TELEVISION & CABLE FACTBOOK
VOLUME 78

Albert Warren
Editor & Publisher 1961-2006

Paul L. Warren, Chairman & Publisher
Daniel Y. Warren, President & Editor

EDITORIAL & BUSINESS HEADQUARTERS
2115 Ward Court, N.W., Washington, D.C. 20037
Phones: 202-872-9200; 800-771-9202
Fax: 202-318-8350
E-mail: info@warren-news.com
Web site: http://www.warren-news.com

Editorial-Factbook/Directories
Michael C. Taliaferro, Managing Editor & Assistant Publisher—Directories
Gaye Nail Lins, Associate Managing Editor
Susan Seiler, Assistant Managing Editor
Kari Danner, Senior Editor & Editorial Supervisor
Colleen M. Crosby, Senior Editor & Editorial Supervisor
Robert T. Dwyer, Senior Research Editor
Marla Shephard, Senior Editor

Advertising -- Factbook/Directories
Richard Nordin, Director of Advertising
Phone: 703-819-7976
Fax: 202-478-5135
E-mail: richard@groupnordin.com

Editorial-News
R. Michael Feazel, Executive Editor
Howard Buskirk, Senior Editor
Anne Veigle, Senior Editor
Dinesh Kumar, Senior Editor
Jonathan Make, Senior Editor
Greg Piper, Associate Editor
Josh Wein, Associate Editor
Adam Bender, Assistant Editor
Yu-Ting Wang, Assistant Editor
Leslie Cantu, Assistant Editor
Tim Warren, Assistant Editor
Dawson B Nail, Executive Editor *Emeritus*
Louis Trager, Consulting News Editor
Dugie Standeford, European Correspondent
Scott Billquist, Geneva Correspondent

Business
Brig Easley, Exec. Vice President & Controller
Deborah Jacobs, Information Systems Manager
Gregory E. Jones, Database/Network Manager
Gina Storr, Director of Sales & Marketing Support
Katrina McCray, Senior Sales & Marketing Support Specialist
Loriane Taylor, Sales & Marketing Support Assistant
Gregory Robinson, Sales & Marketing Support Assistant

Sales
William R. Benton, Sales Director
Agnes Mannarelli, Account Manager
Jim Sharp, Account Manager
Brooke Mowry, Account Manager
Norlie Lin, Account Manager

NEW YORK BUREAU
276 Fifth Avenue, Suite 1002, New York, N.Y. 10001
Phone: 212-686-5410
Fax: 212-889-5097

Editorial
Paul Gluckman, Bureau Chief
Stephen A. Booth, Senior Editor
Mark Seavy, Senior Editor
Jeff Berman, Senior Editor
Razia Mahadeo, Editorial Assistant

Publications & Services of Warren Communications News

TELEVISION & CABLE FACTBOOK: ONLINE

CABLE & STATION COVERAGE ATLAS ON CD-ROM
Published Annually

COMMUNICATIONS DAILY

CONSUMER ELECTRONICS DAILY

GREEN ELECTRONICS DAILY

PUBLIC BROADCASTING REPORT
Published Biweekly

SATELLITE WEEK

TELECOM A.M.
Daily News Service

WARREN'S WASHINGTON INTERNET DAILY

WASHINGTON TELECOM NEWSWIRE
Daily News Service

ISBN: 1-57696-062-5
ISSN: 0732-8648

Index to Sections
Television & Cable Factbook No. 78

Professional Cards

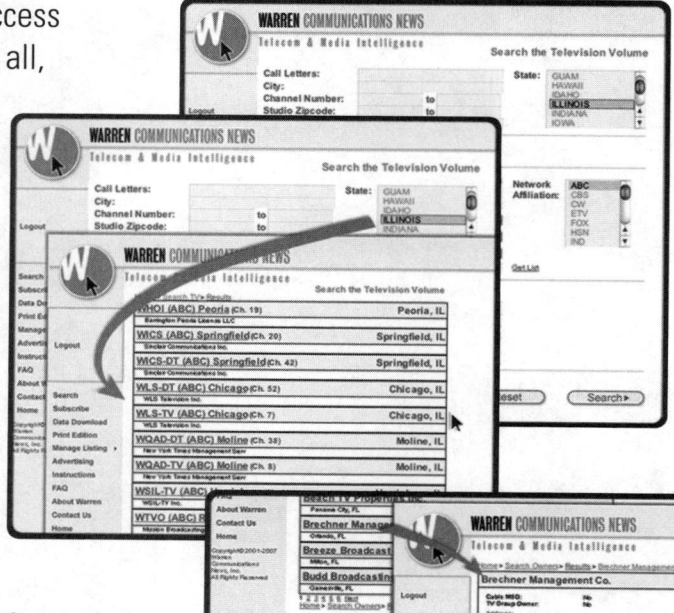

Index to Contents
Television & Cable Factbook No. 78

Index to Contents

CABLE & TV STATION COVERAGE

Atlas 2010

The perfect companion to the Television & Cable Factbook
To order call 800-771-9202 or visit www.warren-news.com

Index to Contents

D

Index to Contents

G

Index to Contents

I

J

K

CABLE & TV STATION COVERAGE

Atlas 2010

The perfect companion to the Television & Cable Factbook
To order call 800-771-9202 or visit www.warren-news.com

N

Index to Contents

Factbook Online

TELEVISION & CABLE

continuous updates | fully searchable | easy to use

For more information call **800-771-9202** or visit **www.warren-news.com**

Index to Contents

Index to Contents

U

V

CABLE & TV STATION COVERAGE

Atlas 2010

The perfect companion to the Television & Cable Factbook

To order call 800-771-9202 or visit www.warren-news.com

W

Index to Contents

Index to Advertisers
Stations Volume

U.S. Television Station Index

Data updated to October 1, 2009 unless otherwise indicated. Includes personnel, facilities and other data.

THE STATE PAGES

Following the map of each state, rankings for Nielsen's Designated Market Area Television Households are shown if they are available. DMA Household Rank is established by Nielsen.

Operating commercial and educational TV stations by VHF and UHF are shown for each state in a status report as of October 1, 2009.

STATION PAGES

CALL LETTERS: Due to the delayed conversion to digital format, most stations in this edition of the Factbook appear with a "-DT" suffix. A complete list of post-conversion call letters were not available at press time. Please refer to the Online Factbook (http://www.tvcablefactbook.com) for the most current information.

Rates, personnel and other data supplied by stations.

STATION POWER: Powers shown are Effective Radiated Powers (ERP).

NIELSEN DATA: The individual stations show Total TV Households, both cable and non-cable, Average Weekly Circulation totals and an Average Daily Circulation total. For definitions of Nielsen terms, consult Description of Station section. These totals shown for circulation within the station DMA and outside it.

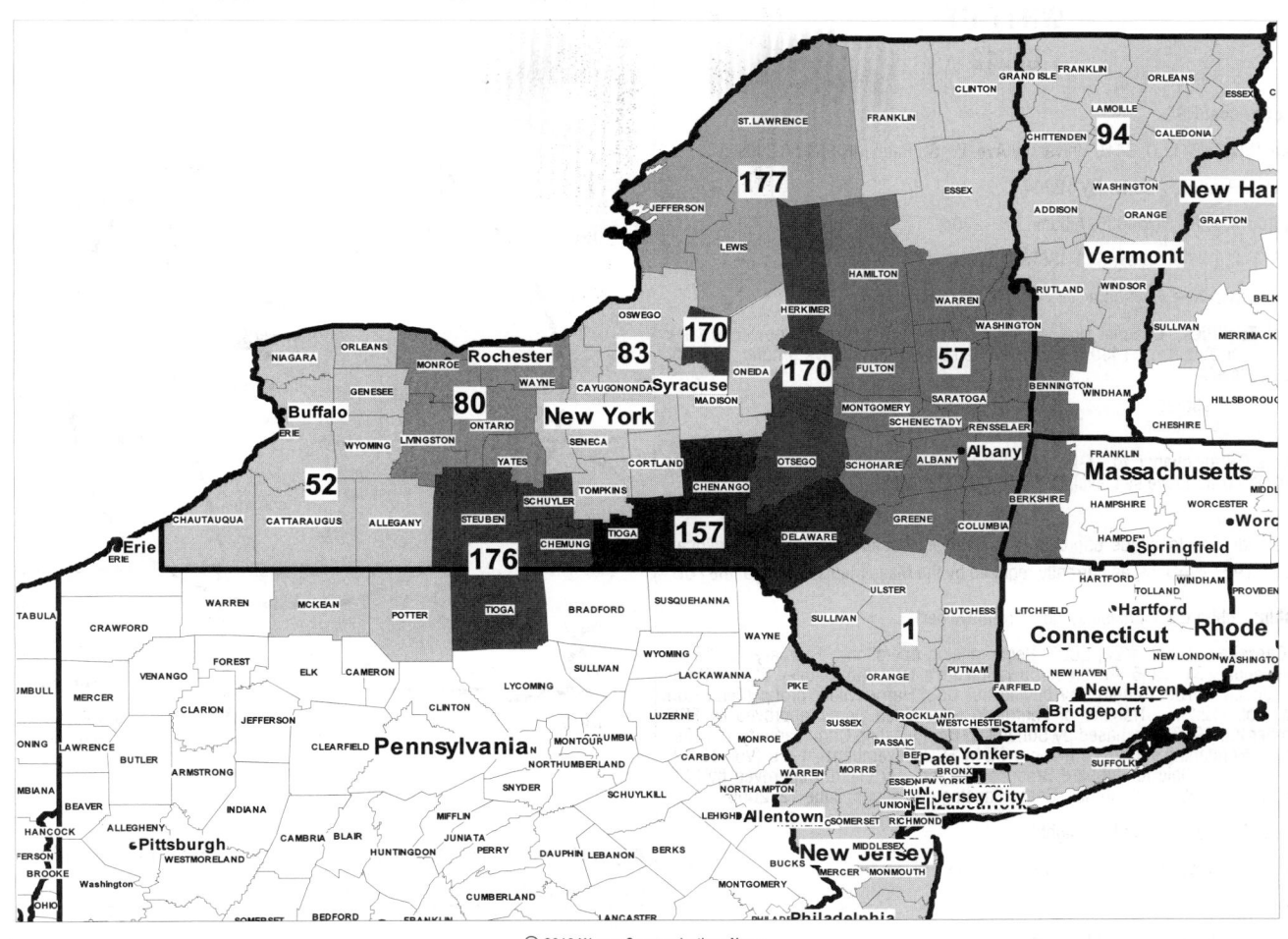

© 2010 Warren Communications News

MARKET	NIELSEN DMA TV HOUSEHOLDS	RANK	MARKET AREA COMMERCIAL STATIONS
New York, NY	7,493,530	1	WABC-DT (7); WCBS-DT (56); WFTY-DT (23); WFUT-DT (53); WLNY-DT (57); WMBC-DT (18); WNBC-DT (28); WNJU-DT (36); WNYW-DT (44); WPIX-DT (11); WPXN-TV (31); WRNN-DT (48); WSAH-DT (42); WTBY-DT (27); WWOR-DT (38); WXTV-DT (40)
Buffalo, NY	633,220	52	WGRZ (33); WIVB-DT (39); WKBW-DT (38); WNLO-DT (32); WNYB-DT (26); WNYO-DT (49); WPXJ-TV (23); WUTV-DT (14)
Albany-Schenectady-Troy, NY	554,070	57	WCDC-DT (36); WCWN-DT (43); WNYA-DT (13); WNYT-DT (12); WRGB-DT (6); WTEN-DT (26); WXXA-DT (7); WYPX-TV (50)
Rochester, NY	392,190	80	WHAM-DT (13); WHEC-DT (10); WROC-DT (45); WUHF-DT (28)
Syracuse, NY	385,440	83	WNYS-DT (44); WSPX-TV (15); WSTM-DT (54); WSYR-DT (17); WSYT-DT (19); WTVH-DT (47)
Burlington, VT-Plattsburgh, NY	330,650	94	WCAX-DT (53); WFFF-DT (43); WNNE-DT (25); WPTZ-DT (14); WVNY-DT (13)
Binghamton, NY	137,240	157	WBNG-DT (7); WICZ-DT (8); WIVT-DT (34)
Utica, NY	104,890	170	WFXV-DT (27); WKTV-DT (29); WUTR-DT (30)
Elmira (Corning), NY	95,790	176	WENY-DT (36); WETM-DT (18); WFBT-DT (14); WYDC-DT (48)
Watertown, NY	93,970	177	WWNY-DT (7); WWTI-DT (21)

New York Station Totals as of October 1, 2009

	VHF	UHF	TOTAL
Commercial Television	10	37	47
Educational Television	0	11	11
	10	48	58

WNYT-DT
Ch. 12

Network Service: NBC.

Licensee: WNYT-TV LLC, 3415 University Ave. W, St. Paul, MN 55114-2099.

Studio: 15 N Pearl St, Albany, NY 12204.

Mailing Address: PO Box 4035, Albany, NY 12204.

Phone: 518-436-4791. **Fax:** 518-436-8524.

Web Site: http://www.wnyt.com

Technical Facilities: Channel No. 12 (204-210 MHz). Authorized power: 9.1-kw visual, aural. Antenna: 1430-ft above av. terrain, 489-ft. above ground, 2270-ft. above sea level.

Latitude	42°	37'	31"
Longitude	74°	00'	38"

Requests CP for change to 15-kw visual, 1427-ft above av. terrain, 489-ft. above ground, 2270-ft. above sea level; BPCDT-20080620ADA.

Note: Latitude and longitude coordinates shown are based on the North American Datum of 1927 (NAD 27) as currently required by the Mass Media Bureau of the FCC.

Ownership: Hubbard Broadcasting Inc. (Group Owner).

Began Operation: October 22, 2003. Began analog operations: February 19, 1954. Left air January 31, 1955. Resumed operation June 15, 1956, Stanley Warner Corp. having acquired 100% control by buying out Col. Harry Wilder group (Television Digest, Vol. 12:24). Transfer of control to Glen Alden Corp. approved by FCC December 22, 1967. Purchased by Sonderling Broadcasting Corp. January 1, 1969. Merger of Sonderling into Viacom approved by FCC November 6, 1979 (Vol. 18:12, 25, 41; 19:46). Sale to Hubbard Broadcasting Inc. by Viacom approved by FCC September 19, 1996 (Vol. 36:35). Ceased analog operations: June 12, 2009.

Represented (legal): Holland & Knight LLP.

Represented (sales): Petry Media Corp.

Personnel:

Stephen P. Baboulis, General Manager.

Tony McManus, Sales Director.

George DeGonzague, Local Sales Manager.

Debbie Reynolds, National Sales Manager.

Paul Lewis, News Director.

Richard E. Klein, Chief Engineer.

Tom Blau, Accounting Manager.

Maryann Ryan, Special Promotion & Program Director.

Steve Robbins, Production Director.

Rob Madeo, Creative Services Director.

Stacy Nguyen, Traffic Manager.

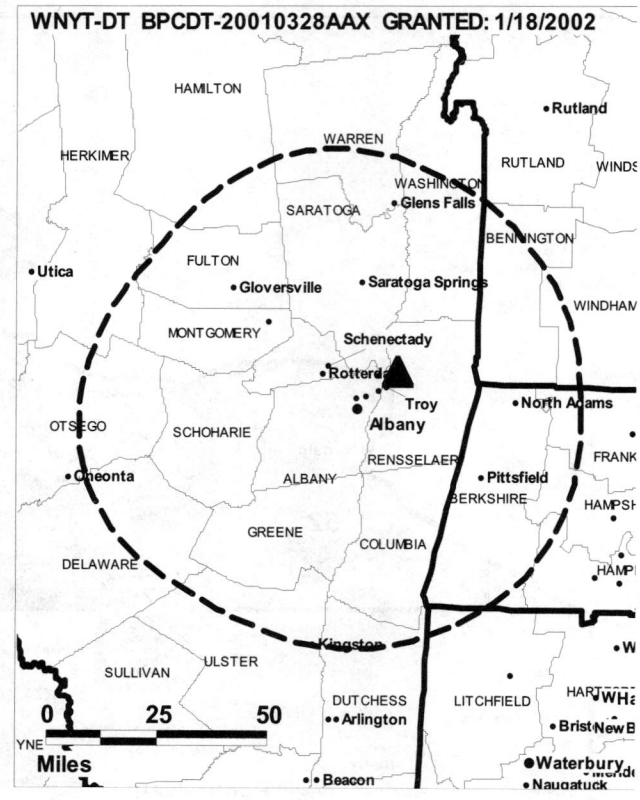

WNYT-DT BPCDT-20010328AAX GRANTED: 1/18/2002

© 2010 Warren Communications News

City of License: Albany. **Station DMA:** Albany-Schenectady-Troy, NY. **Rank:** 57.

Circulation © 2009 Nielsen. Coverage based on Nielsen study.

GrandTotal	Cable TV Households	Non-cable TV Households	Total TV Households
Estimated Station Totals *	433,030	131,510	564,540
Average Weekly Circulation (2009)	288,369	71,810	360,179
Average Daily Circulation (2009)			186,861

Station DMA Total	Cable TV Households	Non-cable TV Households	Total TV Households
Estimated Station Totals *	422,950	131,510	554,460
Average Weekly Circulation (2009)	286,968	71,810	358,778
Average Daily Circulation (2009)			186,549

Other DMA Total	Cable TV Households	Non-cable TV Households	Total TV Households
Estimated Station Totals *	10,080	0	10,080
Average Weekly Circulation (2009)	1,401	0	1,401
Average Daily Circulation (2009)			312

*Estimated station totals are sums of the Nielsen TV and Cable TV household estimates for each county in which the station registers viewing of more than 5% as per the Nielsen Survey Methods.

WTEN-DT
Ch. 26

Network Service: ABC.

Licensee: Young Broadcasting of Albany Inc., Debtor in Possession, PO Box 1800, c/o Brooks, Pierce et al., Raleigh, NC 27602.

Studio: 341 Northern Blvd, Albany, NY 12204.

Mailing Address: 341 Northern Blvd, Albany, NY 12204.

Phone: 518-436-4822. **Fax:** 518-426-4792.

E-mail: jeff.cummings@wten.com

Web Site: http://www.wten.com

Technical Facilities: Channel No. 26 (542-548 MHz). Authorized power: 700-kw max. visual, aural. Antenna: 1398-ft above av. terrain, 456-ft. above ground, 2237-ft. above sea level.

Latitude	42°	37'	31"
Longitude	74°	00'	38"

Note: Latitude and longitude coordinates shown are based on the North American Datum of 1927 (NAD 27) as currently required by the Mass Media Bureau of the FCC.

Ownership: Young Broadcasting Inc., Debtor in Possession (Group Owner).

Began Operation: January 2, 2006. Began analog operations: October 14, 1953 as WROW-RV. Ceased analog operations: June 12, 2009. Sale of 83.4% interest to Lowell Thomas-Frank Smith group approved by FCC November 3, 1954. Station switched from Ch. 41 and changed call letters to WCDA December 1, 1957. Sale by Capital Cities Broadcasting approved by FCC February 24, 1971. Sale to Knight-Ridder by John B. Poole, et al., approved by FCC December 21, 1977. Sale to Young Broadcasting Inc. by Knight-Ridder approved by FCC August 24, 1989. Involuntary assignment to debtor in possession status approved by FCC March 17, 2009. Assignment to Young Broadcasting of Albany Inc. (New Young Broadcasting Holding Co. Inc.) pends.

Represented (legal): Brooks, Pierce, McLendon, Humphrey & Leonard LLP.

Personnel:

Rene LaSpina, President, General Manager & Program Director.

Ron Romines, General Sales Manager.

Mike Bruno, National Sales Manager.

Skeeter Lansing, Chief Engineer & Operations Manager.

Connie Scott, Finance Director.

Dana Dieterle, News Director.

Darlene Hime, Traffic Manager.

City of License: Albany. **Station DMA:** Albany-Schenectady-Troy, NY. **Rank:** 57.

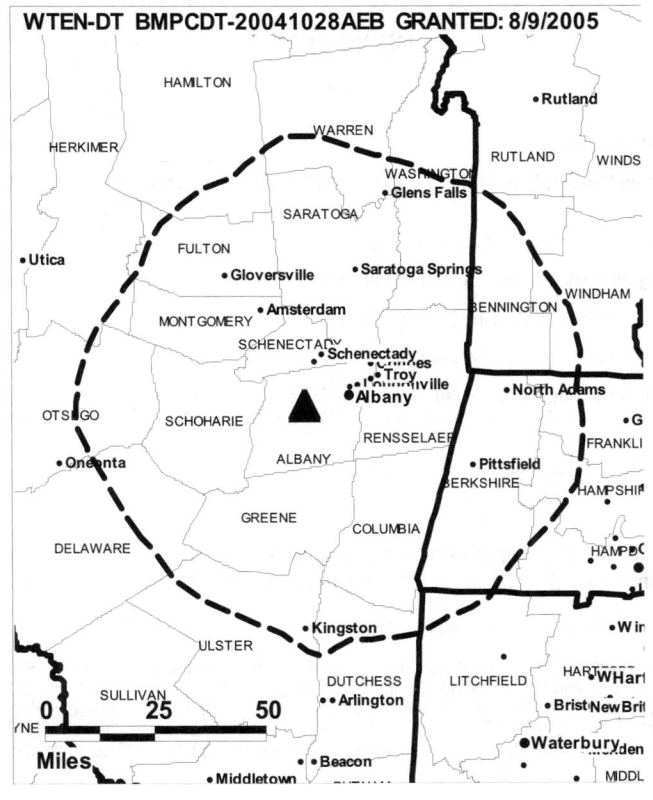

WTEN-DT BMPCDT-20041028AEB GRANTED: 8/9/2005

© 2010 Warren Communications News

Circulation © 2009 Nielsen. Coverage based on Nielsen study.

GrandTotal	Cable TV Households	Non-cable TV Households	Total TV Households
Estimated Station Totals *	435,640	152,550	588,190
Average Weekly Circulation (2009)	277,601	81,005	358,606
Average Daily Circulation (2009)			172,487

Station DMA Total	Cable TV Households	Non-cable TV Households	Total TV Households
Estimated Station Totals *	422,950	131,510	554,460
Average Weekly Circulation (2009)	274,124	79,924	354,048
Average Daily Circulation (2009)			170,885

Other DMA Total	Cable TV Households	Non-cable TV Households	Total TV Households
Estimated Station Totals *	12,690	21,040	33,730
Average Weekly Circulation (2009)	3,477	1,081	4,558
Average Daily Circulation (2009)			1,602

*Estimated station totals are sums of the Nielsen TV and Cable TV household estimates for each county in which the station registers viewing of more than 5% as per the Nielsen Survey Methods.

WXXA-DT
Ch. 7

Network Service: FOX.

Licensee: Newport Television License LLC, 460 Nichols Rd, Ste 250, Kansas City, MO 64112.

Studio: 28 Corporate Cir, Albany, NY 12203.

Mailing Address: 28 Corporate Cir, Albany, NY 12203.

Phone: 518-862-2323. **Fax:** 518-862-0865.

Web Site: http://www.fox23news.com

Technical Facilities: Channel No. 7 (174-180 MHz). Authorized power: 10-kw visual, aural. Antenna: 1424-ft above av. terrain, 489-ft. above ground, 2270-ft. above sea level.

Latitude	42°	37'	31"
Longitude	74°	00'	38"

Note: Latitude and longitude coordinates shown are based on the North American Datum of 1927 (NAD 27) as currently required by the Mass Media Bureau of the FCC.

Ownership: Newport Television LLC (Group Owner).

Began Operation: December 15, 2005. Began analog operations: July 30, 1982. Sale to Heritage Broadcasting Group by James D. Boaz, et al., approved by FCC September 12, 1986. Sale to Clear Channel Television by Heritage Broadcasting Group approved by FCC November 22, 1994. Sale to present owner by Clear Channel Communications Inc. approved by FCC November 29, 2007. Ceased analog operations: June 12, 2009.

Represented (legal): Covington & Burling.

Represented (sales): Katz Media Group.

Personnel:

Sally Stamp, Vice President & General Manager.

Art Hunsinger, News Operations Manager.

Chuck Hunt, Sales Director.

Michael Hendricks, Local Sales Director.

Dan Scher, National Sales Manager.

Sarge Cathrall, Chief Engineer.

Paul Pelliccia, Program Director.

Keith Moran, Creative Services Director & Production Manager.

Penny Kula, Traffic Manager.

Ardelle Hirsch, Community & Client Services Director.

City of License: Albany. **Station DMA:** Albany-Schenectady-Troy, NY. **Rank:** 57.

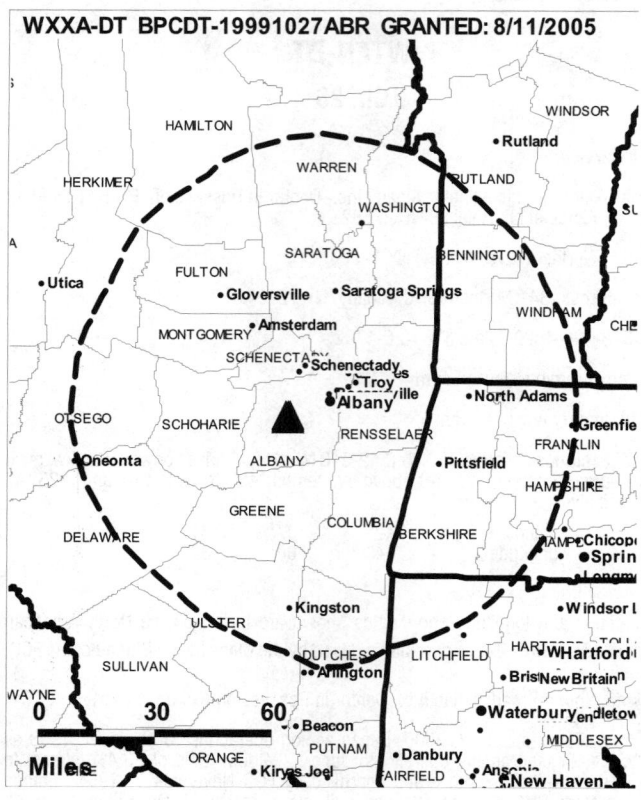

WXXA-DT BPCDT-19991027ABR GRANTED: 8/11/2005

© 2010 Warren Communications News

Circulation © 2009 Nielsen. Coverage based on Nielsen study.

GrandTotal	Cable TV Households	Non-cable TV Households	Total TV Households
Estimated Station Totals *	422,950	141,410	564,360
Average Weekly Circulation (2009)	245,023	61,813	306,836
Average Daily Circulation (2009)			110,165

Station DMA Total	Cable TV Households	Non-cable TV Households	Total TV Households
Estimated Station Totals *	422,950	131,510	554,460
Average Weekly Circulation (2009)	245,023	61,209	306,232
Average Daily Circulation (2009)			110,096

Other DMA Total	Cable TV Households	Non-cable TV Households	Total TV Households
Estimated Station Totals *	0	9,900	9,900
Average Weekly Circulation (2009)	0	604	604
Average Daily Circulation (2009)			69

*Estimated station totals are sums of the Nielsen TV and Cable TV household estimates for each county in which the station registers viewing of more than 5% as per the Nielsen Survey Methods.

WYPX-DT
Ch. 50

Network Service: ION.

Licensee: ION Media Albany License Inc., Debtor in Possession, 601 Clearwater Park Rd, West Palm Beach, FL 33401-6233.

Studio: One Charles Blvd, Guiderland, NY 12084.

Mailing Address: One Charles Blvd, Guilderland, NY 12084.

Phone: 518-464-0143. **Fax:** 518-464-0633.

E-mail: reneeosterlitz@ionmedia.com

Web Site: http://www.ionmedia.com

Technical Facilities: Channel No. 50 (686-692 MHz). Authorized power: 450-kw max. visual, aural. Antenna: 679-ft above av. terrain, 675-ft. above ground, 1420-ft. above sea level.

Latitude	42°	59'	04"
Longitude	74°	10'	56"

Transmitter: 0.6-mi. NE of intersection of State Hwy. 30 & County Hwy. 39.

Note: Latitude and longitude coordinates shown are based on the North American Datum of 1927 (NAD 27) as currently required by the Mass Media Bureau of the FCC.

Ownership: ION Media Networks Inc., Debtor in Possession (Group Owner).

Began Operation: September 15, 2004. Began analog operations: December 14, 1987. Involuntary assignment to debtor in possession status approved by FCC June 5, 2009. Transfer of control by ION Media Networks Inc. from Paxson Management Corp. & Lowell W. Paxson to CIG Media LLC approved by FCC December 31, 2007. On September 6, 2007, station ceased analog operations. Earlier that day station received permission from the FCC to end analog operations and operate in digital format only. Sale to Urban Television LLC pends. Sale to present owner (then Paxson Communications Corp.) by Cornerstone Television Inc. approved by FCC May 22, 1996. Sale to Cornerstone Television Inc. by Amsterdam Broadcasting Inc. approved by FCC May 8, 1992. Sale to Amsterdam Broadcasting Inc. by Beacon Broadcasting Inc. approved by FCC September 30, 1986. Sale to Beacon Broadcasting Inc. by G & M Broadcasting Inc. approved by FCC May 20, 1985. Ceased analog operations: September 7, 2007.

Represented (legal): Dow Lohnes PLLC.

Personnel:

Renee Osterlitz, Station Operatons & Traffic Manager.

Claude Pine, Chief Engineer.

City of License: Amsterdam. **Station DMA:** Albany-Schenectady-Troy, NY. **Rank:** 57.

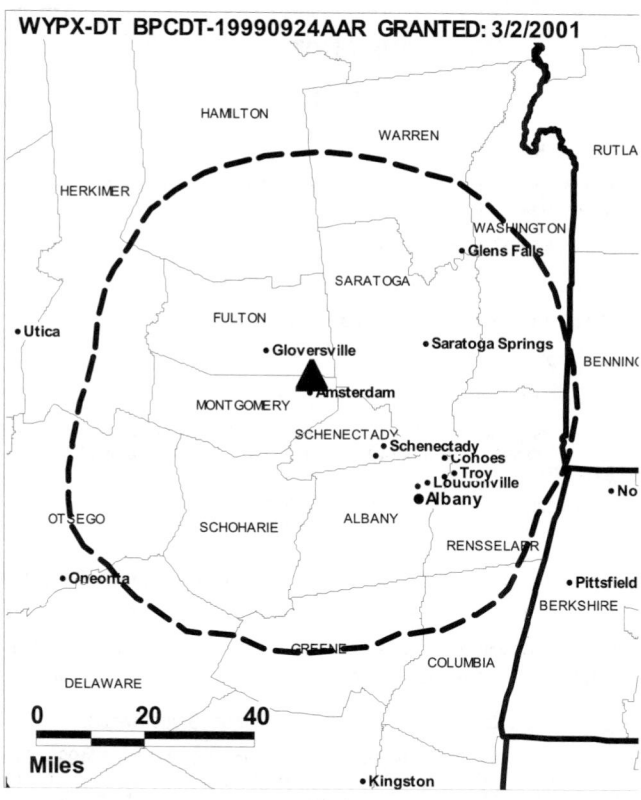

WYPX-DT BPCDT-19990924AAR GRANTED: 3/2/2001

© 2010 Warren Communications News

Circulation © 2009 Nielsen. Coverage based on Nielsen study.

GrandTotal	Cable TV Households	Non-cable TV Households	Total TV Households
Estimated Station Totals *	215,160	5,600	220,760
Average Weekly Circulation (2009)	14,295	526	14,821
Average Daily Circulation (2009)			2,670

Station DMA Total	Cable TV Households	Non-cable TV Households	Total TV Households
Estimated Station Totals *	215,160	5,600	220,760
Average Weekly Circulation (2009)	14,295	526	14,821
Average Daily Circulation (2009)			2,670

*Estimated station totals are sums of the Nielsen TV and Cable TV household estimates for each county in which the station registers viewing of more than 5% as per the Nielsen Survey Methods.

WPXJ-DT
Ch. 23

Network Service: ION.

Grantee: ION Media Buffalo License Inc., Debtor in Possession, 601 Clearwater Park Rd, West Palm Beach, FL 33401-6233.

Studio: 726 Exchange St, Buffalo, NY 14210.

Mailing Address: 726 Exchange St, Ste 605, Buffalo, NY 14210.

Phone: 716-852-1818; 800-380-2658. **Fax:** 716-852-8288.

E-mail: patriciawolfsohn@ionmedia.com

Web Site: http://www.ionmedia.com

Technical Facilities: Channel No. 23 (524-530 MHz). Authorized power: 455-kw max. visual, aural. Antenna: 906-ft above av. terrain, 971-ft. above ground, 1921-ft. above sea level.

Latitude	42°	53'	42"
Longitude	78°	00'	56"

Transmitter: Approx. 0.62-mi. SW of the intersection of Roger & Perry Rds., N of Pavil.

Note: Latitude and longitude coordinates shown are based on the North American Datum of 1927 (NAD 27) as currently required by the Mass Media Bureau of the FCC.

Ownership: ION Media Networks Inc., Debtor in Possession (Group Owner).

Began Operation: June 12, 2009. Began analog operations: September 1, 1998. Sale to Urban Television LLC pends. Involuntary assignment to debtor in possession status approved by FCC June 5, 2009. Transfer of control by ION Media Networks Inc. from Paxson Management Corp. & Lowell W. Paxson to CIG Media LLC approved by FCC December 31, 2007. Paxson Communications Corp. became ION Media Networks Inc. on June 26, 2006. Received FCC approval August 1, 2005 to surrender its digital allotment on Channel 53 and flash cut to digital transmission on its analog Channel 51 at a future date. Sale of permit to Paxson Communications Corp. by Fant Broadcasting Co. LLC approved by FCC July 15, 1997. Ceased analog operations: June 12, 2009.

Represented (legal): Dow Lohnes PLLC.

Represented (engineering): du Treil, Lundin & Rackley Inc.

Personnel:

Barbara Lipka, Station Operations Manager.

Kevin Wright, Chief Engineer.

Patty Wolfsohn, Traffic Manager.

City of License: Batavia. **Station DMA:** Buffalo, NY. **Rank:** 52.

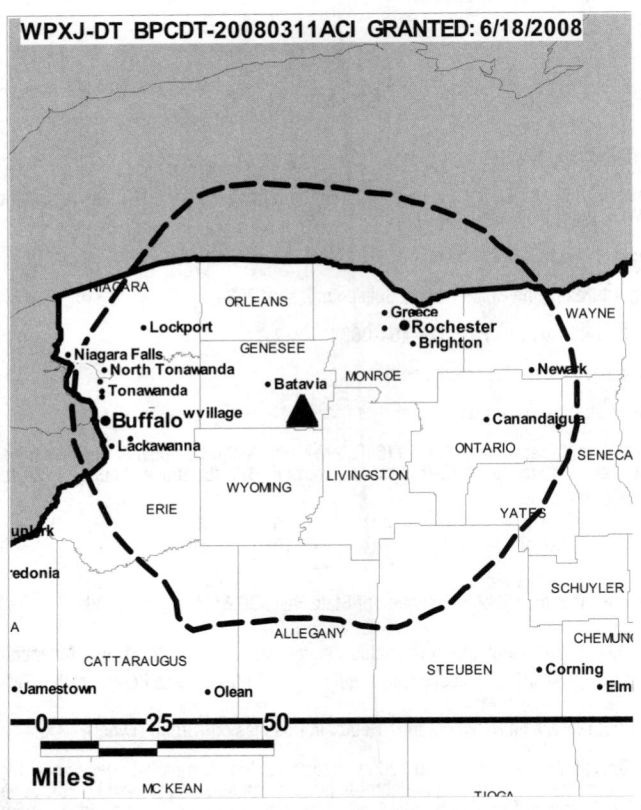

WPXJ-DT BPCDT-20080311ACI GRANTED: 6/18/2008

© 2010 Warren Communications News

Circulation © 2009 Nielsen. Coverage based on Nielsen study.

GrandTotal	Cable TV Households	Non-cable TV Households	Total TV Households
Estimated Station Totals *	309,580	22,760	332,340
Average Weekly Circulation (2009)	22,827	1,482	24,309
Average Daily Circulation (2009)			4,632

Station DMA Total	Cable TV Households	Non-cable TV Households	Total TV Households
Estimated Station Totals *	309,580	22,760	332,340
Average Weekly Circulation (2009)	22,827	1,482	24,309
Average Daily Circulation (2009)			4,632

*Estimated station totals are sums of the Nielsen TV and Cable TV household estimates for each county in which the station registers viewing of more than 5% as per the Nielsen Survey Methods.

WFBT-DT

Ch. 14

Network Service: IND.

Grantee: William H. Walker III, PO Box 1341, Highland, NY 12528.

Mailing Address: PO Box 1341, Highland, NY 12528.

Phone: 914-883-5546.

Technical Facilities: Channel No. 14 (470-476 MHz). Authorized power: 0.676-kw max. visual, aural. Antenna: 643-ft above av. terrain, 241-ft. above ground, 2093-ft. above sea level.

Latitude	42°	18'	33"
Longitude	77°	13'	17"

Transmitter: Intersection of Rtes. 226 & 415, Savona.

Note: Latitude and longitude coordinates shown are based on the North American Datum of 1927 (NAD 27) as currently required by the Mass Media Bureau of the FCC.

Ownership: William H. Walker III.

Began Operation: April 16, 2009. Station went directly to digital broadcast; no analog application.

Represented (legal): Gammon & Grange PC.

City of License: Bath. **Station DMA:** Elmira (Corning), NY. **Rank:** 176.

Nielsen Data: Not available.

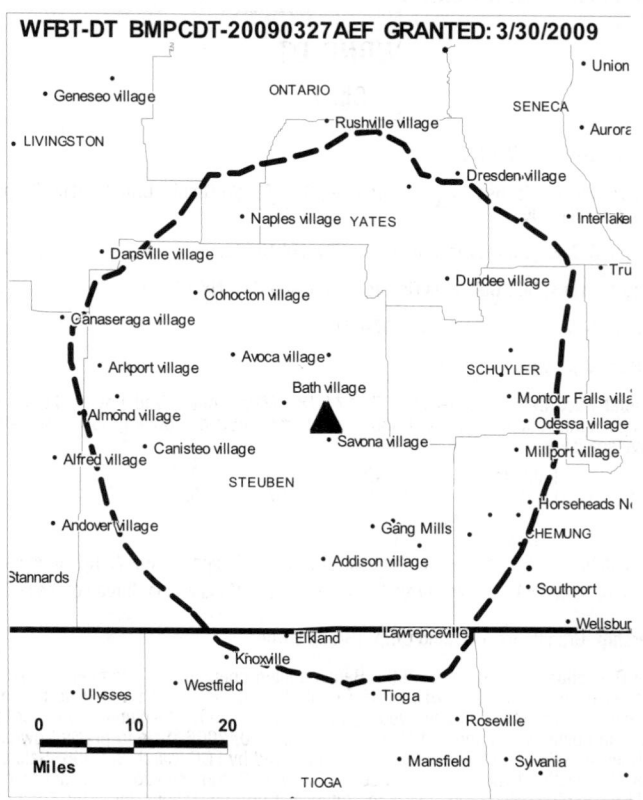

WFBT-DT BMPCDT-20090327AEF GRANTED: 3/30/2009

© 2010 Warren Communications News

WBNG-DT
Ch. 7

Network Service: CW, CBS.

Licensee: WBNG License Inc., 767 3rd Ave., 34th Fl, c/o Granite Broadcasting Corp., New York, NY 10017.

Studio: 560 Columbia Dr, Ste 1, Johnson City, NY 13790.

Mailing Address: 560 Columbia Dr, Ste 1, Johnson City, NY 13790.

Phone: 607-729-8812. **Fax:** 607-797-6211.

Web Site: http://www.wbng.com

Technical Facilities: Channel No. 7 (174-180 MHz). Authorized power: 20.4-kw visual, aural. Antenna: 1122-ft above av. terrain, 660-ft. above ground, 2425-ft. above sea level.

Latitude	42°	03'	31"
Longitude	75°	57'	06"

Note: Latitude and longitude coordinates shown are based on the North American Datum of 1927 (NAD 27) as currently required by the Mass Media Bureau of the FCC.

Ownership: Granite Broadcasting Corp. (Group Owner).

Began Operation: September 9, 2003. Began analog operations: December 1, 1949. Transfer from W. Don Cornwell to SP Granite LLC (Silver Point Capital) as part of Chapter 11 reorganization approved by FCC May 21, 2007. Involuntary transfer to debtor in possession approved by FCC December 20, 2006. Sale to present owner by Television Station Group Holdings LLC approved by FCC March 8, 2006. Sale to Television Station Group Holdings LLC by Gateway Communications Inc. approved by FCC October 27, 2000. Sale to Gateway Communications Inc. by Triangle Publications approved by FCC September 20, 1972. Previous sale to Triangle by John C. Clark interests approved by FCC May 4, 1955. Ceased analog operations: February 17, 2009.

Represented (legal): Akin, Gump, Strauss, Hauer & Feld LLP.

Represented (sales): TeleRep Inc.

Personnel:

Greg Catlin, General Manager.

Bob Krummenacher, Vice President & Station Manager.

Denise Edmister, National Sales Manager.

Michael Calkins, Chief Engineer.

Kim Peskal, Business Manager.

Kate Garger, Program Director.

Christina Rockhill, Creative Services Director & Production Manager.

Janet Heatherman, Traffic Manager.

City of License: Binghamton. **Station DMA:** Binghamton, NY. **Rank:** 157.

WBNG-DT BPCDT-19991029AFF GRANTED: 12/18/2001

© 2010 Warren Communications News

Circulation © 2009 Nielsen. Coverage based on Nielsen study.

GrandTotal	Cable TV Households	Non-cable TV Households	Total TV Households
Estimated Station Totals *	255,440	86,500	341,940
Average Weekly Circulation (2009)	131,417	17,289	148,706
Average Daily Circulation (2009)			78,364

Station DMA Total	Cable TV Households	Non-cable TV Households	Total TV Households
Estimated Station Totals *	100,220	38,710	138,930
Average Weekly Circulation (2009)	79,661	13,944	93,605
Average Daily Circulation (2009)			57,897

Other DMA Total	Cable TV Households	Non-cable TV Households	Total TV Households
Estimated Station Totals *	155,220	47,790	203,010
Average Weekly Circulation (2009)	51,756	3,345	55,101
Average Daily Circulation (2009)			20,467

*Estimated station totals are sums of the Nielsen TV and Cable TV household estimates for each county in which the station registers viewing of more than 5% as per the Nielsen Survey Methods.

WICZ-DT
Ch. 8

Network Service: FOX.

Licensee: Stainless Broadcasting LP, 2111 University Park Dr, Ste 650, Okemos, MI 48864-6913.

Studio: 4600 Vestal Pkwy E, Vestal, NY 13850.

Mailing Address: 4600 Vestal Pkwy. E, Vestal, NY 13850.

Phone: 607-770-4040. **Fax:** 607-798-7950.

Web Site: http://www.wicz.com

Technical Facilities: Channel No. 8 (180-186 MHz). Authorized power: 7.9-kw visual, aural. Antenna: 1217-ft above av. terrain, 886-ft. above ground, 2511-ft. above sea level.

Latitude	42°	03'	22"
Longitude	75°	56'	39"

Note: Latitude and longitude coordinates shown are based on the North American Datum of 1927 (NAD 27) as currently required by the Mass Media Bureau of the FCC.

Ownership: Stainless Broadcasting LP.

Began Operation: May 1, 2002. Began analog operations: November 1, 1957. Sale to present owner by Stainless Enterprises of Pennsylvania approved by FCC July 15, 1997. Sale to Stainless Enterprises of Pennsylvania by Binghamton Press (Gannett) approved by FCC February 22, 1971 (Television Digest, Vol. 10:31). Ceased analog operations: June 12, 2009.

Represented (legal): Leventhal, Senter & Lerman PLLC.

Represented (sales): Continental Television Sales.

Personnel:

Brian Brady, President.

John Leet, General Manager.

Su Neubauer, News Director.

Wayne Gordon, General Sales Manager.

Tony McMahon, National Sales Manager.

Mike Melnyk, Chief Engineer.

Rose Mary Gaeta, Business Manager.

Vernon Rowlands, Program & Promotion Director.

Marianne McGoff, Traffic Manager.

City of License: Binghamton. **Station DMA:** Binghamton, NY. **Rank:** 157.

WICZ-DT BMPCDT-20051109AAA GRANTED: 1/20/2006

© 2010 Warren Communications News

Circulation © 2009 Nielsen. Coverage based on Nielsen study.

GrandTotal	Cable TV Households	Non-cable TV Households	Total TV Households
Estimated Station Totals *	170,320	44,760	215,080
Average Weekly Circulation (2009)	75,493	10,165	85,658
Average Daily Circulation (2009)			29,737

Station DMA Total	Cable TV Households	Non-cable TV Households	Total TV Households
Estimated Station Totals *	100,220	30,060	130,280
Average Weekly Circulation (2009)	59,993	9,309	69,302
Average Daily Circulation (2009)			26,011

Other DMA Total	Cable TV Households	Non-cable TV Households	Total TV Households
Estimated Station Totals *	70,100	14,700	84,800
Average Weekly Circulation (2009)	15,500	856	16,356
Average Daily Circulation (2009)			3,726

*Estimated station totals are sums of the Nielsen TV and Cable TV household estimates for each county in which the station registers viewing of more than 5% as per the Nielsen Survey Methods.

WIVT-DT
Ch. 34

Network Service: ABC.

Licensee: Newport Television License LLC, 460 Nichols Rd, Ste 250, Kansas City, MO 64112.

Studio: 203 Ingraham Hill Rd, Binghamton, NY 13903.

Mailing Address: 203 Ingraham Hill Rd, Binghamton, NY 13903.

Phone: 607-723-7464. **Fax:** 607-723-1034.

E-mail: SharonGozalkowski@clearchannel.com

Web Site: http://www.newschannel34.com

Technical Facilities: Channel No. 34 (590-596 MHz). Authorized power: 345-kw max. visual, aural. Antenna: 912-ft above av. terrain, 531-ft. above ground, 2201-ft. above sea level.

Latitude	42°	03'	39"
Longitude	75°	56'	36"

Note: Latitude and longitude coordinates shown are based on the North American Datum of 1927 (NAD 27) as currently required by the Mass Media Bureau of the FCC.

Ownership: Newport Television LLC (Group Owner).

Began Operation: June 16, 2003. Standard and High Definition. Station broadcasting digitally on its analog channel allotment. Began analog operations: November 24, 1962. Transfer of control to Arthur, Hessen and Lazare by Alfred E. Anscomb (53.13%) and James E. Greeley (10.4%) approved by FCC August 17, 1966. Sale to Pinnacle Communications Inc. approved by FCC August 7, 1978. Sale to Citadel Communications approved by FCC August 6, 1986. Sale to US Broadcast Group approved by FCC January 23, 1996. Sale to The Ackerley Group by US Broadcast Group approved by FCC July 29, 1998. In stock swap, Clear Channel Broadcasting Inc. acquired The Ackerley Group. FCC approved deal May 29, 2002. Sale to present owner by Clear Channel Communications Inc. approved by FCC November 29, 2007. Ceased analog operations: June 12, 2009.

Represented (sales): Blair Television.

Represented (legal): Covington & Burling.

Personnel:

John Birchall, Vice President & General Manager.

Jim Ehmke, News Director.

John King, Chief Engineer.

Jim LaVasser, Promotion & Program Director.

Boyd Chapman, Traffic Manager.

City of License: Binghamton. **Station DMA:** Binghamton, NY. **Rank:** 157.

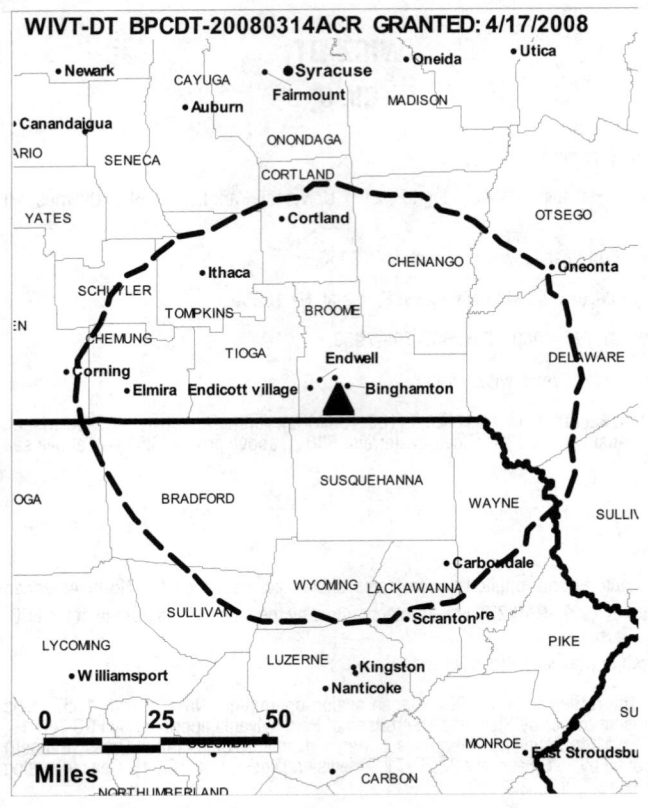

WIVT-DT BPCDT-20080314ACR GRANTED: 4/17/2008

© 2010 Warren Communications News

Circulation © 2009 Nielsen. Coverage based on Nielsen study.

GrandTotal	Cable TV Households	Non-cable TV Households	Total TV Households
Estimated Station Totals *	147,790	35,770	183,560
Average Weekly Circulation (2009)	65,209	8,345	73,554
Average Daily Circulation (2009)			29,068

Station DMA Total	Cable TV Households	Non-cable TV Households	Total TV Households
Estimated Station Totals *	100,220	30,060	130,280
Average Weekly Circulation (2009)	57,636	7,905	65,541
Average Daily Circulation (2009)			27,289

Other DMA Total	Cable TV Households	Non-cable TV Households	Total TV Households
Estimated Station Totals *	47,570	5,710	53,280
Average Weekly Circulation (2009)	7,573	440	8,013
Average Daily Circulation (2009)			1,779

*Estimated station totals are sums of the Nielsen TV and Cable TV household estimates for each county in which the station registers viewing of more than 5% as per the Nielsen Survey Methods.

WGRZ
Ch. 33

Network Service: NBC.

Licensee: Multimedia Entertainment Inc., 7950 Jones Branch Dr, c/o Gannett Co., McLean, VA 22102.

Studio: 259 Delaware Ave, Buffalo, NY 14202.

Mailing Address: 259 Delaware Ave, Buffalo, NY 14202.

Phone: 716-849-2222. **Fax:** 716-849-7600.

E-mail: pharris@wgrz.gannett.com

Web Site: http://www.wgrz.com

Technical Facilities: Channel No. 33 (584-590 MHz). Authorized power: 480-kw max. visual, aural. Antenna: 968-ft above av. terrain, 874-ft. above ground, 2227-ft. above sea level.

Latitude	42°	43'	07"
Longitude	78°	33'	47"

Note: Latitude and longitude coordinates shown are based on the North American Datum of 1927 (NAD 27) as currently required by the Mass Media Bureau of the FCC.

Ownership: Gannett Co. Inc. (Group Owner).

Began Operation: August 1, 2002. High Definition. Began analog operations: August 14, 1954. Sale to Taft by Transcontinent Television Corp. approved by FCC February 19, 1964 (Television Digest, Vol 3:15, 16, 31; 4:8). Sale to General Cinema Corp. by Taft Broadcasting in exchange for WCIX(TV) Ch.6, Miami, FL approved by FCC February 24, 1983. Sale to Robert N. Smith, William S. Reyner, George D. Lilly, et al., approved by FCC July 31, 1986 (Vol. 26:13; 40). Sale to Tak Communications Inc. approved by FCC June 24, 1988 (Vol. 28:19). Sale to Michael Eskridge approved by FCC January 27, 1993. License reassigned in 1994. Sale to Argyle Television Inc. approved by FCC April 20, 1995 (Vol. 35:9, 44). Swap with WZZM-TV, Grand Rapids for Gannett Broadcasting Group's KOCO-TV, Oklahoma City & WLWT, Cincinnati approved by FCC January 27, 1997 (Vol. 36:49; 37:5, 6). Ceased analog operations: June 12, 2009.

Represented (sales): Blair Television.

Personnel:

Joe Toellner, President & General Manager.

Mark Manders, General Sales Manager.

Julie Mecklenburg, Local Sales Manager.

David Luka, National Sales Manager.

Ellen Crooke, Vice President, News & Strategic Iniatives.

Boomer Connell, Vice President, Technology & Operations.

Patty Krzeminiski, Vice President, Business & Innovation.

Paulette Harris, Program Administrator.

Michael Morano, Research Director.

Marilyn Teranova, Traffic Manager.

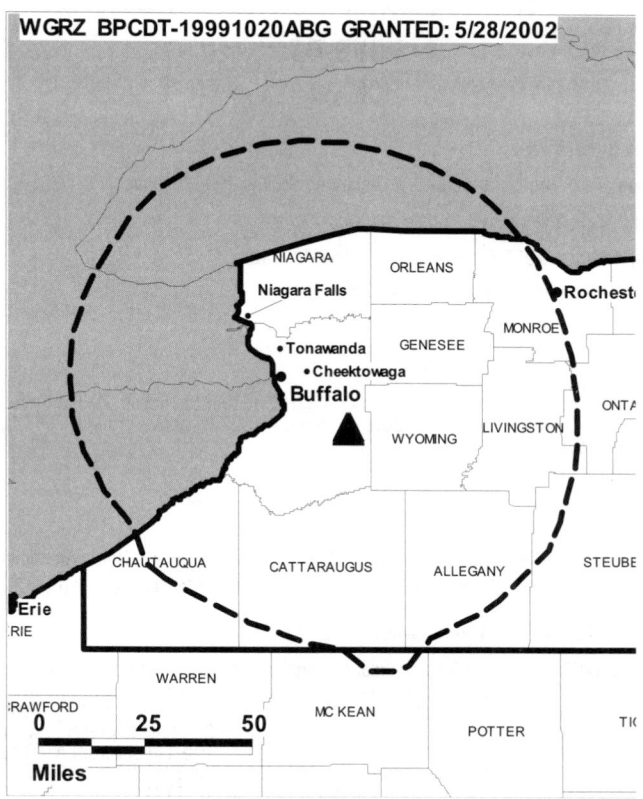

© 2010 Warren Communications News

City of License: Buffalo. **Station DMA:** Buffalo, NY. **Rank:** 52.

Circulation © 2009 Nielsen. Coverage based on Nielsen study.

GrandTotal	Cable TV Households	Non-cable TV Households	Total TV Households
Estimated Station Totals *	403,870	247,690	651,560
Average Weekly Circulation (2009)	285,663	162,213	447,876
Average Daily Circulation (2009)			240,804

Station DMA Total	Cable TV Households	Non-cable TV Households	Total TV Households
Estimated Station Totals *	383,430	247,690	631,120
Average Weekly Circulation (2009)	282,908	162,213	445,121
Average Daily Circulation (2009)			240,191

Other DMA Total	Cable TV Households	Non-cable TV Households	Total TV Households
Estimated Station Totals *	20,440	0	20,440
Average Weekly Circulation (2009)	2,755	0	2,755
Average Daily Circulation (2009)			613

*Estimated station totals are sums of the Nielsen TV and Cable TV household estimates for each county in which the station registers viewing of more than 5% as per the Nielsen Survey Methods.

WIVB-DT
Ch. 39

Network Service: CBS.

Licensee: WIVB Broadcasting LLC, 4 Richmond Sq, Ste 200, Providence, RI 02906.

Studio: 2077 Elmwood Ave, Buffalo, NY 14207.

Mailing Address: 2077 Elmwood Ave, Buffalo, NY 14207.

Phone: 716-874-4410. **Fax:** 716-879-4896.

E-mail: wivb@wivb.com

Web Site: http://www.wivb.com

Technical Facilities: Channel No. 39 (320-626 MHz). Authorized power: 790-kw max. visual, aural. Antenna: 1368-ft above av. terrain, 1027-ft. above ground, 2667-ft. above sea level.

Latitude	42°	39'	33"
Longitude	78°	37'	33"

Note: Latitude and longitude coordinates shown are based on the North American Datum of 1927 (NAD 27) as currently required by the Mass Media Bureau of the FCC.

Ownership: LIN TV Corp. (Group Owner).

Began Operation: June 9, 2002. Standard Definition. Began analog operations: May 14, 1948. Sale to Howard Publications Inc. by Buffalo Evening News approved by FCC September 16, 1977 (Television Digest, Vol. 17:22). Sale to King World Productions approved by FCC October 13, 1988 (Vol. 28:26). Sale to present owner by FCC August 7, 1995 (Vol. 35:23). Sale of controlling interest in LIN from AT&T to Hicks, Muse, Tate & Furst approved by FCC March 2, 1998 (Vol. 37:33, 42; 38:2, 10). Sale to Chancellor Media Corp. cancelled (Vol. 38:28; 39:12). Ceased analog operations: June 12, 2009.

Represented (sales): Blair Television.

Personnel:

Chris Musial, President & General Manager.

Ed Bassler, Sales Director.

Rosalyn Mercio, Local Sales Manager.

Tad O'Rourke, National Sales Manager.

Joseph Schlaerth, News Director.

Dennis Majewicz, Engineering Director.

Diane Breen, Program Coordinator.

Daniel Myers, Marketing & Promotion Director.

Diana Threet, Traffic Manager.

Tim Baxter, New Media Director.

Angela Miles, Public Relations Director.

City of License: Buffalo. **Station DMA:** Buffalo, NY. **Rank:** 52.

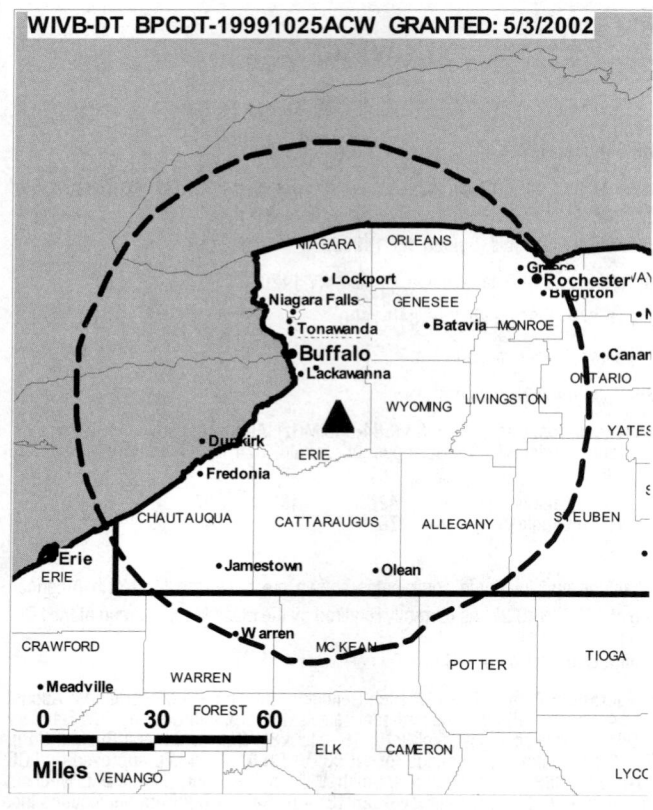

WIVB-DT BPCDT-19991025ACW GRANTED: 5/3/2002

© 2010 Warren Communications News

Circulation © 2009 Nielsen. Coverage based on Nielsen study.

GrandTotal	Cable TV Households	Non-cable TV Households	Total TV Households
Estimated Station Totals *	439,500	247,690	687,190
Average Weekly Circulation (2009)	293,923	179,472	473,395
Average Daily Circulation (2009)			255,297

Station DMA Total	Cable TV Households	Non-cable TV Households	Total TV Households
Estimated Station Totals *	383,430	247,690	631,120
Average Weekly Circulation (2009)	289,169	179,472	468,641
Average Daily Circulation (2009)			253,899

Other DMA Total	Cable TV Households	Non-cable TV Households	Total TV Households
Estimated Station Totals *	56,070	0	56,070
Average Weekly Circulation (2009)	4,754	0	4,754
Average Daily Circulation (2009)			1,398

*Estimated station totals are sums of the Nielsen TV and Cable TV household estimates for each county in which the station registers viewing of more than 5% as per the Nielsen Survey Methods.

WKBW-DT
Ch. 38

Network Service: ABC.

Licensee: WKBW-TV License Inc., 767 3rd Ave., 34th Fl, c/o Granite Broadcasting Corp., New York, NY 10017.

Studio: 7 Broadcast Plaza, Buffalo, NY 14202.

Mailing Address: 7 Broadcast Plaza, Buffalo, NY 14202.

Phone: 716-845-6100. **Fax:** 716-845-1855.

Web Site: http://www.wkbw.com

Technical Facilities: Channel No. 38 (614-620 MHz). Authorized power: 358-kw max. visual, aural. Antenna: 1420-ft above av. terrain, 1037-ft. above ground, 2772-ft. above sea level.

Latitude	42°	38'	14.8"
Longitude	78°	37'	11.9"

Note: Latitude and longitude coordinates shown are based on the North American Datum of 1927 (NAD 27) as currently required by the Mass Media Bureau of the FCC.

Ownership: Granite Broadcasting Corp. (Group Owner).

Began Operation: December 15, 2005. Began analog operations: November 30, 1958. Transfer from W. Don Cornwell to SP Granite LLC (Silver Point Capital) as part of Chapter 11 reorganization approved by FCC May 21, 2007. Involuntary transfer to debtor in possession approved by FCC December 20, 2006. Sale to present owner by Queen City III LP approved by FCC June 7, 1995. Sale to Queen City III LP by Capital Cities Communications Inc. approved by FCC November 14, 1985. Ceased analog operations: June 12, 2009.

Represented (legal): Akin, Gump, Strauss, Hauer & Feld LLP.

Represented (sales): TeleRep Inc.

Personnel:

Bill Ransom, President & General Manager.

Michael R. Nurse, General Sales Manager.

Bill Payer, News Director.

Mike Anger, Chief Engineer.

Ken Koller, Business Manager.

John DiSciullo, Programming & Creative Services Director.

Mark Rivero, Research Director.

Debbie Morrison, Traffic Manager.

City of License: Buffalo. **Station DMA:** Buffalo, NY. **Rank:** 52.

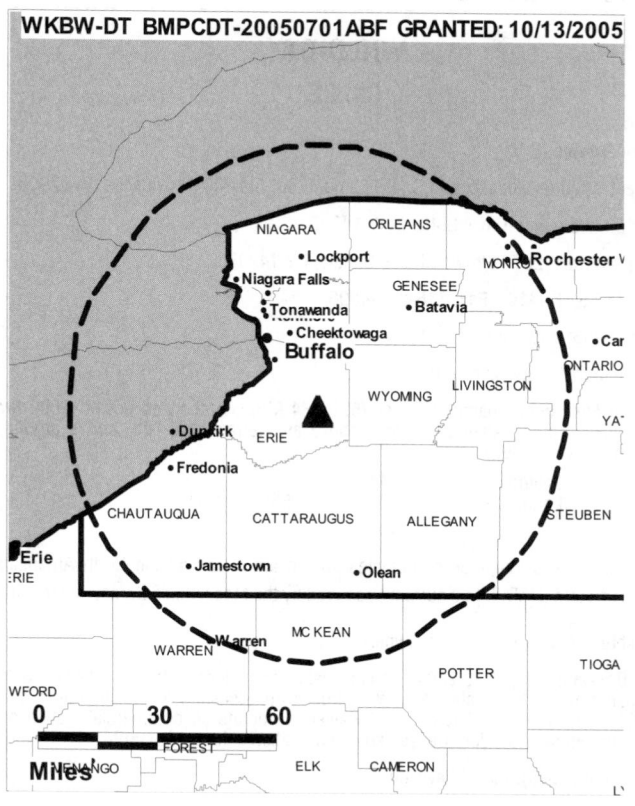

WKBW-DT BMPCDT-20050701ABF GRANTED: 10/13/2005

© 2010 Warren Communications News

Circulation © 2009 Nielsen. Coverage based on Nielsen study.

GrandTotal	Cable TV Households	Non-cable TV Households	Total TV Households
Estimated Station Totals *	417,500	247,690	665,190
Average Weekly Circulation (2009)	271,508	164,385	435,893
Average Daily Circulation (2009)			216,276

Station DMA Total	Cable TV Households	Non-cable TV Households	Total TV Households
Estimated Station Totals *	383,430	247,690	631,120
Average Weekly Circulation (2009)	265,627	164,385	430,012
Average Daily Circulation (2009)			215,009

Other DMA Total	Cable TV Households	Non-cable TV Households	Total TV Households
Estimated Station Totals *	34,070	0	34,070
Average Weekly Circulation (2009)	5,881	0	5,881
Average Daily Circulation (2009)			1,267

*Estimated station totals are sums of the Nielsen TV and Cable TV household estimates for each county in which the station registers viewing of more than 5% as per the Nielsen Survey Methods.

WNLO-DT
Ch. 32

Network Service: CW.

Licensee: WIVB Broadcasting LLC, 4 Richmond Sq, Ste 200, Providence, RI 02906.

Studio: 2077 Elmwood Ave, Buffalo, NY 14207.

Mailing Address: 2077 Elmwood Ave, Buffalo, NY 14207.

Phone: 716-874-4410. **Fax:** 716-879-4896.

E-mail: wivb@wivb.com

Web Site: http://www.wivb.com

Technical Facilities: Channel No. 32 (578-584 MHz). Authorized power: 1000-kw max. visual, aural. Antenna: 994-ft above av. terrain, 1004-ft. above ground, 1581-ft. above sea level.

Latitude	43°	01'	48"
Longitude	78°	55'	15"

Note: Latitude and longitude coordinates shown are based on the North American Datum of 1927 (NAD 27) as currently required by the Mass Media Bureau of the FCC.

Ownership: LIN TV Corp. (Group Owner).

Began Operation: April 1, 2004. Began analog operations: May 13, 1987. Sale to present owner by Western New York Public Broadcasting Association approved by FCC June 6, 2001. LIN recieved waiver to operate as commercial station on non-commercial allocation. Ceased analog operations: June 12, 2009.

Represented (sales): Blair Television.

Personnel:

Chris Musial, General Manager.

Ed Bassler, Sales Director.

Rosalyn Mercio, Local Sales Manager.

Tad O'Rourke, National Sales Manager.

Joseph Schlaerth, News Director.

Dennis Majewicz, Engineering Director.

Diane Breen, Program Coordinator.

Daniel G. Myers, Marketing & Promotions Director.

Diana Threet, Traffic Manager.

Tim Baxter, New Media Director.

Angela Miles, Administrative Assistant.

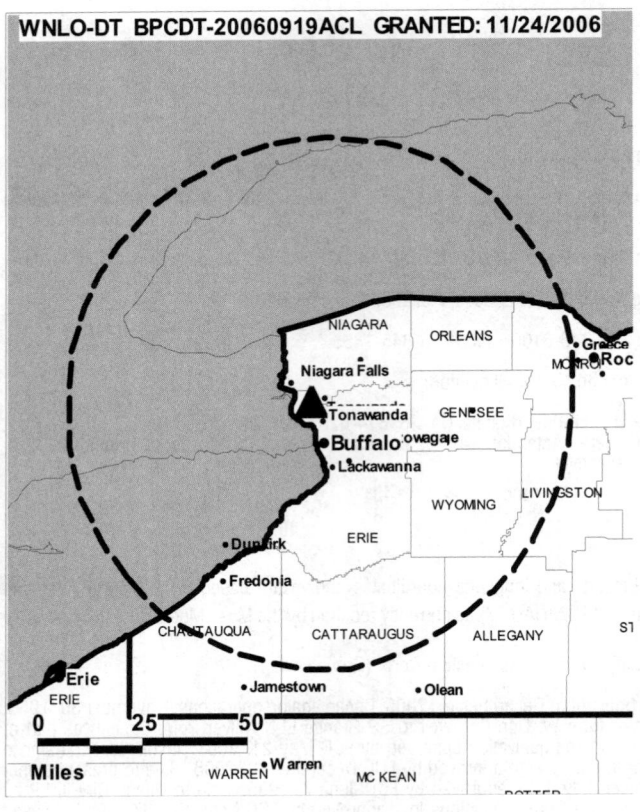

WNLO-DT BPCDT-20060919ACL GRANTED: 11/24/2006

© 2010 Warren Communications News

City of License: Buffalo. **Station DMA:** Buffalo, NY. **Rank:** 52.

Circulation © 2009 Nielsen. Coverage based on Nielsen study.

GrandTotal	Cable TV Households	Non-cable TV Households	Total TV Households
Estimated Station Totals *	372,080	247,690	619,770
Average Weekly Circulation (2009)	114,022	86,860	200,882
Average Daily Circulation (2009)			75,825

Station DMA Total	Cable TV Households	Non-cable TV Households	Total TV Households
Estimated Station Totals *	372,080	247,690	619,770
Average Weekly Circulation (2009)	114,022	86,860	200,882
Average Daily Circulation (2009)			75,825

*Estimated station totals are sums of the Nielsen TV and Cable TV household estimates for each county in which the station registers viewing of more than 5% as per the Nielsen Survey Methods.

WNYO-DT
Ch. 49

Network Service: MNT.

Licensee: New York Television Inc., 10706 Beaver Dam Rd, Cockeysville, MD 21030.

Studio: 699 Hertel Ave, Ste 100, Buffalo, NY 14207-2341.

Mailing Address: 699 Hertel Ave, Ste 100, Buffalo, NY 14207.

Phone: 716-875-4949. **Fax:** 716-875-4919.

E-mail: dsancher@wnyo.spgnet.com

Web Site: http://www.mytvbuffalo.com/

Technical Facilities: Channel No. 49 (680-686 MHz). Authorized power: 198-kw max. visual, aural. Antenna: 1234-ft above av. terrain, 1021-ft. above ground, 2421-ft. above sea level.

Latitude	42°	46'	58"
Longitude	78°	27'	28"

Note: Latitude and longitude coordinates shown are based on the North American Datum of 1927 (NAD 27) as currently required by the Mass Media Bureau of the FCC.

Ownership: Sinclair Broadcast Group Inc. (Group Owner).

Began Operation: December 4, 2006. Station broadcasting digitally on its analog channel allotment. Began analog operations: September 1, 1987. Ceased analog operations: June 12, 2009.

Represented (sales): Katz Media Group.

Personnel:

Nick Magnini, General Manager.

Jose Chapa, General Sales Manager.

Bruce Wilde, Chief Engineer.

John Glemb, Business Manager.

Candice Zoeller, Production & Promotion Manager.

Debbie Coulter, Traffic Manager.

Diane Fancher, Human Resources Director.

City of License: Buffalo. **Station DMA:** Buffalo, NY. **Rank:** 52.

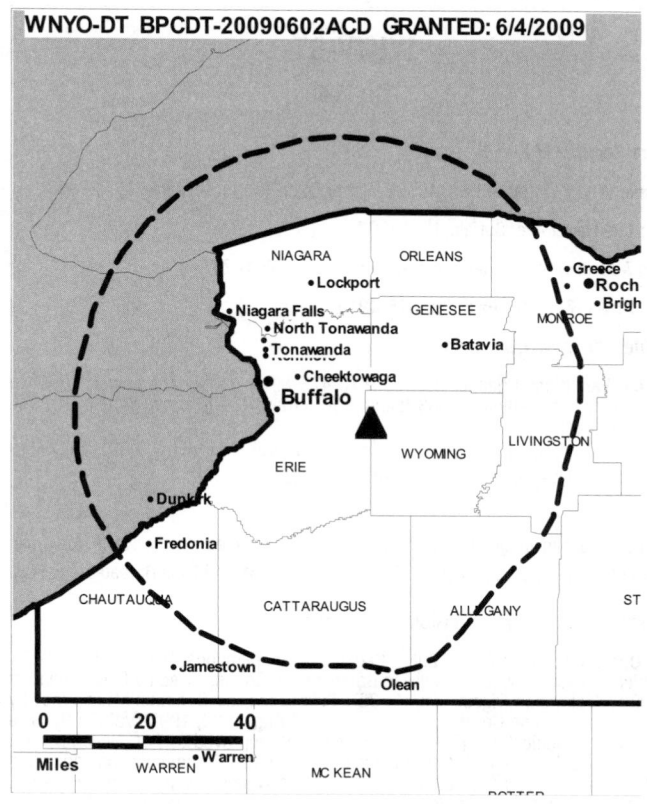

WNYO-DT BPCDT-20090602ACD GRANTED: 6/4/2009

© 2010 Warren Communications News

Circulation © 2009 Nielsen. Coverage based on Nielsen study.

GrandTotal	Cable TV Households	Non-cable TV Households	Total TV Households
Estimated Station Totals *	372,080	247,690	619,770
Average Weekly Circulation (2009)	83,051	52,341	135,392
Average Daily Circulation (2009)			42,635

Station DMA Total	Cable TV Households	Non-cable TV Households	Total TV Households
Estimated Station Totals *	372,080	247,690	619,770
Average Weekly Circulation (2009)	83,051	52,341	135,392
Average Daily Circulation (2009)			42,635

*Estimated station totals are sums of the Nielsen TV and Cable TV household estimates for each county in which the station registers viewing of more than 5% as per the Nielsen Survey Methods.

WUTV-DT
Ch. 14

Network Service: FOX.

Licensee: WUTV Licensee LLC, 10706 Beaver Dam Rd, Cockeysville, MD 21030.

Studio: 699 Hertel Ave, Buffalo, NY 14207.

Mailing Address: 699 Hertel Ave, Ste 100, Buffalo, NY 14207.

Phone: 716-447-3200. **Fax:** 716-875-4919.

Web Site: http://www.wutv.com

Technical Facilities: Channel No. 14 (470-476 MHz). Authorized power: 1000-kw max. visual, aural. Antenna: 983-ft above av. terrain, 984-ft. above ground, 1573-ft. above sea level.

Latitude	43°	01'	32"
Longitude	78°	55'	43"

Note: Latitude and longitude coordinates shown are based on the North American Datum of 1927 (NAD 27) as currently required by the Mass Media Bureau of the FCC.

Ownership: Sinclair Broadcast Group Inc. (Group Owner).

Began Operation: November 3, 2006. Began analog operations: December 21, 1970. Transfer to present owner by Sullivan Broadcasting Co. approved by FCC December 10, 2001 (Television Digest, Vol. 41:38). Sale to Sinclair Communications Inc. by Sullivan Broadcasting Co. was cancelled by FCC August 20, 1999 (Vol. 38:9). Sale to ABRY Communications (Sullivan Broadcasting), approved by FCC December 15, 1995 (Vol. 36:4). Sale to Act III Broadcasting by Citadel Communications approved by FCC June 13, 1990 (Vol. 29:36; 30:26). Sale to Whitehaven by Herman Pease, et al., & subsequent sale to Citadel approved by FCC August 31, 1984. Sale to Herman Pease, et al., by Ultravision Broadcasting Co. (F. R. Burczynski, et al.) approved by FCC February 10, 1978 (Vol. 17:31). Ceased analog operations: February 17, 2009.

Represented (sales): Katz Media Group.

Personnel:

Nick Magnini, General Manager.

Jose Chapa, General Sales Manager.

Bruce Wilde, Chief Engineer.

Robert J. Bart, Business Manager.

Mike Bullen, Program Director.

Candice Zoeller, Promotion Manager.

Dave Samson, Production Manager.

Debbie Coulter, Traffic Manager.

Diane Fancher, Human Resources Manager.

City of License: Buffalo. **Station DMA:** Buffalo, NY. **Rank:** 52.

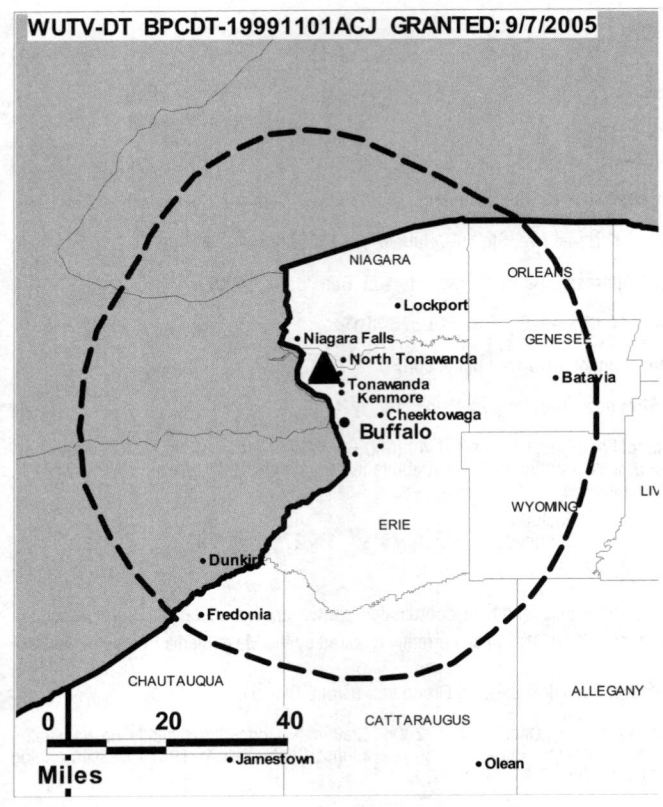

WUTV-DT BPCDT-19991101ACJ GRANTED: 9/7/2005

© 2010 Warren Communications News

Circulation © 2009 Nielsen. Coverage based on Nielsen study.

GrandTotal	Cable TV Households	Non-cable TV Households	Total TV Households
Estimated Station Totals *	392,610	247,690	640,300
Average Weekly Circulation (2009)	213,503	122,536	336,039
Average Daily Circulation (2009)			119,042

Station DMA Total	Cable TV Households	Non-cable TV Households	Total TV Households
Estimated Station Totals *	380,590	247,690	628,280
Average Weekly Circulation (2009)	212,397	122,536	334,933
Average Daily Circulation (2009)			118,886

Other DMA Total	Cable TV Households	Non-cable TV Households	Total TV Households
Estimated Station Totals *	12,020	0	12,020
Average Weekly Circulation (2009)	1,106	0	1,106
Average Daily Circulation (2009)			156

*Estimated station totals are sums of the Nielsen TV and Cable TV household estimates for each county in which the station registers viewing of more than 5% as per the Nielsen Survey Methods.

WWNY-DT
Ch. 7

Network Service: CBS.

Licensee: United Communications Corp., 120 Arcade St, Watertown, NY 13601.

Studio: 120 Arcade St, Watertown, NY 13601.

Mailing Address: 120 Arcade St, Watertown, NY 13601.

Phone: 315-788-3800. **Fax:** 315-782-7468.

Web Site: http://www.wwnytv.com

Technical Facilities: Channel No. 7 (174-180 MHz). Authorized power: 24.9-kw visual, aural. Antenna: 718-ft above av. terrain, 538-ft. above ground, 1634-ft. above sea level.

Latitude	43°	57'	15"
Longitude	75°	35'	45"

Note: Latitude and longitude coordinates shown are based on the North American Datum of 1927 (NAD 27) as currently required by the Mass Media Bureau of the FCC.

Ownership: United Communications Corp. (Group Owner).

Began Operation: May 1, 2002. Station broadcasting digitally on its analog channel allotment. Began analog operations: October 22, 1954. Ceased analog operations: February 17, 2009.

Represented (sales): Continental Television Sales.

Represented (legal): Wood, Maines & Nolan Chartered.

Represented (engineering): Cavell, Mertz & Associates Inc.

Personnel:

Cathy Pircsuk, General Manager.

Patrick Powers, Sales Manager.

Scott Atkinson, News Director.

Dave Monroe, Chief Engineer.

Robin Davis, Business Manager.

Jim Corbin, Program Director.

Kelley Shepard, Promotion Director.

Barbara Lavarnway, Traffic Manager.

City of License: Carthage. **Station DMA:** Watertown, NY. **Rank:** 177.

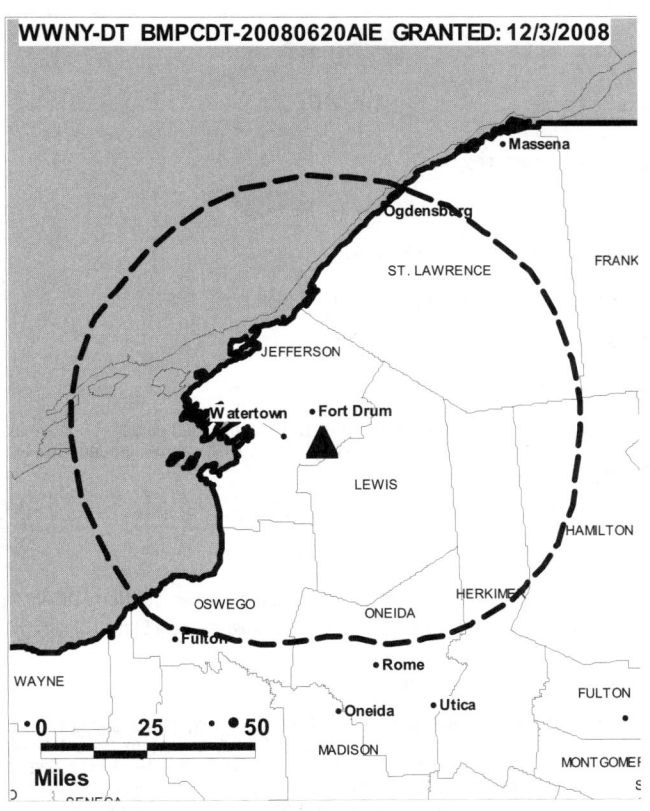

WWNY-DT BMPCDT-20080620AIE GRANTED: 12/3/2008

© 2010 Warren Communications News

Circulation © 2009 Nielsen. Coverage based on Nielsen study.

GrandTotal	Cable TV Households	Non-cable TV Households	Total TV Households
Estimated Station Totals *	65,320	29,640	94,960
Average Weekly Circulation (2009)	50,610	16,852	67,462
Average Daily Circulation (2009)			43,293

Station DMA Total	Cable TV Households	Non-cable TV Households	Total TV Households
Estimated Station Totals *	65,320	29,640	94,960
Average Weekly Circulation (2009)	50,610	16,852	67,462
Average Daily Circulation (2009)			43,293

*Estimated station totals are sums of the Nielsen TV and Cable TV household estimates for each county in which the station registers viewing of more than 5% as per the Nielsen Survey Methods.

WYDC-DT
Ch. 48

Network Service: MNT, FOX.

Grantee: WYDC Inc., 33 E Market St, Corning, NY 14830.

Studio: 33 E Market St, Corning, NY 14830.

Mailing Address: 33 E. Market St, Corning, NY 14830.

Phone: 607-937-5000. **Fax:** 607-937-4019.

Web Site: http://www.wydctv.com

Technical Facilities: Channel No. 48 (674-680 MHz). Authorized power: 7.6-kw max. visual, aural. Antenna: 1096-ft above av. terrain, 774-ft. above ground, 2454-ft. above sea level.

Latitude	42°	08'	30"
Longitude	77°	04'	39"

Note: Latitude and longitude coordinates shown are based on the North American Datum of 1927 (NAD 27) as currently required by the Mass Media Bureau of the FCC.

Ownership: WYDC Inc. (Group Owner).

Began Operation: April 1, 2002. Station broadcasting digitally on its analog channel allotment. Began analog operations: September 6, 1994. Sale to current owner by Standfast Broadcasting Corp. approved by FCC November 19, 1997. Sale to Standfast Broadcasting Corp. by Cornerstone Television Inc. approved by FCC February 28, 1994. Sale to Cornerstone Television Inc. by Dr. Robert P. Walker approved by FCC August 31, 1992. Sale to Dr. Robert P. Walker by Rural New York Broadcasting (David W. Rinehart) approved by FCC October 24, 1988. Sale to Rural New York Broadcasting (David W. Rinehart) by J. Michael Mangione approved by FCC October 24, 1988. Ceased analog operations: February 17, 2009.

Represented (legal): Drinker Biddle.

Represented (engineering): Cohen Dippell & Everist PC.

Personnel:

Bill Christian, President, General Manager & Chief Engineer.

Jared Lampman, General Sales Manager.

Jennifer L. Mattison, Program Director & Business Manager.

Mark Speck, On-Air Promotion Director.

David Scott, Production Manager.

Robin Pickering, Traffic Manager.

City of License: Corning. **Station DMA:** Elmira (Corning), NY. **Rank:** 176.

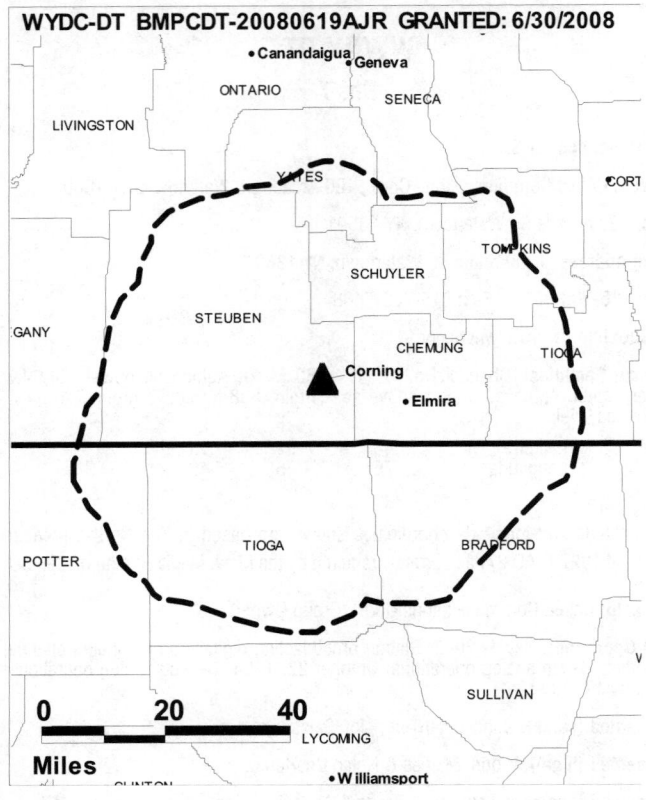

WYDC-DT BMPCDT-20080619AJR GRANTED: 6/30/2008

© 2010 Warren Communications News

Circulation © 2009 Nielsen. Coverage based on Nielsen study.

GrandTotal	Cable TV Households	Non-cable TV Households	Total TV Households
Estimated Station Totals *	71,820	22,800	94,620
Average Weekly Circulation (2009)	29,917	2,037	31,954
Average Daily Circulation (2009)			9,115

Station DMA Total	Cable TV Households	Non-cable TV Households	Total TV Households
Estimated Station Totals *	67,540	22,800	90,340
Average Weekly Circulation (2009)	29,326	2,037	31,363
Average Daily Circulation (2009)			9,055

Other DMA Total	Cable TV Households	Non-cable TV Households	Total TV Households
Estimated Station Totals *	4,280	0	4,280
Average Weekly Circulation (2009)	591	0	591
Average Daily Circulation (2009)			60

*Estimated station totals are sums of the Nielsen TV and Cable TV household estimates for each county in which the station registers viewing of more than 5% as per the Nielsen Survey Methods.

WENY-DT
Ch. 36

Network Service: CW, ABC.

Grantee: Lilly Broadcasting LLC, 2 Eastleigh Ln, Natick, MA 01760.

Studio: 474 Old Ithaca Rd, Horseheads, NY 14845.

Mailing Address: 474 Old Ithaca Rd, Horseheads, NY 14845.

Phone: 607-739-3636. **Fax:** 607-739-1418.

Web Site: http://www.weny.com

Technical Facilities: Channel No. 36 (602-608 MHz). Authorized power: 75-kw max. visual, aural. Antenna: 1122-ft above av. terrain, 774-ft. above ground, 2454-ft. above sea level.

Latitude	42°	08'	31"
Longitude	77°	04'	40"

Note: Latitude and longitude coordinates shown are based on the North American Datum of 1927 (NAD 27) as currently required by the Mass Media Bureau of the FCC.

Ownership: Lilly Broadcasting Holdings LLC (Group Owner).

Began Operation: February 9, 2009. Station broadcasting digitally on its analog channel allotment. Began analog operations: November 19, 1969. Ceased analog operations: February 9, 2009.

Represented (sales): TeleRep Inc.

Personnel:

Pete Veto, General Manager & Programming & National Sales Manager.

Sharon Ewsuk, General Sales & Local Sales Manager.

Brian Lilly, Vice President.

Scott Cook, News Director.

Mark Saia, Chief Engineer.

Lisa Flora, Business Manager.

Patrick Reilly, Promotion Director.

Bruce Hauver, Production Director.

Dan Beach, Traffic Manager.

City of License: Elmira. **Station DMA:** Elmira (Corning), NY. **Rank:** 176.

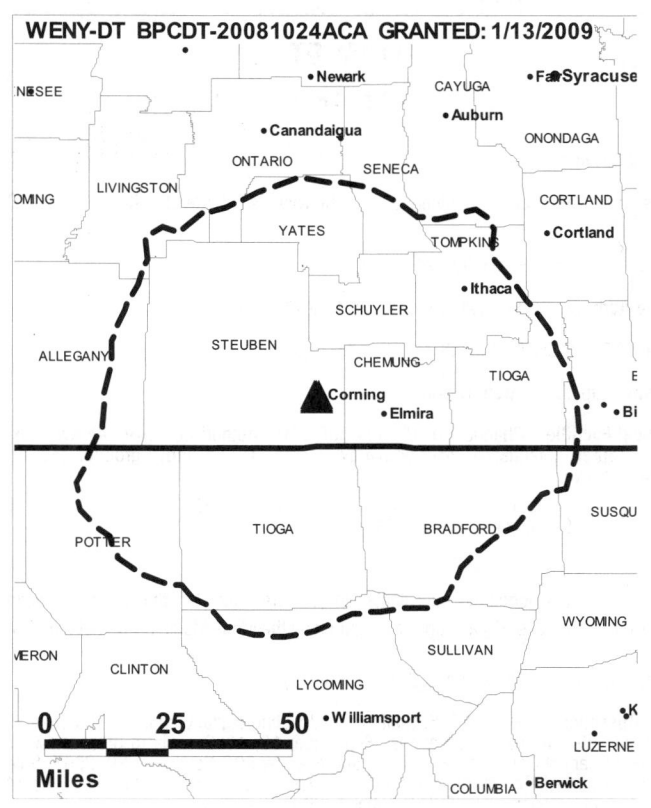

WENY-DT BPCDT-20081024ACA GRANTED: 1/13/2009

© 2010 Warren Communications News

Circulation © 2009 Nielsen. Coverage based on Nielsen study.

GrandTotal	Cable TV Households	Non-cable TV Households	Total TV Households
Estimated Station Totals *	121,210	28,550	149,760
Average Weekly Circulation (2009)	42,903	3,512	46,415
Average Daily Circulation (2009)			17,888

Station DMA Total	Cable TV Households	Non-cable TV Households	Total TV Households
Estimated Station Totals *	67,540	28,550	96,090
Average Weekly Circulation (2009)	37,073	3,512	40,585
Average Daily Circulation (2009)			16,876

Other DMA Total	Cable TV Households	Non-cable TV Households	Total TV Households
Estimated Station Totals *	53,670	0	53,670
Average Weekly Circulation (2009)	5,830	0	5,830
Average Daily Circulation (2009)			1,012

*Estimated station totals are sums of the Nielsen TV and Cable TV household estimates for each county in which the station registers viewing of more than 5% as per the Nielsen Survey Methods.

WETM-DT
Ch. 18

Network Service: NBC.

Licensee: Newport Television License LLC, 460 Nichols Rd, Ste 250, Kansas City, MO 64112.

Studio: 101 E Water St, Elmira, NY 14901.

Mailing Address: PO Box 1207, Elmira, NY 14902.

Phone: 607-733-5518. **Fax:** 607-734-1176.

Web Site: http://www.wetmtv.com

Technical Facilities: Channel No. 18 (494-500 MHz). Authorized power: 45-kw max. visual, aural. Antenna: 1234-ft above av. terrain, 817-ft. above ground, 2523-ft. above sea level.

Latitude	42°	06'	22"
Longitude	76°	52'	17"

Note: Latitude and longitude coordinates shown are based on the North American Datum of 1927 (NAD 27) as currently required by the Mass Media Bureau of the FCC.

Ownership: Newport Television LLC (Group Owner).

Began Operation: June 26, 2006. Station broadcasting digitally on its analog channel allotment. Began analog operations: September 10, 1956. Sale to present owner by Clear Channel Communications Inc. approved by FCC November 29, 2007. Sale to Clear Channel Communications Inc. by Smith Television License Holdings of New York LLC approved by FCC October 1, 2004. Sale to Smith Television License Holdings of New York LLC by Times Mirror Co. approved by FCC April 17, 1986. Previous sale to Times Mirror Co. by Newhouse Broadcasting Corp. approved by FCC March 27, 1980. Ceased analog operations: June 12, 2009.

Represented (legal): Covington & Burling.

Represented (sales): Blair Television.

Personnel:

Randy Reid, Vice President & General Manager.

Bob Cibulsky, General Sales Manager.

Steve Lucarelli, National Sales Manager.

Scott Nichols, News Director.

Chris Zell, Chief Engineer.

Scott Iddings, Marketing & Production Director.

Donna Roberts, Traffic Coordinator.

City of License: Elmira. **Station DMA:** Elmira (Corning), NY. **Rank:** 176.

© 2010 Warren Communications News

Circulation © 2009 Nielsen. Coverage based on Nielsen study.

GrandTotal	Cable TV Households	Non-cable TV Households	Total TV Households
Estimated Station Totals *	97,930	49,380	147,310
Average Weekly Circulation (2009)	60,348	8,173	68,521
Average Daily Circulation (2009)			41,727

Station DMA Total	Cable TV Households	Non-cable TV Households	Total TV Households
Estimated Station Totals *	67,540	28,550	96,090
Average Weekly Circulation (2009)	50,965	6,851	57,816
Average Daily Circulation (2009)			36,195

Other DMA Total	Cable TV Households	Non-cable TV Households	Total TV Households
Estimated Station Totals *	30,390	20,830	51,220
Average Weekly Circulation (2009)	9,383	1,322	10,705
Average Daily Circulation (2009)			5,532

*Estimated station totals are sums of the Nielsen TV and Cable TV household estimates for each county in which the station registers viewing of more than 5% as per the Nielsen Survey Methods.

WNYB-DT
Ch. 26

Network Service: IND.

Licensee: Faith Broadcasting Network Inc., PO Box 1010, Marion, IL 62959-1010.

Studio: 5775 Big Tree Rd, Orchard Park, NY 14127.

Mailing Address: 5775 Big Tree Rd, Orchard Park, NY 14127.

Phone: 716-662-2659. **Fax:** 716-667-2499.

Web Site: http://www.tct.tv

Technical Facilities: Channel No. 26 (542-548 MHz). Authorized power: 234-kw max. visual, aural. Antenna: 1519-ft above av. terrain, 1027-ft. above ground, 2815-ft. above sea level.

Latitude	42°	23'	36"
Longitude	79°	13'	44"

Requests CP for change to 1000-kw max. visual; BPCDT-20080619AFD.

Note: Latitude and longitude coordinates shown are based on the North American Datum of 1927 (NAD 27) as currently required by the Mass Media Bureau of the FCC.

Ownership: Faith Broadcasting Network Inc.

Began Operation: February 6, 2006. Station broadcasting digitally on its analog channel allotment. Began analog operations: September 24, 1988. Left air 1991. Sale to Tri-State Christian TV Inc. by Grant Television Inc. approved by FCC March 1, 1996, when Grant traded CP to Tri-State for WNYO-TV, Buffalo, NY. WNYB returned to air January 10, 1997. Sale to present owner by Tri-State Christian TV Inc. approved by FCC May 7, 2002. Ceased analog operations: June 12, 2009.

Represented (legal): Colby M. May.

Personnel:

Loren Sperrey, Station Manager.

Michael McManus, Chief Engineer.

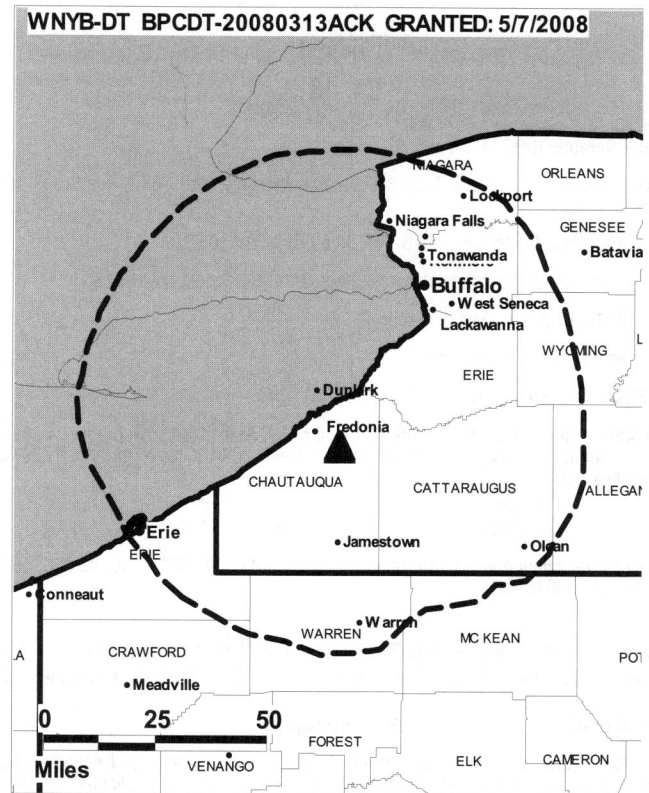

WNYB-DT BPCDT-20080313ACK GRANTED: 5/7/2008

© 2010 Warren Communications News

City of License: Jamestown. **Station DMA:** Buffalo, NY. **Rank:** 52.

Nielsen Data: Not available.

WRNN-DT
Ch. 48

Network Service: IND.

Licensee: WRNN License Co. LLC, 800 Westchester Ave, Ste S-640, Rye Brook, NY 10573.

Studio: 800 Westchester Ave, Ste S-640, Rye Brook, NY 10573.

Mailing Address: 800 Westchester Ave, Ste S-640, Rye Brook, NY 10573.

Phone: 914-417-2700. **Fax:** 914-696-0276.

E-mail: pcorsentino@rnntv.com

Web Site: http://www.rnntv.com

Technical Facilities: Channel No. 48 (674-680 MHz). Authorized power: 950-kw max. visual, aural. Antenna: 1240-ft above av. terrain, 304-ft. above ground, 1709-ft. above sea level.

Latitude	41°	29'	18.3"
Longitude	73°	56'	54.4"

Holds CP for change to 835-kw max. visual; lat. 41° 29' 18", long. 73° 56' 56", BPCDT-20080616AED.

Note: Latitude and longitude coordinates shown are based on the North American Datum of 1927 (NAD 27) as currently required by the Mass Media Bureau of the FCC.

Ownership: WRNN-TV Associates LP (Group Owner).

Began Operation: September 26, 2003. Began analog operations: December 15, 1985. On August 26th, 2004, WRNN-TV ceased analog operations; license returned to FCC September 1, 2004.

Represented (legal): Wiley Rein LLP.

Personnel:

Christian French, Vice President & Chief Executive Officer.

Danny Kischel, Operations Director.

Sal Martirano, General Sales Manager.

Phil Corsentino, News Director.

Rhonda Thorne, Human Resources Director.

Michelle Cannizzo, Consumer Program Director.

Mary Lou Pitcher, Consumer Program Director.

City of License: Kingston. **Station DMA:** New York, NY. **Rank:** 1.

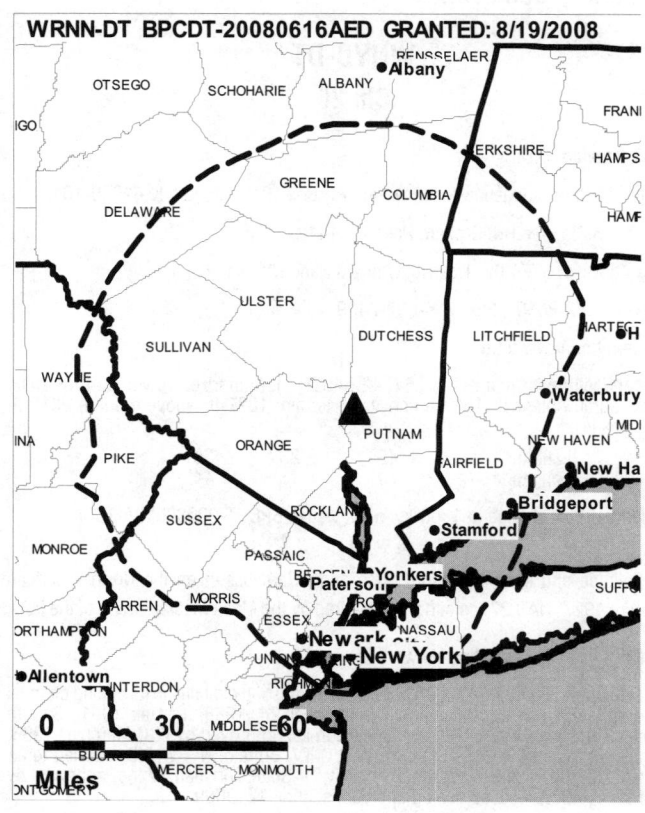

WRNN-DT BPCDT-20080616AED GRANTED: 8/19/2008

© 2010 Warren Communications News

Circulation © 2009 Nielsen. Coverage based on Nielsen study.

GrandTotal	Cable TV Households	Non-cable TV Households	Total TV Households
Estimated Station Totals *	416,930	9,970	426,900
Average Weekly Circulation (2009)	31,376	658	32,034
Average Daily Circulation (2009)			4,659

Station DMA Total	Cable TV Households	Non-cable TV Households	Total TV Households
Estimated Station Totals *	416,930	9,970	426,900
Average Weekly Circulation (2009)	31,376	658	32,034
Average Daily Circulation (2009)			4,659

*Estimated station totals are sums of the Nielsen TV and Cable TV household estimates for each county in which the station registers viewing of more than 5% as per the Nielsen Survey Methods.

WABC-DT
Ch. 7

Network Service: ABC.

Licensee: American Broadcasting Companies Inc., 77 W 66th St, 16th Fl, New York, NY 10023.

Studio: 7 Lincoln Sq, New York, NY 10023.

Mailing Address: 7 Lincoln Sq, New York, NY 10023.

Phone: 212-456-7000; 212-456-3173. **Fax:** 212-456-2381.

Web Site: http://7online.com

Technical Facilities: Channel No. 7 (174-180 MHz). Authorized power: 11.69-kw visual, aural. Antenna: 1329-ft above av. terrain, 1322-ft. above ground, 1373-ft. above sea level.

Latitude	40°	44'	54"
Longitude	73°	59'	10"

Requests CP for change to 27-kw visual; BPCDT-20090626ABL.

Requests modification of CP for change to 5.59-kw visual, 1657-ft above av. terrain, 1686-ft. above ground, 1700-ft. above sea level; lat. 40° 42' 36.4", long. 74° 00' 48.8", BMPCDT-20080620AMV.

Note: Latitude and longitude coordinates shown are based on the North American Datum of 1927 (NAD 27) as currently required by the Mass Media Bureau of the FCC.

Satellite Earth Stations: Vertex, 4.7-meter Ku-band; Andrew, 5.6-meter Ku-band; M/A-Com, Andrew receivers.

Ownership: Disney Enterprises Inc. (Group Owner).

Began Operation: June 29, 2001. Standard Definition. Station broadcasting digitally on its analog channel allotment. Operations terminated due to World Trade Center attacks September 11, 2001. Resumed operations October 30, 2003. Began analog operations: August 10, 1948. Sale to present owner by Capital Cities/ABC Inc. approved by FCC February 8, 1996. Ceased analog operations: June 12, 2009.

Personnel:

Rebecca S. Campbell, President & General Manager.

Pat Liguori, Senior Vice President, Research, ABC Owned TV Stations.

Kenny Plotnik, Vice President & News Director.

Art Moore, Vice President & Programming Director.

Bill Beam, Vice President, Engineering.

Richard Graham, Vice President, Finance & Business Affairs.

Scott Simensky, Vice President & General Sales Manager.

Iris Osman, Vice President & Local Sales Manager.

Alyson Rozner, Vice President, Marketing.

Janine DiCarlo, Vice President, Marketing.

City of License: New York. **Station DMA:** New York, NY. **Rank:** 1.

© 2010 Warren Communications News

Circulation © 2009 Nielsen. Coverage based on Nielsen study.

GrandTotal	Cable TV Households	Non-cable TV Households	Total TV Households
Estimated Station Totals *	6,231,420	2,144,080	8,375,500
Average Weekly Circulation (2009)	3,894,344	917,628	4,811,972
Average Daily Circulation (2009)			2,376,339

Station DMA Total	Cable TV Households	Non-cable TV Households	Total TV Households
Estimated Station Totals *	5,717,640	1,148,600	6,866,240
Average Weekly Circulation (2009)	3,801,339	818,502	4,619,841
Average Daily Circulation (2009)			2,323,571

Other DMA Total	Cable TV Households	Non-cable TV Households	Total TV Households
Estimated Station Totals *	513,780	995,480	1,509,260
Average Weekly Circulation (2009)	93,005	99,126	192,131
Average Daily Circulation (2009)			52,768

*Estimated station totals are sums of the Nielsen TV and Cable TV household estimates for each county in which the station registers viewing of more than 5% as per the Nielsen Survey Methods.

WCBS-DT
Ch. 56

Network Service: CBS.

Licensee: CBS Broadcasting Inc., 2000 K St NW, Ste 725, Washington, DC 20006.

Studio: 524 W 57th St, New York, NY 10019.

Mailing Address: 524 W 57th St, New York, NY 10019.

Phone: 212-975-4321. **Fax:** 212-975-9387.

Web Site: http://www.wcbstv.com

Technical Facilities: Channel No. 56 (722-728 MHz). Authorized power: 349-kw max. visual, aural. Antenna: 1302-ft above av. terrain, 1296-ft. above ground, 1345-ft. above sea level.

Latitude	40°	44'	54"
Longitude	73°	59'	10"

Requests modification of CP for change to 225-kw max. visual, 1703-ft above av. terrain, 1726-ft. above ground, 1740-ft. above sea level; lat. 40° 42' 46", long. 74° 00' 49", BMPCDT-20080619AAZ.

Holds CP for change to channel number 33, 284-kw max. visual, 1302-ft above av. terrain, 1296-ft. above ground, 1347-ft. above sea level; BPCDT-20080523AEI.

Note: Latitude and longitude coordinates shown are based on the North American Datum of 1927 (NAD 27) as currently required by the Mass Media Bureau of the FCC.

Ownership: CBS Corp. (Group Owner).

Began Operation: November 1, 1998. Began analog operations: July 1, 1941. Ceased analog operations: June 12, 2009.

Personnel:

Peter Dunn, President & General Manager.

Joel Goldberg, Senior Vice President & Program Director.

David Friend, Vice President & News Director.

Bruce Brauer, Vice President, Creative Services, Advertising & Promotion.

Steve Pair, Vice President, Engineering.

Allan Clack, General Sales Manager.

Larry Manogue, Sales Operations Manager.

Rich Lacourciere, Local Sales Manager.

Vincent McCarthy, Local Sales Manager.

Rick McGuire, Sports & New Business Sales Director.

Franca Braatz, Special Events & New Operations Director.

Sharon Persaud, Public Affairs Director.

John Auerbach, Managing Editor, News.

Valerie Feder, Assistant News Director.

Kathleen Kelly, Human Resources Director.

Dan Shelley, Digital Media Director.

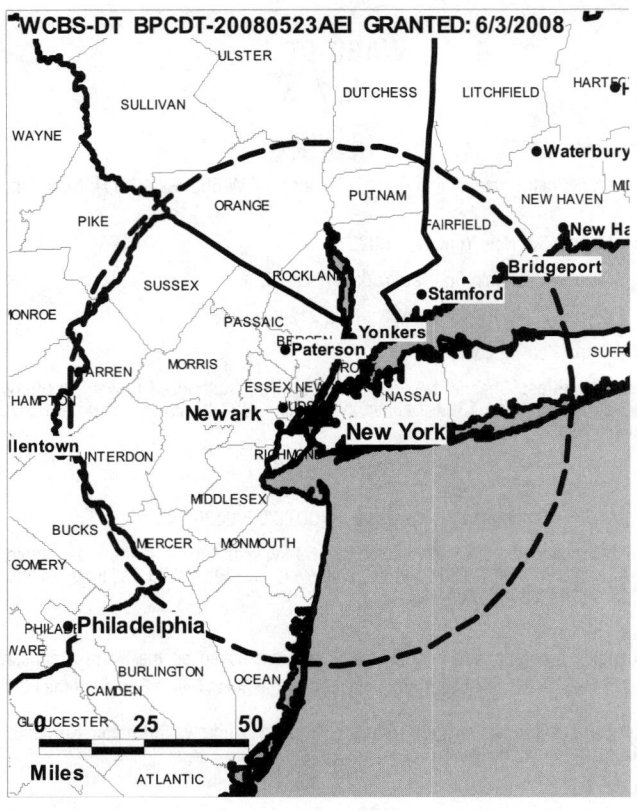

© 2010 Warren Communications News

Pam Teran, Controller.

City of License: New York. **Station DMA:** New York, NY. **Rank:** 1.

Circulation © 2009 Nielsen. Coverage based on Nielsen study.

GrandTotal	Cable TV Households	Non-cable TV Households	Total TV Households
Estimated Station Totals *	6,259,530	2,388,100	8,647,630
Average Weekly Circulation (2009)	3,966,214	864,644	4,830,858
Average Daily Circulation (2009)			2,152,295

Station DMA Total	Cable TV Households	Non-cable TV Households	Total TV Households
Estimated Station Totals *	5,717,640	1,148,600	6,866,240
Average Weekly Circulation (2009)	3,874,820	738,185	4,613,005
Average Daily Circulation (2009)			2,095,513

Other DMA Total	Cable TV Households	Non-cable TV Households	Total TV Households
Estimated Station Totals *	541,890	1,239,500	1,781,390
Average Weekly Circulation (2009)	91,394	126,459	217,853
Average Daily Circulation (2009)			56,782

*Estimated station totals are sums of the Nielsen TV and Cable TV household estimates for each county in which the station registers viewing of more than 5% as per the Nielsen Survey Methods.

WNBC-DT
Ch. 28

Network Service: NBC.

Grantee: NBC Telemundo License Co., 1299 Pennsylvania Ave NW, 11th Fl, c/o NBC Inc., Washington, DC 20004.

Studio: 30 Rockefeller Plaza, New York, NY 10112.

Mailing Address: 30 Rockefeller Plaza, New York, NY 10112.

Phone: 212-664-4444. **Fax:** 212-664-2994.

E-mail: anna.carbonell@nbcuni.com

Web Site: http://www.nbcnewyork.com

Technical Facilities: Channel No. 28 (554-560 MHz). Authorized power: 200.2-kw max. visual, aural. Antenna: 1302-ft above av. terrain, 1296-ft. above ground, 1347-ft. above sea level.

Latitude	40°	41'	54"
Longitude	73°	59'	10"

Note: Latitude and longitude coordinates shown are based on the North American Datum of 1927 (NAD 27) as currently required by the Mass Media Bureau of the FCC.

Ownership: NBC Universal (Group Owner).

Began Operation: July 3, 2001. High Definition. Began analog operations: July 1, 1941. Sale of parent RCA Corp. to General Electric Co. approved by FCC June 5, 1986. Ceased analog operations: June 12, 2009.

Personnel:

Tom O'Brien, President & General Manager.

Vickie Burns, Vice President, News & Content.

David Hyman, Vice President, Creative Services & Programming.

Anna Carbonell, Vice President, Press & Public Affairs.

Robert Harnaga, Vice President, Sales.

Geline Midouin, Vice President, Human Resources.

Kathy Mosolino, Technical & Operations Director.

Evan Kutner, Research Director.

City of License: New York. **Station DMA:** New York, NY. **Rank:** 1.

WNBC-DT BPCDT-20080314ACO GRANTED: 3/31/2008

© 2010 Warren Communications News

Circulation © 2009 Nielsen. Coverage based on Nielsen study.

GrandTotal	Cable TV Households	Non-cable TV Households	Total TV Households
Estimated Station Totals *	6,451,420	2,019,680	8,471,100
Average Weekly Circulation (2009)	3,862,492	802,897	4,665,389
Average Daily Circulation (2009)			2,037,777

Station DMA Total	Cable TV Households	Non-cable TV Households	Total TV Households
Estimated Station Totals *	5,717,640	1,122,570	6,840,210
Average Weekly Circulation (2009)	3,725,518	712,411	4,437,929
Average Daily Circulation (2009)			1,979,099

Other DMA Total	Cable TV Households	Non-cable TV Households	Total TV Households
Estimated Station Totals *	733,780	897,110	1,630,890
Average Weekly Circulation (2009)	136,974	90,486	227,460
Average Daily Circulation (2009)			58,678

*Estimated station totals are sums of the Nielsen TV and Cable TV household estimates for each county in which the station registers viewing of more than 5% as per the Nielsen Survey Methods.

WNYW-DT
Ch. 44

Network Service: FOX.

Licensee: Fox Television Stations Inc., 5151 Wisconsin Ave. NW, c/o Molly Pauker, Washington, DC 20016.

Studio: 205 E 67th St, New York, NY 10065.

Mailing Address: 205 E 67th St, New York, NY 10065.

Phone: 212-452-5555. **Fax:** 212-452-5512.

Web Site: http://www.myfoxny.com

Technical Facilities: Channel No. 44 (650-656 MHz). Authorized power: 246-kw max. visual, aural. Antenna: 1207-ft above av. terrain, 1198-ft. above ground, 1250-ft. above sea level.

Latitude	40°	44'	54"
Longitude	73°	59'	10"

Holds CP for change to 500-kw max. visual, 1391-ft above av. terrain, 1384-ft. above ground, 1435-ft. above sea level; BPCDT-20080620AJQ.

Note: Latitude and longitude coordinates shown are based on the North American Datum of 1927 (NAD 27) as currently required by the Mass Media Bureau of the FCC.

Ownership: Fox Television Holdings Inc. (Group Owner).

Began Operation: May 1, 1999. Began analog operations: May 2, 1944 as a Du Mont station. Du Mont Broadcasting Corp. was spun off by Allen B. Du Mont Laboratories Inc. on December 2, 1955, to its common stockholders of record on November 14, 1955, pursuant to FCC consent of November 17, 1955. Its name was changed to Metropolitan Broadcasting Corp. on May 13, 1958. March 28, 1961, parent company name became Metromedia Inc. Sale to present owner by Metromedia approved by FCC November 14, 1985 (Television Digest, Vol. 25:18, 39, 46). Ceased analog operations: June 12, 2009.

Represented (legal): Skadden, Arps, Slate, Meagher & Flom LLP.

Personnel:

Lew Leone, Vice President & General Manager.

Al Shjarback, Vice President, Engineering & Operations.

Patrick Paolini, Vice President & Sales Director.

Daniel Carlin, Vice President, Programming & Research.

Matt Ohnemus, Vice President & Creative Director.

Rob Schu, National Sales Manager.

Sue Rosenberg, Business Manager.

Ronica Harris, Producer.

Rena Popp, Assistant News Director.

Tony Yee, Research Director.

Violet Chew, Traffic Manager.

Iris Sierra, Human Resourses Director.

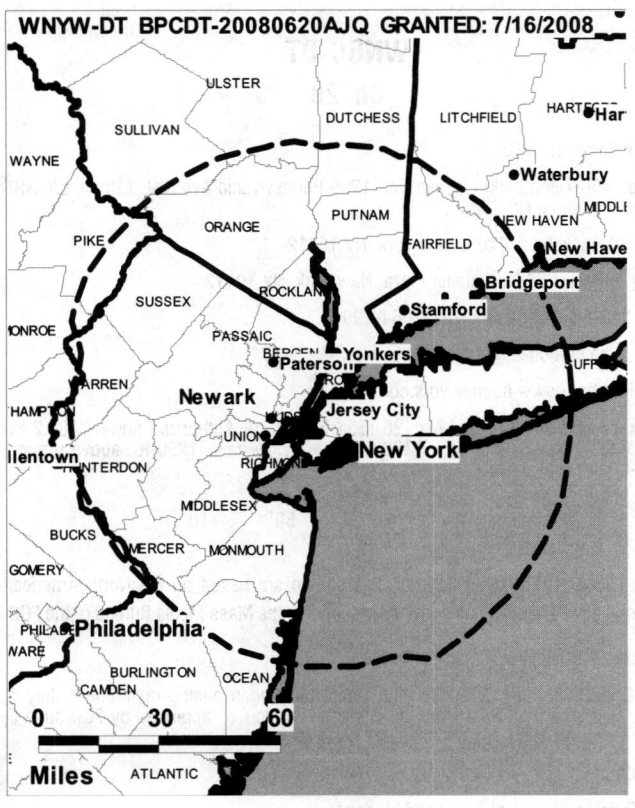

© 2010 Warren Communications News

City of License: New York. **Station DMA:** New York, NY. **Rank:** 1.

Circulation © 2009 Nielsen. Coverage based on Nielsen study.

GrandTotal	Cable TV Households	Non-cable TV Households	Total TV Households
Estimated Station Totals *	6,518,600	2,413,940	8,932,540
Average Weekly Circulation (2009)	3,766,226	920,519	4,686,745
Average Daily Circulation (2009)			1,737,203

Station DMA Total	Cable TV Households	Non-cable TV Households	Total TV Households
Estimated Station Totals *	5,717,640	1,148,600	6,866,240
Average Weekly Circulation (2009)	3,588,201	789,148	4,377,349
Average Daily Circulation (2009)			1,670,558

Other DMA Total	Cable TV Households	Non-cable TV Households	Total TV Households
Estimated Station Totals *	800,960	1,265,340	2,066,300
Average Weekly Circulation (2009)	178,025	131,371	309,396
Average Daily Circulation (2009)			66,645

*Estimated station totals are sums of the Nielsen TV and Cable TV household estimates for each county in which the station registers viewing of more than 5% as per the Nielsen Survey Methods.

WPIX-DT
Ch. 11

Network Service: CW.

Grantee: WPIX Inc., Debtor-In-Possession, 220 E 42nd St, New York, NY 10017.

Studio: 220 E 42nd St, New York, NY 10017.

Mailing Address: 220 E 42nd St, New York, NY 10017.

Phone: 212-949-1100. **Fax:** 212-210-2591.

Web Site: http://cw11.trb.com/

Technical Facilities: Channel No. 11 (198-204 MHz). Authorized power: 9.1-kw visual, aural. Antenna: 1329-ft above av. terrain, 1322-ft. above ground, 1373-ft. above sea level.

Latitude	40°	44'	54"
Longitude	73°	59'	10"

Requests modification of CP for change to 5.5-kw visual, 1660-ft above av. terrain, 1686-ft. above ground, 1699-ft. above sea level; lat. 40° 42' 46", long. 74° 00' 49", BMPCDT-20080620ALB.

Note: Latitude and longitude coordinates shown are based on the North American Datum of 1927 (NAD 27) as currently required by the Mass Media Bureau of the FCC.

Ownership: Tribune Broadcasting Co., Debtor-In-Possession (Group Owner).

Began Operation: July 19, 2001. Station broadcasting digitally on its analog channel allotment. Began analog operations: June 15, 1948. Involuntary assignment to debtor-in-possession status approved by FCC December 24, 2008. Transfer of control from public shareholders of the Tribune Co. to Tribune Employee Stock Ownership Plan approved by FCC November 30, 2007. Ceased analog operations: June 12, 2009.

Represented (legal): Sidley Austin LLP.

Represented (sales): TeleRep Inc.

Personnel:

Betty Ellen Berlamino, President & General Manager.

Laurel Light, Operations Director.

Bob Marra, General Sales Manager.

Debbie Presser, Local Sales Manager.

Adam Shapiro, National & Local Sales Manager.

Karen Scott, News Director.

Cathy Davis, Finance Director.

Ari Pitchenik, Promotion Manager.

Carlos Austin, Local Production & Community Affairs Director.

Steve Schussel, Research Director.

John Zeigler, Creative Services Director.

V. Jean Maye, Human Resources Director.

© 2010 Warren Communications News

City of License: New York. **Station DMA:** New York, NY. **Rank:** 1.

Circulation © 2009 Nielsen. Coverage based on Nielsen study.

GrandTotal	Cable TV Households	Non-cable TV Households	Total TV Households
Estimated Station Totals *	6,788,040	1,999,910	8,787,950
Average Weekly Circulation (2009)	3,006,304	716,963	3,723,267
Average Daily Circulation (2009)			1,309,514

Station DMA Total	Cable TV Households	Non-cable TV Households	Total TV Households
Estimated Station Totals *	5,717,640	1,148,600	6,866,240
Average Weekly Circulation (2009)	2,812,255	648,411	3,460,666
Average Daily Circulation (2009)			1,256,063

Other DMA Total	Cable TV Households	Non-cable TV Households	Total TV Households
Estimated Station Totals *	1,070,400	851,310	1,921,710
Average Weekly Circulation (2009)	194,049	68,552	262,601
Average Daily Circulation (2009)			53,451

*Estimated station totals are sums of the Nielsen TV and Cable TV household estimates for each county in which the station registers viewing of more than 5% as per the Nielsen Survey Methods.

WPXN-DT
Ch. 31

Network Service: ION.

Grantee: ION Media License Co. LLC, Debtor in Possession, 601 Clearwater Park Rd, West Palm Beach, FL 33401-6233.

Studio: 1330 Avenue of the Americas, 32nd Fl, New York, NY 10019.

Mailing Address: 1330 Avenue of the Americas, 32nd Fl, New York, NY 10019.

Phone: 212-757-3100; 212-664-6202. **Fax:** 212-956-2661.

E-mail: jackdavidson@ionmedia.com

Web Site: http://www.ionmedia.com

Technical Facilities: Channel No. 31 (572-578 MHz). Authorized power: 349-kw max. visual, aural. Antenna: 1302-ft above av. terrain, 1296-ft. above ground, 1347-ft. above sea level.

Latitude	40°	44'	54"
Longitude	73°	59'	10"

Requests modification of CP for change to 285-kw max. visual; BMPCDT-20080620ALZ.

Note: Latitude and longitude coordinates shown are based on the North American Datum of 1927 (NAD 27) as currently required by the Mass Media Bureau of the FCC.

Ownership: ION Media Networks Inc., Debtor in Possession (Group Owner).

Began Operation: April 30, 2008. Station broadcasting digitally on its analog channel allotment. Station operating under Special Temporary Authority at 100-kw max. visual. Began analog operations: November 1, 1962. Sale to Urban Television LLC pends. Involuntary assignment to debtor in possession status approved by FCC June 5, 2009. Transfer of control by ION Media Networks Inc. from Paxson Management Corp. & Lowell W. Paxson to CIG Media LLC approved by FCC December 31, 2007. Paxson Communications Corp. became ION Media Networks Inc. on June 26, 2006. Sale to Paxson Communications Corp. by ITT- Dow Jones Television approved by FCC March 4, 1998. Sale to ITT-Dow Jones Television by WNYC Communications Group approved by FCC May 17, 1996. Ceased analog operations: June 12, 2009.

Represented (legal): Dow Lohnes PLLC.

Personnel:

Joseph Koker, Vice President.

Mildred Diaz, Station Operations Manager.

Jack Davidson, Chief Engineer.

Jennifer Etros, Traffic Manager.

City of License: New York. **Station DMA:** New York, NY. **Rank:** 1.

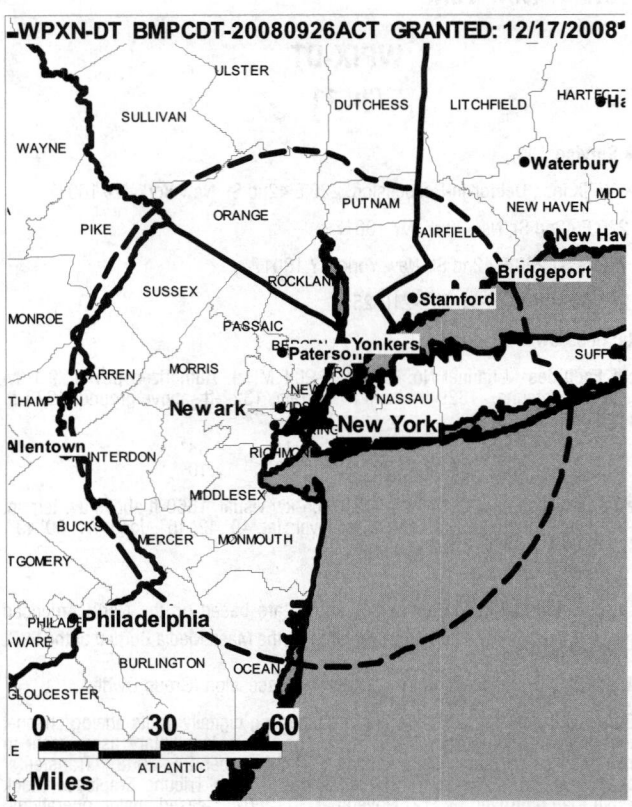

WPXN-DT BMPCDT-20080926ACT GRANTED: 12/17/2008

© 2010 Warren Communications News

Circulation © 2009 Nielsen. Coverage based on Nielsen study.

GrandTotal	Cable TV Households	Non-cable TV Households	Total TV Households
Estimated Station Totals *	5,593,030	941,580	6,534,610
Average Weekly Circulation (2009)	814,390	136,455	950,845
Average Daily Circulation (2009)			197,587

Station DMA Total	Cable TV Households	Non-cable TV Households	Total TV Households
Estimated Station Totals *	5,593,030	941,580	6,534,610
Average Weekly Circulation (2009)	814,390	136,455	950,845
Average Daily Circulation (2009)			197,587

*Estimated station totals are sums of the Nielsen TV and Cable TV household estimates for each county in which the station registers viewing of more than 5% as per the Nielsen Survey Methods.

WPTZ-DT
Ch. 14

Network Service: NBC.

Licensee: Hearst-Argyle Stations Inc., PO Box 1800, c/o Brooks, Pierce et al., Raleigh, NC 27602.

Studios: 5 Television Dr, Plattsburgh, NY 12901; 553 Roosevelt Hwy, Colchester, VT 05446.

Mailing Address: 5 Television Dr, Plattsburgh, NY 12901.

Phone: 518-561-5555. **Fax:** 518-561-5940.

Web Site: http://www.wptz.com

Technical Facilities: Channel No. 14 (470-476 MHz). Authorized power: 650-kw max. visual, aural. Antenna: 2772-ft above av. terrain, 151-ft. above ground, 4167-ft. above sea level.

| Latitude | 44° | 31' | 32" |
| Longitude | 72° | 48' | 58" |

Note: Latitude and longitude coordinates shown are based on the North American Datum of 1927 (NAD 27) as currently required by the Mass Media Bureau of the FCC.

Ownership: Hearst-Argyle Television Inc. (Group Owner).

Began Operation: November 14, 2006. Began analog operations: December 8, 1954. Hearst-Argyle received approval from the FCC May 26, 2009 to become privately owned by The Hearst Corp. Station, along with Sunrise Television's KSBW & WNNE, was swapped for Hearst-Argyle's WDTN & WNAC-TV. FCC approved deal July 1, 1998. In 1997, Sunrise Television purchased station from Sinclair Communications. Sinclair purchased station through trustee William G. Evans after News Corp. had bought Heritage Communications. Merger of Rollins Communications with Heritage Communications approved by FCC February 9, 1987. Sale to Rollins Communications by Carl F. Stohn group approved by FCC March 28, 1956. Ceased analog operations: February 17, 2009.

Represented (legal): Brooks, Pierce, McLendon, Humphrey & Leonard LLP.

Represented (sales): Eagle Television Sales.

Personnel:

Paul Sands, President & General Manager.

James Gratton, Operations Manager & Program Director.

Bruce Lawson, General Sales Manager.

Kyle Grimes, News Director.

Pete James, Local Sales Manager.

Steve Herberg, Controller.

Susan Acklen, Promotion Manager.

Dave Fleming, Production Manager.

Laura Lareau, Traffic Manager.

City of License: North Pole. **Station DMA:** Burlington, VT-Plattsburgh, NY. **Rank:** 94.

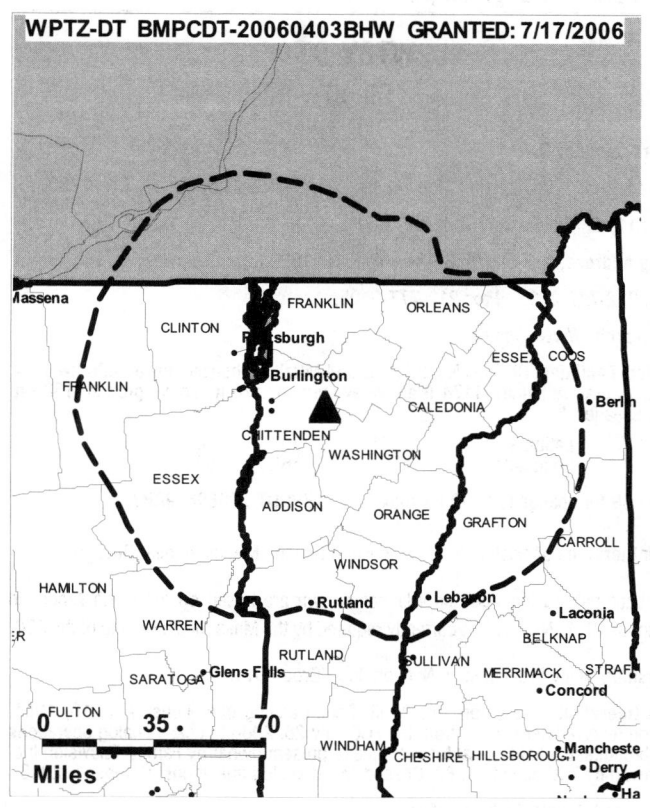

© 2010 Warren Communications News

Circulation © 2009 Nielsen. Coverage based on Nielsen study.

GrandTotal	Cable TV Households	Non-cable TV Households	Total TV Households
Estimated Station Totals *	154,490	162,140	316,630
Average Weekly Circulation (2009)	96,853	83,322	180,175
Average Daily Circulation (2009)			90,898

Station DMA Total	Cable TV Households	Non-cable TV Households	Total TV Households
Estimated Station Totals *	126,710	162,140	288,850
Average Weekly Circulation (2009)	86,602	83,322	169,924
Average Daily Circulation (2009)			87,814

Other DMA Total	Cable TV Households	Non-cable TV Households	Total TV Households
Estimated Station Totals *	27,780	0	27,780
Average Weekly Circulation (2009)	10,251	0	10,251
Average Daily Circulation (2009)			3,084

*Estimated station totals are sums of the Nielsen TV and Cable TV household estimates for each county in which the station registers viewing of more than 5% as per the Nielsen Survey Methods.

WTBY-DT
Ch. 27

Network Service: TBN.

Licensee: Trinity Broadcasting Network Inc., 2442 Michelle Dr, Tustin, CA 92780.

Studio: 111 E 15th St, New York, NY 10003.

Mailing Address: 117 E. 57th St, New York, NY 10003.

Phone: 212-777-2120. **Fax:** 212-777-0405.

Web Site: http://www.tbn.org

Technical Facilities: Channel No. 27 (548-554 MHz). Authorized power: 800-kw max. visual, aural. Antenna: 1174-ft above av. terrain, 176-ft. above ground, 1586-ft. above sea level.

Latitude	41°	29'	20"
Longitude	73°	56'	53"

Holds CP for change to 1000-kw max. visual; BPCDT-20080619ABY.

Transmitter: Side of existing tower atop North Beacon Mountain, near Beacon.

Note: Latitude and longitude coordinates shown are based on the North American Datum of 1927 (NAD 27) as currently required by the Mass Media Bureau of the FCC.

Ownership: Trinity Broadcasting Network Inc. (Group Owner).

Began Operation: September 30, 2003. Began analog operations: April 19, 1981. Station received permission from the FCC July 28, 2008 to cease analog operations and broadcast only in digital format. Sale to present owner by Family Television Inc. approved by FCC June 2, 1982. Ceased eased analog operations: October 1, 2008.

Represented (legal): Colby M. May.

Personnel:

Chris Elia, Station Manager.

Eb Tesfalidet, Chief Engineer.

Mike Hughes, Traffic Manager.

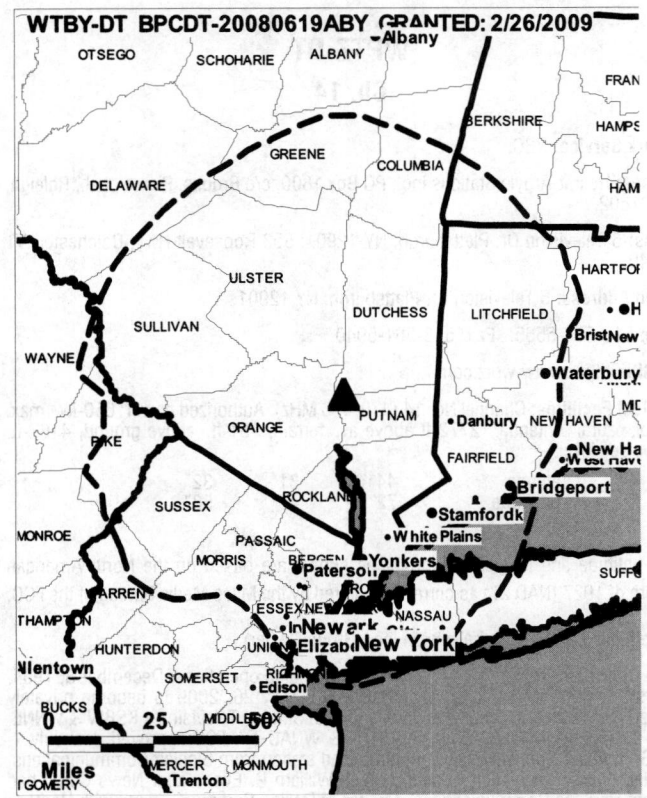

© 2010 Warren Communications News

City of License: Poughkeepsie. **Station DMA:** New York, NY. **Rank:** 1.

Nielsen Data: Not available.

WLNY-DT
Ch. 57

Network Service: IND.

Licensee: WLNY LP, 270 S Service Rd, Ste 55, Melville, NY 11747-2337.

Studio: 270 S Service Rd, Ste 55, Melville, NY 11747-2337.

Mailing Address: 270 S Service Rd, Ste 55, Melville, NY 11747.

Phone: 631-777-8855. **Fax:** 631-777-8180.

E-mail: scullen@wlnytv.com

Web Site: http://www.wlnytv.com

Technical Facilities: Channel No. 57 (728-734 MHz). Authorized power: 425-kw max. visual, aural. Antenna: 635-ft above av. terrain, 613-ft. above ground, 703-ft. above sea level.

Latitude	40°	53'	50"
Longitude	72°	54'	56"

Holds CP for change to 1000-kw max. visual, 633-ft above av. terrain, 620-ft. above ground, 710-ft. above sea level; BMPCDT-20080721ABJ.

Transmitter: 315 Wading River Hollow Rd., Ridge.

Note: Latitude and longitude coordinates shown are based on the North American Datum of 1927 (NAD 27) as currently required by the Mass Media Bureau of the FCC.

Ownership: WLNY Holdings Inc. (Group Owner).

Began Operation: May 1, 2002. Standard Definition. Began analog operations: April 28, 1985. Station received approval September 21, 2005 from FCC to cease analog broadcasting. Ceased analog operations January 1, 2006.

Represented (legal): Cohn & Marks LLP.

Personnel:

David Feinblatt, President & General Manager.

Marvin R. Chauvin, Chief Executive Officer & Program Director.

Elliot Simmons, Vice President & Sales Director.

Gerard Diorio, Vice President & Operations Manager.

Andrew Starr, Vice President, New York & National Sales Manager.

Richard Rose, News Director.

Richard Mulliner, Engineering Director.

Cathy Burkas, Business Manager.

John Lorefice, Promotion Director.

Debbie Ortiz, Production Manager.

Rosie Miranda, Traffic Manager.

Janet Greeley, Office Manager.

Susan Cullen, Executive Assistant.

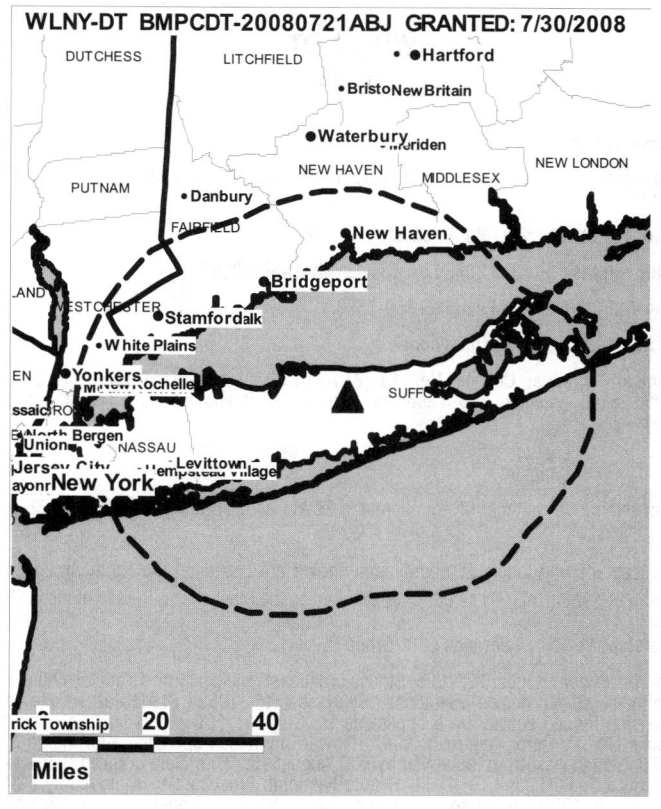

© 2010 Warren Communications News

City of License: Riverhead. **Station DMA:** New York, NY. **Rank:** 1.

Circulation © 2009 Nielsen. Coverage based on Nielsen study.

GrandTotal	Cable TV Households	Non-cable TV Households	Total TV Households
Estimated Station Totals *	4,882,730	921,270	5,804,000
Average Weekly Circulation (2009)	1,070,407	134,675	1,205,082
Average Daily Circulation (2009)			322,027

Station DMA Total	Cable TV Households	Non-cable TV Households	Total TV Households
Estimated Station Totals *	4,868,840	921,270	5,790,110
Average Weekly Circulation (2009)	1,069,546	134,675	1,204,221
Average Daily Circulation (2009)			321,958

Other DMA Total	Cable TV Households	Non-cable TV Households	Total TV Households
Estimated Station Totals *	13,890	0	13,890
Average Weekly Circulation (2009)	861	0	861
Average Daily Circulation (2009)			69

*Estimated station totals are sums of the Nielsen TV and Cable TV household estimates for each county in which the station registers viewing of more than 5% as per the Nielsen Survey Methods.

WHAM-DT
Ch. 13

Network Service: CW, ABC.

Licensee: Newport Television License LLC, 460 Nichols Rd, Ste 250, Kansas City, MO 64112.

Studio: 4225 W Henrietta Rd, Rochester, NY 14623.

Mailing Address: PO Box 20555, Rochester, NY 14602-0555.

Phone: 585-334-8700. **Fax:** 585-359-1570.

Web Site: http://www.13wham.com

Technical Facilities: Channel No. 13 (210-216 MHz). Authorized power: 10.5-kw visual, aural. Antenna: 499-ft above av. terrain, 318-ft. above ground, 991-ft. above sea level.

Latitude	43°	08'	07"
Longitude	77°	35'	03"

Requests modification of CP for change to 30-kw visual; BMPCDT-20080801AZE.

Note: Latitude and longitude coordinates shown are based on the North American Datum of 1927 (NAD 27) as currently required by the Mass Media Bureau of the FCC.

Ownership: Newport Television LLC (Group Owner).

Began Operation: August 12, 2005. Station broadcasting digitally on its analog channel allotment. Began analog operations: September 15, 1962. Started as an interim operation owned equally by 8 applicants for Ch. 13. FCC granted application of Flower City TV Corp. August 3, 1967. Flower City began operation after March 1, 1970. Sale to Post Corp. approved by FCC August 15, 1977. Sale to Gillett Holdings approved by FCC June 19, 1984. Sale to Falmouth Broadcasting approved by FCC February 8, 1990 but not consummated. Sale to VS & A-Hughes Inc. approved by FCC May 15, 1991. Sale to Guy Gannett Communications Inc. approved by FCC January 31, 1995. Sale to Sinclair Communications Inc., who subsequently sold station to The Ackerley Group, approved by FCC April 12, 1999. In stock swap, Clear Channel Broadcasting Inc. acquired The Ackerley Group. FCC approved deal May 29, 2002. Sale to present owner by Clear Channel Communications Inc. approved by FCC November 29, 2007. Ceased analog operations: June 12, 2009.

Represented (sales): Blair Television.

Represented (legal): Covington & Burling.

Personnel:

Chuck Samuels, Vice President & General Manager.

Dave DiProsa, General Sales Manager.

Mark Zeger, National Sales Manager.

Stephen Dawe, News Director.

Ted McWharf, Engineering Co-Manager.

Stan Manson, Engineering Co-Manager.

Kevin Kalvitis, Promotions Director.

Jeff Starkweather, Marketing Director.

Craig D. Heslor, Production Manager.

Charlotte Clarke, Community Affairs Director.

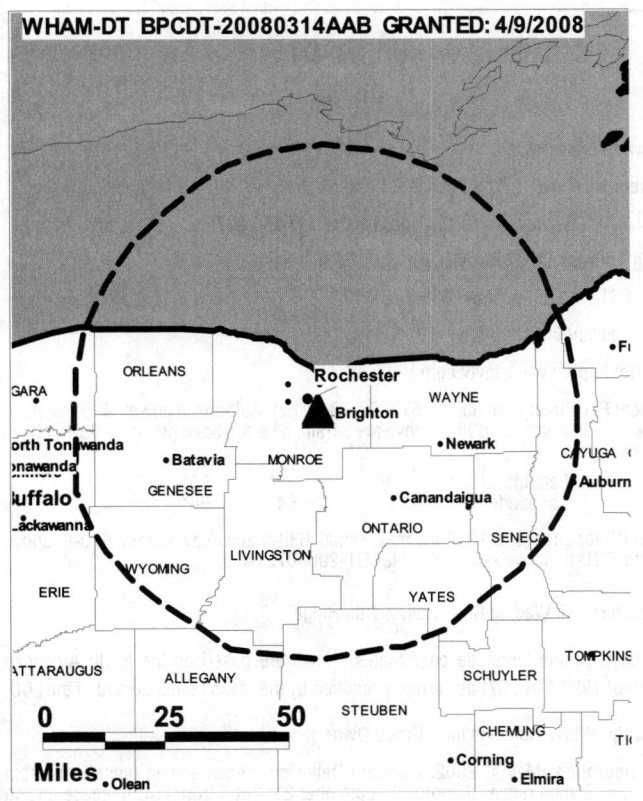

© 2010 Warren Communications News

City of License: Rochester. **Station DMA:** Rochester, NY. **Rank:** 80.

Circulation © 2009 Nielsen. Coverage based on Nielsen study.

GrandTotal	Cable TV Households	Non-cable TV Households	Total TV Households
Estimated Station Totals *	332,580	147,510	480,090
Average Weekly Circulation (2009)	197,592	86,398	283,990
Average Daily Circulation (2009)			142,704

Station DMA Total	Cable TV Households	Non-cable TV Households	Total TV Households
Estimated Station Totals *	267,730	122,860	390,590
Average Weekly Circulation (2009)	182,852	81,896	264,748
Average Daily Circulation (2009)			133,882

Other DMA Total	Cable TV Households	Non-cable TV Households	Total TV Households
Estimated Station Totals *	64,850	24,650	89,500
Average Weekly Circulation (2009)	14,740	4,502	19,242
Average Daily Circulation (2009)			8,822

*Estimated station totals are sums of the Nielsen TV and Cable TV household estimates for each county in which the station registers viewing of more than 5% as per the Nielsen Survey Methods.

WHEC-DT
Ch. 10

Network Service: NBC.

Licensee: Hubbard Broadcasting Inc., 3415 University Ave. W, St. Paul, MN 55114-2099.

Studio: 191 East Ave, Rochester, NY 14604.

Mailing Address: 191 East Ave, Rochester, NY 14604.

Phone: 585-546-5670. **Fax:** 585-454-7433.

Web Site: http://www.10nbc.com

Technical Facilities: Channel No. 10 (192-198 MHz). Authorized power: 18.1-kw visual, aural. Antenna: 502-ft above av. terrain, 307-ft. above ground, 988-ft. above sea level.

Latitude	43°	08'	07"
Longitude	77°	35'	02"

Requests modification of CP for change to 30-kw visual; BMPCDT-20080620ABS.

Note: Latitude and longitude coordinates shown are based on the North American Datum of 1927 (NAD 27) as currently required by the Mass Media Bureau of the FCC.

Ownership: Hubbard Broadcasting Inc. (Group Owner).

Began Operation: October 27, 2005. Station broadcasting digitally on its analog channel allotment. Began analog operations: November 1, 1953. Initial broadcast was as a time-share outlet on Ch. 10 with WVET-TV. It acquired WVET-TV's half of the channel and became a full time outlet following FCC approval of the transfer on August 1, 1961. Sale to BENI Broadcasting of Rochester Inc. by Gannett Co. approved by FCC June 7, 1979. Sale to Viacom International Inc. by BENI Broadcasting of Rochester Inc. approved by FCC October 18, 1983. Hubbard Broadcasting acquired station along with WNYT(TV), Albany in exchange for WTOG-TV, St. Petersburg-Tampa. FCC approved swap September 19, 1996. Ceased analog operations: June 12, 2009.

Represented (legal): Holland & Knight LLP.

Represented (sales): Petry Media Corp.

Personnel:

Arnold Klinsky, Vice President & General Manager.

Marilynn Burruto, General Sales Manager.

Mike Goldrick, News Director.

John Walsh, Chief Engineer.

Joseph Lafornara, Business Manager.

Lynette Carrol Baker, Program Director.

Rob Vandenbergh, Promotion Director.

Sherron Sheridan, Traffic Manager.

City of License: Rochester. **Station DMA:** Rochester, NY. **Rank:** 80.

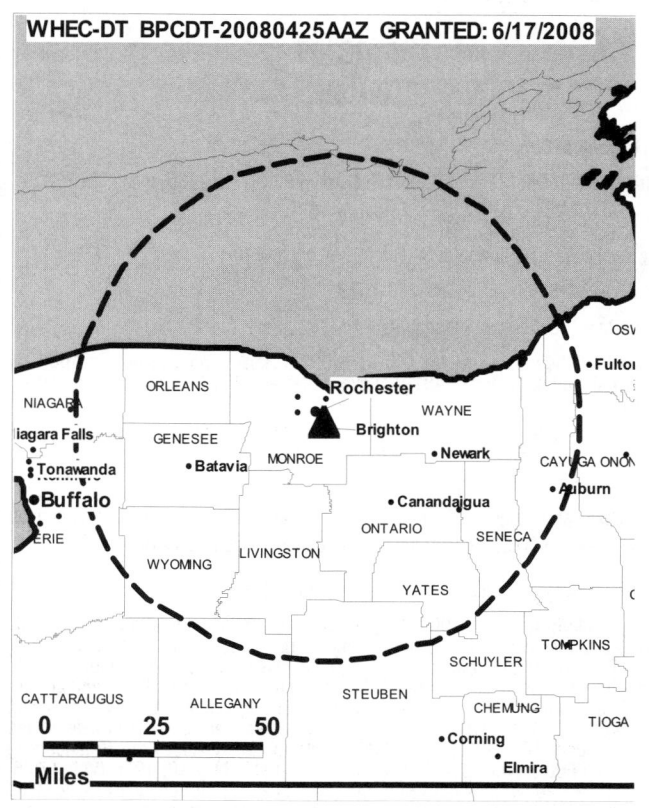

WHEC-DT BPCDT-20080425AAZ GRANTED: 6/17/2008

© 2010 Warren Communications News

Circulation © 2009 Nielsen. Coverage based on Nielsen study.

GrandTotal	Cable TV Households	Non-cable TV Households	Total TV Households
Estimated Station Totals *	332,580	143,920	476,500
Average Weekly Circulation (2009)	196,975	90,081	287,056
Average Daily Circulation (2009)			140,216

Station DMA Total	Cable TV Households	Non-cable TV Households	Total TV Households
Estimated Station Totals *	267,730	122,860	390,590
Average Weekly Circulation (2009)	181,345	85,618	266,963
Average Daily Circulation (2009)			130,911

Other DMA Total	Cable TV Households	Non-cable TV Households	Total TV Households
Estimated Station Totals *	64,850	21,060	85,910
Average Weekly Circulation (2009)	15,630	4,463	20,093
Average Daily Circulation (2009)			9,305

*Estimated station totals are sums of the Nielsen TV and Cable TV household estimates for each county in which the station registers viewing of more than 5% as per the Nielsen Survey Methods.

WROC-DT
Ch. 45

Network Service: CBS.

Licensee: Nexstar Finance Inc., 909 Lake Carolyn Pkwy, Ste 1450, Irving, TX 75039.

Studio: 201 Humboldt St, Rochester, NY 14610.

Mailing Address: 201 Humboldt St, Rochester, NY 14610.

Phone: 585-224-8888. **Fax:** 585-288-7679.

Web Site: http://rochesterhomepage.net

Technical Facilities: Channel No. 45 (656-662 MHz). Authorized power: 1000-kw max. visual, aural. Antenna: 401-ft above av. terrain, 204-ft. above ground, 885-ft. above sea level.

Latitude	43°	08'	07"
Longitude	77°	35'	02"

Note: Latitude and longitude coordinates shown are based on the North American Datum of 1927 (NAD 27) as currently required by the Mass Media Bureau of the FCC.

Ownership: Nexstar Broadcasting Group Inc. (Group Owner).

Began Operation: April 18, 2006. Began analog operations: June 11, 1949. Sale to present owner by Sunrise Broadcasting Corp. approved by FCC December 9, 1999. Sale to Smith Broadcasting Group dismissed March 31, 1999. Sale to Sunrise Broadcasting Corp. by Smith Broadcasting approved by FCC February 26, 1997. Sale to Smith Broadcasting approved by FCC September 29, 1995 (Television Digest, Vol. 35:17, 41). Sale to Television Station Partners by Ziff Corp. approved by FCC January 18, 1983 (Vol. 22:30). Sale to Ziff by Rust Craft Broadcasting approved by FCC March 22, 1979. FCC approved sale May 10, 1978 (Vol. 17:26, 27, 36, 38; 18:20, 31). Sale to Rust Craft Broadcasting by Veterans Broadcasting approved by FCC February 10, 1965 (Vol. 4:39, 46; 5:7). Previous sale to Veterans Broadcasting by Transcontinent TV Corp. approved by FCC November 15, 1961. Sale to Transcontinent by Stromberg-Carlson division of General Dynamics Corp. approved by FCC July 18, 1956 (Vol. 12:24, 29). Ceased analog operations: June 12, 2009.

Represented (legal): Drinker Biddle.

Represented (sales): Katz Media Group.

Personnel:

Louis Gattozzi, Vice President & General Manager.

Don Loy, Station Manager & Programming Manager.

Bob McCaughey, Sales Director.

Wendy Bello, Local Sales Manager.

E. J. Reynolds, National Sales Manager.

Eric Melenbacker, Chief Engineer.

Bonnie Alaimo, Business Manager & Human Resources Director.

Scott Shambley, Promotion Manager.

Dan McCarty, Traffic Manager.

City of License: Rochester. **Station DMA:** Rochester, NY. **Rank:** 80.

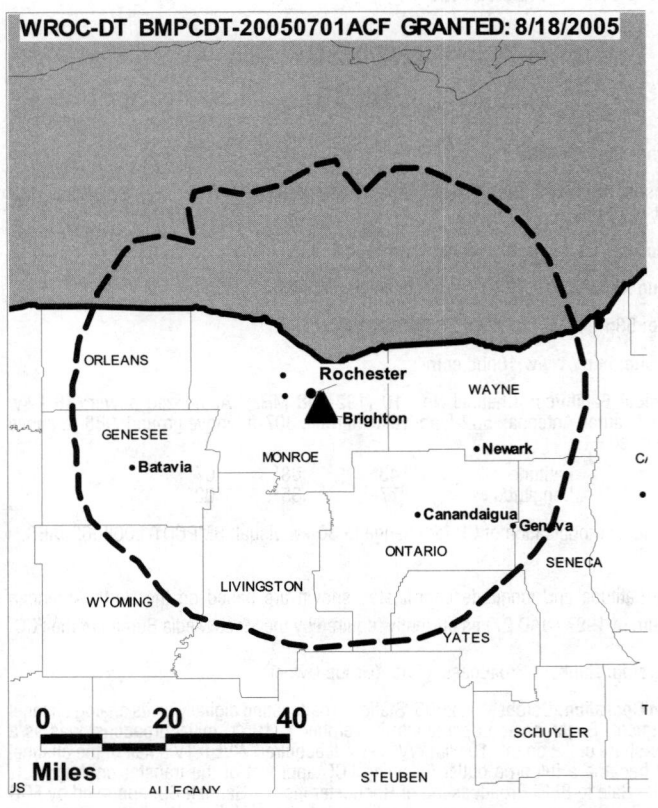

© 2010 Warren Communications News

Circulation © 2009 Nielsen. Coverage based on Nielsen study.

GrandTotal	Cable TV Households	Non-cable TV Households	Total TV Households
Estimated Station Totals *	340,780	147,510	488,290
Average Weekly Circulation (2009)	211,380	90,998	302,378
Average Daily Circulation (2009)			148,817

Station DMA Total	Cable TV Households	Non-cable TV Households	Total TV Households
Estimated Station Totals *	267,730	122,860	390,590
Average Weekly Circulation (2009)	186,240	85,634	271,874
Average Daily Circulation (2009)			135,908

Other DMA Total	Cable TV Households	Non-cable TV Households	Total TV Households
Estimated Station Totals *	73,050	24,650	97,700
Average Weekly Circulation (2009)	25,140	5,364	30,504
Average Daily Circulation (2009)			12,909

*Estimated station totals are sums of the Nielsen TV and Cable TV household estimates for each county in which the station registers viewing of more than 5% as per the Nielsen Survey Methods.

WUHF-DT
Ch. 28

Network Service: FOX.

Licensee: WUHF Licensee LLC, 10706 Beaver Dam Rd, Cockeysville, MD 21030.

Studio: 201 Humboldt St, Rochester, NY 14610.

Mailing Address: 201 Humboldt St, Rochester, NY 14610.

Phone: 585-224-8888. **Fax:** 585-654-8044.

E-mail: lgattozzi@rochesterhomepage.net

Web Site: http://rochesterhomepage.net

Technical Facilities: Channel No. 28 (554-560 MHz). Authorized power: 320-kw max. visual, aural. Antenna: 528-ft above av. terrain, 293-ft. above ground, 1003-ft. above sea level.

Latitude	43°	08'	05"
Longitude	77°	35'	07"

Note: Latitude and longitude coordinates shown are based on the North American Datum of 1927 (NAD 27) as currently required by the Mass Media Bureau of the FCC.

Ownership: Sinclair Broadcast Group Inc. (Group Owner).

Began Operation: September 16, 2005. Began analog operations: January 27, 1980. Ceased analog operations: February 17, 2009.

Represented (sales): Katz Media Group.

Personnel:

Louis Gattozzi, Vice President & General Manager.

Don Roberts, Station Manager.

Don Loy, Operations Manager.

Wendy Bello, Local Sales Manager.

E. J. Reynolds, National Sales Manager.

Jerry Walsh, News Director.

Eric Melenbaker, Chief Engineer.

Bonnie Alaimo, Business Manager.

Scott Shambly, Promotion Director.

Dan McCarty, Traffic Manager.

City of License: Rochester. **Station DMA:** Rochester, NY. **Rank:** 80.

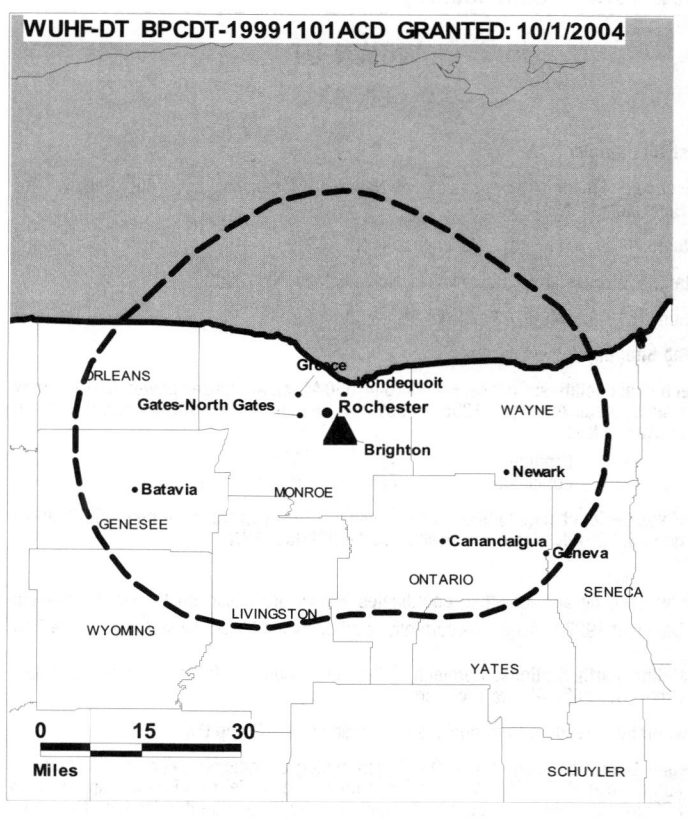

© 2010 Warren Communications News

Circulation © 2009 Nielsen. Coverage based on Nielsen study.

GrandTotal	Cable TV Households	Non-cable TV Households	Total TV Households
Estimated Station Totals *	332,510	130,860	463,370
Average Weekly Circulation (2009)	161,671	72,976	234,647
Average Daily Circulation (2009)			89,689

Station DMA Total	Cable TV Households	Non-cable TV Households	Total TV Households
Estimated Station Totals *	267,730	122,860	390,590
Average Weekly Circulation (2009)	148,737	71,808	220,545
Average Daily Circulation (2009)			85,290

Other DMA Total	Cable TV Households	Non-cable TV Households	Total TV Households
Estimated Station Totals *	64,780	8,000	72,780
Average Weekly Circulation (2009)	12,934	1,168	14,102
Average Daily Circulation (2009)			4,399

*Estimated station totals are sums of the Nielsen TV and Cable TV household estimates for each county in which the station registers viewing of more than 5% as per the Nielsen Survey Methods.

WCWN-DT
Ch. 43

Network Service: CW.

Licensee: Freedom Broadcasting of New York Licensee LLC, 1400 Balltown Rd, Schenectady, NY 12309.

Studio: 1400 Balltown Rd, Schenectady, NY 12309.

Mailing Address: 1400 Balltown Rd, Schenectady, NY 12309.

Phone: 518-381-4900. **Fax:** 518-381-3770.

Web Site: http://www.cwalbany.com

Technical Facilities: Channel No. 43 (644-650 MHz). Authorized power: 676-kw max. visual, aural. Antenna: 1355-ft above av. terrain, 413-ft. above ground, 2194-ft. above sea level.

Latitude	42°	37'	31"
Longitude	74°	00'	38"

Holds CP for change to 600-kw max. visual, 1398-ft above av. terrain, 456-ft. above ground, 2237-ft. above sea level; BPCDT-20080620ABN.

Note: Latitude and longitude coordinates shown are based on the North American Datum of 1927 (NAD 27) as currently required by the Mass Media Bureau of the FCC.

Satellite Earth Stations: Comtech, 3.8-meter; Andrew, 10-meter; Standard Agile Omni, Scientific-Atlanta receivers.

Ownership: Freedom Communications Holdings Inc. (Group Owner).

Began Operation: June 30, 2005. Began analog operations: December 3, 1984 as commercial station WUSV. Transfer of control to U. Bertram Ellis Jr. approved by FCC July 3, 1986 but not consummated. Sale by Union Street Video Inc., Debtor-in-Possession, to WMHT Educational Telecommunications approved by FCC July 24, 1987. Suspended operation July 31, 1991. Resumed operation September 27, 1993. Sale to Sinclair Communications Inc. by WMHT Educational Telecommunications and subsequent operation as a commercial station approved by FCC December 30, 1998; but application was later withdrawn. Sale to Tribune Broadcasting Co. by WMHT Educational Telecommunications and subsequent operation as a commercial station approved by FCC September 7, 1999. Sale to present owner by Tribune Broadcasting Co. approved by FCC November 22, 2006. Ceased analog operations: June 12, 2009.

Represented (legal): Latham & Watkins.

Personnel:

Robert Furlong, Vice President & General Manager.

Rob Croteau, Local & Regional Sales Manager.

Bob Hewitt, National Sales Manager.

Fred Lass, Chief Engineer.

Joe Rosemarino, Controller.

Lisa Jackson, News Director.

Christine Boisvert, Sales Development Director.

Karen Olmstead, Traffic Manager.

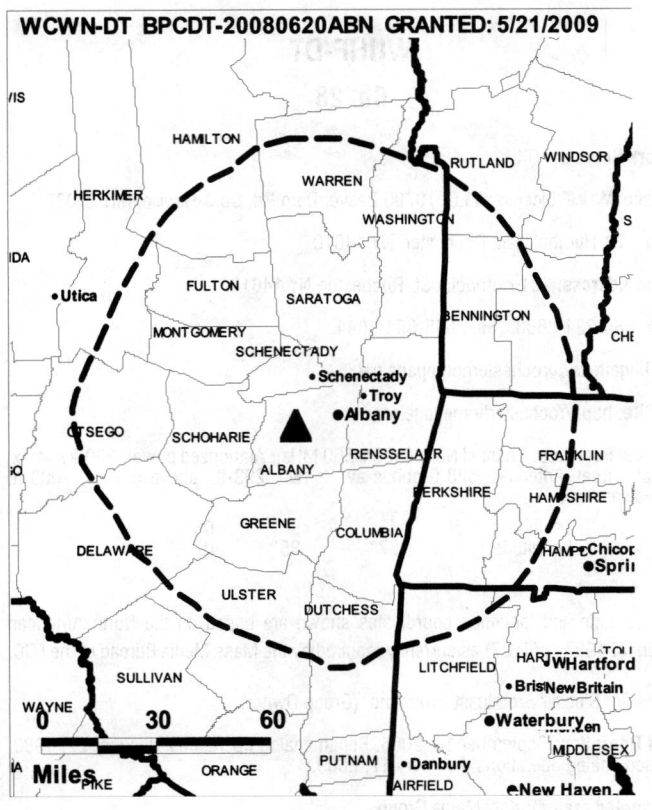

WCWN-DT BPCDT-20080620ABN GRANTED: 5/21/2009

© 2010 Warren Communications News

Shirley Perryman, Human Resources Director.

City of License: Schenectady. **Station DMA:** Albany-Schenectady-Troy, NY.

Rank: 57.

Circulation © 2009 Nielsen. Coverage based on Nielsen study.

GrandTotal	Cable TV Households	Non-cable TV Households	Total TV Households
Estimated Station Totals *	422,950	131,510	554,460
Average Weekly Circulation (2009)	101,099	31,084	132,183
Average Daily Circulation (2009)			38,126

Station DMA Total	Cable TV Households	Non-cable TV Households	Total TV Households
Estimated Station Totals *	422,950	131,510	554,460
Average Weekly Circulation (2009)	101,099	31,084	132,183
Average Daily Circulation (2009)			38,126

*Estimated station totals are sums of the Nielsen TV and Cable TV household estimates for each county in which the station registers viewing of more than 5% as per the Nielsen Survey Methods.

WRGB-DT
Ch. 6

Network Service: CBS.

Licensee: Freedom Broadcasting of New York Licensee LCC, 1400 Balltown Rd, Schenectady, NY 12309.

Studio: 1400 Balltown Rd, Schenectady, NY 12309.

Mailing Address: 1400 Balltown Rd, Schenectady, NY 12309.

Phone: 518-346-6666. **Fax:** 518-346-6249.

Web Site: http://www.cbs6albany.com

Technical Facilities: Channel No. 6 (82-88 MHz). Authorized power: 4.64-kw visual, aural. Antenna: 1299-ft above av. terrain, 362-ft. above ground, 2143-ft. above sea level.

Latitude	42°	37'	31"
Longitude	74°	00'	38"

Requests CP for change to 30.2-kw visual, 1286-ft above av. terrain, 348-ft. above ground, 2129-ft. above sea level; BPCDT-20090622ABV.

Note: Latitude and longitude coordinates shown are based on the North American Datum of 1927 (NAD 27) as currently required by the Mass Media Bureau of the FCC.

Ownership: Freedom Communications Holdings Inc. (Group Owner).

Began Operation: July 5, 2006. Station broadcasting digitally on its analog channel allotment. Began analog operations: February 26, 1942. Originally began as experimental station WGY in 1928; on air since November 6, 1939. Sale to Unicom Inc. by General Electric Broadcasting Co. approved by FCC June 30, 1983 (Television Digest, Vol. 22:48; 23:18). Sale to Freedom Broadcasting Inc. approved by FCC January 6, 1986 (Vol. 25:31, 44). Sale to present owner by Freedom Broadcasting Inc. approved by FCC April 1, 2004. Ceased analog operations: June 12, 2009.

Represented (legal): Latham & Watkins.

Represented (sales): TeleRep Inc.

Personnel:

Bob Furlong, Vice President, General Manager & Program Director.

Robert Epstein, General Sales Manager.

Corey Ausfeld, Local Sales Manager.

Bob Hewitt, National Sales Manager.

Lisa Jackson, News Director.

Fred Lass, Engineering Director.

Joe Rosemarino, Business Manager.

Tim Pennings, Promotion Director & Creative Services Manager.

Bill Brandt, Production Manager.

Karen Olmstead, Traffic Manager.

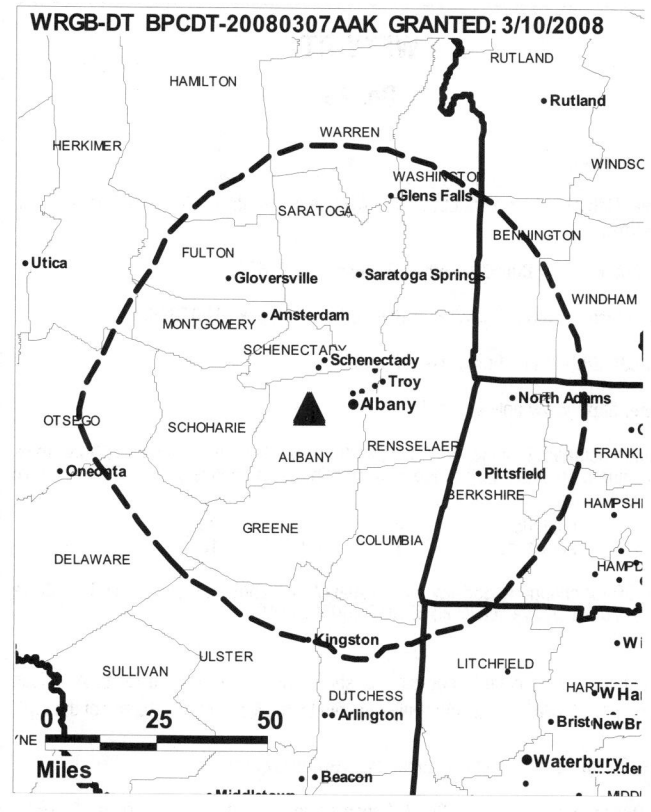

© 2010 Warren Communications News

City of License: Schenectady. **Station DMA:** Albany-Schenectady-Troy, NY.

Rank: 57.

Circulation © 2009 Nielsen. Coverage based on Nielsen study.

GrandTotal	Cable TV Households	Non-cable TV Households	Total TV Households
Estimated Station Totals *	459,430	171,100	630,530
Average Weekly Circulation (2009)	292,478	81,771	374,249
Average Daily Circulation (2009)			191,702

Station DMA Total	Cable TV Households	Non-cable TV Households	Total TV Households
Estimated Station Totals *	422,950	131,510	554,460
Average Weekly Circulation (2009)	284,489	79,343	363,832
Average Daily Circulation (2009)			187,329

Other DMA Total	Cable TV Households	Non-cable TV Households	Total TV Households
Estimated Station Totals *	36,480	39,590	76,070
Average Weekly Circulation (2009)	7,989	2,428	10,417
Average Daily Circulation (2009)			4,373

*Estimated station totals are sums of the Nielsen TV and Cable TV household estimates for each county in which the station registers viewing of more than 5% as per the Nielsen Survey Methods.

WFTY-DT
Ch. 23

Network Service: TEL.

Licensee: Univision New York LLC, 1999 Avenue of the Stars, Ste 3050, Los Angeles, CA 90067.

Studio: 500 Frank W Burr Blvd, 6th Fl, Teaneck, NJ 07666.

Mailing Address: 500 Frank W. Burr Blvd, 6th Fl, Teaneck, NJ 07666.

Phone: 201-287-4141. **Fax:** 201-287-9423.

Web Site: http://www.univision.net

Technical Facilities: Channel No. 23 (524-530 MHz). Authorized power: 150-kw max. visual, aural. Antenna: 668-ft above av. terrain, 610-ft. above ground, 750-ft. above sea level.

Latitude	40°	53'	23"
Longitude	72°	57'	13"

Holds CP for change to 655-kw max. visual, 718-ft above av. terrain, 656-ft. above ground, 797-ft. above sea level; BPCDT-20080613ACJ.

Note: Latitude and longitude coordinates shown are based on the North American Datum of 1927 (NAD 27) as currently required by the Mass Media Bureau of the FCC.

Ownership: Univision Communications Inc. (Group Owner).

Began Operation: January 13, 2003. Began analog operations: November 18, 1973. Left air June 20, 1975; resumed operations December 15, 1979. Began subscription TV operation January 11, 1980. Sale to Wometco Enterprises Inc. approved by FCC November 18, 1980. Transfer of control to WBC Broadcasting approved by FCC April 16, 1984. Resumed full-time commercial operation June 1, 1985. Sale to USA Broadcasting approved by FCC September 16, 1986. Sale to present owner by USA Broadcasting approved by FCC May 21, 2001. Transfer of control to Broadcasting Media Partners Inc. approved by FCC March 27, 2007. Ceased analog operations: June 12, 2009.

Represented (legal): Covington & Burling.

Personnel:

Ramon Pineda, Vice President & General Manager.

Adriana Ruiz-Lopez, Public Relations Manager.

City of License: Smithtown. **Station DMA:** New York, NY. **Rank:** 1.

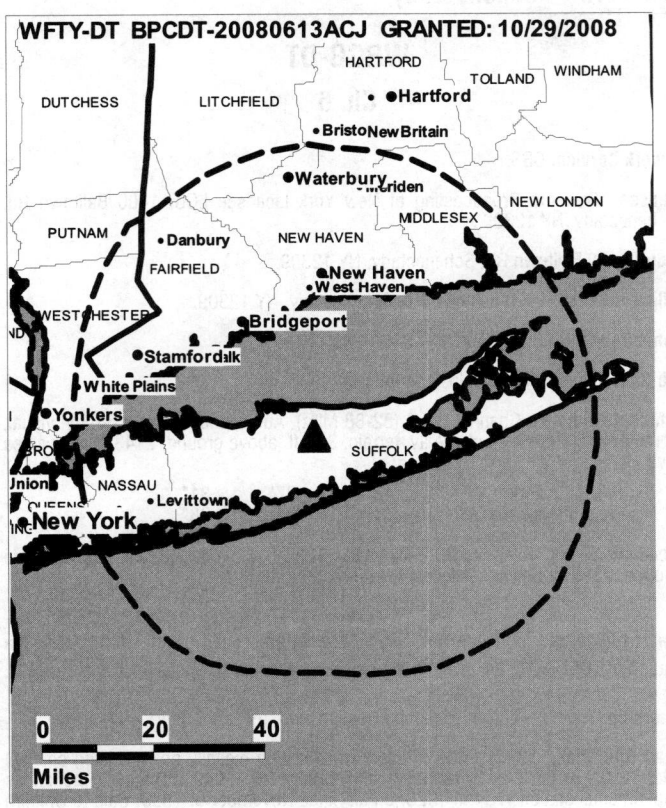

© 2010 Warren Communications News

Circulation © 2009 Nielsen. Coverage based on Nielsen study.

GrandTotal	Cable TV Households	Non-cable TV Households	Total TV Households
Estimated Station Totals *	0	34,400	34,400
Average Weekly Circulation (2009)	0	2,786	2,786
Average Daily Circulation (2009)			69

Station DMA Total	Cable TV Households	Non-cable TV Households	Total TV Households
Estimated Station Totals *	0	34,400	34,400
Average Weekly Circulation (2009)	0	2,786	2,786
Average Daily Circulation (2009)			69

*Estimated station totals are sums of the Nielsen TV and Cable TV household estimates for each county in which the station registers viewing of more than 5% as per the Nielsen Survey Methods.

WNYS-DT
Ch. 44

Network Service: MNT.

Licensee: RKM Media Inc., 137 Spyglass Ln, Fayetteville, NY 13066.

Studio: 1000 James St, Syracuse, NY 13203.

Mailing Address: 1000 James St, Syracuse, NY 13203.

Phone: 315-472-6800. **Fax:** 315-471-8889.

Web Site: http://www.wnys43.com/

Technical Facilities: Channel No. 44 (650-656 MHz). Authorized power: 680-kw max. visual, aural. Antenna: 1460-ft above av. terrain, 991-ft. above ground, 2621-ft. above sea level.

Latitude	42°	52'	50"
Longitude	76°	12'	00"

Note: Latitude and longitude coordinates shown are based on the North American Datum of 1927 (NAD 27) as currently required by the Mass Media Bureau of the FCC.

Ownership: RKM Media Inc. (Group Owner).

Began Operation: May 3, 2006. Began analog operations: October 1, 1989. Ceased analog operations: February 17, 2009. Sale to Salt of the Earth Broadcasting Corp. by Christian Discerner Inc. approved by FCC January 28, 1988. Transfer of control from Donna C. Kimble to Craig L. Fox approved by FCC September 20, 1994. Sale to Metro TV Inc. by Salt of the Earth Broadcasting Corp. approved by FCC August 15, 1995. Sale to present owner by Metro TV Inc. approved by FCC May 23, 1996.

Represented (legal): Rubin, Winston, Diercks, Harris & Cooke LLP.

Represented (sales): Katz Media Group.

Personnel:

Ron Philips, President.

Aaron Olander, Group & General Manager.

Donald O'Connor, General Sales Manager.

Kyrsten Bellen, National Sales Manager.

Vinnie Lopez, Chief Engineer.

Mike Asiedu, Business Manager.

Linda Deeb, Program Director.

Ed Sautter, Promotion Director.

Joan Liscenski, Traffic Manager.

City of License: Syracuse. **Station DMA:** Syracuse, NY. **Rank:** 83.

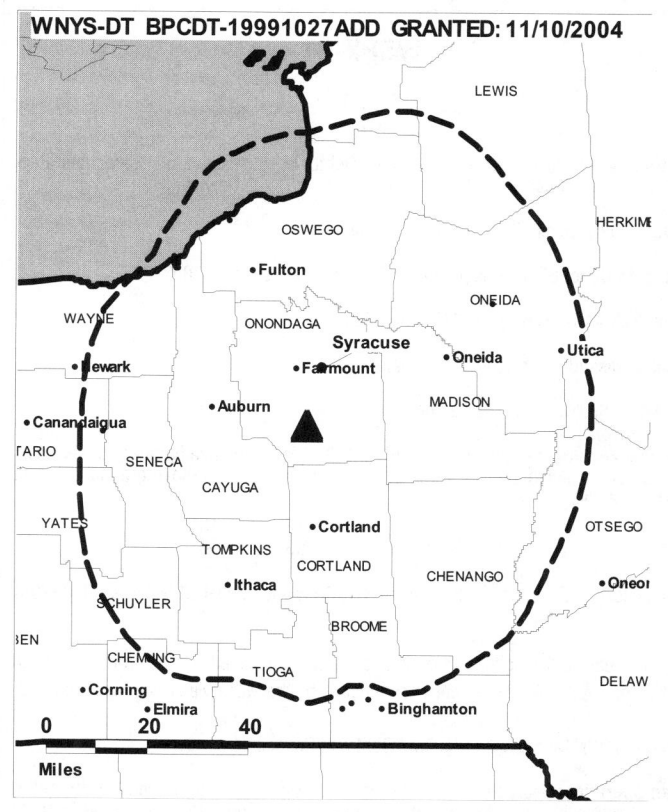

WNYS-DT BPCDT-19991027ADD GRANTED: 11/10/2004

© 2010 Warren Communications News

Circulation © 2009 Nielsen. Coverage based on Nielsen study.

GrandTotal	Cable TV Households	Non-cable TV Households	Total TV Households
Estimated Station Totals *	284,040	136,350	420,390
Average Weekly Circulation (2009)	63,642	23,099	86,741
Average Daily Circulation (2009)			26,080

Station DMA Total	Cable TV Households	Non-cable TV Households	Total TV Households
Estimated Station Totals *	284,040	103,960	388,000
Average Weekly Circulation (2009)	63,642	21,001	84,643
Average Daily Circulation (2009)			25,811

Other DMA Total	Cable TV Households	Non-cable TV Households	Total TV Households
Estimated Station Totals *	0	32,390	32,390
Average Weekly Circulation (2009)	0	2,098	2,098
Average Daily Circulation (2009)			269

*Estimated station totals are sums of the Nielsen TV and Cable TV household estimates for each county in which the station registers viewing of more than 5% as per the Nielsen Survey Methods.

WSPX-DT

Ch. 15

Grantee: ION Media Syracuse License Inc., Debtor in Possession, 601 Clearwater Park Rd, West Palm Beach, FL 33401-6233.

Studio: 6508-B Basile Rowe E, East Syracuse, NY 13057.

Mailing Address: 6508-B Basile Rowe E, East Syracuse, NY 13057.

Phone: 315-414-0178. **Fax:** 315-414-0482.

E-mail: melissadragicevich@ionmedia.com

Web Site: http://www.ionmedia.com

Technical Facilities: Channel No. 15 (476-482 MHz). Authorized power: 27-kw max. visual, aural. Antenna: 1243-ft above av. terrain, 1152-ft. above ground, 1723-ft. above sea level.

Latitude	43°	18'	18"
Longitude	76°	03'	00"

Requests modification of CP for change to 270-kw max. visual; BMPCDT-20080620AIU.

Note: Latitude and longitude coordinates shown are based on the North American Datum of 1927 (NAD 27) as currently required by the Mass Media Bureau of the FCC.

Ownership: ION Media Networks Inc., Debtor in Possession.

Began Operation: February 13, 2009. Began analog operations: December 30, 1998. Sale of remaining 51% to Paxson Communications Corp. from Syracuse Minority TV Inc. (Herbert Washington, et al.) approved by FCC April 29, 1999. Paxson Communications Corp. became ION Media Networks Inc. on June 26. 2006. Transfer of control by ION Media Networks Inc. from Paxson Management Corp. & Lowell W. Paxson to CIG Media LLC approved by FCC December 31, 2007. Involuntary assignment to debtor in possession status approved by FCC June 5, 2009. Ceased analog operations: June 12, 2009.

Represented (legal): Dow Lohnes PLLC.

Personnel:

Margo McCaffery, Station Operations Manager.

Al Szablak, Chief Engineer.

Melissa Dragicevich, Traffic Manager.

City of License: Syracuse. **Station DMA:** Syracuse, NY. **Rank:** 83.

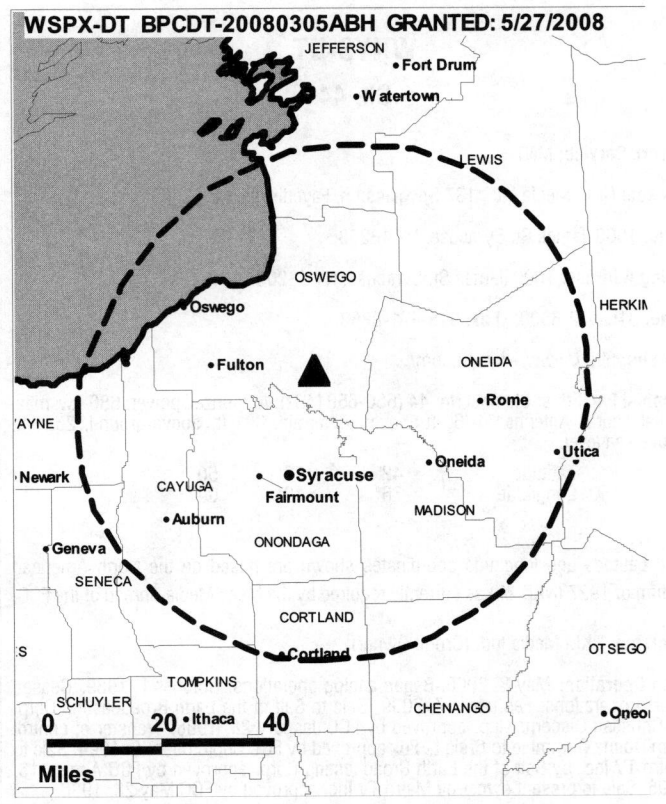

WSPX-DT BPCDT-20080305ABH GRANTED: 5/27/2008

© 2010 Warren Communications News

Circulation © 2009 Nielsen. Coverage based on Nielsen study.

GrandTotal	Cable TV Households	Non-cable TV Households	Total TV Households
Estimated Station Totals *	249,650	58,410	308,060
Average Weekly Circulation (2009)	17,693	4,516	22,209
Average Daily Circulation (2009)			4,662

Station DMA Total	Cable TV Households	Non-cable TV Households	Total TV Households
Estimated Station Totals *	249,650	58,410	308,060
Average Weekly Circulation (2009)	17,693	4,516	22,209
Average Daily Circulation (2009)			4,662

*Estimated station totals are sums of the Nielsen TV and Cable TV household estimates for each county in which the station registers viewing of more than 5% as per the Nielsen Survey Methods.

WSTM-DT
Ch. 54

Network Service: NBC.

Licensee: Barrington Syracuse License LLC, 2500 W Higgins Rd, Ste 880, Hoffman Estates, IL 60195.

Studio: 1030 James St, Syracuse, NY 13203.

Mailing Address: 1030 James St, Syracuse, NY 13203.

Phone: 315-477-9400; 315-474-5000. **Fax:** 315-474-5082.

Web Site: http://www.wstm.com

Technical Facilities: Channel No. 54 (710-716 MHz). Authorized power: 185-kw max. visual, aural. Antenna: 1329-ft above av. terrain, 886-ft. above ground, 2303-ft. above sea level.

Latitude	42°	56'	42"
Longitude	76°	07'	07"

Holds CP for change to channel number 24, 210-kw max. visual, 1289-ft above av. terrain, 843-ft. above ground, 2260-ft. above sea level; BPCDT-20080320ACI.

Note: Latitude and longitude coordinates shown are based on the North American Datum of 1927 (NAD 27) as currently required by the Mass Media Bureau of the FCC.

Ownership: Pilot Group LP (Group Owner).

Began Operation: February 17, 2006. Began analog operations: February 15, 1950. Sale to Times Mirror Co. by Newhouse Broadcasting Corp. approved by FCC March 27, 1980. Sale to SJL Broadcast Management Corp. approved by FCC April 17, 1986. Sale to Federal Broadcasting approved by FCC August 12, 1992. Sale to Raycom Media Inc. by Federal Broadcasting approved by FCC September 24, 1996. Sale to present owner by Raycom Media Inc. approved by FCC June 13, 2006. Ceased analog operations: June 12, 2009.

Represented (legal): Paul Hastings.

Represented (sales): TeleRep Inc.

Personnel:

Chris Geiger, Vice President & General Manager.

David Rhea, General Sales Manager.

Judy Fitzgerald, National Sales Director.

Peggy Phillip, News Director.

Jim Marco, Chief Engineer.

Nancy Liddy, Business Manager.

Bill Green, Production Manager.

Pam Sanson, Traffic Manager.

Laura Hand, Community Relations Director.

City of License: Syracuse. **Station DMA:** Syracuse, NY. **Rank:** 83.

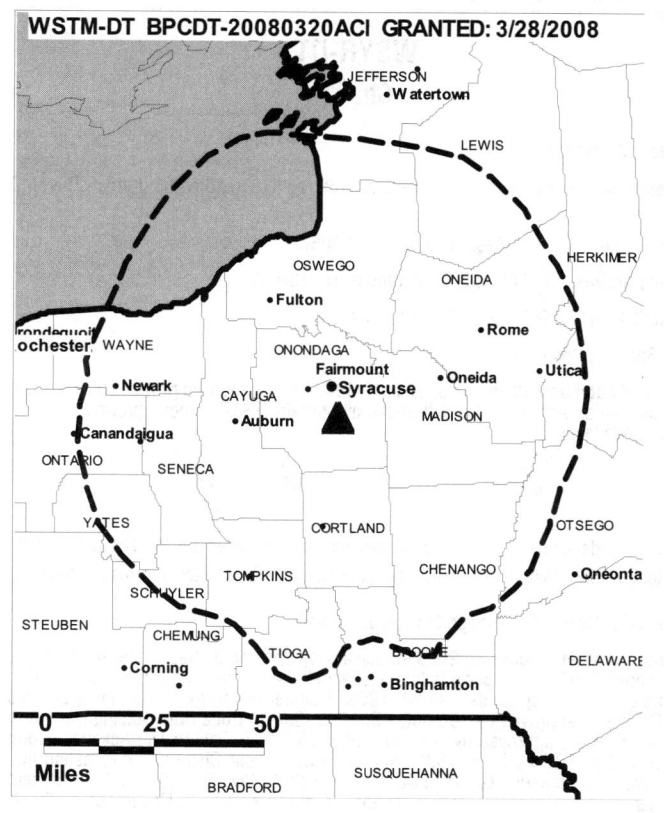

WSTM-DT BPCDT-20080320ACI GRANTED: 3/28/2008

© 2010 Warren Communications News

Circulation © 2009 Nielsen. Coverage based on Nielsen study.

GrandTotal	Cable TV Households	Non-cable TV Households	Total TV Households
Estimated Station Totals *	416,440	183,270	599,710
Average Weekly Circulation (2009)	220,440	73,279	293,719
Average Daily Circulation (2009)			138,717

Station DMA Total	Cable TV Households	Non-cable TV Households	Total TV Households
Estimated Station Totals *	284,040	103,960	388,000
Average Weekly Circulation (2009)	187,474	62,420	249,894
Average Daily Circulation (2009)			122,141

Other DMA Total	Cable TV Households	Non-cable TV Households	Total TV Households
Estimated Station Totals *	132,400	79,310	211,710
Average Weekly Circulation (2009)	32,966	10,859	43,825
Average Daily Circulation (2009)			16,576

*Estimated station totals are sums of the Nielsen TV and Cable TV household estimates for each county in which the station registers viewing of more than 5% as per the Nielsen Survey Methods.

WSYR-DT
Ch. 17

Network Service: ABC.

Licensee: Newport Television License LLC, 460 Nichols Rd, Ste 250, Kansas City, MO 64112.

Studio: 5904 Bridge St, East Syracuse, NY 13057.

Mailing Address: 5904 Bridge St, Syracuse, NY 13057.

Phone: 315-446-9999. **Fax:** 315-446-0045.

Web Site: http://www.9wsyr.com

Technical Facilities: Channel No. 17 (488-494 MHz). Authorized power: 105-kw max. visual, aural. Antenna: 1319-ft above av. terrain, 735-ft. above ground, 2320-ft. above sea level.

Latitude	42°	56'	42"
Longitude	76°	01'	28"

Note: Latitude and longitude coordinates shown are based on the North American Datum of 1927 (NAD 27) as currently required by the Mass Media Bureau of the FCC.

Ownership: Newport Television LLC (Group Owner).

Began Operation: August 12, 2003. Began analog operations: September 9, 1962 as a joint operation by ten applicants for the channel. Assignment of CP granted by FCC to a merger of five applicants May 24, 1968. Transfer of control from other applicants to Outlet Co. approved by FCC July 19, 1972. Sale to Coca Cola Bottling Co., Larry H. Israel, et al., approved by FCC November 15, 1977. Sale to The Ackerley Group approved by FCC April 16, 1982. In stock swap, Clear Channel Broadcasting Inc. acquired The Ackerley Group. FCC approved deal May 29, 2002. Sale to present owner by Clear Channel Communications Inc. approved by FCC November 29, 2007. Ceased analog operations: June 12, 2009.

Represented (sales): Blair Television.

Represented (legal): Covington & Burling.

Personnel:

Theresa Underwood, Vice President & General Manager.

Dale Parker, Sales Manager.

Todd Guard, Sales Manager.

Bill Evans, Sales Director.

Jim Tortora, News & Content Director.

Craig Riker, Chief Engineer.

Jennifer Wilson, Business Manager.

Vincent Spicola, Program Manager, Newport Television.

Michael Cleland, Creative Services Director.

Boyd Chapman, Traffic Manager.

City of License: Syracuse. **Station DMA:** Syracuse, NY. **Rank:** 83.

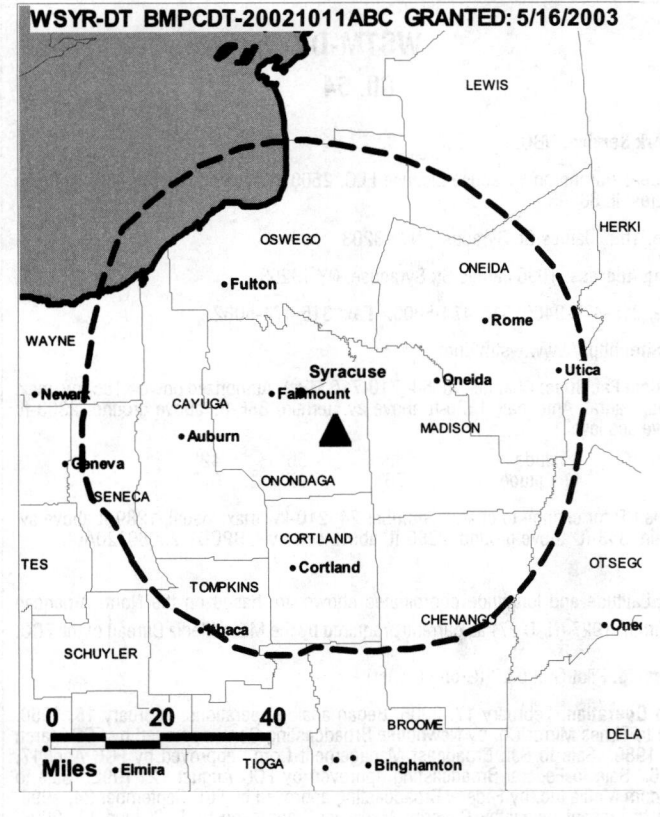

WSYR-DT BMPCDT-20021011ABC GRANTED: 5/16/2003

© 2010 Warren Communications News

Circulation © 2009 Nielsen. Coverage based on Nielsen study.

GrandTotal	Cable TV Households	Non-cable TV Households	Total TV Households
Estimated Station Totals *	376,410	183,270	559,680
Average Weekly Circulation (2009)	212,167	73,334	285,501
Average Daily Circulation (2009)			145,497

Station DMA Total	Cable TV Households	Non-cable TV Households	Total TV Households
Estimated Station Totals *	284,040	103,960	388,000
Average Weekly Circulation (2009)	193,217	62,980	256,197
Average Daily Circulation (2009)			134,863

Other DMA Total	Cable TV Households	Non-cable TV Households	Total TV Households
Estimated Station Totals *	92,370	79,310	171,680
Average Weekly Circulation (2009)	18,950	10,354	29,304
Average Daily Circulation (2009)			10,634

*Estimated station totals are sums of the Nielsen TV and Cable TV household estimates for each county in which the station registers viewing of more than 5% as per the Nielsen Survey Methods.

WSYT-DT
Ch. 19

Network Service: FOX.

Licensee: Sinclair Communications Inc., 10706 Beaver Dam Rd, Cockeysville, MD 21030.

Studio: 1000 James St, Syracuse, NY 13203.

Mailing Address: 1000 James St, Syracuse, NY 13203.

Phone: 315-472-6800. **Fax:** 315-471-8889.

Web Site: http://www.wsyt68.com

Technical Facilities: Channel No. 19 (500-506 MHz). Authorized power: 621-kw max. visual, aural. Antenna: 1460-ft above av. terrain, 991-ft. above ground, 2621-ft. above sea level.

Latitude	42°	52'	50"
Longitude	76°	12'	00"

Note: Latitude and longitude coordinates shown are based on the North American Datum of 1927 (NAD 27) as currently required by the Mass Media Bureau of the FCC.

Ownership: Sinclair Broadcast Group Inc. (Group Owner).

Began Operation: June 30, 2005. Began analog operations: February 15, 1986. Operated part-time until April 5, 1987. Sale to Max Media Properties LLC by Thomas Flatley approved by FCC June 8, 1990. Sale to present owner from Max Media Properties LLC approved by FCC June 26, 1998 (Television Digest, Vol. 37:49). Ceased analog operations: February 17, 2009.

Represented (sales): Katz Media Group.

Personnel:

Aaron Olander, Vice President & Group Manager.

Bob Christiano, Operation & Controller Supervisor.

Donald J. O'Conner, General Sales Manager.

Ed Kampf, Local Sales Manager.

Kyrsten Bellen, National Sales Manager.

Vinnie Lopez, Chief Engineer.

Mike Asideu, Business Manager.

Linda Deeb, Program Coordinator.

Ed Sautter, Promotion Director.

Peter Spartano, Creative Services Director.

Joan Lescenski, Traffic Manager.

City of License: Syracuse. **Station DMA:** Syracuse, NY. **Rank:** 83.

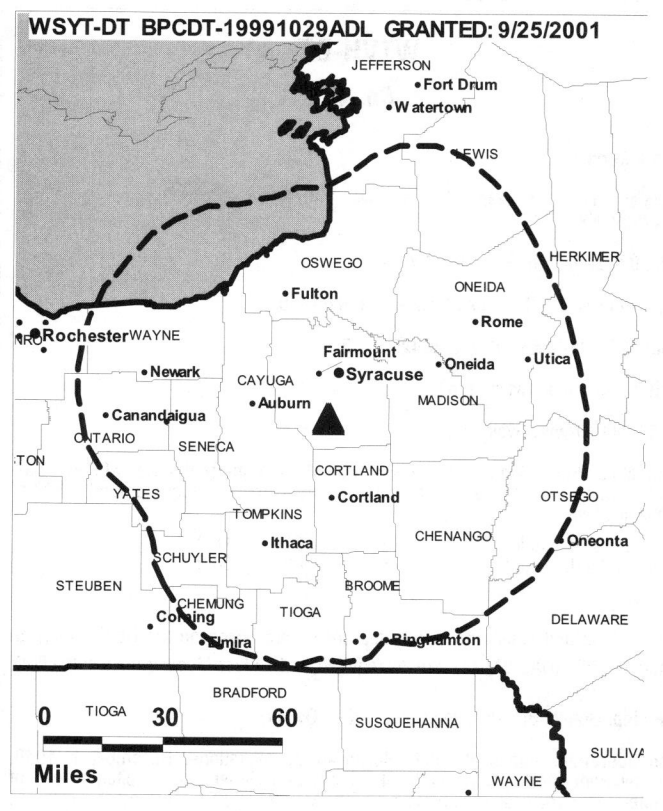

WSYT-DT BPCDT-19991029ADL GRANTED: 9/25/2001

© 2010 Warren Communications News

Circulation © 2009 Nielsen. Coverage based on Nielsen study.

GrandTotal	Cable TV Households	Non-cable TV Households	Total TV Households
Estimated Station Totals *	316,240	156,080	472,320
Average Weekly Circulation (2009)	164,662	46,130	210,792
Average Daily Circulation (2009)			74,180

Station DMA Total	Cable TV Households	Non-cable TV Households	Total TV Households
Estimated Station Totals *	284,040	103,960	388,000
Average Weekly Circulation (2009)	160,667	41,565	202,232
Average Daily Circulation (2009)			72,017

Other DMA Total	Cable TV Households	Non-cable TV Households	Total TV Households
Estimated Station Totals *	32,200	52,120	84,320
Average Weekly Circulation (2009)	3,995	4,565	8,560
Average Daily Circulation (2009)			2,163

*Estimated station totals are sums of the Nielsen TV and Cable TV household estimates for each county in which the station registers viewing of more than 5% as per the Nielsen Survey Methods.

WTVH-DT
Ch. 47

Network Service: CBS.

Licensee: WTVH License Inc., 767 3rd Ave., 34th Fl, c/o Granite Broadcasting Corp., New York, NY 10017.

Studio: 980 James St, Syracuse, NY 13203.

Mailing Address: 980 James St, Syracuse, NY 13203.

Phone: 315-425-5555. **Fax:** 315-425-5525.

E-mail: lvanalstyne@wtvh.com

Web Site: http://www.wtvh.com

Technical Facilities: Channel No. 47 (668-674 MHz). Authorized power: 500-kw max. visual, aural. Antenna: 952-ft above av. terrain, 528-ft. above ground, 1888-ft. above sea level.

Latitude	42°	57'	18.8"
Longitude	76°	06'	34.3"

Note: Latitude and longitude coordinates shown are based on the North American Datum of 1927 (NAD 27) as currently required by the Mass Media Bureau of the FCC.

Ownership: Granite Broadcasting Corp. (Group Owner).

Began Operation: August 9, 2006. Began analog operations: December 1, 1948. Transfer from W. Don Cornwell to SP Granite LLC (Silver Point Capital) as part of Chapter 11 reorganization approved by FCC May 21, 2007. Involuntary transfer to debtor in possession approved by FCC December 20, 2006. Sale to present owner by Meredith Corp. approved by FCC August 9, 1993. Ceased analog operations: June 12, 2009.

Represented (legal): Akin, Gump, Strauss, Hauer & Feld LLP.

Personnel:

Matthew Rosenfeld, President & General Manager.

John Nizamis, Local Sales Manager.

Amy Collins, National Sales Manager.

Greg Catlin, News Director.

Kevin Wright, Chief Engineer.

Vikki Hooper, Business Manager.

Nicole Pooler, Promotion Coordinator.

Laura Cherchio, Traffic & Program Manager.

City of License: Syracuse. **Station DMA:** Syracuse, NY. **Rank:** 83.

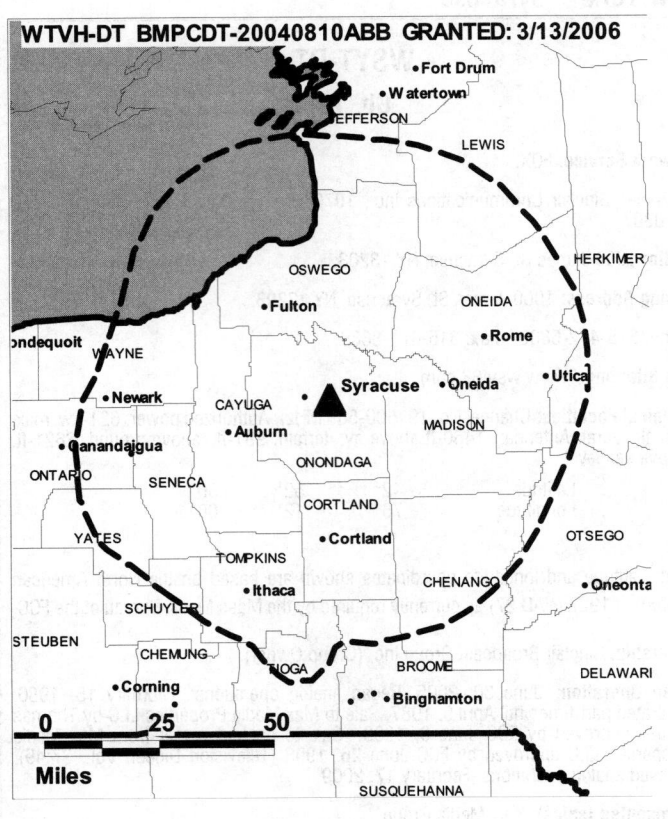

WTVH-DT BMPCDT-20040810ABB GRANTED: 3/13/2006

© 2010 Warren Communications News

Circulation © 2009 Nielsen. Coverage based on Nielsen study.

GrandTotal	Cable TV Households	Non-cable TV Households	Total TV Households
Estimated Station Totals *	416,420	188,870	605,290
Average Weekly Circulation (2009)	224,030	72,069	296,099
Average Daily Circulation (2009)			133,558

Station DMA Total	Cable TV Households	Non-cable TV Households	Total TV Households
Estimated Station Totals *	284,040	103,960	388,000
Average Weekly Circulation (2009)	180,925	61,186	242,111
Average Daily Circulation (2009)			111,828

Other DMA Total	Cable TV Households	Non-cable TV Households	Total TV Households
Estimated Station Totals *	132,380	84,910	217,290
Average Weekly Circulation (2009)	43,105	10,883	53,988
Average Daily Circulation (2009)			21,730

*Estimated station totals are sums of the Nielsen TV and Cable TV household estimates for each county in which the station registers viewing of more than 5% as per the Nielsen Survey Methods.

WFXV-DT
Ch. 27

Network Service: FOX.

Grantee: Nexstar License Inc., 909 Lake Carolyn Pkwy, Ste 1450, Irving, TX 75039.

Studio: 5936 Smith Hill Rd, Utica, NY 13503.

Mailing Address: 5956 Smith Hill Rd, Utica, NY 13503.

Phone: 315-272-1322; 315-797-5220. **Fax:** 315-797-5409.

Web Site: http://www.cnyhomepage.com

Technical Facilities: Channel No. 27 (548-554 MHz). Authorized power: 1000-kw max. visual, aural. Antenna: 692-ft above av. terrain, 285-ft. above ground, 1505-ft. above sea level.

Latitude	43°	08'	43"
Longitude	75°	10'	35"

Note: Latitude and longitude coordinates shown are based on the North American Datum of 1927 (NAD 27) as currently required by the Mass Media Bureau of the FCC.

Ownership: Nexstar Broadcasting Group Inc. (Group Owner).

Began Operation: May 13, 2005. Began analog operations: December 9, 1986. Merger of Quorum Broadcast Holdings Inc. into present owner approved by FCC October 30, 2003. Ceased analog operations: June 12, 2009.

Represented (legal): Drinker Biddle.

Represented (sales): Katz Media Group.

Personnel:

Steve Merren, Vice President & General Manager.

Domenick Cecconi, Programming Director.

Stephen Ventura, Sales Director.

Bob Hajec, Chief Engineer.

Frank Guarnieri, Business Manager.

Rick Lewis, Promotions & Creative Services Director.

City of License: Utica. **Station DMA:** Utica, NY. **Rank:** 170.

Digital cable and TV coverage maps. Visit www.warren-news.com/mediaprints.htm

MediaPrints™
Map a Winning Business Strategy

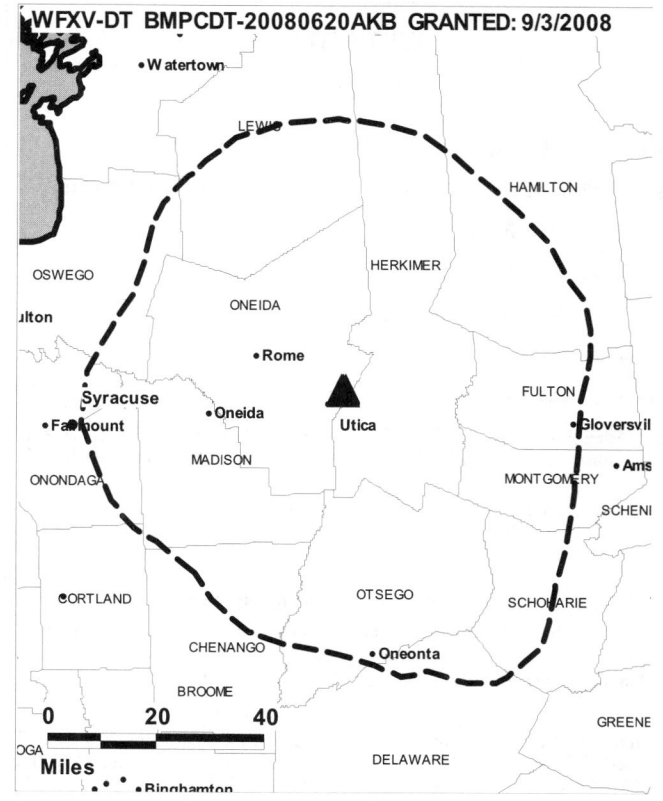

WFXV-DT BMPCDT-20080620AKB GRANTED: 9/3/2008

© 2010 Warren Communications News

Circulation © 2009 Nielsen. Coverage based on Nielsen study.

GrandTotal	Cable TV Households	Non-cable TV Households	Total TV Households
Estimated Station Totals *	146,500	36,920	183,420
Average Weekly Circulation (2009)	48,575	5,246	53,821
Average Daily Circulation (2009)			16,111

Station DMA Total	Cable TV Households	Non-cable TV Households	Total TV Households
Estimated Station Totals *	79,010	17,370	96,380
Average Weekly Circulation (2009)	37,517	2,950	40,467
Average Daily Circulation (2009)			13,117

Other DMA Total	Cable TV Households	Non-cable TV Households	Total TV Households
Estimated Station Totals *	67,490	19,550	87,040
Average Weekly Circulation (2009)	11,058	2,296	13,354
Average Daily Circulation (2009)			2,994

*Estimated station totals are sums of the Nielsen TV and Cable TV household estimates for each county in which the station registers viewing of more than 5% as per the Nielsen Survey Methods.

WKTV-DT
Ch. 29

Network Service: NBC, CW.

Licensee: Smith Media License Holdings LLC, 1215 Cole St, St. Louis, MO 63106.

Studio: 5936 Smith Hill Rd, Utica, NY 13503.

Mailing Address: PO Box 2, Utica, NY 13503.

Phone: 315-733-0404. **Fax:** 315-793-3498.

E-mail: fabbadessa@wktv.com

Web Site: http://www.wktv.com

Technical Facilities: Channel No. 29 (560-566 MHz). Authorized power: 708-kw max. visual, aural. Antenna: 1319-ft above av. terrain, 955-ft. above ground, 2270-ft. above sea level.

Latitude	43°	06'	09"
Longitude	74°	56'	27"

Note: Latitude and longitude coordinates shown are based on the North American Datum of 1927 (NAD 27) as currently required by the Mass Media Bureau of the FCC.

Ownership: Smith Media License Holdings LLC (Group Owner).

Began Operation: May 1, 2006. Began analog operations: December 1, 1949. Sale to Harron Communications Corp. by Kallet Theatres principals approved by FCC December 30, 1958 (Television Digest, Vol. 14:45, 46, 49; 15:1). Transfer of control to Smith Television of New York Inc. approved by FCC May 27, 1992. Sale to present owner by Smith Television of New York License Holdings LLC approved by FCC November 8, 2004. Ceased analog operations: February 17, 2009.

Represented (legal): Dow Lohnes PLLC.

Represented (sales): Continental Television Sales.

Personnel:

Michael Granados, President.

Vic Vetters, Vice President & General Manager.

Frank Abbadessa, Sales Manager.

Tom McNicholl, Chief Engineer.

Steve McMurray, News Director.

Tom Coyne, Program Director.

Dave Streeter, Operations Manager.

Carleen Battista, Traffic Manager.

City of License: Utica. **Station DMA:** Utica, NY. **Rank:** 170.

WKTV-DT BMPCDT-20020404AAF GRANTED: 5/28/2004

© 2010 Warren Communications News

Circulation © 2009 Nielsen. Coverage based on Nielsen study.

GrandTotal	Cable TV Households	Non-cable TV Households	Total TV Households
Estimated Station Totals *	160,850	53,850	214,700
Average Weekly Circulation (2009)	77,767	13,942	91,709
Average Daily Circulation (2009)			54,441

Station DMA Total	Cable TV Households	Non-cable TV Households	Total TV Households
Estimated Station Totals *	79,010	27,270	106,280
Average Weekly Circulation (2009)	59,808	9,655	69,463
Average Daily Circulation (2009)			43,912

Other DMA Total	Cable TV Households	Non-cable TV Households	Total TV Households
Estimated Station Totals *	81,840	26,580	108,420
Average Weekly Circulation (2009)	17,959	4,287	22,246
Average Daily Circulation (2009)			10,529

*Estimated station totals are sums of the Nielsen TV and Cable TV household estimates for each county in which the station registers viewing of more than 5% as per the Nielsen Survey Methods.

WUTR-DT
Ch. 30

Network Service: ABC.

Licensee: Mission Broadcasting Inc., 544 Red Rock Dr, Wadsworth, OH 44281.

Studio: 5936 Smith Hill Rd, Utica, NY 13503.

Mailing Address: 5956 Smith Hill Rd, Utica, NY 13503.

Phone: 315-797-5220. **Fax:** 315-797-5409.

Web Site: http://www.cnyhomepage.com

Technical Facilities: Channel No. 30 (566-572 MHz). Authorized power: 50-kw max. visual, aural. Antenna: 745-ft above av. terrain, 341-ft. above ground, 1562-ft. above sea level.

Latitude	43°	08'	43"
Longitude	75°	10'	35"

Note: Latitude and longitude coordinates shown are based on the North American Datum of 1927 (NAD 27) as currently required by the Mass Media Bureau of the FCC.

Ownership: Mission Broadcasting Inc. (Group Owner).

Began Operation: October 13, 2003. Began analog operations: February 28, 1970. Sale to Park Acquisition Inc. approved by FCC March 27, 1995. Sale to Media General Inc. approved by FCC November 22, 1996. Sale to Utica Television Partners LLC by Media General Inc. approved by FCC June 18, 1997. Sale to The Ackerley Group by Utica Television Partners LLC approved by FCC January 11, 2000. In stock swap, Clear Channel Broadcasting Inc. acquired The Ackerley Group. FCC approved deal May 29, 2002. Sale to present owner by Clear Channel Broadcasting Inc. approved by FCC March 5, 2004. Ceased analog operations: June 12, 2009.

Represented (sales): Katz Media Group.

Represented (legal): Drinker Biddle.

Personnel:

Steve Merren, General Manager.

Diane Siembab, Station Manager.

Stephen Ventura, Sales Manager.

Mike Moran, Chief Engineer.

Frank Guarnieri, Business Manager.

Domenick Cecconi, Program Director & Traffic Manager.

Rick Lewis, Promotions & Creative Services Director.

City of License: Utica. **Station DMA:** Utica, NY. **Rank:** 170.

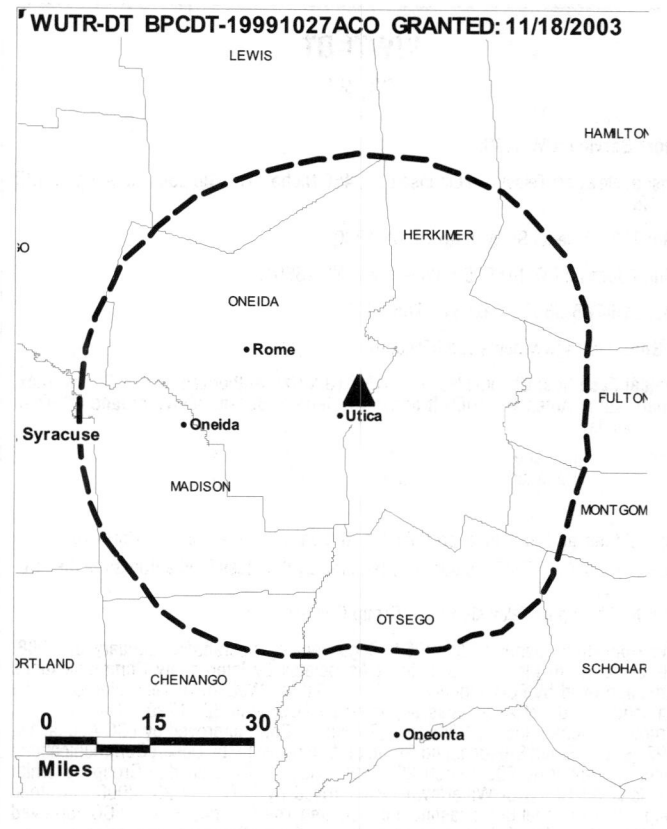

WUTR-DT BPCDT-19991027ACO GRANTED: 11/18/2003

© 2010 Warren Communications News

Circulation © 2009 Nielsen. Coverage based on Nielsen study.

GrandTotal	Cable TV Households	Non-cable TV Households	Total TV Households
Estimated Station Totals *	125,590	27,870	153,460
Average Weekly Circulation (2009)	49,273	4,582	53,855
Average Daily Circulation (2009)			21,019

Station DMA Total	Cable TV Households	Non-cable TV Households	Total TV Households
Estimated Station Totals *	79,010	17,370	96,380
Average Weekly Circulation (2009)	42,346	3,742	46,088
Average Daily Circulation (2009)			19,026

Other DMA Total	Cable TV Households	Non-cable TV Households	Total TV Households
Estimated Station Totals *	46,580	10,500	57,080
Average Weekly Circulation (2009)	6,927	840	7,767
Average Daily Circulation (2009)			1,993

*Estimated station totals are sums of the Nielsen TV and Cable TV household estimates for each county in which the station registers viewing of more than 5% as per the Nielsen Survey Methods.

WWTI-DT
Ch. 21

Network Service: CW, ABC.

Licensee: Newport Television License LLC, 460 Nichols Rd, Ste 250, Kansas City, MO 64112.

Studio: 1222 Arsenal St, Watertown, NY 13601.

Mailing Address: PO Box 6250, Watertown, NY 13601.

Phone: 315-785-8850. **Fax:** 315-785-0127.

Web Site: http://www.newswatch50.com

Technical Facilities: Channel No. 21 (512-518 MHz). Authorized power: 25-kw max. visual, aural. Antenna: 1086-ft above av. terrain, 801-ft. above ground, 2297-ft. above sea level.

Latitude	43°	52'	47"
Longitude	75°	43'	12"

Note: Latitude and longitude coordinates shown are based on the North American Datum of 1927 (NAD 27) as currently required by the Mass Media Bureau of the FCC.

Ownership: Newport Television LLC (Group Owner).

Began Operation: January 28, 2004. Began analog operations: January 3, 1988. Sale of permit to Moreland Broadcast Associates by Intercounty Communications Corp. approved by FCC January 16, 1986. Sale to Watertown Television Corp. by Moreland Broadcast Associates approved by FCC June 22, 1990. Sale to Desert Communications V Inc. by Watertown Television Corp. approved by FCC August 18, 1992. Sale to Smith Broadcasting Group of Watertown LP by Desert Communications V Inc. approved by FCC March 29, 1996. Sale to The Ackerley Group by Smith Broadcasting Group of Watertown LP approved by FCC May 25, 2000. In stock swap, Clear Channel Broadcasting Inc. acquired The Ackerley Group. FCC approved deal May 29, 2002. Sale to present owner by Clear Channel Communications Inc. approved by FCC November 29, 2007. Ceased analog operations: June 12, 2009.

Represented (sales): Blair Television.

Represented (legal): Covington & Burling.

Personnel:

David J. Males, General Manager.

Peter Downey, Sales Manager.

John Moore, News Director.

Keith Rudes, Chief Engineer.

Vince Spicolo, Program Director.

Bobby Walker, Production & Creative Services Director.

City of License: Watertown. **Station DMA:** Watertown, NY. **Rank:** 177.

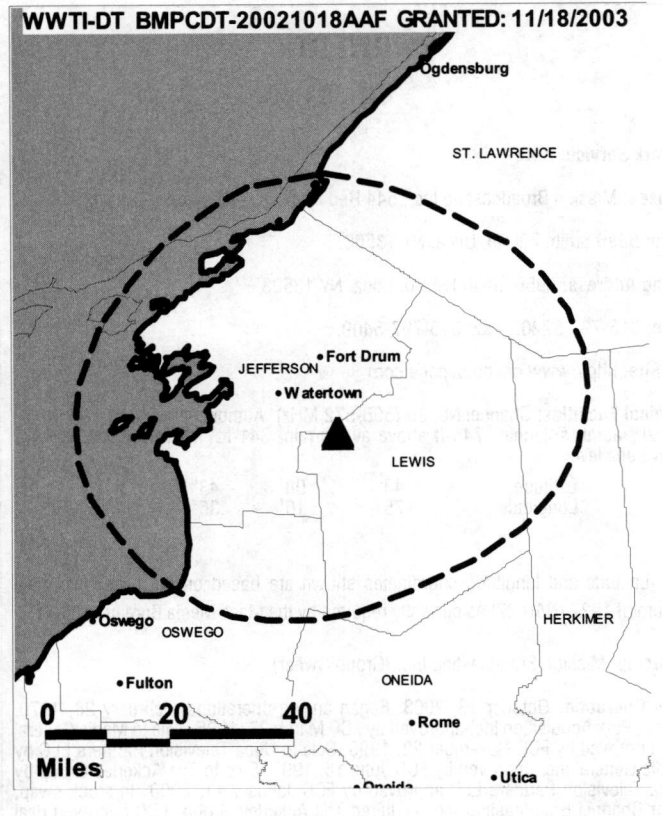

WWTI-DT BMPCDT-20021018AAF GRANTED: 11/18/2003

© 2010 Warren Communications News

Circulation © 2009 Nielsen. Coverage based on Nielsen study.

GrandTotal	Cable TV Households	Non-cable TV Households	Total TV Households
Estimated Station Totals *	65,320	29,640	94,960
Average Weekly Circulation (2009)	31,654	6,280	37,934
Average Daily Circulation (2009)			15,547

Station DMA Total	Cable TV Households	Non-cable TV Households	Total TV Households
Estimated Station Totals *	65,320	29,640	94,960
Average Weekly Circulation (2009)	31,654	6,280	37,934
Average Daily Circulation (2009)			15,547

*Estimated station totals are sums of the Nielsen TV and Cable TV household estimates for each county in which the station registers viewing of more than 5% as per the Nielsen Survey Methods.

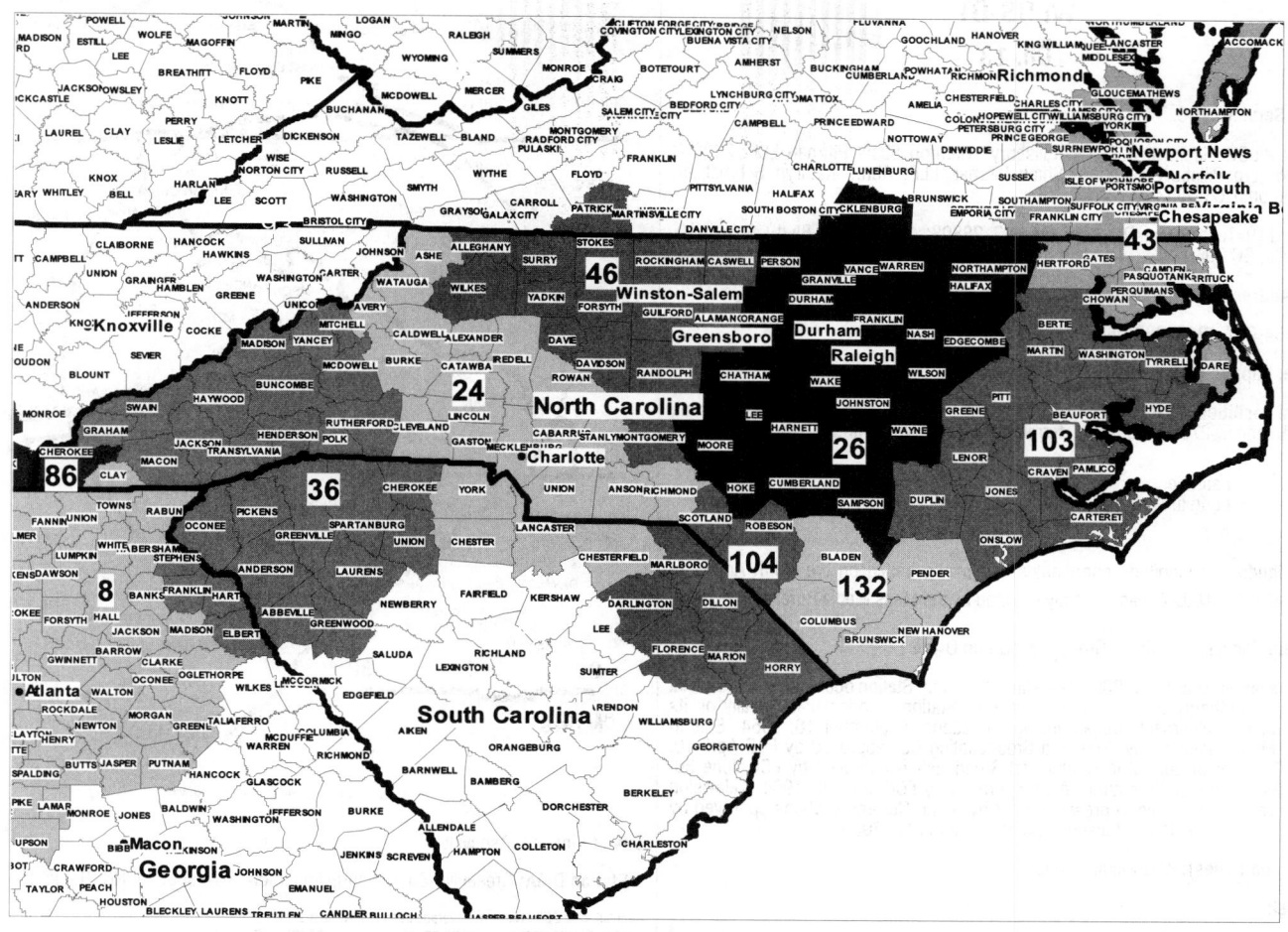

© 2010 Warren Communications News

MARKET	NIELSEN DMA TV HOUSEHOLDS	RANK	MARKET AREA COMMERCIAL STATIONS
Atlanta, GA	2,387,520	8	WAGA-DT (27); WATL-DT (25); WGCL-DT (19); WHSG-DT (44); WPCH-DT (20); WPXA-TV (51); WSB-DT (39); WUPA-DT (43); WUVG-DT (48); WXIA-DT (10)
Charlotte, NC	1,147,910	24	WAXN-DT (50); WBTV-DT (23); WCCB-DT (27); WCNC-DT (22); WHKY-DT (40); WJZY-DT (47); WMYT-DT (39); WSOC-DT (34)
Raleigh-Durham (Fayetteville), NC	1,107,820	26	WFPX-TV (36); WLFL-DT (27); WNCN-DT (17); WRAL-DT (53); WRAY-DT (42); WRAZ-DT (49); WRDC-DT (28); WRPX-TV (15); WTVD-DT (11); WUVC-DT (38)
Greenville-Spartanburg-Anderson, SC-Asheville, NC	865,810	36	WGGS-DT (16); WHNS-DT (21); WLOS-DT (13); WMYA-DT (14); WNEG-DT (24); WSPA-DT (7); WYCW-DT (45); WYFF-DT (59)
Norfolk-Portsmouth-Newport News, VA	709,880	43	WAVY-DT (31); WGNT-DT (50); WHRE-DT (7); WPXV-TV (46); WSKY-DT (4); WTKR-DT (40); WTVZ-DT (33); WVBT-DT (29); WVEC (13)
Greensboro-High Point-Winston Salem, NC	691,380	46	WCWG-DT (19); WFMY-DT (51); WGHP-DT (8); WGPX-TV (14); WLXI (43); WMYV-DT (33); WXII-DT (31); WXLV-DT (29)
Chattanooga, TN	365,400	86	WDEF-DT (12); WDSI-DT (40); WELF-DT (16); WFLI-DT (42); WRCB-DT (13); WTVC-DT (9)
Greenville-New Bern-Washington, NC	290,280	103	WCTI-DT (12); WEPX-TV (51); WFXI-DT (8); WITN-DT (32); WNCT-DT (10); WPXU-TV (34)
Myrtle Beach-Florence, SC	287,400	104	WBTW-DT (13); WFXB-DT (18); WMBF-DT (32); WPDE-DT (16)
Wilmington, NC	189,950	132	WECT-DT (44); WSFX-DT (30); WWAY-DT (46)

North Carolina Station Totals as of October 1, 2009

	VHF	UHF	TOTAL
Commercial Television	7	30	37
Educational Television	1	11	12
	8	41	49

WLOS-DT
Ch. 13

Network Service: ABC.

Grantee: WLOS Licensee LLC, c/o Pillsbury Winthrop Shaw Pittman LLP, 2300 N St. NW, c/o Pillsbury Winthrop Shaw Pittman LLP, Attn.: Kathryn Schmeltzer, Washington, DC 20037-1128.

Studios: 110 Technology Dr, Asheville, NC 28803; 100 Verdae Blvd., Suite 410, Greenville, SC 29607.

Mailing Address: 110 Technology Dr, Asheville, NC 28803.

Phone: 864-297-1313; 828-684-1340. **Fax:** 864-297-8085.

Web Site: http://www.wlos.com

Technical Facilities: Channel No. 13 (210-216 MHz). Authorized power: 50-kw visual, aural. Antenna: 2799-ft above av. terrain, 305-ft. above ground, 6024-ft. above sea level.

Latitude	35°	25'	32"
Longitude	82°	45'	25"

Note: Latitude and longitude coordinates shown are based on the North American Datum of 1927 (NAD 27) as currently required by the Mass Media Bureau of the FCC.

Ownership: Sinclair Broadcast Group Inc. (Group Owner).

Began Operation: October 1, 2002. Standard Definition. Station operating under Special Temporary Authority at 13.6-kw max. visual. Station broadcasting digitally on its analog channel allotment. Began analog operations: September 18, 1954. Sale to Anchor Media Holdings by Wometco Broadcasting Co. approved by FCC April 10, 1987. Transfer of control to Continental Broadcasting approved by FCC June 30, 1993. Sale to Better Communications approved by FCC July 20, 1994 (Television Digest, Vol. 34:20). Sale to present owner by Better Communications approved by FCC June 27, 1997. Ceased analog operations: June 12, 2009.

Represented (sales): Katz Media Group.

Personnel:

Jack Connors, General Manager.

Audra Swain, General Sales Manager.

Donna Daniels, Local Sales Manager.

James Crout, Local Sales Manager.

Courtney Youngblood, National Sales Manager.

Julie Fries, News Director.

Rollin Tompkins, Chief Engineer.

Darrell Rhoden, Business Manager.

Guy Chancey, Program & Promotion Director.

Debbie Barnstable, Research Director.

Sarah Ferris, Traffic Manager.

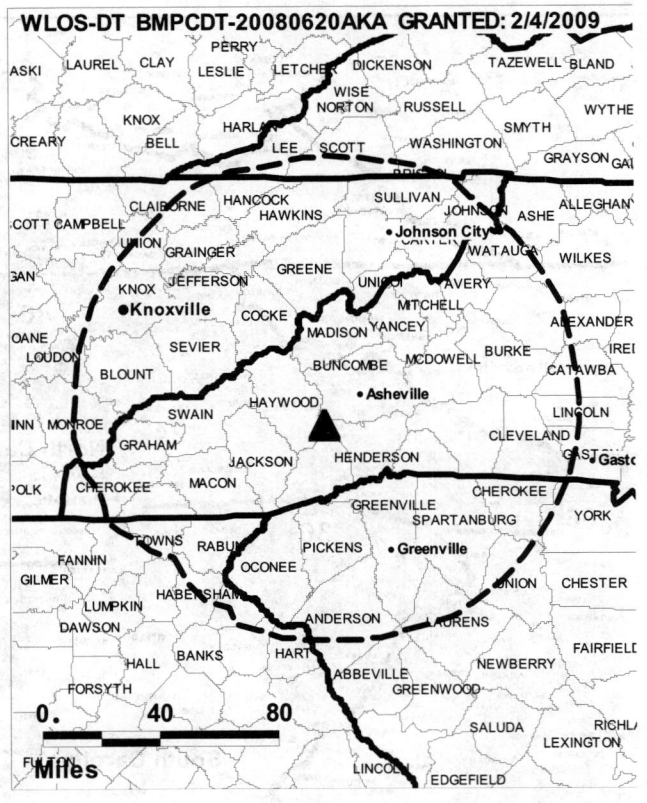

© 2010 Warren Communications News

City of License: Asheville.

Station DMA: Greenville-Spartanburg-Anderson, SC-Asheville, NC. **Rank:** 36.

Circulation © 2009 Nielsen. Coverage based on Nielsen study.

GrandTotal	Cable TV Households	Non-cable TV Households	Total TV Households
Estimated Station Totals *	443,590	467,420	911,010
Average Weekly Circulation (2009)	264,495	251,581	516,076
Average Daily Circulation (2009)			252,763

Station DMA Total	Cable TV Households	Non-cable TV Households	Total TV Households
Estimated Station Totals *	395,190	436,900	832,090
Average Weekly Circulation (2009)	252,163	248,476	500,639
Average Daily Circulation (2009)			250,047

Other DMA Total	Cable TV Households	Non-cable TV Households	Total TV Households
Estimated Station Totals *	48,400	30,520	78,920
Average Weekly Circulation (2009)	12,332	3,105	15,437
Average Daily Circulation (2009)			2,716

*Estimated station totals are sums of the Nielsen TV and Cable TV household estimates for each county in which the station registers viewing of more than 5% as per the Nielsen Survey Methods.

WYCW-DT
Ch. 45

Network Service: CW.

Grantee: Media General Communications Holdings LLC, 333 E Franklin St, Richmond, VA 23219.

Studio: 250 International Dr., Spartanburg, SC 29303.

Mailing Address: PO Box 1717, Spartanburg, SC 29304.

Phone: 864-576-7777. **Fax:** 864-595-4615.

E-mail: ringram@wasu.com

Web Site: http://www.carolinascw.com

Technical Facilities: Channel No. 45 (656-662 MHz). Authorized power: 1000-kw max. visual, aural. Antenna: 1821-ft above av. terrain, 696-ft. above ground, 4121-ft. above sea level.

Latitude	35°	13'	20"
Longitude	82°	32'	58"

Note: Latitude and longitude coordinates shown are based on the North American Datum of 1927 (NAD 27) as currently required by the Mass Media Bureau of the FCC.

Ownership: Media General Inc. (Group Owner).

Began Operation: March 8, 2002. Began analog operations: June 1, 1986. Due to financial & technical difficulties, station ceased operations from early 1991 until April 1994, when it resumed service at reduced power. On January 17, 1996, storm caused tower to collapse. Station resumed operations August 1996. Sale to present owner by Pappas Telecasting Companies approved by FCC January 15, 2002. Ceased analog operations: February 17, 2009.

Personnel:

Phil Lane, Vice President & General Manager.

Randy Ingram, Station & General Sales Manager.

Kelly Oliver, Local Sales Manager.

Alex Bongiorno, News Director.

Ron Peeler, Chief Engineer.

Laura Nunamacher, Business Manager.

Shukriyyah Fareed, Program Director.

Megan Hannigan, Promotion & Public Affairs Manager.

Jessica Heysek, Production Manager.

Gladys Davis, Traffic Manager.

City of License: Asheville.

Station DMA: Greenville-Spartanburg-Anderson, SC-Asheville, NC. **Rank:** 36.

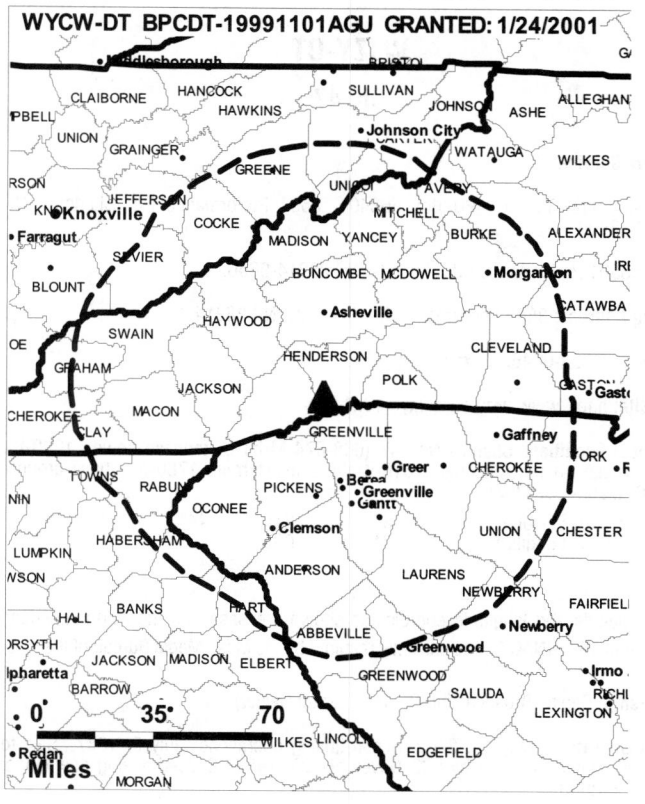

© 2010 Warren Communications News

Circulation © 2009 Nielsen. Coverage based on Nielsen study.

GrandTotal	Cable TV Households	Non-cable TV Households	Total TV Households
Estimated Station Totals *	387,560	430,940	818,500
Average Weekly Circulation (2009)	83,932	84,395	168,327
Average Daily Circulation (2009)			58,890

Station DMA Total	Cable TV Households	Non-cable TV Households	Total TV Households
Estimated Station Totals *	382,360	424,100	806,460
Average Weekly Circulation (2009)	83,316	83,786	167,102
Average Daily Circulation (2009)			58,710

Other DMA Total	Cable TV Households	Non-cable TV Households	Total TV Households
Estimated Station Totals *	5,200	6,840	12,040
Average Weekly Circulation (2009)	616	609	1,225
Average Daily Circulation (2009)			180

*Estimated station totals are sums of the Nielsen TV and Cable TV household estimates for each county in which the station registers viewing of more than 5% as per the Nielsen Survey Methods.

WJZY-DT
Ch. 47

Network Service: CW.

Grantee: WJZY-TV Inc., PO Box 668400, 3501 Performance Rd, Charlotte, NC 28266-8400.

Studio: 3501 Performance Rd, Charlotte, NC 28214-9056.

Mailing Address: 3501 Performance Rd, Charlotte, NC 28214.

Phone: 704-398-0046. **Fax:** 704-393-8407.

Web Site: http://www.wjzy.com/days/18.shtml

Technical Facilities: Channel No. 47 (668-674 MHz). Authorized power: 1000-kw max. visual, aural. Antenna: 1816-ft above av. terrain, 1780-ft. above ground, 2586-ft. above sea level.

| Latitude | 35° | 21' | 44" |
| Longitude | 81° | 09' | 19" |

Note: Latitude and longitude coordinates shown are based on the North American Datum of 1927 (NAD 27) as currently required by the Mass Media Bureau of the FCC.

Ownership: Capitol Broadcasting Co. Inc. (Group Owner).

Began Operation: May 14, 2002. Began analog operations: July 8, 1987. Sale to present owner approved by FCC November 20, 1987. Ceased analog operations: June 12, 2009.

Represented (legal): Holland & Knight LLP.

Represented (sales): TeleRep Inc.

Personnel:

Will Davis, Vice President & General Manager.

Shawn Harris, General Sales Manager.

Matthew Livoti, Local Sales Manager.

Don Travis, National Sales Manager.

John Bishop, Engineering Manager.

Jacqueline Draper, Business Manager.

Joe Heaton, Promotion & Marketing Manager.

Mary Sellars, Traffic Manager.

City of License: Belmont. **Station DMA:** Charlotte, NC. **Rank:** 24.

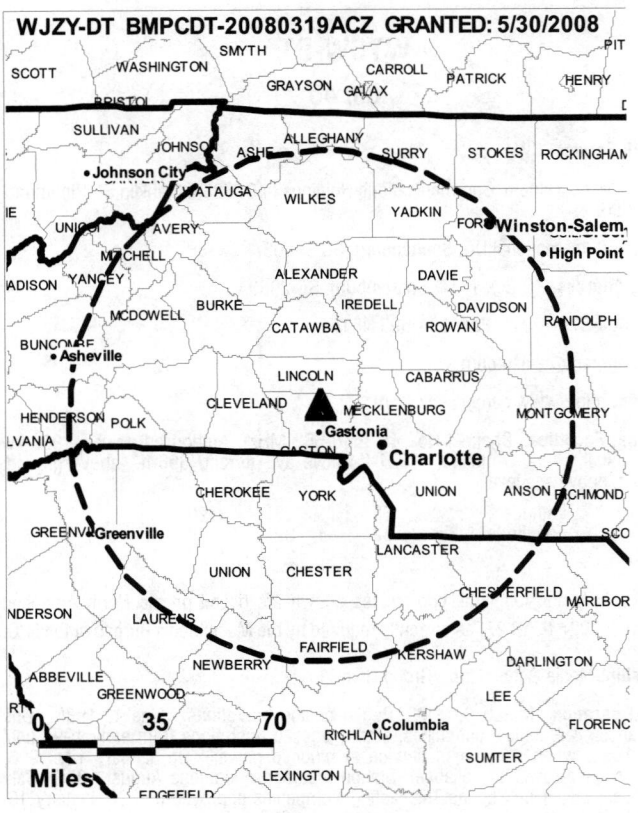

WJZY-DT BMPCDT-20080319ACZ GRANTED: 5/30/2008

© 2010 Warren Communications News

Circulation © 2009 Nielsen. Coverage based on Nielsen study.

GrandTotal	Cable TV Households	Non-cable TV Households	Total TV Households
Estimated Station Totals *	696,380	506,140	1,202,520
Average Weekly Circulation (2009)	175,313	130,846	306,159
Average Daily Circulation (2009)			104,294

Station DMA Total	Cable TV Households	Non-cable TV Households	Total TV Households
Estimated Station Totals *	659,510	447,320	1,106,830
Average Weekly Circulation (2009)	168,265	125,480	293,745
Average Daily Circulation (2009)			100,569

Other DMA Total	Cable TV Households	Non-cable TV Households	Total TV Households
Estimated Station Totals *	36,870	58,820	95,690
Average Weekly Circulation (2009)	7,048	5,366	12,414
Average Daily Circulation (2009)			3,725

*Estimated station totals are sums of the Nielsen TV and Cable TV household estimates for each county in which the station registers viewing of more than 5% as per the Nielsen Survey Methods.

WGPX-TV
Ch. 14

Network Service: ION.

Licensee: ION Media Greensboro License Inc., Debtor in Possession, 601 Clearwater Park Rd, West Palm Beach, FL 33401-6233.

Studio: 1114 N. O'Henry Blvd, Greensboro, NC 27405.

Mailing Address: 1114 N. O'Henry Blvd, Greensboro, NC 27405.

Phone: 336-272-9227. **Fax:** 336-272-9298.

E-mail: stephanieblack@ionmedia.com

Web Site: http://www.ionmedia.com

Technical Facilities: Channel No. 14 (470-476 MHz). Authorized power: 95-kw max. visual, aural. Antenna: 699-ft above av. terrain, 690-ft. above ground, 1428-ft. above sea level.

Latitude	36°	14'	54"
Longitude	79°	39'	21"

Holds CP for change to 1000-kw max. visual, 784-ft above av. terrain, 773-ft. above ground, 1511-ft. above sea level; BPCDT-20080620AFW.

Transmitter: Approx. 0.62-mi. at 71 degrees T from US. Hwy 29 & Benaja Rd. intersection.

Note: Latitude and longitude coordinates shown are based on the North American Datum of 1927 (NAD 27) as currently required by the Mass Media Bureau of the FCC.

Ownership: ION Media Networks Inc., Debtor in Possession (Group Owner).

Began Operation: January 3, 2006. Began analog operations: August 7, 1984. Sale to Kearn family members by National Group Telecommunications of Burlington Inc. approved by FCC August 18, 1983. Sale of 20% interest to Carmelo Selestre from Kearn family members approved by FCC November 7, 1984. Sale to Television Communications Inc. (Jack Rehburg, et al.,) approved by FCC November 20, 1985. Sale to Paxson Communications Corp. by Television Communications Inc. approved by FCC July 15, 1996. Paxson Communications Corp. became ION Media Networks Inc. on June 26, 2006. Transfer of control by ION Media Networks Inc. from Paxson Management Corp. & Lowell W. Paxson to CIG Media LLC approved by FCC December 31, 2007. Involuntary assignment to debtor in possession status approved by FCC June 5, 2009. Sale to Urban Television LLC pends. Ceased analog operations: June 12, 2009.

Represented (legal): Dow Lohnes PLLC.

Represented (engineering): du Treil, Lundin & Rackley Inc.

Personnel:

Dana Lambert, Station Operations Manager.

Steven Hall, Chief Engineer.

Stephanie Black, Traffic Manager.

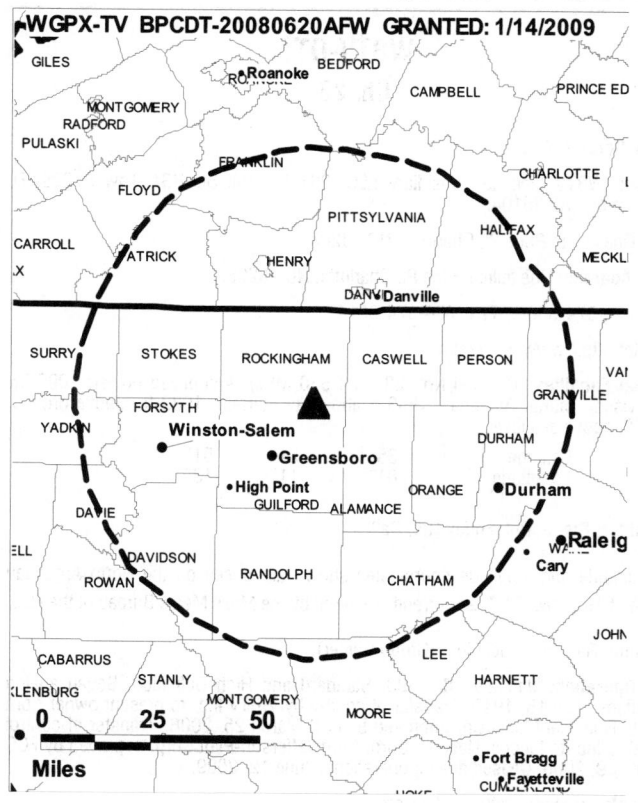

© 2010 Warren Communications News

City of License: Burlington.

Station DMA: Greensboro-High Point-Winston Salem, NC. **Rank:** 46.

Circulation © 2009 Nielsen. Coverage based on Nielsen study.

GrandTotal	Cable TV Households	Non-cable TV Households	Total TV Households
Estimated Station Totals *	409,160	167,950	577,110
Average Weekly Circulation (2009)	38,904	15,279	54,183
Average Daily Circulation (2009)			13,101

Station DMA Total	Cable TV Households	Non-cable TV Households	Total TV Households
Estimated Station Totals *	409,160	167,950	577,110
Average Weekly Circulation (2009)	38,904	15,279	54,183
Average Daily Circulation (2009)			13,101

*Estimated station totals are sums of the Nielsen TV and Cable TV household estimates for each county in which the station registers viewing of more than 5% as per the Nielsen Survey Methods.

WBTV-DT
Ch. 23

Network Service: CBS.

Licensee: WBTV License Subsidiary LLC, 201 Monroe St, RSA Tower, 20th Fl, Montgomery, AL 36104.

Studio: One Julian Price Pl, Charlotte, NC 28208.

Mailing Address: One Julian Price Pl, Charlotte, NC 28208.

Phone: 704-374-3500. **Fax:** 704-374-3614.

Web Site: http://www.wbtv.com

Technical Facilities: Channel No. 23 (524-530 MHz). Authorized power: 1000-kw max. visual, aural. Antenna: 1853-ft above av. terrain, 1932-ft. above ground, 2650-ft. above sea level.

Latitude	35°	21'	51"
Longitude	81°	11'	13"

Transmitter: Rte. 3, Bob Friday Rd., Dallas.

Note: Latitude and longitude coordinates shown are based on the North American Datum of 1927 (NAD 27) as currently required by the Mass Media Bureau of the FCC.

Ownership: Raycom Media Inc. (Group Owner).

Began Operation: January 18, 1998. Standard and High Definition. Began analog operations: July 15, 1949. Transfer of control by WBTV Inc. to present owner from Lincoln Financial Media Co. approved by FCC March 25, 2008. Transfer of control by WBTV Inc. to Lincoln National Corp. from Jefferson-Pilot Corp. approved by FCC February 9, 2006. Ceased analog operations: June 12, 2009.

Represented (sales): Petry Media Corp.

Represented (legal): Covington & Burling.

Personnel:

John Shreves, President.

Mary MacMillan, Senior Vice President & General Manager.

Ellen Sondee, Vice President, Finance.

Matt Aaron, General Sales Manager.

Amy Spainhour, Local Sales Manager.

Michal Campbell, Local Sales Manager.

Patti Goodnight, National Sales Manager.

Dennis Milligan, News Director.

Don Shaw, Operations Director.

Shelly Hill, Programming & Marketing Director.

John Steed, Production Manager.

Calvin Riddle, Traffic Manager.

City of License: Charlotte. **Station DMA:** Charlotte, NC. **Rank:** 24.

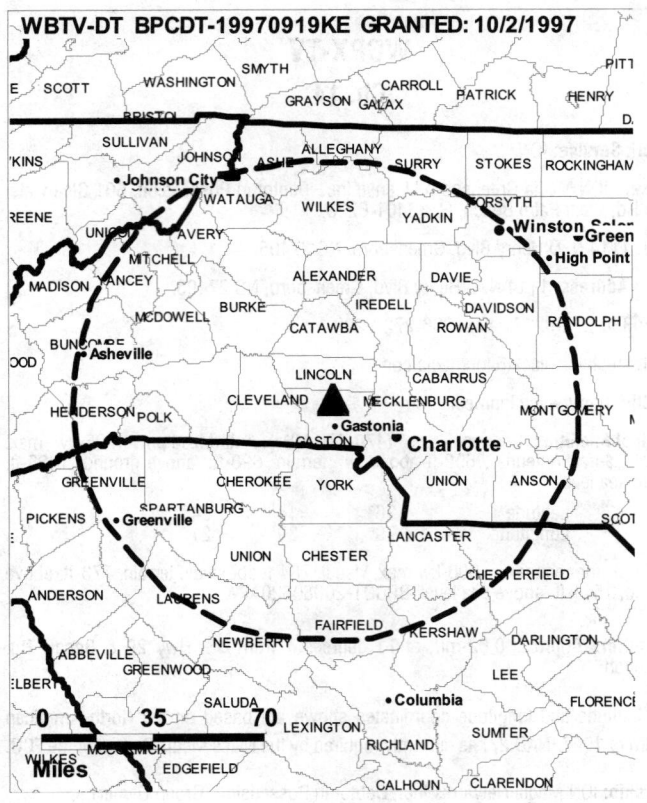

WBTV-DT BPCDT-19970919KE GRANTED: 10/2/1997

© 2010 Warren Communications News

Circulation © 2009 Nielsen. Coverage based on Nielsen study.

GrandTotal	Cable TV Households	Non-cable TV Households	Total TV Households
Estimated Station Totals *	697,450	549,910	1,247,360
Average Weekly Circulation (2009)	441,805	297,815	739,620
Average Daily Circulation (2009)			361,100

Station DMA Total	Cable TV Households	Non-cable TV Households	Total TV Households
Estimated Station Totals *	659,510	456,670	1,116,180
Average Weekly Circulation (2009)	432,535	285,784	718,319
Average Daily Circulation (2009)			352,620

Other DMA Total	Cable TV Households	Non-cable TV Households	Total TV Households
Estimated Station Totals *	37,940	93,240	131,180
Average Weekly Circulation (2009)	9,270	12,031	21,301
Average Daily Circulation (2009)			8,480

*Estimated station totals are sums of the Nielsen TV and Cable TV household estimates for each county in which the station registers viewing of more than 5% as per the Nielsen Survey Methods.

WCCB-DT
Ch. 27

Network Service: FOX.

Licensee: North Carolina Broadcasting Partners, One Television Pl, c/o Leon Porter, Charlotte, NC 28205.

Studio: One Television Pl, Charlotte, NC 28205.

Mailing Address: One Television Pl, Charlotte, NC 28205.

Phone: 704-372-1800. **Fax:** 704-332-7941.

E-mail: raylette@foxcharlotte.tv

Web Site: http://www.foxcharlotte.tv

Technical Facilities: Channel No. 27 (548-554 MHz). Authorized power: 83.2-kw max. visual, aural. Antenna: 1201-ft above av. terrain, 1099-ft. above ground, 1880-ft. above sea level.

Latitude	35°	16'	01"
Longitude	80°	44'	05"

Transmitter: Newell-Hickory Rd.

Note: Latitude and longitude coordinates shown are based on the North American Datum of 1927 (NAD 27) as currently required by the Mass Media Bureau of the FCC.

Ownership: Bahakel Communications Ltd. (Group Owner).

Began Operation: November 1, 2000. Standard Definition. Began analog operations: December 7, 1953. Hugh Deadwyler acquired station as WAYS-TV from G. W. Dowdy & associates for token $4 in December 1954, then took station off air March 15, 1955. While in off-air CP status, Deadwyler sold station to Century Advertising, of which he was part owner. Resumed operation September 5, 1961. Century took station off air May 16, 1963. Sale to present owner, who changed call letters from WUTV & resumed operation November 1, 1964, approved by FCC August 20, 1964. Ceased analog operations: June 12, 2009.

Represented (legal): Dow Lohnes PLLC.

Represented (sales): Eagle Television Sales.

Personnel:

Beverly Bahakel Poston, Executive Vice President & Chief Executive Officer.

John Hutchinson, Vice President & General Manager.

Bob Davis, Operations Manager & Engineering Director.

Gaston Bates, General Sales Manager.

Annie Cordell, Local Sales Manager.

Chris Gray, National Sales Manager.

Ken White, News Director.

Rick Aylette, Chief Engineer.

Cathy Hodges, Business Manager.

Kimberly Seegars, Assistant Program Director.

Jeff Arrowood, Program & Promotion Director.

Rick Gamertsfelder, Production Manager.

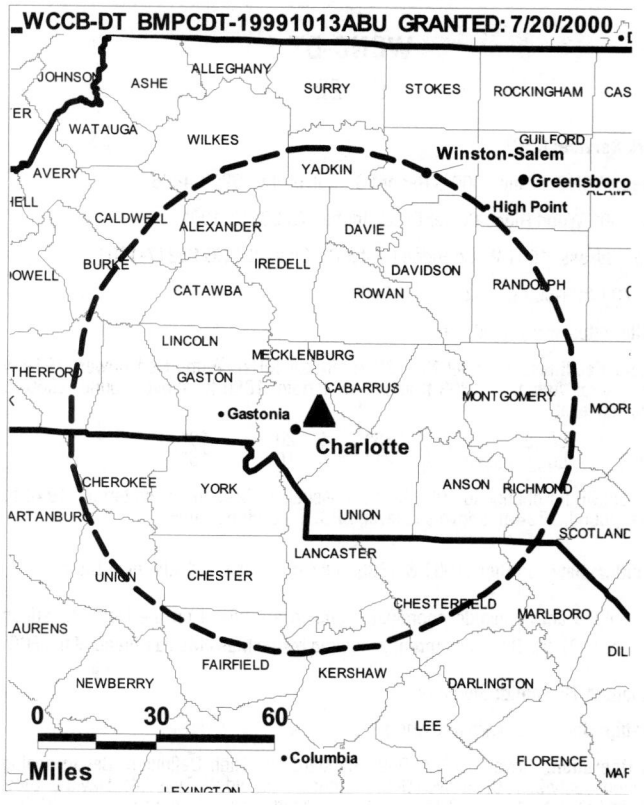

© 2010 Warren Communications News

Lou Mauney, Traffic Manager.

City of License: Charlotte. **Station DMA:** Charlotte, NC. **Rank:** 24.

Circulation © 2009 Nielsen. Coverage based on Nielsen study.

GrandTotal	Cable TV Households	Non-cable TV Households	Total TV Households
Estimated Station Totals *	679,060	465,160	1,144,220
Average Weekly Circulation (2009)	380,554	255,527	636,081
Average Daily Circulation (2009)			217,189

Station DMA Total	Cable TV Households	Non-cable TV Households	Total TV Households
Estimated Station Totals *	659,510	456,670	1,116,180
Average Weekly Circulation (2009)	373,263	254,542	627,805
Average Daily Circulation (2009)			215,305

Other DMA Total	Cable TV Households	Non-cable TV Households	Total TV Households
Estimated Station Totals *	19,550	8,490	28,040
Average Weekly Circulation (2009)	7,291	985	8,276
Average Daily Circulation (2009)			1,884

*Estimated station totals are sums of the Nielsen TV and Cable TV household estimates for each county in which the station registers viewing of more than 5% as per the Nielsen Survey Methods.

WCNC-DT
Ch. 22

Network Service: NBC.

Licensee: WCNC-TV Inc., 400 S Record St, Dallas, TX 75202-4806.

Studio: 1001 Wood Ridge Center Dr, Charlotte, NC 28217-1901.

Mailing Address: 1001 Wood Ridge Center Dr, Charlotte, NC 28217-1901.

Phone: 704-329-3636. **Fax:** 704-357-4980.

Web Site: http://www.nbc6.com

Technical Facilities: Channel No. 22 (518-524 MHz). Authorized power: 791-kw visual, aural. Antenna: 1893-ft above av. terrain, 1880-ft. above ground, 2666-ft. above sea level.

Latitude	35°	20'	49"
Longitude	81°	10'	15"

Requests CP for change to 1000-kw max. visual, 1952-ft above av. terrain, 1942-ft. above ground, 2728-ft. above sea level; BPCDT-20080617AEH.

Transmitter: Between Rtes. 1001 & 1805, 0.87-mi. N of Rte. 1804, near Dallas.

Note: Latitude and longitude coordinates shown are based on the North American Datum of 1927 (NAD 27) as currently required by the Mass Media Bureau of the FCC.

Multichannel TV Sound: Stereo only.

Ownership: Belo Corp. (Group Owner).

Began Operation: November 1, 1999. Standard and High Definition. Began analog operations: July 9, 1967 as WCTU-TV, owned by Harold W. Twisdale, David L. Steel Sr. & others. Sale to R. E. Turner by Emil F. Kratt, Receiver, approved by FCC July 27, 1970. Sale to Westinghouse Broadcasting & Cable approved by FCC March 17, 1980 (Television Digest, Vol. 19:21). Sale to Odyssey Partners approved by FCC November 23, 1984 (Vol. 24:15). Sale to Providence Journal Broadcasting approved by FCC November 1, 1988. Sale to present owner by Providence Journal Broadcasting approved by FCC February 28, 1997. (Vol. 36:40, 37:9). Ceased analog operations: June 12, 2009.

Represented (engineering): Smith & Fisher.

Personnel:

Timothy J. Morrissey, President & General Manager.

Ann Marie Young, Sales Director.

Sherri Brennen, Local Sales Manager.

Jon Barcelo, National Sales Manager.

Mary Alvarez, News Director.

Steve Kiser, Chief Engineer.

Janice Harward, Business Manager & Controller.

John Rice, Program & Promotion Director.

City of License: Charlotte. **Station DMA:** Charlotte, NC. **Rank:** 24.

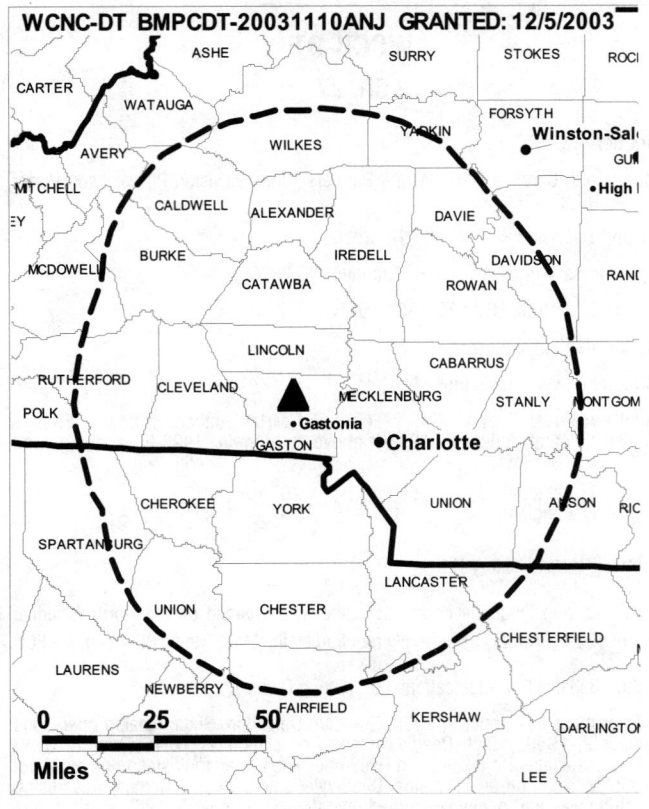

WCNC-DT BMPCDT-20031110ANJ GRANTED: 12/5/2003

© 2010 Warren Communications News

Circulation © 2009 Nielsen. Coverage based on Nielsen study.

GrandTotal	Cable TV Households	Non-cable TV Households	Total TV Households
Estimated Station Totals *	667,960	508,530	1,176,490
Average Weekly Circulation (2009)	382,388	245,348	627,736
Average Daily Circulation (2009)			270,846

Station DMA Total	Cable TV Households	Non-cable TV Households	Total TV Households
Estimated Station Totals *	656,540	456,670	1,113,210
Average Weekly Circulation (2009)	381,196	241,638	622,834
Average Daily Circulation (2009)			269,302

Other DMA Total	Cable TV Households	Non-cable TV Households	Total TV Households
Estimated Station Totals *	11,420	51,860	63,280
Average Weekly Circulation (2009)	1,192	3,710	4,902
Average Daily Circulation (2009)			1,544

*Estimated station totals are sums of the Nielsen TV and Cable TV household estimates for each county in which the station registers viewing of more than 5% as per the Nielsen Survey Methods.

WSOC-DT
Ch. 34

Network Service: ABC.

Licensee: WSOC Television Inc., 6205 Peachtree Dunwoody Rd, Atlanta, GA 30328.

Studio: 1901 N Tryon St, Charlotte, NC 28206.

Mailing Address: PO Box 34665, Charlotte, NC 28234.

Phone: 704-338-9999. **Fax:** 704-335-4961.

Web Site: http://www.wsoctv.com

Technical Facilities: Channel No. 34 (590-596 MHz). Authorized power: 1000-kw max. visual, aural. Antenna: 1142-ft above av. terrain, 997-ft. above ground, 1854-ft. above sea level.

Latitude	35°	15'	41"
Longitude	80°	43'	38"

Transmitter: 7735 Plaza Rd.

Note: Latitude and longitude coordinates shown are based on the North American Datum of 1927 (NAD 27) as currently required by the Mass Media Bureau of the FCC.

Satellite Earth Stations: Transmitter Harris; Satcom Technologies, 5.5-meter Ku-band; Scientific-Atlanta, 7-meter; Satcom Technologies, 7.3-meter Ku-band; Satcom Technologies, 7.3-meter C-band; Scientific-Atlanta receivers.

Ownership: Cox Enterprises Inc. (Group Owner).

Began Operation: October 22, 1999. High Definition. Began analog operations: April 28, 1957. Sale to present owner by E. E. Jones & associates approved by FCC April 8, 1959 (Television Digest, Vol. 15:5, 15). Ceased analog operations: June 12, 2009.

Represented (sales): TeleRep Inc.

Represented (legal): Dow Lohnes PLLC.

Personnel:

Joe Pomilla, Vice President & General Manager.

Paul Briggs, General Sales Manager.

Andrea Moore, National Sales Manager.

Robin Whitmeyer, News Director.

Ted Hand, Chief Engineer.

Shawn Pack, Controller.

Kay Hall, Program Director.

Sally Ganz, Promotion & Creative Services Director.

Patricia Marsden, Research Director.

Kierstin Bouilil, Traffic Manager.

City of License: Charlotte. **Station DMA:** Charlotte, NC. **Rank:** 24.

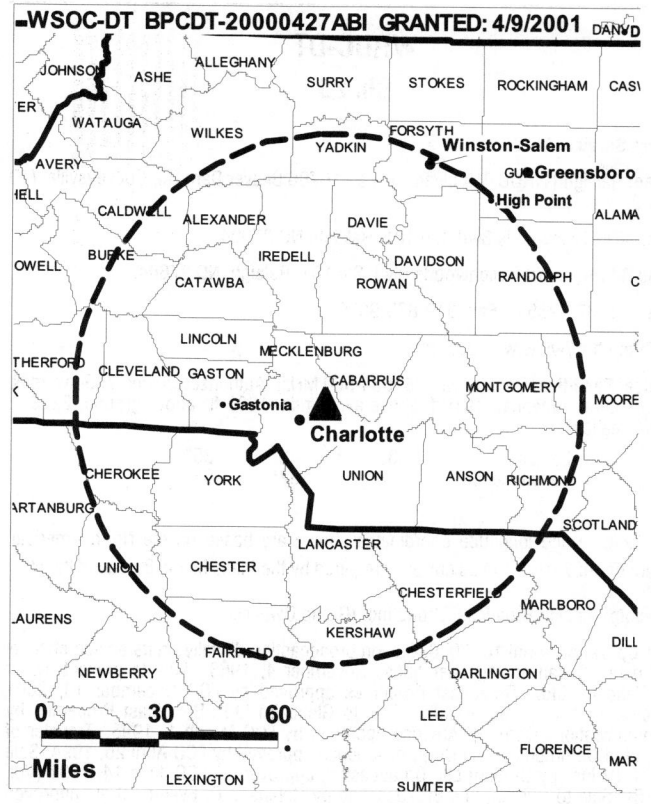

© 2010 Warren Communications News

Circulation © 2009 Nielsen. Coverage based on Nielsen study.

GrandTotal	Cable TV Households	Non-cable TV Households	Total TV Households
Estimated Station Totals *	686,170	529,990	1,216,160
Average Weekly Circulation (2009)	457,252	304,196	761,448
Average Daily Circulation (2009)			392,642

Station DMA Total	Cable TV Households	Non-cable TV Households	Total TV Households
Estimated Station Totals *	659,510	456,670	1,116,180
Average Weekly Circulation (2009)	453,676	289,982	743,658
Average Daily Circulation (2009)			385,581

Other DMA Total	Cable TV Households	Non-cable TV Households	Total TV Households
Estimated Station Totals *	26,660	73,320	99,980
Average Weekly Circulation (2009)	3,576	14,214	17,790
Average Daily Circulation (2009)			7,061

*Estimated station totals are sums of the Nielsen TV and Cable TV household estimates for each county in which the station registers viewing of more than 5% as per the Nielsen Survey Methods.

WRDC-DT
Ch. 28

Network Service: MNT.

Grantee: Raleigh (WRDC-TV) Licensee Inc., 10706 Beaver Dam Rd, Cockeysville, MD 21030.

Studio: 3012 Highwoods Blvd, Ste 101, Raleigh, NC 27604.

Mailing Address: 3012 Highwoods Blvd, Ste 101, Raleigh, NC 27604.

Phone: 919-872-2854. **Fax:** 919-873-9079.

Web Site: http://www.wrdc28.com

Technical Facilities: Channel No. 28 (554-560 MHz). Authorized power: 725-kw max. visual, aural. Antenna: 1919-ft above av. terrain, 1900-ft. above ground, 2223-ft. above sea level.

Latitude	35°	40'	35"
Longitude	78°	32'	08"

Note: Latitude and longitude coordinates shown are based on the North American Datum of 1927 (NAD 27) as currently required by the Mass Media Bureau of the FCC.

Ownership: Sinclair Broadcast Group Inc. (Group Owner).

Began Operation: April 10, 2006. Station broadcasting digitally on its analog channel allotment. Began analog operations: November 4, 1968. Sale to present owner by Glencairn Ltd. Broadcast Properties approved by FCC December 10, 2001 (Television Digest, Vol. 41:38). Sale to Glencairn Ltd. Broadcast Properties by Communications Corp. of America approved by FCC March 1, 1995. Transfer of control to Communications Corp. of America approved by FCC April 26, 1994. Sale to FSF TV Inc. by Durham Life Broadcasting approved by FCC June 14, 1991 (Vol. 31:15). Sale to Durham Life Broadcasting by Robinson O. Everett, et al., approved by FCC May 19, 1977 (Vol. 17:5). Ceased analog operations: February 17, 2009.

Represented (sales): Katz Media Group.

Represented (legal): Pillsbury Winthrop Shaw Pittman LLP.

Personnel:

Neal Davis, General Manager & General Sales Manager.

Lon Goldman, Local Sales Manager.

Clif Wallace, Local Sales Manager.

Devon Brewer, Local Sales Manager.

Gary Todd, Engineering Director.

Richard Bellamy, Credit Manager.

Scott Bradsher, Program Director.

Kim Rivenbark, Promotion Director.

Valerie Venable, Commercial Production Manager.

Sandy Rudd, Traffic Manager.

City of License: Durham. **Station DMA:** Raleigh-Durham (Fayetteville), NC. **Rank:** 26.

WRDC-DT BMPCDT-20080620AJU GRANTED: 2/19/2009

© 2010 Warren Communications News

Circulation © 2009 Nielsen. Coverage based on Nielsen study.

GrandTotal	Cable TV Households	Non-cable TV Households	Total TV Households
Estimated Station Totals *	620,000	471,580	1,091,580
Average Weekly Circulation (2009)	101,555	95,798	197,353
Average Daily Circulation (2009)			70,888

Station DMA Total	Cable TV Households	Non-cable TV Households	Total TV Households
Estimated Station Totals *	613,650	419,370	1,033,020
Average Weekly Circulation (2009)	100,688	92,114	192,802
Average Daily Circulation (2009)			69,972

Other DMA Total	Cable TV Households	Non-cable TV Households	Total TV Households
Estimated Station Totals *	6,350	52,210	58,560
Average Weekly Circulation (2009)	867	3,684	4,551
Average Daily Circulation (2009)			916

*Estimated station totals are sums of the Nielsen TV and Cable TV household estimates for each county in which the station registers viewing of more than 5% as per the Nielsen Survey Methods.

WTVD-DT
Ch. 11

Network Service: ABC.

Licensee: WTVD Television LLC, 77 W 66th St, 16th Fl, New York, NY 10023.

Studio: 411 Liberty St, Durham, NC 27701.

Mailing Address: 411 Liberty St, Durham, NC 27701.

Phone: 919-683-1111. **Fax:** 919-682-7476.

Web Site: http://www.abc11.com

Technical Facilities: Channel No. 11 (198-204 MHz). Authorized power: 20.7-kw visual, aural. Antenna: 2018-ft above av. terrain, 1965-ft. above ground, 2284-ft. above sea level.

Latitude	35°	40'	05"
Longitude	78°	31'	59"

Transmitter: Near Hwy. 70, 4-mi. NW of Clayton.

Note: Latitude and longitude coordinates shown are based on the North American Datum of 1927 (NAD 27) as currently required by the Mass Media Bureau of the FCC.

Ownership: Disney Enterprises Inc. (Group Owner).

Began Operation: October 30, 1999. Standard and High Definition. Station broadcasting digitally on its analog channel allotment. Began analog operations: September 2, 1954. Sale to present owner by Capital Cities/ABC approved by FCC February 8, 1996. Sale to Durham TV Co. Inc. (controlled by Lowell Thomas interests & Capital Cities Communications Corp.) by principal stockholders Harmon L. & Virginia D. Duncan, J. Floyd Fletcher and WDNC (AM) approved by FCC May 22, 1957 (Television Digest, Vol. 13:14, 21). Ceased analog operations: June 12, 2009.

Personnel:

John Idler, President & General Manager.

Tim D. Alwran, General Sales Manager.

Andy Lashbrooke, Local Sales Manager.

Rob Elmore, News Director.

Curtis Meredith, Chief Engineer.

Ed O'Connor, Business Manager.

Curtis Miles, Creative Services Director.

Darryl Furges, Production Supervisor.

Amy Lorenzen, Traffic Manager.

Mimi Sigel, Executive Secretary.

City of License: Durham. **Station DMA:** Raleigh-Durham (Fayetteville), NC. **Rank:** 26.

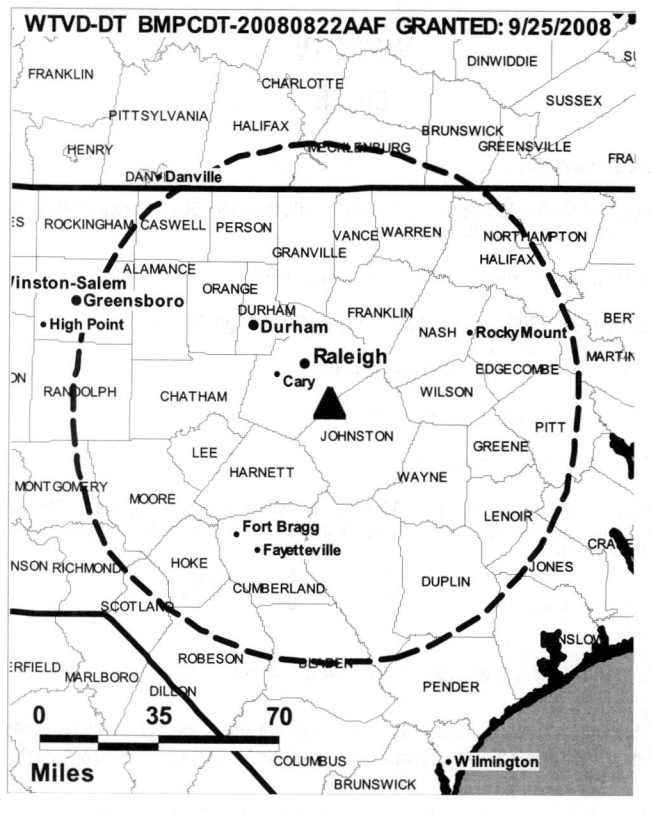

© 2010 Warren Communications News

Circulation © 2009 Nielsen. Coverage based on Nielsen study.

GrandTotal	Cable TV Households	Non-cable TV Households	Total TV Households
Estimated Station Totals *	706,610	494,510	1,201,120
Average Weekly Circulation (2009)	445,218	280,227	725,445
Average Daily Circulation (2009)			370,923

Station DMA Total	Cable TV Households	Non-cable TV Households	Total TV Households
Estimated Station Totals *	628,560	419,370	1,047,930
Average Weekly Circulation (2009)	413,013	269,735	682,748
Average Daily Circulation (2009)			353,768

Other DMA Total	Cable TV Households	Non-cable TV Households	Total TV Households
Estimated Station Totals *	78,050	75,140	153,190
Average Weekly Circulation (2009)	32,205	10,492	42,697
Average Daily Circulation (2009)			17,155

*Estimated station totals are sums of the Nielsen TV and Cable TV household estimates for each county in which the station registers viewing of more than 5% as per the Nielsen Survey Methods.

WFPX-TV
Ch. 36

Network Service: ION.

Licensee: ION Media License Co. LLC, Debtor in Possession, 601 Clearwater Park Rd, West Palm Beach, FL 33401-6233.

Studio: 19234 NC 71 Hwy N, Lumber Bridge, NC 28357.

Mailing Address: 3209 Gresham Lake Rd, Ste 151, Raleigh, NC 27615.

Phone: 910-843-3884. **Fax:** 910-843-2873.

E-mail: michellebarnhill@ionmedia.com

Web Site: http://www.ionmedia.com

Technical Facilities: Channel No. 36 (602-608 MHz). Authorized power: 1000-kw max. visual, aural. Antenna: 794-ft above av. terrain, 794-ft. above ground, 984-ft. above sea level.

Latitude	34°	53'	05"
Longitude	79°	04'	29"

Transmitter: Off Rte. 71, approx. 0.31-mi. SW of Lumber Bridge.

Note: Latitude and longitude coordinates shown are based on the North American Datum of 1927 (NAD 27) as currently required by the Mass Media Bureau of the FCC.

Ownership: ION Media Networks Inc., Debtor in Possession (Group Owner).

Began Operation: November 1, 2002. Standard Definition. Began analog operations: March 4, 1985. Sale to Urban Television LLC pends. Involuntary assignment to debtor in possession status approved by FCC June 5, 2009. Transfer of control by ION Media Networks Inc. from Paxson Management Corp. & Lowell W. Paxson to CIG Media LLC approved by FCC December 31, 2007. Paxson Communications Corp. became ION Media Networks Inc. on June 26, 2006. Sale to Paxson Communications Corp. by Fayetteville-Cumberland Telecasters Inc. approved by FCC October 20, 1997. Involuntary assignment to debtor in possession status approved by FCC December 30, 1992. Ceased analog operations: June 12, 2009.

Represented (legal): Dow Lohnes PLLC.

Personnel:

Michelle Barnhill, Station Operations Manager.

Sam Garfield, Contract Engineer.

Deborah Howard, Traffic Manager.

City of License: Fayetteville. **Station DMA:** Raleigh-Durham (Fayetteville), NC.

Rank: 26.

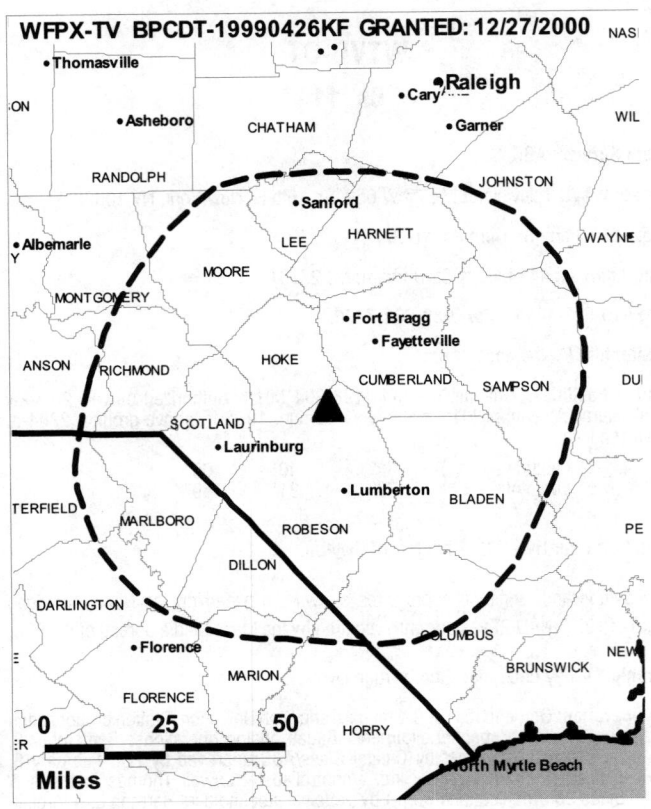

WFPX-TV BPCDT-19990426KF GRANTED: 12/27/2000

© 2010 Warren Communications News

Circulation © 2009 Nielsen. Coverage based on Nielsen study.

GrandTotal	Cable TV Households	Non-cable TV Households	Total TV Households
Estimated Station Totals *	150,620	38,790	189,410
Average Weekly Circulation (2009)	19,092	4,059	23,151
Average Daily Circulation (2009)			4,795

Station DMA Total	Cable TV Households	Non-cable TV Households	Total TV Households
Estimated Station Totals *	115,960	0	115,960
Average Weekly Circulation (2009)	16,102	0	16,102
Average Daily Circulation (2009)			3,256

Other DMA Total	Cable TV Households	Non-cable TV Households	Total TV Households
Estimated Station Totals *	34,660	38,790	73,450
Average Weekly Circulation (2009)	2,990	4,059	7,049
Average Daily Circulation (2009)			1,539

*Estimated station totals are sums of the Nielsen TV and Cable TV household estimates for each county in which the station registers viewing of more than 5% as per the Nielsen Survey Methods.

WUVC-DT
Ch. 38

Network Service: UNV.

Licensee: WUVC License Partnership GP, 1999 Avenue of the Stars, Ste 3050, Los Angeles, CA 90067.

Studio: 230 Donaldson St, Fayetteville, NC 28301.

Mailing Address: 230 Donaldson St, Fayetteville, NC 28301.

Phone: 910-323-4040. **Fax:** 910-323-3924.

Web Site: http://www.univision.net

Technical Facilities: Channel No. 38 (614-620 MHz). Authorized power: 500-kw max. visual, aural. Antenna: 1670-ft above av. terrain, 1549-ft. above ground, 1949-ft. above sea level.

Latitude	35°	30'	44"
Longitude	78°	58'	41"

Holds CP for change to 1000-kw max. visual, 1844-ft above av. terrain, 1722-ft. above ground, 2122-ft. above sea level; lat. 35° 30' 43", long. 78° 58' 42", BPCDT-20090630ABX.

Note: Latitude and longitude coordinates shown are based on the North American Datum of 1927 (NAD 27) as currently required by the Mass Media Bureau of the FCC.

Ownership: Univision Communications Inc. (Group Owner).

Began Operation: May 1, 2002. Began analog operations: June 1, 1981. Transfer of control to Broadcasting Media Partners Inc. approved by FCC March 27, 2007. Transfer of control to present owner by Bahakel Communications Ltd. approved by FCC February 6, 2003. Sale to Bahakel Communications Ltd. by Allied Communications Co. Inc. approved by FCC February 19, 1998. Sale to Allied Communications Co. Inc. by Elbert M. Boyd Jr., T. Y. Baker, et al., approved by FCC January 13, 1994. Sale to Delta Broadcasting Inc. by Ocie F. Murray Jr., Interim Trustee approved by FCC March 20, 1991. Involuntary assignment to Ocie F. Murray Jr., Interim Trustee by SJL of North Carolina Associates LP approved by FCC February 15, 1991. Sale to SJL of North Carolina Assoc. by Norman Suttler, et al. (Fayetteville Television Inc.), approved by FCC June 20, 1985. Ceased analog operations: June 12, 2009.

Represented (legal): Covington & Burling.

Represented (sales): Continental Television Sales.

Personnel:

Michael Munoz, General Manager.

Enrique Delcampo, Local Sales Manager.

Todd Schlacater, National Sales Manager.

William Acevedo, Chief Engineer.

Kevin Booker, Promotion & Production Director.

Fernando D. Romero, Promotion Assistant.

Maria Tajman, Traffic Manager.

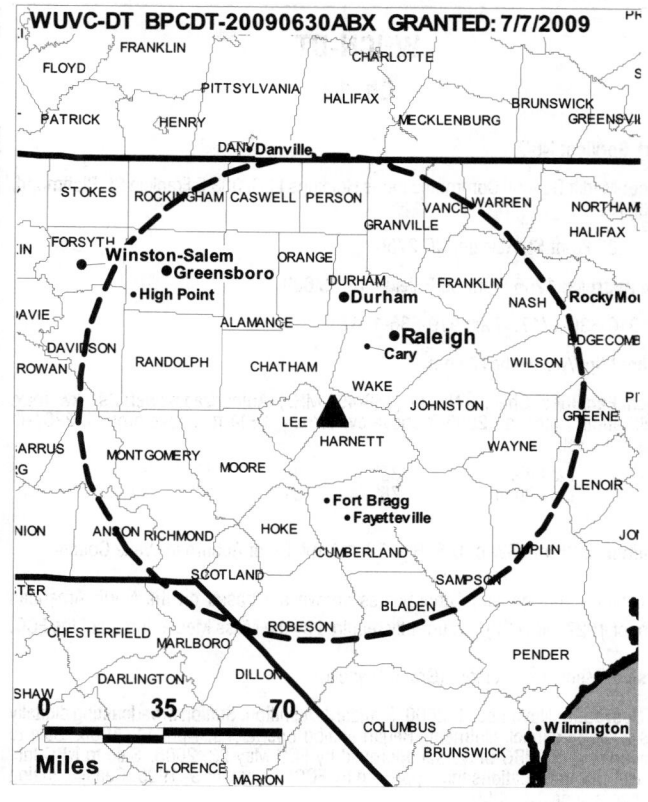

© 2010 Warren Communications News

Yvonne Cerna, Community Affairs Manager.

City of License: Fayetteville. **Station DMA:** Raleigh-Durham (Fayetteville), NC.

Rank: 26.

Circulation © 2009 Nielsen. Coverage based on Nielsen study.

GrandTotal	Cable TV Households	Non-cable TV Households	Total TV Households
Estimated Station Totals *	3,980	111,370	115,350
Average Weekly Circulation (2009)	693	6,863	7,556
Average Daily Circulation (2009)			4,134

Station DMA Total	Cable TV Households	Non-cable TV Households	Total TV Households
Estimated Station Totals *	3,980	111,370	115,350
Average Weekly Circulation (2009)	693	6,863	7,556
Average Daily Circulation (2009)			4,134

*Estimated station totals are sums of the Nielsen TV and Cable TV household estimates for each county in which the station registers viewing of more than 5% as per the Nielsen Survey Methods.

WNCN-DT
Ch. 17

Network Service: NBC.

Licensee: Media General Communications Holdings LLC, 333 E Franklin St, Richmond, VA 23219.

Studio: 1205 Front St, Raleigh, NC 27609.

Mailing Address: 1205 Front St, Raleigh, NC 27609.

Phone: 919-836-1717. **Fax:** 919-836-1747.

Web Site: http://www.nbc17.com

Technical Facilities: Channel No. 17 (488-494 MHz). Authorized power: 291-kw max. visual, aural. Antenna: 2005-ft above av. terrain, 1904-ft. above ground, 2264-ft. above sea level.

Latitude	35°	40'	29"
Longitude	78°	31'	40"

Transmitter: 0.25-mi. SW of U.S. Rte. 70, 1.7-mi. SE of Auburn in Wake County.

Note: Latitude and longitude coordinates shown are based on the North American Datum of 1927 (NAD 27) as currently required by the Mass Media Bureau of the FCC.

Ownership: Media General Inc. (Group Owner).

Began Operation: November 1, 2000. Standard Definition. Station broadcasting digitally on its analog channel allotment. Began analog operations: April 11, 1988. Sale to present owner by NBC Universal approved by FCC May 23, 2006. Sale to NBC Inc. by Outlet Communications Inc. approved by FCC November 9, 1995. Ceased analog operations: June 12, 2009.

Represented (legal): Dow Lohnes PLLC.

Personnel:

Barry Leffler, General Manager.

Carol Ward, General Sales Manager.

Nick Clark, Local & National Sales Manager.

Cory Jackson, Local Sales Manager.

Shuneca Harrington, Local Sales Manager.

Nannette Wilson, Vice President, News.

Ira Lilly, Operations & Engineering Director.

Doug Hamilton, Finance & Administration Director.

Mary Ann Balbo, Marketing Manager.

Beverly Pigford, Traffic Manager.

Richard Bouchez, Creative Services Director.

Jennifer Williams, Results Director.

Tammy LeGlue, Research Director.

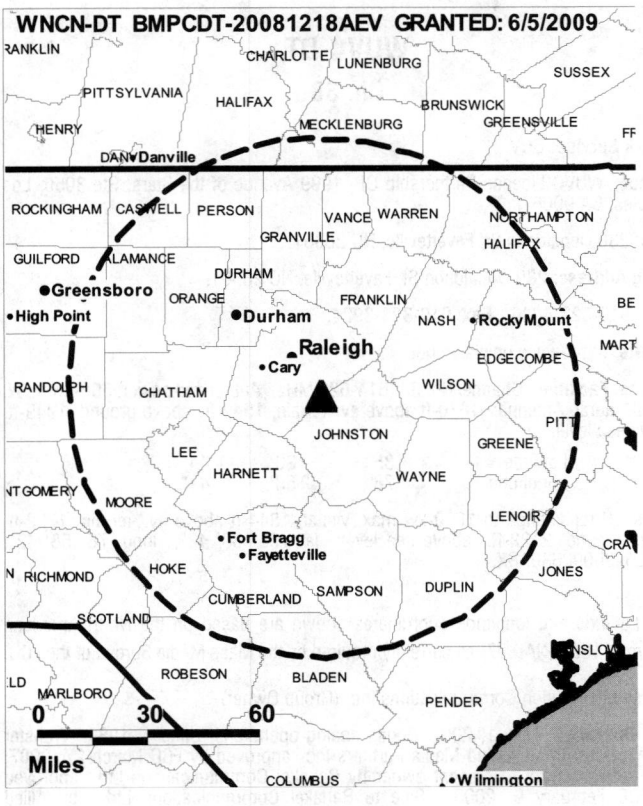

WNCN-DT BMPCDT-20081218AEV GRANTED: 6/5/2009

© 2010 Warren Communications News

City of License: Goldsboro. **Station DMA:** Raleigh-Durham (Fayetteville), NC.

Rank: 26.

Circulation © 2009 Nielsen. Coverage based on Nielsen study.

GrandTotal	Cable TV Households	Non-cable TV Households	Total TV Households
Estimated Station Totals *	618,530	435,510	1,054,040
Average Weekly Circulation (2009)	262,560	199,208	461,768
Average Daily Circulation (2009)			172,291

Station DMA Total	Cable TV Households	Non-cable TV Households	Total TV Households
Estimated Station Totals *	618,530	419,370	1,037,900
Average Weekly Circulation (2009)	262,560	197,465	460,025
Average Daily Circulation (2009)			171,887

Other DMA Total	Cable TV Households	Non-cable TV Households	Total TV Households
Estimated Station Totals *	0	16,140	16,140
Average Weekly Circulation (2009)	0	1,743	1,743
Average Daily Circulation (2009)			404

*Estimated station totals are sums of the Nielsen TV and Cable TV household estimates for each county in which the station registers viewing of more than 5% as per the Nielsen Survey Methods.

WFMY-DT
Ch. 51

Network Service: CBS.

Licensee: WFMY Television Corp., 1615 Phillips Ave, Greensboro, NC 27405.

Studio: 1615 Phillips Ave, Greensboro, NC 27405.

Mailing Address: Box TV-2, Greensboro, NC 27420.

Phone: 336-379-9369. **Fax:** 336-273-2444.

E-mail: dbriscoe@wfmy.gennett.com

Web Site: http://www.wfmynews2.com

Technical Facilities: Channel No. 51 (692-698 MHz). Authorized power: 1000-kw max. visual, aural. Antenna: 1866-ft above av. terrain, 1863-ft. above ground, 2598-ft. above sea level.

Latitude	35°	52'	13"
Longitude	79°	50'	25"

Transmitter: 6252 David Country Rd.

Note: Latitude and longitude coordinates shown are based on the North American Datum of 1927 (NAD 27) as currently required by the Mass Media Bureau of the FCC.

Ownership: Gannett Co. Inc. (Group Owner).

Began Operation: April 1, 2002. High Definition. Began analog operations: September 22, 1949. Sale to present owner by Harte-Hanks Communications Gannett Co. January 21, 1988 (Television Digest, Vol. 27:49; 28:6). Sale to Harte-Hanks Communications by Landmark Communications approved by FCC October 29, 1976 (Vol. 16:27). Sale to Landmark by former owners of Greensboro News Co. approved by FCC December 18, 1964 (Vol. 4:36, 49, 51). Ceased analog operations: June 12, 2009.

Represented (sales): Blair Television.

Personnel:

Deborah Hooper, President & General Manager.

Deana Coble, Engineering & Operations Director.

Bill Lancaster, General Sales Manager.

Gina Katzmark, News Director.

Larry Schell, Business Manager.

David Briscoe, Program Director.

David Reeve, Promotion & Marketing Director.

Kristy Robinson, Traffic Manager.

City of License: Greensboro.

Station DMA: Greensboro-High Point-Winston Salem, NC. **Rank:** 46.

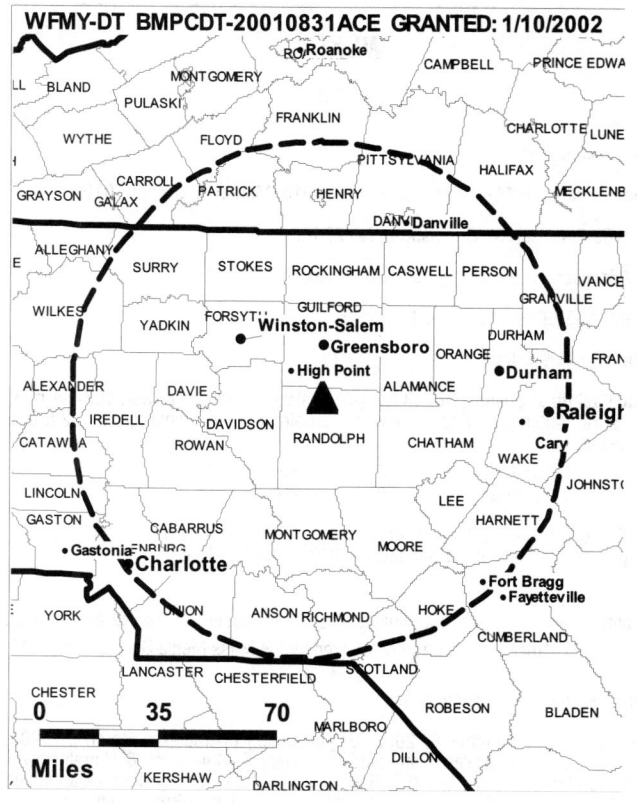

WFMY-DT BMPCDT-20010831ACE GRANTED: 1/10/2002

© 2010 Warren Communications News

Circulation © 2009 Nielsen. Coverage based on Nielsen study.

GrandTotal	Cable TV Households	Non-cable TV Households	Total TV Households
Estimated Station Totals *	492,530	387,360	879,890
Average Weekly Circulation (2009)	318,171	179,806	497,977
Average Daily Circulation (2009)			261,824

Station DMA Total	Cable TV Households	Non-cable TV Households	Total TV Households
Estimated Station Totals *	425,060	251,860	676,920
Average Weekly Circulation (2009)	305,552	159,839	465,391
Average Daily Circulation (2009)			250,334

Other DMA Total	Cable TV Households	Non-cable TV Households	Total TV Households
Estimated Station Totals *	67,470	135,500	202,970
Average Weekly Circulation (2009)	12,619	19,967	32,586
Average Daily Circulation (2009)			11,490

*Estimated station totals are sums of the Nielsen TV and Cable TV household estimates for each county in which the station registers viewing of more than 5% as per the Nielsen Survey Methods.

WLXI
Ch. 43

Network Service: IND.

Licensee: Radiant Life Ministries Inc., PO Box 1010, Marion, IL 62959-1010.

Studio: 2109 Patterson St, Greensboro, NC 27407.

Mailing Address: 2109 Patterson St, Greensboro, NC 27407.

Phone: 336-855-5610. **Fax:** 336-855-3645.

Web Site: http://www.tct.tv

Technical Facilities: Channel No. 43 (644-650 MHz). Authorized power: 105-kw max. visual, aural. Antenna: 1723-ft above av. terrain, 1720-ft. above ground, 2459-ft. above sea level.

Latitude	35°	52'	02"
Longitude	79°	49'	26"

Holds CP for change to 130-kw max. visual, 1729-ft above av. terrain, 1719-ft. above ground, 2458-ft. above sea level; BPCDT-20080619AII.

Note: Latitude and longitude coordinates shown are based on the North American Datum of 1927 (NAD 27) as currently required by the Mass Media Bureau of the FCC.

Ownership: Radiant Life Ministries Inc.

Began Operation: September 6, 2002. Began analog operations: March 5, 1984. Transfer of control to William Satterfield from Gary S. Smithwick & Harrell Powell Jr. approved by FCC May 23, 1985. Sale to Trinity Broadcasting Network approved by FCC February 24, 1986. Sale to present owner by Trinity Broadcasting Network approved by FCC October 7, 1991. Ceased analog operations: June 12, 2009.

Represented (legal): Colby M. May.

Personnel:

Garth Coonce, President.

Larry L. Patton, General Manager & Station & Local Sales Manager.

Santosh Aghamkar, Production Manager.

Gil Couch, Chief Engineer.

Karen Patton, Programming & Traffic Manager.

City of License: Greensboro.

Station DMA: Greensboro-High Point-Winston Salem, NC. **Rank:** 46.

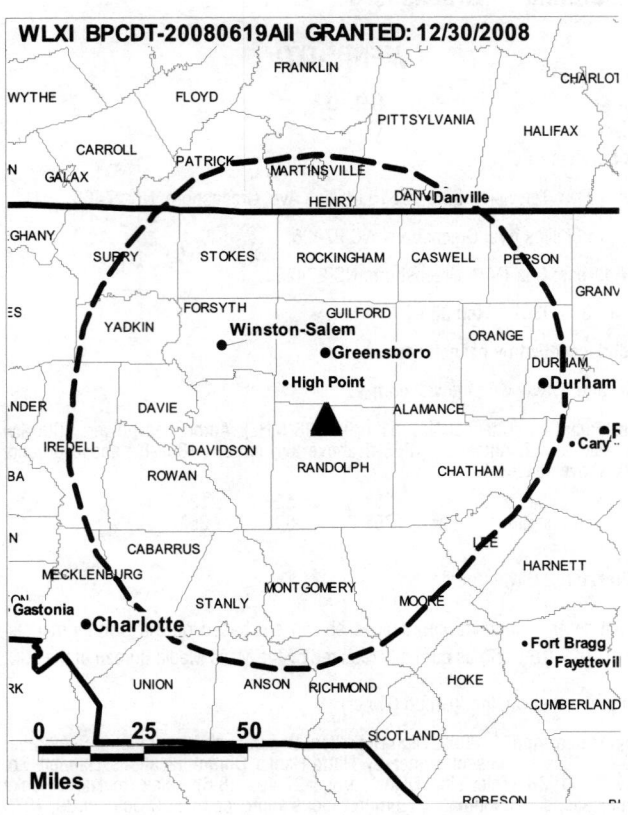

© 2010 Warren Communications News

Circulation © 2009 Nielsen. Coverage based on Nielsen study.

GrandTotal	Cable TV Households	Non-cable TV Households	Total TV Households
Estimated Station Totals *	315,680	0	315,680
Average Weekly Circulation (2009)	20,001	0	20,001
Average Daily Circulation (2009)			4,513

Station DMA Total	Cable TV Households	Non-cable TV Households	Total TV Households
Estimated Station Totals *	315,680	0	315,680
Average Weekly Circulation (2009)	20,001	0	20,001
Average Daily Circulation (2009)			4,513

*Estimated station totals are sums of the Nielsen TV and Cable TV household estimates for each county in which the station registers viewing of more than 5% as per the Nielsen Survey Methods.

WMYV-DT
Ch. 33

Network Service: MNT.

Licensee: WUPN Licensee Inc., 10706 Beaver Dam Rd, Cockeysville, MD 21030.

Studio: 3500 Myer Lee Dr, Winston-Salem, NC 27101.

Mailing Address: 3500 Myer Lee Dr, Winston-Salem, NC 27101.

Phone: 336-274-4848; 336-722-4545. **Fax:** 336-723-8217.

Web Site: http://www.my48.tv/

Technical Facilities: Channel No. 33 (584-590 MHz). Authorized power: 700-kw max. visual, aural. Antenna: 1886-ft above av. terrain, 1872-ft. above ground, 2610-ft. above sea level.

Latitude	35°	52'	03"
Longitude	79°	49'	26"

Note: Latitude and longitude coordinates shown are based on the North American Datum of 1927 (NAD 27) as currently required by the Mass Media Bureau of the FCC.

Ownership: Sinclair Broadcast Group Inc. (Group Owner).

Began Operation: April 29, 2002. Standard Definition. Began analog operations: May 9, 1981. Sale to Edward H. Herlihy approved by FCC June 7, 1985 but not consummated (Television Digest, Vol. 25:13). Sale to Mission Broadcasting Inc. by Guilford Telecasters Inc. approved by FCC June 28, 1996. Sale to present owner by Mission Broadcasting Inc. approved by FCC December 10, 2001 (Vol. 41:38). Ceased analog operations: February 17, 2009.

Represented (sales): Katz Media Group.

Personnel:

Ron Inman, General Manager.

Fran McCrae, General Sales Manager.

Dave Farshing, National Sales Manager.

Sean Hollern, Local Sales Manager.

Jim Hartline, Chief Engineer.

Chris Hummel, Business Manager.

Jeannette Pruitt, Program Director.

Trina Samson, Promotion Manager.

Jay Paul, Production Manager.

Melissa Perry, Research Director.

Dana Baker, Traffic Manager.

City of License: Greensboro.

Station DMA: Greensboro-High Point-Winston Salem, NC. **Rank:** 46.

Circulation © 2009 Nielsen. Coverage based on Nielsen study.

GrandTotal	Cable TV Households	Non-cable TV Households	Total TV Households
Estimated Station Totals *	419,050	257,800	676,850
Average Weekly Circulation (2009)	84,516	52,691	137,207
Average Daily Circulation (2009)			49,322

Station DMA Total	Cable TV Households	Non-cable TV Households	Total TV Households
Estimated Station Totals *	414,860	251,860	666,720
Average Weekly Circulation (2009)	84,101	52,240	136,341
Average Daily Circulation (2009)			49,248

Other DMA Total	Cable TV Households	Non-cable TV Households	Total TV Households
Estimated Station Totals *	4,190	5,940	10,130
Average Weekly Circulation (2009)	415	451	866
Average Daily Circulation (2009)			74

*Estimated station totals are sums of the Nielsen TV and Cable TV household estimates for each county in which the station registers viewing of more than 5% as per the Nielsen Survey Methods.

WEPX-TV
Ch. 51

Network Service: MNT, ION.

Grantee: ION Media Greenville License Inc., Debtor in Possession, 601 Clearwater Park Rd, West Palm Beach, FL 33401-6233.

Studio: 1301 S Glenburnie Rd, New Bern, NC 28562.

Mailing Address: 1301 S Glenburnie Rd, New Bern, NC 28562.

Phone: 252-636-2550. **Fax:** 252-633-7851.

E-mail: lisastroud@ionmedia.com

Web Site: http://www.ionmedia.com

Technical Facilities: Channel No. 51 (692-698 MHz). Authorized power: 143-kw max. visual, aural. Antenna: 505-ft above av. terrain, 473-ft above ground, 541-ft above sea level.

Latitude	35°	24'	09"
Longitude	77°	25'	10"

Note: Latitude and longitude coordinates shown are based on the North American Datum of 1927 (NAD 27) as currently required by the Mass Media Bureau of the FCC.

Ownership: ION Media Networks Inc., Debtor in Possession (Group Owner).

Began Operation: February 10, 2009. Began analog operations: December 1, 2998. Involuntary assignment to debtor in possession status approved by FCC June 5, 2009. Transfer of control by ION Media Networks Inc. from Paxson Management Corp. & Lowell W. Paxson to CIG Media LLC approved by FCC December 31, 2007. Paxson Communications Corp. became ION Media Networks Inc. on June 26, 2006. Sale to Paxson Communications Corp. by Equity Broadcasting Corp. approved by FCC April 13, 1999. Ceased analog operations: June 12, 2009.

Represented (legal): Dow Lohnes PLLC.

Personnel:

Lisa Stroud, Station Operations Manager.

Tammy Mason, Traffic Manager.

Sam Garfield, Contract Engineer.

City of License: Greenville. **Station DMA:** Greenville-New Bern-Washington, NC.

Rank: 103.

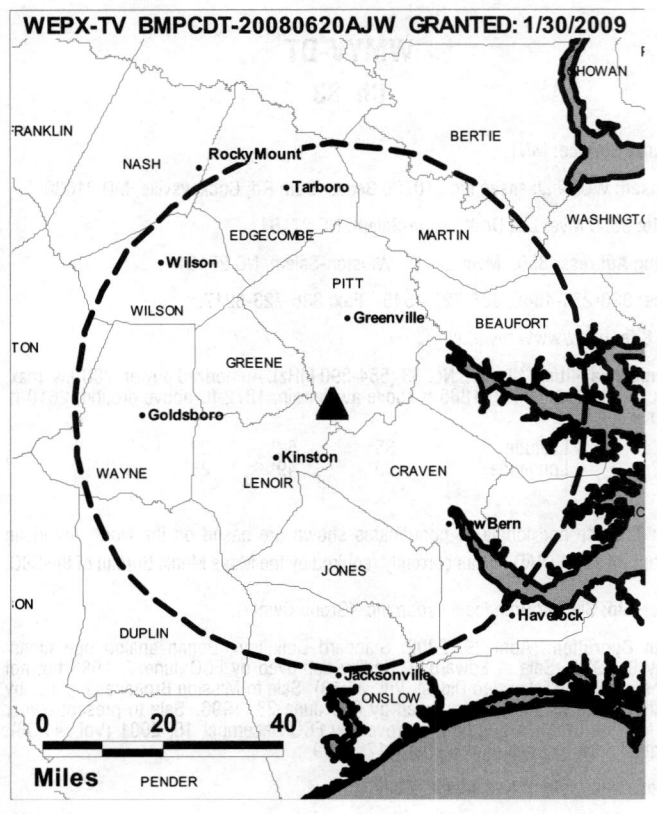

WEPX-TV BMPCDT-20080620AJW GRANTED: 1/30/2009

© 2010 Warren Communications News

Circulation © 2009 Nielsen. Coverage based on Nielsen study.

GrandTotal	Cable TV Households	Non-cable TV Households	Total TV Households
Estimated Station Totals *	68,560	22,750	91,310
Average Weekly Circulation (2009)	6,456	1,274	7,730
Average Daily Circulation (2009)			1,306

Station DMA Total	Cable TV Households	Non-cable TV Households	Total TV Households
Estimated Station Totals *	68,560	22,750	91,310
Average Weekly Circulation (2009)	6,456	1,274	7,730
Average Daily Circulation (2009)			1,306

*Estimated station totals are sums of the Nielsen TV and Cable TV household estimates for each county in which the station registers viewing of more than 5% as per the Nielsen Survey Methods.

WNCT-DT
Ch. 10

Network Service: CW, CBS.

Grantee: Media General Communications Holdings LLC, 333 E Franklin St, Richmond, VA 23219.

Studio: 3221 S. Evans St, Greenville, NC 27834.

Mailing Address: 3221 S. Evans St, Greenville, NC 27834.

Phone: 252-355-8500. **Fax:** 252-355-8568.

Web Site: http://www.wnct.com

Technical Facilities: Channel No. 10 (192-198 MHz). Authorized power: 35-kw visual, aural. Antenna: 1886-ft above av. terrain, 1894-ft. above ground, 1920-ft. above sea level.

Latitude	35°	21'	55"
Longitude	77°	23'	38"

Transmitter: Hwy 118, 2.5-mi. E of Grifton.

Note: Latitude and longitude coordinates shown are based on the North American Datum of 1927 (NAD 27) as currently required by the Mass Media Bureau of the FCC.

Ownership: Media General Inc. (Group Owner).

Began Operation: May 1, 2002. Began analog operations: December 22, 1953. Sale by Carolina Broadcasting System Inc. approved by FCC February 7, 1962 (Television Digest, Vol. 2:7). Sale to Park Acquisition approved by FCC March 27, 1995. Sale to present owner by Park Acquisition approved by FCC November 22, 1996. (Vol. 36:31). Ceased analog operations: June 12, 2009.

Represented (legal): Dow Lohnes PLLC.

Represented (engineering): du Treil, Lundin & Rackley Inc.

Personnel:

Vickie Jones, Vice President & General Manager.

Adam Henning, News Director.

Bertie Cartwright, Chief Engineer.

William Morrisette, Business Manager.

Shirley Dale, Program Coordinator.

Wade F. Poorman, Production Manager.

Ashley Cannon, Traffic Manager.

City of License: Greenville. **Station DMA:** Greenville-New Bern-Washington, NC.

Rank: 103.

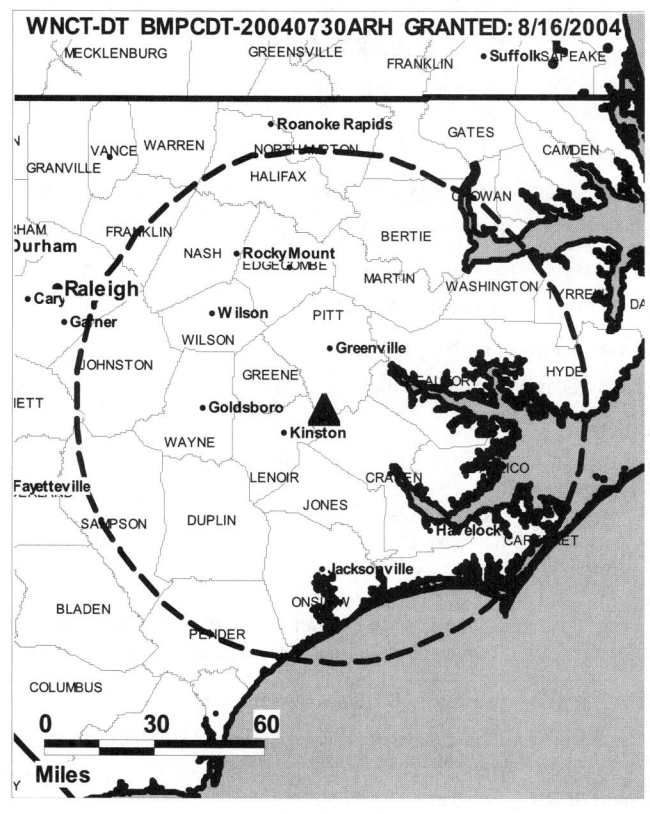

© 2010 Warren Communications News

Circulation © 2009 Nielsen. Coverage based on Nielsen study.

GrandTotal	Cable TV Households	Non-cable TV Households	Total TV Households
Estimated Station Totals *	280,860	191,190	472,050
Average Weekly Circulation (2009)	147,872	84,690	232,562
Average Daily Circulation (2009)			117,212

Station DMA Total	Cable TV Households	Non-cable TV Households	Total TV Households
Estimated Station Totals *	159,160	109,910	269,070
Average Weekly Circulation (2009)	100,168	72,055	172,223
Average Daily Circulation (2009)			86,536

Other DMA Total	Cable TV Households	Non-cable TV Households	Total TV Households
Estimated Station Totals *	121,700	81,280	202,980
Average Weekly Circulation (2009)	47,704	12,635	60,339
Average Daily Circulation (2009)			30,676

*Estimated station totals are sums of the Nielsen TV and Cable TV household estimates for each county in which the station registers viewing of more than 5% as per the Nielsen Survey Methods.

WHKY-DT
Ch. 40

Network Service: IND.

Licensee: Long Communications LLC, 526 Main Ave. SE, Hickory, NC 28602-1103.

Studio: 526 Main Ave. SE, Hickory, NC 28602-1103.

Mailing Address: 526 Main Ave. SE, Hickory, NC 28602.

Phone: 828-322-5115. **Fax:** 828-322-8256.

Web Site: http://www.whky.com

Technical Facilities: Channel No. 40 (626-632 MHz). Authorized power: 600-kw max. visual, aural. Antenna: 597-ft above av. terrain, 462-ft. above ground, 1631-ft. above sea level.

Latitude	35°	43'	59"
Longitude	81°	19'	51"

Holds CP for change to 950-kw max. visual, 823-ft above av. terrain, 164-ft. above ground, 1906-ft. above sea level; lat. 35° 39' 28", long. 81° 24' 24", BPCDT-20080619AAH.

Note: Latitude and longitude coordinates shown are based on the North American Datum of 1927 (NAD 27) as currently required by the Mass Media Bureau of the FCC.

Ownership: Long Communications LLC (Group Owner).

Began Operation: April 6, 2002. Standard Definition. Began analog operations: February 14, 1968. Ceased analog operations: February 17, 2009.

Represented (legal): Hardy, Carey, Chautin & Balkin LLP.

Represented (engineering): du Treil, Lundin & Rackley Inc.

Personnel:

Tom Long, General Manager & Engineering Director.

Jeff Long, Station & Program Director.

Patty Guthrie, General Sales Manager.

Jim Karas, News Director.

Heather Isenhour, Office & Traffic Manager.

Eric Stafford, Promotion & Production Manager.

Jason Savage, Sports Director.

City of License: Hickory. **Station DMA:** Charlotte, NC. **Rank:** 24.

© 2010 Warren Communications News

Circulation © 2009 Nielsen. Coverage based on Nielsen study.

GrandTotal	Cable TV Households	Non-cable TV Households	Total TV Households
Estimated Station Totals *	0	18,980	18,980
Average Weekly Circulation (2009)	0	949	949
Average Daily Circulation (2009)			95

Station DMA Total	Cable TV Households	Non-cable TV Households	Total TV Households
Estimated Station Totals *	0	18,980	18,980
Average Weekly Circulation (2009)	0	949	949
Average Daily Circulation (2009)			95

*Estimated station totals are sums of the Nielsen TV and Cable TV household estimates for each county in which the station registers viewing of more than 5% as per the Nielsen Survey Methods.

WGHP-DT
Ch. 8

Network Service: FOX.

Licensee: Community Television of North Carolina License LLC, 1717 Dixie Hwy, Ste 650, Fort Wright, KY 41011.

Studio: 2005 Francis St, High Point, NC 27263.

Mailing Address: HP-8, High Point, NC 27261.

Phone: 336-841-8888; 336-841-6397. **Fax:** 336-841-8051.

Web Site: http://www.myfoxwghp.com

Technical Facilities: Channel No. 8 (180-186 MHz). Authorized power: 18.75-kw visual, aural. Antenna: 1306-ft above av. terrain, 1217-ft. above ground, 2002-ft. above sea level.

Latitude	35°	48'	46"
Longitude	79°	50'	29"

Note: Latitude and longitude coordinates shown are based on the North American Datum of 1927 (NAD 27) as currently required by the Mass Media Bureau of the FCC.

Ownership: Local TV Holdings LLC (Group Owner).

Began Operation: March 25, 2002. Station broadcasting digitally on its analog channel allotment. Began analog operations: October 14, 1963. Sale to Gulf Broadcast Group by Southern Broadcasting Co. approved by FCC June 16, 1978. Sale to Taft TV & Radio by Gulf approved by FCC May 30, 1985. Sale to Taft Broadcasting Partners LP approved by FCC October 2, 1987. Sale to Great American TV & Radio approved by FCC December 18, 1991. Sale to New World Communications Group approved by FCC July 15, 1994. Sale to Fox Television Stations Inc. by New World Communications Group approved by FCC June 7, 1995. Sale to present owner by Fox Television Stations Inc. approved by FCC June 9, 2008. Ceased analog operations: June 12, 2009.

Represented (legal): Dow Lohnes PLLC.

Personnel:

Karen Adams, Vice President & General Manager.

RaMona Alexander, Vice President, Sales.

Bob Ladka, Vice President, Finance & Administration.

Karen Koutsky, Vice President, News.

Ross Mason, Vice President, Engineering & Operations.

Tim Taylor, Vice President, Creative Services.

Steve Palcsak, National Sales Manager.

Dawn Redding, Local Sales Manager.

Michael Allred, Engineering & Operations Manager.

Susan Davis, Program Director.

Ryan Jessup, Research Director.

Karen Mittman, Traffic Manager.

Becky Austin, Accounting Manager.

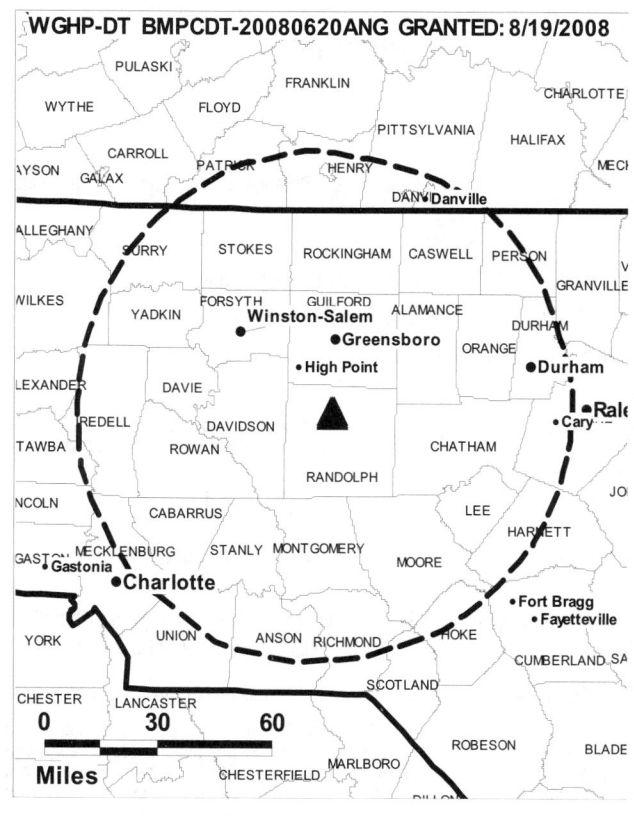

© 2010 Warren Communications News

City of License: High Point.

Station DMA: Greensboro-High Point-Winston Salem, NC. **Rank:** 46.

Circulation © 2009 Nielsen. Coverage based on Nielsen study.

GrandTotal	Cable TV Households	Non-cable TV Households	Total TV Households
Estimated Station Totals *	494,650	469,380	964,030
Average Weekly Circulation (2009)	297,813	193,774	491,587
Average Daily Circulation (2009)			225,102

Station DMA Total	Cable TV Households	Non-cable TV Households	Total TV Households
Estimated Station Totals *	425,060	251,860	676,920
Average Weekly Circulation (2009)	287,561	164,813	452,374
Average Daily Circulation (2009)			213,152

Other DMA Total	Cable TV Households	Non-cable TV Households	Total TV Households
Estimated Station Totals *	69,590	217,520	287,110
Average Weekly Circulation (2009)	10,252	28,961	39,213
Average Daily Circulation (2009)			11,950

*Estimated station totals are sums of the Nielsen TV and Cable TV household estimates for each county in which the station registers viewing of more than 5% as per the Nielsen Survey Methods.

WPXU-DT
Ch. 34

Network Service: MNT, ION.

Licensee: ION Media Jacksonville License Inc., Debtor in Possession, 601 Clearwater Park Rd, West Palm Beach, FL 33401-6233.

Studio: 1301 S Glenburnie Rd, New Bern, NC 28562.

Mailing Address: 1301 S Glenburnie Rd, New Bern, NC 28562.

Phone: 252-636-2550; 877-391-6216. **Fax:** 252-633-7851.

E-mail: tammymason@ionmedia.com

Web Site: http://www.ionmedia.com

Technical Facilities: Channel No. 34 (590-596 MHz). Authorized power: 600-kw max. visual, aural. Antenna: 653-ft above av. terrain, 640-ft. above ground, 669-ft. above sea level.

Latitude	34°	31'	10"
Longitude	77°	26'	52"

Holds CP for change to 1000-kw max. visual; BPCDT-20080620AGG.

Note: Latitude and longitude coordinates shown are based on the North American Datum of 1927 (NAD 27) as currently required by the Mass Media Bureau of the FCC.

Ownership: ION Media Networks Inc., Debtor in Possession (Group Owner).

Began Operation: September 1, 2002. Standard Definition. Began analog operations: July 26, 1999. Involuntary assignment to debtor in possession status approved by FCC June 5, 2009. Transfer of control by ION Media Networks Inc. from Paxson Management Corp. & Lowell W. Paxson to CIG Media LLC approved by FCC December 31, 2007. Paxson Communications Corp. became ION Media Networks Inc. on June 26, 2006. Sale to Paxson Communications Corp. from GOCOM Communications LLC approved by FCC October 1, 1999. Sale to GOCOM Communications LLC by Local Television Associates Inc. approved by FCC March 31, 1995. Ceased analog operations: June 12, 2009.

Represented (legal): Dow Lohnes PLLC.

Personnel:

Tammy Mason, Traffic Manager.

Sam Garfield, Contract Engineer.

City of License: Jacksonville. **Station DMA:** Greenville-New Bern-Washington, NC.

Rank: 103.

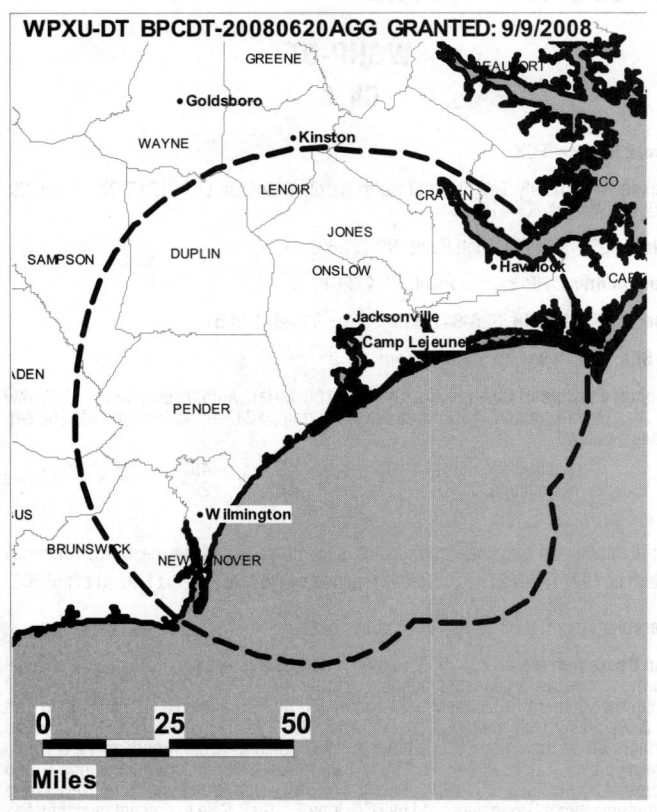

WPXU-DT BPCDT-20080620AGG GRANTED: 9/9/2008

© 2010 Warren Communications News

Circulation © 2009 Nielsen. Coverage based on Nielsen study.

GrandTotal	Cable TV Households	Non-cable TV Households	Total TV Households
Estimated Station Totals *	36,030	12,540	48,570
Average Weekly Circulation (2009)	3,387	702	4,089
Average Daily Circulation (2009)			739

Station DMA Total	Cable TV Households	Non-cable TV Households	Total TV Households
Estimated Station Totals *	36,030	0	36,030
Average Weekly Circulation (2009)	3,387	0	3,387
Average Daily Circulation (2009)			576

Other DMA Total	Cable TV Households	Non-cable TV Households	Total TV Households
Estimated Station Totals *	0	12,540	12,540
Average Weekly Circulation (2009)	0	702	702
Average Daily Circulation (2009)			163

*Estimated station totals are sums of the Nielsen TV and Cable TV household estimates for each county in which the station registers viewing of more than 5% as per the Nielsen Survey Methods.

WAXN-DT
Ch. 50

Network Service: IND.

Licensee: WSOC Television Inc., 6205 Peachtree Dunwoody Rd, Atlanta, GA 30328.

Studio: 1901 N Tryon St, Charlotte, NC 28206.

Mailing Address: PO Box 34665, Charlotte, NC 28234.

Phone: 704-338-9999. **Fax:** 704-335-4941.

Web Site: http://www.action64.com

Technical Facilities: Channel No. 50 (686-692 MHz). Authorized power: 200-kw max. visual, aural. Antenna: 1155-ft above av. terrain, 1011-ft. above ground, 1867-ft. above sea level.

Latitude	35°	15'	41"
Longitude	80°	43'	38"

Holds CP for change to 150-kw max. visual, 1194-ft above av. terrain, 1050-ft. above ground, 1906-ft. above sea level; BMPCDT-20090505ABO.

Transmitter: N of Plaza Ext., 1.4-mi. SSE of Newell.

Note: Latitude and longitude coordinates shown are based on the North American Datum of 1927 (NAD 27) as currently required by the Mass Media Bureau of the FCC.

Ownership: Cox Enterprises Inc. (Group Owner).

Began Operation: April 1, 2002. Standard Definition. Began analog operations: October 15, 1994. Sale to Kannapolis Television Co. by Community Action Communications approved by FCC October 31, 1995. Sale to present owner by Kannapolis Television Co. approved by FCC January 31, 2000. Ceased analog operations: February 17, 2009.

Personnel:

Joe Pomilla, Vice President & General Manager.

Chad Kemper, General Sales Manager.

Colleen Kirk, National Sales Manager.

Robin Whitmeyer, News Director.

Ted Hand, Chief Engineer.

Shawn Pack, Controller.

Kay Hall, Program Director.

Mike Sussman, Promotion.

Brian Phillippi, Traffic Manager.

City of License: Kannapolis. **Station DMA:** Charlotte, NC. **Rank:** 24.

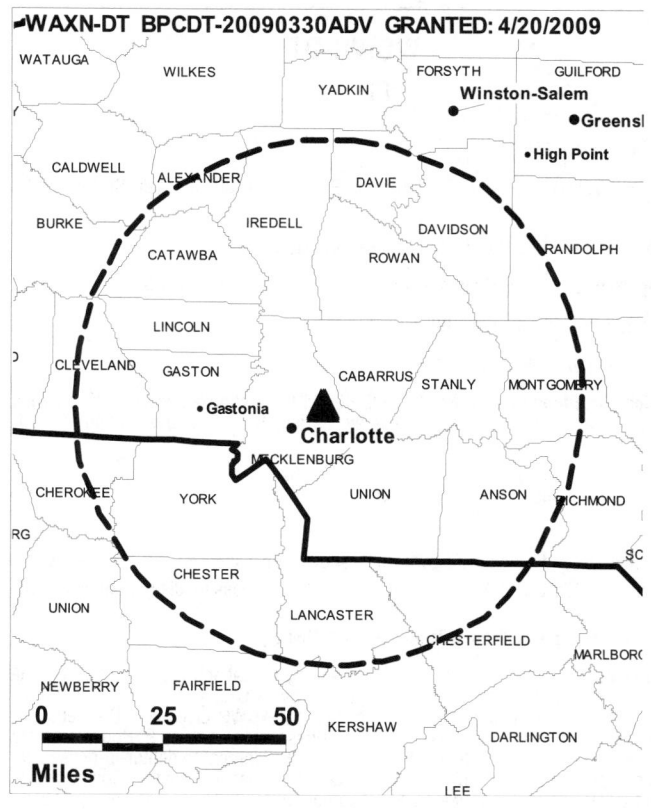

WAXN-DT BPCDT-20090330ADV GRANTED: 4/20/2009

© 2010 Warren Communications News

Circulation © 2009 Nielsen. Coverage based on Nielsen study.

GrandTotal	Cable TV Households	Non-cable TV Households	Total TV Households
Estimated Station Totals *	656,540	465,160	1,121,700
Average Weekly Circulation (2009)	150,342	74,702	225,044
Average Daily Circulation (2009)			81,056

Station DMA Total	Cable TV Households	Non-cable TV Households	Total TV Households
Estimated Station Totals *	656,540	456,670	1,113,210
Average Weekly Circulation (2009)	150,342	74,176	224,518
Average Daily Circulation (2009)			80,971

Other DMA Total	Cable TV Households	Non-cable TV Households	Total TV Households
Estimated Station Totals *	0	8,490	8,490
Average Weekly Circulation (2009)	0	526	526
Average Daily Circulation (2009)			85

*Estimated station totals are sums of the Nielsen TV and Cable TV household estimates for each county in which the station registers viewing of more than 5% as per the Nielsen Survey Methods.

WCWG-DT
Ch. 19

Network Service: CW.

Licensee: WCWG License LLC - Debtor-in-Possession, 301 W Main St, Visalia, CA 93291.

Studio: 622-G Guilford College Rd, Greensboro, NC 27409.

Mailing Address: 622-G Guilford College Rd, Greensboro, NC 27409.

Phone: 336-510-2020. **Fax:** 336-517-2020.

Web Site: http://www.wcwg20.com

Technical Facilities: Channel No. 19 (500-506 MHz). Authorized power: 800-kw max. visual, aural. Antenna: 1890-ft above av. terrain, 1873-ft. above ground, 2612-ft. above sea level.

Latitude	35°	52'	02"
Longitude	79°	49'	26"

Note: Latitude and longitude coordinates shown are based on the North American Datum of 1927 (NAD 27) as currently required by the Mass Media Bureau of the FCC.

Ownership: E. Roger Williams, Trustee (Group Owner).

Began Operation: April 12, 2007. Began analog operations: April 2, 1986. Sale to TTBG/WCWG License Sub LLC approved by FCC July 1, 2009, but not yet consummated. Involuntary transfer of control by WCWG License LLC - Debtor-in-Posession from Harry J. Pappas, Debtor-in-Possession, et al. to E. Roger Williams, Trustee approved by FCC September 17, 2008. Assignment to debtor-in-possession status approved by FCC July 3, 2008. Sale to Pappas Telecasting Companies by Christian TV Network approved by FCC February 9, 1996. Ceased analog operations: June 12, 2009.

Represented (legal): Davis Wright Tremaine LLP.

Represented (sales): TeleRep Inc.

Personnel:

Rosalie Drake, General Manager.

Steve Flint, Sales Manager.

Kathy Iskow, National Sales Manager.

Lindsay Bold, Chief Engineer.

Jennifer Woods, Business Manager.

David Edrington, Program Director & Production Manager.

Dave Shelly, Marketing & Promotion Director.

Cheronda Jones, Traffic Manager.

City of License: Lexington. **Station DMA:** Greensboro-High Point-Winston Salem, NC.

Rank: 46.

© 2010 Warren Communications News

Circulation © 2009 Nielsen. Coverage based on Nielsen study.

GrandTotal	Cable TV Households	Non-cable TV Households	Total TV Households
Estimated Station Totals *	426,470	353,900	780,370
Average Weekly Circulation (2009)	81,833	61,462	143,295
Average Daily Circulation (2009)			50,684

Station DMA Total	Cable TV Households	Non-cable TV Households	Total TV Households
Estimated Station Totals *	423,910	251,860	675,770
Average Weekly Circulation (2009)	81,446	53,983	135,429
Average Daily Circulation (2009)			48,967

Other DMA Total	Cable TV Households	Non-cable TV Households	Total TV Households
Estimated Station Totals *	2,560	102,040	104,600
Average Weekly Circulation (2009)	387	7,479	7,866
Average Daily Circulation (2009)			1,717

*Estimated station totals are sums of the Nielsen TV and Cable TV household estimates for each county in which the station registers viewing of more than 5% as per the Nielsen Survey Methods.

WSKY-DT
Ch. 4

Network Service: IND.

Grantee: Sky Television LLC, PO Box 269, Kitty Hawk, NC 27949.

Studio: 258-B Foster Forbes Rd, Powells Point, NC 27966.

Mailing Address: 920 Corporate Ln, Chesapeake, VA 23320.

Phone: 757-382-0004; 800-414-0911. **Fax:** 252-491-9277.

Web Site: http://www.wsky4.com

Technical Facilities: Channel No. 4 (66-72 MHz). Authorized power: 12-kw visual, aural. Antenna: 899-ft above av. terrain, 899-ft. above ground, 912-ft. above sea level.

| Latitude | 36° | 31' | 14.45" |
| Longitude | 76° | 18' | 16.22" |

Holds CP for change to channel number 9, 85-kw visual, 1004-ft above av. terrain, 1004-ft. above ground, 1017-ft. above sea level; BMPCDT-20080616AAG.

Note: Latitude and longitude coordinates shown are based on the North American Datum of 1927 (NAD 27) as currently required by the Mass Media Bureau of the FCC.

Ownership: Sky Television LLC.

Began Operation: February 17, 2009. Began analog operations: October 1, 2001. Sale to present owner by DanBeth Communications Inc. approved by FCC August 19, 2002. March 2007 high winds destroyed transmitter facilities; station granted Special Temporary Authority to remain silent. Station ceased analog operations after deciding to flash-cut to digital rather than renew the lease to its analog facilities.

Personnel:

Glenn V. Holterhaus, President & General Manager.

Jackie Smullen, Vice President, Business & Traffic Manager.

Tom Powers, Operations Manager & Chief Engineer.

Ruthi Lee, General Sales Manager.

Ed Marlowe, Program Director.

City of License: Manteo. **Station DMA:** Norfolk-Portsmouth-Newport News, VA.

Rank: 43.

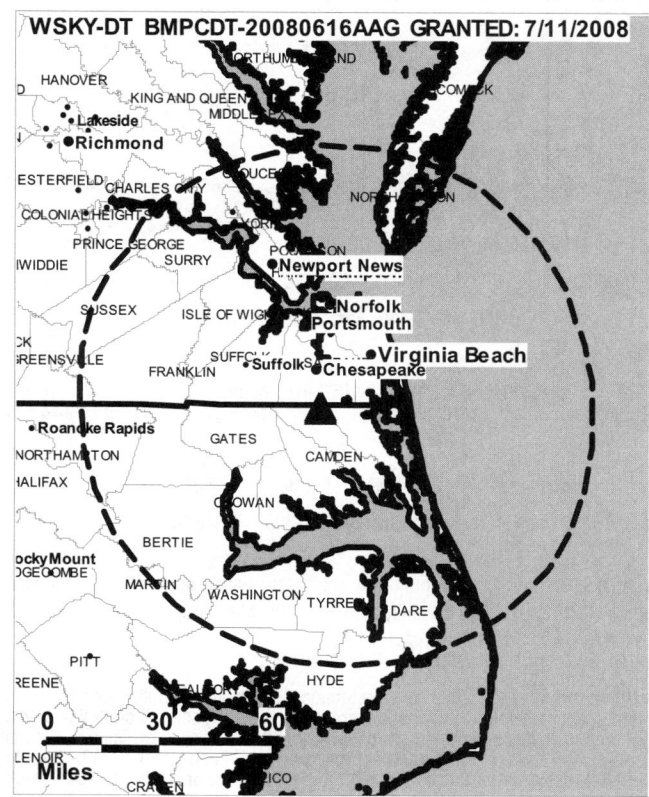

WSKY-DT BMPCDT-20080616AAG GRANTED: 7/11/2008

© 2010 Warren Communications News

Circulation © 2009 Nielsen. Coverage based on Nielsen study.

GrandTotal	Cable TV Households	Non-cable TV Households	Total TV Households
Estimated Station Totals *	495,300	33,880	529,180
Average Weekly Circulation (2009)	50,260	2,740	53,000
Average Daily Circulation (2009)			15,425

Station DMA Total	Cable TV Households	Non-cable TV Households	Total TV Households
Estimated Station Totals *	491,470	33,880	525,350
Average Weekly Circulation (2009)	49,765	2,740	52,505
Average Daily Circulation (2009)			15,393

Other DMA Total	Cable TV Households	Non-cable TV Households	Total TV Households
Estimated Station Totals *	3,830	0	3,830
Average Weekly Circulation (2009)	495	0	495
Average Daily Circulation (2009)			32

*Estimated station totals are sums of the Nielsen TV and Cable TV household estimates for each county in which the station registers viewing of more than 5% as per the Nielsen Survey Methods.

WFXI-DT
Ch. 8

Network Service: MNT, FOX.

Licensee: Esteem Broadcasting of North Carolina LLC, 13865 E Elliott Dr, Marshall, IL 62441.

Studio: 5441 Hwy 70 E, Morehead City, NC 28557.

Mailing Address: PO Box 2069, Morehead City, NC 28557.

Phone: 252-240-0888; 800-849-3699. **Fax:** 252-240-2028.

Web Site: http://www.fox8fox14.com

Technical Facilities: Channel No. 8 (180-186 MHz). Authorized power: 42-kw visual, aural. Antenna: 812-ft above av. terrain, 810-ft. above ground, 815-ft. above sea level.

Latitude	34°	53'	01"
Longitude	76°	30'	22.3"

Holds CP for change to 22.4-kw visual; BPCDT-20090701ADM.

Note: Latitude and longitude coordinates shown are based on the North American Datum of 1927 (NAD 27) as currently required by the Mass Media Bureau of the FCC.

Ownership: Esteem Broadcasting LLC (Group Owner).

Began Operation: July 25, 2007. Station broadcasting digitally on its analog channel allotment. Began analog operations: November 6, 1989. Transfer of control by Local Television Associates Inc. from John W. Gainey III & Frederick J. McCune to Ramon N. Redford Jr. & Anne T. Munden approved by FCC February 6, 1990. Sale to GOCOM Television LP by Local Television Associates Inc. approved by FCC March 31, 1995. Merger of GOCOM Communications LLC with Grapevine Communications Inc. to form GOCOM Holdings LLC approved by FCC November 1, 1999. GOCOM Holdings LLC later renamed Piedmont Television Holdings LLC. Sale to present owner by Piedmont Television Holdings LLC approved by FCC November 1, 2007. Ceased analog operations: June 12, 2009.

Represented (legal): Drinker Biddle.

Represented (sales): Katz Media Group.

Personnel:

Don Fisher, General Manager.

Lisa Leonard, Sales Director.

Jennifer Hagan, National Sales Manager.

Andy Kozik, Chief Engineer.

Marla Liguori, Business Manager.

Linda Murphy, Program Manager.

Walt Young, Promotion Director.

Scott Foley, Production Manager.

Ron Taintor, Creative Services Director.

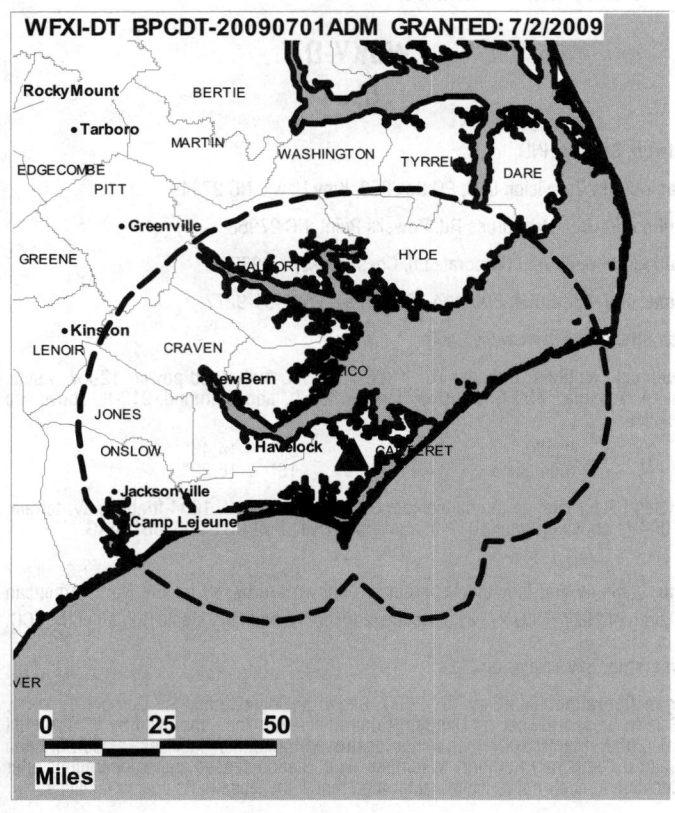

© 2010 Warren Communications News

Sandy Fulcher, Traffic Manager.

City of License: Morehead City. **Station DMA:** Greenville-New Bern-Washington, NC.

Rank: 103.

Circulation © 2009 Nielsen. Coverage based on Nielsen study.

GrandTotal	Cable TV Households	Non-cable TV Households	Total TV Households
Estimated Station Totals *	100,030	109,910	209,940
Average Weekly Circulation (2009)	42,685	19,888	62,573
Average Daily Circulation (2009)			19,905

Station DMA Total	Cable TV Households	Non-cable TV Households	Total TV Households
Estimated Station Totals *	100,030	109,910	209,940
Average Weekly Circulation (2009)	42,685	19,888	62,573
Average Daily Circulation (2009)			19,905

*Estimated station totals are sums of the Nielsen TV and Cable TV household estimates for each county in which the station registers viewing of more than 5% as per the Nielsen Survey Methods.

WCTI-DT
Ch. 12

Network Service: ABC.

Licensee: Newport License Holdings Inc., 280 Park Ave, 25 Fl, E Tower, New York, NY 10017.

Studio: 225 Glenburnie Dr., New Bern, NC 28561.

Mailing Address: PO Box 12325, New Bern, NC 28561.

Phone: 252-638-1212. **Fax:** 252-637-4141.

Web Site: http://www.wcti12.com

Technical Facilities: Channel No. 12 (204-210 MHz). Authorized power: 32.8-kw visual, aural. Antenna: 1932-ft above av. terrain, 1929-ft. above ground, 1975-ft. above sea level.

Latitude	35°	06'	15"
Longitude	77°	20'	12"

Note: Latitude and longitude coordinates shown are based on the North American Datum of 1927 (NAD 27) as currently required by the Mass Media Bureau of the FCC.

Ownership: Bonten Media Group LLC.

Began Operation: March 1, 2001. Standard Definition. Station broadcasting digitally on its analog channel allotment. Began analog operations: September 7, 1963. Transfer to present owner by Newport License Holdings Inc. approved by FCC April 24, 2007. Sale to Newport License Holdings Inc. by Lamco Communications Inc. approved by FCC April 29, 2004. Sale to Lamco Communications Inc. by Diversified Communications approved by FCC August 2, 1993. Sale to Diversified by Heritage Broadcasting approved by FCC February 24, 1986. Sale to Heritage by Malrite Communications Group approved by FCC June 7, 1983. Sale to Malrite by Continental TV approved by FCC October 14, 1976. Sale to Continental TV by Piedmont TV Corp. (Nathan Frank & Thomsland Inc.) approved by FCC April 15, 1969. Ceased analog operations: June 12, 2009.

Represented (legal): Covington & Burling.

Represented (sales): Continental Television Sales.

Personnel:

Jim Ottolin, Vice President & General Manager.

Rich Bunard, General Sales Manager.

Debbie Deskins, Local Sales Manager.

Ingrid Johansen, News Director.

Ken Hughes, Chief Engineer.

Joni Thompson, Business Manager.

Carolyn Stevens, Program Director.

Dan Flaxer, Promotion Director.

Erik Hardtle, Production & Web Operations Director.

Nancy Hughes, Traffic Manager.

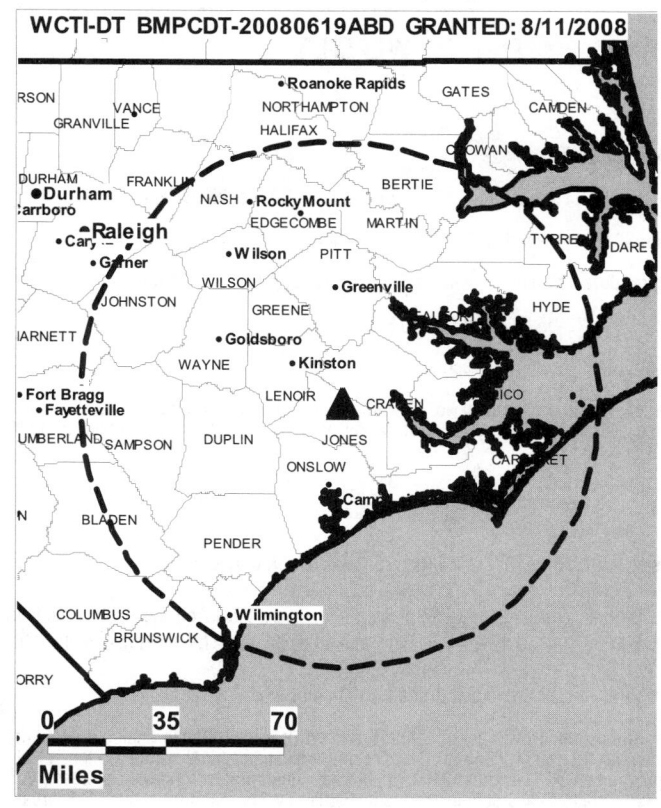

© 2010 Warren Communications News

City of License: New Bern. **Station DMA:** Greenville-New Bern-Washington, NC.

Rank: 103.

Circulation © 2009 Nielsen. Coverage based on Nielsen study.

GrandTotal	Cable TV Households	Non-cable TV Households	Total TV Households
Estimated Station Totals *	171,150	160,080	331,230
Average Weekly Circulation (2009)	97,721	65,056	162,777
Average Daily Circulation (2009)			75,818

Station DMA Total	Cable TV Households	Non-cable TV Households	Total TV Households
Estimated Station Totals *	159,160	109,910	269,070
Average Weekly Circulation (2009)	96,228	59,544	155,772
Average Daily Circulation (2009)			73,988

Other DMA Total	Cable TV Households	Non-cable TV Households	Total TV Households
Estimated Station Totals *	11,990	50,170	62,160
Average Weekly Circulation (2009)	1,493	5,512	7,005
Average Daily Circulation (2009)			1,830

*Estimated station totals are sums of the Nielsen TV and Cable TV household estimates for each county in which the station registers viewing of more than 5% as per the Nielsen Survey Methods.

WLFL-DT
Ch. 27

Network Service: CW.

Grantee: WLFL Licensee Inc., 10706 Beaver Dam Rd, Cockeysville, MD 21030.

Studio: 3012 Highwoods Blvd, Ste 101, Raleigh, NC 27604.

Mailing Address: 3012 Highwoods Blvd, Ste 101, Raleigh, NC 27604.

Phone: 919-872-9535. **Fax:** 919-878-6588.

Web Site: http://www.wlfl22.com

Technical Facilities: Channel No. 27 (548-554 MHz). Authorized power: 725-kw max. visual, aural. Antenna: 2001-ft above av. terrain, 1903-ft. above ground, 2263-ft. above sea level.

Latitude	35°	40'	28"
Longitude	78°	31'	40"

Transmitter: 0.25-mi. SW of US Rte. 70, 1.74-mi. SE of Auburn.

Note: Latitude and longitude coordinates shown are based on the North American Datum of 1927 (NAD 27) as currently required by the Mass Media Bureau of the FCC.

Ownership: Sinclair Broadcast Group Inc. (Group Owner).

Began Operation: November 1, 2002. Standard Definition. Began analog operations: December 18, 1981. Sale to S & F Communications by N. Grant Cotton, et al., approved by FCC December 21, 1984 but not consummated (Television Digest, Vol. 24:39). Sale to TVX Broadcast Group by Family TV Corp. approved by FCC February 10, 1986 (Vol. 25:50; 26:17). Sale to Paramount Group approved by FCC in 1989 (Vol. 29:38). Sale to present owner by Paramount Group approved by FCC November 22, 1994 (Vol. 34:33, 43). Ceased analog operations: February 17, 2009.

Represented (sales): Katz Media Group.

Personnel:

Neal Davis, General Manager & General Sales Manager.

Clif Wallace, Local Sales Manager.

Gary Todd, Chief Engineer.

Richard Bellamy, Business Manager.

Scott Bradsher, Program Director.

Kim Rivenbark, Promotion Manager.

Valerie Venable, Production Director.

Sandy Rudd, Traffic Manager.

City of License: Raleigh. **Station DMA:** Raleigh-Durham (Fayetteville), NC. **Rank:** 26.

© 2010 Warren Communications News

Circulation © 2009 Nielsen. Coverage based on Nielsen study.

GrandTotal	Cable TV Households	Non-cable TV Households	Total TV Households
Estimated Station Totals *	649,530	454,830	1,104,360
Average Weekly Circulation (2009)	151,134	134,010	285,144
Average Daily Circulation (2009)			94,962

Station DMA Total	Cable TV Households	Non-cable TV Households	Total TV Households
Estimated Station Totals *	628,560	419,370	1,047,930
Average Weekly Circulation (2009)	149,194	131,709	280,903
Average Daily Circulation (2009)			94,039

Other DMA Total	Cable TV Households	Non-cable TV Households	Total TV Households
Estimated Station Totals *	20,970	35,460	56,430
Average Weekly Circulation (2009)	1,940	2,301	4,241
Average Daily Circulation (2009)			923

*Estimated station totals are sums of the Nielsen TV and Cable TV household estimates for each county in which the station registers viewing of more than 5% as per the Nielsen Survey Methods.

WRAL-DT
Ch. 53

Network Service: CBS.

Licensee: Capitol Broadcasting Co. Inc., PO Box 12000, Raleigh, NC 27605.

Studio: 2619 Western Blvd, Raleigh, NC 27606.

Mailing Address: PO Box 12000, Raleigh, NC 27605.

Phone: 919-821-8555; 800-532-5343. **Fax:** 919-821-8554.

Web Site: http://www.wral.com

Technical Facilities: Channel No. 53 (704-710 MHz). Authorized power: 1000-kw max. visual, aural. Antenna: 2064-ft above av. terrain, 1915-ft. above ground, 2326-ft. above sea level.

Latitude	35°	40'	29"
Longitude	78°	31'	40"

Holds CP for change to channel number 48, 2064-ft above av. terrain, 1965-ft. above ground, 2325-ft. above sea level; BMPCDT-20080618AAD.

Transmitter: 5033 TV Tower Rd., Garner.

Note: Latitude and longitude coordinates shown are based on the North American Datum of 1927 (NAD 27) as currently required by the Mass Media Bureau of the FCC.

Multichannel TV Sound: Stereo only.

Ownership: Capitol Broadcasting Co. Inc. (Group Owner).

Began Operation: April 16, 2000. High Definition. Began analog operations: December 15, 1956. Ceased analog operations: June 12, 2009.

Represented (sales): TeleRep Inc.

Represented (legal): Holland & Knight LLP.

Personnel:

James F. Goodmon, President & Chief Executive Officer.

James Hefner, General Manager.

James Farmer, Operations Manager.

Quinn Koontz, Sales Director.

Laura Stillman, National Sales Manager.

David Lyles, Local Sales Manager.

Rick Gall, News Director.

Shelly Leslie, Promotion Manager.

John Harris, Program Director.

Ty Reedes, Traffic Manager.

Peter Sockett, Chief Engineer.

Leah Chauncey, Business Manager.

Debbie Strange, Assistant Promotion Manager.

WRAL-DT BMPCDT-20080618AAD GRANTED: 9/3/2008

© 2010 Warren Communications News

City of License: Raleigh. **Station DMA:** Raleigh-Durham (Fayetteville), NC. **Rank:** 26.

Circulation © 2009 Nielsen. Coverage based on Nielsen study.

GrandTotal	Cable TV Households	Non-cable TV Households	Total TV Households
Estimated Station Totals *	785,870	500,410	1,286,280
Average Weekly Circulation (2009)	462,323	301,049	763,372
Average Daily Circulation (2009)			397,498

Station DMA Total	Cable TV Households	Non-cable TV Households	Total TV Households
Estimated Station Totals *	628,560	419,370	1,047,930
Average Weekly Circulation (2009)	423,240	292,973	716,213
Average Daily Circulation (2009)			383,240

Other DMA Total	Cable TV Households	Non-cable TV Households	Total TV Households
Estimated Station Totals *	157,310	81,040	238,350
Average Weekly Circulation (2009)	39,083	8,076	47,159
Average Daily Circulation (2009)			14,258

*Estimated station totals are sums of the Nielsen TV and Cable TV household estimates for each county in which the station registers viewing of more than 5% as per the Nielsen Survey Methods.

WRAZ-DT
Ch. 49

Network Service: FOX.

Grantee: WRAZ-TV Inc., PO Box 12000, Raleigh, NC 27605.

Studio: 2619 Western Blvd, Raleigh, NC 27606.

Mailing Address: PO Box 30050, Durham, NC 27702.

Phone: 919-595-5050. **Fax:** 919-595-5028.

Web Site: http://www.fox50.com; http://www.myfoxraleigh.com

Technical Facilities: Channel No. 49 (680-686 MHz). Authorized power: 1000-kw max. visual, aural. Antenna: 2018-ft above av. terrain, 1916-ft. above ground, 2276-ft. above sea level.

Latitude	35°	40'	29"
Longitude	78°	31'	40"

Transmitter: 5033 TV Tower Rd.

Note: Latitude and longitude coordinates shown are based on the North American Datum of 1927 (NAD 27) as currently required by the Mass Media Bureau of the FCC.

Ownership: Capitol Broadcasting Co. Inc. (Group Owner).

Began Operation: May 1, 2000. High Definition. Began analog operations: September 7, 1995. Sale Carolina Broadcasting System Inc. by Tar Heel Broadcasting approved by FCC June 28, 1996. Sale to present owner by Carolina Broadcasting System Inc. approved by FCC March 29, 2000. Ceased analog operations: June 12, 2009.

Represented (legal): Holland & Knight LLP.

Represented (engineering): Cohen Dippell & Everist PC.

Personnel:

James Goodmon, President & Chief Executive Officer.

Tommy Schenck, General Manager.

Evelyn Booker, General Sales Manager.

Niel Sollod, Local Sales Manager.

Matthew Donegan, National Sales Manager.

Rick Gaul, News Director.

Jimmy Gamble, Chief Engineer.

Leah Chauncey, Business Manager.

Joanne Stanley, Program Director.

Kevin Kolbe, Promotion Director.

Gerald Belton, Research Director.

Kris Trautner, Traffic Manager.

City of License: Raleigh. **Station DMA:** Raleigh-Durham (Fayetteville), NC. **Rank:** 26.

© 2010 Warren Communications News

Circulation © 2009 Nielsen. Coverage based on Nielsen study.

GrandTotal	Cable TV Households	Non-cable TV Households	Total TV Households
Estimated Station Totals *	652,050	432,690	1,084,740
Average Weekly Circulation (2009)	323,127	216,183	539,310
Average Daily Circulation (2009)			194,425

Station DMA Total	Cable TV Households	Non-cable TV Households	Total TV Households
Estimated Station Totals *	628,560	419,370	1,047,930
Average Weekly Circulation (2009)	321,493	215,517	537,010
Average Daily Circulation (2009)			193,923

Other DMA Total	Cable TV Households	Non-cable TV Households	Total TV Households
Estimated Station Totals *	23,490	13,320	36,810
Average Weekly Circulation (2009)	1,634	666	2,300
Average Daily Circulation (2009)			502

*Estimated station totals are sums of the Nielsen TV and Cable TV household estimates for each county in which the station registers viewing of more than 5% as per the Nielsen Survey Methods.

WRPX-TV
Ch. 15

Network Service: ION.

Licensee: ION Media Raleigh License Inc., Debtor in Possession, 601 Clearwater Park Rd, West Palm Beach, FL 33401-6233.

Studio: 3209 Gresham Lake Rd, Ste 151, Raleigh, NC 27615.

Mailing Address: 3209 Gresham Lake Rd, Ste 151, Raleigh, NC 27615.

Phone: 919-827-4801. **Fax:** 919-876-1415.

E-mail: deborahhoward@ionmedia.com

Web Site: http://www.ionmedia.com

Technical Facilities: Channel No. 15 (476-482 MHz). Authorized power: 180-kw max. visual, aural. Antenna: 1161-ft above av. terrain, 1135-ft. above ground, 1460-ft. above sea level.

Latitude	36°	06'	11"
Longitude	78°	11'	29"

Transmitter: Off Wester Farm Rte. 4, near Louisburg.

Note: Latitude and longitude coordinates shown are based on the North American Datum of 1927 (NAD 27) as currently required by the Mass Media Bureau of the FCC.

Ownership: ION Media Networks Inc., Debtor in Possession (Group Owner).

Began Operation: May 10, 2002. Standard Definition. Began analog operations: July 5, 1989. Sale to Urban Television LLC pends. Involuntary assignment to debtor in possession status approved by FCC June 5, 2009. Transfer of control by ION Media Networks Inc. from Paxson Management Corp. & Lowell W. Paxson to CIG Media LLC approved by FCC December 31, 2007. Paxson Communications Corp. became ION Media Networks Inc. on June 26, 2006. Sale to Paxson Communications Corp. by DP Media Inc. approved by FCC February 25, 2000. Sale to DP Media Inc. by Roberts Broadcasting Co. approved by FCC June 9, 1997. Sale to Roberts Broadcasting Co. by Family Broadcasting Enterprises approved by FCC September 19, 1995. Ceased analog operations: June 12, 2009.

Represented (legal): Dow Lohnes PLLC.

Represented (engineering): du Treil, Lundin & Rackley Inc.

Personnel:

Michelle Barnhill, Station Operations Manager.

Deborah Howard, Traffic Manager.

Sam Garfield, Contract Engineer.

City of License: Rocky Mount. **Station DMA:** Raleigh-Durham (Fayetteville), NC.

Rank: 26.

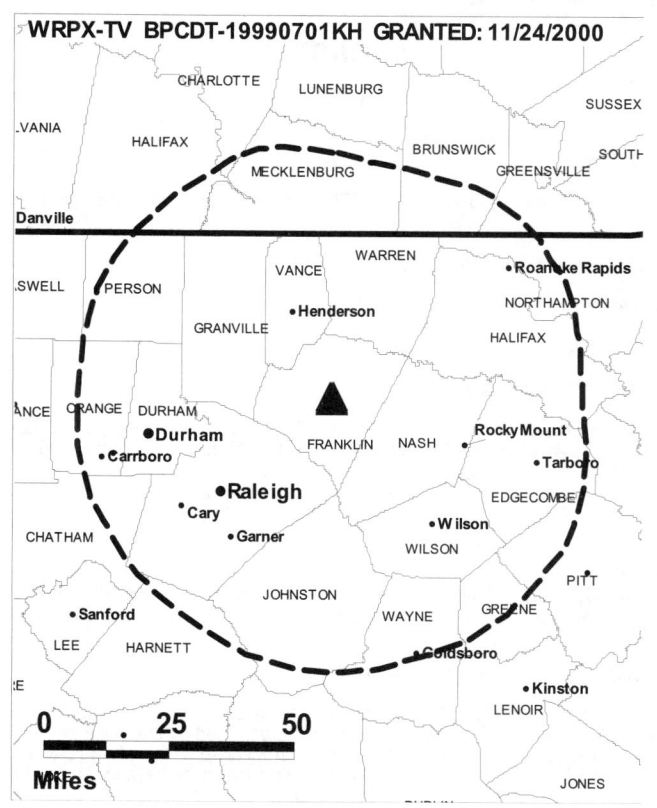

© 2010 Warren Communications News

Circulation © 2009 Nielsen. Coverage based on Nielsen study.

GrandTotal	Cable TV Households	Non-cable TV Households	Total TV Households
Estimated Station Totals *	477,590	182,150	659,740
Average Weekly Circulation (2009)	31,807	14,974	46,781
Average Daily Circulation (2009)			12,356

Station DMA Total	Cable TV Households	Non-cable TV Households	Total TV Households
Estimated Station Totals *	477,590	182,150	659,740
Average Weekly Circulation (2009)	31,807	14,974	46,781
Average Daily Circulation (2009)			12,356

*Estimated station totals are sums of the Nielsen TV and Cable TV household estimates for each county in which the station registers viewing of more than 5% as per the Nielsen Survey Methods.

WITN-DT
Ch. 32

Network Service: NBC.

Grantee: Gray Television Licensee LLC, 1750 K St NW, Ste 1200, Washington, DC 20006.

Studio: PO Box 468, 3057 Hwy 17 S, Washington, NC 27889.

Mailing Address: PO Box 468, Washington, NC 27889.

Phone: 252-946-3131. **Fax:** 252-946-8177.

Web Site: http://www.witntv.com

Technical Facilities: Channel No. 32 (578-584 MHz). Authorized power: 795-kw max. visual, aural. Antenna: 1949-ft above av. terrain, 1959-ft. above ground, 1987-ft. above sea level.

Latitude	35°	21'	55"
Longitude	77°	23'	38"

Note: Latitude and longitude coordinates shown are based on the North American Datum of 1927 (NAD 27) as currently required by the Mass Media Bureau of the FCC.

Ownership: Gray Television Inc. (Group Owner).

Began Operation: June 12, 2006. Began analog operations: September 28, 1955. Sale to AFLAC Inc. by W. R. Roberson Jr., et al., approved by FCC June 26, 1985 (Television Digest, Vol. 25:8). Sale to Raycom Media-U.S. Inc. by AFLAC Inc. approved by FCC March 21, 1997. Sale to present owner by Raycom Media-U.S. Inc. approved by FCC July 28, 1997. Ceased analog operations: June 12, 2009.

Represented (legal): Wiley Rein LLP.

Represented (sales): Blair Television.

Personnel:

Chris Mossman, Vice President & General Manager.

Mark Gentner, General & Local Sales Manager.

Meredith Cutler, National Sales Coordinator.

Stephanie Shoop, News Director.

Jeff Pearce, Chief Engineer.

Michael Riddle, Program & Promotion Director.

Tom Midyette, Production Manager.

Chris Edwards, Media Manager.

City of License: Washington. **Station DMA:** Greenville-New Bern-Washington, NC.

Rank: 103.

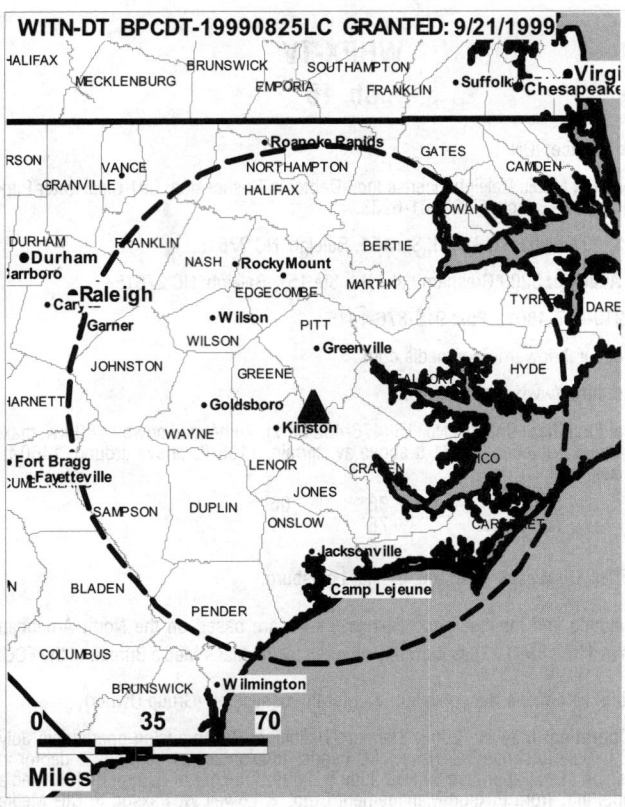

WITN-DT BPCDT-19990825LC GRANTED: 9/21/1999

© 2010 Warren Communications News

Circulation © 2009 Nielsen. Coverage based on Nielsen study.

GrandTotal	Cable TV Households	Non-cable TV Households	Total TV Households
Estimated Station Totals *	285,050	165,240	450,290
Average Weekly Circulation (2009)	141,775	81,901	223,676
Average Daily Circulation (2009)			110,314

Station DMA Total	Cable TV Households	Non-cable TV Households	Total TV Households
Estimated Station Totals *	159,160	109,910	269,070
Average Weekly Circulation (2009)	99,557	73,375	172,932
Average Daily Circulation (2009)			89,162

Other DMA Total	Cable TV Households	Non-cable TV Households	Total TV Households
Estimated Station Totals *	125,890	55,330	181,220
Average Weekly Circulation (2009)	42,218	8,526	50,744
Average Daily Circulation (2009)			21,152

*Estimated station totals are sums of the Nielsen TV and Cable TV household estimates for each county in which the station registers viewing of more than 5% as per the Nielsen Survey Methods.

WECT-DT
Ch. 44

Network Service: NBC.

Licensee: WECT License Subsidiary LLC, 201 Monroe St, RSA Tower, 20th Fl, Montgomery, AL 36104.

Studio: 322 Shipyard Blvd, Wilmington, NC 28412.

Mailing Address: 322 Shipyard Blvd, Wilmington, NC 28412.

Phone: 910-791-8070; 910-791-6681. **Fax:** 910-392-1509.

Web Site: http://www.wect.com

Technical Facilities: Channel No. 44 (650-656 MHz). Authorized power: 575-kw max. visual, aural. Antenna: 919-ft above av. terrain, 927-ft. above ground, 963-ft. above sea level.

Latitude	34°	19'	16"
Longitude	78°	13'	43"

Requests CP for change to 710-kw max. visual, 1936-ft above av. terrain, 1926-ft. above ground, 1989-ft. above sea level; lat. 34° 07' 53", long. 78° 11' 17", BPCDT-20080505ABJ.

Note: Latitude and longitude coordinates shown are based on the North American Datum of 1927 (NAD 27) as currently required by the Mass Media Bureau of the FCC.

Ownership: Raycom Media Inc. (Group Owner).

Began Operation: April 15, 2004. Began analog operations: April 9, 1954. Sale of 60% of stock to WNCT & James Jackson by Richard A. Dunlea & wife approved by FCC December 11, 1957. Sale to News Press & Gazette Co. approved by FCC November 21, 1986. Sale to New Vision Television approved by FCC November 15, 1993. Sale to Ellis Communications approved by FCC February 10, 1995. Sale to present owner by Ellis Communications approved by FCC July 26, 1996. On September 8, 2008 the station voluntarily ceased analog programming to test the transition to digital television. Ceased analog operations: September 30, 2008.

Represented (legal): Covington & Burling.

Personnel:

Gary McNair, General Manager.

Dan Ullmer, Chief Engineer.

Mark Mendenhall, General Sales Manager.

David Toma, Marketing Director.

Eric Scott, Program Director.

City of License: Wilmington. **Station DMA:** Wilmington, NC. **Rank:** 132.

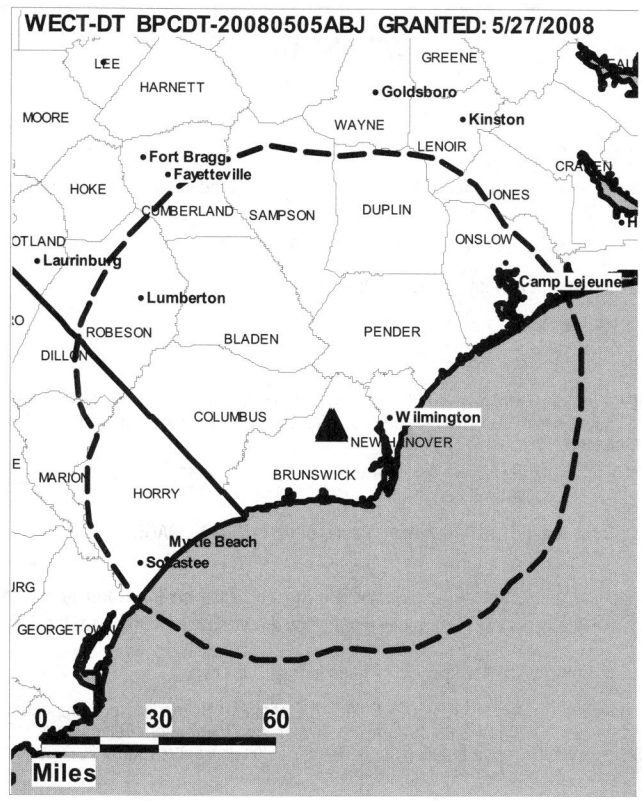

WECT-DT BPCDT-20080505ABJ GRANTED: 5/27/2008

© 2010 Warren Communications News

Circulation © 2009 Nielsen. Coverage based on Nielsen study.

GrandTotal	Cable TV Households	Non-cable TV Households	Total TV Households
Estimated Station Totals *	427,710	76,930	504,640
Average Weekly Circulation (2009)	153,707	40,166	193,873
Average Daily Circulation (2009)			94,453

Station DMA Total	Cable TV Households	Non-cable TV Households	Total TV Households
Estimated Station Totals *	126,690	60,790	187,480
Average Weekly Circulation (2009)	93,897	38,665	132,562
Average Daily Circulation (2009)			76,946

Other DMA Total	Cable TV Households	Non-cable TV Households	Total TV Households
Estimated Station Totals *	301,020	16,140	317,160
Average Weekly Circulation (2009)	59,810	1,501	61,311
Average Daily Circulation (2009)			17,507

*Estimated station totals are sums of the Nielsen TV and Cable TV household estimates for each county in which the station registers viewing of more than 5% as per the Nielsen Survey Methods.

WSFX-DT
Ch. 30

Network Service: FOX.

Licensee: Southeastern Media Holdings Inc., 3500 Colonnade Pkwy, Ste 600, Birmingham, AL 35243.

Studio: 322 Shipyard Blvd, Wilmington, NC 28412.

Mailing Address: 322 Shipyard Blvd, Wilmington, NC 28412.

Phone: 910-343-8826. **Fax:** 910-791-9406.

Web Site: http://www.wsfx.com

Technical Facilities: Channel No. 30 (566-572 MHz). Authorized power: 80-kw max. visual, aural. Antenna: 1936-ft above av. terrain, 1926-ft. above ground, 1989-ft. above sea level.

Latitude	34°	07'	53"
Longitude	78°	11'	17"

Holds CP for change to 190-kw max. visual; BPCDT-20080929AGO.

Note: Latitude and longitude coordinates shown are based on the North American Datum of 1927 (NAD 27) as currently required by the Mass Media Bureau of the FCC.

Ownership: Community Newspaper Holdings Inc. (Group Owner).

Began Operation: March 11, 2002. Standard Definition. Began analog operations: September 24, 1984. Sale to present owner by Wilmington Telecasters Inc. (Robinson Everett, Jacob Froelich Jr. & George Lyles Jr.) approved by FCC August 5, 2003. Ceased analog operations: September 8, 2008.

Represented (legal): Fletcher, Heald & Hildreth PLC.

Represented (sales): Katz Media Group.

Personnel:

Thom Postema, Vice President & General Manager.

Julie Tames, Local Sales Manager.

Mark Mendenhall, National Sales Manager.

Raeford Brown, News Director.

Dan Ullmer, Chief Engineer.

Clara Dittmer, Business Manager.

Mary Southerland, Program Director.

David Toma, Promotion Director.

Doug Norment, Production Manager.

Kimberly Herring, Traffic Manager.

City of License: Wilmington. **Station DMA:** Wilmington, NC. **Rank:** 132.

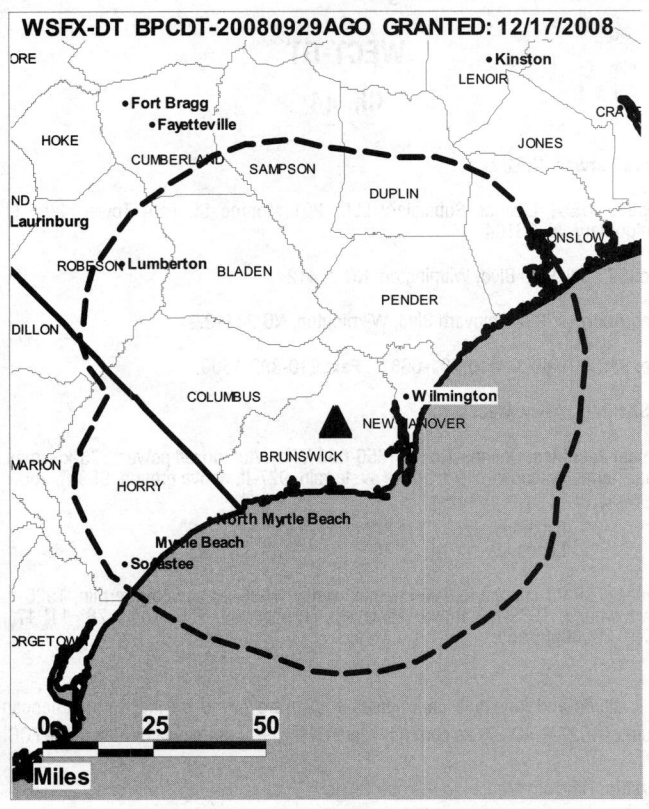

WSFX-DT BPCDT-20080929AGO GRANTED: 12/17/2008

© 2010 Warren Communications News

Circulation © 2009 Nielsen. Coverage based on Nielsen study.

GrandTotal	Cable TV Households	Non-cable TV Households	Total TV Households
Estimated Station Totals *	162,720	76,930	239,650
Average Weekly Circulation (2009)	75,387	31,620	107,007
Average Daily Circulation (2009)			39,750

Station DMA Total	Cable TV Households	Non-cable TV Households	Total TV Households
Estimated Station Totals *	126,690	60,790	187,480
Average Weekly Circulation (2009)	70,703	30,668	101,371
Average Daily Circulation (2009)			38,563

Other DMA Total	Cable TV Households	Non-cable TV Households	Total TV Households
Estimated Station Totals *	36,030	16,140	52,170
Average Weekly Circulation (2009)	4,684	952	5,636
Average Daily Circulation (2009)			1,187

*Estimated station totals are sums of the Nielsen TV and Cable TV household estimates for each county in which the station registers viewing of more than 5% as per the Nielsen Survey Methods.

WWAY-DT
Ch. 46

Network Service: ABC.

Licensee: WWAY-TV LLC, 27 Abercorn St, Savannah, GA 31401-2715.

Studio: 615 N. Front St, Wilmington, NC 28401.

Mailing Address: 615 N. Front St, Wilmington, NC 28401.

Phone: 910-762-8581. **Fax:** 910-762-8367.

Web Site: http://www.wwaytv3.com

Technical Facilities: Channel No. 46 (662-668 MHz). Authorized power: 1000-kw max. visual, aural. Antenna: 1936-ft above av. terrain, 1926-ft. above ground, 1988-ft. above sea level.

Latitude	34°	07'	53"
Longitude	78°	11'	17"

Note: Latitude and longitude coordinates shown are based on the North American Datum of 1927 (NAD 27) as currently required by the Mass Media Bureau of the FCC.

Ownership: Morris Multimedia Inc. (Group Owner).

Began Operation: October 21, 2003. Began analog operations: October 30, 1964. Sale to present owner by Raycom Media Inc. to comply with FCC's duopoly rules approved by FCC February 23, 2006. Sale to Raycom Media Inc. by Cosmos Broadcasting Corp. approved by FCC January 17, 2006. Sale to Cosmos Broadcasting Corp. by Hillside Broadcasting of North Carolina Inc. approved by FCC December 18, 1998. Transfer by Hillside Broadcasting from Mario Beza to Kelso Investment Assoc. V LP approved by FCC June 20, 1997. Sale to Hillside Broadcasting of North Carolina Inc. by CLG Media approved by FCC March 30, 1995. CLG Media of Wilmington Inc. (Chrysler Capital Corp.) assumed control from Sterling TV of Wilmington Inc. (Adams Communications) January 5, 1993. Sale to Adams TV approved by FCC July 11, 1988. Sale to Price Communications Corp. by Clay Communications approved by FCC June 23, 1987. Sale to Cape Fear Telecasting Inc. (William G. Broadfoot Jr., Charles B. Britt, Ferebee Sledge & Craig Wall) approved by FCC August 28, 1968. Left air temporarily January 24, 1981 when plane collided with tower. Ceased analog operations: September 8, 2008.

Represented (legal): Fletcher, Heald & Hildreth PLC.

Represented (sales): Continental Television Sales.

Personnel:

Andy Combs, Vice President & General Manager.

Derek Brown, General Sales Manager.

Tim Horton, Creative Services Director.

Paul Paolcelli, News Director.

Billy Stratton, Chief Engineer.

Kimberly Franklin, Business Manager & Human Resources Director.

Brenda Covey, Program & Traffic Manager.

Ryan Pope, Promotion Director.

Tim Kasenter, Production Manager.

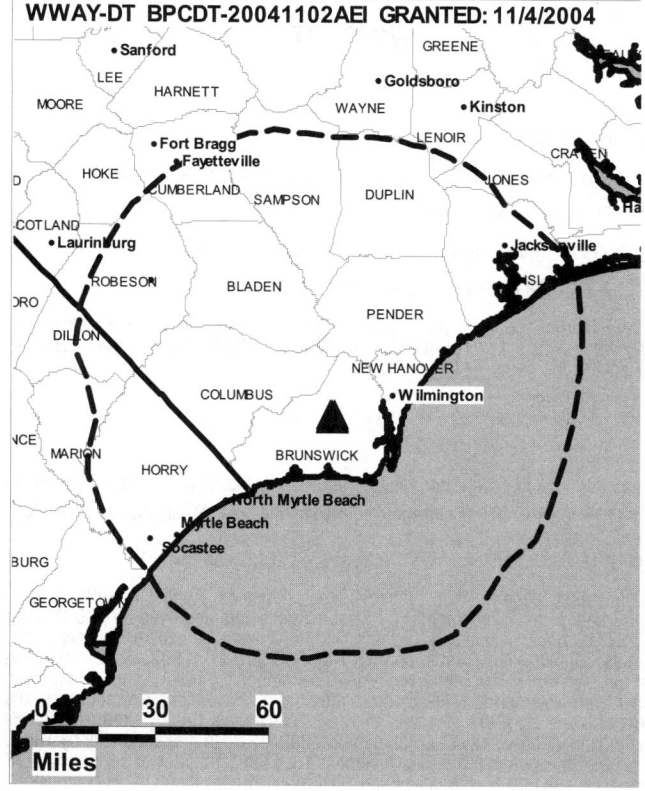

© 2010 Warren Communications News

City of License: Wilmington. **Station DMA:** Wilmington, NC. **Rank:** 132.

Circulation © 2009 Nielsen. Coverage based on Nielsen study.

GrandTotal	Cable TV Households	Non-cable TV Households	Total TV Households
Estimated Station Totals *	166,610	76,930	243,540
Average Weekly Circulation (2009)	81,145	28,757	109,902
Average Daily Circulation (2009)			48,825

Station DMA Total	Cable TV Households	Non-cable TV Households	Total TV Households
Estimated Station Totals *	126,690	60,790	187,480
Average Weekly Circulation (2009)	75,991	27,579	103,570
Average Daily Circulation (2009)			47,159

Other DMA Total	Cable TV Households	Non-cable TV Households	Total TV Households
Estimated Station Totals *	39,920	16,140	56,060
Average Weekly Circulation (2009)	5,154	1,178	6,332
Average Daily Circulation (2009)			1,666

*Estimated station totals are sums of the Nielsen TV and Cable TV household estimates for each county in which the station registers viewing of more than 5% as per the Nielsen Survey Methods.

WRAY-DT
Ch. 42

Network Service: IND.

Licensee: MTB Raleigh Licensee LLC, 449 Broadway, New York, NY 10013.

Studio: 4909 Expressway Dr, Ste E, Wilson, NC 27893.

Mailing Address: 4909 Expressway Dr, Ste E, Wilson, NC 27893.

Phone: 252-243-0584. **Fax:** 252-237-6290.

Technical Facilities: Channel No. 42 (638-644 MHz). Authorized power: 873-kw max. visual, aural. Antenna: 1768-ft above av. terrain, 1739-ft. above ground, 1978-ft. above sea level.

Latitude	35°	49'	53"
Longitude	78°	08'	50"

Note: Latitude and longitude coordinates shown are based on the North American Datum of 1927 (NAD 27) as currently required by the Mass Media Bureau of the FCC.

Ownership: Multicultural Television Broadcasting LLC (Group Owner).

Began Operation: June 2, 2006. Began analog operations: August 7, 1995. Sale to Global Broadcasting Systems Inc. by Wilson Telecasters approved by FCC October 22, 1997. Global Broadcasting Systems filed for Chapter 11 bankruptcy; transfer to S. James Coopersmith, Trustee approved by FCC July 30, 1997. Sale to Shop At Home Inc. by Coopersmith approved by FCC December 10, 1997. Shop At Home Inc. became Summit America Television Inc. after The E. W. Scripps Co. acquired 70% interest October 31, 2002. Transfer to The E. W. Scripps Co. by Summit America Television Inc. approved by FCC February 27, 2004. Sale to present owner by The E. W. Scripps Co. approved by FCC November 15, 2006. Transfer of control by MTB Raleigh Licensee LLC from Multicultural Television Broadcasting LLC to Multicultural Capital Trust (Lee W. Shubert LC, Trustee) approved by FCC January 14, 2009. Ceased analog operations: February 17, 2009.

Represented (legal): Leventhal, Senter & Lerman PLLC.

Personnel:

Harold Rabinowitz, General Manager & Chief Engineer.

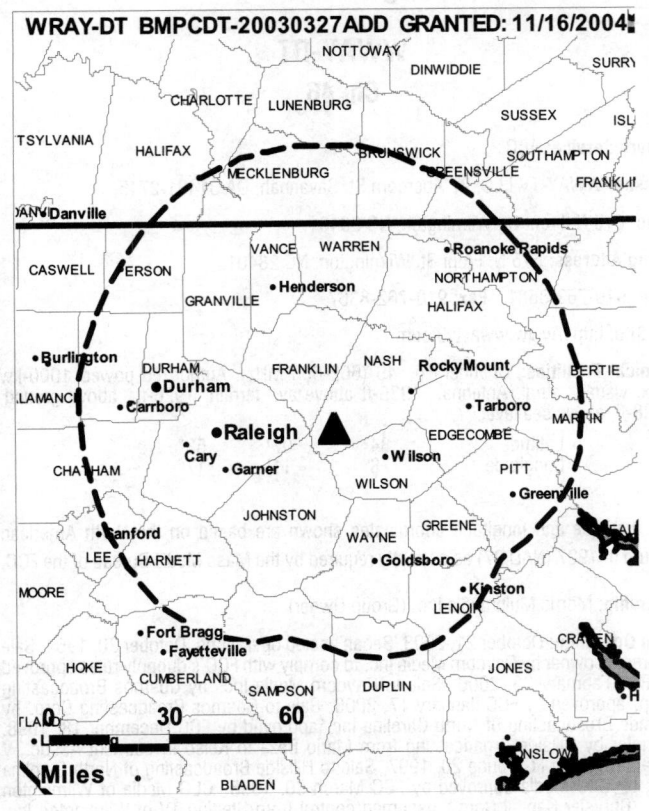

WRAY-DT BMPCDT-20030327ADD GRANTED: 11/16/2004

© 2010 Warren Communications News

City of License: Wilson. **Station DMA:** Raleigh-Durham (Fayetteville), NC. **Rank:** 26.

Nielsen Data: Not available.

WXII-DT
Ch. 31

Network Service: NBC.

Licensee: WXII Hearst-Argyle Television Inc., PO Box 1800, c/o Brooks, Pierce et al., Raleigh, NC 27602.

Studio: 700 Coliseum Dr, Winston-Salem, NC 27106.

Mailing Address: PO Box 11847, Winston-Salem, NC 27116.

Phone: 336-721-9944. **Fax:** 336-721-0856.

Web Site: http://www.wxii12.com

Technical Facilities: Channel No. 31 (572-578 MHz). Authorized power: 815-kw max. visual, aural. Antenna: 1877-ft above av. terrain, 525-ft. above ground, 2926-ft. above sea level.

Latitude	36°	22'	31"
Longitude	80°	22'	26"

Note: Latitude and longitude coordinates shown are based on the North American Datum of 1927 (NAD 27) as currently required by the Mass Media Bureau of the FCC.

Ownership: Hearst-Argyle Television Inc. (Group Owner).

Began Operation: March 19, 2002. High Definition. Began analog operations: September 30, 1953. Sale to Multimedia Inc. by Triangle Broadcasting Corp. approved by FCC September 7, 1972. Exchanged by Multimedia with WFBC-TV, Greenville, SC for KSDK, St. Louis, MO 1981-82. Sale to present owner by Pulitzer Publishing Co. approved by FCC November 24, 1998. Hearst-Argyle received approval from the FCC May 26, 2009 to become privately owned by The Hearst Corp. Ceased analog operations: June 12, 2009.

Represented (legal): Brooks, Pierce, McLendon, Humphrey & Leonard LLP.

Represented (sales): Eagle Television Sales.

Personnel:

Henry E. Price, General Manager.

Michael Pulitzer Jr., Station Manager & Public Service Director.

Matt Bowman, Local Sales Manager.

Barry Klaus, News Director.

John Norvell, Engineering Director.

Julie Hall, Business Manager.

Mark Strand, Marketing & Promotion Director.

Lisa Eldridge, Research Director.

Xavia Beverley, Traffic Manager.

City of License: Winston-Salem.

Station DMA: Greensboro-High Point-Winston Salem, NC. **Rank:** 46.

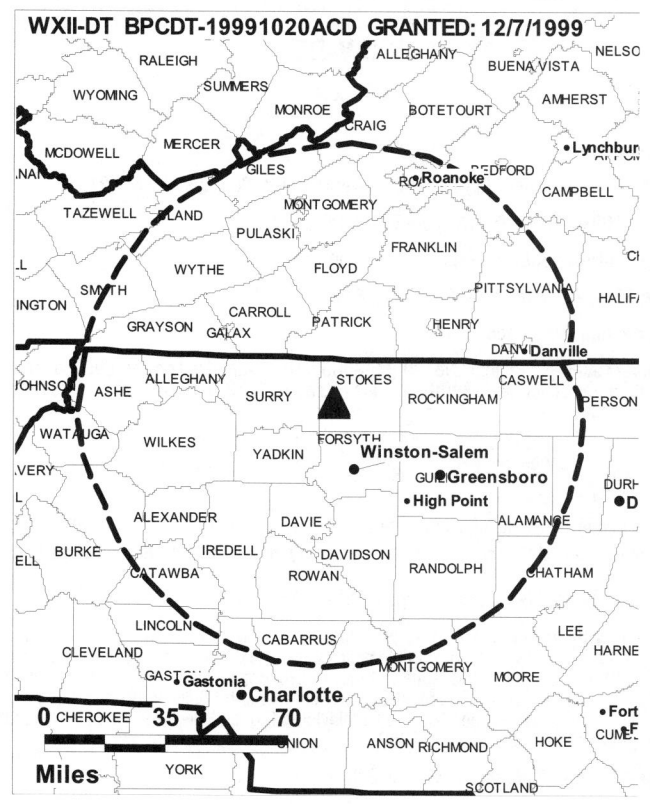

© 2010 Warren Communications News

Circulation © 2009 Nielsen. Coverage based on Nielsen study.

GrandTotal	Cable TV Households	Non-cable TV Households	Total TV Households
Estimated Station Totals *	475,030	393,940	868,970
Average Weekly Circulation (2009)	304,446	169,198	473,644
Average Daily Circulation (2009)			244,269

Station DMA Total	Cable TV Households	Non-cable TV Households	Total TV Households
Estimated Station Totals *	425,060	251,860	676,920
Average Weekly Circulation (2009)	285,032	155,491	440,523
Average Daily Circulation (2009)			231,322

Other DMA Total	Cable TV Households	Non-cable TV Households	Total TV Households
Estimated Station Totals *	49,970	142,080	192,050
Average Weekly Circulation (2009)	19,414	13,707	33,121
Average Daily Circulation (2009)			12,947

*Estimated station totals are sums of the Nielsen TV and Cable TV household estimates for each county in which the station registers viewing of more than 5% as per the Nielsen Survey Methods.

WXLV-DT
Ch. 29

Network Service: ABC.

Grantee: WXLV Licensee LLC, 10706 Beaver Dam Rd, Cockeysville, MD 21030.

Studio: 3500 Myer Lee Dr, Winston-Salem, NC 27101.

Mailing Address: 3500 Myer Lee Dr, Winston-Salem, NC 27101.

Phone: 336-722-4848; 336-722-4545. **Fax:** 336-723-8217.

Web Site: http://www.abc45.com

Technical Facilities: Channel No. 29 (560-566 MHz). Authorized power: 990-kw max. visual, aural. Antenna: 1890-ft above av. terrain, 1873-ft. above ground, 2612-ft. above sea level.

Latitude	35°	52'	03"
Longitude	79°	49'	26"

Note: Latitude and longitude coordinates shown are based on the North American Datum of 1927 (NAD 27) as currently required by the Mass Media Bureau of the FCC.

Ownership: Sinclair Broadcast Group Inc. (Group Owner).

Began Operation: April 1, 2002. Standard Definition. Began analog operations: September 23, 1979. Sale to Act III Broadcasting by TVX Broadcast Group approved by FCC December 17, 1986. Sale to Sullivan Broadcasting Co. by Act III approved by FCC December 15, 1995. Transfer to present owner by Sullivan Broadcasting Co. approved by FCC December 10, 2001 (Television Digest, Vol. 38:9; 41:38). Ceased analog operations: February 17, 2009.

Represented (engineering): Lawrence Behr Associates Inc.

Represented (sales): Katz Media Group.

Personnel:

Ron Inman, General Manager.

Fran McCrae, General Sales Manager.

Sean Hollern, Local Sales Manager.

Dave Farshing, National Sales Manager.

Jim Hartline, Chief Engineer.

Chris Hummel, Business Manager.

Jeanette Pruitt, Program Director.

Trina Samson, Promotion Director.

Jay Paul, Production Manager.

Melissa Perry, Research Director.

Dana Baker, Traffic Manager.

City of License: Winston-Salem.

Station DMA: Greensboro-High Point-Winston Salem, NC. **Rank:** 46.

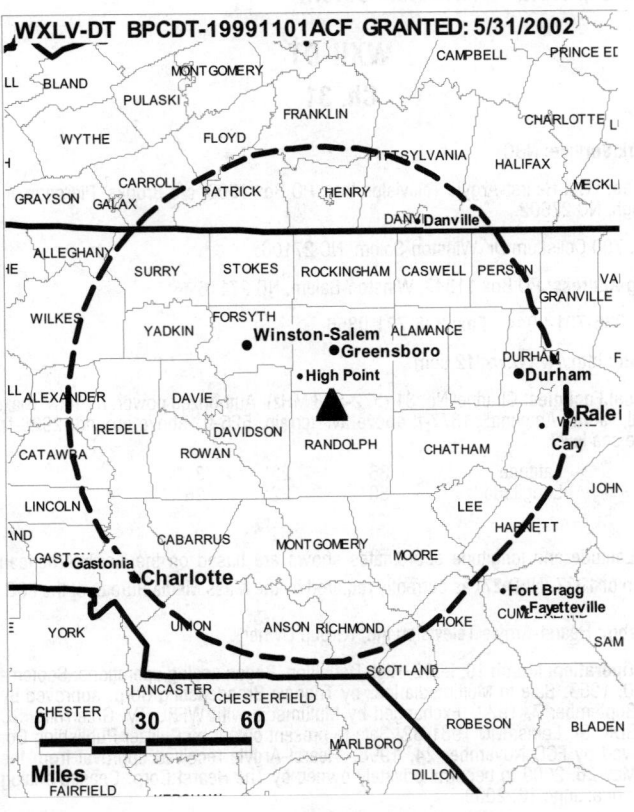

© 2010 Warren Communications News

Circulation © 2009 Nielsen. Coverage based on Nielsen study.

GrandTotal	Cable TV Households	Non-cable TV Households	Total TV Households
Estimated Station Totals *	426,790	293,950	720,740
Average Weekly Circulation (2009)	210,209	93,923	304,132
Average Daily Circulation (2009)			109,259

Station DMA Total	Cable TV Households	Non-cable TV Households	Total TV Households
Estimated Station Totals *	423,130	251,860	674,990
Average Weekly Circulation (2009)	208,283	91,167	299,450
Average Daily Circulation (2009)			108,463

Other DMA Total	Cable TV Households	Non-cable TV Households	Total TV Households
Estimated Station Totals *	3,660	42,090	45,750
Average Weekly Circulation (2009)	1,926	2,756	4,682
Average Daily Circulation (2009)			796

*Estimated station totals are sums of the Nielsen TV and Cable TV household estimates for each county in which the station registers viewing of more than 5% as per the Nielsen Survey Methods.

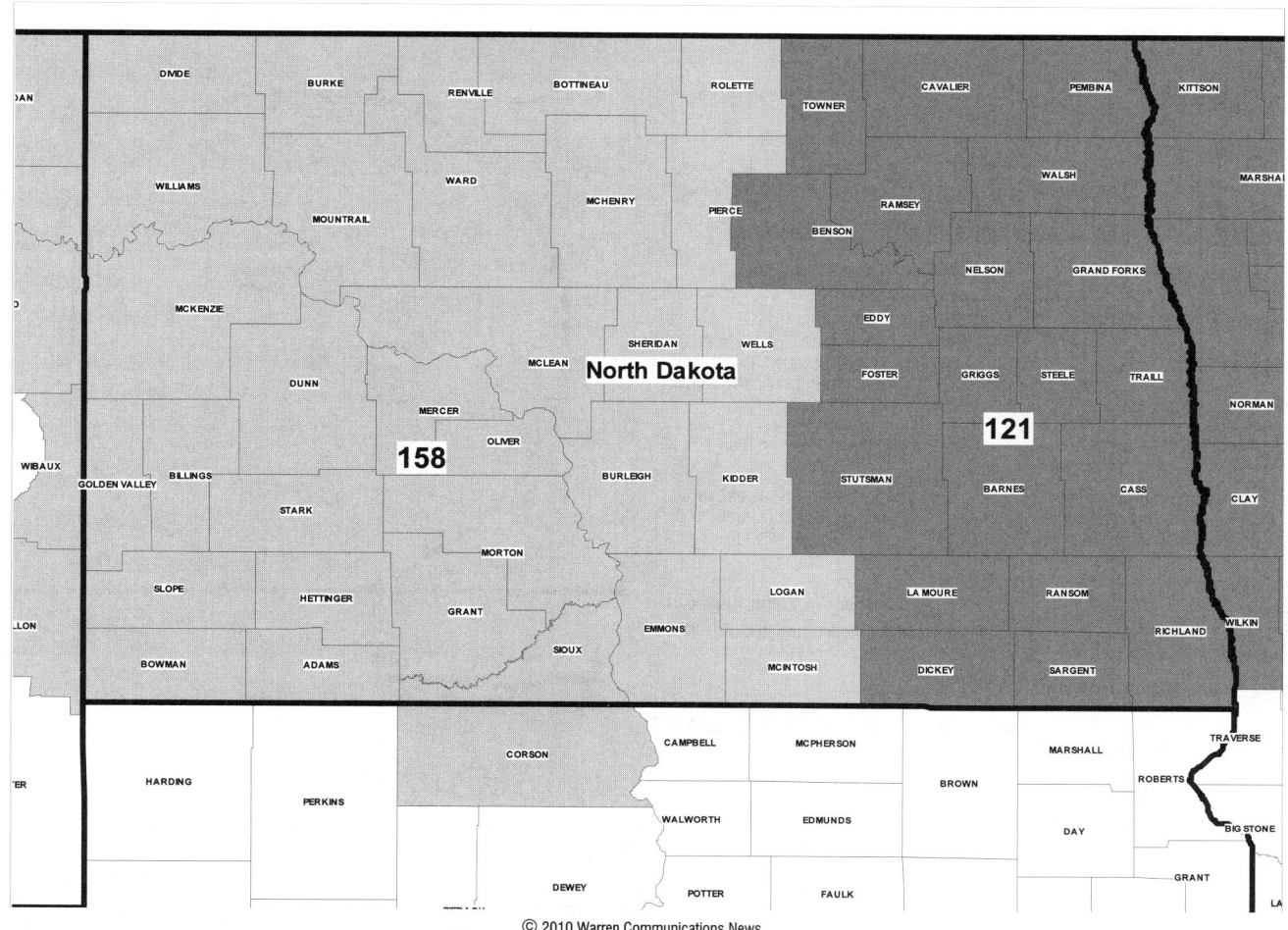

© 2010 Warren Communications News

MARKET	NIELSEN DMA TV HOUSEHOLDS	RANK	MARKET AREA COMMERCIAL STATIONS
Fargo-Valley City, ND	240,330	121	KBRR-DT (10); KJRR-DT (7); KVLY-DT (44); KVRR-DT (19); KXJB-DT (38); WDAY-DT (21); WDAZ-DT (8)
Minot-Bismarck-Dickinson, ND	136,540	158	KBMY-DT (16); KFYR-DT (31); KMCY-DT (14); KMOT-DT (10); KNDX-DT (26); KQCD-DT (7); KUMV-DT (8); KXMA-DT (19); KXMB-DT (12); KXMC-DT (13); KXMD-DT (14); KXND-DT (24)

North Dakota Station Totals as of October 1, 2009

	VHF	UHF	TOTAL
Commercial Television	7	11	18
Educational Television	2	6	8
	9	17	26

KBMY-DT
Ch. 16

Network Service: ABC.

Licensee: KBMY-KMCY LLC, 101 N 5th St, Fargo, ND 58102.

Studio: 3128 E Broadway Ave, Bismarck, ND 58501.

Mailing Address: PO Box 7277, Bismarck, ND 58507-7277.

Phone: 701-223-1700. **Fax:** 701-258-0886.

Web Site: http://www.abc17.tv

Technical Facilities: Channel No. 16 (482-488 MHz). Authorized power: 1.6-kw max. visual, aural. Antenna: 23-ft above av. terrain, 89-ft. above ground, 1775-ft. above sea level.

Latitude	46°	48'	23"
Longitude	100°	44'	36"

Holds CP for change to channel number 17, 75-kw max. visual, 951-ft above av. terrain, 614-ft. above ground, 2844-ft. above sea level; lat. 46° 35' 15", long. 100° 48' 20", BMPCDT-20090625AAC.

Note: Latitude and longitude coordinates shown are based on the North American Datum of 1927 (NAD 27) as currently required by the Mass Media Bureau of the FCC.

Ownership: Forum Communications Co. (Group Owner).

Began Operation: March 29, 2007. Began analog operations: March 31, 1985. Ceased analog operations: June 12, 2009.

Represented (legal): Wiley Rein LLP.

Represented (sales): Katz Media Group.

Personnel:

Gary O'Halloran, General Manager.

Tony Kruckenberg, Chief Engineer.

Susan Eider, Program & Promotion Director.

Terri Benson, Station Manager.

Scott Loerch, Production Manager.

City of License: Bismarck. **Station DMA:** Minot-Bismarck-Dickinson, ND. **Rank:** 158.

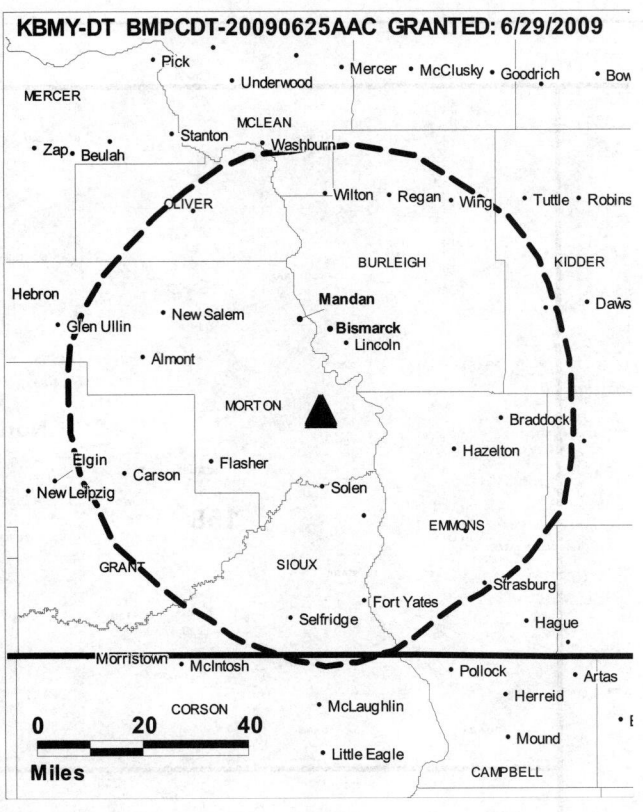

KBMY-DT BMPCDT-20090625AAC GRANTED: 6/29/2009

© 2010 Warren Communications News

Circulation © 2009 Nielsen. Coverage based on Nielsen study.

GrandTotal	Cable TV Households	Non-cable TV Households	Total TV Households
Estimated Station Totals *	45,430	37,230	82,660
Average Weekly Circulation (2009)	19,280	8,147	27,427
Average Daily Circulation (2009)			8,315

Station DMA Total	Cable TV Households	Non-cable TV Households	Total TV Households
Estimated Station Totals *	45,430	37,230	82,660
Average Weekly Circulation (2009)	19,280	8,147	27,427
Average Daily Circulation (2009)			8,315

*Estimated station totals are sums of the Nielsen TV and Cable TV household estimates for each county in which the station registers viewing of more than 5% as per the Nielsen Survey Methods.

KFYR-DT
Ch. 31

Network Service: NBC.

Licensee: Hoak Media of Dakota License LLC, 500 Crescent Ct, Ste 200, Dallas, TX 75201-7808.

Studio: 200 N 4th St, Bismark, ND 58501.

Mailing Address: PO Box 1738, Bismarck, ND 58502.

Phone: 701-255-5757. **Fax:** 701-255-8220.

Web Site: http://www.kfyrtv.com

Technical Facilities: Channel No. 31 (572-578 MHz). Authorized power: 500-kw max. visual, aural. Antenna: 1276-ft above av. terrain, 892-ft. above ground, 3163-ft. above sea level.

Latitude	46°	36'	20"
Longitude	100°	48'	22"

Note: Latitude and longitude coordinates shown are based on the North American Datum of 1927 (NAD 27) as currently required by the Mass Media Bureau of the FCC.

Ownership: Hoak Media LLC (Group Owner).

Began Operation: November 8, 2007. Began analog operations: December 19, 1953. Sale to present owner by North Dakota Television License Sub LLC approved by FCC November 16, 2006. Sale to North Dakota Television License Sub LLC by Smith Broadcasting Group Inc. approved by FCC October 8, 2002. Sale to Smith Broadcasting Group Inc. by Sunrise Television Partners LP approved by FCC May 20, 2002. Ceased analog operations: February 17, 2009.

Represented (legal): Akin, Gump, Strauss, Hauer & Feld LLP.

Represented (sales): Blair Television.

Personnel:

Dick Heidt, General Manager.

Jim Sande, Operations & Programming Manager.

Barry Schumaier, General Sales Manager.

Monica Hannan, News Director.

Brian Funk, Chief Engineer.

Tom Hertz, Business Manager.

LuWanna Ondracek, Promotion Director.

Kathy Scherr, Traffic Manager.

City of License: Bismarck. **Station DMA:** Minot-Bismarck-Dickinson, ND. **Rank:** 158.

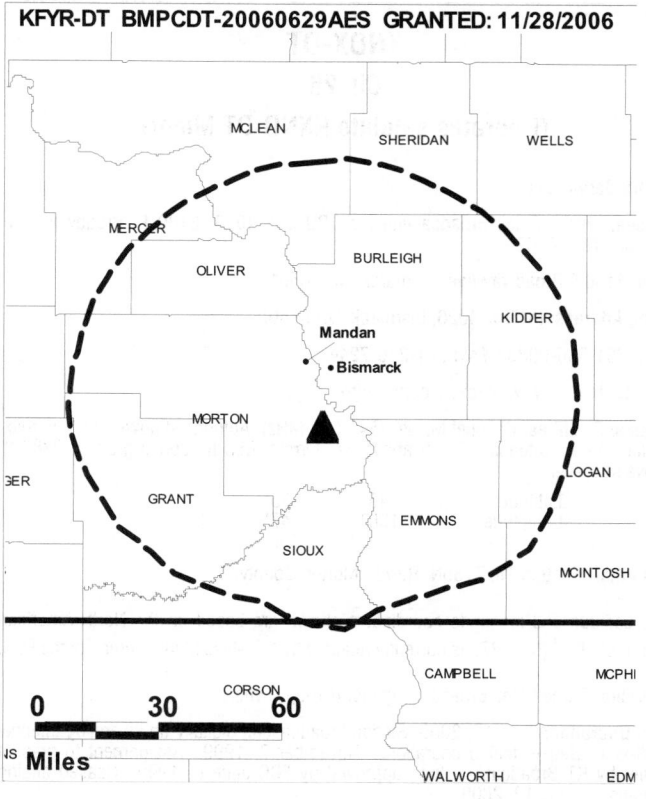

KFYR-DT BMPCDT-20060629AES GRANTED: 11/28/2006

© 2010 Warren Communications News

Circulation © 2009 Nielsen. Coverage based on Nielsen study.

GrandTotal	Cable TV Households	Non-cable TV Households	Total TV Households
Estimated Station Totals *	52,380	40,610	92,990
Average Weekly Circulation (2009)	35,440	13,956	49,396
Average Daily Circulation (2009)			28,138

Station DMA Total	Cable TV Households	Non-cable TV Households	Total TV Households
Estimated Station Totals *	45,520	39,110	84,630
Average Weekly Circulation (2009)	33,640	13,839	47,479
Average Daily Circulation (2009)			27,605

Other DMA Total	Cable TV Households	Non-cable TV Households	Total TV Households
Estimated Station Totals *	6,860	1,500	8,360
Average Weekly Circulation (2009)	1,800	117	1,917
Average Daily Circulation (2009)			533

*Estimated station totals are sums of the Nielsen TV and Cable TV household estimates for each county in which the station registers viewing of more than 5% as per the Nielsen Survey Methods.

KNDX-DT
Ch. 26
(Operates satellite KXND-DT Minot)

Network Service: FOX.

Licensee: Prime Cities Broadcasting Inc., PO Box 4026, 3130 E. Broadway Ave, Bismark, ND 58502.

Studio: 3130 E Broadway Ave, Bismarck, ND 58501.

Mailing Address: PO Box 4026, Bismarck, ND 58502.

Phone: 701-355-0026. **Fax:** 701-250-7244.

Web Site: http://www.myfoxbis.com/myfox

Technical Facilities: Channel No. 26 (542-548 MHz). Authorized power: 50-kw max. visual, aural. Antenna: 984-ft above av. terrain, 663-ft. above ground, 2883-ft. above sea level.

Latitude	46°	35'	23"
Longitude	100°	47'	39"

Transmitter: Section 18, T135N, R80W, Morton County.

Note: Latitude and longitude coordinates shown are based on the North American Datum of 1927 (NAD 27) as currently required by the Mass Media Bureau of the FCC.

Ownership: Prime Cities Broadcasting Inc. (Group Owner).

Began Operation: June 12, 2009. Station broadcasting digitally on its analog channel allotment. Began analog operations: November 7, 1999. Assignment to present owner by KT Broadcasting Inc. approved by FCC June 8, 1999. Ceased analog operations: June 12, 2009.

Represented (sales): Katz Media Group.

Represented (legal): Borsari & Paxson.

Personnel:

Gary O'Halloran, General Manager.

Terri Benson, Local Sales Manager.

Richard Farley, Chief Engineer.

Harold Heit, Business Manager.

Jessie Wald, Program Director & Traffic Manager.

Jodene Friesz, Promotion Director.

Scott Loerch, Production Manager & Creative Services Director.

City of License: Bismarck. **Station DMA:** Minot-Bismarck-Dickinson, ND. **Rank:** 158.

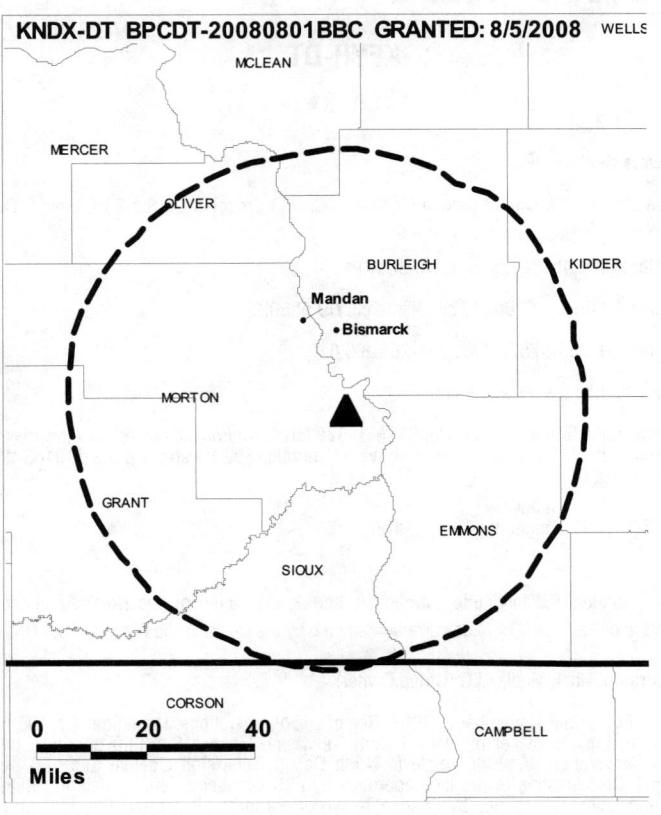

KNDX-DT BPCDT-20080801BBC GRANTED: 8/5/2008

© 2010 Warren Communications News

Circulation © 2009 Nielsen. Coverage based on Nielsen study.

GrandTotal	Cable TV Households	Non-cable TV Households	Total TV Households
Estimated Station Totals *	46,000	30,290	76,290
Average Weekly Circulation (2009)	20,363	6,252	26,615
Average Daily Circulation (2009)			8,879

Station DMA Total	Cable TV Households	Non-cable TV Households	Total TV Households
Estimated Station Totals *	46,000	30,290	76,290
Average Weekly Circulation (2009)	20,363	6,252	26,615
Average Daily Circulation (2009)			8,879

*Estimated station totals are sums of the Nielsen TV and Cable TV household estimates for each county in which the station registers viewing of more than 5% as per the Nielsen Survey Methods.

KXMB-DT
Ch. 12

Network Service: CBS.

Licensee: Reiten Television Inc., PO Box 1617, 1811 N 15th St, Bismarck, ND 58501.

Studio: 1811 N 15th St, Bismarck, ND 58501.

Mailing Address: PO Box 1617, Bismarck, ND 58502-1617.

Phone: 701-223-9197. **Fax:** 701-223-3320.

Web Site: http://www.kxmb.com

Technical Facilities: Channel No. 12 (204-210 MHz). Authorized power: 19.1-kw visual, aural. Antenna: 1458-ft above av. terrain, 1152-ft. above ground, 3371-ft. above sea level.

Latitude	46°	35'	12"
Longitude	100°	48'	20"

Note: Latitude and longitude coordinates shown are based on the North American Datum of 1927 (NAD 27) as currently required by the Mass Media Bureau of the FCC.

Ownership: Reiten Television (Group Owner).

Began Operation: March 18, 2002. High Definition. Station broadcasting digitally on its analog channel allotment. Began analog operations: November 19, 1955. Sale to present owner by KXJB-TV, Valley City-Fargo approved by FCC January 27, 1971 (Television Digest, Vol. 11:5). Ceased analog operations: June 12, 2009.

Represented (sales): Continental Television Sales.

Personnel:

Tim Reiten, General Manager.

Julie Bernhardt, National & Regional Sales Manager.

Bruce Dintelman, Local Sales Manager.

David Lenertz, Corporate Local Sales Manager.

Tom Gerhardt, News Director.

Rocky Hefty, Chief Engineer.

Jeanine Rambough, Program, Promotion, Production & Special Events Director.

Kathy Nagel, Traffic Manager.

Kathleen Reiten, Public Service Director.

City of License: Bismarck. **Station DMA:** Minot-Bismarck-Dickinson, ND. **Rank:** 158.

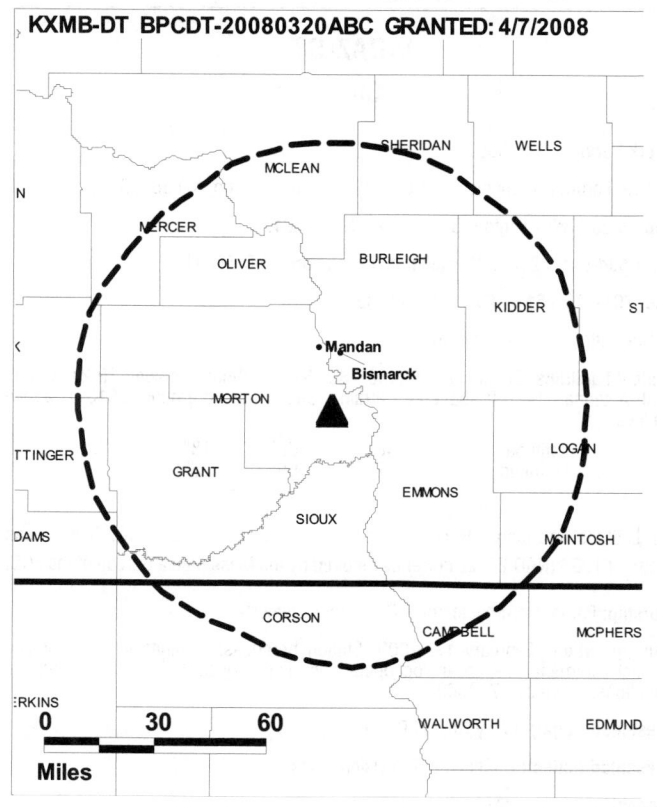

KXMB-DT BPCDT-20080320ABC GRANTED: 4/7/2008

© 2010 Warren Communications News

Circulation © 2009 Nielsen. Coverage based on Nielsen study.

GrandTotal	Cable TV Households	Non-cable TV Households	Total TV Households
Estimated Station Totals *	39,430	15,240	54,670
Average Weekly Circulation (2009)	28,238	7,356	35,594
Average Daily Circulation (2009)			19,722

Station DMA Total	Cable TV Households	Non-cable TV Households	Total TV Households
Estimated Station Totals *	38,770	15,240	54,010
Average Weekly Circulation (2009)	27,939	7,356	35,295
Average Daily Circulation (2009)			19,668

Other DMA Total	Cable TV Households	Non-cable TV Households	Total TV Households
Estimated Station Totals *	660	0	660
Average Weekly Circulation (2009)	299	0	299
Average Daily Circulation (2009)			54

*Estimated station totals are sums of the Nielsen TV and Cable TV household estimates for each county in which the station registers viewing of more than 5% as per the Nielsen Survey Methods.

WDAZ-DT
Ch. 8

Network Service: CW, ABC.

Licensee: Forum Communications Co., 301 8th St. S, Fargo, ND 58103.

Studio: 2220 S Washington, Grand Forks, ND 58201.

Mailing Address: 2220 S. Washington, Grand Forks, ND 58201.

Phone: 701-775-2511. **Fax:** 701-746-8565.

Web Site: http://www.wdaz.com

Technical Facilities: Channel No. 8 (180-186 MHz). Authorized power: 19-kw visual, aural. Antenna: 1480-ft above av. terrain, 1391-ft. above ground, 2913-ft. above sea level.

Latitude	48°	08'	18"
Longitude	97°	59'	35"

Note: Latitude and longitude coordinates shown are based on the North American Datum of 1927 (NAD 27) as currently required by the Mass Media Bureau of the FCC.

Ownership: Forum Communications Co. (Group Owner).

Began Operation: February 17, 2009. Station broadcasting digitally on its analog channel allotment. Began analog operations: February 8, 1967. Ceased analog operations: February 17, 2009.

Represented (legal): Wiley Rein LLP.

Represented (sales): Continental Television Sales.

Personnel:

Robert Kerr, General Manager.

Rob Horken, Sales Manager.

Brad Durick, Account Executive.

Cassie Walder, News Director.

Jeff Awes, Chief Engineer.

Angela Cary, Promotions & Creative Services Director.

Mike Derman, Operations Director.

Jodi Mishler, Administrative Assistant.

Jim L. Johnson, Production Director.

City of License: Devils Lake. **Station DMA:** Fargo-Valley City, ND. **Rank:** 121.

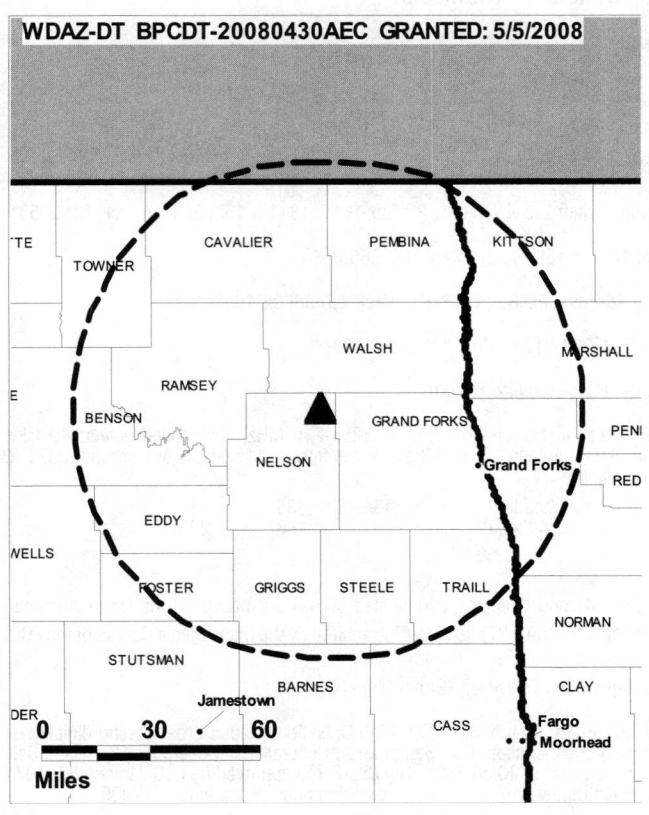

WDAZ-DT BPCDT-20080430AEC GRANTED: 5/5/2008

© 2010 Warren Communications News

Circulation © 2009 Nielsen. Coverage based on Nielsen study.

GrandTotal	Cable TV Households	Non-cable TV Households	Total TV Households
Estimated Station Totals *	52,520	46,550	99,070
Average Weekly Circulation (2009)	35,924	16,537	52,461
Average Daily Circulation (2009)			30,059

Station DMA Total	Cable TV Households	Non-cable TV Households	Total TV Households
Estimated Station Totals *	52,520	46,550	99,070
Average Weekly Circulation (2009)	35,924	16,537	52,461
Average Daily Circulation (2009)			30,059

*Estimated station totals are sums of the Nielsen TV and Cable TV household estimates for each county in which the station registers viewing of more than 5% as per the Nielsen Survey Methods.

KQCD-DT
Ch. 7

Network Service: NBC.

Grantee: Hoak Media of Dakota License LLC, 500 Crescent Ct, Ste 200, Dallas, TX 75201-7808.

Studio: 373 21st St E, Bismark, ND 58501.

Mailing Address: 373 21st St. E, Bismarck, ND 58501.

Phone: 701-483-7777. **Fax:** 701-483-8231.

Web Site: http://www.kqcd.com

Technical Facilities: Channel No. 7 (174-180 MHz). Authorized power: 11.3-kw visual, aural. Antenna: 673-ft above av. terrain, 587-ft. above ground, 3258-ft. above sea level.

Latitude	46°	56'	53"
Longitude	102°	59'	25"

Note: Latitude and longitude coordinates shown are based on the North American Datum of 1927 (NAD 27) as currently required by the Mass Media Bureau of the FCC.

Ownership: Hoak Media LLC (Group Owner).

Began Operation: February 17, 2009. Station broadcasting digitally on its analog channel allotment. Began analog operations: July 28, 1980. Sale to present owner by North Dakota Television License Sub LLC approved by FCC November 16, 2006. Sale to North Dakota Television License Sub LLC by Smith Broadcasting Group Inc. approved by FCC October 8, 2002. Sale to Smith Broadcasting Group Inc. by Sunrise Television Partners LP approved by FCC February 28, 2002. Ceased analog operations: February 17, 2009.

Represented (legal): Akin, Gump, Strauss, Hauer & Feld LLP.

Personnel:

Dick Heidt, General Manager.

Jim Sande, Operations & Program Manager.

Barry Schumaier, General Sales Manager.

Monica Hannan, News Director.

Brian Funk, Chief Engineer.

Tom Hertz, Business Manager.

LuWanna Ondracek, Promotion Director.

Kathy Scherr, Traffic Manager.

City of License: Dickinson. **Station DMA:** Minot-Bismarck-Dickinson, ND. **Rank:** 158.

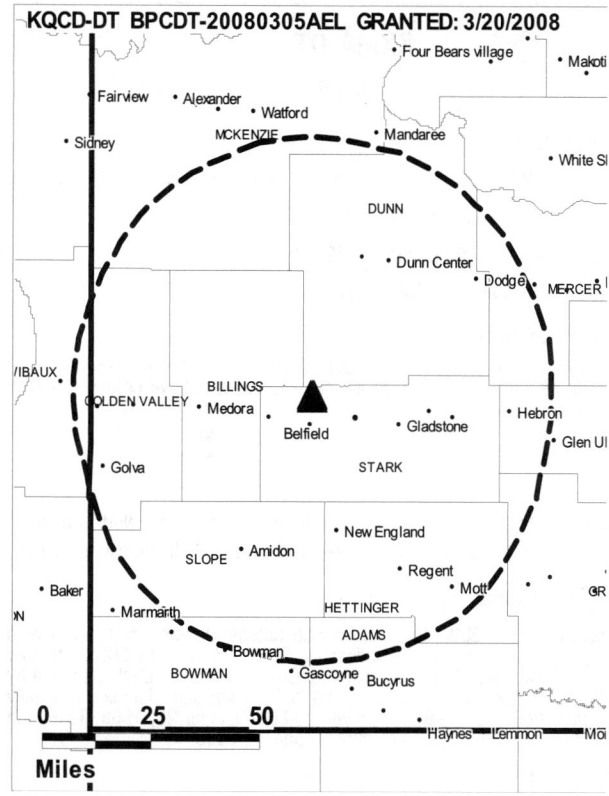

KQCD-DT BPCDT-20080305AEL GRANTED: 3/20/2008

© 2010 Warren Communications News

Circulation © 2009 Nielsen. Coverage based on Nielsen study.

GrandTotal	Cable TV Households	Non-cable TV Households	Total TV Households
Estimated Station Totals *	7,230	3,890	11,120
Average Weekly Circulation (2009)	6,058	2,524	8,582
Average Daily Circulation (2009)			5,807

Station DMA Total	Cable TV Households	Non-cable TV Households	Total TV Households
Estimated Station Totals *	7,230	3,890	11,120
Average Weekly Circulation (2009)	6,058	2,524	8,582
Average Daily Circulation (2009)			5,807

*Estimated station totals are sums of the Nielsen TV and Cable TV household estimates for each county in which the station registers viewing of more than 5% as per the Nielsen Survey Methods.

KXMA-DT
Ch. 19

Network Service: CBS.

Grantee: Reiten Television Inc., PO Box B, 1625 W Villard, Dickinson, ND 58602.

Studio: 1625 W Villard, Dickinson, ND 58601.

Mailing Address: PO Box B, Dickinson, ND 58602.

Phone: 701-483-1400. **Fax:** 701-483-1401.

Web Site: http://www.kxma.com

Technical Facilities: Channel No. 19 (500-506 MHz). Authorized power: 150-kw max. visual, aural. Antenna: 712-ft above av. terrain, 459-ft. above ground, 3389-ft. above sea level.

Latitude	46°	43'	35"
Longitude	102°	54'	57"

Note: Latitude and longitude coordinates shown are based on the North American Datum of 1927 (NAD 27) as currently required by the Mass Media Bureau of the FCC.

Ownership: Reiten Television (Group Owner).

Began Operation: June 5, 2006. Began analog operations: October 15, 1956. Sale to present owner by Northern Plains Broadcasting Group approved by FCC December 4, 1984. Sale to Northern Plains Broadcasting Group by Stanley Deck approved by FCC April 22, 1983. Sale to Deck by Dickinson Radio Association, increasing Stanley Deck's holdings from 5% to 99%, approved by FCC October 25, 1966 (Television Digest, Vol. 6:44). Ceased analog operations: June 12, 2009.

Represented (sales): Continental Television Sales.

Personnel:

Tim Reiten, General Manager.

Darren Lenertz, Corporate Local Sales Manager.

Bruce Dintelman, Local Sales Manager.

Julie Bernhardt, National & Regional Sales Manager.

Tom Gerhardt, News Director.

Rocky Hefty, Chief Engineer.

Bill Kohler, Assistant Engineer.

Mark Enderle, Production Manager & Creative Services Director.

Kathleen Reiten, Public Service Director.

City of License: Dickinson. **Station DMA:** Minot-Bismarck-Dickinson, ND. **Rank:** 158.

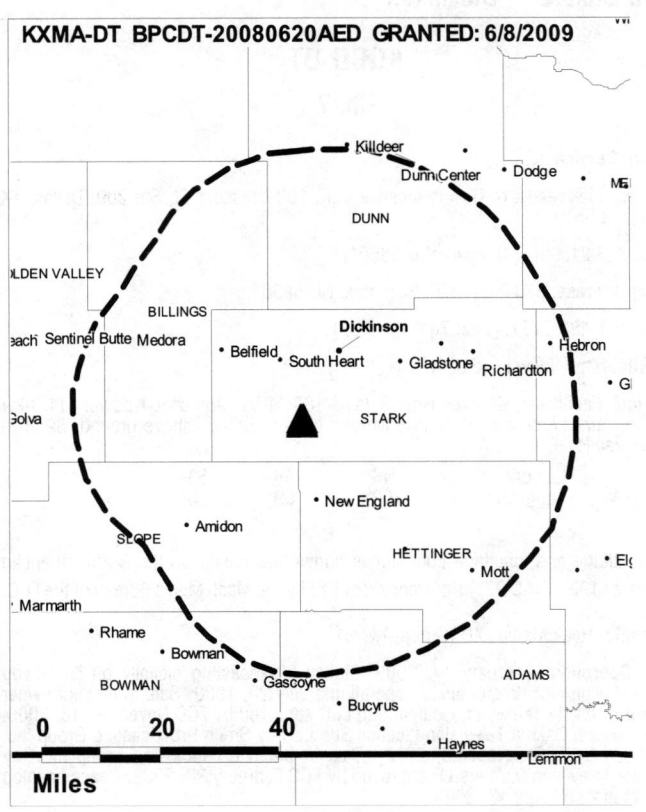

KXMA-DT BPCDT-20080620AED GRANTED: 6/8/2009

© 2010 Warren Communications News

Circulation © 2009 Nielsen. Coverage based on Nielsen study.

GrandTotal	Cable TV Households	Non-cable TV Households	Total TV Households
Estimated Station Totals *	7,230	3,450	10,680
Average Weekly Circulation (2009)	4,278	1,145	5,423
Average Daily Circulation (2009)			2,386

Station DMA Total	Cable TV Households	Non-cable TV Households	Total TV Households
Estimated Station Totals *	7,230	3,450	10,680
Average Weekly Circulation (2009)	4,278	1,145	5,423
Average Daily Circulation (2009)			2,386

*Estimated station totals are sums of the Nielsen TV and Cable TV household estimates for each county in which the station registers viewing of more than 5% as per the Nielsen Survey Methods.

KVLY-DT
Ch. 44

Network Service: NBC.

Licensee: Hoak Media of Dakota License LLC, 500 Crescent Ct, Ste 200, Dallas, TX 75201-7808.

Studios: 1350 21st Ave S, Fargo, ND 58103; 600 DeMers Ave, Grand Forks, ND 58208.

Mailing Address: PO Box 1878, Fargo, ND 58107.

Phone: 701-237-5211; 701-772-3481. **Fax:** 701-232-0493.

Web Site: http://www.kvlytv11.com

Technical Facilities: Channel No. 44 (650-656 MHz). Authorized power: 356-kw max. visual, aural. Antenna: 1890-ft above av. terrain, 1896-ft. above ground, 2871-ft. above sea level.

Latitude	47°	20'	32"
Longitude	97°	17'	20"

Note: Latitude and longitude coordinates shown are based on the North American Datum of 1927 (NAD 27) as currently required by the Mass Media Bureau of the FCC.

Ownership: Hoak Media LLC (Group Owner).

Began Operation: April 30, 2007. Began analog operations: October 11, 1959. Sale to present owner by North Dakota Television License Sub LLC approved by FCC November 16, 2006. Sale to North Dakota Television License Sub LLC by Smith Broadcasting Group Inc. approved by FCC October 8, 2002. Sale to Smith Broadcasting Group Inc. by Sunrise Television Partners LP approved by FCC February 28, 2002. Transfer of control to Smith Broadcasting Partners LP approved by FCC July 12, 2000; equity interest retained by Sunrise Television Partners LP. Sale to Sunrise Television Partners LP by Meyer Broadcasting Co. approved by FCC August 13, 1998. Sale to Meyer Broadcasting Co. from Spokane Television approved by FCC January 20, 1995. Sale to Spokane Television approved by FCC December 23, 1968. Sale of control to Natco by Polaris Corp. approved by FCC September 23, 1966. Sale of control to Polaris by North Dakota Broadcasting approved by FCC July 25, 1962. Ceased analog operations: February 16, 2009.

Represented (sales): Blair Television.

Represented (legal): Akin, Gump, Strauss, Hauer & Feld LLP.

Personnel:

Charley Johnson, General Manager.

Jeff Petrik, Operations Manager & Program Director.

Ron Westrick, Director of Sales.

Doug Jenson, Chief Engineer.

Lynette Samuelson, Business Manager.

Pam Petrik, Creative Services & Promotion Director.

Carol Gillett, Traffic Manager.

City of License: Fargo. **Station DMA:** Fargo-Valley City, ND. **Rank:** 121.

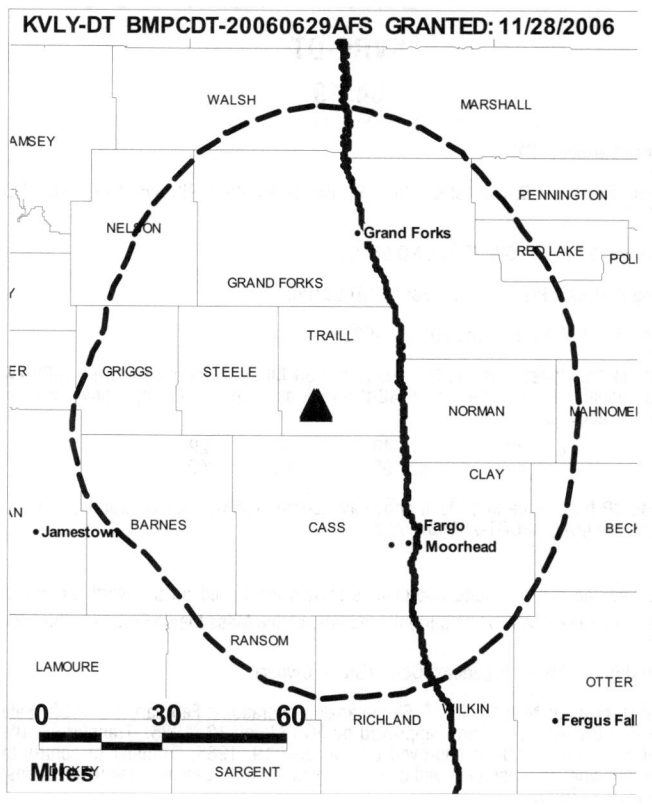

KVLY-DT BMPCDT-20060629AFS GRANTED: 11/28/2006

© 2010 Warren Communications News

Circulation © 2009 Nielsen. Coverage based on Nielsen study.

GrandTotal	Cable TV Households	Non-cable TV Households	Total TV Households
Estimated Station Totals *	133,530	99,530	233,060
Average Weekly Circulation (2009)	88,625	60,952	149,577
Average Daily Circulation (2009)			81,769

Station DMA Total	Cable TV Households	Non-cable TV Households	Total TV Households
Estimated Station Totals *	118,580	97,420	216,000
Average Weekly Circulation (2009)	87,782	60,807	148,589
Average Daily Circulation (2009)			81,615

Other DMA Total	Cable TV Households	Non-cable TV Households	Total TV Households
Estimated Station Totals *	14,950	2,110	17,060
Average Weekly Circulation (2009)	843	145	988
Average Daily Circulation (2009)			154

*Estimated station totals are sums of the Nielsen TV and Cable TV household estimates for each county in which the station registers viewing of more than 5% as per the Nielsen Survey Methods.

KVRR-DT
Ch. 19

Network Service: FOX.

Grantee: Red River Broadcast Co. LLC, PO Box 9115, 4015 9th Ave. SW, Fargo, ND 58106.

Studio: 4015 9th Ave SW, Fargo, ND 58103.

Mailing Address: PO Box 9115, Fargo, ND 58106.

Phone: 701-277-1515. **Fax:** 701-277-9656.

Technical Facilities: Channel No. 19 (500-506 MHz). Authorized power: 1000-kw max. visual, aural. Antenna: 1142-ft above av. terrain, 960-ft. above ground, 2414-ft. above sea level.

Latitude	46°	40'	29"
Longitude	96°	13'	40"

Holds CP for change to 1243-ft above av. terrain, 1063-ft. above ground, 2517-ft. above sea level; BPCDT-20080317AII.

Note: Latitude and longitude coordinates shown are based on the North American Datum of 1927 (NAD 27) as currently required by the Mass Media Bureau of the FCC.

Ownership: Red River Broadcast Corp. (Group Owner).

Began Operation: May 14, 2007. Began analog operations: February 14, 1983. Sale to Fargo Broadcasting Corp. approved by FCC March 12, 1985. Transfer of 50% control to John W. Boler approved by FCC July 19, 1985. Transfer of control to present owner by Boler approved by FCC August 4, 1987. Ceased analog operations: February 1, 2009.

Represented (engineering): du Treil, Lundin & Rackley Inc.

Represented (legal): Holland & Knight LLP.

Represented (sales): Katz Media Group.

Personnel:

Ro Grignon, President.

Myron Kunin, Chief Executive Officer.

Kathy Lau, Vice President & General Manager.

Ed Beiswenger, General & Local Sales Manager.

Dave Hoffman, Chief Engineer.

Jim Shaw, News Director.

Candice Kassenborg, Business Manager.

Jill Heacox, Traffic Manager.

City of License: Fargo. **Station DMA:** Fargo-Valley City, ND. **Rank:** 121.

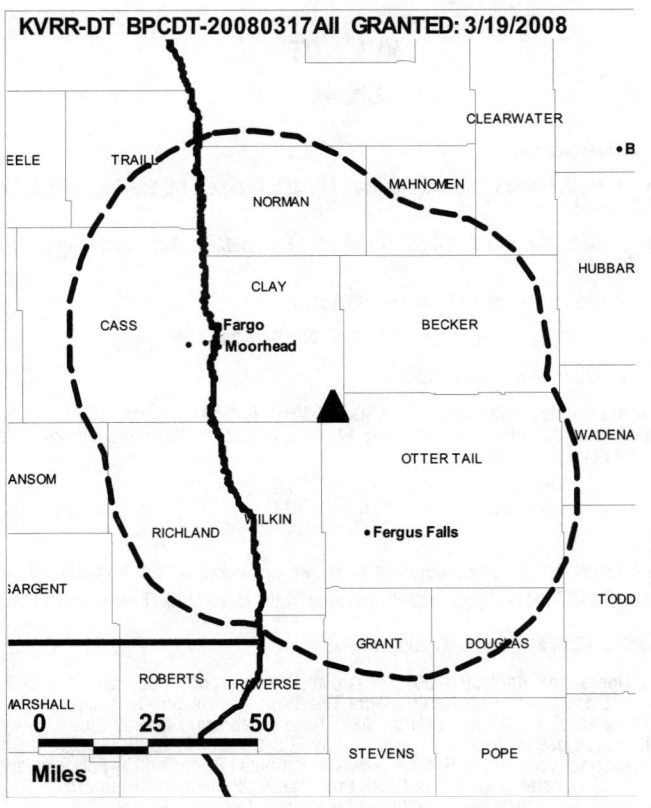

KVRR-DT BPCDT-20080317AII GRANTED: 3/19/2008

© 2010 Warren Communications News

Circulation © 2009 Nielsen. Coverage based on Nielsen study.

GrandTotal	Cable TV Households	Non-cable TV Households	Total TV Households
Estimated Station Totals *	75,510	100,600	176,110
Average Weekly Circulation (2009)	40,499	47,589	88,088
Average Daily Circulation (2009)			31,726

Station DMA Total	Cable TV Households	Non-cable TV Households	Total TV Households
Estimated Station Totals *	63,960	97,420	161,380
Average Weekly Circulation (2009)	37,742	47,206	84,948
Average Daily Circulation (2009)			30,822

Other DMA Total	Cable TV Households	Non-cable TV Households	Total TV Households
Estimated Station Totals *	11,550	3,180	14,730
Average Weekly Circulation (2009)	2,757	383	3,140
Average Daily Circulation (2009)			904

*Estimated station totals are sums of the Nielsen TV and Cable TV household estimates for each county in which the station registers viewing of more than 5% as per the Nielsen Survey Methods.

WDAY-DT
Ch. 21

Network Service: CW, ABC.

Licensee: Forum Communications Co., 301 8th St. S, Fargo, ND 58103.

Studio: 301 8th St S, Fargo, ND 58103.

Mailing Address: PO Box 2466, Fargo, ND 58108.

Phone: 701-237-6500. **Fax:** 701-241-5358.

Web Site: http://www.wday.com

Technical Facilities: Channel No. 21 (512-518 MHz). Authorized power: 1000-kw max. visual, aural. Antenna: 1056-ft above av. terrain, 1070-ft. above ground, 2014-ft. above sea level.

Latitude	47°	00'	28"
Longitude	97°	12'	02"

Note: Latitude and longitude coordinates shown are based on the North American Datum of 1927 (NAD 27) as currently required by the Mass Media Bureau of the FCC.

Ownership: Forum Communications Co. (Group Owner).

Began Operation: December 22, 2006. Began analog operations: June 1, 1953. Sale of remaining 55.56% interest to Fargo Forum (owned by the Black family) by E. C. & Marie E. Reineke approved by FCC July 20, 1960 by FCC (Television Digest, Vol. 16:31). Ceased analog operations: June 12, 2009.

Represented (sales): Continental Television Sales.

Personnel:

William C. Marcil, President.

Mark Prather, General Manager.

Susan Eider, Operations Manager.

Carol Anhorn, General Sales Manager.

Jeff Nelson, News Director.

Bonnie Reberg, Business Manager.

Dave Wee, Promotion Director.

Bernie Just, Traffic Manager.

City of License: Fargo. **Station DMA:** Fargo-Valley City, ND. **Rank:** 121.

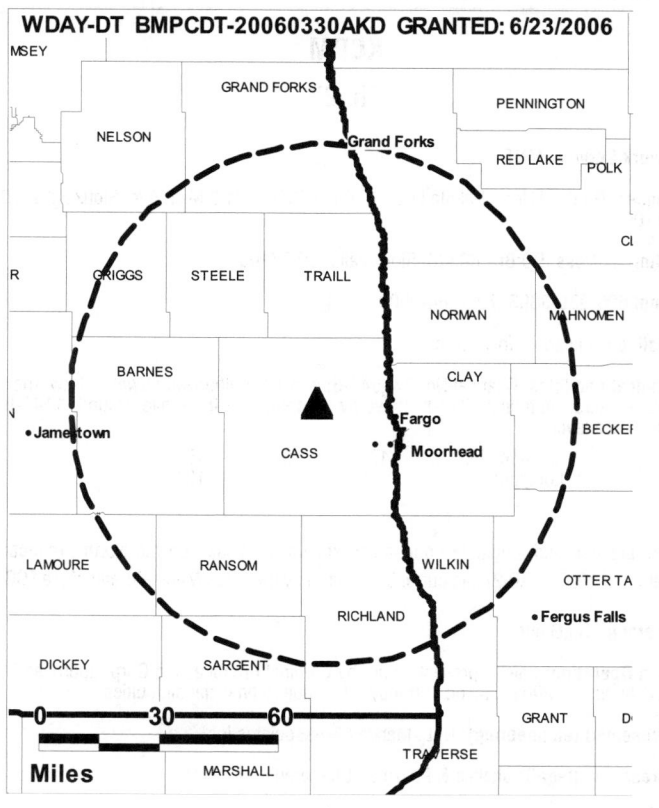

WDAY-DT BMPCDT-20060330AKD GRANTED: 6/23/2006

© 2010 Warren Communications News

Circulation © 2009 Nielsen. Coverage based on Nielsen study.

GrandTotal	Cable TV Households	Non-cable TV Households	Total TV Households
Estimated Station Totals *	86,160	93,140	179,300
Average Weekly Circulation (2009)	56,312	48,947	105,259
Average Daily Circulation (2009)			56,037

Station DMA Total	Cable TV Households	Non-cable TV Households	Total TV Households
Estimated Station Totals *	85,220	89,960	175,180
Average Weekly Circulation (2009)	56,242	48,564	104,806
Average Daily Circulation (2009)			55,976

Other DMA Total	Cable TV Households	Non-cable TV Households	Total TV Households
Estimated Station Totals *	940	3,180	4,120
Average Weekly Circulation (2009)	70	383	453
Average Daily Circulation (2009)			61

*Estimated station totals are sums of the Nielsen TV and Cable TV household estimates for each county in which the station registers viewing of more than 5% as per the Nielsen Survey Methods.

KCPM
Ch. 27

Network Service: MNT.

Licensee: G.I.G. of North Dakota LLC, PO Box 88336, 101 S Main Ave, Sioux Falls, SD 57109.

Mailing Address: PO Box 88336, Sioux Falls, SD 57109.

Phone: 605-335-3393; 701-364-9900.

E-mail: erica.keane@foxtv.com

Technical Facilities: Channel No. 27 (548-554 MHz). Authorized power: 18-kw max. visual, aural. Antenna: 314-ft above av. terrain, 315-ft. above ground, 1141-ft. above sea level.

Latitude	47°	57'	45"
Longitude	97°	03'	12"

Note: Latitude and longitude coordinates shown are based on the North American Datum of 1927 (NAD 27) as currently required by the Mass Media Bureau of the FCC.

Ownership: G.I.G. Inc.

Began Operation: Sale to present owner by Cardinal Broadcasting Corp. approved by FCC August 7, 2001. Station currently off air due to financial difficulties.

Represented (engineering): D. L. Markley & Associates Inc.

Represented (legal): Shainis & Peltzman Chartered.

City of License: Grand Forks. **Station DMA:** Fargo-Valley City, ND. **Rank:** 121.

Nielsen Data: Not available.

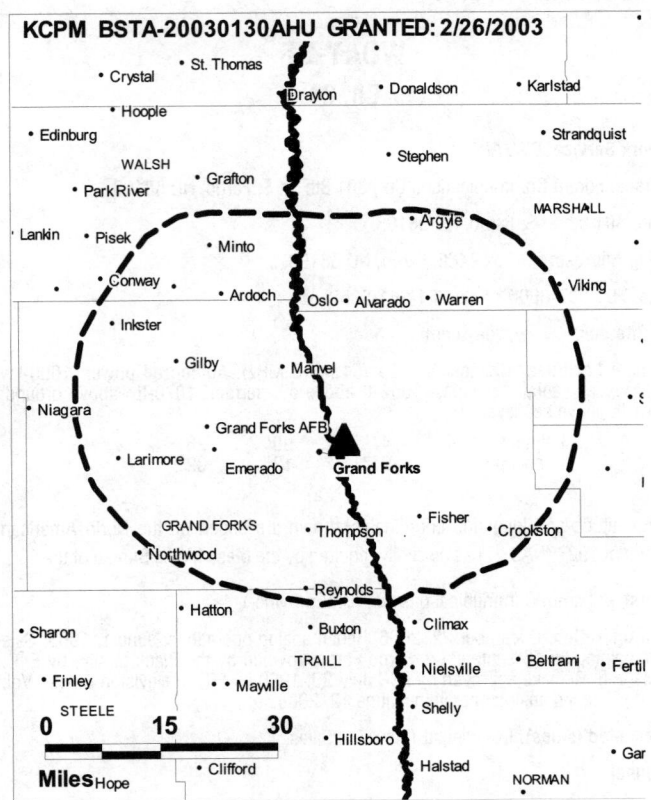

© 2010 Warren Communications News

KJRR-DT
Ch. 7

Network Service: FOX.

Grantee: Red River Broadcast Co. LLC, PO Box 9115, 4015 9th Ave. SW, Fargo, ND 58106.

Studio: 4015 9th Ave SW, Fargo, ND 58103.

Mailing Address: PO Box 9115, Fargo, ND 58106.

Phone: 701-277-1515. **Fax:** 701-277-1830.

Technical Facilities: Channel No. 7 (174-180 MHz). Authorized power: 21.3-kw visual, aural. Antenna: 443-ft above av. terrain, 449-ft. above ground, 1944-ft. above sea level.

Latitude	46°	55'	27"
Longitude	98°	46'	19"

Note: Latitude and longitude coordinates shown are based on the North American Datum of 1927 (NAD 27) as currently required by the Mass Media Bureau of the FCC.

Ownership: Red River Broadcast Corp. (Group Owner).

Began Operation: February 1, 2009. Station broadcasting digitally on its analog channel allotment. Began analog operations: October 7, 1988. Ceased analog operations: February 1, 2009.

Represented (engineering): du Treil, Lundin & Rackley Inc.

Represented (legal): Holland & Knight LLP.

Personnel:

Ro Grignon, President.

Myron Kunin, Chief Executive Officer.

Kathy Lau, Vice President & General Manager.

Ed Beiswenger, Local Sales Manager.

Dave Hoffman, Chief Engineer.

Jill Heacox, Traffic Manager.

Candice Kassenborg, Business Manager.

Jim Shaw, News Director.

City of License: Jamestown. **Station DMA:** Fargo-Valley City, ND. **Rank:** 121.

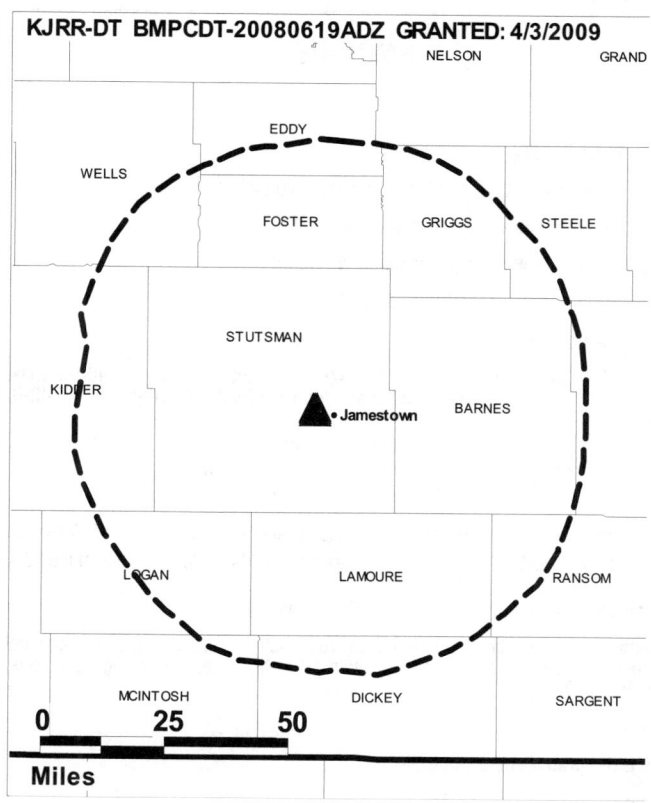

KJRR-DT BMPCDT-20080619ADZ GRANTED: 4/3/2009

© 2010 Warren Communications News

Circulation © 2009 Nielsen. Coverage based on Nielsen study.

GrandTotal	Cable TV Households	Non-cable TV Households	Total TV Households
Estimated Station Totals *	9,150	5,340	14,490
Average Weekly Circulation (2009)	4,251	492	4,743
Average Daily Circulation (2009)			1,555

Station DMA Total	Cable TV Households	Non-cable TV Households	Total TV Households
Estimated Station Totals *	9,150	4,620	13,770
Average Weekly Circulation (2009)	4,251	446	4,697
Average Daily Circulation (2009)			1,546

Other DMA Total	Cable TV Households	Non-cable TV Households	Total TV Households
Estimated Station Totals *	0	720	720
Average Weekly Circulation (2009)	0	46	46
Average Daily Circulation (2009)			9

*Estimated station totals are sums of the Nielsen TV and Cable TV household estimates for each county in which the station registers viewing of more than 5% as per the Nielsen Survey Methods.

KMCY-DT
Ch. 14

Network Service: ABC.

Grantee: KBMY-KMCY LLC, 101 N 5th St, Fargo, ND 58102.

Studio: 3128 E Broadway Ave, Bismarck, ND 58501.

Mailing Address: PO Box 7277, Bismarck, ND 58507.

Phone: 701-223-1700. **Fax:** 701-258-0886.

Web Site: http://www.abc14.tv

Technical Facilities: Channel No. 14 (470-476 MHz). Authorized power: 40-kw max. visual, aural. Antenna: 712-ft above av. terrain, 623-ft. above ground, 2743-ft. above sea level.

Latitude	48°	03'	11"
Longitude	101°	23'	05"

Note: Latitude and longitude coordinates shown are based on the North American Datum of 1927 (NAD 27) as currently required by the Mass Media Bureau of the FCC.

Ownership: Forum Communications Co. (Group Owner).

Began Operation: February 3, 2009. Station broadcasting digitally on its analog channel allotment. Began analog operations: June 19, 1985. Ceased analog operations: February 17, 2009.

Personnel:

Gary O'Halloran, General Manager.

Terri Benson, General Sales Manager.

Tony Kruckenberg, Chief Engineer.

Susan Eider, Program Director.

Scott Loerch, Production Manager.

City of License: Minot. **Station DMA:** Minot-Bismarck-Dickinson, ND. **Rank:** 158.

Digital cable and TV coverage maps.
Visit www.warren-news.com/mediaprints.htm

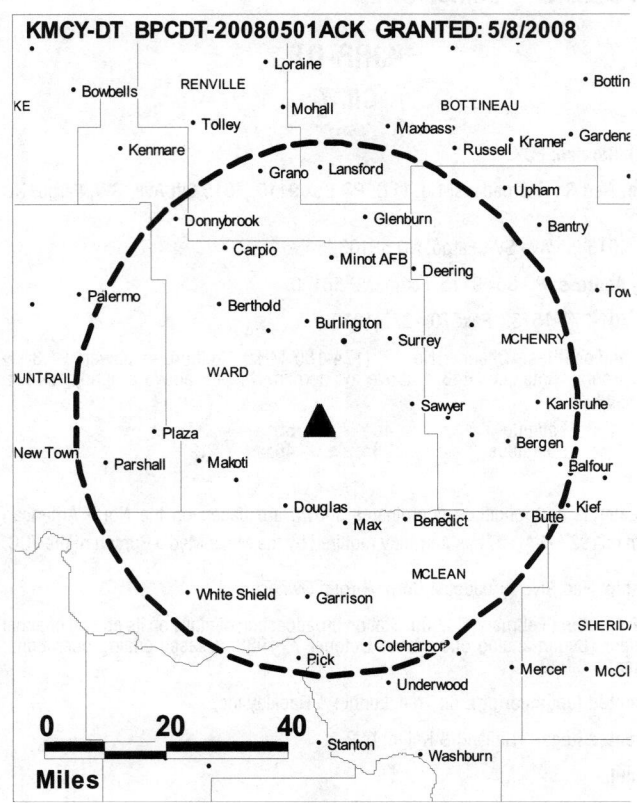

KMCY-DT BPCDT-20080501ACK GRANTED: 5/8/2008

© 2010 Warren Communications News

Circulation © 2009 Nielsen. Coverage based on Nielsen study.

GrandTotal	Cable TV Households	Non-cable TV Households	Total TV Households
Estimated Station Totals *	32,370	20,130	52,500
Average Weekly Circulation (2009)	12,851	4,295	17,146
Average Daily Circulation (2009)			5,491

Station DMA Total	Cable TV Households	Non-cable TV Households	Total TV Households
Estimated Station Totals *	32,370	20,130	52,500
Average Weekly Circulation (2009)	12,851	4,295	17,146
Average Daily Circulation (2009)			5,491

*Estimated station totals are sums of the Nielsen TV and Cable TV household estimates for each county in which the station registers viewing of more than 5% as per the Nielsen Survey Methods.

KMOT-DT
Ch. 10

Network Service: NBC.

Grantee: Hoak Media of Dakota License LLC, 500 Crescent Ct, Ste 200, Dallas, TX 75201-7808.

Studio: 1800 SW 16th St, Minot, ND 58701.

Mailing Address: PO Box 1120, Minot, ND 58702-1120.

Phone: 701-852-4101. **Fax:** 701-838-8195.

Web Site: http://www.kmot.com

Technical Facilities: Channel No. 10 (192-198 MHz). Authorized power: 7.69-kw visual, aural. Antenna: 679-ft above av. terrain, 653-ft. above ground, 2409-ft. above sea level.

Latitude	48°	12'	56"
Longitude	101°	19'	05"

Note: Latitude and longitude coordinates shown are based on the North American Datum of 1927 (NAD 27) as currently required by the Mass Media Bureau of the FCC.

Ownership: Hoak Media LLC (Group Owner).

Began Operation: January 20, 2009. Station broadcasting digitally on its analog channel allotment. Began analog operations: January 20, 1958. Sale to present owner by North Dakota Television License Sub LLC approved by FCC November 16, 2006. Sale to North Dakota Television License Sub LLC by Smith Broadcasting Group Inc. approved by FCC October 8, 2002. Sale to Smith Broadcasting Group Inc. by Sunrise Television Partners LP approved by FCC February 28, 2002. Ceased analog operations: January 20, 2009.

Represented (legal): Akin, Gump, Strauss, Hauer & Feld LLP.

Personnel:

Tom Ross, Station & General Sales Manager.

Greg Bakke, Chief Engineer.

City of License: Minot. **Station DMA:** Minot-Bismarck-Dickinson, ND. **Rank:** 158.

KMOT-DT BPCDT-20080314AAE GRANTED: 5/1/2008

© 2010 Warren Communications News

Circulation © 2009 Nielsen. Coverage based on Nielsen study.

GrandTotal	Cable TV Households	Non-cable TV Households	Total TV Households
Estimated Station Totals *	23,070	18,180	41,250
Average Weekly Circulation (2009)	17,597	5,993	23,590
Average Daily Circulation (2009)			12,843

Station DMA Total	Cable TV Households	Non-cable TV Households	Total TV Households
Estimated Station Totals *	23,070	18,180	41,250
Average Weekly Circulation (2009)	17,597	5,993	23,590
Average Daily Circulation (2009)			12,843

*Estimated station totals are sums of the Nielsen TV and Cable TV household estimates for each county in which the station registers viewing of more than 5% as per the Nielsen Survey Methods.

KXMC-DT
Ch. 13

Network Service: CBS.

Licensee: Reiten Television Inc., PO Box 1686, Minot, ND 58702.

Studio: 3425 S Broadway, Minot, ND 58701.

Mailing Address: PO Box 1686, Minot, ND 58702.

Phone: 701-852-2104. **Fax:** 701-838-1050.

Web Site: http://www.kxmc.com

Technical Facilities: Channel No. 13 (210-216 MHz). Authorized power: 16.1-kw visual, aural. Antenna: 1096-ft above av. terrain, 1033-ft. above ground, 3098-ft. above sea level.

Latitude	48°	03'	00"
Longitude	101°	20'	32"

Note: Latitude and longitude coordinates shown are based on the North American Datum of 1927 (NAD 27) as currently required by the Mass Media Bureau of the FCC.

Ownership: Reiten Television (Group Owner).

Began Operation: October 7, 2003. Station broadcasting digitally on its analog channel allotment. Began analog operations: April 4, 1953. Sale to present owner by North Dakota Broadcasting Co. Inc. approved by FCC October 20, 1959 (Television Digest, Vol. 15:37, 43). Ceased analog operations: June 12, 2009.

Represented (sales): Continental Television Sales.

Personnel:

Tim Reiten, President.

David Reiten, General Manager.

Terry Greuel, Production Manager.

Julie Bernhardt, Corporate Sales Manager.

Darren Lenertz, Local Sales Manager & Promotion Director.

Jay Atwood, National & Regional Sales Manager.

Jim Olson, News Director.

Bob Turneau, Chief Engineer.

Linda Sand, Program & Traffic Manager.

City of License: Minot. **Station DMA:** Minot-Bismarck-Dickinson, ND. **Rank:** 158.

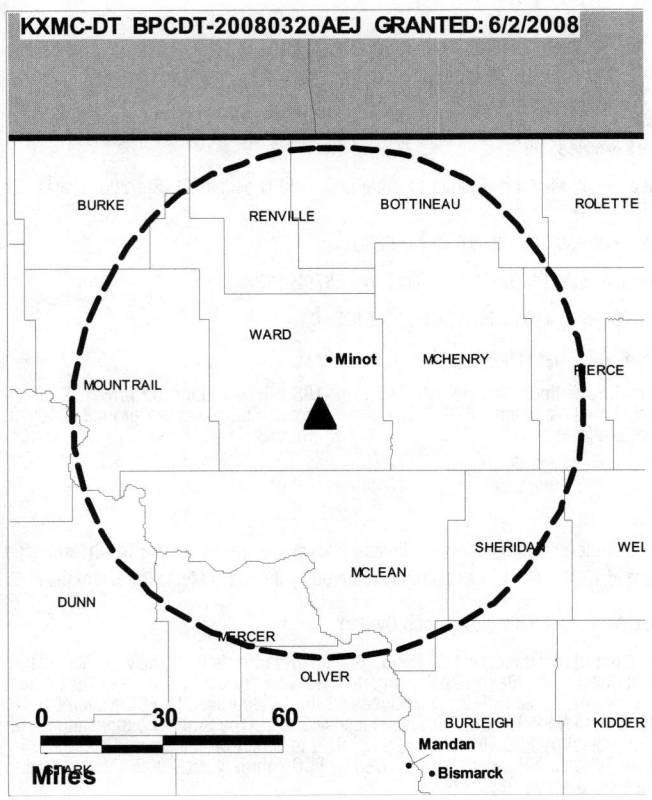

KXMC-DT BPCDT-20080320AEJ GRANTED: 6/2/2008

© 2010 Warren Communications News

Circulation © 2009 Nielsen. Coverage based on Nielsen study.

GrandTotal	Cable TV Households	Non-cable TV Households	Total TV Households
Estimated Station Totals *	24,860	29,880	54,740
Average Weekly Circulation (2009)	20,913	11,340	32,253
Average Daily Circulation (2009)			21,435

Station DMA Total	Cable TV Households	Non-cable TV Households	Total TV Households
Estimated Station Totals *	24,860	29,880	54,740
Average Weekly Circulation (2009)	20,913	11,340	32,253
Average Daily Circulation (2009)			21,435

*Estimated station totals are sums of the Nielsen TV and Cable TV household estimates for each county in which the station registers viewing of more than 5% as per the Nielsen Survey Methods.

KXND-DT
Ch. 24
(Satellite of KNDX-DT Bismarck)

Network Service: FOX.

Licensee: Prime Cities Broadcasting Inc., PO Box 4026, 3130 E. Broadway Ave, Bismark, ND 58502.

Studio: 605 31st Ave SW, Ste A, Minot, ND 58702.

Mailing Address: 605 31st Ave SW, Ste A, Minot, ND 58702.

Phone: 701-858-0024; 701-355-0026. **Fax:** 701-838-8473.

Web Site: http://www.myfoxminot.com

Technical Facilities: Channel No. 24 (530-536 MHz). Authorized power: 50-kw max. visual, aural. Antenna: 784-ft above av. terrain, 663-ft. above ground, 2842-ft. above sea level.

Latitude	48°	03'	14"
Longitude	101°	26'	03"

Transmitter: SW 0.25 of SE quarter of Section 23, Township 153N, Range 48W, Ward County.

Note: Latitude and longitude coordinates shown are based on the North American Datum of 1927 (NAD 27) as currently required by the Mass Media Bureau of the FCC.

Ownership: Prime Cities Broadcasting Inc. (Group Owner).

Began Operation: June 12, 2009. Station broadcasting digitally on its analog channel allotment. Began analog operations: November 15, 1999. Assignment to present owner by KT Broadcasting Inc. approved by FCC June 8, 1999. Ceased analog operations: June 12, 2009.

Represented (sales): Katz Media Group.

Represented (legal): Borsari & Paxson.

Personnel:

Gary O'Halloran, General Manager.

Jamie Schepp, Station & Local Sales Manager.

Richard Farley, Chief Engineer.

Harold Heit, Business Manager.

Jessie Wald, Program Director & Traffic Manager.

Jodene Friesz, Promotion Director.

Scott Loerch, Production Manager & Creative Services Director.

City of License: Minot. **Station DMA:** Minot-Bismarck-Dickinson, ND. **Rank:** 158.

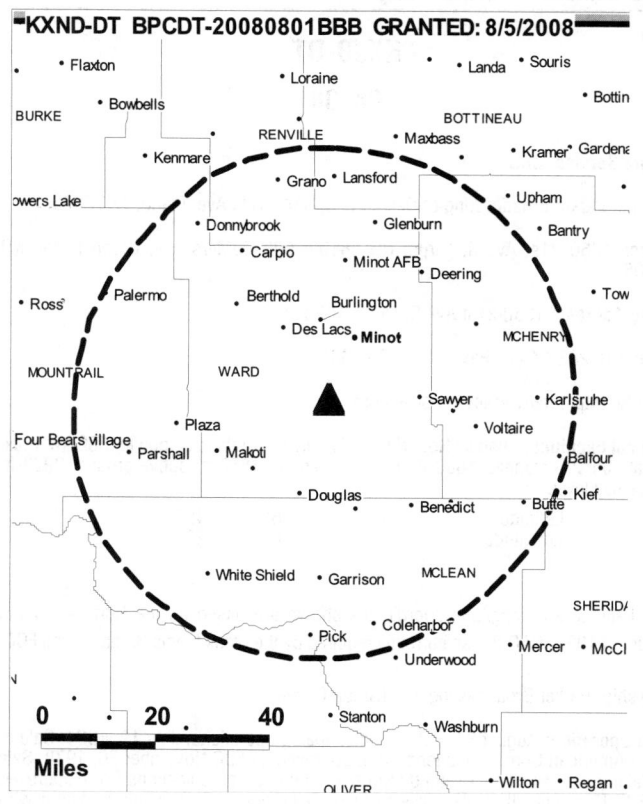

KXND-DT BPCDT-20080801BBB GRANTED: 8/5/2008

© 2010 Warren Communications News

Circulation © 2009 Nielsen. Coverage based on Nielsen study.

GrandTotal	Cable TV Households	Non-cable TV Households	Total TV Households
Estimated Station Totals *	31,720	21,360	53,080
Average Weekly Circulation (2009)	16,372	5,956	22,328
Average Daily Circulation (2009)			7,777

Station DMA Total	Cable TV Households	Non-cable TV Households	Total TV Households
Estimated Station Totals *	31,720	21,360	53,080
Average Weekly Circulation (2009)	16,372	5,956	22,328
Average Daily Circulation (2009)			7,777

*Estimated station totals are sums of the Nielsen TV and Cable TV household estimates for each county in which the station registers viewing of more than 5% as per the Nielsen Survey Methods.

KXJB-DT
Ch. 38

Network Service: CBS.

Licensee: Parker Broadcasting of Dakota LLC, 5341 Tate Ave, Plano, TX 75093.

Studios: 1350 21st Ave S, Fargo, ND 58103; 600 DeMers Ave, Grand Forks, ND 58208.

Mailing Address: 1350 21st Ave S, Fargo, ND 58103.

Phone: 701-282-0444. **Fax:** 701-282-0743.

Web Site: http://www.valleynewslive.com

Technical Facilities: Channel No. 38 (614-620 MHz). Authorized power: 382-kw max. visual, aural. Antenna: 1880-ft above av. terrain, 1857-ft. above ground, 2923-ft. above sea level.

Latitude	47°	16'	45"
Longitude	97°	20'	26"

Note: Latitude and longitude coordinates shown are based on the North American Datum of 1927 (NAD 27) as currently required by the Mass Media Bureau of the FCC.

Ownership: Parker Broadcasting Inc. (Group Owner).

Began Operation: August 31, 2006. Began analog operations: July 12, 1954. Sale to North American Communications Corp. approved by FCC November 30, 1978. Sale to Catamount Broadcast Group by North American Communications Corp. approved by FCC December 8, 1999. Sale to Spirit Television LLC (Michael A. Wach) who then immediately sold station to current owner approved by FCC November 7, 2006. Ceased analog operations: February 16, 2009.

Represented (sales): Continental Television Sales.

Personnel:

Charley Johnson, General Manager.

Ron Westrick, Director of Sales.

Pam Petrik, Promotion & Creative Services Director.

Carol Gillette, Traffic Manager.

Jeremiah Moerke, News Director.

Ron Barr, Chief Engineer.

Jeff Petrik, Operations Manager.

Lynette L. Samuelson, Business Manager.

City of License: Valley City. **Station DMA:** Fargo-Valley City, ND. **Rank:** 121.

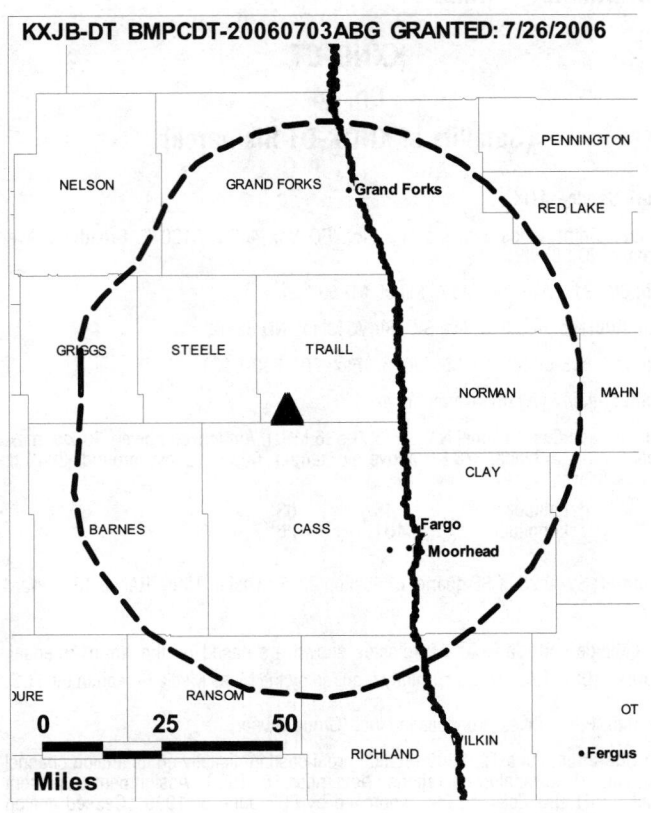

KXJB-DT BMPCDT-20060703ABG GRANTED: 7/26/2006

© 2010 Warren Communications News

Circulation © 2009 Nielsen. Coverage based on Nielsen study.

GrandTotal	Cable TV Households	Non-cable TV Households	Total TV Households
Estimated Station Totals *	119,520	101,440	220,960
Average Weekly Circulation (2009)	77,257	53,293	130,550
Average Daily Circulation (2009)			62,934

Station DMA Total	Cable TV Households	Non-cable TV Households	Total TV Households
Estimated Station Totals *	118,580	97,420	216,000
Average Weekly Circulation (2009)	77,187	52,864	130,051
Average Daily Circulation (2009)			62,846

Other DMA Total	Cable TV Households	Non-cable TV Households	Total TV Households
Estimated Station Totals *	940	4,020	4,960
Average Weekly Circulation (2009)	70	429	499
Average Daily Circulation (2009)			88

*Estimated station totals are sums of the Nielsen TV and Cable TV household estimates for each county in which the station registers viewing of more than 5% as per the Nielsen Survey Methods.

KUMV-DT
Ch. 8

Network Service: NBC.

Grantee: Hoak Media of Dakota License LLC, 500 Crescent Ct, Ste 200, Dallas, TX 75201-7808.

Studio: 602 Main St, Williston, ND 58801.

Mailing Address: PO Box 1287, Williston, ND 58801.

Phone: 701-572-4676. **Fax:** 701-572-0118.

Web Site: http://www.kumv.com

Technical Facilities: Channel No. 8 (180-186 MHz). Authorized power: 6-kw visual, aural. Antenna: 1050-ft above av. terrain, 840-ft. above ground, 3183-ft. above sea level.

Latitude	48°	08'	02"
Longitude	103°	51'	36"

Note: Latitude and longitude coordinates shown are based on the North American Datum of 1927 (NAD 27) as currently required by the Mass Media Bureau of the FCC.

Ownership: Hoak Media LLC (Group Owner).

Began Operation: February 17, 2009. Station broadcasting digitally on its analog channel allotment. Began analog operations: February 11, 1957. Sale to present owner by North Dakota Television License Sub LLC approved by FCC November 16, 2006. Sale to North Dakota Television License Sub LLC by Smith Broadcasting Group Inc. approved by FCC October 8, 2002. Sale to Smith Broadcasting Group Inc. by Sunrise Television Partners LP approved by FCC February 28, 2002. Ceased analog operations: February 17, 2009.

Represented (legal): Akin, Gump, Strauss, Hauer & Feld LLP.

Personnel:

Deborah Burton, Station Manager & Local Sales Manager.

Brian Funk, Chief Engineer.

City of License: Williston. **Station DMA:** Minot-Bismarck-Dickinson, ND. **Rank:** 158.

KUMV-DT BPCDT-20080307AAQ GRANTED: 6/17/2008

© 2010 Warren Communications News

Circulation © 2009 Nielsen. Coverage based on Nielsen study.

GrandTotal	Cable TV Households	Non-cable TV Households	Total TV Households
Estimated Station Totals *	12,500	9,460	21,960
Average Weekly Circulation (2009)	7,992	3,090	11,082
Average Daily Circulation (2009)			6,679

Station DMA Total	Cable TV Households	Non-cable TV Households	Total TV Households
Estimated Station Totals *	9,940	6,430	16,370
Average Weekly Circulation (2009)	6,633	2,756	9,389
Average Daily Circulation (2009)			5,896

Other DMA Total	Cable TV Households	Non-cable TV Households	Total TV Households
Estimated Station Totals *	2,560	3,030	5,590
Average Weekly Circulation (2009)	1,359	334	1,693
Average Daily Circulation (2009)			783

*Estimated station totals are sums of the Nielsen TV and Cable TV household estimates for each county in which the station registers viewing of more than 5% as per the Nielsen Survey Methods.

KXMD-DT
Ch. 14

Network Service: CBS.

Grantee: Reiten Television Inc., PO Box 790, Williston, ND 58801-0790.

Studio: 1802 13th Ave W, Williston, ND 58801.

Mailing Address: PO Box 790, Williston, ND 58802.

Phone: 701-572-2345. **Fax:** 701-572-0658.

Web Site: http://www.kxmd.com

Technical Facilities: Channel No. 14 (470-476 MHz). Authorized power: 100-kw max. visual, aural. Antenna: 843-ft above av. terrain, 715-ft. above ground, 3012-ft. above sea level.

Latitude	48°	08'	30"
Longitude	103°	53'	34"

Note: Latitude and longitude coordinates shown are based on the North American Datum of 1927 (NAD 27) as currently required by the Mass Media Bureau of the FCC.

Ownership: Reiten Television (Group Owner).

Began Operation: April 10, 2006. Began analog operations: October 25, 1969. Ceased analog operations: June 12, 2009.

Represented (sales): Continental Television Sales.

Personnel:

David Reiten, General Manager.

Julie Bernhardt, Corporate Sales Director.

Darren Lenertz, Corporate Local Sales Manager.

Jim Olson, News Director.

Russell Larson, Production Manager.

City of License: Williston. **Station DMA:** Minot-Bismarck-Dickinson, ND. **Rank:** 158.

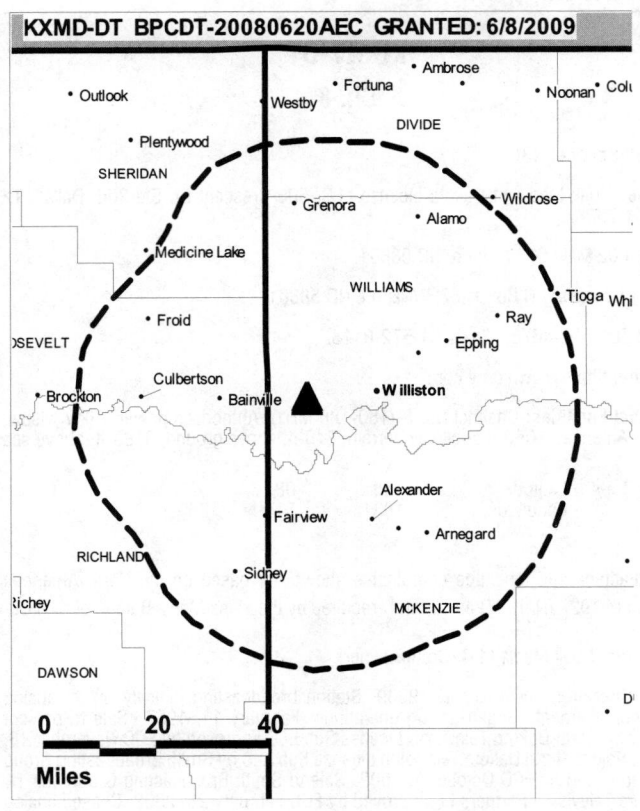

KXMD-DT BPCDT-20080620AEC GRANTED: 6/8/2009

© 2010 Warren Communications News

Circulation © 2009 Nielsen. Coverage based on Nielsen study.

GrandTotal	Cable TV Households	Non-cable TV Households	Total TV Households
Estimated Station Totals *	9,940	6,430	16,370
Average Weekly Circulation (2009)	5,179	2,441	7,620
Average Daily Circulation (2009)			3,284

Station DMA Total	Cable TV Households	Non-cable TV Households	Total TV Households
Estimated Station Totals *	9,940	6,430	16,370
Average Weekly Circulation (2009)	5,179	2,441	7,620
Average Daily Circulation (2009)			3,284

*Estimated station totals are sums of the Nielsen TV and Cable TV household estimates for each county in which the station registers viewing of more than 5% as per the Nielsen Survey Methods.

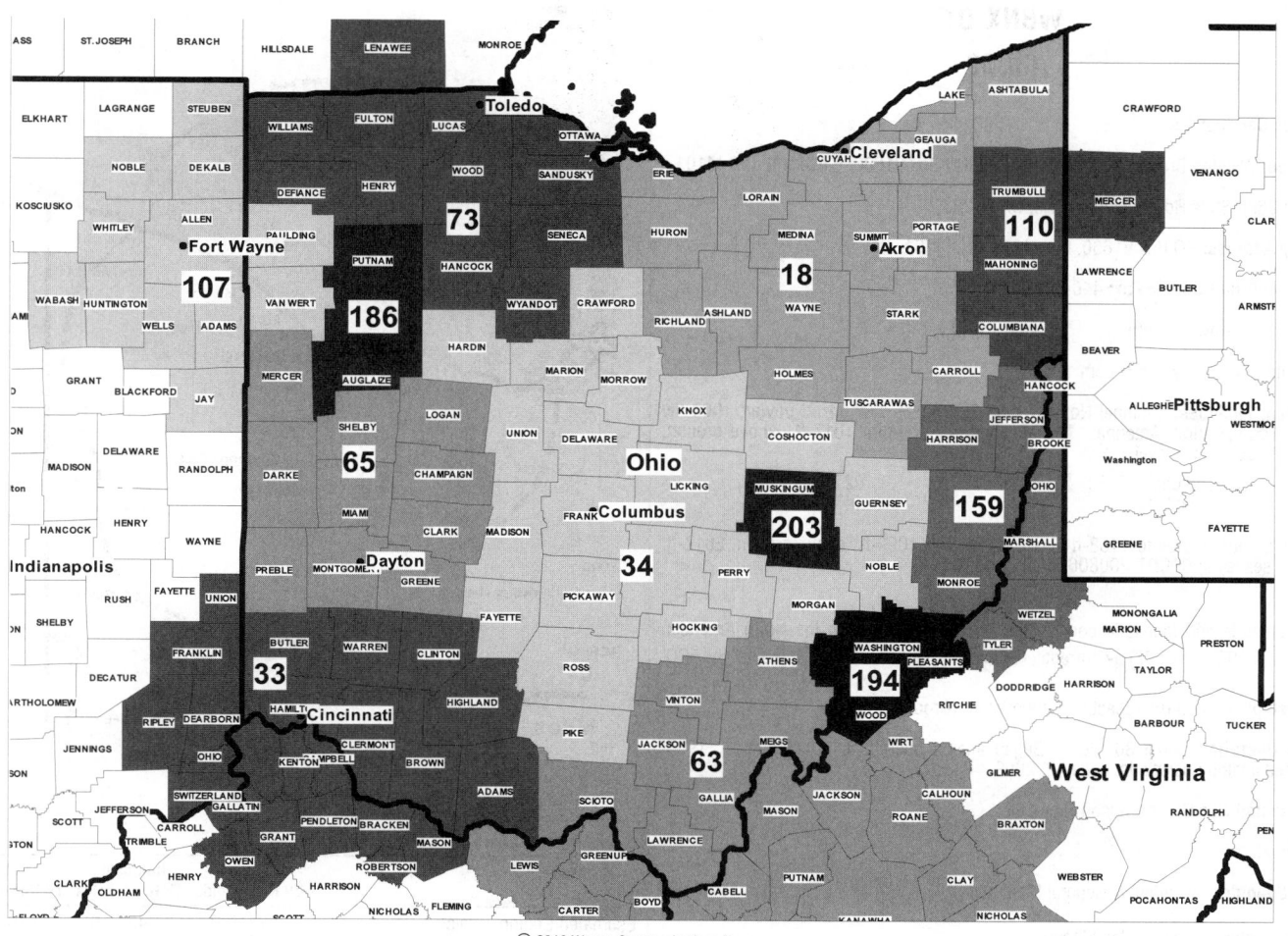

© 2010 Warren Communications News

MARKET	NIELSEN DMA TV HOUSEHOLDS	RANK	MARKET AREA COMMERCIAL STATIONS
Cleveland-Akron (Canton), OH.	1,520,750	18	WBNX-DT (30); WDLI-DT (39); WEWS-DT (15); WGGN-DT (42); WJW-DT (8); WKYC (2); WMFD-DT (12); WOIO-DT (10); WQHS-DT (34); WRLM (47); WUAB-DT (28); WVPX-TV (23)
Cincinnati, OH.	918,670	33	WCPO-DT (10); WKRC-DT (12); WLWT-DT (35); WSTR-DT (33); WXIX-DT (29)
Columbus, OH.	904,030	34	WBNS-DT (21); WCMH-DT (14); WSFJ-DT (24); WSYX-DT (13); WTTE-DT (36); WWHO-DT (46)
Charleston-Huntington, WV.	501,530	63	WCHS-DT (41); WLPX-TV (39); WOWK-DT (13); WQCW-DT (17); WSAZ-DT (23); WTSF-DT (44); WVAH-DT (19)
Dayton, OH.	482,590	65	WBDT-DT (26); WDTN-DT (50); WHIO-DT (41); WKEF-DT (51); WKOI-DT (39); WRGT-DT (30)
Toledo, OH.	423,100	73	WLMB-DT (5); WNWO-DT (49); WTOL-DT (11); WTVG-DT (13); WUPW-DT (46)
Fort Wayne, IN.	273,860	107	WANE-DT (31); WFFT-DT (36); WINM-DT (12); WISE-DT (19); WPTA-DT (24)
Youngstown, OH.	266,560	110	WFMJ-DT (20); WKBN-DT (41); WYTV-DT (36)
Wheeling, WV-Steubenville, OH.	133,110	159	WTOV-DT (9); WTRF-DT (7)
Lima, OH.	71,380	186	WLIO-DT (8); WTLW-DT (44)
Parkersburg, WV.	64,060	194	WTAP-DT (49)
Zanesville, OH.	32,350	203	WHIZ-DT (40)

Ohio Station Totals as of October 1, 2009

	VHF	UHF	TOTAL
Commercial Television	12	28	40
Educational Television	0	12	12
	12	40	52

WBNX-DT
Ch. 30

Network Service: CW.

Licensee: Winston Broadcasting Network Inc., PO Box 91660, Cleveland, OH 44101.

Studio: 2690 State Rd, Cuyahoga Falls, OH 44223.

Mailing Address: PO Box 91660, Cleveland, OH 44101.

Phone: 440-843-5555. **Fax:** 440-842-5597.

E-mail: akeith@wbnx.com

Web Site: http://www.wbnx.com

Technical Facilities: Channel No. 30 (566-572 MHz). Authorized power: 1000-kw max. visual, aural. Antenna: 1087-ft above av. terrain, 1017-ft. above ground, 1935-ft. above sea level.

Latitude	41°	23'	02"
Longitude	81°	41'	44"

Holds CP for change to 1168-ft above av. terrain, 1099-ft. above ground, 2017-ft. above sea level; BPCDT-20080619AFL.

Note: Latitude and longitude coordinates shown are based on the North American Datum of 1927 (NAD 27) as currently required by the Mass Media Bureau of the FCC.

Ownership: Winston Broadcasting Network Inc. (Group Owner).

Began Operation: April 30, 2007. Began analog operations: December 1, 1985. Ceased analog operations: June 12, 2009.

Represented (legal): Thompson Hine LLP.

Personnel:

Lou Spangler, President & General Manager.

Eddie Brown, General Sales Manager.

Don Richardson, Chief Engineer.

Julie Wertheimer, Public Service Director.

Dave Armstrong, Production Manager.

Patty Armstrong, Research Director.

Howard Keith, Creative Services Director.

Colleen Metheney, Traffic & Billing Manager.

Kerry DiFranco, Events Coordinator.

City of License: Akron. **Station DMA:** Cleveland-Akron (Canton), OH. **Rank:** 18.

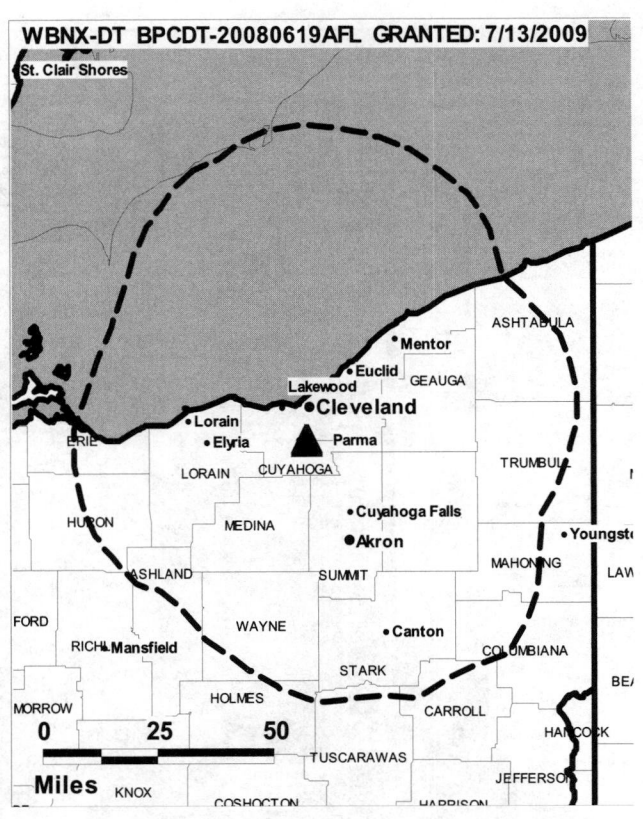

© 2010 Warren Communications News

Circulation © 2009 Nielsen. Coverage based on Nielsen study.

GrandTotal	Cable TV Households	Non-cable TV Households	Total TV Households
Estimated Station Totals *	1,071,360	448,610	1,519,970
Average Weekly Circulation (2009)	320,574	156,354	476,928
Average Daily Circulation (2009)			162,230

Station DMA Total	Cable TV Households	Non-cable TV Households	Total TV Households
Estimated Station Totals *	1,067,420	436,370	1,503,790
Average Weekly Circulation (2009)	319,589	155,418	475,007
Average Daily Circulation (2009)			162,084

Other DMA Total	Cable TV Households	Non-cable TV Households	Total TV Households
Estimated Station Totals *	3,940	12,240	16,180
Average Weekly Circulation (2009)	985	936	1,921
Average Daily Circulation (2009)			146

*Estimated station totals are sums of the Nielsen TV and Cable TV household estimates for each county in which the station registers viewing of more than 5% as per the Nielsen Survey Methods.

WVPX-TV
Ch. 23

Network Service: ION.

Licensee: ION Media Akron License Inc., Debtor in Possession, 601 Clearwater Park Rd, West Palm Beach, FL 33401-6233.

Studio: 1333 Lakeside Ave, Cleveland, OH 44114.

Mailing Address: 1333 Lakeside Ave, Cleveland, OH 44114.

Phone: 330-535-4104; 216-344-7465. **Fax:** 330-535-4835.

E-mail: jamesthomas@ionmedia.com

Web Site: http://www.ionmedia.com

Technical Facilities: Channel No. 23 (524-530 MHz). Authorized power: 317-kw max. visual, aural. Antenna: 971-ft above av. terrain, 925-ft. above ground, 2015-ft. above sea level.

Latitude	41°	03'	53"
Longitude	81°	34'	59"

Holds CP for change to 1000-kw max. visual, 988-ft above av. terrain, 925-ft. above ground, 2015-ft. above sea level; BMPCDT-20080619AEG.

Note: Latitude and longitude coordinates shown are based on the North American Datum of 1927 (NAD 27) as currently required by the Mass Media Bureau of the FCC.

Multichannel TV Sound: Stereo and separate audio program.

Satellite Earth Stations: Transmitter RCA; Comtech, 3-meter; Andrew, 5-meter.

Ownership: ION Media Networks Inc., Debtor in Possession (Group Owner).

Began Operation: June 12, 2009. Station broadcasting digitally on its analog channel allotment. Began analog operations: June 7, 1953. Ceased analog operations: June 12, 2009. Sale to Urban Television LLC pends. Involuntary assignment to debtor in possession status approved by FCC June 5, 2009. Transfer of control by ION Media Networks Inc. from Paxson Management Corp. & Lowell W. Paxson to CIG Media LLC approved by FCC December 31, 2007. Sale to ION Media Networks Inc. (then Paxson Communications Corp.) by ValueVision International approved by FCC December 8, 1995. Sale to ValueVision International by Group One Broadcasting LP approved by FCC in February 15, 1994. Sale to Group One Broadcasting LP by Summit Radio Corp. approved by FCC December 23, 1986. Ceased analog operations: June 12, 2009.

Represented (legal): Dow Lohnes PLLC.

Personnel:

Latonya Pettit, Station Operations Manager.

James Thomas, Chief Engineer.

Amy Sheridan, Traffic Manager.

City of License: Akron. **Station DMA:** Cleveland-Akron (Canton), OH. **Rank:** 18.

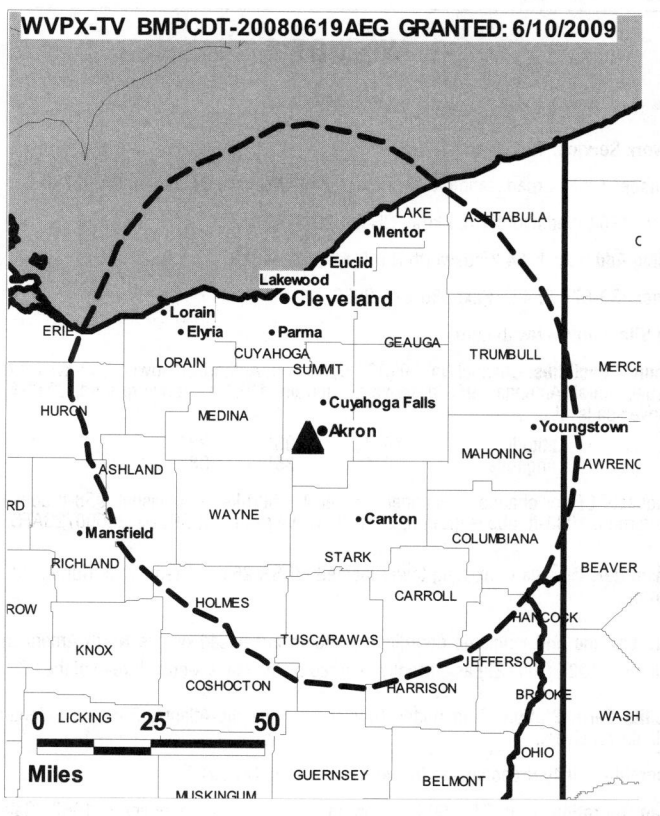

© 2010 Warren Communications News

Circulation © 2009 Nielsen. Coverage based on Nielsen study.

GrandTotal	Cable TV Households	Non-cable TV Households	Total TV Households
Estimated Station Totals *	1,069,780	231,940	1,301,720
Average Weekly Circulation (2009)	108,978	21,716	130,694
Average Daily Circulation (2009)			31,161

Station DMA Total	Cable TV Households	Non-cable TV Households	Total TV Households
Estimated Station Totals *	1,067,420	231,940	1,299,360
Average Weekly Circulation (2009)	108,777	21,716	130,493
Average Daily Circulation (2009)			31,152

Other DMA Total	Cable TV Households	Non-cable TV Households	Total TV Households
Estimated Station Totals *	2,360	0	2,360
Average Weekly Circulation (2009)	201	0	201
Average Daily Circulation (2009)			9

*Estimated station totals are sums of the Nielsen TV and Cable TV household estimates for each county in which the station registers viewing of more than 5% as per the Nielsen Survey Methods.

WDLI-DT
Ch. 39

Network Service: TBN.

Licensee: Trinity Broadcasting Network Inc., 2442 Michelle Dr, Tustin, CA 92780.

Studio: 1764 Wadsworth Rd, Akron, OH 44320-3142.

Mailing Address: 1764 Wadsworth Rd, Akron, OH 44320.

Phone: 330-875-5542. **Fax:** 330-875-9986.

Web Site: http://www.tbn.org

Technical Facilities: Channel No. 39 (320-626 MHz). Authorized power: 200-kw max. visual, aural. Antenna: 958-ft above av. terrain, 1034-ft. above ground, 2011-ft. above sea level.

Latitude	41°	03'	20"
Longitude	81°	35'	38"

Requests CP for change to channel number 49, 900-kw max. visual, 958-ft above av. terrain, 1033-ft. above ground, 2008-ft. above sea level; BPCDT-20090723AFG.

Transmitter: On side of existing tower located off SR 261, 0.68-mi W of Romig Rd., Norton.

Note: Latitude and longitude coordinates shown are based on the North American Datum of 1927 (NAD 27) as currently required by the Mass Media Bureau of the FCC.

Satellite Earth Station: Transmitter Townsend; Scientific-Atlanta, 5-meter; Scientific-Atlanta receivers.

Ownership: Trinity Broadcasting Network Inc. (Group Owner).

Began Operation: April 21, 2003. Began analog operations: January 1, 1967. Sale to present owner by David Livingstone Missionary Foundation Inc. approved by FCC March 5, 1986. Sale to David Livingstone Missionary Foundation Inc. by PTL approved by FCC December 8, 1982. Sale to PTL by Janson Industries approved by FCC August 5, 1977 (Television Digest, Vol. 17:35, 37). Ceased analog operations: June 12, 2009.

Represented (legal): Colby M. May.

Personnel:

Joanne Mann, Station Manager.

Dale K. Osborn, Chief Engineer.

Susan K. Harris, Production Manager.

Aaron Donnelly, Traffic Director.

Carol L. Keefer, Public Affairs Coordinator.

City of License: Canton. **Station DMA:** Cleveland-Akron (Canton), OH. **Rank:** 18.

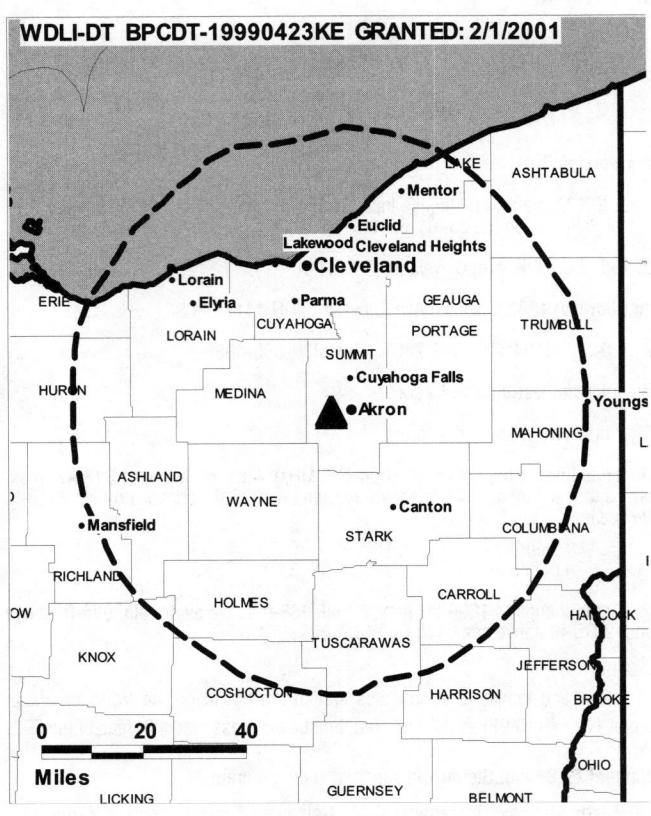

WDLI-DT BPCDT-19990423KE GRANTED: 2/1/2001

© 2010 Warren Communications News

Circulation © 2009 Nielsen. Coverage based on Nielsen study.

GrandTotal	Cable TV Households	Non-cable TV Households	Total TV Households
Estimated Station Totals *	328,780	0	328,780
Average Weekly Circulation (2009)	19,600	0	19,600
Average Daily Circulation (2009)			4,074

Station DMA Total	Cable TV Households	Non-cable TV Households	Total TV Households
Estimated Station Totals *	328,780	0	328,780
Average Weekly Circulation (2009)	19,600	0	19,600
Average Daily Circulation (2009)			4,074

*Estimated station totals are sums of the Nielsen TV and Cable TV household estimates for each county in which the station registers viewing of more than 5% as per the Nielsen Survey Methods.

WRLM
(formerly WOAC)
Ch. 47

Network Service: IND.

Licensee: Radiant Life Ministries Inc., PO Box 1010, Marion, IL 62959-1010.

Studio: 4385 Sherman Rd, Kent, OH 44240.

Mailing Address: 4385 Sherman Rd, Kent, OH 44240.

Phone: 330-677-6760. **Fax:** 330-677-1954.

Technical Facilities: Channel No. 47 (668-674 MHz). Authorized power: 1000-kw max. visual, aural. Antenna: 440-ft above av. terrain, 423-ft. above ground, 1549-ft. above sea level.

Latitude	41°	06'	33"
Longitude	81°	20'	10"

Note: Latitude and longitude coordinates shown are based on the North American Datum of 1927 (NAD 27) as currently required by the Mass Media Bureau of the FCC.

Ownership: Radiant Life Ministries Inc. (Group Owner).

Began Operation: February 22, 2006. Began analog operations: March 1, 1982. Sale to present owner by MTB Cleveland Licensee LLC approved by FCC June 10, 2009. Transfer of control by MTB Cleveland Licensee LLC from Multicultural Television Broadcasting LLC to Multicultural Capital Trust (Lee W. Shubert LC, Trustee) approved by FCC January 14, 2009. Sale to Multicultural Television Broadcasting LLC by The E. W. Scripps Co. approved by FCC November 15, 2006. Transfer to The E. W. Scripps Co. by Summit America Television Inc. approved by FCC February 27, 2004. Shop At Home Inc. became Summit America Television Inc. after The E. W. Scripps Co. acquired 70% interest October 31, 2002. Sale to Shop At Home Inc. by Whitehead Media Inc. approved by FCC January 23, 1998. Proposed sale to Global Broadcasting Systems Inc. dismissed by FCC September 12, 1997. Sale to Whitehead Media Inc. by Canton 67 Ltd. approved by FCC September 6, 1995. Sale to Discovery Broadcasting Systems Inc. by Canton 67 Ltd. approved by FCC June 20, 1985, but not consummated. Ceased analog operations: February 17, 2009.

Represented (legal): Colby M. May.

Personnel:

Glenn Foldessy, General Manager & Chief Engineer.

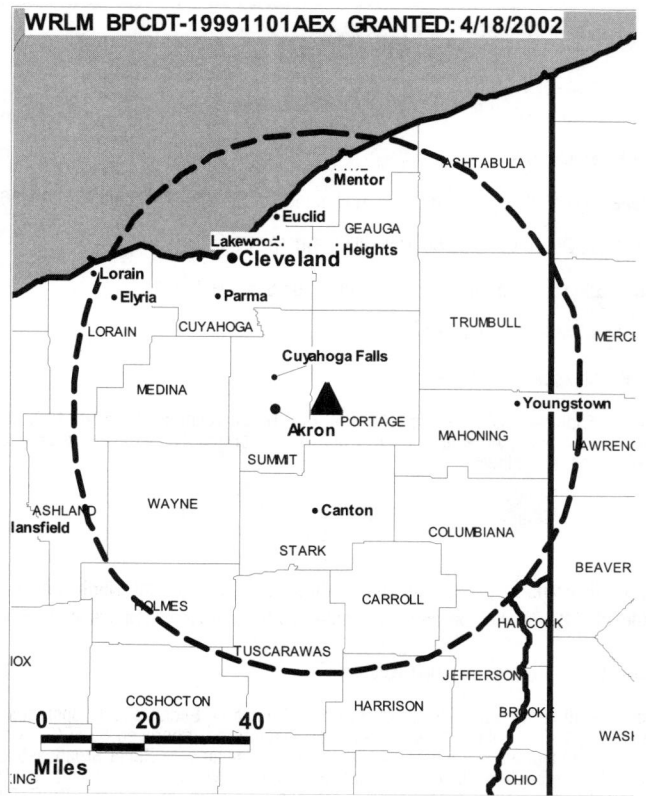

WRLM BPCDT-19991101AEX GRANTED: 4/18/2002

© 2010 Warren Communications News

Josh Rule, Traffic Director.

City of License: Canton. **Station DMA:** Cleveland-Akron (Canton), OH. **Rank:** 18.

Nielsen Data: Not available.

WWHO-DT
Ch. 46

Network Service: CW.

Licensee: WWHO Broadcasting LLC, 4 Richmond Sq, Ste 200, Providence, RI 02906.

Studio: 1160 Dublin Rd, Ste 500, Columbus, OH 43215.

Mailing Address: 1160 Dublin Rd, Ste 500, Columbus, OH 43215.

Phone: 614-485-5300. **Fax:** 614-485-5339.

Web Site: http://www.wwhotv.com/

Technical Facilities: Channel No. 46 (662-668 MHz). Authorized power: 1000-kw max. visual, aural. Antenna: 1076-ft above av. terrain, 1053-ft. above ground, 1824-ft. above sea level.

Latitude	39°	35'	20"
Longitude	83°	06'	44"

Note: Latitude and longitude coordinates shown are based on the North American Datum of 1927 (NAD 27) as currently required by the Mass Media Bureau of the FCC.

Ownership: LIN TV Corp. (Group Owner).

Began Operation: October 25, 2002. Standard Definition. Began analog operations: August 31, 1987. Sale to present owner by Viacom Inc. approved by FCC March 23, 2005. Station was acquired by Viacom Inc. in swap with Outlet Broadcasting. Outlet exercised option and acquired station along with WLWC(TV) New Bedford, MA from Fant Broadcasting, then swapped stations plus cash for Viacom's WVIT(TV) New Britain, CT. FCC approved deal November 6, 1997. Ceased analog operations: February 17, 2009.

Represented (legal): Covington & Burling.

Represented (sales): Katz Media Group.

Personnel:

Ellen Daly, General Manager.

Matt Smith, National Sales Manager.

Angie O'Brien, Local Sales Manager.

Mark Seekins, Chief Engineer.

Lance Carwhile, Programming Director.

Dierdre Conley, Promotion & Creative Services Director.

Lynn Tedrow, Traffic Manager.

City of License: Chillicothe. **Station DMA:** Columbus, OH. **Rank:** 34.

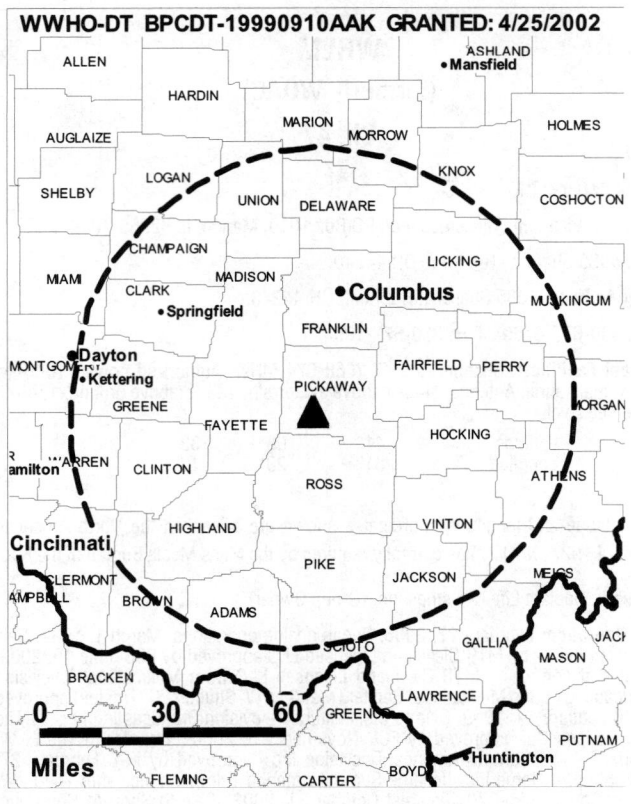

WWHO-DT BPCDT-19990910AAK GRANTED: 4/25/2002

© 2010 Warren Communications News

Circulation © 2009 Nielsen. Coverage based on Nielsen study.

GrandTotal	Cable TV Households	Non-cable TV Households	Total TV Households
Estimated Station Totals *	651,590	304,910	956,500
Average Weekly Circulation (2009)	128,647	56,786	185,433
Average Daily Circulation (2009)			62,754

Station DMA Total	Cable TV Households	Non-cable TV Households	Total TV Households
Estimated Station Totals *	609,140	279,210	888,350
Average Weekly Circulation (2009)	123,904	54,991	178,895
Average Daily Circulation (2009)			60,882

Other DMA Total	Cable TV Households	Non-cable TV Households	Total TV Households
Estimated Station Totals *	42,450	25,700	68,150
Average Weekly Circulation (2009)	4,743	1,795	6,538
Average Daily Circulation (2009)			1,872

*Estimated station totals are sums of the Nielsen TV and Cable TV household estimates for each county in which the station registers viewing of more than 5% as per the Nielsen Survey Methods.

WCPO-DT
Ch. 10

Network Service: ABC.

Licensee: Scripps Howard Broadcasting Co., PO Box 5380, 312 Walnut St, 28th Fl, Cincinnati, OH 45201.

Studio: 1720 Gilbert Ave, Cincinnati, OH 45202.

Mailing Address: 1720 Gilbert Ave, Cincinnati, OH 45202.

Phone: 513-721-9900; 513-852-4047. **Fax:** 513-721-6052.

Web Site: http://www.wcpo.com

Technical Facilities: Channel No. 10 (192-198 MHz). Authorized power: 16.3-kw visual, aural. Antenna: 892-ft above av. terrain, 735-ft. above ground, 1578-ft. above sea level.

Latitude	39°	07'	30"
Longitude	84°	29'	56"

Holds CP for change to 28-kw visual, 1001-ft above av. terrain, 843-ft. above ground, 1686-ft. above sea level; BPCDT-20090723ADV.

Note: Latitude and longitude coordinates shown are based on the North American Datum of 1927 (NAD 27) as currently required by the Mass Media Bureau of the FCC.

Ownership: E. W. Scripps Co. (Group Owner).

Began Operation: December 15, 1998. Standard and High Definition. Began analog operations: July 26, 1949. Ceased analog operations: June 12, 2009.

Represented (sales): HRP: Television Station Representative.

Represented (legal): Baker Hostetler LLP.

Personnel:

William S. Fee, Vice President & General Manager.

Darrell Calloway, General Sales Manager.

Rob Schuck, Local Sales Manager.

Brad Wagner, National Sales Manager.

Bob Morford, News Director.

Debbie Cook, Business Manager.

Sheila Obermeyer, Creative Services & Marketing Director.

Marilyn Stephens, Traffic Manager.

Marquitashua Meachem, Assistant to General Manager.

Mona Morrow, Public Affairs Director.

Nancy Morgan, Administrative Assistant.

City of License: Cincinnati. **Station DMA:** Cincinnati, OH. **Rank:** 33.

WCPO-DT BPCDT-20090723ADV GRANTED: 8/17/2009

© 2010 Warren Communications News

Circulation © 2009 Nielsen. Coverage based on Nielsen study.

GrandTotal	Cable TV Households	Non-cable TV Households	Total TV Households
Estimated Station Totals *	553,080	383,130	936,210
Average Weekly Circulation (2009)	392,130	258,810	650,940
Average Daily Circulation (2009)			342,810

Station DMA Total	Cable TV Households	Non-cable TV Households	Total TV Households
Estimated Station Totals *	533,630	346,500	880,130
Average Weekly Circulation (2009)	386,551	255,844	642,395
Average Daily Circulation (2009)			340,658

Other DMA Total	Cable TV Households	Non-cable TV Households	Total TV Households
Estimated Station Totals *	19,450	36,630	56,080
Average Weekly Circulation (2009)	5,579	2,966	8,545
Average Daily Circulation (2009)			2,152

*Estimated station totals are sums of the Nielsen TV and Cable TV household estimates for each county in which the station registers viewing of more than 5% as per the Nielsen Survey Methods.

WKRC-DT
Ch. 12

Network Service: CW, CBS.

Licensee: Newport Television License LLC, 460 Nichols Rd, Ste 250, Kansas City, MO 64112.

Studio: 1906 Highland Ave, Cincinnati, OH 45219.

Mailing Address: 1906 Highland Ave., Cincinnati, OH 45219.

Phone: 513-763-5500. **Fax:** 513-763-5474.

Web Site: http://www.wkrc.com

Technical Facilities: Channel No. 12 (204-210 MHz). Authorized power: 15.55-kw visual, aural. Antenna: 1001-ft above av. terrain, 942-ft. above ground, 1717-ft. above sea level.

Latitude	39°	06'	59"
Longitude	84°	30'	07"

Transmitter: 1906 Highland Ave.

Note: Latitude and longitude coordinates shown are based on the North American Datum of 1927 (NAD 27) as currently required by the Mass Media Bureau of the FCC.

Ownership: Newport Television LLC (Group Owner).

Began Operation: February 14, 2001. High Definition. Station broadcasting digitally on its analog channel allotment. Began analog operations: April 4, 1949. Sale by Taft TV & Radio approved by FCC October 2, 1987. Sale to Jacor Communications Inc. approved by FCC September 17, 1996. Sale to Clear Channel Communications Inc. from Jacor Communications approved by FCC April 29, 1999. Sale to present owner by Clear Channel Communications Inc. approved by FCC November 29, 2007. Ceased analog operations: June 12, 2009.

Represented (sales): Katz Media Group.

Represented (legal): Covington & Burling.

Represented (engineering): Cohen Dippell & Everist PC.

Personnel:

Steve Minium, Interim General Manager.

Jim Connell, National Sales Manager.

Elbert Tucker, News Director.

Hank Hundemer, Chief Engineer.

Rob Vertrees, Business Manager.

Rick Wagar, Program & Production Manager.

Melissa Benoit, Research & Marketing Director.

Jennifer Bucheit, Marketing & Creative Services Director.

Darrin McCullah, Traffic Manager.

City of License: Cincinnati. **Station DMA:** Cincinnati, OH. **Rank:** 33.

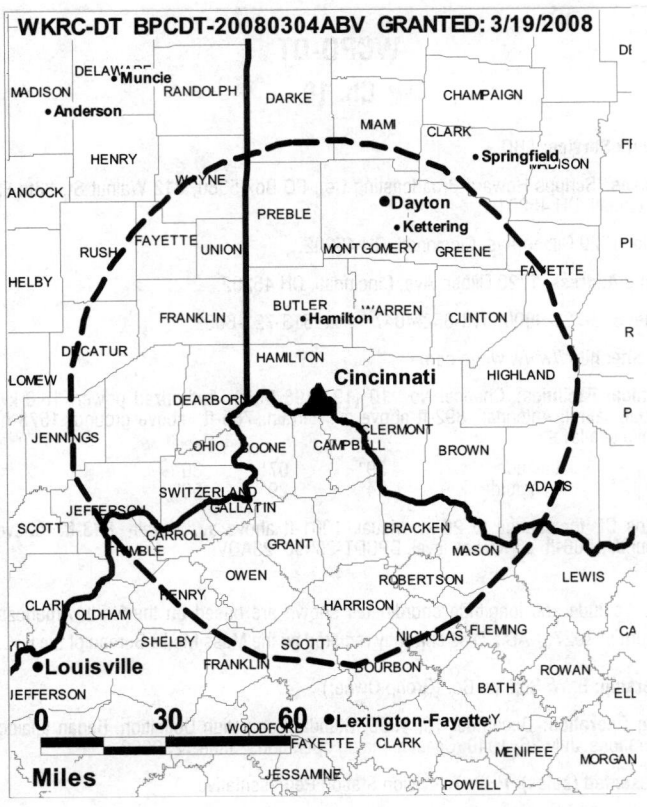

WKRC-DT BPCDT-20080304ABV GRANTED: 3/19/2008

© 2010 Warren Communications News

Circulation © 2009 Nielsen. Coverage based on Nielsen study.

GrandTotal	Cable TV Households	Non-cable TV Households	Total TV Households
Estimated Station Totals *	743,970	364,740	1,108,710
Average Weekly Circulation (2009)	395,167	252,381	647,548
Average Daily Circulation (2009)			314,117

Station DMA Total	Cable TV Households	Non-cable TV Households	Total TV Households
Estimated Station Totals *	533,630	346,500	880,130
Average Weekly Circulation (2009)	366,241	250,931	617,172
Average Daily Circulation (2009)			307,540

Other DMA Total	Cable TV Households	Non-cable TV Households	Total TV Households
Estimated Station Totals *	210,340	18,240	228,580
Average Weekly Circulation (2009)	28,926	1,450	30,376
Average Daily Circulation (2009)			6,577

*Estimated station totals are sums of the Nielsen TV and Cable TV household estimates for each county in which the station registers viewing of more than 5% as per the Nielsen Survey Methods.

WLWT-DT
Ch. 35

Network Service: NBC.

Licensee: Ohio/Oklahoma Hearst-Argyle Television Inc., PO Box 1800, c/o Brooks, Pierce et al., Raleigh, NC 27602.

Studio: 1700 Young St, Cincinnati, OH 45202.

Mailing Address: 1700 Young St, Cincinnati, OH 45202.

Phone: 513-412-5000. **Fax:** 513-412-6121.

Web Site: http://www.wlwt.com

Technical Facilities: Channel No. 35 (596-602 MHz). Authorized power: 1000-kw max. visual, aural. Antenna: 1019-ft above av. terrain, 868-ft. above ground, 1706-ft. above sea level.

Latitude	39°	07'	27"
Longitude	84°	31'	18"

Transmitter: 2222 Chicksaw St.

Note: Latitude and longitude coordinates shown are based on the North American Datum of 1927 (NAD 27) as currently required by the Mass Media Bureau of the FCC.

Ownership: Hearst-Argyle Television Inc. (Group Owner).

Began Operation: February 1, 1998. Began analog operations: February 9, 1948. Sale to Multimedia by Avco Broadcasting Corp. approved by FCC January 16, 1976. Sale to Gannett by Multimedia approved by FCC November 30, 1995. Trade with Gannett-owned KOCO-TV Oklahoma City, OK to Argyle Television Inc. for WGRZ-TV Buffalo, NY & WZZM-TV Grand Rapids, MI approved by FCC January 27, 1997. Argyle merger with Hearst Corp. to form present owner approved by FCC June 2, 1997. Hearst-Argyle received approval from the FCC May 26, 2009 to become privately owned by The Hearst Corp. Ceased analog operations: June 12, 2009.

Represented (legal): Brooks, Pierce, McLendon, Humphrey & Leonard LLP.

Represented (sales): Eagle Television Sales.

Represented (engineering): Cavell, Mertz & Associates Inc.

Personnel:

Richard J. Dyer, President & General Manager.

Mark DiAngelo, General Sales Manager.

Randy Grossert, Local Sales Manager.

Trey Dolle, National Sales Manager.

Brennan Donnellan, News Director.

Paul Nowakowski, Chief Engineer.

Tracy Ahlers, Controller.

Lisa Snell, Programming & Human Resources Manager.

Matt Lewis, Promotion & Creative Services Director.

City of License: Cincinnati. **Station DMA:** Cincinnati, OH. **Rank:** 33.

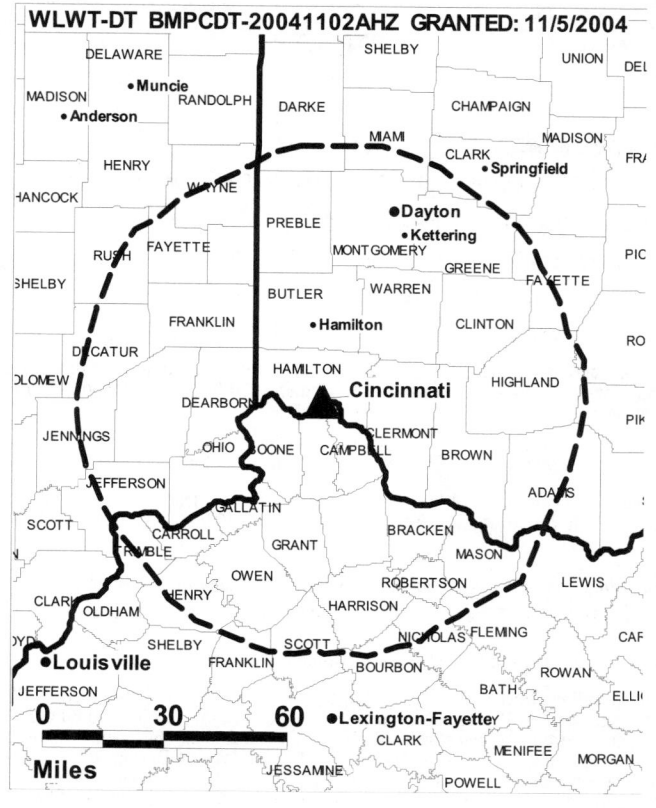

© 2010 Warren Communications News

Circulation © 2009 Nielsen. Coverage based on Nielsen study.

GrandTotal	Cable TV Households	Non-cable TV Households	Total TV Households
Estimated Station Totals *	591,720	378,710	970,430
Average Weekly Circulation (2009)	355,848	233,367	589,215
Average Daily Circulation (2009)			261,590

Station DMA Total	Cable TV Households	Non-cable TV Households	Total TV Households
Estimated Station Totals *	533,630	346,500	880,130
Average Weekly Circulation (2009)	342,789	230,647	573,436
Average Daily Circulation (2009)			257,280

Other DMA Total	Cable TV Households	Non-cable TV Households	Total TV Households
Estimated Station Totals *	58,090	32,210	90,300
Average Weekly Circulation (2009)	13,059	2,720	15,779
Average Daily Circulation (2009)			4,310

*Estimated station totals are sums of the Nielsen TV and Cable TV household estimates for each county in which the station registers viewing of more than 5% as per the Nielsen Survey Methods.

WSTR-DT
Ch. 33

Network Service: MNT.

Grantee: WSTR Licensee Inc., 10706 Beaver Dam Rd, Cockeysville, MD 21030.

Studio: 5177 Fishwick Dr, Cincinnati, OH 45216.

Mailing Address: 5177 Fishwick Dr, Cincinnati, OH 45216.

Phone: 513-641-4400. **Fax:** 513-242-2633.

Web Site: http://www.my64.tv

Technical Facilities: Channel No. 33 (584-590 MHz). Authorized power: 900-kw max. visual, aural. Antenna: 993-ft above av. terrain, 820-ft. above ground, 1720-ft. above sea level.

Latitude	39°	12'	01"
Longitude	84°	31'	22"

Requests modification of CP for change to 360-kw max. visual, 1106-ft above av. terrain, 932-ft. above ground, 1827-ft. above sea level; BMPCDT-20080620AHH.

Note: Latitude and longitude coordinates shown are based on the North American Datum of 1927 (NAD 27) as currently required by the Mass Media Bureau of the FCC.

Ownership: Sinclair Broadcast Group Inc. (Group Owner).

Began Operation: November 6, 2002. Began analog operations: January 28, 1980. Began subscription TV operation February 1, 1980. Sale to HEN Inc. by Buford TV Inc. approved by FCC December 28, 1982. Sale to Channel 64 Joint Venture by HEN Inc. approved by FCC November 14, 1984 (Television Digest, Vol. 24:25). Discontinued subscription TV operation January 1985. Sale to Channel 64 Acquisition Inc. approved by FCC February 9, 1988. Sale to ABRY Communications by Channel 64 Acquisition Inc. approved by FCC September 22, 1989. Sale to present owner by ABRY Communications approved by FCC July 8, 1996. Ceased analog operations: February 17, 2009.

Represented (sales): Katz Media Group.

Personnel:

Jon Lawhead, General Manager.

Terry Roberts, Chief Engineer.

Mark Ramey, Promotion Director.

City of License: Cincinnati. **Station DMA:** Cincinnati, OH. **Rank:** 33.

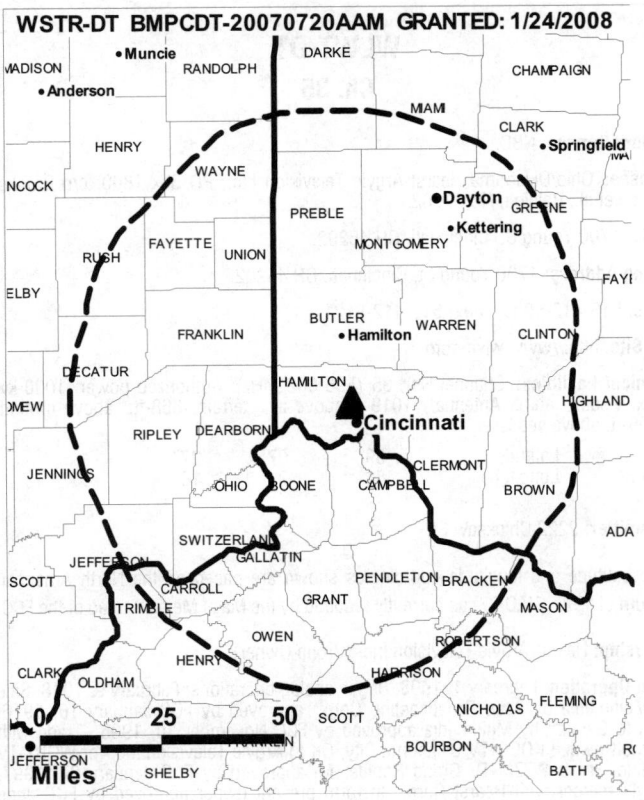

WSTR-DT BMPCDT-20070720AAM GRANTED: 1/24/2008

© 2010 Warren Communications News

Circulation © 2009 Nielsen. Coverage based on Nielsen study.

GrandTotal	Cable TV Households	Non-cable TV Households	Total TV Households
Estimated Station Totals *	534,260	353,900	888,160
Average Weekly Circulation (2009)	108,497	82,160	190,657
Average Daily Circulation (2009)			69,962

Station DMA Total	Cable TV Households	Non-cable TV Households	Total TV Households
Estimated Station Totals *	530,570	346,500	877,070
Average Weekly Circulation (2009)	107,991	81,783	189,774
Average Daily Circulation (2009)			69,862

Other DMA Total	Cable TV Households	Non-cable TV Households	Total TV Households
Estimated Station Totals *	3,690	7,400	11,090
Average Weekly Circulation (2009)	506	377	883
Average Daily Circulation (2009)			100

*Estimated station totals are sums of the Nielsen TV and Cable TV household estimates for each county in which the station registers viewing of more than 5% as per the Nielsen Survey Methods.

WEWS-DT
Ch. 15

Network Service: ABC.

Licensee: Scripps Howard Broadcasting Co., PO Box 5380, 312 Walnut St, 28th Fl, Cincinnati, OH 45201.

Studio: 1717 E 12th St, Cleveland, OH 44115.

Mailing Address: 3001 Euclid Ave, Cleveland, OH 44115.

Phone: 216-431-5555. **Fax:** 216-361-1762.

Web Site: http://www.newsnet5.com

Technical Facilities: Channel No. 15 (476-482 MHz). Authorized power: 870-kw max. visual, aural. Antenna: 935-ft above av. terrain, 719-ft. above ground, 1814-ft. above sea level.

| Latitude | 41° | 22' | 26" |
| Longitude | 81° | 43' | 04" |

Holds CP for change to 1000-kw max. visual, 1017-ft above av. terrain, 801-ft. above ground, 1897-ft. above sea level; BMPCDT-20080620AGC.

Transmitter: 7080 State Rd., Parma.

Note: Latitude and longitude coordinates shown are based on the North American Datum of 1927 (NAD 27) as currently required by the Mass Media Bureau of the FCC.

Ownership: E. W. Scripps Co. (Group Owner).

Began Operation: September 13, 1999. Began analog operations: December 17, 1947. Ceased analog operations: June 12, 2009.

Represented (sales): Eagle Television Sales.

Represented (legal): Baker Hostetler LLP.

Personnel:

Victoria Gedrys Regan, Vice President & General Manager.

Jim Rini, General Sales Manager.

Joe Fishleigh, Local Sales Manager.

Jim Scott, Acting News Director.

Berry Pinney, Engineering Director.

Mary Reed, Business Manager.

Gary A. Stark, Program & Research Director.

Peter Noll, Marketing Director.

Al McQueen, Commercial Production Director.

Dan Coyle, Creative Services Director.

Paul Crow, Traffic Manager.

Moreen Bailey-Frater, Community Affairs Director.

Ryan Donchess, Operations Manager.

Mike Sulzman, Assistant Engineering Director.

WEWS-DT BMPCDT-20080620AGC GRANTED: 11/12/2008

© 2010 Warren Communications News

City of License: Cleveland. **Station DMA:** Cleveland-Akron (Canton), OH. **Rank:** 18.

Circulation © 2009 Nielsen. Coverage based on Nielsen study.

GrandTotal	Cable TV Households	Non-cable TV Households	Total TV Households
Estimated Station Totals *	1,221,660	502,310	1,723,970
Average Weekly Circulation (2009)	804,598	321,607	1,126,205
Average Daily Circulation (2009)			552,174

Station DMA Total	Cable TV Households	Non-cable TV Households	Total TV Households
Estimated Station Totals *	1,067,420	436,370	1,503,790
Average Weekly Circulation (2009)	769,694	316,616	1,086,310
Average Daily Circulation (2009)			539,857

Other DMA Total	Cable TV Households	Non-cable TV Households	Total TV Households
Estimated Station Totals *	154,240	65,940	220,180
Average Weekly Circulation (2009)	34,904	4,991	39,895
Average Daily Circulation (2009)			12,317

*Estimated station totals are sums of the Nielsen TV and Cable TV household estimates for each county in which the station registers viewing of more than 5% as per the Nielsen Survey Methods.

WJW-DT
Ch. 8

Network Service: FOX.

Licensee: Community Television of Ohio License LLC, 1717 Dixie Hwy, Ste 650, Fort Wright, KY 41011.

Studio: 5800 S Marginal Rd, Cleveland, OH 44103.

Mailing Address: 5800 S. Marginal Rd, Cleveland, OH 44103.

Phone: 216-431-8888. **Fax:** 216-432-4282.

Web Site: http://www.fox8cleveland.com

Technical Facilities: Channel No. 8 (180-186 MHz). Authorized power: 30-kw visual, aural. Antenna: 1122-ft above av. terrain, 837-ft. above ground, 1998-ft. above sea level.

Latitude	41°	21'	48"
Longitude	81°	42'	58"

Note: Latitude and longitude coordinates shown are based on the North American Datum of 1927 (NAD 27) as currently required by the Mass Media Bureau of the FCC.

Ownership: Local TV Holdings LLC (Group Owner).

Began Operation: October 1, 1999. High Definition. Station broadcasting digitally on its analog channel allotment. Began analog operations: December 17, 1949. Sale to Storer Communications by Empire Coil Co. Inc. (Herbert Mayer) approved by FCC October 27, 1954. Sale to SCI Television Inc. by Storer Communications approved by FCC August 20, 1987. Transfer to Clifford E. Eley, Trustee approved by FCC September 1, 1992. Transfer to New World Communications Group approved by FCC April 13, 1993. Transfer to Fox Television Stations Inc. by New World Communications Group approved by FCC November 7, 1996. Sale to present owner by Fox Television Stations Inc. approved by FCC June 9, 2008. Ceased analog operations: June 12, 2009.

Represented (legal): Dow Lohnes PLLC.

Personnel:

Greg Easterly, Vice President & General Manager.

Tom Creter, Vice President, Engineering.

Susan Pace, Vice President, Finance.

Kevin Salyer, Vice President, Programming & Promotion.

Paul Perozeni, General Sales Manager.

Barb Toth, Local Sales Manager.

Paul Bodamer, National Sales Manager.

Sonya Thompson, News Director.

Janice Nimergutt, Traffic Manager.

Elzoria Smith, Human Resources Manager.

City of License: Cleveland. **Station DMA:** Cleveland-Akron (Canton), OH. **Rank:** 18.

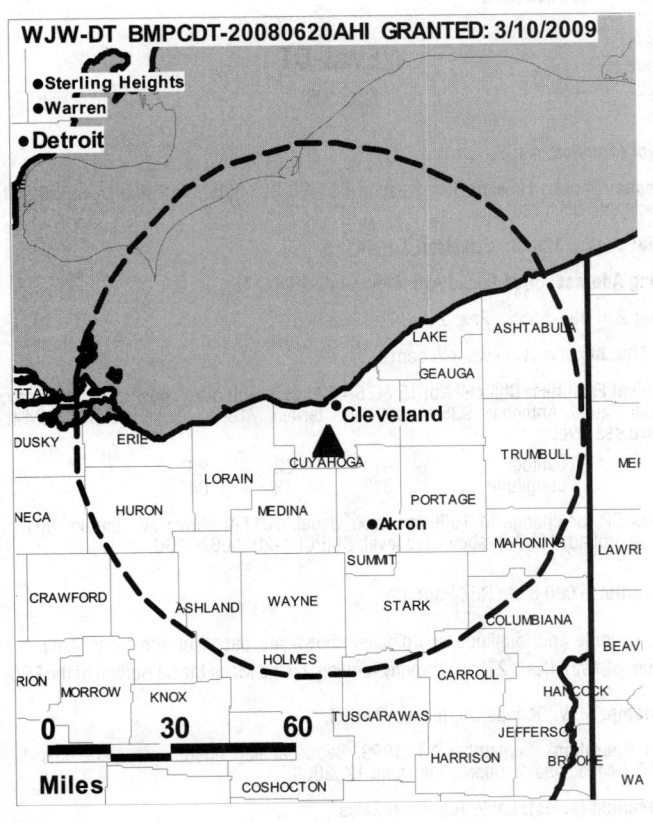

© 2010 Warren Communications News

Circulation © 2009 Nielsen. Coverage based on Nielsen study.

GrandTotal	Cable TV Households	Non-cable TV Households	Total TV Households
Estimated Station Totals *	1,194,520	494,130	1,688,650
Average Weekly Circulation (2009)	816,663	337,513	1,154,176
Average Daily Circulation (2009)			556,417

Station DMA Total	Cable TV Households	Non-cable TV Households	Total TV Households
Estimated Station Totals *	1,067,420	436,370	1,503,790
Average Weekly Circulation (2009)	778,955	331,255	1,110,210
Average Daily Circulation (2009)			542,115

Other DMA Total	Cable TV Households	Non-cable TV Households	Total TV Households
Estimated Station Totals *	127,100	57,760	184,860
Average Weekly Circulation (2009)	37,708	6,258	43,966
Average Daily Circulation (2009)			14,302

*Estimated station totals are sums of the Nielsen TV and Cable TV household estimates for each county in which the station registers viewing of more than 5% as per the Nielsen Survey Methods.

WKYC
Ch. 2

Network Service: NBC.

Licensee: WKYC Holdings Inc., 7950 Jones Branch Dr, c/o Gannett Co., McLean, VA 22102.

Studio: 1333 Lakeside Ave, Cleveland, OH 44114.

Mailing Address: 1333 Lakeside Ave, Cleveland, OH 44114.

Phone: 216-344-3333. **Fax:** 216-344-3314.

Web Site: http://www.wkyc.com

Technical Facilities: Channel No. 2 (54-60 MHz). Authorized power: 8-kw visual, aural. Antenna: 971-ft above av. terrain, 824-ft. above ground, 1864-ft. above sea level.

Latitude	41°	23'	10"
Longitude	81°	41'	21"

Holds CP for change to channel number 17, 868-kw max. visual, 1008-ft above av. terrain, 861-ft. above ground, 1901-ft. above sea level; BPCDT-20080402ACS.

Transmitter: 6600 Broadview Rd., Parma.

Note: Latitude and longitude coordinates shown are based on the North American Datum of 1927 (NAD 27) as currently required by the Mass Media Bureau of the FCC.

Ownership: Gannett Co. Inc. (Group Owner).

Began Operation: June 15, 1999. High Definition. Began analog operations: October 31, 1948. Outlet was originally NBC owned-&-operated. Transfer to Westinghouse approved by FCC December 21, 1955 effective January 15, 1956 (Television Digest, Vol. 11:21; 12:3). Transfered from Westinghouse back to NBC under order by FCC February 17, 1965 (Vol. 5:7, 8, 25). Transfer of control from NBC to Multimedia Inc. approved by FCC December 24, 1990 (Vol. 30:12, 53). Transfer of control from Multimedia to Gannett November 30, 1995 (Vol. 35:25, 31). Ceased analog operations: June 12, 2009.

Represented (sales): Blair Television.

Represented (engineering): Cohen Dippell & Everist PC.

Personnel:

Brooke Spectorsky, President & General Manager.

Ann Ruhlin, Operations Manager.

Dana Nagel, Local Sales Manager.

Jill Slavens, National Sales Manager.

Rita Andolsen, Vice President, News.

Mike Szabo, Chief Engineer.

Larry Giele, Chief Financial Officer.

Terry Moir, Program Director.

Micki Burnes, Marketing & Promotion Director.

Debbie Pfister, Traffic Manager.

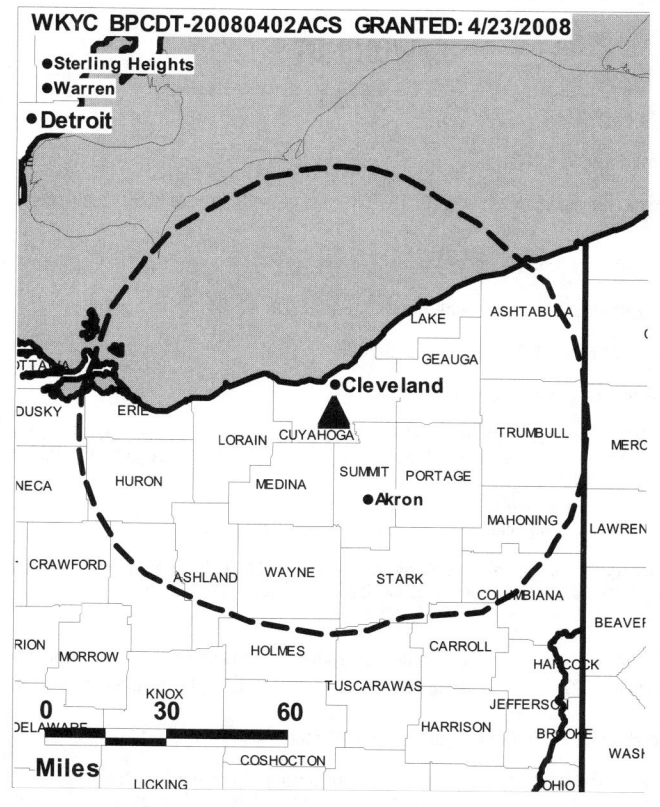

© 2010 Warren Communications News

City of License: Cleveland. **Station DMA:** Cleveland-Akron (Canton), OH. **Rank:** 18.

Circulation © 2009 Nielsen. Coverage based on Nielsen study.

GrandTotal	Cable TV Households	Non-cable TV Households	Total TV Households
Estimated Station Totals *	1,159,210	494,130	1,653,340
Average Weekly Circulation (2009)	813,779	309,134	1,122,913
Average Daily Circulation (2009)			551,191

Station DMA Total	Cable TV Households	Non-cable TV Households	Total TV Households
Estimated Station Totals *	1,067,420	436,370	1,503,790
Average Weekly Circulation (2009)	793,609	304,403	1,098,012
Average Daily Circulation (2009)			544,321

Other DMA Total	Cable TV Households	Non-cable TV Households	Total TV Households
Estimated Station Totals *	91,790	57,760	149,550
Average Weekly Circulation (2009)	20,170	4,731	24,901
Average Daily Circulation (2009)			6,870

*Estimated station totals are sums of the Nielsen TV and Cable TV household estimates for each county in which the station registers viewing of more than 5% as per the Nielsen Survey Methods.

WQHS-DT
Ch. 34

Network Service: UNV.

Licensee: Univision Cleveland LLC, 1999 Avenue of the Stars, Ste 3050, Los Angeles, CA 90067.

Studio: 2861 W Ridgewood Dr, Parma, OH 44134.

Mailing Address: 2861 W. Ridgewood Dr, Parma, OH 44134.

Phone: 440-888-0061. **Fax:** 440-888-7023.

Web Site: http://www.univision.net

Technical Facilities: Channel No. 34 (590-596 MHz). Authorized power: 525-kw max. visual, aural. Antenna: 1095-ft above av. terrain, 913-ft. above ground, 1932-ft. above sea level.

| Latitude | 41° | 22' | 58" |
| Longitude | 81° | 42' | 07" |

Requests CP for change to 690-kw max. visual, 1186-ft above av. terrain, 1004-ft. above ground, 2023-ft. above sea level; BPCDT-20090629ACU.

Note: Latitude and longitude coordinates shown are based on the North American Datum of 1927 (NAD 27) as currently required by the Mass Media Bureau of the FCC.

Ownership: Univision Communications Inc. (Group Owner).

Began Operation: October 27, 2003. Began analog operations: January 13, 1981. Transfer of control to Broadcasting Media Partners Inc. approved by FCC March 27, 2007. Sale to present owner by USA Broadcasting approved by FCC May 21, 2001. Sale to USA Broadcasting by Channel Communications approved by FCC November 6, 1986. Sale to Channel Communications Inc. by Cleveland Associates Co. approved by FCC July 26, 1984. Sale to Cleveland Associates approved by FCC November 26, 1980. Ceased analog operations: June 12, 2009.

Represented (legal): Covington & Burling.

Personnel:

Rolo Duartes, General Manager.

Jose Godur, Sales Manager.

David E. Smith, Chief Engineer.

Bud Bush, Traffic Manager & Assistant Chief Engineer.

City of License: Cleveland. **Station DMA:** Cleveland-Akron (Canton), OH. **Rank:** 18.

© 2010 Warren Communications News

Circulation © 2009 Nielsen. Coverage based on Nielsen study.

GrandTotal	Cable TV Households	Non-cable TV Households	Total TV Households
Estimated Station Totals *	38,750	34,800	73,550
Average Weekly Circulation (2009)	2,402	1,929	4,331
Average Daily Circulation (2009)			1,346

Station DMA Total	Cable TV Households	Non-cable TV Households	Total TV Households
Estimated Station Totals *	38,750	34,800	73,550
Average Weekly Circulation (2009)	2,402	1,929	4,331
Average Daily Circulation (2009)			1,346

*Estimated station totals are sums of the Nielsen TV and Cable TV household estimates for each county in which the station registers viewing of more than 5% as per the Nielsen Survey Methods.

WBNS-DT
Ch. 21

Network Service: CBS.

Licensee: WBNS-TV Inc., 770 Twin Rivers Dr., Columbus, OH 43215.

Studio: 770 Twin Rivers Dr, Columbus, OH 43215.

Mailing Address: PO Box 1010, Columbus, OH 43216.

Phone: 614-460-3700. **Fax:** 614-460-3789.

Web Site: http://www.10tv.com

Technical Facilities: Channel No. 21 (512-518 MHz). Authorized power: 1000-kw max. visual, aural, 915-ft. above ground, 997-ft. above sea level.

	Latitude	39°	58'	16"
	Longitude	83°	01'	40"

Requests CP for change to 1700-kw max. visual, 915-ft above av. terrain, 999-ft. above ground, 1719-ft. above sea level; BPCDT-20080620ANA.

Transmitter: 770 Twin Rivers Dr.

Note: Latitude and longitude coordinates shown are based on the North American Datum of 1927 (NAD 27) as currently required by the Mass Media Bureau of the FCC.

Ownership: Dispatch Broadcast Group (Group Owner).

Began Operation: September 5, 1998. High Definition. Began analog operations: October 5, 1949. Ceased analog operations: June 12, 2009.

Represented (sales): Katz Media Group.

Represented (legal): Sidley Austin LLP.

Represented (engineering): Cohen Dippell & Everist PC.

Personnel:

Thomas Griesdorn, Vice President & General Manager.

Frank Willson, Operations Director.

Mike Berry, Broadcast Operations Manager.

Chuck DeVendra, Sales Director.

Jon Myers, Local Sales Manager.

Pat Wise, National Sales Manager.

Paul Ballinger, Local Sales Manager.

Butch Moore, Sports Sales Manager.

John Cardenas, News Director.

Angela Pace, Community Affairs Director.

Pat Ingram, Engineering Director.

Patty Williams, Business Manager.

Beth Johnson, Program Coordinator.

Doug Jones, On-Air Promotions Manager.

Tim Londergan, Research Director.

WBNS-DT BPCDT-20000425AAZ GRANTED: 6/4/2001

© 2010 Warren Communications News

Christopher Brown, Creative Services Director.

Carol Triplett, Traffic Manager.

City of License: Columbus. **Station DMA:** Columbus, OH. **Rank:** 34.

Circulation © 2009 Nielsen. Coverage based on Nielsen study.

GrandTotal	Cable TV Households	Non-cable TV Households	Total TV Households
Estimated Station Totals *	944,320	391,610	1,335,930
Average Weekly Circulation (2009)	561,790	223,262	785,052
Average Daily Circulation (2009)			410,049

Station DMA Total	Cable TV Households	Non-cable TV Households	Total TV Households
Estimated Station Totals *	613,080	279,210	892,290
Average Weekly Circulation (2009)	452,754	209,049	661,803
Average Daily Circulation (2009)			359,617

Other DMA Total	Cable TV Households	Non-cable TV Households	Total TV Households
Estimated Station Totals *	331,240	112,400	443,640
Average Weekly Circulation (2009)	109,036	14,213	123,249
Average Daily Circulation (2009)			50,432

*Estimated station totals are sums of the Nielsen TV and Cable TV household estimates for each county in which the station registers viewing of more than 5% as per the Nielsen Survey Methods.

WCMH-DT
Ch. 14

Network Service: NBC.

Licensee: Media General Communications Holdings LLC, 333 E Franklin St, Richmond, VA 23219.

Studio: 3165 Olentangy River Rd, Columbus, OH 43202.

Mailing Address: PO Box 4, Columbus, OH 43216.

Phone: 614-263-4444. **Fax:** 614-447-9107.

Web Site: http://www.nbc4i.com

Technical Facilities: Channel No. 14 (470-476 MHz). Authorized power: 902-kw max. visual, aural. Antenna: 866-ft above av. terrain, 941-ft. above ground, 1661-ft. above sea level.

Latitude	39°	58'	16"
Longitude	83°	01'	40"

Note: Latitude and longitude coordinates shown are based on the North American Datum of 1927 (NAD 27) as currently required by the Mass Media Bureau of the FCC.

Ownership: Media General Inc. (Group Owner).

Began Operation: July 28, 2006. Standard Definition. Began analog operations: April 3, 1949. Sale to The Outlet Co. by Avco Broadcasting Corp. approved by FCC December 22, 1975. Sale to Rockefiler Group Inc. by The Outlet Co. approved by FCC November 23, 1983. Sale to Seward Acquisition Corp. (Outlet Communications Inc.) by Rockefeller Group Inc. approved by FCC April 29, 1986. Sale to NBC Inc. by The Outlet Co. approved by FCC November 13, 1995. Sale to present owner by NBC Universal approved by FCC May 23, 2006. Ceased analog operations: June 12, 2009.

Represented (legal): Dow Lohnes PLLC.

Personnel:

Dan Bradley, General Manager.

Michael W. Cash, Vice President, Sales.

Stan Sanders, Vice President, News.

Janna Buckey, Vice President, Creative Services.

Ken Lubker, Local Sales Manager.

Julee Clark, National Sales Manager.

Debra Grivois, Engineering & Operations Director.

Eric Ongaro, Finance Director.

Jean Nemeti, Programming & Community Relations Director.

Dana Pearson, Marketing Services Manager.

Robin Reichard, Traffic Manager.

Reema Karmi, Human Resources Director.

Traci Hogue, General Manager, Interactive Media, nbc41.com.

WCMH-DT BPCDT-19991101ADH GRANTED: 6/7/2000

© 2010 Warren Communications News

City of License: Columbus. **Station DMA:** Columbus, OH. **Rank:** 34.

Circulation © 2009 Nielsen. Coverage based on Nielsen study.

GrandTotal	Cable TV Households	Non-cable TV Households	Total TV Households
Estimated Station Totals *	790,810	319,650	1,110,460
Average Weekly Circulation (2009)	454,496	194,200	648,696
Average Daily Circulation (2009)			318,386

Station DMA Total	Cable TV Households	Non-cable TV Households	Total TV Households
Estimated Station Totals *	613,080	279,210	892,290
Average Weekly Circulation (2009)	408,689	188,746	597,435
Average Daily Circulation (2009)			298,321

Other DMA Total	Cable TV Households	Non-cable TV Households	Total TV Households
Estimated Station Totals *	177,730	40,440	218,170
Average Weekly Circulation (2009)	45,807	5,454	51,261
Average Daily Circulation (2009)			20,065

*Estimated station totals are sums of the Nielsen TV and Cable TV household estimates for each county in which the station registers viewing of more than 5% as per the Nielsen Survey Methods.

WSYX-DT
Ch. 13

Network Service: MNT, ABC.

Licensee: WSYX Licensee Corp., 10706 Beaver Dam Rd, Cockeysville, MD 21030.

Studio: 1261 Dublin Rd, Columbus, OH 43215.

Mailing Address: 1261 Dublin Rd, Columbus, OH 43215.

Phone: 614-481-6666. **Fax:** 614-481-6624.

Web Site: http://www.wsyx6.com

Technical Facilities: Channel No. 13 (210-216 MHz). Authorized power: 59-kw visual, aural. Antenna: 938-ft above av. terrain, 1001-ft. above ground, 1716-ft. above sea level.

Latitude	39°	56'	14"
Longitude	83°	01'	16"

Note: Latitude and longitude coordinates shown are based on the North American Datum of 1927 (NAD 27) as currently required by the Mass Media Bureau of the FCC.

Ownership: Sinclair Broadcast Group Inc. (Group Owner).

Began Operation: October 21, 2002. Began analog operations: September 29, 1949. Sale to Taft Broadcasting by Picture Waves Inc. approved by FCC February 25, 1953 (Television Digest, Vol. 9:9). Sale to Anchor Media Holdings Ltd. approved by FCC December 3, 1987. Transfer of control to Continental Broadcasting Ltd. approved by FCC June 30, 1993. Sale to Better Communications Inc. approved by FCC July 29, 1994 (Vol. 34:20). Sale to present owner from Better Communications approved by FCC July 23, 1993 (Vol. 38:16, 30). Ceased analog operations: June 12, 2009.

Represented (sales): Katz Media Group.

Personnel:

Dan Mellon, General Manager & Station Manager.

Dan Carpenter, Engineering & Operations Director.

Tony D'Angelo, Sales Director.

Lorie Luthman, General Sales Manager.

Jimmy Grilli, Local Sales Director.

Mike Jenkins, National Sales Manager.

Lyn Tolan, News Director.

Pat Richter, Business Affairs Director.

Rick White, Programming Coordinator.

Mike Hansen, Promotion & Marketing Director.

Stephanie Springfedt, Production Manager.

Harshita Patel, Research Director.

Linda Seiler, Traffic Manager.

City of License: Columbus. **Station DMA:** Columbus, OH. **Rank:** 34.

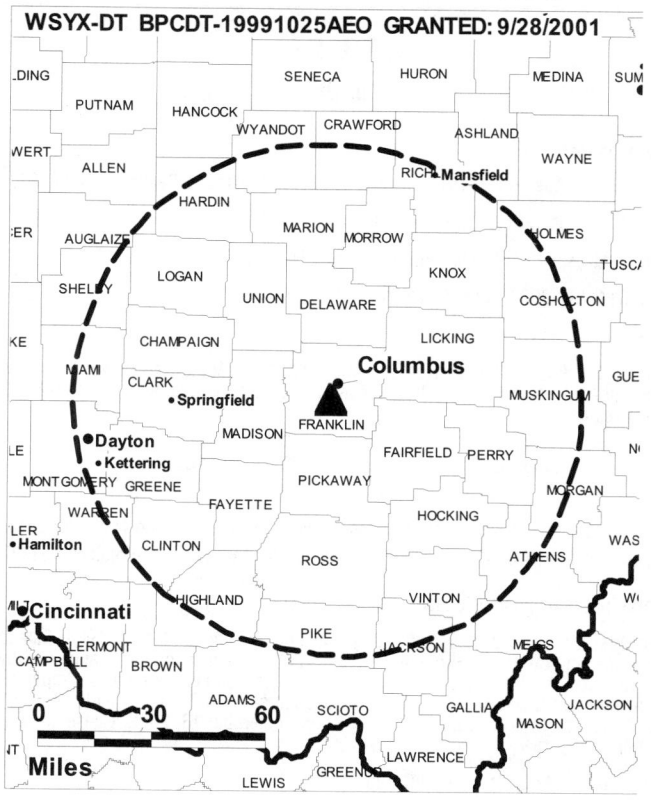

WSYX-DT BPCDT-19991025AEO GRANTED: 9/28/2001

© 2010 Warren Communications News

Circulation © 2009 Nielsen. Coverage based on Nielsen study.

GrandTotal	Cable TV Households	Non-cable TV Households	Total TV Households
Estimated Station Totals *	834,570	327,110	1,161,680
Average Weekly Circulation (2009)	448,940	183,119	632,059
Average Daily Circulation (2009)			256,055

Station DMA Total	Cable TV Households	Non-cable TV Households	Total TV Households
Estimated Station Totals *	613,080	279,210	892,290
Average Weekly Circulation (2009)	383,829	174,833	558,662
Average Daily Circulation (2009)			232,766

Other DMA Total	Cable TV Households	Non-cable TV Households	Total TV Households
Estimated Station Totals *	221,490	47,900	269,390
Average Weekly Circulation (2009)	65,111	8,286	73,397
Average Daily Circulation (2009)			23,289

*Estimated station totals are sums of the Nielsen TV and Cable TV household estimates for each county in which the station registers viewing of more than 5% as per the Nielsen Survey Methods.

WTTE-DT
Ch. 36

Network Service: FOX.

Grantee: Columbus (WTTE-TV) Licensee Inc., 2000 W. 41st St, Baltimore, MD 21211.

Studio: 1261 Dublin Rd, Columbus, OH 43215.

Mailing Address: 1261 Dublin Rd, Columbus, OH 43215.

Phone: 614-481-6666. **Fax:** 614-481-6828.

Web Site: http://www.wtte28.com

Technical Facilities: Channel No. 36 (602-608 MHz). Authorized power: 1000-kw max. visual, aural. Antenna: 889-ft above av. terrain, 951-ft. above ground, 1667-ft. above sea level.

Latitude	39°	56'	14"
Longitude	83°	01'	16"

Note: Latitude and longitude coordinates shown are based on the North American Datum of 1927 (NAD 27) as currently required by the Mass Media Bureau of the FCC.

Ownership: Cunningham Broadcasting Corp. (Group Owner).

Began Operation: October 28, 2002. Began analog operations: June 1, 1984. Sale to Glencairn Ltd. Broadcast Properties by Sinclair Communications Inc. approved by FCC October 24, 1997. Sale to present owner by Glencairn Ltd. Broadcast Properties approved by FCC December 10, 2001. Proposed sales to Sinclair Broadcast Group Inc. dismissed by FCC February 26, 2004 and September 13, 2002. Ceased analog operations: February 17, 2009.

Represented (sales): Katz Media Group.

Personnel:

Dan Mellon, General Manager.

Dan Carpenter, Engineering & Operations Director.

Tony D'Angelo, Sales Director.

Keith Dailey, Local Sales Manager.

Jeff Avon, National Sales Manager.

Lyn Tolan, News Director.

Pat Righter, Business Affairs Director.

Rick White, Programming Coordinator.

Mike Hansen, Promotion & Marketing Director.

Harshita Patel, Research Director.

Linda Seiler, Traffic Manager.

Zoe Ann Del Borrell, Community Affairs Director.

City of License: Columbus. **Station DMA:** Columbus, OH. **Rank:** 34.

WTTE-DT BPCDT-19991029AGZ GRANTED: 4/5/2002

© 2010 Warren Communications News

Circulation © 2009 Nielsen. Coverage based on Nielsen study.

GrandTotal	Cable TV Households	Non-cable TV Households	Total TV Households
Estimated Station Totals *	710,520	334,190	1,044,710
Average Weekly Circulation (2009)	416,416	181,003	597,419
Average Daily Circulation (2009)			248,249

Station DMA Total	Cable TV Households	Non-cable TV Households	Total TV Households
Estimated Station Totals *	613,080	279,210	892,290
Average Weekly Circulation (2009)	391,843	173,199	565,042
Average Daily Circulation (2009)			236,597

Other DMA Total	Cable TV Households	Non-cable TV Households	Total TV Households
Estimated Station Totals *	97,440	54,980	152,420
Average Weekly Circulation (2009)	24,573	7,804	32,377
Average Daily Circulation (2009)			11,652

*Estimated station totals are sums of the Nielsen TV and Cable TV household estimates for each county in which the station registers viewing of more than 5% as per the Nielsen Survey Methods.

WDTN-DT
Ch. 50

Network Service: NBC.

Licensee: WDTN Broadcasting LLC, 4 Richmond Sq, Ste 200, Providence, RI 02906.

Studio: 4595 S. Dixie Ave, Dayton, OH 45439.

Mailing Address: 4595 S Dixie Ave, Dayton, OH 45439.

Phone: 937-293-2101. **Fax:** 937-294-6542.

Web Site: http://www.wdtn.com

Technical Facilities: Channel No. 50 (686-692 MHz). Authorized power: 1000-kw max. visual, aural. Antenna: 1060-ft above av. terrain, 978-ft. above ground, 1932-ft. above sea level.

Latitude	39°	43'	07"
Longitude	84°	15'	22"

Note: Latitude and longitude coordinates shown are based on the North American Datum of 1927 (NAD 27) as currently required by the Mass Media Bureau of the FCC.

Ownership: LIN TV Corp. (Group Owner).

Began Operation: December 17, 2002. Began analog operations: March 15, 1949. Sale to Trustees of Grinnell College by Avco Broadcasting Corp. approved by FCC April 28, 1976 (Television Digest, Vol. 15:25). Sale to Hearst Television by Trustees of Grinnell College approved by FCC July 16, 1981 (Vol. 20:21; 21:29). Merger with Argyle Television Inc. approved by FCC June 2, 1997 (Vol. 37:13, 29, 35). Station, along with Hearst-Argyle's WNAC-TV, was swapped for Sunrise Television's KSBW, WNNE & WPTZ (Vol. 38:8). FCC approved deal July 2, 1998. Transfer of station control to Smith Broadcasting Partners LP approved by FCC July 12, 2000; equity interest maintained by Sunrise Television Partners LP. Transfer to present owner by Smith Broadcasting Partners LP & Sunrise Television Partners LP approved by FCC April 17, 2002. Ceased analog operations: June 12, 2009.

Represented (sales): Blair Television.

Personnel:

Lisa Barhorst, Vice President & General Manager.

Alison Wilkerson, General Sales Manager.

Joe Mulligan, National Sales Manager.

Steve Diorio, News Director.

Jim Atkinson, Chief Engineer.

Jason Doyle, Creative Services Director.

Janice Barney, Traffic Manager.

Sharon Howard, Community Affairs.

City of License: Dayton. **Station DMA:** Dayton, OH. **Rank:** 65.

© 2010 Warren Communications News

Circulation © 2009 Nielsen. Coverage based on Nielsen study.

GrandTotal	Cable TV Households	Non-cable TV Households	Total TV Households
Estimated Station Totals *	405,030	230,450	635,480
Average Weekly Circulation (2009)	205,683	124,841	330,524
Average Daily Circulation (2009)			158,615

Station DMA Total	Cable TV Households	Non-cable TV Households	Total TV Households
Estimated Station Totals *	314,440	169,350	483,790
Average Weekly Circulation (2009)	191,804	111,926	303,730
Average Daily Circulation (2009)			147,806

Other DMA Total	Cable TV Households	Non-cable TV Households	Total TV Households
Estimated Station Totals *	90,590	61,100	151,690
Average Weekly Circulation (2009)	13,879	12,915	26,794
Average Daily Circulation (2009)			10,809

*Estimated station totals are sums of the Nielsen TV and Cable TV household estimates for each county in which the station registers viewing of more than 5% as per the Nielsen Survey Methods.

WHIO-DT
Ch. 41

Network Service: CBS.

Licensee: Miami Valley Broadcasting Corp., PO Box 1206, Dayton, OH 45401.

Studio: 1414 Wilmington Ave, Dayton, OH 45420.

Mailing Address: 1414 Wilmington Ave, Dayton, OH 45420.

Phone: 937-259-2111. **Fax:** 937-259-2001.

Web Site: http://www.whiotv.com

Technical Facilities: Channel No. 41 (632-638 MHz). Authorized power: 1000-kw max. visual, aural. Antenna: 951-ft above av. terrain, 869-ft. above ground, 1821-ft. above sea level.

Latitude	39°	44'	02"
Longitude	84°	14'	53"

Holds CP for change to 1142-ft above av. terrain, 1060-ft. above ground, 2011-ft. above sea level; BPCDT-20080619ACK.

Note: Latitude and longitude coordinates shown are based on the North American Datum of 1927 (NAD 27) as currently required by the Mass Media Bureau of the FCC.

Multichannel TV Sound: Stereo and separate audio program.

Ownership: Cox Enterprises Inc. (Group Owner).

Began Operation: December 1, 2001. High Definition. Began analog operations: February 26, 1949. Ceased analog operations: June 12, 2009.

Represented (legal): Dow Lohnes PLLC.

Personnel:

Harry Delaney, Vice President & General Manager.

James Cosby, General Sales Manager.

John Adams, Local Sales Manager.

John Condit, Local Sales Manager.

Michelle Montague, National Sales Manager.

David Bennallack, News Director.

Chuck Eastman, Chief Engineer.

Eric Zwarg, Controller.

Fantein Kerckaert, Program Director.

Tony Getts, Promotion Director.

Mark McConnell, Production Manager.

Tracy Pyles, Traffic Manager.

City of License: Dayton. **Station DMA:** Dayton, OH. **Rank:** 65.

WHIO-DT BPCDT-20080619ACK GRANTED: 6/9/2009

© 2010 Warren Communications News

Circulation © 2009 Nielsen. Coverage based on Nielsen study.

GrandTotal	Cable TV Households	Non-cable TV Households	Total TV Households
Estimated Station Totals *	566,560	314,780	881,340
Average Weekly Circulation (2009)	315,778	165,633	481,411
Average Daily Circulation (2009)			277,430

Station DMA Total	Cable TV Households	Non-cable TV Households	Total TV Households
Estimated Station Totals *	314,440	169,350	483,790
Average Weekly Circulation (2009)	245,624	140,354	385,978
Average Daily Circulation (2009)			232,808

Other DMA Total	Cable TV Households	Non-cable TV Households	Total TV Households
Estimated Station Totals *	252,120	145,430	397,550
Average Weekly Circulation (2009)	70,154	25,279	95,433
Average Daily Circulation (2009)			44,622

*Estimated station totals are sums of the Nielsen TV and Cable TV household estimates for each county in which the station registers viewing of more than 5% as per the Nielsen Survey Methods.

WKEF-DT
Ch. 51

Network Service: ABC.

Licensee: WKEF Licensee LP, 10706 Beaver Dam Rd, Cockeysville, MD 21030.

Studios: 45 Broadcast Plaza, Dayton, OH 45408; 1731 Soldiers Home Rd, Dayton, OH 45418.

Mailing Address: 1731 Soldiers Home Rd, Dayton, OH 45418.

Phone: 937-263-4500. **Fax:** 937-268-5265.

Web Site: http://www.daytonsnewssource.com

Technical Facilities: Channel No. 51 (692-698 MHz). Authorized power: 137-kw max. visual, aural. Antenna: 1171-ft above av. terrain, 1125-ft. above ground, 2021-ft. above sea level.

Latitude	39°	43'	28"
Longitude	84°	15'	18"

Requests CP for change to 570-kw max. visual, 1152-ft above av. terrain, 1125-ft. above ground, 2021-ft. above sea level; BPCDT-20090320AGS.

Note: Latitude and longitude coordinates shown are based on the North American Datum of 1927 (NAD 27) as currently required by the Mass Media Bureau of the FCC.

Ownership: Sinclair Broadcast Group Inc. (Group Owner).

Began Operation: June 16, 2005. Began analog operations: September 27, 1964. Sale to Adams Communications by Springfield TV Corp. approved by FCC January 9, 1984 (Television Digest, Vol. 23:35). Sale to KT Communications Ltd. Partnership III by Adams approved by FCC February 23, 1989. FCC granted assignment to CitiCorp. September 20, 1994. Sale to Max Media by KT Communications approved by FCC May 5, 1995. Sale to present owner from Max Media approved by FCC August 24, 1999 (Vol. 37:49). Ceased analog operations: June 12, 2009.

Represented (legal): Pillsbury Winthrop Shaw Pittman LLP.

Represented (sales): Millennium Sales & Marketing.

Personnel:

Dean Ditmer, General Manager.

Roland Martel, Chief Engineer & Operations Manager.

Branden Frantz, General Sales Manager.

Marissa Dillon, National Sales Manager.

Pat Casey, News Director.

Jim Ahrns, Business Manager.

Michelle Steinbrugge, Program & Research Director.

Jason Matlock, Promotion Manager.

Mike Thomas, Production Manager.

Lisa Robbins, Traffic Manager.

City of License: Dayton. **Station DMA:** Dayton, OH. **Rank:** 65.

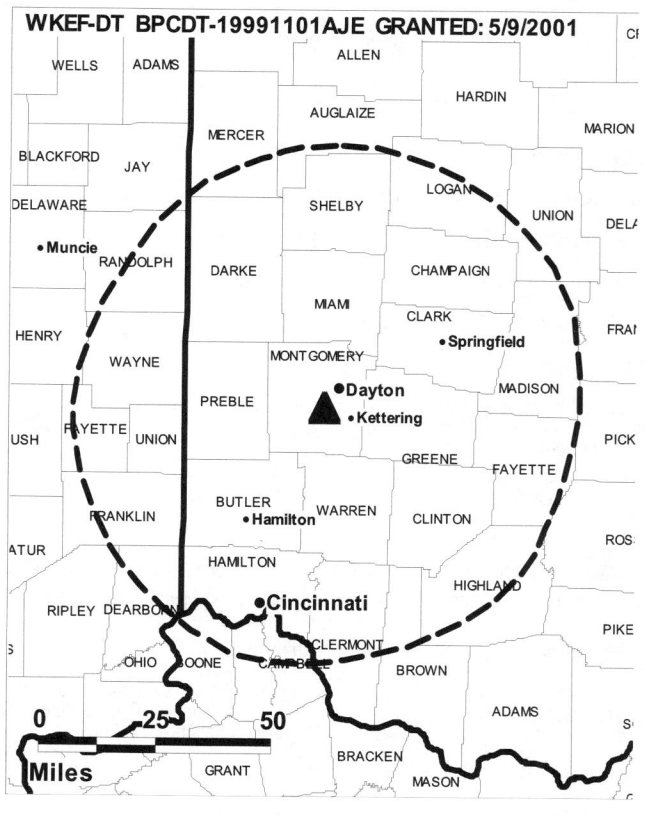

WKEF-DT BPCDT-19991101AJE GRANTED: 5/9/2001

© 2010 Warren Communications News

Circulation © 2009 Nielsen. Coverage based on Nielsen study.

GrandTotal	Cable TV Households	Non-cable TV Households	Total TV Households
Estimated Station Totals *	486,790	292,210	779,000
Average Weekly Circulation (2009)	220,987	126,715	347,702
Average Daily Circulation (2009)			145,091

Station DMA Total	Cable TV Households	Non-cable TV Households	Total TV Households
Estimated Station Totals *	314,440	169,350	483,790
Average Weekly Circulation (2009)	191,207	109,447	300,654
Average Daily Circulation (2009)			128,057

Other DMA Total	Cable TV Households	Non-cable TV Households	Total TV Households
Estimated Station Totals *	172,350	122,860	295,210
Average Weekly Circulation (2009)	29,780	17,268	47,048
Average Daily Circulation (2009)			17,034

*Estimated station totals are sums of the Nielsen TV and Cable TV household estimates for each county in which the station registers viewing of more than 5% as per the Nielsen Survey Methods.

WRGT-DT
Ch. 30

Network Service: MNT, FOX.

Grantee: WRGT Licensee LLC, 2000 W. 41st St, Baltimore, MD 21211.

Studio: 45 Broadcast Plaza, Dayton, OH 45408.

Mailing Address: 45 Broadcast Plaza, Dayton, OH 45408.

Phone: 937-263-4500. **Fax:** 937-268-5265.

Web Site: http://www.fox45.com

Technical Facilities: Channel No. 30 (566-572 MHz). Authorized power: 425-kw max. visual, aural. Antenna: 1152-ft above av. terrain, 1125-ft. above ground, 2021-ft. above sea level.

Latitude	39°	43'	28"
Longitude	84°	15'	18"

Note: Latitude and longitude coordinates shown are based on the North American Datum of 1927 (NAD 27) as currently required by the Mass Media Bureau of the FCC.

Ownership: Cunningham Broadcasting Corp. (Group Owner).

Began Operation: June 21, 2005. Began analog operations: September 23, 1984. Proposed sales to Sinclair Broadcast Group Inc. dismissed by FCC February 26, 2004 and September 13, 2002. Ceased analog operations: June 12, 2009.

Represented (sales): Katz Media Group.

Represented (legal): Pillsbury Winthrop Shaw Pittman LLP.

Personnel:

Dean Ditmer, General Manager.

Roland Martel, Chief Engineer & Operations Manager.

Branden Frantz, General Sales Manager.

Marissa Dillon, National Sales Manager.

Pat Casey, News Director.

Jim Ahrns, Business Manager.

Michelle Steinbrugge, Program & Research Director.

Jason Matlock, Promotion Director.

Mike Thomas, Production Manager.

Lisa Robbins, Traffic Manager.

City of License: Dayton. **Station DMA:** Dayton, OH. **Rank:** 65.

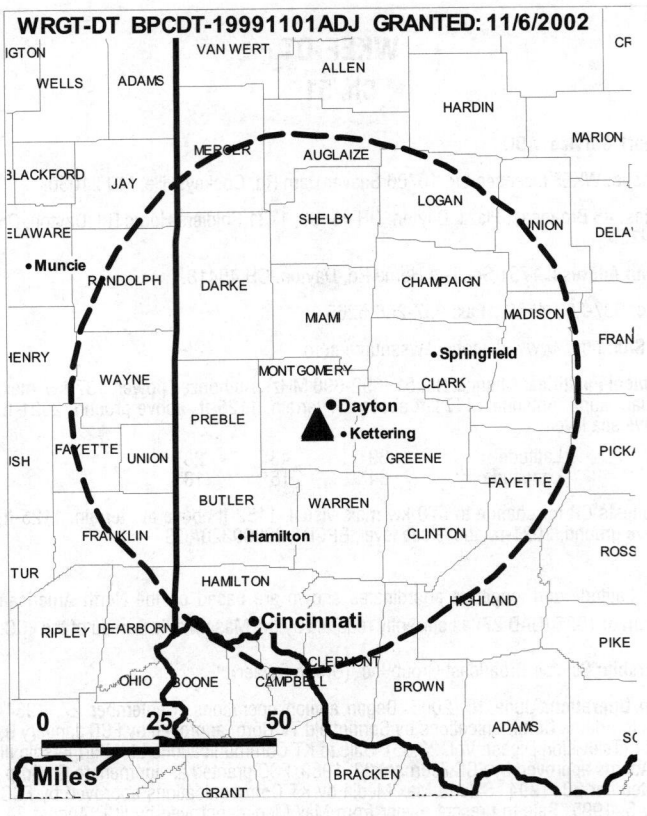

© 2010 Warren Communications News

Circulation © 2009 Nielsen. Coverage based on Nielsen study.

GrandTotal	Cable TV Households	Non-cable TV Households	Total TV Households
Estimated Station Totals *	493,930	296,490	790,420
Average Weekly Circulation (2009)	196,541	119,106	315,647
Average Daily Circulation (2009)			112,984

Station DMA Total	Cable TV Households	Non-cable TV Households	Total TV Households
Estimated Station Totals *	314,440	169,350	483,790
Average Weekly Circulation (2009)	167,531	103,763	271,294
Average Daily Circulation (2009)			98,428

Other DMA Total	Cable TV Households	Non-cable TV Households	Total TV Households
Estimated Station Totals *	179,490	127,140	306,630
Average Weekly Circulation (2009)	29,010	15,343	44,353
Average Daily Circulation (2009)			14,556

*Estimated station totals are sums of the Nielsen TV and Cable TV household estimates for each county in which the station registers viewing of more than 5% as per the Nielsen Survey Methods.

WLIO-DT
Ch. 8

Network Service: NBC, CW.

Grantee: Lima Communications Corp., PO Box 1689, 1424 Rice Ave, Lima, OH 45802.

Studio: 1424 Rice Ave, Lima, OH 45805.

Mailing Address: PO Box 1689, Lima, OH 45802.

Phone: 419-228-8835. **Fax:** 419-229-7091.

E-mail: kevin@wlio.com

Web Site: http://www.wlio.com

Technical Facilities: Channel No. 8 (180-186 MHz). Authorized power: 27.5-kw visual, aural. Antenna: 486-ft above av. terrain, 455-ft. above ground, 1325-ft. above sea level.

Latitude	40°	44'	51"
Longitude	84°	07'	54.5"

Note: Latitude and longitude coordinates shown are based on the North American Datum of 1927 (NAD 27) as currently required by the Mass Media Bureau of the FCC.

Ownership: Block Communications Inc. (Group Owner).

Began Operation: September 23, 2002. Began analog operations: March 30, 1953. Sale to present owner by WLOK Inc. approved by FCC January 19, 1972. Previous sale by Pixley & Case families approved by FCC December 1, 1954 (Television Digest, Vol. 10:44, 49). Ceased analog operations: June 12, 2009.

Represented (sales): Continental Television Sales.

Personnel:

Bruce A. Opperman, President & General Manager.

David E. Plaugher, Chief Financial Officer & Station Manager.

Kevin Creamer, Vice President & General Sales Manager.

Lon Tegels, News Director.

Frederick R. Vobbe, Vice President, Engineering.

Kylie Fortman, Program & Promotion Director.

Tony Unverferth, Sales & Marketing Assistant.

Terry L. Johns, Production Manager.

Mary Griffin, Traffic Manager.

City of License: Lima. **Station DMA:** Lima, OH. **Rank:** 186.

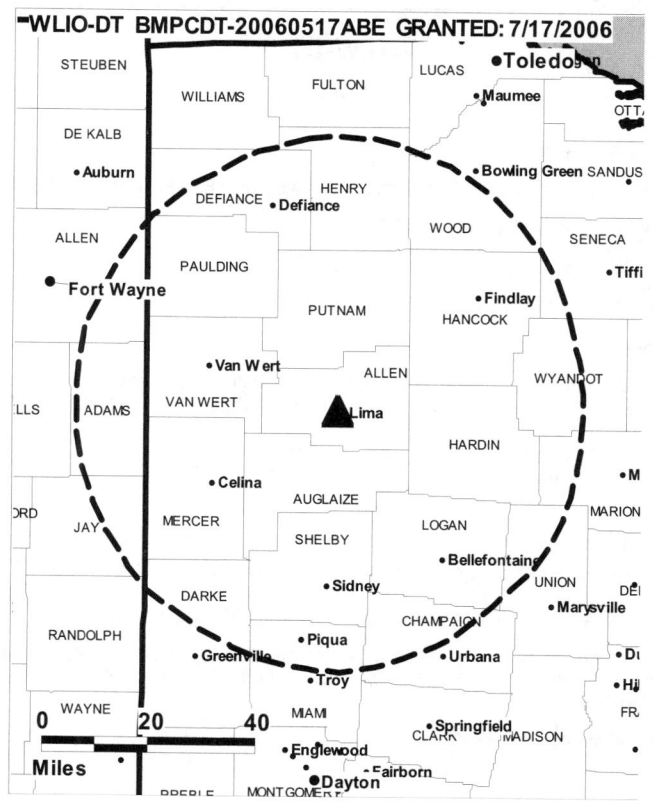

© 2010 Warren Communications News

Circulation © 2009 Nielsen. Coverage based on Nielsen study.

GrandTotal	Cable TV Households	Non-cable TV Households	Total TV Households
Estimated Station Totals *	156,280	63,120	219,400
Average Weekly Circulation (2009)	60,870	20,261	81,131
Average Daily Circulation (2009)			46,770

Station DMA Total	Cable TV Households	Non-cable TV Households	Total TV Households
Estimated Station Totals *	50,690	20,000	70,690
Average Weekly Circulation (2009)	39,230	12,563	51,793
Average Daily Circulation (2009)			32,849

Other DMA Total	Cable TV Households	Non-cable TV Households	Total TV Households
Estimated Station Totals *	105,590	43,120	148,710
Average Weekly Circulation (2009)	21,640	7,698	29,338
Average Daily Circulation (2009)			13,921

*Estimated station totals are sums of the Nielsen TV and Cable TV household estimates for each county in which the station registers viewing of more than 5% as per the Nielsen Survey Methods.

WTLW-DT
Ch. 44

Network Service: IND.

Licensee: American Christian Television Services Inc., 1844 Baty Rd, Lima, OH 45807.

Studio: 1844 Baty Rd, Lima, OH 45807.

Mailing Address: 1844 Baty Rd, Lima, OH 45807.

Phone: 419-339-4444; 800-234-9859. **Fax:** 419-339-1736.

Web Site: http://www.wtlw.com

Technical Facilities: Channel No. 44 (650-656 MHz). Authorized power: 165-kw max. visual, aural. Antenna: 679-ft above av. terrain, 682-ft. above ground, 1509-ft. above sea level.

Latitude	40°	45'	47"
Longitude	84°	10'	59"

Note: Latitude and longitude coordinates shown are based on the North American Datum of 1927 (NAD 27) as currently required by the Mass Media Bureau of the FCC.

Ownership: American Christian Television Services Inc. (Group Owner).

Began Operation: December 9, 2008. Station broadcasting digitally on its analog channel allotment. Began analog operations: June 13, 1982. Ceased analog operations: January 2009.

Represented (legal): Wiley Rein LLP.

Personnel:

Kevin Bowers, General Manager & Program Director.

Wayne Getz, Operations & Production Manager.

Gary Cooper, General Sales Manager.

Rick Corcoran, Chief Engineer.

San Brauen, Business Manager.

Kelly Getz, Traffic Manager.

City of License: Lima. **Station DMA:** Lima, OH. **Rank:** 186.

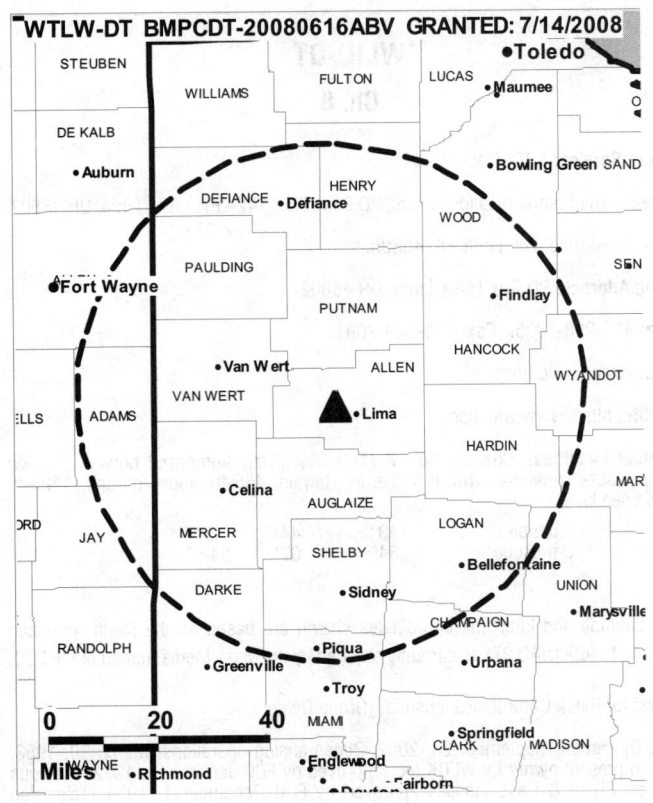

WTLW-DT BMPCDT-20080616ABV GRANTED: 7/14/2008

© 2010 Warren Communications News

Circulation © 2009 Nielsen. Coverage based on Nielsen study.

GrandTotal	Cable TV Households	Non-cable TV Households	Total TV Households
Estimated Station Totals *	99,030	63,120	162,150
Average Weekly Circulation (2009)	12,231	6,734	18,965
Average Daily Circulation (2009)			5,716

Station DMA Total	Cable TV Households	Non-cable TV Households	Total TV Households
Estimated Station Totals *	50,690	20,000	70,690
Average Weekly Circulation (2009)	6,421	3,195	9,616
Average Daily Circulation (2009)			2,814

Other DMA Total	Cable TV Households	Non-cable TV Households	Total TV Households
Estimated Station Totals *	48,340	43,120	91,460
Average Weekly Circulation (2009)	5,810	3,539	9,349
Average Daily Circulation (2009)			2,902

*Estimated station totals are sums of the Nielsen TV and Cable TV household estimates for each county in which the station registers viewing of more than 5% as per the Nielsen Survey Methods.

WUAB-DT
Ch. 28

Network Service: MNT.

Licensee: WOIO License Subsidiary LLC, 201 Monroe St, RSA Tower, 20th Fl, Montgomery, AL 36104.

Studio: 1717 E 12th St, Cleveland, OH 44114.

Mailing Address: 1717 E. 12th St, Cleveland, OH 44114.

Phone: 216-771-1943; 800-929-0132. **Fax:** 216-515-7152.

Web Site: http://www.my43.net

Technical Facilities: Channel No. 28 (554-560 MHz). Authorized power: 200.3-kw max. visual, aural. Antenna: 1106-ft above av. terrain, 912-ft. above ground, 1965-ft. above sea level.

Latitude	41°	22'	45"
Longitude	81°	43'	12"

Transmitter: 4800 Bruening Dr., 0.36-mi. W of State Rd. 94, Parma.

Note: Latitude and longitude coordinates shown are based on the North American Datum of 1927 (NAD 27) as currently required by the Mass Media Bureau of the FCC.

Ownership: Raycom Media Inc. (Group Owner).

Began Operation: May 16, 2002. Began analog operations: September 15, 1968. Sale to present owner by Cannell Cleveland LP approved by FCC January 24, 2000. Sale to Cannell Cleveland LP by Gaylord Broadcasting approved by FCC June 19, 1990. Sale to Gaylord by United Artists Broadcasting & Kaiser Broadcasting Co. approved by FCC June 30, 1977. Ceased analog operations: June 12, 2009.

Represented (legal): Covington & Burling.

Represented (engineering): Cohen Dippell & Everist PC.

Personnel:

Bill Applegate, Vice President & General Manager.

Lynda King, General Sales Manager.

Isadoro Aguinaga, Local Sales Manager.

Dan Salamone, News Director.

Bob Maupin, Chief Engineer.

Karen Bizjak, Business Manager.

Lisa McManus, Program Director.

Rob Boenau, Marketing & Promotion Director.

James Stunek, Production Director & Broadcast Operations.

Jean Niznik, Traffic Manager.

Emily Davis, Community Affairs Director.

Judy Smith, Assistant to the General Manager.

City of License: Lorain. **Station DMA:** Cleveland-Akron (Canton), OH. **Rank:** 18.

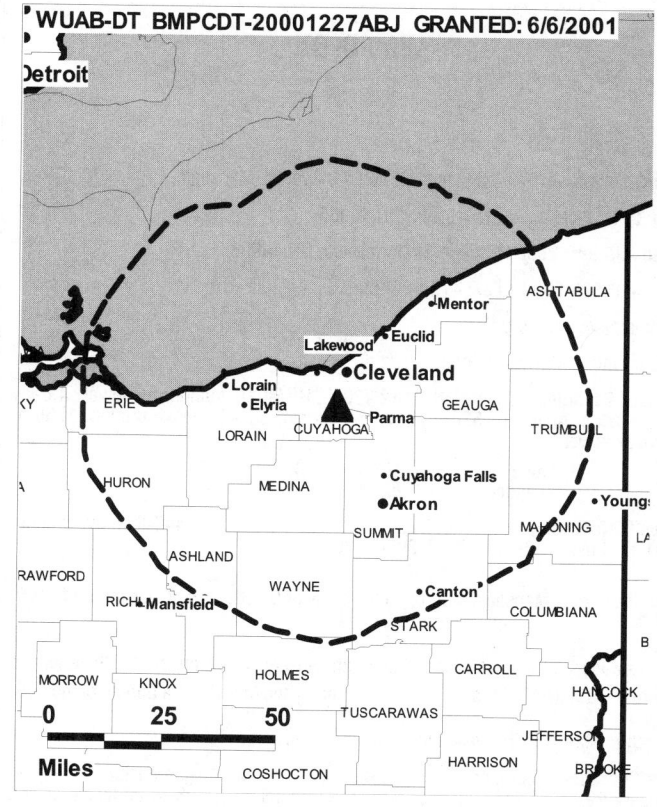

© 2010 Warren Communications News

Circulation © 2009 Nielsen. Coverage based on Nielsen study.

GrandTotal	Cable TV Households	Non-cable TV Households	Total TV Households
Estimated Station Totals *	1,266,010	450,750	1,716,760
Average Weekly Circulation (2009)	452,014	185,387	637,401
Average Daily Circulation (2009)			221,962

Station DMA Total	Cable TV Households	Non-cable TV Households	Total TV Households
Estimated Station Totals *	1,067,420	436,370	1,503,790
Average Weekly Circulation (2009)	425,074	184,436	609,510
Average Daily Circulation (2009)			216,327

Other DMA Total	Cable TV Households	Non-cable TV Households	Total TV Households
Estimated Station Totals *	198,590	14,380	212,970
Average Weekly Circulation (2009)	26,940	951	27,891
Average Daily Circulation (2009)			5,635

*Estimated station totals are sums of the Nielsen TV and Cable TV household estimates for each county in which the station registers viewing of more than 5% as per the Nielsen Survey Methods.

WMFD-DT
Ch. 12

Network Service: IND.

Licensee: Mid-State Television Inc., 2900 Park Ave. W, Mansfield, OH 44906-1062.

Studio: 2900 Park Ave W, Mansfield, OH 44906.

Mailing Address: 2900 Park Ave. W, Mansfield, OH 44906.

Phone: 419-529-5900. **Fax:** 419-529-2319.

E-mail: larrys@wnfd.org

Web Site: http://www.wmfd.com

Technical Facilities: Channel No. 12 (204-210 MHz). Authorized power: 4.8-kw visual, aural. Antenna: 528-ft above av. terrain, 387-ft. above ground, 1768-ft. above sea level.

Latitude	40°	45'	50"
Longitude	82°	37'	04"

Holds CP for change to 14-kw visual, 591-ft above av. terrain, 449-ft. above ground, 1831-ft. above sea level; BPCDT-20040526ABT.

Transmitter: W of Mansfield, approx. 0.24-mi. N of US Rte. 305 & 0.3-mi. E of Lewis Rd.

Note: Latitude and longitude coordinates shown are based on the North American Datum of 1927 (NAD 27) as currently required by the Mass Media Bureau of the FCC.

Ownership: Mid-State Television Inc. (Group Owner).

Began Operation: February 15, 1999. Standard Definition. Began analog operations: February 29, 1988. FCC granted station STA April 17, 2008 to terminate analog operations in order to complete construction of its post-transition DTV facilities.

Represented (legal): Fletcher, Heald & Hildreth PLC.

Represented (engineering): du Treil, Lundin & Rackley Inc.

Personnel:

Gunther Meisse, President & General Manager.

Glenn Cheesnan, Vice President, Sales.

Scott Goodwin, Sales Manager.

Bob Miller, National Sales Manager.

Larry Stine, News Manager.

Wayne Fick, Chief Engineer.

Kelly Bauer, Program Director & Traffic Manager.

City of License: Mansfield. **Station DMA:** Cleveland-Akron (Canton), OH. **Rank:** 18.

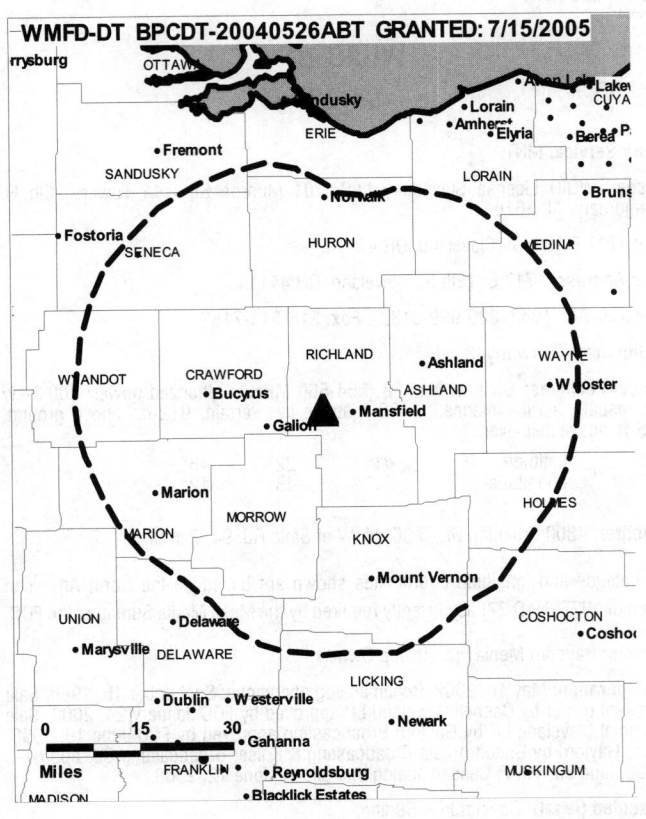

WMFD-DT BPCDT-20040526ABT GRANTED: 7/15/2005

© 2010 Warren Communications News

Circulation © 2009 Nielsen. Coverage based on Nielsen study.

GrandTotal	Cable TV Households	Non-cable TV Households	Total TV Households
Estimated Station Totals *	12,940	5,140	18,080
Average Weekly Circulation (2009)	906	678	1,584
Average Daily Circulation (2009)			434

Other DMA Total	Cable TV Households	Non-cable TV Households	Total TV Households
Estimated Station Totals *	12,940	5,140	18,080
Average Weekly Circulation (2009)	906	678	1,584
Average Daily Circulation (2009)			434

*Estimated station totals are sums of the Nielsen TV and Cable TV household estimates for each county in which the station registers viewing of more than 5% as per the Nielsen Survey Methods.

WSFJ-DT
Ch. 24

Network Service: IND.

Licensee: Trinity Christian Center of Santa Ana Inc., PO Box C-11949, Santa Ana, CA 92711.

Studio: 3948 Townsfair Way, Ste 220, Columbus, OH 43219.

Mailing Address: 3948 Townsfair Way, Ste 220, Columbus, OH 43219.

Phone: 614-416-6080; 800-517-5151. **Fax:** 614-416-6345.

Web Site: http://www.gtn51.com

Technical Facilities: Channel No. 24 (530-536 MHz). Authorized power: 1000-kw max. visual, aural. Antenna: 436-ft above av. terrain, 279-ft. above ground, 1516-ft. above sea level.

Latitude	40°	04'	44"
Longitude	82°	41'	42"

Note: Latitude and longitude coordinates shown are based on the North American Datum of 1927 (NAD 27) as currently required by the Mass Media Bureau of the FCC.

Ownership: Trinity Broadcasting Network Inc. (Group Owner).

Began Operation: January 1, 2002. Began analog operations: March 9, 1980. Ceased analog operations: June 12, 2009.

Represented (legal): Colby M. May.

Personnel:

Richard Schilg, President & Chief Executive Officer.

John Schneider, Business Development Director.

Angel Boulis, Chief Financial Officer.

Elaine Kistler, General & Local Sales Manager.

Mike Hevel, Sales Director.

Rob Kasper, Chief Operating Officer, Guardian Studios.

Dave Wilson, Programming & Operations Director.

City of License: Newark. **Station DMA:** Columbus, OH. **Rank:** 34.

Digital cable and TV coverage maps.
Visit www.warren-news.com/mediaprints.htm

MediaPrints™
Map a Winning Business Strategy

WSFJ-DT BPCDT-19991101AHH GRANTED: 5/14/2002

© 2010 Warren Communications News

Circulation © 2009 Nielsen. Coverage based on Nielsen study.

GrandTotal	Cable TV Households	Non-cable TV Households	Total TV Households
Estimated Station Totals *	473,590	147,530	621,120
Average Weekly Circulation (2009)	27,059	9,381	36,440
Average Daily Circulation (2009)			11,949

Station DMA Total	Cable TV Households	Non-cable TV Households	Total TV Households
Estimated Station Totals *	450,390	147,530	597,920
Average Weekly Circulation (2009)	25,481	9,381	34,862
Average Daily Circulation (2009)			11,624

Other DMA Total	Cable TV Households	Non-cable TV Households	Total TV Households
Estimated Station Totals *	23,200	0	23,200
Average Weekly Circulation (2009)	1,578	0	1,578
Average Daily Circulation (2009)			325

*Estimated station totals are sums of the Nielsen TV and Cable TV household estimates for each county in which the station registers viewing of more than 5% as per the Nielsen Survey Methods.

WQCW-DT

Ch. 17

Network Service: CW.

Licensee: Mountain TV LLC, 220 Salters Creek Rd, Hampton, VA 23661.

Studio: 800 Gallia St, Ste 430, Portsmouth, OH 45662.

Mailing Address: Ste 200, 400 Capitol St, Charleston, WV 25301.

Phone: 740-353-3391; 304-344-9729. **Fax:** 740-353-3372.

Web Site: http://www.tristatescw.com

Technical Facilities: Channel No. 17 (488-494 MHz). Authorized power: 50-kw max. visual, aural. Antenna: 1175-ft above av. terrain, 850-ft. above ground, 1953-ft. above sea level.

Latitude	38°	45'	42"
Longitude	83°	03'	41"

Holds CP for change to 1000-kw max. visual, 1299-ft above av. terrain, 1068-ft. above ground, 2039-ft. above sea level; lat. 38° 30' 21", long. 82° 12' 33", BPCDT-20080618ADI.

Note: Latitude and longitude coordinates shown are based on the North American Datum of 1927 (NAD 27) as currently required by the Mass Media Bureau of the FCC.

Ownership: Mountain TV LLC.

Began Operation: June 30, 2006. Began analog operations: May 8, 1988. Sale to Kenneth W. Russell (Television Properties Inc.) by Janesville Broadcasting Co. approved by FCC July 8, 1985. Left air 1989. Returned to air October 1998. Transfer of control of Television Properties Inc. to Commonwealth Broadcasting Group Inc. by Kenneth W. Russell approved by FCC July 11, 2002. Sale of remaining interest to Commonwealth Broadcasting Group Inc. approved by FCC November 15, 2006. Sale to present owner by Commonwealth Broadcasting Group Inc. approved by FCC February 23, 2007. Ceased analog operations: June 12, 2009.

Represented (legal): Brooks, Pierce, McLendon, Humphrey & Leonard LLP.

Personnel:

William White, General Manager.

Vince Wardell, General Sales Manager.

John Davis, Chief Engineer.

Charles Carey, Chief Master Controller.

Adrienne O'Harra, Traffic Director.

Dennie Large, Production, Marketing & Promotion Manager.

City of License: Portsmouth. **Station DMA:** Charleston-Huntington, WV. **Rank:** 63.

WQCW-DT BPCDT-20080618ADI GRANTED: 3/25/2009

© 2010 Warren Communications News

Circulation © 2009 Nielsen. Coverage based on Nielsen study.

GrandTotal	Cable TV Households	Non-cable TV Households	Total TV Households
Estimated Station Totals *	289,950	175,300	465,250
Average Weekly Circulation (2009)	48,305	19,350	67,655
Average Daily Circulation (2009)			16,242

Station DMA Total	Cable TV Households	Non-cable TV Households	Total TV Households
Estimated Station Totals *	273,660	175,300	448,960
Average Weekly Circulation (2009)	45,854	19,350	65,204
Average Daily Circulation (2009)			15,887

Other DMA Total	Cable TV Households	Non-cable TV Households	Total TV Households
Estimated Station Totals *	16,290	0	16,290
Average Weekly Circulation (2009)	2,451	0	2,451
Average Daily Circulation (2009)			355

*Estimated station totals are sums of the Nielsen TV and Cable TV household estimates for each county in which the station registers viewing of more than 5% as per the Nielsen Survey Methods.

WGGN-DT
Ch. 42

Network Service: TBN.

Grantee: Christian Faith Broadcast Inc., PO Box 247, 3809 Maple Ave, Castalia, OH 44824.

Studio: 3809 Maple Ave, Castalia, OH 44824.

Mailing Address: PO Box 2397, Sandusky, OH 44870.

Phone: 419-684-5311. **Fax:** 419-684-5378.

Web Site: http://www.wggn.tv

Technical Facilities: Channel No. 42 (638-644 MHz). Authorized power: 450-kw visual, aural. Antenna: 928-ft above av. terrain, 961-ft. above ground, 1933-ft. above sea level.

Latitude	41°	04'	30"
Longitude	82°	27'	05"

Note: Latitude and longitude coordinates shown are based on the North American Datum of 1927 (NAD 27) as currently required by the Mass Media Bureau of the FCC.

Ownership: Christian Faith Broadcast Inc. (Group Owner).

Began Operation: November 14, 2002. Began analog operations: December 5, 1982. Ceased analog operations: June 12, 2009.

Personnel:

Shelby Gillam, President.

Rusty Yost, Vice President & Chief Engineer.

Richard Hawkins, General Manager.

Jeff Ferback, Local Sales Manager.

Roy Bilman, Traffic Coordinator.

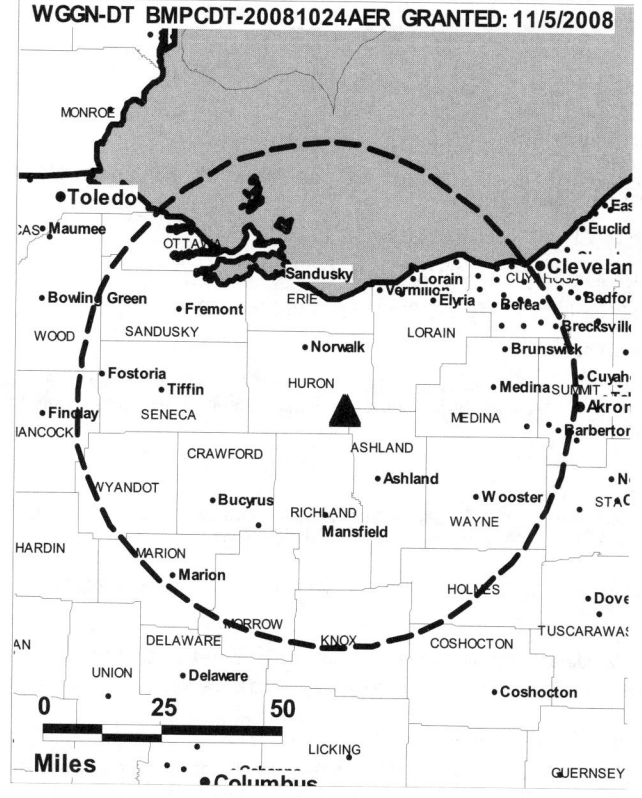

© 2010 Warren Communications News

City of License: Sandusky. **Station DMA:** Cleveland-Akron (Canton), OH. **Rank:** 18.

Nielsen Data: Not available.

WOIO-DT
Ch. 10

Network Service: CBS.

Licensee: WOIO License Subsidiary LLC, 201 Monroe St, RSA Tower, 20th Fl, Montgomery, AL 36104.

Studio: 1717 E 12th St, Cleveland, OH 44114.

Mailing Address: 1717 E. 12th St, Cleveland, OH 44114.

Phone: 216-771-1943; 800-929-0132. **Fax:** 216-515-7152.

Web Site: http://www.woio.com

Technical Facilities: Channel No. 10 (192-198 MHz). Authorized power: 3.5-kw visual, aural. Antenna: 997-ft above av. terrain, 960-ft. above ground, 1860-ft. above sea level.

Latitude	41°	23'	15"
Longitude	81°	41'	43"

Holds CP for change to 10.3-kw visual, 1184-ft above av. terrain, 1114-ft. above ground, 2014-ft. above sea level; BPCDT-20080620AKW.

Transmitter: 0.3-mi. S of Ridgewood Dr., 0.55-mi. W of Broadview Rd./Rte. 176, Parma.

Note: Latitude and longitude coordinates shown are based on the North American Datum of 1927 (NAD 27) as currently required by the Mass Media Bureau of the FCC.

Ownership: Raycom Media Inc. (Group Owner).

Began Operation: November 1, 1999. High Definition. Began analog operations: May 19, 1985. Sale to present owner by Milton S. Maltz approved by FCC August 13, 1998. Ceased analog operations: June 12, 2009.

Represented (sales): TeleRep Inc.

Represented (legal): Covington & Burling.

Personnel:

Bill Applegate, Vice President & General Manager.

Lynda King, General Sales Manager.

Renee Morley, Local Sales Manager.

Dan Salamone, News Director.

Bob Maupin, Chief Engineer.

Jim Stunek, Broadcast Operations Director.

Karen Bizjak, Business Manager.

Lisa McManus, Program Director.

Rob Boenau, Marketing & Promotions Director.

Jean Niznik, Traffic Manager.

Emily Davis, Community Affairs Director.

Judy Smith, Assistant to the General Manager.

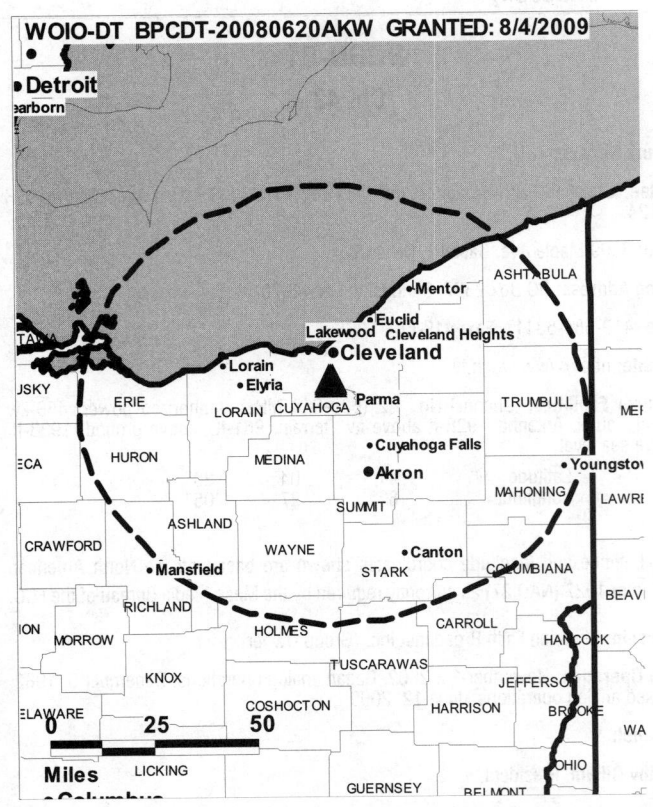

WOIO-DT BPCDT-20080620AKW GRANTED: 8/4/2009

© 2010 Warren Communications News

City of License: Shaker Heights. **Station DMA:** Cleveland-Akron (Canton), OH.

Rank: 18.

Circulation © 2009 Nielsen. Coverage based on Nielsen study.

GrandTotal	Cable TV Households	Non-cable TV Households	Total TV Households
Estimated Station Totals *	1,129,460	452,710	1,582,170
Average Weekly Circulation (2009)	689,752	302,103	991,855
Average Daily Circulation (2009)			440,760

Station DMA Total	Cable TV Households	Non-cable TV Households	Total TV Households
Estimated Station Totals *	1,067,420	436,370	1,503,790
Average Weekly Circulation (2009)	678,895	299,973	978,868
Average Daily Circulation (2009)			438,133

Other DMA Total	Cable TV Households	Non-cable TV Households	Total TV Households
Estimated Station Totals *	62,040	16,340	78,380
Average Weekly Circulation (2009)	10,857	2,130	12,987
Average Daily Circulation (2009)			2,627

*Estimated station totals are sums of the Nielsen TV and Cable TV household estimates for each county in which the station registers viewing of more than 5% as per the Nielsen Survey Methods.

WBDT-DT
Ch. 26

Network Service: CW.

Grantee: ACME Television Licenses of Ohio LLC, 10829 Olive Blvd, Ste 202, St. Louis, MO 63141.

Studio: 2589 Corporate Pl, Miamisburg, OH 45342.

Mailing Address: 2589 Corporate Pl, Miamisburg, OH 45342.

Phone: 937-384-9226. **Fax:** 937-384-7392.

E-mail: melanie.simon@daytonswb.com

Web Site: http://www.daytonscw.com

Technical Facilities: Channel No. 26 (542-548 MHz). Authorized power: 770-kw max. visual, aural. Antenna: 1145-ft above av. terrain, 1119-ft. above ground, 2014-ft. above sea level.

Latitude	39°	43'	28"
Longitude	84°	15'	18"

Note: Latitude and longitude coordinates shown are based on the North American Datum of 1927 (NAD 27) as currently required by the Mass Media Bureau of the FCC.

Ownership: ACME Communications Inc. (Group Owner).

Began Operation: March 15, 2003. Standard Definition. Station broadcasting digitally on its analog channel allotment. Began analog operations: September 21, 1980. Ceased analog operations: June 12, 2009.

Personnel:

John Hannon, Vice President & General Manager.

Melanie Simon, General Sales Manager.

Billie Adkins, National Sales Manager.

Al Schmidt, Chief Engineer.

Bonnie Meyers, Business Manager.

Greg Abbott, Programming Director.

Brian Mercer, Marketing & Research Director.

Mike Shearer, Production Director.

Shasta Scarberry, Creative Services Director.

Reggie Stone, Traffic Manager.

City of License: Springfield. **Station DMA:** Dayton, OH. **Rank:** 65.

© 2010 Warren Communications News

Circulation © 2009 Nielsen. Coverage based on Nielsen study.

GrandTotal	Cable TV Households	Non-cable TV Households	Total TV Households
Estimated Station Totals *	387,150	294,190	681,340
Average Weekly Circulation (2009)	88,458	84,842	173,300
Average Daily Circulation (2009)			64,645

Station DMA Total	Cable TV Households	Non-cable TV Households	Total TV Households
Estimated Station Totals *	314,440	169,350	483,790
Average Weekly Circulation (2009)	81,665	72,949	154,614
Average Daily Circulation (2009)			60,152

Other DMA Total	Cable TV Households	Non-cable TV Households	Total TV Households
Estimated Station Totals *	72,710	124,840	197,550
Average Weekly Circulation (2009)	6,793	11,893	18,686
Average Daily Circulation (2009)			4,493

*Estimated station totals are sums of the Nielsen TV and Cable TV household estimates for each county in which the station registers viewing of more than 5% as per the Nielsen Survey Methods.

WTOV-DT
Ch. 9

Network Service: NBC.

Licensee: WTOV Inc., 6205 Peachtree Dunwoody Rd, Atlanta, GA 30328.

Studio: 9 Red Donley Plaza, Steubenville, OH 43952.

Sales Office: Riley Bldg., 14th & Chapline Sts., 6th Floor, Wheeling, WV 26003.

Mailing Address: PO Box 9999, Steubenville, OH 43952-6799.

Phone: 740-282-9999; 740-282-0911. **Fax:** 740-282-0439.

E-mail: wtov@wtov.com

Web Site: http://www.wtov9.com

Technical Facilities: Channel No. 9 (186-192 MHz). Authorized power: 23-kw visual, aural. Antenna: 925-ft above av. terrain, 869-ft. above ground, 1965-ft. above sea level.

Latitude	40°	20'	33"
Longitude	80°	37'	14"

Note: Latitude and longitude coordinates shown are based on the North American Datum of 1927 (NAD 27) as currently required by the Mass Media Bureau of the FCC.

Ownership: Cox Enterprises Inc. (Group Owner).

Began Operation: November 26, 2002. Station broadcasting digitally on its analog channel allotment. Began analog operations: December 10, 1953. Transfer of stations from WSTV Inc. and WPIT Inc. to United Printers & Publishers, later Rust Craft Greeting Cards Inc., approved by FCC November 8, 1961 (Television Digest, Vol. 17:30, 33; 2:14). Sale to Ziff Corp. by Rust Craft approved by FCC May 10, 1978 (Vol. 17:26, 27, 36; 18:20, 41). Sale to Television Station Partners (I. Martin Pompadur, et al.,) by Ziff Corp. approved by FCC January 18, 1983 (Vol. 22:30). Sale to Smith Broadcasting by Television Station Partners approved by FCC September 29, 1995 (Vol. 35:17, 41). Sale to Smith Acquisition Co. approved by FCC December 13, 1996. Sale to present owner by Smith Acquisition Co. approved by FCC September 22, 2000 (Vol. 40:29). Ceased analog operations: June 12, 2009.

Represented (legal): Dow Lohnes PLLC.

Represented (sales): TeleRep Inc.

Personnel:

Tim McCoy, Vice President & General Manager.

Michael Seachman, Operations & Engineering Director.

Tom Pleva, General Sales Manager.

Brandon Gobel, News Director.

Don Fogle, Chief Engineer.

Chuck Robinson, Controller.

Kristin Murdock, Promotion & Marketing Director.

Michelle Lehita, Traffic Coordinator.

Mary Sue Gallabrese, Human Resources Administrator.

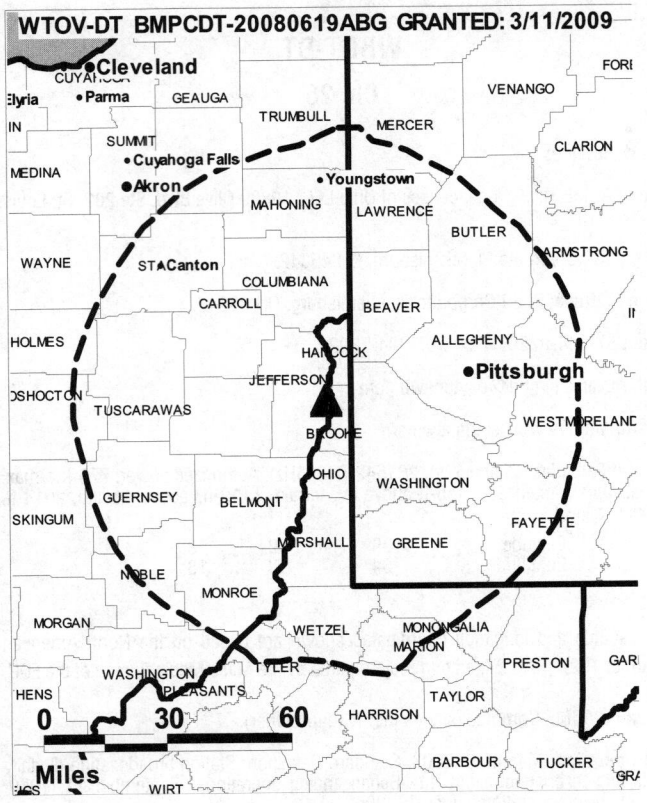

© 2010 Warren Communications News

City of License: Steubenville. **Station DMA:** Wheeling, WV-Steubenville, OH.

Rank: 159.

Circulation © 2009 Nielsen. Coverage based on Nielsen study.

GrandTotal	Cable TV Households	Non-cable TV Households	Total TV Households
Estimated Station Totals *	206,960	89,730	296,690
Average Weekly Circulation (2009)	102,700	22,313	125,013
Average Daily Circulation (2009)			72,117

Station DMA Total	Cable TV Households	Non-cable TV Households	Total TV Households
Estimated Station Totals *	98,310	35,390	133,700
Average Weekly Circulation (2009)	80,375	17,267	97,642
Average Daily Circulation (2009)			61,908

Other DMA Total	Cable TV Households	Non-cable TV Households	Total TV Households
Estimated Station Totals *	108,650	54,340	162,990
Average Weekly Circulation (2009)	22,325	5,046	27,371
Average Daily Circulation (2009)			10,209

*Estimated station totals are sums of the Nielsen TV and Cable TV household estimates for each county in which the station registers viewing of more than 5% as per the Nielsen Survey Methods.

WLMB-DT
Ch. 5

Network Service: IND.

Licensee: Dominion Broadcasting Inc., PO Box 908, 26693 Eckel Rd, Perrysburg, OH 43552.

Studio: 825 Capital Commons Dr, Toledo, OH 43615.

Mailing Address: 825 Capital Commons Dr, Toledo, OH 43615.

Phone: 419-720-9562. **Fax:** 419-720-9563.

E-mail: bmyerholtz@wlmb.com

Web Site: http://www.wlmb.com

Technical Facilities: Channel No. 5 (76-82 MHz). Authorized power: 10-kw visual, aural. Antenna: 509-ft above av. terrain, 512-ft. above ground, 1247-ft. above sea level.

Latitude	41°	44'	41"
Longitude	84°	01'	06"

Note: Latitude and longitude coordinates shown are based on the North American Datum of 1927 (NAD 27) as currently required by the Mass Media Bureau of the FCC.

Ownership: Dominion Broadcasting Inc. (Group Owner).

Began Operation: May 2, 2002. Began analog operations: October 19, 1998. Ceased analog operations: June 12, 2009.

Represented (legal): Wiley Rein LLP.

Represented (engineering): du Treil, Lundin & Rackley Inc.

Personnel:

Jamey R. Schmitz, Chief Executive Officer & General Manager.

Curt Miller, Sales Manager.

Eric Jingst, Chief Engineer.

Brooke Myerholtz, Program & Traffic Director.

Aaron Darr, Production Director & Executive Producer.

Shawn Rames, Office Manager.

Mike Rumschlag, Outreach & Special Events.

City of License: Toledo. **Station DMA:** Toledo, OH. **Rank:** 73.

TELEVISION & CABLE
Factbook Online
continuous updates   fully searchable   easy to use

For more information call **800-771-9202** or visit **www.warren-news.com**

WLMB-DT BPCDT-19991027ADB GRANTED: 9/22/2003

© 2010 Warren Communications News

Circulation © 2009 Nielsen. Coverage based on Nielsen study.

GrandTotal	Cable TV Households	Non-cable TV Households	Total TV Households
Estimated Station Totals *	230,130	49,620	279,750
Average Weekly Circulation (2009)	19,007	3,673	22,680
Average Daily Circulation (2009)			5,898

Station DMA Total	Cable TV Households	Non-cable TV Households	Total TV Households
Estimated Station Totals *	194,920	49,620	244,540
Average Weekly Circulation (2009)	14,465	3,673	18,138
Average Daily Circulation (2009)			4,983

Other DMA Total	Cable TV Households	Non-cable TV Households	Total TV Households
Estimated Station Totals *	35,210	0	35,210
Average Weekly Circulation (2009)	4,542	0	4,542
Average Daily Circulation (2009)			915

*Estimated station totals are sums of the Nielsen TV and Cable TV household estimates for each county in which the station registers viewing of more than 5% as per the Nielsen Survey Methods.

WNWO-DT
Ch. 49

Network Service: NBC.

Licensee: Barrington Toledo License LLC, 2500 W Higgins Rd, Ste 880, Hoffman Estates, IL 60195.

Studio: 300 S Byrne Rd, Toledo, OH 43615.

Mailing Address: 300 S. Byrne Rd, Toledo, OH 43615.

Phone: 419-535-0024. **Fax:** 419-535-0202.

E-mail: sweiss@nbc24.com

Web Site: http://www.nbc24.com

Technical Facilities: Channel No. 49 (680-686 MHz). Authorized power: 302.3-kw max. visual, aural. Antenna: 1334-ft above av. terrain, 1345-ft. above ground, 1924-ft. above sea level.

Latitude	41°	40'	03"
Longitude	83°	21'	22"

Transmitter: 833 N. Cousino Rd. at Arquette Rd., 5.8-mi. E of Toledo.

Note: Latitude and longitude coordinates shown are based on the North American Datum of 1927 (NAD 27) as currently required by the Mass Media Bureau of the FCC.

Ownership: Pilot Group LP (Group Owner).

Began Operation: February 8, 2001. High Definition. Began analog operations: May 3, 1966. Sale to Toledo Television Investors LP by The First National Bank of Boston, which took control from D. H. Overmyer Telecasting Co. Inc. approved by FCC January 31, 1986. Sale to Malrite Communications Group Inc. by Toledo Television Investors LP approved by FCC August 12, 1996. Sale to Raycom Media Inc. by Malrite Communications Group Inc. approved by FCC August 13, 1998. Sale to present owner by Raycom Media Inc. approved by FCC June 13, 2006, but not yet consummated. Ceased analog operations: June 12, 2009.

Represented (sales): TeleRep Inc.

Represented (legal): Paul Hastings.

Personnel:

Jon Skorburg, General Manager.

Sam Weiss, Local Sales Manager.

Kim Jakubowski, National Sales Manager.

Pat Livingston, News Director.

Harold Thompson, Chief Engineer.

Vickie Scott, Business Manager.

Jack Scott, Promotion Director & Production Manager.

Jon Hageali, Traffic Manager.

City of License: Toledo. **Station DMA:** Toledo, OH. **Rank:** 73.

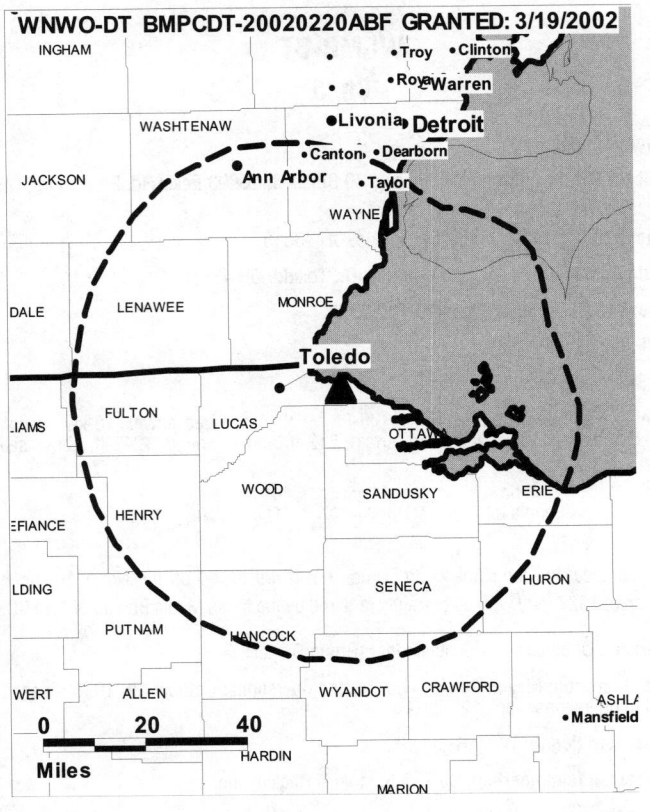

© 2010 Warren Communications News

Circulation © 2009 Nielsen. Coverage based on Nielsen study.

GrandTotal	Cable TV Households	Non-cable TV Households	Total TV Households
Estimated Station Totals *	332,080	254,460	586,540
Average Weekly Circulation (2009)	161,117	112,507	273,624
Average Daily Circulation (2009)			106,846

Station DMA Total	Cable TV Households	Non-cable TV Households	Total TV Households
Estimated Station Totals *	246,530	179,360	425,890
Average Weekly Circulation (2009)	138,328	97,911	236,239
Average Daily Circulation (2009)			92,084

Other DMA Total	Cable TV Households	Non-cable TV Households	Total TV Households
Estimated Station Totals *	85,550	75,100	160,650
Average Weekly Circulation (2009)	22,789	14,596	37,385
Average Daily Circulation (2009)			14,762

*Estimated station totals are sums of the Nielsen TV and Cable TV household estimates for each county in which the station registers viewing of more than 5% as per the Nielsen Survey Methods.

WTOL-DT
Ch. 11

Network Service: CBS.

Licensee: WTOL License Subsidiary LLC, 201 Monroe St, RSA Tower, 20th Fl, Montgomery, AL 36104.

Studio: 730 N Summit St, Toledo, OH 43604.

Mailing Address: 730 N. Summit St, Toledo, OH 43604.

Phone: 419-248-1111. **Fax:** 419-248-1177.

Web Site: http://www.wtol.com

Technical Facilities: Channel No. 11 (198-204 MHz). Authorized power: 16.9-kw visual, aural. Antenna: 1001-ft above av. terrain, 1005-ft. above ground, 1585-ft. above sea level.

Latitude	41°	40'	22"
Longitude	83°	22'	47"

Note: Latitude and longitude coordinates shown are based on the North American Datum of 1927 (NAD 27) as currently required by the Mass Media Bureau of the FCC.

Ownership: Raycom Media Inc. (Group Owner).

Began Operation: April 29, 2002. Standard and High Definition. Station broadcasting digitally on its analog channel allotment. Began analog operations: December 5, 1958. Sale to present owner by Cosmos Broadcasting Corp. approved by FCC January 17, 2006. Sale to Cosmos Broadcasting Corp. by Frazier Reams and associates approved by FCC March 10, 1965. Ceased analog operations: June 12, 2009.

Represented (legal): Covington & Burling.

Personnel:

Bob Chirdon, Vice President & General Manager.

Steve Israel, Operations & Program Manager.

Linda Blackburn, General Sales Manager.

Sue Strayer, Local Sales Manager.

Nancy Bright, National Sales Manager.

Mitch Jacob, News Director.

Steve Crum, Chief Engineer.

Jim Bowe, Engineering Supervisor.

Jenny Thomas, Assistant Regional Controller.

Rob Boenau, Marketing Director.

Bethany Moseley, Sales Research Director.

Bill Stewart, Creative Services Director.

Mary Anne McAuley, Traffic Manager.

City of License: Toledo. **Station DMA:** Toledo, OH. **Rank:** 73.

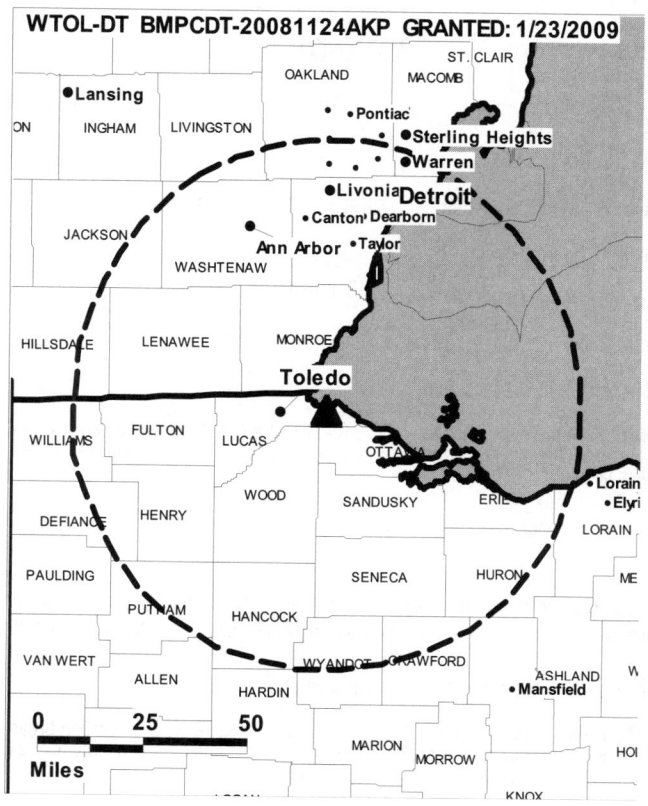

WTOL-DT BMPCDT-20081124AKP GRANTED: 1/23/2009

© 2010 Warren Communications News

Circulation © 2009 Nielsen. Coverage based on Nielsen study.

GrandTotal	Cable TV Households	Non-cable TV Households	Total TV Households
Estimated Station Totals *	350,230	254,460	604,690
Average Weekly Circulation (2009)	243,180	149,175	392,355
Average Daily Circulation (2009)			213,815

Station DMA Total	Cable TV Households	Non-cable TV Households	Total TV Households
Estimated Station Totals *	246,530	179,360	425,890
Average Weekly Circulation (2009)	194,843	125,722	320,565
Average Daily Circulation (2009)			179,729

Other DMA Total	Cable TV Households	Non-cable TV Households	Total TV Households
Estimated Station Totals *	103,700	75,100	178,800
Average Weekly Circulation (2009)	48,337	23,453	71,790
Average Daily Circulation (2009)			34,086

*Estimated station totals are sums of the Nielsen TV and Cable TV household estimates for each county in which the station registers viewing of more than 5% as per the Nielsen Survey Methods.

WTVG-DT
Ch. 13

Network Service: ABC.

Licensee: WTVG Inc., 77 W 66th St, 16th Fl, New York, NY 10023.

Studio: 4247 Dorr St, Toledo, OH 43607.

Mailing Address: 4247 Dorr St, Toledo, OH 43607.

Phone: 419-531-1313; 419-534-3858. **Fax:** 419-531-1399.

Web Site: http://www.13abc.com

Technical Facilities: Channel No. 13 (210-216 MHz). Authorized power: 14.6-kw visual, aural. Antenna: 1002-ft above av. terrain, 1012-ft. above ground, 1593-ft. above sea level.

Latitude	41°	41'	00"
Longitude	83°	24'	49"

Note: Latitude and longitude coordinates shown are based on the North American Datum of 1927 (NAD 27) as currently required by the Mass Media Bureau of the FCC.

Ownership: Disney Enterprises Inc. (Group Owner).

Began Operation: September 19, 2002. Standard and High Definition. Station broadcasting digitally on its analog channel allotment. Began analog operations: July 21, 1948. Ceased analog operations: June 12, 2009.

Personnel:

David Zamichow, President & General Manager.

Barbara Vaughn, Vice President & Chief Financial Officer.

Tami Rost, Program & Operations Manager.

Mary Gerken, Sales Director.

Bob Silver, Local Sales Manager.

Brian Trauring, News Director.

Barry Gries, Chief Engineer.

Matt Black, Production Manager.

Kevin Boyer, Traffic Manager.

Earnestine Weathers, Community Affairs Director.

City of License: Toledo. **Station DMA:** Toledo, OH. **Rank:** 73.

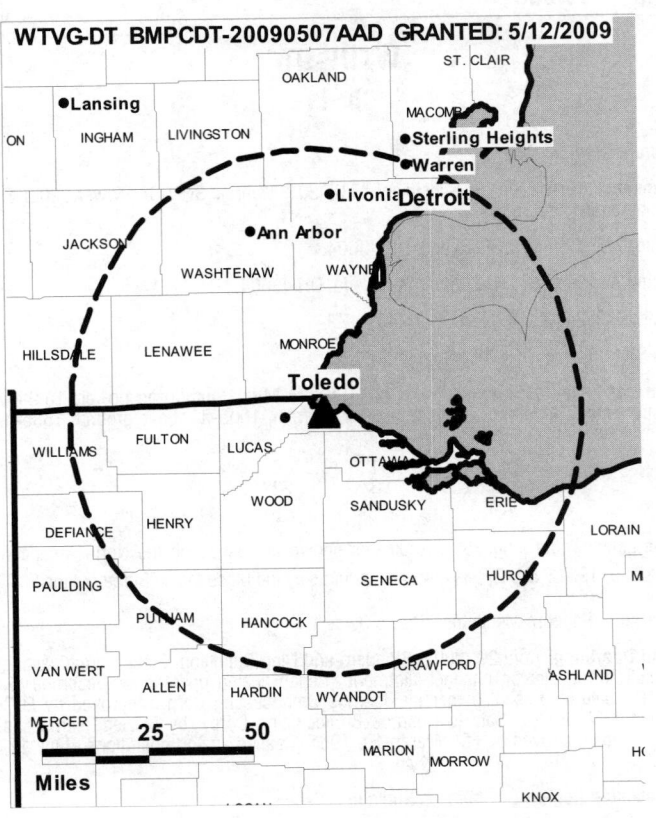

WTVG-DT BMPCDT-20090507AAD GRANTED: 5/12/2009

© 2010 Warren Communications News

Circulation © 2009 Nielsen. Coverage based on Nielsen study.

GrandTotal	Cable TV Households	Non-cable TV Households	Total TV Households
Estimated Station Totals *	367,690	298,180	665,870
Average Weekly Circulation (2009)	230,599	148,291	378,890
Average Daily Circulation (2009)			200,462

Station DMA Total	Cable TV Households	Non-cable TV Households	Total TV Households
Estimated Station Totals *	246,530	179,360	425,890
Average Weekly Circulation (2009)	184,765	122,725	307,490
Average Daily Circulation (2009)			170,597

Other DMA Total	Cable TV Households	Non-cable TV Households	Total TV Households
Estimated Station Totals *	121,160	118,820	239,980
Average Weekly Circulation (2009)	45,834	25,566	71,400
Average Daily Circulation (2009)			29,865

*Estimated station totals are sums of the Nielsen TV and Cable TV household estimates for each county in which the station registers viewing of more than 5% as per the Nielsen Survey Methods.

WUPW-DT
Ch. 46

Network Service: FOX.

Licensee: WUPW Broadcasting LLC, 4 Richmond Sq, Ste 200, Providence, RI 02906.

Studio: Four Seagate, Toledo, OH 43604.

Mailing Address: Four Seagate, Toledo, OH 43604.

Phone: 419-244-3600. **Fax:** 419-244-8842.

E-mail: rcedoz@foxtoledo.com

Web Site: http://www.foxtoledo.com

Technical Facilities: Channel No. 46 (662-668 MHz). Authorized power: 110-kw max. visual, aural. Antenna: 1168-ft above av. terrain, 1168-ft. above ground, 1765-ft. above sea level.

Latitude	41°	39'	22"
Longitude	83°	26'	41"

Requests CP for change to 200-kw max. visual, 1168-ft above av. terrain, 1168-ft. above ground, 1763-ft. above sea level; BPCDT-20080619AJB.

Note: Latitude and longitude coordinates shown are based on the North American Datum of 1927 (NAD 27) as currently required by the Mass Media Bureau of the FCC.

Ownership: LIN TV Corp. (Group Owner).

Began Operation: April 11, 2003. Began analog operations: September 22, 1985. Ceased analog operations: June 12, 2009.

Represented (sales): Blair Television.

Personnel:

Ray Maselli, President & General Manager.

Gary Yoder, General Sales Manager.

Brian Lorenzen, Local Sales Manager.

Steve Pietras, Chief Engineer & Operations Manager.

Maria Castonzo, Business Manager.

Cathy Stoner, Program Director.

Betsy Russell, Promotion Director.

Tom Ovacek, Production & Creative Services Director.

Jessica McClaslin, Traffic Manager.

City of License: Toledo. **Station DMA:** Toledo, OH. **Rank:** 73.

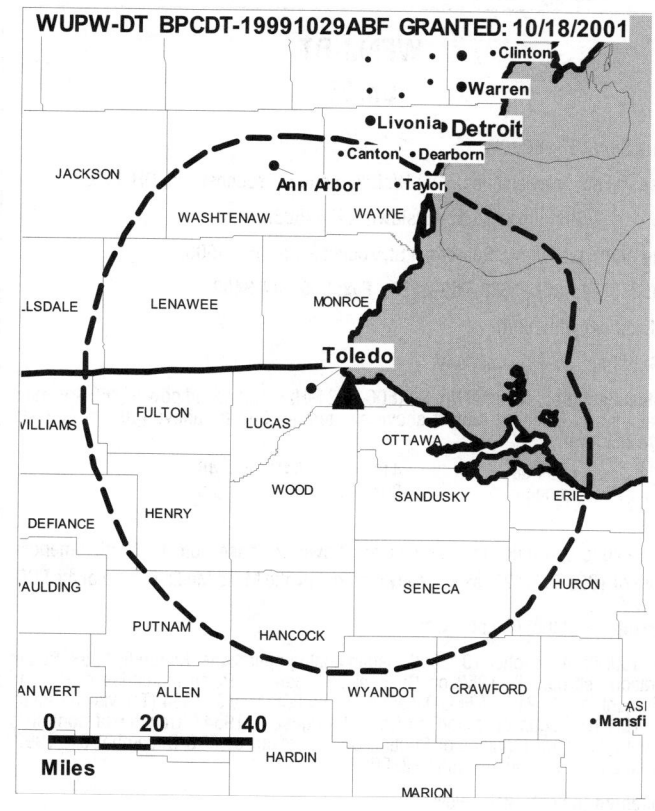

WUPW-DT BPCDT-19991029ABF GRANTED: 10/18/2001

© 2010 Warren Communications News

Circulation © 2009 Nielsen. Coverage based on Nielsen study.

GrandTotal	Cable TV Households	Non-cable TV Households	Total TV Households
Estimated Station Totals *	332,080	238,950	571,030
Average Weekly Circulation (2009)	149,562	113,692	263,254
Average Daily Circulation (2009)			94,561

Station DMA Total	Cable TV Households	Non-cable TV Households	Total TV Households
Estimated Station Totals *	246,530	179,360	425,890
Average Weekly Circulation (2009)	127,636	99,887	227,523
Average Daily Circulation (2009)			79,786

Other DMA Total	Cable TV Households	Non-cable TV Households	Total TV Households
Estimated Station Totals *	85,550	59,590	145,140
Average Weekly Circulation (2009)	21,926	13,805	35,731
Average Daily Circulation (2009)			14,775

*Estimated station totals are sums of the Nielsen TV and Cable TV household estimates for each county in which the station registers viewing of more than 5% as per the Nielsen Survey Methods.

WFMJ-DT
Ch. 20

Network Service: NBC, CW.

Grantee: WFMJ Television Inc., 101 W. Boardman St, Youngstown, OH 44503.

Studio: 101 W Boardman St, Youngstown, OH 44503.

Mailing Address: 101 W. Boardman St, Youngstown, OH 44503.

Phone: 330-744-8611; 888-769-2473. **Fax:** 330-744-3402.

E-mail: kbric@wfmj.com

Web Site: http://www.wfmj.com/

Technical Facilities: Channel No. 20 (506-512 MHz). Authorized power: 460-kw max. visual, aural. Antenna: 966-ft above av. terrain, 988-ft. above ground, 2021-ft. above sea level.

Latitude	41°	04'	48"
Longitude	80°	38'	25"

Note: Latitude and longitude coordinates shown are based on the North American Datum of 1927 (NAD 27) as currently required by the Mass Media Bureau of the FCC.

Ownership: NPM Inc. (Group Owner).

Began Operation: October 13, 2006. Began analog operations: March 8, 1953. Began operation February 8, 1952 on Channel 73. Sale by Polan Industries of CP and equipment for Ch. 21 to WFMJ-TV approved by FCC May 5, 1954 (Television Digest, Vol. 10:19). Began operation on Ch. 21 August 7, 1954. Transfer of control to present owner from Vindicator Printing Co. approved by FCC December 31, 1992. Ceased analog operations: June 12, 2009.

Represented (sales): Blair Television.

Personnel:

Betty H. Brown Jagnow, President.

John Grdic, General Manager, Station Manager & Program Director.

Jack Grdic, Local & Regional Sales Manager.

Kathy Brickman, National Sales Manager.

Mona Alexander, News Director.

Bob Flis, Chief Engineer.

Kathy Duganne, Controller.

Jack Stevenson, Marketing Director.

Joe Romano, Promotion Director.

JoLynn Mullally, Production Manager.

Amy Williams, Traffic Manager.

Cindy Fularz, Human Resources Director.

Madonna Pinkard, Community Relations Director.

City of License: Youngstown. **Station DMA:** Youngstown, OH. **Rank:** 110.

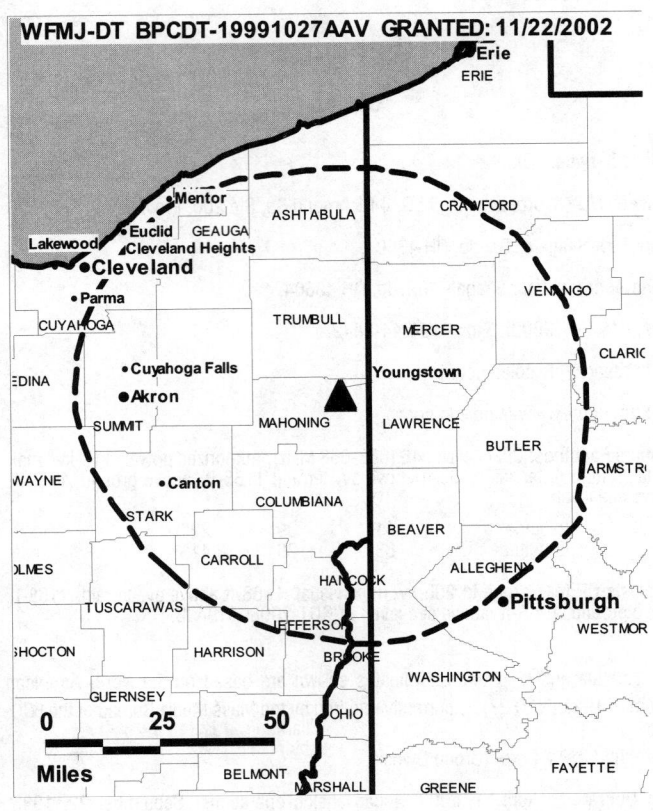

© 2010 Warren Communications News

Circulation © 2009 Nielsen. Coverage based on Nielsen study.

GrandTotal	Cable TV Households	Non-cable TV Households	Total TV Households
Estimated Station Totals *	264,010	169,110	433,120
Average Weekly Circulation (2009)	143,294	68,926	212,220
Average Daily Circulation (2009)			115,633

Station DMA Total	Cable TV Households	Non-cable TV Households	Total TV Households
Estimated Station Totals *	181,500	87,430	268,930
Average Weekly Circulation (2009)	130,507	61,209	191,716
Average Daily Circulation (2009)			107,400

Other DMA Total	Cable TV Households	Non-cable TV Households	Total TV Households
Estimated Station Totals *	82,510	81,680	164,190
Average Weekly Circulation (2009)	12,787	7,717	20,504
Average Daily Circulation (2009)			8,233

*Estimated station totals are sums of the Nielsen TV and Cable TV household estimates for each county in which the station registers viewing of more than 5% as per the Nielsen Survey Methods.

WKBN-DT
Ch. 41

Network Service: CBS.

Grantee: NVT Youngstown Licensee LLC, Debtor in Possession, 3500 Lenox Rd, Ste 640, Atlanta, GA 30326.

Studio: 3930 Sunset Blvd, Youngstown, OH 44512.

Mailing Address: 3930 Sunset Blvd, Youngstown, OH 44512.

Phone: 330-782-1144. **Fax:** 330-782-3504.

E-mail: dcoy@wkbn.com

Web Site: http://www.wkbn.com/

Technical Facilities: Channel No. 41 (632-638 MHz). Authorized power: 700-kw max. visual, aural. Antenna: 1371-ft above av. terrain, 1332-ft. above ground, 2438-ft. above sea level.

Latitude	41°	03'	24"
Longitude	80°	38'	44"

Note: Latitude and longitude coordinates shown are based on the North American Datum of 1927 (NAD 27) as currently required by the Mass Media Bureau of the FCC.

Ownership: New Vision Television LLC, Debtor in Possession (Group Owner).

Began Operation: April 27, 2006. Began analog operations: January 11, 1953. Ceased analog operations: June 12, 2009. W. P. Williamson Jr. increased holdings from 60% to 100% in 1958 by purchasing 40% held by publisher of Cleveland Plain Dealer and News for undisclosed amount and retiring stock to treasury. Sale to GOCOM Communications LLC from WKBN Broadcasting Corp., and subsequent merger with Grapevine Communications Inc., to form GOCOM Holdings LLC approved by FCC November 1, 1999. GOCOM Holdings LLC later renamed Piedmont Television Holdings LLC. Sale to present owner by Piedmont Television Holdings LLC approved by FCC January 8, 2007. Involuntary assignment of license to Debtor in Possession status approved by FCC July 24, 2009.

Represented (legal): Wiley Rein LLP.

Represented (sales): Continental Television Sales.

Personnel:

David Coy, General Manager.

Nicolette Manuel, Local Sales Manager.

Jill Duffy, National Sales Manager.

Gary Coursen, News Director.

Tom Zocolo, Chief Engineer.

Marion Sweely, Business Manager.

John Amann Jr., Marketing, Promotion & Production Director.

Phyllis Rappach, Program Director.

Jo-Lynn Ortenzio, Creative Services & Production Manager.

Sandy Dota, Traffic Manager.

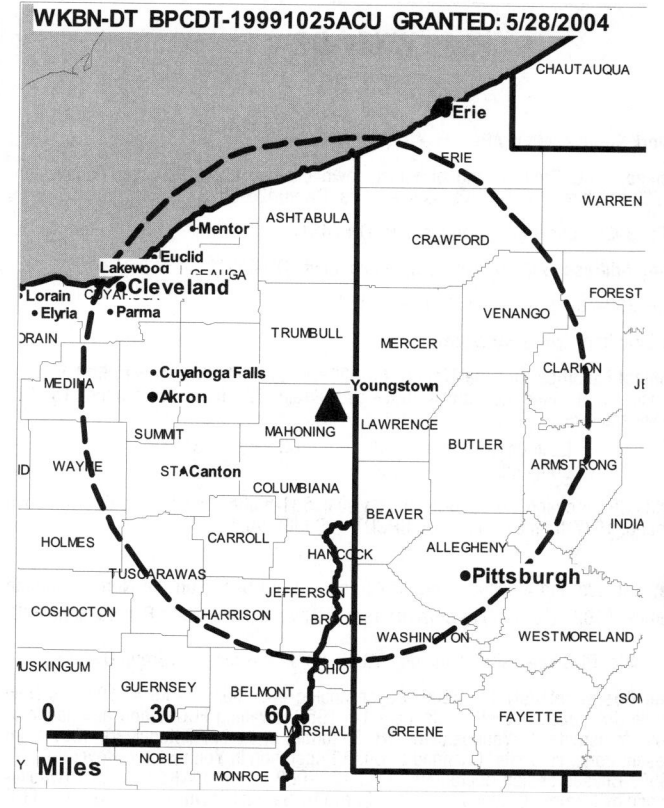

© 2010 Warren Communications News

City of License: Youngstown. **Station DMA:** Youngstown, OH. **Rank:** 110.

Circulation © 2009 Nielsen. Coverage based on Nielsen study.

GrandTotal	Cable TV Households	Non-cable TV Households	Total TV Households
Estimated Station Totals *	280,030	185,870	465,900
Average Weekly Circulation (2009)	134,025	66,387	200,412
Average Daily Circulation (2009)			103,135

Station DMA Total	Cable TV Households	Non-cable TV Households	Total TV Households
Estimated Station Totals *	181,500	87,430	268,930
Average Weekly Circulation (2009)	122,476	59,268	181,744
Average Daily Circulation (2009)			96,786

Other DMA Total	Cable TV Households	Non-cable TV Households	Total TV Households
Estimated Station Totals *	98,530	98,440	196,970
Average Weekly Circulation (2009)	11,549	7,119	18,668
Average Daily Circulation (2009)			6,349

*Estimated station totals are sums of the Nielsen TV and Cable TV household estimates for each county in which the station registers viewing of more than 5% as per the Nielsen Survey Methods.

WYTV-DT
Ch. 36

Network Service: MNT, ABC.

Licensee: PBC Broadcasting of Youngstown License LLC, Debtor in Possession, 11766 Wilshire Blvd, Ste 405, Los Angeles, CA 90025-6573.

Studio: 3930 Sunset Blvd, Youngstown, OH 44512.

Mailing Address: 3930 Sunset Blvd, Youngstown, OH 44512.

Phone: 330-782-1144. **Fax:** 330-782-8154.

Web Site: http://www.wytv.com

Technical Facilities: Channel No. 36 (602-608 MHz). Authorized power: 50-kw max. visual, aural. Antenna: 486-ft above av. terrain, 528-ft. above ground, 1552-ft. above sea level.

Latitude	41°	03'	43"
Longitude	80°	38'	07"

Holds CP for change to 1000-kw max. visual, 581-ft above av. terrain, 622-ft. above ground, 1647-ft. above sea level; BPCDT-20080620ALJ.

Note: Latitude and longitude coordinates shown are based on the North American Datum of 1927 (NAD 27) as currently required by the Mass Media Bureau of the FCC.

Ownership: PBC Television Holdings LLC, Debtor in Possession (Group Owner).

Began Operation: July 11, 2006. Began analog operations: April 4, 1953 as New Castle, PA outlet, but left air January 14, 1955, awaiting FCC action on petition to move transmitter to Youngstown, OH. Resumed operation October 30, 1957 from present transmitter site. Changed to Ch. 33 operation in Youngstown November 26, 1959. Ceased analog operations: June 12, 2009. Sale to WKST-TV Inc. (wholly-owned by Communications Industries Corp.) by Samuel Townsend approved by FCC April 12, 1961. Sale to Edwin G. Richter Jr., Edgewood Investment, Adam Young, Howard D. Duncan Jr., et al., by WKST-TV Inc. approved by FCC February 5, 1965. Sale to Adams-Russell Co. by Edwin G. Richter Jr., Edgewood Investment, Adam Young, Howard D. Duncan Jr., et al., approved by FCC September 12, 1970. Sale to A. Richard Benedek & Robert L. Dudley by Adams-Russell Co. approved by FCC April 15, 1983. Sale of Dudley's 50% to Benedek approved by FCC November 25, 1985. Sale to Chelsey Broadcasting Co. LLC by Benedek Broadcasting Co. LLC approved by FCC August 29, 2002. Sale to present owner by Chelsey Broadcasting Co. LLC approved by FCC July 30, 2007. Involuntary assignment of license to Debtor in Possession status approved by FCC July 24, 2009.

Represented (legal): Drinker Biddle.

Represented (sales): Blair Television.

Personnel:

David Coy, General Manager.

Nikki Manuel, General Sales Manager.

Pat Springer, Regional Sales Manager.

Tom Zocolo, Chief Engineer.

Marion Sweely, Business Manager.

Becky Hambrick, Programming.

John Amann Jr., Marketing & Promotion Director.

Sandy Dota, Traffic Manager.

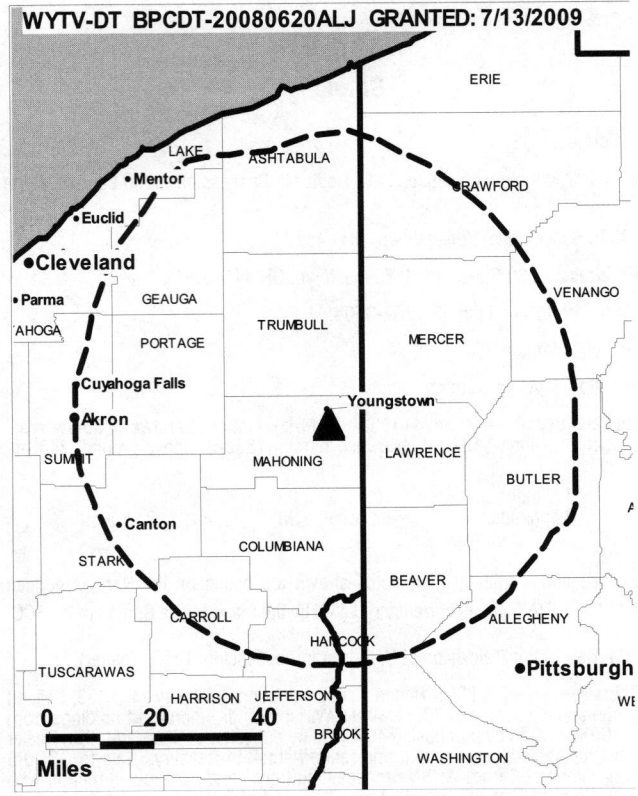

© 2010 Warren Communications News

City of License: Youngstown. **Station DMA:** Youngstown, OH. **Rank:** 110.

Circulation © 2009 Nielsen. Coverage based on Nielsen study.

GrandTotal	Cable TV Households	Non-cable TV Households	Total TV Households
Estimated Station Totals *	333,800	117,210	451,010
Average Weekly Circulation (2009)	126,334	55,479	181,813
Average Daily Circulation (2009)			78,990

Station DMA Total	Cable TV Households	Non-cable TV Households	Total TV Households
Estimated Station Totals *	181,500	87,430	268,930
Average Weekly Circulation (2009)	111,160	53,368	164,528
Average Daily Circulation (2009)			74,766

Other DMA Total	Cable TV Households	Non-cable TV Households	Total TV Households
Estimated Station Totals *	152,300	29,780	182,080
Average Weekly Circulation (2009)	15,174	2,111	17,285
Average Daily Circulation (2009)			4,224

*Estimated station totals are sums of the Nielsen TV and Cable TV household estimates for each county in which the station registers viewing of more than 5% as per the Nielsen Survey Methods.

WHIZ-DT
Ch. 40

Network Service: NBC.

Grantee: Southeastern Ohio Television System, 629 Downard Rd, Zanesville, OH 43701.

Studio: 629 Downard Rd, Zanesville, OH 43701.

Mailing Address: 629 Downard Rd, Zanesville, OH 43701.

Phone: 740-452-5431; 740-453-0361. **Fax:** 740-452-6553.

Web Site: http://www.whiznews.com

Technical Facilities: Channel No. 40 (626-632 MHz). Authorized power: 620-kw max. visual, aural. Antenna: 554-ft above av. terrain, 476-ft. above ground, 1386-ft. above sea level.

Latitude	39°	55'	42"
Longitude	81°	59'	07"

Note: Latitude and longitude coordinates shown are based on the North American Datum of 1927 (NAD 27) as currently required by the Mass Media Bureau of the FCC.

Ownership: Southeastern Ohio Television System (Group Owner).

Began Operation: February 21, 2008. Station off air June 16, 2006 due to antenna failure; returned to air at reduced power late January 2007. Began analog operations: May 23, 1953. Ceased analog operations due to equipment failure July 25, 2008; did not return to air.

Represented (sales): Continental Television Sales.

Personnel:

H. C. Littick, President.

Brian Wagner, Vice President & Station Manager.

Doug Pickrell, General & Local Sales Manager.

George Hiotis, News Director.

Dan Slentz, Chief Engineer.

Scott Lauka, Controller.

Brian Wagner, Program Director.

Gary Earich, Production Manager.

Carolyn Rider, Traffic Manager.

City of License: Zanesville. **Station DMA:** Zanesville, OH. **Rank:** 203.

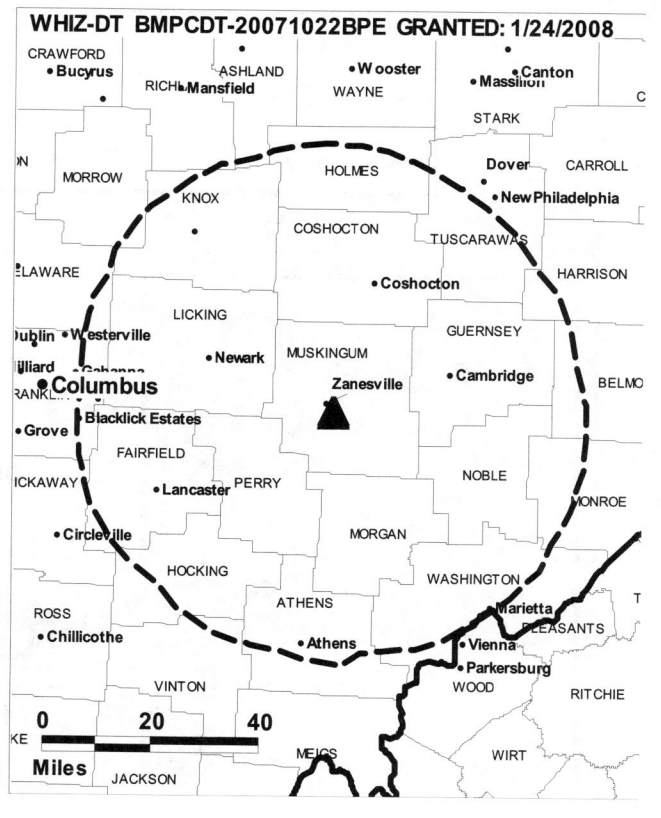

© 2010 Warren Communications News

Circulation © 2009 Nielsen. Coverage based on Nielsen study.

GrandTotal	Cable TV Households	Non-cable TV Households	Total TV Households
Estimated Station Totals *	112,950	37,160	150,110
Average Weekly Circulation (2009)	31,266	8,347	39,613
Average Daily Circulation (2009)			19,472

Station DMA Total	Cable TV Households	Non-cable TV Households	Total TV Households
Estimated Station Totals *	23,200	9,350	32,550
Average Weekly Circulation (2009)	15,753	5,965	21,718
Average Daily Circulation (2009)			12,890

Other DMA Total	Cable TV Households	Non-cable TV Households	Total TV Households
Estimated Station Totals *	89,750	27,810	117,560
Average Weekly Circulation (2009)	15,513	2,382	17,895
Average Daily Circulation (2009)			6,582

*Estimated station totals are sums of the Nielsen TV and Cable TV household estimates for each county in which the station registers viewing of more than 5% as per the Nielsen Survey Methods.

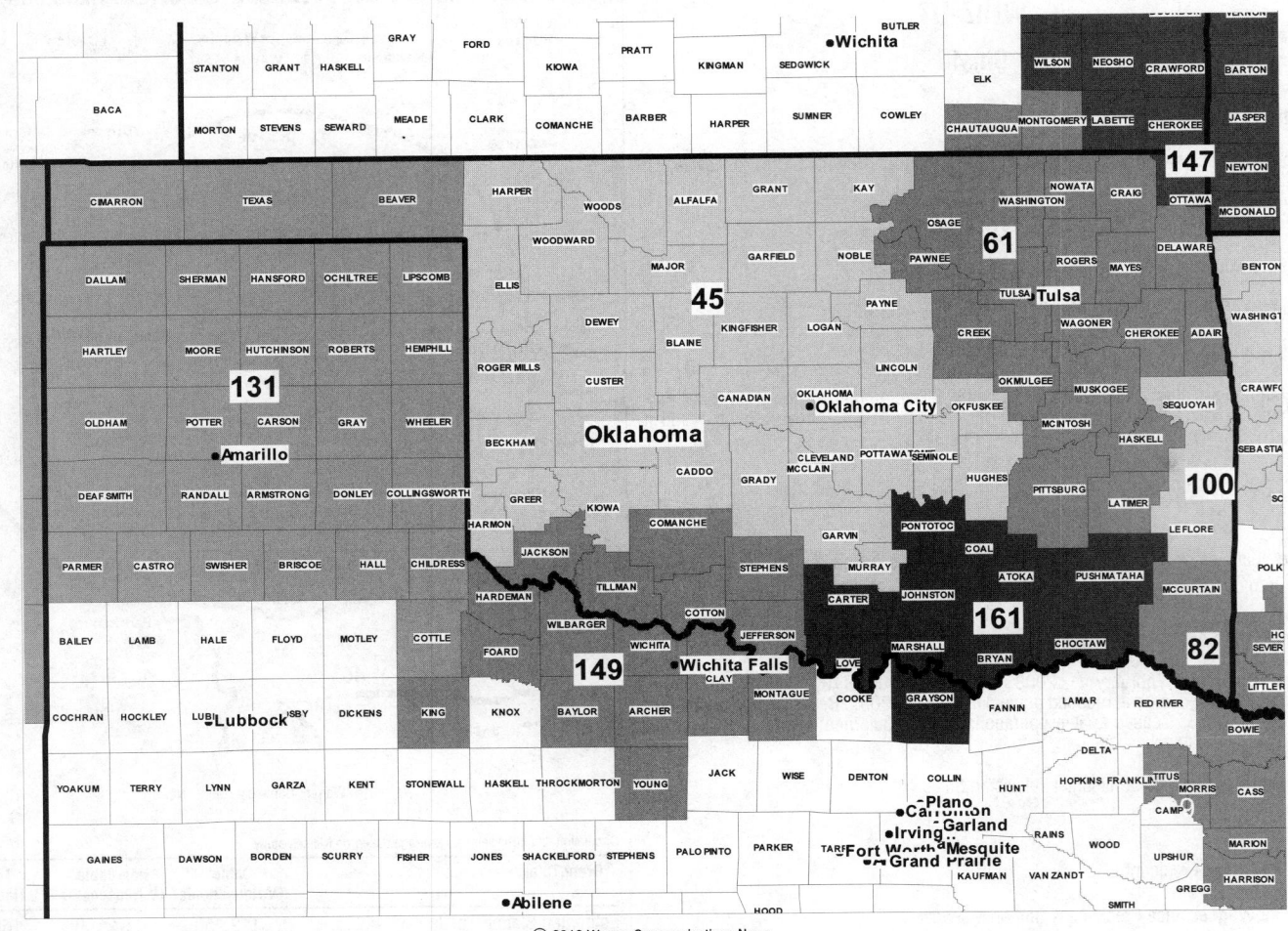

© 2010 Warren Communications News

MARKET	NIELSEN DMA TV HOUSEHOLDS	RANK	MARKET AREA COMMERCIAL STATIONS
Oklahoma City, OK	694,030	45	KAUT-DT (40); KFOR-DT (27); KOCB-DT (33); KOCM-DT (46); KOCO-DT (7); KOKH-DT (24); KOPX-TV (50); KSBI-DT (51); KTBO-DT (15); KTUZ-DT (29); KWTV-DT (9)
Tulsa, OK	528,070	61	KDOR-DT (17); KGEB-DT (49); KJRH-DT (56); KMYT-DT (42); KOKI-DT (22); KOTV-DT (55); KQCW-DT (20); KTPX-TV (28); KTUL-DT (58); KWHB-DT (47)
Shreveport, LA	386,180	82	KMSS-DT (34); KPXJ-DT (21); KSHV-DT (44); KSLA-DT (17); KTAL-DT (15); KTBS-DT (28)
Fort Smith-Fayetteville-Springdale-Rogers, AR	298,330	100	KFSM-DT (18); KFTA-DT (27); KHBS-DT (21); KHOG-DT (15); KNWA-DT (50); KWOG-DT (39)
Amarillo, TX	192,490	131	KAMR-DT (19); KCIT-DT (15); KEYU-DT (31); KFDA-DT (10); KPTF-DT (18); KVIH-DT (12); KVII-DT (7)
Joplin, MO-Pittsburg, KS	155,670	147	KFJX-DT (13); KOAM-DT (7); KODE-DT (43); KSNF-DT (46)
Wichita Falls, TX & Lawton, OK	154,450	149	KAUZ-DT (22); KFDX-DT (28); KJTL-DT (15); KSWO-DT (11)
Sherman, TX-Ada, OK	127,990	161	KTEN-DT (26); KXII-DT (12)

Oklahoma Station Totals as of October 1, 2009

	VHF	UHF	TOTAL
Commercial Television	3	20	23
Educational Television	3	2	5
	6	22	28

KTEN-DT
Ch. 26

Network Service: NBC, CW.

Grantee: Channel 49 Acquisition Corp., PO Box 1800, c/o Brooks, Pierce et al., Raleigh, NC 27602.

Studios: 124 E Main, Ste 2, Ada, TX 74820; 10 Highpoint Cir, Denison, TX 75021.

Mailing Address: 10 Highpoint Cir, Denison, TX 75021.

Phone: 580-436-5836; 580-223-1632. **Fax:** 580-332-1619.

Web Site: http://www.kten.com

Technical Facilities: Channel No. 26 (542-548 MHz). Authorized power: 1000-kw max. visual, aural. Antenna: 1398-ft above av. terrain, 1325-ft. above ground, 2205-ft. above sea level.

Latitude	34°	21'	34"
Longitude	96°	33'	34"

Note: Latitude and longitude coordinates shown are based on the North American Datum of 1927 (NAD 27) as currently required by the Mass Media Bureau of the FCC.

Ownership: Lockwood Broadcasting Inc.

Began Operation: June 29, 2006. Began analog operations: April 28, 1954. Sale to present owner by KTEN Television LP approved by FCC May 28, 1998. Sale to KTEN Television LP approved by FCC July 20, 1994. Assignment of license to Trustee granted by FCC February 8, 1993. Transfer of control to Eastern Oklahoma Television Co. Inc. approved by FCC November 16, 1988. Sale to TV 10, et al., by Bill Hoover, et al., approved by FCC January 25, 1985. Ceased analog operations: June 12, 2009.

Represented (legal): Brooks, Pierce, McLendon, Humphrey & Leonard LLP.

Represented (sales): Continental Television Sales.

Personnel:

Otis Pickett, General Manager.

Asa Jessee, Station Manager.

Ken Braswell, General Sales Manager.

David Robberson, Local Sales Director.

Steve Korioth, News Director.

David Hebert, Chief Engineer.

Karen Lewis, Business Manager.

Courtney Russ, Promotion Director.

Stacy Maxwell, Production Manager.

City of License: Ada. **Station DMA:** Sherman, TX-Ada, OK. **Rank:** 161.

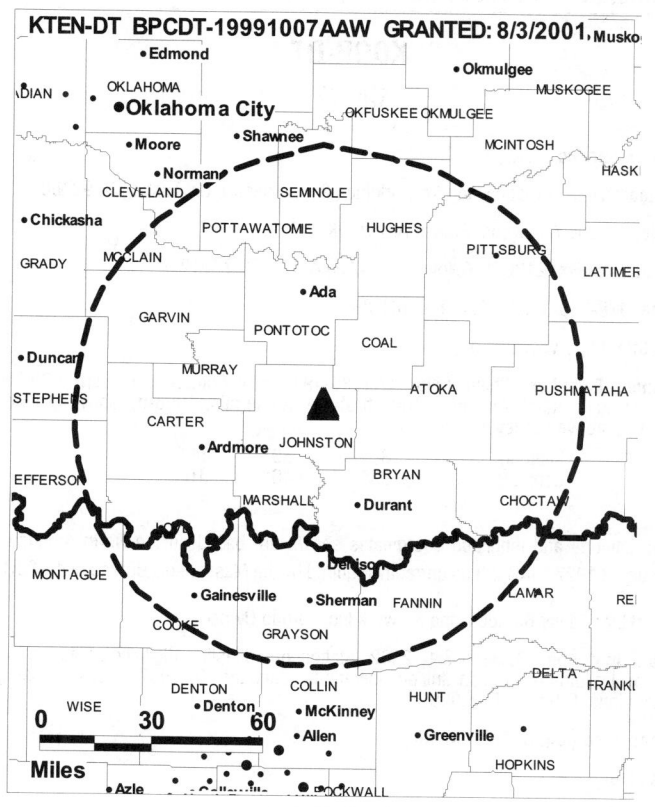

KTEN-DT BPCDT-19991007AAW GRANTED: 8/3/2001.

© 2010 Warren Communications News

Circulation © 2009 Nielsen. Coverage based on Nielsen study.

GrandTotal	Cable TV Households	Non-cable TV Households	Total TV Households
Estimated Station Totals *	72,900	82,240	155,140
Average Weekly Circulation (2009)	37,960	37,762	75,722
Average Daily Circulation (2009)			35,655

Station DMA Total	Cable TV Households	Non-cable TV Households	Total TV Households
Estimated Station Totals *	51,310	68,090	119,400
Average Weekly Circulation (2009)	31,078	36,336	67,414
Average Daily Circulation (2009)			33,134

Other DMA Total	Cable TV Households	Non-cable TV Households	Total TV Households
Estimated Station Totals *	21,590	14,150	35,740
Average Weekly Circulation (2009)	6,882	1,426	8,308
Average Daily Circulation (2009)			2,521

*Estimated station totals are sums of the Nielsen TV and Cable TV household estimates for each county in which the station registers viewing of more than 5% as per the Nielsen Survey Methods.

KDOR-DT
Ch. 17

Network Service: TBN.

Licensee: Trinity Broadcasting Network Inc., 2442 Michelle Dr, Tustin, CA 92780.

Studio: 2120 N Yellowood, Broken Arrow, OK 74012.

Mailing Address: 2120 N. Yellowood, Broken Arrow, OK 74012.

Phone: 918-250-0777. **Fax:** 918-461-8817.

Web Site: http://www.tbn.org

Technical Facilities: Channel No. 17 (488-494 MHz). Authorized power: 1000-kw max. visual, aural. Antenna: 1043-ft above av. terrain, 1056-ft. above ground, 1716-ft. above sea level.

Latitude	36°	30'	59"
Longitude	95°	46'	10"

Note: Latitude and longitude coordinates shown are based on the North American Datum of 1927 (NAD 27) as currently required by the Mass Media Bureau of the FCC.

Ownership: Trinity Broadcasting Network Inc. (Group Owner).

Began Operation: December 1, 2002. Station broadcasting digitally on its analog channel allotment. Began analog operations: January 10, 1987. Ceased analog operations: February 17, 2009.

Represented (legal): Colby M. May.

Personnel:

Craig Nelson, General Manager & Traffic Manager.

Eb Tesfalidet, Chief Engineer.

Michelle Gustafson, Public Affairs.

City of License: Bartlesville. **Station DMA:** Tulsa, OK. **Rank:** 61.

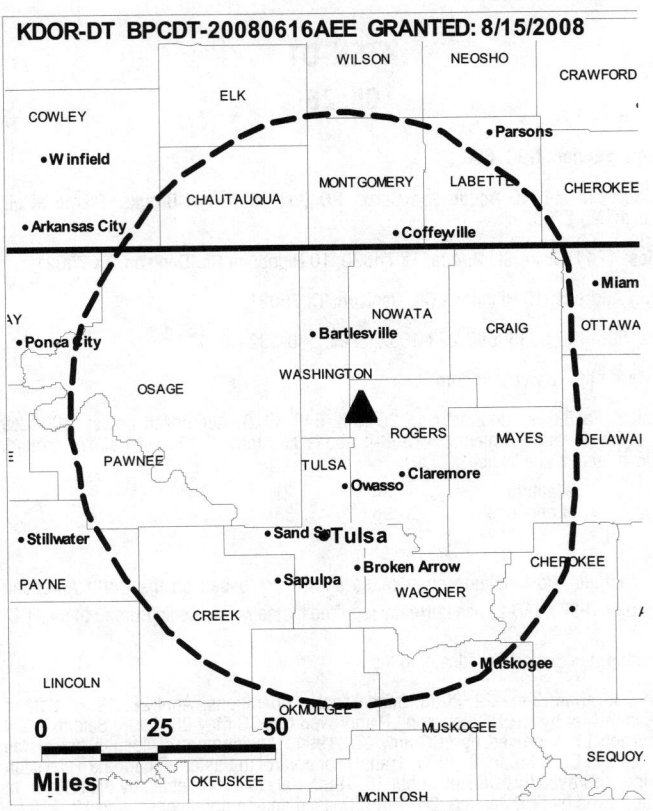

KDOR-DT BPCDT-20080616AEE GRANTED: 8/15/2008

© 2010 Warren Communications News

Circulation © 2009 Nielsen. Coverage based on Nielsen study.

GrandTotal	Cable TV Households	Non-cable TV Households	Total TV Households
Estimated Station Totals *	33,860	0	33,860
Average Weekly Circulation (2009)	2,093	0	2,093
Average Daily Circulation (2009)			316

Station DMA Total	Cable TV Households	Non-cable TV Households	Total TV Households
Estimated Station Totals *	33,860	0	33,860
Average Weekly Circulation (2009)	2,093	0	2,093
Average Daily Circulation (2009)			316

*Estimated station totals are sums of the Nielsen TV and Cable TV household estimates for each county in which the station registers viewing of more than 5% as per the Nielsen Survey Methods.

KSWO-DT
Ch. 11

Network Service: ABC.

Grantee: KSWO Television Co. Inc., PO Box 708, Lawton, OK 73502.

Studio: 1401 SE 60th St, Lawton, OK 73501.

Mailing Address: PO Box 708, Lawton, OK 73502.

Phone: 580-355-7000. **Fax:** 580-357-3811.

Web Site: http://www.kswo.com

Technical Facilities: Channel No. 11 (198-204 MHz). Authorized power: 138-kw visual, aural. Antenna: 1074-ft above av. terrain, 1002-ft. above ground, 2142-ft. above sea level.

Latitude	34°	12'	55"
Longitude	98°	43'	13"

Note: Latitude and longitude coordinates shown are based on the North American Datum of 1927 (NAD 27) as currently required by the Mass Media Bureau of the FCC.

Ownership: Drewry Communications (Group Owner).

Began Operation: July 7, 2006. Began analog operations: March 8, 1953. Sale to KSWO License Co. LLC (London Broadcasting Co. Inc.) approved by FCC November 5, 2008, but never consummated. Ceased analog operations: February 17, 2009.

Represented (legal): Davis Wright Tremaine LLP.

Represented (sales): Petry Media Corp.

Personnel:

Robert Drewry, President.

Larry Patton, Vice President & General Manager.

Mike Raite, Creative Services Director.

John Brandt, Production Manager.

Gail Martinson, Traffic Manager.

Mike Taylor, Operations & Program Director.

Cindy Coleman, General Sales Manager.

David Bradley, News Director.

Joe Bartnik, Chief Engineer.

Todd Young, Promotion Director.

City of License: Lawton. **Station DMA:** Wichita Falls, TX & Lawton, OK. **Rank:** 149.

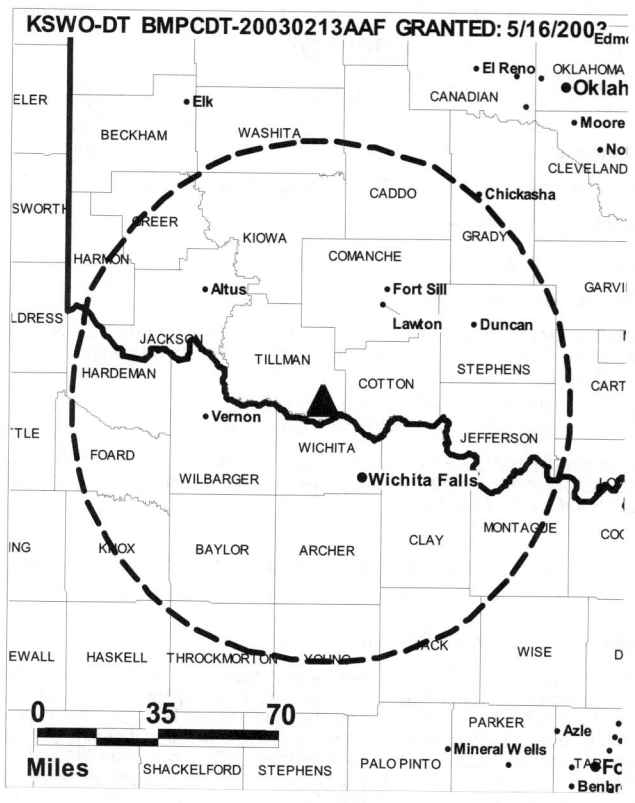

© 2010 Warren Communications News

Circulation © 2009 Nielsen. Coverage based on Nielsen study.

GrandTotal	Cable TV Households	Non-cable TV Households	Total TV Households
Estimated Station Totals *	86,410	86,700	173,110
Average Weekly Circulation (2009)	47,426	43,275	90,701
Average Daily Circulation (2009)			47,452

Station DMA Total	Cable TV Households	Non-cable TV Households	Total TV Households
Estimated Station Totals *	71,490	83,960	155,450
Average Weekly Circulation (2009)	45,497	42,993	88,490
Average Daily Circulation (2009)			46,759

Other DMA Total	Cable TV Households	Non-cable TV Households	Total TV Households
Estimated Station Totals *	14,920	2,740	17,660
Average Weekly Circulation (2009)	1,929	282	2,211
Average Daily Circulation (2009)			693

*Estimated station totals are sums of the Nielsen TV and Cable TV household estimates for each county in which the station registers viewing of more than 5% as per the Nielsen Survey Methods.

KQCW-DT
Ch. 20

Network Service: CW.

Grantee: Griffin Licensing LLC, 7401 N Kelley Ave, Oklahoma City, OK 73111-8420.

Mailing Address: 302 S Frankfort, Tulsa, OK 74120.

Phone: 918-732-6000.

Web Site: http://www.cw12.com

Technical Facilities: Channel No. 20 (506-512 MHz). Authorized power: 550-kw max. visual, aural. Antenna: 827-ft above av. terrain, 752-ft. above ground, 1512-ft. above sea level.

Latitude	35°	45'	08"
Longitude	95°	48'	15"

Requests modification of CP for change to 1000-kw max. visual, 1634-ft above av. terrain, 1557-ft. above ground, 2267-ft. above sea level; lat. 36° 01' 15", long. 95° 40' 32", BMPCDT-20080620AMN.

Note: Latitude and longitude coordinates shown are based on the North American Datum of 1927 (NAD 27) as currently required by the Mass Media Bureau of the FCC.

Ownership: Griffin Communications LLC.

Began Operation: February 17, 2009. Began analog operations: September 12, 1999. Transfer of control from KM Communications Inc. (Myoung Hwa Bae), Northwest Television Inc. & Todd P. Robinson (jointly 100% to 51%) to Tulsa Communications LLC (0% to 49%) approved by FCC October 13, 1998. Transfer of control to Tulsa Communications Inc. (Cascade Broadcasting Group LLC) of remaining 51% interest approved by FCC June 1, 1999. Sale to present owner by Cascade Broadcasting Group LLC approved by FCC November 22, 2005. Ceased analog operations: February 17, 2009.

Represented (legal): Wilkinson Barker Knauer LLP.

City of License: Muskogee. **Station DMA:** Tulsa, OK. **Rank:** 61.

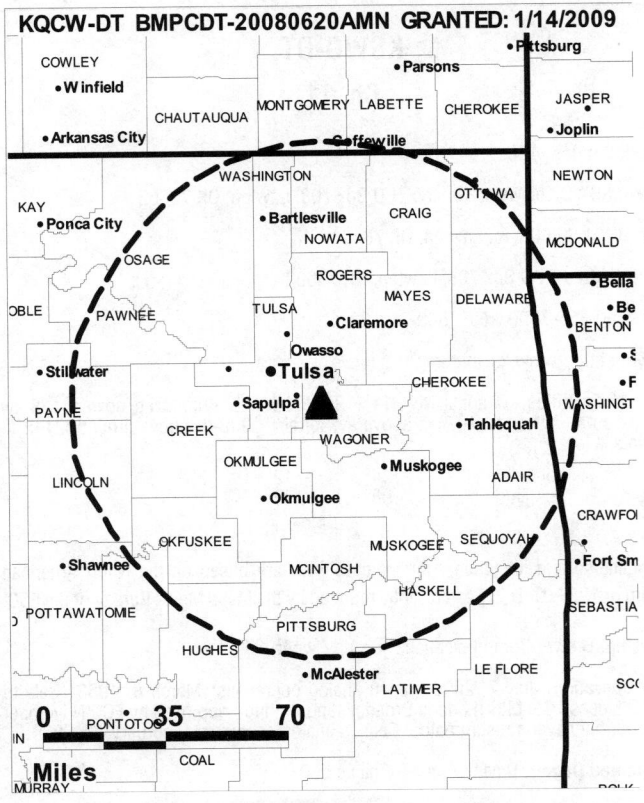

KQCW-DT BMPCDT-20080620AMN GRANTED: 1/14/2009

© 2010 Warren Communications News

Circulation © 2009 Nielsen. Coverage based on Nielsen study.

GrandTotal	Cable TV Households	Non-cable TV Households	Total TV Households
Estimated Station Totals *	274,170	233,460	507,630
Average Weekly Circulation (2009)	61,518	65,521	127,039
Average Daily Circulation (2009)			43,863

Station DMA Total	Cable TV Households	Non-cable TV Households	Total TV Households
Estimated Station Totals *	268,910	233,460	502,370
Average Weekly Circulation (2009)	59,977	65,521	125,498
Average Daily Circulation (2009)			43,768

Other DMA Total	Cable TV Households	Non-cable TV Households	Total TV Households
Estimated Station Totals *	5,260	0	5,260
Average Weekly Circulation (2009)	1,541	0	1,541
Average Daily Circulation (2009)			95

*Estimated station totals are sums of the Nielsen TV and Cable TV household estimates for each county in which the station registers viewing of more than 5% as per the Nielsen Survey Methods.

KOCM-DT
Ch. 46

Network Service: IND.

Licensee: Word of God Fellowship Inc., 3901 Hwy 121 S, Bedford, TX 76021-3009.

Mailing Address: 3901 Hwy 121 S, Bedford, TX 76021.

Phone: 817-571-1229.

Web Site: http://www.daystar.com

Technical Facilities: Channel No. 46 (662-668 MHz). Authorized power: 50-kw max. visual, aural. Antenna: 1365-ft above av. terrain, 1401-ft. above ground, 2503-ft. above sea level.

Latitude	35°	35'	52"
Longitude	97°	29'	22"

Note: Latitude and longitude coordinates shown are based on the North American Datum of 1927 (NAD 27) as currently required by the Mass Media Bureau of the FCC.

Ownership: Word of God Fellowship Inc. (Group Owner).

Began Operation: June 12, 2009. Station broadcasting digitally on its analog channel allotment. Began analog operations: February 7, 2003. Sale to present owner by Norman TV (Cyril H. Miller) approved by FCC August 19, 2002. Ceased analog operations: June 12, 2009.

Represented (legal): Koerner & Olender PC.

City of License: Norman. **Station DMA:** Oklahoma City, OK. **Rank:** 45.

TELEVISION & CABLE
Factbook Online

FULLY SEARCHABLE • CONTINUOUSLY UPDATED • DISCOUNT RATES FOR PRINT PURCHASERS

For more information call **800-771-9202** or visit **www.warren-news.com**

Digital cable and TV coverage maps.
Visit www.warren-news.com/mediaprints.htm

MediaPrints™
Map a Winning Business Strategy

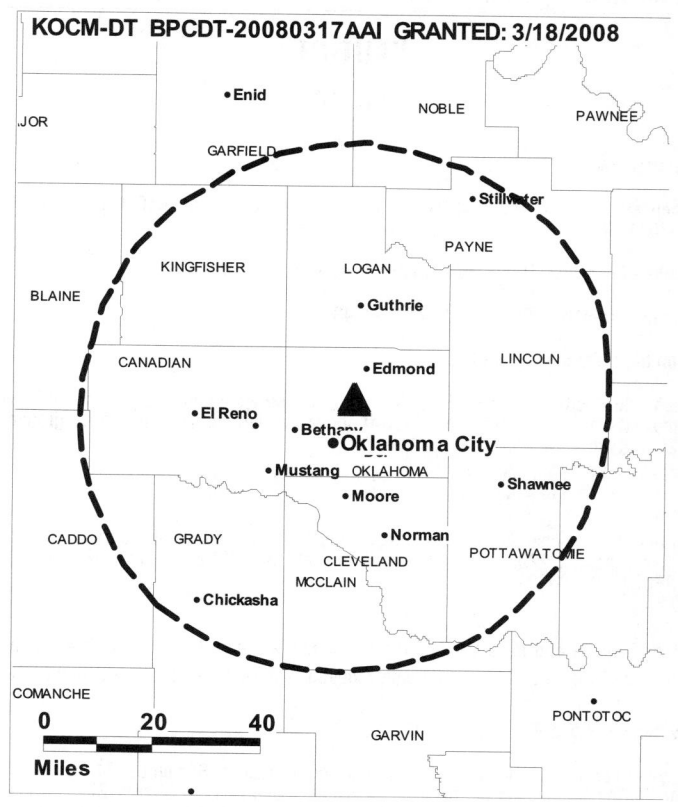

KOCM-DT BPCDT-20080317AAI GRANTED: 3/18/2008

© 2010 Warren Communications News

Circulation © 2009 Nielsen. Coverage based on Nielsen study.

GrandTotal	Cable TV Households	Non-cable TV Households	Total TV Households
Estimated Station Totals *	15,260	7,290	22,550
Average Weekly Circulation (2009)	1,311	459	1,770
Average Daily Circulation (2009)			116

Station DMA Total	Cable TV Households	Non-cable TV Households	Total TV Households
Estimated Station Totals *	15,260	7,290	22,550
Average Weekly Circulation (2009)	1,311	459	1,770
Average Daily Circulation (2009)			116

*Estimated station totals are sums of the Nielsen TV and Cable TV household estimates for each county in which the station registers viewing of more than 5% as per the Nielsen Survey Methods.

KAUT-DT
Ch. 40

Network Service: MNT.

Licensee: Local TV Oklahoma License LLC, 1717 Dixie Hwy, Ste 650, Fort Wright, KY 41011.

Mailing Address: 11901 N Eastern Ave, Oklahoma City, OK 73131.

Phone: 405-516-4300. **Fax:** 405-516-4343.

Web Site: http://www.ok43.com

Technical Facilities: Channel No. 40 (626-632 MHz). Authorized power: 1000-kw max. visual, aural. Antenna: 1433-ft above av. terrain, 1474-ft. above ground, 2576-ft. above sea level.

Latitude	35°	35'	51.9"
Longitude	97°	29'	22.1"

Holds CP for change to 925-kw max. visual, 1558-ft above av. terrain, 1572-ft. above ground, 2703-ft. above sea level; lat. 35° 35' 22", long. 97° 29' 02", BPCDT-20080620AFC.

Note: Latitude and longitude coordinates shown are based on the North American Datum of 1927 (NAD 27) as currently required by the Mass Media Bureau of the FCC.

Ownership: Local TV Holdings LLC.

Began Operation: April 24, 2006. Began analog operations: September 24, 1980. Sale to Rollins Telecasting by Ina S. Autry Estate, Gene Autry & Stanley B. Schneider, co-executors, approved by FCC April 10, 1985. Sale to Heritage Media approved by FCC September 18, 1986. Sale to Oklahoma Educational Television Authority approved by FCC June 27, 1991. Station operated as an ETV 1991-1998. Sale to Viacom Inc. as a commercial station approved by FCC July 8, 1998. Sale to The New York Times Co. by Viacom Inc. approved by FCC November 3, 2005. Sale to present owner by The New York Times Co. approved by FCC March 9, 2007. Ceased analog operations: February 17, 2009.

Represented (legal): Dow Lohnes PLLC.

Personnel:

Wes Milbourn, General Sales Manager.

Tom Heston, Local Sales Manager.

Tina Heston, National Sales Manager.

William Nichols, Chief Engineer.

Brian Hill, Promotion Director.

Christy Jones, Community Affairs Director.

City of License: Oklahoma City. **Station DMA:** Oklahoma City, OK. **Rank:** 45.

KAUT-DT BPCDT-20080620AFC GRANTED: 9/2/2008

© 2010 Warren Communications News

Circulation © 2009 Nielsen. Coverage based on Nielsen study.

GrandTotal	Cable TV Households	Non-cable TV Households	Total TV Households
Estimated Station Totals *	376,780	286,980	663,760
Average Weekly Circulation (2009)	62,695	72,551	135,246
Average Daily Circulation (2009)			51,360

Station DMA Total	Cable TV Households	Non-cable TV Households	Total TV Households
Estimated Station Totals *	373,020	279,710	652,730
Average Weekly Circulation (2009)	62,321	72,086	134,407
Average Daily Circulation (2009)			51,265

Other DMA Total	Cable TV Households	Non-cable TV Households	Total TV Households
Estimated Station Totals *	3,760	7,270	11,030
Average Weekly Circulation (2009)	374	465	839
Average Daily Circulation (2009)			95

*Estimated station totals are sums of the Nielsen TV and Cable TV household estimates for each county in which the station registers viewing of more than 5% as per the Nielsen Survey Methods.

KFOR-DT
Ch. 27

Network Service: NBC.

Licensee: Local TV Oklahoma License LLC, 1717 Dixie Hwy, Ste 650, Fort Wright, KY 41011.

Studio: 444 E Britton Rd, Oklahoma City, OK 73114.

Mailing Address: 444 E. Britton Rd, Oklahoma City, OK 73114.

Phone: 405-424-4444. **Fax:** 405-478-6206.

E-mail: timothy.morrissey@kfor.com

Web Site: http://www.kfor.com

Technical Facilities: Channel No. 27 (548-554 MHz). Authorized power: 790-kw max. visual, aural. Antenna: 1604-ft above av. terrain, 1608-ft. above ground, 2717-ft. above sea level.

Latitude	35°	35'	52"
Longitude	97°	29'	22"

Transmitter: N.E. 122nd St. & N. Kelly Ave.

Note: Latitude and longitude coordinates shown are based on the North American Datum of 1927 (NAD 27) as currently required by the Mass Media Bureau of the FCC.

Ownership: Local TV Holdings LLC (Group Owner).

Began Operation: May 1, 2002. Standard and High Definition. Began analog operations: June 6, 1949. Sale to present owner by The New York Times Co. approved by FCC March 9, 2007. Sale to The New York Times Co. by Palmer Communications approved by FCC July 9, 1996. Sale to Palmer Communications by Knight-Ridder approved by FCC May 8, 1989. Sale to Knight-Ridder by Evening News Assn. approved by FCC January 13, 1986. Sale to Evening News Assn. by Gaylord Broadcasting Co. approved by FCC October 29, 1975. Ceased analog operations: June 12, 2009.

Represented (sales): Katz Media Group.

Represented (legal): Dow Lohnes PLLC.

Personnel:

Mary Ann Eckstein, Senior Vice President & News Director.

Luanne Stuart, Vice President & Creative Services Director.

Wes Milbourn, General Sales Manager.

Bob Ablah, Chief Engineer.

Jill Fraim, Sales, Marketing & Research Director.

Hank Hughes, Production Manager.

Sandy Moyers, Traffic Manager.

Tom Heston, Local Sales Manager.

Tina Dawson, National Sales Manager.

Christy Jones, Program Coordinator.

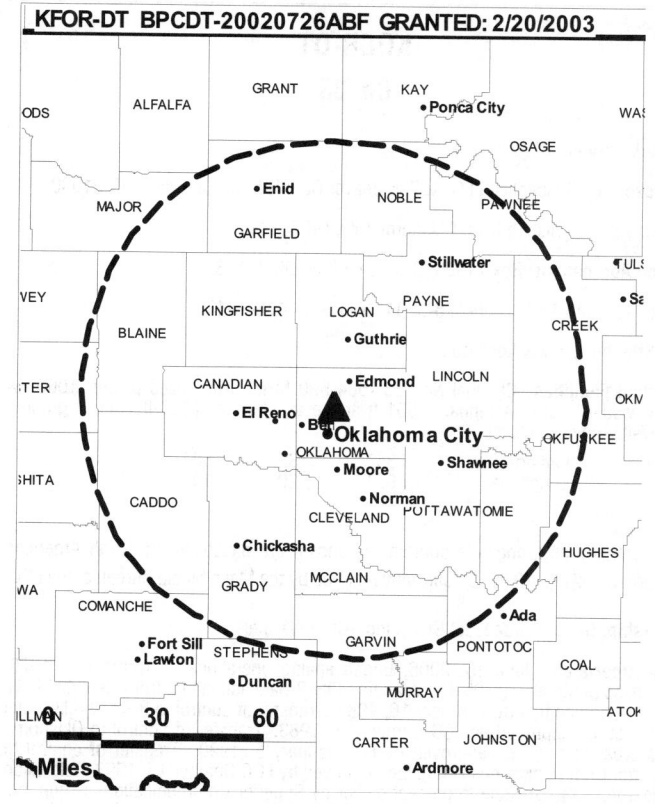

© 2010 Warren Communications News

City of License: Oklahoma City. **Station DMA:** Oklahoma City, OK. **Rank:** 45.

Circulation © 2009 Nielsen. Coverage based on Nielsen study.

GrandTotal	Cable TV Households	Non-cable TV Households	Total TV Households
Estimated Station Totals *	455,680	301,980	757,660
Average Weekly Circulation (2009)	274,102	189,932	464,034
Average Daily Circulation (2009)			249,382

Station DMA Total	Cable TV Households	Non-cable TV Households	Total TV Households
Estimated Station Totals *	375,140	279,710	654,850
Average Weekly Circulation (2009)	251,166	187,046	438,212
Average Daily Circulation (2009)			240,590

Other DMA Total	Cable TV Households	Non-cable TV Households	Total TV Households
Estimated Station Totals *	80,540	22,270	102,810
Average Weekly Circulation (2009)	22,936	2,886	25,822
Average Daily Circulation (2009)			8,792

*Estimated station totals are sums of the Nielsen TV and Cable TV household estimates for each county in which the station registers viewing of more than 5% as per the Nielsen Survey Methods.

KOCB-DT
Ch. 33

Network Service: CW.

Licensee: KOCB Licensee LLC, 10706 Beaver Dam Rd, Cockeysville, MD 21030.

Studio: 1228 E Wilshire Blvd, Oklahoma City, OK 73111.

Mailing Address: PO Box 14925, Oklahoma City, OK 73113.

Phone: 405-843-2525; 405-478-3434. **Fax:** 405-478-4343.

Web Site: http://www.kocb.com

Technical Facilities: Channel No. 33 (584-590 MHz). Authorized power: 1000-kw max. visual, aural. Antenna: 1501-ft above av. terrain, 1527-ft. above ground, 2657-ft. above sea level.

Latitude	35°	32'	58"
Longitude	97°	29'	18"

Note: Latitude and longitude coordinates shown are based on the North American Datum of 1927 (NAD 27) as currently required by the Mass Media Bureau of the FCC.

Ownership: Sinclair Broadcast Group Inc. (Group Owner).

Began Operation: June 15, 2006. Began analog operations: November 1, 1979. Purchase of remaining 80% by Oklahoma City Broadcasting Inc. from General Media Corp. approved by FCC February 16, 1983. Transfer of control to Beverly Hills Hotel Corp., et al., approved by FCC October 21, 1983. Transfer of control to Oklahoma City Broadcasting Co. approved by FCC January 5, 1990. Transfer of control to Superior Communications Group Inc. approved by FCC October 15, 1993 (Television Digest Vol. 33:35). Sale to present owner by Superior Communications Group Inc. approved by FCC April 26, 1996 (Vol. 36:11). Ceased analog operations: February 17, 2009.

Represented (sales): Katz Media Group.

Personnel:

John Rossi, General Manager.

Joe Merideth, Sales Director.

Tim Murphy, Local Sales Manager.

Jerry Klingveil, National Sales Manager.

Steve Bottkol, Engineering Director.

Dave Grogan, Business Manager.

CeCe Smith, Program Director.

Stephanie Sims, Promotion & Creative Services Director.

Brett Thomas, Traffic Manager.

City of License: Oklahoma City. **Station DMA:** Oklahoma City, OK. **Rank:** 45.

KOCB-DT BMPCDT-20020813ABE GRANTED: 5/6/2003

© 2010 Warren Communications News

Circulation © 2009 Nielsen. Coverage based on Nielsen study.

GrandTotal	Cable TV Households	Non-cable TV Households	Total TV Households
Estimated Station Totals *	384,570	298,790	683,360
Average Weekly Circulation (2009)	120,617	90,831	211,448
Average Daily Circulation (2009)			77,429

Station DMA Total	Cable TV Households	Non-cable TV Households	Total TV Households
Estimated Station Totals *	373,020	279,710	652,730
Average Weekly Circulation (2009)	119,759	89,314	209,073
Average Daily Circulation (2009)			76,960

Other DMA Total	Cable TV Households	Non-cable TV Households	Total TV Households
Estimated Station Totals *	11,550	19,080	30,630
Average Weekly Circulation (2009)	858	1,517	2,375
Average Daily Circulation (2009)			469

*Estimated station totals are sums of the Nielsen TV and Cable TV household estimates for each county in which the station registers viewing of more than 5% as per the Nielsen Survey Methods.

KOCO-DT
Ch. 7

Network Service: ABC.

Grantee: Ohio/Oklahoma Hearst-Argyle Television Inc., PO Box 1800, c/o Brooks, Pierce et al., Raleigh, NC 27602.

Studio: 1300 E Britton Rd, Oklahoma City, OK 73131.

Mailing Address: 1300 E Britton Rd, Oklahoma City, OK 73131.

Phone: 405-478-3000. **Fax:** 405-478-6675.

Web Site: http://www.koco.com

Technical Facilities: Channel No. 7 (174-180 MHz). Authorized power: 48-kw visual, aural. Antenna: 1486-ft above av. terrain, 1476-ft. above ground, 2641-ft. above sea level.

Latitude	35°	33'	45"
Longitude	97°	29'	24"

Note: Latitude and longitude coordinates shown are based on the North American Datum of 1927 (NAD 27) as currently required by the Mass Media Bureau of the FCC.

Ownership: Hearst-Argyle Television Inc. (Group Owner).

Began Operation: November 1, 2002. Began analog operations: June 19, 1954. Sale to L. E. Caster (75%) & Ashley L. Robinson (25%) by Streets Electronics Inc. approved by FCC December 11, 1957. Transfer to Caster Estate, et al., approved by FCC March 5, 1958. Sale to Capital Investments Co. (Cimarron Television Corp.) approved by FCC 1961. Transfer to Combined Communications approved by FCC June 7, 1979. Merger of Combined with Gannett Co. approved by FCC June 7, 1979. Trade by Gannett with WLWT-TV Cincinnati, OH to Argyle Television Inc. for WGRZ-TV Buffalo, NY & WZZM-TV Grand Rapids, MI approved by FCC January 27, 1997. Merger with Hearst Corp. to form present owner approved by FCC June 2, 1997. Hearst-Argyle received approval from the FCC May 26, 2009 to become privately owned by The Hearst Corp. Ceased analog operations: June 12, 2009.

Represented (legal): Brooks, Pierce, McLendon, Humphrey & Leonard LLP.

Represented (sales): Eagle Television Sales.

Personnel:

Brent Hensley, President & General Manager.

Tom Comerford, General Sales Manager.

Shayne Vigil, Local Sales Manager.

Nicole Winston, National Sales Manager.

Stephanie Croswait, News Director.

David Evans, Chief Engineer.

Patricia Ronne, Controller.

Lisa Kaitcer, Program Coordinator.

Randal Gage, Promotion & Creative Services Director.

Stella McDaniel, Traffic Manager.

City of License: Oklahoma City. **Station DMA:** Oklahoma City, OK. **Rank:** 45.

KOCO-DT BPCDT-20080616ABL GRANTED: 7/10/2008

© 2010 Warren Communications News

Circulation © 2009 Nielsen. Coverage based on Nielsen study.

GrandTotal	Cable TV Households	Non-cable TV Households	Total TV Households
Estimated Station Totals *	418,670	297,180	715,850
Average Weekly Circulation (2009)	276,501	187,871	464,372
Average Daily Circulation (2009)			230,646

Station DMA Total	Cable TV Households	Non-cable TV Households	Total TV Households
Estimated Station Totals *	375,140	279,710	654,850
Average Weekly Circulation (2009)	264,744	185,408	450,152
Average Daily Circulation (2009)			225,101

Other DMA Total	Cable TV Households	Non-cable TV Households	Total TV Households
Estimated Station Totals *	43,530	17,470	61,000
Average Weekly Circulation (2009)	11,757	2,463	14,220
Average Daily Circulation (2009)			5,545

*Estimated station totals are sums of the Nielsen TV and Cable TV household estimates for each county in which the station registers viewing of more than 5% as per the Nielsen Survey Methods.

KOKH-DT
Ch. 24

Network Service: FOX.

Licensee: KOKH Licensee LLC, c/o Shaw Pittman, 2300 N St. NW, c/o Pillsbury Winthrop Shaw Pittman LLP, Attn.: Kathryn Schmeltzer, Washington, DC 20037-1128.

Studio: 1228 E Wilshire Blvd, Oklahoma City, OK 73111.

Mailing Address: PO Box 14925, Oklahoma City, OK 73113.

Phone: 405-843-2525. **Fax:** 405-478-4343.

Web Site: http://www.kokh.com

Technical Facilities: Channel No. 24 (530-536 MHz). Authorized power: 1000-kw max. visual, aural. Antenna: 1561-ft above av. terrain, 1586-ft. above ground, 2716-ft. above sea level.

Latitude	35°	32'	58"
Longitude	97°	29'	18"

Note: Latitude and longitude coordinates shown are based on the North American Datum of 1927 (NAD 27) as currently required by the Mass Media Bureau of the FCC.

Ownership: Sinclair Broadcast Group Inc. (Group Owner).

Began Operation: December 7, 2004. Began analog operations: February 2, 1959. Initially operated as a non-commercial, educational station. Sale to John Blair & Co. by Independent School District No. 89 of Oklahoma City approved by FCC June 6, 1979 (Television Digest, Vol. 19:25). Resumed operation as commercial station October 1, 1979. Sale by Blair to Gillett Broadcasting approved by FCC December 30, 1986. Transfer to Busse Broadcasting approved by FCC July 31, 1987. Sale to George Gillett and subsequent sale to Heritage Media Corp. approved by FCC June 27, 1991 (Vol. 30:49, 31:23). Sale to News Corp., who then spun-off station to Sinclair Communications approved by FCC 1997. Sale to Sullivan Broadcasting Co. by Sinclair Communications approved by FCC 1998. Sale to Glencairn Ltd. Broadcast Properties dismissed by applicant July 23, 2001 (Vol. 39:47, 48). Sale to present owner by Sullivan Broadcasting Co. approved by FCC December 10, 2001. Ceased analog operations: February 17, 2009.

Represented (sales): Katz Media Group.

Represented (legal): Pillsbury Winthrop Shaw Pittman LLP.

Personnel:

John Rossi, General Manager.

Joe Merideth, Sales Director.

Tim Murphy, Local Sales Manager.

Jerry Klingveil, National Sales Manager.

Steve Bottkol, Engineering Director.

Dave Grogan, Business Manager.

CeCe Smith, Program Director.

Stephanie Sims, Promotion & Creative Services Director.

Brett Thomas, Traffic Manager.

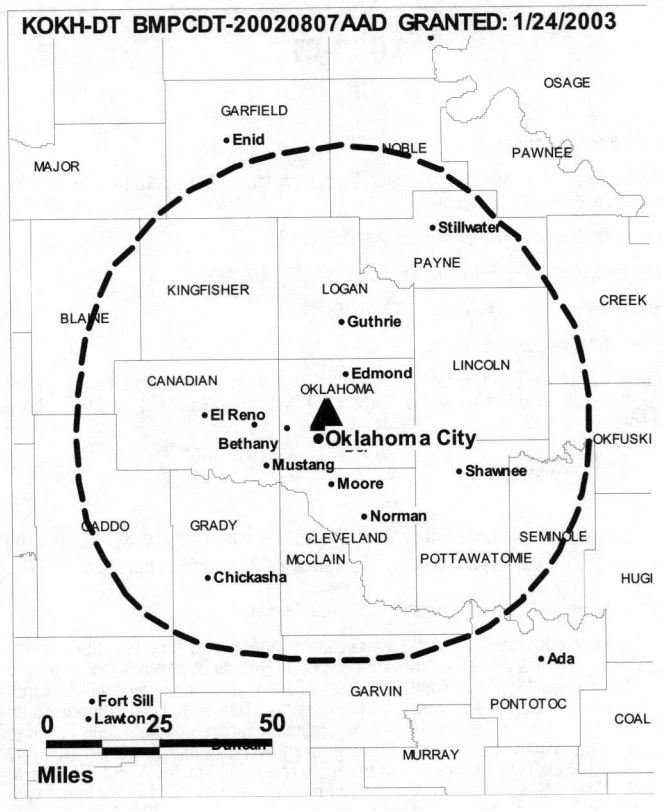

KOKH-DT BMPCDT-20020807AAD GRANTED: 1/24/2003

© 2010 Warren Communications News

City of License: Oklahoma City. **Station DMA:** Oklahoma City, OK. **Rank:** 45.

Circulation © 2009 Nielsen. Coverage based on Nielsen study.

GrandTotal	Cable TV Households	Non-cable TV Households	Total TV Households
Estimated Station Totals *	414,830	295,380	710,210
Average Weekly Circulation (2009)	193,981	146,035	340,016
Average Daily Circulation (2009)			123,490

Station DMA Total	Cable TV Households	Non-cable TV Households	Total TV Households
Estimated Station Totals *	369,530	279,710	649,240
Average Weekly Circulation (2009)	185,093	144,425	329,518
Average Daily Circulation (2009)			120,681

Other DMA Total	Cable TV Households	Non-cable TV Households	Total TV Households
Estimated Station Totals *	45,300	15,670	60,970
Average Weekly Circulation (2009)	8,888	1,610	10,498
Average Daily Circulation (2009)			2,809

*Estimated station totals are sums of the Nielsen TV and Cable TV household estimates for each county in which the station registers viewing of more than 5% as per the Nielsen Survey Methods.

KOPX-TV
Ch. 50

Network Service: ION.

Licensee: ION Media Oklahoma City License Inc., Debtor in Possession, 601 Clearwater Park Rd, West Palm Beach, FL 33401-6233.

Studio: 13424 Railway Dr, Oklahoma City, OK 73114.

Mailing Address: 13424 Railway Dr, Oklahoma City, OK 73114.

Phone: 405-751-6800. **Fax:** 405-478-1789.

E-mail: phillipbrooks@ionmedia.com

Web Site: http://www.ionmedia.com

Technical Facilities: Channel No. 50 (686-692 MHz). Authorized power: 200-kw max. visual, aural. Antenna: 1585-ft above av. terrain, 1617-ft. above ground, 2723-ft. above sea level.

Latitude	35°	35'	52"
Longitude	97°	29'	22"

Transmitter: Intersection of Kelly Ave. & 122nd St.

Note: Latitude and longitude coordinates shown are based on the North American Datum of 1927 (NAD 27) as currently required by the Mass Media Bureau of the FCC.

Ownership: ION Media Networks Inc., Debtor in Possession (Group Owner).

Began Operation: November 1, 2002. Standard Definition. Began analog operations: August 6, 1996. Sale to Urban Television LLC pends. Involuntary assignment to debtor in possession status approved by FCC June 5, 2009. Transfer of control by ION Media Networks Inc. from Paxson Management Corp. & Lowell W. Paxson to CIG Media LLC approved by FCC December 31, 2007. Paxson Communications Corp. became ION Media Networks Inc. on June 26, 2006. Sale to Paxson Communications Corp. by Aracelis Ortiz approved by FCC September 27, 1996. Sale to Aracelis Ortiz by Faith Pleases God Church Corp. approved by FCC March 30, 1994. Sale to Faith Pleases God Church Corp. by Mendoza Broadcasting Ltd. approved by FCC March 15, 1990. Ceased analog operations: June 12, 2009.

Represented (sales): Katz Media Group.

Represented (legal): Dow Lohnes PLLC.

Represented (engineering): du Treil, Lundin & Rackley Inc.

Personnel:

Phillip Brooks, Station Operations Manager.

Les Moorman, Traffic Manager.

City of License: Oklahoma City. **Station DMA:** Oklahoma City, OK. **Rank:** 45.

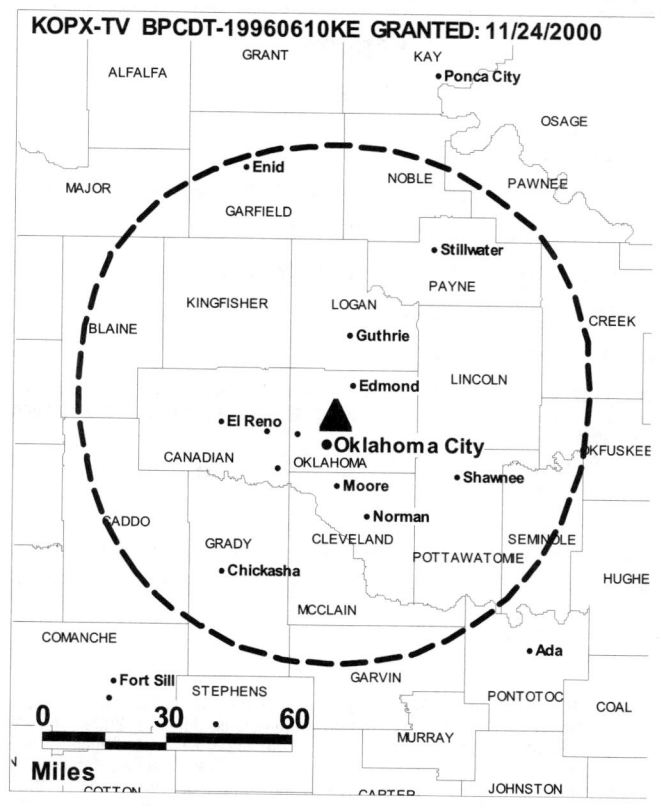

KOPX-TV BPCDT-19960610KE GRANTED: 11/24/2000

© 2010 Warren Communications News

Circulation © 2009 Nielsen. Coverage based on Nielsen study.

GrandTotal	Cable TV Households	Non-cable TV Households	Total TV Households
Estimated Station Totals *	334,940	254,510	589,450
Average Weekly Circulation (2009)	24,526	28,179	52,705
Average Daily Circulation (2009)			13,013

Station DMA Total	Cable TV Households	Non-cable TV Households	Total TV Households
Estimated Station Totals *	334,940	254,510	589,450
Average Weekly Circulation (2009)	24,526	28,179	52,705
Average Daily Circulation (2009)			13,013

*Estimated station totals are sums of the Nielsen TV and Cable TV household estimates for each county in which the station registers viewing of more than 5% as per the Nielsen Survey Methods.

KSBI-DT
Ch. 51

Network Service: IND.

Grantee: Family Broadcasting Group Inc., PO Box 95188, Oklahoma City, OK 73143.

Studio: 1350 SE 82nd St, Oklahoma City, OK 73149.

Mailing Address: PO Box 95188, Oklahoma City, OK 73142.

Phone: 405-631-7335. **Fax:** 405-631-7367.

Web Site: http://www.ksbitv.com

Technical Facilities: Channel No. 51 (692-698 MHz). Authorized power: 1000-kw max. visual, aural. Antenna: 1502-ft above av. terrain, 1540-ft. above ground, 2646-ft. above sea level.

Latitude	35°	35'	52"
Longitude	97°	29'	22"

Note: Latitude and longitude coordinates shown are based on the North American Datum of 1927 (NAD 27) as currently required by the Mass Media Bureau of the FCC.

Multichannel TV Sound: Stereo only.

Ownership: Family Broadcasting Group Inc. (Group Owner).

Began Operation: February 1, 2003. Standard and High Definition. Began analog operations: October 31, 1988. Ceased analog operations: June 12, 2009. Transfer of control by Family Broadcasting Group Inc. from Brady M. Brus, Angela Brus & Seekfirst Media Partners LLC to Aubrey K. McClendon & Ward Family Enterprises LP pends.Transfer of control by Family Broadcasting Group Inc. from Brady M. Brus, Angela Brus & Seekfirst Media Partners LLC to Aubrey K. McClendon & Ward Family Enterprises LP dismissed by FCC April 1, 2009. Sale to Family Broadcasting Group Inc. by Locke Supply Co. approved by FCC January 12, 2004. Transfer of control by Locke Supply Co. from Wanda Locke McKenzie to Locke Supply Co. Employee Stock Option Plan approved by FCC December 12, 2000. Involuntary transfer by Locke Supply Co. from Don J. Locke (deceased) to Wanda Locke McKenzie, Estate Administrator approved by FCC November 17, 2000.

Represented (sales): Lighthouse Media Inc.

Represented (legal): Booth Freret Imlay & Tepper PC.

Personnel:

Brady Brus, General Manager.

Tiffany Hardeman, General & Local Sales Manager.

Bill Robinson, Director of Engineering & Operations.

Fatma Altamim, Program Director.

Angela Graham, Traffic Manager.

Julie Mills, Controller.

City of License: Oklahoma City. **Station DMA:** Oklahoma City, OK. **Rank:** 45.

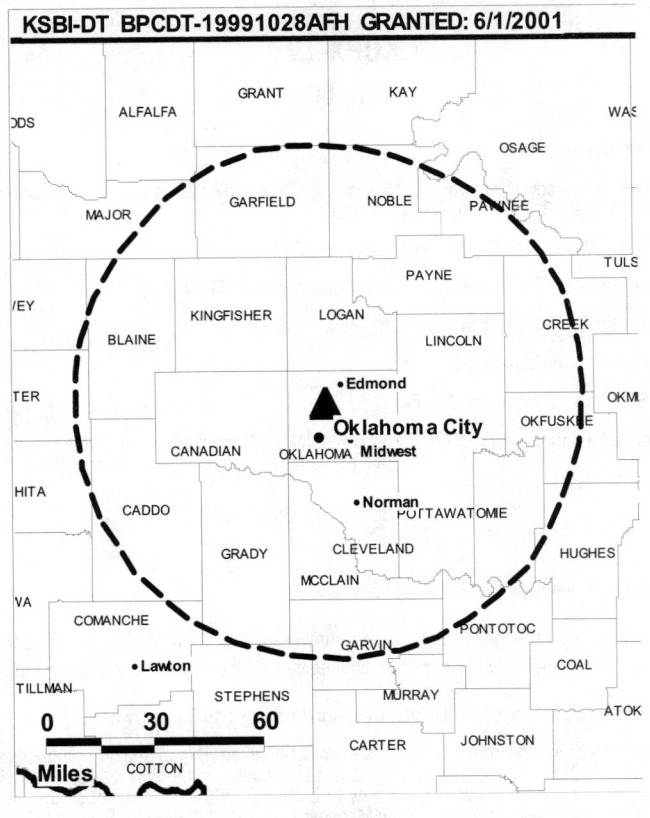

KSBI-DT BPCDT-19991028AFH GRANTED: 6/1/2001

© 2010 Warren Communications News

Circulation © 2009 Nielsen. Coverage based on Nielsen study.

GrandTotal	Cable TV Households	Non-cable TV Households	Total TV Households
Estimated Station Totals *	273,200	258,000	531,200
Average Weekly Circulation (2009)	26,334	35,214	61,548
Average Daily Circulation (2009)			22,126

Station DMA Total	Cable TV Households	Non-cable TV Households	Total TV Households
Estimated Station Totals *	272,220	258,000	530,220
Average Weekly Circulation (2009)	26,157	35,214	61,371
Average Daily Circulation (2009)			22,120

Other DMA Total	Cable TV Households	Non-cable TV Households	Total TV Households
Estimated Station Totals *	980	0	980
Average Weekly Circulation (2009)	177	0	177
Average Daily Circulation (2009)			6

*Estimated station totals are sums of the Nielsen TV and Cable TV household estimates for each county in which the station registers viewing of more than 5% as per the Nielsen Survey Methods.

KTBO-DT
Ch. 15

Network Service: TBN.

Licensee: Trinity Broadcasting Network Inc., 2442 Michelle Dr, Tustin, CA 92780.

Studio: 1600 E Hefner Rd, Oklahoma City, OK 73131.

Mailing Address: 1600 E. Hefner Rd, Oklahoma City, OK 73131.

Phone: 405-848-1414. **Fax:** 405-843-5040.

Web Site: http://www.tbn.org

Technical Facilities: Channel No. 15 (476-482 MHz). Authorized power: 500-kw max. visual, aural. Antenna: 1175-ft above av. terrain, 1152-ft. above ground, 2323-ft. above sea level.

Latitude	35°	34'	35"
Longitude	97°	29'	09"

Holds CP for change to 700-kw max. visual; BPCDT-20080619ACZ.

Transmitter: 0.5-mi. SW of intersection of Eastern Ave. & 108th St. NE.

Note: Latitude and longitude coordinates shown are based on the North American Datum of 1927 (NAD 27) as currently required by the Mass Media Bureau of the FCC.

Ownership: Trinity Broadcasting Network Inc. (Group Owner).

Began Operation: December 1, 2002. Began analog operations: March 6, 1981. Ceased analog operations: June 12, 2009.

Represented (legal): Colby M. May.

Personnel:

Linda Cook, General Manager.

Ken Howerton, Chief Engineer.

Dave Waters, Traffic Manager.

Tami Froh, Public Affairs Director.

City of License: Oklahoma City. **Station DMA:** Oklahoma City, OK. **Rank:** 45.

continuous updates   fully searchable   easy to use

For more information call **800-771-9202** or visit **www.warren-news.com**

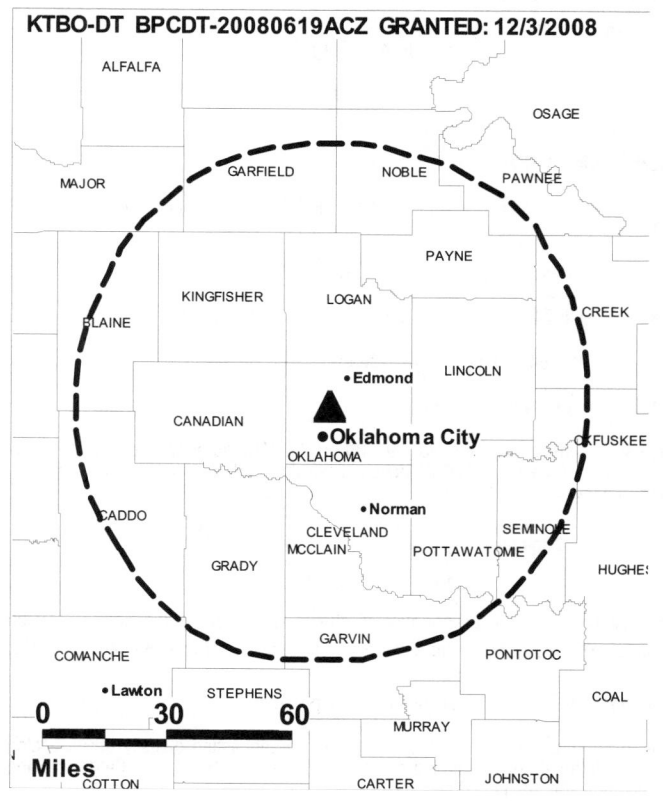

© 2010 Warren Communications News

Circulation © 2009 Nielsen. Coverage based on Nielsen study.

GrandTotal	Cable TV Households	Non-cable TV Households	Total TV Households
Estimated Station Totals *	227,760	118,480	346,240
Average Weekly Circulation (2009)	14,185	6,299	20,484
Average Daily Circulation (2009)			6,652

Station DMA Total	Cable TV Households	Non-cable TV Households	Total TV Households
Estimated Station Totals *	227,760	118,480	346,240
Average Weekly Circulation (2009)	14,185	6,299	20,484
Average Daily Circulation (2009)			6,652

*Estimated station totals are sums of the Nielsen TV and Cable TV household estimates for each county in which the station registers viewing of more than 5% as per the Nielsen Survey Methods.

KWTV-DT
Ch. 9

Network Service: CBS.

Licensee: Griffin OKC Licensing LLC, 7401 N Kelley Ave, Oklahoma City, OK 73111-8420.

Studio: 7401 N Kelley Ave, Oklahoma City, OK 73111.

Mailing Address: 7401 N. Kelley Ave, Oklahoma City, OK 73111.

Phone: 405-843-6641. **Fax:** 405-841-3693.

Web Site: http://www.news9.com

Technical Facilities: Channel No. 9 (186-192 MHz). Authorized power: 62.2-kw visual, aural. Antenna: 1526-ft above av. terrain, 1530-ft. above ground, 2690-ft. above sea level.

Latitude	35°	32'	58"
Longitude	97°	29'	49"

Note: Latitude and longitude coordinates shown are based on the North American Datum of 1927 (NAD 27) as currently required by the Mass Media Bureau of the FCC.

Ownership: Griffin Communications LLC (Group Owner).

Began Operation: December 23, 2003. Station broadcasting digitally on its analog channel allotment. Began analog operations: December 20, 1953. Ceased analog operations: February 17, 2009.

Represented (legal): Holland & Knight LLP.

Represented (sales): TeleRep Inc.

Personnel:

Rob Krier, Vice President & General Manager.

Wade Deaver, General Sales Manager.

Blaise Labbe, News Director.

Julie Cameron, Engineering Director.

Dennis Kelly, Business Manager.

Kim Eubank, Program Director.

Paul Greeley, Advertising & Marketing Director.

Randy Cassimus, Production Director.

City of License: Oklahoma City. **Station DMA:** Oklahoma City, OK. **Rank:** 45.

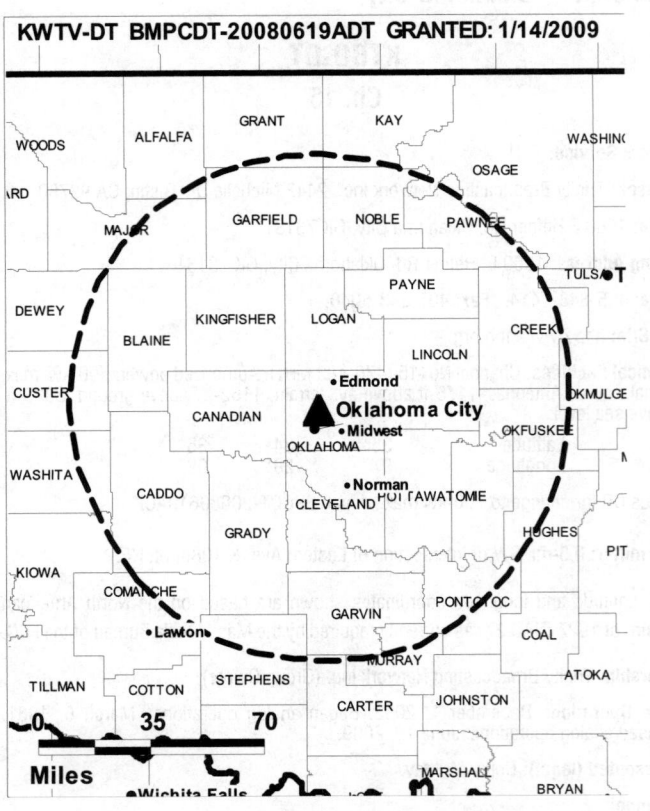

KWTV-DT BMPCDT-20080619ADT GRANTED: 1/14/2009

© 2010 Warren Communications News

Circulation © 2009 Nielsen. Coverage based on Nielsen study.

GrandTotal	Cable TV Households	Non-cable TV Households	Total TV Households
Estimated Station Totals *	458,080	329,380	787,460
Average Weekly Circulation (2009)	279,360	200,361	479,721
Average Daily Circulation (2009)			250,028

Station DMA Total	Cable TV Households	Non-cable TV Households	Total TV Households
Estimated Station Totals *	375,140	279,710	654,850
Average Weekly Circulation (2009)	259,862	196,003	455,865
Average Daily Circulation (2009)			239,939

Other DMA Total	Cable TV Households	Non-cable TV Households	Total TV Households
Estimated Station Totals *	82,940	49,670	132,610
Average Weekly Circulation (2009)	19,498	4,358	23,856
Average Daily Circulation (2009)			10,089

*Estimated station totals are sums of the Nielsen TV and Cable TV household estimates for each county in which the station registers viewing of more than 5% as per the Nielsen Survey Methods.

KTPX-TV
Ch. 28

Network Service: ION.

Licensee: ION Media Tulsa License Inc., Debtor in Possession, 601 Clearwater Park Rd, West Palm Beach, FL 33401-6233.

Studio: 5800 E Skelly Dr, Ste 101, Tulsa, OK 74135.

Mailing Address: 5800 E Skelly Dr, Ste 101, Tulsa, OK 74135.

Phone: 918-664-1044; 800-729-2677. **Fax:** 918-664-1483.

E-mail: tomneedham@ionmedia.com

Web Site: http://www.ionmedia.com

Technical Facilities: Channel No. 28 (554-560 MHz). Authorized power: 1000-kw max. visual, aural. Antenna: 718-ft above av. terrain, 551-ft. above ground, 1480-ft. above sea level.

Latitude	35°	50'	02"
Longitude	96°	07'	28"

Note: Latitude and longitude coordinates shown are based on the North American Datum of 1927 (NAD 27) as currently required by the Mass Media Bureau of the FCC.

Ownership: ION Media Networks Inc., Debtor in Possession (Group Owner).

Began Operation: April 1, 2002. Standard Definition. Began analog operations: August 31, 1998. Sale to Urban Television LLC pends. Involuntary assignment to debtor in possession status approved by FCC June 5, 2009. Transfer of control by ION Media Networks Inc. from Paxson Management Corp. & Lowell W. Paxson to CIG Media LLC approved by FCC December 31, 2007. Paxson Communications Corp. became ION Media Networks Inc. on June 26, 2006. Sale of remaining 51% interest to Paxson Communications Corp. by Broadcasting Systems Inc. approved by FCC September 26, 1997. Sale to Broadcasting Systems Inc. by KGLB Television Inc. approved by FCC December 24, 1991. Sale to KGLB Television Inc. by Brewer Communications Inc. approved by FCC August 13, 1987. Ceased analog operations: June 12, 2009.

Represented (legal): Dow Lohnes PLLC.

Personnel:

Peter De Les Denier, Station Operations Manager.

Tom Needham, Chief Engineer.

Janeen Rode, Traffic Manager.

City of License: Okmulgee. **Station DMA:** Tulsa, OK. **Rank:** 61.

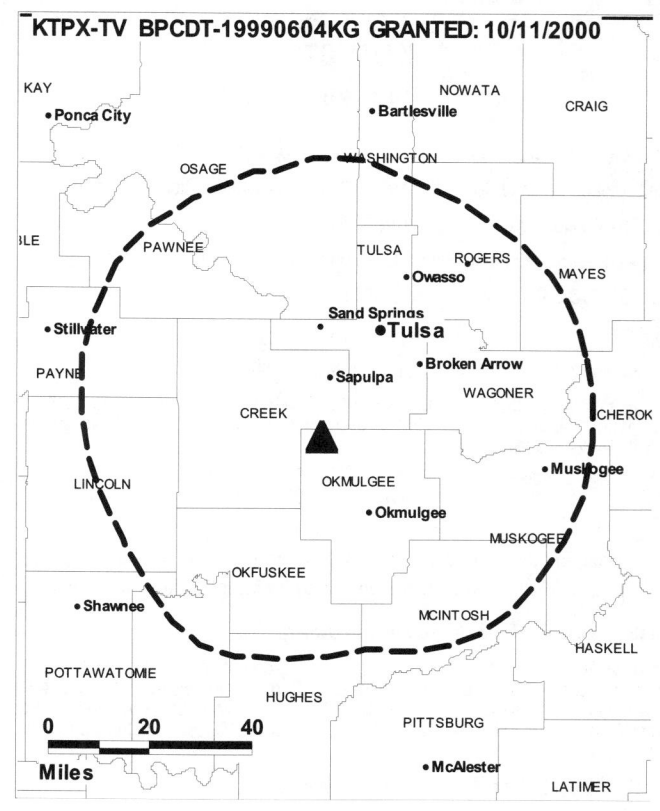

KTPX-TV BPCDT-19990604KG GRANTED: 10/11/2000

© 2010 Warren Communications News

Circulation © 2009 Nielsen. Coverage based on Nielsen study.

GrandTotal	Cable TV Households	Non-cable TV Households	Total TV Households
Estimated Station Totals *	249,070	180,310	429,380
Average Weekly Circulation (2009)	19,578	16,655	36,233
Average Daily Circulation (2009)			9,429

Station DMA Total	Cable TV Households	Non-cable TV Households	Total TV Households
Estimated Station Totals *	249,070	180,310	429,380
Average Weekly Circulation (2009)	19,578	16,655	36,233
Average Daily Circulation (2009)			9,429

*Estimated station totals are sums of the Nielsen TV and Cable TV household estimates for each county in which the station registers viewing of more than 5% as per the Nielsen Survey Methods.

KTUZ-DT
Ch. 29

Network Service: TMO.

Grantee: Oklahoma Land Co. LLC, 5101 S. Shields, Oklahoma City, OK 73129.

Studio: 501 Shields Blvd, Oklahoma City, OK 73129.

Mailing Address: 501 Shields Blvd, Oklahoma City, OK 73129.

Phone: 405-616-5500. **Fax:** 405-616-5511.

E-mail: armando.r@tylermedia.com

Web Site: http://www.ktuztv.com/engine/emw.exe/*qshome=sp

Technical Facilities: Channel No. 29 (560-566 MHz). Authorized power: 1000-kw max. visual, aural. Antenna: 1555-ft above av. terrain, 1570-ft. above ground, 2715-ft. above sea level.

Latitude	35°	33'	36"
Longitude	97°	29'	07"

Note: Latitude and longitude coordinates shown are based on the North American Datum of 1927 (NAD 27) as currently required by the Mass Media Bureau of the FCC.

Ownership: Oklahoma Land Co. LLC (Group Owner).

Began Operation: November 5, 2008. Began analog operations: November 10, 2000. Sale to present owner by Equity Braodcasting Corp. approved by FCC August 10, 2004. Sale Equity Broadcasting Corp. by OKC-30 Television LLC (Myoung Hwa Bae & Pete E. Warren III) approved by FCC July 28, 2000. Ceased analog operations: June 12, 2009.

Represented (legal): Putbrese, Hunsaker & Trent PC.

Personnel:

Armando Rubio, General Manager & Program Director.

Robert Erickson, Chief Engineer.

Lee Redick, General Sales Manager.

Azalea Samarripa, Traffic Manager.

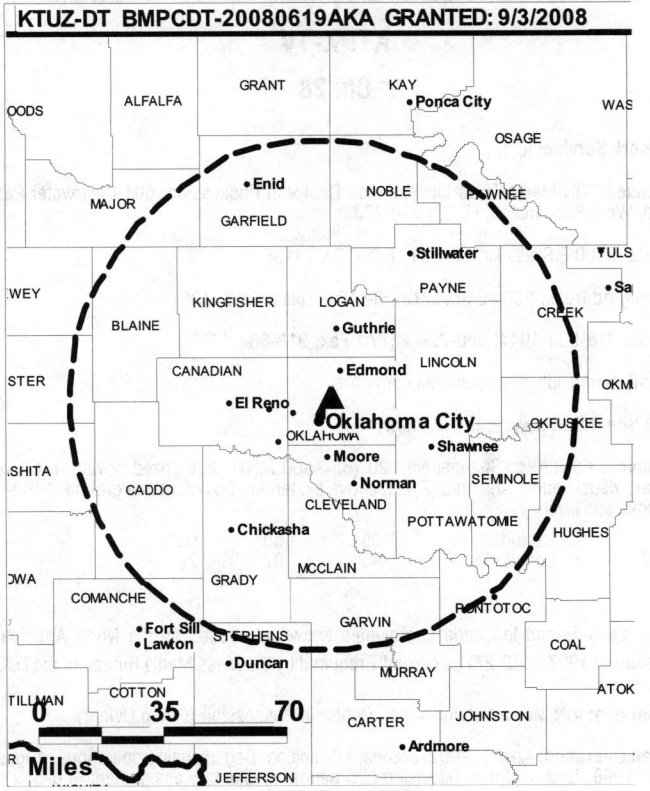

© 2010 Warren Communications News

City of License: Shawnee. **Station DMA:** Oklahoma City, OK. **Rank:** 45.

Nielsen Data: Not available.

KGEB-DT
Ch. 49

Network Service: IND.

Licensee: University Broadcasting Inc., 7777 S Lewis Ave, Tulsa, OK 74171.

Studio: 7777 S Lewis Ave, Tulsa, OK 74171.

Mailing Address: PO Box 7777, Tulsa, OK 74101.

Phone: 918-488-5300. **Fax:** 918-495-7388.

E-mail: cbeverly@oru.edu

Web Site: http://www.kgeb.net

Technical Facilities: Channel No. 49 (680-686 MHz). Authorized power: 50-kw max. visual, aural. Antenna: 597-ft above av. terrain, 673-ft. above ground, 1296-ft. above sea level.

Latitude	36°	02'	35"
Longitude	95°	57'	11"

Note: Latitude and longitude coordinates shown are based on the North American Datum of 1927 (NAD 27) as currently required by the Mass Media Bureau of the FCC.

Ownership: Oral Roberts U.

Began Operation: June 1, 2006. Began analog operations: January 24, 1996. Sale to present owner by Golden Eagle Communications Inc. approved by FCC August 3, 1995. Sale to Golden Eagle Communications Inc. by Native American Broadcasting, LP approved by FCC March 22, 1994. Ceased analog operations: February 17, 2009.

Represented (engineering): du Treil, Lundin & Rackley Inc.

Represented (legal): Hardy, Carey, Chautin & Balkin LLP.

Personnel:

Walter H. Richardson, General Manager.

Amy Calvert, Vice President, Marketing & Sales.

William P. Lee, Engineering Director.

Chris Vanover, Traffic Manager.

Charmaine Lee, Creative Services Director.

City of License: Tulsa. **Station DMA:** Tulsa, OK. **Rank:** 61.

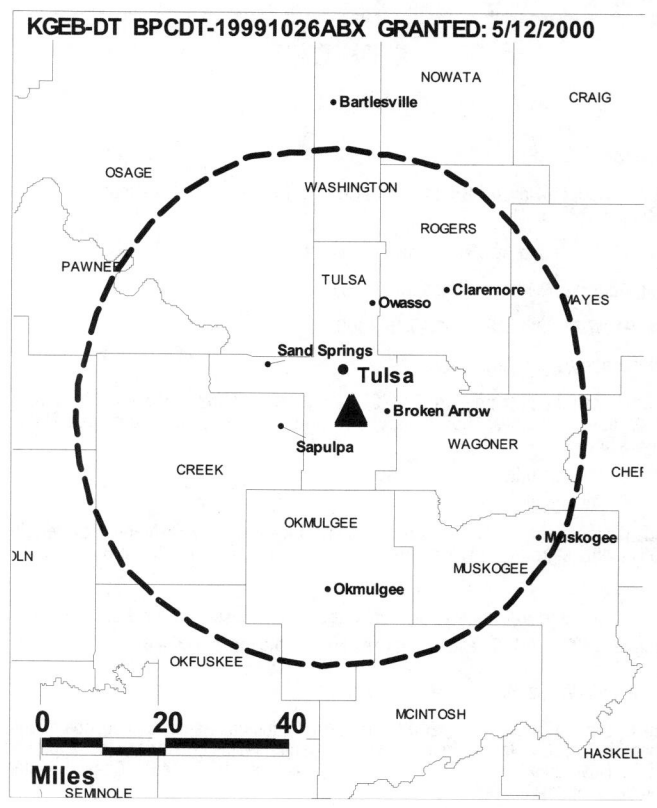

KGEB-DT BPCDT-19991026ABX GRANTED: 5/12/2000

© 2010 Warren Communications News

Circulation © 2009 Nielsen. Coverage based on Nielsen study.

GrandTotal	Cable TV Households	Non-cable TV Households	Total TV Households
Estimated Station Totals *	29,350	0	29,350
Average Weekly Circulation (2009)	2,022	0	2,022
Average Daily Circulation (2009)			256

Station DMA Total	Cable TV Households	Non-cable TV Households	Total TV Households
Estimated Station Totals *	29,350	0	29,350
Average Weekly Circulation (2009)	2,022	0	2,022
Average Daily Circulation (2009)			256

*Estimated station totals are sums of the Nielsen TV and Cable TV household estimates for each county in which the station registers viewing of more than 5% as per the Nielsen Survey Methods.

KJRH-DT
Ch. 56

Network Service: NBC.

Licensee: Scripps Howard Broadcasting Co., PO Box 5380, 312 Walnut St, 28th Fl, Cincinnati, OH 45201.

Studio: 3701 S Peoria Ave, Tulsa, OK 74105-3269.

Mailing Address: PO Box 2, Tulsa, OK 74101.

Phone: 918-743-2222. **Fax:** 918-748-1460.

Web Site: http://www.kjrh.com

Technical Facilities: Channel No. 56 (722-728 MHz). Authorized power: 800-kw max. visual, aural. Antenna: 1657-ft above av. terrain, 1579-ft. above ground, 2290-ft. above sea level.

Latitude	35°	01'	15"
Longitude	95°	40'	32"

Holds CP for change to channel number 8, 15.9-kw visual, 1878-ft above av. terrain, 1803-ft. above ground, 2513-ft. above sea level; BPCDT-20080228ABB.

Note: Latitude and longitude coordinates shown are based on the North American Datum of 1927 (NAD 27) as currently required by the Mass Media Bureau of the FCC.

Ownership: E. W. Scripps Co. (Group Owner).

Began Operation: January 1, 2002. Standard Definition. Began analog operations: December 5, 1954. Sale to present owner by Central Plains Enterprises Inc. approved by FCC November 25, 1970 (Television Digest, Vol. 10:24, 48). Ceased analog operations: June 12, 2009.

Represented (sales): Eagle Television Sales.

Personnel:

Michael J. Vrabac, Vice President & General Manager.

Randy Smith, Local Sales Manager.

Ross Greenawalt, Production Manager.

Karen Framel, Research Director.

Samantha Knowlton, Creative Services Director.

Blake Etter, Traffic Manager.

Rick Cohn, General Sales Manager.

Darlene Mahler, National Sales Manager.

Steve Weinstein, News Director.

Dale Vennes, Engineering Director.

Cara Palmer, Business Manager.

City of License: Tulsa. **Station DMA:** Tulsa, OK. **Rank:** 61.

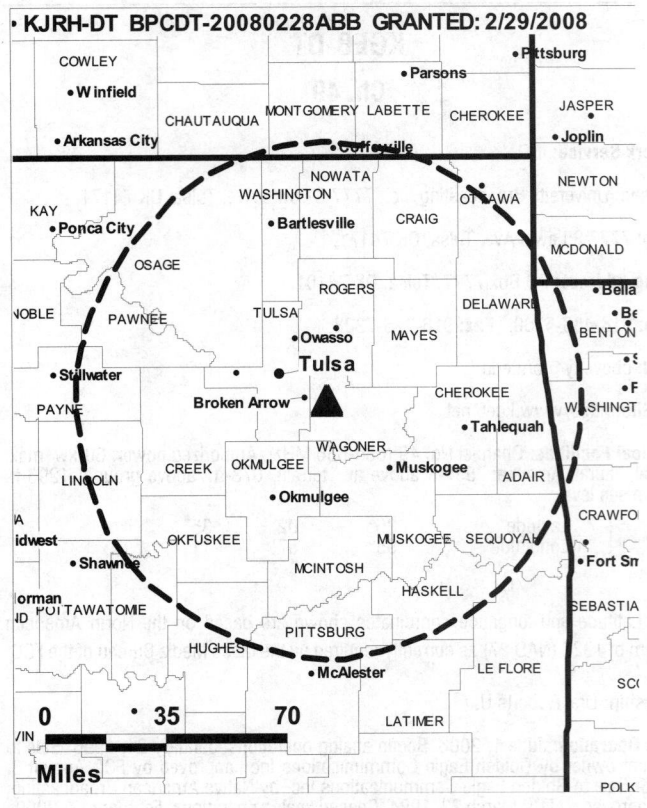

© 2010 Warren Communications News

Circulation © 2009 Nielsen. Coverage based on Nielsen study.

GrandTotal	Cable TV Households	Non-cable TV Households	Total TV Households
Estimated Station Totals *	302,620	257,490	560,110
Average Weekly Circulation (2009)	183,600	145,877	329,477
Average Daily Circulation (2009)			163,540

Station DMA Total	Cable TV Households	Non-cable TV Households	Total TV Households
Estimated Station Totals *	269,880	233,460	503,340
Average Weekly Circulation (2009)	177,308	143,733	321,041
Average Daily Circulation (2009)			160,730

Other DMA Total	Cable TV Households	Non-cable TV Households	Total TV Households
Estimated Station Totals *	32,740	24,030	56,770
Average Weekly Circulation (2009)	6,292	2,144	8,436
Average Daily Circulation (2009)			2,810

*Estimated station totals are sums of the Nielsen TV and Cable TV household estimates for each county in which the station registers viewing of more than 5% as per the Nielsen Survey Methods.

KMYT-DT
Ch. 42

Network Service: MNT.

Licensee: Newport Television License LLC, 460 Nichols Rd, Ste 250, Kansas City, MO 64112.

Studio: 2625 S Memorial Dr, Tulsa, OK 74129.

Mailing Address: 2625 S Memorial Dr, Ste A, Tulsa, OK 74129.

Phone: 918-491-0023. **Fax:** 918-491-6650.

Web Site: http://www.my41tulsa.com

Technical Facilities: Channel No. 42 (638-644 MHz). Authorized power: 900-kw max. visual, aural. Antenna: 1250-ft above av. terrain, 1167-ft. above ground, 1877-ft. above sea level.

Latitude	36°	01'	36"
Longitude	95°	40'	44"

Note: Latitude and longitude coordinates shown are based on the North American Datum of 1927 (NAD 27) as currently required by the Mass Media Bureau of the FCC.

Ownership: Newport Television LLC (Group Owner).

Began Operation: November 12, 2002. Began analog operations: March 18, 1981. Analog station left air February 1, 1989. Sale of interest held by Ray L. Beindorf to Armstrong Investment Co. approved by FCC April 26, 1989. Sale to R.D.S. Broadcasting Inc. approved by FCC August 27, 1990. Station resumed operation May 6, 1991. Sale to MGA Broadcasting Inc. by R.D.S. Broadcasting Inc. approved by FCC May 13, 1997. Sale to Clear Channel Communications Inc. by MGA Broadcasting Inc. approved by FCC March 9, 2000. Sale to present owner by Clear Channel Communications Inc. approved by FCC November 29, 2007. Ceased analog operations: February 17, 2009.

Represented (legal): Covington & Burling.

Represented (sales): Katz Media Group.

Personnel:

Holly Allen, General Manager.

Jim Hanning, Sales Director.

Stephanie Spry, Local Sales Manager.

Kari Barrett, National Sales Manager.

Melanie Henry, News Director.

Brian Egan, Chief Engineer.

Amie Price, Business Manager.

Chooi Ning, Program Director.

Ted Gonderman, Production Supervisor.

Deedra Determan, Marketing Director.

Kristi Littledave, Sales Research Director.

Joan King, Traffic Manager.

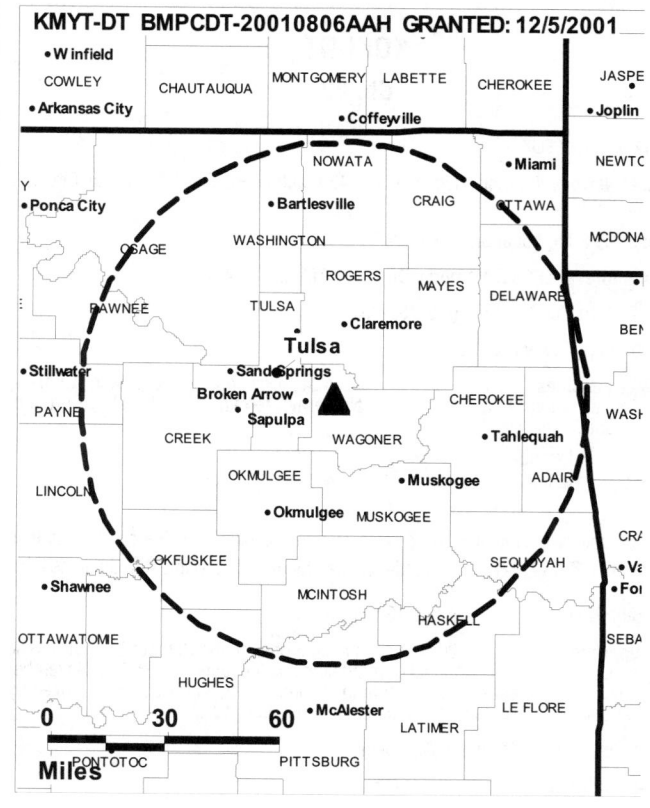

© 2010 Warren Communications News

City of License: Tulsa. **Station DMA:** Tulsa, OK. **Rank:** 61.

Circulation © 2009 Nielsen. Coverage based on Nielsen study.

GrandTotal	Cable TV Households	Non-cable TV Households	Total TV Households
Estimated Station Totals *	281,280	233,460	514,740
Average Weekly Circulation (2009)	44,837	47,597	92,434
Average Daily Circulation (2009)			32,189

Station DMA Total	Cable TV Households	Non-cable TV Households	Total TV Households
Estimated Station Totals *	268,910	233,460	502,370
Average Weekly Circulation (2009)	43,420	47,597	91,017
Average Daily Circulation (2009)			31,964

Other DMA Total	Cable TV Households	Non-cable TV Households	Total TV Households
Estimated Station Totals *	12,370	0	12,370
Average Weekly Circulation (2009)	1,417	0	1,417
Average Daily Circulation (2009)			225

*Estimated station totals are sums of the Nielsen TV and Cable TV household estimates for each county in which the station registers viewing of more than 5% as per the Nielsen Survey Methods.

KOKI-DT
Ch. 22

Network Service: FOX.

Licensee: Newport Television License LLC, 460 Nichols Rd, Ste 250, Kansas City, MO 64112.

Studio: 2625 S Memorial Dr, Tulsa, OK 74129.

Mailing Address: 2625 S Memorial Dr, Ste A, Tulsa, OK 74129.

Phone: 918-491-0023. **Fax:** 918-388-0516.

Web Site: http://www.fox23.com

Technical Facilities: Channel No. 22 (518-524 MHz). Authorized power: 1000-kw max. visual, aural. Antenna: 1316-ft above av. terrain, 1237-ft. above ground, 1944-ft. above sea level.

Latitude	36°	01'	36"
Longitude	95°	40'	44"

Note: Latitude and longitude coordinates shown are based on the North American Datum of 1927 (NAD 27) as currently required by the Mass Media Bureau of the FCC.

Ownership: Newport Television LLC (Group Owner).

Began Operation: October 1, 2002. Began analog operations: October 26, 1980. Sale to present owner by Clear Channel Communications Inc. approved by FCC November 29, 2007. Sale to Clear Channel Communications Inc. by Tulsa 23 LP approved by FCC February 7, 1990. Ceased analog operations: June 12, 2009.

Represented (legal): Covington & Burling.

Represented (sales): Katz Media Group.

Personnel:

Holly Allen, Vice President & General Manager.

Jim Hanning, Sales Director.

Stephanie Spry, Local Sales Manager.

Matt Rolison, New Media Sales Manager.

Kari Barrett, National Sales Manager.

Kristi Littledave, Sales Research Director.

Melanie Henry, News Director.

Brian Egan, Chief Engineer.

Amie Price, Business Manager.

Chooi Ning, Program Director.

Amber Musselman, Marketing Manager.

Ted Gonderman, Production Supervisor.

Joan King, Traffic Manager.

City of License: Tulsa. **Station DMA:** Tulsa, OK. **Rank:** 61.

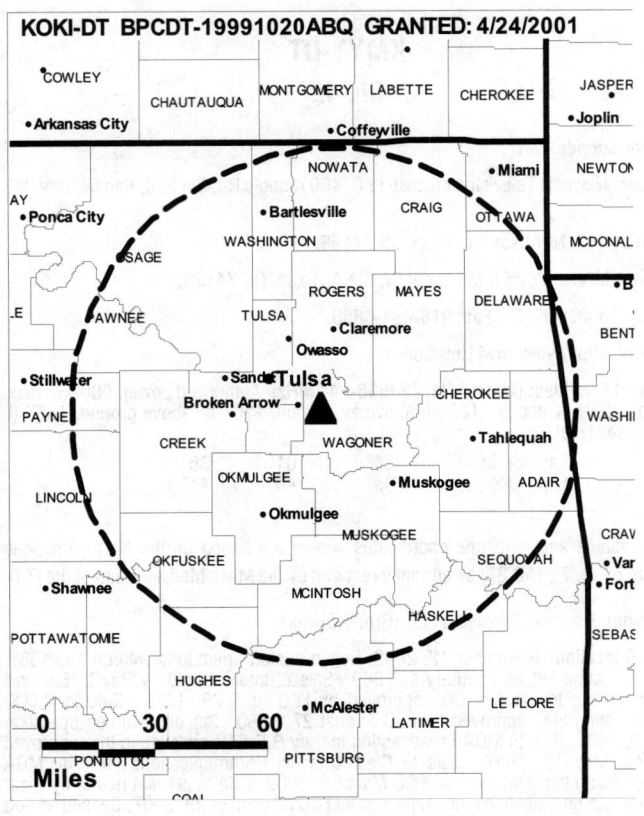

KOKI-DT BPCDT-19991020ABQ GRANTED: 4/24/2001

© 2010 Warren Communications News

Circulation © 2009 Nielsen. Coverage based on Nielsen study.

GrandTotal	Cable TV Households	Non-cable TV Households	Total TV Households
Estimated Station Totals *	289,200	245,340	534,540
Average Weekly Circulation (2009)	152,411	135,984	288,395
Average Daily Circulation (2009)			112,863

Station DMA Total	Cable TV Households	Non-cable TV Households	Total TV Households
Estimated Station Totals *	269,880	233,460	503,340
Average Weekly Circulation (2009)	148,829	134,973	283,802
Average Daily Circulation (2009)			112,228

Other DMA Total	Cable TV Households	Non-cable TV Households	Total TV Households
Estimated Station Totals *	19,320	11,880	31,200
Average Weekly Circulation (2009)	3,582	1,011	4,593
Average Daily Circulation (2009)			635

*Estimated station totals are sums of the Nielsen TV and Cable TV household estimates for each county in which the station registers viewing of more than 5% as per the Nielsen Survey Methods.

KOTV-DT
Ch. 55

Network Service: CBS.

Licensee: Griffin Licensing LLC, 7401 N Kelley Ave, Oklahoma City, OK 73111-8420.

Studio: 302 S Frankfort Ave, Tulsa, OK 74120.

Mailing Address: PO Box 6, Tulsa, OK 74101.

Phone: 918-732-6000. **Fax:** 918-732-6185.

Web Site: http://www.newson6.com

Technical Facilities: Channel No. 55 (716-722 MHz). Authorized power: 970-kw max. visual, aural. Antenna: 1609-ft above av. terrain, 1536-ft. above ground, 2247-ft. above sea level.

Latitude	36°	01'	15"
Longitude	95°	40'	32"

Holds CP for change to channel number 45, 840-kw max. visual, 1825-ft above av. terrain, 1747-ft. above ground, 2457-ft. above sea level; BPCDT-20080317AEZ.

Note: Latitude and longitude coordinates shown are based on the North American Datum of 1927 (NAD 27) as currently required by the Mass Media Bureau of the FCC.

Ownership: Griffin Communications LLC (Group Owner).

Began Operation: May 1, 2002. Began analog operations: October 22, 1949. Ceased analog operations: February 17, 2009. Sale to General Television Co. (Jack D. Wrather & mother, 50%; Maria Helen Alvarez, 50%) approved by FCC July 13, 1952. Sale to Corinthian Broadcasting approved by FCC May 13, 1954. Merger of Corinthian Broadcasting with Dun & Bradstreet approved by FCC April 14, 1971. Sale to Belo Corp. by Corinthian approved by FCC November 22, 1983. Sale to present owner by Belo Corp. approved by FCC December 6, 2000.

Represented (legal): Wilkinson Barker Knauer LLP.

Represented (sales): TeleRep Inc.

Personnel:

Regina Moon, Vice President & Chief Operating Officer.

John Trook, Sales Director.

Shawn Jordan, National Sales Manager.

Ron Harig, News Director.

Stephanie Hill, Executive Producer.

Gerald Weaver, Engineering Director.

Cheryl Sutton, Business Manager.

Donita Quesnel, Marketing Director.

John Quesnel, Production Manager.

Linda Mason, Traffic Manager.

City of License: Tulsa. **Station DMA:** Tulsa, OK. **Rank:** 61.

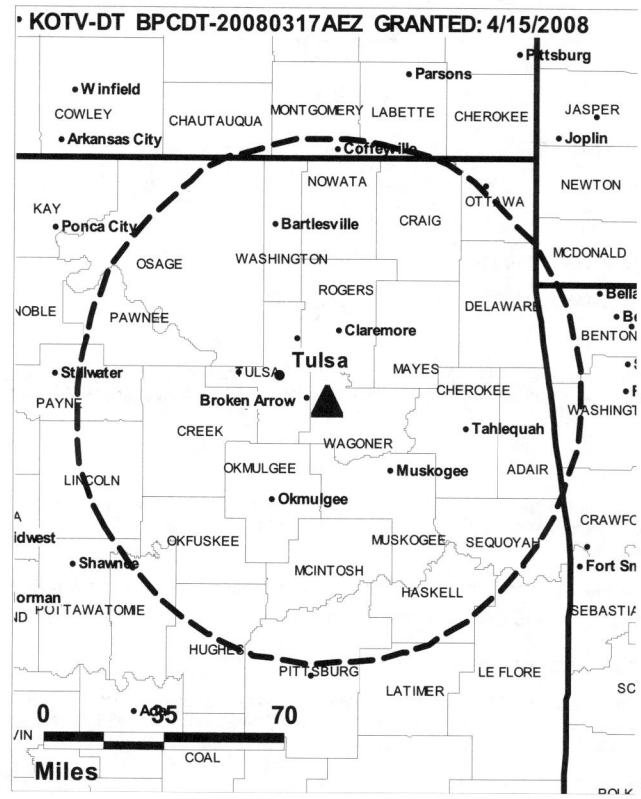

KOTV-DT BPCDT-20080317AEZ GRANTED: 4/15/2008

© 2010 Warren Communications News

Circulation © 2009 Nielsen. Coverage based on Nielsen study.

GrandTotal	Cable TV Households	Non-cable TV Households	Total TV Households
Estimated Station Totals *	287,830	280,350	568,180
Average Weekly Circulation (2009)	202,384	174,671	377,055
Average Daily Circulation (2009)			208,357

Station DMA Total	Cable TV Households	Non-cable TV Households	Total TV Households
Estimated Station Totals *	269,880	233,460	503,340
Average Weekly Circulation (2009)	195,795	171,068	366,863
Average Daily Circulation (2009)			204,685

Other DMA Total	Cable TV Households	Non-cable TV Households	Total TV Households
Estimated Station Totals *	17,950	46,890	64,840
Average Weekly Circulation (2009)	6,589	3,603	10,192
Average Daily Circulation (2009)			3,672

*Estimated station totals are sums of the Nielsen TV and Cable TV household estimates for each county in which the station registers viewing of more than 5% as per the Nielsen Survey Methods.

KTUL-DT
Ch. 58

Network Service: ABC.

Licensee: KTUL LLC, 3333 S 29th West Ave, Tulsa, OK 74107.

Studio: 3333 S 29th West Ave, Tulsa, OK 74107.

Mailing Address: PO Box 8, Tulsa, OK 74101-0008.

Phone: 918-445-8888; 918-445-9362. **Fax:** 918-445-9354.

Web Site: http://www.ktul.com

Technical Facilities: Channel No. 58 (734-740 MHz). Authorized power: 6.9-kw max. visual, aural. Antenna: 1779-ft above av. terrain, 1740-ft. above ground, 2384-ft. above sea level.

Latitude	35°	58'	08"
Longitude	95°	36'	55"

Holds CP for change to channel number 10, 15-kw visual, 1896-ft above av. terrain, 1860-ft. above ground, 2503-ft. above sea level; BPCDT-20080620AGA.

Note: Latitude and longitude coordinates shown are based on the North American Datum of 1927 (NAD 27) as currently required by the Mass Media Bureau of the FCC.

Ownership: Allbritton Communications Co. (Group Owner).

Began Operation: May 19, 2003. Began analog operations: September 18, 1954. Sale to present owner by Leake TV Inc. approved by FCC February 14, 1983 (Television Digest, Vol. 22:45). Ceased analog operations: June 12, 2009.

Represented (sales): Continental Television Sales.

Personnel:

Pat Baldwin, President & General Manager.

Roger Herring, Operations Manager & Chief Engineer.

Huey Ward, General Sales Manager.

Terri Walker, Local Sales Manager.

Carol Jones, National Sales Manager.

Carlton Houston, News Director.

Amy Miller, Program Director.

Deborah Kurin, Marketing Director.

Doug Bonebrake, Production Supervisor.

Larry Nitz, Promotion Director.

Terri Adcock, Traffic Manager.

Troy Wilborn, Business Manager.

City of License: Tulsa. **Station DMA:** Tulsa, OK. **Rank:** 61.

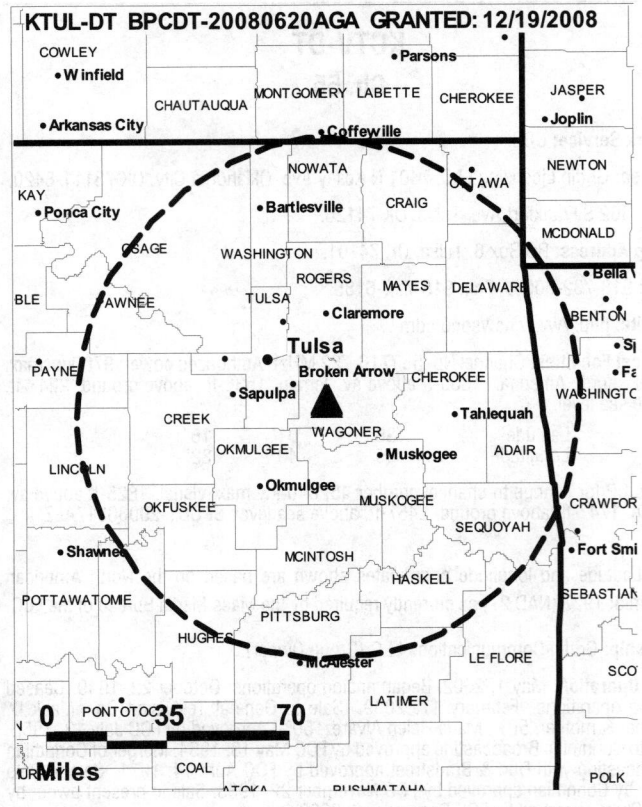

KTUL-DT BPCDT-20080620AGA GRANTED: 12/19/2008

© 2010 Warren Communications News

Circulation © 2009 Nielsen. Coverage based on Nielsen study.

GrandTotal	Cable TV Households	Non-cable TV Households	Total TV Households
Estimated Station Totals *	449,640	274,800	724,440
Average Weekly Circulation (2009)	213,971	163,923	377,894
Average Daily Circulation (2009)			175,332

Station DMA Total	Cable TV Households	Non-cable TV Households	Total TV Households
Estimated Station Totals *	269,880	233,460	503,340
Average Weekly Circulation (2009)	178,142	160,064	338,206
Average Daily Circulation (2009)			164,942

Other DMA Total	Cable TV Households	Non-cable TV Households	Total TV Households
Estimated Station Totals *	179,760	41,340	221,100
Average Weekly Circulation (2009)	35,829	3,859	39,688
Average Daily Circulation (2009)			10,390

*Estimated station totals are sums of the Nielsen TV and Cable TV household estimates for each county in which the station registers viewing of more than 5% as per the Nielsen Survey Methods.

KWHB-DT
Ch. 47

Network Service: IND.

Licensee: LeSea Broadcasting of Tulsa Inc., PO Box 12, 61300 S Ironwood Rd, South Bend, IN 46624.

Studio: 8835 S Memorial, Tulsa, OK 74133.

Mailing Address: 8835 S. Memorial Dr, Tulsa, OK 74133.

Phone: 918-254-4701. **Fax:** 918-254-5614.

E-mail: mzubeck@leasea.com

Web Site: http://www.kwhb.com

Technical Facilities: Channel No. 47 (668-674 MHz). Authorized power: 1000-kw max. visual, aural. Antenna: 1503-ft above av. terrain, 1424-ft. above ground, 2134-ft. above sea level.

Latitude	36°	01'	15"
Longitude	95°	40'	32"

Note: Latitude and longitude coordinates shown are based on the North American Datum of 1927 (NAD 27) as currently required by the Mass Media Bureau of the FCC.

Ownership: LeSea Broadcasting Corp. (Group Owner).

Began Operation: February 21, 2003. Standard Definition. Station broadcasting digitally on its analog channel allotment. Began analog operations: July 20, 1985. Sale as KTCT to present owner by Kearn family approved by FCC May 14, 1986. Ceased analog operations: February 17, 2009.

Personnel:

Kevin Krebbs, General Manager.

Dennis Hendrickson, Program, Traffic & Office Manager.

Anita Repp, Senior Account Manager.

Jim Hobbs, Chief Engineer.

Lori Stowers, Account Manager.

Peter Osteen, Account Manager.

Mike Zubeck, Production Manager.

City of License: Tulsa. **Station DMA:** Tulsa, OK. **Rank:** 61.

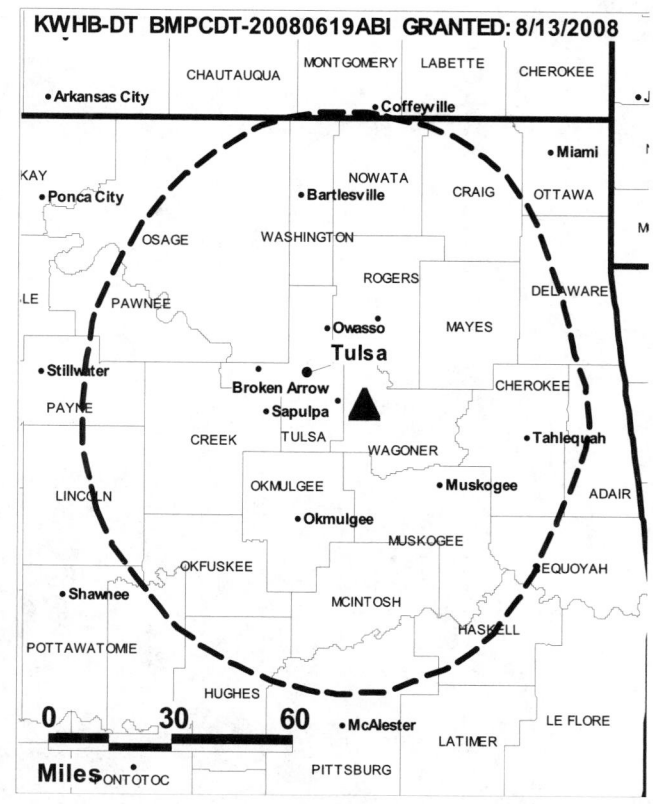

KWHB-DT BMPCDT-20080619ABI GRANTED: 8/13/2008

© 2010 Warren Communications News

Circulation © 2009 Nielsen. Coverage based on Nielsen study.

GrandTotal	Cable TV Households	Non-cable TV Households	Total TV Households
Estimated Station Totals *	229,980	151,560	381,540
Average Weekly Circulation (2009)	15,600	11,075	26,675
Average Daily Circulation (2009)			7,098

Station DMA Total	Cable TV Households	Non-cable TV Households	Total TV Households
Estimated Station Totals *	229,980	151,560	381,540
Average Weekly Circulation (2009)	15,600	11,075	26,675
Average Daily Circulation (2009)			7,098

*Estimated station totals are sums of the Nielsen TV and Cable TV household estimates for each county in which the station registers viewing of more than 5% as per the Nielsen Survey Methods.

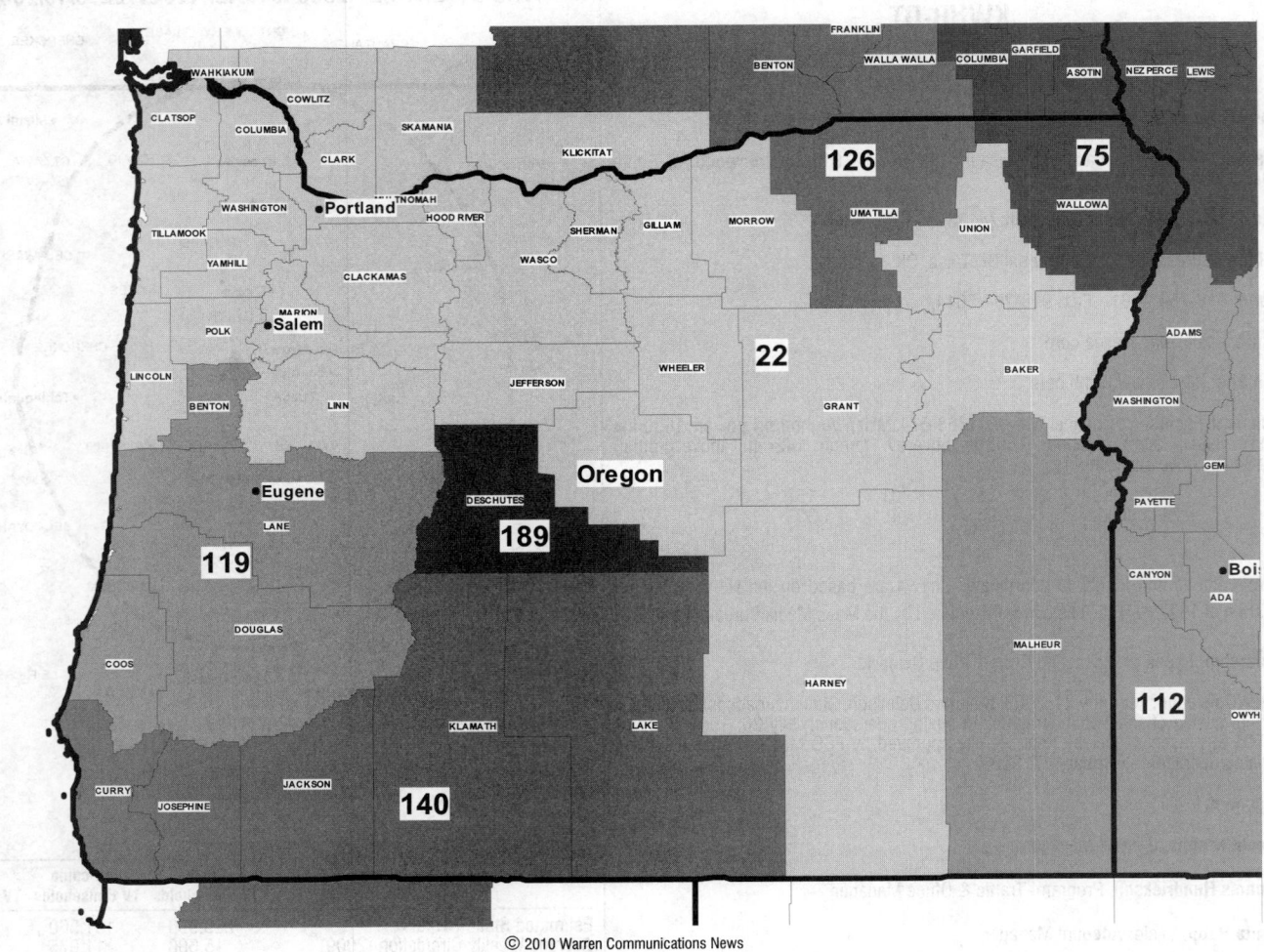

© 2010 Warren Communications News

MARKET	NIELSEN DMA TV HOUSEHOLDS	RANK	MARKET AREA COMMERCIAL STATIONS
Portland, OR	1,188,770	22	KATU-DT (43); KGW-DT (8); KNMT-DT (45); KOIN-DT (40); KPDX-DT (48); KPTV-DT (12); KPXG-TV (22); KRCW-DT (33); KUNP-DT (16)
Spokane, WA	419,350	75	KAYU-DT (28); KGPX-TV (34); KHQ-DT (15); KLEW-DT (32); KREM (20); KSKN-DT (36); KXLY-DT (13)
Boise, ID	262,800	112	KBCI-DT (28); KIVI-TV (24); KKJB-DT (39); KNIN-DT (10); KTRV-DT (13); KTVB-DT (7)
Eugene, OR	241,730	119	KCBY-DT (11); KEZI-DT (9); KLSR-DT (31); KMCB-DT (22); KMTR-DT (17); KPIC-DT (19); KTCW-DT (45); KTVC-DT (18); KVAL-DT (13)
Yakima-Pasco-Richland-Kennewick, WA	219,510	126	KAPP-DT (14); KEPR-DT (18); KFFX-DT (11); KIMA-DT (33); KNDO-DT (16); KNDU-DT (26); KVEW-DT (44)
Medford-Klamath Falls, OR	172,900	140	KBLN-DT (30); KDKF-DT (29); KDRV-DT (12); KMVU-DT (26); KOBI-DT (5); KOTI-DT (13); KTVL-DT (10)
Bend, OR	66,980	189	KOHD-DT (51); KTVZ-DT (18)

Oregon Station Totals as of October 1, 2009

	VHF	UHF	TOTAL
Commercial Television	10	17	27
Educational Television	5	2	7
	15	19	34

KOHD-DT
Ch. 51

Network Service: ABC.

Licensee: Three Sisters Broadcasting LLC, PO Box 7009, Eugene, OR 97401.

Mailing Address: 63049 Lower Meadow Dr, Bend, OR 97701.

Phone: 541-749-5151.

Web Site: http://www.kohd.com

Technical Facilities: Channel No. 51 (692-698 MHz). Authorized power: 84.1-kw max. visual, aural. Antenna: 675-ft above av. terrain, 200-ft. above ground, 4419-ft. above sea level.

Latitude	44°	04'	40.6"
Longitude	121°	19'	56.9"

Note: Latitude and longitude coordinates shown are based on the North American Datum of 1927 (NAD 27) as currently required by the Mass Media Bureau of the FCC.

Ownership: Chambers Communications Corp. (Group Owner).

Began Operation: September 9, 2006. Station flash-cut to digital operation; no analog facitilies constructed.

Represented (legal): Katten Muchin Rosenman LLP.

Personnel:

Jerry Upham, General Manager.

Nicole Moye, News Director.

Neiko Bernardo, Chief Engineer.

Bryan Johnson, Creative Services Director.

City of License: Bend. **Station DMA:** Bend, OR. **Rank:** 189.

KOHD-DT BMPCDT-20060721ABO GRANTED: 8/21/2006

© 2010 Warren Communications News

Circulation © 2009 Nielsen. Coverage based on Nielsen study.

GrandTotal	Cable TV Households	Non-cable TV Households	Total TV Households
Estimated Station Totals *	44,600	23,400	68,000
Average Weekly Circulation (2009)	22,890	4,001	26,891
Average Daily Circulation (2009)			10,207

Station DMA Total	Cable TV Households	Non-cable TV Households	Total TV Households
Estimated Station Totals *	41,430	23,400	64,830
Average Weekly Circulation (2009)	22,621	4,001	26,622
Average Daily Circulation (2009)			10,178

Other DMA Total	Cable TV Households	Non-cable TV Households	Total TV Households
Estimated Station Totals *	3,170	0	3,170
Average Weekly Circulation (2009)	269	0	269
Average Daily Circulation (2009)			29

*Estimated station totals are sums of the Nielsen TV and Cable TV household estimates for each county in which the station registers viewing of more than 5% as per the Nielsen Survey Methods.

KTVZ-DT

Ch. 18

Network Service: NBC, CW.

Grantee: NPG of Oregon Inc., 825 Edmond St, c/o New Press & Gazette Co., St. Joseph, MO 64501.

Studio: 62990 O.B. Riley Rd, Bend, OR 97701.

Mailing Address: PO Box 6038, Bend, OR 97708.

Phone: 541-383-2121. **Fax:** 541-382-1616.

Web Site: http://www.ktvz.com

Technical Facilities: Channel No. 18 (494-500 MHz). Authorized power: 28-kw max. visual, aural. Antenna: 646-ft above av. terrain, 167-ft. above ground, 4383-ft. above sea level.

Latitude	44°	04'	40"
Longitude	121°	19'	49"

Holds CP for change to channel number 21, 250-kw max. visual; BMPCDT-20080612ABU.

Note: Latitude and longitude coordinates shown are based on the North American Datum of 1927 (NAD 27) as currently required by the Mass Media Bureau of the FCC.

Ownership: News Press & Gazette Co. (Group Owner).

Began Operation: October 18, 2007. Station operating under Special Temporary Authority a 13-kw max. visual. Station broadcasting digitally on its analog channel allotment. Began analog operations: November 6, 1977. Sale to present owner by Northwest Broadcasting LP approved by FCC April 17, 2002. Sale to Northwest Broadcasting LP by Stainless Enterprises of Pennsylvania approved by FCC July 15, 1997. Sale to Stainless Enterprises of Pennsylvania by Sierra Cascade Communications Inc. approved by FCC October 30, 1986. Ceased analog operations: June 12, 2009.

Represented (sales): Continental Television Sales.

Personnel:

Chris Gallu, General Manager.

John Geertsen, Production Manager.

Lonnie Harden, Local Sales Manager.

Mike Bothwell, News Director.

Kristie Wilharm, Traffic Manager.

City of License: Bend. **Station DMA:** Bend, OR. **Rank:** 189.

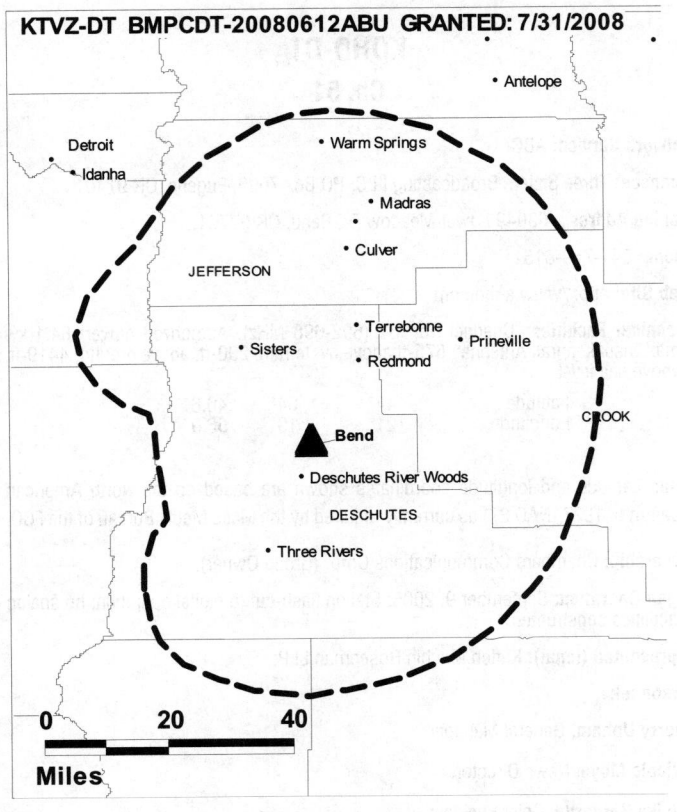

KTVZ-DT BMPCDT-20080612ABU GRANTED: 7/31/2008

© 2010 Warren Communications News

Circulation © 2009 Nielsen. Coverage based on Nielsen study.

GrandTotal	Cable TV Households	Non-cable TV Households	Total TV Households
Estimated Station Totals *	45,390	29,740	75,130
Average Weekly Circulation (2009)	34,856	11,723	46,579
Average Daily Circulation (2009)			26,551

Station DMA Total	Cable TV Households	Non-cable TV Households	Total TV Households
Estimated Station Totals *	41,430	23,400	64,830
Average Weekly Circulation (2009)	32,440	10,132	42,572
Average Daily Circulation (2009)			24,052

Other DMA Total	Cable TV Households	Non-cable TV Households	Total TV Households
Estimated Station Totals *	3,960	6,340	10,300
Average Weekly Circulation (2009)	2,416	1,591	4,007
Average Daily Circulation (2009)			2,499

*Estimated station totals are sums of the Nielsen TV and Cable TV household estimates for each county in which the station registers viewing of more than 5% as per the Nielsen Survey Methods.

KCBY-DT
Ch. 11

Network Service: CBS.

Licensee: Fisher Broadcasting-Oregon TV LLC, 600 University St, Ste 1525, Seattle, WA 98101.

Studio: 3451 Broadway, North Bend, OR 97459.

Mailing Address: PO Box 1156, Coos Bay, OR 97420.

Phone: 541-269-1111. **Fax:** 541-269-7464.

Web Site: http://www.kcby.com

Technical Facilities: Channel No. 11 (198-204 MHz). Authorized power: 5-kw visual, aural. Antenna: 630-ft above av. terrain, 180-ft. above ground, 1037-ft. above sea level.

Latitude	43°	23'	26"
Longitude	124°	07'	46"

Note: Latitude and longitude coordinates shown are based on the North American Datum of 1927 (NAD 27) as currently required by the Mass Media Bureau of the FCC.

Ownership: Fisher Communications Inc. (Group Owner).

Began Operation: May 7, 2007. Station broadcasting digitally on its analog channel allotment. Began analog operations: October 1, 1960. Sale to Retlaw Enterprises Inc. by Northwest Television Inc. approved by FCC March 29, 1996. Sale to present owner from Retlaw Enterprises Inc. approved by FCC April 20, 1999. Ceased analog operations: June 12, 2009.

Represented (sales): Katz Media Group.

Represented (legal): Pillsbury Winthrop Shaw Pittman LLP.

Personnel:

Greg Raschio, General Manager.

Ken Croes, Station Manager, General & Local Sales Manager.

Dino Francois, Promotion Director.

Bob Whitsett, Creative Services Director.

Sara Halka, Traffic Manager.

Tim Novotny, News Director.

Dan Stoe, Chief Engineer.

Paul Greene, Program Director.

City of License: Coos Bay. **Station DMA:** Eugene, OR. **Rank:** 119.

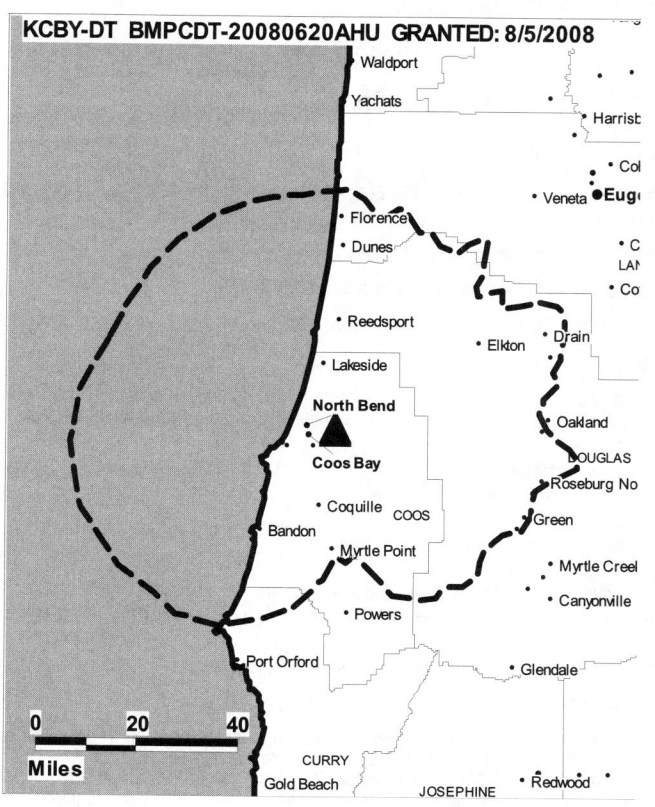

© 2010 Warren Communications News

Circulation © 2009 Nielsen. Coverage based on Nielsen study.

GrandTotal	Cable TV Households	Non-cable TV Households	Total TV Households
Estimated Station Totals *	25,710	14,510	40,220
Average Weekly Circulation (2009)	11,652	2,684	14,336
Average Daily Circulation (2009)			7,749

Station DMA Total	Cable TV Households	Non-cable TV Households	Total TV Households
Estimated Station Totals *	25,710	14,510	40,220
Average Weekly Circulation (2009)	11,652	2,684	14,336
Average Daily Circulation (2009)			7,749

*Estimated station totals are sums of the Nielsen TV and Cable TV household estimates for each county in which the station registers viewing of more than 5% as per the Nielsen Survey Methods.

KMCB-DT
Ch. 22

Network Service: NBC.

Licensee: Newport Television License LLC, 460 Nichols Rd, Ste 250, Kansas City, MO 64112.

Studio: 2455 Maple Leaf, North Bend, OR 97459.

Mailing Address: 2455 Maple Leaf, North Bend, OR 97459.

Phone: 541-746-1600. **Fax:** 541-747-0866.

Web Site: http://www.kmtr.com

Technical Facilities: Channel No. 22 (518-524 MHz). Authorized power: 10-kw max. visual, aural. Antenna: 587-ft above av. terrain, 115-ft. above ground, 994-ft. above sea level.

Latitude	43°	23'	39"
Longitude	124°	07'	56"

Transmitter: Noah Butte, 4.8-mi. NE of Coos Bay.

Note: Latitude and longitude coordinates shown are based on the North American Datum of 1927 (NAD 27) as currently required by the Mass Media Bureau of the FCC.

Multichannel TV Sound: Stereo and separate audio program.

Ownership: Newport Television LLC (Group Owner).

Began Operation: July 17, 2003. Began analog operations: July 8, 1991. Sale to Wicks Broadcast Group LP by KMTR Inc. approved by FCC October 17, 1995. Sale to The Ackerley Group from Wicks Broadcast Group LP approved by FCC March 12, 1999. In stock swap, Clear Channel Broadcasting Inc. acquired The Ackerley Group. FCC approved deal May 29, 2002. Sale to present owner by Clear Channel Communications Inc. approved by FCC November 29, 2007. Ceased analog operations: June 12, 2009.

Represented (sales): Blair Television.

Represented (legal): Covington & Burling.

Personnel:

Cambra Ward, Vice President & General Manager.

Scott Prentice, Operations Manager & Chief Engineer.

Mike Chisholm, General Sales Manager.

Jill Wiliams, Local Sales Manager.

John Wagner, National Sales Manager.

Robert McMichaels, News Director.

Leslie Bristow, Production, Promotion & Creative Services Director.

Melanie Rush, Traffic Manager.

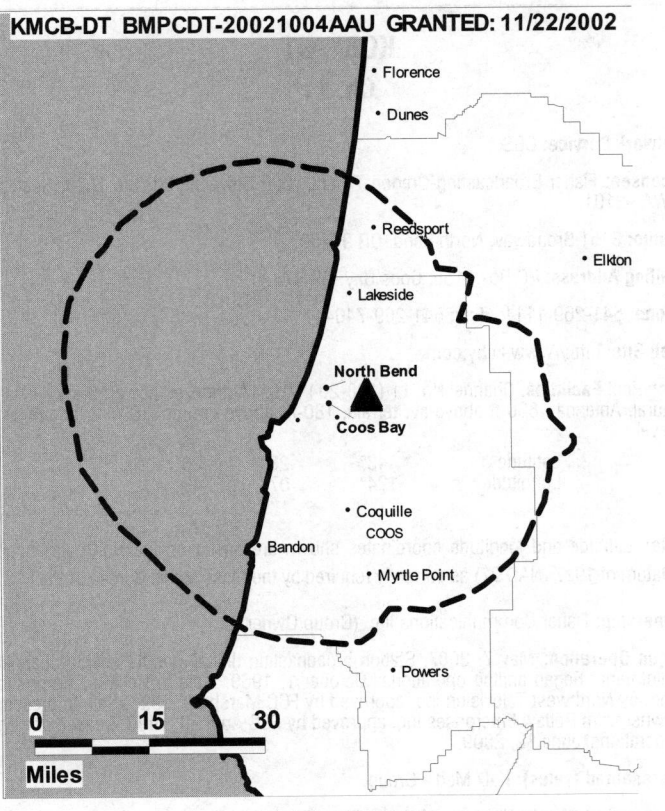

KMCB-DT BMPCDT-20021004AAU GRANTED: 11/22/2002

© 2010 Warren Communications News

City of License: Coos Bay. **Station DMA:** Eugene, OR. **Rank:** 119.

Circulation © 2009 Nielsen. Coverage based on Nielsen study.

GrandTotal	Cable TV Households	Non-cable TV Households	Total TV Households
Estimated Station Totals *	12,100	14,510	26,610
Average Weekly Circulation (2009)	4,005	769	4,774
Average Daily Circulation (2009)			1,756

Station DMA Total	Cable TV Households	Non-cable TV Households	Total TV Households
Estimated Station Totals *	12,100	14,510	26,610
Average Weekly Circulation (2009)	4,005	769	4,774
Average Daily Circulation (2009)			1,756

*Estimated station totals are sums of the Nielsen TV and Cable TV household estimates for each county in which the station registers viewing of more than 5% as per the Nielsen Survey Methods.

KEZI-DT
Ch. 9

Network Service: ABC.

Licensee: KEZI Inc., PO Box 7009, Eugene, OR 97401.

Studio: 2940 Chad Dr, Eugene, OR 97408.

Mailing Address: PO Box 7009, Eugene, OR 97401.

Phone: 541-485-5611. **Fax:** 541-342-1568.

Web Site: http://www.kezi.com

Technical Facilities: Channel No. 9 (186-192 MHz). Authorized power: 43.9-kw visual, aural. Antenna: 1750-ft above av. terrain, 429-ft. above ground, 2539-ft. above sea level.

Latitude	44°	06'	57"
Longitude	122°	59'	57"

Note: Latitude and longitude coordinates shown are based on the North American Datum of 1927 (NAD 27) as currently required by the Mass Media Bureau of the FCC.

Ownership: Chambers Communications Corp. (Group Owner).

Began Operation: March 15, 2007. Station broadcasting digitally on its analog channel allotment. Began analog operations: December 19, 1960. Sale to present owner approved by FCC August 10, 1983. Ceased analog operations: February 17, 2009.

Personnel:

Mark Hatfield, President & General Manager.

Catherine Hatfield, General Sales Manager.

Beth Cookson, National & Regional Sales Coordinator.

Gary Darigol, News Director.

Dennis Hunt, Chief Engineer.

Michelle Johannon, Marketing & Promotion Director.

Pepper Smelser, Traffic Manager.

City of License: Eugene. **Station DMA:** Eugene, OR. **Rank:** 119.

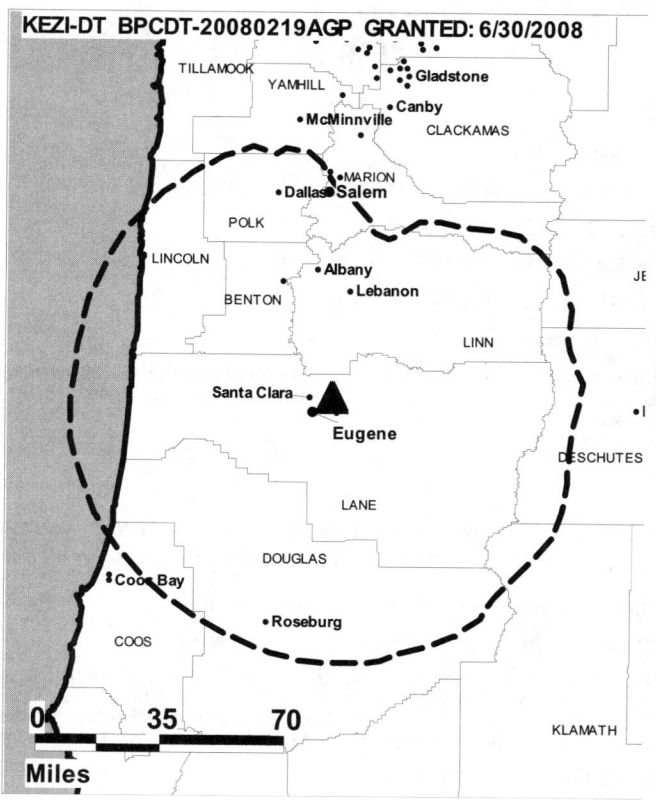

KEZI-DT BPCDT-20080219AGP GRANTED: 6/30/2008

© 2010 Warren Communications News

Circulation © 2009 Nielsen. Coverage based on Nielsen study.

GrandTotal	Cable TV Households	Non-cable TV Households	Total TV Households
Estimated Station Totals *	125,110	148,320	273,430
Average Weekly Circulation (2009)	66,211	66,967	133,178
Average Daily Circulation (2009)			60,462

Station DMA Total	Cable TV Households	Non-cable TV Households	Total TV Households
Estimated Station Totals *	104,770	125,920	230,690
Average Weekly Circulation (2009)	58,645	65,377	124,022
Average Daily Circulation (2009)			56,658

Other DMA Total	Cable TV Households	Non-cable TV Households	Total TV Households
Estimated Station Totals *	20,340	22,400	42,740
Average Weekly Circulation (2009)	7,566	1,590	9,156
Average Daily Circulation (2009)			3,804

*Estimated station totals are sums of the Nielsen TV and Cable TV household estimates for each county in which the station registers viewing of more than 5% as per the Nielsen Survey Methods.

KLSR-DT
Ch. 31

Network Service: FOX.

Licensee: California Oregon Broadcasting Inc., PO Box 1489, Medford, OR 97501.

Studio: 2940 Chad Dr, Eugene, OR 97408.

Mailing Address: 2940 Chad Dr, Eugene, OR 97408.

Phone: 541-683-3434. **Fax:** 541-683-8016.

Web Site: http://www.myfoxeugene.com/myfox

Technical Facilities: Channel No. 31 (572-578 MHz). Authorized power: 88-kw max. visual, aural. Antenna: 1220-ft above av. terrain, 580-ft. above ground, 1876-ft. above sea level.

Latitude	44°	00'	04"
Longitude	123°	06'	45"

Note: Latitude and longitude coordinates shown are based on the North American Datum of 1927 (NAD 27) as currently required by the Mass Media Bureau of the FCC.

Multichannel TV Sound: Stereo and separate audio program.

Ownership: California-Oregon Broadcasting Inc. (Group Owner).

Began Operation: May 1, 2002. Began analog operations: October 30, 1991. Sale to present owner approved by FCC September 1, 1994 (Television Digest, Vol. 34:5). Transfer of control from Carol Anne Smullin Brown to Patricia C. Smullin approved by FCC March 30, 2001. Ceased analog operations: February 17, 2009.

Represented (sales): Blair Television.

Represented (legal): Wiley Rein LLP.

Represented (engineering): Lohnes & Culver.

Personnel:

Mark Metzger, General Manager.

Christina Breen, Local Sales Manager.

Malissa Bare, Local Sales Manager.

Matthew Hilton, Local Sales Manager.

Steve Woodward, Local Sales Manager.

David Fenley, Local Sales Manager.

Scott Bonnell, National Sales Manager.

Bob Broderick, News & Promotion Director.

Tim Hershiser, Chief Engineer.

Kathy Wofford, Business Manager.

Sandra Dornon-Belmont, Program Director.

Marc Belmont, Creative Services Director.

Jeannie Crane, Traffic Manager.

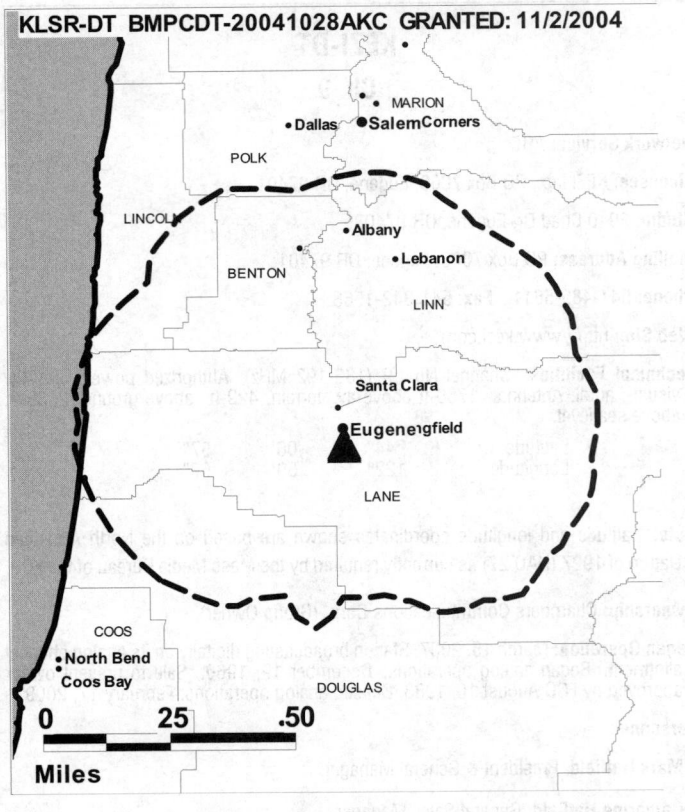

KLSR-DT BMPCDT-20041028AKC GRANTED: 11/2/2004

© 2010 Warren Communications News

City of License: Eugene. **Station DMA:** Eugene, OR. **Rank:** 119.

Circulation © 2009 Nielsen. Coverage based on Nielsen study.

GrandTotal	Cable TV Households	Non-cable TV Households	Total TV Households
Estimated Station Totals *	137,210	148,320	285,530
Average Weekly Circulation (2009)	60,899	57,616	118,515
Average Daily Circulation (2009)			39,602

Station DMA Total	Cable TV Households	Non-cable TV Households	Total TV Households
Estimated Station Totals *	116,870	125,920	242,790
Average Weekly Circulation (2009)	58,906	55,802	114,708
Average Daily Circulation (2009)			38,405

Other DMA Total	Cable TV Households	Non-cable TV Households	Total TV Households
Estimated Station Totals *	20,340	22,400	42,740
Average Weekly Circulation (2009)	1,993	1,814	3,807
Average Daily Circulation (2009)			1,197

*Estimated station totals are sums of the Nielsen TV and Cable TV household estimates for each county in which the station registers viewing of more than 5% as per the Nielsen Survey Methods.

KMTR-DT
Ch. 17

Network Service: NBC, CW.

Licensee: Newport Television License LLC, 460 Nichols Rd, Ste 250, Kansas City, MO 64112.

Studio: 3825 International Ct, Springfield, OR 97477.

Mailing Address: 3825 International Court, Springfield, OR 97477.

Phone: 541-746-1600. **Fax:** 541-747-0866.

Web Site: http://www.kmtr.com

Technical Facilities: Channel No. 17 (488-494 MHz). Authorized power: 70-kw max. visual, aural. Antenna: 1552-ft above av. terrain, 236-ft. above ground, 2346-ft. above sea level.

Latitude	44°	06'	57"
Longitude	122°	59'	57"

Note: Latitude and longitude coordinates shown are based on the North American Datum of 1927 (NAD 27) as currently required by the Mass Media Bureau of the FCC.

Ownership: Newport Television LLC (Group Owner).

Began Operation: June 18, 2003. Began analog operations: October 4, 1982. Transfer of control to KMTR Inc. approved by FCC Jan. 16, 1984. Sale to Wicks Broadcast Group LP approved by FCC October 17, 1995. Sale to The Ackerley Group by Wicks Broadcast Group LP approved by FCC March 12, 1999. In stock swap, Clear Channel Broadcasting Inc. acquired The Ackerley Group. FCC approved deal May 29, 2002. Sale to present owner by Clear Channel Communications Inc. approved by FCC November 29, 2007. Ceased analog operations: June 12, 2009.

Represented (sales): Blair Television.

Represented (legal): Covington & Burling.

Personnel:

Cambra Ward, Vice President & General Manager.

Scott Prentice, Operations Manager & Chief Engineer.

Mike Chisholm, General Sales Manager.

John Wagner, National Sales Manager.

Robert McMichaels, News Director.

Leslie Bristow, Production, Creative Services & Promotion Director.

Melanie Rush, Traffic Manager.

City of License: Eugene. **Station DMA:** Eugene, OR. **Rank:** 119.

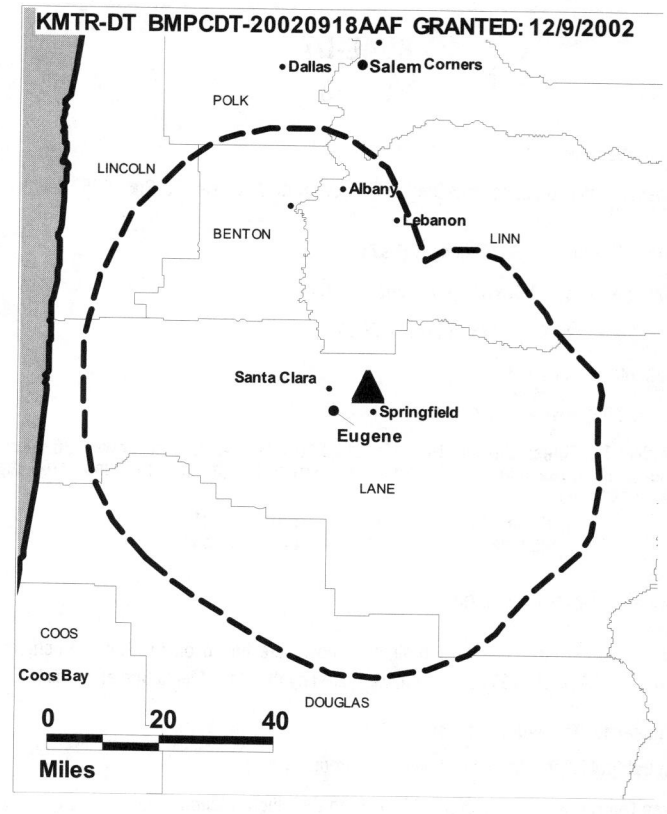

KMTR-DT BMPCDT-20020918AAF GRANTED: 12/9/2002

© 2010 Warren Communications News

Circulation © 2009 Nielsen. Coverage based on Nielsen study.

GrandTotal	Cable TV Households	Non-cable TV Households	Total TV Households
Estimated Station Totals *	125,110	148,320	273,430
Average Weekly Circulation (2009)	60,309	64,086	124,395
Average Daily Circulation (2009)			51,313

Station DMA Total	Cable TV Households	Non-cable TV Households	Total TV Households
Estimated Station Totals *	104,770	125,920	230,690
Average Weekly Circulation (2009)	54,288	62,540	116,828
Average Daily Circulation (2009)			48,364

Other DMA Total	Cable TV Households	Non-cable TV Households	Total TV Households
Estimated Station Totals *	20,340	22,400	42,740
Average Weekly Circulation (2009)	6,021	1,546	7,567
Average Daily Circulation (2009)			2,949

*Estimated station totals are sums of the Nielsen TV and Cable TV household estimates for each county in which the station registers viewing of more than 5% as per the Nielsen Survey Methods.

KVAL-DT
Ch. 13

Network Service: CBS.

Licensee: Fisher Broadcasting-Oregon TV LLC, 600 University St, Ste 1525, Seattle, WA 98101.

Studio: 4575 Blanton Rd, Eugene, OR 97405.

Mailing Address: PO Box 1313, Eugene, OR 97440.

Phone: 541-342-4961. **Fax:** 541-342-2635.

E-mail: olson@kval.com

Web Site: http://www.kval.com

Technical Facilities: Channel No. 13 (210-216 MHz). Authorized power: 30.6-kw visual, aural. Antenna: 1147-ft above av. terrain, 807-ft. above ground, 2102-ft. above sea level.

Latitude	44°	00'	07"
Longitude	123°	06'	53"

Transmitter: 4575 Blanton Rd.

Note: Latitude and longitude coordinates shown are based on the North American Datum of 1927 (NAD 27) as currently required by the Mass Media Bureau of the FCC.

Multichannel TV Sound: Planned.

Ownership: Fisher Communications Inc. (Group Owner).

Began Operation: December 12, 2001. High Definition. Station broadcasting digitally on its analog channel allotment. Began analog operations: April 15, 1954. Sale to Retlaw Enterprises Inc. by Northwest Television Inc. approved by FCC March 29, 1996. Sale to present owner by Retlaw Enterprises Inc. approved by FCC April 20, 1999. Ceased analog operations: June 12, 2009.

Represented (sales): Katz Media Group.

Represented (legal): Pillsbury Winthrop Shaw Pittman LLP.

Personnel:

Greg Raschio, Vice President & General Manager.

Steve Murray, General Sales Manager.

Dan Stoe, Chief Engineer.

Paul Greene, Program Director.

Dino Francois, Promotion Director.

Wade Hughes, Production Manager.

Sheryl Knox, Traffic Manager.

City of License: Eugene. **Station DMA:** Eugene, OR. **Rank:** 119.

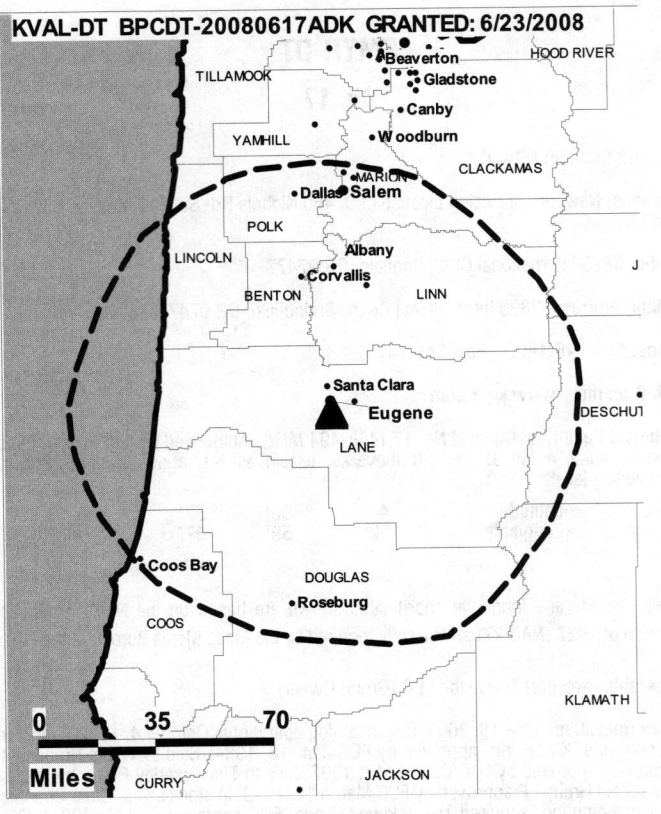

KVAL-DT BPCDT-20080617ADK GRANTED: 6/23/2008

© 2010 Warren Communications News

Circulation © 2009 Nielsen. Coverage based on Nielsen study.

GrandTotal	Cable TV Households	Non-cable TV Households	Total TV Households
Estimated Station Totals *	152,930	148,320	301,250
Average Weekly Circulation (2009)	70,095	64,495	134,590
Average Daily Circulation (2009)			61,353

Station DMA Total	Cable TV Households	Non-cable TV Households	Total TV Households
Estimated Station Totals *	91,160	125,920	217,080
Average Weekly Circulation (2009)	56,621	62,882	119,503
Average Daily Circulation (2009)			55,919

Other DMA Total	Cable TV Households	Non-cable TV Households	Total TV Households
Estimated Station Totals *	61,770	22,400	84,170
Average Weekly Circulation (2009)	13,474	1,613	15,087
Average Daily Circulation (2009)			5,434

*Estimated station totals are sums of the Nielsen TV and Cable TV household estimates for each county in which the station registers viewing of more than 5% as per the Nielsen Survey Methods.

KBLN-DT
Ch. 30

Network Service: IND.

Licensee: Better Life Television Inc., PO Box 766, Grants Pass, OR 97528.

Studio: 1360 NE 9th St, Grants Pass, OR 97526-1324.

Mailing Address: PO Box 766, Grants Pass, OR 97528-0066.

Phone: 541-474-3089; 877-741-2588. **Fax:** 541-474-9409.

Web Site: http://www.betterlifetv.tv

Technical Facilities: Channel No. 30 (566-572 MHz). Authorized power: 2-kw max. visual, aural. Antenna: 2146-ft above av. terrain, 121-ft. above ground, 3891-ft. above sea level.

Latitude	42°	22'	56"
Longitude	123°	16'	29"

Note: Latitude and longitude coordinates shown are based on the North American Datum of 1927 (NAD 27) as currently required by the Mass Media Bureau of the FCC.

Ownership: Better Life Television Inc.

Began Operation: February 17, 2009. Station broadcasting digitally on its analog channel allotment. Began analog operations: October 15, 2001. Ceased analog operations: February 17, 2001.

Personnel:

Ron Davis, General Manager.

Marta Davis, Station Manager.

Bill Whitt, Chief Engineer.

Sarai Romani, Marketing & Programing Director.

City of License: Grants Pass. **Station DMA:** Medford-Klamath Falls, OR. **Rank:** 140.

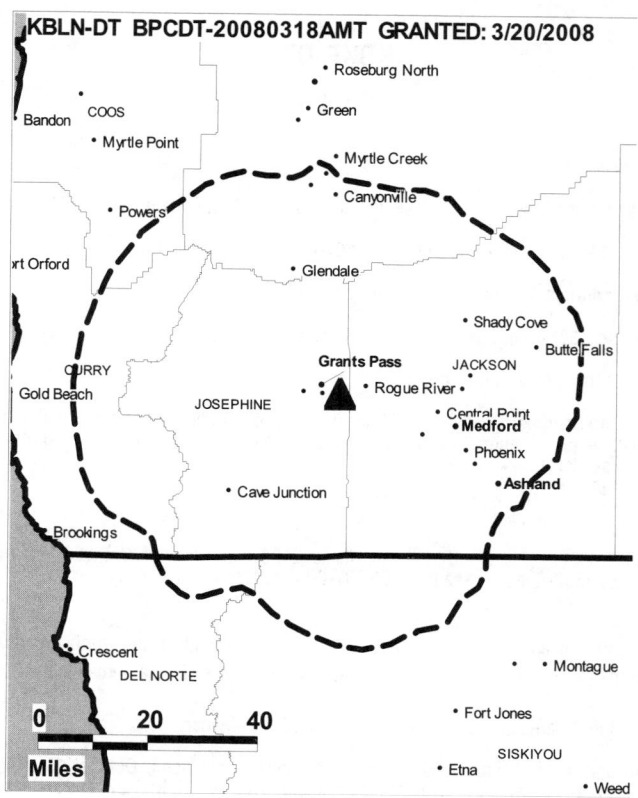

KBLN-DT BPCDT-20080318AMT GRANTED: 3/20/2008

© 2010 Warren Communications News

Nielsen Data: Not available.

KDKF-DT

Ch. 29

Network Service: ABC.

Licensee: Soda Mountain Broadcasting Inc., PO Box 7009, Eugene, OR 97401.

Studio: 231 E Main St, Klamath Falls, OR 97601.

Mailing Address: PO Box 4220, Medford, OR 97501.

Phone: 541-882-5648; 541-888-3131. **Fax:** 541-883-8931.

Web Site: http://www.kdrv.com

Technical Facilities: Channel No. 29 (560-566 MHz). Authorized power: 5-kw max. visual, aural. Antenna: 2136-ft above av. terrain, 13-ft. above ground, 6447-ft. above sea level.

Latitude	42°	05'	50"
Longitude	121°	37'	59"

Holds CP for change to 4.87-kw max. visual, 2136-ft above av. terrain, 129-ft. above ground, 6562-ft. above sea level; BPCDT-20060221AGL.

Note: Latitude and longitude coordinates shown are based on the North American Datum of 1927 (NAD 27) as currently required by the Mass Media Bureau of the FCC.

Ownership: Chambers Communications Corp. (Group Owner).

Began Operation: February 15, 2008. Began analog operations: October 15, 1989. Sale to present owner by Love Broadcasting approved by FCC May 27, 1993. Ceased analog operations: February 17, 2009.

Personnel:

Renard Maiuri, General Manager.

Rick Carrara, Operations Manager & Chief Engineer.

Jack McCauley, Local Sales Manager.

Dan Hill, Local Sales Manager.

Rick Howard, News Director.

Matt Valladao, Senior Director.

Geoffrey Riley, Creative Services Director.

City of License: Klamath Falls. **Station DMA:** Medford-Klamath Falls, OR. **Rank:** 140.

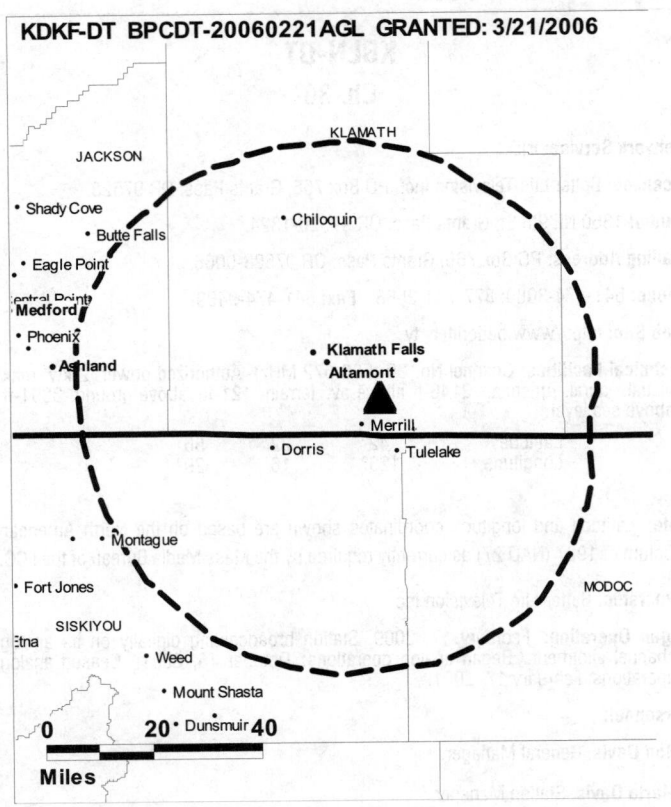

KDKF-DT BPCDT-20060221AGL GRANTED: 3/21/2006

© 2010 Warren Communications News

Circulation © 2009 Nielsen. Coverage based on Nielsen study.

GrandTotal	Cable TV Households	Non-cable TV Households	Total TV Households
Estimated Station Totals *	11,940	17,360	29,300
Average Weekly Circulation (2009)	6,765	1,819	8,584
Average Daily Circulation (2009)			4,524

Station DMA Total	Cable TV Households	Non-cable TV Households	Total TV Households
Estimated Station Totals *	11,940	17,360	29,300
Average Weekly Circulation (2009)	6,765	1,819	8,584
Average Daily Circulation (2009)			4,524

*Estimated station totals are sums of the Nielsen TV and Cable TV household estimates for each county in which the station registers viewing of more than 5% as per the Nielsen Survey Methods.

KOTI-DT
Ch. 13

Network Service: NBC.

Licensee: California-Oregon Broadcasting Inc., PO Box 1489, Medford, OR 97501.

Studio: 222 S 7th St, Box 2K, Klamath Falls, OR 97601.

Mailing Address: PO Box 1489, Medford, OR 97501.

Phone: 541-882-2222. **Fax:** 541-883-7664.

E-mail: rwise@kobi5.com

Web Site: http://www.localnewscomesfirst.com

Technical Facilities: Channel No. 13 (210-216 MHz). Authorized power: 9-kw max. visual, aural. Antenna: 2162-ft above av. terrain, 115-ft. above ground, 6526-ft. above sea level.

Latitude	42°	05'	48"
Longitude	121°	37'	57"

Note: Latitude and longitude coordinates shown are based on the North American Datum of 1927 (NAD 27) as currently required by the Mass Media Bureau of the FCC.

Satellite Earth Station: Transmitter Harris; Paraclipse, 4.5-meter.

Ownership: California-Oregon Broadcasting Inc.

Began Operation: May 1, 2002. Began analog operations: August 13, 1956. Ceased analog operations: February 17, 2009.

Represented (sales): Blair Television.

Represented (legal): Wiley Rein LLP.

Represented (engineering): Lohnes & Culver.

Personnel:

Patricia C. Smullin, President.

Robert Wise, Vice President & General Manager.

Dennis Siewert, General Sales Manager.

Laryl Noble, Acting News Director.

Steve Aase, Chief Engineer.

Donna Rodriguez, Program Director & Traffic Manager.

Scott Gee, Promotion Director.

City of License: Klamath Falls. **Station DMA:** Medford-Klamath Falls, OR. **Rank:** 140.

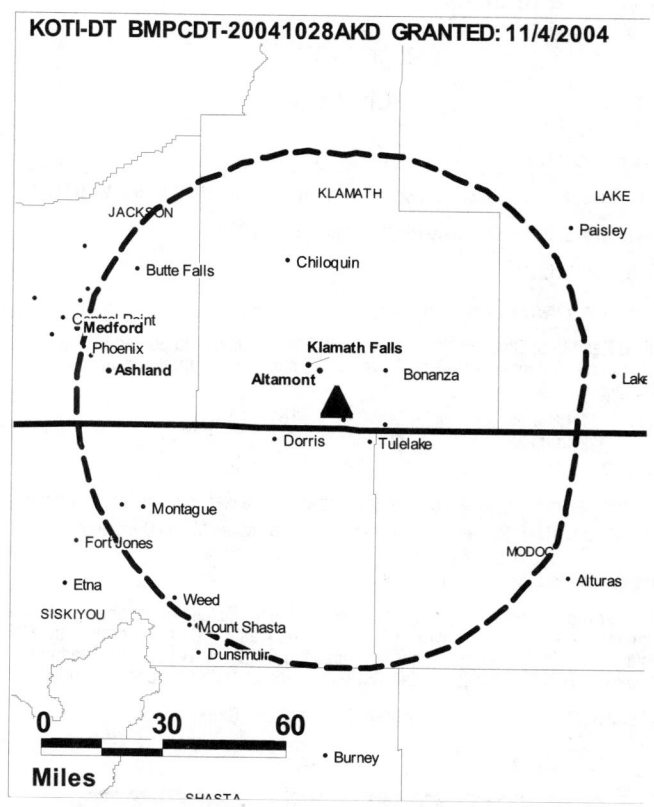

KOTI-DT BMPCDT-20041028AKD GRANTED: 11/4/2004

© 2010 Warren Communications News

Circulation © 2009 Nielsen. Coverage based on Nielsen study.

GrandTotal	Cable TV Households	Non-cable TV Households	Total TV Households
Estimated Station Totals *	11,940	17,360	29,300
Average Weekly Circulation (2009)	6,738	1,684	8,422
Average Daily Circulation (2009)			4,252

Station DMA Total	Cable TV Households	Non-cable TV Households	Total TV Households
Estimated Station Totals *	11,940	17,360	29,300
Average Weekly Circulation (2009)	6,738	1,684	8,422
Average Daily Circulation (2009)			4,252

*Estimated station totals are sums of the Nielsen TV and Cable TV household estimates for each county in which the station registers viewing of more than 5% as per the Nielsen Survey Methods.

KUNP-DT
Ch. 16

Network Service: UNV.

Grantee: Fisher Radio Regional Group, 100 4th Ave N, Ste 510, Seattle, WA 98109.

Mailing Address: 2153 NE Sandy Blvd, Portland, OR 97323.

Phone: 503-231-4222.

Web Site: http://www.kunptv.com

Technical Facilities: Channel No. 16 (482-488 MHz). Authorized power: 50-kw max. visual, aural. Antenna: 2536-ft above av. terrain, 56-ft. above ground, 7175-ft. above sea level.

Latitude	45°	18'	35"
Longitude	117°	43'	57"

Note: Latitude and longitude coordinates shown are based on the North American Datum of 1927 (NAD 27) as currently required by the Mass Media Bureau of the FCC.

Ownership: Fisher Communications Inc.

Began Operation: June 12, 2009. Station broadcasting digitally on its analog channel allotment. Sale to present owner by Equity Broadcasting Corp. approved by FCC February 28, 2006. Sale to Equity Broadcasting Corp. by WinStar Le Grande Inc. approved by FCC October 20, 2000. Ceased analog operations: June 12, 2009.

City of License: La Grande. **Station DMA:** Portland, OR. **Rank:** 22.

MediaPrints™
Map a Winning Business Strategy

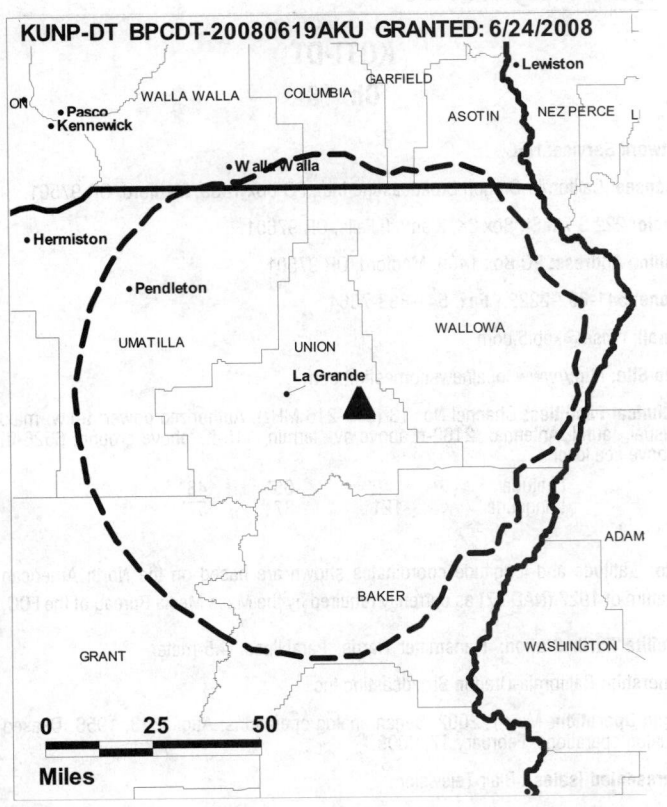

KUNP-DT BPCDT-20080619AKU GRANTED: 6/24/2008

© 2010 Warren Communications News

Circulation © 2009 Nielsen. Coverage based on Nielsen study.

GrandTotal	Cable TV Households	Non-cable TV Households	Total TV Households
Estimated Station Totals *	80,190	0	80,190
Average Weekly Circulation (2009)	6,287	0	6,287
Average Daily Circulation (2009)			2,635

Station DMA Total	Cable TV Households	Non-cable TV Households	Total TV Households
Estimated Station Totals *	80,190	0	80,190
Average Weekly Circulation (2009)	6,287	0	6,287
Average Daily Circulation (2009)			2,635

*Estimated station totals are sums of the Nielsen TV and Cable TV household estimates for each county in which the station registers viewing of more than 5% as per the Nielsen Survey Methods.

KDRV-DT
Ch. 12

Network Service: ABC.

Licensee: Soda Mountain Broadcasting Inc., PO Box 7009, Eugene, OR 97401.

Studio: 1090 Knutson Ave, Medford, OR 97504.

Mailing Address: PO Box 4220, Medford, OR 97501.

Phone: 541-773-1212. **Fax:** 541-779-9261.

Web Site: http://www.kdrv.com

Technical Facilities: Channel No. 12 (204-210 MHz). Authorized power: 16.9-kw visual, aural. Antenna: 2700-ft above av. terrain, 157-ft. above ground, 5410-ft. above sea level.

Latitude	42°	41'	30"
Longitude	123°	13'	44"

Note: Latitude and longitude coordinates shown are based on the North American Datum of 1927 (NAD 27) as currently required by the Mass Media Bureau of the FCC.

Ownership: Chambers Communications Corp. (Group Owner).

Began Operation: April 22, 2003. Station broadcasting digitally on its analog allotment. Began analog operations: February 26, 1984. Sale to present owner by Love Broadcasting approved by FCC May 27, 1993. Sale to Love Broadcasting by Dunbar, Carpenter, et al. approved by FCC July 16, 1987. Ceased analog operations: February 17, 2009.

Represented (sales): Katz Media Group.

Represented (engineering): McClanathan & Associates Inc.

Represented (legal): Pillsbury Winthrop Shaw Pittman LLP.

Represented (sales): Canadian Communications Co.

Personnel:

Renard Maiuri, General Manager.

Jack McCauley, Local Sales Manager.

Rick Carrara, Operations Manager & Chief Engineer.

Matt Valladao, Senior Director.

Rick Howard, News Director.

City of License: Medford. **Station DMA:** Medford-Klamath Falls, OR. **Rank:** 140.

TELEVISION & CABLE
Factbook Online

| continuous updates | fully searchable | easy to use |

For more information call **800-771-9202** or visit **www.warren-news.com**

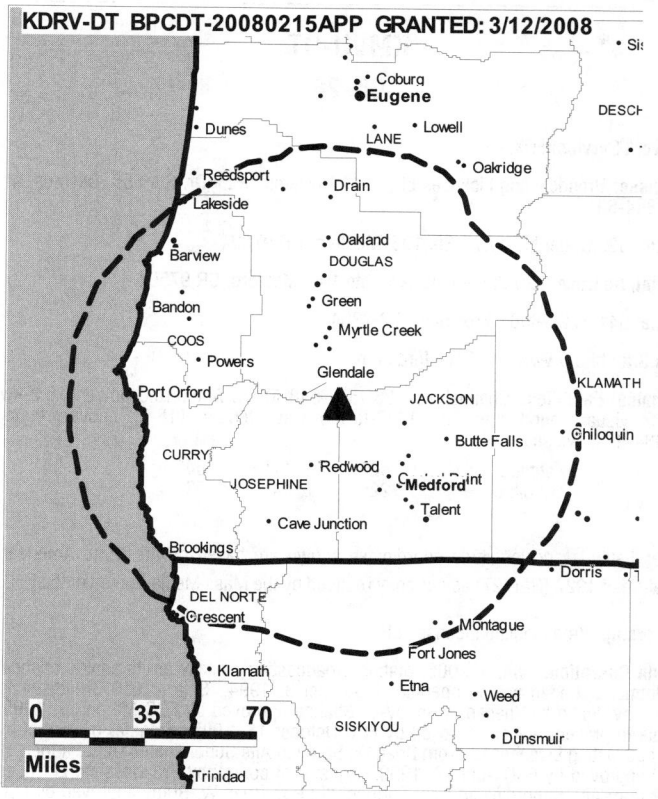

KDRV-DT BPCDT-20080215APP GRANTED: 3/12/2008

© 2010 Warren Communications News

Circulation © 2009 Nielsen. Coverage based on Nielsen study.

GrandTotal	Cable TV Households	Non-cable TV Households	Total TV Households
Estimated Station Totals *	80,860	96,630	177,490
Average Weekly Circulation (2009)	44,550	51,987	96,537
Average Daily Circulation (2009)			51,447

Station DMA Total	Cable TV Households	Non-cable TV Households	Total TV Households
Estimated Station Totals *	74,410	96,630	171,040
Average Weekly Circulation (2009)	44,066	51,987	96,053
Average Daily Circulation (2009)			51,357

Other DMA Total	Cable TV Households	Non-cable TV Households	Total TV Households
Estimated Station Totals *	6,450	0	6,450
Average Weekly Circulation (2009)	484	0	484
Average Daily Circulation (2009)			90

*Estimated station totals are sums of the Nielsen TV and Cable TV household estimates for each county in which the station registers viewing of more than 5% as per the Nielsen Survey Methods.

KMVU-DT
Ch. 26

Network Service: FOX.

Licensee: Broadcasting Licenses LP, 2111 University Park Dr, Ste 650, Okemos, MI 48864-6913.

Studio: 820 Crater Lake Ave, Ste 105, Medford, OR 97504.

Mailing Address: 820 Crater Lake Ave, Ste 105, Medford, OR 97504.

Phone: 541-772-2600. **Fax:** 541-772-7364.

Web Site: http://www.fox26medford.com

Technical Facilities: Channel No. 26 (542-548 MHz). Authorized power: 16.2-kw max. visual, aural. Antenna: 1447-ft above av. terrain, 118-ft. above ground, 3934-ft. above sea level.

Latitude	42°	17'	54"
Longitude	122°	44'	53"

Note: Latitude and longitude coordinates shown are based on the North American Datum of 1927 (NAD 27) as currently required by the Mass Media Bureau of the FCC.

Ownership: Broadcasting Licenses LP.

Began Operation: April 3, 2006. Station broadcasting digitally on its analog channel allotment. Began analog operations: August 8, 1994. Sale to 914 Broadcasting Inc. by Junko K. Shehan & Bobby C. Shehan approved by FCC March 11, 1995. Sale to present owner approved by FCC October 16, 1995. Transfer of control by Broadcasting Licenses LP from Brian W. Brady to Alta Subordinated Debt Partners III LP approved by FCC April 17, 1996. Transfer of control by Broadcasting Licenses LP from Alta Subordinated Debt Partners III LP to Brian W. Brady approved by FCC September 19, 2007. Ceased analog operations: February 17, 2009.

Represented (legal): Leventhal, Senter & Lerman PLLC.

Represented (sales): Continental Television Sales.

Personnel:

Cary Jones, General Manager.

John Glaser, General & National Sales Manager.

Paula Robertson, Local Sales Manager.

Mike Gary, Chief Engineer.

Antoinette Vizzeni, Business Manager.

Dalin Armstrong, Programming Coordinator.

Talin Davis, Promotion Director.

Eric Singer, Creative Services Director.

Lucy Zack, Traffic Manager.

City of License: Medford. **Station DMA:** Medford-Klamath Falls, OR. **Rank:** 140.

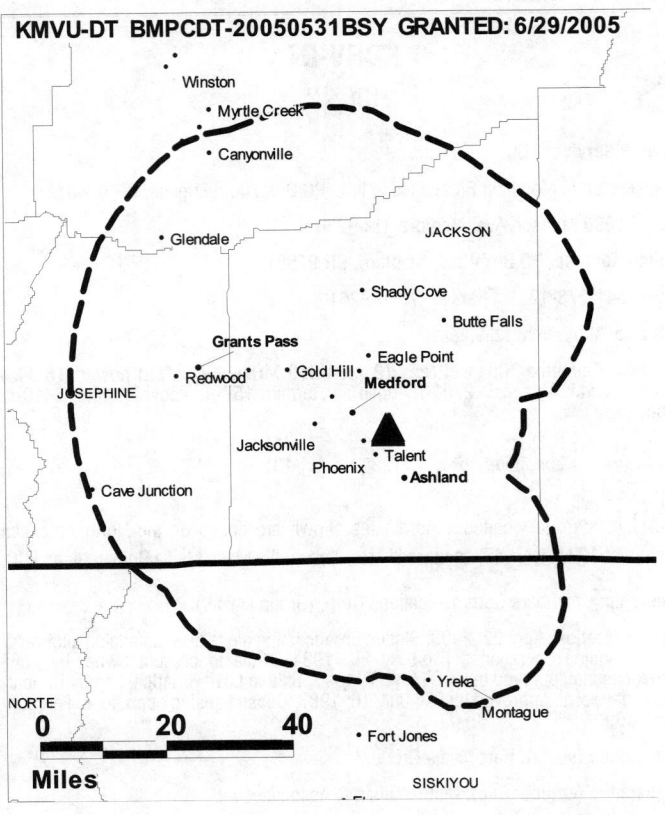

KMVU-DT BMPCDT-20050531BSY GRANTED: 6/29/2005

© 2010 Warren Communications News

Circulation © 2009 Nielsen. Coverage based on Nielsen study.

GrandTotal	Cable TV Households	Non-cable TV Households	Total TV Households
Estimated Station Totals *	81,650	96,630	178,280
Average Weekly Circulation (2009)	37,331	44,716	82,047
Average Daily Circulation (2009)			28,510

Station DMA Total	Cable TV Households	Non-cable TV Households	Total TV Households
Estimated Station Totals *	75,200	96,630	171,830
Average Weekly Circulation (2009)	36,692	44,716	81,408
Average Daily Circulation (2009)			28,407

Other DMA Total	Cable TV Households	Non-cable TV Households	Total TV Households
Estimated Station Totals *	6,450	0	6,450
Average Weekly Circulation (2009)	639	0	639
Average Daily Circulation (2009)			103

*Estimated station totals are sums of the Nielsen TV and Cable TV household estimates for each county in which the station registers viewing of more than 5% as per the Nielsen Survey Methods.

KOBI-DT
Ch. 5

Network Service: NBC.

Licensee: California Oregon Broadcasting Inc., PO Box 1489, Medford, OR 97501.

Studio: 125 S Fir St, Medford, OR 97501.

Mailing Address: PO Box 1489, Medford, OR 97501.

Phone: 541-779-5555. **Fax:** 541-779-5564.

Web Site: http://www.localnewscomesfirst.com

Technical Facilities: Channel No. 5 (76-82 MHz). Authorized power: 5.4-kw visual, aural. Antenna: 2700-ft above av. terrain, 128-ft. above ground, 5384-ft. above sea level.

Latitude	42°	41'	30"
Longitude	123°	13'	46"

Requests CP for change to 6.35-kw visual, 2700-ft above av. terrain, 289-ft. above ground, 5407-ft. above sea level; lat. 42° 41' 49", long. 123° 13' 39", BPCDT-20090813AAO.

Note: Latitude and longitude coordinates shown are based on the North American Datum of 1927 (NAD 27) as currently required by the Mass Media Bureau of the FCC.

Ownership: California-Oregon Broadcasting Inc. (Group Owner).

Began Operation: October 11, 2006. Station broadcasting digitally on its analog channel allotment. Began analog operations: August 1, 1953. Ceased analog operations: February 17, 2009.

Represented (sales): Blair Television.

Personnel:

Patricia C. Smullin, President.

Robert Wise, Vice President & General Manager.

Scott Gee, Promotion Director.

Dennis Siewert, General Sales Manager.

Laryl Noble, Acting News Director.

Steve Aase, Chief Engineer.

Donna Rodriquez, Program Director & Traffic Manager.

City of License: Medford. **Station DMA:** Medford-Klamath Falls, OR. **Rank:** 140.

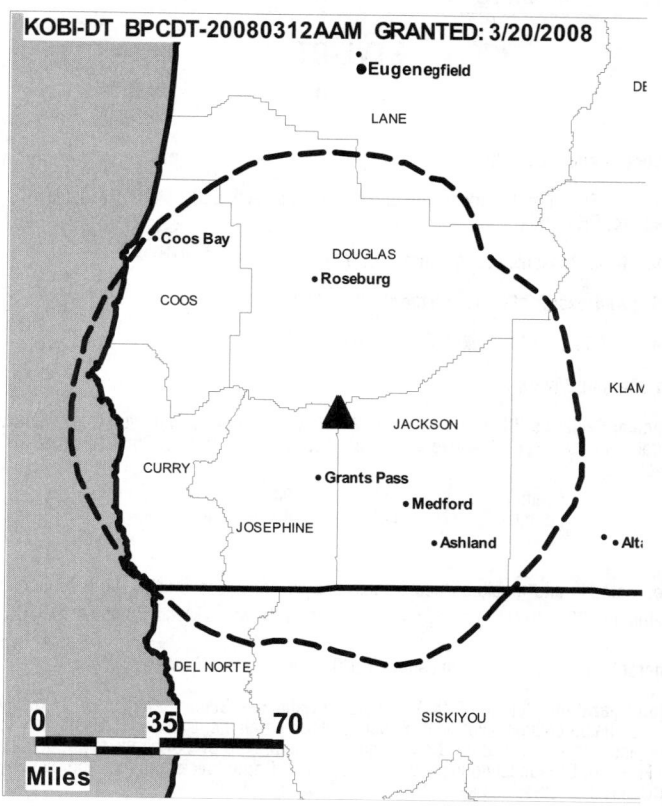

KOBI-DT BPCDT-20080312AAM GRANTED: 3/20/2008

© 2010 Warren Communications News

Circulation © 2009 Nielsen. Coverage based on Nielsen study.

GrandTotal	Cable TV Households	Non-cable TV Households	Total TV Households
Estimated Station Totals *	95,420	99,680	195,100
Average Weekly Circulation (2009)	51,546	47,404	98,950
Average Daily Circulation (2009)			35,897

Station DMA Total	Cable TV Households	Non-cable TV Households	Total TV Households
Estimated Station Totals *	63,260	96,630	159,890
Average Weekly Circulation (2009)	37,899	47,233	85,132
Average Daily Circulation (2009)			33,086

Other DMA Total	Cable TV Households	Non-cable TV Households	Total TV Households
Estimated Station Totals *	32,160	3,050	35,210
Average Weekly Circulation (2009)	13,647	171	13,818
Average Daily Circulation (2009)			2,811

*Estimated station totals are sums of the Nielsen TV and Cable TV household estimates for each county in which the station registers viewing of more than 5% as per the Nielsen Survey Methods.

KTVL-DT
Ch. 10

Network Service: CW, CBS.

Licensee: Freedom Broadcasting of Oregon Licensee LLC, 1440 Rossanley Dr, Medford, OR 97501.

Studio: 1440 Rossanley Dr, Medford, OR 97501.

Mailing Address: PO Box 10, Medford, OR 97501.

Phone: 541-773-7373. **Fax:** 541-779-0451.

Web Site: http://www.ktvl.com

Technical Facilities: Channel No. 10 (192-198 MHz). Authorized power: 9-kw visual, aural. Antenna: 3284-ft above av. terrain, 125-ft. above ground, 7582-ft. above sea level.

Latitude	42°	04'	52"
Longitude	122°	43'	09"

Note: Latitude and longitude coordinates shown are based on the North American Datum of 1927 (NAD 27) as currently required by the Mass Media Bureau of the FCC.

Ownership: Freedom Communications Holdings Inc. (Group Owner).

Began Operation: October 7, 2002. Standard Definition. Station broadcasting digitally on its analog channel allotment. Began analog operations: October 3, 1961. Sale to present owner by Freedom Broadcasting Inc. approved by FCC April 1, 2004. Sale to Freedom Broadcasting Inc. by Sierra/Cascade Communications Inc. approved by FCC July 17, 1981. Ceased analog operations: June 12, 2009.

Represented (legal): Latham & Watkins.

Represented (sales): TeleRep Inc.

Personnel:

Kingsley Kelley, Vice President & General Manager.

Bruce Workman, Local Sales Manager.

Lila Hampton, National Sales Manager.

Manny Fantis, News Director.

Carl Randall, Chief Engineer.

Sheila Georgetti, Program Coordinator.

Mike Gantenbein, Promotion Director.

Tammy Cordonier, Traffic Manager.

Tammy Cordonier, Traffic Manager.

City of License: Medford. **Station DMA:** Medford-Klamath Falls, OR. **Rank:** 140.

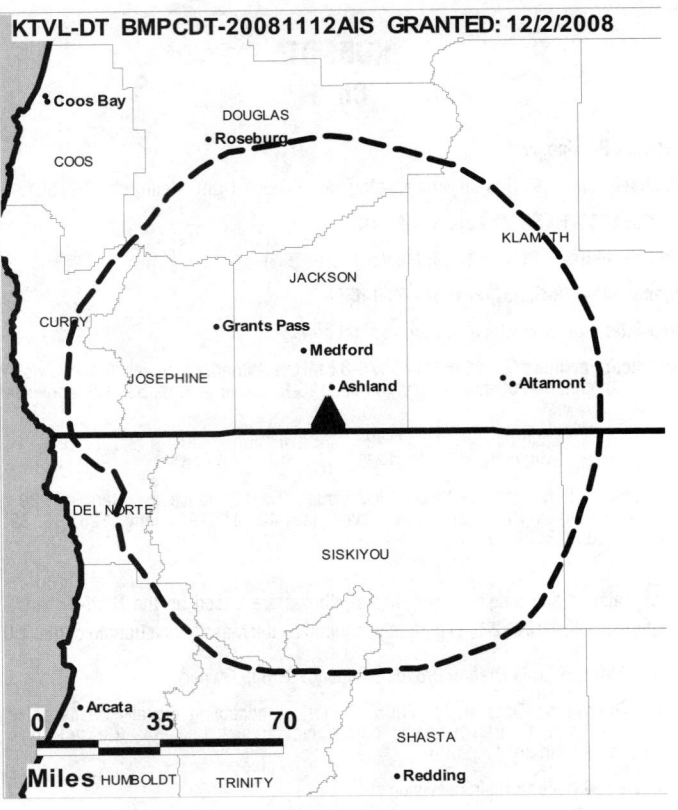

KTVL-DT BMPCDT-20081112AIS GRANTED: 12/2/2008

© 2010 Warren Communications News

Circulation © 2009 Nielsen. Coverage based on Nielsen study.

GrandTotal	Cable TV Households	Non-cable TV Households	Total TV Households
Estimated Station Totals *	81,650	96,630	178,280
Average Weekly Circulation (2009)	47,607	47,766	95,373
Average Daily Circulation (2009)			43,045

Station DMA Total	Cable TV Households	Non-cable TV Households	Total TV Households
Estimated Station Totals *	75,200	96,630	171,830
Average Weekly Circulation (2009)	47,226	47,766	94,992
Average Daily Circulation (2009)			42,981

Other DMA Total	Cable TV Households	Non-cable TV Households	Total TV Households
Estimated Station Totals *	6,450	0	6,450
Average Weekly Circulation (2009)	381	0	381
Average Daily Circulation (2009)			64

*Estimated station totals are sums of the Nielsen TV and Cable TV household estimates for each county in which the station registers viewing of more than 5% as per the Nielsen Survey Methods.

KFFX-DT
Ch. 11

Network Service: FOX.

Licensee: Mountain Licenses LP, 2111 University Park Dr, Ste 650, Okemos, MI 48864-6913.

Studio: 2509 W. Falls Ave., Kennewick, WA 99336.

Mailing Address: 2509 W. Falls Ave, Kennewick, WA 99336.

Phone: 509-735-1700. **Fax:** 509-735-1004.

Web Site: http://www.fox11tricities.com

Technical Facilities: Channel No. 11 (198-204 MHz). Authorized power: 60-kw visual, aural. Antenna: 1549-ft above av. terrain, 220-ft. above ground, 5709-ft. above sea level.

Latitude	45°	44'	51"
Longitude	118°	02'	11"

Note: Latitude and longitude coordinates shown are based on the North American Datum of 1927 (NAD 27) as currently required by the Mass Media Bureau of the FCC.

Ownership: Mountain Licenses LP (Group Owner).

Began Operation: November 7, 2005. Station broadcasting digitally on its analog channel allotment. Began analog operations: January 11, 1999. Transfer of control by Mountain Licenses LP from Alta Subordinated Debt Partners III LP to Brian W. Brady approved by FCC September 19, 2007. Sale to present owner by Communications Properties Inc. approved by FCC September 27, 2000. Ceased analog operations: February 17, 2009.

Represented (legal): Leventhal, Senter & Lerman PLLC.

Represented (sales): Katz Media Group.

Personnel:

Jon Rand, General Manager.

Glenn Rausch, Station Manager.

Brent Phillipy, General Sales Manager.

Lynn Creager, National & Regional Sales Manager.

Ron Sweatte, Chief Engineer.

Chloe Houser, Promotion & Marketing Director.

Rick Andrycha, Program Director.

Robin Lenell, Traffic Manager.

City of License: Pendleton. **Station DMA:** Yakima-Pasco-Richland-Kennewick, WA.

Rank: 126.

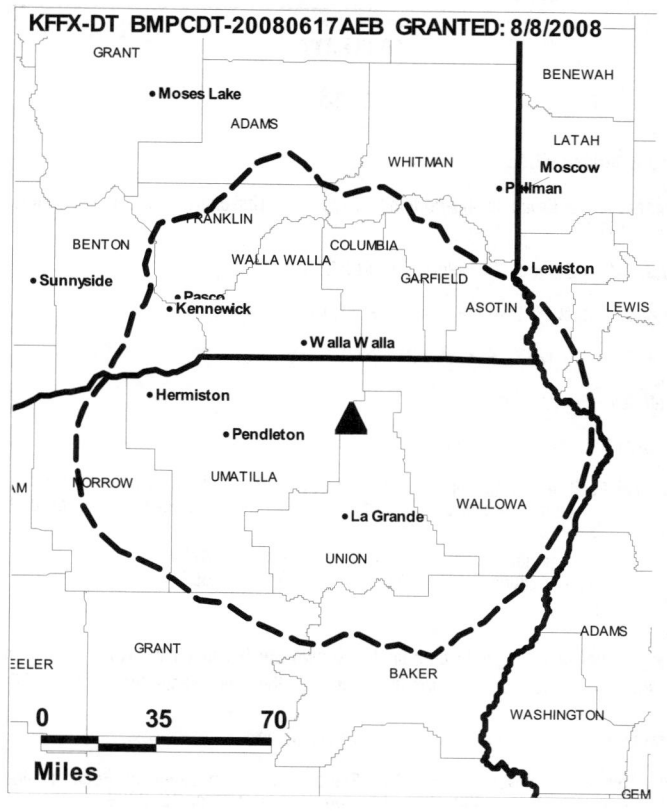

KFFX-DT BMPCDT-20080617AEB GRANTED: 8/8/2008

© 2010 Warren Communications News

Circulation © 2009 Nielsen. Coverage based on Nielsen study.

GrandTotal	Cable TV Households	Non-cable TV Households	Total TV Households
Estimated Station Totals *	60,040	127,890	187,930
Average Weekly Circulation (2009)	29,040	23,338	52,378
Average Daily Circulation (2009)			16,002

Station DMA Total	Cable TV Households	Non-cable TV Households	Total TV Households
Estimated Station Totals *	56,470	127,890	184,360
Average Weekly Circulation (2009)	28,701	23,338	52,039
Average Daily Circulation (2009)			15,916

Other DMA Total	Cable TV Households	Non-cable TV Households	Total TV Households
Estimated Station Totals *	3,570	0	3,570
Average Weekly Circulation (2009)	339	0	339
Average Daily Circulation (2009)			86

*Estimated station totals are sums of the Nielsen TV and Cable TV household estimates for each county in which the station registers viewing of more than 5% as per the Nielsen Survey Methods.

KATU-DT
Ch. 43

Network Service: ABC.

Licensee: Fisher Broadcasting-Portland TV LLC, 600 University St, Ste 1525, Seattle, WA 98101.

Studio: 2153 NE Sandy Blvd, Portland, OR 97232.

Mailing Address: PO Box 2, Portland, OR 97207.

Phone: 503-231-4222. **Fax:** 503-231-4233.

E-mail: juliem@katu.com

Web Site: http://www.katu.com

Technical Facilities: Channel No. 43 (644-650 MHz). Authorized power: 1000-kw max. visual, aural. Antenna: 1719-ft above av. terrain, 955-ft. above ground, 2015-ft. above sea level.

Latitude	45°	30'	57"
Longitude	122°	43'	59"

Note: Latitude and longitude coordinates shown are based on the North American Datum of 1927 (NAD 27) as currently required by the Mass Media Bureau of the FCC.

Ownership: Fisher Communications Inc. (Group Owner).

Began Operation: November 15, 1998. Standard and High Definition. Began analog operations: March 15, 1962. Ceased analog operations: June 12, 2009.

Represented (sales): Katz Media Group.

Represented (legal): Pillsbury Winthrop Shaw Pittman LLP.

Represented (engineering): du Treil, Lundin & Rackley Inc.

Personnel:

John Tamerlano, Vice President & General Manager.

Jo Anne James, General Sales Manager.

Greg Miller, Local Sales Manager.

Don Pratt, News Director.

Alan Batdorf, Chief Engineer.

Julie Mespelt, Programming Director.

Steve Denari, Creative Services Director.

City of License: Portland. **Station DMA:** Portland, OR. **Rank:** 22.

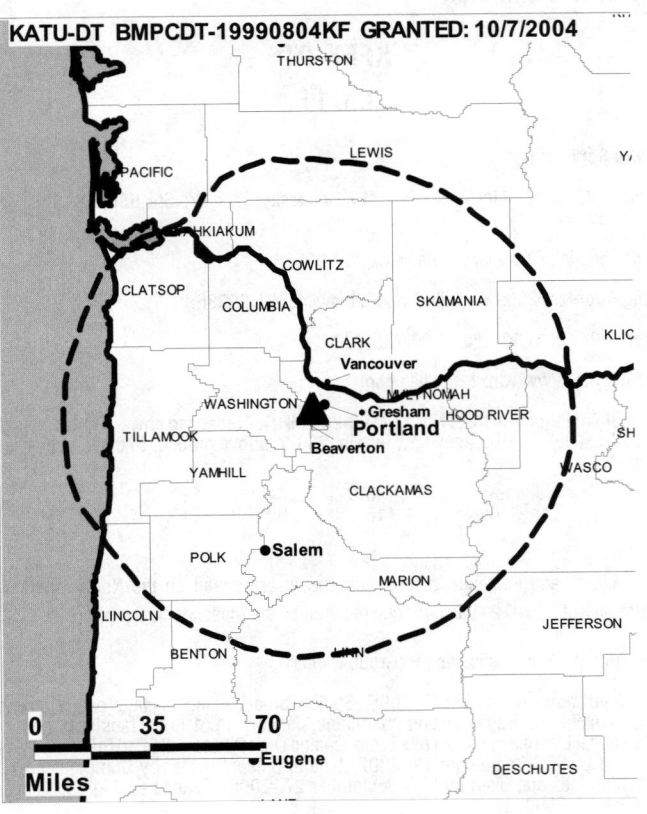

KATU-DT BMPCDT-19990804KF GRANTED: 10/7/2004

© 2010 Warren Communications News

Circulation © 2009 Nielsen. Coverage based on Nielsen study.

GrandTotal	Cable TV Households	Non-cable TV Households	Total TV Households
Estimated Station Totals *	702,090	522,740	1,224,830
Average Weekly Circulation (2009)	416,109	303,853	719,962
Average Daily Circulation (2009)			333,721

Station DMA Total	Cable TV Households	Non-cable TV Households	Total TV Households
Estimated Station Totals *	660,830	484,920	1,145,750
Average Weekly Circulation (2009)	400,055	296,784	696,839
Average Daily Circulation (2009)			325,966

Other DMA Total	Cable TV Households	Non-cable TV Households	Total TV Households
Estimated Station Totals *	41,260	37,820	79,080
Average Weekly Circulation (2009)	16,054	7,069	23,123
Average Daily Circulation (2009)			7,755

*Estimated station totals are sums of the Nielsen TV and Cable TV household estimates for each county in which the station registers viewing of more than 5% as per the Nielsen Survey Methods.

KGW-DT
Ch. 8

Network Service: NBC.

Licensee: KGW-TV Inc., 400 S Record St, Dallas, TX 75202-4806.

Studio: 1501 SW Jefferson St, Portland, OR 97201.

Mailing Address: 1501 S.W. Jefferson St, Portland, OR 97201.

Phone: 503-226-5000. **Fax:** 503-226-5059.

Web Site: http://www.kgw.com

Technical Facilities: Channel No. 8 (180-186 MHz). Authorized power: 25-kw visual, aural. Antenna: 1719-ft above av. terrain, 892-ft. above ground, 2015-ft. above sea level.

Latitude	45°	31'	21"
Longitude	122°	44'	45"

Requests modification of CP for change to 45-kw visual; BMPCDT-20080620AHM.

Note: Latitude and longitude coordinates shown are based on the North American Datum of 1927 (NAD 27) as currently required by the Mass Media Bureau of the FCC.

Ownership: Belo Corp. (Group Owner).

Began Operation: February 4, 2000. High Definition. Station broadcasting digitally on its analog channel allotment. Began analog operations: December 15, 1956. Ceased analog operations: June 12, 2009.

Represented (engineering): du Treil, Lundin & Rackley Inc.

Represented (sales): HRP: Television Station Representative.

Personnel:

Deborah Wilson, President & General Manager.

Mark Handweiger, National Sales Manager.

Rod Gramer, News Director.

Eric Dausman, Engineering Director.

Caryn Lilley, Controller.

Brenda Buratti, Program & Public Affairs Director.

City of License: Portland. **Station DMA:** Portland, OR. **Rank:** 22.

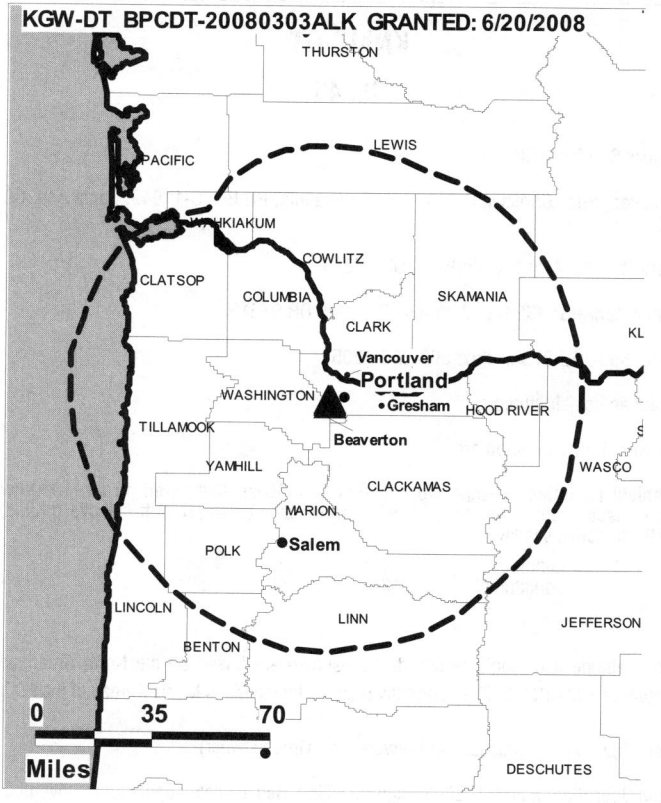

© 2010 Warren Communications News

Circulation © 2009 Nielsen. Coverage based on Nielsen study.

GrandTotal	Cable TV Households	Non-cable TV Households	Total TV Households
Estimated Station Totals *	703,470	522,740	1,226,210
Average Weekly Circulation (2009)	439,944	324,632	764,576
Average Daily Circulation (2009)			356,920

Station DMA Total	Cable TV Households	Non-cable TV Households	Total TV Households
Estimated Station Totals *	660,830	484,920	1,145,750
Average Weekly Circulation (2009)	424,148	321,810	745,958
Average Daily Circulation (2009)			351,646

Other DMA Total	Cable TV Households	Non-cable TV Households	Total TV Households
Estimated Station Totals *	42,640	37,820	80,460
Average Weekly Circulation (2009)	15,796	2,822	18,618
Average Daily Circulation (2009)			5,274

*Estimated station totals are sums of the Nielsen TV and Cable TV household estimates for each county in which the station registers viewing of more than 5% as per the Nielsen Survey Methods.

KNMT-DT
Ch. 45

Network Service: TBN.

Licensee: Trinity Christian Center of Santa Ana Inc., PO Box C-11949, Santa Ana, CA 92711.

Studio: 432 NE 74th Ave, Portland, OR 97213.

Mailing Address: 432 N.E. 74th Ave, Portland, OR 97213.

Phone: 503-252-0792. **Fax:** 503-256-4205.

E-mail: acarbajal@tbn.org

Web Site: http://www.tbn.org

Technical Facilities: Channel No. 45 (656-662 MHz). Authorized power: 1000-kw max. visual, aural. Antenna: 1493-ft above av. terrain, 732-ft. above ground, 1791-ft. above sea level.

Latitude	45°	30'	58"
Longitude	122°	43'	59"

Note: Latitude and longitude coordinates shown are based on the North American Datum of 1927 (NAD 27) as currently required by the Mass Media Bureau of the FCC.

Ownership: Trinity Broadcasting Network Inc. (Group Owner).

Began Operation: March 1, 2003. High Definition. Began analog operations: November 16, 1989. Pro forma assignment to present owner by National Minority TV Inc. approved by FCC August 6, 2008. Sale to National Minority TV Inc. by Greater Portland Broadcasting Corp. approved by FCC October 27, 1988. Ceased analog operations: June 12, 2009.

Represented (legal): Colby M. May.

Personnel:

Jane Duff, President & General Manager.

Adolfo Carbajal, Station Manager.

Stephen Hendrix, Chief Engineer.

Bonnie Gulding, Traffic Manager.

City of License: Portland. **Station DMA:** Portland, OR. **Rank:** 22.

KNMT-DT BMPCDT-20050121AFG GRANTED: 11/30/2005

© 2010 Warren Communications News

Circulation © 2009 Nielsen. Coverage based on Nielsen study.

GrandTotal	Cable TV Households	Non-cable TV Households	Total TV Households
Estimated Station Totals *	73,260	0	73,260
Average Weekly Circulation (2009)	4,133	0	4,133
Average Daily Circulation (2009)			1,006

Station DMA Total	Cable TV Households	Non-cable TV Households	Total TV Households
Estimated Station Totals *	73,260	0	73,260
Average Weekly Circulation (2009)	4,133	0	4,133
Average Daily Circulation (2009)			1,006

*Estimated station totals are sums of the Nielsen TV and Cable TV household estimates for each county in which the station registers viewing of more than 5% as per the Nielsen Survey Methods.

KOIN-DT
Ch. 40

Network Service: CBS.

Licensee: NVT Portland Licensee LLC, Debtor in Possession, 3500 Lenox Rd, Ste 640, Atlanta, GA 30326.

Studio: 222 SW Columbia St, Portland, OR 97201.

Mailing Address: 222 S.W. Columbia St, Portland, OR 97201.

Phone: 503-464-0600. **Fax:** 503-464-0717.

Web Site: http://www.koin.com

Technical Facilities: Channel No. 40 (626-632 MHz). Authorized power: 1000-kw max. visual, aural. Antenna: 1717-ft above av. terrain, 953-ft. above ground, 2012-ft. above sea level.

Latitude	45°	30'	58"
Longitude	122°	43'	58"

Transmitter: 5516 S.W. Barnes Rd.

Note: Latitude and longitude coordinates shown are based on the North American Datum of 1927 (NAD 27) as currently required by the Mass Media Bureau of the FCC.

Ownership: New Vision Television LLC, Debtor in Possession (Group Owner).

Began Operation: December 16, 1999. Standard and High Definition. Began analog operations: October 15, 1953. Ceased analog operations: June 12, 2009. Sale to Lee Enterprises Inc. by Newhouse Broadcasting Corp. and M. M. Tonkon & Harvey Benson, trustees, approved by FCC August 26, 1977. Transfer to Emmis Communications Corp. by Lee Enterprises Inc. approved by FCC September 27, 2000. Sale to Montecito Broadcast Group LLC by Emmis Communications Corp. approved by FCC December 19, 2005. Sale to present owner by Montecito Broadcast Group LLC approved by FCC October 30, 2007. Involuntary assignment of license to Debtor in Possession status approved by FCC July 24, 2009.

Represented (legal): Wiley Rein LLP.

Represented (engineering): Hammett & Edison Inc.

Personnel:

Chris Sehring, General Manager.

Lynn Bailie, Sales Director.

Scott Brock, National Sales Manager.

Vern Alvin, Local Sales Manager.

Lynn Heider, News Director.

David Bird, Engineering Director.

Doug Miller, Finance & Administration Director.

Nichole Myers, Program Director.

Rick Brown, Production Manager.

Roger O'Conner, Creative Services Director.

Carl Gonzales, Traffic Manager.

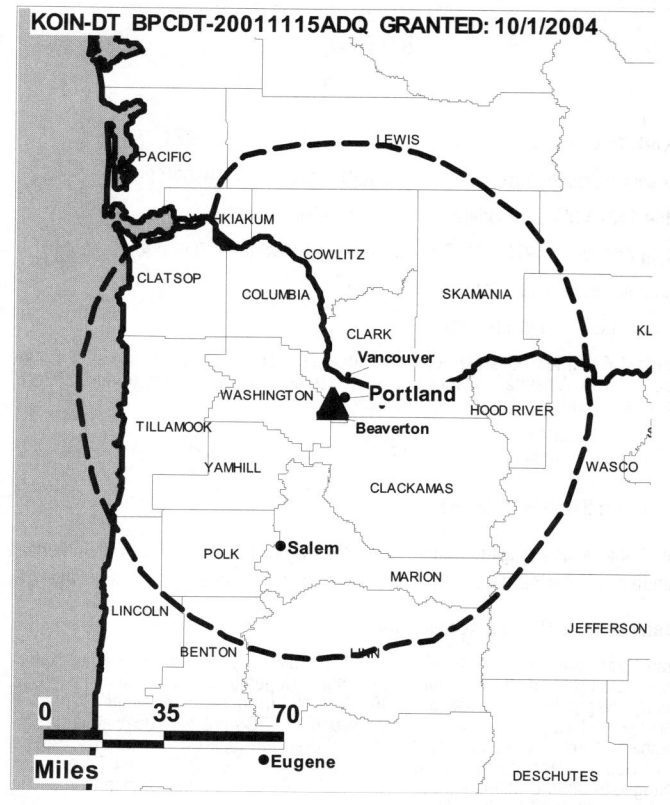

KOIN-DT BPCDT-20011115ADQ GRANTED: 10/1/2004

© 2010 Warren Communications News

City of License: Portland. **Station DMA:** Portland, OR. **Rank:** 22.

Circulation © 2009 Nielsen. Coverage based on Nielsen study.

GrandTotal	Cable TV Households	Non-cable TV Households	Total TV Households
Estimated Station Totals *	732,940	529,630	1,262,570
Average Weekly Circulation (2009)	425,756	309,664	735,420
Average Daily Circulation (2009)			315,569

Station DMA Total	Cable TV Households	Non-cable TV Households	Total TV Households
Estimated Station Totals *	660,830	484,920	1,145,750
Average Weekly Circulation (2009)	403,372	302,543	705,915
Average Daily Circulation (2009)			304,579

Other DMA Total	Cable TV Households	Non-cable TV Households	Total TV Households
Estimated Station Totals *	72,110	44,710	116,820
Average Weekly Circulation (2009)	22,384	7,121	29,505
Average Daily Circulation (2009)			10,990

*Estimated station totals are sums of the Nielsen TV and Cable TV household estimates for each county in which the station registers viewing of more than 5% as per the Nielsen Survey Methods.

KPTV-DT
Ch. 12

Network Service: FOX.

Licensee: Meredith Corp., 1716 Locust St, Des Moines, IA 50309-3203.

Studio: 14975 NW Greenbrier Pkwy, Beaverton, OR 97006.

Mailing Address: 14975 N.W. Greenbrier Pkwy, Beaverton, OR 97006.

Phone: 503-906-1249. **Fax:** 503-548-6920.

Web Site: http://www.kptv.com

Technical Facilities: Channel No. 12 (204-210 MHz). Authorized power: 24.5-kw visual, aural. Antenna: 1736-ft above av. terrain, 1027-ft. above ground, 2020-ft. above sea level.

Latitude	45°	31'	19"
Longitude	122°	44'	53"

Transmitter: 212 N.W. Miller Rd.

Note: Latitude and longitude coordinates shown are based on the North American Datum of 1927 (NAD 27) as currently required by the Mass Media Bureau of the FCC.

Ownership: Meredith Corp. (Group Owner).

Began Operation: June 30, 2000. Standard Definition. Station broadcasting digitally on its analog channel allotment. Began analog operations: September 20, 1952. George Haggarty's purchase of KLOR (Ch. 12) from Henry A. White-Stephen E. Thompson-Julius L. Meier Jr. group approved by FCC April 17, 1957; at same time Haggarty purchased KPTV (Ch. 27) from Storer and took Ch. 27 off air. Transfer from George Haggarty to NAFI Corp. approved July 22, 1959 (NAFI Corp. name changed to Chris-Craft Industries Inc.). Transfer of stock of Chris-Craft Industries Inc. by shareholders to Baldwin-Montrose Chemical Co. Inc. bringing holdings to 35% approved November 8, 1967. Later Baldwin-Montrose merged into Chris-Craft. Sale to Fox Televison Stations Inc. by Chris-Craft Industries Inc. approved by FCC July 23, 2001. Station was swapped for Meredith Corp.'s WOGX(TV) Ocala-Gainesville, FL and WOFL(TV) Orlando, FL. FCC approved deal May 14, 2002. Ceased analog operations: June 12, 2009.

Represented (legal): Dow Lohnes PLLC.

Represented (sales): TeleRep Inc.

Personnel:

Patrick McCreery, Vice President & General Manager.

Greg Flock, General Sales Manager.

Andy Delaporte, Local Sales Manager.

Dannell Bostick, National Sales Manager.

Steve Benedict, Chief Engineer.

Tito Carlos, Business Manager.

John Concillo, Program Director.

Matthew Hyatt, Promotion & Creative Services Director.

Terry Demming, Production Manager.

Mary Warner, Traffic Manager.

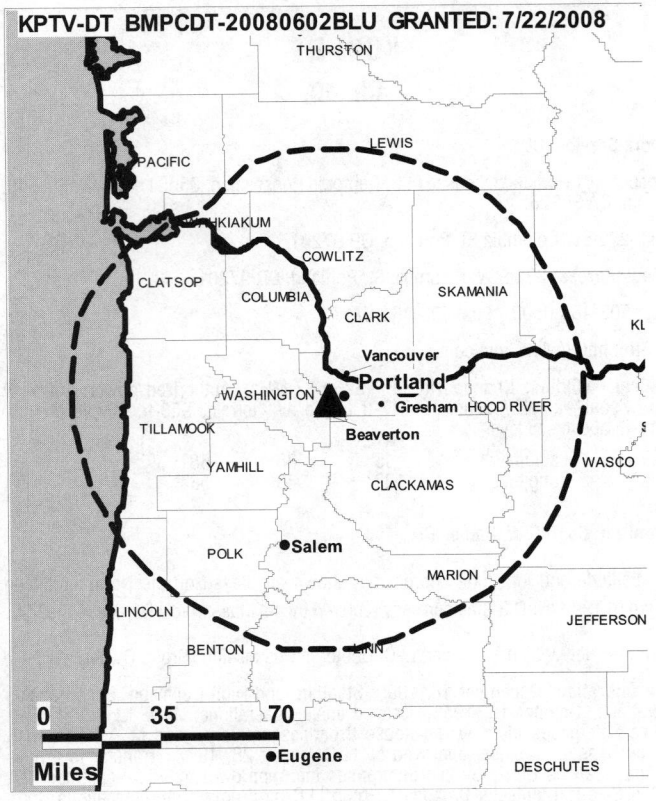

KPTV-DT BMPCDT-20080602BLU GRANTED: 7/22/2008

© 2010 Warren Communications News

City of License: Portland. **Station DMA:** Portland, OR. **Rank:** 22.

Circulation © 2009 Nielsen. Coverage based on Nielsen study.

GrandTotal	Cable TV Households	Non-cable TV Households	Total TV Households
Estimated Station Totals *	696,210	547,000	1,243,210
Average Weekly Circulation (2009)	369,679	301,860	671,539
Average Daily Circulation (2009)			272,901

Station DMA Total	Cable TV Households	Non-cable TV Households	Total TV Households
Estimated Station Totals *	657,660	484,920	1,142,580
Average Weekly Circulation (2009)	360,520	298,122	658,642
Average Daily Circulation (2009)			269,620

Other DMA Total	Cable TV Households	Non-cable TV Households	Total TV Households
Estimated Station Totals *	38,550	62,080	100,630
Average Weekly Circulation (2009)	9,159	3,738	12,897
Average Daily Circulation (2009)			3,281

*Estimated station totals are sums of the Nielsen TV and Cable TV household estimates for each county in which the station registers viewing of more than 5% as per the Nielsen Survey Methods.

KPIC-DT
Ch. 19

Network Service: CBS.

Licensee: South West Oregon TV Broadcasting Corp., 100 4th Ave N, Ste 510, Seattle, WA 98109.

Studio: 655 W Umpqua, Roseburg, OR 97470.

Mailing Address: PO Box 1345, Roseburg, OR 94740.

Phone: 541-672-4481. **Fax:** 541-672-4482.

Web Site: http://www.kpic.com

Technical Facilities: Channel No. 19 (500-506 MHz). Authorized power: 50-kw max. visual, aural. Antenna: 899-ft above av. terrain, 102-ft. above ground, 1591-ft. above sea level.

Latitude	43°	14'	08"
Longitude	123°	19'	18"

Holds CP for change to 958-ft above av. terrain, 161-ft. above ground, 1650-ft. above sea level; BPCDT-20080618ATJ.

Note: Latitude and longitude coordinates shown are based on the North American Datum of 1927 (NAD 27) as currently required by the Mass Media Bureau of the FCC.

Multichannel TV Sound: Planned.

Ownership: California-Oregon Broadcasting Inc. (Group Owner); Fisher Communications Inc. (Group Owner).

Began Operation: March 1, 2002. Began analog operations: April 1, 1956. Ceased analog operations: June 12, 2009.

Represented (sales): Katz Media Group.

Represented (legal): Pillsbury Winthrop Shaw Pittman LLP.

Personnel:

Greg Raschio, General Manager.

Connie Williamson, Station Manager.

Ann Baker, General & Local Sales Manager.

Dan Bain, News Director.

Mike Hill, Chief Engineer.

Paul Green, Program Director.

Dino Francois, Promotion Director.

Peter Smith, Production Manager & Creative Services Director.

Terry Lee, Traffic Manager.

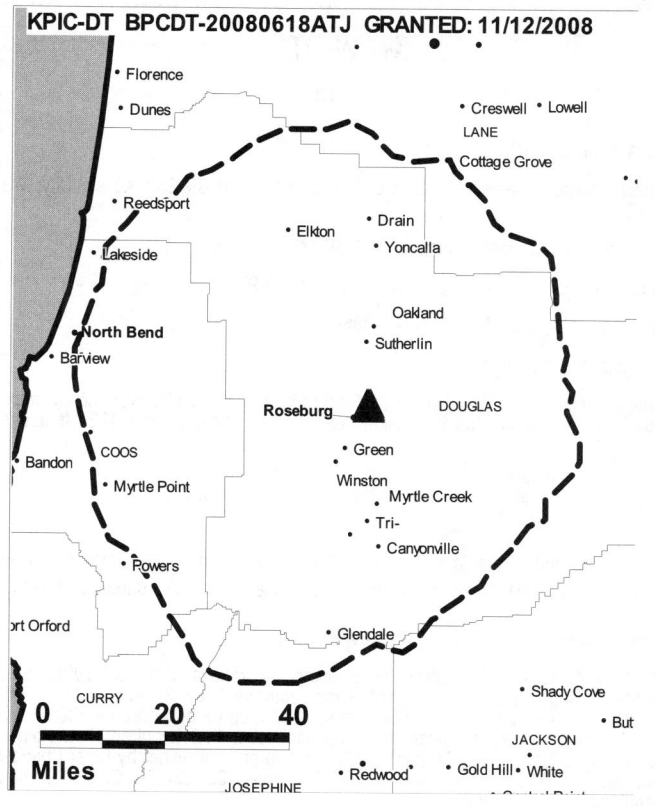

KPIC-DT BPCDT-20080618ATJ GRANTED: 11/12/2008

© 2010 Warren Communications News

City of License: Roseburg. **Station DMA:** Eugene, OR. **Rank:** 119.

Circulation © 2009 Nielsen. Coverage based on Nielsen study.

GrandTotal	Cable TV Households	Non-cable TV Households	Total TV Households
Estimated Station Totals *	13,610	28,570	42,180
Average Weekly Circulation (2009)	9,745	4,971	14,716
Average Daily Circulation (2009)			9,406

Station DMA Total	Cable TV Households	Non-cable TV Households	Total TV Households
Estimated Station Totals *	13,610	28,570	42,180
Average Weekly Circulation (2009)	9,745	4,971	14,716
Average Daily Circulation (2009)			9,406

*Estimated station totals are sums of the Nielsen TV and Cable TV household estimates for each county in which the station registers viewing of more than 5% as per the Nielsen Survey Methods.

KTCW-DT
Ch. 45

Network Service: NBC.

Licensee: Newport Television License LLC, 460 Nichols Rd, Ste 250, Kansas City, MO 64112.

Studio: 1004 SE Stephens, Rosenburg, OR 97470.

Mailing Address: 1004 SE Stephens, Rosenburg, OR 97470.

Phone: 541-746-1600. **Fax:** 541-747-0866.

Web Site: http://www.kmtr.com

Technical Facilities: Channel No. 45 (656-662 MHz). Authorized power: 12-kw max. visual, aural. Antenna: 358-ft above av. terrain, 56-ft. above ground, 1227-ft. above sea level.

Latitude	43°	12'	22"
Longitude	123°	21'	56"

Note: Latitude and longitude coordinates shown are based on the North American Datum of 1927 (NAD 27) as currently required by the Mass Media Bureau of the FCC.

Ownership: Newport Television LLC (Group Owner).

Began Operation: June 18, 2003. Began analog operations: April 20, 1992. Sale to Wicks Broadcast Group LP by KMTR Inc. approved by FCC October 10, 1995. Sale to The Ackerley Group by Wicks Broadcast Group LP approved by FCC March 12, 1999. In stock swap, Clear Channel Broadcasting Inc. acquired The Ackerley Group. FCC approved deal May 29, 2002. Sale to present owner by Clear Channel Communications Inc. approved by FCC November 29, 2007. Ceased analog operations: June 12, 2009.

Represented (legal): Covington & Burling.

Personnel:

Cambra Ward, Vice President & General Manager.

Scott Prentice, Operations Manager & Chief Engineer.

Mike Chisholm, General Sales Manager.

John Wagner, National Sales Manager.

Robert McMichaels, News Director.

Leslie Bristow, Production, Creative Services & Promotion Director.

Melanie Rush, Traffic Manager.

City of License: Roseburg. **Station DMA:** Eugene, OR. **Rank:** 119.

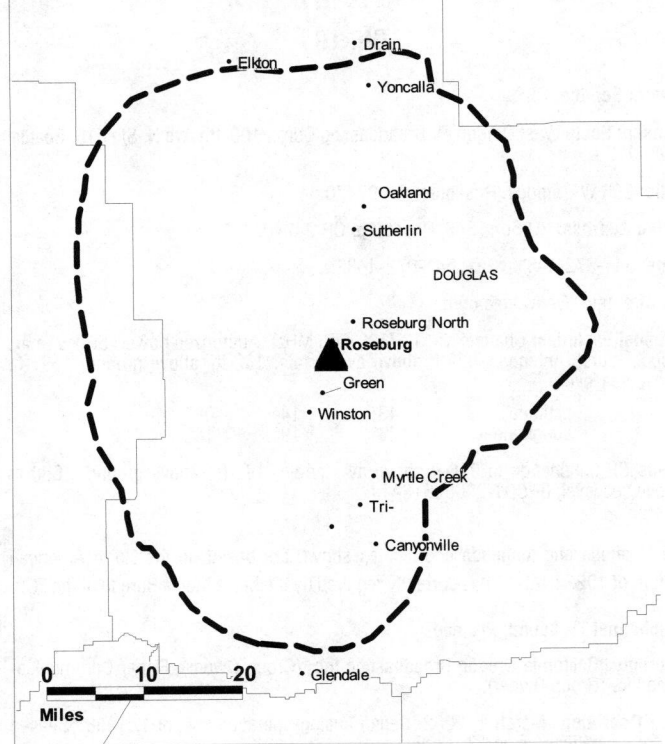

KTCW-DT BMPCDT-20020918AAE GRANTED: 12/9/2002

© 2010 Warren Communications News

Circulation © 2009 Nielsen. Coverage based on Nielsen study.

GrandTotal	Cable TV Households	Non-cable TV Households	Total TV Households
Estimated Station Totals *	13,610	28,570	42,180
Average Weekly Circulation (2009)	3,702	2,543	6,245
Average Daily Circulation (2009)			2,193

Station DMA Total	Cable TV Households	Non-cable TV Households	Total TV Households
Estimated Station Totals *	13,610	28,570	42,180
Average Weekly Circulation (2009)	3,702	2,543	6,245
Average Daily Circulation (2009)			2,193

*Estimated station totals are sums of the Nielsen TV and Cable TV household estimates for each county in which the station registers viewing of more than 5% as per the Nielsen Survey Methods.

KTVC-DT
Ch. 18

Network Service: IND.

Licensee: Better Life Television Inc., PO Box 766, Grants Pass, OR 97528.

Mailing Address: PO Box 766, c/o Better Life Television Inc., Grants Pass, OR 97528.

Phone: 541-474-3089.

Technical Facilities: Channel No. 18 (494-500 MHz). Authorized power: 50-kw max. visual, aural. Antenna: 698-ft above av. terrain, 93-ft. above ground, 1581-ft. above sea level.

Latitude	43°	14'	09"
Longitude	123°	19'	16"

Holds CP for change to 35-kw max. visual, 721-ft above av. terrain, 115-ft. above ground, 1604-ft. above sea level; lat. 43° 14' 08", long. 123° 19' 18", BPCDT-20061013ADM.

Note: Latitude and longitude coordinates shown are based on the North American Datum of 1927 (NAD 27) as currently required by the Mass Media Bureau of the FCC.

Ownership: Better Life Television Inc. (Group Owner).

Began Operation: July 19, 2006. Began analog operations: July 18, 1994. Ceased analog operations: June 12, 2009. Transfer of control from Estate of John E. Field to Johanna Broadcasting Inc. (Ronald & Brenda L. Lee) approved by FCC October 26, 1995. Transfer of control from Ronald & Brenda L. Lee to John J. Kolego, Carl Reifenstein, James Bowen, Patrick M. Orsini, Gareth Plank & Mike Carney approved by FCC December 13, 2000. Sale to Equity Broadcasting Corp. by Johanna Broadcasting Inc. (John J. Kolego, et al.) approved by FCC November 30, 2001. Station returned to air September 1, 2002. Equity Broadcasting Corp. merged with Coconut Palm Acquisition Corp., becoming Equity Media Holdings Corp. FCC approved deal March 27, 2007. Assignment of license to Debtor in Possession status approved by FCC February 4, 2009. Sale to present owner by Equity Media Holdings Corp. approved by FCC June 10, 2009.

Represented (sales): Continental Television Sales.

City of License: Roseburg. **Station DMA:** Eugene, OR. **Rank:** 119.

TELEVISION & CABLE
Factbook Online

| continuous updates | fully searchable | easy to use |

For more information call **800-771-9202** or visit **www.warren-news.com**

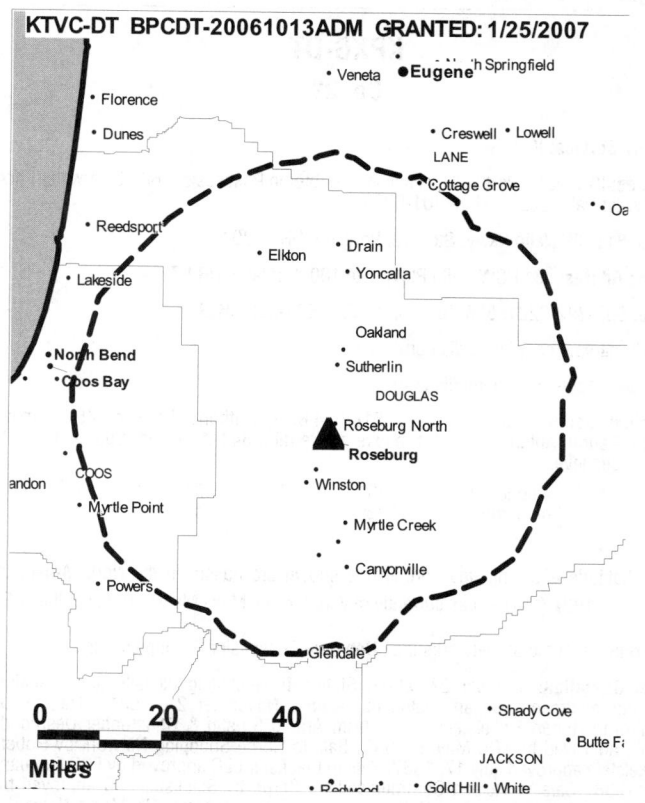

KTVC-DT BPCDT-20061013ADM GRANTED: 1/25/2007

© 2010 Warren Communications News

Circulation © 2009 Nielsen. Coverage based on Nielsen study.

GrandTotal	Cable TV Households	Non-cable TV Households	Total TV Households
Estimated Station Totals *	116,870	113,030	229,900
Average Weekly Circulation (2009)	8,488	6,109	14,597
Average Daily Circulation (2009)			4,187

Station DMA Total	Cable TV Households	Non-cable TV Households	Total TV Households
Estimated Station Totals *	116,870	113,030	229,900
Average Weekly Circulation (2009)	8,488	6,109	14,597
Average Daily Circulation (2009)			4,187

*Estimated station totals are sums of the Nielsen TV and Cable TV household estimates for each county in which the station registers viewing of more than 5% as per the Nielsen Survey Methods.

KPXG-DT
Ch. 22

Network Service: ION.

Licensee: ION Media Portland License Inc., Debtor in Possession, 601 Clearwater Park Rd, West Palm Beach, FL 33401-6233.

Studio: 811 SW Naito Pkwy, Ste 100, Portland, OR 97204.

Mailing Address: 811 SW Naito Pkwy, Ste 100, Portland, OR 97204.

Phone: 503-222-2221; 866-467-2922. **Fax:** 503-222-4613.

E-mail: marypierce@ionmedia.com

Web Site: http://www.ionmedia.com

Technical Facilities: Channel No. 22 (518-524 MHz). Authorized power: 745-kw max. visual, aural. Antenna: 1673-ft above av. terrain, 844-ft. above ground, 1967-ft. above sea level.

Latitude	45°	31'	21"
Longitude	122°	44'	45"

Note: Latitude and longitude coordinates shown are based on the North American Datum of 1927 (NAD 27) as currently required by the Mass Media Bureau of the FCC.

Ownership: ION Media Networks Inc., Debtor in Possession (Group Owner).

Began Operation: October 27, 2004. Station broadcasting digitally on its analog channel allotment. Began analog operations: November 21, 1981. Transfer of control to Robert Finkelstein, et al., from Arnold Brustin & Christopher Desmond, et al., approved by FCC May 8, 1985. Sale to Home Shopping Network by Robert Finkelstein approved July 17, 1987. Sale to Blackstar LLC approved by FCC February 18, 1988. Sale to Paxson Communications Corp. by Blackstar LLC approved by FCC May 14, 1998. Paxson Communications Corp. became ION Media Networks Inc. on June 26, 2006. Transfer of control by ION Media Networks Inc. from Paxson Management Corp. & Lowell W. Paxson to CIG Media LLC approved by FCC December 31, 2007. Involuntary assignment to debtor in possession status approved by FCC June 5, 2009. Sale to Urban Television LLC pends. Ceased analog operations: December 3, 2008.

Represented (legal): Dow Lohnes PLLC.

Personnel:

Linda Messana, Station Operations Manager.

James Kelly, Chief Engineer.

Mary Pierce, Traffic Manager.

City of License: Salem. **Station DMA:** Portland, OR. **Rank:** 22.

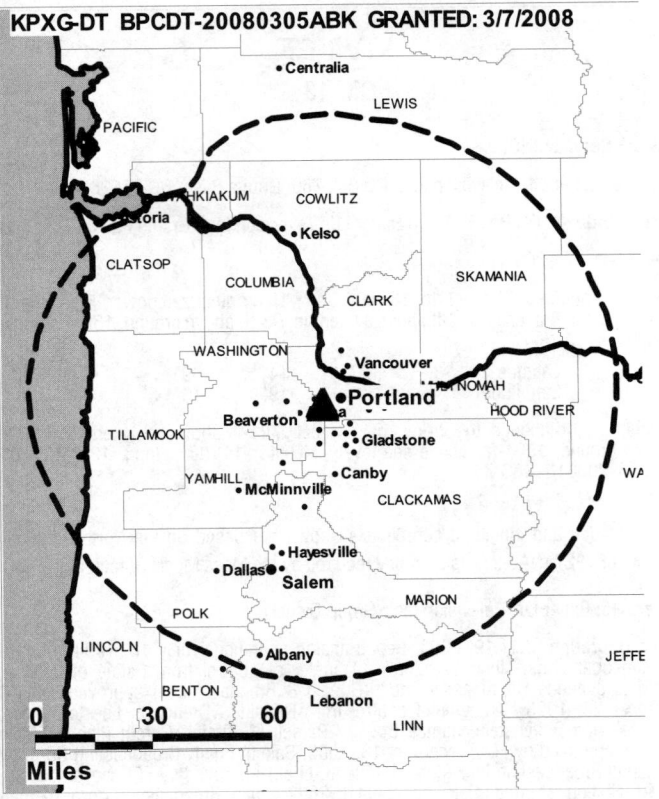

KPXG-DT BPCDT-20080305ABK GRANTED: 3/7/2008

© 2010 Warren Communications News

Circulation © 2009 Nielsen. Coverage based on Nielsen study.

GrandTotal	Cable TV Households	Non-cable TV Households	Total TV Households
Estimated Station Totals *	632,300	411,600	1,043,900
Average Weekly Circulation (2009)	56,219	33,875	90,094
Average Daily Circulation (2009)			20,310

Station DMA Total	Cable TV Households	Non-cable TV Households	Total TV Households
Estimated Station Totals *	611,840	411,600	1,023,440
Average Weekly Circulation (2009)	55,114	33,875	88,989
Average Daily Circulation (2009)			20,146

Other DMA Total	Cable TV Households	Non-cable TV Households	Total TV Households
Estimated Station Totals *	20,460	0	20,460
Average Weekly Circulation (2009)	1,105	0	1,105
Average Daily Circulation (2009)			164

*Estimated station totals are sums of the Nielsen TV and Cable TV household estimates for each county in which the station registers viewing of more than 5% as per the Nielsen Survey Methods.

KRCW-DT
Ch. 33

Network Service: CW.

Licensee: Tribune Broadcast Holdings Inc., Debtor-In-Possession, 10255 SW Arctic Dr, Beaverton, OR 97005.

Studio: 10255 SW Arctic Dr, Beaverton, OR 97005.

Mailing Address: 10255 S.W. Arctic Dr, Beaverton, OR 97005.

Phone: 503-644-3232. **Fax:** 503-626-3576.

E-mail: vickyg@wb32tv.com

Web Site: http://portlandscw.trb.com

Technical Facilities: Channel No. 33 (584-590 MHz). Authorized power: 750-kw max. visual, aural. Antenna: 1717-ft above av. terrain, 953-ft. above ground, 2012-ft. above sea level.

Latitude	45°	30'	58"
Longitude	122°	43'	58"

Holds CP for change to 1000-kw max. visual, 1716-ft above av. terrain, 951-ft. above ground, 2011-ft. above sea level; BPCDT-20080619AKY.

Transmitter: Tualatin Mountains, Multnomah County.

Note: Latitude and longitude coordinates shown are based on the North American Datum of 1927 (NAD 27) as currently required by the Mass Media Bureau of the FCC.

Ownership: Tribune Broadcasting Co., Debtor-In-Possession (Group Owner).

Began Operation: August 30, 2003. Standard Definition. Began analog operations: May 8, 1989. Sale to Glen Chambers, et al., by Willamette Valley Broadcasting approved by FCC July 17, 1991. Station left air in 1992. Resumed operation September 13, 1994. Sale to Victor Ives, et al., approved by FCC September 16, 1994. Transfer of control from Victor Ives, et al. to Peregrine Communications Ltd. approved by FCC September 28, 1995. Sale to ACME Communications Inc. by Peregrine Communications Ltd. approved by FCC May 15, 1997. ACME Communications Inc. went public September 30, 1999. Sale to present owner by ACME Communications Inc. approved by FCC March 14, 2003. Transfer of control from public shareholders of the Tribune Co. to Tribune Employee Stock Ownership Plan approved by FCC November 30, 2007. Involuntary assignment to debtor-in-possession status approved by FCC December 24, 2008. Ceased analog operations: June 12, 2009.

Represented (legal): Sidley Austin LLP.

Represented (engineering): Cohen Dippell & Everist PC.

Personnel:

Pam Pearson, Vice President & General Manager.

Steve Martino, Program Coordinator.

Jeremy Berk, General Sales Manager.

Trey Yant, Sales Manager.

Pat Shearer, Chief Engineer.

Sharon Silverman, Controller.

Nik Miles, Local Marketing Manager.

© 2010 Warren Communications News

City of License: Salem. **Station DMA:** Portland, OR. **Rank:** 22.

Circulation © 2009 Nielsen. Coverage based on Nielsen study.

GrandTotal	Cable TV Households	Non-cable TV Households	Total TV Households
Estimated Station Totals *	648,620	497,810	1,146,430
Average Weekly Circulation (2009)	182,006	145,438	327,444
Average Daily Circulation (2009)			116,964

Station DMA Total	Cable TV Households	Non-cable TV Households	Total TV Households
Estimated Station Totals *	648,620	484,920	1,133,540
Average Weekly Circulation (2009)	182,006	144,265	326,271
Average Daily Circulation (2009)			116,809

Other DMA Total	Cable TV Households	Non-cable TV Households	Total TV Households
Estimated Station Totals *	0	12,890	12,890
Average Weekly Circulation (2009)	0	1,173	1,173
Average Daily Circulation (2009)			155

*Estimated station totals are sums of the Nielsen TV and Cable TV household estimates for each county in which the station registers viewing of more than 5% as per the Nielsen Survey Methods.

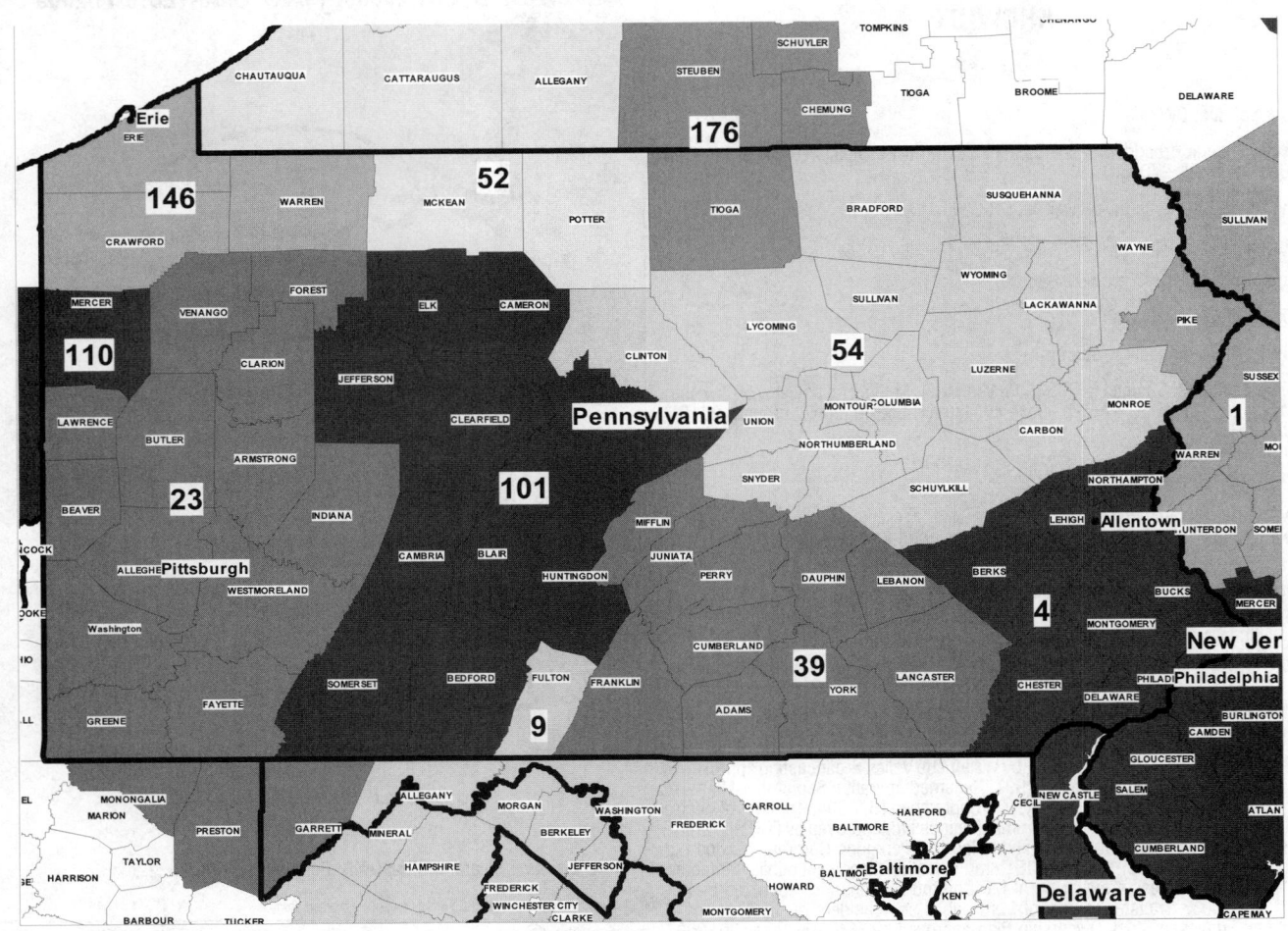

© 2010 Warren Communications News

MARKET	NIELSEN DMA TV HOUSEHOLDS	RANK	MARKET AREA COMMERCIAL STATIONS
New York, NY	7,493,530	1	WABC-DT (7); WCBS-DT (56); WFTY-DT (23); WFUT-DT (53); WLNY-DT (57); WMBC-DT (18); WNBC-DT (28); WNJU-DT (36); WNYW-DT (44); WPIX-DT (11); WPXN-TV (31); WRNN-DT (48); WSAH-DT (42); WTBY-DT (27); WWOR-DT (38); WXTV-DT (40)
Philadelphia, PA	2,955,190	4	KYW-DT (26); WBPH-DT (9); WCAU-DT (67); WFMZ-DT (46); WGTW-DT (27); WMCN-DT (44); WMGM-DT (36); WPHL-DT (17); WPPX-TV (31); WPSG-DT (32); WPVI-DT (6); WTVE-DT (25); WTXF-DT (42); WUVP-DT (65); WWSI-DT (49)
Washington, DC (Hagerstown, MD)	2,335,040	9	WDCA-DT (35); WDCW-DT (50); WFDC-DT (15); WHAG-DT (55); WJAL-DT (39); WJLA-DT (7); WPXW-TV (43); WRC-DT (48); WSSS-TV (1); WTTG-DT (36); WUSA-DT (9); WWPX-TV (12)
Pittsburgh, PA	1,154,950	23	KDKA-DT (25); WPCB-DT (50); WPCW-DT (11); WPGH-DT (43); WPMY-DT (42); WPXI-DT (48); WQEX-DT (26); WTAE-DT (51)
Harrisburg-Lancaster-Lebanon-York, PA	743,420	39	WGAL-DT (8); WGCB-DT (30); WHP-DT (21); WHTM-DT (10); WLYH-DT (23); WPMT-DT (47)
Buffalo, NY	633,220	52	WGRZ (33); WIVB-DT (39); WKBW-DT (38); WNLO-DT (32); WNYB-DT (26); WNYO-DT (49); WPXJ-TV (23); WUTV-DT (14)
Wilkes Barre-Scranton, PA	593,480	54	WBRE-DT (11); WNEP-DT (49); WOLF-DT (45); WQMY-DT (29); WQPX-TV (32); WSWB-DT (31); WYOU-DT (13)
Johnstown-Altoona-State College, PA	294,350	101	WATM-DT (24); WJAC-DT (34); WKBS-DT (46); WTAJ-DT (32); WWCP-DT (8)
Youngstown, OH	266,560	110	WFMJ-DT (20); WKBN-DT (41); WYTV-DT (36)
Erie, PA	156,520	146	WFXP-DT (22); WICU-DT (12); WJET-DT (24); WSEE-DT (16)
Elmira (Corning), NY	95,790	176	WENY-DT (36); WETM-DT (18); WFBT-DT (14); WYDC-DT (48)

Pennsylvania Station Totals as of October 1, 2009

	VHF	UHF	TOTAL
Commercial Television	9	30	39
Educational Television	1	6	7
	10	36	46

WFMZ-DT
Ch. 46

Network Service: IND.

Licensee: Maranatha Broadcasting Co. Inc., 300 E Rock Rd, Allentown, PA 18103.

Studios: 225 Court St, Reading, PA 19601; 300 E Rock Rd, Allentown, PA 18103-7599.

Mailing Address: 300 E Rock Rd, Allentown, PA 18103-7599.

Phone: 610-797-4530. **Fax:** 610-791-2288.

Web Site: http://www.wfmz.com

Technical Facilities: Channel No. 46 (662-668 MHz). Authorized power: 400-kw max. visual, aural. Antenna: 1086-ft above av. terrain, 653-ft. above ground, 1581-ft. above sea level.

Latitude	40°	33'	52"
Longitude	75°	26'	24"

Holds CP for change to 800-kw max. visual; BPCDT-20080619AKZ.

Transmitter: E. Rock Rd.

Note: Latitude and longitude coordinates shown are based on the North American Datum of 1927 (NAD 27) as currently required by the Mass Media Bureau of the FCC.

Multichannel TV Sound: Stereo and separate audio program.

Ownership: Maranatha Broadcasting Co. (Group Owner).

Began Operation: June 1, 1999. Standard Definition. Began analog operations: November 25, 1976. Ceased analog operations: June 12, 2009.

Personnel:

Richard C. Dean, Chief Executive Officer.

Barry N. Fisher, President & General Manager.

Mike Kulp, Chief Financial Officer.

Kevin Arndt, Sales Manager.

Brad Rinehart, Assistant General Manager & News Director.

Brian Dewalt, Chief Engineer.

Dave Tavernier, Promotions Director.

Charles Gale, Traffic Manager.

City of License: Allentown. **Station DMA:** Philadelphia, PA. **Rank:** 4.

WFMZ-DT BPCDT-20080619AKZ GRANTED: 7/24/2009

© 2010 Warren Communications News

Circulation © 2009 Nielsen. Coverage based on Nielsen study.

GrandTotal	Cable TV Households	Non-cable TV Households	Total TV Households
Estimated Station Totals *	1,989,810	564,100	2,553,910
Average Weekly Circulation (2009)	328,273	90,968	419,241
Average Daily Circulation (2009)			143,481

Station DMA Total	Cable TV Households	Non-cable TV Households	Total TV Households
Estimated Station Totals *	1,850,450	564,100	2,414,550
Average Weekly Circulation (2009)	313,308	90,968	404,276
Average Daily Circulation (2009)			139,537

Other DMA Total	Cable TV Households	Non-cable TV Households	Total TV Households
Estimated Station Totals *	139,360	0	139,360
Average Weekly Circulation (2009)	14,965	0	14,965
Average Daily Circulation (2009)			3,944

*Estimated station totals are sums of the Nielsen TV and Cable TV household estimates for each county in which the station registers viewing of more than 5% as per the Nielsen Survey Methods.

WATM-DT
Ch. 24

Network Service: ABC.

Licensee: Palm Television LP, One Cityplace Dr, Ste 570, c/o CBIZ Business Solutions of St. Louis, St. Louis, MO 63141.

Studios: 1450 Scalp Ave, Johnstown, PA 15904; 1107 E Walton Ave, Altoona, PA 16602.

Mailing Address: 1450 Scalp Ave, Johnstown, PA 15904.

Phone: 814-266-8088; 814-949-8823. **Fax:** 814-266-7749.

E-mail: jbrazille@fox8tv.com

Web Site: http://www.abc23.com

Technical Facilities: Channel No. 24 (530-536 MHz). Authorized power: 1000-kw max. visual, aural. Antenna: 1020-ft above av. terrain, 212-ft. above ground, 2742-ft. above sea level.

Latitude	40°	34'	06"
Longitude	78°	26'	38"

Note: Latitude and longitude coordinates shown are based on the North American Datum of 1927 (NAD 27) as currently required by the Mass Media Bureau of the FCC.

Ownership: Gregory P. Filandrinos (Group Owner).

Began Operation: January 1, 2002. Began analog operations: November 28, 1974. Sale to Smith Broadcasting Group Inc. by John R. Powley approved by FCC October 25, 1985. Sale to Auburn Television Group Inc. approved by FCC December 19, 1989 but not consummated. Sale to present owner by Smith Broacasting Group Inc. approved by FCC August 17, 1999. Ceased analog operations: February 17, 2009.

Personnel:

Frank Quitoni, President & General Manager.

Bill Creager, Local Sales Manager.

Jim Pastore, National & Regional Sales Manager.

Jim Penna, News Director.

Dan Owens, Chief Engineer.

Brian Durham, Business Manager.

Ed Cunard, Program Coordinator.

Jill Brazill, Promotion Manager.

Jill Ream, Production Manager.

Brenda Pentz, Traffic Manager.

City of License: Altoona. **Station DMA:** Johnstown-Altoona-State College, PA.

Rank: 101.

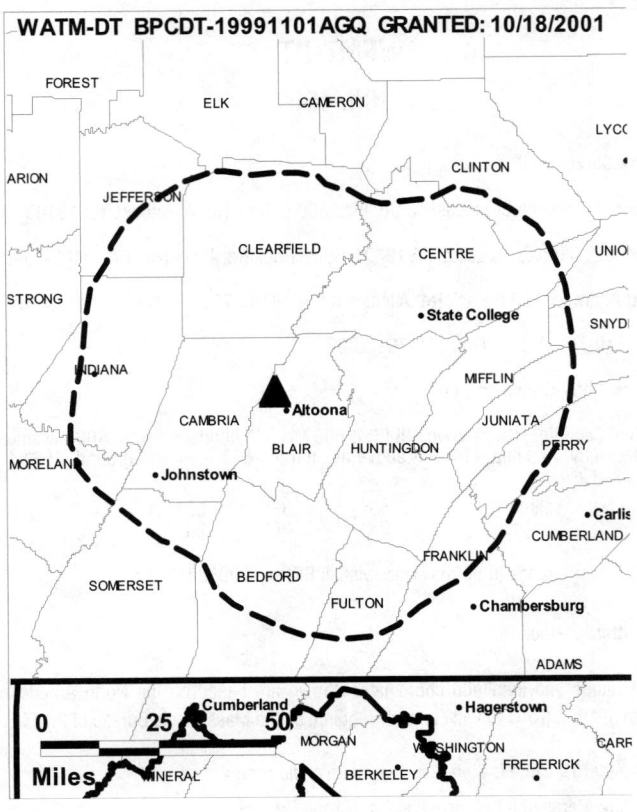

WATM-DT BPCDT-19991101AGQ GRANTED: 10/18/2001

© 2010 Warren Communications News

Circulation © 2009 Nielsen. Coverage based on Nielsen study.

GrandTotal	Cable TV Households	Non-cable TV Households	Total TV Households
Estimated Station Totals *	182,410	117,170	299,580
Average Weekly Circulation (2009)	85,882	44,517	130,399
Average Daily Circulation (2009)			49,070

Station DMA Total	Cable TV Households	Non-cable TV Households	Total TV Households
Estimated Station Totals *	182,410	109,260	291,670
Average Weekly Circulation (2009)	85,882	42,737	128,619
Average Daily Circulation (2009)			48,936

Other DMA Total	Cable TV Households	Non-cable TV Households	Total TV Households
Estimated Station Totals *	0	7,910	7,910
Average Weekly Circulation (2009)	0	1,780	1,780
Average Daily Circulation (2009)			134

*Estimated station totals are sums of the Nielsen TV and Cable TV household estimates for each county in which the station registers viewing of more than 5% as per the Nielsen Survey Methods.

WKBS-DT
Ch. 46

Network Service: IND.

Licensee: Cornerstone Television Inc., One Signal Hill Dr, Wall, PA 15148-1499.

Studio: 354 Lookout Ave, Dysart, PA 16636.

Mailing Address: One Signal Hill Dr, Wall, PA 15148-1499.

Phone: 412-824-3930. **Fax:** 412-824-5442.

Web Site: http://www.ctvn.org

Technical Facilities: Channel No. 46 (662-668 MHz). Authorized power: 50-kw max. visual, aural. Antenna: 1014-ft above av. terrain, 175-ft. above ground, 2892-ft. above sea level.

Latitude	40°	34'	12"
Longitude	78°	26'	26"

Holds CP for change to 200-kw max. visual; BPCDT-20080620ACM.

Note: Latitude and longitude coordinates shown are based on the North American Datum of 1927 (NAD 27) as currently required by the Mass Media Bureau of the FCC.

Ownership: Cornerstone Television Inc. (Group Owner).

Began Operation: June 29, 2006. Began analog operations: October 1, 1985. Ceased analog operations: June 12, 2009.

Personnel:

Ron Henbree, President & Chief Executive Officer.

Roger Wilson, Chief Engineer.

De De Hayes, Vice President, Programming.

Allyson Hayes, Promotion Director.

Steve Johnson, Operations Manager.

City of License: Altoona. **Station DMA:** Johnstown-Altoona-State College, PA.

Rank: 101.

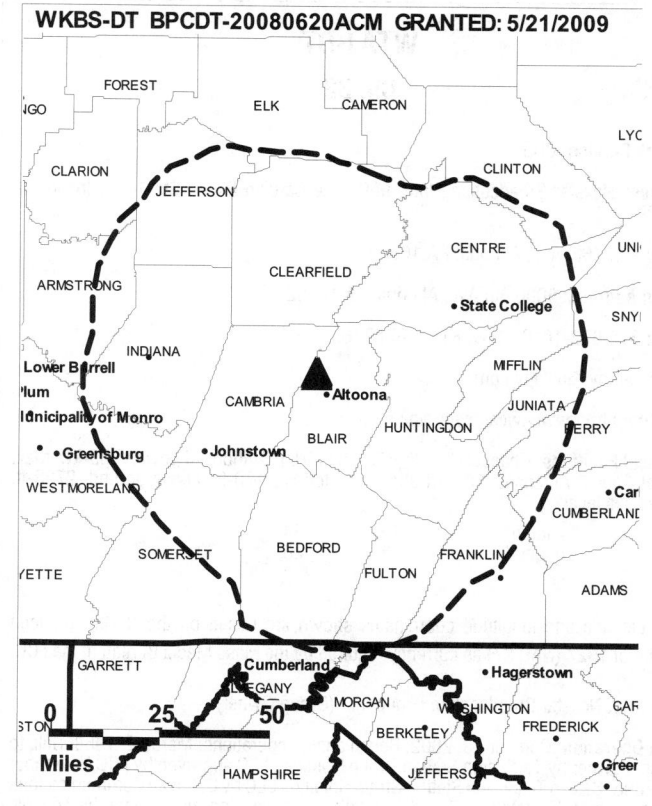

WKBS-DT BPCDT-20080620ACM GRANTED: 5/21/2009

© 2010 Warren Communications News

Circulation © 2009 Nielsen. Coverage based on Nielsen study.

GrandTotal	Cable TV Households	Non-cable TV Households	Total TV Households
Estimated Station Totals *	26,010	0	26,010
Average Weekly Circulation (2009)	2,185	0	2,185
Average Daily Circulation (2009)			400

Station DMA Total	Cable TV Households	Non-cable TV Households	Total TV Households
Estimated Station Totals *	26,010	0	26,010
Average Weekly Circulation (2009)	2,185	0	2,185
Average Daily Circulation (2009)			400

*Estimated station totals are sums of the Nielsen TV and Cable TV household estimates for each county in which the station registers viewing of more than 5% as per the Nielsen Survey Methods.

WTAJ-DT
Ch. 32

Network Service: CBS.

Licensee: Nexstar Broadcasting Inc., 909 Lake Carolyn Pkwy, Ste 1450, Irving, TX 75039.

Studio: 5000 6th Ave, Altoona, PA 16602.

Mailing Address: 5000 6th Ave, Altoona, PA 16602.

Phone: 814-942-1010. **Fax:** 814-946-8746.

E-mail: ostrow@wtajtv.com

Web Site: http://www.wearecentralpa.com

Technical Facilities: Channel No. 32 (578-584 MHz). Authorized power: 883-kw max. visual, aural. Antenna: 1001-ft above av. terrain, 170-ft. above ground, 2723-ft. above sea level.

Latitude	40°	34'	01"
Longitude	78°	26'	30"

Note: Latitude and longitude coordinates shown are based on the North American Datum of 1927 (NAD 27) as currently required by the Mass Media Bureau of the FCC.

Ownership: Nexstar Broadcasting Group Inc. (Group Owner).

Began Operation: October 23, 2002. Began analog operations: March 1, 1953. Sale to present owner by Television Station Group Holdings LLC approved by FCC November 15, 2006. Sale to Television Station Group Holdings LLC by Gateway Communications approved by FCC October 27, 2000. Sale to Gateway Communications by Triangle Publications approved by FCC September 20, 1972. Previous sale by William F Gable Co. dept. store approved by FCC January 11, 1956. Ceased analog operations: June 12, 2009.

Represented (legal): Drinker Biddle.

Represented (sales): Katz Media Group.

Personnel:

Phil Dubrow, Vice President & General Manager.

Susie Gutshall, Local Sales Manager.

Tony Degol, News Director.

Randy Chamberlin, Chief Engineer.

Dave Beeney, Production & Marketing Manager.

Jolane Whiteford, Traffic Manager.

City of License: Altoona. **Station DMA:** Johnstown-Altoona-State College, PA.

Rank: 101.

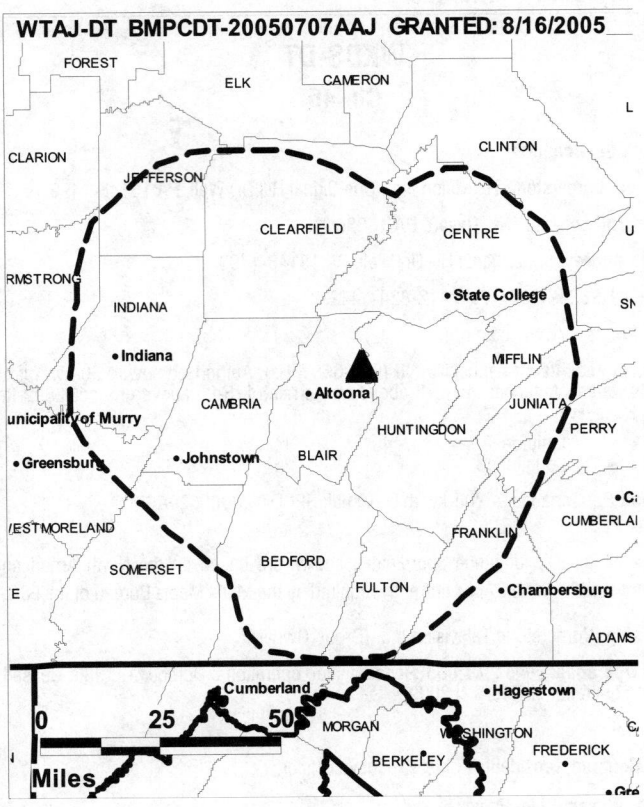

© 2010 Warren Communications News

Circulation © 2009 Nielsen. Coverage based on Nielsen study.

GrandTotal	Cable TV Households	Non-cable TV Households	Total TV Households
Estimated Station Totals *	261,820	136,580	398,400
Average Weekly Circulation (2009)	153,869	71,851	225,720
Average Daily Circulation (2009)			126,051

Station DMA Total	Cable TV Households	Non-cable TV Households	Total TV Households
Estimated Station Totals *	182,410	109,260	291,670
Average Weekly Circulation (2009)	131,556	68,869	200,425
Average Daily Circulation (2009)			116,380

Other DMA Total	Cable TV Households	Non-cable TV Households	Total TV Households
Estimated Station Totals *	79,410	27,320	106,730
Average Weekly Circulation (2009)	22,313	2,982	25,295
Average Daily Circulation (2009)			9,671

*Estimated station totals are sums of the Nielsen TV and Cable TV household estimates for each county in which the station registers viewing of more than 5% as per the Nielsen Survey Methods.

WBPH-DT
Ch. 9

Network Service: IND.

Licensee: Sonshine Family TV Inc., 813 N Fenwick St, Allentown, PA 18109.

Studio: 813 N Fenwick St, Allentown, PA 18109.

Mailing Address: PO Box 4455, Bethlehem, PA 18018.

Phone: 610-433-4400. **Fax:** 610-433-8251.

Web Site: http://www.wbph.org

Technical Facilities: Channel No. 9 (186-192 MHz). Authorized power: 3.2-kw visual, aural. Antenna: 932-ft above av. terrain, 481-ft. above ground, 1411-ft. above sea level.

Latitude	40°	33'	52"
Longitude	75°	26'	24"

Holds CP for change to 89-kw visual; BPCDT-20080619ALA.

Note: Latitude and longitude coordinates shown are based on the North American Datum of 1927 (NAD 27) as currently required by the Mass Media Bureau of the FCC.

Ownership: Sonshine Family TV Inc. (Group Owner).

Began Operation: August 6, 2006. Began analog operations: December 27, 1990. Ceased analog operations: June 12, 2009.

Personnel:

Patricia F. Huber, General Manager.

Daniel Huber, Chief Engineer.

City of License: Bethlehem. **Station DMA:** Philadelphia, PA. **Rank:** 4.

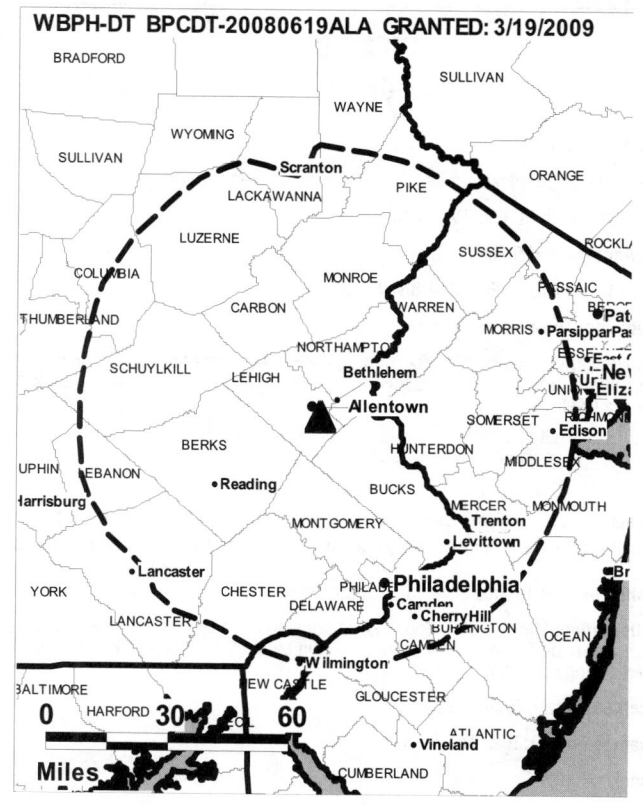

WBPH-DT BPCDT-20080619ALA GRANTED: 3/19/2009

© 2010 Warren Communications News

Circulation © 2009 Nielsen. Coverage based on Nielsen study.

GrandTotal	Cable TV Households	Non-cable TV Households	Total TV Households
Estimated Station Totals *	99,320	0	99,320
Average Weekly Circulation (2009)	14,103	0	14,103
Average Daily Circulation (2009)			1,887

Station DMA Total	Cable TV Households	Non-cable TV Households	Total TV Households
Estimated Station Totals *	99,320	0	99,320
Average Weekly Circulation (2009)	14,103	0	14,103
Average Daily Circulation (2009)			1,887

*Estimated station totals are sums of the Nielsen TV and Cable TV household estimates for each county in which the station registers viewing of more than 5% as per the Nielsen Survey Methods.

WFXP-DT
Ch. 22

Network Service: FOX.

Grantee: Mission Broadcasting Inc., 544 Red Rock Dr, Wadsworth, OH 44281.

Studio: 8455 Peach St, Erie, PA 16509.

Mailing Address: 8425 Peach St, Erie, PA 16509.

Phone: 814-864-2400. **Fax:** 814-864-5393.

Web Site: http://www.yourerie.com

Technical Facilities: Channel No. 22 (518-524 MHz). Authorized power: 850-kw max. visual, aural. Antenna: 938-ft above av. terrain, 717-ft. above ground, 2022-ft. above sea level.

Latitude	42°	02'	25"
Longitude	80°	04'	09"

Note: Latitude and longitude coordinates shown are based on the North American Datum of 1927 (NAD 27) as currently required by the Mass Media Bureau of the FCC.

Ownership: Mission Broadcasting Inc. (Group Owner).

Began Operation: May 1, 2003. Began analog operations: September 2, 1986. Sale to present owner by Bastet Broadcasting Inc. approved by FCC September 17, 2002. Ceased analog operations: June 12, 2009.

Represented (legal): Drinker Biddle.

Represented (sales): Blair Television.

Personnel:

Tim Dunst, General Manager.

Steve Freifeld, General Sales Manager.

Beverly A. Joyce, Program Director.

Lou Baxter, News Director.

Chuck Jennings, Chief Engineer.

Amy Kingen, Business Manager.

Leslie Sadley, Operations Manager & Creative Services Director.

Cheri Chase, Traffic Manager.

City of License: Erie. **Station DMA:** Erie, PA. **Rank:** 146.

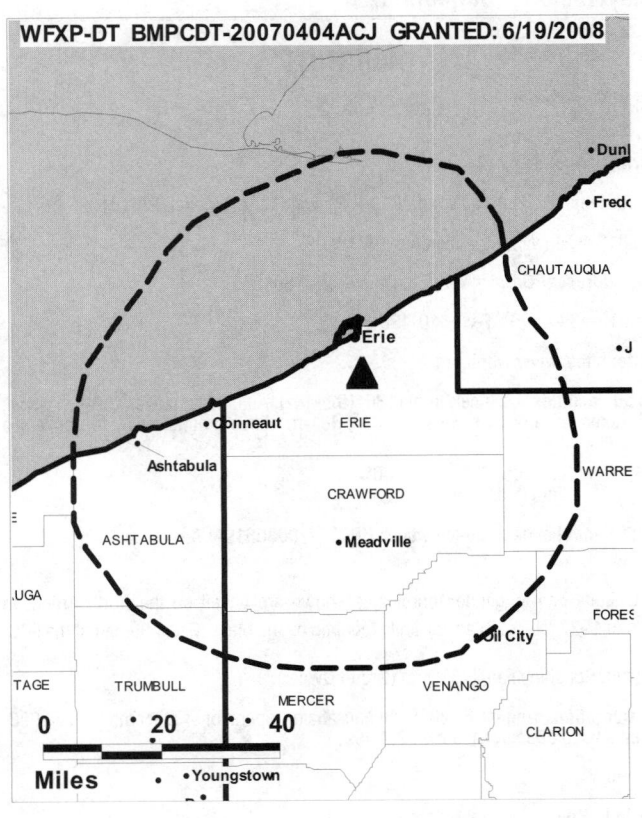

WFXP-DT BMPCDT-20070404ACJ GRANTED: 6/19/2008

© 2010 Warren Communications News

Circulation © 2009 Nielsen. Coverage based on Nielsen study.

GrandTotal	Cable TV Households	Non-cable TV Households	Total TV Households
Estimated Station Totals *	120,260	76,700	196,960
Average Weekly Circulation (2009)	59,011	35,130	94,141
Average Daily Circulation (2009)			34,787

Station DMA Total	Cable TV Households	Non-cable TV Households	Total TV Households
Estimated Station Totals *	90,780	66,830	157,610
Average Weekly Circulation (2009)	52,172	34,321	86,493
Average Daily Circulation (2009)			32,151

Other DMA Total	Cable TV Households	Non-cable TV Households	Total TV Households
Estimated Station Totals *	29,480	9,870	39,350
Average Weekly Circulation (2009)	6,839	809	7,648
Average Daily Circulation (2009)			2,636

*Estimated station totals are sums of the Nielsen TV and Cable TV household estimates for each county in which the station registers viewing of more than 5% as per the Nielsen Survey Methods.

WICU-DT
Ch. 12

Network Service: NBC.

Grantee: SJL of Pennsylvania License Subsidiary LLC, 3514 State St, Erie, PA 16508-2834.

Studio: 3514 State St, Erie, PA 16508.

Mailing Address: 3514 State St, Erie, PA 16508.

Phone: 814-454-5201; 800-533-8812. **Fax:** 814-455-0703.

Web Site: http://www.wicu12.com

Technical Facilities: Channel No. 12 (204-210 MHz). Authorized power: 5.4-kw visual, aural. Antenna: 1006-ft above av. terrain, 758-ft. above ground, 2133-ft. above sea level.

Latitude	42°	03'	50"
Longitude	80°	00'	21"

Note: Latitude and longitude coordinates shown are based on the North American Datum of 1927 (NAD 27) as currently required by the Mass Media Bureau of the FCC.

Ownership: SJL Communications Inc.

Began Operation: May 2, 2002. Standard Definition. Station broadcasting digitally on its analog channel allotment. Began analog operations: March 15, 1949. Sale to present owner by Lamb & Schweir interests approved by FCC July 12, 1996. Ceased analog operations: June 12, 2009.

Represented (legal): Latham & Watkins.

Represented (sales): Continental Television Sales.

Personnel:

Brian Lilly, General Manager.

Matt Filippi, Sales Director.

Pete Veto, National Sales Manager.

Phil Hayes, News Director.

John Wilkosz, Chief Engineer.

Mike Wolf, Business Manager.

Paula Randolph, Program Director.

Coreen Scott, Promotion & Production Director.

Kathy Earley, Traffic Manager.

City of License: Erie. **Station DMA:** Erie, PA. **Rank:** 146.

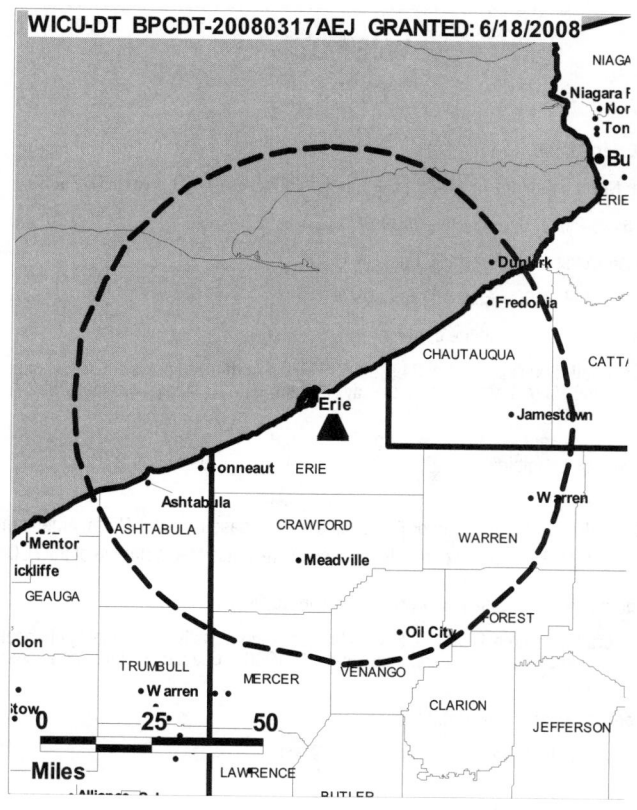

© 2010 Warren Communications News

Circulation © 2009 Nielsen. Coverage based on Nielsen study.

GrandTotal	Cable TV Households	Non-cable TV Households	Total TV Households
Estimated Station Totals *	178,720	106,000	284,720
Average Weekly Circulation (2009)	82,370	46,157	128,527
Average Daily Circulation (2009)			65,189

Station DMA Total	Cable TV Households	Non-cable TV Households	Total TV Households
Estimated Station Totals *	90,780	66,830	157,610
Average Weekly Circulation (2009)	64,783	42,201	106,984
Average Daily Circulation (2009)			56,197

Other DMA Total	Cable TV Households	Non-cable TV Households	Total TV Households
Estimated Station Totals *	87,940	39,170	127,110
Average Weekly Circulation (2009)	17,587	3,956	21,543
Average Daily Circulation (2009)			8,992

*Estimated station totals are sums of the Nielsen TV and Cable TV household estimates for each county in which the station registers viewing of more than 5% as per the Nielsen Survey Methods.

WJET-DT
Ch. 24

Network Service: ABC.

Grantee: Nexstar Finance Inc., 909 Lake Carolyn Pkwy, Ste 1450, Irving, TX 75039.

Studio: 8425 Peach St, Erie, PA 16509.

Mailing Address: 8425 Peach St, Erie, PA 16509.

Phone: 814-864-2400. **Fax:** 814-868-3041.

Web Site: http://www.yourerie.com

Technical Facilities: Channel No. 24 (530-536 MHz). Authorized power: 523-kw max. visual, aural. Antenna: 997-ft above av. terrain, 777-ft. above ground, 2082-ft. above sea level.

Latitude	42°	02'	25"
Longitude	80°	04'	09"

Note: Latitude and longitude coordinates shown are based on the North American Datum of 1927 (NAD 27) as currently required by the Mass Media Bureau of the FCC.

Ownership: Nexstar Broadcasting Group Inc. (Group Owner).

Began Operation: March 17, 2003. Station broadcasting digitally on its analog channel allotment. Began analog operations: April 3, 1966. Ceased analog operations: February 17, 2009.

Represented (legal): Drinker Biddle.

Represented (sales): Katz Media Group.

Personnel:

Tim Dunst, Vice President & General Manager.

Leslie Sadley, Operations, Production & Promotion Manager.

Steve Freifeld, General Sales Manager.

Bob Bach, Local Sales Manager.

Lou Baxter, News Director.

Chuck Jennings, Chief Engineer.

Cheri Chase, Traffic Manager.

City of License: Erie. **Station DMA:** Erie, PA. **Rank:** 146.

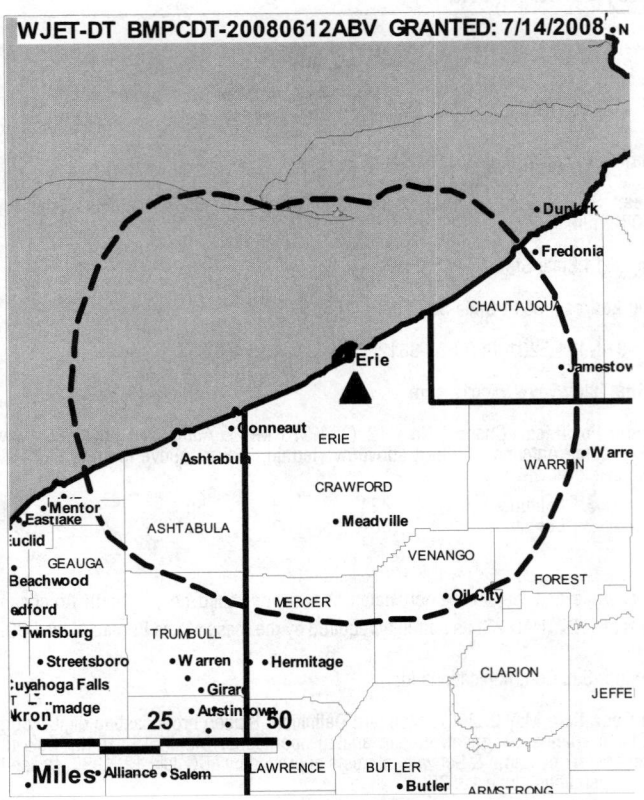

WJET-DT BMPCDT-20080612ABV GRANTED: 7/14/2008

© 2010 Warren Communications News

Circulation © 2009 Nielsen. Coverage based on Nielsen study.

GrandTotal	Cable TV Households	Non-cable TV Households	Total TV Households
Estimated Station Totals *	133,270	106,000	239,270
Average Weekly Circulation (2009)	86,059	48,081	134,140
Average Daily Circulation (2009)			75,351

Station DMA Total	Cable TV Households	Non-cable TV Households	Total TV Households
Estimated Station Totals *	90,780	66,830	157,610
Average Weekly Circulation (2009)	70,889	45,481	116,370
Average Daily Circulation (2009)			68,495

Other DMA Total	Cable TV Households	Non-cable TV Households	Total TV Households
Estimated Station Totals *	42,490	39,170	81,660
Average Weekly Circulation (2009)	15,170	2,600	17,770
Average Daily Circulation (2009)			6,856

*Estimated station totals are sums of the Nielsen TV and Cable TV household estimates for each county in which the station registers viewing of more than 5% as per the Nielsen Survey Methods.

WSEE-DT
Ch. 16

Network Service: CW, CBS.

Grantee: Initial Broadcasting of Pennsylvania License Subsidiary LLC, 2 Eastleigh Ln, Natick, MA 01760.

Studio: 1220 Peach St, Erie, PA 16501.

Mailing Address: 1220 Peach St, Erie, PA 16501.

Phone: 814-455-7575; 814-454-3500. **Fax:** 814-454-2564.

Web Site: http://www.wsee.tv

Technical Facilities: Channel No. 16 (482-488 MHz). Authorized power: 75-kw max. visual, aural. Antenna: 889-ft above av. terrain, 640-ft. above ground, 2014-ft. above sea level.

Latitude	42°	03'	52"
Longitude	80°	00'	19"

Note: Latitude and longitude coordinates shown are based on the North American Datum of 1927 (NAD 27) as currently required by the Mass Media Bureau of the FCC.

Ownership: Kevin T. Lilly.

Began Operation: September 1, 2007. Began analog operations: April 25, 1954. Sale to present owner by WSEE Holdings Inc. approved by FCC October 2, 2002. Transfer of control by WSEE Holdings Inc. to William Mustard, Trustee from James L. Winston, Trustee approved by FCC July 20, 2001. Sale to WSEE Holdings Inc. by Northstar approved by FCC October 25, 1996. Sale to Northstar Television Group by Federal Broadcast Corp. by FCC September 19, 1989. Sale to Federal Broadcast Corp. approved by FCC September 30, 1987 (Television Digest, Vol. 27:33). Sale by MTT Sales Inc. approved by FCC December 13, 1985. Sale to MMT by Gillett Broadcasting approved by FCC April 16, 1982. Sale to Gillett by Great Lakes Television Co. approved by FCC July 19, 1978. Ceased analog operations: February 17, 2009.

Represented (legal): Latham & Watkins.

Personnel:

John Christianson, General Manager & News Director.

Tracy Stufft, Station, Program & Operations Manager.

Douglas Beers, Sales Manager.

John Wilkosz, Chief Engineer.

Mike Wolf, Controller & Business Manager.

Sean Murphy, Promotion & Creative Services Director.

Paula Randolph, Traffic Manager.

City of License: Erie. **Station DMA:** Erie, PA. **Rank:** 146.

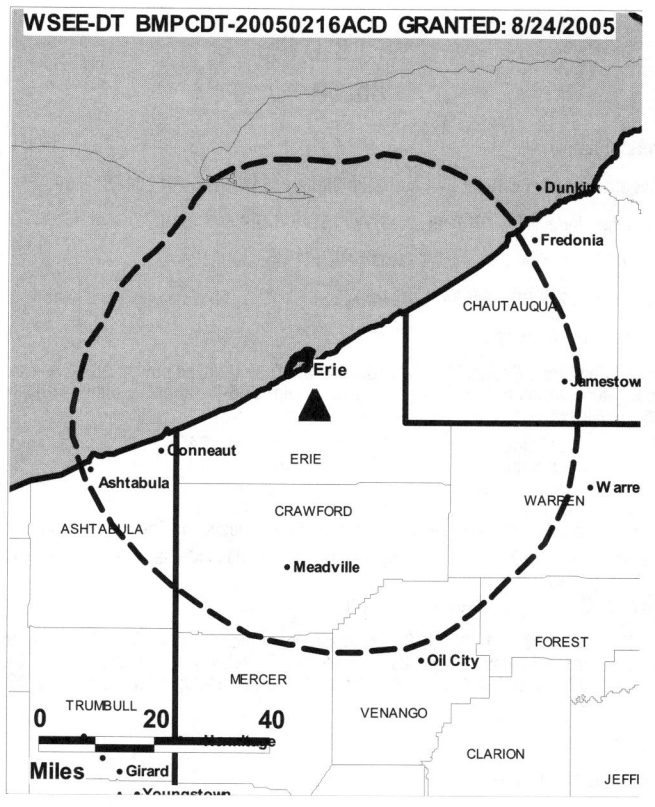

© 2010 Warren Communications News

Circulation © 2009 Nielsen. Coverage based on Nielsen study.

GrandTotal	Cable TV Households	Non-cable TV Households	Total TV Households
Estimated Station Totals *	173,350	76,700	250,050
Average Weekly Circulation (2009)	83,384	36,608	119,992
Average Daily Circulation (2009)			54,809

Station DMA Total	Cable TV Households	Non-cable TV Households	Total TV Households
Estimated Station Totals *	90,780	66,830	157,610
Average Weekly Circulation (2009)	64,677	35,483	100,160
Average Daily Circulation (2009)			49,870

Other DMA Total	Cable TV Households	Non-cable TV Households	Total TV Households
Estimated Station Totals *	82,570	9,870	92,440
Average Weekly Circulation (2009)	18,707	1,125	19,832
Average Daily Circulation (2009)			4,939

*Estimated station totals are sums of the Nielsen TV and Cable TV household estimates for each county in which the station registers viewing of more than 5% as per the Nielsen Survey Methods.

WPCB-DT
Ch. 50

Network Service: IND.

Licensee: Cornerstone Television Inc., One Signal Hill Dr, Wall, PA 15148-1499.

Studio: One Signal Hill Dr, Rte 48, Wall, PA 15148-1499.

Mailing Address: One Signal Hill Dr, Wall, PA 15148-1499.

Phone: 412-824-3930. **Fax:** 412-824-5442.

Web Site: http://www.ctvn.org

Technical Facilities: Channel No. 50 (686-692 MHz). Authorized power: 362-kw max. visual, aural. Antenna: 866-ft above av. terrain, 705-ft. above ground, 1903-ft. above sea level.

Latitude	40°	23'	34"
Longitude	79°	46'	54"

Note: Latitude and longitude coordinates shown are based on the North American Datum of 1927 (NAD 27) as currently required by the Mass Media Bureau of the FCC.

Ownership: Cornerstone Television Inc. (Group Owner).

Began Operation: May 1, 2003. Began analog operations: April 15, 1979. Sale to Paxson Communications Corp. by Cornerstone Television Inc. approved by FCC December 29, 1999, but never consummated. Ceased analog operations: June 12, 2009.

Personnel:

Ron Hembree, President.

Chuck Alexander, Senior Vice President & Chief Financial Officer.

Blake Richert, Vice President, Engineering.

De De Hayes, Vice President, Programming.

Tom McGough, Sales Manager.

Alison Hayes, Marketing & Promotion Director.

Steve Johnson, Production Manager.

Martha Helmstadter, Traffic Manager.

City of License: Greensburg. **Station DMA:** Pittsburgh, PA. **Rank:** 23.

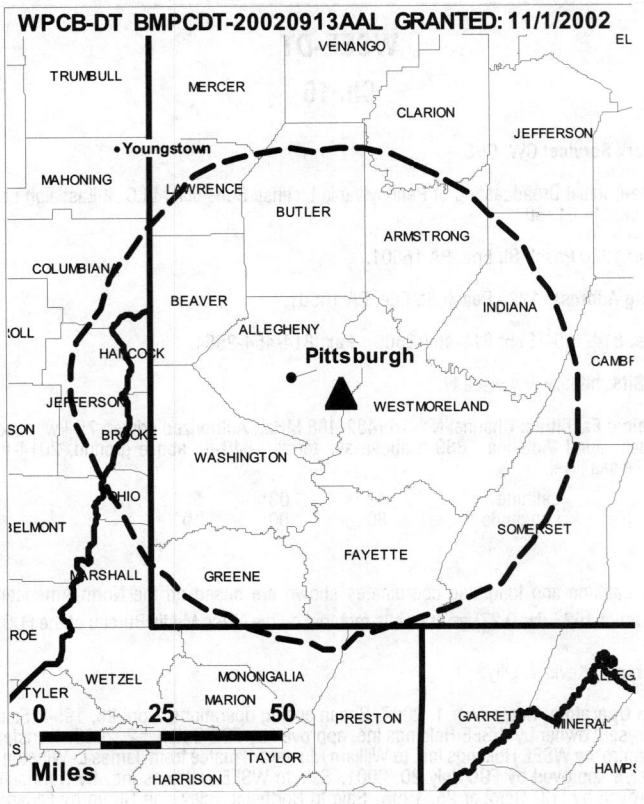

WPCB-DT BMPCDT-20020913AAL GRANTED: 11/1/2002

© 2010 Warren Communications News

Circulation © 2009 Nielsen. Coverage based on Nielsen study.

GrandTotal	Cable TV Households	Non-cable TV Households	Total TV Households
Estimated Station Totals *	95,070	44,710	139,780
Average Weekly Circulation (2009)	6,629	2,526	9,155
Average Daily Circulation (2009)			1,784

Station DMA Total	Cable TV Households	Non-cable TV Households	Total TV Households
Estimated Station Totals *	57,640	25,420	83,060
Average Weekly Circulation (2009)	4,379	1,398	5,777
Average Daily Circulation (2009)			1,020

Other DMA Total	Cable TV Households	Non-cable TV Households	Total TV Households
Estimated Station Totals *	37,430	19,290	56,720
Average Weekly Circulation (2009)	2,250	1,128	3,378
Average Daily Circulation (2009)			764

*Estimated station totals are sums of the Nielsen TV and Cable TV household estimates for each county in which the station registers viewing of more than 5% as per the Nielsen Survey Methods.

WHP-DT
Ch. 21

Network Service: MNT, CBS.

Licensee: Newport Television License LLC, 460 Nichols Rd, Ste 250, Kansas City, MO 64112.

Studio: 3300 N. 6th Street, Harrisburg, PA 17110.

Mailing Address: 3300 N. 6th St, Harrisburg, PA 17110.

Phone: 717-238-2100. **Fax:** 717-238-8744.

E-mail: sherrytaylor@clearchannel.com

Web Site: http://www.whptv.com

Technical Facilities: Channel No. 21 (512-518 MHz). Authorized power: 450-kw max. visual, aural. Antenna: 1211-ft above av. terrain, 463-ft. above ground, 1772-ft. above sea level.

Latitude	40°	20'	43"
Longitude	76°	52'	09"

Note: Latitude and longitude coordinates shown are based on the North American Datum of 1927 (NAD 27) as currently required by the Mass Media Bureau of the FCC.

Ownership: Newport Television LLC (Group Owner).

Began Operation: May 8, 2002. Station broadcasting digitally on its analog channel allotment. Began analog operations: April 15, 1953. Sale to present owner by Clear Channel Communications Inc. approved by FCC November 29, 2007. Transfer of control by WHP Television Ltd. Partnership to Clear Channel Communications Inc. from Becker Television Inc. & Growth Media Inc. approved by FCC September 13, 1995. Sale to WHP Television Ltd. Partnership by WHP Inc. approved by FCC August 18, 1993. Ceased analog operations: June 12, 2009.

Represented (legal): Covington & Burling.

Represented (sales): Katz Media Group.

Personnel:

Lou Castriota, Operations & Programming Director.

Scott Beaver, Sales Director.

Marian Stanislawczk, Local Sales Manager.

Stu Brenner, National Sales Manager.

Caroline Imler, News Director.

Rob Hershey, Chief Engineer.

Susan Ruch, Business Manager.

Taylor Miller, Program Coordinator.

Brett Freitag, Promotion, Production & Creative Services Director.

Danielle DeRitis, Traffic Manager.

City of License: Harrisburg. **Station DMA:** Harrisburg-Lancaster-Lebanon-York, PA.

Rank: 39.

WHP-DT BMPCDT-20080606AEJ GRANTED: 6/9/2008

© 2010 Warren Communications News

Circulation © 2009 Nielsen. Coverage based on Nielsen study.

GrandTotal	Cable TV Households	Non-cable TV Households	Total TV Households
Estimated Station Totals *	546,310	249,010	795,320
Average Weekly Circulation (2009)	294,373	114,305	408,678
Average Daily Circulation (2009)			183,564

Station DMA Total	Cable TV Households	Non-cable TV Households	Total TV Households
Estimated Station Totals *	512,790	226,090	738,880
Average Weekly Circulation (2009)	290,709	112,607	403,316
Average Daily Circulation (2009)			181,431

Other DMA Total	Cable TV Households	Non-cable TV Households	Total TV Households
Estimated Station Totals *	33,520	22,920	56,440
Average Weekly Circulation (2009)	3,664	1,698	5,362
Average Daily Circulation (2009)			2,133

*Estimated station totals are sums of the Nielsen TV and Cable TV household estimates for each county in which the station registers viewing of more than 5% as per the Nielsen Survey Methods.

WHTM-DT

Ch. 10

Network Service: ABC.

Licensee: Harrisburg Television Inc., 3235 Hoffman St, Harrisburg, PA 17110.

Studio: 3235 Hoffman St, Harrisburg, PA 17110.

Mailing Address: PO Box 5860, Harrisburg, PA 17110.

Phone: 717-236-2727; 717-236-1444. **Fax:** 717-232-5272.

Web Site: http://www.abc27.com

Technical Facilities: Channel No. 10 (192-198 MHz). Authorized power: 16.2-kw visual, aural. Antenna: 1021-ft above av. terrain, 460-ft. above ground, 1540-ft. above sea level.

Latitude	40°	18'	58"
Longitude	76°	57'	01"

Holds CP for change to 19.7-kw visual, 1135-ft above av. terrain, 577-ft. above ground, 1657-ft. above sea level; BPCDT-20080620AGL.

Note: Latitude and longitude coordinates shown are based on the North American Datum of 1927 (NAD 27) as currently required by the Mass Media Bureau of the FCC.

Ownership: Allbritton Communications Co. (Group Owner).

Began Operation: August 14, 2004. Began analog operations: June 19, 1953 on Ch. 71. May 15, 1957 FCC authorized WTPA to purchase transmitter & tower of off-air WCMB-TV and to switch to Ch. 27, Ch. 71 being assigned to WCMB-TV. Sale to Times Mirror Co. by Newhouse Broadcasting approved by FCC March 27, 1980. Sale to Smith Broadcasting Group Inc. by Times Mirror approved by FCC April 17, 1986. Sale to Price Communications by Smith Broadcasting approved by FCC March 31, 1994. Sale to present owner by Price Communications approved by FCC February 29, 1996. Ceased analog operations: June 12, 2009.

Represented (sales): Continental Television Sales.

Personnel:

Joseph Lewin, President & General Manager.

Robert Saylor III, General Sales Manager.

Larry Maloney, Local Sales Manager.

Paul Roda, National Sales Manager.

Dennis Fisher, News Director.

Mark O'Lingy, Chief Engineer.

Sharon Chambers, Controller.

Randy Whitaker, Marketing Director.

Betty Bryan, Promotion Director.

Barry Mechling, Production Manager.

Brian Hauf, Creative Services Director.

Nikki Bender, Traffic Manager.

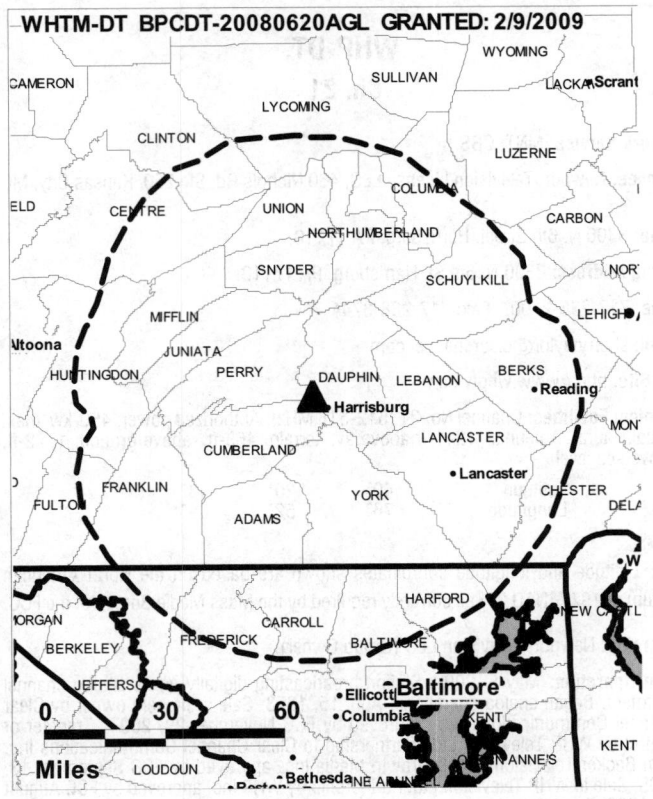

© 2010 Warren Communications News

City of License: Harrisburg. **Station DMA:** Harrisburg-Lancaster-Lebanon-York, PA.

Rank: 39.

Circulation © 2009 Nielsen. Coverage based on Nielsen study.

GrandTotal	Cable TV Households	Non-cable TV Households	Total TV Households
Estimated Station Totals *	546,310	249,010	795,320
Average Weekly Circulation (2009)	287,801	112,612	400,413
Average Daily Circulation (2009)			184,555

Station DMA Total	Cable TV Households	Non-cable TV Households	Total TV Households
Estimated Station Totals *	512,790	226,090	738,880
Average Weekly Circulation (2009)	284,507	111,066	395,573
Average Daily Circulation (2009)			182,489

Other DMA Total	Cable TV Households	Non-cable TV Households	Total TV Households
Estimated Station Totals *	33,520	22,920	56,440
Average Weekly Circulation (2009)	3,294	1,546	4,840
Average Daily Circulation (2009)			2,066

*Estimated station totals are sums of the Nielsen TV and Cable TV household estimates for each county in which the station registers viewing of more than 5% as per the Nielsen Survey Methods.

WOLF-DT
Ch. 45

Network Service: MNT, FOX, CW.

Licensee: New Age Media of Pennsylvania License LLC, 46 Public Square, Wilkes-Barre, PA 18701.

Studio: 1181 Hwy. 315, Plains, PA 18702.

Mailing Address: 1181 Hwy. 315, Plains, PA 18702.

Phone: 570-970-5600. **Fax:** 570-970-5601.

Web Site: http://www.myfoxnepa.com

Technical Facilities: Channel No. 45 (656-662 MHz). Authorized power: 420-kw max. visual, aural. Antenna: 1601-ft above av. terrain, 764-ft. above ground, 2864-ft. above sea level.

Latitude	41°	11'	00"
Longitude	75°	52'	10"

Note: Latitude and longitude coordinates shown are based on the North American Datum of 1927 (NAD 27) as currently required by the Mass Media Bureau of the FCC.

Ownership: New Age Media (Group Owner).

Began Operation: September 6, 2005. Began analog operations: June 3, 1985. Sale to present owner by The PSC Liquidating Trust approved by FCC January 4, 2007. Competing sale to MM Licensing-Wilkes-Barre LLC dismissed by FCC January 23, 2007. Transfer of control to The PSC Liquidating Trust by Pegasus Communications Corp. approved by FCC April 19, 2005. Involuntary assignment of license to WOLF License Corp., Debtor-In-Possession approved by FCC December 23, 2004. Ceased analog operations: June 12, 2009.

Represented (legal): Leventhal, Senter & Lerman PLLC.

Represented (sales): Petry Media Corp.

Represented (engineering): du Treil, Lundin & Rackley Inc.

Personnel:

Jon Cadman, General Manager.

Dan Mecca, National Sales Manager.

Rich Chofey, Chief Engineer.

Marianne Musto, Business Manager.

Linda Greenwald, Program Director.

Bob Spager, Local Sales Manager.

Becky Sinke, Production Manager.

Steve Phillips, Creative Services Director.

Lisa Miller, Traffic Manager.

City of License: Hazleton. **Station DMA:** Wilkes Barre-Scranton, PA. **Rank:** 54.

WOLF-DT BMPCDT-20050106AAO GRANTED: 1/28/2005

© 2010 Warren Communications News

Circulation © 2009 Nielsen. Coverage based on Nielsen study.

GrandTotal	Cable TV Households	Non-cable TV Households	Total TV Households
Estimated Station Totals *	389,380	212,650	602,030
Average Weekly Circulation (2009)	218,455	104,109	322,564
Average Daily Circulation (2009)			114,059

Station DMA Total	Cable TV Households	Non-cable TV Households	Total TV Households
Estimated Station Totals *	379,400	212,650	592,050
Average Weekly Circulation (2009)	217,916	104,109	322,025
Average Daily Circulation (2009)			113,939

Other DMA Total	Cable TV Households	Non-cable TV Households	Total TV Households
Estimated Station Totals *	9,980	0	9,980
Average Weekly Circulation (2009)	539	0	539
Average Daily Circulation (2009)			120

*Estimated station totals are sums of the Nielsen TV and Cable TV household estimates for each county in which the station registers viewing of more than 5% as per the Nielsen Survey Methods.

WPCW-DT

Ch. 11

Network Service: CW.

Grantee: Pittsburgh Television Station WNPA Inc., 2175 K St. NW, Suite 350, Washington, DC 20037.

Phone: 412-575-2200. **Fax:** 412-575-2871.

Web Site: http://www.wpcwtv.com

Technical Facilities: Channel No. 11 (198-204 MHz). Authorized power: 30-kw visual, aural. Antenna: 849-ft above av. terrain, 486-ft. above ground, 1851-ft. above sea level.

Latitude	40°	29'	38"
Longitude	80°	01'	09"

Note: Latitude and longitude coordinates shown are based on the North American Datum of 1927 (NAD 27) as currently required by the Mass Media Bureau of the FCC.

Ownership: CBS Corp.

Began Operation: June 12, 2009. Began analog operations: October 15, 1953. Ceased analog operations: June 12, 2009.

Personnel:

Chris Pike, Vice President & General Manager.

David Patterson, Chief Engineer.

City of License: Jeannette. **Station DMA:** Pittsburgh, PA. **Rank:** 23.

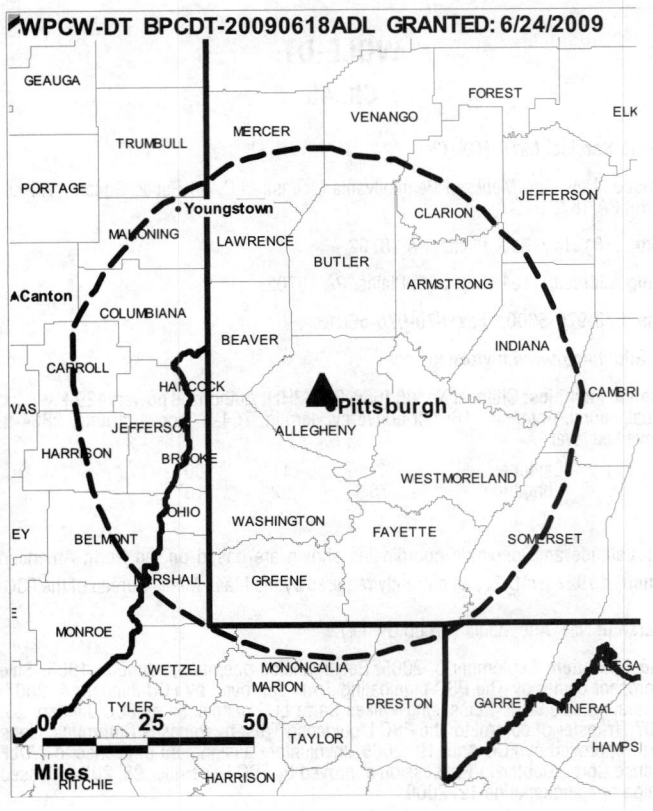

WPCW-DT BPCDT-20090618ADL GRANTED: 6/24/2009

© 2010 Warren Communications News

Circulation © 2009 Nielsen. Coverage based on Nielsen study.

GrandTotal	Cable TV Households	Non-cable TV Households	Total TV Households
Estimated Station Totals *	988,500	405,450	1,393,950
Average Weekly Circulation (2009)	240,428	91,926	332,354
Average Daily Circulation (2009)			109,717

Station DMA Total	Cable TV Households	Non-cable TV Households	Total TV Households
Estimated Station Totals *	850,800	300,710	1,151,510
Average Weekly Circulation (2009)	213,918	75,584	289,502
Average Daily Circulation (2009)			97,774

Other DMA Total	Cable TV Households	Non-cable TV Households	Total TV Households
Estimated Station Totals *	137,700	104,740	242,440
Average Weekly Circulation (2009)	26,510	16,342	42,852
Average Daily Circulation (2009)			11,943

*Estimated station totals are sums of the Nielsen TV and Cable TV household estimates for each county in which the station registers viewing of more than 5% as per the Nielsen Survey Methods.

WJAC-DT
Ch. 34

Network Service: NBC.

Licensee: WPXI Inc., 6205 Peachtree Dunwoody Rd, Atlanta, GA 30328.

Studio: 49 Old Hickory Lane, Johnstown, PA 15905-3373.

Mailing Address: 49 Old Hickory Ln, Johnstown, PA 15905.

Phone: 814-255-7600; 814-255-7616. **Fax:** 814-255-3958.

Web Site: http://www.wjactv.com

Technical Facilities: Channel No. 34 (590-596 MHz). Authorized power: 1000-kw max. visual, aural. Antenna: 1266-ft above av. terrain, 328-ft. above ground, 2986-ft. above sea level.

| Latitude | 40° | 22' | 17" |
| Longitude | 78° | 58' | 56" |

Holds CP for change to 1273-ft above av. terrain, 335-ft. above ground, 2992-ft. above sea level; BPCDT-20080619ADU.

Note: Latitude and longitude coordinates shown are based on the North American Datum of 1927 (NAD 27) as currently required by the Mass Media Bureau of the FCC.

Ownership: Cox Enterprises Inc. (Group Owner).

Began Operation: November 23, 2005. Began analog operations: September 15, 1949. Ceased analog operations: June 12, 2009.

Represented (sales): TeleRep Inc.

Personnel:

Richard Schrott, Vice President & General Manager.

Debbie Miller, Local Sales Manager.

Rob Schmidt, Local Sales Manager.

Phil Johnson, National Sales Manager.

Pam Dennis, News Director.

Rob Abele, Chief Engineer.

Dennis Vickroy, Business Manager.

Jim Edwards, Promotion & Marketing Director.

Rahna Harris, Traffic Manager.

Nancy Shull, Human Resources Director.

City of License: Johnstown. **Station DMA:** Johnstown-Altoona-State College, PA.

Rank: 101.

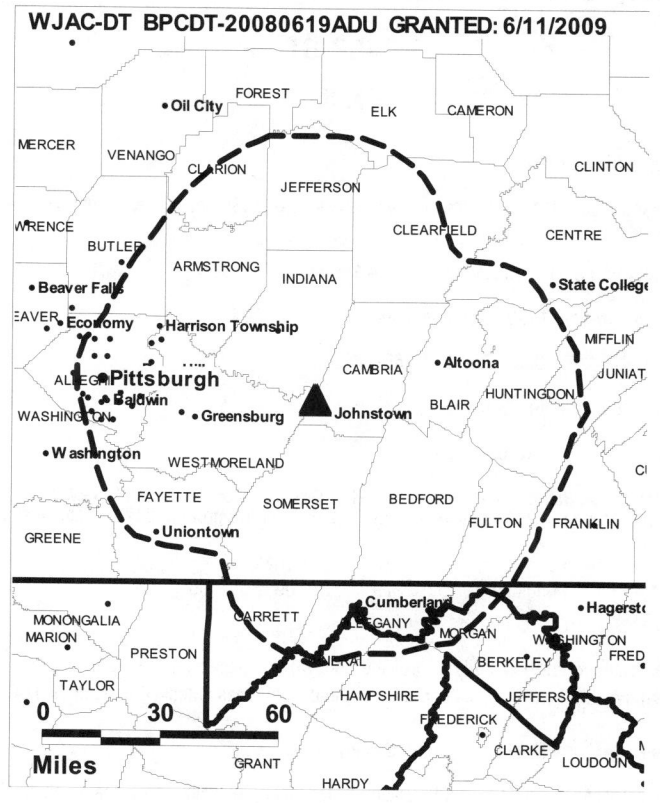

WJAC-DT BPCDT-20080619ADU GRANTED: 6/11/2009

© 2010 Warren Communications News

Circulation © 2009 Nielsen. Coverage based on Nielsen study.

GrandTotal	Cable TV Households	Non-cable TV Households	Total TV Households
Estimated Station Totals *	379,420	204,180	583,600
Average Weekly Circulation (2009)	182,906	78,364	261,270
Average Daily Circulation (2009)			139,109

Station DMA Total	Cable TV Households	Non-cable TV Households	Total TV Households
Estimated Station Totals *	182,410	109,260	291,670
Average Weekly Circulation (2009)	135,747	66,557	202,304
Average Daily Circulation (2009)			113,658

Other DMA Total	Cable TV Households	Non-cable TV Households	Total TV Households
Estimated Station Totals *	197,010	94,920	291,930
Average Weekly Circulation (2009)	47,159	11,807	58,966
Average Daily Circulation (2009)			25,451

*Estimated station totals are sums of the Nielsen TV and Cable TV household estimates for each county in which the station registers viewing of more than 5% as per the Nielsen Survey Methods.

WWCP-DT
Ch. 8

Network Service: FOX.

Licensee: Peak Media of Pennsylvania Licensee LLC, 1430 Scalp Ave, Johnstown, PA 15904.

Studio: 1450 Scalp Ave., Johnstown, PA 15904.

Mailing Address: 1450 Scalp Ave, Johnstown, PA 15904.

Phone: 814-266-8088. **Fax:** 814-266-7749.

E-mail: ecunard@fox8tv.com

Web Site: http://www.fox8tv.com

Technical Facilities: Channel No. 8 (180-186 MHz). Authorized power: 9.3-kw visual, aural. Antenna: 1207-ft above av. terrain, 276-ft. above ground, 3175-ft. above sea level.

Latitude	40°	10'	53"
Longitude	79°	09'	05"

Note: Latitude and longitude coordinates shown are based on the North American Datum of 1927 (NAD 27) as currently required by the Mass Media Bureau of the FCC.

Ownership: Larry D. Marcus (Group Owner).

Began Operation: June 6, 2005. Station broadcasting digitally on its analog channel allotment. Began analog operations: October 13, 1986. Ceased analog operations: February 17, 2009.

Personnel:

Frank Quitoni, President & General Manager.

Bill Creager, Local Sales Manager.

Jim Pastore, National & Regional Sales Manager.

Dan Owens, Chief Engineer.

Brian Durham, Business Manager.

Jill Ream, Production & Programming Coordinator.

Jill Brazill, Promotion Manager.

Brenda Pentz, Traffic Manager.

City of License: Johnstown. **Station DMA:** Johnstown-Altoona-State College, PA.

Rank: 101.

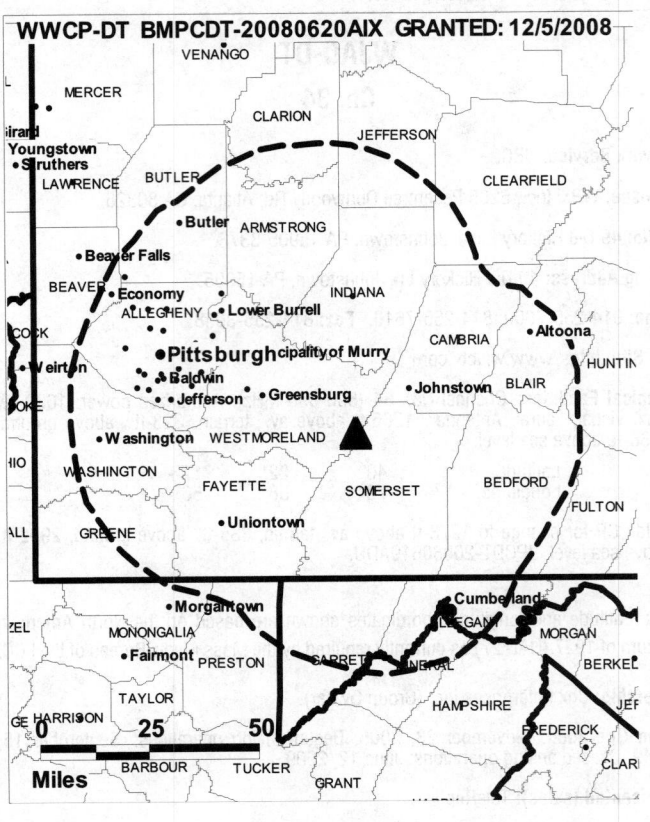

© 2010 Warren Communications News

Circulation © 2009 Nielsen. Coverage based on Nielsen study.

GrandTotal	Cable TV Households	Non-cable TV Households	Total TV Households
Estimated Station Totals *	217,790	215,320	433,110
Average Weekly Circulation (2009)	108,941	54,809	163,750
Average Daily Circulation (2009)			50,239

Station DMA Total	Cable TV Households	Non-cable TV Households	Total TV Households
Estimated Station Totals *	182,410	109,260	291,670
Average Weekly Circulation (2009)	99,983	45,455	145,438
Average Daily Circulation (2009)			46,532

Other DMA Total	Cable TV Households	Non-cable TV Households	Total TV Households
Estimated Station Totals *	35,380	106,060	141,440
Average Weekly Circulation (2009)	8,958	9,354	18,312
Average Daily Circulation (2009)			3,707

*Estimated station totals are sums of the Nielsen TV and Cable TV household estimates for each county in which the station registers viewing of more than 5% as per the Nielsen Survey Methods.

WGAL-DT
Ch. 8

Network Service: NBC.

Licensee: WGAL Hearst-Argyle Television Inc., PO Box 1800, c/o Brooks, Pierce et al., Raleigh, NC 27602.

Studios: 1300 Columbia Ave., Lancaster, PA 17603; 333 Market St., Harrisburg, PA 17105.

Mailing Address: PO Box 7127, Lancaster, PA 17604-7127.

Phone: 717-393-5851. **Fax:** 717-393-9484.

Web Site: http://www.thewgalchannel.com

Technical Facilities: Channel No. 8 (180-186 MHz). Authorized power: 7.5-kw visual, aural. Antenna: 1375-ft above av. terrain, 785-ft. above ground, 1827-ft. above sea level.

Latitude	40°	02'	04"
Longitude	76°	37'	08"

Holds CP for change to 14.1-kw visual; BPCDT-20090710AKB.

Transmitter: 1320 Tower Rd., Hallam.

Note: Latitude and longitude coordinates shown are based on the North American Datum of 1927 (NAD 27) as currently required by the Mass Media Bureau of the FCC.

Ownership: Hearst-Argyle Television Inc. (Group Owner).

Began Operation: November 3, 2001. Standard and High Definition. Station broadcasting digitally on its analog channel allotment. Began analog operations: March 18, 1949. Sale to Pulitzer Publishing Co. by Steinman Stations approved by FCC October 5, 1978. Sale to present owner by Pulitzer approved by FCC November 24, 1998. Hearst-Argyle received approval from the FCC May 26, 2009 to become privately owned by The Hearst Corp. Ceased analog operations: June 12, 2009.

Represented (legal): Brooks, Pierce, McLendon, Humphrey & Leonard LLP.

Represented (sales): Eagle Television Sales.

Personnel:

Paul D. Quinn, President & General Manager.

Bob Good, Assistant General Manager & Operations Director.

Nancy Tulli, General Sales Manager.

Andrew Scheid, Local Sales Manager.

Palmer Brown, Website Sales Manager.

Paul Ladrow, National Sales Manager.

Dan O'Donnell, News Director.

Robert B. Good Jr., Chief Engineer.

Collette Leonard, Business Manager.

Heather Bruce, Program Director.

John Baldwin, Marketing & Promotion Director.

Kim Groff, Traffic Manager.

© 2010 Warren Communications News

City of License: Lancaster. **Station DMA:** Harrisburg-Lancaster-Lebanon-York, PA.

Rank: 39.

Circulation © 2009 Nielsen. Coverage based on Nielsen study.

GrandTotal	Cable TV Households	Non-cable TV Households	Total TV Households
Estimated Station Totals *	865,280	242,940	1,108,220
Average Weekly Circulation (2009)	464,838	151,774	616,612
Average Daily Circulation (2009)			315,567

Station DMA Total	Cable TV Households	Non-cable TV Households	Total TV Households
Estimated Station Totals *	512,790	226,090	738,880
Average Weekly Circulation (2009)	366,058	150,072	516,130
Average Daily Circulation (2009)			286,225

Other DMA Total	Cable TV Households	Non-cable TV Households	Total TV Households
Estimated Station Totals *	352,490	16,850	369,340
Average Weekly Circulation (2009)	98,780	1,702	100,482
Average Daily Circulation (2009)			29,342

*Estimated station totals are sums of the Nielsen TV and Cable TV household estimates for each county in which the station registers viewing of more than 5% as per the Nielsen Survey Methods.

WLYH-DT
Ch. 23

Network Service: CW.

Licensee: Nexstar Broadcasting Inc., 909 Lake Carolyn Pkwy, Ste 1450, Irving, TX 75039.

Studio: 3300 N. 6th St., Harrisburg, PA 17110.

Mailing Address: 3300 N. 6th St, Harrisburg, PA 17110.

Phone: 717-238-2100; 717-273-4697. **Fax:** 717-238-2135.

Web Site: http://www.cw15.com/

Technical Facilities: Channel No. 23 (524-530 MHz). Authorized power: 500-kw max. visual, aural. Antenna: 1250-ft above av. terrain, 919-ft. above ground, 1797-ft. above sea level.

Latitude	40°	15'	45"
Longitude	76°	27'	51"

Note: Latitude and longitude coordinates shown are based on the North American Datum of 1927 (NAD 27) as currently required by the Mass Media Bureau of the FCC.

Ownership: Nexstar Broadcasting Group Inc. (Group Owner).

Began Operation: May 1, 2002. Began analog operations: October 9, 1953. Left air October 16, 1954. Sold to Triangle Publications by radio WLBR-Lebanon News interests and station resumed operation May 2, 1957. Sale to Gateway Communications by Triangle approved by FCC September 20, 1972. Sale to Television Station Group Holdings LLC by Gateway Communications approved by FCC October 27, 2000. Sale to present owner by Television Station Group Holdings LLC approved by FCC November 15, 2006. Ceased analog operations: February 17, 2009.

Represented (legal): Drinker Biddle.

Represented (sales): Katz Media Group.

Personnel:

Jim Berman, Vice President & General Manager.

Lou Castriota, Operations & Programming Director.

Scott Beavers, Sales Director.

Megan Shaffer, Local Sales Manager.

Stu Brenner, National Sales Manager.

Caroline Imler, News Director.

Rob Hershey, Chief Engineer.

Susan Ruch, Business Manager.

Brett Freitag, Creative Services, Production & Promotion Director.

Danielle DeRitis, Traffic Manager.

City of License: Lancaster. **Station DMA:** Harrisburg-Lancaster-Lebanon-York, PA.

Rank: 39.

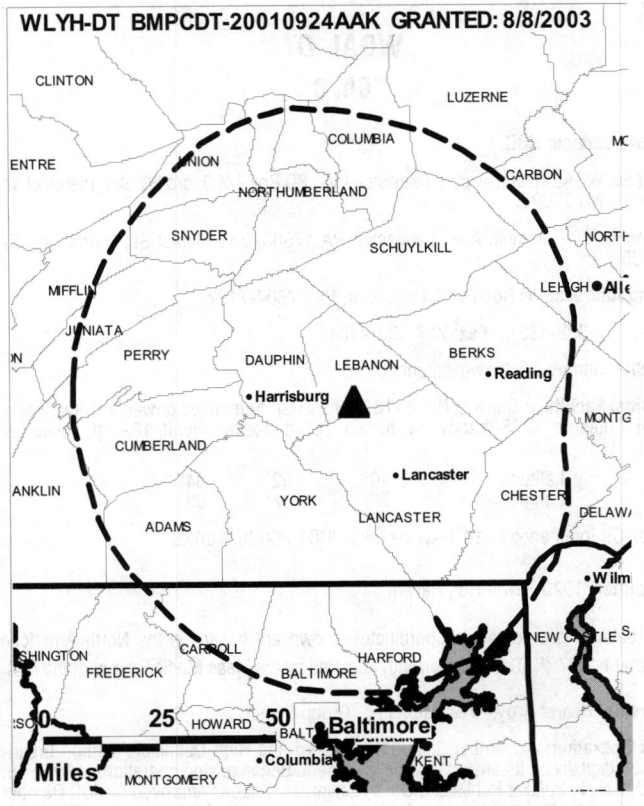

WLYH-DT BMPCDT-20010924AAK GRANTED: 8/8/2003

© 2010 Warren Communications News

Circulation © 2009 Nielsen. Coverage based on Nielsen study.

GrandTotal	Cable TV Households	Non-cable TV Households	Total TV Households
Estimated Station Totals *	703,960	226,090	930,050
Average Weekly Circulation (2009)	129,469	56,192	185,661
Average Daily Circulation (2009)			47,979

Station DMA Total	Cable TV Households	Non-cable TV Households	Total TV Households
Estimated Station Totals *	512,790	226,090	738,880
Average Weekly Circulation (2009)	109,647	56,192	165,839
Average Daily Circulation (2009)			44,333

Other DMA Total	Cable TV Households	Non-cable TV Households	Total TV Households
Estimated Station Totals *	191,170	0	191,170
Average Weekly Circulation (2009)	19,822	0	19,822
Average Daily Circulation (2009)			3,646

*Estimated station totals are sums of the Nielsen TV and Cable TV household estimates for each county in which the station registers viewing of more than 5% as per the Nielsen Survey Methods.

KYW-DT
Ch. 26

Network Service: CBS.

Grantee: CBS Broadcasting Inc., 2000 K St. NW, Ste 725, Washington, DC 20006.

Studio: 1555 Hamilton St, Philadelphia, PA 19130.

Mailing Address: 1555 Hamilton St, Philadelphia, PA 19130.

Phone: 215-977-5300. **Fax:** 215-977-5658.

E-mail: mcelwee@kyw.com

Web Site: http://cbs3.com

Technical Facilities: Channel No. 26 (542-548 MHz). Authorized power: 786-kw max. visual, aural. Antenna: 1360-ft above av. terrain, 1200-ft. above ground, 1442-ft. above sea level.

Latitude	40°	02'	39"
Longitude	75°	14'	26"

Holds CP for change to 790-kw max. visual, 1230-ft above av. terrain, 1201-ft. above ground, 1444-ft. above sea level; lat. 40° 02' 33", long. 75° 14' 33", BPCDT-20080620ABO.

Transmitter: Culp St. & Domino Lane.

Note: Latitude and longitude coordinates shown are based on the North American Datum of 1927 (NAD 27) as currently required by the Mass Media Bureau of the FCC.

Ownership: CBS Corp. (Group Owner).

Began Operation: October 29, 1998. Began analog operations: September 1, 1941. Sold to Westinghouse Broadcasting by Philco Corp. in 1953 (Television Digest, Vol. 9:8, 22); then transferred to NBC in deal approved by FCC December 21, 1955 (Vol. 11:2, 12:3). Transfer from NBC back to Westinghouse under order by FCC approved by FCC February 17, 1965 (Vol. 5:7, 8, 25). Sale to CBS Inc. by Westinghouse approved by FCC August 16, 1995 (Vol. 35:34). Sale to present owner by CBS Inc. approved by FCC May 3, 2000. Ceased analog operations: June 12, 2009.

Personnel:

Michael Colleran, General Manager.

Rich Paleski, Broadcast Operations & Engineering Director.

Karen Gilligan, Sales Director.

Roy Coddington, National Sales Manager.

Susan Schiller, News Director.

Brad Risch, Broadcast Operations Manager.

Kathleen Gorman, Business Manager.

Perry Casciato, Programming Director.

Dominick Nardo, Creative Services & Marketing Director.

Sharon Walz-Kelley, Research Director.

Hilary Hand, Traffic Operations Director.

Joanne Calabria, Communications Director.

KYW-DT BPCDT-20080620ABO GRANTED: 8/11/2008

© 2010 Warren Communications News

Rachel Ferguson, Community Services Manager.

City of License: Philadelphia. **Station DMA:** Philadelphia, PA. **Rank:** 4.

Circulation © 2009 Nielsen. Coverage based on Nielsen study.

GrandTotal	Cable TV Households	Non-cable TV Households	Total TV Households
Estimated Station Totals *	2,824,700	697,600	3,522,300
Average Weekly Circulation (2009)	1,660,205	461,421	2,121,626
Average Daily Circulation (2009)			1,008,470

Station DMA Total	Cable TV Households	Non-cable TV Households	Total TV Households
Estimated Station Totals *	2,223,790	649,450	2,873,240
Average Weekly Circulation (2009)	1,567,506	458,086	2,025,592
Average Daily Circulation (2009)			974,276

Other DMA Total	Cable TV Households	Non-cable TV Households	Total TV Households
Estimated Station Totals *	600,910	48,150	649,060
Average Weekly Circulation (2009)	92,699	3,335	96,034
Average Daily Circulation (2009)			34,194

*Estimated station totals are sums of the Nielsen TV and Cable TV household estimates for each county in which the station registers viewing of more than 5% as per the Nielsen Survey Methods.

WCAU-DT
Ch. 67

Network Service: NBC.

Licensee: NBC Telemundo License Co., 1299 Pennsylvania Ave NW, 11th Fl, c/o NBC Inc., Washington, DC 20004.

Studio: 10 Monument Rd, Bala Cynwyd, PA 19004.

Mailing Address: 10 Monument Rd, Bala Cynwyd, PA 19004.

Phone: 610-668-5510. **Fax:** 610-668-5618.

E-mail: eva.blackwell@nbc.com

Web Site: http://www.nbc10.com

Technical Facilities: Channel No. 67 (788-794 MHz). Authorized power: 759-kw max. visual, aural. Antenna: 1125-ft above av. terrain, 1066-ft. above ground, 1349-ft. above sea level.

Latitude	40°	02'	31"
Longitude	75°	14'	12"

Holds CP for change to channel number 34, 700-kw max. visual, 1313-ft above av. terrain, 1231-ft. above ground, 1523-ft. above sea level; lat. 40° 02' 30", long. 75° 14' 11", BPCDT-20080620AKG.

Transmitter: Domino Lane & Fowler St.

Note: Latitude and longitude coordinates shown are based on the North American Datum of 1927 (NAD 27) as currently required by the Mass Media Bureau of the FCC.

Ownership: NBC Universal (Group Owner).

Began Operation: December 4, 1998. Began analog operations: March 15, 1948. Sale to NBC in exchange for KCNC-TV Denver, CO, license for Ch. 4 Miami, FL, KUTV Salt Lake City, UT & other considerations approved by FCC July 19, 1995 (Television Digest, Vol. 34:29, 35, 48, 52; 35:31). Sale to CBS by Philadelphia Bulletin interests approved by FCC July 23, 1958 (Vol. 13:51; 14:1, 18, 27, 30). Ceased analog operations: June 12, 2009.

Personnel:

Dennis Bianchi, President & General Manager.

Joe Collins, Vice President, Sales.

Chris Blackman, Vice President, News.

Lauren Bacitalupi, Vice President, Creative Services.

Kevin Hungate, Local Sales Manager.

Jim Barger, Engineering & Operations Director.

Tim Cabrey, National Sales Manager.

Judy LaFountaine, National Sales Manager.

Tim O'Sullivan, Chief Engineer.

Greg McNicholas, Finance Director.

Lawana Scales, Program Director.

Joan Erle, Research Director.

Kathy Johnson, Traffic Manager.

WCAU-DT BPCDT-20080620AKG GRANTED: 3/4/2009

© 2010 Warren Communications News

Joanne Wilder, Community Affairs & Public Relations Manager.

City of License: Philadelphia. **Station DMA:** Philadelphia, PA. **Rank:** 4.

Circulation © 2009 Nielsen. Coverage based on Nielsen study.

GrandTotal	Cable TV Households	Non-cable TV Households	Total TV Households
Estimated Station Totals *	3,005,770	653,430	3,659,200
Average Weekly Circulation (2009)	1,618,101	470,872	2,088,973
Average Daily Circulation (2009)			906,166

Station DMA Total	Cable TV Households	Non-cable TV Households	Total TV Households
Estimated Station Totals *	2,223,790	649,450	2,873,240
Average Weekly Circulation (2009)	1,503,248	470,673	1,973,921
Average Daily Circulation (2009)			875,535

Other DMA Total	Cable TV Households	Non-cable TV Households	Total TV Households
Estimated Station Totals *	781,980	3,980	785,960
Average Weekly Circulation (2009)	114,853	199	115,052
Average Daily Circulation (2009)			30,631

*Estimated station totals are sums of the Nielsen TV and Cable TV household estimates for each county in which the station registers viewing of more than 5% as per the Nielsen Survey Methods.

WPHL-DT
Ch. 17

Network Service: MNT.

Licensee: Tribune Television Co., Debtor-In-Possession, 5001 Wynnefield Ave, Philadelphia, PA 19131.

Studio: 5001 Wynnefield Ave., Philadelphia, PA 19131.

Mailing Address: 5001 Wynnefield Ave, Philadelphia, PA 19131.

Phone: 215-878-1700. **Fax:** 215-879-3665.

E-mail: ramara@tribune.com

Web Site: http://myphl17.trb.com/

Technical Facilities: Channel No. 17 (488-494 MHz). Authorized power: 645-kw max. visual, aural. Antenna: 1063-ft above av. terrain, 1056-ft. above ground, 1276-ft. above sea level.

Latitude	40°	02'	30"
Longitude	75°	14'	23"

Note: Latitude and longitude coordinates shown are based on the North American Datum of 1927 (NAD 27) as currently required by the Mass Media Bureau of the FCC.

Ownership: Tribune Broadcasting Co., Debtor-In-Possession (Group Owner).

Began Operation: October 31, 2002. Standard Definition. Station broadcasting digitally on its analog channel allotment. Began analog operations: July 17, 1960. Left air August 1, 1962. Resumed operation September 17, 1965. Sale to U.S. Communications (AVC Corp.) approved by FCC December 6, 1967. Sale to Providence Journal by AVC Corp. approved by FCC November 16, 1978. Sale to Taft Broadcasting Partners LP by Providence Journal approved by FCC October 23, 1987. Transfer of control to present owner from Taft Broadcasting Partners LP approved by FCC April 17, 1992. Transfer of control from public shareholders of the Tribune Co. to Tribune Employee Stock Ownership Plan approved by FCC November 30, 2007. Involuntary assignment to debtor-in-possession status approved by FCC December 24, 2008. Ceased analog operations: June 12, 2009.

Represented (legal): Sidley Austin LLP.

Represented (sales): TeleRep Inc.

Personnel:

Vincent Giannini, Vice President & General Manager.

Patrick Loftus, General Sales Manager.

Josh Nair, Local Sales Manager.

Dave Yost, National Sales Manager.

Mike Hort, Engineering Manager.

David Mayersky, Controller.

Jackie Green, Programming & Community Affairs Coordinator.

Sabrina Andrews, Promotion Manager.

Wendy Kaiser, Creative Services Director.

Denise Jeitles, Traffic Manager.

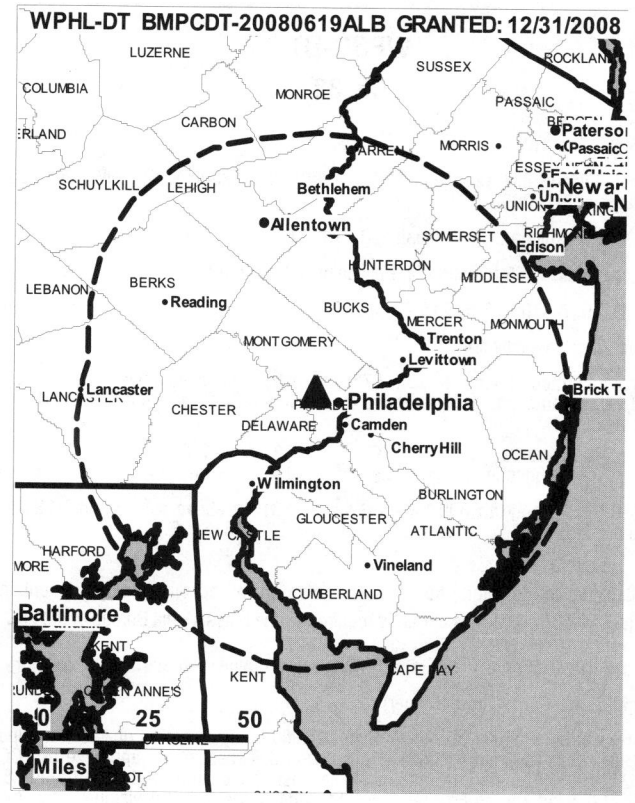

© 2010 Warren Communications News

City of License: Philadelphia. **Station DMA:** Philadelphia, PA. **Rank:** 4.

Circulation © 2009 Nielsen. Coverage based on Nielsen study.

GrandTotal	Cable TV Households	Non-cable TV Households	Total TV Households
Estimated Station Totals *	3,206,510	653,430	3,859,940
Average Weekly Circulation (2009)	1,117,993	347,814	1,465,807
Average Daily Circulation (2009)			520,809

Station DMA Total	Cable TV Households	Non-cable TV Households	Total TV Households
Estimated Station Totals *	2,223,790	649,450	2,873,240
Average Weekly Circulation (2009)	1,003,357	347,615	1,350,972
Average Daily Circulation (2009)			498,120

Other DMA Total	Cable TV Households	Non-cable TV Households	Total TV Households
Estimated Station Totals *	982,720	3,980	986,700
Average Weekly Circulation (2009)	114,636	199	114,835
Average Daily Circulation (2009)			22,689

*Estimated station totals are sums of the Nielsen TV and Cable TV household estimates for each county in which the station registers viewing of more than 5% as per the Nielsen Survey Methods.

WPSG-DT
Ch. 32

Network Service: CW.

Licensee: Philadelphia Television Station WPSG Inc., 2000 K St. NW, Ste 725, Washington, DC 20006.

Studio: 1555 Hamilton St, Philadelphia, PA 19130.

Mailing Address: 1555 Hamilton St, Philadelphia, PA 19130.

Phone: 215-977-5700. **Fax:** 215-677-5789.

Web Site: http://cwphilly.com/

Technical Facilities: Channel No. 32 (578-584 MHz). Authorized power: 25-kw max. visual, aural. Antenna: 1299-ft above av. terrain, 1224-ft. above ground, 1516-ft. above sea level.

Latitude	40°	02'	30"
Longitude	75°	14'	11"

Holds CP for change to 800-kw max. visual, 1312-ft above av. terrain, 1234-ft. above ground, 1526-ft. above sea level; BPCDT-20080616ABE.

Note: Latitude and longitude coordinates shown are based on the North American Datum of 1927 (NAD 27) as currently required by the Mass Media Bureau of the FCC.

Satellite Earth Stations: Prodelin, 4.5-meter; Microdyne, 7-meter.

Ownership: CBS Corp. (Group Owner).

Began Operation: October 30, 2002. High Definition. Began analog operations: June 15, 1981. Sale to Grant Broadcasting by Leon S. Gross, et al., approved by FCC April 24, 1985. Transfer to Combined Broadcasting Inc. approved by FCC June 8, 1988. Proposed sale to Fox Television Stations dismissed (Television Digest Vol. 33:34; 34:10). Sale to present owner approved by FCC August 24, 1995 (Vol. 34:43, 35:20). Ceased analog operations: June 12, 2009.

Represented (sales): Katz Media Group.

Personnel:

Michael Colleran, President & General Manager.

Robin Magyar, Station Manager.

John Braun, General Sales Manager.

Mitch Klein, Local Sales Manager.

Patrick Furlong, National Sales Manager.

Marc Musgrove, Chief Engineer.

Kathleen Gorman, Business Manager.

Perry Casciato, Program Director.

Ed Marshall, Marketing Director.

Leanne Hinkle, Promotion Director.

Sharon Walz-Zelley, Research Director.

Todd Ballantyne, Creative Services Director.

Hilary Hand, Traffic Operations Director.

© 2010 Warren Communications News

City of License: Philadelphia. **Station DMA:** Philadelphia, PA. **Rank:** 4.

Circulation © 2009 Nielsen. Coverage based on Nielsen study.

GrandTotal	Cable TV Households	Non-cable TV Households	Total TV Households
Estimated Station Totals *	2,349,530	649,450	2,998,980
Average Weekly Circulation (2009)	953,766	297,475	1,251,241
Average Daily Circulation (2009)			398,238

Station DMA Total	Cable TV Households	Non-cable TV Households	Total TV Households
Estimated Station Totals *	2,223,790	649,450	2,873,240
Average Weekly Circulation (2009)	939,668	297,475	1,237,143
Average Daily Circulation (2009)			395,896

Other DMA Total	Cable TV Households	Non-cable TV Households	Total TV Households
Estimated Station Totals *	125,740	0	125,740
Average Weekly Circulation (2009)	14,098	0	14,098
Average Daily Circulation (2009)			2,342

*Estimated station totals are sums of the Nielsen TV and Cable TV household estimates for each county in which the station registers viewing of more than 5% as per the Nielsen Survey Methods.

WPVI-DT
Ch. 6

Network Service: ABC.

Grantee: ABC Inc., 77 W 66th St, 17th Fl, New York, NY 10023-6201.

Studio: 4100 City Ave., Philadelphia, PA 19131.

Mailing Address: 4100 City Ave, Philadelphia, PA 19131.

Phone: 215-878-9700. **Fax:** 215-581-4515.

E-mail: Bob.Liga@abc.com

Web Site: http://www.6abc.com

Technical Facilities: Channel No. 6 (82-88 MHz). Authorized power: 7.65-kw visual, aural. Antenna: 1089-ft above av. terrain, 1073-ft. above ground, 1325-ft. above sea level.

Latitude	40°	02'	39"
Longitude	75°	14'	26"

Requests CP for change to 30.2-kw visual; BPCDT-20090617ADQ.

Note: Latitude and longitude coordinates shown are based on the North American Datum of 1927 (NAD 27) as currently required by the Mass Media Bureau of the FCC.

Ownership: Disney Enterprises Inc. (Group Owner).

Began Operation: November 1, 1998. Standard and High Definition. Station broadcasting digitally on its analog channel allotment. Began analog operations: September 13, 1947. Sale to Capital Cities/ABC Inc. by Triangle Publications approved by FCC February 24, 1971 (Television Digest, Vol. 10:8, 9; 11:9). Sale to present owner by Capital Cities/ABC Inc. approved by FCC February 8, 1996. Ceased analog operations: June 12, 2009.

Personnel:

Bernie Prazenica, President & General Manager.

James Aronow, Vice President & Sales Director.

Carla Carpenter, Vice President & News Director.

Bob Liga, Local Sales Manager.

Dirk Ohley, National Sales Manager.

Tim Gianettino, National Sales Manager.

Hank Volpe, Engineering Director.

Cindy Torres, Business Manager.

Paula McDermott, Marketing Manager.

Terry Belford, Production Manager.

Elliot Cohen, Research Director.

Mike Monsell, Creative Services Director.

Stacy Silver, Traffic Manager.

Linda Munich, Public Affairs Director.

© 2010 Warren Communications News

City of License: Philadelphia. **Station DMA:** Philadelphia, PA. **Rank:** 4.

Circulation © 2009 Nielsen. Coverage based on Nielsen study.

GrandTotal	Cable TV Households	Non-cable TV Households	Total TV Households
Estimated Station Totals *	2,973,110	666,470	3,639,580
Average Weekly Circulation (2009)	1,906,493	488,143	2,394,636
Average Daily Circulation (2009)			1,289,025

Station DMA Total	Cable TV Households	Non-cable TV Households	Total TV Households
Estimated Station Totals *	2,223,790	649,450	2,873,240
Average Weekly Circulation (2009)	1,708,464	487,149	2,195,613
Average Daily Circulation (2009)			1,229,884

Other DMA Total	Cable TV Households	Non-cable TV Households	Total TV Households
Estimated Station Totals *	749,320	17,020	766,340
Average Weekly Circulation (2009)	198,029	994	199,023
Average Daily Circulation (2009)			59,141

*Estimated station totals are sums of the Nielsen TV and Cable TV household estimates for each county in which the station registers viewing of more than 5% as per the Nielsen Survey Methods.

WTXF-DT
Ch. 42

Network Service: FOX.

Licensee: Fox Television Stations Inc., 444 N Capitol St NW, Ste 740, c/o Dianne Smith (News Corp.), Washington, DC 20001.

Studio: 330 Market St., Philadelphia, PA 19106.

Mailing Address: 330 Market St, Philadelphia, PA 19106.

Phone: 215-925-2929. **Fax:** 215-982-5494.

Web Site: http://www.myfoxphilly.com

Technical Facilities: Channel No. 42 (638-644 MHz). Authorized power: 1000-kw max. visual, aural. Antenna: 921-ft above av. terrain, 907-ft. above ground, 1132-ft. above sea level.

Latitude	40°	02'	26"
Longitude	75°	14'	19"

Holds CP for change to 260-kw visual, 1125-ft above av. terrain, 1109-ft. above ground, 1334-ft. above sea level; BMPCDT-20090520AGI.

Requests modification of CP for change to 620-kw max. visual; BMPCDT-20080616AAQ.

Note: Latitude and longitude coordinates shown are based on the North American Datum of 1927 (NAD 27) as currently required by the Mass Media Bureau of the FCC.

Ownership: Fox Television Holdings Inc. (Group Owner).

Began Operation: October 16, 2007. Began analog operations: May 16, 1965. Sale to Taft Broadcasting approved by FCC May 7, 1969 (Television Digest, Vol. 9:21). Sale to TVX Broadcast Group by Taft approved by FCC February 20, 1987 (Vol. 27:9, 14, 15). Sale to Paramount Communications Inc. by TVX Broadcast Group approved by FCC April 22, 1990. Sale to present owner by Viacom International approved by FCC August 14, 1995 (Vol. 34:36, 43, 48, 49, 50; 35:20). Ceased analog operations: June 12, 2009.

Represented (legal): Skadden, Arps, Slate, Meagher & Flom LLP.

Personnel:

Michael Renda, Vice President & General Manager.

Vinnie Manzi, Vice President, Sales.

Steve James, Vice President, Engineering.

Audrey Fish, Vice President, Creative Services.

Bernadette Prudente, Vice President, Finance.

Lisa Oswald, Local Sales Manager.

Joseph Rooney, National Sales Manager.

Kingsley Smith, News Director.

Maria Degnan, Program Supervisor.

George Cummings, Production & Operations Manager.

Merl Wilmore, Traffic Manager.

© 2010 Warren Communications News

City of License: Philadelphia. **Station DMA:** Philadelphia, PA. **Rank:** 4.

Circulation © 2009 Nielsen. Coverage based on Nielsen study.

GrandTotal	Cable TV Households	Non-cable TV Households	Total TV Households
Estimated Station Totals *	2,908,810	653,430	3,562,240
Average Weekly Circulation (2009)	1,611,176	458,003	2,069,179
Average Daily Circulation (2009)			808,908

Station DMA Total	Cable TV Households	Non-cable TV Households	Total TV Households
Estimated Station Totals *	2,223,790	649,450	2,873,240
Average Weekly Circulation (2009)	1,492,952	457,804	1,950,756
Average Daily Circulation (2009)			780,644

Other DMA Total	Cable TV Households	Non-cable TV Households	Total TV Households
Estimated Station Totals *	685,020	3,980	689,000
Average Weekly Circulation (2009)	118,224	199	118,423
Average Daily Circulation (2009)			28,264

*Estimated station totals are sums of the Nielsen TV and Cable TV household estimates for each county in which the station registers viewing of more than 5% as per the Nielsen Survey Methods.

KDKA-DT
Ch. 25

Network Service: CBS.

Licensee: CBS Broadcasting Inc., 2000 K St. NW, Ste 725, Washington, DC 20006.

Studio: One Gateway Center, Pittsburgh, PA 15222.

Mailing Address: One Gateway Center, Pittsburgh, PA 15222.

Phone: 412-575-2200. **Fax:** 412-575-2871.

Web Site: http://www.kdka.com

Technical Facilities: Channel No. 25 (536-542 MHz). Authorized power: 1000-kw max. visual, aural. Antenna: 1020-ft above av. terrain, 656-ft. above ground, 2021-ft. above sea level.

Latitude	40°	29'	38"
Longitude	80°	01'	09"

Note: Latitude and longitude coordinates shown are based on the North American Datum of 1927 (NAD 27) as currently required by the Mass Media Bureau of the FCC.

Ownership: CBS Corp. (Group Owner).

Began Operation: April 7, 2000. Began analog operations: January 11, 1949 as WDTV. Sale to Westinghouse by DuMont Laboratories approved by FCC January 5, 1955 (Television Digest, Vol. 10:49; 11:2). Sale to present owner by CBS Inc. approved by FCC May 3, 2000. Ceased analog operations: June 12, 2009.

Represented (legal): Leventhal, Senter & Lerman PLLC.

Personnel:

Chris Pike, Vice President & General Manager.

Chris Cotugno, General Sales Manager.

Bob Schoeppner, National Sales Manager.

John Verrilli, News Director.

Mark Etzi, Broadcast & Engineering Director.

Tina Beon, Promotion & Marketing Director.

Jamie Meyerson, Production Manager.

Jodi Clave, Traffic Manager.

City of License: Pittsburgh. **Station DMA:** Pittsburgh, PA. **Rank:** 23.

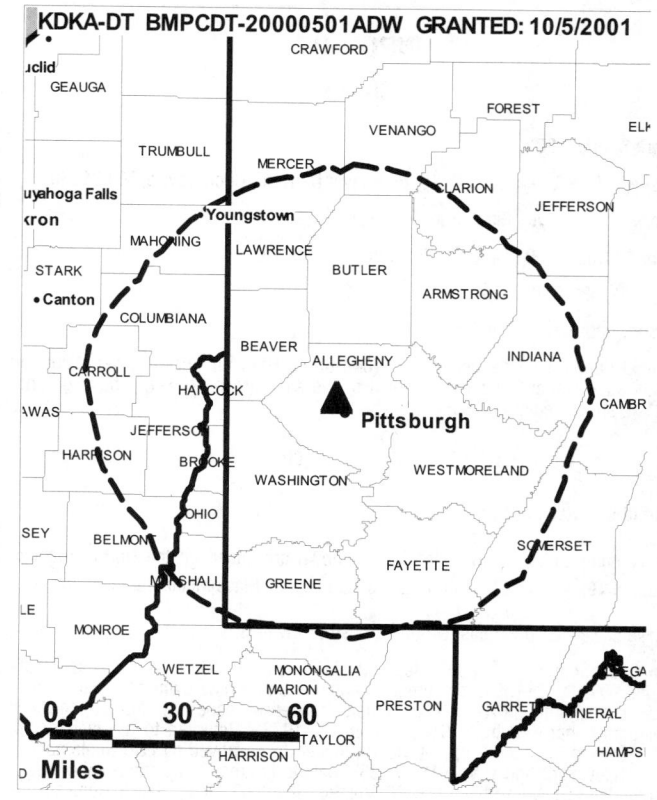

KDKA-DT BMPCDT-20000501ADW GRANTED: 10/5/2001

© 2010 Warren Communications News

Circulation © 2009 Nielsen. Coverage based on Nielsen study.

GrandTotal	Cable TV Households	Non-cable TV Households	Total TV Households
Estimated Station Totals *	1,197,200	395,790	1,592,990
Average Weekly Circulation (2009)	716,908	225,499	942,407
Average Daily Circulation (2009)			501,394

Station DMA Total	Cable TV Households	Non-cable TV Households	Total TV Households
Estimated Station Totals *	853,690	300,710	1,154,400
Average Weekly Circulation (2009)	627,897	215,814	843,711
Average Daily Circulation (2009)			466,511

Other DMA Total	Cable TV Households	Non-cable TV Households	Total TV Households
Estimated Station Totals *	343,510	95,080	438,590
Average Weekly Circulation (2009)	89,011	9,685	98,696
Average Daily Circulation (2009)			34,883

*Estimated station totals are sums of the Nielsen TV and Cable TV household estimates for each county in which the station registers viewing of more than 5% as per the Nielsen Survey Methods.

WPGH-DT
Ch. 43

Network Service: FOX.

Licensee: WPGH Licensee LLC, 10706 Beaver Dam Rd, Cockeysville, MD 21030.

Studio: 750 Ivory Ave., Pittsburgh, PA 15214.

Mailing Address: 750 Ivory Ave, Pittsburgh, PA 15214.

Phone: 412-931-5300. **Fax:** 412-931-8029.

Web Site: http://www.wpgh53.com

Technical Facilities: Channel No. 43 (644-650 MHz). Authorized power: 1000-kw max. visual, aural. Antenna: 1024-ft above av. terrain, 705-ft. above ground, 2021-ft. above sea level.

Latitude	40°	29'	43"
Longitude	80°	00'	18"

Transmitter: 750 Ivory Ave.

Note: Latitude and longitude coordinates shown are based on the North American Datum of 1927 (NAD 27) as currently required by the Mass Media Bureau of the FCC.

Ownership: Sinclair Broadcast Group Inc. (Group Owner).

Began Operation: April 1, 2002. Began analog operations: July 14, 1953 as WKJF-TV, left air July 2, 1954. Resumed operations under new ownership February 1, 1969; left air August 16, 1971. Transfer to Henry Posner Jr. from Receiver in Bankruptcy approved by FCC December 12, 1973. Returned to air January 14, 1974. Sale to Meredith Corp. by Henry Posner Jr. approved by FCC September 8, 1978 (Television Digest, Vol. 18:17, 38). Sale to Lorimar-Telepictures by Meredith approved by FCC November 12, 1986 (Vol. 26:29, 46, 52; 27:2). Sale to Renaissance Communications by Lorimar approved by FCC November 23, 1988 (Vol. 29:3). Sale to present owner by Renaissance approved by FCC June 21, 1991. Ceased analog operations: February 17, 2009.

Represented (sales): Katz Media Group.

Represented (legal): Pillsbury Winthrop Shaw Pittman LLP.

Personnel:

Alan Frank, General Manager.

Jim Lipiano, Sales Director.

Rich Cook, Local Sales Manager.

Tom Yorgen, National Sales Manager.

Kerry Check, Chief Engineer.

Wendy Shust, Business Manager.

Rob DePascale, Program Coordinator.

Dan Zimmerman, Creative Services Director.

Brandy Brueckner, Traffic Manager.

City of License: Pittsburgh. **Station DMA:** Pittsburgh, PA. **Rank:** 23.

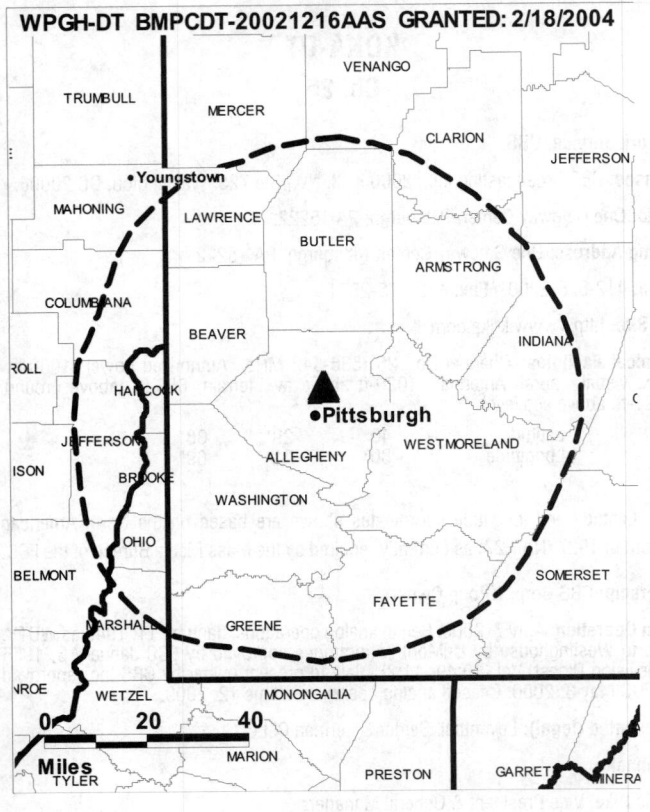

WPGH-DT BMPCDT-20021216AAS GRANTED: 2/18/2004

© 2010 Warren Communications News

Circulation © 2009 Nielsen. Coverage based on Nielsen study.

GrandTotal	Cable TV Households	Non-cable TV Households	Total TV Households
Estimated Station Totals *	974,150	356,140	1,330,290
Average Weekly Circulation (2009)	458,285	152,419	610,704
Average Daily Circulation (2009)			205,726

Station DMA Total	Cable TV Households	Non-cable TV Households	Total TV Households
Estimated Station Totals *	853,690	300,710	1,154,400
Average Weekly Circulation (2009)	432,294	147,484	579,778
Average Daily Circulation (2009)			197,267

Other DMA Total	Cable TV Households	Non-cable TV Households	Total TV Households
Estimated Station Totals *	120,460	55,430	175,890
Average Weekly Circulation (2009)	25,991	4,935	30,926
Average Daily Circulation (2009)			8,459

*Estimated station totals are sums of the Nielsen TV and Cable TV household estimates for each county in which the station registers viewing of more than 5% as per the Nielsen Survey Methods.

WPMY-DT
Ch. 42

Network Service: MNT.

Licensee: WCWB Licensee LLC, 2300 N St. NW, c/o Pillsbury Winthrop Shaw Pittman LLP, Attn.: Kathryn Schmeltzer, Washington, DC 20037-1128.

Studio: 750 Ivory Ave., Pittsburgh, PA 15214.

Mailing Address: 750 Ivory Ave, Pittsburgh, PA 15214.

Phone: 412-931-5300. **Fax:** 412-931-4284.

Web Site: http://www.mypittsburghtv.com/

Technical Facilities: Channel No. 42 (638-644 MHz). Authorized power: 1000-kw max. visual, aural. Antenna: 1033-ft above av. terrain, 711-ft. above ground, 2030-ft. above sea level.

Latitude	40°	29'	43"
Longitude	80°	00'	17"

Note: Latitude and longitude coordinates shown are based on the North American Datum of 1927 (NAD 27) as currently required by the Mass Media Bureau of the FCC.

Ownership: Sinclair Broadcast Group Inc. (Group Owner).

Began Operation: June 7, 2006. Began analog operations: September 29, 1978. Sale to present owner by Glencairn Ltd. Broadcat Properties approved by FCC December 10, 2001 (Television Digest, Vol. 41:38). Sale to Glencairn Ltd. Broadcast Properties by Commercial Radio Institute approved by FCC June 21, 1991. Ceased analog operations: February 17, 2009.

Represented (sales): Katz Media Group.

Represented (legal): Pillsbury Winthrop Shaw Pittman LLP.

Personnel:

Alan Frank, General Manager.

Jim Lipiano, Sales Director.

Rich Cook, Local Sales Manager.

Tom Yorgen, National Sales Manager.

Kerry Check, Chief Engineer.

Wendy Shust, Regional Controller.

Rob DePascale, Program Coordinator.

Dan Zimmerman, Creative Services Manager.

Brandy Brueckner, Traffic Manager.

City of License: Pittsburgh. **Station DMA:** Pittsburgh, PA. **Rank:** 23.

WPMY-DT BMPCDT-20000428ABY GRANTED: 5/28/2004

© 2010 Warren Communications News

Circulation © 2009 Nielsen. Coverage based on Nielsen study.

GrandTotal	Cable TV Households	Non-cable TV Households	Total TV Households
Estimated Station Totals *	936,350	318,070	1,254,420
Average Weekly Circulation (2009)	135,698	50,650	186,348
Average Daily Circulation (2009)			58,159

Station DMA Total	Cable TV Households	Non-cable TV Households	Total TV Households
Estimated Station Totals *	846,550	300,710	1,147,260
Average Weekly Circulation (2009)	128,066	49,438	177,504
Average Daily Circulation (2009)			56,592

Other DMA Total	Cable TV Households	Non-cable TV Households	Total TV Households
Estimated Station Totals *	89,800	17,360	107,160
Average Weekly Circulation (2009)	7,632	1,212	8,844
Average Daily Circulation (2009)			1,567

*Estimated station totals are sums of the Nielsen TV and Cable TV household estimates for each county in which the station registers viewing of more than 5% as per the Nielsen Survey Methods.

WPXI-DT
Ch. 48

Network Service: NBC, IND.

Licensee: WPXI Inc., 6205 Peachtree Dunwoody Rd, Atlanta, GA 30328.

Studio: 4145 Evergreen Rd, Pittsburgh, PA 15214.

Mailing Address: 4145 Evergreen Rd, Pittsburgh, PA 15214.

Phone: 412-237-1100. **Fax:** 412-237-1333.

Web Site: http://www.wpxi.com

Technical Facilities: Channel No. 48 (674-680 MHz). Authorized power: 1000-kw max. visual, aural. Antenna: 948-ft above av. terrain, 764-ft. above ground, 1965-ft. above sea level.

Latitude	40°	27'	48"
Longitude	80°	00'	16"

Note: Latitude and longitude coordinates shown are based on the North American Datum of 1927 (NAD 27) as currently required by the Mass Media Bureau of the FCC.

Ownership: Cox Enterprises Inc. (Group Owner).

Began Operation: December 7, 2000. High Definition. Began analog operations: September 1, 1957. Sale to present owner by co-owners Pittsburgh Post-Gazette & Sun Telegraph and H. Kenneth Brennen & family approved by FCC November 20, 1964 (Television Digest, Vol. 4:36, 47). Ceased analog operations: June 12, 2009.

Represented (sales): TeleRep Inc.

Represented (legal): Dow Lohnes PLLC.

Personnel:

Ray Carter, Vice President & General Manager.

Darren Moore, Local Sales Manager.

Sandy Merritt, Local Sales Manager.

Phil Johnson, National Sales Manager.

Darryl Griffin, National Sales Manager.

Corrie Harding, News Director.

Annette Parks, Engineering Director.

Ann Glausser, Controller.

Mark Barash, Program Director.

Dave Taynor, Production Manager.

Karen Lah, Creative Services Director.

Dawn Wojtaszek, Traffic Manager.

City of License: Pittsburgh. **Station DMA:** Pittsburgh, PA. **Rank:** 23.

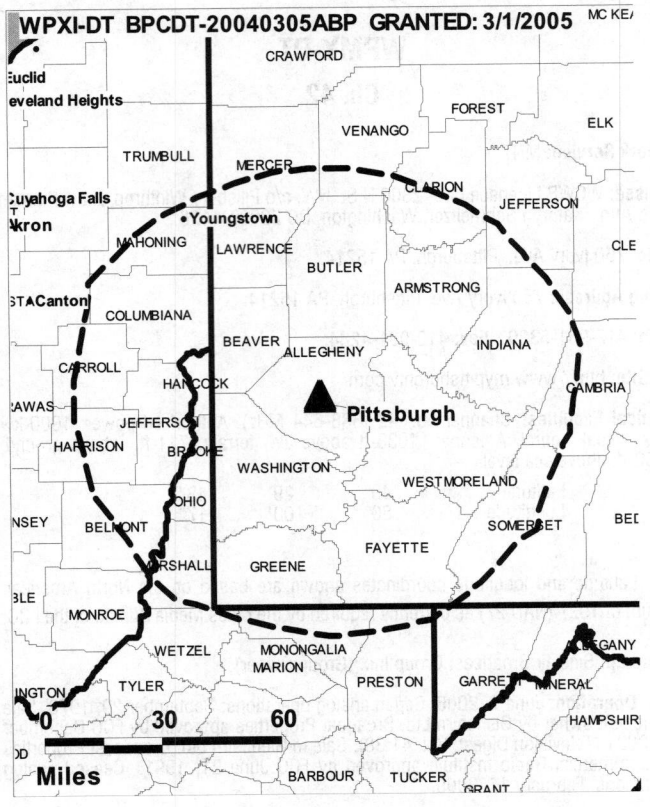

WPXI-DT BPCDT-20040305ABP GRANTED: 3/1/2005

© 2010 Warren Communications News

Circulation © 2009 Nielsen. Coverage based on Nielsen study.

GrandTotal	Cable TV Households	Non-cable TV Households	Total TV Households
Estimated Station Totals *	1,110,540	395,790	1,506,330
Average Weekly Circulation (2009)	645,522	226,439	871,961
Average Daily Circulation (2009)			440,032

Station DMA Total	Cable TV Households	Non-cable TV Households	Total TV Households
Estimated Station Totals *	853,690	300,710	1,154,400
Average Weekly Circulation (2009)	591,276	216,411	807,687
Average Daily Circulation (2009)			417,811

Other DMA Total	Cable TV Households	Non-cable TV Households	Total TV Households
Estimated Station Totals *	256,850	95,080	351,930
Average Weekly Circulation (2009)	54,246	10,028	64,274
Average Daily Circulation (2009)			22,221

*Estimated station totals are sums of the Nielsen TV and Cable TV household estimates for each county in which the station registers viewing of more than 5% as per the Nielsen Survey Methods.

WQEX-DT
Ch. 26

Network Service: IND.

Licensee: WQED Multimedia, 4802 5th Ave, Pittsburgh, PA 15213.

Studio: 4802 5th Ave., Pittsburgh, PA 15213.

Mailing Address: 4802 5th Ave, Pittsburgh, PA 15213.

Phone: 412-622-1300. **Fax:** 412-622-1488.

Web Site: http://www.wqed.org

Technical Facilities: Channel No. 26 (542-548 MHz). Authorized power: 50-kw max. visual, aural. Antenna: 699-ft above av. terrain, 545-ft. above ground, 1709-ft. above sea level.

Latitude	40°	26'	46"
Longitude	79°	57'	51"

Holds CP for change to channel number 38, 500-kw visual; BMPCDT-20080620AAM.

Note: Latitude and longitude coordinates shown are based on the North American Datum of 1927 (NAD 27) as currently required by the Mass Media Bureau of the FCC.

Ownership: WQED Multimedia.

Began Operation: August 1, 2004. Began analog operations: March 20, 1959. Ceased analog operations: February 17, 2009.

Represented (legal): Leventhal, Senter & Lerman PLLC.

Personnel:

Deborah Acklin, Executive Vice President & General Manager.

Lilli Mosco, Vice President, Membership & Development.

Dorothy Frank, Vice President, Sales & Underwriting.

Betsy Benson, Vice President, Publishing.

George Hazimanolis, Senior Director, Corporate Communications.

Kate St. John, Information Technology Director.

WQEX-DT BMPCDT-20080620AAM GRANTED: 7/16/2008

© 2010 Warren Communications News

Keyola Panza, Distribution & Client Services Director.

City of License: Pittsburgh. **Station DMA:** Pittsburgh, PA. **Rank:** 23.

Nielsen Data: Not available.

WTAE-DT
Ch. 51

Network Service: ABC.

Licensee: WTAE Hearst-Argyle Television Inc., PO Box 1800, c/o Brooks, Pierce et al., Raleigh, NC 27602.

Studio: 400 Ardmore Blvd., Pittsburgh, PA 15221.

Mailing Address: 400 Ardmore Blvd, Pittsburgh, PA 15221.

Phone: 412-242-4300. **Fax:** 412-244-4628.

Web Site: http://www.thepittsburghchannel.com

Technical Facilities: Channel No. 51 (692-698 MHz). Authorized power: 1000-kw max. visual, aural. Antenna: 896-ft above av. terrain, 942-ft. above ground, 1926-ft. above sea level.

Latitude	40°	16'	49"
Longitude	79°	48'	11"

Note: Latitude and longitude coordinates shown are based on the North American Datum of 1927 (NAD 27) as currently required by the Mass Media Bureau of the FCC.

Ownership: Hearst-Argyle Television Inc. (Group Owner).

Began Operation: February 1, 1999. High Definition. Began analog operations: September 14, 1958. Hearst acquired 100% control after its purchase of 50% from Earl F. Reed and Irwin D. Wolf, as trustees for a stockholders group. Purchase approved by FCC August 1, 1962. Merger with Argyle Television Inc. to form present owner approved by FCC June 2, 1997. Hearst-Argyle received approval from the FCC May 26, 2009 to become privately owned by The Hearst Corp. Ceased analog operations: June 12, 2009.

Represented (legal): Brooks, Pierce, McLendon, Humphrey & Leonard LLP.

Represented (sales): Eagle Television Sales.

Personnel:

Rick Henry, President & General Manager.

Robert Bee, General Sales Manager.

Tim Devito, Local Sales Manager.

Cindy DeLuca, Local Sales Manager.

Ryan Raughter, National Sales Manager.

Bob Longo, News Director.

Dave Kasperek, Engineering Director.

Kurt Haase, Assistant Chief Engineer.

Maria Zabarella, Business Manager.

Leslie Wojdowski, Marketing Director.

Cindy DeLuca, Business Development Director.

Tammy Laughlin, Production Manager.

Sherry Carpenter, Creative Services Director.

Lou Ann Russell, Traffic Manager.

WTAE-DT BPCDT-20000421AAP GRANTED: 4/23/2004

© 2010 Warren Communications News

City of License: Pittsburgh. **Station DMA:** Pittsburgh, PA. **Rank:** 23.

Circulation © 2009 Nielsen. Coverage based on Nielsen study.

GrandTotal	Cable TV Households	Non-cable TV Households	Total TV Households
Estimated Station Totals *	1,193,010	422,620	1,615,630
Average Weekly Circulation (2009)	716,593	219,432	936,025
Average Daily Circulation (2009)			465,482

Station DMA Total	Cable TV Households	Non-cable TV Households	Total TV Households
Estimated Station Totals *	853,690	300,710	1,154,400
Average Weekly Circulation (2009)	593,623	207,190	800,813
Average Daily Circulation (2009)			418,646

Other DMA Total	Cable TV Households	Non-cable TV Households	Total TV Households
Estimated Station Totals *	339,320	121,910	461,230
Average Weekly Circulation (2009)	122,970	12,242	135,212
Average Daily Circulation (2009)			46,836

*Estimated station totals are sums of the Nielsen TV and Cable TV household estimates for each county in which the station registers viewing of more than 5% as per the Nielsen Survey Methods.

WTVE-DT
Ch. 25

Network Service: IND.

Licensee: WTVE License Co. LLC, 800 Westchester Ave, Ste S-640, Rye Brook, NY 10573.

Studio: 1729 N. 11th St., Reading, PA 19604.

Mailing Address: 1729 N. 11th St, Reading, PA 19604.

Phone: 610-921-9181. **Fax:** 610-921-9139.

Web Site: http://www.wtve.com

Technical Facilities: Channel No. 25 (536-542 MHz). Authorized power: 0.63-kw max. visual, aural. Antenna: 718-ft above av. terrain, 80-ft. above ground, 1180-ft. above sea level.

Latitude	40°	21'	15"
Longitude	75°	53'	56"

Holds CP for change to 126-kw max. visual, 1241-ft above av. terrain, 1163-ft. above ground, 1455-ft. above sea level; lat. 40° 02' 29.56", long. 75° 14' 12.89", BMPCDT-20081027ACR.

Note: Latitude and longitude coordinates shown are based on the North American Datum of 1927 (NAD 27) as currently required by the Mass Media Bureau of the FCC.

Ownership: WRNN-TV Associates LP (Group Owner).

Began Operation: March 23, 2004. Began analog operations: May 4, 1980. Sale to present owner by Reading Broadcasting Inc., Debtor-In-Possession approved by FCC May 12, 2008. Involuntary transfer of control by Reading Broadcasting Inc., Debtor-In-Possession to George L. Miller, Trustee from company shareholders approved by FCC January 24, 2007. Involuntary transfer of control by Reading Broadcasting Inc. to Reading Broadcasting Inc., Debtor-In-Possession approved by FCC November 18, 2005. Ceased analog operations: November 24, 2008.

Represented (engineering): du Treil, Lundin & Rackley Inc.

Represented (legal): Covington & Burling.

Personnel:

George Mattmiller, General Manager & Sales Manager.

Kim Bradley, Program & Production Manager.

Chris Weyandt, Traffic Manager.

City of License: Reading. **Station DMA:** Philadelphia, PA. **Rank:** 4.

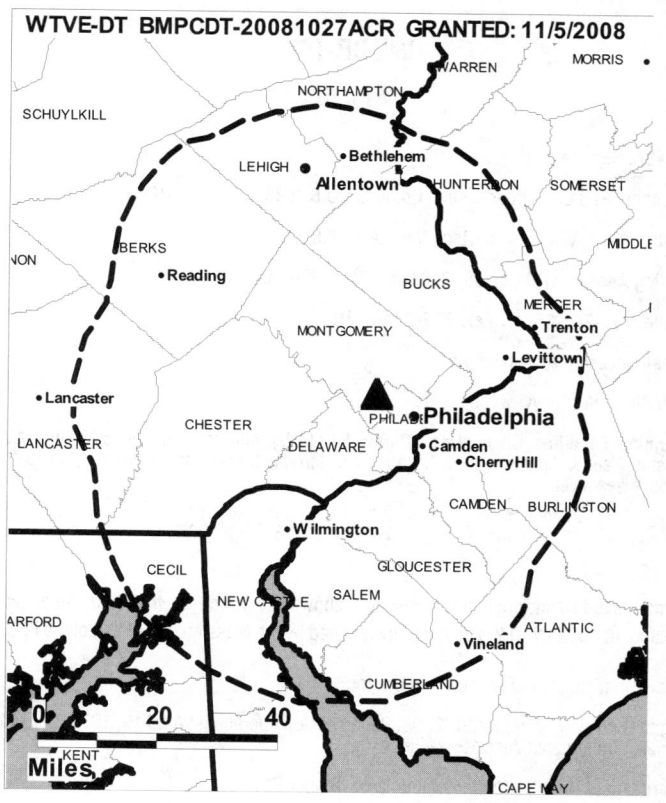

© 2010 Warren Communications News

Circulation © 2009 Nielsen. Coverage based on Nielsen study.

GrandTotal	Cable TV Households	Non-cable TV Households	Total TV Households
Estimated Station Totals *	0	48,300	48,300
Average Weekly Circulation (2009)	0	2,845	2,845
Average Daily Circulation (2009)			190

Station DMA Total	Cable TV Households	Non-cable TV Households	Total TV Households
Estimated Station Totals *	0	48,300	48,300
Average Weekly Circulation (2009)	0	2,845	2,845
Average Daily Circulation (2009)			190

*Estimated station totals are sums of the Nielsen TV and Cable TV household estimates for each county in which the station registers viewing of more than 5% as per the Nielsen Survey Methods.

WGCB-DT
Ch. 30

Network Service: IND.

Licensee: Red Lion Broadcasting Co. Inc., PO Box 88, Red Lion, PA 17356-0088.

Studio: 2900 Windsor Rd., Red Lion, PA 17356.

Mailing Address: PO Box 88, Red Lion, PA 17356-0088.

Phone: 717-246-1681. **Fax:** 717-244-9316.

E-mail: jpeeling@wgcbtv.com

Web Site: http://www.wgcbtv.com

Technical Facilities: Channel No. 30 (566-572 MHz). Authorized power: 500-kw max. visual, aural. Antenna: 572-ft above av. terrain, 299-ft. above ground, 1183-ft. above sea level.

Latitude	39°	54'	18"
Longitude	76°	35'	00"

Note: Latitude and longitude coordinates shown are based on the North American Datum of 1927 (NAD 27) as currently required by the Mass Media Bureau of the FCC.

Ownership: Red Lion Broadcasting Co. Inc.

Began Operation: October 11, 2005. Began analog operations: April 19, 1979. Ceased analog operations: June 12, 2009.

Represented (legal): Booth Freret Imlay & Tepper PC.

Personnel:

John H. Norris, President & General Manager.

Anne Norris, Vice President.

Gordon Moul, National Sales Manager.

Donald Horst, Chief Engineer.

John Peeling, Program Director.

Jerry Jacobs, Marketing Director.

George Montgomery, Production Manager.

City of License: Red Lion. **Station DMA:** Harrisburg-Lancaster-Lebanon-York, PA.

Rank: 39.

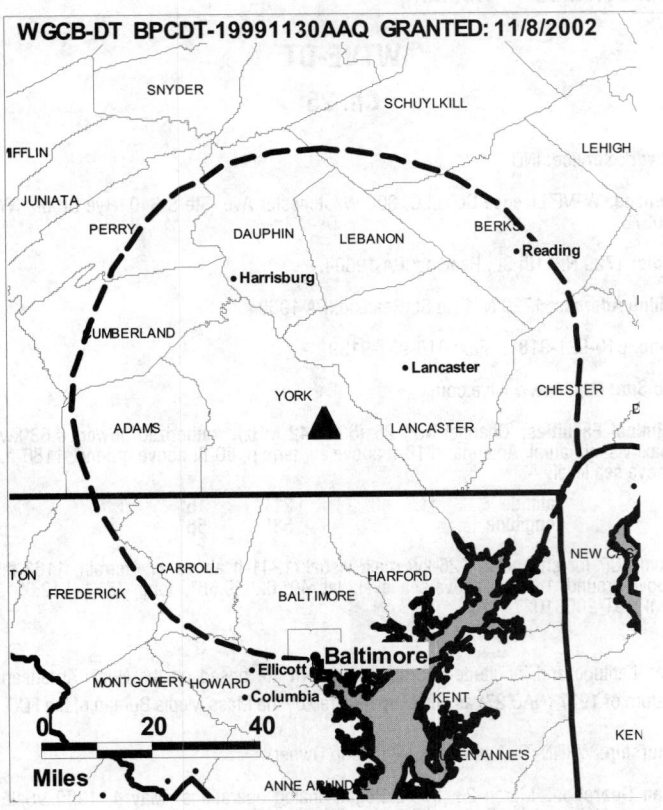

WGCB-DT BPCDT-19991130AAQ GRANTED: 11/8/2002

© 2010 Warren Communications News

Circulation © 2009 Nielsen. Coverage based on Nielsen study.

GrandTotal	Cable TV Households	Non-cable TV Households	Total TV Households
Estimated Station Totals *	172,100	119,000	291,100
Average Weekly Circulation (2009)	12,239	8,894	21,133
Average Daily Circulation (2009)			6,419

Station DMA Total	Cable TV Households	Non-cable TV Households	Total TV Households
Estimated Station Totals *	172,100	119,000	291,100
Average Weekly Circulation (2009)	12,239	8,894	21,133
Average Daily Circulation (2009)			6,419

*Estimated station totals are sums of the Nielsen TV and Cable TV household estimates for each county in which the station registers viewing of more than 5% as per the Nielsen Survey Methods.

WNEP-DT
Ch. 49

Network Service: ABC.

Licensee: Local TV Pennsylvania License LLC, 1717 Dixie Hwy, Ste 650, Fort Wright, KY 41011.

Studio: 16 Montage Mountain Rd., Moosic, PA 18507.

Mailing Address: 16 Montage Mountain Rd, Moosic, PA 18507.

Phone: 570-346-7474; 800-982-4374. **Fax:** 570-347-0359.

Web Site: http://www.wnep.com/

Technical Facilities: Channel No. 49 (680-686 MHz). Authorized power: 100-kw max. visual, aural. Antenna: 1660-ft above av. terrain, 827-ft. above ground, 2100-ft. above sea level.

Latitude	41°	11'	00"
Longitude	75°	52'	10"

Holds CP for change to channel number 50, 500-kw visual, 1696-ft above av. terrain, 817-ft. above ground, 2953-ft. above sea level; lat. 41° 10' 57", long. 75° 52' 15", BPCDT-20090311AAG.

Transmitter: 300-ft. from present WNEP-TV site.

Note: Latitude and longitude coordinates shown are based on the North American Datum of 1927 (NAD 27) as currently required by the Mass Media Bureau of the FCC.

Satellite Earth Stations: Transmitter Comark/Harris; Prodelin, 4-meter; Scientific-Atlanta, 5-meter; Scientific-Atlanta, 11-meter; Standard Communications, Scientific-Atlanta receivers.

Ownership: Local TV Holdings LLC (Group Owner).

Began Operation: May 8, 2002. Standard and High Definition. Began analog operations: February 9, 1954. Sale to present owner by The New York Times Co. approved by FCC March 9, 2007. Sale to The New York Times Co. by NEP Communications approved by FCC October 29, 1985. Sale to NEP by Taft Broadcasting approved by FCC October 30, 1973. Sale to Taft by Transcontinent Television Corp.'s subsidiary, Northeastern Pennsylvania Broadcasting Inc., approved by FCC February 19, 1964. Merger & transfer of WARM-TV, Scranton (Ch. 16) and WILK-TV, Wilkes-Barre, PA (Ch. 34) into Northeastern Pennsylvania Broadcasting Inc. approved by FCC February 12, 1958. Ceased analog operations: February 17, 2009.

Represented (legal): Dow Lohnes PLLC.

Represented (sales): Katz Media Group.

Personnel:

Chuck Morgan, President & General Manager.

Ed Hart, Local Sales Manager.

Mike Last, Sales Manager.

Mike Morkavage, Chief Engineer.

Erik Farmer, Marketing & Research Director.

Laurie LeMaster, Promotion Director.

Dave Lewandoski, Production Manager.

Ann Oliver, Traffic Manager.

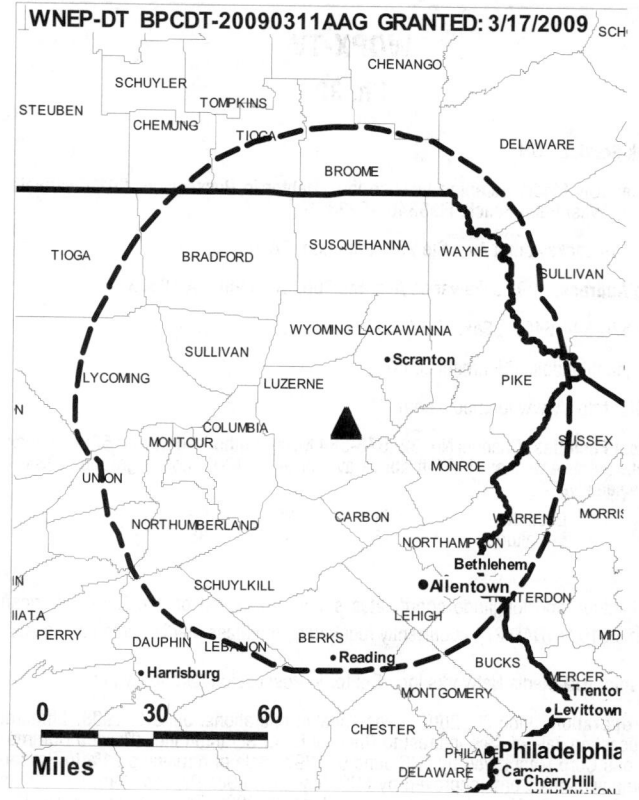

© 2010 Warren Communications News

Debbie Drechin, Program Director.

City of License: Scranton. **Station DMA:** Wilkes Barre-Scranton, PA. **Rank:** 54.

Circulation © 2009 Nielsen. Coverage based on Nielsen study.

GrandTotal	Cable TV Households	Non-cable TV Households	Total TV Households
Estimated Station Totals *	620,730	218,400	839,130
Average Weekly Circulation (2009)	354,663	150,087	504,750
Average Daily Circulation (2009)			302,806

Station DMA Total	Cable TV Households	Non-cable TV Households	Total TV Households
Estimated Station Totals *	379,400	212,650	592,050
Average Weekly Circulation (2009)	304,817	149,725	454,542
Average Daily Circulation (2009)			291,133

Other DMA Total	Cable TV Households	Non-cable TV Households	Total TV Households
Estimated Station Totals *	241,330	5,750	247,080
Average Weekly Circulation (2009)	49,846	362	50,208
Average Daily Circulation (2009)			11,673

*Estimated station totals are sums of the Nielsen TV and Cable TV household estimates for each county in which the station registers viewing of more than 5% as per the Nielsen Survey Methods.

WQPX-TV
Ch. 32

Network Service: ION.

Licensee: ION Media Scranton License Inc., Debtor in Possession, 601 Clearwater Park Rd, West Palm Beach, FL 33401-6233.

Studio: 409 Lackawanna Ave, Ste 700, Scranton, PA 18503.

Mailing Address: 409 Lackawanna Ave, Ste 700, Scranton, PA 18503.

Phone: 570-344-6400. **Fax:** 570-344-3303.

E-mail: jeanbiondollo@ionmedia.com

Web Site: http://www.ionmedia.com

Technical Facilities: Channel No. 32 (578-584 MHz). Authorized power: 528-kw max. visual, aural. Antenna: 1161-ft above av. terrain, 248-ft. above ground, 2338-ft. above sea level.

Latitude	41°	26'	06"
Longitude	75°	43'	35"

Note: Latitude and longitude coordinates shown are based on the North American Datum of 1927 (NAD 27) as currently required by the Mass Media Bureau of the FCC.

Ownership: ION Media Networks Inc., Debtor in Possession (Group Owner).

Began Operation: June 29, 2006. Began analog operations: June 1, 1998. Ehrhardt Broadcasting sale of 49% interest to Channel 64 of Scranton Inc. (Paxson Communications Corp.) approved by FCC June 9, 1997. Sale of remaining 51% to Paxson Communications Corp. approved by FCC July 31, 1998. Paxson Communications Corp. became ION Media Networks Inc. on June 26, 2006. Transfer of control by ION Media Networks Inc. from Paxson Management Corp. & Lowell W. Paxson to CIG Media LLC approved by FCC December 31, 2007. Involuntary assignment to debtor in possession status approved by FCC June 5, 2009. Ceased analog operations: June 12, 2009.

Represented (legal): Dow Lohnes PLLC.

Represented (sales): Katz Media Group.

Represented (engineering): du Treil, Lundin & Rackley Inc.

Personnel:

Regina Lanzo, Station Operations Manager.

Robert Andrade, Chief Engineer.

Jean Biondollo, Traffic Manager.

City of License: Scranton. **Station DMA:** Wilkes Barre-Scranton, PA. **Rank:** 54.

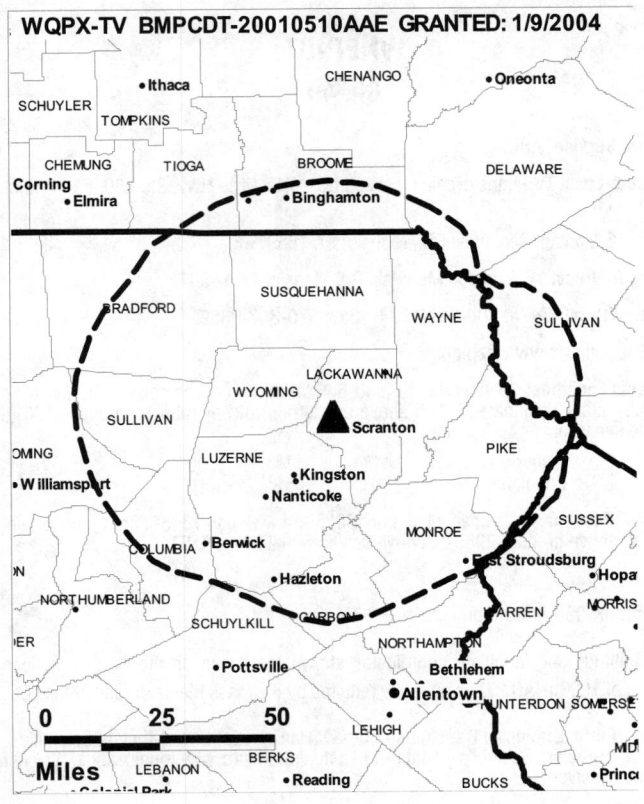

WQPX-TV BMPCDT-20010510AAE GRANTED: 1/9/2004

© 2010 Warren Communications News

Circulation © 2009 Nielsen. Coverage based on Nielsen study.

GrandTotal	Cable TV Households	Non-cable TV Households	Total TV Households
Estimated Station Totals *	322,840	12,340	335,180
Average Weekly Circulation (2009)	21,956	623	22,579
Average Daily Circulation (2009)			3,619

Station DMA Total	Cable TV Households	Non-cable TV Households	Total TV Households
Estimated Station Totals *	322,840	12,340	335,180
Average Weekly Circulation (2009)	21,956	623	22,579
Average Daily Circulation (2009)			3,619

*Estimated station totals are sums of the Nielsen TV and Cable TV household estimates for each county in which the station registers viewing of more than 5% as per the Nielsen Survey Methods.

WSWB-DT
Ch. 31

Network Service: CW.

Licensee: MPS Media of Scranton License LLC, 1181 Hwy 315, Wilkes-Barre, PA 18702.

Studio: 1181 Hwy. 315, Plains, PA 18702.

Mailing Address: 1181 Hwy. 315, Plains, PA 18702.

Phone: 570-970-3800; 570-970-5600. **Fax:** 570-970-5604.

Web Site: http://www.myfoxnepa.com

Technical Facilities: Channel No. 31 (572-578 MHz). Authorized power: 100-kw max. visual, aural. Antenna: 1155-ft above av. terrain, 259-ft. above ground, 2320-ft. above sea level.

Latitude	41°	26'	09"
Longitude	75°	43'	46"

Transmitter: 0.75-mi. NW of Community Dr. & Beacon Dr. intersection.

Note: Latitude and longitude coordinates shown are based on the North American Datum of 1927 (NAD 27) as currently required by the Mass Media Bureau of the FCC.

Ownership: Eugene J. Brown (Group Owner).

Began Operation: August 18, 2006. Began analog operations: June 6, 1985. Sale to present owner by Mystic Television Broadcast Group Inc. approved by FCC January 30, 2007. Competing sale to Bluenose Television of Scranton LLC dismissed by FCC January 24, 2007. Sale to Mystic Television Broadcast Group Inc. by KB Prime Media LLC approved by FCC October 18, 2005. Pegasus Satellite Communications Inc. amended its application making Mystic Television assignee. Ceased analog operations: December 8, 2008.

Represented (sales): Petry Media Corp.

Represented (legal): Fletcher, Heald & Hildreth PLC.

Represented (engineering): du Treil, Lundin & Rackley Inc.

Personnel:

Aldo Cardoni, General Manager.

Jon Cadman, Station Manager.

Dan Mecca, National Sales Director.

Rich Chofey, Chief Engineer.

Marianne Mustu, Business Manager.

Linda Greenwald, Program Director.

Steve Phillips, Creative Services Director.

Becky Sinke, Production Manager.

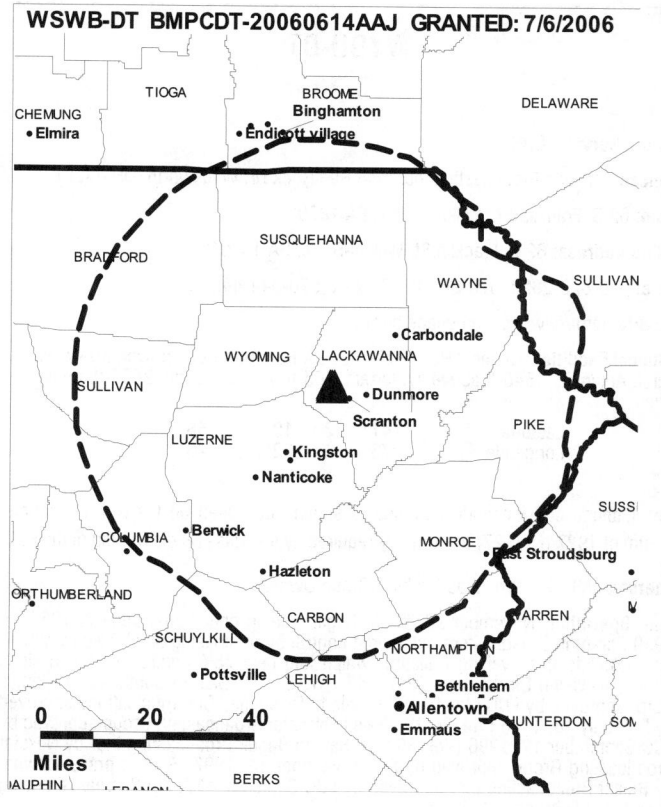

WSWB-DT BMPCDT-20060614AAJ GRANTED: 7/6/2006

© 2010 Warren Communications News

Lisa Miller, Traffic Manager.

City of License: Scranton. **Station DMA:** Wilkes Barre-Scranton, PA. **Rank:** 54.

Circulation © 2009 Nielsen. Coverage based on Nielsen study.

GrandTotal	Cable TV Households	Non-cable TV Households	Total TV Households
Estimated Station Totals *	379,400	212,650	592,050
Average Weekly Circulation (2009)	65,998	43,843	109,841
Average Daily Circulation (2009)			29,213

Station DMA Total	Cable TV Households	Non-cable TV Households	Total TV Households
Estimated Station Totals *	379,400	212,650	592,050
Average Weekly Circulation (2009)	65,998	43,843	109,841
Average Daily Circulation (2009)			29,213

*Estimated station totals are sums of the Nielsen TV and Cable TV household estimates for each county in which the station registers viewing of more than 5% as per the Nielsen Survey Methods.

WYOU-DT
Ch. 13

Network Service: CBS.

Licensee: Mission Broadcasting Inc., 544 Red Rock Dr, Wadsworth, OH 44281.

Studio: 62 S. Franklin St., Wilkes-Barre, PA 18701.

Mailing Address: 62 S. Franklin St, Wilkes-Barre, PA 18701.

Phone: 570-823-2828; 570-961-2222. **Fax:** 570-344-4484.

Web Site: http://www.pahomepage.com

Technical Facilities: Channel No. 13 (210-216 MHz). Authorized power: 30-kw visual, aural. Antenna: 1545-ft above av. terrain, 705-ft. above ground, 2805-ft. above sea level.

Latitude	41°	10'	58"
Longitude	75°	52'	26"

Note: Latitude and longitude coordinates shown are based on the North American Datum of 1927 (NAD 27) as currently required by the Mass Media Bureau of the FCC.

Ownership: Mission Broadcasting Inc. (Group Owner).

Began Operation: November 23, 2005. Began analog operations: June 7, 1953. In 1959 Scranton Broadcasters reacquired control by purchasing stock held by WCAU Inc. (Philadelphia Evening Bulletin), which had held 75% control of station since 1956 (Television Digest, Vol. 12:31, 42; 15:16, 22). Sale to Southeastern Capital Corp. approved by FCC May 9, 1984. Sale to Diversified Communications approved by FCC July 18, 1986 (Vol. 26:23). Sale to Nexstar Broadcasting Group approved by FCC September 12, 1996 (Vol. 36:26). Sale to Bastet Broadcasting Inc. by Nexstar Broadcasting Group approved by FCC November 14, 1997. Sale to present owner by Bastet Broadcasting Inc. approved by FCC September 17, 2002. Ceased analog operations: February 17, 2009.

Represented (legal): Drinker Biddle.

Represented (sales): Blair Television.

Personnel:

Gina Schreiber, General Manager.

Randy Williams, Operations & Production Manager.

Jennifer Mican, Local Sales Manager.

Robin Ziska, National Sales Manager.

Ron Krisulevicz, News Director.

Rick Stolpe, Chief Engineer.

Tiffany Kulig, Business Manager.

Sue Kalinowski, Program Director.

Sean Finn, Promotion Director.

Shannon Lesniak, Creative Services Director.

John Yost, Traffic Manager.

City of License: Scranton. **Station DMA:** Wilkes Barre-Scranton, PA. **Rank:** 54.

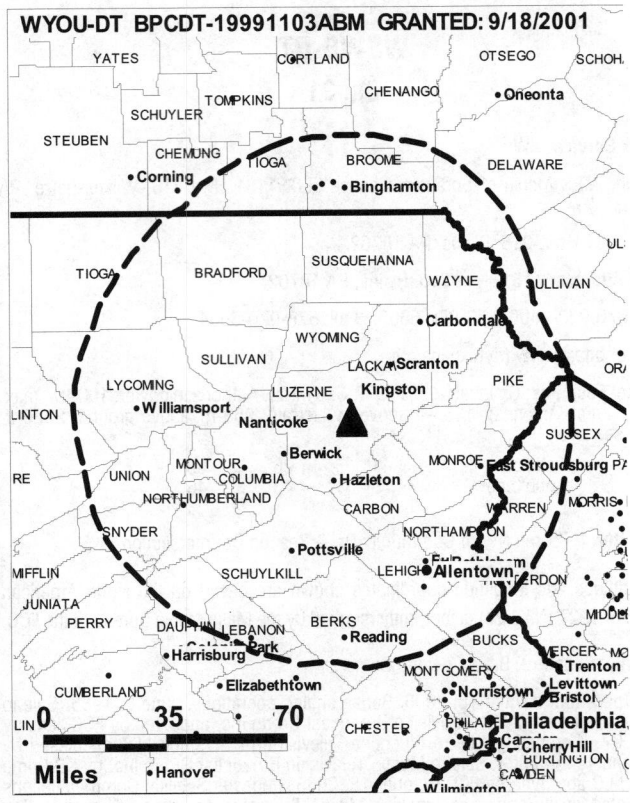

WYOU-DT BPCDT-19991103ABM GRANTED: 9/18/2001

© 2010 Warren Communications News

Circulation © 2009 Nielsen. Coverage based on Nielsen study.

GrandTotal	Cable TV Households	Non-cable TV Households	Total TV Households
Estimated Station Totals *	389,380	212,650	602,030
Average Weekly Circulation (2009)	220,157	116,587	336,744
Average Daily Circulation (2009)			151,855

Station DMA Total	Cable TV Households	Non-cable TV Households	Total TV Households
Estimated Station Totals *	379,400	212,650	592,050
Average Weekly Circulation (2009)	218,021	116,587	334,608
Average Daily Circulation (2009)			151,286

Other DMA Total	Cable TV Households	Non-cable TV Households	Total TV Households
Estimated Station Totals *	9,980	0	9,980
Average Weekly Circulation (2009)	2,136	0	2,136
Average Daily Circulation (2009)			569

*Estimated station totals are sums of the Nielsen TV and Cable TV household estimates for each county in which the station registers viewing of more than 5% as per the Nielsen Survey Methods.

WBRE-DT
Ch. 11

Network Service: NBC.

Licensee: Nexstar Broadcasting of Northeastern Pennsylvania LLC, Ste 1400, 5215 N O'Connor Blvd, Irving, TX 75039.

Studio: 62 S. Franklin St., Wilkes-Barre, PA 18701-1201.

Mailing Address: PO Box 28, Wilkes-Barre, PA 18773.

Phone: 570-823-2828; 800-358-9273. **Fax:** 570-823-4523.

Web Site: http://www.pahomepage.com

Technical Facilities: Channel No. 11 (198-204 MHz). Authorized power: 30-kw visual, aural. Antenna: 1545-ft above av. terrain, 705-ft. above ground, 2805-ft. above sea level.

Latitude	41°	10'	58"
Longitude	75°	52'	26"

Note: Latitude and longitude coordinates shown are based on the North American Datum of 1927 (NAD 27) as currently required by the Mass Media Bureau of the FCC.

Ownership: Nexstar Broadcasting Group Inc. (Group Owner).

Began Operation: November 1, 2002. Began analog operations: January 1, 1953. Sale to WBRE Associates (Northeastern Television Investors) by David M. Baltimore & family approved by FCC May 24, 1984 (Television Digest, Vol. 24:9). Sale to Adams Communications approved by FCC June 22, 1989 but not consummated (Vol. 29:17). Sale to present owner by Northeastern Television Investors approved by FCC November 14, 1997. Ceased analog operations: February 17, 2009.

Represented (legal): Drinker Biddle.

Represented (sales): Katz Media Group.

Personnel:

Louis J. Abitabilo, Vice President & General Manager.

Randy Williams, Station Manager.

Paul Smedley, Local Sales Manager.

Ron Krisulevicz, News Director.

Tiffany Kulig, Business Manager.

Shannon Lesniak, Creative Services Director.

John Yost, Traffic Director.

City of License: Wilkes-Barre. **Station DMA:** Wilkes Barre-Scranton, PA. **Rank:** 54.

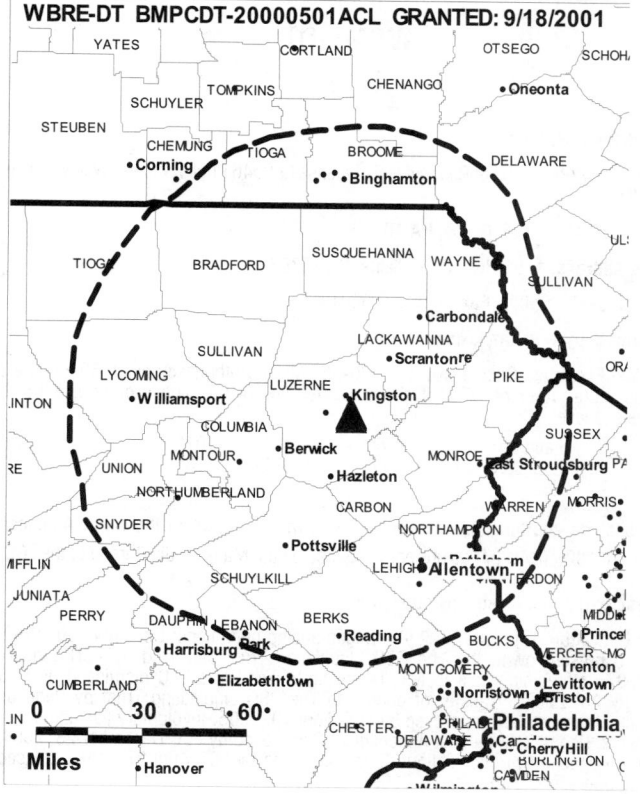

WBRE-DT BMPCDT-20000501ACL GRANTED: 9/18/2001

© 2010 Warren Communications News

Circulation © 2009 Nielsen. Coverage based on Nielsen study.

GrandTotal	Cable TV Households	Non-cable TV Households	Total TV Households
Estimated Station Totals *	427,840	212,650	640,490
Average Weekly Circulation (2009)	245,167	117,488	362,655
Average Daily Circulation (2009)			175,109

Station DMA Total	Cable TV Households	Non-cable TV Households	Total TV Households
Estimated Station Totals *	379,400	212,650	592,050
Average Weekly Circulation (2009)	241,237	117,488	358,725
Average Daily Circulation (2009)			174,418

Other DMA Total	Cable TV Households	Non-cable TV Households	Total TV Households
Estimated Station Totals *	48,440	0	48,440
Average Weekly Circulation (2009)	3,930	0	3,930
Average Daily Circulation (2009)			691

*Estimated station totals are sums of the Nielsen TV and Cable TV household estimates for each county in which the station registers viewing of more than 5% as per the Nielsen Survey Methods.

WQMY-DT
Ch. 29

Network Service: MNT.

Grantee: New Age Media of Pennsylvania License LLC, 46 Public Square, Wilkes-Barre, PA 18701.

Studio: 1181 Hwy. 315, Plains, PA 18702.

Mailing Address: 1181 Hwy. 315, Plains, PA 18702.

Phone: 570-970-5600. **Fax:** 570-970-5601.

Web Site: http://www.myfoxnepa.com

Technical Facilities: Channel No. 29 (560-566 MHz). Authorized power: 50-kw max. visual, aural. Antenna: 797-ft above av. terrain, 140-ft. above ground, 1768-ft. above sea level.

Latitude	41°	12'	01"
Longitude	77°	07'	13"

Note: Latitude and longitude coordinates shown are based on the North American Datum of 1927 (NAD 27) as currently required by the Mass Media Bureau of the FCC.

Ownership: New Age Media (Group Owner).

Began Operation: February 20, 2009. Began analog operations: December 30, 1992. Sale to present owner by The PSC Liquidating Trust approved by FCC January 4, 2007. Competing sale to MM Licensing-Wilkes-Barre LLC dismissed by FCC January 23, 2007. Transfer of control to The PSC Liquidating Trust by Pegasus Communications Corp. approved by FCC April 19, 2005. Involuntary assignment of license to Pegasus Broadcast Associates LP approved by FCC December 23, 2004. Sale to Pegasus Communications Corp. approved by FCC April 27, 1993. Ceased analog operations: February 17, 2009.

Represented (legal): Leventhal, Senter & Lerman PLLC.

Represented (engineering): du Treil, Lundin & Rackley Inc.

Personnel:

Jon Cadman, General Manager.

Dan Mecca, National Sales Manager.

Bob Spager, Local Sales Manager.

Rich Chofey, Chief Engineer.

Marianne Musto, Business Manager.

Steve Philips, Creative Services Director.

Becky Sinke, Production Manager.

Lisa Miller, Traffic Manager.

City of License: Williamsport. **Station DMA:** Wilkes Barre-Scranton, PA. **Rank:** 54.

WQMY-DT BMPCDT-20081113AEW GRANTED: 12/11/2008

© 2010 Warren Communications News

Circulation © 2009 Nielsen. Coverage based on Nielsen study.

GrandTotal	Cable TV Households	Non-cable TV Households	Total TV Households
Estimated Station Totals *	200,070	24,650	224,720
Average Weekly Circulation (2009)	14,859	1,505	16,364
Average Daily Circulation (2009)			3,774

Station DMA Total	Cable TV Households	Non-cable TV Households	Total TV Households
Estimated Station Totals *	200,070	24,650	224,720
Average Weekly Circulation (2009)	14,859	1,505	16,364
Average Daily Circulation (2009)			3,774

*Estimated station totals are sums of the Nielsen TV and Cable TV household estimates for each county in which the station registers viewing of more than 5% as per the Nielsen Survey Methods.

WPMT-DT
Ch. 47

Network Service: FOX.

Licensee: Tribune Television Co., Debtor-In-Possession, 2005 S Queen St, York, PA 17403-4806.

Studio: 2005 S. Queen St., York, PA 17403-4806.

Mailing Address: 2005 S. Queen St, York, PA 17403-4806.

Phone: 717-843-0043. **Fax:** 717-843-9741.

Web Site: http://www.fox43.com

Technical Facilities: Channel No. 47 (668-674 MHz). Authorized power: 933-kw max. visual, aural. Antenna: 1263-ft above av. terrain, 814-ft. above ground, 1713-ft. above sea level.

Latitude	40°	01'	38"
Longitude	76°	36'	00"

Note: Latitude and longitude coordinates shown are based on the North American Datum of 1927 (NAD 27) as currently required by the Mass Media Bureau of the FCC.

Ownership: Tribune Broadcasting Co., Debtor-In-Possession (Group Owner).

Began Operation: December 24, 2004. Began analog operations: December 21, 1952. Involuntary assignment to debtor-in-possession status approved by FCC December 24, 2008. Transfer of control from public shareholders of the Tribune Co. to Tribune Employee Stock Ownership Plan approved by FCC November 30, 2007. Sale to present owner by Renaissance Communications approved by FCC March 20, 1997. Sale to Renaissance Communications by Westport-York Assoc. approved by FCC March 30, 1990. Sale to Westport-York Assoc. by Mohawk Broadcasting approved by FCC September 12, 1986. Sale to Mohawk Broadcasting by Susquehanna Broadcasting (Louis J. Appell) approved by FCC December 30, 1982. Ceased analog operations: June 12, 2009.

Represented (legal): Sidley Austin LLP.

Personnel:

Larry Delia, General Manager.

Matt Uhl, General & National Sales Manager.

Bryon Shumaker, Local Sales Manager.

Jim DePury, News Director.

Jim Myers, Engineering Director.

Timothy L. Koller, Business Manager.

Sandy Halk, Program Coordinator.

David Farish, Promotion & Creative Services Director.

Rick Geisler, Production Manager.

Cindy Jansky, Traffic Manager.

City of License: York. **Station DMA:** Harrisburg-Lancaster-Lebanon-York, PA.

Rank: 39.

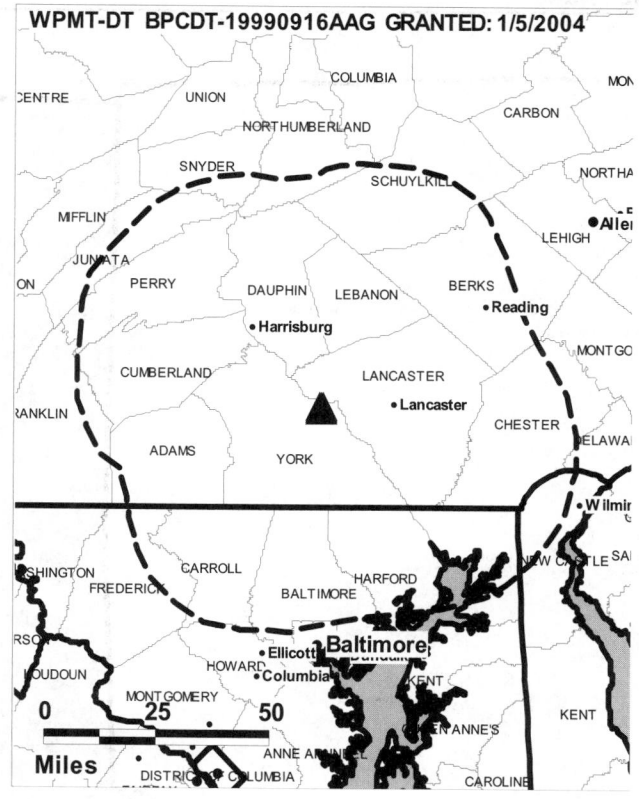

WPMT-DT BPCDT-19990916AAG GRANTED: 1/5/2004

© 2010 Warren Communications News

Circulation © 2009 Nielsen. Coverage based on Nielsen study.

GrandTotal	Cable TV Households	Non-cable TV Households	Total TV Households
Estimated Station Totals *	630,270	232,720	862,990
Average Weekly Circulation (2009)	319,285	129,319	448,604
Average Daily Circulation (2009)			164,532

Station DMA Total	Cable TV Households	Non-cable TV Households	Total TV Households
Estimated Station Totals *	512,790	226,090	738,880
Average Weekly Circulation (2009)	290,677	128,755	419,432
Average Daily Circulation (2009)			158,660

Other DMA Total	Cable TV Households	Non-cable TV Households	Total TV Households
Estimated Station Totals *	117,480	6,630	124,110
Average Weekly Circulation (2009)	28,608	564	29,172
Average Daily Circulation (2009)			5,872

*Estimated station totals are sums of the Nielsen TV and Cable TV household estimates for each county in which the station registers viewing of more than 5% as per the Nielsen Survey Methods.

Rhode Island

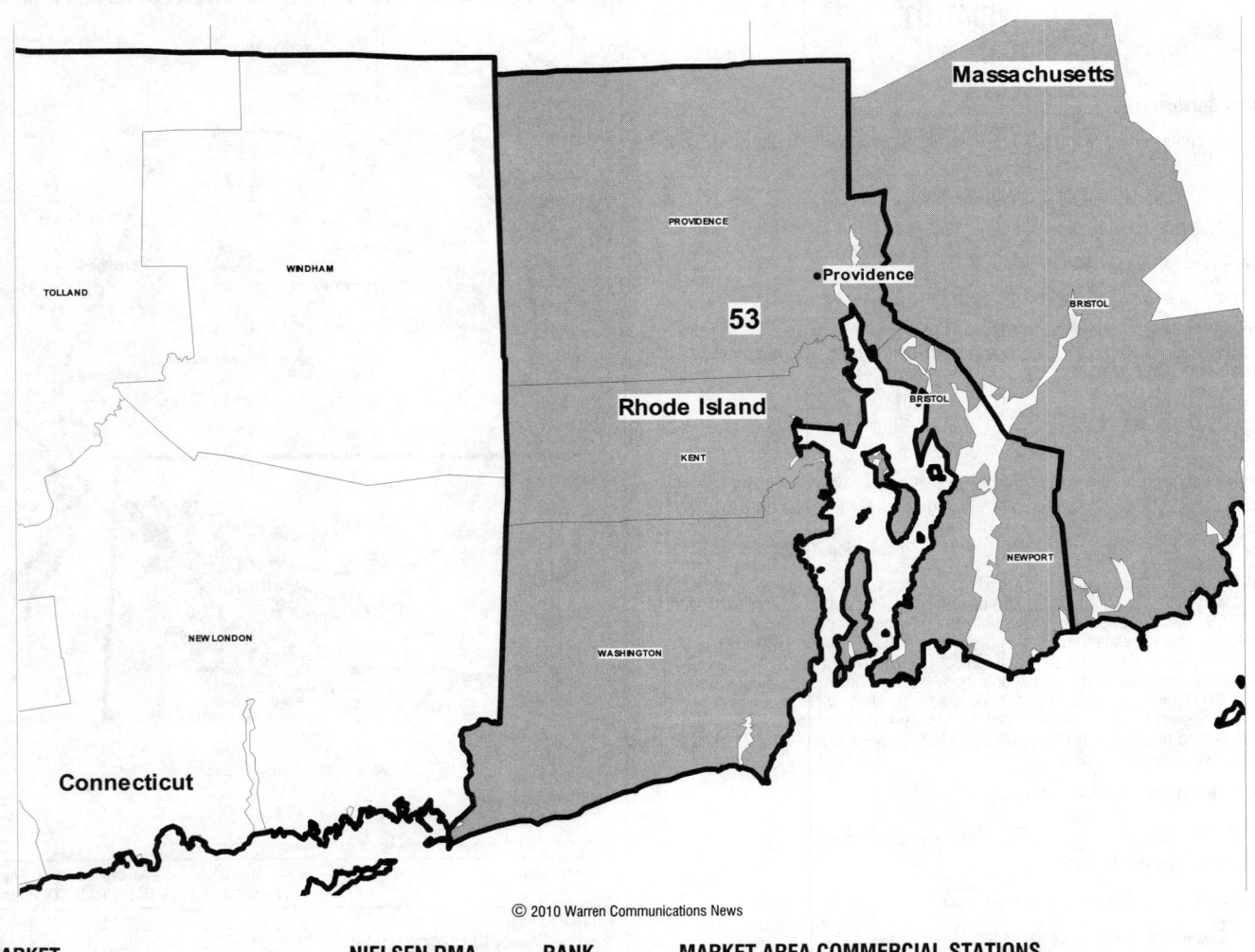

© 2010 Warren Communications News

MARKET	NIELSEN DMA TV HOUSEHOLDS	RANK	MARKET AREA COMMERCIAL STATIONS
Providence, RI-New Bedford, MA	619,610	53	WJAR-DT (51); WLNE-DT (49); WLWC-DT (22); WNAC-DT (54); WPRI-DT (13); WPXQ-TV (17)

Rhode Island Station Totals as of October 1, 2009

	VHF	UHF	TOTAL
Commercial Television	1	3	4
Educational Television	0	1	1
	1	4	5

WPXQ-TV
Ch. 17

Network Service: ION.

Licensee: Ocean State Television LLC, Debtor in Possession, 601 Clearwater Park Rd, West Palm Beach, FL 33401-6233.

Studio: 3 Shaws Cove, Ste 226, New London, CT 06320.

Mailing Address: 3 Shaw's Cove, Ste 226, New London, CT 06320.

Phone: 860-444-2626. **Fax:** 860-440-2601.

E-mail: aaronkaplan@ionmedia.com

Web Site: http://www.ionmedia.com

Technical Facilities: Channel No. 17 (488-494 MHz). Authorized power: 1000-kw max. visual, aural. Antenna: 748-ft above av. terrain, 589-ft. above ground, 978-ft. above sea level.

Latitude	41°	29'	41"
Longitude	71°	47'	06"

Note: Latitude and longitude coordinates shown are based on the North American Datum of 1927 (NAD 27) as currently required by the Mass Media Bureau of the FCC.

Ownership: ION Media Networks Inc., Debtor in Possession (Group Owner).

Began Operation: August 1, 2005. Began analog operations: April 2, 1992. Left air 1995. Sale of 50% interest by Offshore Broadcasting Corp. to Paxson Communications Corp. approved by FCC August 2, 1996. Station returned to air June 1, 1998. Transfer of remaining 50% interest to Paxson Communications Corp. approved by FCC June 15, 2000. Paxson Communications Corp. became ION Media Networks Inc. on June 26, 2006. Transfer of control by ION Media Networks Inc. from Paxson Management Corp. & Lowell W. Paxson to CIG Media LLC approved by FCC December 31, 2007. Involuntary assignment to debtor in possession status approved by FCC June 5, 2009. Ceased analog operations: February 17, 2009.

Represented (legal): Dow Lohnes PLLC.

Personnel:

Deborah Reed-Iler, Station Operations Manager.

Robert Tiodor, Chief Engineer.

Aaron Kaplan, Traffic Manager.

City of License: Block Island. **Station DMA:** Providence, RI-New Bedford, MA.

Rank: 53.

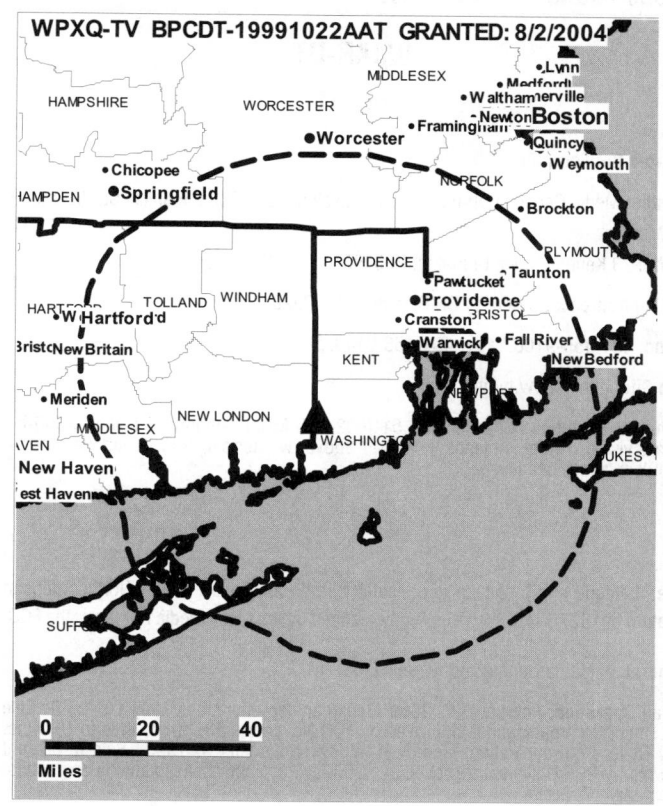

© 2010 Warren Communications News

Circulation © 2009 Nielsen. Coverage based on Nielsen study.

GrandTotal	Cable TV Households	Non-cable TV Households	Total TV Households
Estimated Station Totals *	474,280	22,150	496,430
Average Weekly Circulation (2009)	27,669	1,584	29,253
Average Daily Circulation (2009)			6,234

Station DMA Total	Cable TV Households	Non-cable TV Households	Total TV Households
Estimated Station Totals *	474,280	22,150	496,430
Average Weekly Circulation (2009)	27,669	1,584	29,253
Average Daily Circulation (2009)			6,234

*Estimated station totals are sums of the Nielsen TV and Cable TV household estimates for each county in which the station registers viewing of more than 5% as per the Nielsen Survey Methods.

Rhode Island — Providence

WJAR-DT
Ch. 51

Network Service: NBC.

Grantee: Media General Communications Holdings LLC, 333 E Franklin St, Richmond, VA 23219.

Studio: 23 Kenney Drive, Cranston, RI 02920.

Mailing Address: 23 Kenney Dr, Cranston, RI 02920.

Phone: 401-455-9100. **Fax:** 401-455-9140.

Web Site: http://www.turnto10.com

Technical Facilities: Channel No. 51 (692-698 MHz). Authorized power: 1000-kw max. visual, aural. Antenna: 1004-ft above av. terrain, 900-ft. above ground, 1098-ft. above sea level.

Latitude	41°	51'	54"
Longitude	71°	17'	15"

Note: Latitude and longitude coordinates shown are based on the North American Datum of 1927 (NAD 27) as currently required by the Mass Media Bureau of the FCC.

Ownership: Media General Inc. (Group Owner).

Began Operation: February 17, 2009. Began analog operations: July 10, 1949. Sale to Outlet Communications approved by FCC November 23, 1983. Sale to NBC Inc. by Outlet Communications approved by FCC November 9, 1995. Sale to present owner by NBC Universal approved by FCC May 23, 2006. Ceased analog operations: February 17, 2009.

Represented (legal): Dow Lohnes PLLC.

Personnel:

Lisa Churchville, President & General Manager.

Jeff Walkes, Vice President, Sales.

Betty-Jo Cugine, Vice President, News.

Stephen Del Pico, Local Sales Manager.

Valerie McCain, National Sales Manager.

Clark Smith, Chief Engineer.

Craig Sasges, Business Manager.

Elaine Moy-Gederman, Program & Research Manager.

Barbara Beresford, Promotion Director.

City of License: Providence. **Station DMA:** Providence, RI-New Bedford, MA.

Rank: 53.

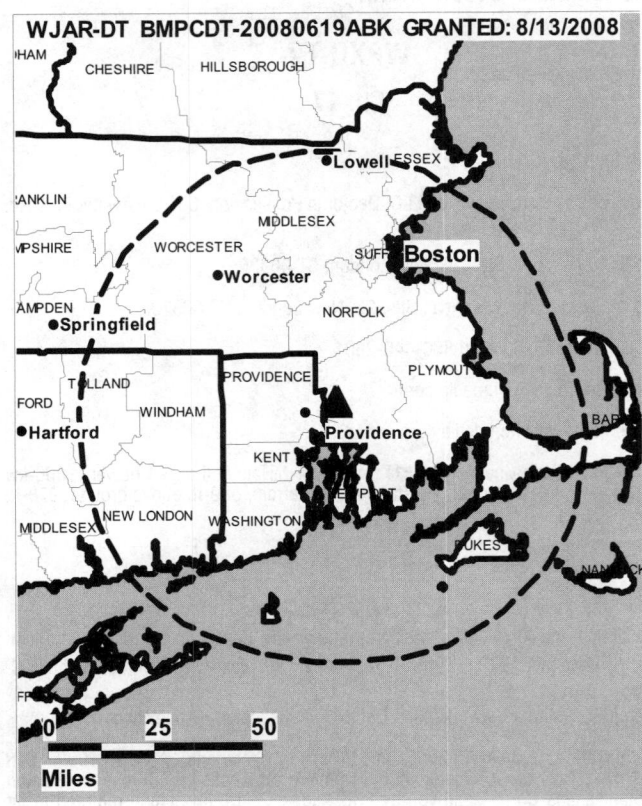

WJAR-DT BMPCDT-20080619ABK GRANTED: 8/13/2008

© 2010 Warren Communications News

Circulation © 2009 Nielsen. Coverage based on Nielsen study.

GrandTotal	Cable TV Households	Non-cable TV Households	Total TV Households
Estimated Station Totals *	1,319,840	220,610	1,540,450
Average Weekly Circulation (2009)	483,983	80,916	564,899
Average Daily Circulation (2009)			281,656

Station DMA Total	Cable TV Households	Non-cable TV Households	Total TV Households
Estimated Station Totals *	517,410	105,170	622,580
Average Weekly Circulation (2009)	351,081	70,503	421,584
Average Daily Circulation (2009)			241,908

Other DMA Total	Cable TV Households	Non-cable TV Households	Total TV Households
Estimated Station Totals *	802,430	115,440	917,870
Average Weekly Circulation (2009)	132,902	10,413	143,315
Average Daily Circulation (2009)			39,748

*Estimated station totals are sums of the Nielsen TV and Cable TV household estimates for each county in which the station registers viewing of more than 5% as per the Nielsen Survey Methods.

WNAC-DT
Ch. 54

Network Service: FOX.

Licensee: WNAC LLC, 34 Main St, Wenham, MA 01984.

Studio: 25 Catamore Blvd., East Providence, RI 02914.

Mailing Address: 25 Catamore Blvd, East Providence, RI 02914.

Phone: 401-438-7200. **Fax:** 401-434-3761.

Web Site: http://www.myfoxprovidence.com

Technical Facilities: Channel No. 54 (710-716 MHz). Authorized power: 1000-kw max. visual, aural. Antenna: 968-ft above av. terrain, 886-ft. above ground, 1060-ft. above sea level.

Latitude	41°	52'	14"
Longitude	71°	17'	45"

Holds CP for change to channel number 12, 30-kw visual, 1001-ft above av. terrain, 934-ft. above ground, 1099-ft. above sea level; lat. 41° 52' 36", long. 71° 16' 57", BMPCDT-20080620AAU.

Note: Latitude and longitude coordinates shown are based on the North American Datum of 1927 (NAD 27) as currently required by the Mass Media Bureau of the FCC.

Ownership: Timothy G. Sheehan (Group Owner).

Began Operation: October 25, 2004. Began analog operations: December 1, 1981. Sale to Providence Television Ltd. Partnership by C. W. Murchison Jr. approved by FCC December 9, 1983. Sale to Sudbrink Broadcasting by Providence Television Ltd. Partnership approved by FCC July 14, 1986. Sale to Price Communications Corp. by Sudbrink Broadcasting approved by FCC May 10, 1988 (Television Digest, Vol. 28:12). Sale to Northstar TV Group by Price Communications Corp. approved by FCC September 11, 1989. Sale to Argyle Television by Northstar TV Group approved by FCC November 7, 1994 (Vol. 34:37; 35:2). Merger with Hearst Corp. approved by FCC June 2, 1997 (Vol. 37:13, 35). Station, along with Hearst-Argyle's WDTN, was swapped for Sunrise Television's KSBW, WNNE & WPTZ (Vol. 38:8). FCC approved deal July 1, 1998. Sale to LIN Television Corp. by Smith Acquisition Co. approved by FCC May 30, 2001. Sale to present owner by LIN Television Corp. approved by FCC April 17, 2002. Ceased analog operations: February 17, 2009.

Represented (legal): Dow Lohnes PLLC.

Represented (sales): Blair Television.

Personnel:

Jay Howell, President & General Manager.

Patrick Wholey, General Sales Manager.

John Macek, Local Sales Manager.

Nancy Mayers, National Sales Manager.

Joseph Abouzeid, News Director.

William Hague, Chief Engineer.

Pamela Brennan, Programming Director.

Susan Tracy-Durant, Creative Services Director.

Christine Peabody, Community Affairs Director.

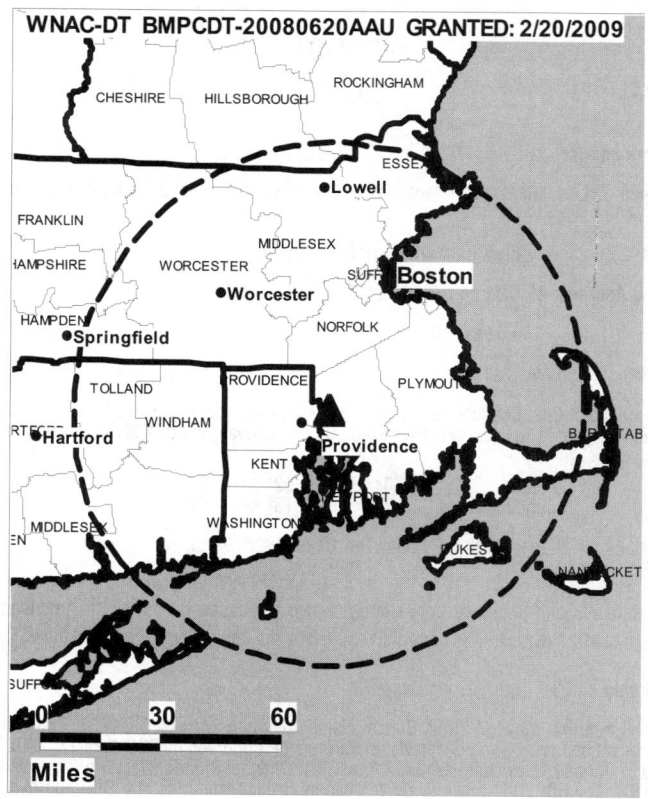

© 2010 Warren Communications News

City of License: Providence. **Station DMA:** Providence, RI-New Bedford, MA.

Rank: 53.

Circulation © 2009 Nielsen. Coverage based on Nielsen study.

GrandTotal	Cable TV Households	Non-cable TV Households	Total TV Households
Estimated Station Totals *	517,410	145,190	662,600
Average Weekly Circulation (2009)	263,752	48,032	311,784
Average Daily Circulation (2009)			104,330

Station DMA Total	Cable TV Households	Non-cable TV Households	Total TV Households
Estimated Station Totals *	517,410	105,170	622,580
Average Weekly Circulation (2009)	263,752	45,751	309,503
Average Daily Circulation (2009)			104,010

Other DMA Total	Cable TV Households	Non-cable TV Households	Total TV Households
Estimated Station Totals *	0	40,020	40,020
Average Weekly Circulation (2009)	0	2,281	2,281
Average Daily Circulation (2009)			320

*Estimated station totals are sums of the Nielsen TV and Cable TV household estimates for each county in which the station registers viewing of more than 5% as per the Nielsen Survey Methods.

WPRI-DT
Ch. 13

Network Service: CBS.

Licensee: TVL Broadcasting of Rhode Island LLC, 4 Richmond Sq, Ste 200, Providence, RI 02906.

Studio: 25 Catamore Blvd, East Providence, RI 02914.

Mailing Address: 25 Catamore Blvd, East Providence, RI 02914.

Phone: 401-438-7200. **Fax:** 401-434-3761.

Web Site: http://www.wpri.com

Technical Facilities: Channel No. 13 (210-216 MHz). Authorized power: 18-kw visual, aural. Antenna: 1001-ft above av. terrain, 932-ft. above ground, 1097-ft. above sea level.

Latitude	41°	52'	36"
Longitude	71°	16'	57"

Holds CP for change to 30-kw visual; BPCDT-20080619AHJ.

Note: Latitude and longitude coordinates shown are based on the North American Datum of 1927 (NAD 27) as currently required by the Mass Media Bureau of the FCC.

Ownership: LIN TV Corp. (Group Owner).

Began Operation: May 26, 2004. Began analog operations: March 27, 1955. Transfer to present owner by Sunrise Television Partners LP approved by FCC April 17, 2002. Sale to Sunrise Television Partners LP by Clear Channel Broadcasting Inc. approved by FCC May 30, 2001. Sale to Clear Channel Broadcasting Inc. by CBS approved by FCC June 11, 1996 (Television Digest, Vol. 36:16). Sale to CBS by Narragansett approved by FCC June 22, 1995 (Vol. 34:50, 35:10, 19). Sale to Narragansett Television LP by Knight-Ridder Broadcasting approved by FCC April 26, 1989 (Vol. 29:9). Sale to Knight-Ridder by Poole Broadcasting approved by FCC December 21, 1977 (Vol. 16:26). Sale to Poole by Capital Cities Broadcasting approved by FCC June 15, 1967. Sale to Capital Cities by William S. Cherry & associates approved by FCC March 11, 1959 (Vol. 14:51; 15:11). Ceased analog operations: February 17, 2009.

Represented (sales): Blair Television.

Personnel:

Jay Howell, President & General Manager.

Patrick Wholey, General Sales Manager.

Mike Martinelli, Local Sales Manager.

Patti St. Pierre, National Sales Manager.

Joseph Abouzeid, News Director.

William Hague, Chief Engineer.

Pam Brennan, Program Director.

Susan Tracy-Durant, Creative Services Director.

Christine Peabody, Community Affairs Director.

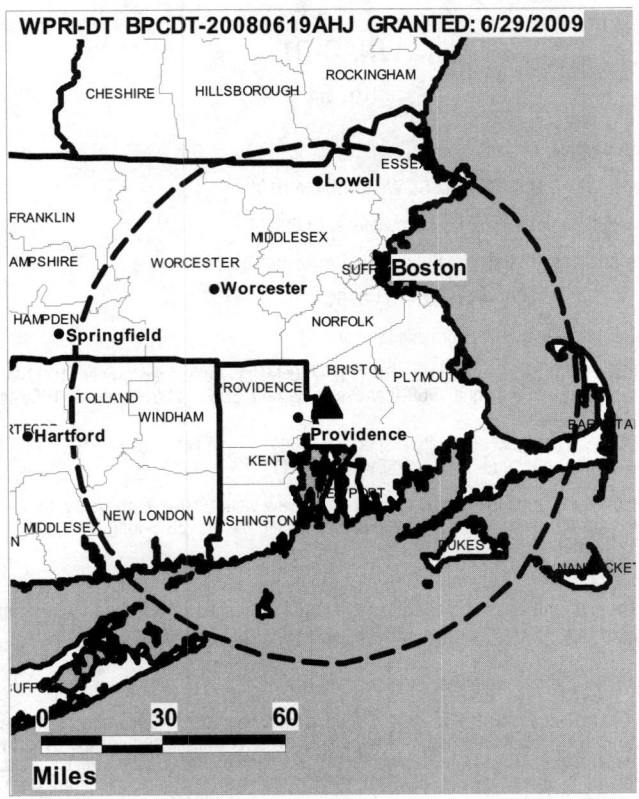

WPRI-DT BPCDT-20080619AHJ GRANTED: 6/29/2009

© 2010 Warren Communications News

City of License: Providence. **Station DMA:** Providence, RI-New Bedford, MA.

Rank: 53.

Circulation © 2009 Nielsen. Coverage based on Nielsen study.

GrandTotal	Cable TV Households	Non-cable TV Households	Total TV Households
Estimated Station Totals *	848,820	160,720	1,009,540
Average Weekly Circulation (2009)	356,478	69,311	425,789
Average Daily Circulation (2009)			202,812

Station DMA Total	Cable TV Households	Non-cable TV Households	Total TV Households
Estimated Station Totals *	517,410	105,170	622,580
Average Weekly Circulation (2009)	326,399	63,902	390,301
Average Daily Circulation (2009)			191,222

Other DMA Total	Cable TV Households	Non-cable TV Households	Total TV Households
Estimated Station Totals *	331,410	55,550	386,960
Average Weekly Circulation (2009)	30,079	5,409	35,488
Average Daily Circulation (2009)			11,590

*Estimated station totals are sums of the Nielsen TV and Cable TV household estimates for each county in which the station registers viewing of more than 5% as per the Nielsen Survey Methods.

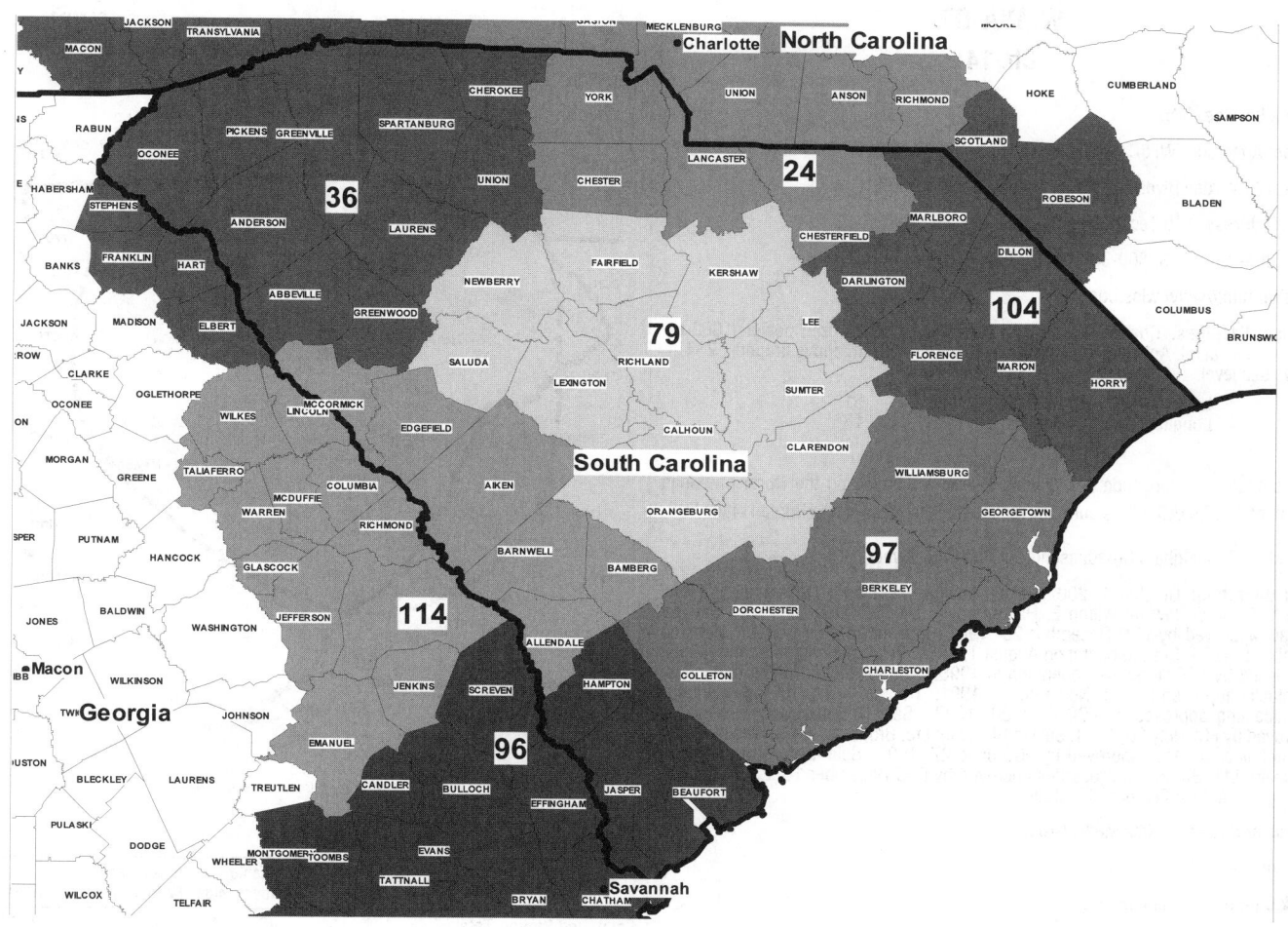

© 2010 Warren Communications News

MARKET	NIELSEN DMA TV HOUSEHOLDS	RANK	MARKET AREA COMMERCIAL STATIONS
Charlotte, NC...............................	1,147,910	24	WAXN-DT (50); WBTV-DT (23); WCCB-DT (27); WCNC-DT (22); WHKY-DT (40); WJZY-DT (47); WMYT-DT (39); WSOC-DT (34)
Greenville-Spartanburg-Anderson, SC-Asheville, NC ...	865,810	36	WGGS-DT (16); WHNS-DT (21); WLOS-DT (13); WMYA-DT (14); WNEG-DT (24); WSPA-DT (7); WYCW-DT (45); WYFF-DT (59)
Columbia, SC	398,620	79	WACH-DT (48); WIS-DT (10); WKTC-DT (39); WLTX-DT (17); WOLO-DT (8); WZRB-DT (47)
Savannah, GA...............................	322,030	96	WGSA-DT (35); WJCL-DT (22); WSAV-DT (39); WTGS-DT (28); WTOC-DT (11)
Charleston, SC	311,190	97	WCBD-DT (50); WCIV-DT (34); WCSC-DT (52); WMMP-DT (36); WTAT-DT (24)
Myrtle Beach-Florence, SC	287,400	104	WBTW-DT (13); WFXB-DT (18); WMBF-DT (32); WPDE-DT (16)
Augusta, GA-Aiken, SC	255,950	114	WAGT-DT (30); WFXG-DT (31); WJBF-DT (42); WRDW-DT (12)

South Carolina Station Totals as of October 1, 2009

	VHF	UHF	TOTAL
Commercial Television	4	18	22
Educational Television	3	8	11
	7	26	33

WMYA-DT
Ch. 14

Network Service: MNT.

Grantee: Anderson (WFBC-TV) Licensee Inc., 2000 W. 41st St, Baltimore, MD 21211.

Studio: 100 Verdae Blvd., Suite 410, Greenville, SC 29607.

Mailing Address: 110 Technology Dr, Asheville, NC 28803.

Phone: 864-297-1313; 800-338-0130. **Fax:** 864-297-8085.

Web Site: http://www.wlos.com

Technical Facilities: Channel No. 14 (470-476 MHz). Authorized power: 1000-kw max. visual, aural. Antenna: 940-ft above av. terrain, 937-ft. above ground, 1734-ft. above sea level.

Latitude	34°	38'	51"
Longitude	82°	16'	13"

Note: Latitude and longitude coordinates shown are based on the North American Datum of 1927 (NAD 27) as currently required by the Mass Media Bureau of the FCC.

Ownership: Cunningham Broadcasting Corp. (Group Owner).

Began Operation: October 1, 2002. Began analog operations: December 1, 1953. Sale to Frank Outlaw by Wilton E. Hall approved by FCC May 31, 1978. Sale by Outlaw approved by FCC December 28, 1982. Left air 1983; resumed operation October 1, 1984. Ceased operation August 1, 1989. Proposed sale to Anchor Media dismissed by FCC. Resumed operation in 1990. Sale to Anchor Media remanded, eventually approved by FCC November 1, 1991. Transfer of control to Continental Broadcasting approved by FCC June 30, 1993. Sale to Better Communications approved by FCC July 20, 1994. Sale to Glencairn Ltd. Broadcast Properties by Better Communications Inc. approved by FCC June 27, 1997. Sale to present owner by Glencairn Ltd. Broadcast Properties approved by FCC December 10, 2001. Ceased analog operations: February 17, 2009.

Represented (sales): Katz Media Group.

Personnel:

Jack Connors, General Manager.

Audra Swain, General Sales Manager.

Greg Conner, Local Sales Manager.

Julie Fries, News Director.

Rollin Tompkins, Chief Engineer.

Darrell Rhoden, Business Manager.

Guy Chancey, Program & Promotions Manager.

Sarah Ferris, Traffic Manager.

Vicki Merck, Community Affairs Director.

City of License: Anderson.

Station DMA: Greenville-Spartanburg-Anderson, SC-Asheville, NC. **Rank:** 36.

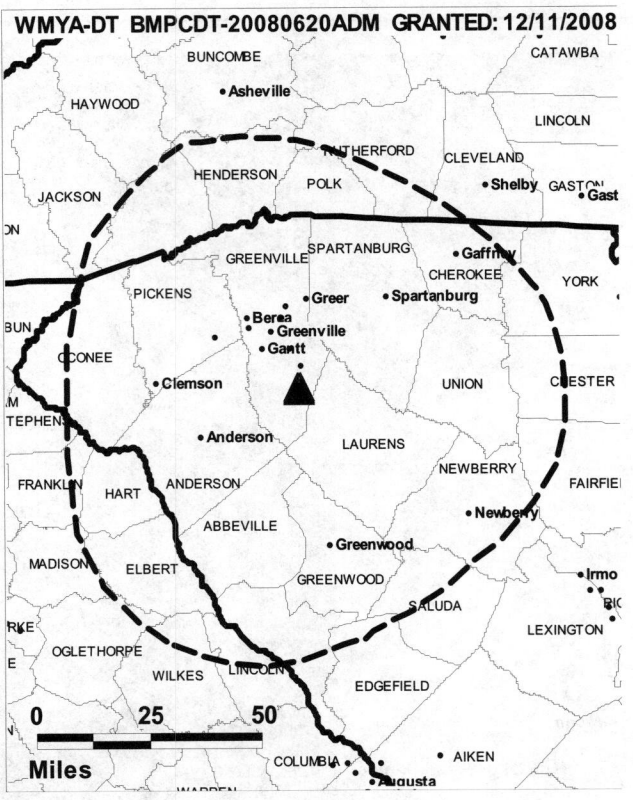

WMYA-DT BMPCDT-20080620ADM GRANTED: 12/11/2008

© 2010 Warren Communications News

Circulation © 2009 Nielsen. Coverage based on Nielsen study.

GrandTotal	Cable TV Households	Non-cable TV Households	Total TV Households
Estimated Station Totals *	401,100	417,640	818,740
Average Weekly Circulation (2009)	70,197	54,975	125,172
Average Daily Circulation (2009)			42,262

Station DMA Total	Cable TV Households	Non-cable TV Households	Total TV Households
Estimated Station Totals *	390,700	410,800	801,500
Average Weekly Circulation (2009)	68,897	54,366	123,263
Average Daily Circulation (2009)			41,898

Other DMA Total	Cable TV Households	Non-cable TV Households	Total TV Households
Estimated Station Totals *	10,400	6,840	17,240
Average Weekly Circulation (2009)	1,300	609	1,909
Average Daily Circulation (2009)			364

*Estimated station totals are sums of the Nielsen TV and Cable TV household estimates for each county in which the station registers viewing of more than 5% as per the Nielsen Survey Methods.

WCBD-DT
Ch. 50

Network Service: NBC, CW.

Grantee: Media General Communications Holdings LLC, 333 E Franklin St, Richmond, VA 23219.

Studio: 210 W. Coleman Blvd., Mount Pleasant, SC 29464.

Mailing Address: 210 W. Coleman Blvd, Mount Pleasant, SC 29464.

Phone: 843-884-2222. **Fax:** 843-884-6624.

Web Site: http://www.wcbd.com

Technical Facilities: Channel No. 50 (686-692 MHz). Authorized power: 1000-kw max. visual, aural. Antenna: 1906-ft above av. terrain, 1903-ft. above ground, 1919-ft. above sea level.

Latitude	32°	56'	24"
Longitude	79°	41'	45"

Transmitter: 5404 Sewee Rd., Ameridan.

Note: Latitude and longitude coordinates shown are based on the North American Datum of 1927 (NAD 27) as currently required by the Mass Media Bureau of the FCC.

Ownership: Media General Inc. (Group Owner).

Began Operation: April 12, 2003. Began analog operations: September 25, 1954. Sale to present owner by State Record Co. approved by FCC December 28, 1982 (Television Digest, Vol. 22:27). Sale to State Record by Reeves Telecom Corp. approved by FCC May 26, 1971 (Vol. 10:42). Transfer of control from J. Drayton Hastie family to Reeves approved by FCC July 14, 1960 (Vol. 16:29). Ceased analog operations: June 12, 2009.

Personnel:

Rick Lipps, Vice President & General Manager.

Lowell Beckner, Operations Manager & Chief Engineer.

Patrick Ryal, General Sales Manager.

Karen Simms, Local Sales Manager.

Dan Fabrizio, News Director.

Laura Hartin, Business Manager.

Mark Bradley, Program Director & Promotions & Marketing Manager.

Steve Blanchard, National Sales Manager.

Brooke Katz, Sales Promotion Coordinator.

Craig Dominique, Production Director.

Brenda Powell, Traffic Manager.

City of License: Charleston. **Station DMA:** Charleston, SC. **Rank:** 97.

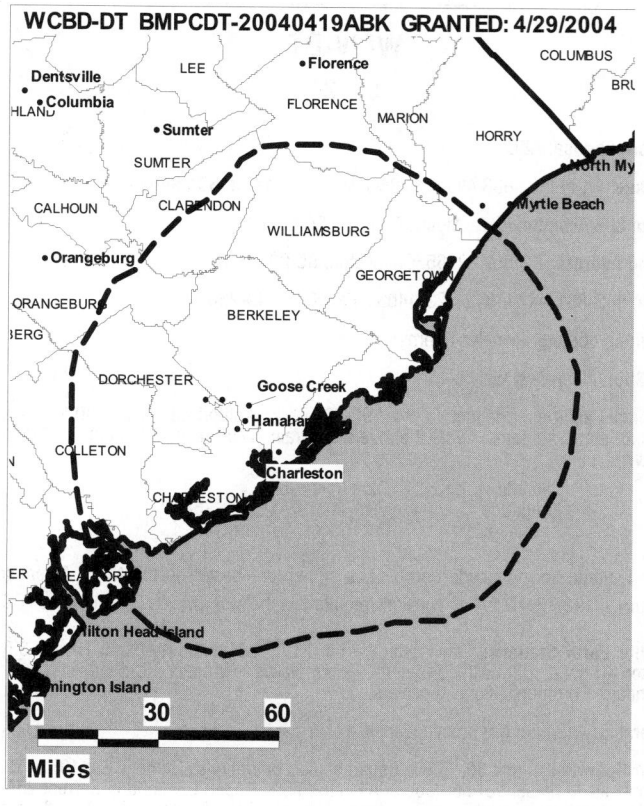

WCBD-DT BMPCDT-20040419ABK GRANTED: 4/29/2004

© 2010 Warren Communications News

Circulation © 2009 Nielsen. Coverage based on Nielsen study.

GrandTotal	Cable TV Households	Non-cable TV Households	Total TV Households
Estimated Station Totals *	248,280	129,770	378,050
Average Weekly Circulation (2009)	130,023	65,912	195,935
Average Daily Circulation (2009)			96,653

Station DMA Total	Cable TV Households	Non-cable TV Households	Total TV Households
Estimated Station Totals *	202,630	104,980	307,610
Average Weekly Circulation (2009)	124,591	64,331	188,922
Average Daily Circulation (2009)			94,215

Other DMA Total	Cable TV Households	Non-cable TV Households	Total TV Households
Estimated Station Totals *	45,650	24,790	70,440
Average Weekly Circulation (2009)	5,432	1,581	7,013
Average Daily Circulation (2009)			2,438

*Estimated station totals are sums of the Nielsen TV and Cable TV household estimates for each county in which the station registers viewing of more than 5% as per the Nielsen Survey Methods.

WCIV-DT
Ch. 34

Network Service: ABC.

Licensee: WCIV Inc., 888 Allbritton Blvd, Mount Pleasant, SC 29464.

Studio: 888 Allbritton Blvd., Mount Pleasant, SC 29464.

Mailing Address: PO Box 22165, Charleston, SC 29413-2165.

Phone: 843-881-4444; 843-723-4403. **Fax:** 843-849-2507.

E-mail: cgroome@abcnews4.com

Web Site: http://www.wciv.com

Technical Facilities: Channel No. 34 (590-596 MHz). Authorized power: 630-kw max. visual, aural. Antenna: 1713-ft above av. terrain, 1706-ft. above ground, 1722-ft. above sea level.

Latitude	32°	55'	28"
Longitude	79°	41'	58"

Note: Latitude and longitude coordinates shown are based on the North American Datum of 1927 (NAD 27) as currently required by the Mass Media Bureau of the FCC.

Satellite Earth Stations: Transmitter Harris; RCA, 3.5-meter Ku-band; Harris, 3.5-meter Ku-band; Comtech, 5-meter C-band; Harris, 10-meter Ku-band; Vertex, Standard Communications receivers.

Ownership: Allbritton Communications Co.

Began Operation: June 30, 2006. Began analog operations: October 23, 1962. Pro forma sale to present owner (Joe L. Allbritton 75%; Robert L. Allbritton & Trust 25%) by Allbritton Communications Co. (Joe L. Allbritton 51%; Robert L. Allbritton & Trust 49%) approved by FCC September 25, 2008. Sale to Allbritton Communications Co. by Washington Star Communications finalized in 1976. Sale to Washington Star Communications by First Charleston Corp. approved by FCC October 5, 1966. Ceased analog operations: June 12, 2009.

Represented (sales): Continental Television Sales.

Personnel:

Suzanne McNay Teagle, President & General Manager.

Tim Greeney, Marketing & Promotion Director.

Chuck Groome, Local Sales Manager.

Octavia Walker, National Sales Manager.

Jim Church, Vice President, Operations.

Eva Wicks, Business Manager.

Deborah Jackson, Program Director.

Sybil Blanton, Traffic Manager.

City of License: Charleston. **Station DMA:** Charleston, SC. **Rank:** 97.

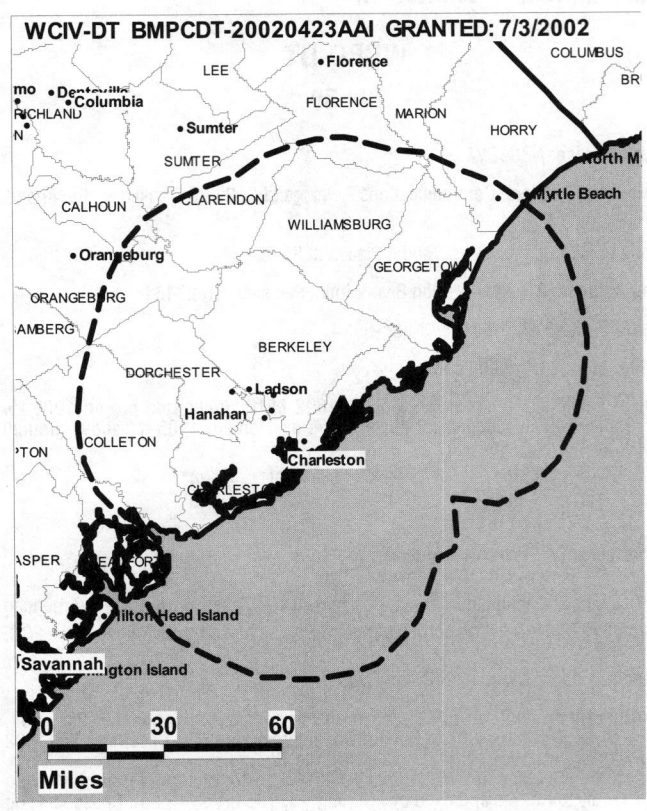

WCIV-DT BMPCDT-20020423AAI GRANTED: 7/3/2002

© 2010 Warren Communications News

Circulation © 2009 Nielsen. Coverage based on Nielsen study.

GrandTotal	Cable TV Households	Non-cable TV Households	Total TV Households
Estimated Station Totals *	250,310	109,440	359,750
Average Weekly Circulation (2009)	118,912	58,101	177,013
Average Daily Circulation (2009)			72,151

Station DMA Total	Cable TV Households	Non-cable TV Households	Total TV Households
Estimated Station Totals *	202,630	104,980	307,610
Average Weekly Circulation (2009)	111,152	57,780	168,932
Average Daily Circulation (2009)			70,114

Other DMA Total	Cable TV Households	Non-cable TV Households	Total TV Households
Estimated Station Totals *	47,680	4,460	52,140
Average Weekly Circulation (2009)	7,760	321	8,081
Average Daily Circulation (2009)			2,037

*Estimated station totals are sums of the Nielsen TV and Cable TV household estimates for each county in which the station registers viewing of more than 5% as per the Nielsen Survey Methods.

WCSC-DT
Ch. 52

Network Service: CBS.

Licensee: WCSC License Subsidiary LLC, 201 Monroe St, RSA Tower, 20th Fl, Montgomery, AL 36104.

Studio: 2126 Charlie Hall Blvd., Charleston, SC 29414.

Mailing Address: 2126 Charlie Hall Blvd, Charleston, SC 29414.

Phone: 843-402-5555. **Fax:** 843-402-5579.

Web Site: http://www.wcsc.com

Technical Facilities: Channel No. 52 (698-704 MHz). Authorized power: 1000-kw max. visual, aural. Antenna: 1709-ft above av. terrain, 1706-ft. above ground, 1722-ft. above sea level.

Latitude	32°	55'	28"
Longitude	79°	41'	58"

Note: Latitude and longitude coordinates shown are based on the North American Datum of 1927 (NAD 27) as currently required by the Mass Media Bureau of the FCC.

Ownership: Raycom Media Inc. (Group Owner).

Began Operation: October 26, 2002. Standard and High Definition. Began analog operations: June 19, 1953. Ceased analog operations: June 12, 2009. Transfer of control by WCSC Inc. from Lincoln Financial Media Co. to Raycom Media Inc. approved by FCC March 25, 2008. Transfer of control by WCSC Inc. to Lincoln National Corp. from Jefferson-Pilot Corp. approved by FCC February 9, 2006. Sale to Jefferson-Pilot Corp. by General Electric Capital Corp. approved by FCC September 3, 1993. Sale to General Electric Capital Corp. by Crump Communications Inc. approved by FCC July 24, 1991. Sale to Anchor Media Holdings Ltd. by Crump Communications Inc. dismissed by FCC April 2, 1990. Sale to Crump Communications Inc. by John M. Rivers Sr., John M. Rivers Jr., Martha R. Rivers, et al., approved by FCC September 1, 1987.

Represented (legal): Covington & Burling.

Represented (sales): Petry Media Corp.

Personnel:

Rita Scott, General Manager.

Sandy Smith, General Sales Manager.

Robin Kienzle, Local Sales Manager.

Mary Rigby, News Director.

Mike Guthrie, Engineering Director.

Lowell Knouff, Assistant Engineer.

Brian Stephenson, Controller.

Amanda Childs, Promotion Director.

James P. DeMauro, Production Manager.

Libby Keller, Traffic Director.

Kelly Ennis, Human Resources Manager.

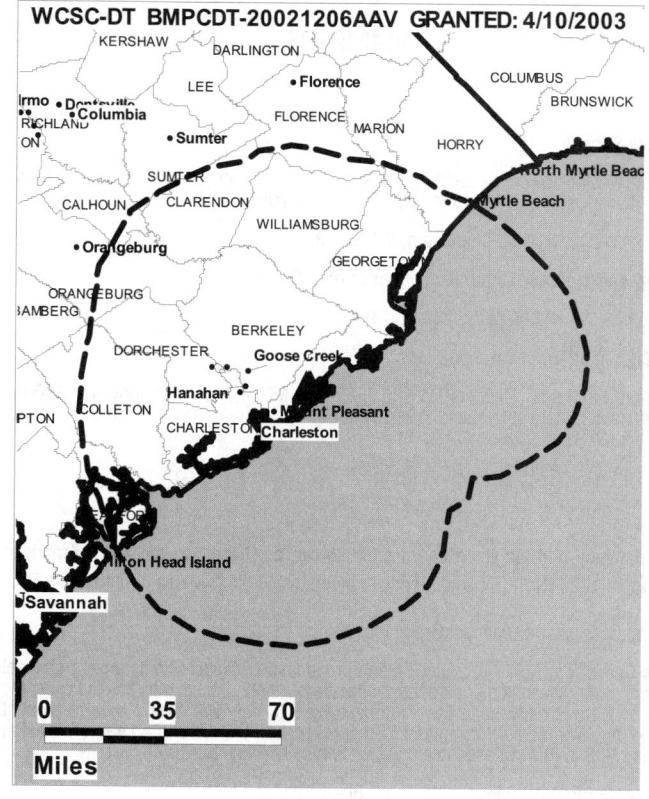

WCSC-DT BMPCDT-20021206AAV GRANTED: 4/10/2003

© 2010 Warren Communications News

City of License: Charleston. **Station DMA:** Charleston, SC. **Rank:** 97.

Circulation © 2009 Nielsen. Coverage based on Nielsen study.

GrandTotal	Cable TV Households	Non-cable TV Households	Total TV Households
Estimated Station Totals *	373,030	115,110	488,140
Average Weekly Circulation (2009)	158,120	73,639	231,759
Average Daily Circulation (2009)			115,348

Station DMA Total	Cable TV Households	Non-cable TV Households	Total TV Households
Estimated Station Totals *	202,630	104,980	307,610
Average Weekly Circulation (2009)	131,770	72,853	204,623
Average Daily Circulation (2009)			107,679

Other DMA Total	Cable TV Households	Non-cable TV Households	Total TV Households
Estimated Station Totals *	170,400	10,130	180,530
Average Weekly Circulation (2009)	26,350	786	27,136
Average Daily Circulation (2009)			7,669

*Estimated station totals are sums of the Nielsen TV and Cable TV household estimates for each county in which the station registers viewing of more than 5% as per the Nielsen Survey Methods.

WMMP-DT
Ch. 36

Network Service: MNT.

Grantee: WMMP Licensee LP, 2300 N St. NW, c/o Pillsbury Winthrop Shaw Pittman LLP, Attn.: Kathryn Schmeltzer, Washington, DC 20037-1128.

Studio: 4310 Arco Lane, Charleston, SC 29418.

Mailing Address: 4301 Arco Lane, Charleston, SC 29418.

Phone: 843-744-2424. **Fax:** 843-554-9649.

Web Site: http://www.wmmp36.com

Technical Facilities: Channel No. 36 (602-608 MHz). Authorized power: 1000-kw max. visual, aural. Antenna: 1914-ft above av. terrain, 1904-ft. above ground, 1921-ft. above sea level.

Latitude	32°	56'	24"
Longitude	79°	41'	45"

Note: Latitude and longitude coordinates shown are based on the North American Datum of 1927 (NAD 27) as currently required by the Mass Media Bureau of the FCC.

Ownership: Sinclair Broadcast Group Inc. (Group Owner).

Began Operation: April 10, 2006. Station broadcasting digitally on its analog channel allotment. Began analog operations: December 2, 1992. Sale to Max Media Properties LLC by Caro Broadcasting Ltd. approved by FCC July 23, 1996. Sale to present owner by Max Media Properties LLC approved by FCC June 26, 1998 (Television Digest, Vol. 37:49). Ceased analog operations: February 17, 2009.

Represented (legal): Pillsbury Winthrop Shaw Pittman LLP.

Represented (sales): Katz Media Group.

Personnel:

Allison Taylor, General Manager.

Mary Margaret Johnson, Local Sales Manager.

Mike Kordek, Chief Engineer.

Bill Littleton, Program Director.

Jason Lewis, Production Manager.

Sallie Moultrie, Traffic Manager.

Marge Bowen, Administrative Assistant, Human Resources.

City of License: Charleston. **Station DMA:** Charleston, SC. **Rank:** 97.

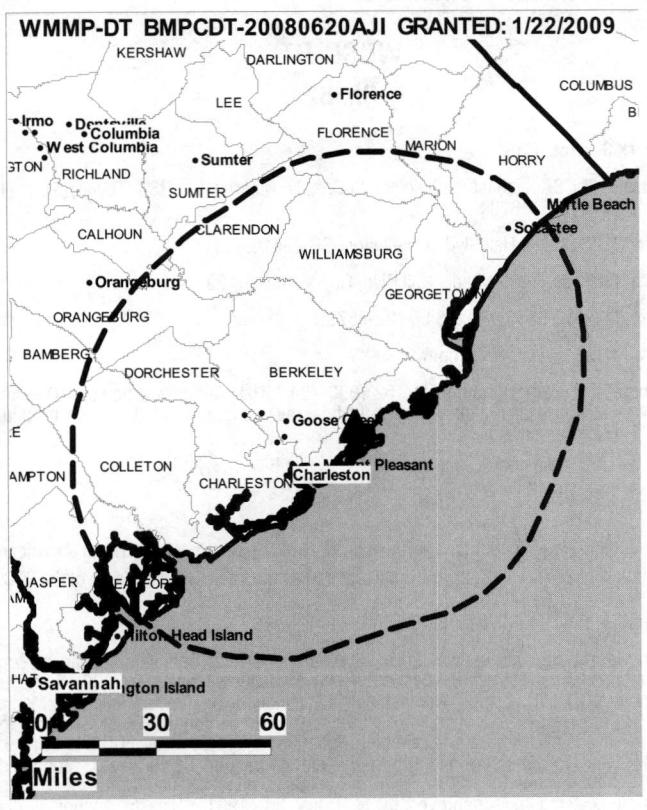

WMMP-DT BMPCDT-20080620AJI GRANTED: 1/22/2009

© 2010 Warren Communications News

Circulation © 2009 Nielsen. Coverage based on Nielsen study.

GrandTotal	Cable TV Households	Non-cable TV Households	Total TV Households
Estimated Station Totals *	202,630	104,980	307,610
Average Weekly Circulation (2009)	30,794	21,609	52,403
Average Daily Circulation (2009)			16,382

Station DMA Total	Cable TV Households	Non-cable TV Households	Total TV Households
Estimated Station Totals *	202,630	104,980	307,610
Average Weekly Circulation (2009)	30,794	21,609	52,403
Average Daily Circulation (2009)			16,382

*Estimated station totals are sums of the Nielsen TV and Cable TV household estimates for each county in which the station registers viewing of more than 5% as per the Nielsen Survey Methods.

WTAT-DT
Ch. 24

Network Service: FOX.

Grantee: WTAT Licensee LLC, 2000 W. 41st St, Baltimore, MD 21211.

Studio: 4301 Arco Lane, Charleston, SC 29418.

Mailing Address: 4301 Arco Lane, Charleston, SC 29418.

Phone: 843-744-2424. **Fax:** 843-554-9649.

Web Site: http://www.wtat24.com

Technical Facilities: Channel No. 24 (530-536 MHz). Authorized power: 1000-kw max. visual, aural. Antenna: 1914-ft above av. terrain, 1904-ft. above ground, 1921-ft. above sea level.

Latitude	32°	56'	24"
Longitude	79°	41'	45"

Note: Latitude and longitude coordinates shown are based on the North American Datum of 1927 (NAD 27) as currently required by the Mass Media Bureau of the FCC.

Ownership: Cunningham Broadcasting Corp. (Group Owner).

Began Operation: April 6, 2006. Station broadcasting digitally on its analog channel allotment. Began analog operations: September 7, 1985. Proposed sales to Sinclair Broadcast Group Inc. dismissed by FCC February 26, 2004 and September 13, 2002. Ceased analog operations: February 17, 2009.

Represented (sales): Katz Media Group.

Represented (legal): Pillsbury Winthrop Shaw Pittman LLP.

Personnel:

Allison Taylor, General Manager.

Mary Margaret Johnson, Local Sales Manager.

Mike Kordek, Chief Engineer.

Bill Littleton, Program Director.

Jason Lewis, Production Manager.

Sallie Moultrie, Traffic Manager.

Marge Bowen, Administrative Assistant & Human Resources Director.

City of License: Charleston. **Station DMA:** Charleston, SC. **Rank:** 97.

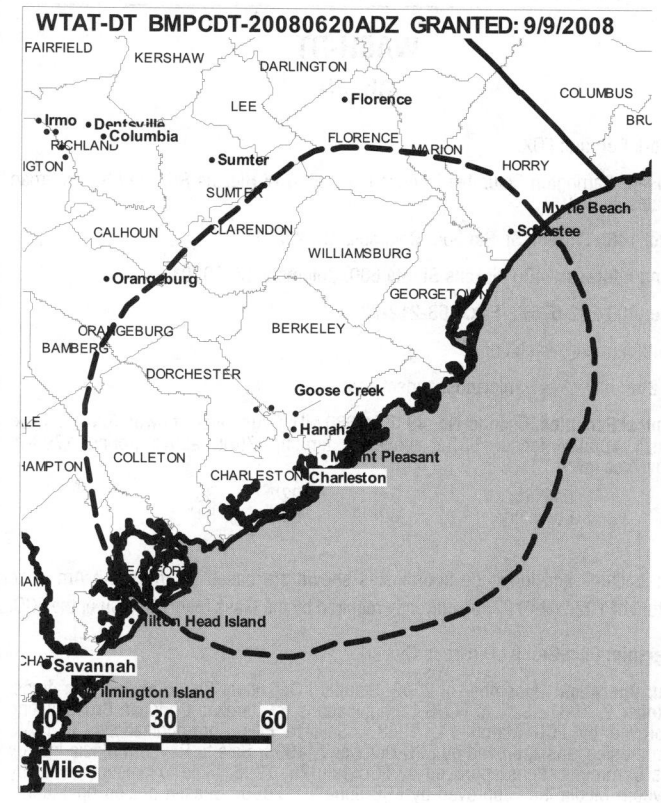

© 2010 Warren Communications News

Circulation © 2009 Nielsen. Coverage based on Nielsen study.

GrandTotal	Cable TV Households	Non-cable TV Households	Total TV Households
Estimated Station Totals *	202,630	113,610	316,240
Average Weekly Circulation (2009)	96,747	52,402	149,149
Average Daily Circulation (2009)			55,073

Station DMA Total	Cable TV Households	Non-cable TV Households	Total TV Households
Estimated Station Totals *	202,630	104,980	307,610
Average Weekly Circulation (2009)	96,747	51,962	148,709
Average Daily Circulation (2009)			54,892

Other DMA Total	Cable TV Households	Non-cable TV Households	Total TV Households
Estimated Station Totals *	0	8,630	8,630
Average Weekly Circulation (2009)	0	440	440
Average Daily Circulation (2009)			181

*Estimated station totals are sums of the Nielsen TV and Cable TV household estimates for each county in which the station registers viewing of more than 5% as per the Nielsen Survey Methods.

WACH-DT
Ch. 48

Network Service: FOX.

Licensee: Barrington Columbia License LLC, 2500 W Higgins Rd, Ste 880, Hoffman Estates, IL 60195.

Studio: 1400 Pickens St, Ste 600, Columbia, SC 29201.

Mailing Address: 1400 Pickens St, Ste 600, Columbia, SC 29201.

Phone: 803-252-5757. **Fax:** 803-212-7270.

E-mail: jfarmer@wach.com

Web Site: http://www.midlandsconnect.com

Technical Facilities: Channel No. 48 (674-680 MHz). Authorized power: 520-kw max. visual, aural. Antenna: 587-ft above av. terrain, 475-ft. above ground, 1793-ft. above sea level.

Latitude	34°	02'	38"
Longitude	80°	59'	51"

Note: Latitude and longitude coordinates shown are based on the North American Datum of 1927 (NAD 27) as currently required by the Mass Media Bureau of the FCC.

Ownership: Pilot Group LP (Group Owner).

Began Operation: December 4, 2002. Standard Definition. Began analog operations: October 2, 1981. Sale to FCVS Comunications by Carolina Christian Broadcasting approved by FCC March 14, 1988. Sale to Ellis Communications by FCVS Communications approved by FCC October 7, 1993. Sale to Raycom Media Inc. by Ellis Communications approved by FCC July 26, 1996. Sale to present owner by Raycom Media Inc. approved by FCC June 13, 2006. Ceased analog operations: June 12, 2009.

Represented (legal): Paul Hastings.

Represented (sales): TeleRep Inc.

Personnel:

Scott McBride, President & Chief Executive Officer.

Phil Shreves, Chief Engineer.

Cheri Spetz, General Sales Manager.

Reese Barkley, Program Director.

City of License: Columbia. **Station DMA:** Columbia, SC. **Rank:** 79.

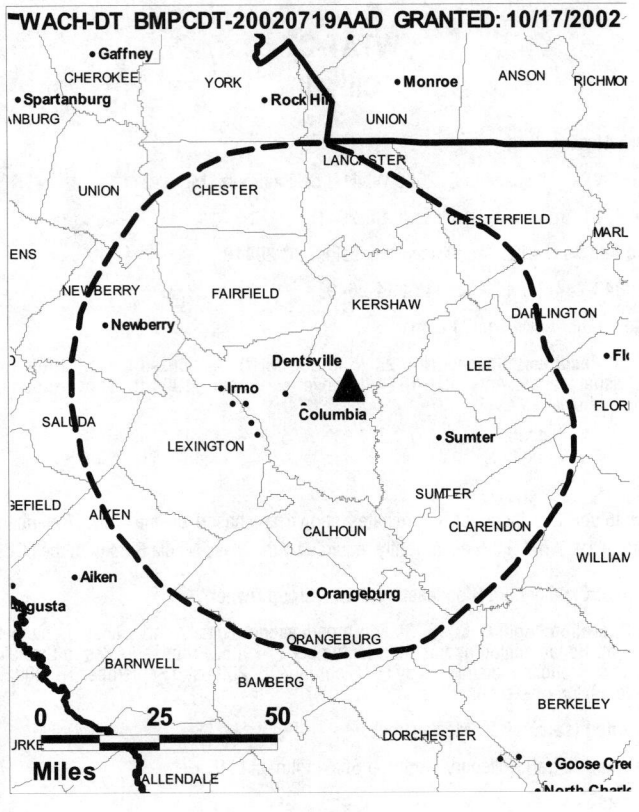

WACH-DT BMPCDT-20020719AAD GRANTED: 10/17/2002

© 2010 Warren Communications News

Circulation © 2009 Nielsen. Coverage based on Nielsen study.

GrandTotal	Cable TV Households	Non-cable TV Households	Total TV Households
Estimated Station Totals *	212,420	208,980	421,400
Average Weekly Circulation (2009)	112,528	98,511	211,039
Average Daily Circulation (2009)			76,089

Station DMA Total	Cable TV Households	Non-cable TV Households	Total TV Households
Estimated Station Totals *	196,430	189,690	386,120
Average Weekly Circulation (2009)	109,469	96,767	206,236
Average Daily Circulation (2009)			74,454

Other DMA Total	Cable TV Households	Non-cable TV Households	Total TV Households
Estimated Station Totals *	15,990	19,290	35,280
Average Weekly Circulation (2009)	3,059	1,744	4,803
Average Daily Circulation (2009)			1,635

*Estimated station totals are sums of the Nielsen TV and Cable TV household estimates for each county in which the station registers viewing of more than 5% as per the Nielsen Survey Methods.

WIS-DT
Ch. 10

Network Service: NBC.

Licensee: WIS License Subsidiary LLC, 201 Monroe St, RSA Tower, 20th Fl, Montgomery, AL 36104.

Studio: 1111 Bull St., Columbia, SC 29201.

Mailing Address: PO Box 367, Columbia, SC 29201.

Phone: 803-799-1010. **Fax:** 803-758-1155.

Web Site: http://www.wistv.com

Technical Facilities: Channel No. 10 (192-198 MHz). Authorized power: 57-kw visual, aural. Antenna: 1578-ft above av. terrain, 1489-ft. above ground, 1841-ft. above sea level.

Latitude	34°	07'	29"
Longitude	80°	45'	23"

Note: Latitude and longitude coordinates shown are based on the North American Datum of 1927 (NAD 27) as currently required by the Mass Media Bureau of the FCC.

Ownership: Raycom Media Inc. (Group Owner).

Began Operation: January 30, 2003. Standard and High Definition. Station broadcasting digitally on its analog channel allotment. Began analog operations: November 7, 1953. Sale to present owner by Cosmos Broadcasting Corp. approved by FCC January 17, 2006. Ceased analog operations: June 12, 2009.

Represented (sales): HRP: Television Station Representative.

Represented (legal): Covington & Burling.

Personnel:

Mel Stebbins, General Manager.

Tina Blacklocke, Station Manager & News Director.

Brent Lane, General Sales Manager.

Lynette Lander, Local Sales Manager.

Sally Rodgers, National & Regional Sales Manager.

Ken Thayer, Chief Engineer.

Quentin Kenny, Business Manager.

Barry Ahrendt, Program & Promotion Director.

Bryan Reeves, Production Manager.

Joyce Murphy, Traffic Manager.

City of License: Columbia. **Station DMA:** Columbia, SC. **Rank:** 79.

WIS-DT BMPCDT-20090304ADP GRANTED: 3/17/2009

© 2010 Warren Communications News

Circulation © 2009 Nielsen. Coverage based on Nielsen study.

GrandTotal	Cable TV Households	Non-cable TV Households	Total TV Households
Estimated Station Totals *	468,890	378,540	847,430
Average Weekly Circulation (2009)	195,016	158,341	353,357
Average Daily Circulation (2009)			193,024

Station DMA Total	Cable TV Households	Non-cable TV Households	Total TV Households
Estimated Station Totals *	196,430	189,690	386,120
Average Weekly Circulation (2009)	149,073	133,861	282,934
Average Daily Circulation (2009)			166,608

Other DMA Total	Cable TV Households	Non-cable TV Households	Total TV Households
Estimated Station Totals *	272,460	188,850	461,310
Average Weekly Circulation (2009)	45,943	24,480	70,423
Average Daily Circulation (2009)			26,416

*Estimated station totals are sums of the Nielsen TV and Cable TV household estimates for each county in which the station registers viewing of more than 5% as per the Nielsen Survey Methods.

WLTX-DT
Ch. 17

Network Service: CBS.

Licensee: Pacific & Southern Co. Inc., 7950 Jones Branch Dr, c/o Gannett Co., McLean, VA 22102.

Studio: 6027 Garners Ferry Rd., Columbia, SC 29209.

Mailing Address: 6027 Garners Ferry Rd, Columbia, SC 29209.

Phone: 803-776-3600. **Fax:** 803-695-3714.

Web Site: http://www.wltx.com

Technical Facilities: Channel No. 17 (488-494 MHz). Authorized power: 1000-kw max. visual, aural. Antenna: 1640-ft above av. terrain, 1569-ft. above ground, 1911-ft. above sea level.

Latitude	34°	05'	49"
Longitude	80°	45'	51"

Note: Latitude and longitude coordinates shown are based on the North American Datum of 1927 (NAD 27) as currently required by the Mass Media Bureau of the FCC.

Satellite Earth Stations: Transmitter RCA; RCA, 3.6-meter Ku-band; ChannelMaster, 3.6-meter C-band; Scientific-Atlanta, 4.6-meter C-band; Scientific-Atlanta, 7-meter C-band; Scientific-Atlanta, ChannelMaster receivers.

Ownership: Gannett Co. Inc. (Group Owner).

Began Operation: May 3, 2002. High Definition. Began analog operations: September 1, 1953. Broadcast on Ch. 67 for first eight years. Shifted to Ch. 19 on June 30, 1961. Sale to Lewis Broadcasting Corp. by Palmetto Radio Corp. approved by FCC February 22, 1978 (Television Digest, Vol. 18:9). Sale to present owner by Lewis Broadcasting Corp. approved by FCC April 29, 1998. Ceased analog operations: June 12, 2009.

Represented (sales): Blair Television.

Personnel:

Rich O'Dell, President & General Manager.

Bob Heinzelmann, General & National Sales Manager.

Mike Garber, News Director.

Keely Richardson, Business Manager.

Jim Hays, Creative Services Director.

Barry Anderson, Production Manager.

Tom Gillespie, Traffic Manager.

City of License: Columbia. **Station DMA:** Columbia, SC. **Rank:** 79.

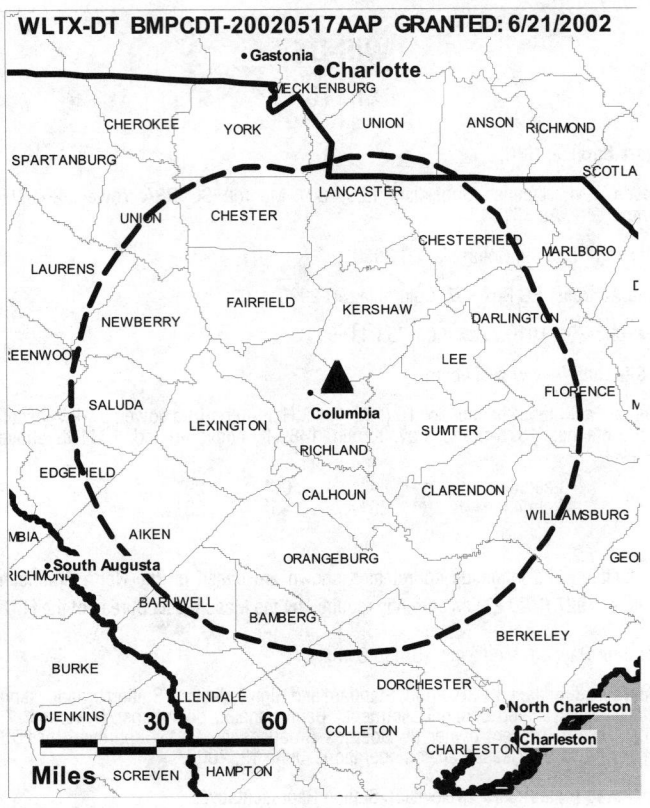

© 2010 Warren Communications News

Circulation © 2009 Nielsen. Coverage based on Nielsen study.

GrandTotal	Cable TV Households	Non-cable TV Households	Total TV Households
Estimated Station Totals *	196,430	258,360	454,790
Average Weekly Circulation (2009)	129,068	127,192	256,260
Average Daily Circulation (2009)			125,149

Station DMA Total	Cable TV Households	Non-cable TV Households	Total TV Households
Estimated Station Totals *	196,430	189,690	386,120
Average Weekly Circulation (2009)	129,068	119,654	248,722
Average Daily Circulation (2009)			123,605

Other DMA Total	Cable TV Households	Non-cable TV Households	Total TV Households
Estimated Station Totals *	0	68,670	68,670
Average Weekly Circulation (2009)	0	7,538	7,538
Average Daily Circulation (2009)			1,544

*Estimated station totals are sums of the Nielsen TV and Cable TV household estimates for each county in which the station registers viewing of more than 5% as per the Nielsen Survey Methods.

WOLO-DT
Ch. 8

Network Service: ABC.

Licensee: South Carolina Broadcasting Partners, One Television Pl, c/o Leon Porter, Charlotte, NC 28205.

Studio: 5807 Shakespeare Rd., Columbia, SC 29223.

Mailing Address: PO Box 4217, Columbia, SC 29240.

Phone: 803-754-7525. **Fax:** 803-754-6147.

Web Site: http://www.abccolumbia.com

Technical Facilities: Channel No. 8 (180-186 MHz). Authorized power: 43.7-kw visual, aural. Antenna: 1736-ft above av. terrain, 1729-ft. above ground, 1765-ft. above sea level.

Latitude	34°	06'	58"
Longitude	80°	45'	51"

Note: Latitude and longitude coordinates shown are based on the North American Datum of 1927 (NAD 27) as currently required by the Mass Media Bureau of the FCC.

Ownership: Bahakel Communications Ltd. (Group Owner).

Began Operation: October 1, 2002. Standard and High Definition. Began analog operations: October 1, 1961. Sale to present owner by First Carolina Corp. approved by FCC May 5, 1964. Ceased analog operations: June 12, 2009.

Represented (legal): Dow Lohnes PLLC.

Represented (sales): Continental Television Sales.

Personnel:

Chris Bailey, Vice President & General Manager.

Jim Babb, Executive Vice President, Television & Cable.

David Aiken, Operations & Program Manager.

Brandt Minnick, General Sales Manager.

Christy Vaughn, News Director.

Jeff Wright, Chief Engineer.

Marty White, Business Manager.

Scott Moore, Creative Services Manager.

Gwen White, Traffic Manager.

City of License: Columbia. **Station DMA:** Columbia, SC. **Rank:** 79.

WOLO-DT BPCDT-19990713KH GRANTED: 8/15/2000

© 2010 Warren Communications News

Circulation © 2009 Nielsen. Coverage based on Nielsen study.

GrandTotal	Cable TV Households	Non-cable TV Households	Total TV Households
Estimated Station Totals *	199,030	208,980	408,010
Average Weekly Circulation (2009)	116,739	104,072	220,811
Average Daily Circulation (2009)			94,313

Station DMA Total	Cable TV Households	Non-cable TV Households	Total TV Households
Estimated Station Totals *	196,430	189,690	386,120
Average Weekly Circulation (2009)	116,440	102,454	218,894
Average Daily Circulation (2009)			93,940

Other DMA Total	Cable TV Households	Non-cable TV Households	Total TV Households
Estimated Station Totals *	2,600	19,290	21,890
Average Weekly Circulation (2009)	299	1,618	1,917
Average Daily Circulation (2009)			373

*Estimated station totals are sums of the Nielsen TV and Cable TV household estimates for each county in which the station registers viewing of more than 5% as per the Nielsen Survey Methods.

WZRB-DT
Ch. 47

Network Service: CW.

Licensee: Roberts Broadcasting USA LLC, 1408 N Kingshighway Blvd, Ste 300, St. Louis, MO 63113.

Studio: 1747 Cushman Dr, Columbia, SC 29204.

Mailing Address: 1747 Cushman Dr, Columbia, SC 29204.

Phone: 803-714-2347. **Fax:** 803-691-3848.

Web Site: http://www.cw47columbia.com/

Technical Facilities: Channel No. 47 (668-674 MHz). Authorized power: 240-kw max. visual, aural. Antenna: 630-ft above av. terrain, 518-ft. above ground, 898-ft. above sea level.

Latitude	34°	02'	38"
Longitude	80°	59'	51"

Note: Latitude and longitude coordinates shown are based on the North American Datum of 1927 (NAD 27) as currently required by the Mass Media Bureau of the FCC.

Ownership: Steven C. Roberts (Group Owner); Michael V. Roberts (Group Owner).

Began Operation: February 17, 2009. Station broadcasting digitally on its analog channel allotment. Began analog operations: January 1, 2005. Ceased analog operations: February 17, 2009.

Personnel:

Dody Yarborough, General Manager.

Rick Sprott, Chief Engineer.

Robin Jackson, National Sales Manager.

Brian Payne, Production Manager.

City of License: Columbia. **Station DMA:** Columbia, SC. **Rank:** 79.

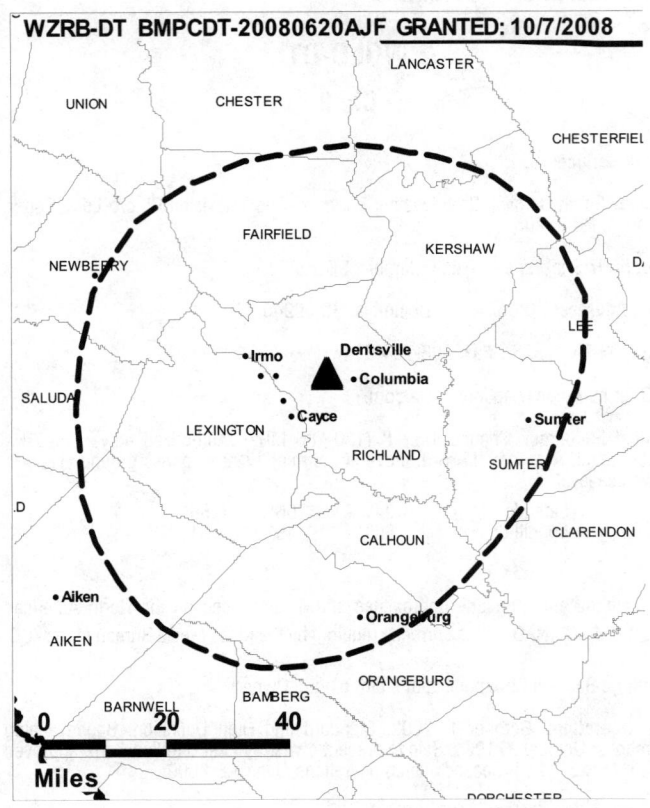

WZRB-DT BMPCDT-20080620AJF GRANTED: 10/7/2008

© 2010 Warren Communications News

Circulation © 2009 Nielsen. Coverage based on Nielsen study.

GrandTotal	Cable TV Households	Non-cable TV Households	Total TV Households
Estimated Station Totals *	191,230	189,690	380,920
Average Weekly Circulation (2009)	41,204	41,874	83,078
Average Daily Circulation (2009)			24,822

Station DMA Total	Cable TV Households	Non-cable TV Households	Total TV Households
Estimated Station Totals *	191,230	189,690	380,920
Average Weekly Circulation (2009)	41,204	41,874	83,078
Average Daily Circulation (2009)			24,822

*Estimated station totals are sums of the Nielsen TV and Cable TV household estimates for each county in which the station registers viewing of more than 5% as per the Nielsen Survey Methods.

WBTW-DT
Ch. 13

Network Service: MNT, CBS.

Grantee: Media General Communications Holdings LLC, 333 E Franklin St, Richmond, VA 23219.

Studio: 3430 N. TV Rd., Florence, SC 29501.

Mailing Address: 3430 N. TV Rd, Florence, SC 29501.

Phone: 843-317-1313; 843-293-1301. **Fax:** 843-317-1422.

Web Site: http://www.wbtw.com

Technical Facilities: Channel No. 13 (210-216 MHz). Authorized power: 31.6-kw visual, aural. Antenna: 1962-ft above av. terrain, 1948-ft. above ground, 2064-ft. above sea level.

Latitude	34°	22'	04"
Longitude	79°	19'	21"

Note: Latitude and longitude coordinates shown are based on the North American Datum of 1927 (NAD 27) as currently required by the Mass Media Bureau of the FCC.

Multichannel TV Sound: Stereo only.

Ownership: Media General Inc. (Group Owner).

Began Operation: January 5, 2002. Station broadcasting digitally on its analog channel allotment. Began analog operations: October 18, 1954. Sale to present owner by Spartan Communications Inc. approved by FCC March 22, 2000. Sale to Spartan Communications Inc. by Daily Telegraph Printing Co. approved by FCC June 12, 1984 (Television Digest, Vol. 24:15). Sale to Daily Telegraph Printing Co. by Jefferson Standard Life Insurance Co. approved by FCC February 28, 1968 (Vol. 7:43; 8:10). Ceased analog operations: June 12, 2009.

Represented (sales): HRP: Television Station Representative.

Represented (legal): Dow Lohnes PLLC.

Personnel:

Michael Caplan, Vice President & General Manager.

Brian Lang, General Sales Manager.

John Vincent, Local Sales Manager.

Scott Chaskin, Local Sales Manager.

David Hart, News Director.

Scott Johnson, Chief Engineer.

James Bethea, Business Manager.

Chuck Spruill, Creative Services Director.

Sandra Sellers, Traffic Manager.

Angela McCravin, Community Affairs Director.

City of License: Florence. **Station DMA:** Myrtle Beach-Florence, SC. **Rank:** 104.

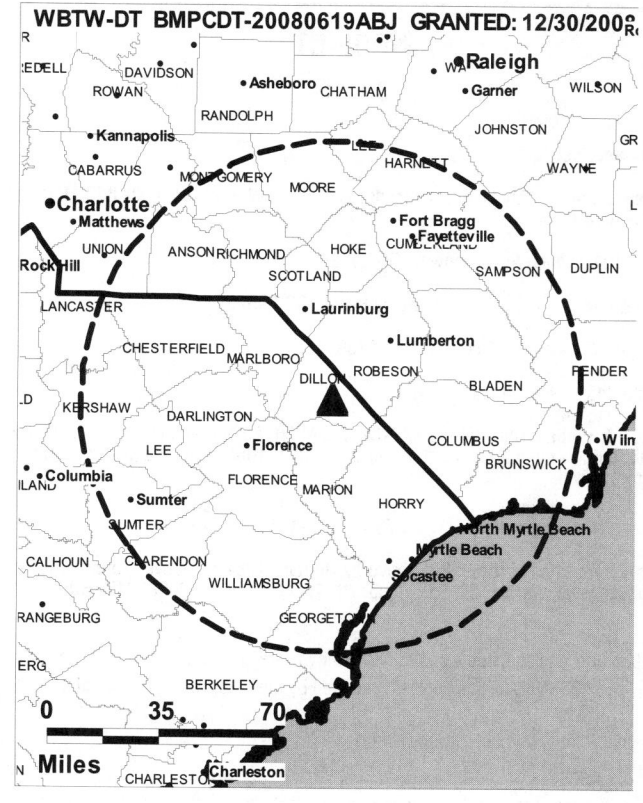

© 2010 Warren Communications News

Circulation © 2009 Nielsen. Coverage based on Nielsen study.

GrandTotal	Cable TV Households	Non-cable TV Households	Total TV Households
Estimated Station Totals *	292,820	190,400	483,220
Average Weekly Circulation (2009)	166,587	87,070	253,657
Average Daily Circulation (2009)			142,804

Station DMA Total	Cable TV Households	Non-cable TV Households	Total TV Households
Estimated Station Totals *	184,020	100,990	285,010
Average Weekly Circulation (2009)	128,770	72,301	201,071
Average Daily Circulation (2009)			118,296

Other DMA Total	Cable TV Households	Non-cable TV Households	Total TV Households
Estimated Station Totals *	108,800	89,410	198,210
Average Weekly Circulation (2009)	37,817	14,769	52,586
Average Daily Circulation (2009)			24,508

*Estimated station totals are sums of the Nielsen TV and Cable TV household estimates for each county in which the station registers viewing of more than 5% as per the Nielsen Survey Methods.

WPDE-DT

Ch. 16

Network Service: ABC.

Licensee: Barrington Myrtle Beach License LLC, 2500 W Higgins Rd, Ste 880, Hoffman Estates, IL 60195.

Studio: 1194 Atlantic Ave., Conway, SC 29526.

Mailing Address: PO Box 51150, Myrtle Beach, SC 29579.

Phone: 843-234-9733. **Fax:** 843-234-9739.

Web Site: http://www.wpde.com

Technical Facilities: Channel No. 16 (482-488 MHz). Authorized power: 421-kw max. visual, aural. Antenna: 1973-ft above av. terrain, 1968-ft. above ground, 2075-ft. above sea level.

Latitude	34°	21'	53"
Longitude	79°	19'	49"

Holds CP for change to 1968-ft above av. terrain, 1962-ft. above ground, 2069-ft. above sea level; lat. 34° 22' 02", long. 79° 19' 49", BPCDT-20080317AHU.

Note: Latitude and longitude coordinates shown are based on the North American Datum of 1927 (NAD 27) as currently required by the Mass Media Bureau of the FCC.

Ownership: Pilot Group LP (Group Owner).

Began Operation: August 15, 2008. Began analog operations: November 22, 1980. Sale to present owner by Diversified Communications approved by FCC December 16, 2005. Sale to Diversified Communications by Eastern Carolinas Broadcasting approved by FCC June 27, 1985. Ceased analog operations: June 12, 2009.

Represented (legal): Paul Hastings.

Represented (sales): Continental Television Sales.

Personnel:

Billy Huggins, Vice President & General Manager.

Lee Camp, General Sales Manager.

Victoria Spechko, News Director.

Mark Olson, Chief Engineer.

Marissa Wilson, Program Manager.

Debra Yost, Accounting & Sales Manager.

Michelle Camp, Commercial Production Manager.

City of License: Florence. **Station DMA:** Myrtle Beach-Florence, SC. **Rank:** 104.

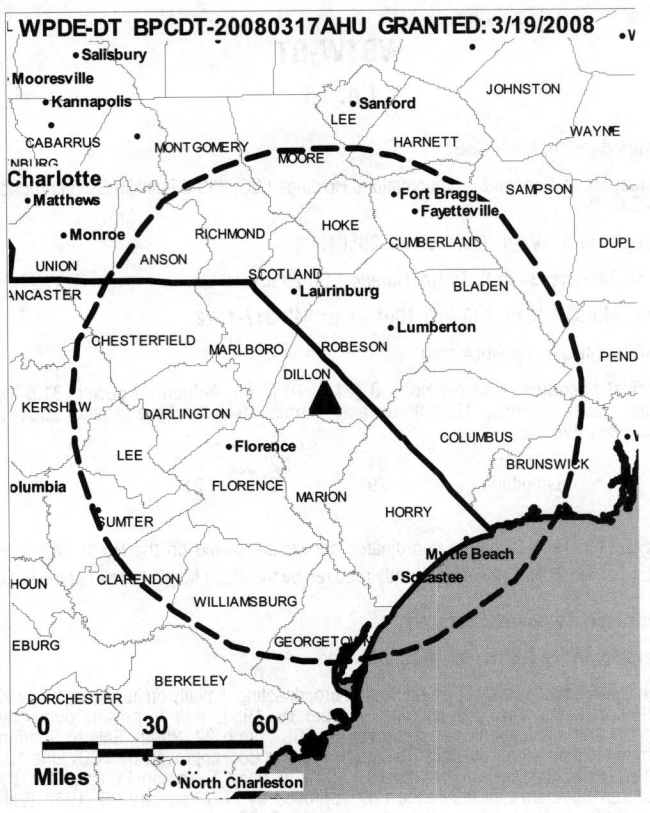

WPDE-DT BPCDT-20080317AHU GRANTED: 3/19/2008

© 2010 Warren Communications News

Circulation © 2009 Nielsen. Coverage based on Nielsen study.

GrandTotal	Cable TV Households	Non-cable TV Households	Total TV Households
Estimated Station Totals *	213,710	161,980	375,690
Average Weekly Circulation (2009)	116,283	60,883	177,166
Average Daily Circulation (2009)			82,261

Station DMA Total	Cable TV Households	Non-cable TV Households	Total TV Households
Estimated Station Totals *	184,020	100,990	285,010
Average Weekly Circulation (2009)	106,844	55,492	162,336
Average Daily Circulation (2009)			76,777

Other DMA Total	Cable TV Households	Non-cable TV Households	Total TV Households
Estimated Station Totals *	29,690	60,990	90,680
Average Weekly Circulation (2009)	9,439	5,391	14,830
Average Daily Circulation (2009)			5,484

*Estimated station totals are sums of the Nielsen TV and Cable TV household estimates for each county in which the station registers viewing of more than 5% as per the Nielsen Survey Methods.

WGGS-DT
Ch. 16

Network Service: IND.

Licensee: Carolina Christian Broadcasting Inc., PO Box 1616, Greenville, SC 29602.

Studio: 3409 Rutherford Rd. Extension, Taylors, SC 29687.

Mailing Address: PO Box 1616, Greenville, SC 29602.

Phone: 864-244-1616. **Fax:** 864-292-8481.

Web Site: http://www.dovebroadcasting.com

Technical Facilities: Channel No. 16 (482-488 MHz). Authorized power: 175-kw max. visual, aural. Antenna: 1181-ft above av. terrain, 167-ft. above ground, 2185-ft. above sea level.

Latitude	34°	56'	26"
Longitude	82°	24'	41"

Requests modification of CP for change to 900-kw max. visual; BMPCDT-20080619AAM.

Note: Latitude and longitude coordinates shown are based on the North American Datum of 1927 (NAD 27) as currently required by the Mass Media Bureau of the FCC.

Ownership: Carolina Christian Broadcasting Co. (Group Owner).

Began Operation: June 27, 2007. Station broadcasting digitally on its analog channel allotment. Began analog operations: October 29, 1972. Ceased analog operations: June 12, 2009.

Personnel:

James H. Thompson, President & General Manager.

Bill Rainey, General Sales Manager.

Dante Thompson, Local Sales Manager.

Pete Littlefield, Chief Engineer.

Kym MacKinnon, Program Director & Traffic Manager.

Greg West, Promotion Director.

Michele Loftis, Production Director.

Derek Myers, Public Affairs Director.

City of License: Greenville.

Station DMA: Greenville-Spartanburg-Anderson, SC-Asheville, NC. **Rank:** 36.

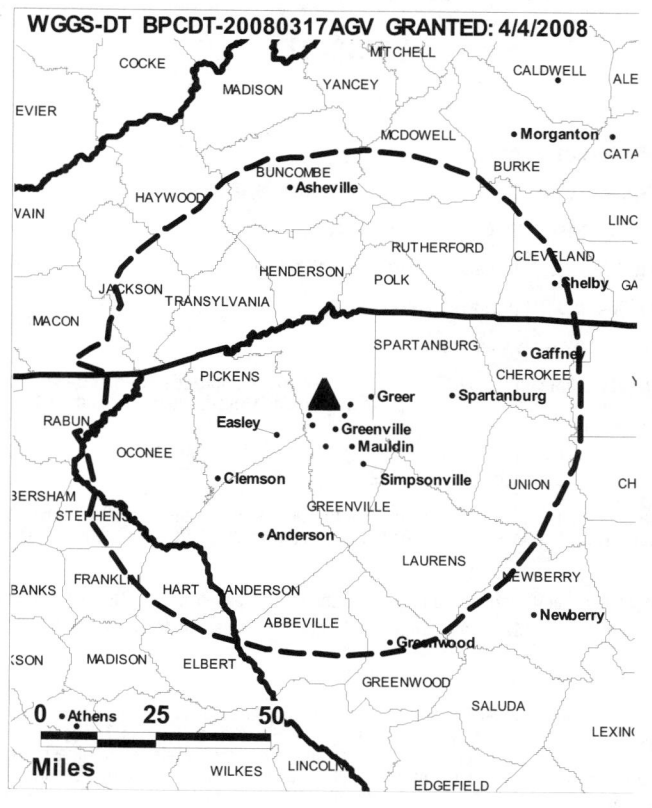

WGGS-DT BPCDT-20080317AGV GRANTED: 4/4/2008

© 2010 Warren Communications News

Circulation © 2009 Nielsen. Coverage based on Nielsen study.

GrandTotal	Cable TV Households	Non-cable TV Households	Total TV Households
Estimated Station Totals *	272,960	249,180	522,140
Average Weekly Circulation (2009)	21,971	19,146	41,117
Average Daily Circulation (2009)			11,048

Station DMA Total	Cable TV Households	Non-cable TV Households	Total TV Households
Estimated Station Totals *	267,760	249,180	516,940
Average Weekly Circulation (2009)	21,560	19,146	40,706
Average Daily Circulation (2009)			11,017

Other DMA Total	Cable TV Households	Non-cable TV Households	Total TV Households
Estimated Station Totals *	5,200	0	5,200
Average Weekly Circulation (2009)	411	0	411
Average Daily Circulation (2009)			31

*Estimated station totals are sums of the Nielsen TV and Cable TV household estimates for each county in which the station registers viewing of more than 5% as per the Nielsen Survey Methods.

WHNS-DT
Ch. 21

Network Service: FOX.

Grantee: Meredith Corp., 1716 Locust St, Des Moines, IA 50309-3203.

Studio: 21 Interstate Ct, Greenville, SC 29615.

Mailing Address: 21 Interstate Ct, Greenville, SC 29615.

Phone: 864-288-2100. **Fax:** 864-297-0728.

Web Site: http://www.whns.com

Technical Facilities: Channel No. 21 (512-518 MHz). Authorized power: 160-kw max. visual, aural. Antenna: 2498-ft above av. terrain, 1583-ft. above ground, 5011-ft. above sea level.

Latitude	35°	10'	56"
Longitude	82°	40'	56"

Requests modification of CP for change to 400-kw max. visual, 2500-ft above av. terrain, 1583-ft. above ground, 5011-ft. above sea level; BMPCDT-20080619AFO.

Note: Latitude and longitude coordinates shown are based on the North American Datum of 1927 (NAD 27) as currently required by the Mass Media Bureau of the FCC.

Ownership: Meredith Corp. (Group Owner).

Began Operation: October 15, 2002. Station broadcasting digitally on its analog channel allotment. Began analog operations: July 5, 1953. Sale to Pappas Telecasting by Thomas Broadcasting approved by FCC July 27, 1979 (Television Digest, Vol. 19:25). Resumed operation April 1, 1984. Sale to Cannell Communications by Pappas Telecasting Companies approved by FCC August 2, 1990 (Vol. 29:47; 30:35). Sale to First Media Television LP by Cannell approved by FCC November 1, 1994. Sale to present owner by First Media Television LP approved by FCC June 20, 1997 (Vol. 37:27). Ceased analog operations: June 12, 2009.

Represented (sales): TeleRep Inc.

Personnel:

Guy Hempel, General Manager.

Jeff Gilbert, General Sales Manager.

Eric Krebs, Local Sales Manager.

Alan DeFlorio, National Sales Manager.

Kyann Lewis, News Director.

Jim Barnes, Chief Engineer.

Phyllis Olson, Controller.

Rhonda Ross, Traffic Manager.

City of License: Greenville.

Station DMA: Greenville-Spartanburg-Anderson, SC-Asheville, NC. **Rank:** 36.

© 2010 Warren Communications News

Circulation © 2009 Nielsen. Coverage based on Nielsen study.

GrandTotal	Cable TV Households	Non-cable TV Households	Total TV Households
Estimated Station Totals *	397,530	461,090	858,620
Average Weekly Circulation (2009)	205,599	227,472	433,071
Average Daily Circulation (2009)			160,723

Station DMA Total	Cable TV Households	Non-cable TV Households	Total TV Households
Estimated Station Totals *	395,190	436,900	832,090
Average Weekly Circulation (2009)	204,658	224,688	429,346
Average Daily Circulation (2009)			159,684

Other DMA Total	Cable TV Households	Non-cable TV Households	Total TV Households
Estimated Station Totals *	2,340	24,190	26,530
Average Weekly Circulation (2009)	941	2,784	3,725
Average Daily Circulation (2009)			1,039

*Estimated station totals are sums of the Nielsen TV and Cable TV household estimates for each county in which the station registers viewing of more than 5% as per the Nielsen Survey Methods.

WYFF-DT
Ch. 59

Network Service: NBC.

Licensee: WYFF Hearst Argyle Television Inc., PO Box 1800, c/o Brooks, Pierce et al., Raleigh, NC 27602.

Studio: Broadcast Place, 505 Rutherford St., Greenville, SC 29609.

Mailing Address: 505 Rutherford St, Greenville, SC 29609.

Phone: 864-242-4404. **Fax:** 864-240-5305.

Web Site: http://www.wyff4.com

Technical Facilities: Channel No. 59 (740-746 MHz). Authorized power: 1000-kw max. visual, aural. Antenna: 1893-ft above av. terrain, 761-ft. above ground, 3848-ft. above sea level.

Latitude	35°	06'	43"
Longitude	82°	36'	24"

Holds CP for change to channel number 36, 1955-ft above av. terrain, 833-ft. above ground, 3921-ft. above sea level; BPCDT-20080317ABT.

Note: Latitude and longitude coordinates shown are based on the North American Datum of 1927 (NAD 27) as currently required by the Mass Media Bureau of the FCC.

Ownership: Hearst-Argyle Television Inc. (Group Owner).

Began Operation: February 18, 2005. Began analog operations: December 31, 1953. Hearst-Argyle received approval from the FCC May 26, 2009 to become privately owned by The Hearst Corp. Sale to present owner by Pulitzer Publishing Co. approved by FCC November 24, 1998. Exchange (with WXII, Winston- Salem, NC) for KSDK, St. Louis, MO approved by FCC February 17, 1983. Transfer to Multimedia Inc. from Southeastern Broadcasting Corp. approved by FCC September 22, 1967. Ceased analog operations: June 12, 2009.

Represented (sales): Eagle Television Sales.

Represented (legal): Brooks, Pierce, McLendon, Humphrey & Leonard LLP.

Personnel:

Michael Hayes, President & General Manager.

John Humphries, General Sales Manager.

Steve Eaton, Local Sales Manager.

Blake Bridges, National Sales Manager.

Justin Antoniotti, News Director.

Douglas Durkee, Broadcast Operations Manager.

Jim Myers, Chief Engineer.

Steve Bomar, Business Manager.

Cathy Petropoulos, Sales & Marketing Director.

Marsa Jarrett, Promotion Manager.

Dan Ross, Production Manager & Programming Director.

Keith Eaker, Research Director.

Melanie Richey, Traffic Manager.

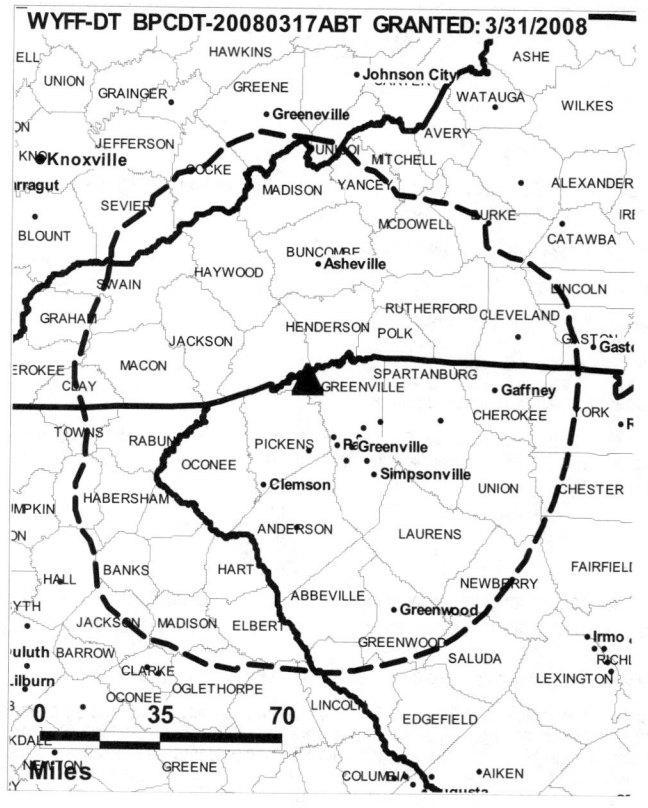

© 2010 Warren Communications News

City of License: Greenville.

Station DMA: Greenville-Spartanburg-Anderson, SC-Asheville, NC. **Rank:** 36.

Circulation © 2009 Nielsen. Coverage based on Nielsen study.

GrandTotal	Cable TV Households	Non-cable TV Households	Total TV Households
Estimated Station Totals *	428,570	438,440	867,010
Average Weekly Circulation (2009)	276,016	272,758	548,774
Average Daily Circulation (2009)			291,173

Station DMA Total	Cable TV Households	Non-cable TV Households	Total TV Households
Estimated Station Totals *	390,980	436,900	827,880
Average Weekly Circulation (2009)	269,828	272,556	542,384
Average Daily Circulation (2009)			289,575

Other DMA Total	Cable TV Households	Non-cable TV Households	Total TV Households
Estimated Station Totals *	37,590	1,540	39,130
Average Weekly Circulation (2009)	6,188	202	6,390
Average Daily Circulation (2009)			1,598

*Estimated station totals are sums of the Nielsen TV and Cable TV household estimates for each county in which the station registers viewing of more than 5% as per the Nielsen Survey Methods.

WTGS-DT
Ch. 28

Network Service: FOX.

Licensee: PBC of Savannah License LLC, Debtor in Possession, 11766 Wilshire Blvd, Ste 405, Los Angeles, CA 90025-6573.

Studio: 10001 Abercorn St, Savannah, GA 31406.

Mailing Address: 10001 Abercorn St, Savannah, GA 31406.

Phone: 912-925-2287; 912-925-0022. **Fax:** 912-925-7026.

E-mail: cstewart@wjcl.com

Web Site: http://www.thecoastalsource.com

Technical Facilities: Channel No. 28 (554-560 MHz). Authorized power: max. visual, aural. Antenna: 1493-ft above av. terrain, 1503-ft. above ground, 1516-ft. above sea level.

Latitude	32°	02'	45"
Longitude	81°	20'	27"

Note: Latitude and longitude coordinates shown are based on the North American Datum of 1927 (NAD 27) as currently required by the Mass Media Bureau of the FCC.

Ownership: PBC Television Holdings LLC, Debtor in Possession (Group Owner).

Began Operation: May 9, 2007. Station broadcasting digitally on its analog channel allotment. Began analog operations: September 1, 1985. Ceased analog operations: February 17, 2009. Involuntary assignment of license to Debtor in Possession status approved by FCC July 24, 2009. Sale to present owner by Brissette Broadcasting of Savannah License LLC approved by FCC July 30, 2007. Sale to Brissette Broadcasting of Savannah License LLC by LP Media Inc. approved by FCC October 28, 1998. Sale to LP Media Inc. by Hilton Head Television Inc. approved by FCC July 15, 1996.

Represented (legal): Drinker Biddle.

Represented (sales): Continental Television Sales.

Personnel:

Lynn Fairbanks, President & General Manager.

Scott Centers, General Sales Manager.

Michael Sullivan, News Director.

Ed Youmans, Chief Engineer.

Erica Scriven, Business Manager.

Morgan Sladick, Program Director.

Chris Hays, Production Manager.

Karon Johnson, Traffic Manager.

City of License: Hardeeville. **Station DMA:** Savannah, GA. **Rank:** 96.

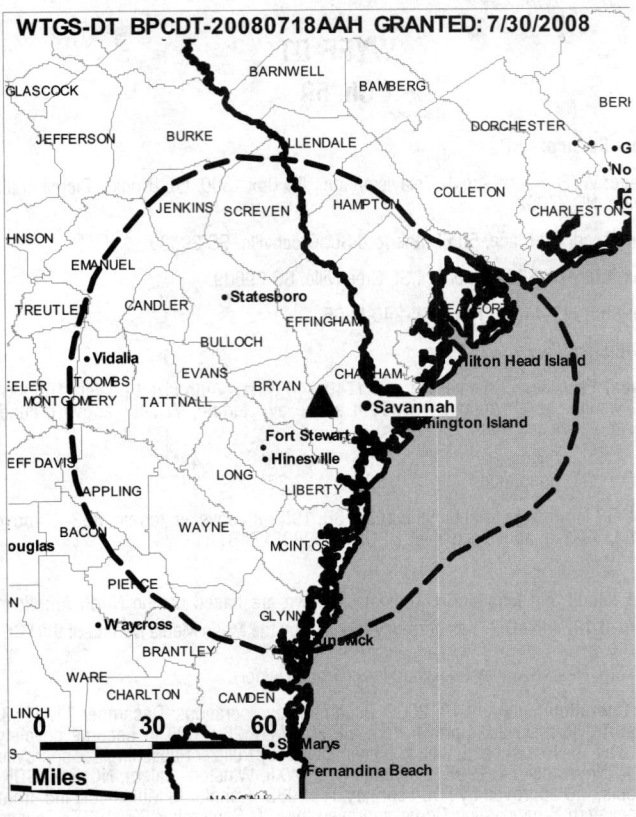

WTGS-DT BPCDT-20080718AAH GRANTED: 7/30/2008

© 2010 Warren Communications News

Circulation © 2009 Nielsen. Coverage based on Nielsen study.

GrandTotal	Cable TV Households	Non-cable TV Households	Total TV Households
Estimated Station Totals *	196,840	114,110	310,950
Average Weekly Circulation (2009)	90,692	50,268	140,960
Average Daily Circulation (2009)			46,146

Station DMA Total	Cable TV Households	Non-cable TV Households	Total TV Households
Estimated Station Totals *	185,020	109,450	294,470
Average Weekly Circulation (2009)	88,878	49,946	138,824
Average Daily Circulation (2009)			45,720

Other DMA Total	Cable TV Households	Non-cable TV Households	Total TV Households
Estimated Station Totals *	11,820	4,660	16,480
Average Weekly Circulation (2009)	1,814	322	2,136
Average Daily Circulation (2009)			426

*Estimated station totals are sums of the Nielsen TV and Cable TV household estimates for each county in which the station registers viewing of more than 5% as per the Nielsen Survey Methods.

WFXB-DT
Ch. 18

Network Service: FOX.

Licensee: Springfield Broadcasting Partners, One Television Pl, c/o Leon Porter, Charlotte, NC 28205.

Studio: 3364 Huger St, Myrtle Beach, SC 29577.

Mailing Address: PO Box 8309, Myrtle Beach, SC 29578.

Phone: 643-828-4300. **Fax:** 843-828-4343.

E-mail: jonjones@wfxb.com

Web Site: http://www.wfxb.com

Technical Facilities: Channel No. 18 (494-500 MHz). Authorized power: 1000-kw max. visual, aural. Antenna: 1506-ft above av. terrain, 1503-ft. above ground, 1579-ft. above sea level.

Latitude	34°	11'	19"
Longitude	79°	11'	00"

Transmitter: 1.5-mi. S of Hwy 76 & State Rd S34-320, Mullins.

Note: Latitude and longitude coordinates shown are based on the North American Datum of 1927 (NAD 27) as currently required by the Mass Media Bureau of the FCC.

Ownership: Bahakel Communications Ltd. (Group Owner).

Began Operation: January 30, 2007. Began analog operations: July 5, 1984. Sale to present owner by GE Media Inc. approved by FCC March 16, 2006. Sale to GE Media Inc. by Carolina Christian Broadcasting Inc. approved by FCC April 12, 1996. Sale to Carolina Christian Broadcasting Inc. approved by FCC November 4, 1981. Ceased analog operations: June 12, 2009.

Represented (legal): Dow Lohnes PLLC.

Represented (sales): Katz Media Group.

Personnel:

Rigby Wilson, Vice President & General Manager.

Pete Sealer, Local Sales Manager, Florence.

Jon Jones, Local Sales Manager, Myrtle Beach.

Ken Theobald, Chief Engineer.

Linda Todd, Business Manager.

Steve Albright, Program Coordinator.

Dave Miligan, Production Manager.

John Lydon, Traffic Coordinator.

City of License: Myrtle Beach. **Station DMA:** Myrtle Beach-Florence, SC. **Rank:** 104.

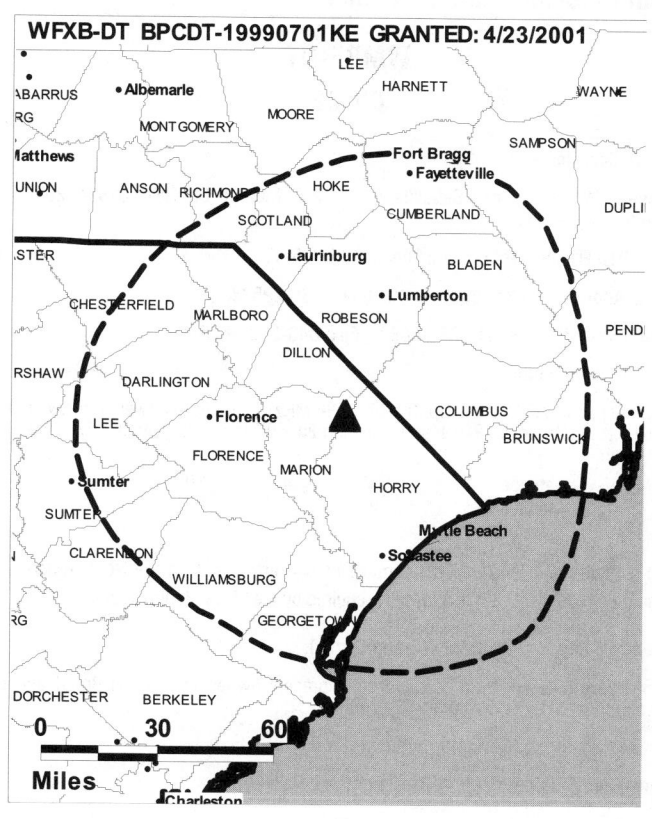

WFXB-DT BPCDT-19990701KE GRANTED: 4/23/2001

© 2010 Warren Communications News

Circulation © 2009 Nielsen. Coverage based on Nielsen study.

GrandTotal	Cable TV Households	Non-cable TV Households	Total TV Households
Estimated Station Totals *	201,560	144,160	345,720
Average Weekly Circulation (2009)	91,982	50,124	142,106
Average Daily Circulation (2009)			48,929

Station DMA Total	Cable TV Households	Non-cable TV Households	Total TV Households
Estimated Station Totals *	184,020	100,990	285,010
Average Weekly Circulation (2009)	88,106	45,988	134,094
Average Daily Circulation (2009)			46,563

Other DMA Total	Cable TV Households	Non-cable TV Households	Total TV Households
Estimated Station Totals *	17,540	43,170	60,710
Average Weekly Circulation (2009)	3,876	4,136	8,012
Average Daily Circulation (2009)			2,366

*Estimated station totals are sums of the Nielsen TV and Cable TV household estimates for each county in which the station registers viewing of more than 5% as per the Nielsen Survey Methods.

WMBF-DT
Ch. 32

Network Service: NBC.

Licensee: WMBF License Subsidiary LLC, 201 Monroe St, RSA Tower, 20th Fl, Montgomery, AL 36104.

Studio: 918 Frontage Rd E, Myrtle Beach, SC 29577.

Mailing Address: PO Box 3579, Myrtle Beach, SC 29578.

Phone: 843-839-9623; 843-661-6683. **Fax:** 843-839-9625.

Web Site: http://wmbftv.com

Technical Facilities: Channel No. 32 (578-584 MHz). Authorized power: 165-kw max. visual, aural. Antenna: 610-ft above av. terrain, 607-ft. above ground, 627-ft. above sea level.

Latitude	33°	43'	50"
Longitude	79°	04'	32"

Note: Latitude and longitude coordinates shown are based on the North American Datum of 1927 (NAD 27) as currently required by the Mass Media Bureau of the FCC.

Ownership: Raycom Media Inc. (Group Owner).

Began Operation: August 8, 2008. Sale to present owner by Cosmos Broadcasting Corp. approved by FCC January 17, 2006.

Represented (legal): Covington & Burling.

Represented (engineering): du Treil, Lundin & Rackley Inc.

Personnel:

Ted Fortenberry, General Manager.

Gary Savage, Chief Engineer.

Eileen Russo, General Sales Manager.

Amanda Leaseburg, Marketing Director.

Megan Jenkins, Program Director.

City of License: Myrtle Beach. **Station DMA:** Myrtle Beach-Florence, SC. **Rank:** 104.

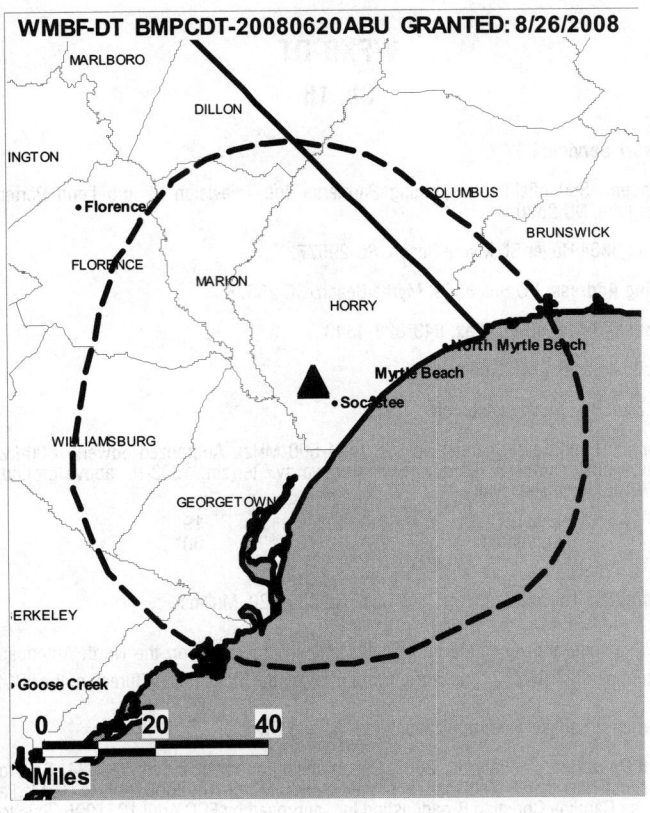

WMBF-DT BMPCDT-20080620ABU GRANTED: 8/26/2008

© 2010 Warren Communications News

Circulation © 2009 Nielsen. Coverage based on Nielsen study.

GrandTotal	Cable TV Households	Non-cable TV Households	Total TV Households
Estimated Station Totals *	200,020	58,050	258,070
Average Weekly Circulation (2009)	49,149	5,889	55,038
Average Daily Circulation (2009)			19,294

Station DMA Total	Cable TV Households	Non-cable TV Households	Total TV Households
Estimated Station Totals *	179,230	58,050	237,280
Average Weekly Circulation (2009)	47,304	5,889	53,193
Average Daily Circulation (2009)			19,060

Other DMA Total	Cable TV Households	Non-cable TV Households	Total TV Households
Estimated Station Totals *	20,790	0	20,790
Average Weekly Circulation (2009)	1,845	0	1,845
Average Daily Circulation (2009)			234

*Estimated station totals are sums of the Nielsen TV and Cable TV household estimates for each county in which the station registers viewing of more than 5% as per the Nielsen Survey Methods.

WMYT-DT
Ch. 39

Network Service: MNT.

Grantee: WMYT-TV Inc., PO Box 668400, 3501 Performance Rd, Charlotte, NC 28266-8400.

Studio: 3501 Performance Rd, Charlotte, NC 28214.

Mailing Address: 3501 Performance Rd, Charlotte, NC 28214.

Phone: 704-398-0046. **Fax:** 704-393-8407.

Web Site: http://www.wmyt12.com/

Technical Facilities: Channel No. 39 (320-626 MHz). Authorized power: 225-kw max. visual, aural. Antenna: 1873-ft above av. terrain, 1844-ft. above ground, 2650-ft. above sea level.

Latitude	35°	21'	44"
Longitude	81°	09'	19"

Note: Latitude and longitude coordinates shown are based on the North American Datum of 1927 (NAD 27) as currently required by the Mass Media Bureau of the FCC.

Ownership: Capitol Broadcasting Co. Inc. (Group Owner).

Began Operation: May 24, 2002. Began analog operations: October 21, 1994. Ceased analog operations: June 12, 2009.

Represented (legal): Holland & Knight LLP.

Personnel:

Will Davis, Vice President & General Manager.

Shawn Harris, General Sales Manager.

Tom Shields, Local Sales Manager.

Don Travis, National Sales Manager.

John Bishop, Engineering Manager.

Jacqueline Draper, Business Manager.

Joe Heaton, Promotion & Marketing Manager.

Mary Sellars, Traffic Manager.

City of License: Rock Hill. **Station DMA:** Charlotte, NC. **Rank:** 24.

Digital cable and TV coverage maps.
Visit www.warren-news.com/mediaprints.htm

MediaPrints™
Map a Winning Business Strategy

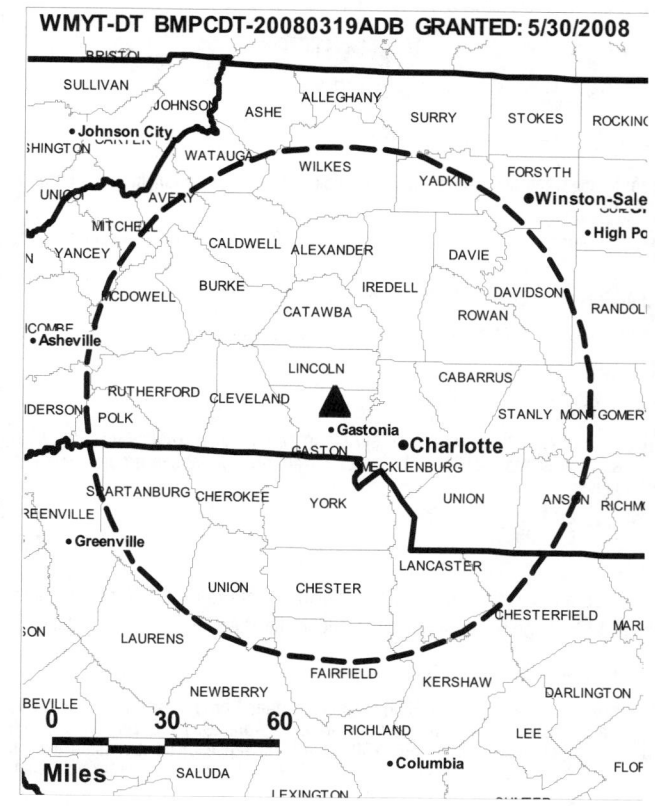

WMYT-DT BMPCDT-20080319ADB GRANTED: 5/30/2008

© 2010 Warren Communications News

Circulation © 2009 Nielsen. Coverage based on Nielsen study.

GrandTotal	Cable TV Households	Non-cable TV Households	Total TV Households
Estimated Station Totals *	649,210	469,880	1,119,090
Average Weekly Circulation (2009)	104,033	80,703	184,736
Average Daily Circulation (2009)			66,095

Station DMA Total	Cable TV Households	Non-cable TV Households	Total TV Households
Estimated Station Totals *	644,890	456,670	1,101,560
Average Weekly Circulation (2009)	103,817	79,501	183,318
Average Daily Circulation (2009)			65,736

Other DMA Total	Cable TV Households	Non-cable TV Households	Total TV Households
Estimated Station Totals *	4,320	13,210	17,530
Average Weekly Circulation (2009)	216	1,202	1,418
Average Daily Circulation (2009)			359

*Estimated station totals are sums of the Nielsen TV and Cable TV household estimates for each county in which the station registers viewing of more than 5% as per the Nielsen Survey Methods.

South Carolina — Spartanburg

WSPA-DT
Ch. 7

Network Service: CBS.

Licensee: Media General Communications Holdings LLC, 333 E Franklin St, Richmond, VA 23219.

Studios: 250 International Dr., Spartanburg, SC 29303; 33 Villa Rd., Greenville, SC 29602.

Mailing Address: PO Box 1717, Spartanburg, SC 29304.

Phone: 864-576-7777; 864-233-7777. **Fax:** 864-587-5430.

E-mail: plane@wspa.com

Web Site: http://www.wspa.com

Technical Facilities: Channel No. 7 (174-180 MHz). Authorized power: 25.7-kw visual, aural. Antenna: 2188-ft above av. terrain, 421-ft. above ground, 3633-ft. above sea level.

Latitude	35°	10'	12"
Longitude	82°	17'	27"

Note: Latitude and longitude coordinates shown are based on the North American Datum of 1927 (NAD 27) as currently required by the Mass Media Bureau of the FCC.

Ownership: Media General Inc. (Group Owner).

Began Operation: June 14, 2000. High Definition. Station broadcasting digitally on its analog channel allotment. Began analog operations: April 29, 1956. Station lost both analog and digital service March 1, 2009 due to collapse of transmission towers from ice storm. Both services were restored March 8th using temporary antennas. Ceased analog operations: June 12, 2009.

Represented (legal): Dow Lohnes PLLC.

Personnel:

Phil Lane, Vice President & General Manager.

Mike Kreaci, General Sales Manager.

Steve Cloy, Local Sales Manager, Greenville.

Alex Bongiorno, News Director.

Ron Peeler, Chief Engineer.

Laura Nunamacher, Business Manager.

Shukriyyah Fareed, Program Coordinator.

Megan Hannigan, Promotion & Public Affairs.

Heather Campbill, Production Manager.

Beth Hitesman, Creative Services Director.

Betty Foster, Traffic Manager.

City of License: Spartanburg.

Station DMA: Greenville-Spartanburg-Anderson, SC-Asheville, NC. **Rank:** 36.

WSPA-DT BMPCDT-20080619ABN GRANTED: 2/6/2009

© 2010 Warren Communications News

Circulation © 2009 Nielsen. Coverage based on Nielsen study.

GrandTotal	Cable TV Households	Non-cable TV Households	Total TV Households
Estimated Station Totals *	553,390	480,070	1,033,460
Average Weekly Circulation (2009)	274,869	283,114	557,983
Average Daily Circulation (2009)			275,427

Station DMA Total	Cable TV Households	Non-cable TV Households	Total TV Households
Estimated Station Totals *	395,190	436,900	832,090
Average Weekly Circulation (2009)	246,645	277,239	523,884
Average Daily Circulation (2009)			264,482

Other DMA Total	Cable TV Households	Non-cable TV Households	Total TV Households
Estimated Station Totals *	158,200	43,170	201,370
Average Weekly Circulation (2009)	28,224	5,875	34,099
Average Daily Circulation (2009)			10,945

*Estimated station totals are sums of the Nielsen TV and Cable TV household estimates for each county in which the station registers viewing of more than 5% as per the Nielsen Survey Methods.

WKTC-DT
Ch. 39

Network Service: MNT.

Licensee: WBHQ Columbia LLC, 120-A Pontiac Business Center Dr, Elgin, SC 29045.

Studio: 120-A Pontiac Business Center Dr., Elgin, SC 29045-9171.

Mailing Address: 120-A Pontiac Business Center Dr, Elgin, SC 29045-9171.

Phone: 803-419-6363. **Fax:** 803-419-6399.

E-mail: sraines@aol.com

Web Site: http://www.wktctv.com/

Technical Facilities: Channel No. 39 (320-626 MHz). Authorized power: 500-kw max. visual, aural. Antenna: 1283-ft above av. terrain, 1280-ft. above ground, 1563-ft. above sea level.

Latitude	34°	06'	58"
Longitude	80°	45'	51"

Note: Latitude and longitude coordinates shown are based on the North American Datum of 1927 (NAD 27) as currently required by the Mass Media Bureau of the FCC.

Ownership: WBHQ Columbia LLC.

Began Operation: October 20, 2007. Began analog operations: September 15, 1997. Sale to present owner by Dove Broadcasting Inc. approved by FCC October 22, 2004. Transfer of remaining 51% interest by C. Fred McLaughlin to Dove Broadcasting Inc. approved by FCC October 15, 1999. Ceased analog operations: February 17, 2009.

Represented (legal): Dickstein Shapiro LLP.

Personnel:

Stephanie Rein, General Manager, General Sales & Business Manager.

Jim McBurney, Chief Engineer.

Anthony Blair, Program & Creative Services Director & Traffic Assistant.

City of License: Sumter. **Station DMA:** Columbia, SC. **Rank:** 79.

WKTC-DT BMPCDT-20040625AAR GRANTED: 8/16/2004

© 2010 Warren Communications News

Circulation © 2009 Nielsen. Coverage based on Nielsen study.

GrandTotal	Cable TV Households	Non-cable TV Households	Total TV Households
Estimated Station Totals *	188,010	190,430	378,440
Average Weekly Circulation (2009)	30,511	25,174	55,685
Average Daily Circulation (2009)			16,770

Station DMA Total	Cable TV Households	Non-cable TV Households	Total TV Households
Estimated Station Totals *	188,010	183,590	371,600
Average Weekly Circulation (2009)	30,511	24,634	55,145
Average Daily Circulation (2009)			16,729

Other DMA Total	Cable TV Households	Non-cable TV Households	Total TV Households
Estimated Station Totals *	0	6,840	6,840
Average Weekly Circulation (2009)	0	540	540
Average Daily Circulation (2009)			41

*Estimated station totals are sums of the Nielsen TV and Cable TV household estimates for each county in which the station registers viewing of more than 5% as per the Nielsen Survey Methods.

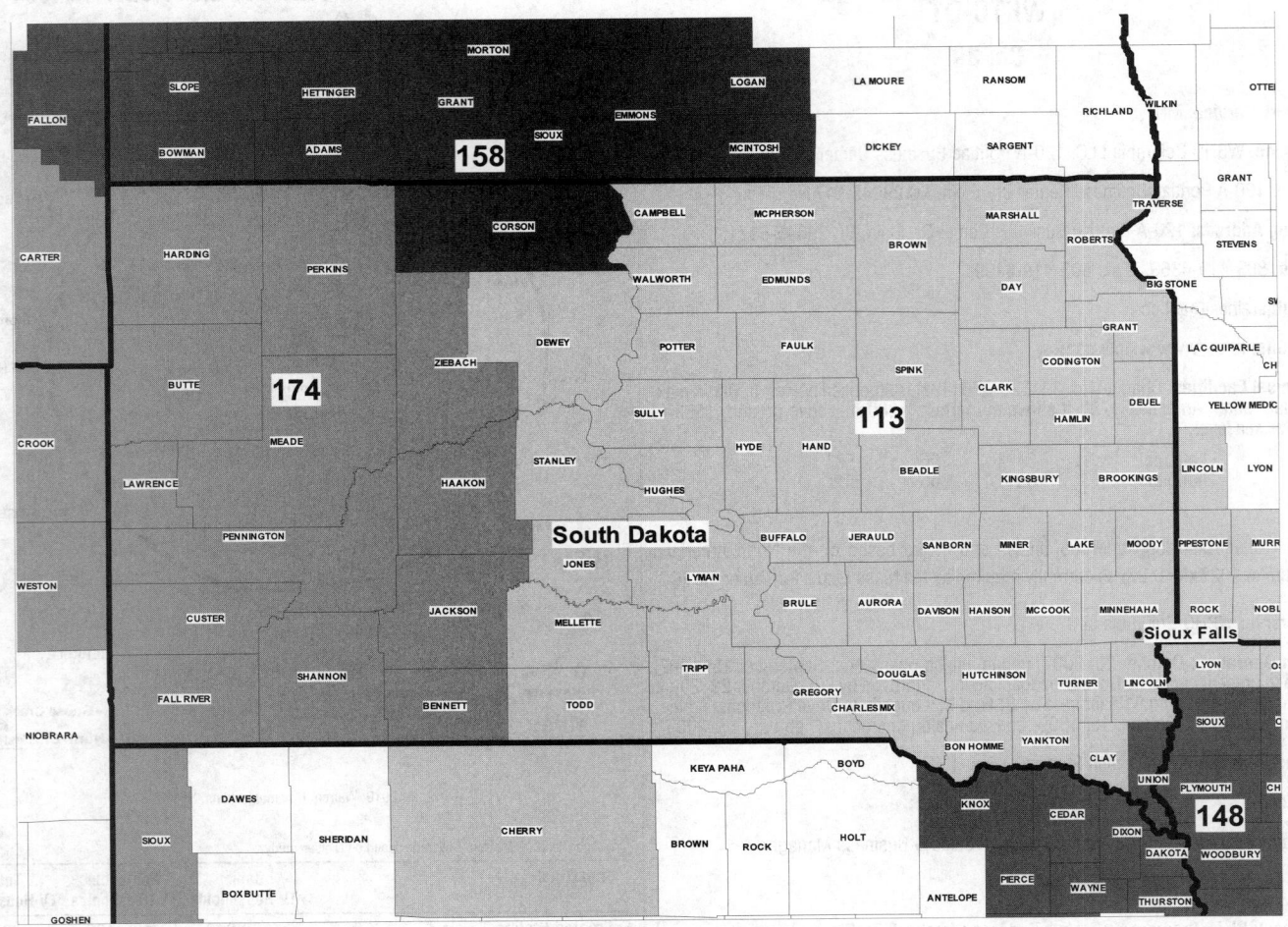

© 2010 Warren Communications News

MARKET	NIELSEN DMA TV HOUSEHOLDS	RANK	MARKET AREA COMMERCIAL STATIONS
Sioux Falls (Mitchell), SD	261,100	113	KABY-DT (9); KDLO-DT (3); KDLT-DT (47); KDLV-DT (26); KELO-DT (11); KPLO-DT (14); KPRY-DT (19); KSFY-DT (13); KTTM-DT (12); KTTW-DT (7); KWSD-DT (36)
Sioux City, IA	154,810	148	KCAU-DT (9); KMEG-DT (39); KPTH-DT (49); KTIV-DT (41)
Minot-Bismarck-Dickinson, ND	136,540	158	KBMY-DT (16); KFYR-DT (31); KMCY-DT (14); KMOT-DT (10); KNDX-DT (26); KQCD-DT (7); KUMV-DT (8); KXMA-DT (19); KXMB-DT (12); KXMC-DT (13); KXMD-DT (14); KXND-DT (24)
Rapid City, SD	98,240	174	KCLO-DT (16); KEVN-DT (7); KHSD-DT (10); KIVV-DT (5); KNBN-DT (21); KOTA-DT (2); KSGW-DT (13)

South Dakota Station Totals as of October 1, 2009

	VHF	UHF	TOTAL
Commercial Television	10	7	17
Educational Television	5	4	9
	15	11	26

KABY-DT
Ch. 9

Network Service: ABC.

Licensee: Hoak Media of Dakota License LLC, 500 Crescent Ct, Ste 200, Dallas, TX 75201-7808.

Studio: 300 N Dakota Ave, Ste 100, Sioux Falls, SD 57104.

Mailing Address: 300 N Dakota Ave, Ste 100, Sioux Falls, SD 57104.

Phone: 605-336-1300; 800-955-5739. **Fax:** 605-336-7936.

E-mail: kmanning@ksfy.com

Web Site: http://www.ksfy.com

Technical Facilities: Channel No. 9 (186-192 MHz). Authorized power: 19.4-kw visual, aural. Antenna: 1401-ft above av. terrain, 1258-ft. above ground, 3027-ft. above sea level.

Latitude	45°	06'	23"
Longitude	97°	53'	57"

Note: Latitude and longitude coordinates shown are based on the North American Datum of 1927 (NAD 27) as currently required by the Mass Media Bureau of the FCC.

Ownership: Hoak Media LLC (Group Owner).

Began Operation: November 18, 2002. Station broadcasting digitally on its analog channel allotment. Began analog operations: November 27, 1958. Sale to present owner by South Dakota Television License Sub LLC approved by FCC November 16, 2006. Sale to South Dakota Television License Sub LLC by Raycom Media Inc. approved by FCC February 27, 2004. Sale to Raycom Media Inc. by Ellis Communications approved by FCC July 26, 1996. Sale to Ellis Communications by New Vision TV approved by FCC December 4, 1994. Sale to New Vision TV by News-Press & Gazette Co. approved by FCC September 7, 1993. Sale to News-Press & Gazette Co. by Forum Publishing approved by FCC November 15, 1985. Sale to Forum Publishing by Gordon H. Ritz, Wheelock Whitney, et al., approved by FCC November 14, 1973. Sale to Gordon H. Ritz, Wheelock Whitney, et. al., by John Boler & others approved by FCC December 23, 1969. Ceased analog operations: February 16, 2009.

Represented (legal): Akin, Gump, Strauss, Hauer & Feld LLP.

Personnel:

Kelly Manning, Vice President, General Manager & Station Manager.

Ryan Welsh, General Sales Manager.

John Shelby, News Director.

Darrel Nelson, Chief Engineer.

Kristen Boyle, Business Manager.

Jeff Bonk, Creative Services Director.

Jeff Morlan, Production Manager.

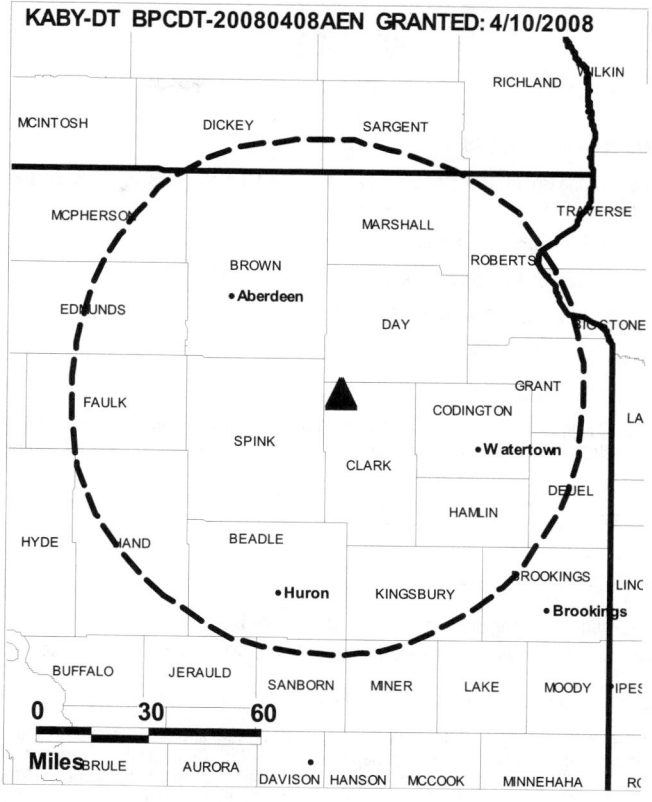

© 2010 Warren Communications News

Tammy Ranum, Traffic Manager.

City of License: Aberdeen. **Station DMA:** Sioux Falls (Mitchell), SD. **Rank:** 113.

Circulation © 2009 Nielsen. Coverage based on Nielsen study.

GrandTotal	Cable TV Households	Non-cable TV Households	Total TV Households
Estimated Station Totals *	32,410	7,580	39,990
Average Weekly Circulation (2009)	18,639	2,031	20,670
Average Daily Circulation (2009)			9,658

Station DMA Total	Cable TV Households	Non-cable TV Households	Total TV Households
Estimated Station Totals *	32,410	7,580	39,990
Average Weekly Circulation (2009)	18,639	2,031	20,670
Average Daily Circulation (2009)			9,658

*Estimated station totals are sums of the Nielsen TV and Cable TV household estimates for each county in which the station registers viewing of more than 5% as per the Nielsen Survey Methods.

KDLO-DT
Ch. 3

Network Service: MNT, CBS.

Licensee: Young Broadcasting of Sioux Falls Inc., Debtor in Possession, PO Box 1800, c/o Brooks, Pierce et al., Raleigh, NC 27602.

Studio: 501 S. Phillips Ave., Sioux Falls, SD 57104.

Mailing Address: 501 S Phillips Ave, Sioux Falls, SD 57104.

Phone: 605-336-1100. **Fax:** 605-357-3350.

E-mail: paulfa@keloland.com

Web Site: http://www.keloland.com

Technical Facilities: Channel No. 3 (60-66 MHz). Authorized power: 14.4-kw visual, aural. Antenna: 1684-ft above av. terrain, 1651-ft. above ground, 3498-ft. above sea level.

Latitude	44°	57'	53"
Longitude	97°	34'	50"

Transmitter: 0.5-mi. N. Garden City.

Note: Latitude and longitude coordinates shown are based on the North American Datum of 1927 (NAD 27) as currently required by the Mass Media Bureau of the FCC.

Ownership: Young Broadcasting Inc., Debtor in Possession (Group Owner).

Began Operation: May 1, 2002. Station broadcasting digitally on its analog channel allotment. Began analog operations: September 24, 1955. Ceased analog operations: June 12, 2009. Assignment to Young Broadcasting of Sioux Falls Inc. (New Young Broadcasting Holding Co. Inc.) pends. Involuntary assignment to debtor in possession status approved by FCC March 17, 2009. Sale to Young Broadcasting Inc. by Midcontinent Television of South Dakota Inc. approved by FCC March 29, 1996.

Represented (legal): Brooks, Pierce, McLendon, Humphrey & Leonard LLP.

Personnel:

Robert Peterson, President & General Manager.

Jay Huizenga, Station Manager.

Jamey Clapp, Production Manager.

Mark Millage, News Director.

John Hertz, Chief Engineer.

Marlin Van Peursem, Finance Director.

Karen Floyd, Program Director.

Paul Farmer, Promotion & Marketing Director.

Misty Farabee, Traffic Manager.

City of License: Florence. **Station DMA:** Sioux Falls (Mitchell), SD. **Rank:** 113.

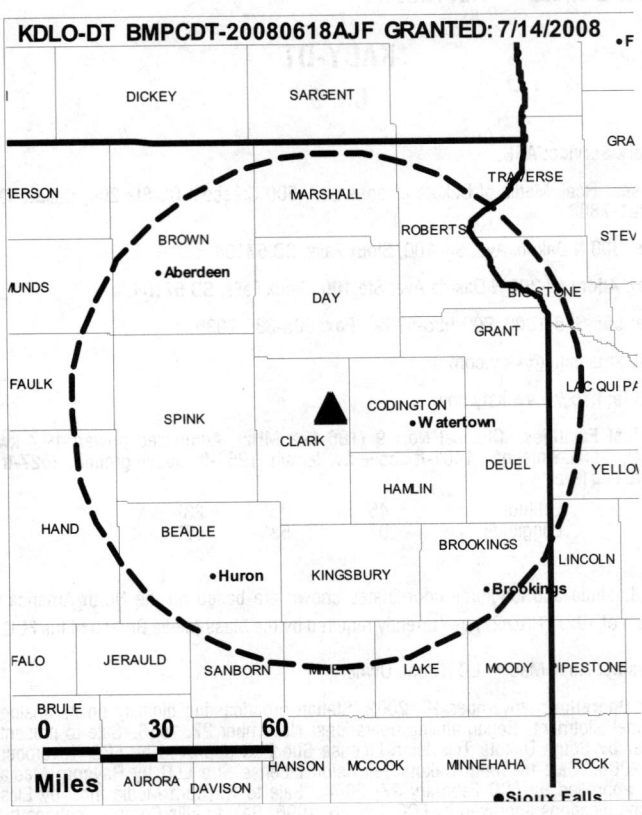

KDLO-DT BMPCDT-20080618AJF GRANTED: 7/14/2008

© 2010 Warren Communications News

Circulation © 2009 Nielsen. Coverage based on Nielsen study.

GrandTotal	Cable TV Households	Non-cable TV Households	Total TV Households
Estimated Station Totals *	33,960	8,120	42,080
Average Weekly Circulation (2009)	19,702	1,579	21,281
Average Daily Circulation (2009)			11,737

Station DMA Total	Cable TV Households	Non-cable TV Households	Total TV Households
Estimated Station Totals *	33,960	7,580	41,540
Average Weekly Circulation (2009)	19,702	1,493	21,195
Average Daily Circulation (2009)			11,725

Other DMA Total	Cable TV Households	Non-cable TV Households	Total TV Households
Estimated Station Totals *	0	540	540
Average Weekly Circulation (2009)	0	86	86
Average Daily Circulation (2009)			12

*Estimated station totals are sums of the Nielsen TV and Cable TV household estimates for each county in which the station registers viewing of more than 5% as per the Nielsen Survey Methods.

KTTM-DT
Ch. 12

Network Service: FOX.

Grantee: Independent Communications Inc., PO Box 5103, 2817 W 11th St, Sioux Falls, SD 57117-5103.

Studio: 2817 W. 11th St., Sioux Falls, SD 57104.

Mailing Address: PO Box 5103, Sioux Falls, SD 57117.

Phone: 605-338-0017. **Fax:** 605-338-7173.

Web Site: http://www.kttw.com

Technical Facilities: Channel No. 12 (204-210 MHz). Authorized power: 5-kw visual, aural. Antenna: 843-ft above av. terrain, 830-ft. above ground, 2145-ft. above sea level.

Latitude	44°	11'	39"
Longitude	98°	19'	05"

Note: Latitude and longitude coordinates shown are based on the North American Datum of 1927 (NAD 27) as currently required by the Mass Media Bureau of the FCC.

Ownership: Independent Communications Inc. (Group Owner).

Began Operation: December 4, 2008. Station broadcasting digitally on its analog channel allotment. Began analog operations: August 31, 1991. Ceased analog operations: November 25, 2008.

Represented (sales): Continental Television Sales.

Personnel:

Ed Hoffman, General Manager & Program Director.

Stacey Sieverding, Sales Manager.

Corey Thompson, Operations & Master Control Manager.

John Bennett, Chief Engineer.

Rodney Bergeson, Production Manager.

City of License: Huron. **Station DMA:** Sioux Falls (Mitchell), SD. **Rank:** 113.

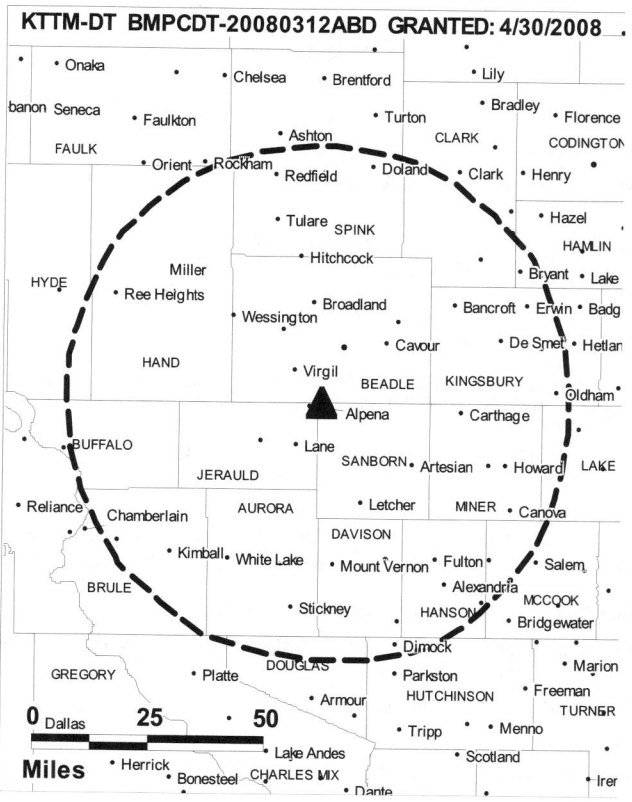

KTTM-DT BMPCDT-20080312ABD GRANTED: 4/30/2008

© 2010 Warren Communications News

Circulation © 2009 Nielsen. Coverage based on Nielsen study.

GrandTotal	Cable TV Households	Non-cable TV Households	Total TV Households
Estimated Station Totals *	26,120	7,640	33,760
Average Weekly Circulation (2009)	7,185	1,585	8,770
Average Daily Circulation (2009)			2,127

Station DMA Total	Cable TV Households	Non-cable TV Households	Total TV Households
Estimated Station Totals *	26,120	7,100	33,220
Average Weekly Circulation (2009)	7,185	1,499	8,684
Average Daily Circulation (2009)			2,109

Other DMA Total	Cable TV Households	Non-cable TV Households	Total TV Households
Estimated Station Totals *	0	540	540
Average Weekly Circulation (2009)	0	86	86
Average Daily Circulation (2009)			18

*Estimated station totals are sums of the Nielsen TV and Cable TV household estimates for each county in which the station registers viewing of more than 5% as per the Nielsen Survey Methods.

KHSD-DT
Ch. 10

Network Service: ABC.

Licensee: Duhamel Broadcasting Enterprises, PO Box 1760, 518 St. Joseph St, Rapid City, SD 57709-1760.

Duhamel Building: 518 St. Joseph St, Rapid City, SD 57701.

Mailing Address: PO Box 1760, Rapid City, SD 57709.

Phone: 605-342-2000. **Fax:** 605-342-7305.

Web Site: http://www.kotatv.com

Technical Facilities: Channel No. 10 (192-198 MHz). Authorized power: 34.8-kw visual, aural. Antenna: 1890-ft above av. terrain, 564-ft. above ground, 7539-ft. above sea level.

Latitude	44°	19'	36"
Longitude	103°	50'	12"

Note: Latitude and longitude coordinates shown are based on the North American Datum of 1927 (NAD 27) as currently required by the Mass Media Bureau of the FCC.

Ownership: Duhamel Broadcasting Enterprises (Group Owner).

Began Operation: August 24, 2005. Began analog operations: November 2, 1966. Ceased analog operations: June 12, 2009.

Represented (sales): Continental Television Sales.

Personnel:

William F. Duhamel, President & General Manager.

Peter A. Duhamel, Vice President.

Helene M. Duhamel, Vice President.

Monte Loos, Operations Manager.

Steve Duffy, National Sales Manager.

Gerry Fenske, Local Sales Manager.

Dan Black, Chief Engineer.

John Petersen, News Director.

Teresa Hofer, Business Manager.

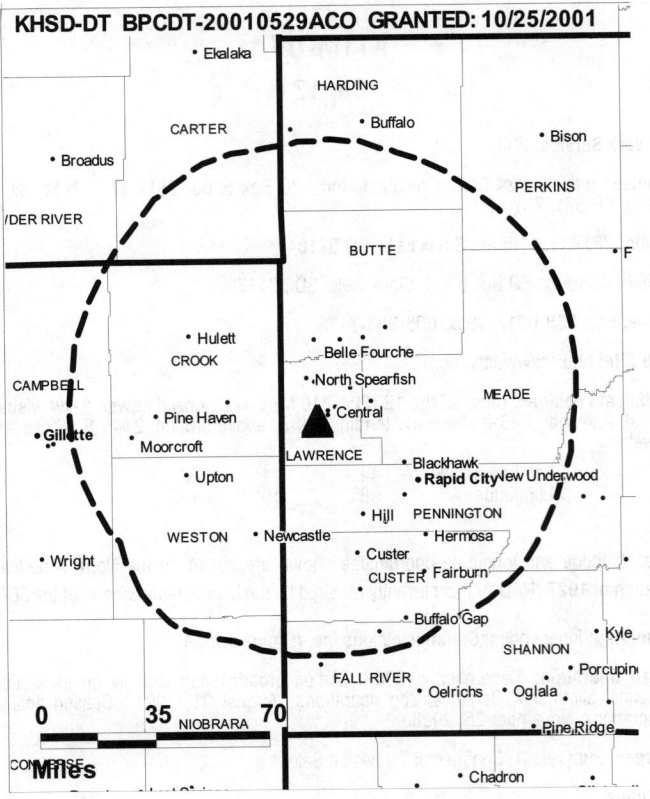

© 2010 Warren Communications News

Dave Bitterman, Production & Creative Service Director.

Doug Loos, Program Director.

Debra Tireman, Traffic Manager.

City of License: Lead. **Station DMA:** Rapid City, SD. **Rank:** 174.

Nielsen Data: Not available.

KIVV-DT
Ch. 5

Network Service: FOX.

Grantee: KEVN Inc., PO Box 677, 2000 Skyline Dr, Rapid City, SD 57709-0677.

Studio: 2000 Skyline Dr., Rapid City, SD 57701.

Mailing Address: PO Box 677, Rapid City, SD 57709.

Phone: 605-394-7777. **Fax:** 605-348-9128.

Web Site: http://www.blackhillsfox.com

Technical Facilities: Channel No. 5 (76-82 MHz). Authorized power: 9.2-kw visual, aural. Antenna: 1841-ft above av. terrain, 591-ft. above ground, 7484-ft. above sea level.

Latitude	44°	19'	30"
Longitude	103°	50'	14"

Note: Latitude and longitude coordinates shown are based on the North American Datum of 1927 (NAD 27) as currently required by the Mass Media Bureau of the FCC.

Ownership: Mission TV LLC (Group Owner).

Began Operation: February 17, 2009. Station broadcasting digitally on its analog channel allotment. Began analog operations: July 11, 1976. Sale to Blackstar LLC by Heritage Media Corp. approved by FCC December 15, 1995. Sale to Silver King Communications Inc. by Blackstar LLC approved by FCC May 14, 1998. Sale to present owner by Silver King Communications Inc. approved by FCC August 26, 1998. KEVN Inc. filed for Chapter 11 bankruptcy November 20, 2003 and emerged July 13, 2005. Ceased analog operations: February 17, 2009.

Personnel:

Bill Reyner, President.

Cindy McNeill, General Manager & General Sales Manager.

Robert A. Slocum, Treasurer & Chief Financial Officer.

Alan Peil, Promotion Director.

Matt Stone, Program Manager.

Dave Downs, Production Manager.

Alissia Hirchert, Traffic Manager.

Jon Fisher, Local Sales Manager.

Jack Caudill, News Director.

Lance Cratty, Chief Engineer.

City of License: Lead. **Station DMA:** Rapid City, SD. **Rank:** 174.

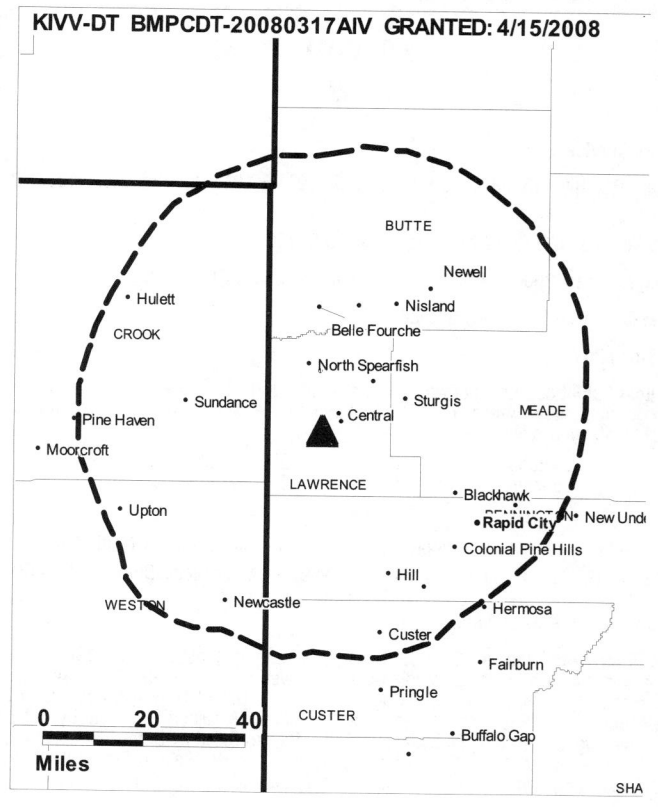

KIVV-DT BMPCDT-20080317AIV GRANTED: 4/15/2008

© 2010 Warren Communications News

Circulation © 2009 Nielsen. Coverage based on Nielsen study.

GrandTotal	Cable TV Households	Non-cable TV Households	Total TV Households
Estimated Station Totals *	1,420	5,660	7,080
Average Weekly Circulation (2009)	247	1,073	1,320
Average Daily Circulation (2009)			208

Station DMA Total	Cable TV Households	Non-cable TV Households	Total TV Households
Estimated Station Totals *	0	5,660	5,660
Average Weekly Circulation (2009)	0	1,073	1,073
Average Daily Circulation (2009)			169

Other DMA Total	Cable TV Households	Non-cable TV Households	Total TV Households
Estimated Station Totals *	1,420	0	1,420
Average Weekly Circulation (2009)	247	0	247
Average Daily Circulation (2009)			39

*Estimated station totals are sums of the Nielsen TV and Cable TV household estimates for each county in which the station registers viewing of more than 5% as per the Nielsen Survey Methods.

KDLV-DT
Ch. 26

Network Service: NBC.

Grantee: Red River Broadcast Co. LLC, PO Box 9115, 4015 9th Ave. SW, Fargo, ND 58106.

Studio: 3600 S. Westport Ave., Sioux Falls, SD 57106.

Mailing Address: 3600 S. Westport Ave, Sioux Falls, SD 57106-6325.

Phone: 605-361-5555. **Fax:** 605-361-7017.

Web Site: http://www.kdlt.com

Technical Facilities: Channel No. 26 (542-548 MHz). Authorized power: 1000-kw max. visual, aural. Antenna: 1043-ft above av. terrain, 1057-ft. above ground, 2481-ft. above sea level.

Latitude	43°	45'	33"
Longitude	98°	24'	44"

Note: Latitude and longitude coordinates shown are based on the North American Datum of 1927 (NAD 27) as currently required by the Mass Media Bureau of the FCC.

Ownership: Red River Broadcast Corp.

Began Operation: October 16, 2008. Began analog operations: June 12, 1960. Sale to present owner by Heritage Media Corp. approved by FCC August 25, 1994. Sale to Heritage Media Corp. by Sherwood L. Corner & Gilbert D. Moyle approved by FCC August 14, 1985. Sale to Sherwood L. Corner & Gilbert D. Moyle by Gillett Broadcasting approved by FCC May 12, 1982. Sale to Gillett by Buford TV approved by FCC January 17, 1978 (Television Digest, Vol. 17:44). Sale to Buford by R. V. Eppel, et al., approved by FCC October 4, 1972. Ceased analog operations: February 1 2009.

Represented (engineering): Cohen Dippell & Everist PC.

Represented (legal): Holland & Knight LLP.

Represented (sales): Katz Media Group.

Personnel:

Myron Kunin, Chief Executive Officer.

Kathy M. Lau, Vice President & Chief Financial Officer.

Mari Ossenfort, General Manager & General & National Sales Manager.

Katie Haffeman, Local Sales Manager.

Amanda Siebert, Promotion Director.

Jeff Johnson, Production Manager.

Paula Mengenhauser, Traffic Manager.

Jen Wahle, News Director.

Don Sturzenbecher, Chief Engineer.

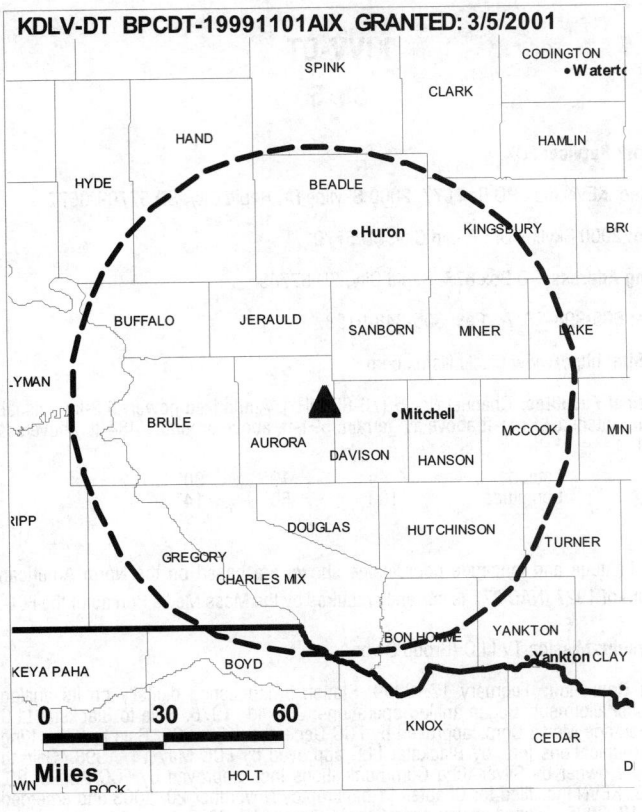

KDLV-DT BPCDT-19991101AIX GRANTED: 3/5/2001

© 2010 Warren Communications News

Susan Enders, Program Director.

City of License: Mitchell. **Station DMA:** Sioux Falls (Mitchell), SD. **Rank:** 113.

Circulation © 2009 Nielsen. Coverage based on Nielsen study.

GrandTotal	Cable TV Households	Non-cable TV Households	Total TV Households
Estimated Station Totals *	13,270	3,110	16,380
Average Weekly Circulation (2009)	4,328	210	4,538
Average Daily Circulation (2009)			1,179

Station DMA Total	Cable TV Households	Non-cable TV Households	Total TV Households
Estimated Station Totals *	13,270	3,110	16,380
Average Weekly Circulation (2009)	4,328	210	4,538
Average Daily Circulation (2009)			1,179

*Estimated station totals are sums of the Nielsen TV and Cable TV household estimates for each county in which the station registers viewing of more than 5% as per the Nielsen Survey Methods.

KPRY-DT
Ch. 19

Network Service: ABC.

Licensee: Hoak Media of Dakota License LLC, 500 Crescent Ct, Ste 200, Dallas, TX 75201-7808.

Studio: 300 N. Dakota Ave., Suite 100, Sioux Falls, SD 57104.

Mailing Address: 300 N Dakota Ave, Ste 100, Sioux Falls, SD 57104.

Phone: 605-336-1300; 800-855-5379. **Fax:** 605-336-7936.

Web Site: http://www.ksfy.com

Technical Facilities: Channel No. 19 (500-506 MHz). Authorized power: 61-kw max. visual, aural. Antenna: 1138-ft above av. terrain, 965-ft. above ground, 3005-ft. above sea level.

Latitude	44°	03'	07"
Longitude	100°	05'	03"

Holds CP for change to 311-kw max. visual; BPCDT-20080602ANS.

Note: Latitude and longitude coordinates shown are based on the North American Datum of 1927 (NAD 27) as currently required by the Mass Media Bureau of the FCC.

Ownership: Hoak Media LLC (Group Owner).

Began Operation: August 6, 2008. Began analog operations: January 30, 1976. Sale to present owner by South Dakota Television License Sub LLC approved by FCC November 16, 2006. Sale to South Dakota Television License Sub LLC by Raycom Media Inc. approved by FCC February 27, 2004. Sale to Raycom Media Inc. by Ellis Communications approved by FCC July 26, 1996. Previous sale to Ellis Communications by New Vision approved by FCC December 21, 1994. Sale to New Vision by News-Press & Gazette Co. approved by FCC September 7, 1993. Sale to News-Press & Gazette Co. approved by FCC November 15, 1985. Ceased analog operations: February 17, 2009.

Represented (legal): Akin, Gump, Strauss, Hauer & Feld LLP.

Personnel:

Kelly Manning, Vice President, General Manager & Station Manager.

Ryan Welsh, General Sales Manager.

John Shelby, News Director.

Darrel Nelson, Chief Engineer.

Kristen Boyle, Business Manager.

Jeff Morlan, Production Manager & Program Director.

Jeff Bonk, Marketing Director.

Tammy Ranum, Traffic Manager.

City of License: Pierre. **Station DMA:** Sioux Falls (Mitchell), SD. **Rank:** 113.

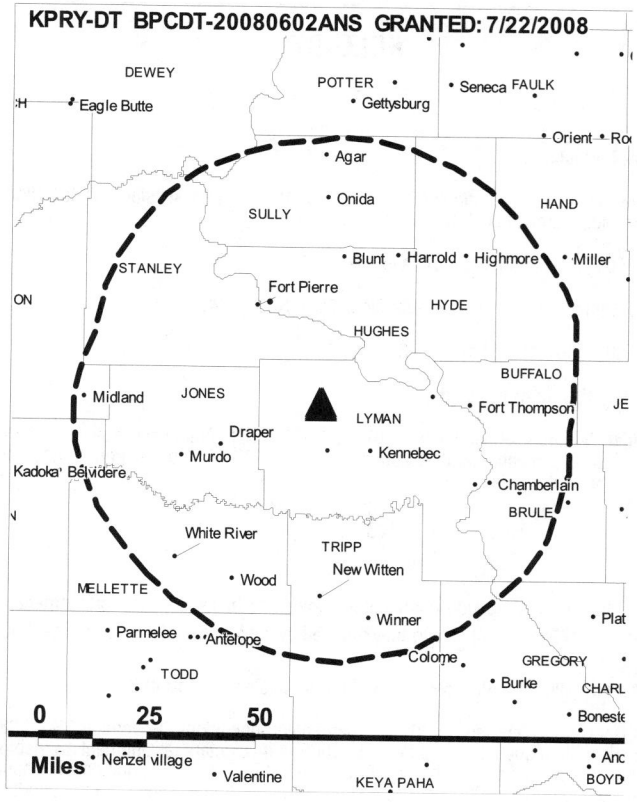

© 2010 Warren Communications News

Circulation © 2009 Nielsen. Coverage based on Nielsen study.

GrandTotal	Cable TV Households	Non-cable TV Households	Total TV Households
Estimated Station Totals *	5,120	2,700	7,820
Average Weekly Circulation (2009)	4,106	381	4,487
Average Daily Circulation (2009)			2,323

Station DMA Total	Cable TV Households	Non-cable TV Households	Total TV Households
Estimated Station Totals *	5,120	1,640	6,760
Average Weekly Circulation (2009)	4,106	318	4,424
Average Daily Circulation (2009)			2,319

Other DMA Total	Cable TV Households	Non-cable TV Households	Total TV Households
Estimated Station Totals *	0	1,060	1,060
Average Weekly Circulation (2009)	0	63	63
Average Daily Circulation (2009)			4

*Estimated station totals are sums of the Nielsen TV and Cable TV household estimates for each county in which the station registers viewing of more than 5% as per the Nielsen Survey Methods.

KCLO-DT

Ch. 16

Network Service: CBS.

Licensee: Young Broadcasting of Rapid City Inc., Debtor in Possession, PO Box 1800, c/o Brooks, Pierce et al., Raleigh, NC 27602.

Studio: 501 S Phillips Ave, Sioux Falls, SD 57104.

Mailing Address: 501 S Phillips Ave, Sioux Falls, SD 57104.

Phone: 605-336-1100. **Fax:** 605-357-3350.

Web Site: http://www.keloland.com

Technical Facilities: Channel No. 16 (482-488 MHz). Authorized power: 150-kw visual, aural. Antenna: 505-ft above av. terrain, 374-ft. above ground, 4153-ft. above sea level.

Latitude	44°	04'	13"
Longitude	103°	15'	01"

Note: Latitude and longitude coordinates shown are based on the North American Datum of 1927 (NAD 27) as currently required by the Mass Media Bureau of the FCC.

Ownership: Young Broadcasting Inc., Debtor in Possession (Group Owner).

Began Operation: February 2, 2006. Began analog operations: November 28, 1988. Ceased analog operations: June 12, 2009. Involuntary assignment to debtor in possession status approved by FCC March 17, 2009. Assignment to Young Broadcasting of Rapid City Inc. (New Young Broadcasting Holding Co. Inc.) pends.

Represented (legal): Brooks, Pierce, McLendon, Humphrey & Leonard LLP.

Personnel:

Robert Peterson, President & General Manager.

Jay Huizenga, Station Manager.

Paul Farmer, Marketing & Promotion Manager.

Jamey Clapp, Operations Director.

Misty Farabee, Traffic Manager.

Mark Millage, News Director.

John Hertz, Chief Engineer.

Marlin Van Peursem, Finance Director.

Karen Floyd, Program Director.

City of License: Rapid City. **Station DMA:** Rapid City, SD. **Rank:** 174.

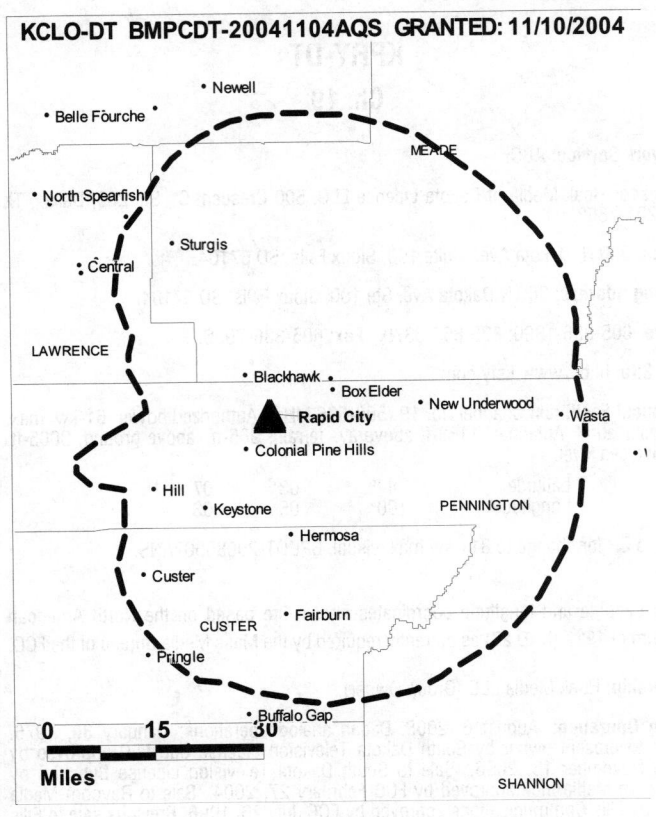

KCLO-DT BMPCDT-20041104AQS GRANTED: 11/10/2004

© 2010 Warren Communications News

Circulation © 2009 Nielsen. Coverage based on Nielsen study.

GrandTotal	Cable TV Households	Non-cable TV Households	Total TV Households
Estimated Station Totals *	50,700	28,330	79,030
Average Weekly Circulation (2009)	28,091	9,509	37,600
Average Daily Circulation (2009)			17,624

Station DMA Total	Cable TV Households	Non-cable TV Households	Total TV Households
Estimated Station Totals *	50,700	26,690	77,390
Average Weekly Circulation (2009)	28,091	9,363	37,454
Average Daily Circulation (2009)			17,609

Other DMA Total	Cable TV Households	Non-cable TV Households	Total TV Households
Estimated Station Totals *	0	1,640	1,640
Average Weekly Circulation (2009)	0	146	146
Average Daily Circulation (2009)			15

*Estimated station totals are sums of the Nielsen TV and Cable TV household estimates for each county in which the station registers viewing of more than 5% as per the Nielsen Survey Methods.

KEVN-DT
Ch. 7

Network Service: FOX.

Grantee: KEVN Inc., PO Box 677, 2000 Skyline Dr, Rapid City, SD 57709-0677.

Studio: 2000 Skyline Dr., Rapid City, SD 57701.

Mailing Address: PO Box 677, Rapid City, SD 57709.

Phone: 605-394-7777. **Fax:** 605-348-9128.

E-mail: lindsayb@kevn.com

Web Site: http://www.blackhillsfox.com

Technical Facilities: Channel No. 7 (174-180 MHz). Authorized power: 43.5-kw visual, aural. Antenna: 669-ft above av. terrain, 587-ft. above ground, 4304-ft. above sea level.

Latitude	44°	04'	00"
Longitude	103°	15'	01"

Note: Latitude and longitude coordinates shown are based on the North American Datum of 1927 (NAD 27) as currently required by the Mass Media Bureau of the FCC.

Satellite Earth Station: Transmitter RCA; Scientific-Atlanta, 7-meter C-band; Scientific-Atlanta receivers.

Ownership: Mission TV LLC (Group Owner).

Began Operation: February 17, 2009. Station broadcasting digitally on its analog channel allotment. Began analog operations: July 11, 1976. Sale to Heritage Media Corp. by Sherwood L. Corner & Gilbert D. Moyle approved by FCC August 14, 1985. Sale to Blackstar LLC by Heritage Media Corp. approved by FCC December 15, 1995. Sale to Silver King Communications Inc. by Blackstar LLC approved by FCC May 14, 1998. Sale to present owner by Silver King approved by FCC August 26, 1998. KEVN Inc. filed for Chapter 11 bankruptcy November 20, 2003, and emerged July 13, 2005. Ceased analog operations: February 17, 2009.

Represented (legal): Hogan & Hartson LLP.

Represented (sales): Katz Media Group.

Personnel:

Bill Reyner, President.

Cynthia McNeill, General Manager & General Sales Manager.

Robert A. Slocum, Treasurer & Chief Financial Officer.

Alan Peil, Promotion Director.

Dave Downs, Production Manager.

Alissia Hirchert, Traffic Manager.

Matt Stone, Program Manager.

Nancy Reber, Local Sales Manager.

Jack Caudill, News Director.

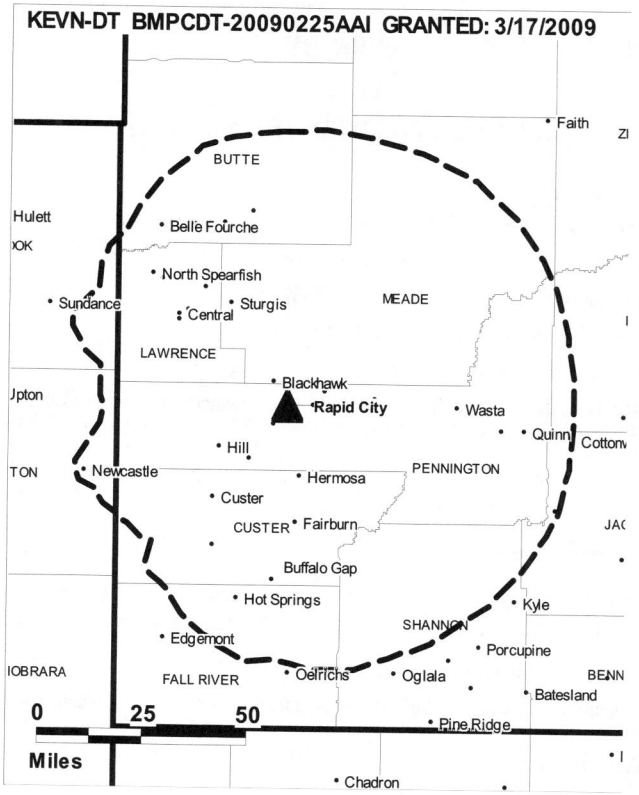

© 2010 Warren Communications News

Lance Cratty, Chief Engineer.

City of License: Rapid City. **Station DMA:** Rapid City, SD. **Rank:** 174.

Circulation © 2009 Nielsen. Coverage based on Nielsen study.

GrandTotal	Cable TV Households	Non-cable TV Households	Total TV Households
Estimated Station Totals *	58,670	26,690	85,360
Average Weekly Circulation (2009)	33,522	10,321	43,843
Average Daily Circulation (2009)			17,487

Station DMA Total	Cable TV Households	Non-cable TV Households	Total TV Households
Estimated Station Totals *	58,670	26,690	85,360
Average Weekly Circulation (2009)	33,522	10,321	43,843
Average Daily Circulation (2009)			17,487

*Estimated station totals are sums of the Nielsen TV and Cable TV household estimates for each county in which the station registers viewing of more than 5% as per the Nielsen Survey Methods.

KNBN-DT
Ch. 21
(Affiliated with KWSD-DT Sioux Falls)

Network Service: NBC.

Licensee: Rapid Broadcasting Co., PO Box 2860, Rapid City, SD 57709.

Studio: 2424 S. Plaza Dr., Rapid City, SD 577002.

Mailing Address: PO Box 9549, Rapid City, SD 57709.

Phone: 605-355-0024. **Fax:** 605-355-0564.

Web Site: http://www.newscenter1.com

Technical Facilities: Channel No. 21 (512-518 MHz). Authorized power: 50-kw max. visual, aural. Antenna: 692-ft above av. terrain, 509-ft. above ground, 4268-ft. above sea level.

Latitude	44°	05'	33"
Longitude	103°	14'	53"

Transmitter: Cowboy Hill.

Note: Latitude and longitude coordinates shown are based on the North American Datum of 1927 (NAD 27) as currently required by the Mass Media Bureau of the FCC.

Ownership: Rapid Broadcasting Co. (Group Owner).

Began Operation: February 6, 2009. Station broadcasting digitally on its analog channel allotment.

Represented (sales): Blair Television.

Represented (legal): Cole, Raywid & Braverman LLP.

Represented (engineering): Graham Brock Inc.

Personnel:

Jim Simpson, General Manager.

Steve Weaver, General Sales Manager.

Tori Robbins, National Sales Manager.

Darren Koehne, Regional Sales Manager.

Jared Eben, Regional News Director.

Donna Houck, Corporate Financial Officer.

Faye Payte, Business Manager.

Wes Des Jardins, Marketing Director.

Mark Walter, Production Manager & Development Director.

Jodi Digmann, Traffic Manager.

Jean Greenwaldt, Promotions Manager.

Bob Nesheim, Engineering Director.

City of License: Rapid City. **Station DMA:** Rapid City, SD. **Rank:** 174.

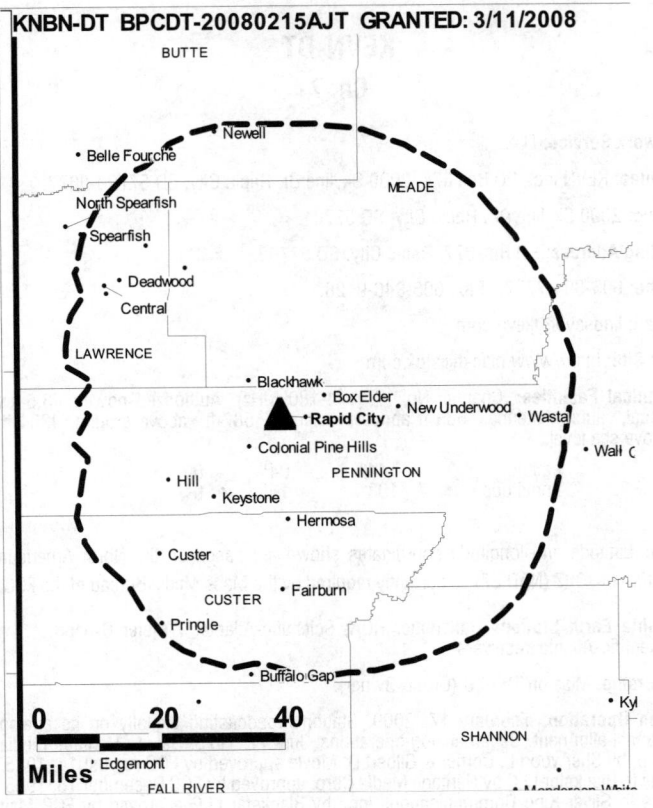

KNBN-DT BPCDT-20080215AJT GRANTED: 3/11/2008

© 2010 Warren Communications News

Circulation © 2009 Nielsen. Coverage based on Nielsen study.

GrandTotal	Cable TV Households	Non-cable TV Households	Total TV Households
Estimated Station Totals *	50,040	28,330	78,370
Average Weekly Circulation (2009)	30,773	8,883	39,656
Average Daily Circulation (2009)			18,276

Station DMA Total	Cable TV Households	Non-cable TV Households	Total TV Households
Estimated Station Totals *	50,040	26,690	76,730
Average Weekly Circulation (2009)	30,773	8,737	39,510
Average Daily Circulation (2009)			18,271

Other DMA Total	Cable TV Households	Non-cable TV Households	Total TV Households
Estimated Station Totals *	0	1,640	1,640
Average Weekly Circulation (2009)	0	146	146
Average Daily Circulation (2009)			5

*Estimated station totals are sums of the Nielsen TV and Cable TV household estimates for each county in which the station registers viewing of more than 5% as per the Nielsen Survey Methods.

KOTA-DT
Ch. 2

Network Service: ABC.

Licensee: Duhamel Broadcasting Enterprises, PO Box 1760, 518 St. Joseph St, Rapid City, SD 57709-1760.

Studio: 518 Saint Joseph St., Rapid City, SD 57701.

Mailing Address: PO Box 1760, Rapid City, SD 57709.

Phone: 605-342-2000. **Fax:** 605-342-7305.

Web Site: http://www.kotatv.com

Technical Facilities: Channel No. 2 (54-60 MHz). Authorized power: 7.1-kw visual, aural. Antenna: 607-ft above av. terrain, 453-ft. above ground, 4249-ft. above sea level.

Latitude	44°	04'	07"
Longitude	103°	15'	03"

Holds CP for change to 18.2-kw visual, 673-ft above av. terrain, 551-ft. above ground, 4311-ft. above sea level; BPCDT-20090702ADI.

Note: Latitude and longitude coordinates shown are based on the North American Datum of 1927 (NAD 27) as currently required by the Mass Media Bureau of the FCC.

Ownership: Duhamel Broadcasting Enterprises (Group Owner).

Began Operation: December 30, 2002. Began analog operations: May 29, 1955. Ceased analog operations: June 12, 2009.

Represented (sales): Continental Television Sales.

Personnel:

William F. Duhamel, President & General Manager.

Peter A. Duhamel, Vice President.

Helene M. Duhamel, Vice President.

Dave Bitterman, Production Director.

Dan Black, Chief Engineer.

Kathy Williamson, Traffic Manager.

Doug Loos, Program Director.

Steve Duffy, General & National Sales Manager.

Gerry Fenske, Local Sales Manager.

John Petersen, News Director.

Teresa Hofer, Business Manager.

Monte Loos, Operations Manager.

City of License: Rapid City. **Station DMA:** Rapid City, SD. **Rank:** 174.

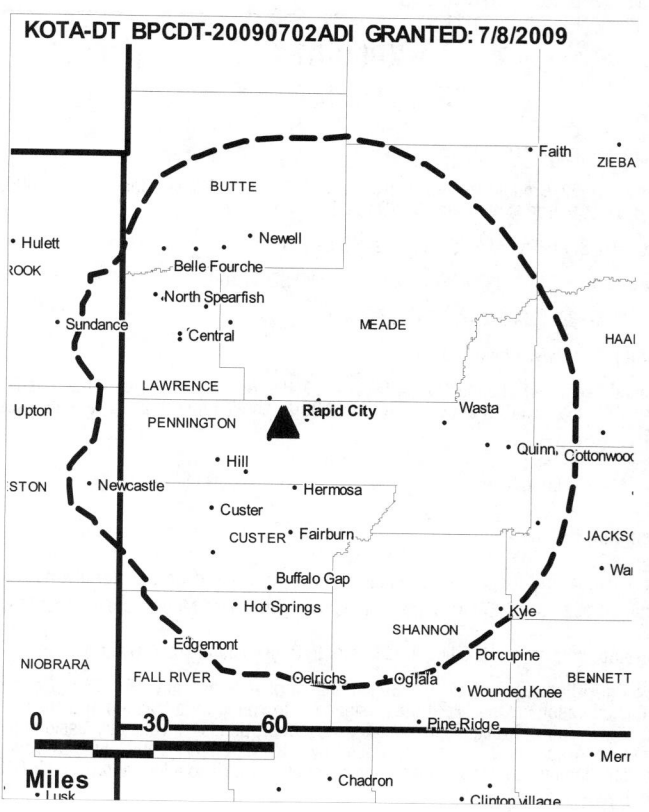

KOTA-DT BPCDT-20090702ADI GRANTED: 7/8/2009

© 2010 Warren Communications News

Circulation © 2009 Nielsen. Coverage based on Nielsen study.

GrandTotal	Cable TV Households	Non-cable TV Households	Total TV Households
Estimated Station Totals *	52,900	28,330	81,230
Average Weekly Circulation (2009)	37,347	14,773	52,120
Average Daily Circulation (2009)			28,737

Station DMA Total	Cable TV Households	Non-cable TV Households	Total TV Households
Estimated Station Totals *	51,480	26,690	78,170
Average Weekly Circulation (2009)	37,032	14,627	51,659
Average Daily Circulation (2009)			28,633

Other DMA Total	Cable TV Households	Non-cable TV Households	Total TV Households
Estimated Station Totals *	1,420	1,640	3,060
Average Weekly Circulation (2009)	315	146	461
Average Daily Circulation (2009)			104

*Estimated station totals are sums of the Nielsen TV and Cable TV household estimates for each county in which the station registers viewing of more than 5% as per the Nielsen Survey Methods.

KPLO-DT
Ch. 14

Network Service: MNT, CBS.

Licensee: Young Broadcasting of Sioux Falls Inc., Debtor in Possession, PO Box 1800, c/o Brooks, Pierce et al., Raleigh, NC 27602.

Studio: 501 S. Phillips Ave., Sioux Falls, SD 57104.

Mailing Address: 501 S Phillips Ave, Sioux Falls, SD 57104.

Phone: 605-336-1100. **Fax:** 605-357-3350.

Web Site: http://www.keloland.com

Technical Facilities: Channel No. 14 (470-476 MHz). Authorized power: 40-kw visual, aural. Antenna: 1043-ft above av. terrain, 600-ft. above ground, 2772-ft. above sea level.

Latitude	43°	57'	57"
Longitude	99°	36'	11"

Transmitter: Reliance.

Note: Latitude and longitude coordinates shown are based on the North American Datum of 1927 (NAD 27) as currently required by the Mass Media Bureau of the FCC.

Ownership: Young Broadcasting Inc., Debtor in Possession (Group Owner).

Began Operation: May 19, 2003. Began analog operations: July 15, 1957. Ceased analog operations: June 12, 2009. Assignment to Young Broadcasting of Sioux Falls Inc. (New Young Broadcasting Holding Co. Inc.) pends. Involuntary assignment to debtor in possession status approved by FCC March 17, 2009. Sale to Young Broadcasting Inc. by Midcontinent Television of South Dakota Inc. approved by FCC March 29, 1996.

Represented (legal): Brooks, Pierce, McLendon, Humphrey & Leonard LLP.

Personnel:

Robert Peterson, President & General Manager.

Jay Huizenga, Station Manager.

Mark Millage, News Director.

John Hertz, Chief Engineer.

Marlin Van Peursem, Finance Director.

Karen Floyd, Program Director.

Paul Farmer, Promotion Manager.

Jamey Clapp, Production Manager.

Misty Farabee, Traffic Manager.

City of License: Reliance. **Station DMA:** Sioux Falls (Mitchell), SD. **Rank:** 113.

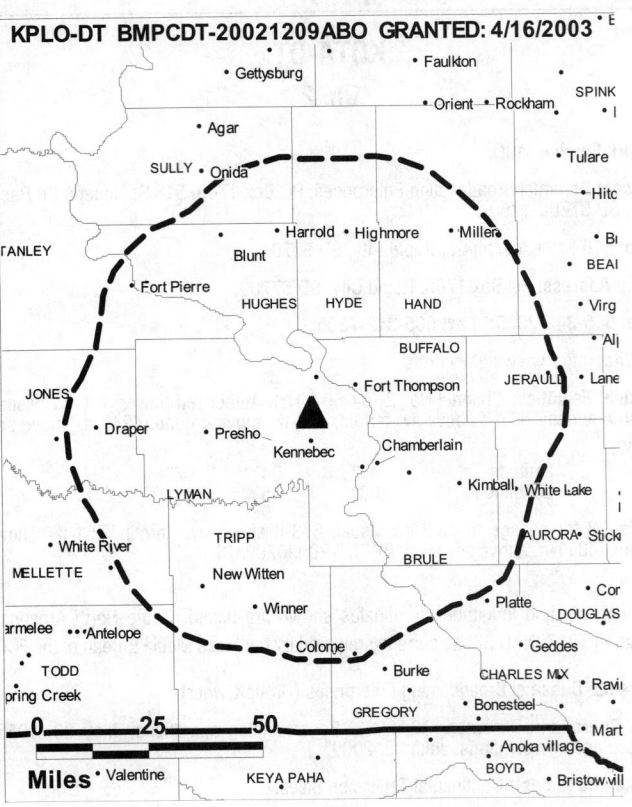

KPLO-DT BMPCDT-20021209ABO GRANTED: 4/16/2003

© 2010 Warren Communications News

Circulation © 2009 Nielsen. Coverage based on Nielsen study.

GrandTotal	Cable TV Households	Non-cable TV Households	Total TV Households
Estimated Station Totals *	5,120	6,460	11,580
Average Weekly Circulation (2009)	3,502	637	4,139
Average Daily Circulation (2009)			2,464

Station DMA Total	Cable TV Households	Non-cable TV Households	Total TV Households
Estimated Station Totals *	5,120	6,460	11,580
Average Weekly Circulation (2009)	3,502	637	4,139
Average Daily Circulation (2009)			2,464

*Estimated station totals are sums of the Nielsen TV and Cable TV household estimates for each county in which the station registers viewing of more than 5% as per the Nielsen Survey Methods.

KDLT-DT
Ch. 47

Network Service: NBC.

Licensee: Red River Broadcast Co. LLC, PO Box 9115, 4015 9th Ave. SW, Fargo, ND 58106.

Studio: 3600 S. Westport Ave., Sioux Falls, SD 57106.

Mailing Address: 3600 S. Westport Ave, Sioux Falls, SD 57106-6325.

Phone: 605-361-5555. **Fax:** 605-361-7017.

Web Site: http://www.kdlt.com

Technical Facilities: Channel No. 47 (668-674 MHz). Authorized power: 1000-kw max. visual, aural. Antenna: 1995-ft above av. terrain, 1965-ft. above ground, 3392-ft. above sea level.

Latitude	43°	30'	18"
Longitude	96°	33'	22"

Note: Latitude and longitude coordinates shown are based on the North American Datum of 1927 (NAD 27) as currently required by the Mass Media Bureau of the FCC.

Ownership: Red River Broadcast Corp. (Group Owner).

Began Operation: August 29, 2005. Began analog operations: September 23, 1998. Ceased analog operations: February 1, 2009.

Represented (engineering): Cohen Dippell & Everist PC.

Represented (legal): Holland & Knight LLP.

Represented (sales): Katz Media Group.

Personnel:

Myron Kunin, Chief Executive Officer.

Kathy M. Lau, Vice President & Chief Financial Officer.

Mari Ossenfort, General Manager & General & National Sales Manager.

Katie Haffeman, Local Sales Manager.

Jen Wahle, News Director.

Don Struzenbecher, Chief Engineer.

Susan Enders, Program Director.

Jeff Johnson, Production Manager.

Stacey Torvik, Traffic Manager.

Amanda Sievert, Promotion Director.

City of License: Sioux Falls. **Station DMA:** Sioux Falls (Mitchell), SD. **Rank:** 113.

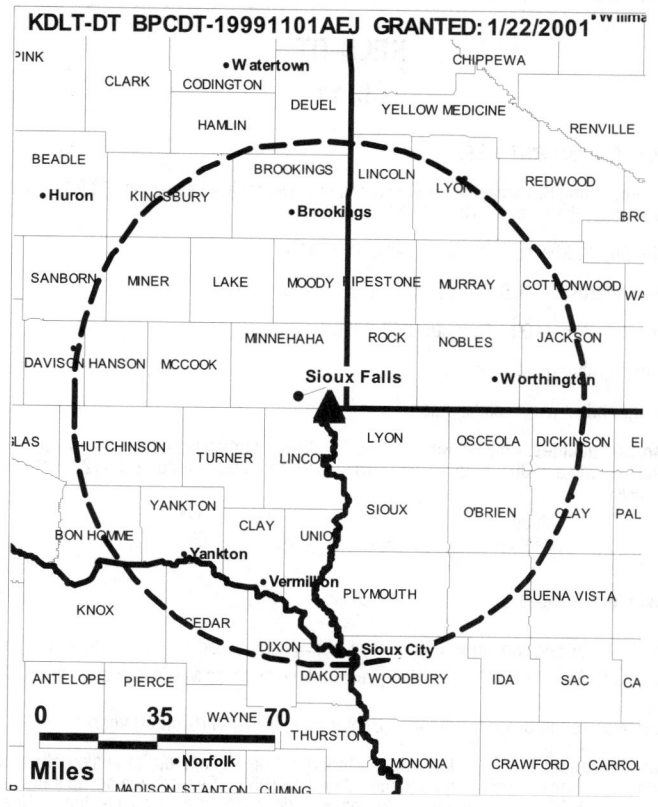

KDLT-DT BPCDT-19991101AEJ GRANTED: 1/22/2001

© 2010 Warren Communications News

Circulation © 2009 Nielsen. Coverage based on Nielsen study.

GrandTotal	Cable TV Households	Non-cable TV Households	Total TV Households
Estimated Station Totals *	152,340	90,020	242,360
Average Weekly Circulation (2009)	76,830	36,840	113,670
Average Daily Circulation (2009)			45,484

Station DMA Total	Cable TV Households	Non-cable TV Households	Total TV Households
Estimated Station Totals *	143,160	63,730	206,890
Average Weekly Circulation (2009)	74,884	34,458	109,342
Average Daily Circulation (2009)			44,407

Other DMA Total	Cable TV Households	Non-cable TV Households	Total TV Households
Estimated Station Totals *	9,180	26,290	35,470
Average Weekly Circulation (2009)	1,946	2,382	4,328
Average Daily Circulation (2009)			1,077

*Estimated station totals are sums of the Nielsen TV and Cable TV household estimates for each county in which the station registers viewing of more than 5% as per the Nielsen Survey Methods.

KELO-DT
Ch. 11

Network Service: MNT, CBS.

Licensee: Young Broadcasting of Sioux Falls Inc., Debtor in Possession, PO Box 1800, c/o Brooks, Pierce et al., Raleigh, NC 27602.

Studio: 501 S. Phillips Ave., Sioux Falls, SD 57104.

Mailing Address: 501 S Phillips Ave, Sioux Falls, SD 57104.

Phone: 605-336-1100. **Fax:** 605-357-3350.

E-mail: mgruber@keloland.com

Web Site: http://www.keloland.com

Technical Facilities: Channel No. 11 (198-204 MHz). Authorized power: 30-kw visual, aural. Antenna: 2001-ft above av. terrain, 1952-ft. above ground, 3412-ft. above sea level.

Latitude	43°	31'	07"
Longitude	96°	32'	05"

Transmitter: Rowena.

Note: Latitude and longitude coordinates shown are based on the North American Datum of 1927 (NAD 27) as currently required by the Mass Media Bureau of the FCC.

Ownership: Young Broadcasting Inc., Debtor in Possession (Group Owner).

Began Operation: May 1, 2002. Station broadcasting digitally on its analog channel allotment. Began analog operations: May 12, 1953. Ceased analog operations: June 12, 2009. Assignment to Young Broadcasting of Sioux Falls Inc. (New Young Broadcasting Holding Co. Inc.) pends. Involuntary assignment to debtor in possession status approved by FCC March 17, 2009. Sale to Young Broadcasting Inc. by Midcontinent Television of South Dakota Inc. approved by FCC March 29, 1996.

Represented (legal): Brooks, Pierce, McLendon, Humphrey & Leonard LLP.

Personnel:

Jay Huizenga, President & General Manager.

Mark Millage, News Director.

John Hertz, Chief Engineer.

Marlin Van Peursem, Finance Director.

Karen Floyd, Program Director.

Paul Farmer, Marketing & Promotion Manager.

Jamey Clapp, Operations Director.

Misty Farabee, Traffic Manager.

City of License: Sioux Falls. **Station DMA:** Sioux Falls (Mitchell), SD. **Rank:** 113.

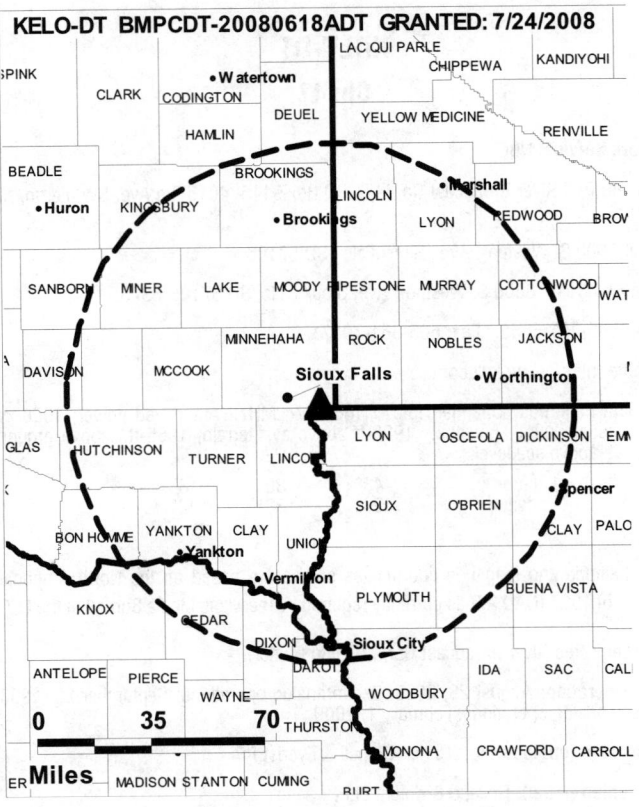

KELO-DT BMPCDT-20080618ADT GRANTED: 7/24/2008

© 2010 Warren Communications News

Circulation © 2009 Nielsen. Coverage based on Nielsen study.

GrandTotal	Cable TV Households	Non-cable TV Households	Total TV Households
Estimated Station Totals *	179,040	86,320	265,360
Average Weekly Circulation (2009)	104,123	54,186	158,309
Average Daily Circulation (2009)			95,819

Station DMA Total	Cable TV Households	Non-cable TV Households	Total TV Households
Estimated Station Totals *	136,720	63,730	200,450
Average Weekly Circulation (2009)	90,611	48,682	139,293
Average Daily Circulation (2009)			88,111

Other DMA Total	Cable TV Households	Non-cable TV Households	Total TV Households
Estimated Station Totals *	42,320	22,590	64,910
Average Weekly Circulation (2009)	13,512	5,504	19,016
Average Daily Circulation (2009)			7,708

*Estimated station totals are sums of the Nielsen TV and Cable TV household estimates for each county in which the station registers viewing of more than 5% as per the Nielsen Survey Methods.

KSFY-DT
Ch. 13

Network Service: ABC.

Licensee: Hoak Media of Dakota License LLC, 500 Crescent Ct, Ste 200, Dallas, TX 75201-7808.

Studio: 300 N. Dakota Ave, Suite 100, Sioux Falls, SD 57104.

Mailing Address: 300 N Dakota Ave, Ste 100, Sioux Falls, SD 57104.

Phone: 605-336-1300; 800-955-5739. **Fax:** 605-336-7936.

E-mail: kmanning@ksfy.com

Web Site: http://www.ksfy.com

Technical Facilities: Channel No. 13 (210-216 MHz). Authorized power: 22.7-kw visual, aural. Antenna: 2001-ft above av. terrain, 1952-ft. above ground, 3411-ft. above sea level.

Latitude	43°	31'	07"
Longitude	96°	32'	05"

Note: Latitude and longitude coordinates shown are based on the North American Datum of 1927 (NAD 27) as currently required by the Mass Media Bureau of the FCC.

Ownership: Hoak Media LLC (Group Owner).

Began Operation: April 4, 2003. Station broadcasting digitally on its analog channel allotment. Began analog operations: July 31, 1960. Sale to present owner by South Dakota Television License Sub LLC approved by FCC November 16, 2006. Sale to South Dakota Television License Sub LLC by Raycom Media Inc. approved by FCC February 27, 2004. Sale to Raycom Media Inc. by Ellis Communications approved by FCC July 26, 1996. Sale to Ellis Communications by New Vision Television approved by FCC February 10, 1995. Sale to New Vision by News-Press & Gazette approved by FCC September 7, 1993. Sale to News-Press & Gazette by Forum Publishing Co. approved by FCC November 15, 1985. Sale to Forum by Gordon H. Ritz, Wheelock Whitney, et al., approved by FCC November 14, 1973. Sale to Ritz & Whitney by former owners approved by FCC August 23, 1965. Ceased analog operations: February 17, 2009.

Represented (legal): Akin, Gump, Strauss, Hauer & Feld LLP.

Represented (sales): TeleRep Inc.

Personnel:

Kelly Manning, General Manager.

Ryan Welsh, General Sales Manager.

John Shelby, News Director.

Darrel Nelson, Chief Engineer.

Kristen Boyle, Business Manager.

Jeff Morlan, Program & Production Director.

Jeff Bonk, Public Relations & Marketing Director.

Tammy Ranum, Traffic Manager.

City of License: Sioux Falls. **Station DMA:** Sioux Falls (Mitchell), SD. **Rank:** 113.

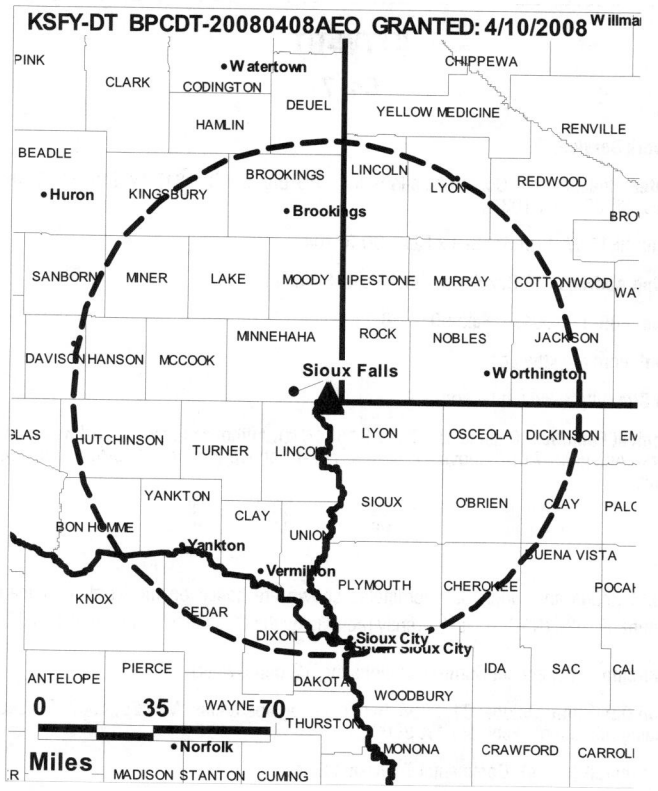

KSFY-DT BPCDT-20080408AEO GRANTED: 4/10/2008

© 2010 Warren Communications News

Circulation © 2009 Nielsen. Coverage based on Nielsen study.

GrandTotal	Cable TV Households	Non-cable TV Households	Total TV Households
Estimated Station Totals *	161,570	82,330	243,900
Average Weekly Circulation (2009)	79,661	44,826	124,487
Average Daily Circulation (2009)			57,506

Station DMA Total	Cable TV Households	Non-cable TV Households	Total TV Households
Estimated Station Totals *	121,530	63,730	185,260
Average Weekly Circulation (2009)	70,181	42,334	112,515
Average Daily Circulation (2009)			53,577

Other DMA Total	Cable TV Households	Non-cable TV Households	Total TV Households
Estimated Station Totals *	40,040	18,600	58,640
Average Weekly Circulation (2009)	9,480	2,492	11,972
Average Daily Circulation (2009)			3,929

*Estimated station totals are sums of the Nielsen TV and Cable TV household estimates for each county in which the station registers viewing of more than 5% as per the Nielsen Survey Methods.

KTTW-DT
Ch. 7

Network Service: FOX.

Grantee: Independent Communications Inc., PO Box 5103, 2817 W 11th St, Sioux Falls, SD 57117-5103.

Studio: 2817 W. 11th St., Sioux Falls, SD 57104.

Mailing Address: PO Box 5103, Sioux Falls, SD 57117.

Phone: 605-338-0017. **Fax:** 605-338-7173.

E-mail: coreyt@kttw.com

Web Site: http://www.httw.com

Technical Facilities: Channel No. 7 (174-180 MHz). Authorized power: 7.5-kw visual, aural. Antenna: 714-ft above av. terrain, 767-ft. above ground, 2119-ft. above sea level.

Latitude	43°	30'	19"
Longitude	96°	34'	19"

Note: Latitude and longitude coordinates shown are based on the North American Datum of 1927 (NAD 27) as currently required by the Mass Media Bureau of the FCC.

Ownership: Independent Communications Inc. (Group Owner).

Began Operation: October 31, 2008. Began analog operations: May 25, 1987. Ceased analog operations: February 17, 2009.

Represented (sales): Continental Television Sales.

Personnel:

Ed Hoffman, General Manager & Program Director.

Stacey Sieverding, Sales Manager.

Corey Thompson, Operations & Master Control Manager.

John Bennett, Chief Engineer.

Rodney Bergeson, Production Manager.

City of License: Sioux Falls. **Station DMA:** Sioux Falls (Mitchell), SD. **Rank:** 113.

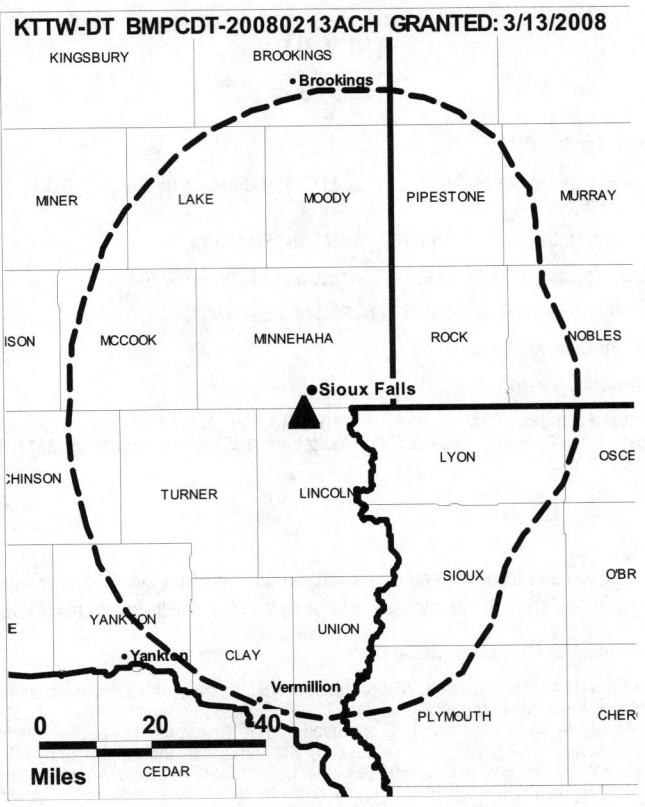

KTTW-DT BMPCDT-20080213ACH GRANTED: 3/13/2008

© 2010 Warren Communications News

Circulation © 2009 Nielsen. Coverage based on Nielsen study.

GrandTotal	Cable TV Households	Non-cable TV Households	Total TV Households
Estimated Station Totals *	143,730	62,610	206,340
Average Weekly Circulation (2009)	52,178	22,410	74,588
Average Daily Circulation (2009)			19,175

Station DMA Total	Cable TV Households	Non-cable TV Households	Total TV Households
Estimated Station Totals *	139,650	62,610	202,260
Average Weekly Circulation (2009)	51,848	22,410	74,258
Average Daily Circulation (2009)			19,102

Other DMA Total	Cable TV Households	Non-cable TV Households	Total TV Households
Estimated Station Totals *	4,080	0	4,080
Average Weekly Circulation (2009)	330	0	330
Average Daily Circulation (2009)			73

*Estimated station totals are sums of the Nielsen TV and Cable TV household estimates for each county in which the station registers viewing of more than 5% as per the Nielsen Survey Methods.

KWSD-DT
Ch. 36
(Affiliated with KNBN-DT Rapid City)

Network Service: CW.

Licensee: J. F. Broadcasting LLC, 23646 Wilderness Canyon Rd, Rapid City, SD 57702.

Studio: 3220 W 57th St, Ste 11, Sioux Falls, SD 57108.

Mailing Address: 3220 W 57th St, Ste 11, Sioux Falls, SD 57108.

Phone: 605-336-3100. **Fax:** 605-338-5484.

Web Site: http://www.siouxfallscw.com

Technical Facilities: Channel No. 36 (602-608 MHz). Authorized power: 150-kw max. visual, aural. Antenna: 754-ft above av. terrain, 807-ft. above ground, 2159-ft. above sea level.

Latitude	43°	30'	19"
Longitude	96°	34'	19"

Transmitter: 1.4-mi. SW of Rowena.

Note: Latitude and longitude coordinates shown are based on the North American Datum of 1927 (NAD 27) as currently required by the Mass Media Bureau of the FCC.

Ownership: James F. Simpson.

Began Operation: July 12, 2006. Station broadcasting digitally on its analog channel allotment. Began analog operations: September 14, 1997. Sale to present owner by Rapid Broadcasting Co. approved by FCC February 28, 2007. Sale to Rapid Broadcasting Co. by Midwest Broadcasting Co. approved by FCC December 14, 2000. Sale to Midwest Broadcasting Co. by Iowa Teleproduction Center Inc. approved by FCC January 23, 1998. Ceased analog operations: June 12, 2009.

Represented (engineering): Graham Brock Inc.

Represented (sales): Blair Television.

Personnel:

Jim Simpson, General Manager.

Mike Smith, Sales Manager.

Cas Dosch, Traffic Manager.

City of License: Sioux Falls. **Station DMA:** Sioux Falls (Mitchell), SD. **Rank:** 113.

Digital cable and TV coverage maps.
Visit www.warren-news.com/mediaprints.htm

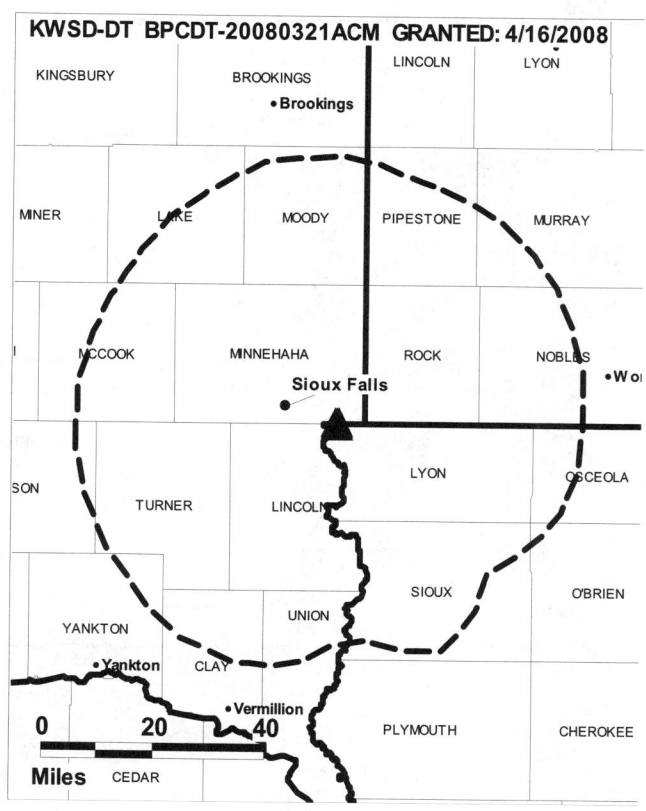

KWSD-DT BPCDT-20080321ACM GRANTED: 4/16/2008

© 2010 Warren Communications News

Circulation © 2009 Nielsen. Coverage based on Nielsen study.

GrandTotal	Cable TV Households	Non-cable TV Households	Total TV Households
Estimated Station Totals *	131,730	54,920	186,650
Average Weekly Circulation (2009)	18,902	8,439	27,341
Average Daily Circulation (2009)			6,093

Station DMA Total	Cable TV Households	Non-cable TV Households	Total TV Households
Estimated Station Totals *	131,730	49,810	181,540
Average Weekly Circulation (2009)	18,902	8,153	27,055
Average Daily Circulation (2009)			6,062

Other DMA Total	Cable TV Households	Non-cable TV Households	Total TV Households
Estimated Station Totals *	0	5,110	5,110
Average Weekly Circulation (2009)	0	286	286
Average Daily Circulation (2009)			31

*Estimated station totals are sums of the Nielsen TV and Cable TV household estimates for each county in which the station registers viewing of more than 5% as per the Nielsen Survey Methods.

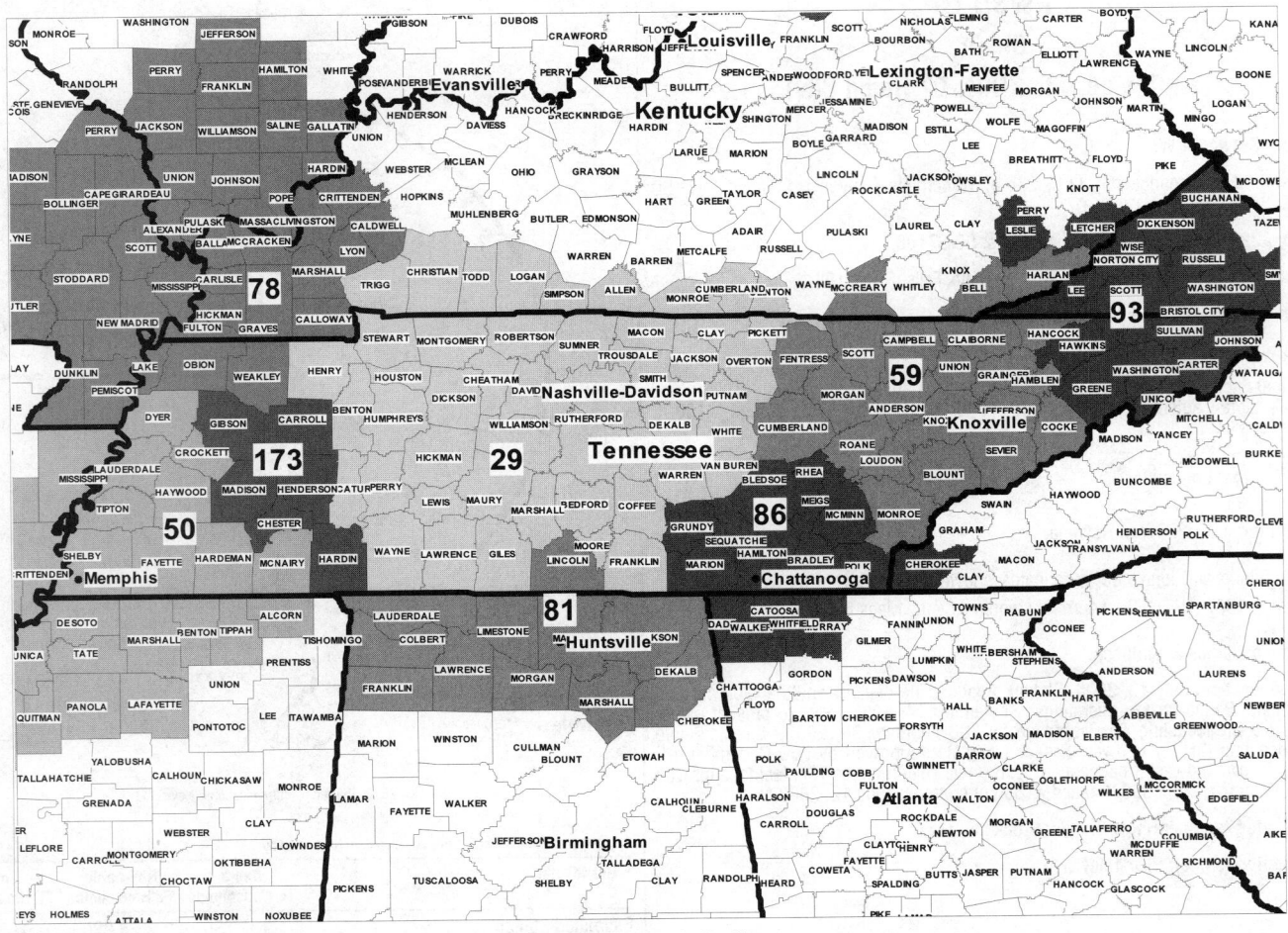

© 2010 Warren Communications News

MARKET	NIELSEN DMA TV HOUSEHOLDS	RANK	MARKET AREA COMMERCIAL STATIONS
Nashville, TN..............................	1,019,010	29	WHTN-DT (38); WJFB-DT (44); WKRN-DT (27); WNAB-DT (23); WNPX-TV (36); WPGD-DT (51); WSMV-DT (10); WTVF-DT (5); WUXP-DT (21); WZTV-DT (15)
Memphis, TN	667,660	50	WBUY-DT (41); WHBQ-DT (13); WLMT-DT (31); WMC-DT (5); WPTY-DT (25); WPXX-TV (51); WREG-DT (28)
Knoxville, TN..............................	552,380	59	WAGV-DT (51); WATE-DT (26); WBIR-DT (10); WBXX-DT (20); WMAK-DT (7); WPXK-TV (23); WTNZ-DT (34); WVLR-DT (48); WVLT-DT (30)
Paducah, KY-Cape Girardeau, MO-Harrisburg, IL......	399,690	78	KBSI-DT (22); KFVS-DT (12); KPOB-DT (15); WDKA-DT (49); WPSD-DT (32); WPXS-DT (21); WSIL-DT (34); WTCT-DT (17)
Huntsville-Decatur (Florence), AL	390,900	81	WAAY-DT (32); WAFF-DT (48); WHDF-DT (14); WHNT-DT (19); WZDX-DT (41)
Chattanooga, TN...........................	365,400	86	WDEF-DT (12); WDSI-DT (40); WELF-DT (16); WFLI-DT (42); WRCB-DT (13); WTVC-DT (9)
Tri-Cities (Bristol, VA-Kingsport-Johnson City, TN)	334,620	93	WCYB-DT (5); WEMT-DT (38); WJHL-DT (11); WKPT-DT (27); WLFG-DT (49)
Jackson, TN	98,250	173	WBBJ-DT (43); WJKT-DT (39)

Tennessee Station Totals as of October 1, 2009

	VHF	UHF	TOTAL
Commercial Television	10	24	34
Educational Television	1	7	8
	11	31	42

WDEF-DT
Ch. 12

Network Service: CBS.

Licensee: WDEF-TV Inc., 27 Abercorn St, Savannah, GA 31401-2715.

Studio: 3300 Broad St., Chattanooga, TN 37408.

Mailing Address: 3300 Broad St, Chattanooga, TN 37408.

Phone: 423-785-1200. **Fax:** 423-785-1271.

Web Site: http://www.wdef.com

Technical Facilities: Channel No. 12 (204-210 MHz). Authorized power: 26-kw visual, aural. Antenna: 1260-ft above av. terrain, 607-ft. above ground, 2516-ft. above sea level.

Latitude	35°	08'	06"
Longitude	85°	19'	25"

Note: Latitude and longitude coordinates shown are based on the North American Datum of 1927 (NAD 27) as currently required by the Mass Media Bureau of the FCC.

Ownership: Morris Multimedia Inc. (Group Owner).

Began Operation: February 6, 2002. High Definition. Station broadcasting digitally on its analog channel allotment. Began analog operations: April 25, 1954. Sale to present owner by Media General Inc. approved by FCC October 6, 2006. Sale to Media General Inc. by Park Acquisition Inc. approved by FCC November 22, 1996 (Television Digest, Vol. 36:31). Transfer of control to Park Acquisition Inc. approved by FCC March 27, 1995. Sale to Park Communications Inc. by Carter M. Parham Group approved by FCC February 28, 1964 (Vol. 4:7). Ceased analog operations: February 17, 2009.

Represented (sales): HRP: Television Station Representative.

Represented (legal): Fletcher, Heald & Hildreth PLC.

Personnel:

Phil Cox, President.

Bill Downs, National Sales Manager.

Tara Dewild, Assistant National Sales Manager.

Dutch Terry, News Director.

Richard McClain, Chief Engineer.

Michael Newberry, Business Manager.

Doris Ellis, Program Director.

Todd Buccelli, Marketing Director.

Kim Beasley, Traffic Manager.

City of License: Chattanooga. **Station DMA:** Chattanooga, TN. **Rank:** 86.

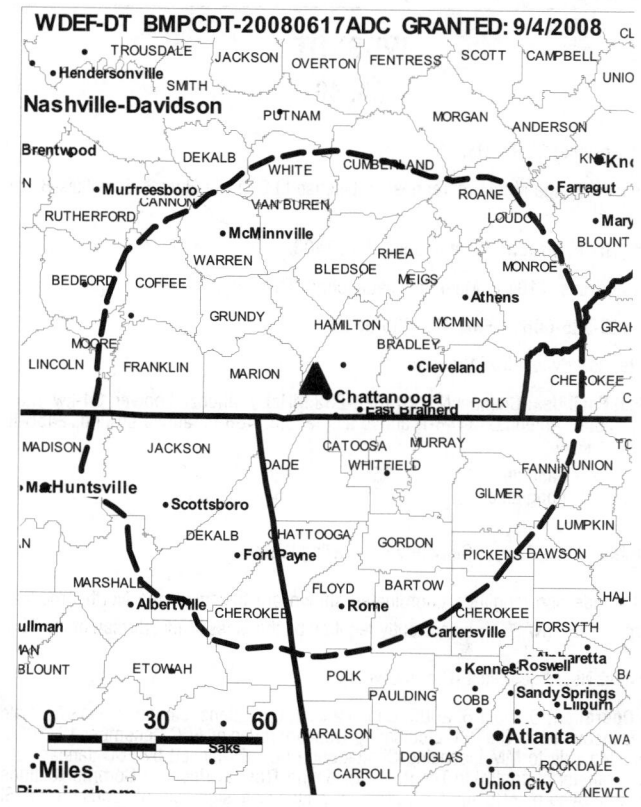

© 2010 Warren Communications News

Circulation © 2009 Nielsen. Coverage based on Nielsen study.

GrandTotal	Cable TV Households	Non-cable TV Households	Total TV Households
Estimated Station Totals *	274,720	198,490	473,210
Average Weekly Circulation (2009)	154,447	84,477	238,924
Average Daily Circulation (2009)			106,228

Station DMA Total	Cable TV Households	Non-cable TV Households	Total TV Households
Estimated Station Totals *	219,630	142,490	362,120
Average Weekly Circulation (2009)	132,443	79,671	212,114
Average Daily Circulation (2009)			97,312

Other DMA Total	Cable TV Households	Non-cable TV Households	Total TV Households
Estimated Station Totals *	55,090	56,000	111,090
Average Weekly Circulation (2009)	22,004	4,806	26,810
Average Daily Circulation (2009)			8,916

*Estimated station totals are sums of the Nielsen TV and Cable TV household estimates for each county in which the station registers viewing of more than 5% as per the Nielsen Survey Methods.

WDSI-DT
Ch. 40

Network Service: MNT, FOX.

Licensee: New Age Media of Tennessee License LLC, 1181 Hwy 315, Wilkes-Barre, PA 18702.

Studio: 1101 E. Main St., Chattanooga, TN 37408.

Mailing Address: 1101 E. Main St, Chattanooga, TN 37408.

Phone: 423-265-0061. **Fax:** 423-265-3636.

Web Site: http://www.fox61tv.com

Technical Facilities: Channel No. 40 (626-632 MHz). Authorized power: 84-kw max. visual, aural. Antenna: 1148-ft above av. terrain, 486-ft. above ground, 2456-ft. above sea level.

Latitude	35°	12'	34"
Longitude	85°	16'	39"

Transmitter: 1129 Sawyer Cemetery Rd., Falling Water.

Note: Latitude and longitude coordinates shown are based on the North American Datum of 1927 (NAD 27) as currently required by the Mass Media Bureau of the FCC.

Ownership: New Age Media (Group Owner).

Began Operation: October 6, 2005. Began analog operations: January 24, 1972. Sale to present owner by The PSC Liquidating Trust approved by FCC December 12, 2006. Competing sale to MM Licensing-Chattanooga LLC dismissed by FCC January 23, 2007. Transfer of control to The PSC Liquidating Trust by Pegasus Communications Corp. approved by FCC April 19, 2005. Involuntary assignment of license to WDSI License Corp., Debtor-In-Possession approved by FCC December 23, 2004. Sale to Pegasus Communications Corp. approved by FCC February 18, 1993. Sale to Donatelli & Klein Inc. by Roy L. Hess, et al., approved by FCC January 30, 1985. Previous sale by Col. Jay Sadow approved by FCC January 18, 1983 (Television Digest, Vol. 22:39). Ceased analog operations: June 12, 2009.

Represented (legal): Leventhal, Senter & Lerman PLLC.

Represented (sales): Petry Media Corp.

Personnel:

Tracye McCarthy, General Manager & General Sales Manager.

Tere Manresa, Local Sales Manager.

Patrick Motley, Chief Engineer.

Ava Moore, Business Manager.

Jenny Giddens, Program Director.

Becky Frank, Marketing & Programming Director.

Tonetta Jones, Traffic Manager.

City of License: Chattanooga. **Station DMA:** Chattanooga, TN. **Rank:** 86.

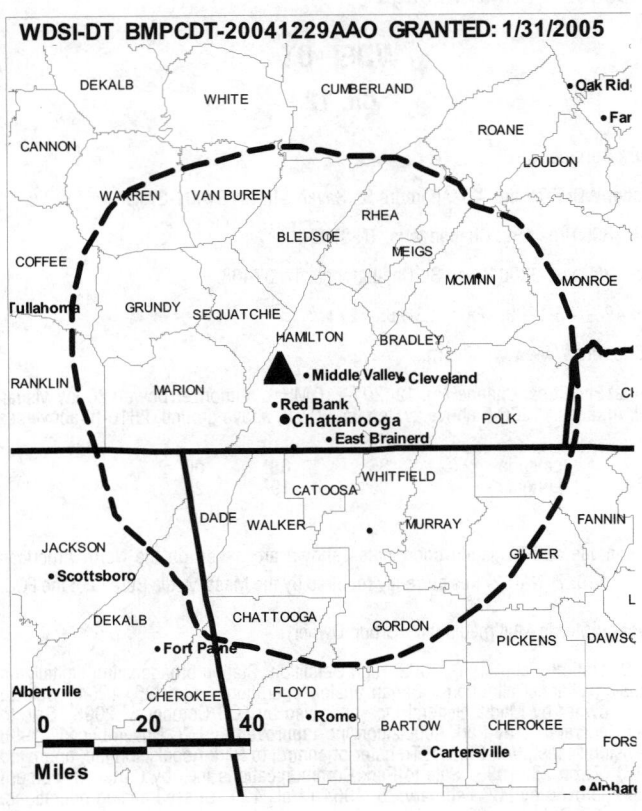

WDSI-DT BMPCDT-20041229AAO GRANTED: 1/31/2005

© 2010 Warren Communications News

Circulation © 2009 Nielsen. Coverage based on Nielsen study.

GrandTotal	Cable TV Households	Non-cable TV Households	Total TV Households
Estimated Station Totals *	228,860	148,650	377,510
Average Weekly Circulation (2009)	112,664	60,291	172,955
Average Daily Circulation (2009)			58,413

Station DMA Total	Cable TV Households	Non-cable TV Households	Total TV Households
Estimated Station Totals *	217,650	142,490	360,140
Average Weekly Circulation (2009)	110,659	58,763	169,422
Average Daily Circulation (2009)			57,970

Other DMA Total	Cable TV Households	Non-cable TV Households	Total TV Households
Estimated Station Totals *	11,210	6,160	17,370
Average Weekly Circulation (2009)	2,005	1,528	3,533
Average Daily Circulation (2009)			443

*Estimated station totals are sums of the Nielsen TV and Cable TV household estimates for each county in which the station registers viewing of more than 5% as per the Nielsen Survey Methods.

WRCB
Ch. 13

Network Service: NBC.

Licensee: Sarkes Tarzian Inc., PO Box 62, 205 N College Ave, Bloomington, IN 47402.

Studio: 900 Whitehall Rd., Chattanooga, TN 37405.

Mailing Address: 900 Whitehall Rd., Chattanooga, TN 37405.

Phone: 423-267-5412. **Fax:** 423-267-6840.

Web Site: http://www.wrcbtv.com

Technical Facilities: Channel No. 13 (210-216 MHz). Authorized power: 34.8-kw max. visual, aural. Antenna: 1099-ft above av. terrain, 269-ft. above ground, 2346-ft. above sea level.

Latitude	35°	09'	40"
Longitude	85°	18'	51"

Holds CP for change to 111-kw visual, 1214-ft. above ground, 381-ft. above sea level; lat. 2457° ' ", BMPCDT-20090323ACN.

Note: Latitude and longitude coordinates shown are based on the North American Datum of 1927 (NAD 27) as currently required by the Mass Media Bureau of the FCC.

Multichannel TV Sound: Stereo only.

Ownership: Sarkes Tarzian Inc. (Group Owner).

Began Operation: May 1, 2001. Began analog operations: May 6, 1956. Sale of 70% to WSTV Inc. by Ramon G. & Helen Patterson approved by FCC November 25, 1959 (Television Digest, Vol. 15:43, 48). Follansbee Steel (interlocking ownership with WSTV Inc.) acquired 30% from H-R Television Inc. early in 1959. Transfer to United Printers & Publishers Inc. (Rust Craft Greeting Cards Inc.) by WSTV Inc. approved by FCC 1961-62. Sale to Ziff-Davis Broadcasting Co. by Rust Craft Broadcasting approved by FCC May 10,1978. Sale to present owner by Ziff-Davis Broadcasting Co. approved by FCC September 29, 1982. Ceased analog operations: June 12, 2009.

Represented (legal): Leventhal, Senter & Lerman PLLC.

Represented (sales): Continental Television Sales.

Personnel:

Thomas R. Tolar Jr., President & General Manager.

Ralph Flynn, Local Sales Manager.

Derrall Stalvey, News Director.

Dan Sommers, Chief Engineer.

Pam Teague, Program Director & Business Manager.

Ronnie Minton, Advertising & Promotion Manager.

Doug Loveridge, Production Manager.

Janet Garner, Traffic Manager.

Kittie Nelson, Executive Assistant.

City of License: Chattanooga. **Station DMA:** Chattanooga, TN. **Rank:** 86.

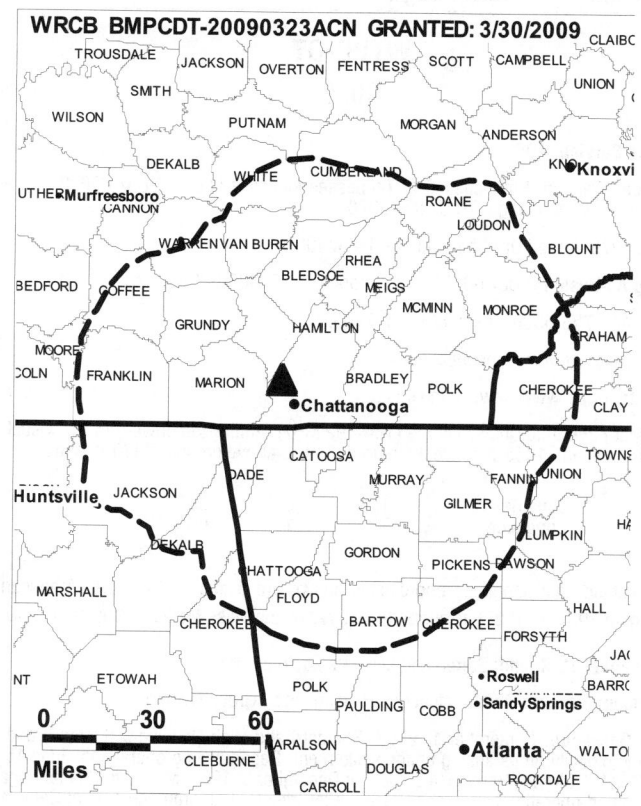

WRCB BMPCDT-20090323ACN GRANTED: 3/30/2009

© 2010 Warren Communications News

Circulation © 2009 Nielsen. Coverage based on Nielsen study.

GrandTotal	Cable TV Households	Non-cable TV Households	Total TV Households
Estimated Station Totals *	283,160	161,970	445,130
Average Weekly Circulation (2009)	149,299	83,760	233,059
Average Daily Circulation (2009)			114,631

Station DMA Total	Cable TV Households	Non-cable TV Households	Total TV Households
Estimated Station Totals *	219,630	142,490	362,120
Average Weekly Circulation (2009)	134,485	80,787	215,272
Average Daily Circulation (2009)			109,713

Other DMA Total	Cable TV Households	Non-cable TV Households	Total TV Households
Estimated Station Totals *	63,530	19,480	83,010
Average Weekly Circulation (2009)	14,814	2,973	17,787
Average Daily Circulation (2009)			4,918

*Estimated station totals are sums of the Nielsen TV and Cable TV household estimates for each county in which the station registers viewing of more than 5% as per the Nielsen Survey Methods.

WTVC-DT
Ch. 9

Network Service: ABC.

Licensee: Freedom Broadcasting of Tennessee Licensee LLC, PO Box 60028, 4279 Benton Dr, Chattanooga, TN 37406-6028.

Studio: 4279 Benton Dr., Chattanooga, TN 37406.

Mailing Address: PO Box 60028, Chattanooga, TN 37406-6028.

Phone: 423-756-5500. **Fax:** 423-757-7400.

E-mail: mcosta@newschannel9.com

Web Site: http://www.newschannel9.com

Technical Facilities: Channel No. 9 (186-192 MHz). Authorized power: 45-kw visual, aural. Antenna: 1056-ft above av. terrain, 239-ft. above ground, 2320-ft. above sea level.

Latitude	35°	09'	38"
Longitude	85°	19'	06"

Note: Latitude and longitude coordinates shown are based on the North American Datum of 1927 (NAD 27) as currently required by the Mass Media Bureau of the FCC.

Multichannel TV Sound: Stereo and separate audio program.

Ownership: Freedom Communications Holdings Inc. (Group Owner).

Began Operation: September 1, 2002. Standard and High Definition. Station broadcasting digitally on its analog channel allotment. Began analog operations: June 15, 1953 as WROM-TV, Rome, GA but left air December 5, 1957. Moved to Chattanooga & resumed operation February 11, 1958 after transfer to Martin Theatres of Georgia Inc. by Dean Covington & associates was approved by FCC October 30, 1957 (Television Digest, Vol. 13:40, 44). Sale to Fuqua Industries by Martin Theatres approved by FCC February 7, 1969. Sale to Belo Broadcasting approved by FCC June 13, 1980. Sale to Freedom Broadcasting Inc. by Belo Broadcasting approved by FCC December 13, 1983 (Vol. 23:42). Sale to present owner by Freedom Broadcasting Inc. approved by FCC April 1, 2004. Ceased analog operations: June 12, 2009.

Represented (legal): Latham & Watkins.

Personnel:

Mike Costa, Vice President & General Manager.

Ted Rudolph, General Sales Manager.

Dennis Brown, Chief Engineer & Operations Manager.

Mike Hood, National Sales Manager.

Tom Henderson, News Director.

Kellye Dillard, Business Manager.

Margie Scott, Programming Coordinator.

Robert Nolan, Promotion & Marketing Director.

Steve Headrick, Production Manager.

Pattie Pendergraph, Traffic Manager.

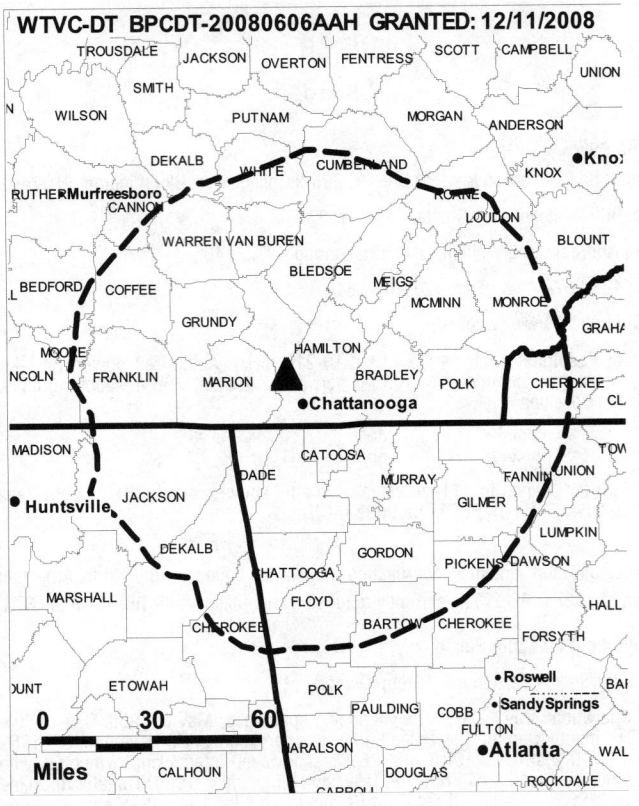

© 2010 Warren Communications News

City of License: Chattanooga. **Station DMA:** Chattanooga, TN. **Rank:** 86.

Circulation © 2009 Nielsen. Coverage based on Nielsen study.

GrandTotal	Cable TV Households	Non-cable TV Households	Total TV Households
Estimated Station Totals *	281,080	189,640	470,720
Average Weekly Circulation (2009)	174,238	93,189	267,427
Average Daily Circulation (2009)			141,002

Station DMA Total	Cable TV Households	Non-cable TV Households	Total TV Households
Estimated Station Totals *	219,630	142,490	362,120
Average Weekly Circulation (2009)	149,873	87,605	237,478
Average Daily Circulation (2009)			128,853

Other DMA Total	Cable TV Households	Non-cable TV Households	Total TV Households
Estimated Station Totals *	61,450	47,150	108,600
Average Weekly Circulation (2009)	24,365	5,584	29,949
Average Daily Circulation (2009)			12,149

*Estimated station totals are sums of the Nielsen TV and Cable TV household estimates for each county in which the station registers viewing of more than 5% as per the Nielsen Survey Methods.

WFLI-DT
Ch. 42

Network Service: CW.

Licensee: MPS Media of Tennessee License LLC, 1181 Hwy 315, Wilkes-Barre, PA 18702.

Studio: 6024 Shallowford Rd., Suite 100, Chattanooga, TN 37421.

Mailing Address: 6024 Shallowford Rd, Ste 100, Chattanooga, TN 37421.

Phone: 423-893-9553. **Fax:** 423-893-9853.

Web Site: http://www.wflitv.com

Technical Facilities: Channel No. 42 (638-644 MHz). Authorized power: 500-kw max. visual, aural. Antenna: 1093-ft above av. terrain, 436-ft. above ground, 2406-ft. above sea level.

Latitude	35°	12'	34"
Longitude	85°	16'	39"

Note: Latitude and longitude coordinates shown are based on the North American Datum of 1927 (NAD 27) as currently required by the Mass Media Bureau of the FCC.

Ownership: Eugene J. Brown (Group Owner).

Began Operation: August 10, 2006. Began analog operations: May 25, 1987. Sale to present owner by Meredith Corp. approved by FCC January 17, 2008. Sale to Meredith Corp. by Lambert Broadcasting of Tennessee approved by FCC July 23, 2004. Sale to Lambert Broadcasting of Tennessee by WFLI-TV Inc. approved by FCC September 4, 1997. Ceased analog operations: December 31, 2009.

Represented (sales): Blair Television.

Represented (legal): Fletcher, Heald & Hildreth PLC.

Represented (engineering): Smith & Fisher.

Personnel:

Tony Thompson, Vice President & General Manager.

Misty Childers, Marketing Director.

Craig Walker, Production Coordinator.

Dan Sommers, Chief Engineer.

Robert Daffron, Program Director.

Laura Wilson, Traffic Manager.

City of License: Cleveland. **Station DMA:** Chattanooga, TN. **Rank:** 86.

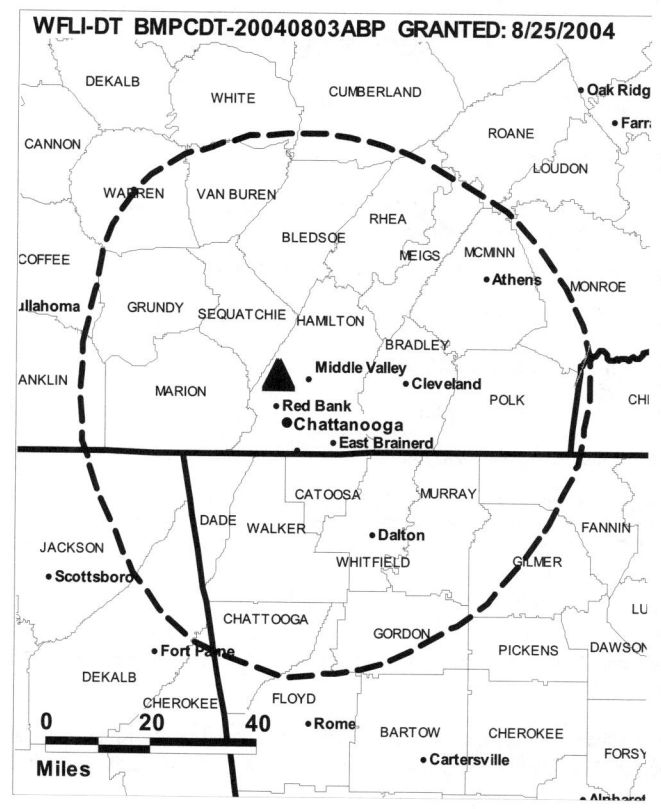

WFLI-DT BMPCDT-20040803ABP GRANTED: 8/25/2004

© 2010 Warren Communications News

Circulation © 2009 Nielsen. Coverage based on Nielsen study.

GrandTotal	Cable TV Households	Non-cable TV Households	Total TV Households
Estimated Station Totals *	226,230	148,650	374,880
Average Weekly Circulation (2009)	50,242	29,643	79,885
Average Daily Circulation (2009)			22,169

Station DMA Total	Cable TV Households	Non-cable TV Households	Total TV Households
Estimated Station Totals *	217,650	142,490	360,140
Average Weekly Circulation (2009)	49,693	28,078	77,771
Average Daily Circulation (2009)			21,854

Other DMA Total	Cable TV Households	Non-cable TV Households	Total TV Households
Estimated Station Totals *	8,580	6,160	14,740
Average Weekly Circulation (2009)	549	1,565	2,114
Average Daily Circulation (2009)			315

*Estimated station totals are sums of the Nielsen TV and Cable TV household estimates for each county in which the station registers viewing of more than 5% as per the Nielsen Survey Methods.

WNPX-TV
Ch. 36

Network Service: ION.

Licensee: ION Media License Co. LLC, Debtor in Possession, 601 Clearwater Park Rd, West Palm Beach, FL 33401-6233.

Studio: 1281 N Mount Juliet Rd, Ste L, Mount Juliet, TN 37122.

Mailing Address: 1281 N Mount Juliet Rd, Ste L, Mount Juliet, TN 37122.

Phone: 615-773-6100. **Fax:** 615-758-4105.

E-mail: lisahorton@ionmedia.com

Web Site: http://www.ionmedia.com

Technical Facilities: Channel No. 36 (602-608 MHz). Authorized power: 733-kw max. visual, aural. Antenna: 1406-ft above av. terrain, 1250-ft. above ground, 2010-ft. above sea level.

Latitude	36°	16'	04.8"
Longitude	86°	47'	44.7"

Transmitter: Approx. 0.75-mi. at 324 degrees T from the intersection of Hackett Rd. & Nabors Hollow.

Note: Latitude and longitude coordinates shown are based on the North American Datum of 1927 (NAD 27) as currently required by the Mass Media Bureau of the FCC.

Ownership: ION Media Networks Inc., Debtor in Possession (Group Owner).

Began Operation: January 28, 2002. Standard Definition. Began analog operations: November 5, 1988. Sale to Steven J. Sweeney by Dove Broadcasting Inc. approved by FCC March 17, 1989. Sale to Inavision Broadcasting Inc. by Steven J. Sweeney approved by FCC June 29, 1993. Sale to Roberts Broadcasting by Inavision approved by FCC November 14, 1996. Sale to Paxson Communications Corp. by Roberts Broadcasting approved by FCC September 4, 1997. Paxson Communications Corp. became ION Media Networks Inc. on June 26, 2006. Transfer of control by ION Media Networks Inc. from Paxson Management Corp. & Lowell W. Paxson to CIG Media LLC approved by FCC December 31, 2007. Involuntary assignment to debtor in possession status approved by FCC June 5, 2009. Sale to Urban Television LLC pends. Ceased analog operations: June 12, 2009.

Represented (legal): Dow Lohnes PLLC.

Represented (engineering): du Treil, Lundin & Rackley Inc.

Personnel:

Lisa Horton, Station Operations & Traffic Manager.

Tim Coucke, Chief Engineer (Acting).

City of License: Cookeville. **Station DMA:** Nashville, TN. **Rank:** 29.

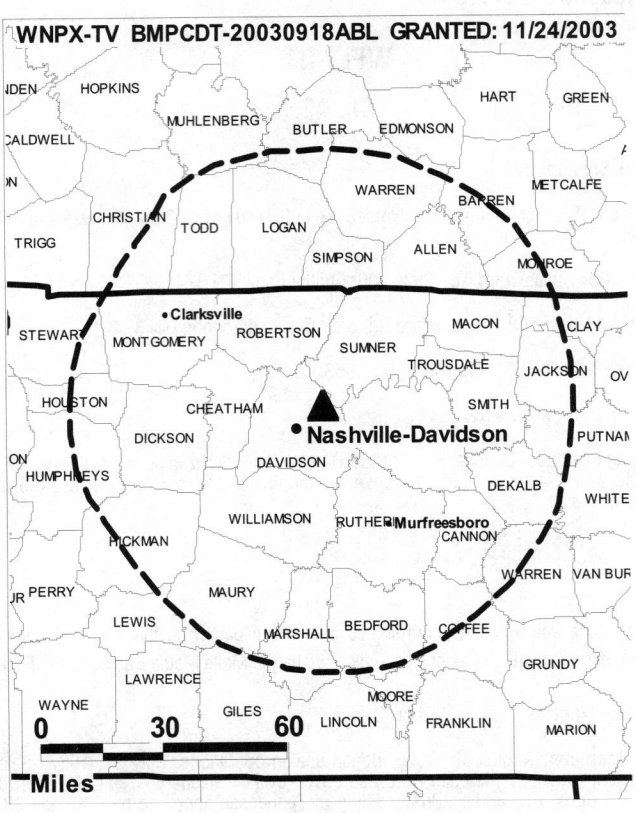

© 2010 Warren Communications News

Circulation © 2009 Nielsen. Coverage based on Nielsen study.

GrandTotal	Cable TV Households	Non-cable TV Households	Total TV Households
Estimated Station Totals *	427,070	29,590	456,660
Average Weekly Circulation (2009)	33,520	2,461	35,981
Average Daily Circulation (2009)			7,221

Station DMA Total	Cable TV Households	Non-cable TV Households	Total TV Households
Estimated Station Totals *	427,070	24,440	451,510
Average Weekly Circulation (2009)	33,520	2,117	35,637
Average Daily Circulation (2009)			7,164

Other DMA Total	Cable TV Households	Non-cable TV Households	Total TV Households
Estimated Station Totals *	0	5,150	5,150
Average Weekly Circulation (2009)	0	344	344
Average Daily Circulation (2009)			57

*Estimated station totals are sums of the Nielsen TV and Cable TV household estimates for each county in which the station registers viewing of more than 5% as per the Nielsen Survey Methods.

WBXX-DT
Ch. 20

Network Service: CW.

Licensee: ACME Television Licenses of Tennessee LLC, 650 Town Center Dr, Ste 850, Costa Mesa, CA 92626.

Studio: 10427 Cogdill Rd., Suite 100, Knoxville, TN 37932.

Mailing Address: 10427 Cogdill Rd, Ste 100, Knoxville, TN 37932.

Phone: 865-777-9220. **Fax:** 865-777-9221.

Web Site: http://www.easttennesseecw.com/

Technical Facilities: Channel No. 20 (506-512 MHz). Authorized power: 652-kw max. visual, aural. Antenna: 2411-ft above av. terrain, 755-ft. above ground, 3995-ft. above sea level.

Latitude	36°	06'	33"
Longitude	84°	20'	17"

Note: Latitude and longitude coordinates shown are based on the North American Datum of 1927 (NAD 27) as currently required by the Mass Media Bureau of the FCC.

Ownership: ACME Communications Inc. (Group Owner).

Began Operation: April 23, 2003. Station broadcasting digitally on its analog channel allotment. Began analog operations: October 3, 1976 as WINT-TV; initial broadcasts were on Ch. 55. Left air 1983; resumed operation on Ch. 20. Left air, date unannounced. Sale to Crossville TV LP approved by FCC February 22, 1996. Resumed operation October 3, 1996. Sale to present owner by Crossville TV LP approved by FCC August 28, 1997. Ceased analog operations: June 12, 2009.

Personnel:

Dan Phillippi, General Manager.

Joanne Marcenkus, General Sales Manager.

Roger McDowell, National Sales Manager.

Ferdy Guidry, Chief Engineer.

Evelyn Cannon, Business Manager.

Teresa Watts-Jackson, Traffic Manager.

Anna Robins, Promotion Director.

Debbie Ogle, Program Manager.

City of License: Crossville. **Station DMA:** Knoxville, TN. **Rank:** 59.

© 2010 Warren Communications News

Circulation © 2009 Nielsen. Coverage based on Nielsen study.

GrandTotal	Cable TV Households	Non-cable TV Households	Total TV Households
Estimated Station Totals *	357,400	245,420	602,820
Average Weekly Circulation (2009)	69,464	53,526	122,990
Average Daily Circulation (2009)			39,978

Station DMA Total	Cable TV Households	Non-cable TV Households	Total TV Households
Estimated Station Totals *	333,380	211,690	545,070
Average Weekly Circulation (2009)	64,607	51,360	115,967
Average Daily Circulation (2009)			38,819

Other DMA Total	Cable TV Households	Non-cable TV Households	Total TV Households
Estimated Station Totals *	24,020	33,730	57,750
Average Weekly Circulation (2009)	4,857	2,166	7,023
Average Daily Circulation (2009)			1,159

*Estimated station totals are sums of the Nielsen TV and Cable TV household estimates for each county in which the station registers viewing of more than 5% as per the Nielsen Survey Methods.

WEMT-DT
Ch. 38

Network Service: FOX.

Licensee: Aurora License Holdings Inc., 2000 K St. NW, Suite 600, c/o Leventhal, Senter & Lerman PLLC, Washington, DC 20006-1809.

Studio: 101 Lee St, Bristol, VA 24201.

Mailing Address: 101 Lee St, Bristol, VA 24201.

Phone: 276-821-9296. **Fax:** 276-645-1555.

E-mail: lwilcher@wemt.sbgnet.com

Web Site: http://www.foxtricities.com

Technical Facilities: Channel No. 38 (614-620 MHz). Authorized power: 1000-kw max. visual, aural. Antenna: 2609-ft above av. terrain, 143-ft. above ground, 4982-ft. above sea level.

Latitude	36°	01'	24"
Longitude	82°	42'	56"

Holds CP for change to 2365-ft above av. terrain, 269-ft. above ground, 4482-ft. above sea level; lat. 36° 26'58", long. 82° 06'29", BPCDT-20090521ADA.

Transmitter: 8684 Viking Mountain Rd.

Note: Latitude and longitude coordinates shown are based on the North American Datum of 1927 (NAD 27) as currently required by the Mass Media Bureau of the FCC.

Ownership: Esteem Broadcasting LLC (Group Owner).

Began Operation: June 6, 2005. Began analog operations: November 8, 1985. Sale to Hawthorne Enterprises Inc. approved by FCC August 23, 1989, but sale never consummated. Sale to East Tennessee Broadcasting Corp. (Michael Perry Thompson, controlling interest) by East Tennessee's Own Inc. (Jay D. Austin, Pres.) approved by FCC September 26, 1989. Sale to Television Marketing Group of Tri-Cities Inc. (Richard Davis) by East Tennessee Broadcasting Corp. approved by FCC March 19, 1992. Sale to Max Media by Television Marketing Group of Tri-Cities Inc. approved by FCC December 6, 1993. Sale to Sinclair Broadcast Group Inc. by Max Media approved by FCC August 26, 1999. Sale to Aurora Broadcasting Inc. by Sinclair Broadcast Group Inc. approved by FCC December 15, 2005. Transfer to present owner by Aurora Broadcasting Inc. approved by FCC April 24, 2007. Ceased analog operations: June 12, 2009.

Represented (legal): Leventhal, Senter & Lerman PLLC.

Represented (sales): Katz Media Group.

Personnel:

Jim McKernan, General Manager & General Sales Manager.

Tony Venable, Operations & Production Director.

Cheryl Stout, National Sales & Traffic Manager & Program Director.

Tom Cupp, Chief Engineer.

Nancy Booher, Business Manager.

Dan Howard, Local Sales Manager.

Gary Leadbetter, Promotion & Community Affairs Director.

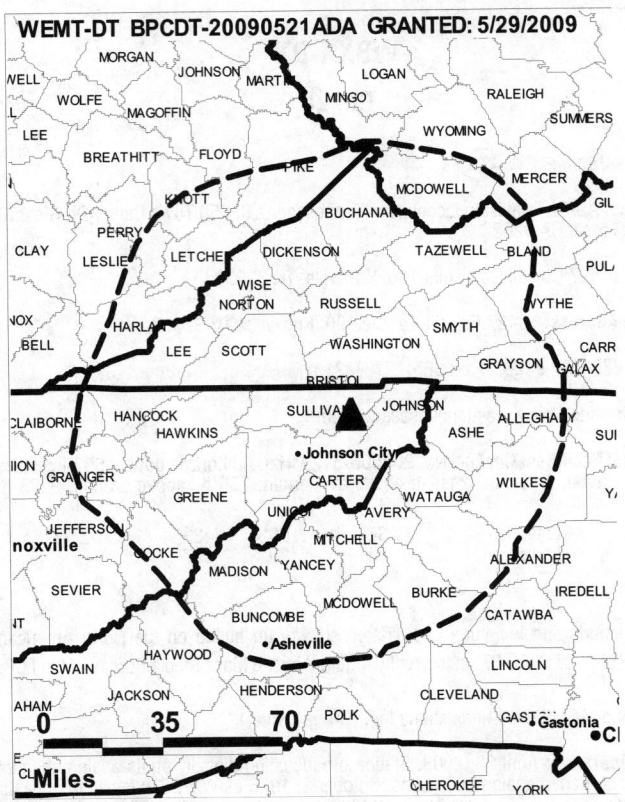

© 2010 Warren Communications News

City of License: Greeneville.

Station DMA: Tri-Cities (Bristol, VA-Kingsport-Johnson City, TN). **Rank:** 93.

Circulation © 2009 Nielsen. Coverage based on Nielsen study.

GrandTotal	Cable TV Households	Non-cable TV Households	Total TV Households
Estimated Station Totals *	241,000	152,230	393,230
Average Weekly Circulation (2009)	101,343	56,554	157,897
Average Daily Circulation (2009)			51,860

Station DMA Total	Cable TV Households	Non-cable TV Households	Total TV Households
Estimated Station Totals *	193,580	129,680	323,260
Average Weekly Circulation (2009)	94,945	54,471	149,416
Average Daily Circulation (2009)			50,179

Other DMA Total	Cable TV Households	Non-cable TV Households	Total TV Households
Estimated Station Totals *	47,420	22,550	69,970
Average Weekly Circulation (2009)	6,398	2,083	8,481
Average Daily Circulation (2009)			1,681

*Estimated station totals are sums of the Nielsen TV and Cable TV household estimates for each county in which the station registers viewing of more than 5% as per the Nielsen Survey Methods.

WPGD-DT
Ch. 51

Network Service: IND.

Licensee: Trinity Broadcasting Network Inc., 2442 Michelle Dr, Tustin, CA 92780.

Studio: 36 Music Village Blvd., Hendersonville, TN 37075.

Mailing Address: One Music Village Blvd, Hendersonville, TN 37075.

Phone: 615-822-1243. **Fax:** 615-822-1642.

Web Site: http://www.tbn.org

Technical Facilities: Channel No. 51 (692-698 MHz). Authorized power: 264-kw max. visual, aural. Antenna: 1368-ft above av. terrain, 1194-ft. above ground, 1973-ft. above sea level.

Latitude	36°	16'	03"
Longitude	86°	47'	44"

Holds CP for change to channel number 33, 1000-kw max. visual, 1352-ft above av. terrain, 1194-ft. above ground, 1954-ft. above sea level; lat. 36° 16' 05", long. 86° 47' 45", BPCDT-20090202BPB.

Note: Latitude and longitude coordinates shown are based on the North American Datum of 1927 (NAD 27) as currently required by the Mass Media Bureau of the FCC.

Ownership: Trinity Broadcasting Network Inc. (Group Owner).

Began Operation: April 4, 2008. Began analog operations: September 24, 1992. Ceased analog operations: June 12, 2009. Sale to All American TV Inc. by Sonlight Broadcasting Systems Inc. approved by FCC June 9, 1997. Sale to present owner by All American TV Inc. approved by FCC May 8, 2000.

Represented (legal): Colby M. May.

Personnel:

Russell Hall, General Manager.

Alan Partlow, Chief Engineer.

Linda Wells, Program Director.

City of License: Hendersonville. **Station DMA:** Nashville, TN. **Rank:** 29.

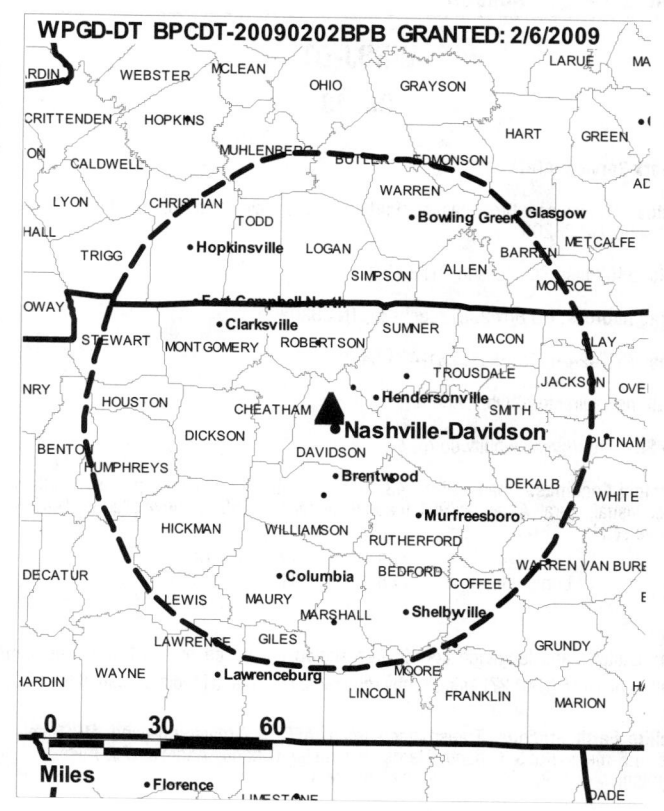

WPGD-DT BPCDT-20090202BPB GRANTED: 2/6/2009

© 2010 Warren Communications News

Circulation © 2009 Nielsen. Coverage based on Nielsen study.

GrandTotal	Cable TV Households	Non-cable TV Households	Total TV Households
Estimated Station Totals *	93,470	0	93,470
Average Weekly Circulation (2009)	5,101	0	5,101
Average Daily Circulation (2009)			1,134

Station DMA Total	Cable TV Households	Non-cable TV Households	Total TV Households
Estimated Station Totals *	93,470	0	93,470
Average Weekly Circulation (2009)	5,101	0	5,101
Average Daily Circulation (2009)			1,134

*Estimated station totals are sums of the Nielsen TV and Cable TV household estimates for each county in which the station registers viewing of more than 5% as per the Nielsen Survey Methods.

WBBJ-DT
Ch. 43

Network Service: ABC.

Grantee: Tennessee Broadcasting Partners, One Television Pl, c/o Leon Porter, Charlotte, NC 28205.

Studio: 346 Muse St, Jackson, TN 38301.

Mailing Address: PO Box 2387, Jackson, TN 38302.

Phone: 731-424-4515. **Fax:** 731-423-5448.

E-mail: newsdirector@wbbjtv.com

Web Site: http://www.wbbjtv.com

Technical Facilities: Channel No. 43 (644-650 MHz). Authorized power: 1000-kw max. visual, aural. Antenna: 991-ft above av. terrain, 955-ft. above ground, 1443-ft. above sea level.

Latitude	35°	38'	16"
Longitude	88°	41'	33"

Note: Latitude and longitude coordinates shown are based on the North American Datum of 1927 (NAD 27) as currently required by the Mass Media Bureau of the FCC.

Satellite Earth Stations: Transmitter Larcan; AFC, 3.7-meter Ku-band; DH Satellite, 4.5-meter Ku & C-band; Harris, 6.1-meter C-band; Andrew, 7.2-meter C-band; M/A-Com, Harris, Andrew receivers.

Ownership: Bahakel Communications Ltd. (Group Owner).

Began Operation: April 14, 2008. Began analog operations: March 6, 1955. Sale to present owner by Dixie Broadcasting (Estate of Aaron B. Robinson, majority owner) approved by FCC August 17, 1966. Ceased analog operations: June 12, 2009.

Represented (legal): Dow Lohnes PLLC.

Personnel:

Jerry K. Moore, Vice President & General Manager.

Mark Brooks, General Sales Manager.

Brad Grantham, News Director.

Randy McCaskill, Engineering Director.

Wayne Thing, Program Director.

Amy Killgore, Traffic Manager.

Thelma Jones, Office Manager.

City of License: Jackson. **Station DMA:** Jackson, TN. **Rank:** 173.

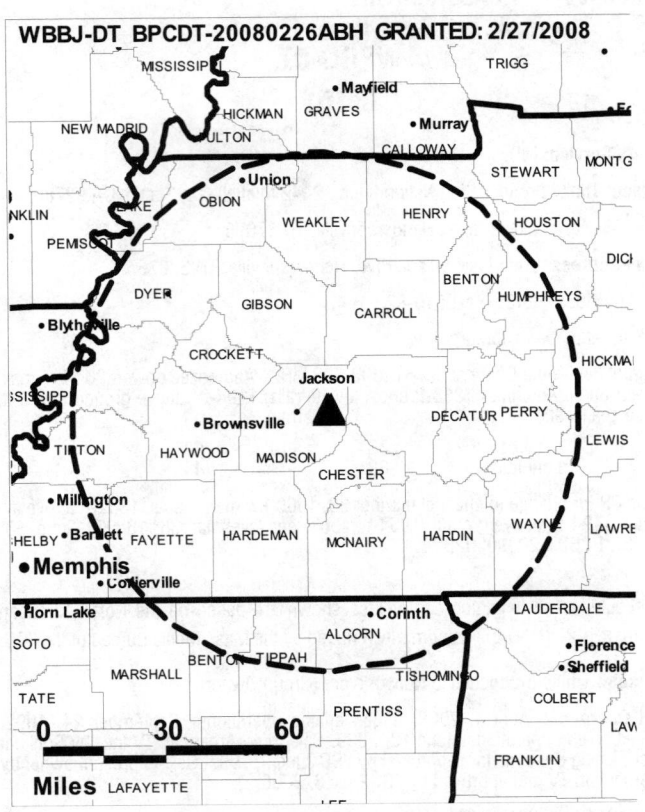

WBBJ-DT BPCDT-20080226ABH GRANTED: 2/27/2008

© 2010 Warren Communications News

Circulation © 2009 Nielsen. Coverage based on Nielsen study.

GrandTotal	Cable TV Households	Non-cable TV Households	Total TV Households
Estimated Station Totals *	110,650	90,590	201,240
Average Weekly Circulation (2009)	73,978	26,306	100,284
Average Daily Circulation (2009)			57,105

Station DMA Total	Cable TV Households	Non-cable TV Households	Total TV Households
Estimated Station Totals *	59,580	38,470	98,050
Average Weekly Circulation (2009)	47,859	17,306	65,165
Average Daily Circulation (2009)			40,299

Other DMA Total	Cable TV Households	Non-cable TV Households	Total TV Households
Estimated Station Totals *	51,070	52,120	103,190
Average Weekly Circulation (2009)	26,119	9,000	35,119
Average Daily Circulation (2009)			16,806

*Estimated station totals are sums of the Nielsen TV and Cable TV household estimates for each county in which the station registers viewing of more than 5% as per the Nielsen Survey Methods.

WJKT-DT
Ch. 39

Network Service: FOX.

Licensee: Newport Television License LLC, 460 Nichols Rd, Ste 250, Kansas City, MO 64112.

Studio: 2701 Union Extended, Suite 100, Memphis, TN 38112.

Mailing Address: PO Box 42087, Memphis, TN 38174.

Phone: 901-323-2430. **Fax:** 901-323-5826.

Web Site: http://www.myeyewitnessnews.com

Technical Facilities: Channel No. 39 (320-626 MHz). Authorized power: 392-kw max. visual, aural. Antenna: 971-ft above av. terrain, 930-ft. above ground, 1310-ft. above sea level.

Latitude	35°	47'	22"
Longitude	89°	06'	14"

Note: Latitude and longitude coordinates shown are based on the North American Datum of 1927 (NAD 27) as currently required by the Mass Media Bureau of the FCC.

Ownership: Newport Television LLC (Group Owner).

Began Operation: March 23, 2005. Began analog operations: April 18, 1985. Sale to present owner by Clear Channel Communications Inc. approved by FCC November 29, 2007. Sale to Clear Channel Communications Inc. by Television Marketing Group of Jackson Inc. approved by FCC September 29, 2000. Sale to Television Marketing Group of Jackson Inc. by Jackson Investment Corp. approved by FCC March 19, 1992. Sale to Jackson Investment Corp. by Star North Communications Inc. approved by FCC December 8, 1989. Sale to Star North Communications Inc. by Golden Circle Broadcasting Inc. approved by FCC October 27, 1988. Transfer of control by Golden Circle Broadcasting Inc. to Lloyd Communications Group Inc. from CLW Communications Group approved by FCC August 20, 1985. Ceased analog operations: June 12, 2009.

Represented (legal): Covington & Burling.

Represented (sales): Katz Media Group.

Personnel:

Jack Peck, General Manager.

Jim Doty, General Sales Manager.

Robyn Callaway, Local Sales Manager.

Jim Turpin, News Director.

Tom Beck, Chief Engineer.

Catherine Floyd, Business Manager.

Hunter Sandlin, Program Director.

Chris Adams, Promotion Manager.

George Davis, Production Manager.

Ahmed Murad, Research Director.

Phyllis Kingery, Traffic Manager.

© 2010 Warren Communications News

City of License: Jackson. **Station DMA:** Jackson, TN. **Rank:** 173.

Circulation © 2009 Nielsen. Coverage based on Nielsen study.

GrandTotal	Cable TV Households	Non-cable TV Households	Total TV Households
Estimated Station Totals *	91,060	87,960	179,020
Average Weekly Circulation (2009)	32,908	10,642	43,550
Average Daily Circulation (2009)			15,598

Station DMA Total	Cable TV Households	Non-cable TV Households	Total TV Households
Estimated Station Totals *	59,580	33,160	92,740
Average Weekly Circulation (2009)	25,404	5,260	30,664
Average Daily Circulation (2009)			9,927

Other DMA Total	Cable TV Households	Non-cable TV Households	Total TV Households
Estimated Station Totals *	31,480	54,800	86,280
Average Weekly Circulation (2009)	7,504	5,382	12,886
Average Daily Circulation (2009)			5,671

*Estimated station totals are sums of the Nielsen TV and Cable TV household estimates for each county in which the station registers viewing of more than 5% as per the Nielsen Survey Methods.

WPXK-TV
Ch. 23

Network Service: ION.

Licensee: ION Media Knoxville License Inc., Debtor in Possession, 601 Clearwater Park Rd, West Palm Beach, FL 33401-6233.

Studio: 9000 Executive Park Dr, Bldg D, Ste 210, Knoxville, TN 37923.

Mailing Address: 9000 Executive Park Dr, Bldg D, Ste 210, Knoxville, TN 37923.

Phone: 865-531-4037. **Fax:** 865-531-4760.

E-mail: hollyjones@ionmedia.com

Web Site: http://www.ionmedia.com

Technical Facilities: Channel No. 23 (524-530 MHz). Authorized power: 18-kw max. visual, aural. Antenna: 1995-ft above av. terrain, 69-ft. above ground, 3602-ft. above sea level.

Latitude	36°	11'	53"
Longitude	84°	13'	51"

Holds CP for change to 1000-kw max. visual, 1736-ft above av. terrain, 1364-ft. above ground, 2757-ft. above sea level; lat. 36° 00' 13", long. 83° 56' 34", BPCDT-20080620AGZ.

Note: Latitude and longitude coordinates shown are based on the North American Datum of 1927 (NAD 27) as currently required by the Mass Media Bureau of the FCC.

Ownership: ION Media Networks Inc., Debtor in Possession (Group Owner).

Began Operation: January 16, 2003. Began analog operations: May 4, 1992. Sale to Urban Television LLC pends. Involuntary assignment to debtor in possession status approved by FCC June 5, 2009. Transfer of control by ION Media Networks Inc. from Paxson Management Corp. & Lowell W. Paxson to CIG Media LLC approved by FCC December 31, 2007. Paxson Communications Corp. became ION Media Networks Inc. on June 26, 2006. Sale to Paxson Communications Corp. by Wayne Marler Crusaders approved by FCC September 23, 1998. Sale to Wayne Marler Crusaders by Pine Mountain Christian Broadcasting Inc. approved by FCC March 2, 1998. Ceased analog operations: June 12, 2009.

Represented (legal): Dow Lohnes PLLC.

Personnel:

Holly Jones, Station Operations & Traffic Manager.

Joe Clary, Chief Engineer.

City of License: Jellico. **Station DMA:** Knoxville, TN. **Rank:** 59.

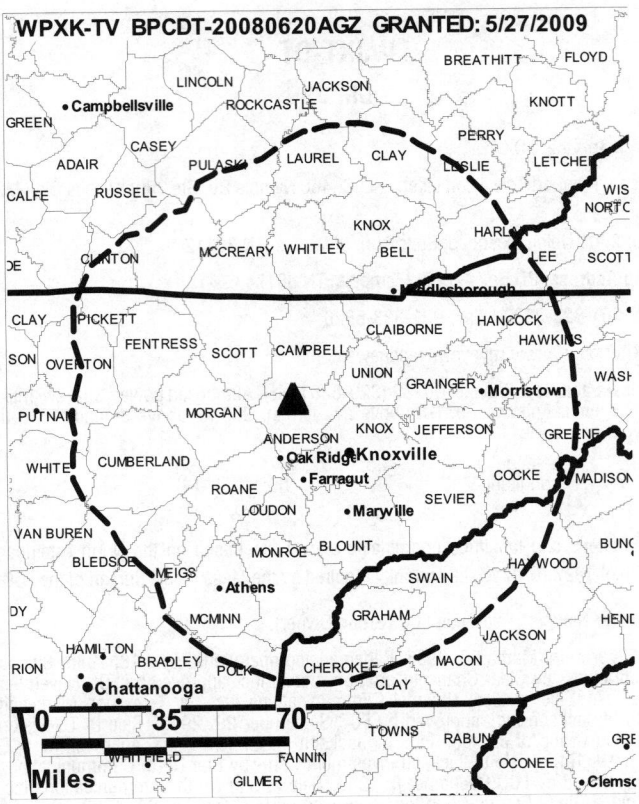

WPXK-TV BPCDT-20080620AGZ GRANTED: 5/27/2009

© 2010 Warren Communications News

Circulation © 2009 Nielsen. Coverage based on Nielsen study.

GrandTotal	Cable TV Households	Non-cable TV Households	Total TV Households
Estimated Station Totals *	252,380	25,380	277,760
Average Weekly Circulation (2009)	16,500	2,204	18,704
Average Daily Circulation (2009)			3,892

Station DMA Total	Cable TV Households	Non-cable TV Households	Total TV Households
Estimated Station Totals *	239,920	20,060	259,980
Average Weekly Circulation (2009)	15,644	1,933	17,577
Average Daily Circulation (2009)			3,692

Other DMA Total	Cable TV Households	Non-cable TV Households	Total TV Households
Estimated Station Totals *	12,460	5,320	17,780
Average Weekly Circulation (2009)	856	271	1,127
Average Daily Circulation (2009)			200

*Estimated station totals are sums of the Nielsen TV and Cable TV household estimates for each county in which the station registers viewing of more than 5% as per the Nielsen Survey Methods.

WJHL-DT
Ch. 11

Network Service: CBS.

Grantee: Media General Communications Holdings LLC, 333 E Franklin St, Richmond, VA 23219.

Studio: 338 E. Main St., Johnson City, TN 37601.

Mailing Address: PO Box 1130, Johnson City, TN 37605-1130.

Phone: 423-926-2151. **Fax:** 423-434-4537.

Web Site: http://www.wjhl.com; http://www.tricities.com

Technical Facilities: Channel No. 11 (198-204 MHz). Authorized power: 25.5-kw visual, aural. Antenna: 2323-ft above av. terrain, 200-ft. above ground, 4370-ft. above sea level.

Latitude	36°	25'	55"
Longitude	82°	08'	15"

Transmitter: Atop Holston Mountain, Carter County.

Note: Latitude and longitude coordinates shown are based on the North American Datum of 1927 (NAD 27) as currently required by the Mass Media Bureau of the FCC.

Satellite Earth Stations: Transmitter NEC; Prodelin, 3.1-meter C-band; AFC, 3.7-meter Ku-band; Scientific-Atlanta, 4.6-meter C-band; Andrew, 4.7-meter Ku-band; Scientific-Atlanta, 7-meter C-band; Scientific-Atlanta, M/A-Com receivers.

Ownership: Media General Inc. (Group Owner).

Began Operation: July 6, 2005. Station broadcasting digitally on its analog channel allotment. Began analog operations: October 26, 1953. Sale to present owner by Park Acquisition Inc. approved by FCC March 21, 1997 (Television Digest, Vol 36:31). Sale to Park Acquisition approved by FCC March 27, 1995. Sale to Park Communications Inc. by W. H. Lancaster Sr. & Jr. approved by FCC June 8, 1964 (Vol. 4:11, 24). Sale of 45% interest to W. H. Lancaster Sr. by S. H. Campbell Jr. family trust approved by FCC 1955-56. Ceased analog operations: June 12, 2009.

Personnel:

Jack D. Dempsey, President & General Manager.

Robin Hodge, Operations & Traffic Manager.

Leesa Wilcher, General Sales Manager.

Jimmy Denton, Local Sales Manager.

Mike Moore, Chief Engineer.

Nancy Mast, Business Manager.

Scott Evans, Production Manager.

City of License: Johnson City.

Station DMA: Tri-Cities (Bristol, VA-Kingsport-Johnson City, TN). **Rank:** 93.

WJHL-DT BMPCDT-20080619ACA GRANTED: 9/2/2008

© 2010 Warren Communications News

Circulation © 2009 Nielsen. Coverage based on Nielsen study.

GrandTotal	Cable TV Households	Non-cable TV Households	Total TV Households
Estimated Station Totals *	218,580	134,250	352,830
Average Weekly Circulation (2009)	140,728	80,049	220,777
Average Daily Circulation (2009)			113,513

Station DMA Total	Cable TV Households	Non-cable TV Households	Total TV Households
Estimated Station Totals *	203,160	129,680	332,840
Average Weekly Circulation (2009)	134,054	79,400	213,454
Average Daily Circulation (2009)			111,993

Other DMA Total	Cable TV Households	Non-cable TV Households	Total TV Households
Estimated Station Totals *	15,420	4,570	19,990
Average Weekly Circulation (2009)	6,674	649	7,323
Average Daily Circulation (2009)			1,520

*Estimated station totals are sums of the Nielsen TV and Cable TV household estimates for each county in which the station registers viewing of more than 5% as per the Nielsen Survey Methods.

WKPT-DT
Ch. 27

Network Service: ABC.

Grantee: Holston Valley Broadcasting Corp., PO Box 1971, Kingsport, TN 37662-1971.

Studio: 222 Commerce St, Kingsport, TN 37660.

Mailing Address: 222 Commerce St, Kingsport, TN 37660.

Phone: 423-246-9578. **Fax:** 423-246-6261.

Web Site: http://www.wkpttv.com

Technical Facilities: Channel No. 27 (548-554 MHz). Authorized power: 200-kw max. visual, aural. Antenna: 2280-ft above av. terrain, 153-ft. above ground, 4326-ft. above sea level.

Latitude	36°	25'	54"
Longitude	82°	08'	15"

Note: Latitude and longitude coordinates shown are based on the North American Datum of 1927 (NAD 27) as currently required by the Mass Media Bureau of the FCC.

Ownership: Holston Valley Broadcasting Corp. (Group Owner).

Began Operation: October 15, 2000. Standard Definition. Began analog operations: August 20, 1969. Ceased analog operations: June 12, 2009.

Represented (legal): Dennis J. Kelly.

Personnel:

George DeVault Jr., President, General Manager & Chief Engineer.

Bette Lawson, Vice President & Treasurer.

Fred Falin, Vice President, Programming.

Art Lanham, General Sales Manager.

Bob Haywood, Local Sales Manager.

Bobby Flowers, Production Manager.

Jerreese Atkinson, Traffic Manager.

City of License: Kingsport.

Station DMA: Tri-Cities (Bristol, VA-Kingsport-Johnson City, TN). **Rank:** 93.

Digital cable and TV coverage maps.
Visit www.warren-news.com/mediaprints.htm

MediaPrints™
Map a Winning Business Strategy

© 2010 Warren Communications News

Circulation © 2009 Nielsen. Coverage based on Nielsen study.

GrandTotal	Cable TV Households	Non-cable TV Households	Total TV Households
Estimated Station Totals *	235,080	129,680	364,760
Average Weekly Circulation (2009)	88,738	45,932	134,670
Average Daily Circulation (2009)			43,294

Station DMA Total	Cable TV Households	Non-cable TV Households	Total TV Households
Estimated Station Totals *	203,160	129,680	332,840
Average Weekly Circulation (2009)	85,279	45,932	131,211
Average Daily Circulation (2009)			42,785

Other DMA Total	Cable TV Households	Non-cable TV Households	Total TV Households
Estimated Station Totals *	31,920	0	31,920
Average Weekly Circulation (2009)	3,459	0	3,459
Average Daily Circulation (2009)			509

*Estimated station totals are sums of the Nielsen TV and Cable TV household estimates for each county in which the station registers viewing of more than 5% as per the Nielsen Survey Methods.

WATE-DT
Ch. 26

Network Service: ABC.

Licensee: WATE GP, Debtor in Possession, PO Box 1800, c/o Brooks, Pierce et al., Raleigh, NC 27602.

Studio: 1306 Broadway NE, Knoxville, TN 37917.

Mailing Address: PO Box 2349, Knoxville, TN 37901.

Phone: 865-637-6666. **Fax:** 865-525-4091.

Web Site: http://www.wate.com

Technical Facilities: Channel No. 26 (542-548 MHz). Authorized power: 930-kw max. visual, aural. Antenna: 1736-ft above av. terrain, 1364-ft. above ground, 2756-ft. above sea level.

Latitude	36°	00'	13"
Longitude	83°	56'	34"

Note: Latitude and longitude coordinates shown are based on the North American Datum of 1927 (NAD 27) as currently required by the Mass Media Bureau of the FCC.

Ownership: Young Broadcasting Inc., Debtor in Possession (Group Owner).

Began Operation: February 26, 2004. Began analog operations: October 1, 1953. Ceased analog operations: June 12, 2009. Sale to Nationwide Communications by Paul Montcastle & associates approved by FCC April 8, 1965. Sale to Young Broadcasting Inc. by Nationwide approved by FCC August 24, 1994. Involuntary assignment to debtor in possession status approved by FCC March 17, 2009. Assignment to WATE GP (New Young Broadcasting Holding Co. Inc.) pends.

Represented (legal): Brooks, Pierce, McLendon, Humphrey & Leonard LLP.

Personnel:

Gwen Kinsey, President & General Manager.

Tony Kahl, General Sales Director.

Jamie Foster, News Director.

Bob Williams, Chief Engineer.

Teresa Sylvia, Business Manager.

Melanie Maassen, Programming Assistant.

Tim Petree, Production Manager.

Mark Bishop, Creative Services Director.

Kim Hammer, Traffic Manager.

City of License: Knoxville. **Station DMA:** Knoxville, TN. **Rank:** 59.

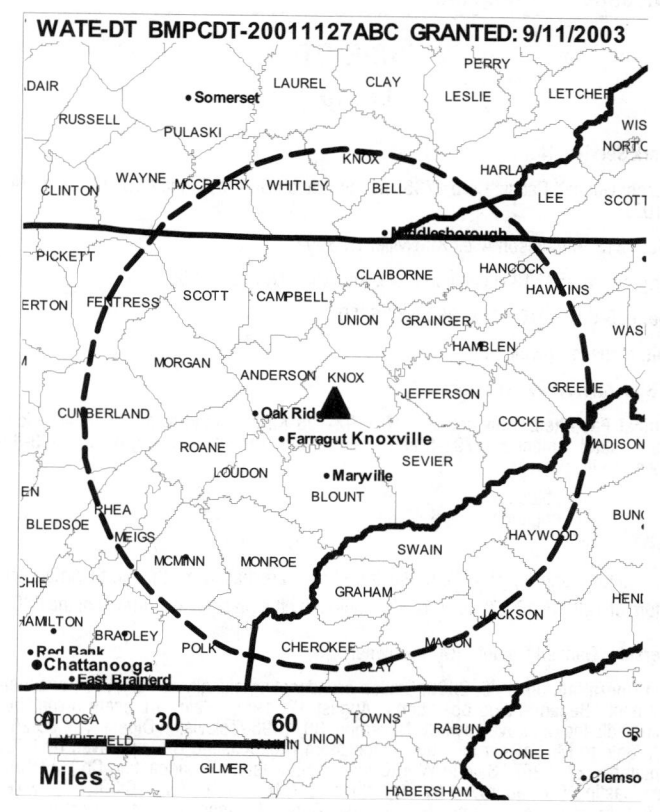

© 2010 Warren Communications News

Circulation © 2009 Nielsen. Coverage based on Nielsen study.

GrandTotal	Cable TV Households	Non-cable TV Households	Total TV Households
Estimated Station Totals *	397,450	245,030	642,480
Average Weekly Circulation (2009)	215,869	135,203	351,072
Average Daily Circulation (2009)			165,638

Station DMA Total	Cable TV Households	Non-cable TV Households	Total TV Households
Estimated Station Totals *	333,380	211,690	545,070
Average Weekly Circulation (2009)	200,736	133,071	333,807
Average Daily Circulation (2009)			160,009

Other DMA Total	Cable TV Households	Non-cable TV Households	Total TV Households
Estimated Station Totals *	64,070	33,340	97,410
Average Weekly Circulation (2009)	15,133	2,132	17,265
Average Daily Circulation (2009)			5,629

*Estimated station totals are sums of the Nielsen TV and Cable TV household estimates for each county in which the station registers viewing of more than 5% as per the Nielsen Survey Methods.

WBIR-DT
Ch. 10

Network Service: NBC.

Licensee: Gannett Pacific Corp., 7950 Jones Branch Dr, c/o Gannett Co., McLean, VA 22102.

Studio: 1513 Hutchinson Ave., Knoxville, TN 37917.

Mailing Address: 1513 Hutchinson Ave, Knoxville, TN 37917-3851.

Phone: 865-637-1010. **Fax:** 865-637-6380.

E-mail: manager@wbir.com

Web Site: http://www.wbir.com

Technical Facilities: Channel No. 10 (192-198 MHz). Authorized power: 40.9-kw visual, aural. Antenna: 1791-ft above av. terrain, 1463-ft. above ground, 2808-ft. above sea level.

Latitude	36°	00'	19"
Longitude	83°	56'	23"

Note: Latitude and longitude coordinates shown are based on the North American Datum of 1927 (NAD 27) as currently required by the Mass Media Bureau of the FCC.

Ownership: Gannett Co. Inc. (Group Owner).

Began Operation: June 30, 2005. Station broadcasting digitally on its analog channel allotment. Began analog operations: August 12, 1956. Sale to present owner by Multimedia Inc. approved by FCC November 30, 1995 (Television Digest, Vol. 35:25, 31). Sale to Multimedia Inc. by Southeastern Broadcasting Co. approved by FCC September 22, 1967. Sale to WMRC Inc. (Southeastern Broadcasting Co.) by Taft Broadcasting Co. approved by FCC November 16, 1960 (Vol. 16:39, 47). Sale of 70% by Gilmore N. Nunn, Mr. & Mrs. Robert L. Ashe & John P. Hart to Taft Broadcasting, which had previously held other 30%, approved by FCC October 29, 1959 (Vol. 15:41, 44). Ceased analog operations: June 12, 2009.

Represented (sales): TeleRep Inc.

Personnel:

Jeffrey H. Lee, President & General Manager.

Debbie Brizendine, General Sales Manager.

Rogan Oliver, Sales Manager.

Allen Koch, Sales Manager.

Bill Shory, News Director.

Gary L. Davis, Chief Engineer.

Linda Vallejos, Business Manager.

David Cowen, Program Director.

Julie Morris, Promotion Director.

Charlie Johnston, Research Director.

Pat Dalton, Traffic Manager.

City of License: Knoxville. **Station DMA:** Knoxville, TN. **Rank:** 59.

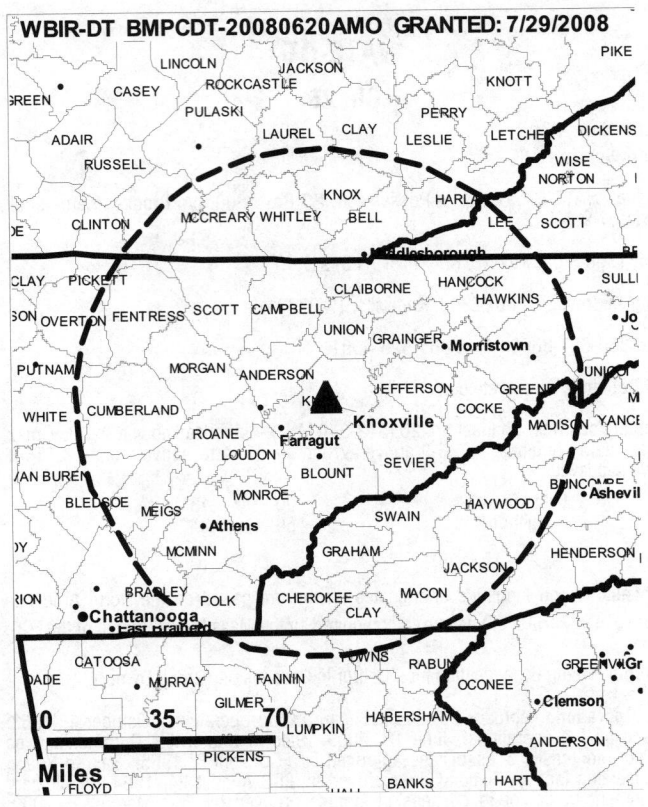

© 2010 Warren Communications News

Circulation © 2009 Nielsen. Coverage based on Nielsen study.

GrandTotal	Cable TV Households	Non-cable TV Households	Total TV Households
Estimated Station Totals *	420,710	248,250	668,960
Average Weekly Circulation (2009)	258,139	155,586	413,725
Average Daily Circulation (2009)			234,345

Station DMA Total	Cable TV Households	Non-cable TV Households	Total TV Households
Estimated Station Totals *	333,380	211,690	545,070
Average Weekly Circulation (2009)	234,026	152,620	386,646
Average Daily Circulation (2009)			224,335

Other DMA Total	Cable TV Households	Non-cable TV Households	Total TV Households
Estimated Station Totals *	87,330	36,560	123,890
Average Weekly Circulation (2009)	24,113	2,966	27,079
Average Daily Circulation (2009)			10,010

*Estimated station totals are sums of the Nielsen TV and Cable TV household estimates for each county in which the station registers viewing of more than 5% as per the Nielsen Survey Methods.

WMAK-DT
Ch. 7

Network Service: IND.

Licensee: Word of God Fellowship Inc., 3901 Hwy 121 S, Bedford, TX 76021-3009.

Mailing Address: 3901 Hwy 121 S, Bedford, TX 76021.

Phone: 865-329-8777. **Fax:** 865-584-9098.

Web Site: http://www.wmaktv.com

Technical Facilities: Channel No. 7 (174-180 MHz). Authorized power: 55-kw visual, aural. Antenna: 1253-ft above av. terrain, 1017-ft. above ground, 2274-ft. above sea level.

Latitude	36°	00'	36"
Longitude	83°	55'	57"

Holds CP for change to 95-kw visual; BPCDT-20080801ASS.

Note: Latitude and longitude coordinates shown are based on the North American Datum of 1927 (NAD 27) as currently required by the Mass Media Bureau of the FCC.

Ownership: Word of God Fellowship Inc.

Began Operation: July 31, 2004. Station launched using digital format. Sale to present owner by Knoxville Channel 7 LLC approved by FCC June 4, 2009. Sale to Richland Broadcasting--Knoxville LLC (Doreen M. Bray) approved by FCC April 28, 2008, but was never consummated.

Represented (legal): Koerner & Olender PC.

Personnel:

David Williams, Station Manager.

Eric East, General Sales Manager.

Tony Bryant, Business Operations Officer.

Bob Glenn, Chief Engineer.

Lorietta Allen, Traffic Manager.

Matt Waters, Promotion & Production Manager.

City of License: Knoxville. **Station DMA:** Knoxville, TN. **Rank:** 59.

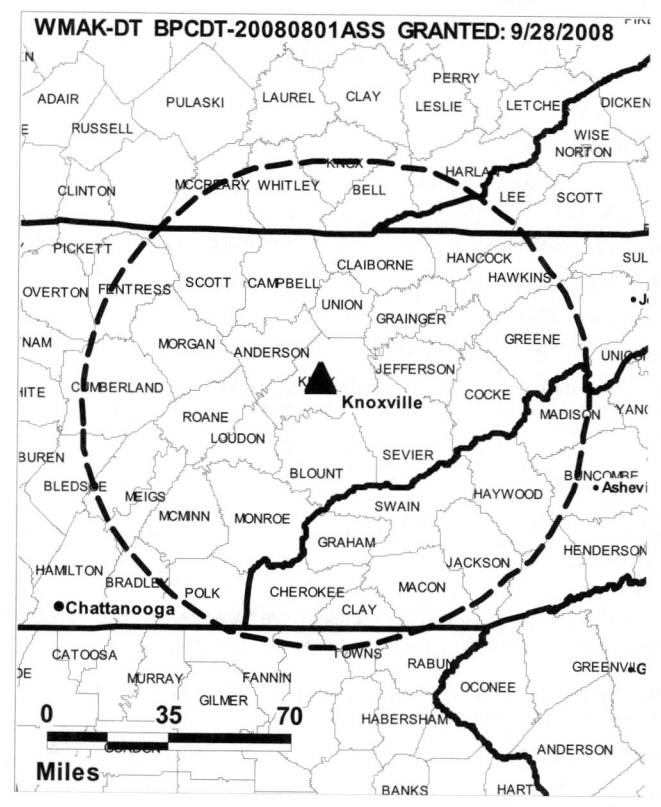

© 2010 Warren Communications News

Circulation © 2009 Nielsen. Coverage based on Nielsen study.

GrandTotal	Cable TV Households	Non-cable TV Households	Total TV Households
Estimated Station Totals *	246,660	112,600	359,260
Average Weekly Circulation (2009)	17,280	9,274	26,554
Average Daily Circulation (2009)			10,285

Station DMA Total	Cable TV Households	Non-cable TV Households	Total TV Households
Estimated Station Totals *	246,660	112,600	359,260
Average Weekly Circulation (2009)	17,280	9,274	26,554
Average Daily Circulation (2009)			10,285

*Estimated station totals are sums of the Nielsen TV and Cable TV household estimates for each county in which the station registers viewing of more than 5% as per the Nielsen Survey Methods.

WTNZ-DT
Ch. 34

Network Service: FOX.

Licensee: WTNZ License Subsidiary LLC, 201 Monroe St, RSA Tower, 20th Fl, Montgomery, AL 36104.

Studio: 9000 Executive Park Dr., Bldg D, Suite 300, Knoxville, TN 37923.

Mailing Address: 9000 Executive Park Dr, Bldg D, Ste 210, Knoxville, TN 37923.

Phone: 865-693-4343. **Fax:** 865-691-6904.

Web Site: http://www.wtnzfox43.com

Technical Facilities: Channel No. 34 (590-596 MHz). Authorized power: 460-kw max. visual, aural. Antenna: 1736-ft above av. terrain, 1356-ft. above ground, 2748-ft. above sea level.

Latitude	36°	00'	13"
Longitude	83°	56'	36"

Holds CP for change to 930-kw max. visual, 1729-ft above av. terrain, 1356-ft. above ground, 2748-ft. above sea level; lat. 36° 00' 13", long. 83° 56' 34", BPCDT-20080619ABZ.

Note: Latitude and longitude coordinates shown are based on the North American Datum of 1927 (NAD 27) as currently required by the Mass Media Bureau of the FCC.

Satellite Earth Stations: AFC, 3-meter Ku-band; Scientific-Atlanta, 4.6-meter C-band; Scientific-Atlanta, Harris receivers.

Ownership: Raycom Media Inc. (Group Owner).

Began Operation: November 4, 2002. Began analog operations: December 31, 1983. Sale to present owner by Ellis Communications approved by FCC July 26, 1996. Sale to Ellis Communications by FCVS Communications approved by FCC October 7, 1993 (Television Digest, Vol. 33:35). Sale to FCVS Communications by Media Central Inc. approved by FCC July 17, 1990. Sale to Media Central by H. Bernard Dixon, et al., approved by FCC October 1, 1985. Ceased analog operations: June 12, 2009.

Represented (legal): Covington & Burling.

Represented (sales): TeleRep Inc.

Personnel:

John Hayes, Vice President & General Manager.

Zach Smith, General Sales Manager.

Doug Koontz, Local Sales Manager.

Sara Foster, National Sales Manager.

Tom Thielmann, Chief Engineer.

Beverly Nettles, Traffic Manager.

Laura Abbott, Program Coordinator.

Doug Wood, Creative Services Director.

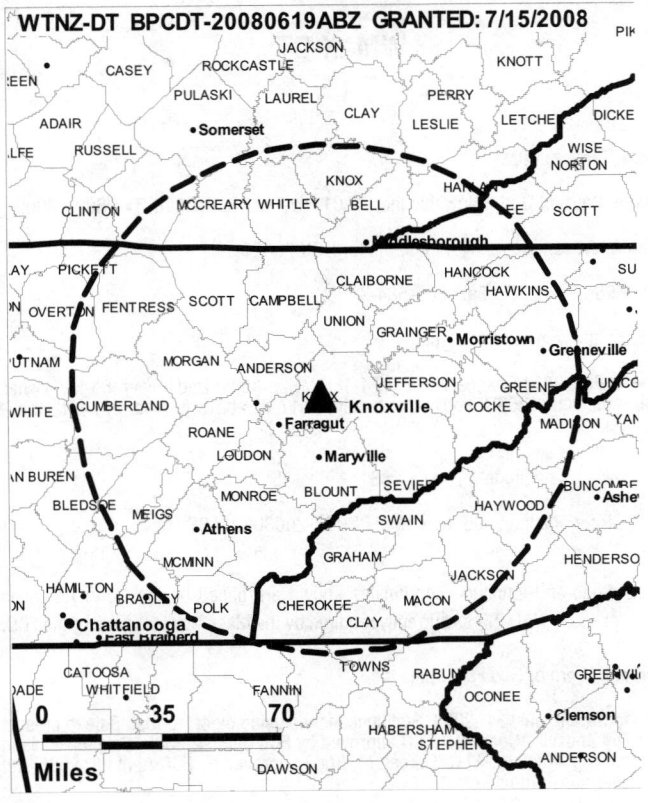

© 2010 Warren Communications News

Kimay Bloch, Marketing Director.

City of License: Knoxville. **Station DMA:** Knoxville, TN. **Rank:** 59.

Circulation © 2009 Nielsen. Coverage based on Nielsen study.

GrandTotal	Cable TV Households	Non-cable TV Households	Total TV Households
Estimated Station Totals *	331,140	211,690	542,830
Average Weekly Circulation (2009)	161,157	97,917	259,074
Average Daily Circulation (2009)			92,209

Station DMA Total	Cable TV Households	Non-cable TV Households	Total TV Households
Estimated Station Totals *	331,140	211,690	542,830
Average Weekly Circulation (2009)	161,157	97,917	259,074
Average Daily Circulation (2009)			92,209

*Estimated station totals are sums of the Nielsen TV and Cable TV household estimates for each county in which the station registers viewing of more than 5% as per the Nielsen Survey Methods.

WVLT-DT
Ch. 30

Network Service: MNT, CBS.

Licensee: Gray Television Licensee LLC, 1750 K St NW, Ste 1200, Washington, DC 20006.

Studio: 6516 Papermill Dr., Knoxville, TN 37919.

Mailing Address: 6516 Papermill Dr, Knoxville, TN 37919.

Phone: 865-450-8888. **Fax:** 865-450-8869.

Web Site: http://www.volunteertv.com

Technical Facilities: Channel No. 30 (566-572 MHz). Authorized power: 398-kw max. visual, aural. Antenna: 1809-ft above av. terrain, 1499-ft. above ground, 2814-ft. above sea level.

Latitude	35°	59'	44"
Longitude	83°	57'	23"

Holds CP for change to 870-kw max. visual; BPCDT-20080618AAM.

Transmitter: 1100 Sharp's Ridge Rd., Knoxville.

Note: Latitude and longitude coordinates shown are based on the North American Datum of 1927 (NAD 27) as currently required by the Mass Media Bureau of the FCC.

Ownership: Gray Television Inc. (Group Owner).

Began Operation: April 30, 2002. Began analog operations: December 6, 1988. Sale to Phipps of Tennessee Inc., et al., by John A. Engelbrecht approved by FCC June 9, 1992. Sale to present owner by John H. Phipps approved by FCC September 27, 1996 (Television Digest, Vol. 35:52; 36:41). Ceased analog operations: June 12, 2009.

Represented (sales): Continental Television Sales.

Represented (legal): Wiley Rein LLP.

Represented (engineering): Cavell, Mertz & Associates Inc.

Personnel:

Christopher Baker, Executive Vice President & General Manager.

Doug Stallard, Executive Vice President, Engineering.

Richard Torbett, General Sales Manager.

Dino Cartwright, Vice President, Promotion & Marketing.

Steve Crabtree, Vice President, News.

Marty Parham, Vice President, Systems & Programming.

Les Phillips, Production Manager.

Jasmine Hatcher, National Sales Manager.

Jeremy Morgan, Business Manager.

Willie McCauley, Local Sales Manager.

City of License: Knoxville. **Station DMA:** Knoxville, TN. **Rank:** 59.

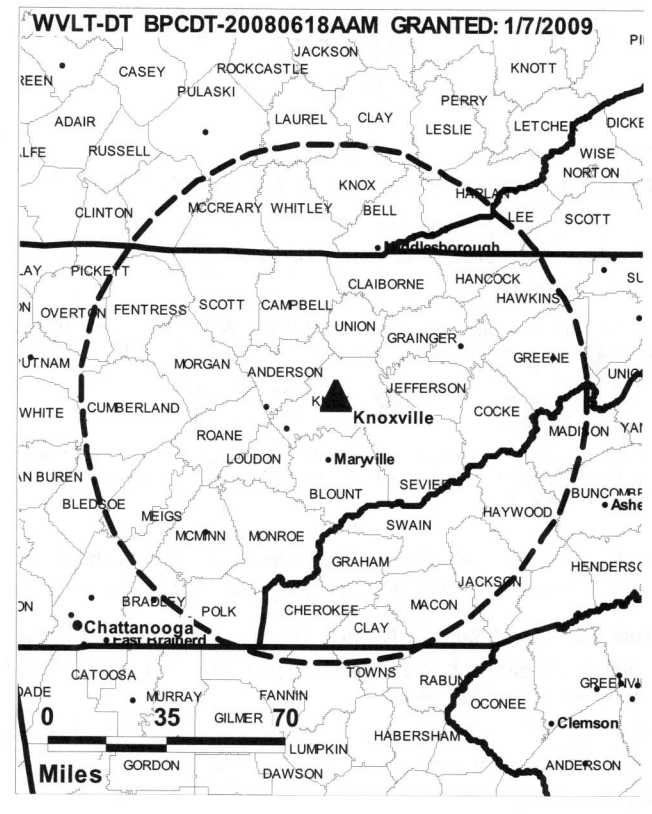

© 2010 Warren Communications News

Circulation © 2009 Nielsen. Coverage based on Nielsen study.

GrandTotal	Cable TV Households	Non-cable TV Households	Total TV Households
Estimated Station Totals *	391,890	238,220	630,110
Average Weekly Circulation (2009)	214,083	134,485	348,568
Average Daily Circulation (2009)			164,403

Station DMA Total	Cable TV Households	Non-cable TV Households	Total TV Households
Estimated Station Totals *	333,380	211,690	545,070
Average Weekly Circulation (2009)	205,608	132,134	337,742
Average Daily Circulation (2009)			160,869

Other DMA Total	Cable TV Households	Non-cable TV Households	Total TV Households
Estimated Station Totals *	58,510	26,530	85,040
Average Weekly Circulation (2009)	8,475	2,351	10,826
Average Daily Circulation (2009)			3,534

*Estimated station totals are sums of the Nielsen TV and Cable TV household estimates for each county in which the station registers viewing of more than 5% as per the Nielsen Survey Methods.

WJFB-DT
Ch. 44

Network Service: IND.

Licensee: Bryant Communications Inc., 200 E Spring St, Lebanon, TN 37087.

Studio: 200 E. Spring St., Lebanon, TN 37087.

Mailing Address: 200 E. Spring St, Lebanon, TN 37087.

Phone: 615-444-8206. **Fax:** 615-444-7592.

Technical Facilities: Channel No. 44 (650-656 MHz). Authorized power: 1000-kw max. visual, aural. Antenna: 528-ft above av. terrain, 259-ft. above ground, 1129-ft. above sea level.

Latitude	36°	09'	13"
Longitude	86°	22'	46"

Holds CP for change to 750-kw max. visual, 1394-ft above av. terrain, 1194-ft. above ground, 1992-ft. above sea level; lat. 36° 15' 50", long. 86° 47' 39", BPCDT-20080619AAQ.

Note: Latitude and longitude coordinates shown are based on the North American Datum of 1927 (NAD 27) as currently required by the Mass Media Bureau of the FCC.

Ownership: Bryant Broadcasting Co. (Group Owner).

Began Operation: February 17, 2009. Began analog operations: July 8, 1987. Ceased analog operations: November 23, 2008.

Personnel:

Dr. Joe F. Bryant, General Manager.

William Bryant, Operations Manager.

Dale Howard, Chief Engineer.

Pat Bryant, Business Manager & Program Director.

City of License: Lebanon. **Station DMA:** Nashville, TN. **Rank:** 29.

WJFB-DT BPCDT-20080619AAQ GRANTED: 10/29/2008

Nielsen Data: Not available.

WHBQ-DT
Ch. 13

Network Service: FOX.

Licensee: Fox Television Stations Inc., 5151 Wisconsin Ave. NW, c/o Molly Pauker, Washington, DC 20016.

Studio: 485 S Highland St, Memphis, TN 38111.

Mailing Address: 485 S Highland St, Memphis, TN 38111.

Phone: 901-320-1313. **Fax:** 901-320-1298.

Web Site: http://www.myfoxmemphis.com

Technical Facilities: Channel No. 13 (210-216 MHz). Authorized power: 95-kw visual, aural. Antenna: 1010-ft above av. terrain, 1043-ft. above ground, 1299-ft. above sea level.

Latitude	35°	10'	29"
Longitude	89°	50'	43"

Note: Latitude and longitude coordinates shown are based on the North American Datum of 1927 (NAD 27) as currently required by the Mass Media Bureau of the FCC.

Multichannel TV Sound: Planned.

SNG Mobile Dish: 4-meter Ku-band.

Ownership: Fox Television Holdings Inc. (Group Owner).

Began Operation: July 10, 2007. Station broadcasting digitally on its analog channel allotment. Began analog operations: September 27, 1953. Ceased analog operations: June 12, 2009.

Represented (legal): Skadden, Arps, Slate, Meagher & Flom LLP.

Represented (sales): Fox Television Stations Inc.

Personnel:

John Koski, Vice President, General Manager & Program Director.

Nichole Henderson, Local Sales Manager.

Tim Moore, National Sales Manager.

Ken Jobe, News Director.

David Bryant, Chief Engineer.

Ozge Kobarik, Marketing Director.

Paul Sloane, Promotion, Creative Services & Public Services Director.

Ethel Sengstacke, Production Manager.

Teddy Scoggins, Traffic Manager.

City of License: Memphis. **Station DMA:** Memphis, TN. **Rank:** 50.

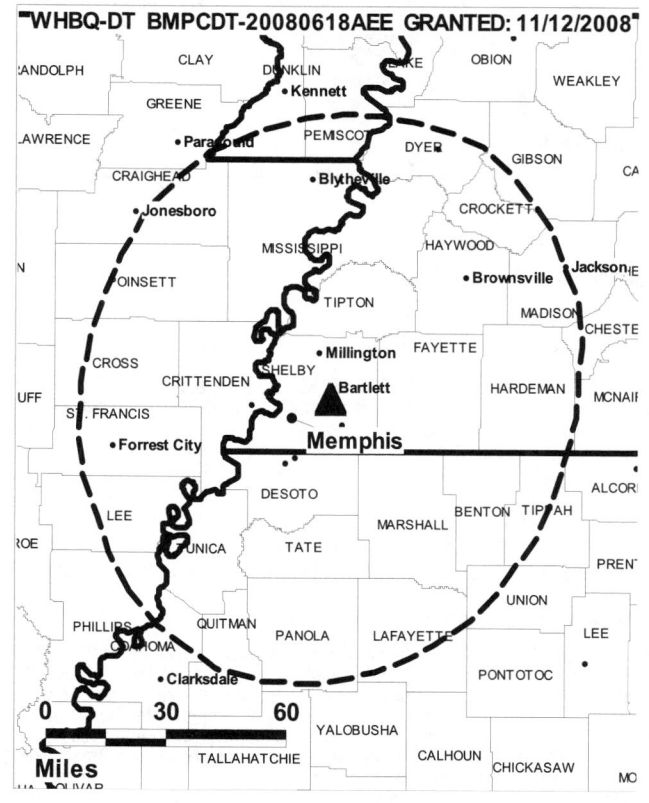

© 2010 Warren Communications News

Circulation © 2009 Nielsen. Coverage based on Nielsen study.

GrandTotal	Cable TV Households	Non-cable TV Households	Total TV Households
Estimated Station Totals *	467,200	395,950	863,150
Average Weekly Circulation (2009)	232,018	209,800	441,818
Average Daily Circulation (2009)			174,702

Station DMA Total	Cable TV Households	Non-cable TV Households	Total TV Households
Estimated Station Totals *	315,230	337,680	652,910
Average Weekly Circulation (2009)	190,590	198,432	389,022
Average Daily Circulation (2009)			161,198

Other DMA Total	Cable TV Households	Non-cable TV Households	Total TV Households
Estimated Station Totals *	151,970	58,270	210,240
Average Weekly Circulation (2009)	41,428	11,368	52,796
Average Daily Circulation (2009)			13,504

*Estimated station totals are sums of the Nielsen TV and Cable TV household estimates for each county in which the station registers viewing of more than 5% as per the Nielsen Survey Methods.

WLMT-DT
Ch. 31

Network Service: CW.

Licensee: Newport Television License LLC, 460 Nichols Rd, Ste 250, Kansas City, MO 64112.

Studio: 2701 Union Ext, Memphis, TN 38112.

Mailing Address: PO Box 42087, Memphis, TN 38174.

Phone: 901-323-2430. **Fax:** 901-323-2430.

Web Site: http://www.myeyewitnessnews.com/

Technical Facilities: Channel No. 31 (572-578 MHz). Authorized power: 871-kw max. visual, aural. Antenna: 1115-ft above av. terrain, 1168-ft. above ground, 1418-ft. above sea level.

Latitude	35°	16'	33"
Longitude	89°	46'	38"

Note: Latitude and longitude coordinates shown are based on the North American Datum of 1927 (NAD 27) as currently required by the Mass Media Bureau of the FCC.

Ownership: Newport Television LLC (Group Owner).

Began Operation: April 27, 2005. Began analog operations: April 18, 1983. Sale to present owner by Clear Channel Communications Inc. approved by FCC November 29, 2007. Sale to Clear Channel Communications Inc. by Television Marketing Group of Memphis Inc. approved by FCC October 20, 2000. Sale to Television Marketing Group of Memphis Inc. by West Tennessee Broadcasting Corp. approved by FCC March 19, 1992. Sale to MT Communications (later West Tennessee Broadcasting Corp.) by TVX of Memphis Inc. approved by FCC March 10, 1989. Assignment of license to Memco Inc. by TVX of Memphis Inc. dismissed by FCC January 25, 1989. Sale to Television Corp. of Memphis by Memphis Area Telecasters approved by FCC August 18, 1982. Transfer of control by Memphis Area Telecasters from TV30 Inc. to Memphis Thirty Inc. approved by FCC October 28, 1981. Ceased analog operations: February 17, 2009.

Represented (legal): Covington & Burling.

Represented (sales): Katz Media Group.

Personnel:

Jack Peck, General Manager.

Jim Doty, General Sales Manager.

Robyn Callaway, Local Sales Manager.

Robert Richardson, National Sales Manager.

Jim Turpin, News Director.

Tom Beck, Chief Engineer.

Catherine Floyd, Business Manager.

Pam Bridges, Program Director.

Tommy Davis, Promotion Manager.

George Davis, Production Manager.

Ahmed Murad, Research Director.

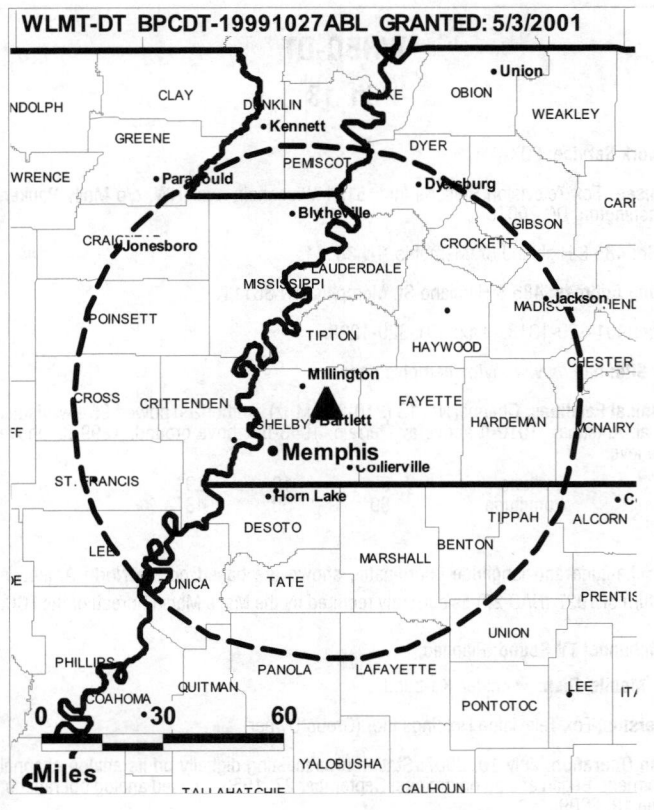

© 2010 Warren Communications News

Phyllis Kingery, Traffic Manager.

City of License: Memphis. **Station DMA:** Memphis, TN. **Rank:** 50.

Circulation © 2009 Nielsen. Coverage based on Nielsen study.

GrandTotal	Cable TV Households	Non-cable TV Households	Total TV Households
Estimated Station Totals *	340,120	369,850	709,970
Average Weekly Circulation (2009)	124,517	112,221	236,738
Average Daily Circulation (2009)			85,656

Station DMA Total	Cable TV Households	Non-cable TV Households	Total TV Households
Estimated Station Totals *	310,910	329,270	640,180
Average Weekly Circulation (2009)	120,972	107,960	228,932
Average Daily Circulation (2009)			84,077

Other DMA Total	Cable TV Households	Non-cable TV Households	Total TV Households
Estimated Station Totals *	29,210	40,580	69,790
Average Weekly Circulation (2009)	3,545	4,261	7,806
Average Daily Circulation (2009)			1,579

*Estimated station totals are sums of the Nielsen TV and Cable TV household estimates for each county in which the station registers viewing of more than 5% as per the Nielsen Survey Methods.

WMC-DT
Ch. 5

Network Service: NBC.

Licensee: WMC License Subsidiary LLC, 201 Monroe St, RSA Tower, 20th Fl, Montgomery, AL 36104.

Studio: 1960 Union Ave., Memphis, TN 38104.

Mailing Address: 1960 Union Ave, Memphis, TN 38104.

Phone: 901-726-0555. **Fax:** 901-278-7633.

Web Site: http://www.wmctv.com

Technical Facilities: Channel No. 5 (76-82 MHz). Authorized power: 34.5-kw visual, aural. Antenna: 1010-ft above av. terrain, 1048-ft. above ground, 1293-ft. above sea level.

Latitude	35°	16'	33"
Longitude	89°	46'	38"

Note: Latitude and longitude coordinates shown are based on the North American Datum of 1927 (NAD 27) as currently required by the Mass Media Bureau of the FCC.

Ownership: Raycom Media Inc. (Group Owner).

Began Operation: May 1, 2002. High Definition. Station broadcasting digitally on its analog channel allotment. Began analog operations: December 11, 148. Sale to Elcom of Memphis Inc. approved by FCC October 7, 1993 (Television Digest, Vol. 33:30). Sale to present owner by Elcom approved by FCC July 26, 1996 (Vol. 36:32). Ceased analog operations: June 12, 2009.

Represented (legal): Covington & Burling.

Represented (sales): TeleRep Inc.

Personnel:

Lee Meredith, Vice President & General Manager.

Gary Macko, General Sales Manager.

Vance Collins, Local Sales Manager.

Tim Seymour, Local Sales Manager.

Tracey Rogers, News Director.

David Evans, Engineering Director.

Rick Roberts, Controller.

Juli Rogers, Program Coordinator.

Chris Conroy, Promotion & Marketing Director.

Jeff Bryant, Creative Services Director.

Shaundra Hill, Traffic Manager.

Craten Armmer, Community Affairs Manager.

City of License: Memphis. **Station DMA:** Memphis, TN. **Rank:** 50.

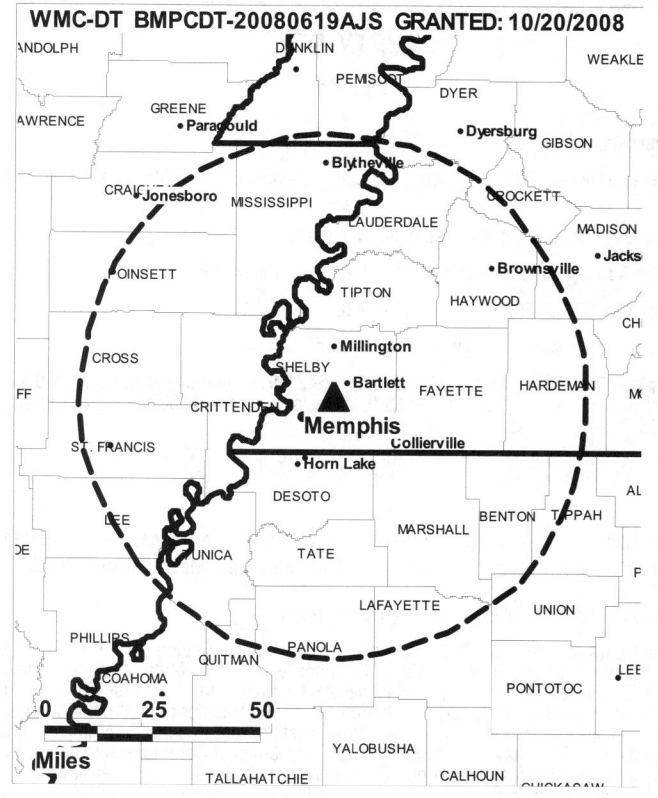

WMC-DT BMPCDT-20080619AJS GRANTED: 10/20/2008

© 2010 Warren Communications News

Circulation © 2009 Nielsen. Coverage based on Nielsen study.

GrandTotal	Cable TV Households	Non-cable TV Households	Total TV Households
Estimated Station Totals *	516,290	399,290	915,580
Average Weekly Circulation (2009)	282,429	229,591	512,020
Average Daily Circulation (2009)			257,368

Station DMA Total	Cable TV Households	Non-cable TV Households	Total TV Households
Estimated Station Totals *	315,230	337,680	652,910
Average Weekly Circulation (2009)	223,171	216,457	439,628
Average Daily Circulation (2009)			235,238

Other DMA Total	Cable TV Households	Non-cable TV Households	Total TV Households
Estimated Station Totals *	201,060	61,610	262,670
Average Weekly Circulation (2009)	59,258	13,134	72,392
Average Daily Circulation (2009)			22,130

*Estimated station totals are sums of the Nielsen TV and Cable TV household estimates for each county in which the station registers viewing of more than 5% as per the Nielsen Survey Methods.

WPTY-DT
Ch. 25

Network Service: ABC.

Licensee: Newport Television License LLC, 460 Nichols Rd, Ste 250, Kansas City, MO 64112.

Studio: 2701 Union Extended, Memphis, TN 38112.

Mailing Address: 2701 Union Extended, Memphis, TN 38112.

Phone: 901-323-2430. **Fax:** 901-323-5826.

Web Site: http://www.myeyewitnessnews.com

Technical Facilities: Channel No. 25 (536-542 MHz). Authorized power: 1000-kw max. visual, aural. Antenna: 1115-ft above av. terrain, 1168-ft. above ground, 1418-ft. above sea level.

Latitude	35°	16'	33"
Longitude	89°	46'	38"

Note: Latitude and longitude coordinates shown are based on the North American Datum of 1927 (NAD 27) as currently required by the Mass Media Bureau of the FCC.

Ownership: Newport Television LLC (Group Owner).

Began Operation: June 28, 2005. Began analog operations: September 10, 1978. Sale to Precht Communications by Martin F. Connelly, Arthur E. Muth, et al., approved by FCC July 23, 1984. Sale to Channel 24 Memphis Ltd. Partnership by Precht Communications approved by FCC March 28, 1986. Transfer of control by Channel 24 Memphis Ltd. Partnership to Chase Broadcasting from Channel 24 Memphis Ltd. approved by FCC May 31, 1988. Sale to Clear Channel Communications Inc. by Chase Broadcasting approved by FCC March 26, 1992. Sale to present owner by Clear Channel Communications Inc. approved by FCC November 29, 2007. Ceased analog operations: June 12, 2009.

Represented (legal): Covington & Burling.

Represented (sales): Katz Media Group.

Personnel:

Jack L. Peck, General Manager.

Marshall Hart, Operations Manager.

Jim Doty, General Sales Manager.

Robert Richardson, National Sales Manager.

Jim Turpin, News Director.

Tom Beck, Chief Engineer.

Catherine Floyd, Business Manager.

Kevin Quinn, Program Director.

Tommy Davis, Promotion Director.

George Davis, Production Manager.

Ahmed Murad, Research Director.

Phyllis Kingery, Traffic Manager.

WPTY-DT BPCDT-19990914AAC GRANTED: 6/1/2001

© 2010 Warren Communications News

City of License: Memphis. **Station DMA:** Memphis, TN. **Rank:** 50.

Circulation © 2009 Nielsen. Coverage based on Nielsen study.

GrandTotal	Cable TV Households	Non-cable TV Households	Total TV Households
Estimated Station Totals *	358,710	382,320	741,030
Average Weekly Circulation (2009)	165,334	178,316	343,650
Average Daily Circulation (2009)			130,757

Station DMA Total	Cable TV Households	Non-cable TV Households	Total TV Households
Estimated Station Totals *	315,230	337,680	652,910
Average Weekly Circulation (2009)	159,542	169,758	329,300
Average Daily Circulation (2009)			126,211

Other DMA Total	Cable TV Households	Non-cable TV Households	Total TV Households
Estimated Station Totals *	43,480	44,640	88,120
Average Weekly Circulation (2009)	5,792	8,558	14,350
Average Daily Circulation (2009)			4,546

*Estimated station totals are sums of the Nielsen TV and Cable TV household estimates for each county in which the station registers viewing of more than 5% as per the Nielsen Survey Methods.

WPXX-DT
Ch. 51

Network Service: MNT, ION.

Grantee: ION Media Memphis License Inc., Debtor in Possession, 601 Clearwater Park Rd, West Palm Beach, FL 33401-6233.

Studio: 5050 Poplar Ave, Ste 909, Memphis, TN 38157.

Mailing Address: 5050 Poplar Ave, Ste 909, Memphis, TN 38157.

Phone: 901-384-9324. **Fax:** 901-384-3157.

E-mail: rubydavis@ionmedia.com

Web Site: http://www.ionmedia.com

Technical Facilities: Channel No. 51 (692-698 MHz). Authorized power: 1000-kw max. visual, aural. Antenna: 978-ft above av. terrain, 988-ft. above ground, 1270-ft. above sea level.

Latitude	35°	12'	41"
Longitude	89°	48'	54"

Note: Latitude and longitude coordinates shown are based on the North American Datum of 1927 (NAD 27) as currently required by the Mass Media Bureau of the FCC.

Ownership: ION Media Networks Inc., Debtor in Possession (Group Owner).

Began Operation: May 1, 2002. Standard Definition. Began analog operations: December 31, 1994. Involuntary assignment to debtor in possession status approved by FCC June 5, 2009. Transfer of control by ION Media Networks Inc. from Paxson Management Corp. & Lowell W. Paxson to CIG Media LLC approved by FCC December 31, 2007. Sale to ION Media Networks Inc. by Flinn Broadcasting Corp. approved by FCC October 25, 2007. Sale to Flinn Broadcasting Corp. by Kyles Broadcasting Ltd. approved by FCC August 27, 1990. Ceased analog operations: June 12, 2009.

Represented (legal): Dow Lohnes PLLC.

Personnel:

Terry Digel, Station Operations Manager.

Charles Meyers, Chief Engineer.

Ruby Davis, Traffic Manager.

City of License: Memphis. **Station DMA:** Memphis, TN. **Rank:** 50.

TELEVISION & CABLE
Factbook Online

| continuous updates | fully searchable | easy to use |

For more information call **800-771-9202** or visit **www.warren-news.com**

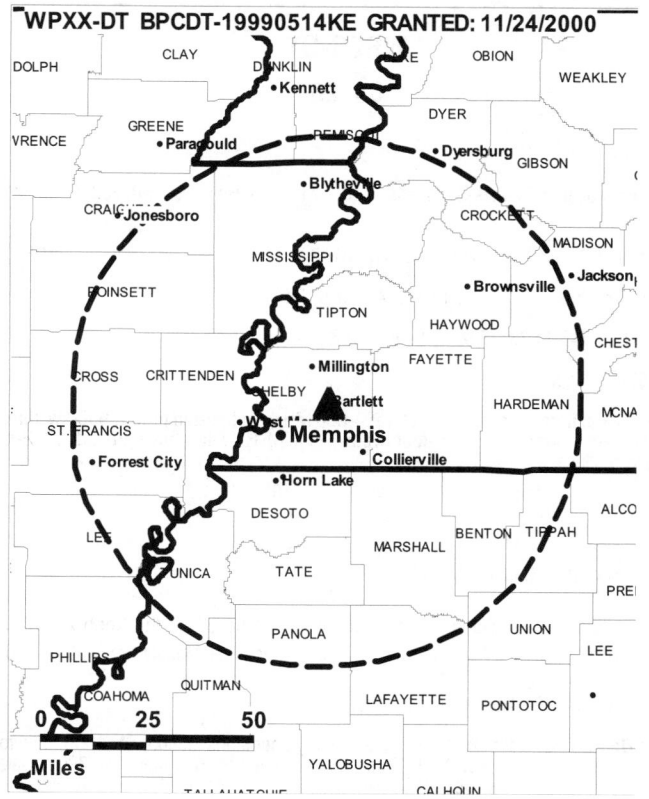

WPXX-DT BPCDT-19990514KE GRANTED: 11/24/2000

© 2010 Warren Communications News

Circulation © 2009 Nielsen. Coverage based on Nielsen study.

GrandTotal	Cable TV Households	Non-cable TV Households	Total TV Households
Estimated Station Totals *	296,110	312,320	608,430
Average Weekly Circulation (2009)	33,013	41,192	74,205
Average Daily Circulation (2009)			21,080

Station DMA Total	Cable TV Households	Non-cable TV Households	Total TV Households
Estimated Station Totals *	294,390	298,570	592,960
Average Weekly Circulation (2009)	32,805	39,980	72,785
Average Daily Circulation (2009)			20,818

Other DMA Total	Cable TV Households	Non-cable TV Households	Total TV Households
Estimated Station Totals *	1,720	13,750	15,470
Average Weekly Circulation (2009)	208	1,212	1,420
Average Daily Circulation (2009)			262

*Estimated station totals are sums of the Nielsen TV and Cable TV household estimates for each county in which the station registers viewing of more than 5% as per the Nielsen Survey Methods.

WREG-DT
Ch. 28

Network Service: CBS.

Licensee: Local TV Tennessee License LLC, 1717 Dixie Hwy, Ste 650, Fort Wright, KY 41011.

Studio: 803 Channel 3 Dr, Memphis, TN 38103.

Mailing Address: 803 Channel 3 Dr, Memphis, TN 38103.

Phone: 901-543-2333. **Fax:** 901-543-2198.

Web Site: http://www.wreg.com

Technical Facilities: Channel No. 28 (554-560 MHz). Authorized power: 906-kw max. visual, aural. Antenna: 1027-ft above av. terrain, 1047-ft. above ground, 1319-ft. above sea level.

Latitude	35°	10'	52"
Longitude	89°	49'	56"

Transmitter: 2105 Charles Bryan Rd.

Note: Latitude and longitude coordinates shown are based on the North American Datum of 1927 (NAD 27) as currently required by the Mass Media Bureau of the FCC.

Ownership: Local TV Holdings LLC (Group Owner).

Began Operation: August 2, 2005. Began analog operations: January 1, 1956. Sale to present owner by The New York Times Co. approved by FCC March 9, 2007. Sale to The New York Times Co. by Cowles Broadcasting approved by FCC August 18, 1971. Sale to Cowles Broadcasting by Hoyt B. Wooten approved by FCC April 24, 1963. Ceased analog operations: June 12, 2009.

Represented (legal): Dow Lohnes PLLC.

Represented (sales): Eagle Television Sales.

Personnel:

Ron Walter, President & General Manager.

Jim Himes, General Sales Manager.

Brett Schutt, National Sales Manager.

Charles Riales, Chief Engineer.

Kim Bowles, Local Sales Manager.

Bruce Moore, News Director.

Randy Culbertson, Controller.

Wes Pollard, Creative Services & Promotion Manager.

City of License: Memphis. **Station DMA:** Memphis, TN. **Rank:** 50.

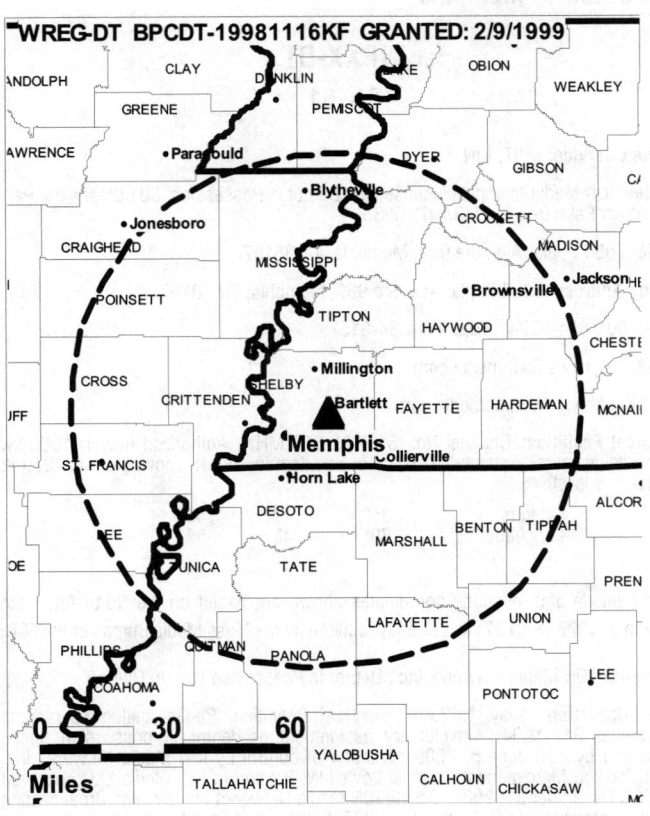

WREG-DT BPCDT-19981116KF GRANTED: 2/9/1999

© 2010 Warren Communications News

Circulation © 2009 Nielsen. Coverage based on Nielsen study.

GrandTotal	Cable TV Households	Non-cable TV Households	Total TV Households
Estimated Station Totals *	464,470	399,210	863,680
Average Weekly Circulation (2009)	287,992	235,773	523,765
Average Daily Circulation (2009)			268,737

Station DMA Total	Cable TV Households	Non-cable TV Households	Total TV Households
Estimated Station Totals *	315,230	337,680	652,910
Average Weekly Circulation (2009)	227,205	222,471	449,676
Average Daily Circulation (2009)			237,881

Other DMA Total	Cable TV Households	Non-cable TV Households	Total TV Households
Estimated Station Totals *	149,240	61,530	210,770
Average Weekly Circulation (2009)	60,787	13,302	74,089
Average Daily Circulation (2009)			30,856

*Estimated station totals are sums of the Nielsen TV and Cable TV household estimates for each county in which the station registers viewing of more than 5% as per the Nielsen Survey Methods.

WHTN-DT
Ch. 38

Network Service: IND.

Licensee: Christian Television Network Inc., 9582 Lebanon Rd, Mount Juliet, TN 37122.

Studio: 9852 Lebanon Rd., Mount Juliet, TN 37122.

Mailing Address: 9852 Lebanon Rd, Mount Juliet, TN 37122.

Phone: 615-754-0039. **Fax:** 615-754-0047.

E-mail: jjarvis@ctnonline.com

Web Site: http://www.ctnonline.com; http://www.ctntv.org

Technical Facilities: Channel No. 38 (614-620 MHz). Authorized power: 1000-kw max. visual, aural. Antenna: 820-ft above av. terrain, 850-ft. above ground, 1421-ft. above sea level.

Latitude	36°	04'	58"
Longitude	86°	25'	52"

Note: Latitude and longitude coordinates shown are based on the North American Datum of 1927 (NAD 27) as currently required by the Mass Media Bureau of the FCC.

Ownership: Christian Television Network Inc. (Group Owner).

Began Operation: June 26, 2006. Began analog operations: December 30, 1983. Sale to Murfreesboro TV Corp. by Channel 39 of Murfreesboro LP approved by FCC August 2, 1985. Sale to present owner by Murfreesboro TV Corp. approved by FCC August 21, 1986. Ceased analog operations: January 20, 2009.

Personnel:

Bob D'Andrea, President.

Monica Schmelter, General Manager.

Ed Lanius, Chief Engineer.

Jacqueline McGirt, Program Director & Traffic Manager.

Carrie Litsey, Office Manager.

Charlie Smith, Production Manager.

Jay Holley, Marketing & Promotions Director.

City of License: Murfreesboro. **Station DMA:** Nashville, TN. **Rank:** 29.

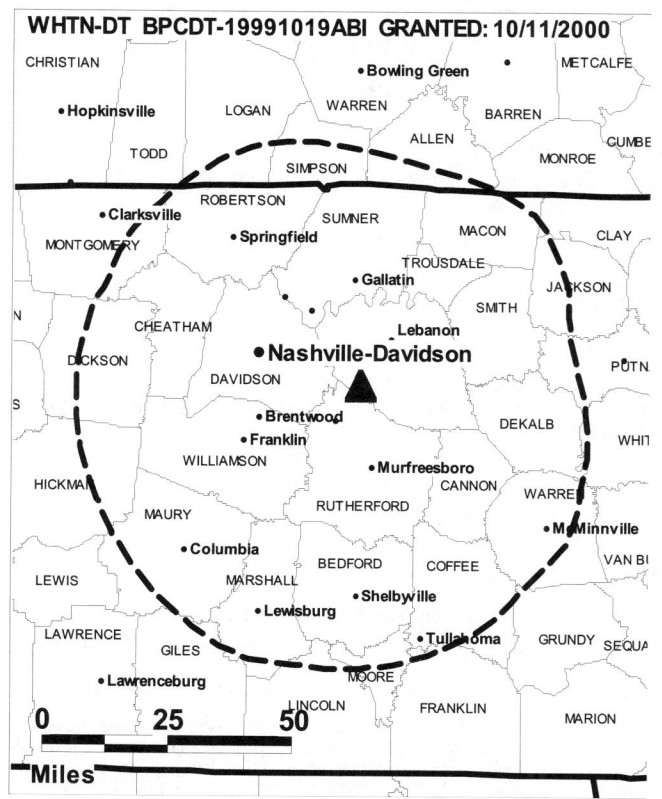

© 2010 Warren Communications News

Circulation © 2009 Nielsen. Coverage based on Nielsen study.

GrandTotal	Cable TV Households	Non-cable TV Households	Total TV Households
Estimated Station Totals *	15,950	33,250	49,200
Average Weekly Circulation (2009)	1,025	2,594	3,619
Average Daily Circulation (2009)			704

Station DMA Total	Cable TV Households	Non-cable TV Households	Total TV Households
Estimated Station Totals *	15,950	33,250	49,200
Average Weekly Circulation (2009)	1,025	2,594	3,619
Average Daily Circulation (2009)			704

*Estimated station totals are sums of the Nielsen TV and Cable TV household estimates for each county in which the station registers viewing of more than 5% as per the Nielsen Survey Methods.

WKRN-DT
Ch. 27

Network Service: ABC.

Licensee: WKRN GP, Debtor in Possession, PO Box 1800, c/o Brooks, Pierce et al., Raleigh, NC 27602.

Studio: 441 Murfreesboro Rd., Nashville, TN 37210.

Mailing Address: 441 Murfreesboro Rd, Nashville, TN 37210.

Phone: 615-259-2200; 615-369-7222. **Fax:** 615-244-2117.

Web Site: http://www.wkrn.com

Technical Facilities: Channel No. 27 (548-554 MHz). Authorized power: 946-kw max. visual, aural. Antenna: 1348-ft above av. terrain, 902-ft. above ground, 2008-ft. above sea level.

Latitude	36°	02'	50"
Longitude	86°	49'	49"

Holds CP for change to 1000-kw max. visual; BMPCDT-20090116ABI.

Transmitter: 1406 Old Hickory Blvd.

Note: Latitude and longitude coordinates shown are based on the North American Datum of 1927 (NAD 27) as currently required by the Mass Media Bureau of the FCC.

Ownership: Young Broadcasting Inc., Debtor in Possession (Group Owner).

Began Operation: May 1, 2002. High Definition. Began analog operations: November 28, 1953. Ceased analog operations: June 12, 2009. Originally broadcast on Ch. 8. Assignment to WKRN GP (New Young Broadcasting Holding Co. inc.) pends. Involuntary assignment to debtor in possession status approved by FCC March 17, 2009. Sale to Young Broadcasting Inc. by Knight-Ridder Broadcasting approved by FCC April 17, 1989. Sale to Knight-Ridder by General Electric Broadcasting Co. approved by FCC September 28, 1983. Sale to General Electric by Louis R. Draughton & associates approved by FCC April 6, 1966.

Represented (legal): Brooks, Pierce, McLendon, Humphrey & Leonard LLP.

Represented (engineering): Cohen Dippell & Everist PC.

Personnel:

Gwen Kinsey, President & General Manager.

Matthew Zelkind, Station Manager & News Director.

Connie Sullivan, General Sales Manager.

Steve Watt, Local Sales Manager.

Scott Piper, National Sales Manager.

Mike McCord, Regional Sales Manager.

Gene Parker, Chief Engineer.

Kathy McElroy, Finance Director.

Michelle Dube, Program & Research Director.

Mike Tarrolly, Marketing Director.

Jane Smith, Traffic Manager.

WKRN-DT BMPCDT-20090116ABI GRANTED: 3/16/2009

© 2010 Warren Communications News

City of License: Nashville. **Station DMA:** Nashville, TN. **Rank:** 29.

Circulation © 2009 Nielsen. Coverage based on Nielsen study.

GrandTotal	Cable TV Households	Non-cable TV Households	Total TV Households
Estimated Station Totals *	569,960	394,900	964,860
Average Weekly Circulation (2009)	330,755	239,505	570,260
Average Daily Circulation (2009)			257,449

Station DMA Total	Cable TV Households	Non-cable TV Households	Total TV Households
Estimated Station Totals *	532,930	369,420	902,350
Average Weekly Circulation (2009)	324,805	237,836	562,641
Average Daily Circulation (2009)			255,676

Other DMA Total	Cable TV Households	Non-cable TV Households	Total TV Households
Estimated Station Totals *	37,030	25,480	62,510
Average Weekly Circulation (2009)	5,950	1,669	7,619
Average Daily Circulation (2009)			1,773

*Estimated station totals are sums of the Nielsen TV and Cable TV household estimates for each county in which the station registers viewing of more than 5% as per the Nielsen Survey Methods.

WNAB-DT
Ch. 23

Network Service: CW.

Licensee: Nashville License Holdings LLC, 100 N Crescent Dr, Ste 200, Beverly Hills, CA 90210.

Studio: 631 Mainstream Dr., Nashville, TN 37228.

Mailing Address: 631 Mainstream Dr, Nashville, TN 37228.

Phone: 615-259-5617. **Fax:** 615-259-3962.

Web Site: http://www.cw58.tv/home/home.html

Technical Facilities: Channel No. 23 (524-530 MHz). Authorized power: 350-kw visual, aural. Antenna: 1204-ft above av. terrain, 1007-ft. above ground, 1805-ft. above sea level.

Latitude	36°	15'	50"
Longitude	86°	47'	39"

Note: Latitude and longitude coordinates shown are based on the North American Datum of 1927 (NAD 27) as currently required by the Mass Media Bureau of the FCC.

Ownership: Lambert Broadcasting of Tennessee (Group Owner).

Began Operation: July 8, 2004. Began analog operations: November 29, 1995. Sale to Speer Communications Holdings I LP by WNAB LP (Ruth Payne Carman) approved by FCC September 23, 1996. Sale to present owner by Speer Communications approved by FCC July 14, 1998. On January 2, 2003, Sinclair Broadcast Group announced that it made an $18,000,000 nonrefundable deposit to buy station. Sale to WNAB Licensee LLC (Sinclair) pends. Ceased analog operations: February 17, 2009.

Represented (sales): Katz Media Group.

Personnel:

Steve Mann, Vice President & General Manager.

Pam Sullivan, Sales Director.

Greg Carr, General Sales Manager.

Ken Smith, News Director.

David Birdsong, Chief Engineer.

Mark Dillon, Station & Regional Business Manager.

Lee Scott, Program & Promotion Director.

Vikki Morris, Traffic Manager.

City of License: Nashville. **Station DMA:** Nashville, TN. **Rank:** 29.

WNAB-DT BMPCDT-20040224ABH GRANTED: 3/12/2004

© 2010 Warren Communications News

Circulation © 2009 Nielsen. Coverage based on Nielsen study.

GrandTotal	Cable TV Households	Non-cable TV Households	Total TV Households
Estimated Station Totals *	534,820	366,570	901,390
Average Weekly Circulation (2009)	101,209	75,607	176,816
Average Daily Circulation (2009)			58,708

Station DMA Total	Cable TV Households	Non-cable TV Households	Total TV Households
Estimated Station Totals *	532,840	366,570	899,410
Average Weekly Circulation (2009)	100,320	75,607	175,927
Average Daily Circulation (2009)			58,653

Other DMA Total	Cable TV Households	Non-cable TV Households	Total TV Households
Estimated Station Totals *	1,980	0	1,980
Average Weekly Circulation (2009)	889	0	889
Average Daily Circulation (2009)			55

*Estimated station totals are sums of the Nielsen TV and Cable TV household estimates for each county in which the station registers viewing of more than 5% as per the Nielsen Survey Methods.

WSMV-DT
Ch. 10

Network Service: TMO, NBC.

Licensee: Meredith Corp., 1716 Locust St, Des Moines, IA 50309-3203.

Studio: 5700 Knob Rd., Nashville, TN 37209.

Mailing Address: 5700 Knob Rd, Nashville, TN 37209.

Phone: 615-353-4444; 615-353-2232. **Fax:** 615-353-2375.

E-mail: dsexton@wsmv.com

Web Site: http://www.wsmv.com

Technical Facilities: Channel No. 10 (192-198 MHz). Authorized power: 42.4-kw visual, aural. Antenna: 1360-ft above av. terrain, 1260-ft. above ground, 675-ft. above sea level.

Latitude	36°	08'	27"
Longitude	86°	51'	56"

Holds CP for change to 60-kw visual, 1355-ft above av. terrain, 1260-ft. above ground, 1935-ft. above sea level; BPCDT-20080619AFW.

Note: Latitude and longitude coordinates shown are based on the North American Datum of 1927 (NAD 27) as currently required by the Mass Media Bureau of the FCC.

Ownership: Meredith Corp. (Group Owner).

Began Operation: October 29, 2002. Began analog operations: September 30, 1950. Sale to present owner by Cook Inlet Communications approved by FCC November 1, 1994 (Television Digest, Vol. 34:34; 35:2). Sale to Cook Inlet Communications by Gillett Broadcasting approved April 17, 1989. Sale to Gillett Broadcasting by NLT Corp. approved by FCC September 14, 1981 (Vol. 21:20). Ceased analog operations: June 12, 2009.

Represented (legal): Dow Lohnes PLLC.

Represented (sales): TeleRep Inc.

Personnel:

Elden A. Hale, Vice President & General Manager.

Vernon Johnson, Operations Manager.

Paul Scott, General Sales Manager.

Pam Vasilevskis, Local Sales Manager.

Brian Mayfield, National Sales Manager.

Brian O'Neal, Chief Engineer.

Teresa McDaniel, Business Manager.

Donna Sexton, Program Coordinator.

Tim Hall, Broadcasting Operations Director.

Mark Ford, Production Supervisor.

Stacy Short, Traffic Manager.

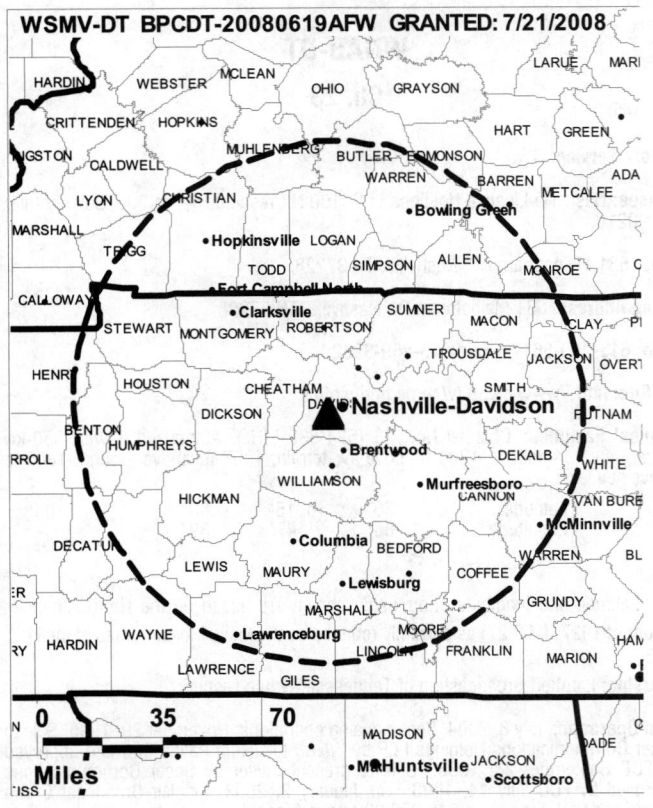

© 2010 Warren Communications News

City of License: Nashville. **Station DMA:** Nashville, TN. **Rank:** 29.

Circulation © 2009 Nielsen. Coverage based on Nielsen study.

GrandTotal	Cable TV Households	Non-cable TV Households	Total TV Households
Estimated Station Totals *	636,400	398,330	1,034,730
Average Weekly Circulation (2009)	377,851	254,037	631,888
Average Daily Circulation (2009)			312,027

Station DMA Total	Cable TV Households	Non-cable TV Households	Total TV Households
Estimated Station Totals *	537,130	369,420	906,550
Average Weekly Circulation (2009)	357,503	251,656	609,159
Average Daily Circulation (2009)			307,233

Other DMA Total	Cable TV Households	Non-cable TV Households	Total TV Households
Estimated Station Totals *	99,270	28,910	128,180
Average Weekly Circulation (2009)	20,348	2,381	22,729
Average Daily Circulation (2009)			4,794

*Estimated station totals are sums of the Nielsen TV and Cable TV household estimates for each county in which the station registers viewing of more than 5% as per the Nielsen Survey Methods.

WTVF-DT
Ch. 5

Network Service: CBS.

Licensee: NewsChannel 5 Network LLC, 474 James Robertson Pkwy, Nashville, TN 37219.

Studio: 474 James Robertson Pkwy, Nashville, TN 37219.

Mailing Address: 474 James Robertson Pkwy, Nashville, TN 37219.

Phone: 615-244-5000. **Fax:** 615-244-9883.

Web Site: http://www.newschannel5.com

Technical Facilities: Channel No. 5 (76-82 MHz). Authorized power: 22-kw visual, aural. Antenna: 1394-ft above av. terrain, 1142-ft. above ground, 2011-ft. above sea level.

Latitude	36°	16'	05"
Longitude	86°	47'	16"

Note: Latitude and longitude coordinates shown are based on the North American Datum of 1927 (NAD 27) as currently required by the Mass Media Bureau of the FCC.

Ownership: Landmark Media Enterprises LLC (Group Owner).

Began Operation: November 15, 2001. High Definition. Station broadcasting digitally on its analog channel allotment. Began analog operations: August 6, 1954. Working control of Life & Casualty Insurance Co. was acquired in 1958 by John D. & Clint W. Murchinson Jr., but FCC didn't approve this transfer of control until July 29, 1959. American General Insurance Co. acquired 100% of the stock of Life & Casualty Insurance Co. on January 1, 1969. Sale to H & C Communications by American General Insurance Co. approved by FCC October 15, 1975. Sale to present owner by H & C Communications approved by FCC September 12, 1991. Transfer of control by NewsChannel 5 Network LLC from Landmark Television Inc. to Bonten Media Group Inc. approved by FCC September 11, 2008, but was never consummated. Ceased analog operations: June 12, 2009.

Represented (sales): Eagle Television Sales.

Represented (legal): Wiley Rein LLP.

Personnel:

Debbie Turner, General Manager.

Lyn Plantinga, Station Manager.

Natalie Ryman, General Sales Manager.

Doris Smith, Local Sales Manager.

Maureen Cleator, New Business Sales Manager.

Kiley Murphy, National Sales Manager.

Mike Cutler, News Director.

Roger Dowdy, Chief Engineer.

Julia Stone, News Business Manager.

Mark Binda, Program Director.

Richard Eller, Promotion Director.

Jeff Bell, Production Manager.

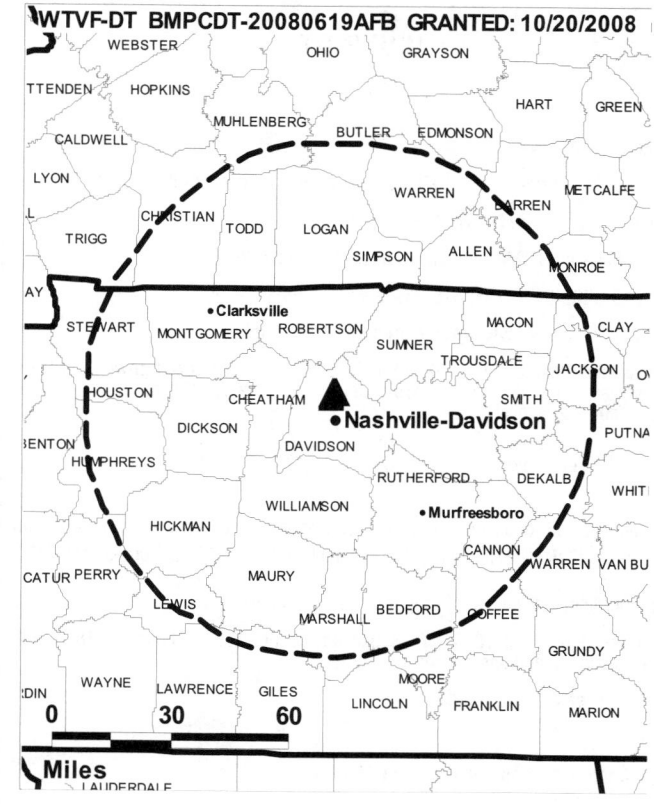

© 2010 Warren Communications News

Julie Hows, Traffic Manager.

City of License: Nashville. **Station DMA:** Nashville, TN. **Rank:** 29.

Circulation © 2009 Nielsen. Coverage based on Nielsen study.

GrandTotal	Cable TV Households	Non-cable TV Households	Total TV Households
Estimated Station Totals *	710,120	421,430	1,131,550
Average Weekly Circulation (2009)	412,343	277,575	689,918
Average Daily Circulation (2009)			358,933

Station DMA Total	Cable TV Households	Non-cable TV Households	Total TV Households
Estimated Station Totals *	537,130	369,420	906,550
Average Weekly Circulation (2009)	368,416	270,395	638,811
Average Daily Circulation (2009)			341,791

Other DMA Total	Cable TV Households	Non-cable TV Households	Total TV Households
Estimated Station Totals *	172,990	52,010	225,000
Average Weekly Circulation (2009)	43,927	7,180	51,107
Average Daily Circulation (2009)			17,142

*Estimated station totals are sums of the Nielsen TV and Cable TV household estimates for each county in which the station registers viewing of more than 5% as per the Nielsen Survey Methods.

WUXP-DT
Ch. 21

Network Service: MNT.

Grantee: WUXP Licensee LLC, 10706 Beaver Dam Rd, Cockeysville, MD 21030.

Studio: 631 Mainstream Dr., Nashville, TN 37228.

Mailing Address: 631 Mainstream Dr, Nashville, TN 37228.

Phone: 615-259-5617. **Fax:** 615-259-3962.

Web Site: http://www.mytv30web.com/home/home.html

Technical Facilities: Channel No. 21 (512-518 MHz). Authorized power: 1000-kw max. visual, aural. Antenna: 1355-ft above av. terrain, 1155-ft. above ground, 1953-ft. above sea level.

Latitude	36°	15'	50"
Longitude	86°	47'	39"

Note: Latitude and longitude coordinates shown are based on the North American Datum of 1927 (NAD 27) as currently required by the Mass Media Bureau of the FCC.

Ownership: Sinclair Broadcast Group Inc. (Group Owner).

Began Operation: April 10, 2006. Began analog operations: February 18, 1984. Ceased analog operations: February 17, 2009.

Represented (sales): Katz Media Group.

Personnel:

Steve Mann, Vice President & General Manager.

Pam Sullivan, Sales Director.

Greg Carr, General Sales Manager.

Dale Bukowski, Local Sales Manager.

David Birdsong, Chief Engineer.

Mark Dillon, Station & Regional Business Manager.

Lee Scott, Program & Promotion Director.

Vikki Morris, Traffic Manager.

City of License: Nashville. **Station DMA:** Nashville, TN. **Rank:** 29.

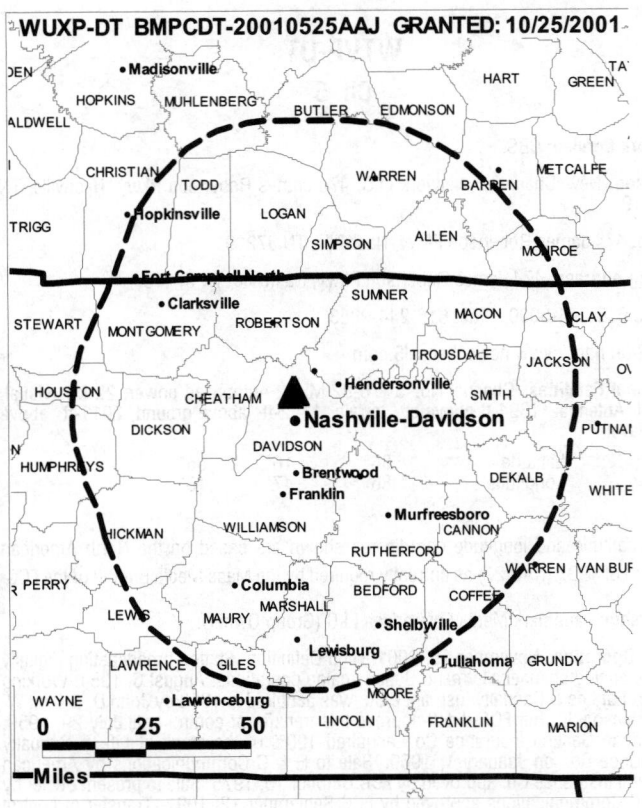

WUXP-DT BMPCDT-20010525AAJ GRANTED: 10/25/2001

© 2010 Warren Communications News

Circulation © 2009 Nielsen. Coverage based on Nielsen study.

GrandTotal	Cable TV Households	Non-cable TV Households	Total TV Households
Estimated Station Totals *	555,680	389,870	945,550
Average Weekly Circulation (2009)	136,033	104,743	240,776
Average Daily Circulation (2009)			88,917

Station DMA Total	Cable TV Households	Non-cable TV Households	Total TV Households
Estimated Station Totals *	528,400	369,420	897,820
Average Weekly Circulation (2009)	130,539	102,878	233,417
Average Daily Circulation (2009)			86,907

Other DMA Total	Cable TV Households	Non-cable TV Households	Total TV Households
Estimated Station Totals *	27,280	20,450	47,730
Average Weekly Circulation (2009)	5,494	1,865	7,359
Average Daily Circulation (2009)			2,010

*Estimated station totals are sums of the Nielsen TV and Cable TV household estimates for each county in which the station registers viewing of more than 5% as per the Nielsen Survey Methods.

WZTV-DT
Ch. 15

Network Service: FOX.

Licensee: WZTV Licensee LLC, 10706 Beaver Dam Rd, Cockeysville, MD 21030.

Studio: 631 Mainstream Dr., Nashville, TN 37228.

Mailing Address: 631 Mainstream Dr, Nashville, TN 37228.

Phone: 615-259-5617. **Fax:** 615-259-3962.

Web Site: http://www.fox17.com

Technical Facilities: Channel No. 15 (476-482 MHz). Authorized power: 1000-kw max. visual, aural. Antenna: 1348-ft above av. terrain, 1148-ft. above ground, 1946-ft. above sea level.

Latitude	36°	15'	50"
Longitude	86°	47'	39"

Note: Latitude and longitude coordinates shown are based on the North American Datum of 1927 (NAD 27) as currently required by the Mass Media Bureau of the FCC.

Ownership: Sinclair Broadcast Group Inc. (Group Owner).

Began Operation: March 9, 2005. Began analog operations: August 5, 1968 as WMCV, station left air March 14, 1971. Sale to Hudson Broadcasting approved by FCC August 1974. Sale to Robert K. Zelle et al., approved by FCC September 30, 1975. Resumed operation March 6, 1976. Sale to Multimedia Inc. by Robert K. Zelle, et al., approved by FCC December 14, 1979 Television Digest, Vol. 19:5; 20:10). Sale to Act III Broadcasting by Multimedia Inc. approved by FCC April 29, 1988 (Vol. 28:5, 12, 26). Sale to Sullivan Broadcasting Co. by Act III Broadcasting approved by FCC December 15, 1995. Transfer to present owner by Sullivan Broadcasting Co. approved by FCC December 10, 2001 (Vol. 41:38). Ceased analog operations: February 17, 2009.

Represented (sales): Katz Media Group.

Personnel:

Steve Mann, Vice President & General Manager.

Pam Sullivan, Sales Director.

Greg Carr, General Sales Manager.

Ken Smith, News Director.

David Birdsong, Chief Engineer.

Mark Dillon, Station & Regional Business Manager.

Lee Scott, Program & Promotion Director.

Vikki Morris, Traffic Manager.

City of License: Nashville. **Station DMA:** Nashville, TN. **Rank:** 29.

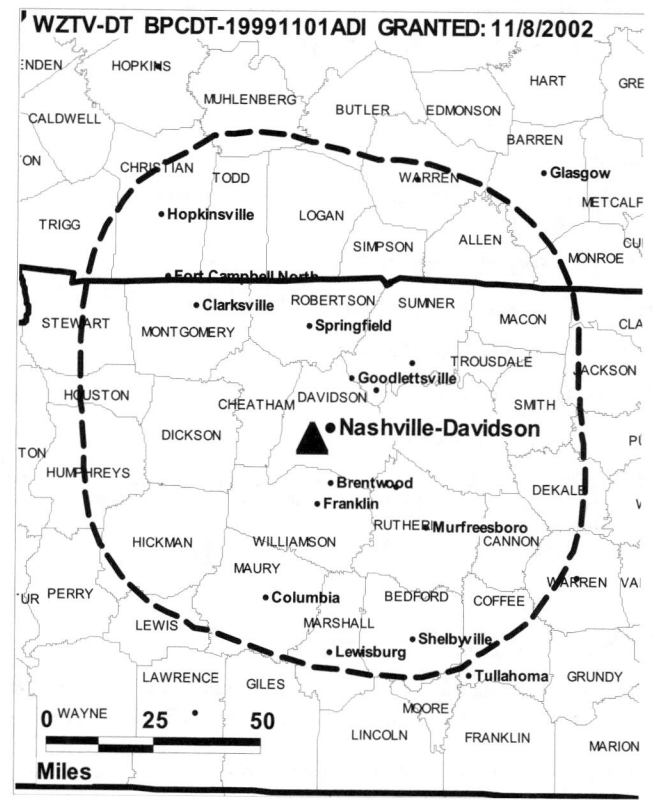

WZTV-DT BPCDT-19991101ADI GRANTED: 11/8/2002

© 2010 Warren Communications News

Circulation © 2009 Nielsen. Coverage based on Nielsen study.

GrandTotal	Cable TV Households	Non-cable TV Households	Total TV Households
Estimated Station Totals *	568,280	371,110	939,390
Average Weekly Circulation (2009)	284,775	200,046	484,821
Average Daily Circulation (2009)			170,451

Station DMA Total	Cable TV Households	Non-cable TV Households	Total TV Households
Estimated Station Totals *	537,130	369,420	906,550
Average Weekly Circulation (2009)	280,335	199,899	480,234
Average Daily Circulation (2009)			169,546

Other DMA Total	Cable TV Households	Non-cable TV Households	Total TV Households
Estimated Station Totals *	31,150	1,690	32,840
Average Weekly Circulation (2009)	4,440	147	4,587
Average Daily Circulation (2009)			905

*Estimated station totals are sums of the Nielsen TV and Cable TV household estimates for each county in which the station registers viewing of more than 5% as per the Nielsen Survey Methods.

WVLR-DT
Ch. 48

Network Service: IND.

Grantee: Volunteer Christian Television Inc., PO Box 6922, 6922 142nd Ave. N, Clearwater, FL 33758.

Studio: 306 Kyker Ferry Rd., Kodak, TN 37764.

Mailing Address: 306 Kyker Ferry Rd, Kodak, TN 37764.

Phone: 865-932-4803. **Fax:** 865-932-4102.

E-mail: jjarvis@ctonline.com

Web Site: http://www.wvlrtv48.com

Technical Facilities: Channel No. 48 (674-680 MHz). Authorized power: 1000-kw max. visual, aural. Antenna: 1411-ft above av. terrain, 280-ft. above ground, 2720-ft. above sea level.

Latitude	36°	15'	30"
Longitude	83°	37'	43"

Transmitter: 950 Blackburn Lane, New Tazewell.

Note: Latitude and longitude coordinates shown are based on the North American Datum of 1927 (NAD 27) as currently required by the Mass Media Bureau of the FCC.

Ownership: Christian Television Network Inc. (Group Owner).

Began Operation: October 1, 2002. Station broadcasting digitally on its analog channel allotment. Sale to present owner by Tazewell Broadcasting LLC approved by FCC January 9, 2002. Ceased analog operations: December 11, 2008.

Represented (legal): Hardy, Carey, Chautin & Balkin LLP.

Personnel:

Bob D'Andrea, President.

Theron P. Woodward, General Manager.

Tom Evensen, Chief Engineer.

Scott Dunkel, Traffic Manager.

Maria Woodward, Assistant Manager & Program Director.

City of License: Tazewell. **Station DMA:** Knoxville, TN. **Rank:** 59.

WVLR-DT BMPCDT-20080925AEP GRANTED: 12/11/2008

© 2010 Warren Communications News

Circulation © 2009 Nielsen. Coverage based on Nielsen study.

GrandTotal	Cable TV Households	Non-cable TV Households	Total TV Households
Estimated Station Totals *	22,520	0	22,520
Average Weekly Circulation (2009)	1,386	0	1,386
Average Daily Circulation (2009)			245

Station DMA Total	Cable TV Households	Non-cable TV Households	Total TV Households
Estimated Station Totals *	22,520	0	22,520
Average Weekly Circulation (2009)	1,386	0	1,386
Average Daily Circulation (2009)			245

*Estimated station totals are sums of the Nielsen TV and Cable TV household estimates for each county in which the station registers viewing of more than 5% as per the Nielsen Survey Methods.

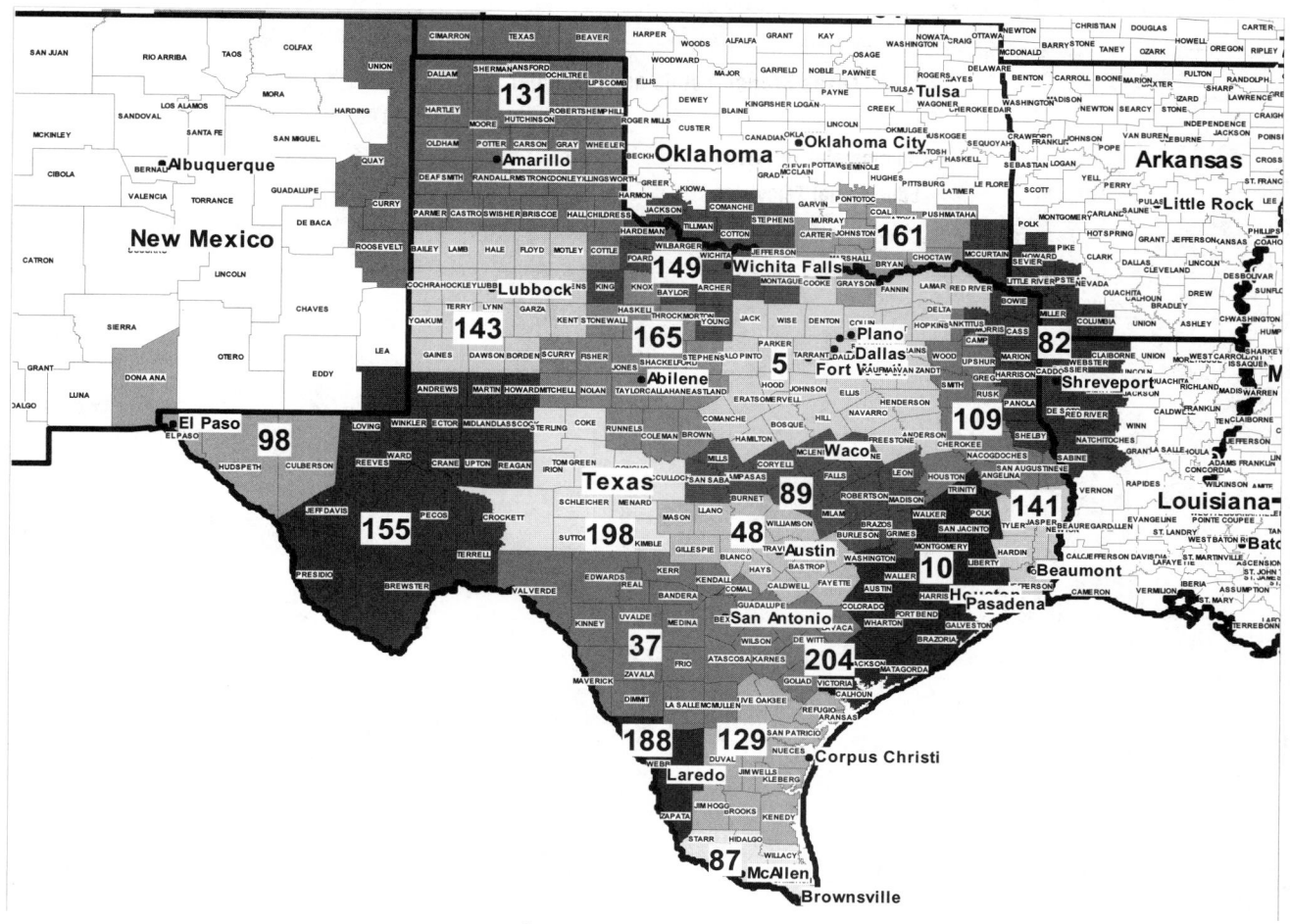

© 2010 Warren Communications News

MARKET	NIELSEN DMA TV HOUSEHOLDS	RANK	MARKET AREA COMMERCIAL STATIONS
Dallas-Fort Worth, TX	2,544,410	5	KDAF-DT (32); KDFI-DT (36); KDFW-DT (35); KDTX-DT (45); KFWD-DT (51); KLDT-DT (54); KMPX-DT (30); KPXD-TV (42); KSTR-DT (48); KTAQ-DT (46); KTVT-DT (11); KTXA-DT (18); KUVN-DT (23); KXAS-DT (41); KXTX-DT (40); WFAA (8)
Houston, TX	2,123,460	10	KAZH-DT (41); KFTH-DT (36); KHOU (11); KIAH-DT (38); KNWS-DT (47); KPRC-DT (35); KPXB-TV (5); KRIV-DT (26); KTBU-DT (42); KTMD-DT (48); KTRK-DT (13); KTXH-DT (19); KXLN-DT (45); KZJL-DT (44)
San Antonio, TX	830,000	37	KABB-DT (30); KENS (55); KMYS-DT (32); KPXL-TV (26); KSAT-DT (12); KTRG-DT (28); KVAW-DT (18); KVDA-DT (38); KWEX-DT (41); WOAI-DT (58)
Austin, TX	678,730	48	KAKW-DT (13); KBVO (27); KCWX-DT (5); KEYE-DT (43); KNIC-DT (18); KNVA-DT (49); KTBC-DT (7); KVUE-DT (33); KXAN-DT (21)
Shreveport, LA	386,180	82	KMSS-DT (34); KPXJ-DT (21); KSHV-DT (44); KSLA-DT (17); KTAL-DT (15); KTBS-DT (28)
Harlingen-Weslaco-Brownsville-McAllen, TX	354,150	87	KGBT-DT (31); KNVO-DT (49); KRGV-DT (13); KTLM-DT (40); KVEO-DT (24)
Waco-Temple-Bryan, TX	339,570	89	KBTX-DT (50); KCEN-DT (9); KWKT-DT (44); KWTX-DT (10); KXXV-DT (26); KYLE-DT (28)
El Paso, TX-Las Cruces, NM	310,760	98	KDBC-DT (18); KFOX-DT (15); KINT-DT (25); KTDO-DT (47); KTFN-DT (51); KTSM-DT (9); KVIA-DT (7)
Tyler-Longview (Lufkin & Nacogdoches), TX	267,890	109	KCEB-DT (51); KETK-DT (22); KFXK-DT (31); KLTV-DT (7); KTRE-DT (9); KYTX-DT (18)
Corpus Christi, TX	199,560	129	KIII-DT (8); KORO-DT (27); KRIS-DT (13); KUQI-DT (38); KZTV-DT (10)
Amarillo, TX	192,490	131	KAMR-DT (19); KCIT-DT (15); KEYU-DT (31); KFDA-DT (10); KPTF-DT (18); KVIH-DT (12); KVII-DT (7)
Beaumont-Port Arthur, TX	167,330	141	KBMT-DT (12); KBTV-DT (40); KFDM-DT (21)
Lubbock, TX	158,360	143	KAMC-DT (27); KCBD-DT (11); KJTV-DT (35); KLBK-DT (40); KLCW-DT (43); KPTB-DT (16)
Wichita Falls, TX & Lawton, OK	154,450	149	KAUZ-DT (22); KFDX-DT (28); KJTL-DT (15); KSWO-DT (11)
Odessa-Midland, TX	143,710	155	KMID-DT (26); KMLM-DT (42); KOSA-DT (7); KPEJ-DT (23); KUPB-DT (18); KUPT-DT (29); KWAB-DT (33); KWES-DT (9); KWWT-DT (30)
Sherman, TX-Ada, OK	127,990	161	KTEN-DT (26); KXII-DT (12)
Abilene-Sweetwater, TX	116,190	165	KPCB-DT (17); KRBC-DT (29); KTAB-DT (24); KTXS-DT (20); KXVA-DT (15)
Laredo, TX	69,790	188	KGNS-DT (8); KLDO-DT (19); KVTV-DT (13)
San Angelo, TX	54,580	198	KIDY-DT (19); KLST-DT (11); KSAN-DT (16)
Victoria, TX	31,560	204	KAVU-DT (15); KVCT-DT (11)

(Continued on next page)

Texas Station Totals as of October 1, 2009

	VHF	UHF	TOTAL
Commercial Television	30	88	118
Educational Television	5	15	20
	35	103	138

KRBC-DT
Ch. 29

Network Service: NBC.

Licensee: Mission Broadcasting Inc., 544 Red Rock Dr, Wadsworth, OH 44281.

Studio: 4510 S 14th St, Abilene, TX 79605.

Mailing Address: 4510 S 14th St, Abilene, TX 79605.

Phone: 325-692-4242. **Fax:** 325-692-8265.

Web Site: http://www.bigcountryhomepage.com

Technical Facilities: Channel No. 29 (560-566 MHz). Authorized power: 1000-kw max. visual, aural. Antenna: 846-ft above av. terrain, 620-ft. above ground, 2828-ft. above sea level.

Latitude	32°	16'	38"
Longitude	99°	35'	51"

Note: Latitude and longitude coordinates shown are based on the North American Datum of 1927 (NAD 27) as currently required by the Mass Media Bureau of the FCC.

Ownership: Mission Broadcasting Inc. (Group Owner).

Began Operation: August 31, 2007. Began analog operations: August 24, 1953. Station ceased operations following the collapse of its tower during an ice storm. FCC granted station Special Temporary Authority to remain silent until modification of permit was granted for station to construct full-power digital facilities. Station then applied for and was granted a license to resume operations. Sale by Abilene Reporter News to Abilene Radio & Television Co. approved by FCC September 16, 1953 (Television Digest, Vol. 9:35, 38). Sale to Sunrise Television Partners LP by Abilene Radio & Television Co. approved by FCC February 10, 1998. Transfer of control to Smith Broadcasting Partners LP approved by FCC July 12, 2000; equity interest retained by Sunrise Television Partners LP. Transfer to LIN TV Corp. by Smith Broadcasting Partners LP & Sunrise Television Partners LP approved by FCC April 17, 2002. Sale to present owner by LIN TV Corp. approved by FCC May 20, 2003. Ceased analog operations: June 12, 2009.

Represented (legal): Drinker Biddle.

Represented (sales): Petry Media Corp.

Personnel:

Eric Thomas, General Manager.

Caron Keesee, Station Manager.

Justin Riggan, Sales Director.

Maxine Little, Local Sales Manager.

Tom Vodak, News Director.

Glen McCandless, Chief Engineer.

Darlene Loza, Business Manager.

Karen Yarbrough, Creative Services & Production Director.

Marian Zett, Traffic & Program Manager.

City of License: Abilene. **Station DMA:** Abilene-Sweetwater, TX. **Rank:** 165.

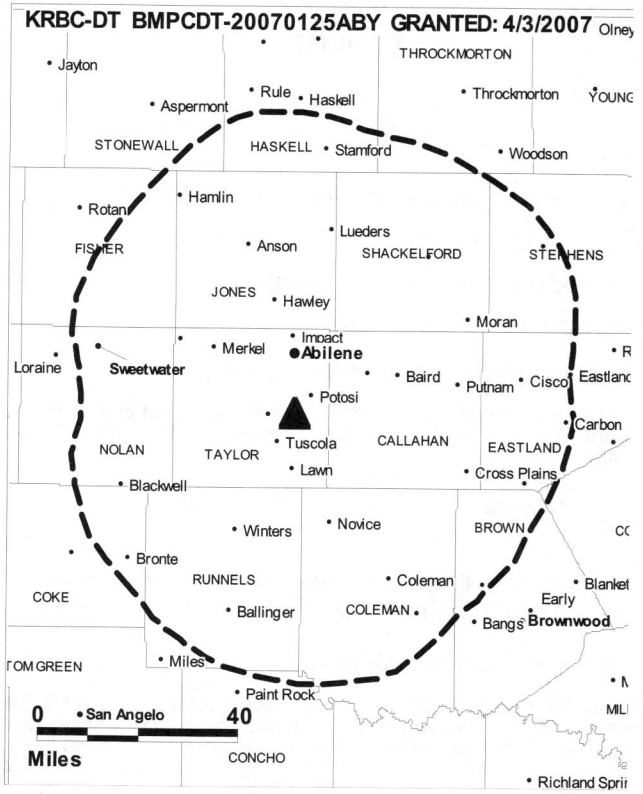

© 2010 Warren Communications News

Circulation © 2009 Nielsen. Coverage based on Nielsen study.

GrandTotal	Cable TV Households	Non-cable TV Households	Total TV Households
Estimated Station Totals *	47,380	67,300	114,680
Average Weekly Circulation (2009)	26,005	33,633	59,638
Average Daily Circulation (2009)			26,227

Station DMA Total	Cable TV Households	Non-cable TV Households	Total TV Households
Estimated Station Totals *	47,210	65,340	112,550
Average Weekly Circulation (2009)	25,835	33,510	59,345
Average Daily Circulation (2009)			26,185

Other DMA Total	Cable TV Households	Non-cable TV Households	Total TV Households
Estimated Station Totals *	170	1,960	2,130
Average Weekly Circulation (2009)	170	123	293
Average Daily Circulation (2009)			42

*Estimated station totals are sums of the Nielsen TV and Cable TV household estimates for each county in which the station registers viewing of more than 5% as per the Nielsen Survey Methods.

KTAB-DT
Ch. 24

Network Service: CBS.

Licensee: Nexstar Finance Inc., 909 Lake Carolyn Pkwy, Ste 1450, Irving, TX 75039.

Studio: 4510 S 14th St, Abilene, TX 79605.

Mailing Address: 4510 S 14th St, Abilene, TX 79605.

Phone: 325-692-4242. **Fax:** 325-691-5822.

Web Site: http://www.bigcountryhomepage.com

Technical Facilities: Channel No. 24 (530-536 MHz). Authorized power: 1000-kw max. visual, aural. Antenna: 846-ft above av. terrain, 620-ft. above ground, 2828-ft. above sea level.

Latitude	32°	16'	38"
Longitude	99°	35'	51"

Note: Latitude and longitude coordinates shown are based on the North American Datum of 1927 (NAD 27) as currently required by the Mass Media Bureau of the FCC.

Ownership: Nexstar Broadcasting Group Inc. (Group Owner).

Began Operation: August 31, 2007. Began analog operations: October 6, 1979. Sale to present owner from Shooting Star Broadcasting approved by FCC July 7, 1999. Sale to Shooting Star Broadcasting from Shamrock Holdings Inc. approved by FCC November 14, 1996. Sale to Shamrock Holdings Inc. by Television Investors Ltd. Partnership approved by FCC November 25, 1986 (Television Digest, Vol. 26:42). Sale to Television Investors Ltd. Partnership by Big Country TV of Abilene Inc. approved by FCC December 31, 1984. Sale to Big Country by William Terry, et al., approved by FCC May 25, 1984. Ceased analog operations: June 12, 2009.

Represented (legal): Drinker Biddle.

Represented (sales): Katz Media Group.

Personnel:

Eric Thomas, Vice President & General Manager.

Saundra Carriker, Local Sales Manager.

David Bacon, News Director.

Glen McCandless, Chief Engineer.

Darlene Loza, Business Manager.

Marian Zett, Traffic & Program Manager.

Tom Vodak, New Media Manager.

City of License: Abilene. **Station DMA:** Abilene-Sweetwater, TX. **Rank:** 165.

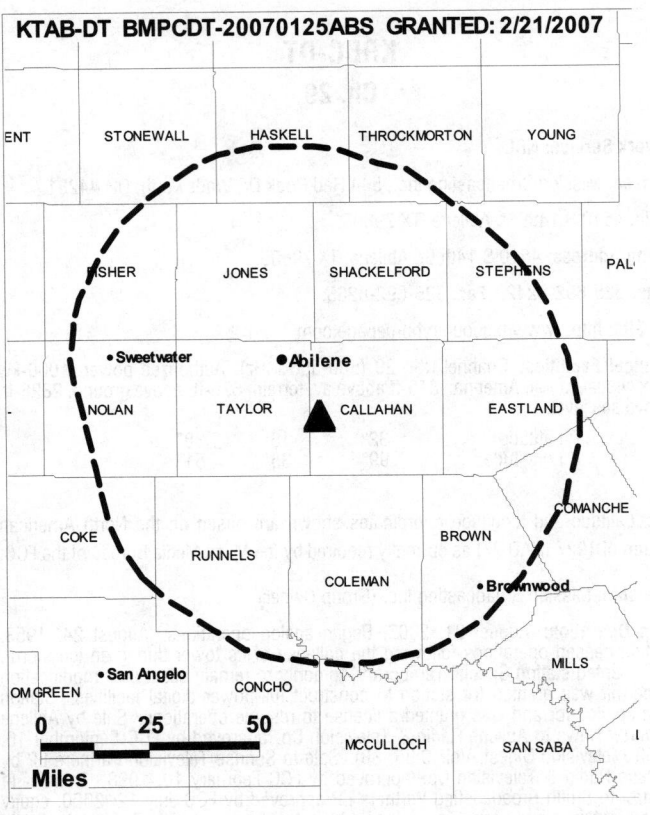

KTAB-DT BMPCDT-20070125ABS GRANTED: 2/21/2007

© 2010 Warren Communications News

Circulation © 2009 Nielsen. Coverage based on Nielsen study.

GrandTotal	Cable TV Households	Non-cable TV Households	Total TV Households
Estimated Station Totals *	47,210	66,510	113,720
Average Weekly Circulation (2009)	30,921	41,174	72,095
Average Daily Circulation (2009)			41,709

Station DMA Total	Cable TV Households	Non-cable TV Households	Total TV Households
Estimated Station Totals *	47,210	65,340	112,550
Average Weekly Circulation (2009)	30,921	41,034	71,955
Average Daily Circulation (2009)			41,675

Other DMA Total	Cable TV Households	Non-cable TV Households	Total TV Households
Estimated Station Totals *	0	1,170	1,170
Average Weekly Circulation (2009)	0	140	140
Average Daily Circulation (2009)			34

*Estimated station totals are sums of the Nielsen TV and Cable TV household estimates for each county in which the station registers viewing of more than 5% as per the Nielsen Survey Methods.

KXVA-DT
Ch. 15

Network Service: FOX.

Licensee: Bayou City Broadcasting LLC, 1300 Post Oak Blvd, Ste 830, Houston, TX 77056.

Studio: 500 Chesnut St, Ste 804, Abilene, TX 79602.

Mailing Address: 500 Chesnut St, Ste 804, Abilene, TX 79602.

Phone: 325-672-5606. **Fax:** 325-676-2437.

Web Site: http://www.myfoxabilene.com

Technical Facilities: Channel No. 15 (476-482 MHz). Authorized power: 165-kw max. visual, aural. Antenna: 978-ft above av. terrain, 770-ft. above ground, 2952-ft. above sea level.

Latitude	32°	16'	31"
Longitude	99°	35'	23"

Note: Latitude and longitude coordinates shown are based on the North American Datum of 1927 (NAD 27) as currently required by the Mass Media Bureau of the FCC.

Ownership: Bayou City Broadcasting LLC (Group Owner).

Began Operation: February 16, 2009. Station broadcasting digitally on its analog channel allotment. Began analog operations: January 30, 2001. Ceased analog operations: February 16, 2009. Sale to present owner by Sage Broadcasting Corp. approved by FCC May 29, 2008. Sale to Sage Broadcasting Corp. by Star Broadcasting Ltd. approved by FCC December 28, 2004.

Represented (legal): Fletcher, Heald & Hildreth PLC.

Represented (sales): Katz Media Group.

Personnel:

Bill Carter, General Manager.

Billie Garver, Account Executive & Officer Manager.

James Tilley, Chief Engineer.

Mike Anderson, Creative Services Director.

City of License: Abilene. **Station DMA:** Abilene-Sweetwater, TX. **Rank:** 165.

TELEVISION & CABLE
Factbook Online

| continuous updates | fully searchable | easy to use |

For more information call **800-771-9202** or visit **www.warren-news.com**

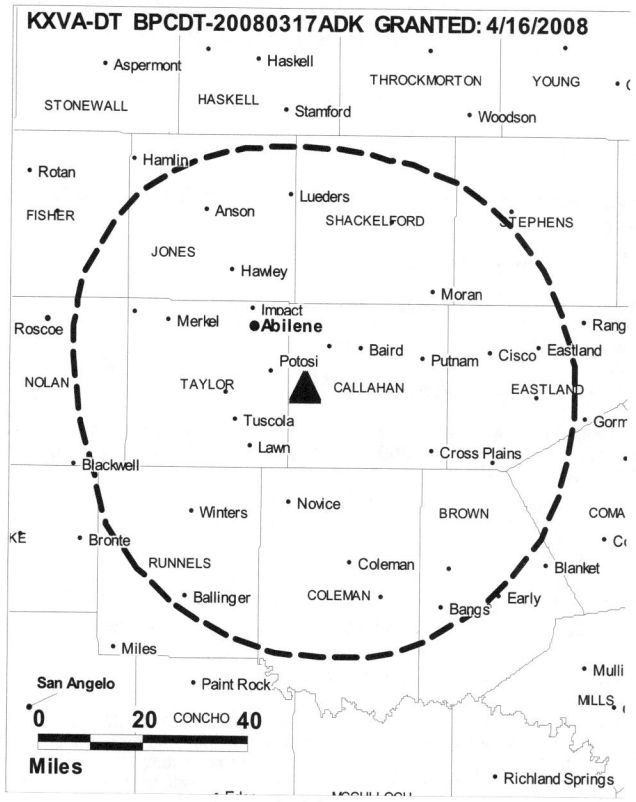

KXVA-DT BPCDT-20080317ADK GRANTED: 4/16/2008

© 2010 Warren Communications News

Circulation © 2009 Nielsen. Coverage based on Nielsen study.

GrandTotal	Cable TV Households	Non-cable TV Households	Total TV Households
Estimated Station Totals *	46,430	66,510	112,940
Average Weekly Circulation (2009)	17,724	25,729	43,453
Average Daily Circulation (2009)			15,196

Station DMA Total	Cable TV Households	Non-cable TV Households	Total TV Households
Estimated Station Totals *	46,430	65,340	111,770
Average Weekly Circulation (2009)	17,724	25,655	43,379
Average Daily Circulation (2009)			15,183

Other DMA Total	Cable TV Households	Non-cable TV Households	Total TV Households
Estimated Station Totals *	0	1,170	1,170
Average Weekly Circulation (2009)	0	74	74
Average Daily Circulation (2009)			13

*Estimated station totals are sums of the Nielsen TV and Cable TV household estimates for each county in which the station registers viewing of more than 5% as per the Nielsen Survey Methods.

KFTH-DT
Ch. 36

Network Service: TEL.

Licensee: Telefutura Houston LLC, 1999 Avenue of the Stars, Ste 3050, Los Angeles, CA 90067.

Studio: 5100 Southwest Frwy, Houston, TX 77056.

Mailing Address: 5100 SW Freeway, Houston, TX 77056.

Phone: 713-662-4545. **Fax:** 713-965-2401.

Web Site: http://www.univision.net

Technical Facilities: Channel No. 36 (602-608 MHz). Authorized power: 1000-kw max. visual, aural. Antenna: 1900-ft above av. terrain, 1885-ft. above ground, 1962-ft. above sea level.

Latitude	29°	34'	15"
Longitude	95°	30'	37"

Note: Latitude and longitude coordinates shown are based on the North American Datum of 1927 (NAD 27) as currently required by the Mass Media Bureau of the FCC.

Ownership: Univision Communications Inc. (Group Owner).

Began Operation: October 1, 2002. Began analog operations: January 27, 1986. Transfer of control to Broadcasting Media Partners Inc. approved by FCC March 27, 2007. Transfer of control to present owner by USA Broadcasting approved by FCC May 21, 2001. Sale to USA Broadcasting by Four Star Broadcasting Inc. approved by FCC October 30, 1986. Ceased analog operations: June 12, 2009.

Represented (legal): Covington & Burling.

Personnel:

Craig Bland, General Manager.

Jose Oti, General Sales Manager.

Melissa McMillon, Local Sales Manager.

Tom Daniels, Chief Engineer.

Mike Mancour, Business Manager.

Sandui Salazar, Program Director & Traffic Manager.

City of License: Alvin. **Station DMA:** Houston, TX. **Rank:** 10.

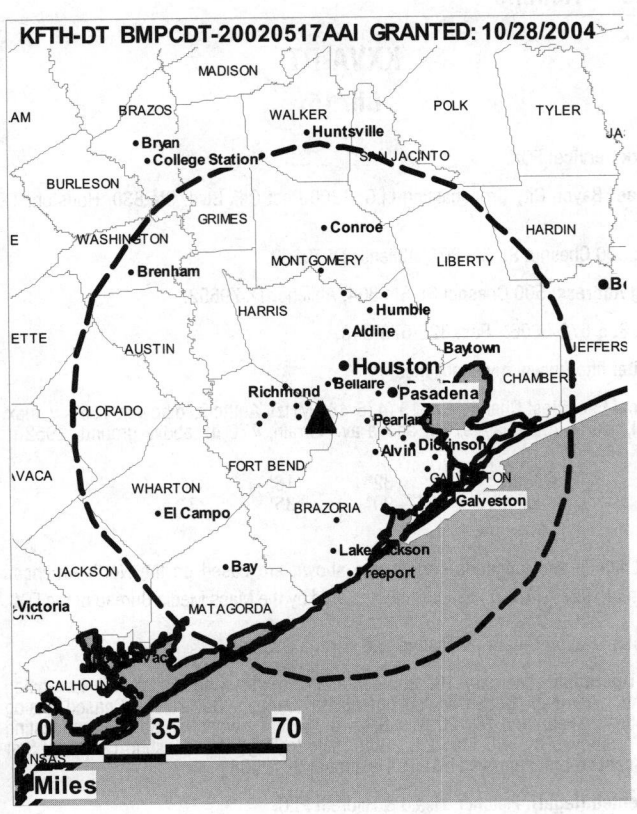

© 2010 Warren Communications News

Circulation © 2009 Nielsen. Coverage based on Nielsen study.

GrandTotal	Cable TV Households	Non-cable TV Households	Total TV Households
Estimated Station Totals *	905,700	802,760	1,708,460
Average Weekly Circulation (2009)	115,975	204,540	320,515
Average Daily Circulation (2009)			162,556

Station DMA Total	Cable TV Households	Non-cable TV Households	Total TV Households
Estimated Station Totals *	905,700	802,760	1,708,460
Average Weekly Circulation (2009)	115,975	204,540	320,515
Average Daily Circulation (2009)			162,556

*Estimated station totals are sums of the Nielsen TV and Cable TV household estimates for each county in which the station registers viewing of more than 5% as per the Nielsen Survey Methods.

KAMR-DT
Ch. 19

Network Service: NBC.

Grantee: Nexstar Finance Inc., 909 Lake Carolyn Pkwy, Ste 1450, Irving, TX 75039.

Studio: 1015 S. Fillmore, Amarillo, TX 79101.

Mailing Address: PO Box 751, Amarillo, TX 79189.

Phone: 806-383-3321. **Fax:** 806-349-9083.

Web Site: http://www.kamr.com

Technical Facilities: Channel No. 19 (500-506 MHz). Authorized power: 400-kw max. visual, aural. Antenna: 1493-ft above av. terrain, 1457-ft. above ground, 4888-ft. above sea level.

Latitude	35°	20'	33"
Longitude	101°	49'	21"

Note: Latitude and longitude coordinates shown are based on the North American Datum of 1927 (NAD 27) as currently required by the Mass Media Bureau of the FCC.

Ownership: Nexstar Broadcasting Group Inc. (Group Owner).

Began Operation: May 19, 2008. Began analog operations: March 18, 1953. Merger of Quorum Broadcast Holdings Inc. into present owner approved by FCC October 30, 2003. Sale to Quorum Broadcast Holdings Inc. by Cannan Communications Inc. approved by FCC February 23, 1999. Sale to Cannan Communications Inc. by Stauffer Publications approved by FCC July 1, 1974 (Television Digest, Vol. 13:43, 14:31). Sale to Stauffer by Globe News Publishing Co. approved by FCC January 12, 1966 (Vol. 5:42; 6:3). Ceased analog operations: June 12, 2009.

Represented (legal): Drinker Biddle.

Represented (sales): Katz Media Group.

Personnel:

Mark McKay, General Manager.

Tim Sturgess, General Sales Manager.

Mike Crowell, Promotion Director.

Dan Morgan, Production Manager.

Kristin Brain, Traffic Manager.

Nylynn Nichols, News Director.

Ken High, Chief Engineer.

James Elza, Business Manager.

City of License: Amarillo. **Station DMA:** Amarillo, TX. **Rank:** 131.

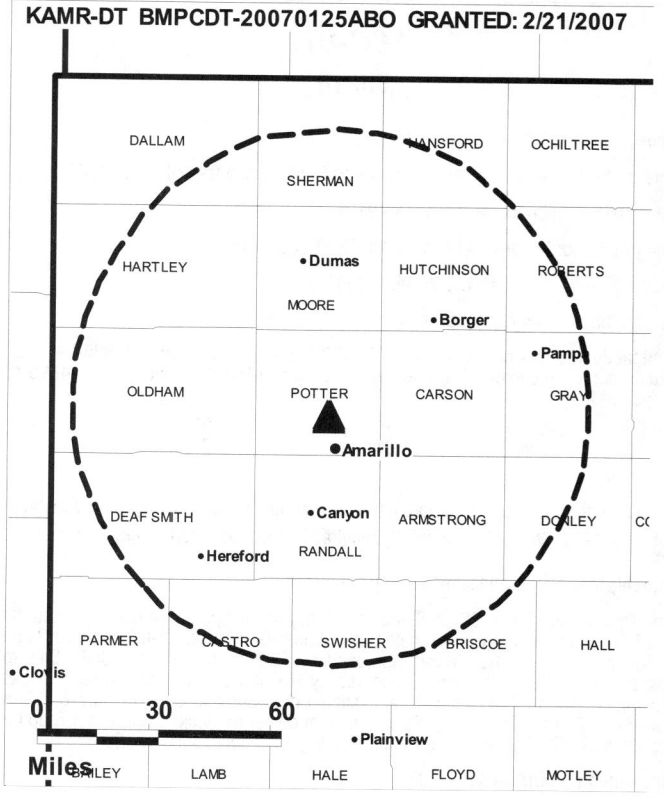

KAMR-DT BMPCDT-20070125ABO GRANTED: 2/21/2007

© 2010 Warren Communications News

Circulation © 2009 Nielsen. Coverage based on Nielsen study.

GrandTotal	Cable TV Households	Non-cable TV Households	Total TV Households
Estimated Station Totals *	73,610	88,710	162,320
Average Weekly Circulation (2009)	40,061	42,185	82,246
Average Daily Circulation (2009)			34,507

Station DMA Total	Cable TV Households	Non-cable TV Households	Total TV Households
Estimated Station Totals *	73,610	88,710	162,320
Average Weekly Circulation (2009)	40,061	42,185	82,246
Average Daily Circulation (2009)			34,507

*Estimated station totals are sums of the Nielsen TV and Cable TV household estimates for each county in which the station registers viewing of more than 5% as per the Nielsen Survey Methods.

KCIT-DT
Ch. 15

Network Service: FOX.

Grantee: Mission Broadcasting Inc., 544 Red Rock Dr, Wadsworth, OH 44281.

Studio: 1015 S. Fillmore, Amarillo, TX 79101.

Mailing Address: PO Box 1414, Amarillo, TX 79105-1414.

Phone: 806-383-3321. **Fax:** 806-349-9083.

Web Site: http://www.myhighplains.com

Technical Facilities: Channel No. 15 (476-482 MHz). Authorized power: 925-kw max. visual, aural. Antenna: 1522-ft above av. terrain, 1460-ft. above ground, 4895-ft. above sea level.

Latitude	35°	20'	33"
Longitude	101°	49'	21"

Note: Latitude and longitude coordinates shown are based on the North American Datum of 1927 (NAD 27) as currently required by the Mass Media Bureau of the FCC.

Ownership: Mission Broadcasting Inc. (Group Owner).

Began Operation: May 1, 2002. Station operating under Special Temporary Authority at 8.5-kw max. visual. Began analog operations: October 29, 1982. Sale to Ralph Wilson Industries by Ray Moran approved by FCC December 11, 1984. Sale to Epic by Ralph Wilson Industries approved by FCC March 11, 1991. Sale to Wicks Broadcast Group LP by Epic Broadcasting Co. approved by FCC July 6, 1995 (Television Digest, Vol. 35:18). Sale to present owner by Wicks Broadcast Group LP approved by FCC April 8, 1999. Ceased analog operations: June 12, 2009.

Represented (legal): Drinker Biddle.

Represented (sales): Katz Media Group.

Personnel:

Mark McKay, General Manager & Program Director.

Tim Sturgess, General Sales Manager.

Stuart Stallard, Local & Regional Sales Manager.

Nylynn Nichols, News Director.

Wesley Wilson, Chief Engineer.

James Elza, Business Manager.

Mike Crowell, Promotion Director.

Dan Morgan, Production Manager.

Kristen Brain, Traffic Manager.

City of License: Amarillo. **Station DMA:** Amarillo, TX. **Rank:** 131.

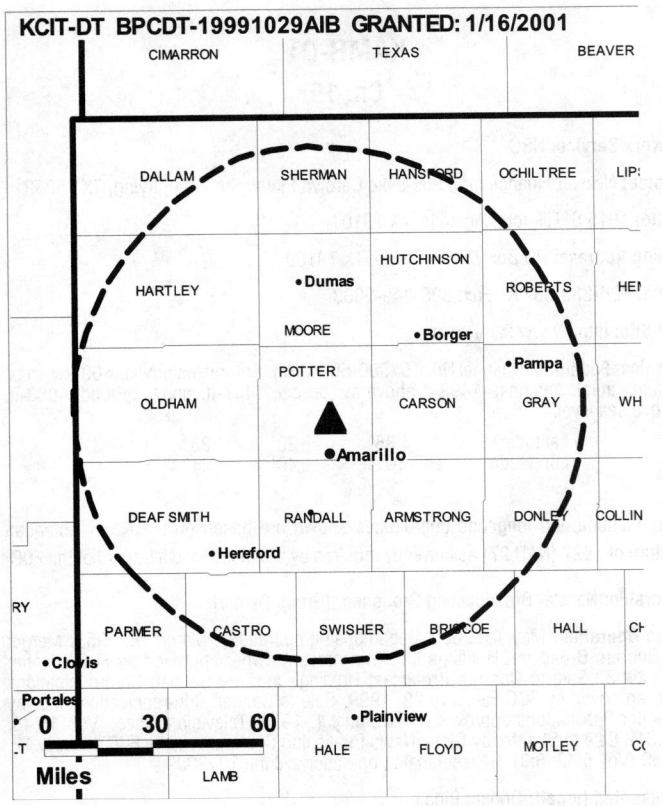

KCIT-DT BPCDT-19991029AIB GRANTED: 1/16/2001

© 2010 Warren Communications News

Circulation © 2009 Nielsen. Coverage based on Nielsen study.

GrandTotal	Cable TV Households	Non-cable TV Households	Total TV Households
Estimated Station Totals *	73,610	88,710	162,320
Average Weekly Circulation (2009)	34,724	40,223	74,947
Average Daily Circulation (2009)			27,115

Station DMA Total	Cable TV Households	Non-cable TV Households	Total TV Households
Estimated Station Totals *	73,610	88,710	162,320
Average Weekly Circulation (2009)	34,724	40,223	74,947
Average Daily Circulation (2009)			27,115

*Estimated station totals are sums of the Nielsen TV and Cable TV household estimates for each county in which the station registers viewing of more than 5% as per the Nielsen Survey Methods.

KFDA-DT
Ch. 10

Network Service: CBS.

Licensee: Panhandle Telecasting LP, PO Box 10, Amarillo, TX 79105-0010.

Studio: 7900 Broadway, Amarillo, TX 79108.

Mailing Address: PO Box 10, Amarillo, TX 79105-0010.

Phone: 806-383-1010. **Fax:** 806-383-7178.

E-mail: mikelee@newschannel10.com

Web Site: http://www.newschannel10.com

Technical Facilities: Channel No. 10 (192-198 MHz). Authorized power: 20.8-kw visual, aural. Antenna: 1529-ft above av. terrain, 1453-ft. above ground, 5003-ft. above sea level.

Latitude	35°	17'	34"
Longitude	101°	50'	42"

Note: Latitude and longitude coordinates shown are based on the North American Datum of 1927 (NAD 27) as currently required by the Mass Media Bureau of the FCC.

Ownership: Drewry Communications (Group Owner).

Began Operation: September 16, 2002. Standard and High Definition. Station broadcasting digitally on its analog channel allotment. Began analog operations: April 4, 1953. Sale of 61% by Sid W. Richardson Foundation to Bass Broadcasting and subsequent transfer of 19.6% by Gene L. Cagle was approved by FCC February 2, 1966. Sale to Midessa Cablevision by Bass Broadcasting approved by FCC August 20, 1976. Sale of 50% by Midessa Television Inc. to Lawton Cablevision Inc. approved by FCC February 27, 1984. Sale to KFDA License Co. LLC (London Broadcasting Co. Inc.) approved by FCC November 5, 2008, but never consummated. Ceased analog operations: June 12, 2009.

Represented (legal): Davis Wright Tremaine LLP.

Represented (sales): Petry Media Corp.

Personnel:

Brent McClure, Vice President & General Manager.

Joyce Austin, Local, National & Regional Sales Manager.

Shawn Verhaus, News Director.

Tim Winn, Chief Engineer.

Tony Smitherman, Promotion & Marketing Director.

Richard Fulkerson, Production Manager.

Tonya Padilla, Traffic & Business Manager.

City of License: Amarillo. **Station DMA:** Amarillo, TX. **Rank:** 131.

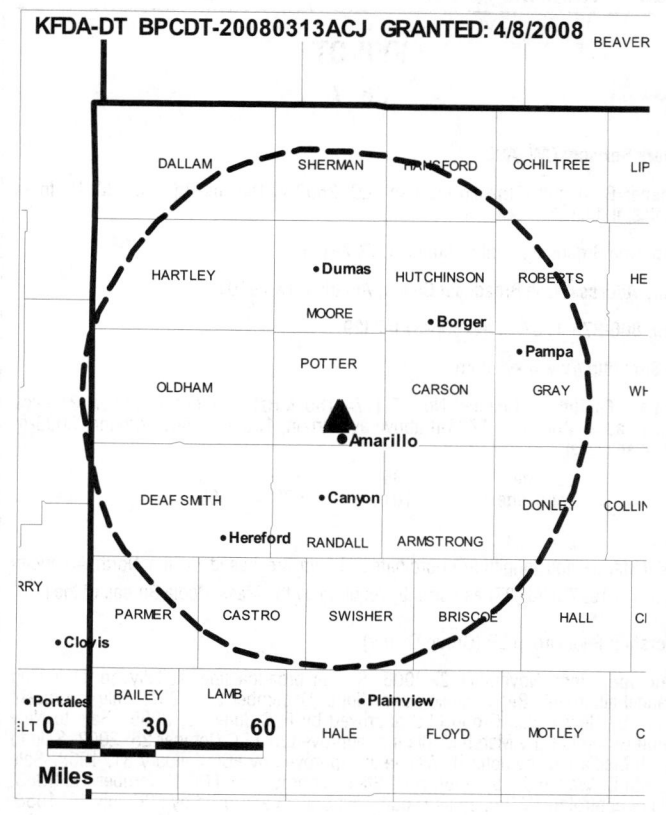

KFDA-DT BPCDT-20080313ACJ GRANTED: 4/8/2008

© 2010 Warren Communications News

Circulation © 2009 Nielsen. Coverage based on Nielsen study.

GrandTotal	Cable TV Households	Non-cable TV Households	Total TV Households
Estimated Station Totals *	76,160	88,710	164,870
Average Weekly Circulation (2009)	51,746	54,271	106,017
Average Daily Circulation (2009)			60,065

Station DMA Total	Cable TV Households	Non-cable TV Households	Total TV Households
Estimated Station Totals *	73,610	88,710	162,320
Average Weekly Circulation (2009)	50,889	54,271	105,160
Average Daily Circulation (2009)			59,986

Other DMA Total	Cable TV Households	Non-cable TV Households	Total TV Households
Estimated Station Totals *	2,550	0	2,550
Average Weekly Circulation (2009)	857	0	857
Average Daily Circulation (2009)			79

*Estimated station totals are sums of the Nielsen TV and Cable TV household estimates for each county in which the station registers viewing of more than 5% as per the Nielsen Survey Methods.

KVII-DT
Ch. 7

Network Service: CW, ABC.

Licensee: Barrington Amarillo License LLC, 2500 W Higgins Rd, Ste 880, Hoffman Estates, IL 60195.

Studio: One Broadcast Center, Amarillo, TX 79101.

Mailing Address: One Broadcast Center, Amarillo, TX 79101.

Phone: 806-373-1787. **Fax:** 806-371-7329.

Web Site: http://www.kvii.com

Technical Facilities: Channel No. 7 (174-180 MHz). Authorized power: 21.9-kw visual, aural. Antenna: 1703-ft above av. terrain, 1581-ft. above ground, 5003-ft. above sea level.

Latitude	35°	22'	30"
Longitude	101°	52'	56"

Note: Latitude and longitude coordinates shown are based on the North American Datum of 1927 (NAD 27) as currently required by the Mass Media Bureau of the FCC.

Ownership: Pilot Group LP (Group Owner).

Began Operation: November 2, 2006. Station broadcasting digitally on its analog channel allotment. Began analog operations: December 21, 1957. Sale to present owner by New Vision Group LLC approved by FCC June 15, 2005. Sale to New Vision Group LLC by Marsh Media Inc. approved by FCC October 25, 2002. Sale to Marsh Media Inc. by John B. Walton Jr. approved by FCC January 31, 1968. Sale to John B. Walton Jr. by Southwest States approved by FCC November 12, 1963. Sale of control to TV Properties (Southwest States) approved by FCC July 16, 1958. Ceased analog operations: June 12, 2009.

Represented (legal): Paul Hastings.

Represented (sales): Continental Television Sales.

Personnel:

Marc Gilmour, General Manager.

Jay Ricci, Operations Manager & News Director.

Chris Knight, Local Sales Manager.

Dean Wilson, Chief Engineer.

Bryan White, Production Manager.

Michelle Cook, Business Manager.

Carla Cooper, Program Director.

Ross White, Creative Services Director.

Margaret Burris, Traffic Manager.

City of License: Amarillo. **Station DMA:** Amarillo, TX. **Rank:** 131.

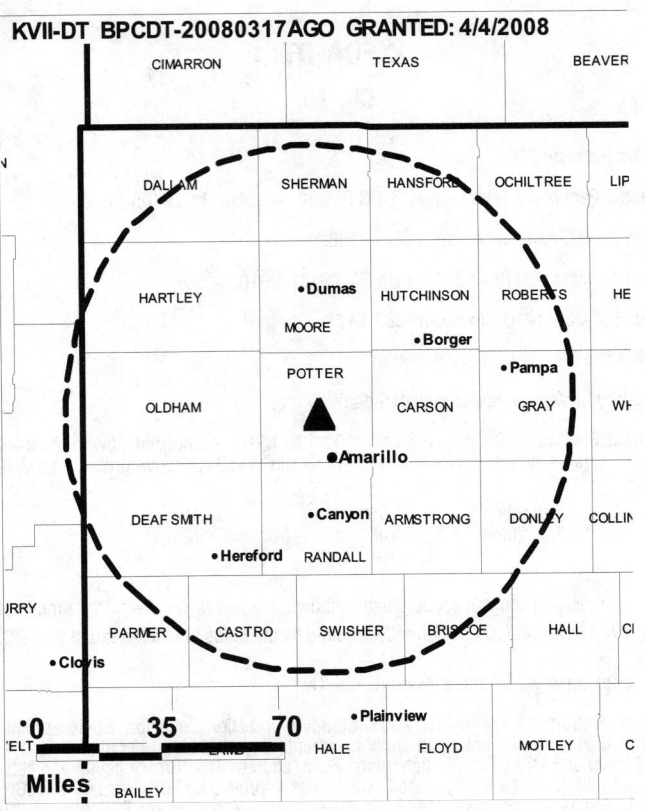

KVII-DT BPCDT-20080317AGO GRANTED: 4/4/2008

© 2010 Warren Communications News

Circulation © 2009 Nielsen. Coverage based on Nielsen study.

GrandTotal	Cable TV Households	Non-cable TV Households	Total TV Households
Estimated Station Totals *	79,860	88,710	168,570
Average Weekly Circulation (2009)	51,185	50,396	101,581
Average Daily Circulation (2009)			53,163

Station DMA Total	Cable TV Households	Non-cable TV Households	Total TV Households
Estimated Station Totals *	73,610	88,710	162,320
Average Weekly Circulation (2009)	50,566	50,396	100,962
Average Daily Circulation (2009)			53,032

Other DMA Total	Cable TV Households	Non-cable TV Households	Total TV Households
Estimated Station Totals *	6,250	0	6,250
Average Weekly Circulation (2009)	619	0	619
Average Daily Circulation (2009)			131

*Estimated station totals are sums of the Nielsen TV and Cable TV household estimates for each county in which the station registers viewing of more than 5% as per the Nielsen Survey Methods.

KPXD-TV
Ch. 42

Network Service: ION.

Licensee: ION Media Dallas License Inc., Debtor in Possession, 601 Clearwater Park Rd, West Palm Beach, FL 33401-6233.

Studio: 600 Six Flags Dr, Ste 652, Arlington, TX 76011.

Mailing Address: 600 Six Flags Dr, Ste 652, Fort Worth, TX 76011.

Phone: 817-633-6843. **Fax:** 817-633-3176.

E-mail: kirahatcher@ionmedia.com

Web Site: http://www.ionmedia.com

Technical Facilities: Channel No. 42 (638-644 MHz). Authorized power: 1000-kw max. visual, aural. Antenna: 1207-ft above av. terrain, 1000-ft. above ground, 1829-ft. above sea level.

Latitude	32°	35'	25"
Longitude	96°	58'	23"

Holds CP for change to 1624-ft above av. terrain, 1476-ft. above ground, 2290-ft. above sea level; lat. 32° 32'36", long. 96° 57'32", BPCDT-20080619AJA.

Note: Latitude and longitude coordinates shown are based on the North American Datum of 1927 (NAD 27) as currently required by the Mass Media Bureau of the FCC.

Ownership: ION Media Networks Inc., Debtor in Possession (Group Owner).

Began Operation: January 1, 2002. Standard and High Definition. Began analog operations: December 21, 1996. Sale to Urban Television LLC pends. Involuntary assignment to debtor in possession status approved by FCC June 5, 2009. Transfer of control by ION Media Networks Inc. from Paxson Management Corp. & Lowell W. Paxson to CIG Media LLC approved by FCC December 31, 2007. Paxson Communications Corp. became ION Media Networks Inc. on June 26, 2006. Transfer of control from United Broadcast Group Ltd. to Paxson Communications Corp. approved by FCC April 4, 1997. Ceased analog operations: June 12, 2009.

Represented (legal): Dow Lohnes PLLC.

Personnel:

Rick Fetter, Station Operations Manager.

David Carr, Chief Engineer.

Kira Hatcher, Traffic Manager.

City of License: Arlington. **Station DMA:** Dallas-Fort Worth, TX. **Rank:** 5.

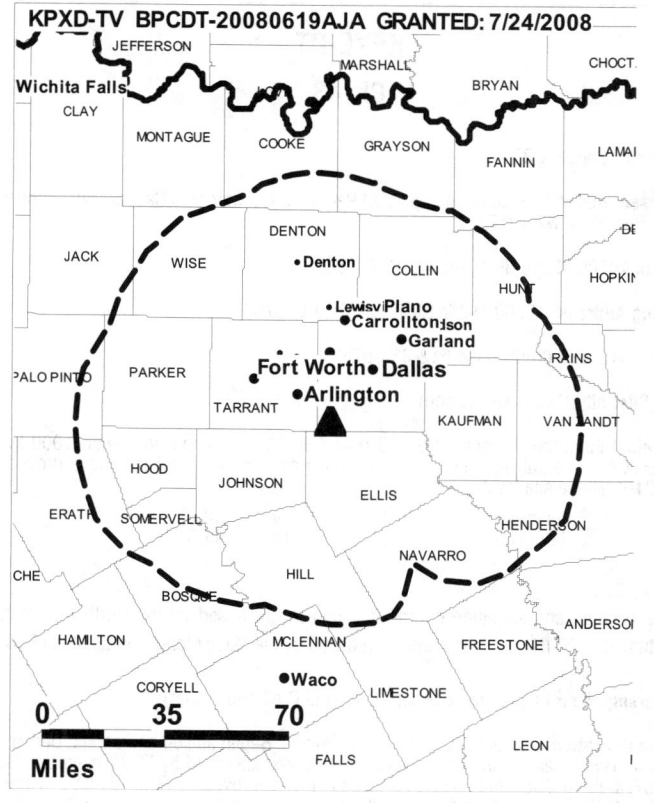

KPXD-TV BPCDT-20080619AJA GRANTED: 7/24/2008

© 2010 Warren Communications News

Circulation © 2009 Nielsen. Coverage based on Nielsen study.

GrandTotal	Cable TV Households	Non-cable TV Households	Total TV Households
Estimated Station Totals *	1,027,350	1,071,780	2,099,130
Average Weekly Circulation (2009)	91,284	164,196	255,480
Average Daily Circulation (2009)			60,683

Station DMA Total	Cable TV Households	Non-cable TV Households	Total TV Households
Estimated Station Totals *	1,027,350	1,071,780	2,099,130
Average Weekly Circulation (2009)	91,284	164,196	255,480
Average Daily Circulation (2009)			60,683

*Estimated station totals are sums of the Nielsen TV and Cable TV household estimates for each county in which the station registers viewing of more than 5% as per the Nielsen Survey Methods.

KEYE-DT
Ch. 43

Network Service: CBS.

Licensee: Austin TV Licensee Corp., 299 Park Ave, c/o Cerberus Capital Management LP, New York, NY 10171.

Studio: 10700 Metric Blvd., Austin, TX 78758.

Mailing Address: 10700 Metric Blvd., Austin, TX 78758.

Phone: 512-835-0042. **Fax:** 512-837-6753.

Web Site: http://www.keyetv.com

Technical Facilities: Channel No. 43 (644-650 MHz). Authorized power: 1000-kw max. visual, aural. Antenna: 1296-ft above av. terrain, 1184-ft. above ground, 2021-ft. above sea level.

Latitude	30°	19'	18.6"
Longitude	97°	48'	11.6"

Note: Latitude and longitude coordinates shown are based on the North American Datum of 1927 (NAD 27) as currently required by the Mass Media Bureau of the FCC.

Ownership: Four Points Media Group Holding LLC (Group Owner).

Began Operation: October 1, 2003. High Definition. Began analog operations: December 4, 1983. Sale to present owner by CBS Corp. approved by FCC November 21, 2007. Sale to CBS Corp. by KBVO License Inc. approved by FCC August 3, 1999. Sal to KBVO License Inc. by Austin Television approved by FCC December 20, 1994. Ceased analog operations: February 17, 2009.

Represented (legal): Wiley Rein LLP.

Personnel:

Amy Villarreal, Vice President & General Manager.

Arthur Smith, Chief Engineer.

Ira Poole, Local Sales Manager.

Fred Lindstrom, National & Regional Sales Manager.

Suzanne Black, News Director.

Dusty Granberry, Engineering Director.

Christy Beadle, Business Manager.

Jessica Tremmell, Traffic Manager.

City of License: Austin. **Station DMA:** Austin, TX. **Rank:** 48.

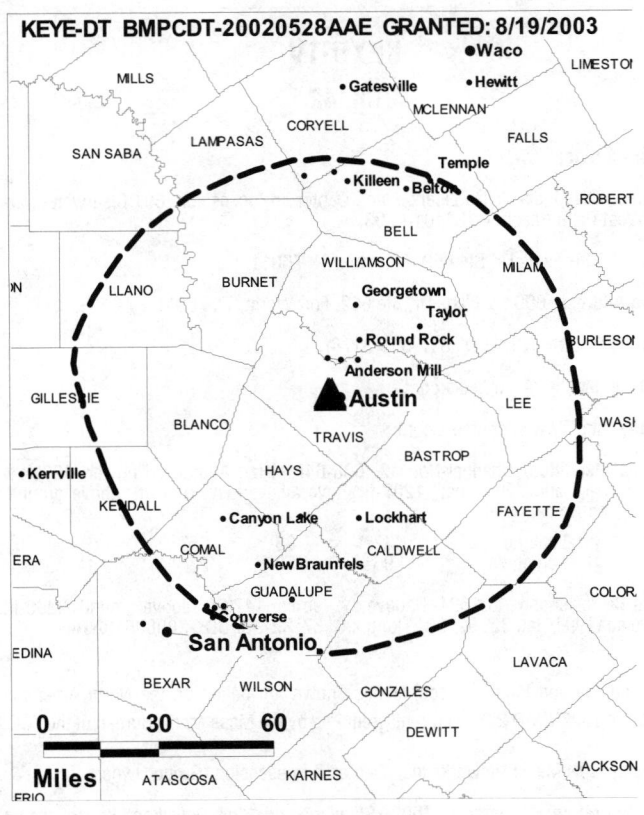

KEYE-DT BMPCDT-20020528AAE GRANTED: 8/19/2003

© 2010 Warren Communications News

Circulation © 2009 Nielsen. Coverage based on Nielsen study.

GrandTotal	Cable TV Households	Non-cable TV Households	Total TV Households
Estimated Station Totals *	433,950	240,390	674,340
Average Weekly Circulation (2009)	236,208	123,070	359,278
Average Daily Circulation (2009)			155,166

Station DMA Total	Cable TV Households	Non-cable TV Households	Total TV Households
Estimated Station Totals *	427,580	225,660	653,240
Average Weekly Circulation (2009)	234,441	121,779	356,220
Average Daily Circulation (2009)			154,044

Other DMA Total	Cable TV Households	Non-cable TV Households	Total TV Households
Estimated Station Totals *	6,370	14,730	21,100
Average Weekly Circulation (2009)	1,767	1,291	3,058
Average Daily Circulation (2009)			1,122

*Estimated station totals are sums of the Nielsen TV and Cable TV household estimates for each county in which the station registers viewing of more than 5% as per the Nielsen Survey Methods.

KNVA-DT
Ch. 49

Network Service: MNT, CW.

Licensee: 54 Broadcasting Inc., 908 W Martin Luther King Blvd, Austin, TX 78701.

Studio: 908 W Martin Luther King Blvd, Austin, TX 78701.

Mailing Address: 908 W Martin Luther King Blvd, Austin, TX 78701.

Phone: 512-478-5400. **Fax:** 512-476-1520.

Web Site: http://www.thecwaustin.com

Technical Facilities: Channel No. 49 (680-686 MHz). Authorized power: 197-kw max. visual, aural. Antenna: 1299-ft above av. terrain, 1161-ft. above ground, 2011-ft. above sea level.

Latitude	30°	19'	33"
Longitude	97°	47'	58"

Holds CP for change to 500-kw max. visual; BPCDT-20080606AAC.

Note: Latitude and longitude coordinates shown are based on the North American Datum of 1927 (NAD 27) as currently required by the Mass Media Bureau of the FCC.

Ownership: 54 Broadcasting Inc. (Group Owner).

Began Operation: August 8, 2008. Began analog operations: August 31, 1994. Ceased analog operations: June 12, 2009. Transfer of control by 54 Broadcasting Inc. from LS Communications Ltd., et al., to Vaughan Media LLC approved by FCC May 27, 2009. Transfer of control by 54 Broadcasting Inc. for LS Communications Ltd. from Rosalie Goldberg to her children (Frank Goldberg, Mark Goldberg, Richard Goldberg & Diane Levy) approved by FCC June 10, 2004.

Represented (legal): Thompson Hine LLP.

Represented (sales): Blair Television.

Personnel:

Eric Lassberg, President & General Manager.

Mark Dunham, Chief Engineer.

Denise Daniels, General Sales Manager.

Tish Saliani, Marketing Director.

Jamie Aragon, Program Director.

City of License: Austin. **Station DMA:** Austin, TX. **Rank:** 48.

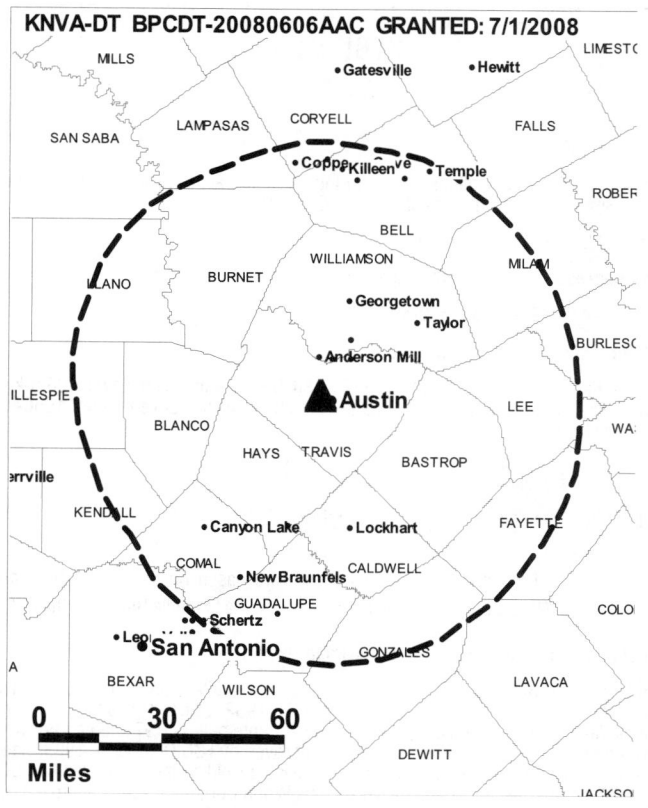

KNVA-DT BPCDT-20080606AAC GRANTED: 7/1/2008

© 2010 Warren Communications News

Circulation © 2009 Nielsen. Coverage based on Nielsen study.

GrandTotal	Cable TV Households	Non-cable TV Households	Total TV Households
Estimated Station Totals *	428,650	236,600	665,250
Average Weekly Circulation (2009)	75,134	63,465	138,599
Average Daily Circulation (2009)			45,204

Station DMA Total	Cable TV Households	Non-cable TV Households	Total TV Households
Estimated Station Totals *	423,690	219,450	643,140
Average Weekly Circulation (2009)	74,654	61,436	136,090
Average Daily Circulation (2009)			44,596

Other DMA Total	Cable TV Households	Non-cable TV Households	Total TV Households
Estimated Station Totals *	4,960	17,150	22,110
Average Weekly Circulation (2009)	480	2,029	2,509
Average Daily Circulation (2009)			608

*Estimated station totals are sums of the Nielsen TV and Cable TV household estimates for each county in which the station registers viewing of more than 5% as per the Nielsen Survey Methods.

KTBC-DT
Ch. 7

Network Service: FOX.

Licensee: NW Communications of Austin Inc., 444 N Capitol St NW, Ste 740, c/o Dianne Smith (News Corp.), Washington, DC 20001.

Studio: 119 E. 10th St., Austin, TX 78701.

Mailing Address: 119 E. 10th St, Austin, TX 78701.

Phone: 512-476-7777. **Fax:** 512-495-7001.

Web Site: http://www.myfoxaustin.com

Technical Facilities: Channel No. 7 (174-180 MHz). Authorized power: 98.6-kw visual, aural. Antenna: 1257-ft above av. terrain, 1046-ft. above ground, 1966-ft. above sea level.

Latitude	30°	18'	35"
Longitude	97°	47'	34"

Holds CP for change to 71.2-kw visual; BMPCDT-20080930BFX.

Note: Latitude and longitude coordinates shown are based on the North American Datum of 1927 (NAD 27) as currently required by the Mass Media Bureau of the FCC.

Ownership: Fox Television Holdings Inc. (Group Owner).

Began Operation: March 2, 2006. Station broadcasting digitally on its analog channel allotment. Began analog operations: November 27, 1952. Sale to Times Mirror Co. by Claudia Taylor Johnson, et al., approved by FCC September 6, 1973. Sale to Argyle Television Holding Inc. by Times Mirror Co. approved by FCC October 6, 1993. Sale to New World Communications by Argyle Television Holding Inc. approved by FCC March 31, 1995. Sale to present owner by New World Communications approved by FCC November 7, 1996. Ceased analog operations: June 12, 2009.

Represented (legal): Skadden, Arps, Slate, Meagher & Flom LLP.

Personnel:

Mark Rodman, President & General Manager.

Jay Jamandre, Operations & Production Manager.

Scott Moore, Local Sales Manager.

Michael Rusinko, National Sales Manager.

Pam Vaught, Vice President & News Director.

Shawn O'Shea, Vice President, Engineering.

Bob Sorrels, Business Manager.

Holly Breaux, Program Director.

Kathie Smith, Creative Services Director.

Gloria Frazier, Traffic Manager.

Rob Cunningham, Community Relations Director.

City of License: Austin. **Station DMA:** Austin, TX. **Rank:** 48.

KTBC-DT BMPCDT-20080930BFX GRANTED: 6/30/2009

© 2010 Warren Communications News

Circulation © 2009 Nielsen. Coverage based on Nielsen study.

GrandTotal	Cable TV Households	Non-cable TV Households	Total TV Households
Estimated Station Totals *	436,900	256,300	693,200
Average Weekly Circulation (2009)	231,780	130,212	361,992
Average Daily Circulation (2009)			135,677

Station DMA Total	Cable TV Households	Non-cable TV Households	Total TV Households
Estimated Station Totals *	427,580	225,660	653,240
Average Weekly Circulation (2009)	230,614	126,485	357,099
Average Daily Circulation (2009)			133,920

Other DMA Total	Cable TV Households	Non-cable TV Households	Total TV Households
Estimated Station Totals *	9,320	30,640	39,960
Average Weekly Circulation (2009)	1,166	3,727	4,893
Average Daily Circulation (2009)			1,757

*Estimated station totals are sums of the Nielsen TV and Cable TV household estimates for each county in which the station registers viewing of more than 5% as per the Nielsen Survey Methods.

KVUE-DT
Ch. 33

Network Service: ABC.

Licensee: KVUE Television Inc., 400 S Record St, Dallas, TX 75202-4806.

Studio: 3201 Steck Ave., Austin, TX 78757.

Mailing Address: PO Box 9927, Austin, TX 78766.

Phone: 512-459-6521. **Fax:** 512-533-2233.

Web Site: http://www.kvue.com

Technical Facilities: Channel No. 33 (584-590 MHz). Authorized power: 1000-kw max. visual, aural. Antenna: 1234-ft above av. terrain, 1124-ft. above ground, 1959-ft. above sea level.

Latitude	30°	19'	18"
Longitude	97°	48'	11"

Note: Latitude and longitude coordinates shown are based on the North American Datum of 1927 (NAD 27) as currently required by the Mass Media Bureau of the FCC.

Ownership: Belo Corp. (Group Owner).

Began Operation: June 24, 2005. Began analog operations: September 12, 1971. Swap of station by Gannett Broadcasting Group for A. H. Belo's KXTV, Sacramento-Stockton, CA approved by FCC April 8, 1999. Sale to Gannett Broadcasting Group by Evening News Association approved by FCC January 13, 1986 (Television Digest, Vol. 26:3). Sale to Evening News by Tolbert Foster, Allen Shivers, et al., approved by FCC September 8, 1978 (Vol. 18:21, 38). Ceased analog operations: June 12, 2009.

Personnel:

Patti C. Smith, President & General Manager.

Hoyt Hill, National Sales Manager.

Randy Rich, Local Sales Manager.

Eric Duncan, Local Sales Manager.

Frank Volpicella, News Director.

Mike Wenglar, Technology Director.

Stacy Smith, Controller & Human Resources Director.

Megan Sullivan, Programming Coordinator.

Mark Willenborg, Creative Services Director.

Brandi Vineyard, Traffic Coordinator.

Lynn Sparks, Community Affairs Manager.

City of License: Austin. **Station DMA:** Austin, TX. **Rank:** 48.

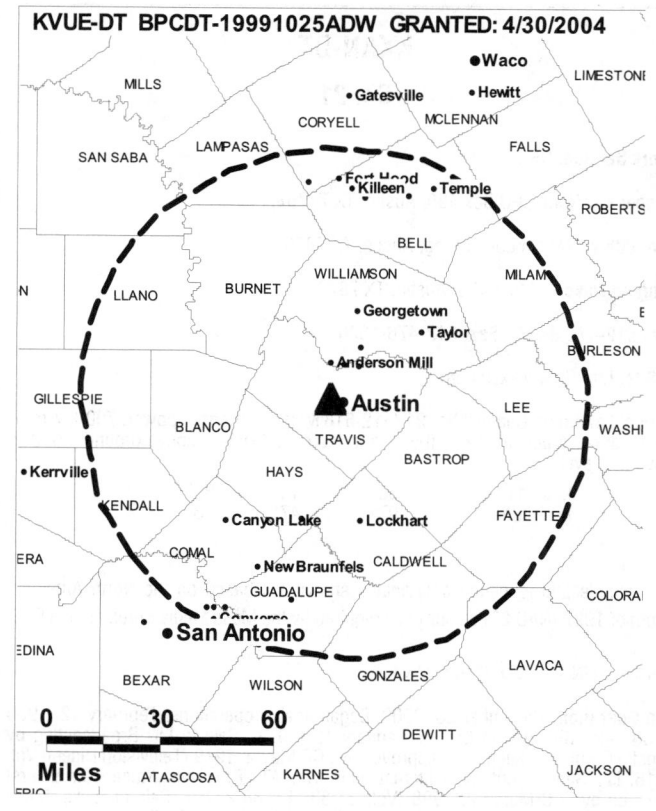

KVUE-DT BPCDT-19991025ADW GRANTED: 4/30/2004

© 2010 Warren Communications News

Circulation © 2009 Nielsen. Coverage based on Nielsen study.

GrandTotal	Cable TV Households	Non-cable TV Households	Total TV Households
Estimated Station Totals *	434,930	239,220	674,150
Average Weekly Circulation (2009)	275,683	137,547	413,230
Average Daily Circulation (2009)			191,635

Station DMA Total	Cable TV Households	Non-cable TV Households	Total TV Households
Estimated Station Totals *	427,580	225,660	653,240
Average Weekly Circulation (2009)	273,625	136,162	409,787
Average Daily Circulation (2009)			190,403

Other DMA Total	Cable TV Households	Non-cable TV Households	Total TV Households
Estimated Station Totals *	7,350	13,560	20,910
Average Weekly Circulation (2009)	2,058	1,385	3,443
Average Daily Circulation (2009)			1,232

*Estimated station totals are sums of the Nielsen TV and Cable TV household estimates for each county in which the station registers viewing of more than 5% as per the Nielsen Survey Methods.

KXAN-DT
Ch. 21

Network Service: NBC.

Licensee: KXAN Inc., PO Box 490, Austin, TX 78767.

Studio: 908 W. Martin Luther King, Austin, TX 78701.

Mailing Address: PO Box 490, Austin, TX 78767.

Phone: 512-476-3636. **Fax:** 512-476-1520.

Web Site: http://www.kxan.com

Technical Facilities: Channel No. 21 (512-518 MHz). Authorized power: 700-kw max. visual, aural. Antenna: 1297-ft above av. terrain, 1163-ft. above ground, 2012-ft. above sea level.

Latitude	30°	19'	33"
Longitude	97°	47'	58"

Note: Latitude and longitude coordinates shown are based on the North American Datum of 1927 (NAD 27) as currently required by the Mass Media Bureau of the FCC.

Ownership: LIN TV Corp. (Group Owner).

Began Operation: December 28, 2000. Began analog operations: February 12, 1965 on Ch. 42. Changed to Ch. 36 January 12, 1973. Sale to LIN Broadcasting by Kingstip Communications Inc. approved by FCC May 2, 1979 (Television Digest, Vol. 18:16, 17). Sale of controlling interest in LIN from AT&T to Hicks, Muse, Tate & Furst approved by FCC March 2, 1998 (Vol. 37:33, 42; 38:2, 19). Sale of Hicks, Muse interest to Chancellor Media Corp. cancelled (Vol. 38:28; 39:12). Ceased analog operations: June 12, 2009.

Represented (sales): Blair Television.

Personnel:

Eric Lassberg, President & General Manager.

Rachel Steading, Operations & Production Manager.

Amy Coplen, National Sales Manager.

Todd Krauss, Local Sales Manager.

Michael Sabac, News Director.

Mark Dunham, Chief Engineer.

Lisa Li, Business Manager.

Jamie Aragon, Traffic Manager & Program Director.

City of License: Austin. **Station DMA:** Austin, TX. **Rank:** 48.

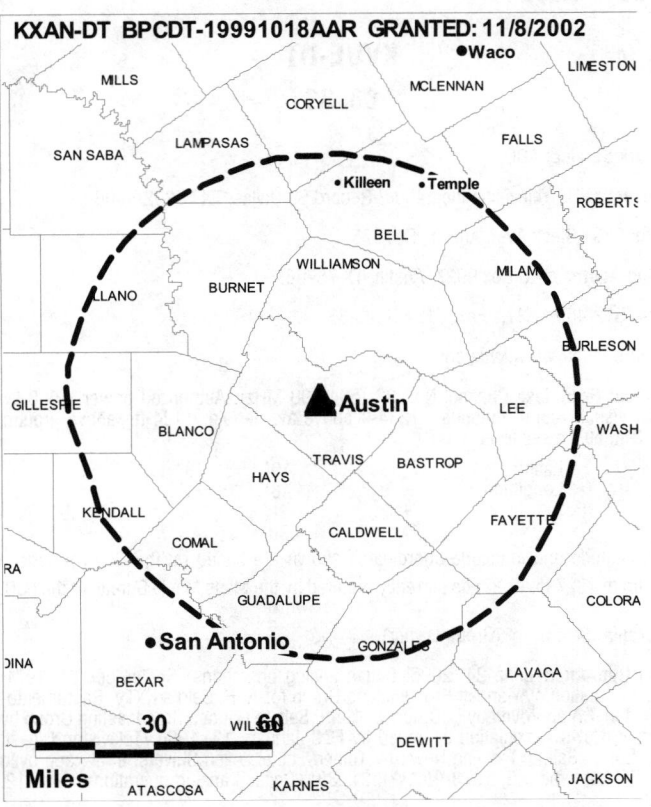

KXAN-DT BPCDT-19991018AAR GRANTED: 11/8/2002

© 2010 Warren Communications News

Circulation © 2009 Nielsen. Coverage based on Nielsen study.

GrandTotal	Cable TV Households	Non-cable TV Households	Total TV Households
Estimated Station Totals *	431,980	241,180	673,160
Average Weekly Circulation (2009)	247,031	136,328	383,359
Average Daily Circulation (2009)			167,813

Station DMA Total	Cable TV Households	Non-cable TV Households	Total TV Households
Estimated Station Totals *	427,580	225,660	653,240
Average Weekly Circulation (2009)	246,587	134,316	380,903
Average Daily Circulation (2009)			167,049

Other DMA Total	Cable TV Households	Non-cable TV Households	Total TV Households
Estimated Station Totals *	4,400	15,520	19,920
Average Weekly Circulation (2009)	444	2,012	2,456
Average Daily Circulation (2009)			764

*Estimated station totals are sums of the Nielsen TV and Cable TV household estimates for each county in which the station registers viewing of more than 5% as per the Nielsen Survey Methods.

KAZH-DT
Ch. 41

Network Service: IND.

Grantee: KAZH License LLC - Debtor-in-Possession, 301 W Main St, Visalia, CA 93291.

Studio: 2620 Fountain View, Suite 485, Houston, TX 77057.

Mailing Address: 2620 Fountain View, Suite 485, Houston, TX 77057.

Phone: 713-783-5741. **Fax:** 713-783-4157.

Web Site: http://www.kazh57.com

Technical Facilities: Channel No. 41 (632-638 MHz). Authorized power: 1000-kw max. visual, aural. Antenna: 1903-ft above av. terrain, 1887-ft. above ground, 1964-ft. above sea level.

Latitude	61°	20'	10.8"
Longitude	149°	30'	48.2"

Note: Latitude and longitude coordinates shown are based on the North American Datum of 1927 (NAD 27) as currently required by the Mass Media Bureau of the FCC.

Ownership: E. Roger Williams, Trustee (Group Owner).

Began Operation: October 15, 2008. Began analog operations: May 18, 1988. Sale to TTBG/KAZH License Sub LLC approved by FCC July 1, 2009, but not yet consummated. Involuntary transfer of control by KAZH License LLC - Debtor-in-Possession from Harry J. Pappas, Debtor-in-Possession, et al. to E. Roger Williams, Trustee approved by FCC September 17, 2008. Assignment to debtor-in-possession status approved by FCC July 3, 2008. Sale to Azteca America Stations Group LLC by Harry J. Pappas was approved by the FCC March 20, 2001, but was never consummated. Ceased analog operations: June 12, 2009.

Represented (legal): Davis Wright Tremaine LLP.

Personnel:

Emilio Nicolas, General Manager.

Rick Cruz-Iago, Sales Manager.

Altaf Boolani, Chief Engineer.

Mario Garcia, Production Manager.

Andrea Robinson, Traffic Manager.

City of License: Baytown. **Station DMA:** Houston, TX. **Rank:** 10.

© 2010 Warren Communications News

Circulation © 2009 Nielsen. Coverage based on Nielsen study.

GrandTotal	Cable TV Households	Non-cable TV Households	Total TV Households
Estimated Station Totals *	817,810	621,140	1,438,950
Average Weekly Circulation (2009)	48,741	82,612	131,353
Average Daily Circulation (2009)			39,822

Station DMA Total	Cable TV Households	Non-cable TV Households	Total TV Households
Estimated Station Totals *	817,810	621,140	1,438,950
Average Weekly Circulation (2009)	48,741	82,612	131,353
Average Daily Circulation (2009)			39,822

*Estimated station totals are sums of the Nielsen TV and Cable TV household estimates for each county in which the station registers viewing of more than 5% as per the Nielsen Survey Methods.

KBMT-DT
Ch. 12

Network Service: ABC.

Licensee: KBMT License Co. LLC, 5052 Addison Cir, Addison, TX 75001.

Studio: 525 Interstate Hwy 10 S, Beaumont, TX 77701.

Mailing Address: 525 Interstate Hwy 10 S, Beaumont, TX 77701.

Phone: 409-833-7512. **Fax:** 409-981-1562.

Web Site: http://www.kbmt12.com

Technical Facilities: Channel No. 12 (204-210 MHz). Authorized power: 18.2-kw visual, aural. Antenna: 1001-ft above av. terrain, 994-ft. above ground, 1020-ft. above sea level.

Latitude	30°	11'	26"
Longitude	93°	53'	08"

Note: Latitude and longitude coordinates shown are based on the North American Datum of 1927 (NAD 27) as currently required by the Mass Media Bureau of the FCC.

Satellite Earth Stations: Transmitter Harris; EASI, 3.7-meter Ku & C-band; AFC, 3.7-meter Ku-band; Harris, 4.5-meter C-band; Andrew, 4.5-meter C-band; Andrew, 7.3-meter C-band; Agile Omni, M/A-Com, Harris, Avantek receivers.

Ownership: London Broadcasting Co. Inc. (Group Owner).

Began Operation: September 15, 2006. Station broadcasting digitally on its analog channel allotment. Began analog operations: June 18, 1961. Ceased analog operations: June 12, 2009. Sale to present owner by Texas Television Inc. approved by FCC June 15, 2009. Sale to Texas Television Inc. by Harbour TV Systems (Liberty National Corp.) approved by FCC October 21, 1976. Transfer of control to Harbour TV Systems from A. O. Banning & William G. Hill Jr. approved by FCC February 11, 1976. Sale to Banning & Hill by Devon Corp. approved by FCC September 28, 1973.

Represented (legal): Wiley Rein LLP.

Represented (sales): Continental Television Sales.

Personnel:

Michael Elrod, General Manager.

Bob Wilson, Local Sales Manager.

Ken Smith, General Sales Manager.

Miles Resnick, News Director.

Elizabeth West, Program Director.

Mark Cormier, Chief Engineer.

William Norman, Production Manager.

City of License: Beaumont. **Station DMA:** Beaumont-Port Arthur, TX. **Rank:** 141.

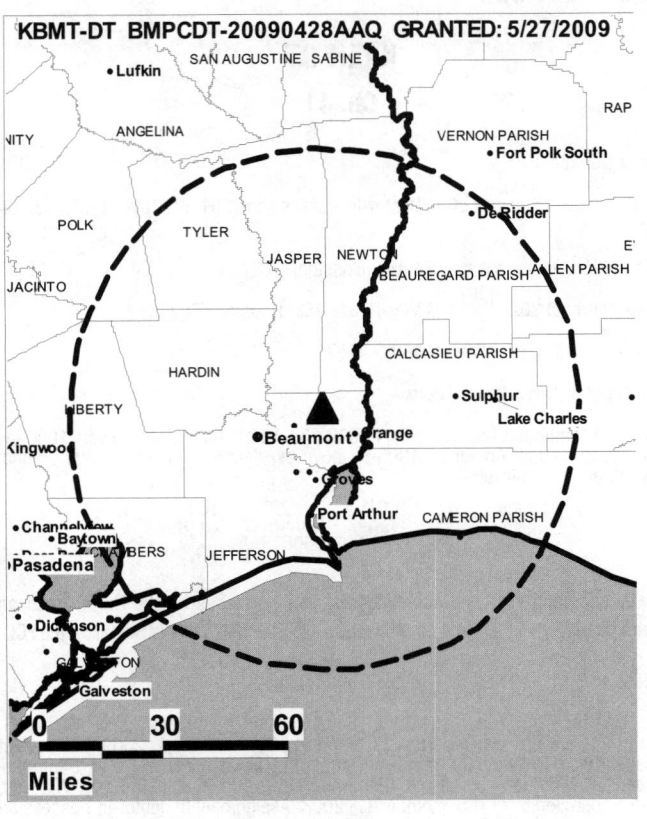

KBMT-DT BMPCDT-20090428AAQ GRANTED: 5/27/2009

© 2010 Warren Communications News

Circulation © 2009 Nielsen. Coverage based on Nielsen study.

GrandTotal	Cable TV Households	Non-cable TV Households	Total TV Households
Estimated Station Totals *	153,300	91,190	244,490
Average Weekly Circulation (2009)	90,995	40,324	131,319
Average Daily Circulation (2009)			59,591

Station DMA Total	Cable TV Households	Non-cable TV Households	Total TV Households
Estimated Station Totals *	96,730	63,490	160,220
Average Weekly Circulation (2009)	64,736	35,873	100,609
Average Daily Circulation (2009)			48,694

Other DMA Total	Cable TV Households	Non-cable TV Households	Total TV Households
Estimated Station Totals *	56,570	27,700	84,270
Average Weekly Circulation (2009)	26,259	4,451	30,710
Average Daily Circulation (2009)			10,897

*Estimated station totals are sums of the Nielsen TV and Cable TV household estimates for each county in which the station registers viewing of more than 5% as per the Nielsen Survey Methods.

KFDM-DT
Ch. 21

Network Service: CW, CBS.

Licensee: Freedom Broadcasting of Texas Licensee LLC, PO Box 7128, Beaumont, TX 77726-7128.

Studio: 2955 Interstate 10 E, Beaumont, TX 77702.

Mailing Address: PO Box 7128, Beaumont, TX 77726.

Phone: 409-892-6622. **Fax:** 409-892-6665.

Web Site: http://www.kfdm.com

Technical Facilities: Channel No. 21 (512-518 MHz). Authorized power: 50-kw max. visual, aural. Antenna: 833-ft above av. terrain, 820-ft. above ground, 840-ft. above sea level.

Latitude	30°	08'	24"
Longitude	93°	58'	44"

Holds CP for change to 350-kw max. visual, 889-ft above av. terrain, 886-ft. above ground, 915-ft. above sea level; BPCDT-20080618AAY.

Note: Latitude and longitude coordinates shown are based on the North American Datum of 1927 (NAD 27) as currently required by the Mass Media Bureau of the FCC.

Ownership: Freedom Communications Holdings Inc. (Group Owner).

Began Operation: January 22, 2003. High Definition. Began analog operations: April 24, 1955. Sale to present owner by Freedom Broadcasting Inc. approved by FCC April 1, 2004. Sale to Freedom Broadcasting Inc. by Belo Broadcasting Corp. approved by FCC December 13, 1983 (Television Digest, Vol. 23:42). Sale to Belo by Beaumont Broadcasting Corp. approved by FCC May 1969 (Vol. 9:19). Ceased analog operations: June 12, 2009.

Represented (engineering): Carl T. Jones Corp.

Represented (legal): Latham & Watkins.

Represented (sales): TeleRep Inc.

Personnel:

Larry Beaulieu, Vice President & General Manager.

C. Rix Garey, General Sales Manager.

Lori Leach, Local Sales Assistant.

Stuart Sepaugh, National Sales Manager.

David Lowell, News Director.

Richard Kihn, Chief Engineer.

Katherine Read, Business Manager.

Penny Peden, Program Scheduling & Executive Assistant.

Gina Hinson, Promotion Director & Production Manager.

City of License: Beaumont. **Station DMA:** Beaumont-Port Arthur, TX. **Rank:** 141.

KFDM-DT BPCDT-20090202AEN GRANTED: 2/6/2009

© 2010 Warren Communications News

Circulation © 2009 Nielsen. Coverage based on Nielsen study.

GrandTotal	Cable TV Households	Non-cable TV Households	Total TV Households
Estimated Station Totals *	161,740	91,190	252,930
Average Weekly Circulation (2009)	92,899	43,210	136,109
Average Daily Circulation (2009)			79,488

Station DMA Total	Cable TV Households	Non-cable TV Households	Total TV Households
Estimated Station Totals *	96,730	63,490	160,220
Average Weekly Circulation (2009)	81,682	40,512	122,194
Average Daily Circulation (2009)			74,992

Other DMA Total	Cable TV Households	Non-cable TV Households	Total TV Households
Estimated Station Totals *	65,010	27,700	92,710
Average Weekly Circulation (2009)	11,217	2,698	13,915
Average Daily Circulation (2009)			4,496

*Estimated station totals are sums of the Nielsen TV and Cable TV household estimates for each county in which the station registers viewing of more than 5% as per the Nielsen Survey Methods.

KWAB-DT
Ch. 33

Network Service: NBC.

Grantee: Midessa Television LP, PO Box 60150, Midland, TX 79711.

Studio: 2500 Kentucky Way, Big Spring, TX 79720.

Mailing Address: PO Box 60150, Midland, TX 79711.

Phone: 432-567-9999. **Fax:** 432-567-9993.

Web Site: http://www.kwes.com

Technical Facilities: Channel No. 33 (584-590 MHz). Authorized power: 33.5-kw max. visual, aural. Antenna: 273-ft above av. terrain, 274-ft. above ground, 2830-ft. above sea level.

Latitude	32°	16'	55"
Longitude	101°	29'	34"

Note: Latitude and longitude coordinates shown are based on the North American Datum of 1927 (NAD 27) as currently required by the Mass Media Bureau of the FCC.

Ownership: Drewry Communications (Group Owner).

Began Operation: November 16, 2004. Began analog operations: January 15, 1958. Sale to KWES License Co. LLC (London Broadcasting Co. Inc.) approved by FCC November 5, 2008, but never consummated. Sale to present owner by James T. Taylor, Receiver approved by FCC September 9, 1991. Assignment to James T. Taylor, Receiver from MSP Television of Midland-Odessa Inc. approved by FCC December 3, 1987. Sale to MSP Television of Midland-Odessa Inc. by Permian Basin Television Corp. approved by FCC November 19, 1985. Sale to Permian Basin Television Corp. approved by FCC April 21, 1980. Ceased analog operations: June 12, 2009.

Represented (legal): Davis Wright Tremaine LLP.

Personnel:

Mac Douglas, General Manager.

Richard Esparza, General Sales Manager.

Chuck Cooper, Chief Engineer.

City of License: Big Spring. **Station DMA:** Odessa-Midland, TX. **Rank:** 155.

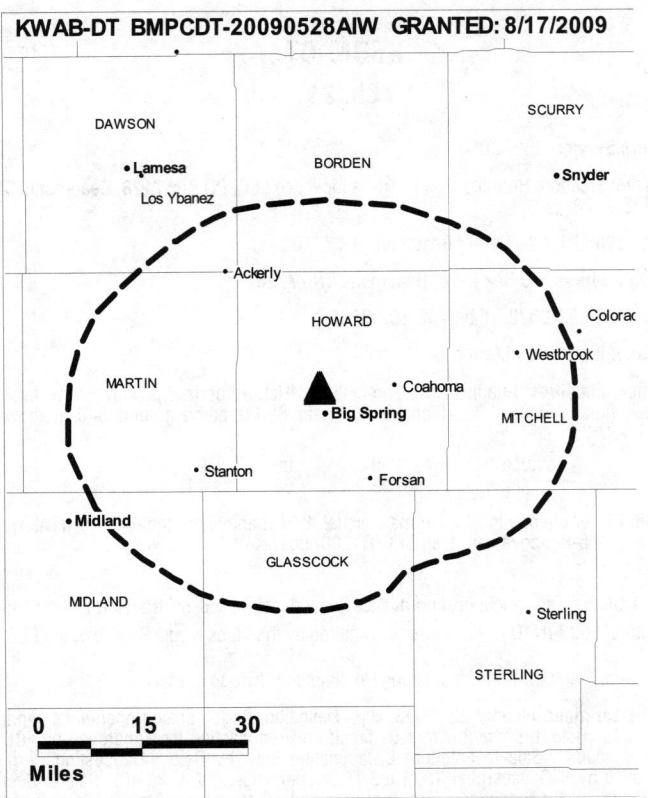

KWAB-DT BMPCDT-20090528AIW GRANTED: 8/17/2009

© 2010 Warren Communications News

Circulation © 2009 Nielsen. Coverage based on Nielsen study.

GrandTotal	Cable TV Households	Non-cable TV Households	Total TV Households
Estimated Station Totals *	780	3,740	4,520
Average Weekly Circulation (2009)	248	628	876
Average Daily Circulation (2009)			234

Station DMA Total	Cable TV Households	Non-cable TV Households	Total TV Households
Estimated Station Totals *	0	3,740	3,740
Average Weekly Circulation (2009)	0	628	628
Average Daily Circulation (2009)			191

Other DMA Total	Cable TV Households	Non-cable TV Households	Total TV Households
Estimated Station Totals *	780	0	780
Average Weekly Circulation (2009)	248	0	248
Average Daily Circulation (2009)			43

*Estimated station totals are sums of the Nielsen TV and Cable TV household estimates for each county in which the station registers viewing of more than 5% as per the Nielsen Survey Methods.

KNIC-DT
Ch. 18

Grantee: Telefutura Partnership of San Antonio, 5999 Center Dr, Ste 4083, Los Angeles, CA 90045.

Mailing Address: 411 E Durango, San Antonio, TX 78204.

Phone: 210-227-4141. **Fax:** 210-227-0469.

Technical Facilities: Channel No. 18 (494-500 MHz). Authorized power: 1000-kw max. visual, aural. Antenna: 656-ft above av. terrain, 552-ft. above ground, 1808-ft. above sea level.

Latitude	29°	41'	48"
Longitude	98°	30'	45"

Note: Latitude and longitude coordinates shown are based on the North American Datum of 1927 (NAD 27) as currently required by the Mass Media Bureau of the FCC.

Ownership: Univision Communications Inc.

Began Operation: June 12, 2009. Began analog operations: October 16, 2006. Transfer of control to Broadcasting Media Partners Inc. approved by FCC March 27, 2007. Ceased analog operations: June 12, 2009.

City of License: Blanco. **Station DMA:** Austin, TX. **Rank:** 48.

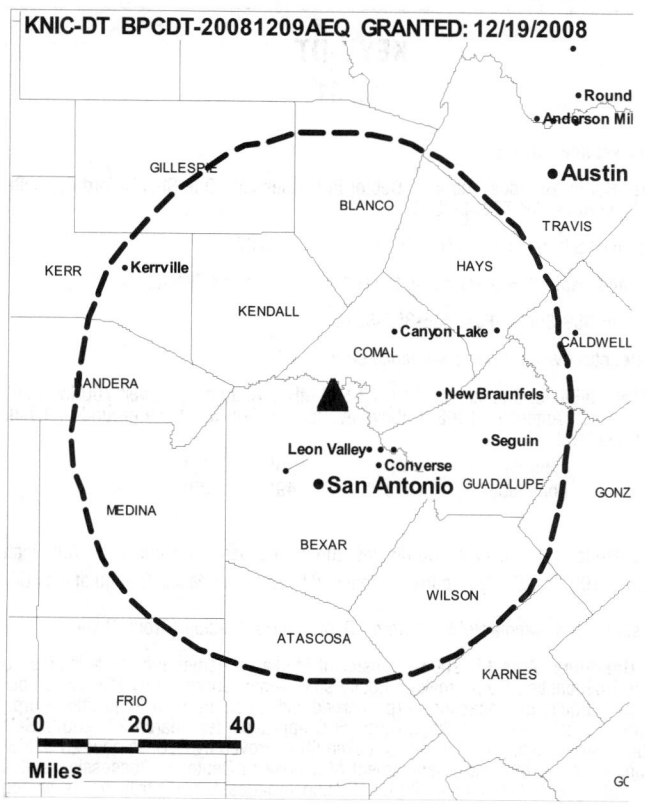

KNIC-DT BPCDT-20081209AEQ GRANTED: 12/19/2008

© 2010 Warren Communications News

Circulation © 2009 Nielsen. Coverage based on Nielsen study.

GrandTotal	Cable TV Households	Non-cable TV Households	Total TV Households
Estimated Station Totals *	19,720	197,400	217,120
Average Weekly Circulation (2009)	2,562	19,537	22,099
Average Daily Circulation (2009)			4,533

Station DMA Total	Cable TV Households	Non-cable TV Households	Total TV Households
Estimated Station Totals *	19,720	197,400	217,120
Average Weekly Circulation (2009)	2,562	19,537	22,099
Average Daily Circulation (2009)			4,533

*Estimated station totals are sums of the Nielsen TV and Cable TV household estimates for each county in which the station registers viewing of more than 5% as per the Nielsen Survey Methods.

KEYU-DT
Ch. 31

Network Service: UNV.

Grantee: Borger Broadcasting Inc., Debtor in Possession, One Shackleford Dr, Suite 400, Little Rock, AR 72211-2545.

Studio: 1616 S Kentucky, Ste D-130, Amarillo, TX 79102.

Mailing Address: 1616 S Kentucky, Ste D-130, Amarillo, TX 79102.

Phone: 806-359-8900. **Fax:** 806-352-8912.

Web Site: http://www.univision-amarillo.com

Technical Facilities: Channel No. 31 (572-578 MHz). Authorized power: 700-kw max. visual, aural. Antenna: 1002-ft above av. terrain, 965-ft. above ground, 4397-ft. above sea level.

Latitude	35°	20'	33"
Longitude	101°	49'	20"

Note: Latitude and longitude coordinates shown are based on the North American Datum of 1927 (NAD 27) as currently required by the Mass Media Bureau of the FCC.

Ownership: Equity Media Holdings Corp., Debtor in Possession (Group Owner).

Began Operation: April 11, 2005. Transfer of Media Properties Inc. 50% interest to Equity Broadcasting Corp., making Equity sole owner, approved by FCC November 22, 2000. Equity Broadcasting Corp. merged with Coconut Palm Acquisition Corp., becoming Equity Media Holdings Corp. FCC approved deal March 27, 2007. Sale to Luken Broadcasting LLC (Harry G. Luken III) approved by FCC October 23, 2008, but not yet consummated. Assignment of license to Debtor in Possession status approved by FCC February 4, 2009. Station broadcasting digitally on its analog channel allotment.

Personnel:

Jim MacDonald, General Manager.

Fernando Ballin, Operations Manager.

City of License: Borger. **Station DMA:** Amarillo, TX. **Rank:** 131.

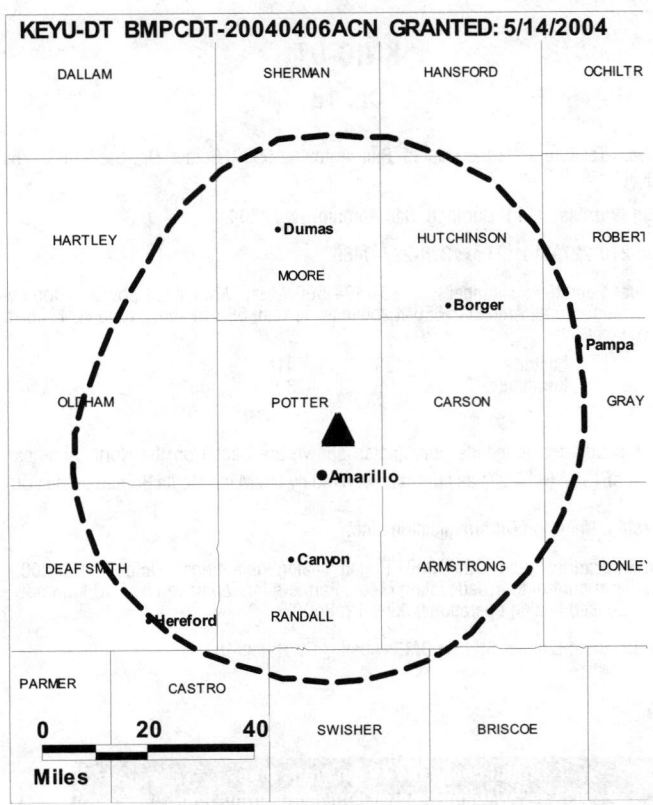

KEYU-DT BMPCDT-20040406ACN GRANTED: 5/14/2004

© 2010 Warren Communications News

Circulation © 2009 Nielsen. Coverage based on Nielsen study.

GrandTotal	Cable TV Households	Non-cable TV Households	Total TV Households
Estimated Station Totals *	34,310	27,450	61,760
Average Weekly Circulation (2009)	4,212	1,662	5,874
Average Daily Circulation (2009)			3,257

Station DMA Total	Cable TV Households	Non-cable TV Households	Total TV Households
Estimated Station Totals *	34,310	27,450	61,760
Average Weekly Circulation (2009)	4,212	1,662	5,874
Average Daily Circulation (2009)			3,257

*Estimated station totals are sums of the Nielsen TV and Cable TV household estimates for each county in which the station registers viewing of more than 5% as per the Nielsen Survey Methods.

KVEO-DT
Ch. 24

Network Service: NBC.

Licensee: ComCorp of Texas License Corp., PO Box 53708, Lafayette, LA 70505-3708.

Studio: 394 N. Expressway, Brownsville, TX 78521.

Mailing Address: 394 N. Expressway, Brownville, TX 78521.

Phone: 956-544-2323. **Fax:** 956-544-4636.

E-mail: programming@kveo.com

Web Site: http://www.kveo.com

Technical Facilities: Channel No. 24 (530-536 MHz). Authorized power: 1000-kw max. visual, aural. Antenna: 1460-ft above av. terrain, 1464-ft. above ground, 1520-ft. above sea level.

Latitude	26°	06'	01"
Longitude	97°	50'	20"

Note: Latitude and longitude coordinates shown are based on the North American Datum of 1927 (NAD 27) as currently required by the Mass Media Bureau of the FCC.

Ownership: Communications Corp. of America (Group Owner).

Began Operation: June 24, 2005. Began analog operations: December 18, 1981. Sale to Valley Broadcasting Co. by Trustee-in-Bankruptcy approved by FCC August 31, 1984. Sale to SouthWest MultiMedia Corp. by Valley Broadcasting Co. approved by FCC November 29, 1985. Sale to Associated Broadcasters Inc. by SouthWest MultiMedia Corp. approved by FCC October 19, 1990. Sale to Communications Corp. of America by Associated Broadcasters Inc. approved by FCC April 29, 1994. Transfer of control from Thomas R. Galloway Sr. to Apollo Capital Management II Inc. & Thomas R. Galloway Sr. jointly approved by FCC April 16, 2004. Ceased analog operations: June 12, 2009.

Represented (legal): Dow Lohnes PLLC.

Represented (sales): Katz Media Group.

Personnel:

William Jorn, General Manager.

Debbie Flores, General Sales Manager.

Peter Hoekzema, Chief Engineer.

Maria Fulford, Business Manager.

Shannon Tetreau, Promotion Director.

Juan Montero, Program Coordinator.

Ray Gomez, Production Manager.

John Joe Hernandez, Traffic Manager.

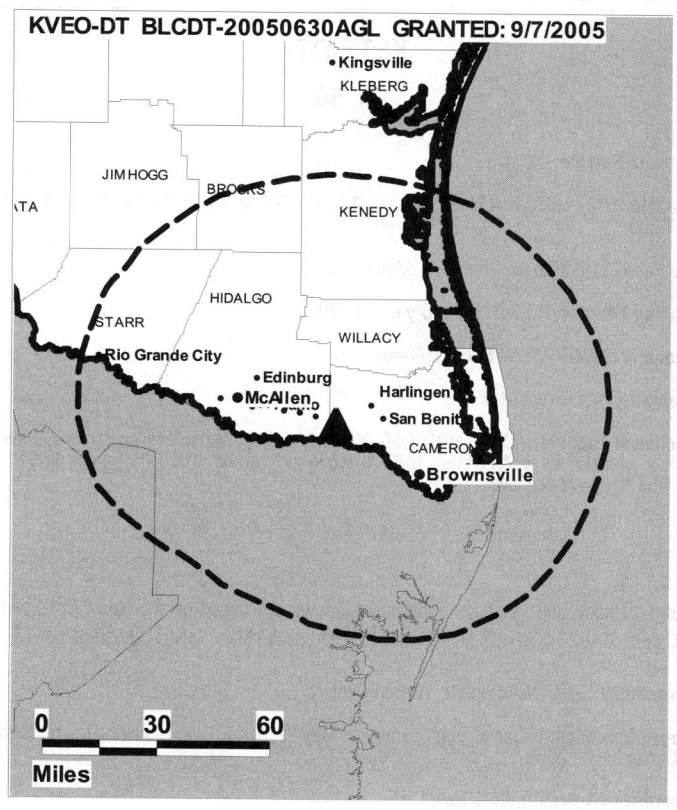

KVEO-DT BLCDT-20050630AGL GRANTED: 9/7/2005

© 2010 Warren Communications News

City of License: Brownsville.

Station DMA: Harlingen-Weslaco-Brownsville-McAllen, TX. **Rank:** 87.

Circulation © 2009 Nielsen. Coverage based on Nielsen study.

GrandTotal	Cable TV Households	Non-cable TV Households	Total TV Households
Estimated Station Totals *	139,180	210,730	349,910
Average Weekly Circulation (2009)	50,796	68,985	119,781
Average Daily Circulation (2009)			47,840

Station DMA Total	Cable TV Households	Non-cable TV Households	Total TV Households
Estimated Station Totals *	139,180	210,730	349,910
Average Weekly Circulation (2009)	50,796	68,985	119,781
Average Daily Circulation (2009)			47,840

*Estimated station totals are sums of the Nielsen TV and Cable TV household estimates for each county in which the station registers viewing of more than 5% as per the Nielsen Survey Methods.

KBTX-DT
Ch. 50

Network Service: CW, CBS.

Grantee: Gray Television Licensee LLC, 1750 K St NW, Ste 1200, Washington, DC 20006.

Studio: 4141 E 29th St, Bryan, TX 77802.

Mailing Address: PO Box 3730, Bryan, TX 77805.

Phone: 979-846-7777. **Fax:** 979-846-1490.

Web Site: http://www.kbtx.com

Technical Facilities: Channel No. 50 (686-692 MHz). Authorized power: 1000-kw max. visual, aural. Antenna: 1664-ft above av. terrain, 1623-ft. above ground, 1955-ft. above sea level.

Latitude	30°	33'	16"
Longitude	96°	01'	51"

Note: Latitude and longitude coordinates shown are based on the North American Datum of 1927 (NAD 27) as currently required by the Mass Media Bureau of the FCC.

Ownership: Gray Television Inc. (Group Owner).

Began Operation: Began analog operations: May 22, 1957. Ceased analog operations: December 1, 2008.

Represented (legal): Wiley Rein LLP.

Represented (sales): Katz Media Group.

Personnel:

Mike Wright, General Manager.

Jon Boaz, General Sales Manager.

Chace Murphy, News Director.

Kris Swearingen, Chief Engineer.

Donna Pittman, Program Director.

Cliff Wallace, Promotions Manager.

Trey Holt, Production Manager.

Margaret Wren, Traffic Manager.

Mandy Riske, Operations Manager.

City of License: Bryan. **Station DMA:** Waco-Temple-Bryan, TX. **Rank:** 89.

KBTX-DT BMPCDT-20080611AAI GRANTED: 12/17/2008

© 2010 Warren Communications News

Circulation © 2009 Nielsen. Coverage based on Nielsen study.

GrandTotal	Cable TV Households	Non-cable TV Households	Total TV Households
Estimated Station Totals *	40,090	96,860	136,950
Average Weekly Circulation (2009)	26,394	22,762	49,156
Average Daily Circulation (2009)			26,790

Station DMA Total	Cable TV Households	Non-cable TV Households	Total TV Households
Estimated Station Totals *	39,300	96,860	136,160
Average Weekly Circulation (2009)	26,301	22,762	49,063
Average Daily Circulation (2009)			26,788

Other DMA Total	Cable TV Households	Non-cable TV Households	Total TV Households
Estimated Station Totals *	790	0	790
Average Weekly Circulation (2009)	93	0	93
Average Daily Circulation (2009)			2

*Estimated station totals are sums of the Nielsen TV and Cable TV household estimates for each county in which the station registers viewing of more than 5% as per the Nielsen Survey Methods.

KYLE-DT
Ch. 28

Network Service: CW.

Grantee: ComCorp of Bryan License Corp., PO Box 53708, Lafayette, LA 70505-3708.

Studio: 2402 Broadmoor Dr., Suite B-101, Bryan, TX 77802.

Mailing Address: 2402 Broadmoor Dr, Ste B-101, Bryan, TX 77802.

Phone: 979-774-1800. **Fax:** 979-774-1901.

Web Site: http://www.kwkt.com

Technical Facilities: Channel No. 28 (554-560 MHz). Authorized power: 50-kw max. visual, aural. Antenna: 722-ft above av. terrain, 640-ft. above ground, 1020-ft. above sea level.

Latitude	30°	41'	18"
Longitude	96°	25'	35"

Note: Latitude and longitude coordinates shown are based on the North American Datum of 1927 (NAD 27) as currently required by the Mass Media Bureau of the FCC.

Ownership: Communications Corp. of America (Group Owner).

Began Operation: July 1, 2008. Station broadcasting digitally on its analog channel allotment. Began analog operations: October 31, 1994. Company emerged from debtor in possession status October 4, 2007. Involuntary transfer of control to debtor in possession approved by FCC August 29, 2006. Transfer of control from Thomas R. Galloway Sr. to Apollo Capital Management II Inc. & Thomas R. Galloway Sr. jointly approved by FCC April 16, 2004. Sale to Communications Corp. of America from Silent Ministry Group Inc. approved by FCC November 19, 1996. Ceased analog operations: February 17, 2009.

Represented (legal): Dow Lohnes PLLC.

Represented (sales): Continental Television Sales.

Personnel:

Ron Crowder, General Manager.

Duane Sartor, Station Manager.

Robin Rice, National Sales Assistant.

Lou Strowger, Chief Engineer.

Edna Williams, Business Manager.

Amy Bishop, Program Director.

Caroline Nelson, Traffic Manager.

City of License: Bryan. **Station DMA:** Waco-Temple-Bryan, TX. **Rank:** 89.

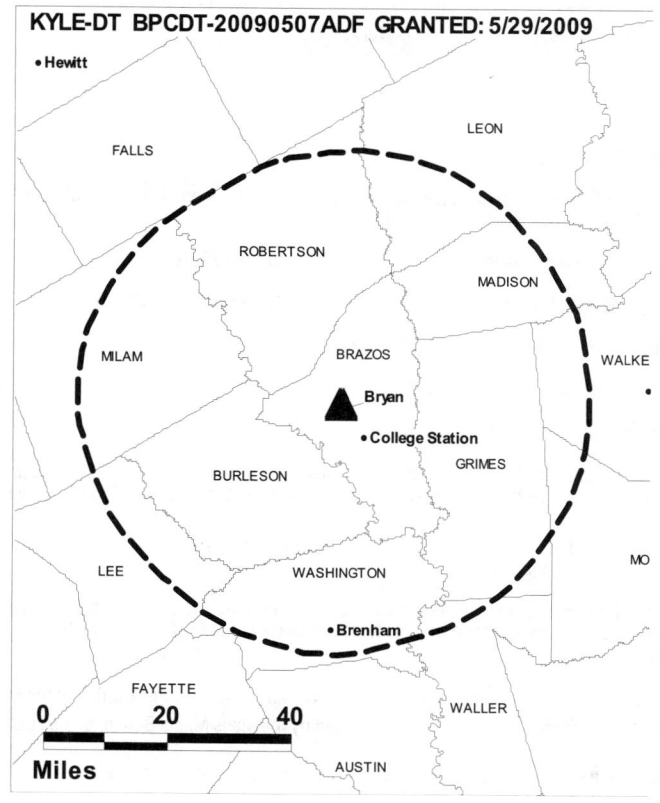

KYLE-DT BPCDT-20090507ADF GRANTED: 5/29/2009

© 2010 Warren Communications News

Circulation © 2009 Nielsen. Coverage based on Nielsen study.

GrandTotal	Cable TV Households	Non-cable TV Households	Total TV Households
Estimated Station Totals *	39,300	45,290	84,590
Average Weekly Circulation (2009)	16,313	6,332	22,645
Average Daily Circulation (2009)			7,594

Station DMA Total	Cable TV Households	Non-cable TV Households	Total TV Households
Estimated Station Totals *	39,300	45,290	84,590
Average Weekly Circulation (2009)	16,313	6,332	22,645
Average Daily Circulation (2009)			7,594

*Estimated station totals are sums of the Nielsen TV and Cable TV household estimates for each county in which the station registers viewing of more than 5% as per the Nielsen Survey Methods.

KPXB-TV
Ch. 5

Network Service: ION.

Licensee: ION Media Houston License Inc., Debtor in Possession, 601 Clearwater Park Rd, West Palm Beach, FL 33401-6233.

Studio: 256 N Sam Houston Pkwy E, Ste 49, Houston, TX 77060.

Mailing Address: 256 N Sam Houston Pkwy E, Ste 49, Houston, TX 77060.

Phone: 281-820-4900. **Fax:** 281-820-3916.

E-mail: alexstroot@ionmedia.com

Web Site: http://www.ionmedia.com

Technical Facilities: Channel No. 5 (76-82 MHz). Authorized power: 9.5-kw visual, aural. Antenna: 1821-ft above av. terrain, 1806-ft. above ground, 1883-ft. above sea level.

Latitude	29°	34'	15"
Longitude	95°	30'	37"

Holds CP for change to channel number 32, 1000-kw max. visual, 1900-ft above av. terrain, 1885-ft. above ground, 1962-ft. above sea level; BMPCDT-20080619AGV.

Note: Latitude and longitude coordinates shown are based on the North American Datum of 1927 (NAD 27) as currently required by the Mass Media Bureau of the FCC.

Ownership: ION Media Networks Inc., Debtor in Possession (Group Owner).

Began Operation: April 1, 2004. Began analog operations: June 16, 1989. Sale to Urban Television LLC pends. Involuntary assignment to debtor in possession status approved by FCC June 5, 2009. Transfer of control by ION Media Networks Inc. from Paxson Management Corp. & Lowell W. Paxson to CIG Media LLC approved by FCC December 31, 2007. Paxson Communications Corp. became ION Media Networks Inc. on June 26, 2006. Sale to Paxson Communications Corp. by San Jacinto TV Corp. approved by FCC May 16, 1995. Ceased analog operations: June 12, 2009.

Represented (legal): Dow Lohnes PLLC.

Personnel:

Alex Stroot, Station Operations Manager.

Bob Mardock, Chief Engineer.

Wendy Weisinger, Traffic Manager.

City of License: Conroe. **Station DMA:** Houston, TX. **Rank:** 10.

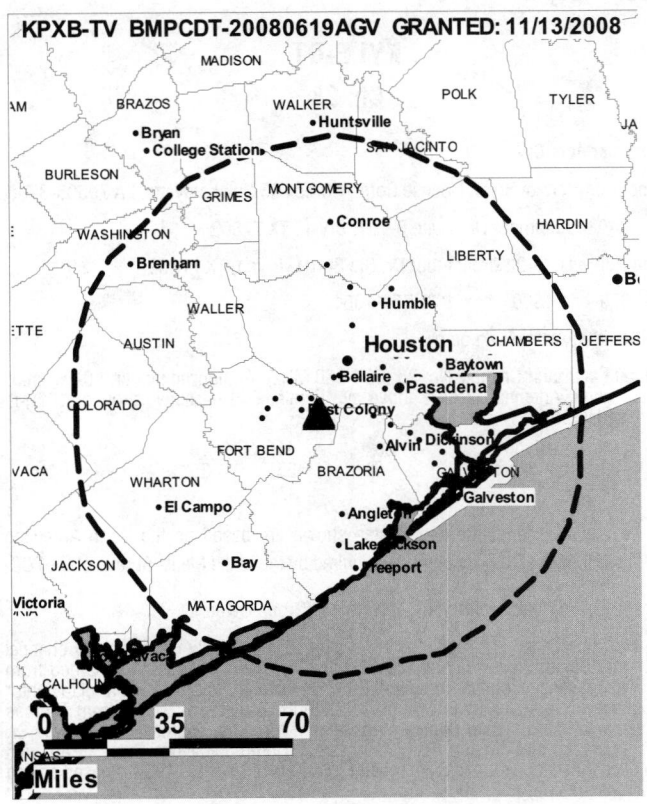

© 2010 Warren Communications News

Circulation © 2009 Nielsen. Coverage based on Nielsen study.

GrandTotal	Cable TV Households	Non-cable TV Households	Total TV Households
Estimated Station Totals *	1,064,690	705,960	1,770,650
Average Weekly Circulation (2009)	132,098	49,048	181,146
Average Daily Circulation (2009)			33,333

Station DMA Total	Cable TV Households	Non-cable TV Households	Total TV Households
Estimated Station Totals *	1,064,690	705,960	1,770,650
Average Weekly Circulation (2009)	132,098	49,048	181,146
Average Daily Circulation (2009)			33,333

*Estimated station totals are sums of the Nielsen TV and Cable TV household estimates for each county in which the station registers viewing of more than 5% as per the Nielsen Survey Methods.

KTBU-DT
Ch. 42

Network Service: IND.

Licensee: Humanity Interested Media LP, 11150 Equity Dr, Houston, TX 77041.

Studio: 11150 Equity Dr, Houston, TX 77041.

Mailing Address: 11150 Equity Dr, Houston, TX 77041.

Phone: 713-351-0755. **Fax:** 713-351-0756.

E-mail: epeterson@ktbu.tv

Web Site: http://www.ktbu.tv

Technical Facilities: Channel No. 42 (638-644 MHz). Authorized power: 1000-kw max. visual, aural. Antenna: 1959-ft above av. terrain, 1946-ft. above ground, 2020-ft. above sea level.

Latitude	29°	33'	44"
Longitude	95°	30'	35"

Note: Latitude and longitude coordinates shown are based on the North American Datum of 1927 (NAD 27) as currently required by the Mass Media Bureau of the FCC.

Ownership: Humanity Interested Media LP (Group Owner).

Began Operation: December 9, 2004. Began analog operations: July 15, 1998. Transfer by Humanity Interested Media LP from Lakewood Church to HIM GP LLC approved by FCC March 20, 2006. Transfer of control from Christ's Church of Conroe Inc. & Montgomery County Media Network Inc. to Channel 55 Broadcasting LLC approved by FCC August 4, 2004. Sale to present licensee by Imagists approved by FCC October 24, 1995. Ceased analog operations: June 12, 2009.

Represented (legal): Garvey Schubert Barer.

Personnel:

Matt Reiff, General Manager.

Phil Lonsway, General Sales Manager.

Erik Peterson, Chief Engineer.

Yvonne Beard, Program & Production Director.

Florence Martinez, Traffic Manager.

City of License: Conroe. **Station DMA:** Houston, TX. **Rank:** 10.

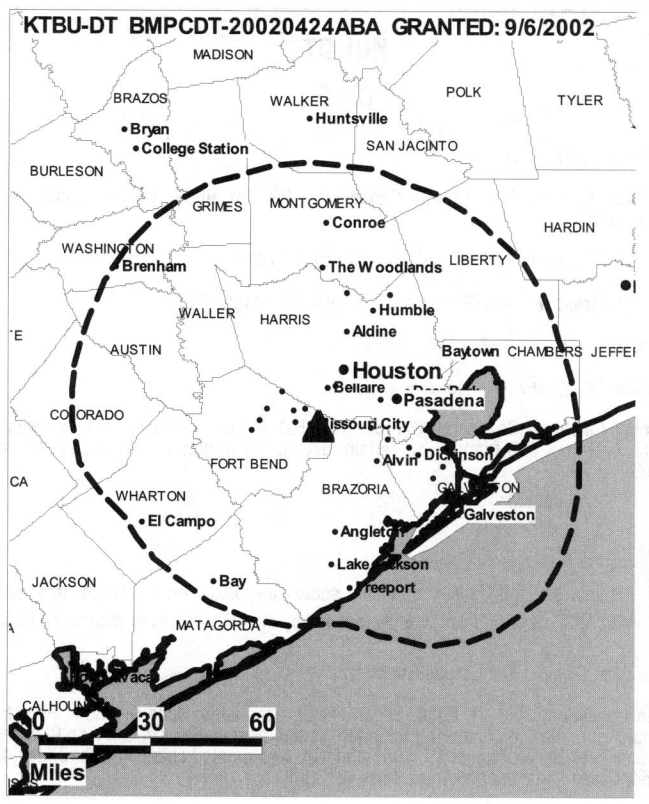

KTBU-DT BMPCDT-20020424ABA GRANTED: 9/6/2002

© 2010 Warren Communications News

Circulation © 2009 Nielsen. Coverage based on Nielsen study.

GrandTotal	Cable TV Households	Non-cable TV Households	Total TV Households
Estimated Station Totals *	1,073,130	896,560	1,969,690
Average Weekly Circulation (2009)	136,206	124,908	261,114
Average Daily Circulation (2009)			55,553

Station DMA Total	Cable TV Households	Non-cable TV Households	Total TV Households
Estimated Station Totals *	1,073,130	896,560	1,969,690
Average Weekly Circulation (2009)	136,206	124,908	261,114
Average Daily Circulation (2009)			55,553

*Estimated station totals are sums of the Nielsen TV and Cable TV household estimates for each county in which the station registers viewing of more than 5% as per the Nielsen Survey Methods.

KIII-DT
Ch. 8

Network Service: ABC.

Licensee: Channel 3 of Corpus Christi Inc., PO Box 6669, Corpus Christi, TX 78466-6669.

Studio: 5002 S Padre Island Dr, Corpus Christi, TX 78411.

Mailing Address: PO Box 6669, Corpus Christi, TX 78466-6669.

Phone: 361-986-8300. **Fax:** 361-986-8507.

Web Site: http://www.kiiitv.com

Technical Facilities: Channel No. 8 (180-186 MHz). Authorized power: 160-kw visual, aural. Antenna: 883-ft above av. terrain, 873-ft. above ground, 925-ft. above sea level.

Latitude	27°	39'	30"
Longitude	97°	36'	04"

Note: Latitude and longitude coordinates shown are based on the North American Datum of 1927 (NAD 27) as currently required by the Mass Media Bureau of the FCC.

Ownership: Channel 3 of Corpus Christi Inc.

Began Operation: July 10, 2006. Began analog operations: June 9, 1954. Prior to transfer of control to Clinton D. McKinnon, station operated as KVDO-TV on Channel 22 until it left the air August 19, 1957 and later was granted change to Ch. 3 May 4, 1964. Ceased analog operations: June 12, 2009.

Represented (legal): Cohn & Marks LLP.

Represented (sales): Continental Television Sales.

Personnel:

Michael McKinnon, President.

Dick Drilling, Vice President & General Manager.

Richard Longoria, News Director.

Ralph Quiroz, Chief Engineer.

Scott Jones, Operations Manager.

Paula Tilton, Traffic Manager.

Larry Hogue, Regional Sales Manager.

Bill Beck, Local Sales Manager.

Joe Hopkins, Business Manager.

City of License: Corpus Christi. **Station DMA:** Corpus Christi, TX. **Rank:** 129.

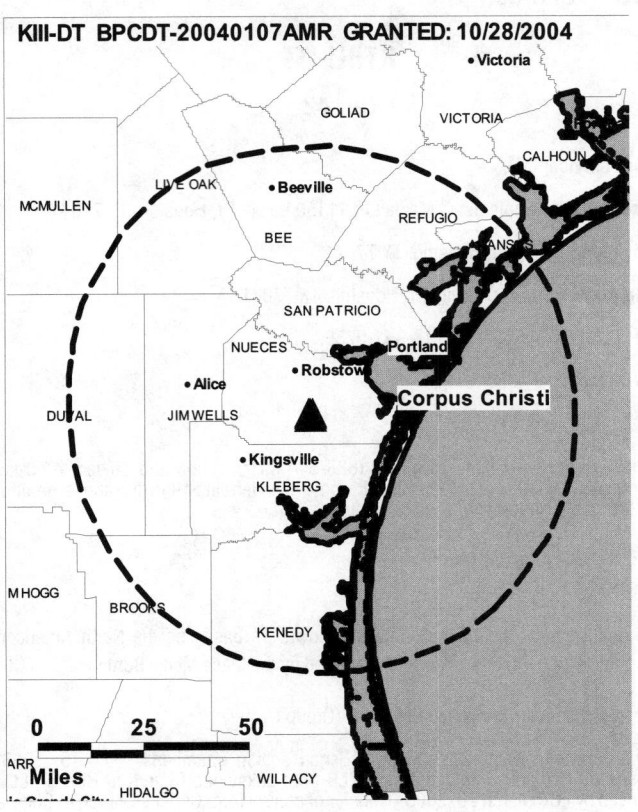

KIII-DT BPCDT-20040107AMR GRANTED: 10/28/2004

© 2010 Warren Communications News

Circulation © 2009 Nielsen. Coverage based on Nielsen study.

GrandTotal	Cable TV Households	Non-cable TV Households	Total TV Households
Estimated Station Totals *	129,550	68,760	198,310
Average Weekly Circulation (2009)	94,603	43,012	137,615
Average Daily Circulation (2009)			79,877

Station DMA Total	Cable TV Households	Non-cable TV Households	Total TV Households
Estimated Station Totals *	126,670	68,760	195,430
Average Weekly Circulation (2009)	93,915	43,012	136,927
Average Daily Circulation (2009)			79,762

Other DMA Total	Cable TV Households	Non-cable TV Households	Total TV Households
Estimated Station Totals *	2,880	0	2,880
Average Weekly Circulation (2009)	688	0	688
Average Daily Circulation (2009)			115

*Estimated station totals are sums of the Nielsen TV and Cable TV household estimates for each county in which the station registers viewing of more than 5% as per the Nielsen Survey Methods.

KORO-DT
Ch. 27

Network Service: UNV.

Licensee: Entravision Holdings LLC, 2425 Olympic Blvd, Ste 6000 W, Santa Monica, CA 90404.

Studio: 102 N. Mesquite, Corpus Christi, TX 78401.

Mailing Address: PO Box 2667, Corpus Christi, TX 78403.

Phone: 361-883-2823. **Fax:** 361-883-2931.

Web Site: http://www.koro.entravision.com/p956.html

Technical Facilities: Channel No. 27 (548-554 MHz). Authorized power: 1000-kw max. visual, aural. Antenna: 943-ft above av. terrain, 934-ft. above ground, 994-ft. above sea level.

Latitude	27°	42'	27.9"
Longitude	97°	37'	59"

Note: Latitude and longitude coordinates shown are based on the North American Datum of 1927 (NAD 27) as currently required by the Mass Media Bureau of the FCC.

Ownership: Entravision Communications Corp. (Group Owner).

Began Operation: June 26, 2006. Began analog operations: April 13, 1977. Ceased analog operations: June 12, 2009.

Personnel:

Anita Saenz-Carvalho, General Manager.

Neyla Barajas, General & Local Sales Manager.

Angel Covarrbuias, News Director.

Alan Hejl, Chief Engineer.

Emma Muniz, Business Manager.

Miracal McGill, Program Director & Traffic Manager.

Russell Rodriguez, Production Manager.

Lorena Portillo, Creative Services Director.

City of License: Corpus Christi. **Station DMA:** Corpus Christi, TX. **Rank:** 129.

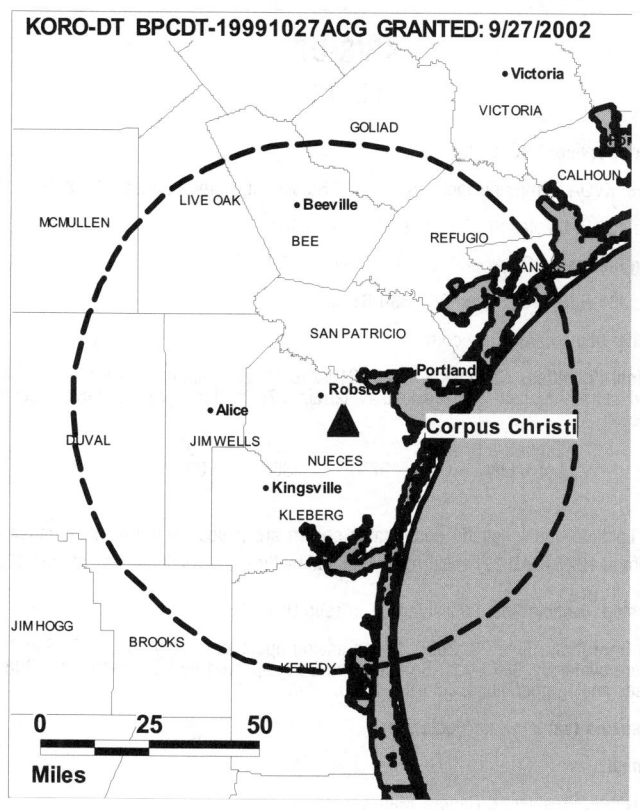

KORO-DT BPCDT-19991027ACG GRANTED: 9/27/2002

© 2010 Warren Communications News

Circulation © 2009 Nielsen. Coverage based on Nielsen study.

GrandTotal	Cable TV Households	Non-cable TV Households	Total TV Households
Estimated Station Totals *	122,310	61,040	183,350
Average Weekly Circulation (2009)	20,156	10,116	30,272
Average Daily Circulation (2009)			18,432

Station DMA Total	Cable TV Households	Non-cable TV Households	Total TV Households
Estimated Station Totals *	122,310	61,040	183,350
Average Weekly Circulation (2009)	20,156	10,116	30,272
Average Daily Circulation (2009)			18,432

*Estimated station totals are sums of the Nielsen TV and Cable TV household estimates for each county in which the station registers viewing of more than 5% as per the Nielsen Survey Methods.

KRIS-DT
Ch. 13

Network Service: NBC, CW.

Grantee: KVOA Communications Inc., 409 S Staples St, Corpus Christi, TX 78401.

Studio: 409 S. Staples St., Corpus Christi, TX 78401.

Mailing Address: PO Box 840, Corpus Christi, TX 78403.

Phone: 361-886-6100. **Fax:** 361-886-6175.

Web Site: http://www.kristv.com

Technical Facilities: Channel No. 13 (210-216 MHz). Authorized power: 46.1-kw visual, aural. Antenna: 786-ft above av. terrain, 775-ft. above ground, 836-ft. above sea level.

Latitude	27°	44'	29”
Longitude	97°	36'	09”

Note: Latitude and longitude coordinates shown are based on the North American Datum of 1927 (NAD 27) as currently required by the Mass Media Bureau of the FCC.

Ownership: Evening Post Publishing Co. (Group Owner).

Began Operation: June 28, 2006. Began analog operations: May 25, 1956. Sale to present owner by Gulf Coast Broadcasting Co. approved by FCC August 7, 1998. Ceased analog operations: June 12, 2009.

Represented (sales): Katz Media Group.

Personnel:

Tim Noble, President & General Manager.

Bob Cleary, National Sales Manager.

Don Grubaugh, Regional Sales Manager.

Sandra Richards, News Director.

Steve West, Chief Engineer.

Alice Galindo, Business Manager.

Joyce Appleby, Program Director.

Jonathan Sosa, Promotion Director.

Madeleine Kerr, Traffic Manager.

Meredith Coplen, New Media Director.

City of License: Corpus Christi. **Station DMA:** Corpus Christi, TX. **Rank:** 129.

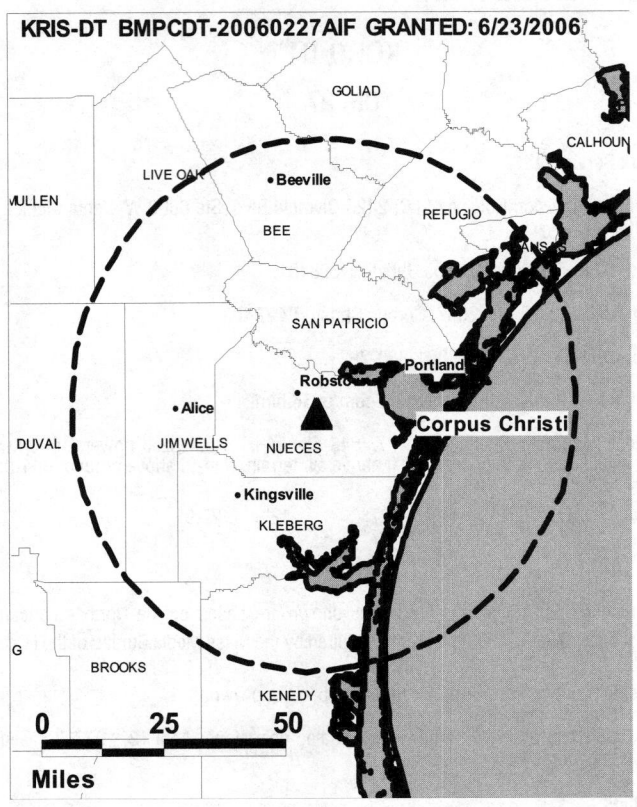

KRIS-DT BMPCDT-20060227AIF GRANTED: 6/23/2006

© 2010 Warren Communications News

Circulation © 2009 Nielsen. Coverage based on Nielsen study.

GrandTotal	Cable TV Households	Non-cable TV Households	Total TV Households
Estimated Station Totals *	126,670	68,760	195,430
Average Weekly Circulation (2009)	88,803	44,326	133,129
Average Daily Circulation (2009)			70,486

Station DMA Total	Cable TV Households	Non-cable TV Households	Total TV Households
Estimated Station Totals *	126,670	68,760	195,430
Average Weekly Circulation (2009)	88,803	44,326	133,129
Average Daily Circulation (2009)			70,486

*Estimated station totals are sums of the Nielsen TV and Cable TV household estimates for each county in which the station registers viewing of more than 5% as per the Nielsen Survey Methods.

KUQI-DT
Ch. 38

Network Service: FOX.

Grantee: High Maintenance Broadcasting LLC, 600 Leopard St, Ste 1924, Corpus Christi, TX 78473.

Studio: 600 Leopard St, Ste 1924, Corpus Christi, TX 78473.

Mailing Address: 600 Leopard St, Ste 1924, Corpus Christi, TX 78473.

Phone: 361-882-1414. **Fax:** 361-882-1973.

E-mail: fred@ktov.com

Technical Facilities: Channel No. 38 (614-620 MHz). Authorized power: 50-kw max. visual, aural. Antenna: 810-ft above av. terrain, 794-ft. above ground, 855-ft. above sea level.

Latitude	27°	45'	31.8"
Longitude	97°	36'	26.3"

Note: Latitude and longitude coordinates shown are based on the North American Datum of 1927 (NAD 27) as currently required by the Mass Media Bureau of the FCC.

Ownership: High Maintenance Broadcasting LLC.

Began Operation: February 16, 2009. Station broadcasting digitally on its analog channel allotment. Began full power analog operations: January 3, 2008; station initially launched at reduced power November 11, 2007. Sale to present owner by Minority Media TV 38 LLC approved by FCC February 8, 2008. Involuntary transfer of control by Minority Media TV 38 LLC from majority owners John Myrl Warren & Phillip Wright to Lee W. Shubert, Receiver approved by FCC May 4, 2006. Ceased analog operations: February 16, 2009.

Personnel:

Don Gillis, General Manager.

Fred Hoffmann, Chief Engineer.

Andrea Rhum, National Sales Manager.

Lori Hoffman, Regional Sales Manager.

Margaret Rodriguez, Traffic Manager.

Patrick Cage, Local Sales Manager.

City of License: Corpus Christi. **Station DMA:** Corpus Christi, TX. **Rank:** 129.

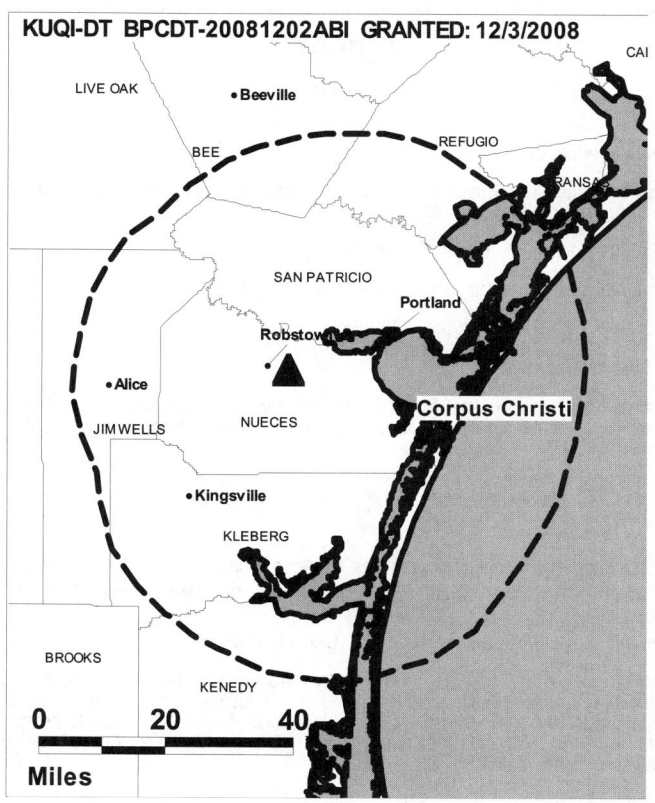

© 2010 Warren Communications News

Circulation © 2009 Nielsen. Coverage based on Nielsen study.

GrandTotal	Cable TV Households	Non-cable TV Households	Total TV Households
Estimated Station Totals *	126,670	67,890	194,560
Average Weekly Circulation (2009)	36,479	15,579	52,058
Average Daily Circulation (2009)			12,390

Station DMA Total	Cable TV Households	Non-cable TV Households	Total TV Households
Estimated Station Totals *	126,670	67,890	194,560
Average Weekly Circulation (2009)	36,479	15,579	52,058
Average Daily Circulation (2009)			12,390

*Estimated station totals are sums of the Nielsen TV and Cable TV household estimates for each county in which the station registers viewing of more than 5% as per the Nielsen Survey Methods.

KZTV-DT
Ch. 10

Network Service: CBS.

Licensee: Eagle Creek Broadcasting of Corpus Christi LLC, 2111 University Park Dr, Ste 650, Okemos, MI 48864-6913.

Studio: 301 Artesian St., Corpus Christi, TX 78401.

Mailing Address: 301 Artesian St, Corpus Christi, TX 78401.

Phone: 361-883-7070. **Fax:** 361-882-8553.

Web Site: http://www.kztv10.com

Technical Facilities: Channel No. 10 (192-198 MHz). Authorized power: 13.5-kw visual, aural. Antenna: 951-ft above av. terrain, 942-ft. above ground, 1002-ft. above sea level.

Latitude	37°	42'	28"
Longitude	97°	37'	59"

Note: Latitude and longitude coordinates shown are based on the North American Datum of 1927 (NAD 27) as currently required by the Mass Media Bureau of the FCC.

Ownership: Eagle Creek Broadcasting LLC (Group Owner).

Began Operation: February 16, 2007. Station broadcasting digitally on its analog channel allotment. Began analog operations: September 30, 1956. Sale to SagamoreHill of Corpus Christi Licenses LLC (Louis Wall) pends. Sale to present owner by K-SIX Television Inc. approved by FCC June 13, 2002. Ceased analog operations: June 12, 2009.

Represented (legal): Leventhal, Senter & Lerman PLLC.

Represented (sales): Katz Media Group.

Personnel:

Billy Brotherton, President, General Manager & Program Director.

Shelly Langhan, General Sales Manager.

Hollis Grizzard, News Director.

Russell Vaughn, Chief Engineer.

John David, Business Manager.

Wade Capps, Promotion Director.

Sherry Lemerond, Traffic Manager.

City of License: Corpus Christi. **Station DMA:** Corpus Christi, TX. **Rank:** 129.

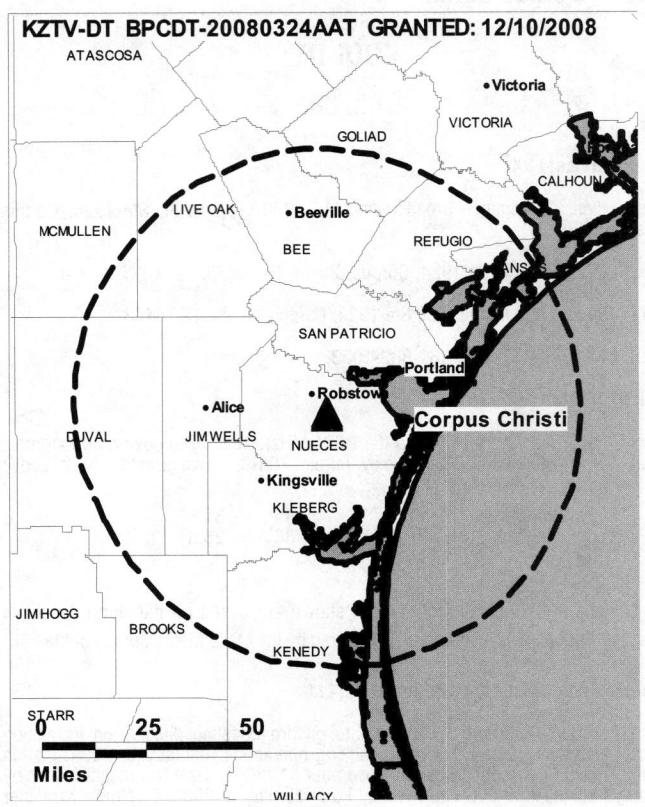

© 2010 Warren Communications News

Circulation © 2009 Nielsen. Coverage based on Nielsen study.

GrandTotal	Cable TV Households	Non-cable TV Households	Total TV Households
Estimated Station Totals *	126,670	68,760	195,430
Average Weekly Circulation (2009)	77,959	38,894	116,853
Average Daily Circulation (2009)			54,749

Station DMA Total	Cable TV Households	Non-cable TV Households	Total TV Households
Estimated Station Totals *	126,670	68,760	195,430
Average Weekly Circulation (2009)	77,959	38,894	116,853
Average Daily Circulation (2009)			54,749

*Estimated station totals are sums of the Nielsen TV and Cable TV household estimates for each county in which the station registers viewing of more than 5% as per the Nielsen Survey Methods.

KDAF-DT
Ch. 32

Network Service: IND, CW.

Licensee: Tribune Television Co., Debtor-In-Possession, 8001 John W Carpenter Frwy, Dallas, TX 75247.

Studio: 8001 John W Carpenter Frwy, Dallas, TX 75247.

Mailing Address: 8001 John W Carpenter Frwy, Dallas, TX 75247.

Phone: 214-252-9233. **Fax:** 214-252-3379.

Web Site: http://cw33.trb.com

Technical Facilities: Channel No. 32 (578-584 MHz). Authorized power: 780-kw max. visual, aural. Antenna: 1762-ft above av. terrain, 1608-ft. above ground, 2422-ft. above sea level.

Latitude	32°	32'	35"
Longitude	96°	57'	32"

Holds CP for change to 1000-kw max. visual, 1762-ft above av. terrain, 1608-ft. above ground, 2421-ft. above sea level; BPCDT-20080620AET.

Transmitter: 2133 Tar Rd., Cedar Hill.

Note: Latitude and longitude coordinates shown are based on the North American Datum of 1927 (NAD 27) as currently required by the Mass Media Bureau of the FCC.

Ownership: Tribune Broadcasting Co., Debtor-In-Possession (Group Owner).

Began Operation: May 11, 2005. Standard Definition. Began analog operations: September 29, 1980. Involuntary assignment to debtor-in-possession status approved by FCC December 24, 2008. Transfer of control from public shareholders of the Tribune Co. to Tribune Employee Stock Ownership Plan approved by FCC November 30, 2007. Sale to present owner by Renaissance Communications Corp. approved by FCC March 20, 1997 (Television Digest, Vol. 36:28; 37:12, 13). Sale to Renaissance Communications Corp. by Fox Television Stations Inc. approved by FCC June 7, 1995 (Vol. 34:48). Sale to Fox Television Stations by Metromedia approved by FCC November 14, 1985. Sale to Metromedia by Sheldon K. Turner and Nolanda Turner Hill approved by FCC November 8, 1983. Ceased analog operations: June 12, 2009.

Represented (legal): Sidley Austin LLP.

Represented (sales): MMT Sales Inc.

Represented (engineering): du Treil, Lundin & Rackley Inc.

Personnel:

Joseph A. Young, Vice President & General Manager.

Steve McDonald, General Sales Manager.

Christopher Daly, Local Sales Manager.

Eric Jasper, Marketing Manager.

David Duitch, News Director.

Roger Vertrees, Creative Services Director.

Rick J. Anderson, Chief Engineer.

Carolyn Hudspeth, Controller.

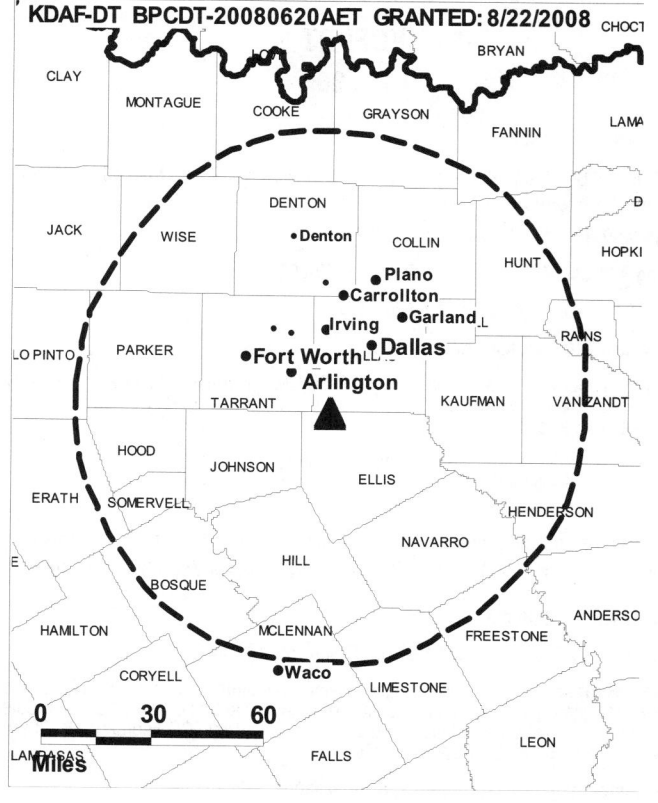

© 2010 Warren Communications News

City of License: Dallas. **Station DMA:** Dallas-Fort Worth, TX. **Rank:** 5.

Circulation © 2009 Nielsen. Coverage based on Nielsen study.

GrandTotal	Cable TV Households	Non-cable TV Households	Total TV Households
Estimated Station Totals *	1,032,710	1,123,360	2,156,070
Average Weekly Circulation (2009)	437,399	533,482	970,881
Average Daily Circulation (2009)			366,810

Station DMA Total	Cable TV Households	Non-cable TV Households	Total TV Households
Estimated Station Totals *	1,030,780	1,093,320	2,124,100
Average Weekly Circulation (2009)	437,191	531,234	968,425
Average Daily Circulation (2009)			366,146

Other DMA Total	Cable TV Households	Non-cable TV Households	Total TV Households
Estimated Station Totals *	1,930	30,040	31,970
Average Weekly Circulation (2009)	208	2,248	2,456
Average Daily Circulation (2009)			664

*Estimated station totals are sums of the Nielsen TV and Cable TV household estimates for each county in which the station registers viewing of more than 5% as per the Nielsen Survey Methods.

KDFI-DT
Ch. 36

Network Service: MNT.

Grantee: NW Communications of Texas Inc., 444 N Capitol St NW, Ste 740, c/o Dianne Smith (News Corp.), Washington, DC 20001.

Studio: 400 N Griffin St., Dallas, TX 75202.

Mailing Address: 400 N Griffin St, Dallas, TX 75202.

Phone: 214-720-4444. **Fax:** 214-720-3177.

Web Site: http://www.kdfi27.com

Technical Facilities: Channel No. 36 (602-608 MHz). Authorized power: 1000-kw max. visual, aural. Antenna: 1624-ft above av. terrain, 1473-ft. above ground, 2287-ft. above sea level.

Latitude	32°	32'	36"
Longitude	96°	57'	32"

Note: Latitude and longitude coordinates shown are based on the North American Datum of 1927 (NAD 27) as currently required by the Mass Media Bureau of the FCC.

Multichannel TV Sound: Planned.

Ownership: Fox Television Holdings Inc. (Group Owner).

Began Operation: May 1, 2002. Began analog operations: January 26, 1981. Pro forma assignment of license to present owner approved by FCC July 26, 1996 Sale to present owner by New Dallas Media Inc. approved by FCC February 18, 2000. Ceased analog operations: June 12, 2009.

Represented (legal): Skadden, Arps, Slate, Meagher & Flom LLP.

Personnel:

Kathy Saunders, Vice President & General Manager.

Andy Alexander, Vice President, Programming & Research.

John Kukla, Vice President, Creative Services.

Mark LeValley, Vice President, Engineering.

Dennis Welsh, Vice President & Sales Director.

Marie Fuhrken, Vice President, Finance.

Jeff Gurley, Vice President & General Sales Manager.

Jarrett Hale, Local Sales Manager.

Joe Foster, Local Sales Manager.

Jennifer Owen-Scott, National Sales Manager.

Mitchell West, Internet Sales Manager.

Maria Barnes, Vice President, News.

Ken Williams, Chief Engineer.

Kay Shera, Traffic Director.

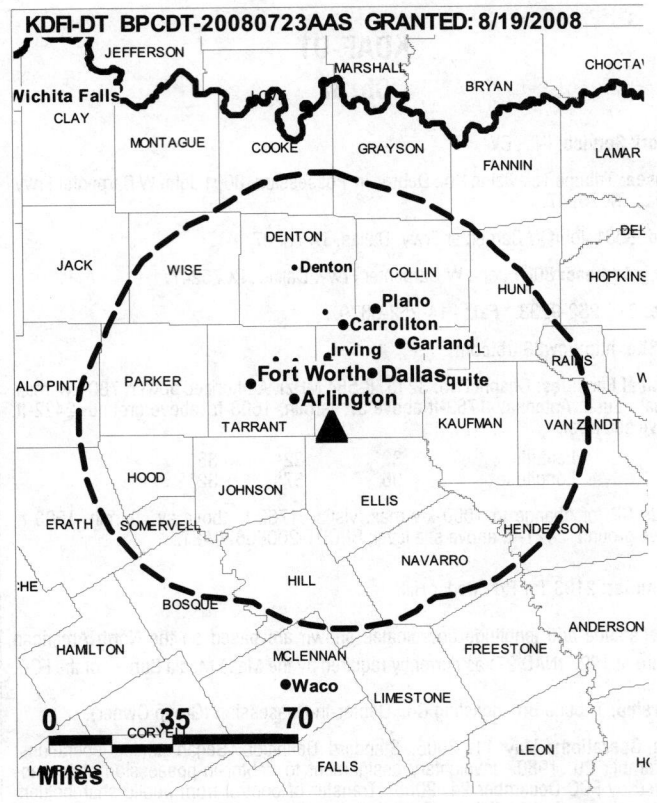

© 2010 Warren Communications News

City of License: Dallas. **Station DMA:** Dallas-Fort Worth, TX. **Rank:** 5.

Circulation © 2009 Nielsen. Coverage based on Nielsen study.

GrandTotal	Cable TV Households	Non-cable TV Households	Total TV Households
Estimated Station Totals *	1,066,740	1,106,510	2,173,250
Average Weekly Circulation (2009)	319,882	414,991	734,873
Average Daily Circulation (2009)			223,464

Station DMA Total	Cable TV Households	Non-cable TV Households	Total TV Households
Estimated Station Totals *	1,038,520	1,100,330	2,138,850
Average Weekly Circulation (2009)	315,318	414,626	729,944
Average Daily Circulation (2009)			222,677

Other DMA Total	Cable TV Households	Non-cable TV Households	Total TV Households
Estimated Station Totals *	28,220	6,180	34,400
Average Weekly Circulation (2009)	4,564	365	4,929
Average Daily Circulation (2009)			787

*Estimated station totals are sums of the Nielsen TV and Cable TV household estimates for each county in which the station registers viewing of more than 5% as per the Nielsen Survey Methods.

KDFW-DT
Ch. 35

Network Service: FOX.

Licensee: NW Communications of Texas Inc., 444 N Capitol St NW, Ste 740, c/o Dianne Smith (News Corp.), Washington, DC 20001.

Studio: 400 N Griffin St., Dallas, TX 75202.

Mailing Address: 400 N Griffin St, Dallas, TX 75202.

Phone: 214-720-4444. **Fax:** 214-720-3177.

Web Site: http://www.myfoxdfw.com

Technical Facilities: Channel No. 35 (596-602 MHz). Authorized power: 857-kw max. visual, aural. Antenna: 1699-ft above av. terrain, 1496-ft. above ground, 2306-ft. above sea level.

Latitude	32°	35'	06"
Longitude	96°	58'	41"

Holds CP for change to 1000-kw max. visual, 1673-ft above av. terrain, 1496-ft. above ground, 2305-ft. above sea level; BPCDT-20080616AAL.

Transmitter: Beltline & Mansfield Rds. intersection, Cedar Hill.

Note: Latitude and longitude coordinates shown are based on the North American Datum of 1927 (NAD 27) as currently required by the Mass Media Bureau of the FCC.

Ownership: Fox Television Holdings Inc. (Group Owner).

Began Operation: September 10, 1998. Began analog operations: December 3, 1949. Sale to Times Mirror Co. by Times Herald Printing Co. along with Dallas-Times Herald, approved by FCC May 15, 1970. Sale to Argyle Television Holding Inc. by Times Mirror Co. approved by FCC August 6, 1993. Sale to New World Communications by Argyle Television Holding Inc. approved by FCC March 31, 1995. Sale to present owner by New World Communications approved by FCC November 7, 1996. Ceased analog operations: June 12, 2009.

Represented (legal): Skadden, Arps, Slate, Meagher & Flom LLP.

Represented (engineering): Smith & Fisher.

Personnel:

Kathy Saunders, Vice President & General Manager.

Andy Alexander, Vice President, Programming & Research.

John Kukla, Vice President, Creative Services.

Marie Fuhrken, Vice President, Finance.

Dennis Welsh, Vice President, Director of Sales.

Mark LeValley, Vice President, Engineering.

Jeff Gurley, Vice President, General Sales Manager.

Jarrett Hale, Local Sales Manager.

Joe Foster, Local Sales Manager.

Maria Barrs, Vice President, News.

Jennifer Owen-Scott, National Sales Manager.

Ken Williams, Chief Engineer.

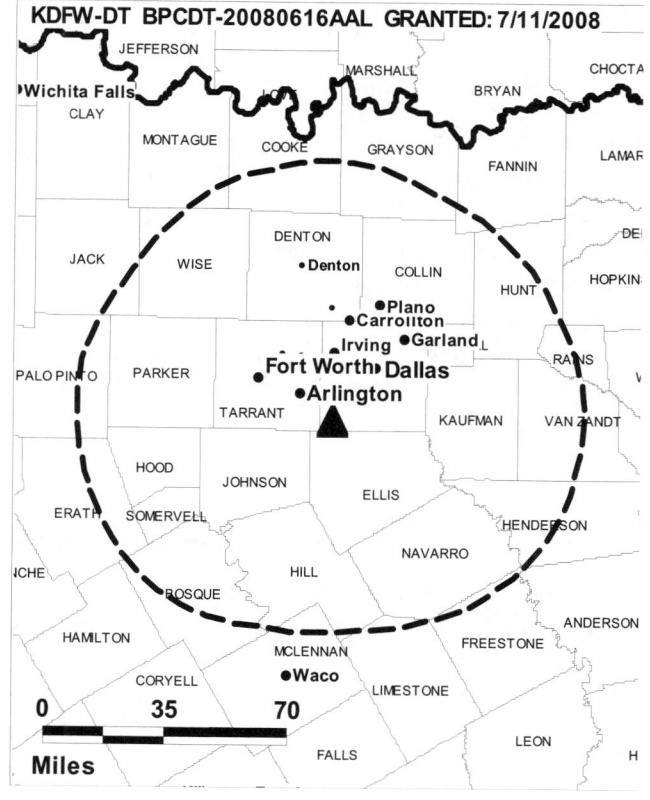

KDFW-DT BPCDT-20080616AAL GRANTED: 7/11/2008

© 2010 Warren Communications News

Kay Shera, Traffic Director.

Mitchell West, Internet Sales Manager.

City of License: Dallas. **Station DMA:** Dallas-Fort Worth, TX. **Rank:** 5.

Circulation © 2009 Nielsen. Coverage based on Nielsen study.

GrandTotal	Cable TV Households	Non-cable TV Households	Total TV Households
Estimated Station Totals *	1,153,390	1,147,660	2,301,050
Average Weekly Circulation (2009)	671,274	743,297	1,414,571
Average Daily Circulation (2009)			617,648

Station DMA Total	Cable TV Households	Non-cable TV Households	Total TV Households
Estimated Station Totals *	1,038,520	1,100,330	2,138,850
Average Weekly Circulation (2009)	642,525	734,580	1,377,105
Average Daily Circulation (2009)			606,091

Other DMA Total	Cable TV Households	Non-cable TV Households	Total TV Households
Estimated Station Totals *	114,870	47,330	162,200
Average Weekly Circulation (2009)	28,749	8,717	37,466
Average Daily Circulation (2009)			11,557

*Estimated station totals are sums of the Nielsen TV and Cable TV household estimates for each county in which the station registers viewing of more than 5% as per the Nielsen Survey Methods.

KDTX-DT
Ch. 45

Network Service: TBN.

Grantee: Trinity Broadcasting Network Inc., 2442 Michelle Dr, Tustin, CA 92780.

Studio: 2823 W Irving Blvd, Irving, TX 75061.

Mailing Address: 2823 W Irving Blvd, Irving, TX 75061.

Phone: 972-313-1333. **Fax:** 972-790-5853.

Web Site: http://www.tbn.org

Technical Facilities: Channel No. 45 (656-662 MHz). Authorized power: 1000-kw max. visual, aural. Antenna: 1621-ft above av. terrain, 1473-ft. above ground, 2287-ft. above sea level.

Latitude	32°	32'	36"
Longitude	96°	57'	32"

Note: Latitude and longitude coordinates shown are based on the North American Datum of 1927 (NAD 27) as currently required by the Mass Media Bureau of the FCC.

Ownership: Trinity Broadcasting Network Inc. (Group Owner).

Began Operation: October 1, 2002. Standard Definition. Began analog operations: February 9, 1987. Ceased analog operations: June 12, 2009.

Represented (legal): Colby M. May.

Personnel:

Steve Fjordbak, Station Manager.

Carl Young, Chief Engineer.

Alicia Garcia, Public Affairs Director.

City of License: Dallas. **Station DMA:** Dallas-Fort Worth, TX. **Rank:** 5.

TELEVISION & CABLE
Factbook Online

FULLY SEARCHABLE • CONTINUOUSLY UPDATED • DISCOUNT RATES FOR PRINT PURCHASERS

For more information call **800-771-9202** or visit **www.warren-news.com**

Digital cable and TV coverage maps.
Visit www.warren-news.com/mediaprints.htm

MediaPrints™
Map a Winning Business Strategy

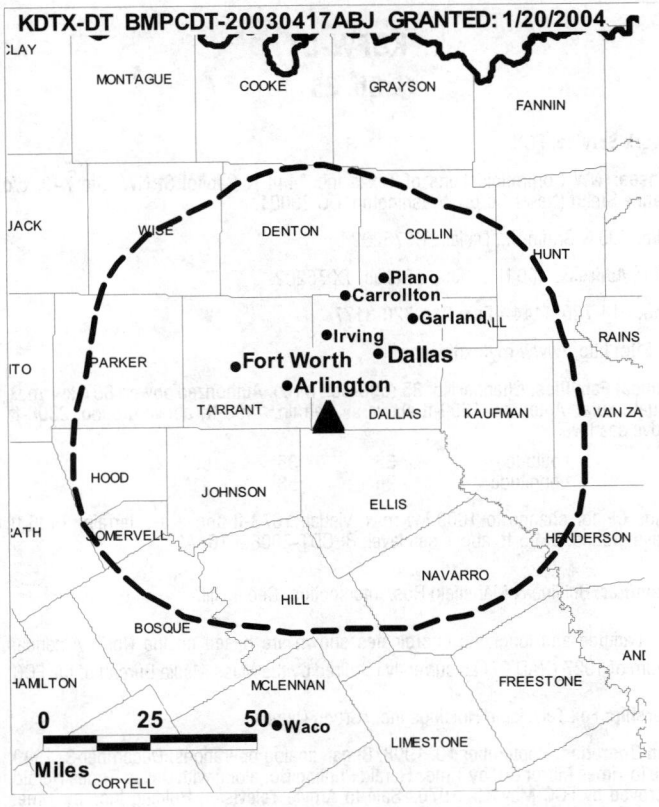

KDTX-DT BMPCDT-20030417ABJ GRANTED: 1/20/2004

© 2010 Warren Communications News

Circulation © 2009 Nielsen. Coverage based on Nielsen study.

GrandTotal	Cable TV Households	Non-cable TV Households	Total TV Households
Estimated Station Totals *	461,630	803,530	1,265,160
Average Weekly Circulation (2009)	31,936	66,178	98,114
Average Daily Circulation (2009)			21,565

Station DMA Total	Cable TV Households	Non-cable TV Households	Total TV Households
Estimated Station Totals *	455,180	803,530	1,258,710
Average Weekly Circulation (2009)	31,465	66,178	97,643
Average Daily Circulation (2009)			21,533

Other DMA Total	Cable TV Households	Non-cable TV Households	Total TV Households
Estimated Station Totals *	6,450	0	6,450
Average Weekly Circulation (2009)	471	0	471
Average Daily Circulation (2009)			32

*Estimated station totals are sums of the Nielsen TV and Cable TV household estimates for each county in which the station registers viewing of more than 5% as per the Nielsen Survey Methods.

KXTX-DT
Ch. 40

Network Service: TMO.

Grantee: NBC Telemundo License Co., 1299 Pennsylvania Ave NW, 11th Fl, c/o NBC Inc., Washington, DC 20004.

Studio: 3100 McKinnon St, Ste 800, Dallas, TX 75201.

Mailing Address: 3100 McKinnon St, Ste 800, Dallas, TX 75201.

Phone: 214-521-3900. **Fax:** 817-654-6528.

Web Site: http://www.telemundodallas.com

Technical Facilities: Channel No. 40 (626-632 MHz). Authorized power: 1000-kw max. visual, aural. Antenna: 1621-ft above av. terrain, 1430-ft. above ground, 2244-ft. above sea level.

Latitude	32°	35'	07"
Longitude	96°	58'	06"

Note: Latitude and longitude coordinates shown are based on the North American Datum of 1927 (NAD 27) as currently required by the Mass Media Bureau of the FCC.

Ownership: NBC Universal (Group Owner).

Began Operation: August 1, 2002. Standard Definition. Began analog operations: February 5, 1968 as KDTV. Donation to United States Media Corp. by Doubleday Broadcasting Co. approved by FCC November 9, 1973. Following transfer, Christian Broadcasting switched to Ch. 39 from Ch. 33, which went dark. Proposed sale to Family Group Broadcasting (Ian N. Wheeler, et al.) dismissed November 24, 1986. Sale to Southwestern Sports Television LP by United States Media Corp. approved by FCC November 13, 2000. Sale to Pappas Telecasting Companies by Southwestern Sports Television LP approved by FCC November 13, 2000 but never consummated. Sale to Telemundo Holdings Inc. by Southwestern Sports Television LP approved by FCC August 31, 2001. Transfer to present owner by Telemundo Holdings Inc. approved by FCC April 10, 2002 (Television Digest, Vol. 42:15). Ceased analog operations: June 12, 2009.

Personnel:

Manuel Abud, Vice President & General Manager.

Joe Jaime, Local Sales Manager.

Andres Chaparro, General Sales Manager.

Jose Flores, News Director.

Joe Rushing, Chief Engineer.

Maria Rios, Business Manager.

Carmen Moreno, Promotion Director.

Bryan McCall, Production Manager.

City of License: Dallas. **Station DMA:** Dallas-Fort Worth, TX. **Rank:** 5.

© 2010 Warren Communications News

Circulation © 2009 Nielsen. Coverage based on Nielsen study.

GrandTotal	Cable TV Households	Non-cable TV Households	Total TV Households
Estimated Station Totals *	853,190	891,980	1,745,170
Average Weekly Circulation (2009)	94,204	161,592	255,796
Average Daily Circulation (2009)			118,284

Station DMA Total	Cable TV Households	Non-cable TV Households	Total TV Households
Estimated Station Totals *	853,190	891,980	1,745,170
Average Weekly Circulation (2009)	94,204	161,592	255,796
Average Daily Circulation (2009)			118,284

*Estimated station totals are sums of the Nielsen TV and Cable TV household estimates for each county in which the station registers viewing of more than 5% as per the Nielsen Survey Methods.

WFAA
Ch. 8

Network Service: ABC.

Licensee: WFAA-TV Inc., 400 S Record St, Dallas, TX 75202-4806.

Studio: 606 Young St., Communications Center, Dallas, TX 75202-4810.

Mailing Address: 606 Young St, Communications Center, Dallas, TX 75202.

Phone: 214-748-9631. **Fax:** 214-977-6590.

Web Site: http://www.wfaa.com

Technical Facilities: Channel No. 8 (180-186 MHz). Authorized power: 45-kw visual, aural. Antenna: 1680-ft above av. terrain, 1499-ft. above ground, 2308-ft. above sea level.

Latitude	32°	35'	06"
Longitude	96°	58'	41"

Transmitter: 1570 W. Beltline Rd., Cedar Hill.

Note: Latitude and longitude coordinates shown are based on the North American Datum of 1927 (NAD 27) as currently required by the Mass Media Bureau of the FCC.

Satellite Earth Stations: Transmitter Harris; Scientific-Atlanta, 5.5-meter Ku-band; Scientific-Atlanta, 7-meter C-band; Scientific-Atlanta receivers.

Ownership: Belo Corp. (Group Owner).

Began Operation: February 27, 1998. Standard Definition. Station broadcasting digitally on its analog channel allotment. Began analog operations: September 17, 1949 as KBTV. Sold to present owner February 1950 (Television Digest, Vol. 6:4, 11). Ceased analog operations: June 12, 2009.

Represented (sales): TeleRep Inc.

Represented (legal): Wiley Rein LLP.

Represented (engineering): Cohen Dippell & Everist PC.

Personnel:

Mike Devlin, President & General Manager.

Deidre Davis, Human Resources Director.

Angela Betasso, Local Sales Manager.

Michael Valentine, Vice President, News.

David Johnson, Engineering Director.

Steve Kennett, Controller.

David Walther, Program Director.

James Glass, Creative Services Director.

Laura Lauskew, Traffic Manager.

Stephanie Walters, Community Relations Director.

City of License: Dallas. **Station DMA:** Dallas-Fort Worth, TX. **Rank:** 5.

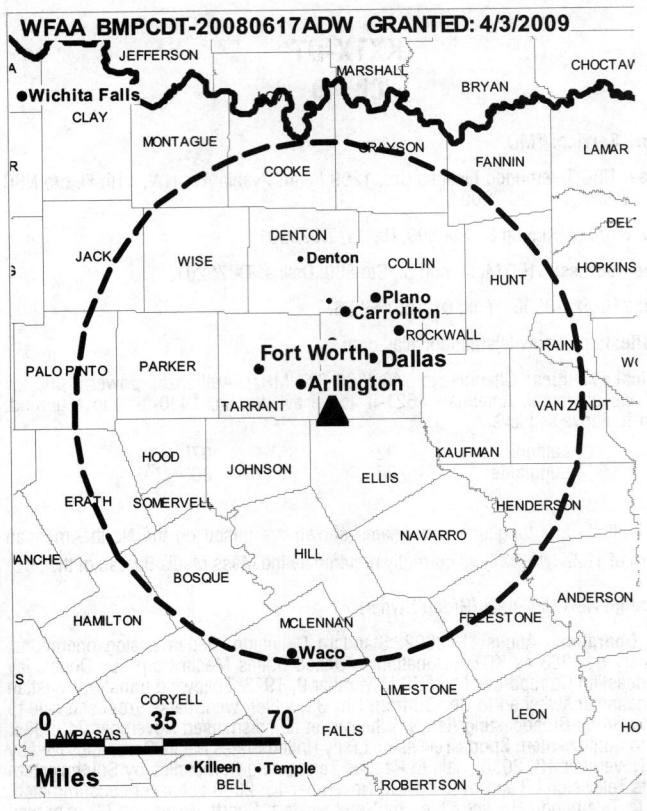

© 2010 Warren Communications News

Circulation © 2009 Nielsen. Coverage based on Nielsen study.

GrandTotal	Cable TV Households	Non-cable TV Households	Total TV Households
Estimated Station Totals *	1,195,260	1,144,620	2,339,880
Average Weekly Circulation (2009)	693,892	775,022	1,468,914
Average Daily Circulation (2009)			666,578

Station DMA Total	Cable TV Households	Non-cable TV Households	Total TV Households
Estimated Station Totals *	1,038,520	1,100,330	2,138,850
Average Weekly Circulation (2009)	652,754	767,114	1,419,868
Average Daily Circulation (2009)			651,358

Other DMA Total	Cable TV Households	Non-cable TV Households	Total TV Households
Estimated Station Totals *	156,740	44,290	201,030
Average Weekly Circulation (2009)	41,138	7,908	49,046
Average Daily Circulation (2009)			15,220

*Estimated station totals are sums of the Nielsen TV and Cable TV household estimates for each county in which the station registers viewing of more than 5% as per the Nielsen Survey Methods.

KMPX-DT
Ch. 30

Network Service: IND.

Licensee: Liberman Television of Dallas License LLC, 1845 Empire Ave, Burbank, CA 91504.

Studio: 4201 Pool Rd., Colleyville, TX 76034.

Mailing Address: 4201 Pool Rd, Colleyville, TX 76034.

Phone: 817-868-2900. **Fax:** 817-868-2929.

Web Site: http://www.kmpx29.tv

Technical Facilities: Channel No. 30 (566-572 MHz). Authorized power: 1000-kw max. visual, aural. Antenna: 1785-ft above av. terrain, 1610-ft. above ground, 2413-ft. above sea level.

Latitude	32°	35'	19"
Longitude	96°	58'	05"

Note: Latitude and longitude coordinates shown are based on the North American Datum of 1927 (NAD 27) as currently required by the Mass Media Bureau of the FCC.

Ownership: Liberman Broadcasting Inc. (Group Owner).

Began Operation: March 17, 2006. Began analog operations: September 15, 1993. Sale to present owner by Word of God Fellowship Inc. approved by FCC October 24, 2003. Ceased analog operations: June 12, 2009.

Represented (legal): Wiley Rein LLP.

Personnel:

Rosa Cuellar-Khraish, General Manager.

Michael Greenspan, National Sales Manager.

Boone Nerren, Regional Sales Manager.

Carlos Alba, Production Director.

Thuy Morahan, Marketing Director.

Dick Liebert, Chief Engineer.

Esmeralda Morales, Business Manager.

Steve Rodriguez, Traffic Manager.

Anthony Guitierrez, Promotions Director.

City of License: Decatur. **Station DMA:** Dallas-Fort Worth, TX. **Rank:** 5.

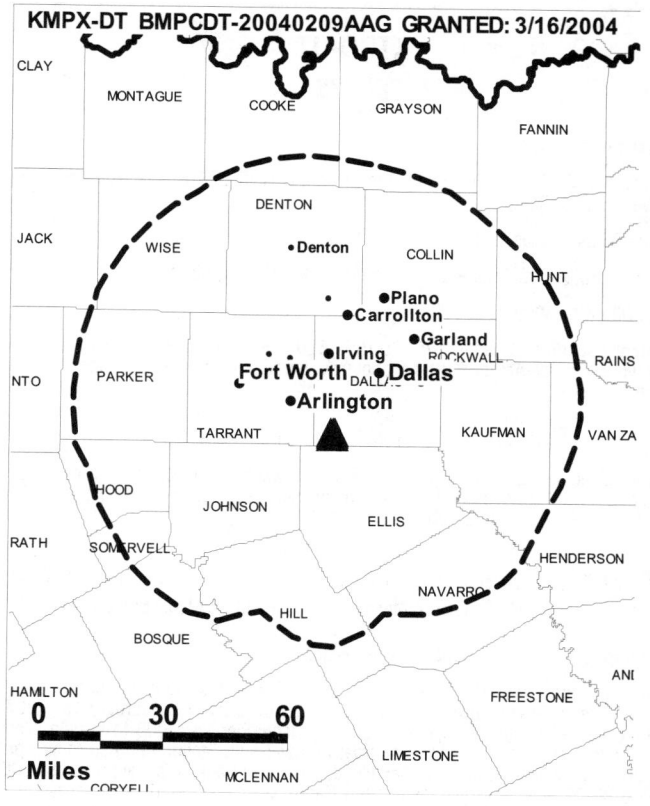

© 2010 Warren Communications News

Circulation © 2009 Nielsen. Coverage based on Nielsen study.

GrandTotal	Cable TV Households	Non-cable TV Households	Total TV Households
Estimated Station Totals *	704,620	796,660	1,501,280
Average Weekly Circulation (2009)	71,697	163,602	235,299
Average Daily Circulation (2009)			104,949

Station DMA Total	Cable TV Households	Non-cable TV Households	Total TV Households
Estimated Station Totals *	704,620	796,660	1,501,280
Average Weekly Circulation (2009)	71,697	163,602	235,299
Average Daily Circulation (2009)			104,949

*Estimated station totals are sums of the Nielsen TV and Cable TV household estimates for each county in which the station registers viewing of more than 5% as per the Nielsen Survey Methods.

KTRG-DT
Ch. 28

Network Service: IND.

Grantee: SATV 10 LLC, Debtor in Possession, 10155 Collins Ave, Ste 1505, Bal Harbour, FL 33154.

Studio: 80 Las Palmas, Del Rio, TX 78841.

Mailing Address: 203 Saint Peter St., Del Rio, TX 78840-4282.

Phone: 830-488-5093.

Technical Facilities: Channel No. 28 (554-560 MHz). Authorized power: 1000-kw max. visual, aural. Antenna: 328-ft above av. terrain, 282-ft. above ground, 1339-ft. above sea level.

| Latitude | 29° | 20' | 39" |
| Longitude | 100° | 51' | 39" |

Requests modification of CP for change to 265-kw max. visual, 2211-ft above av. terrain, 1968-ft. above ground, 3665-ft. above sea level; lat. 29° 28' 10", long. 99° 56' 29", BMPCDT-20080618ACC.

Note: Latitude and longitude coordinates shown are based on the North American Datum of 1927 (NAD 27) as currently required by the Mass Media Bureau of the FCC.

Ownership: SATV 10 LLC, Debtor in Possession.

Began Operation: June 12, 2009. Began analog operations: June 1, 1998. Sale to present owner by Ortiz Broadcasting Corp. approved by FCC February 15, 2007. Station granted Special Temporary Authority December 28, 2005 to remain silent during relocation of facilties to an alternative tower site. Station returned to air April 11, 2008. Involuntary transfer to Ben Floyd, Trustee In Bankruptcy, approved by FCC April 6, 2005. Involuntary transfer from Carlos Ortiz (deceased) to Aracelis Ortiz, Executrix of Carlos Ortiz Estate, approved by FCC March 16, 2001. Sale to Ortiz Broadcasting Corp. by Republic Broadcasting Co. approved by FCC July 24, 1997. Sale to Commonwealth Broadcasting Group Inc. dismissed at request of Republic, September 16, 1996. Transfer within Republic Broadcasting Co. from M. D. Lynch to Thomas Robert Gilchrist approved by FCC September 24, 1993.Assignment to debtor in possession status approved by FCC March 12, 2009. Ceased analog operations: June 12, 2009.

Represented (legal): Rini Coran PC.

Personnel:

Marcos Guajardo, General Manager.

Wes Broadcasting, Chief Engineer.

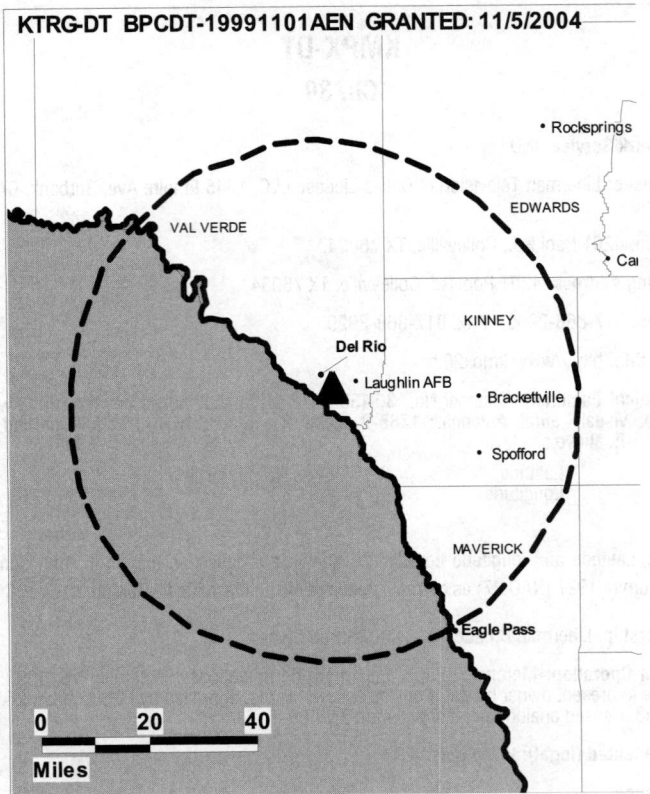

KTRG-DT BPCDT-19991101AEN GRANTED: 11/5/2004

© 2010 Warren Communications News

Paul Libovitz, General Sales Manager.

Patrice Doley, Marketing Director.

Barbara Lawrence, Program Director.

City of License: Del Rio. **Station DMA:** San Antonio, TX. **Rank:** 37.

Nielsen Data: Not available.

KVAW-DT
Ch. 18

Network Service: IND.

Licensee: Dr. Joseph A. Zavaletta, 603 E St Charles St, Brownsville, TX 78520.

Studio: 2524 N Veterans Blvd, Eagle Pass, TX 78852.

Mailing Address: 603 E St Charles St, Brownsville, TX 78520.

Phone: 830-773-3668.

Web Site: http://www.kvaw16.com

Technical Facilities: Channel No. 18 (494-500 MHz). Authorized power: 50-kw max. visual, aural. Antenna: 278-ft above av. terrain, 1063-ft. above ground, 1870-ft. above sea level.

Latitude	28°	43'	32"
Longitude	100°	28'	35"

Requests CP for change to channel number 24, 1000-kw max. visual, 1985-ft above av. terrain, 1965-ft. above ground, 2669-ft. above sea level; lat. 28° 50' 42", long. 99° 33' 22", BPCDT-20080402AAG.

Note: Latitude and longitude coordinates shown are based on the North American Datum of 1927 (NAD 27) as currently required by the Mass Media Bureau of the FCC.

Ownership: Dr. Joseph A. Zavaletta (Group Owner).

Began Operation: March 8, 2007. Began analog operations: June 15, 1991. Sale to present owner by Hispanic Television Network Inc., Debtor in Possession approved by FCC August 23, 2004. Sale to Hispanic Television Network Inc. by Juan Wheeler Jr. approved by FCC February 13, 2001. Station petitioned FCC July 2007 to remain off air due to financial difficulties. Ceased analog operations: June 12, 2009.

Represented (legal): Skadden, Arps, Slate, Meagher & Flom LLP.

Personnel:

Dr. Joseph A. Zavaletta, General Manager.

City of License: Eagle Pass. **Station DMA:** San Antonio, TX. **Rank:** 37.

TELEVISION & CABLE
Factbook Online

| continuous updates | fully searchable | easy to use |

For more information call **800-771-9202** or visit **www.warren-news.com**

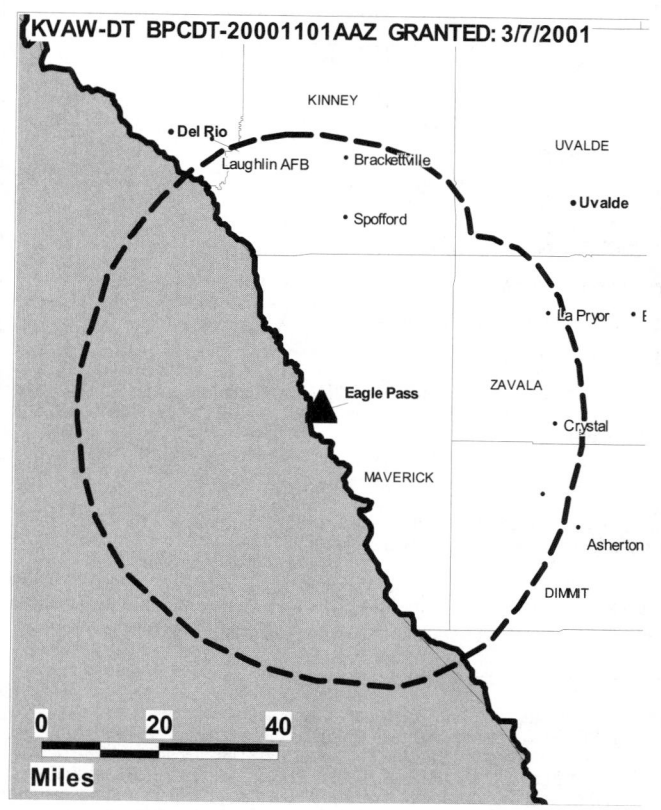

© 2010 Warren Communications News

Circulation © 2009 Nielsen. Coverage based on Nielsen study.

GrandTotal	Cable TV Households	Non-cable TV Households	Total TV Households
Estimated Station Totals *	0	4,440	4,440
Average Weekly Circulation (2009)	0	253	253
Average Daily Circulation (2009)			115

Station DMA Total	Cable TV Households	Non-cable TV Households	Total TV Households
Estimated Station Totals *	0	4,440	4,440
Average Weekly Circulation (2009)	0	253	253
Average Daily Circulation (2009)			115

*Estimated station totals are sums of the Nielsen TV and Cable TV household estimates for each county in which the station registers viewing of more than 5% as per the Nielsen Survey Methods.

KDBC-DT
Ch. 18

Network Service: MNT, CBS.

Licensee: KDBC License LLC - Debtor-in-Possession, 301 W Main St, Visalia, CA 93291.

Studio: 2201 E Wyoming Ave, El Paso, TX 79903.

Mailing Address: 2201 E Wyoming Ave, El Paso, TX 79903.

Phone: 915-496-4444. **Fax:** 915-496-4590.

Web Site: http://www.kdbc.com

Technical Facilities: Channel No. 18 (494-500 MHz). Authorized power: 363-kw max. visual, aural. Antenna: 1299-ft above av. terrain, 175-ft. above ground, 5375-ft. above sea level.

Latitude	31°	47'	46"
Longitude	106°	28'	57"

Holds CP for change to 413-kw max. visual, 1532-ft above av. terrain, 394-ft. above ground, 5594-ft. above sea level; BMPCDT-20090121ABN.

Note: Latitude and longitude coordinates shown are based on the North American Datum of 1927 (NAD 27) as currently required by the Mass Media Bureau of the FCC.

Ownership: E. Roger Williams, Trustee.

Began Operation: August 10, 2005. Began analog operations: December 14, 1952. Sale to TTBG/KDBC License Sub LLC approved by FCC July 1, 2009, but not yet consummated. Involuntary transfer of control by KDBC License LLC - Debtor-in-Possession from Harry J. Pappas, Debtor-in-Possession to E. Roger Williams, Trustee approved by FCC September 17, 2008. Assignment to debtor-in-possession status approved by FCC July 3, 2008. Sale to Pappas Telecasting Companies by Imes Communications approved by FCC January 21, 2004. Sale to Pappas Telecasting by Imes Communications approved by FCC May 31, 2000 but never consummated. Sale to Imes Communications by United Broadcasting Corp. approved by FCC May 10, 1988. Sale to United Broadcasting Corp. by El Paso TV Co. approved by FCC April 21, 1986. Sale to Evening Post Publishing Co. by Doubleday Broadcasting Co. approved by FCC August 30, 1974. Previous sale of Trigg-Vaughn station group to Doubleday approved by FCC February 1, 1967. Sale as KROD-TV-AM to Trigg-Vaughn interests by Dorrance Roderick and family, publisher of El Paso Times, approved by FCC October 29, 1959. Ceased analog operations: June 12, 2009.

Represented (legal): Davis Wright Tremaine LLP.

Represented (sales): Blair Television.

Personnel:

Bram Watkins, General Manager.

Robert Rios, National Sales Manager.

Rick Bagley, News Director.

Don Somen, Chief Engineer.

Margaret Carrillo, Business Manager.

Isabel Castillo, Program Director.

Tim Kruz, Production & Creative Services Director.

Rita Fortini, Traffic Manager.

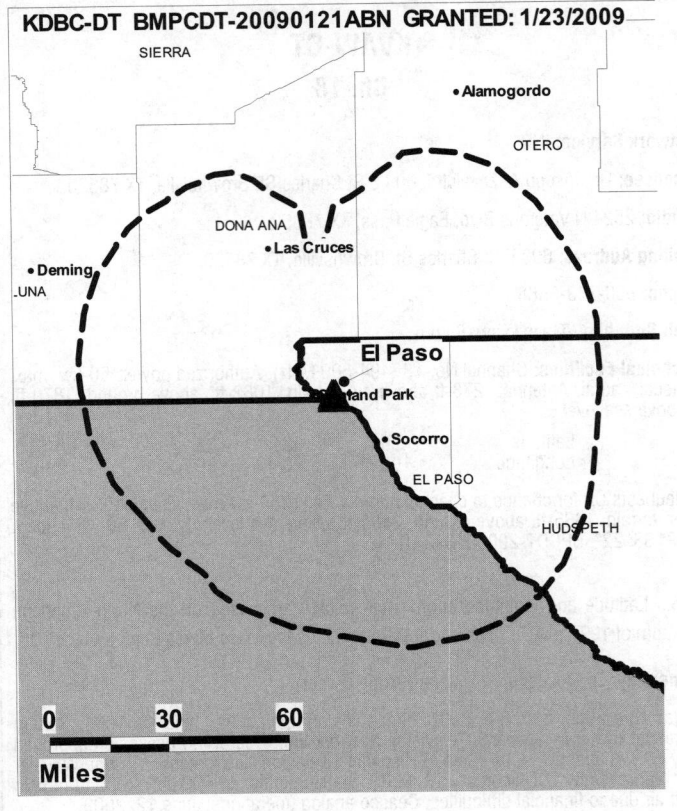

© 2010 Warren Communications News

City of License: El Paso. **Station DMA:** El Paso, TX-Las Cruces, NM. **Rank:** 98.

Circulation © 2009 Nielsen. Coverage based on Nielsen study.

GrandTotal	Cable TV Households	Non-cable TV Households	Total TV Households
Estimated Station Totals *	142,280	195,670	337,950
Average Weekly Circulation (2009)	70,494	60,634	131,128
Average Daily Circulation (2009)			59,683

Station DMA Total	Cable TV Households	Non-cable TV Households	Total TV Households
Estimated Station Totals *	133,920	172,210	306,130
Average Weekly Circulation (2009)	67,095	58,674	125,769
Average Daily Circulation (2009)			57,778

Other DMA Total	Cable TV Households	Non-cable TV Households	Total TV Households
Estimated Station Totals *	8,360	23,460	31,820
Average Weekly Circulation (2009)	3,399	1,960	5,359
Average Daily Circulation (2009)			1,905

*Estimated station totals are sums of the Nielsen TV and Cable TV household estimates for each county in which the station registers viewing of more than 5% as per the Nielsen Survey Methods.

KFOX-DT
Ch. 15

Network Service: FOX.

Licensee: KTVU Partnership, 6004 N. Mesa St, El Paso, TX 79912.

Studio: 6004 N. Mesa, El Paso, TX 79912.

Mailing Address: 6004 N. Mesa, El Paso, TX 79912.

Phone: 915-833-8585. **Fax:** 915-833-8973.

Web Site: http://www.kfoxtv.com

Technical Facilities: Channel No. 15 (476-482 MHz). Authorized power: 1000-kw max. visual, aural. Antenna: 1975-ft above av. terrain, 335-ft. above ground, 6083-ft. above sea level.

Latitude	31°	48'	55"
Longitude	106°	29'	20"

Note: Latitude and longitude coordinates shown are based on the North American Datum of 1927 (NAD 27) as currently required by the Mass Media Bureau of the FCC.

Ownership: KTVU Partnership (Group Owner).

Began Operation: October 31, 2005. Began analog operations: August 1, 1979. Sale to Santa Fe Communications & DeRance Foundation by Cristo Rey Corp. approved by FCC April 20, 1983. Sale to John Mulderrig & David Caparis approved by FCC June 17, 1988. Sale to Cox approved by FCC June 27, 1996 (Television Digest, Vol. 36:21). Ceased analog operations: June 12, 2009.

Represented (legal): Dow Lohnes PLLC.

Represented (sales): TeleRep Inc.

Personnel:

John Witte, Vice President & General Manager.

Kevin Hayes, Local Sales Manager.

Neil Henderson, National Sales Manager.

Elizabeth O'Hara, News Director.

Antonio Castro, Chief Engineer.

Candace MacBlain, Creative Services Director.

Josie Garmon, Traffic Manager.

Armando Maldonado, Business Manager.

Eddie Hernandez, Production Manager.

Nichole Villalobos, Program Director.

City of License: El Paso. **Station DMA:** El Paso, TX-Las Cruces, NM. **Rank:** 98.

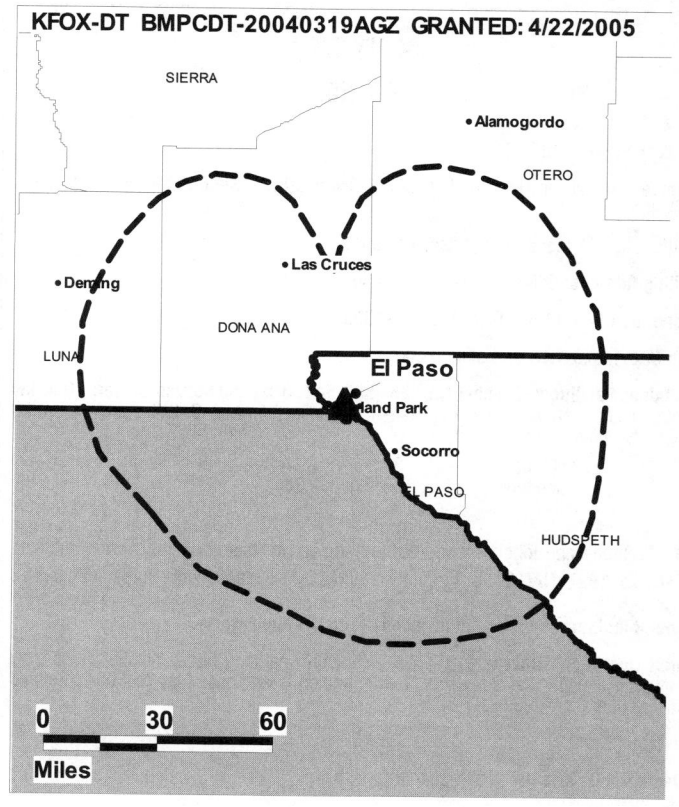

KFOX-DT BMPCDT-20040319AGZ GRANTED: 4/22/2005

© 2010 Warren Communications News

Circulation © 2009 Nielsen. Coverage based on Nielsen study.

GrandTotal	Cable TV Households	Non-cable TV Households	Total TV Households
Estimated Station Totals *	140,910	172,210	313,120
Average Weekly Circulation (2009)	74,440	83,711	158,151
Average Daily Circulation (2009)			64,891

Station DMA Total	Cable TV Households	Non-cable TV Households	Total TV Households
Estimated Station Totals *	133,920	172,210	306,130
Average Weekly Circulation (2009)	72,651	83,711	156,362
Average Daily Circulation (2009)			64,646

Other DMA Total	Cable TV Households	Non-cable TV Households	Total TV Households
Estimated Station Totals *	6,990	0	6,990
Average Weekly Circulation (2009)	1,789	0	1,789
Average Daily Circulation (2009)			245

*Estimated station totals are sums of the Nielsen TV and Cable TV household estimates for each county in which the station registers viewing of more than 5% as per the Nielsen Survey Methods.

KINT-DT
Ch. 25

Network Service: UNV.

Grantee: Entravision Holdings LLC, 2425 Olympic Blvd, Ste 6000 W, Santa Monica, CA 90404.

Studio: 5426 N. Mesa St., El Paso, TX 79912.

Mailing Address: 5426 N. Mesa St, El Paso, TX 79912.

Phone: 915-581-1126. **Fax:** 915-581-1393.

Web Site: http://www.univision26.com

Technical Facilities: Channel No. 25 (536-542 MHz). Authorized power: 1000-kw max. visual, aural. Antenna: 1441-ft above av. terrain, 316-ft. above ground, 5516-ft. above sea level.

Latitude	31°	47'	46"
Longitude	106°	28'	57"

Note: Latitude and longitude coordinates shown are based on the North American Datum of 1927 (NAD 27) as currently required by the Mass Media Bureau of the FCC.

Ownership: Entravision Communications Corp. (Group Owner).

Began Operation: November 17, 2006. Station operating under Special Temporary Authority at 1.8-kw max. visual. Began analog operations: May 5, 1984. Ceased analog operations: June 12, 2009.

Personnel:

David Candelaria, General Manager.

Diana DeLara, General Sales Manager.

Zoltan Csanyi, News Director.

Alfredo Durand, Chief Engineer.

Richard Franco, Chief Financial Officer.

Sylvia Martinez, Program Director.

Abel Rodriguez, Promotion Director.

Gilbert Martinez, Production Manager.

City of License: El Paso. **Station DMA:** El Paso, TX-Las Cruces, NM. **Rank:** 98.

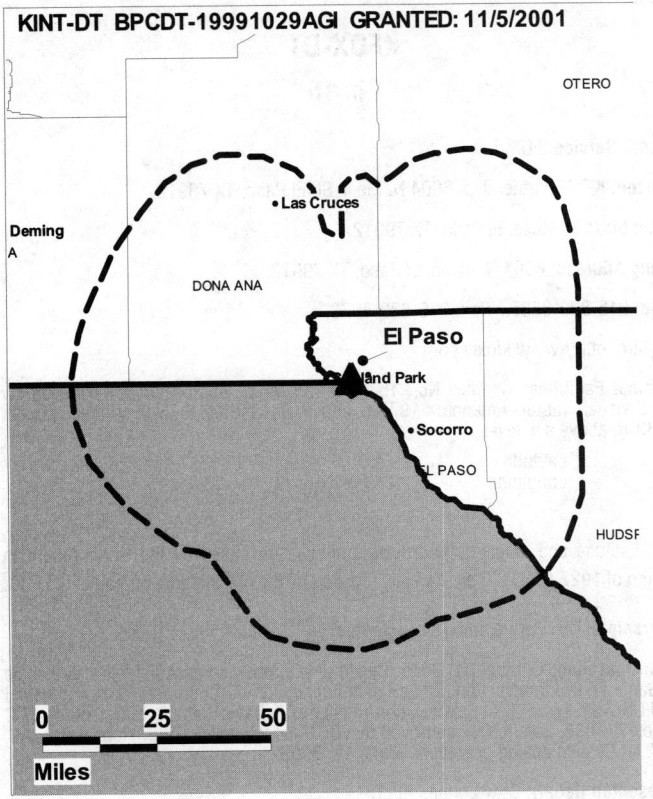

KINT-DT BPCDT-19991029AGI GRANTED: 11/5/2001

© 2010 Warren Communications News

Circulation © 2009 Nielsen. Coverage based on Nielsen study.

GrandTotal	Cable TV Households	Non-cable TV Households	Total TV Households
Estimated Station Totals *	133,920	188,490	322,410
Average Weekly Circulation (2009)	32,068	77,035	109,103
Average Daily Circulation (2009)			69,011

Station DMA Total	Cable TV Households	Non-cable TV Households	Total TV Households
Estimated Station Totals *	133,920	172,210	306,130
Average Weekly Circulation (2009)	32,068	75,912	107,980
Average Daily Circulation (2009)			68,213

Other DMA Total	Cable TV Households	Non-cable TV Households	Total TV Households
Estimated Station Totals *	0	16,280	16,280
Average Weekly Circulation (2009)	0	1,123	1,123
Average Daily Circulation (2009)			798

*Estimated station totals are sums of the Nielsen TV and Cable TV household estimates for each county in which the station registers viewing of more than 5% as per the Nielsen Survey Methods.

KTFN-DT
Ch. 51

Network Service: TEL.

Grantee: Entravision Holdings LLC, 2425 Olympic Blvd, Ste 6000 W, Santa Monica, CA 90404.

Studio: 5426 N. Mesa, El Paso, TX 79912.

Mailing Address: 5426 N. Mesa St, El Paso, TX 79912.

Phone: 915-581-1126. **Fax:** 915-585-4612.

Web Site: http://www.entravision.com

Technical Facilities: Channel No. 51 (692-698 MHz). Authorized power: 70-kw max. visual, aural. Antenna: 1723-ft above av. terrain, 190-ft. above ground, 5794-ft. above sea level.

Latitude	31°	48'	18"
Longitude	106°	28'	59"

Note: Latitude and longitude coordinates shown are based on the North American Datum of 1927 (NAD 27) as currently required by the Mass Media Bureau of the FCC.

Ownership: Entravision Communications Corp. (Group Owner).

Began Operation: November 27, 2006. Began analog operations: June 22, 1991. Ceased analog operations: June 12, 2009.

Personnel:

David Candelaria, Station Manager.

Diana De Lara, General Sales Manager.

Zoltan Csanyi, News Director.

Alfredo Durand, Chief Engineer.

Luz Ramirez, Program Director & Traffic Manager.

Gilbert Martinez, Production Manager.

City of License: El Paso. **Station DMA:** El Paso, TX-Las Cruces, NM. **Rank:** 98.

Digital cable and TV coverage maps.
Visit www.warren-news.com/mediaprints.htm

MediaPrints™
Map a Winning Business Strategy

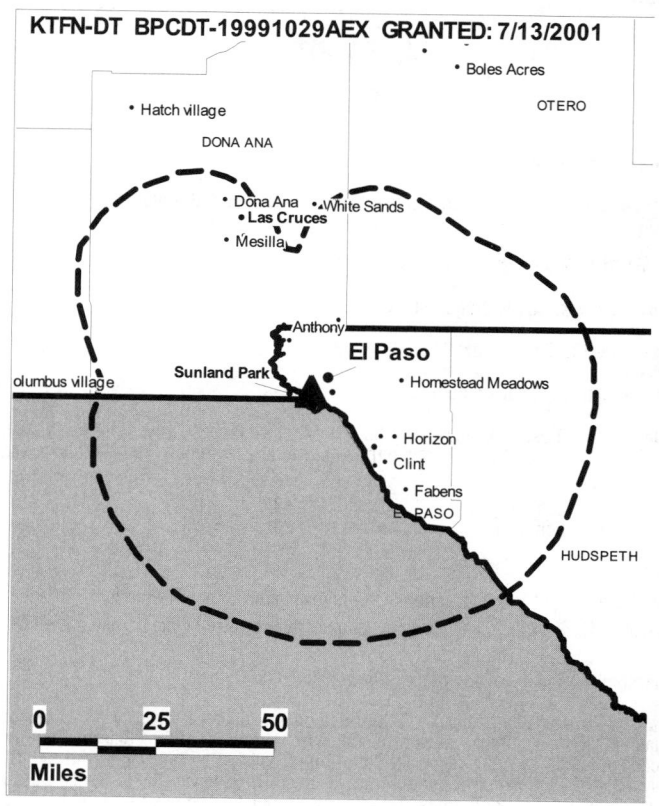

KTFN-DT BPCDT-19991029AEX GRANTED: 7/13/2001

© 2010 Warren Communications News

Circulation © 2009 Nielsen. Coverage based on Nielsen study.

GrandTotal	Cable TV Households	Non-cable TV Households	Total TV Households
Estimated Station Totals *	133,920	172,210	306,130
Average Weekly Circulation (2009)	17,540	36,013	53,553
Average Daily Circulation (2009)			21,772

Station DMA Total	Cable TV Households	Non-cable TV Households	Total TV Households
Estimated Station Totals *	133,920	172,210	306,130
Average Weekly Circulation (2009)	17,540	36,013	53,553
Average Daily Circulation (2009)			21,772

*Estimated station totals are sums of the Nielsen TV and Cable TV household estimates for each county in which the station registers viewing of more than 5% as per the Nielsen Survey Methods.

KTSM-DT
Ch. 9

Network Service: NBC.

Licensee: ComCorp of El Paso License Corp., PO Box 53708, Lafayette, LA 70505-3708.

Studio: 801 N Oregon St, El Paso, TX 79902.

Mailing Address: 801 N Oregon St, El Paso, TX 79902.

Phone: 915-532-5421. **Fax:** 915-532-6793.

Web Site: http://www.ktsm.com

Technical Facilities: Channel No. 9 (186-192 MHz). Authorized power: 34-kw visual, aural. Antenna: 1893-ft above av. terrain, 335-ft. above ground, 5964-ft. above sea level.

Latitude	31°	48'	18"
Longitude	106°	28'	57.6"

Note: Latitude and longitude coordinates shown are based on the North American Datum of 1927 (NAD 27) as currently required by the Mass Media Bureau of the FCC.

Ownership: Communications Corp. of America (Group Owner).

Began Operation: September 13, 2005. Station broadcasting digitally on its analog channel allotment. Began analog operations: January 4, 1953. Sale to Communications Corp. of America by Tri-State Broadcasting Co. Inc. approved by FCC July 23, 1997. Transfer of control from Thomas R. Galloway Sr. to Apollo Capital Management II Inc. & Thomas R. Galloway Sr. jointly approved by FCC April 16, 2004. Involuntary transfer of control to debtor in possession approved by FCC August 29, 2006. Company emerged from debtor in possession status October 4, 2007. Ceased analog operations: June 12, 2009.

Represented (sales): Katz Media Group.

Represented (legal): Dow Lohnes PLLC.

Personnel:

Gary Sotir, General Manager & Program Director.

Deb Hastings, Sales Manager.

Ernie Hartt, Engineering Director.

Kim Bridger, News Director.

Maria Saavedra, Promotion Director.

Raul Martinez, Production Manager.

Mimi Sanchez, Traffic Manager.

City of License: El Paso. **Station DMA:** El Paso, TX-Las Cruces, NM. **Rank:** 98.

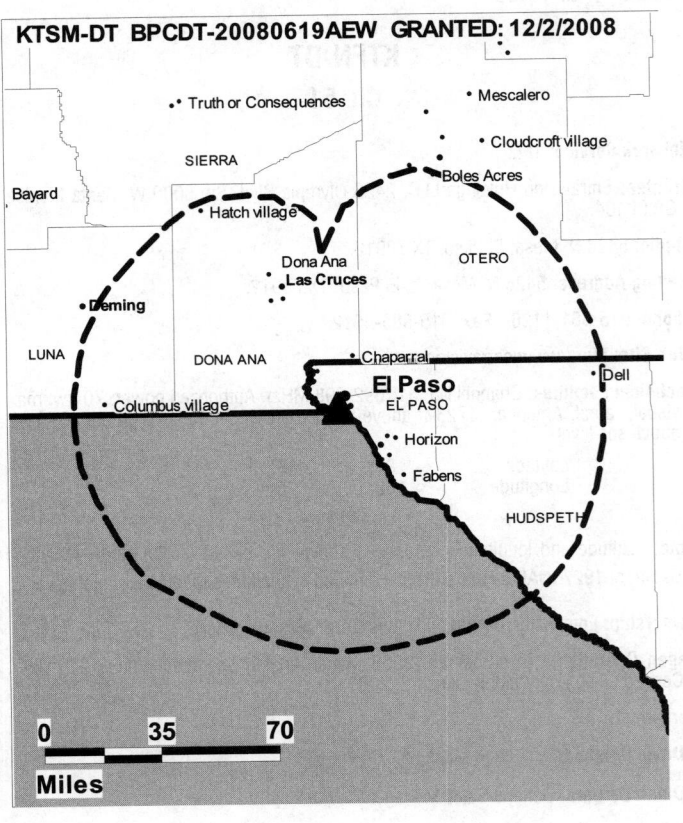

© 2010 Warren Communications News

Circulation © 2009 Nielsen. Coverage based on Nielsen study.

GrandTotal	Cable TV Households	Non-cable TV Households	Total TV Households
Estimated Station Totals *	145,340	179,390	324,730
Average Weekly Circulation (2009)	76,904	80,301	157,205
Average Daily Circulation (2009)			69,212

Station DMA Total	Cable TV Households	Non-cable TV Households	Total TV Households
Estimated Station Totals *	133,920	172,210	306,130
Average Weekly Circulation (2009)	75,032	79,368	154,400
Average Daily Circulation (2009)			68,007

Other DMA Total	Cable TV Households	Non-cable TV Households	Total TV Households
Estimated Station Totals *	11,420	7,180	18,600
Average Weekly Circulation (2009)	1,872	933	2,805
Average Daily Circulation (2009)			1,205

*Estimated station totals are sums of the Nielsen TV and Cable TV household estimates for each county in which the station registers viewing of more than 5% as per the Nielsen Survey Methods.

KVIA-DT
Ch. 7

Network Service: CW, ABC.

Licensee: NPG of Texas LP, 4140 Rio Bravo, El Paso, TX 79902.

Studio: 4140 Rio Bravo St., El Paso, TX 79902.

Mailing Address: 4140 Rio Bravo St, El Paso, TX 79902.

Phone: 915-496-7777. **Fax:** 915-532-0070.

Web Site: http://www.kvia.com

Technical Facilities: Channel No. 7 (174-180 MHz). Authorized power: 32.4-kw visual, aural. Antenna: 1942-ft above av. terrain, 335-ft. above ground, 5964-ft. above sea level.

Latitude	31°	48'	18"
Longitude	106°	28'	58"

Note: Latitude and longitude coordinates shown are based on the North American Datum of 1927 (NAD 27) as currently required by the Mass Media Bureau of the FCC.

Ownership: News Press & Gazette Co. (Group Owner).

Began Operation: February 7, 2006. Station broadcasting digitally on its analog channel allotment. Began analog operations: September 1, 1956 n Ch. 13 which is now an educational outlet. Sale to present owner by Marsh Media Inc. approved by FCC December 9, 1994. Previous sale by John B. Walton Jr. approved by FCC February 24, 1976. Sale to Walton by Joseph Harris & Norman Alexander approved by FCC January 19, 1966 (Television Digest, Vol. 6:4). Sale to Harris & Alexander by McLendon Investment Corp. approved by FCC March 20, 1957 (Vol. 13:12). Ceased analog operations: June 12, 2009.

Represented (sales): Continental Television Sales.

Personnel:

Kevin Lovell, General Manager.

Chris Swann, Operations Manager.

Dan Overstreet, National Sales Manager.

Brenda DeAnda, News Director.

Elias Ventanilla, Chief Engineer.

Mike Sepulveda, Controller.

Karla Huelga, Program & Community Relations Director.

Mark Ross, Promotion Director.

John Ross, Creative Services Director.

Kelly Rubi, Traffic Manager.

City of License: El Paso. **Station DMA:** El Paso, TX-Las Cruces, NM. **Rank:** 98.

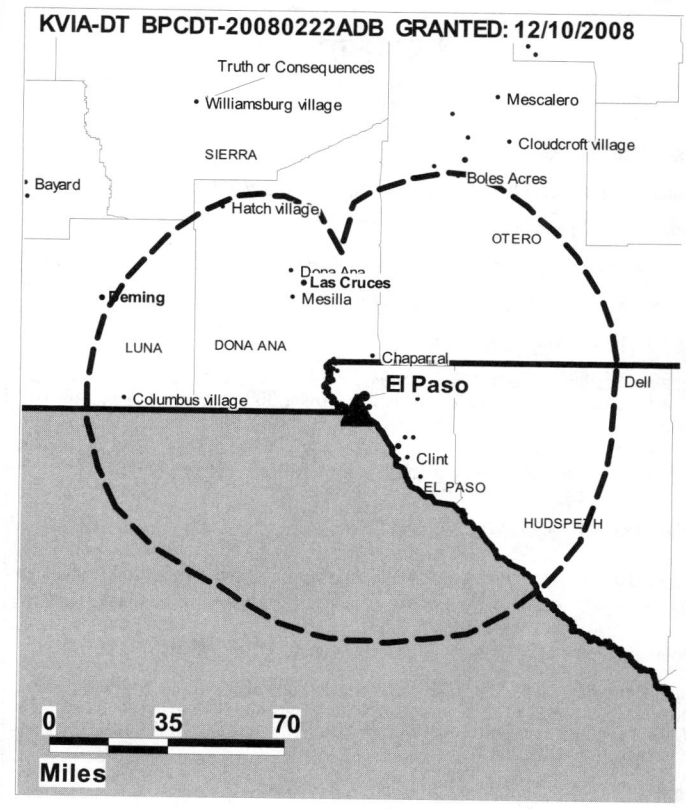

© 2010 Warren Communications News

Circulation © 2009 Nielsen. Coverage based on Nielsen study.

GrandTotal	Cable TV Households	Non-cable TV Households	Total TV Households
Estimated Station Totals *	145,340	195,670	341,010
Average Weekly Circulation (2009)	82,426	85,158	167,584
Average Daily Circulation (2009)			87,573

Station DMA Total	Cable TV Households	Non-cable TV Households	Total TV Households
Estimated Station Totals *	133,920	172,210	306,130
Average Weekly Circulation (2009)	79,113	82,348	161,461
Average Daily Circulation (2009)			84,269

Other DMA Total	Cable TV Households	Non-cable TV Households	Total TV Households
Estimated Station Totals *	11,420	23,460	34,880
Average Weekly Circulation (2009)	3,313	2,810	6,123
Average Daily Circulation (2009)			3,304

*Estimated station totals are sums of the Nielsen TV and Cable TV household estimates for each county in which the station registers viewing of more than 5% as per the Nielsen Survey Methods.

KPTF-DT
Ch. 18

Network Service: IND.

Licensee: Prime Time Christian Broadcasting Inc., PO Box 7708, Midland, TX 79708.

Studio: 2401-B N Main St, Clovis, NM 88101.

Mailing Address: 2401-B N.Main St, Clovis, NM 88101.

Phone: 505-742-1800. **Fax:** 915-563-1736.

Web Site: http://www.ptcbglc.com

Technical Facilities: Channel No. 18 (494-500 MHz). Authorized power: 50-kw max. visual, aural. Antenna: 367-ft above av. terrain, 360-ft. above ground, 4671-ft. above sea level.

Latitude	34°	25'	21"
Longitude	103°	12'	22"

Transmitter: 1.2-mi. W of U.S. 70, S of Clovis, NM.

Note: Latitude and longitude coordinates shown are based on the North American Datum of 1927 (NAD 27) as currently required by the Mass Media Bureau of the FCC.

Ownership: Prime Time Christian Broadcasting Inc. (Group Owner).

Began Operation: June 12, 2009. Began analog operations: April 1, 2001. Station broadcasting digitally on its analog channel allotment, Sale to present owner by Winstar Broadcasting Corp. approved by FCC December 23, 1999. Ceased analog operations: June 12, 2009.

Represented (engineering): du Treil, Lundin & Rackley Inc.

Personnel:

Al Cooper, General Manager.

Jeff Welters, Operations Manager.

City of License: Farwell. **Station DMA:** Amarillo, TX. **Rank:** 131.

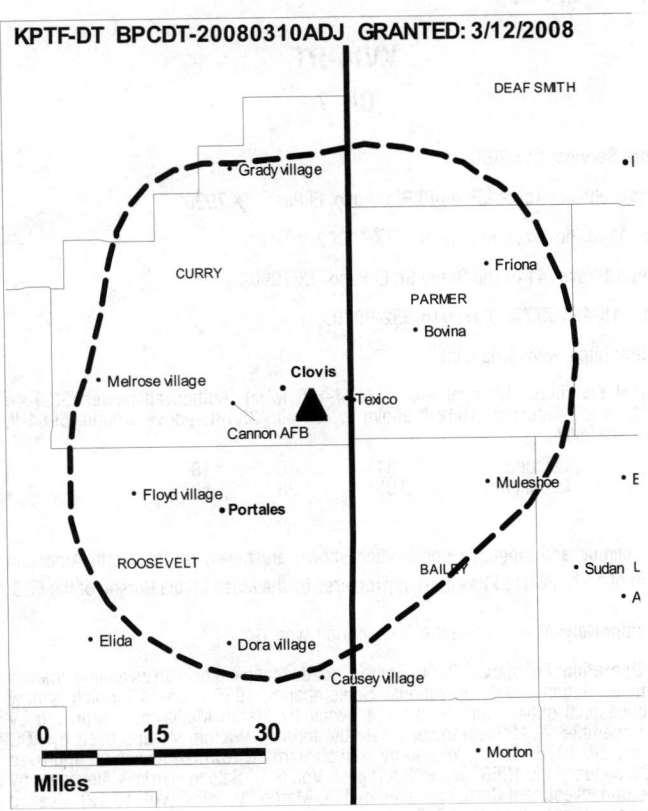

KPTF-DT BPCDT-20080310ADJ GRANTED: 3/12/2008

© 2010 Warren Communications News

Circulation © 2009 Nielsen. Coverage based on Nielsen study.

GrandTotal	Cable TV Households	Non-cable TV Households	Total TV Households
Estimated Station Totals *	24,130	10,300	34,430
Average Weekly Circulation (2009)	1,466	638	2,104
Average Daily Circulation (2009)			310

Station DMA Total	Cable TV Households	Non-cable TV Households	Total TV Households
Estimated Station Totals *	24,130	10,300	34,430
Average Weekly Circulation (2009)	1,466	638	2,104
Average Daily Circulation (2009)			310

*Estimated station totals are sums of the Nielsen TV and Cable TV household estimates for each county in which the station registers viewing of more than 5% as per the Nielsen Survey Methods.

KFWD-DT
Ch. 51

Network Service: IND.

Licensee: HIC Broadcast Inc., 606 Young St, Communications Center, Dallas, TX 75202.

Studio: 606 Young St., Dallas, TX 75202.

Mailing Address: 606 Young St, Communications Center, Dallas, TX 75202.

Phone: 214-977-6780. **Fax:** 214-977-6544.

Web Site: http://www.kfwd.tv

Technical Facilities: Channel No. 51 (692-698 MHz). Authorized power: 375-kw max. visual, aural. Antenna: 1788-ft above av. terrain, 1624-ft. above ground, 2425-ft. above sea level.

Latitude	32°	35'	19"
Longitude	96°	58'	05"

Holds CP for change to channel number 9, 55-kw visual, 1791-ft above av. terrain, 1617-ft. above ground, 2417-ft. above sea level; BMPCDT-20080620AKS.

Transmitter: 1310 Beltline Rd., 0.87-mi. W of Cedar Hill.

Note: Latitude and longitude coordinates shown are based on the North American Datum of 1927 (NAD 27) as currently required by the Mass Media Bureau of the FCC.

Ownership: HIC Broadcast Inc.

Began Operation: May 1, 2002. Standard Definition. Began analog operations: September 1, 1988. Sale to present owner by Ronald Ulloa approved by FCC February 28, 1990. Ceased analog operations: June 12, 2009.

Represented (legal): Dow Lohnes PLLC.

Represented (sales): TeleRep Inc.

Personnel:

Tony Montes, Station Manager.

Steve Brooks, Sales Director.

Derek Ozymy, Local & National Sales Manager.

Walter Chavez, Business Manager.

David Johnson, Technology Director.

City of License: Fort Worth. **Station DMA:** Dallas-Fort Worth, TX. **Rank:** 5.

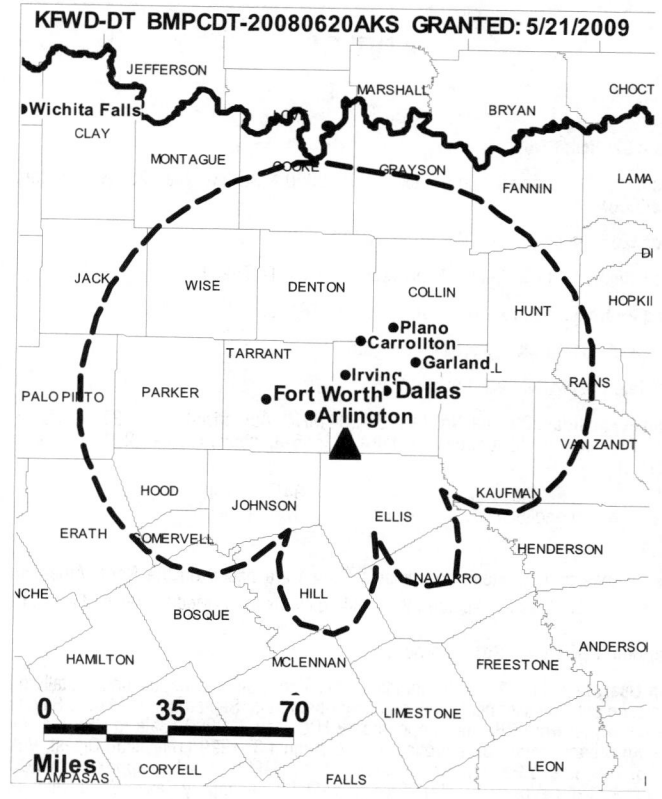

KFWD-DT BMPCDT-20080620AKS GRANTED: 5/21/2009

© 2010 Warren Communications News

Circulation © 2009 Nielsen. Coverage based on Nielsen study.

GrandTotal	Cable TV Households	Non-cable TV Households	Total TV Households
Estimated Station Totals *	1,006,210	1,076,570	2,082,780
Average Weekly Circulation (2009)	145,391	263,718	409,109
Average Daily Circulation (2009)			132,033

Station DMA Total	Cable TV Households	Non-cable TV Households	Total TV Households
Estimated Station Totals *	1,006,210	1,070,390	2,076,600
Average Weekly Circulation (2009)	145,391	263,304	408,695
Average Daily Circulation (2009)			131,940

Other DMA Total	Cable TV Households	Non-cable TV Households	Total TV Households
Estimated Station Totals *	0	6,180	6,180
Average Weekly Circulation (2009)	0	414	414
Average Daily Circulation (2009)			93

*Estimated station totals are sums of the Nielsen TV and Cable TV household estimates for each county in which the station registers viewing of more than 5% as per the Nielsen Survey Methods.

KTVT-DT
Ch. 11

Network Service: CBS.

Licensee: CBS Stations Group of Texas, L.P., 2000 K St. NW, Ste 725, Washington, DC 20006.

Studio: 5233 Bridge St., Fort Worth, TX 76103.

Dallas Office: 10111 N. Central Expressway, Dallas, TX 75231.

Mailing Address: PO Box 2495, Fort Worth, TX 76113.

Phone: 817-451-1111. **Fax:** 817-457-1897.

Web Site: http://www.cbs11tv.com

Technical Facilities: Channel No. 11 (198-204 MHz). Authorized power: 23-kw visual, aural. Antenna: 1708-ft above av. terrain, 1545-ft. above ground, 2344-ft. above sea level.

Latitude	32°	34'	43"
Longitude	96°	57'	12"

Note: Latitude and longitude coordinates shown are based on the North American Datum of 1927 (NAD 27) as currently required by the Mass Media Bureau of the FCC.

Ownership: CBS Corp. (Group Owner).

Began Operation: May 1, 1999. Standard Definition. Station broadcasting digitally on its analog channel allotment. Began analog operations: September 11, 1955. Sale to present owner from CBS Inc. approved by FCC May 3, 2000. Sale to CBS Inc. by Gaylord Broadcasting Co. approved by FCC August 3, 1999 (Television Digest, Vol. 39:16, 42). Sale to Gaylord Broadcasting Co. by NAFI Telecasting approved by FCC August 1, 1962 (Vol. 2:11, 32). Sale to NAFI Telecasting by Texas State Network approved by FCC July 27, 1960 (Vol. 16:21, 31). Ceased analog operations: June 12, 2009.

Represented (sales): HRP: Television Station Representative.

Represented (legal): Leventhal, Senter & Lerman PLLC.

Represented (engineering): Cavell, Mertz & Associates Inc.

Personnel:

Steve Mauldin, President & General Manager.

Gary Schneider, Senior Vice President & Station Manager.

David Hershey, Vice President, Creative Services.

Carla Alexander, Sales Operation Manager.

Adam Levy, General Sales Manager.

Matt Flewelling, Local Sales Manager.

Don Dobbs, Engineering Director.

Ken Foote, Programming Director.

Scott Diener, News Director.

Lori Conrad, Communications Director.

Mike Stewart, Promotions Director.

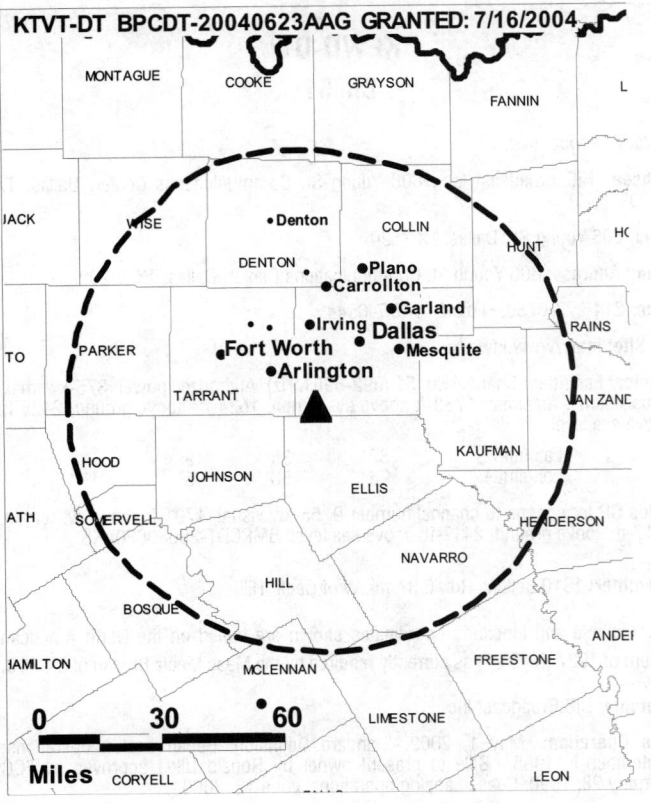

© 2010 Warren Communications News

City of License: Fort Worth. **Station DMA:** Dallas-Fort Worth, TX. **Rank:** 5.

Circulation © 2009 Nielsen. Coverage based on Nielsen study.

GrandTotal	Cable TV Households	Non-cable TV Households	Total TV Households
Estimated Station Totals *	1,077,950	1,144,620	2,222,570
Average Weekly Circulation (2009)	613,998	730,262	1,344,260
Average Daily Circulation (2009)			625,472

Station DMA Total	Cable TV Households	Non-cable TV Households	Total TV Households
Estimated Station Totals *	1,038,520	1,100,330	2,138,850
Average Weekly Circulation (2009)	600,448	722,766	1,323,214
Average Daily Circulation (2009)			617,488

Other DMA Total	Cable TV Households	Non-cable TV Households	Total TV Households
Estimated Station Totals *	39,430	44,290	83,720
Average Weekly Circulation (2009)	13,550	7,496	21,046
Average Daily Circulation (2009)			7,984

*Estimated station totals are sums of the Nielsen TV and Cable TV household estimates for each county in which the station registers viewing of more than 5% as per the Nielsen Survey Methods.

KTXA-DT
Ch. 18

Network Service: IND.

Licensee: Television Station KTXA LP, 5233 Bridge St, Fort Worth, TX 76103.

Studio: 5233 Bridge St., Fort Worth, TX 76103.

Mailing Address: PO Box 2495, Fort Worth, TX 76113.

Phone: 214-743-2100. **Fax:** 214-743-2150.

Web Site: http://www.cbs11tv.com

Technical Facilities: Channel No. 18 (494-500 MHz). Authorized power: 220-kw max. visual, aural. Antenna: 1755-ft above av. terrain, 1608-ft. above ground, 2421-ft. above sea level.

Latitude	32°	32'	35"
Longitude	96°	57'	32"

Holds CP for change to channel number 19, 750-kw visual, 1640-ft above av. terrain, 1480-ft. above ground, 2279-ft. above sea level; lat. 32° 34' 43", long. 96° 57' 12", BMPCDT-20090504AAV.

Transmitter: 2133 Tar Rd., Cedar Hill.

Note: Latitude and longitude coordinates shown are based on the North American Datum of 1927 (NAD 27) as currently required by the Mass Media Bureau of the FCC.

Satellite Earth Stations: Harris, 3-meter C-band; Vertex, 4.6-meter Ku-band; Harris, 6.1-meter C-band; Vertex, Harris receivers.

Ownership: CBS Corp. (Group Owner).

Began Operation: October 16, 2000. High Definition. Began analog operations: January 4, 1981. Sale to TVX, later Paramount Stations Group, by Taft Television & Radio Co. approved by FCC February 20, 1987 (Television Digest, Vol. 27:9, 14, 15). Sale to Taft by Gulf Broadcast Group approved by FCC May 30, 1985 (Vol. 25:5, 20, 22). Sale to Gulf by Sidney L. Schlenker, J. Livingston Kosberg, et. al., approved by FCC December 11, 1984 (Vol. 24:23, 53). Ceased analog operations: June 12, 2009.

Represented (sales): Katz Media Group.

Represented (engineering): du Treil, Lundin & Rackley Inc.

Personnel:

Steve Mauldin, President & General Manager.

Gary Schneider, Senior Vice President & Station Manager.

David Hershey, Vice President, Creative Services.

Julia O'Hickey, Sales Director.

Don Dobbs, Engineering Director.

Ken Foote, Programming Director.

Kimberly Robison, Research Director.

Carla Alexander, Sales Operations Manager.

Lori Conrad, Communications Director.

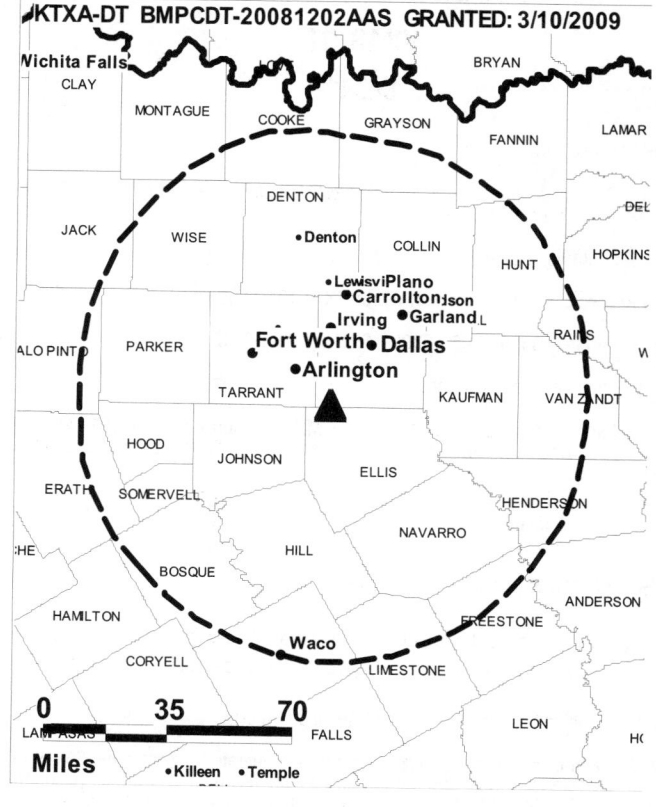

KTXA-DT BMPCDT-20081202AAS GRANTED: 3/10/2009

© 2010 Warren Communications News

City of License: Fort Worth. **Station DMA:** Dallas-Fort Worth, TX. **Rank:** 5.

Circulation © 2009 Nielsen. Coverage based on Nielsen study.

GrandTotal	Cable TV Households	Non-cable TV Households	Total TV Households
Estimated Station Totals *	1,035,400	1,131,950	2,167,350
Average Weekly Circulation (2009)	298,962	484,945	783,907
Average Daily Circulation (2009)			274,441

Station DMA Total	Cable TV Households	Non-cable TV Households	Total TV Households
Estimated Station Totals *	1,030,780	1,100,330	2,131,110
Average Weekly Circulation (2009)	298,346	482,485	780,831
Average Daily Circulation (2009)			273,778

Other DMA Total	Cable TV Households	Non-cable TV Households	Total TV Households
Estimated Station Totals *	4,620	31,620	36,240
Average Weekly Circulation (2009)	616	2,460	3,076
Average Daily Circulation (2009)			663

*Estimated station totals are sums of the Nielsen TV and Cable TV household estimates for each county in which the station registers viewing of more than 5% as per the Nielsen Survey Methods.

KXAS-DT
Ch. 41

Network Service: NBC.

Licensee: Station Venture Operations LP, 1299 Pennsylvania Ave NW, 11th Fl, c/o NBC Inc, Washington, DC 20004.

Studio: 3900 Barnett St, Fort Worth, TX 76103.

Mailing Address: PO Box 1780, Fort Worth, TX 76101-1780.

Phone: 817-429-5555; 817-654-6300. **Fax:** 817-654-6442.

Web Site: http://www.nbcdfw.com

Technical Facilities: Channel No. 41 (632-638 MHz). Authorized power: 891-kw max. visual, aural. Antenna: 1660-ft above av. terrain, 1470-ft above ground, 2284-ft. above sea level.

Latitude	32°	35'	07"
Longitude	96°	58'	06"

Transmitter: 1200 W. Beltline Rd., Cedar Hill.

Note: Latitude and longitude coordinates shown are based on the North American Datum of 1927 (NAD 27) as currently required by the Mass Media Bureau of the FCC.

Ownership: Station Venture Operations LP (Group Owner).

Began Operation: November 1, 1998. Began analog operations: September 29, 1948. Sale to LIN Television Corp. by Carter Publications Inc. (Fort Worth Star-Telegram) approved by FCC May 13, 1974. Transfer of control from AT&T to Hicks, Muse, Tate & Furst, and subsequent assignment to present owner approved by FCC March 2, 1998. Ceased analog operations: June 12, 2009.

Represented (legal): NBC Universal Inc. (Legal).

Represented (engineering): NBC Universal Inc. (Engineering).

Personnel:

Thomas Ehlmann, President & General Manager.

Charles Compagnone, Vice President, Sales.

Brian Hocker, Vice President, Programming & Administration.

Susan Tully, Vice President, Content Development.

Karen Dickens, National Sales Manager.

Larry Watzman, Marketing Director.

Nada Ruddock, Community Affairs Director.

City of License: Fort Worth. **Station DMA:** Dallas-Fort Worth, TX. **Rank:** 5.

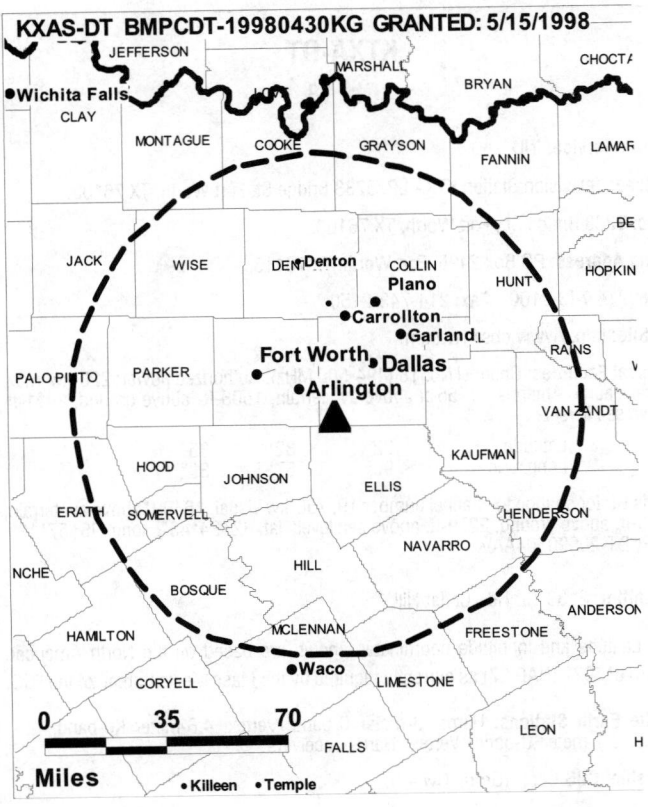

KXAS-DT BMPCDT-19980430KG GRANTED: 5/15/1998

© 2010 Warren Communications News

Circulation © 2009 Nielsen. Coverage based on Nielsen study.

GrandTotal	Cable TV Households	Non-cable TV Households	Total TV Households
Estimated Station Totals *	1,105,030	1,151,780	2,256,810
Average Weekly Circulation (2009)	646,239	728,694	1,374,933
Average Daily Circulation (2009)			607,759

Station DMA Total	Cable TV Households	Non-cable TV Households	Total TV Households
Estimated Station Totals *	1,038,520	1,100,330	2,138,850
Average Weekly Circulation (2009)	633,130	720,886	1,354,016
Average Daily Circulation (2009)			600,383

Other DMA Total	Cable TV Households	Non-cable TV Households	Total TV Households
Estimated Station Totals *	66,510	51,450	117,960
Average Weekly Circulation (2009)	13,109	7,808	20,917
Average Daily Circulation (2009)			7,376

*Estimated station totals are sums of the Nielsen TV and Cable TV household estimates for each county in which the station registers viewing of more than 5% as per the Nielsen Survey Methods.

KCWX-DT
Ch. 5

Network Service: CW.

Grantee: Corridor Television LLC, 111 Congress Ave, Ste 2530, One Congress Pl, Austin, TX 78701.

Phone: 210-366-5000. **Fax:** 210-770-0740.

Web Site: http://www.mysanantonio.com

Technical Facilities: Channel No. 5 (76-82 MHz). Authorized power: 23.7-kw visual, aural. Antenna: 1352-ft above av. terrain, 1102-ft. above ground, 3002-ft. above sea level.

Latitude	30°	08'	13"
Longitude	98°	36'	35"

Holds CP for change to 82.9-kw visual; BPCDT-20090713ACO.

Note: Latitude and longitude coordinates shown are based on the North American Datum of 1927 (NAD 27) as currently required by the Mass Media Bureau of the FCC.

Ownership: Global Information Technologies Inc.

Began Operation: June 12, 2009. Began analog operations: August 3, 2000. Ceased analog operations: June 12, 2009.

City of License: Fredericksburg. **Station DMA:** Austin, TX. **Rank:** 48.

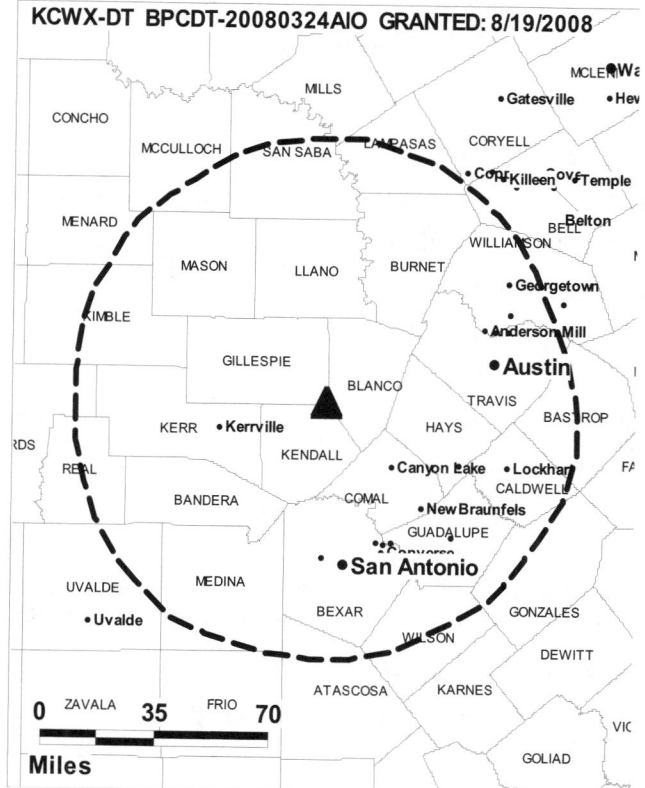

KCWX-DT BPCDT-20080324AIO GRANTED: 8/19/2008

© 2010 Warren Communications News

Circulation © 2009 Nielsen. Coverage based on Nielsen study.

GrandTotal	Cable TV Households	Non-cable TV Households	Total TV Households
Estimated Station Totals *	464,050	275,770	739,820
Average Weekly Circulation (2009)	66,676	25,499	92,175
Average Daily Circulation (2009)			24,281

Station DMA Total	Cable TV Households	Non-cable TV Households	Total TV Households
Estimated Station Totals *	460,160	269,560	729,720
Average Weekly Circulation (2009)	66,373	24,816	91,189
Average Daily Circulation (2009)			24,059

Other DMA Total	Cable TV Households	Non-cable TV Households	Total TV Households
Estimated Station Totals *	3,890	6,210	10,100
Average Weekly Circulation (2009)	303	683	986
Average Daily Circulation (2009)			222

*Estimated station totals are sums of the Nielsen TV and Cable TV household estimates for each county in which the station registers viewing of more than 5% as per the Nielsen Survey Methods.

KTMD-DT
Ch. 48

Network Service: TMO.

Licensee: Telemundo of Texas Partnership LP, 2290 W. 8th Ave, Hialeah, FL 33010.

Studio: 1235 North Loop W, Ste 125, Houston, TX 77008.

Mailing Address: 1235 North Loop W, Ste 125, Houston, TX 77008.

Phone: 713-974-4848. **Fax:** 713-243-7850.

Web Site: http://www.ktmd.com

Technical Facilities: Channel No. 48 (674-680 MHz). Authorized power: 1000-kw max. visual, aural. Antenna: 1959-ft above av. terrain, 1945-ft. above ground, 2022-ft. above sea level.

Latitude	29°	34'	15"
Longitude	95°	30'	37"

Note: Latitude and longitude coordinates shown are based on the North American Datum of 1927 (NAD 27) as currently required by the Mass Media Bureau of the FCC.

Ownership: NBC Universal (Group Owner).

Began Operation: July 29, 2004. Began analog operations: February 1, 1988. Ceased analog operations: June 12, 2009.

Personnel:

Roel Medina, Vice President & General Manager.

Dominic Fails, General Sales Manager.

Gregorio Cerzantes, National Sales Manager.

Jose Flores, News Director.

Linda Stillwell, Business Manager.

Marcello Marini, Program & Public Relations Manager.

Arturo Sovarzo, Production Manager.

Delores Pineda, Traffic Manager.

City of License: Galveston. **Station DMA:** Houston, TX. **Rank:** 10.

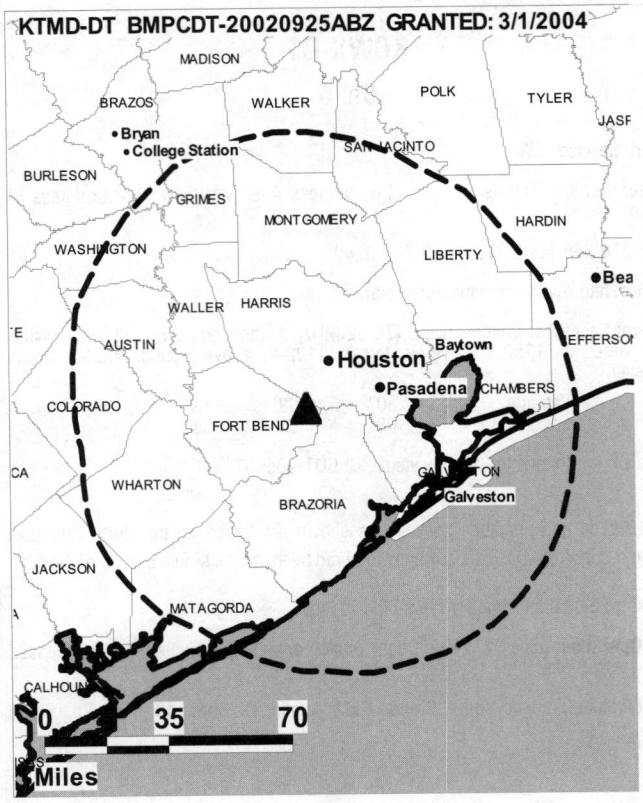

KTMD-DT BMPCDT-20020925ABZ GRANTED: 3/1/2004

© 2010 Warren Communications News

Circulation © 2009 Nielsen. Coverage based on Nielsen study.

GrandTotal	Cable TV Households	Non-cable TV Households	Total TV Households
Estimated Station Totals *	973,050	828,790	1,801,840
Average Weekly Circulation (2009)	115,921	199,319	315,240
Average Daily Circulation (2009)			146,494

Station DMA Total	Cable TV Households	Non-cable TV Households	Total TV Households
Estimated Station Totals *	973,050	828,790	1,801,840
Average Weekly Circulation (2009)	115,921	199,319	315,240
Average Daily Circulation (2009)			146,494

*Estimated station totals are sums of the Nielsen TV and Cable TV household estimates for each county in which the station registers viewing of more than 5% as per the Nielsen Survey Methods.

KUVN-DT
Ch. 23

Network Service: UNV.

Licensee: KUVN License Partnership LP, 1999 Avenue of the Stars, Ste 3050, Los Angeles, CA 90067.

Studio: 2323 Bryan St., Suite 1900, Dallas, TX 75201.

Mailing Address: 2323 Bryan St, Ste 1900, Dallas, TX 75201.

Phone: 214-758-2300. **Fax:** 214-758-2350.

Web Site: http://www.univision.com

Technical Facilities: Channel No. 23 (524-530 MHz). Authorized power: 1000-kw max. visual, aural. Antenna: 1696-ft above av. terrain, 1496-ft. above ground, 2326-ft. above sea level.

Latitude	32°	35'	21"
Longitude	96°	58'	12"

Note: Latitude and longitude coordinates shown are based on the North American Datum of 1927 (NAD 27) as currently required by the Mass Media Bureau of the FCC.

Ownership: Univision Communications Inc. (Group Owner).

Began Operation: October 31, 2002. Standard Definition. Station broadcasting digitally on its analog channel allotment. Began analog operations: September 25, 1986. Transfer of control to Broadcasting Media Partners Inc. approved by FCC March 27, 2007. Sale to present owner by Hallmark Cards Inc. approved by FCC Spetember 30, 1992. Sale to Hallmark Cards Inc. by I am Broadcasting Co., Debtor In Possession approved by FCC June 28, 1988. Ceased analog operations: June 12, 2009.

Represented (legal): Covington & Burling.

Personnel:

Becky Munoz-Diaz, Vice President & General Manager.

Luis Hernadez, General Sales Manager.

Millie Adan-Garza, Local Sales Manager.

Audrey Savage, Local Sales Manager.

Martha Kattan, News Director.

Pamela Gilbert, Business Manager & Controller.

Armando de la Fuente, Promotions & Community Affairs Director.

City of License: Garland. **Station DMA:** Dallas-Fort Worth, TX. **Rank:** 5.

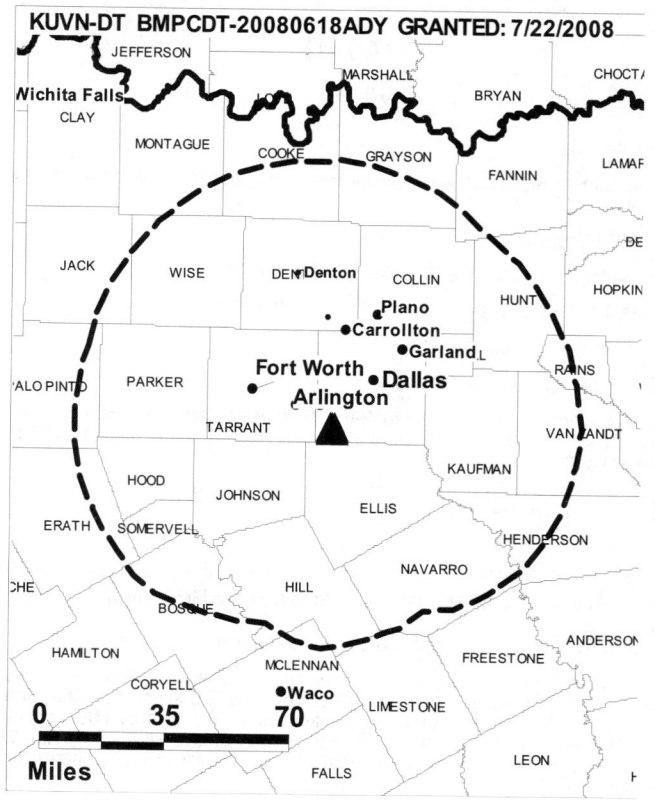

© 2010 Warren Communications News

Circulation © 2009 Nielsen. Coverage based on Nielsen study.

GrandTotal	Cable TV Households	Non-cable TV Households	Total TV Households
Estimated Station Totals *	729,780	1,032,680	1,762,460
Average Weekly Circulation (2009)	103,700	204,782	308,482
Average Daily Circulation (2009)			223,129

Station DMA Total	Cable TV Households	Non-cable TV Households	Total TV Households
Estimated Station Totals *	729,780	1,032,680	1,762,460
Average Weekly Circulation (2009)	103,700	204,782	308,482
Average Daily Circulation (2009)			223,129

*Estimated station totals are sums of the Nielsen TV and Cable TV household estimates for each county in which the station registers viewing of more than 5% as per the Nielsen Survey Methods.

KTAQ-DT
Ch. 46

Network Service: IND.

Licensee: Simons Broadcasting LP, Debtor in Possession, 510 N Valley Mills Dr, Ste 500, Waco, TX 76710.

Studio: 1062 Country Rd 1057, Greenville, TX 75401.

Mailing Address: PO Box 224297, Dallas, TX 75222-4297.

Phone: 903-455-8847; 800-717-0765. **Fax:** 903-455-8891.

E-mail: mcook@shopnbc.com

Web Site: http://www.mikesimons.com

Technical Facilities: Channel No. 46 (662-668 MHz). Authorized power: 600-kw max. visual, aural. Antenna: 1627-ft above av. terrain, 1473-ft. above ground, 2287-ft. above sea level.

Latitude	32°	32'	36"
Longitude	96°	57'	32"

Note: Latitude and longitude coordinates shown are based on the North American Datum of 1927 (NAD 27) as currently required by the Mass Media Bureau of the FCC.

Ownership: Simons Broadcasting LP, Debtor in Possession (Group Owner).

Began Operation: April 14, 2004. Began analog operations: April 1, 1994. Involuntary assignment to debtor in possession status approved by FCC March 19, 2009. Sale to New World Broadcasters Corp. by present owner approved by FCC January 12, 2000, but never consummated. Sale to Simons Broadcasting LP by A.B.W. Communications Inc. approved by FCC March 24, 1992. Ceased analog operations: February 17, 2009.

Represented (legal): Garvey Schubert Barer.

Personnel:

Mike Simons, General Manager.

City of License: Greenville. **Station DMA:** Dallas-Fort Worth, TX. **Rank:** 5.

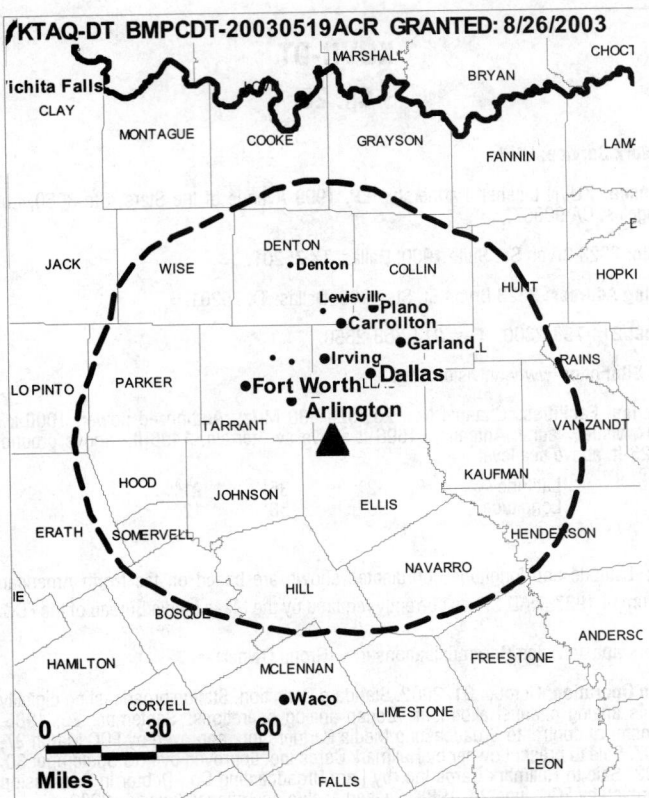

© 2010 Warren Communications News

Nielsen Data: Not available.

KGBT-DT
Ch. 31

Network Service: CBS.

Licensee: Barrington Harlingen Licnese LLC, 2500 W Higgins Rd, Ste 880, Hoffman Estates, IL 60195.

Studio: 9201 W Expy 83, Harlington, TX 78552.

Mailing Address: 9201 W Expy 83, Harlingen, TX 78552.

Phone: 956-366-4400. **Fax:** 956-366-4494.

E-mail: rroberts@kgbt4.com

Web Site: http://www.kgbt4.com

Technical Facilities: Channel No. 31 (572-578 MHz). Authorized power: 1000-kw max. visual, aural. Antenna: 1207-ft above av. terrain, 1201-ft. above ground, 1257-ft. above sea level.

Latitude	26°	08'	56"
Longitude	97°	49'	18"

Note: Latitude and longitude coordinates shown are based on the North American Datum of 1927 (NAD 27) as currently required by the Mass Media Bureau of the FCC.

Ownership: Pilot Group LP (Group Owner).

Began Operation: June 19, 2003. Began analog operations: October 4, 1953. Sale to present owner by Raycom Media Inc. approved by FCC July 18, 2006. Sale to Raycom Media Inc. by Cosmos Broadcasting Corp. approved by FCC January 17, 2006. Sale to Cosmos Broadcasting Corp. by Draper Communications Inc. approved by FCC October 23, 1998. Sale to Draper Communications Inc. by Tichenor Media System Inc. approved by FCC February 7, 1986. Ceased analog operations: June 12, 2009.

Represented (legal): Covington & Burling.

Represented (sales): Continental Television Sales.

Personnel:

Teresa Burgess, Vice President & General Manager.

Robert Ledesma, National Sales Manager.

Randy Roberts, General & National Sales Manager.

Colleen Willis, Local Sales Manager.

Kimberly Wyatt, News Director.

Rick Hutchinson, Chief Engineer.

Beau Pillet, Marketing Director.

Linda Guerrero Diecla, Business Manager.

Patty Chancey, Traffic Manager.

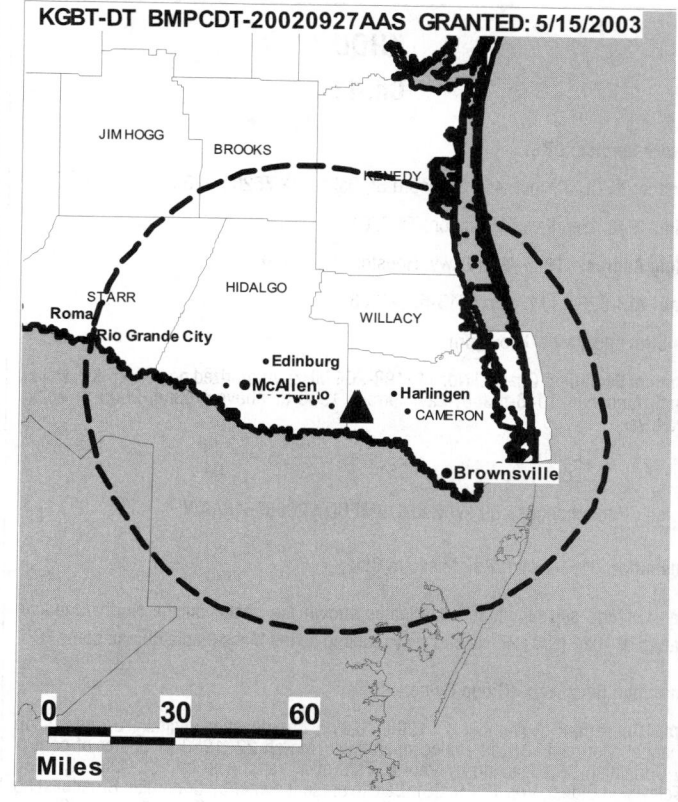

KGBT-DT BMPCDT-20020927AAS GRANTED: 5/15/2003

© 2010 Warren Communications News

City of License: Harlingen.

Station DMA: Harlingen-Weslaco-Brownsville-McAllen, TX. **Rank:** 87.

Circulation © 2009 Nielsen. Coverage based on Nielsen study.

GrandTotal	Cable TV Households	Non-cable TV Households	Total TV Households
Estimated Station Totals *	139,180	210,730	349,910
Average Weekly Circulation (2009)	71,638	76,032	147,670
Average Daily Circulation (2009)			74,497

Station DMA Total	Cable TV Households	Non-cable TV Households	Total TV Households
Estimated Station Totals *	139,180	210,730	349,910
Average Weekly Circulation (2009)	71,638	76,032	147,670
Average Daily Circulation (2009)			74,497

*Estimated station totals are sums of the Nielsen TV and Cable TV household estimates for each county in which the station registers viewing of more than 5% as per the Nielsen Survey Methods.

KHOU
Ch. 11

Network Service: CBS.

Licensee: KHOU-TV Inc., 400 S Record St, Dallas, TX 75202-4806.

Studio: 1945 Allen Pkwy., Houston, TX 77019.

Mailing Address: 1945 Allen Pkwy, Houston, TX 77019.

Phone: 713-526-1111. **Fax:** 713-521-4326.

Web Site: http://www.khou.com

Technical Facilities: Channel No. 11 (198-204 MHz). Authorized power: 25-kw visual, aural. Antenna: 1946-ft above av. terrain, 1936-ft. above ground, 2008-ft. above sea level.

Latitude	29°	33'	40"
Longitude	95°	30'	04"

Holds CP for change to 60-kw visual; BMPCDT-20080618AAW.

Transmitter: 3111 Senior Rd., Missouri City.

Note: Latitude and longitude coordinates shown are based on the North American Datum of 1927 (NAD 27) as currently required by the Mass Media Bureau of the FCC.

Ownership: Belo Corp. (Group Owner).

Began Operation: November 1, 1998. Station broadcasting digitally on its analog channel allotment. Began analog operations: March 22, 1953. Transfer of control to Corinthian Broadcasting by Paul E. Taft, et al., approved by FCC July 11, 1956 (Television Digest, Vol. 12:19, 28). Sale to present owner by Corinthian Broadcasting approved by FCC November 22, 1983. Ceased analog operations: June 12, 2009.

Represented (legal): Wiley Rein LLP.

Represented (sales): TeleRep Inc.

Personnel:

Susan McEldoon, President & General Manager.

Keith Connors, News Director.

Steve Gratzer, National Sales Manager.

Janell Pennington, National Sales Manager.

Miles Cathey, Local Sales Manager.

Frank Peterman, Engineering Director.

David Kobrin, Production Manager.

Lisa Shumate, Marketing Director.

Robyn Hughes, Art Director.

City of License: Houston. **Station DMA:** Houston, TX. **Rank:** 10.

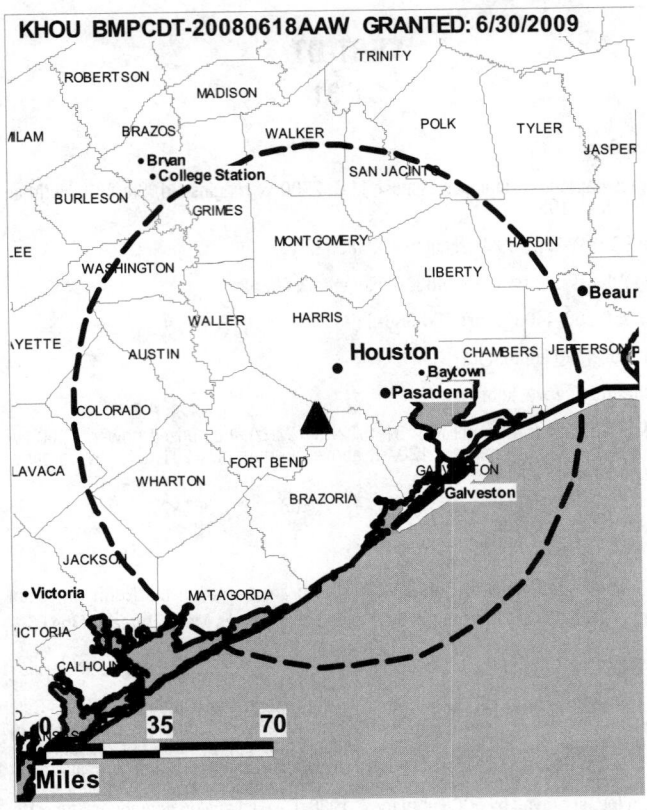

© 2010 Warren Communications News

Circulation © 2009 Nielsen. Coverage based on Nielsen study.

GrandTotal	Cable TV Households	Non-cable TV Households	Total TV Households
Estimated Station Totals *	1,090,290	915,540	2,005,830
Average Weekly Circulation (2009)	724,269	570,015	1,294,284
Average Daily Circulation (2009)			638,394

Station DMA Total	Cable TV Households	Non-cable TV Households	Total TV Households
Estimated Station Totals *	1,073,130	896,560	1,969,690
Average Weekly Circulation (2009)	720,965	568,261	1,289,226
Average Daily Circulation (2009)			636,945

Other DMA Total	Cable TV Households	Non-cable TV Households	Total TV Households
Estimated Station Totals *	17,160	18,980	36,140
Average Weekly Circulation (2009)	3,304	1,754	5,058
Average Daily Circulation (2009)			1,449

*Estimated station totals are sums of the Nielsen TV and Cable TV household estimates for each county in which the station registers viewing of more than 5% as per the Nielsen Survey Methods.

KIAH-DT
Ch. 38

Network Service: CW.

Licensee: KHCW Inc., Debtor-In-Possession, 7700 Westpark Dr, Houston, TX 77063.

Studio: 7700 Westpark Dr., Houston, TX 77063.

Mailing Address: 7700 Westpark Dr, Houston, TX 77063.

Phone: 713-781-3939. **Fax:** 713-781-3441.

Web Site: http://khcw.trb.com

Technical Facilities: Channel No. 38 (614-620 MHz). Authorized power: 1000-kw max. visual, aural. Antenna: 1909-ft above av. terrain, 1887-ft. above ground, 1965-ft. above sea level.

Latitude	29°	34'	06"
Longitude	95°	29'	57"

Holds CP for change to 975-kw max. visual, 1949-ft above av. terrain, 1939-ft. above ground, 2018-ft. above sea level; BPCDT-20080619AKV.

Note: Latitude and longitude coordinates shown are based on the North American Datum of 1927 (NAD 27) as currently required by the Mass Media Bureau of the FCC.

Ownership: Tribune Broadcasting Co., Debtor-In-Possession (Group Owner).

Began Operation: October 22, 2002. Standard Definition. Began analog operations: October 10, 1953 as KNUZ-TV, but left air June 25, 1954. Sale of 80% to WKY-TV by KNUZ Television Co. approved by FCC October 13, 1965. Transfer of remaining 20% approved by FCC June 17, 1966. Resumed operations January 6, 1967. Sale to present owner by Gaylord Broadcasting Co. approved by FCC December 15, 1995. Transfer of control from public shareholders of the Tribune Co. to Tribune Employee Stock Ownership Plan approved by FCC November 30, 2007. Involuntary assignment to debtor-in-possession status approved by FCC December 24, 2008. Ceased analog operations: June 12, 2009.

Represented (legal): Sidley Austin LLP.

Personnel:

Roger Bare, Vice President & General Manager.

Harvey Saxer, General Sales Manager.

Debbie Brizendine, Local Sales Manager.

Melissa McAnelly, National Sales Manager.

Joe Nolan, News Director.

Bob Chase, Engineering & Technology Director.

Feli Wong, Controller.

Jeff Clemons, Marketing & Creative Services Director.

Gail Halvorsen, On-Air Promotion Director.

Yolanda Green, Community Relations Director.

Colin Kirkpatrick, Art Director.

City of License: Houston. **Station DMA:** Houston, TX. **Rank:** 10.

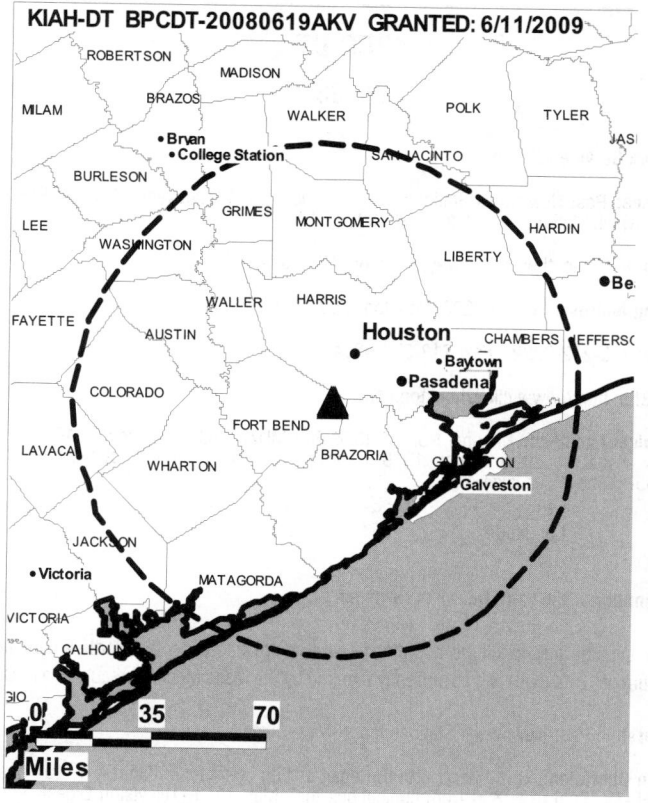

KIAH-DT BPCDT-20080619AKV GRANTED: 6/11/2009

© 2010 Warren Communications News

Circulation © 2009 Nielsen. Coverage based on Nielsen study.

GrandTotal	Cable TV Households	Non-cable TV Households	Total TV Households
Estimated Station Totals *	1,078,130	903,330	1,981,460
Average Weekly Circulation (2009)	451,572	446,414	897,986
Average Daily Circulation (2009)			342,170

Station DMA Total	Cable TV Households	Non-cable TV Households	Total TV Households
Estimated Station Totals *	1,073,130	896,560	1,969,690
Average Weekly Circulation (2009)	451,162	445,981	897,143
Average Daily Circulation (2009)			341,967

Other DMA Total	Cable TV Households	Non-cable TV Households	Total TV Households
Estimated Station Totals *	5,000	6,770	11,770
Average Weekly Circulation (2009)	410	433	843
Average Daily Circulation (2009)			203

*Estimated station totals are sums of the Nielsen TV and Cable TV household estimates for each county in which the station registers viewing of more than 5% as per the Nielsen Survey Methods.

KPRC-DT
Ch. 35

Network Service: NBC.

Licensee: Post-Newsweek Stations, Houston Inc., 550 W Lafayette Blvd, c/o Post-Newsweek Stations Inc., Detroit, MI 48226-3140.

Studio: 8181 Southwest Freeway, Houston, TX 77074.

Mailing Address: PO Box 2222, Houston, TX 77252.

Phone: 713-222-2222. **Fax:** 713-270-9334.

Web Site: http://www.click2houston.com

Technical Facilities: Channel No. 35 (596-602 MHz). Authorized power: 1000-kw max. visual, aural. Antenna: 1919-ft above av. terrain, 1906-ft. above ground, 1985-ft. above sea level.

Latitude	29°	34'	06"
Longitude	95°	29'	57"

Transmitter: 4126 Farm Rd. 2234, Missouri City.

Note: Latitude and longitude coordinates shown are based on the North American Datum of 1927 (NAD 27) as currently required by the Mass Media Bureau of the FCC.

Ownership: Post-Newsweek Stations Inc. (Group Owner).

Began Operation: November 1, 1999. Began analog operations: January 1, 1949 as KLEE-TV. Sold to H & C Communications Inc. May 1950 (Television Digest, Vol. 6:13, 21). Sale to present owner approved by FCC February 28, 1994 (Vol. 33:49). Ceased analog operations: June 12, 2009.

Represented (legal): Covington & Burling.

Personnel:

Larry Blackerby, Vice President & General Manager.

Tammy Dean, Operations & Traffic Manager.

Ben Oldham, General Sales Manager.

Shannon Murphy, Local Sales Manager.

Skip Valet, News Director.

Dale Werner, Broadcast Operations & Engineering Director.

Von Johnson, Business Manager.

Jeff Jandheur, Production Manager.

City of License: Houston. **Station DMA:** Houston, TX. **Rank:** 10.

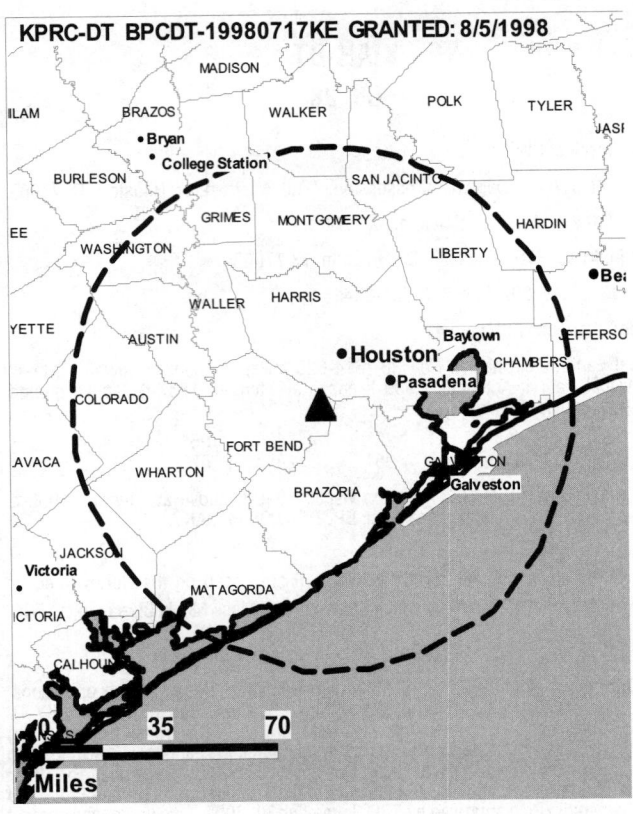

KPRC-DT BPCDT-19980717KE GRANTED: 8/5/1998

© 2010 Warren Communications News

Circulation © 2009 Nielsen. Coverage based on Nielsen study.

GrandTotal	Cable TV Households	Non-cable TV Households	Total TV Households
Estimated Station Totals *	1,106,580	913,470	2,020,050
Average Weekly Circulation (2009)	684,502	446,357	1,130,859
Average Daily Circulation (2009)			482,419

Station DMA Total	Cable TV Households	Non-cable TV Households	Total TV Households
Estimated Station Totals *	1,073,130	896,560	1,969,690
Average Weekly Circulation (2009)	679,823	445,373	1,125,196
Average Daily Circulation (2009)			481,179

Other DMA Total	Cable TV Households	Non-cable TV Households	Total TV Households
Estimated Station Totals *	33,450	16,910	50,360
Average Weekly Circulation (2009)	4,679	984	5,663
Average Daily Circulation (2009)			1,240

*Estimated station totals are sums of the Nielsen TV and Cable TV household estimates for each county in which the station registers viewing of more than 5% as per the Nielsen Survey Methods.

KRIV-DT
Ch. 26

Network Service: FOX.

Licensee: Fox Television Stations Inc., 5151 Wisconsin Ave. NW, c/o Molly Pauker, Washington, DC 20016.

Studio: 4261 Southwest Freeway, Houston, TX 77027.

Mailing Address: 4261 Southwest Freeway, Houston, TX 77027.

Phone: 713-479-2600. **Fax:** 713-479-2859.

Web Site: http://www.myfoxhouston.com

Technical Facilities: Channel No. 26 (542-548 MHz). Authorized power: 1000-kw max. visual, aural. Antenna: 1962-ft above av. terrain, 1946-ft. above ground, 2024-ft. above sea level.

Latitude	29°	34'	28"
Longitude	95°	29'	37"

Transmitter: 5034 McHard Rd., Missouri City; 0.4-mi S of TX Rte. 2234; 0.1-mi W of intersection.

Note: Latitude and longitude coordinates shown are based on the North American Datum of 1927 (NAD 27) as currently required by the Mass Media Bureau of the FCC.

Ownership: Fox Television Holdings Inc. (Group Owner).

Began Operation: November 1, 1999. Standard Definition. Station broadcasting digitally on its analog channel allotment. Began analog operations: August 15, 1971. Sale to present owner by Metromedia approved by FCC November 14, 1985. Sale to Metromedia by Crest Broadcasting approved by FCC April 6, 1978 (Television Digest, Vol. 17:34). Ceased analog operations: June 12, 2009.

Represented (legal): Skadden, Arps, Slate, Meagher & Flom LLP.

Personnel:

D'Artagnan Bebel, Vice President & General Manager.

Charles Hughes, Vice President & Chief Engineer.

Karen Koch, Promotion Manager.

Susie Doucett, Local Sales Manager.

Brian Dodge, National Sales Manager.

Byron Wilkinson, National Sales Manager.

Stan Wasilik, Program Director.

City of License: Houston. **Station DMA:** Houston, TX. **Rank:** 10.

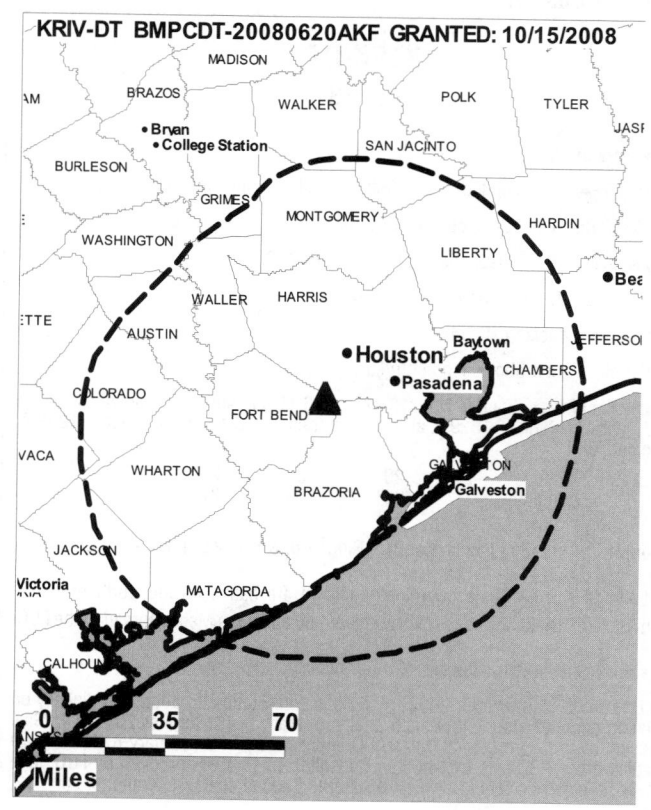

KRIV-DT BMPCDT-20080620AKF GRANTED: 10/15/2008

© 2010 Warren Communications News

Circulation © 2009 Nielsen. Coverage based on Nielsen study.

GrandTotal	Cable TV Households	Non-cable TV Households	Total TV Households
Estimated Station Totals *	1,075,120	903,330	1,978,450
Average Weekly Circulation (2009)	620,328	575,457	1,195,785
Average Daily Circulation (2009)			477,667

Station DMA Total	Cable TV Households	Non-cable TV Households	Total TV Households
Estimated Station Totals *	1,073,130	896,560	1,969,690
Average Weekly Circulation (2009)	619,259	574,794	1,194,053
Average Daily Circulation (2009)			477,397

Other DMA Total	Cable TV Households	Non-cable TV Households	Total TV Households
Estimated Station Totals *	1,990	6,770	8,760
Average Weekly Circulation (2009)	1,069	663	1,732
Average Daily Circulation (2009)			270

*Estimated station totals are sums of the Nielsen TV and Cable TV household estimates for each county in which the station registers viewing of more than 5% as per the Nielsen Survey Methods.

KTRK-DT
Ch. 13

Network Service: ABC.

Licensee: KTRK Television Inc., 77 W 66th St, 16th Fl, New York, NY 10023.

Studio: 3310 Bissonnet St., Houston, TX 77005.

Mailing Address: 3310 Bissonnet St, Houston, TX 77005.

Phone: 713-666-0713. **Fax:** 713-664-0013.

E-mail: susan.buddeke@abc.com

Web Site: http://www.abclocal.go.com/ktrk

Technical Facilities: Channel No. 13 (210-216 MHz). Authorized power: 32.4-kw visual, aural. Antenna: 1929-ft above av. terrain, 1913-ft. above ground, 1992-ft. above sea level.

Latitude	29°	34'	28"
Longitude	95°	29'	37"

Transmitter: 0.4-mi. S of junction of Blue Ridge Rd. & Rte. 2234, Missouri City.

Note: Latitude and longitude coordinates shown are based on the North American Datum of 1927 (NAD 27) as currently required by the Mass Media Bureau of the FCC.

Ownership: Disney Enterprises Inc. (Group Owner).

Began Operation: January 30, 2002. High Definition. Station broadcasting digitally on its analog channel allotment. Began analog operations: November 20, 1954. Sale to present owner from Capital Cities/ABC approved by FCC February 8, 1996. Sale to Capital Cities/ABC Inc. by Houston Consolidated TV Co. approved by FCC June 15, 1967 (Television Digest, Vol. 6:48; 7:25). Ceased analog operations: June 12, 2009.

Personnel:

Henry Florsheim, President & General Manager.

Jerry Lyles, Vice President & General Sales Manager.

Susan Buddeke, Vice President & Marketing Director.

Winfred Frazier, Local & Regional Sales Manager.

Gwen Anderson, Local Sales Manager.

Dave Strickland, News Director.

Chuck Primrose, Chief Engineer.

Kim Nordt-Jackson, Program Director.

Rick Herring, Production Manager.

Tom Ash, Promotion Director.

Trish Zagrzecki, Research & Sales Development Director.

JoAnn Crenshaw, Traffic Manager.

Robin Freese, Executive Producer.

City of License: Houston. **Station DMA:** Houston, TX. **Rank:** 10.

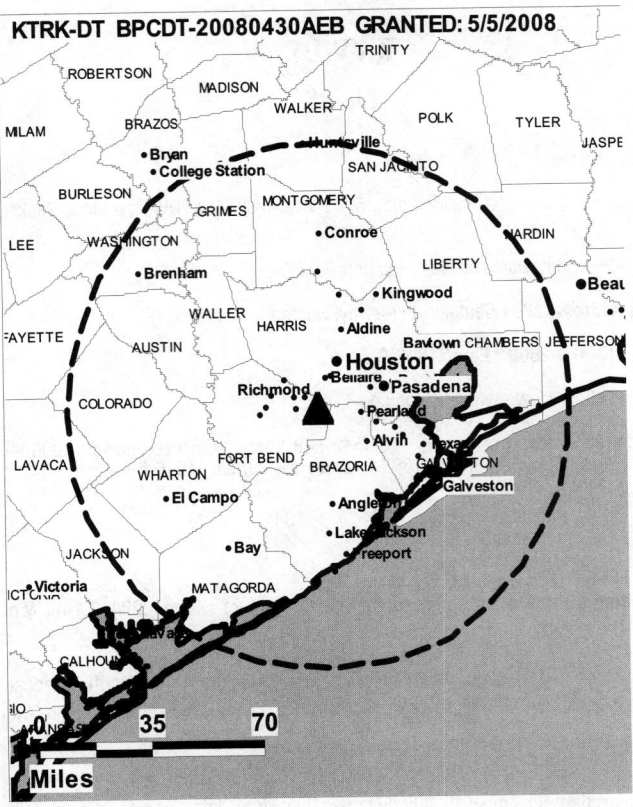

© 2010 Warren Communications News

Circulation © 2009 Nielsen. Coverage based on Nielsen study.

GrandTotal	Cable TV Households	Non-cable TV Households	Total TV Households
Estimated Station Totals *	1,128,920	915,540	2,044,460
Average Weekly Circulation (2009)	722,452	631,747	1,354,199
Average Daily Circulation (2009)			642,589

Station DMA Total	Cable TV Households	Non-cable TV Households	Total TV Households
Estimated Station Totals *	1,073,130	896,560	1,969,690
Average Weekly Circulation (2009)	716,672	630,360	1,347,032
Average Daily Circulation (2009)			640,357

Other DMA Total	Cable TV Households	Non-cable TV Households	Total TV Households
Estimated Station Totals *	55,790	18,980	74,770
Average Weekly Circulation (2009)	5,780	1,387	7,167
Average Daily Circulation (2009)			2,232

*Estimated station totals are sums of the Nielsen TV and Cable TV household estimates for each county in which the station registers viewing of more than 5% as per the Nielsen Survey Methods.

KTXH-DT
Ch. 19

Network Service: MNT.

Licensee: Fox Television Stations Inc., 5151 Wisconsin Ave. NW, c/o Molly Pauker, Washington, DC 20016.

Studio: 4261 Southwest Freeway, Houston, TX 77027.

Mailing Address: 4261 Southwest Freeway, Houston, TX 77027.

Phone: 713-661-2020. **Fax:** 713-479-2859.

Web Site: http://www.mynetworktv.com

Technical Facilities: Channel No. 19 (500-506 MHz). Authorized power: 421-kw max. visual, aural. Antenna: 1955-ft above av. terrain, 1942-ft. above ground, 2017-ft. above sea level.

Latitude	29°	33'	44"
Longitude	95°	30'	35"

Holds CP for change to 1000-kw max. visual; BPCDT-20080619AAW.

Note: Latitude and longitude coordinates shown are based on the North American Datum of 1927 (NAD 27) as currently required by the Mass Media Bureau of the FCC.

Ownership: Fox Television Holdings Inc. (Group Owner).

Began Operation: April 2, 2003. Began analog operations: November 7, 1982. Left air December 7, 1982; resumed operation February 13, 1983. Station, along with WDCA(TV) Washington, DC was swapped for Fox Television Stations Inc.'s KBHK(TV) San Francisco. FCC approved deal October 26, 2001 (Television Digest, Vol. 41:33). Transfer to Viacom International Inc. by Paramount Communications Inc. 1993-1994. Sale to Paramount Communications Inc. by Taft Television & Radio Co. approved by FCC February 20, 1987 (Television Digest, Vol. 27:9, 14, 15). Sale to Taft by Gulf Broadcast Group approved by FCC May 30, 1985 (Vol. 25:5, 20, 22). Sale to Gulf by Peter S. McMullen, Sidney Schlenker, et al., approved by FCC December 11, 1984 (Vol. 24:23, 53). Ceased analog operations: June 12, 2009.

Represented (legal): Skadden, Arps, Slate, Meagher & Flom LLP.

Represented (sales): Katz Media Group.

Personnel:

D'Artagnan Bebel, Vice President & General Manager.

Susie Doucette, Local Sales Manager.

Byron Wilkinson, National Sales Manager.

Brian Dodge, National Sales Manager.

Charles Hughes, Chief Engineer.

Stan Wasilik, Program Director.

Karen Kock, Promotion Director.

Jackie Lebay, Public Affairs Director.

City of License: Houston. **Station DMA:** Houston, TX. **Rank:** 10.

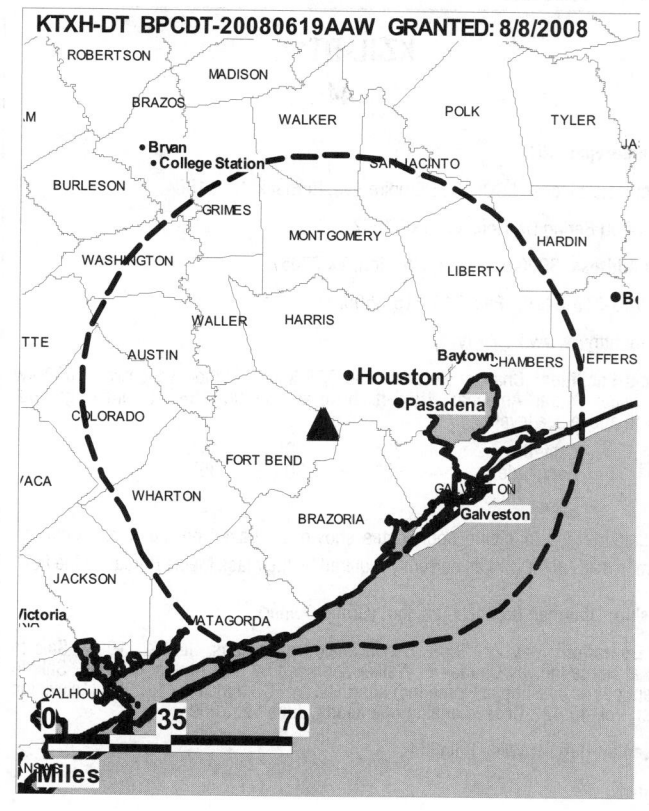

KTXH-DT BPCDT-20080619AAW GRANTED: 8/8/2008

© 2010 Warren Communications News

Circulation © 2009 Nielsen. Coverage based on Nielsen study.

GrandTotal	Cable TV Households	Non-cable TV Households	Total TV Households
Estimated Station Totals *	1,079,200	896,560	1,975,760
Average Weekly Circulation (2009)	356,673	424,863	781,536
Average Daily Circulation (2009)			261,042

Station DMA Total	Cable TV Households	Non-cable TV Households	Total TV Households
Estimated Station Totals *	1,073,130	896,560	1,969,690
Average Weekly Circulation (2009)	355,207	424,863	780,070
Average Daily Circulation (2009)			260,990

Other DMA Total	Cable TV Households	Non-cable TV Households	Total TV Households
Estimated Station Totals *	6,070	0	6,070
Average Weekly Circulation (2009)	1,466	0	1,466
Average Daily Circulation (2009)			52

*Estimated station totals are sums of the Nielsen TV and Cable TV household estimates for each county in which the station registers viewing of more than 5% as per the Nielsen Survey Methods.

KZJL-DT
Ch. 44

Network Service: IND.

Grantee: KZJL License LCC, 1845 Empire Ave, Burbank, CA 91504.

Studio: 3000 Bering Dr, Houston, TX 77057.

Mailing Address: 3000 Bering Dr, Houston, TX 77057.

Phone: 713-315-3400. **Fax:** 713-315-3506.

Web Site: http://www.kzjl61.tv

Technical Facilities: Channel No. 44 (650-656 MHz). Authorized power: 1000-kw max. visual, aural. Antenna: 1898-ft above av. terrain, 1885-ft. above ground, 1960-ft. above sea level.

Latitude	29°	33'	44"
Longitude	95°	30'	35"

Note: Latitude and longitude coordinates shown are based on the North American Datum of 1927 (NAD 27) as currently required by the Mass Media Bureau of the FCC.

Ownership: Liberman Broadcasting Inc. (Group Owner).

Began Operation: May 24, 2006. Began analog operations: June 2, 1995. Sale to Shop at Home Inc. by Charles E. Walker approved by FCC August 6, 1996. Sale to present owner by Shop at Home Inc. approved by FCC January 11, 2001 (Television Digest, Vol. 40:42). Ceased analog operations: June 12, 2009.

Represented (legal): Wiley Rein LLP.

Personnel:

Michael Kromp, General Manager.

Chris Buchanan, Chief Engineer.

Adrian Tonfi, Program Director.

City of License: Houston. **Station DMA:** Houston, TX. **Rank:** 10.

© 2010 Warren Communications News

Circulation © 2009 Nielsen. Coverage based on Nielsen study.

GrandTotal	Cable TV Households	Non-cable TV Households	Total TV Households
Estimated Station Totals *	990,460	844,800	1,835,260
Average Weekly Circulation (2009)	115,381	145,142	260,523
Average Daily Circulation (2009)			89,288

Station DMA Total	Cable TV Households	Non-cable TV Households	Total TV Households
Estimated Station Totals *	990,460	844,800	1,835,260
Average Weekly Circulation (2009)	115,381	145,142	260,523
Average Daily Circulation (2009)			89,288

*Estimated station totals are sums of the Nielsen TV and Cable TV household estimates for each county in which the station registers viewing of more than 5% as per the Nielsen Survey Methods.

KSTR-DT
Ch. 48

Network Service: TEL.

Licensee: Telefutura Dallas LLC, 1999 Avenue of the Stars, Ste 3050, Los Angeles, CA 90067.

Studio: 2323 Bryan St., Suite 1900, Dallas, TX 75201.

Mailing Address: 2323 Bryan St, Ste 1900, Dallas, TX 75201.

Phone: 214-758-2300; 214-954-4900. **Fax:** 214-758-2324.

Web Site: http://www.univision.net

Technical Facilities: Channel No. 48 (674-680 MHz). Authorized power: 225-kw max. visual, aural. Antenna: 1755-ft above av. terrain, 1608-ft. above ground, 1824-ft. above sea level.

Latitude	32°	32'	35"
Longitude	96°	57'	32"

Holds CP for change to 1000-kw max. visual, 1755-ft above av. terrain, 1608-ft. above ground, 2422-ft. above sea level; BPCDT-20080618AEK.

Transmitter: Beltline Rd., 1-mi. W of Cedar Hill.

Note: Latitude and longitude coordinates shown are based on the North American Datum of 1927 (NAD 27) as currently required by the Mass Media Bureau of the FCC.

Ownership: Univision Communications Inc. (Group Owner).

Began Operation: August 28, 2003. Standard Definition. Began analog operations: April 17, 1984. Sale to USA Broadcasting Inc. by Cela Inc. approved by FCC April 7, 1987. Transfer of control to present owner by USA Broadcasting Inc. approved by FCC May 21, 2001. Transfer of control to Broadcasting Media Partners Inc. approved by FCC March 27, 2007. Ceased analog operations: January 12, 2009.

Represented (legal): Covington & Burling.

Represented (engineering): John F. X. Browne & Associates PC.

Personnel:

Rebecca Munoz-Diaz, General Manager.

Luis Hernandez, General Sales Manager.

Audrey Savage, Local Sales Manager.

Millie Adan-Garza, Local Sales Manager.

Carlos Perez, Local Sales Manager.

Armando de la Fuente, Promotion Director.

Jessica Hernadez, Traffic Manager.

City of License: Irving. **Station DMA:** Dallas-Fort Worth, TX. **Rank:** 5.

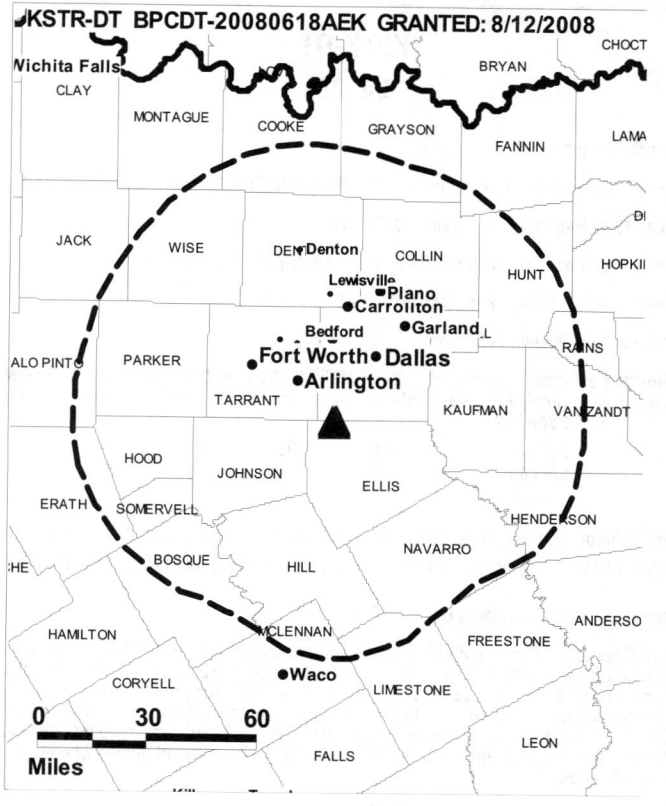

© 2010 Warren Communications News

Circulation © 2009 Nielsen. Coverage based on Nielsen study.

GrandTotal	Cable TV Households	Non-cable TV Households	Total TV Households
Estimated Station Totals *	878,970	796,660	1,675,630
Average Weekly Circulation (2009)	97,143	161,015	258,158
Average Daily Circulation (2009)			126,978

Station DMA Total	Cable TV Households	Non-cable TV Households	Total TV Households
Estimated Station Totals *	878,970	796,660	1,675,630
Average Weekly Circulation (2009)	97,143	161,015	258,158
Average Daily Circulation (2009)			126,978

*Estimated station totals are sums of the Nielsen TV and Cable TV household estimates for each county in which the station registers viewing of more than 5% as per the Nielsen Survey Methods.

KETK-DT
Ch. 22

Network Service: NBC.

Licensee: ComCorp of Tyler License Corp., PO Box 53708, Lafayette, LA 70505-3708.

Studio: 4300 Richmond Rd., Tyler, TX 75703.

Mailing Address: 4300 Richmond Rd, Tyler, TX 75703.

Phone: 903-581-5656. **Fax:** 903-561-1648.

Web Site: http://www.nbc56.com

Technical Facilities: Channel No. 22 (518-524 MHz). Authorized power: 1000-kw max. visual, aural. Antenna: 1505-ft above av. terrain, 1367-ft. above ground, 1948-ft. above sea level.

Latitude	32°	03'	40"
Longitude	95°	18'	50"

Note: Latitude and longitude coordinates shown are based on the North American Datum of 1927 (NAD 27) as currently required by the Mass Media Bureau of the FCC.

Ownership: Communications Corp. of America.

Began Operation: June 16, 2006. Began analog operations: March 9, 1987. Company emerged from debtor in possession status October 4, 2007. Involuntary transfer of control to debtor in possession approved by FCC August 29, 2006. Sale to Communications Corp. of America by Sinclair Broadcast Group Inc. approved by FCC November 12, 2004. Transfer of control to Sinclair Broadcast Group Inc. by Max Media Properties LLC approved by FCC June 29, 1998. Ceased analog operations: June 12, 2009.

Represented (legal): Dow Lohnes PLLC.

Represented (sales): Katz Media Group.

Personnel:

Dave Tillery, General Manager.

Eric Jontra, General Sales Manager.

Neal Barton, News Director.

Johnny Cummings, Chief Engineer.

Brandi Blalock, Business Manager.

Suzanne Calhoun, Local Sales Manager.

Yolanda Clater, Program Director.

Scott Shellhorse, Production Manager.

Connie Jobe, Traffic Manager.

City of License: Jacksonville.

Station DMA: Tyler-Longview (Lufkin & Nacogdoches), TX. **Rank:** 109.

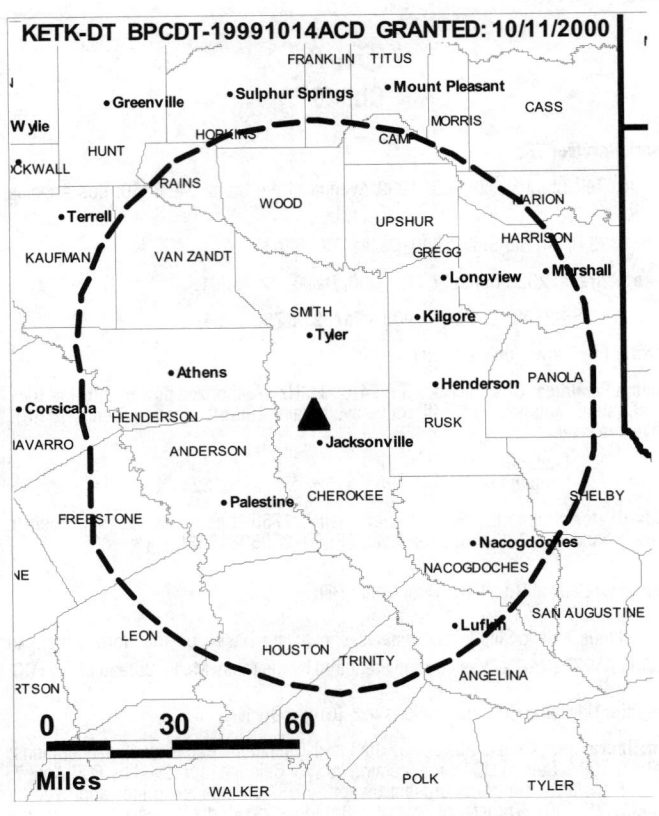

KETK-DT BPCDT-19991014ACD GRANTED: 10/11/2000

© 2010 Warren Communications News

Circulation © 2009 Nielsen. Coverage based on Nielsen study.

GrandTotal	Cable TV Households	Non-cable TV Households	Total TV Households
Estimated Station Totals *	116,080	173,370	289,450
Average Weekly Circulation (2009)	57,307	72,149	129,456
Average Daily Circulation (2009)			52,207

Station DMA Total	Cable TV Households	Non-cable TV Households	Total TV Households
Estimated Station Totals *	89,140	149,670	238,810
Average Weekly Circulation (2009)	45,360	69,557	114,917
Average Daily Circulation (2009)			49,014

Other DMA Total	Cable TV Households	Non-cable TV Households	Total TV Households
Estimated Station Totals *	26,940	23,700	50,640
Average Weekly Circulation (2009)	11,947	2,592	14,539
Average Daily Circulation (2009)			3,193

*Estimated station totals are sums of the Nielsen TV and Cable TV household estimates for each county in which the station registers viewing of more than 5% as per the Nielsen Survey Methods.

KNWS-DT
Ch. 47

Network Service: IND.

Grantee: Johnson Broadcasting Inc.-Debtor-in-Possession, 8440 Westpark Dr, Houston, TX 77063.

Studio: 8440 Westpark Dr., Houston, TX 77063.

Mailing Address: 8440 Westpark Dr, Houston, TX 77063.

Phone: 713-974-5151. **Fax:** 713-974-5188.

Web Site: http://www.knws51.com

Technical Facilities: Channel No. 47 (668-674 MHz). Authorized power: 1000-kw max. visual, aural. Antenna: 1959-ft above av. terrain, 1945-ft. above ground, 2022-ft. above sea level.

Latitude	29°	34'	15"
Longitude	95°	30'	37"

Note: Latitude and longitude coordinates shown are based on the North American Datum of 1927 (NAD 27) as currently required by the Mass Media Bureau of the FCC.

Ownership: Douglas R. Johnson (Group Owner).

Began Operation: January 1, 2003. Standard and High Definition. Station operating under Special Temporary Authority at 11.9-kw max. visual. Began analog operations: November 3, 1993. Transfer of control to debtor-in-possession status was approved by FCC October 10, 2008. Ceased analog operations: June 12, 2009.

Represented (legal): Smithwick & Belendiuk PC.

Personnel:

Doug Johnson, General Manager.

Kevin Ford, Operations Director.

Jack Dabbah, Station & Sales Manager.

Rod Rodriquez, Local Sales Manager.

Andrew Bicknell, Chief Engineer.

Anna Grinvalds, Business Manager.

Tenesa Thompson, Traffic Manager & PSA Director.

City of License: Katy. **Station DMA:** Houston, TX. **Rank:** 10.

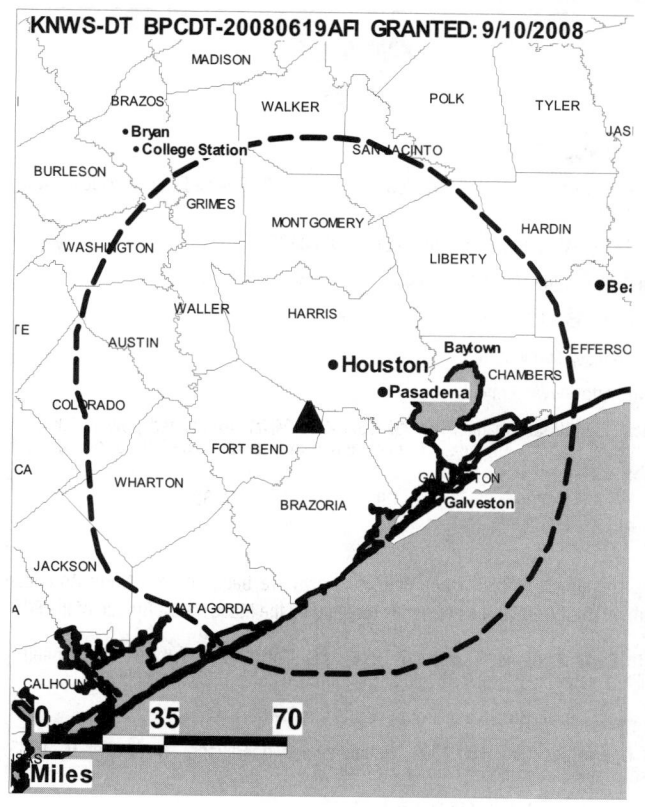

© 2010 Warren Communications News

Circulation © 2009 Nielsen. Coverage based on Nielsen study.

GrandTotal	Cable TV Households	Non-cable TV Households	Total TV Households
Estimated Station Totals *	1,064,690	853,780	1,918,470
Average Weekly Circulation (2009)	164,433	96,179	260,612
Average Daily Circulation (2009)			52,839

Station DMA Total	Cable TV Households	Non-cable TV Households	Total TV Households
Estimated Station Totals *	1,064,690	853,780	1,918,470
Average Weekly Circulation (2009)	164,433	96,179	260,612
Average Daily Circulation (2009)			52,839

*Estimated station totals are sums of the Nielsen TV and Cable TV household estimates for each county in which the station registers viewing of more than 5% as per the Nielsen Survey Methods.

KMYS-DT
Ch. 32

Network Service: MNT.

Licensee: San Antonio (KRRT-TV) Licensee Inc., 10706 Beaver Dam Rd, Cockeysville, MD 21030.

Studio: 4335 N.W. Loop 410, San Antonio, TX 78229.

Mailing Address: 4335 N.W. Loop 410, San Antonio, TX 78229.

Phone: 210-366-1129. **Fax:** 210-377-4758.

E-mail: dradla@sbgtv.com

Web Site: http://www.kmys.tv

Technical Facilities: Channel No. 32 (578-584 MHz). Authorized power: 1000-kw max. visual, aural. Antenna: 1741-ft above av. terrain, 1527-ft. above ground, 3023-ft. above sea level.

Latitude	29°	36'	38"
Longitude	98°	53'	33"

Note: Latitude and longitude coordinates shown are based on the North American Datum of 1927 (NAD 27) as currently required by the Mass Media Bureau of the FCC.

Satellite Earth Stations: Transmitter PYE; U.S. Tower, 2-meter Ku-band; United Satellite Systems, 5-meter C-band; Scientific-Atlanta, Collins receivers.

Ownership: Sinclair Broadcast Group Inc. (Group Owner).

Began Operation: May 15, 2003. Began analog operations: November 6, 1985. Ceased analog operations: February 17, 2009.

Represented (sales): Katz Media Group.

Represented (legal): Pillsbury Winthrop Shaw Pittman LLP.

Personnel:

John Seabers, General Manager.

David Ostmo, Operations Director.

Dean Radla, Sales Director.

Yesenia Rivas, Local Sales Manager.

Gwen Frames, National Sales Manager.

Yvette Reyna, Sales Promotion Director.

Mike Guerrero, Chief Engineer.

Renae Flood, Regional Business Manager.

David Howitt, Marketing Director.

Azalia Hoetling, Promotion Director.

Debra Smith, Traffic Manager.

City of License: Kerrville. **Station DMA:** San Antonio, TX. **Rank:** 37.

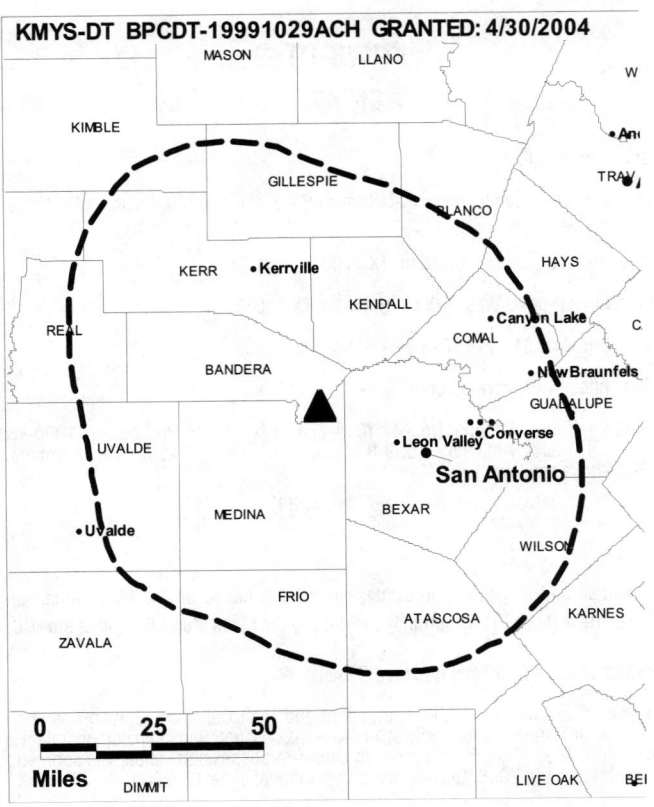

KMYS-DT BPCDT-19991029ACH GRANTED: 4/30/2004

© 2010 Warren Communications News

Circulation © 2009 Nielsen. Coverage based on Nielsen study.

GrandTotal	Cable TV Households	Non-cable TV Households	Total TV Households
Estimated Station Totals *	493,180	282,720	775,900
Average Weekly Circulation (2009)	105,992	66,766	172,758
Average Daily Circulation (2009)			57,854

Station DMA Total	Cable TV Households	Non-cable TV Households	Total TV Households
Estimated Station Totals *	489,290	276,510	765,800
Average Weekly Circulation (2009)	105,677	66,089	171,766
Average Daily Circulation (2009)			57,440

Other DMA Total	Cable TV Households	Non-cable TV Households	Total TV Households
Estimated Station Totals *	3,890	6,210	10,100
Average Weekly Circulation (2009)	315	677	992
Average Daily Circulation (2009)			414

*Estimated station totals are sums of the Nielsen TV and Cable TV household estimates for each county in which the station registers viewing of more than 5% as per the Nielsen Survey Methods.

KAKW-DT
Ch. 13

Network Service: UNV.

Licensee: KAKW License Partnership LP, 1999 Avenue of the Stars, Ste 3050, Los Angeles, CA 90067.

Studio: 8803 Woodway Dr, Waco, TX 76712-2344.

Mailing Address: 2233 W North Loop Blvd, Austin, TX 78756.

Phone: 512-453-8899. **Fax:** 512-533-2888.

Web Site: http://www.univision.com

Technical Facilities: Channel No. 13 (210-216 MHz). Authorized power: 45-kw visual, aural. Antenna: 1588-ft above av. terrain, 1565-ft. above ground, 2700-ft. above sea level.

Latitude	30°	43'	34"
Longitude	97°	59'	23"

Holds CP for change to 39-kw visual, 1814-ft above av. terrain, 1791-ft. above ground, 2926-ft. above sea level; BPCDT-20090630ACH.

Note: Latitude and longitude coordinates shown are based on the North American Datum of 1927 (NAD 27) as currently required by the Mass Media Bureau of the FCC.

Ownership: Univision Communications Inc. (Group Owner).

Began Operation: September 8, 2006. Began analog operations: May 31, 1996. Transfer of control to Broadcasting Media Partners Inc. approved by FCC March 27, 2007. Sale to present owner by White Knight Holding Inc. approved by FCC December 10, 2001. Sale to White Knight Holding Inc. by 62 Broadcasting Inc. approved by FCC July 24, 1995. Ceased analog operations: June 12, 2009.

Represented (legal): Covington & Burling.

Represented (sales): Continental Television Sales.

Personnel:

Susan Kelly, Local Sales Manager.

Ramsey Elia, National Sales Manager.

Kenneth Barnett, Chief Engineer.

Kathy Lebrun, Business Manager.

Elizabeth Villarreal, Traffic Manager.

City of License: Killeen. **Station DMA:** Austin, TX. **Rank:** 48.

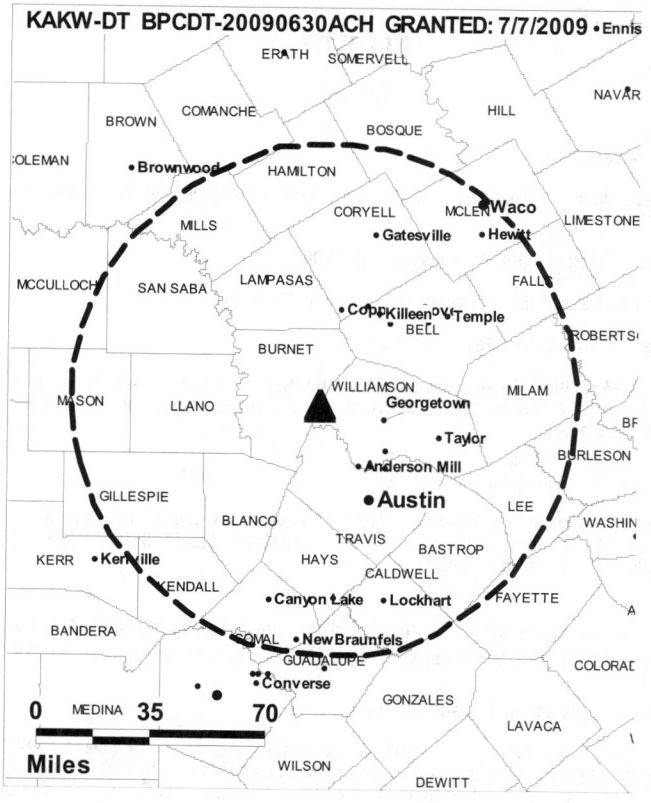

KAKW-DT BPCDT-20090630ACH GRANTED: 7/7/2009

© 2010 Warren Communications News

Circulation © 2009 Nielsen. Coverage based on Nielsen study.

GrandTotal	Cable TV Households	Non-cable TV Households	Total TV Households
Estimated Station Totals *	310,570	123,020	433,590
Average Weekly Circulation (2009)	18,494	8,624	27,118
Average Daily Circulation (2009)			17,429

Station DMA Total	Cable TV Households	Non-cable TV Households	Total TV Households
Estimated Station Totals *	310,570	112,450	423,020
Average Weekly Circulation (2009)	18,494	8,096	26,590
Average Daily Circulation (2009)			17,344

Other DMA Total	Cable TV Households	Non-cable TV Households	Total TV Households
Estimated Station Totals *	0	10,570	10,570
Average Weekly Circulation (2009)	0	528	528
Average Daily Circulation (2009)			85

*Estimated station totals are sums of the Nielsen TV and Cable TV household estimates for each county in which the station registers viewing of more than 5% as per the Nielsen Survey Methods.

KLDT-DT
Ch. 54

Network Service: IND.

Licensee: Johnson Broadcasting of Dallas Inc.-Debtor-in-Possession, 8440 Westpark Dr, Houston, TX 77063.

Studio: 2450 Rockbrook Dr., Lewisville, TX 75067.

Mailing Address: 2450 Rockbrook Dr, Lewisville, TX 75067.

Phone: 713-974-5151. **Fax:** 713-974-5188.

Technical Facilities: Channel No. 54 (710-716 MHz). Authorized power: 75-kw max. visual, aural. Antenna: 1621-ft above av. terrain, 1473-ft. above ground, 2287-ft. above sea level.

Latitude	32°	32'	36"
Longitude	96°	57'	32"

Holds CP for change to channel number 39, 1000-kw max. visual, 1673-ft above av. terrain, 1489-ft. above ground, 2303-ft. above sea level; lat. 32° 35' 07", long. 96° 58' 06", BPCDT-20080619AEY.

Note: Latitude and longitude coordinates shown are based on the North American Datum of 1927 (NAD 27) as currently required by the Mass Media Bureau of the FCC.

Ownership: Douglas R. Johnson (Group Owner).

Began Operation: February 1, 2003. Began analog operations: October 1, 1997. Transfer of control to debtor-in-possession status was approved by FCC October 10, 2008. Sale to Hispanic Television Network Inc. approved by FCC August 7, 2000, but never consummated. On November 17, 2006, station received permission from the FCC to end analog operations and operate in digital format only. Ceased analog operations: January 1, 2007.

Represented (sales): Smithwick & Belendiuk PC.

Personnel:

Douglas Johnson, General Manager.

Andrew Bicknell, Chief Engineer.

Tenesa Randell Thompson, Traffic Manager.

Jack Dabbah, General Sales Manager.

Anna Grinvalds, Business Manager.

City of License: Lake Dallas. **Station DMA:** Dallas-Fort Worth, TX. **Rank:** 5.

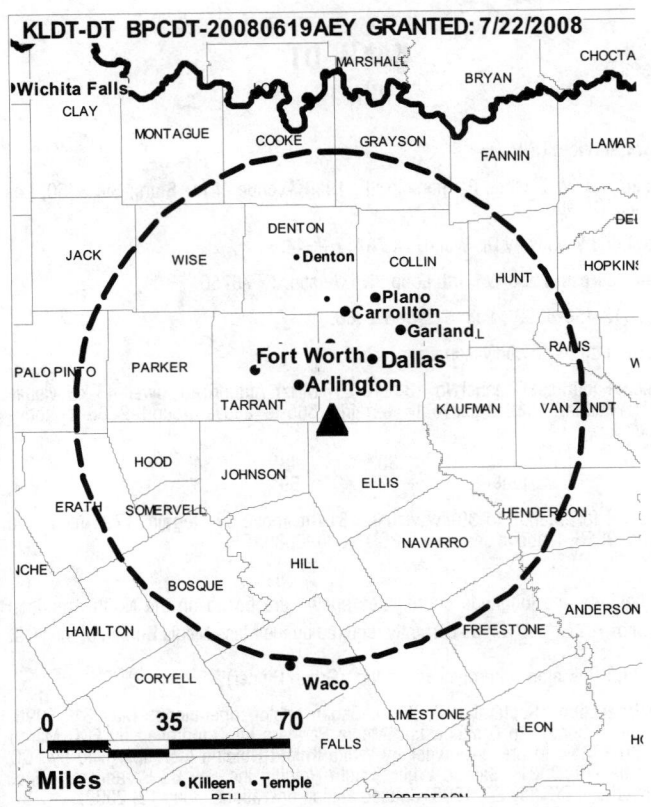

KLDT-DT BPCDT-20080619AEY GRANTED: 7/22/2008

© 2010 Warren Communications News

Circulation © 2009 Nielsen. Coverage based on Nielsen study.

GrandTotal	Cable TV Households	Non-cable TV Households	Total TV Households
Estimated Station Totals *	0	8,450	8,450
Average Weekly Circulation (2009)	0	608	608
Average Daily Circulation (2009)			42

Station DMA Total	Cable TV Households	Non-cable TV Households	Total TV Households
Estimated Station Totals *	0	8,450	8,450
Average Weekly Circulation (2009)	0	608	608
Average Daily Circulation (2009)			42

*Estimated station totals are sums of the Nielsen TV and Cable TV household estimates for each county in which the station registers viewing of more than 5% as per the Nielsen Survey Methods.

KGNS-DT
Ch. 8

Network Service: NBC, CW.

Grantee: SagamoreHill Broadcasting of Texas LLC, 3825 Inverness Way, Augusta, GA 30907.

Studio: 120 W. Del Mar Blvd., Laredo, TX 78045.

Mailing Address: PO Box 2829, Laredo, TX 78044.

Phone: 956-727-8888. **Fax:** 956-727-5336.

Web Site: http://www.pro8news.com

Technical Facilities: Channel No. 8 (180-186 MHz). Authorized power: 20-kw visual, aural. Antenna: 1024-ft above av. terrain, 1033-ft. above ground, 1517-ft. above sea level.

Latitude	27°	40'	21"
Longitude	99°	39'	51"

Note: Latitude and longitude coordinates shown are based on the North American Datum of 1927 (NAD 27) as currently required by the Mass Media Bureau of the FCC.

Ownership: SagamoreHill Broadcasting LLC (Group Owner).

Began Operation: December 8, 2006. Station broadcasting digitally on its analog channel allotment. Began analog operations: January 5, 1956. Transfer by partners H. C. Avery Jr. & David H. Cole to Donald W. Reynolds approved by FCC July 30, 1958 (Television Digest, Vol. 14:28, 32). Sale to T. Frank Smith Jr., et al., approved by FCC October 4, 1977. Sale to Burke Broadcasting approved by FCC October 28, 1983; rescinded November 2, 1983; granted December 15, 1983. Federal court subsequently ordered that Burke sell station back to Gulf Coast Broadcasting Co., to be followed by sale to Century Development Corp. (Malcolm I. Glazer). Sale to present owner by The Malcolm Glazer Trust approved by FCC September 28, 2004. Ceased analog operations: June 12, 2009.

Represented (legal): Wiley Rein LLP.

Represented (sales): Continental Television Sales.

Personnel:

Carlos H. Salinas, Vice President & General Manager.

Jose Luis Salinas, Production Manager.

Ramiro Saucedo, Creative Services Director.

Olga Ramirez, Traffic Manager & Programming Director.

Juan Cue, Local Sales Manager.

Raymond Gomez, News Director.

David York, Chief Engineer.

Priscilla Flores, Business Manager.

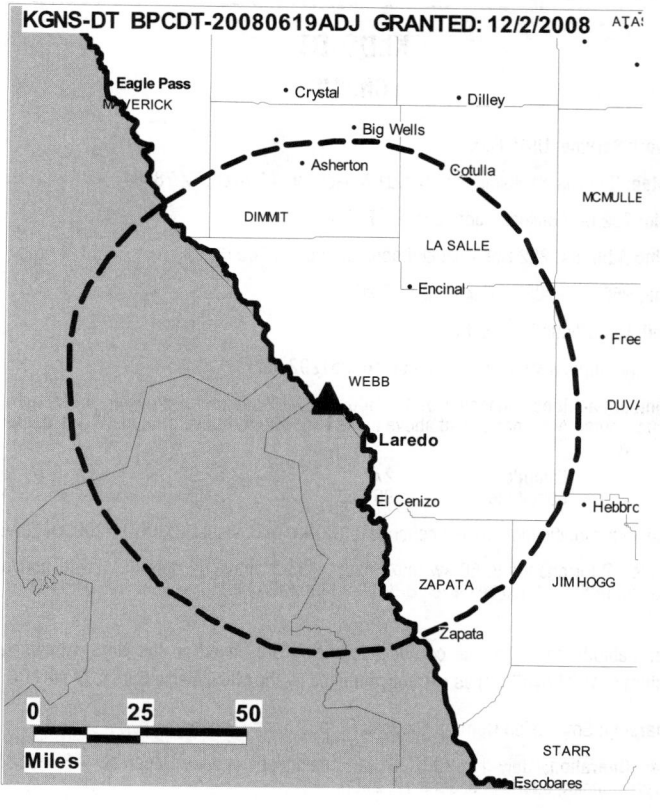

© 2010 Warren Communications News

City of License: Laredo. **Station DMA:** Laredo, TX. **Rank:** 188.

Circulation © 2009 Nielsen. Coverage based on Nielsen study.

GrandTotal	Cable TV Households	Non-cable TV Households	Total TV Households
Estimated Station Totals *	41,140	26,970	68,110
Average Weekly Circulation (2009)	25,146	8,521	33,667
Average Daily Circulation (2009)			20,147

Station DMA Total	Cable TV Households	Non-cable TV Households	Total TV Households
Estimated Station Totals *	41,140	26,970	68,110
Average Weekly Circulation (2009)	25,146	8,521	33,667
Average Daily Circulation (2009)			20,147

*Estimated station totals are sums of the Nielsen TV and Cable TV household estimates for each county in which the station registers viewing of more than 5% as per the Nielsen Survey Methods.

KLDO-DT
Ch. 19

Network Service: UNV, FOX.

Grantee: Entravision Holdings LLC, 801 N Jackson, McAllen, TX 78504.

Studio: 222 Bob Bullock Loop, Laredo, TX 78043.

Mailing Address: 222 Bob Bullock Loop, Laredo, TX 78043.

Phone: 956-727-0027. **Fax:** 956-727-2673.

E-mail: kldoproduction@entravision.com

Web Site: http://www.kldo.entravision.com/p1292.html

Technical Facilities: Channel No. 19 (500-506 MHz). Authorized power: 5-kw max. visual, aural. Antenna: 359-ft above av. terrain, 400-ft. above ground, 873-ft. above sea level.

Latitude	27°	39'	52.9"
Longitude	99°	36'	24.9"

Requests modification of CP for change to 150-kw max. visual; BMPCDT-20090713ACI.

Holds CP for change to 50-kw max. visual, 433-ft above av. terrain, 475-ft. above ground, 948-ft. above sea level; BPCDT-20090212AAT.

Note: Latitude and longitude coordinates shown are based on the North American Datum of 1927 (NAD 27) as currently required by the Mass Media Bureau of the FCC.

Ownership: Entravision Communications Corp. (Group Owner).

Began Operation: July 17, 2007. Began analog operations: December 18, 1984. Ceased analog operations: June 12, 2009.

Personnel:

Terry Elena Ordaz, General Manager & General Sales Manager.

Loretta Bafidis, Local Sales Manager.

Jeanette Puig, National Sales Manager.

Angel Covarrubias, News Director.

Joe Martinez, Chief Engineer.

Elizabeth Canavati, Business Manager.

Ime Valenzuele, Promotion Director.

Bill Teogarcia, Production Manager.

Gloria Arechiga, Traffic Manager.

City of License: Laredo. **Station DMA:** Laredo, TX. **Rank:** 188.

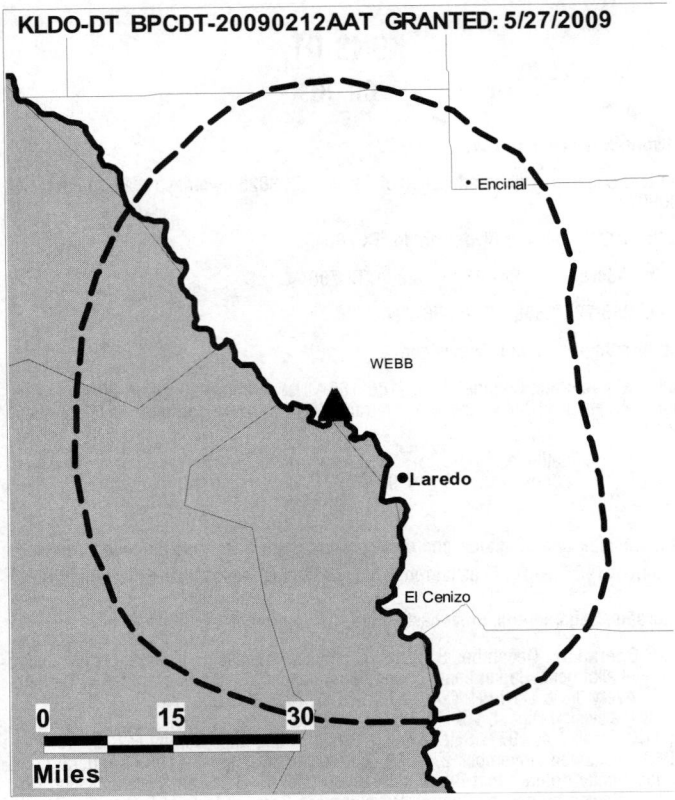

KLDO-DT BPCDT-20090212AAT GRANTED: 5/27/2009

© 2010 Warren Communications News

Circulation © 2009 Nielsen. Coverage based on Nielsen study.

GrandTotal	Cable TV Households	Non-cable TV Households	Total TV Households
Estimated Station Totals *	41,140	26,970	68,110
Average Weekly Circulation (2009)	24,683	17,691	42,374
Average Daily Circulation (2009)			25,764

Station DMA Total	Cable TV Households	Non-cable TV Households	Total TV Households
Estimated Station Totals *	41,140	26,970	68,110
Average Weekly Circulation (2009)	24,683	17,691	42,374
Average Daily Circulation (2009)			25,764

*Estimated station totals are sums of the Nielsen TV and Cable TV household estimates for each county in which the station registers viewing of more than 5% as per the Nielsen Survey Methods.

KVTV-DT
Ch. 13

Network Service: CBS.

Licensee: Eagle Creek Broadcasting of Laredo LLC, 2111 University Park Dr, Ste 650, Okemos, MI 48864-6913.

Studio: 2600 Shea St, Laredo, TX 78040.

Mailing Address: 2600 Shea St, Laredo, TX 78040.

Phone: 956-727-1300. **Fax:** 956-712-0185.

Technical Facilities: Channel No. 13 (210-216 MHz). Authorized power: 3-kw visual, aural. Antenna: 932-ft above av. terrain, 996-ft. above ground, 1411-ft. above sea level.

Latitude	27°	31'	12"
Longitude	99°	31'	19"

Note: Latitude and longitude coordinates shown are based on the North American Datum of 1927 (NAD 27) as currently required by the Mass Media Bureau of the FCC.

Ownership: Eagle Creek Broadcasting LLC (Group Owner).

Began Operation: October 15, 2007. Station broadcasting digitally on its analog channel allotment. Began analog operations: December 28, 1973. Ceased analog operations: November 30, 2008.

Represented (legal): Leventhal, Senter & Lerman PLLC.

Represented (sales): Katz Media Group.

Personnel:

Billy Brotherton, President, General Manager & Program Director.

Shelly Langhan, General Sales Manager.

Hollis Grizzard, News Director.

Russell Vaughn, Chief Engineer.

John David, Business Manager.

Wade Capps, Promotion Director.

Sherry Lemerond, Traffic Manager.

City of License: Laredo. **Station DMA:** Laredo, TX. **Rank:** 188.

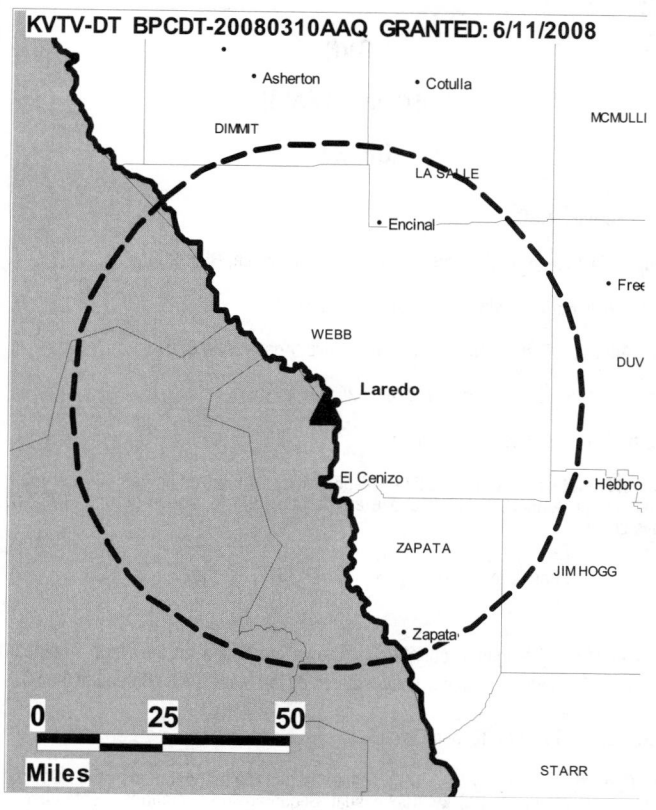

KVTV-DT BPCDT-20080310AAQ GRANTED: 6/11/2008

© 2010 Warren Communications News

Circulation © 2009 Nielsen. Coverage based on Nielsen study.

GrandTotal	Cable TV Households	Non-cable TV Households	Total TV Households
Estimated Station Totals *	41,140	26,970	68,110
Average Weekly Circulation (2009)	13,759	5,155	18,914
Average Daily Circulation (2009)			8,019

Station DMA Total	Cable TV Households	Non-cable TV Households	Total TV Households
Estimated Station Totals *	41,140	26,970	68,110
Average Weekly Circulation (2009)	13,759	5,155	18,914
Average Daily Circulation (2009)			8,019

*Estimated station totals are sums of the Nielsen TV and Cable TV household estimates for each county in which the station registers viewing of more than 5% as per the Nielsen Survey Methods.

KBVO
(formerly KXAM)
Ch. 27

Network Service: NBC.

Grantee: KXAN Inc., 4 Richmond Sq, Ste 200, Providence, RI 02906.

Studio: 908 W Martin L King Blvd., Austin, TX 78701.

Mailing Address: 908 W Martin Luther King Blvd, Austin, TX 78701.

Phone: 512-476-3636. **Fax:** 512-476-1520.

Web Site: http://www.kxam14.com

Technical Facilities: Channel No. 27 (548-554 MHz). Authorized power: 660-kw max. visual, aural. Antenna: 817-ft above av. terrain, 394-ft. above ground, 1932-ft. above sea level.

Latitude	30°	40'	36"
Longitude	98°	33'	59"

Note: Latitude and longitude coordinates shown are based on the North American Datum of 1927 (NAD 27) as currently required by the Mass Media Bureau of the FCC.

Ownership: LIN TV Corp. (Group Owner).

Began Operation: February 27, 2003. Station began digital operations under Special Temporary Authority at 125-kw max. visual. Began analog operations: September 6, 1991. Ceased analog operations: June 12, 2009. Sale of controlling interest in LIN from AT&T to Hicks, Muse, Tate & Furst approved by FCC March 2, 1998. Proposed transfer of control from Ranger Equity Partners LP to Chancellor Media dismissed by FCC March 15, 1999.

Personnel:

Eric Lassberg, President & General Manager.

Mark Dunham, Chief Engineer.

Denise Daniels, General Sales Manager.

Tish Saliani, Marketing Director.

Jamie Aragon, Program Director.

City of License: Llano. **Station DMA:** Austin, TX. **Rank:** 48.

© 2010 Warren Communications News

Circulation © 2009 Nielsen. Coverage based on Nielsen study.

GrandTotal	Cable TV Households	Non-cable TV Households	Total TV Households
Estimated Station Totals *	8,640	17,510	26,150
Average Weekly Circulation (2009)	1,795	1,285	3,080
Average Daily Circulation (2009)			1,646

Station DMA Total	Cable TV Households	Non-cable TV Households	Total TV Households
Estimated Station Totals *	8,170	17,510	25,680
Average Weekly Circulation (2009)	1,657	1,285	2,942
Average Daily Circulation (2009)			1,641

*Estimated station totals are sums of the Nielsen TV and Cable TV household estimates for each county in which the station registers viewing of more than 5% as per the Nielsen Survey Methods.

KCEB-DT
Ch. 51

Network Service: CW.

Grantee: Estes Broadcasting LLC, 910 Travis St, Ste 2030, Houston, TX 77002.

Mailing Address: 701 N Access Rd, Longview, TX 75602.

Phone: 903-236-0051. **Fax:** 903-753-6637.

Technical Facilities: Channel No. 51 (692-698 MHz). Authorized power: 1000-kw max. visual, aural. Antenna: 1243-ft above av. terrain, 1175-ft. above ground, 1693-ft. above sea level.

Latitude	32°	15'	36"
Longitude	94°	57'	02"

Note: Latitude and longitude coordinates shown are based on the North American Datum of 1927 (NAD 27) as currently required by the Mass Media Bureau of the FCC.

Ownership: Estes Broadcasting LLC.

Began Operation: June 12, 2009. Began analog operations: July 20, 2003. Transfer of control to Dimension Enterprises Ltd. (Charles H. Chatelain) from JMI Services Inc. approved by FCC November 24, 2003. Ceased analog operations: June 12, 2009.

City of License: Longview.

Station DMA: Tyler-Longview (Lufkin & Nacogdoches), TX. **Rank:** 109.

FULLY SEARCHABLE • CONTINUOUSLY UPDATED • DISCOUNT RATES FOR PRINT PURCHASERS

For more information call **800-771-9202** or visit **www.warren-news.com**

Digital cable and TV coverage maps.
Visit www.warren-news.com/mediaprints.htm

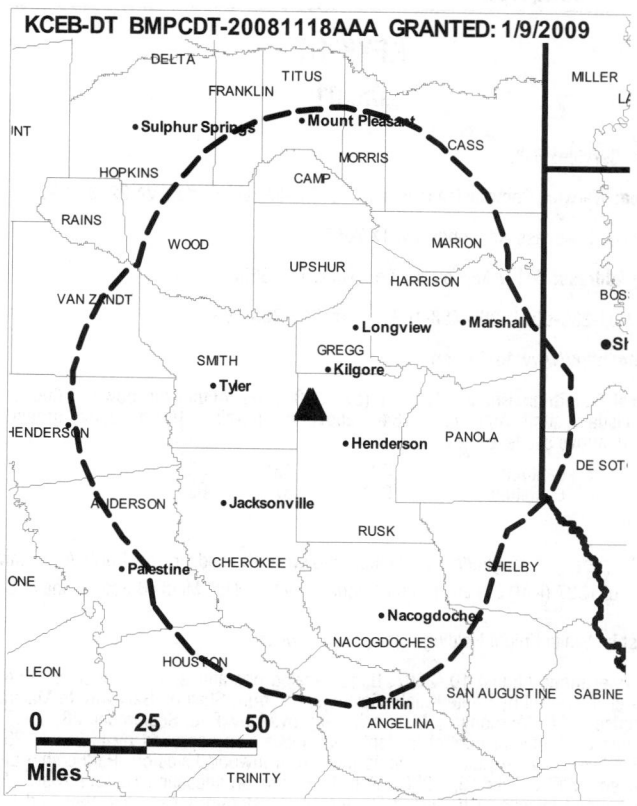

KCEB-DT BMPCDT-20081118AAA GRANTED: 1/9/2009

© 2010 Warren Communications News

Circulation © 2009 Nielsen. Coverage based on Nielsen study.

GrandTotal	Cable TV Households	Non-cable TV Households	Total TV Households
Estimated Station Totals *	106,580	130,320	236,900
Average Weekly Circulation (2009)	17,833	11,937	29,770
Average Daily Circulation (2009)			7,113

Station DMA Total	Cable TV Households	Non-cable TV Households	Total TV Households
Estimated Station Totals *	102,110	112,680	214,790
Average Weekly Circulation (2009)	17,290	10,455	27,745
Average Daily Circulation (2009)			6,715

Other DMA Total	Cable TV Households	Non-cable TV Households	Total TV Households
Estimated Station Totals *	4,470	17,640	22,110
Average Weekly Circulation (2009)	543	1,482	2,025
Average Daily Circulation (2009)			398

*Estimated station totals are sums of the Nielsen TV and Cable TV household estimates for each county in which the station registers viewing of more than 5% as per the Nielsen Survey Methods.

KFXK-DT
Ch. 31

Network Service: FOX.

Licensee: Warwick Communications Inc., 9257 Bailey Ln, Fairfax, VA 22031-1903.

Studio: 701 N Access Rd, Longview, TX 75602.

Mailing Address: 701 N Access Rd, Longview, TX 75602.

Phone: 903-236-0051; 903-758-1691. **Fax:** 903-753-6637.

Web Site: http://www.fox51.com

Technical Facilities: Channel No. 31 (572-578 MHz). Authorized power: 1000-kw max. visual, aural. Antenna: 1184-ft above av. terrain, 1109-ft. above ground, 1631-ft. above sea level.

Latitude	32°	15'	35"
Longitude	94°	57'	02"

Note: Latitude and longitude coordinates shown are based on the North American Datum of 1927 (NAD 27) as currently required by the Mass Media Bureau of the FCC.

Ownership: White Knight Holdings Inc. (Group Owner).

Began Operation: August 10, 2007. Began analog operations: September 9, 1984. Transfer of control by White Knight Holdings Inc. from Sheldon Galloway to Malara Enterprises LLC (Anthony J. Malara III) approved by FCC September 28, 2007. Involuntary transfer of control to debtor in possession approved by FCC July 25, 2006. Sale to White Knight Holdings Inc. from Inwood Investors Partnership LP approved by FCC July 16, 1998. Sale to Kamin Broadcasting Co./Longview LP (later Inwood Investors) by Jason R. Searcy, Trustee-In-Bankruptcy approved by FCC November 8, 1990. Assignment to Jason R. Searcy, Trustee-In-Bankruptcy from KLMG-TV Inc., Debtor In Possession approved by FCC November 9, 1989. Involuntary assignment to KLMG-TV Debtor In Possession approved by FCC June 30, 1987. Ceased analog operations: June 12, 2009.

Represented (legal): WolfBlock.

Represented (sales): Katz Media Group.

Personnel:

Dave Tillery, General Manager.

David Bailey, Local Sales Manager.

Dan Trent, Engineering Director.

Drew Balch, Program Director.

Mindy Countryman, Promotion Director.

Connie Jobe, Traffic Manager.

City of License: Longview.

Station DMA: Tyler-Longview (Lufkin & Nacogdoches), TX. **Rank:** 109.

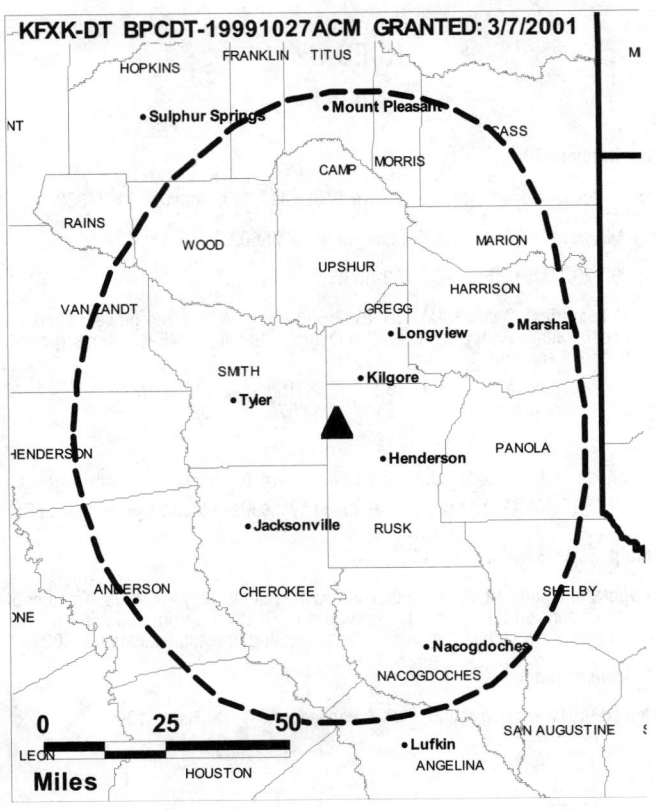

KFXK-DT BPCDT-19991027ACM GRANTED: 3/7/2001

© 2010 Warren Communications News

Circulation © 2009 Nielsen. Coverage based on Nielsen study.

GrandTotal	Cable TV Households	Non-cable TV Households	Total TV Households
Estimated Station Totals *	116,730	179,410	296,140
Average Weekly Circulation (2009)	43,938	63,181	107,119
Average Daily Circulation (2009)			35,134

Station DMA Total	Cable TV Households	Non-cable TV Households	Total TV Households
Estimated Station Totals *	102,110	149,670	251,780
Average Weekly Circulation (2009)	38,668	60,264	98,932
Average Daily Circulation (2009)			33,090

Other DMA Total	Cable TV Households	Non-cable TV Households	Total TV Households
Estimated Station Totals *	14,620	29,740	44,360
Average Weekly Circulation (2009)	5,270	2,917	8,187
Average Daily Circulation (2009)			2,044

*Estimated station totals are sums of the Nielsen TV and Cable TV household estimates for each county in which the station registers viewing of more than 5% as per the Nielsen Survey Methods.

KAMC-DT
Ch. 27

Network Service: ABC.

Grantee: Mission Broadcasting Inc., 544 Red Rock Dr, Wadsworth, OH 44281.

Studio: 7403 S University Ave, Lubbock, TX 79423-1424.

Mailing Address: 7403 S University Ave, Lubbock, TX 79423.

Phone: 806-745-2345; 806-745-2828. **Fax:** 806-748-1080.

Web Site: http://www.kamc28.com

Technical Facilities: Channel No. 27 (548-554 MHz). Authorized power: 1000-kw max. visual, aural. Antenna: 720-ft above av. terrain, 706-ft. above ground, 3935-ft. above sea level.

Latitude	33°	31'	33"
Longitude	101°	52'	07"

Note: Latitude and longitude coordinates shown are based on the North American Datum of 1927 (NAD 27) as currently required by the Mass Media Bureau of the FCC.

Ownership: Mission Broadcasting Inc. (Group Owner).

Began Operation: February 8, 2008. Began analog operations: November 11, 1968. Transfer of control to McAlister TV Enterprises Inc. approved by FCC March 24, 1975. Assignment of license to Intercontinental Pacific Group Inc. (Douglas Wolf) & subsequent sale to Burr-Hawkins Media Inc. approved by FCC November 24, 1998. Transfer to VHR Broadcasting Inc. by Burr-Hawkins Media Inc. approved by FCC December 29, 1998. Sale to Kenos Broadcasting Inc. (David Smith) by VHR Broadcasting Inc. approved by FCC December 17, 2003. Pro forma assignment of license to present owner by Kenos Broadcasting Inc. (David Smith) approved by FCC December 22, 2003. Ceased analog operations: February 17, 2009.

Represented (legal): Drinker Biddle.

Represented (sales): Blair Television.

Represented (engineering): Cavell, Mertz & Associates Inc.

Personnel:

Greg McAlister, General Manager.

Charles Spaugh, Operations & Program Director.

Eric Thomas, Sales Director.

Jason Henry, Sales Manager.

Mike Randolph, Chief Engineer.

Joyce Kelley, Business Manager.

Russ Poteet, News Director.

Jeff Pitner, Promotion & Marketing Director.

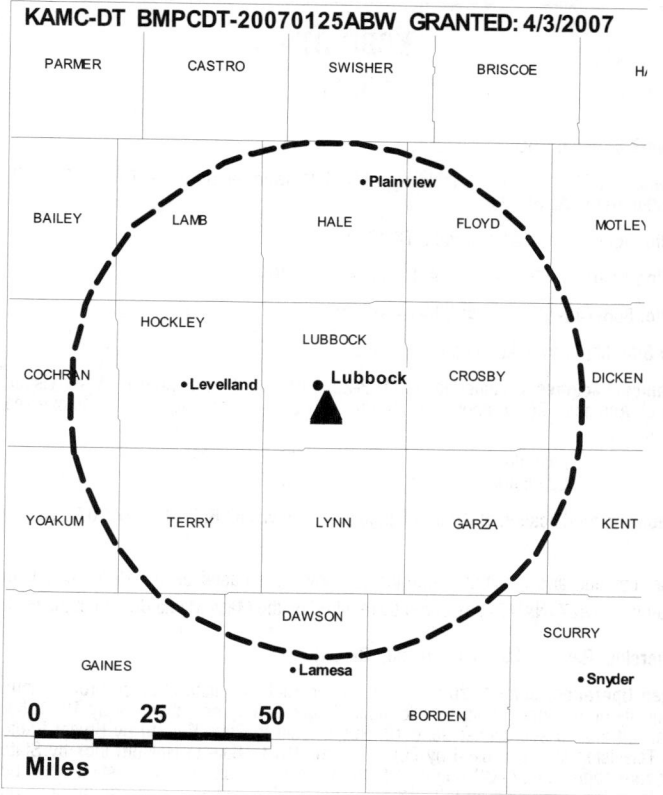

KAMC-DT BMPCDT-20070125ABW GRANTED: 4/3/2007

© 2010 Warren Communications News

City of License: Lubbock. **Station DMA:** Lubbock, TX. **Rank:** 143.

Circulation © 2009 Nielsen. Coverage based on Nielsen study.

GrandTotal	Cable TV Households	Non-cable TV Households	Total TV Households
Estimated Station Totals *	66,080	82,540	148,620
Average Weekly Circulation (2009)	38,269	45,442	83,711
Average Daily Circulation (2009)			35,526

Station DMA Total	Cable TV Households	Non-cable TV Households	Total TV Households
Estimated Station Totals *	66,080	82,540	148,620
Average Weekly Circulation (2009)	38,269	45,442	83,711
Average Daily Circulation (2009)			35,526

*Estimated station totals are sums of the Nielsen TV and Cable TV household estimates for each county in which the station registers viewing of more than 5% as per the Nielsen Survey Methods.

KCBD-DT
Ch. 11

Network Service: NBC.

Licensee: KCBD License Subsidiary LLC, 201 Monroe St, RSA Tower, 20th Fl, Montgomery, AL 36104.

Studio: 5600 Avenue A., Lubbock, TX 79404.

Mailing Address: 5600 Avenue A, Lubbock, TX 79404.

Phone: 806-744-1414. **Fax:** 806-744-0449.

Web Site: http://www.kcbd.com

Technical Facilities: Channel No. 11 (198-204 MHz). Authorized power: 15-kw visual, aural. Antenna: 761-ft above av. terrain, 757-ft. above ground, 3957-ft. above sea level.

Latitude	33°	32'	32"
Longitude	101°	50'	14"

Requests modification of CP for change to 41-kw visual; BMPCDT-20090722ACC.

Note: Latitude and longitude coordinates shown are based on the North American Datum of 1927 (NAD 27) as currently required by the Mass Media Bureau of the FCC.

Ownership: Raycom Media Inc. (Group Owner).

Began Operation: June 1, 2002. Standard and High Definition. Station broadcasting digitally on its analog channel allotment. Began analog operations: May 10, 1953. Ceased analog operations: June 12, 2009. Sale to State Record by Bryant Radio & Television Inc. approved by FCC May 26, 1971. Sale to Holsum Inc. by State Record approved by FCC August 12, 1983. Sale to Cosmos Broadcasting Corp. by Holsum Inc. approved by FCC February 17, 2000. Transfer of control by Cosmos Broadcasting Corp. from shareholders of The Liberty Corp. to Raycom Media Inc. approved by FCC January 17, 2006.

Represented (legal): Covington & Burling.

Represented (sales): Continental Television Sales.

Personnel:

Dan Jackson, Vice President & General Manager.

Josh Young, Operations & Promotion Director.

Beverly McBeath, General Sales Manager.

Diane Harlan, Local Sales Manager.

Benji Snead, News Director.

Ricky Price, Chief Engineer.

Linda London, Business Manager.

Jennifer Stephenson, Program Director.

Michelle Doggett, Traffic Manager.

City of License: Lubbock. **Station DMA:** Lubbock, TX. **Rank:** 143.

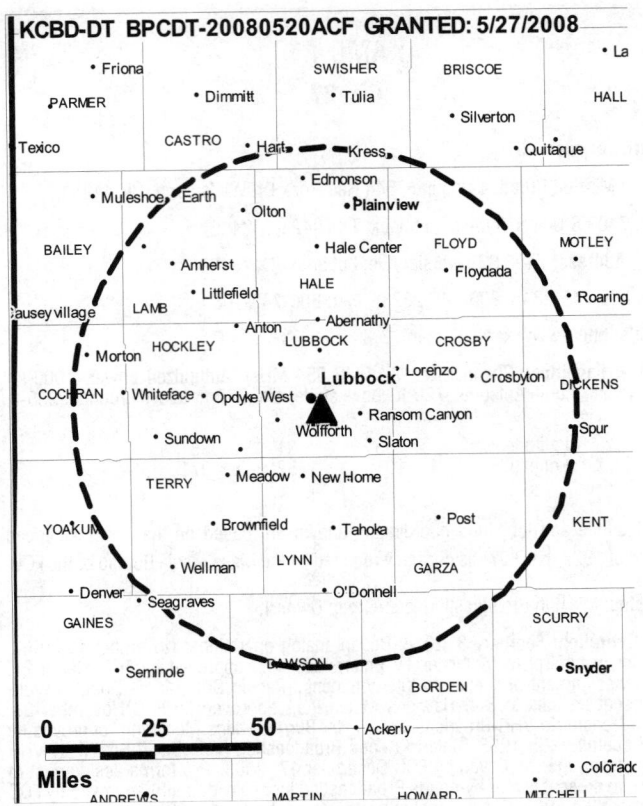

KCBD-DT BPCDT-20080520ACF GRANTED: 5/27/2008

© 2010 Warren Communications News

Circulation © 2009 Nielsen. Coverage based on Nielsen study.

GrandTotal	Cable TV Households	Non-cable TV Households	Total TV Households
Estimated Station Totals *	69,690	82,540	152,230
Average Weekly Circulation (2009)	49,505	57,957	107,462
Average Daily Circulation (2009)			64,591

Station DMA Total	Cable TV Households	Non-cable TV Households	Total TV Households
Estimated Station Totals *	66,320	82,540	148,860
Average Weekly Circulation (2009)	47,571	57,957	105,528
Average Daily Circulation (2009)			63,944

Other DMA Total	Cable TV Households	Non-cable TV Households	Total TV Households
Estimated Station Totals *	3,370	0	3,370
Average Weekly Circulation (2009)	1,934	0	1,934
Average Daily Circulation (2009)			647

*Estimated station totals are sums of the Nielsen TV and Cable TV household estimates for each county in which the station registers viewing of more than 5% as per the Nielsen Survey Methods.

KJTV-DT
Ch. 35

Network Service: FOX.

Grantee: Ramar Communications Inc., PO Box 3757, Lubbock, TX 79452-3757.

Studio: 9800 University Ave., Lubbock, TX 79423.

Mailing Address: PO Box 3757, Lubbock, TX 79452.

Phone: 806-745-3434. **Fax:** 806-748-1949.

Web Site: http://www.myfoxlubbock.com

Technical Facilities: Channel No. 35 (596-602 MHz). Authorized power: 1000-kw max. visual, aural. Antenna: 899-ft above av. terrain, 925-ft. above ground, 4132-ft. above sea level.

Latitude	33°	30'	08"
Longitude	101°	52'	20"

Note: Latitude and longitude coordinates shown are based on the North American Datum of 1927 (NAD 27) as currently required by the Mass Media Bureau of the FCC.

Ownership: Ramar Communications Inc. (Group Owner).

Began Operation: January 31, 2007. Began analog operations: December 10, 1981. Ceased analog operations: February 17, 2009.

Represented (legal): Leventhal, Senter & Lerman PLLC.

Represented (sales): Katz Media Group.

Personnel:

Brad Moran, President & General Manager.

Ray Moran, General Partner.

Marcie Reno, Promotion Director.

Jeff Klotzman, News Director.

Sherry Saffle, General Sales Manager.

Stephanie Fox, Regional Sales Manager.

Donna Campbell, Business Manager.

Traci Thorne, Program Director.

City of License: Lubbock. **Station DMA:** Lubbock, TX. **Rank:** 143.

TELEVISION & CABLE
Factbook Online

| continuous updates | fully searchable | easy to use |

For more information call **800-771-9202** or visit **www.warren-news.com**

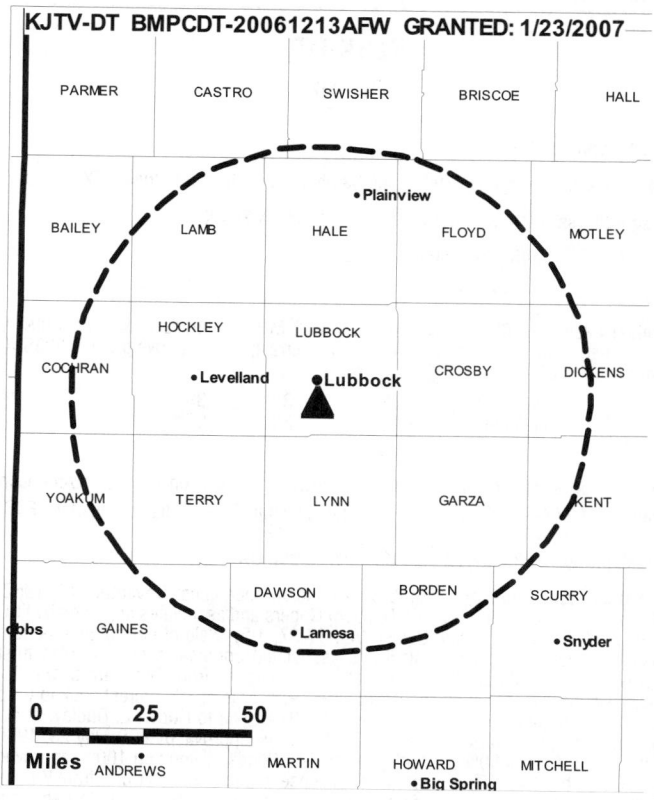

© 2010 Warren Communications News

Circulation © 2009 Nielsen. Coverage based on Nielsen study.

GrandTotal	Cable TV Households	Non-cable TV Households	Total TV Households
Estimated Station Totals *	81,460	90,720	172,180
Average Weekly Circulation (2009)	33,612	40,402	74,014
Average Daily Circulation (2009)			26,761

Station DMA Total	Cable TV Households	Non-cable TV Households	Total TV Households
Estimated Station Totals *	66,080	82,540	148,620
Average Weekly Circulation (2009)	28,894	39,887	68,781
Average Daily Circulation (2009)			25,317

Other DMA Total	Cable TV Households	Non-cable TV Households	Total TV Households
Estimated Station Totals *	15,380	8,180	23,560
Average Weekly Circulation (2009)	4,718	515	5,233
Average Daily Circulation (2009)			1,444

*Estimated station totals are sums of the Nielsen TV and Cable TV household estimates for each county in which the station registers viewing of more than 5% as per the Nielsen Survey Methods.

KLBK-DT
Ch. 40

Network Service: CBS.

Grantee: Nexstar Finance Inc., 909 Lake Carolyn Pkwy, Ste 1450, Irving, TX 75039.

Mailing Address: 7403 S University Ave, Lubbock, TX 79423.

Phone: 806-745-2345. **Fax:** 806-748-2250.

Web Site: http://www.klbk.com

Technical Facilities: Channel No. 40 (626-632 MHz). Authorized power: 1000-kw max. visual, aural. Antenna: 720-ft above av. terrain, 706-ft. above ground, 3935-ft. above sea level.

Latitude	33°	31'	33"
Longitude	101°	52'	07"

Note: Latitude and longitude coordinates shown are based on the North American Datum of 1927 (NAD 27) as currently required by the Mass Media Bureau of the FCC.

Ownership: Nexstar Broadcasting Group Inc. (Group Owner).

Began Operation: February 8, 2008. Began analog operations: November 13, 1952. Sale to Grayson Enterprises by W. D. (Dub) Rogers and associates approved by FCC October 11, 1961 (Television Digest, Vol. 17:27; 1:5). Sale of control to Theodore Shanbaum, Ellis Carp, Lee Optical and associated companies pension plan trust approved by FCC March 25, 1964. Sale of 1/3 interest from Ellis Carp to Dal-Tex Optical Co. Inc. approved by FCC March 19, 1971. Sale of 1/3 interest back to Carp by Dal-Tex approved by FCC December 24, 1974. Sale to Robert L. Dudley, et al., conditionally approved by FCC March 27, 1980; full approval by FCC May 23, 1980 (Vol. 20:13). Sale of 50% by Dudley to Charles Woods, giving him 100%, approved by FCC October 14, 1983. Assignment of license to BankAmerica Corp. from Woods Communications Group Inc. approved by FCC March 16, 1993. Sale to Petracom Equity Partners LP by Banam Broadcasting Inc. approved by FCC May 31, 1995. Sale to Quorum Broadcast Holdings Inc. by Petracom Equity Partners LP approved by FCC May 4, 1998 (Vol. 37:37). Merger of Quorum Broadcast Holdings Inc. into present owner approved by FCC October 30, 2003. Ceased analog operations: February 17, 2009.

Represented (legal): Drinker Biddle.

Represented (sales): Katz Media Group.

Personnel:

Greg McAllister, General Manager.

Chuck Spaugh, Operations & Program Director.

Eric Thomas, Sales Director.

Cindy Gilstrap, Sales Manager.

Russ Poteet, News Director.

Mike Randolph, Chief Engineer.

Jeff Pitner, Promotion Director.

Joyce Kelly, Business Manager.

City of License: Lubbock. **Station DMA:** Lubbock, TX. **Rank:** 143.

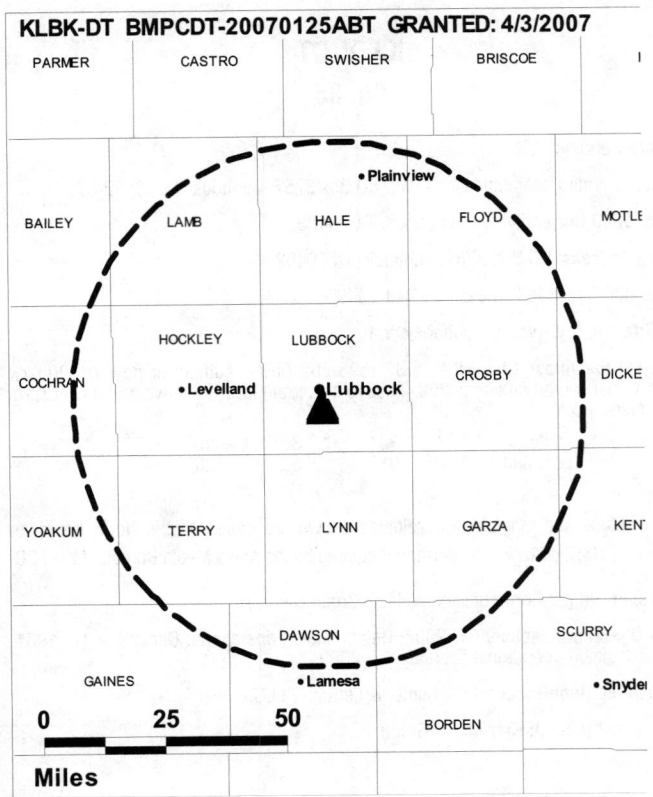

KLBK-DT BMPCDT-20070125ABT GRANTED: 4/3/2007

© 2010 Warren Communications News

Circulation © 2009 Nielsen. Coverage based on Nielsen study.

GrandTotal	Cable TV Households	Non-cable TV Households	Total TV Households
Estimated Station Totals *	66,770	82,540	149,310
Average Weekly Circulation (2009)	38,590	45,283	83,873
Average Daily Circulation (2009)			38,241

Station DMA Total	Cable TV Households	Non-cable TV Households	Total TV Households
Estimated Station Totals *	63,400	82,540	145,940
Average Weekly Circulation (2009)	37,734	45,283	83,017
Average Daily Circulation (2009)			38,012

Other DMA Total	Cable TV Households	Non-cable TV Households	Total TV Households
Estimated Station Totals *	3,370	0	3,370
Average Weekly Circulation (2009)	856	0	856
Average Daily Circulation (2009)			229

*Estimated station totals are sums of the Nielsen TV and Cable TV household estimates for each county in which the station registers viewing of more than 5% as per the Nielsen Survey Methods.

KPTB-DT
Ch. 16

Network Service: IND.

Licensee: Prime Time Christian Broadcasting Inc., PO Box 7708, Midland, TX 79708.

Studio: 1330 44th St., Lubbock, TX 79412.

Mailing Address: PO Box 12388, Lubbock, TX 79404.

Phone: 806-747-4997; 800-707-0420. **Fax:** 915-563-1736.

Web Site: http://www.ptcbglc.com

Technical Facilities: Channel No. 16 (482-488 MHz). Authorized power: 50-kw max. visual, aural. Antenna: 272-ft above av. terrain, 282-ft. above ground, 3456-ft. above sea level.

Latitude	33°	33'	12"
Longitude	101°	49'	13"

Note: Latitude and longitude coordinates shown are based on the North American Datum of 1927 (NAD 27) as currently required by the Mass Media Bureau of the FCC.

Ownership: Prime Time Christian Broadcasting Inc. (Group Owner).

Began Operation: February 27, 2009. Station broadcasting digitally on its analog channel allotment. Began analog operations: June 10, 1996. Ceased analog operations: February 17, 2009.

Personnel:

Al Cooper, President & General Manager.

Matt Montgomery, Chief Engineer.

City of License: Lubbock. **Station DMA:** Lubbock, TX. **Rank:** 143.

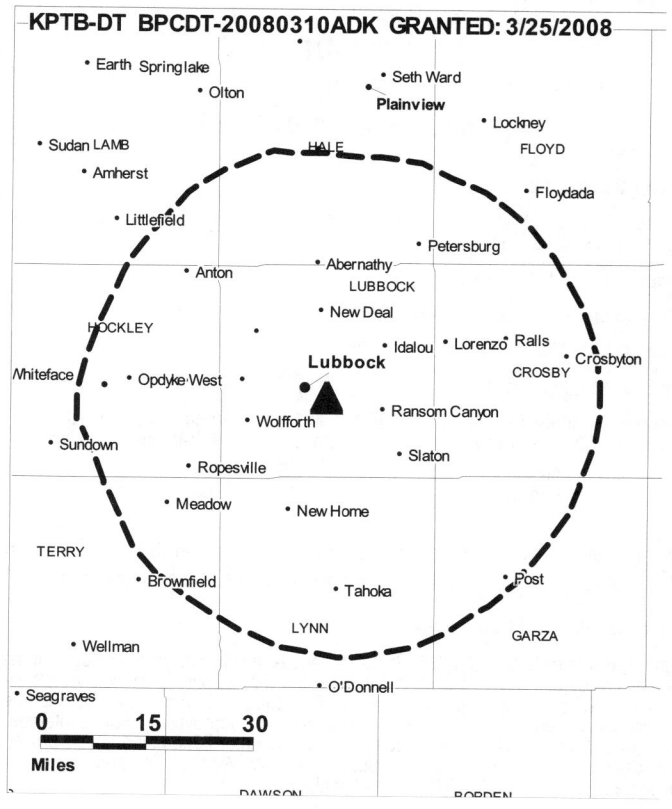

KPTB-DT BPCDT-20080310ADK GRANTED: 3/25/2008

© 2010 Warren Communications News

Circulation © 2009 Nielsen. Coverage based on Nielsen study.

GrandTotal	Cable TV Households	Non-cable TV Households	Total TV Households
Estimated Station Totals *	5,050	0	5,050
Average Weekly Circulation (2009)	343	0	343
Average Daily Circulation (2009)			60

Station DMA Total	Cable TV Households	Non-cable TV Households	Total TV Households
Estimated Station Totals *	2,600	0	2,600
Average Weekly Circulation (2009)	191	0	191
Average Daily Circulation (2009)			13

Other DMA Total	Cable TV Households	Non-cable TV Households	Total TV Households
Estimated Station Totals *	2,450	0	2,450
Average Weekly Circulation (2009)	152	0	152
Average Daily Circulation (2009)			47

*Estimated station totals are sums of the Nielsen TV and Cable TV household estimates for each county in which the station registers viewing of more than 5% as per the Nielsen Survey Methods.

KTRE-DT
Ch. 9
(Satellite of KLTV-DT Tyler)

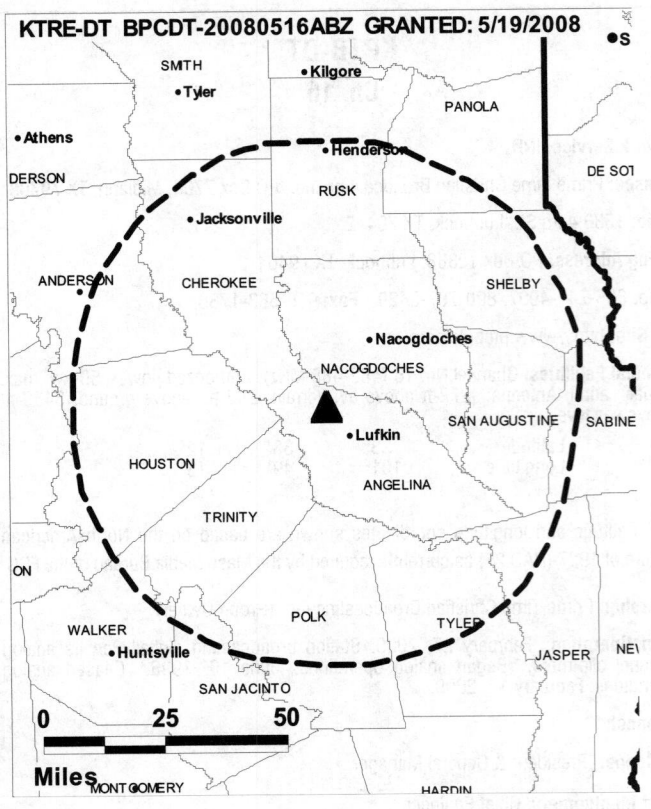

KTRE-DT BPCDT-20080516ABZ GRANTED: 5/19/2008

© 2010 Warren Communications News

Network Service: ABC.

Licensee: KLTV/KTRE License Subsidiary LLC, 201 Monroe St, RSA Tower, 20th Fl, Montgomery, AL 36104.

Studio: 358 TV Rd., Pollok, TX 75969.

Mailing Address: PO Box 729, Lufkin, TX 75902-0729.

Phone: 936-853-5873. **Fax:** 936-853-3084.

Web Site: http://www.ktre.com

Technical Facilities: Channel No. 9 (186-192 MHz). Authorized power: visual, aural. Antenna: 669-ft above av. terrain, 520-ft. above ground, 932-ft. above sea level.

Latitude	31°	25'	09"
Longitude	94°	48'	03"

Note: Latitude and longitude coordinates shown are based on the North American Datum of 1927 (NAD 27) as currently required by the Mass Media Bureau of the FCC.

Ownership: Raycom Media Inc. (Group Owner).

Began Operation: October 9, 2005. Station broadcasting digitally on its analog channel allotment. Began analog operations: August 31, 1955. Sale to present owner by Cosmos Broadcasting Corp. approved by FCC January 17, 2006. Sale to Cosmos Broadcasting Corp. by Civic Communications Corp. approved by FCC September 25, 2000. Sale to Civic Communications Corp. by Buford Television Inc. approved by FCC February 16, 1989. Sale to Buford by R. W. Wortham Jr. and associates approved by FCC July 18, 1962. Ceased analog operations: June 12, 2009.

Represented (sales): Katz Media Group.

Represented (legal): Covington & Burling.

Represented (sales): Continental Television Sales.

Personnel:

Artie L. Bedard, General Manager.

Lane Lowery, Production Department Director.

Randy Robinson, General Sales Manager.

Tina Alexander, News Director.

Steve Halsell, Chief Engineer.

Glenda London, Business Manager.

Cathy Carmichael, Program Director.

Mike Wiggins, Promotion Director.

James Moore, Marketing Manager.

Lea Ann Hendrick, Public Service Director.

City of License: Lufkin. **Station DMA:** Tyler-Longview (Lufkin & Nacogdoches), TX.

Rank: 109.

Circulation © 2009 Nielsen. Coverage based on Nielsen study.

GrandTotal	Cable TV Households	Non-cable TV Households	Total TV Households
Estimated Station Totals *	39,840	30,860	70,700
Average Weekly Circulation (2009)	22,891	7,855	30,746
Average Daily Circulation (2009)			17,862

Station DMA Total	Cable TV Households	Non-cable TV Households	Total TV Households
Estimated Station Totals *	29,850	30,860	60,710
Average Weekly Circulation (2009)	19,507	7,855	27,362
Average Daily Circulation (2009)			17,567

Other DMA Total	Cable TV Households	Non-cable TV Households	Total TV Households
Estimated Station Totals *	9,990	0	9,990
Average Weekly Circulation (2009)	3,384	0	3,384
Average Daily Circulation (2009)			295

*Estimated station totals are sums of the Nielsen TV and Cable TV household estimates for each county in which the station registers viewing of more than 5% as per the Nielsen Survey Methods.

KNVO-DT
Ch. 49

Network Service: UNV.

Licensee: Entravision Holdings LLC, 11900 Olympic Blvd, Ste 590, Los Angeles, CA 90064.

Studio: 801 N Jackson Rd, McAllen, TX 78501-9306.

Mailing Address: 801 N Jackson Rd, McAllen, TX 78501-9306.

Phone: 956-687-4848. **Fax:** 956-687-7784.

Web Site: http://www.knvo.com

Technical Facilities: Channel No. 49 (680-686 MHz). Authorized power: 1000-kw max. visual, aural. Antenna: 937-ft above av. terrain, 942-ft. above ground, 1019-ft. above sea level.

Latitude	26°	05'	18"
Longitude	98°	03'	44"

Note: Latitude and longitude coordinates shown are based on the North American Datum of 1927 (NAD 27) as currently required by the Mass Media Bureau of the FCC.

Ownership: Entravision Communications Corp. (Group Owner).

Began Operation: June 26, 2006. Began analog operations: October 12, 1992. Sale to present owner by Valley Channel 48 approved by FCC September 11, 1996. Ceased analog operations: June 12, 2009.

Personnel:

Larry Safir, General Manager.

Harry Thielman, Chief Engineer.

Joel Olivarez, General Sales Manager.

City of License: McAllen. **Station DMA:** Harlingen-Weslaco-Brownsville-McAllen, TX.

Rank: 87.

Digital cable and TV coverage maps.
Visit www.warren-news.com/mediaprints.htm

MediaPrints™
Map a Winning Business Strategy

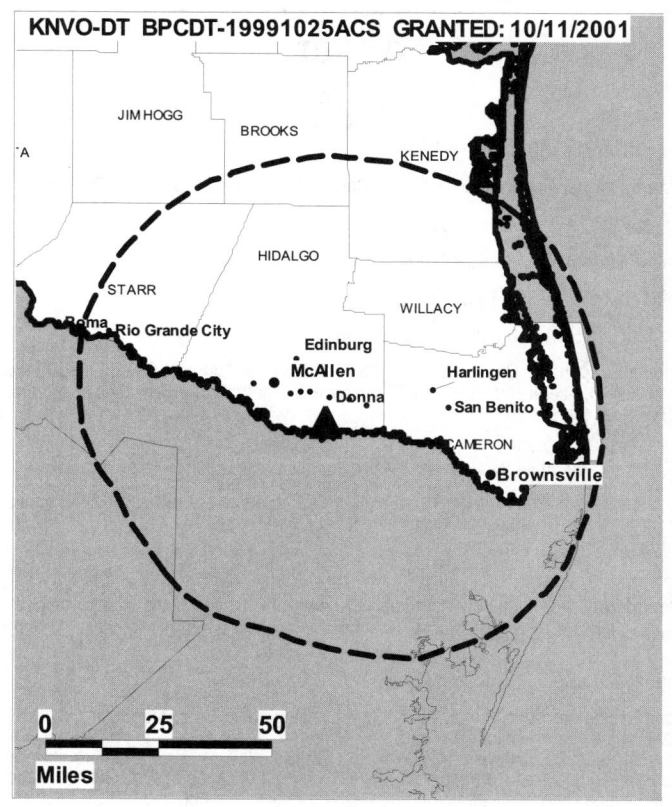

KNVO-DT BPCDT-19991025ACS GRANTED: 10/11/2001

© 2010 Warren Communications News

Circulation © 2009 Nielsen. Coverage based on Nielsen study.

GrandTotal	Cable TV Households	Non-cable TV Households	Total TV Households
Estimated Station Totals *	139,180	210,730	349,910
Average Weekly Circulation (2009)	54,661	99,109	153,770
Average Daily Circulation (2009)			99,819

Station DMA Total	Cable TV Households	Non-cable TV Households	Total TV Households
Estimated Station Totals *	139,180	210,730	349,910
Average Weekly Circulation (2009)	54,661	99,109	153,770
Average Daily Circulation (2009)			99,819

*Estimated station totals are sums of the Nielsen TV and Cable TV household estimates for each county in which the station registers viewing of more than 5% as per the Nielsen Survey Methods.

KMID-DT
Ch. 26

Network Service: ABC.

Grantee: Nexstar Finance Inc., 909 Lake Carolyn Pkwy, Ste 1450, Irving, TX 75039.

Studio: 3200 La Force Blvd., Midland, TX 79711.

Mailing Address: PO Box 60230, Midland, TX 79711.

Phone: 432-563-2222. **Fax:** 432-563-5819.

Web Site: http://www.permianbasin360.com

Technical Facilities: Channel No. 26 (542-548 MHz). Authorized power: 1000-kw max. visual, aural. Antenna: 1060-ft above av. terrain, 1076-ft. above ground, 3986-ft. above sea level.

Latitude	32°	05'	11"
Longitude	102°	17'	10"

Requests modification of CP for change to 902-ft above av. terrain, 910-ft. above ground, 3824-ft. above sea level; lat. 32° 05' 51", long. 102° 17' 21", BMPCDT-20081208ADC.

Note: Latitude and longitude coordinates shown are based on the North American Datum of 1927 (NAD 27) as currently required by the Mass Media Bureau of the FCC.

Ownership: Nexstar Broadcasting Group Inc. (Group Owner).

Began Operation: November 1, 2002. Began analog operations: December 18, 1953. Sale to Lorimar-Telepictures Corp. by Midessa TV Co. Inc. approved by FCC January 4, 1984 (Television Digest, Vol. 23:38). Sale to Davis-Goldfarb Co. by Lorimar-Telepictures Corp. approved by FCC February 12, 1988 (Vol. 28:7). Sale to Cottonwood Communications LLC by Davis-Goldfarb Co. approved by FCC February 13, 1995 (Vol. 35:30). Sale to GOCOM Communications LLC by Cottonwood Communications LLC approved by FCC September 18, 1997 (Vol. 37:37). Merger with Grapevine Communications Inc. approved by FCC November 1, 1999. Sale to present owner by GOCOM Holdings LLC approved by FCC July 31, 2000. Ceased analog operations: June 12, 2009.

Represented (legal): Drinker Biddle.

Represented (sales): Katz Media Group.

Personnel:

Jerry Jones, Vice President & General Manager.

Randall Whan, Operations Manager.

Shane Boing, General Sales Manager.

Kirk Keller, Local Sales Manager.

Mel Hudman, News Director.

Glenn Edwards, Chief Engineer.

Juanita Dannenberg, Controller.

Kay Harden, Program Director.

Katrina Kingston, Traffic & Programming Manager.

Wayne Wagner, Promotions Manager.

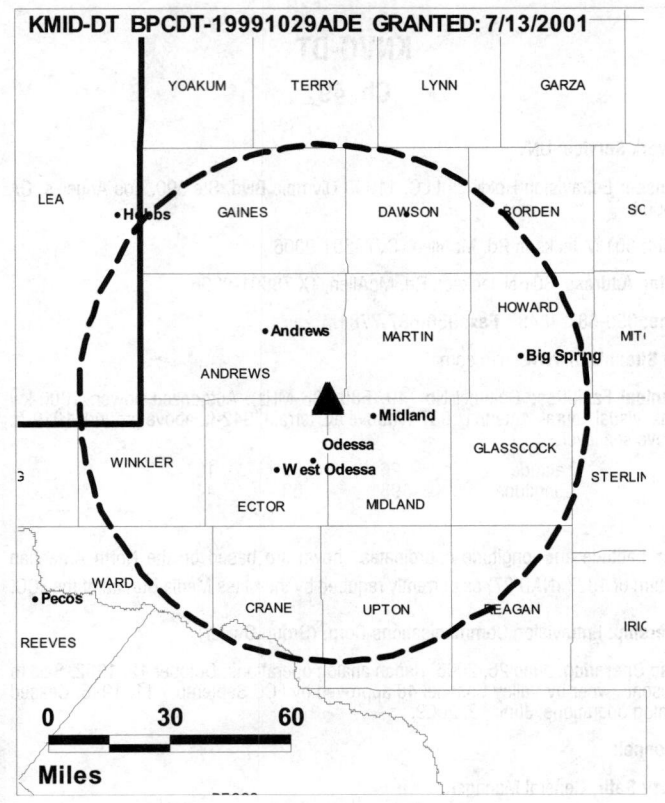

KMID-DT BPCDT-19991029ADE GRANTED: 7/13/2001

© 2010 Warren Communications News

City of License: Midland. **Station DMA:** Odessa-Midland, TX. **Rank:** 155.

Circulation © 2009 Nielsen. Coverage based on Nielsen study.

GrandTotal	Cable TV Households	Non-cable TV Households	Total TV Households
Estimated Station Totals *	102,150	44,030	146,180
Average Weekly Circulation (2009)	54,561	15,985	70,546
Average Daily Circulation (2009)			28,765

Station DMA Total	Cable TV Households	Non-cable TV Households	Total TV Households
Estimated Station Totals *	90,310	42,150	132,460
Average Weekly Circulation (2009)	48,997	15,680	64,677
Average Daily Circulation (2009)			27,631

Other DMA Total	Cable TV Households	Non-cable TV Households	Total TV Households
Estimated Station Totals *	11,840	1,880	13,720
Average Weekly Circulation (2009)	5,564	305	5,869
Average Daily Circulation (2009)			1,134

*Estimated station totals are sums of the Nielsen TV and Cable TV household estimates for each county in which the station registers viewing of more than 5% as per the Nielsen Survey Methods.

KUPB-DT
Ch. 18

Network Service: UNV.

Licensee: Entravision Midland Holdings LLC, 2809 Maxwell, Midland, TX 79705.

Studio: 10313 W. County Rd. 117, Midland, TX 79711-1907.

Mailing Address: 10313 W. County Rd. 117, Midland, TX 79711-1907.

Phone: 432-563-1826. **Fax:** 432-563-0215.

Web Site: http://www.univision.com

Technical Facilities: Channel No. 18 (494-500 MHz). Authorized power: 1000-kw max. visual, aural. Antenna: 922-ft above av. terrain, 951-ft. above ground, 3957-ft. above sea level.

Latitude	31°	50'	19"
Longitude	102°	31'	59"

Transmitter: 0.9-mi. NE of Hwys. 1213 & 349.

Note: Latitude and longitude coordinates shown are based on the North American Datum of 1927 (NAD 27) as currently required by the Mass Media Bureau of the FCC.

Ownership: Entravision Communications Corp. (Group Owner).

Began Operation: June 12, 2009. Station broadcasting digitally on its analog channel allotment. Began analog operations: May 14, 2001. Ceased analog operations: June 12, 2009.

Represented (legal): Thompson Hine LLP.

Personnel:

Leticia Martinez, General Manager & General Sales Manager.

Eddie Sills, Chief Engineer.

Roy Bermea, Program Director & Traffic Manager.

Rogelio Ramirez, News Director.

Brian Goldbard, Production Manager.

City of License: Midland. **Station DMA:** Odessa-Midland, TX. **Rank:** 155.

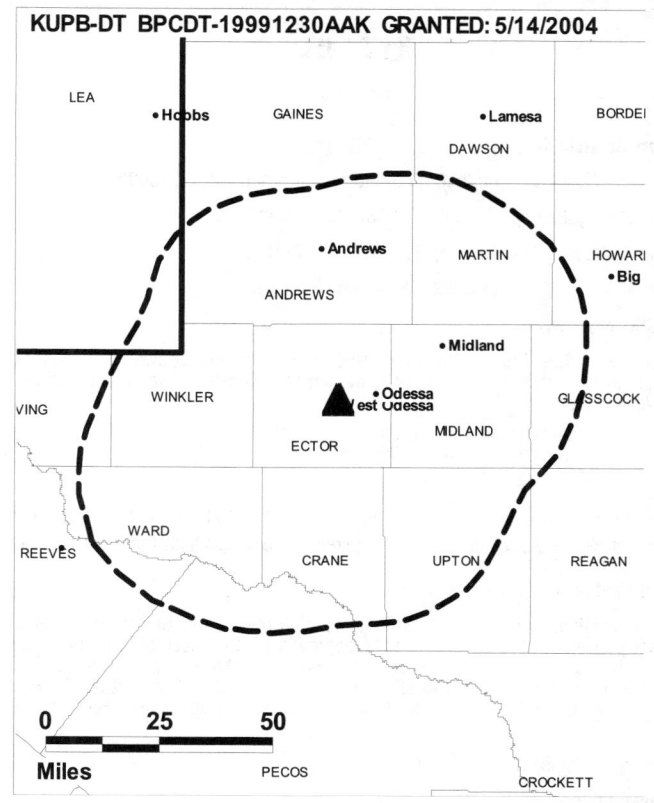

KUPB-DT BPCDT-19991230AAK GRANTED: 5/14/2004

© 2010 Warren Communications News

Circulation © 2009 Nielsen. Coverage based on Nielsen study.

GrandTotal	Cable TV Households	Non-cable TV Households	Total TV Households
Estimated Station Totals *	94,090	33,910	128,000
Average Weekly Circulation (2009)	10,751	5,575	16,326
Average Daily Circulation (2009)			9,384

Station DMA Total	Cable TV Households	Non-cable TV Households	Total TV Households
Estimated Station Totals *	87,890	33,910	121,800
Average Weekly Circulation (2009)	9,320	5,575	14,895
Average Daily Circulation (2009)			8,953

Other DMA Total	Cable TV Households	Non-cable TV Households	Total TV Households
Estimated Station Totals *	6,200	0	6,200
Average Weekly Circulation (2009)	1,431	0	1,431
Average Daily Circulation (2009)			431

*Estimated station totals are sums of the Nielsen TV and Cable TV household estimates for each county in which the station registers viewing of more than 5% as per the Nielsen Survey Methods.

KYTX-DT
Ch. 18

Network Service: IND, CBS.

Licensee: KYTX License Co. LLC, 5052 Addison Cir, Addison, TX 75001.

Studio: 2211 ESE Loop 323, Tyler, TX 75701.

Mailing Address: 2211 ESE Loop 323, Tyler, TX 75701.

Phone: 903-581-2211. **Fax:** 903-581-4769.

Web Site: http://www.cbs19.tv

Technical Facilities: Channel No. 18 (494-500 MHz). Authorized power: 640-kw max. visual, aural. Antenna: 1499-ft above av. terrain, 1545-ft. above ground, 1876-ft. above sea level.

Latitude	31°	54'	20"
Longitude	95°	05'	05"

Note: Latitude and longitude coordinates shown are based on the North American Datum of 1927 (NAD 27) as currently required by the Mass Media Bureau of the FCC.

Ownership: London Broadcasting Co. Inc.

Began Operation: August 10, 2007. Began analog operations: September 1, 1991. Sale to present owner by Max Media LLC approved by FCC December 21, 2007. Sale to Max Media LLC by KLSB Television LLC (Brian E. Cobb, et al.) approved by FCC December 15, 2003. Sale to KLSB Television LLC (Brian E. Cobb, et al.) by Paul Lucci approved by FCC August 5, 2003. Ceased analog operations: February 17, 2009.

Represented (legal): Wiley Rein LLP.

Represented (sales): Katz Media Group.

Personnel:

Philip Hurley, President & General Manager.

John Gaston, Station Manager.

Kent Dominique, Creative Services Director.

Chesley Bryan, National Sales Manager.

Moe Strout, Engineering Director.

Nancy Denton, Business Manager.

Margaret Strout, Program & Traffic Manager.

Jeremy G. Butler, Promotion Manager.

Kevin Meyer, Production Manager.

Carol Daniels, Personnel Director.

Dan Delgado, News Director.

Jeradee Zips, Community Relations Director.

City of License: Nacogdoches.

Station DMA: Tyler-Longview (Lufkin & Nacogdoches), TX. **Rank:** 109.

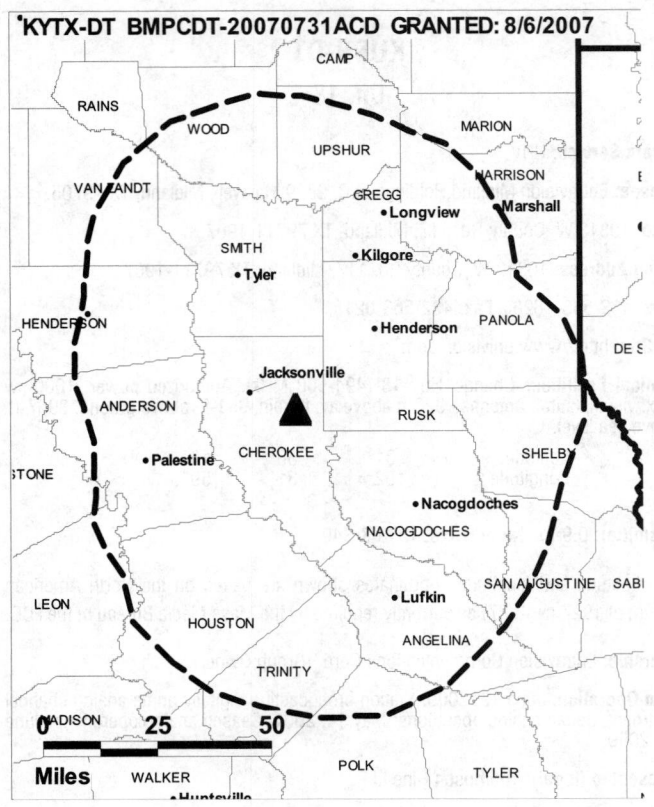

© 2010 Warren Communications News

Circulation © 2009 Nielsen. Coverage based on Nielsen study.

GrandTotal	Cable TV Households	Non-cable TV Households	Total TV Households
Estimated Station Totals *	114,060	175,730	289,790
Average Weekly Circulation (2009)	53,460	62,898	116,358
Average Daily Circulation (2009)			48,560

Station DMA Total	Cable TV Households	Non-cable TV Households	Total TV Households
Estimated Station Totals *	103,140	149,670	252,810
Average Weekly Circulation (2009)	51,900	61,502	113,402
Average Daily Circulation (2009)			47,597

Other DMA Total	Cable TV Households	Non-cable TV Households	Total TV Households
Estimated Station Totals *	10,920	26,060	36,980
Average Weekly Circulation (2009)	1,560	1,396	2,956
Average Daily Circulation (2009)			963

*Estimated station totals are sums of the Nielsen TV and Cable TV household estimates for each county in which the station registers viewing of more than 5% as per the Nielsen Survey Methods.

KMLM-DT
Ch. 42

Network Service: IND.

Licensee: Prime Time Christian Broadcasting Inc., PO Box 7708, Midland, TX 79708.

Studio: 12706 W Hwy 80E, Odessa, TX 79765.

Mailing Address: PO Box 61000, Midland, TX 79711.

Phone: 432-563-0420. **Fax:** 432-563-1736.

Web Site: http://www.godslearningchannel.com

Technical Facilities: Channel No. 42 (638-644 MHz). Authorized power: 50-kw max. visual, aural. Antenna: 476-ft above av. terrain, 469-ft. above ground, 3393-ft. above sea level.

Latitude	32°	02'	54"
Longitude	102°	18'	04"

Note: Latitude and longitude coordinates shown are based on the North American Datum of 1927 (NAD 27) as currently required by the Mass Media Bureau of the FCC.

Ownership: Prime Time Christian Broadcasting Inc. (Group Owner).

Began Operation: December 24, 2008. Station broadcasting digitally on its analog channel allotment. Began analog operations: October 17, 1988. Ceased analog operations: November 19, 2008.

Personnel:

Al Cooper, President.

Amy Posey, General Manager.

Dave Whitley, Traffic Manager.

Matt Montgomery, Chief Engineer.

City of License: Odessa. **Station DMA:** Odessa-Midland, TX. **Rank:** 155.

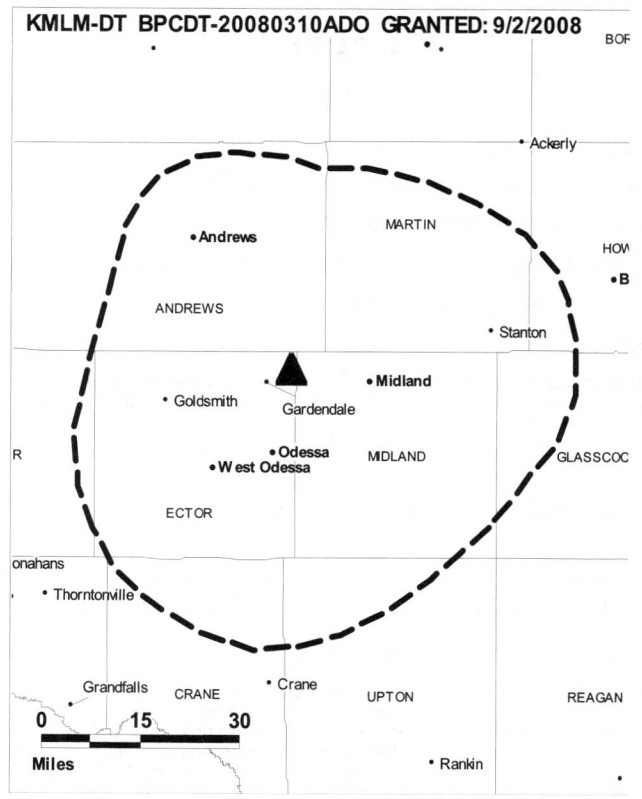

KMLM-DT BPCDT-20080310ADO GRANTED: 9/2/2008

© 2010 Warren Communications News

Circulation © 2009 Nielsen. Coverage based on Nielsen study.

GrandTotal	Cable TV Households	Non-cable TV Households	Total TV Households
Estimated Station Totals *	19,050	0	19,050
Average Weekly Circulation (2009)	1,781	0	1,781
Average Daily Circulation (2009)			394

Station DMA Total	Cable TV Households	Non-cable TV Households	Total TV Households
Estimated Station Totals *	15,770	0	15,770
Average Weekly Circulation (2009)	1,589	0	1,589
Average Daily Circulation (2009)			366

Other DMA Total	Cable TV Households	Non-cable TV Households	Total TV Households
Estimated Station Totals *	3,280	0	3,280
Average Weekly Circulation (2009)	192	0	192
Average Daily Circulation (2009)			28

*Estimated station totals are sums of the Nielsen TV and Cable TV household estimates for each county in which the station registers viewing of more than 5% as per the Nielsen Survey Methods.

KOSA-DT
Ch. 7

Network Service: MNT, CBS.

Grantee: ICA Broadcasting I Ltd., 700 N. Grant St, Odessa, TX 79761.

Studio: 4101 E. 42nd St., Suite J7, Odessa, TX 79762.

Mailing Address: 4101 E. 42nd St, Ste J7, Box 107, Odessa, TX 79762.

Phone: 432-580-5672. **Fax:** 432-580-8010.

Web Site: http://www.cbs7kosa.com

Technical Facilities: Channel No. 7 (174-180 MHz). Authorized power: 13.1-kw visual, aural. Antenna: 741-ft above av. terrain, 685-ft. above ground, 3820-ft. above sea level.

Latitude	31°	51'	50"
Longitude	102°	34'	41"

Holds CP for change to 48-kw visual; BMPCDT-20080620AJT.

Note: Latitude and longitude coordinates shown are based on the North American Datum of 1927 (NAD 27) as currently required by the Mass Media Bureau of the FCC.

Ownership: ICA Broadcasting LLC (Group Owner).

Began Operation: May 24, 2002. Station broadcasting digitally on its analog channel allotment. Began analog operations: January 1, 1956. Sale to Forward by Doubleday Broadcasting Co. approved by FCC September 11, 1973. Transfer of control to Wesray Communications Corp. approved by FCC August 16, 1984. Sale to International Broadcasting Co. approved by FCC February 27, 1986 but not consummated. Sale of Forward stations to Adams Communications approved by FCC December 23, 1987. Sale to Brissette Broadcasting Inc. by Adams Communications approved by FCC December 24, 1991. Sale to Benedek Broadcasting Co. LLC by Brissette Broadcasting approved by FCC May 22, 1996 (Television Digest, Vol. 35:37, 52). Sale to present owner by Benedek Broadcasting Co. LLC approved by FCC March 10, 2000 (Vol. 40:1). Ceased analog operations: June 12, 2009.

Represented (sales): Continental Television Sales.

Personnel:

Barry Marks, General Manager.

Dale Palmer, General & Local Sales Manager.

Jose Gaona, News Director.

Jim McKinnon, Chief Engineer.

Cynthia Terry, Business & Traffic Manager.

Rick McGee, Program Director.

Molly Maytubby, Promotion Manager.

Danny Jordan, Production Manager.

City of License: Odessa. **Station DMA:** Odessa-Midland, TX. **Rank:** 155.

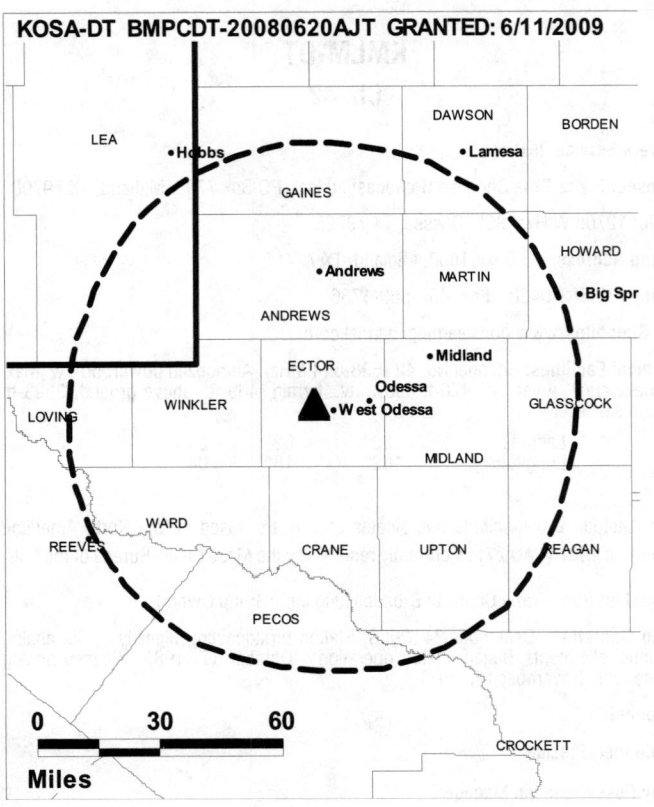

KOSA-DT BMPCDT-20080620AJT GRANTED: 6/11/2009

© 2010 Warren Communications News

Circulation © 2009 Nielsen. Coverage based on Nielsen study.

GrandTotal	Cable TV Households	Non-cable TV Households	Total TV Households
Estimated Station Totals *	105,650	44,880	150,530
Average Weekly Circulation (2009)	65,772	20,274	86,046
Average Daily Circulation (2009)			44,233

Station DMA Total	Cable TV Households	Non-cable TV Households	Total TV Households
Estimated Station Totals *	90,310	43,500	133,810
Average Weekly Circulation (2009)	58,685	20,186	78,871
Average Daily Circulation (2009)			42,124

Other DMA Total	Cable TV Households	Non-cable TV Households	Total TV Households
Estimated Station Totals *	15,340	1,380	16,720
Average Weekly Circulation (2009)	7,087	88	7,175
Average Daily Circulation (2009)			2,109

*Estimated station totals are sums of the Nielsen TV and Cable TV household estimates for each county in which the station registers viewing of more than 5% as per the Nielsen Survey Methods.

KPEJ-DT
Ch. 23

Network Service: FOX.

Licensee: ComCorp of Texas License Corp., PO Box 53708, Lafayette, LA 70505-3708.

Studio: 1550 W. Interstate 20, Odessa, TX 79763.

Mailing Address: PO Box 11009, Odessa, TX 79760.

Phone: 432-580-0024. **Fax:** 432-337-6306.

Web Site: http://www.kpejtv.com

Technical Facilities: Channel No. 23 (524-530 MHz). Authorized power: 600-kw max. visual, aural. Antenna: 1093-ft above av. terrain, 1102-ft. above ground, 4016-ft. above sea level.

Latitude	32°	05'	51"
Longitude	102°	17'	21"

Note: Latitude and longitude coordinates shown are based on the North American Datum of 1927 (NAD 27) as currently required by the Mass Media Bureau of the FCC.

Ownership: Communications Corp. of America (Group Owner).

Began Operation: June 29, 2006. Began analog operations: June 16, 1986. Sale to Associated Broadcasters by SWMM/Odessa-Midland Corp. approved by FCC October 31, 1990. Sale to Communications Corp. of America by Associated Broadcasters Inc. approved by FCC February 13, 1995. Transfer of control from Thomas R. Galloway Sr. to Apollo Capital Management II Inc. & Thomas R. Galloway Sr. jointly approved by FCC April 16, 2004. Involuntary transfer of control to debtor in possession approved by FCC August 29, 2006. Company emerged from debtor in possession status October 4, 2007. Ceased analog operations: June 12, 2009.

Represented (legal): Dow Lohnes PLLC.

Represented (sales): Katz Media Group.

Personnel:

Laura Wolf, General Manager.

Sylvia Holcomb, Local Sales Manager.

Elma Westphall, National Sales Assistant.

Doug Faltus, Chief Engineer.

Tina Plumlee, Business Manager.

Jayne Faltus, Program Director.

Cliff Voake, Promotion Director.

Sergio Ramos, Production Manager.

Rhonda Starnes, Traffic Manager.

City of License: Odessa. **Station DMA:** Odessa-Midland, TX. **Rank:** 155.

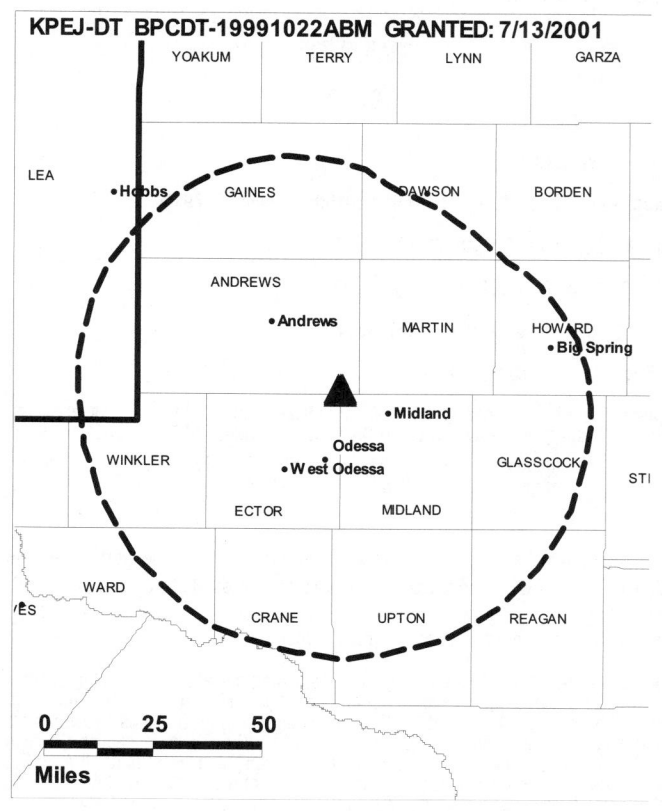

© 2010 Warren Communications News

Circulation © 2009 Nielsen. Coverage based on Nielsen study.

GrandTotal	Cable TV Households	Non-cable TV Households	Total TV Households
Estimated Station Totals *	95,030	44,030	139,060
Average Weekly Circulation (2009)	39,674	14,596	54,270
Average Daily Circulation (2009)			16,172

Station DMA Total	Cable TV Households	Non-cable TV Households	Total TV Households
Estimated Station Totals *	90,310	42,150	132,460
Average Weekly Circulation (2009)	38,753	14,177	52,930
Average Daily Circulation (2009)			15,737

Other DMA Total	Cable TV Households	Non-cable TV Households	Total TV Households
Estimated Station Totals *	4,720	1,880	6,600
Average Weekly Circulation (2009)	921	419	1,340
Average Daily Circulation (2009)			435

*Estimated station totals are sums of the Nielsen TV and Cable TV household estimates for each county in which the station registers viewing of more than 5% as per the Nielsen Survey Methods.

KWES-DT
Ch. 9

Network Service: NBC.

Grantee: Midessa Television LP, PO Box 60150, Midland, TX 79711.

Studio: 11320 County Rd. 127 W, Midland, TX 79711.

Mailing Address: PO Box 60150, Midland, TX 79711.

Phone: 432-567-9999. **Fax:** 432-567-9994.

Web Site: http://www.kwes.com

Technical Facilities: Channel No. 9 (186-192 MHz). Authorized power: visual, aural. Antenna: 1284-ft above av. terrain, 1039-ft. above ground, 4431-ft. above sea level.

Latitude	31°	59'	17"
Longitude	102°	52'	41"

Note: Latitude and longitude coordinates shown are based on the North American Datum of 1927 (NAD 27) as currently required by the Mass Media Bureau of the FCC.

Ownership: Drewry Communications (Group Owner).

Began Operation: May 24, 2004. Station broadcasting digitally on its analog channel allotment. Began analog operations: December 1, 1958. Moved to new site and higher power February 1, 1963. Sale to Grayson Enterprises by Tri-Cities Broadcasters (John B. Walton) approved by FCC February 12, 1969. Distress sale to Permian Basin TV Corp. conditionally approved by FCC March 27, 1980; full grant April 22, 1980. Sale to MSP Television of Midland-Odessa approved by FCC November 19, 1985. Sale to present owner by MSP Television approved by FCC September 9, 1991. Sale to KWES License Co. LLC (London Broadcasting Co. Inc.) approved by FCC November 5, 2008, but never consummated. Ceased analog operations: June 12, 2009.

Represented (legal): Davis Wright Tremaine LLP.

Represented (sales): Petry Media Corp.

Personnel:

Mac Douglas, General Manager.

Richard Esparza, General Sales Manager.

Mark Kurtz, News Director.

Valarie Leonard, Business Manager.

Chuck Cooper, Chief Engineer.

Christina Taylor, Creative Services Director.

Lonnie Richardson, Production Manager.

City of License: Odessa. **Station DMA:** Odessa-Midland, TX. **Rank:** 155.

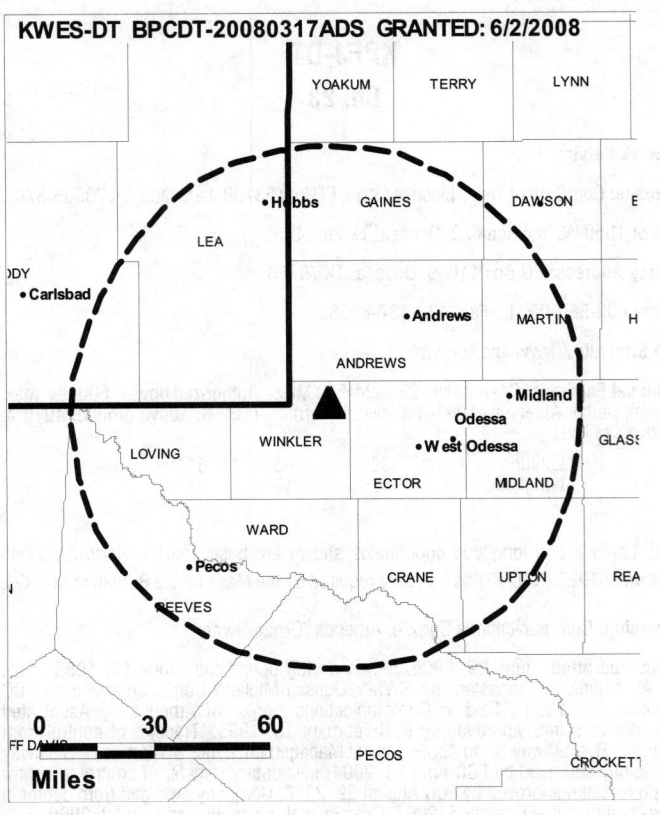

KWES-DT BPCDT-20080317ADS GRANTED: 6/2/2008

© 2010 Warren Communications News

Circulation © 2009 Nielsen. Coverage based on Nielsen study.

GrandTotal	Cable TV Households	Non-cable TV Households	Total TV Households
Estimated Station Totals *	105,650	45,380	151,030
Average Weekly Circulation (2009)	65,731	18,248	83,979
Average Daily Circulation (2009)			43,075

Station DMA Total	Cable TV Households	Non-cable TV Households	Total TV Households
Estimated Station Totals *	90,310	43,500	133,810
Average Weekly Circulation (2009)	58,295	18,133	76,428
Average Daily Circulation (2009)			41,358

Other DMA Total	Cable TV Households	Non-cable TV Households	Total TV Households
Estimated Station Totals *	15,340	1,880	17,220
Average Weekly Circulation (2009)	7,436	115	7,551
Average Daily Circulation (2009)			1,717

*Estimated station totals are sums of the Nielsen TV and Cable TV household estimates for each county in which the station registers viewing of more than 5% as per the Nielsen Survey Methods.

KWWT-DT
Ch. 30

Network Service: CW.

Licensee: WinStar Odessa Inc., 2100 N Palm Canyon Dr, Ste B-103, Palm Springs, CA 92262.

Studio: 10751 E Browder Rd, Gardendale, TX 79758.

Mailing Address: PO Box 60339, Midland, TX 79711.

Phone: 432-563-5795. **Fax:** 432-563-4343.

Technical Facilities: Channel No. 30 (566-572 MHz). Authorized power: 50-kw max. visual, aural. Antenna: 482-ft above av. terrain, 486-ft. above ground, 3403-ft. above sea level.

Latitude	32°	02'	52.5"
Longitude	102°	17'	44"

Note: Latitude and longitude coordinates shown are based on the North American Datum of 1927 (NAD 27) as currently required by the Mass Media Bureau of the FCC.

Ownership: JB Broadcasting Inc.

Began Operation: Station broadcasting digitally on its analog channel allotment. Began analog operations: December 3, 2001. Transfer to present owner by Paxson Communications Corp. approved by FCC April 3, 2001. Sale of remaining 51% interest by WinStar Communications Inc. to Paxson Communications Corp. approved by FCC September 4, 1998. Ceased analog operations: June 12, 2009.

Represented (legal): Dow Lohnes PLLC.

Represented (engineering): du Treil, Lundin & Rackley Inc.

Personnel:

J. Gordon Lunn, General Manager.

Glena Thart, Sales Manager.

Doug Faltus, Chief Engineer.

City of License: Odessa. **Station DMA:** Odessa-Midland, TX. **Rank:** 155.

Digital cable and TV coverage maps.
Visit www.warren-news.com/mediaprints.htm

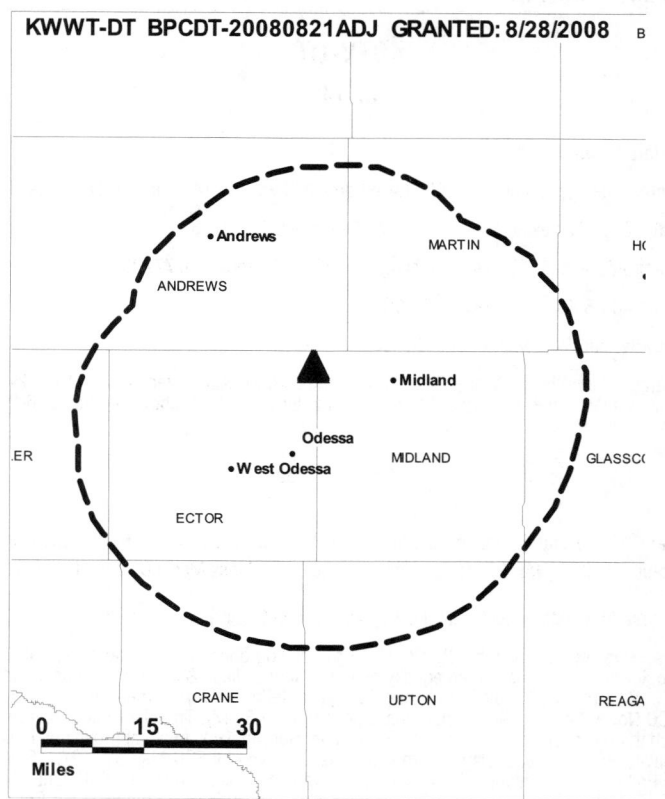

KWWT-DT BPCDT-20080821ADJ GRANTED: 8/28/2008

© 2010 Warren Communications News

Circulation © 2009 Nielsen. Coverage based on Nielsen study.

GrandTotal	Cable TV Households	Non-cable TV Households	Total TV Households
Estimated Station Totals *	88,630	37,050	125,680
Average Weekly Circulation (2009)	13,820	4,671	18,491
Average Daily Circulation (2009)			4,848

Station DMA Total	Cable TV Households	Non-cable TV Households	Total TV Households
Estimated Station Totals *	88,630	37,050	125,680
Average Weekly Circulation (2009)	13,820	4,671	18,491
Average Daily Circulation (2009)			4,848

*Estimated station totals are sums of the Nielsen TV and Cable TV household estimates for each county in which the station registers viewing of more than 5% as per the Nielsen Survey Methods.

KBTV-DT
Ch. 40

Network Service: FOX.

Grantee: Nexstar Finance Inc., 909 Lake Carolyn Pkwy, Ste 1450, Irving, TX 75039.

Studio: 6155 Eastex Freeway, Suite 300, Beaumont, TX 77706.

Mailing Address: 6155 Eastex Freeway, Ste 300, Beaumont, TX 77706.

Phone: 409-840-4444. **Fax:** 409-899-4590.

Web Site: http://www.setxhomepage.com

Technical Facilities: Channel No. 40 (626-632 MHz). Authorized power: 1000-kw max. visual, aural. Antenna: 829-ft above av. terrain, 826-ft. above ground, 846-ft. above sea level.

Latitude	30°	09'	20"
Longitude	93°	59'	10"

Note: Latitude and longitude coordinates shown are based on the North American Datum of 1927 (NAD 27) as currently required by the Mass Media Bureau of the FCC.

Ownership: Nexstar Broadcasting Group Inc. (Group Owner).

Began Operation: November 22, 2002. Began analog operations: October 22, 1957. Originally station was owned equally by Port Arthur College & Jefferson Amusement Co. Sale of its 50% by Port Arthur College to Jefferson Amusement approved by FCC November 15, 1965 (Television Digest, Vol. 5:43, 47). Transfer of control from Jefferson Amusement to Robert H. Park, Janet Gordon Jack, et al., approved by FCC May 1, 1969. Sale to Clay Communications approved by FCC May 31, 1973. Sale to Price Communications Corp. by Clay Communications approved by FCC June 23, 1987 (Vol. 27:21). Sale to US Broadcast Group by Price Communications Corp. approved by FCC November 9, 1995 (Vol. 35:35). Sale to present owner by US Broadcast Group approved by FCC November 6, 1997. Ceased analog operations: June 12, 2009.

Represented (legal): Drinker Biddle.

Represented (sales): Katz Media Group.

Personnel:

Van Greer, General Manager.

Brad Dawson, General Sales Manager.

Paul Bergen, News Director.

Rick Tallent, Chief Engineer.

Gery Meyer, Business Manager.

Barbara Nixon, Programming & Community Affairs Director.

Lori Winzer, Creative Services Director.

Margie Redkey, Traffic Manager.

City of License: Port Arthur. **Station DMA:** Beaumont-Port Arthur, TX. **Rank:** 141.

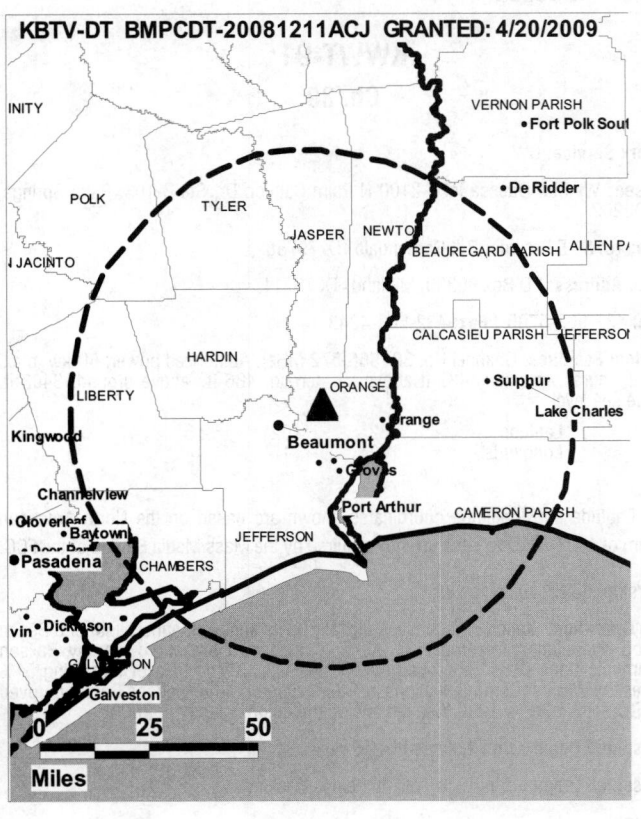

© 2010 Warren Communications News

Circulation © 2009 Nielsen. Coverage based on Nielsen study.

GrandTotal	Cable TV Households	Non-cable TV Households	Total TV Households
Estimated Station Totals *	149,030	107,200	256,230
Average Weekly Circulation (2009)	61,243	34,264	95,507
Average Daily Circulation (2009)			38,244

Station DMA Total	Cable TV Households	Non-cable TV Households	Total TV Households
Estimated Station Totals *	96,730	63,490	160,220
Average Weekly Circulation (2009)	55,961	28,128	84,089
Average Daily Circulation (2009)			34,686

Other DMA Total	Cable TV Households	Non-cable TV Households	Total TV Households
Estimated Station Totals *	52,300	43,710	96,010
Average Weekly Circulation (2009)	5,282	6,136	11,418
Average Daily Circulation (2009)			3,558

*Estimated station totals are sums of the Nielsen TV and Cable TV household estimates for each county in which the station registers viewing of more than 5% as per the Nielsen Survey Methods.

KTLM-DT
Ch. 40

Network Service: TMO.

Grantee: Sunbelt Multimedia Co., 3900 N 10th St, 7th Fl, McAllen, TX 78501.

Studio: 3900 N. 10th St., 7th Floor, McAllen, TX 78501.

Mailing Address: 3900 N 10th St, 7th Fl, McAllen, TX 78501.

Phone: 956-686-0040. **Fax:** 956-686-0770.

E-mail: bjorn@ktlm-tv.com

Web Site: http://www.ktlmtv.com

Technical Facilities: Channel No. 40 (626-632 MHz). Authorized power: 355-kw max. visual, aural. Antenna: 1893-ft above av. terrain, 1886-ft. above ground, 2297-ft. above sea level.

Latitude	26°	31'	01"
Longitude	98°	39'	07"

Note: Latitude and longitude coordinates shown are based on the North American Datum of 1927 (NAD 27) as currently required by the Mass Media Bureau of the FCC.

Ownership: Sunbelt Multimedia Co.

Began Operation: March 17, 2003. Station broadcasting digitally on its analog channel allotment. Began analog operations: August 1, 1999. Transfer of control from Antonio Falcon to Sam F. Vale approved by FCC August 12, 2005. Sale to present owner from Starr County Historical Foundation Inc. approved by FCC March 30, 2000. Ceased analog operations: June 12, 2009.

Represented (legal): Wood, Maines & Nolan Chartered.

Personnel:

Marta Muniz, Vice President & General Manager.

Yolanda Velacruz, News Director.

Flora Tano, Business Manager.

Noel Duran, Program & Production Manager.

Lupita Varga, Traffic Manager.

City of License: Rio Grande City.

Station DMA: Harlingen-Weslaco-Brownsville-McAllen, TX. **Rank:** 87.

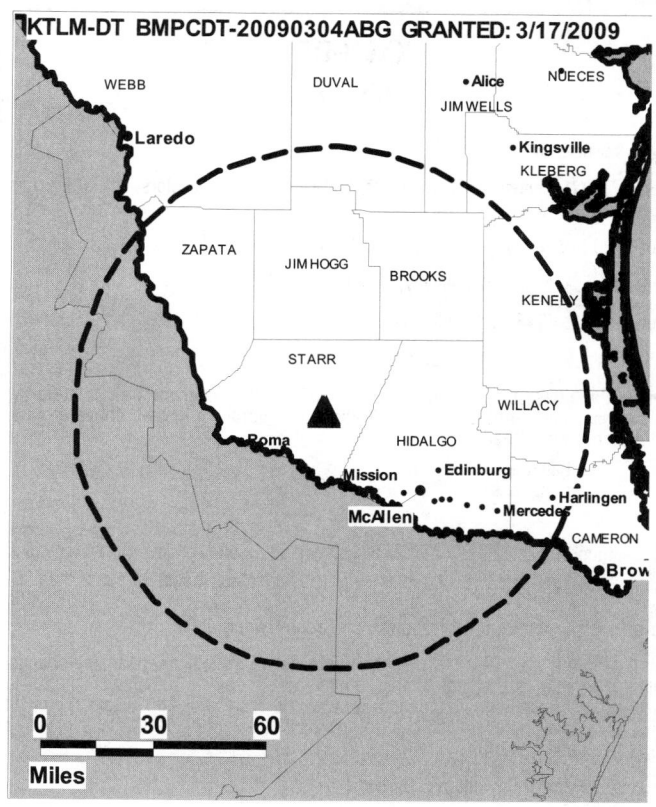

KTLM-DT BMPCDT-20090304ABG GRANTED: 3/17/2009

© 2010 Warren Communications News

Circulation © 2009 Nielsen. Coverage based on Nielsen study.

GrandTotal	Cable TV Households	Non-cable TV Households	Total TV Households
Estimated Station Totals *	139,180	215,180	354,360
Average Weekly Circulation (2009)	34,974	59,219	94,193
Average Daily Circulation (2009)			49,231

Station DMA Total	Cable TV Households	Non-cable TV Households	Total TV Households
Estimated Station Totals *	139,180	210,730	349,910
Average Weekly Circulation (2009)	34,974	58,508	93,482
Average Daily Circulation (2009)			49,037

Other DMA Total	Cable TV Households	Non-cable TV Households	Total TV Households
Estimated Station Totals *	0	4,450	4,450
Average Weekly Circulation (2009)	0	711	711
Average Daily Circulation (2009)			194

*Estimated station totals are sums of the Nielsen TV and Cable TV household estimates for each county in which the station registers viewing of more than 5% as per the Nielsen Survey Methods.

KXLN-DT
Ch. 45

Network Service: UNV.

Licensee: KXLN License Partnership LP, 1999 Avenue of the Stars, Ste 3050, Los Angeles, CA 90067.

Studio: 5100 SW Freeway, Houston, TX 77056.

Mailing Address: 5100 SW Freeway, Houston, TX 77056.

Phone: 713-662-4545. **Fax:** 713-965-2701.

Web Site: http://www.univision.com

Technical Facilities: Channel No. 45 (656-662 MHz). Authorized power: 1000-kw max. visual, aural. Antenna: 1949-ft above av. terrain, 1929-ft. above ground, 2004-ft. above sea level.

Latitude	29°	33'	44"
Longitude	95°	30'	35"

Note: Latitude and longitude coordinates shown are based on the North American Datum of 1927 (NAD 27) as currently required by the Mass Media Bureau of the FCC.

Ownership: Univision Communications Inc. (Group Owner).

Began Operation: May 22, 2003. Station broadcasting digitally on its analog channel allotment. Began analog operations: September 1, 1987. Transfer of control to Broadcasting Media Partners Inc. approved by FCC March 27, 2007. Sale to present owner by Pueblo Broadcasting Corp. approved by FCC July 20, 1994. Ceased analog operations: June 12, 2009.

Represented (legal): Covington & Burling.

Personnel:

Craig Bland, Senior Vice President & General Manager.

Jose Oti, Vice President & General Sales Manager.

Chris Brown, Vice President & Controller.

Charlie Lozano, Promotion Director.

Chas Wilson, National Sales Manager.

Kath Blanco, National Sales Manager.

Mike Thomas, Local Sales Manager.

Rey Chavez, News Director.

Tom Daniels, Chief Engineer.

Cindy Chisum, Program & Traffic Manager.

Ray Sepeda, Production Manager.

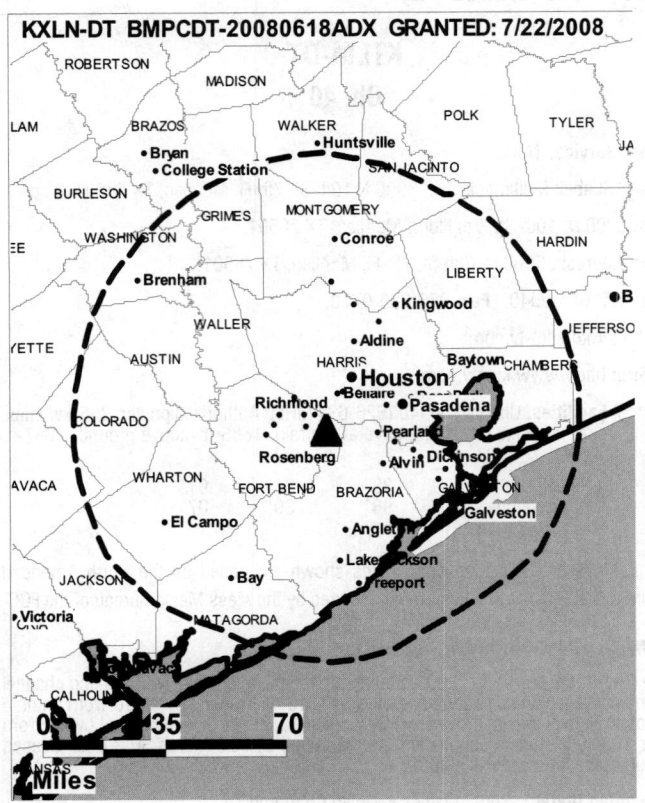

© 2010 Warren Communications News

City of License: Rosenberg. **Station DMA:** Houston, TX. **Rank:** 10.

Circulation © 2009 Nielsen. Coverage based on Nielsen study.

GrandTotal	Cable TV Households	Non-cable TV Households	Total TV Households
Estimated Station Totals *	905,700	828,790	1,734,490
Average Weekly Circulation (2009)	146,560	256,364	402,924
Average Daily Circulation (2009)			280,026

Station DMA Total	Cable TV Households	Non-cable TV Households	Total TV Households
Estimated Station Totals *	905,700	828,790	1,734,490
Average Weekly Circulation (2009)	146,560	256,364	402,924
Average Daily Circulation (2009)			280,026

*Estimated station totals are sums of the Nielsen TV and Cable TV household estimates for each county in which the station registers viewing of more than 5% as per the Nielsen Survey Methods.

KIDY-DT
Ch. 19

Network Service: FOX.

Grantee: Bayou City Broadcasting LLC, 1300 Post Oak Blvd, Ste 830, Houston, TX 77056.

Studio: 406 S. Irving, San Angelo, TX 76903.

Mailing Address: 406 S. Irving St, San Angelo, TX 76903.

Phone: 325-655-6006. **Fax:** 325-655-8461.

Web Site: http://www.foxsanangelo.com

Technical Facilities: Channel No. 19 (500-506 MHz). Authorized power: 700-kw max. visual, aural. Antenna: 784-ft above av. terrain, 830-ft. above ground, 2864-ft. above sea level.

Latitude	31°	35'	21"
Longitude	100°	31'	00"

Note: Latitude and longitude coordinates shown are based on the North American Datum of 1927 (NAD 27) as currently required by the Mass Media Bureau of the FCC.

Ownership: Bayou City Broadcasting LLC (Group Owner).

Began Operation: February 16, 2009. Began analog operations: May 12, 1984. Ceased analog operations: February 5, 2009. Sale to present owner by Sage Broadcasting Corp. approved by FCC May 29, 2008.

Represented (legal): Fletcher, Heald & Hildreth PLC.

Represented (sales): Katz Media Group.

Personnel:

DuJuan McCoy, President & General Manager.

Amy Zetman, Production Manager.

Teddye Read, National & Local Sales Manager.

Charles Sherrill, Chief Engineer.

Billie Garver, Business Manager.

City of License: San Angelo. **Station DMA:** San Angelo, TX. **Rank:** 198.

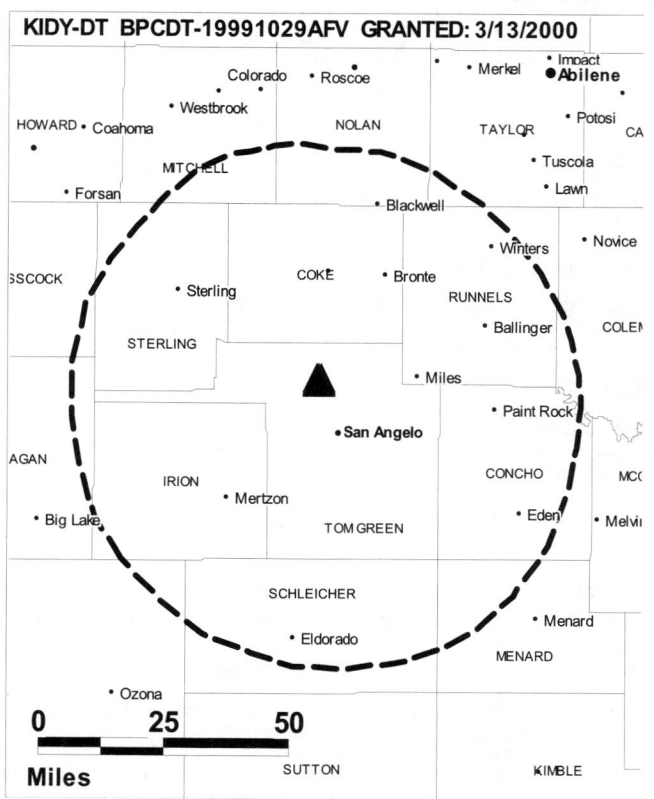

KIDY-DT BPCDT-19991029AFV GRANTED: 3/13/2000

© 2010 Warren Communications News

Circulation © 2009 Nielsen. Coverage based on Nielsen study.

GrandTotal	Cable TV Households	Non-cable TV Households	Total TV Households
Estimated Station Totals *	29,900	23,020	52,920
Average Weekly Circulation (2009)	15,512	7,438	22,950
Average Daily Circulation (2009)			7,618

Station DMA Total	Cable TV Households	Non-cable TV Households	Total TV Households
Estimated Station Totals *	29,900	23,020	52,920
Average Weekly Circulation (2009)	15,512	7,438	22,950
Average Daily Circulation (2009)			7,618

*Estimated station totals are sums of the Nielsen TV and Cable TV household estimates for each county in which the station registers viewing of more than 5% as per the Nielsen Survey Methods.

KLST-DT
Ch. 11

Network Service: CBS.

Grantee: Nexstar Broadcasting Inc., 909 Lake Carolyn Pkwy, Ste 1450, Irving, TX 75039.

Studio: 2800 Armstrong, San Angelo, TX 76903.

Mailing Address: 2800 Armstrong St, San Angelo, TX 76903.

Phone: 325-949-8800. **Fax:** 325-658-4006.

Web Site: http://www.conchovalleyhomepage.com

Technical Facilities: Channel No. 11 (198-204 MHz). Authorized power: 18.8-kw visual, aural. Antenna: 1425-ft above av. terrain, 1440-ft. above ground, 3265-ft. above sea level.

Latitude	31°	22'	01"
Longitude	100°	02'	48"

Note: Latitude and longitude coordinates shown are based on the North American Datum of 1927 (NAD 27) as currently required by the Mass Media Bureau of the FCC.

Ownership: Nexstar Broadcasting Group Inc. (Group Owner).

Began Operation: February 17, 2009. Began analog operations: June 26, 1953. Transfer of 74% to KGKL and R. H. Simmons approved by FCC March 13, 1957 (Television Digest, Vol. 13:2, 11). Transfer of 49% from KGKL to Big Spring Broadcasting Co. effective March 25, 1959. Transfer to Westex TV Co. approved by FCC December 4, 1962. Sale to T. B. Lanford (Jewell Television Corp.) by Houston H. & Edward H. Harte & A. L. Hall approved by FCC January 20, 1971. Transfer of control from Lanford estate approved by FCC June 13, 1994. Sale to present owner by Jewell Television Corp. approved by FCC September 2, 2004. Ceased analog operations: February 17, 2009.

Represented (legal): Drinker Biddle.

Represented (sales): Katz Media Group.

Personnel:

Tom Stovall, General Manager & Program Director.

Albert Guttierrez, General Sales Manager.

Julie Andreopulos, Regional Sales Manager.

Kathy Munoz, News Director.

Len Martinez, Chief Engineer.

Chad Wilson, Promotion Director.

Sherri Scott, Traffic Manager.

City of License: San Angelo. **Station DMA:** San Angelo, TX. **Rank:** 198.

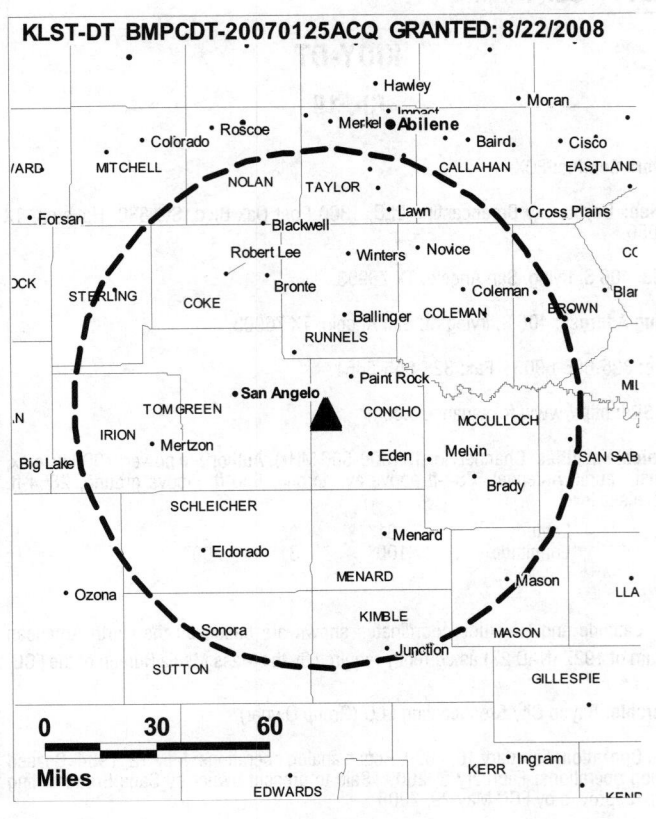

KLST-DT BMPCDT-20070125ACQ GRANTED: 8/22/2008

© 2010 Warren Communications News

Circulation © 2009 Nielsen. Coverage based on Nielsen study.

GrandTotal	Cable TV Households	Non-cable TV Households	Total TV Households
Estimated Station Totals *	32,370	25,920	58,290
Average Weekly Circulation (2009)	22,057	11,850	33,907
Average Daily Circulation (2009)			20,116

Station DMA Total	Cable TV Households	Non-cable TV Households	Total TV Households
Estimated Station Totals *	29,900	23,020	52,920
Average Weekly Circulation (2009)	21,651	11,403	33,054
Average Daily Circulation (2009)			19,705

Other DMA Total	Cable TV Households	Non-cable TV Households	Total TV Households
Estimated Station Totals *	2,470	2,900	5,370
Average Weekly Circulation (2009)	406	447	853
Average Daily Circulation (2009)			411

*Estimated station totals are sums of the Nielsen TV and Cable TV household estimates for each county in which the station registers viewing of more than 5% as per the Nielsen Survey Methods.

KSAN-DT
Ch. 16

Network Service: NBC.

Grantee: Mission Broadcasting Inc., 544 Red Rock Dr, Wadsworth, OH 44281.

Studio: 2800 Armstrong St, San Angelo, TX 79604.

Mailing Address: 2800 Armstrong St, San Angelo, TX 79604.

Phone: 325-949-8800. **Fax:** 325-655-3040.

Web Site: http://www.conchovalleyhomepage.com

Technical Facilities: Channel No. 16 (482-488 MHz). Authorized power: 1000-kw max. visual, aural. Antenna: 524-ft above av. terrain, 351-ft. above ground, 2601-ft. above sea level.

Latitude	31°	37'	22"
Longitude	100°	26'	14"

Note: Latitude and longitude coordinates shown are based on the North American Datum of 1927 (NAD 27) as currently required by the Mass Media Bureau of the FCC.

Ownership: Mission Broadcasting Inc. (Group Owner).

Began Operation: February 17, 2009. Began analog operations: February 8, 1962. Sale to present owner by LIN TV Corp. approved by FCC May 20, 2003. Ceased analog operations: February 17, 2009.

Represented (sales): Blair Television.

Represented (legal): Drinker Biddle.

Personnel:

Thomas Stovall, General Manager.

Len Martinez, Chief Engineer.

Albert Guiterrez, Sales Director.

Sherry Scott, Station Manager.

Kathy Munoz, News Director.

City of License: San Angelo. **Station DMA:** San Angelo, TX. **Rank:** 198.

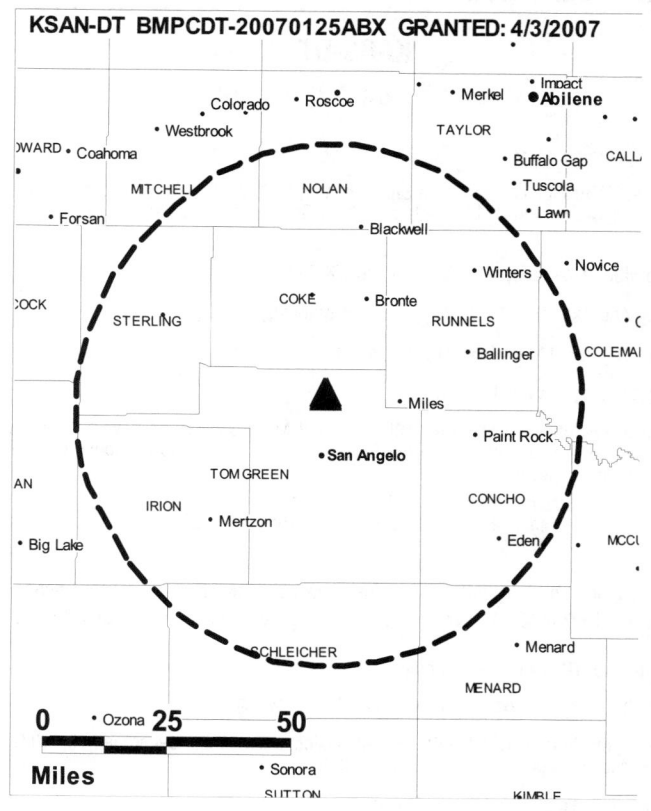

KSAN-DT BMPCDT-20070125ABX GRANTED: 4/3/2007

© 2010 Warren Communications News

Circulation © 2009 Nielsen. Coverage based on Nielsen study.

GrandTotal	Cable TV Households	Non-cable TV Households	Total TV Households
Estimated Station Totals *	29,730	25,920	55,650
Average Weekly Circulation (2009)	17,344	8,705	26,049
Average Daily Circulation (2009)			11,592

Station DMA Total	Cable TV Households	Non-cable TV Households	Total TV Households
Estimated Station Totals *	29,730	23,020	52,750
Average Weekly Circulation (2009)	17,344	8,427	25,771
Average Daily Circulation (2009)			11,467

Other DMA Total	Cable TV Households	Non-cable TV Households	Total TV Households
Estimated Station Totals *	0	2,900	2,900
Average Weekly Circulation (2009)	0	278	278
Average Daily Circulation (2009)			125

*Estimated station totals are sums of the Nielsen TV and Cable TV household estimates for each county in which the station registers viewing of more than 5% as per the Nielsen Survey Methods.

KABB-DT
Ch. 30

Network Service: FOX.

Grantee: KABB Licensee LLC, c/o Shaw Pittman LLP, 2300 N St. NW, c/o Pillsbury Winthrop Shaw Pittman LLP, Attn.: Kathryn Schmeltzer, Washington, DC 20037-1128.

Studio: 4335 N.W. Loop 410, San Antonio, TX 78229.

Mailing Address: 4335 N.W. Loop 410, San Antonio, TX 78229.

Phone: 210-366-1129. **Fax:** 210-377-4758.

Web Site: http://www.kabb.com

Technical Facilities: Channel No. 30 (566-572 MHz). Authorized power: 1000-kw max. visual, aural. Antenna: 1447-ft above av. terrain, 1483-ft. above ground, 1982-ft. above sea level.

Latitude	29°	17'	28"
Longitude	98°	16'	12"

Note: Latitude and longitude coordinates shown are based on the North American Datum of 1927 (NAD 27) as currently required by the Mass Media Bureau of the FCC.

Multichannel TV Sound: Stereo only.

Ownership: Sinclair Broadcast Group Inc. (Group Owner).

Began Operation: May 1, 2002. Began analog operations: December 16, 1987. Ceased analog operations: February 17, 2009.

Represented (sales): Katz Media Group.

Personnel:

John Seabers, General Manager.

David Ostmo, Operations Director.

Dean Radla, Sales Director.

Robert Canales, Local Sales Manager.

Jimmy Cola, National Sales Manager.

Greg Koelfgen, News Director.

Mike Guerrero, Chief Engineer.

Renae Flood, Business Manager.

Yvette Reyna, Sales Promotion Director.

David Howitt, Marketing Director.

Teddy Scoggins, Traffic Manager.

City of License: San Antonio. **Station DMA:** San Antonio, TX. **Rank:** 37.

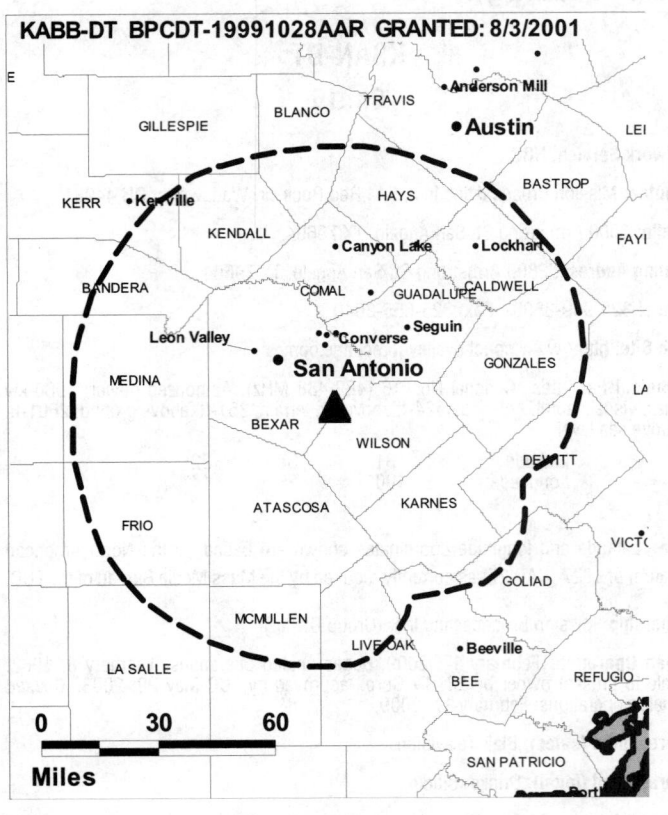

KABB-DT BPCDT-19991028AAR GRANTED: 8/3/2001

© 2010 Warren Communications News

Circulation © 2009 Nielsen. Coverage based on Nielsen study.

GrandTotal	Cable TV Households	Non-cable TV Households	Total TV Households
Estimated Station Totals *	534,390	304,940	839,330
Average Weekly Circulation (2009)	233,179	144,459	377,638
Average Daily Circulation (2009)			136,865

Station DMA Total	Cable TV Households	Non-cable TV Households	Total TV Households
Estimated Station Totals *	495,470	277,850	773,320
Average Weekly Circulation (2009)	225,894	141,753	367,647
Average Daily Circulation (2009)			135,165

Other DMA Total	Cable TV Households	Non-cable TV Households	Total TV Households
Estimated Station Totals *	38,920	27,090	66,010
Average Weekly Circulation (2009)	7,285	2,706	9,991
Average Daily Circulation (2009)			1,700

*Estimated station totals are sums of the Nielsen TV and Cable TV household estimates for each county in which the station registers viewing of more than 5% as per the Nielsen Survey Methods.

KENS
Ch. 55

Network Service: CBS.

Licensee: KENS-TV Inc., 400 S Record St, Dallas, TX 75202-4806.

Studio: 5400 Fredericksburg Rd., San Antonio, TX 78229.

Mailing Address: Box TV 5, San Antonio, TX 78229.

Phone: 210-366-5000. **Fax:** 210-377-0740.

E-mail: rmcgann@kens5.com

Web Site: http://www.mysanantonio.com

Technical Facilities: Channel No. 55 (716-722 MHz). Authorized power: 825-kw max. visual, aural. Antenna: 1460-ft above av. terrain, 1463-ft. above ground, 1982-ft. above sea level.

Latitude	29°	16'	11"
Longitude	98°	15'	55"

Holds CP for change to channel number 39, 1000-kw max. visual, 1447-ft above av. terrain, 1450-ft. above ground, 1969-ft. above sea level; BPCDT-20080303ALJ.

Note: Latitude and longitude coordinates shown are based on the North American Datum of 1927 (NAD 27) as currently required by the Mass Media Bureau of the FCC.

Ownership: Belo Corp. (Group Owner).

Began Operation: April 15, 2002. Standard Definition. Began analog operations: February 15, 1950. Sale to present owner by E. W. Scripps Co. approved by FCC December 2, 1997. Sale to E. W. Scripps Co. by Harte-Hanks Communications Inc. approved by FCC September 5, 1997 (Television Digest, Vol. 37:21). Transfer to Harte-Hanks Communications Inc. from owner of San Antonio Express and News approved by FCC July 3, 1962. Sale to San Antonio Express and News by Storer Broadcasting Co., which acquired it in October 1951, approved by FCC October 27, 1954 (Vol. 7:30, 41; 10:15, 22, 26, 44). Ceased analog operations: June 12, 2009.

Represented (sales): TeleRep Inc.

Represented (legal): Wiley Rein LLP.

Personnel:

Robert McGann, Vice President & General Manager.

Rebecca Walker, General Sales Manager & Program Director.

Sara Fulmer, Local Sales Manager.

Jana Willborn, National Sales Manager.

Kurt Davis, News Director.

Frank Peterman, Chief Engineer.

Susan Lynch, Controller.

Ellen Lansing, Marketing Director.

Amy Oranday, Traffic Manager.

City of License: San Antonio. **Station DMA:** San Antonio, TX. **Rank:** 37.

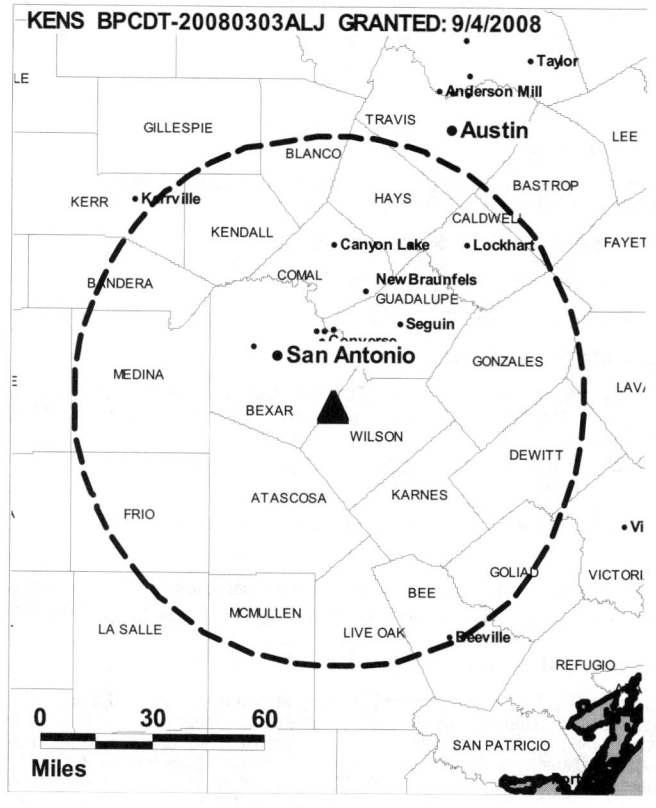

© 2010 Warren Communications News

Circulation © 2009 Nielsen. Coverage based on Nielsen study.

GrandTotal	Cable TV Households	Non-cable TV Households	Total TV Households
Estimated Station Totals *	602,890	299,610	902,500
Average Weekly Circulation (2009)	315,220	167,572	482,792
Average Daily Circulation (2009)			247,353

Station DMA Total	Cable TV Households	Non-cable TV Households	Total TV Households
Estimated Station Totals *	495,470	277,850	773,320
Average Weekly Circulation (2009)	291,789	164,099	455,888
Average Daily Circulation (2009)			236,884

Other DMA Total	Cable TV Households	Non-cable TV Households	Total TV Households
Estimated Station Totals *	107,420	21,760	129,180
Average Weekly Circulation (2009)	23,431	3,473	26,904
Average Daily Circulation (2009)			10,469

*Estimated station totals are sums of the Nielsen TV and Cable TV household estimates for each county in which the station registers viewing of more than 5% as per the Nielsen Survey Methods.

KSAT-DT
Ch. 12

Network Service: ABC.

Licensee: Post-Newsweek Stations, San Antonio Inc., 550 W Lafayette Blvd, c/o Post-Newsweek Stations Inc., Detroit, MI 48226-3140.

Studio: 1408 N. St. Mary's St., San Antonio, TX 78215.

Mailing Address: PO Box 2478, San Antonio, TX 78298.

Phone: 210-351-1200. **Fax:** 210-351-1328.

Web Site: http://www.ksat.com

Technical Facilities: Channel No. 12 (204-210 MHz). Authorized power: 17.6-kw visual, aural. Antenna: 1493-ft above av. terrain, 1469-ft. above ground, 2011-ft. above sea level.

Latitude	29°	16'	11"
Longitude	98°	15'	31"

Holds CP for change to 22.2-kw visual; BPCDT-20090630ABA.

Note: Latitude and longitude coordinates shown are based on the North American Datum of 1927 (NAD 27) as currently required by the Mass Media Bureau of the FCC.

Ownership: Post-Newsweek Stations Inc. (Group Owner).

Began Operation: May 1, 2002. High Definition. Station broadcasting digitally on its analog channel allotment. Began analog operations: January 21, 1957. Sale to present owner by H & C Communications Inc. approved by FCC February 28, 1994 (Television Digest, Vol. 33:49). Sale to H & C Communications Inc. by Rockefeller Group Inc. approved by FCC April 29, 1986 (Vol. 26:6, 12). Sale to Rockefeller Group by Outlet Co. approved by FCC November 23, 1983 (Vol. 23:19, 22; 24:6). Sale to Outlet Co. by Mission Telecasting Corp. approved by FCC November 22, 1967. Ceased analog operations: June 12, 2009.

Represented (legal): Covington & Burling.

Personnel:

James E. Joslyn, Vice President & General Manager.

Randy Schmidt, General Sales Manager.

Scot Allen Laird, Chief Engineer.

City of License: San Antonio. **Station DMA:** San Antonio, TX. **Rank:** 37.

Digital cable and TV coverage maps.
Visit www.warren-news.com/mediaprints.htm

MediaPrints™
Map a Winning Business Strategy

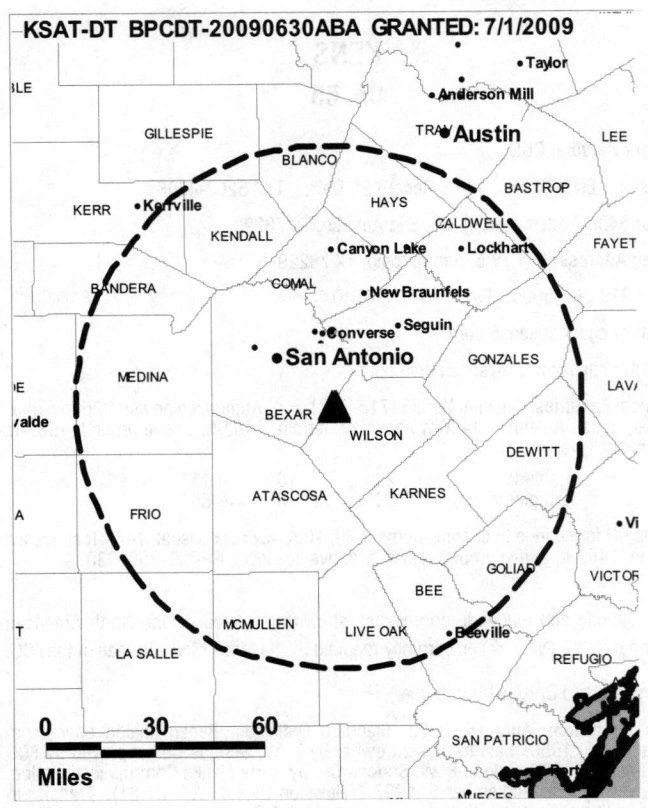

KSAT-DT BPCDT-20090630ABA GRANTED: 7/1/2009

0   30   60 Miles

© 2010 Warren Communications News

Circulation © 2009 Nielsen. Coverage based on Nielsen study.

GrandTotal	Cable TV Households	Non-cable TV Households	Total TV Households
Estimated Station Totals *	583,200	300,630	883,830
Average Weekly Circulation (2009)	349,043	189,647	538,690
Average Daily Circulation (2009)			285,263

Station DMA Total	Cable TV Households	Non-cable TV Households	Total TV Households
Estimated Station Totals *	495,470	277,850	773,320
Average Weekly Circulation (2009)	330,879	186,709	517,588
Average Daily Circulation (2009)			278,679

Other DMA Total	Cable TV Households	Non-cable TV Households	Total TV Households
Estimated Station Totals *	87,730	22,780	110,510
Average Weekly Circulation (2009)	18,164	2,938	21,102
Average Daily Circulation (2009)			6,584

*Estimated station totals are sums of the Nielsen TV and Cable TV household estimates for each county in which the station registers viewing of more than 5% as per the Nielsen Survey Methods.

KVDA-DT
Ch. 38

Network Service: TMO.

Licensee: NBC Telemundo License Co., 1299 Pennsylvania Ave NW, 11th Fl, c/o NBC Inc., Washington, DC 20004.

Studio: 6234 San Pedro, San Antonio, TX 78216.

Mailing Address: 6234 San Pedro, San Antonio, TX 78216.

Phone: 210-340-8860. **Fax:** 210-341-3962.

Technical Facilities: Channel No. 38 (614-620 MHz). Authorized power: 1000-kw max. visual, aural. Antenna: 1358-ft above av. terrain, 1361-ft. above ground, 1886-ft. above sea level.

Latitude	29°	17'	38.5"
Longitude	98°	15'	30.7"

Note: Latitude and longitude coordinates shown are based on the North American Datum of 1927 (NAD 27) as currently required by the Mass Media Bureau of the FCC.

Ownership: NBC Universal (Group Owner).

Began Operation: October 15, 2002. Standard Definition. Began analog operations: September 10, 1989. Ceased analog operations: June 12, 2009.

Personnel:

Roel Medina, Vice President & General Manager.

Linda Stillwell, Business & Operations Manager.

James Dickens, Local Sales Manager.

Roger Topping, Chief Engineer.

Beatrice Pitts, Program & Traffic Manager.

Maricela Arce, Promotion Director.

City of License: San Antonio. **Station DMA:** San Antonio, TX. **Rank:** 37.

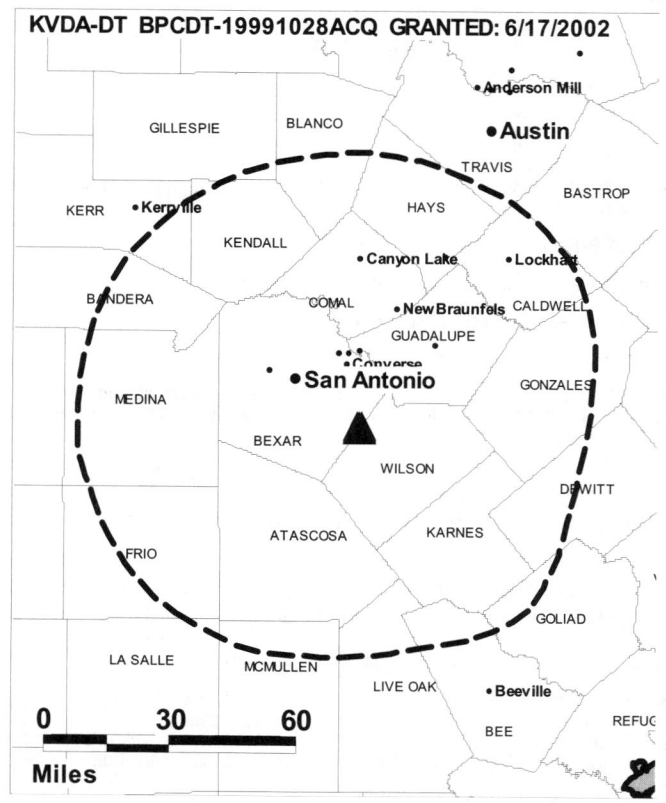

KVDA-DT BPCDT-19991028ACQ GRANTED: 6/17/2002

© 2010 Warren Communications News

Circulation © 2009 Nielsen. Coverage based on Nielsen study.

GrandTotal	Cable TV Households	Non-cable TV Households	Total TV Households
Estimated Station Totals *	431,230	204,050	635,280
Average Weekly Circulation (2009)	36,631	21,518	58,149
Average Daily Circulation (2009)			26,920

Station DMA Total	Cable TV Households	Non-cable TV Households	Total TV Households
Estimated Station Totals *	430,570	204,050	634,620
Average Weekly Circulation (2009)	36,586	21,518	58,104
Average Daily Circulation (2009)			26,914

Other DMA Total	Cable TV Households	Non-cable TV Households	Total TV Households
Estimated Station Totals *	660	0	660
Average Weekly Circulation (2009)	45	0	45
Average Daily Circulation (2009)			6

*Estimated station totals are sums of the Nielsen TV and Cable TV household estimates for each county in which the station registers viewing of more than 5% as per the Nielsen Survey Methods.

KWEX-DT
Ch. 41

Network Service: UNV.

Licensee: KWEX License Partnership LP, 1999 Avenue of the Stars, Ste 3050, Los Angeles, CA 90067.

Studio: 411 E. Durango, San Antonio, TX 78204.

Mailing Address: 411 E. Durango, San Antonio, TX 78204.

Phone: 210-227-4141. **Fax:** 210-227-0469.

Web Site: http://www.univision.net

Technical Facilities: Channel No. 41 (632-638 MHz). Authorized power: 580-kw max. visual, aural. Antenna: 1417-ft above av. terrain, 1421-ft. above ground, 1946-ft. above sea level.

Latitude	29°	17'	38"
Longitude	98°	15'	31"

Requests CP for change to 1000-kw max. visual; BPCDT-20090626ACY.

Note: Latitude and longitude coordinates shown are based on the North American Datum of 1927 (NAD 27) as currently required by the Mass Media Bureau of the FCC.

Ownership: Univision Communications Inc. (Group Owner).

Began Operation: January 26, 2004. Station broadcasting digitally on its analog channel allotment. Began analog operations: June 10, 1955. Sale as KUAL-TV by Raul A. Cortez and associates approved by FCC December 6, 1961. Sale to Hallmark Cards (Univision Holdings) by Spanish International Communications Corp.approved by FCC June 12, 1987. Sale to Perenchio TV Inc. by Hallmark Cards Inc. approved by FCC September 30, 1992. Transfer of control to Broadcasting Media Partners Inc. approved by FCC March 27, 2007. Ceased analog operations: June 12, 2009.

Represented (legal): Covington & Burling.

Personnel:

David Loving, Vice President & General Manager.

Tony Canales, General Sales Manager.

Becki Garcia, Local Sales Manager.

Teri Palos, Local Sales Manager.

Marti Gamer, National Sales Manager.

Robert Sarabia, National Sales Manager.

Samuel Belilty, News Director.

Rafael Monzon, Chief Engineer.

Lydia Luna-Buchman, Business Manager.

Angie Ruiz, Program Director.

Pamela Senuta-Hughes, Marketing Director.

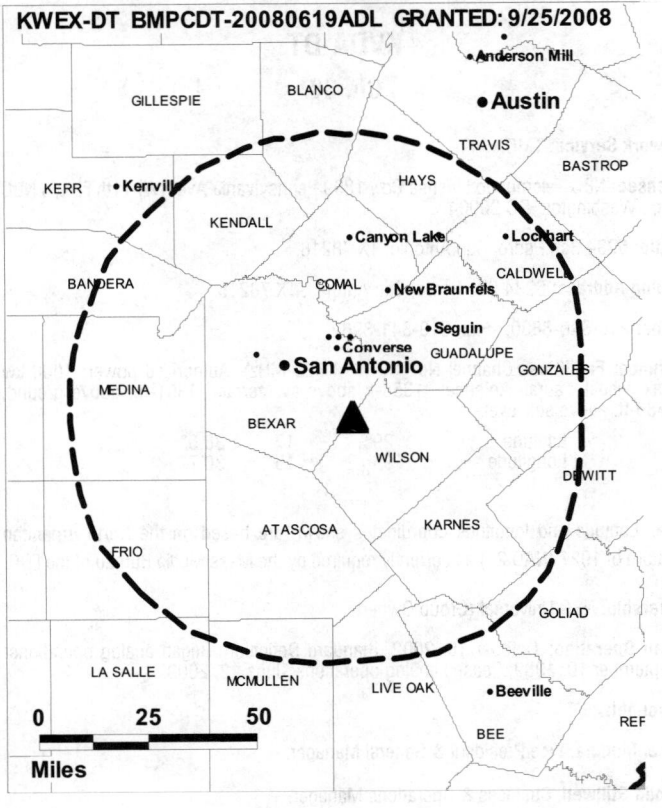

© 2010 Warren Communications News

Amparo Ortiz, Promotion Manager & Community Affairs Director.

Roland Davila, Production Manager.

City of License: San Antonio. **Station DMA:** San Antonio, TX. **Rank:** 37.

Circulation © 2009 Nielsen. Coverage based on Nielsen study.

GrandTotal	Cable TV Households	Non-cable TV Households	Total TV Households
Estimated Station Totals *	483,940	245,000	728,940
Average Weekly Circulation (2009)	83,528	47,686	131,214
Average Daily Circulation (2009)			84,450

Station DMA Total	Cable TV Households	Non-cable TV Households	Total TV Households
Estimated Station Totals *	483,940	245,000	728,940
Average Weekly Circulation (2009)	83,528	47,686	131,214
Average Daily Circulation (2009)			84,450

*Estimated station totals are sums of the Nielsen TV and Cable TV household estimates for each county in which the station registers viewing of more than 5% as per the Nielsen Survey Methods.

WOAI-DT
Ch. 58

Network Service: NBC.

Licensee: High Plains Broadcasting License Co. LLC, PO Box 288, 120 Oak Dr, Kaw City, OK 74641.

Studio: 1031 Navarro St., San Antonio, TX 78205.

Mailing Address: PO Box 2641, San Antonio, TX 78299.

Phone: 210-226-4444. **Fax:** 210-476-1016.

Web Site: http://www.woai.com

Technical Facilities: Channel No. 58 (734-740 MHz). Authorized power: 776-kw max. visual, aural. Antenna: 1499-ft above av. terrain, 1506-ft. above ground, 2025-ft. above sea level.

Latitude	29°	16'	11"
Longitude	98°	15'	55"

Holds CP for change to channel number 48, 905-kw max. visual, 1499-ft above av. terrain, 1506-ft. above ground, 2024-ft. above sea level; BPCDT-20080304AAH.

Note: Latitude and longitude coordinates shown are based on the North American Datum of 1927 (NAD 27) as currently required by the Mass Media Bureau of the FCC.

Ownership: High Plains Broadcasting Inc. (Group Owner).

Began Operation: April 3, 2002. High Definition. Began analog operations: December 11, 1949. Sale to present owner by Newport Television License LLC approved by FCC September 12, 2008. Sale to Newport Television License LLC by Clear Channel Communications Inc. approved by FCC November 29, 2007. To comply with Justice Dept. consent decree, Fox swapped station with KTVX Salt Lake City, UT for Clear Channel Broadcasting's KFTC Bemidji, MN & WFTC Minneapolis-St. Paul, MN. FCC approved deal September 21, 2001. Sale to Fox Television Stations Inc. by United Television Inc. approved by FCC July 23, 2001. Sale to United Television Inc. by Avco Broadcasting Corp. approved by FCC September 18, 1975. Sale to Avco by Hugh Halff Jr. & associates approved by FCC September 15, 1965. Ceased analog operations: June 12, 2009.

Represented (sales): Katz Media Group.

Represented (legal): Pillsbury Winthrop Shaw Pittman LLP.

Personnel:

Linda Danna, Interim General Manager & Sales Director.

Tod Terry, New Media Sales Director.

Velma Garcia, National Sales Manager.

David Walker, Local Sales Manager.

Aaron Ramey, News Director.

Becky Wilson, Business Manager.

Carolyn Mastin, Program Director.

Robert Dodd, Production Director.

Elizabeth Guzman, Research Director.

Greg Derkowski, Creative Services Director.

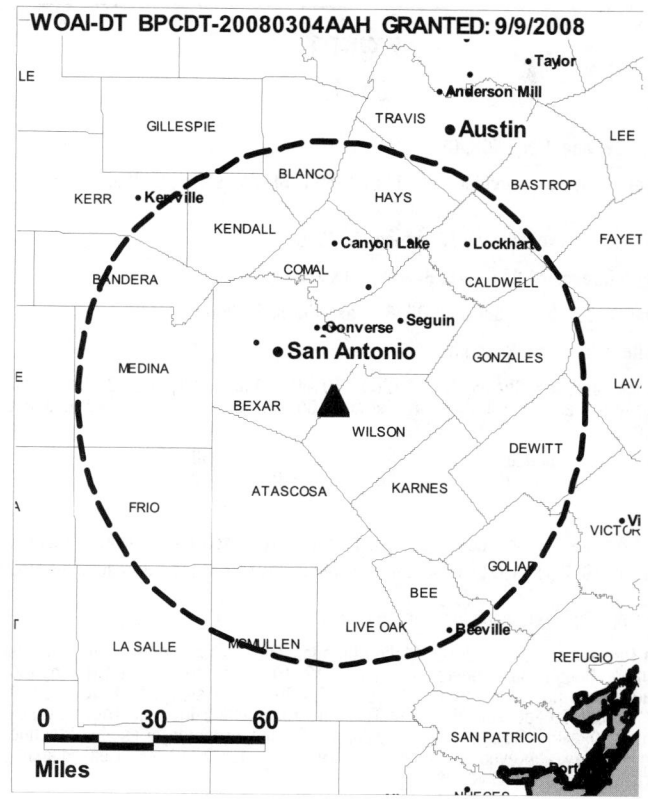

WOAI-DT BPCDT-20080304AAH GRANTED: 9/9/2008

© 2010 Warren Communications News

Josie Rios, Traffic Manager.

City of License: San Antonio. **Station DMA:** San Antonio, TX. **Rank:** 37.

Circulation © 2009 Nielsen. Coverage based on Nielsen study.

GrandTotal	Cable TV Households	Non-cable TV Households	Total TV Households
Estimated Station Totals *	499,360	289,670	789,030
Average Weekly Circulation (2009)	271,288	154,407	425,695
Average Daily Circulation (2009)			196,741

Station DMA Total	Cable TV Households	Non-cable TV Households	Total TV Households
Estimated Station Totals *	495,470	277,850	773,320
Average Weekly Circulation (2009)	270,510	152,522	423,032
Average Daily Circulation (2009)			195,605

Other DMA Total	Cable TV Households	Non-cable TV Households	Total TV Households
Estimated Station Totals *	3,890	11,820	15,710
Average Weekly Circulation (2009)	778	1,885	2,663
Average Daily Circulation (2009)			1,136

*Estimated station totals are sums of the Nielsen TV and Cable TV household estimates for each county in which the station registers viewing of more than 5% as per the Nielsen Survey Methods.

KXII-DT
Ch. 12

Network Service: MNT, FOX, CBS.

Licensee: Gray Television Licensee LLC, 1750 K St NW, Ste 1200, Washington, DC 20006.

KXII-DT: 4201 Texoma Pkwy., Sherman, TX 75090.

Mailing Address: PO Box 1175, Sherman, TX 75091.

Phone: 903-892-8123; 580-223-0946. **Fax:** 903-893-7858.

Web Site: http://www.kxii.com

Technical Facilities: Channel No. 12 (204-210 MHz). Authorized power: 36-kw visual, aural. Antenna: 1790-ft above av. terrain, 1659-ft. above ground, 2549-ft. above sea level.

Latitude	34°	01'	58"
Longitude	96°	48'	00"

Note: Latitude and longitude coordinates shown are based on the North American Datum of 1927 (NAD 27) as currently required by the Mass Media Bureau of the FCC.

Ownership: Gray Television Inc. (Group Owner).

Began Operation: April 8, 2002. Station broadcasting digitally on its analog channel allotment. Began analog operations: August 12, 1956. Sale to present owner by KXII Broadcasters Inc. approved by FCC June 29, 1999 (Television Digest, Vol. 39:16). Sale to KXII Broadcasters Inc. by Texoma Broadcasters Inc. approved by FCC October 30, 1986. Sale to Texoma by John E. Riesen, executor for estate of founder John F. Easley, approved by FCC June 17, 1959 (Vol. 15:17, 23, 25). Ceased analog operations: February 17, 2009.

Represented (sales): Katz Media Group.

Represented (legal): Wiley Rein LLP.

Personnel:

Rick Dean, General Manager.

Randy Wells, Chief Engineer, Studio.

Dennis Kite, Chief Engineer, Remote Facility.

Todd Bates, General Sales Manager.

Bryan Norman, Production Manager.

City of License: Sherman. **Station DMA:** Sherman, TX-Ada, OK. **Rank:** 161.

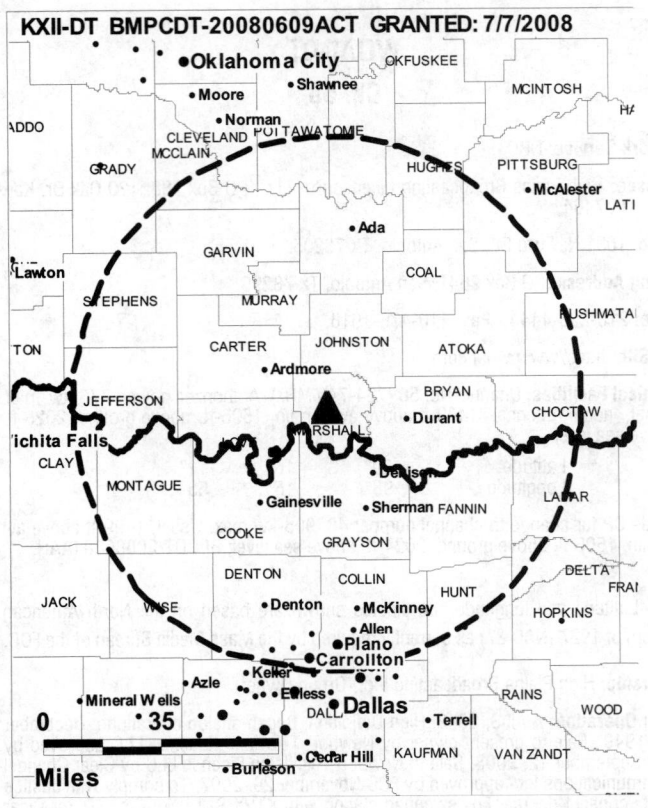

KXII-DT BMPCDT-20080609ACT GRANTED: 7/7/2008

© 2010 Warren Communications News

Circulation © 2009 Nielsen. Coverage based on Nielsen study.

GrandTotal	Cable TV Households	Non-cable TV Households	Total TV Households
Estimated Station Totals *	55,820	71,040	126,860
Average Weekly Circulation (2009)	36,804	41,812	78,616
Average Daily Circulation (2009)			47,193

Station DMA Total	Cable TV Households	Non-cable TV Households	Total TV Households
Estimated Station Totals *	51,310	68,090	119,400
Average Weekly Circulation (2009)	35,711	41,659	77,370
Average Daily Circulation (2009)			46,738

Other DMA Total	Cable TV Households	Non-cable TV Households	Total TV Households
Estimated Station Totals *	4,510	2,950	7,460
Average Weekly Circulation (2009)	1,093	153	1,246
Average Daily Circulation (2009)			455

*Estimated station totals are sums of the Nielsen TV and Cable TV household estimates for each county in which the station registers viewing of more than 5% as per the Nielsen Survey Methods.

Texas — Snyder

KPCB-DT
Ch. 17

Network Service: IND.

Licensee: Prime Time Christian Broadcasting Inc., PO Box 7708, Midland, TX 79708.

Studio: 88 E County Rd 112, Snyder, TX 79549.

Mailing Address: PO Box 61000, Midland, TX 79711.

Phone: 325-573-9517; 432-563-0420.

Web Site: http://www.ptcbglc.com

Technical Facilities: Channel No. 17 (488-494 MHz). Authorized power: 5-kw max. visual, aural. Antenna: 443-ft above av. terrain, 322-ft. above ground, 2820-ft. above sea level.

Latitude	32°	46'	52"
Longitude	100°	53'	52"

Note: Latitude and longitude coordinates shown are based on the North American Datum of 1927 (NAD 27) as currently required by the Mass Media Bureau of the FCC.

Ownership: Prime Time Christian Broadcasting Inc. (Group Owner).

Began Operation: July 20, 2006. Station broadcasting digitally on its analog channel allotment. Began analog operations: March 24, 1997.

Personnel:

Al Cooper, General Manager.

Jeff Tveit, Chief Engineer.

City of License: Snyder. **Station DMA:** Abilene-Sweetwater, TX. **Rank:** 165.

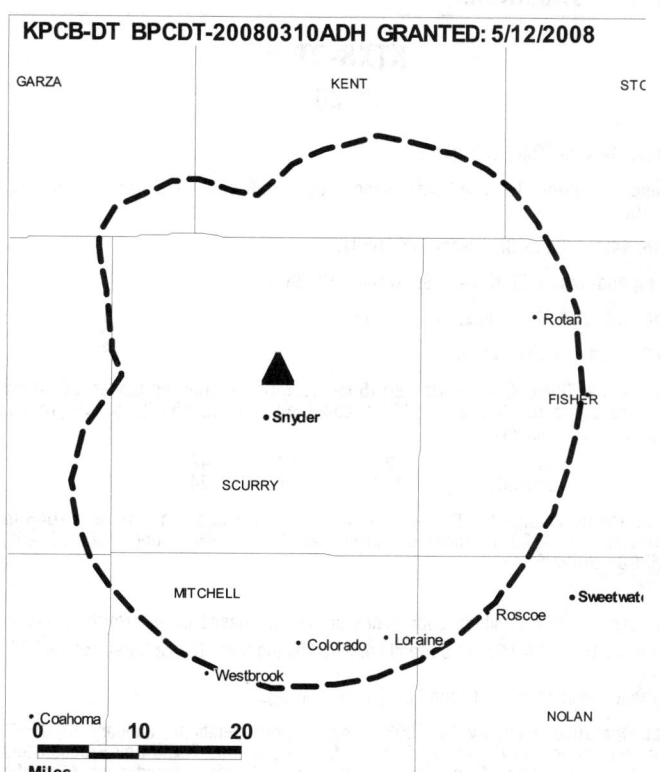

KPCB-DT BPCDT-20080310ADH GRANTED: 5/12/2008

© 2010 Warren Communications News

Circulation © 2009 Nielsen. Coverage based on Nielsen study.

GrandTotal	Cable TV Households	Non-cable TV Households	Total TV Households
Estimated Station Totals *	3,830	2,900	6,730
Average Weekly Circulation (2009)	342	191	533
Average Daily Circulation (2009)			113

Station DMA Total	Cable TV Households	Non-cable TV Households	Total TV Households
Estimated Station Totals *	3,830	2,900	6,730
Average Weekly Circulation (2009)	342	191	533
Average Daily Circulation (2009)			113

*Estimated station totals are sums of the Nielsen TV and Cable TV household estimates for each county in which the station registers viewing of more than 5% as per the Nielsen Survey Methods.

Digital cable and TV coverage maps. Visit www.warren-news.com/mediaprints.htm

MediaPrints™ Map a Winning Business Strategy

2010 Edition

A-1267

KTXS-DT
Ch. 20

Network Service: TMO, CW, ABC.

Licensee: BlueStone License Holdings Inc., 280 Park Ave, 25 Fl, E Tower, New York, NY 10017.

Studio: 4420 N Clack St, Abilene, TX 79601.

Mailing Address: 4420 N Clack St, Abilene, TX 79601.

Phone: 325-677-2281. **Fax:** 325-676-9231.

Web Site: http://www.ktxs.com

Technical Facilities: Channel No. 20 (506-512 MHz). Authorized power: 26.44-kw max. visual, aural. Antenna: 1152-ft above av. terrain, 751-ft. above ground, 3231-ft. above sea level.

Latitude	32°	24'	47"
Longitude	100°	06'	24"

Holds CP for change to 700-kw max. visual, 1441-ft above av. terrain, 1043-ft. above ground, 3523-ft. above sea level; lat. 32° 24' 48", long. 100° 06' 25", BMPCDT-20080619ABA.

Note: Latitude and longitude coordinates shown are based on the North American Datum of 1927 (NAD 27) as currently required by the Mass Media Bureau of the FCC.

Ownership: Bonten Media Group LLC (Group Owner).

Began Operation: February 15, 2008. Began analog operations: January 30, 1956. Operation by former owners A. R. Elam & Associates as Texas Key Broadcasters Inc. (to whom Grayson Enterprises leased equipment) was terminated when transfer of all Texas Key stock to Grayson Enterprises was approved by FCC June 15, 1966. For sale to Prima Inc., see KLBK-TV, Lubbock, TX. Sale to S. M. Moore Jr. by Prima approved by FCC July 25, 1983. Sale to SouthWest MultiMedia Corp. approved by FCC October 30, 1985. Sale to Lamco Communications Inc. by SouthWest MultiMedia Corp. approved by FCC November 25, 1986. Sale to BlueStone TV Holdings Inc. by Lamco Communications Inc. approved by FCC April 29, 2004. Transfer to present owner by BlueStone TV Holdings Inc. approved by FCC April 24, 2007. Ceased analog operations: June 12, 2009.

Represented (legal): Covington & Burling.

Represented (sales): Petry Media Corp.

Personnel:

Jackie Rutledge, General Manager.

Jorge Montoya, General Sales Director.

Brad Bullington, Local Sales Manager.

George Levesque, News Director.

Leland Olhausen, Chief Engineer.

Eddie Sides, Business Manager.

Sylvia Holmes, Program Director.

David Caldwell, Creative Services Manager.

Susan Acuna, Production Manager.

Sylvia Holmes, Programming Director.

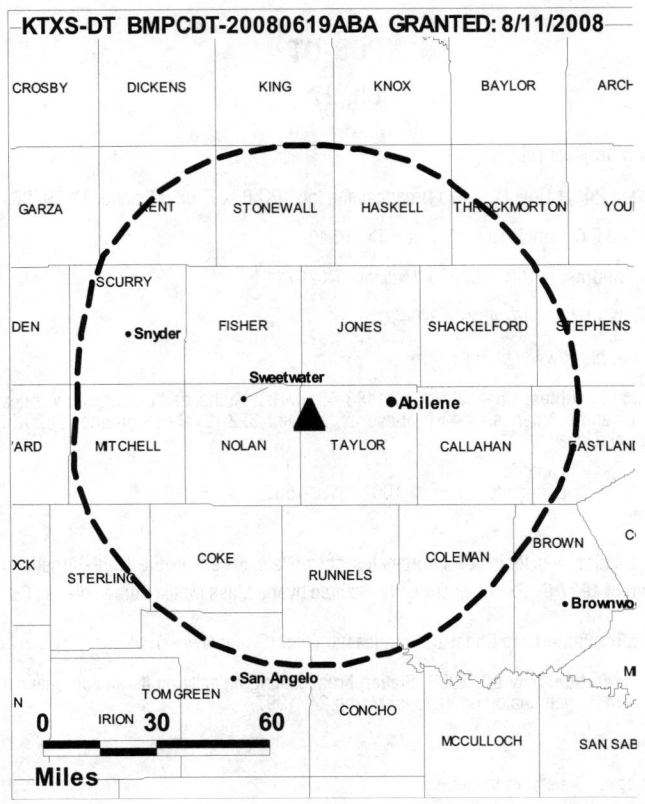

© 2010 Warren Communications News

City of License: Sweetwater. **Station DMA:** Abilene-Sweetwater, TX. **Rank:** 165.

Circulation © 2009 Nielsen. Coverage based on Nielsen study.

GrandTotal	Cable TV Households	Non-cable TV Households	Total TV Households
Estimated Station Totals *	49,960	83,180	133,140
Average Weekly Circulation (2009)	30,373	42,418	72,791
Average Daily Circulation (2009)			36,846

Station DMA Total	Cable TV Households	Non-cable TV Households	Total TV Households
Estimated Station Totals *	47,210	65,340	112,550
Average Weekly Circulation (2009)	29,079	40,243	69,322
Average Daily Circulation (2009)			35,962

Other DMA Total	Cable TV Households	Non-cable TV Households	Total TV Households
Estimated Station Totals *	2,750	17,840	20,590
Average Weekly Circulation (2009)	1,294	2,175	3,469
Average Daily Circulation (2009)			884

*Estimated station totals are sums of the Nielsen TV and Cable TV household estimates for each county in which the station registers viewing of more than 5% as per the Nielsen Survey Methods.

KCEN-DT
Ch. 9

Network Service: NBC.

Licensee: KCEN License Co. LLC, 5052 Addison Cir, Addison, TX 75001.

Studio: 314 I-35 S, Eddy, TX 76524.

Mailing Address: PO Box 6103, Temple, TX 76503-6103.

Phone: 254-773-6868; 254-859-5481. **Fax:** 254-859-4004.

Web Site: http://www.kcentv.com

Technical Facilities: Channel No. 9 (186-192 MHz). Authorized power: 25-kw visual, aural. Antenna: 1729-ft above av. terrain, 1726-ft. above ground, 2329-ft. above sea level.

Latitude	31°	16'	24"
Longitude	97°	13'	14"

Note: Latitude and longitude coordinates shown are based on the North American Datum of 1927 (NAD 27) as currently required by the Mass Media Bureau of the FCC.

Ownership: London Broadcasting Co. Inc. (Group Owner).

Began Operation: October 10, 2002. Standard Definition. Began analog operations: November 1, 1953. Sale to present owner by Channel 6 Inc. approved by FCC April 1, 2009. Ceased analog operations: February 17, 2009.

Represented (legal): Wiley Rein LLP.

Represented (sales): Blair Television.

Personnel:

Anyse Sue Mayborn, President.

W. Randy Odil, Vice President & General Manager.

Becky Kueck, General Sales Manager.

Melva Williams, National Sales Manager.

Don Bradley, News Director.

Dan Archer, Chief Engineer.

Randy Shenkir, Business Manager.

Christina Mejia, Promotion Director.

C. J. Davis, Production Director.

City of License: Temple. **Station DMA:** Waco-Temple-Bryan, TX. **Rank:** 89.

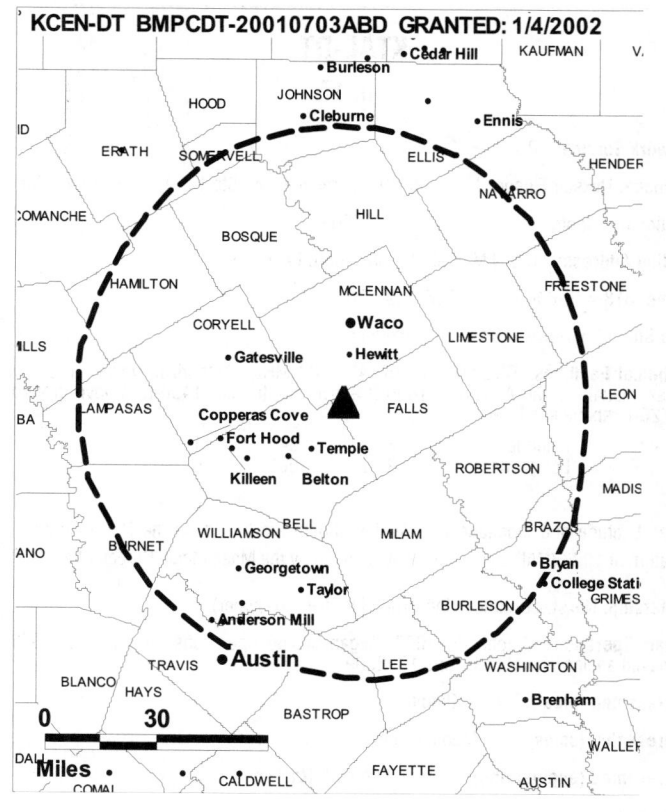

KCEN-DT BMPCDT-20010703ABD GRANTED: 1/4/2002

© 2010 Warren Communications News

Circulation © 2009 Nielsen. Coverage based on Nielsen study.

GrandTotal	Cable TV Households	Non-cable TV Households	Total TV Households
Estimated Station Totals *	189,820	126,990	316,810
Average Weekly Circulation (2009)	89,207	70,962	160,169
Average Daily Circulation (2009)			73,110

Station DMA Total	Cable TV Households	Non-cable TV Households	Total TV Households
Estimated Station Totals *	182,370	126,990	309,360
Average Weekly Circulation (2009)	88,417	70,962	159,379
Average Daily Circulation (2009)			72,999

Other DMA Total	Cable TV Households	Non-cable TV Households	Total TV Households
Estimated Station Totals *	7,450	0	7,450
Average Weekly Circulation (2009)	790	0	790
Average Daily Circulation (2009)			111

*Estimated station totals are sums of the Nielsen TV and Cable TV household estimates for each county in which the station registers viewing of more than 5% as per the Nielsen Survey Methods.

KTAL-DT
Ch. 15

Network Service: NBC.

Licensee: Nexstar Finance Inc., 909 Lake Carolyn Pkwy, Ste 1450, Irving, TX 75039.

Studio: 132 Central Mall, Texarkana, TX 75503.

Mailing Address: 3150 N Market St, Shreveport, LA 71107.

Phone: 318-629-6000. **Fax:** 318-629-6001.

Web Site: http://www.arklatexhomepage.com

Technical Facilities: Channel No. 15 (476-482 MHz). Authorized power: 1000-kw max. visual, aural. Antenna: 1490-ft above av. terrain, 1430-ft. above ground, 1726-ft. above sea level.

Latitude	32°	54'	11"
Longitude	94°	00'	20"

Note: Latitude and longitude coordinates shown are based on the North American Datum of 1927 (NAD 27) as currently required by the Mass Media Bureau of the FCC.

Ownership: Nexstar Broadcasting Group Inc. (Group Owner).

Began Operation: October 5, 2007. Began analog operations: August 16, 1953. Ceased analog operations: June 12, 2009.

Represented (legal): Drinker Biddle.

Represented (sales): Katz Media Group.

Represented (engineering): du Treil, Lundin & Rackley Inc.

Personnel:

Mark Cummings, Vice President & General Manager.

Cheryl Olive, General Sales Manager.

Janelle Williamson, Local Sales Manager, Texarkana.

Joey Stephens, Local Sales Manager, Shreveport.

Jessica Pace, Regional Sales Manager.

Paul Bergen, News Director.

Kevin Southern, Chief Engineer.

Rhonda Randolph, Business Manager.

Chunte Robinson, Program Director.

Michael Thomas, Marketing & Promotion Director.

C. L. Key, Production Manager.

Sandra Lewis, Traffic Manager.

City of License: Texarkana. **Station DMA:** Shreveport, LA. **Rank:** 82.

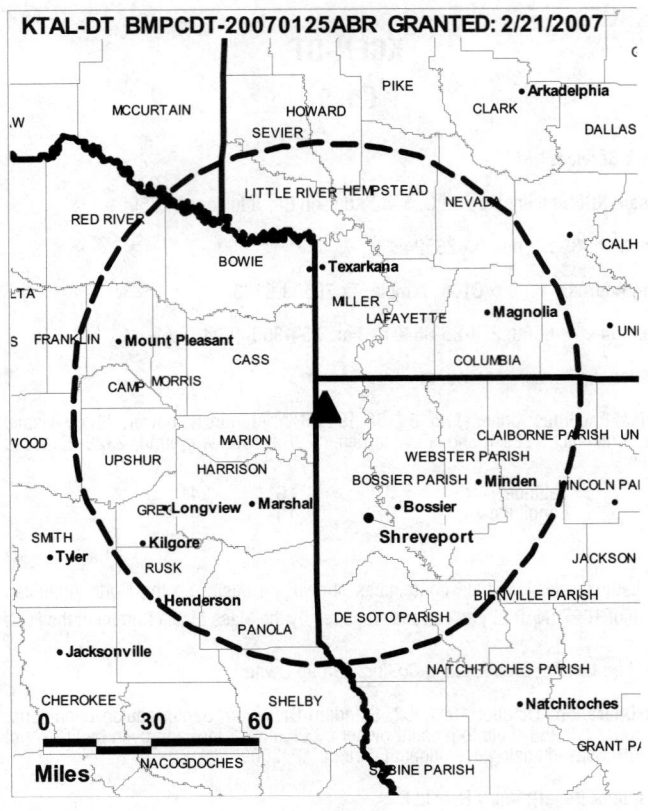

KTAL-DT BMPCDT-20070125ABR GRANTED: 2/21/2007

© 2010 Warren Communications News

Circulation © 2009 Nielsen. Coverage based on Nielsen study.

GrandTotal	Cable TV Households	Non-cable TV Households	Total TV Households
Estimated Station Totals *	157,900	237,770	395,670
Average Weekly Circulation (2009)	72,860	112,462	185,322
Average Daily Circulation (2009)			78,006

Station DMA Total	Cable TV Households	Non-cable TV Households	Total TV Households
Estimated Station Totals *	132,230	218,330	350,560
Average Weekly Circulation (2009)	70,239	110,616	180,855
Average Daily Circulation (2009)			76,943

Other DMA Total	Cable TV Households	Non-cable TV Households	Total TV Households
Estimated Station Totals *	25,670	19,440	45,110
Average Weekly Circulation (2009)	2,621	1,846	4,467
Average Daily Circulation (2009)			1,063

*Estimated station totals are sums of the Nielsen TV and Cable TV household estimates for each county in which the station registers viewing of more than 5% as per the Nielsen Survey Methods.

KLTV-DT
Ch. 7
(Operates satellite KTRE-DT Lufkin)

Network Service: ABC.

Licensee: KLTV/KTRE License Subsidiary LLC, 201 Monroe St, RSA Tower, 20th Fl, Montgomery, AL 36104.

Studio: 105 W. Ferguson, Tyler, TX 75702.

Mailing Address: PO Box 957, Tyler, TX 75710.

Phone: 903-597-5588. **Fax:** 903-510-7847.

Web Site: http://www.kltv.com

Technical Facilities: Channel No. 7 (174-180 MHz). Authorized power: 66-kw visual, aural. Antenna: 984-ft above av. terrain, 1030-ft. above ground, 1380-ft. above sea level.

Latitude	32°	32'	23"
Longitude	95°	13'	12"

Note: Latitude and longitude coordinates shown are based on the North American Datum of 1927 (NAD 27) as currently required by the Mass Media Bureau of the FCC.

Ownership: Raycom Media Inc. (Group Owner).

Began Operation: November 3, 2005. Station broadcasting digitally on its analog channel allotment. Began analog operations: October 14, 1954. Sale to present owner by Cosmos Broadcasting Corp. approved by FCC January 17, 2006. Ceased analog operations: June 12, 2009.

Represented (legal): Covington & Burling.

Represented (sales): Continental Television Sales.

Personnel:

Brad Streit, General Manager.

Pat Stacey, General Sales Manager.

Mary Ryan, National Sales Manager.

Kenny Boles, News Director.

Butch Adair, Chief Engineer.

Glenda London, Business Manager.

Cathy Carmichael, Program Director.

Greta Neal, Traffic Supervisor.

City of License: Tyler. **Station DMA:** Tyler-Longview (Lufkin & Nacogdoches), TX.

Rank: 109.

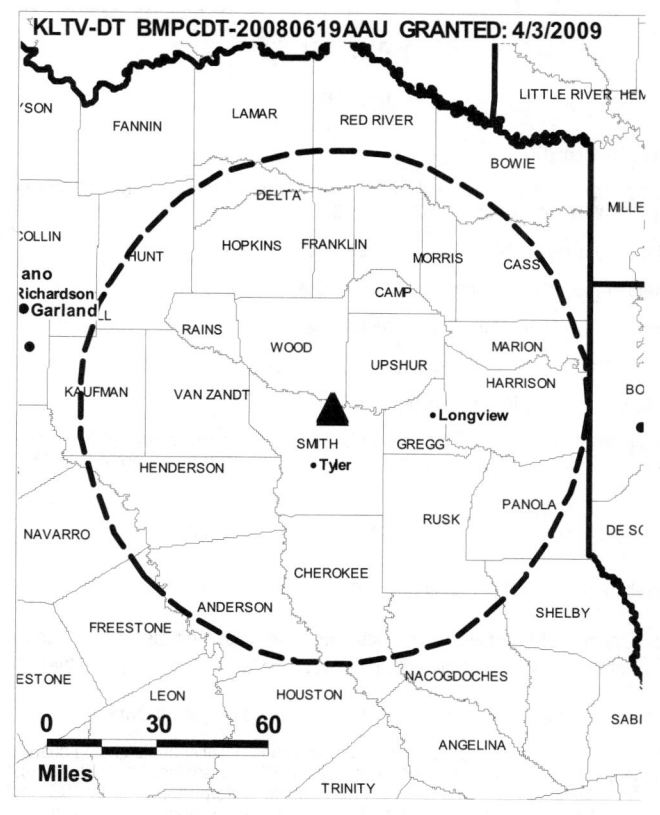

© 2010 Warren Communications News

Circulation © 2009 Nielsen. Coverage based on Nielsen study.

GrandTotal	Cable TV Households	Non-cable TV Households	Total TV Households
Estimated Station Totals *	102,060	175,130	277,190
Average Weekly Circulation (2009)	74,562	101,848	176,410
Average Daily Circulation (2009)			101,790

Station DMA Total	Cable TV Households	Non-cable TV Households	Total TV Households
Estimated Station Totals *	78,290	149,670	227,960
Average Weekly Circulation (2009)	62,050	98,323	160,373
Average Daily Circulation (2009)			96,615

Other DMA Total	Cable TV Households	Non-cable TV Households	Total TV Households
Estimated Station Totals *	23,770	25,460	49,230
Average Weekly Circulation (2009)	12,512	3,525	16,037
Average Daily Circulation (2009)			5,175

*Estimated station totals are sums of the Nielsen TV and Cable TV household estimates for each county in which the station registers viewing of more than 5% as per the Nielsen Survey Methods.

KPXL-TV
Ch. 26

Network Service: ION.

Licensee: ION Media San Antonio License Inc., Debtor in Possession, 601 Clearwater Park Rd, West Palm Beach, FL 33401-6233.

Studio: 6100 Bandera Rd, Ste 304, San Antonio, TX 78238.

Mailing Address: 6100 Bandera Rd, Ste 304, San Antonio, TX 78238.

Phone: 210-682-2626. **Fax:** 210-682-3155.

E-mail: angelabetancur@ionmedia.com

Web Site: http://www.ionmedia.com

Technical Facilities: Channel No. 26 (542-548 MHz). Authorized power: 228-kw max. visual, aural. Antenna: 1709-ft above av. terrain, 1470-ft. above ground, 3018-ft. above sea level.

Latitude	29°	37'	11"
Longitude	99°	02'	55"

Transmitter: 16.8-mi. N of Hondo Ranch Rd.

Note: Latitude and longitude coordinates shown are based on the North American Datum of 1927 (NAD 27) as currently required by the Mass Media Bureau of the FCC.

Ownership: ION Media Networks Inc., Debtor in Possession (Group Owner).

Began Operation: June 12, 2009. Station broadcasting digitally on its analog channel allotment. Began analog operations: February 19, 1999. Transfer of minority interest from Dr. Joseph Zavaletta to Paxson Communications Corp. approved by FCC April 17, 1998. Transfer of remaining interest to Paxson Communications Corp. approved by FCC June 24, 1999. Paxson Communications Corp. became ION Media Networks Inc. on June 26, 2006. Transfer of control by ION Media Networks Inc. from Paxson Management Corp. & Lowell W. Paxson to CIG Media LLC approved by FCC December 31, 2007. Involuntary assignment to debtor in possession status approved by FCC June 5, 2009. Sale to Urban Television LLC pends. Ceased analog operations: June 12, 2009.

Represented (legal): Dow Lohnes PLLC.

Represented (sales): Katz Media Group.

Personnel:

Kathy Williams, Station Operations Manager.

Marcus Potier, Chief Engineer.

Angela Betancur, Traffic Manager.

City of License: Uvalde. **Station DMA:** San Antonio, TX. **Rank:** 37.

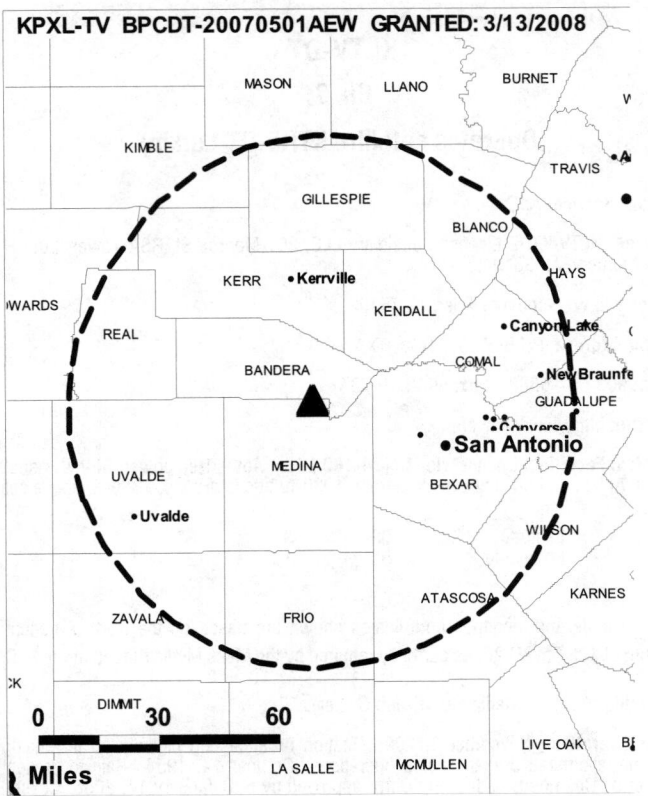

KPXL-TV BPCDT-20070501AEW GRANTED: 3/13/2008

© 2010 Warren Communications News

Circulation © 2009 Nielsen. Coverage based on Nielsen study.

GrandTotal	Cable TV Households	Non-cable TV Households	Total TV Households
Estimated Station Totals *	457,390	18,010	475,400
Average Weekly Circulation (2009)	27,629	2,031	29,660
Average Daily Circulation (2009)			6,252

Station DMA Total	Cable TV Households	Non-cable TV Households	Total TV Households
Estimated Station Totals *	457,390	18,010	475,400
Average Weekly Circulation (2009)	27,629	2,031	29,660
Average Daily Circulation (2009)			6,252

*Estimated station totals are sums of the Nielsen TV and Cable TV household estimates for each county in which the station registers viewing of more than 5% as per the Nielsen Survey Methods.

KAVU-DT
Ch. 15

Network Service: ABC.

Grantee: Saga Broadcasting LLC, 73 Kercheval Ave, Grosse Pointe Farms, MI 48236.

Studio: 3808 N. Navarro, Victoria, TX 77901.

Mailing Address: 3808 N. Navarro, Victoria, TX 77901.

Phone: 361-575-2500. **Fax:** 361-575-2255.

Web Site: http://www.myvictoriaonline.com

Technical Facilities: Channel No. 15 (476-482 MHz). Authorized power: 900-kw max. visual, aural. Antenna: 1024-ft above av. terrain, 1010-ft. above ground, 1152-ft. above sea level.

Latitude	28°	50'	42"
Longitude	97°	07'	33"

Note: Latitude and longitude coordinates shown are based on the North American Datum of 1927 (NAD 27) as currently required by the Mass Media Bureau of the FCC.

Multichannel TV Sound: Stereo and separate audio program.

LMA: Local marketing agreement with KVCT-DT Victoria.

Ownership: Saga Communications Inc. (Group Owner).

Began Operation: June 27, 2006. Began analog operations: July 21, 1982. Ceased analog operations: February 17, 2009.

Represented (sales): Continental Television Sales.

Personnel:

Jeff Pryor, President & General Manager.

John Garcia, Operations Manager.

Doug Tisdale, News Director.

Kevin John, Chief Engineer.

Mike Wall, Business Manager.

Rebecca Sarlls, Program Director.

Sean McBride, Promotions Manager.

Dave Winston, Creative Director.

Jennifer Rosales, Traffic Manager.

City of License: Victoria. **Station DMA:** Victoria, TX. **Rank:** 204.

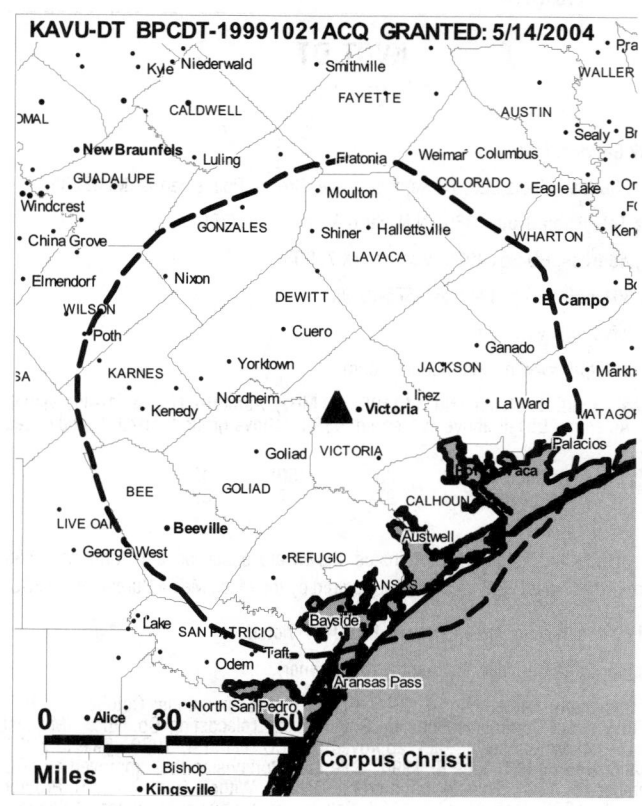

© 2010 Warren Communications News

Circulation © 2009 Nielsen. Coverage based on Nielsen study.

GrandTotal	Cable TV Households	Non-cable TV Households	Total TV Households
Estimated Station Totals *	21,890	18,590	40,480
Average Weekly Circulation (2009)	15,929	6,609	22,538
Average Daily Circulation (2009)			13,468

Station DMA Total	Cable TV Households	Non-cable TV Households	Total TV Households
Estimated Station Totals *	20,480	10,780	31,260
Average Weekly Circulation (2009)	15,585	5,864	21,449
Average Daily Circulation (2009)			12,879

Other DMA Total	Cable TV Households	Non-cable TV Households	Total TV Households
Estimated Station Totals *	1,410	7,810	9,220
Average Weekly Circulation (2009)	344	745	1,089
Average Daily Circulation (2009)			589

*Estimated station totals are sums of the Nielsen TV and Cable TV household estimates for each county in which the station registers viewing of more than 5% as per the Nielsen Survey Methods.

KVCT-DT
Ch. 11

Network Service: FOX.

Grantee: Surtsey Media LLC, 73 Kercheval Ave, Grosse Pointe Farms, MI 48236.

Victoria Television Group: 3808 N Navarro, Victoria, TX 77901.

Mailing Address: PO Box 4929, Victoria, TX 77903.

Phone: 361-575-2500. **Fax:** 361-575-2255.

E-mail: jpryor@kavutv.com

Web Site: http://www.myvictoriaonline.com

Technical Facilities: Channel No. 11 (198-204 MHz). Authorized power: 18-kw visual, aural. Antenna: 951-ft above av. terrain, 938-ft. above ground, 1079-ft. above sea level.

Latitude	28°	50'	42"
Longitude	97°	07'	33"

Note: Latitude and longitude coordinates shown are based on the North American Datum of 1927 (NAD 27) as currently required by the Mass Media Bureau of the FCC.

LMA: Local marketing agreement with KAVU-DT Victoria.

Ownership: Dana Christian Raymant (Group Owner).

Began Operation: September 14, 2006. Began analog operations: October 1, 1969. Sale to Victoria Communications by South Texas Telecasting Co. Inc. (Michael D. & C. Dan McKinnon, et. al.) approved by FCC March 4, 1976. Sale to KVCT Inc. approved by FCC June 8, 1990. Sale to VictoriaVision Inc. approved by FCC December 20, 1994. Transfer of control to Dana R. Withers from Gerald R. Proctor approved by FCC September 22, 1998. Sale to present owner by VictoriaVision Inc. approved by FCC April 26, 1999. Ceased analog operations: June 12, 2009.

Represented (legal): Fletcher, Heald & Hildreth PLC.

Represented (sales): Continental Television Sales.

Personnel:

Jeff Pryor, General Manager.

Kevin John, Chief Engineer.

John Garcia, Production Manager.

Sean McBride, Promotion Director.

Rebecca Sarlls, Program Director.

Carol Fox, Local Sales Manager.

Jennifer Rosales, Traffic Manager.

City of License: Victoria. **Station DMA:** Victoria, TX. **Rank:** 204.

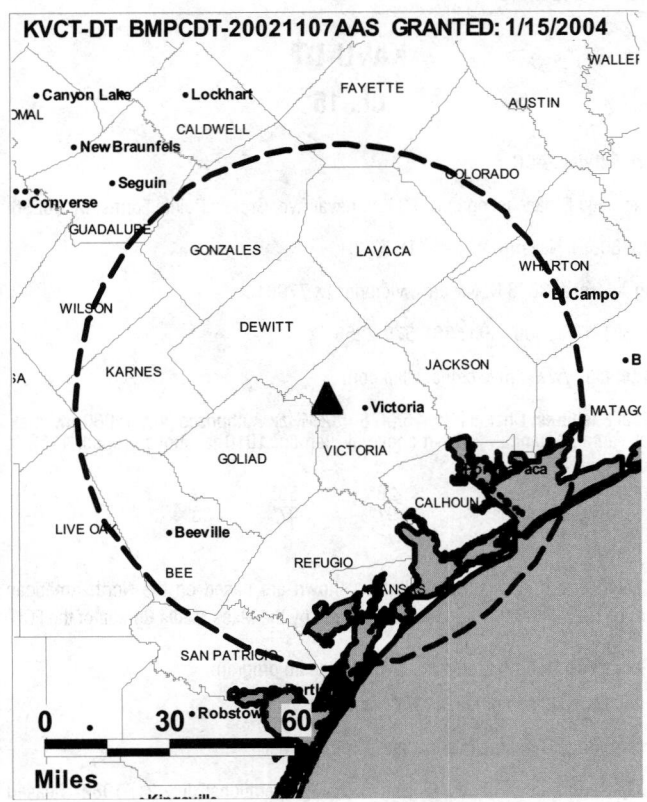

© 2010 Warren Communications News

Circulation © 2009 Nielsen. Coverage based on Nielsen study.

GrandTotal	Cable TV Households	Non-cable TV Households	Total TV Households
Estimated Station Totals *	20,480	10,780	31,260
Average Weekly Circulation (2009)	9,134	3,169	12,303
Average Daily Circulation (2009)			4,501

Station DMA Total	Cable TV Households	Non-cable TV Households	Total TV Households
Estimated Station Totals *	20,480	10,780	31,260
Average Weekly Circulation (2009)	9,134	3,169	12,303
Average Daily Circulation (2009)			4,501

*Estimated station totals are sums of the Nielsen TV and Cable TV household estimates for each county in which the station registers viewing of more than 5% as per the Nielsen Survey Methods.

KWKT-DT
Ch. 44

Network Service: MNT, FOX.

Licensee: ComCorp of Texas License Corp., PO Box 53708, Lafayette, LA 70505-3708.

Studio: 8803 Woodway Dr., Waco, TX 76712.

Mailing Address: PO Box 2544, Waco, TX 76702.

Phone: 254-776-3844. **Fax:** 254-776-8032.

E-mail: mkeese@kwkt.com

Web Site: http://www.kwkt.com

Technical Facilities: Channel No. 44 (650-656 MHz). Authorized power: 135-kw max. visual, aural. Antenna: 1829-ft above av. terrain, 1672-ft. above ground, 2499-ft. above sea level.

Latitude	31°	18'	53"
Longitude	97°	19'	36"

Note: Latitude and longitude coordinates shown are based on the North American Datum of 1927 (NAD 27) as currently required by the Mass Media Bureau of the FCC.

Ownership: Communications Corp. of America (Group Owner).

Began Operation: February 17, 2009. Station broadcasting digitally on its analog channel allotment. Began analog operations: March 13, 1988. Company emerged from debtor in possession status October 4, 2007. Involuntary transfer of control to debtor in possession approved by FCC August 29, 2006. Transfer of control from Thomas R. Galloway Sr. to Apollo Capital Management II Inc. & Thomas R. Galloway Sr. jointly approved by FCC April 16, 2004. Sale to Communications Corp. of America by Associated Broadcasters Inc. approved by FCC April 29, 1994. Sale to Associated Broadcasters Inc. by SouthWest MultiMedia/Waco Corp. approved by FCC October 31, 1990. Ceased analog operations: February 17, 2009.

Represented (legal): Dow Lohnes PLLC.

Represented (sales): Continental Television Sales.

Personnel:

Ron Crowder, General Manager.

Duane Sartor, Station Manager.

Mike Keese, General Sales Manager.

Robin Rice, National Sales Assistant.

Lou Strowger, Chief Engineer.

Edna Williams, Business Manager.

Amy Bishop, Program Director.

Caroline Nelson, Traffic Manager.

City of License: Waco. **Station DMA:** Waco-Temple-Bryan, TX. **Rank:** 89.

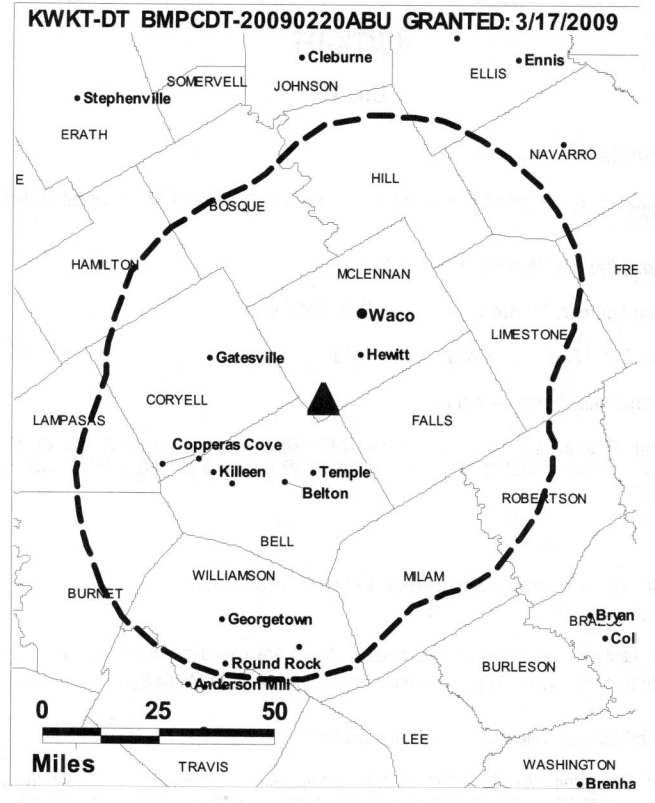

KWKT-DT BMPCDT-20090220ABU GRANTED: 3/17/2009

© 2010 Warren Communications News

Circulation © 2009 Nielsen. Coverage based on Nielsen study.

GrandTotal	Cable TV Households	Non-cable TV Households	Total TV Households
Estimated Station Totals *	144,050	137,930	281,980
Average Weekly Circulation (2009)	58,239	57,475	115,714
Average Daily Circulation (2009)			36,715

Station DMA Total	Cable TV Households	Non-cable TV Households	Total TV Households
Estimated Station Totals *	144,050	126,990	271,040
Average Weekly Circulation (2009)	58,239	56,851	115,090
Average Daily Circulation (2009)			36,540

Other DMA Total	Cable TV Households	Non-cable TV Households	Total TV Households
Estimated Station Totals *	0	10,940	10,940
Average Weekly Circulation (2009)	0	624	624
Average Daily Circulation (2009)			175

*Estimated station totals are sums of the Nielsen TV and Cable TV household estimates for each county in which the station registers viewing of more than 5% as per the Nielsen Survey Methods.

KWTX-DT
Ch. 10

Network Service: CW, CBS.

Licensee: Gray Television Licensee LLC, 1750 K St NW, Ste 1200, Washington, DC 20006.

Studio: 6700 American Plaza, Waco, TX 76712.

Mailing Address: PO Box 2636, Waco, TX 76702-2636.

Phone: 254-776-1330. **Fax:** 245-751-1088.

Web Site: http://www.kwtx.com

Technical Facilities: Channel No. 10 (192-198 MHz). Authorized power: 26-kw visual, aural. Antenna: 1821-ft above av. terrain, 1630-ft. above ground, 2483-ft. above sea level.

Latitude	31°	19'	19"
Longitude	97°	19'	02"

Holds CP for change to 39-kw visual; BPCDT-20090601AUH.

Note: Latitude and longitude coordinates shown are based on the North American Datum of 1927 (NAD 27) as currently required by the Mass Media Bureau of the FCC.

Ownership: Gray Television Inc. (Group Owner).

Began Operation: May 15, 2001. High Definition. Station broadcasting digitally on its analog channel allotment. Began analog operations: April 3, 1955. Ceased analog operations: February 17, 2009.

Represented (legal): Wiley Rein LLP.

Represented (sales): Katz Media Group.

Personnel:

Jason Effinger, Regional Vice President & General Manager.

Virgil Teter, Vice President, News.

Ken Musgrave, Operations Manager.

Bob Bunch, General & Local Sales Manager.

Pam Samford, National Sales Manager.

Kathryn Yglecias, News Director.

Larry Brown, Chief Engineer.

City of License: Waco. **Station DMA:** Waco-Temple-Bryan, TX. **Rank:** 89.

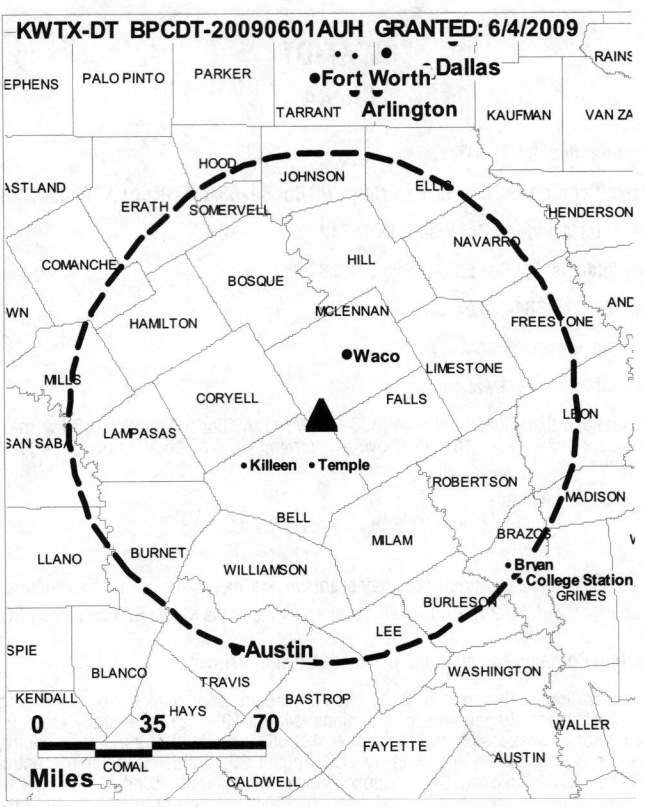

KWTX-DT BPCDT-20090601AUH GRANTED: 6/4/2009

© 2010 Warren Communications News

Circulation © 2009 Nielsen. Coverage based on Nielsen study.

GrandTotal	Cable TV Households	Non-cable TV Households	Total TV Households
Estimated Station Totals *	156,150	126,990	283,140
Average Weekly Circulation (2009)	96,266	72,422	168,688
Average Daily Circulation (2009)			87,491

Station DMA Total	Cable TV Households	Non-cable TV Households	Total TV Households
Estimated Station Totals *	143,660	126,990	270,650
Average Weekly Circulation (2009)	94,510	72,422	166,932
Average Daily Circulation (2009)			87,304

Other DMA Total	Cable TV Households	Non-cable TV Households	Total TV Households
Estimated Station Totals *	12,490	0	12,490
Average Weekly Circulation (2009)	1,756	0	1,756
Average Daily Circulation (2009)			187

*Estimated station totals are sums of the Nielsen TV and Cable TV household estimates for each county in which the station registers viewing of more than 5% as per the Nielsen Survey Methods.

KXXV-DT
Ch. 26

Network Service: TMO, ABC.

Licensee: Centex Television LP, PO Box 2522, Waco, TX 76702.

Studio: 1909 S. New Rd., Waco, TX 76711.

Mailing Address: PO Box 2522, Waco, TX 76702.

Phone: 254-754-2525. **Fax:** 254-757-1119.

Web Site: http://www.kxxv.com

Technical Facilities: Channel No. 26 (542-548 MHz). Authorized power: 1000-kw max. visual, aural. Antenna: 1842-ft above av. terrain, 1706-ft. above ground, 2502-ft. above sea level.

Latitude	31°	20'	16"
Longitude	97°	18'	36"

Note: Latitude and longitude coordinates shown are based on the North American Datum of 1927 (NAD 27) as currently required by the Mass Media Bureau of the FCC.

Ownership: Drewry Communications (Group Owner).

Began Operation: June 30, 2005. Standard Definition. Began analog operations: March 22, 1985. Sale to KXXV License Co. LLC (London Broadcasting Co. Inc.) approved by FCC November 5, 2008, but never consummated. Sale to present owner by Shamrock Broadcasting Inc. approved by FCC October 7, 1994. Sale to Shamrock Holdings by Robert Mann, et al., approved by FCC October 1, 1987 (Television Digest, Vol. 27:20). Ceased analog operations: February 17 2009.

Represented (legal): Davis Wright Tremaine LLP.

Represented (sales): Petry Media Corp.

Personnel:

Mike Lee, General Manager.

Jeff Armstrong, Local Sales Manager.

Jennifer McCutchan, National Sales Manager.

Dennis Kinney, News Director.

Randy Lee, Chief Engineer.

Anna Holyfield, Traffic Manager & Program Director.

City of License: Waco. **Station DMA:** Waco-Temple-Bryan, TX. **Rank:** 89.

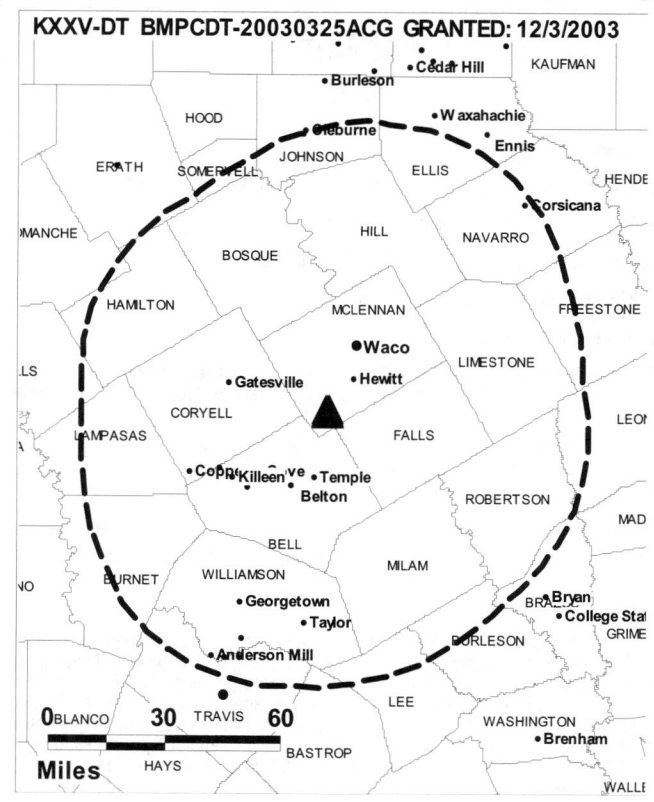

KXXV-DT BMPCDT-20030325ACG GRANTED: 12/3/2003

© 2010 Warren Communications News

Circulation © 2009 Nielsen. Coverage based on Nielsen study.

GrandTotal	Cable TV Households	Non-cable TV Households	Total TV Households
Estimated Station Totals *	150,940	126,990	277,930
Average Weekly Circulation (2009)	81,052	69,115	150,167
Average Daily Circulation (2009)			63,639

Station DMA Total	Cable TV Households	Non-cable TV Households	Total TV Households
Estimated Station Totals *	143,660	126,990	270,650
Average Weekly Circulation (2009)	79,421	69,115	148,536
Average Daily Circulation (2009)			63,508

Other DMA Total	Cable TV Households	Non-cable TV Households	Total TV Households
Estimated Station Totals *	7,280	0	7,280
Average Weekly Circulation (2009)	1,631	0	1,631
Average Daily Circulation (2009)			131

*Estimated station totals are sums of the Nielsen TV and Cable TV household estimates for each county in which the station registers viewing of more than 5% as per the Nielsen Survey Methods.

KRGV-DT
Ch. 13

Network Service: ABC.

Licensee: Mobile Video Tapes Inc., PO Box 5, Weslaco, TX 78599-0005.

Studio: 900 E. Expressway, Weslaco, TX 78596.

Mailing Address: PO Box 5, Weslaco, TX 78599-0005.

Phone: 956-968-5555. **Fax:** 956-973-5003.

Web Site: http://www.newschannel5.tv

Technical Facilities: Channel No. 13 (210-216 MHz). Authorized power: 57-kw visual, aural. Antenna: 1457-ft above av. terrain, 1460-ft. above ground, 1513-ft. above sea level.

Latitude	26°	06'	02"
Longitude	97°	50'	21"

Note: Latitude and longitude coordinates shown are based on the North American Datum of 1927 (NAD 27) as currently required by the Mass Media Bureau of the FCC.

Ownership: Mobile Video Tapes Inc.

Began Operation: October 8, 2002. High Definition. Began analog operations: April 10, 1954. Sale to present owner by Kenco Enterprises approved by FCC January 28, 1964 (Television Digest, Vol. 4:5). Sale to Kenco Enterprises by LBJ Co. approved by FCC October 18, 1961 (Vol. 17:35). LBJ Co. acquired full control of TV and radio when FCC approved sale of 50% by O. L. Taylor (Vol. 14:12, 14). Original 50% of TV acquired by LBJ from Taylor after FCC approved transfer April 4, 1956 (Vol. 12:11, 14), with LBJ exercising option April 1, 1957 on 50% of radio. Ceased analog operations: June 12, 2009.

Represented (sales): Blair Television.

Represented (legal): Cohn & Marks LLP.

Represented (engineering): du Treil, Lundin & Rackley Inc.

Personnel:

John Kittleman, General Manager.

Danny Aguilar, General Sales Manager.

Jim Chancey, Local Sales Manager.

Debbie Nott, National Sales Manager.

Jenny Martinez, News Director.

Chuck Salge, Chief Engineer.

Romeo Rodriguez, Controller.

Michelle Martone, Program Director.

Jerry Berg, Promotion Director.

Jay Leal, Production Director.

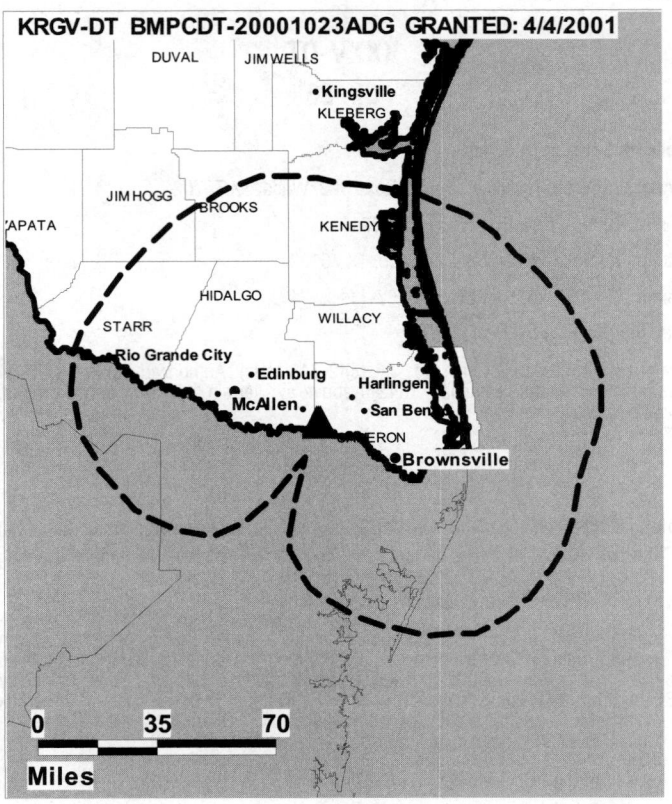

© 2010 Warren Communications News

Ginger Walker, Traffic Manager.

City of License: Weslaco. **Station DMA:** Harlingen-Weslaco-Brownsville-McAllen, TX.

Rank: 87.

Circulation © 2009 Nielsen. Coverage based on Nielsen study.

GrandTotal	Cable TV Households	Non-cable TV Households	Total TV Households
Estimated Station Totals *	139,180	210,730	349,910
Average Weekly Circulation (2009)	87,526	94,428	181,954
Average Daily Circulation (2009)			107,424

Station DMA Total	Cable TV Households	Non-cable TV Households	Total TV Households
Estimated Station Totals *	139,180	210,730	349,910
Average Weekly Circulation (2009)	87,526	94,428	181,954
Average Daily Circulation (2009)			107,424

*Estimated station totals are sums of the Nielsen TV and Cable TV household estimates for each county in which the station registers viewing of more than 5% as per the Nielsen Survey Methods.

KAUZ-DT
Ch. 22

Network Service: CW, CBS.

Grantee: Hoak Media of Wichita Falls License LLC, 500 Crescent Ct, Ste 200, Dallas, TX 75201-7808.

Studio: One Broadcast Ave., Wichita Falls, TX 76309.

Mailing Address: PO Box 2130, Wichita Falls, TX 76307.

Phone: 941-322-6957. **Fax:** 940-761-3331.

Web Site: http://www.kauz.com/

Technical Facilities: Channel No. 22 (518-524 MHz). Authorized power: 433-kw max. visual, aural. Antenna: 1020-ft above av. terrain, 994-ft. above ground, 2008-ft. above sea level.

Latitude	33°	54'	04"
Longitude	98°	32'	21"

Note: Latitude and longitude coordinates shown are based on the North American Datum of 1927 (NAD 27) as currently required by the Mass Media Bureau of the FCC.

Ownership: Hoak Media LLC (Group Owner).

Began Operation: January 1, 2003. Began analog operations: March 1, 1953 as KWFT-TV. Sale to present owner by Chelsey Broadcasting Co. LLC approved by FCC October 10, 2003. Sale to Chelsey Broadcasting Co. LLC by Benedek Broadcasting Co. LLC approved by FCC August 29, 2002. Sale to Benedek Broadcasting Co. LLC by Brissette Broadcasting approved by FCC May 22, 1996. Sale to Brissette Broadcasting by Adams Communications approved by FCC December 24, 1991. Sale to Adams Communications by Ray Clymer & W. Erle White approved by FCC January 5, 1984. Sale to Clymer & White approved by FCC May 30, 1978. Sale by Bass Bros. approved by FCC September 19, 1974. Sale to Bass Bros. by Mid-New York Broadcasting (Paul F. Harron) approved by FCC April 10, 1968. Sale to Mid-New York Broadcasting by Sidney A. Grayson & associates approved by FCC March 13, 1963. Transfer to Sidney A. Grayson group by E. H. Rowley theatre chain family & Kenyon Brown approved by FCC January 11, 1956. Ceased analog operations: June 12, 2009.

Represented (legal): Akin, Gump, Strauss, Hauer & Feld LLP.

Represented (sales): Petry Media Corp.

Personnel:

Michael Delier, General Manager.

Randy Blake, Local Sales Manager.

Dan Garcia, News Director.

Bill Lewis, Chief Engineer.

Gary Lucas, Business Manager.

Tiffany Childs, Program Manager.

Jackie McCartney, Promotion Manager.

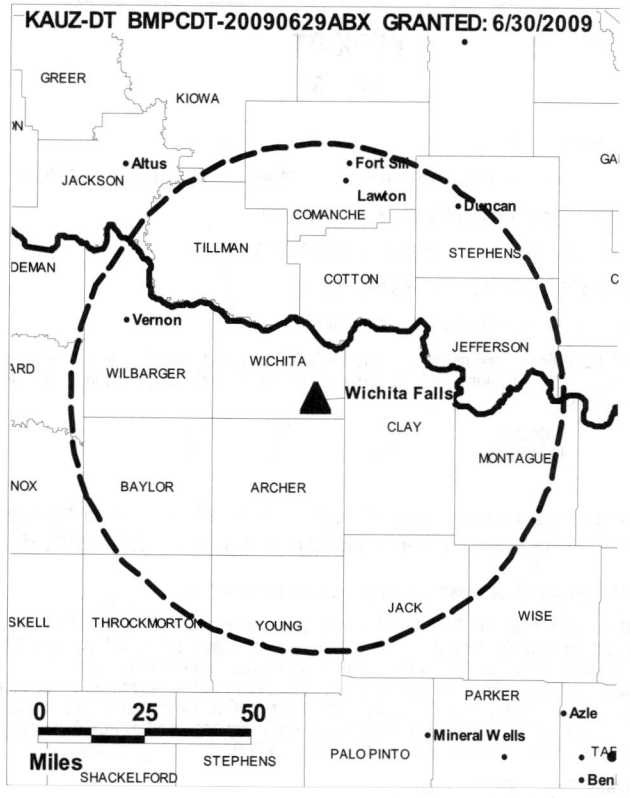

KAUZ-DT BMPCDT-20090629ABX GRANTED: 6/30/2009

© 2010 Warren Communications News

City of License: Wichita Falls. **Station DMA:** Wichita Falls, TX & Lawton, OK.

Rank: 149.

Circulation © 2009 Nielsen. Coverage based on Nielsen study.

GrandTotal	Cable TV Households	Non-cable TV Households	Total TV Households
Estimated Station Totals *	71,490	83,960	155,450
Average Weekly Circulation (2009)	45,611	43,279	88,890
Average Daily Circulation (2009)			45,072

Station DMA Total	Cable TV Households	Non-cable TV Households	Total TV Households
Estimated Station Totals *	71,490	83,960	155,450
Average Weekly Circulation (2009)	45,611	43,279	88,890
Average Daily Circulation (2009)			45,072

*Estimated station totals are sums of the Nielsen TV and Cable TV household estimates for each county in which the station registers viewing of more than 5% as per the Nielsen Survey Methods.

KFDX-DT
Ch. 28

Network Service: NBC.

Grantee: Nexstar Finance Inc., 909 Lake Carolyn Pkwy, Ste 1450, Irving, TX 75039.

Studio: 4500 Seymour Hwy, Witchita Falls, TX 76309.

Mailing Address: 4500 Seymour Hwy, Wichita Falls, TX 76309.

Phone: 940-691-0003. **Fax:** 940-691-0330.

Web Site: http://www.texomashomepage.com

Technical Facilities: Channel No. 28 (554-560 MHz). Authorized power: 1000-kw max. visual, aural. Antenna: 884-ft above av. terrain, 873-ft. above ground, 1877-ft. above sea level.

Latitude	33°	53'	23"
Longitude	98°	33'	30"

Note: Latitude and longitude coordinates shown are based on the North American Datum of 1927 (NAD 27) as currently required by the Mass Media Bureau of the FCC.

Ownership: Nexstar Broadcasting Group Inc. (Group Owner).

Began Operation: February 2, 2009. Began analog operations: March 13, 1953. Sale to Clay Communications by Darrold A. Cannan, et al., approved by FCC January 27, 1971 (Television Digest, Vol. 11:5). Sale to Price Communications Corp. by Clay Communications approved by FCC June 23, 1987 (Vol. 27:21). Sale to US Broadcast Group by Price Communications Corp. approved by FCC November 9, 1995 (Vol. 35:35). Sale to present owner from US Broadcast Group approved by FCC November 6, 1997. Ceased analog operations: February 17, 2009.

Represented (legal): Drinker Biddle.

Represented (sales): Katz Media Group.

Personnel:

Julie Pruett, Vice President & General Manager.

Greg Collier, Operations Manager.

Wayne Reed, General Sales Manager.

Britt Milstead, Local Sales Manager.

Chris Huston, News Director.

Terry Porter, Chief Engineer.

Phyllis Vaughn, Business Manager.

Carolyn Schrick, Production Manager.

Chad Johnson, Creative Director.

Troy Short, Promotion Manager.

Donna Parter, Traffic Manager.

City of License: Wichita Falls. **Station DMA:** Wichita Falls, TX & Lawton, OK.

Rank: 149.

KFDX-DT BMPCDT-20070621ABP GRANTED: 10/4/2007

© 2010 Warren Communications News

Circulation © 2009 Nielsen. Coverage based on Nielsen study.

GrandTotal	Cable TV Households	Non-cable TV Households	Total TV Households
Estimated Station Totals *	72,160	83,960	156,120
Average Weekly Circulation (2009)	44,892	46,784	91,676
Average Daily Circulation (2009)			48,981

Station DMA Total	Cable TV Households	Non-cable TV Households	Total TV Households
Estimated Station Totals *	71,030	83,960	154,990
Average Weekly Circulation (2009)	44,778	46,784	91,562
Average Daily Circulation (2009)			48,976

Other DMA Total	Cable TV Households	Non-cable TV Households	Total TV Households
Estimated Station Totals *	1,130	0	1,130
Average Weekly Circulation (2009)	114	0	114
Average Daily Circulation (2009)			5

*Estimated station totals are sums of the Nielsen TV and Cable TV household estimates for each county in which the station registers viewing of more than 5% as per the Nielsen Survey Methods.

KJTL-DT
Ch. 15

Network Service: FOX.

Grantee: Mission Broadcasting Inc., 544 Red Rock Dr, Wadsworth, OH 44281.

Studio: 4500 Seymour Hwy, Wichita Falls, TX 76309.

Mailing Address: 4500 Seymour Hwy, Wichita Falls, TX 76309.

Phone: 940-691-0003. **Fax:** 940-691-4856.

Web Site: http://www.texomashomepage.com

Technical Facilities: Channel No. 15 (476-482 MHz). Authorized power: 1000-kw max. visual, aural. Antenna: 863-ft above av. terrain, 833-ft. above ground, 1941-ft. above sea level.

Latitude	34°	12'	05"
Longitude	98°	43'	45"

Note: Latitude and longitude coordinates shown are based on the North American Datum of 1927 (NAD 27) as currently required by the Mass Media Bureau of the FCC.

Ownership: Mission Broadcasting Inc. (Group Owner).

Began Operation: February 27, 2009. Began analog operations: May 14, 1985. Sold to Wichita Fall Television Ltd. by Janet T. Lee, et al., approved by FCC August 1986. Sale to BSP Broadcasting approved by FCC June 29, 1989. Sale to Wicks Broadcast Group LP by Epic Broadcasting Co. approved by FCC July 6, 1995 (Television Digest, Vol. 35:18). Sale to present owner by Wicks Broadcast Group LP approved by FCC April 8, 1999. Ceased analog operations: February 17, 2009.

Represented (legal): Drinker Biddle.

Represented (sales): Blair Television.

Personnel:

Stephanie Reed, General Manager.

Wayne Reed, General Sales Manager.

Rhonda Wright, Local Sales Manager.

Sharon Davis, National Sales Manager.

Terry Porter, Chief Engineer.

Phyllis Vaughn, Business Manager.

Troy Short, Promotion Manager.

Debra Parish, Traffic Manager.

Chris Huston, News Director.

Chad Johnson, Creative Services Director.

Greg Collier, Operations Manager.

Carolyn Schrick, Production Manager.

City of License: Wichita Falls. **Station DMA:** Wichita Falls, TX & Lawton, OK.

Rank: 149.

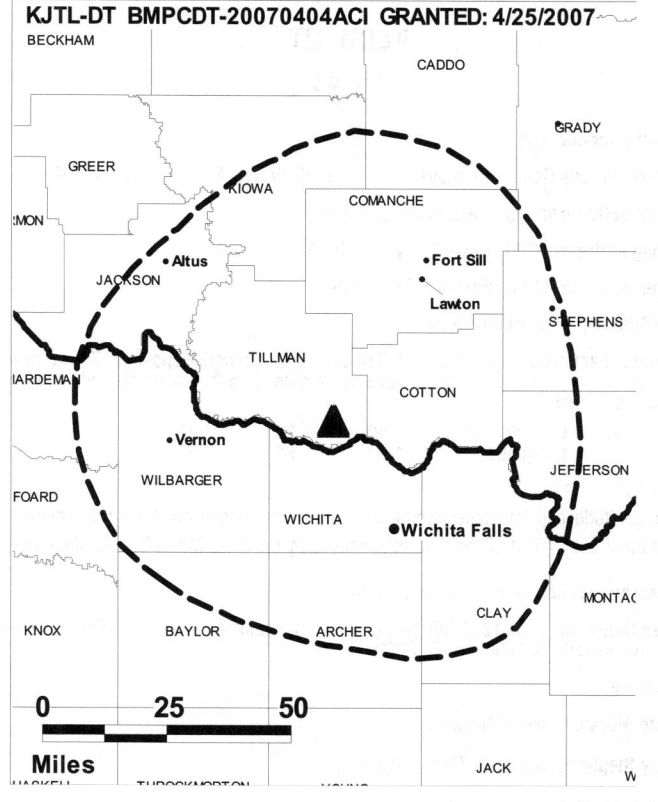

KJTL-DT BMPCDT-20070404ACI GRANTED: 4/25/2007

© 2010 Warren Communications News

Circulation © 2009 Nielsen. Coverage based on Nielsen study.

GrandTotal	Cable TV Households	Non-cable TV Households	Total TV Households
Estimated Station Totals *	75,670	83,960	159,630
Average Weekly Circulation (2009)	29,998	33,284	63,282
Average Daily Circulation (2009)			20,779

Station DMA Total	Cable TV Households	Non-cable TV Households	Total TV Households
Estimated Station Totals *	71,490	83,960	155,450
Average Weekly Circulation (2009)	29,423	33,284	62,707
Average Daily Circulation (2009)			20,718

Other DMA Total	Cable TV Households	Non-cable TV Households	Total TV Households
Estimated Station Totals *	4,180	0	4,180
Average Weekly Circulation (2009)	575	0	575
Average Daily Circulation (2009)			61

*Estimated station totals are sums of the Nielsen TV and Cable TV household estimates for each county in which the station registers viewing of more than 5% as per the Nielsen Survey Methods.

KLCW-DT
Ch. 43

Network Service: CW.

Grantee: Woods Communications Corp., One WCOV Ave, Montgomery, AL 36111.

Studio: 9800 University Ave, Lubbock, TX 79424.

Mailing Address: 9800 University Ave, Lubbock, TX 79424.

Phone: 806-745-3434. **Fax:** 806-748-1949.

Web Site: http://www.lubbockcw.com

Technical Facilities: Channel No. 43 (644-650 MHz). Authorized power: 179-kw max. visual, aural. Antenna: 919-ft above av. terrain, 925-ft. above ground, 4132-ft. above sea level.

Latitude	33°	30'	08"
Longitude	101°	52'	20"

Note: Latitude and longitude coordinates shown are based on the North American Datum of 1927 (NAD 27) as currently required by the Mass Media Bureau of the FCC.

Ownership: Woods Communications Corp.

Began Operation: April 12, 2008. Began analog operations: February 9, 2001. Ceased analog operations: February 17, 2009.

Personnel:

Brad Moran, General Manager.

Amy Stephens, Station & Traffic Manager.

Tee Thomas, Chief Engineer.

Sherry Saffle, General Sales Manager.

Traci Thorne, Program Director.

Marcie Reno, Promotion Director & Production Manager.

City of License: Wolfforth. **Station DMA:** Lubbock, TX. **Rank:** 143.

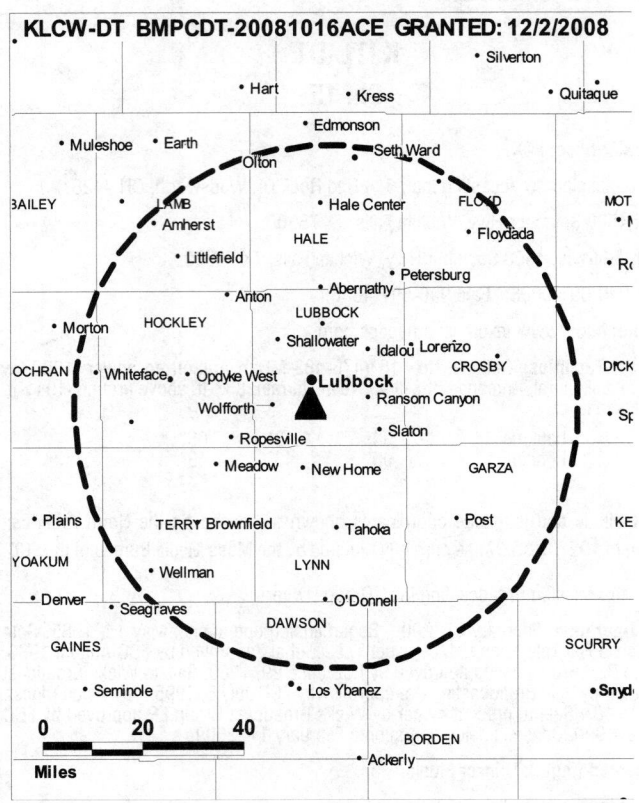

KLCW-DT BMPCDT-20081016ACE GRANTED: 12/2/2008

© 2010 Warren Communications News

Circulation © 2009 Nielsen. Coverage based on Nielsen study.

GrandTotal	Cable TV Households	Non-cable TV Households	Total TV Households
Estimated Station Totals *	62,730	82,540	145,270
Average Weekly Circulation (2009)	9,150	16,533	25,683
Average Daily Circulation (2009)			7,136

Station DMA Total	Cable TV Households	Non-cable TV Households	Total TV Households
Estimated Station Totals *	62,730	82,540	145,270
Average Weekly Circulation (2009)	9,150	16,533	25,683
Average Daily Circulation (2009)			7,136

*Estimated station totals are sums of the Nielsen TV and Cable TV household estimates for each county in which the station registers viewing of more than 5% as per the Nielsen Survey Methods.

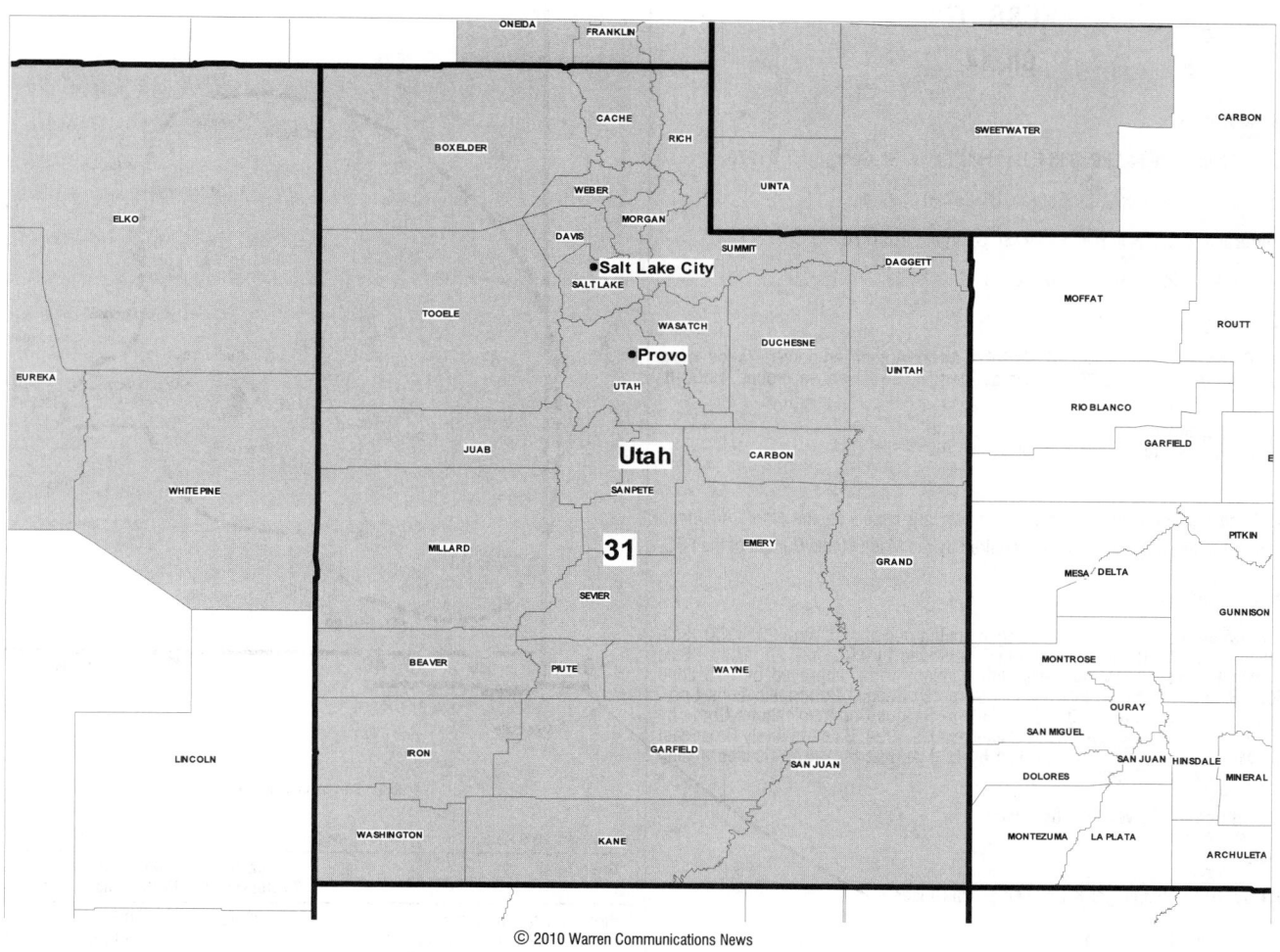

© 2010 Warren Communications News

MARKET	NIELSEN DMA TV HOUSEHOLDS	RANK	MARKET AREA COMMERCIAL STATIONS
Salt Lake City, UT	944,060	31	KBNY-DT (27); KCSG-DT (14); KENV-DT (10); KGWR-DT (13); KJZZ-DT (46); KPNZ-DT (24); KSL-DT (38); KSTU-DT (28); KTMW-DT (20); KTVX-DT (40); KUCW-DT (48); KUPX-TV (29); KUSG-DT (9); KUTH-DT (32); KUTV-DT (34); KVNV-DT (3)

Utah Station Totals as of October 1, 2009

	VHF	UHF	TOTAL
Commercial Television	1	11	12
Educational Television	0	5	5
	1	16	17

KCSG-DT
Ch. 14

Network Service: IND.

Grantee: Southwest Media LLC, 845 E Red Hills Pkwy, St. George, UT 84770.

Studio: 845 E Red Hills Pkwy, St. George, UT 84770.

Mailing Address: 845 E Red Hills Pkwy, St. George, UT 84770.

Phone: 435-634-7500. **Fax:** 435-674-2774.

Web Site: http://www.kcsg.com

Technical Facilities: Channel No. 14 (470-476 MHz). Authorized power: 25-kw max. visual, aural. Antenna: 1263-ft above av. terrain, 56-ft. above ground, 8350-ft. above sea level.

Latitude	37°	38'	22"
Longitude	113°	02'	00"

Note: Latitude and longitude coordinates shown are based on the North American Datum of 1927 (NAD 27) as currently required by the Mass Media Bureau of the FCC.

Ownership: Southwest Media LLC.

Began Operation: February 17, 2009. Began analog operations: April 23, 1990. Sale to present owner by Broadcast West LLC approved by FCC July 20, 2005. Sale to Broadcast West LLC by Bonneville International Corp. approved by FCC June 3, 2002. Sale to Bonneville International Corp. by Seagull Communications Corp. approved by FCC December 10, 1997. Sale to Seagull Communications Corp. by Liberty Broadcast Co. approved by FCC January 19, 1994. Sale to Liberty Broadcast Co. by Michael Glenn Golden approved by FCC August 5, 1987. Ceased analog operations: February 17, 2009.

Represented (legal): Garvey Schubert Barer.

Personnel:

Ray Hardy, General Manager & Chief Financial Officer.

Lani Purri, Promotion Director.

Jim Nagy, News Director.

Amy Palmer, Traffic Manager.

David Hudson, Operations Manager.

Kimberly Cooper, General Sales Manager.

City of License: Cedar City. **Station DMA:** Salt Lake City, UT. **Rank:** 31.

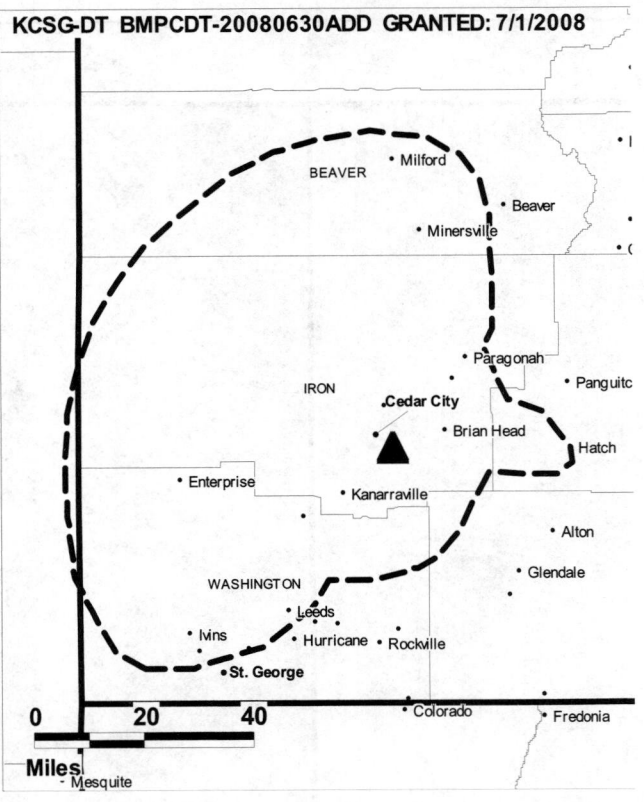

KCSG-DT BMPCDT-20080630ADD GRANTED: 7/1/2008

© 2010 Warren Communications News

Circulation © 2009 Nielsen. Coverage based on Nielsen study.

GrandTotal	Cable TV Households	Non-cable TV Households	Total TV Households
Estimated Station Totals *	20,150	60,580	80,730
Average Weekly Circulation (2009)	4,176	3,629	7,805
Average Daily Circulation (2009)			2,171

Station DMA Total	Cable TV Households	Non-cable TV Households	Total TV Households
Estimated Station Totals *	20,150	60,580	80,730
Average Weekly Circulation (2009)	4,176	3,629	7,805
Average Daily Circulation (2009)			2,171

*Estimated station totals are sums of the Nielsen TV and Cable TV household estimates for each county in which the station registers viewing of more than 5% as per the Nielsen Survey Methods.

KPNZ-DT
Ch. 24

Network Service: IND.

Licensee: KRCA License LLC, 1845 Empire Ave, Burbank, CA 91504.

Studio: 150 N. Wright Brothers. Dr, Suite 520, Salt Lake City, UT 84116.

Mailing Address: 150 N. Wright Brothers Dr, Ste 520, Salt Lake City, UT 84116.

Phone: 801-519-2424. **Fax:** 801-359-1272.

Technical Facilities: Channel No. 24 (530-536 MHz). Authorized power: 450-kw max. visual, aural. Antenna: 4032-ft above av. terrain, 197-ft. above ground, 9232-ft. above sea level.

| Latitude | 40° | 39' | 33" |
| Longitude | 112° | 12' | 07" |

Note: Latitude and longitude coordinates shown are based on the North American Datum of 1927 (NAD 27) as currently required by the Mass Media Bureau of the FCC.

Ownership: Liberman Broadcasting Inc. (Group Owner).

Began Operation: June 12, 2009. Station broadcasting digitally on its analog channel allotment. Began analog operations: December 6, 1998. Sale to present owner by Utah Communications LLC approved by FCC November 19, 2007. Ceased analog operations: June 12, 2009.

Represented (engineering): Cavell, Mertz & Associates Inc.

Represented (legal): Latham & Watkins.

Personnel:

Roger Mills, Chief Engineer.

Christy Loader, Program Director & Traffic Manager.

City of License: Ogden. **Station DMA:** Salt Lake City, UT. **Rank:** 31.

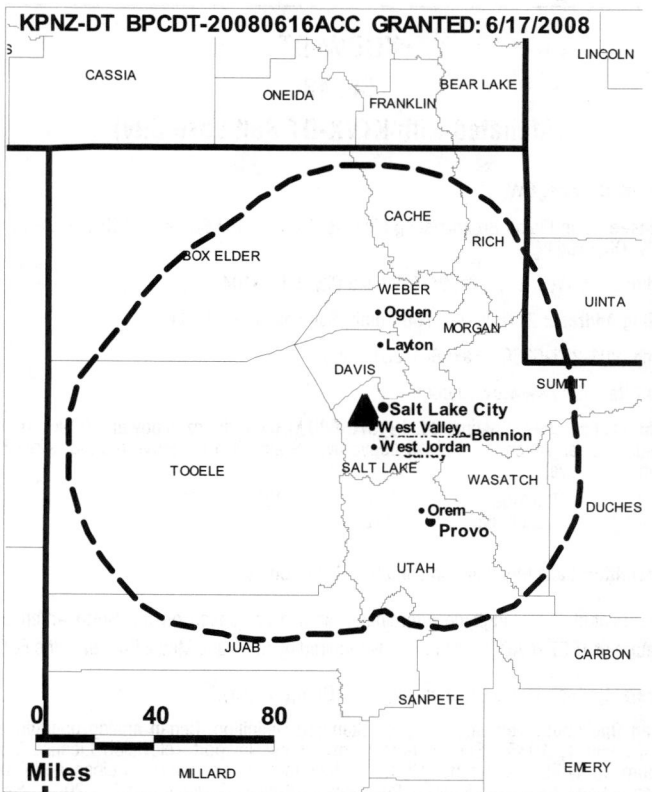

KPNZ-DT BPCDT-20080616ACC GRANTED: 6/17/2008

© 2010 Warren Communications News

Nielsen Data: Not available.

KUCW-DT
Ch. 48
(Affiliated with KTVX-DT Salt Lake City)

Network Service: CW.

Licensee: High Plains Broadcasting License Co. LLC, PO Box 288, 120 Oak Dr, Kaw City, OK 74641.

Studio: 2175 West 1700 South, Salt Lake City, UT 84104.

Mailing Address: 2175 West 1700 South, Salt Lake City, UT 84104.

Phone: 801-281-0330. **Fax:** 801-281-4503.

Web Site: http://www.cw30.com

Technical Facilities: Channel No. 48 (674-680 MHz). Authorized power: 200-kw max. visual, aural. Antenna: 4124-ft above av. terrain, 256-ft. above ground, 9291-ft. above sea level.

Latitude	40°	39'	33"
Longitude	112°	12'	07"

Transmitter: Lake Mountain Antenna Site, Lehi County.

Note: Latitude and longitude coordinates shown are based on the North American Datum of 1927 (NAD 27) as currently required by the Mass Media Bureau of the FCC.

Ownership: High Plains Broadcasting Inc. (Group Owner).

Began Operation: February 1, 2002. Standard Definition. Began analog operations: November 1, 1985. Sale to present owner by Newport Television License LLC approved by FCC September 12, 2008. Sale to Newport Television License LLC by Clear Channel Communications Inc. approved by FCC November 29, 2007. Sale to Clear Channel Communications Inc. by ACME Television Licenses of Utah LLC approved by FCC March 22, 2006. Sale to ACME Television Licenses of Utah LLC by Roberts Broadcasting approved by FCC April 29, 1999. Sale to Roberts Broadcasting by Paxson Communications Corp. approved by FCC March 30, 1999. Sale to Paxson Communications Corp. by Alpha & Omega Communications Inc. approved by FCC November 6, 1996. Sale to Miracle Rock Church (later Alpha & Omega Communications Inc.) by Scott Stuart, Receiver for Ogden Television Inc. approved by FCC July 14, 1993. Involuntary assignment to Scott Stuart as Receiver by Ogden Television Inc. approved by FCC February 22, 1993. Ceased analog operations: June 12, 2009.

Represented (legal): Pillsbury Winthrop Shaw Pittman LLP.

Personnel:

Kalvin Pike, Interim General Manager & General Sales Manager.

Steve Fowles, Local Sales Manager.

Barbara Syphus, National Sales Manager.

Bob Lyon, Chief Engineer.

Ida Anderson, Business Manager.

Cade Wilbur, Program Manager.

Dennis Elsbury, Promotion & Creative Services Director.

Mike Spiecha, Production Manager.

Shara Meredith, Traffic Manager.

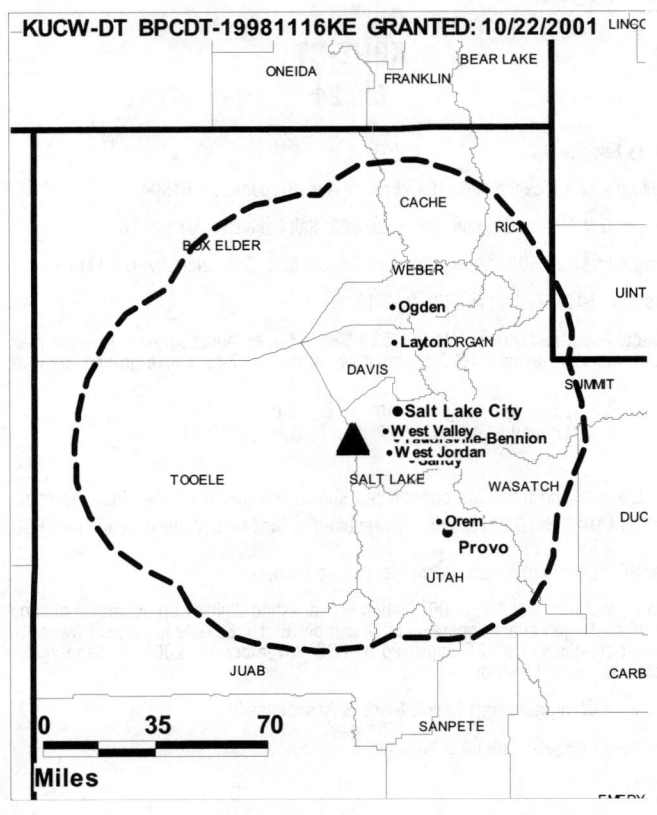

KUCW-DT BPCDT-19981116KE GRANTED: 10/22/2001

© 2010 Warren Communications News

City of License: Ogden. **Station DMA:** Salt Lake City, UT. **Rank:** 31.

Circulation © 2009 Nielsen. Coverage based on Nielsen study.

GrandTotal	Cable TV Households	Non-cable TV Households	Total TV Households
Estimated Station Totals *	374,230	475,140	849,370
Average Weekly Circulation (2009)	84,791	121,241	206,032
Average Daily Circulation (2009)			67,892

Station DMA Total	Cable TV Households	Non-cable TV Households	Total TV Households
Estimated Station Totals *	373,400	475,140	848,540
Average Weekly Circulation (2009)	84,593	121,241	205,834
Average Daily Circulation (2009)			67,883

Other DMA Total	Cable TV Households	Non-cable TV Households	Total TV Households
Estimated Station Totals *	830	0	830
Average Weekly Circulation (2009)	198	0	198
Average Daily Circulation (2009)			9

*Estimated station totals are sums of the Nielsen TV and Cable TV household estimates for each county in which the station registers viewing of more than 5% as per the Nielsen Survey Methods.

KUPX-TV
Ch. 29

Network Service: ION.

Licensee: ION Media Salt Lake City License Inc., Debtor in Possession, 601 Clearwater Park Rd, West Palm Beach, FL 33401-6233.

Studio: 466 C Lawndale Dr, Salt Lake City, UT 84115.

Mailing Address: 466 C Lawndale Dr, Salt Lake City, UT 84115.

Phone: 801-474-0016. **Fax:** 801-463-9667.

E-mail: jimobin@ionmedia.com

Web Site: http://www.ionmedia.com

Technical Facilities: Channel No. 29 (560-566 MHz). Authorized power: 530-kw max. visual, aural. Antenna: 3842-ft above av. terrain, 194-ft. above ground, 9045-ft. above sea level.

Latitude	40°	39'	12"
Longitude	112°	12'	06"

Note: Latitude and longitude coordinates shown are based on the North American Datum of 1927 (NAD 27) as currently required by the Mass Media Bureau of the FCC.

Ownership: ION Media Networks Inc., Debtor in Possession (Group Owner).

Began Operation: May 10, 2002. Standard Definition. Began analog operations: April 21, 1998. Sale to Roberts Broadcasting by Royal Television of Utah Inc. approved by FCC February 22, 1996. Roberts Broadcasting sale of minority interest to Acme Television Holdings LLC approved by FCC October 20, 1997. Transfer of remaining interest from Roberts Broadcasting to minority owner Acme Television Holdings LLC approved by FCC January 26, 1999. Trade of station from Acme to Paxson Communications Corp. for KUWB, Ogden, UT, approved by FCC March 30, 1999. Paxson Communications Corp. became ION Media Networks Inc. June 26, 2006. Transfer of control by ION Media Networks Inc. from Paxson Management Corp. & Lowell W. Paxson to CIG Media LLC approved by FCC December 31, 2007. Involuntary assignment to debtor in possession status approved by FCC June 5, 2009. Sale to Urban Television LLC pends. Ceased analog operations: June 12, 2009.

Represented (legal): Dow Lohnes PLLC.

Represented (engineering): du Treil, Lundin & Rackley Inc.

Personnel:

Jim Obin, Station Operations & Traffic Manager.

James Elmer, Master Contol Operator.

Larry O'Donnell, Chief Engineer.

City of License: Provo. **Station DMA:** Salt Lake City, UT. **Rank:** 31.

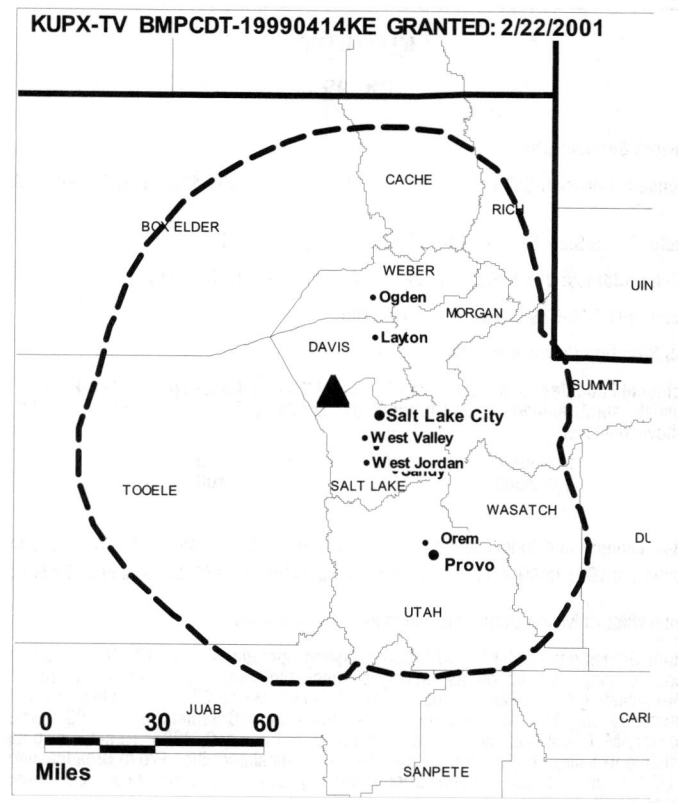

KUPX-TV BMPCDT-19990414KE GRANTED: 2/22/2001

© 2010 Warren Communications News

Circulation © 2009 Nielsen. Coverage based on Nielsen study.

GrandTotal	Cable TV Households	Non-cable TV Households	Total TV Households
Estimated Station Totals *	256,460	310,010	566,470
Average Weekly Circulation (2009)	17,359	22,666	40,025
Average Daily Circulation (2009)			9,193

Station DMA Total	Cable TV Households	Non-cable TV Households	Total TV Households
Estimated Station Totals *	256,460	310,010	566,470
Average Weekly Circulation (2009)	17,359	22,666	40,025
Average Daily Circulation (2009)			9,193

*Estimated station totals are sums of the Nielsen TV and Cable TV household estimates for each county in which the station registers viewing of more than 5% as per the Nielsen Survey Methods.

KUTH-DT
Ch. 32

Network Service: UNV.

Licensee: Univision Salt Lake City LLC, 5999 Center Dr, Ste 4083, Los Angeles, CA 90045.

Studio: 215 S State St, Ste 100-A, Salt Lake City, UT 84111.

Mailing Address: 215 S State St, Ste 100-A, Salt Lake City, UT 84111.

Phone: 801-519-9784. **Fax:** 801-519-9785.

Web Site: http://www.univision-utah.com

Technical Facilities: Channel No. 32 (578-584 MHz). Authorized power: 194-kw max. visual, aural. Antenna: 2664-ft above av. terrain, 125-ft. above ground, 7582-ft. above sea level.

Latitude	40°	16'	45"
Longitude	111°	56'	00"

Note: Latitude and longitude coordinates shown are based on the North American Datum of 1927 (NAD 27) as currently required by the Mass Media Bureau of the FCC.

Ownership: Univision Communications Inc. (Group Owner).

Began Operation: April 17, 2003. Began analog operations: April 17, 2003. Station broadcasting digitally on its analog channel allotment. Transfer of control to Broadcasting Media Partners Inc. approved by FCC March 27, 2007. Sale to present owner by Gary M. Cocola Family Trust approved by FCC September 13, 2004. Sale to Gary M. Cocola Family Trust approved by FCC January 9, 2003. To settle dispute relating to sale of permit, the 12 members of original permittee Provo Broadcasting LLC conducted closed auction. Cocola was high bidder. Ceased analog operations: June 12, 2009.

Represented (legal): Pillsbury Winthrop Shaw Pittman LLP.

Personnel:

Bob Jay, Station Development Manager.

German Rodriguez, Production Manager.

Rene Torcatty, News Director.

Anthony Tsosie, Chief Engineer.

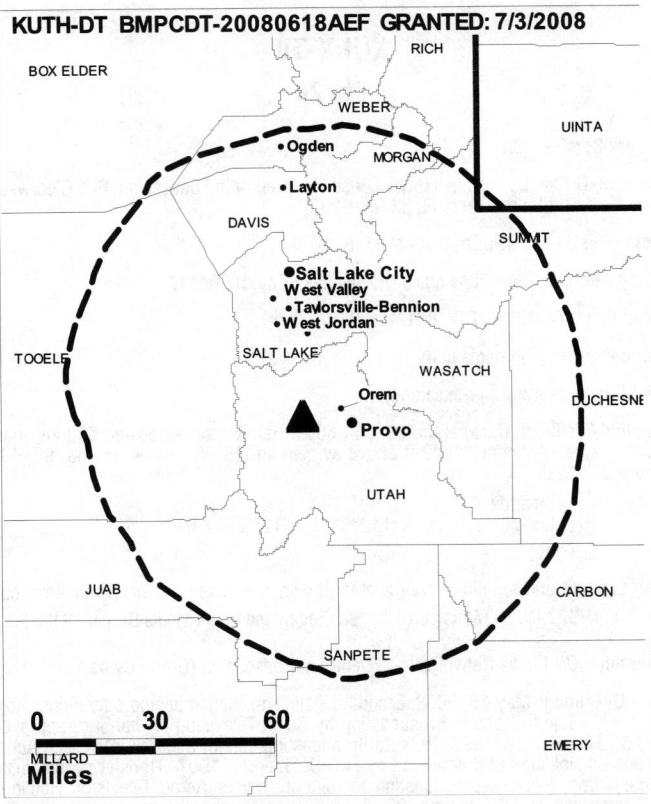

KUTH-DT BMPCDT-20080618AEF GRANTED: 7/3/2008

© 2010 Warren Communications News

Maria Barrios, Business Manager.

Marcella Kuck, Traffic Director.

City of License: Provo. **Station DMA:** Salt Lake City, UT. **Rank:** 31.

Nielsen Data: Not available.

KJZZ-DT
Ch. 46

Network Service: MNT.

Licensee: Larry H. Miller Communications Corp., 5181 Amelia Earhart Dr, Salt Lake City, UT 84116-2869.

Studio: 5181 Amelia Earhart Dr., Salt Lake City, UT 84116.

Mailing Address: 5181 Amelia Earhart Dr, Salt Lake City, UT 84116.

Phone: 801-537-1414. **Fax:** 801-238-6414.

Web Site: http://www.kjzz.com

Technical Facilities: Channel No. 46 (662-668 MHz). Authorized power: 200-kw max. visual, aural. Antenna: 4153-ft above av. terrain, 287-ft. above ground, 9319-ft. above sea level.

Latitude	40°	39'	33"
Longitude	112°	12'	07"

Note: Latitude and longitude coordinates shown are based on the North American Datum of 1927 (NAD 27) as currently required by the Mass Media Bureau of the FCC.

Ownership: Larry H. Miller Communications Corp. (Group Owner).

Began Operation: November 1, 2002. Standard Definition. Began analog operations: February 14, 1989. Sale to present owner by American TV of Utah approved by FCC February 22, 1993. Larry H Miller died February 20, 2009. Involuntary transfer of control to Karen G Miller, Personal Representative approved by FCC March 30, 2009. Ceased analog operations: June 12, 2009.

Represented (legal): Leventhal, Senter & Lerman PLLC.

Represented (sales): Blair Television.

Personnel:

Chris Baum, Station & General Sales Manager.

Lynn Lamb, Local Sales Manager.

Michael Grover, Chief Engineer.

Randy Wright, Controller.

Bob Quigley, Program Director.

Janalee Clements, Marketing Director.

Dean Paynter, Production Director.

City of License: Salt Lake City. **Station DMA:** Salt Lake City, UT. **Rank:** 31.

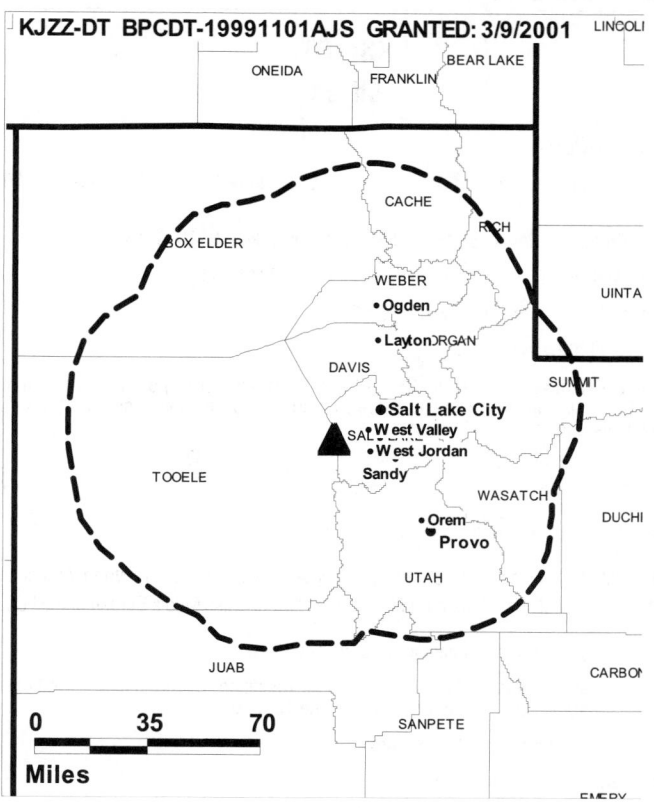

KJZZ-DT BPCDT-19991101AJS GRANTED: 3/9/2001

© 2010 Warren Communications News

Circulation © 2009 Nielsen. Coverage based on Nielsen study.

GrandTotal	Cable TV Households	Non-cable TV Households	Total TV Households
Estimated Station Totals *	374,030	491,600	865,630
Average Weekly Circulation (2009)	101,135	145,918	247,053
Average Daily Circulation (2009)			79,525

Station DMA Total	Cable TV Households	Non-cable TV Households	Total TV Households
Estimated Station Totals *	368,720	480,830	849,550
Average Weekly Circulation (2009)	100,426	145,080	245,506
Average Daily Circulation (2009)			79,173

Other DMA Total	Cable TV Households	Non-cable TV Households	Total TV Households
Estimated Station Totals *	5,310	10,770	16,080
Average Weekly Circulation (2009)	709	838	1,547
Average Daily Circulation (2009)			352

*Estimated station totals are sums of the Nielsen TV and Cable TV household estimates for each county in which the station registers viewing of more than 5% as per the Nielsen Survey Methods.

KSL-DT
Ch. 38

Network Service: NBC.

Licensee: Bonneville Holding Co., 55 N 300 W, Broadcast House, Salt Lake City, UT 84180.

Studio: Broadcast House, 55 North 300 West, Salt Lake City, UT 84180.

Mailing Address: PO Box 1160, Salt Lake City, UT 84110-1160.

Phone: 801-575-5555. **Fax:** 801-575-5561.

Web Site: http://www.ksl.com

Technical Facilities: Channel No. 38 (614-620 MHz). Authorized power: 546-kw max. visual, aural. Antenna: 4157-ft above av. terrain, 289-ft. above ground, 9324-ft. above sea level.

Latitude	40°	39'	33"
Longitude	112°	12'	07"

Transmitter: Farnsworth Peak, 6.2-mi. SW of Magna.

Note: Latitude and longitude coordinates shown are based on the North American Datum of 1927 (NAD 27) as currently required by the Mass Media Bureau of the FCC.

Ownership: Bonneville International Corp. (Group Owner).

Began Operation: October 28, 1999. Standard Definition. Began analog operations: June 1, 1949. Ceased analog operations: June 12, 2009.

Represented (sales): Petry Media Corp.

Personnel:

Greg James, Senior Vice President & Station Manager.

Mark Wiest, Vice President, Sales.

Con Psarras, Vice President, News & News Director.

Steve Poulsen, Vice President, Marketing & Promotions.

Brent Robinson, Chief Engineer.

Mark Palmer, Business Manager.

Michelle Kettle, Program Director.

Vickie Bojanski, Traffic Manager.

City of License: Salt Lake City. **Station DMA:** Salt Lake City, UT. **Rank:** 31.

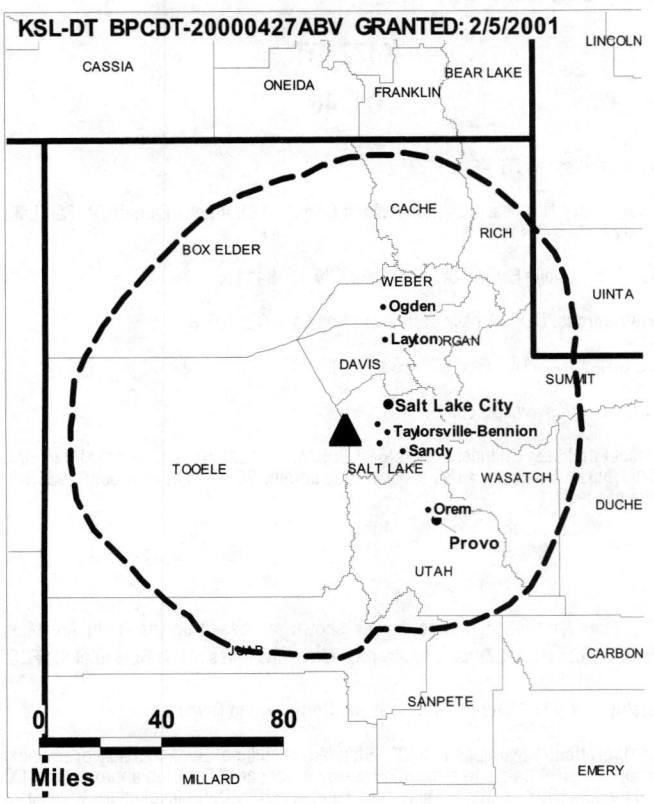

KSL-DT BPCDT-20000427ABV GRANTED: 2/5/2001

© 2010 Warren Communications News

Circulation © 2009 Nielsen. Coverage based on Nielsen study.

GrandTotal	Cable TV Households	Non-cable TV Households	Total TV Households
Estimated Station Totals *	426,230	483,890	910,120
Average Weekly Circulation (2009)	245,485	333,929	579,414
Average Daily Circulation (2009)			279,853

Station DMA Total	Cable TV Households	Non-cable TV Households	Total TV Households
Estimated Station Totals *	373,400	482,260	855,660
Average Weekly Circulation (2009)	239,397	333,818	573,215
Average Daily Circulation (2009)			278,862

Other DMA Total	Cable TV Households	Non-cable TV Households	Total TV Households
Estimated Station Totals *	52,830	1,630	54,460
Average Weekly Circulation (2009)	6,088	111	6,199
Average Daily Circulation (2009)			991

*Estimated station totals are sums of the Nielsen TV and Cable TV household estimates for each county in which the station registers viewing of more than 5% as per the Nielsen Survey Methods.

KSTU-DT
Ch. 28

Network Service: FOX.

Licensee: Community Television of Utah License LLC, 1717 Dixie Hwy, Ste 650, Fort Wright, KY 41011.

Studio: 5020 W. Amelia Earhart Dr., Salt Lake City, UT 84116.

Mailing Address: 5020 W. Amelia Earhart Dr, Salt Lake City, UT 84116.

Phone: 801-532-1300; 801-536-1313. **Fax:** 801-536-1325.

E-mail: rbodley@fox13.com

Web Site: http://www.myfoxutah.com

Technical Facilities: Channel No. 28 (554-560 MHz). Authorized power: 350-kw max. visual, aural. Antenna: 3970-ft above av. terrain, 168-ft. above ground, 9134-ft. above sea level.

Latitude	40°	39'	33"
Longitude	112°	12'	08"

Holds CP for change to 3970-ft above av. terrain, 167-ft. above ground, 9134-ft. above sea level; BPCDT-20081216BKJ.

Note: Latitude and longitude coordinates shown are based on the North American Datum of 1927 (NAD 27) as currently required by the Mass Media Bureau of the FCC.

Ownership: Local TV Holdings LLC (Group Owner).

Began Operation: May 1, 2002. Standard Definition. Began analog operations: October 24, 1978 on channel 20; began operation on channel 13 November 2, 1987. Sale to present owner by Fox Television Stations Inc. approved by FCC June 9, 2008. Sale to Fox Television Stations Inc. by MWT Corp., Northstar Communications Inc., et al., approved by FCC February 16, 1990. Sale to MWT Corp., et al., by Adams Communications approved by FCC September 9, 1987. Sale to Adams Communications by Springfield Television Corp. approved by FCC January 9, 1984. Ceased analog operations: June 12, 2009.

Represented (legal): Dow Lohnes PLLC.

Personnel:

Tim Ermish, General Manager.

Kirt Burton, General Sales Manager.

Linda Gates, Local Sales Manager.

Kent Carson, National Sales Manager.

Renai Bodley, News Director.

Al Schultz, Chief Engineer.

Melanie Say, Program Director.

Tammy Bryant, Traffic Manager.

City of License: Salt Lake City. **Station DMA:** Salt Lake City, UT. **Rank:** 31.

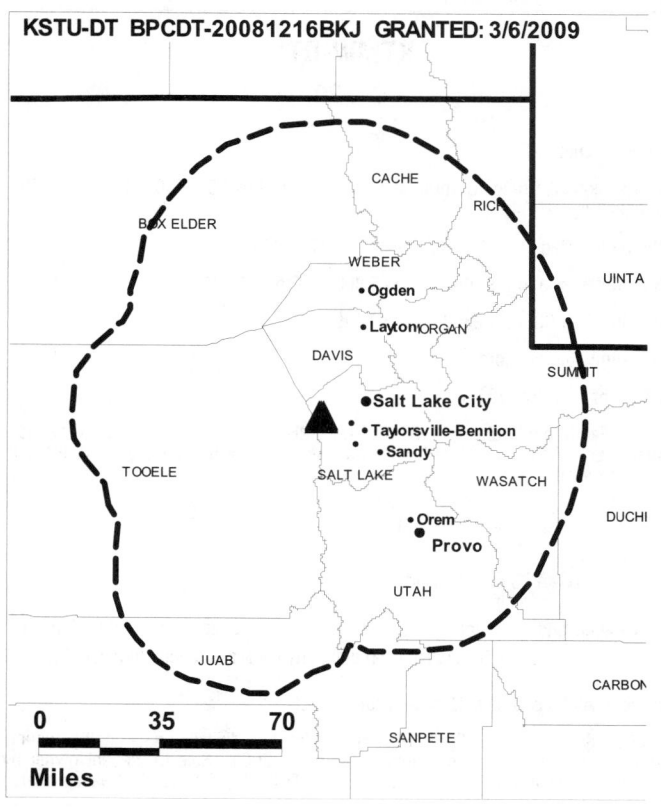

KSTU-DT BPCDT-20081216BKJ GRANTED: 3/6/2009

© 2010 Warren Communications News

Circulation © 2009 Nielsen. Coverage based on Nielsen study.

GrandTotal	Cable TV Households	Non-cable TV Households	Total TV Households
Estimated Station Totals *	374,720	483,890	858,610
Average Weekly Circulation (2009)	194,406	284,881	479,287
Average Daily Circulation (2009)			193,034

Station DMA Total	Cable TV Households	Non-cable TV Households	Total TV Households
Estimated Station Totals *	373,400	482,260	855,660
Average Weekly Circulation (2009)	194,064	284,674	478,738
Average Daily Circulation (2009)			192,795

Other DMA Total	Cable TV Households	Non-cable TV Households	Total TV Households
Estimated Station Totals *	1,320	1,630	2,950
Average Weekly Circulation (2009)	342	207	549
Average Daily Circulation (2009)			239

*Estimated station totals are sums of the Nielsen TV and Cable TV household estimates for each county in which the station registers viewing of more than 5% as per the Nielsen Survey Methods.

KTMW-DT
Ch. 20

Network Service: IND.

Licensee: Alpha & Omega Communications LLC, PO Box 352, 530 E 100 S, No. 204, Salt Lake City, UT 84110.

Studio: 314 S. Redwood Rd., Salt Lake City, UT 84014.

Mailing Address: 314 S Redwood Rd, Salt Lake City, UT 84014.

Phone: 801-973-9838. **Fax:** 801-973-7145.

E-mail: ktmw20@aol.com

Web Site: http://www.tv20.tv

Technical Facilities: Channel No. 20 (506-512 MHz). Authorized power: 530-kw max. visual, aural. Antenna: 3842-ft above av. terrain, 194-ft. above ground, 9045-ft. above sea level.

Latitude	40°	39'	12"
Longitude	112°	12'	06"

Transmitter: 0.5-mi. S of Farnsworth Peak.

Note: Latitude and longitude coordinates shown are based on the North American Datum of 1927 (NAD 27) as currently required by the Mass Media Bureau of the FCC.

Ownership: Alpha & Omega Communications LLC.

Began Operation: June 12, 2009. Station broadcasting digitally on its analog channel allotment. Began analog operations: March 31, 2001. Sale to present owner by Channel 20 Television Co. LLC approved by FCC May 29, 2003. Ceased analog operations: June 12, 2009.

Represented (legal): Wood, Maines & Nolan Chartered.

Represented (sales): Apex Media Sales.

Personnel:

Danny Ermel, General Manager & Program Manager.

Sean O'Brien, Chief Engineer.

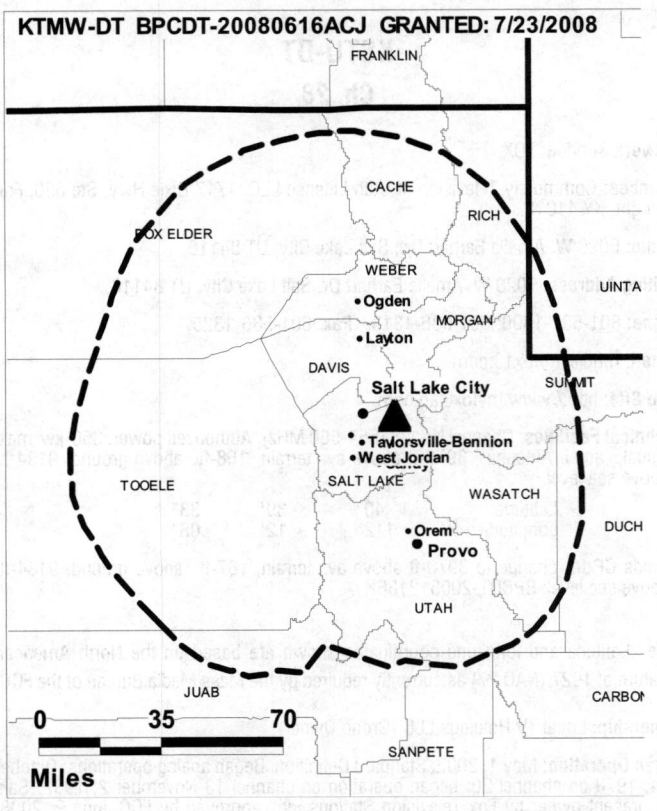

KTMW-DT BPCDT-20080616ACJ GRANTED: 7/23/2008

© 2010 Warren Communications News

Bob Whitney, Business Manager.

City of License: Salt Lake City. **Station DMA:** Salt Lake City, UT. **Rank:** 31.

Nielsen Data: Not available.

KTVX-DT
Ch. 40
(Affiliated with KUCW-DT Ogden)

Network Service: ABC.

Licensee: Newport Television License LLC, 460 Nichols Rd, Ste 250, Kansas City, MO 64112.

Studio: 2175 West 1700 South, Salt Lake City, UT 84104.

Mailing Address: 2175 West 1700 South, Salt Lake City, UT 84104.

Phone: 801-975-4444. **Fax:** 801-975-4442.

E-mail: tclay@4utah.com

Web Site: http://www.abc4.com

Technical Facilities: Channel No. 40 (626-632 MHz). Authorized power: 475.7-kw visual, aural. Antenna: 4121-ft above av. terrain, 255-ft. above ground, 9290-ft. above sea level.

Latitude	40°	39'	33"
Longitude	112°	12'	07"

Note: Latitude and longitude coordinates shown are based on the North American Datum of 1927 (NAD 27) as currently required by the Mass Media Bureau of the FCC.

Multichannel TV Sound: Stereo only.

Ownership: Newport Television LLC (Group Owner).

Began Operation: October 24, 2003. Began analog operations: July 1, 1948. Proposed sale to High Plains Broadcasting Inc. (James H. Martin) withdrawn August 22, 2008. Sale to present owner by Clear Channel Communications Inc. approved by FCC November 29, 2007. To comply with Justice Dept. consent decree, Fox swapped station with KMOL-TV San Antonio, TX for Clear Channel Broadcasting's KFTC Bemidji, MN & WFTC Minneapolis-St. Paul, MN. FCC approved deal September 21, 2001. Sale to Fox Television Stations Inc. by United Television Inc. approved by FCC July 23, 2001. Sale to United Television Inc. by Screen Gems Stations Inc., subsidiary of Columbia Pictures Industries Inc., approved by FCC August 12, 1975. Sale to Screen Gems by TLF Broadcasters Inc. (Time Inc.) approved by FCC November 5, 1959. Sale to Time Inc. by Intermountain Broadcasting & Television Corp. (S. S. Fox, et al.) approved by FCC June 24, 1953. Ceased analog operations: June 12, 2009.

Represented (legal): Covington & Burling.

Personnel:

Kalvin Pike, Interim General Manager & General Sales Manager.

M'Kay McGrath, Local Sales Manager.

Jon Fischer, News Director.

Robert Lyon, Chief Engineer.

Ida Anderson, Business Manager.

Mike Spiecha, Production Manager.

Dennis Elsbury, Marketing Director.

Shara Meredith, Traffic Manager.

Karen Zabriskie, Program Manager.

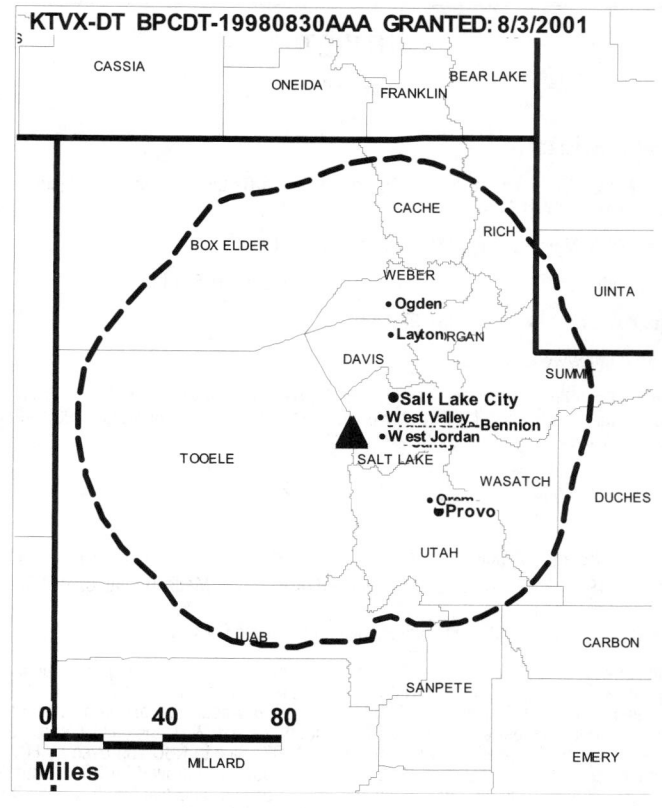

© 2010 Warren Communications News

City of License: Salt Lake City. **Station DMA:** Salt Lake City, UT. **Rank:** 31.

Circulation © 2009 Nielsen. Coverage based on Nielsen study.

GrandTotal	Cable TV Households	Non-cable TV Households	Total TV Households
Estimated Station Totals *	374,230	482,260	856,490
Average Weekly Circulation (2009)	196,723	269,823	466,546
Average Daily Circulation (2009)			183,688

Station DMA Total	Cable TV Households	Non-cable TV Households	Total TV Households
Estimated Station Totals *	373,400	482,260	855,660
Average Weekly Circulation (2009)	196,454	269,823	466,277
Average Daily Circulation (2009)			183,653

Other DMA Total	Cable TV Households	Non-cable TV Households	Total TV Households
Estimated Station Totals *	830	0	830
Average Weekly Circulation (2009)	269	0	269
Average Daily Circulation (2009)			35

*Estimated station totals are sums of the Nielsen TV and Cable TV household estimates for each county in which the station registers viewing of more than 5% as per the Nielsen Survey Methods.

KUTV-DT
Ch. 34

Network Service: CBS.

Licensee: SLC TV Licensee Corp., 299 Park Ave, c/o Cerberus Capital Management LP, New York, NY 10171.

Studio: 299 S. Main St., Suite 150, Salt Lake City, UT 84111.

Mailing Address: 299 S. Main St, Ste 150, Salt Lake City, UT 84111.

Phone: 801-973-3000. **Fax:** 801-973-3369.

Web Site: http://www.kutv.com

Technical Facilities: Channel No. 34 (590-596 MHz). Authorized power: 423-kw max. visual, aural. Antenna: 4157-ft above av. terrain, 289-ft. above ground, 9324-ft. above sea level.

Latitude	40°	39'	33"
Longitude	112°	12'	07"

Note: Latitude and longitude coordinates shown are based on the North American Datum of 1927 (NAD 27) as currently required by the Mass Media Bureau of the FCC.

Ownership: Four Points Media Group Holding LLC (Group Owner).

Began Operation: January 15, 2002. High Definition. Began analog operations: September 10, 1954. Sale to KUTV Inc. by Frank C. Carman, Grant R. Wrathall & Kearns-Tribune Corp. approved by FCC March 7, 1956. Acquisition of Kearns-Tribune Corp. minority interest approved by FCC January 29, 1972. Transfer of control to VS & A Hughes approved by FCC October 18, 1993. Sale to NBC approved by FCC February 28, 1995. Transfer of control to CBS/Group W approved by FCC August 16, 1995. Sale to Viacom International Inc. from CBS Inc. approved by FCC May 3, 2000. Viacom created CBS Corp. June 14, 2005. Sale to present owner by CBS Corp. approved by FCC November 21, 2007. Ceased analog operations: June 12, 2009.

Represented (legal): Wiley Rein LLP.

Personnel:

Dave Phillips, Vice President & General Manager.

Scott Jones, Operations Director.

Kent Crawford, Sales Director.

Doug Beck, Local Sales Manager.

Mark Crowther, National Sales Manager.

Tanya Vea, News Director.

Kip Greene, Chief Engineer.

Rori Pickott, Business Manager.

Amber Williams, Program Director & Traffic Manager.

City of License: Salt Lake City. **Station DMA:** Salt Lake City, UT. **Rank:** 31.

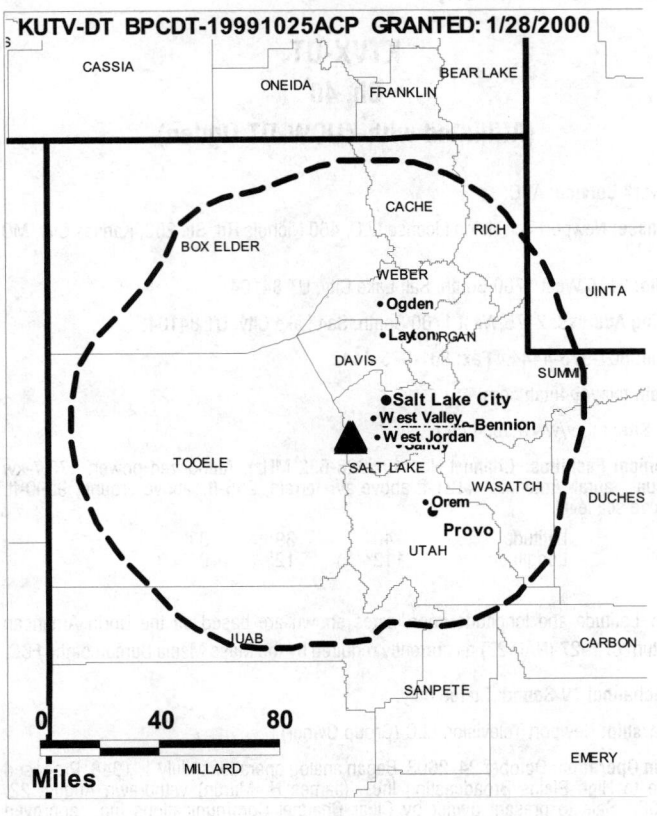

KUTV-DT BPCDT-19991025ACP GRANTED: 1/28/2000

© 2010 Warren Communications News

Circulation © 2009 Nielsen. Coverage based on Nielsen study.

GrandTotal	Cable TV Households	Non-cable TV Households	Total TV Households
Estimated Station Totals *	374,230	482,260	856,490
Average Weekly Circulation (2009)	223,277	289,146	512,423
Average Daily Circulation (2009)			252,337

Station DMA Total	Cable TV Households	Non-cable TV Households	Total TV Households
Estimated Station Totals *	373,400	482,260	855,660
Average Weekly Circulation (2009)	223,045	289,146	512,191
Average Daily Circulation (2009)			252,310

Other DMA Total	Cable TV Households	Non-cable TV Households	Total TV Households
Estimated Station Totals *	830	0	830
Average Weekly Circulation (2009)	232	0	232
Average Daily Circulation (2009)			27

*Estimated station totals are sums of the Nielsen TV and Cable TV household estimates for each county in which the station registers viewing of more than 5% as per the Nielsen Survey Methods.

KUSG-DT
Ch. 9

Network Service: IND.

Licensee: SLC TV Licensee Corp., 299 Park Ave, c/o Cerberus Capital Management LP, New York, NY 10171.

Studio: 299 S. Main St., Suite 150, Salt Lake City, UT 84111.

Mailing Address: 299 S. Main St, Ste 150, Salt Lake City, UT 84111.

Phone: 801-973-3000. **Fax:** 435-773-6324.

Web Site: http://www.kutv.com

Technical Facilities: Channel No. 9 (186-192 MHz). Authorized power: 3.2-kw visual, aural. Antenna: 141-ft above av. terrain, 23-ft. above ground, 3166-ft. above sea level.

Latitude	37°	03'	48"
Longitude	113°	34'	23"

Note: Latitude and longitude coordinates shown are based on the North American Datum of 1927 (NAD 27) as currently required by the Mass Media Bureau of the FCC.

Ownership: Four Points Media Group Holding LLC (Group Owner).

Began Operation: November 11, 2002. High Definition. Began analog operations: August 11, 1999. Sale to Viacom International Inc. from CBS Inc. approved by FCC May 3, 2000. Viacom created CBS Corp. June 14, 2005. Sale to present owner by CBS Corp. approved by FCC November 21, 2007. Ceased analog operations: June 12, 2009.

Represented (legal): Wiley Rein LLP.

Personnel:

David Phillips, Vice President & General Manager.

Scott Jones, Operations Director.

Kent Crawford, Sales Director.

Doug Beck, Local Sales Manager.

Mark Crowther, National Sales Manager.

Tanya Vea, News Director.

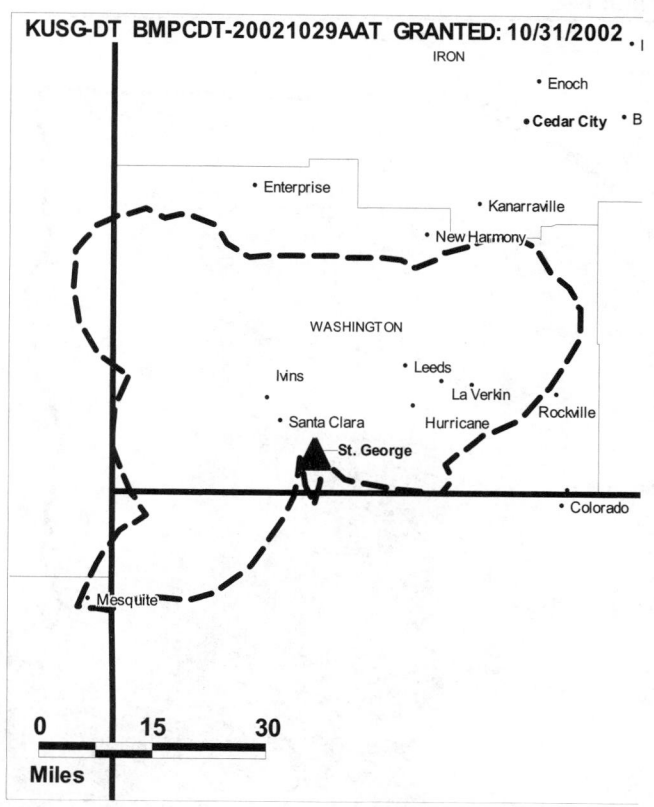

© 2010 Warren Communications News

Kip Greene, Engineering Director.

Rori Pickott, Business Manager.

Amber Williams, Program Director & Traffic Manager.

City of License: St. George. **Station DMA:** Salt Lake City, UT. **Rank:** 31.

Nielsen Data: Not available.

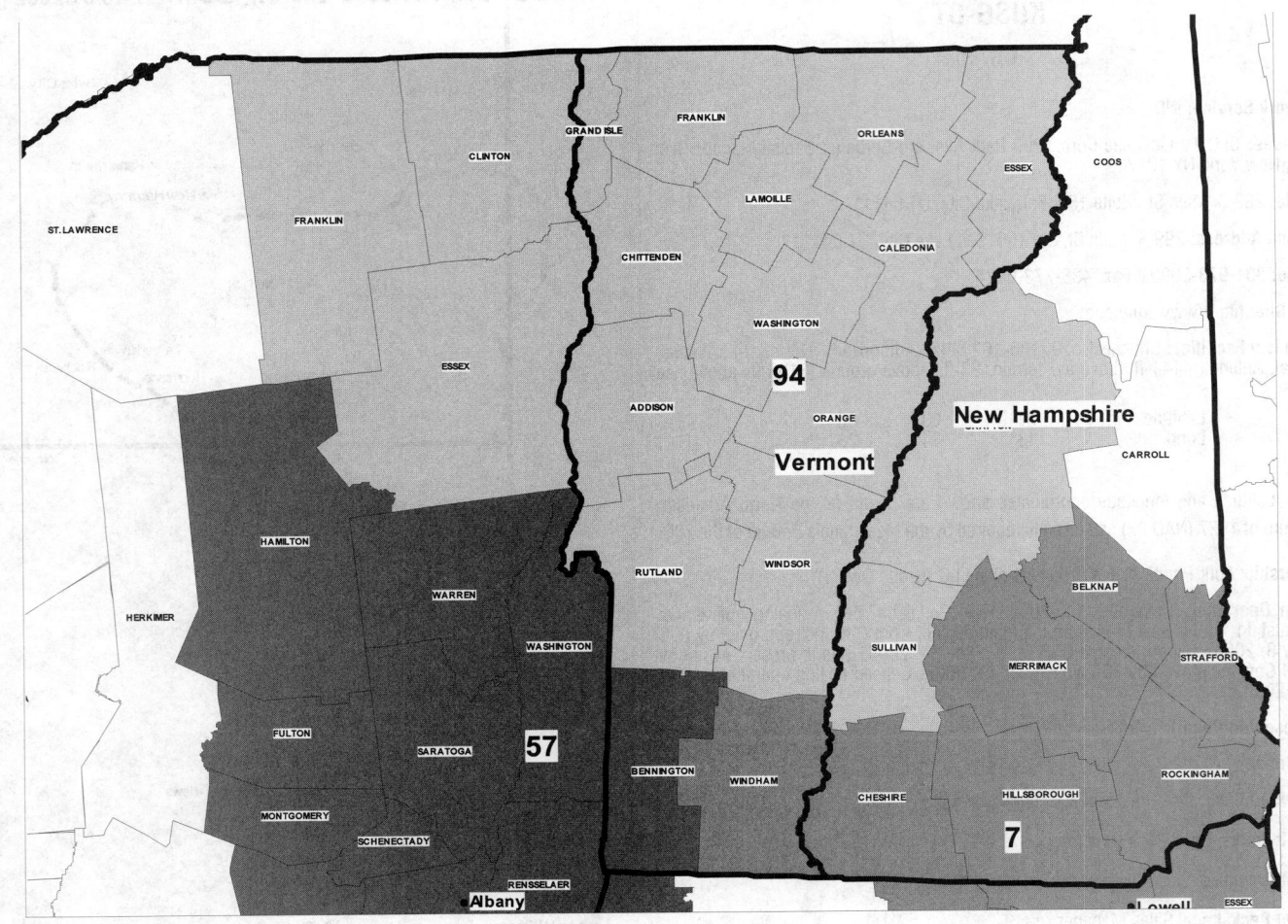

© 2010 Warren Communications News

MARKET	NIELSEN DMA TV HOUSEHOLDS	RANK	MARKET AREA COMMERCIAL STATIONS
Boston, MA-Manchester, NH....................	2,410,180	7	WBPX-TV (32); WBZ-DT (30); WCVB-DT (20); WDPX-TV (40); WFXT-DT (31); WHDH-DT (7); WLVI-DT (41); WMFP-DT (18); WMUR-DT (9); WNEU-DT (34); WPXG-TV (33); WSBK-DT (39); WUNI-DT (29); WUTF-DT (23); WWDP-DT (52); WZMY-DT (35)
Albany-Schenectady-Troy, NY..................	554,070	57	WCDC-DT (36); WCWN-DT (43); WNYA-DT (13); WNYT-DT (12); WRGB-DT (6); WTEN-DT (26); WXXA-DT (7); WYPX-TV (50)
Burlington, VT-Plattsburgh, NY	330,650	94	WCAX-DT (53); WFFF-DT (43); WNNE-DT (25); WPTZ-DT (14); WVNY-DT (13)

Vermont Station Totals as of October 1, 2009

	VHF	UHF	TOTAL
Commercial Television	1	3	4
Educational Television	1	3	4
	2	6	8

WCAX-DT
Ch. 53

Network Service: CBS.

Licensee: Mount Mansfield Television Inc., PO Box 608, Burlington, VT 05402.

Studio: 30 Joy Dr., South Burlington, VT 05403.

Mailing Address: PO Box 4508, Burlington, VT 05406-4508.

Phone: 802-652-6300. **Fax:** 802-652-6319.

Web Site: http://www.wcax.com

Technical Facilities: Channel No. 53 (704-710 MHz). Authorized power: 628-kw max. visual, aural. Antenna: 2772-ft above av. terrain, 151-ft. above ground, 4167-ft. above sea level.

Latitude	44°	31'	32"
Longitude	72°	48'	58"

Requests modification of CP for change to 550-kw max. visual; BMPCDT-20080616ADK.

Holds CP for change to channel number 22, 443-kw max. visual; BPCDT-20080317AEE.

Note: Latitude and longitude coordinates shown are based on the North American Datum of 1927 (NAD 27) as currently required by the Mass Media Bureau of the FCC.

Ownership: Mount Mansfield Television Inc. (Group Owner).

Began Operation: October 30, 2006. Began analog operations: September 3, 1954. Ceased analog operations: February 17, 2009.

Personnel:

Peter R. Martin, President & General Manager.

Bruce Grindle, General Sales Manager.

Judith Fisher, Local Sales Manager.

Marselis Parsons, News Director.

Joe Tymecki, Chief Engineer.

Peg Doolin, Business Manager.

Meredith Neary, Program & Public Services Coordinator.

Phil Scharf, Commercial Director & Production Supervisor.

Jim Strader, Creative Services Director.

Brenda Bouvier, Technical Manager.

City of License: Burlington. **Station DMA:** Burlington, VT-Plattsburgh, NY. **Rank:** 94.

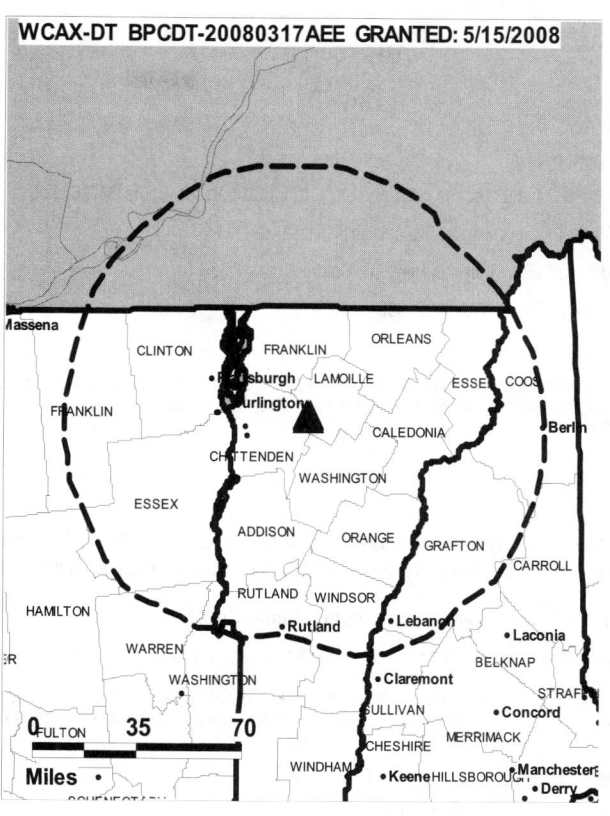

WCAX-DT BPCDT-20080317AEE GRANTED: 5/15/2008

© 2010 Warren Communications News

Circulation © 2009 Nielsen. Coverage based on Nielsen study.

GrandTotal	Cable TV Households	Non-cable TV Households	Total TV Households
Estimated Station Totals *	183,530	162,140	345,670
Average Weekly Circulation (2009)	118,737	100,788	219,525
Average Daily Circulation (2009)			118,202

Station DMA Total	Cable TV Households	Non-cable TV Households	Total TV Households
Estimated Station Totals *	166,000	162,140	328,140
Average Weekly Circulation (2009)	114,025	100,788	214,813
Average Daily Circulation (2009)			116,972

Other DMA Total	Cable TV Households	Non-cable TV Households	Total TV Households
Estimated Station Totals *	17,530	0	17,530
Average Weekly Circulation (2009)	4,712	0	4,712
Average Daily Circulation (2009)			1,230

*Estimated station totals are sums of the Nielsen TV and Cable TV household estimates for each county in which the station registers viewing of more than 5% as per the Nielsen Survey Methods.

WFFF-DT
Ch. 43

Network Service: FOX.

Licensee: Smith Media License Holdings LLC, 1215 Cole St, St. Louis, MO 63106.

Studio: 298 Mountain View Dr., Colcheser, VT 05446.

Mailing Address: 298 Mountain View Dr, Colchester, VT 05446.

Phone: 802-660-9333. **Fax:** 802-660-8673.

Web Site: http://www.fox44.net

Technical Facilities: Channel No. 43 (644-650 MHz). Authorized power: 47-kw max. visual, aural. Antenna: 2753-ft above av. terrain, 125-ft. above ground, 4137-ft. above sea level.

Latitude	44°	31'	33"
Longitude	72°	48'	57"

Note: Latitude and longitude coordinates shown are based on the North American Datum of 1927 (NAD 27) as currently required by the Mass Media Bureau of the FCC.

Ownership: Smith Media License Holdings LLC (Group Owner).

Began Operation: June 29, 2007. Began analog operations: August 31, 1997. Sale to present owner by Smith Broadcasting of Vermont LLC approved by FCC November 8, 2004. Sale to Smith Broadcasting of Vermont LLC by Champlain Valley Telecasting Inc. approved by FCC November 30, 1998. Ceased analog operations: February 17, 2009.

Represented (legal): Dow Lohnes PLLC.

Represented (sales): Katz Media Group.

Personnel:

Ken Kasz, Operations Director.

Vic Vetters, General Manager.

Leigh Gross, National Sales & Traffic Manager.

Gena Boyden, General Sales Manager.

Matt Servis, Chief Engineer.

City of License: Burlington. **Station DMA:** Burlington, VT-Plattsburgh, NY. **Rank:** 94.

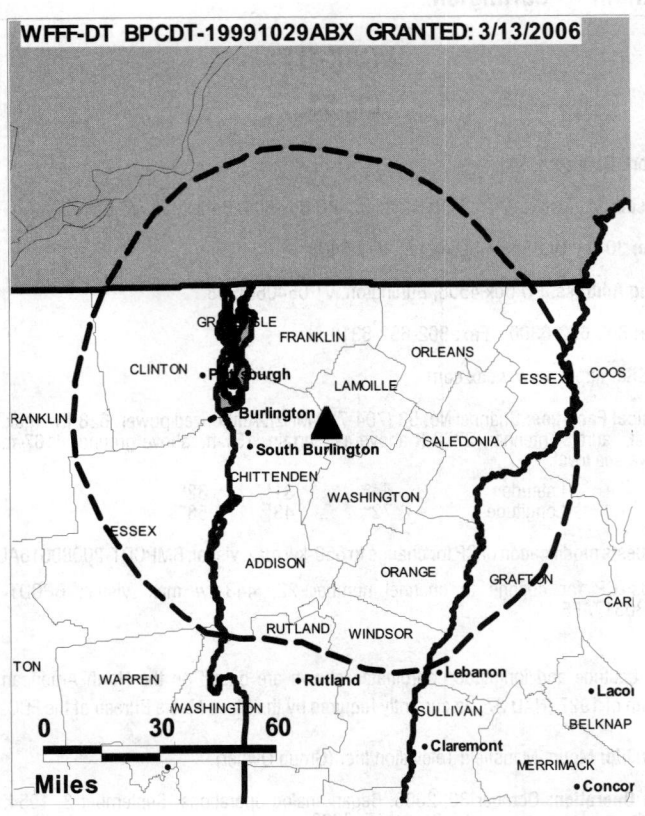

WFFF-DT BPCDT-19991029ABX GRANTED: 3/13/2006

© 2010 Warren Communications News

Circulation © 2009 Nielsen. Coverage based on Nielsen study.

GrandTotal	Cable TV Households	Non-cable TV Households	Total TV Households
Estimated Station Totals *	209,100	162,140	371,240
Average Weekly Circulation (2009)	77,080	61,676	138,756
Average Daily Circulation (2009)			44,577

Station DMA Total	Cable TV Households	Non-cable TV Households	Total TV Households
Estimated Station Totals *	166,000	162,140	328,140
Average Weekly Circulation (2009)	74,106	61,676	135,782
Average Daily Circulation (2009)			43,715

Other DMA Total	Cable TV Households	Non-cable TV Households	Total TV Households
Estimated Station Totals *	43,100	0	43,100
Average Weekly Circulation (2009)	2,974	0	2,974
Average Daily Circulation (2009)			862

*Estimated station totals are sums of the Nielsen TV and Cable TV household estimates for each county in which the station registers viewing of more than 5% as per the Nielsen Survey Methods.

WVNY-DT
Ch. 13

Network Service: ABC.

Licensee: Lambert Broadcasting of Burlington LLC, 100 N Crescent Dr, Ste 200, Beverly Hills, CA 90210.

Studio: 298 Mountain View Dr, Colchester, VT 05446.

Mailing Address: 298 Mountain View Dr, Colchester, VT 05446.

Phone: 802-660-9333. **Fax:** 802-660-8673.

Web Site: http://www.abc22.com

Technical Facilities: Channel No. 13 (210-216 MHz). Authorized power: 10-kw visual, aural. Antenna: 2726-ft above av. terrain, 98-ft. above ground, 4111-ft. above sea level.

Latitude	44°	31'	33"
Longitude	72°	48'	57"

Note: Latitude and longitude coordinates shown are based on the North American Datum of 1927 (NAD 27) as currently required by the Mass Media Bureau of the FCC.

Ownership: Michael Lambert.

Began Operation: November 9, 2006. Began analog operations: April 19, 1968. Left air April 2, 1971; resumed operation September 17, 1971. Sale to International TV Corp. (Donald G. Martin, et al.) by Vermont-New York TV Inc. approved by FCC April 17, 1974. Sale to Citadel Communications by International TV Corp. approved by FCC October 18, 1982. Sale to U.S. Broadcast Group LP by Citadel Communications approved by FCC November 9, 1995. Sale to C-22 FCC Licensee Subsidiary LLC by U.S. Broadcast group approved by FCC April 23, 1998. Sale to present owner by C-22 FCC Licensee Subsidiary LLC approved by FCC May 20, 2005. Ceased analog operations: February 17, 2009.

Represented (legal): Covington & Burling.

Represented (sales): Continental Television Sales.

Personnel:

Vic Vetters, General Manager.

Ken Kasz, Operations Director.

Gena Boyden, General Sales Manager.

Matt Servis, Chief Engineer.

Ethan Bond, Business Manager.

Leigh Gross, Traffic Manager.

City of License: Burlington. **Station DMA:** Burlington, VT-Plattsburgh, NY. **Rank:** 94.

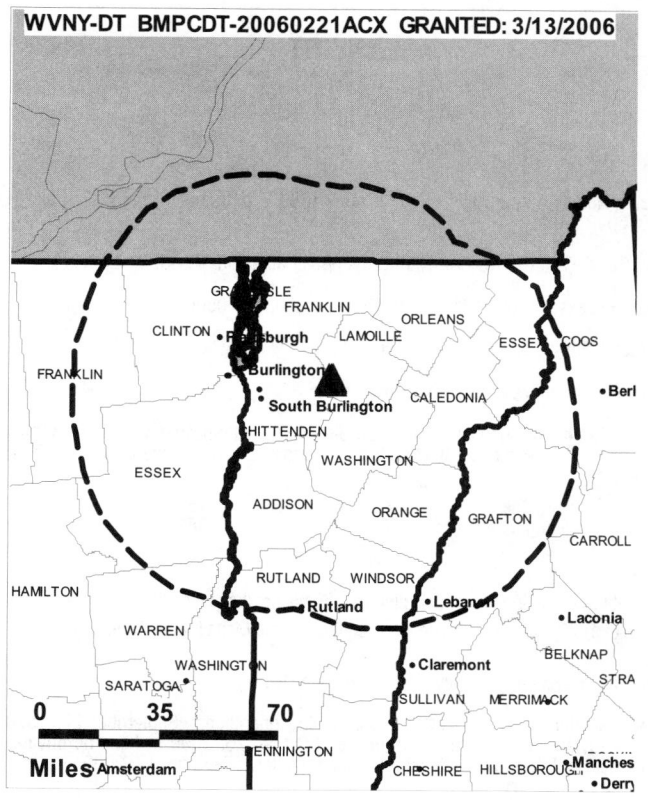

WVNY-DT BMPCDT-20060221ACX GRANTED: 3/13/2006

© 2010 Warren Communications News

Circulation © 2009 Nielsen. Coverage based on Nielsen study.

GrandTotal	Cable TV Households	Non-cable TV Households	Total TV Households
Estimated Station Totals *	166,000	162,140	328,140
Average Weekly Circulation (2009)	69,444	61,121	130,565
Average Daily Circulation (2009)			44,654

Station DMA Total	Cable TV Households	Non-cable TV Households	Total TV Households
Estimated Station Totals *	166,000	162,140	328,140
Average Weekly Circulation (2009)	69,444	61,121	130,565
Average Daily Circulation (2009)			44,654

*Estimated station totals are sums of the Nielsen TV and Cable TV household estimates for each county in which the station registers viewing of more than 5% as per the Nielsen Survey Methods.

WNNE-DT
Ch. 25

Network Service: NBC.

Licensee: Hearst-Argyle Stations Inc., PO Box 1800, c/o Brooks, Pierce et al., Raleigh, NC 27602.

Studio: 203 DeWitt Dr., PO Box 1310, White River Junction, VT 05001-2027.

Mailing Address: PO Box 1310, White River Junction, VT 05001.

Phone: 802-295-3100. **Fax:** 802-295-3983.

Web Site: http://www.wnne.com

Technical Facilities: Channel No. 25 (536-542 MHz). Authorized power: 117-kw max. visual, aural. Antenna: 2136-ft above av. terrain, 266-ft. above ground, 3127-ft. above sea level.

Latitude	43°	26'	15"
Longitude	72°	27'	08"

Note: Latitude and longitude coordinates shown are based on the North American Datum of 1927 (NAD 27) as currently required by the Mass Media Bureau of the FCC.

Ownership: Hearst-Argyle Television Inc. (Group Owner).

Began Operation: July 27, 2005. Began analog operations: September 27, 1978. Hearst-Argyle received approval from the FCC May 26, 2009 to become privately owned by The Hearst Corp. Ceased analog operations: February 17, 2009.

Represented (legal): Brooks, Pierce, McLendon, Humphrey & Leonard LLP.

Represented (sales): Eagle Television Sales.

Personnel:

Paul Sands, President & General Manager.

Bruce Lawson, General Sales Manager.

Pete James, Local Sales Manager.

Kyle Grimes, News Director.

James Gratton, Operations Manager & Program Director.

Steve Herberg, Controller.

Dave Fleming, Production Manager.

Susan Acklen, Promotion Manager.

Laura Lareau, Traffic Manager.

City of License: Hartford. **Station DMA:** Burlington, VT-Plattsburgh, NY. **Rank:** 94.

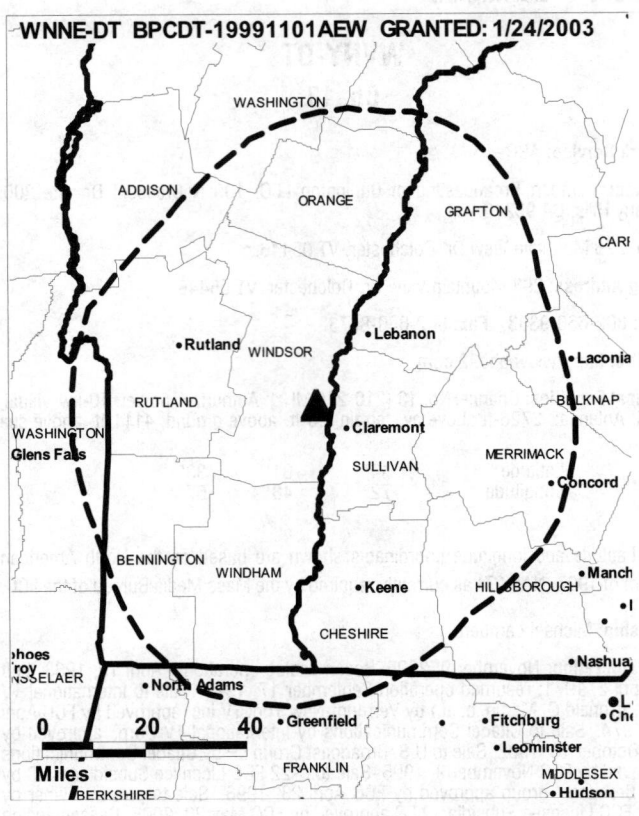

WNNE-DT BPCDT-19991101AEW GRANTED: 1/24/2003

© 2010 Warren Communications News

Circulation © 2009 Nielsen. Coverage based on Nielsen study.

GrandTotal	Cable TV Households	Non-cable TV Households	Total TV Households
Estimated Station Totals *	135,020	82,670	217,690
Average Weekly Circulation (2009)	31,007	14,281	45,288
Average Daily Circulation (2009)			17,225

Station DMA Total	Cable TV Households	Non-cable TV Households	Total TV Households
Estimated Station Totals *	74,040	82,670	156,710
Average Weekly Circulation (2009)	16,628	14,281	30,909
Average Daily Circulation (2009)			13,325

Other DMA Total	Cable TV Households	Non-cable TV Households	Total TV Households
Estimated Station Totals *	60,980	0	60,980
Average Weekly Circulation (2009)	14,379	0	14,379
Average Daily Circulation (2009)			3,900

*Estimated station totals are sums of the Nielsen TV and Cable TV household estimates for each county in which the station registers viewing of more than 5% as per the Nielsen Survey Methods.

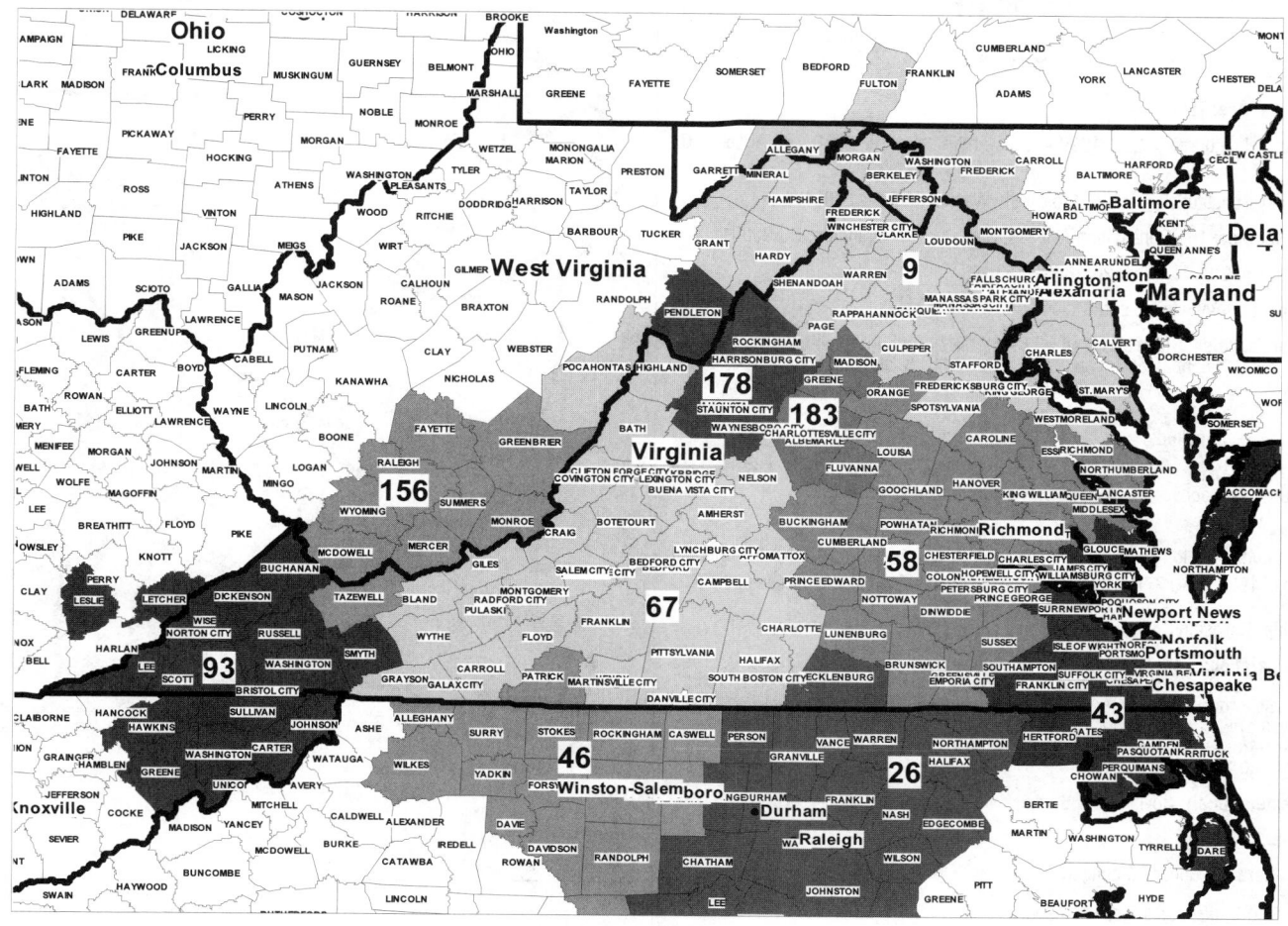

© 2010 Warren Communications News

MARKET	NIELSEN DMA TV HOUSEHOLDS	RANK	MARKET AREA COMMERCIAL STATIONS
Washington, DC (Hagerstown, MD)...............	2,335,040	9	WDCA-DT (35); WDCW-DT (50); WFDC-DT (15); WHAG-DT (55); WJAL-DT (39); WJLA-DT (7); WPXW-TV (43); WRC-DT (48); WSSS-TV (1); WTTG-DT (36); WUSA-DT (9); WWPX-TV (12)
Raleigh-Durham (Fayetteville), NC.................	1,107,820	26	WFPX-TV (36); WLFL-DT (27); WNCN-DT (17); WRAL-DT (53); WRAY-DT (42); WRAZ-DT (49); WRDC-DT (28); WRPX-TV (15); WTVD-DT (11); WUVC-DT (38)
Norfolk-Portsmouth-Newport News, VA.............	709,880	43	WAVY-DT (31); WGNT-DT (50); WHRE-DT (7); WPXV-TV (46); WSKY-DT (4); WTKR-DT (40); WTVZ-DT (33); WVBT-DT (29); WVEC (13)
Greensboro-High Point-Winston Salem, NC..........	691,380	46	WCWG-DT (19); WFMY-DT (51); WGHP-DT (8); WGPX-TV (14); WLXI (43); WMYV-DT (33); WXII-DT (31); WXLV-DT (29)
Richmond-Petersburg, VA........................	553,950	58	WRIC-DT (22); WRLH-DT (26); WTVR-DT (25); WUPV-DT (47); WWBT-DT (12)
Roanoke-Lynchburg, VA.........................	461,220	67	WDBJ-DT (18); WDRL-DT (24); WFXR-DT (17); WPXR-DT (36); WSET-DT (13); WSLS-DT (30); WWCW-DT (20)
Tri-Cities (Bristol, VA-Kingsport-Johnson City, TN)	334,620	93	WCYB-DT (5); WEMT-DT (38); WJHL-DT (11); WKPT-DT (27); WLFG-DT (49)
Bluefield-Beckley-Oak Hill, WV	142,570	156	WLFB-DT (40); WOAY-DT (50); WVNS-DT (8); WVVA-DT (46)
Harrisonburg, VA..............................	93,400	178	WHSV-DT (49)
Charlottesville, VA............................	75,920	183	WCAV-DT (19); WVIR-DT (32)

Virginia Station Totals as of October 1, 2009

	VHF	UHF	TOTAL
Commercial Television	5	22	27
Educational Television	2	8	10
	7	30	37

WFDC-DT
Ch. 15

Network Service: TEL.

Licensee: Telefutura D.C. LLC, 1999 Avenue of the Stars, Ste 3050, Los Angeles, CA 90067.

Studio: 101 Constitution Ave NW, Ste L-100, Washington, DC 20001.

Mailing Address: 101 Constitution Ave NW, Ste L-100, Washington, DC 20001.

Phone: 202-522-8640. **Fax:** 202-898-1753.

Web Site: http://www.wfdc.entravision.com

Technical Facilities: Channel No. 15 (476-482 MHz). Authorized power: 325-kw max. visual, aural. Antenna: 568-ft above av. terrain, 410-ft. above ground, 797-ft. above sea level.

Latitude	38°	56'	24"
Longitude	77°	04'	54"

Holds CP for change to 1000-kw max. visual, 745-ft above av. terrain, 587-ft. above ground, 974-ft. above sea level; BPCDT-20080618AKE.

Note: Latitude and longitude coordinates shown are based on the North American Datum of 1927 (NAD 27) as currently required by the Mass Media Bureau of the FCC.

Ownership: Univision Communications Inc. (Group Owner).

Began Operation: February 15, 2007. Began analog operations: August 3, 1993. Transfer of control to Broadcasting Media Partners Inc. approved by FCC March 27, 2007. Sale to present owner by Urban Broadcasting Corp., Debtor-in-Possession approved by FCC June 1, 2001. Involuntary assignment to Urban Broadcasting Corp., Debtor-in-Possession approved by FCC March 28, 2001. Ceased analog operations: June 12, 2009.

Represented (legal): Covington & Burling.

Personnel:

Rudy Guernica, General Manager.

Oscar Rodriquez, Local Sales Manager.

Erin Dawson, National Sales Manager.

Fred Willard, Chief Engineer.

Mini Capers, Business Manager.

Mauricio Rosales, Traffic Manager.

Ernesto Clavijo, News Director.

City of License: Arlington. **Station DMA:** Washington, DC (Hagerstown, MD).

Rank: 9.

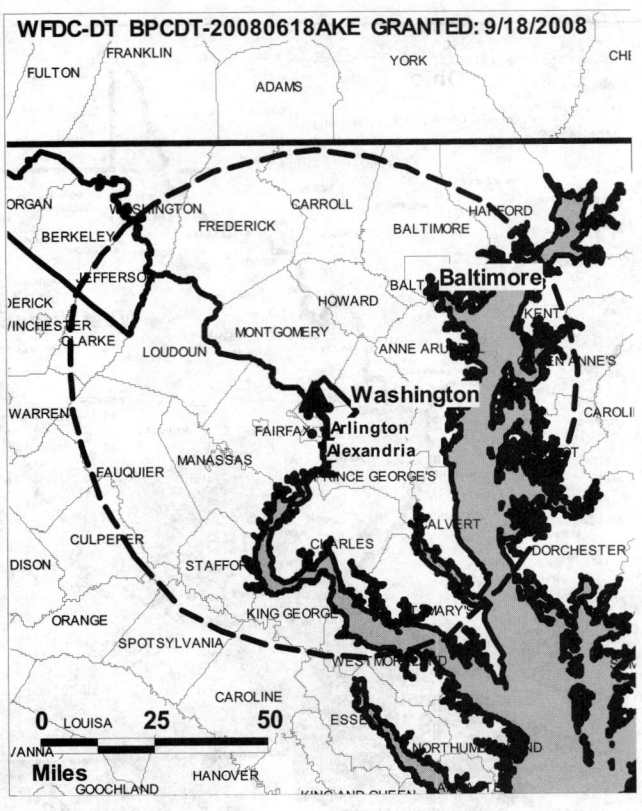

WFDC-DT BPCDT-20080618AKE GRANTED: 9/18/2008

© 2010 Warren Communications News

Circulation © 2009 Nielsen. Coverage based on Nielsen study.

GrandTotal	Cable TV Households	Non-cable TV Households	Total TV Households
Estimated Station Totals *	894,280	355,920	1,250,200
Average Weekly Circulation (2009)	67,836	52,135	119,971
Average Daily Circulation (2009)			66,332

Station DMA Total	Cable TV Households	Non-cable TV Households	Total TV Households
Estimated Station Totals *	894,280	355,920	1,250,200
Average Weekly Circulation (2009)	67,836	52,135	119,971
Average Daily Circulation (2009)			66,332

*Estimated station totals are sums of the Nielsen TV and Cable TV household estimates for each county in which the station registers viewing of more than 5% as per the Nielsen Survey Methods.

WUPV-DT
Ch. 47

Network Service: CW.

Licensee: Southeastern Media Holdings Inc., 3500 Colonnade Pkwy, Ste 600, Birmingham, AL 35243.

Studio: 3301 W Broad St, Richmond, VA 23230.

Mailing Address: 3301 W Broad St, Richmond, VA 23230.

Phone: 804-254-3600. **Fax:** 804-342-5746.

Web Site: http://www.cwrichmond.tv/

Technical Facilities: Channel No. 47 (668-674 MHz). Authorized power: 1000-kw max. visual, aural. Antenna: 817-ft above av. terrain, 830-ft. above ground, 925-ft. above sea level.

Latitude	37°	44'	31"
Longitude	77°	15'	15"

Note: Latitude and longitude coordinates shown are based on the North American Datum of 1927 (NAD 27) as currently required by the Mass Media Bureau of the FCC.

Ownership: Community Newspaper Holdings Inc.

Began Operation: February 9, 2006. Began analog operations: March 9, 1990. Sale to Bell Broadcasting by Christel Broadcasting approved by FCC February 7, 1997. Sale to TV-65 Broadcasting LLC by Bell Broadcasting approved by FCC July 18, 1997. Sale to present owner by TV-65 Broadcasting LLC approved by FCC November 3, 2006. Ceased analog operations: June 12, 2009.

Represented (legal): Fletcher, Heald & Hildreth PLC.

Represented (sales): Blair Television.

Personnel:

John Rezabeck, General Manager & General Sales Manager.

David Hayes, Local Sales Manager.

Gene Todd, Chief Engineer.

Tiffany Humphrey, Business Manager.

Blake Peddicord, Program Director.

City of License: Ashland. **Station DMA:** Richmond-Petersburg, VA. **Rank:** 58.

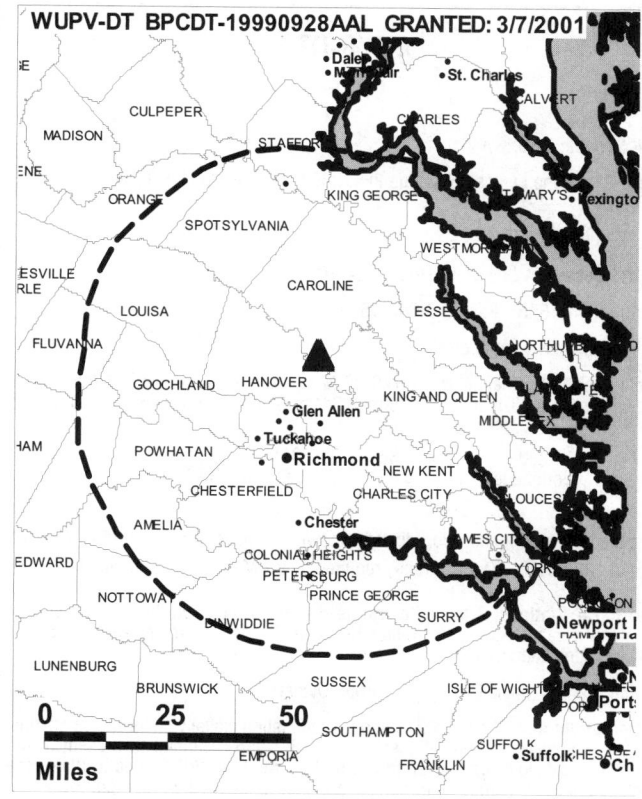

WUPV-DT BPCDT-19990928AAL GRANTED: 3/7/2001

© 2010 Warren Communications News

Circulation © 2009 Nielsen. Coverage based on Nielsen study.

GrandTotal	Cable TV Households	Non-cable TV Households	Total TV Households
Estimated Station Totals *	299,740	217,200	516,940
Average Weekly Circulation (2009)	73,804	51,425	125,229
Average Daily Circulation (2009)			43,325

Station DMA Total	Cable TV Households	Non-cable TV Households	Total TV Households
Estimated Station Totals *	299,740	211,970	511,710
Average Weekly Circulation (2009)	73,804	50,970	124,774
Average Daily Circulation (2009)			43,247

Other DMA Total	Cable TV Households	Non-cable TV Households	Total TV Households
Estimated Station Totals *	0	5,230	5,230
Average Weekly Circulation (2009)	0	455	455
Average Daily Circulation (2009)			78

*Estimated station totals are sums of the Nielsen TV and Cable TV household estimates for each county in which the station registers viewing of more than 5% as per the Nielsen Survey Methods.

WCYB-DT
Ch. 5

Network Service: NBC, CW.

Licensee: BlueStone License Holdings Inc., 280 Park Ave, 25 Fl, E Tower, New York, NY 10017.

Studio: 101 Lee St., Bristol, VA 24201.

Mailing Address: 101 Lee St, Bristol, VA 24201.

Phone: 276-645-1555. **Fax:** 276-645-1513.

Web Site: http://www.wcyb.com

Technical Facilities: Channel No. 5 (76-82 MHz). Authorized power: 7.1-kw visual, aural. Antenna: 2438-ft above av. terrain, 341-ft. above ground, 4554-ft. above sea level.

Latitude	36°	26'	57.8"
Longitude	82°	06'	29.2"

Note: Latitude and longitude coordinates shown are based on the North American Datum of 1927 (NAD 27) as currently required by the Mass Media Bureau of the FCC.

Satellite Earth Stations: Transmitter Harris; Harris, 3-meter Ku-band; Comtech, 3.8-meter Ku-band; Harris, 6.1-meter Ku-band; Harris, 6.1-meter C-band; Standard Communications, Harris receivers.

Ownership: Bonten Media Group LLC (Group Owner).

Began Operation: August 12, 2002. Station broadcasting digitally on its analog channel allotment. Began analog operations: August 13, 1956. Transfer to present owner by BlueStone TV Holdings Inc. approved by FCC April 24, 2007. Sale to BlueStone TV Holdings Inc. by Lamco Communications Inc. approved by FCC April 29, 2004. Sale to Lamco Communications Inc. by Starr Broadcasting Group approved by FCC March 17, 1977 (Television Digest, Vol. 16:33). Sale to Starr by Robert H. Smith, J. Fey Rogers, Charles M. Gore & Harry M. Daniel approved by FCC November 12, 1970 (Vol. 10:6, 46). Ceased analog operations: June 12, 2009.

Represented (legal): Covington & Burling.

Represented (sales): Petry Media Corp.

Personnel:

Jim McKernan, General Manager.

Jim Bowman, Sales Manager.

Dan Howard, Local Sales Manager.

Steve Hawkins, News Manager.

Tom Cupp, Engineering Manager.

Nancy Booher, Business Manager.

Cheryl Stout, Program Manager & Traffic Manager.

Tony Venable, Promotion & Production Manager.

City of License: Bristol.

Station DMA: Tri-Cities (Bristol, VA-Kingsport-Johnson City, TN). **Rank:** 93.

WCYB-DT BMPCDT-20020808AAK GRANTED: 12/9/2002

© 2010 Warren Communications News

Circulation © 2009 Nielsen. Coverage based on Nielsen study.

GrandTotal	Cable TV Households	Non-cable TV Households	Total TV Households
Estimated Station Totals *	252,310	155,240	407,550
Average Weekly Circulation (2009)	160,142	93,217	253,359
Average Daily Circulation (2009)			143,862

Station DMA Total	Cable TV Households	Non-cable TV Households	Total TV Households
Estimated Station Totals *	203,160	129,680	332,840
Average Weekly Circulation (2009)	146,822	90,963	237,785
Average Daily Circulation (2009)			138,863

Other DMA Total	Cable TV Households	Non-cable TV Households	Total TV Households
Estimated Station Totals *	49,150	25,560	74,710
Average Weekly Circulation (2009)	13,320	2,254	15,574
Average Daily Circulation (2009)			4,999

*Estimated station totals are sums of the Nielsen TV and Cable TV household estimates for each county in which the station registers viewing of more than 5% as per the Nielsen Survey Methods.

WCAV-DT
Ch. 19

Network Service: CBS.

Licensee: Gray Television Licensee LLC, 1750 K St NW, Ste 1200, Washington, DC 20006.

Studio: 999 2nd St SE, Charlottesville, VA 22902.

Mailing Address: 999 2nd St SE, Charlottesville, VA 22902.

Phone: 434-242-1919; 434-220-7522. **Fax:** 434-220-0398.

E-mail: jim.mccabe@wcav.tv

Web Site: http://www.wcav.tv

Technical Facilities: Channel No. 19 (500-506 MHz). Authorized power: 155-kw max. visual, aural. Antenna: 1068-ft above av. terrain, 164-ft. above ground, 1619-ft. above sea level.

Latitude	37°	59'	03"
Longitude	78°	28'	52"

Note: Latitude and longitude coordinates shown are based on the North American Datum of 1927 (NAD 27) as currently required by the Mass Media Bureau of the FCC.

Ownership: Gray Television Inc. (Group Owner).

Began Operation: February 9, 2009. Station broadcasting digitally on its analog channel allotment. Sale to present owner by Charlottesville Broadcasting Corp. approved by FCC May 28, 2004. Transfer of control by Charlottesville Broadcasting Corp. from Susan M. Bechtel (25% to 2%) & Laurie G. Cole (25% to 0) to Margot Polivy (45% to 88%) & Marilyn Marcosson (5% to 10%) approved by FCC March 9, 2004. Ceased analog operations: February 9, 2009.

Represented (legal): Wiley Rein LLP.

Personnel:

Roger Burchett, General Manager.

Daniel Adams, Marketing & Promotions Manager.

City of License: Charlottesville. **Station DMA:** Charlottesville, VA. **Rank:** 183.

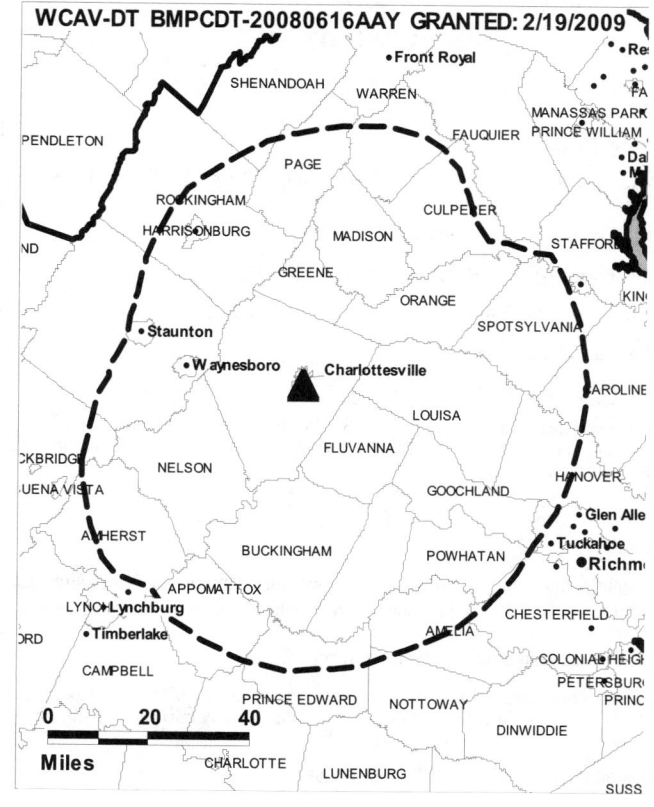

WCAV-DT BMPCDT-20080616AAY GRANTED: 2/19/2009

© 2010 Warren Communications News

Circulation © 2009 Nielsen. Coverage based on Nielsen study.

GrandTotal	Cable TV Households	Non-cable TV Households	Total TV Households
Estimated Station Totals *	48,810	55,210	104,020
Average Weekly Circulation (2009)	23,475	15,063	38,538
Average Daily Circulation (2009)			15,785

Station DMA Total	Cable TV Households	Non-cable TV Households	Total TV Households
Estimated Station Totals *	41,840	34,760	76,600
Average Weekly Circulation (2009)	22,336	13,462	35,798
Average Daily Circulation (2009)			14,370

Other DMA Total	Cable TV Households	Non-cable TV Households	Total TV Households
Estimated Station Totals *	6,970	20,450	27,420
Average Weekly Circulation (2009)	1,139	1,601	2,740
Average Daily Circulation (2009)			1,415

*Estimated station totals are sums of the Nielsen TV and Cable TV household estimates for each county in which the station registers viewing of more than 5% as per the Nielsen Survey Methods.

WVIR-DT
Ch. 32

Network Service: NBC, CW.

Licensee: Virginia Broadcasting Corp., PO Box 769, 503 E Market St, Charlottesville, VA 22902-0503.

Studio: 503 E Market St, Charlottesville, VA 22902.

Mailing Address: PO Box 769, Charlottesville, VA 22902.

Phone: 434-220-2900; 540-886-0934. **Fax:** 434-220-2904.

E-mail: hwright@nbc29.com

Web Site: http://www.nbc29.com

Technical Facilities: Channel No. 32 (578-584 MHz). Authorized power: 1000-kw max. visual, aural. Antenna: 1207-ft above av. terrain, 286-ft. above ground, 1758-ft. above sea level.

Latitude	37°	59'	02"
Longitude	78°	28'	53"

Note: Latitude and longitude coordinates shown are based on the North American Datum of 1927 (NAD 27) as currently required by the Mass Media Bureau of the FCC.

Ownership: Waterman Broadcasting Corp. (Group Owner).

Began Operation: October 15, 2002. Began analog operations: March 11, 1973. Sale to present owner by Harold B. Wright Jr., et al., approved by FCC October 30, 1986. Ceased analog operations: February 17, 2009.

Represented (sales): Continental Television Sales.

Personnel:

Harold B. Wright Jr., Vice President & General Manager.

Jim Fernald, General Sales Manager.

Tom Maloy, National & Regional Sales Manager.

Jaye Urgo, Local Sales Manager.

Neal Bennett, News Director.

Bob Jenkins, Chief Engineer.

Pam Mills, Business Manager.

Ben Moore, Operations Manager.

Devin Swanson, Marketing Assistant.

Terri Warren, Production Coordinator.

Ralph Tobias, Program Director.

Laura VanMeter, Traffic Manager.

City of License: Charlottesville. **Station DMA:** Charlottesville, VA. **Rank:** 183.

WVIR-DT BMPCDT-20040730AGY GRANTED: 8/30/2004

© 2010 Warren Communications News

Circulation © 2009 Nielsen. Coverage based on Nielsen study.

GrandTotal	Cable TV Households	Non-cable TV Households	Total TV Households
Estimated Station Totals *	112,280	107,350	219,630
Average Weekly Circulation (2009)	68,052	33,361	101,413
Average Daily Circulation (2009)			55,324

Station DMA Total	Cable TV Households	Non-cable TV Households	Total TV Households
Estimated Station Totals *	41,840	34,760	76,600
Average Weekly Circulation (2009)	32,250	20,882	53,132
Average Daily Circulation (2009)			32,340

Other DMA Total	Cable TV Households	Non-cable TV Households	Total TV Households
Estimated Station Totals *	70,440	72,590	143,030
Average Weekly Circulation (2009)	35,802	12,479	48,281
Average Daily Circulation (2009)			22,984

*Estimated station totals are sums of the Nielsen TV and Cable TV household estimates for each county in which the station registers viewing of more than 5% as per the Nielsen Survey Methods.

WDRL-DT
Ch. 24

Network Service: IND.

Licensee: MNE Broadcasting LLC, PO Box 370, Danville, VA 24540.

MNE Broadcasting LLC: Ste T-5, 5001 Airport Rd, Roanoke, VA 24014.

Mailing Address: PO Box 14005, Roanoke, VA 24038.

Phone: 540-366-2424. **Fax:** 540-366-7530.

E-mail: joe@wdrl-tv.com

Web Site: http://www.wdrl-tv.com

Technical Facilities: Channel No. 24 (530-536 MHz). Authorized power: 63-kw max. visual, aural. Antenna: 1240-ft above av. terrain, 167-ft. above ground, 2128-ft. above sea level.

Latitude	37°	00'	37"
Longitude	79°	34'	17"

Note: Latitude and longitude coordinates shown are based on the North American Datum of 1927 (NAD 27) as currently required by the Mass Media Bureau of the FCC.

Ownership: MNE Broadcasting LLC.

Began Operation: May 17, 2006. Station broadcasting digitally on its analog channel allotment. Began analog operations: August 16, 1994. Ceased analog operations: February 17, 2009. Sale to N. Thomas Eaton by William R. Morer (Danville Communications) approved by FCC Septrember 20, 1990. Sale to Danville Television Partnership (Melvin N. Eleazer & Caroline K. Powley) approved by FCC June 12 1992. During bankruptcy court proceedings, it was determined Caroline K. Powley never formed partnership with Melvin N. Eleazer. He was awarded full custody of station by court and proposed assignment to Eleazer was dismissed by FCC October 14, 1999. Involuntary transfer to debtor-in-possession approved by FCC April 9, 2003. Emergence from Chapter 13 bankruptcy and pro forma assignment to present owner approved by FCC August 29, 2006. Proposed sale to Liberty University Inc. dismissed by FCC June 10, 2008. Sale to Living Faith Ministries Inc. approved by FCC May 14, 2009, but not yet consummated.

Represented (legal): Borsari & Paxson.

Personnel:

Melvin N. Eleazer, Chief Executive Officer, General Manager & Station Manager.

Dave Ross, Sales & Traffic Manager.

Larry Smith, National Sales Manager.

Dave Spruell, Operations & Program Director.

Tammy Taylor, Business Manager.

Nele Kirt, Production Manager.

City of License: Danville. **Station DMA:** Roanoke-Lynchburg, VA. **Rank:** 67.

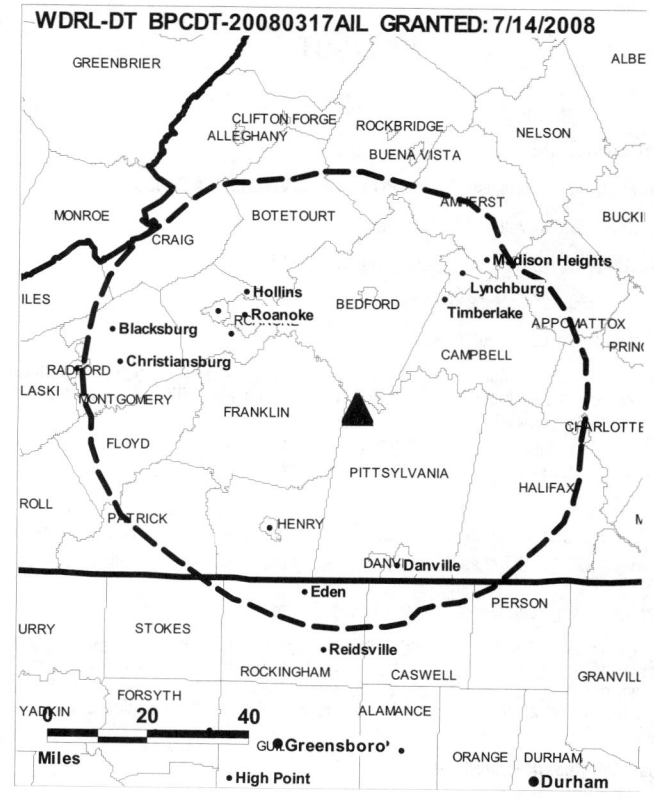

WDRL-DT BPCDT-20080317AIL GRANTED: 7/14/2008

© 2010 Warren Communications News

Circulation © 2009 Nielsen. Coverage based on Nielsen study.

GrandTotal	Cable TV Households	Non-cable TV Households	Total TV Households
Estimated Station Totals *	153,860	80,480	234,340
Average Weekly Circulation (2009)	12,163	5,224	17,387
Average Daily Circulation (2009)			3,708

Station DMA Total	Cable TV Households	Non-cable TV Households	Total TV Households
Estimated Station Totals *	151,580	80,480	232,060
Average Weekly Circulation (2009)	11,939	5,224	17,163
Average Daily Circulation (2009)			3,702

Other DMA Total	Cable TV Households	Non-cable TV Households	Total TV Households
Estimated Station Totals *	2,280	0	2,280
Average Weekly Circulation (2009)	224	0	224
Average Daily Circulation (2009)			6

*Estimated station totals are sums of the Nielsen TV and Cable TV household estimates for each county in which the station registers viewing of more than 5% as per the Nielsen Survey Methods.

WLFG-DT
Ch. 49

Network Service: IND.

Licensee: Living Faith Ministries Inc., PO Box 151, Vansant, VA 24656.

Studio: 8594 Hidden Valley Rd., Abingdon, VA 24210.

Mailing Address: PO Box 1867, Abingdon, VA 24212.

Phone: 540-676-3806. **Fax:** 540-676-3572.

Web Site: http://www.livingfaithtv.com

Technical Facilities: Channel No. 49 (680-686 MHz). Authorized power: 1000-kw max. visual, aural. Antenna: 2172-ft above av. terrain, 167-ft. above ground, 4347-ft. above sea level.

Latitude	36°	49'	47"
Longitude	82°	04'	45"

Note: Latitude and longitude coordinates shown are based on the North American Datum of 1927 (NAD 27) as currently required by the Mass Media Bureau of the FCC.

Ownership: Living Faith Ministries Inc. (Group Owner).

Began Operation: October 25, 2007. Began analog operations: January 1, 1995. Transfer of control from Tookland Pentecostal Church to Living Faith Broadcasting Inc. approved by FCC March 31, 2005. Involuntary transfer of control to Official Board dismissed at filer's request December 3, 2004. Ceased analog operations: May 30, 2007.

Represented (legal): PennStuart.

Personnel:

Michael D. Smith, President.

Marvin W. McGeorge, Sales Manager.

Wayne Price, Chief Engineer.

Lisa Smith, Chief Financial Officer & Promotion Director.

Sue Howington, Traffic Manager.

City of License: Grundy.

Station DMA: Tri-Cities (Bristol, VA-Kingsport-Johnson City, TN). **Rank:** 93.

Digital cable and TV coverage maps.
Visit www.warren-news.com/mediaprints.htm

MediaPrints™
Map a Winning Business Strategy

WLFG-DT BPCDT-19991029AGK GRANTED: 2/23/2001

© 2010 Warren Communications News

Circulation © 2009 Nielsen. Coverage based on Nielsen study.

GrandTotal	Cable TV Households	Non-cable TV Households	Total TV Households
Estimated Station Totals *	223,190	30,460	253,650
Average Weekly Circulation (2009)	18,419	1,987	20,406
Average Daily Circulation (2009)			4,465

Station DMA Total	Cable TV Households	Non-cable TV Households	Total TV Households
Estimated Station Totals *	196,390	30,460	226,850
Average Weekly Circulation (2009)	16,030	1,987	18,017
Average Daily Circulation (2009)			3,903

Other DMA Total	Cable TV Households	Non-cable TV Households	Total TV Households
Estimated Station Totals *	26,800	0	26,800
Average Weekly Circulation (2009)	2,389	0	2,389
Average Daily Circulation (2009)			562

*Estimated station totals are sums of the Nielsen TV and Cable TV household estimates for each county in which the station registers viewing of more than 5% as per the Nielsen Survey Methods.

WVEC
Ch. 13

Network Service: ABC.

Licensee: WVEC Television Inc., 613 Woodis Ave, Norfolk, VA 23510.

Studios: 774 Settler's Landing Rd., Hampton, VA 23669; 613 Woodis Ave., Norfolk, VA 23510.

Mailing Address: 613 Woodis Ave, Norfolk, VA 23510.

Phone: 757-625-1313; 757-628-5888. **Fax:** 757-628-6530.

Web Site: http://www.wvec.com

Technical Facilities: Channel No. 13 (210-216 MHz). Authorized power: 35-kw visual, aural. Antenna: 1191-ft above av. terrain, 1184-ft. above ground, 1208-ft. above sea level.

Latitude	36°	48'	59"
Longitude	76°	28'	06"

Note: Latitude and longitude coordinates shown are based on the North American Datum of 1927 (NAD 27) as currently required by the Mass Media Bureau of the FCC.

Multichannel TV Sound: Stereo only.

Ownership: Belo Corp. (Group Owner).

Began Operation: April 3, 2002. Standard and High Definition. Station broadcasting digitally on its analog channel allotment. Began analog operations: September 19, 1953 on Ch. 15; switched to Ch. 13 November 13, 1959. Ceased analog operations: June 12, 2009. Sale to Corinthian Broadcasting by Thomas P. Chisman, et al., approved by FCC February 12, 1980. Sale to present owner by Corinthian Broadcasting approved by FCC November 29, 1983.

Represented (sales): TeleRep Inc.

Represented (engineering): Cohen Dippell & Everist PC.

Personnel:

Tod A. Smith, President & General Manager.

Amy Warren, Sales & Marketing Director.

John Witte, Local Sales Manager.

Rich LeBenson, Executive News Director.

John Dolize, Engineering Director.

Chris Parker, Controller.

Deb Shollenberger, Program Director.

Wendy Juren, Community Marketing Director.

Greg Brauer, Production Manager.

Matthew Earl, Creative Services Manager.

City of License: Hampton. **Station DMA:** Norfolk-Portsmouth-Newport News, VA.

Rank: 43.

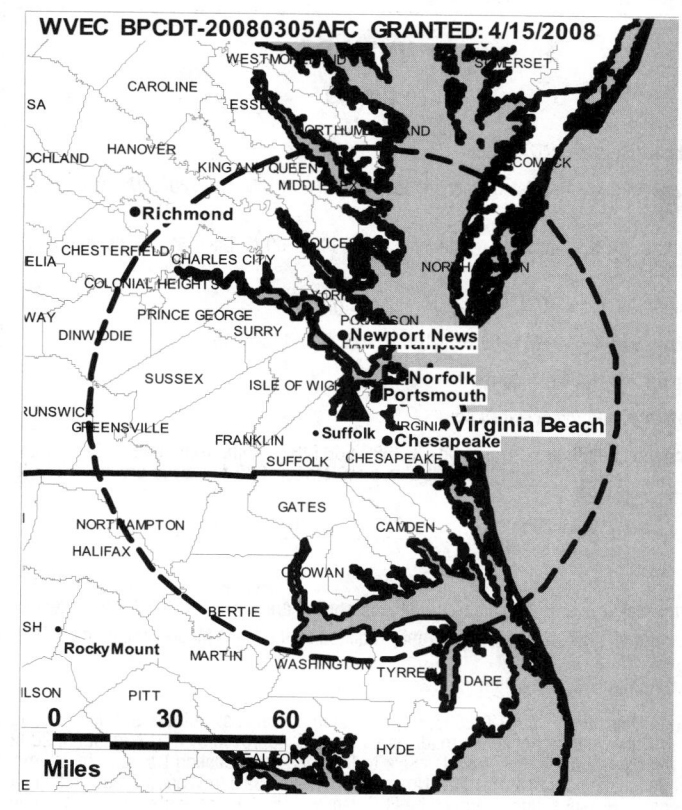

© 2010 Warren Communications News

Circulation © 2009 Nielsen. Coverage based on Nielsen study.

GrandTotal	Cable TV Households	Non-cable TV Households	Total TV Households
Estimated Station Totals *	508,520	208,270	716,790
Average Weekly Circulation (2009)	364,716	140,785	505,501
Average Daily Circulation (2009)			268,268

Station DMA Total	Cable TV Households	Non-cable TV Households	Total TV Households
Estimated Station Totals *	502,950	199,810	702,760
Average Weekly Circulation (2009)	363,432	139,584	503,016
Average Daily Circulation (2009)			267,135

Other DMA Total	Cable TV Households	Non-cable TV Households	Total TV Households
Estimated Station Totals *	5,570	8,460	14,030
Average Weekly Circulation (2009)	1,284	1,201	2,485
Average Daily Circulation (2009)			1,133

*Estimated station totals are sums of the Nielsen TV and Cable TV household estimates for each county in which the station registers viewing of more than 5% as per the Nielsen Survey Methods.

WHSV-DT
Ch. 49

Network Service: MNT, ABC.

Licensee: Gray Television Licensee LLC, 1750 K St NW, Ste 1200, Washington, DC 20006.

Studios: 29 N. Central Ave., Staunton, VA 24401; 50 N. Main St., Harrisonburg, VA 22802.

Mailing Address: 50 N. Main St, Harrisonburg, VA 22802.

Phone: 540-433-9191; 888-801-1883. **Fax:** 540-433-4028.

E-mail: tjones@whsv.com

Web Site: http://www.whsv.com

Technical Facilities: Channel No. 49 (680-686 MHz). Authorized power: 65-kw max. visual, aural. Antenna: 2096-ft above av. terrain, 289-ft. above ground, 3245-ft. above sea level.

Latitude	38°	36'	05"
Longitude	78°	37'	57"

Note: Latitude and longitude coordinates shown are based on the North American Datum of 1927 (NAD 27) as currently required by the Mass Media Bureau of the FCC.

Ownership: Gray Television Inc. (Group Owner).

Began Operation: April 13, 2006. Began analog operations: October 9, 1953. Sale to present owner by Benedek Broadcasting Co. LLC approved by FCC August 29, 2002 (Television Digest, Vol. 42:14). Sale to Benedek Broadcasting Co. LLC by Worrell Broadcasting approved by FCC November 5, 1986. Sale to Worrell Broadcasting by Gilmore Broadcasting approved by FCC January 15, 1976; transfer completed June 3, 1976. Sale to Gilmore Broadcasting by Evening Star and Hamilton Shea approved by FCC August 9, 1965 (Vol. 5:23, 33). Sale of 50% by Transcontinent Corp. & 1% by Hamilton Shea to the Evening Star Broadcasting Co. approved by FCC September 23, 1959 (Vol. 15:30, 32, 39). Sale to Transcontinent Corp. & Hamilton Shea as co-equal owners by Frederick L. Allman approved by FCC May 29, 1956 (Vol. 12:15, 22). Station ceased analog operations: February 17, 2009.

Represented (legal): Wiley Rein LLP.

Represented (sales): Continental Television Sales.

Personnel:

Tracey Jones, Vice President & General Manager.

Michael Dunlap, Chief Engineer & Operations Manager.

Jamey Hansbrough, General Sales Manager.

Ed Reams, News Director.

Meta Franzenburg, Business Manager.

Jeremy Harmon, Promotion, Creative Services & Production Manager.

Tina Wood, Traffic Manager & Program Director.

City of License: Harrisonburg. **Station DMA:** Harrisonburg, VA. **Rank:** 178.

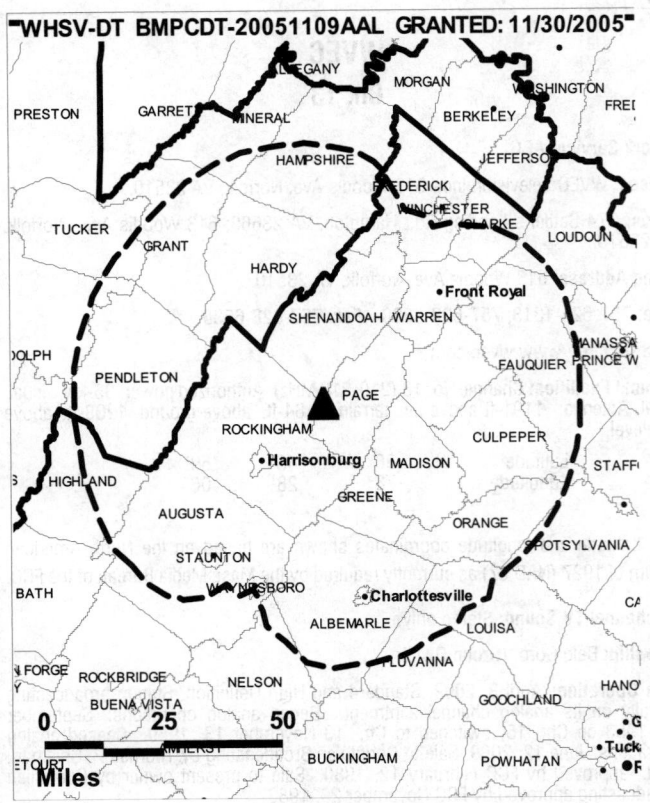

© 2010 Warren Communications News

Circulation © 2009 Nielsen. Coverage based on Nielsen study.

GrandTotal	Cable TV Households	Non-cable TV Households	Total TV Households
Estimated Station Totals *	85,530	49,530	135,060
Average Weekly Circulation (2009)	58,840	18,827	77,667
Average Daily Circulation (2009)			40,937

Station DMA Total	Cable TV Households	Non-cable TV Households	Total TV Households
Estimated Station Totals *	55,390	37,510	92,900
Average Weekly Circulation (2009)	41,600	16,924	58,524
Average Daily Circulation (2009)			33,654

Other DMA Total	Cable TV Households	Non-cable TV Households	Total TV Households
Estimated Station Totals *	30,140	12,020	42,160
Average Weekly Circulation (2009)	17,240	1,903	19,143
Average Daily Circulation (2009)			7,283

*Estimated station totals are sums of the Nielsen TV and Cable TV household estimates for each county in which the station registers viewing of more than 5% as per the Nielsen Survey Methods.

WSET-DT
Ch. 13

Network Service: ABC.

Licensee: WSET Inc., 2320 Langhorne Rd, Lynchburg, VA 24501.

Studio: 2320 Langhorne Rd, Lynchburg, VA 24501.

Mailing Address: PO Box 11588, Lynchburg, VA 24506-1588.

Phone: 434-528-1313. **Fax:** 434-847-0458.

E-mail: dcoleman@wset.com

Web Site: http://www.wset.com

Technical Facilities: Channel No. 13 (210-216 MHz). Authorized power: 28.7-kw visual, aural. Antenna: 2051-ft above av. terrain, 1178-ft. above ground, 3097-ft. above sea level.

Latitude	37°	18'	54"
Longitude	79°	38'	06"

Transmitter: Thaxton Mountain, 15-mi. E of Roanoke.

Note: Latitude and longitude coordinates shown are based on the North American Datum of 1927 (NAD 27) as currently required by the Mass Media Bureau of the FCC.

Ownership: Allbritton Communications Co. (Group Owner).

Began Operation: May 1, 2002. Station broadcasting digitally on its analog channel allotment. Began analog operations: February 8, 1953. Sale to present owner by Evening Star Broadcasting Co. approved by FCC May 5, 1976. Sale to Evening Star by Lynchburg Broadcasting Co. approved by FCC August 23, 1965 (Television Digest, Vol. 5:25, 35). Ceased analog operations: June 12, 2009.

Represented (sales): Continental Television Sales.

Represented (legal): Sidley Austin LLP.

Represented (engineering): Cavell, Mertz & Associates Inc.

Personnel:

Randall Smith, President.

George Kayes, General Sales Manager.

Linda Ottinger, Local Sales Manager.

Bill Foy, News Director.

Matt Leslie, Finance Director & Traffic Manager.

Debbie Coleman, Administration Director.

John Crumpler, Promotion, Audience Development & Graphic Arts Director.

K. C. Spiron, Operations Manager.

Wade Campbell, Commercial Production Coordinator.

Paul Glover, Technology Manager.

City of License: Lynchburg. **Station DMA:** Roanoke-Lynchburg, VA. **Rank:** 67.

WSET-DT BMPCDT-20080620AIR GRANTED: 2/6/2009

© 2010 Warren Communications News

Circulation © 2009 Nielsen. Coverage based on Nielsen study.

GrandTotal	Cable TV Households	Non-cable TV Households	Total TV Households
Estimated Station Totals *	215,560	245,830	461,390
Average Weekly Circulation (2009)	118,508	120,478	238,986
Average Daily Circulation (2009)			113,557

Station DMA Total	Cable TV Households	Non-cable TV Households	Total TV Households
Estimated Station Totals *	205,200	224,940	430,140
Average Weekly Circulation (2009)	117,122	119,094	236,216
Average Daily Circulation (2009)			112,764

Other DMA Total	Cable TV Households	Non-cable TV Households	Total TV Households
Estimated Station Totals *	10,360	20,890	31,250
Average Weekly Circulation (2009)	1,386	1,384	2,770
Average Daily Circulation (2009)			793

*Estimated station totals are sums of the Nielsen TV and Cable TV household estimates for each county in which the station registers viewing of more than 5% as per the Nielsen Survey Methods.

WWCW-DT
Ch. 20

Network Service: FOX, CW.

Grantee: GB Lynchburg Licensing LLC, 915 Middle River Dr, Ste 409, Fort Lauderdale, FL 33304.

Studio: 2618 Colonial Ave SW, Roanoke, VA 24015.

Mailing Address: PO Box 2127, Roanoke, VA 24009.

Phone: 540-344-2127; 434-239-2700. **Fax:** 540-345-1912.

Web Site: http://www.fox2127.com

Technical Facilities: Channel No. 20 (506-512 MHz). Authorized power: 916-kw max. visual, aural. Antenna: 1641-ft above av. terrain, 869-ft. above ground, 2752-ft. above sea level.

Latitude	37°	19'	14"
Longitude	79°	37'	58"

Note: Latitude and longitude coordinates shown are based on the North American Datum of 1927 (NAD 27) as currently required by the Mass Media Bureau of the FCC.

Ownership: Grant Co. Inc. (Group Owner).

Began Operation: March 1, 2002. Standard Definition. Began analog operations: March 23, 1986. Ceased analog operations: June 12, 2009.

Represented (legal): Wilkinson Barker Knauer LLP.

Personnel:

Ralph Claussen, General Manager & General Sales Manager.

Glen Gunnussen, Chief Engineer.

Deborah Saunders, Business Manager.

Joe Spencer, Program Director.

Debbie Reardon, Promotion & Marketing Director.

Mike Hanger, Production Manager.

Sherri Parrish, Traffic Director.

City of License: Lynchburg. **Station DMA:** Roanoke-Lynchburg, VA. **Rank:** 67.

© 2010 Warren Communications News

Circulation © 2009 Nielsen. Coverage based on Nielsen study.

GrandTotal	Cable TV Households	Non-cable TV Households	Total TV Households
Estimated Station Totals *	52,490	96,120	148,610
Average Weekly Circulation (2009)	20,227	10,296	30,523
Average Daily Circulation (2009)			9,849

Station DMA Total	Cable TV Households	Non-cable TV Households	Total TV Households
Estimated Station Totals *	52,490	96,120	148,610
Average Weekly Circulation (2009)	20,227	10,296	30,523
Average Daily Circulation (2009)			9,849

*Estimated station totals are sums of the Nielsen TV and Cable TV household estimates for each county in which the station registers viewing of more than 5% as per the Nielsen Survey Methods.

WPXW-TV
Ch. 43

Network Service: ION.

Licensee: ION Media Washington License Inc., Debtor in Possession, 601 Clearwater Park Rd, West Palm Beach, FL 33401-6233.

Studio: 6199 Old Arrington Ln, Fairfax Station, VA 22039.

Mailing Address: 6199 Old Arrington Ln, Fairfax Station, VA 22039.

Phone: 703-503-7966; 888-466-1702. **Fax:** 703-503-1225.

E-mail: tanyalewis@ionmedia.com

Web Site: http://www.ionmedia.com

Technical Facilities: Channel No. 43 (644-650 MHz). Authorized power: 90-kw max. visual, aural. Antenna: 623-ft above av. terrain, 461-ft. above ground, 443-ft. above sea level.

| Latitude | 38° | 47' | 16" |
| Longitude | 77° | 19' | 47" |

Holds CP for change to channel number 34, 1000-kw max. visual, 846-ft above av. terrain, 663-ft. above ground, 1073-ft. above sea level; lat. 38° 57' 01", long. 77° 04' 47", BMPCDT-20080620AML.

Transmitter: 6110 Ox Rd. (Rte. 123), Fairfax Station.

Note: Latitude and longitude coordinates shown are based on the North American Datum of 1927 (NAD 27) as currently required by the Mass Media Bureau of the FCC.

Ownership: ION Media Networks Inc., Debtor in Possession (Group Owner).

Began Operation: April 18, 2001. Standard Definition. Began analog operations: March 26, 1978. Sale to Urban Television LLC pends. Involuntary assignment to debtor in possession status approved by FCC June 5, 2009. Transfer of control by ION Media Networks Inc. from Paxson Management Corp. & Lowell W. Paxson to CIG Media LLC approved by FCC December 31, 2007. Paxson Communications Corp. became ION Media Networks Inc. on June 26, 2006. Sale to Paxson Communications Corp. by VVI Manassas Inc. approved by FCC April 16, 1997. Sale to VVI Manassas Inc. by National Capital Christian Broadcasting Inc. approved by FCC January 27, 1994. Ceased analog operations: June 12, 2009.

Represented (sales): Dow Lohnes PLLC.

Personnel:

Tanya Lewis, Traffic Manager.

City of License: Manassas. **Station DMA:** Washington, DC (Hagerstown, MD).

Rank: 9.

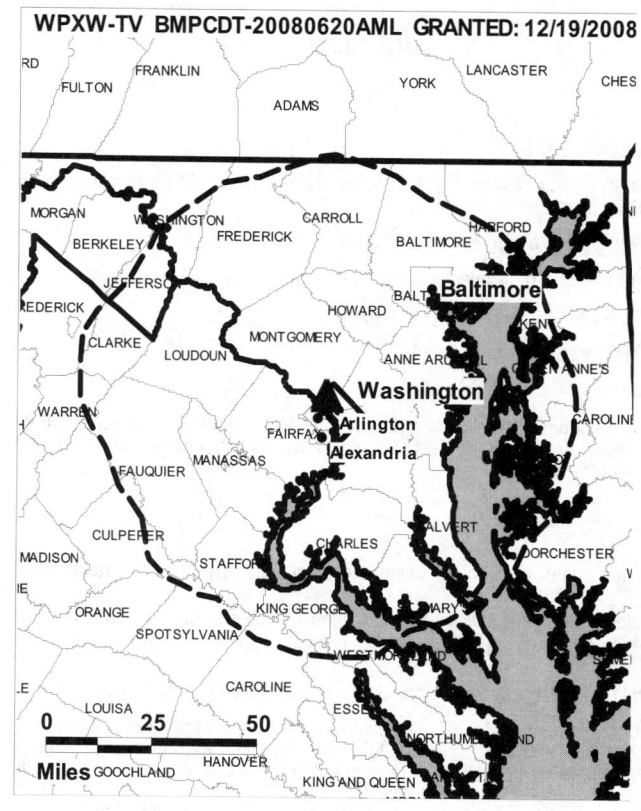

WPXW-TV BMPCDT-20080620AML GRANTED: 12/19/2008

© 2010 Warren Communications News

Circulation © 2009 Nielsen. Coverage based on Nielsen study.

GrandTotal	Cable TV Households	Non-cable TV Households	Total TV Households
Estimated Station Totals *	1,036,050	322,710	1,358,760
Average Weekly Circulation (2009)	99,751	26,479	126,230
Average Daily Circulation (2009)			21,124

Station DMA Total	Cable TV Households	Non-cable TV Households	Total TV Households
Estimated Station Totals *	1,029,340	322,710	1,352,050
Average Weekly Circulation (2009)	99,111	26,479	125,590
Average Daily Circulation (2009)			21,059

Other DMA Total	Cable TV Households	Non-cable TV Households	Total TV Households
Estimated Station Totals *	6,710	0	6,710
Average Weekly Circulation (2009)	640	0	640
Average Daily Circulation (2009)			65

*Estimated station totals are sums of the Nielsen TV and Cable TV household estimates for each county in which the station registers viewing of more than 5% as per the Nielsen Survey Methods.

WPXV-TV
Ch. 46

Network Service: ION.

Licensee: ION Media License Co. LLC, Debtor in Possession, 601 Clearwater Park Rd, West Palm Beach, FL 33401-6233.

Studio: 230 Clearfield Ave., Suite 104, Virginia Beach, VA 23462.

Mailing Address: 230 Clearfield Ave, Ste 104, Virginia Beach, VA 23462.

Phone: 757-499-1261. **Fax:** 757-499-1679.

E-mail: cindyarthur@ionmedia.com

Web Site: http://www.ionmedia.com

Technical Facilities: Channel No. 46 (662-668 MHz). Authorized power: 1000-kw max. visual, aural. Antenna: 1181-ft above av. terrain, 1168-ft. above ground, 1191-ft. above sea level.

Latitude	36°	48'	31"
Longitude	76°	30'	13"

Transmitter: Approx. 0.19-mi. NE of intersection of State Hwy. 337 & Sportsman Blvd.

Note: Latitude and longitude coordinates shown are based on the North American Datum of 1927 (NAD 27) as currently required by the Mass Media Bureau of the FCC.

Ownership: ION Media Networks Inc., Debtor in Possession (Group Owner).

Began Operation: April 1, 2002. Standard Definition. Began analog operations: May 29, 1989. Sale to Urban Television LLC pends. Involuntary assignment to debtor in possession status approved by FCC June 5, 2009. Transfer of control by ION Media Networks Inc. from Paxson Management Corp. & Lowell W. Paxson to CIG Media LLC approved by FCC December 31, 2007. Paxson Communications Corp. became ION Media Networks Inc. on June 26, 2006. Sale to Paxson Communications Corp. by Lockwood Broadcasting Inc. approved by FCC December 18, 1997. Sale to Lockwood Broadcasting Inc. by Tidewater Christian Communications Corp. approved by FCC December 31, 1996. Ceased analog operations: June 12, 2009.

Represented (legal): Dow Lohnes PLLC.

Represented (sales): Blair Television.

Represented (engineering): du Treil, Lundin & Rackley Inc.

Personnel:

Rhonda Nelson, Station Operations Manager.

Joseph Brown, Chief Engineer.

Cindy Arthur, Traffic Manager.

City of License: Norfolk. **Station DMA:** Norfolk-Portsmouth-Newport News, VA.

Rank: 43.

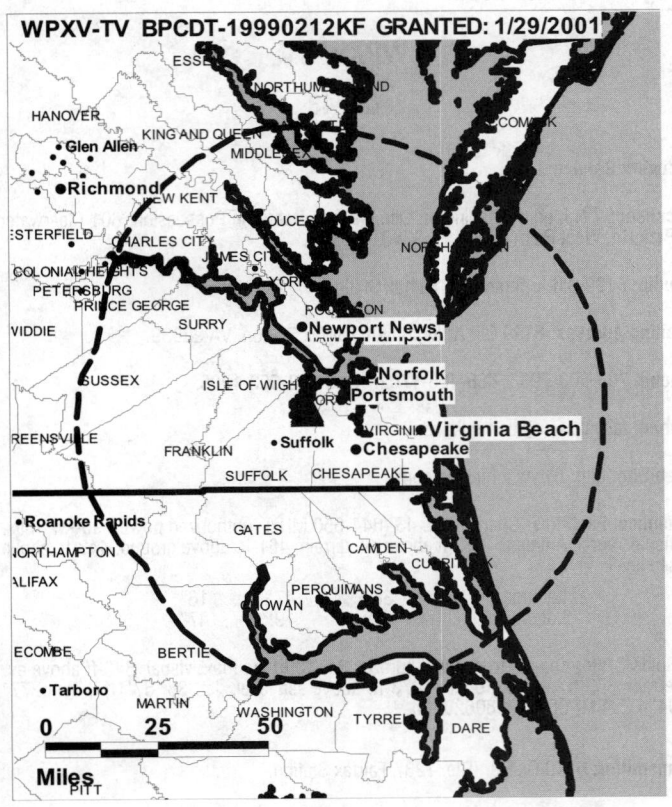

WPXV-TV BPCDT-19990212KF GRANTED: 1/29/2001

© 2010 Warren Communications News

Circulation © 2009 Nielsen. Coverage based on Nielsen study.

GrandTotal	Cable TV Households	Non-cable TV Households	Total TV Households
Estimated Station Totals *	331,890	165,130	497,020
Average Weekly Circulation (2009)	21,838	17,865	39,703
Average Daily Circulation (2009)			8,917

Station DMA Total	Cable TV Households	Non-cable TV Households	Total TV Households
Estimated Station Totals *	331,890	165,130	497,020
Average Weekly Circulation (2009)	21,838	17,865	39,703
Average Daily Circulation (2009)			8,917

*Estimated station totals are sums of the Nielsen TV and Cable TV household estimates for each county in which the station registers viewing of more than 5% as per the Nielsen Survey Methods.

WTKR-DT
Ch. 40

Network Service: CBS.

Licensee: Local TV Virginia Licensee LLC, 1717 Dixie Hwy, Ste 650, Fort Wright, KY 41011.

Studio: 720 Boush St., Norfolk, VA 23510.

Mailing Address: 720 Boush St, Norfolk, VA 23510.

Phone: 757-446-1000; 800-375-0901. **Fax:** 757-446-1376.

Web Site: http://www.wtkr.com

Technical Facilities: Channel No. 40 (626-632 MHz). Authorized power: 950-kw max. visual, aural. Antenna: 1237-ft above av. terrain, 1224-ft. above ground, 1247-ft. above sea level.

Latitude	36°	48'	31"
Longitude	76°	30'	13"

Transmitter: 37020 Namsemond Pkwy., Suffolk.

Note: Latitude and longitude coordinates shown are based on the North American Datum of 1927 (NAD 27) as currently required by the Mass Media Bureau of the FCC.

Ownership: Local TV Holdings LLC (Group Owner).

Began Operation: March 11, 2002. High Definition. Began analog operations: April 2, 1950. Sale to Knight-Ridder by Landmark Television approved by FCC January 16, 1981. Sale to Narragansett Television approved by FCC April 26, 1989. Sale to The New York Times Co. by Narragansett Television approved by FCC May 3, 1995. Sale to present owner by The New York Times Co. approved by FCC March 9, 2007. Ceased analog operations: June 12, 2009.

Represented (legal): Dow Lohnes PLLC.

Represented (sales): Eagle Television Sales.

Personnel:

David Bunnell, President & General Manager.

Cindi Dove, General Sales Manager.

Shane Moreland, News Director.

Sam Barclay, Chief Engineer.

Jennifer Crabtree, Controller.

Towanda Porter, Program Manager.

Kristie Flynn, Research & Marketing Director.

William Varnier, Creative Services Director.

Bob Wilkes, Traffic Manager.

City of License: Norfolk. **Station DMA:** Norfolk-Portsmouth-Newport News, VA.

Rank: 43.

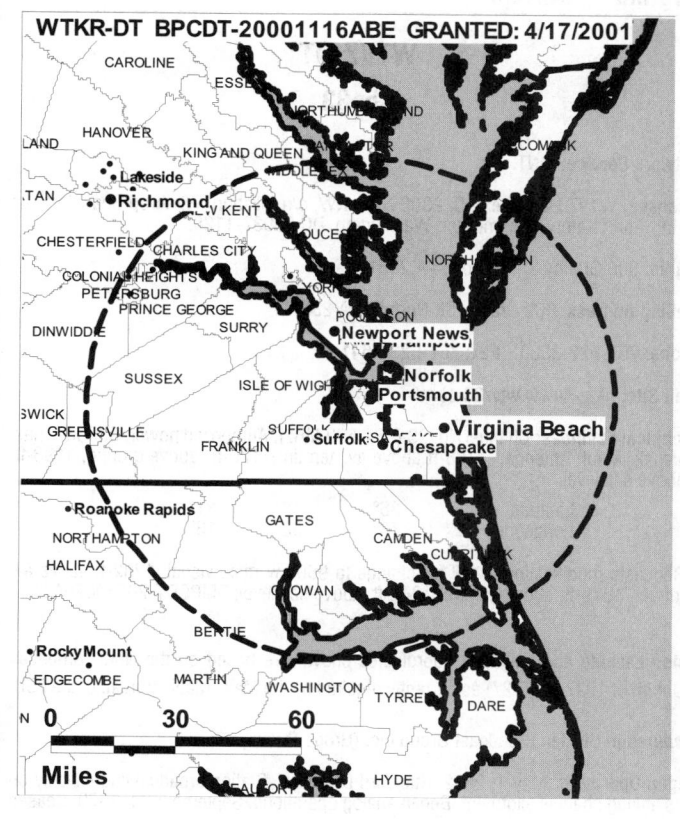

© 2010 Warren Communications News

Circulation © 2009 Nielsen. Coverage based on Nielsen study.

GrandTotal	Cable TV Households	Non-cable TV Households	Total TV Households
Estimated Station Totals *	514,810	216,890	731,700
Average Weekly Circulation (2009)	297,716	112,765	410,481
Average Daily Circulation (2009)			181,974

Station DMA Total	Cable TV Households	Non-cable TV Households	Total TV Households
Estimated Station Totals *	502,950	199,810	702,760
Average Weekly Circulation (2009)	294,684	111,325	406,009
Average Daily Circulation (2009)			179,957

Other DMA Total	Cable TV Households	Non-cable TV Households	Total TV Households
Estimated Station Totals *	11,860	17,080	28,940
Average Weekly Circulation (2009)	3,032	1,440	4,472
Average Daily Circulation (2009)			2,017

*Estimated station totals are sums of the Nielsen TV and Cable TV household estimates for each county in which the station registers viewing of more than 5% as per the Nielsen Survey Methods.

WTVZ-DT
Ch. 33

Network Service: MNT.

Licensee: WTVZ Licensee LLC, 2300 N St. NW, c/o Pillsbury Winthrop Shaw Pittman LLP, Attn.: Kathryn Schmeltzer, Washington, DC 20037-1128.

Studio: 900 Granby St., Norfolk, VA 23510.

Mailing Address: 900 Granby St, Norfolk, VA 23510.

Phone: 757-622-3333. **Fax:** 757-623-1541.

Web Site: http://www.wtvz33.com/

Technical Facilities: Channel No. 33 (584-590 MHz). Authorized power: 905-kw max. visual, aural. Antenna: 1183-ft above av. terrain, 1170-ft. above ground, 1193-ft. above sea level.

Latitude	36°	48'	31"
Longitude	76°	30'	13"

Requests modification of CP for change to 960-kw max. visual, 1232-ft above av. terrain, 1219-ft. above ground, 1242-ft. above sea level; BMPCDT-20080620AJZ.

Note: Latitude and longitude coordinates shown are based on the North American Datum of 1927 (NAD 27) as currently required by the Mass Media Bureau of the FCC.

Ownership: Sinclair Broadcast Group Inc. (Group Owner).

Began Operation: May 1, 2002. Standard Definition. Station broadcasting digitally on its analog channel allotment. Began analog operations: September 24, 1979. Ceased analog operations: February 17, 2009.

Represented (sales): Katz Media Group.

Personnel:

Bill Scaffide, General Manager.

Paul Rossi, General Sales Manager.

Pam Simpson, Local Sales Manager.

Bill Barber, Chief Engineer.

Stacy Fuller, Controller.

Donny Lowe, Promotion Director.

John Doughtie, Production Director.

Bonnie Philtrantz, Traffic Manager.

City of License: Norfolk. **Station DMA:** Norfolk-Portsmouth-Newport News, VA.

Rank: 43.

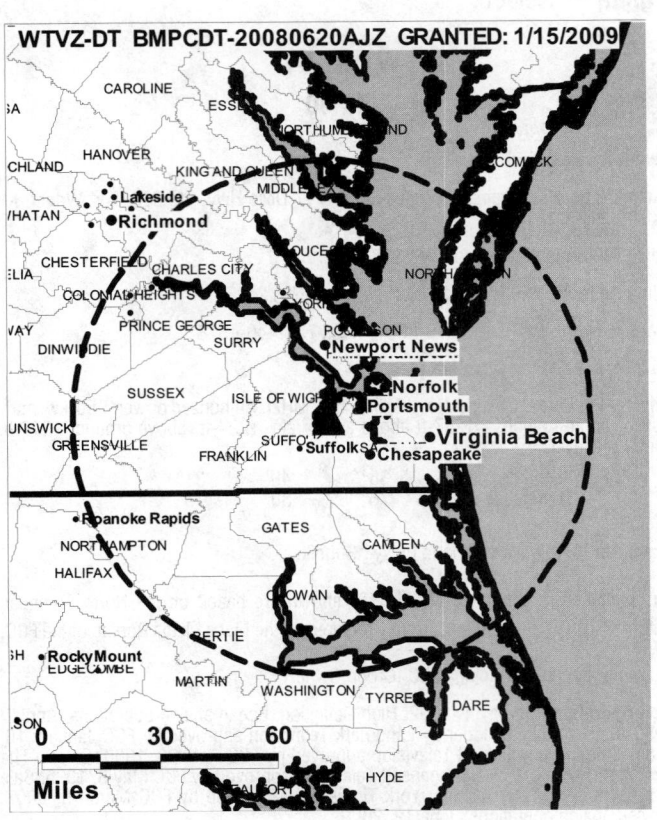

© 2010 Warren Communications News

Circulation © 2009 Nielsen. Coverage based on Nielsen study.

GrandTotal	Cable TV Households	Non-cable TV Households	Total TV Households
Estimated Station Totals *	500,750	208,270	709,020
Average Weekly Circulation (2009)	126,489	64,417	190,906
Average Daily Circulation (2009)			72,046

Station DMA Total	Cable TV Households	Non-cable TV Households	Total TV Households
Estimated Station Totals *	498,760	199,810	698,570
Average Weekly Circulation (2009)	126,358	63,833	190,191
Average Daily Circulation (2009)			71,946

Other DMA Total	Cable TV Households	Non-cable TV Households	Total TV Households
Estimated Station Totals *	1,990	8,460	10,450
Average Weekly Circulation (2009)	131	584	715
Average Daily Circulation (2009)			100

*Estimated station totals are sums of the Nielsen TV and Cable TV household estimates for each county in which the station registers viewing of more than 5% as per the Nielsen Survey Methods.

WRIC-DT
Ch. 22

Network Service: ABC.

Licensee: Young Broadcasting of Richmond Inc., Debtor in Possession, PO Box 1800, c/o Brooks, Pierce et al., Raleigh, NC 27602.

Studio: 301 Arboretum Place, Richmond, VA 23236.

Mailing Address: 301 Arboretum Pl, Richmond, VA 23236-3464.

Phone: 804-330-8888. **Fax:** 804-330-8882.

Web Site: http://www.wric.com

Technical Facilities: Channel No. 22 (518-524 MHz). Authorized power: 450-kw max. visual, aural. Antenna: 727-ft above av. terrain, 737-ft. above ground, 1317-ft. above sea level.

Latitude	37°	30'	45"
Longitude	77°	36'	05"

Holds CP for change to 850-kw max. visual, 1077-ft above av. terrain, 934-ft. above ground, 1292-ft. above sea level; BPCDT-20080618ADU.

Note: Latitude and longitude coordinates shown are based on the North American Datum of 1927 (NAD 27) as currently required by the Mass Media Bureau of the FCC.

Ownership: Young Broadcasting Inc., Debtor in Possession (Group Owner).

Began Operation: November 11, 2002. Began analog operations: August 15, 1955. Ceased analog operations: June 12, 2009. Sale to Nationwide Communications Inc. by Thomas G. Tinsley Jr. & Assoc. approved by FCC in 1968. Sale to Young Broadcasting Inc. by Nationwide approved by FCC August 24, 1994. Involuntary assignment to debtor in possession status approved by FCC March 17, 2009. Assignment to Young Broadcasting of Richmond Inc. (New Young Broadcasting Holding Co. Inc.) pends.

Represented (legal): Brooks, Pierce, McLendon, Humphrey & Leonard LLP.

Personnel:

Robert M. Peterson, Vice President & General Manager.

David Weems, General Sales Manager.

Carl Archacki, Local Sales Manager.

Lisa Melton, News Director.

Darrell Chaney, Chief Engineer.

Regina Crockett, Finance Director.

Bill Blank, Program Manager.

Steve Bays, Promotion Director.

Mike Laffey, Production Manager.

Dixon Johnston, Creative Services Director.

Marie Mickie, Traffic Manager.

City of License: Petersburg. **Station DMA:** Richmond-Petersburg, VA. **Rank:** 58.

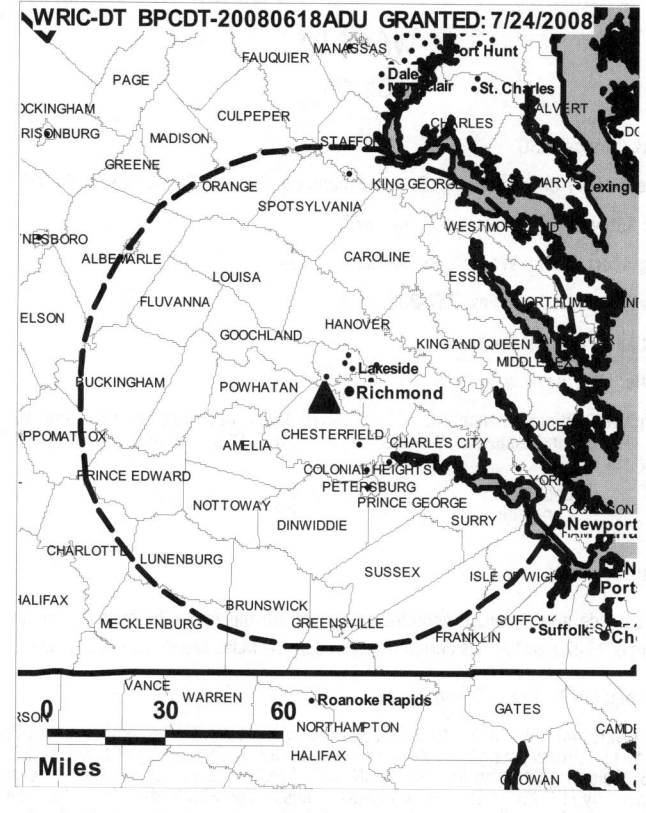

WRIC-DT BPCDT-20080618ADU GRANTED: 7/24/2008

© 2010 Warren Communications News

Circulation © 2009 Nielsen. Coverage based on Nielsen study.

GrandTotal	Cable TV Households	Non-cable TV Households	Total TV Households
Estimated Station Totals *	371,350	221,090	592,440
Average Weekly Circulation (2009)	206,230	144,230	350,460
Average Daily Circulation (2009)			159,855

Station DMA Total	Cable TV Households	Non-cable TV Households	Total TV Households
Estimated Station Totals *	307,370	211,970	519,340
Average Weekly Circulation (2009)	192,891	142,437	335,328
Average Daily Circulation (2009)			157,874

Other DMA Total	Cable TV Households	Non-cable TV Households	Total TV Households
Estimated Station Totals *	63,980	9,120	73,100
Average Weekly Circulation (2009)	13,339	1,793	15,132
Average Daily Circulation (2009)			1,981

*Estimated station totals are sums of the Nielsen TV and Cable TV household estimates for each county in which the station registers viewing of more than 5% as per the Nielsen Survey Methods.

WAVY-DT
Ch. 31

Network Service: NBC.

Licensee: WAVY Broadcasting LLC, 4 Richmond Sq, Ste 200, Providence, RI 02906.

Studio: 300 Wavy St., Portsmouth, VA 23704.

Mailing Address: 300 Wavy St, Portsmouth, VA 23704.

Phone: 757-393-1010. **Fax:** 757-399-7628.

E-mail: john.cochrane@wavy.com

Web Site: http://www.wavy.com

Technical Facilities: Channel No. 31 (572-578 MHz). Authorized power: 1000-kw max. visual, aural. Antenna: 919-ft above av. terrain, 919-ft. above ground, 942-ft. above sea level.

Latitude	36°	49'	14"
Longitude	76°	30'	41"

Transmitter: Kings Hwy., Driver.

Note: Latitude and longitude coordinates shown are based on the North American Datum of 1927 (NAD 27) as currently required by the Mass Media Bureau of the FCC.

Ownership: LIN TV Corp. (Group Owner).

Began Operation: March 30, 2001. Began analog operations: September 1, 1957. Sale to LIN Broadcasting by Tidewater Teleradio Inc. approved by FCC March 27, 1968. Sale of controlling interest in LIN from AT&T to Hicks, Muse, Tate & Furst approved by FCC March 2, 1998 (Television Digest, Vol. 37:33, 42; 38:2, 10). Sale to Chancellor Media Corp. dismissed by FCC 1999 (Vol. 38:28; 39:12). Ceased analog operations: June 12, 2009.

Represented (legal): Covington & Burling.

Represented (engineering): du Treil, Lundin & Rackley Inc.

Represented (sales): Blair Television.

Personnel:

Doug Davis, President & General Manager.

John Cochrane, General Sales Manager.

Nick Hasenecz, Local Sales Manager.

Kathy Hostetter, News Director.

Les Garrenton, Engineering Director.

Joe Weller, Program Coordinator.

Judy Triska, Marketing & Promotion Director.

Dave Whitener, Production Manager.

Eather White, Traffic Manager.

Rosetta Rolan, Public Affairs Director.

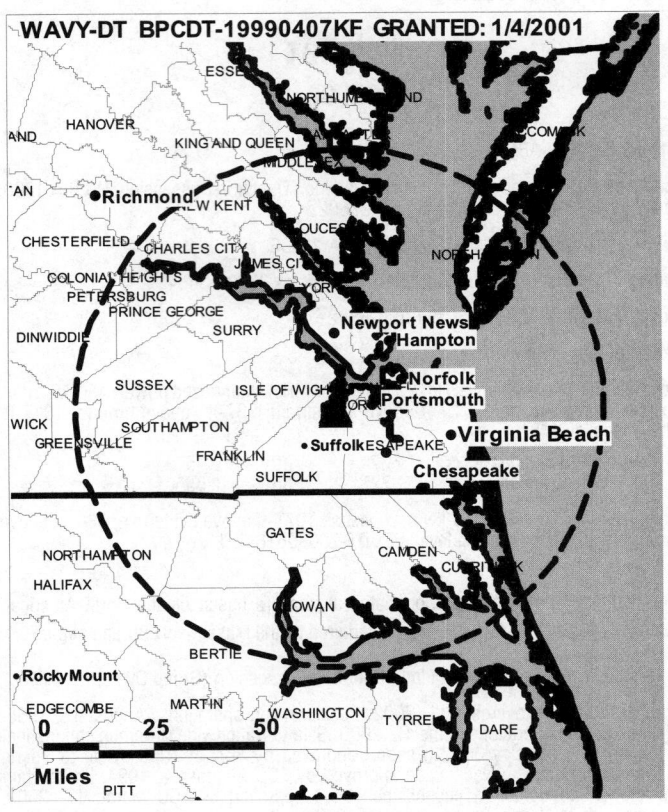

© 2010 Warren Communications News

City of License: Portsmouth. **Station DMA:** Norfolk-Portsmouth-Newport News, VA.

Rank: 43.

Circulation © 2009 Nielsen. Coverage based on Nielsen study.

GrandTotal	Cable TV Households	Non-cable TV Households	Total TV Households
Estimated Station Totals *	515,460	211,680	727,140
Average Weekly Circulation (2009)	336,697	133,315	470,012
Average Daily Circulation (2009)			235,921

Station DMA Total	Cable TV Households	Non-cable TV Households	Total TV Households
Estimated Station Totals *	502,950	199,810	702,760
Average Weekly Circulation (2009)	333,239	132,291	465,530
Average Daily Circulation (2009)			234,128

Other DMA Total	Cable TV Households	Non-cable TV Households	Total TV Households
Estimated Station Totals *	12,510	11,870	24,380
Average Weekly Circulation (2009)	3,458	1,024	4,482
Average Daily Circulation (2009)			1,793

*Estimated station totals are sums of the Nielsen TV and Cable TV household estimates for each county in which the station registers viewing of more than 5% as per the Nielsen Survey Methods.

WGNT-DT
Ch. 50

Network Service: CW.

Licensee: Viacom Broadcasting of Seattle Inc., 2175 K St. NW, Suite 350, Washington, DC 20037.

Studio: 1318 Spratley St., Portsmouth, VA 23704.

Mailing Address: 1318 Spratley St, Portsmouth, VA 23704.

Phone: 757-393-2501. **Fax:** 757-393-6353.

Web Site: http://cw27.com/

Technical Facilities: Channel No. 50 (686-692 MHz). Authorized power: 800-kw max. visual, aural. Antenna: 866-ft above av. terrain, 861-ft. above ground, 883-ft. above sea level.

Latitude	36°	48'	43"
Longitude	76°	27'	45"

Holds CP for change to 1000-kw max. visual, 1004-ft above av. terrain, 997-ft. above ground, 1019-ft. above sea level; BPCDT-20080616ABC.

Note: Latitude and longitude coordinates shown are based on the North American Datum of 1927 (NAD 27) as currently required by the Mass Media Bureau of the FCC.

Ownership: CBS Corp. (Group Owner).

Began Operation: July 15, 2002. High Definition. Began analog operations: October 1, 1961 as a non-commercial religious station. Began commercial operation July 1967. Sale to Centennial Communications Inc. approved by FCC May 22, 1989. Sale to present owner by Centennial Communications Inc. approved by FCC October 17, 1997. Ceased analog operations: June 12, 2009.

Personnel:

Steve Soldinger, Vice President & General Manager.

John Erkenbrack, Station, Business & General Sales Manager.

Brigette Ward, Local Sales Manager.

Chuck Martin, National Sales Manager.

George Randell, Chief Engineer.

Chris Wolf, Programming & Creative Services Director.

Chris Johnson, Program Coordinator.

Patrick Anderson, On-Air Promotion Coordinator.

Jonathan Young, Production Coordinator.

Diane Hall, Traffic Manager.

Kafi Rouse, Public Affairs Director.

City of License: Portsmouth. **Station DMA:** Norfolk-Portsmouth-Newport News, VA.

Rank: 43.

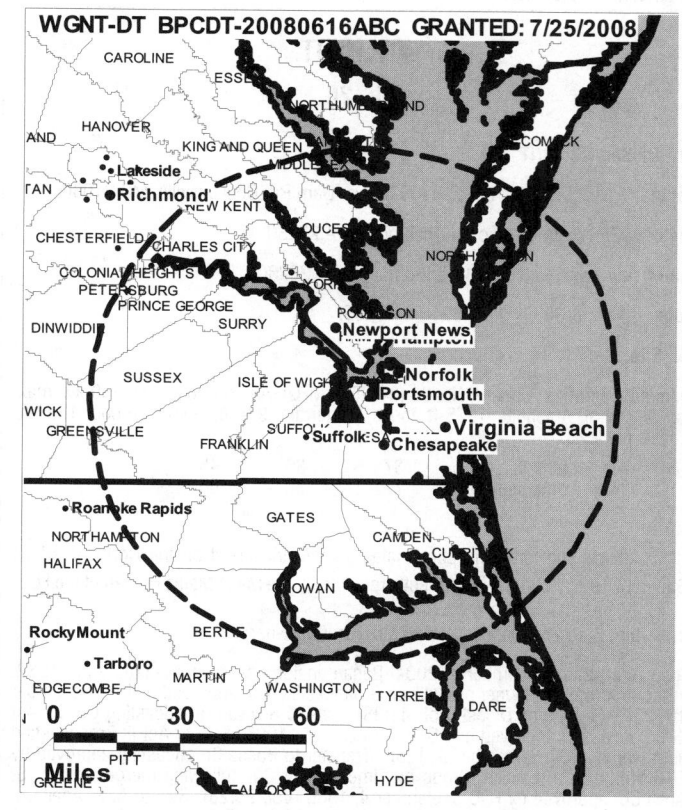

WGNT-DT BPCDT-20080616ABC GRANTED: 7/25/2008

© 2010 Warren Communications News

Circulation © 2009 Nielsen. Coverage based on Nielsen study.

GrandTotal	Cable TV Households	Non-cable TV Households	Total TV Households
Estimated Station Totals *	516,960	205,380	722,340
Average Weekly Circulation (2009)	179,030	89,426	268,456
Average Daily Circulation (2009)			104,611

Station DMA Total	Cable TV Households	Non-cable TV Households	Total TV Households
Estimated Station Totals *	502,950	199,810	702,760
Average Weekly Circulation (2009)	172,924	88,930	261,854
Average Daily Circulation (2009)			103,431

Other DMA Total	Cable TV Households	Non-cable TV Households	Total TV Households
Estimated Station Totals *	14,010	5,570	19,580
Average Weekly Circulation (2009)	6,106	496	6,602
Average Daily Circulation (2009)			1,180

*Estimated station totals are sums of the Nielsen TV and Cable TV household estimates for each county in which the station registers viewing of more than 5% as per the Nielsen Survey Methods.

WRLH-DT
Ch. 26

Network Service: MNT, FOX.

Grantee: WRLH Licensee LLC, 10706 Beaver Dam Rd, Cockeysville, MD 21030.

Studio: 1925 Westmoreland St., Richmond, VA 23230.

Mailing Address: PO Box 11169, Richmond, VA 23230.

Phone: 804-358-3535. **Fax:** 804-358-1495.

Web Site: http://www.fox35.com

Technical Facilities: Channel No. 26 (542-548 MHz). Authorized power: 800-kw max. visual, aural. Antenna: 1075-ft above av. terrain, 934-ft. above ground, 1292-ft. above sea level.

Latitude	37°	30'	45"
Longitude	77°	36'	05"

Note: Latitude and longitude coordinates shown are based on the North American Datum of 1927 (NAD 27) as currently required by the Mass Media Bureau of the FCC.

Ownership: Sinclair Broadcast Group Inc. (Group Owner).

Began Operation: December 7, 2004. Began analog operations: February 20, 1982. Transfer to present owner by Sullivan Broadcasting Co. approved by FCC December 10, 2001 (Television Digest, Vol. 41:38). Sale to Sullivan Broadcasting Co. by Act III Broadcasting approved by FCC December 15, 1995. Sale to Act III Broadcasting approved by FCC September 9, 1988. Transfer to Busse Broadcasting approved by FCC 1987. Sale to Gillett Group by Times Mirror Co. following merger with A. S. Abell Co. approved by FCC September 4, 1986 (Vol. 26:28). Sale to A. S. Abell Co. by Television Corp. of Richmond approved by FCC April 24, 1985. Ceased analog operations: February 17, 2009.

Represented (sales): Katz Media Group.

Personnel:

Steven Genett, General Manager.

Jerry Hogan, General Sales Manager.

Brandon Richards, News Director.

Charles Rause, Chief Engineer.

Julie Dyer, Business Manager.

Linda Strickland, Program Director.

Jay Endicott, Production Director.

Mark Bartholomew, Creative Services Manager.

Brenda Thomas, Traffic Manager.

City of License: Richmond. **Station DMA:** Richmond-Petersburg, VA. **Rank:** 58.

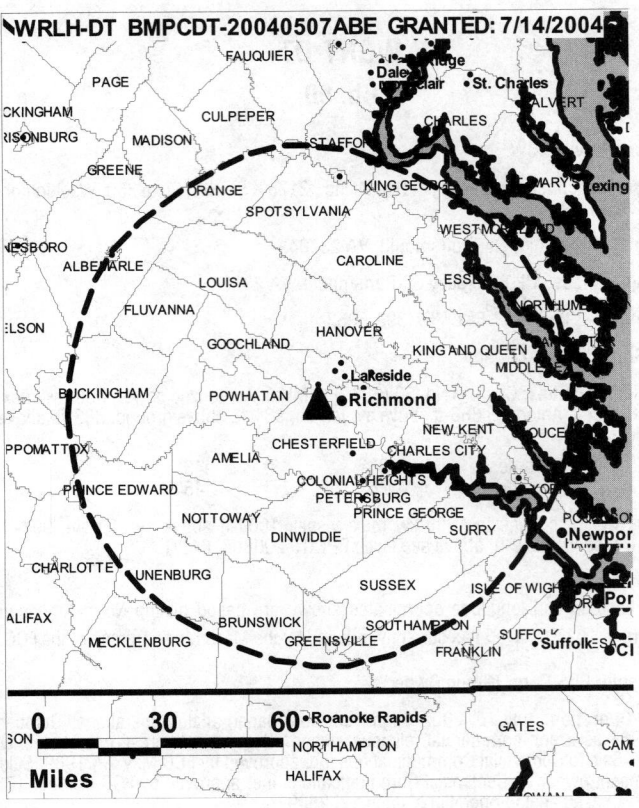

WRLH-DT BMPCDT-20040507ABE GRANTED: 7/14/2004

© 2010 Warren Communications News

Circulation © 2009 Nielsen. Coverage based on Nielsen study.

GrandTotal	Cable TV Households	Non-cable TV Households	Total TV Households
Estimated Station Totals *	308,200	221,090	529,290
Average Weekly Circulation (2009)	168,213	121,145	289,358
Average Daily Circulation (2009)			108,492

Station DMA Total	Cable TV Households	Non-cable TV Households	Total TV Households
Estimated Station Totals *	307,370	211,970	519,340
Average Weekly Circulation (2009)	167,869	119,078	286,947
Average Daily Circulation (2009)			108,010

Other DMA Total	Cable TV Households	Non-cable TV Households	Total TV Households
Estimated Station Totals *	830	9,120	9,950
Average Weekly Circulation (2009)	344	2,067	2,411
Average Daily Circulation (2009)			482

*Estimated station totals are sums of the Nielsen TV and Cable TV household estimates for each county in which the station registers viewing of more than 5% as per the Nielsen Survey Methods.

WTVR-DT
Ch. 25

Network Service: CBS.

Licensee: Community Television of Alabama License LLC, 1717 Dixie Hwy, Ste 650, Fort Wright, KY 41011.

Studio: 3301 W. Broad St., Richmond, VA 23230.

Mailing Address: PO Box 11064, Richmond, VA 23230.

Phone: 804-254-3600. **Fax:** 804-254-3697.

Web Site: http://www.wtvr.com

Technical Facilities: Channel No. 25 (536-542 MHz). Authorized power: 410-kw max. visual, aural. Antenna: 1138-ft above av. terrain, 995-ft. above ground, 1353-ft. above sea level.

Latitude	37°	30'	45"
Longitude	77°	36'	05"

Note: Latitude and longitude coordinates shown are based on the North American Datum of 1927 (NAD 27) as currently required by the Mass Media Bureau of the FCC.

Multichannel TV Sound: Stereo only.

Satellite Earth Stations: Transmitter NEC; Comtech, 5.2-meter Ku & C-band; Comtech, 5.2-meter C-band.

Ownership: Local TV Holdings LLC (Group Owner).

Began Operation: October 16, 2002. Standard and High Definition. Began analog operations: April 15, 1948. Sale to Park Communications by Wilbur M. Havens approved by FCC October 13, 1965. Transfer of control of Park Acquisition to John Fiorini & Gary Knapp approved by FCC March 27, 1995. Sale to Media General by Park Acquisition approved by FCC November 22, 1996. Media General swap of WTVR-TV with Ellis Communications (Raycom Media) for WSAV-TV Savannah, GA, WHLT Hattiesburg & WJTV Jackson, MS approved by FCC July 23, 1997. Due to acquistion of WWBT(TV) Richmond, VA, Raycom Media sold WTVR-TV to Community Television of Alabama License LLC to comply with FCC's duopoly rules. FCC approved sale March 12, 2009. Ceased analog operations: June 12, 2009.

Represented (legal): Dow Lohnes PLLC.

Represented (sales): TeleRep Inc.

Personnel:

Peter Maroney, Vice President & General Manager.

Don Cox, Engineering & Operations Director.

Steven Hayes, General Sales Manager.

Steve Young, Local Sales Manager.

James Taguchi, National Sales Manager.

Chip Mahaney, News Director.

Tricia Thurman, Business Manager.

Blake Peddicord, Program Coordinator.

Bill Anderson, Marketing Director.

Cherie Miller, Research Director.

Jessica Noll Messervy, Local Program Director.

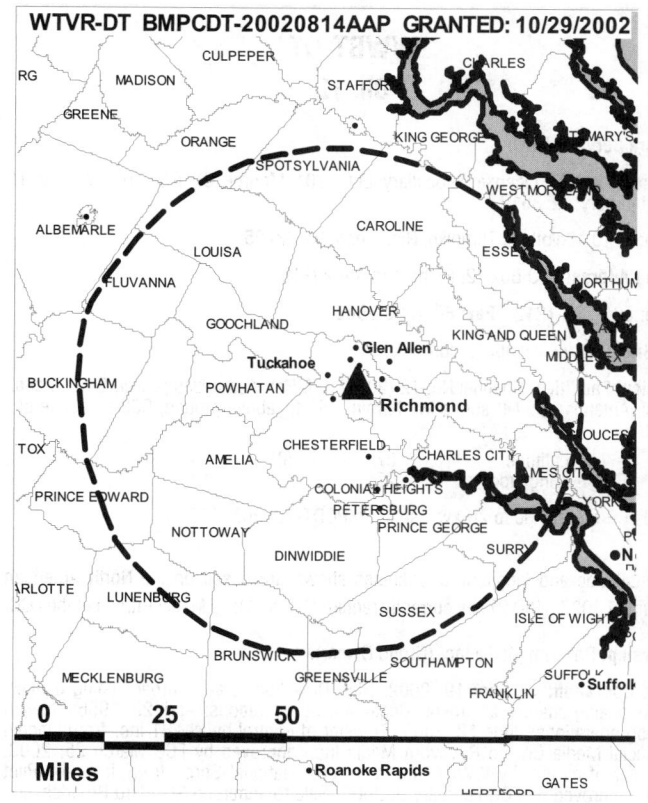

© 2010 Warren Communications News

Shane Rogers, Traffic Manager.

City of License: Richmond. **Station DMA:** Richmond-Petersburg, VA. **Rank:** 58.

Circulation © 2009 Nielsen. Coverage based on Nielsen study.

GrandTotal	Cable TV Households	Non-cable TV Households	Total TV Households
Estimated Station Totals *	383,200	225,010	608,210
Average Weekly Circulation (2009)	204,458	136,116	340,574
Average Daily Circulation (2009)			149,646

Station DMA Total	Cable TV Households	Non-cable TV Households	Total TV Households
Estimated Station Totals *	307,370	211,970	519,340
Average Weekly Circulation (2009)	184,893	134,022	318,915
Average Daily Circulation (2009)			144,891

Other DMA Total	Cable TV Households	Non-cable TV Households	Total TV Households
Estimated Station Totals *	75,830	13,040	88,870
Average Weekly Circulation (2009)	19,565	2,094	21,659
Average Daily Circulation (2009)			4,755

*Estimated station totals are sums of the Nielsen TV and Cable TV household estimates for each county in which the station registers viewing of more than 5% as per the Nielsen Survey Methods.

WWBT-DT
Ch. 12

Network Service: NBC.

Licensee: WWBT License Subsidiary LLC, 201 Monroe St, RSA Tower, 20th Fl, Montgomery, AL 36104.

Studio: 5710 Midlothian Turnpike, Richmond, VA 23225.

Mailing Address: PO Box 12, Richmond, VA 23218.

Phone: 804-230-1212. **Fax:** 804-230-2500.

Web Site: http://www.nbc12.com

Technical Facilities: Channel No. 12 (204-210 MHz). Authorized power: 6-kw visual, aural. Antenna: 794-ft above av. terrain, 757-ft. above ground, 968-ft. above sea level.

Latitude	37°	30'	23"
Longitude	77°	30'	12"

Holds CP for change to 26-kw visual; BMPCDT-20090724ADI.

Note: Latitude and longitude coordinates shown are based on the North American Datum of 1927 (NAD 27) as currently required by the Mass Media Bureau of the FCC.

Ownership: Raycom Media Inc. (Group Owner).

Began Operation: January 19, 2002. High Definition. Station broadcasting digitally on its analog channel allotment. Began analog operations: April 29, 1956. Ceased analog operations: June 12, 2009. Transfer of control by WWBT Inc. from Lincoln Financial Media Co. to Raycvom Media Inc. approved by FCC March 25, 2008. Transfer of control by WWBT Inc. to Lincoln National Corp. from Jefferson-Pilot Corp. approved by FCC February 9, 2006. Sale to Jefferson Standard Broadcasting by Richmond Television Corp. approved by FCC October 16, 1968.

Represented (legal): Covington & Burling.

Represented (sales): Petry Media Corp.

Personnel:

Don Richards, Vice President & General Manager.

W. Henry Boze, Vice President, Engineering & Television.

Kym Grinnage, General Sales Manager.

Jeff Hoyt, Sales Manager.

Bruce Tinoco, Chief Engineer.

Christine Markowitz, Business Manager.

Joanne Cardwell, Program Director.

Dawn Young, Sales Promotion Director.

Rae Maupin, Creative Services Supervisor.

Maureen Turgeon, Traffic Manager.

City of License: Richmond. **Station DMA:** Richmond-Petersburg, VA. **Rank:** 58.

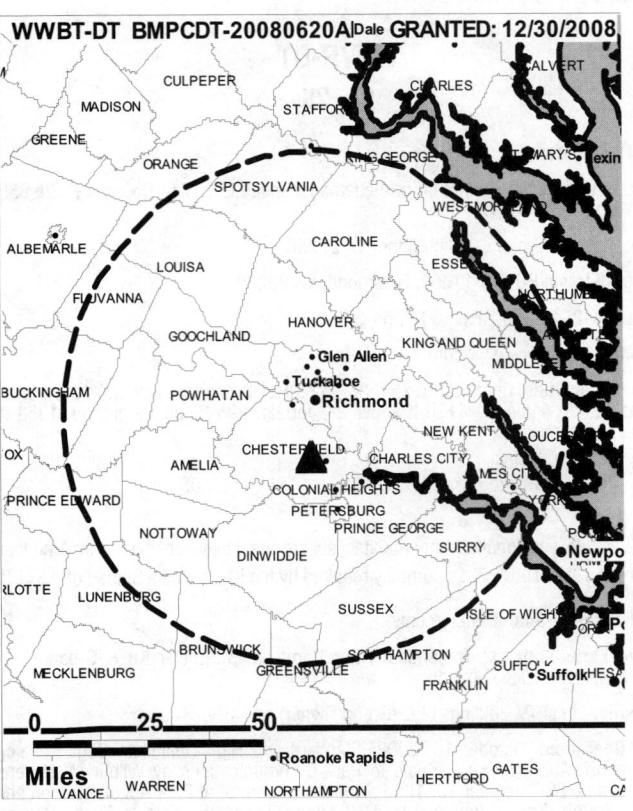

WWBT-DT BMPCDT-20080620A Dale GRANTED: 12/30/2008

© 2010 Warren Communications News

Circulation © 2009 Nielsen. Coverage based on Nielsen study.

GrandTotal	Cable TV Households	Non-cable TV Households	Total TV Households
Estimated Station Totals *	397,350	222,450	619,800
Average Weekly Circulation (2009)	228,238	146,816	375,054
Average Daily Circulation (2009)			204,757

Station DMA Total	Cable TV Households	Non-cable TV Households	Total TV Households
Estimated Station Totals *	307,370	211,970	519,340
Average Weekly Circulation (2009)	219,702	145,193	364,895
Average Daily Circulation (2009)			203,060

Other DMA Total	Cable TV Households	Non-cable TV Households	Total TV Households
Estimated Station Totals *	89,980	10,480	100,460
Average Weekly Circulation (2009)	8,536	1,623	10,159
Average Daily Circulation (2009)			1,697

*Estimated station totals are sums of the Nielsen TV and Cable TV household estimates for each county in which the station registers viewing of more than 5% as per the Nielsen Survey Methods.

WDBJ-DT
Ch. 18

Network Service: MNT, CBS.

Licensee: WDBJ Television Inc., PO Box 7, Roanoke, VA 24022-0007.

Studio: 2807 Hershberger Rd., Roanoke, VA 24017.

Mailing Address: PO Box 7, Roanoke, VA 24022-0007.

Phone: 540-344-7000. **Fax:** 540-344-5097.

E-mail: kzuber@wdbj7.com

Web Site: http://www.wdbj7.com

Technical Facilities: Channel No. 18 (494-500 MHz). Authorized power: 460-kw max. visual, aural. Antenna: 1988-ft above av. terrain, 125-ft. above ground, 3884-ft. above sea level.

Latitude	37°	11'	42"
Longitude	80°	09'	23"

Holds CP for change to 675-kw max. visual; BPCDT-20090622ADU.

Transmitter: 8187 Honeysuckle Lane.

Note: Latitude and longitude coordinates shown are based on the North American Datum of 1927 (NAD 27) as currently required by the Mass Media Bureau of the FCC.

Satellite Earth Stations: Transmitter Harris; AFC, 3.7-meter Ku-band; Scientific-Atlanta, 4.6-meter Ku-band; Andrew, 5.6-meter Ku-band; Harris, 6.1-meter C-band; Scientific-Atlanta, 7-meter C-band; Scientific-Atlanta, M/A-Com, Harris receivers.

Ownership: Schurz Communications Inc. (Group Owner).

Began Operation: April 29, 2002. High Definition. Began analog operations: October 3, 1955. Sale to present owner by Times World Corp. approved by FCC October 29, 1969 (Television Digest, Vol. 9:44). Ceased analog operations: June 12, 2009.

Represented (sales): HRP: Television Station Representative.

Represented (legal): Fletcher, Heald & Hildreth PLC.

Personnel:

Jeffrey A. Marks, President & General Manager.

Carl Guffey, Operations & Engineering Director.

Ray Sullivan, General & National Sales Manager.

Lolly Quigley, Local Sales Manager.

Amy Morris, News Director.

Alan Novitsky, Engineering Manager.

Angela McCaskill, Business Manager.

Mike Bell, Programming & Promotion Director.

Kelly Zuber, Digital Media Director.

Mark Layman, Production Manager.

Debra Bell, Traffic Manager.

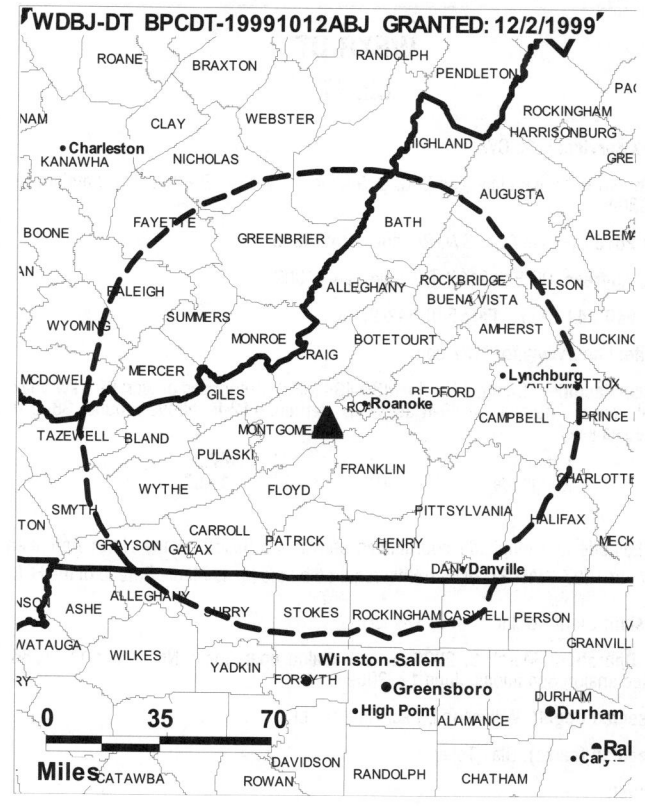

© 2010 Warren Communications News

City of License: Roanoke. **Station DMA:** Roanoke-Lynchburg, VA. **Rank:** 67.

Circulation © 2009 Nielsen. Coverage based on Nielsen study.

GrandTotal	Cable TV Households	Non-cable TV Households	Total TV Households
Estimated Station Totals *	292,790	291,950	584,740
Average Weekly Circulation (2009)	167,102	153,867	320,969
Average Daily Circulation (2009)			176,819

Station DMA Total	Cable TV Households	Non-cable TV Households	Total TV Households
Estimated Station Totals *	207,760	224,940	432,700
Average Weekly Circulation (2009)	143,712	149,217	292,929
Average Daily Circulation (2009)			167,070

Other DMA Total	Cable TV Households	Non-cable TV Households	Total TV Households
Estimated Station Totals *	85,030	67,010	152,040
Average Weekly Circulation (2009)	23,390	4,650	28,040
Average Daily Circulation (2009)			9,749

*Estimated station totals are sums of the Nielsen TV and Cable TV household estimates for each county in which the station registers viewing of more than 5% as per the Nielsen Survey Methods.

WFXR-DT
Ch. 17

Network Service: FOX, CW.

Grantee: GB Roanoke Licensing LLC, 915 Middle River Dr, Ste 409, Fort Lauderdale, FL 33304.

Studio: 2618 Colonial Ave., SW, Roanoke, VA 24015.

Mailing Address: PO Box 2127, Roanoke, VA 24009.

Phone: 540-344-2127. **Fax:** 540-342-2753.

Web Site: http://www.fox2127.com

Technical Facilities: Channel No. 17 (488-494 MHz). Authorized power: 695-kw max. visual, aural. Antenna: 1949-ft above av. terrain, 112-ft. above ground, 3845-ft. above sea level.

Latitude	37°	11'	47.3"
Longitude	80°	09'	15.5"

Note: Latitude and longitude coordinates shown are based on the North American Datum of 1927 (NAD 27) as currently required by the Mass Media Bureau of the FCC.

Ownership: Grant Co. Inc. (Group Owner).

Began Operation: March 3, 2006. Began analog operations: November 11, 1986. Ceased analog operations: June 12, 2009.

Represented (legal): Wilkinson Barker Knauer LLP.

Represented (sales): Blair Television.

Personnel:

Ralph Claussen, General Manager & National Sales Manager.

Deb Saunders, Assistant Station Manager & Business Manager.

Glenn Gunnussen, Chief Engineer.

Joe Spencer, Program Director.

Debbie Reardon, Promotion Director.

Mike Hanger, Production Manager.

Sherri Parrish, Traffic Manager.

City of License: Roanoke. **Station DMA:** Roanoke-Lynchburg, VA. **Rank:** 67.

WFXR-DT BPCDT-20080619AJU GRANTED: 1/8/2009

© 2010 Warren Communications News

Circulation © 2009 Nielsen. Coverage based on Nielsen study.

GrandTotal	Cable TV Households	Non-cable TV Households	Total TV Households
Estimated Station Totals *	204,910	224,940	429,850
Average Weekly Circulation (2009)	95,087	99,916	195,003
Average Daily Circulation (2009)			71,307

Station DMA Total	Cable TV Households	Non-cable TV Households	Total TV Households
Estimated Station Totals *	203,060	224,940	428,000
Average Weekly Circulation (2009)	94,710	99,916	194,626
Average Daily Circulation (2009)			71,269

Other DMA Total	Cable TV Households	Non-cable TV Households	Total TV Households
Estimated Station Totals *	1,850	0	1,850
Average Weekly Circulation (2009)	377	0	377
Average Daily Circulation (2009)			38

*Estimated station totals are sums of the Nielsen TV and Cable TV household estimates for each county in which the station registers viewing of more than 5% as per the Nielsen Survey Methods.

WPXR-TV
Ch. 36

Network Service: ION.

Licensee: ION Media License Co. LLC, Debtor in Possession, 601 Clearwater Park Rd, West Palm Beach, FL 33401-6233.

Studio: 401 3rd St SW, Roanoke, VA 24011.

Mailing Address: 401 3rd St SW, Roanoke, VA 24011.

Phone: 540-857-0038. **Fax:** 540-345-8568.

E-mail: shirleybundy@ionmedia.com

Web Site: http://www.ionmedia.com

Technical Facilities: Channel No. 36 (602-608 MHz). Authorized power: 700-kw max. visual, aural. Antenna: 2044-ft above av. terrain, 180-ft. above ground, 3940-ft. above sea level.

Latitude	37°	11'	37"
Longitude	80°	09'	25"

Note: Latitude and longitude coordinates shown are based on the North American Datum of 1927 (NAD 27) as currently required by the Mass Media Bureau of the FCC.

Ownership: ION Media Networks Inc., Debtor in Possession (Group Owner).

Began Operation: April 1, 2002. Standard Definition. Began analog operations: January 3, 1986. Involuntary assignment to debtor in possession status approved by FCC June 5, 2009. Transfer of control by ION Media Networks Inc. from Paxson Management Corp. & Lowell W. Paxson to CIG Media LLC approved by FCC December 31, 2007. Paxson Communications Corp. became ION Media Networks Inc. on June 26, 2006. Sale to Paxson Communications Corp. by Vine & Branch Inc. approved by FCC August 21, 1997. Ceased analog operations: June 12, 2009.

Represented (legal): Dow Lohnes PLLC.

Personnel:

Shirley Bundy, Station Operations Manager.

George Stein, Chief Engineer.

Genia Wright, Traffic Manager.

City of License: Roanoke. **Station DMA:** Roanoke-Lynchburg, VA. **Rank:** 67.

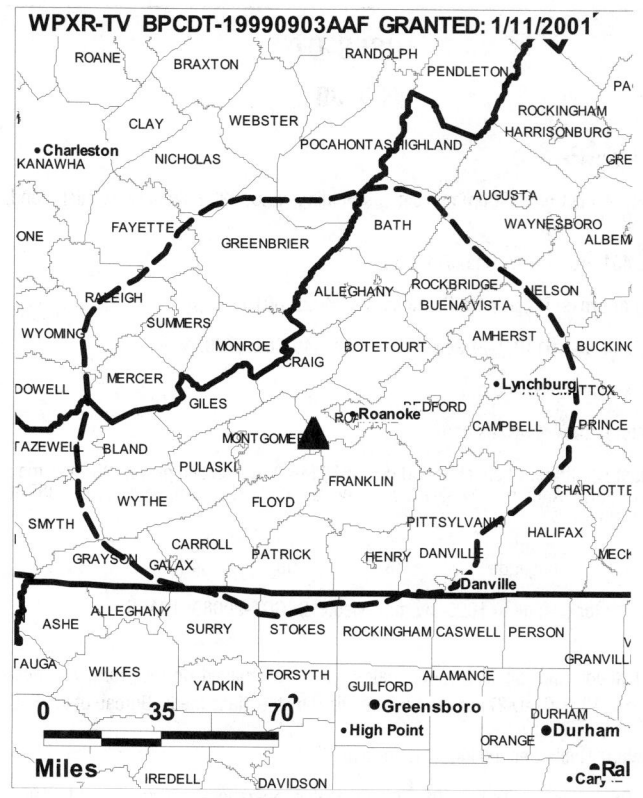

WPXR-TV BPCDT-19990903AAF GRANTED: 1/11/2001

© 2010 Warren Communications News

Circulation © 2009 Nielsen. Coverage based on Nielsen study.

GrandTotal	Cable TV Households	Non-cable TV Households	Total TV Households
Estimated Station Totals *	191,720	21,360	213,080
Average Weekly Circulation (2009)	23,347	2,029	25,376
Average Daily Circulation (2009)			4,480

Station DMA Total	Cable TV Households	Non-cable TV Households	Total TV Households
Estimated Station Totals *	191,720	21,360	213,080
Average Weekly Circulation (2009)	23,347	2,029	25,376
Average Daily Circulation (2009)			4,480

*Estimated station totals are sums of the Nielsen TV and Cable TV household estimates for each county in which the station registers viewing of more than 5% as per the Nielsen Survey Methods.

WSLS-DT
Ch. 30

Network Service: NBC.

Grantee: Media General Communications Holdings LLC, 333 E Franklin St, Richmond, VA 23219.

Studio: 401 3rd St. SW, Roanoke, VA 24011.

Mailing Address: PO Box 10, Roanoke, VA 24022-0010.

Phone: 540-981-9110; 540-981-9126. **Fax:** 540-981-9709.

E-mail: kmohn@wsls.com

Web Site: http://www.wsls.com

Technical Facilities: Channel No. 30 (566-572 MHz). Authorized power: 950-kw max. visual, aural. Antenna: 1942-ft above av. terrain, 136-ft. above ground, 3857-ft. above sea level.

Latitude	37°	12'	03"
Longitude	80°	08'	54"

Holds CP for change to 1000-kw max. visual; BPCDT-20080619ABS.

Note: Latitude and longitude coordinates shown are based on the North American Datum of 1927 (NAD 27) as currently required by the Mass Media Bureau of the FCC.

Ownership: Media General Inc. (Group Owner).

Began Operation: July 1, 2005. Began analog operations: December 11, 1952. Sale to Park Communications by Shenandoah Life Insurance Co. approved by FCC September 10, 1969 (Television Digest, Vol. 9:36, 37). Transfer of control of Park Acquisition to John Fiorini & Gary Knapp approved by FCC March 27, 1995. Sale to present owner by Park Acquisition approved by FCC November 22, 1996 (Vol. 36:31). Ceased analog operations: June 12, 2009.

Personnel:

Warren Fiihr, Vice President & General Manager.

Bruce Bryan, General Sales Manager.

Melissa Preas, News Director.

Ricky Williams, Chief Engineer.

Judy Ralph, Program & Human Resources Director.

Kevin Kirkalde, Marketing Director.

Mike Wright, Creative Services Supervisor.

Angela Combs, Traffic Manager.

City of License: Roanoke. **Station DMA:** Roanoke-Lynchburg, VA. **Rank:** 67.

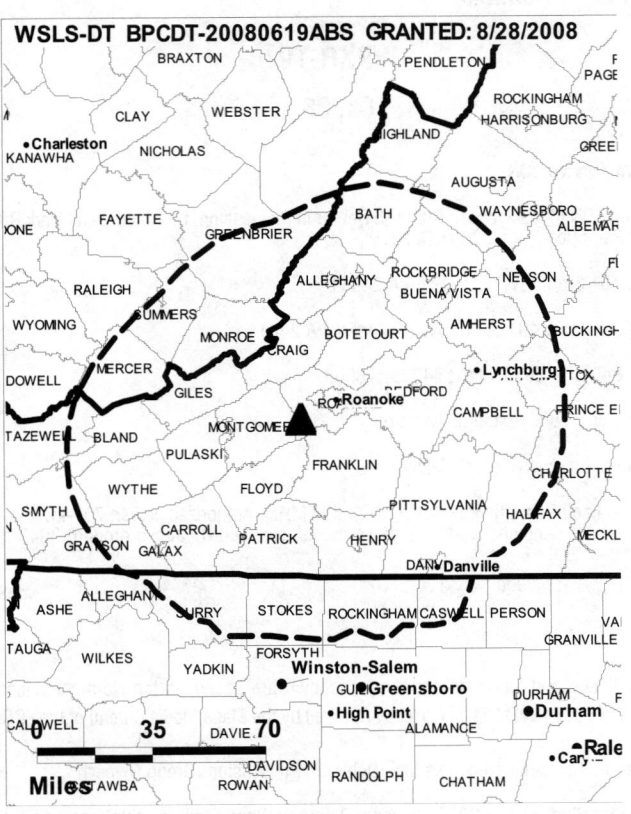

© 2010 Warren Communications News

Circulation © 2009 Nielsen. Coverage based on Nielsen study.

GrandTotal	Cable TV Households	Non-cable TV Households	Total TV Households
Estimated Station Totals *	254,340	243,290	497,630
Average Weekly Circulation (2009)	131,675	137,110	268,785
Average Daily Circulation (2009)			130,914

Station DMA Total	Cable TV Households	Non-cable TV Households	Total TV Households
Estimated Station Totals *	207,760	224,940	432,700
Average Weekly Circulation (2009)	126,549	135,756	262,305
Average Daily Circulation (2009)			129,221

Other DMA Total	Cable TV Households	Non-cable TV Households	Total TV Households
Estimated Station Totals *	46,580	18,350	64,930
Average Weekly Circulation (2009)	5,126	1,354	6,480
Average Daily Circulation (2009)			1,693

*Estimated station totals are sums of the Nielsen TV and Cable TV household estimates for each county in which the station registers viewing of more than 5% as per the Nielsen Survey Methods.

WHRE-DT
Ch. 7

Network Service: TBN.

Grantee: Copeland Channel 21 LLC, 168 Business Park Dr, Ste 200, Virginia Beach, VA 23462.

Studio: 5200 Hampton Blvd, Norfolk, VA 23508.

Mailing Address: 5200 Hampton Blvd, Norfolk, VA 23508.

Phone: 757-605-2602.

Technical Facilities: Channel No. 7 (174-180 MHz). Authorized power: 85-kw visual, aural. Antenna: 1017-ft above av. terrain, 1014-ft. above ground, 1037-ft. above sea level.

Latitude	36°	48'	31"
Longitude	76°	30'	12"

Note: Latitude and longitude coordinates shown are based on the North American Datum of 1927 (NAD 27) as currently required by the Mass Media Bureau of the FCC.

Ownership: Robert O. Copeland.

Began Operation: June 12, 2009. Began analog operations: March 27, 2006. Ceased analog operations: June 12, 2009.

City of License: Virginia Beach.

Station DMA: Norfolk-Portsmouth-Newport News, VA. **Rank:** 43.

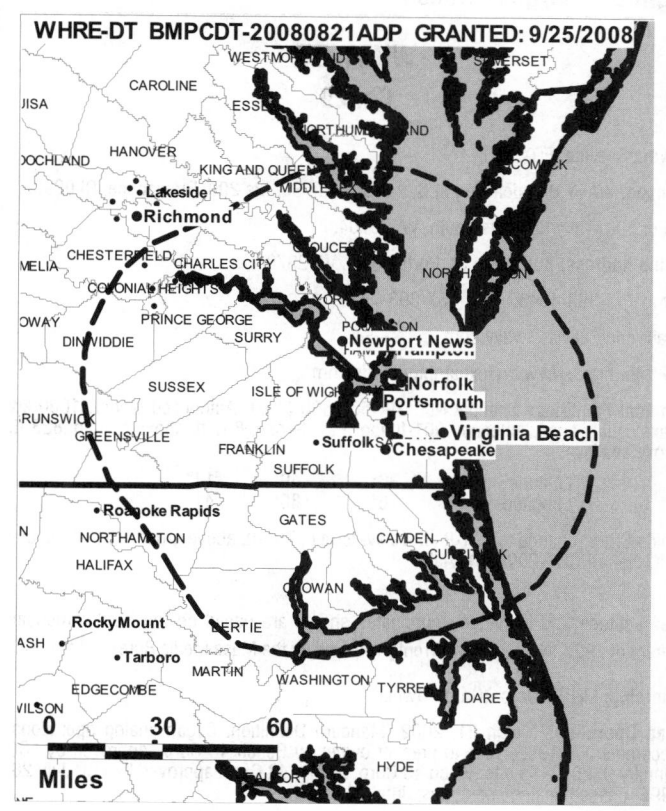

© 2010 Warren Communications News

Circulation © 2009 Nielsen. Coverage based on Nielsen study.

GrandTotal	Cable TV Households	Non-cable TV Households	Total TV Households
Estimated Station Totals *	98,480	66,050	164,530
Average Weekly Circulation (2009)	8,585	4,749	13,334
Average Daily Circulation (2009)			4,225

Station DMA Total	Cable TV Households	Non-cable TV Households	Total TV Households
Estimated Station Totals *	98,480	66,050	164,530
Average Weekly Circulation (2009)	8,585	4,749	13,334
Average Daily Circulation (2009)			4,225

*Estimated station totals are sums of the Nielsen TV and Cable TV household estimates for each county in which the station registers viewing of more than 5% as per the Nielsen Survey Methods.

WVBT-DT
Ch. 29

Network Service: FOX.

Licensee: WAVY Broadcasting LLC, 4 Richmond Sq, Ste 200, Providence, RI 02906.

Studio: 300 Wavy St, Portsmouth, VA 23704.

Mailing Address: 300 Wavy St, Portsmouth, VA 23704.

Phone: 757-393-4343. **Fax:** 757-393-7615.

E-mail: doug.davis@wavy.com

Web Site: http://www.myfoxhamptonroads.com

Technical Facilities: Channel No. 29 (560-566 MHz). Authorized power: 1000-kw max. visual, aural. Antenna: 801-ft above av. terrain, 801-ft. above ground, 823-ft. above sea level.

Latitude	36°	49'	14"
Longitude	76°	30'	41"

Holds CP for change to 791-ft above av. terrain, 791-ft. above ground, 814-ft. above sea level; BPCDT-20080619AJD.

Note: Latitude and longitude coordinates shown are based on the North American Datum of 1927 (NAD 27) as currently required by the Mass Media Bureau of the FCC.

Ownership: LIN TV Corp. (Group Owner).

Began Operation: March 21, 2002. Standard Definition. Began analog operations: December 17, 1992. Sale to present owner by Beach 43 Corp. approved by FCC January 9, 2002. Sale to Beach 43 Corp. by The 43 Corp. approved by FCC July 28, 1995. Ceased analog operations: June 12, 2009.

Represented (sales): Blair Television.

Personnel:

Doug Davis, Vice President & General Manager.

Nick Hasenecz, Local Sales Manager.

Andy Hilton, National Sales Manager.

Kathy Hostetter, News Director.

David Seals, Assistant News Director.

Les Garrenton, Engineering Director.

Lisa Hansen, Regional Business Manager.

Judy Triska, Promotion Director.

Latonya Hunter, Research Development Director.

David Whitbner Jr., Production Director.

Eather White, Traffic Manager.

City of License: Virginia Beach.

Station DMA: Norfolk-Portsmouth-Newport News, VA. **Rank:** 43.

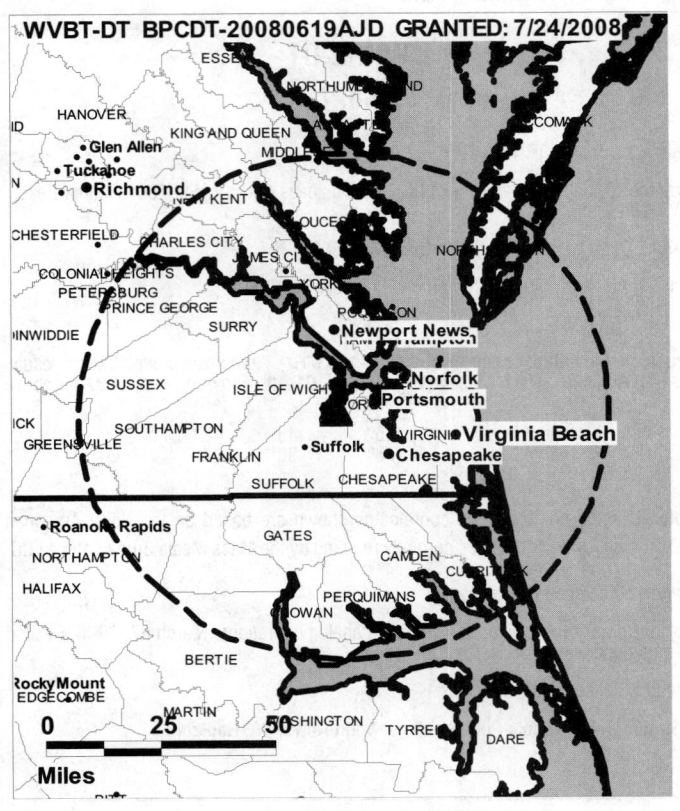

WVBT-DT BPCDT-20080619AJD GRANTED: 7/24/2008

© 2010 Warren Communications News

Circulation © 2009 Nielsen. Coverage based on Nielsen study.

GrandTotal	Cable TV Households	Non-cable TV Households	Total TV Households
Estimated Station Totals *	502,950	205,380	708,330
Average Weekly Circulation (2009)	263,019	103,390	366,409
Average Daily Circulation (2009)			123,276

Station DMA Total	Cable TV Households	Non-cable TV Households	Total TV Households
Estimated Station Totals *	502,950	199,810	702,760
Average Weekly Circulation (2009)	263,019	103,000	366,019
Average Daily Circulation (2009)			123,192

Other DMA Total	Cable TV Households	Non-cable TV Households	Total TV Households
Estimated Station Totals *	0	5,570	5,570
Average Weekly Circulation (2009)	0	390	390
Average Daily Circulation (2009)			84

*Estimated station totals are sums of the Nielsen TV and Cable TV household estimates for each county in which the station registers viewing of more than 5% as per the Nielsen Survey Methods.

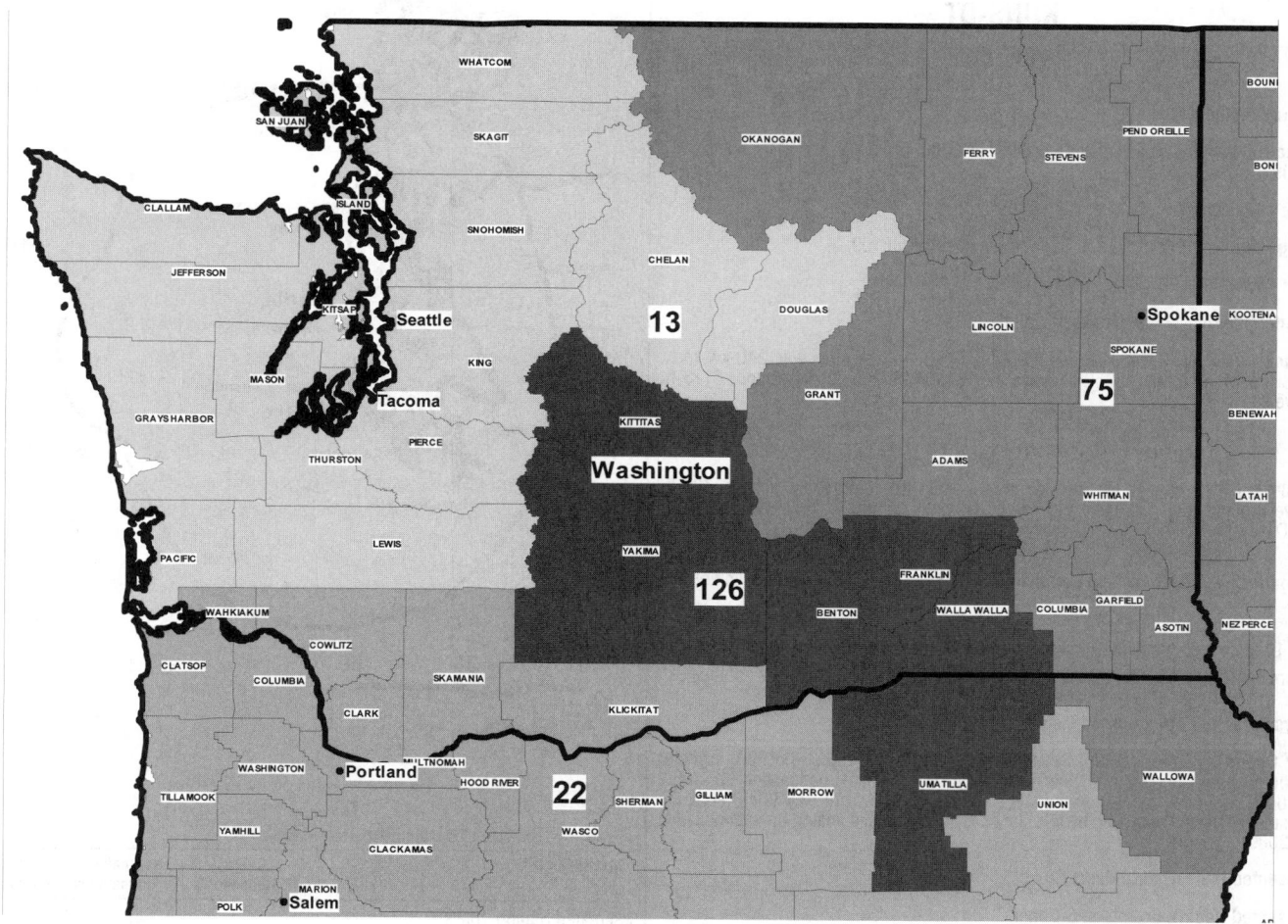

© 2010 Warren Communications News

MARKET	NIELSEN DMA TV HOUSEHOLDS	RANK	MARKET AREA COMMERCIAL STATIONS
Seattle-Tacoma, WA	1,833,990	13	KBCB-DT (19); KCPQ-DT (13); KHCV-DT (44); KING-DT (48); KIRO-DT (39); KMYQ-DT (25); KOMO-DT (38); KONG (31); KSTW-DT (11); KTBW-DT (14); KUNS-DT (50); KVOS-DT (35); KWPX-TV (33)
Portland, OR	1,188,770	22	KATU-DT (43); KGW-DT (8); KNMT-DT (45); KOIN-DT (40); KPDX-DT (48); KPTV-DT (12); KPXG-TV (22); KRCW-DT (33); KUNP-DT (16)
Spokane, WA	419,350	75	KAYU-DT (28); KGPX-TV (34); KHQ-DT (15); KLEW-DT (32); KREM (20); KSKN-DT (36); KXLY-DT (13)
Yakima-Pasco-Richland-Kennewick, WA.	219,510	126	KAPP-DT (14); KEPR-DT (18); KFFX-DT (11); KIMA-DT (33); KNDO-DT (16); KNDU-DT (26); KVEW-DT (44)

Washington Station Totals as of October 1, 2009

	VHF	UHF	TOTAL
Commercial Television	3	23	26
Educational Television	2	6	8
	5	29	34

KUNS-DT
Ch. 50

Network Service: UNV.

Licensee: Fisher Broadcasting-Bellevue TV LLC, 100 4th Ave N, Ste 510, Seattle, WA 98109.

Studio: 140 Fourth Ave, Seattle, WA 98109.

Mailing Address: 100 4th Ave N, Ste 510, Seattle, WA 98109.

Phone: 206-404-4199. **Fax:** 206-404-4422.

Web Site: http://www.univisionseattle.com

Technical Facilities: Channel No. 50 (686-692 MHz). Authorized power: 240-kw max. visual, aural. Antenna: 2359-ft above av. terrain, 279-ft. above ground, 3123-ft. above sea level.

| Latitude | 47° | 30' | 17" |
| Longitude | 121° | 58' | 04" |

Requests CP for change to 1000-kw max. visual, 801-ft above av. terrain, 486-ft. above ground, 936-ft. above sea level; lat. 47° 37' 55", long. 122° 21' 09", BPCDT-20080620AGX.

Transmitter: W. Tiger Mountain Communications Site, 2-mi. SW of intersection of 203 & I-90.

Note: Latitude and longitude coordinates shown are based on the North American Datum of 1927 (NAD 27) as currently required by the Mass Media Bureau of the FCC.

Ownership: Fisher Communications Inc. (Group Owner).

Began Operation: July 7, 2006. Began analog operations: August 8, 1999. Transfer of control from Christopher J. Racine (75% to 0) to Fisher Broadcasting Co. (25% to 100%) approved by FCC August 11, 2006. Transfer from Ray Wick, et al. to Christopher Racine approved by FCC July 14, 2000. Ceased analog operations: June 12, 2009.

Represented (sales): Katz Media Group.

Represented (legal): Covington & Burling.

Personnel:

James Clayton, General Manager.

John Barrett, Chief Engineer.

Janene Drafs, General Sales Manager.

Denise M. Llanes Cabo, Sales Assistant.

City of License: Bellevue. **Station DMA:** Seattle-Tacoma, WA. **Rank:** 13.

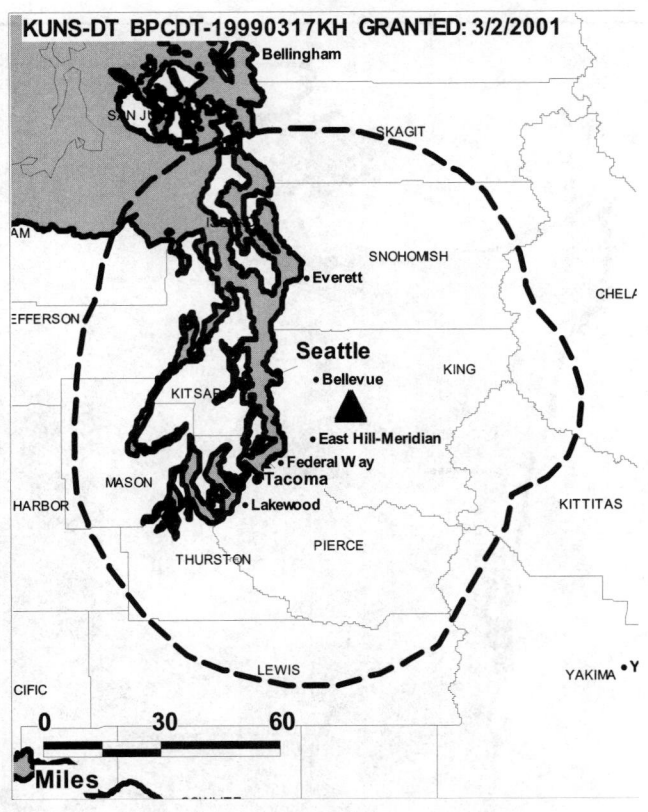

KUNS-DT BPCDT-19990317KH GRANTED: 3/2/2001

© 2010 Warren Communications News

Circulation © 2009 Nielsen. Coverage based on Nielsen study.

GrandTotal	Cable TV Households	Non-cable TV Households	Total TV Households
Estimated Station Totals *	0	87,450	87,450
Average Weekly Circulation (2009)	0	5,293	5,293
Average Daily Circulation (2009)			1,293

Station DMA Total	Cable TV Households	Non-cable TV Households	Total TV Households
Estimated Station Totals *	0	87,450	87,450
Average Weekly Circulation (2009)	0	5,293	5,293
Average Daily Circulation (2009)			1,293

*Estimated station totals are sums of the Nielsen TV and Cable TV household estimates for each county in which the station registers viewing of more than 5% as per the Nielsen Survey Methods.

KWPX-DT
Ch. 33

Network Service: ION.

Licensee: ION Media License Co. LLC, Debtor in Possession, 601 Clearwater Park Rd, West Palm Beach, FL 33401-6233.

KWPX-DT: 8112-C 304th Ave SE, Preston, WA 98050.

Mailing Address: 8112-C 304th Ave SE, Preston, WA 98050.

Phone: 425-222-6010. **Fax:** 425-222-6032.

E-mail: terryspring@ionmedia.com

Web Site: http://www.ionmedia.com

Technical Facilities: Channel No. 33 (584-590 MHz). Authorized power: 400-kw max. visual, aural. Antenna: 2349-ft above av. terrain, 272-ft. above ground, 3111-ft. above sea level.

Latitude	47°	30'	17"
Longitude	121°	58'	06"

Note: Latitude and longitude coordinates shown are based on the North American Datum of 1927 (NAD 27) as currently required by the Mass Media Bureau of the FCC.

Ownership: ION Media Networks Inc., Debtor in Possession (Group Owner).

Began Operation: October 28, 2002. Standard Definition. Began analog operations: May 17, 1989. Sale to NW TV Inc. by Robert Gill Communications LP approved by FCC January 6, 1995. Left air, date unreported. Resumed operation November 1, 1995. Sale to ValueVision International by NW TV Inc. approved by FCC January 26, 1996. Sale to Paxson Communications Corp. by ValueVision International approved by FCC February 2, 1998. Paxson Communications Corp. became ION Media Networks Inc. on June 26, 2006. Transfer of control by ION Media Networks Inc. from Paxson Management Corp. & Lowell W. Paxson to CIG Media LLC approved by FCC December 31, 2007. Involuntary assignment to debtor in possession status approved by FCC June 5, 2009. Sale to Urban Television LLC pends. Ceased analog operations: February 17, 2009.

Represented (legal): Dow Lohnes PLLC.

Represented (engineering): du Treil, Lundin & Rackley Inc.

Personnel:

Monica Nelsen, Station Operations Manager.

Terry Spring, Chief Engineer.

Erin Larson, Traffic Manager.

City of License: Bellevue. **Station DMA:** Seattle-Tacoma, WA. **Rank:** 13.

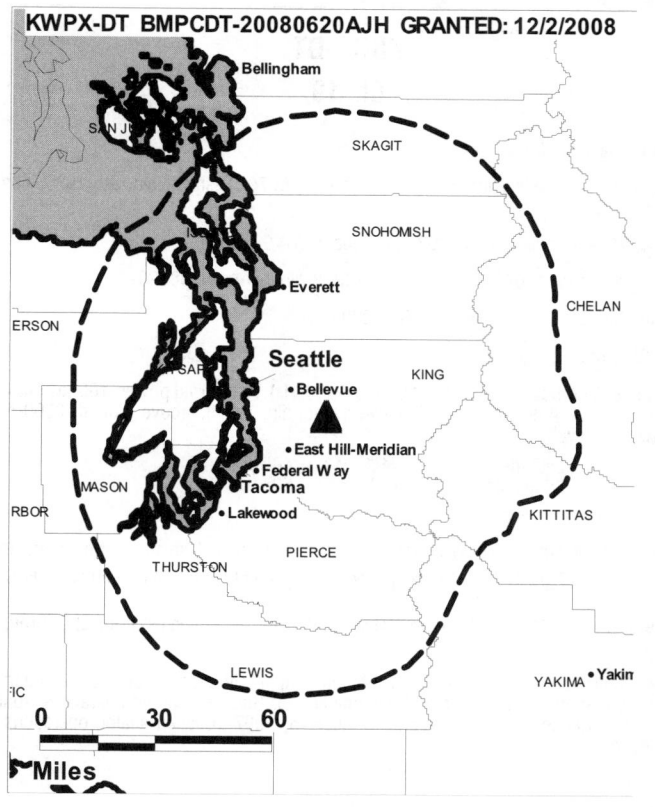

KWPX-DT BMPCDT-20080620AJH GRANTED: 12/2/2008

© 2010 Warren Communications News

Circulation © 2009 Nielsen. Coverage based on Nielsen study.

GrandTotal	Cable TV Households	Non-cable TV Households	Total TV Households
Estimated Station Totals *	1,251,870	252,100	1,503,970
Average Weekly Circulation (2009)	161,026	14,994	176,020
Average Daily Circulation (2009)			33,957

Station DMA Total	Cable TV Households	Non-cable TV Households	Total TV Households
Estimated Station Totals *	1,251,870	252,100	1,503,970
Average Weekly Circulation (2009)	161,026	14,994	176,020
Average Daily Circulation (2009)			33,957

*Estimated station totals are sums of the Nielsen TV and Cable TV household estimates for each county in which the station registers viewing of more than 5% as per the Nielsen Survey Methods.

KBCB-DT
Ch. 19

Network Service: IND.

Licensee: World Television of Washington LLC, 5670 Wilshire Blvd, Ste 1300, Los Angeles, CA 90036.

Studio: 4164 Meridian St, Ste 102, Bellingham, WA 98226.

Mailing Address: 4164 Meridian St, Ste 102, Bellingham, WA 98226.

Phone: 360-647-8842. **Fax:** 360-647-9204.

Web Site: http://www.kbcbtv.com

Technical Facilities: Channel No. 19 (500-506 MHz). Authorized power: 165-kw max. visual, aural. Antenna: 2484-ft above av. terrain, 487-ft. above ground, 2600-ft. above sea level.

Latitude	48°	40'	46"
Longitude	122°	50'	31"

Note: Latitude and longitude coordinates shown are based on the North American Datum of 1927 (NAD 27) as currently required by the Mass Media Bureau of the FCC.

Ownership: Frank Washington (Group Owner); Venture Technologies Group LLC (Group Owner).

Began Operation: January 12, 2004. Station temporarily ceased operations January 2006 due to electrical problem at transmitter site. Station resumed operations April 9, 2008. Began analog operations: August 15, 1997. Ceased analog operations: February 17, 2009.

Personnel:

Andy Wilcoxson, Station Manager & Chief Engineer.

Karen Phelps, General Sales Manager & Program Director.

City of License: Bellingham. **Station DMA:** Seattle-Tacoma, WA. **Rank:** 13.

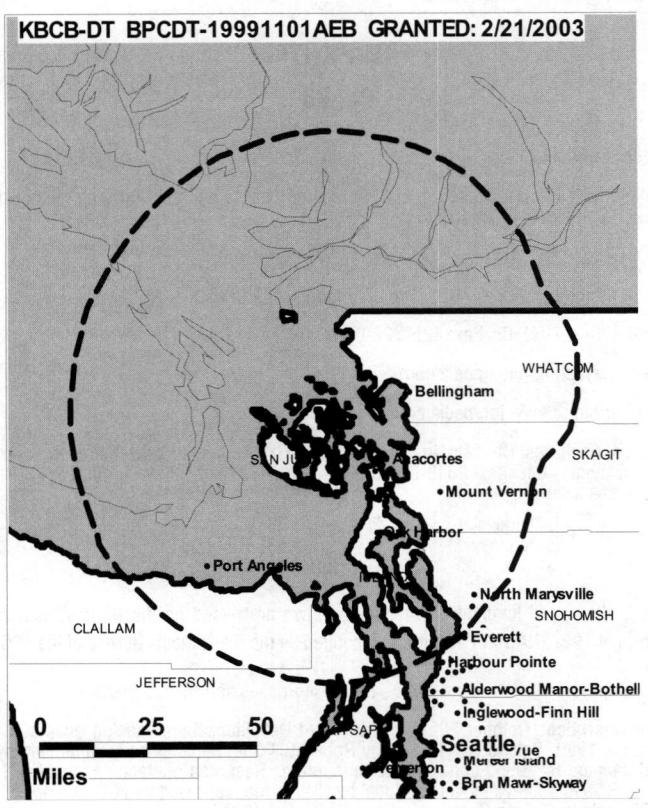

KBCB-DT BPCDT-19991101AEB GRANTED: 2/21/2003

© 2010 Warren Communications News

Nielsen Data: Not available.

KVOS-DT
Ch. 35

Network Service: IND.

Grantee: Newport Television LLC, 50 Kennedy Plz, 18th Fl, Providence, RI 02903.

Studio: 1151 Ellis St., Bellingham, WA 98225.

Mailing Address: 1151 Ellis St, Bellingham, WA 98225.

Phone: 360-671-1212. **Fax:** 360-647-0824.

Web Site: http://www.kvos.com

Technical Facilities: Channel No. 35 (596-602 MHz). Authorized power: 580-kw max. visual, aural. Antenna: 2621-ft above av. terrain, 468-ft. above ground, 2738-ft. above sea level.

Latitude	48°	40'	50"
Longitude	122°	50'	22"

Note: Latitude and longitude coordinates shown are based on the North American Datum of 1927 (NAD 27) as currently required by the Mass Media Bureau of the FCC.

Satellite Earth Stations: Transmitter NEC; Microdyne, 7-meter; Harris, 7-meter; Microdyne receivers.

Ownership: Newport Television LLC (Group Owner).

Began Operation: February 1, 2003. Standard Definition. Began analog operations: May 23, 1953. Sale to LK Station Group LLC (Barbara Laurence, et al.) by Newport Television Inc. approved by FCC February 27, 2008, but never consummated. Sale to present owner by Clear Channel Communications Inc. approved by FCC November 29, 2007. In stock swap, Clear Channel Broadcasting Inc. acquired The Ackerley Group. FCC approved deal May 29, 2002. Sale to The Ackerley Group approved by FCC June 5, 1985. Sale to Wometco Enterprises Inc. by Rogan Jones & associates approved by FCC March 29, 1961. Ceased analog operations: February 17, 2009.

Represented (legal): Covington & Burling.

Personnel:

David P. Reid, President & General Manager.

T. J. Hunt, Local Sales Manager.

Sabrina Hlebichuk, National Sales Manager.

Jim Ross, Sales Manager.

Joe Bates, News Coordinator.

John Franz, Chief Engineer.

Joan McCauley, Controller.

Ian Grant, Research & Development Director.

Joyce Lorenz, Traffic Manager.

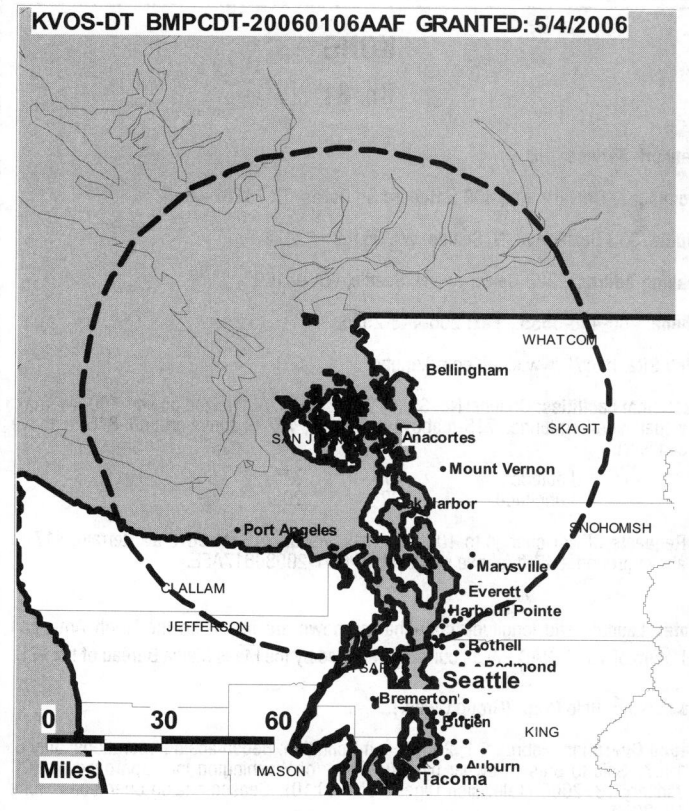

KVOS-DT BMPCDT-20060106AAF GRANTED: 5/4/2006

© 2010 Warren Communications News

City of License: Bellingham. **Station DMA:** Seattle-Tacoma, WA. **Rank:** 13.

Circulation © 2009 Nielsen. Coverage based on Nielsen study.

GrandTotal	Cable TV Households	Non-cable TV Households	Total TV Households
Estimated Station Totals *	296,290	127,170	423,460
Average Weekly Circulation (2009)	39,917	13,437	53,354
Average Daily Circulation (2009)			17,225

Station DMA Total	Cable TV Households	Non-cable TV Households	Total TV Households
Estimated Station Totals *	296,290	127,170	423,460
Average Weekly Circulation (2009)	39,917	13,437	53,354
Average Daily Circulation (2009)			17,225

*Estimated station totals are sums of the Nielsen TV and Cable TV household estimates for each county in which the station registers viewing of more than 5% as per the Nielsen Survey Methods.

KONG
Ch. 31

Network Service: IND.

Licensee: KONG-TV Inc., 400 S Record St, Dallas, TX 75202-4806.

Studio: 333 Dexter Ave. N, Seattle, WA 98109.

Mailing Address: 333 Dexter Ave N, Seattle, WA 98109.

Phone: 206-448-5555. **Fax:** 206-448-2525.

Web Site: http://www.king5.com/kongtv

Technical Facilities: Channel No. 31 (572-578 MHz). Authorized power: 700-kw max. visual, aural. Antenna: 715-ft above av. terrain, 417-ft. above ground, 846-ft. above sea level.

Latitude	47°	37'	55"
Longitude	122°	20'	59"

Requests CP for change to 1000-kw max. visual, 715-ft above av. terrain, 417-ft. above ground, 847-ft. above sea level; BPCDT-20080617AEE.

Note: Latitude and longitude coordinates shown are based on the North American Datum of 1927 (NAD 27) as currently required by the Mass Media Bureau of the FCC.

Ownership: Belo Corp. (Group Owner).

Began Operation: February 1, 2002. High Definition. Began analog operations: July 8, 1997. Sale to present owner by Zeus Corp. of Washington Inc. approved by FCC January 18, 2000 (Television Digest, Vol. 40:10). Ceased analog operations: June 12, 2009.

Personnel:

Ray Heacox, President & General Manager.

Luke Hublou, Local Sales Manager.

Mitch Boyle, National Sales Manager.

Mark Ginther, News Director.

Kathy Palmer, Chief Engineer.

Sheldon Lee, Business Manager.

Erin Twelker, Traffic Manager.

City of License: Everett. **Station DMA:** Seattle-Tacoma, WA. **Rank:** 13.

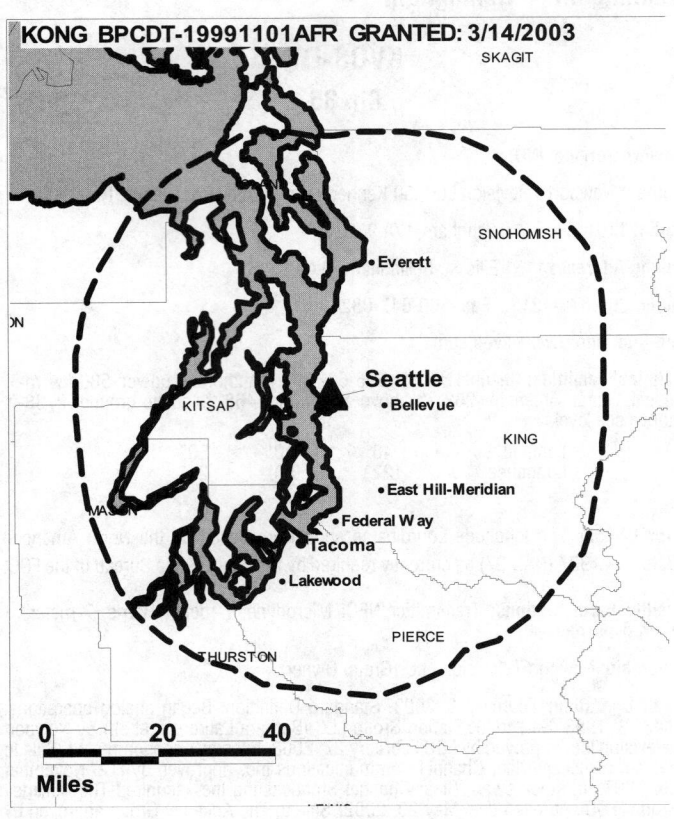

KONG BPCDT-19991101AFR GRANTED: 3/14/2003

© 2010 Warren Communications News

Circulation © 2009 Nielsen. Coverage based on Nielsen study.

GrandTotal	Cable TV Households	Non-cable TV Households	Total TV Households
Estimated Station Totals *	1,251,870	491,370	1,743,240
Average Weekly Circulation (2009)	515,025	165,968	680,993
Average Daily Circulation (2009)			217,711

Station DMA Total	Cable TV Households	Non-cable TV Households	Total TV Households
Estimated Station Totals *	1,251,870	491,370	1,743,240
Average Weekly Circulation (2009)	515,025	165,968	680,993
Average Daily Circulation (2009)			217,711

*Estimated station totals are sums of the Nielsen TV and Cable TV household estimates for each county in which the station registers viewing of more than 5% as per the Nielsen Survey Methods.

KVEW-DT
Ch. 44

Network Service: MNT, ABC.

Grantee: Apple Valley Broadcasting Inc., 1610 S 24th Ave, Yakima, WA 98902-5719.

Studio: 601 N. Edison, Kennewick, WA 99336.

Mailing Address: 601 N. Edison, Yakima, WA 99336.

Phone: 509-735-8369. **Fax:** 509-735-7889.

E-mail: mikeb@kvewtv.com

Web Site: http://www.kvewtv.com

Technical Facilities: Channel No. 44 (650-656 MHz). Authorized power: 160-kw max. visual, aural. Antenna: 1325-ft above av. terrain, 243-ft. above ground, 2372-ft. above sea level.

Latitude	46°	06'	12"
Longitude	119°	07'	57"

Note: Latitude and longitude coordinates shown are based on the North American Datum of 1927 (NAD 27) as currently required by the Mass Media Bureau of the FCC.

Satellite Earth Station: Transmitter NEC; M/A-Com, 5-meter; M/A-Com, Avantek receivers.

Ownership: Morgan Murphy Media (Group Owner).

Began Operation: May 1, 2002. Began analog operations: October 29, 1970. Ceased analog operations: February 17, 2009.

Represented (legal): Rini Coran PC.

Personnel:

Elizabeth Murphy Burns, President.

Darrell Blue, Vice President, Government Affairs & Community Relations.

Brian Paul, General Manager.

Lynn Kinuko Nishimoto, Sales Director.

Shane Pierone, Local Sales Manager.

Neil Bennett, Chief Engineer.

Bob Cole, Business Manager.

Nancy Guin, Promotion & Traffic Manager.

John Wilkerson, Production Manager.

Mike Balmelli, News Director.

Cheryl Senpel, Program & Human Resources Director.

City of License: Kennewick. **Station DMA:** Yakima-Pasco-Richland-Kennewick, WA.

Rank: 126.

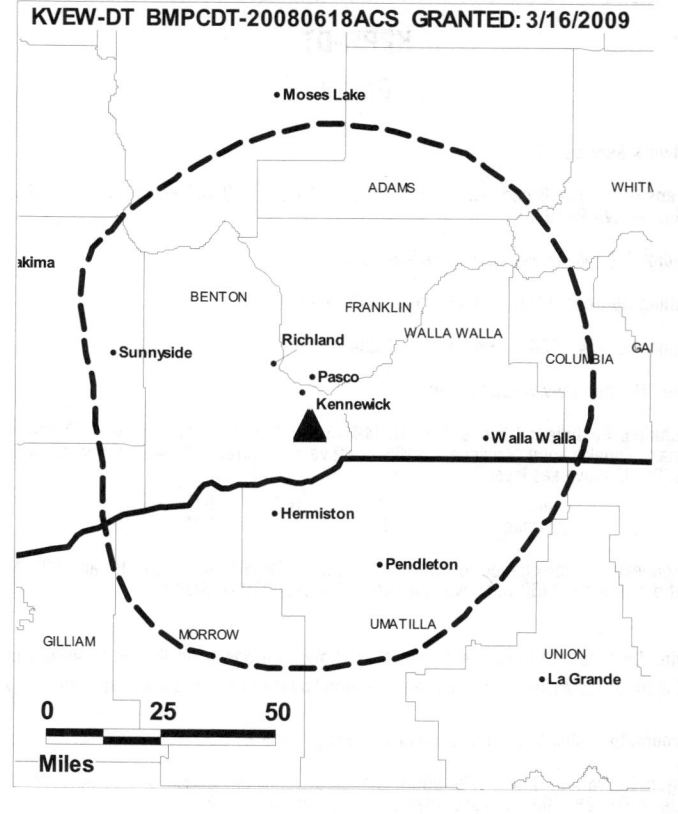

KVEW-DT BMPCDT-20080618ACS GRANTED: 3/16/2009

© 2010 Warren Communications News

Circulation © 2009 Nielsen. Coverage based on Nielsen study.

GrandTotal	Cable TV Households	Non-cable TV Households	Total TV Households
Estimated Station Totals *	57,870	127,890	185,760
Average Weekly Circulation (2009)	32,019	37,134	69,153
Average Daily Circulation (2009)			25,220

Station DMA Total	Cable TV Households	Non-cable TV Households	Total TV Households
Estimated Station Totals *	56,470	127,890	184,360
Average Weekly Circulation (2009)	31,941	37,134	69,075
Average Daily Circulation (2009)			25,217

Other DMA Total	Cable TV Households	Non-cable TV Households	Total TV Households
Estimated Station Totals *	1,400	0	1,400
Average Weekly Circulation (2009)	78	0	78
Average Daily Circulation (2009)			3

*Estimated station totals are sums of the Nielsen TV and Cable TV household estimates for each county in which the station registers viewing of more than 5% as per the Nielsen Survey Methods.

KEPR-DT
Ch. 18

Network Service: CBS.

Licensee: Fisher Broadcasting-Washington TV LLC, 600 University St, Ste 1525, Seattle, WA 98101.

Studio: 2807 W. Lewis St., Pasco, WA 99301.

Mailing Address: PO Box 2648, Pasco, WA 99302-2648.

Phone: 509-547-0547. **Fax:** 540-547-2845.

Web Site: http://www.keprtv.com

Technical Facilities: Channel No. 18 (494-500 MHz). Authorized power: 32.43-kw max. visual, aural. Antenna: 1166-ft above av. terrain, 290-ft. above ground, 2325-ft. above sea level.

Latitude	46°	05'	51"
Longitude	119°	11'	29"

Requests CP for change to 83-kw max. visual, 1204-ft above av. terrain, 331-ft. above ground, 2366-ft. above sea level; BPCDT-20080617ADA.

Note: Latitude and longitude coordinates shown are based on the North American Datum of 1927 (NAD 27) as currently required by the Mass Media Bureau of the FCC.

Ownership: Fisher Communications Inc. (Group Owner).

Began Operation: March 27, 2002. Standard Definition. Began analog operations: December 28, 1954. Ceased analog operations: June 12, 2009.

Represented (engineering): Hammett & Edison Inc.

Represented (legal): Pillsbury Winthrop Shaw Pittman LLP.

Represented (sales): Katz Media Group.

Personnel:

Ken Messer, Vice President & General Manager.

David Praga, Station & Local Sales Manager.

Cris Headley, Operations & Traffic Manager.

Steve Crow, General Sales Manager.

Robin Wojtanik, News Director.

John Housholder, Chief Engineer.

City of License: Pasco. **Station DMA:** Yakima-Pasco-Richland-Kennewick, WA.

Rank: 126.

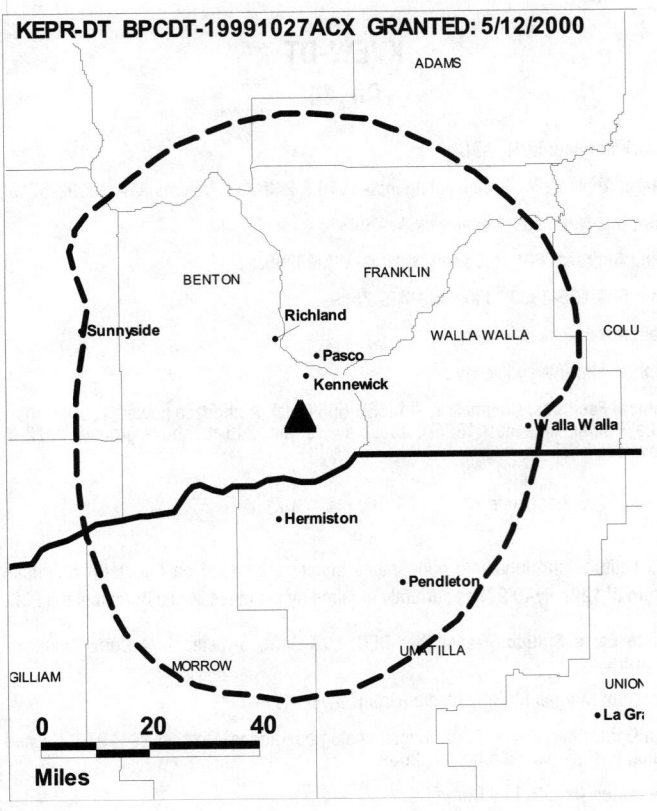

KEPR-DT BPCDT-19991027ACX GRANTED: 5/12/2000

© 2010 Warren Communications News

Circulation © 2009 Nielsen. Coverage based on Nielsen study.

GrandTotal	Cable TV Households	Non-cable TV Households	Total TV Households
Estimated Station Totals *	57,870	118,990	176,860
Average Weekly Circulation (2009)	34,217	24,091	58,308
Average Daily Circulation (2009)			24,449

Station DMA Total	Cable TV Households	Non-cable TV Households	Total TV Households
Estimated Station Totals *	56,470	118,990	175,460
Average Weekly Circulation (2009)	34,139	24,091	58,230
Average Daily Circulation (2009)			24,434

Other DMA Total	Cable TV Households	Non-cable TV Households	Total TV Households
Estimated Station Totals *	1,400	0	1,400
Average Weekly Circulation (2009)	78	0	78
Average Daily Circulation (2009)			15

*Estimated station totals are sums of the Nielsen TV and Cable TV household estimates for each county in which the station registers viewing of more than 5% as per the Nielsen Survey Methods.

KNDU-DT
Ch. 26

Network Service: NBC.

Grantee: KHQ Inc., PO Box 8088, 4202 S Regal St, Spokane, WA 99203-8088.

Studio: 3312 W. Kennewick Ave., Kennewick, WA 99336.

Mailing Address: 3312 W. Kennewick Ave, Kennewick, WA 99336.

Phone: 509-737-6700. **Fax:** 509-737-6767.

Web Site: http://www.kndu.com

Technical Facilities: Channel No. 26 (542-548 MHz). Authorized power: 150-kw max. visual, aural. Antenna: 1319-ft above av. terrain, 190-ft. above ground, 2352-ft. above sea level.

Latitude	46°	06'	12"
Longitude	119°	07'	49"

Note: Latitude and longitude coordinates shown are based on the North American Datum of 1927 (NAD 27) as currently required by the Mass Media Bureau of the FCC.

Ownership: Cowles Co. (Group Owner).

Began Operation: August 1, 2008. Station operating under Special Temporary Authority at 33-kw max. visual. Began analog operations: October 10, 1961. Ceased analog operations: February 17, 2009.

Represented (sales): Blair Television.

Personnel:

Paul Dughi, General Manager.

Larry Forsgren, General Sales Manager.

Sherry Bissell, National Sales Manager.

Christine Brown, News Director.

Bill Lynner, Chief Engineer.

Susan Martinez, Program & Traffic Manager.

Scott Morgan, Promotion Manager.

Jim Tippett, Production Manager.

City of License: Richland. **Station DMA:** Yakima-Pasco-Richland-Kennewick, WA.

Rank: 126.

TELEVISION & CABLE
Factbook Online

| continuous updates | fully searchable | easy to use |

For more information call **800-771-9202** or visit **www.warren-news.com**

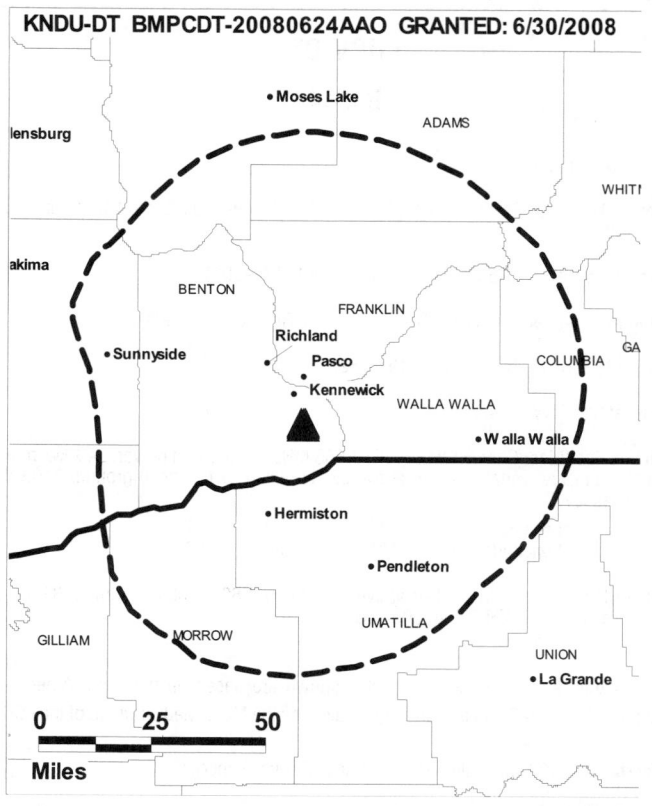

KNDU-DT BMPCDT-20080624AAO GRANTED: 6/30/2008

© 2010 Warren Communications News

Circulation © 2009 Nielsen. Coverage based on Nielsen study.

GrandTotal	Cable TV Households	Non-cable TV Households	Total TV Households
Estimated Station Totals *	57,870	127,890	185,760
Average Weekly Circulation (2009)	37,177	53,333	90,510
Average Daily Circulation (2009)			40,881

Station DMA Total	Cable TV Households	Non-cable TV Households	Total TV Households
Estimated Station Totals *	56,470	127,890	184,360
Average Weekly Circulation (2009)	37,099	53,333	90,432
Average Daily Circulation (2009)			40,860

Other DMA Total	Cable TV Households	Non-cable TV Households	Total TV Households
Estimated Station Totals *	1,400	0	1,400
Average Weekly Circulation (2009)	78	0	78
Average Daily Circulation (2009)			21

*Estimated station totals are sums of the Nielsen TV and Cable TV household estimates for each county in which the station registers viewing of more than 5% as per the Nielsen Survey Methods.

KHCV-DT
Ch. 44

Network Service: IND.

Licensee: North Pacific International TV Inc., 9825 Willows Rd NE, Ste 140, Redmond, WA 98052.

Studio: 9825 Willows Rd NE, Ste 140, Redmond, WA 98052.

Mailing Address: 9825 Willows Rd NE, Ste 140, Redmond, WA 98052.

Phone: 425-497-1515. **Fax:** 425-497-8629.

Web Site: http://www.tv45.tv

Technical Facilities: Channel No. 44 (650-656 MHz). Authorized power: 240-kw max. visual, aural. Antenna: 2342-ft above av. terrain, 259-ft. above ground, 3103-ft. above sea level.

Latitude	47°	30'	17"
Longitude	121°	58'	06"

Holds CP for change to 2329-ft above av. terrain, 262-ft. above ground, 3100-ft. above sea level; BPCDT-20080609AAG.

Note: Latitude and longitude coordinates shown are based on the North American Datum of 1927 (NAD 27) as currently required by the Mass Media Bureau of the FCC.

Ownership: North Pacific International TV Inc. (Group Owner).

Began Operation: January 25, 2008. Began analog operations: January 1, 1999. Ceased analog operations: February 17, 2009.

Represented (legal): Hatfield & Dawson.

Represented (engineering): Irwin, Campbell & Tannenwald PC.

Personnel:

Kenneth Casey, President.

Charlene Casey, Station Manager Chief Financial Officer.

Tony Austin, Chief Engineer.

Charlene Weh, Program & Development Director.

City of License: Seattle. **Station DMA:** Seattle-Tacoma, WA. **Rank:** 13.

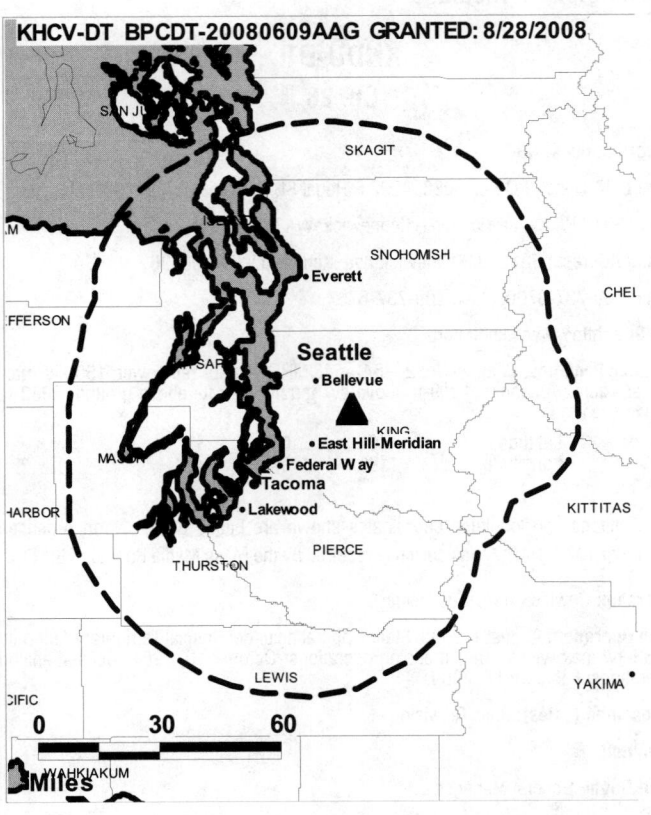

KHCV-DT BPCDT-20080609AAG GRANTED: 8/28/2008

© 2010 Warren Communications News

Circulation © 2009 Nielsen. Coverage based on Nielsen study.

GrandTotal	Cable TV Households	Non-cable TV Households	Total TV Households
Estimated Station Totals *	0	16,430	16,430
Average Weekly Circulation (2009)	0	1,429	1,429
Average Daily Circulation (2009)			148

Station DMA Total	Cable TV Households	Non-cable TV Households	Total TV Households
Estimated Station Totals *	0	16,430	16,430
Average Weekly Circulation (2009)	0	1,429	1,429
Average Daily Circulation (2009)			148

*Estimated station totals are sums of the Nielsen TV and Cable TV household estimates for each county in which the station registers viewing of more than 5% as per the Nielsen Survey Methods.

KING-DT
Ch. 48

Network Service: NBC.

Licensee: King Broadcasting Co., 400 S Record St, Dallas, TX 75202-4806.

Studio: 333 Dexter Ave. N, Seattle, WA 98109.

Mailing Address: 333 Dexter Ave N, Seattle, WA 98109.

Phone: 206-448-5555; 206-448-4521. **Fax:** 206-448-3195.

Web Site: http://www.king5.com

Technical Facilities: Channel No. 48 (674-680 MHz). Authorized power: 960-kw max. visual, aural. Antenna: 784-ft above av. terrain, 485-ft. above ground, 915-ft. above sea level.

Latitude	47°	37'	55"
Longitude	122°	20'	59"

Holds CP for change to 1000-kw max. visual, 843-ft above av. terrain, 545-ft. above ground, 975-ft. above sea level; BPCDT-20080617AED.

Transmitter: Queen Anne Hill, 301 Galer St.

Note: Latitude and longitude coordinates shown are based on the North American Datum of 1927 (NAD 27) as currently required by the Mass Media Bureau of the FCC.

Ownership: Belo Corp. (Group Owner).

Began Operation: October 1, 1998. High Definition. Began analog operations: November 25, 1948 as KRSC-TV. Sale to King Broadcasting Co. approved by FCC August 1949 (Television Digest, Vol. 5:20, 23, 30). Sale to Providence Journal approved by FCC August 27, 1991 (Vol. 30:35; 31:9, 29). Sale to present owner by Providence Journal approved by FCC February 28, 1997 (Vol. 36:40; 37:9). Ceased analog operations: June 12, 2009.

Represented (sales): TeleRep Inc.

Represented (legal): Wiley Rein LLP.

Represented (engineering): Smith & Fisher.

Personnel:

Ray Heacox, President & General Manager.

Luke Hublou, Local Sales Manager.

Mitch Boyle, National Sales Manager.

Mark Ginther, News Director.

Kathy Palmer, Engineering Director.

Sheldon Lee, Business Manager.

Erin Twelker, Traffic Manager.

City of License: Seattle. **Station DMA:** Seattle-Tacoma, WA. **Rank:** 13.

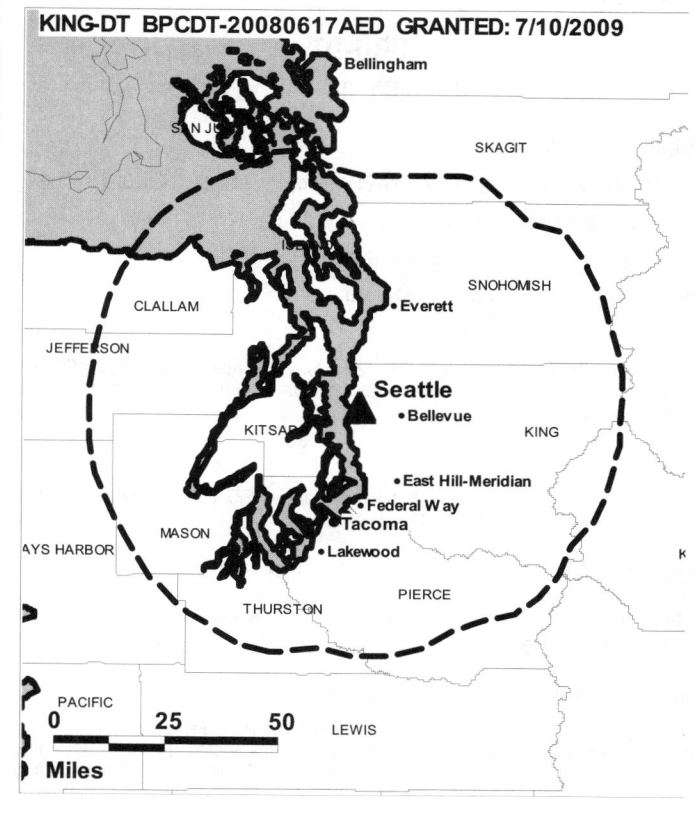

KING-DT BPCDT-20080617AED GRANTED: 7/10/2009

© 2010 Warren Communications News

Circulation © 2009 Nielsen. Coverage based on Nielsen study.

GrandTotal	Cable TV Households	Non-cable TV Households	Total TV Households
Estimated Station Totals *	1,295,570	501,640	1,797,210
Average Weekly Circulation (2009)	907,380	352,465	1,259,845
Average Daily Circulation (2009)			639,260

Station DMA Total	Cable TV Households	Non-cable TV Households	Total TV Households
Estimated Station Totals *	1,251,870	491,370	1,743,240
Average Weekly Circulation (2009)	896,070	351,541	1,247,611
Average Daily Circulation (2009)			635,743

Other DMA Total	Cable TV Households	Non-cable TV Households	Total TV Households
Estimated Station Totals *	43,700	10,270	53,970
Average Weekly Circulation (2009)	11,310	924	12,234
Average Daily Circulation (2009)			3,517

*Estimated station totals are sums of the Nielsen TV and Cable TV household estimates for each county in which the station registers viewing of more than 5% as per the Nielsen Survey Methods.

KIRO-DT
Ch. 39

Network Service: IND, CBS.

Licensee: KIRO-TV Inc., 6205 Peachtree Dunwoody Rd, Atlanta, GA 30328.

Studio: 2807 3rd Ave., Seattle, WA 98121.

Mailing Address: 2807 3rd Ave, Seattle, WA 98121.

Phone: 206-728-7777. **Fax:** 206-441-8230.

Web Site: http://www.kirotv.com

Technical Facilities: Channel No. 39 (320-626 MHz). Authorized power: 1000-kw max. visual, aural. Antenna: 755-ft above av. terrain, 489-ft. above ground, 889-ft. above sea level.

Latitude	47°	38'	01"
Longitude	122°	21'	20"

Requests CP for change to 843-ft above av. terrain, 577-ft. above ground, 977-ft. above sea level; BPCDT-20080619AAP.

Transmitter: SE Corner of Queen Anne Ave. & W. Garfield St.

Note: Latitude and longitude coordinates shown are based on the North American Datum of 1927 (NAD 27) as currently required by the Mass Media Bureau of the FCC.

Ownership: Cox Enterprises Inc. (Group Owner).

Began Operation: April 1, 1999. Began analog operations: February 8, 1958. Sale to Bonneville International by Saul Haas & associates approved by FCC December 17, 1963. Sale to A. H. Belo Corp. approved by FCC January 27, 1995. Sale to present owner from A. H. Belo Corp. approved by FCC April 16, 1997. Ceased analog operations: June 12, 2009.

Represented (legal): Dow Lohnes PLLC.

Represented (engineering): Hammett & Edison Inc.

Personnel:

Eric Lerner, Vice President & General Manager.

Michael Poth, Sales Operations Director.

Sandy Zogg, General Sales Manager.

Holly Grambihler, Local Sales Manager.

David Blakely, National Sales Manager.

Todd Mokhtari, News Director.

John Walters, Engineering & Technical Operations Director.

Pat Otis, Chief Engineer.

Heidi Copes, Controller.

Therese Wieler, Program Director.

Scott Gee, Creative Services Director.

Janeen Gutierrez, Operations & Traffic Director.

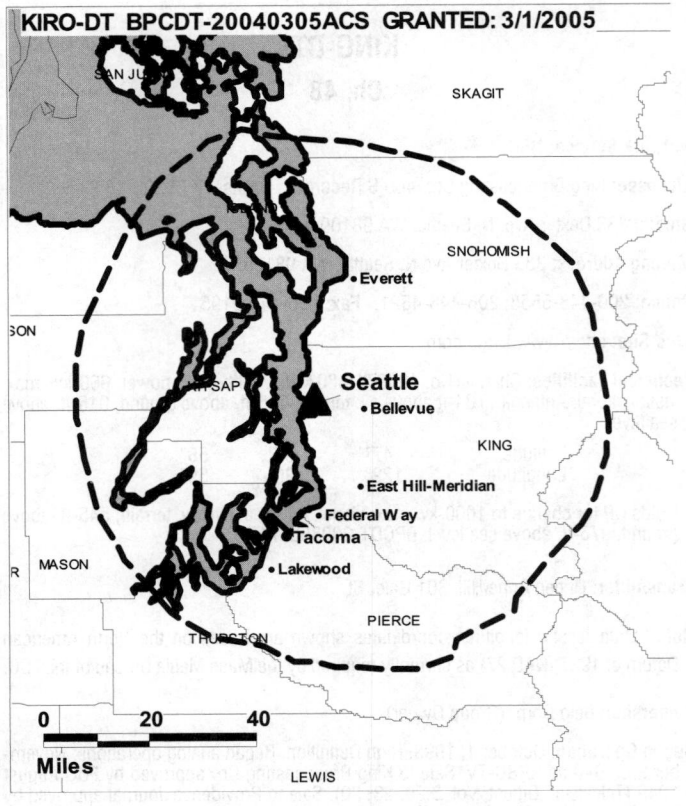

KIRO-DT BPCDT-20040305ACS GRANTED: 3/1/2005

© 2010 Warren Communications News

City of License: Seattle. **Station DMA:** Seattle-Tacoma, WA. **Rank:** 13.

Circulation © 2009 Nielsen. Coverage based on Nielsen study.

GrandTotal	Cable TV Households	Non-cable TV Households	Total TV Households
Estimated Station Totals *	1,267,840	500,270	1,768,110
Average Weekly Circulation (2009)	814,989	309,893	1,124,882
Average Daily Circulation (2009)			502,460

Station DMA Total	Cable TV Households	Non-cable TV Households	Total TV Households
Estimated Station Totals *	1,251,870	491,370	1,743,240
Average Weekly Circulation (2009)	812,391	309,377	1,121,768
Average Daily Circulation (2009)			501,770

Other DMA Total	Cable TV Households	Non-cable TV Households	Total TV Households
Estimated Station Totals *	15,970	8,900	24,870
Average Weekly Circulation (2009)	2,598	516	3,114
Average Daily Circulation (2009)			690

*Estimated station totals are sums of the Nielsen TV and Cable TV household estimates for each county in which the station registers viewing of more than 5% as per the Nielsen Survey Methods.

KMYQ-DT
Ch. 25

Network Service: MNT.

Grantee: Tribune Television Holdings Inc., Debtor-In-Possession, 1813 Westlake Ave N, Seattle, WA 98109-2706.

Studio: 1813 Westlake Ave. N, Seattle, WA 98109.

Mailing Address: 1813 Westlake Ave. N, Seattle, WA 98109-2706.

Phone: 206-674-1313. **Fax:** 206-674-1777.

Web Site: http://myq2.trb.com

Technical Facilities: Channel No. 25 (536-542 MHz). Authorized power: 1000-kw max. visual, aural. Antenna: 951-ft above av. terrain, 659-ft. above ground, 1070-ft. above sea level.

Latitude	47°	36'	57"
Longitude	122°	18'	26"

Note: Latitude and longitude coordinates shown are based on the North American Datum of 1927 (NAD 27) as currently required by the Mass Media Bureau of the FCC.

Ownership: Tribune Broadcasting Co., Debtor-In-Possession (Group Owner).

Began Operation: January 18, 2002. Began analog operations: June 22, 1985. Sale to Dudley Communications Corp. by United States Television Seattle Ltd. Partnership approved by FCC September 29, 1988. Sale to Emmis Broadcasting Corp. by Dudley Communications Corp. approved by FCC March 20, 1998. Emmis subsequently swapped station, along with WXMI Grand Rapids, for Tribune Broadcasting's WQCD (FM), New York. Swap approved by FCC March 20, 1998. Station was first put in hands of John D. Dudley, trustee, but because of ownership rule changes, FCC approved Tribune control January 18, 2000. Transfer of control from public shareholders of the Tribune Co. to Tribune Employee Stock Ownership Plan approved by FCC November 30, 2007. Involuntary assignment to debtor-in-possession status approved by FCC December 24, 2008. Ceased analog operations: June 12, 2009.

Represented (legal): Sidley Austin LLP.

Represented (sales): TeleRep Inc.

Personnel:

Pamela Pearson, Vice President & General Manager.

Paul Rennie, General & National Sales Manager.

Michael Goodman, Engineering Director.

Sharon Silverman, Business Manager.

Natalie Grant, Program Manager.

Jule Ferkingstad, Program Coordinator.

Jamie McDowell, Creative Services Manager.

Wendy Anderson, Traffic Manager.

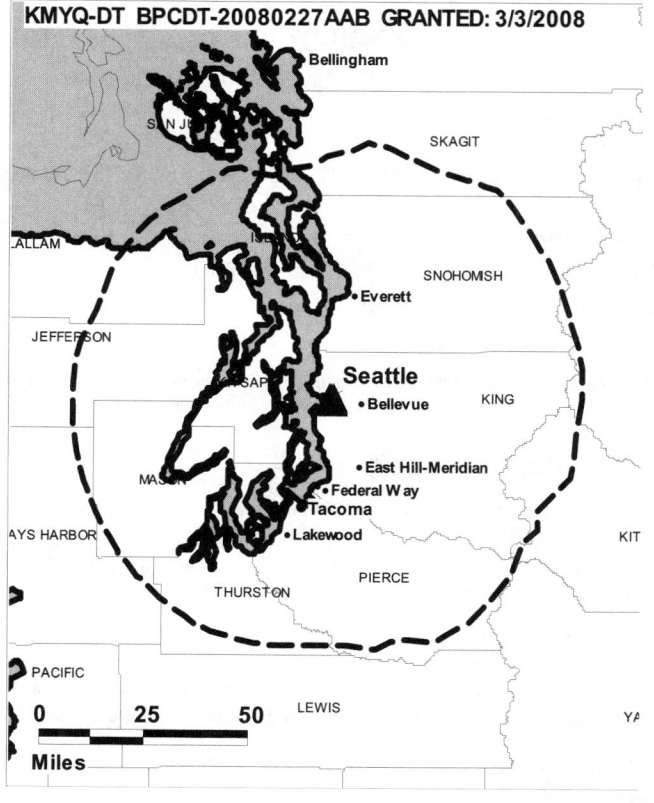

KMYQ-DT BPCDT-20080227AAB GRANTED: 3/3/2008

© 2010 Warren Communications News

City of License: Seattle. **Station DMA:** Seattle-Tacoma, WA. **Rank:** 13.

Circulation © 2009 Nielsen. Coverage based on Nielsen study.

GrandTotal	Cable TV Households	Non-cable TV Households	Total TV Households
Estimated Station Totals *	1,251,870	491,370	1,743,240
Average Weekly Circulation (2009)	373,742	148,183	521,925
Average Daily Circulation (2009)			140,727

Station DMA Total	Cable TV Households	Non-cable TV Households	Total TV Households
Estimated Station Totals *	1,251,870	491,370	1,743,240
Average Weekly Circulation (2009)	373,742	148,183	521,925
Average Daily Circulation (2009)			140,727

*Estimated station totals are sums of the Nielsen TV and Cable TV household estimates for each county in which the station registers viewing of more than 5% as per the Nielsen Survey Methods.

KOMO-DT
Ch. 38

Network Service: ABC.

Licensee: Fisher Broadcasting-Seattle TV LLC, 600 University St, Ste 1525, Seattle, WA 98101.

Studio: 140 4th Ave. N, Seattle, WA 98109.

Mailing Address: 100 4th Ave N, Ste 510, Seattle, WA 98109.

Phone: 206-404-4000. **Fax:** 206-404-4422.

Web Site: http://www.komotv.com

Technical Facilities: Channel No. 38 (614-620 MHz). Authorized power: 810-kw max. visual, aural. Antenna: 1000-ft above av. terrain, 551-ft. above ground, 449-ft. above sea level.

| Latitude | 42° | 37' | 55" |
| Longitude | 121° | 21' | 09" |

Holds CP for change to 880-kw visual, 850-ft above av. terrain, 535-ft. above ground, 984-ft. above sea level; BPCDT-20090527AAF.

Requests CP for change to 1000-kw max. visual, 850-ft above av. terrain, 535-ft. above ground, 985-ft. above sea level; BPCDT-20080620AHD.

Transmitter: 157 Galer St.

Note: Latitude and longitude coordinates shown are based on the North American Datum of 1927 (NAD 27) as currently required by the Mass Media Bureau of the FCC.

Multichannel TV Sound: Stereo and separate audio program.

Ownership: Fisher Communications Inc. (Group Owner).

Began Operation: January 1, 1997. Began analog operations: December 10, 1953. Sale of 1/3 to Fisher's Blend Station (making it 100% owner) by Theodore Gamble & C. Howard Lane consummated in April 1959. Ceased analog operations: June 12, 2009.

Represented (sales): Katz Media Group.

Represented (legal): Pillsbury Winthrop Shaw Pittman LLP.

Represented (engineering): du Treil, Lundin & Rackley Inc.

Personnel:

James Clayton, Vice President & General Manager.

Janene Drafs, General Sales Manager.

Patty Dean, Local Sales Manager.

Jaquinci Brackett, Local Sales Manager.

Holly Gauntt, News Director.

Mark Simonson, Chief Engineer.

Dennis Hanson, Production Director.

Scott Altus, Creative Services Director.

Caren Redd, Traffic Manager.

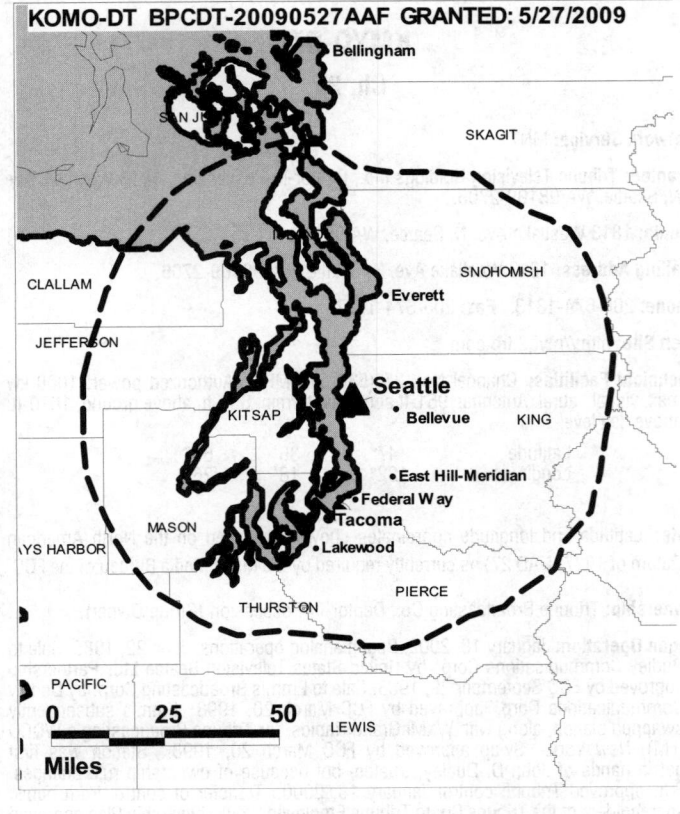

KOMO-DT BPCDT-20090527AAF GRANTED: 5/27/2009

© 2010 Warren Communications News

City of License: Seattle. **Station DMA:** Seattle-Tacoma, WA. **Rank:** 13.

Circulation © 2009 Nielsen. Coverage based on Nielsen study.

GrandTotal	Cable TV Households	Non-cable TV Households	Total TV Households
Estimated Station Totals *	1,274,820	500,270	1,775,090
Average Weekly Circulation (2009)	857,427	318,855	1,176,282
Average Daily Circulation (2009)			554,165

Station DMA Total	Cable TV Households	Non-cable TV Households	Total TV Households
Estimated Station Totals *	1,251,870	491,370	1,743,240
Average Weekly Circulation (2009)	853,737	318,348	1,172,085
Average Daily Circulation (2009)			552,812

Other DMA Total	Cable TV Households	Non-cable TV Households	Total TV Households
Estimated Station Totals *	22,950	8,900	31,850
Average Weekly Circulation (2009)	3,690	507	4,197
Average Daily Circulation (2009)			1,353

*Estimated station totals are sums of the Nielsen TV and Cable TV household estimates for each county in which the station registers viewing of more than 5% as per the Nielsen Survey Methods.

KAYU-DT
Ch. 28

Network Service: FOX.

Licensee: Mountain Licenses LP, 2111 University Park Dr, Ste 650, Okemos, MI 48864-6913.

Studio: 4600 S Regal St, Spokane, WA 99223.

Mailing Address: 4600 S Regal St, Spokane, WA 99223.

Phone: 509-448-2828. **Fax:** 509-448-3815.

Web Site: http://www.kayutv.com

Technical Facilities: Channel No. 28 (554-560 MHz). Authorized power: 91.4-kw max. visual, aural. Antenna: 1972-ft above av. terrain, 795-ft. above ground, 4371-ft. above sea level.

Latitude	47°	34'	44"
Longitude	117°	17'	46"

Requests modification of CP for change to 445-kw max. visual; BMPCDT-20080617ADY.

Note: Latitude and longitude coordinates shown are based on the North American Datum of 1927 (NAD 27) as currently required by the Mass Media Bureau of the FCC.

Ownership: Mountain Licenses LP (Group Owner).

Began Operation: September 7, 2005. Station broadcasting digitally on its analog channel allotment. Began analog operations: October 31, 1982. Sale to Bingham Communications by Robert J. Hamacher, et al., approved by FCC January 29, 1988 but never consummated. Sale to present owner approved by FCC October 19, 1995. Transfer of control by Mountain Licenses LP from Brian W. Brady to Alta Subordinated Debt Partners III LP approved by FCC April 17, 1996. Transfer of control by Mountain Licenses LP from Alta Subordinated Debt Partners III LP to Brian W. Brady approved by FCC September 19, 2007. Ceased analog operations: February 16, 2009.

Represented (legal): Leventhal, Senter & Lerman PLLC.

Represented (sales): Katz Media Group.

Personnel:

Jon Rand, General Manager.

Tom Holcomb, Local Sales Manager.

Jonathan Mitchell, News Director.

Ron Sweatte, Chief Engineer.

Tom Manning, Assistant Engineer.

Rick Andrycha, Program Director.

Kim Rogge, Promotion Director.

Robin Lenell, Traffic Manager.

Cassandra Jones, Community Affairs.

City of License: Spokane. **Station DMA:** Spokane, WA. **Rank:** 75.

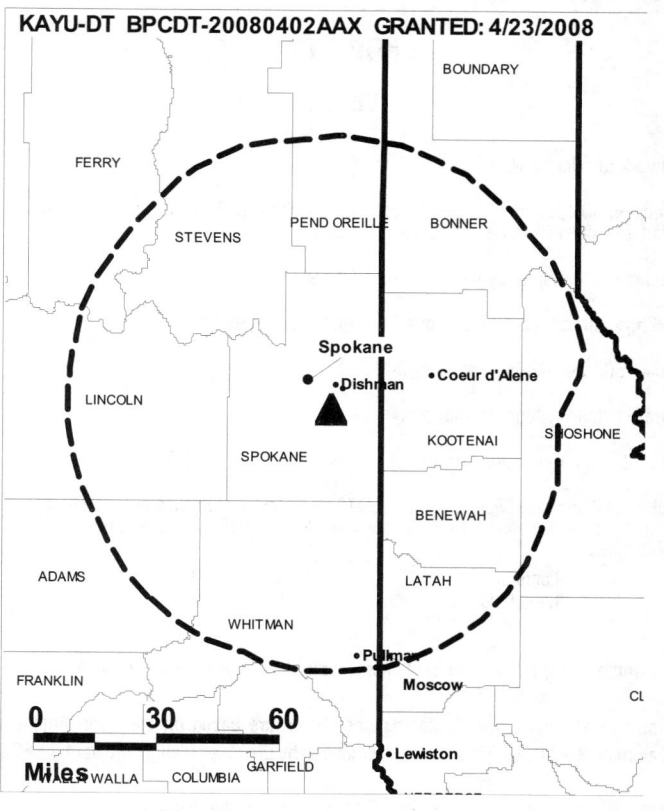

KAYU-DT BPCDT-20080402AAX GRANTED: 4/23/2008

© 2010 Warren Communications News

Circulation © 2009 Nielsen. Coverage based on Nielsen study.

GrandTotal	Cable TV Households	Non-cable TV Households	Total TV Households
Estimated Station Totals *	167,680	231,180	398,860
Average Weekly Circulation (2009)	92,574	100,677	193,251
Average Daily Circulation (2009)			64,607

Station DMA Total	Cable TV Households	Non-cable TV Households	Total TV Households
Estimated Station Totals *	167,680	212,440	380,120
Average Weekly Circulation (2009)	92,574	99,553	192,127
Average Daily Circulation (2009)			64,438

Other DMA Total	Cable TV Households	Non-cable TV Households	Total TV Households
Estimated Station Totals *	0	18,740	18,740
Average Weekly Circulation (2009)	0	1,124	1,124
Average Daily Circulation (2009)			169

*Estimated station totals are sums of the Nielsen TV and Cable TV household estimates for each county in which the station registers viewing of more than 5% as per the Nielsen Survey Methods.

KGPX-TV

Ch. 34

Network Service: ION.

Licensee: ION Media Spokane License Inc., Debtor in Possession, 601 Clearwater Park Rd, West Palm Beach, FL 33401-6233.

Studio: 1201 W Sprague Ave, Spokane, WA 99201.

Mailing Address: 1201 W Sprague Ave, Spokane, WA 99201.

Phone: 509-340-3405. **Fax:** 509-340-3417.

E-mail: mitchwasson@ionmedia.com

Web Site: http://www.ionmedia.com

Technical Facilities: Channel No. 34 (590-596 MHz). Authorized power: 104-kw max. visual, aural. Antenna: 1476-ft above av. terrain, 535-ft. above ground, 3760-ft. above sea level.

Latitude	47°	36'	04"
Longitude	117°	17'	53"

Transmitter: Krell Hill, 2.5-mi. E of intersection of Palouse Hwy. & 57th Ave.

Note: Latitude and longitude coordinates shown are based on the North American Datum of 1927 (NAD 27) as currently required by the Mass Media Bureau of the FCC.

Ownership: ION Media Networks Inc., Debtor in Possession (Group Owner).

Began Operation: June 12, 2009. Station broadcasting digitally on its analog channel allotment. Began analog operations: August 1, 1999. Sale to Urban Television LLC pends. Involuntary assignment to debtor in possession status approved by FCC June 5, 2009. Transfer of control by ION Media Networks Inc. from Paxson Management Corp. & Lowell W. Paxson to CIG Media LLC approved by FCC December 31, 2007. Paxson Communications Corp. became ION Media Networks Inc. on June 26, 2006. Ceased analog operations: June 12, 2009.

Represented (legal): Dow Lohnes PLLC.

Personnel:

Amber Morales, Station Operations & Traffic Manager.

Mitch Wasson, Chief Engineer.

City of License: Spokane. **Station DMA:** Spokane, WA. **Rank:** 75.

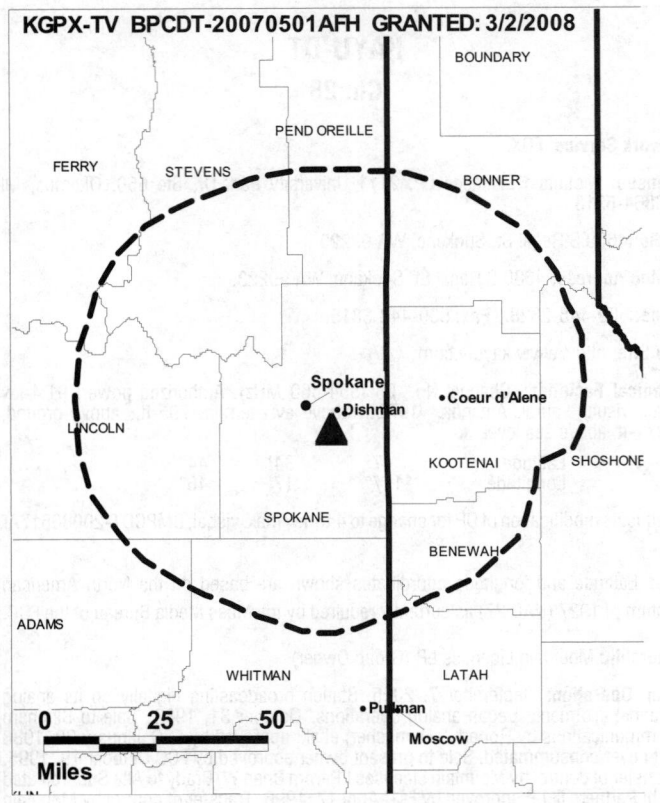

KGPX-TV BPCDT-20070501AFH GRANTED: 3/2/2008

© 2010 Warren Communications News

Circulation © 2009 Nielsen. Coverage based on Nielsen study.

GrandTotal	Cable TV Households	Non-cable TV Households	Total TV Households
Estimated Station Totals *	144,820	91,330	236,150
Average Weekly Circulation (2009)	10,552	6,479	17,031
Average Daily Circulation (2009)			3,474

Station DMA Total	Cable TV Households	Non-cable TV Households	Total TV Households
Estimated Station Totals *	144,820	91,330	236,150
Average Weekly Circulation (2009)	10,552	6,479	17,031
Average Daily Circulation (2009)			3,474

*Estimated station totals are sums of the Nielsen TV and Cable TV household estimates for each county in which the station registers viewing of more than 5% as per the Nielsen Survey Methods.

KHQ-DT
Ch. 15

Network Service: NBC.

Licensee: KHQ Inc., PO Box 600, 1201 W Sprague Ave, Spokane, WA 99210-0600.

Studio: 1201 W. Sprague Ave., Spokane, WA 99201.

Mailing Address: Box 600, Spokane, WA 99201.

Phone: 509-448-6000. **Fax:** 509-448-4694.

E-mail: patricia.mcrae@khq.com

Web Site: http://www.khq.com

Technical Facilities: Channel No. 15 (476-482 MHz). Authorized power: 424.7-kw max. visual, aural. Antenna: 1708-ft above av. terrain, 599-ft. above ground, 4244-ft. above sea level.

Latitude	47°	34'	53"
Longitude	117°	17'	47"

Requests modification of CP for change to 1000-kw max. visual; BMPCDT-20090708AGE.

Holds CP for change to channel number 7, 45.1-kw visual, 2142-ft above av. terrain, 860-ft. above ground, 4505-ft. above sea level; lat. 47° 34'52", long. 117° 17'47", BPCDT-20080314ABV.

Transmitter: Tower Mountain, Spokane.

Note: Latitude and longitude coordinates shown are based on the North American Datum of 1927 (NAD 27) as currently required by the Mass Media Bureau of the FCC.

Ownership: Cowles Co. (Group Owner).

Began Operation: June 30, 2005. Began analog operations: December 20, 1952. Ceased analog operations: February 17, 2009.

Represented (sales): Blair Television.

Personnel:

Patricia McRae, Vice President & Station Manager.

Bill Storms, General Sales Manager.

Brian Sullivan, Local Sales Manager.

Mike Dugger, National Sales Manager & Program Director.

Jonathan Mitchell, News Director.

Paul Caryl, Chief Engineer.

Paula Bauer, Accounting Manager.

Traci Zeravica, Web Producer.

Doug Miles, Production Manager.

Louise Hansen, Community Affairs.

City of License: Spokane. **Station DMA:** Spokane, WA. **Rank:** 75.

KHQ-DT BPCDT-20080314ABV GRANTED: 3/19/2008

© 2010 Warren Communications News

Circulation © 2009 Nielsen. Coverage based on Nielsen study.

GrandTotal	Cable TV Households	Non-cable TV Households	Total TV Households
Estimated Station Totals *	184,430	212,440	396,870
Average Weekly Circulation (2009)	122,625	130,326	252,951
Average Daily Circulation (2009)			123,563

Station DMA Total	Cable TV Households	Non-cable TV Households	Total TV Households
Estimated Station Totals *	167,680	212,440	380,120
Average Weekly Circulation (2009)	117,824	130,326	248,150
Average Daily Circulation (2009)			122,482

Other DMA Total	Cable TV Households	Non-cable TV Households	Total TV Households
Estimated Station Totals *	16,750	0	16,750
Average Weekly Circulation (2009)	4,801	0	4,801
Average Daily Circulation (2009)			1,081

*Estimated station totals are sums of the Nielsen TV and Cable TV household estimates for each county in which the station registers viewing of more than 5% as per the Nielsen Survey Methods.

KREM
Ch. 20

Network Service: CBS.

Licensee: King Broadcasting Co., 400 S Record St, Dallas, TX 75202-4806.

Studio: 4103 S. Regal St., Spokane, WA 99223.

Mailing Address: 4103 S Regal St, Spokane, WA 99223.

Phone: 509-448-2000. **Fax:** 509-448-2090.

Web Site: http://www.krem.com

Technical Facilities: Channel No. 20 (506-512 MHz). Authorized power: 893-kw max. visual, aural. Antenna: 2103-ft above av. terrain, 794-ft. above ground, 4403-ft. above sea level.

Latitude	47°	35'	41"
Longitude	117°	17'	53"

Requests CP for change to 1000-kw visual, 2205-ft above av. terrain, 896-ft. above ground, 4505-ft. above sea level; BPCDT-20080617AEA.

Note: Latitude and longitude coordinates shown are based on the North American Datum of 1927 (NAD 27) as currently required by the Mass Media Bureau of the FCC.

Ownership: Belo Corp. (Group Owner).

Began Operation: June 23, 2005. Began analog operations: October 29, 1954. Sale to King Broadcasting by founder Louis Wasmer approved by FCC September 25, 1957 (Television Digest, Vol. 13:28, 39, 51). Sale to Providence Journal approved by FCC August 27, 1991 (Vol. 30:35; 31:9, 29). Sale to present owner by Providence Journal approved by FCC February 28, 1997 (Vol. 36:40; 37:9). Ceased analog operations: June 12, 2009.

Represented (sales): TeleRep Inc.

Personnel:

Jamie Aitken, President & General Manager.

John W. Souza, Engineering Director.

Bruce Felt, Special Projects Coordinator.

Dan Lamphere, Operations & Production Manager.

Susan Miller, Sales Director.

Chris Larum, Local Sales Manager.

Noah Cooper, News Director.

Boyd Lundberg, Chief Engineer.

Barbara Grant, Business Manager.

Terry Coker, Program Director.

Ariel Carter, Research Analyst.

Dan Weig, Creative Services Manager.

Jessica Taylor, Traffic Manager.

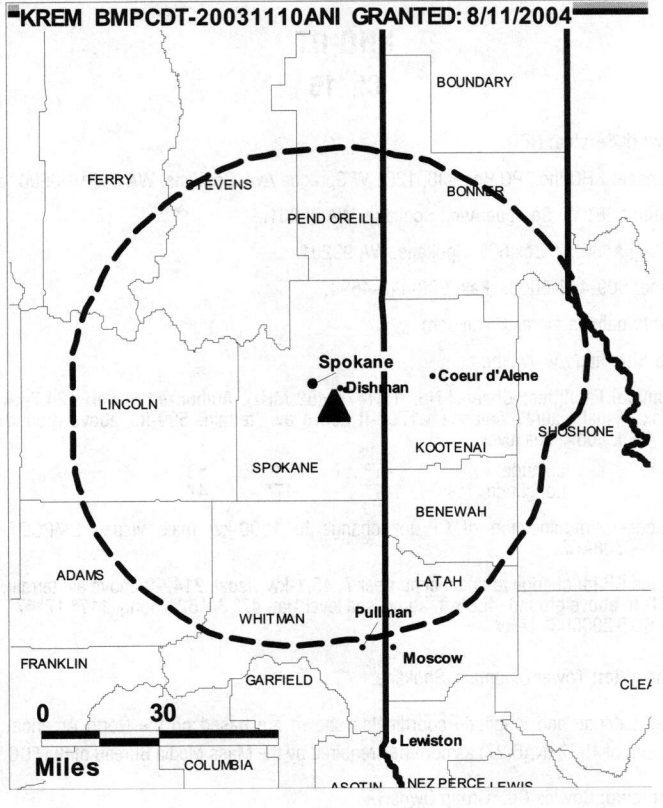

KREM BMPCDT-20031110ANI GRANTED: 8/11/2004

© 2010 Warren Communications News

City of License: Spokane. **Station DMA:** Spokane, WA. **Rank:** 75.

Circulation © 2009 Nielsen. Coverage based on Nielsen study.

GrandTotal	Cable TV Households	Non-cable TV Households	Total TV Households
Estimated Station Totals *	200,770	239,600	440,370
Average Weekly Circulation (2009)	129,138	130,282	259,420
Average Daily Circulation (2009)			124,083

Station DMA Total	Cable TV Households	Non-cable TV Households	Total TV Households
Estimated Station Totals *	167,680	212,440	380,120
Average Weekly Circulation (2009)	115,463	128,286	243,749
Average Daily Circulation (2009)			118,878

Other DMA Total	Cable TV Households	Non-cable TV Households	Total TV Households
Estimated Station Totals *	33,090	27,160	60,250
Average Weekly Circulation (2009)	13,675	1,996	15,671
Average Daily Circulation (2009)			5,205

*Estimated station totals are sums of the Nielsen TV and Cable TV household estimates for each county in which the station registers viewing of more than 5% as per the Nielsen Survey Methods.

KSKN-DT
Ch. 36

Network Service: CW.

Licensee: KSKN Television Inc., c/o Belo Corp., 400 S Record St, Dallas, TX 75202-4806.

Studio: 4103 S. Regal St., Spokane, WA 99223.

Mailing Address: 4103 S Regal St, Spokane, WA 99223.

Phone: 509-448-2000. **Fax:** 509-448-2090.

Web Site: http://www.krem.com

Technical Facilities: Channel No. 36 (602-608 MHz). Authorized power: 250-kw max. visual, aural. Antenna: 2041-ft above av. terrain, 732-ft. above ground, 4340-ft. above sea level.

Latitude	47°	35'	41"
Longitude	117°	17'	53"

Holds CP for change to 1000-kw max. visual, 2103-ft above av. terrain, 794-ft. above ground, 4403-ft. above sea level; BPCDT-20080617AEM.

Note: Latitude and longitude coordinates shown are based on the North American Datum of 1927 (NAD 27) as currently required by the Mass Media Bureau of the FCC.

Ownership: Belo Corp. (Group Owner).

Began Operation: January 13, 2005. Began analog operations: December 18, 1983. Sale to Sun Continental Group by Broadcast Vision TV approved by FCC November 27, 1985. Left air 1988. Sale to Whitehead Broadcasting by Sun Continental Group approved by FCC 1988. Sale to KSKN-TV Inc. by Whitehead Broadcasting approved by FCC February 15, 1991. Resumed operation October 3, 1994. Transfer by KSKN-TV Inc. to Judy Querio by Mel Querio Estate approved by FCC February 18, 1999. Sale to present owner by KSKN-TV Inc. approved by FCC August 24, 2001. Ceased analog operations: June 12, 2009.

Personnel:

Jamie Aitken, President & General Manager.

Dan Lamphere, Operations & Production Manager.

Susan Miller, General & National Sales Manager.

R. J. Merritt, Local Sales Manager.

Noah Cooper, News Director.

Boyd Lundberg, Chief Engineer.

Barbara Grant, Business Manager.

Terry Coker, Program Director.

Bruce Felt, Special Projects Coordinator.

Ariel Carter, Research Analyst.

Dan Weig, Creative Services Manager.

Jessica Taylor, Traffic Manager.

City of License: Spokane. **Station DMA:** Spokane, WA. **Rank:** 75.

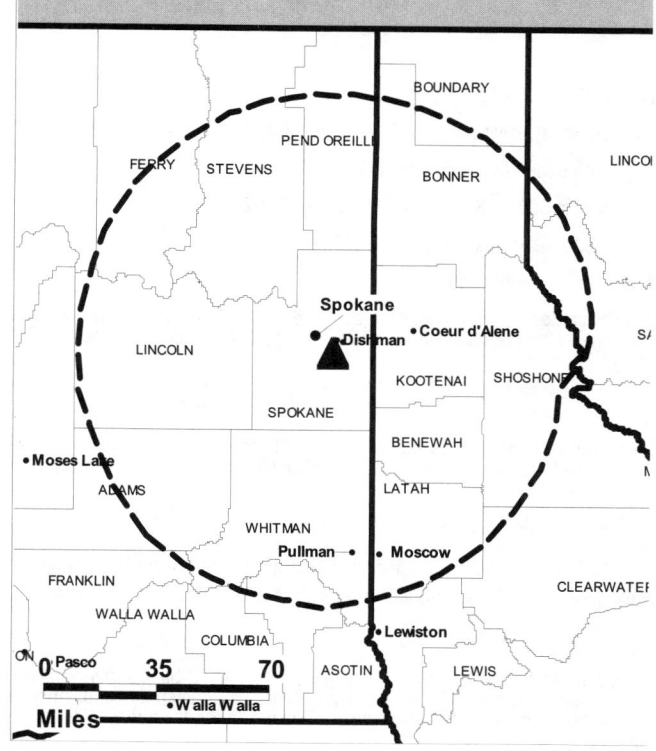

KSKN-DT BPCDT-20080617AEM GRANTED: 7/31/2009

© 2010 Warren Communications News

Circulation © 2009 Nielsen. Coverage based on Nielsen study.

GrandTotal	Cable TV Households	Non-cable TV Households	Total TV Households
Estimated Station Totals *	153,980	220,860	374,840
Average Weekly Circulation (2009)	38,098	48,504	86,602
Average Daily Circulation (2009)			26,087

Station DMA Total	Cable TV Households	Non-cable TV Households	Total TV Households
Estimated Station Totals *	153,980	212,440	366,420
Average Weekly Circulation (2009)	38,098	47,704	85,802
Average Daily Circulation (2009)			26,003

Other DMA Total	Cable TV Households	Non-cable TV Households	Total TV Households
Estimated Station Totals *	0	8,420	8,420
Average Weekly Circulation (2009)	0	800	800
Average Daily Circulation (2009)			84

*Estimated station totals are sums of the Nielsen TV and Cable TV household estimates for each county in which the station registers viewing of more than 5% as per the Nielsen Survey Methods.

KXLY-DT
Ch. 13

Network Service: MNT, ABC.

Licensee: Spokane Television Inc., 500 W Boone Ave, Spokane, WA 99201.

Studio: 500 W. Boone Ave., Spokane, WA 99201.

Mailing Address: 500 W. Boone Ave, Spokane, WA 99201.

Phone: 509-324-4000. **Fax:** 509-328-5274.

Web Site: http://www.kxly.com

Technical Facilities: Channel No. 13 (210-216 MHz). Authorized power: 23.3-kw visual, aural. Antenna: 3071-ft above av. terrain, 177-ft. above ground, 6037-ft. above sea level.

Latitude	47°	55'	18"
Longitude	117°	06'	48"

Requests CP for change to 35-kw visual, 2215-ft above av. terrain, 518-ft. above ground, 4879-ft. above sea level; BPCDT-20080619ACJ.

Transmitter: Mount Spokane, 23-mi. NE of Central Spokane.

Note: Latitude and longitude coordinates shown are based on the North American Datum of 1927 (NAD 27) as currently required by the Mass Media Bureau of the FCC.

Multichannel TV Sound: Stereo only.

Satellite Earth Stations: Satcom Technologies, 9.1-meter C-band; Andrew, 4.6-meter Ku-band; Andrew, 4.5-meter C-band; Vertex, 4.6-meter Ku-band; Andrew, 4.6-meter Ku-band; Satcom Technologies, 7-meter C-band; Andrew, 7.3-meter C-band.

SNG Mobile Dish: Andrew, 2.4-meter Ku-band.

Ownership: Morgan Murphy Media (Group Owner).

Began Operation: April 1, 1999. High Definition. Began analog operations: January 16, 1953. Sale to present owner by Joseph Harris & Norman E. Alexander approved by FCC January 17, 1962 (Television Digest, Vol. 17:34; 2:4, 6, 7). Sale to Harris & Alexander by Symons Broadcasting Co. (E. B. Craney) & Bing Crosby approved by FCC January 6, 1954 (Vol. 9:49; 10:2). Ceased analog operations: February 17, 2009.

Personnel:

Stephen R. Herling, Executive Vice President & General Manager.

Catherine Bruntlett, Research Development Director.

Terri Christensen, Creative Services Director.

Nancy Guin, Traffic Manager.

Teddie Gibbon, Vice President & Station Manager.

Debbie Sieverding, Local Sales Manager.

Brent Phillipy, National & Regional Sales Manager.

Tim A. Anderson, Engineering Director.

Bob Cole, Business Manager.

Jerry Post, Television News Director.

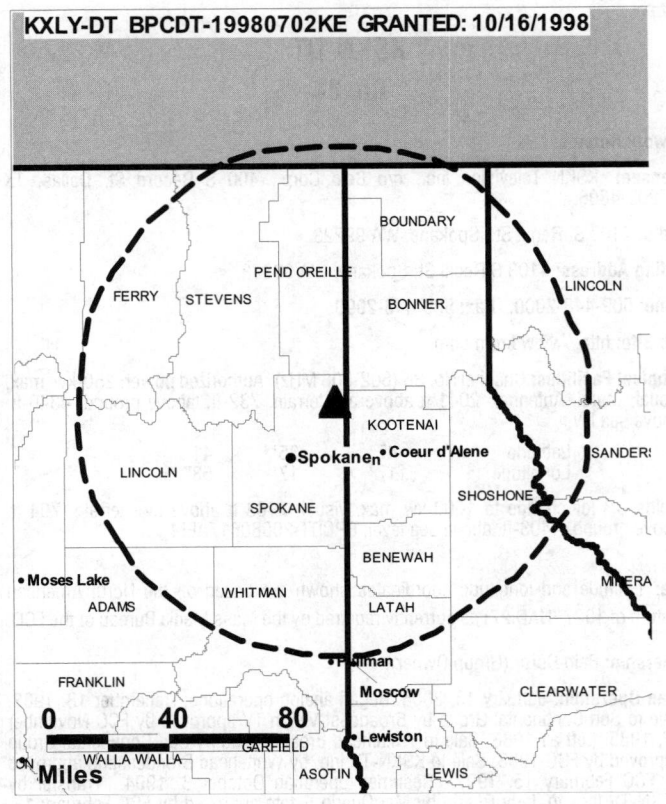

KXLY-DT BPCDT-19980702KE GRANTED: 10/16/1998

© 2010 Warren Communications News

David Lee, Promotions Manager.

City of License: Spokane. **Station DMA:** Spokane, WA. **Rank:** 75.

Circulation © 2009 Nielsen. Coverage based on Nielsen study.

GrandTotal	Cable TV Households	Non-cable TV Households	Total TV Households
Estimated Station Totals *	203,070	212,440	415,510
Average Weekly Circulation (2009)	110,690	115,158	225,848
Average Daily Circulation (2009)			97,270

Station DMA Total	Cable TV Households	Non-cable TV Households	Total TV Households
Estimated Station Totals *	167,210	212,440	379,650
Average Weekly Circulation (2009)	104,413	115,158	219,571
Average Daily Circulation (2009)			96,356

Other DMA Total	Cable TV Households	Non-cable TV Households	Total TV Households
Estimated Station Totals *	35,860	0	35,860
Average Weekly Circulation (2009)	6,277	0	6,277
Average Daily Circulation (2009)			914

*Estimated station totals are sums of the Nielsen TV and Cable TV household estimates for each county in which the station registers viewing of more than 5% as per the Nielsen Survey Methods.

KCPQ-DT
Ch. 13

Network Service: FOX.

Licensee: Tribune Television Northwest Inc., Debtor-In-Possession, 1813 Westlake Ave N, Seattle, WA 98109-2706.

Studio: 1813 Westlake Ave., Seattle, WA 98109-2706.

Mailing Address: 1813 Westlake Ave. N, Seattle, WA 98109-2706.

Phone: 206-674-1313. **Fax:** 206-674-1777.

Web Site: http://q13.trb.com

Technical Facilities: Channel No. 13 (210-216 MHz). Authorized power: 30-kw visual, aural. Antenna: 2001-ft above av. terrain, 669-ft. above ground, 2356-ft. above sea level.

Latitude	47°	32'	53"
Longitude	122°	48'	22"

Transmitter: Gold Mountain, 6.5-mi. W of Bremerton.

Note: Latitude and longitude coordinates shown are based on the North American Datum of 1927 (NAD 27) as currently required by the Mass Media Bureau of the FCC.

Ownership: Tribune Broadcasting Co., Debtor-In-Possession (Group Owner).

Began Operation: August 1, 2001. Standard Definition. Station broadcasting digitally on its analog channel allotment. Began analog operations: August 2, 1953. Commercial station left air December 13, 1974. Sale to Clover Park School District No. 400 approved by FCC September 9, 1975. Resumed operation as an educational station January 4, 1976. Sale to Kelly Broadcasting Co. approved by FCC December 4, 1979. Resumed operation as a commercial station November 4, 1980. Station was sold to Meredith Broadcasting, who then swapped KCPQ for Tribune Broadcasting's WGNX, Atlanta, GA. FCC approved deal February 22, 1999. Transfer of control from public shareholders of the Tribune Co. to Tribune Employee Stock Ownership Plan approved by FCC November 30, 2007. Involuntary assignment to debtor-in-possession status approved by FCC December 24, 2008. Ceased analog operations: June 12, 2009.

Represented (sales): HRP: Television Station Representative.

Represented (legal): Sidley Austin LLP.

Personnel:

Pamela Pearson, Vice President & General Manager.

Paul Rennie, Sales Director.

Steve Krayzik, News Director.

Michael Goodman, Engineering Director.

Sharon Silverman, Finance Director.

Natalie Grant, Program Manager.

Sheri Ligouri, Program Coordinator.

Jamie McDowell, Creative Services Director.

Wendy Anderson, Traffic Manager.

City of License: Tacoma. **Station DMA:** Seattle-Tacoma, WA. **Rank:** 13.

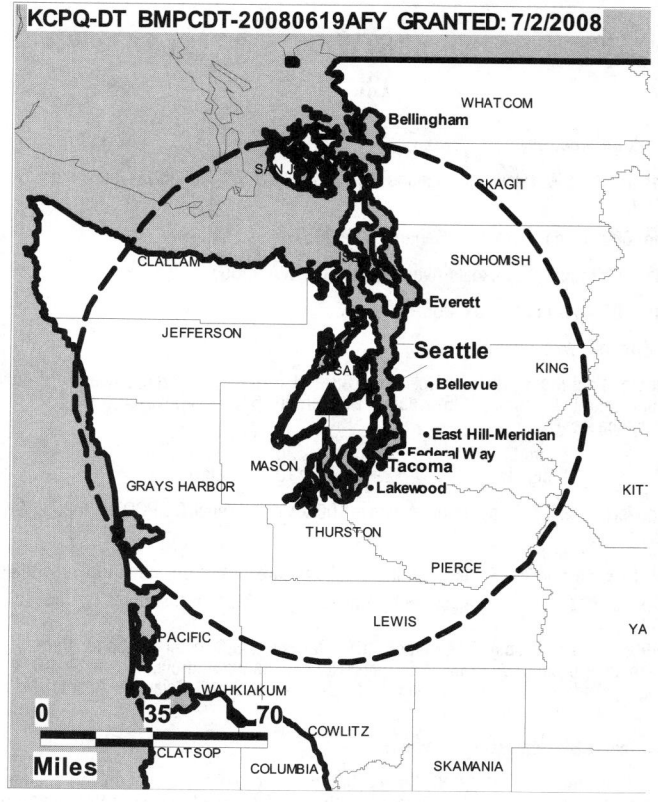

© 2010 Warren Communications News

Circulation © 2009 Nielsen. Coverage based on Nielsen study.

GrandTotal	Cable TV Households	Non-cable TV Households	Total TV Households
Estimated Station Totals *	1,253,960	500,270	1,754,230
Average Weekly Circulation (2009)	735,579	303,599	1,039,178
Average Daily Circulation (2009)			400,656

Station DMA Total	Cable TV Households	Non-cable TV Households	Total TV Households
Estimated Station Totals *	1,251,870	491,370	1,743,240
Average Weekly Circulation (2009)	735,462	302,442	1,037,904
Average Daily Circulation (2009)			400,385

Other DMA Total	Cable TV Households	Non-cable TV Households	Total TV Households
Estimated Station Totals *	2,090	8,900	10,990
Average Weekly Circulation (2009)	117	1,157	1,274
Average Daily Circulation (2009)			271

*Estimated station totals are sums of the Nielsen TV and Cable TV household estimates for each county in which the station registers viewing of more than 5% as per the Nielsen Survey Methods.

KSTW-DT
Ch. 11

Network Service: CW.

Licensee: The CW Television Stations Inc., 2175 K St NW, Ste 350, Washington, DC 20037.

Studio: 602 Oakdale Ave. SW, Renton, WA 98057.

Mailing Address: 602 Oakdale Ave. SW, Renton, WA 98057.

Phone: 206-441-1111. **Fax:** 206-861-8915.

Web Site: http://kstw.com

Technical Facilities: Channel No. 11 (198-204 MHz). Authorized power: 12.5-kw visual, aural. Antenna: 905-ft above av. terrain, 610-ft. above ground, 1021-ft. above sea level.

Latitude	47°	36'	55.6"
Longitude	122°	18'	28.5"

Requests modification of CP for change to 100-kw max. visual; BMPCDT-20080617ACH.

Note: Latitude and longitude coordinates shown are based on the North American Datum of 1927 (NAD 27) as currently required by the Mass Media Bureau of the FCC.

Satellite Earth Stations: Transmitter RCA; Comtech, 3.8-meter Ku-band; Vertex, 4.5-meter Ku-band; Andrew, 4.5-meter Ku & C-band; Andrew, 7.3-meter Ku & C-band; Andrew, 10-meter C-band; Standard Agile Omni, Scientific-Atlanta, M/A-Com, Andrew receivers.

Ownership: CBS Corp. (Group Owner).

Began Operation: July 8, 2005. Station broadcasting digitally on its analog channel allotment. Began analog operations: March 1, 1953. Sale to Gaylord Broadcasting Co. by Tribune Publishing Co. approved by FCC January 30, 1974. Sale to present owner from Gaylord Broadcasting approved by FCC April 4, 1997. Ceased analog operations: June 12, 2009.

Represented (legal): CBS Television Network (Legal Services).

Personnel:

Ron Longinotti, Vice President & General Manager.

Steve Gahler, Vice President, Station Manager & Sales Director.

Amber Stelzer, National Sales Manager.

Dave Gregory, Local Sales Manager.

Jeff McDiarmid, Local Sales Manager.

Howard Shack, Production Manager.

Carl Larson, Controller.

Ann Essman, Traffic Assistant.

Dean Poor, Creative Services Director.

Megan Temple, Marketing Director.

Kathy Walker, Program Director.

Ron Diotte, Chief Engineer.

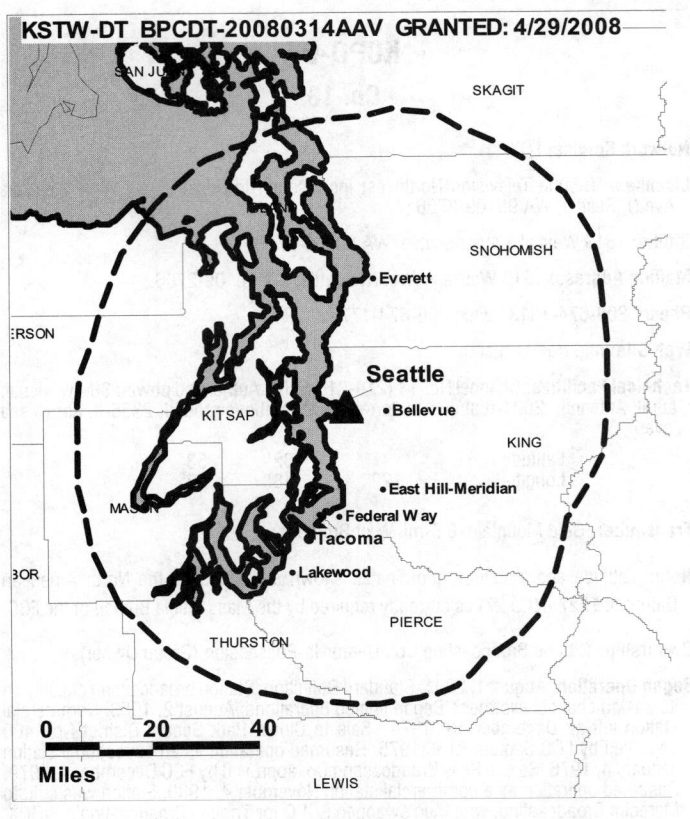

KSTW-DT BPCDT-20080314AAV GRANTED: 4/29/2008

© 2010 Warren Communications News

City of License: Tacoma. **Station DMA:** Seattle-Tacoma, WA. **Rank:** 13.

Circulation © 2009 Nielsen. Coverage based on Nielsen study.

GrandTotal	Cable TV Households	Non-cable TV Households	Total TV Households
Estimated Station Totals *	1,261,630	491,370	1,753,000
Average Weekly Circulation (2009)	441,417	184,512	625,929
Average Daily Circulation (2009)			182,466

Station DMA Total	Cable TV Households	Non-cable TV Households	Total TV Households
Estimated Station Totals *	1,251,870	491,370	1,743,240
Average Weekly Circulation (2009)	439,719	184,512	624,231
Average Daily Circulation (2009)			182,309

Other DMA Total	Cable TV Households	Non-cable TV Households	Total TV Households
Estimated Station Totals *	9,760	0	9,760
Average Weekly Circulation (2009)	1,698	0	1,698
Average Daily Circulation (2009)			157

*Estimated station totals are sums of the Nielsen TV and Cable TV household estimates for each county in which the station registers viewing of more than 5% as per the Nielsen Survey Methods.

KTBW-DT
Ch. 14

Network Service: TBN.

Licensee: Trinity Broadcasting Network Inc., 2442 Michelle Dr, Tustin, CA 92780.

Studio: 1909 S 341st Pl, Federal Way, WA 98003.

Mailing Address: 1909 S 341st Pl, Federal Way, WA 98003.

Phone: 253-927-7770. **Fax:** 253-874-7432.

E-mail: dmccord@tbn.org

Web Site: http://www.tbn.org

Technical Facilities: Channel No. 14 (470-476 MHz). Authorized power: 90-kw max. visual, aural. Antenna: 1552-ft above av. terrain, 236-ft. above ground, 1906-ft. above sea level.

Latitude	47°	32'	50"
Longitude	122°	47'	40"

Requests CP for change to 575-kw max. visual; BPCDT-20080619ADM.

Transmitter: Existing tower atop Gold Mountain, near Bremerton.

Note: Latitude and longitude coordinates shown are based on the North American Datum of 1927 (NAD 27) as currently required by the Mass Media Bureau of the FCC.

Ownership: Trinity Broadcasting Network Inc. (Group Owner).

Began Operation: June 15, 2006. Began analog operations: March 30, 1984. Sale to present owner by Family Broadcasting Co. approved by FCC October 25, 1984. Ceased analog operations: June 12, 2009.

Represented (legal): Colby M. May.

Represented (engineering): Smith & Fisher.

Personnel:

Mary Jane Allen, General Manager.

Gene Glasunow, Engineering Director.

Denise McCord, Program Administrator.

Greg Frederickson, Traffic Manager.

City of License: Tacoma. **Station DMA:** Seattle-Tacoma, WA. **Rank:** 13.

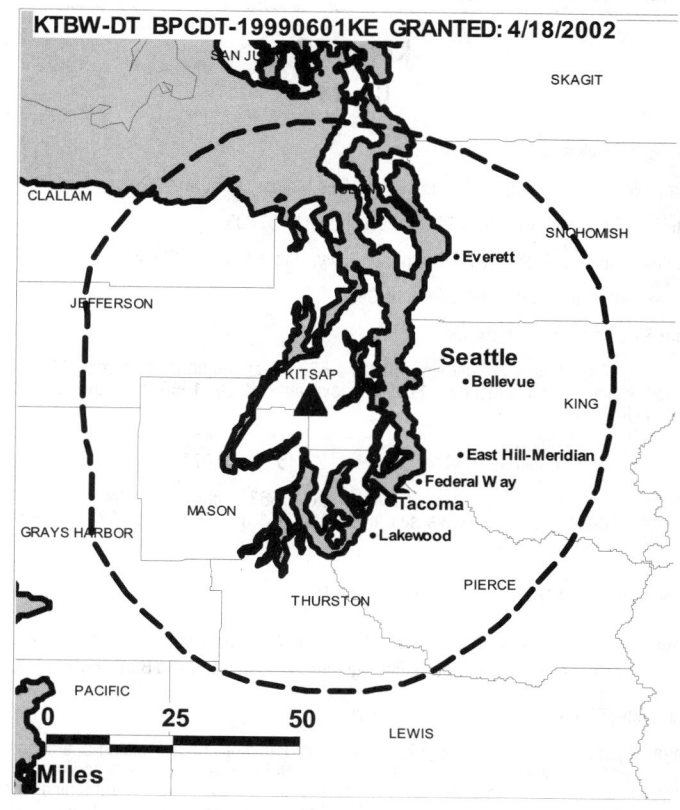

KTBW-DT BPCDT-19990601KE GRANTED: 4/18/2002

© 2010 Warren Communications News

Circulation © 2009 Nielsen. Coverage based on Nielsen study.

GrandTotal	Cable TV Households	Non-cable TV Households	Total TV Households
Estimated Station Totals *	457,080	16,160	473,240
Average Weekly Circulation (2009)	32,456	1,034	33,490
Average Daily Circulation (2009)			7,009

Station DMA Total	Cable TV Households	Non-cable TV Households	Total TV Households
Estimated Station Totals *	457,080	16,160	473,240
Average Weekly Circulation (2009)	32,456	1,034	33,490
Average Daily Circulation (2009)			7,009

*Estimated station totals are sums of the Nielsen TV and Cable TV household estimates for each county in which the station registers viewing of more than 5% as per the Nielsen Survey Methods.

KPDX-DT
Ch. 48

Network Service: MNT.

Licensee: Meredith Corp., 1716 Locust St, Des Moines, IA 50309-3203.

Studio: 14975 NW Greenbrier Pkwy, Beaverton, OR 97006.

Mailing Address: 14975 N.W. Greenbrier Pkwy, Beaverton, OR 97006.

Phone: 503-906-1249. **Fax:** 503-548-6910.

Web Site: http://www.kpdx.com

Technical Facilities: Channel No. 48 (674-680 MHz). Authorized power: 1000-kw max. visual, aural. Antenna: 1739-ft above av. terrain, 1050-ft. above ground, 2018-ft. above sea level.

Latitude	45°	31'	22"
Longitude	122°	45'	07"

Holds CP for change to channel number 30, 1683-ft above av. terrain, 974-ft. above ground, 1967-ft. above sea level; lat. 45° 31' 19", long. 122° 44' 53", BMPCDT-20080619AGD.

Transmitter: 211 N.W. Miller Rd., Portland, OR.

Note: Latitude and longitude coordinates shown are based on the North American Datum of 1927 (NAD 27) as currently required by the Mass Media Bureau of the FCC.

Ownership: Meredith Corp. (Group Owner).

Began Operation: November 2, 1999. Standard Definition. Began analog operations: October 1, 1983. Sale to present owner by KPDX License Partnership approved by FCC June 20, 1997. Sale to KPDX License Partnership by Cannell Communications LP approved by FCC November 1, 1994. Sale to Cannell Communications LP by Columbia River Television Inc. approved by FCC November 6, 1992. Transfer of control by Columbia River Television Inc. to Jack F. Matranga from Camellia City Telecasters Inc. approved by FCC December 12, 1986. Transfer of control by Columbia River Television Inc. to Camellia City Telecasters Inc. from Al Angelo Jr., Richard N. Bolton, et al., approved by FCC October 18, 1982. Ceased analog operations: June 12, 2009.

Personnel:

Patrick McCreery, Vice President & General Manager.

Greg Flock, General Sales Manager.

Andy Delaporte, Local Sales Manager.

Dannell Bostick, National Sales Manager.

Steve Benedict, Chief Engineer.

Tito Carlos, Business Manager.

John Concillo, Programming & Broadcast Operations Director.

Matthew Hyatt, Promotion & Creative Services Director.

Terry Demming, Production Manager.

Mary Warner, Traffic Manager.

Morgan Home, Administrative Assistant to the General Manager.

KPDX-DT BMPCDT-20080619AGD GRANTED: 7/21/2008

© 2010 Warren Communications News

City of License: Vancouver. **Station DMA:** Portland, OR. **Rank:** 22.

Circulation © 2009 Nielsen. Coverage based on Nielsen study.

GrandTotal	Cable TV Households	Non-cable TV Households	Total TV Households
Estimated Station Totals *	661,620	508,320	1,169,940
Average Weekly Circulation (2009)	122,018	107,477	229,495
Average Daily Circulation (2009)			83,176

Station DMA Total	Cable TV Households	Non-cable TV Households	Total TV Households
Estimated Station Totals *	660,830	484,920	1,145,750
Average Weekly Circulation (2009)	121,723	105,745	227,468
Average Daily Circulation (2009)			82,857

Other DMA Total	Cable TV Households	Non-cable TV Households	Total TV Households
Estimated Station Totals *	790	23,400	24,190
Average Weekly Circulation (2009)	295	1,732	2,027
Average Daily Circulation (2009)			319

*Estimated station totals are sums of the Nielsen TV and Cable TV household estimates for each county in which the station registers viewing of more than 5% as per the Nielsen Survey Methods.

KAPP-DT
Ch. 14

Network Service: MNT, ABC.

Licensee: Apple Valley Broadcasting Inc., 1610 S 24th Ave, Yakima, WA 98902-5719.

Studio: 1610 S 24th Ave, Yakima, WA 98902.

Mailing Address: PO Box 10208, Yakima, WA 98902.

Phone: 509-453-0351. **Fax:** 509-453-3623.

E-mail: brianp@kapptv.com

Web Site: http://www.kapptv.com

Technical Facilities: Channel No. 14 (470-476 MHz). Authorized power: 160-kw max. visual, aural. Antenna: 961-ft above av. terrain, 148-ft. above ground, 2123-ft. above sea level.

Latitude	46°	31'	57"
Longitude	120°	30'	37"

Note: Latitude and longitude coordinates shown are based on the North American Datum of 1927 (NAD 27) as currently required by the Mass Media Bureau of the FCC.

Ownership: Morgan Murphy Media (Group Owner).

Began Operation: November 1, 2006. Began analog operations: September 21, 1970. Ceased analog operations: February 17, 2009.

Represented (legal): Rini Coran PC.

Personnel:

Elizabeth Murphy Burns, President.

Brian Paul, General Manager.

Darrell Blue, Vice President, Government Affairs & Community Relations.

Lynn Kinuko Nishimoto, Sales Director.

Shane Pierone, Local Sales Manager.

Mike Balmelli, News Director.

Neil Bennett, Chief Engineer.

Bob Cole, Business Manager.

Cheryl Senpel, Program & Human Resources Director.

John Wilkerson, Production Manager.

Nancy Guin, Traffic Manager.

City of License: Yakima. **Station DMA:** Yakima-Pasco-Richland-Kennewick, WA.

Rank: 126.

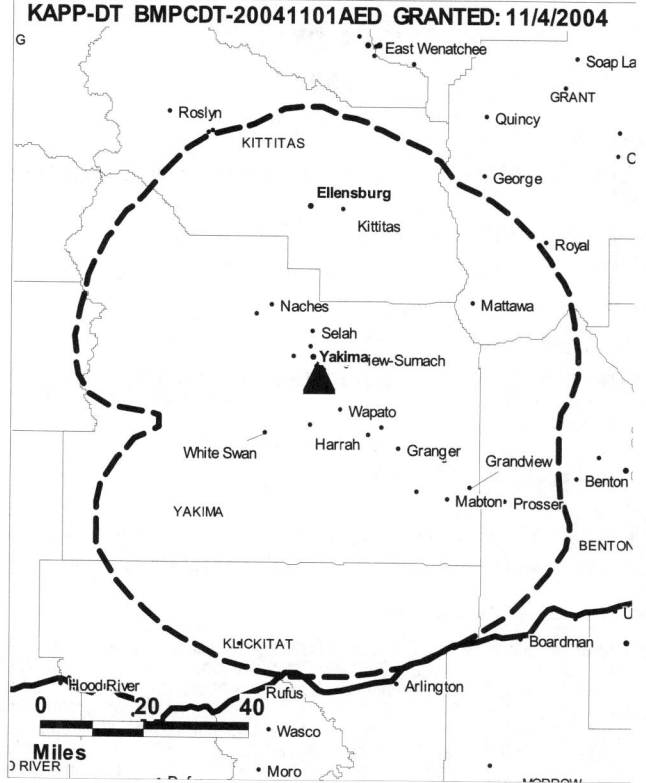

KAPP-DT BMPCDT-20041101AED GRANTED: 11/4/2004

© 2010 Warren Communications News

Circulation © 2009 Nielsen. Coverage based on Nielsen study.

GrandTotal	Cable TV Households	Non-cable TV Households	Total TV Households
Estimated Station Totals *	32,420	127,890	160,310
Average Weekly Circulation (2009)	16,215	31,965	48,180
Average Daily Circulation (2009)			17,771

Station DMA Total	Cable TV Households	Non-cable TV Households	Total TV Households
Estimated Station Totals *	32,420	127,890	160,310
Average Weekly Circulation (2009)	16,215	31,965	48,180
Average Daily Circulation (2009)			17,771

*Estimated station totals are sums of the Nielsen TV and Cable TV household estimates for each county in which the station registers viewing of more than 5% as per the Nielsen Survey Methods.

KIMA-DT
Ch. 33

Network Service: CBS.

Grantee: Fisher Broadcasting-Washington TV LLC, 600 University St, Ste 1525, Seattle, WA 98101.

Studio: 2801 Terrace Heights Dr., Yakima, WA 98901.

Mailing Address: PO Box 702, Yakima, WA 98907.

Phone: 509-575-0029. **Fax:** 509-248-1218.

Web Site: http://www.kimatv.com

Technical Facilities: Channel No. 33 (584-590 MHz). Authorized power: 100-kw max. visual, aural. Antenna: 958-ft above av. terrain, 144-ft. above ground, 2144-ft. above sea level.

Latitude	46°	31'	58"
Longitude	120°	30'	33"

Note: Latitude and longitude coordinates shown are based on the North American Datum of 1927 (NAD 27) as currently required by the Mass Media Bureau of the FCC.

Ownership: Fisher Communications Inc. (Group Owner).

Began Operation: March 29, 2002. Standard Definition. Began analog operations: July 19, 1953. Sale to present owner by Retlaw Enterprises Inc. approved by FCC April 20, 1999. Sale to Retlaw Enterprises Inc. by NWG Broadcasting Co. approved by FCC November 25, 1986. Sale to NWG Broadcasting by Filmways Inc. approved by FCC August 30, 1972. Merger of Filmways Inc. & Cascade Broadcasting approved by FCC July 23, 1969. Sale to Cascade Broadcasting by A. W. Talbot & Ralph Sundquist, et al., approved by FCC February 21, 1962. Ceased analog operations: June 12, 2009.

Represented (engineering): Hammett & Edison Inc.

Represented (legal): Pillsbury Winthrop Shaw Pittman LLP.

Represented (sales): Katz Media Group.

Personnel:

Larry Roberts, Vice President & Acting General Manager.

Karla Griffin, Operations Manager.

Steve Crow, National Sales Manager.

Ryan Messer, Local Sales Manager.

Robin Wojtanik, News Director.

Cliff Grady, Chief Engineer.

Cheryl Menke, Business Manager.

Darlene Johnson, Programming Director.

Reed Hansen, Creative Services Director.

Nadine Stillwaugh, Traffic Manager.

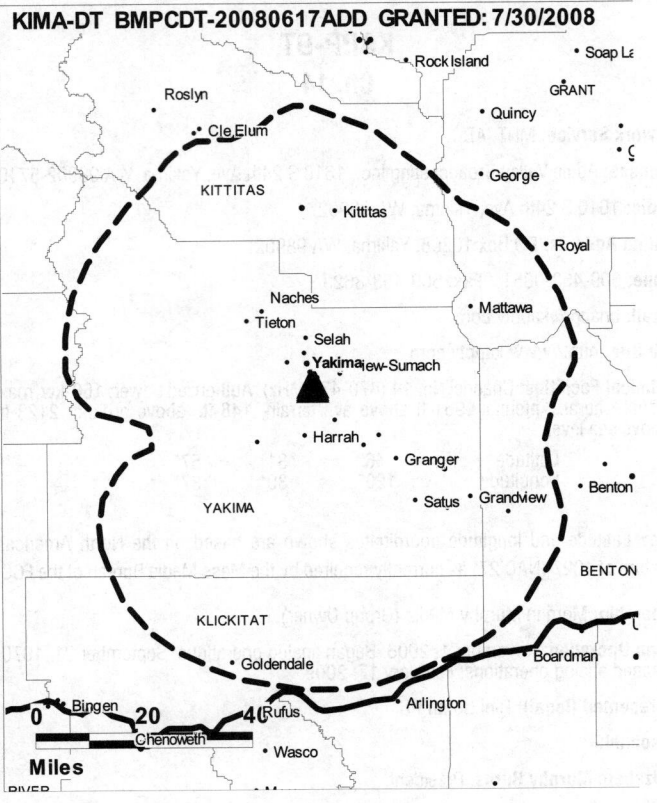

KIMA-DT BMPCDT-20080617ADD GRANTED: 7/30/2008

© 2010 Warren Communications News

Dane Pierone, Promotions Director.

City of License: Yakima. **Station DMA:** Yakima-Pasco-Richland-Kennewick, WA.

Rank: 126.

Circulation © 2009 Nielsen. Coverage based on Nielsen study.

GrandTotal	Cable TV Households	Non-cable TV Households	Total TV Households
Estimated Station Totals *	32,420	127,890	160,310
Average Weekly Circulation (2009)	19,917	42,758	62,675
Average Daily Circulation (2009)			28,908

Station DMA Total	Cable TV Households	Non-cable TV Households	Total TV Households
Estimated Station Totals *	32,420	127,890	160,310
Average Weekly Circulation (2009)	19,917	42,758	62,675
Average Daily Circulation (2009)			28,908

*Estimated station totals are sums of the Nielsen TV and Cable TV household estimates for each county in which the station registers viewing of more than 5% as per the Nielsen Survey Methods.

KNDO-DT
Ch. 16

Network Service: NBC.

Grantee: KHQ Inc., PO Box 8088, 4202 S Regal St, Spokane, WA 99203-8088.

Studio: 1608 S. 24th Ave., Yakima, WA 98902.

Mailing Address: 1608 S. 24th Ave, Yakima, WA 98902.

Phone: 509-225-2300. **Fax:** 509-225-2331.

Web Site: http://www.kndo.com

Technical Facilities: Channel No. 16 (482-488 MHz). Authorized power: 50-kw max. visual, aural. Antenna: 873-ft above av. terrain, 82-ft. above ground, 2032-ft. above sea level.

Latitude	46°	31'	59"
Longitude	120°	30'	26"

Holds CP for change to 150-kw max. visual, 873-ft above av. terrain, 131-ft. above ground, 2082-ft. above sea level; BMPCDT-20080624AAP.

Note: Latitude and longitude coordinates shown are based on the North American Datum of 1927 (NAD 27) as currently required by the Mass Media Bureau of the FCC.

Ownership: Cowles Co. (Group Owner).

Began Operation: Began analog operations: October 15, 1959. Sale to Hugh E. Davis, et al., by Ralph Tronsrud approved by FCC February 1, 1961 (Television Digest, Vol. 16:34; 17:6). Sale to Farragut Communications approved by FCC January 29, 1988 (Vol. 27:51). Sale to Federal Broadcasting Co. approved by FCC December 11, 1995. Sale to Raycom Media Inc. by Federal Broadcasting approved by FCC September 24, 1996. Sale to present owner from Raycom Media Inc. approved by FCC June 17, 1999. Ceased analog operations: February 17, 2009.

Represented (sales): Blair Television.

Personnel:

Paul Dughi, General Manager.

Larry Forsgren, General Sales Manager.

Jennifer Bliesner, Local Sales Manager.

Sherri Bissell, National Sales Manager.

Christine Brown, News Director.

Mark Kennedy, Chief Engineer.

Melissa Waite, Business Manager.

Susan Martinez, Program Director & Traffic Manager.

Jim Tippett, Production Director.

KNDO-DT BMPCDT-20080624AAP GRANTED: 7/25/2008

© 2010 Warren Communications News

City of License: Yakima. **Station DMA:** Yakima-Pasco-Richland-Kennewick, WA.

Rank: 126.

Circulation © 2009 Nielsen. Coverage based on Nielsen study.

GrandTotal	Cable TV Households	Non-cable TV Households	Total TV Households
Estimated Station Totals *	32,420	58,350	90,770
Average Weekly Circulation (2009)	19,568	18,792	38,360
Average Daily Circulation (2009)			18,765

Station DMA Total	Cable TV Households	Non-cable TV Households	Total TV Households
Estimated Station Totals *	32,420	58,350	90,770
Average Weekly Circulation (2009)	19,568	18,792	38,360
Average Daily Circulation (2009)			18,765

*Estimated station totals are sums of the Nielsen TV and Cable TV household estimates for each county in which the station registers viewing of more than 5% as per the Nielsen Survey Methods.

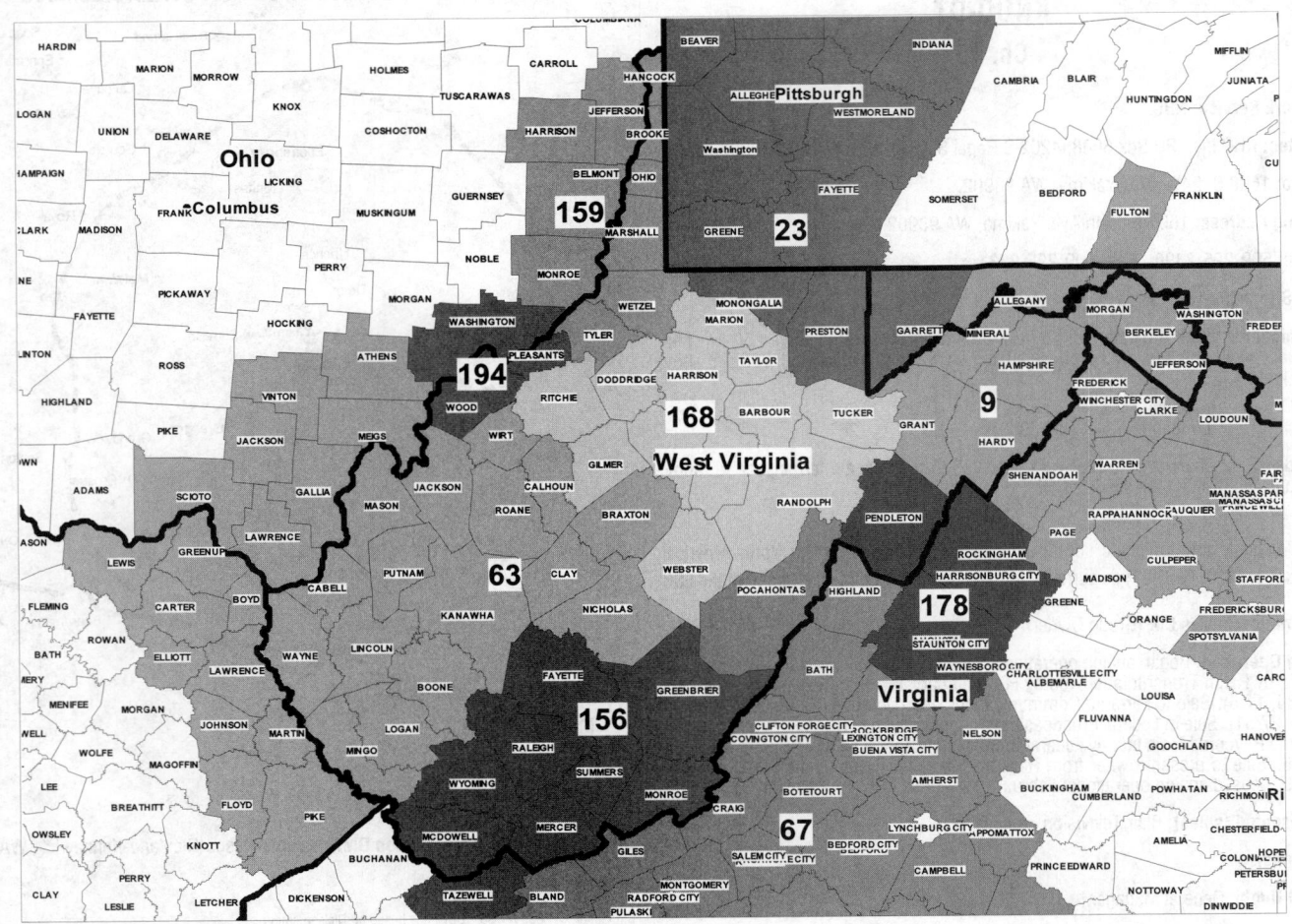

© 2010 Warren Communications News

MARKET	NIELSEN DMA TV HOUSEHOLDS	RANK	MARKET AREA COMMERCIAL STATIONS
Washington, DC (Hagerstown, MD)...............	2,335,040	9	WDCA-DT (35); WDCW-DT (50); WFDC-DT (15); WHAG-DT (55); WJAL-DT (39); WJLA-DT (7); WPXW-TV (43); WRC-DT (48); WSSS-TV (1); WTTG-DT (36); WUSA-DT (9); WWPX-TV (12)
Pittsburgh, PA................................	1,154,950	23	KDKA-DT (25); WPCB-DT (50); WPCW-DT (11); WPGH-DT (43); WPMY-DT (42); WPXI-DT (48); WQEX-DT (26); WTAE-DT (51)
Charleston-Huntington, WV	501,530	63	WCHS-DT (41); WLPX-TV (39); WOWK-DT (13); WQCW-DT (17); WSAZ-DT (23); WTSF-DT (44); WVAH-DT (19)
Roanoke-Lynchburg, VA	461,220	67	WDBJ-DT (18); WDRL-DT (24); WFXR-DT (17); WPXR-TV (36); WSET-DT (13); WSLS-DT (30); WWCW-DT (20)
Bluefield-Beckley-Oak Hill, WV	142,570	156	WLFB-DT (40); WOAY-DT (50); WVNS-DT (8); WVVA-DT (46)
Wheeling, WV-Steubenville, OH..................	133,110	159	WTOV-DT (9); WTRF-DT (7)
Clarksburg-Weston, WV	110,050	168	WBOY-DT (12); WDTV-DT (5); WVFX-DT (10)
Harrisonburg, VA.............................	93,400	178	WHSV-DT (49)
Parkersburg, WV.............................	64,060	194	WTAP-DT (49)

West Virginia Station Totals as of October 1, 2009

	VHF	UHF	TOTAL
Commercial Television	7	8	15
Educational Television	1	2	3
	8	10	18

WLFB-DT
Ch. 40

Network Service: IND.

Licensee: Living Faith Ministries Inc., PO Box 151, Vansant, VA 24656.

Studio: 8594 Hidden Valley Rd., Abingdon, VA 24210.

Mailing Address: PO Box 1867, Abingdon, VA 24212.

Phone: 276-676-3806. **Fax:** 276-676-3572.

Web Site: http://www.livingfaithtv.com

Technical Facilities: Channel No. 40 (626-632 MHz). Authorized power: 1000-kw max. visual, aural. Antenna: 1283-ft above av. terrain, 177-ft. above ground, 4009-ft. above sea level.

Latitude	37°	13'	08"
Longitude	81°	15'	39"

Note: Latitude and longitude coordinates shown are based on the North American Datum of 1927 (NAD 27) as currently required by the Mass Media Bureau of the FCC.

Ownership: Living Faith Ministries Inc. (Group Owner).

Began Operation: October 12, 2006. Station broadcasting digitally on its analog channel allotment. Began analog operations: November 2, 2000. Transfer of control from Tookland Pentecostal Church to Living Faith Broadcasting Inc. approved by FCC March 31, 2005. Involuntary transfer of control to Official Board dismissed at filer's request December 3, 2004. Ceased analog operations: June 12, 2009.

Represented (legal): PennStuart.

Personnel:

Michael D. Smith, President.

Marvin W. McGeorge, Sales Manager.

Wayne Price, Chief Engineer.

Lisa Smith, Chief Financial Officer & Promotion Director.

Sue Howington, Traffic Manager.

City of License: Bluefield. **Station DMA:** Bluefield-Beckley-Oak Hill, WV. **Rank:** 156.

TELEVISION & CABLE
Factbook Online

continuous updates   fully searchable   easy to use

For more information call **800-771-9202** or visit **www.warren-news.com**

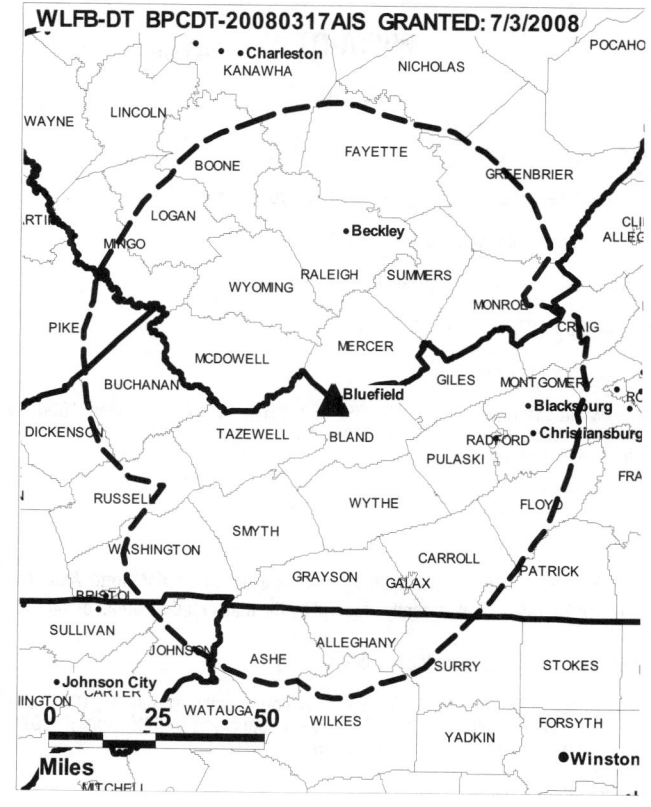

WLFB-DT BPCDT-20080317AIS GRANTED: 7/3/2008

© 2010 Warren Communications News

Circulation © 2009 Nielsen. Coverage based on Nielsen study.

GrandTotal	Cable TV Households	Non-cable TV Households	Total TV Households
Estimated Station Totals *	28,240	0	28,240
Average Weekly Circulation (2009)	2,699	0	2,699
Average Daily Circulation (2009)			617

Station DMA Total	Cable TV Households	Non-cable TV Households	Total TV Households
Estimated Station Totals *	24,890	0	24,890
Average Weekly Circulation (2009)	2,347	0	2,347
Average Daily Circulation (2009)			587

Other DMA Total	Cable TV Households	Non-cable TV Households	Total TV Households
Estimated Station Totals *	3,350	0	3,350
Average Weekly Circulation (2009)	352	0	352
Average Daily Circulation (2009)			30

*Estimated station totals are sums of the Nielsen TV and Cable TV household estimates for each county in which the station registers viewing of more than 5% as per the Nielsen Survey Methods.

WVVA-DT
Ch. 46

Network Service: NBC, CW.

Grantee: WVVA Television Inc., 130-138 S 5th St, Quincy, IL 62301.

Studio: 3052 Big Laurel Hwy., Bluefield, WV 24701.

Mailing Address: PO Box 1930, Bluefield, WV 24701.

Phone: 304-325-5487. **Fax:** 304-327-5586.

Web Site: http://www.wvva.com

Technical Facilities: Channel No. 46 (662-668 MHz). Authorized power: 1000-kw max. visual, aural. Antenna: 1220-ft above av. terrain, 143-ft. above ground, 3811-ft. above sea level.

Latitude	37°	15'	20.7"
Longitude	81°	10'	54"

Note: Latitude and longitude coordinates shown are based on the North American Datum of 1927 (NAD 27) as currently required by the Mass Media Bureau of the FCC.

Ownership: Quincy Newspapers Inc. (Group Owner).

Began Operation: September 28, 2006. Began analog operations: July 31, 1955. Sale to present owner by Daily Telegraph Printing Co. approved by FCC April 9, 1979. Ceased analog operations: February 17, 2009.

Represented (sales): Blair Television.

Personnel:

Frank Brady, General Manager.

Charity Holman, Local Sales Representative.

Yvonne Moses, Regional Sales Manager.

Kathy Mitchell, National Sales Manager.

Greg Carter, News Director.

Danny Via, Chief Engineer.

Wanda Davidson, Business Manager.

Dustin Long, Program & Promotion Director.

Tom Moses, Production Manager.

Audrey Williams, Traffic Manager.

City of License: Bluefield. **Station DMA:** Bluefield-Beckley-Oak Hill, WV. **Rank:** 156.

WVVA-DT BMPCDT-20060707ABJ GRANTED: 9/22/2006

© 2010 Warren Communications News

Circulation © 2009 Nielsen. Coverage based on Nielsen study.

GrandTotal	Cable TV Households	Non-cable TV Households	Total TV Households
Estimated Station Totals *	119,360	44,760	164,120
Average Weekly Circulation (2009)	67,623	8,182	75,805
Average Daily Circulation (2009)			43,162

Station DMA Total	Cable TV Households	Non-cable TV Households	Total TV Households
Estimated Station Totals *	95,250	44,760	140,010
Average Weekly Circulation (2009)	65,044	8,182	73,226
Average Daily Circulation (2009)			42,757

Other DMA Total	Cable TV Households	Non-cable TV Households	Total TV Households
Estimated Station Totals *	24,110	0	24,110
Average Weekly Circulation (2009)	2,579	0	2,579
Average Daily Circulation (2009)			405

*Estimated station totals are sums of the Nielsen TV and Cable TV household estimates for each county in which the station registers viewing of more than 5% as per the Nielsen Survey Methods.

WCHS-DT
Ch. 41

Network Service: ABC.

Licensee: WCHS Licensee LLC, 10706 Beaver Dam Rd, Cockeysville, MD 21030.

Studio: 1301 Piedmont Rd., Charleston, WV 25301.

Mailing Address: PO Box 11138, Charleston, WV 25339-1138.

Phone: 304-346-5358. **Fax:** 304-346-4765.

E-mail: lbarna@sbgnet.com

Web Site: http://www.wchstv.com

Technical Facilities: Channel No. 41 (632-638 MHz). Authorized power: 475-kw max. visual, aural. Antenna: 1687-ft above av. terrain, 1418-ft. above ground, 2467-ft. above sea level.

Latitude	38°	24'	28"
Longitude	81°	54'	13"

Note: Latitude and longitude coordinates shown are based on the North American Datum of 1927 (NAD 27) as currently required by the Mass Media Bureau of the FCC.

Ownership: Sinclair Broadcast Group Inc. (Group Owner).

Began Operation: June 14, 2005. Began analog operations: August 16, 1954. Sale to present owner by William G. Evans, trustee for Heritage Media Corp., approved by FCC October 8, 1997 (Television Digest, Vol. 37:29). Sale to Heritage Media Corp. by Rollins Communications approved by FCC September 19, 1986. Sale to Rollins by Tierney Co. approved by FCC September 28, 1960 (Vol. 16:29, 40). Ceased analog operations: June 12, 2009.

Represented (sales): Katz Media Group.

Personnel:

Alan Frank, Regional Manager.

Harold Cooper, General Manager.

Bob Butterfield, Local Sales Manager.

Raymond Beckner, Engineering Director.

John Sandoro, Business Manager.

Lori Margurt, Program Director.

Paul Fox, Promotion Director.

Bob Bratton, Production Manager.

Jo Corey, Public Service Director.

City of License: Charleston. **Station DMA:** Charleston-Huntington, WV. **Rank:** 63.

WCHS-DT BMPCDT-20030717AAB GRANTED: 5/28/2004

© 2010 Warren Communications News

Circulation © 2009 Nielsen. Coverage based on Nielsen study.

GrandTotal	Cable TV Households	Non-cable TV Households	Total TV Households
Estimated Station Totals *	407,540	231,110	638,650
Average Weekly Circulation (2009)	219,098	107,908	327,006
Average Daily Circulation (2009)			142,086

Station DMA Total	Cable TV Households	Non-cable TV Households	Total TV Households
Estimated Station Totals *	278,140	201,780	479,920
Average Weekly Circulation (2009)	169,569	105,401	274,970
Average Daily Circulation (2009)			125,463

Other DMA Total	Cable TV Households	Non-cable TV Households	Total TV Households
Estimated Station Totals *	129,400	29,330	158,730
Average Weekly Circulation (2009)	49,529	2,507	52,036
Average Daily Circulation (2009)			16,623

*Estimated station totals are sums of the Nielsen TV and Cable TV household estimates for each county in which the station registers viewing of more than 5% as per the Nielsen Survey Methods.

WLPX-DT
Ch. 39

Network Service: ION.

Licensee: ION Media Charleston License Inc., Debtor in Possession, 601 Clearwater Park Rd, West Palm Beach, FL 33401-6233.

Studio: 600-C Prestige Dr., Hurricane, WV 25526.

Mailing Address: 600-C Prestige Dr, Hurricane, WV 25526.

Phone: 304-760-1029. **Fax:** 304-760-1036.

E-mail: stevenstanley@ionmedia.com

Web Site: http://www.ionmedia.com

Technical Facilities: Channel No. 39 (320-626 MHz). Authorized power: 1000-kw max. visual, aural. Antenna: 1148-ft above av. terrain, 909-ft. above ground, 1929-ft. above sea level.

Latitude	38°	28'	12"
Longitude	86°	46'	35"

Transmitter: Approx. 1.5-mi. N of the intersection of County Rds. 31 & 38.

Note: Latitude and longitude coordinates shown are based on the North American Datum of 1927 (NAD 27) as currently required by the Mass Media Bureau of the FCC.

Ownership: ION Media Networks Inc., Debtor in Possession (Group Owner).

Began Operation: May 1, 2002. Began analog operations: August 31, 1998. Involuntary assignment to debtor in possession status approved by FCC June 5, 2009. Transfer of control by ION Media Networks Inc. from Paxson Management Corp. & Lowell W. Paxson to CIG Media LLC approved by FCC December 31, 2007. Paxson Communications Corp. became ION Media Networks Inc. on June 26, 2006. Transfer of control to Paxson Communications Corp. by William L. Kepper approved by FCC October 28, 1998. Ceased analog operations: June 12, 2009.

Represented (legal): Dow Lohnes PLLC.

Represented (engineering): du Treil, Lundin & Rackley Inc.

Personnel:

Steven Stanley, Station Operations & Traffic Manager.

Gene Monday, Chief Engineer.

City of License: Charleston. **Station DMA:** Charleston-Huntington, WV. **Rank:** 63.

WLPX-DT BPCDT-19990513KH GRANTED: 2/22/2001

© 2010 Warren Communications News

Circulation © 2009 Nielsen. Coverage based on Nielsen study.

GrandTotal	Cable TV Households	Non-cable TV Households	Total TV Households
Estimated Station Totals *	165,960	33,400	199,360
Average Weekly Circulation (2009)	15,667	2,411	18,078
Average Daily Circulation (2009)			3,290

Station DMA Total	Cable TV Households	Non-cable TV Households	Total TV Households
Estimated Station Totals *	164,600	33,400	198,000
Average Weekly Circulation (2009)	15,549	2,411	17,960
Average Daily Circulation (2009)			3,285

Other DMA Total	Cable TV Households	Non-cable TV Households	Total TV Households
Estimated Station Totals *	1,360	0	1,360
Average Weekly Circulation (2009)	118	0	118
Average Daily Circulation (2009)			5

*Estimated station totals are sums of the Nielsen TV and Cable TV household estimates for each county in which the station registers viewing of more than 5% as per the Nielsen Survey Methods.

WVAH-DT
Ch. 19

Network Service: FOX.

Grantee: WVAH Licensee LLC, 2000 W. 41st St, Baltimore, MD 21211.

Studio: 11 Broadcast Plaza, Huntington, WV 25526.

Mailing Address: 11 Broadcast Plaza, Hurricane, WV 25526.

Phone: 304-757-0011. **Fax:** 304-757-7533.

E-mail: tcole@sbgnet.com

Web Site: http://www.wvah.com

Technical Facilities: Channel No. 19 (500-506 MHz). Authorized power: 475-kw max. visual, aural. Antenna: 1687-ft above av. terrain, 1418-ft. above ground, 2467-ft. above sea level.

Latitude	38°	24'	28"
Longitude	81°	54'	13"

Note: Latitude and longitude coordinates shown are based on the North American Datum of 1927 (NAD 27) as currently required by the Mass Media Bureau of the FCC.

Ownership: Cunningham Broadcasting Corp. (Group Owner).

Began Operation: June 21, 2005. Began analog operations: September 19, 1982. Proposed sales to Sinclair Broadcast Group Inc. dismissed by FCC February 26, 2004 and September 13, 2002. Ceased analog operations: June 12, 2009.

Represented (sales): Katz Media Group.

Personnel:

Alan Frank, General Manager.

Harold Cooper, Sales Director.

Bob Butterfield, Local Sales Manager.

Raymond Beckner, Engineering Director.

John Sandoro, Business Manager.

Lori Margurt, Program Director.

Paul Fox, Promotion Director.

Bob Bratton, Production Manager.

Jo Corey, Public Service Director.

City of License: Charleston. **Station DMA:** Charleston-Huntington, WV. **Rank:** 63.

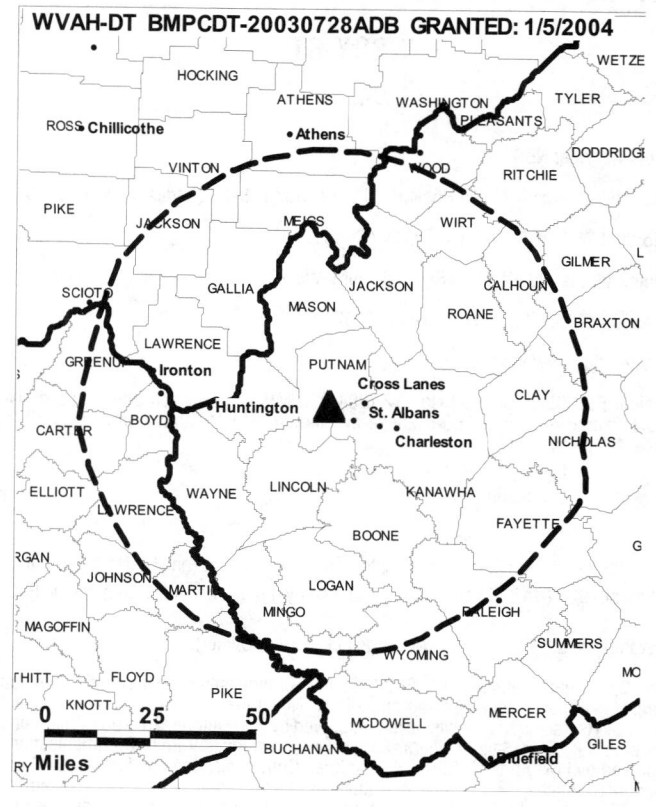

WVAH-DT BMPCDT-20030728ADB GRANTED: 1/5/2004

© 2010 Warren Communications News

Circulation © 2009 Nielsen. Coverage based on Nielsen study.

GrandTotal	Cable TV Households	Non-cable TV Households	Total TV Households
Estimated Station Totals *	419,190	218,560	637,750
Average Weekly Circulation (2009)	189,332	106,509	295,841
Average Daily Circulation (2009)			110,181

Station DMA Total	Cable TV Households	Non-cable TV Households	Total TV Households
Estimated Station Totals *	278,140	201,780	479,920
Average Weekly Circulation (2009)	147,265	104,774	252,039
Average Daily Circulation (2009)			98,873

Other DMA Total	Cable TV Households	Non-cable TV Households	Total TV Households
Estimated Station Totals *	141,050	16,780	157,830
Average Weekly Circulation (2009)	42,067	1,735	43,802
Average Daily Circulation (2009)			11,308

*Estimated station totals are sums of the Nielsen TV and Cable TV household estimates for each county in which the station registers viewing of more than 5% as per the Nielsen Survey Methods.

WBOY-DT

Ch. 12

Network Service: NBC.

Grantee: West Virginia Media Holdings LLC, PO Box 11848, Charleston, WV 25339.

Studio: 904 W. Pike St., Clarksburg, WV 26301.

Mailing Address: 904 W. Pike St, Clarksburg, WV 26301.

Phone: 304-623-3311. **Fax:** 304-624-6152.

Web Site: http://www.wboy.com

Technical Facilities: Channel No. 12 (204-210 MHz). Authorized power: 12.25-kw visual, aural. Antenna: 860-ft above av. terrain, 571-ft. above ground, 2023-ft. above sea level.

Latitude	39°	17'	06"
Longitude	80°	19'	46"

Note: Latitude and longitude coordinates shown are based on the North American Datum of 1927 (NAD 27) as currently required by the Mass Media Bureau of the FCC.

Ownership: West Virginia Media Holdings LLC (Group Owner).

Began Operation: February 17, 2009. Station broadcasting digitally on its analog channel allotment. Began analog operations: November 17, 1957. Sale to present owner by Hearst-Argyle Television Inc. approved by FCC October 25, 2001 (Television Digest, Vol.41:38). Sale to Hearst-Argyle Television Inc. by Imes Communications approved by FCC April 26, 2001. Sale to Imes Communications by Fortnightly Corp. (Marion R. Ascoli, Max Ascoli & Nathan W. Levin) approved by FCC November 5, 1976. Sale to Fortnightly Corp. by Rust Craft Broadcasting Co. approved by FCC March 11,1964 (Television Digest, Vol. 3:12, 46; 4:11). Sale to Rust Craft Broadcasting Co. Inc. by WSTV Inc. approved by FCC 1961-1962. Ceased analog operations: February 17, 2009.

Represented (sales): Petry Media Corp.

Personnel:

Larry Cottrill, Vice President & General Manager.

George Boggs, General Sales Manager.

Aaron Williams, News Director.

Robert Hardman, Chief Engineer.

Tom Gaudino, Business Manager.

Amanda Leaseburg, Promotions Manager.

Shawn Geiger, Production Manager.

Virginia Richison, Traffic Manager.

City of License: Clarksburg. **Station DMA:** Clarksburg-Weston, WV. **Rank:** 168.

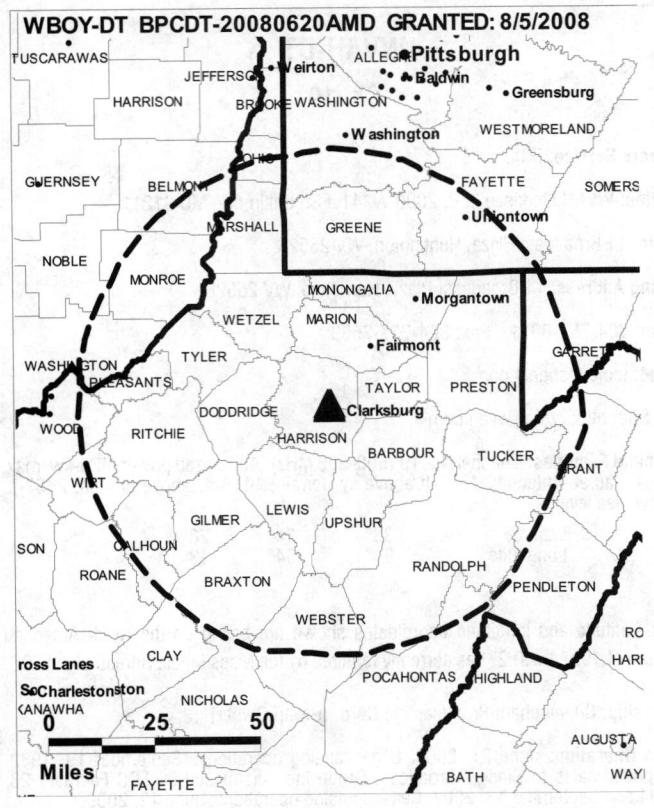

WBOY-DT BPCDT-20080620AMD GRANTED: 8/5/2008

© 2010 Warren Communications News

Circulation © 2009 Nielsen. Coverage based on Nielsen study.

GrandTotal	Cable TV Households	Non-cable TV Households	Total TV Households
Estimated Station Totals *	97,750	74,250	172,000
Average Weekly Circulation (2009)	65,266	26,599	91,865
Average Daily Circulation (2009)			56,197

Station DMA Total	Cable TV Households	Non-cable TV Households	Total TV Households
Estimated Station Totals *	56,950	42,530	99,480
Average Weekly Circulation (2009)	44,844	23,858	68,702
Average Daily Circulation (2009)			42,944

Other DMA Total	Cable TV Households	Non-cable TV Households	Total TV Households
Estimated Station Totals *	40,800	31,720	72,520
Average Weekly Circulation (2009)	20,422	2,741	23,163
Average Daily Circulation (2009)			13,253

*Estimated station totals are sums of the Nielsen TV and Cable TV household estimates for each county in which the station registers viewing of more than 5% as per the Nielsen Survey Methods.

WVFX-DT
Ch. 10

Network Service: FOX, CW.

Grantee: Withers Broadcasting Co. of Clarksburg LLC, PO Box 1508, Mount Vernon, IL 62864-1508.

Studio: 775 W Pike St, Clarksburg, WV 26301.

Mailing Address: PO Box 1475, Clarksburg, WV 26301.

Phone: 304-622-9839. **Fax:** 304-623-9021.

Web Site: http://www.wvfx.com

Technical Facilities: Channel No. 10 (192-198 MHz). Authorized power: 30-kw visual, aural. Antenna: 771-ft above av. terrain, 594-ft. above ground, 1955-ft. above sea level.

Latitude	39°	18'	02"
Longitude	80°	20'	37"

Note: Latitude and longitude coordinates shown are based on the North American Datum of 1927 (NAD 27) as currently required by the Mass Media Bureau of the FCC.

Ownership: W. Russell Withers Jr. (Group Owner).

Began Operation: February 20, 2004. Began analog operations: February 8, 1981. Sale to present owner by Davis Television Inc. approved by FCC March 31, 2008. Sale to Davis Television Inc. by Channel 49 Acquisition Corp. approved by FCC November 24, 1998. Sale to Channel 49 Acquisition Corp. by Christian Communications Center Inc. approved by FCC July 2, 1998. Ceased analog operations: June 12, 2009.

Represented (legal): Dennis J. Kelly.

Represented (sales): Blair Television.

Personnel:

Tim DeFazio, General Manager & General Sales Manager.

Mike McGougan, Chief Engineer.

Trisha Scott, Business Manager.

Kathy Busceker, Program & Promotion Director.

Patrick Coleman, Production Manager.

Barb Scott, Traffic Manager.

City of License: Clarksburg. **Station DMA:** Clarksburg-Weston, WV. **Rank:** 168.

Digital cable and TV coverage maps.
Visit www.warren-news.com/mediaprints.htm

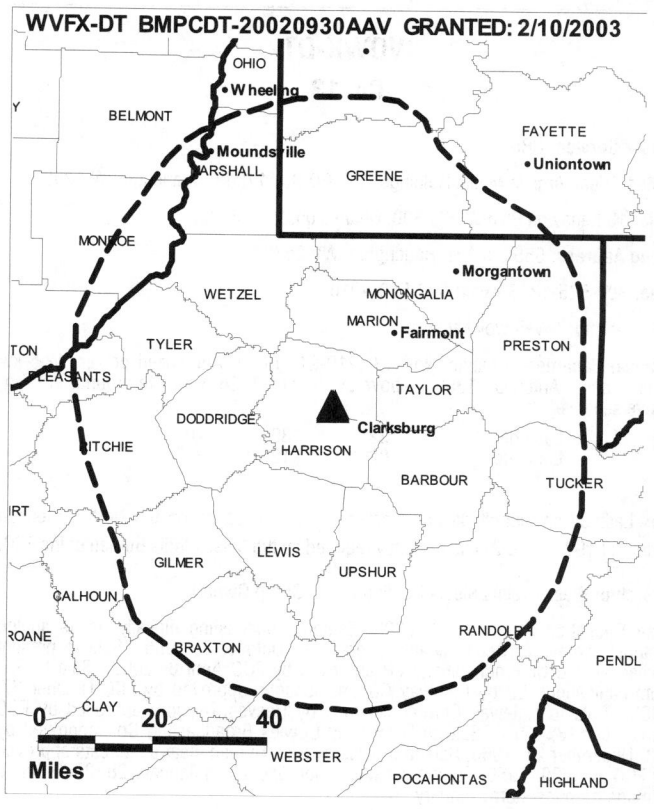

WVFX-DT BMPCDT-20020930AAV GRANTED: 2/10/2003

© 2010 Warren Communications News

Circulation © 2009 Nielsen. Coverage based on Nielsen study.

GrandTotal	Cable TV Households	Non-cable TV Households	Total TV Households
Estimated Station Totals *	92,040	42,530	134,570
Average Weekly Circulation (2009)	34,732	10,736	45,468
Average Daily Circulation (2009)			12,362

Station DMA Total	Cable TV Households	Non-cable TV Households	Total TV Households
Estimated Station Totals *	55,590	42,530	98,120
Average Weekly Circulation (2009)	26,950	10,736	37,686
Average Daily Circulation (2009)			11,110

Other DMA Total	Cable TV Households	Non-cable TV Households	Total TV Households
Estimated Station Totals *	36,450	0	36,450
Average Weekly Circulation (2009)	7,782	0	7,782
Average Daily Circulation (2009)			1,252

*Estimated station totals are sums of the Nielsen TV and Cable TV household estimates for each county in which the station registers viewing of more than 5% as per the Nielsen Survey Methods.

WOWK-DT
Ch. 13

Network Service: CBS.

Grantee: West Virginia Media Holdings LLC, PO Box 11848, Charleston, WV 25339.

Studio: 13 Kanawha Blvd W, Ste 300, Charleston, WV 25302.

Mailing Address: 555 5th Ave, Huntington, WV 25701.

Phone: 304-525-1313. **Fax:** 304-529-4910.

Web Site: http://www.wowktv.com

Technical Facilities: Channel No. 13 (210-216 MHz). Authorized power: 12.5-kw visual, aural. Antenna: 1358-ft above av. terrain, 1126-ft. above ground, 2097-ft. above sea level.

Latitude	32°	30'	20"
Longitude	82°	12'	32"

Note: Latitude and longitude coordinates shown are based on the North American Datum of 1927 (NAD 27) as currently required by the Mass Media Bureau of the FCC.

Ownership: West Virginia Media Holdings LLC (Group Owner).

Began Operation: October 24, 2005. Station broadcasting digitally on its analog channel allotment. Began analog operations: October 2, 1955. Sale to present owner by SJL Communications LP approved by FCC April 8, 2002. Sale to SJL Communications LP by Gateway Communications approved by FCC October 27, 2000. Sale to Gateway Communications by Reeves Telecom approved by FCC September 13, 1974. Sale to Reeves by Cowles Broadcasting Co. approved by FCC December 21, 1960. Sale to Cowles by S. J. Hyman theatre interests approved by FCC June 20, 1956. Station ceased analog operations January 28, 2009 due to damage from ice storm January 26.

Represented (legal): Bryan Cave LLP.

Represented (engineering): Cohen Dippell & Everist PC.

Represented (sales): Petry Media Corp.

Personnel:

Bray Cary, President & Chief Executive Officer.

John Fawcett, General Manager.

Chris Leister, General Sales Manager.

Brent Cowen, Local Sales Manager.

Scott Sterling, National Sales Manager.

Charlotte Cowen, Regional Sales Manager.

Ron Miller, News Director.

Bill Galloway, Chief Engineer.

M. J. Coss, Program Director.

Allen Payne, Production Manager.

City of License: Huntington. **Station DMA:** Charleston-Huntington, WV. **Rank:** 63.

© 2010 Warren Communications News

Circulation © 2009 Nielsen. Coverage based on Nielsen study.

GrandTotal	Cable TV Households	Non-cable TV Households	Total TV Households
Estimated Station Totals *	349,620	226,550	576,170
Average Weekly Circulation (2009)	172,029	103,675	275,704
Average Daily Circulation (2009)			117,621

Station DMA Total	Cable TV Households	Non-cable TV Households	Total TV Households
Estimated Station Totals *	276,720	201,780	478,500
Average Weekly Circulation (2009)	148,519	101,269	249,788
Average Daily Circulation (2009)			109,552

Other DMA Total	Cable TV Households	Non-cable TV Households	Total TV Households
Estimated Station Totals *	72,900	24,770	97,670
Average Weekly Circulation (2009)	23,510	2,406	25,916
Average Daily Circulation (2009)			8,069

*Estimated station totals are sums of the Nielsen TV and Cable TV household estimates for each county in which the station registers viewing of more than 5% as per the Nielsen Survey Methods.

WSAZ-DT
Ch. 23

Network Service: NBC, MNT.

Grantee: Gray Television Licensee LLC, 1750 K St NW, Ste 1200, Washington, DC 20006.

Studios: 645 5th Ave., Huntington, WV 25701; 111 Columbia Ave., Charleston, WV 25302.

Mailing Address: 645 5th Ave, Huntington, WV 25701.

Phone: 304-697-4780; 304-344-3521. **Fax:** 304-690-3061.

Web Site: http://www.wsaz.com

Technical Facilities: Channel No. 23 (524-530 MHz). Authorized power: max. visual, aural. Antenna: 1203-ft above av. terrain, 922-ft. above ground, 1933-ft. above sea level.

Latitude	38°	30'	36"
Longitude	82°	13'	10"

Note: Latitude and longitude coordinates shown are based on the North American Datum of 1927 (NAD 27) as currently required by the Mass Media Bureau of the FCC.

Satellite Earth Stations: Transmitter RCA; Pinzone, 5-meter Ku-band; Pinzone, 5-meter C-band; SatCom, 5.5-meter C-band; Pinzone, M/A-Com, Harris, DX Engineering receivers.

Ownership: Gray Television Inc. (Group Owner).

Began Operation: November 15, 2002. Began analog operations: October 14, 1949. Sale to present owner by Emmis Communications Corp. approved by FCC November 29, 2005. Sale to Emmis Communications Corp. by Lee Enterprises Inc. approved by FCC September 27, 2000. Sale to Lee Enterprises Inc. by Capital Cities Broadcasting approved by FCC February 1971. Previous sale by Goodwill Stations Inc. approved by FCC July 29, 1964. Sale to Goodwill Stations by Huntington Publishing Co. & Mrs. Eugene Katz approved by FCC March 20, 1961. Ceased analog operations: February 17, 2009.

Represented (legal): Wiley Rein LLP.

Represented (sales): Continental Television Sales.

Personnel:

Donald Ray, Vice President & General Manager.

Rebecca Swan, General Sales Manager.

Charlie Boush, National Sales Manager.

Scott Saxton, News Manager.

Aaron Withrow, Engineering Manager.

Barbara Gunn, Controller.

Edwin Lake, Promotions & Creative Services Manager.

Jack Deakin, Interactive Media Director.

City of License: Huntington. **Station DMA:** Charleston-Huntington, WV. **Rank:** 63.

© 2010 Warren Communications News

Circulation © 2009 Nielsen. Coverage based on Nielsen study.

GrandTotal	Cable TV Households	Non-cable TV Households	Total TV Households
Estimated Station Totals *	384,950	214,200	599,150
Average Weekly Circulation (2009)	218,197	139,261	357,458
Average Daily Circulation (2009)			213,989

Station DMA Total	Cable TV Households	Non-cable TV Households	Total TV Households
Estimated Station Totals *	278,140	201,780	479,920
Average Weekly Circulation (2009)	196,888	138,281	335,169
Average Daily Circulation (2009)			207,330

Other DMA Total	Cable TV Households	Non-cable TV Households	Total TV Households
Estimated Station Totals *	106,810	12,420	119,230
Average Weekly Circulation (2009)	21,309	980	22,289
Average Daily Circulation (2009)			6,659

*Estimated station totals are sums of the Nielsen TV and Cable TV household estimates for each county in which the station registers viewing of more than 5% as per the Nielsen Survey Methods.

WVNS-DT
Ch. 8

Network Service: CBS.

Grantee: West Virginia Media Holdings LLC, PO Box 11848, Charleston, WV 25339.

Studio: 141 Old Cline Rd., Ghent, WV 25843.

Mailing Address: PO Box 509, Ghent, WV 25843.

Phone: 304-787-5959. **Fax:** 304-787-2440.

Web Site: http://www.cbs59.com

Technical Facilities: Channel No. 8 (180-186 MHz). Authorized power: 3.86-kw visual, aural. Antenna: 1893-ft above av. terrain, 256-ft. above ground, 4131-ft. above sea level.

Latitude	37°	46'	22"
Longitude	80°	42'	25"

Note: Latitude and longitude coordinates shown are based on the North American Datum of 1927 (NAD 27) as currently required by the Mass Media Bureau of the FCC.

Ownership: West Virginia Media Holdings LLC (Group Owner).

Began Operation: August 1, 2005. Began analog operations: August 11, 1995. Station went off air in early 1996; resumed operation December 21, 1996. Sale to present owner by High Mountain Broadcasting Corp. approved by FCC January 9, 2003. Sale to High Mountain Broadcasting Corp. by WVGV Television Corp. approved by FCC April 4, 1996. Ceased analog operations: February 17, 2009.

Represented (legal): Willkie Farr & Gallagher LLP.

Represented (sales): Petry Media Corp.

Personnel:

John Fawcett, General Manager.

Jeff Morrison, Operations & Promotion Director.

Mark Ford, General Sales Manager.

Christy Buckland, News Director.

Gary Kirk, Chief Engineer.

Debbie Holstein, Accounts Receivable.

Donnie Aliff, Production Manager.

Cyndi Patrick, Traffic Manager.

City of License: Lewisburg. **Station DMA:** Bluefield-Beckley-Oak Hill, WV. **Rank:** 156.

WVNS-DT BMPCDT-20040608ABO GRANTED: 7/14/2004

© 2010 Warren Communications News

Circulation © 2009 Nielsen. Coverage based on Nielsen study.

GrandTotal	Cable TV Households	Non-cable TV Households	Total TV Households
Estimated Station Totals *	95,250	19,190	114,440
Average Weekly Circulation (2009)	48,560	2,619	51,179
Average Daily Circulation (2009)			21,293

Station DMA Total	Cable TV Households	Non-cable TV Households	Total TV Households
Estimated Station Totals *	95,250	19,190	114,440
Average Weekly Circulation (2009)	48,560	2,619	51,179
Average Daily Circulation (2009)			21,293

*Estimated station totals are sums of the Nielsen TV and Cable TV household estimates for each county in which the station registers viewing of more than 5% as per the Nielsen Survey Methods.

WWPX-TV
Ch. 12

Network Service: ION.

Licensee: ION Media Martinsburg License Inc., Debtor in Possession, 601 Clearwater Park Rd, West Palm Beach, FL 33401-6233.

Studio: 74 Swinging Bridge Rd, Martinsburg, WV 25403.

Mailing Address: 6199 Old Arrington Ln, Fairfax Station, VA 22039.

Phone: 703-503-7966; 888-466-1702. **Fax:** 703-503-1225.

E-mail: tanyalewis@ionmedia.com

Web Site: http://www.ionline.com

Technical Facilities: Channel No. 12 (204-210 MHz). Authorized power: 23-kw visual, aural. Antenna: 1030-ft above av. terrain, 243-ft. above ground, 1703-ft. above sea level.

Latitude	39°	27'	27"
Longitude	78°	03'	52"

Note: Latitude and longitude coordinates shown are based on the North American Datum of 1927 (NAD 27) as currently required by the Mass Media Bureau of the FCC.

Ownership: ION Media Networks Inc., Debtor in Possession (Group Owner).

Began Operation: October 31, 2002. Began analog operations: October 1, 1991. Sale to Flying A Communications Inc. by WEWV Inc. approved by FCC June 15, 1990. Sale to Paxson Communications Corp. by Flying A Communications LP, Gary A. Rosen, Trustee approved by FCC August 23, 1995. Station went off air; resumed operation August 1, 1996. Sale to DP Media Inc. by Paxson Communications Inc. approved by FCC April 16, 1997. Sale to Paxson Communications Corp. by DP Media Inc. approved by FCC June 1, 2000. Paxson Communications Corp. became ION Media Networks Inc. on June 26, 2006. Transfer of control by ION Media Networks Inc. from Paxson Management Corp. & Lowell W. Paxson to CIG Media LLC approved by FCC December 31, 2007. Involuntary assignment to debtor in possession status approved by FCC June 5, 2009. Ceased analog operations: June 12, 2009.

Represented (legal): Dow Lohnes PLLC.

Personnel:

Tanya Lewis, Traffic Manager.

City of License: Martinsburg. **Station DMA:** Washington, DC (Hagerstown, MD).

Rank: 9.

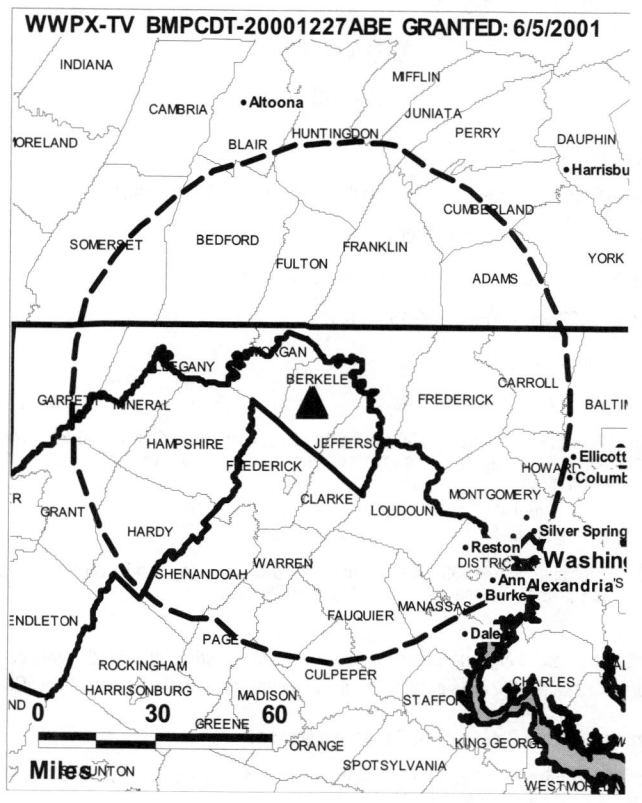

WWPX-TV BMPCDT-20001227ABE GRANTED: 6/5/2001

© 2010 Warren Communications News

Circulation © 2009 Nielsen. Coverage based on Nielsen study.

GrandTotal	Cable TV Households	Non-cable TV Households	Total TV Households
Estimated Station Totals *	158,020	38,940	196,960
Average Weekly Circulation (2009)	21,167	3,107	24,274
Average Daily Circulation (2009)			4,522

Station DMA Total	Cable TV Households	Non-cable TV Households	Total TV Households
Estimated Station Totals *	158,020	38,940	196,960
Average Weekly Circulation (2009)	21,167	3,107	24,274
Average Daily Circulation (2009)			4,522

*Estimated station totals are sums of the Nielsen TV and Cable TV household estimates for each county in which the station registers viewing of more than 5% as per the Nielsen Survey Methods.

WOAY-DT
Ch. 50

Network Service: ABC.

Licensee: Thomas Broadcasting Co., PO Box 3001, Oak Hill, WV 25901.

Studio: Rte. 16 S, Oak Hill, WV 25901.

Mailing Address: PO Box 3001, Oak Hill, WV 25901.

Phone: 304-469-3361. **Fax:** 304-465-1420.

E-mail: amarra@woay.com

Web Site: http://www.woay.com

Technical Facilities: Channel No. 50 (686-692 MHz). Authorized power: 600-kw max. visual, aural. Antenna: 656-ft above av. terrain, 565-ft. above ground, 2565-ft. above sea level.

Latitude	37°	57'	26"
Longitude	81°	09'	03"

Holds CP for change to 1000-kw max. visual, 778-ft above av. terrain, 693-ft. above ground, 2693-ft. above sea level; BPCDT-20080619AID.

Note: Latitude and longitude coordinates shown are based on the North American Datum of 1927 (NAD 27) as currently required by the Mass Media Bureau of the FCC.

Ownership: Thomas Broadcasting Co. (Group Owner).

Began Operation: April 23, 2007. Began analog operations: December 3, 1954. Ceased analog operations: June 12, 2009.

Represented (legal): Fletcher, Heald & Hildreth PLC.

Represented (engineering): Cavell, Mertz & Associates Inc.

Represented (sales): Continental Television Sales.

Personnel:

Robert R. Thomas III, President.

Al Marra, General Manager.

Joetta Kelly Oliver, General & Local Sales Manager.

Joe Wynne, National Sales & Traffic Manager.

Bob Brunner, News Director.

Jim Martin, Chief Engineer.

Andy Kahle, Promotion Manager.

Timothy Naylor, Production Manager.

City of License: Oak Hill. **Station DMA:** Bluefield-Beckley-Oak Hill, WV. **Rank:** 156.

WOAY-DT BPCDT-2008061AID GRANTED: 8/28/2008

© 2010 Warren Communications News

Circulation © 2009 Nielsen. Coverage based on Nielsen study.

GrandTotal	Cable TV Households	Non-cable TV Households	Total TV Households
Estimated Station Totals *	110,870	21,610	132,480
Average Weekly Circulation (2009)	53,896	5,336	59,232
Average Daily Circulation (2009)			23,474

Station DMA Total	Cable TV Households	Non-cable TV Households	Total TV Households
Estimated Station Totals *	95,250	21,610	116,860
Average Weekly Circulation (2009)	50,833	5,336	56,169
Average Daily Circulation (2009)			22,962

Other DMA Total	Cable TV Households	Non-cable TV Households	Total TV Households
Estimated Station Totals *	15,620	0	15,620
Average Weekly Circulation (2009)	3,063	0	3,063
Average Daily Circulation (2009)			512

*Estimated station totals are sums of the Nielsen TV and Cable TV household estimates for each county in which the station registers viewing of more than 5% as per the Nielsen Survey Methods.

WTAP-DT
Ch. 49

Network Service: NBC, MNT, FOX.

Licensee: Gray Television Licensee LLC, 1750 K St NW, Ste 1200, Washington, DC 20006.

Studio: One Television Plaza, Parkersburg, WV 26101.

Mailing Address: One Television Pl, Parkersburg, WV 26101.

Phone: 304-485-4588. **Fax:** 304-422-3920.

E-mail: bruce.layman@wtap.com

Web Site: http://www.wtap.com

Technical Facilities: Channel No. 49 (680-686 MHz). Authorized power: 47.4-kw max. visual, aural. Antenna: 633-ft above av. terrain, 440-ft. above ground, 1407-ft. above sea level.

Latitude	39°	20'	59"
Longitude	81°	33'	56"

Requests CP for change to 1000-kw max. visual, 643-ft above av. terrain, 440-ft. above ground, 1410-ft. above sea level; lat. 39° 21' 00", long. 81° 33' 56", BPCDT-20080617ABQ.

Note: Latitude and longitude coordinates shown are based on the North American Datum of 1927 (NAD 27) as currently required by the Mass Media Bureau of the FCC.

Ownership: Gray Television Inc. (Group Owner).

Began Operation: January 15, 2004. High Definition. Began analog operations: October 8, 1953. Sale to present owner by Benedek Broadcasting Co. LLC approved by FCC August 29, 2002 (Television Digest, Vol. 42:14). Sale to Benedek Broadcasting Co. LLC by CMA Communications Inc. (Robert E. Richardson, et al.), approved by FCC October 3, 1979 (Vol. 19:44). Sale to CMA Communications by R. L. Drake Co. approved by FCC November 1974. Sale to Broadcasting Services Inc. by Zanesville Times-Recorder & Signal approved by FCC November 2, 1967. Sale to Zanesville Times-Recorder & Signal by Frank Baer-Howard Chernoff group approved by FCC March 30, 1955 (Vol. 11:10, 14). Ceased analog operations: February 17, 2009.

Represented (legal): Wiley Rein LLP.

Represented (sales): Continental Television Sales.

Personnel:

Roger Sheppard, Vice President & Station Manager.

Shane Vass, Sales Manager.

Bruce Layman, News Director.

Joyce Ancrile, Program & Promotion Director.

Larry White, Production Manager.

Jeff Nutter, Creative Services Director.

Tammy Lockhart, Traffic Manager.

City of License: Parkersburg. **Station DMA:** Parkersburg, WV. **Rank:** 194.

WTAP-DT BPCDT-20080617ABQ GRANTED: 4/13/2009

© 2010 Warren Communications News

Circulation © 2009 Nielsen. Coverage based on Nielsen study.

GrandTotal	Cable TV Households	Non-cable TV Households	Total TV Households
Estimated Station Totals *	70,010	18,060	88,070
Average Weekly Circulation (2009)	40,977	6,870	47,847
Average Daily Circulation (2009)			29,539

Station DMA Total	Cable TV Households	Non-cable TV Households	Total TV Households
Estimated Station Totals *	45,700	18,060	63,760
Average Weekly Circulation (2009)	38,037	6,870	44,907
Average Daily Circulation (2009)			29,010

Other DMA Total	Cable TV Households	Non-cable TV Households	Total TV Households
Estimated Station Totals *	24,310	0	24,310
Average Weekly Circulation (2009)	2,940	0	2,940
Average Daily Circulation (2009)			529

*Estimated station totals are sums of the Nielsen TV and Cable TV household estimates for each county in which the station registers viewing of more than 5% as per the Nielsen Survey Methods.

WDTV-DT
Ch. 5

Network Service: CBS.

Grantee: Withers Broadcasting Co. of West Virginia, PO Box 480, 5 Television Dr, Bridgeport, WV 26330.

Studio: 5 Television Dr., Bridgeport, WV 26330.

Mailing Address: PO Box 480, Bridgeport, WV 26330.

Phone: 304-848-5000. **Fax:** 304-842-7501.

E-mail: bscott@wdtv.com

Web Site: http://www.wdtv.com

Technical Facilities: Channel No. 5 (76-82 MHz). Authorized power: 10-kw visual, aural. Antenna: 787-ft above av. terrain, 614-ft. above ground, 1973-ft. above sea level.

Latitude	39°	18'	02"
Longitude	80°	20'	37"

Note: Latitude and longitude coordinates shown are based on the North American Datum of 1927 (NAD 27) as currently required by the Mass Media Bureau of the FCC.

Ownership: W. Russell Withers Jr. (Group Owner).

Began Operation: July 19, 2005. Station broadcasting digitally on its analog channel allotment. Began analog operations: June 22, 1960. Sale to present owner by Broadcasting Industries of West Virginia approved by FCC April 5, 1973. Transfer of control to William A. Meehan, Receiver, by Broadcast Industries of West Virginia approved by FCC June 30, 1971. Sale to Broadcast Industries (formerly Medallion Pictures) by J. Patrick Beacom, Thomas P. Johnson & George W. Eby approved by FCC August 24, 1966 (Television Digest, Vol. 6:34, 35). Ceased analog operations: June 12, 2009.

Represented (sales): Continental Television Sales.

Personnel:

Tim DeFazio, General Manager & General Sales Manager.

Howard Spurlock, Local Sales Manager.

Scott Snyder, News Director.

Dave Compton, Chief Engineer.

Barbara Scott, Business & Traffic Manager.

Nathan Allen, Program Director.

Caffie Busdeker, Promotion Director.

John Breen, Production Manager.

City of License: Weston. **Station DMA:** Clarksburg-Weston, WV. **Rank:** 168.

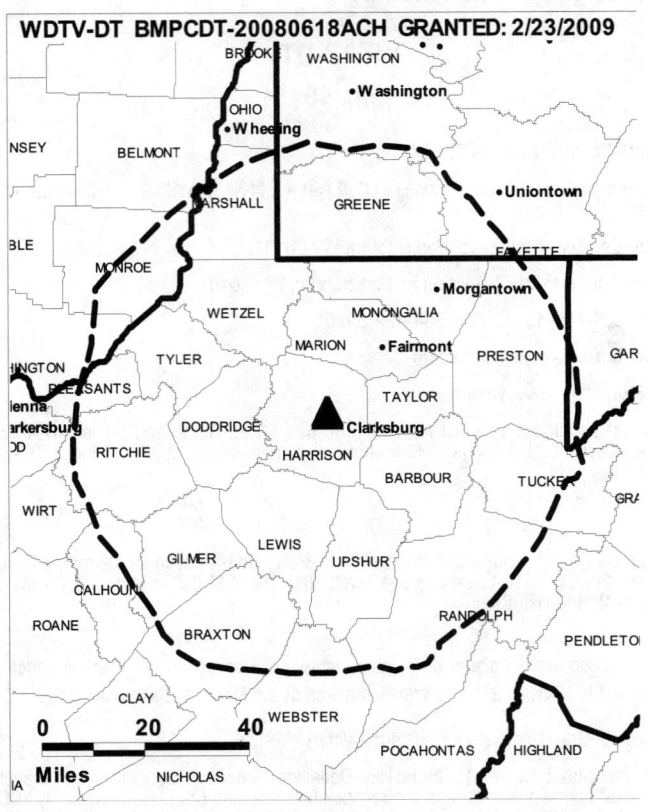

© 2010 Warren Communications News

Circulation © 2009 Nielsen. Coverage based on Nielsen study.

GrandTotal	Cable TV Households	Non-cable TV Households	Total TV Households
Estimated Station Totals *	100,760	59,930	160,690
Average Weekly Circulation (2009)	49,164	24,265	73,429
Average Daily Circulation (2009)			35,292

Station DMA Total	Cable TV Households	Non-cable TV Households	Total TV Households
Estimated Station Totals *	56,950	42,530	99,480
Average Weekly Circulation (2009)	35,010	22,470	57,480
Average Daily Circulation (2009)			30,122

Other DMA Total	Cable TV Households	Non-cable TV Households	Total TV Households
Estimated Station Totals *	43,810	17,400	61,210
Average Weekly Circulation (2009)	14,154	1,795	15,949
Average Daily Circulation (2009)			5,170

*Estimated station totals are sums of the Nielsen TV and Cable TV household estimates for each county in which the station registers viewing of more than 5% as per the Nielsen Survey Methods.

WTRF-DT
Ch. 7

Network Service: CBS.

Grantee: West Virginia Media Holdings LLC, PO Box 11848, Charleston, WV 25339.

Studio: 96 16th St., Wheeling, WV 26003-0744.

Mailing Address: 96 16th St, Wheeling, WV 26003.

Phone: 304-232-7777. **Fax:** 304-232-4975.

Web Site: http://www.wtrf.com

Technical Facilities: Channel No. 7 (174-180 MHz). Authorized power: 25.4-kw visual, aural. Antenna: 961-ft above av. terrain, 707-ft. above ground, 1991-ft. above sea level.

Latitude	40°	03'	41"
Longitude	80°	45'	08"

Note: Latitude and longitude coordinates shown are based on the North American Datum of 1927 (NAD 27) as currently required by the Mass Media Bureau of the FCC.

Ownership: West Virginia Media Holdings LLC (Group Owner).

Began Operation: February 17, 2009. Broadcasting digitally on its analog channel allotment. Began analog operations: October 24, 1953. Sale to present owner by Benedek Broadcasting Co. LLC approved by FCC March 12, 2002 (Television Digest, Vol. 42:14). Transfer of control to Benedek Broadcasting Co. LLC from Brissette Broadcasting approved by FCC May 22, 1996 (Vol. 35:37, 52). Sale to Brissette Broadcasting Corp. by Adams Communications approved by FCC December 24, 1991. Sale to Adams Communications by Wesray Corp. approved by FCC December 23, 1987. Sale to Wesray Corp. by Forward Communications approved by FCC August 16, 1984. Transfer of control to Forward Communications from Albert V. Dix family approved by FCC February 28, 1969. Forward assumed control April 8, 1969. Previously, Dix family increased holdings from 30% to 90% by stock purchases from Wheeling Intelligencer and News Register (30%) and Thomas Bloch family & estate after FCC approved transfer of control December 17, 1958 (Vol. 14:46, 48, 52). Ceased analog operations: February 17 2009.

Represented (sales): Petry Media Corp.

Personnel:

Roger Lyons, General Manager.

Charlotte Cohen, General Sales Manager.

Brenda Danehart, News Director.

Brad Stanford, Chief Engineer.

Tom Guadino, Human Resources Manager.

M. J. Coss, Program & Traffic Manager.

Jane Dombroski, Promotion Manager.

City of License: Wheeling. **Station DMA:** Wheeling, WV-Steubenville, OH. **Rank:** 159.

© 2010 Warren Communications News

Circulation © 2009 Nielsen. Coverage based on Nielsen study.

GrandTotal	Cable TV Households	Non-cable TV Households	Total TV Households
Estimated Station Totals *	135,790	43,680	179,470
Average Weekly Circulation (2009)	73,029	12,433	85,462
Average Daily Circulation (2009)			44,131

Station DMA Total	Cable TV Households	Non-cable TV Households	Total TV Households
Estimated Station Totals *	98,310	35,390	133,700
Average Weekly Circulation (2009)	63,029	11,795	74,824
Average Daily Circulation (2009)			41,061

Other DMA Total	Cable TV Households	Non-cable TV Households	Total TV Households
Estimated Station Totals *	37,480	8,290	45,770
Average Weekly Circulation (2009)	10,000	638	10,638
Average Daily Circulation (2009)			3,070

*Estimated station totals are sums of the Nielsen TV and Cable TV household estimates for each county in which the station registers viewing of more than 5% as per the Nielsen Survey Methods.

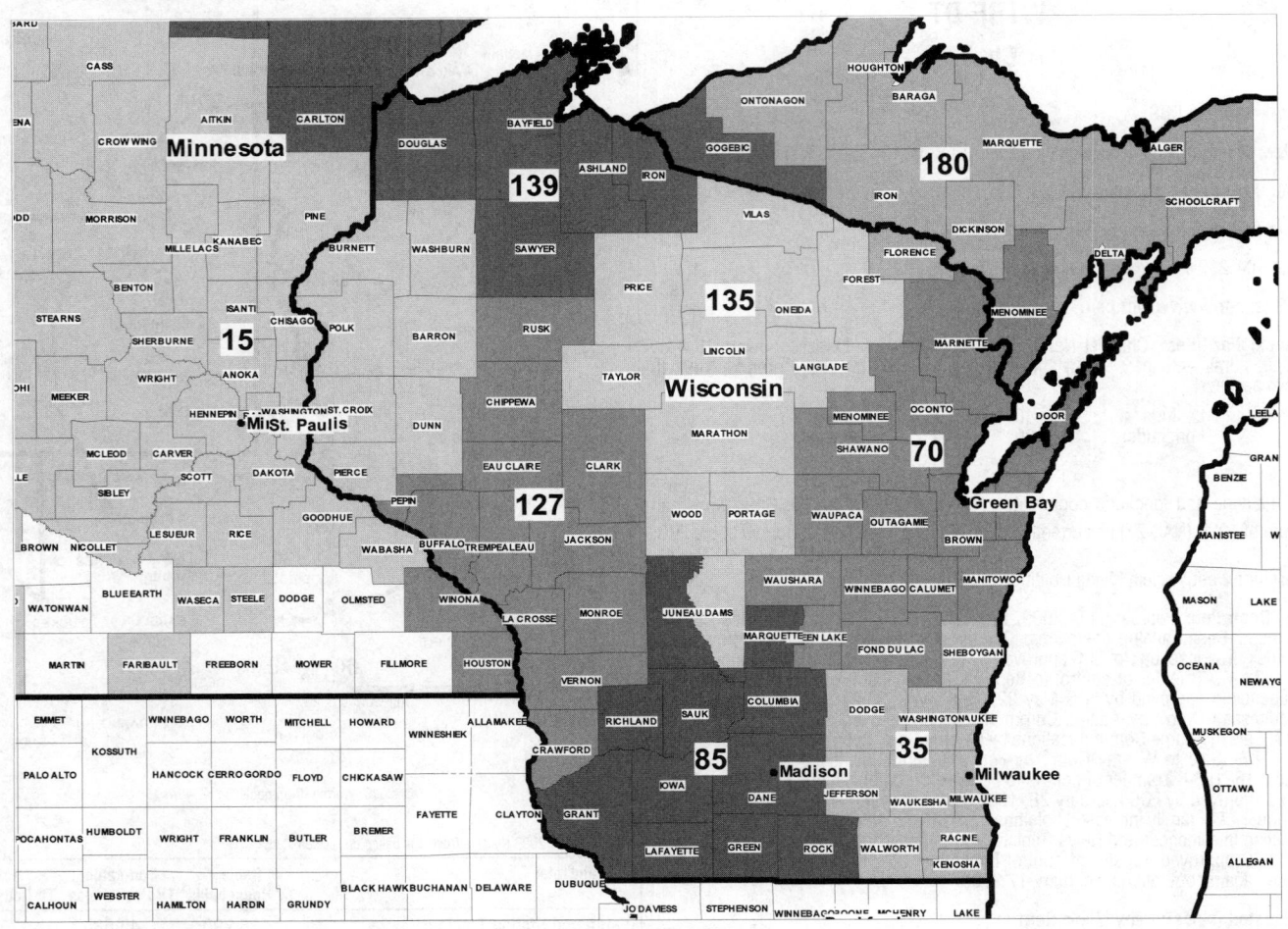

© 2010 Warren Communications News

MARKET	NIELSEN DMA TV HOUSEHOLDS	RANK	MARKET AREA COMMERCIAL STATIONS
Minneapolis-St. Paul, MN	1,732,050	15	KARE-DT (11); KCCO-DT (7); KCCW-DT (12); KFTC-DT (26); KMSP-DT (9); KPXM-TV (40); KRWF-DT (27); KSAX-DT (42); KSTC-DT (45); KSTP-DT (50); WCCO-DT (32); WFTC-DT (29); WUCW-DT (22)
Milwaukee, WI	901,790	35	WBME-DT (48); WCGV-DT (25); WDJT-DT (46); WISN-DT (34); WITI-DT (33); WPXE-TV (40); WTMJ-DT (28); WVCY-DT (22); WVTV-DT (18); WWRS-DT (43)
Green Bay-Appleton, WI	443,420	70	WACY-TV (27); WBAY-DT (23); WFRV-DT (39); WGBA-TV (41); WIWB-DT (21); WLUK-DT (11)
Madison, WI	377,260	85	WBUW-DT (32); WISC-DT (50); WKOW-DT (26); WMSN-DT (11); WMTV-DT (19)
La Crosse-Eau Claire, WI	214,820	127	WEAU-DT (13); WEUX-DT (49); WKBT-DT (8); WLAX-DT (17); WQOW-DT (15); WXOW-DT (48)
Wausau-Rhinelander, WI	184,720	135	WAOW-DT (9); WFXS-DT (31); WJFW-DT (16); WSAW-DT (7); WTPX-TV (46); WYOW-DT (28)
Duluth, MN-Superior, WI	174,360	139	KBJR-DT (19); KDLH-DT (33); KQDS-DT (17); KRII-DT (11); WDIO-DT (10); WIRT-DT (13)
Marquette, MI	88,490	180	WBKP-DT (5); WBUP-DT (10); WDHS-DT (8); WJMN-DT (48); WLUC-DT (35); WZMQ-DT (19)

Wisconsin Station Totals as of October 1, 2009

	VHF	UHF	TOTAL
Commercial Television	6	28	34
Educational Television	1	7	8
	7	35	42

WTPX-DT
Ch. 46

Network Service: ION.

Licensee: ION Media Wausau License Inc., Debtor in Possession, 601 Clearwater Park Rd, West Palm Beach, FL 33401-6233.

Studio: 6161 N Flint Rd, Ste F, Glendale, WI 53209.

Mailing Address: 6161 N Flint Rd, Ste F, Glendale, WI 53209.

Phone: 414-247-0117. **Fax:** 414-247-1302.

E-mail: shirleyzyniecki@ionmedia.com

Web Site: http://www.ionline.tv

Technical Facilities: Channel No. 46 (662-668 MHz). Authorized power: 50-kw max. visual, aural. Antenna: 938-ft above av. terrain, 860-ft. above ground, 2329-ft. above sea level.

Latitude	45°	03'	22"
Longitude	89°	27'	54"

Note: Latitude and longitude coordinates shown are based on the North American Datum of 1927 (NAD 27) as currently required by the Mass Media Bureau of the FCC.

Ownership: ION Media Networks Inc., Debtor in Possession (Group Owner).

Began Operation: November 15, 2001. Station went straight to digital broadcast after analog CP conversion. Involuntary assignment to debtor in possession status approved by FCC June 5, 2009. Transfer of control by ION Media Networks Inc. from Paxson Management Corp. & Lowell W. Paxson to CIG Media LLC approved by FCC December 31, 2007. Paxson Communications Corp. became ION Media Networks Inc. on June 26, 2006. Conversion of analog CP to digital operation approved by FCC October 4, 2001. Sale to Paxson Communications Corp. by Price Communications Corp. approved by FCC April 18, 2000. Sale to Paxson Communications Corp. by Price Communications Corp. approved by FCC April 18, 2000.

Represented (legal): Dow Lohnes PLLC.

Personnel:

Laurie Lau, Station Operations Manager.

Paul Freel, Chief Engineer.

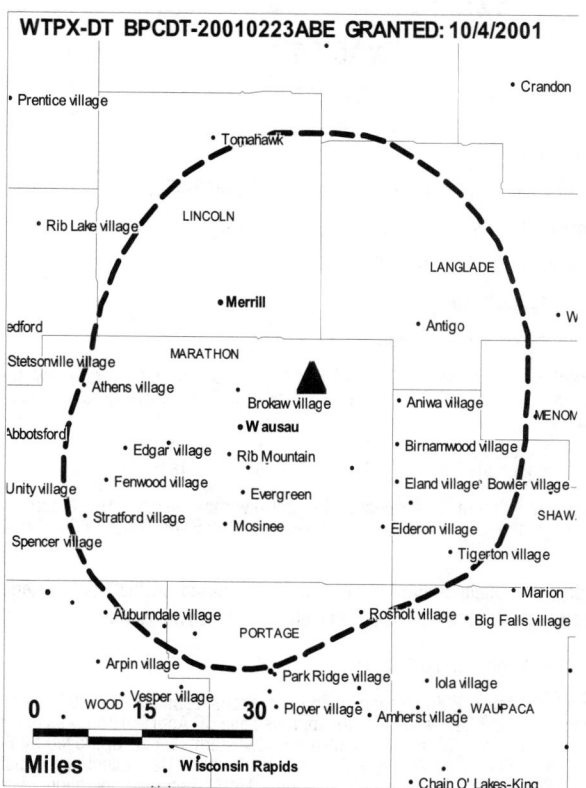

WTPX-DT BPCDT-20010223ABE GRANTED: 10/4/2001

© 2010 Warren Communications News

Shirley Zyniecki, Traffic Manager.

City of License: Antigo. **Station DMA:** Wausau-Rhinelander, WI. **Rank:** 135.

Nielsen Data: Not available.

WACY-TV
Ch. 27

Network Service: MNT.

Grantee: Ace TV Inc., 1391 North Rd, Green Bay, WI 54313-5723.

Mailing Address: 1391 North Rd, Green Bay, WI 54313.

Phone: 920-490-0320. **Fax:** 920-494-9550.

E-mail: genmgr@upn32.com

Web Site: http://www.mynew32.com

Technical Facilities: Channel No. 27 (548-554 MHz). Authorized power: 50-kw max. visual, aural. Antenna: 975-ft above av. terrain, 785-ft. above ground, 1775-ft. above sea level.

| Latitude | 44° | 21' | 30" |
| Longitude | 87° | 58' | 48" |

Requests modification of CP for change to 1000-kw max. visual, 1199-ft above av. terrain, 1009-ft. above ground, 1999-ft. above sea level; BMPCDT-20080620AHO.

Note: Latitude and longitude coordinates shown are based on the North American Datum of 1927 (NAD 27) as currently required by the Mass Media Bureau of the FCC.

Ownership: Ace TV Inc. (Group Owner).

Began Operation: May 1, 2002. Began analog operations: January 15, 1984. Transfer of control to Appleton Midwestern TV Ltd. approved by FCC April 9, 1985. Assignment to Richard D. Ellenburg, Trustee by Appleton Midwestern TV Ltd. approved by FCC November 18, 1991. Sale to present owner by Richard De. Ellenburg, Trustee approved by FCC August 3, 1992. Left air August 1993. Resumed operation June 3, 1994. Shirley Martin assumed control of ACE after death of Carl J. Martin in 2000. Ceased analog operations: June 12, 2009.

Represented (sales): Petry Media Corp.

Personnel:

Warren Glover, General Manager & Program Director.

Dave Drissen, Chief Engineer.

Joe Poss, General Sales Manager.

Ken Ambrosius, Marketing Director.

City of License: Appleton. **Station DMA:** Green Bay-Appleton, WI. **Rank:** 70.

TELEVISION & CABLE
Factbook Online

| continuous updates | fully searchable | easy to use |

For more information call **800-771-9202** or visit **www.warren-news.com**

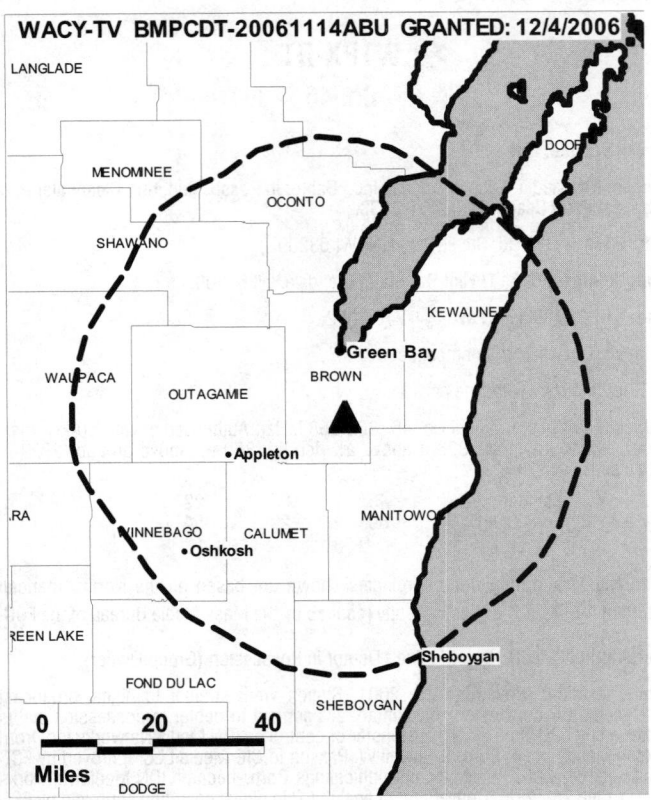

WACY-TV BMPCDT-20061114ABU GRANTED: 12/4/2006

© 2010 Warren Communications News

Circulation © 2009 Nielsen. Coverage based on Nielsen study.

GrandTotal	Cable TV Households	Non-cable TV Households	Total TV Households
Estimated Station Totals *	221,230	214,290	435,520
Average Weekly Circulation (2009)	39,330	56,637	95,967
Average Daily Circulation (2009)			29,504

Station DMA Total	Cable TV Households	Non-cable TV Households	Total TV Households
Estimated Station Totals *	217,100	214,290	431,390
Average Weekly Circulation (2009)	38,681	56,637	95,318
Average Daily Circulation (2009)			29,423

Other DMA Total	Cable TV Households	Non-cable TV Households	Total TV Households
Estimated Station Totals *	4,130	0	4,130
Average Weekly Circulation (2009)	649	0	649
Average Daily Circulation (2009)			81

*Estimated station totals are sums of the Nielsen TV and Cable TV household estimates for each county in which the station registers viewing of more than 5% as per the Nielsen Survey Methods.

WEUX-DT
Ch. 49

Network Service: FOX.

Grantee: GM Chippewa Falls Licensing LLC, 915 Middle River Dr, Ste 409, Fort Lauderdale, FL 33304.

Studio: 800 Wisconsin St., Building 2, Suite 101, PO Box 60, Eau Claire, WI 54701.

Mailing Address: PO Box 259, La Crosse, WI 54603.

Phone: 715-831-2548. **Fax:** 715-831-2550.

Web Site: http://www.fox25fox48.com

Technical Facilities: Channel No. 49 (680-686 MHz). Authorized power: 1000-kw max. visual, aural. Antenna: 731-ft above av. terrain, 472-ft. above ground, 1736-ft. above sea level.

Latitude	44°	57'	24"
Longitude	91°	40'	03"

Note: Latitude and longitude coordinates shown are based on the North American Datum of 1927 (NAD 27) as currently required by the Mass Media Bureau of the FCC.

Ownership: Grant Co. Inc. (Group Owner).

Began Operation: October 24, 2008. Began analog operations: March 8, 1993. Sale to present owner by Aries Telecommunication Corp. approved by FCC December 15, 1995. Sale to Aries Telecommunication Corp. by Family Group Ltd. III approved by FCC February 28, 1992. Sale to Aries Telecommunication Corp. by Family Group Ltd. III approved by FCC April 9, 1991, but was never consummated. Sale to Krypton Broadcast Corp. by Family Group Ltd. III approved by FCC May 17, 1989, but was never consummated. Ceased analog operations: February 17, 2009.

Represented (legal): Wilkinson Barker Knauer LLP.

Personnel:

Bob Weinstein, Station Manager.

Steve Wroth, Local & Regional Sales Manager.

Mark Burg, Chief Engineer.

Kenny Ammerman, Business Manager.

Barb Quillan, Program Director.

Pat Stiphout, Promotion Director.

Eric Barczak, Traffic Manager.

City of License: Chippewa Falls. **Station DMA:** La Crosse-Eau Claire, WI. **Rank:** 127.

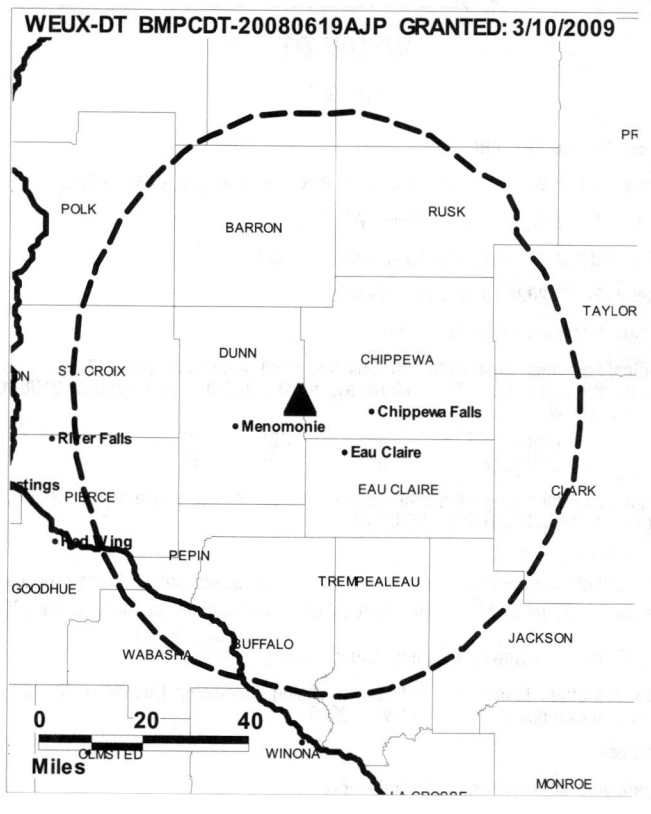

WEUX-DT BMPCDT-20080619AJP GRANTED: 3/10/2009

© 2010 Warren Communications News

Circulation © 2009 Nielsen. Coverage based on Nielsen study.

GrandTotal	Cable TV Households	Non-cable TV Households	Total TV Households
Estimated Station Totals *	68,360	59,620	127,980
Average Weekly Circulation (2009)	31,466	10,637	42,103
Average Daily Circulation (2009)			15,380

Station DMA Total	Cable TV Households	Non-cable TV Households	Total TV Households
Estimated Station Totals *	48,730	51,500	100,230
Average Weekly Circulation (2009)	23,501	9,257	32,758
Average Daily Circulation (2009)			12,886

Other DMA Total	Cable TV Households	Non-cable TV Households	Total TV Households
Estimated Station Totals *	19,630	8,120	27,750
Average Weekly Circulation (2009)	7,965	1,380	9,345
Average Daily Circulation (2009)			2,494

*Estimated station totals are sums of the Nielsen TV and Cable TV household estimates for each county in which the station registers viewing of more than 5% as per the Nielsen Survey Methods.

WYOW-DT
Ch. 28

Network Service: CW, ABC.

Grantee: WAOW-WYOW Television Inc., PO Box 909, Quincy, IL 62306-0909.

Studio: 528 Pine St, Ste B, Eagle River, WI 54521.

Mailing Address: PO Box 2705, Eagle River, WI 54521.

Phone: 715-477-2020. **Fax:** 715-477-2438.

Web Site: http://www.wyowtv34.com

Technical Facilities: Channel No. 28 (554-560 MHz). Authorized power: 70-kw max. visual, aural. Antenna: 472-ft above av. terrain, 426-ft. above ground, 2106-ft. above sea level.

Latitude	45°	46'	30"
Longitude	89°	14'	55"

Requests CP for change to 535-ft above av. terrain, 489-ft. above ground, 2169-ft. above sea level; BPCDT-20090630ACN.

Note: Latitude and longitude coordinates shown are based on the North American Datum of 1927 (NAD 27) as currently required by the Mass Media Bureau of the FCC.

Ownership: Quincy Newspapers Inc. (Group Owner).

Began Operation: March 15, 2006. Began analog operations: December 22, 1996. Ceased analog operations: February 17 2009.

Personnel:

Laurin Jorstad, President & General Manager.

Kathy Silk, General Sales Manager.

Joe Tessmer, National Sales Manager.

Randy Winter, News Director & Production Manager.

Russ Crass, Chief Engineer.

Tara Marshal, Program Director & Traffic Manager.

Mark Oliver, Promotion Director.

Tricia Schairer, Human Resources Manager.

City of License: Eagle River. **Station DMA:** Wausau-Rhinelander, WI. **Rank:** 135.

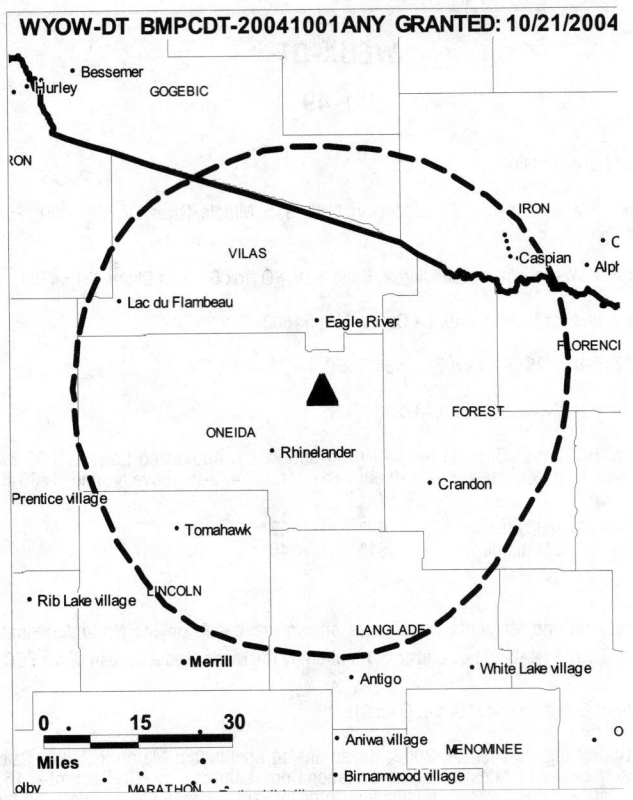

WYOW-DT BMPCDT-20041001ANY GRANTED: 10/21/2004

© 2010 Warren Communications News

Circulation © 2009 Nielsen. Coverage based on Nielsen study.

GrandTotal	Cable TV Households	Non-cable TV Households	Total TV Households
Estimated Station Totals *	19,970	15,870	35,840
Average Weekly Circulation (2009)	5,709	2,774	8,483
Average Daily Circulation (2009)			3,966

Station DMA Total	Cable TV Households	Non-cable TV Households	Total TV Households
Estimated Station Totals *	15,000	15,870	30,870
Average Weekly Circulation (2009)	5,156	2,774	7,930
Average Daily Circulation (2009)			3,835

Other DMA Total	Cable TV Households	Non-cable TV Households	Total TV Households
Estimated Station Totals *	4,970	0	4,970
Average Weekly Circulation (2009)	553	0	553
Average Daily Circulation (2009)			131

*Estimated station totals are sums of the Nielsen TV and Cable TV household estimates for each county in which the station registers viewing of more than 5% as per the Nielsen Survey Methods.

WEAU-DT
Ch. 13

Network Service: NBC.

Grantee: Gray Television Licensee LLC, 1750 K St NW, Ste 1200, Washington, DC 20006.

Studio: 1907 S. Hastings Way, Eau Claire, WI 54701.

Mailing Address: PO Box 47, Eau Claire, WI 54702-0047.

Phone: 715-835-1313; 715-832-3474. **Fax:** 715-832-0246.

E-mail: info@weau.com

Web Site: http://www.weau.com

Technical Facilities: Channel No. 13 (210-216 MHz). Authorized power: 29.9-kw visual, aural. Antenna: 2005-ft above av. terrain, 1947-ft. above ground, 3044-ft. above sea level.

Latitude	44°	39'	50"
Longitude	90°	57'	40"

Note: Latitude and longitude coordinates shown are based on the North American Datum of 1927 (NAD 27) as currently required by the Mass Media Bureau of the FCC.

Ownership: Gray Television Inc. (Group Owner).

Began Operation: February 17, 2009. Station broadcasting digitally on its analog channel allotment. Began analog operations: December 17, 1953. Station sold to Cosmos Broadcasting Corp. by Busse Broadcasting Corp. Cosmos then swapped station for Gray Communications Systems WALB-TV, Albany, GA. Deal approved by FCC July 30, 1998 (Television Digest: 38:3, 8). Transfer of control within Busse Broadcasting Corp. to Mikael Salovaara & Alfred C. Eckert III from Lawrence A. Busse in reorganization approved by FCC May 2, 1995. Sale to Richard Benedek by Busse Broadcasting approved by FCC April 6, 1990 (Vol. 30:13), but never consummated. Sale to Busse Broadcasting by Gillett Broadcasting approved by FCC July 31, 1987. Sale to Gillett Broadcasting by Post Corp. approved by FCC June 19, 1984. Sale to Post Corp. by Morgan Murphy interest approved by FCC May 16, 1962 (Vol. 2:4, 21). Ceased analog operations: February 17, 2009.

Represented (legal): Wiley Rein LLP.

Personnel:

Terry McHugh, President & General Manager.

Tom Benson, Production Manager.

Wendy Gustofson, General & Local Sales Manager.

Glen Mabie, News Director.

Ron Wiedemeier, Chief Engineer.

Mary Berg, Business Manager.

Deanne Brott, Traffic Manager.

Jolene Jensen, Community Affairs Director & Programming Assistant.

City of License: Eau Claire. **Station DMA:** La Crosse-Eau Claire, WI. **Rank:** 127.

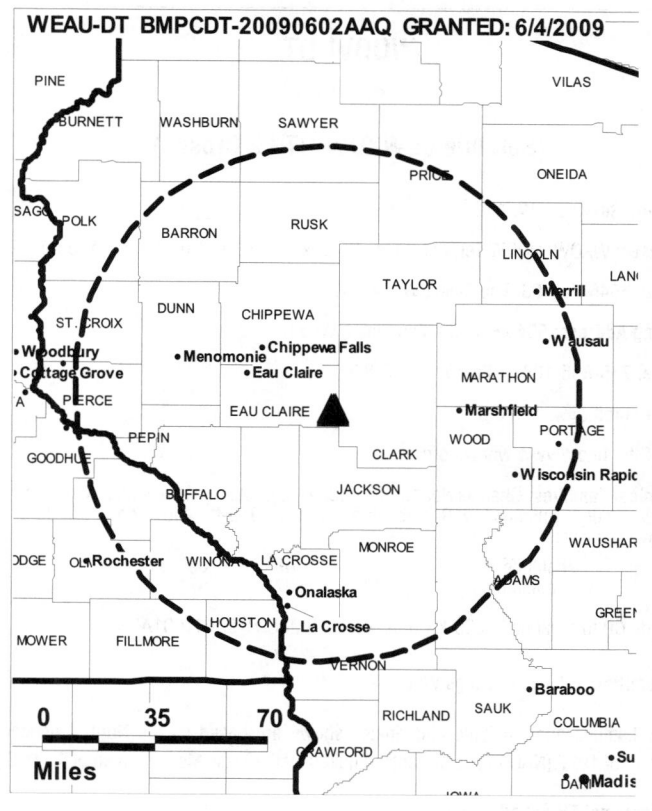

© 2010 Warren Communications News

Circulation © 2009 Nielsen. Coverage based on Nielsen study.

GrandTotal	Cable TV Households	Non-cable TV Households	Total TV Households
Estimated Station Totals *	200,120	184,190	384,310
Average Weekly Circulation (2009)	97,152	72,463	169,615
Average Daily Circulation (2009)			86,453

Station DMA Total	Cable TV Households	Non-cable TV Households	Total TV Households
Estimated Station Totals *	112,950	102,660	215,610
Average Weekly Circulation (2009)	69,840	59,601	129,441
Average Daily Circulation (2009)			70,825

Other DMA Total	Cable TV Households	Non-cable TV Households	Total TV Households
Estimated Station Totals *	87,170	81,530	168,700
Average Weekly Circulation (2009)	27,312	12,862	40,174
Average Daily Circulation (2009)			15,628

*Estimated station totals are sums of the Nielsen TV and Cable TV household estimates for each county in which the station registers viewing of more than 5% as per the Nielsen Survey Methods.

WQOW-DT
Ch. 15
(Satellite of WXOW-DT La Crosse)

Network Service: CW, ABC.

Licensee: WXOW/WQOW Television Inc., PO Box C-4019, La Crosse, WI 54602-4019.

Studio: 5545 Hwy 93, Eau Claire, WI 54701.

Mailing Address: 5545 Hwy 93, Eau Claire, WI 54701.

Phone: 715-835-1881. **Fax:** 715-835-8009.

E-mail: croth@wxow.com

Web Site: http://www.wqow.com

Technical Facilities: Channel No. 15 (476-482 MHz). Authorized power: 250-kw max. visual, aural. Antenna: 919-ft above av. terrain, 942-ft. above ground, 1831-ft. above sea level.

Latitude	44°	48'	00"
Longitude	91°	27'	57"

Holds CP for change to 200-kw max. visual; BMPCDT-20041001AOM.

Transmitter: 1907 S. Hastings Way.

Note: Latitude and longitude coordinates shown are based on the North American Datum of 1927 (NAD 27) as currently required by the Mass Media Bureau of the FCC.

Multichannel TV Sound: Stereo only.

Ownership: Quincy Newspapers Inc. (Group Owner).

Began Operation: October 1, 2002. High Definition. Began analog operations: September 22, 1980. Sale to Tak Communications (Sharad Tak) by Liberty Broadcasting approved by FCC January 7, 1985 (Television Digest, Vol. 24:43). Assignment of license to Operating Agent granted January 27, 1993. Sale to Shockley Communications Corp. approved by FCC September 27, 1995. Sale to present owner by Shockley Communications Corp. approved by FCC April 17, 2001 (Vol. 41:23). Ceased analog operations: February 17, 2009.

Represented (sales): Blair Television.

Represented (legal): Wilkinson Barker Knauer LLP.

Personnel:

Dave Booth, Vice President & General Manager.

Mark Golden, Station & Sales Manager.

Dave White, Chief Engineer.

Deborah Simonis, Program Director.

City of License: Eau Claire. **Station DMA:** La Crosse-Eau Claire, WI. **Rank:** 127.

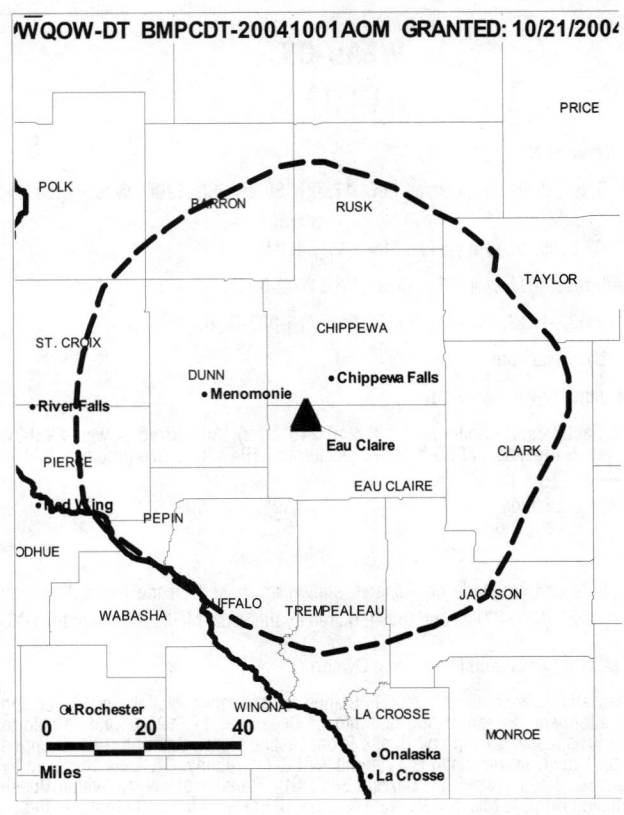

WQOW-DT BMPCDT-20041001AOM GRANTED: 10/21/2004

© 2010 Warren Communications News

Circulation © 2009 Nielsen. Coverage based on Nielsen study.

GrandTotal	Cable TV Households	Non-cable TV Households	Total TV Households
Estimated Station Totals *	75,400	61,580	136,980
Average Weekly Circulation (2009)	30,971	11,798	42,769
Average Daily Circulation (2009)			18,696

Station DMA Total	Cable TV Households	Non-cable TV Households	Total TV Households
Estimated Station Totals *	46,680	53,460	100,140
Average Weekly Circulation (2009)	24,191	10,824	35,015
Average Daily Circulation (2009)			16,334

Other DMA Total	Cable TV Households	Non-cable TV Households	Total TV Households
Estimated Station Totals *	28,720	8,120	36,840
Average Weekly Circulation (2009)	6,780	974	7,754
Average Daily Circulation (2009)			2,362

*Estimated station totals are sums of the Nielsen TV and Cable TV household estimates for each county in which the station registers viewing of more than 5% as per the Nielsen Survey Methods.

WWAZ-DT
Ch. 44

Network Service: IND.

Licensee: WMMF License LLC, 500 S. Chinowth Rd, Visalia, CA 93277.

Studio: 254 Winnebago Dr., Fond du Lac, WI 54935.

Mailing Address: PO Box 2326, Fond du Lac, WI 54936.

Phone: 920-921-6368. **Fax:** 920-907-8330.

Technical Facilities: Channel No. 44 (650-656 MHz). Authorized power: 700-kw max. visual, aural. Antenna: 640-ft above av. terrain, 469-ft. above ground, 1611-ft. above sea level.

Latitude	26°	20'	88"
Longitude	88°	31'	29"

Note: Latitude and longitude coordinates shown are based on the North American Datum of 1927 (NAD 27) as currently required by the Mass Media Bureau of the FCC.

Ownership: Pappas Telecasting Companies (Group Owner).

Began Operation: Began analog operations: March 1, 1995. Left air, date unreported. Resumed analog operation December 4, 2000. Ceased analog operations January 15th 2008 due to financial constraints. Station received permission from the FCC on July 28, 2008 to permanently cease analog operations and broadcast only in digital format. Station was operating digitally under Special Temporary Authority at 1.8-kw max. visual. Ceased digital operations January 12, 2009 due to financial constraints.

Personnel:

Howard Shrier, General Manager.

Edward Bok, Chief Engineer.

Debbie Sweeney, Program Director.

Lisa Moriarty, Receptionist.

City of License: Fond du Lac. **Station DMA:** Green Bay-Appleton, WI. **Rank:** 70.

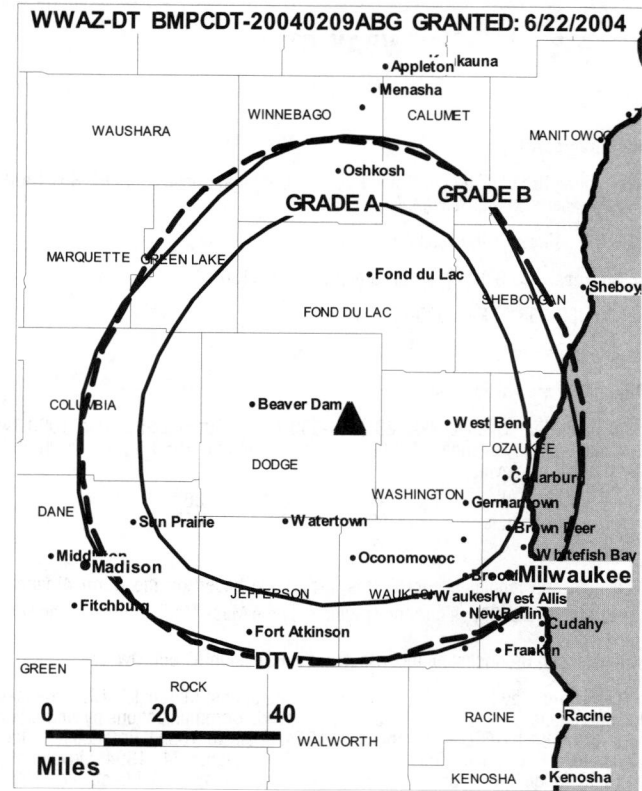

WWAZ-DT BMPCDT-20040209ABG GRANTED: 6/22/2004

© 2010 Warren Communications News

Nielsen Data: Not available.

WBAY-DT
Ch. 23

Network Service: ABC.

Licensee: Young Broadcasting of Green Bay Inc., Debtor in Possession, PO Box 1800, c/o Brooks, Pierce et al., Raleigh, NC 27602.

Studio: 115 S Jefferson St, Green Bay, WI 54301.

Mailing Address: 115 S Jefferson St, Green Bay, WI 54301.

Phone: 920-432-3331. **Fax:** 920-438-3355.

E-mail: rkrieghoff@wbay.com

Web Site: http://www.wbay.com

Technical Facilities: Channel No. 23 (524-530 MHz). Authorized power: 1000-kw max. visual, aural. Antenna: 1220-ft above av. terrain, 1066-ft. above ground, 1965-ft. above sea level.

Latitude	44°	24'	36"
Longitude	88°	00'	06"

Note: Latitude and longitude coordinates shown are based on the North American Datum of 1927 (NAD 27) as currently required by the Mass Media Bureau of the FCC.

Ownership: Young Broadcasting Inc., Debtor in Possession (Group Owner).

Began Operation: May 31, 2002. Began analog operations: March 17, 1953. Ceased analog operations: June 12, 2009. Sale to Nationwide Communications by Norbertine Fathers approved by FCC December 30, 1974. Sale to Young Broadcasting Inc. by Nationwide Communications approved by FCC August 24, 1994. Involuntary assignment to debtor in possession status approved by FCC March 17, 2009. Assignment to Young Broadcasting of Green Bay Inc. (New Young Broadcasting Holding Co. Inc.) pends.

Represented (legal): Brooks, Pierce, McLendon, Humphrey & Leonard LLP.

Personnel:

Don Carmichael, General Manager.

Dick Millhiser, Program & Operations Manager.

Steve Lavin, General Sales Manager.

Jonie Paye, National Sales Manager.

Tom McCarey, News Director.

Greg Tadyshak, Chief Engineer.

Peggy Wilcox, Business Manager.

Pam Jessen, Promotion & Public Service Director.

John Franken, Production Manager.

Willy Olson, Traffic Manager.

City of License: Green Bay. **Station DMA:** Green Bay-Appleton, WI. **Rank:** 70.

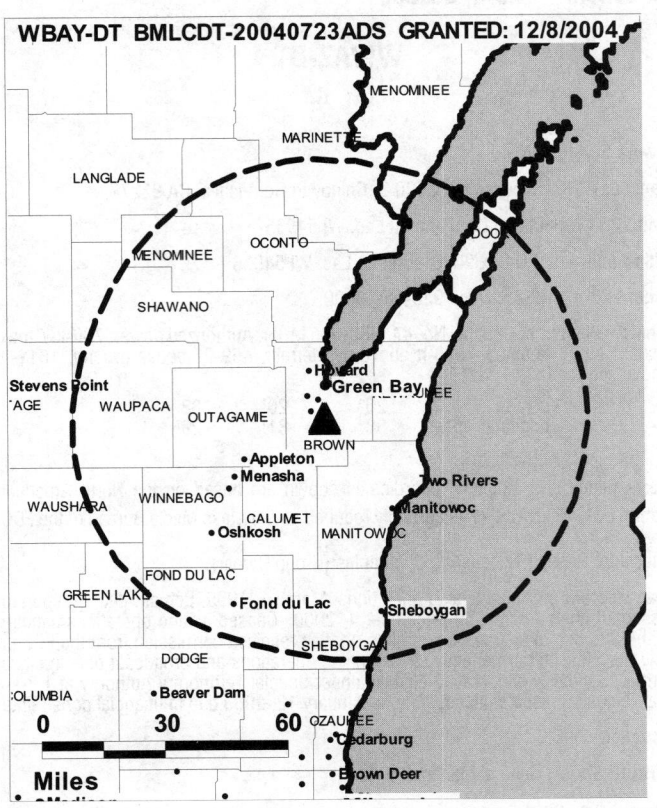

© 2010 Warren Communications News

Circulation © 2009 Nielsen. Coverage based on Nielsen study.

GrandTotal	Cable TV Households	Non-cable TV Households	Total TV Households
Estimated Station Totals *	274,390	260,140	534,530
Average Weekly Circulation (2009)	166,712	157,737	324,449
Average Daily Circulation (2009)			167,064

Station DMA Total	Cable TV Households	Non-cable TV Households	Total TV Households
Estimated Station Totals *	220,300	222,510	442,810
Average Weekly Circulation (2009)	156,547	154,812	311,359
Average Daily Circulation (2009)			162,455

Other DMA Total	Cable TV Households	Non-cable TV Households	Total TV Households
Estimated Station Totals *	54,090	37,630	91,720
Average Weekly Circulation (2009)	10,165	2,925	13,090
Average Daily Circulation (2009)			4,609

*Estimated station totals are sums of the Nielsen TV and Cable TV household estimates for each county in which the station registers viewing of more than 5% as per the Nielsen Survey Methods.

WFRV-DT
Ch. 39

Network Service: CBS.

Licensee: WFRV and WJMN Television Station Inc., 2175 K St NW, Ste 350, Washington, DC 20037.

Studios: 320 Patriot Dr, Little Chute, WI 54140; 1181 E Mason St, Green Bay, WI 54301.

Mailing Address: PO Box 19055, Green Bay, WI 54307-9055.

Phone: 920-437-5411. **Fax:** 920-437-4576.

E-mail: mitchede@wfrv.cbs.com

Web Site: http://www.wfrv.com

Technical Facilities: Channel No. 39 (320-626 MHz). Authorized power: 1000-kw max. visual, aural. Antenna: 1194-ft above av. terrain, 1126-ft. above ground, 2016-ft. above sea level.

Latitude	44°	20'	01"
Longitude	87°	58'	56"

Note: Latitude and longitude coordinates shown are based on the North American Datum of 1927 (NAD 27) as currently required by the Mass Media Bureau of the FCC.

Ownership: Liberty Media Corp. (Group Owner).

Began Operation: February 12, 2002. High Definition. Began analog operations: May 21, 1955. Transfer to present owner by CBS Corp. approved by FCC April 6, 2007. Purchase of CBS Inc. by Viacom Inc. approved by FCC May 3, 2000. Sale to CBS Inc. by Midwest Communications approved by FCC December 19, 1991. Sale to Midwest Communications by Orion Broadcasting approved by FCC August 14, 1981. Sale to Orion by S. N. Pickard group approved by FCC January 4, 1961. Ceased analog operations: February 17, 2009.

Represented (legal): Nelson Mullins Riley & Scarborough LLP.

Represented (sales): TeleRep Inc.

Personnel:

Perry Kidder, President & General Manager.

Dave Stewart, Vice President & Controller.

Dale Mitchell, Technical Operations, Marketing & Engineering Director.

Jackie Stewart, General Sales Manager.

Kit Overlock, Local Sales Manager.

H. Lee Hitter, News Director.

Jaci Haakonson, Program & Research Manager.

Gretchen Mattingly, Production Manager.

Jill Harkoff, Traffic Manager.

City of License: Green Bay. **Station DMA:** Green Bay-Appleton, WI. **Rank:** 70.

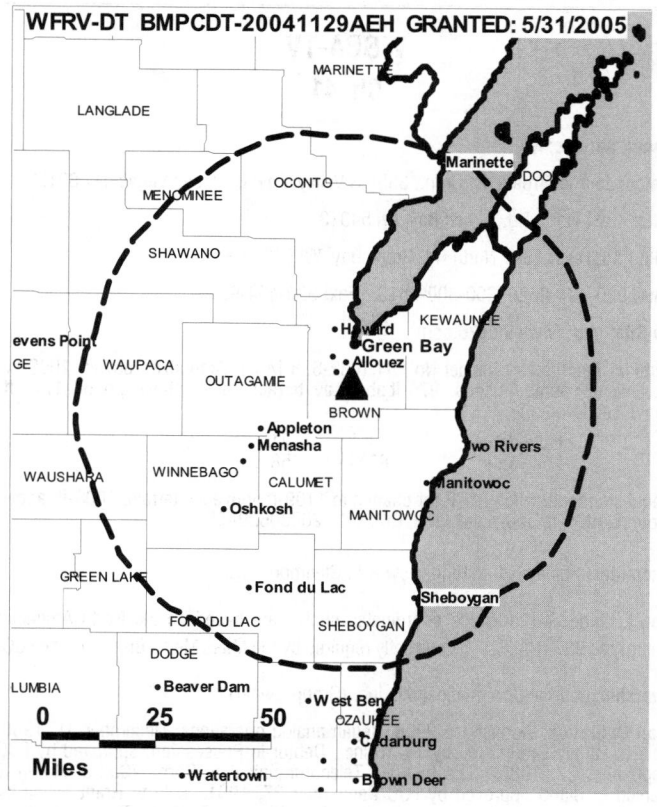

WFRV-DT BMPCDT-20041129AEH GRANTED: 5/31/2005

© 2010 Warren Communications News

Circulation © 2009 Nielsen. Coverage based on Nielsen study.

GrandTotal	Cable TV Households	Non-cable TV Households	Total TV Households
Estimated Station Totals *	292,080	264,870	556,950
Average Weekly Circulation (2009)	161,534	156,907	318,441
Average Daily Circulation (2009)			150,721

Station DMA Total	Cable TV Households	Non-cable TV Households	Total TV Households
Estimated Station Totals *	220,300	222,510	442,810
Average Weekly Circulation (2009)	148,950	153,792	302,742
Average Daily Circulation (2009)			144,852

Other DMA Total	Cable TV Households	Non-cable TV Households	Total TV Households
Estimated Station Totals *	71,780	42,360	114,140
Average Weekly Circulation (2009)	12,584	3,115	15,699
Average Daily Circulation (2009)			5,869

*Estimated station totals are sums of the Nielsen TV and Cable TV household estimates for each county in which the station registers viewing of more than 5% as per the Nielsen Survey Methods.

WGBA-TV
Ch. 41

Network Service: NBC.

Grantee: Journal Broadcast Corp., 3355 S Valley View Blvd, Las Vegas, NV 89102.

Studio: 1391 North Rd., Green Bay, WI 54313.

Mailing Address: 1391 North Rd, Green Bay, WI 54313.

Phone: 920-494-2626; 800-800-6619. **Fax:** 920-494-9550.

Web Site: http://www.nbc26.com

Technical Facilities: Channel No. 41 (632-638 MHz). Authorized power: 1000-kw max. visual, aural. Antenna: 975-ft above av. terrain, 785-ft. above ground, 1775-ft. above sea level.

Latitude	44°	21'	30"
Longitude	87°	58'	48"

Requests modification of CP for change to 1199-ft above av. terrain, 1009-ft. above ground, 1999-ft. above sea level; BMPCDT-20080620AEI.

Transmitter: Shirley Rd. at Ridgeview Rd., Glenmore Twp.

Note: Latitude and longitude coordinates shown are based on the North American Datum of 1927 (NAD 27) as currently required by the Mass Media Bureau of the FCC.

Ownership: Journal Communications Inc. (Group Owner).

Began Operation: August 13, 2008. Began analog operations: December 31, 1980. Sale to Family Group Ltd. by TV-26 Inc., Debtor-in-Possession, approved by FCC September 27, 1985. Sale to Aries Telecommunication Corp. (Carl J. Martin & Donald E. Clark) approved by FCC September 27, 1991. Sale to Grant Media by Aries Telecommunication Corp. approved by FCC July 29, 1992. Transfer to Aries Telecommunication Corp. by Grant Media approved by FCC June 27, 1997. Sale to present owner by Aries Telecommunication Corp. approved by FCC August 23, 2004. Ceased analog operations: June 12, 2009.

Represented (legal): Hogan & Hartson LLP.

Represented (sales): Petry Media Corp.

Personnel:

Guyanne Taylor, Vice President & General Manager.

Tanya Atkinson, National Sales Manager.

Megan Rushmore, News Director.

Dave Driesser, Assistant Chief Engineer.

Cheri Hendricks, Business Manager.

Willie Garrett, Promotion & Creative Services Director.

Erik Berger, Commercial Producer.

Patty Gamboa, Traffic Manager.

City of License: Green Bay. **Station DMA:** Green Bay-Appleton, WI. **Rank:** 70.

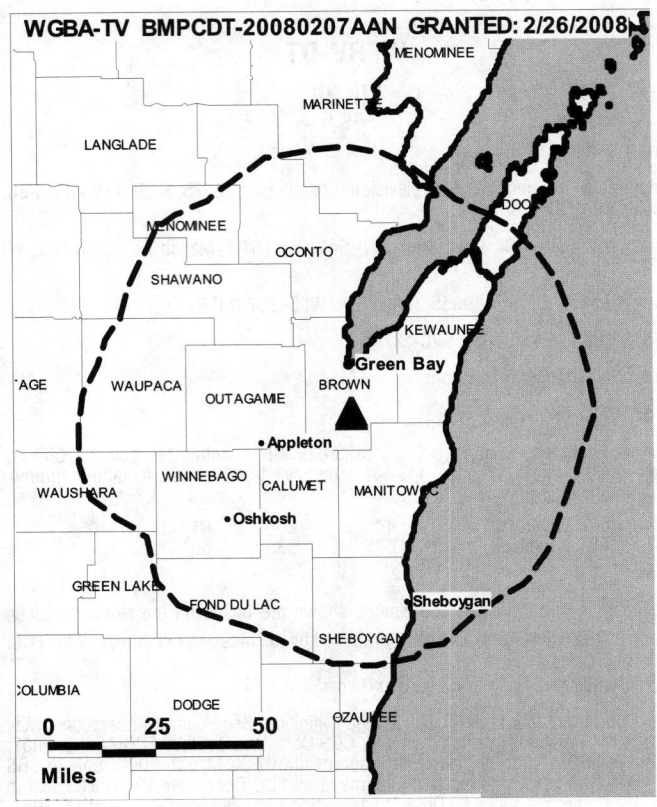

© 2010 Warren Communications News

Circulation © 2009 Nielsen. Coverage based on Nielsen study.

GrandTotal	Cable TV Households	Non-cable TV Households	Total TV Households
Estimated Station Totals *	252,790	244,110	496,900
Average Weekly Circulation (2009)	120,137	127,571	247,708
Average Daily Circulation (2009)			101,277

Station DMA Total	Cable TV Households	Non-cable TV Households	Total TV Households
Estimated Station Totals *	220,300	222,510	442,810
Average Weekly Circulation (2009)	116,845	126,050	242,895
Average Daily Circulation (2009)			99,931

Other DMA Total	Cable TV Households	Non-cable TV Households	Total TV Households
Estimated Station Totals *	32,490	21,600	54,090
Average Weekly Circulation (2009)	3,292	1,521	4,813
Average Daily Circulation (2009)			1,346

*Estimated station totals are sums of the Nielsen TV and Cable TV household estimates for each county in which the station registers viewing of more than 5% as per the Nielsen Survey Methods.

WLUK-DT
Ch. 11

Network Service: FOX.

Licensee: LIN of Wisconsin LLC, 4 Richmond Sq, Ste 200, Providence, RI 02906.

Studio: 787 Lombardi Ave., Green Bay, WI 54304.

Mailing Address: 787 Lombardi Ave, Green Bay, WI 54304.

Phone: 920-494-8711; 800-242-8067. **Fax:** 920-494-8782.

Web Site: http://www.myfoxnewswisconsin.com

Technical Facilities: Channel No. 11 (198-204 MHz). Authorized power: 17.19-kw visual, aural. Antenna: 1260-ft above av. terrain, 1129-ft. above ground, 2017-ft. above sea level.

Latitude	44°	24'	32"
Longitude	87°	59'	31"

Note: Latitude and longitude coordinates shown are based on the North American Datum of 1927 (NAD 27) as currently required by the Mass Media Bureau of the FCC.

Ownership: LIN TV Corp. (Group Owner).

Began Operation: January 20, 2003. Standard Definition. Station broadcasting digitally on its analog channel allotment. Began analog operations: August 9, 1954. Sale to present owner by Emmis Communications Corp. approved by FCC November 29, 2005. Sale to Emmis Communications Corp. by Silver King Communications Inc. approved by FCC June 23, 1998. Sale to Silver King Communications Inc. by SF Broadcasting approved by FCC August 16, 1996. Sale to SF Broadcasting by Busse Broadcasting Co. approved by FCC April 27, 1995. Sale to Busse Broadcasting Co. by Gillett Broadcasting approved by FCC July 31, 1987. Sale to Gillett Broadcasting by Post Corp. approved by FCC June 19, 1984. Sale to Post Corp. by M & M Broadcasting Co. Inc. approved by FCC January 6, 1965. Sale to M & M Broadcasting by W. E. Walker (50%), J. D. Mackin (23.3%) & associates approved by FCC March 19, 1958. Ceased analog operations: June 12, 2009.

Represented (legal): Covington & Burling.

Represented (sales): Continental Television Sales.

Personnel:

Jay Zollar, Vice President, General Manager & Program Director.

Tori Grant Welhouse, General Sales Manager.

Paul Cappelle, Local Sales Manager.

Juli Buehler, News Director.

Mike Nipps, Chief Engineer.

Robert Elliott, Regional Business Manager, LIN TV.

Pat Krohlow, Promotion & Marketing Director.

Karen Blazejewski, Traffic Manager.

City of License: Green Bay. **Station DMA:** Green Bay-Appleton, WI. **Rank:** 70.

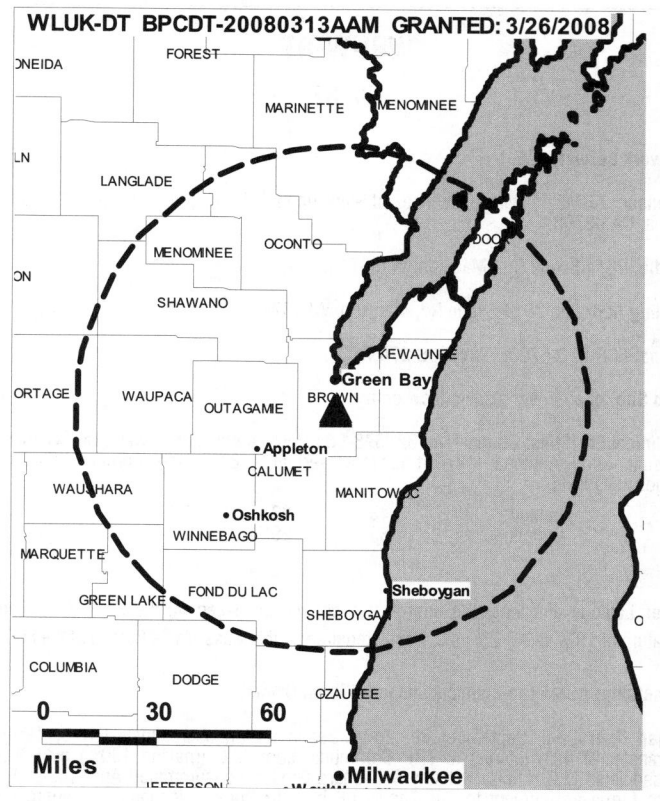

© 2010 Warren Communications News

Circulation © 2009 Nielsen. Coverage based on Nielsen study.

GrandTotal	Cable TV Households	Non-cable TV Households	Total TV Households
Estimated Station Totals *	338,120	266,630	604,750
Average Weekly Circulation (2009)	197,951	173,636	371,587
Average Daily Circulation (2009)			181,701

Station DMA Total	Cable TV Households	Non-cable TV Households	Total TV Households
Estimated Station Totals *	220,300	222,510	442,810
Average Weekly Circulation (2009)	162,902	169,402	332,304
Average Daily Circulation (2009)			169,433

Other DMA Total	Cable TV Households	Non-cable TV Households	Total TV Households
Estimated Station Totals *	117,820	44,120	161,940
Average Weekly Circulation (2009)	35,049	4,234	39,283
Average Daily Circulation (2009)			12,268

*Estimated station totals are sums of the Nielsen TV and Cable TV household estimates for each county in which the station registers viewing of more than 5% as per the Nielsen Survey Methods.

WBUW-DT
Ch. 32

Network Service: CW.

Licensee: ACME Television Licenses of Madison LLC, 2101 E. 4th St, Ste 202, Santa Ana, CA 92705.

Studio: 2814 Syene Rd., Madison, WI 53713.

Mailing Address: 2814 Syene Rd, Madison, WI 53713.

Phone: 608-270-5700. **Fax:** 608-270-5717.

Web Site: http://www.madisonscw.com/

Technical Facilities: Channel No. 32 (578-584 MHz). Authorized power: 200-kw max. visual, aural. Antenna: 1270-ft above av. terrain, 1181-ft. above ground, 2247-ft. above sea level.

Latitude	43°	03'	03"
Longitude	89°	29'	13"

Note: Latitude and longitude coordinates shown are based on the North American Datum of 1927 (NAD 27) as currently required by the Mass Media Bureau of the FCC.

Ownership: ACME Communications Inc. (Group Owner).

Began Operation: September 30, 2004. Began analog operations: July 5, 1999. Transfer of 49% interest to TRP Communications LLC (making 100%) by LSLG Associates LLC (Lucille Salhany & Leonard Grossi) consummated April 14, 2000. Pro forma assignment to Puri Family LP by TRP Communications LLC approved by FCC October 24, 2000. Involuntary assignment to Michael E. Kepler, Trustee, approved by FCC January 11, 2002. Sale to present owner by Michael Kepler, Trustee, Puri Family LP approved by FCC June 7, 2002. Ceased analog operations: February 17, 2009.

Personnel:

Tom Keeler, General Manager & General Sales Manager.

Eric Krieghoff, National Sales Manager.

Vanessa Younger, Local Sales Manager.

Eugene Cooper, Program Director.

Corey Udler, Promotions Manager.

Mark Albright, Traffic Manager.

Fred Moore, Chief Engineer.

Dave Riche, Production Director.

City of License: Janesville. **Station DMA:** Madison, WI. **Rank:** 85.

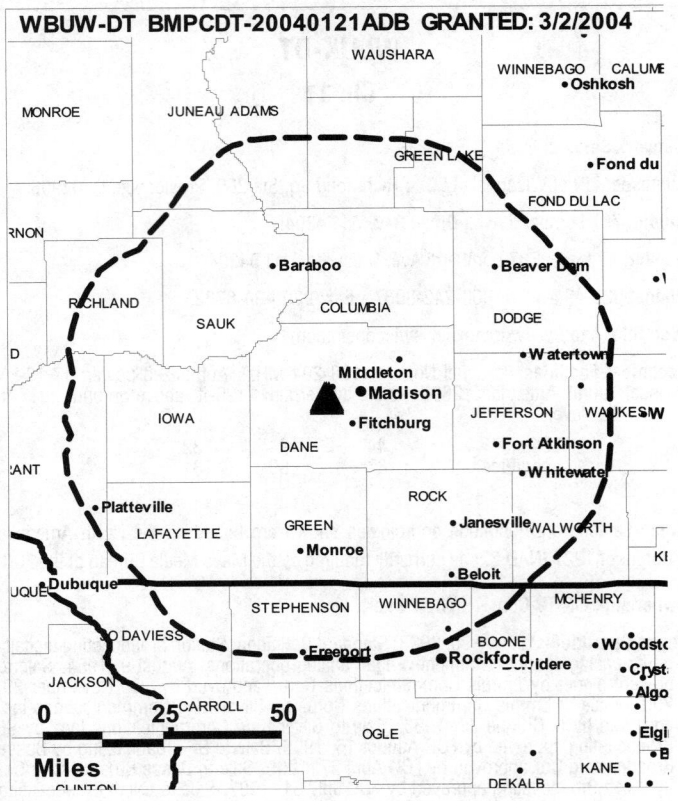

WBUW-DT BMPCDT-20040121ADB GRANTED: 3/2/2004

© 2010 Warren Communications News

Circulation © 2009 Nielsen. Coverage based on Nielsen study.

GrandTotal	Cable TV Households	Non-cable TV Households	Total TV Households
Estimated Station Totals *	204,970	226,530	431,500
Average Weekly Circulation (2009)	34,197	47,967	82,164
Average Daily Circulation (2009)			24,257

Station DMA Total	Cable TV Households	Non-cable TV Households	Total TV Households
Estimated Station Totals *	187,420	180,520	367,940
Average Weekly Circulation (2009)	31,986	43,461	75,447
Average Daily Circulation (2009)			22,425

Other DMA Total	Cable TV Households	Non-cable TV Households	Total TV Households
Estimated Station Totals *	17,550	46,010	63,560
Average Weekly Circulation (2009)	2,211	4,506	6,717
Average Daily Circulation (2009)			1,832

*Estimated station totals are sums of the Nielsen TV and Cable TV household estimates for each county in which the station registers viewing of more than 5% as per the Nielsen Survey Methods.

WPXE-TV
Ch. 40

Network Service: ION.

Licensee: ION Media Milwaukee License Inc., Debtor in Possession, 601 Clearwater Park Rd, West Palm Beach, FL 33401-6233.

Studio: 6161 N Flint Rd, Ste F, Glendale, WI 53209.

Mailing Address: 6161 N Flint Rd, Ste F, Glendale, WI 53209.

Phone: 414-247-0117. **Fax:** 414-247-1302.

E-mail: shirleyzyniecki@ionmedia.com

Web Site: http://www.ionmedia.com

Technical Facilities: Channel No. 40 (626-632 MHz). Authorized power: 830-kw max. visual, aural. Antenna: 1175-ft above av. terrain, 1201-ft. above ground, 1827-ft. above sea level.

Latitude	43°	05'	44"
Longitude	87°	54'	17"

Note: Latitude and longitude coordinates shown are based on the North American Datum of 1927 (NAD 27) as currently required by the Mass Media Bureau of the FCC.

Multichannel TV Sound: Stereo only.

Ownership: ION Media Networks Inc., Debtor in Possession (Group Owner).

Began Operation: February 5, 2004. Began analog operations: June 1, 1988. Sale to Urban Television LLC pends. Involuntary assignment to debtor in possession status approved by FCC June 5, 2009. Transfer of control by ION Media Networks Inc. from Paxson Management Corp. & Lowell W. Paxson to CIG Media LLC approved by FCC December 31, 2007. Paxson Communications Corp. became ION Media Networks Inc. on June 26, 2006. Sale to Paxson Communications Corp. by DP Media Inc. approved by FCC February 18, 2000. Sale to DP Media Inc. by Paxson Communications Corp. approved by FCC March 30, 1998. Sale to Paxson Communications Corp. by Channel 55 of Milwaukee Inc. approved by FCC February 7, 1997. Sale to Channel 55 of Milwaukee Inc. (then Christian Network Inc.) by LeSea Broadcasting Corp. approved by FCC June 30, 1995. Sale to Lab Partners by LeSea Braodcasting Corp. approved by FCC July 29, 1992, but never consummated. Sale to LeSea Broadcasting Corp. by Midwest Broadcast Associates Ltd. approved by FCC May 30, 1986. Ceased analog operations: June 12, 2009.

Represented (legal): Dow Lohnes PLLC.

Personnel:

Laurie Lau, Station Operations Manager.

Paul Freel, Chief Engineer.

Shirley Zyniecki, Traffic Manager.

City of License: Kenosha. **Station DMA:** Milwaukee, WI. **Rank:** 35.

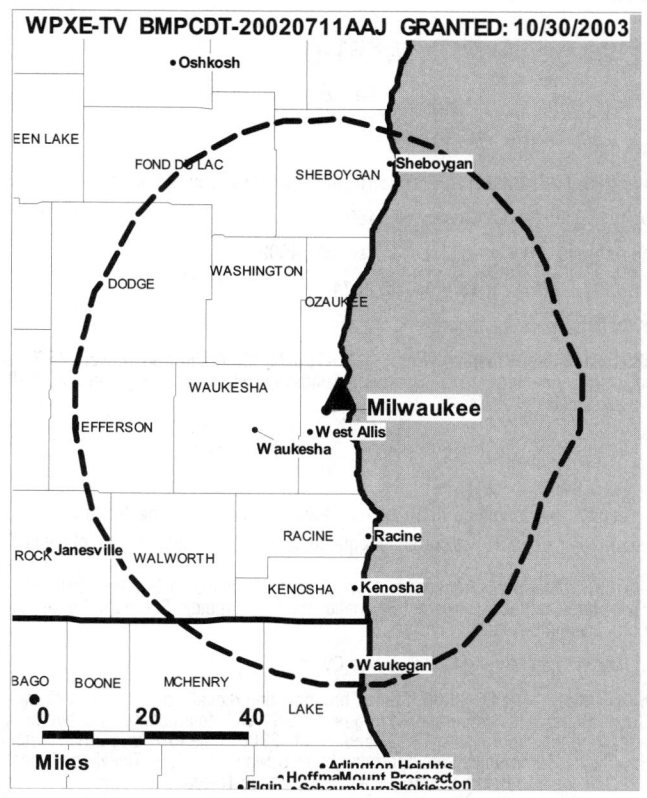

WPXE-TV BMPCDT-20020711AAJ GRANTED: 10/30/2003

© 2010 Warren Communications News

Circulation © 2009 Nielsen. Coverage based on Nielsen study.

GrandTotal	Cable TV Households	Non-cable TV Households	Total TV Households
Estimated Station Totals *	433,200	312,500	745,700
Average Weekly Circulation (2009)	28,160	21,696	49,856
Average Daily Circulation (2009)			11,961

Station DMA Total	Cable TV Households	Non-cable TV Households	Total TV Households
Estimated Station Totals *	430,030	252,470	682,500
Average Weekly Circulation (2009)	27,735	18,694	46,429
Average Daily Circulation (2009)			11,519

Other DMA Total	Cable TV Households	Non-cable TV Households	Total TV Households
Estimated Station Totals *	3,170	60,030	63,200
Average Weekly Circulation (2009)	425	3,002	3,427
Average Daily Circulation (2009)			442

*Estimated station totals are sums of the Nielsen TV and Cable TV household estimates for each county in which the station registers viewing of more than 5% as per the Nielsen Survey Methods.

WKBT-DT
Ch. 8

Network Service: MNT, CBS.

Grantee: QueenB Television LLC, 7025 Raymond Rd, Madison, WI 53719.

Studio: 141 S. 6th St., La Crosse, WI 54601.

Mailing Address: PO Box 1867, La Crosse, WI 54602.

Phone: 608-782-4678. **Fax:** 608-782-4674.

Web Site: http://www.wkbt.com

Technical Facilities: Channel No. 8 (180-186 MHz). Authorized power: 25.7-kw visual, aural. Antenna: 1525-ft above av. terrain, 1546-ft. above ground, 2370-ft. above sea level.

Latitude	44°	05'	28.1"
Longitude	91°	20'	16.5"

Note: Latitude and longitude coordinates shown are based on the North American Datum of 1927 (NAD 27) as currently required by the Mass Media Bureau of the FCC.

Satellite Earth Stations: Transmitter RCA; Scientific-Atlanta, 4.6-meter; DH Satellite, 5-meter; Comtech, 5-meter; Scientific-Atlanta, 7-meter; Standard Communications, Scientific-Atlanta receivers.

Ownership: Morgan Murphy Media (Group Owner).

Began Operation: June 26, 2006. Station broadcasting digitally on its analog channel allotment. Began analog operations: August 1, 1954. Sale to present owner by Young Broadcasting Inc. approved by FCC January 11, 2000. Sale to Young Broadcasting Inc. by Backe Communications approved by FCC May 14, 1986 (Television Digest, Vol. 25:15). Sale to Backe Communications by Gross Telecasting approved by FCC April 26, 1984 (Vol. 24:12). Sale to Gross Telecasting by La Crosse Tribune, Dahl family & others approved by FCC December 10, 1969 (Vol. 9:24, 50). Ceased analog operations: February 17, 2009.

Personnel:

Scott Chorski, Vice President & General Manager.

Barb Pervisky, General Sales Manager & Sales Director.

Cindy Taerud-Forkes, Local Sales Manager.

Brian Voight, Production Coordinator.

Anne Paape, News Director.

Dennis McSorley, Chief Engineer.

Marsha Olson, Business Manager & Human Resources.

Maria Roswall, Program Director.

Chad Busta, Promotion Manager.

Jeff Voves, Creative Services Manager.

Larry Johnson, Traffic Manager.

Lynn Zee Dokken-Knox, Web Manager, Special Projects & Community Services Manager.

City of License: La Crosse. **Station DMA:** La Crosse-Eau Claire, WI. **Rank:** 127.

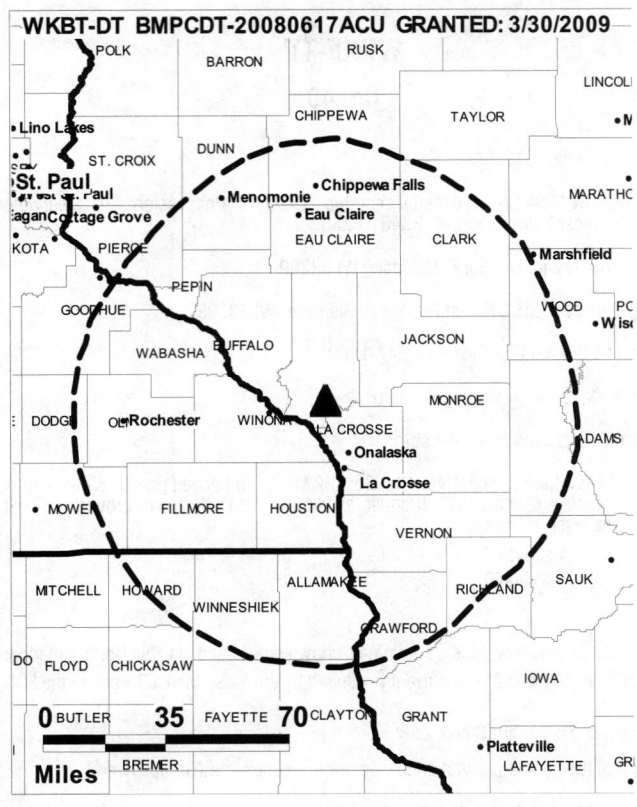

WKBT-DT BMPCDT-20080617ACU GRANTED: 3/30/2009

© 2010 Warren Communications News

Circulation © 2009 Nielsen. Coverage based on Nielsen study.

GrandTotal	Cable TV Households	Non-cable TV Households	Total TV Households
Estimated Station Totals *	152,430	122,340	274,770
Average Weekly Circulation (2009)	85,245	56,441	141,686
Average Daily Circulation (2009)			70,795

Station DMA Total	Cable TV Households	Non-cable TV Households	Total TV Households
Estimated Station Totals *	112,950	102,660	215,610
Average Weekly Circulation (2009)	74,990	53,783	128,773
Average Daily Circulation (2009)			66,769

Other DMA Total	Cable TV Households	Non-cable TV Households	Total TV Households
Estimated Station Totals *	39,480	19,680	59,160
Average Weekly Circulation (2009)	10,255	2,658	12,913
Average Daily Circulation (2009)			4,026

*Estimated station totals are sums of the Nielsen TV and Cable TV household estimates for each county in which the station registers viewing of more than 5% as per the Nielsen Survey Methods.

WLAX-DT
Ch. 17

Network Service: FOX.

Grantee: GM La Crosse Licensing LLC, 915 Middle River Dr, Ste 409, Fort Lauderdale, FL 33304.

Studio: 1305 Interchange Place, La Crosse, WI 54603.

Mailing Address: 1305 Interchange Pl, La Crosse, WI 54603.

Phone: 608-781-0025. **Fax:** 608-783-2520.

Web Site: http://www.fox25fox48.com

Technical Facilities: Channel No. 17 (488-494 MHz). Authorized power: 852-kw max. visual, aural. Antenna: 975-ft above av. terrain, 651-ft. above ground, 1857-ft. above sea level.

Latitude	43°	48'	16.14"
Longitude	91°	22'	19.29"

Note: Latitude and longitude coordinates shown are based on the North American Datum of 1927 (NAD 27) as currently required by the Mass Media Bureau of the FCC.

Ownership: Grant Co. Inc. (Group Owner).

Began Operation: November 5, 2008. Began analog operations: November 10, 1986. Sale to TV-26 Inc. by Quarterview Inc. approved by FCC November 1, 1984. Sale to Family Group Ltd. III by TV-26 Inc. approved by FCC September 27, 1985. Sale to Krypton Broadcasting Corp. by Family Group Ltd. III approved by FCC May 17, 1989, but was never consummated. Sale to Aries Telecommunications Corp. by Family Group Ltd. III approved by FCC September 27, 1991. Sale to Donald E. Clark by Aries Telecommunications Corp. approved by FCC July 29, 1992. Sale to present owner by Donald E. Clark approved by FCC December 15, 1995. Ceased analog operations: February 17, 2009.

Represented (legal): Wilkinson Barker Knauer LLP.

Represented (sales): Petry Media Corp.

Personnel:

Bob Weinstein, Station & General Sales Manager.

Steve Wroth, Local & Regional Sales Manager.

Mark G. Burg, Engineering Director.

Kenny Ammerman, Business Manager.

Barb Quillin, Program Director.

Pat Stipout, Promotions Manager.

Bill Stoneberg, Production Manager.

Eric Barczak, Traffic Director.

City of License: La Crosse. **Station DMA:** La Crosse-Eau Claire, WI. **Rank:** 127.

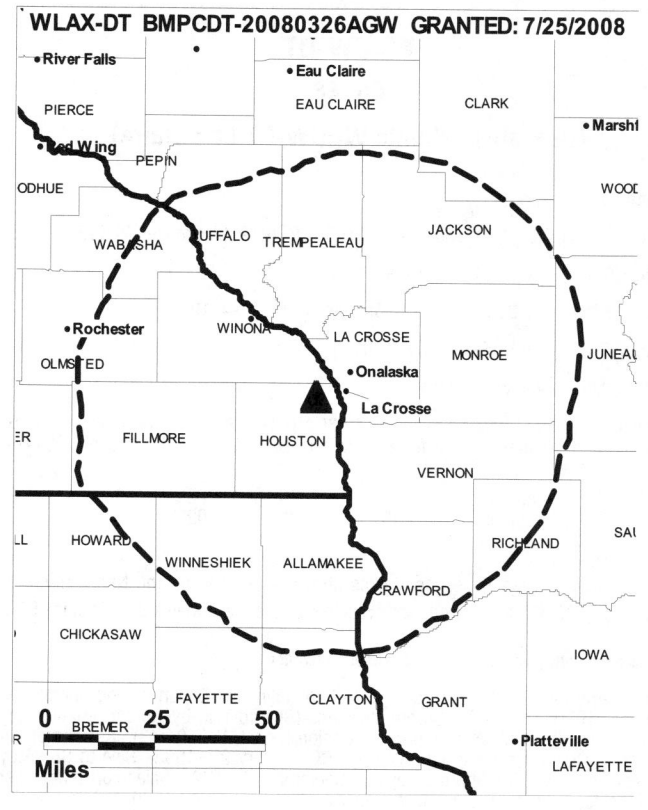

WLAX-DT BMPCDT-20080326AGW GRANTED: 7/25/2008

© 2010 Warren Communications News

Circulation © 2009 Nielsen. Coverage based on Nielsen study.

GrandTotal	Cable TV Households	Non-cable TV Households	Total TV Households
Estimated Station Totals *	108,900	115,690	224,590
Average Weekly Circulation (2009)	46,689	45,945	92,634
Average Daily Circulation (2009)			31,003

Station DMA Total	Cable TV Households	Non-cable TV Households	Total TV Households
Estimated Station Totals *	85,080	102,660	187,740
Average Weekly Circulation (2009)	42,567	44,074	86,641
Average Daily Circulation (2009)			29,217

Other DMA Total	Cable TV Households	Non-cable TV Households	Total TV Households
Estimated Station Totals *	23,820	13,030	36,850
Average Weekly Circulation (2009)	4,122	1,871	5,993
Average Daily Circulation (2009)			1,786

*Estimated station totals are sums of the Nielsen TV and Cable TV household estimates for each county in which the station registers viewing of more than 5% as per the Nielsen Survey Methods.

WXOW-DT
Ch. 48
(Operates satellite WQOW-DT Eau Claire)

Network Service: CW, ABC.

Grantee: WXOW/WQOW Television Inc., PO Box C-4019, La Crosse, WI 54602-4019.

Studio: 3705 County Hwy 25, La Crescent, MN 55947.

Mailing Address: PO Box C-4019, La Crosse, WI 54602-4019.

Phone: 507-895-9969. **Fax:** 507-895-8124.

Web Site: http://www.wxow.com

Technical Facilities: Channel No. 48 (674-680 MHz). Authorized power: 371-kw max. visual, aural. Antenna: 1142-ft above av. terrain, 787-ft. above ground, 2014-ft. above sea level.

Latitude	43°	48'	23"
Longitude	91°	22'	02"

Note: Latitude and longitude coordinates shown are based on the North American Datum of 1927 (NAD 27) as currently required by the Mass Media Bureau of the FCC.

Ownership: Quincy Newspapers Inc. (Group Owner).

Began Operation: August 20, 2002. Standard Definition. Began analog operations: March 7, 1970. Sale to Tak Communications (Sharad Tak) by Liberty Broadcasting approved by FCC January 7, 1985 (Television Digest, Vol. 24:43). Assignment of license to Operating Agent approved by FCC January 27, 1993. Sale to Shockley Communications Corp. approved by FCC September 27, 1995. Sale to present owner by Shockley Communications Corp. approved by FCC April 17, 2001 (Vol. 41:23). Ceased analog operations: February 17, 2009.

Represented (sales): Blair Television.

Represented (legal): Wilkinson Barker Knauer LLP.

Personnel:

Thomas A. Oakley, Chief Executive Officer.

Ralph M. Oakley, Chief Operating Officer.

David Booth, General Manager.

Brian Schumacher, General Sales Manager.

Sean Dwyer, News Director.

Dave White, Chief Engineer.

Deborah Simonis, Program & Traffic Director.

Laramie McClurg, Promotion Director.

Mitch Moths, Production Manager.

City of License: La Crosse. **Station DMA:** La Crosse-Eau Claire, WI. **Rank:** 127.

WXOW-DT BMPCDT-20090113ABG GRANTED: 3/16/2009

© 2010 Warren Communications News

Circulation © 2009 Nielsen. Coverage based on Nielsen study.

GrandTotal	Cable TV Households	Non-cable TV Households	Total TV Households
Estimated Station Totals *	94,470	115,690	210,160
Average Weekly Circulation (2009)	48,175	43,288	91,463
Average Daily Circulation (2009)			41,249

Station DMA Total	Cable TV Households	Non-cable TV Households	Total TV Households
Estimated Station Totals *	73,670	102,660	176,330
Average Weekly Circulation (2009)	45,999	41,723	87,722
Average Daily Circulation (2009)			40,254

Other DMA Total	Cable TV Households	Non-cable TV Households	Total TV Households
Estimated Station Totals *	20,800	13,030	33,830
Average Weekly Circulation (2009)	2,176	1,565	3,741
Average Daily Circulation (2009)			995

*Estimated station totals are sums of the Nielsen TV and Cable TV household estimates for each county in which the station registers viewing of more than 5% as per the Nielsen Survey Methods.

WISC-DT
Ch. 50

Network Service: MNT, CBS.

Grantee: Television Wisconsin Inc., PO Box 44965, Madison, WI 53744-4965.

Studio: 7025 Raymond Rd., Madison, WI 53719.

Mailing Address: PO Box 44965, Madison, WI 53744-4965.

Phone: 608-271-4321. **Fax:** 608-278-5569.

E-mail: jsommers@wisctv.com

Web Site: http://www.channel3000.com

Technical Facilities: Channel No. 50 (686-692 MHz). Authorized power: 380.2-kw max. visual, aural. Antenna: 1529-ft above av. terrain, 1388-ft. above ground, 2514-ft. above sea level.

Latitude	43°	03'	21"
Longitude	89°	32'	06"

Note: Latitude and longitude coordinates shown are based on the North American Datum of 1927 (NAD 27) as currently required by the Mass Media Bureau of the FCC.

Ownership: Morgan Murphy Media (Group Owner).

Began Operation: January 4, 2001. High Definition. Began analog operations: June 24, 1956. Ceased analog operations: February 17, 2009.

Personnel:

Elizabeth Murphy Burns, President.

David Sanks, Vice President & General Manager.

Tom Bier, Station Manager & Executive News Director.

Mark Friesch, General & Local Sales Manager.

Leonard Charles, Chief Engineer.

Glen Krieg, Chief Financial Officer & Business Manager.

Jill Sommers, Program & Operations Director.

Nan Roach, Promotion & Marketing Director.

Rieva Everhart, Traffic Manager.

City of License: Madison. **Station DMA:** Madison, WI. **Rank:** 85.

Digital cable and TV coverage maps.
Visit www.warren-news.com/mediaprints.htm

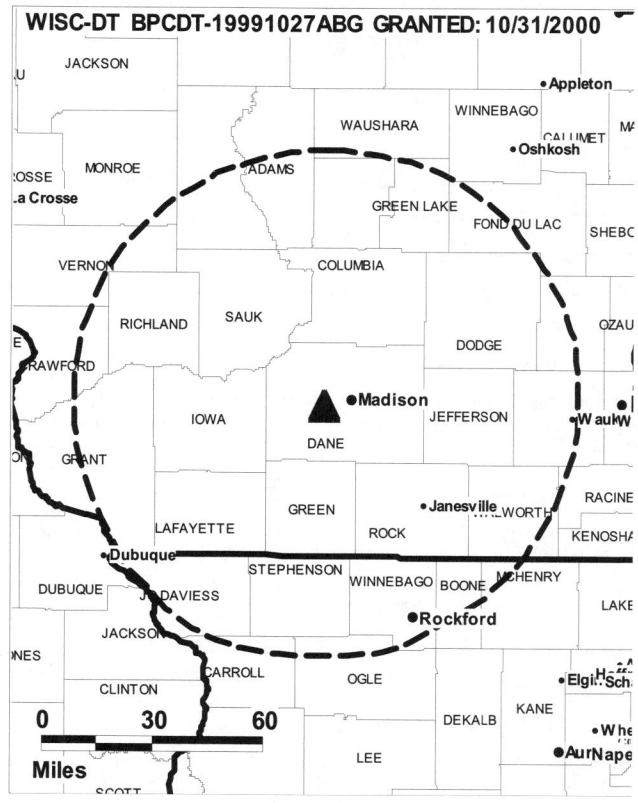

© 2010 Warren Communications News

Circulation © 2009 Nielsen. Coverage based on Nielsen study.

GrandTotal	Cable TV Households	Non-cable TV Households	Total TV Households
Estimated Station Totals *	245,410	260,660	506,070
Average Weekly Circulation (2009)	145,874	131,964	277,838
Average Daily Circulation (2009)			139,178

Station DMA Total	Cable TV Households	Non-cable TV Households	Total TV Households
Estimated Station Totals *	188,650	190,090	378,740
Average Weekly Circulation (2009)	128,485	120,387	248,872
Average Daily Circulation (2009)			125,329

Other DMA Total	Cable TV Households	Non-cable TV Households	Total TV Households
Estimated Station Totals *	56,760	70,570	127,330
Average Weekly Circulation (2009)	17,389	11,577	28,966
Average Daily Circulation (2009)			13,849

*Estimated station totals are sums of the Nielsen TV and Cable TV household estimates for each county in which the station registers viewing of more than 5% as per the Nielsen Survey Methods.

WKOW-DT
Ch. 26

Network Service: ABC.

Licensee: WKOW Television Inc., PO Box 909, Quincy, IL 62306-0909.

Studio: 5727 Tokay Blvd., Madison, WI 53719.

Mailing Address: 5727 Tokay Blvd, Madison, WI 52719.

Phone: 608-274-1234. **Fax:** 608-274-9514.

E-mail: dkuehn@wkowtv.com

Web Site: http://www.wkowtv.com

Technical Facilities: Channel No. 26 (542-548 MHz). Authorized power: 171-kw max. visual, aural. Antenna: 1493-ft above av. terrain, 1352-ft. above ground, 2477-ft. above sea level.

Latitude	43°	03'	21"
Longitude	89°	32'	06"

Holds CP for change to 1000-kw max. visual, 1493-ft above av. terrain, 1352-ft. above ground, 2478-ft. above sea level; BPCDT-20080619AEK.

Transmitter: 8559 Mineral Point Rd., Verona.

Note: Latitude and longitude coordinates shown are based on the North American Datum of 1927 (NAD 27) as currently required by the Mass Media Bureau of the FCC.

Ownership: Quincy Newspapers Inc. (Group Owner).

Began Operation: November 1, 1998. Began analog operations: June 30, 1953. Sale to present owner by Shockley Communications Corp. approved by FCC April 17, 2001 (Television Digest, Vol. 41:23). Sale to Shockley Communications Corp. by Operating Agent approved by FCC September 27, 1995. Assignment of license to Operating Agent granted by FCC January 27, 1993. Sale to Tak Communications (Sharad Tak) by Liberty Broadcasting approved by FCC January 7, 1985 (Vol. 24:43). Sale to Liberty Broadcasting by Horizons Communications approved by FCC September 20, 1978 (Vol. 18:24). Sale to Horizons Communications by Midcontinent Broadcasting Co. (Joseph L. Floyd, N. L. Bentson & Edmund R. Ruben) approved by FCC September 9, 1970 (Vol. 10:37). Sale to Midcontinent Broadcasting Co. by Monona Broadcasting Co. approved by FCC July 20, 1960 (Vol. 16:24, 26, 30). Ceased analog operations: February 17, 2009.

Represented (sales): Continental Television Sales.

Represented (legal): Rosenman & Colin LLP.

Personnel:

Kevin Harlan, General Manager.

Dave Kuehn, General Sales Manager.

Keith Triller, Local Sales Manager.

Julia Stein-Barnes, National Sales Manager.

Al Zobel, News Director.

Steve Zimmerman, Chief Engineer.

Jessica Miller, Program Director.

Darin Eidson, Promotion Director.

Bob Goessling, Production Manager.

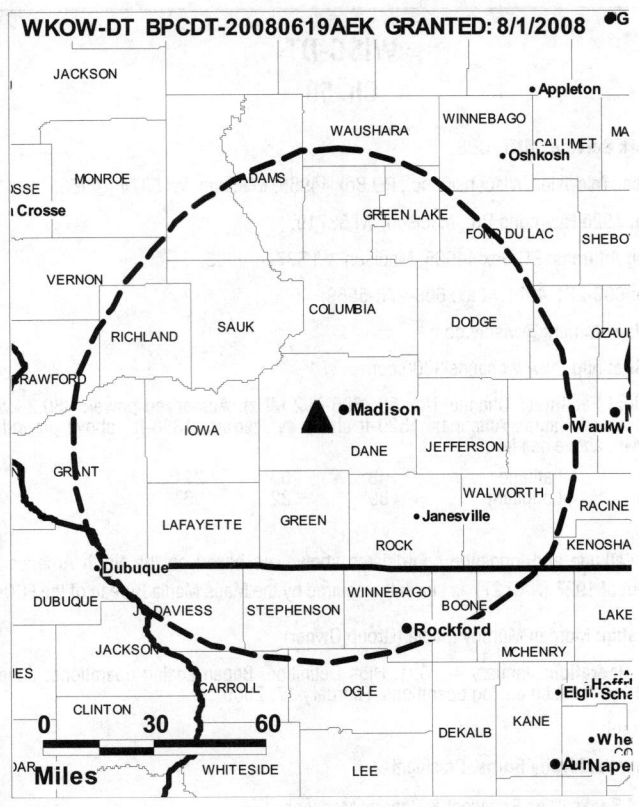

WKOW-DT BPCDT-20080619AEK GRANTED: 8/1/2008

© 2010 Warren Communications News

Maurice Scott, Traffic Manager.

City of License: Madison. **Station DMA:** Madison, WI. **Rank:** 85.

Circulation © 2009 Nielsen. Coverage based on Nielsen study.

GrandTotal	Cable TV Households	Non-cable TV Households	Total TV Households
Estimated Station Totals *	230,520	250,640	481,160
Average Weekly Circulation (2009)	121,395	126,563	247,958
Average Daily Circulation (2009)			112,807

Station DMA Total	Cable TV Households	Non-cable TV Households	Total TV Households
Estimated Station Totals *	188,650	190,090	378,740
Average Weekly Circulation (2009)	112,952	116,323	229,275
Average Daily Circulation (2009)			104,195

Other DMA Total	Cable TV Households	Non-cable TV Households	Total TV Households
Estimated Station Totals *	41,870	60,550	102,420
Average Weekly Circulation (2009)	8,443	10,240	18,683
Average Daily Circulation (2009)			8,612

*Estimated station totals are sums of the Nielsen TV and Cable TV household estimates for each county in which the station registers viewing of more than 5% as per the Nielsen Survey Methods.

WMSN-DT
Ch. 11

Network Service: FOX.

Licensee: WMSN Licensee LLC, 10706 Beaver Dam Rd, Cockeysville, MD 21030.

Studio: 7847 Big Sky Dr., Madison, WI 53719.

Mailing Address: 7847 Big Sky Dr, Madison, WI 53719.

Phone: 608-833-0047. **Fax:** 608-833-5055.

E-mail: kjohnson@wkowtv.com

Web Site: http://www.fox47.com

Technical Facilities: Channel No. 11 (198-204 MHz). Authorized power: 15-kw visual, aural. Antenna: 1545-ft above av. terrain, 1411-ft. above ground, 2536-ft. above sea level.

Latitude	43°	03'	21"
Longitude	89°	32'	06"

Holds CP for change to channel number 49, 280-kw max. visual, 1539-ft above av. terrain, 1398-ft. above ground, 2524-ft. above sea level; BPCDT-20090209AGC.

Note: Latitude and longitude coordinates shown are based on the North American Datum of 1927 (NAD 27) as currently required by the Mass Media Bureau of the FCC.

Ownership: Sinclair Broadcast Group Inc. (Group Owner).

Began Operation: November 18, 2004. Began analog operations: June 8, 1986. Ceased analog operations: June 12, 2009.

Represented (sales): Katz Media Group.

Personnel:

Kerry Johnson, General Manager.

Joan Kelner, General Sales Manager.

Al Zobel, News Director.

Kerry Maki, Chief Engineer.

Sheryl Nelson, Regional Controller.

Colin Campbell, Program Coordinator.

Audra Johnson, Promotion Manager.

Mitch Proctor, Creative Services Director.

Carol Poole, Traffic Manager.

Debra Lorenz, Administrative Assistant.

City of License: Madison. **Station DMA:** Madison, WI. **Rank:** 85.

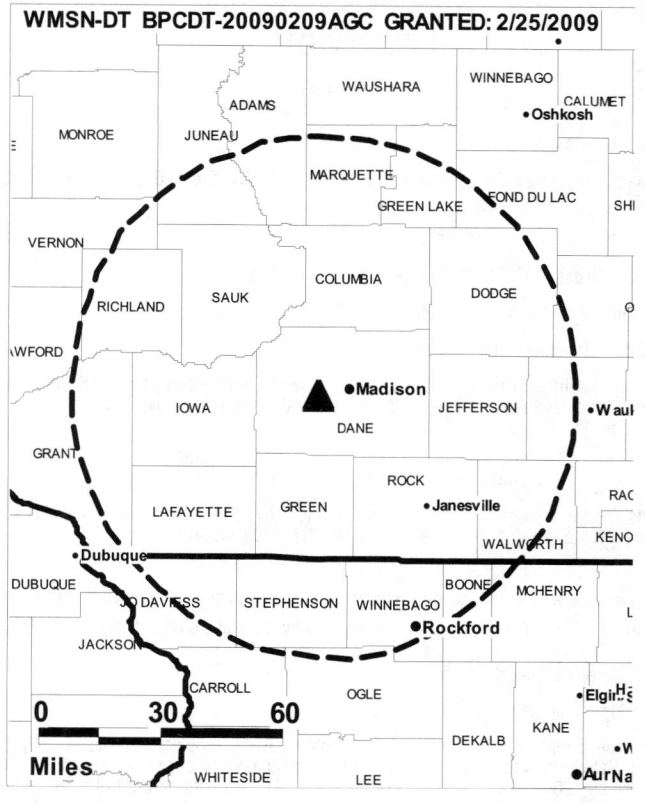

WMSN-DT BPCDT-20090209AGC GRANTED: 2/25/2009

© 2010 Warren Communications News

Circulation © 2009 Nielsen. Coverage based on Nielsen study.

GrandTotal	Cable TV Households	Non-cable TV Households	Total TV Households
Estimated Station Totals *	239,950	252,060	492,010
Average Weekly Circulation (2009)	110,821	120,302	231,123
Average Daily Circulation (2009)			81,912

Station DMA Total	Cable TV Households	Non-cable TV Households	Total TV Households
Estimated Station Totals *	188,650	190,090	378,740
Average Weekly Circulation (2009)	100,633	109,168	209,801
Average Daily Circulation (2009)			75,217

Other DMA Total	Cable TV Households	Non-cable TV Households	Total TV Households
Estimated Station Totals *	51,300	61,970	113,270
Average Weekly Circulation (2009)	10,188	11,134	21,322
Average Daily Circulation (2009)			6,695

*Estimated station totals are sums of the Nielsen TV and Cable TV household estimates for each county in which the station registers viewing of more than 5% as per the Nielsen Survey Methods.

WMTV-DT
Ch. 19

Network Service: NBC.

Licensee: Gray Television Licensee LLC, 1750 K St NW, Ste 1200, Washington, DC 20006.

Studio: 615 Forward Dr., Madison, WI 53711.

Mailing Address: 615 Forward Dr, Madison, WI 53711.

Phone: 608-274-1515. **Fax:** 608-271-5193.

Web Site: http://www.nbc15.com

Technical Facilities: Channel No. 19 (500-506 MHz). Authorized power: 56-kw max. visual, aural. Antenna: 1269-ft above av. terrain, 1181-ft. above ground, 2247-ft. above sea level.

Latitude	43°	03'	03"
Longitude	89°	29'	13"

Holds CP for change to 155-kw max. visual, 1361-ft above av. terrain, 1273-ft. above ground, 2339-ft. above sea level; BPCDT-20080609ABR.

Note: Latitude and longitude coordinates shown are based on the North American Datum of 1927 (NAD 27) as currently required by the Mass Media Bureau of the FCC.

Multichannel TV Sound: Stereo only.

Ownership: Gray Television Inc. (Group Owner).

Began Operation: April 5, 2001. High Definition. Began analog operations: July 8, 1953. Sale to present owner from Benedek Broadcasting Co. LLC approved by FCC August 29, 2002 (Television Digest, Vol. 42:14). Transfer of control to Benedek Broadcasting Co. LLC from Brissette Broadcasting approved by FCC May 22, 1996 (Vol. 35:37, 52), but Trustee Philip A. Jones operated station until revised ownership rules allowed Benedek to acquire. FCC approved control on January 11, 2000. Sale to Brissette by Adams Communications approved by FCC December 24, 1991. Sale to Adams Communications by Wesray Corp. approved by FCC December 23, 1987. Sale to Wesray Corp. by Forward Communications Corp. approved by FCC August 16, 1984. Sale to Forward by Lee P. Loomis approved by FCC May 15, 1963 (Vol. 3:20). Sale to Loomis by WTVJ interests (Mitchell Wolfson) approved by FCC April 2, 1958 (Vol. 14:10, 14). Sale to WTVJ interests by founding GeraldA. Bartell family approved by FCC July 25, 1957 (Vol. 13:26, 30). Ceased analog operations: February 17, 2009.

Represented (sales): Continental Television Sales.

Represented (legal): Wiley Rein LLP.

Personnel:

Robert Smith, General Manager & Station Manager.

Curt Molander, General Sales Manager.

Don Vesely, Local Sales Manager.

Sara McCormack, National Sales Manager.

Chris Gegg, News Director.

Tom Weeden, Chief Engineer.

Dave Lobenstein, Business Manager.

Ellen Buss, Program Director.

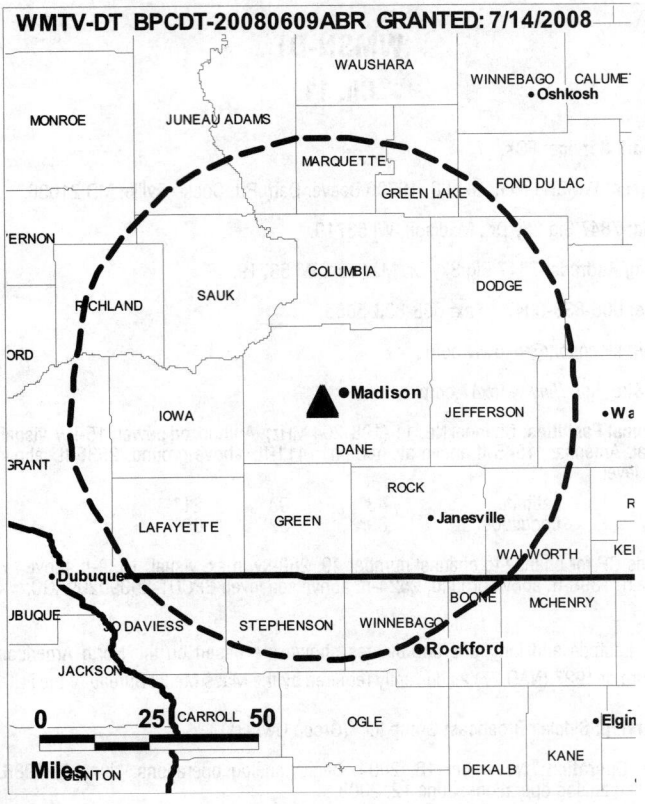

WMTV-DT BPCDT-20080609ABR GRANTED: 7/14/2008

© 2010 Warren Communications News

Jeff Shields, Creative Services Director.

City of License: Madison. **Station DMA:** Madison, WI. **Rank:** 85.

Circulation © 2009 Nielsen. Coverage based on Nielsen study.

GrandTotal	Cable TV Households	Non-cable TV Households	Total TV Households
Estimated Station Totals *	242,550	250,290	492,840
Average Weekly Circulation (2009)	140,261	138,400	278,661
Average Daily Circulation (2009)			137,679

Station DMA Total	Cable TV Households	Non-cable TV Households	Total TV Households
Estimated Station Totals *	188,650	190,090	378,740
Average Weekly Circulation (2009)	123,026	127,129	250,155
Average Daily Circulation (2009)			122,500

Other DMA Total	Cable TV Households	Non-cable TV Households	Total TV Households
Estimated Station Totals *	53,900	60,200	114,100
Average Weekly Circulation (2009)	17,235	11,271	28,506
Average Daily Circulation (2009)			15,179

*Estimated station totals are sums of the Nielsen TV and Cable TV household estimates for each county in which the station registers viewing of more than 5% as per the Nielsen Survey Methods.

WWRS-DT
Ch. 43

Network Service: TBN.

Grantee: Trinity Christian Center of Santa Ana Inc., PO Box C-11949, Santa Ana, CA 92711.

Studio: N6707 Madison Rd, Iron Ridge, WI 53035.

Mailing Address: PO Box 267, Mayville, WI 53050.

Phone: 920-387-9052. **Fax:** 920-387-9053.

Web Site: http://www.nmtv.org

Technical Facilities: Channel No. 43 (644-650 MHz). Authorized power: 300-kw max. visual, aural. Antenna: 610-ft above av. terrain, 413-ft. above ground, 1572-ft. above sea level.

Latitude	43°	26'	11"
Longitude	88°	31'	34"

Requests CP for change to 1000-kw max. visual, 656-ft above av. terrain, 466-ft. above ground, 1624-ft. above sea level; BPCDT-20080618ATT.

Note: Latitude and longitude coordinates shown are based on the North American Datum of 1927 (NAD 27) as currently required by the Mass Media Bureau of the FCC.

Ownership: Trinity Broadcasting Network Inc. (Group Owner).

Began Operation: November 1, 2002. Standard Definition. Began analog operations: February 1, 1999. Pro forma assignment to present owner by National Minority TV Inc. approved by FCC August 6, 2008. Sale to Mayville Communications Inc. (later National Minority TV Inc.) by TV-52 Inc. approved by FCC December 17, 1998. Original sale to Mayville Communications Inc. dismissed by FCC December 18, 1996 at request of TV 52 Inc. Sale to TV-52 Inc. by Pacer Televison Co. approved by FCC April 15, 1993. Involuntary pro forma transfer by Pacer Television Inc. from Wayne R. Stenz, deceased to Esate of Wayne R. Stenz, Jean L. Danor Execturix approved by FCC October 4, 1991. Ceased analog operations: June 12, 2009.

Represented (legal): Colby M. May.

Personnel:

Dinah Calhoun, Station Manager.

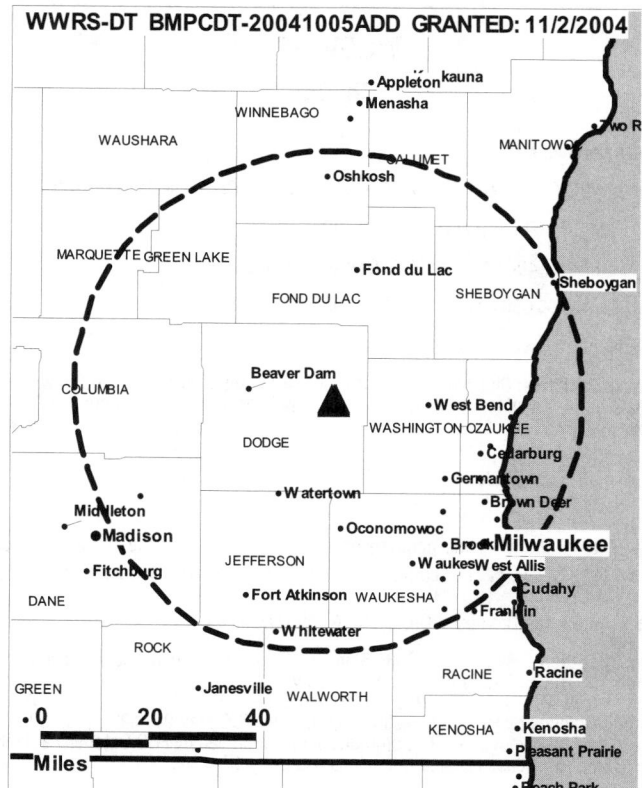

© 2010 Warren Communications News

Gary Wallace, Chief Engineer.

City of License: Mayville. **Station DMA:** Milwaukee, WI. **Rank:** 35.

Nielsen Data: Not available.

WCGV-DT
Ch. 25

Network Service: MNT.

Grantee: WCGV Licensee Inc., 10706 Beaver Dam Rd, Cockeysville, MD 21030.

Studio: 4041 N. 35th St., Milwaukee, WI 53216.

Mailing Address: 4041 N. 35th St, Milwaukee, WI 53216.

Phone: 414-442-7050. **Fax:** 414-874-1898.

Web Site: http://www.thattvwebsite.com

Technical Facilities: Channel No. 25 (536-542 MHz). Authorized power: 625-kw max. visual, aural. Antenna: 1116-ft above av. terrain, 1135-ft. above ground, 1763-ft. above sea level.

Latitude	43°	05'	44"
Longitude	87°	54'	17"

Note: Latitude and longitude coordinates shown are based on the North American Datum of 1927 (NAD 27) as currently required by the Mass Media Bureau of the FCC.

Ownership: Sinclair Broadcast Group Inc. (Group Owner).

Began Operation: March 21, 2003. Standard Definition. Began analog operations: March 19, 1980. Sale to HR Broadcasting by Byron Lasky, Howard Heckel, et al., approved by FCC July 14, 1986 (Television Digest, Vol. 26:26). Sale to ABRY Communications by HR Broadcasting approved by FCC May 20, 1994 (Vol. 30:24). Sale to present owner by ABRY Communications approved by FCC October 19, 1990 (Vol. 33:3, 35). Ceased analog operations: February 17, 2009.

Represented (sales): Katz Media Group.

Personnel:

David Ford, General Manager.

Mark Martin, Sales Director.

Robert Krieghoff, Local Sales Manager.

Sue Trotman, National Sales Manager.

Dennis Brechlin, Chief Engineer.

Wally Koepke, Business Manager.

Jim Seeley, Program Director.

Jason VanAcker, Promotion Director.

Paul Rudolph, Production Manager.

Kay Mazurkiewicz, Traffic Manager.

Bev Captain, Human Resources Manager & Assistant to General Manager.

City of License: Milwaukee. **Station DMA:** Milwaukee, WI. **Rank:** 35.

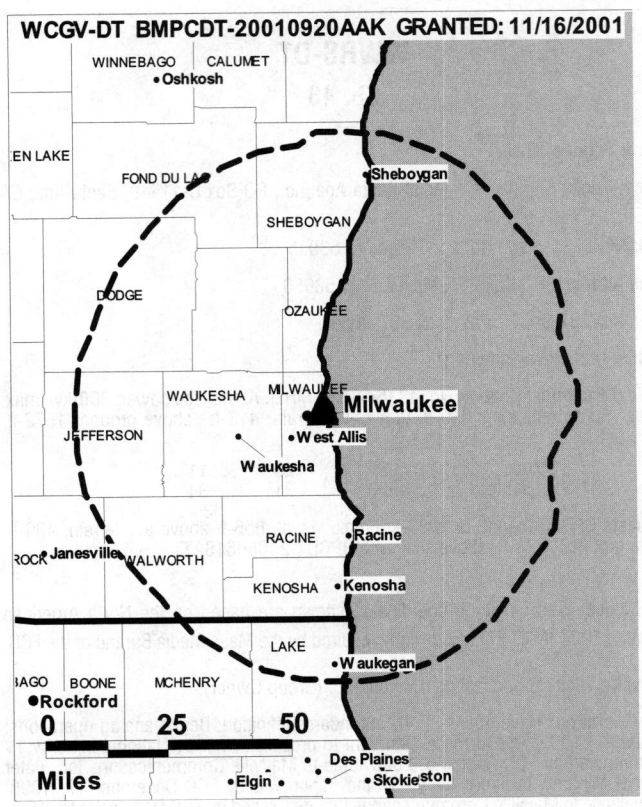

WCGV-DT BMPCDT-20010920AAK GRANTED: 11/16/2001

© 2010 Warren Communications News

Circulation © 2009 Nielsen. Coverage based on Nielsen study.

GrandTotal	Cable TV Households	Non-cable TV Households	Total TV Households
Estimated Station Totals *	580,650	363,880	944,530
Average Weekly Circulation (2009)	96,609	90,296	186,905
Average Daily Circulation (2009)			68,313

Station DMA Total	Cable TV Households	Non-cable TV Households	Total TV Households
Estimated Station Totals *	558,030	347,320	905,350
Average Weekly Circulation (2009)	93,487	88,938	182,425
Average Daily Circulation (2009)			67,098

Other DMA Total	Cable TV Households	Non-cable TV Households	Total TV Households
Estimated Station Totals *	22,620	16,560	39,180
Average Weekly Circulation (2009)	3,122	1,358	4,480
Average Daily Circulation (2009)			1,215

*Estimated station totals are sums of the Nielsen TV and Cable TV household estimates for each county in which the station registers viewing of more than 5% as per the Nielsen Survey Methods.

WDJT-DT
Ch. 46

Network Service: CBS.

Licensee: WDJT-TV Limited Partnership, 26 N Halsted St, Chicago, IL 60661.

Studio: 809 S. 60th St., Milwaukee, WI 53214.

Mailing Address: 809 S. 60th St, Milwaukee, WI 53214.

Phone: 414-777-5800. **Fax:** 414-777-5802.

Web Site: http://www.cbs58.com

Technical Facilities: Channel No. 46 (662-668 MHz). Authorized power: 1000-kw max. visual, aural. Antenna: 1056-ft above av. terrain, 1143-ft. above ground, 1766-ft. above sea level.

Latitude	43°	06'	42"
Longitude	87°	55'	50"

Transmitter: 5201 N. Milwaukee River Pkwy.

Note: Latitude and longitude coordinates shown are based on the North American Datum of 1927 (NAD 27) as currently required by the Mass Media Bureau of the FCC.

Ownership: Weigel Broadcasting Co. (Group Owner).

Began Operation: July 20, 2005. Began analog operations: November 1, 1988. Ceased analog operations: June 12, 2009.

Represented (legal): Cohn & Marks LLP.

Personnel:

Jim Hall, General Manager.

John Davis, Local Sales Manager.

Adam Leston, National Sales Manager.

Grant Uitti, News Director.

Dan Dyer, Chief Engineer.

Kyle Hart, Program Manager.

Dale Palecek, Promotion Director.

Bob Moore, Research Director.

Gloria Cervantes, Traffic Manager.

Christina Camps, Human Resources Director.

City of License: Milwaukee. **Station DMA:** Milwaukee, WI. **Rank:** 35.

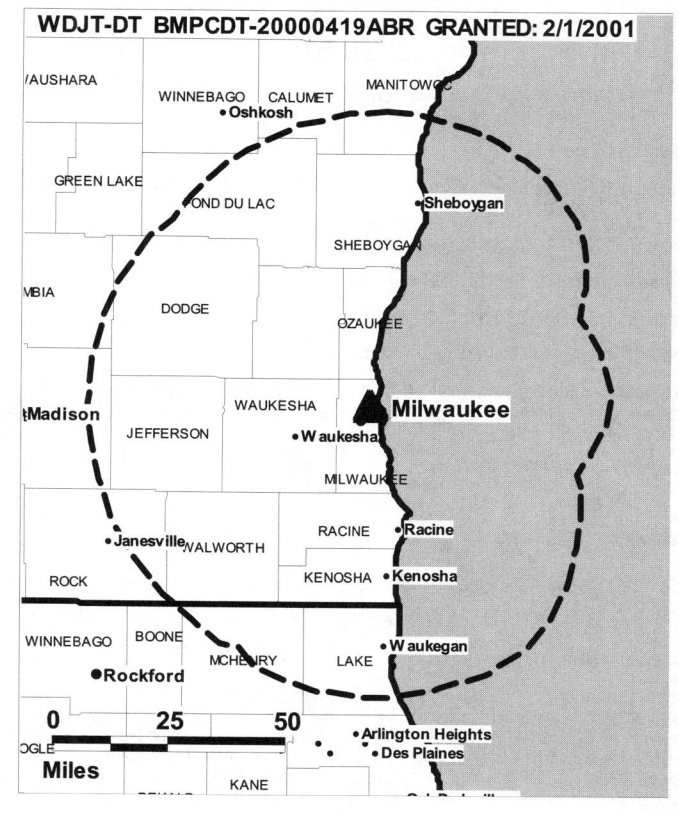

WDJT-DT BMPCDT-20000419ABR GRANTED: 2/1/2001

© 2010 Warren Communications News

Circulation © 2009 Nielsen. Coverage based on Nielsen study.

GrandTotal	Cable TV Households	Non-cable TV Households	Total TV Households
Estimated Station Totals *	583,850	378,380	962,230
Average Weekly Circulation (2009)	320,075	181,678	501,753
Average Daily Circulation (2009)			222,808

Station DMA Total	Cable TV Households	Non-cable TV Households	Total TV Households
Estimated Station Totals *	558,030	347,320	905,350
Average Weekly Circulation (2009)	314,413	178,970	493,383
Average Daily Circulation (2009)			220,569

Other DMA Total	Cable TV Households	Non-cable TV Households	Total TV Households
Estimated Station Totals *	25,820	31,060	56,880
Average Weekly Circulation (2009)	5,662	2,708	8,370
Average Daily Circulation (2009)			2,239

*Estimated station totals are sums of the Nielsen TV and Cable TV household estimates for each county in which the station registers viewing of more than 5% as per the Nielsen Survey Methods.

WISN-DT
Ch. 34

Network Service: ABC.

Licensee: WISN Hearst-Argyle Television Inc., PO Box 1800, c/o Brooks, Pierce et al., Raleigh, NC 27602.

Studio: 759 N. 19th St., Milwaukee, WI 53233.

Mailing Address: PO Box 402, Milwaukee, WI 53201-0402.

Phone: 414-342-8812. **Fax:** 414-342-6490.

Web Site: http://www.themilwaukeechannel.com

Technical Facilities: Channel No. 34 (590-596 MHz). Authorized power: 863-kw max. visual, aural. Antenna: 863-ft above av. terrain, 945-ft. above ground, 1568-ft. above sea level.

Latitude	43°	06'	42"
Longitude	87°	55'	42"

Transmitter: 5201 Milwaukee River Pkwy.

Note: Latitude and longitude coordinates shown are based on the North American Datum of 1927 (NAD 27) as currently required by the Mass Media Bureau of the FCC.

Ownership: Hearst-Argyle Television Inc. (Group Owner).

Began Operation: April 12, 2005. Began analog operations: October 27, 1954. Station's first call letters were WTVW. Sale to Hearst Broadcast Group by group headed by L. F. Gran, Paul A. Pratt & Loron Thurwachter approved by FCC March 2, 1955. Merger of Hearst with Argyle Television Inc. to form present owner approved by FCC June 2, 1997. Hearst-Argyle received approval from the FCC May 26, 2009 to become privately owned by The Hearst Corp. Ceased analog operations: June 12, 2009.

Represented (legal): Brooks, Pierce, McLendon, Humphrey & Leonard LLP.

Represented (sales): Eagle Television Sales.

Represented (engineering): Cavell, Mertz & Associates Inc.

Personnel:

Jan Wade, President & General Manager.

Pete Monfre, Vice President, Sales.

Dan Joerres, Local Sales Manager.

Lori Walden, News Director.

Tony Coleman, Engineering Director.

Jim Kurz, Controller.

Dean Maytag, Broadcast Services & Program Director.

Jim Windsor, Promotion & Community Services Director.

Sue Samuelson, Traffic Manager.

City of License: Milwaukee. **Station DMA:** Milwaukee, WI. **Rank:** 35.

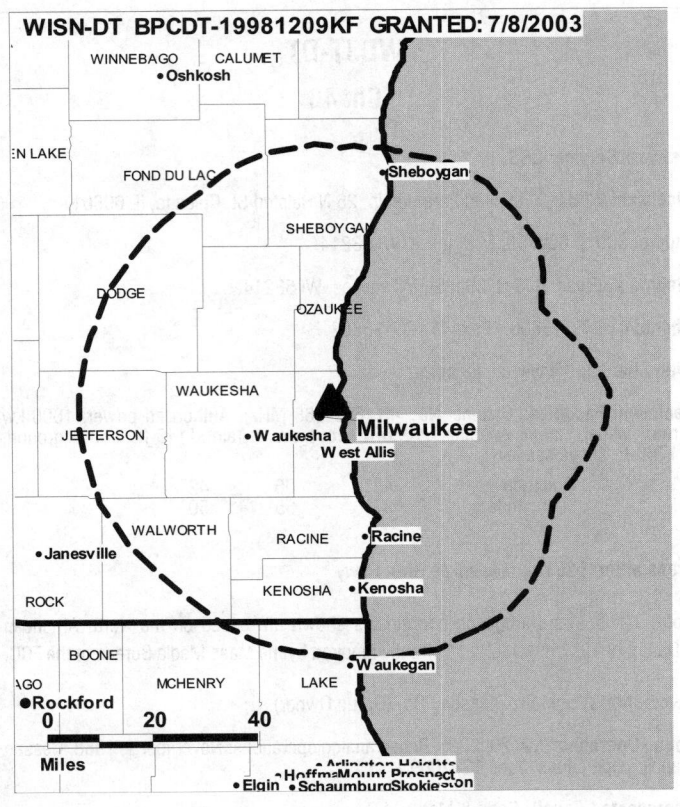

WISN-DT BPCDT-19981209KF GRANTED: 7/8/2003

© 2010 Warren Communications News

Circulation © 2009 Nielsen. Coverage based on Nielsen study.

GrandTotal	Cable TV Households	Non-cable TV Households	Total TV Households
Estimated Station Totals *	626,390	363,880	990,270
Average Weekly Circulation (2009)	362,525	232,393	594,918
Average Daily Circulation (2009)			293,816

Station DMA Total	Cable TV Households	Non-cable TV Households	Total TV Households
Estimated Station Totals *	558,030	347,320	905,350
Average Weekly Circulation (2009)	351,052	229,512	580,564
Average Daily Circulation (2009)			289,046

Other DMA Total	Cable TV Households	Non-cable TV Households	Total TV Households
Estimated Station Totals *	68,360	16,560	84,920
Average Weekly Circulation (2009)	11,473	2,881	14,354
Average Daily Circulation (2009)			4,770

*Estimated station totals are sums of the Nielsen TV and Cable TV household estimates for each county in which the station registers viewing of more than 5% as per the Nielsen Survey Methods.

WITI-DT
Ch. 33

Network Service: FOX.

Licensee: Community Television of Wisconsin License LLC, 1717 Dixie Hwy, Ste 650, Fort Wright, KY 41011.

Studio: 9001 N. Green Bay Rd., Milwaukee, WI 53209.

Mailing Address: 9001 N. Green Bay Rd, Milwaukee, WI 53209.

Phone: 414-355-6666. **Fax:** 414-355-7853.

Web Site: http://www.myfoxmilwaukee.com

Technical Facilities: Channel No. 33 (584-590 MHz). Authorized power: 980-kw max. visual, aural. Antenna: 948-ft above av. terrain, 961-ft. above ground, 1591-ft. above sea level.

Latitude	43°	05'	26"
Longitude	87°	53'	50"

Holds CP for change to 1000-kw max. visual, 997-ft above av. terrain, 1050-ft. above ground, 1680-ft. above sea level; BMPCDT-20081204ADM.

Note: Latitude and longitude coordinates shown are based on the North American Datum of 1927 (NAD 27) as currently required by the Mass Media Bureau of the FCC.

Ownership: Local TV Holdings LLC (Group Owner).

Began Operation: May 1, 2002. Standard Definition. Began analog operations: May 21, 1956. Sale to current owner by Fox Television Stations Inc. approved by FCC June 9, 2008. Transfer of control to Fox Television Stations Inc. by New World Communications Group approved by FCC November 7, 1996. Ceased analog operations: June 12, 2009.

Represented (legal): Dow Lohnes PLLC.

Personnel:

Chuck Steinmetz, General Manager.

Mike Neale, General & Local Sales Manager.

Jim Lemon, Vice President & News Director.

John Workman, Vice President, Engineering & Operations.

Parveen Hughes, Vice President, Finance.

Hailey Puffer, Program Coordinator.

Eric Steele, Research Director.

Lori Wucherer, Vice President, Creative Services.

Terri Graske, Traffic Manager.

City of License: Milwaukee. **Station DMA:** Milwaukee, WI. **Rank:** 35.

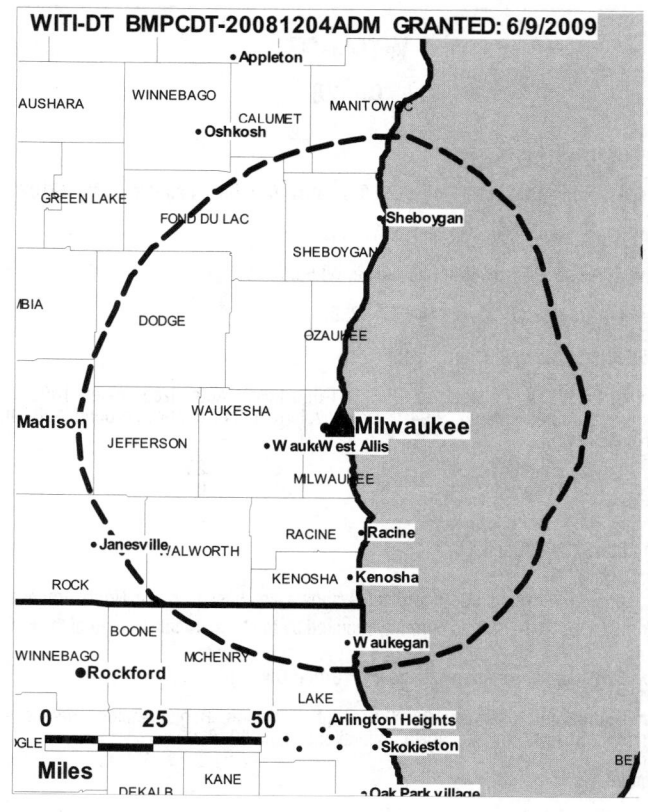

WITI-DT BMPCDT-20081204ADM GRANTED: 6/9/2009

© 2010 Warren Communications News

Circulation © 2009 Nielsen. Coverage based on Nielsen study.

GrandTotal	Cable TV Households	Non-cable TV Households	Total TV Households
Estimated Station Totals *	583,850	363,880	947,730
Average Weekly Circulation (2009)	387,964	230,899	618,863
Average Daily Circulation (2009)			279,797

Station DMA Total	Cable TV Households	Non-cable TV Households	Total TV Households
Estimated Station Totals *	558,030	347,320	905,350
Average Weekly Circulation (2009)	381,946	228,067	610,013
Average Daily Circulation (2009)			276,571

Other DMA Total	Cable TV Households	Non-cable TV Households	Total TV Households
Estimated Station Totals *	25,820	16,560	42,380
Average Weekly Circulation (2009)	6,018	2,832	8,850
Average Daily Circulation (2009)			3,226

*Estimated station totals are sums of the Nielsen TV and Cable TV household estimates for each county in which the station registers viewing of more than 5% as per the Nielsen Survey Methods.

WTMJ-DT
Ch. 28

Network Service: NBC.

Licensee: Journal Broadcast Corp., 3355 S Valley View Blvd, Las Vegas, NV 89102.

Studio: 720 E. Capitol Dr., Milwaukee, WI 53212.

Mailing Address: PO Box 693, Milwaukee, WI 53201.

Phone: 414-332-9611. **Fax:** 414-967-5255.

Web Site: http://www.touchtmj4.com

Technical Facilities: Channel No. 28 (554-560 MHz). Authorized power: 1000-kw max. visual, aural. Antenna: 894-ft above av. terrain, 944-ft. above ground, 1581-ft. above sea level.

Latitude	43°	05'	29"
Longitude	87°	54'	07"

Transmitter: 720 E. Capitol Dr.

Note: Latitude and longitude coordinates shown are based on the North American Datum of 1927 (NAD 27) as currently required by the Mass Media Bureau of the FCC.

Ownership: Journal Communications Inc. (Group Owner).

Began Operation: November 3, 2000. High Definition. Began analog operations: December 3, 1947. Ceased analog operations: June 12, 2009.

Personnel:

Steve Wexler, Executive Vice President, Journal Broadcast Group & General Manager.

Jim Thomas, Vice President, Marketing & Programming.

Mark LeGrand, General Sales Manager.

Mike O'Brien, Local Sales Manager.

Lon Rudolph, National Sales Manager.

Bill Berra, News Director.

Kent Aschenbrenner, Engineering Director.

Alyssa Kroll, Business Manager.

Brenda Serio, Program Manager.

Gregg Schraufnagel, Creative Services & Marketing.

Leon DeRoune, Production Manager.

Tim McCormack, Traffic Manager.

City of License: Milwaukee. **Station DMA:** Milwaukee, WI. **Rank:** 35.

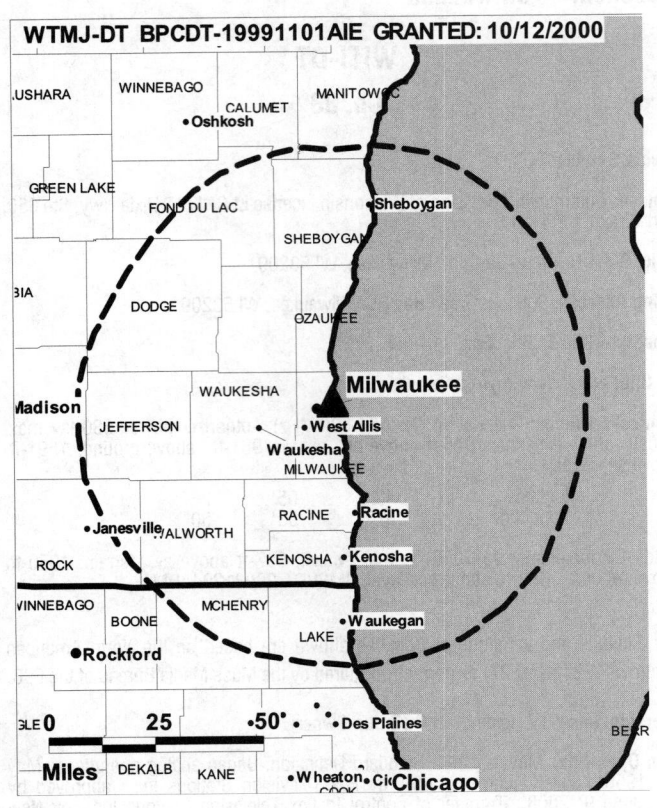

WTMJ-DT BPCDT-19991101AIE GRANTED: 10/12/2000

© 2010 Warren Communications News

Circulation © 2009 Nielsen. Coverage based on Nielsen study.

GrandTotal	Cable TV Households	Non-cable TV Households	Total TV Households
Estimated Station Totals *	641,560	363,880	1,005,440
Average Weekly Circulation (2009)	384,964	225,326	610,290
Average Daily Circulation (2009)			302,486

Station DMA Total	Cable TV Households	Non-cable TV Households	Total TV Households
Estimated Station Totals *	558,030	347,320	905,350
Average Weekly Circulation (2009)	367,456	222,478	589,934
Average Daily Circulation (2009)			295,249

Other DMA Total	Cable TV Households	Non-cable TV Households	Total TV Households
Estimated Station Totals *	83,530	16,560	100,090
Average Weekly Circulation (2009)	17,508	2,848	20,356
Average Daily Circulation (2009)			7,237

*Estimated station totals are sums of the Nielsen TV and Cable TV household estimates for each county in which the station registers viewing of more than 5% as per the Nielsen Survey Methods.

WVCY-DT
Ch. 22

Network Service: IND.

Licensee: VCY America Inc., 3434 W Kilbourn Ave, Milwaukee, WI 53208.

Studio: 2700 W. Vliet St., Milwaukee, WI 53208.

Mailing Address: 3434 W. Kilbourn Ave, Milwaukee, WI 53208.

Phone: 414-935-3000; 800-729-9829. **Fax:** 414-935-3015.

Web Site: http://www.vcyamerica.org

Technical Facilities: Channel No. 22 (518-524 MHz). Authorized power: 196-kw max. visual, aural. Antenna: 938-ft above av. terrain, 965-ft. above ground, 1593-ft. above sea level.

Latitude	43°	05'	46"
Longitude	87°	54'	15"

Note: Latitude and longitude coordinates shown are based on the North American Datum of 1927 (NAD 27) as currently required by the Mass Media Bureau of the FCC.

Ownership: VCY America Inc. (Group Owner).

Began Operation: June 19, 2006. Began analog operations: January 1, 1983. Ceased analog operations: February 17, 2009.

Represented (legal): Wiley Rein LLP.

Personnel:

Vic Eliason, General Manager.

Andy Eliason, Chief Engineer.

Jim Schneider, Program Director.

City of License: Milwaukee. **Station DMA:** Milwaukee, WI. **Rank:** 35.

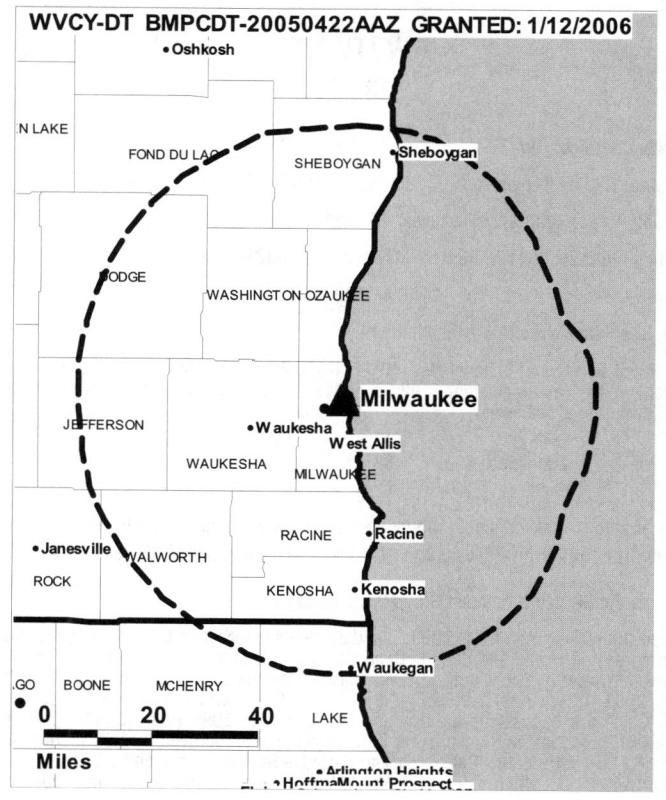

WVCY-DT BMPCDT-20050422AAZ GRANTED: 1/12/2006

© 2010 Warren Communications News

Circulation © 2009 Nielsen. Coverage based on Nielsen study.

GrandTotal	Cable TV Households	Non-cable TV Households	Total TV Households
Estimated Station Totals *	0	162,950	162,950
Average Weekly Circulation (2009)	0	8,148	8,148
Average Daily Circulation (2009)			1,467

Station DMA Total	Cable TV Households	Non-cable TV Households	Total TV Households
Estimated Station Totals *	0	162,950	162,950
Average Weekly Circulation (2009)	0	8,148	8,148
Average Daily Circulation (2009)			1,467

*Estimated station totals are sums of the Nielsen TV and Cable TV household estimates for each county in which the station registers viewing of more than 5% as per the Nielsen Survey Methods.

WVTV-DT
Ch. 18

Network Service: CW.

Grantee: WVTV Licensee Inc., 10706 Beaver Dam Rd, Cockeysville, MD 21030.

Studio: 4041 N. 35th St., Milwaukee, WI 53216.

Mailing Address: 4041 N. 35th St, Milwaukee, WI 53216.

Phone: 414-442-7050. **Fax:** 414-874-1899.

Web Site: http://www.thattvwebsite.com

Technical Facilities: Channel No. 18 (494-500 MHz). Authorized power: 1000-kw max. visual, aural. Antenna: 992-ft above av. terrain, 1011-ft. above ground, 1639-ft. above sea level.

Latitude	43°	05'	44"
Longitude	87°	54'	17"

Note: Latitude and longitude coordinates shown are based on the North American Datum of 1927 (NAD 27) as currently required by the Mass Media Bureau of the FCC.

Ownership: Sinclair Broadcast Group Inc. (Group Owner).

Began Operation: March 21, 2003. Standard Definition. Station broadcasting digitally on its analog channel allotment. Began analog operations: July 20, 1959. Sale to present owner by Glencairn Ltd. Broadcast Properties approved by FCC December 10, 2001 (Television Digest, Vol. 41:38). Sale to Glencairn Ltd. Broadcast Properties by Gaylord Broadcasting approved by FCC June 20, 1995 (Vol. 33:34). Sale to Gaylord Broadcasting by Harold & Bernard Sampson approved by FCC March 24, 1966 (Vol. 5:45; 6:13). Sale of 51% to Harold & Bernard Sampson by Gene Posner approved by FCC August 9, 1962 (Vol. 2:26). Ceased analog operations: February 17, 2009.

Represented (sales): Katz Media Group.

Represented (legal): Pillsbury Winthrop Shaw Pittman LLP.

Personnel:

David Ford, General Manager.

Mark Martin, Sales Director.

Amy Cousland, Local Sales Manager.

Sue Trotman, National Sales Manager.

Dennis Brechlin, Engineering Director.

Wally Koepke, Business Manager.

Jim Seeley, Program Director.

Jason Van Acker, Promotion Director.

Paul Rudolph, Production & Operations Manager.

Kay Mazurkiewicz, Traffic Manager.

City of License: Milwaukee. **Station DMA:** Milwaukee, WI. **Rank:** 35.

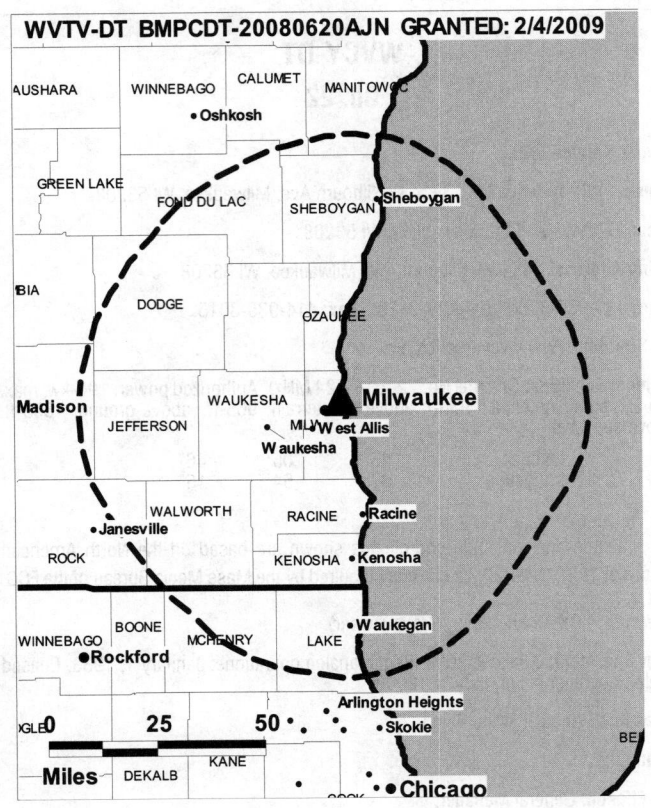

© 2010 Warren Communications News

Circulation © 2009 Nielsen. Coverage based on Nielsen study.

GrandTotal	Cable TV Households	Non-cable TV Households	Total TV Households
Estimated Station Totals *	595,820	363,880	959,700
Average Weekly Circulation (2009)	120,823	106,513	227,336
Average Daily Circulation (2009)			81,068

Station DMA Total	Cable TV Households	Non-cable TV Households	Total TV Households
Estimated Station Totals *	558,030	347,320	905,350
Average Weekly Circulation (2009)	117,440	105,105	222,545
Average Daily Circulation (2009)			79,837

Other DMA Total	Cable TV Households	Non-cable TV Households	Total TV Households
Estimated Station Totals *	37,790	16,560	54,350
Average Weekly Circulation (2009)	3,383	1,408	4,791
Average Daily Circulation (2009)			1,231

*Estimated station totals are sums of the Nielsen TV and Cable TV household estimates for each county in which the station registers viewing of more than 5% as per the Nielsen Survey Methods.

WBME-DT
Ch. 48

Network Service: IND.

Licensee: TV-49 Inc., 4311 E Oakwood Rd, Oak Creek, WI 53154.

Studio: 4311 E. Oakwood Rd., Oak Creek, WI 53154.

Mailing Address: PO Box 92, Oak Creek, WI 53154.

Phone: 414-764-4953. **Fax:** 414-764-5190.

Technical Facilities: Channel No. 48 (674-680 MHz). Authorized power: 62-kw max. visual, aural. Antenna: 489-ft above av. terrain, 436-ft. above ground, 1135-ft. above sea level.

Latitude	42°	51'	18"
Longitude	87°	50'	41"

Holds CP for change to 500-kw max. visual, 984-ft above av. terrain, 1030-ft. above ground, 1654-ft. above sea level; lat. 43° 06' 42", long. 87° 55' 50", BMPCDT-20090709ABY.

Note: Latitude and longitude coordinates shown are based on the North American Datum of 1927 (NAD 27) as currently required by the Mass Media Bureau of the FCC.

Ownership: Weigel Broadcasting Co. (Group Owner).

Began Operation: December 11, 2006. Began analog operations: January 27, 1990. Transfer of control by TV-49 Inc. from Joel J. Kinlow to Weigel Broadcasting Co. approved by FCC September 12, 2007. Ceased analog operations: June 12, 2009.

Represented (engineering): du Treil, Lundin & Rackley Inc.

Represented (legal): Denise B. Moline.

Personnel:

Joel Kinlow, General Manager.

Bruce Herzog, Chief Engineer.

City of License: Racine. **Station DMA:** Milwaukee, WI. **Rank:** 35.

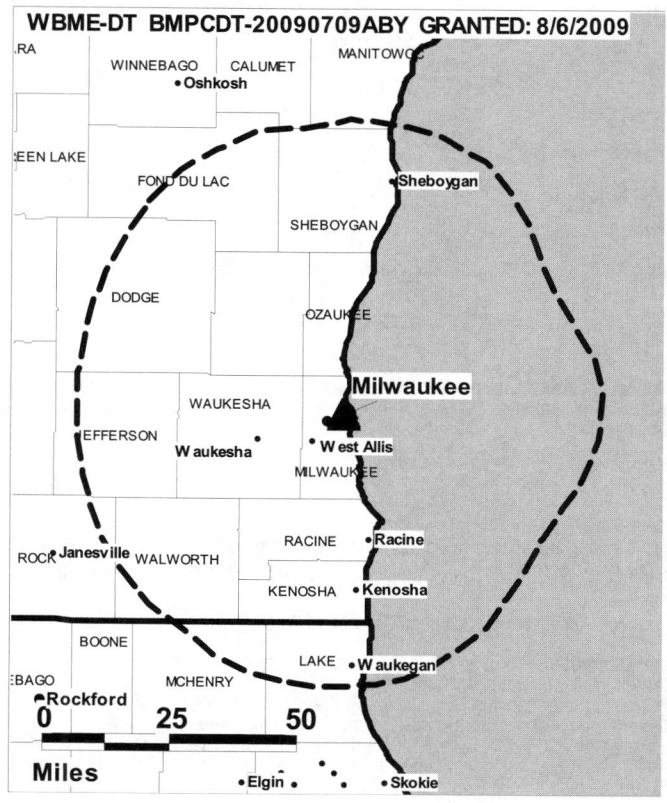

WBME-DT BMPCDT-20090709ABY GRANTED: 8/6/2009

© 2010 Warren Communications News

Circulation © 2009 Nielsen. Coverage based on Nielsen study.

GrandTotal	Cable TV Households	Non-cable TV Households	Total TV Households
Estimated Station Totals *	531,010	252,420	783,430
Average Weekly Circulation (2009)	55,149	22,335	77,484
Average Daily Circulation (2009)			31,637

Station DMA Total	Cable TV Households	Non-cable TV Households	Total TV Households
Estimated Station Totals *	531,010	252,420	783,430
Average Weekly Circulation (2009)	55,149	22,335	77,484
Average Daily Circulation (2009)			31,637

*Estimated station totals are sums of the Nielsen TV and Cable TV household estimates for each county in which the station registers viewing of more than 5% as per the Nielsen Survey Methods.

WJFW-DT
Ch. 16

Network Service: NBC.

Licensee: Northland Television LLC, 885 3rd Ave, 34th Fl, New York, NY 10022.

Studio: 3217 County Trunk G, Rhinelander, WI 54501.

Mailing Address: PO Box 858, Rhinelander, WI 54501-0858.

Phone: 715-365-8812. **Fax:** 715-365-8810.

Web Site: http://www.wjfw.com

Technical Facilities: Channel No. 16 (482-488 MHz). Authorized power: 269-kw max. visual, aural. Antenna: 1188-ft above av. terrain, 1168-ft. above ground, 2812-ft. above sea level.

Latitude	45°	40'	03"
Longitude	89°	12'	29"

Note: Latitude and longitude coordinates shown are based on the North American Datum of 1927 (NAD 27) as currently required by the Mass Media Bureau of the FCC.

Ownership: Rockfleet Broadcasting LP (Group Owner).

Began Operation: February 22, 2007. Began analog operations: October 20, 1966. Ceased analog operations: February 17, 2009. Left air November 17, 1968 following destruction of transmitter by plane crash. Resumed operation September 10, 1969. Distress sale to minority-owned Seaway Communications Inc. by Alvin O'Konski approved by FCC April 20, 1979. Sale to present owner (Randall D. Smith & Jeffrey Smith) from Seaway Communications Inc. approved by FCC April 23, 1998. Transfer of control by present owner from Rockfleet Holdings Inc. to R. Joseph Fuchs approved by FCC July 15, 2008.

Represented (legal): Wiley Rein LLP.

Represented (sales): Blair Television.

Personnel:

Gil Buettner, General Manager & General Sales Manager.

Greg Buzzell, Chief Engineer.

City of License: Rhinelander. **Station DMA:** Wausau-Rhinelander, WI. **Rank:** 135.

Digital cable and TV coverage maps.
Visit www.warren-news.com/mediaprints.htm

MediaPrints™
Map a Winning Business Strategy

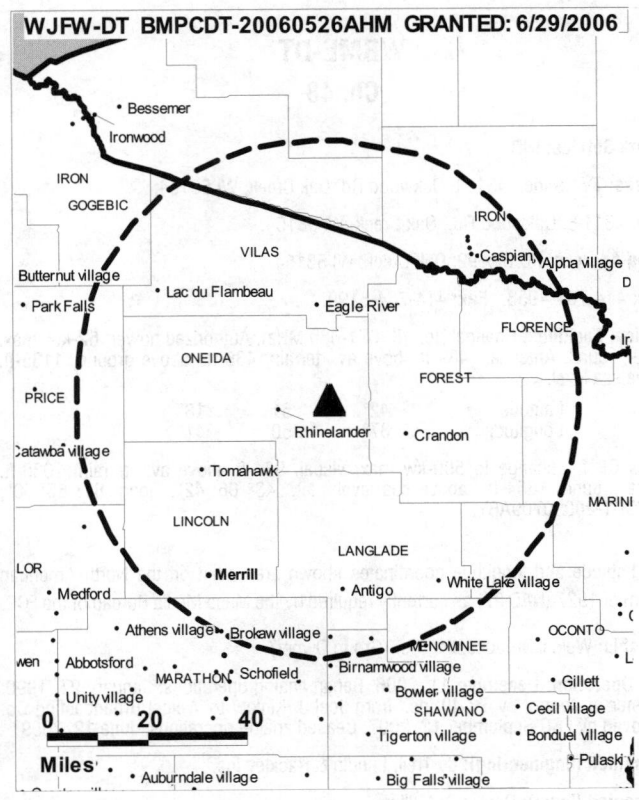

© 2010 Warren Communications News

Circulation © 2009 Nielsen. Coverage based on Nielsen study.

GrandTotal	Cable TV Households	Non-cable TV Households	Total TV Households
Estimated Station Totals *	95,610	113,410	209,020
Average Weekly Circulation (2009)	39,640	43,857	83,497
Average Daily Circulation (2009)			37,479

Station DMA Total	Cable TV Households	Non-cable TV Households	Total TV Households
Estimated Station Totals *	84,690	99,530	184,220
Average Weekly Circulation (2009)	36,566	41,847	78,413
Average Daily Circulation (2009)			35,963

Other DMA Total	Cable TV Households	Non-cable TV Households	Total TV Households
Estimated Station Totals *	10,920	13,880	24,800
Average Weekly Circulation (2009)	3,074	2,010	5,084
Average Daily Circulation (2009)			1,516

*Estimated station totals are sums of the Nielsen TV and Cable TV household estimates for each county in which the station registers viewing of more than 5% as per the Nielsen Survey Methods.

KBJR-DT
Ch. 19
(Operates satellite KRII-DT Chisholm)

Network Service: NBC, MNT.

Licensee: KBJR License Inc., 767 3rd Ave., 34th Fl, c/o Granite Broadcasting Corp., New York, NY 10017.

Studio: 246 S Lake Ave, Duluth, MN 55802.

Mailing Address: 246 S Lake Ave, Duluth, MN 55802.

Phone: 218-720-9600. **Fax:** 218-720-9699.

Web Site: http://www.northlandsnewscenter.com

Technical Facilities: Channel No. 19 (500-506 MHz). Authorized power: 384-kw max. visual, aural. Antenna: 1023-ft above av. terrain, 785-ft. above ground, 2029-ft. above sea level.

Latitude	46°	47'	21.3"
Longitude	92°	06'	50.7"

Note: Latitude and longitude coordinates shown are based on the North American Datum of 1927 (NAD 27) as currently required by the Mass Media Bureau of the FCC.

Ownership: Granite Broadcasting Corp. (Group Owner).

Began Operation: January 15, 2003. Standard and High Definition. Began analog operations: February 23, 1954. Sale to RJR Communications by Northwest Publications Inc. approved by FCC September 5, 1974. Sale to present owner approved by FCC September 12, 1988. Involuntary transfer to debtor in possession approved by FCC December 20, 2006. Transfer from W. Don Cornwell to SP Granite LLC (Silver Point Capital) as part of Chapter 11 reorganization approved by FCC May 21, 2007. Ceased analog operations: February 17, 2009.

Represented (legal): Akin, Gump, Strauss, Hauer & Feld LLP.

Represented (sales): Continental Television Sales.

Personnel:

Robert J. Wilmers, President & General Manager.

David Jensch, Vice President & Station Manager.

Carl Keller, National Sales Manager.

Todd Wentworth, General Sales Manager.

Joe Biondi, Local Sales Manager.

Larry Erickson, Chief Engineer.

Rita Johnson, Business Manager.

Barbara Wentworth, Program Manager.

Nate Stoltman, Promotion & Production Manager.

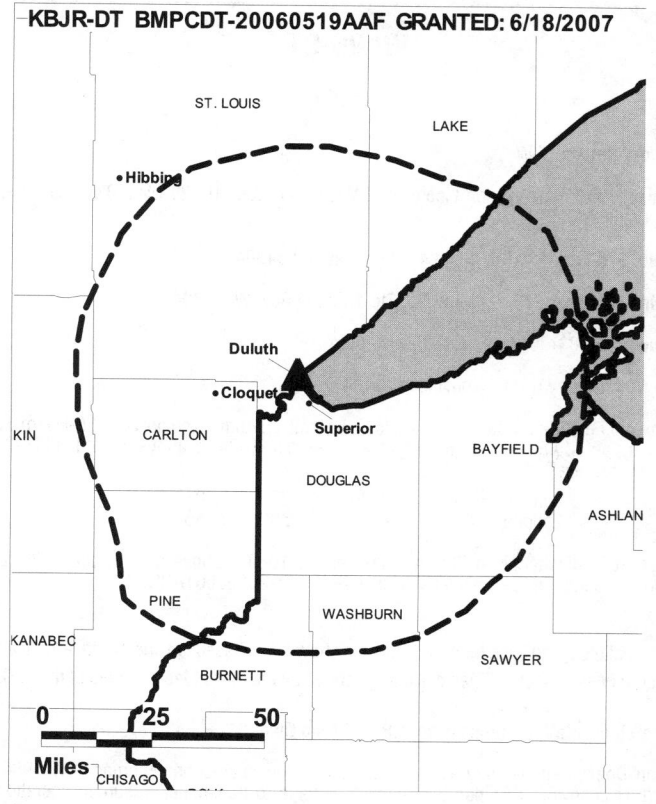

KBJR-DT BMPCDT-20060519AAF GRANTED: 6/18/2007

© 2010 Warren Communications News

Mary Rhodes, Traffic Manager.

City of License: Superior. **Station DMA:** Duluth, MN-Superior, WI. **Rank:** 139.

Circulation © 2009 Nielsen. Coverage based on Nielsen study.

GrandTotal	Cable TV Households	Non-cable TV Households	Total TV Households
Estimated Station Totals *	67,670	103,020	170,690
Average Weekly Circulation (2009)	40,537	67,068	107,605
Average Daily Circulation (2009)			59,399

Station DMA Total	Cable TV Households	Non-cable TV Households	Total TV Households
Estimated Station Totals *	67,670	103,020	170,690
Average Weekly Circulation (2009)	40,537	67,068	107,605
Average Daily Circulation (2009)			59,399

*Estimated station totals are sums of the Nielsen TV and Cable TV household estimates for each county in which the station registers viewing of more than 5% as per the Nielsen Survey Methods.

WIWB-DT
Ch. 21

Network Service: CW.

Licensee: ACME Television Licenses of Wisconsin LLC, 10829 Olive Blvd, Ste 202, St. Louis, MO 63141.

Studio: 975 Parkview Rd., Suite 4, Green Bay, WI 54304.

Mailing Address: 975 Parkview Rd, Ste 4, Green Bay, WI 54304.

Phone: 920-983-9014. **Fax:** 920-983-9424.

Web Site: http://www.wisconsinscw.com

Technical Facilities: Channel No. 21 (512-518 MHz). Authorized power: 450-kw mzx. visual, aural. Antenna: 1089-ft above av. terrain, 1024-ft. above ground, 1115-ft. above sea level.

Latitude	44°	20'	01"
Longitude	87°	58'	56"

Holds CP for change to 800-kw max. visual, 1089-ft above av. terrain, 1020-ft. above ground, 1912-ft. above sea level; BMPCDT-20090601AQN.

Note: Latitude and longitude coordinates shown are based on the North American Datum of 1927 (NAD 27) as currently required by the Mass Media Bureau of the FCC.

Ownership: ACME Communications Inc. (Group Owner).

Began Operation: January 1, 2004. Began analog operations: February 22, 1984. Left air July 28, 1987 due to extensive damage to transmitter; resumed operation December 27, 1988. Left air again July 1991; resumed operation February 5, 1997. Sale to Paxson Communications Corp. from VCY/America Inc. approved by FCC July 23, 1997 (Television Digest, Vol. 37:19). Sale to present owner from Paxson Communications Corp. approved by FCC June 14, 1999. Ceased analog operations: February 17, 2009.

Personnel:

Stephen M. Shanks, Vice President & General Manager.

Todd Ziegler, Local Sales Manager.

Tim Brusky, Chief Engineer.

Jim Parfitt, Business Manager.

Aaron White, Program Director.

Jeff Bartel, Promotion Director.

Brent Gulsvig, Production Manager.

Heidi Gillis, Traffic Manager.

City of License: Suring. **Station DMA:** Green Bay-Appleton, WI. **Rank:** 70.

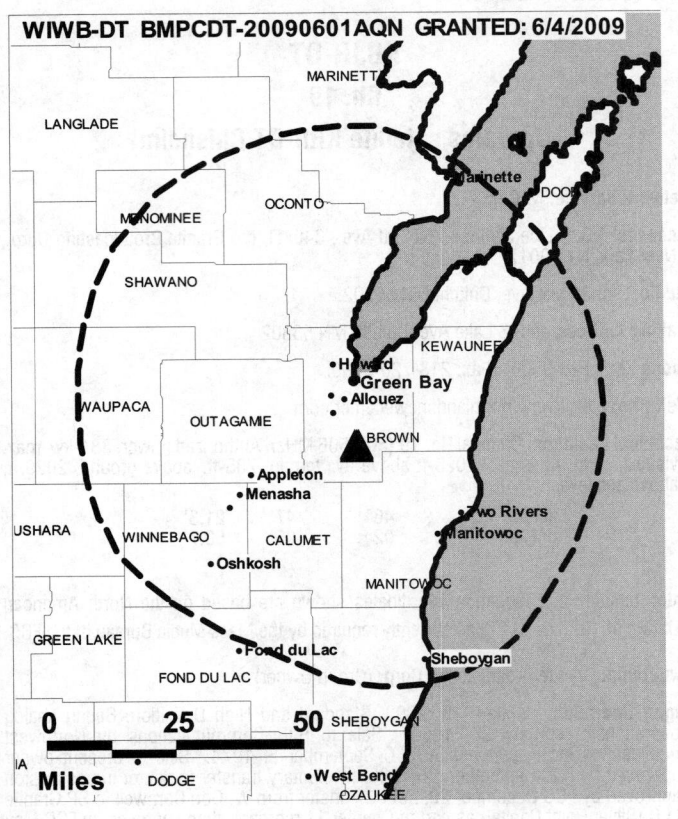

WIWB-DT BMPCDT-20090601AQN GRANTED: 6/4/2009

© 2010 Warren Communications News

Circulation © 2009 Nielsen. Coverage based on Nielsen study.

GrandTotal	Cable TV Households	Non-cable TV Households	Total TV Households
Estimated Station Totals *	211,380	228,770	440,150
Average Weekly Circulation (2009)	41,565	56,367	97,932
Average Daily Circulation (2009)			28,778

Station DMA Total	Cable TV Households	Non-cable TV Households	Total TV Households
Estimated Station Totals *	211,380	222,510	433,890
Average Weekly Circulation (2009)	41,565	55,929	97,494
Average Daily Circulation (2009)			28,697

Other DMA Total	Cable TV Households	Non-cable TV Households	Total TV Households
Estimated Station Totals *	0	6,260	6,260
Average Weekly Circulation (2009)	0	438	438
Average Daily Circulation (2009)			81

*Estimated station totals are sums of the Nielsen TV and Cable TV household estimates for each county in which the station registers viewing of more than 5% as per the Nielsen Survey Methods.

WAOW-DT
Ch. 9

Network Service: CW, ABC.

Grantee: WAOW-WYOW Television Inc., PO Box 909, Quincy, IL 62306-0909.

Studio: 1908 Grand Ave, Wausau, WI 54403.

Mailing Address: 1908 Grand Ave, Wausau, WI 54403.

Phone: 715-842-2251. **Fax:** 715-848-0195.

E-mail: rcrass@waow.com

Web Site: http://www.waow.com

Technical Facilities: Channel No. 9 (186-192 MHz). Authorized power: 31.6-kw visual, aural. Antenna: 1207-ft above av. terrain, 571-ft. above ground, 2474-ft. above sea level.

Latitude	44°	55'	14"
Longitude	89°	41'	28"

Note: Latitude and longitude coordinates shown are based on the North American Datum of 1927 (NAD 27) as currently required by the Mass Media Bureau of the FCC.

Ownership: Quincy Newspapers Inc. (Group Owner).

Began Operation: June 28, 2006. Station broadcasting digitally on its analog channel allotment. Began analog operations: May 7, 1965. Sale to Tak Communications (Sharad Tak) by Liberty Broadcasting approved by FCC January 7, 1985 (Television Digest, Vol. 24:43). Assignment of license to Operating Agent approved by FCC January 27, 1993. Sale to Shockley Communications Corp. approved by FCC September 27, 1995. Sale to present owner by Shockley Communications Corp. approved by FCC April 17, 2001 (Vol. 41:23). Ceased analog operations: February 17 2009.

Represented (sales): Continental Television Sales.

Personnel:

Laurin Jorstad, Vice President & General Manager.

Kathy Silk, General Sales Manager.

Randy Winter, News Director.

Russ Crass, Chief Engineer.

Tara Marshal, Program & Traffic Manager.

Mark Oliver, Promotion Director.

Tricia Schairer, Human Resources Director.

City of License: Wausau. **Station DMA:** Wausau-Rhinelander, WI. **Rank:** 135.

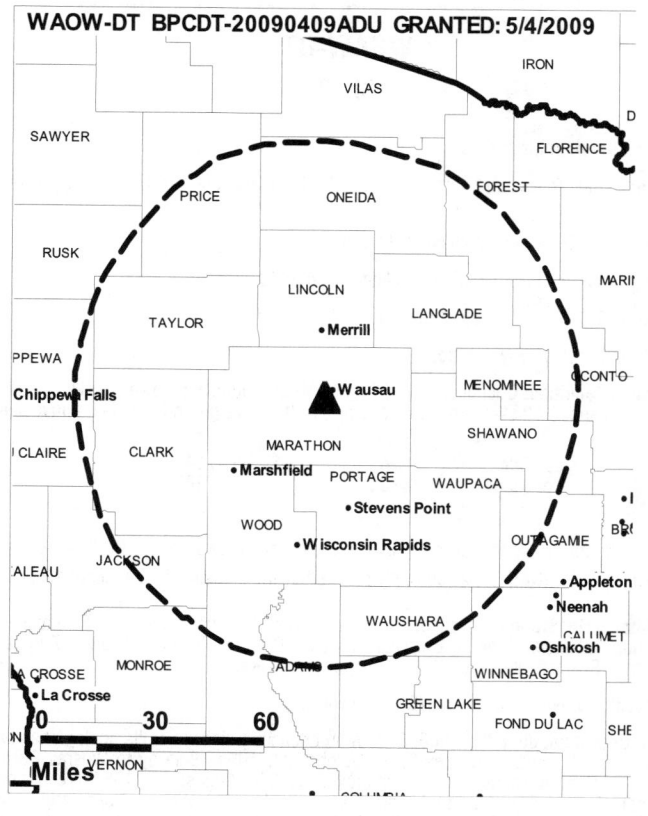

WAOW-DT BPCDT-20090409ADU GRANTED: 5/4/2009

© 2010 Warren Communications News

Circulation © 2009 Nielsen. Coverage based on Nielsen study.

GrandTotal	Cable TV Households	Non-cable TV Households	Total TV Households
Estimated Station Totals *	96,180	118,470	214,650
Average Weekly Circulation (2009)	56,415	72,130	128,545
Average Daily Circulation (2009)			73,753

Station DMA Total	Cable TV Households	Non-cable TV Households	Total TV Households
Estimated Station Totals *	84,690	99,530	184,220
Average Weekly Circulation (2009)	54,593	67,597	122,190
Average Daily Circulation (2009)			70,101

Other DMA Total	Cable TV Households	Non-cable TV Households	Total TV Households
Estimated Station Totals *	11,490	18,940	30,430
Average Weekly Circulation (2009)	1,822	4,533	6,355
Average Daily Circulation (2009)			3,652

*Estimated station totals are sums of the Nielsen TV and Cable TV household estimates for each county in which the station registers viewing of more than 5% as per the Nielsen Survey Methods.

WSAW-DT
Ch. 7

Network Service: MNT, CBS.

Grantee: Gray Television Licensee LLC, 1750 K St NW, Ste 1200, Washington, DC 20006.

Studio: 1114 Grand Ave, Wausau, WI 54403.

Mailing Address: 1114 Grand Ave, Wausau, WI 54403.

Phone: 715-845-4211. **Fax:** 715-845-2649.

Web Site: http://www.wsaw.com

Technical Facilities: Channel No. 7 (174-180 MHz). Authorized power: 72-kw visual, aural. Antenna: 1224-ft above av. terrain, 591-ft. above ground, 2491-ft. above sea level.

Latitude	44°	55'	14"
Longitude	89°	41'	28"

Note: Latitude and longitude coordinates shown are based on the North American Datum of 1927 (NAD 27) as currently required by the Mass Media Bureau of the FCC.

Satellite Earth Stations: Transmitter RCA; Vertex, 4.6-meter Ku-band; Scientific-Atlanta, 4.6-meter C-band; Comtech, 5-meter C-band; Scientific-Atlanta, 7-meter C-band; Scientific-Atlanta, RCA, M/A-Com receivers.

Ownership: Gray Television Inc. (Group Owner).

Began Operation: June 27, 2006. Station broadcasting digitally on its analog channel allotment. Began analog operations: October 24, 1954. Sale by to Wesray Corp. Forward Communications Corp. approved by FCC August 16, 1984 (Television Digest, Vol. 23:44). Sale to Adams Communications by Wesray Corp. approved by FCC December 23, 1987. Sale to Brissette Broadcasting Corp. by Adams Communications approved by FCC December 24, 1991. Transfer of control to Benedek Broadcasting Co. LLC by Brissette Broadcasting Corp. approved by FCC May 22, 1996 (Vol. 35:37, 52). Sale to present owner by Benedek Broadcasting Co. LLC approved by FCC August 29, 2002 (Vol. 42:14). Ceased analog operations: February 17, 2009.

Represented (sales): Continental Television Sales.

Represented (legal): Wiley Rein LLP.

Personnel:

Al Lancaster, Vice President & General Manager.

Judy Stark, Local Sales Manager.

Sara McCormack, National Sales Manager.

Susan Ramsett, News Director.

Chad Myers, Chief Engineer.

Michael Beebe, Creative Services Director.

Patti Shook, Operations Director.

Dan Froelich, Promotions Director.

Cindy Cachavake, Traffic Manager.

WSAW-DT BMPCDT-20080620AKR GRANTED: 4/21/2009

© 2010 Warren Communications News

City of License: Wausau. **Station DMA:** Wausau-Rhinelander, WI. **Rank:** 135.

Circulation © 2009 Nielsen. Coverage based on Nielsen study.

GrandTotal	Cable TV Households	Non-cable TV Households	Total TV Households
Estimated Station Totals *	109,980	132,230	242,210
Average Weekly Circulation (2009)	66,487	79,281	145,768
Average Daily Circulation (2009)			80,322

Station DMA Total	Cable TV Households	Non-cable TV Households	Total TV Households
Estimated Station Totals *	84,690	99,530	184,220
Average Weekly Circulation (2009)	61,079	73,213	134,292
Average Daily Circulation (2009)			74,698

Other DMA Total	Cable TV Households	Non-cable TV Households	Total TV Households
Estimated Station Totals *	25,290	32,700	57,990
Average Weekly Circulation (2009)	5,408	6,068	11,476
Average Daily Circulation (2009)			5,624

*Estimated station totals are sums of the Nielsen TV and Cable TV household estimates for each county in which the station registers viewing of more than 5% as per the Nielsen Survey Methods.

WFXS-DT
Ch. 31

Network Service: FOX.

Grantee: Davis Television Wausau LLC, 2121 Avenue of the Stars, Ste 2800, Los Angeles, CA 90067.

Mailing Address: 1000 N 3rd St, Wausau, WI 54403.

Phone: 715-847-1155. **Fax:** 715-847-1156.

Web Site: http://www.myfoxwausau.com

Technical Facilities: Channel No. 31 (572-578 MHz). Authorized power: 685-kw max. visual, aural. Antenna: 1066-ft above av. terrain, 994-ft. above ground, 2464-ft. above sea level.

Latitude	45°	03'	22"
Longitude	89°	27'	54"

Note: Latitude and longitude coordinates shown are based on the North American Datum of 1927 (NAD 27) as currently required by the Mass Media Bureau of the FCC.

Ownership: Davis Television Inc.

Began Operation: February 17, 2009. Began analog operations: December 1, 1999. Ceased analog operations: February 17 2009.

Personnel:

Robert Raff, President & General Manager.

JanEl Daul, General Sales Manager.

Patrick Mahon, Chief Engineer.

City of License: Wittenberg. **Station DMA:** Wausau-Rhinelander, WI. **Rank:** 135.

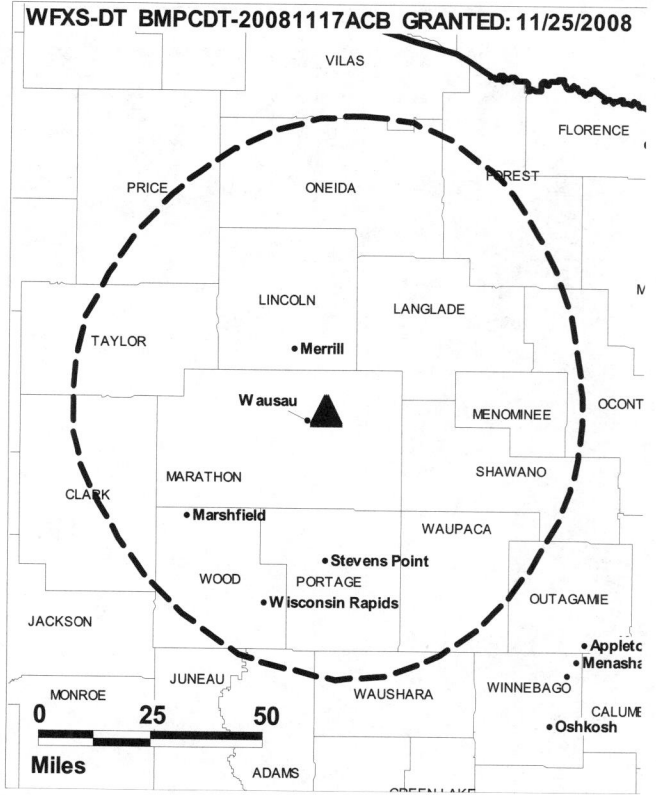

© 2010 Warren Communications News

Circulation © 2009 Nielsen. Coverage based on Nielsen study.

GrandTotal	Cable TV Households	Non-cable TV Households	Total TV Households
Estimated Station Totals *	89,920	132,230	222,150
Average Weekly Circulation (2009)	43,347	45,384	88,731
Average Daily Circulation (2009)			24,681

Station DMA Total	Cable TV Households	Non-cable TV Households	Total TV Households
Estimated Station Totals *	84,690	99,530	184,220
Average Weekly Circulation (2009)	42,557	42,766	85,323
Average Daily Circulation (2009)			23,943

Other DMA Total	Cable TV Households	Non-cable TV Households	Total TV Households
Estimated Station Totals *	5,230	32,700	37,930
Average Weekly Circulation (2009)	790	2,618	3,408
Average Daily Circulation (2009)			738

*Estimated station totals are sums of the Nielsen TV and Cable TV household estimates for each county in which the station registers viewing of more than 5% as per the Nielsen Survey Methods.

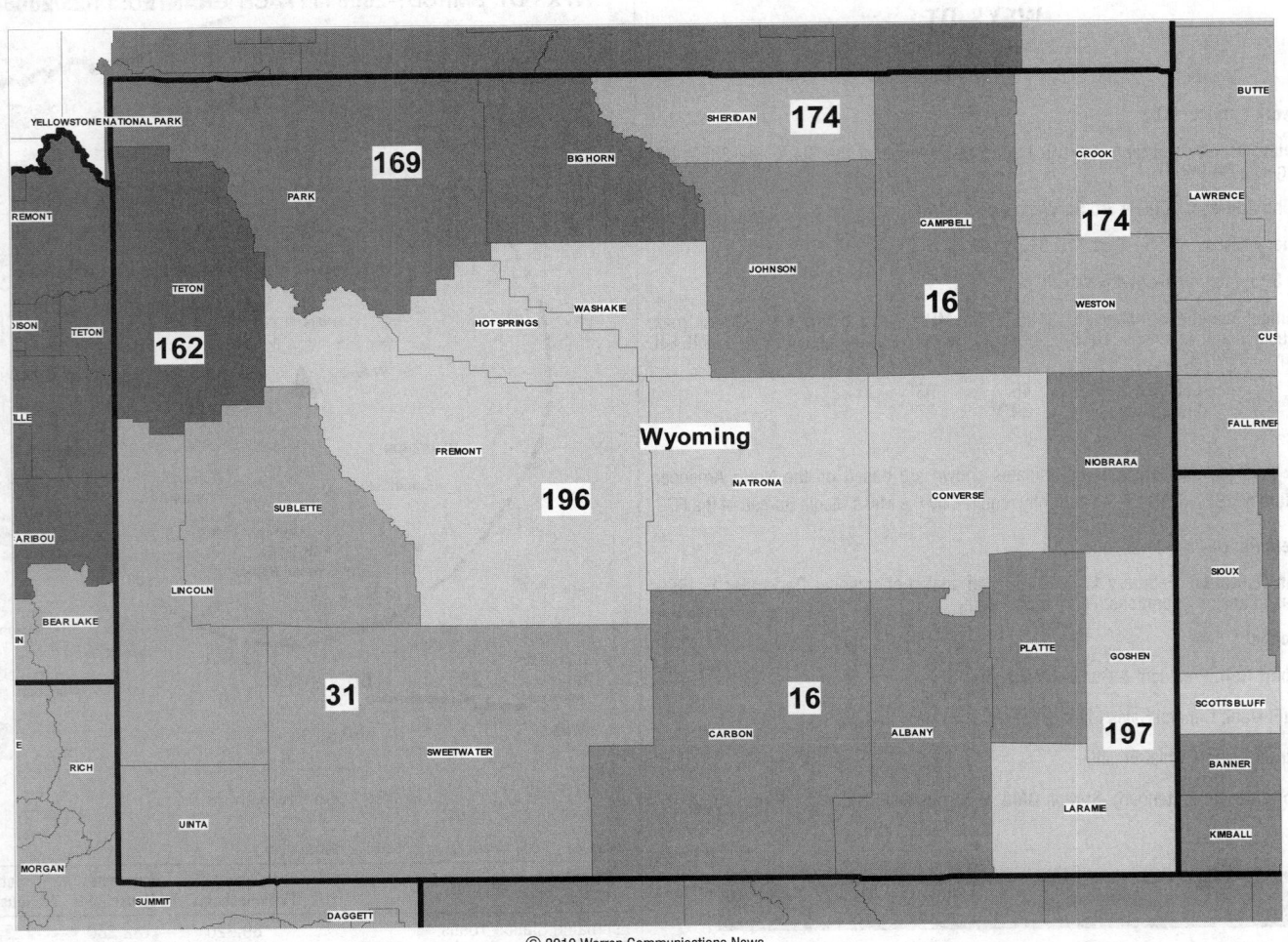

© 2010 Warren Communications News

MARKET	NIELSEN DMA TV HOUSEHOLDS	RANK	MARKET AREA COMMERCIAL STATIONS
Denver, CO	1,539,380	16	KCDO-TV (23); KCEC-DT (51); KCNC-DT (35); KDEN-DT (29); KDVR-DT (32); KFCT-DT (21); KFNR-DT (9); KMGH-DT (7); KPJR-DT (38); KPXC-TV (43); KREG-DT (23); KTFD-DT (15); KTVD-DT (19); KUSA-DT (9); KWGN-DT (34); KWHD-DT (46)
Salt Lake City, UT	944,060	31	KBNY-DT (27); KCSG-DT (14); KENV-DT (10); KGWR-DT (13); KJZZ-DT (46); KPNZ-DT (24); KSL-DT (38); KSTU-DT (28); KTMW-DT (20); KTVX-DT (40); KUCW-DT (48); KUPX-TV (29); KUSG-DT (9); KUTH-DT (32); KUTV-DT (34); KVNV-DT (3)
Idaho Falls-Pocatello, ID-Jackson, WY	126,880	162	KBEO-DT (11); KFXP-DT (31); KIDK-DT (36); KIFI-DT (8); KJWY-DT (2); KPIF-DT (15); KPVI-DT (23)
Billings, MT	107,420	169	KHMT-DT (22); KSVI-DT (18); KTVQ-DT (10); KULR-DT (11); KYUS-DT (3)
Rapid City, SD	98,240	174	KCLO-DT (16); KEVN-DT (7); KHSD-DT (10); KIVV-DT (5); KNBN-DT (21); KOTA-DT (2); KSGW-DT (13)
Casper-Riverton, WY	55,620	196	KCWY-DT (12); KCWY-DT (12); KFNB-DT (20); KFNE-DT (10); KGWC-DT (14); KGWL-DT (7); KTWO-DT (17)
Cheyenne, WY-Scottsbluff, NE	54,710	197	KDUH-DT (7); KGWN-DT (30); KLWY-DT (27); KQCK-DT (11); KSTF-DT (29); KTUW-DT (16)

Wyoming Station Totals as of October 1, 2009

	VHF	UHF	TOTAL
Commercial Television	9	5	14
Educational Television	3	0	3
	12	5	17

KCWY-DT
Ch. 12

Network Service: NBC.

Grantee: Bozeman Trail Communications Co., 1500 Foremaster Lane, Las Vegas, NV 89101.

Mailing Address: PO Box 1540, Mills, WY 82644.

Phone: 307-577-0013. **Fax:** 307-577-5251.

Web Site: http://www.nbcforwyoming.com

Technical Facilities: Channel No. 12 (204-210 MHz). Authorized power: 3.2-kw visual, aural. Antenna: 1875-ft above av. terrain, 220-ft. above ground, 8242-ft. above sea level.

Latitude	42°	44'	37"
Longitude	106°	18'	24"

Note: Latitude and longitude coordinates shown are based on the North American Datum of 1927 (NAD 27) as currently required by the Mass Media Bureau of the FCC.

Ownership: Sunbelt Communications Co.

Began Operation: June 12, 2009. Began analog operations: February 21, 2001. Transfer of control from Uhlmann/Latshaw Broadcasting LLC (51% to 0) to Bozeman Trail Communications Co. (Sunbelt Communications Co.) (49% to 100%) dismissed by FCC February 5, 2004 due to failure of parties to include copy of stock purchase agreement. Parties have since refiled application with necessary documentation. Transfer approved by FCC July 29, 2005. Acquisition of 49% interest by Bozeman Trail Communications Co. granted by FCC September 1, 1998. Ceased analog operations: June 12, 2009.

City of License: Casper. **Station DMA:** Casper-Riverton, WY. **Rank:** 196.

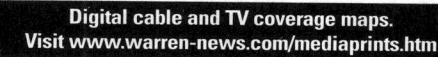

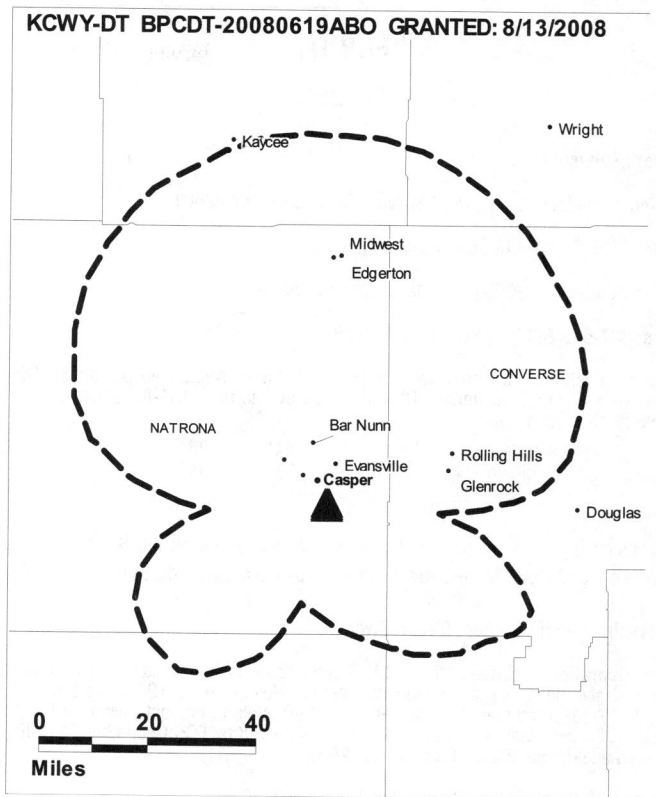

KCWY-DT BPCDT-20080619ABO GRANTED: 8/13/2008

© 2010 Warren Communications News

Circulation © 2009 Nielsen. Coverage based on Nielsen study.

GrandTotal	Cable TV Households	Non-cable TV Households	Total TV Households
Estimated Station Totals *	63,260	22,340	85,600
Average Weekly Circulation (2009)	23,135	9,790	32,925
Average Daily Circulation (2009)			16,824

Station DMA Total	Cable TV Households	Non-cable TV Households	Total TV Households
Estimated Station Totals *	34,090	20,250	54,340
Average Weekly Circulation (2009)	20,338	9,686	30,024
Average Daily Circulation (2009)			16,337

Other DMA Total	Cable TV Households	Non-cable TV Households	Total TV Households
Estimated Station Totals *	29,170	2,090	31,260
Average Weekly Circulation (2009)	2,797	104	2,901
Average Daily Circulation (2009)			487

*Estimated station totals are sums of the Nielsen TV and Cable TV household estimates for each county in which the station registers viewing of more than 5% as per the Nielsen Survey Methods.

KFNB-DT

Ch. 20

Network Service: FOX.

Grantee: WyoMedia Corp., 1856 Skyview Dr, Casper, WY 82601.

Studio: 1856 Skyview Dr., Casper, WY 82601.

Mailing Address: 1856 Skyview Dr, Casper, WY 82601.

Phone: 307-577-5923. **Fax:** 307-577-5928.

Technical Facilities: Channel No. 20 (506-512 MHz). Authorized power: 52.4-kw max. visual, aural. Antenna: 1837-ft above av. terrain, 164-ft. above ground, 8185-ft. above sea level.

Latitude	42°	44'	26"
Longitude	106°	21'	34"

Note: Latitude and longitude coordinates shown are based on the North American Datum of 1927 (NAD 27) as currently required by the Mass Media Bureau of the FCC.

Ownership: Wyomedia Corp. (Group Owner).

Began Operation: February 17, 2009. Station broadcasting digitally on its analog channel allotment. Began analog operations: November 1, 1984. Left air April 25, 1989; resumed operation January 22, 1990. Sale to present owner by Casper Channel 20 Inc., Mark R. Nalbone, Receiver approved by FCC December 11, 1991. Ceased analog operations: February 17, 2009.

Represented (legal): Irwin, Campbell & Tannenwald PC.

Represented (sales): Continental Television Sales.

Personnel:

Mark Nalbone, General Manager.

Judy Lewis, General & Local Sales Manager.

Terry Lane, Chief Engineer.

Tony Lattea, Business & Traffic Manager.

Nicole Lane, Program Director.

Joe Lowndes, Promotions Director.

City of License: Casper. **Station DMA:** Casper-Riverton, WY. **Rank:** 196.

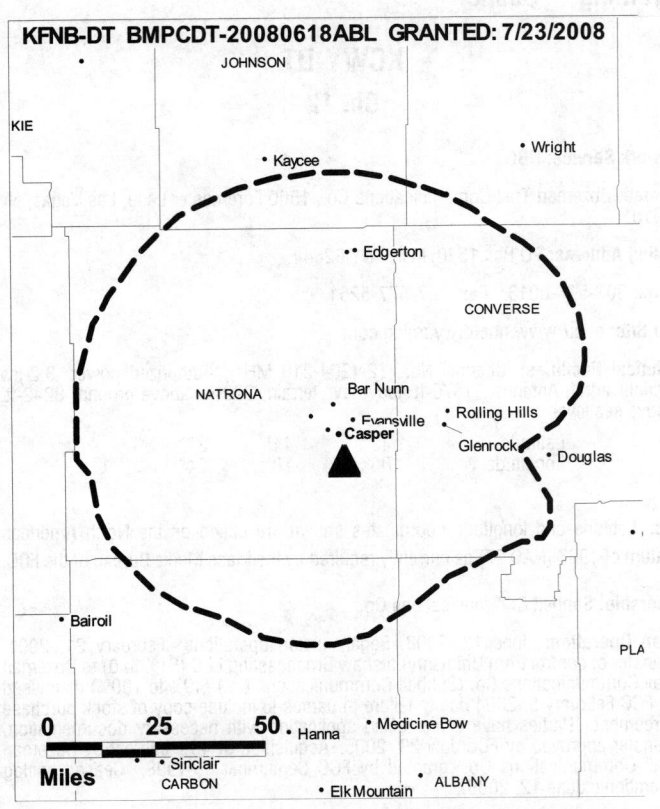

© 2010 Warren Communications News

Circulation © 2009 Nielsen. Coverage based on Nielsen study.

GrandTotal	Cable TV Households	Non-cable TV Households	Total TV Households
Estimated Station Totals *	23,910	20,250	44,160
Average Weekly Circulation (2009)	9,731	6,416	16,147
Average Daily Circulation (2009)			4,024

Station DMA Total	Cable TV Households	Non-cable TV Households	Total TV Households
Estimated Station Totals *	23,910	20,250	44,160
Average Weekly Circulation (2009)	9,731	6,416	16,147
Average Daily Circulation (2009)			4,024

*Estimated station totals are sums of the Nielsen TV and Cable TV household estimates for each county in which the station registers viewing of more than 5% as per the Nielsen Survey Methods.

KGWC-DT
Ch. 14

Network Service: CBS.

Grantee: Mark III Media Inc., 2312 Sagewood, Casper, WY 82601.

Studio: 1856 Skyview Dr., Casper, WY 82601.

Mailing Address: 1856 Skyview Dr, Casper, WY 82601.

Phone: 307-577-5923. **Fax:** 307-234-4005.

E-mail: joanturner@kgwn.tv

Technical Facilities: Channel No. 14 (470-476 MHz). Authorized power: 53.3-kw max. visual, aural. Antenna: 1844-ft above av. terrain, 164-ft. above ground, 8185-ft. above sea level.

Latitude	42°	44'	26"
Longitude	106°	21'	34"

Note: Latitude and longitude coordinates shown are based on the North American Datum of 1927 (NAD 27) as currently required by the Mass Media Bureau of the FCC.

Ownership: Mark III Media Inc. (Group Owner).

Began Operation: February 17, 2009. Station broadcasting digitally on its analog channel allotment. Began analog operations: August 12, 1980. Ceased analog operations: February 17, 2009. Sale to present owner by Chelsey Broadcasting Co. LLC approved by FCC May 31, 2005. Sale to Chelsey Broadcasting Co. LLC by Benedek Broadcasting Co. LLC approved by FCC August 29, 2002. Sale to Benedek Broadcasting Co. LLC by Morris Communications approved by FCC April 12, 1996. Sale to Morris Communications by Stauffer Communications Inc. approved by FCC May 2, 1995. Sale to Stauffer Communications Inc. by Rocky Mountain Communications Network approved by FCC August 25, 1986.

Represented (legal): Borsari & Paxson.

Represented (sales): Continental Television Sales.

Personnel:

Mark Nalbone, General Manager.

T. J. Corson, Operations Manager.

Terry Lane, Chief Engineer.

Judy Lewis, General Sales Manager.

Brandi Hancock, Program Director.

City of License: Casper. **Station DMA:** Casper-Riverton, WY. **Rank:** 196.

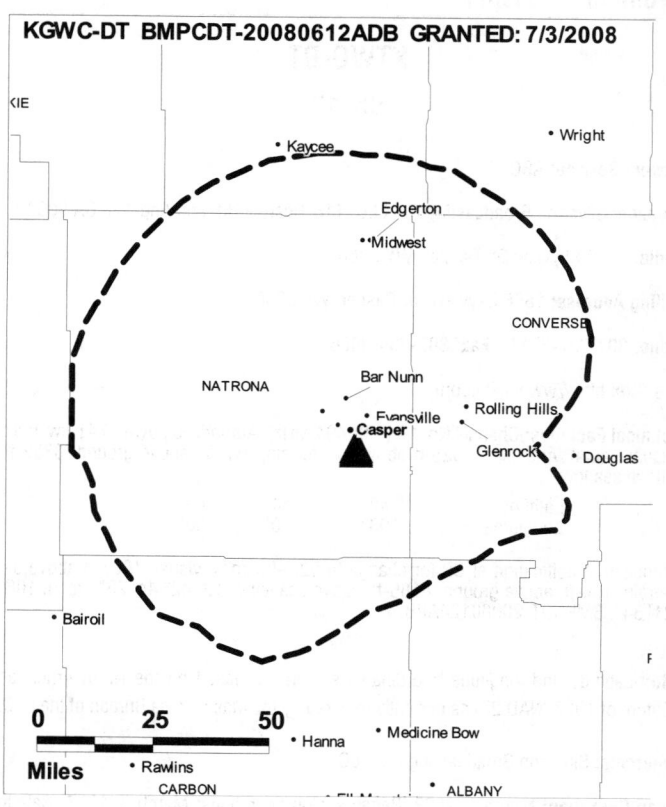

KGWC-DT BMPCDT-20080612ADB GRANTED: 7/3/2008

© 2010 Warren Communications News

Circulation © 2009 Nielsen. Coverage based on Nielsen study.

GrandTotal	Cable TV Households	Non-cable TV Households	Total TV Households
Estimated Station Totals *	23,910	20,250	44,160
Average Weekly Circulation (2009)	13,039	9,121	22,160
Average Daily Circulation (2009)			9,114

Station DMA Total	Cable TV Households	Non-cable TV Households	Total TV Households
Estimated Station Totals *	23,910	20,250	44,160
Average Weekly Circulation (2009)	13,039	9,121	22,160
Average Daily Circulation (2009)			9,114

*Estimated station totals are sums of the Nielsen TV and Cable TV household estimates for each county in which the station registers viewing of more than 5% as per the Nielsen Survey Methods.

KTWO-DT
Ch. 17

Network Service: ABC.

Licensee: Silverton Broadcasting Co. LLC, 116 Tigertail Rd, Los Angeles, CA 90049.

Studio: 1896 Skyview Dr, Casper, WY 82601.

Mailing Address: 1856 Skyview Dr, Casper, WY 82601.

Phone: 307-237-3711. **Fax:** 307-234-9866.

Web Site: http://www.k2tv.com

Technical Facilities: Channel No. 17 (488-494 MHz). Authorized power: 741-kw max. visual, aural. Antenna: 1928-ft above av. terrain, 242-ft. above ground, 8352-ft. above sea level.

Latitude	42°	44'	03"
Longitude	103°	20'	00"

Requests modification of CP for change to 52.9-kw max. visual, 1837-ft above av. terrain, 164-ft. above ground, 8185-ft. above sea level; lat. 42° 44' 26", long. 106° 21' 34", BMPCDT-20080124ABB.

Note: Latitude and longitude coordinates shown are based on the North American Datum of 1927 (NAD 27) as currently required by the Mass Media Bureau of the FCC.

Ownership: Silverton Broadcasting Co. LLC.

Began Operation: March 1, 2003. Began analog operations: March 8, 1957. Sale to Wooster Republican Printing Co. by Harriscope Broadcasting Corp. approved by FCC December 12, 1986. Sale to Eastern Broadcasting Corp. approved by FCC September 6, 1994. Sale to Grapevine Communications Inc. from Eastern Broadcasting Corp. approved by FCC July 2, 1997. Merger with GOCOM Communications LLC to form GOCOM Holdings LLC approved by FCC November 1, 1999. Sale to Wyoming Channel 2 Inc. by GOCOM Holdings LLC approved by FCC March 26, 2001. Sale to K-Two TV of Wyoming Inc. (Cheryl Kaupp) dismissed per applicant's request May 4, 2005. Sale to present owner by Wyoming Channel 2 Inc. approved by FCC May 31, 2006. Ceased analog operations: February 17, 2009.

Represented (legal): Drinker Biddle.

Represented (sales): Katz Media Group.

Personnel:

Kristi Lockard, General Manager.

Terry Lane, Chief Engineer.

Julie Ledger, Traffic & Program Manager.

Jennifer Mason, Local Sales Manager.

City of License: Casper. **Station DMA:** Casper-Riverton, WY. **Rank:** 196.

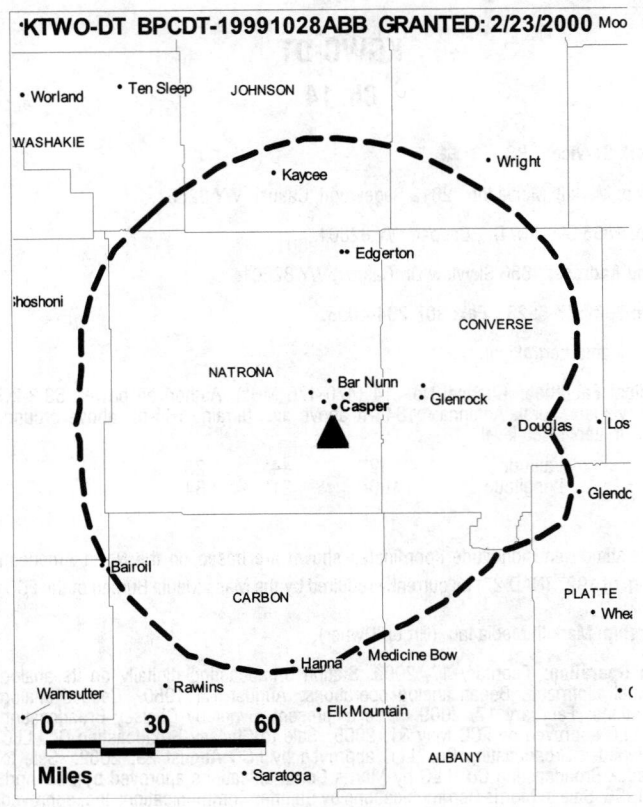

KTWO-DT BPCDT-19991028ABB GRANTED: 2/23/2000 Moo

© 2010 Warren Communications News

Circulation © 2009 Nielsen. Coverage based on Nielsen study.

GrandTotal	Cable TV Households	Non-cable TV Households	Total TV Households
Estimated Station Totals *	76,720	29,230	105,950
Average Weekly Circulation (2009)	34,084	9,848	43,932
Average Daily Circulation (2009)			17,790

Station DMA Total	Cable TV Households	Non-cable TV Households	Total TV Households
Estimated Station Totals *	34,090	20,250	54,340
Average Weekly Circulation (2009)	19,963	8,986	28,949
Average Daily Circulation (2009)			13,543

Other DMA Total	Cable TV Households	Non-cable TV Households	Total TV Households
Estimated Station Totals *	42,630	8,980	51,610
Average Weekly Circulation (2009)	14,121	862	14,983
Average Daily Circulation (2009)			4,247

*Estimated station totals are sums of the Nielsen TV and Cable TV household estimates for each county in which the station registers viewing of more than 5% as per the Nielsen Survey Methods.

KGWN-DT
Ch. 30

Network Service: CW, CBS.

Grantee: SagamoreHill Broadcasting of Wyoming/Northern Colorado LLC, 2 Embarcadero Center, 23rd Fl, San Francisco, CA 94111.

Studio: 2923 E. Lincolnway, Cheyenne, WY 82001.

Mailing Address: 2923 E Lincoln Way, Cheyenne, WY 82001.

Phone: 307-634-7755. **Fax:** 307-638-0182.

E-mail: joanturner@kgwn.tv

Web Site: http://www.kgwn.tv

Technical Facilities: Channel No. 30 (566-572 MHz). Authorized power: 459-kw max. visual, aural. Antenna: 531-ft above av. terrain, 388-ft. above ground, 7167-ft. above sea level.

Latitude	41°	06'	01"
Longitude	105°	00'	23"

Note: Latitude and longitude coordinates shown are based on the North American Datum of 1927 (NAD 27) as currently required by the Mass Media Bureau of the FCC.

Ownership: SagamoreHill Broadcasting LLC (Group Owner).

Began Operation: March 27, 2007. Began analog operations: March 22, 1954. Sale as KFBC-TV to Lamb Communications by Frontier Broadcasting Co. approved by FCC July 6, 1972 (Television Digest, Vol. 11:47; 12:28). Sale to Burke Broadcasting approved by FCC October 14, 1983. Sale to Stauffer Communications Inc. by Burke Broadcasting approved by FCC July 8, 1986 (Vol. 26:13). Sale to Morris Communications by Stauffer Communications approved by FCC May 22, 1995. Sale to Benedek Broadcasting Co. LLC by Morris Communications approved by FCC April 12, 1996 (Vol. 35:49). Sale to Chelsey Broadcasting Co. LLC by Benedek Broadcasting Co. LLC approved by FCC August 8, 2002 (Vol. 42:14). Sale to present owner by Chelsey Broadcasting Co. LLC approved by FCC December 22, 2003. Ceased analog operations: June 12, 2009.

Represented (legal): Wiley Rein LLP.

Represented (sales): Continental Television Sales.

Personnel:

Joan Turner-Doyle, General Manager.

Dusty Thein, General Sales Manager.

Tony Schaefer, Engineering Director.

Jeff Pearson, Production Manager.

Barbara Parenti, Program Director.

Tricia Murphy, Marketing & Promotion Manager.

Keith Yosten, Chief Engineer.

Tregg White, News Director.

City of License: Cheyenne. **Station DMA:** Cheyenne, WY-Scottsbluff, NE. **Rank:** 197.

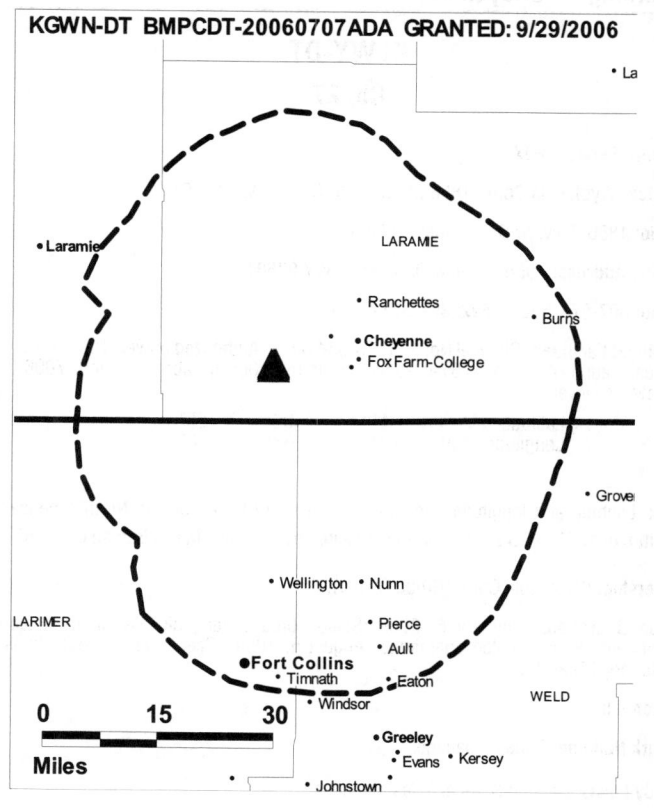

KGWN-DT BMPCDT-20060707ADA GRANTED: 9/29/2006

© 2010 Warren Communications News

Circulation © 2009 Nielsen. Coverage based on Nielsen study.

GrandTotal	Cable TV Households	Non-cable TV Households	Total TV Households
Estimated Station Totals *	37,670	19,420	57,090
Average Weekly Circulation (2009)	19,495	9,697	29,192
Average Daily Circulation (2009)			14,704

Station DMA Total	Cable TV Households	Non-cable TV Households	Total TV Households
Estimated Station Totals *	26,500	19,420	45,920
Average Weekly Circulation (2009)	17,250	9,697	26,947
Average Daily Circulation (2009)			14,168

Other DMA Total	Cable TV Households	Non-cable TV Households	Total TV Households
Estimated Station Totals *	11,170	0	11,170
Average Weekly Circulation (2009)	2,245	0	2,245
Average Daily Circulation (2009)			536

*Estimated station totals are sums of the Nielsen TV and Cable TV household estimates for each county in which the station registers viewing of more than 5% as per the Nielsen Survey Methods.

KLWY-DT
Ch. 27

Network Service: FOX.

Grantee: WyoMedia Corp., 1856 Skyview Dr, Casper, WY 82601.

Studio: 1856 Skyview Dr., Casper, WY 82601.

Mailing Address: 1856 Skyview Dr, Casper, WY 82601.

Phone: 307-577-5923. **Fax:** 307-577-5928.

Technical Facilities: Channel No. 27 (548-554 MHz). Authorized power: 169-kw max. visual, aural. Antenna: 761-ft above av. terrain, 605-ft. above ground, 7006-ft. above sea level.

Latitude	41°	02'	55"
Longitude	104°	53'	28"

Note: Latitude and longitude coordinates shown are based on the North American Datum of 1927 (NAD 27) as currently required by the Mass Media Bureau of the FCC.

Ownership: Wyomedia Corp. (Group Owner).

Began Operation: February 6, 2009. Station broadcasting digitally on its analog allotment. Began analog operations: August 5, 1994. Ceased analog operations: February 17, 2009.

Personnel:

Mark Nalbone, General Manager.

Judy Lewis, General & Local Sales Manager.

Terry Lane, Chief Engineer.

Nicole Lane, Program Director.

Joe Lowndes, Promotion Director.

Tim Haase, Production Manager.

Tony Lattea, Traffic Manager.

City of License: Cheyenne. **Station DMA:** Cheyenne, WY-Scottsbluff, NE. **Rank:** 197.

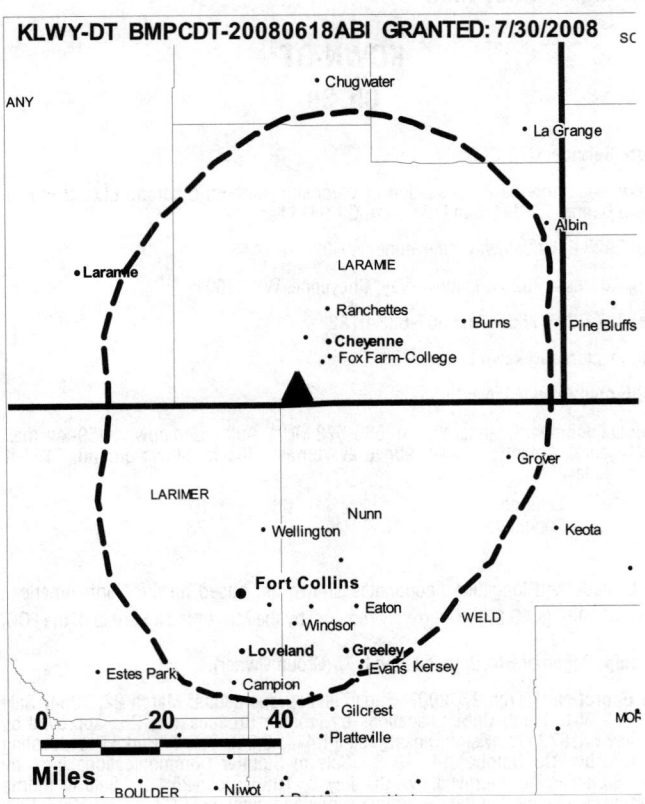

KLWY-DT BMPCDT-20080618ABI GRANTED: 7/30/2008

© 2010 Warren Communications News

Circulation © 2009 Nielsen. Coverage based on Nielsen study.

GrandTotal	Cable TV Households	Non-cable TV Households	Total TV Households
Estimated Station Totals *	35,620	19,420	55,040
Average Weekly Circulation (2009)	14,057	5,868	19,925
Average Daily Circulation (2009)			6,226

Station DMA Total	Cable TV Households	Non-cable TV Households	Total TV Households
Estimated Station Totals *	34,700	19,420	54,120
Average Weekly Circulation (2009)	13,942	5,868	19,810
Average Daily Circulation (2009)			6,203

Other DMA Total	Cable TV Households	Non-cable TV Households	Total TV Households
Estimated Station Totals *	920	0	920
Average Weekly Circulation (2009)	115	0	115
Average Daily Circulation (2009)			23

*Estimated station totals are sums of the Nielsen TV and Cable TV household estimates for each county in which the station registers viewing of more than 5% as per the Nielsen Survey Methods.

KQCK-DT
Ch. 11

Network Service: IND.

Licensee: Denver Broadcasting Inc., Debtor in Possession, One Shackleford Dr, Suite 400, Little Rock, AR 72211-2545.

Studio: 200 W 24th, Ste 303, Cheyenne, WY 82001.

Mailing Address: 200 W 24th, Ste 303, Cheyenne, WY 82001.

Phone: 307-638-8738; 501-219-2400. **Fax:** 307-637-8304.

Technical Facilities: Channel No. 11 (198-204 MHz). Authorized power: 16-kw visual, aural. Antenna: 2133-ft above av. terrain, 49-ft. above ground, 7182-ft. above sea level.

Latitude	40°	32'	47"
Longitude	105°	11'	50"

Holds CP for change to 18-kw visual, 1308-ft above av. terrain, 49-ft. above ground, 7192-ft. above sea level; BPCDT-20080620AAP.

Note: Latitude and longitude coordinates shown are based on the North American Datum of 1927 (NAD 27) as currently required by the Mass Media Bureau of the FCC.

Ownership: Equity Media Holdings Corp., Debtor in Possession (Group Owner).

Began Operation: May 7, 2004. Began analog operations: August 28, 1987. Ceased analog operations: June 12, 2009. Sale to Eastern Broadcasting Corp. by Wooster Republican Printing Co. approved by FCC September 6, 1994. Sale to Grapevine Communications Inc. from Eastern Broadcasting Corp. approved by FCC July 2, 1997 (Television Digest, Vol. 37:12). Merger with GOCOM Communications LLC to GOCOM Holdings LLC approved by FCC November 1, 1999. Sale to Equity Broadcasting Corp. by GOCOM Holdings LLC approved by FCC March 26, 2001. Equity Broadcasting Corp. merged with Coconut Palm Acquisition Corp., becoming Equity Media Holdings Corp. FCC approved deal March 27, 2007. Assignment of license to Debtor in Possession status approved by FCC February 4, 2009. Sale to VB Denver LLC (Valley Bank, Larry Henson, president) pends.

Represented (sales): Katz Media Group.

Personnel:

Mick Burge, General Manager.

Jim Hawks, General Sales Manager.

Dale Roberts, Engineering Director.

City of License: Cheyenne. **Station DMA:** Cheyenne, WY-Scottsbluff, NE. **Rank:** 197.

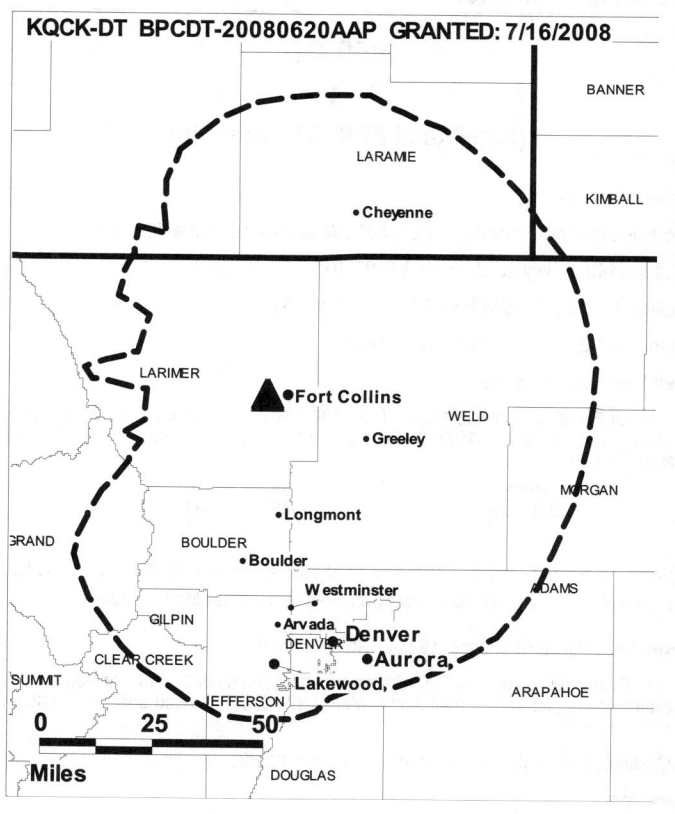

KQCK-DT BPCDT-20080620AAP GRANTED: 7/16/2008

© 2010 Warren Communications News

Circulation © 2009 Nielsen. Coverage based on Nielsen study.

GrandTotal	Cable TV Households	Non-cable TV Households	Total TV Households
Estimated Station Totals *	26,500	19,420	45,920
Average Weekly Circulation (2009)	3,298	2,702	6,000
Average Daily Circulation (2009)			1,682

Other DMA Total	Cable TV Households	Non-cable TV Households	Total TV Households
Estimated Station Totals *	26,500	19,420	45,920
Average Weekly Circulation (2009)	3,298	2,702	6,000
Average Daily Circulation (2009)			1,682

*Estimated station totals are sums of the Nielsen TV and Cable TV household estimates for each county in which the station registers viewing of more than 5% as per the Nielsen Survey Methods.

KBEO-DT
Ch. 11
(Satellite of KPIF-DT Pocatello)

Network Service: IND.

Licensee: Pocatello Channel 15 LLC, 3654 W Jarvis Ave, Skokie, IL 60076.

Studio: 1140 W Hwy 22, Jackson, WY 83001.

Mailing Address: 1140 W Hwy 22, Jackson, WY 83001.

Phone: 847-647-0864. **Fax:** 847-674-9188.

Web Site: http://www.kbeo.net

Technical Facilities: Channel No. 11 (198-204 MHz). Authorized power: 30-kw max. visual, aural. Antenna: 1978-ft above av. terrain, 180-ft. above ground, 10980-ft. above sea level.

Latitude	43°	38'	14"
Longitude	110°	38'	03"

Note: Latitude and longitude coordinates shown are based on the North American Datum of 1927 (NAD 27) as currently required by the Mass Media Bureau of the FCC.

Ownership: Pocatello Channel 15 LLC (Group Owner).

Began Operation: June 12, 2009. Station broadcasting digitally on its analog channel allotment. Began analog operations: March 30, 2001. Ceased analog operations: June 12, 2009.

Represented (legal): Irwin, Campbell & Tannenwald PC.

Personnel:

Kevin Bae, General Manager.

City of License: Jackson. **Station DMA:** Idaho Falls-Pocatello, ID-Jackson, WY.

Rank: 162.

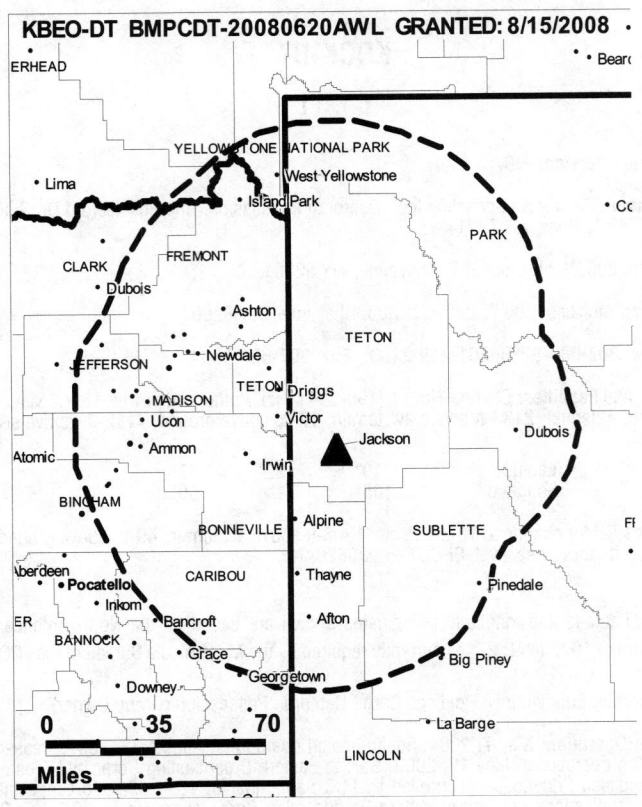

© 2010 Warren Communications News

Nielsen Data: Not available.

KJWY-DT
Ch. 2

Network Service: NBC.

Grantee: PMCM TV LLC, 63 W Parish Rd, Concord, NH 03301.

Studio: 970 W Broadway, Ste 204, Jackson, WY 83001.

Mailing Address: PO Box 7454, Jackson, WY 83002.

Phone: 307-733-2066. **Fax:** 307-733-4834.

Web Site: http://www.kjwy2.com

Technical Facilities: Channel No. 2 (54-60 MHz). Authorized power: 0.27-kw visual, aural. Antenna: 1097-ft above av. terrain, 27-ft. above ground, 8708-ft. above sea level.

Latitude	43°	29'	25"
Longitude	110°	57'	20"

Note: Latitude and longitude coordinates shown are based on the North American Datum of 1927 (NAD 27) as currently required by the Mass Media Bureau of the FCC.

Ownership: PMCM TV LLC (Group Owner).

Began Operation: April 13, 2009. Station broadcasting digitally on its analog channel allotment. Began analog operations: January 9, 1991. Ceased analog operations: June 12, 2009. Sale to Sunbelt Communications Co. by Ambassador Media Corp. approved by FCC September 29, 1995. Sale to present owner by Sunbelt Communications Co. approved by FCC June 10, 2009.

Represented (legal): Fletcher, Heald & Hildreth PLC.

Represented (sales): Blair Television.

Personnel:

Bill Fouch, Executive Vice President & General Manager.

Christel Rahme, Station, General Sales & Business Manager.

John Ehrhart, News Director.

Robin Estopinal, Chief Engineer.

Barbara Monroy, Program Director & Traffic Manager.

Jonathan Cook, Production Manager.

City of License: Jackson. **Station DMA:** Idaho Falls-Pocatello, ID-Jackson, WY.

Rank: 162.

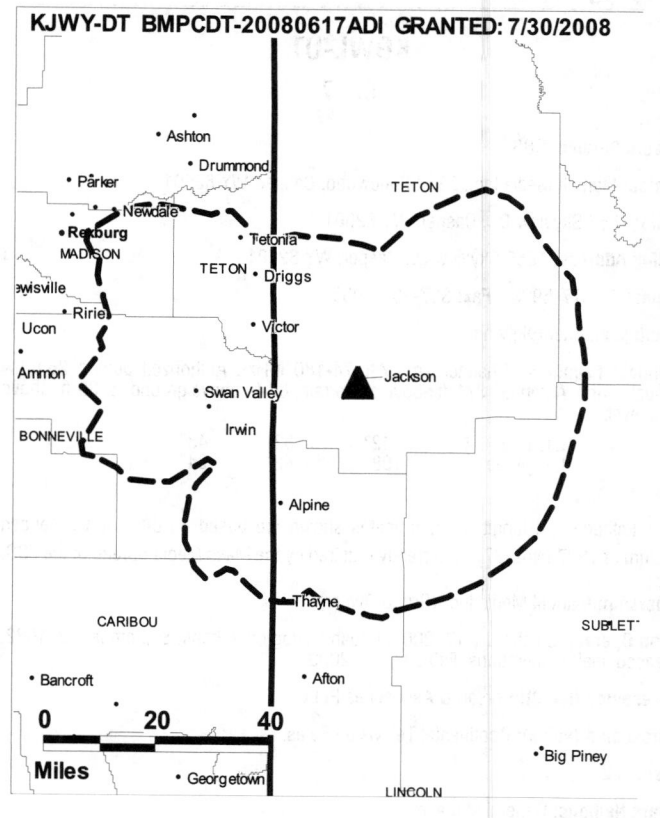

KJWY-DT BMPCDT-20080617ADI GRANTED: 7/30/2008

© 2010 Warren Communications News

Circulation © 2009 Nielsen. Coverage based on Nielsen study.

GrandTotal	Cable TV Households	Non-cable TV Households	Total TV Households
Estimated Station Totals *	5,360	0	5,360
Average Weekly Circulation (2009)	2,675	0	2,675
Average Daily Circulation (2009)			691

Station DMA Total	Cable TV Households	Non-cable TV Households	Total TV Households
Estimated Station Totals *	5,360	0	5,360
Average Weekly Circulation (2009)	2,675	0	2,675
Average Daily Circulation (2009)			691

*Estimated station totals are sums of the Nielsen TV and Cable TV household estimates for each county in which the station registers viewing of more than 5% as per the Nielsen Survey Methods.

KGWL-DT
Ch. 7

Network Service: CBS.

Grantee: Mark III Media Inc., 2312 Sagewood, Casper, WY 82601.

Studio: 1856 Skyview Dr., Casper, WY 82601.

Mailing Address: 1856 Skyview Dr, Casper, WY 82601.

Phone: 307-577-5923. **Fax:** 307-234-4005.

E-mail: joanturner@kgwn.tv

Technical Facilities: Channel No. 7 (174-180 MHz). Authorized power: 26.8-kw visual, aural. Antenna: 371-ft above av. terrain, 89-ft. above ground, 5935-ft. above sea level.

Latitude	42°	53'	43"
Longitude	108°	43'	34"

Note: Latitude and longitude coordinates shown are based on the North American Datum of 1927 (NAD 27) as currently required by the Mass Media Bureau of the FCC.

Ownership: Mark III Media Inc. (Group Owner).

Began Operation: February 17, 2009. Began analog operations: September 12, 1982. Ceased analog operations: February 17, 2009.

Represented (legal): Borsari & Associates PLLC.

Represented (sales): Continental Television Sales.

Personnel:

Mark Nalbone, General Manager.

Judy Lewis, General Sales Manager.

Terry Lane, Director of Engineering.

Nicole Lane, Program Director.

City of License: Lander. **Station DMA:** Casper-Riverton, WY. **Rank:** 196.

Digital cable and TV coverage maps.
Visit www.warren-news.com/mediaprints.htm

MediaPrints™
Map a Winning Business Strategy

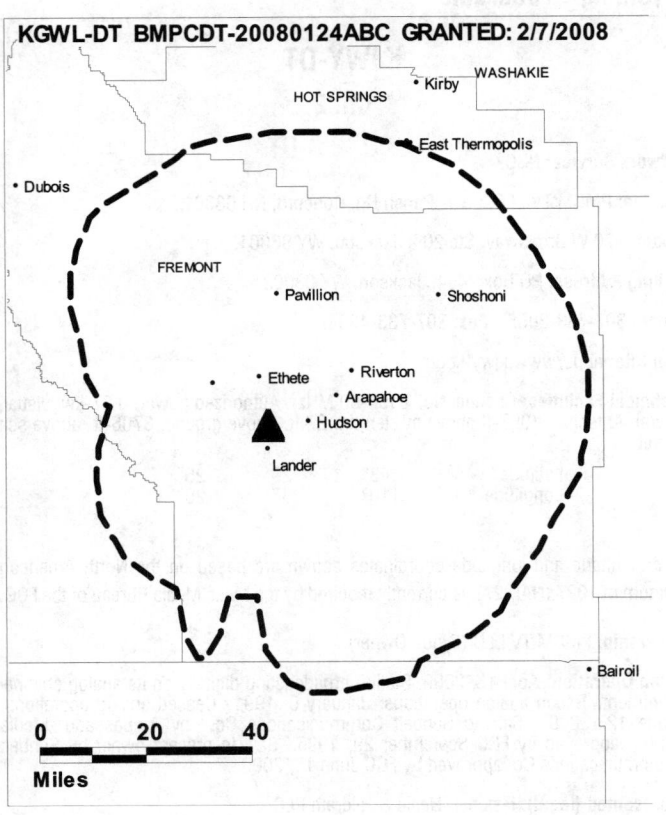

KGWL-DT BMPCDT-20080124ABC GRANTED: 2/7/2008

© 2010 Warren Communications News

Circulation © 2009 Nielsen. Coverage based on Nielsen study.

GrandTotal	Cable TV Households	Non-cable TV Households	Total TV Households
Estimated Station Totals *	10,180	7,100	17,280
Average Weekly Circulation (2009)	5,004	405	5,409
Average Daily Circulation (2009)			2,584

Station DMA Total	Cable TV Households	Non-cable TV Households	Total TV Households
Estimated Station Totals *	10,180	7,100	17,280
Average Weekly Circulation (2009)	5,004	405	5,409
Average Daily Circulation (2009)			2,584

*Estimated station totals are sums of the Nielsen TV and Cable TV household estimates for each county in which the station registers viewing of more than 5% as per the Nielsen Survey Methods.

KFNR-DT
Ch. 9
(Satellite of KFNB-DT Casper)

Network Service: FOX.

Grantee: Wyomedia, 1856 Skyview Dr, Casper, WY 82601.

Studio: 1856 Skyview Dr., Casper, WY 82601.

Mailing Address: 1856 Skyview Dr, Casper, WY 82601.

Phone: 307-577-5923. **Fax:** 307-577-5928.

Technical Facilities: Channel No. 9 (186-192 MHz). Authorized power: 0.978-kw visual, aural. Antenna: 168-ft above av. terrain, 30-ft. above ground, 7234-ft. above sea level.

Latitude	41°	46'	16"
Longitude	107°	14'	15"

Note: Latitude and longitude coordinates shown are based on the North American Datum of 1927 (NAD 27) as currently required by the Mass Media Bureau of the FCC.

Ownership: Wyomedia Corp. (Group Owner).

Began Operation: October 13, 2008. Began analog operations: April 16, 1986. Sale to present owner by First National Broadcasting Corp. approved by FCC February 10, 2009. Station ceased analog operations October 13, 2008.

Represented (legal): Drinker Biddle.

Represented (sales): Continental Television Sales.

Personnel:

Mark Nalbone, General Manager.

Judy Lewis, General & Local Sales Manager.

Terry Lane, Chief Engineer.

Tony Lattea, Business Manager & Traffic Manager.

Nicole Lane, Program Director.

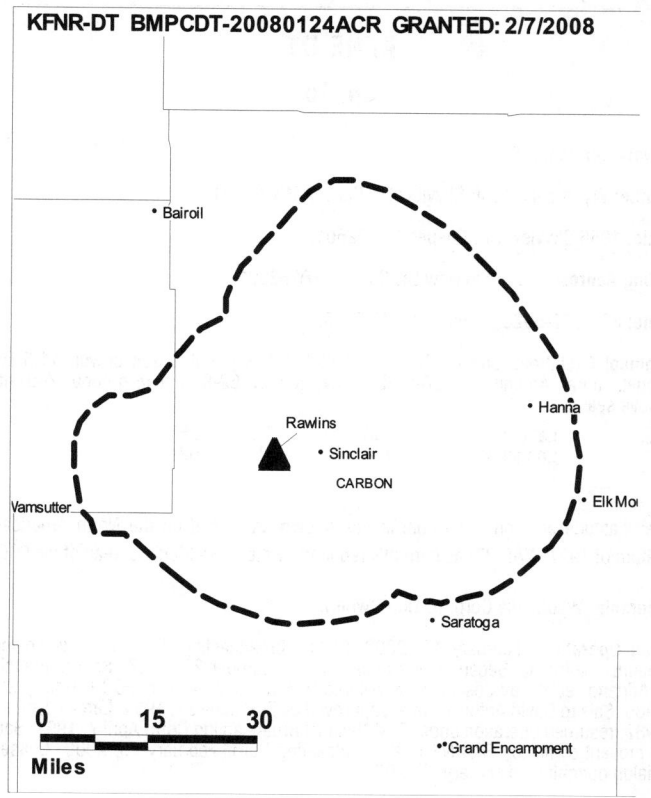

KFNR-DT BMPCDT-20080124ACR GRANTED: 2/7/2008

© 2010 Warren Communications News

Joe Lowndes, Promotion Director.

Tim Haase, Production Manager.

City of License: Rawlins. **Station DMA:** Denver, CO. **Rank:** 16.

Nielsen Data: Not available.

KFNE-DT
Ch. 10

Network Service: FOX.

Grantee: Wyomedia, 1856 Skyview Dr, Casper, WY 82601.

Studio: 1856 Skyview Dr., Casper, WY 82601.

Mailing Address: 1856 Skyview Dr, Casper, WY 82601.

Phone: 307-577-5923. **Fax:** 307-577-5928.

Technical Facilities: Channel No. 10 (192-198 MHz). Authorized power: 11.3-kw visual, aural. Antenna: 1726-ft above av. terrain, 62-ft. above ground, 7497-ft. above sea level.

Latitude	43°	27'	26"
Longitude	108°	12'	02"

Note: Latitude and longitude coordinates shown are based on the North American Datum of 1927 (NAD 27) as currently required by the Mass Media Bureau of the FCC.

Ownership: Wyomedia Corp. (Group Owner).

Began Operation: February 17, 2009. Station broadcasting digitally on its analog channel allotment. Began analog operations: December 22, 1957. Sale to Francis D'Addario, et al., by Joseph P. & Mildred V. Ernst approved by FCC February 28, 1980. Sale to David Antoniak, et al., approved by FCC June 27, 1984. Left air January 1987; resumed operation under First National Broadcasting Corp. April 7, 1991. Sale to present owner by First National Broadcasting Corp. February 10, 2009. Ceased analog operations: February 17, 2009.

Represented (legal): Drinker Biddle.

Represented (sales): Continental Television Sales.

Personnel:

Mark Nalbone, General Manager.

Judy Lewis, General & Local Sales Manager.

Terry Lane, Chief Engineer.

Tony Lattea, Business & Traffic Manager.

Nicole Lane, Program Director.

Joe Lowndes, Promotions Manager.

City of License: Riverton. **Station DMA:** Casper-Riverton, WY. **Rank:** 196.

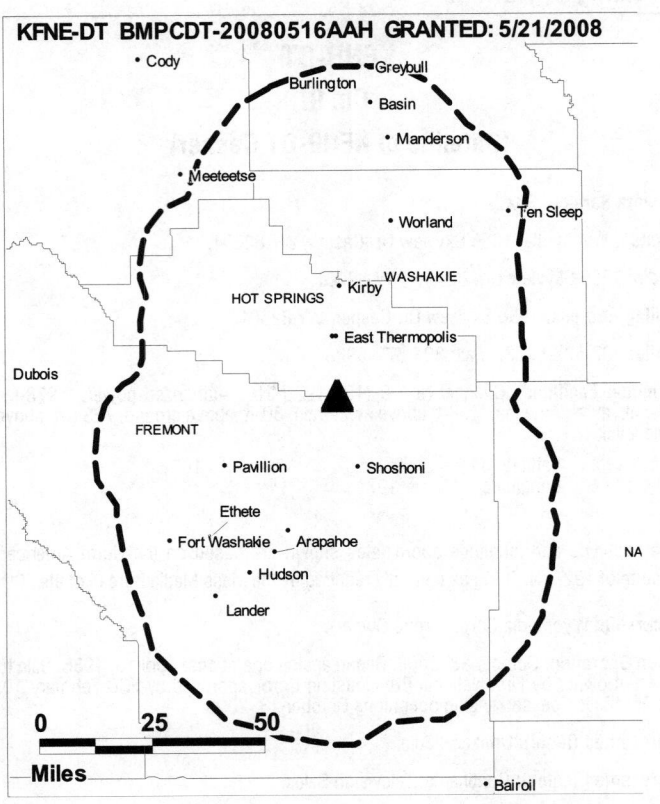

KFNE-DT BMPCDT-20080516AAH GRANTED: 5/21/2008

© 2010 Warren Communications News

Circulation © 2009 Nielsen. Coverage based on Nielsen study.

GrandTotal	Cable TV Households	Non-cable TV Households	Total TV Households
Estimated Station Totals *	10,180	8,170	18,350
Average Weekly Circulation (2009)	3,904	427	4,331
Average Daily Circulation (2009)			1,503

Station DMA Total	Cable TV Households	Non-cable TV Households	Total TV Households
Estimated Station Totals *	10,180	8,170	18,350
Average Weekly Circulation (2009)	3,904	427	4,331
Average Daily Circulation (2009)			1,503

*Estimated station totals are sums of the Nielsen TV and Cable TV household estimates for each county in which the station registers viewing of more than 5% as per the Nielsen Survey Methods.

KGWR-DT
Ch. 13

Network Service: CBS.

Grantee: Mark III Media Inc., 2312 Sagewood, Casper, WY 82601.

Studio: 1856 Skyview Dr., Casper, WY 82601.

Mailing Address: 1856 Skyview Dr, Casper, WY 82601.

Phone: 307-577-5923. **Fax:** 307-234-4005.

E-mail: joanturner@kgwn.tv

Technical Facilities: Channel No. 13 (210-216 MHz). Authorized power: 14.2-kw visual, aural. Antenna: 1624-ft above av. terrain, 148-ft. above ground, 8694-ft. above sea level.

Latitude	41°	26'	21"
Longitude	109°	06'	42"

Note: Latitude and longitude coordinates shown are based on the North American Datum of 1927 (NAD 27) as currently required by the Mass Media Bureau of the FCC.

Ownership: Mark III Media Inc. (Group Owner).

Began Operation: February 17, 2009. Station broadcasting digitally on its analog channel allotment. Began analog operations: October 21, 1977. Sale of KTUX to Rocky Mountain Communications by Gerald E. & Linda K. Devine approved by FCC July 13, 1982. Resumed operation as KWWY January 27, 1983. Sale to Stauffer Communications Inc. approved August 25, 1986. Sale to Morris Communications Corp. approved by FCC May 2, 1995. Sale to Benedek Broadcasting Co. LLC by Morris Communications approved by FCC April 12, 1996. Sale to Chelsey Broadcasting Co. LLC by Benedek Broadcasting Co. LLC approved by FCC August 29, 2002. Sale to present owner by Chelsey Broadcasting Co. LLC approved by FCC May 31, 2006. Ceased analog operations: February 17, 2009.

Represented (legal): Borsari & Associates PLLC.

Represented (sales): Continental Television Sales.

Personnel:

Mark Nalbone, General Manager.

Judy Lewis, General Sales Manager.

Terry Lane, Engineering Director.

Nicole Lane, Program Director.

City of License: Rock Springs. **Station DMA:** Salt Lake City, UT. **Rank:** 31.

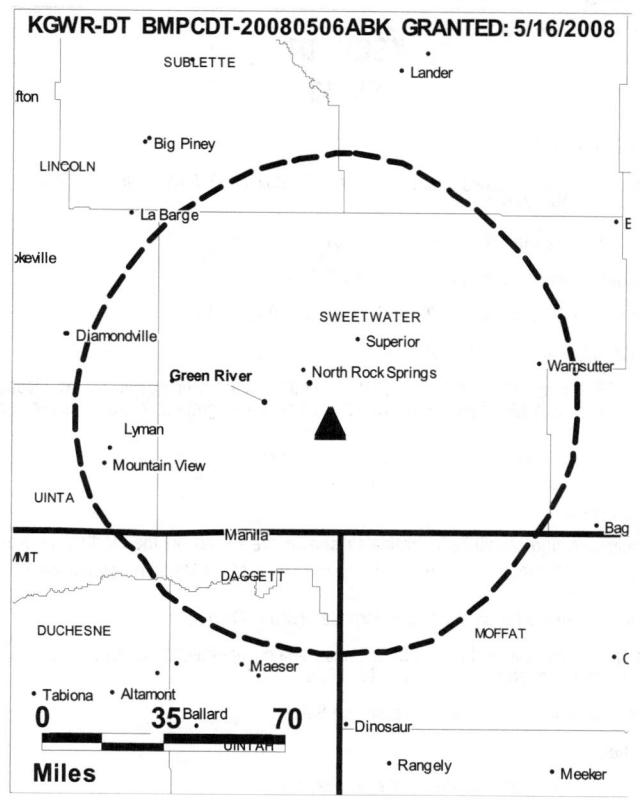

KGWR-DT BMPCDT-20080506ABK GRANTED: 5/16/2008

© 2010 Warren Communications News

Circulation © 2009 Nielsen. Coverage based on Nielsen study.

GrandTotal	Cable TV Households	Non-cable TV Households	Total TV Households
Estimated Station Totals *	8,960	0	8,960
Average Weekly Circulation (2009)	1,299	0	1,299
Average Daily Circulation (2009)			349

Other DMA Total	Cable TV Households	Non-cable TV Households	Total TV Households
Estimated Station Totals *	8,960	0	8,960
Average Weekly Circulation (2009)	1,299	0	1,299
Average Daily Circulation (2009)			349

*Estimated station totals are sums of the Nielsen TV and Cable TV household estimates for each county in which the station registers viewing of more than 5% as per the Nielsen Survey Methods.

KSGW-DT
Ch. 13

Network Service: ABC.

Licensee: Duhamel Broadcasting Enterprises, PO Box 1760, 518 St. Joseph St, Rapid City, SD 57709-1760.

Studio: 518 St. Joseph St., Rapid City, SD 57709.

Mailing Address: PO Box 1760, Rapid City, SD 57709.

Phone: 605-342-2000; 307-672-5335. **Fax:** 605-342-7305.

Web Site: http://www.kotatv.com

Technical Facilities: Channel No. 13 (210-216 MHz). Authorized power: 50-kw visual, aural. Antenna: 1220-ft above av. terrain, 118-ft. above ground, 7798-ft. above sea level.

Latitude	44°	37'	20"
Longitude	107°	06'	57"

Note: Latitude and longitude coordinates shown are based on the North American Datum of 1927 (NAD 27) as currently required by the Mass Media Bureau of the FCC.

Ownership: Duhamel Broadcasting Enterprises (Group Owner).

Began Operation: December 6, 2005. Began analog operations: October 28, 1977. Ceased analog operations: February 17, 2009.

Represented (sales): Continental Television Sales.

Personnel:

William F. Duhamel, President & General Manager.

Peter Duhamel, Vice President.

Steve Duffy, General Sales Manager.

Gerry Fenske, Local Sales Manager.

Dan Black, Chief Engineer.

John Petersen, News Director.

Teresa Hofer, Business Manager.

Monte Loos, Operations Director.

David Bitterman, Production Director.

Doug Loos, Program Director.

Kathy Williamson, Traffic Manager.

City of License: Sheridan. **Station DMA:** Rapid City, SD. **Rank:** 174.

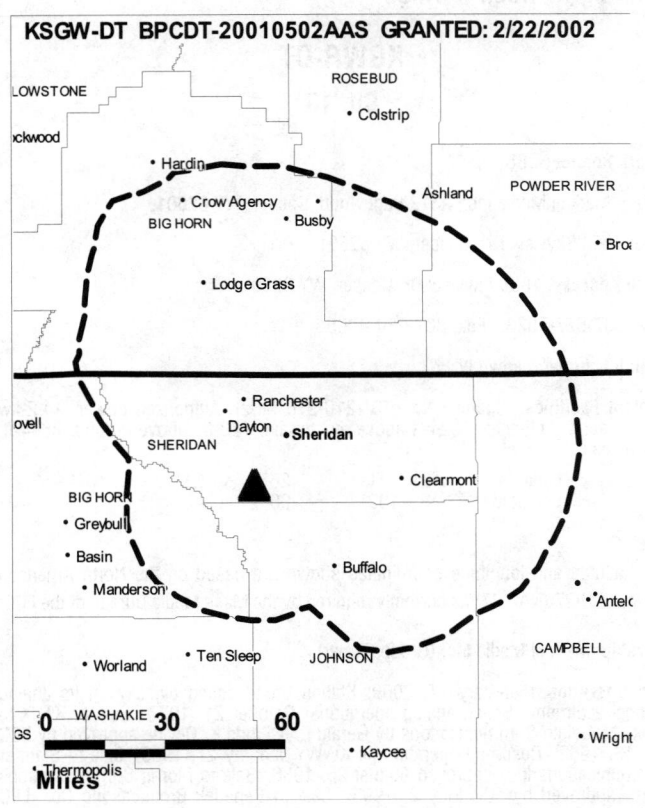

KSGW-DT BPCDT-20010502AAS GRANTED: 2/22/2002

© 2010 Warren Communications News

Circulation © 2009 Nielsen. Coverage based on Nielsen study.

GrandTotal	Cable TV Households	Non-cable TV Households	Total TV Households
Estimated Station Totals *	7,190	4,820	12,010
Average Weekly Circulation (2009)	3,243	1,205	4,448
Average Daily Circulation (2009)			2,282

Station DMA Total	Cable TV Households	Non-cable TV Households	Total TV Households
Estimated Station Totals *	7,190	4,820	12,010
Average Weekly Circulation (2009)	3,243	1,205	4,448
Average Daily Circulation (2009)			2,282

*Estimated station totals are sums of the Nielsen TV and Cable TV household estimates for each county in which the station registers viewing of more than 5% as per the Nielsen Survey Methods.

KUAM-DT
Ch. 8

Network Service: NBC.

Grantee: Pacific Telestations Inc., 600 Harmon Loop Rd, Suite 102, Dededo, GU 96912.

Mailing Address: PO Box 368, Agana, GU 63932.

Phone: 671-637-5826.

Web Site: http://www.kuam.com

Technical Facilities: Channel No. 8 (180-186 MHz). Authorized power: 3.5-kw visual, aural. Antenna: 997-ft above av. terrain, 92-ft. above ground, 1125-ft. above sea level.

Latitude	13°	25'	53"
Longitude	144°	42'	36"

Ownership: Micronesia Broadcasting Corp. (Group Owner).

Began Operation: February 17, 2009. After digital transition, analog operations will continue on K28HS Agana. Station broadcasting digitally on its analog channel allotment. Began analog operations: August 5, 1956.

City of License: Agana. **Station DMA:** Guam. **Rank:** 0.

Nielsen Data: Not available.

KTGM-DT

Ch. 14

Network Service: ABC.

Grantee: Sorensen Television Systems Inc., 111 Chalan Santo Papa, Ste 800, Hagatna, GU 96910.

Mailing Address: 692 N Marine Dr, Ste 308, Tamuning, GU 96911.

Phone: 671-649-8814.

Technical Facilities: Channel No. 14 (470-476 MHz). Authorized power: 41-kw max. visual, aural. Antenna: 551-ft above av. terrain, 118-ft. above ground, 758-ft. above sea level.

Latitude	13°	29'	17"
Longitude	144°	49'	30"

Ownership: Sorensen Television Systems Inc.

Began Operation: Station broadcasting digitally on its analog channel allotment. Began analog operations: October 19, 1987. Sale to present owner by Island Broadcasting Inc. approved by FCC October 11, 2005. Ceased analog operations: February 17, 2009.

Represented (legal): Kaye Scholer LLP.

City of License: Tamuning. **Station DMA:** Guam. **Rank:** 0.

Nielsen Data: Not available.

WQHA-DT
Ch. 50

Network Service: IND.

Licensee: Concilio Mision Cristiana Fuente de Agua Viva Inc., PO Box 4039, Marginal Baldorioty de Castro, Carolina, PR 00984.

Studio: 24 B St. Urb-Ind., Carolina, PR 00979.

Mailing Address: PO Box 4039, Carolina, PR 00984-4039.

Phone: 787-625-5858. **Fax:** 787-750-6440.

Web Site: http://www.fuentedeaguaviva.org

Technical Facilities: Channel No. 50 (686-692 MHz). Authorized power: 50-kw max. visual, aural. Antenna: 1125-ft above av. terrain, 184-ft. above ground, 1332-ft. above sea level.

Latitude	18°	19'	07"
Longitude	67°	10'	48"

Note: Latitude and longitude coordinates shown are based on the North American Datum of 1927 (NAD 27) as currently required by the Mass Media Bureau of the FCC.

Ownership: Concilio Mision Cristiana Fuente de Agua Viva Inc. (Group Owner).

Began Operation: July 7, 2006. Station broadcasting digitally on its analog channel allotment. Began analog operations: November 1, 1995. Ceased analog operations: June 12, 2009.

Personnel:

Oton Font, General Manager.

Edwin Rodriguez, Sales Manager.

City of License: Aguada. **Station DMA:** Puerto Rico. **Rank:** 0.

Nielsen Data: Not available.

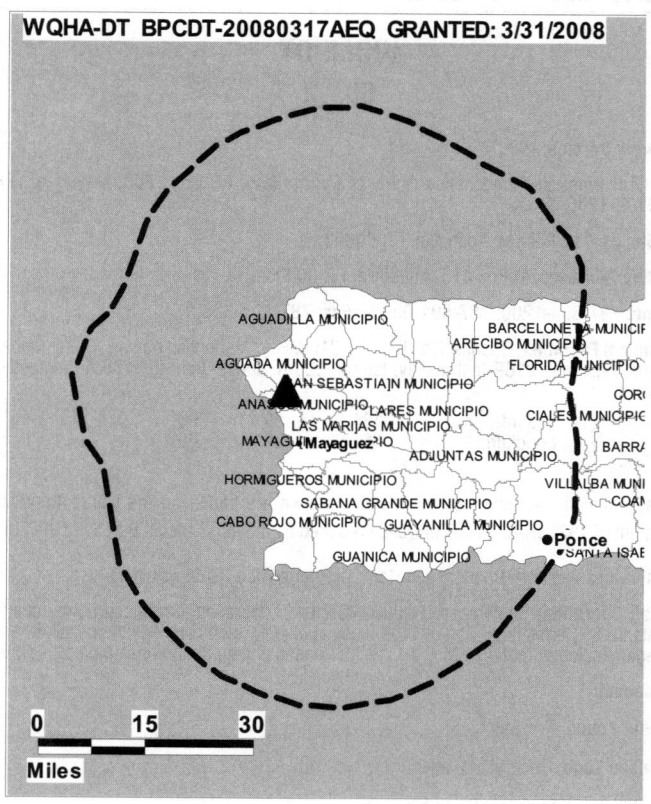

© 2010 Warren Communications News

WOLE-DT
Ch. 12

Network Service: IND.

Grantee: Western Broadcasting Corp. of Puerto Rico, PO Box 1200, Mayaguez, PR 00709-1200.

Studio: St. 111 Palmar, Aguadilla, PR 00603.

Mailing Address: PO Box 415, Aguadilla, PR 00605.

Phone: 787-833-1200; 787-891-0390. **Fax:** 787-891-3380.

Technical Facilities: Channel No. 12 (204-210 MHz). Authorized power: 47-kw visual, aural. Antenna: 2169-ft above av. terrain, 223-ft. above ground, 3176-ft. above sea level.

Latitude	18°	09'	00"
Longitude	66°	59'	00"

Note: Latitude and longitude coordinates shown are based on the North American Datum of 1927 (NAD 27) as currently required by the Mass Media Bureau of the FCC.

Ownership: Western Broadcasting Corp. of Puerto Rico (Group Owner).

Began Operation: September 16, 2002. Currently operating at reduced power due to antenna system failure. Station broadcasting digitally on its analog channel allotment. Began analog operations: May 10, 1960. Ceased analog operations: June 12, 2009.

Personnel:

Irwin Young, President.

Wilson Lugo, General Manager.

M. Milagros Acevedo, Sales Manager.

Doel Oriol, Chief Engineer.

Milagros Acevedo, Traffic Manager.

City of License: Aguadilla. **Station DMA:** Puerto Rico. **Rank:** 0.

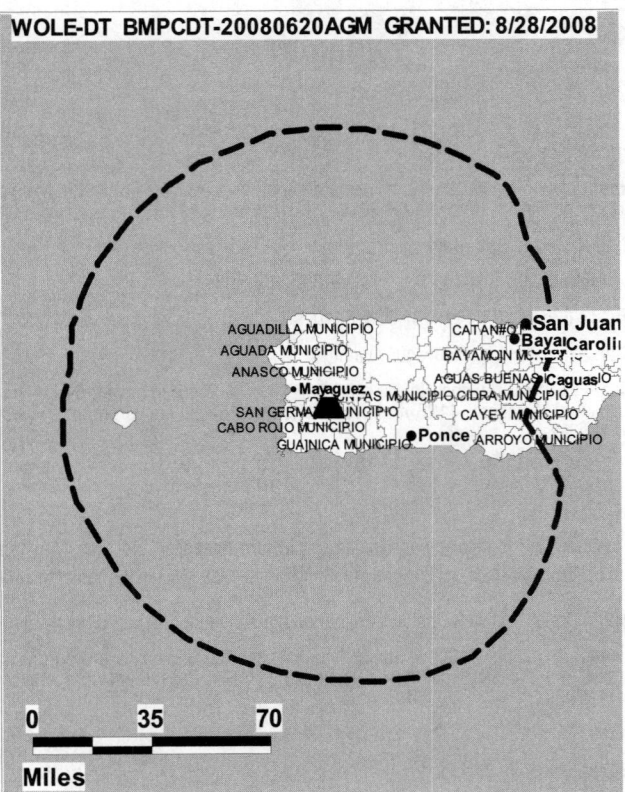

WOLE-DT BMPCDT-20080620AGM GRANTED: 8/28/2008

© 2010 Warren Communications News

Nielsen Data: Not available.

WVEO-DT
Ch. 17

Network Service: IND.

Grantee: International Broadcasting Corp., Calle Bori 1554, Urb. Antonsanti, San Juan, PR 00927-6113.

Mailing Address: Aptdo. 1569, Par. Zagrado Corazon de Jesus, Quebradillas, PR 00678.

Technical Facilities: Channel No. 17 (488-494 MHz). Authorized power: 42-kw max. visual, aural, 1220-ft. above ground, 184-ft. above sea level.

Latitude	1398°	18'	19"
Longitude	06°	67'	10"

Transmitter: 42.

Note: Latitude and longitude coordinates shown are based on the North American Datum of 1927 (NAD 27) as currently required by the Mass Media Bureau of the FCC.

Ownership: Pedro Roman Collazo (Group Owner).

Began Operation: November 16, 2007. Began analog operations: October 7, 1974. Sale to CaribeVision Station Group LLC dismissed by FCC May 1, 2007. Sale to Esperanza Television LLC (William S. Reyner) approved by FCC July 23, 2001, but never consummated. Ceased analog operations: June 12, 2009.

Represented (legal): Irwin, Campbell & Tannenwald PC.

City of License: Aguadilla. **Station DMA:** Puerto Rico. **Rank:** 0.

Nielsen Data: Not available.

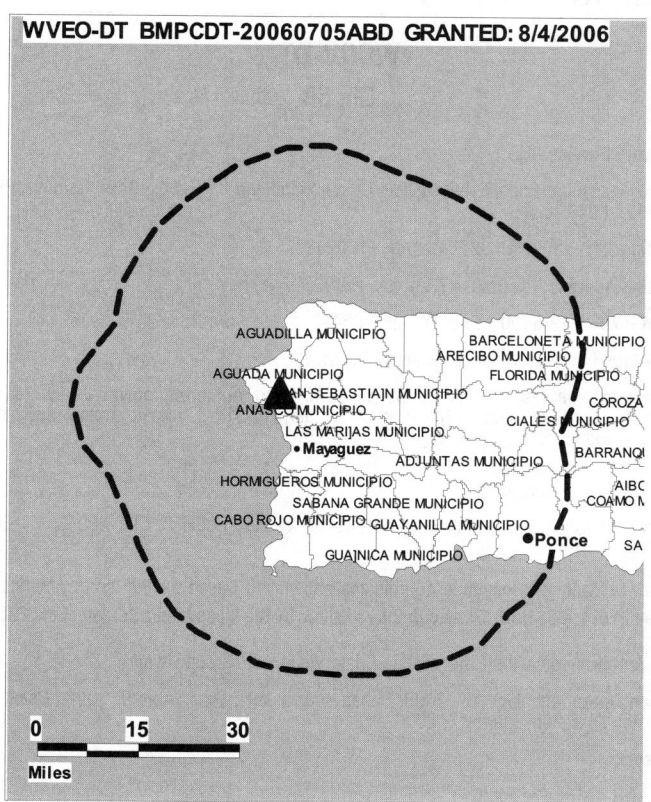

WVEO-DT BMPCDT-20060705ABD GRANTED: 8/4/2006

WCCV-DT
Ch. 53

Network Service: IND.

Licensee: Asociacion Evangelistica Cristo Viene Inc., PO Box 949, Camuy, PR 00627-0949.

Studio: Carr. No. 2, km 92.6, Camuy, PR 00627.

Mailing Address: PO Box 949, Camuy, PR 00627-0949.

Phone: 787-262-5400. **Fax:** 787-262-0541.

Web Site: http://www.cdminternacional.com

Technical Facilities: Channel No. 53 (704-710 MHz). Authorized power: 25-kw max. visual, aural. Antenna: 1968-ft above av. terrain, 512-ft. above ground, 3563-ft. above sea level.

Latitude	18°	14'	06"
Longitude	66°	45'	36"

Holds CP for change to channel number 46, 50-kw max. visual; BPCDT-20080317AEO.

Note: Latitude and longitude coordinates shown are based on the North American Datum of 1927 (NAD 27) as currently required by the Mass Media Bureau of the FCC.

Ownership: Asociacion Evangelistica Cristo Viene Inc. (Group Owner).

Began Operation: June 21, 2006. Began analog operations: April 9, 1982. Ceased analog operations: June 12, 2009.

Personnel:

Jose J. Avila, President.

Esteban Parebes, General Manager.

Frank Martinez, Sales Manager & Marketing Director.

Jorge Figueroa, Chief Engineer.

Sandra Ramos, Program Director.

Rafael Acevedo, Production Manager.

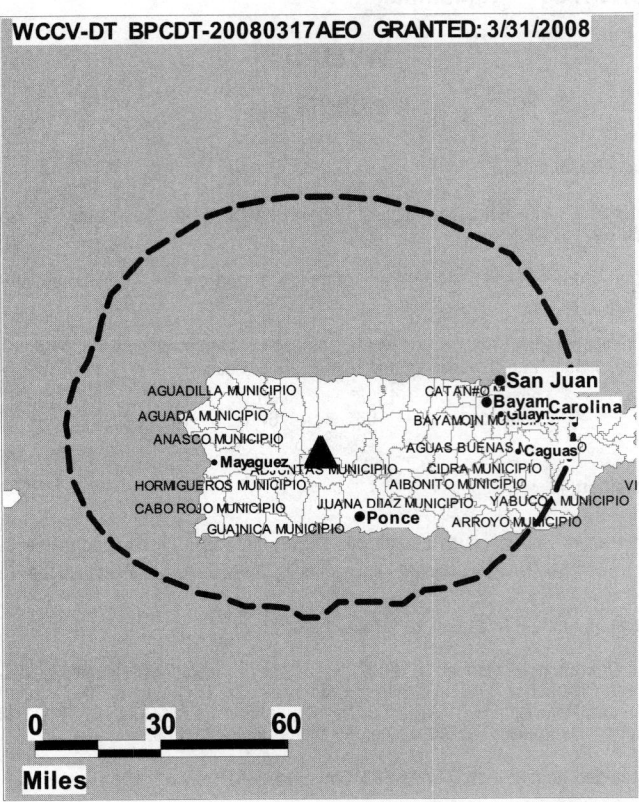

WCCV-DT BPCDT-20080317AEO GRANTED: 3/31/2008

© 2010 Warren Communications News

Ariel Vargas, Traffic Manager.

City of License: Arecibo. **Station DMA:** Puerto Rico. **Rank:** 0.

Nielsen Data: Not available.

WMEI-DT
Ch. 14

Network Service: IND.

Grantee: CMCG Puerto Rico License LLC, 900 Laskin Rd, Virginia Beach, VA 23451.

Phone: 809-743-0988.

Technical Facilities: Channel No. 14 (470-476 MHz). Authorized power: 315-kw max. visual, aural. Antenna: 2733-ft above av. terrain, 421-ft. above ground, 4358-ft. above sea level.

Latitude	18°	09'	17.1"
Longitude	66°	33'	16.4"

Note: Latitude and longitude coordinates shown are based on the North American Datum of 1927 (NAD 27) as currently required by the Mass Media Bureau of the FCC.

Ownership: Max Media X LLC; Power Television International LLC.

Began Operation: February 17, 2009. Began analog operations: November 29, 2006. Ceased analog operations: January 19, 2009. Sale to present owners by Hector Negroni Cartagena approved by FCC February 17, 2006. Proposed sale to Signal Television (Jose J. Arzuaga & Juan G. Padin) dismissed by FCC May 10, 2005. Proposed sale to Teleamericas Network Inc. dismissed by FCC February 26, 1999. Ceased analog operations: January 19, 2009.

Represented (legal): Garvey Schubert Barer.

City of License: Arecibo. **Station DMA:** Puerto Rico. **Rank:** 0.

Nielsen Data: Not available.

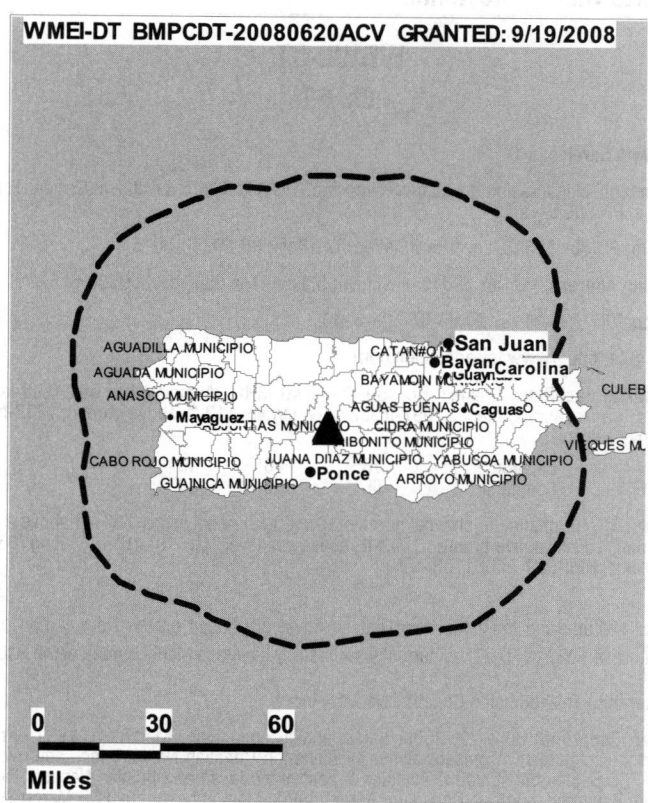

© 2010 Warren Communications News

WDWL-DT
Ch. 59

Network Service: IND.

Licensee: Teleadoracion Christian Network Inc., PO Box 50615, Levittown Station, Toa Baja, PR 00950-0615.

Studio: PO Box 50615, Levittown Station, Toa Baja, PR 00950-0615.

Mailing Address: PO Box 50615, Levittown Station, Toa Baja, PR 00950-0615.

Phone: 787-795-8113. **Fax:** 787-795-8140.

Web Site: http://www.teleadoracion.com

Technical Facilities: Channel No. 59 (740-746 MHz). Authorized power: 0.55-kw max. visual, aural. Antenna: 997-ft above av. terrain, 112-ft. above ground, 1732-ft. above sea level.

Latitude	18°	16'	40"
Longitude	66°	06'	38"

Holds CP for change to channel number 30, 100-kw max. visual, 1027-ft above av. terrain, 108-ft. above ground, 1749-ft. above sea level; lat. 18° 16' 49", long. 66° 06' 35", BMPCDT-20081103ACW.

Note: Latitude and longitude coordinates shown are based on the North American Datum of 1927 (NAD 27) as currently required by the Mass Media Bureau of the FCC.

Ownership: Teleadoracion Christian Network Inc.

Began Operation: June 22, 2006. Began analog operations: March 25, 1991. Pro forma assignment to present owner by Bayamon Christian Network Inc. approved by FCC September 2, 2008. Transfer of control by Bayamon Christian Network Inc. from Bayamon to Iglesia Christiana Amor y Verdad Inc. approved by FCC March 29, 1995. Ceased analog operations: June 12, 2009.

Represented (legal): Fletcher, Heald & Hildreth PLC.

Personnel:

Zoraida Justiniano, General Manager.

Jesus Belec, General Sales Manager.

David Baez, Chief Engineer & Production Manager.

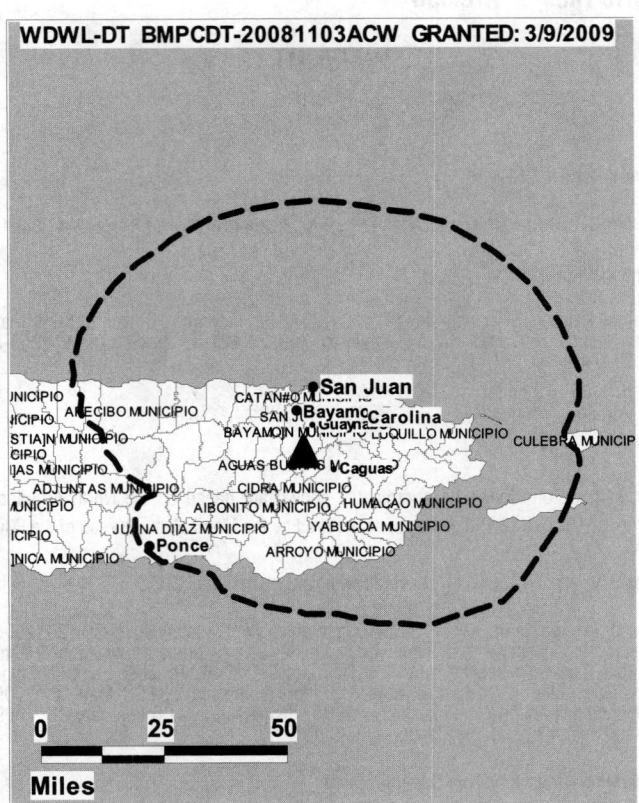

WDWL-DT BMPCDT-20081103ACW GRANTED: 3/9/2009

© 2010 Warren Communications News

Rosa Pereles, Program Director.

City of License: Bayamon. **Station DMA:** Puerto Rico. **Rank:** 0.

Nielsen Data: Not available.

WLII-DT
Ch. 11

Network Service: UNV.

Licensee: WLII/WSUR License Partnership GP, 1999 Avenue of the Stars, Ste 3050, Los Angeles, CA 90067.

Studio: Calle Carazo, No. 62, Guaynabo, PR 00969.

Mailing Address: PO Box 7888, Guaynabo, PR 00970.

Phone: 787-620-1111. **Fax:** 787-300-5003.

Web Site: http://univision.centenialpr.net

Technical Facilities: Channel No. 11 (198-204 MHz). Authorized power: 38-kw visual, aural. Antenna: 1165-ft above av. terrain, 210-ft. above ground, 1880-ft. above sea level.

Latitude	18°	16'	54"
Longitude	66°	06'	46"

Note: Latitude and longitude coordinates shown are based on the North American Datum of 1927 (NAD 27) as currently required by the Mass Media Bureau of the FCC.

Ownership: Univision Communications Inc. (Group Owner).

Began Operation: March 28, 2003. Station broadcasting digitally on its analog channel allotment. Began analog operations: April 22, 1960. Transfer of control to Broadcasting Media Partners Inc. approved by FCC March 27, 2007. Transfer to present owner by Raycom Media Inc. approved by FCC May 23, 2005. Transfer to Univision Communications Inc. by Raycom Media Inc. approved by FCC August 20, 2001, but sale never consummated. Transfer to Raycom Media Inc. by Milton S. Maltz approved by FCC August 13, 1998. Sale to Estrella Brilliante Ltd. Co-Partnership by Teleonce Corp. approved by FCC August 5, 1991. Ceased analog operations: June 12, 2009.

Represented (legal): Covington & Burling.

Personnel:

Larry Sands, General Manager.

Modesto Delgado, Operations Manager.

Carlos Pagan, General Sales Manager.

Susanne Ramirez de Arellano, News Director.

Andres Diaz, Chief Engineer.

Jorge Pietri, Business Manager.

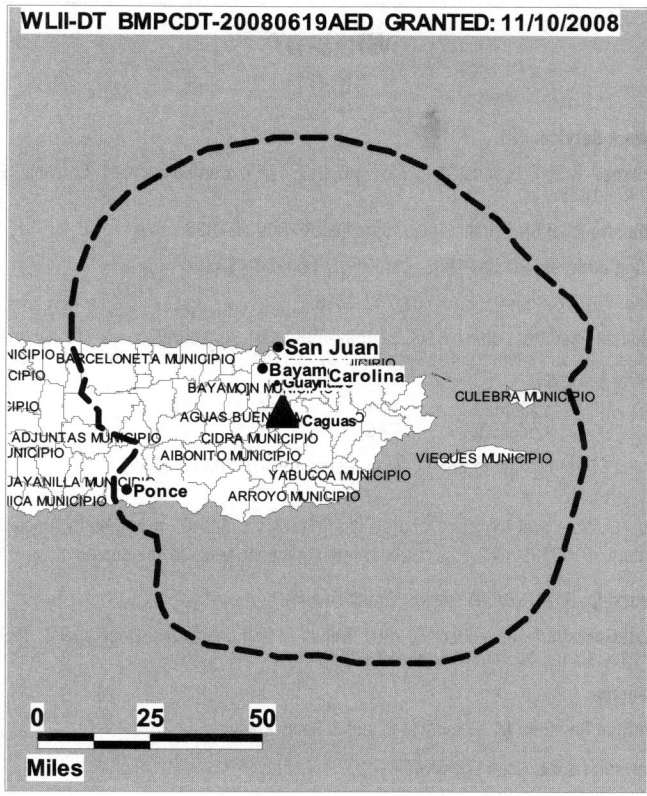

© 2010 Warren Communications News

Jessica Rodriquez, Program Director.

Gerardo Oliveras, Promotion Manager.

Manuel Santiago, Production Manager.

Nancy Guzman, Traffic Manager.

City of License: Caguas. **Station DMA:** Puerto Rico. **Rank:** 0.

Nielsen Data: Not available.

WRFB-DT
Ch. 51

Network Service: IND.

Licensee: R & F Broadcasting Inc., PO Box 1833, Cermica Annex, Carolina, PR 00984-1833.

Studio: No 21 B St, Sabana Abajo, Carolina, PR 00984-1825.

Mailing Address: PO Box 1833, Carolina, PR 00984-1833.

Phone: 787-762-5500. **Fax:** 787-752-1825.

Technical Facilities: Channel No. 51 (692-698 MHz). Authorized power: 16-kw max. visual, aural. Antenna: 1847-ft above av. terrain, 180-ft. above ground, 2592-ft. above sea level.

Latitude	18°	16'	44"
Longitude	65°	51'	12"

Holds CP for change to 256-kw max. visual; BPCDT-20081118AEZ.

Note: Latitude and longitude coordinates shown are based on the North American Datum of 1927 (NAD 27) as currently required by the Mass Media Bureau of the FCC.

Ownership: R. & F. Broadcasting (Group Owner).

Began Operation: November 16, 2007. Began analog operations: December 1, 1998. Ceased analog operations: June 12, 2009.

Personnel:

Enrique Sanchez Jr., General Manager & Sales Manager.

German Lanzo, Chief Engineer.

Blanche deSanchez, Program Director.

Michelle Diaz, Marketing Director.

Sandra de Sanchez, Promotion Director.

City of License: Carolina. **Station DMA:** Puerto Rico. **Rank:** 0.

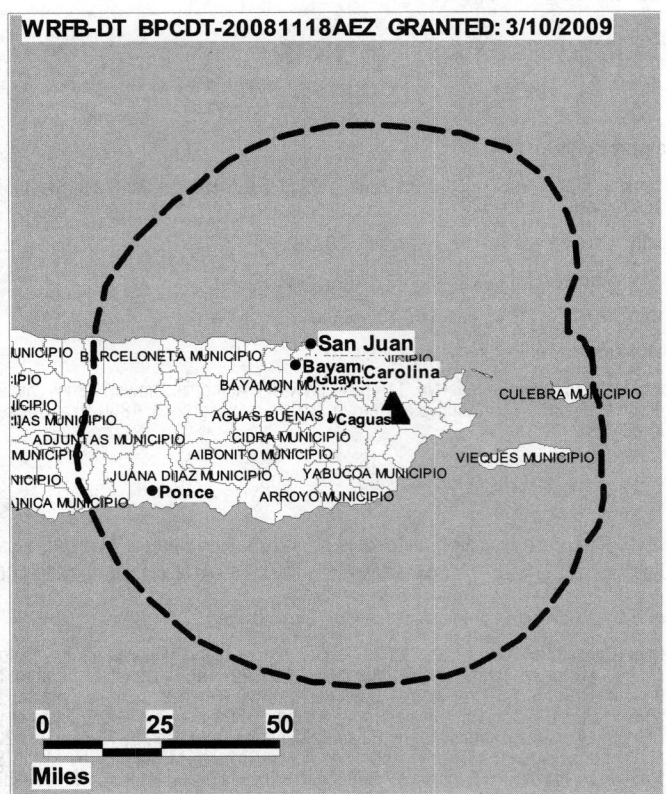

WRFB-DT BPCDT-20081118AEZ GRANTED: 3/10/2009

© 2010 Warren Communications News

Nielsen Data: Not available.

WORO-DT
Ch. 13

Network Service: IND.

Licensee: The Catholic Apostolic & Roman Church In Puerto Rico, PO Box 9021967, San Juan, PR 00902-1967.

Studio: 50 Calle del Cristo, San Juan, PR 00901.

Mailing Address: PO Box 9021967, San Juan, PR 00902-1967.

Phone: 787-727-7373. **Fax:** 787-723-4040.

Technical Facilities: Channel No. 13 (210-216 MHz). Authorized power: 38-kw visual, aural. Antenna: 2805-ft above av. terrain, 184-ft. above ground, 3481-ft. above sea level.

Latitude	18°	18'	36"
Longitude	65°	47'	41"

Note: Latitude and longitude coordinates shown are based on the North American Datum of 1927 (NAD 27) as currently required by the Mass Media Bureau of the FCC.

Ownership: The Catholic, Apostolic & Roman Church In Puerto Rico.

Began Operation: October 24, 2004. Station broadcasting digitally on its analog channel allotment. Began analog operations: December 22, 1984. Sale to present owner by WPRV-TV Inc. approved by FCC August 29, 1994. Ceased analog operations: February 17, 2009.

Represented (legal): du Treil, Lundin & Rackley Inc.

Represented (legal): Reynolds & Manning.

City of License: Fajardo. **Station DMA:** Puerto Rico. **Rank:** 0.

Nielsen Data: Not available.

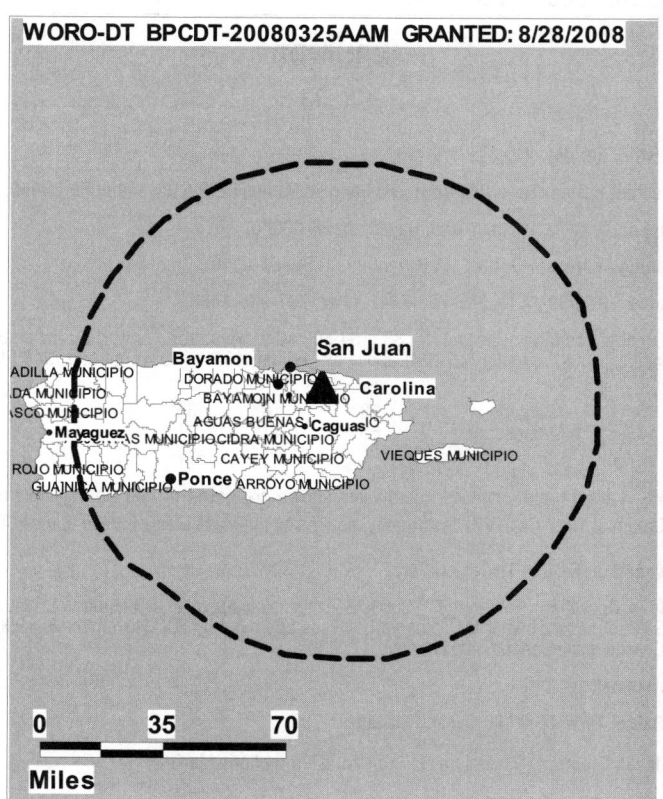

© 2010 Warren Communications News

WRUA-DT
Ch. 33

Network Service: IND.

Grantee: Eastern Television Corp., via Rexville, Ramos EE-22, Bayamon, PR 00960.

Studio: Carretera 167, km 18.9, Bayamon, PR 00960.

Mailing Address: PO Box 310, Bayamon, PR 00960-0310.

Phone: 787-999-1480; 787-797-3447. **Fax:** 787-999-1488.

Technical Facilities: Channel No. 33 (584-590 MHz). Authorized power: 50-kw max. visual, aural. Antenna: 2782-ft above av. terrain, 167-ft. above ground, 3465-ft. above sea level.

Latitude	18°	18'	36"
Longitude	65°	47'	41"

Note: Latitude and longitude coordinates shown are based on the North American Datum of 1927 (NAD 27) as currently required by the Mass Media Bureau of the FCC.

Ownership: Eastern Television Corp.

Began Operation: February 17, 2009. Began analog operations: February 1, 1995. Sale to present owner by Damarys de Jesus approved by FCC November 8, 1999. Ceased analog operations: February 17, 2009.

Personnel:

Rafael Torres Padilla, General Manager.

Jesus Espinoza, General Sales, Program & Promotions Manager.

Mickey Linares, Chief Engineer.

City of License: Fajardo. **Station DMA:** Puerto Rico. **Rank:** 0.

Nielsen Data: Not available.

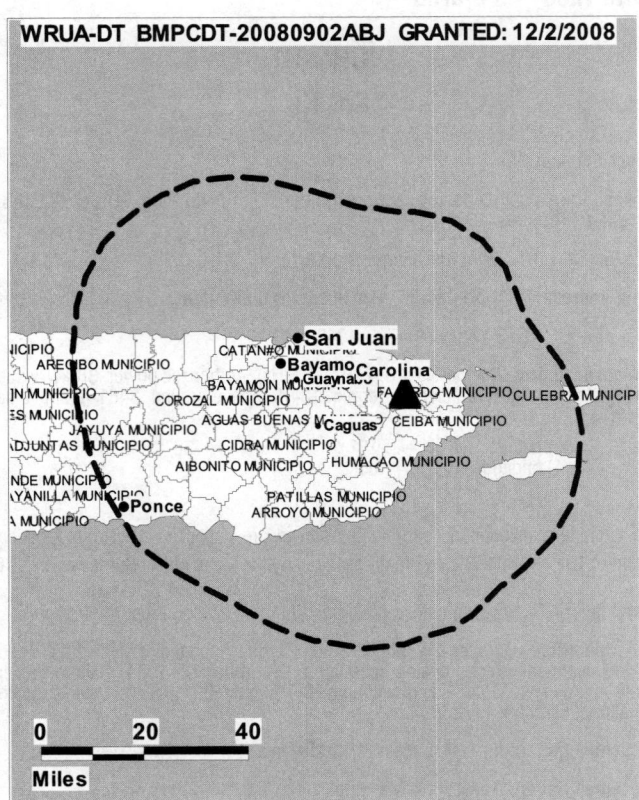

WRUA-DT BMPCDT-20080902ABJ GRANTED: 12/2/2008

WIDP-DT

Ch. 45

Network Service: IND.

Licensee: Ebenezer Broadcasting Group Inc., PO Box 21065, San Juan, PR 00928.

Mailing Address: PO Box 20165, San Juan, PR 00928.

Phone: 787-763-6363.

Technical Facilities: Channel No. 45 (656-662 MHz). Authorized power: 50.1-kw max. visual, aural. Antenna: 2070-ft above av. terrain, 236-ft. above ground, 2759-ft. above sea level.

Latitude	18°	16'	44"
Longitude	65°	51'	10"

Note: Latitude and longitude coordinates shown are based on the North American Datum of 1927 (NAD 27) as currently required by the Mass Media Bureau of the FCC.

Ownership: Ebenezer Broadcasting Group Inc. (Group Owner).

Began Operation: December 15, 2007. Began analog operations: April 16, 1999. Ceased analog operations: June 12, 2009.

City of License: Guayama. **Station DMA:** Puerto Rico. **Rank:** 0.

Nielsen Data: Not available.

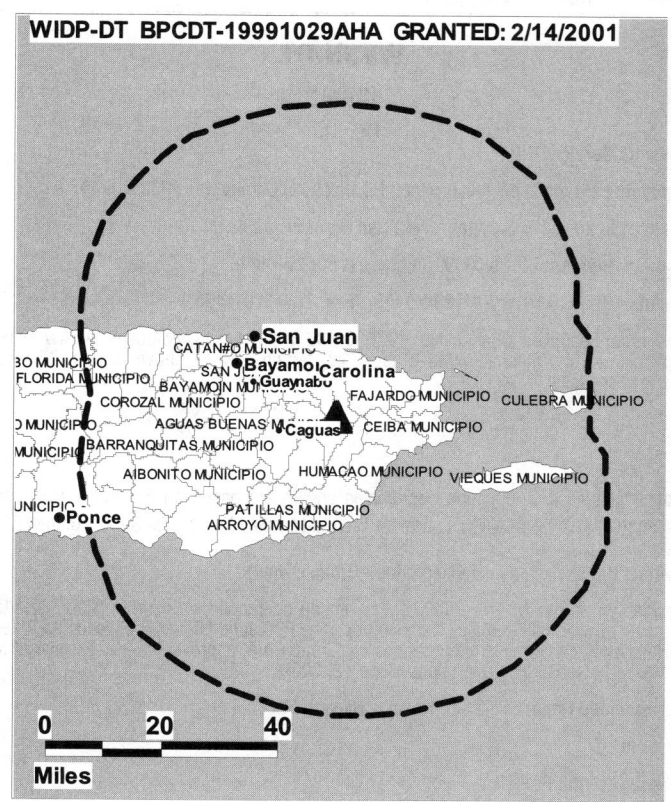

WIDP-DT BPCDT-19991029AHA GRANTED: 2/14/2001

© 2010 Warren Communications News

WVSN-DT
Ch. 49

Network Service: IND.

Grantee: La Cadena del Milagro Inc., PO Box 949, Camuy, PR 00627-0949.

Studio: No 20, 1415 S Caparra Terr, San Juan, PR 00906.

Mailing Address: PO Box 949, Camuy, PR 00627-0949.

Phone: 787-262-5416; 787-898-5120. **Fax:** 787-820-4496.

Technical Facilities: Channel No. 49 (680-686 MHz). Authorized power: 46-kw max. visual, aural. Antenna: 2044-ft above av. terrain, 210-ft. above ground, 2733-ft. above sea level.

Latitude	18°	16'	44"
Longitude	65°	51'	10"

Note: Latitude and longitude coordinates shown are based on the North American Datum of 1927 (NAD 27) as currently required by the Mass Media Bureau of the FCC.

Ownership: La Cadena del Milagro Inc. (Group Owner).

Began Operation: May 8, 2008. Began analog operations: August 1, 1990. Sale to present owner by Tito Atiles Natal approved by FCC June 15, 2000. Sale to Tito Atiles Natal by Bocanegra/Gerald Broadcasting Group Corp. approved by FCC February 15, 1001. Ceased analog operations: June 12, 2009.

Represented (legal): Fletcher, Heald & Hildreth PLC.

Personnel:

Jose J. Avila, President.

Esteban Pasedes, General Manager.

George Figueroa, Chief Engineer.

City of License: Humacao. **Station DMA:** Puerto Rico. **Rank:** 0.

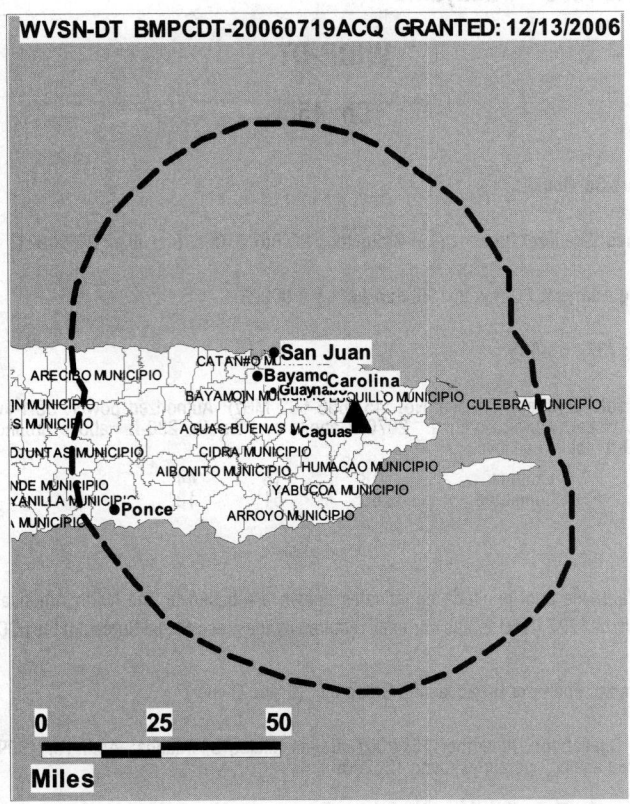

WVSN-DT BMPCDT-20060719ACQ GRANTED: 12/13/2006

© 2010 Warren Communications News

Nielsen Data: Not available.

WNJX-DT
Ch. 23

Network Service: IND.

Grantee: Televicentro of Puerto Rico LLC, 4 Richmond Sq, Ste 200, Providence, RI 02906.

Studio: St. Rd. 19, km 0.5, San Juan, PR 00966.

Mailing Address: PO Box 362050, San Juan, PR 00936-2050.

Phone: 787-792-4444. **Fax:** 787-782-8060.

Web Site: http://www.televicentropr.com

Technical Facilities: Channel No. 23 (524-530 MHz). Authorized power: 400-kw max. visual, aural. Antenna: 2274-ft above av. terrain, 328-ft. above ground, 3281-ft. above sea level.

Latitude	18°	09'	00"
Longitude	66°	59'	00"

Note: Latitude and longitude coordinates shown are based on the North American Datum of 1927 (NAD 27) as currently required by the Mass Media Bureau of the FCC.

Ownership: InterMedia Partners VII LP (Group Owner).

Began Operation: October 29, 2008. Began analog operations: April 27, 1986. Transfer of control from LIN TV Corp. to present owner approved by FCC February 2, 2007. Ceased analog operations: June 12, 2009.

Represented (legal): Willkie Farr & Gallagher LLP.

Personnel:

Jose Ramos, General Manager.

Enrique Cruz, Executive Vice President & News Director.

Jose Guerra, Vice President, Engineering.

Jimmy Arteaja, Vice President, Programming & Promotion.

Jonathan Garcia, Vice President, Sales & Marketing.

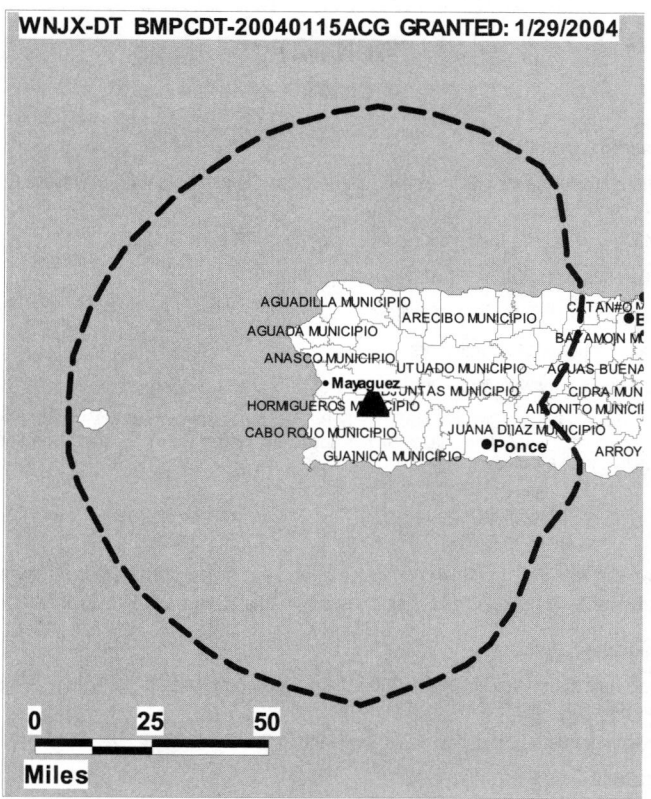

Maggie Alonso, Vice President, Production.

City of License: Mayaguez. **Station DMA:** Puerto Rico. **Rank:** 0.

Nielsen Data: Not available.

WORA-DT
Ch. 29

Network Service: IND.

Grantee: Telecinco Inc., PO Box 43, Ave Gonzalez Clemente No 449, Mayaguez, PR 00681-0043.

Studio: Ave Gonzalez Clemente, No 449, Mayaguez, PR 00681-0043.

Mailing Address: PO Box 43, Mayaguez, PR 00681-0043.

Phone: 787-831-5555; 787-721-4054. **Fax:** 787-833-0075.

E-mail: csepulveda@woratv.com

Web Site: http://www.woratv.com

Technical Facilities: Channel No. 29 (560-566 MHz). Authorized power: 1000-kw max. visual, aural. Antenna: 2081-ft above av. terrain, 271-ft. above ground, 3091-ft. above sea level.

Latitude	18°	09'	03.2"
Longitude	66°	59'	21.4"

Note: Latitude and longitude coordinates shown are based on the North American Datum of 1927 (NAD 27) as currently required by the Mass Media Bureau of the FCC.

Ownership: Telecinco Inc.

Began Operation: November 18, 2008. Began analog operations: October 1, 1955. Ceased analog operations: June 12, 2009.

Represented (legal): Fletcher, Heald & Hildreth PLC.

Personnel:

Alfredo Ramirez de Arellano, President.

Jose A. Toro, General Manager.

Jose A. Vizcarrondo, Vice President & Operations Director.

Carlos Sepulveda, News Director.

Fred Toledo, Engineering Director.

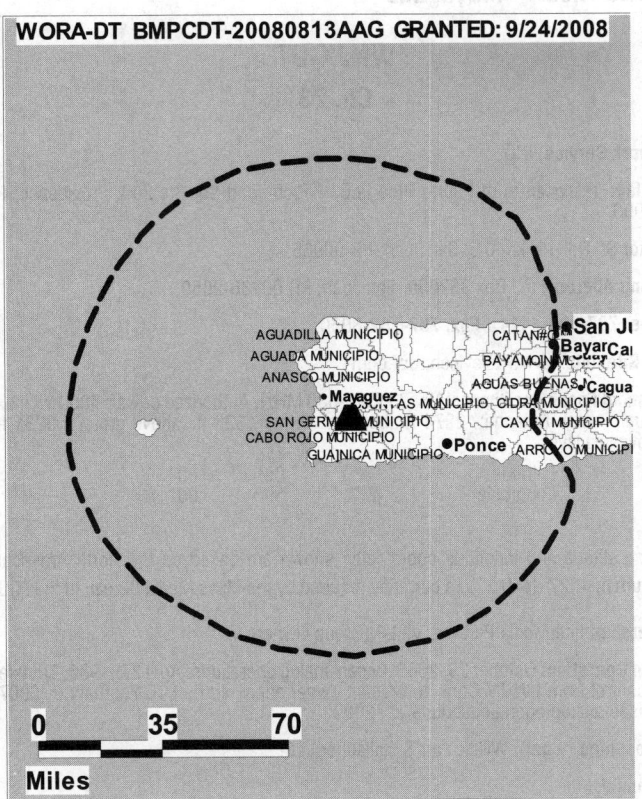

WORA-DT BMPCDT-20080813AAG GRANTED: 9/24/2008

City of License: Mayaguez.

Nielsen Data: Not available.

WECN-DT
Ch. 18

Network Service: IND.

Grantee: Encuentro Christian Network, PO Box 310, Bayamon, PR 00960-0310.

Studio: Hwy 167, km 18.9, Bayamon, PR 00960.

Mailing Address: PO Box 310, Bayamon, PR 00960-0310.

Phone: 787-999-1480; 787-797-3447. **Fax:** 787-999-1487.

Technical Facilities: Channel No. 18 (494-500 MHz). Authorized power: 50-kw max. visual, aural. Antenna: 466-ft above av. terrain, 131-ft. above ground, 1722-ft. above sea level.

Latitude	18°	17'	34"
Longitude	66°	16'	02"

Note: Latitude and longitude coordinates shown are based on the North American Datum of 1927 (NAD 27) as currently required by the Mass Media Bureau of the FCC.

Ownership: Encuentro Christian Network Corp. (Group Owner).

Began Operation: February 17, 2009. Began analog operations: January 1, 1989. Station off air October 16, 2007 due to technical problems. Returned to air May 13, 2008 at reduced power. Sale to WPBD License Corp. (Pegasus Communications Corp.) approved by FCC May 15, 2001, but never consummated. Sale to present owner by Art Broadcasting Corp. approved by FCC September 2, 1987. Ceased analog operations: February 17, 2009.

Personnel:

Rafael Torres Padilla, General Manager.

Jesus Espinoza, General Sales Manager.

Mickey Linares Perez, Chief Engineer.

Mirium Guzman Rodriguez, Program & Production Director.

Raphael Gonzales, Traffic Manager.

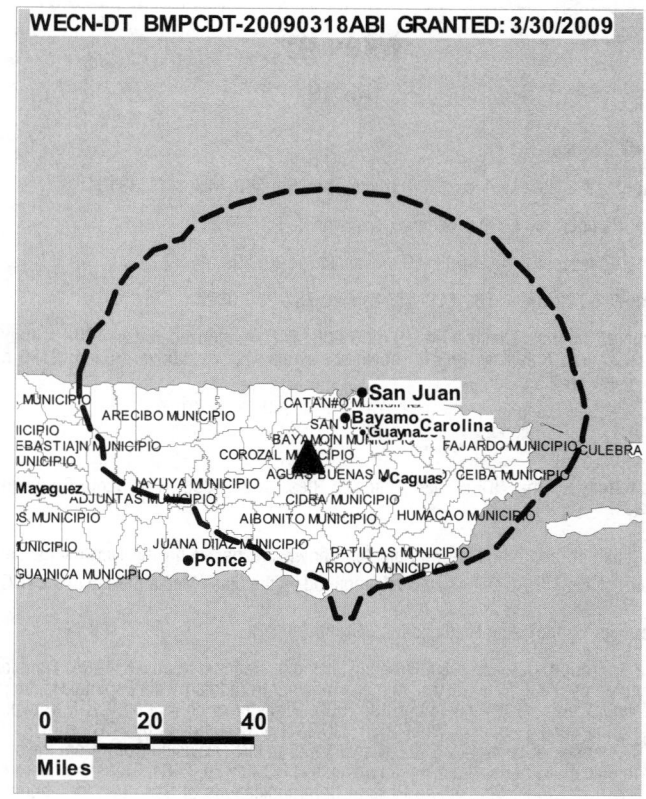

WECN-DT BMPCDT-20090318ABI GRANTED: 3/30/2009

© 2010 Warren Communications News

City of License: Naranjito. **Station DMA:** Puerto Rico. **Rank:** 0.

Nielsen Data: Not available.

WKPV-DT
Ch. 19

Network Service: IND.

Grantee: S & E Network Inc., 1401 Brickell Ave, Ste 500, Miami, FL 33131.

Studio: Hippodromo el Commadante, Canovanas, PR 00729.

Mailing Address: PO Box 10001, Canovanas, PR 00729.

Phone: 787-722-2424; 561-659-4754. **Fax:** 787-256-0320.

Technical Facilities: Channel No. 19 (500-506 MHz). Authorized power: 700-kw max. visual, aural. Antenna: 883-ft above av. terrain, 102-ft. above ground, 2136-ft. above sea level.

Latitude	18°	04'	49"
Longitude	66°	44'	53"

Transmitter: 1.7-mi. NW of intersection of Rtes. 132 & 386, N of Santo Domingo, Penuelas.

Note: Latitude and longitude coordinates shown are based on the North American Datum of 1927 (NAD 27) as currently required by the Mass Media Bureau of the FCC.

Ownership: CaribeVision Holdings Inc. (Group Owner).

Began Operation: October 1, 2008. Began analog operations: August 6, 1985. Transfer of control by S & E Network Inc. to present owner from Intermedia Espanol Holdings LLC approved by FCC September 20, 2007. Transfer of control by S & E Network Inc. to Intermedia Partners VII LP from LIN TV Corp. approved by FCC February 2, 2007. Transfer of control by S & E Network Inc. to LIN Television Corp. from Paxson Communications of San Juan Inc. approved by FCC July 20, 2001. Transfer of control by S & E Networks Inc. where Paxson Communications of San Juan Inc. bought out Housing Development Associates SE approved by FCC December 4, 1996. Transfer of control by S & E Network Inc. to Housing Development Associates SE & Paxson Communications of San Juan Inc. from Housing Development Associates SE approved by FCC July 12, 1996. Sale to S & E Network Inc. (then Interstate General Properties LP SE) from Multi-Media Television Inc., approved by FCC September 14, 1994. Sale to Multi-Media Television Inc. from Maria Esther Rivera approved by FCC October 31, 1985. Sale to Maria Esther Rivera from Norman E. Parkhurst III approved by FCC September 27, 1984. Sale to Patricia O'Reilly-Diaz from Norman E. Parkhurst III dismissed by FCC August 14, 1984. Ceased analog operations: June 12, 2009.

Represented (legal): Fletcher, Heald & Hildreth PLC.

Personnel:

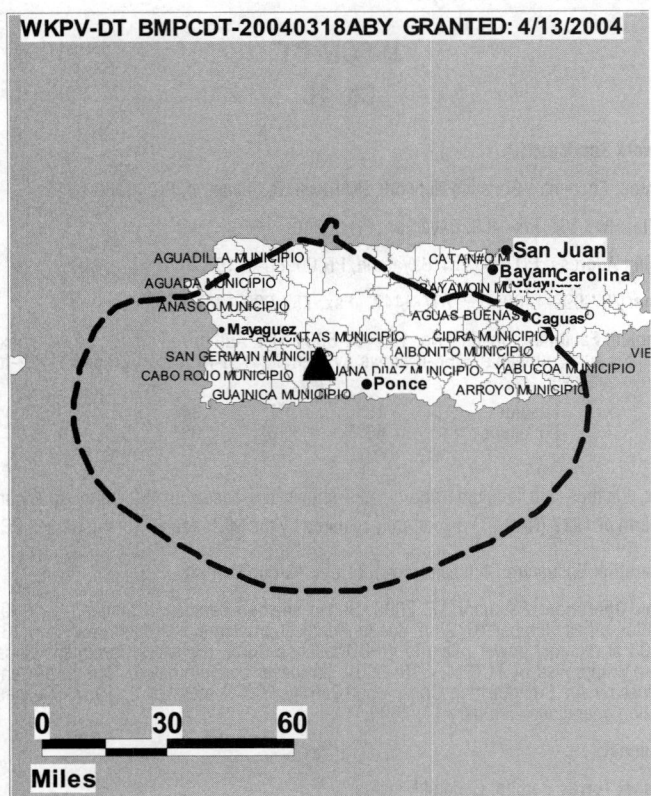

WKPV-DT BMPCDT-20040318ABY GRANTED: 4/13/2004

© 2010 Warren Communications News

Jose Ramos, President & General Manager.

Enrique Cruz, Executive Vice President & News Director.

Jonathan Garcia, Vice President, Sales & Marketing.

City of License: Ponce. **Station DMA:** Puerto Rico. **Rank:** 0.

Nielsen Data: Not available.

WSTE-DT
Ch. 8

Network Service: IND.

Licensee: WLII/WSUR License Partnership GP, 5999 Center Dr, Ste 4083, Los Angeles, CA 90045.

Studio: Calle Carazo No 62, Guaynabo, PR 00969.

Mailing Address: PO Box 7088, Guaynabo, PR 00970.

Phone: 787-724-7777. **Fax:** 787-300-5000.

E-mail: wcostanzo@supersiete.com

Technical Facilities: Channel No. 8 (180-186 MHz). Authorized power: 50-kw visual, aural. Antenna: 289-ft above av. terrain, 220-ft. above ground, 1059-ft. above sea level.

Latitude	18°	02'	52"
Longitude	66°	39'	16"

Requests CP for change to channel number 7, 3.2-kw visual; BPCDT-20080528AAQ.

Note: Latitude and longitude coordinates shown are based on the North American Datum of 1927 (NAD 27) as currently required by the Mass Media Bureau of the FCC.

Ownership: Univision Communications Inc. (Group Owner).

Began Operation: June 15, 2007. Began analog operations: February 2, 1958. Sale to present owner by Siete Grande Television Inc. approved by FCC October 11, 2007. Sale to Siete Grande Television Inc. by Channel 7 Inc. approved by FCC August 5, 1991. Transfer of control to Channel 7 Inc. by L. Thomas Muniz approved by FCC September 27, 1985. Ceased analog operations: June 12, 2009.

Represented (legal): Pillsbury Winthrop Shaw Pittman LLP.

Personnel:

Larry Sands, General Manager.

Andres Diaz, Chief Engineer.

Jorge Pietri, Controller.

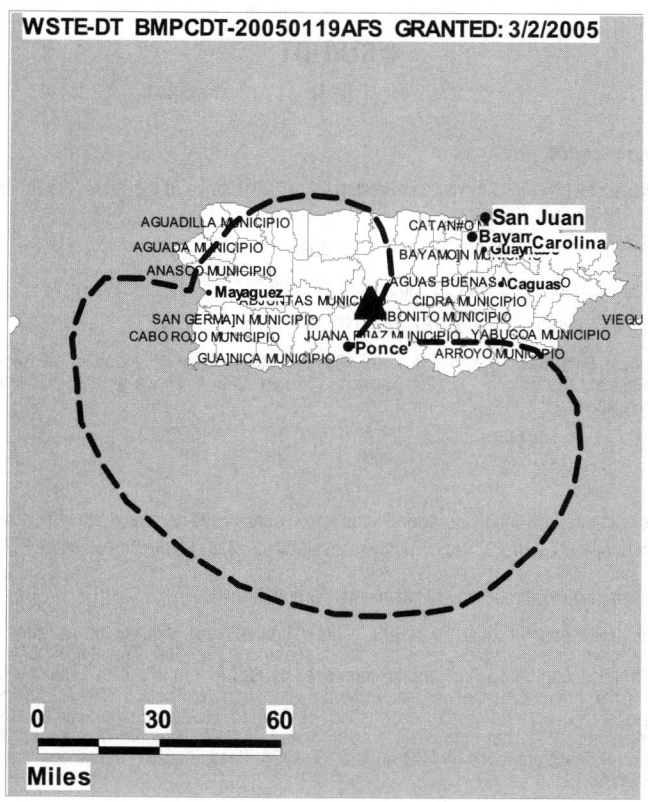

© 2010 Warren Communications News

Nancy Guzman, Traffic Manager.

City of License: Ponce. **Station DMA:** Puerto Rico. **Rank:** 0.

Nielsen Data: Not available.

WSUR-DT
Ch. 9

Network Service: UNV.

Licensee: WLII/WSUR License Partnership GP, 1999 Avenue of the Stars, Ste 3050, Los Angeles, CA 90067.

Studio: Calle Carazo, No 62, Guaynabo, PR 00969.

Mailing Address: PO Box 7888, Guaynabo, PR 00970.

Phone: 787-620-1111. **Fax:** 787-300-5101.

Technical Facilities: Channel No. 9 (186-192 MHz). Authorized power: 21.6-kw visual, aural. Antenna: 2812-ft above av. terrain, 266-ft. above ground, 4531-ft. above sea level.

Latitude	18°	10'	09"
Longitude	66°	34'	36"

Note: Latitude and longitude coordinates shown are based on the North American Datum of 1927 (NAD 27) as currently required by the Mass Media Bureau of the FCC.

Ownership: Univision Communications Inc. (Group Owner).

Began Operation: August 19, 2003. Station broadcasting digitally on its analog channel allotment. Began analog operations: February 20, 1958. Transfer of control to Broadcasting Media Partners Inc. approved by FCC March 27, 2007. Transfer of control to present owner by Raycom Media Inc. approved by FCC May 23, 2005. Transfer to Univision Communications Inc. by Raycom Media Inc. approved by FCC August 20, 2001, but sale never consummated. Sale to Raycom Media Inc. by Milton S. Maltz approved by FCC August 13, 1998. Ceased analog operations: June 12, 2009.

Represented (legal): Covington & Burling.

Personnel:

Larry Sands, General Manager.

Modesto Delgado, Operations Manager.

Carlos Pagan, General Sales Manager.

Susanne Ramirez de Arellano, News Director.

Andres Diaz, Chief Engineer.

Jorge Pietri, Business Manager.

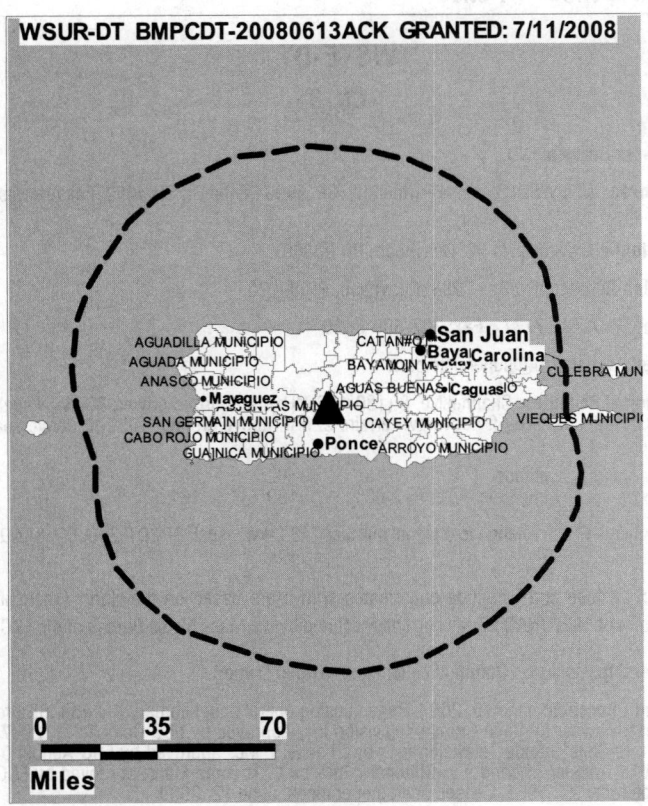

WSUR-DT BMPCDT-20080613ACK GRANTED: 7/11/2008

© 2010 Warren Communications News

Jessica Rodiguez, Program Director.

Gerardo Oliveras, Promotion Manager.

Manuel Santiago, Production Manager.

Nancy Guzman, Traffic Manager.

City of License: Ponce. **Station DMA:** Puerto Rico. **Rank:** 0.

Nielsen Data: Not available.

WTIN-DT
Ch. 15

Network Service: IND.

Grantee: Televicentro of Puerto Rico LLC, 4 Richmond Sq, Ste 200, Providence, RI 02906.

Mailing Address: 10th St., B-19, Valpariso, Toa Baja, PR 00949.

Phone: 787-848-5250.

Technical Facilities: Channel No. 15 (476-482 MHz). Authorized power: 380.2-kw max. visual, aural. Antenna: 2753-ft above av. terrain, 141-ft. above ground, 4439-ft. above sea level.

Latitude	18°	10'	10"
Longitude	66°	34'	36"

Note: Latitude and longitude coordinates shown are based on the North American Datum of 1927 (NAD 27) as currently required by the Mass Media Bureau of the FCC.

Ownership: InterMedia Partners VII LP (Group Owner).

Began Operation: October 13, 2008. Began analog operations: December 27, 1985. Transfer of control from LIN TV Corp. to present owner approved by FCC February 2, 2007. Sale to LIN TV Corp. by Laura Nicolau approved by FCC April 27, 2004. Ceased analog operations: June 12, 2009.

Represented (legal): Willkie Farr & Gallagher LLP.

Personnel:

Jose Ramos, President & General Manager.

Enrique Cruz, Executive Vice President & News Director.

Jonathan Garcia, Vice President, Sales & Marketing.

Jose Guerra, Chief Engineer.

City of License: Ponce. **Station DMA:** Puerto Rico. **Rank:** 0.

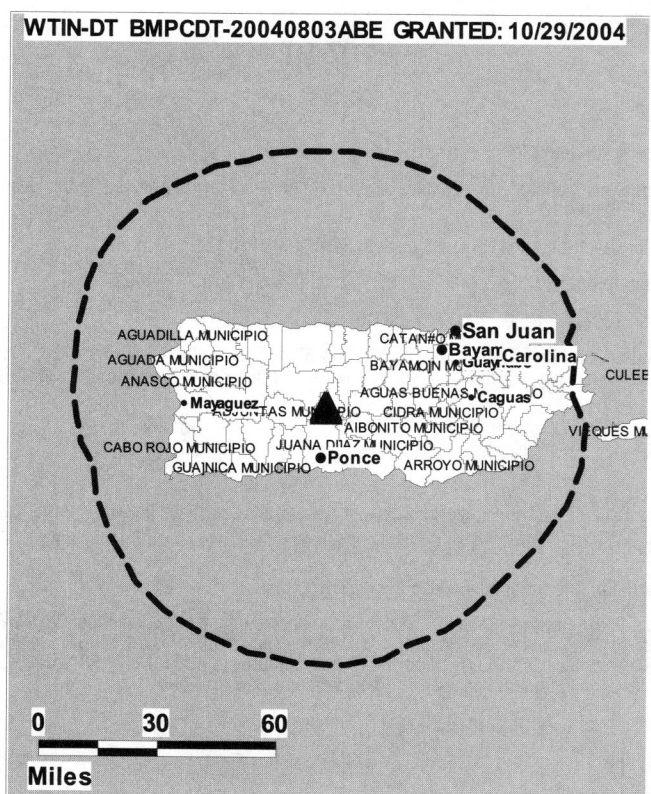

WTIN-DT BMPCDT-20040803ABE GRANTED: 10/29/2004

© 2010 Warren Communications News

Nielsen Data: Not available.

WVOZ-DT
Ch. 47

Network Service: IND.

Grantee: International Broadcasting Corp., Calle Bori 1554, Urb. Antonsanti, San Juan, PR 00927-6113.

Studio: Calle Bori 1554, Urb. Antonsanti, San Juan, PR 00927.

Mailing Address: Calle Bori 1554, Urb. Antonsanti, San Juan, PR 00927.

Phone: 787-274-1800. **Fax:** 787-281-9758.

Technical Facilities: Channel No. 47 (668-674 MHz). Authorized power: 50.1-kw max. visual, aural. Antenna: 810-ft above av. terrain, 98-ft. above ground, 2034-ft. above sea level.

Latitude	18°	04'	50"
Longitude	66°	44'	50"

Note: Latitude and longitude coordinates shown are based on the North American Datum of 1927 (NAD 27) as currently required by the Mass Media Bureau of the FCC.

Ownership: Pedro Roman Collazo (Group Owner).

Began Operation: November 16, 2007. Began analog operations: December 29 1987. Sale to CaribeVision Station Group LLC dismissed by FCC May 1, 2007. Sale to Esperanza Television LLC (William S. Reyner) approved by FCC July 23, 2001 but never consummated. Ceased analog operations: June 12, 2009.

Represented (legal): Irwin, Campbell & Tannenwald PC.

Personnel:

Pedro Roman Collazo, President.

Margarita Nacario, General Manager.

Rey Moreira, Chief Engineer.

City of License: Ponce. **Station DMA:** Puerto Rico. **Rank:** 0.

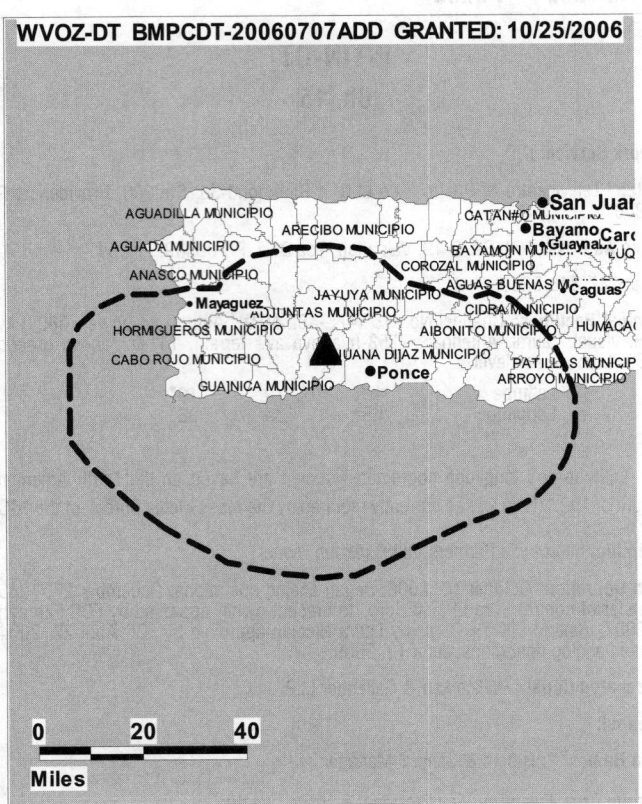

WVOZ-DT BMPCDT-20060707ADD GRANTED: 10/25/2006

Nielsen Data: Not available.

WAPA-DT
Ch. 27

Network Service: IND.

Licensee: Televicentro of Puerto Rico LLC, 4 Richmond Sq, Ste 200, Providence, RI 02906.

Studio: State Rd 19, Km 0.5, San Juan, PR 00657.

Mailing Address: PO Box 362050, San Juan, PR 00936-2050.

Phone: 787-792-4444. **Fax:** 787-782-7825.

Web Site: http://www.televicentropr.com

Technical Facilities: Channel No. 27 (548-554 MHz). Authorized power: 1000-kw max. visual, aural. Antenna: 2605-ft above av. terrain, 787-ft. above ground, 3743-ft. above sea level.

Latitude	18°	06'	42"
Longitude	66°	03'	05"

Note: Latitude and longitude coordinates shown are based on the North American Datum of 1927 (NAD 27) as currently required by the Mass Media Bureau of the FCC.

Ownership: InterMedia Partners VII LP (Group Owner).

Began Operation: June 20, 2006. Began analog operations: March 5, 1954. Transfer of control from LIN TV Corp. to present owner approved by FCC February 2, 2007. Ceased analog operations: June 12, 2009.

Represented (legal): Willkie Farr & Gallagher LLP.

Represented (sales): Blair Television.

Personnel:

Jose Ramos, President & General Manager.

Enrique Cruz, Executive Vice President & News Director.

Jonathan Garcia, Vice President, Sales & Marketing.

Jose Guerra, Vice President, Engineering.

Margarita Millan, Vice President, Programming & Promotion.

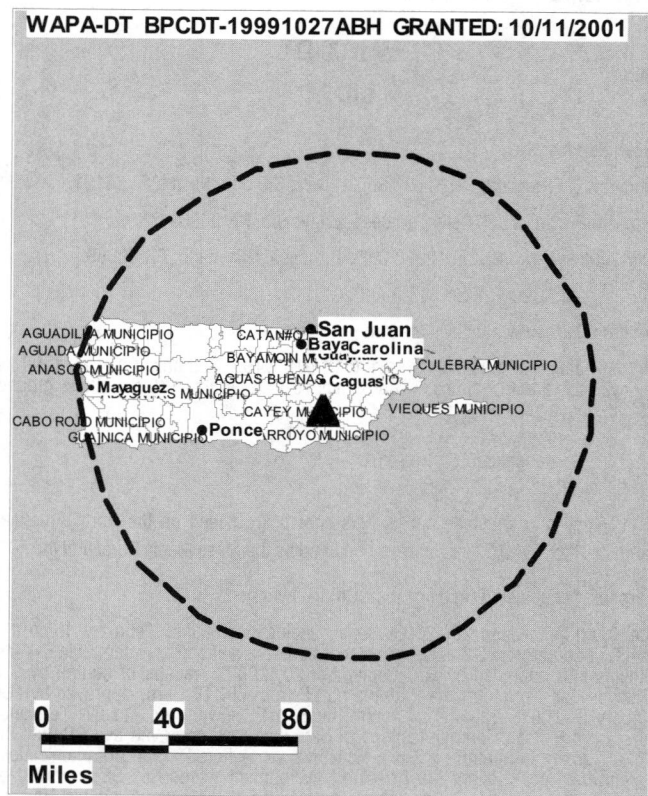

© 2010 Warren Communications News

Maggie Alonso, Vice President, Production.

Maria Rodriguez, Station Manager.

City of License: San Juan. **Station DMA:** Puerto Rico. **Rank:** 0.

Nielsen Data: Not available.

WJPX-DT
Ch. 21

Network Service: IND.

Licensee: S & E Network Inc., 1401 Brickell Ave, Ste 500, Miami, FL 33131.

Studio: Urb Bucare, 2020 Calle Turquesa, Guaynabo, PR 00969.

Mailing Address: Urb Bucare, 2020 Calle Turquesa, Guaynabo, PR 00969.

Phone: 787-999-3200. **Fax:** 787-999-3201.

Web Site: http://www.caribevision.com

Technical Facilities: Channel No. 21 (512-518 MHz). Authorized power: 1000-kw max. visual, aural. Antenna: 1850-ft above av. terrain, 160-ft. above ground, 2558-ft. above sea level.

Latitude	18°	16'	45"
Longitude	65°	51'	14"

Note: Latitude and longitude coordinates shown are based on the North American Datum of 1927 (NAD 27) as currently required by the Mass Media Bureau of the FCC.

Ownership: CaribeVision Holdings Inc. (Group Owner).

Began Operation: June 20, 2006. Began analog operations: February 15, 1987. Transfer of control by S & E Network Inc. to present owner from Intermedia Espanol Holdings LLC approved by FCC September 20, 2007. Transfer of control by S & E Network Inc. to Intermedia Partners VII LP from LIN TV Corp. approved by FCC February 2, 2007. Transfer of control by S & E Network Inc. to LIN Television Corp. from Paxson Communications of San Juan Inc. approved by FCC July 20, 2001. Transfer of control by S & E Networks Inc. where Paxson Communications of San Juan Inc. bought out Housing Development Associates SE approved by FCC December 4, 1996. Transfer of control by S & E Network Inc. to Housing Development Associates SE & Paxson Communications of San Juan Inc. from Housing Development Associates SE approved by FCC July 12, 1996. Sale to S & E Network Inc. (then Interstate General Properties LP SE) from Jem Communications Inc. approved by FCC September 14, 1994. Ceased analog operations: June 12, 2009.

Represented (legal): Fletcher, Heald & Hildreth PLC.

Personnel:

Mayda Nazaro, General Manager & General Sales Manager.

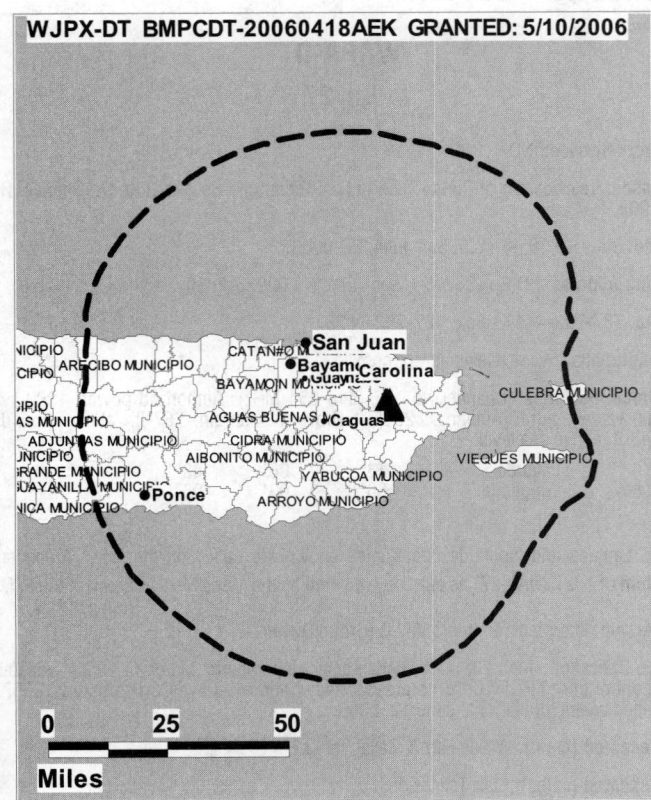

WJPX-DT BMPCDT-20060418AEK GRANTED: 5/10/2006

© 2010 Warren Communications News

Jorge Figueroa, Chief Engineer.

City of License: San Juan. **Station DMA:** Puerto Rico. **Rank:** 0.

Nielsen Data: Not available.

WKAQ-DT
Ch. 28

Network Service: TMO.

Licensee: NBC Telemundo License Co., 1299 Pennsylvania Ave NW, 11th Fl, c/o NBC Inc., Washington, DC 20004.

Studio: 383 Roosevelt Ave., Hato Rey, PR 00919.

Mailing Address: PO Box 366222, San Juan, PR 00936-6222.

Phone: 305-889-7989; 787-758-2222. **Fax:** 787-641-2182.

Web Site: http://www.telemundopr.com

Technical Facilities: Channel No. 28 (554-560 MHz). Authorized power: 924-kw max. visual, aural. Antenna: 2710-ft above av. terrain, 930-ft. above ground, 3874-ft. above sea level.

Latitude	18°	06'	55"
Longitude	66°	03'	11"

Note: Latitude and longitude coordinates shown are based on the North American Datum of 1927 (NAD 27) as currently required by the Mass Media Bureau of the FCC.

Ownership: NBC Universal (Group Owner).

Began Operation: January 31, 2002. Began analog operations: March 28, 1954. Ceased analog operations: June 12, 2009.

Personnel:

Hilary Hattler, Vice President & General Manager.

Froyd Rivera, Station Manager.

Juan Miguel Muniz, News Director.

Jose Medina, Chief Engineer.

Ileana Santiago, Program Director.

Raymond Bozi, Marketing Manager.

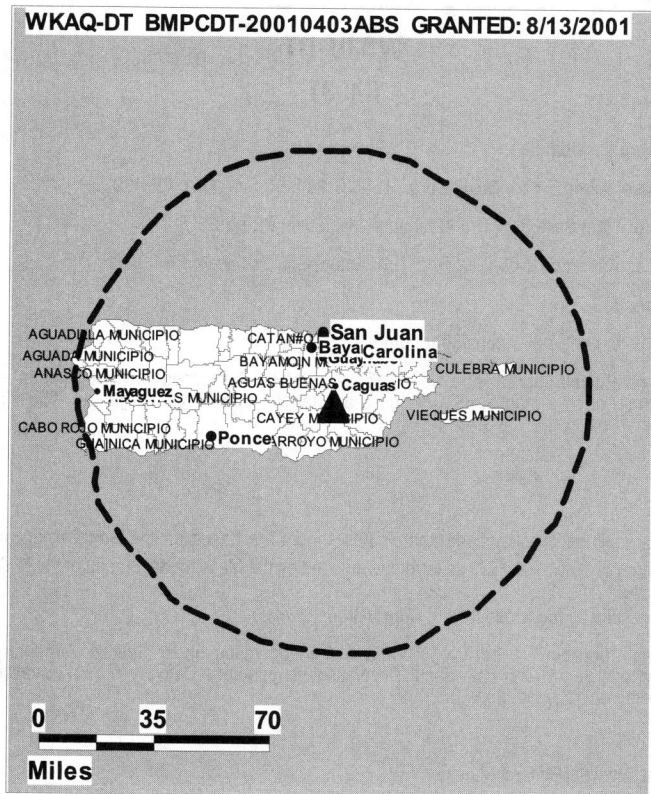

WKAQ-DT BMPCDT-20010403ABS GRANTED: 8/13/2001

Awilda Rivera, Traffic Manager.

City of License: San Juan. **Station DMA:** Puerto Rico. **Rank:** 0.

Nielsen Data: Not available.

WSJU-DT
Ch. 31

Network Service: IND.

Grantee: Aerco Broadcasting Corp., 1508 Calle Bori, San Juan, PR 00927.

Studio: 1508 Calle Bori, Urb Antonsanil, San Juan, PR 00927.

Mailing Address: 1508 Calle Bori, Urb. Antonsanil, San Juan, PR 00927.

Phone: 809-756-8700.

Web Site: http://www.canal30pr.com

Technical Facilities: Channel No. 31 (572-578 MHz). Authorized power: 66-kw max. visual, aural. Antenna: 876-ft above av. terrain, 105-ft. above ground, 1581-ft. above sea level.

Latitude	18°	16'	30"
Longitude	66°	05'	36"

Note: Latitude and longitude coordinates shown are based on the North American Datum of 1927 (NAD 27) as currently required by the Mass Media Bureau of the FCC.

Ownership: Aerco Broadcasting Corp. (Group Owner).

Began Operation: February 5, 2004. Station operating under Special Temporary Authority at 5.45-kw max. visual. Began analog operations: January 1, 1987. Ceased analog operations: June 12, 2009.

Personnel:

Luz Alvarez, General Manager.

City of License: San Juan. **Station DMA:** Puerto Rico. **Rank:** 0.

Nielsen Data: Not available.

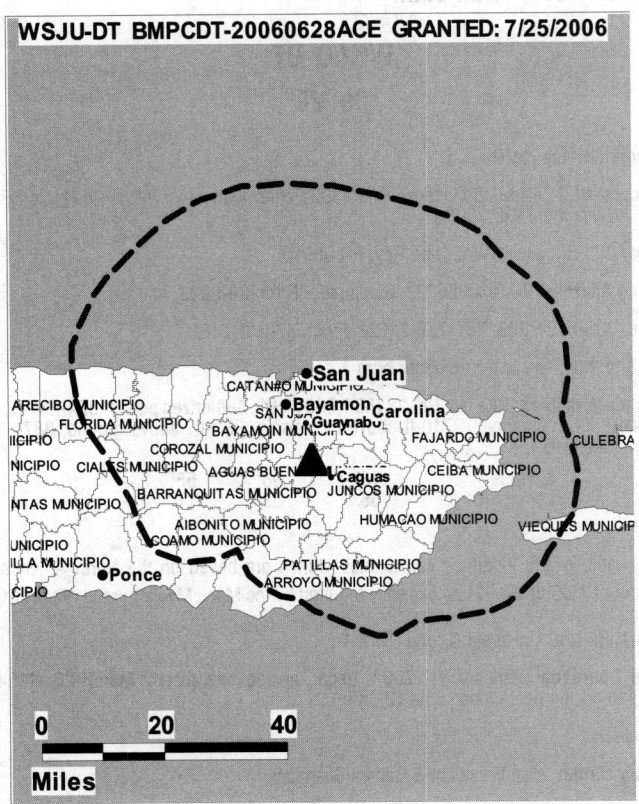

WSJU-DT BMPCDT-20060628ACE GRANTED: 7/25/2006

© 2010 Warren Communications News

WTCV-DT
Ch. 32

Network Service: IND.

Licensee: International Broadcasting Corp., Calle Bori 1554, Urb. Antonsanti, San Juan, PR 00927-6113.

Studio: Urb Antonsanti, Calle Bori 1554, San Juan, PR 00927.

Mailing Address: Urb. Antonsanti, Calle Bori 1554, San Juan, PR 00927.

Phone: 787-274-1800. **Fax:** 787-281-9758.

Technical Facilities: Channel No. 32 (578-584 MHz). Authorized power: 3.9-kw max. visual, aural. Antenna: 951-ft above av. terrain, 180-ft. above ground, 1657-ft. above sea level.

Latitude	18°	16'	30"
Longitude	66°	05'	36"

Holds CP for change to 50-kw max. visual, 2779-ft above av. terrain, 167-ft. above ground, 3465-ft. above sea level; lat. 18° 18' 36", long. 65° 47' 41", BPCDT-20070125AAX.

Note: Latitude and longitude coordinates shown are based on the North American Datum of 1927 (NAD 27) as currently required by the Mass Media Bureau of the FCC.

Ownership: Pedro Roman Collazo (Group Owner).

Began Operation: July 20, 2004. Began analog operations: July 29, 1984. Sale to CaribeVision Station Group LLC dismissed by FCC May 1, 2007. Sale to Esperanza Television LLC (William S. Reyner) approved by FCC July 23, 2001, but never consummated. Ceased analog operations: February 17, 2009.

Represented (legal): Irwin, Campbell & Tannenwald PC.

Personnel:

Margarita Nazario, General Manager.

Hector Collazo, Assistant Manager & Controller.

Reinaldo Moreira, Chief Engineer.

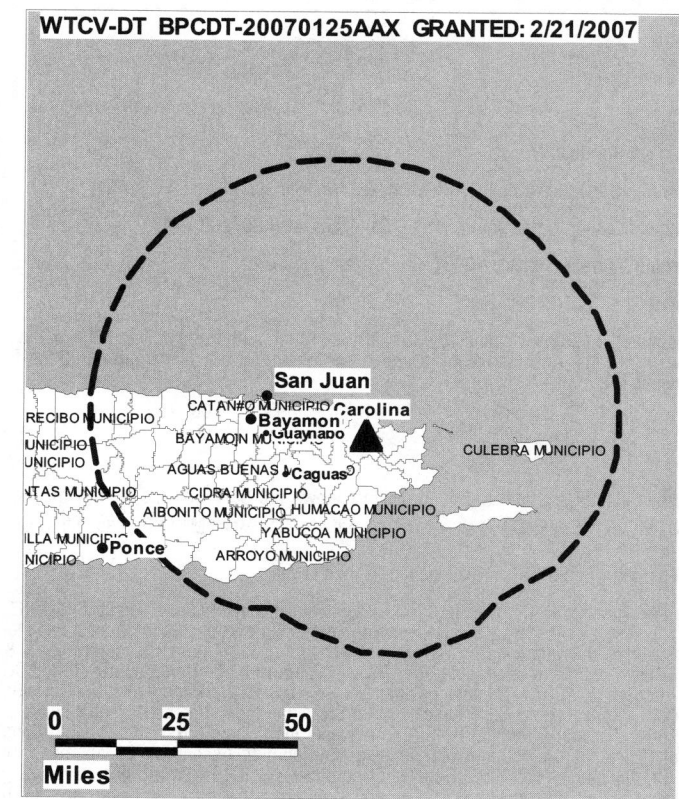

WTCV-DT BPCDT-20070125AAX GRANTED: 2/21/2007

© 2010 Warren Communications News

City of License: San Juan. **Station DMA:** Puerto Rico. **Rank:** 0.

Nielsen Data: Not available.

WJWN-DT
Ch. 39

Network Service: IND.

Grantee: S & E Network Inc., 1401 Brickell Ave, Ste 500, Miami, FL 33131.

Studio: Hippodromo el Commadante, Canovanas, PR 00729.

Mailing Address: PO Box 10001, Canovanas, PR 00729.

Phone: 787-722-2424. **Fax:** 787-256-0320.

Technical Facilities: Channel No. 39 (320-626 MHz). Authorized power: 700-kw max. visual, aural. Antenna: 2057-ft above av. terrain, 171-ft. above ground, 3064-ft. above sea level.

Latitude	18°	09'	00"
Longitude	66°	59'	00"

Note: Latitude and longitude coordinates shown are based on the North American Datum of 1927 (NAD 27) as currently required by the Mass Media Bureau of the FCC.

Ownership: CaribeVision Holdings Inc. (Group Owner).

Began Operation: October 10, 2008. Began analog operations: January 1, 1987. Transfer of control by S & E Network Inc. to present owner from Intermedia Espanol Holdings LLC approved by FCC September 20, 2007. Transfer of control by S & E Network Inc. to Intermedia Partners VII LP from LIN TV Corp. approved by FCC February 2, 2007. Transfer of control by S & E Network Inc. to LIN Television Corp. from Paxson Communications of San Juan Inc. approved by FCC July 20, 2001. Transfer of control by S & E Networks Inc. where Paxson Communications of San Juan Inc. bought out Housing Development Associates SE approved by FCC December 4, 1996. Transfer of control by S & E Network Inc. to Housing Development Associates SE & Paxson Communications of San Juan Inc. from Housing Development Associates SE approved by FCC July 12, 1996. Sale to S & E Network Inc. (then Interstate General Properties LP SE) from Tele 38 Inc. approved by FCC September 14, 1994. Transfer of control by Tele 38 Inc. to Haydee Diaz from Jose Cordero & Nayda Nicolau de Colon approved by FCC July 17, 1987. Pro forma sale to Tele 38 Inc. from Jose Cordero & Nayda Nicolau de Colon approved by FCC March 7, 1986. Ceased analog operations: June 12, 2009.

Represented (legal): Fletcher, Heald & Hildreth PLC.

Personnel:

Jose Ramos, President & General Manager.

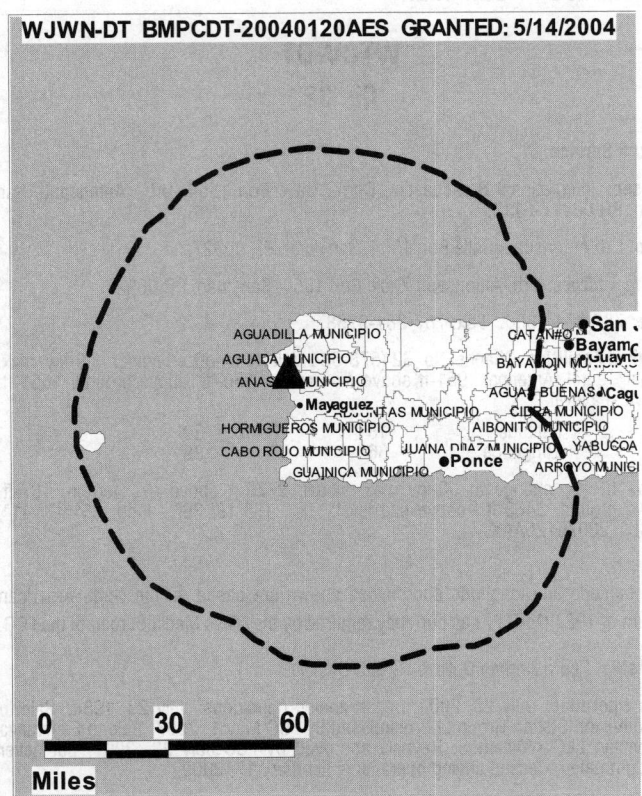

WJWN-DT BMPCDT-20040120AES GRANTED: 5/14/2004

Enrique Cruz, Executive Vice President & News Director.

Jonathan Garcia, Vice President, Sales & Marketing.

City of License: San Sebastian. **Station DMA:** Puerto Rico. **Rank:** 0.

Nielsen Data: Not available.

WIRS-DT
Ch. 41

Network Service: IND.

Grantee: CaribeVision Station Group LLC, 1401 Brickell Ave, Ste 500, Miami, FL 33131.

Mailing Address: PO Box 310, Bayamon, PR 00960-0310.

Phone: 787-797-3447. **Fax:** 787-799-6444.

Technical Facilities: Channel No. 41 (632-638 MHz). Authorized power: 185-kw max. visual, aural. Antenna: 2730-ft above av. terrain, 126-ft. above ground, 4424-ft. above sea level.

Latitude	18°	10'	10"
Longitude	66°	34'	36"

Note: Latitude and longitude coordinates shown are based on the North American Datum of 1927 (NAD 27) as currently required by the Mass Media Bureau of the FCC.

Ownership: CaribeVision Holdings Inc. (Group Owner).

Began Operation: October 5, 2008. Began analog operations: December 1, 1991. Sale to present owners by InterMedia Partners VII LP approved by FCC September 20, 2007. Transfer of control by Televicentro of Puerto Rico LLC to InterMedia Partners VII LP from LIN TV Corp. approved by FCC February 2, 2007. Sale to LIN TV Corp. by Maranatha Christian Network approved by FCC December 11, 2003. Ceased analog operations: June 12, 2009.

Represented (legal): Fletcher, Heald & Hildreth PLC.

Personnel:

Jose Ramos, President & General Manager.

Enrique Cruz, Executive Vice President & News Director.

Jonathan Garcia, Vice President, Sales & Marketing.

City of License: Yauco. **Station DMA:** Puerto Rico. **Rank:** 0.

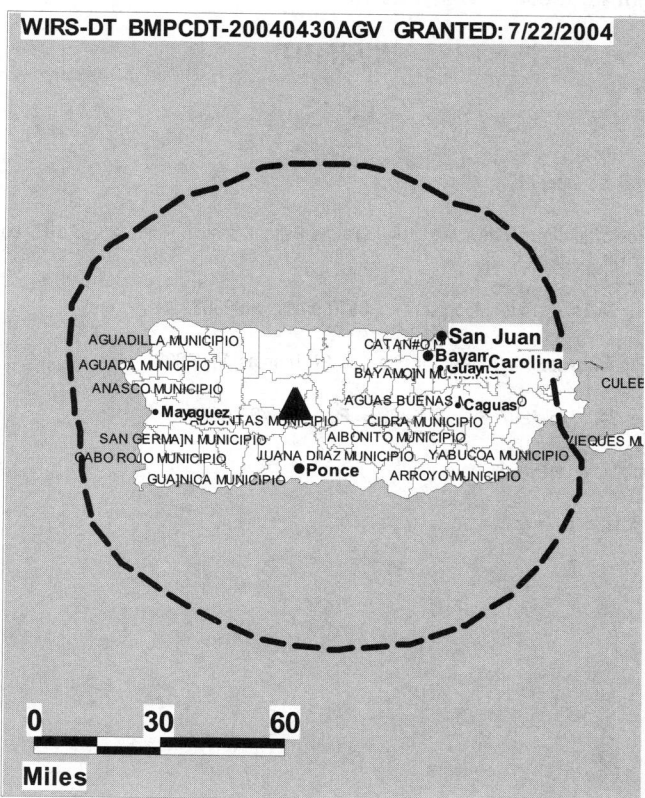

WIRS-DT BMPCDT-20040430AGV GRANTED: 7/22/2004

© 2010 Warren Communications News

Nielsen Data: Not available.

WVXF-DT

Ch. 17

Network Service: IND.

Grantee: Storefront Television, 1040 N. Las Palmas Ave, Building 25, 3rd Fl, Los Angeles, CA 90038.

Studio: 2A Estate Peter Mountain Top, St. Thomas, VI 00802.

Mailing Address: 8000 Nisky Ctr, Ste 714, St. Thomas, VI 00802.

Phone: 340-775-1297; 323-934-8283. **Fax:** 787-793-0371.

E-mail: victoria@wvxftv.com

Web Site: http://www.wvxftv.com

Technical Facilities: Channel No. 17 (488-494 MHz). Authorized power: 4.2-kw max. visual, aural. Antenna: 1489-ft above av. terrain, 59-ft. above ground, 1539-ft. above sea level.

Latitude	18°	21'	26"
Longitude	64°	56'	50"

Ownership: Storefront Television LLC (Group Owner).

Began Operation: June 12, 2009. Station broadcasting digitally on its analog channel allotment. Sale to present owner by Atlantic Properties Corp. approved by FCC September 27, 2004. Ceased analog operations: June 12, 2009.

Represented (legal): Womble, Carlyle, Sandridge & Rice.

Personnel:

Keith Bass, General Manager & Chief Engineer.

Dario Martinez, Sales Manager.

City of License: Charlotte Amalie.

Nielsen Data: Not available.

WZVI-DT

Ch. 43

Network Service: ABC.

Licensee: Marri Broadcasting LP, 607 14th St NW, Ste 900, c/o Thomas J. Dougherty, Washington, DC 20005-2018.

Mailing Address: 607 14th St NW, Ste 900, c/o Thomas J. Dougherty Jr., Washington, DC 20005-2018.

Phone: 202-508-5836.

E-mail: tdougherty@kilpatrickstockton.com

Technical Facilities: Channel No. 43 (644-650 MHz). Authorized power: 1.4-kw max. visual, aural. Antenna: 92-ft above av. terrain, 24-ft. above ground, 122-ft. above sea level.

Latitude	18°	20'	43.1"
Longitude	64°	55'	45.2"

Ownership: Marri Broadcasting Corp. (Group Owner).

Began Operation: May 17, 2004. Station was built as a digital-only station with no analog operations.

Represented (legal): Gardner Carton & Douglas.

Represented (engineering): Smith & Fisher.

City of License: Charlotte Amalie. **Station DMA:** Virgin Islands. **Rank:** 0.

Nielsen Data: Not available.

WCVI-DT
Ch. 50

Network Service: CW.

Grantee: Virgin Blue Inc., PO Box 24027, Gallows Bay, Christiansted, VI 00824.

Studio: One K, Little Princess, St. Croix, VI 00724.

Mailing Address: PO Box 24027, Christiansted, VI 00824.

Phone: 340-718-9927. **Fax:** 340-718-0712.

Web Site: http://www.wcvi.tv

Technical Facilities: Channel No. 50 (686-692 MHz). Authorized power: 0.656-kw max. visual, aural. Antenna: 1242-ft above av. terrain, 331-ft. above ground, 459-ft. above sea level.

Latitude	17°	44'	53"
Longitude	64°	43'	40"

Ownership: Virgin Blue Inc.

Began Operation: June 12, 2009. Began analog operations: March 7, 2000. Ceased analog operations: June 12, 2009.

Personnel:

Victor Gold, General Manager, Chief Engineer & Business Manager.

Marty Adamshick, Program Director & Traffic Manager.

City of License: Christiansted. **Station DMA:** Virgin Islands. **Rank:** 0.

Nielsen Data: Not available.

WSVI-DT
Ch. 20

Network Service: ABC.

Grantee: Alpha Broadcasting Corp., PO Box 8 ABC, Sunny Isle Shopping Center, Christiansted, VI 00823.

Studio: Sunny Isle Shopping Center, Christiansted, St. Croix, VI 00823.

Mailing Address: PO Box 6000, Christiansted, St. Croix, VI 00823.

Phone: 340-778-5008. **Fax:** 340-778-5011.

Web Site: http://home.att.net/~davidlampel/Newschannel8.htm

Technical Facilities: Channel No. 20 (506-512 MHz). Authorized power: 1.1-kw max. visual, aural. Antenna: 951-ft above av. terrain, 102-ft. above ground, 1092-ft. above sea level.

Latitude	17°	45'	21"
Longitude	64°	47'	56"

Ownership: Alpha Broadcasting Corp.

Began Operation: October 30, 2003. Began analog operations: November 10, 1965. Ceased analog operations: June 12, 2009.

Personnel:

David Lampel, President & General Manager.

Ruby Vidal, Office Manager.

Glen Dratte, Operations Manager.

Chester Benjamin, Chief Engineer.

Stephen Francis, Sports Director.

City of License: Christiansted. **Station DMA:** Virgin Islands. **Rank:** 0.

Nielsen Data: Not available.

Public/Educational TV Stations

Personnel, facilities and other data as of October 1, 2009

Alabama

WBIQ-DT
Birmingham
Ch. 10

Licensee: Alabama Educational Television Commission, 2112 11th Ave S, Ste 400, Birmingham, AL 35205.

Studios: 2112 11th Ave S, Ste 400, Birmingham, AL 35205; 1255 Madison Ave, Montgomery, AL 36107.

Mailing Address: 2112 11th Ave S, Ste 400, Birmingham, AL 35205.

Phones: 205-328-8756; 800-239-5233. **Fax:** 205-251-2192.

Web Site: http://www.aptv.org

Technical Facilities: Channel No. 10 (192-198 MHz). Authorized power: 3-kw visual, aural. Antenna: 1398-ft above av. terrain, 1072-ft. above ground, 2019-ft. above sea level.

Latitude	33°	29'	04"
Longitude	86°	48'	25"

Note: Latitude and longitude coordinates shown are based on the North American Datum of 1927 (NAD 27) as currently required by the Mass Media Bureau of the FCC.

Ownership: Alabama Educational Television Commission.

Began Operation: February 17, 2009. Station broadcasting digitally on its analog channel allotment. Began analog operations: April 28, 1955. Ceased analog operations: February 17, 2009.

Personnel:

Allan Pizzato, Executive Director.

Charlie Grantham, Chief Operating Officer.

Jon Beans, News Director.

Wendel Wood, Broadcast Engineering Director.

Pauline Howland, Deputy Director & Chief Financial Officer.

Dorothy McDonald, Assistant Programming Director.

Mike McKenzie, Public Information & Promotions Director.

Duane Johnson, Special Events Manager.

John Brady, Development Director.

Bob Corley, Montgomery Production Center Director.

WIIQ-DT
Demopolis
Ch. 19

Licensee: Alabama Educational Television Commission, 2112 11th Ave S, Ste 400, Birmingham, AL 35205.

Studios: 1255 Madison Ave, Montgomery, AL 36107; 2112 11th Ave S, Ste 400, Birmingham, AL 35205.

Mailing Address: 2112 11th Ave S, Ste 400, Birmingham, AL 35205.

Phones: 205-328-8756; 800-239-5233. **Fax:** 205-251-2192.

Web Site: http://www.aptv.org

Technical Facilities: Channel No. 19 (500-506 MHz). Authorized power: 1000-kw max. visual, aural. Antenna: 1063-ft above av. terrain, 971-ft. above ground, 1204-ft. above sea level.

Latitude	32°	21'	45"
Longitude	87°	52'	04"

Holds CP for change to 1067-ft above av. terrain, 972-ft. above ground, 1205-ft. above sea level lat. 32° 21' 45", long. 87° 52' 30.5"; BPEDT-20090422AAZ.

Transmitter: 6-mi. NW of Linden.

Note: Latitude and longitude coordinates shown are based on the North American Datum of 1927 (NAD 27) as currently required by the Mass Media Bureau of the FCC.

Ownership: Alabama Educational Television Commission.

Began Operation: October 15, 2003. Began analog operations: September 13, 1970. Ceased analog operations: February 17, 2009.

Personnel:

Allan Pizzato, Executive Director.

Charlie Grantham, Chief Operating Officer.

Jon Beans, News Director.

Wendel Wood, Broadcast Engineering Director.

Pauline Howland, Deputy Director & Chief Financial Officer.

Dorothy McDonald, Assistant Programming Director.

Mike McKenzie, Public Information & Promotions Director.

Duane Johnson, Special Events Manager.

John Brady, Development Director.

Bob Corley, Montgomery Production Center Director.

WDIQ-DT
Dozier
Ch. 11

Licensee: Alabama Educational Television Commission, 2112 11th Ave S, Ste 400, Birmingham, AL 35205.

Studio: 2112 11th Ave S, Ste 400, Birmingham, AL 35205.

Mailing Address: 2112 11th Ave S, Ste 400, Birmingham, AL 35205.

Phones: 205-328-8756; 800-239-5233. **Fax:** 205-251-2192.

Web Site: http://www.aptv.org

Technical Facilities: Channel No. 11 (198-204 MHz). Authorized power: 1.3-kw visual, aural. Antenna: 702-ft above av. terrain, 561-ft. above ground, 1066-ft. above sea level.

Latitude	31°	33'	16"
Longitude	86°	23'	32"

Holds CP for change to channel number 10, 30-kw visual, 738-ft above av. terrain, 595-ft. above ground, 1100-ft. above sea level; BMPEDT-20080619AGY.

Note: Latitude and longitude coordinates shown are based on the North American Datum of 1927 (NAD 27) as currently required by the Mass Media Bureau of the FCC.

Ownership: Alabama Educational Television Commission.

Began Operation: June 18, 2006. Began analog operations: August 8, 1956. Ceased analog operations: February 17, 2009.

Personnel:

Allan Pizzato, Executive Director.

Charlie Grantham, Chief Operating Officer.

Jon Beans, News Director.

Wendel Wood, Broadcast Engineering Director.

Pauline Howland, Deputy Director & Chief Financial Officer.

Dorothy McDonald, Assistant Programming Director.

Mike McKenzie, Public Information & Promotions Director.

Duane Johnson, Special Events Manager.

John Brady, Development Director.

Bob Corley, Montgomery Production Center Director.

WFIQ-DT
Florence
Ch. 22

Licensee: Alabama Educational Television Commission, 2112 11th Ave S, Ste 400, Birmingham, AL 35205.

WDIQ-DT
Dozier
Ch. 11

Studios: 1255 Madison Ave, Montgomery, AL 36107; 2112 11th Ave S, Ste 400, Birmingham, AL 35205.

Mailing Address: 2112 11th Ave S, Ste 400, Birmingham, AL 35205.

Phones: 205-328-8756; 800-239-5233. **Fax:** 205-251-2192.

Web Site: http://www.aptv.org

Technical Facilities: Channel No. 22 (518-524 MHz). Authorized power: 418.8-kw max. visual, aural. Antenna: 681-ft above av. terrain, 508-ft. above ground, 1413-ft. above sea level.

Latitude	34°	34'	41"
Longitude	87°	47'	02"

Holds CP for change to 650-kw max. visual; BPEDT-20080619AGU.

Transmitter: Hwy. 65, 4-mi. NE of Frankfort.

Note: Latitude and longitude coordinates shown are based on the North American Datum of 1927 (NAD 27) as currently required by the Mass Media Bureau of the FCC.

Ownership: Alabama Educational Television Commission.

Began Operation: February 17, 2009. Began analog operations: August 9, 1967. Ceased analog operations: February 17, 2009.

Personnel:

Allan Pizzato, Executive Director.

Charlie Grantham, Chief Operating Officer.

Jon Beans, News Director.

Wendel Wood, Broadcast Engineering Director.

Pauline Howland, Deputy Director & Chief Financial Officer.

Dorothy McDonald, Assistant Programming Director.

Mike McKenzie, Public Information & Promotions Director.

Duane Johnson, Special Events Manager.

Bob Corley, Montgomery Production Center Director.

John Brady, Development Director.

WHIQ-DT
Huntsville
Ch. 24

Licensee: Alabama Educational Television Commission, 2112 11th Ave S, Ste 400, Birmingham, AL 35205.

Studios: 2112 11th Ave S, Ste 400, Birmingham, AL 35205; 1255 Madison Ave, Montgomery, AL 36107.

Mailing Address: 2112 11th Ave S, Ste 400, Birmingham, AL 35205.

Phones: 205-328-8756; 800-239-5233. **Fax:** 205-251-2192.

Web Site: http://www.aptv.org

Technical Facilities: Channel No. 24 (530-536 MHz). Authorized power: 396-kw max. visual, aural. Antenna: 1110-ft above av. terrain, 292-ft. above ground, 1890-ft. above sea level.

Latitude	34°	44'	13"
Longitude	86°	31'	45"

Transmitter: 706 Read Dr. SE.

Note: Latitude and longitude coordinates shown are based on the North American Datum of 1927 (NAD 27) as currently required by the Mass Media Bureau of the FCC.

Ownership: Alabama Educational Television Commission.

Began Operation: February 17, 2009. Began analog operations: November 15, 1965. Ceased analog operations: February 17, 2009.

Personnel:

Allan Pizzato, Executive Director.

Charlie Grantham, Chief Operating Officer.

Jon Beans, News Director.

Wendel Wood, Broadcast Engineering Director.

Pauline Howland, Deputy Director & Chief Financial Officer.

Dorothy McDonald, Assistant Programming Director.

Mike McKenzie, Public Information & Promotions Director.

Duane Johnson, Special Events Manager.

John Brady, Development Director.

Bob Corley, Montgomery Production Center Director.

WGIQ-DT
Louisville
Ch. 44

Licensee: Alabama Educational Television Commission, 2112 11th Ave S, Ste 400, Birmingham, AL 35205.

Studios: 1255 Madison Ave, Montgomery, AL 36107; 2112 11th Ave S, Ste 400, Birmingham, AL 35205.

Mailing Address: 2112 11th Ave S, Ste 400, Birmingham, AL 35205.

Phones: 205-328-8756; 800-239-5233. **Fax:** 205-251-2192.

Web Site: http://www.aptv.org

Technical Facilities: Channel No. 44 (650-656 MHz). Authorized power: 925-kw max. visual, aural. Antenna: 860-ft above av. terrain, 689-ft. above ground, 1276-ft. above sea level.

Latitude	31°	43'	04"
Longitude	85°	26'	03"

Transmitter: TV Tower Rd., 0.37-mi. W of Texasville.

Note: Latitude and longitude coordinates shown are based on the North American Datum of 1927 (NAD 27) as currently required by the Mass Media Bureau of the FCC.

Ownership: Alabama Educational Television Commission.

Began Operation: December 31, 2002. Began analog operations: September 9, 1968. Ceased analog operations: February 17, 2009.

Personnel:

Allan Pizzato, Executive Director.

Charlie Grantham, Chief Operating Officer.

Jon Beans, News Director.

Wendel Wood, Broadcast Engineering Director.

Pauline Howland, Deputy Director & Chief Financial Officer.

Dorothy McDonald, Assistant Programming Director.

Mike McKenzie, Public Information & Promotions Director.

Duane Johnson, Special Events Manager.

John Brady, Development Director.

Bob Corley, Montgomery Production Center Director.

WEIQ-DT
Mobile
Ch. 41

Licensee: Alabama Educational Television Commission, 2112 11th Ave S, Ste 400, Birmingham, AL 35205.

Studio: 2112 11th Ave S, Ste 400, Birmingham, AL 35205.

Mailing Address: 2112 11th Ave S, Ste 400, Birmingham, AL 35205.

Phones: 205-328-8756; 800-239-5233. **Fax:** 205-251-2192.

Web Site: http://www.aptv.org

Technical Facilities: Channel No. 41 (632-638 MHz). Authorized power: 199-kw max. visual, aural. Antenna: 607-ft above av. terrain, 518-ft. above ground, 686-ft. above sea level.

Latitude	30°	39'	33"
Longitude	87°	53'	33"

Holds CP for change to 1000-kw max. visual; BPEDT-20080619AGR.

Transmitter: 0.6-mi. S of U.S. Hwy. 31, Spanish Fort.

Note: Latitude and longitude coordinates shown are based on the North American Datum of 1927 (NAD 27) as currently required by the Mass Media Bureau of the FCC.

Ownership: Alabama Educational Television Commission.

Began Operation: April 30, 2003. Began analog operations: November 18, 1964. Ceased analog operations: February 17, 2009.

Personnel:

Allan Pizzato, Executive Director.

Charlie Grantham, Chief Operating Officer.

Jon Beans, News Director.

Wendel Wood, Broadcast Engineering Director.

Pauline Howland, Deputy Director & Chief Financial Officer.

Dorothy McDonald, Assistant Programming Director.

Mike McKenzie, Public Information & Promotions Director.

Duane Johnson, Special Events Manager.

John Brady, Development Director.

Bob Corley, Montgomery Production Center Director.

WAIQ-DT
Montgomery
Ch. 27

Licensee: Alabama Educational Television Commission, 2112 11th Ave S, Ste 400, Birmingham, AL 35205.

Studio: 1255 Madison Ave, Montgomery, AL 36107.

Mailing Address: 2112 11th Ave S, Ste 400, Birmingham, AL 35205.

Phones: 205-328-8756; 800-239-5233. **Fax:** 205-251-2192.

Web Site: http://www.aptv.org

Technical Facilities: Channel No. 27 (548-554 MHz). Authorized power: 600-kw max. visual, aural. Antenna: 586-ft above av. terrain, 534-ft. above ground, 780-ft. above sea level.

Latitude	32°	22'	55"
Longitude	86°	17'	33"

Transmitter: 1300 Upper Wetumpka Rd.

Note: Latitude and longitude coordinates shown are based on the North American Datum of 1927 (NAD 27) as currently required by the Mass Media Bureau of the FCC.

Ownership: Alabama Educational Television Commission.

Began Operation: January 1, 2002. Began analog operations: December 18, 1962. Ceased analog operations: February 17, 2009.

Personnel:

Allan Pizzato, Executive Director.

Charlie Grantham, Chief Operating Officer.

Jon Beans, News Director.

Wendel Wood, Broadcast Engineering Director.

Pauline Howland, Deputy Director & Chief Financial Officer.

Dorothy McDonald, Assistant Programming Director.

Mike McKenzie, Public Information & Promotions Director.

Duane Johnson, Special Events Manager.

John Brady, Development Director.

Bob Corley, Montgomery Production Center Director.

WCIQ-DT
Mount Cheaha State Park
Ch. 7

Licensee: Alabama Educational Television Commission, 2112 11th Ave S, Ste 400, Birmingham, AL 35205.

Dorothy McDonald, Assistant Programming Director.

Mike McKenzie, Public Information & Promotions Director.

Duane Johnson, Special Events Manager.

John Brady, Development Director.

Bob Corley, Montgomery Production Center Director.

Studio: 2112 11th Ave S, Ste 400, Birmingham, AL 35205.

Mailing Address: 2112 11th Ave S, Ste 400, Birmingham, AL 35205.

Phones: 205-328-8756; 800-239-5233. **Fax:** 205-251-2192.

Web Site: http://www.aptv.org

Technical Facilities: Channel No. 7 (174-180 MHz). Authorized power: 34.8-kw visual, aural. Antenna: 1889-ft above av. terrain, 532-ft. above ground, 2881-ft. above sea level.

Latitude	33°	29'	06"
Longitude	85°	48'	32"

Note: Latitude and longitude coordinates shown are based on the North American Datum of 1927 (NAD 27) as currently required by the Mass Media Bureau of the FCC.

Ownership: Alabama Educational Television Commission.

Began Operation: November 8, 2006. Station broadcasting digitally on its analog channel allotment. Began analog operations: January 7, 1955. Ceased analog operations: February 17, 2009.

Personnel:

Allan Pizzato, Executive Director.

Charlie Grantham, Chief Operating Officer.

Jon Beans, News Director.

Wendel Wood, Broadcast Engineering Director.

Pauline Howland, Deputy Director & Chief Financial Officer.

Dorothy McDonald, Assistant Programming Director.

Mike McKenzie, Public Information & Promotions Director.

Duane Johnson, Special Events Manager.

John Brady, Development Director.

Bob Corley, Montgomery Production Center Director.

Alaska

KAKM-DT
Anchorage
Ch. 8

Licensee: Alaska Public Telecommunications Inc., 3877 University Dr, Anchorage, AK 99508.

Studio: 3877 University Dr, Anchorage, AK 99508.

Mailing Address: 3877 University Dr, Anchorage, AK 99508.

Phone: 907-550-8400. **Fax:** 907-550-8401.

Web Site: http://www.kakm.org

Technical Facilities: Channel No. 8 (180-186 MHz). Authorized power: 50-kw visual, aural. Antenna: 787-ft above av. terrain, 774-ft. above ground, 890-ft. above sea level.

Latitude	61°	25'	22"
Longitude	149°	52'	20"

Note: Latitude and longitude coordinates shown are based on the North American Datum of 1927 (NAD 27) as currently required by the Mass Media Bureau of the FCC.

Ownership: Alaska Public Telecommunications Inc.

Began Operation: January 4, 2007. Began analog operations: May 7, 1975. Ceased analog operations: June 12, 2009.

Personnel:

Steve Lindbeck, General Manager.

Bob Dickinson, Chief Engineer.

Karen Olstad, Finance Director.

Veronica Dent, Program & Production Director.

Will Peterson, Development Director.

KUAC-DT
Fairbanks
Ch. 9

Licensee: U. of Alaska, PO Box 755620, Fairbanks, AK 99775.

Studio: U. of Alaska, Theatre Bldg, 312 Tanana Dr, Ste 202, Fairbanks, AK 99775-5620.

Mailing Address: PO Box 755620, U of Alaska Fairbanks, Fairbanks, AK 99775-5620.

Phone: 907-474-7491. **Fax:** 907-474-5064.

Web Site: http://www.kuac.org

Technical Facilities: Channel No. 9 (186-192 MHz). Authorized power: 30-kw visual, aural. Antenna: 554-ft above av. terrain, 117-ft. above ground, 1417-ft. above sea level.

Latitude	64°	54'	42"
Longitude	147°	46'	38"

Transmitter: Bender Mountain, off Farmer's Loop & Ski Boot Hill Rds.

Note: Latitude and longitude coordinates shown are based on the North American Datum of 1927 (NAD 27) as currently required by the Mass Media Bureau of the FCC.

Satellite Earth Station: Harris; Vertex, 8.2-meter Ku-band.

Ownership: U. of Alaska.

Began Operation: May 1, 2003. Station broadcasting digitally on its analog channel allotment. Began analog operations: December 22, 1971. Ceased analog operations: June 12, 2009.

Personnel:

Greg Petrowich, General Manager.

Mark Anderson, Chief Engineer.

Patty Dyer-Smith, Finance & Administration Director.

Claudia Clark, Program Coordinator.

Gretchen Gordon, Development & Outreach Director.

KTOO-DT
Juneau
Ch. 10

Licensee: Capital Community Broadcasting Inc., 360 Egan Dr, Juneau, AK 99801.

Studio: 360 Egan Dr, Juneau, AK 99801-1746.

Mailing Address: 360 Egan Dr, Juneau, AK 99801.

Phone: 907-586-1670. **Fax:** 907-586-3612.

Web Site: http://www.ktoo.org

Technical Facilities: Channel No. 10 (192-198 MHz). Authorized power: 1-kw visual, aural. Antenna: Minus 1191-ft above av. terrain, 72-ft. above ground, 121-ft. above sea level.

Latitude	58°	17'	56"
Longitude	134°	24'	07"

Note: Latitude and longitude coordinates shown are based on the North American Datum of 1927 (NAD 27) as currently required by the Mass Media Bureau of the FCC.

Ownership: Capital Community Broadcasting Inc.

Began Operation: July 30, 2004. Began analog operations: October 1, 1978. Ceased analog operations: June 12, 2009.

Personnel:

Bill Legere, President & General Manager.

James Mahan, Station Manager.

Will Judy, Information Technology Director.

Lise Paradis, Business Manager.

John Beiler, Development Director.

Mandy Judy, Office Manager.

Arizona

KDTP-DT
Holbrook
Ch. 11

Grantee: Community Television Educators Inc., 3901 Hwy 121 S, Bedford, TX 76021-3009.

Mailing Address: 3901 Hwy 121 S, Bedford, TX 76021.

Phone: 817-571-1229.

Web Site: http://www.daystar.com

Technical Facilities: Channel No. 11 (198-204 MHz). Authorized power: 160-kw visual, aural. Antenna: 997-ft above av. terrain, 525-ft. above ground, 8130-ft. above sea level.

Latitude	34°	23'	19"
Longitude	110°	59'	36"

Note: Latitude and longitude coordinates shown are based on the North American Datum of 1927 (NAD 27) as currently required by the Mass Media Bureau of the FCC.

Ownership: Community Television Educators Inc.

Began Operation: June 12, 2009. Station broadcasting digitally on its analog channel allotment. Began analog operations: January 2, 2001. Station swapped analog allocation and City of License with KPHZ. FCC approved switch October 5, 2005 and CPs were granted April 11, 2006. Ceased analog operations: June 12, 2009.

KAET-DT
Phoenix
Ch. 8

Licensee: Arizona State Board of Regents for Arizona State U., PO Box 871405, Tempe, AZ 85287-1405.

Studio: Stauffer Hall, B-Wing, 10th St & Myrtle, Tempe, AZ 85281.

Mailing Address: PO Box 871405, Tempe, AZ 85287-1405.

Phone: 480-965-8888. **Fax:** 480-965-1000.

Web Site: http://www.azpbs.org

Technical Facilities: Channel No. 8 (180-186 MHz). Authorized power: 40-kw visual, aural. Antenna: 1801-ft above av. terrain, 308-ft. above ground, 2992-ft. above sea level.

Latitude	33°	20'	00"
Longitude	112°	03'	49"

Note: Latitude and longitude coordinates shown are based on the North American Datum of 1927 (NAD 27) as currently required by the Mass Media Bureau of the FCC.

Ownership: Arizona State Board of Regents for Arizona State U.

Began Operation: April 17, 2001. Station broadcasting digitally on its analog channel allotment. Began analog operations: January 30, 1961. Ceased analog operations: June 12, 2009.

Personnel:

Greg Giczi, General Manager.

Beth Vershure, Station Manager.

Mike Philipsen, News Director.

Gilbert Aykroyd, Engineering Manager.

Ray G. Murdock, Business Manager.

Nancy Southgate, Program Manager.

John Booth, Production Manager.

Kelly McCullough, Marketing & Development Director & Associate General Manager.

John Menzies, Creative Services Director.

KUAS-DT
Tucson
Ch. 28

Licensee: Arizona Board of Regents, U. of Arizona, PO Box 210151, Tucson, AZ 85721.

Studio: Modern Languages Bldg, U. of Arizona, 1423 E University Blvd, Tucson, AZ 85721.

Mailing Address: 1423 E University Blvd, U. of Arizona, Modern Languages Bldg, Tucson, AZ 85721.

Phone: 520-621-5828. **Fax:** 520-621-3360.

Email: janderson@kuat.arizona.edu **Web Site:** http://www.kuat.org

Technical Facilities: Channel No. 28 (554-560 MHz). Authorized power: 50-kw max. visual, aural. Antenna: 584-ft above av. terrain, 31-ft. above ground, 3129-ft. above sea level.

Latitude	32°	12'	53"
Longitude	111°	00'	21"

Note: Latitude and longitude coordinates shown are based on the North American Datum of 1927 (NAD 27) as currently required by the Mass Media Bureau of the FCC.

Ownership: U. of Arizona.

Began Operation: October 1, 2002. Began analog operations: July 18, 1988. Ceased analog operations: June 12, 2009.

Personnel:

Jack Gibson, General Manager.

David Ross, Technical Services.

Martin Camacho, Business Development Specialist.

Peter Michaels, News Director.

Frank Fregoso, Chief Engineer.

John Kelley, Assistant General Manager & Program Manager.

Fran Sherlock, Production Manager.

KUAT-DT
Tucson
Ch. 30

Licensee: Arizona Board of Regents, U. of Arizona, PO Box 210151, Tucson, AZ 85721.

Studio: Modern Languages Bldg, U. of Arizona, 1423 E University Blvd, Tucson, AZ 85721.

Mailing Address: 1423 E University Blvd, U. of Arizona, Modern Languages Bldg, Tucson, AZ 85721.

Phone: 520-621-5828. **Fax:** 520-621-3360.

Web Site: http://www.kuat.org

Technical Facilities: Channel No. 30 (566-572 MHz). Authorized power: 667.5-kw max. visual, aural. Antenna: 3583-ft above av. terrain, 163-ft. above ground, 8698-ft. above sea level.

Latitude	32°	24'	55"
Longitude	110°	42'	51"

Note: Latitude and longitude coordinates shown are based on the North American Datum of 1927 (NAD 27) as currently required by the Mass Media Bureau of the FCC.

Ownership: U. of Arizona.

Began Operation: July 27, 2004. Began analog operations: March 8, 1959. Ceased analog operations: June 12, 2009.

Personnel:

Jack Gibson, General Manager.

David Ross, Technical Services.

Martin Camacho, Business Development Specialist.

Peter Michaels, News Director.

Frank Fregoso, Chief Engineer.

John Kelley, Assistant General Manager & Program Manager.

Fran Sherlock, Production Manager.

Arkansas

KETG-DT
Arkadelphia
Ch. 13

Licensee: Arkansas ETV Commission, 350 S Donaghey Ave, Conway, AR 72034.

Studio: 350 S Donaghey Ave, Conway, AR 72034.

Mailing Address: PO Box 1250, Conway, AR 72033.

Phones: 501-682-2386; 501-450-1727. **Fax:** 501-682-4122.

Web Site: http://www.aetn.org

Technical Facilities: Channel No. 13 (210-216 MHz). Authorized power: 7.3-kw visual, aural. Antenna: 1048-ft above av. terrain, 1024-ft. above ground, 1262-ft. above sea level.

Latitude	33°	54'	26"
Longitude	93°	06'	46"

Holds CP for change to 13.85-kw visual, 1030-ft above av. terrain, 1024-ft. above ground, 1262-ft. above sea level; BPEDT-20080620AFO.

Note: Latitude and longitude coordinates shown are based on the North American Datum of 1927 (NAD 27) as currently required by the Mass Media Bureau of the FCC.

Ownership: Arkansas ETV Commission.

Began Operation: June 1, 2004. Began analog operations: October 2, 1976. Ceased analog operations: June 12, 2009.

Personnel:

Allen Weatherly, Executive Director.

Tony Brooks, Deputy Director.

DeWayne Wilbur, Operations Director.

Gary Schultz, Engineering Director.

Donna Smith, Finance & Administration Director.

Kathy Atkinson, Program Director.

Carole Adornetto, Production Director.

Mike McCullars, Research & Special Projects Director.

Mona Dixon, Development Director.

Kathleen Stafford, Learning Services Director.

Ron Johnson, Communications Director.

Kevin Lewis, Informational Technology Director.

KETZ-DT
El Dorado
Ch. 12

Licensee: Arkansas ETV Commission, 350 S Donaghey Ave, Conway, AR 72034.

Studio: 350 S Donaghey Ave, Conway, AR 72034.

Mailing Address: PO Box 1250, Conway, AR 72033.

Phone: 501-682-2386. **Fax:** 501-682-4122.

Web Site: http://www.aetn.org

Technical Facilities: Channel No. 12 (204-210 MHz). Authorized power: 7.2-kw visual, aural. Antenna: 1765-ft above av. terrain, 1739-ft. above ground, 1867-ft. above sea level.

Latitude	33°	04'	41"
Longitude	92°	13'	41"

Holds CP for change to channel number 10, 16.2-kw visual lat. 33° 4' 41", long. 92° 13' 30"; BMPEDT-20090324ACT.

Note: Latitude and longitude coordinates shown are based on the North American Datum of 1927 (NAD 27) as currently required by the Mass Media Bureau of the FCC.

Ownership: Arkansas ETV Commission.

Began Operation: May 17, 2006. Station went directly to digital broadcast; no analog channel.

Personnel:

Allen Weatherly, Executive Director.

Tony Brooks, Deputy Director.

DeWayne Wilbur, Operations Director.

Gary Schultz, Engineering Director.

Donna Smith, Finance & Administation Director.

Kathy Atkinson, Program Director.

Mona Dixon, Development Director.

Carole Adornetto, Production Manager.

Mike McCullars, Research & Special Projects Director.

Kathleen Stafford, Learning Services Director.

Ron Johnson, Communications Director.

Kevin Lewis, Information Technology Director.

KAFT-DT
Fayetteville
Ch. 9

Licensee: Arkansas ETV Commission, 350 S Donaghey Ave, Conway, AR 72034.

Studio: 350 S Donaghey Ave, Conway, AR 72034.

Mailing Address: PO Box 1250, Conway, AR 72033.

Phones: 501-682-2386; 501-450-1727. **Fax:** 501-682-4122.

Web Site: http://www.aetn.org

Technical Facilities: Channel No. 9 (186-192 MHz). Authorized power: 19-kw visual, aural. Antenna: 1644-ft above av. terrain, 1065-ft. above ground, 3375-ft. above sea level.

Latitude	35°	48'	53"
Longitude	94°	01'	41"

Holds CP for change to 37.9-kw visual, 1650-ft above av. terrain, 1065-ft. above ground, 3375-ft. above sea level; BPEDT-20080620AFK.

Note: Latitude and longitude coordinates shown are based on the North American Datum of 1927 (NAD 27) as currently required by the Mass Media Bureau of the FCC.

Ownership: Arkansas ETV Commission.

Began Operation: May 18, 2004. Began analog operations: September 18, 1976. Ceased analog operations: June 12, 2009.

Personnel:

Allen Weatherly, Executive Director.

Tony Brooks, Deputy Director.

DeWayne Wilbur, Operations Director.

Gary Schultz, Engineering Director.

Donna Smith, Finance & Administration Director.

Kathy Atkinson, Program Director.

Mona Dixon, Development Director.

Carole Adornetto, Production Director.

Mike McCullars, Research & Special Projects Director.

Kathleen Stafford, Learning Services Director.

Ron Johnson, Communications Director.

Kevin Lewis, Informational Technology Director.

KTEJ-DT
Jonesboro
Ch. 20

Licensee: Arkansas ETV Commission, 350 S Donaghey Ave, Conway, AR 72034.

Studio: 350 S Donaghey Ave, Conway, AR 72034.

Mailing Address: PO Box 1250, Conway, AR 72033.

Phones: 501-682-2386; 501-450-1727. **Fax:** 501-682-4122.

Web Site: http://www.aetn.org

Technical Facilities: Channel No. 20 (506-512 MHz). Authorized power: 50-kw max. visual, aural. Antenna: 1018-ft above av. terrain, 933-ft. above ground, 1313-ft. above sea level.

Latitude	35°	54'	14"
Longitude	90°	46'	14"

Holds CP for change to 419-kw max. visual, 1017-ft above av. terrain, 933-ft. above ground, 1313-ft. above sea level; BPEDT-20080620AFN.

Note: Latitude and longitude coordinates shown are based on the North American Datum of 1927 (NAD 27) as currently required by the Mass Media Bureau of the FCC.

Ownership: Arkansas ETV Commission.

Began Operation: June 3, 2004. Began analog operations: May 1, 1976. Ceased analog operations: February 17, 2009.

Personnel:

Allen Weatherly, Executive Director.

Tony Brooks, Deputy Director.

DeWayne Wilbur, Operations Director.

Gary Schultz, Engineering Director.

Donna Smith, Finance & Administration Director.

Kathy Atkinson, Program Director.

Mona Dixon, Development Director.

Carole Adornetto, Production Manager.

Mike McCullars, Research & Special Projects Director.

Kathleen Stafford, Learning Services Director.

Ron Johnson, Communications Director.

Kevin Lewis, Information Technology Director.

KETS-DT
Little Rock
Ch. 5

Licensee: Arkansas ETV Commission, 350 S Donaghey Ave, Conway, AR 72034.

Studio: 350 S Donaghey Ave, Conway, AR 72034.

Mailing Address: PO Box 1250, Conway, AR 72033.

Phones: 501-682-2386; 501-450-1727. **Fax:** 501-682-4122.

Web Site: http://www.aetn.org

Technical Facilities: Channel No. 5 (76-82 MHz). Authorized power: 2.1-kw visual, aural. Antenna: 1798-ft above av. terrain, 1732-ft. above ground, 2070-ft. above sea level.

Latitude	34°	26'	31"
Longitude	92°	13'	03"

Holds CP for change to channel number 7, 26.73-kw visual, 1795-ft above av. terrain, 1732-ft. above ground, 2070-ft. above sea level; BPEDT-20080317AHV.

Note: Latitude and longitude coordinates shown are based on the North American Datum of 1927 (NAD 27) as currently required by the Mass Media Bureau of the FCC.

Ownership: Arkansas ETV Commission.

Began Operation: May 27, 2004. Off air January 2008 due to tower collapse. Resumed digital operations prior to February 17, 2009. Began analog operations: December 4, 1966. Ceased analog operations: January 26, 2009.

Personnel:

Allen Weatherly, Executive Director.

Tony Brooks, Deputy Director.

DeWayne Wilbur, Operations Director.

Gary Schultz, Engineering Director.

Donna Smith, Finance & Administration Director.

Kathy Atkinson, Program Director.

Mona Dixon, Development Director.

Carole Adornetto, Production Director.

Mike McCullars, Research & Special Projects Director.

Kathleen Stafford, Learning Services Director.

Ron Johnson, Communications Director.

Kevin Lewis, Informational Technology Director.

KKAP-DT
Little Rock
Ch. 36

Licensee: Educational Broadcasting Corp., 3901 Hwy 121 S, Bedford, TX 76021-3009.

Mailing Address: 3901 Hwy 121 S, Bedford, TX 76021.

Phone: 817-571-1229. **Fax:** 817-571-7458.

Technical Facilities: Channel No. 36 (602-608 MHz). Authorized power: 1000-kw max. visual, aural. Antenna: 1296-ft above av. terrain, 656-ft. above ground, 1709-ft. above sea level.

Latitude	34°	47'	56"
Longitude	92°	29'	45"

Note: Latitude and longitude coordinates shown are based on the North American Datum of 1927 (NAD 27) as currently required by the Mass Media Bureau of the FCC.

Ownership: Educational Broadcasting Corporation.

Began Operation: June 12, 2009. Station broadcasting digitally on its analog channel allotment. Began analog operations: May 4, 2001. Ceased analog operations: June 12, 2009.

KEMV-DT
Mountain View
Ch. 13

Licensee: Arkansas ETV Commission, 350 S Donaghey Ave, Conway, AR 72034.

Studio: 350 S Donaghey Ave, Conway, AR 72034.

Mailing Address: PO Box 1250, Conway, AR 72033.

Phones: 501-682-2386; 501-450-1727. **Fax:** 501-682-4122.

Web Site: http://www.aetn.org

Technical Facilities: Channel No. 13 (210-216 MHz). Authorized power: 4.05-kw visual, aural. Antenna: 1336-ft above av. terrain, 889-ft. above ground, 2409-ft. above sea level.

Latitude	35°	48'	47"
Longitude	92°	17'	24"

Holds CP for change to 12.1-kw visual, 1398-ft above av. terrain, 951-ft. above ground, 2471-ft. above sea level; BPEDT-20080620AFQ.

Note: Latitude and longitude coordinates shown are based on the North American Datum of 1927 (NAD 27) as currently required by the Mass Media Bureau of the FCC.

Ownership: Arkansas ETV Commission.

Began Operation: May 20, 2004. Began analog operations: November 16, 1980. Ceased analog operations: June 12, 2009.

Personnel:

Allen Weatherly, Executive Director.

Tony Brooks, Deputy Director.

DeWayne Wilbur, Operations Director.

Gary Schultz, Engineering Director.

Donna Smith, Finance & Administration Director.

Kathy Atkinson, Program Director.

Mona Dixon, Development Director.

Carole Adornetto, Production Director.

Mike McCullars, Research & Special Projects Director.

Kathleen Stafford, Learning Services Director.

Ron Johnson, Communications Director.

Kevin Lewis, Informational Technology Director.

California

KBSV-DT
Ceres
Ch. 15

Grantee: Bet-Nahrain Inc., PO Box 4116, Modesto, CA 95352.

Studio: 3119 S Central Ave, Ceres, CA 95307.

Mailing Address: PO Box 4116, Modesto, CA 95352.

Phones: 209-537-0933; 209-538-4130. **Fax:** 209-538-2795.

Web Site: http://www.betnahrain.org/kbsv/kbsv.htm

Technical Facilities: Channel No. 15 (476-482 MHz). Authorized power: 18.6-kw max. visual, aural. Antenna: 495-ft above av. terrain, 66-ft. above ground, 1129-ft. above sea level.

Latitude	37°	29'	32.3"
Longitude	121°	13'	27.8"

Holds CP for change to 0.421-kw max. visual, 1888-ft above av. terrain, 36-ft. above ground, 3298-ft. above sea level lat. 37° 30' 28", long. 121° 22' 20.2"; BMPEDT-20081002ABR.

Note: Latitude and longitude coordinates shown are based on the North American Datum of 1927 (NAD 27) as currently required by the Mass Media Bureau of the FCC.

Ownership: Bet-Nahrain Inc.

Began Operation: February 14, 2006. Began analog operations: April 14, 1996. Ceased analog operations: June 12, 2009.

Personnel:

Sargon Dadesho, General Manager.

Shemiran Daniali, Vice President.

Richard Green, Chief Engineer.

Jannet Shamon, Mass Media Director.

Lena Lazar, Secretary.

KRCB-DT
Cotati
Ch. 23

Licensee: Rural California Broadcasting Corp., 5850 LaBath Ave, Rohnert Park, CA 94928.

Studio: 5850 LaBath Ave, Rohnert Park, CA 94928.

Mailing Address: 5850 LaBath Ave, Rohnert Park, CA 94928.

Phones: 707-584-2000; 800-287-2722. **Fax:** 707-585-1363.

Email: cindy_armstrong@krcb.org **Web Site:** http://www.krcb.org

Technical Facilities: Channel No. 23 (524-530 MHz). Authorized power: 105-kw max. visual, aural. Antenna: 2068-ft above av. terrain, 194-ft. above ground, 2635-ft. above sea level.

Latitude	38°	20'	54.7"
Longitude	122°	34'	37.5"

Holds CP for change to 299-kw max. visual; BPEDT-20080617AEI.

Note: Latitude and longitude coordinates shown are based on the North American Datum of 1927 (NAD 27) as currently required by the Mass Media Bureau of the FCC.

Ownership: Rural California Broadcasting Corp.

Began Operation: November 7, 2008. Began analog operations: December 2, 1984. Ceased analog operations: June 12, 2009.

Personnel:

Nancy Dobbs, President & Chief Executive Officer.

Stan Marvin, TV Production Director & Underwriting Manager.

Larry Stratton, Chief Engineer.

Sandy Price, Business Manager.

KEET-DT
Eureka
Ch. 11

Licensee: Redwood Empire Public Television Inc., PO Box 13, Eureka, CA 95502-0013.

Studio: 7246 Humboldt Hill Rd, Eureka, CA 95503.

Mailing Address: PO Box 13, Eureka, CA 95502-0013.

Phone: 707-445-0813. **Fax:** 707-445-8977.

Email: rschoenher@keet-tv.org **Web Site:** http://www.keet.org

Technical Facilities: Channel No. 11 (198-204 MHz). Authorized power: 38.4-kw visual, aural. Antenna: 1803-ft above av. terrain, 419-ft. above ground, 3069-ft. above sea level.

Latitude	40°	43'	38.9"
Longitude	123°	58'	17"

Note: Latitude and longitude coordinates shown are based on the North American Datum of 1927 (NAD 27) as currently required by the Mass Media Bureau of the FCC.

Ownership: Redwood Empire Public TV Inc.

Began Operation: February 17, 2009. Began analog operations: April 14, 1969. Ceased analog operations: February 17, 2009.

Personnel:

Ronald Schoenherr, Executive Director.

Karen Barnes, Assistant Manager & Programming Director.

Jeffrey Reinus, Underwriting Executive.

Joel M. Householter, Engineering Director.

Claire Reynolds, Community Relations & Outreach.

Therese Buck, Traffic Manager.

KVPT-DT
Fresno
Ch. 40

Licensee: Valley Public Television Inc., 1544 Van Ness Ave, Fresno, CA 93721.

Studio: 1544 Van Ness Ave, Fresno, CA 93721.

Mailing Address: 1544 Van Ness Ave, Fresno, CA 93721.

Phone: 559-266-1800. **Fax:** 559-650-1880.

Web Site: http://www.kvpt.org

Technical Facilities: Channel No. 40 (626-632 MHz). Authorized power: 250-kw max. visual, aural. Antenna: 2290-ft above av. terrain, 220-ft. above ground, 3615-ft. above sea level.

Latitude	36°	44'	45"
Longitude	119°	16'	51.6"

Note: Latitude and longitude coordinates shown are based on the North American Datum of 1927 (NAD 27) as currently required by the Mass Media Bureau of the FCC.

Ownership: Valley Public Television Inc.

Began Operation: September 1, 2004. Began analog operations: April 10, 1977. Ceased analog operations: February 17, 2009.

Personnel:

Paula Castadio, President & Chief Executive Officer.

Rodger Hixon, Chief Engineer.

Phyllis Brotherton, Senior Vice President & Chief Financial Officer.

Jerry Lee, Vice President, Programming & Communications.

David Getchell, Chief Development Officer.

Bob Tyrcha, Senior Producer.

Steven Lee, Traffic Manager.

Nancy Anderson, Membership Manager.

Denise Lanier, Educational Services & Outreach Coordinator.

KOCE-DT
Huntington Beach
Ch. 48

Licensee: KOCE-TV Foundation, 15751 Gothard St, Huntington Beach, CA 92647.

Studio: 15751 Gothard St, Huntington Beach, CA 92647.

Mailing Address: PO Box 2476, 15751 Gothard St, Huntington Beach, CA 92647.

Phone: 714-861-4300. **Fax:** 714-842-5790.

Web Site: http://www.koce.org

Technical Facilities: Channel No. 48 (674-680 MHz). Authorized power: 1000-kw max. visual, aural. Antenna: 3113-ft above av. terrain, 322-ft. above ground, 6029-ft. above sea level.

Latitude	34°	13'	35"
Longitude	118°	03'	57"

Note: Latitude and longitude coordinates shown are based on the North American Datum of 1927 (NAD 27) as currently required by the Mass Media Bureau of the FCC.

Ownership: KOCE-TV Foundation.

Began Operation: May 1, 2003. Began analog operations: November 20, 1972. Sale to present owner by Coast Community College District approved by FCC September 9, 2004. Ceased analog operations: June 12, 2009.

Personnel:

Mel Rogers, President & General Manager.

Ed Miskevich, Vice President & Station Manager.

Roger Yoakum, Chief Engineer.

Pat Petric, Broadcast Manager & Program Director.

Kurt Mische, Advancement Director.

Nicole Quirk, Traffic Manager.

Suzanne White, Viewer Services Director.

KCET-DT
Los Angeles
Ch. 28

Licensee: Community TV of Southern California, 4401 Sunset Blvd, Los Angeles, CA 90027.

Studio: 4401 Sunset Blvd, Los Angeles, CA 90027.

Mailing Address: 4401 Sunset Blvd, Los Angeles, CA 90027.

Phone: 323-666-6500. **Fax:** 323-953-5523.

Email: nrishagen@kcet.org **Web Site:** http://www.kcet.org

Technical Facilities: Channel No. 28 (554-560 MHz). Authorized power: 155-kw max. visual, aural. Antenna: 3039-ft above av. terrain, 330-ft. above ground, 5989-ft. above sea level.

| Latitude | 34° | 13' | 26" |
| Longitude | 118° | 03' | 44" |

Requests modification of CP for change to 220-kw max. visual; BMPEDT-20090206ACI.

Transmitter: 47 Audio Rd., Mount Wilson antenna farm, 15.5-mi. NE of Los Angeles.

Note: Latitude and longitude coordinates shown are based on the North American Datum of 1927 (NAD 27) as currently required by the Mass Media Bureau of the FCC.

Ownership: Community TV of Southern California.

Began Operation: April 1, 2002. Station broadcasting digitally on its analog channel allotment. Began analog operations: September 28, 1964. Ceased analog operations: June 12, 2009.

Personnel:

Al Jerome, President & Chief Executive Officer.

Deborah Hinton, Executive Vice President, Operations & Chief Financial Officer.

Laurel Lambert, Senior Vice President, Communications.

Mary Mazur, Senior Vice President, Programming & Production.

Susan Reardon, Senior Vice President & General Counsel.

Nancy Rishagen, Senior Vice President, Development.

Shawn Aminian, Vice President, Information Technology & Chief Information Officer.

Lourdes Nunez-Burgess, Vice President, Human Resources.

Jackie Kain, Vice President, New Media.

Gordon Bell, Vice President, Engineering & Operations.

Renee Williams, Vice President, Membership Marketing.

Val Zavala, Vice President, News & Public Affairs.

KLCS-DT
Los Angeles
Ch. 41

Licensee: Los Angeles Unified School District, PO Box 3307, Los Angeles, CA 90051.

Studio: 1061 W Temple St, Los Angeles, CA 90012.

Mailing Address: 1061 W Temple St, Los Angeles, CA 90012.

Phone: 213-241-4000. **Fax:** 213-481-1019.

Email: sabrina.thomas@lausd.net **Web Site:** http://www.klcs.org

Technical Facilities: Channel No. 41 (632-638 MHz). Authorized power: 162-kw max. visual, aural. Antenna: 2955-ft above av. terrain, 167-ft. above ground, 5823-ft. above sea level.

| Latitude | 34° | 13' | 26" |
| Longitude | 118° | 03' | 45" |

Requests modification of CP for change to 1000-kw max. visual; BMPEDT-20080620AIZ.

Holds CP for change to 156-kw max. visual, 2958-ft above av. terrain, 170-ft. above ground, 5826-ft. above sea level; BPEDT-20080326AJE.

Note: Latitude and longitude coordinates shown are based on the North American Datum of 1927 (NAD 27) as currently required by the Mass Media Bureau of the FCC.

Ownership: Los Angeles City Board of Education.

Began Operation: July 17, 2003. Began analog operations: November 5, 1973. Ceased analog operations: June 12, 2009.

Personnel:

Janalyn Glymph, General Manager.

Jorge Briseno, Classroom Instructional TV Director.

Sabrina Fair Thomas, Operations & Programming Director.

KIXE-DT
Redding
Ch. 9

Grantee: Northern California Educational TV Assn. Inc., 603 N. Market St, Redding, CA 96003.

Studio: 603 N Market St, Redding, CA 96003.

Mailing Address: 603 N Market St, Redding, CA 96003.

Phone: 530-243-5493. **Fax:** 530-243-7443.

Web Site: http://www.kixe.org

Technical Facilities: Channel No. 9 (186-192 MHz). Authorized power: 15-kw visual, aural. Antenna: 3579-ft above av. terrain, 86-ft. above ground, 6267-ft. above sea level.

| Latitude | 40° | 36' | 09" |
| Longitude | 122° | 39' | 01" |

Note: Latitude and longitude coordinates shown are based on the North American Datum of 1927 (NAD 27) as currently required by the Mass Media Bureau of the FCC.

Ownership: Northern California Educational TV Assn. Inc.

Began Operation: August 20, 2008. Station broadcasting digitally on its analog channel allotment. Began analog operations: October 5, 1964. Ceased analog operations: August 20, 2008.

Personnel:

Myron Tisdel, General Manager.

Mike Lampella, Operations Manager.

Susan Maxey, Chief Engineer.

Renee Cooper, Business & Personnel Manager.

Anne Kerns, Development Director.

Mike Herger, Production Manager.

Pauline Horne, Membership Coordinator.

Rob Keenan, Content Director.

Kitty Conners, Volunteer Coordinator.

KVIE-DT
Sacramento
Ch. 53

Licensee: KVIE Inc., PO Box 6, Sacramento, CA 95812-0006.

Studio: 2595 Capitol Oaks Dr, Sacramento, CA 95833.

Mailing Address: PO Box 6, Sacramento, CA 95812-0006.

Phones: 916-929-5843; 800-347-5843. **Fax:** 916-929-7215.

Web Site: http://www.kvie.org

Technical Facilities: Channel No. 53 (704-710 MHz). Authorized power: 360-kw max. visual, aural. Antenna: 1857-ft above av. terrain, 1860-ft. above ground, 1862-ft. above sea level.

| Latitude | 38° | 16' | 18" |
| Longitude | 121° | 30' | 18" |

Holds CP for change to channel number 9, 33-kw visual, 1958-ft above av. terrain, 1960-ft. above ground, 1962-ft. above sea level; BMPEDT-20080516ABR.

Transmitter: 1400 Twin Cities Rd., Walnut Grove.

Note: Latitude and longitude coordinates shown are based on the North American Datum of 1927 (NAD 27) as currently required by the Mass Media Bureau of the FCC.

Ownership: KVIE Inc.

Began Operation: July 6, 2006. Began analog operations: February 23, 1959. Ceased analog operations: June 12, 2009.

Personnel:

David Lowe, Interim President & General Manager.

Mike Sanford, Vice President, Content Production.

Michael Wall, Vice President, Technology.

Michelle Kuo Harris, Chief Financial Officer.

Margaret Stigers, Program & Broadcast Operations Director.

J. Greenberg, Executive Producer, Local Production.

KVCR-DT
San Bernardino
Ch. 26

Licensee: San Bernardino Community College District, 701 S. Mt. Vernon Ave, San Bernardino, CA 92410.

Studio: 701 S Mount Vernon Ave, San Bernardino, CA 92410-2798.

Mailing Address: 701 S Mt Vernon Ave, San Bernardino, CA 92410.

Phone: 909-384-4444. **Fax:** 909-885-2116.

Web Site: http://www.kvcr.org

Technical Facilities: Channel No. 26 (542-548 MHz). Authorized power: 475-kw max. visual, aural. Antenna: 1672-ft above av. terrain, 174-ft. above ground, 3125-ft. above sea level.

| Latitude | 33° | 57' | 57" |
| Longitude | 117° | 17' | 05" |

Transmitter: 10550 Box Springs Mountain Rd., Moreno Valley.

Note: Latitude and longitude coordinates shown are based on the North American Datum of 1927 (NAD 27) as currently required by the Mass Media Bureau of the FCC.

Ownership: San Bernardino Community College District.

Began Operation: May 1, 2003. Began analog operations: September 11, 1962. Ceased analog operations: June 12, 2009.

Personnel:

Larry Ciecalone, General Manager.

Kenn Couch, Station Manager.

Tom Guptill, Chief Engineer.

Benjamin Holland, Program Director.

Al Gondos, Producer & Director.

Lillian Vasquez, Marketing & Promotions Director.

Gina Guerrero, Executive Secretary.

KPBS-DT
San Diego
Ch. 30

Grantee: Board of Trustees, California State U. for San Diego State U., 5200 Campanile Dr, MC 5400, San Diego, CA 92182.

Studio: 5200 Campanile Dr, San Diego, CA 92182.

Mailing Address: 5200 Campanile Dr, San Diego State U., San Diego, CA 92182.

Phone: 619-594-1515. **Fax:** 619-594-3812.

Web Site: http://www.kpbs.org

Technical Facilities: Channel No. 30 (566-572 MHz). Authorized power: 350-kw max. visual, aural. Antenna: 1862-ft above av. terrain, 167-ft. above ground, 2661-ft. above sea level.

Latitude	32°	41'	53"
Longitude	116°	56'	03"

Note: Latitude and longitude coordinates shown are based on the North American Datum of 1927 (NAD 27) as currently required by the Mass Media Bureau of the FCC.

Ownership: California State U. for San Diego State U.

Began Operation: November 21, 2001. High Definition. Began analog operations: June 25, 1967. Ceased analog operations: June 12, 2009.

Personnel:

Doug Myrland, General Manager.

Nancy Worlie, Communications Director.

Leon Messenie, Chief Engineer.

Tom Karlo, Associate General Manager, Business, Finance & Operations.

Keith York, Program Director.

Deanna Martin Mackey, Associate General Manager, Marketing, Education & New Media.

Stephanie Bergsma, Development Director.

Anna Bunge, Traffic Manager.

KMTP-DT
San Francisco
Ch. 33

Grantee: Minority Television Project Inc., 1504 Bryant St, San Francisco, CA 94103.

Studio: 1504 Bryant St, San Francisco, CA 94103.

Mailing Address: 1504 Bryant St, San Francisco, CA 94103.

Phones: 415-777-3232; 650 254 1233. **Fax:** 415-552-3209.

Web Site: http://www.kmtp.org

Technical Facilities: Channel No. 33 (584-590 MHz). Authorized power: 500-kw max. visual, aural. Antenna: 1627-ft above av. terrain, 883-ft. above ground, 1715-ft. above sea level.

Latitude	37°	45'	19"
Longitude	122°	27'	06"

Note: Latitude and longitude coordinates shown are based on the North American Datum of 1927 (NAD 27) as currently required by the Mass Media Bureau of the FCC.

Ownership: Minority Television Project/Channel 32.

Began Operation: May 1, 2002. Standard Definition. Began analog operations: August 31, 1991. Ceased analog operations: June 12, 2009.

Personnel:

Booker Wade, General Manager.

Will Washington, Chief Engineer.

Arlene Stevens, Program Director.

KQED-DT
San Francisco
Ch. 30

Licensee: Northern California Public Broadcasting Inc., 2601 Mariposa St, San Francisco, CA 94110-1426.

Studio: 2601 Mariposa St, San Francisco, CA 94110-1426.

Mailing Address: 2601 Mariposa St, San Francisco, CA 94110-1426.

Phone: 415-864-2000. **Fax:** 415-553-2254.

Email: kacord@kqed.org **Web Site:** http://www.kqed.org/dtv

Technical Facilities: Channel No. 30 (566-572 MHz). Authorized power: 777-kw max. visual, aural. Antenna: 1434-ft above av. terrain, 702-ft. above ground, 1535-ft. above sea level.

Latitude	37°	45'	19"
Longitude	122°	27'	06"

Holds CP for change to 710-kw max. visual, 1679-ft above av. terrain, 946-ft. above ground, 1780-ft. above sea level; BPEDT-20080314ACI.

Transmitter: Sutro Tower, One La Avanzada Ave., San Francisco.

Note: Latitude and longitude coordinates shown are based on the North American Datum of 1927 (NAD 27) as currently required by the Mass Media Bureau of the FCC.

Multichannel TV Sound: Stereo and separate audio program.

Satellite Earth Stations: Harris; Standard Components; General Instrument.

Ownership: Northern California Public Broadcasting Inc.

Began Operation: April 1, 2000. Began analog operations: April 2, 1954. Current owner previously known as KQED Inc. Ceased analog operations: June 12, 2009.

Personnel:

Jeff Clarke, President & Chief Executive Officer.

Jeff Nemy, Chief Financial Officer.

Linda O'Bryon, Executive Vice President & Chief Content Officer.

Michael Isip, Vice President & Executive Director, TV & Educational Services.

Donald W. Derheim, Executive Vice President, Marketing.

Mitzie Kelly, Controller.

Margaret Berry, General Counsel & Corporate Secretary.

Lee Young, Engineering Manager.

Scott Walton, Communications Director.

KTEH-DT
San Jose
Ch. 50

Licensee: Northern California Public Broadcasting Inc., 2601 Mariposa St, San Francisco, CA 94110-1426.

Studio: 1585 Schallenberger Rd, San Jose, CA 95131.

Mailing Address: 1585 Schallenberger Rd, San Jose, CA 95131.

Phone: 408-795-5400. **Fax:** 408-995-5446.

Web Site: http://www.kteh.org

Technical Facilities: Channel No. 50 (686-692 MHz). Authorized power: 290-kw max. visual, aural. Antenna: 2172-ft above av. terrain, 476-ft. above ground, 2915-ft. above sea level.

Latitude	37°	29'	17"
Longitude	121°	51'	59"

Holds CP for change to 1000-kw max. visual, 2172-ft above av. terrain, 473-ft. above ground, 2912-ft. above sea level; BPEDT-20080620AKJ.

Transmitter: Monument Peak, 4.5-mi. NW of Milpitas.

Note: Latitude and longitude coordinates shown are based on the North American Datum of 1927 (NAD 27) as currently required by the Mass Media Bureau of the FCC.

Ownership: Northern California Public Broadcasting Inc.

Began Operation: August 1, 2004. Began analog operations: October 19, 1964. Sale to present owner (previously known as KQED Inc.) by KTEH Foundation approved by FCC July 28, 2006. Ceased analog operations: June 12, 2009.

Personnel:

Jeff Clarke, President.

Becca King-Reed, General Manager & Executive Producer.

Larry Voytilla, Chief Engineer.

Elizabeth Sharpe-Ramirez, Ready to Learn Coordinator.

Ken Patterson, Broadcast Scheduling Manager.

KCSM-DT
San Mateo
Ch. 43

Licensee: San Mateo County Community College District, 1700 W. Hillsdale Blvd, San Mateo, CA 94402.

Studio: 1700 W Hillsdale Blvd, San Mateo, CA 94402.

Mailing Address: 1700 W. Hillsdale Blvd, San Mateo, CA 94402.

Phone: 650-574-6586. **Fax:** 650-524-6975.

Web Site: http://www.kcsm.org

Technical Facilities: Channel No. 43 (644-650 MHz). Authorized power: 536-kw max. visual, aural. Antenna: 1404-ft above av. terrain, 673-ft. above ground, 1507-ft. above sea level.

Latitude	37°	45'	19.3"
Longitude	122°	27'	06.1"

Holds CP for change to 500-kw max. visual, 1678-ft above av. terrain, 946-ft. above ground, 1780-ft. above sea level; BPEDT-20080825AAV.

Transmitter: 900 Radio Rd., Bldg. 9, Tower 10, Daly City, San Bruno Mountain State Park.

Note: Latitude and longitude coordinates shown are based on the North American Datum of 1927 (NAD 27) as currently required by the Mass Media Bureau of the FCC.

Ownership: San Mateo County Community College District.

Began Operation: August 22, 2003. Began analog operations: October 12, 1964. Due to difficulties in renewing its transmitter site lease, ceased analog operations May 17, 2004.

Personnel:

Marilyn Lawrence, Station Manager.

Don Heckler, Chief Engineer.

James Ball, Business Manager.

Steve Opson, Program Director.

Sinclair Crockett, Development Executive & External Affairs Director.

Dante Betteo, Executive Producer.

Michele Muller, Technology Director.

KNXT-DT
Visalia
Ch. 50

Licensee: Diocese of Fresno Education Corp., 1550 N Fresno St, Fresno, CA 93703.

Studio: 1550 N Fresno St, Fresno, CA 93703.

Mailing Address: 1550 N. Fresno St, Fresno, CA 93703.

Phone: 559-448-7440. **Fax:** 559-488-7444.

Web Site: http://www.knxt.tv

Technical Facilities: Channel No. 50 (686-692 MHz). Authorized power: 185-kw max. visual, aural. Antenna: 2736-ft above av. terrain, 167-ft. above ground, 6053-ft. above sea level.

Latitude	36°	17'	14"
Longitude	118°	50'	17"

Note: Latitude and longitude coordinates shown are based on the North American Datum of 1927 (NAD 27) as currently required by the Mass Media Bureau of the FCC.

Ownership: Diocese of Fresno Education Corp.

Began Operation: July 6, 2006. Began analog operations: November 2, 1986. Ceased analog operations: June 12, 2009.

Personnel:

Colin Dougherty, General Manager.

Gary Temple, Chief Engineer.

Halfrid Nelson, Development Director.

Rosa Maria Henry, Operations Supervisor.

Susan Gibson, Traffic Manager.

Daniel Lopez, Production Supervisor.

KQET-DT
Watsonville
Ch. 25

Licensee: Northern California Public Broadcasting Inc., 2601 Mariposa St, San Francisco, CA 94110-1426.

Studio: 1585 Schallenberger Rd, San Jose, CA 95131.

Mailing Address: 1585 Schallenberger Rd, San Jose, CA 95131.

Phone: 408-795-5400. **Fax:** 408-995-5446.

Web Site: http://www.kteh.org

Technical Facilities: Channel No. 25 (536-542 MHz). Authorized power: 81.1-kw max. visual, aural. Antenna: 2292-ft above av. terrain, 153-ft. above ground, 3230-ft. above sea level.

Latitude	36°	45'	22.9"
Longitude	121°	30'	04.9"

Note: Latitude and longitude coordinates shown are based on the North American Datum of 1927 (NAD 27) as currently required by the Mass Media Bureau of the FCC.

Ownership: Northern California Public Broadcasting Inc.

Began Operation: March 1, 2003. Station broadcasting digitally on its analog channel allotment. Began analog operations: November 19, 1989. Left air, date unreported due to financial difficulties. Returned to air September 28, 2001. Sale to present owner (previously known as KQED Inc.) by KTEH Foundation approved by FCC July 28, 2006. Ceased analog operations: June 12, 2009.

Personnel:

Jeff Clarke, President.

Becca King-Reid, General Manager & Executive Producer.

Larry Voytilla, Engineering Director.

Ken Patterson, Broadcast Scheduling Manager.

Colorado

KBDI-DT
Broomfield
Ch. 13

Grantee: Colorado Public Television Inc., 2900 Welton St, First Fl, Denver, CO 80205.

Studio: 2900 Welton St, First Fl, Denver, CO 80205.

Mailing Address: 2900 Welton St, First Fl, Denver, CO 80205.

Phones: 303-296-1212; 800-727-8812. **Fax:** 303-296-6650.

Web Site: http://www.kbdi.org

Technical Facilities: Channel No. 13 (210-216 MHz). Authorized power: 34.4-kw visual, aural. Antenna: 2428-ft above av. terrain, 77-ft. above ground, 11510-ft. above sea level.

Latitude	39°	40'	55"
Longitude	105°	29'	49"

Note: Latitude and longitude coordinates shown are based on the North American Datum of 1927 (NAD 27) as currently required by the Mass Media Bureau of the FCC.

Ownership: Colorado Public Television Inc.

Began Operation: May 1, 2003. Began analog operations: February 22, 1980. Ceased analog operations: February 17, 2009.

Personnel:

Willard Roland, President & General Manager.

Kim Johnson, Vice President, Broadcast Operations.

Kirby McClure, Traffic & Communications Manager.

Paula DeGroat, Business Manager.

Brad Haug, Program Manager.

Darrow Hodges, Vice President, Marketing & Development.

Paula Roth, Corporate Support Director.

Dominic Dezzutti, Production Manager.

Shari Bernson, Membership Director.

KRMA-DT
Denver
Ch. 18

Licensee: Rocky Mountain Public Broadcasting Network Inc., 1089 Bannock St, Denver, CO 80204-9972.

Studio: 1089 Bannock St, Denver, CO 80204.

Mailing Address: 1089 Bannock St, Denver, CO 80204.

Phone: 303-892-6666. **Fax:** 303-620-5600.

Email: claudia_dunning@krma.pbs.org **Web Site:** http://www.krma.org

Technical Facilities: Channel No. 18 (494-500 MHz). Authorized power: 1000-kw max. visual, aural. Antenna: 1115-ft above av. terrain, 85-ft. above ground, 7746-ft. above sea level.

Latitude	39°	40'	25"
Longitude	105°	13'	01"

Holds CP for change to 1129-ft above av. terrain, 85-ft. above ground, 7746-ft. above sea level; BMPEDT-20080825AAI.

Note: Latitude and longitude coordinates shown are based on the North American Datum of 1927 (NAD 27) as currently required by the Mass Media Bureau of the FCC.

Ownership: Rocky Mountain Public Broadcasting Network Inc.

Began Operation: December 1, 1999. High Definition. Began analog operations: January 30, 1956. Ceased analog operations: June 12, 2009.

Personnel:

James Morgese, President & General Manager.

John Anderson, Chief Engineer.

Bill Wengert, Administration & Finance Director.

Donna Sanford, Program & Production Director.

Pam Osborne, Marketing & Communications Director.

Suzanne Banning, Development Director.

Michelle Mesmith, Traffic Manager.

Cynthia Hessin, Executive Producer, Public Affairs.

KRMT-DT
Denver
Ch. 40

Licensee: Word of God Fellowship Inc., 3901 Hwy 121 S, Bedford, TX 76021-3009.

Studio: 12014 W 64th Ave, Arvada, CO 80004.

Mailing Address: 12014 W. 64th Ave, Arvada, CO 80004.

Phone: 303-423-4141. **Fax:** 303-424-0571.

Web Site: http://www.daystar.com

Technical Facilities: Channel No. 40 (626-632 MHz). Authorized power: 74.8-kw max. visual, aural. Antenna: 1129-ft above av. terrain, 151-ft. above ground, 7999-ft. above sea level.

Latitude	39°	35'	59"
Longitude	105°	12'	35"

Holds CP for change to 1000-kw max. visual; BPEDT-20080619AAR.

Transmitter: End of S. Turkey Creek Rd. Extension.

Note: Latitude and longitude coordinates shown are based on the North American Datum of 1927 (NAD 27) as currently required by the Mass Media Bureau of the FCC.

Ownership: Word of God Fellowship Inc.

Began Operation: December 21, 2006. Began analog operations: August 20, 1988. Ceased analog operations: June 12, 2009.

Personnel:

Robert Saraduke, Operations Manager.

Kevin Russell, Facility Manager.

KRMU-DT
Durango
Ch. 20

Grantee: Rocky Mountain Public Broadcasting Network Inc., 1089 Bannock St, Denver, CO 80204-9972.

Studio: 1089 Bannock St, Denver, CO 80204.

Mailing Address: 1089 Bannock St, Denver, CO 80204.

Phone: 303-892-6666. **Fax:** 303-620-5600.

Email: claudia_dunning@krma.pbs.org **Web Site:** http://www.krma.org

Technical Facilities: Channel No. 20 (506-512 MHz). Authorized power: 12.6-kw max. visual, aural. Antenna: 427-ft above av. terrain, 49-ft. above ground, 7753-ft. above sea level.

Latitude	37°	15'	46"
Longitude	107°	53'	58"

Note: Latitude and longitude coordinates shown are based on the North American Datum of 1927 (NAD 27) as currently required by the Mass Media Bureau of the FCC.

Ownership: Rocky Mountain Public Broadcasting Network Inc.

Began Operation: July 8, 2005. Station operating digitally on its analog channel allotment; no analog broadcast.

Personnel:

James Morgese, President & General Manager.

John Anderson, Chief Engineer.

Bill Wengert, Administration & Finance Director.

Donna Sanford, Program & Production Director.

Pam Osborne, Marketing & Communications Director.

Suzanne Banning, Development Director.

Michelle Mesmith, Traffic Manager.

Cynthia Hessin, Executive Producer, Public Affairs.

KRMJ-DT
Grand Junction
Ch. 18

Licensee: Rocky Mountain Public Broadcasting Network Inc., 1089 Bannock St, Denver, CO 80204-9972.

Studio: 2520 Blichmann, Grand Junction, CO 81505.

Mailing Address: 1089 Bannock St, Denver, CO 80204.

Phone: 303-892-6666. **Fax:** 303-620-5600.

Email: john_anderson@krma.pbs.org **Web Site:** http://www.rmpbs.org

Technical Facilities: Channel No. 18 (494-500 MHz). Authorized power: 50-kw max. visual, aural. Antenna: 1342-ft above av. terrain, 151-ft. above ground, 7231-ft. above sea level.

Latitude	39°	03'	58"
Longitude	108°	44'	43"

Note: Latitude and longitude coordinates shown are based on the North American Datum of 1927 (NAD 27) as currently required by the Mass Media Bureau of the FCC.

Ownership: Rocky Mountain Public Broadcasting Network Inc.

Began Operation: June 29, 2006. Station broadcasting digitally on its analog channel allotment. Began analog operations: January 1, 1997. Ceased analog operations prior to original digital transition date of February 17, 2009.

Personnel:

James Morgese, President & General Manager.

John Anderson, Chief Engineer.

Bill Wengert, Administration & Finance Director.

Donna Sanford, Program & Production Director.

Pam Osborne, Marketing & Communications Director.

Suzanne Banning, Development Director.

Michelle Mesmith, Traffic Manager.

Cynthia Hessin, Executive Producer, Public Affairs.

KTSC-DT
Pueblo
Ch. 8

Licensee: Rocky Mountain Public Broadcasting Network Inc., 1089 Bannock St, Denver, CO 80204-9972.

Studio: 2200 Bonforte Blvd, Pueblo, CO 81001.

Mailing Address: 1089 Bannock St, Denver, CO 80204.

Phone: 303-892-6666. **Fax:** 303-620-5600.

Email: customer_service@ktsc.pbs.org **Web Site:** http://www.rmpbs.org

Technical Facilities: Channel No. 8 (180-186 MHz). Authorized power: 22.4-kw visual, aural. Antenna: 2362-ft above av. terrain, 322-ft. above ground, 9731-ft. above sea level.

Latitude	38°	44'	43"
Longitude	104°	51'	39"

Note: Latitude and longitude coordinates shown are based on the North American Datum of 1927 (NAD 27) as currently required by the Mass Media Bureau of the FCC.

Ownership: Rocky Mountain Public Broadcasting Network Inc.

Began Operation: July 26, 2006. Station broadcasting digitally on its analog channel allotment. Began analog operations: February 3, 1971. Ceased analog operations: June 12, 2009.

Personnel:

James Morgese, President & General Manager.

John Anderson, Chief Engineer.

Bill Wengert, Administration & Finance Director.

Donna Sanford, Program & Production Director.

Pam Osborne, Marketing & Communications Director.

Suzanne Banning, Development Director.

Cynthia Hessin, Executive Producer, Public Affairs.

Michelle Mesmith, Traffic Manager.

KRMZ-DT
Steamboat Springs
Ch. 10

Licensee: Rocky Mountain Public Broadcasting Network Inc., 1089 Bannock St, Denver, CO 80204-9972.

Studio: 1089 Bannock St, Denver, CO 80204.

Mailing Address: 1089 Bannock St, Denver, CO 80204.

Phone: 303-892-6666. **Fax:** 303-620-5600.

Email: claudia_dunning@krma.pbs.org **Web Site:** http://www.rmpbs.org

Technical Facilities: Channel No. 10 (192-198 MHz). Authorized power: 0.481-kw visual, aural. Antenna: 575-ft above av. terrain, 53-ft. above ground, 8308-ft. above sea level.

Latitude	40°	27'	43"
Longitude	106°	50'	57"

Note: Latitude and longitude coordinates shown are based on the North American Datum of 1927 (NAD 27) as currently required by the Mass Media Bureau of the FCC.

Ownership: Rocky Mountain Public Broadcasting Network Inc.

Began Operation: July 11, 2006. Began analog operations: March 1, 1988. Sale to F & I TV Inc. approved by FCC January 15, 1992. Sale to Green TV Corp. by F & I TV Inc. approved by FCC June 1, 1995. Sale to Council Tree Communications by Green TV Corp. approved by FCC March 8, 2000. Sale to Telemundo Holdings Inc. by Council Tree Communications approved by FCC November 17, 2000. Transfer to NBC Universal by Telemundo Holdings Inc. approved by FCC April 10, 2002. KMAS-TV was knocked off air late November 2006 due to severe weather. Sale to present owner by NBC Universal approved by FCC February 2, 2007. After sale, station converted to non-commercial status. Station returned to air September 13, 2007. Ceased analog operations: February 17, 2009.

Personnel:

James Morgese, President & General Manager.

John Anderson, Chief Engineer.

Bill Wengert, Administration & Finance Director.

Donna Sanford, Program & Production Director.

Pam Osborne, Marketing & Communications Director.

Suzanne Banning, Development Director.

Michelle Mesmith, Traffic Manager.

Cynthia Hessin, Executive Producer, Public Affairs.

Connecticut

WEDW-DT
Bridgeport
Ch. 49

Licensee: Connecticut Public Broadcasting Inc., 1049 Asylum Ave, Hartford, CT 06105.

Studio: 1049 Asylum Ave, Hartford, CT 06105.

Mailing Address: 1049 Asylum Ave, Hartford, CT 06105.

Phones: 860-278-5310; 203-777-7506. **Fax:** 860-275-7483.

Web Site: http://www.cptv.org

Technical Facilities: Channel No. 49 (680-686 MHz). Authorized power: 91-kw max. visual, aural. Antenna: 728-ft above av. terrain, 476-ft. above ground, 1004-ft. above sea level.

Latitude	41°	16'	44"
Longitude	73°	11'	08"

Note: Latitude and longitude coordinates shown are based on the North American Datum of 1927 (NAD 27) as currently required by the Mass Media Bureau of the FCC.

Satellite Earth Station: Comark; Vertex, 8.2-meter Ku-band; Scientific-Atlanta receivers.

Ownership: Connecticut Public Broadcasting Inc.

Began Operation: February 17, 2009. Station broadcasting digitally on its analog channel allotment. Began analog operations: December 17, 1967. Ceased analog operations: February 17, 2009.

Personnel:

Jerry Franklin, President & Chief Executive Officer.

John Dankosky, News Director.

Joe Zareski, Chief Engineer.

Meg Sakellarides, Senior Vice President & Chief Financial Officer.

Larry Rifkin, Senior Vice President & National Programming Officer.

Jay Whitsett, Senior Vice President, Programming & Station Manager.

Nancy Bauer, Vice President, Sales & Corporate Sponsorships.

Dean Orton, Senior Vice President, Development & Media Services.

Joanne Whitehead, Program Director, CPTV.

Phyllis Serafin, Marketing Services Manager.

Carol Sisco, Corporate Communications Director.

WEDH-DT
Hartford
Ch. 45

Grantee: Connecticut Public Broadcasting Inc., 1049 Asylum Ave, Hartford, CT 06105.

Studio: 1049 Asylum Av, Hartford, CT 06105.

Mailing Address: 1049 Asylum Ave, Hartford, CT 06105.

Phones: 860-278-5310; 203-777-7506. **Fax:** 860-275-7483.

Web Site: http://www.cptv.org

Technical Facilities: Channel No. 45 (656-662 MHz). Authorized power: 490-kw max. visual, aural. Antenna: 1657-ft above av. terrain, 1273-ft. above ground, 1982-ft. above sea level.

Latitude	41°	42'	13"
Longitude	72°	49'	57"

Note: Latitude and longitude coordinates shown are based on the North American Datum of 1927 (NAD 27) as currently required by the Mass Media Bureau of the FCC.

Ownership: Connecticut Public Broadcasting Inc.

Began Operation: June 12, 2009. Began analog operations: October 1, 1962. Ceased analog operations: June 12, 2009.

Personnel:

Jerry Franklin, President & Chief Executive Officer.

Joe Zareski, Chief Engineer.

John Danokosky, News Director.

Meg Sakellarides, Senior Vice President & Chief Financial Officer.

Larry Rifkin, Senior Vice President & National Programming Officer.

Jay Whitsett, Senior Vice President, Programming & Station Manager.

Nancy Bauer, Vice President, Sales & Corporate Sponsorships.

Dean Orton, Senior Vice President, Development & Media Services.

Joanne Whitehead, Program Director, CPTV.

Phyllis Serafin, Marketing Services Manager.

Carol Sisco, Corporate Communications Director.

WEDY-DT
New Haven
Ch. 6

Grantee: Connecticut Public Broadcasting Inc., 1049 Asylum Ave, Hartford, CT 06105.

Studio: 1049 Asylum Ave, Hartford, CT 06105.

Mailing Address: 1049 Asylum Ave, Hartford, CT 06105.

Phone: 860-278-5310. **Fax:** 860-275-7483.

Web Site: http://www.cptv.org

Technical Facilities: Channel No. 6 (82-88 MHz). Authorized power: 0.4-kw visual, aural. Antenna: 289-ft above av. terrain, 89-ft. above ground, 340-ft. above sea level.

Latitude	41°	19'	42"
Longitude	72°	54'	25"

Note: Latitude and longitude coordinates shown are based on the North American Datum of 1927 (NAD 27) as currently required by the Mass Media Bureau of the FCC.

Ownership: Connecticut Public Broadcasting Inc.

Began Operation: June 12, 2009. Began analog operations: December 1, 1974. Ceased analog operations: July 31, 2005 due to equipment failure.

Personnel:

Jerry Franklin, President & Chief Executive Officer.

Larry Rifkin, Senior Vice President & National Programming Officer.

Meg Sakellarides, Senior Vice President & Chief Financial Officer.

Jay Whitsett, Senior Vice President, Programming.

Dean Orton, Senior Vice President, Development & Media Services.

Nancy Bauer, Vice President, Sales & Corporate Sponsorships.

Carol Sisco, Corporate Communications Director.

John Dankosky, News Director.

Joe Zareski, Chief Engineer.

Joann Whitehead, Program Manager, CPTV.

Phyllis Serafin, Marketing Services Manager.

WEDN-DT
Norwich
Ch. 45

Licensee: Connecticut Public Broadcasting Inc., 1049 Asylum Ave, Hartford, CT 06105.

Studio: 1049 Asylum Ave, Hartford, CT 06105.

Mailing Address: 1049 Asylum Ave, Hartford, CT 06105.

Phones: 860-278-5310; 203-277-7506. **Fax:** 860-275-7483.

Web Site: http://www.cptv.org

Technical Facilities: Channel No. 45 (656-662 MHz). Authorized power: 200-kw max. visual, aural. Antenna: 630-ft above av. terrain, 423-ft. above ground, 933-ft. above sea level.

| Latitude | 41° | 31' | 14" |
| Longitude | 72° | 10' | 03" |

Holds CP for change to channel number 9, 4.2-kw visual, 630-ft above av. terrain, 423-ft. above ground, 932-ft. above sea level; BPEDT-20080619AFA.

Note: Latitude and longitude coordinates shown are based on the North American Datum of 1927 (NAD 27) as currently required by the Mass Media Bureau of the FCC.

Ownership: Connecticut Public Broadcasting Inc.

Began Operation: April 25, 2003. Began analog operations: March 5, 1967. Ceased analog operations: June 12, 2009.

Personnel:

Jerry Franklin, President & Chief Executive Officer.

John Dankosky, News Director.

Joe Zareski, Chief Engineer.

Meg Sakellarides, Senior Vice President & Chief Financial Officer.

Larry Rifkin, Senior Vice President & National Programming Officer.

Jay Whitsett, Senior Vice President, Programming & Station Manager.

Nancy Bauer, Vice President, Sales & Corporate Sponsorships.

Dean Orton, Senior Vice President, Development & Media Services.

Joann Whitehead, Program Manager, CPTV.

Carol Sisco, Corporate Comunications Director.

Phyllis Serafin, Marketing Services Manager.

Delaware

WDPB-DT
Seaford
Ch. 44

Licensee: WHYY Inc., 625 Orange St, Wilmington, DE 19801.

Studio: 625 Orange St, Wilmington, DE 19801.

Mailing Address: 150 N. 6th St, Independence Mall West, Philadelphia, PA 19106.

Phones: 302-888-1200; 215-351-1200. **Fax:** 302-575-0346.

Web Site: http://www.whyy.org

Technical Facilities: Channel No. 44 (650-656 MHz). Authorized power: 98-kw max. visual, aural. Antenna: 643-ft above av. terrain, 643-ft. above ground, 673-ft. above sea level.

| Latitude | 38° | 39' | 15" |
| Longitude | 75° | 36' | 42" |

Note: Latitude and longitude coordinates shown are based on the North American Datum of 1927 (NAD 27) as currently required by the Mass Media Bureau of the FCC.

Ownership: WHYY Inc.

Began Operation: June 24, 2005. Began analog operations: December 4, 1981. Ceased analog operations: June 12, 2009.

Personnel:

William J. Marrazzo, President & Chief Executive Officer.

Christine Dempsey, Vice President & Chief Content Officer.

Bruce Flamm, Vice President & Chief Operations Officer.

William J. Weber, Vice President & Chief Technology Officer.

Kerri Hanlon, Vice President & Chief Marketing Officer.

Micheline Boudreau, News Director.

John Doran, Chief Engineer.

Kevin Yashioka, Business Manager.

Art Ellis, Promotion Director.

Susan M. Poglinco, Children's Services Director.

John Lamb, Traffic Manager.

WHYY-DT
Wilmington
Ch. 12

Grantee: WHYY Inc., 150 N 6th St, Philadelphia, PA 19106.

Studios: 625 Orange St, Wilmington, DE 19801; Independence Mall West, 150 N. 6th St, Philadelphia, PA 19106.

Mailing Address: 150 N. 6th St, Independence Mall West, PA 19106.

Phones: 215-351-1200; 302-888-1200. **Fax:** 215-351-0398.

Web Site: http://www.whyy.org

Technical Facilities: Channel No. 12 (204-210 MHz). Authorized power: 20-kw visual, aural. Antenna: 965-ft above av. terrain, 958-ft. above ground, 1178-ft. above sea level.

| Latitude | 40° | 02' | 30" |
| Longitude | 75° | 14' | 23" |

Transmitter: 329 Domino Lane, Philadelphia, PA.

Note: Latitude and longitude coordinates shown are based on the North American Datum of 1927 (NAD 27) as currently required by the Mass Media Bureau of the FCC.

Ownership: WHYY Inc.

Began Operation: March 17, 2003. High Definition. Station broadcasting digitally on its analog channel allotment. Began analog operations: September 12, 1963. Ceased analog operations: June 12, 2009.

Personnel:

William J. Marrazzo, President & Chief Executive Officer.

Christine Dempsey, Vice President & Chief Content Officer.

Bruce Flamm, Vice President & Chief Operating Officer.

Micheline Boudreau, News Director.

William J. Weber, Vice President & Chief Technology Officer.

Kerri Hanlon, Vice President & Chief Marketing Officer.

John Doran, Chief Engineer.

Kevin Yashioka, Business Manager.

Art Ellis, Promotion Director.

John Lamb, Traffic Manager.

Susan M. Poglinco, Children's Services Director.

District of Columbia

WETA-DT
Washington
Ch. 27

Licensee: Greater Washington Educational Telecommunications Assn., PO Box 2626, 2775 S Quincy St, Arlington, VA 22206.

Studio: 2775 S. Quincy St., Arlington, VA 22206.

Mailing Address: 2775 S. Quincy St, Arlington, VA 22206.

Phone: 703-998-2600. **Fax:** 703-998-3401.

Web Site: http://www.weta.org

Technical Facilities: Channel No. 27 (548-554 MHz). Authorized power: 90-kw max. visual, aural. Antenna: 833-ft above av. terrain, 663-ft. above ground, 1073-ft. above sea level.

| Latitude | 38° | 57' | 01" |
| Longitude | 77° | 04' | 47" |

Transmitter: 5217 19th Rd. N, Arlington, VA.

Note: Latitude and longitude coordinates shown are based on the North American Datum of 1927 (NAD 27) as currently required by the Mass Media Bureau of the FCC.

Ownership: Greater Washington Educational Telecommunications Association.

Began Operation: November 1, 1998. Began analog operations: October 2, 1961. Ceased analog operations: June 12, 2009.

Personnel:

Sharon Percy Rockefeller, President & Chief Executive Officer.

Frank Fitzmaurice, General Manager.

Kevin Harris, Vice President & Station Manager.

Joseph Bruns, Executive Vice President & Chief Operating Officer.

Katherine Benson, Vice President, Eastern Sales.

Jeff Beiber, Vice President, News & Public Affairs Programming.

Lew Zager, Vice President, Technology.

Polly Heath, Senior Vice President & Chief Financial Officer.

Joe Cook, Vice President, Chief Financial Officer.

Dalton Delan, Executive Vice President & Chief Programming Officer.

David Thompson, Vice President, Cultural Programming & New Media.

Karen Fritz, Vice President, Programming Development & Syndication.

Cathy Sterling, Vice President, Development.

Susan Richmond, Senior Vice President, Individual Giving.

Mary Stewart, Vice President, Communications.

Lisa Lindstrom Delaney, Vice President, Legal Matters.

Fern Barrow, Community Affairs.

WHUT-DT
Washington
Ch. 33

Grantee: Howard U., 2222 4th St. NW, Washington, DC 20059.

Studio: 2222 4th St., NW, Washington, DC 20059.

Mailing Address: 2222 4th St. NW, Washington, DC 20059.

Phone: 202-806-3200. **Fax:** 202-806-3300.

Web Site: http://www.whut.org

Technical Facilities: Channel No. 33 (584-590 MHz). Authorized power: 1000-kw max. visual, aural. Antenna: 833-ft above av. terrain, 664-ft. above ground, 1073-ft. above sea level.

| Latitude | 38° | 57' | 01" |
| Longitude | 77° | 04' | 47" |

Note: Latitude and longitude coordinates shown are based on the North American Datum of 1927 (NAD 27) as currently required by the Mass Media Bureau of the FCC.

Ownership: Howard University.

Began Operation: October 18, 2007. Began analog operations: November 17, 1980. Ceased analog operations: June 12, 2009.

Personnel:

Jennifer Lawson, General Manager & Business Manager.

Luma Haj, Operations Director.

David Martin, Chief Engineer.

Diane Robertson, Programming Director.

Cody Cox, Production Manager.

Kim Johnson, Research Librarian.

Florida

WBEC-DT
Boca Raton
Ch. 40

Grantee: School Board of Broward County, FL, 14444 66th St. N, Clearwater, FL 33764.

Mailing Address: 6600 SW Nova Dr, Fort Lauderdale, FL 33317.

Phone: 754-321-1000. **Fax:** 754-321-1180.

Web Site: http://www.becon.tv

Technical Facilities: Channel No. 40 (626-632 MHz). Authorized power: 1000-kw max. visual, aural. Antenna: 935-ft above av. terrain, 932-ft. above ground, 943-ft. above sea level.

Latitude	25°	59'	08.7"
Longitude	80°	11'	37.1"

Note: Latitude and longitude coordinates shown are based on the North American Datum of 1927 (NAD 27) as currently required by the Mass Media Bureau of the FCC.

Ownership: School Board of Broward County, Florida.

Began Operation: December 20, 2007. Began analog operations: May 19, 2000. Ceased analog operations: June 12, 2009.

Personnel:

Chris Bartch, Station Manager.

Andy Furlong, Engineering Manager.

Noel Hyatt, Marketing Coordinator.

Tom Ford, Traffic Manager.

Eric Powell, Production Manager.

WBCC-DT
Cocoa
Ch. 30

Licensee: Brevard Community College, 1519 Clearlake Rd, Cocoa, FL 32922.

Studio: 1519 Clearlake Rd, Cocoa, FL 32922.

Mailing Address: 1519 Clearlake Rd, Cocoa, FL 32922.

Phone: 321-433-7110. **Fax:** 321-433-7154.

Web Site: http://www.wbcctv.org

Technical Facilities: Channel No. 30 (566-572 MHz). Authorized power: 182-kw max. visual, aural. Antenna: 1542-ft above av. terrain, 1516-ft. above ground, 1640-ft. above sea level.

Latitude	28°	35'	12"
Longitude	81°	04'	58"

Note: Latitude and longitude coordinates shown are based on the North American Datum of 1927 (NAD 27) as currently required by the Mass Media Bureau of the FCC.

Ownership: Brevard Community College.

Began Operation: April 30, 2003. Began analog operations: June 18, 1987. Ceased analog operations: February 17, 2009.

Personnel:

Dr. James Drake, District President.

Joe Williams, Associate Vice President, Telecommunication.

Phillip Wallace, General Manager.

Anthony Padgett, Chief Engineer.

Doug Grover, Production Manager.

Glenn Brady, Traffic Manager.

WGCU-DT
Fort Myers
Ch. 31

Licensee: State Board of Regents acting for & on behalf of Florida Gulf Coast U., 10501 FGCU Blvd. S, Fort Myers, FL 33965.

Studio: 10501 FGCU Blvd. S, Fort Meyers, FL 33965-6565.

Mailing Address: 10501 FGCU Blvd. S, Fort Myers, FL 33965-6565.

Phone: 239-590-2300. **Fax:** 239-590-2310.

Web Site: http://www.wgcu.org

Technical Facilities: Channel No. 31 (572-578 MHz). Authorized power: 50-kw max. visual, aural. Antenna: 906-ft above av. terrain, 900-ft. above ground, 930-ft. above sea level.

Latitude	26°	48'	54"
Longitude	81°	45'	43"

Holds CP for change to 63-kw max. visual; BPEDT-20080317AFZ.

Note: Latitude and longitude coordinates shown are based on the North American Datum of 1927 (NAD 27) as currently required by the Mass Media Bureau of the FCC.

Ownership: Florida Gulf Coast U. Board of Regents.

Began Operation: February 26, 2003. Began analog operations: August 15, 1983. Ceased analog operations: June 12, 2009.

Personnel:

Kathleen B. Davey, General Manager.

Amy Tardif, Station Manager & News Director.

Rick Carroll, Chief Engineer.

Iris Gerstle, Finance Director.

Toby Cooke, Program & Promotion Director.

Sheri Coleman, Television Production Services Director.

Sharon Striker, Traffic Manager.

WTCE-DT
Fort Pierce
Ch. 38

Licensee: Jacksonville Educators Broadcasting Inc., 10902 S Wilcrest Dr, Houston, TX 77099.

Studio: 3601 N. 25th St, Fort Pierce, FL 34946-8604.

Mailing Address: 3601 N. 25th St, Fort Pierce, FL 34946-8604.

Phone: 772-489-2701. **Fax:** 772-489-6833.

Web Site: http://www.wtce.tv

Technical Facilities: Channel No. 38 (614-620 MHz). Authorized power: 756-kw max. visual, aural. Antenna: 974-ft above av. terrain, 968-ft. above ground, 984-ft. above sea level.

Latitude	27°	01'	32"
Longitude	80°	10'	43"

Holds CP for change to 1000-kw max. visual; BPEDT-20080618ACY.

Note: Latitude and longitude coordinates shown are based on the North American Datum of 1927 (NAD 27) as currently required by the Mass Media Bureau of the FCC.

Ownership: Jacksonville Educators Broadcasting Inc.

Began Operation: February 24, 2003. Began analog operations: May 9, 1990. Ceased analog operations: June 12, 2009.

Personnel:

Charles Massi, General Manager.

Steve Chan, Chief Engineer.

Marina Santos, Office Manager.

WUFT-DT
Gainesville
Ch. 36

Grantee: Board of Trustees, State of Florida, acting for and on behalf of the U. of Florida, PO Box 118405, 2200 Weimer Hall, Gainesville, FL 32611-8405.

Studio: 1200 Weimer Hall, U. of Florida, Gainesville, FL 32611.

Mailing Address: PO Box 118405, Gainesville, FL 32611.

Phone: 352-392-5551. **Fax:** 352-392-5731.

Web Site: http://www.wuft.org

Technical Facilities: Channel No. 36 (602-608 MHz). Authorized power: 1000-kw max. visual, aural. Antenna: 863-ft above av. terrain, 807-ft. above ground, 988-ft. above sea level.

Latitude	29°	42'	34"
Longitude	82°	23'	40"

Transmitter: 4732 N.W. 53rd Ave.

Note: Latitude and longitude coordinates shown are based on the North American Datum of 1927 (NAD 27) as currently required by the Mass Media Bureau of the FCC.

Ownership: U. of Florida.

Began Operation: March 4, 2004. Began analog operations: November 17, 1958. Ceased analog operations: June 12, 2009.

Personnel:

Larry Dankner, Interim General Manager.

Titus Rush, Station Manager.

Tim Brueckner, Operations Director.

Mark Leeps, News Director.

Robert Carr, Engineering Director.

Bob Wood, Engineering Manager.

LaWanna Duncan, Finance & Administration Director.

Jodi Floyd, Program Director & Viewer Services Coordinator.

Susan Wagner, Communications Director.

Brent Williams, Development Director.

Frank Counts, Executive Producer.

Merline Durant, Traffic Manager.

Harvey Ward, Corporate Support Director.

Debbie Booth, Membership Manager.

WJCT-DT
Jacksonville
Ch. 7

Licensee: WJCT Inc., 100 Festival Park Ave, Jacksonville, FL 32202.

Studio: 100 Festival Park Ave, Jacksonville, FL 32202.

Mailing Address: 100 Festival Park Ave, Jacksonville, FL 32202.

Phone: 904-353-7770. **Fax:** 904-353-4830.

Web Site: http://www.wjct.org

Technical Facilities: Channel No. 7 (174-180 MHz). Authorized power: 18-kw visual, aural. Antenna: 991-ft above av. terrain, 1001-ft. above ground, 1010-ft. above sea level.

Latitude	30°	16'	51"
Longitude	81°	34'	12"

Note: Latitude and longitude coordinates shown are based on the North American Datum of 1927 (NAD 27) as currently required by the Mass Media Bureau of the FCC.

Ownership: WJCT Inc.

Began Operation: September 27, 2004. Station broadcasting digitally on its analog channel allotment. Began analog operations: September 10, 1958. Ceased analog operations: June 12, 2009.

Personnel:

Michael T. Boylan, President & Chief Executive Officer.

Rick Johnson, Senior Vice President, TV/FM.

Bob Culkeen, Vice President, Technology & Operations.

Jocelyn Enriques, Vice President, Finance.

Geri Cirillo, Vice President, Corporate Support.

Carla Marlier, Vice President, External Affairs.

Melanie Carriere, Membership Services Manager.

WJEB-DT
Jacksonville
Ch. 44

Licensee: Jacksonville Educators Broadcasting Inc., PO Box 5219, Jacksonville, FL 32247.

Studio: 3101 Emerson Expwy, Jacksonville, FL 32207-4965.

Mailing Address: PO Box 5219, Jacksonville, FL 32247-5219.

Phone: 904-399-8413. **Fax:** 904-399-8423.

Web Site: http://www.wjeb.org

Technical Facilities: Channel No. 44 (650-656 MHz). Authorized power: 715-kw max. visual, aural. Antenna: 771-ft above av. terrain, 758-ft. above ground, 786-ft. above sea level.

Latitude	30°	16'	34"
Longitude	81°	33'	53"

Holds CP for change to 1000-kw max. visual, 945-ft above av. terrain, 932-ft. above ground, 962-ft. above sea level lat. 30° 16' 34", long. 81° 33' 52"; BPEDT-20080618ADQ.

Note: Latitude and longitude coordinates shown are based on the North American Datum of 1927 (NAD 27) as currently required by the Mass Media Bureau of the FCC.

Ownership: Jacksonville Educators Broadcasting Inc.

Began Operation: March 13, 2006. Began analog operations: May 29, 1991. Ceased analog operations: June 12, 2009.

Personnel:

Collette Snowden, Station Manager.

Clayton Roney, Chief Operator.

Marcia Yarborough, Traffic Manager.

Carolyn Rentrope, Public Affairs Director.

WTGL-DT
Leesburg
Ch. 46

Licensee: Good Life Broadcasting Inc., 653 W. Michigan St., Orlando, FL 32805.

Studio: 31 Skyline Dr, Lake Mary, FL 32746.

Mailing Address: 31 Skyline Dr, Lake Mary, FL 32746.

Phone: 407-215-6745. **Fax:** 407-215-6789.

Web Site: http://www.tv45.org

Technical Facilities: Channel No. 46 (662-668 MHz). Authorized power: 660-kw max. visual, aural. Antenna: 1686-ft above av. terrain, 1653-ft. above ground, 1720-ft. above sea level.

Latitude	28°	35'	12"
Longitude	81°	04'	58"

Holds CP for change to 1000-kw max. visual, 1686-ft above av. terrain, 1654-ft. above ground, 1719-ft. above sea level; BPEDT-20080612AAG.

Note: Latitude and longitude coordinates shown are based on the North American Datum of 1927 (NAD 27) as currently required by the Mass Media Bureau of the FCC.

Ownership: Good Life Broadcasting Inc.

Began Operation: September 9, 2005. Began analog operations: December 12, 2000. Ceased analog operations: February 17, 2009.

Personnel:

Ken Mikesell, President & General Manager.

Ed Griffis, General Sales Manager.

WLRN-DT
Miami
Ch. 20

Licensee: School Board of Dade County, 172 N.E. 15th St, Miami, FL 33132.

Studio: 172 NE 15th St, Miami, FL 33132.

Mailing Address: 172 NE 15th St, Miami, FL 33132.

Phone: 305-995-1717. **Fax:** 305-995-2299.

Email: mgonzalez@wlrn.org **Web Site:** http://www.wlrn.org

Technical Facilities: Channel No. 20 (506-512 MHz). Authorized power: 625-kw max. visual, aural. Antenna: 988-ft above av. terrain, 984-ft. above ground, 994-ft. above sea level.

Latitude	25°	58'	46"
Longitude	80°	11'	46"

Holds CP for change to 870-kw max. visual; BPEDT-20080609AAM.

Transmitter: 3300 S.W. 52nd Ave., Pembroke Park, Broward County.

Note: Latitude and longitude coordinates shown are based on the North American Datum of 1927 (NAD 27) as currently required by the Mass Media Bureau of the FCC.

Ownership: School Board of Dade County/ WLRN-TV.

Began Operation: April 11, 2003. Began analog operations: September 7, 1962. Ceased analog operations: June 12, 2009.

Personnel:

John LaBonia, General Manager.

Bernadette Siy, Station, Program & Traffic Manager.

Michael Peyton, Sales Manager.

Irina Allemende, News Director.

Mario Barrios, Chief Engineer.

Eileen Reilly, Finance Supervisor.

Chip Richards, Production Manager.

Adrienne Kennedy, Special Projects Manager.

Ginette Grey, Communications Director.

WPBT-DT
Miami
Ch. 18

Grantee: Community TV Foundation of South Florida Inc., 14901 NE 20th Ave, Miami, FL 33181.

Studio: 14901 NE 20th Ave, Miami, FL 33181.

Mailing Address: PO Box 610002, Miami, FL 33261-0002.

Phone: 305-949-8321. **Fax:** 305-944-4211.

Web Site: http://www.channel2.org

Technical Facilities: Channel No. 18 (494-500 MHz). Authorized power: 1000-kw max. visual, aural. Antenna: 1014-ft above av. terrain, 1014-ft. above ground, 1020-ft. above sea level.

Latitude	25°	57'	30"
Longitude	80°	12'	44"

Transmitter: 695 N.W. 199th St.

Note: Latitude and longitude coordinates shown are based on the North American Datum of 1927 (NAD 27) as currently required by the Mass Media Bureau of the FCC.

Ownership: Community TV Foundation of South Florida Inc.

Began Operation: July 5, 2001. High Definition. Began analog operations: August 12, 1955. Ceased analog operations: June 12, 2009.

Personnel:

Rick Schneider, President & Chief Executive Officer.

Delores Sukhdeo, Chief Operating Officer & Station Manager.

Rodney Ward, Executive Vice President, NBR Enterprises & News.

Diane Arlotta, Vice President, Administrative Services.

Graham Simmons, Senior Vice President, Engineering & Operations.

Bernard Cottle, Facilities Operations Supervisor.

Gene Talley, Chief Engineer.

Shirley C. Carroll, Senior Vice President, Finance.

Neal Hecker, Program Director.

Bradley Hurlburt, Senior Vice President, Development & Marketing.

WDSC-DT
New Smyrna Beach
Ch. 33

Licensee: Daytona State College Inc., 1200 W International Speedway Blvd, Daytona Beach, FL 32114.

Studio: 1200 International Speedway Blvd, Ste B400, Daytona Beach, FL 32114.

Mailing Address: PO Box 9245, Daytona Beach, FL 32120-9245.

Phones: 386-506-4415; 800-638-9238. **Fax:** 386-506-4427.

Email: dunnb@dbcc.edu **Web Site:** http://www.wceu.org

Technical Facilities: Channel No. 33 (584-590 MHz). Authorized power: 308-kw max. visual, aural. Antenna: 161-ft above av. terrain, 158-ft. above ground, 164-ft. above sea level.

Latitude	28°	36'	35"
Longitude	81°	03'	35"

Transmitter: 2.9-mi. N 90 degrees E of Lake Pickett.

Note: Latitude and longitude coordinates shown are based on the North American Datum of 1927 (NAD 27) as currently required by the Mass Media Bureau of the FCC.

Ownership: Daytona Beach Community College.

Began Operation: January 20, 2005. Began analog operations: February 8, 1988. Ceased analog operations: July 2008.

Personnel:

Bruce Dunn, Associate Vice President & General Manager.

JoAnne Osha, Underwriting Director & Corporate Support.

Bill Schwartz, Chief Engineer.

B. J. Lackey, Traffic Manager.

Mike Rentnelli, Production Manager.

Brian Long, Engineering Assistant.

Andy Chalanick, Educational Services Director.

WMFE-DT
Orlando
Ch. 23

Grantee: Community Communications Inc., 11510 E. Colonial Dr, Orlando, FL 32817-4699.

Studio: 11510 E Colonial Dr, Orlando, FL 32817-4699.

Mailing Address: 11510 E. Colonial Dr, Orlando, FL 32817-4699.

Phone: 407-273-2300. **Fax:** 407-273-3613.

Web Site: http://www.wmfe.org

Technical Facilities: Channel No. 23 (524-530 MHz). Authorized power: 950-kw max. visual, aural. Antenna: 1247-ft above av. terrain, 1220-ft. above ground, 1286-ft. above sea level.

Latitude	28°	36'	08"
Longitude	81°	05'	37"

Transmitter: Approx. 3.5-mi. N of Bithlo.

Note: Latitude and longitude coordinates shown are based on the North American Datum of 1927 (NAD 27) as currently required by the Mass Media Bureau of the FCC.

Ownership: Community Communications Inc.-Florida.

Began Operation: February 17, 2009. Began analog operations: March 15, 1965. Ceased analog operations: February 17, 2009.

Personnel:

Sherry Alexander, Senior Vice President, Administration & Finance.

Jose A. Fajardo, President & Chief Executive Officer.

Mike Simmons, Chief Engineer.

Dale Spear, Chief Operating Officer.

Jack Church, Vice President, Marketing.

Keith Hastings, Production Director.

Julia Downs, Human Resources Director.

Catherine McManus, Senior Vice President & Chief Philanthropy Officer.

WFSG-DT
Panama City
Ch. 38

Licensee: Board of Regents of Florida, acting for & on behalf of Florida State U., 1600 Red Barber Plz, Tallahassee, FL 32310.

Studio: 1600 Red Barber Plaza, Tallahassee, FL 32310-6068.

Mailing Address: 1600 Red Barber Plaza, Tallahassee, FL 32310.

Phone: 850-487-3170. **Fax:** 850-487-3093.

Web Site: http://www.wfsu.org

Technical Facilities: Channel No. 38 (614-620 MHz). Authorized power: 49.2-kw max. visual, aural. Antenna: 450-ft above av. terrain, 407-ft. above ground, 473-ft. above sea level.

Latitude	30°	22'	02"
Longitude	85°	55'	28"

Holds CP for change to 158-kw max. visual, 436-ft above av. terrain, 407-ft. above ground, 472-ft. above sea level; BPEDT-20080620AFH.

Transmitter: Steelfield Rd., 5.2-mi. NW of West Bay.

Note: Latitude and longitude coordinates shown are based on the North American Datum of 1927 (NAD 27) as currently required by the Mass Media Bureau of the FCC.

Ownership: Florida State U.

Began Operation: July 3, 2002. Began analog operations: July 22, 1988. Ceased analog operations: February 17, 2009.

Personnel:

Patrick Keating, General Manager.

Sarah Schuetz, Program & Operations Manager.

Barry Fitzpatrick, Engineering Director.

Ray Chamberlain, Chief Engineer.

Denison Graham, Business Manager.

Beckie Hamilton, Program Manager.

Jannie Whitt, Promotion Director.

John Kwak, Development Director.

Mike Dunn, Production Director.

Michelle Thorpe, Membership Manager.

Marie Quick, Assistant to the General Manager.

Mike Arnold, Art Director.

WSRE-DT
Pensacola
Ch. 31

Licensee: District Board of Trustees, 1000 College Blvd, Pensacola Jr. College, Pensacola, FL 32504.

Studio: 1000 College Blvd, Pensacola, FL 32504.

Mailing Address: 1000 College Blvd, Pensacola, FL 32504.

Phone: 850-484-1200. **Fax:** 850-484-1255.

Email: rmcarthur@wsre.org **Web Site:** http://www.wsre.org

Technical Facilities: Channel No. 31 (572-578 MHz). Authorized power: 1000-kw max. visual, aural. Antenna: 1801-ft above av. terrain, 1831-ft. above ground, 1936-ft. above sea level.

| Latitude | 30° | 36' | 40.3" |
| Longitude | 87° | 36' | 26.9" |

Note: Latitude and longitude coordinates shown are based on the North American Datum of 1927 (NAD 27) as currently required by the Mass Media Bureau of the FCC.

Ownership: Pensacola Jr. College District Board of Trustees.

Began Operation: July 3, 2001. Began analog operations: September 11, 1967. Ceased analog operations: February 17, 2009.

Personnel:

Sandy Cesaretti Ray, General Manager.

Darryl Harrison, Chief Engineer.

Karen Pope, Business Manager & Controller.

Robin McArthur, Marketing & Promotion Manager.

Janie Stewart, Underwriting & Special Events Manager.

Jill Hubbs, Educational Services & Outreach Director.

WFSU-DT
Tallahassee
Ch. 32

Licensee: Board of Regents of Florida, acting for & on behalf of Florida State U., 1600 Red Barber Plz, Tallahassee, FL 32310.

Studio: 1600 Red Barber Plaza, Tallahassee, FL 32310-6068.

Mailing Address: 1600 Red Barber Plaza, Tallahassee, FL 32310.

Phone: 850-487-3170. **Fax:** 850-487-3093.

Web Site: http://www.wfsu.org

Technical Facilities: Channel No. 32 (578-584 MHz). Authorized power: 937.8-kw max. visual, aural. Antenna: 776-ft above av. terrain, 794-ft. above ground, 919-ft. above sea level.

| Latitude | 30° | 21' | 31.21" |
| Longitude | 84° | 36' | 38.23" |

Transmitter: Junction of National Forest Rds. 344 & 344B, 6.9-mi. SW of Holland.

Note: Latitude and longitude coordinates shown are based on the North American Datum of 1927 (NAD 27) as currently required by the Mass Media Bureau of the FCC.

Ownership: Florida State U.

Began Operation: July 30, 2003. Began analog operations: September 20, 1960. Ceased analog operations: February 17, 2009.

Personnel:

Patrick Keating, General Manager.

Sarah Schuetz, Operations & Programming Director.

Barry Fitzpatrick, Engineering Director.

Ray Chamberlain, Chief Engineer.

Denison Graham, Business Manager.

Beckie Hamilton, Program Manager.

Jannie Whitt, Promotion Director.

John Kwak, Development Director.

Mike Dunn, Production Director.

Michelle Thorpe, Membership Manager.

Marie Quick, Assistant to the General Manager.

Mike Arnold, Art Director.

WEDU-DT
Tampa
Ch. 54

Licensee: Florida West Coast Public Broadcasting Inc., 1300 North Blvd, Tampa, FL 33607.

Studio: 1300 North Blvd, Tampa, FL 33607.

Mailing Address: 1300 North Blvd, Tampa, FL 33607.

Phones: 813-254-9338; 800-354-9338. **Fax:** 813-253-0826.

Web Site: http://www.wedu.org

Technical Facilities: Channel No. 54 (710-716 MHz). Authorized power: 387-kw max. visual, aural. Antenna: 1487-ft above av. terrain, 1479-ft. above ground, 1555-ft. above sea level.

| Latitude | 27° | 50' | 50" |
| Longitude | 82° | 15' | 50" |

Holds CP for change to channel number 13, 25-kw visual, 1545-ft above av. terrain, 1537-ft. above ground, 1613-ft. above sea level; BPEDT-20080317ACK.

Transmitter: 14021 Boyette Rd., 4-mi. ESE of Riverview.

Note: Latitude and longitude coordinates shown are based on the North American Datum of 1927 (NAD 27) as currently required by the Mass Media Bureau of the FCC.

Ownership: Florida West Coast Public Broadcasting Inc.

Began Operation: November 3, 2006. Began analog operations: October 27, 1958. Ceased analog operations: February 17, 2009.

Personnel:

Richard M. Lobo, President & Chief Executive Officer.

Leah Brainard, Vice President, Administration.

Jack Conley, Operation Services Director.

Frank Wolynski, Vice President, Engineering & Operations.

Miguel Amador, Chief Engineer.

Patrick Perkins, Chief Financial Officer.

Claire O'Connor-Solomon, Vice President, Annual Giving & Outreach.

Angela Jones, Traffic Coordinator.

Sartura Shuman, Education Outreach Coordinator.

WUSF-DT
Tampa
Ch. 34

Licensee: U. of South Florida, Board of Regents, 4202 E. Fowler Ave, Tampa, FL 33620.

Studio: 4202 E Fowler Ave, TVB 100, Tampa, FL 33620.

Mailing Address: 4202 E Fowler Ave, TVB 100, Tampa, FL 33620.

Phones: 813-974-8700; 800-741-9090. **Fax:** 813-974-5016.

Web Site: http://www.wusf.org

Technical Facilities: Channel No. 34 (590-596 MHz). Authorized power: 475-kw max. visual, aural. Antenna: 1486-ft above av. terrain, 1480-ft. above ground, 1558-ft. above sea level.

| Latitude | 27° | 50' | 52" |
| Longitude | 82° | 15' | 48" |

Note: Latitude and longitude coordinates shown are based on the North American Datum of 1927 (NAD 27) as currently required by the Mass Media Bureau of the FCC.

Ownership: U. of South Florida Board of Trustees.

Began Operation: March 19, 2003. Began analog operations: September 12, 1966. Ceased analog operations: June 12, 2009.

Personnel:

Jo Ann Urofsky, General Manager.

Tom Dollenmayer, Station Manager.

Mike Martin, Chief Engineer.

Susan Geiger, Program Manager.

Scot Kaufman, Sales Manager.

Margaret Fuesy, Marketing Director.

Gary Byrd, IntellisMedia Director.

Jorge Cunha, Production Manager.

Patricia Hickok, Membership Services Manager.

WXEL-DT
West Palm Beach
Ch. 27

Licensee: Barry Telecommunications Inc., PO Box 6607, West Palm Beach, FL 33405.

Studio: 3401 S Congress Ave, Boynton Beach, FL 33426.

Mailing Address: PO Box 6607, West Palm Beach, FL 33405.

Phones: 561-737-8000; 800-915-9935. **Fax:** 561-369-3067.

Email: lrowand@wxel.org **Web Site:** http://www.wxel.org

Technical Facilities: Channel No. 27 (548-554 MHz). Authorized power: 400-kw max. visual, aural. Antenna: 1444-ft above av. terrain, 1440-ft. above ground, 1456-ft. above sea level.

| Latitude | 26° | 34' | 37" |
| Longitude | 80° | 14' | 32" |

Note: Latitude and longitude coordinates shown are based on the North American Datum of 1927 (NAD 27) as currently required by the Mass Media Bureau of the FCC.

Ownership: Barry Telecommunications Inc.

Began Operation: July 4, 2004. Began analog operations: July 8, 1982. Sale to WXEL Public Broadcasting Corp. dismissed by FCC June 4, 2008. Ceased analog operations: June 12, 2009.

Personnel:

Jerry Carr, President, General Manager & Chief Executive Officer.

Bernie Henneberg, Vice President, Finance.

Mike Maville, Chief Engineer.

Lee Rowand, Creative Services & Program Director.

Bill Wasko, Production Manager.

JoAnne Cole Fulop, Traffic Manager.

Marlene Figuroa, Community Affairs Director.

Amy Fruchtman, Membership Director.

Ross Cooper, Sales Underwriting Manager.

Georgia

WGTV-DT
Athens
Ch. 8

Grantee: Georgia Public Telecommunications Commission, 260 14th St NW, Atlanta, GA 30318.

Studio: 260 14th St NW, Atlanta, GA 30318.

Mailing Address: 260 14th St NW, Atlanta, GA 30318.

Phones: 404-685-2400; 800-222-6006. **Fax:** 404-685-2491.

Web Site: http://www.gpb.org

Technical Facilities: Channel No. 8 (180-186 MHz). Authorized power: 21-kw visual, aural. Antenna: 1083-ft above av. terrain, 361-ft. above ground, 1990-ft. above sea level.

| Latitude | 33° | 48' | 18" |
| Longitude | 84° | 08' | 40" |

Transmitter: 2 Robert E. Lee Blvd., atop Stone Mountain.

Note: Latitude and longitude coordinates shown are based on the North American Datum of 1927 (NAD 27) as currently required by the Mass Media Bureau of the FCC.

Ownership: Georgia Public Telecommunications Commission.

Began Operation: January 18, 2008. Station broadcasting digitally on its analog channel allotment. Began analog operations: May 23, 1960. Ceased analog operations February 17, 2009.

Personnel:

Nancy Hall, Interim Executive Director.

Bob Houghton, General Manager.

Robert Olive, Assistant General Manager.

Mark Fehlig, Technical & Engineering Services Director.

Bonnie Bean, Chief Financial Officer.

Carol Fisk, GPB Productions Director.

Melvin Jones, Human Resources Director.

Michael Nixon, Information Technology & Education Services Director.

Mandy Wilson, Communications & Community Services.

Nancy Zintak, Communications & Marketing.

WATC-DT
Atlanta
Ch. 41

Licensee: Community Television Inc., 1862 Enterprise Dr, Norcross, GA 30115.

Studio: 1852 Enterprise Dr, Norcross, GA 30093.

Mailing Address: 1852 Enterprise Dr, Norcross, GA 30093.

Phone: 770-300-9828. Fax: 770-300-9838.

Email: watc@mindspring.com Web Site: http://www.watc.tv

Technical Facilities: Channel No. 41 (632-638 MHz). Authorized power: 165-kw max. visual, aural. Antenna: 1047-ft above av. terrain, 171-ft. above ground, 2054-ft. above sea level.

| Latitude | 34° | 03' | 59" |
| Longitude | 84° | 27' | 17" |

Holds CP for change to 750-kw max. visual, 1040-ft above av. terrain, 171-ft. above ground, 2054-ft. above sea level; BPEDT-20080619AIR.

Note: Latitude and longitude coordinates shown are based on the North American Datum of 1927 (NAD 27) as currently required by the Mass Media Bureau of the FCC.

Ownership: Community Television Inc.

Began Operation: September 12, 2007. Began analog operations: April 14, 1996. Transfer of control from James Thompson, et al. to James Thompson et al. approved by FCC January 30, 2004. Station ceased analog operations: February 17, 2009.

Personnel:

James Thompson, President & General Manager.

Scott Wills, Chief Engineer.

John Broomall, General Sales & Underwriting Manager.

Greg West, Programming Director.

Vincent Thompson, Production Manager.

Pat Mathis, Business Manager.

WPBA-DT
Atlanta
Ch. 21

Licensee: Board of Education of the City of Atlanta, 210 Pryor St. SW, Atlanta, GA 30335.

Studio: 740 Bismark Dr. NE, Atlanta, GA 30324.

Mailing Address: 740 Bismark Rd NE, Atlanta, GA 30324.

Phone: 678-686-0321. Fax: 678-686-0356.

Web Site: http://www.wpba.org

Technical Facilities: Channel No. 21 (512-518 MHz). Authorized power: 55.4-kw max. visual, aural. Antenna: 872-ft above av. terrain, 821-ft. above ground, 1801-ft. above sea level.

| Latitude | 33° | 45' | 32" |
| Longitude | 84° | 20' | 07" |

Note: Latitude and longitude coordinates shown are based on the North American Datum of 1927 (NAD 27) as currently required by the Mass Media Bureau of the FCC.

Satellite Earth Station: Harris; Scientific-Atlanta, 10-meter; Scientific-Atlanta, Collins receivers.

Ownership: Board of Education of the City of Atlanta.

Began Operation: January 1, 2005. Began analog operations: February 17, 1958. Ceased analog operations: June 12, 2009.

Personnel:

Milton Clipper, President & Chief Executive Officer.

John Weatherford, Senior Vice President, Public Broadcasting Atlanta.

Mike Halpin, Senior Vice President, DTV.

Dustin Lecate, Station Manager.

Reed Haggard, Sales & Underwriting Director.

John York, Engineering Director.

Irene Wreen, Chief Financial Officer.

Monique Williams, Finance Director.

Kenneth Brown, Human Resources Director.

Wayne Sharpe, New Media Director.

WNGH-DT
Chatsworth
Ch. 33

Grantee: Georgia Public Telecommunications Commission, 260 14th St NW, Atlanta, GA 30318.

Studio: 260 14th St NW, Atlanta, GA 30318.

Mailing Address: 260 14th St NW, Atlanta, GA 30318.

Phones: 404-685-2400; 800-222-6006. Fax: 404-685-2591.

Email: mkillingsworth@gpb.org Web Site: http://www.gpb.org

Technical Facilities: Channel No. 33 (584-590 MHz). Authorized power: 426-kw max. visual, aural. Antenna: 1762-ft above av. terrain, 246-ft. above ground, 2963-ft. above sea level.

| Latitude | 34° | 45' | 06" |
| Longitude | 84° | 42' | 54" |

Transmitter: Cohutta Mountain, 3-mi. ESE of Chatsworth, 2765 Fort Mountain State Park Rd.

Note: Latitude and longitude coordinates shown are based on the North American Datum of 1927 (NAD 27) as currently required by the Mass Media Bureau of the FCC.

Ownership: Georgia Public Telecommunications Commission.

Began Operation: May 19, 2008. Began analog operations: January 30, 1967. Ceased analog operations: February 17, 2009.

Personnel:

Nancy Hall, Interim Executive Director.

Bob Houghton, General Manager.

Robert Olive, Assistant General Manager.

Mark Fehlig, Technical & Engineering Services Director.

Bonnie Bean, Chief Financial Officer.

Carol Fisk, GPB Productions Director.

Melvin Jones, Human Resources Director.

Michael Nixon, Informational Technology & Education Services Director.

Mandy Wilson, Communications & Community Services.

Nancy Zintak, Communications & Marketing.

WMUM-DT
Cochran
Ch. 7

Grantee: Georgia Public Telecommunications Commission, 260 14th St NW, Atlanta, GA 30318.

Studio: 260 14th St NW, Atlanta, GA 30318.

Mailing Address: 260 14th St NW, Atlanta, GA 30318.

Phones: 404-685-2400; 800-222-6006. Fax: 404-685-2591.

Email: mfehlig@gpb.org Web Site: http://www.gpb.org

Technical Facilities: Channel No. 7 (174-180 MHz). Authorized power: 31-kw visual, aural. Antenna: 1088-ft above av. terrain, 1050-ft. above ground, 1431-ft. above sea level.

| Latitude | 32° | 28' | 11" |
| Longitude | 83° | 15' | 17" |

Transmitter: Salem Cary Rd., off Hwy. 26, 7.5-mi. NE of Cochran.

Note: Latitude and longitude coordinates shown are based on the North American Datum of 1927 (NAD 27) as currently required by the Mass Media Bureau of the FCC.

Ownership: Georgia Public Telecommunications Commission.

Began Operation: May 1, 2003. Began analog operations: January 1, 1968. Ceased analog operations: February 17, 2009.

Personnel:

Nancy Hall, Interim Executive Director.

Bob Houghton, General Manager.

Robert Olive, Assistant General Manager.

Mark Fehlig, Technical & Engineering Services Director.

Bonnie Bean, Chief Financial Officer.

Carol Fisk, GPB Productions Director.

Melvin Jones, Human Resources Director.

Michael Nixon, Informational Technology & Education Services Director.

Mandy Wilson, Communications & Community Services.

Nancy Zintak, Communications & Marketing.

WJSP-DT
Columbus
Ch. 23

Grantee: Georgia Public Telecommunications Commission, 260 14th St NW, Atlanta, GA 30318.

Studio: 260 14th St NW, Atlanta, GA 30318.

Mailing Address: 260 14th St NW, Atlanta, GA 30318.

Phones: 404-685-2400; 800-222-6006. Fax: 404-685-2591.

Web Site: http://www.gpb.org

Technical Facilities: Channel No. 23 (524-530 MHz). Authorized power: 177-kw max. visual, aural. Antenna: 1457-ft above av. terrain, 1014-ft. above ground, 2313-ft. above sea level.

| Latitude | 32° | 51' | 08" |
| Longitude | 84° | 42' | 04" |

Note: Latitude and longitude coordinates shown are based on the North American Datum of 1927 (NAD 27) as currently required by the Mass Media Bureau of the FCC.

Ownership: Georgia Public Telecommunications Commission.

Began Operation: May 1, 2003. Began analog operations: August 10, 1964. Ceased analog operations: February 17, 2009.

Personnel:

Nancy Hall, Interim Executive Director.

Bob Houghton, General Manager.

Robert Olive, Assistant General Manager.

Mark Fehlig, Technical & Engineering Services Director.

Bonnie Bean, Chief Financial Officer.

Carol Fisk, GPB Productions Director.

Mandy Wilson, Communications & Community Services.

Melvin Jones, Human Resources Director.

Michael Nixon, Information Technology & Education Services Director.

Nancy Zintak, Communications & Marketing.

WACS-DT
Dawson
Ch. 8

Grantee: Georgia Public Telecommunications Commission, 260 14th St NW, Atlanta, GA 30318.

Studio: 260 14th St NW, Atlanta, GA 30318.

Mailing Address: 260 14th St NW, Atlanta, GA 30318.

Phones: 404-685-2400; 800-222-6006. Fax: 404-685-2591.

Email: mfehlig@gpb.org Web Site: http://www.gpb.org

Technical Facilities: Channel No. 8 (180-186 MHz). Authorized power: 4.7-kw visual, aural. Antenna: 1093-ft above av. terrain, 1056-ft. above ground, 1526-ft. above sea level.

Latitude	31°	56'	15"
Longitude	84°	33'	15"

Note: Latitude and longitude coordinates shown are based on the North American Datum of 1927 (NAD 27) as currently required by the Mass Media Bureau of the FCC.

Ownership: Georgia Public Telecommunications Commission.

Began Operation: May 1, 2003. Began analog operations: March 6, 1967. Ceased analog operations February 17, 2009.

Personnel:

Nancy Hall, Interim Executive Director.

Bob Houghton, General Manager.

Robert Olive, Assistant General Manager.

Mark Fehlig, Technical & Engineering Services Director.

Bonnie Bean, Chief Financial Officer.

Carol Fisk, GPB Productions Director.

Melvin Jones, Human Resources Director.

Michael Nixon, Informational Technology & Education Services Director.

Mandy Wilson, Communications & Community Services.

Nancy Zintak, Communications & Marketing.

WABW-DT
Pelham
Ch. 6

Grantee: Georgia Public Telecommunications Commission, 260 14th St NW, Atlanta, GA 30318.

Studio: 260 14th St NW, Atlanta, GA 30318.

Mailing Address: 260 14th St NW, Atlanta, GA 30318.

Phones: 404-685-2400; 800-222-6006. Fax: 404-685-2591.

Web Site: http://www.gpb.org

Technical Facilities: Channel No. 6 (82-88 MHz). Authorized power: 0.52-kw visual, aural. Antenna: 555-ft above av. terrain, 504-ft. above ground, 829-ft. above sea level.

Latitude	31°	08'	05"
Longitude	84°	06'	16"

Holds CP for change to 10.5-kw visual, 1243-ft above av. terrain, 1192-ft. above ground, 1517-ft. above sea level; BMPEDT-20080619AKP.

Note: Latitude and longitude coordinates shown are based on the North American Datum of 1927 (NAD 27) as currently required by the Mass Media Bureau of the FCC.

Ownership: Georgia Public Telecommunications Commission.

Began Operation: May 30, 2008. Began analog operations: January 2, 1967. Ceased analog operations February 17, 2009.

Personnel:

Nancy Hall, Interim Executive Director.

Bob Houghton, General Manager.

Robert Olive, Assistant General Manager.

Mark Fehlig, Technical & Engineering Services Director.

Bonnie Bean, Chief Financial Officer.

Carol Fisk, GPB Production Director.

Melvin Jones, Human Resources Director.

Michael Nixon, Informational Technology & Educational Services Director.

Mandy Wilson, Communications & Community Services.

Nancy Zintak, Communications & Marketing.

WVAN-DT
Savannah
Ch. 9

Grantee: Georgia Public Telecommunications Commission, 260 14th St NW, Atlanta, GA 30318.

Studio: 260 14th St NW, Atlanta, GA 30318.

Mailing Address: 260 14th St NW, Atlanta, GA 30318.

Phones: 404-685-2400; 800-222-6006. Fax: 404-685-2591.

Web Site: http://www.gpb.org

Technical Facilities: Channel No. 9 (186-192 MHz). Authorized power: 20-kw visual, aural. Antenna: 1274-ft above av. terrain, 1261-ft. above ground, 1356-ft. above sea level.

Latitude	32°	08'	48"
Longitude	81°	37'	05"

Note: Latitude and longitude coordinates shown are based on the North American Datum of 1927 (NAD 27) as currently required by the Mass Media Bureau of the FCC.

Ownership: Georgia Public Telecommunications Commission.

Began Operation: May 16, 2008. Station broadcasting digitally on its analog channel allotment. Began analog operations: September 17, 1963. Ceased analog operations: June 12, 2009.

Personnel:

Nancy Hall, Interim Executive Director.

Bob Houghton, General Manager.

Robert Olive, Assistant General Manager.

Mark G. Fehlig, Technical & Engineering Services Director.

Bonnie Bean, Chief Financial Officer.

Carol Fisk, GPB Production Director.

Melvin Jones, Human Resources Director.

Michael Nixon, Information Technology & Education Services Director.

Mandy Wilson, Communications & Community Services.

Nancy Zintac, Communications & Marketing.

WXGA-DT
Waycross
Ch. 8

Grantee: Georgia Public Telecommunications Commission, 260 14th St NW, Atlanta, GA 30318.

Studio: 260 14th St NW, Atlanta, GA 30318.

Mailing Address: 260 14th St NW, Atlanta, GA 30318.

Phones: 404-685-2400; 800-222-6006. Fax: 404-685-2591.

Email: mfehlig@gpb.org Web Site: http://www.gpb.org

Technical Facilities: Channel No. 8 (180-186 MHz). Authorized power: 35.3-kw visual, aural. Antenna: 1010-ft above av. terrain, 1013-ft. above ground, 1173-ft. above sea level.

Latitude	31°	13'	17"
Longitude	82°	34'	24"

Transmitter: 6433 TV Tower Rd., Millwood.

Note: Latitude and longitude coordinates shown are based on the North American Datum of 1927 (NAD 27) as currently required by the Mass Media Bureau of the FCC.

Ownership: Georgia Public Telecommunications Commission.

Began Operation: February 17, 2009. Station broadcasting digitally on its analog channel allotment. Began analog operations: November 19, 1961. Ceased analog operations: February 17, 2009.

Personnel:

Nancy Hall, Interim Executive Director.

Bob Houghton, General Manager.

Robert Olive, Assistant General Manager.

Bonnie Bean, Chief Financial Officer.

Mark G. Fehlig, Technical & Engineering Services Director.

Carol Fisk, GPB Production Manager.

Melvin Jones, Human Resources Director.

Michael Nixon, Information Technology & Educational Services Director.

Mandy Wilson, Communications & Community Services.

Nancy Zintak, Communications & Marketing.

WCES-DT
Wrens
Ch. 6

Grantee: Georgia Public Telecommunications Commission, 260 14th St NW, Atlanta, GA 30318.

Studio: 260 14th St NW, Atlanta, GA 30318.

Mailing Address: 260 14th St NW, Atlanta, GA 30318.

Phones: 404-685-2400; 800-222-6006. Fax: 404-685-2591.

Email: mfehlig@gpb.org Web Site: http://www.gpb.org

Technical Facilities: Channel No. 6 (82-88 MHz). Authorized power: 7.9-kw visual, aural. Antenna: 1409-ft above av. terrain, 1350-ft. above ground, 1785-ft. above sea level.

Latitude	33°	15'	33"
Longitude	82°	17'	09"

Note: Latitude and longitude coordinates shown are based on the North American Datum of 1927 (NAD 27) as currently required by the Mass Media Bureau of the FCC.

Ownership: Georgia Public Telecommunications Commission.

Began Operation: February 17, 2009. Began analog operations: September 12, 1966. Ceased analog operations: February 17, 2009.

Personnel:

Nancy Hall, Interim Executive Director.

Bob Houghton, General Manager.

Robert Olive, Assistant General Manager.

Mark Fehlig, Technical & Engineering Services Director.

Bonnie Bean, Chief Financial Officer.

Carol Fisk, GPB Production Director.

Melvin Jones, Human Resources Director.

Michael Nixon, Information Technology & Educational Services Director.

Mandy Wilson, Communications & Community Services.

Nancy Zintak, Communications & Marketing.

Hawaii

KALO-DT
Honolulu
Ch. 38

Grantee: One Love Outreach Inc., PO Box 283177, Honolulu, HI 96828.

Studio: 875 Waimanu St, Ste 110, Honolulu, HI 96813.

Mailing Address: PO Box 8969, Honolulu, HI 96830.

Phone: 808-596-8897. **Fax:** 808-596-2646.

Web Site: http://www.kalo-tv.com

Technical Facilities: Channel No. 38 (614-620 MHz). Authorized power: 155-kw max. visual, aural. Antenna: 1893-ft above av. terrain, 40-ft. above ground, 2321-ft. above sea level.

Latitude	21°	23'	44.5"
Longitude	158°	05'	58"

Note: Latitude and longitude coordinates shown are based on the North American Datum of 1927 (NAD 27) as currently required by the Mass Media Bureau of the FCC.

Ownership: One Love Outreach Inc.

Began Operation: January 15, 2009. Station broadcasting digitally on its analog channel allotment. Began analog operations: July 9, 1999. Sale to present owner by Pacifica Broadcasting Co. approved by FCC August 18, 2009. Ceased analog operations: January 15, 2009.

Personnel:

Chris Racine, President & General Manager.

Ken Wooley, Chief Engineer.

KHET-DT
Honolulu
Ch. 11

Licensee: Hawaii Public Television Foundation, PO Box 11673, Honolulu, HI 96828.

Studio: 2350 Dole St, Honolulu, HI 96822.

Mailing Address: PO Box 11673, Honolulu, HI 96828.

Phones: 808-973-1000; 808-973-1087. **Fax:** 808-973-1090.

Web Site: http://www.pbshawaii.org

Technical Facilities: Channel No. 11 (198-204 MHz). Authorized power: 28.7-kw visual, aural. Antenna: 2051-ft above av. terrain, 150-ft. above ground, 2630-ft. above sea level.

Latitude	21°	17'	46.4"
Longitude	157°	50'	35.9"

Requests CP for change to lat. 21° 24' 3", long. 158° 6' 10"; BPEDT-20090708ABF.

Note: Latitude and longitude coordinates shown are based on the North American Datum of 1927 (NAD 27) as currently required by the Mass Media Bureau of the FCC.

Ownership: Hawaii Public Television Foundation.

Began Operation: May 16, 2006. Station broadcasting digitally on its analog channel allotment. Began analog operations: April 15, 1966. Ceased analog operations: January 15, 2009.

Personnel:

Leslie Wilcox, President & Chief Executive Officer.

Stephen Komori, Vice President, Technical Services.

Karen Yamamoto, Senior Vice President, Administration.

Lucy Ahn, Vice President, Corporate Support.

Lisa Levine, Vice President, Membership.

Robert Pennybacker, Vice President, Creative Services.

Linda Brock, Vice President, Programming & Community Relations.

KWBN-DT
Honolulu
Ch. 43

Licensee: Ho'Ona'Auao Community TV Inc., 3901 Hwy 121 S, Bedford, TX 76021-3009.

Mailing Address: 3901 Hwy 121 S, Bedford, TX 76021.

Phones: 817-571-1229; 808-591-9556. **Fax:** 808-591-9225.

Email: dtorres@daystar.com **Web Site:** http://www.daystar.com

Technical Facilities: Channel No. 43 (644-650 MHz). Authorized power: 6.46-kw max. visual, aural. Antenna: 1893-ft above av. terrain, 69-ft. above ground, 2349-ft. above sea level.

Latitude	21°	23'	45"
Longitude	158°	05'	58"

Holds CP for change to 22-kw max. visual; BPEDT-20080618AUB.

Note: Latitude and longitude coordinates shown are based on the North American Datum of 1927 (NAD 27) as currently required by the Mass Media Bureau of the FCC.

Ownership: Ho' Ona' Auao Community Television Inc.

Began Operation: August 17, 2005. Began analog operations: October 1, 1996. FCC granted station Special Temporary Authority to remain silent due to major power supply failure. Station returned to air October 2007. Ceased analog operations: January 15, 2009.

Personnel:

Arnold Torres, General Manager.

David Thompson, Chief Engineer.

KMEB-DT
Wailuku
Ch. 10

Grantee: Hawaii Public Television Foundation, 2350 Dole St, Honolulu, HI 96822.

Studio: 2350 Dole St, Honolulu, HI 96822.

Mailing Address: PO Box 11673, Honolulu, HI 96828.

Phones: 808-973-1000; 808-973-1087. **Fax:** 808-973-1090.

Web Site: http://www.pbshawaii.org

Technical Facilities: Channel No. 10 (192-198 MHz). Authorized power: 21.2-kw visual, aural. Antenna: 2451-ft above av. terrain, 161-ft. above ground, 4626-ft. above sea level.

Latitude	20°	39'	37"
Longitude	156°	21'	46"

Note: Latitude and longitude coordinates shown are based on the North American Datum of 1927 (NAD 27) as currently required by the Mass Media Bureau of the FCC.

Ownership: Hawaii Public Television Foundation.

Began Operation: January 15, 2009. Station broadcasting digitally on its analog channel allotment. Began analog operations: September 22, 1966. Ceased analog operations: January 15, 2009.

Personnel:

Leslie Wilcox, President & Chief Executive Officer.

Stephen Komori, Vice President, Technical Services.

Karen Yamamoto, Senior Vice President, Administration.

Lisa Levine, Vice President, Membership.

Lucy Ahn, Vice President, Corporate Support.

Robert Pennybacker, Vice President, Creative Services.

Linda Brock, Vice President, Programming & Community Relations.

Idaho

KAID-DT
Boise
Ch. 21

Licensee: Idaho State Board of Education, 1455 N Orchard St, Boise, ID 83706-2239.

Studio: 1455 N Orchard St, Boise, ID 83706.

Mailing Address: 1455 N Orchard St, Boise, ID 83706.

Phones: 208-373-7220; 800-543-6868. **Fax:** 208-373-7245.

Web Site: http://www.idahoptv.org

Technical Facilities: Channel No. 21 (512-518 MHz). Authorized power: 725-kw max. visual, aural. Antenna: 2815-ft above av. terrain, 307-ft. above ground, 7364-ft. above sea level.

Latitude	43°	45'	21"
Longitude	116°	05'	54"

Note: Latitude and longitude coordinates shown are based on the North American Datum of 1927 (NAD 27) as currently required by the Mass Media Bureau of the FCC.

Ownership: Idaho State Board of Education.

Began Operation: September 24, 2001. Standard Definition. Began analog operations: December 31, 1971. Ceased analog operations: June 12, 2009.

Personnel:

Peter W. Morrill, General Manager.

Sandy Sutherland, Underwriting Director.

Joan Cartan-Hansen, News Director.

Rich Van Genderen, Technology Director.

Phillip Kottraba, Business Manager.

Ron Pisaneschi, Program Director.

Kim Philipps, Marketing Director.

Bruce Reichert, Production Manager.

Anne Peterson, Public Information Director.

KCDT-DT
Coeur d'Alene
Ch. 45

Licensee: Idaho State Board of Education, 1455 N Orchard St, Boise, ID 83706-2239.

Studio: 1455 N Orchard St, Boise, ID 83706.

Mailing Address: 1455 N Orchard St, Boise, ID 83706.

Phones: 208-373-7220; 208-885-1226. **Fax:** 208-373-7245.

Web Site: http://www.idahoptv.org

Technical Facilities: Channel No. 45 (656-662 MHz). Authorized power: 38-kw max. visual, aural. Antenna: 1526-ft above av. terrain, 88-ft. above ground, 4149-ft. above sea level.

Latitude	47°	43'	54"
Longitude	116°	43'	47"

Holds CP for change to 54.7-kw max. visual; BPEDT-20080620AGN.

Note: Latitude and longitude coordinates shown are based on the North American Datum of 1927 (NAD 27) as currently required by the Mass Media Bureau of the FCC.

Ownership: Idaho State Board of Education.

Began Operation: August 5, 2003. Began analog operations: September 22, 1992. Ceased analog operations: June 12, 2009.

Personnel:

Peter Morrill, General Manager.

Kris Freeland, Station Manager.

Sandy Sutherland, Underwriting Account Executive.

Joan Cartan-Hansen, News Director.

Richard Van Genderen, Technology Director.

Ken Segota, Chief Engineer.

Phillip Kottraba, Business Manager.

Ron Pisaneschi, Program Director.

Kim Philipps, Marketing Director.

Bruce Reichert, Production Director.

Anne Peterson, Public Information Director.

KUID-DT
Moscow
Ch. 12

Licensee: Idaho State Board of Education, 1455 N Orchard St, Boise, ID 83706-2239.

Studio: Radio-TV Center, U. of Idaho, Moscow, ID 83844.

Mailing Address: 1455 N Orchard St, Boise, ID 83706.

Phones: 208-885-1226; 208-373-7220. **Fax:** 208-373-7245.

Web Site: http://www.idahoptv.org

Technical Facilities: Channel No. 12 (204-210 MHz). Authorized power: 78-kw visual, aural. Antenna: 1114-ft above av. terrain, 292-ft. above ground, 3891-ft. above sea level.

Latitude	46°	40'	54"
Longitude	116°	58'	13"

Note: Latitude and longitude coordinates shown are based on the North American Datum of 1927 (NAD 27) as currently required by the Mass Media Bureau of the FCC.

Ownership: Idaho State U.

Began Operation: March 31, 2003. Began analog operations: September 6, 1965. Ceased analog operations: June 12, 2009.

Personnel:

Peter Morrill, General Manager.

Kris Freeland, Station Manager.

Sandy Sutherland, Underwriting Account Executive.

Joan Cartan-Hansen, News Director.

Richard Van Genderen, Technology Director.

Ken Segota, Chief Engineer.

Phillip Kottraba, Business Manager.

Ron Pisaneschi, Program Director.

Kim Philipps, Marketing Director.

Bruce Reichert, Production Manager.

Anne Peterson, Public Information Director.

KISU-DT
Pocatello
Ch. 17

Licensee: Idaho State Board of Education, 1455 N Orchard St, Boise, ID 83706-2239.

Studio: PO Box 8111, Bldg 62, Idaho State U. Campus, Pocatello, ID 83209.

Mailing Address: 1455 N Orchard St, Boise, ID 83706.

Phones: 208-373-7220; 800-543-6868. **Fax:** 208-373-7245.

Web Site: http://www.idahoptv.org

Technical Facilities: Channel No. 17 (488-494 MHz). Authorized power: 189-kw max. visual, aural. Antenna: 1480-ft above av. terrain, 85-ft. above ground, 6620-ft. above sea level.

Latitude	43°	30'	04"
Longitude	112°	39'	41"

Holds CP for change to 378.4-kw max. visual, 1460-ft above av. terrain, 80-ft. above ground, 6753-ft above sea level lat. 43° 30' 2", long. 112° 39' 36"; BPEDT-20080620AGK.

Note: Latitude and longitude coordinates shown are based on the North American Datum of 1927 (NAD 27) as currently required by the Mass Media Bureau of the FCC.

Ownership: Idaho State Board of Education.

Began Operation: January 17, 2003. Began analog operations: July 7, 1971. Ceased analog operations: June 12, 2009.

Personnel:

Peter Morrill, General Manager.

Chris Grayson, Station Coordinator & Development Director.

Sandy Sutherland, Underwriting Account Executive.

Joan Cartan-Hansen, News Director.

Richard Van Genderen, Technology Director.

Dave Turnmire, Chief Engineer.

Phillip Kottraba, Business Manager.

Ron Pisaneschi, Program Director.

Kim Philipps, Marketing Director.

Bruce Reichert, Production Manager.

Anne Peterson, Public Information Director.

KIPT-DT
Twin Falls
Ch. 22

Licensee: Idaho State Board of Education, 1455 N Orchard St, Boise, ID 83706-2239.

Studio: 1455 N Orchard St, Boise, ID 83706.

Mailing Address: 1455 N Orchard St, Boise, ID 83706.

Phones: 208-373-7220; 800-543-6868. **Fax:** 208-373-7245.

Web Site: http://www.idahoptv.org

Technical Facilities: Channel No. 22 (518-524 MHz). Authorized power: 50-kw max. visual, aural. Antenna: 597-ft above av. terrain, 150-ft. above ground, 4441-ft. above sea level.

Latitude	42°	43'	46.2"
Longitude	114°	24'	53.4"

Holds CP for change to 77.98-kw max. visual; BPEDT-20080620AGQ.

Note: Latitude and longitude coordinates shown are based on the North American Datum of 1927 (NAD 27) as currently required by the Mass Media Bureau of the FCC.

Ownership: Idaho State Board of Education.

Began Operation: April 28, 2003. Standard and High Definition. Began analog operations: January 17, 1992. Ceased analog operations: June 12, 2009.

Personnel:

Peter Morrill, General Manager.

Sandy Sutherland, Underwriting Account Executive.

Joan Cartan-Hansen, News Director.

Rich Van Genderen, Technology Director.

Phillip Kottraba, Business Manager.

Ron Pisaneschi, Program Director.

Kim Philipps, Marketing Director.

Bruce Reichert, Production Manager.

Anne Peterson, Public Information Director.

Illinois

WSIU-DT
Carbondale
Ch. 8

Licensee: Board of Trustees of Southern Illinois U., Communications Bldg., Room 1003, SIU Mailcode 6602, Carbondale, IL 62901-6602.

Studio: 1100 Lincoln Dr, Communications Bldg, Rm 1065, Carbondale, IL 62901-6602.

Mailing Address: 1100 Lincoln Dr, MC 6602, Communications Bldg, Rm 1003, Carbondale, IL 62901-6602.

Phones: 618-453-4343; 866-498-5561. **Fax:** 618-453-6186.

Email: Candis_Isberner@wsiu.pbs.org **Web Site:** http://www.wsiu.org

Technical Facilities: Channel No. 8 (180-186 MHz). Authorized power: 53-kw visual, aural. Antenna: 890-ft above av. terrain, 861-ft. above ground, 1347-ft. above sea level.

Latitude	38°	06'	11"
Longitude	89°	14'	40"

Note: Latitude and longitude coordinates shown are based on the North American Datum of 1927 (NAD 27) as currently required by the Mass Media Bureau of the FCC.

Ownership: Board of Trustees of Southern Illinois U.

Began Operation: December 15, 2005. Station broadcasting digitally on its analog channel allotment. Began analog operations: November 6, 1961. Ceased analog operations: January 30, 2009.

Personnel:

Delores Kerstein, Interim Executive Director & Finance Director.

Robert Henderson, Operations Director & Production Manager.

Jim Gee, News Director.

Terry Harvey, Technology Director.

Trina Thomas, Program & On-Air Promotions Coordinator.

Renee Dillard, Marketing Director & Membership Development.

Monica Tichenor, Print Promotion Coordinator.

Kevin Boucher, Traffic Manager.

WEIU-DT
Charleston
Ch. 50

Licensee: Eastern Illinois U., 600 Lincoln Ave, Radio & Television Center, Charleston, IL 61920.

Studio: 600 Lincoln Ave, 1521 Buzzard Hall, Charleston, IL 61920.

Mailing Address: 600 Lincoln Ave, 1521 Buzzard Hall, Charleston, IL 61920.

Phones: 217-581-5956; 877-727-9348. **Fax:** 217-581-6650.

Web Site: http://www.weiu.net

Technical Facilities: Channel No. 50 (686-692 MHz). Authorized power: 255-kw max. visual, aural. Antenna: 479-ft above av. terrain, 472-ft. above ground, 1153-ft. above sea level.

Latitude	39°	34'	15"
Longitude	88°	18'	25.5"

Note: Latitude and longitude coordinates shown are based on the North American Datum of 1927 (NAD 27) as currently required by the Mass Media Bureau of the FCC.

Ownership: Eastern Illinois U.

Began Operation: February 17, 2009. Standard Definition. Began analog operations: July 1, 1986. Ceased analog operations: February 17, 2009.

Personnel:

Denis Roche, General Manager.

Kelly Runyon, News Director.

Kevin Armstrong, Chief Engineer.

Brenda Good, Administration & Finance Director.

Linda Kingery, Program Director.

Lori Casey, Production Director.

Mack White, Traffic & Continuity Manager.

Ke'an Rogers, Publicity Promotions Specialist.

John Wiley, Specialist Corporate Fundraising.

Jeni Huckstep, Ready to Lead in Literacy Coordinator.

WTTW-DT
Chicago
Ch. 47

Grantee: Window to the World Communications Inc., 5400 N. St. Louis Ave, Chicago, IL 60625.

Studio: 5400 N St. Louis Ave, Chicago, IL 60625-4698.

Mailing Address: 5400 N. St. Louis Ave, Chicago, IL 60625-4698.

Phone: 773-583-5000.

Web Site: http://www.wttw.com

Technical Facilities: Channel No. 47 (668-674 MHz). Authorized power: 300-kw max. visual, aural. Antenna: 1526-ft above av. terrain, 1526-ft. above ground, 2119-ft. above sea level.

Latitude	41°	52'	44"
Longitude	87°	38'	10"

Transmitter: Sears Tower, 233 S. Wacker Dr.

Note: Latitude and longitude coordinates shown are based on the North American Datum of 1927 (NAD 27) as currently required by the Mass Media Bureau of the FCC.

Ownership: Window to the World Communications Inc.

Began Operation: April 4, 2002. Standard Definition. Began analog operations: September 5, 1955. Ceased analog operations: June 12, 2009.

Personnel:

Daniel J. Schmidt, President & Chief Executive Officer.

Ron Yergovich, Senior Vice President, Engineering & Technology.

Reese P. Marcusson, Executive Vice President & Chief Financial Officer.

Parke Richeson, Senior Vice President, Finance & Business Development.

Joanie Bayhack, Vice President, Corporate Communications & Direct Marketing.

Greg Cameron, Executive Vice President, Development.

Donna L. Davies, Senior Vice President, Development.

V. J. McAleer, Vice President, Production & Community Partnerships.

WYCC-DT
Chicago
Ch. 21

Licensee: Board of Trustees of Community College District No. 508, County of Cook, 226 W. Jackson Blvd, Ste 922, Chicago, IL 60606.

Studio: 6258 S Union Ave, Chicago, IL 60621.

Mailing Address: 6258 S Union Ave, Chicago, IL 60621.

Phones: 773-838-7878; 773-838-7961. **Fax:** 773-783-2906.

Web Site: http://www.wycc.tv

Technical Facilities: Channel No. 21 (512-518 MHz). Authorized power: 98.9-kw max. visual, aural. Antenna: 1240-ft above av. terrain, 1237-ft. above ground, 593-ft. above sea level.

Latitude	41°	53'	56"
Longitude	87°	37'	23"

Note: Latitude and longitude coordinates shown are based on the North American Datum of 1927 (NAD 27) as currently required by the Mass Media Bureau of the FCC.

Ownership: Board of Trustees, Community College No. 508.

Began Operation: April 30, 2003. Began analog operations: September 20, 1965. Ceased analog operations: June 12, 2009.

Personnel:

Arthur Wood, Interim General Manager.

Thaddeus Szymanski, Chief Engineer.

Cynthia Syperek, Program Manager.

Jim Kirwan, Creative Services Director.

Mike McKenna, Traffic Manager.

Alisa Clarke, Membership Manager.

WSEC-DT
Jacksonville
Ch. 15

Licensee: West Central Illinois Educational Telecommunications Corp., PO Box 6248, Springfield, IL 62708.

Studio: 1475 E Plummer Blvd, Chatham, IL 62629.

Mailing Address: PO Box 6248, Springfield, IL 62708.

Phones: 217-483-7887; 800-232-3605. **Fax:** 217-483-1112.

Email: mbates@wsec.tv **Web Site:** http://www.tkn.tv

Technical Facilities: Channel No. 15 (476-482 MHz). Authorized power: 75-kw max. visual, aural. Antenna: 968-ft above av. terrain, 945-ft. above ground, 1617-ft. above sea level.

Latitude	39°	36'	09"
Longitude	90°	02'	47"

Note: Latitude and longitude coordinates shown are based on the North American Datum of 1927 (NAD 27) as currently required by the Mass Media Bureau of the FCC.

Ownership: West Central Illinois Educational Telecommunications Corp.

Began Operation: October 31, 2003. Began analog operations: August 11, 1984. Ceased analog operations: June 12, 2009.

Personnel:

Jerold Gruebel, President & Chief Executive Officer.

Richard Plotkin, Vice President, Engineering & Production.

Mary Jane Bates, Business Manager & Executive Assistant.

Scott Troehler, Senior Producer & Director, Local Programming.

Stephanie Cole, Programming & Traffic Coordinator.

Amy Evans, Membership Coordinator.

WMEC-DT
Macomb
Ch. 21

Licensee: West Central Illinois Educational Telecommunications Corp., PO Box 6248, Springfield, IL 62708.

Studio: 1475 E Plummer Blvd, Chatham, IL 62629.

Mailing Address: PO Box 6248, Springfield, IL 62708.

Phones: 217-483-7887; 800-232-3605. **Fax:** 217-483-1112.

Email: mbates@wsec.tv **Web Site:** http://www.wmec.tv/

Technical Facilities: Channel No. 21 (512-518 MHz). Authorized power: 75-kw max. visual, aural. Antenna: 430-ft above av. terrain, 466-ft. above ground, 1066-ft. above sea level.

Latitude	40°	23'	54"
Longitude	90°	43'	55"

Note: Latitude and longitude coordinates shown are based on the North American Datum of 1927 (NAD 27) as currently required by the Mass Media Bureau of the FCC.

Ownership: West Central Illinois Educational Telecommunications Corp.

Began Operation: February 17, 2009. Began analog operations: October 1, 1984. Ceased analog operations: February 17, 2009.

Personnel:

Jerold Gruebel, President & Chief Executive Officer.

Rich Plotkin, Vice President, Engineering & Production.

Mary Jane Bates, Business Manager & Executive Assistant.

Scott Troehler, Senior Producer & Director, Local Programming.

Stephanie Cole, Programming & Traffic Coordinator.

Amy Evans, Membership Coordinator.

WQPT-DT
Moline
Ch. 23

Licensee: Black Hawk College, 6600 34th Ave, Moline, IL 61265.

Studio: 6600 34th Ave, Moline, IL 61265.

Mailing Address: 6600 34th Ave, Moline, IL 61265.

Phones: 309-796-2424; 800-747-2430. **Fax:** 309-796-2484.

Email: bestr@bhc.edu **Web Site:** http://www.wqpt.org

Technical Facilities: Channel No. 23 (524-530 MHz). Authorized power: 80-kw max. visual, aural. Antenna: 883-ft above av. terrain, 866-ft. above ground, 1619-ft. above sea level.

Latitude	41°	18'	44"
Longitude	90°	22'	45"

Note: Latitude and longitude coordinates shown are based on the North American Datum of 1927 (NAD 27) as currently required by the Mass Media Bureau of the FCC.

Ownership: Black Hawk College.

Began Operation: July 2, 2003. Began analog operations: November 2, 1983. Sale to Greater Quad Cities Telecommunication Corp. approved by FCC June 30, 2009, but not yet consummated. Ceased analog operations: June 12, 2009.

Personnel:

Rick Best, General Manager.

Terry Wynn, Acting Chief Engineer.

Cathryn Lass, Business Manager.

Jerry Myers, Programming Manager.

Lora Adams, Chief Development Officer.

Paul Magnuson, Production Manager.

Richard Diamond, Traffic Manager.

Candy Eastman, Membership Coordinator.

Bea Brasel, Special Events Coordinator.

Susan McPeters, Public Affairs Director.

Ana Kehoe, Educational Outreach.

WUSI-DT
Olney
Ch. 19

Licensee: Board of Trustees of Southern Illinois U., Communications Bldg., Room 1003, SIU Mailcode 6602, Carbondale, IL 62901-6602.

Studio: Southern Illinois U., Communications Bldg., Rm 1003, Carbondale, IL 62901-6602.

Mailing Address: 1100 Lincoln Dr, MC 6602, Communications Bldg, Rm 1003, Carbondale, IL 62901-6602.

Phones: 618-453-4343; 866-498-5561. **Fax:** 618-453-6816.

Web Site: http://www.wsiu.org

Technical Facilities: Channel No. 19 (500-506 MHz). Authorized power: 46-kw max. visual, aural. Antenna: 931-ft above av. terrain, 949-ft. above ground, 1419-ft. above sea level.

Latitude	38°	50'	19"
Longitude	88°	07'	47"

Note: Latitude and longitude coordinates shown are based on the North American Datum of 1927 (NAD 27) as currently required by the Mass Media Bureau of the FCC.

Satellite Earth Station: Harris; Gardiner C-band; Standard Components, Scientific-Atlanta, International Satellite receivers.

Ownership: Board of Trustees of Southern Illinois U.

Began Operation: June 19, 2006. Began analog operations: August 19, 1968. Ceased analog operations: February 17, 2009.

Personnel:

Delores Kerstein, Acting General Manager, Finance & Administrative Director.

Terry Harvey, Technology Director.

Trina Thomas, Program Director.

Monica Tichenor, Promotion & Public Service Director.

Renee Dillard, Development & Membership Director.

Kevin Boucher, Traffic Manager.

WTVP-DT
Peoria
Ch. 46

Licensee: Illinois Valley Public Telecommunications Corp., 1501 W. Bradley Ave, Peoria, IL 61606.

Studio: 101 State St, Peoria, IL 61602-1547.

Mailing Address: 101 State St, Peoria, IL 61602-1547.

Phones: 309-677-4747; 800-837-4747. **Fax:** 309-677-4730.

Web Site: http://www.wtvp.org

Technical Facilities: Channel No. 46 (662-668 MHz). Authorized power: 190-kw max. visual, aural. Antenna: 709-ft above av. terrain, 577-ft. above ground, 1322-ft. above sea level.

Latitude	40°	37'	44"
Longitude	89°	34'	12"

Transmitter: Cole Hollow Rd. at I-474.

Note: Latitude and longitude coordinates shown are based on the North American Datum of 1927 (NAD 27) as currently required by the Mass Media Bureau of the FCC.

Ownership: Illinois Valley Public Telecommunications Corp.

Began Operation: November 1, 2001. Began analog operations: June 27, 1971. Ceased analog operations: February 17, 2009.

Personnel:

Chet Tomczyk, President & Chief Executive Officer.

Jackie Luebcke, Operations Manager.

David Schenk, Vice President, Engineering.

James Jordan, Senior Engineer & Chief Operator.

Carol Gray, Controller.

Linda Miller, Vice President, Programming.

Stacey Tomczyk, Promotion Director.

William Baker, Executive Producer.

Ben Bier, Traffic Coordinator.

Mark Lasswell, IT Director.

WQEC-DT
Quincy
Ch. 34

Licensee: West Central Illinois Educational Telecommunications Corp., PO Box 3303, Quincy, IL 62301.

Studio: 1475 E Plummer Blvd, Chatham, IL 62629.

Mailing Address: PO Box 3303, Springfield, IL 62708.

Phones: 217-483-7887; 800-232-3605. Fax: 217-483-1112.

Email: jgruebel@wsec.tv Web Site: http://www.tkn.tv

Technical Facilities: Channel No. 34 (590-596 MHz). Authorized power: 58.6-kw max. visual, aural. Antenna: 502-ft above av. terrain, 427-ft above ground, 1139-ft. above sea level.

Latitude	39°	58'	41"
Longitude	91°	18'	32"

Note: Latitude and longitude coordinates shown are based on the North American Datum of 1927 (NAD 27) as currently required by the Mass Media Bureau of the FCC.

Ownership: West Central Illinois Educational Telecommunications Corp.

Began Operation: July 14, 2004. Began analog operations: March 9, 1985. Ceased analog operations: February 17, 2009.

Personnel:

Dr. Jerold Gruebel, President & Chief Executive Officer.

Rich Plotkin, Vice President, Operations, Engineering & Production.

Mary Jane Bates, Business Manager.

Stephanie Cole, Programming & Traffic Director.

Scott Troehler, Senior Producer & Director, Local Programming.

Amy Evans, Membership Coordinator.

WILL-DT
Urbana
Ch. 9

Licensee: Board of Trustees of the U. of Illinois, 300 N. Goodwin Ave, Urbana, IL 61801.

Studio: 300 N Goodwin Ave, Campbell Hall, Urbana, IL 61801-2316.

Mailing Address: 300 N Goodwin Ave, Campbell Hall, Urbana, IL 61801-2316.

Phone: 217-333-1070. Fax: 217-244-6386.

Web Site: http://www.will.uiuc.edu

Technical Facilities: Channel No. 9 (186-192 MHz). Authorized power: 30-kw visual, aural. Antenna: 991-ft above av. terrain, 988-ft. above ground, 1676-ft. above sea level.

Latitude	40°	02'	18"
Longitude	88°	40'	10"

Note: Latitude and longitude coordinates shown are based on the North American Datum of 1927 (NAD 27) as currently required by the Mass Media Bureau of the FCC.

Satellite Earth Station: RCA; Collins, 10-meter C-band; Collins receivers.

Ownership: U. of Illinois.

Began Operation: February 21, 2006. Began analog operations: August 1, 1955. Ceased analog operations: June 12, 2009.

Personnel:

Mark Leonard, General Manager & Broadcasting Director.

Carl Caldwell, Station Manager.

Richard Finney, Chief Engineer.

David Thiel, Program Director.

Kate Dobrovolony, Marketing Director.

George Hauenstein, Development Director.

Tim Hartin, Production Manager.

Lillie Buck, Traffic Manager.

Rita Schulte, Membership Director.

Anita Stein, Viewer Services Manager.

Indiana

WTIU-DT
Bloomington
Ch. 14

Licensee: Trustees of Indiana U., 900 E. 7th Street, M-19, Bloomington, IN 47405.

Studio: Radio-TV Center, Indiana U., Bloomington, IN 47405-5501.

Mailing Address: Radio-TV Center, Indiana U, Bloomington, IN 47405-5501.

Phone: 812-855-5900. Fax: 812-855-0729.

Email: amwesley@indiana.edu Web Site: http://www.wtiu.indiana.edu

Technical Facilities: Channel No. 14 (470-476 MHz). Authorized power: 224-kw max. visual, aural. Antenna: 725-ft above av. terrain, 627-ft. above ground, 1434-ft. above sea level.

Latitude	39°	08'	31"
Longitude	86°	29'	43"

Holds CP for change to 1000-kw max. visual, 725-ft above av. terrain, 627-ft. above ground, 1433-ft. above sea level; BPEDT-20080620ACT.

Note: Latitude and longitude coordinates shown are based on the North American Datum of 1927 (NAD 27) as currently required by the Mass Media Bureau of the FCC.

Ownership: Indiana U. Trustees.

Began Operation: May 20, 2003. Began analog operations: March 3, 1969. Ceased analog operations: June 12, 2009.

Personnel:

Perry Metz, General Manager.

Phil Meyer, Station Manager.

Barrie Zimmerman, Operations & Engineering Director.

Chuck Carney, News Director.

Brad Howard, Chief Engineer.

Virginia Metzger, Chief Financial Officer.

Brent Molnar, On-Air Promotion & Program Manager.

Ann Wesley, Marketing & External Relations Director.

Judy Witt, Production Development Director.

Steve Solie, Production Manager.

Mary Ducette, Ready to Learn Coordinator.

Tom Dukeman, Underwriting Director.

Joan Padawan, Membership Marketing Coordinator.

WNIN-DT
Evansville
Ch. 9

Licensee: Tri-State Public Teleplex Inc., 405 Carpenter St, Evansville, IN 47708.

Studio: 405 Carpenter St, Evansville, IN 47708.

Mailing Address: 405 Carpenter St, Evansville, IN 47708.

Phone: 812-423-2973. Fax: 812-428-7548.

Web Site: http://www.wnin.org

Technical Facilities: Channel No. 9 (186-192 MHz). Authorized power: 19-kw visual, aural. Antenna: 997-ft above av. terrain, 899-ft. above ground, 1403-ft. above sea level.

Latitude	37°	59'	01"
Longitude	87°	16'	13"

Transmitter: New Hope Rd., Pelzer.

Note: Latitude and longitude coordinates shown are based on the North American Datum of 1927 (NAD 27) as currently required by the Mass Media Bureau of the FCC.

Ownership: Southwest Indiana Public Broadcasting Inc.

Began Operation: April 22, 2003. Station broadcasting digitally on its analog channel allotment. Began analog operations: March 15, 1970. Ceased analog operations: June 12, 2009.

Personnel:

David L. Dial, President & General Manager.

Bonnie Rheinhardt, Vice President, Programming & Operations.

Josh Bozeman, Operations Director.

Wayne Aldridge, Studio Operations Supervisor.

Tonya Wolf, Corporate Sales & Promotion Manager.

Don Hollinsworth, Chief Engineer.

Carlin Beckman, Finance & Administration Director.

Dorothy Arrigo, Membership Coordinator.

Suzanne Hudson-Smith, Vice President, Development.

Jason Bumm, Production Manager.

Brenda Ricker, TV Traffic & Operations Director.

Sheryl Flaherty, Member Services Manager.

WFWA-DT
Fort Wayne
Ch. 40

Licensee: Fort Wayne Public Television Inc., 2501 E. Coliseum Blvd, Fort Wayne, IN 46805.

Studio: 2501 E Coliseum Blvd, Fort Wayne, IN 46805.

Mailing Address: PO Box 39, Fort Wayne, IN 46801-0039.

Phone: 260-484-8839. Fax: 260-482-3632.

Email: rogerrhodes@wfwa.org Web Site: http://www.wfwa.org

Technical Facilities: Channel No. 40 (626-632 MHz). Authorized power: 90-kw max. visual, aural. Antenna: 725-ft above av. terrain, 718-ft. above ground, 1532-ft. above sea level.

Latitude	41°	06'	13"
Longitude	85°	11'	28"

Requests CP for change to 153-kw max. visual; BPEDT-20080617ADU.

Note: Latitude and longitude coordinates shown are based on the North American Datum of 1927 (NAD 27) as currently required by the Mass Media Bureau of the FCC.

Ownership: Fort Wayne Public Television Inc.

Began Operation: February 17, 2009. Began analog operations: December 5, 1986. Ceased analog operations: February 17, 2009.

Personnel:

Bruce Haines, President & General Manager.

Richard Bienz, Vice President, Finance & Administration.

Toni Kayumi, Vice President, Marketing & Development.

Claudia Johnson, Broadcast Manager.

Matt Kyle, Chief Engineer.

Mark Ryan, Promotion Manager.

Candy Worthington, Membership Services Coordinator.

WYIN-DT
Gary
Ch. 17

Licensee: Northwest Indiana Public Broadcasting Inc., 8625 Indiana Pl, Merrillville, IN 46410.

Studio: 8625 Indiana Pl, Merrillville, IN 46410.

Mailing Address: 8625 Indiana Pl, Merrillville, IN 46410.

Phones: 219-756-5656; 800-276-5656. **Fax:** 219-755-4312.

Web Site: http://www.lakeshoreptv.com

Technical Facilities: Channel No. 17 (488-494 MHz). Authorized power: 300-kw max. visual, aural. Antenna: 951-ft above av. terrain, 922-ft. above ground, 1647-ft. above sea level.

Latitude	41°	20'	56"
Longitude	87°	24'	02"

Note: Latitude and longitude coordinates shown are based on the North American Datum of 1927 (NAD 27) as currently required by the Mass Media Bureau of the FCC.

Ownership: Northwest Indiana Public Broadcasting Inc.

Began Operation: March 9, 2004. Began analog operations: November 15, 1987. Ceased analog operations: June 12, 2009.

Personnel:

Thomas E. Carroll, President & Chief Executive Officer.

Bonnie Pollock, Sales Director.

Todd Haver, News Director.

Henry Ruhweidel, Chief Engineer.

Mary Lewis, Business Manager.

Katherine Prochno, Program Director.

Megan Ciszewski, Special Events & Marketing Director.

Matt Franklin, Production Manager.

Craig Johnson, Traffic Manager.

Kristie Hughes, Membership Manager.

WDTI-DT
Indianapolis
Ch. 44

Licensee: Indianapolis Community Television Inc., 3901 Hwy 121 S, Bedford, TX 76021-3009.

Tower: 4703 Lester, Indianapolis, IN 46205.

Mailing Address: 3901 Hwy 121 S, Bedford, TX 76021.

Phones: 800-329-0029; 817-571-1229. **Fax:** 817-571-7458.

Web Site: http://www.daystar.com

Technical Facilities: Channel No. 44 (650-656 MHz). Authorized power: 28-kw max. visual, aural. Antenna: 961-ft above av. terrain, 965-ft. above ground, 1800-ft. above sea level.

Latitude	39°	53'	40"
Longitude	86°	12'	21"

Holds CP for change to 1000-kw max. visual; BPEDT-20080617AEQ.

Note: Latitude and longitude coordinates shown are based on the North American Datum of 1927 (NAD 27) as currently required by the Mass Media Bureau of the FCC.

Ownership: Indianapolis Community Television Inc.

Began Operation: June 30, 2004. Began analog operations: June 1, 1992. Station received approval from the FCC November 10, 2008 to cease analog operations and broadcast only in digital format. Sale to present owner by Butler University approved by FCC August 2, 2004. Ceased analog operations: November 10, 2008.

WFYI-DT
Indianapolis
Ch. 21

Licensee: Metropolitan Indianapolis Public Broadcasting Inc., 1401 N. Meridian St, Indianapolis, IN 46202-2389.

Studio: 1401 N Meridian St, Indianapolis, IN 46202-2389.

Mailing Address: 1630 N Meridian St, Indianapolis, IN 46202-1429.

Phone: 317-636-2020. **Fax:** 317-633-7418.

Web Site: http://www.wfyi.org

Technical Facilities: Channel No. 21 (512-518 MHz). Authorized power: 200-kw max. visual, aural. Antenna: 774-ft above av. terrain, 781-ft. above ground, 1611-ft. above sea level.

Latitude	39°	53'	59"
Longitude	86°	12'	01"

Holds CP for change to 225-kw max. visual, 828-ft above av. terrain, 836-ft. above ground, 1666-ft. above sea level lat. 39° 53' 57", long. 86° 12' 2"; BPEDT-20081219AEH.

Note: Latitude and longitude coordinates shown are based on the North American Datum of 1927 (NAD 27) as currently required by the Mass Media Bureau of the FCC.

Ownership: Metropolitan Indianapolis Public Broadcasting Inc.

Began Operation: March 10, 2003. Began analog operations: October 4, 1970. Ceased analog operations: June 12, 2009.

Personnel:

Lloyd Wright, President & Chief Executive Officer.

Alan Cloe, Executive Vice President.

Jeanelle Adamak, Executive Vice President.

Mary Hartnett, Radio News Director.

Steve Jensen, Vice President, Broadcast Operations.

Anthony Lorenz, Vice President, Finance & Chief Financial Officer.

Brad Boyd, Vice President, Corporate Development.

David DeMunbrun, Production Operations Director.

Alan Carmack, Television Program Manager.

Rena Barraclough, Vice President, Communications.

WIPB-DT
Muncie
Ch. 23

Grantee: Ball State U., Edmund F. Ball Bldg, Muncie, IN 47306.

Studio: Edmund F. Ball Bldg, Ball State U., Muncie, IN 47306.

Mailing Address: Ball State U, Edmund F. Ball Bldg, Muncie, IN 47306.

Phone: 765-285-1249. **Fax:** 765-285-5548.

Web Site: http://www.bsu.edu/wipb

Technical Facilities: Channel No. 23 (524-530 MHz). Authorized power: 250-kw max. visual, aural. Antenna: 807-ft above av. terrain, 823-ft. above ground, 1818-ft. above sea level.

Latitude	40°	05'	37"
Longitude	85°	23'	32"

Note: Latitude and longitude coordinates shown are based on the North American Datum of 1927 (NAD 27) as currently required by the Mass Media Bureau of the FCC.

Ownership: Ball State U.

Began Operation: February 17, 2009. Began analog operations: May 8, 1953. Ceased analog operations: February 17, 2009.

Personnel:

Alice J. Cheney, General Manager.

Robert Fairchild, Chief Engineer.

Marty Gors, Business Manager.

Sue Bunner, Program Director.

Lori Georgi, Promotion Director.

Shannon Farber, Development Director.

Alan Gordon, Production Manager.

Wanda Refler, Traffic Manager.

WNIT-DT
South Bend
Ch. 35

Licensee: Michiana Public Broadcasting Corp., PO Box 3434, Elkhart, IN 46515-3434.

Studio: 2300 Charger Blvd, Elkhart, IN 46514.

Mailing Address: PO Box 3434, Elkhart, IN 46515-3434.

Phone: 574-675-9648. **Fax:** 574-262-8497.

Web Site: http://www.wnit.org

Technical Facilities: Channel No. 35 (596-602 MHz). Authorized power: 50-kw max. visual, aural. Antenna: 1092-ft above av. terrain, 1010-ft. above ground, 1885-ft. above sea level.

Latitude	41°	36'	49"
Longitude	86°	11'	20"

Holds CP for change to 85-kw max. visual; BPEDT-20081103ACU.

Note: Latitude and longitude coordinates shown are based on the North American Datum of 1927 (NAD 27) as currently required by the Mass Media Bureau of the FCC.

Ownership: Michiana Public Broadcasting Corp.

Began Operation: April 30, 2003. Standard and High Definition. Began analog operations: February 18, 1974. On March 12, 2008, analog broadcasts ceased after transmitter failure. Station was granted an STA by the FCC May 15, 2008 to terminate analog operations.

Personnel:

Mary Pruess, President & General Manager.

Brian Hoover, Broadcast Operations Director & Chief Engineer.

Amy L. Cassidy, Assistant General Manager for Support Services.

Angela Moisenko, Program Director.

Kori Schenk, Graphic Designer.

Diane Marlow, Traffic Coordinator.

Doug Farmwald, Content & Outreach Director.

Cindy McCraner, Membership Manager.

WVUT-DT
Vincennes
Ch. 22

Licensee: Board of Trustees for Vincennes U., 1002 N. First St, Vincennes, IN 47591.

Studio: 1200 N 2nd St, Vincennes, IN 47591.

Mailing Address: 1200 N. 2nd St, Vincennes, IN 47591.

Phone: 812-888-4345. **Fax:** 812-882-2237.

Web Site: http://www.vubroadcasting.org

Technical Facilities: Channel No. 22 (518-524 MHz). Authorized power: 57-kw max. visual, aural. Antenna: 538-ft above av. terrain, 489-ft. above ground, 989-ft. above sea level.

Latitude	38°	39'	06"
Longitude	87°	28'	37"

Note: Latitude and longitude coordinates shown are based on the North American Datum of 1927 (NAD 27) as currently required by the Mass Media Bureau of the FCC.

Ownership: Vincennes U.

Began Operation: September 30, 2002. Station broadcasting digitally on its analog channel allotment. Began analog operations: May 25, 1964. Ceased analog operations: June 12, 2009.

Personnel:

Al Rerko, General Manager & Business Manager.

John Szink, News Director.

James Evans, Chief Engineer.

Sharon Kiefer, Program, Promotion & Traffic Manager.

Jill Ballinger, Production Manager.

Rebecca Clark, Producer & Director, Remote Productions.

Julie Sievers, Producer & Director, Remote Productions.

Tony Cloyd, News & Sports Producer.

Iowa

KEFB-DT
Ames
Ch. 34

Licensee: Family Educational Broadcasting Inc., PO Box 201, Huxley, IA 50124-0201.

Studio: PO Box 201, Huxley, IA 50124-0201.

Mailing Address: PO Box 201, Huxley, IA 50124.

Phone: 515-597-3138.

Technical Facilities: Channel No. 34 (590-596 MHz). Authorized power: 37.23-kw max. visual, aural. Antenna: 505-ft above av. terrain, 472-ft. above ground, 1522-ft. above sea level.

Latitude	41°	58'	49"
Longitude	93°	44'	23"

Transmitter: 2175 260th St., 1.3-mi. W of Napier.

Note: Latitude and longitude coordinates shown are based on the North American Datum of 1927 (NAD 27) as currently required by the Mass Media Bureau of the FCC.

Ownership: Family Educational Broadcasting Inc.

Began Operation: June 12, 2009. Station broadcasting digitally on its analog channel allotment. Began analog operations: October 25, 2005. Ceased analog operations: June 12, 2009.

KBIN-DT
Council Bluffs
Ch. 33

Licensee: Iowa Public Broadcasting Board, PO Box 6450, Johnston, IA 50131-6450.

Studio: 6450 Corporate Dr, Johnston, IA 50131.

Mailing Address: PO Box 6450, Johnston, IA 50131-6450.

Phones: 515-242-3100; 800-532-1290. Fax: 515-242-5404.

Web Site: http://www.iptv.org

Technical Facilities: Channel No. 33 (584-590 MHz). Authorized power: 200-kw max. visual, aural. Antenna: 322-ft above av. terrain, 141-ft. above ground, 1391-ft. above sea level.

Latitude	41°	15'	15"
Longitude	95°	50'	08"

Note: Latitude and longitude coordinates shown are based on the North American Datum of 1927 (NAD 27) as currently required by the Mass Media Bureau of the FCC.

Ownership: Iowa Public Television.

Began Operation: May 1, 2003. Standard Definition. Began analog operations: September 7, 1975. Ceased analog operations: June 12, 2009.

Personnel:

Daniel K. Miller, Executive Director & General Manager.

Rebecca Ketcherside, Operations Manager.

William Hayes, Engineering Director.

Kris Houston, Administration Director.

Molly M. Phillips, Communications Director.

Susan Moritz, Foundation President.

Wayne Bruns, Production Manager, Local Programming.

Fran Cleaver, Traffic Manager.

Terry Rinehart, Education Director.

KQIN-DT
Davenport
Ch. 34

Grantee: Iowa Public Broadcasting Board, PO Box 6450, Johnston, IA 50131-6450.

Studio: 6450 Corporate Dr, Johnston, IA 50131.

Mailing Address: PO Box 6450, Johnston, IA 50131-6450.

Phones: 515-242-3100; 800-532-1290. Fax: 515-242-5404.

Web Site: http://www.iptv.org

Technical Facilities: Channel No. 34 (590-596 MHz). Authorized power: 368-kw max. visual, aural. Antenna: 764-ft above av. terrain, 748-ft. above ground, 1501-ft. above sea level.

Latitude	41°	18'	44"
Longitude	90°	22'	46"

Note: Latitude and longitude coordinates shown are based on the North American Datum of 1927 (NAD 27) as currently required by the Mass Media Bureau of the FCC.

Ownership: Iowa Public Broadcasting Board.

Began Operation: May 1, 2003. Began analog operations: December 16, 1991. Ceased analog operations: June 12, 2009.

Personnel:

Daniel K. Miller, Executive Director.

Rebecca Ketcherside, Operations Manager.

William T. Hayes, Engineering Director.

Kris Houston, Administration Director.

Molly M. Phillips, Communications Director.

Susan Moritz, Foundation President.

Wayne Bruns, Production Manager, Local Programming.

Fran Cleaver, Traffic Manager.

Terry Rinehart, Education Director.

KDIN-DT
Des Moines
Ch. 11

Licensee: Iowa Public Broadcasting Board, PO Box 6450, Johnston, IA 50131-6450.

Studio: 6450 Corporate Dr, Johnston, IA 50131.

Mailing Address: PO Box 6450, Johnston, IA 50131-6450.

Phones: 515-242-3100; 800-532-1290. Fax: 515-242-5404.

Web Site: http://www.iptv.org

Technical Facilities: Channel No. 11 (198-204 MHz). Authorized power: 22.5-kw visual, aural. Antenna: 1968-ft above av. terrain, 1942-ft. above ground, 2930-ft. above sea level.

Latitude	41°	48'	33"
Longitude	93°	36'	53"

Note: Latitude and longitude coordinates shown are based on the North American Datum of 1927 (NAD 27) as currently required by the Mass Media Bureau of the FCC.

Ownership: Iowa Public Television.

Began Operation: October 1, 2000. Station broadcasting digitally on its analog channel allotment. Began analog operations: April 27, 1959. Ceased analog operations: June 12, 2009.

Personnel:

Daniel K. Miller, Executive Director.

Rebecca Ketcherside, Operations Manager.

William Hayes, Engineering Director.

Kris Houston, Administration Director.

Molly M. Phillips, Communications Director.

Susan Moritz, Foundation President.

Wayne Bruns, Production Manager, Local Programming.

Fran Cleaver, Traffic Manager.

Terry Rinehart, Education Director.

KTIN-DT
Fort Dodge
Ch. 25

Licensee: Iowa Public Broadcasting Board, PO Box 6450, Johnston, IA 50131-6450.

Studio: 6450 Corporate Dr, Johnston, IA 50131.

Mailing Address: PO Box 6450, Johnston, IA 50131-6450.

Phones: 515-242-3100; 800-532-1290. Fax: 515-242-5404.

Web Site: http://www.iptv.org

Technical Facilities: Channel No. 25 (536-542 MHz). Authorized power: 600-kw max. visual, aural. Antenna: 1165-ft above av. terrain, 1166-ft. above ground, 2334-ft. above sea level.

Latitude	42°	49'	03"
Longitude	94°	24'	41"

Note: Latitude and longitude coordinates shown are based on the North American Datum of 1927 (NAD 27) as currently required by the Mass Media Bureau of the FCC.

Ownership: Iowa Public Television.

Began Operation: August 21, 2007. Began analog operations: April 8, 1977. Ceased analog operations: June 12, 2009.

Personnel:

Daniel K. Miller, Executive Director & General Manager.

Kris Houston, Director of Administration.

Rebecca Ketcherside, Operations Manager.

Susan Moritz, Foundation President.

Bill Hayes, Engineering Director.

Molly M. Phillips, Communications Director.

Wayne Bruns, Production Manager of Local Programming.

Fran Cleaver, Traffic Manager.

Terry Rinehart, Education Director.

KIIN-DT
Iowa City
Ch. 12

Grantee: Iowa Public Broadcasting Board, PO Box 6450, Johnston, IA 50131-6450.

Studio: 6450 Corporate Dr, Johnston, IA 50131.

Mailing Address: PO Box 6450, Johnston, IA 50131-6450.

Phones: 515-242-3100; 800-532-1290. Fax: 515-242-5404.

Web Site: http://www.iptv.org

Technical Facilities: Channel No. 12 (204-210 MHz). Authorized power: 17.8-kw visual, aural. Antenna: 1440-ft above av. terrain, 1394-ft. above ground, 2194-ft. above sea level.

Latitude	41°	43'	15"
Longitude	91°	20'	29.4"

Requests modification of CP for change to 57-kw visual; BMPEDT-20080620AHR.

Note: Latitude and longitude coordinates shown are based on the North American Datum of 1927 (NAD 27) as currently required by the Mass Media Bureau of the FCC.

Ownership: Iowa Public Television.

Began Operation: June 7, 2007. Station broadcasting digitally on its analog channel allotment. Began analog operations: February 8, 1970. Ceased analog operations: June 12, 2009.

Personnel:

Daniel K. Miller, Executive Director & General Manager.

Rebecca Ketcherside, Operations Manager.

William Hayes, Engineering Director.

Kris Houston, Administration Director.

Molly M. Phillips, Communications Director.

Susan Moritz, Foundation President.

Wayne Bruns, Production Manager, Local Programming.

Fran Cleaver, Traffic Manager.

Terry Rinehart, Education Director.

KYIN-DT
Mason City
Ch. 18

Licensee: Iowa Public Broadcasting Board, PO Box 6450, Johnston, IA 50131-6450.

Studio: 6450 Corporate Dr, Johnston, IA 50131.

Mailing Address: PO Box 6450, Johnston, IA 50131-6450.

Phones: 515-242-3100; 800-532-1290. Fax: 515-242-5404.

Email: janice@iptv.org Web Site: http://www.iptv.org

Technical Facilities: Channel No. 18 (494-500 MHz). Authorized power: 250-kw max. visual, aural. Antenna: 1471-ft above av. terrain, 1475-ft. above ground, 2750-ft. above sea level.

Latitude	43°	28'	32"
Longitude	92°	42'	29"

Holds CP for change to 533-kw max. visual; BPEDT-20080620AFL.

Note: Latitude and longitude coordinates shown are based on the North American Datum of 1927 (NAD 27) as currently required by the Mass Media Bureau of the FCC.

Ownership: Iowa Public Television.

Began Operation: September 13, 2007. Began analog operations: May 14, 1977. Ceased analog operations: June 12, 2009.

Personnel:

Daniel K. Miller, Executive Director.

Rebecca Ketcherside, Operations Manager.

William Hayes, Engineering Director.

Kris Houston, Administration Director.

Molly M. Phillips, Communications Director.

Susan Moritz, Foundation President.

Wayne Bruns, Production Manager, Local Programming.

Fran Cleaver, Traffic Manager.

Terry Rinehart, Education Director.

KHIN-DT
Red Oak
Ch. 35

Licensee: Iowa Public Broadcasting Board, PO Box 6450, Johnston, IA 50131-6450.

Studio: 6450 Corporate Dr, Johnstown, IA 50131.

Mailing Address: PO Box 6450, Johnston, IA 50131-6450.

Phones: 515-242-3100; 800-532-1290. **Fax:** 515-242-5404.

Web Site: http://www.iptv.org

Technical Facilities: Channel No. 35 (596-602 MHz). Authorized power: 600-kw max. visual, aural. Antenna: 1558-ft above av. terrain, 1480-ft. above ground, 2808-ft. above sea level.

Latitude	41°	20'	40"
Longitude	95°	15'	21"

Note: Latitude and longitude coordinates shown are based on the North American Datum of 1927 (NAD 27) as currently required by the Mass Media Bureau of the FCC.

Ownership: Iowa Public Television.

Began Operation: October 21, 2005. Began analog operations: September 7, 1975. Ceased analog operations: June 12, 2009.

Personnel:

Daniel Miller, Executive Director & General Manager.

Rebecca Ketcherside, Operations Manager.

Bill Hayes, Engineering Director.

Kris Houston, Administration Director.

Molly M. Phillips, Communications Director.

Susan Moritz, Foundation President.

Wayne Bruns, Production Manager, Local Programming.

Fran Cleaver, Traffic Manager.

Terry Rinehart, Education Director.

KSIN-DT
Sioux City
Ch. 28

Licensee: Iowa Public Broadcasting Board, PO Box 6450, Johnston, IA 50131-6450.

Studio: 6450 Corporate Dr, Johnston, IA 50131.

Mailing Address: PO Box 6450, Johnston, IA 50131-6450.

Phones: 515-242-3100; 800-532-1290. **Fax:** 515-242-5404.

Web Site: http://www.iptv.org

Technical Facilities: Channel No. 28 (554-560 MHz). Authorized power: 400-kw max. visual, aural. Antenna: 1143-ft above av. terrain, 944-ft. above ground, 2365-ft. above sea level.

Latitude	42°	30'	53"
Longitude	96°	18'	15"

Note: Latitude and longitude coordinates shown are based on the North American Datum of 1927 (NAD 27) as currently required by the Mass Media Bureau of the FCC.

Ownership: Iowa Public Television.

Began Operation: July 1, 2004. Began analog operations: January 4, 1975. Ceased analog operations: June 12, 2009.

Personnel:

Daniel K. Miller, Executive Director.

Rebecca Ketcherside, Operations Manager.

William Hayes, Engineering Director.

Kris Houston, Administration Director.

Molly M. Phillips, Communications Director.

Susan Moritz, Foundation President.

Wayne Bruns, Production Manager, Local Programming.

Fran Cleaver, Traffic Manager.

Terry Rinehart, Education Director.

KRIN-DT
Waterloo
Ch. 35

Licensee: Iowa Public Broadcasting Board, PO Box 6450, Johnston, IA 50131-6450.

Studio: 6450 Corporate Dr, Johnston, IA 50131.

Mailing Address: PO Box 6450, Johnston, IA 50131-6450.

Phones: 515-242-3100; 800-532-1290. **Fax:** 515-242-5404.

Web Site: http://www.iptv.org

Technical Facilities: Channel No. 35 (596-602 MHz). Authorized power: 250-kw max. visual, aural. Antenna: 1916-ft above av. terrain, 1811-ft. above ground, 2828-ft. above sea level.

Latitude	42°	18'	59"
Longitude	91°	51'	31"

Note: Latitude and longitude coordinates shown are based on the North American Datum of 1927 (NAD 27) as currently required by the Mass Media Bureau of the FCC.

Ownership: Iowa Public Television.

Began Operation: February 17, 2005. Began analog operations: December 15, 1974. Ceased analog operations: June 12, 2009.

Personnel:

Daniel K. Miller, Executive Director.

Rebecca Ketcherside, Operations Manager.

William Hayes, Engineering Director.

Kris Houston, Administration Director.

Molly M. Phillips, Communications Director.

Susan Moritz, Foundation President.

Wayne Bruns, Production Manager, Local Programming.

Fran Cleaver, Traffic Manager.

Terry Rinehart, Education Director.

Kansas

KWKS-DT
Colby
Ch. 19

Licensee: Smoky Hills Public Television Corp., PO Box 9, 604 Elm St, Bunker Hill, KS 67626-0009.

Studio: 604 Elm St, Bunker Hill, KS 67626.

Mailing Address: PO Box 9, Bunker Hill, KS 67626.

Phone: 785-483-6990. **Fax:** 785-483-4605.

Web Site: http://www.shptv.org

Technical Facilities: Channel No. 19 (500-506 MHz). Authorized power: 464-kw max. visual, aural. Antenna: 1257-ft above av. terrain, 1224-ft. above ground, 4666-ft. above sea level.

Latitude	39°	14'	31"
Longitude	101°	21'	38"

Note: Latitude and longitude coordinates shown are based on the North American Datum of 1927 (NAD 27) as currently required by the Mass Media Bureau of the FCC.

Ownership: Smoky Hills Public Television Corp.

Began Operation: July 26, 2007. Station went directly to digital broadcast; no analog application.

Personnel:

Lawrence Holden, Chief Executive Officer & General Manager.

Terry Cutler, Chief Engineer.

Brian Pertl, Engineering Assistant.

Debra Creamer, Administration & Finance Director.

Mary Pat Waymaster, Broadcasting Director.

Jane Habinger, Marketing & Communications Director.

Glenna Letsch, Traffic Coordinator.

Dale Staab, Corporate Support Representative.

Susan Penka, Corporate Support Representative.

Malinda Walker, Membership Services Director.

Michael Quade, Production Specialist.

KDCK-DT
Dodge City
Ch. 21

Licensee: Smoky Hills Public Television Corp., PO Box 9, 604 Elm St, Bunker Hill, KS 67626-0009.

Studio: 604 Elm St, Bunker Hill, KS 67626.

Mailing Address: PO Box 9, Bunker Hill, KS 67626.

Phone: 785-483-6990. **Fax:** 785-483-4605.

Web Site: http://www.shptv.org

Technical Facilities: Channel No. 21 (512-518 MHz). Authorized power: 8.42-kw max. visual, aural. Antenna: 325-ft above av. terrain, 372-ft. above ground, 2926-ft. above sea level.

Latitude	37°	49'	33"
Longitude	100°	10'	40"

Note: Latitude and longitude coordinates shown are based on the North American Datum of 1927 (NAD 27) as currently required by the Mass Media Bureau of the FCC.

Ownership: Smoky Hills Public Television Corp.

Began Operation: June 1, 2007. Station broadcasting digitally on its analog allotment. Began analog operations: March 3, 1998. Ceased analog operations: June 1, 2007.

Personnel:

Lawrence Holden, Chief Executive Officer & General Manager.

Terry Cutler, Chief Engineer.

Brian Pertl, Engineering Assistant.

Debra Creamer, Administration & Finance Director.

Mary Pat Waymaster, Broadcasting Director.

Jane Habinger, Marketing & Communications Director.

Glenna Letsch, Traffic Coordinator.

Dale Staab, Corporate Support Representative.

Susan Penka, Corporate Support Representative.

Malinda Walker, Membership Services Director.

Michael Quade, Production Specialist.

KOOD-DT
Hays
Ch. 16

Licensee: Smoky Hills Public Television Corp., PO Box 9, 604 Elm St, Bunker Hill, KS 67626-0009.

Studio: 604 Elm St, Bunker Hill, KS 67626.

Mailing Address: PO Box 9, Bunker Hill, KS 67626.

Phone: 785-483-6990. **Fax:** 785-483-4605.

Web Site: http://www.shptv.org

Technical Facilities: Channel No. 16 (482-488 MHz). Authorized power: 496-kw max. visual, aural. Antenna: 997-ft above av. terrain, 961-ft. above ground, 2802-ft. above sea level.

	Latitude	38°	46'	16"
	Longitude	98°	44'	16"

Note: Latitude and longitude coordinates shown are based on the North American Datum of 1927 (NAD 27) as currently required by the Mass Media Bureau of the FCC.

Ownership: Smoky Hills Public Television Corp.

Began Operation: March 15, 2003. Standard and High Definition. Began analog operations: November 10, 1982. Ceased analog operations: February 17, 2009.

Personnel:

Lawrence Holden, Chief Executive Officer & General Manager.

Terry Cutler, Chief Engineer.

Brian Pertl, Engineering Assistant.

Debra Creamer, Administration & Finance Director.

Mary Pat Waymaster, Broadcasting Director.

Glenna Letsch, Traffic Coordinator.

Dale Staab, Corporate Support Representative.

Malinda Walker, Membership Services Director.

Susan Penka, Corporate Support Representative.

Michael Quade, Production Specialist.

Jane Habinger, Marketing & Communications Director.

KPTS-DT
Hutchinson
Ch. 8

Licensee: Kansas Public Telecommunications Service Inc., 320 W. 21st St. N, Wichita, KS 67203.

Studio: 320 W 21st St. N, Wichita, KS 67203-2499.

Mailing Address: 320 W 21st St N, Wichita, KS 67203-2499.

Phones: 316-838-3090; 800-794-8498. **Fax:** 316-838-8586.

Web Site: http://www.kpts.org

Technical Facilities: Channel No. 8 (180-186 MHz). Authorized power: 32-kw visual, aural. Antenna: 801-ft above av. terrain, 742-ft. above ground, 2312-ft. above sea level.

	Latitude	38°	03'	21"
	Longitude	97°	46'	35"

Note: Latitude and longitude coordinates shown are based on the North American Datum of 1927 (NAD 27) as currently required by the Mass Media Bureau of the FCC.

Ownership: Kansas Public Telecommunications Service Inc.

Began Operation: April 1, 2003. Standard and High Definition. Station broadcasting digitally on its analog channel allotment. Began analog operations: January 5, 1970. Ceased analog operations: January 5, 2009.

Personnel:

Dave McClintock, Interim General Manager & Technology Director.

Carolyn Potter, Administration Manager.

Jesse Huxman, Content Director.

David Brewer, Program Manager.

Bob Locke, Chief Engineer.

Molly Fox, Development Director.

Pat McKaig, Controller.

Kelly Wilkerson, Promotions Manager.

Gabe Juhnke, Production Manager.

KSWK-DT
Lakin
Ch. 8

Licensee: Smoky Hills Public Television Corp., PO Box 9, 604 Elm St, Bunker Hill, KS 67626-0009.

Studio: 604 Elm St, Bunker Hill, KS 67626.

Mailing Address: PO Box 9, Bunker Hill, KS 67626.

Phone: 785-483-6990. **Fax:** 785-483-4605.

Web Site: http://www.shptv.org

Technical Facilities: Channel No. 8 (180-186 MHz). Authorized power: 33-kw visual, aural. Antenna: 502-ft above av. terrain, 479-ft. above ground, 3484-ft. above sea level.

	Latitude	37°	49'	40"
	Longitude	101°	06'	35"

Note: Latitude and longitude coordinates shown are based on the North American Datum of 1927 (NAD 27) as currently required by the Mass Media Bureau of the FCC.

Ownership: Smoky Hills Public Television Corp.

Began Operation: December 1, 2005. Began analog operations: March 15, 1989. Ceased analog operations: February 17, 2009.

Personnel:

Lawrence Holden, Chief Executive Officer & General Manager.

Terry Cutler, Chief Engineer.

Brian Pertl, Engineering Assistant.

Debra Creamer, Administration & Finance Director.

Mary Pat Waymaster, Broadcasting Director.

Jane Habiger, Marketing & Communications Director.

Glenna Letsch, Traffic Coordinator.

Dale Staab, Corporate Support Representative.

Malinda Walker, Membership Services Director.

Susan Penka, Corporate Support Representative.

Michael Quade, Production Specialist.

KTWU-DT
Topeka
Ch. 11

Licensee: Washburn U. of Topeka, 1700 SW College Ave, Topeka, KS 66621-1100.

Studio: 19th & Jewell Ave, Topeka, KS 66621-1100.

Mailing Address: 1700 College Ave, Topeka, KS 66621-1100.

Phones: 785-670-1111; 800-866-5895. **Fax:** 785-670-1112.

Web Site: http://ktwu.washburn.edu

Technical Facilities: Channel No. 11 (198-204 MHz). Authorized power: 25-kw visual, aural. Antenna: 991-ft above av. terrain, 901-ft. above ground, 1982-ft. above sea level.

	Latitude	39°	03'	50"
	Longitude	95°	45'	49"

Holds CP for change to 38-kw visual, 991-ft above av. terrain, 901-ft. above ground, 1980-ft. above sea level; BPEDT-20090728ACW.

Note: Latitude and longitude coordinates shown are based on the North American Datum of 1927 (NAD 27) as currently required by the Mass Media Bureau of the FCC.

Ownership: Washburn U.

Began Operation: February 17, 2009. Station broadcasting digitally on its analog channel allotment. Began analog operations: October 21, 1965. Ceased analog operations: February 17, 2009.

Personnel:

Eugene Williams, Chief Executive Officer & General Manager.

Duane Loyd, Chief Engineer.

Val VanDerSluis, Program Director.

Kevin Goodman, Marketing & Promotion Director.

Dave Kendall, Production Director.

Cindy Barry, Development Director.

Mary Livingston, Traffic Director.

Kentucky

WKAS-DT
Ashland
Ch. 26

Licensee: Kentucky Authority for ETV, 600 Cooper Dr, Lexington, KY 40502-2296.

Studio: 600 Cooper Dr, Lexington, KY 40502-2296.

Mailing Address: 600 Cooper Dr, Lexington, KY 40502-2296.

Phones: 859-258-7000; 800-432-0951. **Fax:** 859-258-7399.

Email: tbischoff@ket.org **Web Site:** http://www.ket.org

Technical Facilities: Channel No. 26 (542-548 MHz). Authorized power: 61.3-kw max. visual, aural. Antenna: 449-ft above av. terrain, 344-ft. above ground, 1151-ft. above sea level.

	Latitude	38°	27'	44"
	Longitude	82°	37'	12"

Transmitter: DeBord St.

Note: Latitude and longitude coordinates shown are based on the North American Datum of 1927 (NAD 27) as currently required by the Mass Media Bureau of the FCC.

Ownership: Kentucky Authority for ETV.

Began Operation: March 17, 2002. Standard Definition. Began analog operations: September 23, 1968. Ceased analog operations: June 12, 2009.

Personnel:

Malcolm Wall, Executive Director.

Michele Ripley, President, Commonwealth Fund for KET.

Linda Hume, Deputy Executive Director, Administration & Support.

Bill Wilson, Deputy Executive Director, Education & Outreach.

Shae Hopkins, Deputy Executive Director, Programming & Production.

Mike Clark, Technology Director.

Rick Melton, Studio Engineering Director.

Robert Ball, Transmission Systems Director.

Craig Cornwell, Programming Director.

Kathy Quinn, Education Director.

Tim Bischoff, Marketing Director.

Mike Brower, Production Director.

WKGB-DT
Bowling Green
Ch. 48

Grantee: Kentucky Authority for ETV, 600 Cooper Dr, Lexington, KY 40502-2296.

Studio: 600 Cooper Dr, Lexington, KY 40502-2296.

Mailing Address: 600 Cooper Dr, Lexington, KY 40502-2296.

Phones: 859-258-7000; 800-432-0951. **Fax:** 859-258-7399.

Email: tbischoff@ket.org **Web Site:** http://www.ket.org

Technical Facilities: Channel No. 48 (674-680 MHz). Authorized power: 54.8-kw max. visual, aural. Antenna: 768-ft above av. terrain, 548-ft. above ground, 1306-ft. above sea level.

	Latitude	37°	05'	22"
	Longitude	86°	38'	05"

Note: Latitude and longitude coordinates shown are based on the North American Datum of 1927 (NAD 27) as currently required by the Mass Media Bureau of the FCC.

Ownership: Kentucky Authority for ETV.

Began Operation: February 28, 2002. Standard Definition. Began analog operations: September 23, 1968. Ceased analog operations: June 12, 2009.

Personnel:

Malcolm Wall, Executive Director.

Bill Wilson, Deputy Executive Director, Education & Outreach.

Mike Clark, Technology Planning Director.

Craig Cornwell, Programming Director.

Shae Hopkins, Deputy Executive Director, Programming & Production.

Tim Bischoff, Marketing Director.

Robert Ball, Transmission Systems Director.

Linda Hume, Deputy Executive Director, Administration & Support.

Rick Melton, Studio Engineering Director.

Kathy Quinn, Education Director.

Mike Brower, Production Director.

Michele Ripley, President, Commonwealth Fund for KET.

WKYU-DT
Bowling Green
Ch. 18

Licensee: Western Kentucky U., 1906 College Heights Blvd, No. 11034, Bowling Green, KY 42101-1034.

Studio: 1906 College Heights Blvd, No. 11034, Bowling Green, KY 42101-1034.

Mailing Address: 1906 College Heights Blvd, No 11034, Bowling Green, KY 42101-1034.

Phones: 270-745-2400; 800-599-2424. **Fax:** 270-745-2084.

Web Site: http://www.wkyupbs.org

Technical Facilities: Channel No. 18 (494-500 MHz). Authorized power: 61-kw max. visual, aural. Antenna: 580-ft above av. terrain, 400-ft. above ground, 1140-ft. above sea level.

| Latitude | 37° | 03' | 49" |
| Longitude | 86° | 26' | 07" |

Note: Latitude and longitude coordinates shown are based on the North American Datum of 1927 (NAD 27) as currently required by the Mass Media Bureau of the FCC.

Ownership: Western Kentucky U.

Began Operation: February 17, 2009. Began analog operations: February 21, 1989. Ceased analog operations: February 17, 2009.

Personnel:

Linda Gerofsky, Station Manager.

Justin Davis, Operations Manager.

Roger Hall, Acting Chief Engineer.

Rita Isenberg, Business Manager.

Linda Oldham, Program Director.

David Brinkley, Senior Producer & Director.

Terry Reagan, Development Director.

Dana Divine, Traffic Manager.

Jack A. Hanes, Educational Telecommunications Director.

WCVN-DT
Covington
Ch. 24

Licensee: Kentucky Authority for ETV, 600 Cooper Dr, Lexington, KY 40502-2296.

Studio: 600 Cooper Dr, Lexington, KY 40502-2296.

Mailing Address: 600 Cooper Dr, Lexington, KY 40502-2296.

Phones: 859-258-7000; 800-432-0951. **Fax:** 859-258-7399.

Email: tbischoff@ket.org **Web Site:** http://www.ket.org

Technical Facilities: Channel No. 24 (530-536 MHz). Authorized power: 53.5-kw max. visual, aural. Antenna: 384-ft above av. terrain, 269-ft. above ground, 1099-ft. above sea level.

| Latitude | 39° | 01' | 50" |
| Longitude | 84° | 30' | 23" |

Note: Latitude and longitude coordinates shown are based on the North American Datum of 1927 (NAD 27) as currently required by the Mass Media Bureau of the FCC.

Ownership: Kentucky Authority for ETV.

Began Operation: January 24, 2002. Standard Definition. Began analog operations: September 8, 1969. Ceased analog operations: June 12, 2009.

Personnel:

Malcolm Wall, Executive Director.

Michele Ripley, President, Commonwealth Fund for KET.

Bill Wilson, Deputy Executive Director, Education & Outreach.

Linda Hume, Deputy Executive Director, Administration & Support.

Shae Hopkins, Deputy Executive Director, Programming & Production.

Rick Melton, Studio Engineering Director.

Craig Cornwell, Programming Director.

Timothy Bischoff, Marketing Director.

Robert Ball, Transmission Systems Director.

Mike Clark, Technology Planning Director.

Kathy Quinn, Education Director.

Mike Brower, Production Director.

WKZT-DT
Elizabethtown
Ch. 43

Licensee: Kentucky Authority for ETV, 600 Cooper Dr, Lexington, KY 40502-2296.

Studio: 600 Cooper Dr, Lexington, KY 40502-2296.

Mailing Address: 600 Cooper Dr, Lexington, KY 40502-2296.

Phones: 859-258-7000; 800-432-0951. **Fax:** 859-258-7399.

Email: tbischoff@ket.org **Web Site:** http://www.ket.org

Technical Facilities: Channel No. 43 (644-650 MHz). Authorized power: 61-kw max. visual, aural. Antenna: 584-ft above av. terrain, 571-ft. above ground, 1348-ft. above sea level.

| Latitude | 37° | 40' | 55" |
| Longitude | 85° | 50' | 31" |

Note: Latitude and longitude coordinates shown are based on the North American Datum of 1927 (NAD 27) as currently required by the Mass Media Bureau of the FCC.

Ownership: Kentucky Authority for ETV.

Began Operation: December 17, 2001. Standard Definition. Began analog operations: September 23, 1968. Ceased analog operations: June 12, 2009.

Personnel:

Malcolm Wall, Executive Director.

Michele Ripley, President, Commonwealth Fund for KET.

Linda Hume, Deputy Executive Director, Administration & Support.

Bill Wilson, Deputy Executive Director, Education & Outreach.

Shae Hopkins, Deputy Executive Director, Programming & Production.

Mike Clark, Technology Director.

Rick Melton, Studio Engineering Director.

Robert Ball, Transmission Systems Director.

Craig Cornwell, Programming Director.

Kathy Quinn, Education Director.

Mike Brower, Production Director.

Tim Bischoff, Marketing Director.

WKHA-DT
Hazard
Ch. 16

Grantee: Kentucky Authority for ETV, 600 Cooper Dr, Lexington, KY 40502-2296.

Studio: 600 Cooper Dr, Lexington, KY 40502-2296.

Mailing Address: 600 Cooper Dr, Lexington, KY 40502-2296.

Phones: 859-258-7000; 800-432-0951. **Fax:** 859-258-7399.

Email: tbischoff@ket.org **Web Site:** http://www.ket.org

Technical Facilities: Channel No. 16 (482-488 MHz). Authorized power: 53.2-kw max. visual, aural. Antenna: 1211-ft above av. terrain, 528-ft. above ground, 2526-ft. above sea level.

| Latitude | 37° | 11' | 35" |
| Longitude | 83° | 11' | 17" |

Note: Latitude and longitude coordinates shown are based on the North American Datum of 1927 (NAD 27) as currently required by the Mass Media Bureau of the FCC.

Ownership: Kentucky Authority for ETV.

Began Operation: January 29, 2002. Began analog operations: December 16, 1968. Ceased analog operations: June 12, 2009.

Personnel:

Malcolm Wall, Executive Director.

Bill Wilson, Deputy Executive Director, Education & Outreach.

Mike Clark, Technology Planning Director.

Craig Cornwell, Programming Director.

Shae Hopkins, Deputy Executive Director, Programming & Production.

Tim Bischoff, Marketing Director.

Robert Ball, Transmission Systems Director.

Linda Hume, Deputy Executive Director, Administration & Support.

Rick Melton, Studio Engineering Director.

Mike Brower, Production Director.

Michele Ripley, President, Commonwealth Fund for KET.

Kathy Quinn, Education Director.

WKLE-DT
Lexington
Ch. 42

Licensee: Kentucky Authority for ETV, 600 Cooper Dr, Lexington, KY 40502-2296.

Studio: 600 Cooper Dr, Lexington, KY 40502-2296.

Mailing Address: 600 Cooper Dr, Lexington, KY 40502-2296.

Phones: 859-258-7000; 800-432-0951. **Fax:** 856-258-7399.

Email: tbischoff@ket.org **Web Site:** http://www.ket.org

Technical Facilities: Channel No. 42 (638-644 MHz). Authorized power: 45.8-kw max. visual, aural. Antenna: 845-ft above av. terrain, 788-ft. above ground, 1703-ft. above sea level.

| Latitude | 37° | 52' | 45" |
| Longitude | 84° | 19' | 33" |

Note: Latitude and longitude coordinates shown are based on the North American Datum of 1927 (NAD 27) as currently required by the Mass Media Bureau of the FCC.

Ownership: Kentucky Authority for ETV.

Began Operation: November 14, 2001. Standard Definition. Began analog operations: September 23, 1968. Ceased analog operations: June 12, 2009.

Personnel:

Malcolm Wall, Executive Director.

Michele Ripley, President, Commonwealth Fund for KET.

Bill Wilson, Deputy Executive Director, Education & Outreach.

Mike Clark, Technology & Support Director.

Craig Cornwell, Programming Director.

Shae Hopkins, Deputy Executive Director, Programming & Production.

Tim Bischoff, Marketing Director.

Robert Ball, Transmission Systems Director.

Linda Hume, Deputy Executive Director, Administration & Support.

Rick Melton, Studio Engineering Director.

Kathy Quinn, Education Director.

Mike Brower, Production Director.

WKMJ-DT
Louisville
Ch. 38

Licensee: Kentucky Authority for ETV, 600 Cooper Dr, Lexington, KY 40502-2296.

Studio: 600 Cooper Dr, Lexington, KY 40502-2296.

Mailing Address: 600 Cooper Dr, Lexington, KY 40502-2296.

Phones: 859-258-7000; 800-432-0951. **Fax:** 859-258-7399.

Email: tbischoff@ket.org **Web Site:** http://www.ket.org

Technical Facilities: Channel No. 38 (614-620 MHz). Authorized power: 61.6-kw max. visual, aural. Antenna: 715-ft above av. terrain, 367-ft. above ground, 1345-ft. above sea level.

Latitude	38°	22'	01"
Longitude	85°	49'	54"

Note: Latitude and longitude coordinates shown are based on the North American Datum of 1927 (NAD 27) as currently required by the Mass Media Bureau of the FCC.

Ownership: Kentucky Authority for ETV.

Began Operation: April 1, 2003. Began analog operations: September 2, 1970. Ceased analog operations: June 12, 2009.

Personnel:

Malcolm Wall, Executive Director.

Michele Ripley, President, Commonwealth Fund for KET.

Linda Hume, Deputy Executive Director, Administration & Support.

Bill Wilson, Deputy Executive Director, Education & Outreach.

Shae Hopkins, Deputy Executive Director, Programming & Production.

Mike Clark, Technology Director.

Rick Melton, Studio Engineering Director.

Robert Ball, Transmission Systems Director.

Craig Cornwell, Programming Director.

Kathy Quinn, Education Director.

Mike Brower, Production Director.

Tim Bischoff, Marketing Director.

WKPC-DT
Louisville
Ch. 17

Licensee: Kentucky Authority for ETV, 600 Cooper Dr, Lexington, KY 40502-2296.

Studio: 600 Cooper Dr, Lexington, KY 40502-2296.

Mailing Address: 600 Cooper Dr, Lexington, KY 40502-2296.

Phones: 859-258-7000; 800-432-0951. **Fax:** 859-258-7399.

Email: tbischoff@ket.org **Web Site:** http://www.ket.org

Technical Facilities: Channel No. 17 (488-494 MHz). Authorized power: 60.3-kw max. visual, aural. Antenna: 778-ft above av. terrain, 423-ft. above ground, 1401-ft. above sea level.

Latitude	38°	22'	01"
Longitude	85°	49'	54"

Transmitter: Bald Knob, 3.1-mi. N of New Albany on Bald Knob Rd.

Note: Latitude and longitude coordinates shown are based on the North American Datum of 1927 (NAD 27) as currently required by the Mass Media Bureau of the FCC.

Ownership: Kentucky Authority for ETV.

Began Operation: August 25, 1999. Began analog operations: September 8, 1958. Ceased analog operations: June 12, 2009.

Personnel:

Malcolm Wall, Executive Director.

Michele Ripley, President, Commonwealth Fund for KET.

Bill Wilson, Deputy Executive Director, Education & Outreach.

Mike Clark, Technology Planning Director.

Craig Cornwell, Programming Director.

Shae Hopkins, Deputy Executive Director, Programming & Production.

Tim Bischoff, Marketing Director.

Robert Ball, Transmission Systems Director.

Linda Hume, Deputy Executive Director, Administration & Support.

Rick Melton, Studio Engineering Director.

Kathy Quinn, Education Director.

Mike Brower, Production Director.

WKMA-DT
Madisonville
Ch. 42

Licensee: Kentucky Authority for ETV, 600 Cooper Dr, Lexington, KY 40502-2296.

Studio: 600 Cooper Dr, Lexington, KY 40502-2296.

Mailing Address: 600 Cooper Dr, Lexington, KY 40502-2296.

Phones: 859-258-7000; 800-432-0951. **Fax:** 859-258-7399.

Email: tbischoff@ket.org **Web Site:** http://www.ket.org

Technical Facilities: Channel No. 42 (638-644 MHz). Authorized power: 55.1-kw max. visual, aural. Antenna: 978-ft above av. terrain, 915-ft. above ground, 1467-ft. above sea level.

Latitude	37°	11'	21"
Longitude	87°	30'	49"

Note: Latitude and longitude coordinates shown are based on the North American Datum of 1927 (NAD 27) as currently required by the Mass Media Bureau of the FCC.

Ownership: Kentucky Authority for ETV.

Began Operation: February 28, 2003. Standard Definition. Began analog operations: August 23, 1968. Ceased analog operations: June 12, 2009.

WKMR-DT
Morehead
Ch. 15

Licensee: Kentucky Authority for ETV, 600 Cooper Dr, Lexington, KY 40502-2296.

Studio: 600 Cooper Dr, Lexington, KY 40502-2296.

Mailing Address: 600 Cooper Dr, Lexington, KY 40502-2296.

Phones: 859-258-7000; 800-432-0951. **Fax:** 859-258-7399.

Email: tbischoff@ket.org **Web Site:** http://www.ket.org

Technical Facilities: Channel No. 15 (476-482 MHz). Authorized power: 51.4-kw max. visual, aural. Antenna: 948-ft above av. terrain, 538-ft. above ground, 1926-ft. above sea level.

Latitude	38°	10'	38"
Longitude	83°	24'	17"

Note: Latitude and longitude coordinates shown are based on the North American Datum of 1927 (NAD 27) as currently required by the Mass Media Bureau of the FCC.

Ownership: Kentucky Authority for ETV.

Began Operation: January 24, 2002. Began analog operations: September 23, 1968. Ceased analog operations: June 12, 2009.

Personnel:

Malcolm Wall, Executive Director.

Michele Ripley, President, Commonwealth Fund for KET.

Linda Hume, Deputy Executive Director, Administration & Support.

Bill Wilson, Deputy Executive Director, Education & Outreach.

Shae Hopkins, Deputy Executive Director, Programming & Production.

Mike Clark, Technology Director.

Rick Melton, Studio Engineering Director.

Robert Ball, Transmission Systems Director.

Craig Cornwell, Programming Director.

Kathy Quinn, Education Director.

Mike Brower, Production Director.

Tim Bischoff, Marketing Director.

WKMU-DT
Murray
Ch. 36

Licensee: Kentucky Authority for ETV, 600 Cooper Dr, Lexington, KY 40502-2296.

Studio: 600 Cooper Dr, Lexington, KY 40502-2296.

Mailing Address: 600 Cooper Dr, Lexington, KY 40502-2296.

Phones: 859-258-7000; 800-432-0951. **Fax:** 859-258-7399.

Email: tbischoff@ket.org **Web Site:** http://www.ket.org

Technical Facilities: Channel No. 36 (602-608 MHz). Authorized power: 56.9-kw max. visual, aural. Antenna: 614-ft above av. terrain, 581-ft. above ground, 1109-ft. above sea level.

Latitude	36°	41'	34"
Longitude	88°	32'	11"

Note: Latitude and longitude coordinates shown are based on the North American Datum of 1927 (NAD 27) as currently required by the Mass Media Bureau of the FCC.

Ownership: Kentucky Authority for ETV.

Began Operation: February 21, 2002. Standard Definition. Began analog operations: October 9, 1968. Ceased analog operations: June 12, 2009.

Personnel:

Malcolm Wall, Executive Director.

Michele Ripley, President, Commonwealth Fund for KET.

Linda Hume, Deputy Executive Director, Administration & Support.

Bill Wilson, Deputy Executive Director, Education & Outreach.

Shae Hopkins, Deputy Executive Director, Programming & Production.

Mike Clark, Technology Director.

Rick Melton, Studio Engineering Director.

Robert Ball, Transmission Systems Director.

Craig Cornwell, Programming Director.

Kathy Quinn, Education Director.

Mike Brower, Production Director.

Tim Bischoff, Marketing Director.

WKOH-DT
Owensboro
Ch. 30

Licensee: Kentucky Authority for ETV, 600 Cooper Dr, Lexington, KY 40502-2296.

Studio: 600 Cooper Dr, Lexington, KY 40502-2296.

Mailing Address: 600 Cooper Dr, Lexington, KY 40502-2296.

Phones: 859-258-7000; 800-432-0951. **Fax:** 859-258-7399.

Email: tbischoff@ket.org **Web Site:** http://www.ket.org

Personnel (WKMA-DT):

Malcolm Wall, Executive Director.

Michele Ripley, President, Commonwealth Fund for KET.

Linda Hume, Deputy Executive Director, Administration & Support.

Bill Wilson, Deputy Executive Director, Education & Outreach.

Shae Hopkins, Deputy Executive Director, Programming & Production.

Mike Clark, Technology Director.

Rick Melton, Studio Engineering Director.

Robert Ball, Transmission Systems Director.

Craig Cornwell, Programming Director.

Kathy Quinn, Education Director.

Mike Brower, Production Director.

Technical Facilities: Channel No. 30 (566-572 MHz). Authorized power: 63.3-kw max. visual, aural. Antenna: 407-ft above av. terrain, 420-ft. above ground, 794-ft. above sea level.

Latitude	37°	51'	07"
Longitude	87°	19'	44"

Note: Latitude and longitude coordinates shown are based on the North American Datum of 1927 (NAD 27) as currently required by the Mass Media Bureau of the FCC.

Ownership: Kentucky Authority for ETV.

Began Operation: February 12, 2002. Standard Definition. Began analog operations: August 30, 1979. Ceased analog operations: June 12, 2009.

Personnel:

Malcolm Wall, Executive Director.

Michele Ripley, President, Commonwealth Fund for KET.

Bill Wilson, Deputy Executive Director, Education & Outreach.

Mike Clark, Technology Planning Director.

Craig Cornwell, Programming Director.

Shae Hopkins, Deputy Executive Director, Programming & Production.

Tim Bischoff, Marketing Director.

Robert Ball, Transmission Systems Director.

Linda Hume, Deputy Executive Director, Administration & Support.

Rick Melton, Studio Engineering Director.

Kathy Quinn, Education Director.

Mike Brower, Production Director.

WKON-DT
Owenton
Ch. 44

Licensee: Kentucky Authority for ETV, 600 Cooper Dr, Lexington, KY 40502-2296.

Studio: 600 Cooper Dr, Lexington, KY 40502-2296.

Mailing Address: 600 Cooper Dr, Lexington, KY 40502-2296.

Phones: 859-258-7000; 800-432-0951. **Fax:** 859-258-7399.

Email: tbischoff@ket.org **Web Site:** http://www.ket.org

Technical Facilities: Channel No. 44 (650-656 MHz). Authorized power: 49.7-kw max. visual, aural. Antenna: 702-ft above av. terrain, 531-ft. above ground, 1489-ft. above sea level.

Latitude	38°	31'	31"
Longitude	84°	48'	39"

Note: Latitude and longitude coordinates shown are based on the North American Datum of 1927 (NAD 27) as currently required by the Mass Media Bureau of the FCC.

Ownership: Kentucky Authority for ETV.

Began Operation: November 16, 2001. Standard Definition. Began analog operations: September 23, 1968. Ceased analog operations: June 12, 2009.

Personnel:

Malcolm Wall, Executive Director.

Michele Ripley, President, Commonwealth Fund for KET.

Linda Hume, Deputy Executive Director, Administration & Support.

Bill Wilson, Deputy Executive Director, Education & Outreach.

Shae Hopkins, Deputy Executive Director, Programming & Production.

Mike Clark, Technology Director.

Rick Melton, Studio Engineering Director.

Robert Ball, Transmission Systems Director.

Craig Cornwell, Programming Director.

Kathy Quinn, Education Director.

Mike Brower, Production Director.

Tim Bischoff, Marketing Director.

WKPD-DT
Paducah
Ch. 41

Licensee: Kentucky Authority for ETV, 600 Cooper Dr, Lexington, KY 40502-2296.

Studio: 600 Cooper Dr, Lexington, KY 40502-2296.

Mailing Address: 600 Cooper Dr, Lexington, KY 40502-2296.

Phones: 859-258-7000; 800-432-0951. **Fax:** 859-258-7399.

Email: tbischoff@ket.org **Web Site:** http://www.ket.org

Technical Facilities: Channel No. 41 (632-638 MHz). Authorized power: 55.7-kw max. visual, aural. Antenna: 469-ft above av. terrain, 472-ft. above ground, 843-ft. above sea level.

Latitude	37°	05'	39"
Longitude	88°	40'	20"

Note: Latitude and longitude coordinates shown are based on the North American Datum of 1927 (NAD 27) as currently required by the Mass Media Bureau of the FCC.

Ownership: Kentucky Authority for ETV.

Began Operation: February 21, 2002. Standard Definition. Began analog operations: May 31, 1971. Ceased analog operations: June 12, 2009.

Personnel:

Malcolm Wall, Executive Director.

Michele Ripley, President, Commonwealth Fund for KET.

Linda Hume, Deputy Executive Director, Administration & Support.

Bill Wilson, Deputy Executive Director, Education & Outreach.

Shae Hopkins, Deputy Executive Director, Programming & Production.

Mike Clark, Technology Director.

Rick Melton, Studio Engineering Director.

Robert Ball, Transmission Systems Director.

Craig Cornwell, Programming Director.

Kathy Quinn, Education Director.

Mike Brower, Production Director.

Tim Bischoff, Marketing Director.

WKPI-DT
Pikeville
Ch. 24

Licensee: Kentucky Authority for ETV, 600 Cooper Dr, Lexington, KY 40502-2296.

Studio: 600 Cooper Dr, Lexington, KY 40502-2296.

Mailing Address: 600 Cooper Dr, Lexington, KY 40502-2296.

Phones: 859-258-7000; 800-432-0951. **Fax:** 859-258-7399.

Email: tbischoff@ket.org **Web Site:** http://www.ket.org

Technical Facilities: Channel No. 24 (530-536 MHz). Authorized power: 50.4-kw max. visual, aural. Antenna: 1388-ft above av. terrain, 85-ft. above ground, 2920-ft. above sea level.

Latitude	37°	17'	06"
Longitude	82°	31'	28"

Note: Latitude and longitude coordinates shown are based on the North American Datum of 1927 (NAD 27) as currently required by the Mass Media Bureau of the FCC.

Ownership: Kentucky Authority for ETV.

Began Operation: March 8, 2002. Began analog operations: January 13, 1969. Ceased analog operations: June 12, 2009.

Personnel:

Malcolm Wall, Executive Director.

Michelle Ripley, President, Commonwealth Fund for KET.

Linda Hume, Deputy Executive Director, Administration & Support.

Bill Wilson, Deputy Executive Director, Education & Outreach.

Shae Hopkins, Deputy Executive Director, Programming & Production.

Mike Clark, Technology Director.

Rick Melton, Studio Engineering Director.

Robert Ball, Transmission Systems Director.

Craig Cornwell, Programming Director.

Kathy Quinn, Education Director.

Mike Brower, Production Director.

Tim Bischoff, Marketing Director.

WKSO-DT
Somerset
Ch. 14

Licensee: Kentucky Authority for ETV, 600 Cooper Dr, Lexington, KY 40502-2296.

Studio: 600 Cooper Dr, Lexington, KY 40502-2296.

Mailing Address: 600 Cooper Dr, Lexington, KY 40502-2296.

Phones: 859-258-7000; 800-432-0951. **Fax:** 859-258-7399.

Email: tbischoff@ket.org **Web Site:** http://www.ket.org

Technical Facilities: Channel No. 14 (470-476 MHz). Authorized power: 53.3-kw max. visual, aural. Antenna: 1407-ft above av. terrain, 906-ft. above ground, 2431-ft. above sea level.

Latitude	37°	10'	03"
Longitude	84°	49'	30"

Note: Latitude and longitude coordinates shown are based on the North American Datum of 1927 (NAD 27) as currently required by the Mass Media Bureau of the FCC.

Ownership: Kentucky Authority for ETV.

Began Operation: February 28, 2002. Began analog operations: September 23, 1968. Ceased analog operations: June 12, 2009.

Personnel:

Malcolm Wall, Executive Director.

Michele Ripley, President, Commonwealth Fund for KET.

Linda Hume, Deputy Executive Director, Administration & Support.

Bill Wilson, Deputy Executive Director, Education & Outreach.

Shae Hopkins, Deputy Executive Director, Programming & Production.

Mike Clark, Technology Director.

Rick Melton, Studio Engineering Director.

Robert Ball, Transmission Systems Director.

Craig Cornwell, Programming Director.

Kathy Quinn, Education Director.

Mike Brower, Production Director.

Tim Bischoff, Marketing Director.

Louisiana

KLPA-DT
Alexandria
Ch. 26

Licensee: Louisiana ETV Authority, 7733 Perkins Rd, Baton Rouge, LA 70810.

Studio: 7733 Perkins Rd, Baton Rouge, LA 70810.

Mailing Address: 7733 Perkins Rd, Baton Rouge, LA 70810.

Phones: 225-767-5660; 800-272-8161. **Fax:** 225-767-4299.

Email: grant1ed@mail.cmich.edu **Web Site:** http://www.lpb.org

Technical Facilities: Channel No. 26 (542-548 MHz). Authorized power: 76-kw max. visual, aural. Antenna: 1355-ft above av. terrain, 1299-ft. above ground, 1519-ft. above sea level.

Latitude	31°	33'	56"
Longitude	92°	32'	50"

Note: Latitude and longitude coordinates shown are based on the North American Datum of 1927 (NAD 27) as currently required by the Mass Media Bureau of the FCC.

Ownership: Louisiana ETV Authority.

Began Operation: September 1, 2004. Began analog operations: July 1, 1983. Ceased analog operations: June 12, 2009.

Personnel:

Beth Courtney, President & Chief Executive Officer.

Randy Ward, Director of Engineering.

Fred Christiansen, Assistant Director of Engineering, Transmission.

Tom Woodside, Operations Manager.

C. C. Copeland, Assistant Director of Engineering, Operations.

Jennifer Howze, Program Director.

Bob Neese, Promotions Manager.

Clay Fourier, Executive Producer.

Dorothy Efferson, Human Resources Director.

Terri Crocket, Friends of LPB Executive Manager.

Joanne Gaudet, Business Services Director.

Ellen Wydra, Educational Services Director.

Ken Miller, Production Manager.

WLPB-DT
Baton Rouge
Ch. 25

Licensee: Louisiana ETV Authority, 7733 Perkins Rd, Baton Rouge, LA 70810.

Studio: 7733 Perkins Rd, Baton Rouge, LA 70810.

Mailing Address: 7733 Perkins Rd, Baton Rouge, LA 70810.

Phones: 225-767-5660; 800-272-8161. Fax: 225-767-4299.

Web Site: http://www.lpb.org

Technical Facilities: Channel No. 25 (536-542 MHz). Authorized power: 200-kw max. visual, aural. Antenna: 968-ft above av. terrain, 968-ft. above ground, 988-ft. above sea level.

| Latitude | 30° | 22' | 22" |
| Longitude | 91° | 12' | 16" |

Holds CP for change to 357-kw max. visual, 1020-ft above av. terrain, 1020-ft. above ground, 1039-ft. above sea level; BMPEDT-20081008ADB.

Note: Latitude and longitude coordinates shown are based on the North American Datum of 1927 (NAD 27) as currently required by the Mass Media Bureau of the FCC.

Ownership: Louisiana ETV Authority.

Began Operation: September 26, 2000. Began analog operations: September 6, 1975. Ceased analog operations: June 12, 2009.

Personnel:

Beth Courtney, President & Chief Executive Officer.

Tom Woodside, Operations Manager.

Randy Ward, Director of Engineering.

Fred Christiansen, Assistant Director of Engineering, Transmission.

C. C. Copeland, Assistant Director of Engineering, Operations.

Ken Miller, Production Manager.

Jennifer Howze, Program Director.

Bob Neese, Promotions Manager.

Clay Fourier, Executive Producer.

Dorothy Efferson, Human Resources Director.

Terri Crocket, Friends of LPB Executive Manager.

Joanne Gaudet, Business Services Director.

Ellen Wydra, Educational Services Director.

KLPB-DT
Lafayette
Ch. 23

Licensee: Louisiana ETV Authority, 7733 Perkins Rd, Baton Rouge, LA 70810.

Studio: 7733 Perkins Rd, Baton Rouge, LA 70810.

Mailing Address: 7733 Perkins Rd, Baton Rouge, LA 70810.

Phones: 225-767-5660; 800-272-8161. Fax: 225-767-4299.

Email: grant1ed@mail.cmich.edu Web Site: http://www.lpb.org

Technical Facilities: Channel No. 23 (524-530 MHz). Authorized power: 50-kw max. visual, aural. Antenna: 1520-ft above av. terrain, 1526-ft. above ground, 1552-ft. above sea level.

| Latitude | 30° | 19' 19.3" |
| Longitude | 92° | 16' 58.5" |

Note: Latitude and longitude coordinates shown are based on the North American Datum of 1927 (NAD 27) as currently required by the Mass Media Bureau of the FCC.

Ownership: Louisiana ETV Authority.

Began Operation: November 17, 2003. Began analog operations: May 13, 1981. Ceased analog operations: June 12, 2009.

Personnel:

Beth Courtney, President & Chief Executive Officer.

Tom Woodside, Operations Manager.

Randy Ward, Director of Engineering.

Fred Christiansen, Assistant Director of Engineering, Transmission.

C. C. Copeland, Assistant Director of Engineering, Operations.

Jennifer Howze, Program Director.

Bob Neese, Promotion Manager.

Clay Fourier, Executive Producer.

Dorothy Efferson, Human Resources Director.

Terri Crocket, Friends of LPB Executive Manager.

Joanne Gaudet, Business Services Director.

Ellen Wydra, Educational Services Director.

Ken Miller, Production Manager.

KLTL-DT
Lake Charles
Ch. 20

Licensee: Louisiana ETV Authority, 7733 Perkins Rd, Baton Rouge, LA 70810.

Studio: 7733 Perkins Rd, Baton Rouge, LA 70810.

Mailing Address: 7733 Perkins Rd, Baton Rouge, LA 70810.

Phones: 225-767-5660; 800-272-8161. Fax: 225-767-4299.

Email: grant1ed@mail.cmich.edu Web Site: http://www.lpb.org

Technical Facilities: Channel No. 20 (506-512 MHz). Authorized power: 55-kw max. visual, aural. Antenna: 981-ft above av. terrain, 978-ft. above ground, 1008-ft. above sea level.

| Latitude | 30° | 23' | 46" |
| Longitude | 93° | 00' | 03" |

Holds CP for change to 131.4-kw max. visual; BMPEDT-20090508ABP.

Note: Latitude and longitude coordinates shown are based on the North American Datum of 1927 (NAD 27) as currently required by the Mass Media Bureau of the FCC.

Ownership: Louisiana ETV Authority.

Began Operation: September 14, 2004. Began analog operations: May 5, 1981. Ceased analog operations: June 12, 2009.

Personnel:

Beth Courtney, President & Chief Executive Officer.

Tom Woodside, Operations Manager.

Randy Ward, Director of Engineering.

Fred Christiansen, Assistant Director of Engineering, Transmission.

C. C. Copeland, Assistant Director of Engineering, Operations.

Ken Miller, Production Manager.

Jennifer Howze, Program Director.

Bob Neese, Promotions Manager.

Clay Fourier, Executive Producer.

Dorothy Efferson, Human Resources Director.

Terri Crocket, Friends of LPB Executive Manager.

Joanne Gaudet, Business Services Director.

Ellen Wydra, Educational Services Director.

KLTM-DT
Monroe
Ch. 13

Licensee: Louisiana ETV Authority, 7733 Perkins Rd, Baton Rouge, LA 70810.

Studio: 7733 Perkins Rd, Baton Rouge, LA 70810.

Mailing Address: 7733 Perkins Rd, Baton Rouge, LA 70810.

Phones: 225-767-5660; 800-272-8161. Fax: 225-767-4299.

Email: grant1ed@mail.cmich.edu Web Site: http://www.lpb.org

Technical Facilities: Channel No. 13 (210-216 MHz). Authorized power: 17.2-kw visual, aural. Antenna: 1785-ft above av. terrain, 1807-ft. above ground, 1870-ft. above sea level.

| Latitude | 32° | 11' | 50" |
| Longitude | 92° | 04' | 14" |

Note: Latitude and longitude coordinates shown are based on the North American Datum of 1927 (NAD 27) as currently required by the Mass Media Bureau of the FCC.

Ownership: Louisiana ETV Authority.

Began Operation: August 18, 2004. Station broadcasting digitally on its analog channel allotment. Began analog operations: September 8, 1976. Ceased analog operations: June 12, 2009.

Personnel:

Beth Courtney, President & Chief Executive Officer.

Tom Woodside, Operations Manager.

Randy Ward, Director of Engineering.

Fred Christiansen, Assistant Director of Engineering, Transmission.

C. C. Copeland, Assistant Director of Engineering, Operations.

Ken Miller, Production Manager.

Jennifer Howze, Program Director.

Bob Neese, Promotion Director.

Clay Fourier, Executive Producer.

Dorothy Efferson, Human Resources Director.

Terri Crocket, Friends of LPB Executive Manager.

Joanne Gaudet, Business Services Director.

Ellen Wydra, Educational Services Director.

WLAE-DT
New Orleans
Ch. 31

Grantee: Educational Broadcasting Foundation Inc., 3330 N. Causeway Blvd, Ste 345, Metairie, LA 70002.

Studio: 3330 N Causeway Blvd, Ste 345, New Orleans, LA 70002.

Mailing Address: 3330 N Causeway Blvd, Ste 345, Metairie, LA 70002.

Phones: 504-866-7411; 800-725-7411. Fax: 504-840-9838.

Web Site: http://www.pbs.org/wlae

Technical Facilities: Channel No. 31 (572-578 MHz). Authorized power: 200-kw max. visual, aural. Antenna: 899-ft above av. terrain, 899-ft. above ground, 899-ft. above sea level.

| Latitude | 29° | 58' | 57" |
| Longitude | 89° | 57' | 09" |

Transmitter: 2 Bayou Bienvenue Paris Rd., Chalmette.

Note: Latitude and longitude coordinates shown are based on the North American Datum of 1927 (NAD 27) as currently required by the Mass Media Bureau of the FCC.

Ownership: WLAE Educational Broadcasting Foundation Inc.

Began Operation: April 1, 2007. Began analog operations: July 8, 1984. Ceased analog operations: January 19, 2009.

Personnel:

Father Tom Chambers, President.

Ron Yager, Vice President & General Manager.

Jim Dotson, Vice President & General Manager, WLAE Productions.

David Snowdy, Facility Technical Officer.

Douglas Curry, Senior Technology Officer.

Rene Michel, Development Director.

Ana Maria Uribe, Production Coordinator.

Kathleen Kerr, Personnel Manager.

WYES-DT
New Orleans
Ch. 11

Licensee: Greater New Orleans ETV Foundation, PO Box 24026, New Orleans, LA 70184.

Studio: 916 Navarre Ave, New Orleans, LA 70124.

Mailing Address: PO Box 24026, New Orleans, LA 70184.

Phone: 504-486-5511. Fax: 504-483-8408.

Email: jim@yesproductions.com Web Site: http://www.wyes.org

Technical Facilities: Channel No. 11 (198-204 MHz). Authorized power: 70.8-kw visual, aural. Antenna: 1008-ft above av. terrain, 1007-ft above ground, 1010-ft above sea level.

Latitude	29°	57'	13"
Longitude	89°	56'	58"

Holds CP for change to 104-kw visual, 1004-ft above av. terrain, 1003-ft. above ground, 1006-ft. above sea level; BPEDT-20080620AEW.

Note: Latitude and longitude coordinates shown are based on the North American Datum of 1927 (NAD 27) as currently required by the Mass Media Bureau of the FCC.

Ownership: Greater New Orleans ETV Foundation.

Began Operation: July 29, 2004. Began analog operations: April 1, 1957. Hurricane Katrina knocked station off air September 2005; resumed operations December 2005. Ceased analog operations: June 12, 2009.

Personnel:

Randall Feldman, President & General Manager.

Jim Tapley, General Sales Manager.

Fred Barrett, Chief Engineer.

Beth Utterback, Program Director.

Aislinn Hinyup, Promotion Manager.

Kirk Demoruelle, Operations & Traffic Manager.

KLTS-DT
Shreveport
Ch. 24

Licensee: Louisiana ETV Authority, 7733 Perkins Rd, Baton Rouge, LA 70810.

Studio: 7733 Perkins Rd, Baton Rouge, LA 70810.

Mailing Address: 7733 Perkins Rd, Baton Rouge, LA 70810.

Phones: 225-767-5660; 800-272-8161. Fax: 225-767-4299.

Web Site: http://www.lpb.org

Technical Facilities: Channel No. 24 (530-536 MHz). Authorized power: 350-kw max. visual, aural. Antenna: 1070-ft above av. terrain, 1039-ft. above ground, 1289-ft. above sea level.

Latitude	32°	40'	39.6"
Longitude	93°	55'	30.1"

Note: Latitude and longitude coordinates shown are based on the North American Datum of 1927 (NAD 27) as currently required by the Mass Media Bureau of the FCC.

Ownership: Louisiana ETV Authority.

Began Operation: February 14, 2002. Standard Definition. Station broadcasting digitally on its analog channel allotment. Began analog operations: August 9, 1978. Ceased analog operations: June 12, 2009.

Personnel:

Beth Courtney, President & Chief Executive Officer.

Tom Woodside, Operations Manager.

Randy Ward, Director of Engineering.

Fred Christiansen, Assistant Director of Engineering, Transmission.

C. C. Copeland, Assistant Director of Engineering, Operations.

Ken Miller, Production Manager.

Jennifer Howze, Program Director.

Bob Neese, Promotion Director.

Clay Fourier, Executive Producer.

Dorothy Efferson, Human Resources Director.

Terri Crocket, Friends of LPB Executive Manager.

Joanne Gaudet, Business Services Director.

Ellen Wydra, Educational Services Director.

Maine

WCBB-DT
Augusta
Ch. 10

Licensee: Maine Public Broadcasting Corp., 1450 Lisbon St, Lewiston, ME 04240.

Studio: 65 Texas Ave, Bangor, ME 04401.

Mailing Address: 1450 Libson St, Lewiston, ME 04240.

Phones: 207-783-9101; 800-884-1717. Fax: 207-783-5193.

Web Site: http://www.mpbn.net

Technical Facilities: Channel No. 10 (192-198 MHz). Authorized power: 13.32-kw visual, aural. Antenna: 997-ft above av. terrain, 581-ft. above ground, 1269-ft. above sea level.

Latitude	44°	09'	15"
Longitude	70°	00'	37"

Holds CP for change to 30-kw visual; BMPEDT-20080620ALG.

Note: Latitude and longitude coordinates shown are based on the North American Datum of 1927 (NAD 27) as currently required by the Mass Media Bureau of the FCC.

Ownership: Maine Public Broadcasting Corp.

Began Operation: May 21, 2002. Station broadcasting digitally on its analog channel allotment. Began analog operations: November 13, 1961. Ceased analog operations: January 11, 2009.

Personnel:

Jim Dowe, President & General Manager.

Alexander G. Maxwell Jr., Senior Vice President & Chief Technology Officer.

Joe Riley, Vice President, Media Services.

Mary Mayo, Vice President, Development.

Chris F. Amann, Vice President, Administration & Chief Financial Officer.

Jeff Pierce, Promotion Director.

Edward Fowler, Production Manager.

Diane Dillon, Human Resources Director.

WMEA-DT
Biddeford
Ch. 45

Licensee: Maine Public Broadcasting Corp., 65 Texas Ave, Bangor, ME 04401.

Studio: 65 Texas Ave, Bangor, ME 04401.

Mailing Address: 1450 Libson St, Lewiston, ME 04240.

Phones: 207-783-9101; 800-884-1717. Fax: 207-783-5193.

Web Site: http://www.mpbn.net

Technical Facilities: Channel No. 45 (656-662 MHz). Authorized power: 50-kw max. visual, aural. Antenna: 758-ft above av. terrain, 516-ft. above ground, 1146-ft. above sea level.

Latitude	43°	25'	00"
Longitude	70°	48'	17"

Note: Latitude and longitude coordinates shown are based on the North American Datum of 1927 (NAD 27) as currently required by the Mass Media Bureau of the FCC.

Ownership: Maine Public Broadcasting Corp.

Began Operation: May 21, 2002. Standard Definition. Began analog operations: March 15, 1975. Ceased analog operations: January 11, 2009.

Personnel:

Jim Dowe, President & General Manager.

Alexander G. Maxwell, Senior Vice President, Chief Technology Officer.

Joe Riley, Vice President, Media Services.

Mary Mayo, Vice President, Development.

Chris F. Amann, Vice President, Administration & Chief Financial Officer.

Jeff Pierce, Promotion Director.

Edward Fowler, Production Manager.

Diane Dillon, Human Resources Director.

WMED-DT
Calais
Ch. 10

Licensee: Maine Public Broadcasting Corp., 1450 Lisbon St, Lewiston, ME 04240.

Studio: 65 Texas Ave, Bangor, ME 04401.

Mailing Address: 1450 Libson St, Lewiston, ME 04240.

Phones: 207-783-9101; 800-884-1717. Fax: 207-783-5193.

Web Site: http://www.mpbn.net

Technical Facilities: Channel No. 10 (192-198 MHz). Authorized power: 3.5-kw visual, aural. Antenna: 436-ft above av. terrain, 177-ft. above ground, 657-ft. above sea level.

Latitude	45°	01'	45"
Longitude	67°	19'	26"

Transmitter: Conant Hill, 1.6-mi. SSE of Meddybemps.

Note: Latitude and longitude coordinates shown are based on the North American Datum of 1927 (NAD 27) as currently required by the Mass Media Bureau of the FCC.

Ownership: Maine Public Broadcasting Corp.

Began Operation: March 7, 2003. Began analog operations: September 23, 1964. Ceased analog operations: January 11, 2009.

Personnel:

Jim Dowe, President & General Manager.

Alexander G. Maxwell, Senior Vice President, Chief Technology Officer.

Joe Riley, Vice President, Media Services.

Mary Mayo, Vice President, Development.

Chris F. Amann, Vice President, Administration & Chief Financial Officer.

Jeff Pierce, Promotion Director.

Edward Fowler, Production Manager.

Diane Dillon, Human Resources Director.

WMEB-DT
Orono
Ch. 9

Licensee: Maine Public Broadcasting Corp., 1450 Lisbon St, Lewiston, ME 04240.

Studio: 65 Texas Ave, Bangor, ME 04401.

Mailing Address: 1450 Libson St, Lewiston, ME 04240.

Phones: 207-783-9101; 800-884-1717. Fax: 207-783-5193.

Web Site: http://www.mpbn.net

Technical Facilities: Channel No. 9 (186-192 MHz). Authorized power: 15-kw visual, aural. Antenna: 1230-ft above av. terrain, 419-ft. above ground, 1608-ft. above sea level.

Latitude	44°	42'	11"
Longitude	69°	04'	47"

Note: Latitude and longitude coordinates shown are based on the North American Datum of 1927 (NAD 27) as currently required by the Mass Media Bureau of the FCC.

Ownership: Maine Public Broadcasting Corp.

Began Operation: May 21, 2002. Standard Definition. Began analog operations: October 8, 1963. Ceased analog operations: January 11, 2009.

Personnel:

Jim Dowe, President & General Manager.

Alexander G. Maxwell, Senior Vice President, Chief Technology Officer.

Joe Riley, Vice President, Media Services.

Mary Mayo, Vice President, Development.

Chris F. Amann, Vice President, Administration & Chief Financial Officer.

Jeff Pierce, Promotion Director.

Edward Fowler, Production Manager.

Diane Dillon, Human Resources Director.

WMEM-DT
Presque Isle
Ch. 10

Licensee: Maine Public Broadcasting Corp., 1450 Lisbon St, Lewiston, ME 04240.

Studio: 65 Texas Ave, Bangor, ME 04401.

Mailing Address: 1450 Lisbon St, Lewiston, ME 04240.

Phones: 207-783-9101; 800-884-1717. **Fax:** 207-783-5193.

Web Site: http://www.mpbc.org

Technical Facilities: Channel No. 10 (192-198 MHz). Authorized power: 14.5-kw visual, aural. Antenna: 1158-ft above av. terrain, 171-ft. above ground, 1775-ft. above sea level.

Latitude	46°	33'	06"
Longitude	67°	48'	38"

Note: Latitude and longitude coordinates shown are based on the North American Datum of 1927 (NAD 27) as currently required by the Mass Media Bureau of the FCC.

Ownership: Maine Public Broadcasting Corp.

Began Operation: May 8, 2002. Station broadcasting digitally on its analog channel allotment. Began analog operations: February 17, 1964. Ceased analog operations: January 11, 2009.

Personnel:

Jim Dowe, President & General Manager.

Alexander G. Maxwell, Senior Vice President & Chief Technology Officer.

Joe Riley, Vice President, Media Services.

Mary Mayo, Vice President, Development.

Chris F. Amann, Vice President, Administration & Chief Financial Officer.

Jeff Pierce, Promotion Director.

Edward Fowler, Production Manager.

Diane Dillon, Human Resources Director.

Maryland

WMPT-DT
Annapolis
Ch. 42

Licensee: Maryland Public Broadcasting Commission, 11767 Owings Mills Blvd, Owings Mills, MD 21117-1499.

Studio: 11767 Owings Mills Blvd, Owings Mills, MD 21117.

Mailing Address: 11767 Owings Mills Blvd, Owings Mills, MD 21117.

Phone: 410-356-5600. **Fax:** 410-581-4338.

Web Site: http://www.mpt.org

Technical Facilities: Channel No. 42 (638-644 MHz). Authorized power: 150-kw max. visual, aural. Antenna: 948-ft above av. terrain, 879-ft. above ground, 1027-ft. above sea level.

Latitude	39°	00'	36"
Longitude	76°	36'	33"

Holds CP for change to 516-kw max. visual, 951-ft above av. terrain, 879-ft. above ground, 1025-ft. above sea level; BPEDT-20080620AIA.

Transmitter: 1690 Hawkins Rd.

Note: Latitude and longitude coordinates shown are based on the North American Datum of 1927 (NAD 27) as currently required by the Mass Media Bureau of the FCC.

Ownership: Maryland Public Television.

Began Operation: September 3, 2003. Began analog operations: July 16, 1975. Ceased analog operations: June 12, 2009.

Personnel:

Robert Shuman, President & Chief Executive Officer.

Larry Unger, Executive Vice President & Chief Operating Officer.

Gladys Kaplan, Vice President, Facilities & Human Resources.

George Beneman, Vice President, Technology.

Michael Golden, Managing Director, Communications.

Kirby Storms, Managing Director, Engineering.

Marty Jacobs, Vice President & Chief Financial Officer.

Eric Eggleton, Senior Vice President & Chief Content Officer.

Zvi Shoubin, Managing Director, MPT Networks Department.

Joseph L. Krushinsky, Vice President, Institutional Advancement.

Harry Vaughn, Managing Director, Production Operations Department.

Alex Vitalo, Managing Director, Creative Services.

Gail Porter Long, Vice President, Education & Community Outreach.

WMPB-DT
Baltimore
Ch. 29

Licensee: Maryland Public Broadcasting Commission, 11767 Owings Mills Blvd, Owings Mills, MD 21117-1499.

Studio: 11767 Owings Mills Blvd, Owings Mills, MD 21117.

Mailing Address: 11767 Owings Mills Blvd, Owings Mills, MD 21117.

Phone: 410-356-5600. **Fax:** 410-581-4338.

Web Site: http://www.mpt.org

Technical Facilities: Channel No. 29 (560-566 MHz). Authorized power: 14-kw max. visual, aural. Antenna: 1014-ft above av. terrain, 896-ft. above ground, 1522-ft. above sea level.

Latitude	39°	26'	50"
Longitude	76°	46'	48"

Holds CP for change to 42.6-kw max. visual, 1014-ft above av. terrain, 896-ft. above ground, 1524-ft. above sea level; BPEDT-20080620AHW.

Note: Latitude and longitude coordinates shown are based on the North American Datum of 1927 (NAD 27) as currently required by the Mass Media Bureau of the FCC.

Ownership: Maryland Public Television.

Began Operation: October 29, 2003. Began analog operations: October 5, 1969. Ceased analog operations: June 12, 2009.

Personnel:

Robert Shuman, President & Chief Executive Officer.

Larry Unger, Executive Vice President & Chief Operating Officer.

Gladys Kaplan, Vice President, Facilities & Human Resources.

George Beneman, Vice President, Technology.

Eric Eggleton, Senior Vice President & Chief Content Officer.

Michael Golden, Managing Director, Communications.

Kirby Storms, Managing Director, Engineering.

Marty Jacobs, Vice President, Chief Financial Officer.

Zvi Shoubin, Managing Director, MPT Networks Department.

Joseph L. Krushinsky, Vice President, Institutional Advancement.

Harry Vaughn, Managing Director, Production Operations Department.

Alex Vitalo, Managing Director, Creative Services.

Gail Porter Long, Vice President, Education & Community Outreach.

WFPT-DT
Frederick
Ch. 28

Licensee: Maryland Public Broadcasting Commission, 11767 Owings Mills Blvd, Owings Mills, MD 21117-1499.

Studio: 11767 Owings Mills Blvd, Owings Mills, MD 21117.

Mailing Address: 11767 Owings Mills Blvd, Owings Mills, MD 21117.

Phone: 410-356-5600. **Fax:** 410-581-4338.

Web Site: http://www.mpt.org

Technical Facilities: Channel No. 28 (554-560 MHz). Authorized power: 30-kw max. visual, aural. Antenna: 522-ft above av. terrain, 486-ft. above ground, 998-ft. above sea level.

Latitude	39°	15'	37.62"
Longitude	77°	18'	44.65"

Holds CP for change to 41.2-kw max. visual, 518-ft above av. terrain, 486-ft. above ground, 998-ft. above sea level; BPEDT-20080620AHT.

Note: Latitude and longitude coordinates shown are based on the North American Datum of 1927 (NAD 27) as currently required by the Mass Media Bureau of the FCC.

Ownership: Maryland Public Television.

Began Operation: March 2, 2005. Began analog operations: July 4, 1987. Ceased analog operations: June 12, 2009.

Personnel:

Robert Shuman, President & Chief Executive Officer.

Larry Unger, Executive Vice President & Chief Operating Officer.

Gladys Kaplan, Vice President, Facilities & Human Resources.

George Beneman, Vice President, Technology.

Eric Eggleton, Senior Vice President & Chief Content Officer.

Michael Golden, Managing Director, Communications.

Kirby Storms, Managing Director, Engineering.

Marty Jacobs, Vice President & Chief Financial Officer.

Zvi Shoubin, Managing Director, MPT Networks Department.

Joseph L. Krushinsky, Vice President, Institutional Advancement.

Harry Vaughn, Managing Director, Production Operations Department.

Alex Vitalo, Managing Director, Creative Services.

Gail Porter Long, Vice President, Education & Community Outreach.

WWPB-DT
Hagerstown
Ch. 44

Licensee: Maryland Public Broadcasting Commission, 11767 Owings Mills Blvd, Owings Mills, MD 21117-1499.

Studio: 11767 Owings Mills Blvd, Owings Mills, MD 21117.

Mailing Address: 11767 Owings Mills Blvd, Owings Mills, MD 21117.

Phone: 410-356-5600. **Fax:** 410-581-4338.

Web Site: http://www.mpt.org

Technical Facilities: Channel No. 44 (650-656 MHz). Authorized power: 209-kw max. visual, aural. Antenna: 1178-ft above av. terrain, 354-ft. above ground, 1798-ft. above sea level.

| Latitude | 39° | 39' | 04" |
| Longitude | 77° | 58' | 15" |

Holds CP for change to 1000-kw max. visual, 1211-ft above av. terrain, 358-ft. above ground, 1798-ft. above sea level; BPEDT-20080620ANI.

Note: Latitude and longitude coordinates shown are based on the North American Datum of 1927 (NAD 27) as currently required by the Mass Media Bureau of the FCC.

Ownership: Maryland Public Television.

Began Operation: October 29, 2003. Began analog operations: October 5, 1974. Ceased analog operations: June 12, 2009.

Personnel:

Robert Shuman, President & Chief Executive Officer.

Larry Unger, Executive Vice President & Chief Operating Officer.

Gladys Kaplan, Vice President, Facilities & Human Resources.

George Beneman, Vice President of Technology.

Michael Golden, Managing Director, Communications.

Kirby Storms, Managing Director, Engineering.

Marty Jacobs, Vice President & Chief Financial Officer.

Eric Eggleton, Senior Vice President & Chief Content Officer.

Zvi Shoubin, Managing Director, MPT Networks Department.

Joseph L. Krushinsky, Vice President, Institutional Advancement.

Harry Vaughn, Managing Director, Production Operations Department.

Alex Vitalo, Managing Director, Creative Services.

Gail Porter Long, Vice President, Education & Community Outreach.

WGPT-DT
Oakland
Ch. 36

Licensee: Maryland Public Broadcasting Commission, 11767 Owings Mills Blvd, Owings Mills, MD 21117-1499.

Studio: 11767 Owings Mills Blvd, Owings Mills, MD 21117.

Mailing Address: 11767 Owings Mills Blvd, Owings Mills, MD 21117.

Phone: 410-356-5600. **Fax:** 410-581-4338.

Web Site: http://www.mpt.org

Technical Facilities: Channel No. 36 (602-608 MHz). Authorized power: 45-kw max. visual, aural. Antenna: 955-ft above av. terrain, 430-ft. above ground, 3469-ft. above sea level.

| Latitude | 39° | 24' | 14" |
| Longitude | 79° | 17' | 37" |

Holds CP for change to 252-kw max. visual, 935-ft above av. terrain, 430-ft. above ground, 3469-ft. above sea level; BMPEDT-20080620ANK.

Note: Latitude and longitude coordinates shown are based on the North American Datum of 1927 (NAD 27) as currently required by the Mass Media Bureau of the FCC.

Ownership: Maryland Public Television.

Began Operation: July 25, 2005. Station broadcasting digitally on its analog channel allotment. Began analog operations: March 1, 1980. Ceased analog operations: December 8, 2008.

Personnel:

Robert Shuman, President & Chief Executive Officer.

Larry Unger, Executive Vice President & Chief Operating Officer.

Gladys Kaplan, Vice President, Facilities & Human Resources.

George Beneman, Vice President, Technology.

Michael Golden, Managing Director, Communications.

Kirby Storms, Managing Director, Engineering.

Marty Jacobs, Vice President, Chief Financial Officer.

Eric Eggleton, Senior Vice President & Chief Content Officer.

Zvi Shoubin, Managing Director, MPT Networks Department.

Joseph L. Krushinsky, Vice President, Institutional Advancement.

Harry Vaughn, Managing Director, Production Operations Department.

Alex Vitalo, Managing Director, Creative Services.

Gail Porter Long, Vice President, Education & Community Outreach.

WCPB-DT
Salisbury
Ch. 28

Licensee: Maryland Public Broadcasting Commission, 11767 Owings Mills Blvd, Owings Mills, MD 21117-1499.

Studio: 11767 Owings Mills Blvd, Owings Mills, MD 21117.

Mailing Address: 11767 Owings Mills Blvd, Owings Mills, MD 21117.

Phone: 410-356-5600. **Fax:** 410-581-4338.

Web Site: http://www.mpt.org

Technical Facilities: Channel No. 28 (554-560 MHz). Authorized power: 132-kw max. visual, aural. Antenna: 509-ft above av. terrain, 518-ft. above ground, 545-ft. above sea level.

| Latitude | 38° | 23' | 09" |
| Longitude | 75° | 35' | 33" |

Note: Latitude and longitude coordinates shown are based on the North American Datum of 1927 (NAD 27) as currently required by the Mass Media Bureau of the FCC.

Ownership: Maryland Public Television.

Began Operation: February 9, 2009. Station broadcasting digitally on its analog channel allotment. Began analog operations: March 18, 1971. Ceased analog operations: January 20, 2009.

Personnel:

Robert Shuman, President & Chief Executive Officer.

Larry Unger, Executive Vice President & Chief Operating Officer.

Gladys Kaplan, Vice President, Facilities & Human Resources.

George Beneman, Vice President, Technology.

Eric Eggleton, Senior Vice President & Chief Content Officer.

Michael Golden, Managing Director, Communications.

Kirby Storms, Managing Director, Engineering.

Marty Jacobs, Vice President & Chief Financial Officer.

Zvi Shoubin, Managing Director, MPT Networks Department.

Joseph L. Krushinsky, Vice President, Institutional Advancement.

Harry Vaughn, Managing Director, Production Operations Department.

Alex Vitalo, Managing Director, Creative Services.

Gail Porter Long, Vice President, Education & Community Outreach.

Massachusetts

WGBH-DT
Boston
Ch. 19

Licensee: WGBH Educational Foundation, 125 Western Ave, Boston, MA 02134.

Studio: One Guest St, Brighton, MA 02135.

Mailing Address: PO Box 200, Boston, MA 02134.

Phone: 617-300-5400. **Fax:** 617-300-1026.

Web Site: http://www.wgbh.org

Technical Facilities: Channel No. 19 (500-506 MHz). Authorized power: 900-kw max. visual, aural. Antenna: 1214-ft above av. terrain, 1198-ft. above ground, 1352-ft. above sea level.

| Latitude | 42° | 18' | 37" |
| Longitude | 71° | 14' | 14" |

Transmitter: 350 Cedar St., Needham.

Note: Latitude and longitude coordinates shown are based on the North American Datum of 1927 (NAD 27) as currently required by the Mass Media Bureau of the FCC.

Ownership: WGBH Educational Foundation.

Began Operation: December 18, 2002. Began analog operations: May 2, 1955. Ceased analog operations: June 12, 2009.

Personnel:

Jonathan Abbott, President & Chief Executive Officer.

Benjamin Godley, Vice President.

Joseph Igoe, Chief Technology Officer.

David MacCarn, Chief Technologist.

Margaret Drain, Vice President, National Programming.

Chad Davis, Programming Director.

Sharon Corey, Local Development Interactive Director.

Chris Pullman, Vice President, Design.

Jeanne Hopkins, Vice President, Corporate Communications & Government Relations.

WGBX-DT
Boston
Ch. 43

Licensee: WGBH Educational Foundation, 125 Western Ave, Boston, MA 02134.

Studio: One Guest St, Brighton, MA 02135.

Mailing Address: PO Box 200, Boston, MA 02134.

Phone: 617-300-5400. **Fax:** 617-300-1026.

Web Site: http://www.wgbh.org

Technical Facilities: Channel No. 43 (644-650 MHz). Authorized power: 500-kw max. visual, aural. Antenna: 1283-ft above av. terrain, 1270-ft. above ground, 1424-ft. above sea level.

| Latitude | 42° | 18' | 37" |
| Longitude | 71° | 14' | 14" |

Transmitter: 350 Cedar St., Needham.

Note: Latitude and longitude coordinates shown are based on the North American Datum of 1927 (NAD 27) as currently required by the Mass Media Bureau of the FCC.

Ownership: WGBH Educational Foundation.

Began Operation: January 1, 2003. Began analog operations: September 25, 1967. Ceased analog operations: June 12, 2009.

Personnel:

Jonathan Abbott, President & Chief Executive Officer.

Benjamin Godley, Vice President.

Joseph Igoe, Chief Technology Officer.

David MacCarn, Chief Technologist.

Margaret Drain, Vice President, National Programming.

Chad Davis, Programming Director.

Sharon Corey, Local Development Interactive Director.

Chris Pullman, Vice President, Design.

Jeanne Hopkins, Vice President, Corporate Communications & Government Relations.

WGBY-DT
Springfield
Ch. 58

Licensee: WGBH Educational Foundation, 125 Western Ave, Boston, MA 02134.

Studio: 44 Hampden St, Springfield, MA 01103.

Mailing Address: 44 Hampden St, Springfield, MA 01103.

Phone: 413-781-2801. **Fax:** 413-731-5093.

Email: rmiller@wgby.org **Web Site:** http://www.wgby.org

Technical Facilities: Channel No. 58 (734-740 MHz). Authorized power: 50-kw max. visual, aural. Antenna: 965-ft above av. terrain, 92-ft. above ground, 1289-ft. above sea level.

Latitude	42°	14'	29"
Longitude	72°	38'	56"

Holds CP for change to channel number 22, 1004-ft above av. terrain, 124-ft. above ground, 1325-ft. above sea level; BPEDT-20080507ACW.

Transmitter: Mount Tom, Holyoke.

Note: Latitude and longitude coordinates shown are based on the North American Datum of 1927 (NAD 27) as currently required by the Mass Media Bureau of the FCC.

Ownership: WGBH Educational Foundation.

Began Operation: March 1, 2000. Standard Definition. Began analog operations: September 26, 1971. Ceased analog operations: November 5, 2008.

Personnel:

Russell Peotter, Vice President & General Manager.

Raymond Joyce, Deputy General Manager, Marketing & Development.

Lynn Page, Deputy General Manager, Content & Delivery.

Jim Gallerani, Administrative Manager.

Ray Miller, Chief Engineer.

Gary Rivest, Broadcast Operations Manager.

Charley Rose, Marketing Director.

Heather Lavigne, Education & Outreach Director.

Keith Clark, Production Manager.

Jim Madigan, Public Affairs Programs Director.

WYDN-DT
Worcester
Ch. 47

Licensee: Educational Public TV Corp., 3901 Hwy 121 S, Bedford, TX 76021-3009.

Mailing Address: PO Box 1975, San Benito, TX 78586.

Phones: 817-571-1229; 508-363-4800.

Technical Facilities: Channel No. 47 (668-674 MHz). Authorized power: 365-kw max. visual, aural. Antenna: 712-ft above av. terrain, 750-ft. above ground, 100-ft. above sea level.

Latitude	42°	18'	27"
Longitude	71°	13'	27"

Requests CP for change to 1000-kw max. visual; BPEDT-20080618ATX.

Holds CP for change to 50-kw max. visual, 1047-ft above av. terrain, 1037-ft. above ground, 1190-ft. above sea level lat. 42° 18' 37", long. 71° 14' 14"; BPEDT-20080207ANW.

Note: Latitude and longitude coordinates shown are based on the North American Datum of 1927 (NAD 27) as currently required by the Mass Media Bureau of the FCC.

Ownership: Educational Public TV Corp.

Began Operation: April 18, 2005. Began analog operations: May 5, 1999. Ceased analog operations: June 12, 2009.

Michigan

WCML-DT
Alpena
Ch. 57

Licensee: Central Michigan U., 1999 E. Campus Dr, Mount Pleasant, MI 48859.

Studio: 1999 E Campus Dr, Mount Pleasant, MI 48859.

Mailing Address: 1999 E. Campus Dr, Mount Pleasant, MI 48859.

Phone: 989-774-3105. **Fax:** 989-774-4427.

Email: grant1ed@cmich.edu **Web Site:** http://www.wcmu.org

Technical Facilities: Channel No. 57 (728-734 MHz). Authorized power: 200-kw max. visual, aural. Antenna: 1289-ft above av. terrain, 1148-ft. above ground, 2208-ft. above sea level.

Latitude	45°	08'	18"
Longitude	84°	09'	45"

Holds CP for change to channel number 24, 300-kw max. visual; BMPEDT-20090623ABV.

Note: Latitude and longitude coordinates shown are based on the North American Datum of 1927 (NAD 27) as currently required by the Mass Media Bureau of the FCC.

Ownership: Central Michigan U.

Began Operation: September 14, 2005. Began analog operations: November 21, 1975. Ceased analog operations: June 12, 2009.

Personnel:

Edward Grant, General Manager.

Rick Schudiske, Assistant General Manager & Television Director.

Randy Kapenga, Engineering Director.

Kim Walters, Business Operations Manager.

Linda Dielman, Program Director.

Geoff Bartlett, Development Director.

Brian Baker, Director & Production Specialist.

Sharon Periard, Fundraising & Volunteer Coordinator.

Sarah Adams, Public Relations Coordinator, TV Production.

WDCQ-DT
Bad Axe
Ch. 15

Licensee: Delta College, 1961 Delta Rd, University Center, MI 48710.

Studio: 1961 Delta Rd., University Center, MI 48710.

Mailing Address: 1961 Delta Rd, University Center, MI 48710.

Phones: 989-686-9362; 877-472-7677. **Fax:** 989-686-0155.

Email: ceflemin@delta.edu **Web Site:** http://www.delta.edu/broadcasting

Technical Facilities: Channel No. 15 (476-482 MHz). Authorized power: 200-kw max. visual, aural. Antenna: 1014-ft above av. terrain, 1026-ft. above ground, 1627-ft. above sea level.

Latitude	43°	32'	33"
Longitude	83°	39'	37"

Note: Latitude and longitude coordinates shown are based on the North American Datum of 1927 (NAD 27) as currently required by the Mass Media Bureau of the FCC.

Ownership: Delta College.

Began Operation: September 22, 2003. Began analog operations: December 31, 1986. Ceased analog operations: June 12, 2009.

Personnel:

Barry G. Baker, General Manager & Executive Director, Communications Technology.

Tom Garnett, Chief Engineer.

Scott Seeburger, Business & Community Relations Coordinator.

Joseph Yezak, Program Director.

Tom Bennett, Manager, Distance Learning & TV Production.

Chris Fleming, TV Operations Manager.

Debra Haskin, Pledge Producer.

Diane Palm-Osantowski, Development Director.

WCMV-DT
Cadillac
Ch. 17

Licensee: Central Michigan U., 1999 E. Campus Dr, Mount Pleasant, MI 48859.

Studio: 1999 E Campus Dr, Mount Pleasant, MI 48859.

Mailing Address: 1999 E. Campus Dr, Mount Pleasant, MI 48859.

Phone: 989-774-3105. **Fax:** 989-774-4427.

Web Site: http://www.wcmu.org

Technical Facilities: Channel No. 17 (488-494 MHz). Authorized power: 338-kw max. visual, aural. Antenna: 1289-ft above av. terrain, 1214-ft. above ground, 2441-ft. above sea level.

Latitude	44°	44'	53"
Longitude	85°	04'	08"

Note: Latitude and longitude coordinates shown are based on the North American Datum of 1927 (NAD 27) as currently required by the Mass Media Bureau of the FCC.

Ownership: Central Michigan U.

Began Operation: September 14, 2005. Began analog operations: September 7, 1984. Ceased analog operations: June 12, 2009.

Personnel:

Dr. Ed Grant, General Manager.

Rick Schudiske, Assistant General Manager & Director of Television.

Randy Kapenga, Technical Services Director.

Kim Walters, Business Manager.

Linda Dielman, Program Director.

Geoff Bartlett, Development Director.

Brian Baker, Production Manager.

Sarah Adams, Public Relations Coordinator, TV Production.

Sharon Periard, Fundraising & Volunteer Coordinator.

WTVS-DT
Detroit
Ch. 43

Licensee: Detroit Educational TV Foundation Inc., 7441 Second Blvd, Detroit, MI 48202.

Studio: 7441 Second Blvd, Detroit, MI 48202.

Mailing Address: 7441 Second Blvd, Detroit, MI 48202.

Phone: 248-305-3900. **Fax:** 248-305-3988.

Web Site: http://www.dptv.org

Technical Facilities: Channel No. 43 (644-650 MHz). Authorized power: 200-kw max. visual, aural. Antenna: 1043-ft above av. terrain, 1033-ft. above ground, 1696-ft. above sea level.

Latitude	42°	26'	52"
Longitude	83°	10'	23"

Holds CP for change to 600-kw max. visual; BPEDT-20080620AAL.

Transmitter: 20931 Meyers Rd., Oak Park.

Note: Latitude and longitude coordinates shown are based on the North American Datum of 1927 (NAD 27) as currently required by the Mass Media Bureau of the FCC.

Ownership: Detroit Educational Television Foundation.

Began Operation: October 24, 2000. Began analog operations: October 3, 1955. Ceased analog operations: June 12, 2009.

Personnel:

Rich Homberg, General Manager.

Daniel Alpert, Station Manager.

Helge Blucher, Vice President, Engineering & Technology.

Dan Gaitens, Program Director.

Tim Wilson, Corporate Marketing Director.

Diane Bliss, Vice President, Fundraising, Program Development & Industry Relations.

Jeff Forster, Vice President, Production & Station Enterprises.

Joann Havel, Traffic Manager.

Dave Devereaux, Vice President, Communications & Outreach.

WKAR-DT
East Lansing
Ch. 55

Licensee: Board of Trustees, Michigan State U., 450 Administration Building, East Lansing, MI 48824.

Studio: 283 Communications Art Bldg, East Lansing, MI 48824.

Mailing Address: 283 Communications Arts Bldg, Michigan State U, East Lansing, MI 48824.

Phone: 517-432-9527. **Fax:** 517-353-7124.

Email: DeAnne@wkar.org **Web Site:** http://www.wkar.org

Technical Facilities: Channel No. 55 (716-722 MHz). Authorized power: 54.6-kw max. visual, aural. Antenna: 965-ft above av. terrain, 994-ft. above ground, 1847-ft. above sea level.

Latitude	42°	42'	07"
Longitude	84°	24'	48"

Holds CP for change to channel number 40, 425-kw max. visual, 969-ft above av. terrain, 999-ft. above ground, 1851-ft. above sea level; BMPEDT-20080620AIJ.

Note: Latitude and longitude coordinates shown are based on the North American Datum of 1927 (NAD 27) as currently required by the Mass Media Bureau of the FCC.

Ownership: Board of Trustees, Michigan State U.

Began Operation: March 12, 2004. Began analog operations: January 15, 1954. Ceased analog operations: January 4, 2009.

Personnel:

DeAnne Hamilton, General Manager.

Doug Schrems, Station Enterprises Manager.

Kent Wieland, TV Station Manager.

Scott Remington, Production Operations & Facilities Manager.

Bill Morgan, Marketing & Communications Director.

Gary Blievernicht, Chief Engineer.

Nancy Gilleo, Business Manager.

Phil Barrie, Program Manager.

Cindy Herfindahl, Marketing & Development Director.

Jeanie Croope, TV Promotion & Membership Publication.

Timothy Zeko, Executive Producer.

WFUM-DT
Flint
Ch. 28

Licensee: Regents of The U. of Michigan, 535 W William, Ste 110, Flint, MI 48103.

Studio: 303 E Kearsley St, Flint, MI 48502.

Mailing Address: 303 E Kearsley St, Flint, MI 48502.

Phones: 810-762-3028; 800-728-9386. **Fax:** 810-233-6017.

Email: ennaj@umflint.edu **Web Site:** http://www.wfum.org

Technical Facilities: Channel No. 28 (554-560 MHz). Authorized power: 126-kw max. visual, aural. Antenna: 846-ft above av. terrain, 883-ft. above ground, 1804-ft. above sea level.

Latitude	42°	53'	56"
Longitude	83°	27'	41"

Requests modification of CP for change to 500-kw max. visual; BMPEDT-20080617ABY.

Note: Latitude and longitude coordinates shown are based on the North American Datum of 1927 (NAD 27) as currently required by the Mass Media Bureau of the FCC.

Ownership: Regents of the U. of Michigan.

Began Operation: June 1, 2004. Station broadcasting digitally on its analog allotment. Began analog operations: August 23, 1980. Ceased analog operations: November 19, 2008.

Personnel:

Stephen Schram, General Manager.

Jennifer White, Station Manager.

Michael Saunders, Operations Supervisor.

Wayne Henderson, Engineering Director.

Elizabeth Noren, Media Financial Officer.

Larry Jonas, Development Director.

Chris McElroy, Production Director.

Steve Kimbrell, Creative Services Director.

John Vamossy, Programming & Traffic Coordinator.

WGVU-DT
Grand Rapids
Ch. 11

Licensee: Grand Valley State U., 301 W Fulton St, Grand Rapids, MI 49504-6492.

Studio: 301 W Fulton St, Grand Rapids, MI 49504-6492.

Mailing Address: 301 W Fulton St, Grand Rapids, MI 49504-6492.

Phones: 616-331-6666; 800-442-2771. **Fax:** 616-331-6625.

Email: readera@gvsu.edu **Web Site:** http://www.wgvu.org

Technical Facilities: Channel No. 11 (198-204 MHz). Authorized power: 50-kw visual, aural. Antenna: 781-ft above av. terrain, 758-ft. above ground, 1447-ft. above sea level.

Latitude	42°	57'	35"
Longitude	85°	53'	45"

Holds CP for change to 41.5-kw visual, 853-ft above av. terrain, 827-ft. above ground, 1517-ft. above sea level; BPEDT-20090618AAK.

Note: Latitude and longitude coordinates shown are based on the North American Datum of 1927 (NAD 27) as currently required by the Mass Media Bureau of the FCC.

Ownership: Grand Valley State U.

Began Operation: June 30, 2006. Began analog operations: December 17, 1972. Ceased analog operations: June 12, 2009.

Personnel:

Michael T. Walenta, General Manager.

Fred Martino, News & Public Affairs Manager.

Bob Lumbert, Engineering Director.

Carrie Corbin, Program Director.

Pamela Holtz, Promotion Director.

Phil Lane, Production Manager.

Ed Spier, Traffic Manager.

WGVK-DT
Kalamazoo
Ch. 5

Licensee: Grand Valley State U., 301 W Fulton St, Grand Rapids, MI 49504-6492.

Studio: 301 W Fulton St, Grand Rapids, MI 49504-6492.

Mailing Address: 301 W Fulton St, Grand Rapids, MI 49504-6492.

Phones: 616-331-6666; 800-442-2771. **Fax:** 616-331-6625.

Email: readera@gvsu.edu **Web Site:** http://www.wgvu.org

Technical Facilities: Channel No. 5 (76-82 MHz). Authorized power: 10-kw visual, aural. Antenna: 554-ft above av. terrain, 436-ft. above ground, 1417-ft. above sea level.

Latitude	42°	18'	23"
Longitude	85°	39'	25"

Note: Latitude and longitude coordinates shown are based on the North American Datum of 1927 (NAD 27) as currently required by the Mass Media Bureau of the FCC.

Ownership: Grand Valley State U.

Began Operation: June 30, 2006. Began analog operations: October 1, 1984. Ceased analog operations: June 12, 2009.

Personnel:

Michael Walenta, General Manager.

Fred Martino, News Director & Public Affairs Manager.

Bob Lumbert, Chief Engineer.

Carrie Corbin, Program Director.

Pamela Holtz, Promotion Director.

Phil Lane, Production Manager.

Ed Spier, Traffic Manager.

WCMW-DT
Manistee
Ch. 21

Licensee: Central Michigan U., 1999 E. Campus Dr, Mount Pleasant, MI 48859.

Studio: 1999 E Campus Dr, Mount Pleasant, MI 48859.

Mailing Address: 1999 E. Campus Dr, Mount Pleasant, MI 48859.

Phone: 989-774-3105. **Fax:** 989-774-4427.

Web Site: http://www.wcmu.org

Technical Facilities: Channel No. 21 (512-518 MHz). Authorized power: 70-kw max. visual, aural. Antenna: 440-ft above av. terrain, 384-ft. above ground, 1102-ft. above sea level.

Latitude	44°	03'	57"
Longitude	86°	19'	58"

Note: Latitude and longitude coordinates shown are based on the North American Datum of 1927 (NAD 27) as currently required by the Mass Media Bureau of the FCC.

Ownership: Central Michigan U.

Began Operation: September 14, 2005. Station broadcasting digitally on its analog channel allotment. Began analog operations: September 7, 1984. Ceased analog operations: June 12, 2009.

Personnel:

Ed Grant, General Manager.

Rick Schudiske, Assistant General Manager & Director of Television.

Randy Kapenga, Technical Services Director.

Kim Walters, Business Manager.

Linda Dielman, Program Director.

Geoff Bartlett, Development Director.

Brian Baker, Production Manager.

Sarah Adams, Public Relations Coordinator, TV Production.

Sharon Periard, Fundraising & Volunteer Coordinator.

WNMU-DT
Marquette
Ch. 13

Licensee: Board of Control of Northern Michigan U., 1401 Presque Isle Ave, Marquette, MI 49855.

Studio: Learning Resources Bldg., Northern Michigan U., Marquette, MI 49855.

Mailing Address: 1401 Presque Isle Ave, Marquette, MI 49855.

Phones: 906-227-9668; 800-227-9668. **Fax:** 906-227-2905.

Web Site: http://www.nmu.edu/wnmutv

Technical Facilities: Channel No. 13 (210-216 MHz). Authorized power: 15.4-kw visual, aural. Antenna: 1061-ft above av. terrain, 1027-ft. above ground, 2527-ft. above sea level.

Latitude	46°	21'	10.2"
Longitude	87°	51'	14.5"

Note: Latitude and longitude coordinates shown are based on the North American Datum of 1927 (NAD 27) as currently required by the Mass Media Bureau of the FCC.

Ownership: Northern Michigan U.

Began Operation: July 12, 2004. Station broadcasting digitally on its analog channel allotment. Began analog operations: December 28, 1972. Ceased analog operations: June 12, 2009.

Personnel:

Eric Smith, General Manager & Production Manager.

Bruce Turner, Station Manager.

David Bett, Chief Engineer.

Bob Thomson, Producer & Director.

Sonya Chrisman, News Director & Producer.

Marianne Eyer, Membership & Volunteer Supervisor.

WCMU-DT
Mount Pleasant
Ch. 56

Licensee: Central Michigan U., 1999 E. Campus Dr, Mount Pleasant, MI 48859.

Studio: 1999 E Campus Dr, Mount Pleasant, MI 48859.

Mailing Address: 1999 E. Campus Dr, Mount Pleasant, MI 48859.

Phone: 989-774-3105. **Fax:** 989-774-4427.

Web Site: http://www.wcmu.org

Technical Facilities: Channel No. 56 (722-728 MHz). Authorized power: 400-kw max. visual, aural. Antenna: 981-ft above av. terrain, 942-ft. above ground, 2028-ft. above sea level.

Latitude	43°	45'	11"
Longitude	85°	12'	40"

Holds CP for change to channel number 26, 450-kw max. visual; BMPEDT-20080619AFX.

Note: Latitude and longitude coordinates shown are based on the North American Datum of 1927 (NAD 27) as currently required by the Mass Media Bureau of the FCC.

Ownership: Central Michigan U.

Began Operation: September 14, 2005. Began analog operations: March 29, 1967. Ceased analog operations: June 12, 2009.

Personnel:

Ed Grant, General Manager.

Rick Schudiske, Assistant General Manager & Director of Television.

Randy Kapenga, Technical Services Director.

Kim Walters, Business Manager.

Linda Dielman, Program Director.

Brian Baker, Production Manager.

Geoff Bartlett, Development Director.

Sarah Adams, Public Relations Coordinator, TV Production.

Sharon Periard, Fundraising & Volunteer Coordinator.

Minnesota

KWCM-DT
Appleton
Ch. 10

Licensee: West Central Minnesota Educational TV Co., 120 W. Schlieman Ave, Appleton, MN 56208.

Studio: 120 W. Schlieman, Appleton, MN 56208.

Mailing Address: 120 W Schlieman Ave, Appleton, MN 56208.

Phones: 320-289-2622; 800-726-3178. **Fax:** 320-289-2634.

Email: gcerny@pioneer.org **Web Site:** http://www.pioneer.org

Technical Facilities: Channel No. 10 (192-198 MHz). Authorized power: 50-kw visual, aural. Antenna: 1250-ft above av. terrain, 1243-ft. above ground, 2279-ft. above sea level.

Latitude	45°	10'	03"
Longitude	96°	00'	02"

Note: Latitude and longitude coordinates shown are based on the North American Datum of 1927 (NAD 27) as currently required by the Mass Media Bureau of the FCC.

Ownership: West Central Minnesota ETV Corp.

Began Operation: June 19, 2006. Station broadcasting digitally on its analog channel allotment. Began analog operations: January 21, 1966. Ceased analog operations: February 17, 2009.

Personnel:

Les Heen, General Manager.

Jon Panzer, Station Manager & Engineering Director.

Robert Rakow, Broadcast Operations Director.

Matthew Moe, Finance Director.

Shirley Schwarz, Program Director.

Tim Bakken, Production Manager.

KSMQ-DT
Austin
Ch. 20

Licensee: KSMQ Public Service Media Inc., 2000 8th Ave NW, Austin, MN 55912.

Studio: 2000 8th Ave. NW, Austin, MN 55912.

Mailing Address: 2000 8th Ave. NW, Austin, MN 55912.

Phones: 507-433-0678; 800-658-2539. **Fax:** 507-433-0670.

Web Site: http://www.ksmq.org

Technical Facilities: Channel No. 20 (506-512 MHz). Authorized power: 400-kw max. visual, aural. Antenna: 994-ft above av. terrain, 1001-ft. above ground, 2352-ft. above sea level.

Latitude	43°	38'	34"
Longitude	92°	31'	35"

Holds CP for change to 319.2-kw max. visual, 993-ft above av. terrain, 1001-ft. above ground, 2352-ft. above sea level; BMPEDT-20081114AAX.

Note: Latitude and longitude coordinates shown are based on the North American Datum of 1927 (NAD 27) as currently required by the Mass Media Bureau of the FCC.

Ownership: KSMQ Public Service Media Inc.

Began Operation: December 23, 2008. Began analog operations: October 17, 1972. Sale to Southern Minnesota Quality Broadcasting Inc. (now KSMQ Public Service Media Inc.) by Independent School District #492 approved by FCC May 6, 2005. Ceased analog operations: June 12, 2009.

Personnel:

Sandra Session-Robertson, President & Chief Executive Officer.

Pat Stumme, Education & Outreach Coordinator.

Shawn Weitzel, Chief Engineer.

Shirley Blake, Executive Administrative & Membership Assistant.

Michele Hoeper, Traffic Manager.

John Wiedenheft, Producer & Director.

Suzi Stone, Programming & Traffic Manager.

KAWE-DT
Bemidji
Ch. 9

Licensee: Northern Minnesota Public Television Inc., PO Box 9, 1500 Birchmont Dr. NE, Bemidji, MN 56601.

Studio: Deputy Hall, Bemidji State U., Bemidji, MN 56601.

Mailing Address: PO Box 9, 1500 Birchmont Dr NE, Bemidji, MN 56601.

Phone: 218-751-3407. **Fax:** 218-751-3142.

Web Site: http://www.lakelandptv.org

Technical Facilities: Channel No. 9 (186-192 MHz). Authorized power: 14.5-kw visual, aural. Antenna: 1098-ft above av. terrain, 1037-ft. above ground, 2457-ft. above sea level.

Latitude	47°	42'	03"
Longitude	94°	29'	15"

Holds CP for change to 27-kw visual; BMPEDT-20080620AHK.

Note: Latitude and longitude coordinates shown are based on the North American Datum of 1927 (NAD 27) as currently required by the Mass Media Bureau of the FCC.

Ownership: Northern Minnesota Public TV Inc.

Began Operation: October 10, 2003. Station broadcasting digitally on its analog channel allotment. Began analog operations: June 1, 1980. Ceased analog operations: February 17, 2009.

Personnel:

Bill Sanford, General Manager & Engineering Director.

Dennis Weimann, News Director.

Tom Lembrick, Engineering Manager.

Tim McMahon, Broadcast Engineering Manager.

Ron Johnson, Design & Promotion Manager.

Sharon Pugh, Assistant General Manager & Development Director.

Jeff Hanks, Program Manager.

Jess Skala, Traffic & Operations Manager.

KAWB-DT
Brainerd
Ch. 28

Licensee: Northern Minnesota Public Television Inc., PO Box 9, 1500 Birchmont Dr. NE, Bemidji, MN 56601.

Studio: 1500 Birchmont Dr. NE, Bemidji, MN 56601.

Mailing Address: PO Box 9, 1500 Birchmont Dr NE, Bemidji, MN 56601.

Phone: 218-751-3407. **Fax:** 218-751-3142.

Web Site: http://www.lakelandptv.org

Technical Facilities: Channel No. 28 (554-560 MHz). Authorized power: 46.8-kw max. visual, aural. Antenna: 745-ft above av. terrain, 653-ft. above ground, 2024-ft. above sea level.

Latitude	46°	25'	21"
Longitude	94°	27'	42"

Requests CP for change to 137.5-kw max. visual lat. 46° 25' 21", long. 94° 27' 41"; BPEDT-20080620AHQ.

Note: Latitude and longitude coordinates shown are based on the North American Datum of 1927 (NAD 27) as currently required by the Mass Media Bureau of the FCC.

Ownership: Northern Minnesota Public TV Inc.

Began Operation: April 29, 2003. Began analog operations: March 1, 1988. Ceased analog operations: February 17, 2009.

Personnel:

Bill Sanford, General Manager.

Daniel Hegstad, Station Manager.

Dennis Weimann, News Director.

Tom Lembrick, Chief Engineer.

Tim McMahon, Broadcast Engineer.

Ron Johnson, Promotion & Design Services Manager.

Sharon Pugh, Development Director & Assistant General Manager.

Jess Skala, Operations & Traffic Manager.

Jeff Hanks, Program Manager.

KCGE-DT
Crookston
Ch. 16

Licensee: Prairie Public Broadcasting Inc., PO Box 3240, Fargo, ND 58108-3240.

Studio: 207 N 5th St, Fargo, ND 58102.

Mailing Address: PO Box 3240, Fargo, ND 58108-3240.

Phone: 701-241-6900. **Fax:** 701-239-7650.

Web Site: http://www.prairiepublic.org

Technical Facilities: Channel No. 16 (482-488 MHz). Authorized power: 105-kw max. visual, aural. Antenna: 720-ft above av. terrain, 720-ft. above ground, 1625-ft. above sea level.

Latitude	47°	58'	38"
Longitude	96°	36'	18"

Note: Latitude and longitude coordinates shown are based on the North American Datum of 1927 (NAD 27) as currently required by the Mass Media Bureau of the FCC.

Ownership: Prairie Public Broadcasting Inc.

Began Operation: October 1, 2003. Station went directly to digital broadcast; no analog application.

Personnel:

John Harris, President & Chief Executive Officer.

Cheryl Heller, Television Operations Manager.

Jack Anderson, Engineering Director.

Bob Dambach, Program & Production Director.

Marie Lucero, Promotion Manager.

Ann Clark, Director of Development.

Russell Ford-Dunker, Corporate Support Manager.

Morgan Jenkins, Customer Service Coordinator.

Bev Pearson, Education Services.

WDSE-DT
Duluth
Ch. 8

Licensee: Duluth-Superior Area Educational TV Corp., 632 Niagara Ct, Duluth, MN 55811.

Studio: 632 Niagara Ct, Duluth, MN 55811.

Mailing Address: 632 Niagara Court, Duluth, MN 55811.

Phone: 218-724-8567. Fax: 218-724-4269.

Web Site: http://www.wdse.org

Technical Facilities: Channel No. 8 (180-186 MHz). Authorized power: 34-kw visual, aural. Antenna: 968-ft above av. terrain, 735-ft. above ground, 1997-ft. above sea level.

Latitude	46°	47'	30"
Longitude	92°	07'	21"

Note: Latitude and longitude coordinates shown are based on the North American Datum of 1927 (NAD 27) as currently required by the Mass Media Bureau of the FCC.

Ownership: Duluth-Superior Area ETV Corp.

Began Operation: June 30, 2006. Station broadcasting digitally on its analog channel allotment. Began analog operations: September 1, 1964. Ceased analog operations: June 12, 2009.

Personnel:

Allen D. Harmon, President & General Manager.

Ronald F. Anderson, Program & Production Manager.

Jodi Hagen, Promotion & Creative Services Director.

Cheryl Leeper, Development Director.

Patti Alberg, Traffic Manager.

WRPT-DT
Hibbing
Ch. 31

Grantee: Duluth-Superior Area Educational TV Corp., 632 Niagara Ct, Duluth, MN 55811.

Studio: 632 Niagara Ct, Duluth, MN 55811.

Mailing Address: 632 Niagara Court, Duluth, MN 55811.

Phone: 218-724-8567. Fax: 218-724-4269.

Web Site: http://www.wdse.org

Technical Facilities: Channel No. 31 (572-578 MHz). Authorized power: 250-kw max. visual, aural. Antenna: 548-ft above av. terrain, 354-ft. above ground, 1974-ft. above sea level.

Latitude	47°	22'	53"
Longitude	92°	57'	15"

Note: Latitude and longitude coordinates shown are based on the North American Datum of 1927 (NAD 27) as currently required by the Mass Media Bureau of the FCC.

Ownership: Duluth-Superior Area ETV Corp.

Began Operation: February 27, 2009. Station went directly to digital broadcast; no analog application.

Personnel:

Allen Harmon, General Manager.

Julie Deynoer, Sales Director & Business Manager.

Rex Greenwell, Chief Engineer.

Ron Anderson, Program Director.

Greg Grell, Research Director.

Cheryl Leeper, Development Director.

Patty Alberg, Traffic Manager.

KTCA-DT
St. Paul
Ch. 34

Licensee: Twin Cities Public Television Inc., 172 E 4th St, St. Paul, MN 55101.

Studio: 172 E 4th St, St. Paul, MN 55101.

Mailing Address: 172 E. 4th St, St. Paul, MN 55101.

Phone: 651-222-1717. Fax: 651-229-1282.

Email: cmaloney@tpt.org Web Site: http://www.tpt.org

Technical Facilities: Channel No. 34 (590-596 MHz). Authorized power: 662-kw max. visual, aural. Antenna: 1349-ft above av. terrain, 1358-ft. above ground, 2266-ft. above sea level.

Latitude	45°	03'	30"
Longitude	93°	07'	27"

Transmitter: 540 Gramsie Rd., Shoreview.

Note: Latitude and longitude coordinates shown are based on the North American Datum of 1927 (NAD 27) as currently required by the Mass Media Bureau of the FCC.

Multichannel TV Sound: Stereo and separate audio program.

Ownership: Twin Cities Public Television Inc.

Began Operation: July 28, 2006. Began analog operations: September 3, 1957. Ceased analog operations: June 12, 2009.

Personnel:

James R. Pagliarini, President & Chief Executive Officer.

Dan Thomas, Chief Operating Officer.

Glenn Fisher, Vice President, Broadcast Services.

Gerald Richman, Vice President, National Productions.

Bill Hanley, Vice President, Minnesota Productions.

Tom Holter, Program Director.

Scott Thorson, Traffic Manager.

Stephen Usery, Vice President, Marketing.

Scott Holisky, Chief Engineer.

KTCI-DT
St. Paul
Ch. 16

Licensee: Twin Cities Public Television Inc., 172 E. 4th St, St. Paul, MN 55101.

Studio: 172 E 4th St, St. Paul, MN 55101.

Mailing Address: 172 E. 4th St, St. Paul, MN 55101.

Phone: 651-222-1717. Fax: 651-329-1282.

Web Site: http://www.tpt.org

Technical Facilities: Channel No. 16 (482-488 MHz). Authorized power: 50-kw max. visual, aural. Antenna: 1289-ft above av. terrain, 2282-ft. above ground, 2208-ft. above sea level.

Latitude	45°	03'	30"
Longitude	93°	07'	27"

Holds CP for change to channel number 23, 375-kw max. visual, 1355-ft above av. terrain, 1365-ft. above ground, 2274-ft. above sea level; BPEDT-20090716ACS.

Transmitter: 540 Gramsie Rd., Shoreview.

Note: Latitude and longitude coordinates shown are based on the North American Datum of 1927 (NAD 27) as currently required by the Mass Media Bureau of the FCC.

Multichannel TV Sound: Stereo and separate audio program.

Ownership: Twin Cities Public Television Inc.

Began Operation: July 1, 1999. Standard Definition. Began analog operations: May 4, 1965. Ceased analog operations: June 12, 2009.

Personnel:

James R. Pagliarini, President & Chief Executive Officer.

Dan Thomas, Chief Operating Officer.

Glenn Fisher, Vice President, Broadcast Services.

Gerald Richman, Vice President, National Productions.

Bill Hanley, Vice President, Minnesota Productions.

Scott Thorson, Traffic Manager.

Tom Holter, Program Director.

Scott Holisky, Chief Engineer.

Stephen Usery, Vice President, Marketing.

KSMN-DT
Worthington
Ch. 15

Licensee: West Central Minnesota Educational TV Co., 120 W. Schlieman Ave, Appleton, MN 56208.

Studio: 120 W Schlieman Ave, Appleton, MN 56208.

Mailing Address: 120 W Schlieman Ave, Appleton, MN 56208.

Phones: 320-289-2622; 800-276-3178. Fax: 320-289-2634.

Email: gcerny@pioneer.org Web Site: http://www.pioneer.org

Technical Facilities: Channel No. 15 (476-482 MHz). Authorized power: 200-kw max. visual, aural. Antenna: 952-ft above av. terrain, 830-ft. above ground, 2655-ft. above sea level.

Latitude	43°	53'	52"
Longitude	95°	56'	50"

Holds CP for change to 1000-kw max. visual, 1089-ft above av. terrain, 966-ft. above ground, 2791-ft. above sea level; BPEDT-20080620ALP.

Note: Latitude and longitude coordinates shown are based on the North American Datum of 1927 (NAD 27) as currently required by the Mass Media Bureau of the FCC.

Ownership: West Central Minnesota ETV Corp.

Began Operation: December 28, 2005. Began analog operations: December 6, 1996. Ceased analog operations: February 17, 2009.

Personnel:

Les Heen, General Manager.

Jon Panzer, Station Manager & Engineering Director.

Robert Rakow, Broadcast Operations Director.

Matthew Moe, Finance Director.

Shirley Schwarz, Program Director.

Tim Bakken, Production Manager.

Mississippi

WMAH-DT
Biloxi
Ch. 16

Licensee: Mississippi Authority for ETV, 3825 Ridgewood Rd, Jackson, MS 39211.

Studio: 3825 Ridgewood Rd, Jackson, MS 39211.

Mailing Address: 3825 Ridgewood Rd, Jackson, MS 39211.

Phones: 601-432-6565; 800-922-9698. Fax: 601-432-6654.

Email: phyllis.allen@mpbonline.org Web Site: http://www.etv.state.ms.us

Technical Facilities: Channel No. 16 (482-488 MHz). Authorized power: 150-kw max. visual, aural. Antenna: 1565-ft above av. terrain, 1512-ft. above ground, 174-ft. above sea level.

Latitude	30°	45'	18"
Longitude	88°	56'	44"

Requests CP for change to 540-kw max. visual, 1563-ft above av. terrain, 1511-ft. above ground, 1686-ft. above sea level; BPEDT-20080619AGM.

Note: Latitude and longitude coordinates shown are based on the North American Datum of 1927 (NAD 27) as currently required by the Mass Media Bureau of the FCC.

Ownership: Mississippi Authority for ETV.

Began Operation: February 17, 2009. Began analog operations: January 14, 1972. Ceased analog operations: February 17, 2009.

Personnel:

Marie Antoon, Executive Director.

Maggie Gibson, Administration Director.

Teresa Collier, News & Public Affairs Director.

Bob Buie, Technical Services Director.

Jerry Ladd, Chief Network Engineer.

Randy Harris, Business Services Director.

Art Starkey, Program Director.

Jay Woods, Content Development Director.

Darryl Moses, Production Manager.

Brenda Busby, Traffic Manager.

Mari Irby, Public Relations Director.

WMAE-DT
Booneville
Ch. 12

Grantee: Mississippi Authority for ETV, 3825 Ridgewood Rd, Jackson, MS 39211.

Studio: 3825 Ridgewood Rd, Jackson, MS 39211.

Mailing Address: 3825 Ridgewood Rd, Jackson, MS 39211.

Phones: 601-432-6565; 800-922-9698. **Fax:** 501-432-6654.

Email: phyllis.allen@mpbonline.org **Web Site:** http://www.etv.state.ms.us

Technical Facilities: Channel No. 12 (204-210 MHz). Authorized power: 31-kw visual, aural. Antenna: 732-ft above av. terrain, 537-ft. above ground, 1255-ft. above sea level.

Latitude	34°	40'	00"
Longitude	88°	45'	05"

Note: Latitude and longitude coordinates shown are based on the North American Datum of 1927 (NAD 27) as currently required by the Mass Media Bureau of the FCC.

Ownership: Mississippi Authority for ETV.

Began Operation: February 17, 2009. Station broadcasting digitally on its analog channel allotment. Began analog operations: August 11, 1974. Ceased analog operations: February 17, 2009.

Personnel:

Marie Antoon, Executive Director.

Maggie Gibson, Administration Director.

Teresa Collier, News & Public Affairs Director.

Bob Buie, Technical Services Director.

Jerry Ladd, Chief Network Engineer.

Randy Harris, Business Services Director.

Art Starkey, Program Director.

Jay Woods, Content Development Director.

Darryl Moses, Production Manager.

Brenda Busby, Traffic Manager.

Mari Irby, Public Relations Director.

WMAU-DT
Bude
Ch. 18

Licensee: Mississippi Authority for ETV, 3825 Ridgewood Rd, Jackson, MS 39211.

Studio: 3825 Ridgewood Rd, Jackson, MS 39211.

Mailing Address: 3825 Ridgewood Rd, Jackson, MS 39211.

Phones: 601-432-6565; 800-992-9698. **Fax:** 601-432-6654.

Email: phyllis.allen@mpbonline.org **Web Site:** http://www.etv.state.ms.us

Technical Facilities: Channel No. 18 (494-500 MHz). Authorized power: 1000-kw max. visual, aural. Antenna: 1119-ft above av. terrain, 1033-ft. above ground, 1519-ft. above sea level.

Latitude	31°	22'	22"
Longitude	90°	45'	04"

Holds CP for change to 682-kw max. visual, 1115-ft above av. terrain, 1030-ft. above ground, 1516-ft. above sea level; BMPEDT-20090121AHA.

Note: Latitude and longitude coordinates shown are based on the North American Datum of 1927 (NAD 27) as currently required by the Mass Media Bureau of the FCC.

Ownership: Mississippi Authority for ETV.

Began Operation: February 17, 2009. Began analog operations: January 14, 1972. Ceased analog operations: February 17, 2009.

Personnel:

Marie Antoon, Executive Director.

Maggie Gibson, Administration Director.

Teresa Collier, News & Public Affairs Director.

Bob Buie, Technical Services Director.

Jerry Ladd, Chief Network Engineer.

Randy Harris, Business Services Director.

Art Starkey, Program Director.

Jay Woods, Content Development Director.

Darryl Moses, Production Manager.

Brenda Busby, Traffic Manager.

Mari Irby, Public Relations Director.

WMAO-DT
Greenwood
Ch. 25

Grantee: Mississippi Authority for ETV, 3825 Ridgewood Rd, Jackson, MS 39211.

Studio: 3825 Ridgewood Rd, Jackson, MS 39211.

Mailing Address: 3825 Ridgewood Rd, Jackson, MS 39211.

Phones: 601-432-6565; 800-922-9698. **Fax:** 601-432-6654.

Email: phyllis.allen@mpbonline.org **Web Site:** http://www.etv.state.ms.us

Technical Facilities: Channel No. 25 (536-542 MHz). Authorized power: 815-kw max. visual, aural. Antenna: 1041-ft above av. terrain, 1037-ft. above ground, 1152-ft. above sea level.

Latitude	33°	22'	37"
Longitude	90°	32'	32"

Transmitter: 3.2-mi. NE of Inverness.

Note: Latitude and longitude coordinates shown are based on the North American Datum of 1927 (NAD 27) as currently required by the Mass Media Bureau of the FCC.

Ownership: Mississippi Authority for ETV.

Began Operation: February 17, 2009. Began analog operations: September 15, 1972. Ceased analog operations: February 17, 2009.

Personnel:

Marie Antoon, Executive Director.

Maggie Gibson, Administration Director.

Teresa Collier, News & Public Affairs Director.

Bob Buie, Technical Services Director.

Jerry Ladd, Chief Network Engineer.

Randy Harris, Business Services Director.

Art Starkey, Program Director.

Jay Woods, Content Development Director.

Darryl Moses, Production Manager.

Brenda Busby, Traffic Manager.

Mari Irby, Public Relations Director.

WMPN-DT
Jackson
Ch. 20

Grantee: Mississippi Authority for ETV, 3825 Ridgewood Rd, Jackson, MS 39211.

Studio: 3825 Ridgewood Rd, Jackson, MS 39211.

Mailing Address: 3825 Ridgewood Rd, Jackson, MS 39211.

Phones: 601-432-6565; 800-922-9698. **Fax:** 601-432-6654.

Web Site: http://www.etv.state.ms.us

Technical Facilities: Channel No. 20 (506-512 MHz). Authorized power: 400-kw max. visual, aural. Antenna: 1581-ft above av. terrain, 1532-ft. above ground, 1877-ft. above sea level.

Latitude	32°	11'	29"
Longitude	90°	24'	22"

Note: Latitude and longitude coordinates shown are based on the North American Datum of 1927 (NAD 27) as currently required by the Mass Media Bureau of the FCC.

Ownership: Mississippi Authority for ETV.

Began Operation: October 1, 1998. High Definition. Began analog operations: February 1, 1970. Ceased analog operations: February 17, 2009.

Personnel:

Marie Antoon, Executive Director.

Maggie Gibson, Administration Director.

Teresa Collier, News & Public Affairs Director.

Bob Buie, Technical Services Director.

Jerry Ladd, Chief Network Engineer.

Randy Harris, Business Services Director.

Art Starkey, Program Director.

Jay Woods, Content Development Director.

Darryl Moses, Production Manager.

Brenda Busby, Traffic Manager.

Mari Irby, Public Relations Director.

WMAW-DT
Meridian
Ch. 44

Grantee: Mississippi Authority for ETV, 3825 Ridgewood Rd, Jackson, MS 39211.

Studio: 3825 Ridgewood Rd, Jackson, MS 39211.

Mailing Address: 3825 Ridgewood Rd, Jackson, MS 39211.

Phones: 601-432-6565; 800-922-9698. **Fax:** 601-432-6654.

Email: phyllis.allen@mpbonline.org **Web Site:** http://www.etv.state.ms.us

Technical Facilities: Channel No. 44 (650-656 MHz). Authorized power: 880-kw max. visual, aural. Antenna: 1211-ft above av. terrain, 1040-ft. above ground, 1670-ft. above sea level.

Latitude	32°	08'	18"
Longitude	89°	05'	36"

Transmitter: 5.5-mi. W of Rose Hill.

Note: Latitude and longitude coordinates shown are based on the North American Datum of 1927 (NAD 27) as currently required by the Mass Media Bureau of the FCC.

Ownership: Mississippi Authority for ETV.

Began Operation: September 3, 2003. Began analog operations: January 14, 1972. Ceased analog operations: February 17, 2009.

Personnel:

Marie Antoon, Executive Director.

Maggie Gibson, Administration Director.

Teresa Gibson, News & Public Affairs Director.

Bob Buie, Technical Services Director.

Jerry Ladd, Chief Network Engineer.

Randy Harris, Business Services Director.

Art Starkey, Program Director.

Jay Woods, Content Development Director.

Darryl Moses, Production Manager.

Brenda Busby, Traffic Manager.

Mari Irby, Public Relations Director.

WMAB-DT
Mississippi State
Ch. 38

Licensee: Mississippi Authority for ETV, 3825 Ridgewood Rd, Jackson, MS 39211.

Studio: 3825 Ridgewood Rd, Jackson, MS 39211.

Mailing Address: 3825 Ridgewood Rd, Jackson, MS 39211.

Phones: 601-432-6565; 800-922-9698. **Fax:** 601-432-6654.

Email: phyllis.allen@mpbonline.org **Web Site:** http://www.etv.state.ms.us

Technical Facilities: Channel No. 38 (614-620 MHz). Authorized power: 4.3-kw max. visual, aural. Antenna: 1145-ft above av. terrain, 945-ft. above ground, 1611-ft. above sea level.

| Latitude | 33° | 21' | 14" |
| Longitude | 89° | 09' | 00" |

Holds CP for change to channel number 10, 8-kw visual; BPEDT-20080619AGS.

Note: Latitude and longitude coordinates shown are based on the North American Datum of 1927 (NAD 27) as currently required by the Mass Media Bureau of the FCC.

Ownership: Mississippi Authority for ETV.

Began Operation: February 17, 2009. Began analog operations: July 4, 1971. Ceased analog operations: February 17, 2009.

Personnel:

Marie Antoon, Executive Director.

Maggie Gibson, Administration Director.

Teresa Collier, News & Public Affairs Director.

Bob Buie, Technical Services Director.

Jerry Ladd, Chief Network Engineer.

Randy Harris, Business Services Director.

Art Starkey, Program Director.

Jay Woods, Content Development Director.

Darryl Moses, Production Manager.

Brenda Busby, Traffic Manager.

Mari Irby, Public Relations Director.

WMAV-DT
Oxford
Ch. 36

Grantee: Mississippi Authority for ETV, 3825 Ridgewood Rd, Jackson, MS 39211.

Studio: 3825 Ridgewood Rd, Jackson, MS 39211.

Mailing Address: 3825 Ridgewood Rd, Jackson, MS 39211.

Phones: 601-432-6565; 800-922-9698. **Fax:** 601-432-6654.

Email: phyllis.allen@mpbonline.org **Web Site:** http://www.etv.state.ms.us

Technical Facilities: Channel No. 36 (602-608 MHz). Authorized power: 272.5-kw max. visual, aural. Antenna: 1399-ft above av. terrain, 1293-ft. above ground, 1756-ft. above sea level.

| Latitude | 34° | 17' | 28" |
| Longitude | 89° | 42' | 21" |

Note: Latitude and longitude coordinates shown are based on the North American Datum of 1927 (NAD 27) as currently required by the Mass Media Bureau of the FCC.

Ownership: Mississippi Authority for ETV.

Began Operation: February 27, 2003. Began analog operations: May 19, 1972. Ceased analog operations: February 17, 2009.

Personnel:

Marie Antoon, Executive Director.

Maggie Gibson, Administration Director.

Teresa Collier, News & Public Affairs Director.

Bob Buie, Technical Services Director.

Jerry Ladd, Chief Network Engineer.

Randy Harris, Business Services Director.

Art Starkey, Program Director.

Jay Woods, Content Development Director.

Darryl Moses, Production Manager.

Brenda Busby, Traffic Manager.

Mari Irby, Public Relations Director.

Missouri

KOZJ-DT
Joplin
Ch. 25

Licensee: Board of Governors of Missouri State U., 901 S National Ave, Springfield, MO 65897.

Studio: 901 S. National Ave, Springfield, MO 65804.

Mailing Address: 901 S. National Ave, Springfield, MO 65804.

Phone: 417-836-3500. **Fax:** 417-836-3569.

Web Site: http://www.optv.org

Technical Facilities: Channel No. 25 (536-542 MHz). Authorized power: 55-kw max. visual, aural. Antenna: 922-ft above av. terrain, 850-ft. above ground, 1895-ft. above sea level.

| Latitude | 37° | 04' | 37" |
| Longitude | 94° | 32' | 15" |

Transmitter: 1928 W. 13th St.

Note: Latitude and longitude coordinates shown are based on the North American Datum of 1927 (NAD 27) as currently required by the Mass Media Bureau of the FCC.

Ownership: Board of Governors of Missouri State U.

Began Operation: June 20, 2006. Began analog operations: June 1, 1986. Ceased analog operations: June 12, 2009.

Personnel:

Tammy Wiley, General Manager.

Tina Stillwell, Corporate Support Manager.

Brent Moore, Chief Engineer.

Janet Bowman, Office Manager.

Tom Carter, Programming & Production Manager.

Monica Cataldo, Traffic Manager.

Lolita Albers, Educational Services Manager.

Lori Street, Membership Manager.

KCPT-DT
Kansas City
Ch. 18

Licensee: Public Television 19 Inc., 125 E 31st St, Kansas City, MO 64108.

Studio: 125 E 31st St, Kansas City, MO 64108.

Mailing Address: 125 E. 31st St, Kansas City, MO 64108.

Phone: 816-756-3580. **Fax:** 816-931-2500.

Web Site: http://www.kcpt.org

Technical Facilities: Channel No. 18 (494-500 MHz). Authorized power: 55-kw max. visual, aural. Antenna: 1165-ft above av. terrain, 1191-ft. above ground, 2018-ft. above sea level.

| Latitude | 39° | 04' | 59" |
| Longitude | 94° | 28' | 49" |

Holds CP for change to 1000-kw max. visual; BPEDT-20080620ANC.

Transmitter: 2100 Stark St.

Note: Latitude and longitude coordinates shown are based on the North American Datum of 1927 (NAD 27) as currently required by the Mass Media Bureau of the FCC.

Ownership: Public TV 19 Inc.

Began Operation: October 1, 1998. Began analog operations: March 22, 1961. Ceased analog operations: June 12, 2009.

Personnel:

Victor Hogstrom, President & Chief Executive Officer.

Michael Zeller, Vice President, Educational Services.

Jeff Evans, Engineering Director.

Grenetha Baldwin, Program Coordinator & Broadcast Operations Director.

Patti Broderick, Individual Giving Director.

Karen Button, Chief Operations Officer, Promotions & Production.

Bonnie Rabicoff, Vice President, Development & Community Partnerships.

Nick Haines, Public & Executive Affairs Director.

KMOS-DT
Sedalia
Ch. 15

Licensee: Board of Governors of Central Missouri State U., Wood 11, Office of Broadcast Services, Warrensburg, MO 64093.

Studio: Wood Bldg., Central Missouri State U., Warrensburg, MO 64093.

Mailing Address: Central Missouri State U, Wood Bldg, Warrensburg, MO 64093.

Phone: 660-543-4155. **Fax:** 660-543-8863.

Web Site: http://www.kmos.org

Technical Facilities: Channel No. 15 (476-482 MHz). Authorized power: 322-kw max. visual, aural. Antenna: 1978-ft above av. terrain, 1965-ft. above ground, 2838-ft. above sea level.

| Latitude | 38° | 37' | 36" |
| Longitude | 92° | 52' | 03" |

Note: Latitude and longitude coordinates shown are based on the North American Datum of 1927 (NAD 27) as currently required by the Mass Media Bureau of the FCC.

Ownership: Central Missouri State U. Board of Governors.

Began Operation: January 8, 2003. Began analog operations: July 8, 1954. Ceased analog operations: June 12, 2009.

Personnel:

Donald W. Peterson, Broadcasting Services Director.

Fred Hunt, Operations Coordinator.

John Long, Chief Engineer.

Sarah Bailey, Administrative Finance Coordinator.

Dorothy McGrath, TV Programs Manager.

Michael O'Keefe, Program Services Manager.

Roy Millen, Production Coordinator.

Kathy Forste, Traffic Specialist.

Mark Pearce, Corporate & Community Support Coordinator.

KOZK-DT
Springfield
Ch. 23

Licensee: Board of Governors of Missouri State U., 901 S National Ave, Springfield, MO 65897.

Studio: 901 S. National Ave, Springfield, MO 65804.

Mailing Address: 901 S. National Ave, Springfield, MO 65804.

Phone: 417-836-3500. **Fax:** 417-836-3569.

Web Site: http://www.optv.org

Technical Facilities: Channel No. 23 (524-530 MHz). Authorized power: 100-kw max. visual, aural. Antenna: 2024-ft above av. terrain, 1926-ft. above ground, 3491-ft. above sea level.

| Latitude | 37° | 10' | 11" |
| Longitude | 92° | 56' | 30" |

Note: Latitude and longitude coordinates shown are based on the North American Datum of 1927 (NAD 27) as currently required by the Mass Media Bureau of the FCC.

Ownership: Board of Governors of Missouri State U.

Began Operation: September 10, 2003. Began analog operations: January 20, 1975. Ceased analog operations: June 12, 2009.

Personnel:

Tammy Wiley, General Manager.

Tina Stillwell, Corporate Support Manager.

Brent Moore, Chief Engineer.

Janet Bowman, Office Manager.

Tom Carter, Programming & Production Manager.

Monica Cataldo, Traffic Manager.

Lori Street, Membership Manager.

Lolita Albers, Educational Services Manager.

KETC-DT
St. Louis
Ch. 39

Licensee: St. Louis Regional Educational & Public TV Commission, 3655 Olive St, St. Louis, MO 63108-3601.

Studio: 3655 Olive St, St. Louis, MO 63108-3601.

Mailing Address: 3655 Olive St, St. Louis, MO 63108-3601.

Phones: 314-512-9000; 800-729-9966. **Fax:** 314-512-9005.

Web Site: http://www.ketc.org

Technical Facilities: Channel No. 39 (320-626 MHz). Authorized power: 125-kw max. visual, aural. Antenna: 911-ft above av. terrain, 876-ft. above ground, 1452-ft. above sea level.

| Latitude | 38° | 28' | 56" |
| Longitude | 90° | 23' | 53" |

Holds CP for change to 142.5-kw max. visual, 1064-ft above av. terrain, 1029-ft. above ground, 1605-ft. above sea level; BMPEDT-20080617AEP.

Transmitter: 5489 Butler Hill Rd.

Note: Latitude and longitude coordinates shown are based on the North American Datum of 1927 (NAD 27) as currently required by the Mass Media Bureau of the FCC.

Ownership: St. Louis Regional Educational & Public TV Commission.

Began Operation: October 1, 2001. Began analog operations: September 20, 1954. Ceased analog operations: June 12, 2009.

Personnel:

John Galmiche, President & Chief Executive Officer.

Chrys Marlow, Engineering & Operations Director.

Richard Skalski, Senior Vice President, Chief Financial Officer & Chief Operating Officer.

Patricia Kistler, Vice President, Programming.

Beth Savage, Vice President, Development.

John Lindsay, Vice President, National & International Productions.

Patrick Murphy, Vice President, Production.

Terri Gates, Public Relations Manager.

Amy Shaw, Vice President, Education Services.

Don Baggett, Traffic Manager.

Montana

KBGS-TV
Billings
Ch. 16

Grantee: Board of Regents of the Montana University System, Room 183, VCB, Bozeman, MT 59717-3340.

Mailing Address: Room 183, VCB, Bozeman, MT 59717-3340.

Phone: 406-994-3437.

Web Site: http://www.montanapbs.org

Technical Facilities: Channel No. 16 (482-488 MHz). Authorized power: 29.8-kw max. visual, aural. Antenna: 548-ft above av. terrain, 322-ft. above ground, 3989-ft. above sea level.

| Latitude | 45° | 46' | 09.2" |
| Longitude | 108° | 27' | 26.3" |

Note: Latitude and longitude coordinates shown are based on the North American Datum of 1927 (NAD 27) as currently required by the Mass Media Bureau of the FCC.

Ownership: Montana U. System Board of Regents.

Began Operation: June 12, 2009. Station went directly to digital broadcast; no analog application.

Personnel:

Eric Hyyppa, General Manager.

Dean Lawver, Chief Engineer.

KUSM-DT
Bozeman
Ch. 8

Licensee: Montana State U., Visual Communications Bldg, Room 183, Bozeman, MT 59717.

Studio: Visual Communications Bldg. 183, Montana State U., Bozeman, MT 59717.

Mailing Address: Visual Communications Bldg. 183, Montana State U, Bozeman, MT 59717.

Phone: 406-994-3437. **Fax:** 406-994-6545.

Web Site: http://www.montanapbs.org

Technical Facilities: Channel No. 8 (180-186 MHz). Authorized power: 17.9-kw visual, aural. Antenna: 889-ft above av. terrain, 314-ft. above ground, 6925-ft. above sea level.

| Latitude | 45° | 40' | 24" |
| Longitude | 110° | 52' | 02" |

Note: Latitude and longitude coordinates shown are based on the North American Datum of 1927 (NAD 27) as currently required by the Mass Media Bureau of the FCC.

Ownership: Montana U. System Board of Regents.

Began Operation: September 26, 2005. Began analog operations: October 1, 1984. Ceased analog operations: June 12, 2009.

Personnel:

Eric Hyyppa, General Manager.

Kyle Sorenson, Promotion Director.

Paul Heitt-Rennie, Broadcast Operations Manager.

Chris Seifert, Outreach Coordinator.

Dean Lawver, Chief Engineer.

Kathy Brekke, Business Manager.

Gene Brodeur, Program Producer.

Aaron Pruitt, Program Director.

KUFM-DT
Missoula
Ch. 11

Licensee: The U. of Montana, PARTV Bldg., Room 180, Broadcast Media Center, Missoula, MT 59812.

Studio: PARTV 180, 32 Campus Dr, Missoula, MT 59812.

Mailing Address: PARTV 180, 32 Campus Dr, Missoula, MT 59812.

Phone: 406-243-4101. **Fax:** 406-243-3299.

Web Site: http://www.montanapbs.org

Technical Facilities: Channel No. 11 (198-204 MHz). Authorized power: 5.8-kw visual, aural. Antenna: 2079-ft above av. terrain, 102-ft. above ground, 6263-ft. above sea level.

| Latitude | 46° | 48' | 09.3" |
| Longitude | 113° | 58' | 20.6" |

Requests CP for change to 12.3-kw visual; BPEDT-20090617ABA.

Note: Latitude and longitude coordinates shown are based on the North American Datum of 1927 (NAD 27) as currently required by the Mass Media Bureau of the FCC.

Ownership: Montana U. System Board of Regents.

Began Operation: November 28, 2006. Station broadcasting digitally on its analog channel allotment. Began analog operations: January 1, 1997. Ceased analog operations: June 12, 2009.

Personnel:

William Marcus, Station Manager & Program Director.

Daniel Dauterive, Operations Director.

Charles Lubrecht, Engineer.

Doug Drader, Engineer.

Nebraska

KTNE-DT
Alliance
Ch. 13

Licensee: Nebraska Educational Telecommunications Commission, PO Box 83111, Lincoln, NE 68501.

Studio: 1800 N 33rd St, Lincoln, NE 68501.

Mailing Address: PO Box 83111, Lincoln, NE 68501.

Phone: 402-472-3611. **Fax:** 402-472-1785.

Web Site: http://www.mynptv.org

Technical Facilities: Channel No. 13 (210-216 MHz). Authorized power: 27-kw visual, aural. Antenna: 1529-ft above av. terrain, 1436-ft. above ground, 5688-ft. above sea level.

| Latitude | 41° | 50' | 27" |
| Longitude | 103° | 03' | 18" |

Note: Latitude and longitude coordinates shown are based on the North American Datum of 1927 (NAD 27) as currently required by the Mass Media Bureau of the FCC.

Ownership: Nebraska Educational Telecommunications Commission.

Began Operation: March 9, 2004. Station broadcasting digitally on its analog channel allotment. Began analog operations: September 7, 1966. Ceased analog operations: February 17, 2009.

Personnel:

Rod Bates, Network General Manager.

Verle Finke, Production & Operations Manager.

David Feingold, Assistant General Manager, Educational Communications.

Michael Beach, Chief Technology Officer.

Randy Hanson, Business Manager.

Terry Dugas, Acting Program Director.

Kate Templemeyer, Traffic Manager.

KMNE-DT
Bassett
Ch. 7

Licensee: Nebraska Educational Telecommunications Commission, PO Box 83111, Lincoln, NE 68501.

Studio: 1800 N 33rd St, Lincoln, NE 68501.

Mailing Address: PO Box 83111, Lincoln, NE 68501.

Phone: 402-472-3611. **Fax:** 462-472-1785.

Web Site: http://www.mynptv.org

Technical Facilities: Channel No. 7 (174-180 MHz). Authorized power: 27-kw visual, aural. Antenna: 1486-ft above av. terrain, 1473-ft. above ground, 4001-ft. above sea level.

| Latitude | 42° | 20' | 05" |
| Longitude | 99° | 29' | 02" |

Transmitter: 17-mi. S & 2.5-mi. E of Bassett.

Note: Latitude and longitude coordinates shown are based on the North American Datum of 1927 (NAD 27) as currently required by the Mass Media Bureau of the FCC.

Ownership: Nebraska Educational Telecommunications Commission.

Began Operation: October 3, 2008. Station broadcasting digitally on its analog channel allotment. Began analog operations: September 1, 1967. Ceased analog operations: September 30, 2008.

Personnel:

Rod Bates, Network General Manager.

Verle Finke, Production & Operations Manager.

David Feingold, Assistant General Manager, Educational Telecommunications.

Michael Beach, Chief Technology Officer.

Randy Hanson, Business Manager.

Terry Dugas, Acting Program Director.

Kate Templemeyer, Traffic Manager.

KHNE-DT
Hastings
Ch. 14

Licensee: Nebraska Educational Telecommunications Commission, PO Box 83111, Lincoln, NE 68501.

Studio: 1800 N 33rd St, Lincoln, NE 68501.

Mailing Address: PO Box 83111, Lincoln, NE 68501.

Phone: 402-472-3611. **Fax:** 402-472-1785.

Web Site: http://www.mynptv.org

Technical Facilities: Channel No. 14 (470-476 MHz). Authorized power: 200-kw max. visual, aural. Antenna: 1201-ft above av. terrain, 1207-ft. above ground, 3018-ft. above sea level.

| Latitude | 40° | 46' | 20" |
| Longitude | 98° | 05' | 21" |

Transmitter: 3-mi. E of Giltner, Hamilton County.

Note: Latitude and longitude coordinates shown are based on the North American Datum of 1927 (NAD 27) as currently required by the Mass Media Bureau of the FCC.

Ownership: Nebraska Educational Telecommunications Commission.

Began Operation: April 3, 2003. Began analog operations: November 18, 1968. Ceased analog operations: February 17, 2009.

Personnel:

Rod Bates, Network General Manager.

Verle Finke, Production & Operations Manager.

David Feingold, Assistant General Manager, Educational Telecommunications.

Michael Beach, Chief Technology Officer.

Randy Hanson, Business Manager.

Terry Dugas, Acting Program Director.

Kate Templemeyer, Traffic Manager.

KLNE-DT
Lexington
Ch. 26

Licensee: Nebraska Educational Telecommunications Commission, PO Box 83111, Lincoln, NE 68501.

Studio: 1800 N 33rd St, Lincoln, NE 68501.

Mailing Address: PO Box 83111, Lincoln, NE 68501.

Phone: 402-472-3611. **Fax:** 402-472-1785.

Web Site: http://www.mynptv.org

Technical Facilities: Channel No. 26 (542-548 MHz). Authorized power: 375-kw max. visual, aural. Antenna: 1086-ft above av. terrain, 1035-ft. above ground, 3420-ft. above sea level.

| Latitude | 40° | 23' | 05" |
| Longitude | 99° | 27' | 30" |

Transmitter: 1-mi. NE of Atlanta, Phelps County.

Note: Latitude and longitude coordinates shown are based on the North American Datum of 1927 (NAD 27) as currently required by the Mass Media Bureau of the FCC.

Ownership: Nebraska Educational Telecommunications Commission.

Began Operation: June 20, 2007. Began analog operations: September 6, 1965. Ceased analog operations: February 17, 2009.

Personnel:

Rod Bates, Network General Manager.

Verle Finke, Production & Operations Manager.

David Feingold, Assistant General Manager, Educational Telecommunications.

Michael Beach, Chief Technology Officer.

Randy Hanson, Business Manager.

Terry Dugas, Acting Program Director.

Kate Templemeyer, Traffic Manager.

KUON-DT
Lincoln
Ch. 12

Licensee: Nebraska Educational Telecommunications Commission, PO Box 83111, Lincoln, NE 68501.

Studio: 1800 N 33rd St, Lincoln, NE 68501.

Mailing Address: PO Box 83111, Lincoln, NE 68501.

Phone: 402-472-3611. **Fax:** 402-472-1785.

Web Site: http://www.mynptv.org

Technical Facilities: Channel No. 12 (204-210 MHz). Authorized power: 75-kw visual, aural. Antenna: 830-ft above av. terrain, 820-ft. above ground, 1996-ft. above sea level.

| Latitude | 41° | 08' | 18" |
| Longitude | 96° | 27' | 20" |

Note: Latitude and longitude coordinates shown are based on the North American Datum of 1927 (NAD 27) as currently required by the Mass Media Bureau of the FCC.

Ownership: U. of Nebraska.

Began Operation: November 8, 2008. Station broadcasting digitally on its analog channel allotment. Began analog operations: November 1, 1954. Ceased analog operations: October 28, 2008.

Personnel:

Rod Bates, Network General Manager.

David Feingold, Assistant General Manager, Educational Telecommunications.

Verle Finke, Production & Operations Manager.

Michael Beach, Chief Technology Officer.

Randy Hanson, Business Manager.

Terry Dugas, Acting Program Director.

Kate Templemeyer, Traffic Manager.

KRNE-DT
Merriman
Ch. 12

Licensee: Nebraska Educational Telecommunications Commission, PO Box 83111, Lincoln, NE 68501.

Studio: 1800 N 33rd St, Lincoln, NE 68501.

Mailing Address: PO Box 83111, Lincoln, NE 68501.

Phone: 402-472-3611. **Fax:** 402-472-1785.

Web Site: http://www.mynptv.org

Technical Facilities: Channel No. 12 (204-210 MHz). Authorized power: 75-kw visual, aural. Antenna: 1056-ft above av. terrain, 978-ft. above ground, 4518-ft. above sea level.

| Latitude | 42° | 40' | 37" |
| Longitude | 101° | 42' | 39" |

Transmitter: 17-mi. S of Merriman.

Note: Latitude and longitude coordinates shown are based on the North American Datum of 1927 (NAD 27) as currently required by the Mass Media Bureau of the FCC.

Ownership: Nebraska Educational Telecommunications Commission.

Began Operation: April 3, 2003. Station broadcasting digitally on its analog channel allotment. Began analog operations: December 9, 1968. Ceased analog operations: September 1, 2008.

Personnel:

Rod Bates, Network General Manager.

Verle Finke, Production & Operations Manager.

David Feingold, Assistant General Manager, Educational Telecommunications.

Michael Beach, Chief Technology Officer.

Randy Hanson, Business Manager.

Terry Dugas, Acting Program Director.

Kate Templemeyer, Traffic Manager.

KXNE-DT
Norfolk
Ch. 19

Licensee: Nebraska Educational Telecommunications Commission, PO Box 83111, Lincoln, NE 68501.

Studio: 1800 N 33rd St, Lincoln, NE 68501.

Mailing Address: PO Box 83111, Lincoln, NE 68501.

Phone: 402-472-3611. **Fax:** 402-472-1785.

Web Site: http://www.mynptv.org

Technical Facilities: Channel No. 19 (500-506 MHz). Authorized power: 475-kw max. visual, aural. Antenna: 1056-ft above av. terrain, 974-ft. above ground, 2760-ft. above sea level.

| Latitude | 42° | 14' | 15" |
| Longitude | 97° | 16' | 41" |

Note: Latitude and longitude coordinates shown are based on the North American Datum of 1927 (NAD 27) as currently required by the Mass Media Bureau of the FCC.

Ownership: Nebraska Educational Telecommunications Commission.

Began Operation: September 1, 2008. Station broadcasting digitally on its analog channel allotment. Began analog operations: November 10, 1967. Ceased analog operations: November 4, 2008.

Personnel:

Rod Bates, Network General Manager.

Verle Finke, Production & Operations Manager.

David Feingold, Assistant General Manager, Educational Telecommunications.

Steve Lenzen, National Sales Manager.

Bill Ganzel, News Director.

Michael Beach, Chief Technology Officer.

Randy Hanson, Business Manager.

Terry Dugas, Acting Program Director.

Kate Templemeyer, Traffic Manager.

KPNE-DT
North Platte
Ch. 9

Licensee: Nebraska Educational Telecommunications Commission, PO Box 83111, Lincoln, NE 68501.

Studio: 1800 N 33rd St, Lincoln, NE 68501.

Mailing Address: PO Box 83111, Lincoln, NE 68501.

Phone: 402-472-3611. **Fax:** 402-472-1785.

Web Site: http://www.mynptv.org

Technical Facilities: Channel No. 9 (186-192 MHz). Authorized power: 85-kw visual, aural. Antenna: 1096-ft above av. terrain, 1042-ft. above ground, 4251-ft. above sea level.

| Latitude | 41° | 01' | 22" |
| Longitude | 101° | 09' | 14" |

Note: Latitude and longitude coordinates shown are based on the North American Datum of 1927 (NAD 27) as currently required by the Mass Media Bureau of the FCC.

Ownership: Nebraska Educational Telecommunications Commission.

Began Operation: April 3, 2003. Station broadcasting digitally on its analog channel allotment. Began analog operations: September 12, 1966. Ceased analog operations: October 7, 2008.

Personnel:

Rod Bates, Network General Manager.

Verle Finke, Production & Operations Manager.

David Feingold, Assistant General Manager, Educational Telecommunications.

Michael Beach, Chief Technology Officer.

Randy Hanson, Business Manager.

Terry Dugas, Acting Program Director.

Kate Templemeyer, Traffic Manager.

KYNE-DT
Omaha
Ch. 17

Licensee: Nebraska Educational Telecommunications Commission, PO Box 83111, Lincoln, NE 68501.

Studio: 1800 N 33rd St, Lincoln, NE 68501.

Mailing Address: PO Box 83111, Lincoln, NE 68501.

Phone: 402-472-3611. **Fax:** 402-472-1785.

Web Site: http://www.mynptv.org

Technical Facilities: Channel No. 17 (488-494 MHz). Authorized power: 200-kw max. visual, aural. Antenna: 384-ft above av. terrain, 329-ft. above ground, 1480-ft. above sea level.

| Latitude | 41° | 15' | 28" |
| Longitude | 96° | 00' | 32" |

Transmitter: 6-mi. S of Gretna.

Note: Latitude and longitude coordinates shown are based on the North American Datum of 1927 (NAD 27) as currently required by the Mass Media Bureau of the FCC.

Ownership: Nebraska Educational Telecommunications Commission.

Began Operation: April 3, 2003. Began analog operations: October 19, 1965. Ceased analog operations: February 17, 2009.

Personnel:

Rod Bates, Network General Manager.

Verle Finke, Production & Operations Manager.

David Feingold, Assistant General Manager, Educational Telecommunications.

Michael Beach, Chief Technology Officer.

Randy Hanson, Business Manager.

Terry Dugas, Acting Program Director.

Kate Templemeyer, Traffic Manager.

Nevada

KLVX-DT
Las Vegas
Ch. 11

Licensee: Clark County School District, 4210 Channel 10 Dr, Las Vegas, NV 89119.

Studio: 4210 Channel 10 Dr, Las Vegas, NV 89119.

Mailing Address: 4210 Channel 10 Dr, Las Vegas, NV 89119.

Phone: 702-799-1010. **Fax:** 702-799-2960.

Email: taxtell@klvx.org **Web Site:** http://www.vegaspbs.org

Technical Facilities: Channel No. 11 (198-204 MHz). Authorized power: 105-kw visual, aural. Antenna: 1217-ft above av. terrain, 144-ft. above ground, 3494-ft. above sea level.

Latitude	36°	00'	27"
Longitude	115°	00'	24"

Transmitter: Tower 6, Black Mountain antenna farm, 13.6-mi. SE of Las Vegas.

Note: Latitude and longitude coordinates shown are based on the North American Datum of 1927 (NAD 27) as currently required by the Mass Media Bureau of the FCC.

Ownership: Clark County School District.

Began Operation: March 27, 2002. Began analog operations: March 25, 1968. Ceased analog operations: June 12, 2009.

Personnel:

Thomas A. Axtell, General Manager.

Joe Cordova, Chief Television Engineer.

Barbara Merman, Business Manager.

KNPB-DT
Reno
Ch. 15

Licensee: Channel 5 Public Broadcasting Inc., 1670 N Virginia St, Reno, NV 89503.

Studio: 1670 N Virginia St, Reno, NV 89503.

Mailing Address: 1670 N. Virginia St, Reno, NV 89503.

Phone: 775-784-4555. **Fax:** 775-784-1438.

Email: kliff@knpb.org **Web Site:** http://www.knpb.org

Technical Facilities: Channel No. 15 (476-482 MHz). Authorized power: 32.3-kw max. visual, aural. Antenna: 490-ft above av. terrain, 177-ft. above ground, 5606-ft. above sea level.

Latitude	39°	35'	02"
Longitude	119°	47'	55"

Note: Latitude and longitude coordinates shown are based on the North American Datum of 1927 (NAD 27) as currently required by the Mass Media Bureau of the FCC.

Ownership: Channel 5 Public Broadcasting Inc.

Began Operation: September 24, 2003. High Definition. Began analog operations: September 29, 1983. Ceased analog operations: February 17, 2009.

Personnel:

Kliff Kuehl, President & Chief Executive Officer.

Fred Ihlow, Vice President, Technology.

Evelyn Chmura, Technology & Operations Manager.

Loree Daniels, Finance & Administration Director.

Lee Nicholson, Business Manager.

Barbara Harmon, Programming Coordinator & Traffic Manager.

Patricia Miller, Vice President, Programming, Education & Outreach.

Tony Manfredi, Vice President, Marketing & Development.

Dave Santina, Production Manager.

New Hampshire

WENH-DT
Durham
Ch. 11

Licensee: U. of New Hampshire, 268 Mast Rd, Durham, NH 03824-4601.

Studio: 268 Mast Rd, Broadcast Center, Durham, NH 03824.

Mailing Address: 268 Mast Rd, Durham, NH 03824.

Phone: 603-868-1100. **Fax:** 603-868-7552.

Web Site: http://www.nhptv.org

Technical Facilities: Channel No. 11 (198-204 MHz). Authorized power: 30-kw visual, aural. Antenna: 998-ft above av. terrain, 431-ft. above ground, 1517-ft. above sea level.

Latitude	43°	10'	33"
Longitude	71°	12'	29"

Transmitter: Saddleback Mountain.

Note: Latitude and longitude coordinates shown are based on the North American Datum of 1927 (NAD 27) as currently required by the Mass Media Bureau of the FCC.

Ownership: U. of New Hampshire.

Began Operation: February 17, 2009. Station broadcasting digitally on its analog channel allotment. Began analog operations: July 6, 1959. Ceased analog operations: February 17, 2009.

Personnel:

Peter Frid, General Manager & Chief Executive Officer.

Brian Shepperd, Engineering Director.

Chris Whalen, Finance Director.

Hazel Molin, Programming Director.

Dennis Malloy, Development Director.

Susan Adams, Education Technical Coordinator.

Jeff Morris, Corporate Underwriting Director.

WEKW-DT
Keene
Ch. 49

Licensee: U. of New Hampshire, 268 Mast Rd, Durham, NH 03824-4601.

Studio: 268 Mast Rd, Durham, NH 03824-4601.

Mailing Address: 268 Mast Rd, Durham, NH 03824.

Phone: 603-868-1100. **Fax:** 603-868-7552.

Web Site: http://www.nhptv.org

Technical Facilities: Channel No. 49 (680-686 MHz). Authorized power: 43-kw max. visual, aural. Antenna: 1083-ft above av. terrain, 476-ft. above ground, 1993-ft. above sea level.

Latitude	43°	02'	00"
Longitude	72°	22'	04"

Requests CP for change to 112-kw max. visual; BPEDT-20080620AAR.

Note: Latitude and longitude coordinates shown are based on the North American Datum of 1927 (NAD 27) as currently required by the Mass Media Bureau of the FCC.

Ownership: U. of New Hampshire.

Began Operation: May 3, 2002. Began analog operations: May 21, 1968. Ceased analog operations: February 17, 2009.

Personnel:

Peter Frid, General Manager & Chief Executive Officer.

Brian Shepperd, Engineering Director.

Chris Whalen, Finance Director.

Hazel Molin, Programming Director.

Dennis Malloy, Development Director.

Susan Adams, Education Technical Coordinator.

Jeff Morris, Corporate Underwriting Director.

WLED-DT
Littleton
Ch. 48

Licensee: U. of New Hampshire, 268 Mast Rd, Durham, NH 03824-4601.

Studio: 268 Mast Rd, Durham, NH 03824-4601.

Mailing Address: 268 Mast Rd, Durham, NH 03824.

Phone: 603-868-1100. **Fax:** 603-868-7552.

Web Site: http://www.nhptv.org

Technical Facilities: Channel No. 48 (674-680 MHz). Authorized power: 45-kw max. visual, aural. Antenna: 1273-ft above av. terrain, 420-ft. above ground, 2441-ft. above sea level.

Latitude	44°	21'	10"
Longitude	71°	44'	15"

Requests CP for change to 108-kw max. visual, 1282-ft above av. terrain, 422-ft. above ground, 2442-ft. above sea level; BPEDT-20080620AAJ.

Note: Latitude and longitude coordinates shown are based on the North American Datum of 1927 (NAD 27) as currently required by the Mass Media Bureau of the FCC.

Ownership: U. of New Hampshire.

Began Operation: February 17, 2009. Began analog operations: February 8, 1968. Ceased analog operations: February 17, 2009.

Personnel:

Peter Frid, General Manager & Chief Executive Officer.

Brian Shepperd, Engineering Director.

Chris Whalen, Finance Director.

Hazel Molin, Program Director.

Dennis Malloy, Development Director.

Susan Adams, Education Technical Coordinator.

New Jersey

WNJS-DT
Camden
Ch. 22

Licensee: New Jersey Public Broadcasting Authority, PO Box 777, Trenton, NJ 08625-0777.

Studio: 25 S Stockton St, Trenton, NJ 08608.

Mailing Address: PO Box 777, Trenton, NJ 08625-0777.

Phones: 609-777-5000; 973-643-3630. **Fax:** 609-633-2912.

Web Site: http://www.njn.net/television

Technical Facilities: Channel No. 22 (518-524 MHz). Authorized power: 197-kw max. visual, aural. Antenna: 866-ft above av. terrain, 853-ft. above ground, 965-ft. above sea level.

Latitude	39°	43'	41"
Longitude	24°	50'	39"

Holds CP for change to 566-kw max. visual, 869-ft above av. terrain, 853-ft. above ground, 965-ft. above sea level; BPEDT-20080620ALH.

Note: Latitude and longitude coordinates shown are based on the North American Datum of 1927 (NAD 27) as currently required by the Mass Media Bureau of the FCC.

Ownership: New Jersey Public Broadcasting Authority.

Began Operation: June 11, 2007. Began analog operations: October 23, 1972. Ceased analog operations: June 12, 2009.

Personnel:

Elizabeth G. Christopherson, Executive Director & Chief Executive Officer.

Robert Prindible, Deputy Executive Director, Finance & Administration.

William Jobes, News & Public Affairs Director.

Bill Schnorbus, Engineering Director.

Andre Butts, Program Director.

Jo Anne Ruscio, Marketing & Communications Director.

Gerry O'Connor, Senior Vice President, Development.

Janice Selinger, Deputy Executive Director, Production.

Freddie Chisholm, Membership Director.

Stephen Priolo, Underwriter, NJN Foundation.

Ellen Mushinski, Education Initiatives Director.

WNJN-DT
Montclair
Ch. 51

Licensee: New Jersey Public Broadcasting Authority, PO Box 777, Trenton, NJ 08625-0777.

Studio: 25 S Stockton St, Trenton, NJ 08608.

Mailing Address: PO Box 777, Trenton, NJ 08625-0777.

Phones: 609-777-5000; 973-643-3630. **Fax:** 609-633-2912.

Web Site: http://www.njn.net/television

Technical Facilities: Channel No. 51 (692-698 MHz). Authorized power: 200-kw max. visual, aural. Antenna: 764-ft above av. terrain, 591-ft. above ground, 984-ft. above sea level.

Latitude	40°	51'	53"
Longitude	74°	12'	03"

Holds CP for change to 443-kw visual, 778-ft above av. terrain, 591-ft. above ground, 984-ft. above sea level; BPEDT-20080620ALF.

Note: Latitude and longitude coordinates shown are based on the North American Datum of 1927 (NAD 27) as currently required by the Mass Media Bureau of the FCC.

Ownership: New Jersey Public Broadcasting Authority.

Began Operation: October 1, 2001. Standard and High Definition. Began analog operations: June 2, 1973. Ceased analog operations: June 12, 2009.

Personnel:

Elizabeth Christopherson, Executive Director & Chief Executive Officer.

Robert Prindible, Deputy Executive Director, Finance & Administration.

William Jobes, News & Public Affairs Director.

Bill Schnorbus, Engineering Director.

Andre Butts, Program Director.

Jo Anne Ruscio, Marketing & Communications Director.

Gerry O'Connor, Senior Vice President, Development.

Janice Selinger, Deputy Executive Director, Production.

Stephen Priolo, Underwriter, NJN Foundation.

Ellen Mushinski, Education Initiatives Director.

Freddie Chisholm, Membership Director.

WNJB-DT
New Brunswick
Ch. 8

Grantee: New Jersey Public Broadcasting Authority, PO Box 777, Trenton, NJ 08625-0777.

Studio: 25 S Stockton St, Trenton, NJ 08608.

Mailing Address: PO Box 777, Trenton, NJ 08625-0777.

Phones: 609-777-5000; 973-648-3630. **Fax:** 609-633-2912.

Web Site: http://www.njn.net/television

Technical Facilities: Channel No. 8 (180-186 MHz). Authorized power: 17.9-kw visual, aural. Antenna: 705-ft above av. terrain, 374-ft. above ground, 922-ft. above sea level.

Latitude	40°	37'	17"
Longitude	74°	30'	15"

Note: Latitude and longitude coordinates shown are based on the North American Datum of 1927 (NAD 27) as currently required by the Mass Media Bureau of the FCC.

Ownership: New Jersey Public Broadcasting Authority.

Began Operation: April 30, 2003. Began analog operations: June 2, 1973. Ceased analog operations: June 12, 2009.

Personnel:

Elizabeth Christopherson, Executive Director & Chief Executive Officer.

Robert Prindible, Deputy Executive Director, Finance and Administration.

William Jobes, News & Public Affairs Director.

William Schnorbus, Engineering Director.

Andre Butts, Program Director.

Jo Anne Ruscio, Marketing & Communications Director.

Gerry O'Connor, Senior Vice President, Development.

Janice Selinger, Deputy Executive Director of Production.

Freddie Chisholm, Membership Director.

Stephen Priolo, Underwriter, NJN Foundation.

Ellen Mushinski, Education Initiatives Director.

WNET-DT
Newark
Ch. 13

Grantee: WNET.ORG, 450 W 33rd St, 6th Fl, Attn: Vice President & Secretary, New York, NY 10001-2605.

Studio: 450 W 33rd St, New York, NY 10001.

Mailing Address: 450 W. 33rd St, 6th Fl, New York, NY 10001-2605.

Phones: 212-560-1313; 973-643-3315. **Fax:** 212-560-1314.

Web Site: http://www.thirteen.org

Technical Facilities: Channel No. 13 (210-216 MHz). Authorized power: 9.3-kw visual, aural. Antenna: 1329-ft above av. terrain, 1322-ft. above ground, 1373-ft. above sea level.

Latitude	40°	44'	54"
Longitude	73°	59'	10"

Requests modification of CP for change to 4-kw visual, 1663-ft above av. terrain, 1686-ft. above ground, 1700-ft. above sea level lat. 40° 42' 46", long. 74° 0' 49"; BMPCDT-20090709AGX.

Note: Latitude and longitude coordinates shown are based on the North American Datum of 1927 (NAD 27) as currently required by the Mass Media Bureau of the FCC.

Ownership: WNET.ORG.

Began Operation: July 11, 2001. Station broadcasting digitally on its analog channel allotment. Began analog operations: September 16, 1962. Ceased analog operations: June 12, 2009.

Personnel:

Neal Shapiro, President & Chief Operating Officer.

Thomas A. Conway, Vice President, Chief Financial Officer & Treasurer.

Stephen Segaller, Vice President, National Productions.

Ronald Thorpe, Vice President & Education Director.

Barbara Bantivoglio, Vice President, Institutional Advancement.

Ken Devine, Vice President, Media Operations & Chief Information Officer.

Frank Graybill, Chief Engineer.

Catherine Schultheis, Marketing Director & Traffic Manager.

WNJT-DT
Trenton
Ch. 43

Licensee: New Jersey Public Broadcasting Authority, PO Box 777, Trenton, NJ 08625-0777.

Studios: 50 Park Pl, Newark, NJ 07102; 25 S Stockton St, Trenton, NJ 08608.

Mailing Address: PO Box 777, Trenton, NJ 08625-0777.

Phones: 609-777-5000; 973-643-3630. **Fax:** 609-633-2912.

Web Site: http://www.njn.net/television

Technical Facilities: Channel No. 43 (644-650 MHz). Authorized power: 46-kw max. visual, aural. Antenna: 873-ft above av. terrain, 925-ft. above ground, 984-ft. above sea level.

Latitude	40°	16'	58"
Longitude	74°	41'	11"

Holds CP for change to 59.4-kw max. visual; BPEDT-20080620AGH.

Note: Latitude and longitude coordinates shown are based on the North American Datum of 1927 (NAD 27) as currently required by the Mass Media Bureau of the FCC.

Ownership: New Jersey Public Broadcasting Authority.

Began Operation: April 10, 2003. Began analog operations: April 5, 1971. Ceased analog operations: June 12, 2009.

Personnel:

Elizabeth G. Christopherson, Executive Director & Chief Executive Officer.

Robert Prindible, Deputy Executive Director, Finance & Administration.

Janice Selinger, Deputy Executive Director of Production.

William Jobes, News & Public Affairs Director.

Bill Schnorbus, Engineering Director.

Andre Butts, Program Director.

Gerry O'Connor, Senior Vice President, Development.

Freddie Chisholm, Membership Director.

Stephen Priolo, Underwriter, NJN Foundation.

Ellen Mushinski, Education Initiatives Director.

Jo Anne Ruscio, Marketing & Communications Director.

WFME-DT
West Milford
Ch. 29

Licensee: Family Stations of New Jersey Inc., 4135 Northgate Blvd, Ste 1, Sacramento, CA 95834.

Studio: 289 Mount Pleasant Ave, West Orange, NJ 07052.

Mailing Address: 289 Mt. Pleasant Ave, West Orange, NJ 07052.

Phone: 973-736-3600. **Fax:** 973-736-4832.

Web Site: http://www.wfme-tv.com

Technical Facilities: Channel No. 29 (560-566 MHz). Authorized power: 200-kw max. visual, aural. Antenna: 548-ft above av. terrain, 141-ft. above ground, 761-ft. above sea level.

Latitude	40°	47'	18"
Longitude	74°	15'	19"

Transmitter: 289 Mount Pleasant Ave., West Orange.

Note: Latitude and longitude coordinates shown are based on the North American Datum of 1927 (NAD 27) as currently required by the Mass Media Bureau of the FCC.

Ownership: Family Stations Inc.

Began Operation: July 12, 2004. Standard Definition. Began analog operations: March 1, 1996. Ceased analog operations: February 17, 2009.

Personnel:

Harold Camping, President & General Manager.

Charles H. Menut, Station Manager & Chief Engineer.

Jason Frentsos, Public Affairs Director.

New Mexico

KAZQ-DT
Albuquerque
Ch. 17

Licensee: Alpha-Omega Broadcasting of Albuquerque Inc., 4501 Montgomery Blvd. NE, Albuquerque, NM 87109.

Studio: 4501 Montgomery Blvd NE, Albuquerque, NM 87109.

Mailing Address: 4501 Montgomery Blvd. NE, Albuquerque, NM 87109.

Phone: 505-884-8355. **Fax:** 505-884-8367.

Web Site: http://www.kazq32.org

Technical Facilities: Channel No. 17 (488-494 MHz). Authorized power: 65.6-kw max. visual, aural. Antenna: 4091-ft above av. terrain, 110-ft. above ground, 10717-ft. above sea level.

Latitude	35°	12' 51"
Longitude	106°	27' 01"

Note: Latitude and longitude coordinates shown are based on the North American Datum of 1927 (NAD 27) as currently required by the Mass Media Bureau of the FCC.

Ownership: Alpha-Omega Broadcasting of Albuquerque Inc.

Began Operation: October 11, 2005. Began analog operations: October 12, 1987. Ceased analog operations: June 12, 2009.

Personnel:

Brenton Franks, Vice President, Operations.

Jeff Helmers, General Manager.

Rob Ramseyer, Chief Engineer.

Ruth Franks, Operations Director.

Leticia Maturino, Community Affairs Director.

Howard Holley, Production Manager.

Steve Minor, Traffic Manager.

David Staley, Lead Editor.

KNME-DT
Albuquerque
Ch. 25

Licensee: Regents of the U. of New Mexico & The Board of Education of the City of Albuquerque, 1130 University Blvd NE, Albuquerque, NM 87102.

Studio: 1130 University Blvd. NE, Albuquerque, NM 87102.

Mailing Address: 1130 University Blvd. NE, Albuquerque, NM 87102.

Phone: 505-277-2121. **Fax:** 505-277-2191.

Web Site: http://www.knmetv.org

Technical Facilities: Channel No. 25 (536-542 MHz). Authorized power: 250-kw max. visual, aural. Antenna: 4222-ft above av. terrain, 219-ft. above ground, 10829-ft. above sea level.

Latitude	35°	12' 49.7"
Longitude	106°	27' 01.3"

Transmitter: Sandia Crest Electronics Site, near Albuquerque.

Note: Latitude and longitude coordinates shown are based on the North American Datum of 1927 (NAD 27) as currently required by the Mass Media Bureau of the FCC.

Ownership: Board of Education of the City of Albuquerque. Regents of the U. of New Mexico.

Began Operation: November 1, 2001. High Definition. Began analog operations: May 1, 1958. Ceased analog operations: June 12, 2009.

Personnel:

Ted A. Garcia, General Manager & Chief Executive Officer.

Jim Gale, Engineering Director.

Esther Perea, Finance & Administration Director.

Chad Davis, Program Director.

Joan Rebecchi, Advertising & Promotion Manager.

Bill Pinell, Marketing Representative.

Joanne Bachmann, Associate General Manager.

Franz Joachim, Production Manager.

Heidi Brown, Membership Services Manager.

Ed Uman, Educational Services Manager.

John Burch, Membership Services Director.

KRWG-DT
Las Cruces
Ch. 23

Licensee: Regents of New Mexico State U., PO Box 30001, MSC: TV22, New Mexico State U., Las Cruces, NM 88003.

Studio: Milton Hall, Jordan St, PO Box 30001, MSC: TV22, New Mexico State U., Las Cruces, NM 88003.

Mailing Address: PO Box 30001, Room 100, Milton Hall, New Mexico State U, Las Cruces, NM 88003-8001.

Phone: 505-646-2222. **Fax:** 505-646-1924.

Email: CGromatz@nmsu.edu **Web Site:** http://www.krwg-tv.org

Technical Facilities: Channel No. 23 (524-530 MHz). Authorized power: 200-kw max. visual, aural. Antenna: 673-ft above av. terrain, 171-ft. above ground, 5089-ft. above sea level.

Latitude	32°	17' 33"
Longitude	106°	41' 51"

Holds CP for change to 1000-kw max. visual; BPEDT-20080709AHL.

Note: Latitude and longitude coordinates shown are based on the North American Datum of 1927 (NAD 27) as currently required by the Mass Media Bureau of the FCC.

Ownership: Regents of New Mexico State U.

Began Operation: December 14, 2007. Began analog operations: June 29, 1973. Ceased analog operations: June 12, 2009.

Personnel:

Glen Cerny, University Broadcasting Director.

William Saggerson, Chief Engineer.

David Holly, Underwriting Director.

Anthony Casaus, Development Director.

J. D. Jarvis, Production Manager.

April Bond, Marketing Director.

Heidi Seelbach, Program Director.

KENW-DT
Portales
Ch. 32

Licensee: Regents of Eastern New Mexico U., 52 Broadcast Center, Portales, NM 88130-9989.

Studio: 52 Broadcast Center, Portales, NM 88130.

Mailing Address: 52 Broadcast Center, Portales, NM 88130-9989.

Phone: 575-562-2112. **Fax:** 575-562-2590.

Web Site: http://www.kenw.org

Technical Facilities: Channel No. 32 (578-584 MHz). Authorized power: 82.6-kw max. visual, aural. Antenna: 624-ft above av. terrain, 707-ft. above ground, 4065-ft. above sea level.

Latitude	34°	15' 08.1"
Longitude	130°	14' 20.6"

Note: Latitude and longitude coordinates shown are based on the North American Datum of 1927 (NAD 27) as currently required by the Mass Media Bureau of the FCC.

Ownership: Eastern New Mexico U. Board of Regents.

Began Operation: February 19, 2003. Began analog operations: September 1, 1974. Ceased analog operations February 17, 2009.

Personnel:

Duane W. Ryan, Broadcasting Director.

Orlando Ortega, Operations Director.

John Kirby, News Director.

Jeff Burmeister, Broadcast Engineering Director.

Ed Miller, Chief Engineer.

Terri Doerr, Business Manager.

Sheryl Borden, Development Officer.

Linda Stefanovic, Program Director.

Rena Garrett, Development & Promotion Director.

Don Criss, Community Relations & Production Director.

KNMD-DT
Santa Fe
Ch. 9

Licensee: Regents of the U. of New Mexico & Board of Education of the City of Albuquerque, 1130 University Blvd NE, Albuquerque, NM 81702.

Studio: 1130 University Blvd. NE, Albuquerque, NM 87102.

Mailing Address: 1130 University Blvd. NE, Albuquerque, NM 87102.

Phone: 505-277-2121. **Fax:** 505-277-2191.

Web Site: http://www.knmetv.org

Technical Facilities: Channel No. 9 (186-192 MHz). Authorized power: 0.2-kw visual, aural. Antenna: 4071-ft above av. terrain, 46-ft. above ground, 10686-ft. above sea level.

Latitude	35°	12' 45"
Longitude	106°	26' 58"

Requests CP for change to channel number 8, 5.14-kw visual, 4180-ft above av. terrain, 157-ft. above ground, 10790-ft. above sea level lat. 35° 12' 44", long. 106° 26' 57"; BPEDT-20090827ACA.

Note: Latitude and longitude coordinates shown are based on the North American Datum of 1927 (NAD 27) as currently required by the Mass Media Bureau of the FCC.

Ownership: Board of Education of the City of Albuquerque. Regents of the U. of New Mexico.

Began Operation: September 13, 2004. Station went directly to digital broadcast on its original analog allotment.

Personnel:

Ted A. Garcia, Chief Executive Officer & General Manager.

Jim Gale, Engineering Director.

Ester Perea, Finance & Administration Director.

Chad Davis, Program Director.

Bill Pinell, Marketing Representative.

Joan Rebecchi, Advertising & Promotion Manager.

Joanne Bachmann, Associate General Manager.

Franz Joachim, Production Manager.

Heidi Brown, Membership Services Director.

John Burch, Membership Services Manager.

Ed Uman, Education Services Manager.

New York

WSKG-DT
Binghamton
Ch. 42

Licensee: WSKG Public Telecommunications Council, PO Box 3000, Binghamton, NY 13902.

Studio: 601 Gates Rd, Vestal, NY 13850.

Mailing Address: PO Box 3000, Binghamton, NY 13902-3000.

Phone: 607-729-0100. **Fax:** 607-729-7328.

Web Site: http://www.wskg.org

Technical Facilities: Channel No. 42 (638-644 MHz). Authorized power: 50-kw max. visual, aural. Antenna: 1339-ft above av. terrain, 925-ft. above ground, 2635-ft. above sea level.

| Latitude | 42° | 03' | 40" |
| Longitude | 75° | 56' | 45" |

Note: Latitude and longitude coordinates shown are based on the North American Datum of 1927 (NAD 27) as currently required by the Mass Media Bureau of the FCC.

Ownership: WSKG Public Telecommunications Council.

Began Operation: May 25, 2005. Began analog operations: May 12, 1968. Ceased analog operations: June 12, 2009.

Personnel:

Brian Sickora, President & Chief Executive Officer.

Naomi Rupright, Business Office Manager.

Michael Pufky, Chief Engineer.

Stacey Mosteller, Programming Director.

Nancy Christensen, Operations Director.

Bill Jaker, Senior Program Producer.

WNED-DT
Buffalo
Ch. 43

Licensee: Western New York Public Broadcasting Assn., PO Box 1263, Buffalo, NY 14240-1263.

Studio: 140 Lower Terrace, Buffalo, NY 14202.

Mailing Address: PO Box 1263, Buffalo, NY 14240-1263.

Phone: 716-845-7000. **Fax:** 716-845-7036.

Web Site: http://www.wned.org

Technical Facilities: Channel No. 43 (644-650 MHz). Authorized power: 156-kw max. visual, aural. Antenna: 1076-ft above av. terrain, 1086-ft. above ground, 1663-ft. above sea level.

| Latitude | 43° | 01' | 48" |
| Longitude | 78° | 55' | 15" |

Note: Latitude and longitude coordinates shown are based on the North American Datum of 1927 (NAD 27) as currently required by the Mass Media Bureau of the FCC.

Ownership: Western New York Public Broadcasting Association.

Began Operation: August 12, 2003. Began analog operations: March 30, 1959. Ceased analog operations: June 12, 2009.

Personnel:

Donald K. Boswell, President & Chief Executive Officer.

Richard Daly, Senior Vice President, Broadcasting.

Jim DiMino, National Sales Manager.

Jim Ranney, News Director.

Joe Puma, Vice President, Engineering & Technology.

Michael G. Sutton, Vice President, Chief Financial Officer.

Nancy Hammond, Controller.

John Grant, Chief Program Officer.

Sylvia Bennett, Vice President, Development.

Ron Santora, Vice President, Broadcasting & Station Manager.

Darwin McPherson, Corporate Communications Director.

Bree Bishop, Membership Director.

WSKA-DT
Corning
Ch. 30

Licensee: WSKG Public Telecommunications Council, PO Box 3000, Binghamton, NY 13902-3000.

Studio: 601 Gates Rd, Vestal, NY 13850.

Mailing Address: PO Box 3000, Binghamton, NY 13902-3000.

Phone: 607-729-0100. **Fax:** 607-729-7328.

Web Site: http://www.wskg.org

Technical Facilities: Channel No. 30 (566-572 MHz). Authorized power: 25-kw max. visual, aural. Antenna: 1096-ft above av. terrain, 774-ft. above ground, 2454-ft. above sea level.

| Latitude | 42° | 08' | 29.7" |
| Longitude | 77° | 04' | 39.1" |

Note: Latitude and longitude coordinates shown are based on the North American Datum of 1927 (NAD 27) as currently required by the Mass Media Bureau of the FCC.

Ownership: WSKG Public Telecommunications Council.

Began Operation: August 1, 2006. Station went directly to digital broadcast on its analog allotment.

Personnel:

Brian Sickora, President & Chief Executive Officer.

Nancy Christensen, Operations Director.

Michael Pufky, Chief Engineer.

Naomi Rupright, Business Manager.

Stacey Mosteller, Program Director.

Bill Jaker, Senior Program Producer.

WLIW-DT
Garden City
Ch. 21

Licensee: WNET.ORG, 450 W 33rd St, 6th Fl, Attn: Vice President & Secretary, New York, NY 10001-2605.

Studio: Channel 21 Dr, Plainview, NY 11803.

Mailing Address: PO Box 21, Plainview, NY 11803-0021.

Phone: 516-367-2100. **Fax:** 516-692-7629.

Web Site: http://www.wliw.org

Technical Facilities: Channel No. 21 (512-518 MHz). Authorized power: 89.9-kw max. visual, aural. Antenna: 364-ft above av. terrain, 254-ft. above ground, 489-ft. above sea level.

| Latitude | 40° | 47' | 19" |
| Longitude | 73° | 27' | 09" |

Requests modification of CP for change to 251-kw max. visual, 403-ft above av. terrain, 294-ft. above ground, 530-ft. above sea level; BMPEDT-20080620AID.

Transmitter: Channel 21 Dr., Plainview.

Note: Latitude and longitude coordinates shown are based on the North American Datum of 1927 (NAD 27) as currently required by the Mass Media Bureau of the FCC.

Ownership: WNET.ORG.

Began Operation: October 7, 2003. Station broadcasting digitally on its analog channel allotment. Began analog operations: January 14, 1969. Sale to present owner by Long Island Educational Television Council approved by FCC October 16, 2002. Ceased analog operations: June 12, 2009.

Personnel:

Terrel Cass, President & General Manager.

Tom D'Agostino, Engineering Director.

Virin Batra, Finance Director.

Joseph Campbell, Program Director.

Roy Hammond, Production Projects Director.

WNYE-DT
New York
Ch. 24

Grantee: New York City Department of Information Technology & Telecommunications, 75 Park Place, 9th Fl, New York, NY 10007.

Studio: 112 Tillary St, Brooklyn, NY 11201.

Mailing Address: 112 Tillary St, Brooklyn, NY 11201.

Phone: 212-669-7400. **Fax:** 212-669-8448.

Web Site: http://www.nyc.gov/tv

Technical Facilities: Channel No. 24 (530-536 MHz). Authorized power: 151-kw max. visual, aural. Antenna: 1016-ft above av. terrain, 1014-ft. above ground, 1064-ft. above sea level.

| Latitude | 40° | 45' | 22" |
| Longitude | 73° | 59' | 12" |

Note: Latitude and longitude coordinates shown are based on the North American Datum of 1927 (NAD 27) as currently required by the Mass Media Bureau of the FCC.

Ownership: Board of Education of the City of New York.

Began Operation: April 23, 2002. Began analog operations: April 3, 1967. Ceased analog operations: June 12, 2009.

Personnel:

Arick Wierson, General Manager.

Terence M. O'Driscoll, Facilities & Planning Director.

Chang Kim, Chief Engineer.

Trevor Scotland, Business Development Director.

WNPI-DT
Norwood
Ch. 23

Licensee: St. Lawrence Valley Educational TV Council Inc., 1056 Arsenal St, Watertown, NY 13601.

Studio: 1056 Arsenal St, Watertown, NY 13601.

Mailing Address: 1056 Arsenal St, Watertown, NY 13601.

Phone: 315-782-3142. **Fax:** 315-782-2491.

Email: tom_hanley@wpbs.pbs.org **Web Site:** http://www.wpbstv.org

Technical Facilities: Channel No. 23 (524-530 MHz). Authorized power: 40-kw max. visual, aural. Antenna: 793-ft above av. terrain, 724-ft. above ground, 1957-ft. above sea level.

| Latitude | 44° | 29' | 29" |
| Longitude | 74° | 51' | 27" |

Requests CP for change to 60.5-kw max. visual, 794-ft above av. terrain, 725-ft. above ground, 1959-ft. above sea level; BPEDT-20080619ABH.

Note: Latitude and longitude coordinates shown are based on the North American Datum of 1927 (NAD 27) as currently required by the Mass Media Bureau of the FCC.

Ownership: St. Lawrence Valley ETV Council.

Began Operation: July 15, 2005. Began analog operations: September 5, 1971. Ceased analog operations: June 12, 2009.

Personnel:

Thomas F. Hanley, President & General Manager.

Leslie O'Hara, Sales Manager.

Gary Talkiewicz, Technology Director & Chief Engineer.

Lynn Brown, Programming & Development Director.

Joline Furgison, Program Manager.

Tracy Duflo, Production Director.

Cari Knight, Educational Services Manager.

Beth Russell, Staff Accountant.

Julie Weston, Events Manager.

William Tinsley, Website Development.

Lucia Bliss, Major & Planned Giving Manager.

Teresa Rolfe, Volunteer Coordinator.

WCFE-DT
Plattsburgh
Ch. 38

Licensee: Mountain Lake Public Telecommunications Council, 1 Sesame St, Plattsburgh, NY 12901.

Studio: One Sesame St, Plattsburgh, NY 12901.

Mailing Address: One Sesame St, Plattsburgh, NY 12901.

Phone: 518-563-9770. **Fax:** 518-561-1928.

Email: charlie_zarbo@mountainlake.pbs.org **Web Site:** http://www.mountainlake.org

Technical Facilities: Channel No. 38 (614-620 MHz). Authorized power: 100-kw max. visual, aural. Antenna: 2418-ft above av. terrain, 410-ft. above ground, 4062-ft. above sea level.

Latitude 44° 41' 43"
Longitude 73° 53' 00"

Requests CP for change to 200-kw max. visual; BPEDT-20080617ABV.

Holds CP for change to 55-kw max. visual; BPEDT-20080130AJH.

Note: Latitude and longitude coordinates shown are based on the North American Datum of 1927 (NAD 27) as currently required by the Mass Media Bureau of the FCC.

Satellite Earth Stations: Thales; DH Satellite, 5-meter C-band; Vertex, 6.1-meter; Bitlink, Teryon 7500, Standard MT850, DSR 4000 receivers.

Ownership: Mountain Lake Public Telecommunications Council.

Began Operation: February 1, 2004. Began analog operations: March 6, 1977. FCC granted station Special Temporary Authority to remain silent after station was forced off-air April 2007 following the collapse of its transmitter tower. Station resumed operations October 18, 2007. Ceased analog operations: February 17, 2009.

Personnel:

Alice Recore, President & Chief Executive Officer.

Charles Zarbo, Engineering Director.

William T. Rogers, Chief Engineer.

Sharlene F. Petro-Durgan, Business Manager.

Colin A Powers, Production & Programming Director.

Zachary Kowalczyk, Traffic Coordinator.

Jane Owens, Outreach & Education Director.

WXXI-DT
Rochester
Ch. 16

Licensee: WXXI Public Broadcasting Council, PO Box 30021, 280 State St, Rochester, NY 14603.

Studio: 280 State St, Rochester, NY 14603.

Mailing Address: PO Box 30021, Rochester, NY 14603-3021.

Phone: 585-325-7500. **Fax:** 585-258-0335.

Web Site: http://www.wxxi.org

Technical Facilities: Channel No. 16 (482-488 MHz). Authorized power: 180-kw max. visual, aural. Antenna: 427-ft above av. terrain, 239-ft. above ground, 912-ft. above sea level.

Latitude 43° 08' 07"
Longitude 77° 35' 03"

Transmitter: Pinnacle Hill, Brighton.

Note: Latitude and longitude coordinates shown are based on the North American Datum of 1927 (NAD 27) as currently required by the Mass Media Bureau of the FCC.

Satellite Earth Stations: Harris; Comtech, 3.8-meter Ku-band; Andrew, 10-meter C-band; Standard Communications, General Instrument DVB receivers.

Ownership: WXXI Public Broadcasting Council.

Began Operation: November 4, 2004. Began analog operations: September 6, 1966. Ceased analog operations: June 12, 2009.

Personnel:

Norm Silverstein, President & Chief Executive Officer.

Susan Rogers, Executive Vice President.

Eric Fundin, Operations Director.

Elissa Orlando, Vice President, Television.

Kent Hatfield, Vice President, Technology & Operations.

Robert Owens, TV Program Director.

John Overlan, Executive Director, Broadcast Productions.

Jon Haliniak, Creative Director.

Fran Lipani, Human Resources Director.

WMHT-DT
Schenectady
Ch. 34

Licensee: WMHT Educational Telecommunications, PO Box 17, Schenectady, NY 12301-0017.

Studio: 4 Global View, Troy, NY 12180.

Mailing Address: 4 Global View, Troy, NY 12180.

Phones: 518-880-3400; 800-477-9648. **Fax:** 518-880-3409.

Email: ssauer@wmht.org **Web Site:** http://www.wmht.org

Technical Facilities: Channel No. 34 (590-596 MHz). Authorized power: 325-kw max. visual, aural. Antenna: 1398-ft above av. terrain, 456-ft. above ground, 2237-ft. above sea level.

Latitude 42° 37' 31"
Longitude 74° 00' 38"

Note: Latitude and longitude coordinates shown are based on the North American Datum of 1927 (NAD 27) as currently required by the Mass Media Bureau of the FCC.

Ownership: WMHT Educational Telecommunications.

Began Operation: January 8, 2004. Began analog operations: March 26, 1962. Ceased analog operations: June 12, 2009.

Personnel:

Robert Altman, President & General Manager.

Paul Hoagland, Senior Vice President & Station Manager.

David Nicosia, Engineering Operations Manager.

Julie Raskin, Finance & Accounting Director.

Mary Anne Potter, Vice President, Television & Programming Manager.

Scott Sauer, Senior Vice President, Development.

Jayne Robinson, Traffic Coordinator.

Jackie McGinnis, Communications Director.

Katherine Jetter, Vice President, Educational Services.

WCNY-DT
Syracuse
Ch. 25

Licensee: Public Broadcasting Council of Central New York Inc., PO Box 2400, 506 Old Liverpool Rd, Syracuse, NY 13220-2400.

Studio: 506 Old Liverpool Rd, Liverpool, NY 13088.

Mailing Address: PO Box 2400, Syracuse, NY 13220-2400.

Phone: 315-453-2424. **Fax:** 315-451-8824.

Email: pete_headd@wcny.org **Web Site:** http://www.wcny.org

Technical Facilities: Channel No. 25 (536-542 MHz). Authorized power: 97-kw max. visual, aural. Antenna: 1289-ft above av. terrain, 843-ft. above ground, 2260-ft. above sea level.

Latitude 42° 56' 44"
Longitude 76° 07' 07"

Note: Latitude and longitude coordinates shown are based on the North American Datum of 1927 (NAD 27) as currently required by the Mass Media Bureau of the FCC.

Satellite Earth Stations: Thales; Vertex, 6.1-meter Ku-band; Andrew, 11-meter C-band; Collins receivers.

Ownership: The Public Broadcasting Council of Central New York Inc.

Began Operation: April 10, 2003. Began analog operations: December 20, 1965. Ceased analog operations: June 12, 2009.

Personnel:

Robert J. Daino, President & Chief Executive Officer.

Brian Damm, Corporate Communications Director.

Larry Goodsight, Vice President, Sales & Business Development.

John Duffy, Vice President, Technology & Operations.

Dale Wagner, Programming Services Director.

Janeen Bonner, Human Resources Director.

Renee DeVestey, Volunteer Services Director.

WPBS-DT
Watertown
Ch. 41

Licensee: St. Lawrence Valley Educational TV Council Inc., 1056 Arsenal St, Watertown, NY 13601.

Studio: 1056 Arsenal St, Watertown, NY 13601.

WPBS-TV/WNPI-TV: 9 Antares Dr, Ottawa, ON, K2E7V5.

Mailing Address: 1056 Arsenal St, Watertown, NY 13601.

Phones: 315-782-3142; 613-226-2660. **Fax:** 315-782-2491.

Email: tom_hanley@wpbs.pbs.org **Web Site:** http://www.wpbstv.org

Technical Facilities: Channel No. 41 (632-638 MHz). Authorized power: 40-kw max. visual, aural. Antenna: 1214-ft above av. terrain, 914-ft. above ground, 2476-ft. above sea level.

Latitude 43° 51' 46"
Longitude 75° 43' 39"

Holds CP for change to 59-kw max. visual, 1212-ft above av. terrain, 914-ft. above ground, 2477-ft. above sea level; BPEDT-20080619ABP.

Note: Latitude and longitude coordinates shown are based on the North American Datum of 1927 (NAD 27) as currently required by the Mass Media Bureau of the FCC.

Ownership: St. Lawrence Valley ETV Council.

Began Operation: August 11, 2005. Began analog operations: August 9, 1971. Ceased analog operations: June 12, 2009.

Personnel:

Thomas F. Hanley, President & General Manager.

Lynn Brown, Programming & Development Director.

Tracy Duflo, Production Manager.

Joline Furgison, Program Manager.

Beth Russell, Staff Accountant.

Gary Talkiewicz, Chief Engineer & Technology Director.

Leslie O'Hara, Sales Director.

Cari Knight, Educational Services Manager.

Julie Weston, Events Manager.

William Tinsley, Website Development.

Teresa Rolfe, Volunteer Coordinator.

Lucia Bliss, Major & Planned Giving Manager.

North Carolina

WUNF-DT
Asheville
Ch. 25

Licensee: U. of North Carolina, PO Box 14900, Research Triangle Park, NC 27709-4900.

Studio: 10 TW Alexander Dr, Research Triangle Park, NC 27709.

Mailing Address: PO Box 14900, Research Triangle Park, NC 27709-4900.

Phone: 919-549-7000. **Fax:** 919-549-7179.

Web Site: http://www.unctv.org

Technical Facilities: Channel No. 25 (536-542 MHz). Authorized power: 185-kw max. visual, aural. Antenna: 2615-ft above av. terrain, 131-ft. above ground, 5850-ft. above sea level.

Latitude	35°	25'	32"
Longitude	82°	45'	25"

Holds CP for change to 125-kw max. visual, 2677-ft above av. terrain, 194-ft. above ground, 5912-ft. above sea level; BPEDT-20080619AEH.

Note: Latitude and longitude coordinates shown are based on the North American Datum of 1927 (NAD 27) as currently required by the Mass Media Bureau of the FCC.

Ownership: U. of North Carolina.

Began Operation: March 24, 2003. Began analog operations: September 11, 1967. Ceased analog operations: June 12, 2009.

Personnel:

Tom Howe, Director & General Manager.

Carl Davis, Engineering Director & Assistant General Manager.

Diane Lucas, Program Director.

James A. McGurk, Promotions Manager.

Delores James, Assistant General Manager & Development Director.

Bobby Royster, Local Productions Director.

Dennis Dowdy, Traffic Manager.

Kirk Scharfenberg, Human Resources Director.

Steven Volstad, Communications Director.

Kathy Dobbins, Grants Director.

WUNC-DT
Chapel Hill
Ch. 59

Licensee: U. of North Carolina, PO Box 14900, Research Triangle Park, NC 27709-4900.

Studio: 10 TW Alexander Dr, Research Triangle Park, NC 27709.

Mailing Address: PO Box 14900, Research Triangle Park, NC 27709-4900.

Phone: 919-549-7000. **Fax:** 919-549-7179.

Web Site: http://www.unctv.org

Technical Facilities: Channel No. 59 (740-746 MHz). Authorized power: 893.2-kw max. visual, aural. Antenna: 1470-ft above av. terrain, 1204-ft. above ground, 1946-ft. above sea level.

Latitude	35°	51'	59"
Longitude	79°	10'	00"

Holds CP for change to channel number 25, 1000-kw max. visual, 1522-ft above av. terrain, 1257-ft. above ground, 1998-ft. above sea level; BMPEDT-20080617AAK.

Note: Latitude and longitude coordinates shown are based on the North American Datum of 1927 (NAD 27) as currently required by the Mass Media Bureau of the FCC.

Ownership: U. of North Carolina.

Began Operation: December 12, 2001. Standard Definition. Began analog operations: January 8, 1955. Ceased analog operations: June 12, 2009.

Personnel:

Tom Howe, Director & General Manager.

Carl Davis, Engineering Director & Assistant General Manager.

Diane Lucas, Programming Director.

James A. McGurk, Promotions Manager.

Delores James, Assistant General Manager & Development Director.

Bobby Royster, Local Productions Director.

Dennis Dowdy, Traffic Manager.

Kirk Scharfenberg, Human Resources Director.

Steven Volstad, Communications Director.

Kathy Dobbins, Grants Director.

WTVI-DT
Charlotte
Ch. 11

Licensee: Charlotte-Mecklenburg Public Broadcasting Authority, 3242 Commonwealth Ave, Charlotte, NC 28205.

Studio: 3242 Commonwealth Ave, Charlotte, NC 28205.

Mailing Address: 3242 Commonwealth Ave, Charlotte, NC 28205.

Phone: 704-372-2442. **Fax:** 704-335-1358.

Email: tgreen@wtvi.org **Web Site:** http://www.wtvi.org

Technical Facilities: Channel No. 11 (198-204 MHz). Authorized power: 2.2-kw visual, aural. Antenna: 1191-ft above av. terrain, 1142-ft. above ground, 1857-ft. above sea level.

Latitude	35°	17'	14"
Longitude	80°	41'	45"

Holds CP for change to 2.57-kw visual; BPEDT-20080620ALW.

Note: Latitude and longitude coordinates shown are based on the North American Datum of 1927 (NAD 27) as currently required by the Mass Media Bureau of the FCC.

Multichannel TV Sound: Stereo and separate audio program.

Ownership: Charlotte-Mecklenburg Public Bcstg. Authority.

Began Operation: April 1, 2002. Standard Definition. Began analog operations: August 27, 1965. Ceased analog operations: February 17, 2009.

Personnel:

Elsie B. Garner, President & Chief Executive Officer.

Taujauna Howard, Chief Financial Officer.

Tom Green, Chief Engineer.

Eric Davis, Production Director.

Regina Berry, Program & Traffic Operations Manager.

Chad Scott, Chief Development Officer.

Michelle Lewis, Information Technology Manager.

Beverly Dorn-Steele, Educational & Outreach Services Director.

WUNG-DT
Concord
Ch. 44

Licensee: U. of North Carolina, PO Box 14900, Research Triangle Park, NC 27709-4900.

Studio: 10 TW Alexander Dr, Research Triangle Park, NC 27709.

Mailing Address: PO Box 14900, Research Triangle Park, NC 27709-4900.

Phone: 919-549-7000. **Fax:** 919-549-7179.

Web Site: http://www.unctv.org

Technical Facilities: Channel No. 44 (650-656 MHz). Authorized power: 150-kw max. visual, aural. Antenna: 1325-ft above av. terrain, 1322-ft. above ground, 1955-ft. above sea level.

Latitude	35°	21'	30"
Longitude	80°	36'	37"

Holds CP for change to 160-kw max. visual, 1384-ft above av. terrain, 1381-ft. above ground, 2014-ft. above sea level; BPEDT-20080616ACB.

Note: Latitude and longitude coordinates shown are based on the North American Datum of 1927 (NAD 27) as currently required by the Mass Media Bureau of the FCC.

Ownership: U. of North Carolina.

Began Operation: August 6, 2001. Began analog operations: September 11, 1967. Ceased analog operations: June 12, 2009.

Personnel:

Tom Howe, Director & General Manager.

Carl Davis, Engineering Director & Assistant General Manager.

Diane Lucas, Program Director.

James A. McGurk, Promotions Manager.

Delores James, Assistant General Manager & Development Director.

Bobby Royster, Local Productions Director.

Dennis Dowdy, Traffic Manager.

Kirk Scharfenberg, Human Resources Director.

Steven Volstad, Communications Director.

Kathy Dobbins, Grants Director.

WUND-DT
Edenton
Ch. 20

Licensee: U. of North Carolina, PO Box 14900, Research Triangle Park, NC 27709-4900.

Studio: 10 TW Alexander Dr, Research Triangle Park, NC 27709.

Mailing Address: PO Box 14900, Research Triangle Park, NC 27709-4900.

Phone: 919-549-7000. **Fax:** 919-549-7179.

Web Site: http://www.unctv.org

Technical Facilities: Channel No. 20 (506-512 MHz). Authorized power: 543-kw max. visual, aural. Antenna: 1604-ft above av. terrain, 1604-ft. above ground, 1611-ft. above sea level.

Latitude	35°	54'	00"
Longitude	76°	20'	45"

Transmitter: State Rd. 1117, 5-mi. W of Columbia.

Note: Latitude and longitude coordinates shown are based on the North American Datum of 1927 (NAD 27) as currently required by the Mass Media Bureau of the FCC.

Ownership: U. of North Carolina.

Began Operation: November 12, 2001. Standard Definition. Began analog operations: September 10, 1965. Change of city of license from Columbia to Edenton per FCC Report and Order adopted July 21, 2005. Ceased analog operations: June 12, 2009.

Personnel:

Tom Howe, Director & General Manager.

Carl Davis, Engineering Director & Assistant General Manager.

Diane Lucas, Programming Director.

James A. McGurk, Promotions Manager.

Delores James, Assistant General Manager & Development Director.

Bobby Royster, Local Productions Director.

Dennis Dowdy, Traffic Manager.

Kirk Scharfenberg, Human Resources Director.

Steven Volstad, Communications Director.

Kathy Dobbins, Grants Director.

WUNK-DT
Greenville
Ch. 23

Licensee: U. of North Carolina, PO Box 14900, Research Triangle Park, NC 27709-4900.

Studio: 10 TW Alexander Dr, Research Triangle Park, NC 27709.

Mailing Address: PO Box 14900, Research Triangle Park, NC 27709-4900.

Phone: 919-549-7000. **Fax:** 919-549-7179.

Web Site: http://www.unctv.org

Technical Facilities: Channel No. 23 (524-530 MHz). Authorized power: 71-kw max. visual, aural. Antenna: 1086-ft above av. terrain, 1247-ft. above ground, 1325-ft. above sea level.

Latitude	35°	33'	10"
Longitude	77°	36'	06"

Holds CP for change to 700-kw max. visual, 1152-ft above av. terrain, 1138-ft. above ground, 1217-ft. above sea level; BPEDT-20080617AAR.

Note: Latitude and longitude coordinates shown are based on the North American Datum of 1927 (NAD 27) as currently required by the Mass Media Bureau of the FCC.

Ownership: U. of North Carolina.

Began Operation: January 25, 2002. Began analog operations: May 7, 1972. Ceased analog operations: June 12, 2009.

Personnel:

Tom Howe, Director & General Manager.

Carl Davis, Engineering Director & Assistant General Manager.

Diane Lucas, Program Director.

James A. McGurk, Promotions Manager.

Delores James, Assistant General Manager & Development Director.

Bobby Royster, Local Productions Director.

Dennis Dowdy, Traffic Manager.

Kirk Scharfenberg, Human Resources Director.

Steven Volstad, Communications Director.

Kathy Dobbins, Grants Director.

WUNM-DT
Jacksonville
Ch. 19

Licensee: U. of North Carolina, PO Box 14900, Research Triangle Park, NC 27709-4900.

Studio: 10 TW Alexander Dr, Research Triangle Park, NC 27709.

Mailing Address: PO Box 14900, Research Triangle Park, NC 27709-4900.

Phone: 919-549-7000. **Fax:** 919-549-7179.

Email: kstahl@unctv.org **Web Site:** http://www.unctv.org

Technical Facilities: Channel No. 19 (500-506 MHz). Authorized power: 100-kw max. visual, aural. Antenna: 1841-ft above av. terrain, 1841-ft. above ground, 1886-ft. above sea level.

Latitude	35°	05'	15"
Longitude	77°	20'	12"

Note: Latitude and longitude coordinates shown are based on the North American Datum of 1927 (NAD 27) as currently required by the Mass Media Bureau of the FCC.

Ownership: U. of North Carolina.

Began Operation: November 5, 2002. Station broadcasting digitally on its analog channel allotment. Began analog operations: November 16, 1982. Ceased analog operations: June 12, 2009.

Personnel:

Tom Howe, Director & General Manager.

Carl Davis, Engineering Director & Assistant General Manager.

Diane Lucas, Program Director.

James A. McGurk, Promotions Manager.

Delores James, Assistant General Manager & Development Director.

Bobby Royster, Local Productions Director.

Dennis Dowdy, Traffic Manager.

Kirk Scharfenberg, Human Resources Director.

Steven Volstad, Communications Director.

Kathy Dobbins, Grants Director.

WUNE-DT
Linville
Ch. 17

Licensee: U. of North Carolina, PO Box 14900, Research Triangle Park, NC 27709-4900.

Studio: 10 TW Alexander Dr, Research Triangle Park, NC 27709.

Mailing Address: PO Box 14900, Research Triangle Park, NC 27709-4900.

Phone: 919-549-7000. **Fax:** 919-549-7179.

Email: kstahl@unctv.org **Web Site:** http://www.unctv.org

Technical Facilities: Channel No. 17 (488-494 MHz). Authorized power: 100-kw max. visual, aural. Antenna: 1791-ft above av. terrain, 420-ft. above ground, 5026-ft. above sea level.

Latitude	36°	03'	50"
Longitude	81°	50'	33"

Note: Latitude and longitude coordinates shown are based on the North American Datum of 1927 (NAD 27) as currently required by the Mass Media Bureau of the FCC.

Ownership: U. of North Carolina.

Began Operation: December 6, 2001. Station broadcasting digitally on its analog channel allotment. Began analog operations: September 11, 1967. Ceased analog operations: June 12, 2009.

Personnel:

Tom Howe, Director & General Manager.

Carl Davis, Engineering Director & Assistant General Manager.

Diane Lucas, Programming Director.

James A. McGurk, Promotions Manager.

Delores James, Assistant General Manager & Development Director.

Bobby Royster, Local Productions Director.

Dennis Dowdy, Traffic Manager.

Kirk Scharfenberg, Human Resources Director.

Steven Volstad, Communications Director.

Kathy Dobbins, Grants Director.

WUNU-DT
Lumberton
Ch. 31

Licensee: U. of North Carolina, PO Box 14900, Research Triangle Park, NC 27709-4900.

Studio: 10 TW Alexander Dr, Research Triangle Park, NC 27709.

Mailing Address: PO Box 14900, Research Triangle Park, NC 27709-4900.

Phone: 919-549-7000. **Fax:** 919-549-7179.

Web Site: http://www.unctv.org

Technical Facilities: Channel No. 31 (572-578 MHz). Authorized power: 18-kw max. visual, aural. Antenna: 1047-ft above av. terrain, 1033-ft. above ground, 1217-ft. above sea level.

Latitude	35°	47'	50"
Longitude	79°	02'	42"

Holds CP for change to 175-kw max. visual; BMPEDT-20080617AAP.

Transmitter: 7-mi. SSE of intersection of State Rtes. 1006 & 1784, 4-mi. WSW of St. Paul.

Note: Latitude and longitude coordinates shown are based on the North American Datum of 1927 (NAD 27) as currently required by the Mass Media Bureau of the FCC.

Ownership: U. of North Carolina.

Began Operation: August 6, 2001. Station broadcasting digitally on its analog channel allotment. Began analog operations: September 23, 1996. Ceased analog operations: June 12, 2009.

Personnel:

Tom Howe, Director & General Manager.

Carl Davis, Engineering Director & Assistant General Manager.

Diane Lucas, Program Director.

James A. McGurk, Promotions Manager.

Delores James, Assistant General Manager & Development Director.

Bobby Royster, Local Productions Director.

Dennis Dowdy, Traffic Manager.

Kirk Scharfenberg, Human Resources Director.

Steven Volstad, Communications Director.

Kathy Dobbins, Grants Director.

WUNP-DT
Roanoke Rapids
Ch. 36

Licensee: U. of North Carolina, PO Box 14900, Research Triangle Park, NC 27709-4900.

Studio: 10 TW Alexander Dr, Research Triangle Park, NC 27709.

Mailing Address: PO Box 14900, Research Triangle Park, NC 27709-4900.

Phone: 919-549-7000. **Fax:** 919-549-7179.

Web Site: http://www.unctv.org

Technical Facilities: Channel No. 36 (602-608 MHz). Authorized power: 125-kw max. visual, aural. Antenna: 1207-ft above av. terrain, 1135-ft. above ground, 1421-ft. above sea level.

Latitude	36°	17'	27"
Longitude	77°	50'	11"

Transmitter: NC 48, 1.5-mi. NE of NC 561 & NC 48 intersection, Brinkleyville.

Note: Latitude and longitude coordinates shown are based on the North American Datum of 1927 (NAD 27) as currently required by the Mass Media Bureau of the FCC.

Ownership: U. of North Carolina.

Began Operation: February 5, 2002. Station broadcasting digitally on its analog channel allotment. Began analog operations: October 16, 1986. Ceased analog operations: June 12, 2009.

Personnel:

Tom Howe, Director & General Manager.

Carl Davis, Engineering Director & Assistant General Manager.

Diane Lucas, Program Director.

James A. McGurk, Promotions Manager.

Delores James, Assistant General Manager & Development Director.

Bobby Royster, Local Productions Director.

Dennis Dowdy, Traffic Manager.

Kirk Scharfenberg, Human Resources Director.

Steven Volstad, Communications Director.

Kathy Dobbins, Grants Director.

WUNJ-DT
Wilmington
Ch. 29

Licensee: U. of North Carolina, PO Box 14900, Research Triangle Park, NC 27709-4900.

Studio: 10 TW Alexander Dr, Research Triangle Park, NC 27709.

Mailing Address: PO Box 14900, Research Triangle Park, NC 27709-4900.

Phone: 919-549-7000. **Fax:** 919-549-7179.

Web Site: http://www.unctv.org

Technical Facilities: Channel No. 29 (560-566 MHz). Authorized power: 700-kw max. visual, aural. Antenna: 974-ft above av. terrain, 981-ft. above ground, 1017-ft. above sea level.

Latitude	34°	19'	16"
Longitude	78°	13'	43"

Holds CP for change to 1000-kw max. visual, 974-ft above av. terrain, 988-ft. above ground, 1017-ft. above sea level; BPEDT-20080616ACA.

Note: Latitude and longitude coordinates shown are based on the North American Datum of 1927 (NAD 27) as currently required by the Mass Media Bureau of the FCC.

Ownership: U. of North Carolina.

Began Operation: September 13, 2002. Began analog operations: June 4, 1971. Ceased analog operations: February 17, 2009.

Personnel:

Tom Howe, Director & General Manager.

Carl Davis, Engineering Director & Assistant General Manager.

Diane Lucas, Program Director.

James A. McGurk, Promotions Manager.

Delores James, Assistant General Manager & Development Director.

Bobby Royster, Local Productions Director.

Dennis Dowdy, Traffic Manager.

Kirk Scharfenberg, Human Resources Director.

Steven Volstad, Communications Director.

Kathy Dobbins, Grants Director.

WUNL-DT
Winston-Salem
Ch. 32

Licensee: U. of North Carolina, PO Box 14900, Research Triangle Park, NC 27709-4900.

Studio: 10 TW Alexander Dr, Research Triangle Park, NC 27709.

Mailing Address: PO Box 14900, Research Triangle Park, NC 27709-4900.

Phone: 919-549-7000. **Fax:** 919-549-7179.

Web Site: http://www.unctv.org

Technical Facilities: Channel No. 32 (578-584 MHz). Authorized power: 197.5-kw max. visual, aural. Antenna: 1572-ft above av. terrain, 262-ft. above ground, 2624-ft. above sea level.

Latitude	36°	22'	33"
Longitude	80°	22'	18"

Holds CP for change to 400-kw max. visual, 1654-ft above av. terrain, 348-ft. above ground, 2707-ft. above sea level; BPEDT-20080617AAL.

Note: Latitude and longitude coordinates shown are based on the North American Datum of 1927 (NAD 27) as currently required by the Mass Media Bureau of the FCC.

Ownership: U. of North Carolina.

Began Operation: December 8, 2001. Began analog operations: February 22, 1973. Ceased analog operations: June 12, 2009.

Personnel:

Tom Howe, Director & General Manager.

Carl Davis, Engineering Director & Assistant General Manager.

Diane Lucas, Program Director.

James A. McGurk, Promotions Manager.

Delores James, Assistant General Manager & Development Director.

Bobby Royster, Local Productions Director.

Dennis Dowdy, Traffic Manager.

Kirk Scharfenberg, Human Resources Director.

Steven Volstad, Communications Director.

Kathy Dobbins, Grants Director.

North Dakota

KBME-DT
Bismarck
Ch. 22

Licensee: Prairie Public Broadcasting Inc., PO Box 3240, Fargo, ND 58108-3240.

Studio: 207 N 5th St, Fargo, ND 58102.

Mailing Address: PO Box 3240, Fargo, ND 58108-3240.

Phone: 701-241-6900. **Fax:** 701-239-7650.

Web Site: http://www.prairiepublic.org

Technical Facilities: Channel No. 22 (518-524 MHz). Authorized power: 97.33-kw max. visual, aural. Antenna: 1286-ft above av. terrain, 967-ft. above ground, 3188-ft. above sea level.

Latitude	46°	35'	23"
Longitude	100°	48'	02"

Transmitter: 5-mi. E & 2-mi. S of St. Anthony's.

Note: Latitude and longitude coordinates shown are based on the North American Datum of 1927 (NAD 27) as currently required by the Mass Media Bureau of the FCC.

Ownership: Prairie Public Broadcasting Inc.

Began Operation: January 15, 2002. Began analog operations: June 18, 1979. Ceased analog operations: February 17, 2009.

Personnel:

John E. Harris, President & Chief Executive Officer.

Cheryl Heller, Television Operations & Traffic Manager.

Jack Anderson, Engineering Director.

John Gast, Finance Director.

Bob Dambach, Television Director.

Marie Lucero, Promotions Director.

Ann Clark, Development Director.

Russell Ford-Dunker, Corporate Support Manager.

Morgan Jenkins, Customer Service Coordinator.

Bev Pearson, Education Services.

KMDE-DT
Devils Lake
Ch. 25

Licensee: Prairie Public Broadcasting Inc., PO Box 3240, Fargo, ND 58108-3240.

Studio: 207 N 5th St, Fargo, ND 58102.

Mailing Address: PO Box 3240, Fargo, ND 58108-3240.

Phone: 701-241-6900. **Fax:** 701-239-7650.

Web Site: http://www.prairiepublic.org

Technical Facilities: Channel No. 25 (536-542 MHz). Authorized power: 134-kw max. visual, aural. Antenna: 802-ft above av. terrain, 729-ft. above ground, 2350-ft. above sea level.

Latitude	48°	03'	47.8"
Longitude	99°	20'	08.7"

Note: Latitude and longitude coordinates shown are based on the North American Datum of 1927 (NAD 27) as currently required by the Mass Media Bureau of the FCC.

Ownership: Prairie Public Broadcasting Inc.

Began Operation: February 1, 2006. Station went directly to digital broadcast; no analog application.

Personnel:

John E. Harris, President & Chief Executive Officer.

John Gast, Finance Director.

Jack Anderson, Engineering Director.

Cheryl Heller, Television Operations & Traffic Manager.

Bob Dambach, Television Director.

Marie Lucero, Promotions Director.

Ann Clark, Development Director.

Russell Ford-Dunker, Corporate Support Manager.

Morgan Jenkins, Customer Service Coordinator.

Bev Pearson, Education Services.

KDSE-DT
Dickinson
Ch. 9

Licensee: Prairie Public Broadcasting Inc., PO Box 3240, Fargo, ND 58108-3240.

Studio: 207 N 5th St, Fargo, ND 58102.

Mailing Address: PO Box 3240, Fargo, ND 58108-3240.

Phone: 701-241-6900. **Fax:** 701-239-7650.

Web Site: http://www.prairiepublic.org

Technical Facilities: Channel No. 9 (186-192 MHz). Authorized power: 8.35-kw visual, aural. Antenna: 799-ft above av. terrain, 531-ft. above ground, 3462-ft. above sea level.

Latitude	46°	43'	35"
Longitude	102°	54'	57"

Holds CP for change to 30.3-kw visual, 782-ft above av. terrain, 531-ft. above ground, 3462-ft. above sea level; BMPEDT-20080618AEC.

Note: Latitude and longitude coordinates shown are based on the North American Datum of 1927 (NAD 27) as currently required by the Mass Media Bureau of the FCC.

Ownership: Prairie Public Broadcasting Inc.

Began Operation: October 2, 2009. Station broadcasting digitally on its analog channel allotment. Began analog operations: August 4, 1982. Ceased analog operations: October 2, 2009.

Personnel:

John E. Harris, President & Chief Executive Officer.

Cheryl Heller, Television Operations & Traffic Manager.

Jack Anderson, Engineering Director.

John Gast, Finance Director.

Bob Dambach, Television Director.

Marie Lucero, Promotions Director.

Ann Clark, Development Director.

Russell Ford-Dunker, Corporate Support Manager.

Morgan Jenkins, Customer Service Coordinator.

Bev Pearson, Education Services.

KJRE-DT
Ellendale
Ch. 20

Licensee: Prairie Public Broadcasting Inc., PO Box 3240, Fargo, ND 58108-3240.

Studio: 207 N 5th St, Fargo, ND 58102.

Mailing Address: PO Box 3240, Fargo, ND 58108-3240.

Phone: 701-241-6900. **Fax:** 701-239-7650.

Web Site: http://www.prairiepublic.org

Technical Facilities: Channel No. 20 (506-512 MHz). Authorized power: 72.3-kw max. visual, aural. Antenna: 533-ft above av. terrain, 459-ft. above ground, 2429-ft. above sea level.

Latitude	46°	17'	56"
Longitude	98°	51'	56"

Note: Latitude and longitude coordinates shown are based on the North American Datum of 1927 (NAD 27) as currently required by the Mass Media Bureau of the FCC.

Ownership: Prairie Public Broadcasting Inc.

Began Operation: February 17, 2009. Began analog operations: May 11, 1992. Ceased analog operations: February 17, 2009.

Personnel:

John E. Harris, President & Chief Executive Officer.

Cheryl Heller, Television Operations & Traffic Manager.

Jack Anderson, Engineering Director.

John Gast, Finance Director.

Bob Dambach, Television Director.

Marie Lucero, Promotions Director.

Ann Clark, Development Director.

Russell Ford-Dunker, Corporate Support Manager.

Morgan Jenkins, Customer Service Coordinator.

Bev Pearson, Education Services.

KFME-DT
Fargo
Ch. 13

Licensee: Prairie Public Broadcasting Inc., PO Box 3240, Fargo, ND 58108-3240.

Studio: 207 N 5th St, Fargo, ND 58102.

Mailing Address: PO Box 3240, Fargo, ND 58108-3240.

Phone: 701-241-6900. **Fax:** 701-239-7650.

Web Site: http://www.prairiepublic.org

Technical Facilities: Channel No. 13 (210-216 MHz). Authorized power: 29.7-kw visual, aural. Antenna: 1122-ft above av. terrain, 1128-ft. above ground, 2071-ft. above sea level.

Latitude	47°	00'	45"
Longitude	97°	11'	41"

Holds CP for change to 56.2-kw visual; BMPEDT-20081030ABJ.

Transmitter: 1.2-mi. E of Amenia.

Note: Latitude and longitude coordinates shown are based on the North American Datum of 1927 (NAD 27) as currently required by the Mass Media Bureau of the FCC.

Ownership: Prairie Public Broadcasting Inc.

Began Operation: September 9, 2002. Station broadcasting digitally on its analog channel allotment. Began analog operations: January 19, 1964. Ceased analog operations: February 2, 2009.

Personnel:

John E. Harris, President & Chief Executive Officer.

Cheryl Heller, Television Operations & Traffic Manager.

Jack Anderson, Engineering Director.

John Gast, Finance Director.

Bob Dambach, Television Director.

Marie Lucero, Promotions Director.

Ann Clark, Development Director.

Russell Ford-Dunker, Corporate Support Manager.

Morgan Jenkins, Customer Service Coordinator.

Bev Pearson, Education Services.

KGFE-DT
Grand Forks
Ch. 15

Grantee: Prairie Public Broadcasting Inc., PO Box 3240, Fargo, ND 58108-3240.

Studio: 207 N 5th St, Fargo, ND 58102.

Mailing Address: PO Box 3240, Fargo, ND 58108-3240.

Phone: 701-241-6900. Fax: 701-239-7650.

Web Site: http://www.prairiepublic.org

Technical Facilities: Channel No. 15 (476-482 MHz). Authorized power: 22.6-kw max. visual, aural. Antenna: 611-ft above av. terrain, 610-ft. above ground, 1515-ft. above sea level.

Latitude	47°	58'	38"
Longitude	96°	36'	18"

Note: Latitude and longitude coordinates shown are based on the North American Datum of 1927 (NAD 27) as currently required by the Mass Media Bureau of the FCC.

Ownership: Prairie Public Broadcasting Inc.

Began Operation: June 12, 2009. Began analog operations: September 9 , 1974. Ceased analog operations: June 12, 2009.

Personnel:

John E. Harris, President & Chief Executive Officer.

Cheryl Heller, Television Operations & Traffic Manager.

Jack Anderson, Engineering Director.

John Gast, Finance Director.

Bob Dambach, Television Director.

Marie Lucero, Promotions Director.

Ann Clark, Development Director.

Russell Ford-Dunker, Corporate Support Manager.

Morgan Jenkins, Customer Service Coordinator.

Bev Pearson, Education Services.

KSRE-DT
Minot
Ch. 40

Licensee: Prairie Public Broadcasting Inc., PO Box 3240, Fargo, ND 58108-3240.

Studio: 207 N 5th St, Fargo, ND 58102.

Mailing Address: PO Box 3240, Fargo, ND 58108-3240.

Phone: 701-241-6900. Fax: 701-239-7650.

Web Site: http://www.prairiepublic.org

Technical Facilities: Channel No. 40 (626-632 MHz). Authorized power: 146-kw max. visual, aural. Antenna: 818-ft above av. terrain, 750-ft. above ground, 2868-ft. above sea level.

Latitude	48°	03'	02"
Longitude	101°	23'	25"

Note: Latitude and longitude coordinates shown are based on the North American Datum of 1927 (NAD 27) as currently required by the Mass Media Bureau of the FCC.

Ownership: Prairie Public Broadcasting Inc.

Began Operation: October 1, 2003. Began analog operations: January 25, 1980. Ceased analog operations: February 17, 2009.

Personnel:

John E. Harris, President & Chief Executive Officer.

Cheryl Heller, Television Operations & Traffic Manager.

Jack Anderson, Engineering Director.

John Gast, Finance Director.

Bob Dambach, Television Director.

Marie Lucero, Promotions Director.

Ann Clark, Development Director.

Russell Ford-Dunker, Corporate Support Manager.

Morgan Jenkins, Customer Service Coordinator.

Bev Pearson, Education Services.

KWSE-DT
Williston
Ch. 51

Licensee: Prairie Public Broadcasting Inc., PO Box 3240, Fargo, ND 58108-3240.

Studio: 207 N 5th St, Fargo, ND 58102.

Mailing Address: PO Box 3240, Fargo, ND 58108-3240.

Phone: 701-241-6900. Fax: 701-239-7650.

Web Site: http://www.prairiepublic.org

Technical Facilities: Channel No. 51 (692-698 MHz). Authorized power: 53.9-kw max. visual, aural. Antenna: 813-ft above av. terrain, 715-ft. above ground, 3012-ft. above sea level.

Latitude	48°	08'	30"
Longitude	103°	53'	34"

Holds CP for change to channel number 11, 84.9-kw visual, 912-ft above av. terrain, 785-ft. above ground, 3082-ft. above sea level; BPEDT-20090619AAI.

Note: Latitude and longitude coordinates shown are based on the North American Datum of 1927 (NAD 27) as currently required by the Mass Media Bureau of the FCC.

Ownership: Prairie Public Broadcasting Inc.

Began Operation: June 1, 2004. Began analog operations: April 8, 1983. Ceased analog operations: September 1, 2008.

Personnel:

John E. Harris, President & Chief Executive Officer.

Cheryl Heller, Television Operations & Traffic Manager.

Jack Anderson, Engineering Director.

John Gast, Finance Director.

Bob Dambach, Television Director.

Marie Lucero, Promotions Director.

Ann Clark, Development Director.

Russell Ford-Dunker, Corporate Support Manager.

Morgan Jenkins, Customer Service Coordinator.

Bev Pearson, Education Services.

Ohio

WEAO-DT
Akron
Ch. 50

Licensee: Northeastern Educational TV of Ohio Inc., PO Box 5191, 1750 Campus Center Dr, Kent, OH 44240-5191.

Studio: 1750 Campus Center Dr, Kent, OH 44240.

Mailing Address: 1750 Campus Center Dr, Kent, OH 44240.

Phone: 330-677-4549. Fax: 330-678-0688.

Web Site: http://www.pbs4549.org

Technical Facilities: Channel No. 50 (686-692 MHz). Authorized power: 180-kw max. visual, aural. Antenna: 1001-ft above av. terrain, 906-ft. above ground, 2024-ft. above sea level.

Latitude	41°	04'	58"
Longitude	81°	38'	02"

Holds CP for change to 250-kw max. visual, 1001-ft above av. terrain, 906-ft. above ground, 2026-ft. above sea level; BPEDT-20080620AAD.

Note: Latitude and longitude coordinates shown are based on the North American Datum of 1927 (NAD 27) as currently required by the Mass Media Bureau of the FCC.

Ownership: Northeastern Educational Television of Ohio.

Began Operation: September 27, 2004. Began analog operations: September 21, 1975. Ceased analog operations: June 12, 2009.

Personnel:

Trina Cutter, President & Chief Executive Officer.

William O'Neil, Station, Engineering & IT Services Manager.

Lisa Martinez, Vice President, Marketing & Development.

Pat Houck, Traffic Manager.

Jeff Good, Educational Services Director.

WNEO-DT
Alliance
Ch. 45

Licensee: Northeastern Educational TV of Ohio Inc., PO Box 5191, 1750 Campus Center Dr, Kent, OH 44240-5191.

Studio: 1750 Campus Center Dr, Kent, OH 44240.

Mailing Address: PO Box 5191, Kent, OH 44240.

Phone: 330-677-4549. Fax: 330-678-0688.

Web Site: http://www.pbs4549.org

Technical Facilities: Channel No. 45 (656-662 MHz). Authorized power: 44-kw max. visual, aural. Antenna: 830-ft above av. terrain, 735-ft. above ground, 2010-ft. above sea level.

Latitude	40°	54'	23"
Longitude	80°	54'	40"

Holds CP for change to 500-kw max. visual; BMPEDT-20080619AIA.

Note: Latitude and longitude coordinates shown are based on the North American Datum of 1927 (NAD 27) as currently required by the Mass Media Bureau of the FCC.

Ownership: Northeastern Educational Television of Ohio.

Began Operation: May 1, 2003. Digital operations ceased on channel 46 November 12, 2008 and relaunched on channel 45 November 21, 2008. Began analog operations: May 30, 1973. Station ceased analog operations on channel 45 November 19, 2008.

Personnel:

Trina Cutter, President & Chief Executive Officer.

William O'Neil, Station, Engineering & IT Services Manager.

Lisa Martinez, Vice President, Marketing & Development.

Pat Houck, Traffic Manager.

Jeff Good, Educational Services Director.

WOUB-DT
Athens
Ch. 27

Grantee: Ohio U., 9 S College St, Athens, OH 45701.

Studio: 9 S College St, Athens, OH 45701.

Mailing Address: 9 S. College St, Athens, OH 45701.

Phone: 740-593-1771. Fax: 740-593-0240.

Email: carolyn_lewis@woub.pbs.org Web Site: http://www.woub.org

Technical Facilities: Channel No. 27 (548-554 MHz). Authorized power: 250-kw max. visual, aural. Antenna: 795-ft above av. terrain, 837-ft. above ground, 1621-ft. above sea level.

Latitude	39°	18'	52"
Longitude	82°	08'	59"

Note: Latitude and longitude coordinates shown are based on the North American Datum of 1927 (NAD 27) as currently required by the Mass Media Bureau of the FCC.

Ownership: Ohio U.

Began Operation: January 26, 2004. Began analog operations: December 27, 1962. Ceased analog operations: June 12, 2009.

Personnel:

Carolyn Lewis, General Manager.

Steve Skidmore, Technical & IT Operations Director.

David Wiseman, Chief Technology Officer.

Tim Sharp, News Director.

Ted Ross, Engineering Director.

Joan Pittman, Program Services Director.

Jeannie Jeffers, Associate Director, Development & Communications.

Jason Martin, Traffic & Promotion Coordinator.

WBGU-DT
Bowling Green
Ch. 27

Licensee: Bowling Green State U., 245 Troup St, Bowling Green, OH 43403.

Studio: 245 Troup St, Bowling Green, OH 43403.

Mailing Address: 245 Troup St, Bowling Green, OH 43403.

Phone: 419-372-2700. Fax: 419-372-7048.

Web Site: http://www.wbgu.org

Technical Facilities: Channel No. 27 (548-554 MHz). Authorized power: 153-kw max. visual, aural. Antenna: 1050-ft above av. terrain, 1061-ft above ground, 1788-ft. above sea level.

Latitude	41°	08'	12"
Longitude	83°	54'	24"

Note: Latitude and longitude coordinates shown are based on the North American Datum of 1927 (NAD 27) as currently required by the Mass Media Bureau of the FCC.

Ownership: Bowling Green State U.

Began Operation: February 22, 2007. Station broadcasting digitally on its analog channel allotment. Began analog operations: February 10, 1964. Ceased analog operations: February 16, 2009.

Personnel:

Patrick Fitzgerald, General Manager.

Al Bowe, Chief Engineer.

Tina Simon, Business Manager & Development Director.

Tom Cummings, Technical Services Coordinator.

Deb Boyce, Public Relations & Promotion Director.

Denise Kisabeth, Production Manager.

Jennifer Karches, Traffic Manager.

Tony Short, Learning Services Director.

Lisa Wayne, Public Relations & Volunteer Coordinator.

Pat Koehler, Special Events Coordinator.

Julie Albert, Ready to Learn Coordinator.

Cari Tuttle, Member Services Coordinator.

WOUC-DT
Cambridge
Ch. 35

Licensee: Ohio U., 9 S College St, Athens, OH 45701.

Studio: 9 S College St, Athens, OH 45701.

Mailing Address: 9 S. College St, Athens, OH 45701.

Phone: 740-593-1771. Fax: 740-543-0240.

Email: carolyn_lewis@woub.pbs.org Web Site: http://www.woub.org

Technical Facilities: Channel No. 35 (596-602 MHz). Authorized power: 310-kw max. visual, aural. Antenna: 1263-ft above av. terrain, 1175-ft. above ground, 2294-ft. above sea level.

Latitude	40°	05'	32"
Longitude	81°	17'	19"

Note: Latitude and longitude coordinates shown are based on the North American Datum of 1927 (NAD 27) as currently required by the Mass Media Bureau of the FCC.

Ownership: Ohio U.

Began Operation: July 22, 2004. Began analog operations: July 26, 1973. Ceased analog operations: June 12, 2009.

Personnel:

Carolyn Lewis, General Manager.

Steve Skidmore, Technical & IT Operations Director.

David Wiseman, Chief Technology Officer.

Tim Sharp, News Director.

Ted Ross, Engineering Director.

Joan Pittman, Program Services Director.

Jeannie Jeffers, Associate Director, Development & Communications.

Jason Martin, Traffic & Promotion Coordinator.

WCET-DT
Cincinnati
Ch. 34

Licensee: Greater Cincinnati TV Educational Foundation, 1223 Central Pkwy, Cincinnati, OH 45214.

Studio: 1223 Central Pkwy, Cincinnati, OH 45214-2890.

Mailing Address: 1223 Central Pkwy, Cincinnati, OH 45214-2890.

Phone: 513-381-4033. Fax: 513-381-7520.

Email: grace_hill@wcet.pbs.org Web Site: http://www.cetconnect.org

Technical Facilities: Channel No. 34 (590-596 MHz). Authorized power: 400-kw max. visual, aural. Antenna: 1070-ft above av. terrain, 925-ft. above ground, 1762-ft. above sea level.

Latitude	39°	07'	27"
Longitude	84°	31'	18"

Note: Latitude and longitude coordinates shown are based on the North American Datum of 1927 (NAD 27) as currently required by the Mass Media Bureau of the FCC.

Ownership: Public Media Connect.

Began Operation: November 19, 2002. Began analog operations: July 26, 1954. Transfer of control by Greater Cincinnati TV Educational Foundation from Greater Cincinnati TV Educational Foundation to Public Media Connect approved by FCC June 24, 2009. Ceased analog operations: June 12, 2009.

Personnel:

Susan Howarth, President & Chief Executive Officer.

Jack T. Dominick, General Manager.

Tina Hebel, Operations Director & Traffic Manager.

Neil Schmidt, Chief Engineer.

Adam Fischer, Senior Vice President, Finance & Administration.

Grace K. Hill, Program Director.

Colleen Harris, Marketing Manager.

Taylor Feltner, Production Manager.

WVIZ-DT
Cleveland
Ch. 26

Grantee: Ideastream, 4300 Brookpark Rd, Cleveland, OH 44134.

Studio: 1375 Euclid Ave, Cleveland, OH 44115.

Mailing Address: 1375 Euclid Ave, Cleveland, OH 44115.

Phone: 216-916-6100. Fax: 216-916-6090.

Email: engineering@wviz.org Web Site: http://www.wviz.org

Technical Facilities: Channel No. 26 (542-548 MHz). Authorized power: 150-kw max. visual, aural. Antenna: 1105-ft above av. terrain, 897-ft. above ground, 1937-ft. above sea level.

Latitude	41°	23'	10"
Longitude	81°	41'	21"

Note: Latitude and longitude coordinates shown are based on the North American Datum of 1927 (NAD 27) as currently required by the Mass Media Bureau of the FCC.

Ownership: Media Inc.

Began Operation: July 15, 2004. Began analog operations: February 7, 1965. Ceased analog operations: June 12, 2009.

Personnel:

Jerry Wareham, President & Chief Executive Officer.

Kit Jensen, Chief Operating Officer.

Mark Smukler, Station Manager & Senior Director, Content.

Kimberlee Namen, Traffic & Operations Manager.

Dave Molpus, Executive News Director.

David Rodriguez, Engineering Director.

Thomas P. Furnas, Senior Director, Technology.

Robert Calsin, Chief Financial Officer.

David Kanzeg, Program Director.

Maureen Paschke, Senior Director, Marketing.

Kent Geist, Senior Director, Marketing & Development.

Mike Vendeland, Production Manager.

Roy Norris, Senior Director, Educational Services.

WOSU-DT
Columbus
Ch. 38

Licensee: Ohio State U., 2400 Olentangy River Rd, Columbus, OH 43210.

Studio: 2400 Olentangy River Rd, Columbus, OH 43210.

Mailing Address: 2400 Olentangy River Rd, Columbus, OH 43210.

Phones: 614-292-9678; 614-292-7625. Fax: 614-688-3343.

Email: donscott@wosu.org Web Site: http://www.wosu.org

Technical Facilities: Channel No. 38 (614-620 MHz). Authorized power: 250-kw max. visual, aural. Antenna: 955-ft above av. terrain, 971-ft. above ground, 1893-ft. above sea level.

Latitude	40°	09'	33"
Longitude	82°	55'	23"

Holds CP for change to 503-kw max. visual, 1079-ft above av. terrain, 1085-ft. above ground, 2006-ft. above sea level; BPEDT-20080620ADY.

Note: Latitude and longitude coordinates shown are based on the North American Datum of 1927 (NAD 27) as currently required by the Mass Media Bureau of the FCC.

Ownership: Ohio State U.

Began Operation: January 28, 2004. Began analog operations: February 20, 1956. Ceased analog operations: June 12, 2009.

Personnel:

Thomas Rieland, General Manager.

Sheri Walker, Assistant General Manager.

Edwin Clay, TV Station Manager.

Tom Lahr, Chief Engineer.

John Prosek, Broadcast Manager.

Mary Alice Akins, Operations Director.

Stacia Hentz, Program Coordinator.

Jamison Pack, Marketing Director.

Brent Davis, Production Manager.

Cheryl Krebs Petrilla, Public Relations Manager.

Marcelita Haskins, Instructional Services Coordinator.

David Dunham, Development Director.

WPTD-DT
Dayton
Ch. 16

Licensee: Greater Dayton Public Television Inc., 110 S Jefferson St, Dayton, OH 45402-2415.

Studio: 110 S Jefferson St, Dayton, OH 45402-2415.

Mailing Address: 110 S. Jefferson St, Dayton, OH 45402-2415.

Phones: 937-220-1600; 937-220-1611. Fax: 937-220-1642.

Email: david_fogarty@wptd.pbs.org Web Site: http://www.thinktv.org

Technical Facilities: Channel No. 16 (482-488 MHz). Authorized power: 155-kw max. visual, aural. Antenna: 1148-ft above av. terrain, 1132-ft. above ground, 2011-ft. above sea level.

Latitude	39°	43'	16"
Longitude	84°	15'	00"

Requests CP for change to 163-kw max. visual, 1129-ft above av. terrain, 1113-ft. above ground, 1992-ft. above sea level; BPEDT-20090723AEU.

Transmitter: 1.1-air miles W of Layland on State Rte. 41/12.

Note: Latitude and longitude coordinates shown are based on the North American Datum of 1927 (NAD 27) as currently required by the Mass Media Bureau of the FCC.

Ownership: Public Media Connect.

Began Operation: April 29, 2003. Began analog operations: March 20, 1967. Station broadcasting digitally on its analog channel allotment. Transfer of control by Greater Dayton Public Television Inc. from Greater Dayton Public Television Inc. to Public Media Connect approved by FCC June 24, 2009. Ceased analog operations: June 12, 2009.

Personnel:

David M. Fogarty, President & General Manager.

H. Fred Stone, Engineering & Technical Services Director.

Gloria Skurski, Content Development & Broadcast Services Director.

Suzanne O'Brien, Finance & Administration Director.

Jim Wiener, Program Manager.

Kitty Lensman, Marketing & Business Development Director & Production Manager.

Sue Brinson, Promotion & Communications Manager.

Kay High, Development Director.

Gary Greenberg, Educational Services Manager.

Charles Cole, Broadcast Operations & Traffic Manager.

Casimera Sullivan, Corporate Development Manager & Human Resources.

WPTO-DT
Oxford
Ch. 28

Licensee: Greater Dayton Public Television Inc., 110 S Jefferson St, Dayton, OH 45402-2415.

Studio: 110 S Jefferson St, Dayton, OH 45402-2415.

Mailing Address: 110 S. Jefferson St, Dayton, OH 45402-2415.

Phones: 937-220-1600; 937-220-1611. **Fax:** 937-220-1642.

Web Site: http://www.thinktv.org

Technical Facilities: Channel No. 28 (554-560 MHz). Authorized power: 400-kw max. visual, aural. Antenna: 906-ft above av. terrain, 886-ft. above ground, 1614-ft. above sea level.

Latitude	39°	07'	19"
Longitude	84°	32'	52"

Note: Latitude and longitude coordinates shown are based on the North American Datum of 1927 (NAD 27) as currently required by the Mass Media Bureau of the FCC.

Ownership: Public Media Connect.

Began Operation: June 28, 2004. Began analog operations: October 14, 1959. Transfer of control by Greater Dayton Public Television Inc. from Greater Dayton Public Television Inc. to Public Media Connect approved by FCC June 24, 2009. Ceased analog operations: June 12, 2009.

Personnel:

David M. Fogarty, President & General Manager.

H. Fred Stone, Engineering & Technical Services Director.

Gloria Skurski, Content Development & Broadcast Services Director.

Suzanne O'Brien, Finance & Administration Director.

Jim Wiener, Program Manager.

Kitty Lensman, Marketing & Business Development Director & Production Manager.

Sue Brinson, Promotion & Communication Manager.

Kay High, Development Director.

Charles Cole, Broadcast Operations & Traffic Manager.

Gary Greenberg, Educational Services Manager.

Casimera Sullivan, Corporate Development Manager & Human Resources.

WPBO-DT
Portsmouth
Ch. 43

Licensee: Ohio State U., 2400 Olentangy River Rd, Columbus, OH 43210.

Studio: 2400 Olentangy River Rd, Columbus, OH 43210.

Mailing Address: 2400 Olentangy River Rd, Columbus, OH 43210.

Phones: 614-292-9678; 614-292-7625. **Fax:** 614-688-3343.

Web Site: http://www.wosu.org

Technical Facilities: Channel No. 43 (644-650 MHz). Authorized power: 50-kw max. visual, aural. Antenna: 1253-ft above av. terrain, 915-ft. above ground, 2018-ft. above sea level.

Latitude	38°	45'	42"
Longitude	83°	03'	41"

Note: Latitude and longitude coordinates shown are based on the North American Datum of 1927 (NAD 27) as currently required by the Mass Media Bureau of the FCC.

Ownership: Ohio State U.

Began Operation: June 4, 2004. Began analog operations: October 1, 1973. Ceased analog operations: June 12, 2009.

Personnel:

Thomas Rieland, General Manager.

Sheri Walker, Assistant General Manager.

Edwin Clay, TV Station Manager.

Tom Lahr, Chief Engineer.

John Prosek, Broadcast Manager.

Mary Alice Akins, Operations Manager.

Stacia Hentz, Program Coordinator.

Jamison Pack, Marketing Director.

Brent Davis, Production Manager.

David Dunham, Development Director.

Cheryl Krebs Petrilla, Public Relations Manager.

Marcelita Haskins, Instructional Services Coordinator.

WGTE-DT
Toledo
Ch. 29

Licensee: Public Broadcasting Foundation of Northwest Ohio, PO Box 30, Toledo, OH 43697.

Studio: 1270 S Detroit Ave, Toledo, OH 43614.

Mailing Address: PO Box 30, Toledo, OH 43614.

Phones: 419-380-4600; 800-243-9483. **Fax:** 419-380-4710.

Email: jen_homier@wgte.org **Web Site:** http://www.wgte.org

Technical Facilities: Channel No. 29 (560-566 MHz). Authorized power: 49.5-kw max. visual, aural. Antenna: 1027-ft above av. terrain, 1027-ft. above ground, 1621-ft. above sea level.

Latitude	41°	39'	26"
Longitude	83°	25'	55"

Note: Latitude and longitude coordinates shown are based on the North American Datum of 1927 (NAD 27) as currently required by the Mass Media Bureau of the FCC.

Ownership: Public Broadcasting Foundation of Northwest Ohio.

Began Operation: May 1, 2003. Began analog operations: October 10, 1960. Ceased analog operations: February 17, 2009.

Personnel:

Marlon Kiser, President & Chief Executive Officer.

Dan Niedzwiecki, Engineering Director.

Ron Harrison, Finance Manager.

Darren LaShelle, TV Program Manager.

Jen Homier, Marketing Manager.

Jamie Pierman, Production Manager.

Barbara Helsop, Operations Coordinator & Traffic Coordinator.

Betsy Hood, Learning Services Director.

Oklahoma

KWET-DT
Cheyenne
Ch. 8

Licensee: Oklahoma Educational Television Authority, PO Box 14190, Oklahoma City, OK 73113-4190.

Studio: 7401 N Kelley Ave, Oklahoma City, OK 73111.

Mailing Address: PO Box 14190, Oklahoma City, OK 73113.

Phones: 405-848-8501; 800-879-6382. **Fax:** 405-841-9216.

Web Site: http://www.oeta.tv

Technical Facilities: Channel No. 8 (180-186 MHz). Authorized power: 30-kw visual, aural. Antenna: 995-ft above av. terrain, 958-ft. above ground, 3050-ft. above sea level.

Latitude	35°	35'	36"
Longitude	99°	40'	01"

Note: Latitude and longitude coordinates shown are based on the North American Datum of 1927 (NAD 27) as currently required by the Mass Media Bureau of the FCC.

Ownership: Oklahoma Educational Television Authority.

Began Operation: June 1, 2006. Began analog operations: August 1, 1978. Ceased analog operations: June 12, 2009.

Personnel:

John McCarroll, Executive Director.

Earle Connors, Engineering Director.

Bill Thrash, Program Production Deputy Director.

Price Woolridge, Production Manager.

Bill Perry, Field Production Bureau Manager.

Janette Thornbrue, Traffic Manager.

Ashley Barcum, Communications & Public Information.

Ted d'Andriole, Underwriter.

KRSC-DT
Claremore
Ch. 36

Licensee: Board of Regents of the U. of Oklahoma & Rogers State U., 1701 W. Will Rogers Blvd, Claremore, OK 74017-3252.

Studio: 1701 W Will Rogers Blvd, Rogers State U., Claremore, OK 74017-3252.

Mailing Address: 1701 W. Will Rogers Blvd, Claremore, OK 74017-3252.

Phones: 918-343-7657; 800-823-7210. **Fax:** 918-343-7952.

Web Site: http://www.rsupublictv.org

Technical Facilities: Channel No. 36 (602-608 MHz). Authorized power: 144-kw max. visual, aural. Antenna: 837-ft above av. terrain, 810-ft. above ground, 1509-ft. above sea level.

Latitude	36°	24'	03"
Longitude	95°	36'	30"

Note: Latitude and longitude coordinates shown are based on the North American Datum of 1927 (NAD 27) as currently required by the Mass Media Bureau of the FCC.

Ownership: Rogers State U.

Began Operation: October 1, 2006. Began analog operations: June 1, 1987. Ceased analog operations: February 17, 2009.

Personnel:

Dan Schiedel, General Manager.

Juanita Sheppler, Traffic Coordinator.

Jim Mertins, Chief Engineer.

Janice Curtis, Program & Membership Manager.

Dale A. McKinney, Production Manager.

Dawn Tatro, Administrative Assistant.

KOET-DT
Eufaula
Ch. 31

Grantee: Oklahoma Educational Television Authority, PO Box 14190, Oklahoma City, OK 73113-4190.

Studio: 7401 N Kelley Ave, Oklahoma City, OK 73111.

Mailing Address: PO Box 14190, Oklahoma City, OK 73113.

Phones: 405-848-8501; 800-879-6382. **Fax:** 405-841-9216.

Web Site: http://www.oeta.tv

Technical Facilities: Channel No. 31 (572-578 MHz). Authorized power: 1000-kw max. visual, aural. Antenna: 1195-ft above av. terrain, 541-ft. above ground, 1891-ft. above sea level.

Latitude	35°	11'	01"
Longitude	95°	20'	19"

Note: Latitude and longitude coordinates shown are based on the North American Datum of 1927 (NAD 27) as currently required by the Mass Media Bureau of the FCC.

Ownership: Oklahoma Educational Television Authority.

Began Operation: June 1, 2006. Began analog operations: December 1, 1977. Ceased analog operations: June 12, 2009.

Personnel:

John McCarroll, Executive Director.

Ted d'Andriole, Underwriter.

Earle Connors, Engineering Director.

Bill Thrash, Program Production Deputy Director.

Price Woolridge, Production Manager.

Bill Perry, Executive Producer, Documentary Department.

Janette Thornbrue, Traffic Manager.

Ashley Barcum, Communications & Public Information.

KETA-DT
Oklahoma City
Ch. 13

Grantee: Oklahoma Educational Television Authority, PO Box 14190, Oklahoma City, OK 73113-4190.

Studio: 7401 N Kelley Ave, Oklahoma City, OK 73111.

Mailing Address: PO Box 14190, Oklahoma City, OK 73113.

Phones: 405-848-8501; 800-879-6382. **Fax:** 405-841-9216.

Web Site: http://www.oeta.tv

Technical Facilities: Channel No. 13 (210-216 MHz). Authorized power: 50-kw visual, aural. Antenna: 1526-ft above av. terrain, 1530-ft. above ground, 2690-ft. above sea level.

Latitude	35°	32'	58"
Longitude	97°	29'	50"

Note: Latitude and longitude coordinates shown are based on the North American Datum of 1927 (NAD 27) as currently required by the Mass Media Bureau of the FCC.

Satellite Earth Stations: Harris; Harris, 3-meter; Vertex, 6.1-meter Ku-band; Andrew, 10-meter; Standard Communications, Sony, Scientific-Atlanta receivers.

Ownership: Oklahoma Educational Television Authority.

Began Operation: February 17, 2009. Station broadcasting digitally on its analog channel allotment. Began analog operations: April 13, 1956. Ceased analog operations: February 17, 2009.

Personnel:

John McCarroll, Executive Director.

Earle Connors, Engineering Director.

Bill Thrash, Station Manager.

Price Woolridge, Production Manager.

Bill Perry, Executive Producer, Documentary Department.

Janette Thornbrue, Traffic Manager.

Ashley Barcum, Communications & Public Information.

Ted d'Andriole, Underwriter.

KOED-DT
Tulsa
Ch. 11

Licensee: Oklahoma Educational Television Authority, PO Box 14190, Oklahoma City, OK 73113-4190.

Studios: 811 N Sheridan Rd, Tulsa, OK 74115; 7401 N Kelley Ave, Oklahoma City, OK 73111.

Mailing Address: PO Box 14190, Oklahoma City, OK 73113.

Phones: 405-848-8501; 800-879-6382. **Fax:** 405-841-9216.

Email: john.mccarroll@oeta.pbs.org **Web Site:** http://www.oeta.tv

Technical Facilities: Channel No. 11 (198-204 MHz). Authorized power: 35-kw visual, aural. Antenna: 1709-ft above av. terrain, 1640-ft. above ground, 2350-ft. above sea level.

Latitude	36°	01'	15"
Longitude	95°	40'	32"

Note: Latitude and longitude coordinates shown are based on the North American Datum of 1927 (NAD 27) as currently required by the Mass Media Bureau of the FCC.

Ownership: Oklahoma Educational Television Authority.

Began Operation: June 1, 2006. Station broadcasting digitally on its analog channel allotment. Began analog operations: January 12, 1959. Ceased analog operations: February 17, 2009.

Personnel:

John McCarroll, Executive Director.

Earle Connors, Engineering Director.

Bill Thrash, Program Production Deputy Director.

Price Woolridge, Production Manager.

Bill Perry, Executive Producer, Documentary Department.

Janette Thornbrue, Traffic Director.

Ashley Barcum, Communications & Public Information.

Ted d'Andriole, Underwriter.

Oregon

KOAB-DT
Bend
Ch. 11

Licensee: Oregon Public Broadcasting, 7140 SW Macadam Ave, Portland, OR 97219-3099.

Studio: 7140 SW Macadam Ave, Portland, OR 97219-3099.

Mailing Address: 7140 S.W. Macadam Ave, Portland, OR 97219-3099.

Phone: 503-244-9900. **Fax:** 503-293-1919.

Web Site: http://www.opb.org

Technical Facilities: Channel No. 11 (198-204 MHz). Authorized power: 90-kw visual, aural. Antenna: 804-ft above av. terrain, 325-ft. above ground, 4544-ft. above sea level.

Latitude	44°	04'	41"
Longitude	121°	19'	57"

Transmitter: Atop Aubrey Butte, 1.7-mi. NW of central Bend.

Note: Latitude and longitude coordinates shown are based on the North American Datum of 1927 (NAD 27) as currently required by the Mass Media Bureau of the FCC.

Ownership: Oregon Public Broadcasting.

Began Operation: August 23, 2006. Began analog operations: February 24, 1970. Ceased analog operations: June 12, 2009.

Personnel:

Steve Bass, President & Chief Executive Officer.

Jeff Douglas, Senior Vice President & Station Manager.

Dan Metziga, Vice President, Development.

Morgan Holm, Vice President, News & Public Affairs.

Don McKay, Vice President, Engineering.

Jan Heskiss, Chief Financial Officer.

Tom Doggett, Vice President, Television Programming.

Tara Taylor, Vice President, Marketing.

Dave Davis, Vice President, National TV Production.

Debbie Rotich, Vice President, Human Resources.

Carol Howard, Local Public Relations & Promotion Manager.

KOAC-DT
Corvallis
Ch. 7

Licensee: Oregon Public Broadcasting, 7140 SW Macadam Ave, Portland, OR 97219-3099.

Studio: 7140 SW Macadam Ave, Portland, OR 97219-3099.

Mailing Address: 7140 S.W. Macadam Ave, Portland, OR 97219-3099.

Phone: 503-244-9900. **Fax:** 503-293-1919.

Web Site: http://www.opb.org

Technical Facilities: Channel No. 7 (174-180 MHz). Authorized power: 18.1-kw visual, aural. Antenna: 1171-ft above av. terrain, 246-ft. above ground, 1686-ft. above sea level.

Latitude	44°	38'	25"
Longitude	123°	16'	25"

Note: Latitude and longitude coordinates shown are based on the North American Datum of 1927 (NAD 27) as currently required by the Mass Media Bureau of the FCC.

Ownership: Oregon Public Broadcasting.

Began Operation: July 1, 2000. Station broadcasting digitally on its analog channel allotment. Began analog operations: October 7, 1957. Ceased analog operations: June 12, 2009.

Personnel:

Steve Bass, President & Chief Executive Officer.

Jeff Douglas, Senior Vice President & Station Manager.

Dan Metziga, Vice President, Development.

Morgan Holm, Vice President, News & Public Affairs.

Don McKay, Vice President, Engineering.

Jan Heskiss, Chief Financial Officer.

Tom Doggett, Vice President, Television Programming.

Tara Taylor, Vice President, Marketing.

Dave Davis, Vice President, National TV Production.

Debbie Rotich, Vice President, Human Resources.

Carol Howard, Local Public Relations & Promotion Manager.

KEPB-DT
Eugene
Ch. 29

Licensee: Oregon Public Broadcasting, 7140 SW Macadam Ave, Portland, OR 97219-3099.

Studio: 7140 SW Macadam Ave, Portland, OR 97219-3099.

Mailing Address: 7140 S.W. Macadam Ave, Portland, OR 97219-3099.

Phone: 503-244-9900. **Fax:** 503-293-1919.

Web Site: http://www.opb.org

Technical Facilities: Channel No. 29 (560-566 MHz). Authorized power: 100-kw max. visual, aural. Antenna: 1322-ft above av. terrain, 682-ft. above ground, 1978-ft. above sea level.

Latitude	44°	00'	07"
Longitude	123°	06'	53"

Transmitter: Blanton Rd.

Note: Latitude and longitude coordinates shown are based on the North American Datum of 1927 (NAD 27) as currently required by the Mass Media Bureau of the FCC.

Ownership: Oregon Public Broadcasting.

Began Operation: January 27, 2005. Began analog operations: September 27, 1990. Ceased analog operations: June 12, 2009.

Personnel:

Steve Bass, President & Chief Executive Officer.

Jeff Douglas, Senior Vice President & Station Manager.

Dan Metziga, Vice President, Development.

Morgan Holm, Vice President, News & Public Affairs.

Don McKay, Vice President, Engineering.

Jan Heskiss, Chief Financial Officer.

Tom Doggett, Vice President, Television Programming.

Debbie Rotich, Vice President, Human Resources.

Tara Taylor, Vice President, Marketing.

Dave Davis, Vice President, National TV Production.

Carol Howard, Local Public Relations & Promotion Manager.

KFTS-DT
Klamath Falls
Ch. 33

Licensee: Southern Oregon Public Television Inc., 34 S Fir St, Medford, OR 97501.

Studio: 34 S Fir St, Medford, OR 97501.

Mailing Address: PO Box 4688, 34 S Fir St, Medford, OR 97501.

Phones: 541-779-0808; 800-888-1847. **Fax:** 541-779-2178.

Web Site: http://www.soptv.org

Technical Facilities: Channel No. 33 (584-590 MHz). Authorized power: 9.6-kw max. visual, aural. Antenna: 2129-ft above av. terrain, 129-ft above ground, 6493-ft above sea level.

Latitude	42°	05'	50"
Longitude	121°	37'	59"

Note: Latitude and longitude coordinates shown are based on the North American Datum of 1927 (NAD 27) as currently required by the Mass Media Bureau of the FCC.

Ownership: Southern Oregon Public Television Inc.

Began Operation: February 2, 2006. Began analog operations: December 13, 1988. Ceased analog operations: June 12, 2009.

Personnel:

Mark Stanislawski, President & Chief Executive Officer.

Tom Werner, Technology Director.

Brad Fay, Content & Services Director.

Helena Darling, Chief Development Officer & Major Gifts Manager.

Jessey Riley, Production Manager.

Nancy MacRae, Traffic Coordinator.

Bruce Johnson, Media Coordinator.

KTVR-DT
La Grande
Ch. 13

Licensee: Oregon Public Broadcasting, 7140 SW Macadam Ave, Portland, OR 97219-3099.

Studio: 7140 SW Macadam Ave, Portland, OR 97219-3099.

Mailing Address: 7140 S.W. Macadam Ave, Portland, OR 97219-3099.

Phone: 503-244-9900. **Fax:** 503-293-1919.

Web Site: http://www.opb.org

Technical Facilities: Channel No. 13 (210-216 MHz). Authorized power: 16.1-kw visual, aural. Antenna: 2543-ft above av. terrain, 161-ft. above ground, 7195-ft. above sea level.

Latitude	45°	18'	33"
Longitude	117°	43'	54"

Note: Latitude and longitude coordinates shown are based on the North American Datum of 1927 (NAD 27) as currently required by the Mass Media Bureau of the FCC.

Ownership: Oregon Public Broadcasting.

Began Operation: November 1, 2004. Station broadcasting digitally on its analog channel allotment. Began analog operations: December 6, 1964. Ceased analog operations: June 12, 2009.

Personnel:

Steve Bass, President & Chief Executive Officer.

Jeff Douglas, Senior Vice President & Station Manager.

Dan Metziga, Vice President, Development.

Morgan Holm, Vice President, News & Public Affairs.

Don McKay, Vice President, Engineering.

Jan Heskiss, Chief Financial Officer.

Tom Doggett, Vice President, Television Programming.

Tara Taylor, Vice President, Marketing.

Dave Davis, Vice President, National TV Production.

Debbie Rotich, Vice President, Human Resources.

Carol Howard, Local Public Relations & Promotion Manager.

KSYS-DT
Medford
Ch. 8

Grantee: Southern Oregon Public Television Inc., 34 S Fir St, Medford, OR 97501.

Studio: 34 S Fir St, Medford, OR 97501.

Mailing Address: PO Box 4688, 34 S Fir St, Medford, OR 97501.

Phones: 541-779-0808; 800-888-1847. **Fax:** 541-779-2178.

Web Site: http://www.soptv.org

Technical Facilities: Channel No. 8 (180-186 MHz). Authorized power: 16.9-kw visual, aural. Antenna: 2684-ft above av. terrain, 128-ft. above ground, 5390-ft. above sea level.

Latitude	42°	41'	32"
Longitude	123°	13'	45"

Note: Latitude and longitude coordinates shown are based on the North American Datum of 1927 (NAD 27) as currently required by the Mass Media Bureau of the FCC.

Ownership: Southern Oregon Public Television Inc.

Began Operation: June 13, 2003. Standard and High Definition. Station broadcasting digitally on its analog channel allotment. Began analog operations: January 17, 1977. Ceased analog operations: February 17, 2009.

Personnel:

Mark Stanislawski, President & Chief Executive Officer.

Tom Werner, Technology Director.

Brad Fay, Content & Services Director.

Jessey Riley, Production Manager.

Nancy MacRae, Program & Operations Manager.

Bruce Johnson, Media Coordinator.

KOPB-DT
Portland
Ch. 10

Licensee: Oregon Public Broadcasting, 7140 SW Macadam Ave, Portland, OR 97219-3099.

Studio: 7140 SW Macadam Ave, Portland, OR 97219-3099.

Mailing Address: 7140 S.W. Macadam Ave, Portland, OR 97219-3099.

Phone: 503-244-9900. **Fax:** 503-293-1919.

Web Site: http://www.opb.org

Technical Facilities: Channel No. 10 (192-198 MHz). Authorized power: 32.4-kw visual, aural. Antenna: 1719-ft above av. terrain, 896-ft. above ground, 2019-ft. above sea level.

Latitude	45°	31'	21"
Longitude	122°	44'	45"

Transmitter: 299 N.W. Skyline Dr.

Note: Latitude and longitude coordinates shown are based on the North American Datum of 1927 (NAD 27) as currently required by the Mass Media Bureau of the FCC.

Ownership: Oregon Public Broadcasting.

Began Operation: December 6, 2000. Station broadcasting digitally on its analog channel allotment. Began analog operations: February 6, 1961. Ceased analog operations: June 12, 2009.

Personnel:

Steve Bass, President & Chief Executive Officer.

Jeff Douglas, Senior Vice President & Station Manager.

Dan Metziga, Vice President, Development.

Morgan Holm, Vice President, News & Public Affairs.

Don McKay, Vice President, Engineering.

Jan Heskiss, Chief Financial Officer.

Tom Doggett, Vice President, Television Programming.

Tara Taylor, Vice President, Marketing.

Dave Davis, Vice President, National TV Production.

Debbie Rotich, Vice President, Human Resources.

Carol Howard, Local Public Relations & Promotion Manager.

Pennsylvania

WLVT-DT
Allentown
Ch. 39

Licensee: Lehigh Valley Public Telecommunications Corp., 123 Sesame St, Bethlehem, PA 18015-4799.

Studio: 123 Sesame St, Bethlethem, PA 18015-4799.

Mailing Address: 123 Sesame St, Bethlehem, PA 18015-4799.

Phone: 610-867-4677. **Fax:** 610-867-3544.

Web Site: http://www.wlvt.org

Technical Facilities: Channel No. 39 (320-626 MHz). Authorized power: 52-kw max. visual, aural. Antenna: 968-ft above av. terrain, 531-ft. above ground, 1465-ft. above sea level.

Latitude	40°	33'	52"
Longitude	75°	26'	24"

Transmitter: 300 E. Rock Rd.

Note: Latitude and longitude coordinates shown are based on the North American Datum of 1927 (NAD 27) as currently required by the Mass Media Bureau of the FCC.

Satellite Earth Stations: RCA; Vertex, 6.1-meter Ku-band; Andrew, 10-meter C-band; Standard Agile Omni receivers.

Ownership: Lehigh Valley Public Telecommunications Corp.

Began Operation: January 30, 2009. Station broadcasting digitally on its analog channel allotment. Began analog operations: September 7, 1965. Ceased analog operations: January 30, 2009.

Personnel:

Pat Simon, President & Chief Executive Officer.

Amy Burkett, Senior Vice President of Production & News Director.

Lee Ann Rinkenberg, Chief Financial Officer & Human Resources Manager.

Stacey Scholl, Development Director.

Tyler Glenn, Production Manager.

David Smith, Senior Staff Engineer.

WPSU-DT
Clearfield
Ch. 15

Grantee: Pennsylvania State U., 100 Innovation Blvd, 120 Outreach Bldg, University Park, PA 16802.

Studio: 100 Innovation Blvd, 120 Outreach Bldg, University Park, PA 16802.

Mailing Address: 100 Innovation Blvd, 120 Outreach Bldg, University Park, PA 16802.

Phone: 814-865-3333. **Fax:** 814-865-3145.

Web Site: http://www.wpsu.org

Technical Facilities: Channel No. 15 (476-482 MHz). Authorized power: 810-kw max. visual, aural. Antenna: 1354-ft above av. terrain, 948-ft. above ground, 3119-ft. above sea level.

Latitude	41°	07'	20"
Longitude	78°	26'	29.8"

Note: Latitude and longitude coordinates shown are based on the North American Datum of 1927 (NAD 27) as currently required by the Mass Media Bureau of the FCC.

Ownership: The Pennsylvania State U. Board of Trustees.

Began Operation: May 9, 2003. Began analog operations: March 1, 1965. Ceased analog operations: June 12, 2009.

Personnel:

Ted Krichels, General Manager.

Kate Domico, Operations Director.

Russell Rockwell, Chief Engineer.

Anne Marie Doncsecz, Business Manager.

Greg Petersen, Program, Production & Marketing Director.

WQLN-DT
Erie
Ch. 50

Licensee: Public Broadcasting of Northwest Pennsylvania Inc., 8425 Peach St, Erie, PA 16509.

Studio: 8425 Peach St, Erie, PA 16509.

Mailing Address: 8425 Peach St, Erie, PA 16509.

Phone: 814-864-3001. **Fax:** 814-864-4077.

Web Site: http://www.wqln.org

Technical Facilities: Channel No. 50 (686-692 MHz). Authorized power: 39.1-kw max. visual, aural. Antenna: 888-ft above av. terrain, 702-ft. above ground, 2009-ft. above sea level.

Latitude	42°	02'	34"
Longitude	80°	03'	56"

Holds CP for change to 200-kw max. visual; BMPEDT-20000412AAR.

Transmitter: 8425 Peach St., Erie.

Note: Latitude and longitude coordinates shown are based on the North American Datum of 1927 (NAD 27) as currently required by the Mass Media Bureau of the FCC.

Ownership: Public Broadcasting of Northwest Pennsylvania Inc.

Began Operation: December 3, 2001. Began analog operations: August 13, 1967. On September 15, 2008, weather damaged the station's transmission line causing analog broadcasts to cease.

Personnel:

Dwight Miller, President & General Manager.

Tom Pysz, Corporate & Foundation Support Director.

Tracy Ferrier, Vice President & Major Gifts Director.

Kim Young, News Director.

Ed Upton, Engineering Director.

Tom New, Creative Services Director.

Sally Baker, Traffic Assistant.

Kimberly Fabrizio, Educational Services Director.

WITF-DT
Harrisburg
Ch. 36

Licensee: WITF Inc., 1982 Locust Ln, Harrisburg, PA 17105.

Studio: 4801 Lindle Rd, Harrisburg, PA 17111.

Mailing Address: PO Box 2954, Harrisburg, PA 17105.

Phone: 717-236-6000. **Fax:** 717-704-3659.

Email: ron_kain@witf.org **Web Site:** http://www.witf.org

Technical Facilities: Channel No. 36 (602-608 MHz). Authorized power: 50-kw max. visual, aural. Antenna: 1348-ft above av. terrain, 630-ft. above ground, 1939-ft. above sea level.

Latitude	40°	20'	44"
Longitude	76°	52'	07"

Requests CP for change to 124-kw max. visual, 1348-ft above av. terrain, 629-ft. above ground, 1939-ft. above sea level; BPEDT-20080620AMA.

Transmitter: Blue Mountain near Harrisburg, Roberts Valley Rd. Extension.

Note: Latitude and longitude coordinates shown are based on the North American Datum of 1927 (NAD 27) as currently required by the Mass Media Bureau of the FCC.

Ownership: WITF Inc.

Began Operation: August 26, 1998. Began analog operations: November 22, 1964. Ceased analog operations: February 17, 2009.

Personnel:

Kathleen A. Pavelko, President.

Ron Kain, Chief Technology Officer.

Ron Hetrick, Engineering Director.

Tim McMasters, Business Manager.

Craig Cohen, Program Director.

Bob Rich, Vice President, Marketing.

Cara Fry, Vice President, Production.

Kathy Silks, Vice President, Communications.

Kim Hutnik, Volunteer Coordinator.

WYBE-DT
Philadelphia
Ch. 35

Licensee: Independence Public Media of Philadelphia Inc., 8200 Ridge Ave, Philadelphia, PA 19128.

Studio: 8200 Ridge Rd., Philadelphia, PA 19128.

Mailing Address: 8200 Ridge Ave, Philadelphia, PA 19128-1604.

Phone: 215-483-3900. **Fax:** 215-483-6908.

Web Site: http://www.mindtv.org

Technical Facilities: Channel No. 35 (596-602 MHz). Authorized power: 450-kw max. visual, aural. Antenna: 1234-ft above av. terrain, 1155-ft. above ground, 1447-ft. above sea level.

Latitude	40°	02'	30"
Longitude	75°	14'	11"

Note: Latitude and longitude coordinates shown are based on the North American Datum of 1927 (NAD 27) as currently required by the Mass Media Bureau of the FCC.

Ownership: Independence Public Media of Philadelphia Inc.

Began Operation: March 31, 2003. Station broadcasting digitally on its analog channel allotment. Began analog operations: June 10, 1990. Ceased analog operations: June 12, 2009.

Personnel:

Sherri Hope Culver, General Manager.

Kim Brown, New Business Director.

Stuart Jakoda, Engineering Director.

Norman Barnum, Finance Director.

Joni Helton, Program Director.

Shivani Jani, Marketing Director.

Jessica Kegelman, On-Air Promotion Manager.

Stephanie Campbell, Development Director.

Lee Wolfe, Production Director.

Jeff Weir, Traffic Coordinator.

Sheba Verma, Member Services Coordinator.

WQED-DT
Pittsburgh
Ch. 13

Licensee: WQED Multimedia, 4802 5th Ave, Pittsburgh, PA 15213.

Studio: 4802 5th Ave., Pittsburgh, PA 15213.

Mailing Address: 4802 5th Ave, Pittsburgh, PA 15213.

Phones: 412-622-1300; 412-622-6413. **Fax:** 412-622-1488.

Web Site: http://www.wqed.org

Technical Facilities: Channel No. 13 (210-216 MHz). Authorized power: 25-kw visual, aural. Antenna: 689-ft above av. terrain, 528-ft. above ground, 1693-ft. above sea level.

Latitude	40°	26'	46"
Longitude	79°	57'	51"

Note: Latitude and longitude coordinates shown are based on the North American Datum of 1927 (NAD 27) as currently required by the Mass Media Bureau of the FCC.

Satellite Earth Stations: Harris; Vertex, 6.1-meter Ku-band; Andrew, 10-meter C-band; Standard Agile Omni, General Instrument receivers.

Ownership: WQED Multimedia.

Began Operation: September 1, 2002. Station broadcasting digitally on its analog channel allotment. Began analog operations: March 19, 1954. Ceased analog operations: June 12, 2009.

Personnel:

George L. Miles Jr., President & Chief Executive Officer.

Deborah Acklin, Senior Vice President & Chief Content Officer.

Lilli Mosco, Vice President, Membership & Development.

Patty Walker, Vice President, Business & Finance.

Betsy Benson, Vice President, Publishing.

Steve Reubi, Treasurer & Chief Financial Officer.

George Hazimanolis, Corporate Communications Director.

Kate St. John, Information Technology Director.

WVIA-DT
Scranton
Ch. 41

Licensee: Northeastern Pennsylvania ETV Association, 100 WVIA Way, Pittston, PA 18640-6197.

Studio: 100 WVIA Way, Pittston, PA 18640-6197.

Mailing Address: 100 WVIA Way, Pittston, PA 18640-6197.

Phones: 570-826-6144; 570-344-1244. **Fax:** 570-655-1180.

Web Site: http://www.wvia.org

Technical Facilities: Channel No. 41 (632-638 MHz). Authorized power: 200-kw max. visual, aural. Antenna: 1598-ft above av. terrain, 758-ft. above ground, 2861-ft. above sea level.

Latitude	41°	10'	55"
Longitude	75°	52'	17"

Requests CP for change to 171-kw max. visual; BPEDT-20090721AAG.

Holds CP for change to 365-kw max. visual, 1673-ft above av. terrain, 822-ft. above ground, 2925-ft. above sea level lat. 41° 10' 55.3", long. 75° 52' 16.3"; BPEDT-20080619ADK.

Note: Latitude and longitude coordinates shown are based on the North American Datum of 1927 (NAD 27) as currently required by the Mass Media Bureau of the FCC.

Ownership: Northeastern Pennsylvania ETV Association.

Began Operation: January 8, 2001. Began analog operations: September 26, 1966. Ceased analog operations: February 17, 2009.

Personnel:

A. William Kelly, President & Chief Executive Officer.

Dan Mattern, Chief Engineer.

Joe Glynn, Vice President, Engineering.

Lynn Volk, Finance Director.

Thom Curra, Vice President, Television Programming.

Ron Prislupski, Corporate & Business Development Director.

John Koons, Information Systems Manager.

Steve Franco, Webmaster.

George Thomas, Membership Director.

Wendy Wilson, Vice President, Communications.

Puerto Rico

WELU-DT
Aguadilla
Ch. 34

Grantee: Pabellon Educational Broadcasting Inc., PO Box 1093, Hormigueros, PR 00660.

Mailing Address: PO Box 1093, Hormigueros, PR 00660.

Phone: 787-849-4020.

Technical Facilities: Channel No. 34 (590-596 MHz). Authorized power: 250-kw max. visual, aural. Antenna: 1985-ft above av. terrain, 135-ft. above ground, 2943-ft. above sea level.

	Latitude	18°	09'	06"
	Longitude	66°	59'	23"

Note: Latitude and longitude coordinates shown are based on the North American Datum of 1927 (NAD 27) as currently required by the Mass Media Bureau of the FCC.

Ownership: Pabellon Educational Broadcasting.

Began Operation: June 12, 2009. Began analog operations: June 1, 1987. Ceased analog operations: June 12, 2009.

WUJA-DT
Caguas
Ch. 57

Licensee: Caguas Educational TV Inc., PO Box 4039, Marginal Baldorioty de Castro, Carolina, PR 00984.

Studio: 24 B St, Urb. Industrial, Carolina, PR 00979.

Mailing Address: PO Box 4039, Carolina, PR 00984-4039.

Phone: 787-625-5858. **Fax:** 787-750-6440.

Web Site: http://www.fuentedeaguaviva.org

Technical Facilities: Channel No. 57 (728-734 MHz). Authorized power: 2.5-kw max. visual, aural. Antenna: 1017-ft above av. terrain, 131-ft. above ground, 1752-ft. above sea level.

	Latitude	18°	16'	40"
	Longitude	66°	06'	38"

Holds CP for change to channel number 48, 50-kw max. visual, 1024-ft above av. terrain, 102-ft. above ground, 1746-ft. above sea level lat. 18° 16' 48", long. 66° 6' 33"; BPEDT-20080317AET.

Note: Latitude and longitude coordinates shown are based on the North American Datum of 1927 (NAD 27) as currently required by the Mass Media Bureau of the FCC.

Ownership: Caguas Educational TV Inc.

Began Operation: July 7, 2006. Began analog operations: October 27, 1985. Ceased analog operations: June 12, 2009.

Personnel:

Oton Font, General Manager.

Edwin Rodriguez, Sales Manager.

WMTJ-DT
Fajardo
Ch. 16

Grantee: Ana G. Mendez Educational Foundation, PO Box 21345, Rio Peidras, PR 00928.

Studio: Isidoro Colon No 176, km 0.3, San Juan, PR 00928.

Mailing Address: PO Box 21345, San Juan, PR 00928-1345.

Phone: 787-766-2600. **Fax:** 787-250-8546.

Web Site: http://www.suagm.edu

Technical Facilities: Channel No. 16 (482-488 MHz). Authorized power: 140-kw max. visual, aural. Antenna: 2796-ft above av. terrain, 175-ft. above ground, 3472-ft. above sea level.

	Latitude	18°	18'	35"
	Longitude	65°	47'	43"

Requests modification of CP for change to 178-kw max. visual; BMPEDT-20080620AEH.

Note: Latitude and longitude coordinates shown are based on the North American Datum of 1927 (NAD 27) as currently required by the Mass Media Bureau of the FCC.

Ownership: Ana G. Mendez Educational Foundation.

Began Operation: June 12, 2009. Began analog operations: February 2, 1985. Ceased analog operations: June 12, 2009.

Personnel:

Migdalia Torres, General Manager.

Ariel Diaz Osorio, Chief Engineer.

Carmen Pujois, Business Manager.

Mailuz Gerena Aguiar, Program Director.

Rene Sotomayor, Promotion Director.

Luiz Martinez, Production Manager.

Sabatian Natal, Traffic Manager.

WIPM-DT
Mayaguez
Ch. 35

Grantee: Puerto Rico Public Broadcasting Corp., PO Box 190909, Hato Rey, PR 00919-0909.

Studio: Post St., 502-S, Mayaguez, PR 00709.

Mailing Address: PO Box 190909, Hato Rey, PR 00919-0909.

Phones: 787-766-0505; 787-834-0164. **Fax:** 787-765-6720.

Web Site: http://www.tutv.puertorico.pr

Technical Facilities: Channel No. 35 (596-602 MHz). Authorized power: 690-kw max. visual, aural. Antenna: 2211-ft above av. terrain, 325-ft. above ground, 3218-ft. above sea level.

	Latitude	18°	09'	00"
	Longitude	66°	59'	00"

Holds CP for change to 784-kw max. visual; BPEDT-20080619AEV.

Note: Latitude and longitude coordinates shown are based on the North American Datum of 1927 (NAD 27) as currently required by the Mass Media Bureau of the FCC.

Ownership: Commonwealth of Puerto Rico.

Began Operation: June 27, 2006. Began analog operations: March 19, 1961. Ceased analog operations: June 12, 2009.

Personnel:

Yolanda Zabala, President.

Daniel Veallaunuava, Administrative Vice President.

Nora Soto, News Director.

Jorge Gonzalez, Chief Engineer.

Wilma Reyes, Program Director.

Louis Santiago, Marketing Director.

Proue Petrelle, Traffic Manager.

Maritty Lasanta, Public Relations Director.

WQTO-DT
Ponce
Ch. 25

Licensee: Ana G. Mendez Educational Foundation, PO Box 21345, Rio Piedras, PR 00928.

Mailing Address: PO Box 21345, Rio Piedras, PR 00928.

Phone: 787-766-2600. **Fax:** 787-250-8546.

Technical Facilities: Channel No. 25 (536-542 MHz). Authorized power: 200-kw max. visual, aural. Antenna: 1017-ft above av. terrain, 217-ft. above ground, 2234-ft. above sea level.

	Latitude	18°	04'	48"
	Longitude	66°	44'	56"

Holds CP for change to 800-kw max. visual, 1017-ft above av. terrain, 217-ft. above ground, 2235-ft. above sea level; BPEDT-20080620AEL.

Note: Latitude and longitude coordinates shown are based on the North American Datum of 1927 (NAD 27) as currently required by the Mass Media Bureau of the FCC.

Ownership: Ana G. Mendez Educational Foundation.

Began Operation: June 14, 2006. Began analog operations: November 26, 1986. Ceased analog operations: June 12, 2009.

Personnel:

Migdalia Torres, General Manager.

WIPR-DT
San Juan
Ch. 43

Grantee: Puerto Rico Public Broadcasting Corp., PO Box 190909, Hato Rey, PR 00919-0909.

Studio: No 5070 Hostos Ave, Hato Rey, PR 00919.

Mailing Address: PO Box 190909, Hato Rey, PR 00919-0909.

Phone: 787-766-0505. **Fax:** 787-765-6720.

Web Site: http://www.tutv.puertorico.pr

Technical Facilities: Channel No. 43 (644-650 MHz). Authorized power: 1000-kw max. visual, aural. Antenna: 2546-ft above av. terrain, 728-ft. above ground, 3684-ft. above sea level.

	Latitude	18°	06'	42"
	Longitude	66°	03'	05"

Note: Latitude and longitude coordinates shown are based on the North American Datum of 1927 (NAD 27) as currently required by the Mass Media Bureau of the FCC.

Ownership: Commonwealth of Puerto Rico.

Began Operation: July 17, 2007. Began analog operations: January 6, 1958. Ceased analog operations: June 12, 2009.

Personnel:

Yolanda Zabala, President.

Daniel Vealaunuava, Administrative Vice President.

Nora Soto, News Director.

Jorge Gonzalez, Chief Engineer.

Wilma Reyes, Program Director.

Louis Santiago, Marketing Director.

Proue Petrelle, Traffic Manager.

Maritty Lasanta, Public Relations Director.

Rhode Island

WSBE-DT
Providence
Ch. 21

Licensee: Rhode Island Public Telecommunications Authority, 50 Park Lane, Providence, RI 02907.

Studio: 50 Park Lane, Providence, RI 02907-3145.

Mailing Address: 50 Park Lane, Providence, RI 02907-3145.

Phones: 401-222-3636; 800-613-8836. **Fax:** 401-222-3407.

Email: public@ripbs.org **Web Site:** http://www.ripbs.org

Technical Facilities: Channel No. 21 (512-518 MHz). Authorized power: 50-kw max. visual, aural. Antenna: 879-ft above av. terrain, 774-ft. above ground, 971-ft. above sea level.

Latitude	41°	51'	54"
Longitude	71°	17'	15"

Note: Latitude and longitude coordinates shown are based on the North American Datum of 1927 (NAD 27) as currently required by the Mass Media Bureau of the FCC.

Ownership: Rhode Island Public Telecommunications Authority.

Began Operation: May 1, 2006. Began analog operations: June 1, 1967. Ceased analog operations: January 15, 2009.

Personnel:

Robert Fish, President.

David Piccerelli, Vice President & Chief Financial Officer.

Dexter Merry, Broadcast Operations Director.

Gunnar Rieger, Chief Engineer.

Kathryn Larsen, Program Director.

Lucie Houle, Public Information Manager.

Jim Garrett, Producer & Director.

David Marseglia, Production Director.

Chrisann Hyland, Information Systems Manager.

Maria del Pilar Velasquez, Education Services Director.

South Carolina

WEBA-DT
Allendale
Ch. 33

Licensee: South Carolina ETV Commission, 1101 George Rogers Blvd, Columbia, SC 29201.

Studio: 1101 George Rogers Blvd., Columbia, SC 29201.

Mailing Address: PO Box 11000, Columbia, SC 29211-1000.

Phones: 803-737-3200; 803-737-9959. **Fax:** 803-737-3417.

Web Site: http://www.scetv.org

Technical Facilities: Channel No. 33 (584-590 MHz). Authorized power: 427-kw max. visual, aural. Antenna: 792-ft above av. terrain, 772-ft. above ground, 1002-ft. above sea level.

Latitude	33°	11'	15"
Longitude	81°	23'	50"

Note: Latitude and longitude coordinates shown are based on the North American Datum of 1927 (NAD 27) as currently required by the Mass Media Bureau of the FCC.

Ownership: South Carolina ETV Commission.

Began Operation: September 15, 2005. Began analog operations: September 5, 1967. Ceased analog operations: February 17, 2009.

Personnel:

Maurice Bresnahan, President & General Manager.

David Crouch, Senior Vice President, Administration.

Kerry Feduk, Vice President, Broadcast Content.

Hap Griffin, Chief Engineer.

Cheryl Nunnley, Program Manager.

John Bane, Creative Services Director.

Catherine Christman, Vice President, Communications.

Debbie Hamlett, On-Air Fundraising Director.

Lydia Freeman, Ready to Learn.

WJWJ-DT
Beaufort
Ch. 44

Licensee: South Carolina ETV Commission, 1101 George Rogers Blvd, Columbia, SC 29201.

Studio: 1101 George Rogers Blvd, Columbia, SC 29201.

Mailing Address: PO Box 1165, Beaufort, SC 29901.

Phones: 803-737-3200; 843-524-0808. **Fax:** 843-524-1016.

Web Site: http://www.wjwj.org

Technical Facilities: Channel No. 44 (650-656 MHz). Authorized power: 440-kw max. visual, aural. Antenna: 1196-ft above av. terrain, 1200-ft. above ground, 1216-ft. above sea level.

Latitude	32°	42'	42"
Longitude	80°	40'	54"

Note: Latitude and longitude coordinates shown are based on the North American Datum of 1927 (NAD 27) as currently required by the Mass Media Bureau of the FCC.

Ownership: South Carolina ETV Commission.

Began Operation: May 15, 2006. Began analog operations: September 10, 1975. Ceased analog operations: February 17, 2009.

Personnel:

Maurice Bresnahan, President & General Manager.

David Crouch, Senior Vice President, Administration.

Kerry Feduk, Vice President, Broadcast Content.

John Brunelli, Station Manager.

Hap Griffin, Chief Engineer.

Cheryl Nunnley, Program Manager.

Catherine Christman, Vice President, Communications.

Debbie Hamlett, On-Air Fundraising Director.

John Bane, Creative Services Director.

Lydia Freeman, Ready to Learn.

WITV-DT
Charleston
Ch. 7

Licensee: South Carolina ETV Commission, 1101 George Rogers Blvd, Columbia, SC 29201.

Studio: 1101 George Rogers Blvd., Columbia, SC 29201.

Mailing Address: PO Box 11000, Columbia, SC 29211-1000.

Phones: 803-737-3200; 803-737-9959. **Fax:** 803-737-3417.

Web Site: http://www.scetv.org

Technical Facilities: Channel No. 7 (174-180 MHz). Authorized power: 20-kw visual, aural. Antenna: 1843-ft above av. terrain, 1837-ft. above ground, 1853-ft. above sea level.

Latitude	32°	55'	28"
Longitude	79°	41'	58"

Transmitter: 3.4-mi. NE of Ten Mile, Charleston County, E of Rte. 17-701, SE of intersection with Sewee Rd.

Note: Latitude and longitude coordinates shown are based on the North American Datum of 1927 (NAD 27) as currently required by the Mass Media Bureau of the FCC.

Ownership: South Carolina ETV Commission.

Began Operation: January 1, 2002. Standard Definition. Station broadcasting digitally on its analog channel allotment. Began analog operations: January 19, 1964. Ceased analog operations: February 17, 2009.

Personnel:

Maurice Bresnahan, President & General Manager.

David Crouch, Senior Vice President, Administration.

Kerry Feduk, Vice President, Broadcast Content.

Hap Griffin, Chief Engineer.

Cheryl Nunnley, Program Manager.

John Bane, Creative Services Director.

Debbie Hamlett, On-Air Fundraising Director.

Catherine Christman, Vice President, Communications.

Lydia Freeman, Ready to Learn.

WRLK-DT
Columbia
Ch. 32

Licensee: South Carolina ETV Commission, 1101 George Rogers Blvd, Columbia, SC 29201.

Studio: 1101 George Rogers Blvd., Columbia, SC 29201.

Mailing Address: PO Box 11000, Columbia, SC 29211-1000.

Phone: 803-737-3200. **Fax:** 803-737-3417.

Web Site: http://www.scetv.org

Technical Facilities: Channel No. 32 (578-584 MHz). Authorized power: 62-kw max. visual, aural. Antenna: 1036-ft above av. terrain, 977-ft. above ground, 1367-ft. above sea level.

Latitude	34°	07'	06"
Longitude	80°	56'	13"

Holds CP for change to 250-kw max. visual, 1035-ft above av. terrain, 977-ft. above ground, 1368-ft. above sea level; BPEDT-20080620ACO.

Note: Latitude and longitude coordinates shown are based on the North American Datum of 1927 (NAD 27) as currently required by the Mass Media Bureau of the FCC.

Ownership: South Carolina ETV Commission.

Began Operation: February 17, 2009. Began analog operations: September 6, 1966. Ceased analog operations: February 17, 2009.

Personnel:

Maurice Bresnahan, President & General Manager.

David Crouch, Senior Vice President, Administration.

Kerry Feduk, Vice President, Broadcast Content.

Hap Griffin, Chief Engineer.

Cheryl Nunnley, Program Manager.

John Bane, Creative Services Director.

Debbie Hamlett, On-Air Fundraising Director.

Lydia Freeman, Ready to Learn Director.

Catherine Christman, Vice President, Communications.

WHMC-DT
Conway
Ch. 9

Licensee: South Carolina ETV Commission, 1101 George Rogers Blvd, Columbia, SC 29201.

Studio: 1101 George Rogers Blvd., Columbia, SC 29211.

Mailing Address: PO Box 11000, Columbia, SC 29211-1000.

Phones: 803-737-3200; 803-737-9959. **Fax:** 803-737-3417.

Web Site: http://www.scetv.org

Technical Facilities: Channel No. 9 (186-192 MHz). Authorized power: 20-kw visual, aural. Antenna: 753-ft above av. terrain, 739-ft. above ground, 818-ft. above sea level.

Latitude	33°	56'	58"
Longitude	79°	06'	31"

Holds CP for change to 31.8-kw visual; BPEDT-20080620AKP.

Note: Latitude and longitude coordinates shown are based on the North American Datum of 1927 (NAD 27) as currently required by the Mass Media Bureau of the FCC.

Ownership: South Carolina ETV Commission.

Began Operation: August 30, 2005. Began analog operations: September 2, 1980. Ceased analog operations: February 17, 2009.

Personnel:

Maurice Bresnahan, President & General Manager.

David Crouch, Senior Vice President, Administration.

Kerry Feduk, Vice President, Broadcast Content.

Hap Griffin, Chief Engineer.

Cheryl Nunnley, Program Manager.

John Bane, Creative Services Director.

Debbie Hamlett, On-Air Fundraising Director.

Catherine Christman, Vice President, Communications.

Lydia Freeman, Ready to Learn.

WJPM-DT
Florence
Ch. 45

Licensee: South Carolina ETV Commission, 1101 George Rogers Blvd, Columbia, SC 29201.

Studio: 1101 George Rogers Blvd., Columbia, SC 29201.

Mailing Address: PO Box 11000, Columbia, SC 29211-1000.

Phones: 803-737-9959; 803-737-3200. **Fax:** 803-737-3417.

Web Site: http://www.scetv.org

Technical Facilities: Channel No. 45 (656-662 MHz). Authorized power: 45-kw max. visual, aural. Antenna: 795-ft above av. terrain, 779-ft. above ground, 898-ft. above sea level.

Latitude	34°	16'	48"
Longitude	79°	44'	35"

Holds CP for change to 108.9-kw max. visual; BPEDT-20080620ACG.

Note: Latitude and longitude coordinates shown are based on the North American Datum of 1927 (NAD 27) as currently required by the Mass Media Bureau of the FCC.

Ownership: South Carolina ETV Commission.

Began Operation: November 1, 2004. Began analog operations: September 3, 1967. Ceased analog operations: February 17, 2009.

Personnel:

Maurice Bresnahan, President & General Manager.

David Crouch, Senior Vice President, Administration.

Kerry Feduk, Vice President, Broadcast Content.

Hap Griffin, Chief Engineer.

Cheryl Nunnley, Program Manager.

John Bane, Creative Services Director.

Debbie Hamlett, On-Air Fundraising Director.

Lydia Freeman, Ready to Learn.

Catherine Christman, Vice President, Communications.

WNTV-DT
Greenville
Ch. 9

Licensee: South Carolina ETV Commission, 1101 George Rogers Blvd, Columbia, SC 29201.

Studio: 1101 George Rogers Blvd., Columbia, SC 29201.

Mailing Address: PO Box 11000, Columbia, SC 29211-1000.

Phones: 803-737-3200; 803-737-9959. **Fax:** 803-737-3417.

Web Site: http://www.scetv.org

Technical Facilities: Channel No. 9 (186-192 MHz). Authorized power: 65-kw visual, aural. Antenna: 1239-ft above av. terrain, 217-ft. above ground, 2244-ft. above sea level.

Latitude	34°	56'	29"
Longitude	82°	24'	38"

Holds CP for change to 102.3-kw visual; BPEDT-20080620ACK.

Note: Latitude and longitude coordinates shown are based on the North American Datum of 1927 (NAD 27) as currently required by the Mass Media Bureau of the FCC.

Ownership: South Carolina ETV Commission.

Began Operation: February 17, 2009. Began analog operations: September 29, 1963. Ceased analog operations: February 17, 2009.

Personnel:

Maurice Bresnahan, President & General Manager.

David Crouch, Senior Vice President, Administration.

Kerry Feduk, Vice President, Broadcast Content.

Hap Griffin, Chief Engineer.

Cheryl Nunnley, Program Manager.

John Bane, Creative Services Director.

Catherine Christman, Vice President, Communications.

Lydia Freeman, Ready to Learn Director.

Debbie Hamlett, On-Air Fundraising Director.

WNEH-DT
Greenwood
Ch. 18

Licensee: South Carolina ETV Commission, 1101 George Rogers Blvd, Columbia, SC 29201.

Studio: 1101 George Rogers Blvd., Columbia, SC 29201.

Mailing Address: PO Box 11000, Columbia, SC 29211-1000.

Phones: 803-737-3200; 803-737-9959. **Fax:** 803-737-3417.

Web Site: http://www.scetv.org

Technical Facilities: Channel No. 18 (494-500 MHz). Authorized power: 49-kw max. visual, aural. Antenna: 754-ft above av. terrain, 654-ft. above ground, 1351-ft. above sea level.

Latitude	34°	22'	19"
Longitude	82°	10'	05"

Holds CP for change to 106.7-kw max. visual; BPEDT-20080620ACH.

Note: Latitude and longitude coordinates shown are based on the North American Datum of 1927 (NAD 27) as currently required by the Mass Media Bureau of the FCC.

Ownership: South Carolina ETV Commission.

Began Operation: March 24, 2005. Began analog operations: September 10, 1984. Ceased analog operations: February 17, 2009.

Personnel:

Maurice Bresnahan, President & General Manager.

David Crouch, Senior Vice President, Administration.

Kerry Feduk, Vice President, Broadcast Content.

Hap Griffin, Chief Engineer.

Cheryl Nunnley, Programming Manager.

John Bane, Creative Services Director.

Catherine Christman, Vice President, Communications.

Lydia Freeman, Ready to Learn.

Debbie Hamlett, On-Air Fundraising Director.

WNSC-DT
Rock Hill
Ch. 15

Licensee: South Carolina ETV Commission, 1101 George Rogers Blvd, Columbia, SC 29201.

Studio: 452 S. Anderson Rd., Rock Hill, SC 29730.

Mailing Address: PO Box 11766, Rock Hill, SC 29731.

Phones: 803-737-3200; 803-324-3184. **Fax:** 803-737-3417.

Web Site: http://www.wnsc.org

Technical Facilities: Channel No. 15 (476-482 MHz). Authorized power: 403-kw max. visual, aural. Antenna: 694-ft above av. terrain, 622-ft. above ground, 1261-ft. above sea level.

Latitude	34°	50'	23"
Longitude	81°	01'	07"

Note: Latitude and longitude coordinates shown are based on the North American Datum of 1927 (NAD 27) as currently required by the Mass Media Bureau of the FCC.

Ownership: South Carolina ETV Commission.

Began Operation: February 17, 2009. Began analog operations: January 3, 1978. Ceased analog operations: February 17, 2009.

Personnel:

Maurice Bresnahan, President & General Manager.

Tim Coghill, Station Manager.

Kerry Feduk, Vice President, Broadcast Content.

David Crouch, Senior Vice President, Administration.

Hap Griffin, Chief Engineer.

Cheryl Nunnley, Program Manager.

John Bane, Creative Services Director.

Catherine Christman, Vice President, Communications.

Debbie Hamlett, On-Air Fundraising Director.

Lydia Freeman, Ready to Learn Director.

WRET-DT
Spartanburg
Ch. 43

Licensee: South Carolina ETV Commission, 1101 George Rogers Blvd, Columbia, SC 29201.

Studio: PO Box 4069, Spartanburg, SC 29305.

Mailing Address: PO Box 4069, Spartanburg, SC 29305.

Phones: 803-737-3200; 864-503-9371. **Fax:** 803-737-3495.

Web Site: http://www.scetv.org

Technical Facilities: Channel No. 43 (644-650 MHz). Authorized power: 50-kw max. visual, aural. Antenna: 991-ft above av. terrain, 829-ft. above ground, 1645-ft. above sea level.

Latitude	34°	53'	11"
Longitude	81°	49'	16"

Holds CP for change to 106.2-kw max. visual; BPEDT-20080620ACI.

Note: Latitude and longitude coordinates shown are based on the North American Datum of 1927 (NAD 27) as currently required by the Mass Media Bureau of the FCC.

Ownership: South Carolina ETV Commission.

Began Operation: March 17, 2005. Began analog operations: September 8, 1980. Ceased analog operations: February 17, 2009.

Personnel:

Maurice Bresnahan, President & General Manager.

William Richardson, Station Manager.

David Crouch, Senior Vice President, Administration.

Kerry Feduk, Vice President, Broadcast Content.

Hap Griffen, Chief Engineer.

Cheryl Nunnley, Program Manager.

John Bane, Creative Services Director.

Catherine Christman, Vice President, Communications.

Lydia Freeman, Ready to Learn Director.

Debbie Hamlett, On-Air Fundraising Director.

WRJA-DT
Sumter
Ch. 28

Licensee: South Carolina ETV Commission, 1101 George Rogers Blvd, Columbia, SC 29211.

Studio: 18 N. Harvin St., Sumter, SC 29150.

Mailing Address: PO Box 11000, Columbia, SC 29211-1000.

Phones: 803-737-3200; 803-773-5546. **Fax:** 803-737-3417.

Web Site: http://www.scetv.org

Technical Facilities: Channel No. 28 (554-560 MHz). Authorized power: 98.4-kw max. visual, aural. Antenna: 1194-ft above av. terrain, 1161-ft. above ground, 1302-ft. above sea level.

| Latitude | 33° | 52' | 51" |
| Longitude | 80° | 16' | 15" |

Note: Latitude and longitude coordinates shown are based on the North American Datum of 1927 (NAD 27) as currently required by the Mass Media Bureau of the FCC.

Ownership: South Carolina ETV Commission.

Began Operation: November 1, 2003. Began analog operations: September 7, 1975. Ceased analog operations: February 17, 2009.

Personnel:

Maurice Bresnahan, President & General Manager.

David Crouch, Senior Vice President, Administration.

Kerry Feduk, Vice President, Broadcast Content.

Hap Griffin, Chief Engineer.

Cheryl Nunnley, Program Manager.

John Bane, Creative Services Director.

Catherine Christman, Vice President, Communications.

Lydia Freeman, Ready to Learn.

Debbie Hamlett, On-Air Fundraising Director.

South Dakota

KDSD-DT
Aberdeen
Ch. 17

Licensee: South Dakota Board of Directors for Educational Telecommunications, PO Box 5000, Cherry & Dakota Sts, Vermillion, SD 57069-5000.

Studio: 555 N. Dakota St., Vermillion, SD 57069-5000.

Mailing Address: PO Box 5000, Vermillion, SD 57069-5000.

Phones: 605-677-5861; 800-456-0766. **Fax:** 605-677-5010.

Web Site: http://www.sdpb.org

Technical Facilities: Channel No. 17 (488-494 MHz). Authorized power: 19-kw max. visual, aural. Antenna: 1145-ft above av. terrain, 1001-ft. above ground, 2858-ft. above sea level.

| Latitude | 45° | 29' | 54" |
| Longitude | 97° | 40' | 28" |

Holds CP for change to 37.8-kw max. visual; BPEDT-20080618ACL.

Note: Latitude and longitude coordinates shown are based on the North American Datum of 1927 (NAD 27) as currently required by the Mass Media Bureau of the FCC.

Ownership: South Dakota Board of Directors for Educational Telecommunications.

Began Operation: August 12, 2004. Began analog operations: January 1, 1972. Ceased analog operations: February 17, 2009.

Personnel:

Julie Andersen, Executive Director.

Craig Jensen, Operations Director.

Severn Ashes, Engineering Director.

Deborah Larson, Business Manager.

Fritz Miller, Marketing Director.

Carol Robertson, Marketing Manager.

Terry Spencer, Development Director.

Ruth Bylander, Public Relations & Grant Manager.

Bob Bosse, Television Director.

Brad Van Osdel, Production Manager.

Amber Anders, Continuity Director.

Steve Thum, Traffic Manager.

Sherri Rodgers-Conti, Education & Outreach Director.

Dave Foote, Promotion Producer.

Wess Pravecek, Ready To Learn Coordinator.

Steve Rokusek, Outreach Coordinator & Education Specialist.

KESD-DT
Brookings
Ch. 8

Licensee: South Dakota Board of Directors for Educational Telecommunications, PO Box 5000, Cherry & Dakota Sts, Vermillion, SD 57069-5000.

Studio: 555 N. Dakota St., Vermillion, SD 57069.

Mailing Address: PO Box 5000, Vermillion, SD 57069-5000.

Phones: 605-677-5861; 800-456-0760. **Fax:** 605-677-5010.

Email: terry.spencer@sdpb.org **Web Site:** http://www.sdpb.org

Technical Facilities: Channel No. 8 (180-186 MHz). Authorized power: 15-kw visual, aural. Antenna: 751-ft above av. terrain, 757-ft. above ground, 2506-ft. above sea level.

| Latitude | 44° | 20' | 16" |
| Longitude | 97° | 13' | 42" |

Note: Latitude and longitude coordinates shown are based on the North American Datum of 1927 (NAD 27) as currently required by the Mass Media Bureau of the FCC.

Ownership: South Dakota Board of Directors for Educational Telecommunications.

Began Operation: July 8, 2004. Station broadcasting digitally on its analog channel allotment. Began analog operations: February 4, 1968. Ceased analog operations: February 17, 2009.

Personnel:

Julie Andersen, Executive Director.

Terry Spencer, Development Director.

Fritz Miller, Marketing Director.

Carol Robertson, Marketing Manager.

Amber Anders, Continuity Director.

Ruth Bylander, Public Relations & Grants Manager.

Dave Foote, Promotion Producer.

Sherri Rodgers-Conti, Education & Outreach Director.

Wess Pravecek, Ready to Learn Coordinator.

Steve Rokusek, Outreach Coordinator & Education Specialist.

Bob Bosse, Television Director.

Craig Jensen, Operations Director.

Severn Ashes, Engineering Director.

Deborah Larsen, Business Manager.

Brad Van Osdel, Production Manager.

Steve Thum, Traffic Manager.

KPSD-DT
Eagle Butte
Ch. 13

Licensee: South Dakota Board of Directors for Educational Telecommunications, PO Box 5000, Cherry & Dakota Sts, Vermillion, SD 57069-5000.

Studio: 555 N. Dakota St., Vermillion, SD 57069.

Mailing Address: PO Box 5000, Vermillion, SD 57069-5000.

Phones: 605-677-5861; 800-456-0766. **Fax:** 605-677-5010.

Email: terry.spencer@sdpb.org **Web Site:** http://www.sdpb.org

Technical Facilities: Channel No. 13 (210-216 MHz). Authorized power: 27-kw visual, aural. Antenna: 1693-ft above av. terrain, 1683-ft. above ground, 4253-ft. above sea level.

| Latitude | 45° | 03' | 14" |
| Longitude | 102° | 15' | 47" |

Note: Latitude and longitude coordinates shown are based on the North American Datum of 1927 (NAD 27) as currently required by the Mass Media Bureau of the FCC.

Ownership: South Dakota Board of Directors for Educational Telecommunications.

Began Operation: July 14, 2004. Station broadcasting digitally on its analog channel allotment. Began analog operations: September 16, 1974. Ceased analog operations: February 17, 2009.

Personnel:

Julie Andersen, Executive Director.

Terry Spencer, Development Director.

Fritz Miller, Marketing Director.

Carol Robertson, Marketing Manager.

Amber Anders, Continuity Director.

Ruth Bylander, Public Relations & Grants Manager.

Dave Foote, Promotion Producer.

Sherri Rodgers-Conti, Education & Outreach Director.

Wess Pravecek, Ready to Learn Coordinator.

Steve Rokusek, Outreach Coordinator & Education Specialist.

Bob Bosse, Television Director.

Craig Jensen, Operations Director.

Severn Ashes, Engineering Director.

Deborah Larson, Business Manager.

Brad Van Osdel, Production Manager.

Steve Thum, Traffic Manager.

KQSD-DT
Lowry
Ch. 11

Licensee: South Dakota Board of Directors for Educational Telecommunications, PO Box 5000, Cherry & Dakota Sts, Vermillion, SD 57069-5000.

Studio: 555 N. Dakota St., Vermillion, SD 57069.

Mailing Address: PO Box 5000, Vermillion, SD 57069-5000.

Phones: 605-677-5861; 800-456-0766. **Fax:** 605-677-5010.

Email: terry.spencer@sdpb.org **Web Site:** http://www.sdpb.org

Technical Facilities: Channel No. 11 (198-204 MHz). Authorized power: 37-kw visual, aural. Antenna: 1026-ft above av. terrain, 795-ft. above ground, 2970-ft. above sea level.

| Latitude | 45° | 16' | 38" |
| Longitude | 99° | 59' | 10" |

Note: Latitude and longitude coordinates shown are based on the North American Datum of 1927 (NAD 27) as currently required by the Mass Media Bureau of the FCC.

Ownership: South Dakota Board of Directors for Educational Telecommunications.

Began Operation: August 4, 2004. Station broadcasting digitally on its analog channel allotment. Began analog operations: March 9, 1976. Ceased analog operations: February 17, 2009.

Personnel:

Julie Andersen, Executive Director.

Terry Spencer, Development Director.

Fritz Miller, Marketing Director.

Carol Robertson, Marketing Manager.

Amber Anders, Continuity Director.

Ruth Bylander, Public Relations & Grants Manager.

Dave Foote, Promotion Producer.

Sherri Rodgers-Conti, Education & Outreach Director.

Wess Pravecek, Ready to Learn Coordinator.

Steve Rokusek, Outreach Coordinator & Education Specialist.

Bob Bosse, Television Director.

Craig Jensen, Operations Director.

Severn Ashes, Engineering Director.

Deborah Larson, Business Manager.

Brad Van Osdel, Production Manager.

Steve Thum, Traffic Manager.

KZSD-DT
Martin
Ch. 8

Licensee: South Dakota Board of Directors for Educational Telecommunications, PO Box 5000, Cherry & Dakota Sts, Vermillion, SD 57069-5000.

Studio: 555 N. Dakota St., Vermillion, SD 57069.

Mailing Address: PO Box 5000, Vermillion, SD 57069-5000.

Phones: 605-677-5861; 800-456-0760. Fax: 605-677-5010.

Email: terry.spencer@sdpb.org Web Site: http://www.sdpb.org

Technical Facilities: Channel No. 8 (180-186 MHz). Authorized power: 44.7-kw visual, aural. Antenna: 873-ft above av. terrain, 620-ft. above ground, 3718-ft. above sea level.

Latitude	43°	25'	59"
Longitude	101°	33'	16"

Note: Latitude and longitude coordinates shown are based on the North American Datum of 1927 (NAD 27) as currently required by the Mass Media Bureau of the FCC.

Ownership: South Dakota Board of Directors for Educational Telecommunications.

Began Operation: September 10, 2004. Station broadcasting digitally on its analog channel allotment. Began analog operations: February 9, 1978. Ceased analog operations: February 17, 2009.

Personnel:

Julie Andersen, Executive Director.

Terry Spencer, Development Director.

Fritz Miller, Marketing Director.

Carol Robertson, Marketing Manager.

Amber Anders, Continuity Director.

Ruth Bylander, Public Relations & Grants Manager.

Dave Foote, Promotion Producer.

Sherri Rodgers-Conti, Education & Outreach Director.

Wess Pravecek, Ready to Learn Coordinator.

Steve Rokusek, Outreach Coordinator & Education Specialist.

Bob Bosse, Television Director.

Craig Jensen, Operations Director.

Severn Ashes, Engineering Director.

Deborah Larson, Business Manager.

Brad Van Osdel, Production Manager.

Steve Thum, Traffic Manager.

KTSD-DT
Pierre
Ch. 10

Licensee: South Dakota Board of Directors for Educational Telecommunications, PO Box 5000, Cherry & Dakota Sts, Vermillion, SD 57069-5000.

Studio: 555 N. Dakota St., Vermillion, SD 57069.

Mailing Address: PO Box 5000, Vermillion, SD 57069-5000.

Phones: 605-677-5861; 800-456-0766. Fax: 605-667-5010.

Email: fritz.miller@sdpb.org Web Site: http://www.sdpb.org

Technical Facilities: Channel No. 10 (192-198 MHz). Authorized power: 54.7-kw visual, aural. Antenna: 1600-ft above av. terrain, 1263-ft. above ground, 3321-ft. above sea level.

Latitude	43°	58'	05"
Longitude	99°	35'	40"

Note: Latitude and longitude coordinates shown are based on the North American Datum of 1927 (NAD 27) as currently required by the Mass Media Bureau of the FCC.

Ownership: South Dakota Board of Directors for Educational Telecommunications.

Began Operation: July 15, 2004. Station broadcasting digitally on its analog channel allotment. Began analog operations: August 1, 1970. Ceased analog operations: February 17, 2009.

Personnel:

Julie Andersen, Executive Director.

Terry Spencer, Development Director.

Fritz Miller, Marketing Director.

Carol Robertson, Marketing Manager.

Amber Anders, Continuity Director.

Ruth Bylander, Public Relations & Grants Manager.

Dave Foote, Promotion Producer.

Sherri Rodgers-Conti, Education & Outreach Director.

Wess Pravecek, Ready to Learn Coordinator.

Steve Rokusek, Outreach Coordinator & Education Specialist.

Bob Bosse, Television Director.

Craig Jensen, Operations Director.

Severn Ashes, Engineering Director.

Deborah Larson, Business Manager.

Brad Van Osdel, Production Manager.

Steve Thum, Traffic Manager.

KBHE-DT
Rapid City
Ch. 26

Licensee: South Dakota Board of Directors for Educational Telecommunications, PO Box 5000, Cherry & Dakota Sts, Vermillion, SD 57069-5000.

Studio: 555 N. Dakota St., Vermillion, SD 57069.

Mailing Address: PO Box 5000, Vermillion, SD 57069-5000.

Phones: 605-677-5861; 800-456-0766. Fax: 605-677-5010.

Email: wess.pravecek@state.sd.us Web Site: http://www.sdpb.org

Technical Facilities: Channel No. 26 (542-548 MHz). Authorized power: 76.3-kw max. visual, aural. Antenna: 629-ft above av. terrain, 370-ft. above ground, 4202-ft. above sea level.

Latitude	44°	03'	08"
Longitude	103°	14'	34"

Holds CP for change to 79-kw max. visual; BPEDT-20080618ACI.

Note: Latitude and longitude coordinates shown are based on the North American Datum of 1927 (NAD 27) as currently required by the Mass Media Bureau of the FCC.

Ownership: South Dakota Board of Directors for Educational Telecommunications.

Began Operation: April 30, 2003. Began analog operations: September 13, 1967. Ceased analog operations: February 17, 2009.

Personnel:

Julie Andersen, Executive Director.

Terry Spencer, Development Director.

Fritz Miller, Marketing Director.

Carol Robertson, Marketing Manager.

Amber Anders, Continuity Director.

Ruth Bylander, Public Relations & Grant Manager.

Dave Foote, Promotion Producer.

Sherri Rodgers-Conti, Education & Outreach Director.

Wess Pravecek, Ready to Learn Coordinator.

Steve Rokusek, Outreach Coordinator & Education Specialist.

Bob Bosse, Television Director.

Craig Jensen, Operations Director.

Severn Ashes, Engineering Director.

Deborah Larson, Business Manager.

Brad Van Osdel, Production Manager.

Steve Thum, Traffic Manager.

KCSD-DT
Sioux Falls
Ch. 24

Licensee: South Dakota Board of Directors for Educational Telecommunications, PO Box 5000, Cherry & Dakota Sts, Vermillion, SD 57069-5000.

Studio: 555 N. Dakota St., Vermillion, SD 57069.

Mailing Address: PO Box 5000, Vermillion, SD 57069-5000.

Phones: 605-677-5861; 800-456-0766. Fax: 605-677-5010.

Web Site: http://www.sdpb.org

Technical Facilities: Channel No. 24 (530-536 MHz). Authorized power: 29-kw max. visual, aural. Antenna: 246-ft above av. terrain, 180-ft. above ground, 1680-ft. above sea level.

Latitude	43°	34'	28"
Longitude	96°	39'	19"

Holds CP for change to 80.9-kw max. visual; BPEDT-20080618ABO.

Note: Latitude and longitude coordinates shown are based on the North American Datum of 1927 (NAD 27) as currently required by the Mass Media Bureau of the FCC.

Ownership: South Dakota Board of Directors for Educational Telecommunications.

Began Operation: January 24, 2004. Began analog operations: June 13, 1995. Ceased analog operations: February 17, 2009.

Personnel:

Julie Andersen, Executive Director.

Bob Bosse, Television Director.

Craig Jensen, Operations Director.

Severn Ashes, Engineering Director.

Deborah Larson, Business Manager.

Fritz Miller, Marketing Director.

Carol Robertson, Marketing Manager.

Terry Spencer, Development Director.

Ruth Bylander, Public Relations & Grant Manager.

Brad Van Osdel, Production Manager.

Amber Anders, Continuity Director.

Steve Thum, Traffic Manager.

Sherri Rodgers-Conti, Education & Outreach Director.

Dave Foote, Promotion Producer.

Wess Pravecek, Ready To Learn Coordinator.

Steve Rokusek, Outreach Coordinator & Education Specialist.

KUSD-DT
Vermillion
Ch. 34

Licensee: South Dakota Board of Directors for Educational Telecommunications, PO Box 5000, Cherry & Dakota Sts, Vermillion, SD 57069-5000.

Studio: 555 N. Dakota St., Vermillion, SD 57069.

Mailing Address: PO Box 5000, Vermillion, SD 57069-5000.

Phones: 605-677-5861; 800-456-0766. Fax: 605-677-5010.

Email: terry.spencer@sdpb.org Web Site: http://www.sdpb.org

Technical Facilities: Channel No. 34 (590-596 MHz). Authorized power: 236-kw max. visual, aural. Antenna: 669-ft above av. terrain, 518-ft. above ground, 2028-ft. above sea level.

Latitude	43°	03'	01"
Longitude	96°	47'	01"

Holds CP for change to 277-kw max. visual, 768-ft above av. terrain, 617-ft. above ground, 2127-ft. above sea level; BPEDT-20090527AGS.

Note: Latitude and longitude coordinates shown are based on the North American Datum of 1927 (NAD 27) as currently required by the Mass Media Bureau of the FCC.

Ownership: South Dakota Board of Directors for Educational Telecommunications.

Began Operation: July 7, 2004. Began analog operations: July 5, 1961. Ceased analog operations: February 17, 2009.

Personnel:

Julie Andersen, Executive Director.

Terry Spencer, Development Director.

Fritz Miller, Marketing Director.

Carol Robertson, Marketing Manager.

Amber Anders, Continuity Director.

Ruth Bylander, Public Relations & Grants Manager.

Dave Foote, Promotion Producer.

Sherri Rodgers-Conti, Education & Outreach Director.

Wess Pravecek, Ready to Learn Coordinator.

Steve Rokusek, Outreach Coordinator & Education Specialist.

Bob Bosse, Television Director.

Craig Jensen, Operations Director.

Severn Ashes, Engineering Director.

Deborah Larson, Business Manager.

Brad Van Osdel, Production Manager.

Steve Thum, Traffic Manager.

Tennessee

WTCI-DT
Chattanooga
Ch. 29

Licensee: Greater Chattanooga Public Television Corp., 7540 Bonnyshire Dr, Chattanooga, TN 37416.

Studio: 7540 Bonnyshire Dr, Chattanooga, TN 37416.

Mailing Address: 7540 Bonnyshire Dr, Chattanooga, TN 37416.

Phone: 423-629-0045. **Fax:** 423-698-8557.

Web Site: http://www.wtcitv.org

Technical Facilities: Channel No. 29 (560-566 MHz). Authorized power: 200-kw max. visual, aural. Antenna: 1102-ft above av. terrain, 410-ft. above ground, 2422-ft. above sea level.

Latitude	35°	12'	26"
Longitude	85°	16'	52"

Note: Latitude and longitude coordinates shown are based on the North American Datum of 1927 (NAD 27) as currently required by the Mass Media Bureau of the FCC.

Ownership: Greater Chattanooga Public TV Corp.

Began Operation: February 17, 2009. Began analog operations: March 3, 1970. Ceased analog operations: February 17, 2009.

Personnel:

Paul Grove, President & Chief Executive Officer.

Julie Taylor, Vice President, Development.

Bryan D. Fuqua, Vice President, Technical Services.

Peter Delynn, Vice President, Production.

Susan Cates, Business & Office Manager.

Pam Carpenter, Traffic Manager.

Kevin Lusk, Public Information & Community Outreach Director.

Sara Maloney, Membership Director.

WCTE-DT
Cookeville
Ch. 22

Licensee: Upper Cumberland Broadcast Council, PO Box 2040, Cookeville, TN 38502.

Studio: 1151 Stadium Dr., Suite 104, Cookeville, TN 38501.

Mailing Address: PO Box 2040, Cookeville, TN 38502.

Phone: 931-528-2222. **Fax:** 931-372-6284.

Email: dcastle@wcte.org **Web Site:** http://www.wcte.org

Technical Facilities: Channel No. 22 (518-524 MHz). Authorized power: 50-kw max. visual, aural. Antenna: 1386-ft above av. terrain, 766-ft. above ground, 2763-ft. above sea level.

Latitude	36°	10'	26"
Longitude	85°	20'	37"

Holds CP for change to 57-kw max. visual, 1352-ft above av. terrain, 710-ft. above ground, 2707-ft. above sea level; BMPEDT-20090626AAC.

Note: Latitude and longitude coordinates shown are based on the North American Datum of 1927 (NAD 27) as currently required by the Mass Media Bureau of the FCC.

Ownership: Upper Cumberland Broadcast Council.

Began Operation: January 30, 2009. Station broadcasting digitally on its analog channel allotment. Began analog operations: August 21, 1978. Station temporarily ceased operations February 10, 2006 due to electrical system malfunction and was granted Special Temporary Authority to remain silent. Ceased analog operations: January 30, 2009.

Personnel:

Becky Magura, General Manager.

Robert Huddleston, Chief Engineer.

Becky Murdock, Business Manager.

Donna Castle, Program & Promotion Manager.

Jo Ward, Development Director.

Rick Wells, Production Manager.

Sue Gibbons, Traffic Manager.

Joyce Hunter, Special Events Director.

WKOP-DT
Knoxville
Ch. 17

Licensee: East Tennessee Public Communications Corp., 1611 E Magnolia Ave, Knoxville, TN 37917.

Studio: 1611 E. Magnolia Ave., Knoxville, TN 37917.

Mailing Address: 1611 E. Magnolia Ave, Knoxville, TN 37917.

Phones: 865-595-0220; 800-595-0220. **Fax:** 865-595-0300.

Web Site: http://www.etptv.org

Technical Facilities: Channel No. 17 (488-494 MHz). Authorized power: 100-kw max. visual, aural. Antenna: 1809-ft above av. terrain, 1499-ft. above ground, 2814-ft. above sea level.

Latitude	35°	59'	44"
Longitude	83°	47'	23"

Note: Latitude and longitude coordinates shown are based on the North American Datum of 1927 (NAD 27) as currently required by the Mass Media Bureau of the FCC.

Ownership: East Tennessee Public Communications Corp.

Began Operation: April 5, 2004. Began analog operations: August 15, 1990. On June 24, 2008, analog broadcasts ceased after transmitter failure. Station was granted Special Temporary Authority by the FCC July 24, 2008 to terminate analog operations.

Personnel:

Teresa James, President & Chief Executive Officer.

Frank Miller, Vice President, Assistant General Manager & In-School Services Director.

Kurtis Allin, Chief Engineer.

Robert Hutchison, Program Director.

Kelly Hodges, Development Director.

Russ Manning, Production Manager.

Cathy Wilson, Traffic Manager.

Christopher Smith, Public Service Director.

Vickie Lawson, Membership Manager.

Robert Bratton, Underwriting Director.

WLJT-DT
Lexington
Ch. 47

Grantee: West Tennessee Public TV Council Inc., PO Box 966, Martin, TN 32837.

Studio: Communications Bldg., 201 Hurt St, Martin, TN 38238.

Mailing Address: PO Box 966, Martin, TN 38237.

Phones: 731-881-7561; 800-366-9558. **Fax:** 731-881-7566.

Web Site: http://www.wljt.org

Technical Facilities: Channel No. 47 (668-674 MHz). Authorized power: 282-kw max. visual, aural. Antenna: 548-ft above av. terrain, 346-ft. above ground, 1014-ft. above sea level.

Latitude	35°	42'	12"
Longitude	88°	36'	10"

Transmitter: 12.5-mi. NW of Lexington.

Note: Latitude and longitude coordinates shown are based on the North American Datum of 1927 (NAD 27) as currently required by the Mass Media Bureau of the FCC.

Ownership: West Tennessee Public TV Council Inc.

Began Operation: February 17, 2009. Began analog operations: February 13, 1968. Ceased analog operations: February 17, 2009.

Personnel:

Dave Hinman, General Manager.

Katrina Cobb, Broadcast Operations Director.

Walter Swigert, Chief Engineer.

Kenneth Robinson, Engineering Director.

Monica Shumake, Finance & Administration Director.

Darrell Conner, Production Director.

Jack Glisson, Production Engineer.

Sue Lasky, Education, Outreach & Ready-to-Learn Coordinator.

Mandy Hinson, Individual Giving Manager.

Madison Mayo, Marketing Manager.

WKNO-DT
Memphis
Ch. 29

Licensee: Mid-South Public Communications Foundation, PO Box 241880, Memphis, TN 38124-1880.

Studio: 900 Getwell Rd., Memphis, TN 38111.

Mailing Address: PO Box 241880, Memphis, TN 38124.

Phone: 901-458-2521. **Fax:** 901-325-6505.

Web Site: http://www.wkno.org

Technical Facilities: Channel No. 29 (560-566 MHz). Authorized power: 835-kw max. visual, aural. Antenna: 1051-ft above av. terrain, 1021-ft. above ground, 1356-ft. above sea level.

Latitude	35°	09'	16"
Longitude	89°	49'	20"

Transmitter: 7192 Raleigh LaGrange Rd.

Note: Latitude and longitude coordinates shown are based on the North American Datum of 1927 (NAD 27) as currently required by the Mass Media Bureau of the FCC.

Multichannel TV Sound: Stereo and separate audio program.

Ownership: Mid-South Public Communications Foundation.

Began Operation: June 27, 2006. Began analog operations: June 25, 1956. Ceased analog operations: June 12, 2009.

Personnel:

Michael J. LaBonia, President & Chief Executive Officer.

Russ A. Abernathy, Television & Engineering Director.

Arthur Smith, Engineering Manager.

Scott Davidson, Finance & Administration Director.

Debi Robertson, Program Operations Manager.

Jim Eikner, Marketing Manager.

Teri Sullivan, Promotion Director.

Charles McLarty, Development & Communications Director.

Joe Dixon, Productions Unit Manager.

David George, Production Manager.

Becky Kelly, Auction Manager.

WTWV-DT
Memphis
Ch. 14

Licensee: Christian Worldview Broadcasting Corp., 6080 Mount Moriah, Memphis, TN 38115.

Mailing Address: 900 Getwell Rd, Memphis, TN 38111.

Phone: 901-795-1781.

Technical Facilities: Channel No. 14 (470-476 MHz). Authorized power: 20-kw max. visual, aural. Antenna: 787-ft above av. terrain, 801-ft. above ground, 1076-ft. above sea level.

	Latitude	35°	12'	34"
	Longitude	89°	49'	01"

Holds CP for change to channel number 23, 1000-kw max. visual, 856-ft above av. terrain, 869-ft. above ground, 1145-ft. above sea level; BMPEDT-20090113ACJ.

Note: Latitude and longitude coordinates shown are based on the North American Datum of 1927 (NAD 27) as currently required by the Mass Media Bureau of the FCC.

Ownership: Christian Worldview Broadcasting Corp.

Began Operation: June 12, 2009. Sale to present owner by Kaleidoscope Foundation Memphis Inc. approved by FCC March 7, 2006. Station broadcasting digitally on its original analog application; no analog broadcast.

WNPT-DT
Nashville
Ch. 8

Licensee: Nashville Public Television Inc., 161 Rains Ave, Nashville, TN 37203.

Studio: 161 Rains Ave., Nashville, TN 37203-5330.

Mailing Address: 161 Rains Ave, Nashville, TN 37203-5330.

Phones: 615-259-9325; 615-259-9326. Fax: 615-248-6120.

Web Site: http://www.wnpt.net

Technical Facilities: Channel No. 8 (180-186 MHz). Authorized power: 17.65-kw visual, aural. Antenna: 1280-ft above av. terrain, 834-ft. above ground, 1939-ft. above sea level.

	Latitude	36°	02'	49"
	Longitude	86°	49'	49"

Note: Latitude and longitude coordinates shown are based on the North American Datum of 1927 (NAD 27) as currently required by the Mass Media Bureau of the FCC.

Ownership: Nashville Public Television Inc.

Began Operation: June 30, 2006. Station broadcasting digitally on its analog channel allotment. Began analog operations: September 10, 1962. Ceased analog operations: June 12, 2009.

Personnel:

Beth Curley, President & Chief Executive Officer.

Steve Sonnenblick, Chief Engineer.

Kevin Crane, Vice President, Technology & Programming.

Charles Brumbelow, Vice President & Chief Financial Officer.

Justin Harvey, Program Manager.

Gary Shipley, Corporate Marketing Director.

Daniel Tidwell, Vice President, Development & Marketing.

Jim DeMarco, Production Director.

Hugh Brian O'Neill, Creative Services Director.

Jo Ann Scalf, Educational Services Director.

Kimberly Wonsey, Human Resources & Administration Director.

Joe Pagetta, Media Relations Manager.

WETP-DT
Sneedville
Ch. 41

Licensee: East Tennessee Public Communications Corp., 1611 E Magnolia Ave, Knoxville, TN 37917.

Studio: 1611 E. Magnolia Ave., Knoxville, TN 37917.

Mailing Address: 1611 E. Magnolia Ave, Knoxville, TN 37917.

Phones: 865-595-0220; 800-595-0220. Fax: 865-595-0300.

Web Site: http://www.etptv.org

Technical Facilities: Channel No. 41 (632-638 MHz). Authorized power: 445-kw max. visual, aural. Antenna: 1859-ft above av. terrain, 565-ft. above ground, 3220-ft. above sea level.

	Latitude	36°	22'	52"
	Longitude	83°	10'	49"

Note: Latitude and longitude coordinates shown are based on the North American Datum of 1927 (NAD 27) as currently required by the Mass Media Bureau of the FCC.

Ownership: East Tennessee Public Communications Corp.

Began Operation: September 16, 2005. Began analog operations: March 15, 1967. Ceased analog operations: February 17, 2009.

Personnel:

Teresa James, President & Chief Executive Officer.

Frank Miller, Vice President, Assistant General Manager & In-School Services Director.

Kurtis Allin, Chief Engineer.

Robert Hutchison, Program Director.

Kelly Hodges, Development Director.

Russ Manning, Production Manager.

Cathy Wilson, Traffic Manager.

Christopher Smith, Public Service Director.

Vickie Lawson, Membership Manager.

Robert Bratton, Underwriting Director.

Texas

KACV-DT
Amarillo
Ch. 8

Licensee: Amarillo Junior College District, PO Box 447, Amarillo, TX 79178.

Studio: 2408 S. Jackson, Amarillo, TX 79109.

Mailing Address: PO Box 447, Amarillo, TX 79178.

Phones: 806-371-5222; 806-371-5230. Fax: 806-371-5258.

Email: smith-jw@actx.edu Web Site: http://www.kacv.org

Technical Facilities: Channel No. 8 (180-186 MHz). Authorized power: 5-kw visual, aural. Antenna: 1703-ft above av. terrain, 1580-ft. above ground, 5002-ft. above sea level.

	Latitude	35°	22'	30"
	Longitude	101°	52'	56"

Requests CP for change to channel number 9, 30-kw visual, 1306-ft above av. terrain, 1271-ft. above ground, 4703-ft. above sea level lat. 35° 20' 33", long. 101° 49' 21"; BPEDT-20090903AAZ.

Transmitter: 1.4-mi. NNE of U.S. 87 & Givens Ave.

Note: Latitude and longitude coordinates shown are based on the North American Datum of 1927 (NAD 27) as currently required by the Mass Media Bureau of the FCC.

Ownership: Amarillo Junior College.

Began Operation: April 1, 2004. Standard and High Definition. Began analog operations: August 29, 1988. Ceased analog operations February 17, 2009.

Personnel:

Linda Pitner, General Manager.

Charles Proctor, Chief Engineer.

Alan Greer, Business Manager.

Brian Frank, Program Director.

Jill Frank, Promotion Director.

Jackie Smith, Operations Director.

KLRU-DT
Austin
Ch. 22

Licensee: Capital of Texas Public Telecommunications Council, PO Box 7158, Austin, TX 78713.

Studio: 2504-B Whitis Ave., Austin, TX 78712.

Mailing Address: PO Box 7158, Austin, TX 78713.

Phone: 512-471-4811. Fax: 512-471-5561.

Web Site: http://www.klru.org

Technical Facilities: Channel No. 22 (518-524 MHz). Authorized power: 700-kw max. visual, aural. Antenna: 1173-ft above av. terrain, 1125-ft. above ground, 1960-ft. above sea level.

	Latitude	30°	19'	19"
	Longitude	97°	48'	12"

Note: Latitude and longitude coordinates shown are based on the North American Datum of 1927 (NAD 27) as currently required by the Mass Media Bureau of the FCC.

Ownership: Capital of Texas Public Telecommunications Council.

Began Operation: March 5, 2004. Began analog operations: May 3, 1979. Ceased analog operations: June 12, 2009.

Personnel:

Bill Stotesbery, President & Chief Executive Officer.

David Kuipers, Chief Engineer.

Pat Wertz, Vice President, Finance.

Maria Rodriguez, Vice President, Programming.

Maury Sullivan, Vice President, Marketing & Communications.

Stewart Nelson, Traffic Manager.

Shane Guiter, Membership Director.

Linda Schmid, Vice President, Educational Services.

KITU-DT
Beaumont
Ch. 33

Licensee: Community Educational Television Inc., PO Box 721582, Houston, TX 77272.

Studio: 11221 Interstate 10, Orange, TX 77630.

Mailing Address: PO Box 721582, Houston, TX 77272.

Phone: 409-745-3434. Fax: 409-745-4752.

Web Site: http://www.communityedtv.org

Technical Facilities: Channel No. 33 (584-590 MHz). Authorized power: 500-kw max. visual, aural. Antenna: 1024-ft above av. terrain, 1027-ft. above ground, 1050-ft. above sea level.

	Latitude	30°	10'	41"
	Longitude	93°	54'	26"

Holds CP for change to 1000-kw max. visual; BPEDT-20080618ACT.

Note: Latitude and longitude coordinates shown are based on the North American Datum of 1927 (NAD 27) as currently required by the Mass Media Bureau of the FCC.

Ownership: Community Educational Television Inc.

Began Operation: June 30, 2006. Began analog operations: June 20, 1986. Ceased analog operations: June 12, 2009.

Personnel:

Wayne Ozio, Station Manager & Chief Engineer.

Jacqueline Orr, Production Coordinator.

Harold White, Traffic Manager.

Carol Tallent, Public Affairs Director.

KNCT-DT
Belton
Ch. 46

Licensee: Central Texas College, PO Box 1800, Killeen, TX 76540.

Studio: 6200 W. Central Texas Expwy., Killeen, TX 76549.

Mailing Address: PO Box 1800, Killeen, TX 76540.

Phone: 254-526-1176. **Fax:** 254-526-1850.

Web Site: http://www.knct.org

Technical Facilities: Channel No. 46 (662-668 MHz). Authorized power: 500-kw max. visual, aural. Antenna: 1286-ft above av. terrain, 1117-ft. above ground, 2043-ft. above sea level.

Latitude	30°	59'	08.4"
Longitude	97°	37'	50.1"

Note: Latitude and longitude coordinates shown are based on the North American Datum of 1927 (NAD 27) as currently required by the Mass Media Bureau of the FCC.

Ownership: Central Texas College.

Began Operation: April 23, 2008. Station broadcasting digitally on its analog channel allotment. Began analog operations: November 23, 1970. Ceased analog operations: June 12, 2009.

Personnel:

Max Rudolph, General Manager.

Steve Sulzer, Chief Engineer.

Ruth Wedergren, Program Director.

Fred McNeilly, Promotion Director.

Christian Wohlfahrt, Production Manager.

Steve Benger, M/C Supervisor & Traffic Manager.

Pat McCray, Membership Director.

KAMU-DT
College Station
Ch. 12

Licensee: Texas A & M U., 4244 TAMU, College Station, TX 77843.

Studio: Joe H. Moore Communication Center, 4244 TAMU, College Station, TX 77843.

Mailing Address: 4244 TAMU, Joe H. Moore Communication Center, College Station, TX 77843.

Phone: 979-845-5611. **Fax:** 979-845-1643.

Web Site: http://kamu.tamu.edu

Technical Facilities: Channel No. 12 (204-210 MHz). Authorized power: 3.2-kw visual, aural. Antenna: 344-ft above av. terrain, 344-ft. above ground, 659-ft. above sea level.

Latitude	30°	37'	47"
Longitude	96°	20'	33"

Transmitter: Hensel Park, Texas A & M U. campus.

Note: Latitude and longitude coordinates shown are based on the North American Datum of 1927 (NAD 27) as currently required by the Mass Media Bureau of the FCC.

Satellite Earth Stations: Comark; Vertex, 8.1-meter Ku-band; Andrew, 10-meter C-band; Standard Components receivers.

Ownership: Texas A & M U.

Began Operation: March 18, 2003. Began analog operations: February 15, 1970. Ceased analog operations: June 12, 2009.

Personnel:

Dr. Rodney L. Zent, General Manager.

Anjel Vaughn, Assistant Director, Administration.

Jon P. Bennett, Station Manager & Program Director.

Wayne Pecena, Engineering Director.

Ken Nelson, Chief Engineer.

Elaine Hoyak, Development Director.

KEDT-DT
Corpus Christi
Ch. 23

Grantee: South Texas Public Broadcasting System, 4455 S Padre Island Dr, Ste 38, Corpus Christi, TX 78411.

Studio: 4455 S. Padre Island Dr., Suite 38, Corpus Christi, TX 78411.

Mailing Address: 4455 S. Padre Island Dr, Ste 38, Corpus Christi, TX 78411.

Phone: 361-855-2213. **Fax:** 361-855-3877.

Web Site: http://www.kedt.org

Technical Facilities: Channel No. 23 (524-530 MHz). Authorized power: 50-kw max. visual, aural. Antenna: 886-ft above av. terrain, 886-ft. above ground, 935-ft. above sea level.

Latitude	27°	39'	20"
Longitude	97°	33'	55"

Note: Latitude and longitude coordinates shown are based on the North American Datum of 1927 (NAD 27) as currently required by the Mass Media Bureau of the FCC.

Ownership: South Texas Public Broadcasting System.

Began Operation: October 24, 2008. Began analog operations: October 15, 1972. Ceased analog operations: June 12, 2009.

Personnel:

Don Dunlap, President & General Manager.

Cody Blount, Operations & Engineering Director.

Myra Lombardo, Vice President, Administration.

Stewart Jacoby, Program Director.

Jeff Felts, Production Manager.

Donna Frank, Educational Services Director.

Michelle Salazar, Traffic Coordinator.

KERA-DT
Dallas
Ch. 14

Licensee: North Texas Public Broadcasting Inc., 3000 Harry Hines Blvd, Dallas, TX 75201.

Studio: 3000 Harry Hines Blvd., Dallas, TX 75201.

Mailing Address: 3000 Harry Hines Blvd, Dallas, TX 75201.

Phone: 214-871-1390. **Fax:** 214-754-0635.

Web Site: http://www.kera.org/

Technical Facilities: Channel No. 14 (470-476 MHz). Authorized power: 475-kw max. visual, aural. Antenna: 1640-ft above av. terrain, 1479-ft. above ground, 2277-ft. above sea level.

Latitude	32°	34'	43"
Longitude	96°	57'	12"

Transmitter: Approx. 0.7-mi. S of Cedar Hill.

Note: Latitude and longitude coordinates shown are based on the North American Datum of 1927 (NAD 27) as currently required by the Mass Media Bureau of the FCC.

Multichannel TV Sound: Stereo and separate audio program.

Satellite Earth Station: Andrew, 10-meter Ku & C-band; General Instrument receivers.

Ownership: North Texas Public Broadcasting Inc.

Began Operation: December 1, 2000. Began analog operations: September 11, 1960. Ceased analog operations: June 12, 2009.

Personnel:

Mary Anne Alhadeff, President & Chief Executive Officer.

Jason Daisey, Executive Vice President & Chief Operations Officer.

Shelley Kofler, News Director.

David Jones, Vice President, Technology.

Bill Young, Vice President, Programming.

Angela Gieras, Vice President, Membership Development.

Debbie Diaz, Vice President, Corporate Development.

Deanna Collingwood, Interim Senior Vice President, Development.

Sylvia Komatsu, Senior Vice President, Content.

KDTN-DT
Denton
Ch. 43

Licensee: Community Television Educators of DFW Inc., 3901 Hwy 121 S, Bedford, TX 76021-3009.

Studio: 3901 Hwy. 121 S, Bedford, TX 76021.

Mailing Address: 3901 Hwy 121 S, Bedford, TX 76021.

Phone: 817-571-1229. **Fax:** 817-571-7458.

Web Site: http://www.daystar.com

Technical Facilities: Channel No. 43 (644-650 MHz). Authorized power: 1000-kw max. visual, aural. Antenna: 1621-ft above av. terrain, 1474-ft. above ground, 2288-ft. above sea level.

Latitude	32°	32'	35"
Longitude	96°	57'	32"

Note: Latitude and longitude coordinates shown are based on the North American Datum of 1927 (NAD 27) as currently required by the Mass Media Bureau of the FCC.

Ownership: Community Television Educators of DFW Inc.

Began Operation: August 12, 2004. Began analog operations: September 1, 1988. Sale to present owner by North Texas Public Broadcasting Inc. approved by FCC October 24, 2003. Ceased analog operations: June 12, 2009.

Personnel:

Marcus Lamb, President & Chief Executive Officer.

Steve Wilhite, Senior Vice President, Affiliate Relations.

Arnold Torres, Business Administrator.

Jeanette Hawkins, Marketing Director.

KCOS-DT
El Paso
Ch. 13

Licensee: El Paso Public Television Foundation, 500 W. University Ave, El Paso, TX 79968-0650.

Studio: 950 Viscount Blvd, Ste A-440, El Paso, TX 79925.

Mailing Address: PO Box 26668, El Paso, TX 79926.

Phone: 915-590-1313. **Fax:** 915-594-5394.

Web Site: http://www.kcostv.org

Technical Facilities: Channel No. 13 (210-216 MHz). Authorized power: 27-kw visual, aural. Antenna: 850-ft above av. terrain, 259-ft. above ground, 4921-ft. above sea level.

Latitude	31°	47'	15"
Longitude	106°	28'	47"

Requests CP for change to 42-kw visual; BPEDT-20090716ABN.

Note: Latitude and longitude coordinates shown are based on the North American Datum of 1927 (NAD 27) as currently required by the Mass Media Bureau of the FCC.

Ownership: El Paso Public Television Foundation.

Began Operation: July 28, 2006. Station broadcasting digitally on its analog channel allotment. Began analog operations: August 18, 1978. Ceased analog operations: June 12, 2009.

Personnel:

Craig Brush, President & General Manager.

David Echaniz, Engineering Director.

Juan Barrera, Assistant Engineering Director.

Barbara Hakim, Vice President, Business Affairs.

Mike Seymour, Program Manager.

Louis Moreno, Marketing Director.

Jim Heiney, Promotion & Public Relations Director.

Leticia Alderete, Production Manager.

Trashelta Tyler, Traffic Manager.

KSCE-DT
El Paso
Ch. 39

Licensee: Channel 38 Christian TV, 6400 Escondido D, El Paso, TX 79912.

Studio: 6400 Escondido, El Paso, TX 79912.

Mailing Address: 6400 Escondido Dr, El Paso, TX 79912.

Phone: 915-585-8838. Fax: 915-585-8841.

Web Site: http://www.kscetv.com

Technical Facilities: Channel No. 39 (320-626 MHz). Authorized power: 50-kw max. visual, aural. Antenna: 164-ft above av. terrain, 174-ft above ground, 590-ft. above sea level.

Latitude	31°	48'	55"
Longitude	106°	29'	17"

Holds CP for change to 150-kw max. visual, 1827-ft above av. terrain, 299-ft. above ground, 5902-ft. above sea level lat. 31° 48' 19", long. 106° 28' 59"; BPEDT-20080620AAC.

Note: Latitude and longitude coordinates shown are based on the North American Datum of 1927 (NAD 27) as currently required by the Mass Media Bureau of the FCC.

Ownership: Channel 38 Christian TV.

Began Operation: March 31, 2008. Began analog operations: April 15, 1989. Ceased analog operations: June 12, 2009.

Personnel:

Grace Rendall, General Manager.

Mark Stephenson, Traffic Manager.

KLTJ-DT
Galveston
Ch. 23

Grantee: Community TV Educators of Texas Inc., 3901 Hwy 121 S, Bedford, TX 76021-3009.

Studio: 1050 Gemini St., Houston, TX 77058.

Mailing Address: 1050 Gemini St, Houston, TX 77058.

Phone: 281-212-1022. Fax: 281-212-1031.

Web Site: http://www.daystar.com

Technical Facilities: Channel No. 23 (524-530 MHz). Authorized power: 2-kw max. visual, aural. Antenna: 1900-ft above av. terrain, 1883-ft. above ground, 1960-ft. above sea level.

Latitude	29°	34'	15"
Longitude	95°	30'	37"

Holds CP for change to 350-kw max. visual; BPEDT-20080617AAD.

Note: Latitude and longitude coordinates shown are based on the North American Datum of 1927 (NAD 27) as currently required by the Mass Media Bureau of the FCC.

Ownership: Word of God Fellowship Inc.

Began Operation: February 12, 2008. Began analog operations: July 24, 1989. Sale to present owner by Go Inc. approved by FCC October 18, 1999. Ceased analog operations: June 12, 2009.

Personnel:

Nathan Williams, General Manager.

Lugderio D'Orville, Traffic Manager.

Byron Gehret, Production Manager.

D'Andria Banks, Financial Manager.

KLUJ-DT
Harlingen
Ch. 34

Licensee: Community Educational Television Inc., PO Box 721582, Houston, TX 77272.

Studio: 1920 Loop 499, Ste 117, Harlingen, TX 78550.

Mailing Address: 1920 Loop 499, Ste 117, Harlingen, TX 78550.

Phone: 956-425-4225. Fax: 956-412-1740.

Technical Facilities: Channel No. 34 (590-596 MHz). Authorized power: 45-kw max. visual, aural. Antenna: 928-ft above av. terrain, 928-ft. above ground, 978-ft. above sea level.

Latitude	26°	13'	00"
Longitude	97°	46'	48"

Transmitter: Side of KLUJ(TV) tower, 1.5-mi. WSW of intersection of Wilson Tract & Primera.

Note: Latitude and longitude coordinates shown are based on the North American Datum of 1927 (NAD 27) as currently required by the Mass Media Bureau of the FCC.

Ownership: Community Educational Television Inc.

Began Operation: April 2, 2007. Began analog operations: June 25, 1984. Ceased analog operations: June 12, 2009.

Personnel:

Mary Campos, Station Manager.

Andy Mandiola, Chief Engineer.

KMBH-DT
Harlingen
Ch. 38

Licensee: RGV Educational Broadcasting Inc., PO Box 2147, Harlingen, TX 78551.

Studio: 1701 Tennessee Ave., Harlingen, TX 78550.

Mailing Address: PO Box 2147, Harlingen, TX 78551.

Phones: 956-421-4111; 800-433-2522. Fax: 956-421-4150.

Web Site: http://www.kmbh.org

Technical Facilities: Channel No. 38 (614-620 MHz). Authorized power: 1000-kw max. visual, aural. Antenna: 1134-ft above av. terrain, 1130-ft. above ground, 1182-ft. above sea level.

Latitude	26°	07'	14"
Longitude	97°	49'	18"

Note: Latitude and longitude coordinates shown are based on the North American Datum of 1927 (NAD 27) as currently required by the Mass Media Bureau of the FCC.

Ownership: RGV Educational Broadcasting Inc.

Began Operation: December 5, 2003. Began analog operations: April 30, 1982. Ceased analog operations: February 17, 2009.

Personnel:

Pedro Briseno, President & General Manager.

John Ross, Engineering Director.

Dianna Lee Alcalde, Business Manager.

Jesse Mendez, TV Producer.

David Holden, Business Support Manager.

Norma Villarreal, Membership Manager.

Ismael Herrera, TV Producer.

KETH-DT
Houston
Ch. 24

Licensee: Community Educational Television Inc., 10902 S Wilcrest Dr, Houston, TX 77099.

Studio: 10902 S. Wilcrest Dr., Houston, TX 77099.

Mailing Address: 10902 S. Wilcrest Dr, Houston, TX 77099.

Phone: 281-561-5828. Fax: 281-561-9793.

Web Site: http://www.communityedtv.org

Technical Facilities: Channel No. 24 (530-536 MHz). Authorized power: 900-kw max. visual, aural. Antenna: 1900-ft above av. terrain, 1883-ft. above ground, 1960-ft. above sea level.

Latitude	29°	34'	15"
Longitude	95°	30'	37"

Holds CP for change to 1000-kw max. visual, 1903-ft above av. terrain, 1883-ft. above ground, 1960-ft. above sea level; BPEDT-20080620ANS.

Note: Latitude and longitude coordinates shown are based on the North American Datum of 1927 (NAD 27) as currently required by the Mass Media Bureau of the FCC.

Ownership: Community Educational Television Inc.

Began Operation: February 2, 2005. Began analog operations: July 16, 1987. Ceased analog operations: June 12, 2009.

Personnel:

Laura Hanks, Operations Manager.

Rod Hardy, Chief Engineer.

Gil Delaney, Production Manager.

Carlton Ricketts, Traffic Manager.

KUHT-DT
Houston
Ch. 8

Licensee: U. of Houston System, 4343 Elgin St, Houston, TX 77204.

Studio: 4343 Elgin St., Houston, TX 77204.

Mailing Address: 4343 Elgin St, Houston, TX 77204.

Phone: 713-748-8888. Fax: 713-743-8867.

Web Site: http://www.houstonpbs.org

Technical Facilities: Channel No. 8 (180-186 MHz). Authorized power: 34.3-kw visual, aural. Antenna: 1898-ft above av. terrain, 1882-ft. above ground, 1961-ft. above sea level.

Latitude	29°	34'	29"
Longitude	95°	29'	37"

Requests modification of CP for change to 71-kw visual, 1857-ft above av. terrain, 1841-ft. above ground, 1919-ft. above sea level; BMPEDT-20090730ACE.

Transmitter: 4-mi. SE of Missouri City.

Note: Latitude and longitude coordinates shown are based on the North American Datum of 1927 (NAD 27) as currently required by the Mass Media Bureau of the FCC.

Ownership: U. of Houston.

Began Operation: May 1, 2001. Station broadcasting digitally on its analog channel allotment. Began analog operations: May 12, 1953. Ceased analog operations: June 12, 2009.

Personnel:

John Hesse, General Manager.

Steve Pyndus, Operations Director.

Marty Kirkland, Engineering Director.

Bill Anderson, Chief Engineer.

Georgeann Smith, Business & Finance Director.

Ken Lawrence, Program Director.

Gary Nilsen, On-Air Promotion Manager.

Francisco Castro, Production Manager.

Linda Olson, Development Director.

KTXT-DT
Lubbock
Ch. 39

Licensee: Texas Tech U., PO Box 42161, Lubbock, TX 79409.

Studio: 17th St & Indiana Ave, Lubbock, TX 79409.

Mailing Address: PO Box 42161, Lubbock, TX 79409.

Phone: 806-742-2209. Fax: 806-742-1274.

Web Site: http://www.ktxt.org

Technical Facilities: Channel No. 39 (320-626 MHz). Authorized power: 890-kw max. visual, aural. Antenna: 469-ft above av. terrain, 476-ft. above ground, 3701-ft. above sea level.

Latitude	33°	34'	55"
Longitude	101°	53'	25"

Holds CP for change to 665-ft above av. terrain, 672-ft. above ground, 3897-ft. above sea level; BPEDT-20080619AFE.

Note: Latitude and longitude coordinates shown are based on the North American Datum of 1927 (NAD 27) as currently required by the Mass Media Bureau of the FCC.

Ownership: Texas Tech U.

Began Operation: November 24, 2003. Began analog operations: October 16, 1962. Ceased analog operations: February 17, 2009.

Personnel:

Pat Cates, General Manager.

Patricia Guy, Promotion Director.

Kelley Titts, Development Manager.

Sheryl Headlee, Senior Office Assistant.

Natalie Sparks, Outreach Coordinator.

Michelle Dillard, Program & Traffic Manager.

KPBT-DT
Odessa
Ch. 22

Licensee: Permian Basin Public Telecommunications Inc., 550 W Texas Ave, Ste 800, Midland, TX 79764.

Studio: 302 E. 29th St., Odessa, TX 79762.

Mailing Address: PO Box 8940, Midland, TX 79708-8940.

Phone: 432-580-0036. **Fax:** 432-563-5731.

Web Site: http://www.basinpbs.org

Technical Facilities: Channel No. 22 (518-524 MHz). Authorized power: 50-kw max. visual, aural. Antenna: 262-ft above av. terrain, 276-ft. above ground, 3189-ft. above sea level.

Latitude	31°	51'	58"
Longitude	102°	22'	48"

Holds CP for change to channel number 38, 220-kw max. visual; BMPEDT-20080813AEN.

Note: Latitude and longitude coordinates shown are based on the North American Datum of 1927 (NAD 27) as currently required by the Mass Media Bureau of the FCC.

Ownership: Permian Basin Public Telecommunications Inc.

Began Operation: August 19, 2008. Began analog operations: March 24, 1986. Sale to present owner by Ector County Independent School District approved by FCC November 22, 2005. Sale to Ector County Independent School District from Odessa Junior College District approved by FCC January 14, 2004. Ceased analog operations: February 17, 2009.

Personnel:

Dapne Dowdy, General Manager.

Domingo Machuca, Chief Engineer.

Amy Lynch, Program Director & Traffic Manager.

Melissa Burnett, Development Director.

Christie Gesell, Sponsorship Director.

KHCE-DT
San Antonio
Ch. 16

Licensee: San Antonio Community Educational TV Inc., PO Box 721582, Houston, TX 77272.

Studio: 15533 Capital Port Dr., San Antonio, TX 78249.

Mailing Address: PO Box 691246, San Antonio, TX 78269.

Phone: 210-479-0123. **Fax:** 210-492-5679.

Web Site: http://www.khce.org

Technical Facilities: Channel No. 16 (482-488 MHz). Authorized power: 500-kw max. visual, aural. Antenna: 1007-ft above av. terrain, 1001-ft. above ground, 1541-ft. above sea level.

Latitude	29°	17'	24"
Longitude	98°	15'	20"

Requests CP for change to 850-kw max. visual; BPEDT-20080618ARI.

Holds CP for change to 360-kw max. visual, 1076-ft above av. terrain, 1066-ft. above ground, 1606-ft. above sea level; BPEDT-20080313AAS.

Note: Latitude and longitude coordinates shown are based on the North American Datum of 1927 (NAD 27) as currently required by the Mass Media Bureau of the FCC.

Ownership: San Antonio Community Educational TV Inc.

Began Operation: March 1, 2005. Began analog operations: July 9, 1989. Ceased analog operations: June 12, 2009.

Personnel:

Dorcas Rogers, Station Manager.

Adam Mendez, Traffic & Operations Manager.

Sharon Denney, Public Affairs Director.

KLRN-DT
San Antonio
Ch. 9

Licensee: Alamo Public Telecommunications Council, PO Box 9, San Antonio, TX 78291-0009.

Studio: 501 Broadway, San Antonio, TX 78215.

Mailing Address: PO Box 9, San Antonio, TX 78291-0009.

Phone: 210-270-9000. **Fax:** 210-270-9078.

Email: eresendiz@klrn.org **Web Site:** http://www.klrn.org

Technical Facilities: Channel No. 9 (186-192 MHz). Authorized power: 13.6-kw visual, aural. Antenna: 938-ft above av. terrain, 1006-ft. above ground, 1501-ft. above sea level.

Latitude	29°	19'	38.1"
Longitude	98°	21'	17"

Note: Latitude and longitude coordinates shown are based on the North American Datum of 1927 (NAD 27) as currently required by the Mass Media Bureau of the FCC.

Satellite Earth Station: Harris; SatCom, 7-meter C-band; Standard Communications, Scientific-Atlanta receivers.

Ownership: Alamo Public Telecommunications Council.

Began Operation: September 14, 2004. Station broadcasting digitally on its analog channel allotment. Began analog operations: September 10, 1962. Ceased analog operations: June 12, 2009.

Personnel:

Joanne Winik, President & General Manager.

Pete Gonzalez, Vice President, Engineering.

Patrick A. Lopez, Vice President, Financial.

Charles Vaughn, Senior Vice President, Telecommunications & Programming.

Ellen Evans, Vice President, Marketing.

Lisa McGrath, Vice President, Education.

Katrina Kehoe, Public Relations Manager.

KWBU-DT
Waco
Ch. 20

Licensee: Brazos Valley Public Broadcasting Foundation, One Bear Pl, Ste 97296, Waco, TX 76798.

Studio: Castellaw Communications Bldg, Waco, TX 76798.

Mailing Address: 1 Bear Pl, Ste 97296, Waco, TX 76798-7296.

Phone: 254-710-3472. **Fax:** 254-710-3874.

Web Site: http://www.kwbu.org

Technical Facilities: Channel No. 20 (506-512 MHz). Authorized power: 700-kw max. visual, aural. Antenna: 1047-ft above av. terrain, 959-ft. above ground, 1719-ft. above sea level.

Latitude	31°	19'	17"
Longitude	97°	20'	40"

Note: Latitude and longitude coordinates shown are based on the North American Datum of 1927 (NAD 27) as currently required by the Mass Media Bureau of the FCC.

Ownership: Brazos Valley Public Broadcasting Foundation.

Began Operation: June 22, 2006. Began analog operations: May 22, 1989. Ceased analog operations: February 17, 2009.

Personnel:

Polly Anderson, President & Chief Executive Officer.

Clare Paul, Station Manager.

Ashley Kortis, Corporate Support Director.

Anthony Poole, Chief Engineer.

Carla Hervey, Business Affairs Manager.

Loretta Howard, Membership Director.

Utah

KUEN-DT
Ogden
Ch. 36

Licensee: Utah State Board of Regents, 101 S Wasatch Dr, Eccles Broadcast Center, Salt Lake City, UT 84112.

Studio: 101 S Wasatch Dr, U of Utah, Salt Lake City, UT 84112.

Mailing Address: 101 S Wasatch Dr, Eccles Broadcast Center, Salt Lake City, UT 84112.

Phone: 801-581-2999. **Fax:** 801-585-6105.

Web Site: http://www.uen.org/tv

Technical Facilities: Channel No. 36 (602-608 MHz). Authorized power: 200-kw max. visual, aural. Antenna: 4157-ft above av. terrain, 287-ft. above ground, 9322-ft. above sea level.

Latitude	40°	39'	33"
Longitude	112°	12'	07"

Transmitter: Farnsworth Peak, 6.2-mi. SW of Magna.

Note: Latitude and longitude coordinates shown are based on the North American Datum of 1927 (NAD 27) as currently required by the Mass Media Bureau of the FCC.

Ownership: U. of Utah.

Began Operation: April 29, 2003. Began analog operations: December 1, 1986. Ceased analog operations: June 12, 2009.

Personnel:

Laura Hunter, General Manager.

Phillip Titus, Chief Engineer.

Kyle Anderson, Program Director.

Bill Kucera, Promotion & Marketing Director.

KBYU-DT
Provo
Ch. 44

Licensee: Brigham Young U., 2000 Ironton Blvd, Provo, UT 84606.

Studio: Room C-302, Harris Fine Arts Center, Brigham Young U., Provo, UT 84602.

Mailing Address: Brigham Young U., Harris Fine Arts Center C-302, Provo, UT 84602.

Phones: 801-422-8450; 800-298-5298. **Fax:** 801-422-8478.

Email: derek.marquis@byu.edu **Web Site:** http://www.byub.org

Technical Facilities: Channel No. 44 (650-656 MHz). Authorized power: 346-kw max. visual, aural. Antenna: 4124-ft above av. terrain, 256-ft. above ground, 9291-ft. above sea level.

Latitude	40°	39'	33"
Longitude	112°	12'	07"

Holds CP for change to 402.8-kw max. visual; BPEDT-20060120ADA.

Note: Latitude and longitude coordinates shown are based on the North American Datum of 1927 (NAD 27) as currently required by the Mass Media Bureau of the FCC.

Ownership: Brigham Young U.

Began Operation: August 1, 2002. Began analog operations: November 15, 1965. Ceased analog operations: June 12, 2009.

Personnel:

Derek Marquis, Managing Director.

Wes Sims, News Director.

Brandon Smith, Chief Engineer.

Steven V. Sorenson, Finance & Business Administration Director.

Wendy Thomas, Programming Manager.

Alana Tilley, Human Resource Manager.

Daniel Hubbard, Creative & Information Services Manager.

Sterling Van Wagenen, Content & Media Integration Director.

KUES-DT
Richfield
Ch. 19

Licensee: U. of Utah, 101 S Wasatch Dr, Eccles Broadcast Center, Salt Lake City, UT 84112.

Studio: 101 S Wasatch Dr, U of Utah, Salt Lake City, UT 84112.

Mailing Address: 101 S Wasatch Dr, Eccles Broadcast Center, Salt Lake City, UT 84112.

Phones: 801-581-7777; 801-581-3064. **Fax:** 801-587-5096.

Web Site: http://www.kued.org

Technical Facilities: Channel No. 19 (500-506 MHz). Authorized power: 1.2-kw max. visual, 0.33-kw aural. Antenna: 1447-ft above av. terrain, 56-ft. above ground, 8816-ft. above sea level.

Latitude	38°	38'	04"
Longitude	112°	03'	33"

Transmitter: 3.5-mi. E of Monroe.

Note: Latitude and longitude coordinates shown are based on the North American Datum of 1927 (NAD 27) as currently required by the Mass Media Bureau of the FCC.

Multichannel TV Sound: Stereo and separate audio program.

Ownership: U. of Utah.

Began Operation: July 1, 2000. Broadcasting digitally on its analog allotment; no analog broadcast.

Personnel:

Larry S. Smith, General Manager.

Phillip Titus, Chief Engineer.

Scott Chaffin, Broadcasting Director.

Ken Verdoia, Production Director.

Mary Dickson, Creative Services Director.

KUED-DT
Salt Lake City
Ch. 42

Licensee: U. of Utah, 101 S Wasatch Dr, Eccles Broadcast Center, Salt Lake City, UT 84112.

Studio: 101 S Wasatch Dr, U. of Utah, Salt Lake City, UT 84112.

Mailing Address: 101 S Wasatch Dr, Eccles Broadcast Center, Salt Lake City, UT 84112.

Phone: 801-581-7777. **Fax:** 801-587-5096.

Email: cmorris@media.utah.edu **Web Site:** http://www.kued.org

Technical Facilities: Channel No. 42 (638-644 MHz). Authorized power: 239-kw max. visual, aural. Antenna: 4153-ft above av. terrain, 287-ft. above ground, 9322-ft. above sea level.

Latitude	40°	39'	33"
Longitude	112°	12'	07"

Note: Latitude and longitude coordinates shown are based on the North American Datum of 1927 (NAD 27) as currently required by the Mass Media Bureau of the FCC.

Ownership: U. of Utah.

Began Operation: September 1, 2001. Began analog operations: January 20, 1958. Ceased analog operations: June 12, 2009.

Personnel:

Larry S. Smith, General Manager.

Scott Chaffin, Broadcasting Director.

Phillip Titus, Chief Engineer.

Ken Verdoia, Production Director.

Mary Dickson, Creative Services Director.

KUEW-DT
St. George
Ch. 18

Licensee: U. of Utah, 101 S Wasatch Dr, Eccles Broadcast Center, Salt Lake City, UT 84112.

Studio: 101 S Wasatch Dr, U of Utah, Salt Lake City, UT 84112.

Mailing Address: 101 S Wasatch Dr, Eccles Broadcast Center, Salt Lake City, UT 84112.

Phone: 801-581-7777. **Fax:** 801-587-5096.

Web Site: http://www.kued.org

Technical Facilities: Channel No. 18 (494-500 MHz). Authorized power: 1.62-kw max. visual, aural. Antenna: 218-ft above av. terrain, 75-ft. above ground, 3216-ft. above sea level.

Latitude	37°	03'	50"
Longitude	113°	34'	20"

Note: Latitude and longitude coordinates shown are based on the North American Datum of 1927 (NAD 27) as currently required by the Mass Media Bureau of the FCC.

Ownership: U. of Utah.

Began Operation: August 26, 2002. Station went directly to digital broadcast; no analog application.

Personnel:

Larry Smith, General Manager.

Phillip Titus, Chief Engineer.

Mary Dickson, Creative Services Director.

Ken Verdoia, Production Director.

Scott Chaffin, Broadcasting Director.

Vermont

WETK-DT
Burlington
Ch. 32

Licensee: Vermont Public Television, 204 Ethan Allen Ave, Colchester, VT 05446.

Studio: 204 Ethan Allen Ave., Colchester, VT 05446.

Mailing Address: 204 Ethan Allen Ave, Colchester, VT 05446.

Phone: 802-655-4800. **Fax:** 802-655-6593.

Email: llee@vpt.org **Web Site:** http://www.vpt.org

Technical Facilities: Channel No. 32 (578-584 MHz). Authorized power: 90-kw max. visual, aural. Antenna: 2723-ft above av. terrain, 100-ft. above ground, 4110-ft. above sea level.

Latitude	44°	31'	32"
Longitude	72°	48'	51"

Note: Latitude and longitude coordinates shown are based on the North American Datum of 1927 (NAD 27) as currently required by the Mass Media Bureau of the FCC.

Ownership: Vermont ETV Inc.

Began Operation: September 28, 2006. Began analog operations: October 16, 1967. Ceased analog operations: February 17, 2009.

Personnel:

John E. King, President & Chief Executive Officer.

Dan Harvey, Vice President, Production & General Manager.

Ronald A. Whitcomb, Chief Engineer.

Andrea Bergeron, Vice President, Finance & Chief Financial Officer.

Kelly Luoma, Vice President, Programming & Educational Services.

Ann Curran, Marketing & Communications Manager.

Lee Ann Lee, Vice President, Marketing & Development.

WVER-DT
Rutland
Ch. 9

Licensee: Vermont Public Television, 204 Ethan Allen Ave, Colchester, VT 05446.

Studio: 204 Ethan Allen Ave., Colchester, VT 05446.

Mailing Address: 204 Ethan Allen Ave, Colchester, VT 05446.

Phone: 802-655-4800. **Fax:** 802-655-6593.

Email: llee@vpt.org **Web Site:** http://www.vpt.org

Technical Facilities: Channel No. 9 (186-192 MHz). Authorized power: 15-kw visual, aural. Antenna: 1263-ft above av. terrain, 130-ft. above ground, 2105-ft. above sea level.

Latitude	43°	39'	31"
Longitude	73°	06'	25"

Note: Latitude and longitude coordinates shown are based on the North American Datum of 1927 (NAD 27) as currently required by the Mass Media Bureau of the FCC.

Ownership: Vermont ETV Inc.

Began Operation: June 1, 2005. Began analog operations: March 18, 1968. Ceased analog operations: February 17, 2009.

Personnel:

John King, President & Chief Executive Officer.

Dan Harvey, Vice President, Production & General Manager.

Ronald A. Whitcomb, Chief Engineer.

Andrea Bergeron, Vice President, Finance & Chief Financial Officer.

Kelly Luoma, Vice President, Programming & Educational Services.

Lee Ann Lee, Vice President, Marketing & Development.

Ann Curran, Marketing & Communications Manager.

WVTB-DT
St. Johnsbury
Ch. 18

Licensee: Vermont Public Television, 204 Ethan Allen Ave, Colchester, VT 05446.

Studio: 204 Ethan Allen Ave., Colchester, VT 05446.

Mailing Address: 204 Ethan Allen Ave, Colchester, VT 05446.

Phone: 802-655-4800. **Fax:** 802-655-6593.

Email: llee@vpt.org **Web Site:** http://www.vpt.org

Technical Facilities: Channel No. 18 (494-500 MHz). Authorized power: 75-kw max. visual, aural. Antenna: 1936-ft above av. terrain, 99-ft. above ground, 3354-ft. above sea level.

Latitude	44°	34'	16"
Longitude	71°	53'	39"

Holds CP for change to 67-kw max. visual; BPEDT-20071026ABW.

Note: Latitude and longitude coordinates shown are based on the North American Datum of 1927 (NAD 27) as currently required by the Mass Media Bureau of the FCC.

Ownership: Vermont ETV Inc.

Began Operation: August 1, 2006. Began analog operations: February 26, 1968. Ceased analog operations: February 17, 2009.

Personnel:

John E. King, President & Chief Executive Officer.

Dan Harvey, Vice President, Production & General Manager.

Ronald A. Whitcomb, Chief Engineer.

Andrea Bergeron, Vice President, Finance & Chief Financial Officer.

Kelly Luoma, Vice President, Programming & Educational Services.

Lee Ann Lee, Vice President, Marketing & Development.

Ann Curran, Marketing & Communications Manager.

WVTA-DT
Windsor
Ch. 24

Grantee: Vermont Public Television, 204 Ethan Allen Ave, Colchester, VT 05446-3129.

Studio: 204 Ethan Allen Ave., Colchester, VT 05446.

Mailing Address: 204 Ethan Allen Ave, Colchester, VT 05446.

Phone: 802-655-4800. **Fax:** 802-655-6593.

Email: llee@vpt.org **Web Site:** http://www.vpt.org

Technical Facilities: Channel No. 24 (530-536 MHz). Authorized power: 55.7-kw max. visual, aural. Antenna: 2270-ft above av. terrain, 400-ft. above ground, 3260-ft. above sea level.

Latitude	43°	26'	14.7"
Longitude	72°	27'	07.7"

Transmitter: Mount Ascutney.

Note: Latitude and longitude coordinates shown are based on the North American Datum of 1927 (NAD 27) as currently required by the Mass Media Bureau of the FCC.

Ownership: Vermont ETV Inc.

Began Operation: February 17, 2009. Began analog operations: March 18, 1968. Ceased analog operations: February 17, 2009.

Personnel:

John E. King, President & Chief Executive Officer.

Dan Harvey, Vice President, Production & General Manager.

Ronald A. Whitcomb, Chief Engineer.

Andrea Bergeron, Vice President, Finance & Chief Financial Officer.

Kelly Luoma, Vice President, Programming & Educational Services.

Lee Ann Lee, Vice President, Marketing & Development.

Ann Curran, Marketing & Communications Manager.

Virginia

WHTJ-DT
Charlottesville
Ch. 46

Licensee: Commonwealth Public Broadcasting Corp., 23 Sesame St, Richmond, VA 23235.

Studio: 528 E Main St, Charlottesville, VA 22902.

Mailing Address: 528 E Main St, Charlottesville, VA 22902.

Phones: 804-320-1301; 434-295-7671. **Fax:** 434-295-2813.

Web Site: http://www.ideastations.org

Technical Facilities: Channel No. 46 (662-668 MHz). Authorized power: 165-kw max. visual, aural. Antenna: 1088-ft above av. terrain, 236-ft. above ground, 1637-ft. above sea level.

Latitude	37°	58'	59"
Longitude	78°	29'	02"

Holds CP for change to 340-kw max. visual, 1089-ft above av. terrain, 236-ft. above ground, 1637-ft. above sea level; BPEDT-20080610AAP.

Note: Latitude and longitude coordinates shown are based on the North American Datum of 1927 (NAD 27) as currently required by the Mass Media Bureau of the FCC.

Ownership: Commonwealth Public Broadcasting Corp.

Began Operation: August 18, 2005. Began analog operations: May 19, 1989. Ceased analog operations: June 12, 2009.

Personnel:

A. Curtis Monk, President & Chief Executive Officer.

John H. Felton, Executive Vice President & General Manager.

Mark Spiller, Vice President, Engineering.

D. J. Crotteau, WHTJ Station Manager.

Lisa Tait, Vice President, Development & Communications.

David M. DeBarger, Creative Services Director.

Iris Beverly, Vice President, Education Services.

Lynne McCarthy-Jones, Communications Manager.

WNVC-DT
Fairfax
Ch. 57

Licensee: Commonwealth Public Broadcasting Corp., 23 Sesame St, Richmond, VA 23235.

Studio: 8101A Lee Hwy., Falls Church, VA 22042.

Mailing Address: 8101A Lee Hwy, Falls Church, VA 22042.

Phone: 703-770-7100. **Fax:** 703-770-7112.

Web Site: http://www.mhznetworks.org

Technical Facilities: Channel No. 57 (728-734 MHz). Authorized power: 7.3-kw max. visual, aural. Antenna: 570-ft above av. terrain, 500-ft. above ground, 862-ft. above sea level.

Latitude	38°	52'	28"
Longitude	77°	13'	24"

Holds CP for change to channel number 24, 160-kw max. visual, 725-ft above av. terrain, 658-ft. above ground, 1020-ft. above sea level; BMPEDT-20080609ACI.

Note: Latitude and longitude coordinates shown are based on the North American Datum of 1927 (NAD 27) as currently required by the Mass Media Bureau of the FCC.

Ownership: Commonwealth Public Broadcasting Corp.

Began Operation: December 30, 2003. Station ceased digital operations September 1, 2008 to complete construction of facilities. Began analog operations: June 1, 1983. Ceased analog operations: February 16, 2009.

Personnel:

Frederick Thomas, General Manager.

Nancy Sherwood, Manager of Station Relations.

David Hurd, Chief Engineer.

Dave Powell, Engineering Director.

Katie Abell, Program Director.

Stephanie Misar, Marketing Director.

Grant Oines, Business Development Director.

Chris Hunter, Digital Content Creator, Promotion Director & Production Manager.

Chris Arth, Traffic Manager.

WVPY-DT
Front Royal
Ch. 21

Licensee: Shenandoah Valley Educational Television Corp, 298 Port Republic Rd, Harrisonburg, VA 22801-3063.

Studio: 298 Port Republic Rd., Harrisonburg, VA 22801.

Mailing Address: 298 Port Republic Rd, Harrisonburg, VA 22801-3052.

Phones: 540-434-5391; 800-345-9878. **Fax:** 540-434-7084.

Web Site: http://www.wvpt.net

Technical Facilities: Channel No. 21 (512-518 MHz). Authorized power: 50-kw max. visual, aural. Antenna: 1312-ft above av. terrain, 85-ft. above ground, 2195-ft. above sea level.

Latitude	38°	57'	36"
Longitude	78°	19'	52"

Holds CP for change to 100-kw max. visual, 1312-ft above av. terrain, 85-ft. above ground, 2192-ft. above sea level; BPEDT-20081022ACD.

Note: Latitude and longitude coordinates shown are based on the North American Datum of 1927 (NAD 27) as currently required by the Mass Media Bureau of the FCC.

Ownership: Shenandoah Valley Educational TV Corp.

Began Operation: December 20, 2002. Began analog operations: August 22, 1996. Ceased analog operations: June 12, 2009.

Personnel:

Bert Schmidt, President & General Manager.

Tony Mancari, Vice President & Chief Operating Officer.

Tony Barrick, Chief Engineer.

Larry Hedrick, Chief Financial Officer.

Wanda Zimmerman, Program Director.

Gail Smith, Corporate Communications Director.

WNVT-DT
Goldvein
Ch. 30

Licensee: Commonwealth Public Broadcasting Corp., 23 Sesame St, Richmond, VA 23235.

Studio: 8101A Lee Hwy., Falls Church, VA 22042.

Mailing Address: 8101A Lee Hwy, Falls Church, VA 22042.

Phone: 703-770 7100. **Fax:** 703-770-7112.

Web Site: http://www.mhznetworks.org

Technical Facilities: Channel No. 30 (566-572 MHz). Authorized power: 160-kw max. visual, aural. Antenna: 751-ft above av. terrain, 617-ft. above ground, 1016-ft. above sea level.

Latitude	38°	37'	43"
Longitude	77°	26'	21"

Note: Latitude and longitude coordinates shown are based on the North American Datum of 1927 (NAD 27) as currently required by the Mass Media Bureau of the FCC.

Ownership: Commonwealth Public Broadcasting Corp.

Began Operation: December 30, 2003. Began analog operations: March 1, 1972. Ceased analog operations prior to original transition date of February 17, 2009.

Personnel:

Frederick Thomas, General Manager.

Dave Powell, Engineering Director.

David Hurd, Chief Engineer.

Stephanie Misar, Marketing Director.

Chris Hunter, Digital Content Creator, Promotions Director & Production Manager.

Chris Arth, Traffic Manager.

Nancy Sherwood, Station Relations Manager.

Grant Oines, Business Development Director.

WHRO-DT
Hampton-Norfolk
Ch. 16

Licensee: Hampton Roads Educational Telecommunications Assn. Inc, 5200 Hampton Blvd, Norfolk, VA 23508.

Studio: 5200 Hampton Blvd., Norfolk, VA 23508.

Mailing Address: 5200 Hampton Blvd, Norfolk, VA 23508.

Phone: 757-889-9400. **Fax:** 757-489-0007.

Email: diane.rogic@whro.org **Web Site:** http://www.whro.org

Technical Facilities: Channel No. 16 (482-488 MHz). Authorized power: 950-kw max. visual, aural. Antenna: 1183-ft above av. terrain, 1170-ft. above ground, 1193-ft. above sea level.

Latitude	36°	48'	31"
Longitude	76°	30'	13"

Holds CP for change to 1000-kw max. visual lat. 36° 48' 31", long. 76° 30' 12"; BPEDT-20080619ADA.

Transmitter: 3702-B Nansemond Pkwy., State Rte. 337, 1-mi. S of Driver.

Note: Latitude and longitude coordinates shown are based on the North American Datum of 1927 (NAD 27) as currently required by the Mass Media Bureau of the FCC.

Ownership: Hampton Roads Educational Telecommunications Association.

Began Operation: March 20, 2002. Began analog operations: October 2, 1961. Ceased analog operations: February 17, 2009.

Personnel:

John Heimerl, Chief Enterprise Officer.

Lawrence E. Crum, Chief Education Officer.

Diane Rogic, Senior Sales Representative.

Bill Griggs, Sales Manager.

Robert Boone, Chief Engineer.

Colleen Miscally, Business Manager.

Virginia Thumn, Chief Development Officer.

Linda Delgado, Traffic Manager.

Chuck Williams, Information Technology Director.

Brian Callahan, Educational Services Director.

WMSY-DT
Marion
Ch. 42

Licensee: Blue Ridge Public Television Inc., PO Box 13246, Roanoke, VA 24032.

Studio: 1215 McNeil Dr. SW, Roanoke, VA 24015.

Mailing Address: PO Box 13246, Roanoke, VA 24032-4706.

Phone: 540-344-0991. **Fax:** 540-344-2148.

Web Site: http://www.blueridgepbs.org

Technical Facilities: Channel No. 42 (638-644 MHz). Authorized power: 100-kw max. visual, aural. Antenna: 1470-ft above av. terrain, 217-ft. above ground, 3894-ft. above sea level.

Latitude	36°	54'	07"
Longitude	81°	32'	32"

Transmitter: Walker Mountain.

Note: Latitude and longitude coordinates shown are based on the North American Datum of 1927 (NAD 27) as currently required by the Mass Media Bureau of the FCC.

Ownership: Blue Ridge Public Television Inc.

Began Operation: January 1, 2003. Began analog operations: August 1, 1981. Ceased analog operations: June 12, 2009.

Personnel:

Debbie Jordan, Executive Vice President.

James Baum, General Manager.

Erwin Roman, Vice President, Engineering.

Sherry Spradlin, Program Director.

Kate Foreman, Vice President, Advancement.

Will Anderson, Executive Producer.

Sally Pheifer, Traffic Manager.

Carol Jennings, Corporate Communications Manager.

WSBN-DT
Norton
Ch. 32

Licensee: Blue Ridge Public Television Inc., PO Box 13246, Roanoke, VA 24032.

Studio: 1215 McNeil Dr. SW, Roanoke, VA 24015.

Mailing Address: PO Box 13246, Roanoke, VA 24032-4706.

Phone: 540-344-0991. **Fax:** 540-344-2148.

Web Site: http://www.blueridgepbs.org

Technical Facilities: Channel No. 32 (578-584 MHz). Authorized power: 100-kw max. visual, aural. Antenna: 1939-ft above av. terrain, 217-ft. above ground, 4377-ft. above sea level.

Latitude	36°	53'	53"
Longitude	82°	37'	21"

Transmitter: Stone Mountain.

Note: Latitude and longitude coordinates shown are based on the North American Datum of 1927 (NAD 27) as currently required by the Mass Media Bureau of the FCC.

Ownership: Blue Ridge Public Television Inc.

Began Operation: January 1, 2003. Began analog operations: March 30, 1971. Ceased analog operations: June 12, 2009.

Personnel:

Debbie Jordan, Executive Vice President.

James Baum, General Manager.

Erwin Roman, Vice President, Engineering.

Sherry Spradlin, Program Director.

Kate Foreman, Vice President, Advancement.

Will Anderson, Executive Producer.

Sally Pheifer, Traffic Manager.

Carol Jennings, Corporate Communications Manager.

WCVE-DT
Richmond
Ch. 42

Licensee: Commonwealth Public Broadcasting Corp., 23 Sesame St, Richmond, VA 23235.

Studio: 23 Sesame St., Richmond, VA 23235.

Mailing Address: 23 Sesame St, Richmond, VA 23235.

Phone: 804-320-1301. **Fax:** 804-320-8729.

Web Site: http://www.ideastations.org

Technical Facilities: Channel No. 42 (638-644 MHz). Authorized power: 160-kw max. visual, aural. Antenna: 1136-ft above av. terrain, 995-ft. above ground, 1353-ft. above sea level.

Latitude	37°	30'	44"
Longitude	77°	36'	04"

Requests CP for change to 436-kw max. visual, 1135-ft above av. terrain, 994-ft. above ground, 1352-ft. above sea level lat. 37° 30' 45", long. 77° 36' 5"; BPEDT-20080610AAQ.

Note: Latitude and longitude coordinates shown are based on the North American Datum of 1927 (NAD 27) as currently required by the Mass Media Bureau of the FCC.

Ownership: Commonwealth Public Broadcasting Corp.

Began Operation: July 11, 2005. Began analog operations: September 10, 1964. Ceased analog operations: June 12, 2009.

Personnel:

A. Curtis Monk, President & Chief Executive Officer.

John H. Felton, Executive Vice President & General Manager.

Mark Spiller, Vice President, Engineering.

Lisa Tait, Vice President, Development & Communications.

David M. DeBarger, Creative Services Director.

Iris Beverly, Vice President, Education Services.

Lynne McCarthy-Jones, Communications Manager.

WCVW-DT
Richmond
Ch. 44

Licensee: Commonwealth Public Broadcasting Corp., 23 Sesame St, Richmond, VA 23235.

Studio: 23 Sesame St., Richmond, VA 23235.

Mailing Address: 23 Sesame St, Richmond, VA 23235.

Phone: 804-320-1301. **Fax:** 804-320-8729.

Web Site: http://www.ideastations.org

Technical Facilities: Channel No. 44 (650-656 MHz). Authorized power: 100-kw max. visual, aural. Antenna: 1076-ft above av. terrain, 935-ft. above ground, 1293-ft. above sea level.

Latitude	37°	30'	45"
Longitude	77°	36'	05"

Holds CP for change to 112-kw max. visual, 1076-ft above av. terrain, 935-ft. above ground, 1292-ft. above sea level; BPEDT-20080610AAR.

Note: Latitude and longitude coordinates shown are based on the North American Datum of 1927 (NAD 27) as currently required by the Mass Media Bureau of the FCC.

Ownership: Commonwealth Public Broadcasting Corp.

Began Operation: August 1, 2004. Began analog operations: December 24, 1966. Ceased analog operations: June 12, 2009.

Personnel:

A. Curtis Monk, President & Chief Executive Officer.

John H. Felton, Executive Vice President & General Manager.

Mark Spiller, Vice President, Engineering.

Lisa Tait, Vice President, Development & Communications.

David M. DeBarger, Creative Services Director.

Iris Beverly, Vice President, Education Services.

Lynne McCarthy-Jones, Communications Manager.

WBRA-DT
Roanoke
Ch. 3

Licensee: Blue Ridge Public Television Inc., PO Box 13246, Roanoke, VA 24032.

Studio: 1215 McNeil Dr. SW, Roanoke, VA 24015.

Mailing Address: PO Box 13246, Roanoke, VA 24032-4706.

Phone: 540-344-0991. **Fax:** 540-344-2148.

Web Site: http://www.blueridgepbs.org

Technical Facilities: Channel No. 3 (60-66 MHz). Authorized power: 7.25-kw visual, aural. Antenna: 2028-ft above av. terrain, 180-ft. above ground, 3921-ft. above sea level.

Latitude	37°	11'	46"
Longitude	80°	09'	17"

Holds CP for change to 9.8-kw visual, 2015-ft above av. terrain, 180-ft. above ground, 3921-ft. above sea level; BPEDT-20080619ACF.

Transmitter: 8149 Honeysuckle Lane.

Note: Latitude and longitude coordinates shown are based on the North American Datum of 1927 (NAD 27) as currently required by the Mass Media Bureau of the FCC.

Ownership: Blue Ridge Public Television Inc.

Began Operation: April 30, 2003. Began analog operations: August 1, 1967. Ceased analog operations: June 12, 2009.

Personnel:

Debbie Jordan, Executive Vice President.

James Baum, General Manager.

Erwin Roman, Vice President, Engineering.

Sherry Spradlin, Program Director.

Kate Foreman, Vice President, Advancement.

Will Anderson, Executive Producer.

Sally Pheifer, Traffic Manager.

Carol Jennings, Corporate Communications Manager.

WVPT-DT
Staunton
Ch. 11

Licensee: Shenandoah Valley Educational TV Corp., 298 Port Republic Rd, Harrisonburg, VA 22801-3063.

Studio: 298 Port Republic Rd., Harrisonburg, VA 22801.

Mailing Address: 298 Port Republic Rd, Harrisonburg, VA 22801-3052.

Phones: 540-434-5391; 800-345-9878. **Fax:** 540-434-7084.

Web Site: http://www.wvpt.net

Technical Facilities: Channel No. 11 (198-204 MHz). Authorized power: 3.2-kw visual, aural. Antenna: 2231-ft above av. terrain, 33-ft. above ground, 4373-ft. above sea level.

| Latitude | 38° | 09' | 54" |
| Longitude | 79° | 18' | 51" |

Requests CP for change to 10-kw visual; BPEDT-20081022ABK.

Note: Latitude and longitude coordinates shown are based on the North American Datum of 1927 (NAD 27) as currently required by the Mass Media Bureau of the FCC.

Ownership: Shenandoah Valley Educational TV Corp.

Began Operation: October 18, 2001. Began analog operations: September 9, 1968. Ceased analog operations: June 12, 2009.

Personnel:

David Mullins, President & General Manager.

Tony Mancari, Vice President & Chief Operating Officer.

John Harper, Chief Engineer.

Wanda Zimmerman, Program Director.

Gail Smith, Corporate Communications Director.

Washington

KCKA-DT
Centralia
Ch. 19

Licensee: Bates Technical College, 1101 S Yakima Ave, Tacoma, WA 98405.

Studio: 2320 S. 19th St., Tacoma, WA 98405.

Mailing Address: 2320 S. 19th St, Tacoma, WA 98405.

Phone: 253-680-7700. **Fax:** 253-680-7725.

Email: sstanton@kbtc.org **Web Site:** http://www.kbtc.org

Technical Facilities: Channel No. 19 (500-506 MHz). Authorized power: 43.7-kw max. visual, aural. Antenna: 1096-ft above av. terrain, 157-ft. above ground, 1604-ft. above sea level.

| Latitude | 46° | 33' | 16" |
| Longitude | 123° | 03' | 26" |

Requests CP for change to 187-kw max. visual, 1138-ft above av. terrain, 194-ft. above ground, 1640-ft. above sea level; BPEDT-20080620ABA.

Note: Latitude and longitude coordinates shown are based on the North American Datum of 1927 (NAD 27) as currently required by the Mass Media Bureau of the FCC.

Ownership: Bates Technical College.

Began Operation: October 20, 2005. Began analog operations: October 2, 1982. Ceased analog operations: June 12, 2009.

Personnel:

Debbie Emond, General Manager.

Darin Gerchak, Chief Engineer.

Vicki Valdez, Financial Specialist.

Paul Jackson, Development Director.

Connie Wyman, Customer Service Representative & Information Technician.

Jennifer Strachen, Executive Producer.

Phil Kane, Program Director & Traffic Manager.

Michael Peters, Production Assistant.

KWSU-DT
Pullman
Ch. 10

Licensee: Washington State U., PO Box 642530, Murrow Communications Center, Pullman, WA 99164-2530.

Studio: Washington State U., Murrow Communications Center, 1st Fl, Pullman, WA 99164.

Mailing Address: PO Box 642530, Pullman, WA 99164-2530.

Phones: 509-335-6588; 800-922-4220. **Fax:** 509-335-3772.

Web Site: http://www.kwsu.org

Technical Facilities: Channel No. 10 (192-198 MHz). Authorized power: 6.2-kw visual, aural. Antenna: 1339-ft above av. terrain, 266-ft. above ground, 3829-ft. above sea level.

| Latitude | 46° | 51' | 43" |
| Longitude | 117° | 10' | 26" |

Requests modification of CP for change to 35-kw visual; BMPEDT-20080611ACA.

Note: Latitude and longitude coordinates shown are based on the North American Datum of 1927 (NAD 27) as currently required by the Mass Media Bureau of the FCC.

Ownership: Washington State U.

Began Operation: July 21, 2006. Station broadcasting digitally on its analog channel allotment. Began analog operations: September 24, 1962. Ceased analog operations: December 1, 2008.

Personnel:

Tony Wright, Interim General Manager.

Warren Wright, Station Manager.

Katherine Dahmen, Associate General Manager.

Don Peters, Chief Engineer.

Katharine McPherson, Business Manager.

Maya Lessov, Programming Assistant.

Chris Waiting, Production Manager.

KTNW-DT
Richland
Ch. 38

Licensee: Washington State U., PO Box 642530, Murrow Communications Center, Pullman, WA 99164-2530.

Studio: Washington State U., Murrow Communications Center, 1st Fl, Pullman, WA 99164.

Mailing Address: PO Box 642530, Pullman, WA 99164-2530.

Phones: 509-335-6588; 800-922-4220. **Fax:** 509-335-3772.

Web Site: http://www.ktnw.org

Technical Facilities: Channel No. 38 (614-620 MHz). Authorized power: 47.6-kw max. visual, aural. Antenna: 1184-ft above av. terrain, 33-ft. above ground, 2215-ft. above sea level.

| Latitude | 46° | 06' | 12" |
| Longitude | 119° | 07' | 40" |

Holds CP for change to 45.1-kw max. visual, 1210-ft above av. terrain, 56-ft. above ground, 2238-ft. above sea level; BPEDT-20090312AAB.

Transmitter: Jump Off Joe Butte, 8-mi. S of Kennewick.

Note: Latitude and longitude coordinates shown are based on the North American Datum of 1927 (NAD 27) as currently required by the Mass Media Bureau of the FCC.

Ownership: Washington State U.

Began Operation: April 29, 2003. Began analog operations: October 18, 1987. Ceased analog operations: February 17, 2009.

Personnel:

Tony Wright, Interim General Manager.

Warren Wright, Station Manager.

Katherine Dahmen, Associate General Manager.

Don Peters, Chief Engineer.

Katharine McPherson, Business Manager.

Maya Lessov, Programming Assistant.

Chris Waiting, Production Manager.

KCTS-DT
Seattle
Ch. 9

Licensee: KCTS Television, 401 Mercer St, Seattle, WA 98109-4699.

Studio: 401 Mercer St., Seattle, WA 98019.

Mailing Address: 401 Mercer St, Seattle, WA 98109.

Phone: 206-728-6463. **Fax:** 206-443-6691.

Email: jparikh@kcts.org **Web Site:** http://www.kcts.org

Technical Facilities: Channel No. 9 (186-192 MHz). Authorized power: 21.7-kw visual, aural. Antenna: 817-ft above av. terrain, 525-ft. above ground, 935-ft. above sea level.

| Latitude | 47° | 36' | 58" |
| Longitude | 122° | 18' | 28" |

Transmitter: 18th Ave & E Madison St.

Note: Latitude and longitude coordinates shown are based on the North American Datum of 1927 (NAD 27) as currently required by the Mass Media Bureau of the FCC.

Ownership: KCTS Television.

Began Operation: April 10, 1999. Station broadcasting digitally on its analog channel allotment. Began analog operations: December 7, 1954. Ceased analog operations: June 12, 2009.

Personnel:

Bill Mohler, Chief Executive Officer.

Randy Brinson, General Manager.

Monica Reisner, General Counsel.

Cliff Anderson, Engineering Director.

Jay Parikh, Marketing & Development Director.

Michal Anderson Jacob, Finance Director.

Enrique Cerna, Production Manager.

KSPS-DT
Spokane
Ch. 39

Licensee: Spokane School District No. 81, 200 N Bernard St, Spokane, WA 99201.

Studio: 3911 S. Regal St., Spokane, WA 99223.

Mailing Address: 3911 S. Regal St, Spokane, WA 99223.

Phones: 509-354-7800; 800-735-2377. **Fax:** 509-354-7757.

Web Site: http://www.ksps.org

Technical Facilities: Channel No. 39 (320-626 MHz). Authorized power: 21.6-kw max. visual, aural. Antenna: 1831-ft above av. terrain, 531-ft. above ground, 4139-ft. above sea level.

| Latitude | 47° | 34' | 34" |
| Longitude | 117° | 17' | 58" |

Requests CP for change to channel number 7, 45.1-kw visual, 1831-ft above av. terrain, 531-ft. above ground, 4159-ft. above sea level; BPEDT-20090612ADT.

Transmitter: South end of Krell Hill.

Note: Latitude and longitude coordinates shown are based on the North American Datum of 1927 (NAD 27) as currently required by the Mass Media Bureau of the FCC.

Ownership: Spokane School District No. 81.

Began Operation: February 17, 2009. Station plans to broadcast digitally on its analog channel allotment. Began analog operations: April 24, 1967. Ceased analog operations: February 17, 2009.

Personnel:

Claude L. Kistler, General Manager.

William Stanley, Consultant.

Ron Valley, Chief Engineer.

Jim Zimmer, Production Manager.

Patty Starkey, Development Director.

Cary Balzer, Program Director.

KBTC-DT
Tacoma
Ch. 27

Licensee: Bates Technical College, 1101 S Yakima Ave, Tacoma, WA 98405.

Studio: 2320 S. 19th St., Tacoma, WA 98405.

Mailing Address: 2320 S. 19th St, Tacoma, WA 98405.

Phone: 253-680-7700. **Fax:** 253-680-7725.

Web Site: http://www.kbtc.org

Technical Facilities: Channel No. 27 (548-554 MHz). Authorized power: 45-kw max. visual, aural. Antenna: 771-ft above av. terrain, 489-ft. above ground, 899-ft. above sea level.

| Latitude | 47° | 16' | 44" |
| Longitude | 122° | 30' | 42" |

Requests CP for change to 100-kw max. visual; BPEDT-20080620ABF.

Note: Latitude and longitude coordinates shown are based on the North American Datum of 1927 (NAD 27) as currently required by the Mass Media Bureau of the FCC.

Ownership: Bates Technical College.

Began Operation: April 25, 2003. Began analog operations: September 25, 1961. Ceased analog operations: June 12, 2009.

Personnel:

Debbie Emond, General Manager.

Darin Gerchak, Chief Engineer.

Vicki Valdez, Financial Specialist.

Paul Jackson, Development Director.

Connie Wyman, Information Technician & Customer Service Representative.

Michael Peters, Production Assistant.

Phil Kane, Traffic Manager & Program Director.

Jennifer Strachen, Executive Producer.

KWDK-DT
Tacoma
Ch. 42

Licensee: Puget Sound Educational TV, 2200 112th St NW, Bellevue, WA 98004.

Studio: 18014 72nd Ave. S, Kent, WA 98032.

Mailing Address: 18014 72nd Ave. S, Kent, WA 98032.

Phone: 425-251-4313. **Fax:** 425-251-4305.

Web Site: http://www.daystar.com

Technical Facilities: Channel No. 42 (638-644 MHz). Authorized power: 144-kw max. visual, aural. Antenna: 2280-ft above av. terrain, 197-ft. above ground, 2843-ft. above sea level.

| Latitude | 47° | 30' | 17" |
| Longitude | 121° | 58' | 06" |

Transmitter: W. Tiger Mountain.

Note: Latitude and longitude coordinates shown are based on the North American Datum of 1927 (NAD 27) as currently required by the Mass Media Bureau of the FCC.

Ownership: Puget Sound Educational TV.

Began Operation: April 21, 2005. Station received approval from FCC June 20, 2005 to cease analog broadcasting and operate in digital format only.

Personnel:

Terry Spring, Chief Engineer.

KYVE-DT
Yakima
Ch. 21

Licensee: KCTS Television, 401 Mercer St, Seattle, WA 98109-4699.

Studio: 12 S 2nd St, Yakima, WA 98901.

Mailing Address: 12 S 2nd St, Yakima, WA 98901.

Phone: 509-452-4700. **Fax:** 509-452-4704.

Web Site: http://www.kyve.org

Technical Facilities: Channel No. 21 (512-518 MHz). Authorized power: 50-kw max. visual, aural. Antenna: 919-ft above av. terrain, 120-ft. above ground, 2092-ft. above sea level.

| Latitude | 46° | 31' | 58" |
| Longitude | 120° | 30' | 33" |

Transmitter: Ahtanum Ridge Rd, 2-mi. SW of Union Gap.

Note: Latitude and longitude coordinates shown are based on the North American Datum of 1927 (NAD 27) as currently required by the Mass Media Bureau of the FCC.

Ownership: KCTS Television.

Began Operation: September 10, 2003. Began analog operations: November 1, 1962. Ceased analog operations: June 12, 2009.

Personnel:

Ken Messer, General Manager.

Rod Venable, Chief Engineer.

Marilee Sinclair, Business Manager.

West Virginia

WSWP-DT
Grandview
Ch. 10

Grantee: West Virginia Educational Broadcasting Authority, 600 Capitol St, Charleston, WV 25301-1223.

Studio: 600 Capitol St., Charleston, WV 25301.

Mailing Address: PO Box 9004, Beckley, WV 25802-9004.

Phones: 304-254-7840; 304-556-4900. **Fax:** 304-556-4980.

Web Site: http://www.wvptv.org

Technical Facilities: Channel No. 10 (192-198 MHz). Authorized power: 24-kw visual, aural. Antenna: 1043-ft above av. terrain, 445-ft. above ground, 3404-ft. above sea level.

| Latitude | 37° | 53' | 46" |
| Longitude | 80° | 59' | 21" |

Note: Latitude and longitude coordinates shown are based on the North American Datum of 1927 (NAD 27) as currently required by the Mass Media Bureau of the FCC.

Ownership: West Virginia Educational Broadcasting Authority.

Began Operation: July 25, 2003. Station operating under Special Temporary Authority at 35.8-kw max. visual. Began analog operations: November 1, 1970. Ceased analog operations: June 12, 2009.

Personnel:

Dennis Adkins, Executive Director.

Bill Acker, Broadcasting & Technology Director.

Craig Lanham, Programming & Operations Director.

Greg Collard, News & Public Affairs Director.

Jack Wells, Engineering Director.

Mike Meador, Chief Financial Officer.

Marilyn DiVita, Marketing Director.

Mike Youngren, Production Director.

Shawn Patterson, Communications Director.

Peggy Dorsey, Individual Giving Manager.

Danny Wilson, Engineering Maintenance Manager.

Debbie Oleksa, Educational Services Director.

David McClanahan, Engineering Manager.

WPBY-DT
Huntington
Ch. 34

Licensee: West Virginia Educational Broadcasting Authority, 600 Capitol St, Charleston, WV 25301-1223.

Studio: 600 Capital St., Charleston, WV 25301.

Mailing Address: 600 Capitol St, Charleston, WV 25301.

Phone: 304-556-4900. **Fax:** 304-556-4980.

Web Site: http://www.wvpubcast.org

Technical Facilities: Channel No. 34 (590-596 MHz). Authorized power: 60.1-kw max. visual, aural. Antenna: 1241-ft above av. terrain, 1039-ft. above ground, 1979-ft. above sea level.

| Latitude | 38° | 29' | 41" |
| Longitude | 82° | 12' | 03" |

Holds CP for change to 953-kw max. visual, 1243-ft above av. terrain, 1041-ft. above ground, 1981-ft. above sea level; BPEDT-20080619ACN.

Transmitter: 9183 Barkers Ridge Church Rd., Milton.

Note: Latitude and longitude coordinates shown are based on the North American Datum of 1927 (NAD 27) as currently required by the Mass Media Bureau of the FCC.

Ownership: West Virginia Educational Broadcasting Authority.

Began Operation: February 28, 2002. Began analog operations: July 14, 1969. Ceased analog operations: June 12, 2009.

Personnel:

Dennis Adkins, Executive Director.

Bill Acker, Broadcasting & Technology Director.

Craig Lanham, Programming & Operations Director.

Greg Collard, News & Public Affairs Director.

Jack Wells, Engineering Director.

David McClanahan, Engineering Manager.

Mike Meador, Chief Financial Officer.

Marilyn DiVita, Marketing Director.

Peggy Dorsey, Individual Giving Manager.

Mike Youngren, Production Director.

Debbie Oleksa, Educational Services Director.

Danny Wilson, Engineering Maintenance Manager.

Shawn Patterson, Communications Director.

WNPB-DT
Morgantown
Ch. 33

Licensee: West Virginia Educational Broadcasting Authority, 600 Capitol St, Charleston, WV 25301-1223.

Studio: 191 Scott Ave., Morgantown, WV 26508.

Mailing Address: 191 Scott Ave, Morgantown, WV 26508.

Phones: 304-284-1440; 304-556-4900. **Fax:** 304-556-4980.

Web Site: http://www.wvptv.org

Technical Facilities: Channel No. 33 (584-590 MHz). Authorized power: 108-kw max. visual, aural. Antenna: 1446-ft above av. terrain, 416-ft. above ground, 3012-ft. above sea level.

| Latitude | 39° | 41' | 45" |
| Longitude | 79° | 45' | 45" |

Holds CP for change to 615-kw max. visual, 1522-ft above av. terrain, 492-ft. above ground, 3088-ft. above sea level; BMPEDT-20080619ACQ.

Transmitter: Adjacent to Sandy Springs Lookout Tower, 10-mi. NE of Morgantown.

Note: Latitude and longitude coordinates shown are based on the North American Datum of 1927 (NAD 27) as currently required by the Mass Media Bureau of the FCC.

Ownership: West Virginia Educational Broadcasting Authority.

Began Operation: December 30, 2003. Began analog operations: February 23, 1969. Ceased analog operations: June 12, 2009.

Personnel:

Dennis Adkins, Executive Director.

Jack Wells, Engineering Director.

Bill Acker, Broadcasting & Technology Director.

Greg Collard, News & Public Affairs Director.

Danny Wilson, Engineering Maintenance Manager.

Michael Meador, Chief Financial Officer.

Craig Lanham, Program & Operations Director.

Marilyn DiVita, Marketing Director.

Mike Youngren, Production Director.

Debbie Oleksa, Educational Services Director.

David McClanahan, Engineering Manager.

Peggy Dorsey, Individual Giving Manager.

Shawn Patterson, Communications Director.

Wisconsin

WPNE-TV
Green Bay
Ch. 42

Licensee: Educational Communications Board, 3319 W Beltline Hwy, Madison, WI 53713-4296.

Studio: 821 University Ave., Madison, WI 53703.

Mailing Address: 3319 W Beltline Hwy, Madison, WI 53713-4296.

Phones: 608-264-9600; 608-264-9400. Fax: 608-264-9664.

Email: rwundrock@ecb.org Web Site: http://www.ecb.org

Technical Facilities: Channel No. 42 (638-644 MHz). Authorized power: 200-kw max. visual, aural. Antenna: 1230-ft above av. terrain, 1066-ft. above ground, 1966-ft. above sea level.

Latitude	44°	24'	34"
Longitude	88°	00'	06"

Note: Latitude and longitude coordinates shown are based on the North American Datum of 1927 (NAD 27) as currently required by the Mass Media Bureau of the FCC.

Ownership: Wisconsin Educational Communications Board.

Began Operation: May 5, 2004. Began analog operations: September 11, 1972. Ceased analog operations: June 12, 2009.

Personnel:

Gene Purcell, Executive Director.

Kathy Bissen, Executive Producer, News & Public Affairs.

James Steinbach, Production & Program Director.

John H. Ashley Jr., Educational Program Director.

Michael Bridgeman, Promotion Director.

Dennis Behr, Engineering & Operations Administrator.

WHLA-DT
La Crosse
Ch. 30

Licensee: Educational Communications Board, 3319 W Beltline Hwy, Madison, WI 53713-4296.

Studio: 821 University Ave., Madison, WI 53703.

Mailing Address: 3319 W Beltline Hwy, Madison, WI 53713-4296.

Phones: 608-264-9600; 608-264-9400. Fax: 608-264-9664.

Email: rwundrock@ecb.org Web Site: http://www.ecb.org

Technical Facilities: Channel No. 30 (566-572 MHz). Authorized power: 307.5-kw max. visual, aural. Antenna: 1152-ft above av. terrain, 800-ft. above ground, 2018-ft. above sea level.

Latitude	43°	48'	17"
Longitude	91°	22'	06"

Note: Latitude and longitude coordinates shown are based on the North American Datum of 1927 (NAD 27) as currently required by the Mass Media Bureau of the FCC.

Ownership: Wisconsin Educational Communications Board.

Began Operation: May 7, 2004. Began analog operations: December 3, 1973. Ceased analog operations: June 12, 2009.

Personnel:

Gene Purcell, Executive Director.

Kathy Bissen, Executive Producer, News & Public Affairs.

James Steinbach, Program & Production Director.

John H. Ashley Jr., Educational Programming Director.

Michael Bridgeman, Promotion Director.

Dennis Behr, Engineering & Operations Administrator.

WHA-DT
Madison
Ch. 20

Licensee: Board of Regents of the U. of Wisconsin System, 1220 Linden Dr, 1730 Van Hise Hall, Madison, WI 53706.

Studio: 821 University Ave., Madison, WI 53706.

Mailing Address: 821 University Ave, Madison, WI 53706.

Phone: 608-263-2121. Fax: 608-263-9763.

Web Site: http://www.wpt.org

Technical Facilities: Channel No. 20 (506-512 MHz). Authorized power: 200-kw max. visual, aural. Antenna: 1486-ft above av. terrain, 1348-ft. above ground, 2474-ft. above sea level.

Latitude	43°	03'	21"
Longitude	89°	32'	06"

Holds CP for change to 140-kw max. visual; BPEDT-20080620AEM.

Transmitter: Mineral Point Rd., Madison.

Note: Latitude and longitude coordinates shown are based on the North American Datum of 1927 (NAD 27) as currently required by the Mass Media Bureau of the FCC.

Ownership: Regents of the U. of Wisconsin System Board.

Began Operation: May 30, 2002. Began analog operations: May 3, 1954. Ceased analog operations: June 12, 2009.

Personnel:

Malcolm Brett, General Manager.

Kathy Bissen, Production Director.

Richard Taugher, Engineering Director.

Joan Klaski, Business Manager.

James Steinbach, Television Director, Production & Traffic Manager.

Michael Bridgeman, Promotion Director.

John Miskowski, Development Director.

Garry Denny, Program Manager.

Erik Ernst, Promotion Manager.

WHWC-DT
Menomonie
Ch. 27

Licensee: Educational Communications Board, 3319 W Beltline Hwy, Madison, WI 53713-4296.

Studio: 821 University Ave., Madison, WI 53703.

Mailing Address: 3319 W Beltline Hwy, Madison, WI 53713-4296.

Phones: 608-264-9400; 608-264-9600. Fax: 608-264-9664.

Email: wwink@ecb.state.wi.us Web Site: http://www.ecb.org

Technical Facilities: Channel No. 27 (548-554 MHz). Authorized power: 291-kw max. visual, aural. Antenna: 1148-ft above av. terrain, 1170-ft. above ground, 2150-ft. above sea level.

Latitude	45°	02'	49"
Longitude	91°	51'	47"

Note: Latitude and longitude coordinates shown are based on the North American Datum of 1927 (NAD 27) as currently required by the Mass Media Bureau of the FCC.

Ownership: Wisconsin Educational Communications Board.

Began Operation: August 19, 2004. Standard and High Definition. Began analog operations: November 16, 1973. Ceased analog operations: June 12, 2009.

Personnel:

Gene Purcell, Executive Director.

Kathy Bissen, Executive Producer, News & Public Affairs.

James Steinbach, Program & Production Director.

John H. Ashley Jr., Educational Programming Director.

Michael Bridgeman, Promotion Director.

Dennis Behr, Engineering & Operations Administrator.

WMVS-DT
Milwaukee
Ch. 8

Licensee: Milwaukee Area Technical College District Board, 1036 N 8th St, Milwaukee, WI 53233.

Studio: 1036 N. 8th St., Milwaukee, WI 53233.

Mailing Address: 1036 N. 8th St, Milwaukee, WI 53233.

Phone: 414-271-1036. Fax: 414-297-7536.

Email: brombere@matc.edu Web Site: http://www.mptv.org

Technical Facilities: Channel No. 8 (180-186 MHz). Authorized power: 25-kw visual, aural. Antenna: 1161-ft above av. terrain, 1188-ft. above ground, 1816-ft. above sea level.

Latitude	43°	05'	46"
Longitude	87°	54'	15"

Requests CP for change to 32-kw visual; BPEDT-20090310ADU.

Note: Latitude and longitude coordinates shown are based on the North American Datum of 1927 (NAD 27) as currently required by the Mass Media Bureau of the FCC.

Ownership: Milwaukee Area Technical College District Board.

Began Operation: March 6, 2000. Began analog operations: October 28, 1957. Ceased analog operations: June 12, 2009.

Personnel:

Ellis Bromberg, General Manager.

David C. Felland, Engineering Director.

Tom Dvorak, Broadcasting Director.

Darlene Haertlein, Outreach Supervisor.

Scott Rackham, Development Manager.

Raul Galvan, Production Manager.

Amy Sullivan, Traffic Manager.

Kevin Kukowski, TV Technical Facilities Coordinator.

WMVT-DT
Milwaukee
Ch. 35

Licensee: Milwaukee Area Technical College District Board, 1036 N 8th St, Milwaukee, WI 53233.

Studio: 1036 N. 8th St., Milwaukee, WI 53233.

Mailing Address: 1036 N. 8th St, Milwaukee, WI 53233.

Phone: 414-271-1036. Fax: 414-297-7536.

Email: brombere@matc.edu Web Site: http://www.mptv.org

Technical Facilities: Channel No. 35 (596-602 MHz). Authorized power: 500-kw max. visual, aural. Antenna: 1164-ft above av. terrain, 1193-ft. above ground, 1821-ft. above sea level.

Latitude	43°	05'	46"
Longitude	87°	54'	15"

Holds CP for change to 625-kw max. visual; BPEDT-20090310ADX.

Transmitter: 4350 N. Humboldt Ave.

Note: Latitude and longitude coordinates shown are based on the North American Datum of 1927 (NAD 27) as currently required by the Mass Media Bureau of the FCC.

Ownership: Milwaukee Area Technical College District Board.

Began Operation: November 29, 2004. Began analog operations: December 20, 1962. Ceased analog operations: June 12, 2009.

Personnel:

Ellis Bromberg, General Manager.

David C. Felland, Engineering Director.

Tom Dvorak, Broadcasting Director.

Darlene Haerlein, Outreach Supervisor.

Scott Rackham, Development Director.

Raul Galvan, Production Manager.

Amy Sullivan, Traffic Manager.

Kevin Kukowski, TV Technical Facilities Coordinator.

WLEF-DT
Park Falls
Ch. 36

Licensee: Educational Communications Board, 3319 W Beltline Hwy, Madison, WI 53713-4296.

Studio: 821 University Ave., Madison, WI 53706.

Mailing Address: 3319 W Beltline Hwy, Madison, WI 53713-4296.

Phones: 608-264-9600; 608-264-9400. **Fax:** 608-264-9664.

Email: wwink@ecb.state.wi.us **Web Site:** http://www.ecb.org

Technical Facilities: Channel No. 36 (602-608 MHz). Authorized power: 50-kw max. visual, aural. Antenna: 1460-ft above av. terrain, 1470-ft above ground, 3020-ft. above sea level.

Latitude	45°	56'	43"
Longitude	90°	16'	23"

Holds CP for change to 200-kw max. visual; BMPEDT-20080611ABN.

Note: Latitude and longitude coordinates shown are based on the North American Datum of 1927 (NAD 27) as currently required by the Mass Media Bureau of the FCC.

Multichannel TV Sound: Stereo and separate audio program.

Ownership: Wisconsin Educational Communications Board.

Began Operation: February 13, 2009. Station broadcasting digitally on its analog channel allotment. Began analog operations: December 5, 1977. Ceased analog operations: February 2, 2009.

Personnel:

Gene Purcell, Executive Director.

Kathy Bissen, Executive Producer, News & Public Affairs.

James Steinbach, Program Director & Production Manager.

John H. Ashley Jr., Educational Programming Director.

Michael Bridgeman, Promotion Director.

Dennis Behr, Engineering & Operations Administrator.

WHRM-DT
Wausau
Ch. 24

Licensee: Educational Communications Board, 3319 W Beltline Hwy, Madison, WI 53713-4296.

Studio: 821 University Ave., Madison, WI 53703.

Mailing Address: 3319 W Beltline Hwy, Madison, WI 53713-4296.

Phones: 608-264-9600; 608-264-9400. **Fax:** 608-264-9664.

Web Site: http://www.ecb.org

Technical Facilities: Channel No. 24 (530-536 MHz). Authorized power: 172-kw max. visual, aural. Antenna: 1270-ft above av. terrain, 630-ft. above ground, 2529-ft. above sea level.

Latitude	44°	55'	14"
Longitude	89°	41'	28"

Note: Latitude and longitude coordinates shown are based on the North American Datum of 1927 (NAD 27) as currently required by the Mass Media Bureau of the FCC.

Ownership: Wisconsin Educational Communications Board.

Began Operation: October 9, 2003. Began analog operations: October 25, 1975. Ceased analog operations: June 12, 2009.

Personnel:

Gene Purcell, Executive Director.

Dennis Behr, Engineering & Operations Adminstrator.

Kathy Bissen, Executive Producer, News & Public Affairs.

James Steinbach, Program & Production Director.

John H. Ashley Jr., Educational Programming Director.

Michael Bridgeman, Promotion Director.

Wyoming

KPTW-DT
Casper
Ch. 8

Grantee: Central Wyoming College, 2660 Peck Ave, Riverton, WY 82501.

Phones: 307-856-6944; 800-495-9788. **Fax:** 307-856-3893.

Web Site: http://www.wyoptv.org

Technical Facilities: Channel No. 8 (180-186 MHz). Authorized power: 2.3-kw visual, aural. Antenna: 1863-ft above av. terrain, 190-ft. above ground, 8209-ft. above sea level.

Latitude	42°	44'	26"
Longitude	106°	21'	34"

Note: Latitude and longitude coordinates shown are based on the North American Datum of 1927 (NAD 27) as currently required by the Mass Media Bureau of the FCC.

Ownership: Central Wyoming College.

Began Operation: February 17, 2009. Began analog operations: February 28, 2007. Ceased analog operations: February 17, 2009.

Personnel:

Ruby Calvert, General Manager & Programming Director.

Robert Spain, Engineering Director.

Bob Connelly, Chief Engineer.

Dean King, Promotions Producer.

Kyle Nicholoff, Production Manager.

Suze Kanack, Traffic Manager.

Joel Kindle, Operations Manager.

Sonja Fairfield, Administrative Assistant.

KCWC-DT
Lander
Ch. 8

Licensee: Central Wyoming College, 2660 Peck Ave, Riverton, WY 82501.

Studio: Central Wyoming College, 2660 Peck Ave, Riverton, WY 82501.

Mailing Address: 2660 Peck Ave, Riverton, WY 82501.

Phone: 307-856-6944. **Fax:** 307-856-3893.

Web Site: http://www.wyomingpbs.org

Technical Facilities: Channel No. 8 (180-186 MHz). Authorized power: 60-kw visual, aural. Antenna: 1417-ft above av. terrain, 190-ft. above ground, 9121-ft. above sea level.

Latitude	42°	34'	59"
Longitude	108°	42'	36"

Transmitter: Limestone Mountain, 1.5-mi. N of Hwy. 28.

Note: Latitude and longitude coordinates shown are based on the North American Datum of 1927 (NAD 27) as currently required by the Mass Media Bureau of the FCC.

Ownership: Central Wyoming College.

Began Operation: February 26, 2007. Began analog operations: May 10, 1983. Ceased analog operations February 2, 2009 due to equipment failure.

Personnel:

Ruby Calvert, General Manager & Programming Director.

Robert Spain, Engineering Director.

Bob Connelly, Chief Engineer.

Dean King, Promotions Producer.

Kyle Nicholoff, Production Manager.

Suze Kanack, Traffic Manager.

Joel Kindle, Operations Manager.

Sonja Fairfield, Administrative Assistant.

KWYP-DT
Laramie
Ch. 8

Licensee: Central Wyoming College, 2660 Peck Ave, Riverton, WY 82501.

Studio: Central Wyoming College, 2660 Peck Ave, Riverton, WY 82501.

Mailing Address: 2660 Peck Ave, Riverton, WY 82501.

Phone: 307-856-6944. **Fax:** 307-856-3893.

Web Site: http://www.wyomingpbs.org

Technical Facilities: Channel No. 8 (180-186 MHz). Authorized power: 13-kw visual, aural. Antenna: 1010-ft above av. terrain, 85-ft. above ground, 8901-ft. above sea level.

Latitude	41°	18'	35"
Longitude	105°	27'	19"

Note: Latitude and longitude coordinates shown are based on the North American Datum of 1927 (NAD 27) as currently required by the Mass Media Bureau of the FCC.

Ownership: Central Wyoming College.

Began Operation: February 17, 2009. Station broadcasting digitally on its analog channel allotment. Began analog operations: November 1, 2004. Ceased analog operations: February 17, 2009.

Personnel:

Ruby Calvert, General Manager & Programming Director.

Robert Spain, Engineering Director.

Sonja Fairfield, Administrative Assistant.

Bob Connelly, Transmitter Engineer.

Dean King, Promotions Producer.

Kyle Nicholoff, Production Manager.

Suze Kanack, Traffic Manager.

Joel Kindle, Operations Manager.

Guam

KGTF-DT
Agana
Ch. 12

Grantee: Guam Educational Telecommunications Corp., PO Box 21499, Guam Main Facility, Barrigad, GU 96921.

Mailing Address: PO Box 21449, Guam Mail Facility, Agana, GU 96921.

Phone: 671-734-3476. **Fax:** 671-734-2207.

Technical Facilities: Channel No. 12 (204-210 MHz). Authorized power: 54.7-kw visual, aural. Antenna: 583-ft above av. terrain, 138-ft. above ground, 794-ft. above sea level.

Latitude	13°	29' 16.8"	
Longitude	144°	49' 37.3"	

Note: Latitude and longitude coordinates shown are based on the North American Datum of 1927 (NAD 27) as currently required by the Mass Media Bureau of the FCC.

Ownership: Guam Educational Telecommunications Corp.

Began Operation: March 5, 2009. Station broadcasting digitally on its analog channel allotment. Began analog operations: October 30, 1970. Station ceased analog operations: February 16, 2009.

Virgin Islands

WTJX-DT
Charlotte Amalie
Ch. 44

Licensee: Virgin Islands Public Television System, PO Box 7879, St. Thomas, VI 00801.

Studio: 158-159A Haypiece Hill Subbase, St. Thomas, VI 00802.

Mailing Address: PO Box 7879, St. Thomas, VI 00801.

Phone: 340-774-6255. **Fax:** 340-774-7092.

Web Site: http://www.wtjxtv.org

Technical Facilities: Channel No. 44 (650-656 MHz). Authorized power: 50-kw max. visual, aural. Antenna: 1503-ft above av. terrain, 69-ft. above ground, 1549-ft. above sea level.

Latitude	18°	21'	26"
Longitude	64°	56'	50"

Holds CP for change to 50-kw max. visual, 1657-ft above av. terrain, 243-ft. above ground, 1705-ft. above sea level lat. 18° 21' 28", long. 64° 56' 53"; BMPEDT-20080620AFB.

Note: Latitude and longitude coordinates shown are based on the North American Datum of 1927 (NAD 27) as currently required by the Mass Media Bureau of the FCC.

Ownership: Government of the U.S. Virgin Islands.

Began Operation: August 23, 2004. Began analog operations: August 29, 1972. Ceased analog operations: June 12, 2009.

Personnel:

Osbert Potter, Executive Director.
Rupert Smith, Operations Supervisor.
Samuel Jones, Chief Engineer.
Clarina Modeste-Elliott, Business Manager.
Gwendolyn Kelly, Program Manager.
Yvette de Laubanque, Development Officer.
Edwardo Smith, Production Manager.
Angela Gordon, Supervising Producer.
Brenda Stapleton, Traffic Officer.
Petra Phipps, Executive Assistant.

Digital Construction Permits & Applications

Dagger (†) indicates non-commercial station. Diamond (◆) indicates application. Reporting all current FCC grants, applications, changes, etc.

Alabama

Troy (Ch. 48)—WRJM-DT. Network Service: MNT. Josie Park Broadcasting Inc., PO Box 310900, c/o Whit Armstrong, Enterprise Capital Corp., Enterprise, AL 36331. Phone: 334-670-6766. Fax: 334-670-6717. Email: vhodges@wrjm.com. Web site: http://www.wrjm.com. Technical facilities: Channel No. 48 (674-680 MHz). Proposed power: 50-kw max. visual, aural. Antenna: 1130-ft above av. terrain, 977-ft. above ground, 1544-ft. above sea level. Latitude 32° 03' 36.54''. Longitude 85° 57' 01.83''. Ownership: Enterprise Capital Corp. Represented (engineering): Lohnes & Culver. Represented (legal): Putbrese, Hunsaker & Trent PC. Personnel: Don Hess, General Manager; Buddy Johnson, General Sales Manager; Walter Lunsford, Business Manager; Brenda Simechak, Programming Director; Ria Miller, Traffic Manager. Montgomery-Selma, AL DMA. BPCDT-19991101AKR. Grant Date: February 7, 2001. Began analog operations: November 24, 2000. Assignment of license to Southern Venture Capital Group LLC pends. Transfer of control by Walter P. Lunsford, Receiver for Josie Park Broadcasting Inc. from Walter P. Lunsford to Enterprise Capital Corp. approved by FCC December 11, 2008. Involuntary assignment to Walter P. Lunsford as Receiver approved by FCC February 11, 2008. Sale to Josie Park Broadcasting Inc. by Stage Door Development Inc. approved by FCC November 8, 2000. Sale to Stage Door Development Inc. by Shelley Broadcasting Co. Inc., Debtor In Possession approved by FCC January 26, 1993. Involuntary assignment of debtor in possession status to Shelley Broadcasting Co. Inc. approved by FCC November 21, 1989. Ceased analog operations: June 12, 2009. Station unable to make digital transition due lightning strike to transmitter.

California

◆†Sacramento (Ch. 43 ETV)— Calvary Christian Center Inc., PO Box 15010, 2665 Del Paso Blvd, Sacramento, CA 95851. Phone: 916-929-1383. Technical facilities: Channel No. 43 (644-650 MHz). Proposed power: 650-kw max. visual, aural. Antenna: 1163-ft above av. terrain, 177-ft. above ground, 2221-ft. above sea level. Latitude 38° 43' 10''. Longitude 120° 59' 22''. Ownership: Calvary Christian Center Inc. Sacramento-Stockton-Modesto, CA DMA. BNPEDT-20030919AAV. Grant Date: Unreported. Station plans to go directly to digital broadcast; no analog application.

Illinois

Galesburg (Ch. 53)— Northwest Television Inc., 408 Jackson Dr, Sarasota, FL 34236. Phone: 941-388-2400. Technical facilities: Channel No. 53 (704-710 MHz). Proposed power: 1000-kw max. visual, aural. Antenna: 1091-ft above av. terrain, 1067-ft. above ground, 1820-ft. above sea level. Latitude 41° 18' 44'', Longitude 90° 22' 45''. Ownership: Northwest Television Inc. Represented (engineering): Carl E. Smith Consulting Engineers. Represented (legal): Borsari & Paxson. Davenport, IA-Rock Island-Moline, IL DMA. BPCDT-19951215KK. Grant Date: July 20, 2007. Station plans to go directly to digital broadcast; no analog application.

◆†Springfield (Ch. 36 ETV)—Network Service: PBS. West Central Illinois Educational Telecommunications Corp., PO Box 6248, Springfield, IL 62708. Phone: 217-206-6647. Technical facilities: Channel No. 36 (602-608 MHz). Proposed power: 10-kw max. visual, aural. Antenna: 279-ft above av. terrain, 276-ft. above ground, 874-ft. above sea level. Latitude 39° 41' 29'', Longitude 89° 41' 27''. Ownership: West Central Illinois Educational Telecommunications Corp. Champaign & Springfield-Decatur, IL DMA. BPEDT-19960129KH. Grant Date: Unreported. Station plans to go directly to digital broadcast; no analog application.

Minnesota

Duluth (Ch. 27)—KCWV-DT. George S. Flinn III, 275 Goodwyn, Memphis, TN 38111. Phone: 901-375-9324. Technical facilities: Channel No. 27 (548-554 MHz). Proposed power: 63-kw max. visual, aural. Antenna: 751-ft above av. terrain, 518-ft above ground, 1781-ft. above sea level. Latitude 46° 47'30'', Longitude 92° 07'21''. Requests modification of CP for change to 40-kw max. visual, 679-ft above av. terrain, 449-ft. above ground, 1683-ft. above sea level lat. 46° 47' 7'', long. 92° 7' 15''. BMPCDT-20080617ACJ. Ownership: George S. Flinn III. Represented (legal): Stephen C. Simpson. Represented (engineering): du Treil, Lundin & Rackley Inc. Duluth, MN-Superior, WI DMA. BMPCDT-20080221ACC. Grant Date: February 25, 2008. Station plans to go directly to digital broadcast; no analog application. Construction of digital facilities is ongoing.

Mississippi

†Columbus (Ch. 43 ETV)—WMAA-DT. Network Service: ETV. Mississippi Authority for ETV, 3825 Ridgewood Rd, Jackson, MS 39211. Phone: 601-432-6565. Fax: 601-432-6654. Web site: http://www.etv.state.ms.us. Technical facilities: Channel No. 43 (644-650 MHz). Proposed power: 81-kw max. visual, aural. Antenna: 668-ft above av. terrain, 658-ft. above ground, 1595-ft. above sea level. Latitude 33° 50' 31'', Longitude 88° 41' 48''. Ownership: Mississippi Authority for ETV. Represented (legal): Schwartz, Woods & Miller. Represented (engineering): Kessler & Gehman Associates Inc. Personnel: Marie Antoon, Executive Director; Becky Cade, Administration Director; Dick Rizzo, News & Public Affairs Director; Keith Martin, Technical Services Director; Jerry Ladd, Chief Network Engineer; Maggie Gibson, Business Services Director; Art Starkey, Program Director; Gene Edward, Content Development Director; Darryl Moses, Production Manager; Brenda Busby, Traffic Manager; Randy Tinney, Public Relations. Columbus-Tupelo-West Point-Houston, MS DMA. BMPEDT-20020611ABI. Grant Date: June 27, 2002. Station plans to broadcast in digital mode on its analog allotment.

Montana

†Great Falls (Ch. 21 ETV)— Board of Regents of the Montana University System, Room 183, VCB, Bozeman, MT 59717-3340. Phone: 406-994-3437. Technical facilities: Channel No. 21 (512-518 MHz). Proposed power: 23.4-kw max. visual, aural. Antenna: 501-ft above av. terrain, 440-ft. above ground, 3983-ft. above sea level. Latitude 47° 32' 09.2'', Longitude 111° 17' 02.1''. Ownership: Montana U. System Board of Regents. Represented (engineering): Cohen Dippell & Everist PC. Represented (legal): Dow Lohnes PLLC. Great Falls, MT DMA. BNPEDT-20060809AJP. Grant Date: October 12, 2007. Station plans to go directly to digital broadcast; no analog application.

◆†Kalispell (Ch. 46 ETV)— Board of Regents of the Montana University System, Room 183, VCB, Bozeman, MT 59717-3340. Phone: 406-994-3437. Technical facilities: Channel No. 46 (662-668 MHz). Proposed power: 67.1-kw max. visual, aural. Antenna: 2721-ft above av. terrain, 155-ft. above ground, 6835-ft. above sea level. Latitude 48° 00' 48.2''. Longitude 114° 21' 54.5''. Ownership: Montana U. System Board of Regents. Represented (engineering): Cohen Dippell & Everist PC. Represented (legal): Dow Lohnes PLLC. Missoula, MT DMA. BNPEDT-20060809AJQ. Grant Date: Unreported. Station plans to go directly to digital broadcast; no analog application.

◆†Kalispell (Ch. 46 ETV)— Flathead Adventist Radio Inc., 1375 Hwy. 93 N, Kalispell, MT 59901. Phone: 406-250-1226. Technical facilities: Channel No. 46 (662-668 MHz). Proposed power: 180-kw max. visual, aural. Antenna: 2703-ft above av. terrain, 140-ft. above ground, 6827-ft. above sea level. Latitude 48° 00' 48'', Longitude 114° 21' 55''. Ownership: Flathead Adventist Radio Inc. Represented (engineering): Smith & Fisher. Missoula, MT DMA. BNPEDT-20060810ABD. Grant Date: Unreported. Station plans to go directly to digital broadcast; no analog application.

Nevada

Ely (Ch. 27)—KBNY-DT. Nevada Channel 6 Inc., Debtor in Possession, One Shackleford Dr, Suite 400, Little Rock, AR 72211-2545. Phone: 501-221-0400. Technical facilities: Channel No. 27 (548-554 MHz). Proposed power: 300-kw max. visual, aural. Antenna: 1073-ft above av. terrain, 92-ft. above ground, 8090-ft. above sea level. Latitude 39° 15' 58'', Longitude 114° 54'05''. Ownership: Equity Media Holdings Corp., Debtor in Possession. Salt Lake City, UT DMA. BPCDT-20080807AAQ. Grant Date: August 8, 2008. Assignment of permit to Debtor in Possession status approved by FCC February 4, 2009. Equity Broadcasting Corp. merged with Coconut Palm Acquisition Corp., becoming Equity Media Holdings Corp. FCC approved deal March 27, 2007. Analog station never operational.

Goldfield (Ch. 50)—KEGS-DT. Network Service: IND. Nevada Channel 3 Inc., Debtor in Possession, One Shackleford Dr, Suite 400, Little Rock, AR 72211-2545. Phone: 501-219-2400. Technical facilities: Channel No. 50 (686-692 MHz). Proposed power: 30-kw max. visual, aural. Antenna: 1447-ft above av. terrain, 35-ft. above ground, 7135-ft. above sea level. Latitude 38° 03' 05'', Longitude 117° 13' 30''. Ownership: Equity Media Holdings Corp., Debtor in Possession. Las Vegas, NV DMA. BPCDT-20080808AAC. Grant Date: August 11, 2008. Began analog operations: April 11, 2002. Assignment of license to Debtor in Possession status approved by FCC February 4, 2009. Equity Broadcasting Corp. merged with Coconut Palm Acquisition Corp., becoming Equity Media Holdings Corp. FCC approved deal March 27, 2007. Ceased analog operations: June 12, 2009. Station missed digital transition deadline due to financial difficulties and has requested permission from the FCC to remain silent while they obtain a tower lease.

New Mexico

◆†**Hobbs (Ch. 47 ETV)**— ESP Technology Community Broadcasters, 110 Green Meadows, Abilene, TX 79605. Phone: 325-691-0397. Technical facilities: Channel No. 47 (668-674 MHz). Proposed power: 100-kw max. visual, aural. Antenna: 350-ft above av. terrain, 489-ft. above ground, 4107-ft. above sea level. Latitude 32° 43' 28'', Longitude 103° 05' 46''. Ownership: ESP Technology Community Broadcasters. Albuquerque-Santa Fe, NM DMA. BNPEDT-20040526ATP. Grant Date: Unreported. Station plans to go directly to digital broadcast; no analog application.

◆†**Hobbs (Ch. 47 ETV)**— Eastern New Mexico U., 52 Broadcast Center, Portales, NM 88130-9989. Phone: 505-562-2112. Technical facilities: Channel No. 47 (668-674 MHz). Proposed power: 125-kw max. visual, aural. Antenna: 169-ft above av. terrain, 179-ft. above ground, 3857-ft. above sea level. Latitude 32° 45' 40.1'', Longitude 103° 11' 21.7''. Ownership: Eastern New Mexico U. Board of Regents. Albuquerque-Santa Fe, NM DMA. BNPEDT-20040524AOU. Grant Date: Unreported. Station plans to go directly to digital broadcast; no analog application.

New York

Ithaca (Ch. 20)—WNYI-DT. Word of God Fellowship Inc., 3901 Hwy 121 S, Bedford, TX 76021. Phone: 817-571-1229. Technical facilities: Channel No. 20 (506-512 MHz). Proposed power: 60-kw max. visual, aural. Antenna: 801-ft above av. terrain, 367-ft. above ground, 1968-ft. above sea level. Latitude 42° 52' 10'', Longitude 76° 11' 46''. Ownership: Word of God Fellowship Inc. Represented (legal): Koerner & Olender PC. Syracuse, NY DMA. BPCDT-20080620AAS. Grant Date: June 2, 2009. Began analog operations: January 12, 2002. Ceased analog operations: June 12, 2009. Station was unable to make digital transition due to financial difficulties. Sale to present owner by Equity Media Holdings Corp. approved by FCC June 12, 2009. Assignment of license to Debtor in Possession status approved by FCC February 4, 2009. Equity Broadcasting Corp. merged with Coconut Palm Acquisition Corp., becoming Equity Media Holdings Corp. FCC approved deal March 27, 2007. Sale to Equity Broadcasting Corp. by William M. Smith approved by FCC June 25, 2004. Transfer of control from Kevin O'Kane (56% to 0%) & Curt Dunham (20% to 0%) to William M. Smith (20% to 100%) approved by FCC April 3, 2003.

Saranac Lake (Ch. 40)—WNMN-DT. Channel 61 Associates LLC, 4231 Brittany Lane, Sarasota, FL 34233-3702. Phone: 941-371-0272. Technical facilities: Channel No. 40 (626-632 MHz). Proposed power: 50-kw max. visual, aural. Antenna: 1444-ft above av. terrain, 46-ft. above ground, 3182-ft. above sea level. Latitude 44° 09' 35'', Longitude 74° 28' 34''. Ownership: Floyd L. Cox Jr. Represented (legal): Davis Wright Tremaine LLP. Represented (engineering): du Treil, Lundin & Rackley Inc. Burlington, VT-Plattsburgh, NY DMA. BPCDT-20080619ALG. Grant Date: July 7, 2008. Station plans to broadcast digitally on its analog channel allotment. Sale to Twin Valleys Television LLC (Jeff Loper & Harrison Uhl) pends. Due to construction difficulties, digital transition has been delayed.

Springville (Ch. 7)—WNGS-DT. Network Service: IND. Word of God Fellowship Inc., 3901 Hwy 121 S, Bedford, TX 76021. Phone: 716-942-3000. Fax: 716-942-3010. Email: wngsmngr@localnet.com. Technical facilities: Channel No. 7 (174-180 MHz). Proposed power: 15.5-kw max. visual, aural. Antenna: 1348-ft above av. terrain, 963-ft. above ground, 2698-ft. above sea level. Latitude 42° 38' 15'', Longitude 78° 37' 12''. Ownership: Word of God Fellowship Inc. (Group Owner). Represented (legal): Koerner & Olender PC. Personnel: Caroline K. Powley, General Manager & Business Manager; Donna McDonnough, Sales Manager; Ralph Thompson, Chief Engineer; William Smith, Program Manager; Stephen Howe, Promotion & Production Manager; Ralph L. Palmer, Traffic Manager & Control Room Supervisor. Buffalo, NY DMA. BPCDT-20080328AFD. Grant Date: June 23, 2008. Began analog operations: December 15, 1996. Ceased analog operations: June 12, 2009. Station did not meet digital transition deadline due to financial difficulties. Sale to present owner by Equity Media Holdings Corp. approved by FCC June 10, 2009. Assignment of license to Debtor in Possession status approved by FCC February 4, 2009. Equity Broadcasting Corp. merged with Coconut Palm Acquisition Corp., becoming Equity Media Holdings Corp. FCC approved deal March 27, 2007. Sale to Equity Broadcasting Corp. by Unicorn/Springville (Caroline K. Powley) approved by FCC June 25, 2004. Sale to Granite Broadcasting Corp. by Unicorn/Springville (Caroline K. Powley) dismissed by FCC April 30, 2001.

North Carolina

†**Canton (Ch. 27 ETV)**—WUNW-DT. Network Service: ETV. U. of North Carolina, PO Box 14900, Research Triangle Park, NC 27709-4900. Phone: 919-549-7000. Fax: 919-549-7207. Web site: http://www.unctv.org. Technical facilities: Channel No. 27 (548-554 MHz). Proposed power: 0.35-kw max. visual, aural. Antenna: 1555-ft above av. terrain, 69-ft. above ground, 4557-ft. above sea level. Latitude 35° 34' 06'', Longitude 82° 54' 25''. Requests modification of CP for change to 50-kw max. visual. Ownership: U. of North Carolina. Represented (legal): Schwartz, Woods & Miller. Greenville-Spartanburg-Anderson, SC-Asheville, NC DMA. BPEDT-20080402AAN. Grant Date: August 26, 2008. Station plans to broadcast digitally on its original analog channel allotment. Current construction deadline is January 2011.

Greenville (Ch. 47)—WYDO-DT. Network Service: MNT, FOX. Esteem Broadcasting of North Carolina LLC, 13865 E Elliott Dr, Marshall, IL 62441. Phone: 252-756-0814. Fax: 252-240-2028. Email: gdean@fox8fox14.com. Web site: http://www.fox8fox14.com. Technical facilities: Channel No. 47 (668-674 MHz). Proposed power: 200-kw max. visual, aural. Antenna: 1778-ft above av. terrain, 1775-ft. above ground, 1821-ft. above sea level.

Latitude 35° 06' 15'', Longitude 77° 20' 12''. Ownership: Esteem Broadcasting LLC. (Group Owner). Represented (legal): Drinker Biddle. Personnel: Don Fisher, Station Manager; Lisa Leonard, Sales Director; Gary Dean, News Director; Andy Kozik, Chief Engineer; Marla Liguori, Business Manager; Linda Murphy, Program Manager; Walt Young, Promotions Manager; Scott Foley, Production Manager; Ron Taintor, Creative Services Director; Sandy Fulcher, Traffic Manager. Greenville-New Bern-Washington, NC DMA. BMPCDT-20081217AAL. Grant Date: January 6, 2008. Began analog operations: July 30, 1992. Sale to present owner by Piedmont Television Holdings LLC approved by FCC November 1, 2007. Piedmont Television Holdings LLC previously known as GOCOM Holdings LLC. Merger of GOCOM Communications LLC with Grapevine Communications Inc. to form GOCOM Holdings LLC approved by FCC November 1, 1999. Sale to GOCOM Communications LLC by KS Family Television Inc. approved by FCC August 4, 1997. Transfer of control by KS Family Television Inc. from Karl H. Stoll to Frederick J. McCune approved by FCC September 21, 1992. Ceased analog operations: June 12, 2009. Station is completing construction of its digital facilities and anticipates broadcasting in October 2009.

North Dakota

Pembina (Ch. 12)—KNRR-DT. Network Service: FOX. Red River Broadcast Co. LLC, PO Box 9115, 4015 9th Ave. SW, Fargo, ND 58106. Phone: 701-277-1515. Fax: 701-277-1830. Technical facilities: Channel No. 12 (204-210 MHz). Proposed power: 4.44-kw visual, aural. Antenna: 1401-ft above av. terrain, 1413-ft. above ground, 2211-ft. above sea level. Latitude 48° 59' 44'', Longitude 97° 24' 28''. Ownership: Red River Broadcast Corp. (Group Owner). Represented (legal): Holland & Knight LLP. Personnel: Ro Grignon, President; Kathy Lau, Vice President, General Manager & Promotion Director; Myron Kunin, Chief Executive Officer; Ed Beiswenger, General & Local Sales Manager; Dave Hoffman, Chief Engineer; Jim Shaw, News Director; Candice Kassenborg, Business Manager; Jill Heacox, Traffic Manager. Fargo-Valley City, ND DMA. BPCDT-20080520ACJ. Grant Date: January 14, 2009. Station plans to broadcast digitally on its analog channel allotment. Began analog operations: August 11, 1985. Ceased analog operations: June 12, 2009. Station currently silent due to financial difficulties and hopes to be operational by October 18, 2009.

Oklahoma

◆†**Tulsa (Ch. 26 ETV)**—Network Service: ETV. Oral Roberts U., 7777 S Lewis Ave, Tulsa, OK 74171. Phone: 918-495-6383. Fax: 918-495-7388. Web site: http://www.oru.edu. Technical facilities: Channel No. 26 (542-548 MHz). Proposed power: 50-kw max. visual, aural. Antenna: 597-ft above av. terrain, 673-ft. above ground, 1296-ft. above sea level. Latitude 36° 02' 34'', Longitude 95° 57' 11''. Ownership: Oral Roberts U. Represented (legal): Hardy, Carey, Chautin & Balkin LLP. Represented (engineering): du Treil, Lundin & Rackley Inc. Tulsa, OK DMA. BPET-19960621KE. Grant Date: Unreported. Application amended to change from analog 63 to digital 26.

Puerto Rico

Mayaguez (Ch. 22)—WOST-DT. CMCG Puerto Rico License LLC, 900 Laskin Rd, Virginia Beach, VA 23451. Phone: 787-895-2725. Fax: 787-895-9198. Technical facilities: Channel No. 22 (518-524 MHz). Proposed power: 50-kw max. visual, aural. Antenna: 1073-ft above av. terrain, 80-ft. above ground, 1228-ft. above sea level. Latitude 18° 18' 51'', Longitude 67° 11' 24''. Ownership: Max Media X LLC.; Power Television International LLC. Represented (legal): Garvey Schubert Barer. Puerto Rico DMA. BPCDT-20080303AKY. Grant Date: March 25, 2008. Began analog operations: January 20, 2006. Station went off air June 7, 2007 due to possible interference from loss of output filter. Station resumed operations July 16, 2007. Sale to present owners by Signal Broadcasting approved by FCC February 17, 2006. Ceased analog operations: January 19, 2009. Station has completed construction of digital facilities and expects to commence authorized operation by August 2009.

South Carolina

†**Georgetown (Ch. 38 ETV)**—WPJT-DT. Network Service: ETV. Community Television Inc., PO Box 1616, Greenville, SC 29602. Phone: 864-244-1616. Technical facilities: Channel No. 38 (614-620 MHz). Proposed power: 500-kw max. visual, aural. Antenna: 561-ft above av. terrain, 548-ft. above ground, 589-ft. above sea level. Latitude 33° 50' 12'', Longitude 78° 51' 11''. Ownership: Community Television Inc. Columbia, SC DMA. BMPEDT-20040503AFV. Grant Date: November 1, 2004. Station plans to go directly to digital broadcast; analog application never granted.

Utah

Vernal (Ch. 16)—KBCJ-DT. Vernal Broadcasting Inc., Debtor in Possession, One Shackleford Dr, Suite 400, Little Rock, AR 72211-2545. Phone: 520-544-0088. Technical facilities: Channel No. 16 (482-488 MHz). Proposed power: 1000-kw max. visual, aural. Antenna: 2218-ft above av. terrain, 128-ft. above ground, 8337-ft. above sea level. Latitude 40° 21' 22'', Longitude 109° 08' 41''. Ownership: Equity Media Holdings Corp., Debtor in Possession. Salt Lake City, UT DMA. BPCDT-20080331AEG. Grant Date: May 27, 2008. Station never began analog operations. Sale of Kaleidoscope Foundation's 50% interest to Equity Broadcasting Corp. approved by FCC August 21, 1998. Sale of Media Properties LP's 50% interest to Kaleidoscope Foundation Inc. dismissed by FCC at applicant's request May 25, 1999. Transfer of Equity's interest to restructured entity approved by FCC August 23, 1999. Transfer of Media Properties LP's 50% interest to Equity Broadcasting Corp.

approved by FCC May 11, 2001. Equity Broadcasting Corp. merged with Coconut Palm Acquisition Corp., becoming Equity Media Holdings Corp. FCC approved deal March 27, 2007. Assignment of permit to Debtor in Possession status approved by FCC February 4, 2009. Due to the licensee's financial situation, station has applied for an extension for construction of their digital facilities.

West Virginia

◆**Charleston (Ch. 52)**— Pappas Telecasting of America, 500 S. Chinowth Rd, Visalia, CA 93277. Phone: 209-733-7800. Technical facilities: Channel No. 52 (698-704 MHz). Proposed power: 100-kw max. visual, aural. Antenna: 896-ft above av. terrain, 1043-ft. above ground, 2015-ft. above sea level. Latitude 38° 30' 21'', Longitude 82° 12' 33''. Ownership: Pappas Telecasting Companies. (Group Owner). Represented (legal): Fletcher, Heald & Hildreth PLC. Charleston-Huntington, WV DMA. BPCDT-19960722KO. Grant Date: Unreported. Station plans to go directly to digital broadcast; no analog application.

Wisconsin

Crandon (Ch. 12)—WBIJ-DT. Selenka Communications LLC, 1904 Doty St, Oshkosh, WI 54902. Phone: 920-589-2511. Technical facilities: Channel No. 12 (204-210 MHz). Proposed power: 3.2-kw visual, aural. Antenna: 390-ft above av. terrain, 240-ft. above ground, 2064-ft. above sea level. Latitude 45° 34' 23'', Longitude 88° 52' 57''. Ownership: Dennis R. Selenka Estate. Represented (legal): Dickstein Shapiro LLP. Wausau-Rhinelander, WI DMA. BPCDT-20080618ATL. Grant Date: September 5, 2008. Began analog operations: June 21, 2003. Sale to WAOW-WYOW Television Inc. (Quincy Newspapers Inc.) pends. Ceased analog operations: June 12, 2009. Station did not meet transition deadline due to financial difficulties and has requested permission from the FCC to remain silent until December 2009.

Ownership of Commercial Television Stations

Comprises all persons or companies which have interest in commercial television stations. Ownership of all stations is assumed to be 100% unless otherwise noted.

ACCESS.1 COMMUNICATIONS CORP.
11 Penn Plaza, 16th Floor
New York, NY 10001
Phone: 212-714-1000
Officers:
Sydney L. Small, Chairman & Chief Executive Officer
Chesley Maddox-Dorsey, President & Chief Operating Officer
Adriane Gaines, Secretary
Ownership: Sydney L. Small, 50.16%; Chesley Maddox-Dorsey, 5.28%; Adriane Gaines, 3.44%.
Represented (legal): Rubin, Winston, Diercks, Harris & Cooke LLP.
TV Stations:
New Jersey: WMGM-DT Wildwood.
LPTV Stations:
New Jersey: WMGM-LP Atlantic City.
Other Holdings:
Radio: SupeRadio, producer & distributer if radio programming.

ACME COMMUNICATIONS INC.
2101 E. 4th St.
Suite 202A
Santa Ana, CA 92705
Phone: 715-245-9499
E-mail: contactus@newmexicoswbcw.tv
Officers:
Jamie Kellner, Chairman & Chief Executive Officer
Douglas Gealy, President & Chief Operating Officer
Tom Allen, Executive Vice President, Secretary & Chief Financial Officer
Ownership: Gabelli Capital LLC, 10.11%; CEA Capital Partners USA LP, 9.57%; James Collis, 9.57%; Brian McNeill, 9.57%; Cannell Capital LLC, 8.62%; Dimensional Fund Advisors Inc., 7.2%; Alta Communications VI LP, 6.72%; Wynnefield Capital, 5.68%; Jamie Kellner, 4.72%; Douglas Gealy, 3.39%; Thomas D. Allen, 3.38%; Thomas Embrescia, 0.90%.
Represented (legal): O'Melveny & Myers LLP; Dickstein Shapiro LLP.
TV Stations:
New Mexico: KASY-DT Albuquerque; KRWB-DT Roswell; KWBQ-DT Santa Fe.
Ohio: WBDT-DT Springfield.
Tennessee: WBXX-DT Crossville.
Wisconsin: WBUW-DT Janesville; WIWB-DT Suring.
LPTV Stations:
New Mexico: K24CT Alamogordo; K28HB Alamogordo; K23BT Farmington; K17EM Roswell.

ADELL BROADCASTING CORP.
35000 Adell Dr.
Clinton Twp., MI 48045-2814
Phone: 810-790-3838
Fax: 810-790-3841
Officers:
Kevin Adell, Vice President, Operations
D. Sharron Adell, Secretary-Treasurer
Ownership: Franklin Z. Adell Trust, Kevin Adell, Trustee, 86%%; R Antoinette Riley, 5%%; O'Neil D Swanson, 5%%; Ralph G Lameti, 3%%; Horace Sheffield Estate, 1%%.
Represented (legal): William D. Silva.
TV Stations:
Michigan: WADL-DT Mount Clemens.

ALLBRITTON COMMUNICATIONS CO.
1000 Wilson Blvd.
Suite 2700
Arlington, VA 22209
Phone: 703-647-8700
Fax: 703-647-8707
E-mail: jfritz@allbrittontv.com
Officers:
Joe L. Allbritton, Chairman of Executive Committee
Robert L. Allbritton, Chairman & Chief Executive Officer
Lawrence I. Hebert, Vice Chairman
Frederick J. Ryan Jr., Vice Chairman, President & Chief Executive Officer
Jerald N. Fritz, Senior Vice President, Legal & Strategic Affairs
Stephen P. Gibson, Senior Vice President & Chief Financial Officer
Ownership: Joe L Allbritton, 49%; Robert Lewis Allbritton 1996 Trust, 49%; Barbara B. Allbritton 2008 Marital Trust, 2%.
TV Stations:
Alabama: WJSU-DT Anniston; WCFT-DT Tuscaloosa.
Arkansas: KATV-DT Little Rock.
District of Columbia: WJLA-DT Washington.
Oklahoma: KTUL-DT Tulsa.
Pennsylvania: WHTM-DT Harrisburg.
South Carolina: WCIV-DT Charleston.
Virginia: WSET-DT Lynchburg.
LPTV Stations:
Alabama: WBMA-LP Birmingham.
Virginia: W05AA Roanoke.
Newspapers:
Connecticut: Enfield Press
Massachusetts: Longmeadow News, Wallace Pennysaver, The Westfield Evening News (published by Allbritton affiliate Westfield News Advertiser Inc.)

ALPHA & OMEGA COMMUNICATIONS LLC
PO Box 352
Salt Lake City, UT 84110
Phone: 801-973-8820
Ownership: Isaac Max Jaramillo; Patricia Jaramillo; Connie Whitney, 33.3% each.
Represented (legal): Wood, Maines & Nolan Chartered.
TV Stations:
Utah: KTMW-DT Salt Lake City.
LPTV Stations:
Idaho: KCLP-CA Boise.
Utah: K58FT Huntsville; K22IT Provo; K59GS Salt Lake City; K49GD Spanish Fork.

AMERICAN CHRISTIAN TELEVISION SERVICES INC.
1844 Baty Rd.
Lima, OH 45807
Phone: 419-339-4444
Officers:
Jeff Hazel, Chairman
Kevin Bowers, President & Chief Executive Officer
Eugene Lehman, Secretary-Treasurer
Joe Wassink, Chief Financial Officer
Ownership: Jeff Hazel; Eugene Lehman; Peg Schultz; David Halker; Susan Ingraham; Doug Roser; Kevin Bowers; Gary Hempleman; Andrea King; Paul Woehlke.
Represented (legal): Wiley Rein LLP.
TV Stations:
Ohio: WTLW-DT Lima.

ASOCIACION EVANGELISTICA CRISTO VIENE INC.
Box 949
Camuy, PR 00627
Phone: 787-898-5120
Fax: 787-898-0529
Officers:
Jose J. Avila, President
Esther Robles, Secretary
Ownership: Tito Apiles, 25%; Jose J Avila, 25%; Edwin Tavarez, 25%; Vincente Vales, 25%.
TV Stations:
Puerto Rico: WCCV-DT Arecibo.
LPTV Stations:
Puerto Rico: W54AQ Yauco.

ASSOCIATED CHRISTIAN TELEVISION SYSTEM INC.
4520 Parkbreeze Court
Orlando, FL 32808
Phone: 407-298-5555
Officers:
Claud Bowers, Chairman, President & Chief Executive Officer
Angela Courte, Vice President, Operations
P. B. Howell Jr., Vice President
Freeda Bowers, Secretary-Treasurer & Chief Financial Officer
Ownership: Non-profit organization.
Represented (legal): Koerner & Olender PC.
TV Stations:
Florida: WACX-DT Leesburg.
LPTV Stations:
Florida: W40CQ-D Alachua, etc.; W69AY Alachua, etc.; WACX-LP Tallahassee.

BAHAKEL COMMUNICATIONS LTD.
One Television Place
c/o Leon Porter
Charlotte, NC 28205
Phone: 704-372-4434
Web site: www.nesbe.com
Officers:
Beverly Bahakel Poston, Executive Vice President & Chief Operating Officer
Lorraine Lancaster, Senior Vice President & Secretary
Ed Conrad, Senior Vice President & Chief Financial Officer
Russell Schwartz, Senior Vice President, Legal Counsel
Cullie Tarleton, Senior Vice President, TV
Stephen Bahakel, Senior Vice President, Radio
Anna Rufty, Vice President, Human Resources
Bill Naper, Vice President, Engineering & Technology
Ownership: New Voting Stock LLC; NVSLLC ownership:; 2000 Bahakel Descendents Trust; Beverly B. Poston, Sole Investments & Benefits Trustee.
Represented (legal): Moore & Van Allen.
TV Stations:
Alabama: WAKA-DT Selma.
North Carolina: WCCB-DT Charlotte.
South Carolina: WOLO-DT Columbia; WFXB-DT Myrtle Beach.
Tennessee: WBBJ-DT Jackson.
Radio Stations:
Colorado: KILO (FM), KYZK (FM) Colorado Springs
Iowa: KFMW (FM), KOKZ (FM), KWLO (AM), KXEL (AM) Waterloo
Tennessee: WDEF-AM-FM, WDOD-AM-FM Chattanooga

BAYOU CITY BROADCASTING LLC
1300 Post Oak Blvd
Ste 830
Houston, TX 77056
Phone: 281-380-0076
Ownership: Dr. Oliver Hunter, 50%; DuJuan McCoy, 50%.
Represented (legal): Fletcher, Heald & Hildreth PLC.
TV Stations:
Texas: KXVA-DT Abilene; KIDY-DT San Angelo.
LPTV Stations:
Texas: KIDZ-LP Abilene; KIDV-LP Albany; KIDU-LP Brownwood; KIDT-LP Stamford; KIDB-CA Sweetwater.

BAY TELEVISION
5510 W. Gray St. W
Tampa, FL 33609-1054
Phone: 813-886-9882
Fax: 813-880-8100
Officers:
David D. Smith, President & Director
J. Duncan Smith, Vice President, Secretary & Director
Robert E. Smith, Treasurer & Director
Robert L. Simmons, Assistant Secretary & Director
Frederick G. Smith, Assistant Treasurer & Director
Ownership: David D. Smith, 18.75%%. voting; J. Duncan Smith, 18.75%%. voting; Robert E. Smith, 18.75%%. voting; Frederick G. Smith, 18.75%%. voting; Robert L. Simmons, 18.56%%. voting.
TV Stations:
Florida: WTTA-DT St. Petersburg.

BEACH TV PROPERTIES INC.
8317 Front Beach Rd.
Suite 23
Panama City, FL 32407

Phone: 850-234-2773
Officers:
Byron J. Colley Jr., President
Tonita Davis, Secretary-Treasurer
Ownership: Jud Colley, 50%; Tonita Davis, 50%.
TV Stations:
Florida: WAWD-DT Fort Walton Beach; WPCT-DT Panama City Beach.
LPTV Stations:
Florida: WDES-CA Destin; WCAY-LP Key West; W46AN Panama City; WPFN-CA Panama City.
Georgia: WTHC-LP Atlanta.
Louisiana: KNOV-CD New Orleans.

BELO CORP.
Box 655237
Dallas, TX 75265
Phone: 214-977-6606
Fax: 214-977-6603
E-mail: nhulcy@belo.com
Web site: www.belo.com
Officers:
Robert W. Decherd, Chairman
Dunia A. Shive, President & Chief Executive Officer
Dennis A. Williamson, Executive Vice President & Chief Financial Officer
Peter Diaz, Executive Vice President, Television Operations
Guy H. Kerr, Executive Vice President, Law & Government and Secretary
Kathy Clements, Senior Vice President, Television Operations
Russell F Coleman, Senior Vice President & General Counsel
Marian Spitzberg, Senior Vice President, Human Resources
Paul Fry, Vice President, Investor Relations & Corporate Communications
Ownership: Publicly held. On February 8, 2008, all newspaper holdings and related assets were spun-off to a new publicly traded company, A. H. Belo Corp.
TV Stations:
Arizona: KASW-DT Phoenix; KTVK-DT Phoenix; KMSB Tucson; KTTU-DT Tucson.
Idaho: KTVB-DT Boise.
Kentucky: WHAS-DT Louisville.
Louisiana: WWL-DT New Orleans; WUPL-DT Slidell.
Missouri: KMOV-DT St. Louis.
North Carolina: WCNC-DT Charlotte.
Oregon: KGW-DT Portland.
Texas: KVUE-DT Austin; WFAA Dallas; KHOU Houston; KENS San Antonio.
Virginia: WVEC Hampton.
Washington: KONG Everett; KING-DT Seattle; KREM Spokane; KSKN-DT Spokane.
LPTV Stations:
Arizona: K34EE Cottonwood & Prescott; K38AI Cottonwood, etc.; K54GI Flagstaff; K57BO Globe & Miami; K11LC Prescott; K50FV Tucson; K53GM Williams-Ash Fork; K41JE Williams-Ashfork.
Idaho: K05DC Cambridge, etc.; K13GO Cascade; K41FJ Coeur d'Alene; K13GW Council; K05DD Glenns Ferry; K21CC Lewiston; K13SO McCall, etc.; KTFT-LP Twin Falls.
Louisiana: WBXN-CA New Orleans.
North Carolina: W30CR Biscoe; W24AY Lilesville & Wadesboro.
Oregon: K29AZ Newport; K08KN Prineville.
Washington: K35HU Grays River, etc..
Newspapers:
California: La Prensa, The Business Press, The Press-Enterprise, This Week in the Desert (Riverside)
Rhode Island: Rhode Island Monthly, The Providence Journal (Providence)

Texas: al dia, Denton Record Chronicle, Quick, Texas Almanac, The Dallas Morning News (Dallas/Ft. Worth)
Other Holdings:
Cable Network: 24/7 NewsChannel (Boise, ID); Texas Cable News; Local News on Cable (Norfolk-Hampton, VA); NewsWatch on Channel 15 (New Orleans, LA); Northwest Cable News Network
Data service: Belo Interactive Inc..

THOMAS BENSON JR.
5800 Airline Dr
Metairie, LA 70003
Phone: 504-733-0255
Represented (legal): Covington & Burling.
TV Stations:
Louisiana: WVUE-DT New Orleans.

BETTER LIFE TELEVISION INC.
PO Box 776
Grants Pass, OR 97528
Phone: 541-474-3089
Fax: 541-474-9409
E-mail: rondavis@betterlifetv.tv
Web site: www.betterlifetv.tv
Officers:
Robert Heisler, President
Delmer Wagner, Vice President
Ron Davis, Secretary
Don Eisner, Treasurer
Ownership: Keith Babcock; Duane Corwin; Ron Davis; Don Eisner; Glenn Gingery, 5.5%. votes each.; Paul Gordon; Robert L Heisler; Patty Hyland; Walter MacPhee; Bob McReynolds; Olen Nations; Perry Parks; Judy Randahl; Willard Register; Holly Rueb; Richard Surroz; Delmer Wagner; George White.
Represented (legal): Donald E. Martin.
TV Stations:
Oregon: KBLN-DT Grants Pass; KTVC-DT Roseburg.
LPTV Stations:
Oregon: K48GO Cave Junction; K44FH Coos Bay; KAMK-LP Eugene; K22FC Grants Pass; K47GI Grants Pass; K48IW Kalmath; K48HV Klamath Falls; K18GB Medford; K23EX Medford; K25IM Medford; K29GX Merlin; K33GJ Merlin; K47HT Roseburg; K26HS Tillamook.

BLOCK COMMUNICATIONS INC.
6450 Monroe St.
Sylvania, OH 43560
Phones: 419-724-9802; 419-724-6035
Fax: 419-724-6167
Web site: www.blockcommunications.com
Officers:
Allan J Block, Chairman
John R Block, Vice Chairman
Gary J Blair, President
David M. Beihoff, Vice President, Newspaper Operations
Jodi L. Miehls, Assistant Secretary
Ownership: Allan J Block, 25%; John R Block, 25%; William Block Jr., 25%; Karen D. Johnese, 25%. votes.
Represented (legal): Dow Lohnes PLLC.
Cable Systems:
OHIO: SANDUSKY; TOLEDO.
TV Stations:
Idaho: KTRV-DT Nampa.
Illinois: WAND-DT Decatur.
Indiana: WMYO-DT Salem.
Kentucky: WDRB-DT Louisville.
Ohio: WLIO-DT Lima.
LPTV Stations:
Illinois: W31BX-D Danville.
Ohio: WFND-LP Findlay; WLMO-LP Lima; WLQP-LP Lima; WOHL-CA Sylvania.
Newspapers:

Ohio: Toledo Blade
Pennsylvania: Pittsburgh Post-Gazette
Other Holdings:
Outdoor advertising: Community Communications Services, advertising distribution company..

BOISE TELECASTERS LP
706 W. Herndon Ave.
Fresno, CA 93650-1033
Phone: 559-435-7000
Ownership: Cocola Broadcasting Companies LLC, see listing, 51%; Diane D. Dostinich Living Trust, 49%.
Represented (legal): Dow Lohnes PLLC.
TV Stations:
Idaho: KKJB-DT Boise.

BONNEVILLE INTERNATIONAL CORP.
55 North 300 West, Box 1160
Broadcast House
Salt Lake City, UT 84110-1160
Phone: 801-575-7500
Fax: 801-575-7548
Officers:
James B. Jacobson, Chairman
Bruce T. Reese, President & Chief Executive Officer
Robert A. Johnson, Executive Vice President & Chief Operating Officer
Glenn N. Larkin, Senior Vice President & Chief Financial Officer
David K. Redd, Vice President, Secretary & General Counsel
Ownership: Deseret Management Corp.; DMC ownership:; The First Presidency of the Jesus Christ of the Latter-Day Saints..
Represented (legal): Wilkinson Barker Knauer LLP.
TV Stations:
Utah: KSL-DT Salt Lake City.
LPTV Stations:
Utah: K24FE-D Beaver, etc.; K20GJ-D Bloomington; K07ED-D Enterprise; K11QQ-D Hildale, UT & Cane Beds, AZ; K08EN-D Pine Valley, etc.; K05AR-D Rockville; K35FS-D Santa Clara, etc.; K07CG-D Toquerville; K08BO-D Virgin.
Newspapers:
Utah: The Deseret News, Salt Lake City (operated by Deseret News Publishing)
Radio Stations:
Arizona: KMVP (AM), KPKX (FM), KTAR-AM-FM Phoenix
District of Columbia: WTOP (AM), WWWT-AM-FM
Illinois: WDRV (FM), WILV (FM) Chicago; WMVN (FM) East St. Louis; WARH (FM) Granite City; WTMX (FM) Skokie
Kentucky: WYGY (FM) Fort Thomas
Maryland: WFED (AM) Silver Spring
Missouri: WIL-AM-FM St. Louis
Ohio: WKRQ (FM), WUVE-FM Cincinnati; WSWD (FM) Fairfield
Utah: KSF (FM), KSL-AM-FM, KRSP-FM Salt Lake City; KUTR (AM) Taylorsville
Other Holdings:
Production: Video West (Salt Lake City)
Service company: Media/Paymaster Plus Corp. (Salt Lake City) provide payroll and signatory services; Bonneville Entertainment Co. (Los Angeles); Bonneville Communications (Salt Lake City) provides advertising agency services.

BONTEN MEDIA GROUP LLC
280 Park Ave
25th Floor, E Tower
New York, NY 10017
Phone: 212-247-8717
E-mail: info@dchold.com

Officers:
Randall D. Bongarten, President
David M. Wittels, Vice President
Scott Schneider, Vice President
Stephen M. Bassford, Vice President
Kyle N. Cruz, Vice President
Ownership: Diamond Castle Partners IV LP. votes, 69.6% assets; Bonten/DiamondCastle LLC, 29.8%. assets; DCPIVLP & BDCLLC ownership:; DCP IV GP LP, Gen. Partner; DCPIVGPLP ownership:; DCP IV GP-GP LLC, Gen. Partner; DCPIVGPGPLLC ownership:; Michael W. Ranger, Managing Member, 50%. votes; Lawrence M.v.D. Schloss, Managing Member, 50%. votes.
Represented (legal): Covington & Burling.
TV Stations:
California: KAEF-DT Arcata; KRCR-DT Redding.
Montana: KTVM-DT Butte; KCFW-DT Kalispell; KECI-DT Missoula.
North Carolina: WCTI-DT New Bern.
Texas: KTXS-DT Sweetwater.
Virginia: WCYB-DT Bristol.
LPTV Stations:
California: K12JJ Benbow, etc.; K04EZ Big Bend, etc.; K36BT Blue Lake; K05DQ Burney, etc.; K05BR Dunsmuir, etc.; K33DI East Weed; K04EQ Fort Jones, etc.; K20CN Fortuna/Rio Dell; K45DS Freshwater, etc.; K05EQ Green Point, etc.; K25CI Klamath; K27BH Lake Shastina; K02FF Lakehead; K11LD Likely; K05JK Mineral; K03FU Mountain Gate; K15CX Oroville; K05EM Paradise; K51EG South Eureka & Loleta; K34BW Willow Creek; K13LO Yreka, etc..
Idaho: K10HC Mullan.
Montana: K34FI-D Bozeman; K42BZ Bozeman; K51DW Dillon; K02AO Eureka, etc.; K14IU Frenchtown; K10HZ Pony; K02OL Seeley Lake; K35DJ Three Forks; K10HL Virginia City; K09KH Watkins, etc..
Texas: KTES-LP Abilene; KTXE-LP Abilene.

BROADCASTING LICENSES LP
2111 University Park Dr.
Suite 650
Okemos, MI 48864-6913
Phone: 517-347-4111
Ownership: Northwest Broadcasting Inc., Gern. Partner. 100% votes; 1% equity; Broadcasting Communications LLC, Ltd. Partner, 99%. equity; NBI ownership:; Brian W. Brady; BCLLC ownership:; Northwest Broadcasting Inc. 100% votes; 1% equity; Northwest Broadcasting LP, 99%. equity; NBLP ownership:; Northwest Broadcasting Inc., Gen. Partner. 100% votes; 0.07% equity; Brian W. Brady, Ltd. Partner, 99.3% equity; NBI ownership:; Brian W. Brady. Brady is also a principal of Mountain Licenses LP & Stainless Licenses LP, see listings.
TV Stations:
Oregon: KMVU-DT Medford.
LPTV Stations:
California: K41JB Yreka.
Oregon: K31GP Brookings, etc.; K44JB-D Grants Pass; K45ED Grants Pass; K44DZ Klamath Falls.

EUGENE J. BROWN
1181 Hwy 315
Wilkes Barre, PA 18702
Phone: 570-256-7436
Represented (legal): Fletcher, Heald & Hildreth PLC.
TV Stations:
Florida: WNBW-DT Gainesville; WTLF-DT Tallahassee.
Maine: WPME-DT Lewiston.
Pennsylvania: WSWB-DT Scranton.
Tennessee: WFLI-DT Cleveland.

BRYANT BROADCASTING CO.
200 E. Spring St.
Lebanon, TN 37087

Phones: 615-444-7211; 615-444-8206
Fax: 615-444-7215
Ownership: Dr. Joe F Bryant, Chairman, President & Chief Executive Officer.
TV Stations:
Tennessee: WJFB-DT Lebanon.
LPTV Stations:
Tennessee: W11BD Lebanon.

BUDD BROADCASTING CO. INC.
4150 N.W. 93rd Ave.
Gainesville, FL 32653
Phone: 352-371-7772
Fax: 352-371-9353
E-mail: buddman@gru.net
Officers:
Harvey M. Budd, President
Ilene S. Budd, Vice President & Secretary-Treasurer
Ownership: Harvey M Budd, 50%; Ilene Budd, 50%.
Represented (legal): Shainis & Peltzman Chartered.
TV Stations:
Florida: WFXU-DT Live Oak.
LPTV Stations:
Florida: WGVT-LD Gainesville; WNFT-LP Gainesville; WVVQ-LP Jacksonville; WOFT-LP Reddick; WMMF-LP Vero Beach; WGCT-LP Yankeetown; WGCT-LD Zephyrhills.
Kentucky: WKUG-LP Glasgow; WKUT-LP Glasgow.
New York: WKUW-LP Glasgow.

CADILLAC TELECASTING CO.
22713 N Galacia Dr
Sun City West, AZ 85375-2361
Phone: 602-571-1052
E-mail: jrnbolea@aol.com
Ownership: Alexander Bolea, President & Secretary-Treasurer.
Represented (legal): Womble, Carlyle, Sandridge & Rice.
TV Stations:
Michigan: WFQX-DT Cadillac; WFUP-DT Vanderbilt.
LPTV Stations:
Michigan: W43CM Pickford; W61CR Sault Ste. Marie; W54CR Traverse City.

CALIFORNIA-OREGON BROADCASTING INC.
PO Box 1489
125 S. Fir St.
Medford, OR 97501
Phones: 541-779-5555; 1-800-821-8108
Fax: 541-779-1151
Web site: www.kobi5.com
Ownership: Patricia C Smullin, Pres..
Represented (legal): Wiley Rein LLP.
Cable Systems:
OREGON: ENTERPRISE; LA PINE; MADRAS; PRINEVILLE.
TV Stations:
Oregon: KLSR-DT Eugene; KOTI-DT Klamath Falls; KOBI-DT Medford; KPIC-DT Roseburg.
LPTV Stations:
California: K06GS Bieber; K34KJ Crescent City, etc.; K11JM Fall River Mills, etc.; K13HU Fort Jones, etc.; K05ET-D Likely; K47DV South Yreka; K04HE Yreka, etc..
Oregon: K04ER Applegate Valley; K07JT Brookings; K07PP Camas Valley; K43DI Canyonville; K07KT Canyonville, etc.; K07PZ Cave Junction; K07PS Chemult; K06NS-D Chiloquin; K30BN Coos Bay; K36BX Coos Bay; K63DO Coos Bay; K14GW Corvallis; KEVU-LP Eugene; K19GH Eugene, etc.; K65ER Eugene, etc.; K58DA Glendale; K26HO Glide,etc.; K25EN Gold Beach; K02FT Gold Hill; K50FW Grants Pass; K04EY Grants

Pass, etc.; K13JR-D Jacksonville, etc.; K04ES Klamath Falls; K07NR-D Lakeview, etc.; K32DY Medford; K62BE Midland, etc.; K34BV Murphy, etc.; K13HM Myrtle Creek; K13JQ North Bend & Empire; K12IA Oakland, etc.; K08AK Port Orford, etc.; K62DR Roseburg; K03EI Tolo, etc.; K11GH Tri-City, etc.; K32FI Yoncalla.

CAPITOL BROADCASTING CO. INC.
2619 Western Blvd
Raleigh, NC 27606
Phone: 919-890-6000
Fax: 919-890-6095
E-mail: webmaster@cbc-raleigh.com
Web site: www.cbc-raleigh.com
Officers:
Jim Goodmon, President & Chief Executive Officer
Jimmy Goodmon, Vice President, CBC New Media Group
George W. Habel, Vice President, Radio Networks/Sports
Michael D. Hill, Vice President, General Counsel
Ardie Gregory, Vice President, General Manager, WRAL-FM & WCMC-FM
Jim Hefner, Vice President & General Manager, WRAL-TV
Dan McGrath, Vice President, Finance & Treasurer
Vicki Murray, Corporate Secretary
Jan Sharp, Vice President, Human Resources
Tom McLaughlin, Corporate Controller & Assistant Secretary-Assistant Treasurer
Ownership: Capitol Holding Co. Inc., 96.4%; A.J. Fletcher Foundation, 3.6%; CHCI ownership:; James F. Goodmon, 96%.
Represented (legal): Fletcher, Heald & Hildreth PLC.
TV Stations:
North Carolina: WJZY-DT Belmont; WRAL-DT Raleigh; WRAZ-DT Raleigh.
South Carolina: WMYT-DT Rock Hill.
LPTV Stations:
North Carolina: WILM-LD Wilmington.
Radio Stations:
North Carolina: WRAL (FM) Raleigh
Other Holdings:
Telecommunications company (Microspace Communications Corp.).

CARIBEVISION HOLDINGS INC.
1401 Brickell Ave
Ste 500
Miami, FL 33131
Phone: 305-365-2030
Officers:
Alejandro Burillo, Chairman
Carlos Barba, President & Chief Executive Officer
Enrique de la Campa, Vice President & Secretary-Treasurer
Ownership: Barba TV Group LLC, 80.73%; BTVGLLC ownership:; Barba Television Co., 91.65%; Pedro Gonzales, 5.44%; Maria Barba-Farshchian, 2.91%; BTC ownership:; Carlos Barba, 50%; Teresa Barba, 50%.
Represented (legal): Fletcher, Heald & Hildreth PLC.
TV Stations:
Puerto Rico: WKPV-DT Ponce; WJPX-DT San Juan; WJWN-DT San Sebastian; WIRS-DT Yauco.
LPTV Stations:
Florida: WFUN-LP Miami, etc.; WZXZ-CA Orlando.
New Jersey: WPXO-LD East Orange.

CAROLINA CHRISTIAN BROADCASTING CO.
Box 1616
Greenville, SC 29602

Phone: 864-244-1616
Fax: 864-292-8481
Officers:
James H. Thompson, President & General Manager
Norvin C. Duncan, Assistant to the President
Ownership: James H Thompson, 92%; remainder unissued.
Represented (legal): Bechtel & Cole Chartered.
TV Stations:
South Carolina: WGGS-DT Greenville.
LPTV Stations:
North Carolina: WJJV-LP Asheville; W23BQ Asheville, etc.; W31AZ Hendersonville.
South Carolina: W65DS Honea Path.

CATAMOUNT BROADCAST GROUP
71 East Ave.
Norwalk, CT 06851
Phone: 203-852-7164
Fax: 203-852-7163
Officers:
Ralph E. Becker, President & Chief Executive Officer
Daniel J. Duman, Chief Financial Officer
Ownership: BCI Partners Inc., Principal.
Represented (legal): Fletcher, Heald & Hildreth PLC.
TV Stations:
California: KHSL-DT Chico.
LPTV Stations:
California: K04FL Lakeshore, etc.; K49CT Paradise; K54EE Westwood.

THE CATHOLIC, APOSTOLIC & ROMAN CHURCH IN PUERTO RICO
Apartado 9021967
San Juan, PR 00902-1967
Phone: 787-727-7373
Ownership: Archdiocese of San Juan.
Represented (legal): Reynolds & Manning.
TV Stations:
Puerto Rico: WORO-DT Fajardo.

CBS CORP.
51 W. 52nd St.
New York, NY 10019-6188
Phone: 212-975-4321
Fax: 212-975-4516
Web site: www.cbscorporation.com
Officers:
Sumner M. Redstone, Chairman
Leslie Moonves, President & Chief Executive Officer
Anthony G. Ambrosio, Executive Vice President, Human Resources & Administration
Louis J. Briskman, Executive Vice President & General Counsel
Martin D. Franks, Executive Vice President, Planning, Policy & Government Relations
Gil Schwartz, Executive Vice President, Corporate Communications
Martin M. Shea, Executive Vice President, Investor Relations
Susan C. Gordon, Senior Vice President, Corporate Controller & Chief Accounting Officer
Angeline C. Straka, Senior Vice President, Deputy General Counsel & Secretary
Joseph R. Ianniello, Senior Vice President, Finance & Treasurer

Branch Office:
Paramount Stations Group Inc.
5555 Melrose Ave.
Los Angeles, CA 90038
Phone: 323-956-8100
Fax: 323-862-0121

Ownership: NAIRI Inc., 69.5% voting stock; remainder publicly held.%; NI ownership:; National Amusements Inc.; NAI ownership:; The Sumner M. Redstone Trust, 80%; Shari Redstone, 20%.
TV Stations:
California: KCAL-DT Los Angeles; KCBS-DT Los Angeles; KMAX-DT Sacramento; KBCW-DT San Francisco; KPIX-DT San Francisco; KOVR-DT Stockton.
Colorado: KCNC-DT Denver.
Florida: WBFS-DT Miami; WFOR-DT Miami; WTOG-DT St. Petersburg.
Georgia: WUPA-DT Atlanta.
Illinois: WBBM-DT Chicago.
Maryland: WJZ-DT Baltimore.
Massachusetts: WBZ-DT Boston; WSBK-DT Boston.
Michigan: WKBD-DT Detroit; WWJ-DT Detroit.
Minnesota: KCCO-DT Alexandria; WCCO-DT Minneapolis; KCCW-DT Walker.
New York: WCBS-DT New York.
Pennsylvania: WPCW-DT Jeannette; KYW-DT Philadelphia; WPSG-DT Philadelphia; KDKA-DT Pittsburgh.
Texas: KTVT-DT Fort Worth; KTXA-DT Fort Worth.
Virginia: WGNT-DT Portsmouth.
Washington: KSTW-DT Tacoma.
LPTV Stations:
Florida: W61AK Inverness; W23CN Sebring.
Indiana: WBXI-CA Indianapolis.
Utah: K44IZ-D Delta, etc..
Radio Stations:
Arizona: KMLE (FM) Chandler; KOOL-FM, KZON (FM) Phoenix
California: KCBS-AM-FM, KFWB (AM), KLSX (FM), KNX (AM), KRTH (FM), KTWV (FM) Los Angeles; KROQ-FM Pasadena; KQJK (FM) Roseville; KHTK-AM, KNCI (FM), KYMX (FM), KZZO (FM) Sacramento; KFRG (FM) San Bernardino; KSCF (FM), KYXY (FM) San D
Colorado: KIMN-FM, KWLI (FM), KXKL-FM Denver
Connecticut: WTIC-AM-FM, WZMX (FM) Hartford; WRCH (FM) New Britain
District of Columbia: WPGC-AM-FM
Florida: WJHM (FM) Daytona Beach; WOCL (FM) DeLand; WLLD (FM) Holmes Beach; WPBZ (FM) Indiantown; WMBX (FM) Jensen Beach; WNEW (FM) Jupiter; WSJT (FM) Lakeland; WOMX-FM Orlando; WYUU (FM) Safety Harbor; WQYK-AM-FM Seffner; WRBQ (FM) Atlanta
Georgia: WAOK (AM), WVEE (FM), WZGC (FM) Atlanta
Illinois: WBBM-AM-FM, WJMK (FM), WSCR (AM), WUSN (FM), WXRT-FM Chicago; WCFS-FM Elmwood Park
Kansas: KXNT (AM) Topeka
Maryland: WLZL (FM) Annapolis; WJFK-AM-FM, WLIF (FM), WQSR (FM), WWMX (FM) Baltimore; WTGB-FM Bethesda; WHFS (FM) Catonsville; WPGC (AM) Morningside
Massachusetts: WBCN (FM), WBMX (FM), WBZ (AM), WODS (FM), WZLX-FM Boston
Michigan: WOMC (FM), WVMV (FM), WWJ (AM), WXYT-AM-FM, WYCD (FM) Detroit
Minnesota: WCCO (AM), WLTE (FM) Minneapolis; KZJK (FM) St. Louis Park
Missouri: KEZK-FM, KMOX (AM), KYKY (FM) St. Louis
Nevada: KKJ (FM), KMXB (FM) Henderson; KLUC-FM Las Vegas; KSFN (AM) North Las Vegas; KXTE (FM) Pahrump
New York: WCBS-AM-FM, WFAN (AM), WINS (AM), WWFS (FM), WXRK (FM) New York
North Carolina: WFNA (AM), WFNZ (AM), WKQC (FM), WNKS (FM), WSOC-FM Charlotte; WPEG (FM) Concord; WBAV-FM Gastonia; WKRK (FM) Murphy
Ohio: WDOK (FM), WNCX (FM), WQAL (FM) Cleveland
Oregon: KVMX (FM) Banks; KLTH (FM) Lake Oswego; KCMD (FM), KINK-FM, KUFO-FM, KUPL-FM Portland
Pennsylvania: WZPT (FM) New Kensington; KYW (AM), WIP (AM), WPHT (AM), WYSP (FM) Philadelphia; KDKA (AM), WBZW-FM, WDSY-FM Pittsburgh

Texas: KJKK (FM), KLLI (FM), KLUV (FM), KRLD (AM), KVIL (FM) Dallas; KMVK (FM) Fort Worth; KHJZ (FM), KILT-AM-FM Houston; KIKK (AM) Pasadena Washington: KJAQ (FM), KMPS-FM, KPTK (AM), KZOK-FM Seattle; KBKS-FM Tacoma

Other Holdings:
Advertising on out-of-door media: CBS Outdoor.
Broadcast holdings: Caballero Acquisition Inc., see listing.
Consumer Products: CBS Consumer Products.
Digital Media: CBS Digital Media & CSTV Networks.
Publishing holdings: Simon & Schuster.
Television Production & Syndication: CBS Paramount Television & King World.
Theme Parks: Paramount Parks..

CHAMBERS COMMUNICATIONS CORP.
PO Box 7009
2295 Coburg Rd., Suite 200
Eugene, OR 97401
Phone: 541-485-5611
Fax: 541-342-2695
E-mail: mpuckett@adpronetworks.com
Web site: www.chamberscable.com; www.cmc.net/~chambers/
Ownership: Carolyn S Chambers, Chmn. & Chief Exec. Officer, see also Soda Mountain Broadcasting Inc..
Represented (legal): Arnold, Gallagher, Saydack, Percell, Roberts & Potter PC.
Cable Systems:
OREGON: SUNRIVER.
TV Stations:
Oregon: KOHD-DT Bend; KEZI-DT Eugene; KDKF-DT Klamath Falls; KDRV-DT Medford.
LPTV Stations:
Oregon: K11GT College Hill, etc.; K27CL Coos Bay; K07JS North Bend; K04OS Reedsport; K53CU Roseburg.
Other Holdings:
Multimedia: Chambers Production Group, Chambers Multimedia Connection Inc..

CHANNEL 3 OF CORPUS CHRISTI INC.
PO Box 6669
Corpus Christi, TX 78466-6669
Phone: 361-986-8300
Officers:
Michael D. McKinnon, President & Treasurer
James A. Gillece, Vice President & Secretary
Ownership: Michael D. McKinnon, 40.08%; Sandra E. McKinnon, 40%; C. Dan McKinnon, 17.48%; Mark Daniel McKinnon, 1.22%; Michael Dean McKinnon, 1.22%. Michael D., C. Dan, Mark & Michael Dean McKinnon are principals of Texas Television Inc., see listing.
Represented (legal): Cohn & Marks LLP.
TV Stations:
Texas: KIII-DT Corpus Christi.

CHRISTIAN COMMUNICATIONS OF CHICAGOLAND INC.
38 S. Peoria
Chicago, IL 60607
Phone: 312-433-3838
Fax: 312-433-3839
Officers:
Jerry K. Rose, Chairman & Chief Executive Officer
Jim Nichols, Chief Financial Officer
Peter Edgers, Director, Network Operations
Holly Swanson, Cable, Affiliate Director

Branch Office:
San Francisco Office:
400 Tamal Plaza
Corte Madera, CA 94925
Phone: 415-924-7500

Represented (legal): Pillsbury Winthrop Shaw Pittman LLP.
TV Stations:
California: KTLN-DT Novato.
LPTV Stations:
Illinois: WCFC-CA Rockford.
Nevada: KEEN-CA Las Vegas.

CHRISTIAN FAITH BROADCAST INC.
PO Box 247
3809 Maple Ave
Castalia, OH 44824
Phone: 419-684-5311
Fax: 419-684-5378
Officers:
Shelby Gilliam, President
Debra Yost, Secretary
TV Stations:
Michigan: WLLA-DT Kalamazoo.
Ohio: WGGN-DT Sandusky.
LPTV Stations:
Ohio: W33BW Ashland.
Radio Stations:
Ohio: WJKW (FM) Athens, WGGN (FM) Castalia, WLRD (FM) Willard

CHRISTIAN TELEVISION NETWORK INC.
6922 142nd Ave. N
Largo, FL 33771
Phone: 727-535-5622
Fax: 727-531-2497
E-mail: comments@ctnonline.com
Officers:
Robert D'Andrea, President
Virginia Oliver, Secretary
Jimmy Smith, Treasurer
Ownership: Robert D'Andrea; Virginia Oliver; Jimmy Smith; Wayne Wetzel; Robert S. Young, 20%. votes each.
Represented (legal): Hardy, Carey, Chautin & Balkin LLP.
TV Stations:
Florida: WCLF-DT Clearwater; WFGC-DT Palm Beach; WHBR-DT Pensacola; WRXY-DT Tice.
Georgia: WGNM-DT Macon.
Illinois: WTJR-DT Quincy.
Iowa: KFXB-DT Dubuque.
Missouri: KNLJ-DT Jefferson City.
Tennessee: WHTN-DT Murfreesboro; WVLR-DT Tazewell.
LPTV Stations:
Florida: WVUP-CA Tallahassee.
Georgia: WYBU-CA Columbus.
Illinois: WLCF-LD Effingham.

COCOLA BROADCASTING COMPANIES LLC
706 W. Herndon Ave.
Fresno, CA 93650-1033
Phone: 559-435-7000
Fax: 559-435-3201
Web site: www.cocolatv.com
Officers:
Gary M. Cocola, Chairman & Chief Executive Officer
Todd Lopes, President
Colleen Crouch, Administrative Assistant
Ownership: Gary M. Cocola, sole member & manager.
Represented (legal): Dow Lohnes PLLC.
TV Stations:
California: KBBC-DT Bishop; KGMC-DT Clovis.
LPTV Stations:
California: KBFK-LP Bakersfield; KCBT-LP Bakersfield; KPMC-LP Bakersfield; KJOI-LP Caliente; KJKZ-LP Coalinga; KBID-LP Fresno; KHSC-LP Fresno; KJEO-LP Fresno; KMSG-LP Fresno; KSDI-LP Fresno; KVHF-LP Fresno;

KYMB-LD Monterey; KMBY-LP Paso Robles; KVVG-LP Porterville; KRHT-LP Redding; KCWB-LP Reedley; KSAO-LP Sacramento; KKDJ-LP Santa Maria; KWSM-LP Santa Maria; KFAZ-CA Visalia; KMCF-LP Visalia.
Idaho: KBTI-LP Boise; KCBB-LP Boise; KIWB-LP Boise; KKIC-LP Boise; KZAK-LP Boise; KBSE-LP Boise, etc..
Other Holdings:
Boise Telecasters LP, see listing.

PEDRO ROMAN COLLAZO
Calle Bori 1554, Urb. Antonsanti
San Juan, PR 00927-6113
Phone: 787-274-1800
TV Stations:
Puerto Rico: WVEO-DT Aguadilla; WVOZ-DT Ponce; WTCV-DT San Juan.
Radio Stations:
Puerto Rico: WVOZ (AM) San Juan

COMMUNICATIONS CORP. OF AMERICA
Box 53708
Lafayette, LA 70505
Phone: 337-237-1142
Fax: 337-237-1373
Officer:
Steve Pruett, Chief Executive Officer
Ownership: SP ComCorp LLC, 75%; SPCCLLC ownership:; SP ComCorp Investments LLC, Member & Mgr.. 100% votes; SP ComCorp Holdco 1 LLC, Member, 99%. assets; SP ComCorp Holdco 2 LLC, 1%. assets; SPCCILLC ownership:; Edward Mule', 50%. votes; Robert O'Shea, 50%. votes; SPCCH 1 & 2 LLC ownership:; Edward Mule', 40%. votes; Robert O'Shea, 40%. votes; Michael Gatto, 20%. votes.
Represented (legal): Dow Lohnes PLLC.
TV Stations:
Indiana: WEVV-DT Evansville.
Louisiana: WGMB-DT Baton Rouge; KADN-DT Lafayette; KMSS-DT Shreveport.
Mississippi: WNTZ-DT Natchez.
Texas: KVEO-DT Brownsville; KYLE-DT Bryan; KTSM-DT El Paso; KETK-DT Jacksonville; KPEJ-DT Odessa; KWKT-DT Waco.
LPTV Stations:
Louisiana: K47DW Alexandria; WBRL-CA Baton Rouge; K67GL Bunkie; K69HD Church Point; K61GO Hicks; KLAF-LP Lafayette; K51FO Leesville; K54FT New Iberia; KOPP-LP Opelousas.
Texas: K20HD Pecos.

COMMUNITY NEWSPAPER HOLDINGS INC.
3500 Colonnade Pkwy.
Suite 600
Birmingham, AL 35243
Phone: 205-298-7100
Officers:
Donna Barrett, President & Chief Executive Officer
Kevin Kampman, Senior Vice President
Kevin Blevins, Vice President
Lynn Pearson, Vice President & Assistant Secretary
Tom Lindley, Secretary
Ownership: Employee owned..
Represented (legal): Fletcher, Heald & Hildreth PLC.
TV Stations:
Georgia: WFXG-DT Augusta; WXTX-DT Columbus.
North Carolina: WSFX-DT Wilmington.

Virginia: WUPV-DT Ashland.

COMPASS COMMUNICATIONS OF IDAHO INC.
103 Entrance Dr.
Ste 1
Livingston, TX 77351
Phone: 936-328-5960
Fax: 936-328-5970
Officers:
Gerald R. Proctor, President & Treasurer
Gerald S. Rourke, Secretary
Ownership: Gerald R Proctor, 50%; Gerald S Rourke, 50%.
Represented (legal): Fletcher, Heald & Hildreth PLC.
TV Stations:
Idaho: KFXP-DT Pocatello.

CONCILIO MISION CRISTIANA FUENTE DE AGUA VIVA INC.
Box 3986
Carolina, PR 00984-3986
Phone: 787-750-4090
Officers:
Font Radolfo, President
Rosado E. Luis, Secretary
Enarcacion William, Treasurer
Ownership: Rodolfo Font, 33.33%; Luis E Rosado, 33.33%; William Encarnacion, 33.33%.
TV Stations:
Puerto Rico: WQHA-DT Aguada.

CORNERSTONE TELEVISION INC.
One Signal Hill Dr.
Wall, PA 15148-1499
Phone: 412-824-3930
Fax: 412-824-5442
Web site: www.ctvn.org
Officers:
Oleen Eagle, Chief Executive Officer
David Skeba, Vice President & Director, Programming
Blake Richert, Vice President & Director, Engineering
Dee Richert, Secretary
Ron Hembree, Chief Ministerial Officer
Ownership: Non-profit organization.; Michele Agatston; Oleen Eagle; Dr. William Kofmehl; Dr. Mitchel Nickols; Richard Simmons; Gary Tustin, jointly.
Represented (legal): Pillsbury Winthrop Shaw Pittman LLP.
TV Stations:
Pennsylvania: WKBS-DT Altoona; WPCB-DT Greensburg.
LPTV Stations:
Pennsylvania: W35BT Harrisburg; W29CO Sharon.
West Virginia: W21CJ Clarksburg.

COSTA DE ORO TELEVISION INC.
2323 Corinth Ave.
West Los Angeles, CA 90064
Phone: 310-943-5288
Fax: 310-943-5299
Ownership: Walter F Ulloa, Pres. & Chief Exec. Officer. Ulloa also has interest in Biltmore Broadcating & Entravision Communications Corp., see listings.
Represented (legal): Thompson Hine LLP.
TV Stations:
California: KJLA-DT Ventura.
LPTV Stations:
California: KSMV-LP Los Angeles.

COWLES CO.
W 999 Riverside Ave
Spokane, WA 99201-1006
Phone: 509-459-5520
E-mail: q6news@khq.com
Officers:
Elizabeth Allison Cowles, Chairman
William Stacey Cowles, President
Steven R. Rector, Secretary-Treasurer
Ownership: James P Cowles; William Stacey Cowles, Co-Trustees of Various Cowles Family Trusts.
Represented (legal): Skadden, Arps, Slate, Meagher & Flom LLP.
TV Stations:
California: KION-DT Monterey; KCOY-DT Santa Maria.
Washington: KNDU-DT Richland; KHQ-DT Spokane; KNDO-DT Yakima.
LPTV Stations:
California: KMUV-LP Monterey; K44DN Paso Robles; KKFX-CA San Luis Obispo.
Idaho: K18DT Coeur d'Alene; K35BW Lewiston; K48DX Sandpoint.
Newspapers:
Washington: Spokesman Review; Spokane Journal of Business

COX ENTERPRISES INC.
1400 Lake Hearn Dr. NE
Atlanta, GA 30319
Phone: 404-843-5000
Fax: 404-843-5142
Officers:
James C. Kennedy, Chairman
David E. Easterly, Vice Chairman
Jimmy W Hayes, Chief Executive Officer
G. Dennis Berry, President & Chief Operating Officer
Bruce Baker, President, Cox TV
John M. Dyer, Executive Vice President & Chief Financial Officer
John G. Boyette, Senior Vice President, Investments & Administration
Dale Hughes, Senior Vice President, Strategic Investments & Real Estate Planning
Timothy W. Hughes, Senior Vice President, Administration
Alexander V. Netchvolodoff, Senior Vice President, Public Policy

Branch Offices:
Public Policy
1225 19th St. NW
Suite 450
Washington, DC 20036
Phone: 202-296-4933
Newspaper
2000 Pennsylvania Ave. NW
Suite 10000
Washington, DC 20006
Phone: 202-331-0900

Broadcasting
400 N. Capitol St.
Suite 189
Washington, DC 20001
Phone: 202-737-0277
Ownership: Dayton Cox Trust-A, 41.06%; Barbara Cox Anthony Atlanta Trust, 28.94%; Anne Cox Chambers Atlanta Trust, 28.94%.
Represented (legal): Dow Lohnes PLLC.
TV Stations:
Florida: WFTV-DT Orlando; WRDQ-DT Orlando.
Georgia: WSB-DT Atlanta.
North Carolina: WSOC-DT Charlotte; WAXN-DT Kannapolis.
Ohio: WHIO-DT Dayton; WTOV-DT Steubenville.
Pennsylvania: WJAC-DT Johnstown; WPXI-DT Pittsburgh.
Washington: KIRO-DT Seattle.
LPTV Stations:
California: K29AB Monterey, etc.; K12PP South Lake Tahoe.

Nevada: K17CA-D Carson City; K51IA Fallon; K36GL Lovelock; K16GM Yerington.
North Carolina: W06AI Marion.
Pennsylvania: W07CD State College; W42DG-D State College.
Washington: K26IC-D Bremerton; K53AZ Centralia, etc.; K58BW Everett; K67GJ Point Pulley, etc.; K30FL Port Angeles; K54GS Puyallup.
Newspapers:
Colorado: The Daily Sentinel, The Nickel (Grand Junction)
Florida: Palm Beach Daily News; The Palm Beach Post, Florida Pennysaver, LaPalma (West Palm Beach)
Georgia: The Atlanta Journal Constitution, Mundo Hispânico (Atlanta)
Ohio: Dayton Daily News, JournalNews (Hamilton), Western Star (Lebanon), Fairfield Echo (Liberty Township), Pulse-Journal (Mason), The Middletown Journal, Oxford Press, Springfield News-Sun
Texas: Austin American-Statesman, íahora sf!, Lake Travis View (Austin); Bastrop Advertiser; Longview News-Journal; The Lufkin Daily News; The Marshall News Messenger; The Daily Sentinel (Nacogdoches); North Lake Trav
Radio Stations:
Alabama: WAGG (AM), WZZK-FM Birmingham; WNCB (FM) Gardendale; WBPT (FM) Homewood; WBHJ (FM) Midfield; WBHK (FM) Warrior
Connecticut: WEZN-FM Bridgeport; WPLR (FM) New Haven; WFOX (FM), WNLK (AM) Norwalk; WSTC (AM) Stamford
Florida: WFYV-FM Atlantic Beach; WHQT (FM) Coral Gables; WCFB (FM) Daytona Beach; WSUN-FM Holiday; WAPE-FM, WJGL (FM), WMXQ (FM), WOKV-AM-FM Jacksonville; WPYD (FM) Maitland; WEDR (FM), WFLC (FM), WHDR (FM) Miami; WDUV (FM) New
Georgia: WSB-AM-FM Atlanta, WBTS (FM) Dora, WSRV (FM) Gainesville, WALR-FM Greenville
Hawaii: KCCN-FM, KINE-FM, KRTR-AM-FM Honolulu; KPHW (FM) Kaneohe; KKNE (AM) Waipahu
Indiana: WSFR (FM) Corydon
Kentucky: WPTI (FM) Louisville; WRKA (FM), WVEZ (FM) St. Matthews
New York: WBAB (FM) Babylon, WBLI (FM) Patchogue, WCTZ (FM) Port Chester
Ohio: WHIO (AM), WHKO (FM) Dayton; WZLR (FM) Xenia
Oklahoma: KKCM (FM) Sand Springs; KJSR (FM), KRAV-FM, KRMG (AM), KWEN (FM) Tulsa
South Carolina: WJMZ-FM Anderson, WHZT (FM) Seneca
Texas: KTHT (FM) Cleveland; KHPT (FM) Conroe; KHTC (FM) Lake Jackson; KKBQ-FM Pasadena; KCYY (FM), KISS-FM, KKYX (AM), KONO (AM) San Antonio; KSMG (FM) Seguin; KPWT (FM) Terrell Hills
Virginia: WDYL (FM) Chester, WKHK (FM) Colonial Heights, WKLR (FM) Fort Lee, WMXB (FM) Richmond
Other Holdings:
Auction company: Manheim Auctions
Cable advertising representative: CableRep Inc.
Production: Rysher Entertainment
Program source: 10.4% E! Entertainment TV Network
Publishing: Auto Trader, Auto Mart & Truck Trader.
Telecommunications company: Interactive Studios: Cox Interactive Media Inc.
TV Station sales representative: TeleRep Inc.; MMT Sales; Harrington, Righter & Parsons.

CUMBIA ENTERTAINMENT LLC
c/o Charles R. Naftalin, Holland & Knight LLP
2099 Pennsylvania Ave. NW, Suite 100
Washington, DC 20006-6801
Phone: 202-457-7040

E-mail: charles.naftalin@hklaw.com
Officer:
Alejandro Santo Domingo, President & Manager
Ownership: Wepahe Entertainment LLC, 75%; Caracol TV America Corp., 25%; WELLC ownership:; Alejandro Santo Domingo CTAC ownership:; Caracol Television SA (Columbia).
Represented (legal): Holland & Knight LLP.
TV Stations:
Florida: WGEN-DT Key West.
LPTV Stations:
Florida: W39AC Key West; W21CL Marathon; W38AA Marathon; W63AL Marathon; W49CL Miami; WGEN-LP Miami; WDLP-CA Pompano Beach; W64AN Rock Harbor.

CUNNINGHAM BROADCASTING CORP.
2000 W. 41st St.
Baltimore, MD 21211
Phones: 410-662-9688; 410-484-2258
Officers:
Robert L. Simmons, President
Carolyn C. Smith, Vice President
Lisa Asher, Secretary-Treasurer
Ownership: Carolyn C. Smith Cunningham Trust, 7.2%.
Represented (legal): Pillsbury Winthrop Shaw Pittman LLP.
TV Stations:
Maryland: WNUV-DT Baltimore.
Ohio: WTTE-DT Columbus; WRGT-DT Dayton.
South Carolina: WMYA-DT Anderson; WTAT-DT Charleston.
West Virginia: WVAH-DT Charleston.

DISNEY ENTERPRISES INC.
500 S. Buena Vista St.
Burbank, CA 91521
Phone: 818-560-1000
Fax: 818-566-7308
Officers:
George Mitchell, Chairman
Robert Iger, Chief Executive Officer
Tom Stagg, Chief Financial Officer
Lawrence P. Murphy, Executive Vice President, Strategic Planning & Development
Sanford M. Litvack, Senior Executive Vice President & Chief, Corporate Operations
Marsha L. Reed, Vice President & Corporate Secretary
Jack J. Garand, Vice President, Planning & Control
Ownership: The Walt Disney Co..
TV Stations:
California: KFSN-DT Fresno; KABC-DT Los Angeles; KGO-DT San Francisco.
Illinois: WLS-DT Chicago.
Michigan: WJRT-DT Flint.
New York: WABC-DT New York.
North Carolina: WTVD-DT Durham.
Ohio: WTVG-DT Toledo.
Pennsylvania: WPVI-DT Philadelphia.
Texas: KTRK-DT Houston.
Other Holdings:
Book publishing: Hyperion Books; Chilton Book Publishing
Data service: 10% of Netpliance Inc.; Go.com
Magazine: Family PC, Women's Wear Daily, W, Institutional Investor & Multi-Channel News
Motion picture holdings: Miramax
Multimedia: Disney On-Line & Disney Interactive Group
Music publishing: Walt Disney Records & Hollywood Records
Production: Buena Vista Television Group, ESPNSUR
Professional sports team: The Mighty Ducks of Anaheim, professional hockey team &

the Anaheim Angels, professional baseball team.
Publishing: Fairchild Publication Inc.; ABC Inc. publishing operations & Disney Publishing
Retail operation: The Disney Store & The ESPN Store
Satellite programming: Disney Channel; 80% of ESPN, ESPN2 & ESPNews; 79.2% of E! Networks (through partnership with Comcast Cable Communications Inc.); 37.5% of both A & E and the History Channel; 50% of Lifetime Television
Theater: Stage plays
Theme Parks: Disney World & Disney Land. International Parks: Tokyo, Amsterdam & Paris.
Video production: Disney Home Video.

DISPATCH BROADCAST GROUP
Box 1010
Columbus, OH 43216
Phone: 614-460-3700
Fax: 614-460-2812
Officers:
Michael J. Fiorile, President & Chief Executive Officer
Thomas S. Stewart, Vice President & General Manager
Marvin Born, Vice President Engineering
Gerald E. Cary, Chief Financial Officer
Ownership: Dispatch Printing Co..
Represented (legal): Sidley Austin LLP.
TV Stations:
Indiana: WTHR-DT Indianapolis.
Ohio: WBNS-DT Columbus.
LPTV Stations:
Indiana: WALV-CA Indianapolis.
Newspapers:
Ohio: Columbus Dispatch
Radio Stations:
Ohio: WBNS-AM-FM-Columbus

DIVERSIFIED COMMUNICATIONS
121 Free St.
Portland, ME 04101
Phones: 207-842-5400; 207-842-5500
Fax: 207-842-5405
Officers:
Horace A. Hildreth, Chairman
David H. Lowell, President, Chief Executive Officer & Secretary
Michael T. Young, Vice President
Carolyn Catlin Barrett, Vice President
William L. Huggins, Vice President
Paul G. Clancy, Treasurer & Chief Financial Officer
Ownership: Josephine H Detmer, 35%; Horace A Hildreth Jr., 18.9%; Alison Hildreth, 8.9%.
Represented (legal): Irwin, Campbell & Tannenwald PC.
TV Stations:
Florida: WCJB-DT Gainesville.
Maine: WABI-DT Bangor.
Other Holdings:
Magazine: Diversified Publications (National Fisherman, Seafood Business, Work Boat).

DOMINION BROADCASTING INC.
215 Melody Lane
Toledo, OH 43615
Phone: 419-473-7283
Officers:
Larry Whatley, President
Ronald L. Mighell, Vice President
Jerry Toth, Secretary-Treasurer
Ownership: Larry Whatley; Ronald L Mighell; Jamey Schmitz, 33.33%.

TV Stations:
Ohio: WLMB-DT Toledo.

DRAPER HOLDINGS BUSINESS TRUST
1729 N. Salisbury Blvd.
Box 2057
Salisbury, MD 21801
Phone: 410-749-1111
Fax: 410-749-6098
Officers:
Thomas H. Draper, Chairman, President, Chief Executive & Operating Officer
Laura K. Baker, Vice President, Finance, Treasurer & Chief Financial Officer
Rick Jordan, Vice President, Technical Services
Deborah C. Eufemia, Secretary
Bobby Beach, Assistant Secretary & Assistant Treasurer
Ownership: Thomas H. Draper, 66.2%; Bobby O. Beach, 33.8%.
Represented (legal): Covington & Burling.
TV Stations:
Maryland: WBOC-DT Salisbury.

DREWRY COMMUNICATIONS
811 S.W. D Ave.
Lawton, OK 73501
Phone: 580-355-2250
Fax: 580-355-7531
Web site: www.lcisp.com
Officers:
Robert H. Drewry, Vice President
Larry Patton, Vice President
Ownership: Drewry Family, controlling interest. Drewrys also have interest in Adelante Television Limited Partnership & Panhandle Television, see listings.
TV Stations:
Oklahoma: KSWO-DT Lawton.
Texas: KFDA-DT Amarillo; KWAB-DT Big Spring; KWES-DT Odessa; KXXV-DT Waco.
LPTV Stations:
Oklahoma: KSWX-LP Duncan.
Other Holdings:
Radio.

DUHAMEL BROADCASTING ENTERPRISES
Box 1760
Rapid City, SD 57709-1760
Phone: 605-342-2000
Fax: 605-342-7305
Officers:
William F. Duhamel Sr., President & Chief Executive Officer
Dr. Peter A. Duhamel, Vice President
Monte Loos, Chief Operating Officer
Susan Hastings, Chief Financial Officer
Ownership: William F Duhamel Sr., 63%; Dr. Peter A Duhamel, 37%.
Represented (legal): Pillsbury Winthrop Shaw Pittman LLP.
TV Stations:
Nebraska: KDUH-DT Scottsbluff.
South Dakota: KHSD-DT Lead; KOTA-DT Rapid City.
Wyoming: KSGW-DT Sheridan.
LPTV Stations:
Nebraska: K02NT Scottsbluff.
Wyoming: K06JM Gillette.
Radio Stations:
South Dakota: KOTA (AM), KQRQ (FM) Rapid City; KDDX (FM) Spearfish

EAGLE CREEK BROADCASTING LLC
2111 University Park Dr.
Suite 650
Okemos, MI 48864
Phone: 517-347-4141

Officers:
Brian W. Brady, President & Chief Executive Officer
Fred L. Levy, Secretary
William R. Quarles, Treasurer
Imanta Bergmanis, Assistant Secretary
Catherine B. Gardner, Assistant Secretary
Ownership: Alta Communications VIII LP, 86.21%. equity member; ACVIIILP ownership:; Alta Communications VIII Managers LLC, Gen. Partner. 100% votes; ACVIIIMLLC ownership;; Brian W. McNeill, Managing Member, 50%. votes, 25% equity; Timothy L. Dibble, Managing Member, 50%. votes, 25% equity; William P. Egan, 7.5%. equity; William P. Egan 1998 Trust, 7.5%. equity; Estate of David Retik, 7.5%. equity; Robert Emmert, 6.25%. equity; B. Lane McDonald, 6.25%. equity; Phil Thompson, 6.25%. equity; Eileen McCarthy, 5%. equity.
Represented (legal): Leventhal, Senter & Lerman PLLC.
TV Stations:
Texas: KZTV-DT Corpus Christi; KVTV-DT Laredo.
Radio Stations:
Texas: KSIX (AM)

EBENEZER BROADCASTING GROUP INC.
Aptdo 21065
San Juan, PR 00928
Phone: 787-937-4800
Officers:
Rev. Marcos Rivera Cordova, President
Jose Ive Padilla, Vice President
Lizette Portalatin Amador, Secretary
Rev. Cesar A. Perez Corales, Treasurer
Ownership: Lizette Portalatin Amador; Rev. Cesar A. Perez Corales; Rev. Marcos Rivera Cordova; Rev. Moises Flores; Omar Alicea Morales; Jose Ive Padilla; Victor Aldarondo Ruiz; Rev. Ismael Velazquez, board members, 12.5%. votes each.
TV Stations:
Puerto Rico: WIDP-DT Guayama.

ELLIS COMMUNICATIONS GROUP LLC
685 11th St.
Atlanta, GA 30318
Phone: 678-904-0516
Ownership: Bert Ellis, 33.33%. votes, 1.33% assets; Frank K. Bynum Jr., 33.33%. votes; Thomas R. Wall Jr., 33.33%. votes; Kelso KDOC Holdco LLC, 40.61%. assets; KKDOCHLLC & KEPVILLC ownership:; Philip E. Berney; Frank K. Bynum Jr.; James J. Connors I; Michael B. Goldberg; Frank J. Loverro; George E. Matelich; Frank T. Nickell; David I. Wahrhaftig; Thomas R. Wall IV, Managing Members, 11.11%. each.
Represented (legal): Goldberg, Godles, Wiener & Wright.
TV Stations:
California: KDOC-DT Anaheim.

ELLIS COMMUNICATIONS INC.
1180 Northmoor Ct
Atlanta, GA 30327
Phone: 404-229-8080
Officers:
U. Bertram Ellis Jr., President
James Altenbach, Secretary
Ownership: U. Bertram Ellis Jr..
Represented (legal): Goldberg, Godles, Wiener & Wright.
TV Stations:
Nevada: KAME-DT Reno.
LPTV Stations:
California: K23DT Tahoe City.
Nevada: K32GW-D Carson City; K35AX Hawthorne, etc.; K34BL Lovelock.

ENTRAVISION COMMUNICATIONS CORP.
2425 Olympic Blvd.
Suite 6000 W
Santa Monica, CA 90404
Phone: 310-447-3870
Officers:
Walter F. Ulloa, Chairman & Chief Executive Officer
Philip C. Wilkinson, President & Chief Operating Officer
Christopher T. Young, Executive Vice President, Treasurer & Chief Financial Officer
Larry E. Safir, Executive Vice President
Jeffrey A. Liberman, President, Radio Division
Paul A. Zevnik, Secretary
Mark A. Boelke, General Counsel, Vice President, Legal Affairs & Secretary
Ownership: Walter F Ulloa, 12.36%; Philip C Wilkinson, 7.2%; Paul A Zevnik, 4.52%; Univision Communications Inc., 16%; remainder publicly held. See also listings for Biltmore Broadcasting & Costa de Oro Television Inc.
Represented (legal): Thompson Hine LLP.
TV Stations:
California: KVYE-DT El Centro; KSMS-DT Monterey; KPMR-DT Santa Barbara.
Colorado: KCEC-DT Denver; KVSN-DT Pueblo.
Connecticut: WUVN-DT Hartford.
Florida: WVEN-DT Daytona Beach; WVEA-DT Venice.
Kansas: KDCU-DT Derby.
Maryland: WJAL-DT Hagerstown.
Massachusetts: WUNI-DT Worcester.
Nevada: KINC-DT Las Vegas; KREN-DT Reno.
New Mexico: KLUZ-DT Albuquerque.
Texas: KORO-DT Corpus Christi; KINT-DT El Paso; KTFN-DT El Paso; KLDO-DT Laredo; KNVO-DT McAllen; KUPB-DT Midland.
LPTV Stations:
California: KEVC-CA Indio; KVER-CA Indio; K100G Lompoc; KVES-LP Palm Springs; K17GD Paso Robles; KDJT-CA Salinas/Monterey, etc.; KBNT-CA San Diego; KDTF-LP San Diego; KSZZ-LP San Diego; KTCD-LP San Diego; KTSB-LP Santa Barbara; K35ER Santa Maria; KREN-LP Susanville; KHAX-LP Vista.
Colorado: KDVT-LP Denver; K43FN Fort Collins; K54IK Fort Collins; KGHB-CA Pueblo, etc..
Connecticut: WUTH-CA Hartford.
District of Columbia: WMDO-CA Washington.
Florida: W47DA Melbourne; WVCI-LP Orlando; WVEA-LP Tampa.
Nevada: KNNC-LP Battle Mountain; KELV-LP Las Vegas; KNTL-LP Laughlin; KWWB-LP Mesquite, etc.; KNCV-LP Reno; KNVV-LP Reno; KRNS-CA Reno; KPMP-LP Winnemucca.
New Mexico: KTFA-LP Albuquerque.
Texas: KVTF-CA Brownsville; KTIZ-LP Harlingen; KFTN-CA La Feria; KETF-CA Laredo; KXOF-CA Laredo; KBZO-LP Lubbock; KSFE-LP McAllen; KTFV-CA McAllen; KANG-CA San Angelo; KEUS-LP San Angelo.
Radio Stations:
Arizona: KVVA-FM Apache Junction, KMIA (AM) Black Canyon City, KDVA (FM) Buckeye
California: KSSE (FM) Arcadia, KSEH (FM) Brawley, KXSE (FM) Davis, KWST (AM) El Centro, KSSD (FM) Fallbrook, KMXX (FM) Imperial, KCVR (AM) Lodi, KRCX-FM Marysville, KDLE (FM) Newport Beach, KTSE-FM Patterson, KLYY (FM) Riverside, K
Colorado: KPVW (FM) Aspen, KMXA (AM) Aurora, KJMN (FM) Castle Rock, KXPK (FM) Evergreen
Nevada: KRRN (FM) Dolan Springs, KQRT (FM) Las Vegas, KRNV-FM Reno
New Mexico: KRZY-AM-FM Albuquerque
Texas: KKPS (FM) Brownsville, KVLY (FM) Edinburg; KHRO (AM), KINT-FM, KOFX (FM),

KSVE (AM), KYSE (FM) El Paso; KFRQ (FM) Harlingen; KGOL (AM) Humble; KBZO (AM) Lubbock; KNVO-FM Port Isabel; KAIQ (FM) Wollfforth
Other Holdings:
Television holdings: Limited voting interest in licensees of XHAS-TV, San Diego, CA-Tijuana, Mexico & XUPN-TV, Tecate, Baja California, Mexico..

EQUITY MEDIA HOLDINGS CORP., DEBTOR IN POSSESSION
One Shackleford Dr.
Suite 400
Little Rock, AR 72211
Phones: 501-219-2400; 501-221-0400
Fax: 501-221-1101
Officers:
John E. Oxendine, Chief Executive Officer
Larry E Morton, President & Chief Executive Officer, Retro Programming Services Inc.
Gregory W. Fess, Senior Vice President & Chief Operating Officer
Mario B. Ferrari, Chief Strategic Officer
Thomas M Arnost, President & Chief Executive Officer, Equity Broadcasting Corp.
Mark Dvornik, Executive Vice President, Retro Television Network
James H. Hearnsberger, Vice President, Administration & Finance
Patrick Doran, Chief Financial Officer
Glenn Charlesworth, Vice President & Chief Accounting Officer
Lori Withrow, Corporate Secretary
Ownership: Harry G. Luken III, 16.08%; Greg Fess, 5.91%; RPCP Investments LLC, 5.89%. Luken has interest in Luken Broadcasting LLC & Luken Communications LLC, see listings. Equity filed for Chapter 11 bankruptcy protection December 8, 2008. Chief Restructuring Officer is Kim Kelly.
Represented (legal): Irwin, Campbell & Tannenwald PC.
TV Stations:
Nebraska: KTUW-DT Scottsbluff.
Texas: KEYU-DT Borger.
Wyoming: KQCK-DT Cheyenne.
LPTV Stations:
Alabama: W23DJ Dothan; WDTH-LP Dothan.
Arkansas: KHMF-CA Bentonville; K47JG El Dorado; KEGW-LP Fayetteville; KFFS-CA Fayetteville; K32GH Fort Smith; K33HE Fort Smith; K48FL Fort Smith; KFDF-CA Fort Smith; KPBI-CA Fort Smith; KUFS-LP Fort Smith; KWFT-LP Fort Smith; KXUN-LP Fort Smith; KRBF-CA Hindsville; KTVV-LP Hot Springs; KHUG-LP Little Rock; KKYK-CA Little Rock; KLRA-LP Little Rock; KRAH-CA Paris; KWBK-LP Pine Bluff; KEJC-LP Sheridan; KKAF-CA Siloam Springs; KJBW-CA Springdale; KWNL-LP Winslow.
California: KIMG-LP Ventura.
Colorado: KQDK-CA Aurora.
Florida: WFPI-LP Fort Pierce; WBSP-CA Naples; W56EJ Williston; W63DB Williston.
Mississippi: WJXF-LP Jackson.
Missouri: KNJE-LP Aurora; KBBL-CA Springfield.
Montana: KEXI-LP Kalispell.
Oklahoma: K64GJ Lawton; KUOK-CA Norman; KSJF-CA Poteau.
Texas: KAMT-LP Amarillo; KEAT-LP Amarillo; KEYU-LP Amarillo; KUTW-LP Somerville; KWKO-LP Waco; KTWW-LP Wichita Falls; KUWF-LP Wichita Falls.
Wyoming: KDEV-LP Cheyenne; K61DX Laramie; K21CV Rawlins.

ESTEEM BROADCASTING LLC
13865 E Elliott Dr
Marshall, IL 62441
Phone: 217-826-6095
Ownership: David L. Bailey, Pres..
Represented (legal): Drinker Biddle

TV Stations:
North Carolina: WFXI-DT Morehead City.
Tennessee: WEMT-DT Greeneville.
LPTV Stations:
Virginia: W43BO Marion.

EVANGELISTIC ALASKA MISSIONARY FELLOWSHIP
Box 56359
North Pole, AK 99705-1359
Phone: 907-488-2216
Fax: 907-488-5246
Web site: www.mosquitonet.com/~kjnp
Officers:
Genevieve L. Nelson, Chief Executive Officer
Yvonne L. Carriker, President
Ownership: Non-profit corp.--North Pole, AK.
Represented (legal): Fletcher, Heald & Hildreth PLC.
TV Stations:
Alaska: KJNP-DT North Pole.
Radio Stations:
Alaska: KJHA-FM Houston, KJNO (AM) North Pole

EVENING POST PUBLISHING CO.
134 Columbus St.
Charleston, SC 29403-4800
Phone: 843-577-7111
E-mail: publiceditor@postandcourier.com
Officers:
Peter Manigault, Chairman
Ivan V. Anderson Jr., President & Chief Executive Officer
Terrance F. Hurley, TV Group President
Travis O. Rockey, Executive Vice President & Chief Operating Officer
Arthur M. Wilcox, Secretary
James W. Martin, Treasurer & Chief Financial Officer
Mary M. Gilbreth, Assistant Secretary

Branch Office:
Cordillera Communications Inc.
11 E. Superior St.
Suite 518
Duluth, MN 55802
Phone: 218-625-2260
Fax: 218-625-2261
Ownership: Peter Manigault, Principal.
Represented (legal): Dow Lohnes PLLC.
TV Stations:
Arizona: KVOA-DT Tucson.
California: KSBY-DT San Luis Obispo.
Colorado: KOAA-DT Pueblo.
Kentucky: WLEX-DT Lexington.
Louisiana: KATC-DT Lafayette.
Montana: KTVQ-DT Billings; KBZK-DT Bozeman; KXLF-DT Butte; KRTV-DT Great Falls; KPAX-DT Missoula.
Texas: KRIS-DT Corpus Christi.
LPTV Stations:
Arizona: K20FO Sierra Vista.
California: K59CD Santa Barbara.
Montana: K26DE Bozeman; KXLH-LP Helena; K48AI Joplin; K18AJ Kalispell; K45CS Lewistown; K10GF Miles City.
Newspapers:
North Carolina: The Clemmons Courier, Davie County Enterprise, The Salisbury Post
South Carolina: Aiken Standard; The Charleston Mercury, The Post and Courier (Charleston); The Georgetown Times; Goose Creek Gazette; The Journal (James Island-Folly Beach); The (Kingtree) News; The Berkeley Independent (Monck
Texas: The Eagle (Bryan-College Station)
Other Holdings:
Features syndicator: Editor's Press Service Inc. (International)
Service company: White Oak Forestry Corp. (timberland management).

FAITH BROADCASTING NETWORK INC.
Box 1010
Marion, IL 62959-1010
Phone: 618-997-9333
Fax: 618-997-1859
E-mail: cmmay@maylawoffices.com
Officers:
Garth W. Coonce, President
Christina M. Coonce, Vice President
Michael J. Daly, Secretary
Charles Payne, Treasurer
Julie Nolan, Assistant Secretary
Ownership: Non-profit organization--Marion, IL; Garth W. Coonce; Christina M. Coonce; Charles Payne; Victoria Clark; Julie Nolan, 20%. votes, each.
Represented (legal): Colby M. May.
TV Stations:
New York: WNYB-DT Jamestown.
LPTV Stations:
New York: WBNF-CA Buffalo.

54 BROADCASTING INC.
908 W Martin Luther King Blvd
Austin, TX 78701
Phone: 512-478-5400
Ownership: Thomas J Vaughan, 95.51%; LIN Television of Texas LP, 4.49%.
Represented (legal): Thompson Hine LLP.
TV Stations:
Texas: KNVA-DT Austin.

GREGORY P. FILANDRINOS
940 W. Port Plaza
Suite 210
St. Louis, MO 63146
Phone: 314-453-9696
Represented (legal): Irwin, Campbell & Tannenwald PC.
TV Stations:
Pennsylvania: WATM-DT Altoona.

FISHER COMMUNICATIONS INC.
100 4th Ave. N
Suite 510
Seattle, WA 98109
Phone: 206-404-7000
Fax: 206-404-6037
E-mail: info@fsci.com
Web site: www.fsci.com
Officers:
Phelps K. Fisher, Chairman
Colleen B. Brown, President & Chief Executive Officer
Christopher Bellavia, Senior Vice President, General Counsel & Corporate Secretary
Joseph Lovejoy, Acting Chief Financial Officer

Branch Office:
444 N. Capitol St. NW
Suite 601-A
Washington, DC 20001
Phone: 202-783-0322
Ownership: GAMCO Investors Inc., 16.28%; Donald G. Graham Jr., 9.3263%; Reed, Conner & Birdwell LLC, 6.7%; George D. Fisher, 6.1%; Edward A. Gowey, 6%; Robin J. Campbell Knepper, 5.3468%; William H. Gates III, 5.24%; Donald G. Graham III, 5.1884%; O.D. Fisher Investment Co., 5.0228%; TowerView LLC, 5%; Phelps K. Fisher, 3%; GAMCO ownership:; Mario Gabelli, controlling interest; RC&BLLC ownership:; Donn B. Conner; Jeffrey Bronchick, principals; ODFIC ownership:; Donald G. Graham Jr., Pres.; TVLLC ownership:; Daniel R. Tisch, principal.
Represented (legal): Irwin, Campbell & Tannenwald PC.
TV Stations:
California: KBAK-DT Bakersfield.

Idaho: KBCI-DT Boise; KIDK-DT Idaho Falls; KLEW-DT Lewiston.
Oregon: KCBY-DT Coos Bay; KVAL-DT Eugene; KUNP-DT La Grande; KATU-DT Portland; KPIC-DT Roseburg.
Washington: KUNS-DT Bellevue; KEPR-DT Pasco; KOMO-DT Seattle; KIMA-DT Yakima.
LPTV Stations:
California: KBFX-CA Bakersfield.
Idaho: KYUU-LP Boise; K65AZ Burley, etc.; K55GM Cambridge; K11GR Cascade; K10AW Challis; K11CP Fish Creek, etc.; K09HS Glenns Ferry; K13IA Lowman; K10FD McCall, etc.; KXPI-LP Pocatello.
Oregon: K26DB Astoria; K07PP Camas Valley; K45CV Corvallis; K04DR Eugene; K58DA Glendale; K26HO Glide,etc.; K33CP Gold Beach; K10GQ Huntington; K11LS Jordan Valley; K42CZ Lincoln City, etc.; K13HM Myrtle Creek; K12IA Oakland, etc.; KUNP-LP Portland; K54AP Prineville; K29CI Prineville, etc.; K02DB Scottsburg; K18HH The Dalles; K11GH Tri-City, etc..
Washington: KWWA-CA Ellensburg, etc.; KVVK-CA Kennewick, etc.; KORX-CA Walla Walla; KUNW-CA Yakima.
Radio Stations:
Montana: KIKF (FM), KINX (FM) Cascade; KQDI-AM-FM, KXGF (AM) Great Falls
Washington: KOMO (AM), KPLZ-FM, KVI (AM) Seattle

GEORGE S. FLINN JR.
188 S. Bellevue
Suite 222
Memphis, TN 38104
Phone: 901-726-8970
TV Stations:
Florida: WFBD-DT Destin.
Mississippi: WWJX-DT Jackson.
LPTV Stations:
Tennessee: W26CX Memphis.
Other Holdings:
Flinn Broadcasting Corp., see listing..

FORT MYERS BROADCASTING CO.
2824 Palm Beach Blvd.
Fort Myers, FL 33916
Phone: 941-334-1111
Fax: 941-334-0744
Officers:
Brian A. McBride, President & Treasurer
Gary W. Gardner, Vice President
Gerald McBride, Vice President & Secretary
Ownership: Brian A McBride, 29.77%; Maureen McBride, 24.44%; Kathleen McBride Plum, 24.44%; Gerald McBride, 6.67%; Thomas McBride, 6.67%; Edward McBride, 6.67%; Rita McBride, 1.33%.
Represented (legal): Leibowitz & Associates PA.
TV Stations:
Florida: WINK-DT Fort Myers.
Radio Stations:
Florida: WINK-AM-FM Fort Myers, WPTK (AM) Pine Island Center, WTLQ-FM Punta Rassa

FORUM COMMUNICATIONS CO.
Box 2020
Fargo, ND 58103
Phone: 701-235-7311
E-mail: kbmykmcy@btinet.net
Officers:
William C. Marcil, President & Chief Executive Officer
Lloyd Case, Vice President & Chief Operating Officer
Charles Bohnet, Vice President
Jane B. Marcil, Secretary-Treasurer
Ownership: Jane B Marcil; William C Marcil.
Represented (legal): Wiley Rein LLP.

TV Stations:
North Dakota: KBMY-DT Bismarck; WDAZ-DT Devils Lake; WDAY-DT Fargo; KMCY-DT Minot.
LPTV Stations:
Minnesota: K02MM Fergus Falls.
North Dakota: K02DD Jamestown.
Newspapers:
Minnesota: Alexandria Echo Press; The Pioneer (Bemidji); The Pine Journal (Cloquet); Duluth News Tribune; Duluth Budgeteer News; Detroit Lakes Tribune, Becker County Record, Lake Area Press (Detroit Lakes); The Farmington
North Dakota: The Dickinson Press, The Forum (Fargo), Grand Forks Herald, The Jamestown Sun, The West Fargo Pioneer
South Dakota: The Daily Republic (Mitchell)
Wisconsin: Hudson Star-Observer, New Richmond News, Pierce County Herald, River Falls Journal, The Daily Telegram (Superior)
Radio Stations:
North Dakota: WDAY (AM) Fargo

FOUR POINTS MEDIA GROUP HOLDING LLC
299 Park Ave
c/o Cerberus Capital Management LP
New York, NY 10171
Phone: 212-891-2100
Officers:
Christopher A Holt, Vice President
Mark Ploof, Vice President
Richard Reingold, Vice President
Ownership: Four Points Media Group LLC; FPMGLLC ownership:; TV Stations Investors LLC, managing member. 100% votes, not less than 90% assets; TVSILLC ownership:; TV Manager LLC. 100% votes; TVMLLC ownership:; Insulated Members. 100% assets; Stephen Feinberg; IM ownership:; Affiliates of Cerberus Capital Management LP; AOCCMLP ownership:; Stephen Feinberg, managing member%.
Represented (legal): Wiley Rein LLP.
TV Stations:
Florida: WTVX-DT Fort Pierce.
Massachusetts: WLWC-DT New Bedford.
Texas: KEYE-DT Austin.
Utah: KUTV-DT Salt Lake City; KUSG-DT St. George.
LPTV Stations:
Florida: WTCN-CA Palm Beach; WWHB-CA Stuart.
Utah: K53CF Aurora; K22FS-D Beaver, etc.; K31FG Delta, etc.; K03BF Enterprise; K07SC Hildale, UT & Cane Beds, AZ; K43AE Myton, etc.; K09CD Rockville; K49AS Santa Clara; K41FX Spring Glen; K03AL Toquerville; K02AW Virgin.

FOX TELEVISION HOLDINGS INC.
444 N Capitol St NW, Ste 740
c/o Dianne Smith (News Corp.)
Washington, DC 20001
Phone: 202-715-2350
E-mail: mollyp@foxtv.com
Officers:
K. Rupert Murdoch, Chairman & Chief Operating Officer
Lawrence A. Jacobs, Executive Vice President & Secretary
Raymond L. Parrish, Vice President & Assistant Treasurer
Joseph DiScipio, Vice President, Legal & FCC Compliance
Paula M. Wardynski, Vice President
David E. Miller, Treasurer
Bonnie I. Bogin, Assistant Secretary
Elizabeth Casey, Assistant Secretary
Jon Del Barrio, Assistant Secretary
Randall F. Kender, Assistant Secretary
Gary D. Roberts, Assistant Secretary

Branch Offices:
5151 Wisconsin Ave NW
Washington, DC 20016
Phone: 202-244-5151
1211 Avenue of the Americas
21st Fl
New York, NY 10036
Phone: 212-301-3545
Ownership: Fox Entertainment Group Inc., 85.2%. votes, 99.9% equity; K. Rupert Murdoch, 14.8%. votes, 0.1% equity; FEGI ownership:; News Corp.; NC ownership:; K. Rupert Murdoch, Chmn. & Chief Exec. Officer, 5.7%. asserts, 38.6% votes; Murdoch Family Trust, Cruden Financial Services LLC, Trustee, 5.4%. assets; 37.2 % votes; HRH Prince Alwaleed Bin Talal Bin Abdulaziz Alsaud, 1%. assets, 7% votes.
Represented (legal): Skadden, Arps, Slate, Meagher & Flom LLP.
TV Stations:
Arizona: KSAZ-DT Phoenix; KUTP-DT Phoenix.
California: KCOP-DT Los Angeles; KTTV-DT Los Angeles.
District of Columbia: WDCA-DT Washington; WTTG-DT Washington.
Florida: WOGX-DT Ocala; WOFL-DT Orlando; WRBW-DT Orlando; WTVT-DT Tampa.
Georgia: WAGA-DT Atlanta.
Illinois: WFLD-DT Chicago.
Indiana: WPWR-DT Gary.
Maryland: WUTB-DT Baltimore.
Massachusetts: WFXT-DT Boston.
Michigan: WJBK-DT Detroit.
Minnesota: KFTC-DT Bemidji; KMSP-DT Minneapolis; WFTC-DT Minneapolis.
New Jersey: WWOR-DT Secaucus.
New York: WNYW-DT New York.
Pennsylvania: WTXF-DT Philadelphia.
Tennessee: WHBQ-DT Memphis.
Texas: KTBC-DT Austin; KDFI-DT Dallas; KDFW-DT Dallas; KRIV-DT Houston; KTXH-DT Houston.
LPTV Stations:
Alabama: W15AP Gadsden.
Arizona: K16BP Cottonwood; K39FC East Flagstaff, etc.; K28CW Flagstaff; K48GI Flagstaff; K14HG Kingman; K15CR Lake Havasu City; K55BW Madera Peak; K36AE Phoenix; K04AI Prescott; K14HC Prescott; K39IT-D Prescott; K07OJ Snowflake, etc.; K43IE Williams; K09JZ Winslow.
Minnesota: K30DK Bemidji; K48IF Brainerd; K49KQ Little Falls; K33KC Wadena; K49CU Walker.
Radio Stations:
Illinois: WSBC (AM) Chicago, WCFJ (AM) Chicago Heights
Other Holdings:
Television holdings: Equity interest in Davis Television Inc., see listing.

FREEDOM COMMUNICATIONS HOLDINGS INC.
17666 Fitch
Irvine, CA 92614
Phone: 949-253-2313
Fax: 949-253-2349
E-mail: staff@wpecnews12.com
Officers:
Scott N. Flanders, President & Chief Executive Officer
N. Christian Anderson III, Senior Vice President & President, Metro Information Div.
Michael J. Mathieu, Senior Vice President & President, Interactive Division
Jonathan Segal, Senior Vice President & President, Community Newspapers Division
Doreen D. Wade, Senior Vice President & President, Broadcast Division
Marcy E. Bruskin, Vice President, Human Resources & Organizational Development
Richard A. Wallace, Vice President & Secretary
Michael Brown, Vice President & Chief Information Officer

Joanne Norton, Vice President, Shareholder Relations & Assistant Secretary
Rachel L. Sagan, Vice President & General Counsel
Nancy S. Trillo, Vice President, Treasurer & Controller
Katherine Bartzoff, Assistant Secretary
Ownership: Blackstone FC Communications Partners LP, 16.81%. votes; Providence Equity Partners IV LP, 15.93%. votes; Mary Elizabeth Hoiles Bassett, 9.33%. votes; Threshie Ltd., 8.44%. votes; Robin J. Hardie, 6.93%. votes; Janet Baker Nardie, 6.8%. votes; Douglas R. Hardie, 6.39%. votes; Blackstone FC Capital Partners IV LP, 5.6%. votes; Thomas W. Bassett, 5.59%. votes; Richard A. Wallace, 3.75%. votes; David A. Threshie, 0.79%. votes; Raymond C. H. Bryan, 0.36%. votes; BFCCPLP & BFCCPIVLP ownership:; Peter G. Peterson, Founding Member; Stephen A. Schwarzman, Founding Member; PEPIVLP ownership:; Glenn M. Creamer; Jonathan M. Nelson; Paul J. Salem, principals; TL ownership:; Threshie Family Trusts.
Represented (legal): Latham & Watkins.
TV Stations:
Florida: WPEC-DT West Palm Beach.
Michigan: WWMT-DT Kalamazoo; WLAJ-DT Lansing.
New York: WCWN-DT Schenectady; WRGB-DT Schenectady.
Oregon: KTVL-DT Medford.
Tennessee: WTVC-DT Chattanooga.
Texas: KFDM-DT Beaumont.
LPTV Stations:
California: K60AR Alturas; K02CN Dunsmuir, etc.; K06KA Fort Jones, etc.; K06GP Yreka; K53DY Yreka.
Oregon: K02EK Applegate Valley; K04EO Ashland, etc.; K10LR Brookings; K04JQ Butte Falls; K60BJ Carpenterville; K24BV Cave Junction; K02DV Cave Junction, etc.; K48BS Glendale, etc.; K04JZ Gold Hill; K54DM Grants Pass; K40BL Hugo, etc.; K02IC Jacksonville; K07PU Klamath Falls, etc.; K12IH Lakeview; K15HU-D Lakeview; K19HH-D Midland, etc.; K60BH Midland, etc.; K16CU Phoenix & Talent; K47LD-D Phoenix & Talent; K03BZ Rogue River; K04JP Williams.
Newspapers:
Arizona: East Valley Tribune (Mesa); Daily News-Sun (Sun City); The Sun, Bajo El Sol (Yuma)
California: Desert Dispatch (Barstow); Colusa Sun Herald; Corning Observer; Hesperia Star; Appeal-Democrat (Marysville); The Orange County Register; Orland Press Register; The Porterville Recorder, Noticieros Semanal (Port
Colorado: The Gazette (Colorado Springs)
Florida: Holmes County Times-Advertiser (Bonifay), The Crestview News Bulletin, The Destin Log, Northwest Florida Daily News (Fort Walton Beach), Santa Rosa Press Gazette/Santa Rosa Free Press (Milton), The News Herald
Illinois: The Telegraph (Alton), Journal-Courier (Jacksonville)
Indiana: The Tribune (Seymour)
Missouri: The Sedalia Democrat
New Mexico: Clovis News Journal, Portales News-Tribune, Quay County Sun
North Carolina: Times-News (Burlington), The Gaston Gazette, Havelock News, The Daily News (Jacksonville), Free Press (Kinston), Sun Journal (New Bern), The Shelby Star, The Topsail Advertiser (Surf City), Jones Post (Trenton)
Ohio: The Lima News
Texas: The Brownsville Herald, El Nuevo Heraldo (Brownsville), Valley Morning Star, La Estrella (Harlingen); The Monitor, La Frontera (McAllen); Odessa American, El Semanario (Odessa); Mid Valley Town Crier (Weslaco)

Other Holdings:
Magazine: Clinical Geriatrics; CRM Magazine; Field Force Automation; Home HealthCare Consultant; The Journal of Gender Specific Medicine; Latin Trade; MODE Magazine; Revista Latin Trade; Small Business Computing; The Annals of Long-Term Care.

FREE STATE COMMUNICATIONS LLC
609 New Hampshire
Lawrence, KS 66044
Phone: 317-362-4678
E-mail: rrogala@sunflowerbroadband.com
Officer:
Patrick Knorr, Manager
Ownership: Orbiter LLC; OLLC ownership:; The World Company. 100% votes, 94% assets; TWC ownership:; The Dolph C. Simons Jr. GST Trust, 48.6%. votes, 3.4% assets; The Marie Simons GST Trust, 30.1%. votes, 2.1% assets; The Dolph C. Simons Jr. GST Trust of 2004, 21.4%. votes, 1.5% assets.
Represented (legal): Cinnamon Mueller.
TV Stations:
Kansas: KTKA-DT Topeka.

FRONTIER BROADCAST INVESTORS LLC
4311 Wilshire Blvd
Ste 412
Los Angeles, CA 90010
Phone: 323-931-1745
Ownership: Frontier Radio Management Inc., Mgr.. 100% votes; Windsor Square Investors LLC, Member, less than 5%. assets; FRMI ownership:; Jason R. Wolff, Pres. & Secy.; Lucy M. H. Wild, V.P.; WSILLC ownership:; Jason R. Wolff, Managing Member. 100% votes, 20% assets.
Represented (legal): Wiley Rein LLP.
TV Stations:
Georgia: WGXA-DT Macon.

GANNETT CO. INC.
7950 Jones Bridge Dr.
McLean, VA 22107
Phone: 703-854-6899
E-mail: gcishare@gannett.com
Officers:
Craig A. Dubow, Chairman, President & Chief Executive Officer
Dave Lougee, President, Broadcast Division
Garcia C. Martore, Executive Vice President & Chief Financial Officer
Todd A. Mayman, Senior Vice President, Secretary & General Counsel
Christopher W. Baldwin, Vice President, Taxes
Jose A. Berrios, Vice President, Leadership Development & Diversity
Tara J. Connell, Vice President, Corporate Communications
Daniel S. Ehrman Jr., Vice President, Planning & Development
George R. Gavagan, Vice President & Controller
Michael A. Hart, Vice President & Treasurer
Roxanne V. Horning, Vice President, Human Resources
Darryll Green, Vice President, Program Development
Wendell J. Van Lare, Vice President, Senior Labor Counsel
Barbara W. Wall, Vice President, Senior Associate General Counsel
Ownership: Publicly held..
Represented (legal): Wiley Rein LLP.
TV Stations:
Arizona: KNAZ-DT Flagstaff; KPNX-DT Mesa.
Arkansas: KTHV-DT Little Rock.
California: KXTV-DT Sacramento.

Colorado: KTVD-DT Denver; KUSA-DT Denver.
District of Columbia: WUSA-DT Washington.
Florida: WTLV-DT Jacksonville; WJXX-DT Orange Park; WTSP-DT St. Petersburg.
Georgia: WATL-DT Atlanta; WXIA-DT Atlanta; WMAZ-DT Macon.
Maine: WLBZ-DT Bangor; WCSH-DT Portland.
Michigan: WZZM Grand Rapids.
Minnesota: KARE-DT Minneapolis.
Missouri: KSDK-DT St. Louis.
New York: WGRZ Buffalo.
North Carolina: WFMY-DT Greensboro.
Ohio: WKYC Cleveland.
South Carolina: WLTX-DT Columbia.
Tennessee: WBIR-DT Knoxville.
LPTV Stations:
Arizona: K61FB Globe & Miami; KPSN-LP Payson; K06AE Prescott.
Colorado: K47IH Boulder.
Maine: W57AQ Calais; WGCI-LP Skowhegan.
Newspapers:
Alabama: The Montgomery Advertiser
Arizona: The Arizona Republic (Phoenix), Tucson Citizen
Arkansas: Baxter Bulletin (Mountain Home)
California: The Desert Sun (Palm Springs), The Salinas Californian, Tulare Advance-Register, Visalia Times-Delta
Colorado: Fort Collins Coloradoan
Delaware: The News Journal (Wilmington)
Florida: Florida Today (Brevard County), The News-Press (Fort Myers), Pensacola News Journal, Tallahasee Democrat
Guam: Pacific Daily News (Hagatna)
Hawaii: The Honolulu Advertiser
Indiana: The Indianapolis Star, Journal and Courier (Lafayette), The Star Press (Muncie), Palladium-Item (Richmond)
Iowa: The Des Moines Register, Iowa City Press-Citizen
Kentucky: The Courier-Journal (Louisville)
Louisiana: The Town Talk (Alexandria), The Daily Advertiser (Lafayette), The News-Star (Monroe), Daily World (Opelousas), The Times (Shreveport)
Maryland: The Daily Times (Salisbury)
Michigan: Battle Creek Enquirer, Detroit Free Press, Lansing State Journal, Daily Press & Argus (Livingston County), Observer & Eccentric Newspapers (Livonia), Times Herald (Port Huron)
Minnesota: St. Cloud Times
Mississippi: Hattiesburg American, The Clarion-Ledger (Jackson)
Missouri: Springfield News-Leader
Montana: Great Falls Tribune
Nevada: Reno Gazette-Journal
New Jersey: Asbury Park Press, Courier-News (Bridgewater), Courier-Post (Cherry Hill), Home News Tribune (East Brunswick), Daily Record (Morristown), The Daily Journal (Vineland)
New York: Press and Sun-Bulletin (Binghamton), Star-Gazette (Elmira), The Ithaca Journal, Poughkeepsie Journal, Rochester Democrat and Chronicle, The Journal News (Westchester County)
North Carolina: Asheville Citizen-Times
Ohio: Telegraph-Forum (Bucyrus), Chillicothe Gazette, The Cincinnati Enquirer, Newspaper Network of Central Ohio (Columbus), Coshocton Tribune, The News-Messenger (Fremont), Lancaster Eagle-Gazette, News Journal (Man
Oregon: Statesman Journal (Salem)
South Carolina: The Greenville News
South Dakota: Argus Leader (Sioux Falls)
Tennessee: The Leaf-Chronicle (Clarksville), The Jackson Sun, The Daily News Journal (Murfreesboro), The Tennessean (Nashville)
Utah: The Spectrum (St. George)
Vermont: The Burlington Free Press
Virginia: Staunton Daily News-Leader
Wisconsin: The Port-Crescent (Appleton); Action Advertising Inc., The Reporter (Fond du Lac); Green Bay Press-Gazette; Herald Times Reporter (Manitowoc); Marshfield News-Herald; Oshkosh Northwestern; The Sheboygan Press;

Other Holdings:
Magazine: Military Times; Army Times; Armed Forces Journal; Navy Times; Marine Corps Times; Air Force Times; Federal Times; Defense News
National Newspaper: USA Today Over 300 non-daily publications.

THE GAZETTE CO.
Box 816
Cedar Rapids, IA 52401
Phone: 319-398-8422
Fax: 319-398-8378
Officers:
Joe Hladky III, President
Ken Slaughter, Chief Financial Officer
Ownership: Joseph F Hladky III, Trustee of Employee Stock Ownership Trust; John L Donnelly; Kenneth J Slaughter, 38.5%; John M Hladky, 6.55%; Elizabeth T Barry, 6.1%; Alice T Smith, 6.08%; Anne M. Cole Family Trust, 5.59%; Elsie H. Miller Trust, 5.19%; Joseph F Hladkey III, 4.06%; Martin L. Cole InterVivos Trust, 3.93%; Cynthia A Thompson, 3.67%; Nancy L Thompson, 3.67%; Joseph F Hladkey Jr. Estate, 3.28%; Melissa J Sheppard, 3.02%; Kathleen M Spillman, 3.02%; Jane M Hladkey, 2.56%; Robert C Davis Jr., 1.69%.
Represented (legal): Wiley Rein LLP.
TV Stations:
Iowa: KCRG-DT Cedar Rapids.
Newspapers:
Iowa: Cedar Rapids Gazette

G.I.G. INC.
PO Box 88336
Sioux Falls, SD 57109
Phone: 605-335-3393
Officer:
Charles D. Poppen, President
TV Stations:
North Dakota: KCPM Grand Forks.
LPTV Stations:
North Dakota: KVNJ-LP Fargo.
South Dakota: KCPL-LP Rapid City; KCPO-LP Sioux Falls.

GILMORE BROADCASTING CORP.
PO Box 25
Evansville, IN 47701
Phone: 800-879-6523
Officers:
Douglas A. Padgett, President & Chief Operating Officer
Mariette A. Lemieux, Chief Executive Officer & Treasurer
Fred F. Fielding, Executive Vice President & General Counsel
Chistopher J. Shook, Executive Vice President
George H. Lennon III, Secretary
Ownership: National City Bank of Midwest, Trustee of The James S. Gilmore Jr. Revocable Trust. James S Gilmore Jr died December 2000.
Represented (legal): Wiley Rein LLP.
TV Stations:
Indiana: WEHT-DT Evansville.
Other Holdings:
Program source: Jim Gilmore Productions, Evansville, IN.

GLOBAL BROADCASTING LLC
1020 Francisco St
San Francisco, CA 94109
Phone: 202-730-1310
Ownership: Kevin P. O'Brien, President & Chief Executive Officer.
Represented (legal): Harris, Wiltshire & Grannis LLP.

TV Stations:
Massachusetts: WLNE-DT New Bedford.

GOCOM MEDIA OF ILLINOIS LLC
200 Main St
Ste 201B
Hilton Head Island, SC 29926
Phone: 843-342-4405
Officer:
Richard L. Gorman, President & Chief Executive Officer
Ownership: Robinson O. Everett Estate, 58.03%; J. McGregor Everett, 20.57%; GOCOM Broadcasting Corp., 15.64%; James H. Doyle, 2.49%; Peter O'Brien, 1.09%; Daniel J. Duman, 1.08%; C. Randall Stone, 0.54%; GBC ownership:; Richard L. Gorman, Pres. & Treas., 51%; Katherine R. Gorman, Secy., 49%.
Represented (legal): Fletcher, Heald & Hildreth PLC.
TV Stations:
Illinois: WBUI-DT Decatur; WRSP-DT Springfield; WCCU-DT Urbana.

GORMALLY BROADCASTING LLC
1441 Main St
Ste 604
Springfield, MA 01103
Phone: 413-781-8600
E-mail: gormally@comcast.net
Ownership: John J. Gormally, Managing Partner.
Represented (legal): Davis Wright Tremaine LLP.
TV Stations:
Massachusetts: WGGB-DT Springfield.

GRANITE BROADCASTING CORP.
767 3rd Ave
34th Floor
New York, NY 10017-2083
Phone: 212-826-2530
Fax: 212-826-2858
Officers:
Peter Markham, Chairman & Chief Executive Officer
Duane Lammers, Chief Operating Officer
Lawrence I. Wills, Senior Vice President & Chief Financial Officer
Andrea Pagliughi, Assistant Secretary
Ownership: SP Granite LLC, at least 63%; SPGLLC ownership:; SP Granite Investments LLC, sole mgr.. votes, less than 1% assets; SP Granite Holdco 1, 2, 3 LLC, members, over 99%. assets; SPGILLC ownership:; Edward Mule'; Robert O'Shea, 50%. each; SPGH 1-3 LLC ownership:; Edward Mule', 40%. votes; Robert O'Shea, 40%. votes; Michael Gatto, 20%. votes.
Represented (legal): Akin, Gump, Strauss, Hauer & Feld LLP.
TV Stations:
California: KSEE-DT Fresno; KOFY-DT San Francisco.
Illinois: WEEK-DT Peoria.
Indiana: WISE-DT Fort Wayne.
Michigan: WMYD-DT Detroit.
Minnesota: KRII-DT Chisholm.
New York: WBNG-DT Binghamton; WKBW-DT Buffalo; WTVH-DT Syracuse.
Wisconsin: KBJR-DT Superior.

GRANT CO. INC.
915 Middle River Dr.
Suite 409
Fort Lauderdale, FL 33304
Phone: 954-568-2000
Fax: 954-568-2015
Officer:
Benjamin L. Klein, Chief Financial Officer

Ownership: The Milton Grant Living Trust, Jack L. Lewis, Business Trustee. Milton Grant died April 28, 2007.
Represented (legal): Wilkinson Barker Knauer LLP.
TV Stations:
Alabama: WZDX-DT Huntsville.
Iowa: KGCW-DT Burlington; KLJB-DT Davenport.
Virginia: WWCW-DT Lynchburg; WFXR-DT Roanoke.
Wisconsin: WEUX-DT Chippewa Falls; WLAX-DT La Crosse.

GRAY TELEVISION INC.
126 N. Washington St.
Albany, GA 31702-0048
Phones: 229-888-9390; 404-504-9828
Fax: 229-888-9374
Web site: www.graycommunications.com
Officers:
Hilton Howell, Chief Executive Officer
Robert S. Prather Jr., President & Chief Operating Officer
James C. Ryan, Senior Vice President & Chief Financial Officer
Robert A. Beizer, Vice President, Law & Development
Jackson S. Cowart IV, Chief Accounting Officer & Assistant Secretary
Martha E. Gilbert, Assistant Vice President, Benefis
Vance F. Luke, Controller & Assistant Secretary
Ownership: Datasouth Computer Corp., 15.25%; Bull Run Corp., 10.86%; Robert S. Prather Jr., 2.86%; DCC ownership:; Bull Run Corp.; BRC ownership:; J. Mack Robinson, 16.67%; Samuel R. Shapiro, 10.9%; Robinson-Prather Partnership, 7.16%; James W. Busby, 5.72%; W. James Host, 3.16%.
Represented (legal): Venable LLP.
TV Stations:
Alabama: WTVY-DT Dothan.
Colorado: KKTV-DT Colorado Springs; KKCO-DT Grand Junction.
Florida: WJHG-DT Panama City.
Georgia: WRDW-DT Augusta; WCTV-DT Thomasville; WSWG-DT Valdosta.
Illinois: WIFR-DT Freeport.
Indiana: WNDU-DT South Bend.
Kansas: KLBY-DT Colby; KUPK-DT Garden City; WIBW-DT Topeka; KAKE-DT Wichita.
Kentucky: WBKO-DT Bowling Green; WYMT-DT Hazard; WKYT-DT Lexington.
Michigan: WILX-DT Onondaga.
Mississippi: WTOK-DT Meridian.
Nebraska: KGIN-DT Grand Island; KOLN-DT Lincoln; WOWT-DT Omaha.
Nevada: KOLO-DT Reno.
North Carolina: WITN-DT Washington.
Tennessee: WVLT-DT Knoxville.
Texas: KBTX-DT Bryan; KXII-DT Sherman; KWTX-DT Waco.
Virginia: WCAV-DT Charlottesville; WHSV-DT Harrisonburg.
West Virginia: WSAZ-DT Huntington; WTAP-DT Parkersburg.
Wisconsin: WEAU-DT Eau Claire; WMTV-DT Madison; WSAW-DT Wausau.
LPTV Stations:
Colorado: K10LI Canon City; K49JX-D Montrose; K50EZ Montrose; K57CB Romeo, etc..
Kansas: K30GD Great Bend; K25CV Hays; K38GH Russell; K51GC Salina.
Nebraska: K30FV Cambridge; K55AF Cozad; K28GC Gothenburg; K53GC Neligh; K25GM Newport; K57CZ North Platte; K43FX O'Neill; K33FF Wallace.
Nevada: K12IX Austin; K49CK Stead & Lawton.
Texas: K02EQ Paris.
Virginia: WAHU-CA Charlottesville; WAHU-LD Charlottesville; WVAW-LD Charlottesville.
West Virginia: W16CE Charleston.
Wisconsin: W57AR Sayner & Vilas County.
Radio Stations:
Colorado: KRYD-FM

GRIFFIN COMMUNICATIONS LLC
7401 N Kelley Ave
Oklahoma City, OK 73111-8420
Phone: 405-841-9155
Officers:
David F. Griffin, President & Manager
Steve P. Foerster, Vice President
Joyce Reed, Vice President
Ted W. Strickland, Vice President & Chief Financial Officer
Terry Alexander, Secretary
Ownership: Griffin Capital Corp., 65.2%; Griffin Holdings Inc., 34.8%; GCC ownership:; David F. Griffin Revocable Trust, 69.39%; Grace Holly Griffin GST Exempt 2004 Family Trust, 15.22%; John Wilkinson Griffin GST Exempt 2004 Family Trust, 15.22%; GHI ownership:; John Watson Griffin Trust 1, 86.5%; John W. Griffin Irrevocable Children's Trust, 13.5%.
Represented (legal): Holland & Knight LLP.
TV Stations:
Oklahoma: KQCW-DT Muskogee; KWTV-DT Oklahoma City; KOTV-DT Tulsa.
Other Holdings:
LPTV Stations: Oklahoma Community Television LLC, see listing, 99.49% interest.

CHARLES M. HARKER
1150 Foothill Blvd
Ste D
La Canada, CA 91011
Phone: 818-790-9283
E-mail: charlesm@pacbell.net
Represented (legal): David Tillotson.
TV Stations:
Mississippi: WABG-DT Greenwood.
Radio Stations:
Mississippi: WABG (AM)

HEARST-ARGYLE TELEVISION INC.
888 7th Ave.
New York, NY 10106
Phone: 212-887-6800
Fax: 212-887-6875
Officers:
Frank A Bennack Jr, Chairman
David J. Barrett, President & Chief Executive Officer
Harry T. Hawks, Executive Vice President, Chief Financial Officer & Asstistant Secretary
Steven IA. Hobbs, Executive Vice President & Chief Legal & Development Officer
Roger Keating, Senior Vice President, Digital Media
Philip M. Stolz, Senior Vice President
Brian Bracco, Senior Vice President, News
Jonathan C. Mintzer, Vice President, General Counsel & Corporate Secretary
Ownership: Hearst Broadcasting Inc.; HBI ownership:; Hearst Holdings Inc.; HHI ownership:; The Hearst Corp.; THC ownership:; Stock is vested in trust with 13 trustees.
Represented (legal): Clifford Chance; Brooks, Pierce, McLendon, Humphrey & Leonard LLP.
TV Stations:
Arkansas: KHOG-DT Fayetteville; KHBS-DT Fort Smith.
California: KCRA-DT Sacramento; KSBW-DT Salinas; KQCA-DT Stockton.
Florida: WKCF-DT Clermont; WESH-DT Daytona Beach.
Hawaii: KHVO-DT Hilo; KITV-DT Honolulu; KMAU-DT Wailuku.
Iowa: KCCI-DT Des Moines.
Kentucky: WLKY-DT Louisville.
Louisiana: WDSU-DT New Orleans.
Maine: WMTW-DT Poland Spring.
Maryland: WBAL-DT Baltimore.
Massachusetts: WCVB-DT Boston.
Mississippi: WAPT-DT Jackson.

Missouri: KMBC-DT Kansas City.

Nebraska: KETV-DT Omaha.

New Hampshire: WMUR-DT Manchester.

New Mexico: KOAT-DT Albuquerque; KOCT-DT Carlsbad; KOVT-DT Silver City.

New York: WPTZ-DT North Pole.

North Carolina: WXII-DT Winston-Salem.

Ohio: WLWT-DT Cincinnati.

Oklahoma: KOCO-DT Oklahoma City.

Pennsylvania: WGAL-DT Lancaster; WTAE-DT Pittsburgh.

South Carolina: WYFF-DT Greenville.

Vermont: WNNE-DT Hartford.

Wisconsin: WISN-DT Milwaukee.

LPTV Stations:

Arizona: K10IN Chinle; K63AE Many Farms.

Colorado: K45DH Durango.

Georgia: W06AE Clayton, etc..

Hawaii: K51BB Lihue.

New Hampshire: W27BL Berlin; W26CQ Colebrook; W38CB Littleton; WMUR-LP Littleton.

New Mexico: K34CR Alamogordo, etc.; K10CG-D Aztec & Cedar Hill; K09JJ Bloomfield, etc.; K49CZ Caballo; K43BT Carrizozo; K66AE Colfax; K65FJ Crownpoint; K51DS Deming; K28ER Dulce & Lumberton; K19CM Farmington; K62CR Farmington; K52CR Forrest, etc.; K08IJ Gallup; K67BP Gallup; K11EV Grants, etc.; K12NH Hobbs; K66EE Horse Springs; K09AI Las Vegas; K61CN Lordsburg; K57BR Montoya & Newkirk; K46IN Portales; K16CH Raton, etc.; K12OC Red River; K13RK Roswell; K62AL Roswell; K20GU Ruidoso, etc.; K08KX Taos; K60DD Tierra Amarilla.

North Carolina: W08BH Andrews, etc.; W11AX Bat Cave, etc.; W05AR Bryson City, etc.; W09AS Burnsville; W11AU Canton, etc.; W10AL Cherokee, etc.; W03AK Ela, etc.; W06AJ Franklin; W06AI Marion; W10AK Spruce Pine; W02AF Sylva, etc.; W11AH Tryon & Columbus.

Vermont: W27CP White River Junction; W65AM White River Junction.

Radio Stations:

Maryland: WBAL (AM), WIYY (FM) Baltimore

HEARST BROADCASTING INC.

PO Box 1800

c/o Brooks, Pierce, et al.

Raleigh, NC 27602

Phone: 919-839-0300

Officers:

George R. Hearst Jr., Chairman

Frank A. Bennack Jr., Chief Executive Officer

John G. Conomikes, Vice President & General Manager, Broadcasting

David Barrett, Vice President & Deputy General Manager, Broadcasting

Martin Faubell, Vice President Engineering

Ownership: Hearst Television Inc.; HTI ownership;; The Hearst Corp.; THC ownership;; William Randolph Hearst Trust.

Represented (legal): Clifford Chance; Brooks, Pierce, McLendon, Humphrey & Leonard LLP.

TV Stations:

Florida: WMOR-DT Lakeland; WPBF-DT Tequesta.

Missouri: KCWE-DT Kansas City.

Other Holdings:

Program source: 20% of ESPN; 37.5% of both A&E and the History Channel; Through The Hearst Corp., 50% of Lifetime Radio.

HERITAGE BROADCASTING GROUP

Box 627

Cadillac, MI 49601-0627

Phone: 616-775-3478

Fax: 616-775-3671

Officers:

Mario F. Iacobelli, Chairman, President & Chief Operating Officer

William E. Kring, Vice President, Secretary-Treasurer & Chief Financial Officer

Ownership: Mario F Iacobelli.

Represented (legal): Hogan & Hartson LLP.

TV Stations:

Michigan: WWTV-DT Cadillac; WWUP-DT Sault Ste. Marie.

HERO BROADCASTING LLC

14450 Commerce Way

Miami Lakes, FL 33016

Phone: 305-863-5700

E-mail: bbehar@belallc.com

Officers:

Robert Behar, President & Chief Executive Officer

Marisol Messir, Secretary-Treasurer & Chief Financial Officer

Ownership: Robert Behar. votes, 70.6% assets.

Represented (legal): Dow Lohnes PLLC.

TV Stations:

Arizona: KMOH-DT Kingman.

California: KBEH-DT Oxnard.

LPTV Stations:

Arizona: KEJR-LD Phoenix; KEJR-LP Phoenix.

HIC BROADCAST INC.

606 Young St.

Dallas, TX 75202

Phone: 214-977-6780

Officers:

Roland A. Hernandez, President

Enrique Hernandez Jr., Secretary

Ownership: The Hernandez Family Trust, Dated as of 12/12/1988, 50%; Enrique Hernandez Jr., 25%; Roland A Hernandez, 25%.

Represented (legal): Dow Lohnes PLLC.

TV Stations:

Texas: KFWD-DT Fort Worth.

HIGH PLAINS BROADCASTING INC.

Po Box 288

120 Oak Dr

Kaw City, OK 74641

Phone: 580-269-2215

Ownership: James H. Martin, Pres..

Represented (legal): Pillsbury Winthrop Shaw Pittman LLP.

TV Stations:

California: KGET-DT Bakersfield; KGPE-DT Fresno; KFTY-DT Santa Rosa.

Florida: WTEV-DT Jacksonville.

Texas: WOAI-DT San Antonio.

Utah: KUCW-DT Ogden.

LPTV Stations:

Utah: KUWB-LP Bloomington; K40HS Duchesne; K43JF-D Manti/Ephraim; K14LW Myton; K17GT-D Price; K24GK Salina; K48JD Santa Clara & Washington; K51IC-D Spring Glen.

Wyoming: K28DV Evanston; K31FW Mountain View; K45IA Rock Springs.

HOAK MEDIA LLC

500 Crescent Ct

Ste 220

Dallas, TX 75201

Phone: 972-960-4896

Officers:

James M. Hoak, Chairman

Eric Van den Branden, President & Manager

Kelly Slayton, Secretary

Ownership: James M. Hoak, 30.3%. votes; 9.3%. assets; Centennial Hoak Media Inc., 36.4%. votes, 11.4%. assets; Columbia Hoak Partners III Inc., 26.2%. votes, 8.2%. assets; Columbia Hoak Partners III LLC, 5.1%. votes, 1.6%. assets; Lanny Martin, 1.3%. votes, 0.4%. assets; Charles A. Anderson, 0.3%. votes, 0.1%. assets; Richard A. Anderson, 0.3%. votes, 0.1%. assets; Hoak & Co., 0.1%. votes; CHMI ownership;; Duncan T. Butler Jr., 25%. votes, 15% assets; Steven C. Halstedt, 25%. votes, 17% assets; David C. Hull Jr., 25%. votes, 15% assets; Jeffrey H. Schutz, 25%. votes, 15.25% assets; CHPIIII & CHPIIII ownership;; James B. Fleming Jr., 33.3%. votes, 11.21%. assets; R. Philip Herget III, 33.3%. votes, 15.7% assets; Harry F. Hopper III, 33.3%. votes, 27.67% assets; HAC ownership;; James M. Hoak, Chmn., 10%; Nancy J. Hoak, 90%.

Represented (legal): Akin, Gump, Strauss, Hauer & Feld LLP.

TV Stations:

Colorado: KREG-DT Glenwood Springs; KREX-DT Grand Junction; KREY-DT Montrose.

Florida: WMBB-DT Panama City.

Louisiana: KALB-DT Alexandria; KNOE-DT Monroe.

Nebraska: KHAS-DT Hastings; KNOP-DT North Platte.

North Dakota: KFYR-DT Bismarck; KQCD-DT Dickinson; KVLY-DT Fargo; KMOT-DT Minot; KUMV-DT Williston.

South Dakota: KABY-DT Aberdeen; KPRY-DT Pierre; KSFY-DT Sioux Falls.

Texas: KAUZ-DT Wichita Falls.

LPTV Stations:

Arkansas: K18AB El Dorado.

Colorado: K44CA Cimarron Creek, etc.; K09MR Gateway; K07GD-D Glenwood Springs; KGJT-LP Grand Junction; K02HW Grand Valley; K13ML Hotchkiss, etc.; K06GQ Norwood; K02GC Nucla, etc.; K06HZ Paonia; K09QA Paonia, etc.; K03FX Placerville; K03AY Ridgway; K40CS Rulison.

Montana: K13PL Glendive.

Nebraska: K20DK Beaver Lake area; K18DH Broken Bow; K14IY Holdrege; K35AL Lexington; K11TW North Platte; K21CY Ogallala.

South Dakota: K07QL Mitchell.

Radio Stations:

Louisiana: KNOE-AM-FM Monroe

HOUR OF HARVEST INC.

219 Radio Station Loop

Box Y

Beattyville, KY 41311

Phone: 606-464-3600

Fax: 606-464-5021

Officers:

Margaret Drake, President

Jonathan Drake, Vice President

Rachel Drake, Secretary-Treasurer

Ownership: Non-stock corp..

TV Stations:

Kentucky: WLJC-DT Beattyville.

Radio Stations:

Kentucky: WLJC (FM) Beattyville.

HUBBARD BROADCASTING INC.

3415 University Ave.

St. Paul, MN 55114

Phone: 651-642-4212

Fax: 651-642-4103

E-mail: promotion@kstp.com

Officers:

Stanley S. Hubbard, Chairman, President & Chief Executive Officer

Virginia Hubbard Morris, President, Radio Group

Gerald D. Deeney, Vice President

Robert W. Hubbard, Vice President & President, Television Group

Stanley E. Hubbard II, Vice President & President, Hubbard Media Group

John Soucheray, Vice President & General Manager, Hubbard Radio Network

Ronald L. Lindwall, Vice President & Chief Financial Officer

John Mayasich, Vice President, Public Affairs

Harold Crump, Vice President, Corporate Affairs

Kathryn Hubbard Rominski, Secretary

James A. Barnum, Deputy General Counsel

Ownership: Stanley E. Hubbard Grandchildren's Trust, Stanley S. Hubbard, Trustee, 27.61%; Stanley S. Hubbard Trust, Stanley S. Hubbard, Trustee, 17.83%; Stanley E. Hubbard Residuary Trust, Stanley S. Hubbard, Trustee, 16.57%; Stanley S. Hubbard, 15.25%; Stanley E. Hubbard, 6.2%; Kathryn H. Rominski, 6.2%; Julia D. Coyte, 3.44%; Robert W. Hubbard, 3.44%; Virginia H. Morris, 3.44%.

Represented (legal): Holland & Knight LLP.

TV Stations:

Minnesota: KSAX-DT Alexandria; KAAL-DT Austin; WDIO-DT Duluth; WIRT-DT Hibbing; KSTC-DT Minneapolis; KRWF-DT Redwood Falls; KSTP-DT St. Paul.

New Mexico: KOB-DT Albuquerque; KOBF-DT Farmington; KOBR-DT Roswell; KOBG-DT Silver City.

New York: WNYT-DT Albany; WHEC-DT Rochester.

LPTV Stations:

Arizona: K08HQ Chinle; K09XH Ganado; K43GQ Klagetoh; K49ET Many Farms.

Colorado: K46FM Bayfield; K50IV Cortez; K25GE Durango; K40GE Pagosa Springs; K63AN Romeo.

Massachusetts: W38DL Adams, etc.; W28DA Pittsfield, etc.

Minnesota: K28DD Bemidji; K16BQ Brainerd; W61AF Grand Marais; K55BR Grand Portage; K32FY Park Rapids; K57CN Wabasha; K17FE Wadena; K30FZ Willmar.

New Mexico: K31GJ Alamogordo; K20HA Caballo; K30GM Capitan & Ruidoso; K45GJ Carlsbad; K51CN Carrizozo; K56FN Cebolla; K16EX Clovis; K30GJ Colfax; K28GT Crownpoint; K35GY Cuba; K48HL Datil/Horse Springs; K41FM Deming; K30EK Dulce & Lumberton; K31GC Forrest, etc.; K48GD Gallina; K39EW Gallup; K06CU Grants, etc.; K09LQ Guadalupita; K20GT Indian Village; KAEP-LP Las Cruces; K47GV Las Vegas; K27FN Lordsburg; K36GA Lordsburg; K17FK Montoya & Newkirk; K25FI Mora; K06FT Penasco; K09JK Quemado; K09GR Questa; K26DX Raton; K46GL Red River; K06EM Roy; K36DI Santa Rosa; K09KC Santa Rosa Heights; K10MG Socorro; K06LE Taos; K09KJ Tierra Amarilla, etc.; K06IS Tohatchi; K16DL Zuni Pueblo.

New York: W21CP Gloversville.

Radio Stations:

Minnesota: WFMP (FM) Coon Rapids, KSTP-AM-FM St. Paul

Other Holdings:

Data service (Conus Communications).

HUMANITY INTERESTED MEDIA LP

11150 Equity Dr

Houston, TX 77041

Phone: 713-403-6909

E-mail: dwhite@usfrmedia.com

Officers:

Gregory L. Brown, President & Chief Executive Officer of HIM GP

Donna White, Secretary of HIM GP

Ownership: HIM GP LLC, Gen. Partner, 0.1%; Channel 55/42 Operating LP, Ltd. Partner, 99.9%; C55/42OLP & HIMGPLLC ownership:; US Farm & Ranch Supply Co. Inc. dba USFR Media Group; USFRMG ownership:; JJM 1999 Living Trust, 22.96%; LaSalle Cattle Co. Ltd., 20.63%; Stanford Venture Capital Holdings Inc., 10.62%; Media Sports Partnership Ltd., 5.98%; JJM1999LT ownership:; Peter S. McMullen; Patrick J. Gilmartin, Trustees; LCCL ownership:; LaSalle Management LC, General Partner; SVCHI ownership:; Stanford International Band Ltd.; MSPL ownership:; Media Sports Inc., Gen. Partner.
Represented (legal): Fletcher, Heald & Hildreth PLC.
TV Stations:
Texas: KTBU-DT Conroe.

INTERMEDIA PARTNERS VII LP
405 Lexington Ave
48th Floor
New York, NY 10174
Phone: 212-503-2855
Ownership: InterMedia Partners LP, Gen. Partner. votes, 7.8% assets; IMPLP ownership:; HK Capital Partners LLC, Gen. Partner. votes, 7.8% assets; HKCPLLC ownership:; Leo Hindery Jr., 50%. votes, 4.3% assets; Peter Kern, 50%. votes, 3.6% assets.
Represented (legal): Willkie Farr & Gallagher LLP.
TV Stations:
Puerto Rico: WNJX-DT Mayaguez; WTIN-DT Ponce; WAPA-DT San Juan.

INTERNATIONAL MEDIA GROUP
1990 S. Bundy Dr.
Suite 850
Los Angeles, CA 90025
Phone: 310-478-1818
Fax: 310-479-8118
Officers:
Ray Beindorf, Chairman Emeritus
Jon Yasuda, President & Chief Operating Officer
Richard Millet, Vice President, Station Manager
Tony Cortese, Vice President & Chief Financial Officer
Bill Welty, Vice President, Engineering

Branch Office:
New York Sales Office
1180 Avenue of the Americas
New York, NY 10036
Phone: 212-899-5448
Ownership: AMG Intermediate LLC, 69.42%; Ray L. Beindorf, 25.5%; AMGI ownership:; Asian Media Investors I LP, 64.28%; Korea Times Los Angeles Inc., 19.99%; AMI ownership:; GEI Capital III LLC; KTLAI ownership:; Jae Min Chang, Pres., 50%; Jae Ku Change, 50%; GEIC ownership:; Leonard Green, 30.7%; Johnathan Sokoloff, 20.8%; John Danhakl, 18.7%; Peter Nolan, 18.7%; Greg Annick, 8.6%; Jonathan Seiffer, 2.5%.
Represented (legal): Skadden, Arps, Slate, Meagher & Flom LLP.
TV Stations:
California: KSCI-DT Long Beach.
Hawaii: KIKU-DT Honolulu.
LPTV Stations:
California: KUAN-LP Poway, etc..

ION MEDIA NETWORKS INC., DEBTOR IN POSSESSION
601 Clearwater Park Rd.
West Palm Beach, FL 33401-6233
Phone: 561-659-4122
Fax: 561-659-4754
E-mail: pressroom@ionmedia.tv

Web site: www.ionmedia.com
Officers:
R Brandon Burgess, Chairman & Chief Executive Officer
Richard Garcia, Senior Vice President & Chief Financial Officer
Kristine Hunsinger, Senior Vice President, Planning, Scheduling & Acquisitions
Blaine Rominger, Senior Vice President, National, Local, Cable Long-Form Sales
Adam K. Weinstein, Senior Vice President, Secretary & Chief Legal Officer
Stephen P. Appel, President, Sales & Marketing
Douglas C. Barker, President., Bcst. Distribution & Southern Region
Steven J. Friedman, President, Cable
David A. Glenn, President, Engineering
Joseph Koker, President, TV Stations Group
Tammy G. Hedge, Vice President, Chief Accounting Officer & Controller
Brett Jenkins, Vice President, Technology
Robert Marino, Vice President, National Sales
Jeffrey J Quinn, Vice President & Treasurer

Branch Office:
Sales Offices:
1330 Avenue of the Americas
32nd Floor
New York, NY 10019
Phone: 212-603-8451
Fax: 212-956-0920
Ownership: CIG Media LLC; CIGMLLC ownership:; Citadel Wellington LLC, 79%. equity; Citadel Kensington Global Strategies Fund Ltd., 21%. equity; CWLLC & CKGSFL ownership:; Citadel LP; CLP ownership:; Citadel Investment Group LLC, Gen. Partner; CIGLLC ownership:; Kenneth Griffin. Paxson Communications Corp. became ION Media Networks Inc. effective June 26, 2006. ION Media Networks Inc. filed for Chapter 11 bankruptcy protection May 20, 2009.
Represented (legal): Dow Lohnes PLLC.
TV Stations:
Alabama: WPXH-TV Gadsden.
Arizona: KPPX-DT Tolleson.
California: KSPX-TV Sacramento; KPXN-TV San Bernardino; KKPX-TV San Jose.
Colorado: KPXC-DT Denver.
Connecticut: WHPX-DT New London.
Delaware: WPPX-TV Wilmington.
Florida: WXPX-TV Bradenton; WPXP-TV Lake Worth; WOPX-TV Melbourne; WPXM-DT Miami.
Georgia: WPXC-DT Brunswick; WPXA-TV Rome.
Hawaii: KPXO-DT Kaneohe.
Illinois: WCPX-TV Chicago.
Indiana: WIPX-TV Bloomington.
Iowa: KPXR-TV Cedar Rapids; KFPX-TV Newton.
Kentucky: WUPX-DT Morehead.
Louisiana: WPXL-TV New Orleans.
Massachusetts: WBPX-TV Boston; WDPX-TV Vineyard Haven.
Michigan: WPXD-DT Ann Arbor; WZPX-TV Battle Creek.
Minnesota: KPXM-TV St. Cloud.
Missouri: KPXE-TV Kansas City.
New Hampshire: WPXG-TV Concord.
New York: WYPX-DT Amsterdam; WPXJ-DT Batavia; WPXN-DT New York; WSPX-DT Syracuse.
North Carolina: WGPX-TV Burlington; WFPX-TV Fayetteville; WEPX-TV Greenville; WPXU-DT Jacksonville; WRPX-TV Rocky Mount.
Ohio: WVPX-TV Akron.
Oklahoma: KOPX-TV Oklahoma City; KTPX-TV Okmulgee.
Oregon: KPXG-DT Salem.
Pennsylvania: WQPX-TV Scranton.
Rhode Island: WPXQ-TV Block Island.
Tennessee: WNPX-TV Cookeville; WPXK-TV Jellico; WPXX-DT Memphis.
Texas: KPXD-TV Arlington; KPXB-TV Conroe; KPXL-TV Uvalde.

Utah: KUPX-TV Provo.
Virginia: WPXW-TV Manassas; WPXV-TV Norfolk; WPXR-TV Roanoke.
Washington: KWPX-DT Bellevue; KGPX-TV Spokane.
West Virginia: WLPX-DT Charleston; WWPX-TV Martinsburg.
Wisconsin: WTPX-DT Antigo; WPXE-TV Kenosha.
LPTV Stations:
Colorado: KPXH-LP Fort Collins.
Florida: WPXB-LD Daytona Beach; WPXJ-LP Jacksonville.
Indiana: WIPX-LP Indianapolis.
Massachusetts: W40BO Boston; WMPX-LP Dennis.
Michigan: W48AV Detroit.
New York: WPXU-LP Amityville.
Oregon: KPXG-LP Portland.
Tennessee: WNPX-LP Nashville.
Texas: KBPX-LP Houston.

JB BROADCASTING INC.
PO Box 547
Arroyo Grande, CA 93421
Phone: 805-896-7335
Officer:
James L. Primm, President
Ownership: James L Primm, 50%; Charles Meeker, 50%.
TV Stations:
Texas: KWWT-DT Odessa.

DOUGLAS R. JOHNSON
8440 Westpark Dr
Houston, TX 77063
Phone: 713-974-5151
Fax: 713-975-6397
Represented (legal): Smithwick & Belendiuk PC.
TV Stations:
Texas: KNWS-DT Katy; KLDT-DT Lake Dallas.

JOURNAL COMMUNICATIONS INC.
333 W State St
Milwaukee, WI 53203
Phone: 414-332-9611
Fax: 414-967-5400
Officers:
Steven J. Smith, Chairman & Chief Executive Officer
Douglas G. Kiel, President
Paul M. Bonaiuto, Executive Vice President & Chief Financial Officer
Elizabeth F. Brenner, Executive Vice President
Mary Hill Leahy, Senior Vice President, General Counsel, Chief Compliance Officer & Secretary
Anne M. Bauer, Vice President
Carl D. Gardner, Vice President
Mark J. Keefe, Vice President
Kenneth L. Kozminski, Vice President
James P. Prather, Vice President
Steven H. Wexler, Vice President
Karen O. Trickle, Vice President & Treasurer
Ownership: Publicly held..
Represented (legal): Leventhal, Senter & Lerman PLLC.
TV Stations:
Arizona: KWBA-TV Sierra Vista; KGUN-DT Tucson.
California: KMIR-DT Palm Springs.
Florida: WFTX-TV Cape Coral.
Idaho: KNIN-DT Caldwell; KIVI-TV Nampa.
Michigan: WSYM-DT Lansing.
Nebraska: KMTV-TV Omaha.
Nevada: KTNV-TV Las Vegas.
Wisconsin: WGBA-TV Green Bay; WTMJ-DT Milwaukee.
LPTV Stations:
Arizona: K16EO Oro Valley & Tucson.

California: KPSE-LP Palm Springs.
Idaho: K27DX McCall; KSAW-LP Twin Falls.
Michigan: W31BK Menominee.
Nevada: K59EX Laughlin; K42AA Pahrump.
Wisconsin: W22BW Sturgeon Bay.
Newspapers:
Florida: St. John's Recorder (Fruit Cove), Clay Today (Orange Park), Ponte Vedra Recorder (Ponte Vedra Beach), Pelican Press (Sarasota)
Wisconsin: Brookfield News; Cudahy-St. Francis Reminder-Enterprise; Elm Grove Elm Leaves; Franklin Hub; Germantown Banner-Press; Greendale Village Life; Greenfield Observer; Hales Corners Village Hub; Kettle Moraine Index
Radio Stations:
Arizona: KGMG (FM) Oracle; KFFN (AM), KMXZ-FM, KQTH (FM) Tucson.
Idaho: KGEM (FM), KJOT (FM) Boise; KCID (AM), KTHI (FM) Caldwell; KRVB (FM) Nampa; KQXR (FM) Payette
Kansas: KYQQ (FM) Arkansas City; KFXJ (FM) Augusta; KFDI-FM, KFTI (AM), KICT-FM Wichita
Missouri: KZRQ (FM) Mount Vernon; KSPW (FM) Sparta; KSGF (AM), KTTS-FM Springfield
Nebraska: KEZO-FM, KKCD (FM), KQCH (FM), KSRZ (FM), KXSP (AM) Omaha
Oklahoma: KXBL (FM) Henryetta; KFAQ (AM), KVOO-FM Tulsa
Tennessee: WMYU (FM) Karns, WKHT (FM) Knoxville, WQBB (AM) Powell, WWST (FM) Sevierville
Wisconsin: WKTI-FM, WTMJ (AM) Milwaukee

JOVON BROADCASTING CORP.
18600 Oak Park Ave.
Tinley Park, IL 60477
Phone: 708-633-0001
Officers:
Joseph A. Stroud, President
Reginald Jones, Chief Operating Officer
Yvonne M. Stroud, Secretary-Treasurer
Ownership: Joseph A Stroud, 99%; Yvonne M Stroud, 1%.
Represented (legal): Hogan & Hartson LLP.
TV Stations:
Indiana: WJYS-DT Hammond.

KAZT LLC
4343 E. Camelback Rd.
Suite 400
Phoenix, AZ 85018
Phone: 602-957-1650
Fax: 602-224-2284
Ownership: Londen Insurance Group Inc., 99%; Ron Bergamo, 1%; LIG ownership:; Jack Londen, 96.52%; Thomas Londen, 3.48%.
Represented (legal): Pillsbury Winthrop Shaw Pittman LLP.
TV Stations:
Arizona: KAZT-DT Phoenix.
LPTV Stations:
Arizona: K24DK Bullhead City; K43CO Casa Grande; K30DT Flagstaff; K20ID Kingman; K17DA Lake Havasu City; K57HX Mesa; K55EH Phoenix; KAZT-CA Phoenix; K23BY Scottsdale; K29DK Williams; K19CX Yuma.

KETCHIKAN TV LLC
PO Box 348
2539 N Hwy 67
Sedalia, CO 80135
Phone: 303-688-5162
Officer:
David M. Drucker, President
Ownership: David M. Drucker, 75%; ENA Lukes Family Trust, 25%. Drucker also has interest in Cayo Hueso Networks LLC, Denver Digital Television LLC, Echonet Corp., GreenTV Corp. & Polar Communications, see listings.
Represented (legal): Rini Coran PC.

TV Stations:
Alaska: KDMD-DT Anchorage; KUBD-DT Ketchikan; KTNL-DT Sitka.
LPTV Stations:
Alaska: K41DP Anchorage; K45HQ Anchorage; KDMD-LP Fairbanks; KUBD-LP Kodiak.

KM COMMUNICATIONS INC.
3654 W. Jarvis Ave.
Skokie, IL 60076
Phone: 847-674-0864
Fax: 847-674-9188
Officers:
Myoung Hwa Bae, President & Treasurer
Kevin Joel Bae, Secretary
Ownership: Myoung Hwa Bae, see Hapa Media Properties LLC & Pocatello Channel 15 LLC..
Represented (legal): Irwin, Campbell & Tannenwald PC.
TV Stations:
Arizona: KCFG-DT Flagstaff.
Arkansas: KEJB-DT El Dorado.
Iowa: KWKB-DT Iowa City.
LPTV Stations:
Arizona: KWKM-LP Concho; KWSJ-LP Concho; KNLO-LP Holbrook; KPVY-LD Prescott; KVFA-LP Yuma.
California: KRDN-LP Redding.
Georgia: WSKC-CA Atlanta; WWPD-LP Douglas; WPDW-LP Pearson; WPNG-LP Pearson.
Guam: KTKB-LP Tamuning.
Hawaii: KHIK-LP Kailua-Kona.
Illinois: WRDH-LP Ashton; WCRD-LP Carthage; WBKM-LP Chana; WOCH-CA Chicago; WOCK-CA Chicago; WMKB-LP Rochelle.
Indiana: WHFE-LP Sullivan; WIIB-LP Sullivan; WKMF-LP Sullivan; WVGO-LP Sullivan.
Louisiana: W44CE Vidalia.
Pennsylvania: WLEP-LP Erie.
Texas: KTXF-LP Abilene; KPPY-LP Beaumont; KCCG-LP Corpus Christi; KETK-LP Lufkin; KSVH-LP Victoria.
Wisconsin: WMKE-CA Milwaukee.

EDWARD J. KOPLAR
One S Memorial Dr
Ste 2000
St. Louis, MO 63102
Phone: 314-345-1000
E-mail: jim@koplar.com
TV Stations:
Missouri: KRBK-DT Osage Beach.

PAUL H. KOPLIN
1207 Oak St.
Santa Monica, CA 90405
Phone: 323-965-5400
TV Stations:
Illinois: WAOE-DT Peoria.
LPTV Stations:
Iowa: WBQD-LP Davenport.

KTBS INC.
PO Box 44227
312 E. Kings Hwy.
Shreveport, LA 71104
Phone: 318-861-5800
Fax: 318-862-9430
Officers:
Edwin W. Wray, President & General Manager
Helen H. Wray, Vice President
George D. Wray, Vice President
Lois Wray Rowe, Vice President & Secretary-Treasurer
Sherri McCallie, Chief Financial Officer
Ownership: Wray Properties Trust, 26.38%; Lois Wray Rowe; Edwin Newton Wray Jr, Co-Executors of Florence H Wray Estate, 18.87%; Edwin H Wray Jr, 17.37%; Loir Wray Rowe, 16.7%; Jerry Wray, Executor of George D Wray Estate, 13.19%.

Represented (legal): Fletcher, Heald & Hildreth PLC.
TV Stations:
Louisiana: KTBS-DT Shreveport.

KTVU PARTNERSHIP
6205 Peachtree Dunwoody Rd.
Atlanta, GA 30328
Phone: 678-645-0000
Officer:
Andrew A. Merdek, Secretary
Ownership: KTVU Inc., 55%; Anthony Family Partnership, 22.5%; ACC Family Partnership LP, 22.5%; KTVUI ownership:; Cox Broadcasting Inc.; AFC ownership:; Kennedy Children's Trust, James C. Kennedy & R. Dale Hughes, Trustees, 39.19%; Parry-Okeden Children's Trust, Blair K. Parry-Okeden & R. Dale Hughes, Trustees, 26.13%; Blair D. Parry-Okeden Trust, James C. Kennedy & R. Dale Hughes, Trustees, 14.84%; KTVU-JCK Inc., 14.84%; KTVU-BCA Inc., 5%; ACCFPLP ownership:; KTVU-ACC Inc., Gen. Partner, 5%; CBI ownership:; Dayton Cox Trust-A, Barbara Cox Anthony, Anne Cox Chambers & Richard L. Braunstein, Trustees, 41.1%; Anne Cox Chambers Atlanta Trust, Barbara Cox Anthony, Trustee, 28.95%; Barbara Cox Anthony Atlanta Trust, Anne Cox Chambers, Trustee, 28.95%; KTVUACCI ownership:; Anne Cox Chambers; KTVUBCAI ownership:; Barbara Cox Anthony; KTVUJCKI ownership:; James C. Kennedy.
Represented (legal): Dow Lohnes PLLC.
TV Stations:
California: KTVU-DT Oakland; KICU-DT San Jose.
Nevada: KRXI-DT Reno.
Texas: KFOX-DT El Paso.
LPTV Stations:
California: K48LA-D South Lake Tahoe.
Nevada: K22FH Hawthorne; K56IG Nixon; K33IB Silver Springs; K17HB Winnemucca.

LARA KUNKLER
11910 Rosemount Dr.
Fort Myers, FL 33913-8377
Phone: 941-939-6236
TV Stations:
Florida: WZVN-DT Naples.

LAKE SUPERIOR COMMUNITY BROADCASTING CORP.
1390 Bagley St.
Alpena, MI 49707
Phones: 989-356-3434; 906-225-5700
Fax: 989-356-4188; 906-225-5998
Ownership: Stephen A. Marks, Pres..
TV Stations:
Michigan: WBKP-DT Calumet; WBUP-DT Ishpeming.

LAMBERT BROADCASTING OF TENNESSEE
9333 Wilshire Blvd.
Beverly Hills, CA 90210-5404
Phone: 310-551-1900
Ownership: Michael Lambert, see listing, 79%; J.P. Hannan, 14%; Robert Finklestein, 7%.
Represented (legal): Dow Lohnes PLLC.
TV Stations:
Tennessee: WNAB-DT Nashville.

MICHAEL LAMBERT
100 N. Crescent Dr.
Suite 200
Beverly Hills, CA 90210
Phone: 310-385-4200
Represented (legal): Covington & Burling.

TV Stations:
Vermont: WVNY-DT Burlington.
LPTV Stations:
New York: W55AI Lake Placid.
Vermont: W63AD Rutland.
Other Holdings:
TV Stations: Lambert Broadcasting of Tennessee, see listing..

LANDMARK MEDIA ENTERPRISES LLC
150 W Brambleton Ave
Norfolk, VA 23510-2075
Phones: 757-446-2010; 800-446-2004
Fax: 757-446-2489
Web site: www.landmarkcom.com
Officers:
Frank Batten Sr., Chairman of Executive Committee
Frank Batten Jr., Chairman & Chief Executive Officer
Richard F. Barry III, Vice Chairman
Decker Anstrom, President & Chief Operating Officer
Debora Wilson, President, The Weather Channel
R. Bruce Bradley, Executive Vice President, Landmark Publishing Group
Guy Friddell III, Executive Vice President, Corporate Secretary & Counsel
Charlie W. Hill, Executive Vice President, Human Resources
Lemuel E. Lewis, Executive Vice President & Chief Financial Officer
Colleen R. Pittman, Vice President, Finance
Michael Alston, Vice President, Corporate Development & New Ventures
Ownership: Frank Batten Jr. Trust, Frank Batten Jr, Trustee, 36.27%. votes; Fay M. Slover Trust, Bank of America N.A. & Frank Batten, Trustees, 35.10%. votes, 24.37 % assets; Frank Batten 1986 Family Trust, Frank Batten Jr., Trustee, 18.25%. votes; William S. Glennan Trust, J. Allen Tyler, Trustee, 8.42%. votes; 6.52 assets; Frank Batten Trust, Frank Batten, Trustee, 18.47%. assets; Dorothy Batten Rolph Revocable Trust, 5.59%. assets. Formerly Landmark Communications Inc.
Represented (legal): Wiley Rein LLP.
TV Stations:
Nevada: KLAS-DT Las Vegas.
Tennessee: WTVF-DT Nashville.
LPTV Stations:
Nevada: K46GX Henderson; K22DR Laughlin; K48AB Mercury, etc.; K49AB Pahrump.
Newspapers:
Colorado: Metrowest (Brighton), The Canyon Courier (Evergreen), Clear Creek Courant (Idaho Springs), Columbine Community Courier (Littleton), The Hustler (Pine)
Florida: The Visitor (Beverly Hills), Cedar Key Beacon, Chiefland Citizen, The Wakulla News (Crawfordville), Riverland News (Dunnellon), South Marion Citizen (Ocala), Sumter County Times, The Osceola (Tallahasee), Willi
Illinois: Vandalia Leader-Union
Indiana: Mt. Vernon Democrat, Perry County News, Spencer County Journal-Democrat (Rockport)
Iowa: Opinion-Tribune (Glenwood), Red Oak Express
Kentucky: The Kentucky Standard, PLG-TV (Bardstown); Trimble Banner (Bedford); Central Kentucky News-Journal (Campbellsville); Carrollton News-Democrat; Casey County News; Cynthiana Democrat; The News-Enterprise (Elizabe
Maryland: The Capital (Annapolis); Carroll County Times, Community Times (Westminster)
Mississippi: New Albany Gazette
New Mexico: Las Vegas Optic, Los Alamos Monitor

North Carolina: News & Record (Greensboro), Brunswick Beacon (Shallotte)
South Carolina: Chester News and Reporter, The Lancaster News, Pageland Progressive-Journal
Tennessee: LaFollette Press, Morgan County News, Roane County News
Virginia: The Bedford Bulletin, The Gazette (Galax), Declaration (Independence), Loudon Easterner, The Virginian-Pilot (Norfolk), The Roanoke TImes
Other Holdings:
Career Schools: Landmark Education Serivces Inc.
Data Network Service: Continental Broadband Inc.
Databases: Alliant Cooperative Data Solutions LLC
Franchise Broker Service: FranchiseBuyer
Franchise Coordinator: Franchise Solutions
Franchise Referrals: FranchiseOpportunities.com
Magazine: The Cats' Pause (Lexington, KY); Voice of the Hawkeyes (North Liberty, IA); Florida Special Publications (Beverly Hills, FL); Gator Bait (Williston, FL); Real Estate News Citrus (Beverly Hills, FL); Citrus County Chronicle (Crystal River); Inside Indiana (Shelbyville, KY); Tri-State Homes (Cynthiana, KY); Greater Baltimore Homes (Westminster, MD); West Virginia Real Estate Guide (Martinsburg, WV); Eastern Panhandle Real Estate Guide (WV) (Westminster, MD); Eastern Panhandle Homes (WV) (Westminster, MD); Dulles Homes (Westminster, MD); Roane Real Estate Review (Kingston, TN); Carolina Gateway (Lancaster, SC); Homes of York/Adams Counties (PA) (Westminster, MD); Carolina Blue (Durham, NC); Homes & Property (Los Alamos, NM); Huskers Illustrated (Lincoln, NE); Mississippi Homes (New Albany); Real Estate News Hernando/Pasco (Beverly Hills, FL); Guide to Homes (Westminster, MD); Central Kentucky Homes (Elizabethtown, KY); Baltimore/Harford/Cecil Homes (Westminster, MD); Kentucky Homes Bullitt/Nelson/Spencer (Cynthiana, KY); Kentucky Homes Central (Cynthiana, KY); Kentucky Homes Garrard/Lincoln/Rockcastle (Cynthiana, KY); Kentucky Homes Madison/Estill (Cynthiana, KY); Kentucky Homes Northern (Cynthiana, KY); Kentucky Homes Pulaski/Wayne (Cynthiana, KY); Shelby County Home Finder's Guide (Shelbyville, KY); Frederick/Washington Co. Homes (Westminster, MD); Central Maryland Homes (Westminster, MD); 1st Choice Properties (Westminster, MD); Marion/Washington Homes (Lebanon, KY)
On-Demand Video: TotalVid Inc.
On-Line Auction Service: Naxcom.com
On-Line Marketing Services: Q Interactive
Publishing: Trader Publishing Co.; Washingtonian Magazine.

H. CHASE LENFEST
1332 Enterprise Dr.
West Chester, PA 19380
Phone: 610-719-4708
TV Stations:
New Jersey: WMCN-DT Atlantic City.

LESEA BROADCASTING CORP.
61300 S. Ironwood Rd.
South Bend, IN 46614
Phone: 574-291-8200
Fax: 574-291-9043
Officers:
Peter Sumrall, President
Stephen Sumrall, Secretary
David Sumrall, Treasurer
Ownership: David Sumrall; Peter Sumrall; Stephen Sumrall, each, 33.33%.
Represented (legal): Hardy, Carey, Chautin & Balkin LLP.
TV Stations:
Colorado: KWHD-DT Castle Rock.
Hawaii: KWHH-DT Hilo; KWHE-DT Honolulu; KWHM-DT Wailuku.

Indiana: WHMB-DT Indianapolis; WHME-DT South Bend.
Louisiana: WHNO-DT New Orleans.
Oklahoma: KWHB-DT Tulsa.
LPTV Stations:
Colorado: KWHS-LP Colorado Springs.
Indiana: WHCH-LD Chesterton; WHNW-LP Gary; WHVI-LP Valparaiso.
Radio Stations:
Indiana: WHME (FM) South Bend
Other Holdings:
Broadcast Holdings: Shortwave operations.

LIBERMAN BROADCASTING INC.
1845 Empire Ave.
Burbank, CA 91504
Phone: 818-729-5300
E-mail: LBInfo@lbimedia.com
Officers:
Jose Liberman, President
Lenard Liberman, Executive Vice President, Secretary & Chief Financial Officer
Andrew Wallace, Vice President, Midwest National Sales
Ownership: Lenard D. Liberman, 63.13%. votes, 41.03% equity; The Liberman Trust, Jose Liberman Trustee, approximately 30%. votes, approximately 20% equity.
Represented (legal): Latham & Watkins.
TV Stations:
California: KRCA-DT Riverside.
Texas: KMPX-DT Decatur; KZJL-DT Houston.
Utah: KPNZ-DT Ogden.
LPTV Stations:
Arizona: KVPA-LP Phoenix.
California: KSDX-LP San Diego.
Other Holdings:
Radio.

LIBERTY MEDIA CORP.
1200 Liberty Blvd
Englewood, CO 80112
Phone: 720-875-5440
Officers:
John C. Malone, Chairman
Gregory B. Maffei, President & Chief Executive Officer
David J. A. Flowers, Senior Vice President & Treasurer
Albert E. Rosenthaler, Senior Vice President
Christopher W. Shean, Senior Vice President & Controller
Charles Y. Tanabe, Executive Vice President, General Counsel & Secretary
Ownership: John C. Malone, 29.2%. votes, 3.4% assets.
Represented (legal): Nelson Mullins Riley & Scarborough LLP.
TV Stations:
Michigan: WJMN-DT Escanaba.
Wisconsin: WFRV-DT Green Bay.
Other Holdings:
Cable Program Sources: Has interest in QVC, Starz Entertainemnt & News Corp..

LINCOLN BROADCASTING CO.
100 Valley Dr.
Brisbane, CA 94005
Phone: 415-468-2626
Fax: 415-467-7559
Officers:
Lillian L. Howell, Chairman
Lincoln C. Howell, President & Chief Executive Officer
Karen Huynh, Chief Financial Officer
Ownership: Lincoln Television Inc., Gen. Partner; Lillian Lincoln; Lincoln Howell, Ltd. Partners.
Represented (legal): DLA Piper International.

TV Stations:
California: KTSF-DT San Francisco.

LINGARD BROADCASTING CORP.
Box 1732
Tupelo, MS 38802-1732
Phone: 706-369-8180
Officers:
John R. Lingard, President
Dale A. Lingard, Secretary-Treasurer
Ownership: John R Lingard.
TV Stations:
Mississippi: WLOV-DT West Point.

LIN TV CORP.
4 Richmond Sq
Ste 200
Providence, RI 02906
Phone: 401-454-2880
Fax: 401-454-2817
E-mail: edward.munson@lintv.com
Web site: www.lintv.com
Officers:
Vincent L. Sadusky, President & Chief Executive Officer
Scott Blumenthal, Executive Vice President, TV
Richard Schmaeling, Senior Vice President & Chief Financial Officer
Robert Richter, Senior Vice President, New Media
Nicholas Mohamed, Vice President & Controller
Peter E. Maloney, Vice President, Benefits & Special Projects
Edward Munson, Vice President, Station Sales
Denise M. Parent, Vice President & General Counsel

Branch Office:
11 Dupont Circle
Suite 365
Washington, DC 20036
Phone: 202-462-6065
Fax: 202-462-8285
Ownership: Hicks, Muse, Tate & Furst, 70%. voting rights; Publicly held, 30%. voting rights.
Represented (legal): Covington & Burling.
TV Stations:
Alabama: WBPG-DT Gulf Shores; WALA-DT Mobile.
Colorado: KREZ-DT Durango.
Connecticut: WCTX-DT New Haven; WTNH-DT New Haven.
Indiana: WANE-DT Fort Wayne; WISH-DT Indianapolis; WLFI-DT Lafayette; WNDY-DT Marion; WTHI-DT Terre Haute.
Massachusetts: WWLP-DT Springfield.
Michigan: WOTV-DT Battle Creek; WOOD-DT Grand Rapids.
New Mexico: KRQE-DT Albuquerque; KBIM-DT Roswell; KASA-DT Santa Fe.
New York: WIVB-DT Buffalo; WNLO-DT Buffalo.
Ohio: WWHO-DT Chillicothe; WDTN-DT Dayton; WUPW-DT Toledo.
Rhode Island: WPRI-DT Providence.
Texas: KXAN-DT Austin; KBVO Llano.
Virginia: WAVY-DT Portsmouth; WVBT-DT Virginia Beach.
Wisconsin: WLUK-DT Green Bay.
LPTV Stations:
Arizona: K13VW Chinle; K30GL Many Farms; K66BH Navajo Compressor Station.
Colorado: K50FS-D Bayfield; K42DI-D Bayfield & Ignacio; K06JF Cortez; K39AH-D Durango; K31FV-D Durango & Hermosa; K02IL Pagosa Springs; K04NS Pagosa Springs; K31FS Pagosa Springs; K43GT Pagosa Springs; K48HA Pagosa Springs; K66AV Sunetha & Nutria.
Indiana: WIIH-CA Indianapolis.
Massachusetts: WFXQ-CA Springfield.

Michigan: WOBC-CA Battle Creek; W40AN-D Escanaba; WOGC-CA Grand Rapids; WOLP-CA Grand Rapids; WXSP-CA Grand Rapids; WOHO-CA Holland; WOKZ-CA Kalamazoo; WOMS-CA Muskegon.
New Mexico: K27HP Alamogordo; K49FX Alamogordo; K34FU Arrey & Derry; K46FE Artesia; K08FR Aztec; K44GC-D Aztec; K11JO Bloomfield, etc.; K31DR Caballo; K33GD Capitan & Ruidoso; K47FX Carlsbad; K48GY Carrizozo, etc.; K40HC Chama; K44DD Chama; K49BY Clovis; K47DI Coyote Canyon; K44GD Crownpoint; K35HB Deming; K43FU Deming; K40GC Dora; K22GE Dulce; K26EP Dulce & Lumberton; K38EC Eagles Nest; K39EJ Espanola; K21AX Farmington; K29HR-D Farmington; K67CE Gallina; K18HF Gallup; K48GK Gallup; K46FI Grants; K09EP Grants, etc.; K11NV Guadalupita; K18DY Hillsboro; K27GL Hobbs; K50GM Hobbs; K25HJ Hornsby Ranch, etc.; K20GQ Las Vegas; K43FI Las Vegas; K14LO Lordsburg; K29DP Lordsburg; K31HQ Lordsburg; K40HJ Lordsburg; K13OY Mescalero; K22EU Montoya; K06HX Mora; K22EW Mora; K13OX Mud Canyon; K14KO Portales; K40DI Raton; K43GW Raton, etc.; K08ES Red River; K15FT Roswell; K16BZ Ruidoso; K43GL Santa Rosa; K38HR Santa Rosa; K45CU Shiprock; K25DI Silver City; K45EC Silver City; K44HJ Socorro; K12OG Taos; K21FD Taos; K28HM Thoreau; K41FK Tohatchi; K25HV Truth or Consequences; K27BN Truth or Consequences; K44CJ Tucumcari; K48EH Tucumcari; K06BN Wagon Mound; K39FY Zuni.
Texas: KBVO-CA Austin; KHPB-CA Bastrop; KHPF-CA Fredericksburg; KHPX-CA Georgetown; KHPG-CA Giddings; KHPL-CA La Grange; KHPZ-CA Round Rock; KHPM-CA San Marcos.
Virginia: WITD-CA Chesapeake; WPMC-CA Mappsville; WKTD-CA Portsmouth; WBTD-LP Suffolk; WCTX-CA Virginia Beach; WNLO-CA Virginia Beach.
Radio Stations:
Indiana: WTHI-FM; WWVR-FM
Other Holdings:
Broadcast holdings: 54 Broadcasting Inc., see listing, 4.49% interest.; Station Venture Holdings LLC, 20.38% equity interest, limited partner of Station Venture Operations LP, see listing..

LIVING FAITH MINISTRIES INC.
Box 151
Vansant, VA 24656
Phone: 276-676-3806
Officers:
Michael David Smith, President & Chief Executive Officer
Lisa Smith, Executive Vice President
Sue Howington, Secretary
Ownership: Living Faith Broadcasting Inc.; LFBI ownership:; Sue Howington; W. A. Johnson; Joe Macione; Denise McGeorge; James Smith; Lisa Smith; Michael David Smith, Board Members.
Represented (legal): PennStuart.
TV Stations:
Kentucky: WAGV-DT Harlan.
Virginia: WLFG-DT Grundy.
West Virginia: WLFB-DT Bluefield.

LOCAL TV HOLDINGS LLC
1717 Dixie Hwy
Ste 650
Fort Wright, KY 41011
Phone: 859-448-2707
E-mail: klatek@dowlohnes.com
Officers:
Robert L Lawrence, President & Chief Executive Officer
Pamela Taylor, Chief Operating Officer

Theodore Kuhlman, Chief Financial Officer
Benjamin Diesbach, Vice President
Jonathan Friesel, Vice President
Kevin G. Levy, Vice President
Ownership: Oak Hill Capital Partners III LTV A LLC, 39.57%; Oak Hill Capital Partners II LP, 28.27%; Oak Hill Capital Partners LTV C Inc., 15.05%; Local TV B-Corp A Inc., 9.71%; OHCPIIILTVA & OHCPIIILTVC ownership:; J. Taylor Crandall; John Fant; Steven B. Gruber; Kevin G. Levy; Dennis J. Nayden; Ray L. Pinson; Mark A. Wolfson, Mgrs., 14.29%. each; OHCPILP & LTVBCAI ownership:; J. Taylor Crandall; John Fant; Steven B. Gruber; Greg Kent; Kevin G. Levy; Dennis J. Nayden; Ray L. Pinson; Mark A. Wolfson, shareholders, 12.5%. each.
Represented (legal): Dow Lohnes PLLC.
TV Stations:
Alabama: WBRC-DT Birmingham; WHNT-DT Huntsville.
Arkansas: KFSM-DT Fort Smith.
Colorado: KDVR-DT Denver; KFCT-DT Fort Collins.
Illinois: WQAD-DT Moline.
Iowa: WHO-DT Des Moines.
Missouri: WDAF-DT Kansas City; KTVI-DT St. Louis.
North Carolina: WGHP-DT High Point.
Ohio: WJW-DT Cleveland.
Oklahoma: KAUT-DT Oklahoma City; KFOR-DT Oklahoma City.
Pennsylvania: WNEP-DT Scranton.
Tennessee: WREG-DT Memphis.
Utah: KSTU-DT Salt Lake City.
Virginia: WTKR-DT Norfolk; WTVR-DT Richmond.
Wisconsin: WITI-DT Milwaukee.
LPTV Stations:
Alabama: W29AO Anniston.
Arkansas: K67EO Bentonville; K62DQ Fayetteville.
Colorado: K54DK Boulder.
Missouri: K62DA Malden.
Oklahoma: K56FK Alva & Cherokee; K58EM Alva & Cherokee; K60ER Cherokee & Alva; K62EH Cherokee & Alva; K64EA Cherokee & Alva; K16DX Gage; K20BR Gage, etc.; K18BV May, etc.; K22BR May, etc.; K61CW Mooreland, etc.; K49DO Seiling; K51EB Seiling; K53CI Seiling; K55EZ Seiling; K57EA Seiling; K59EE Woodward; K63CF Woodward, etc.; K65CO Woodward, etc.; K67CW Woodward, etc.; K69DH Woodward, etc..
Pennsylvania: W07DC Allentown-Bethlehem; W14CO Clarks Summit, etc.; W26CV Mansfield; W61AG Pottsville, etc.; W40BS Renova; W36BE State College; W39BE State College; W26DE-D Stroudsburg; W10CP Towanda; W15CO-D Towanda; W20AD Williamsport.
Utah: K25HF Heber City; K56BB Juab County (rural); K15FQ-D Milford, etc.; K35OP Park City; K35CK Price; K43CC Santa Clara; KKRP-LP St. George; K22DE Tooele; K17HM Wendover.

JAMES L. LOCKWOOD JR.
Box 1800
Raleigh, NC 27602
Phone: 919-839-0300
Represented (legal): Brooks, Pierce, McLendon, Humphrey & Leonard LLP.
TV Stations:
Alabama: WHDF-DT Florence.
Other Holdings:
TV Stations: Lockwood Broadcasting Inc. & Mountian TV LLC, see listings..

LONDON BROADCASTING CO. INC.
2 Lincoln Centre
5420 LBJ Fwy, Ste 1000
Dallas, TX 75240

Phone: 972-663-8917

Officers:

Ned N. Fleming III, Chairman

Terry E. London, President & Chief Executive Officer

Phillip Hurley, Chief Operating Officer

Carl Kornmeyer, Chief Financial Officer

Barrett N. Bruce, Secretary

Benjamin D. Eakes, Treasurer

Ownership: SunTx LBC Holdings LP, 67.21%; SunTx Fulcrum Fund II--SBIC LP, 30.37%; STLBCHLP ownership:; SunTx Capital Partners II GP, LP, Gen. Partner; STFFII-SBICLP ownership:; SunTx Capital SBIC LP; STCPIIGPLP & STCSBICLP ownership:; Ned N. Fleming III, Pres. & Chief Exec. Officer.

Represented (legal): Wiley Rein LLP.

TV Stations:

Texas: KBMT-DT Beaumont; KYTX-DT Nacogdoches; KCEN-DT Temple.

LPTV Stations:

Oklahoma: KKTM-LP Altus.

Texas: KTMO-LP Amarillo; KMAY-LP Bryan; KTLD-LP Odessa; KTLE-LP Odessa.

LONG COMMUNICATIONS LLC

526 Main Ave. SE
Hickory, NC 28601

Phone: 828-322-5115

Fax: 828-322-8256

Officers:

Thomas E. Long, Member & Manager

Jeffrey B. Long, Member & Manager

Ownership: Thomas E. Long, 49%; Roberta S Long, 41%; Jeffrey B Long, 10%.

Represented (legal): Hardy, Carey, Chautin & Balkin LLP.

TV Stations:

North Carolina: WHKY-DT Hickory.

Radio Stations:

North Carolina: WHKY (AM) Hickory

LOUISIANA CHRISTIAN BROADCASTING INC.

701 Parkwood Dr.
West Monroe, LA 71201

Phone: 318-322-1399

Fax: 318-323-3783

Ownership: Lamb Broadcasting Inc.; LBI ownership:; Joel Dyke; Billy Haisty; Gerald Lewis; Mike Reed, Dirs.

Represented (legal): Hardy, Carey, Chautin & Balkin LLP.

TV Stations:

Louisiana: KMCT-DT West Monroe.

LPTV Stations:

Arkansas: KLMB-LP El Dorado.

Louisiana: WCBZ-LP Baton Rouge.

Mississippi: W24CR Natchez.

PAUL LUCCI

200 College Place
Suite 118
Norfolk, VA 23510

Phone: 757-624-9742

Represented (legal): Smithwick & Belendiuk PC.

TV Stations:

Kentucky: WDKA-DT Paducah.

MALIBU BROADCASTING LLC

Second Generation Pl
3029 Prospect Ave
Cleveland, OH 44115

Phone: 323-965-5400

Ownership: Thomas J Wilson.

Represented (legal): Wiley Rein LLP.

TV Stations:

Illinois: WAOE-DT Peoria.

LPTV Stations:

Illinois: WLFM-LP Chicago.

Iowa: WBQD-LP Davenport.

MARANATHA BROADCASTING CO.

E. Rock Rd.
Allentown, PA 18103

Phone: 610-797-4530

Officers:

Richard C. Dean, President

Barry Fisher, Vice President, TV

David Hinson, Vice President, Radio

Mike Kulp, Chief Financial Officer

Ownership: Richard C Dean, 54%; Jennifer Dean, 8%; Rick Allen Dean, 8%; Wendy Shubert, 8%; Rebecca Watrous, 8%; Barry Fisher, 5%; David G Hinson, 5%; Mike Kulp, 4%.

TV Stations:

Pennsylvania: WFMZ-DT Allentown.

LPTV Stations:

Pennsylvania: W46BL Allentown-Bethlehem.

Radio Stations:

Pennsylvania: WEST (AM)

LARRY D. MARCUS

248 Gay Ave.
Clayton, MO 63105

Phone: 314-727-6670

Fax: 314-727-6680

Represented (legal): Dow Lohnes PLLC.

TV Stations:

Pennsylvania: WWCP-DT Johnstown.

MARRI BROADCASTING CORP.

659 W. 183rd St.
c/o David P. Lampel
New York, NY 10033-3807

Phone: 212-568-8007

Officers:

Harry E. Figgie III, President, Secretary & Assistant Treasurer

David P. Lampel, Executive Vice President

Matthew P. Figgie, Vice President, Treasurer & Assistant Secretary

Ownership: Harry E Figgie III, 25%; David P Lampel; Mark P Figgie, 25%; Matthew P Figgie, 25%; Nancy F Figgie, 20%; Harry E Figgie Jr., 5%.

TV Stations:

Virgin Islands: WZVI-DT Charlotte Amalie.

MAX MEDIA X LLC

900 Laskin Rd.
Virginia Beach, VA 23451

Phone: 757-437-9800

Fax: 757-437-0034

Officer:

A. Eugene Loving Jr., President & Chief Executive Officer

Ownership: Max Media LLC, Member/Mgr., 90%; Max Management X LLC, Member, 10%; MMLLC ownership:; MBG-GG LLC, 42.0345%; MBG Quad-C Investors I Inc., 41.4133%; Aardvarks Also LLC, 6.1967%; Colonnade Max Investors Inc., 4.8671%; Quad-C Max Investors Inc., 4.6799%; MGLLC ownership:; Kenneth Diekroeger, 49.99%. equity, 50% voting; Jesse Rogers, 49.99%. equity, 50% voting; Alan Nichols, 0.0002%. equity; MQIII ownership:; Terrence D. Daniels, Mgr., 29.51%. equity, 50% voting; Gary A. Binning, 20%. equity, 16.67% voting; Stephen M. Burns, 20%. equity, 16.67 voting; Anthony R. Ignaczak, 20%. equity, 16.67 voting; AALLC ownership:; LaMaSa Airwaves LLC, 21.407%; Bay Shore Enterprises LLC, 19.648%; A. Eugene Loving Jr., Secy., 19.648%; Steamboat SPGS LLC, 19.648%; John A. Trinder, Pres., 16.701%; James C. Trinder, 2.947%; CMII ownership:; Commonwealth Investors II LP, 96.37%; Allen B. Rider III, Chmn., Pres. & Chief Exec. Officer, 1.04%; James C. Wheat III, V.P., 1.04%; QCMII ownership:; Terrence C. Daniels, Mgr., 40%. equity, 57.14 voting; Stephen M. Burns, 15%. equity, 10.71% voting; Edward T. Harvey, 15%. equity, 10.71% voting; Anthony R. Ignaczak, 15%. equity, 10.71% voting; Gary A. Binning, 12%. equity, 8.57% voting; MMXLLC ownership:; A Eugene Loving Jr, Chief Exec. Officer, Secy. & Mgr., 20%; Allen B Rider III, Mgr., 20%; Timothy B Robertson, 20%; John A Trinder, Chief Operating Officer, Pres. & Mgr., 20%; David J Wilhelm, V.P., Chief Financial Officer & Asst. Secy., 20%.

Represented (legal): Williams Mullen.

TV Stations:

Kentucky: WNKY-DT Bowling Green.

Maine: WPFO-DT Waterville.

Montana: KULR-DT Billings; KWYB-DT Butte; KFBB-DT Great Falls; KTMF-DT Missoula.

Puerto Rico: WMEI-DT Arecibo.

LPTV Stations:

Montana: KWYB-LP Bozeman; K24FL Columbus; KHBB-LD Helena; KTMF-LP Kalispell; K43DC Lewistown; K66BR Livingston, etc.; K06FE Miles City.

Puerto Rico: WQQZ-CA Ponce; WWKQ-LP Quebradillas.

MCG CAPITAL CORP.

1100 Wilson Blvd
Ste 3000
Arlington, VA 22209

Phone: 703-247-7500

Officers:

Kenneth J. O'Keefe, Chairman

Steven F. Tunney, President & Chief Executive Officer

Robert J. Merrick, Executive Vice President & Chief Investment Officer

Michael R. McDonnell, Executive Vice President, Chief Operating & Financial Officer & Treasurer

B. Hagen Seville, Executive Vice President, Business Development

Derek R. Thomas, Executive Vice President, Risk Management & Underwriting

Samuel G. Rubenstein, Exec. V.P., Gen. Counsel & Chief Legal Officer, Chief Compliance Officer & Corp. Secy.

Robert S. Grazioli, Senior Vice President & Chief Information Officer

John C. Wellons, Senior Vice President, Chief Accounting Officer & Assistant Treasurer

Ownership: Publicly held..

Represented (legal): Dow Lohnes PLLC.

TV Stations:

Hawaii: KGMD-DT Hilo; KGMB-DT Honolulu; KGMV-DT Wailuku.

LPTV Stations:

Hawaii: K69BZ Lihue, etc.; K57BI Waimea.

MCGRAW-HILL BROADCASTING CO. INC.

4600 Air Way
San Diego, CA 92102

Phone: 619-237-6212

Fax: 619-262-8842

Officers:

Darrell K. Brown, President

Bruce Stein, Vice President, Sales

Mark Limbach, Group Controller

Ownership: The McGraw-Hill Companies. The McGraw-Hill Companies also have interest in financial services; information and media services; educational & professional publishing.

Represented (legal): Holland & Knight LLP.

TV Stations:

California: KERO-DT Bakersfield; KGTV-DT San Diego.

Colorado: KMGH-DT Denver.

Indiana: WRTV-DT Indianapolis.

LPTV Stations:

California: KZKC-LP Bakersfield; KZSD-LP San Diego.

Colorado: KZCS-LP Colorado Springs; KZCO-LP Denver; KZFC-LP Windsor.

MEDIA GENERAL INC.

Box 85333
Richmond, VA 23293-0001

Phones: 804-649-6000; 804-649-6103

Officers:

J. Stewart Bryan III, Chairman

Marshall N. Morton, President & Chief Executive Officer

Reid Ashe, Executive Vice President & Chief Operating Officer

Neal F. Fondren, Vice President & President, Interactive Media Division

H. Graham Woodlief Jr., Vice President & President, Publishing Division

James A. Zimmerman, Vice President & President, Broadcast Div.

Lou Anne Nabhan, Vice President, Corporate Communications

George L. Mahoney, Vice President, Secretary & General Counsel

John A. Schauss, Vice President, Finance, Treasurer & Chief Financial Officer

Ownership: Publicly held.

TV Stations:

Alabama: WVTM-DT Birmingham; WKRG-DT Mobile.

Florida: WCWJ-DT Jacksonville; WFLA-DT Tampa.

Georgia: WJBF-DT Augusta; WRBL-DT Columbus; WSAV-DT Savannah.

Mississippi: WHLT-DT Hattiesburg; WJTV-DT Jackson.

North Carolina: WYCW-DT Asheville; WNCN-DT Goldsboro; WNCT-DT Greenville.

Ohio: WCMH-DT Columbus.

Rhode Island: WJAR-DT Providence.

South Carolina: WCBD-DT Charleston; WBTW-DT Florence; WSPA-DT Spartanburg.

Tennessee: WJHL-DT Johnson City.

Virginia: WSLS-DT Roanoke.

LPTV Stations:

North Carolina: W08BP Beaver Dam; W02AG Brevard; W11AN Bryson City, etc.; W02AT Burnsville; W08AO Canton, etc.; W08AT Cherokee, etc.; W09AG Franklin; W08BJ Marion, etc.; W02AH Mars Hill; W08AX Marshall; W10AD Montreat, etc.; W05BI Morehead City; W08BF Spruce Pine, etc.; W09AF Sylva, etc.; W09AD Waynesville; W09AR Weaverville.

South Carolina: W10AJ Greenville.

Newspapers:

Alabama: Dothan Eagle, The Enterprise Ledger, Opelika-Auburn News

Florida: Hernando Today (Brooksville), Jackson County Floridian, Highlands Today (Sebring), The Tampa Tribune

North Carolina: (Concord & Kannapolis) Independent Tribune, The (Eden) Daily News, Hickory Daily Record, The (Marion) McDowell News, The (Morganton) News Herald, The Reidsville Review, Statesville Record & Landmark, Winston-Sa

South Carolina: (Florence) Morning News

Virginia: Bristol Herald Courier, The (Charlottesville) Daily Progress, Culpeper Star-Exponent, Danville Register & Bee, The (Lynchburg) News & Advance, Manassas Journal Messenger, Potomac (Woodbridge) News, Richmond Tim

Radio Stations:
Georgia: WNEG (AM)

Other Holdings:
Data service: TBO.com, timesdispatch.com, JournalNow.com, FlorenceMyrtleBeach.com, Tri-Cities-News.com

Finance service: Media General Financial Services-Richmond

Magazine: Virginia Business Magazine

Printing company: SP Newsprint Co. (33%), Duslin, GA and Newberg, OR.

MEDIA NEWS GROUP INC.
1560 Broadway
Suite 2075
Denver, CO 80202
Phone: 303-563-6395
Officers:
Richard B. Scudder, Chairman
W. Dean Singleton, Vice Chairman, President & Chief Executive Officer
Anthony F. Tierno, Executive Vice President & Chief Operating Officer
Joseph J. Ladovic IV, Executive Vice President & Chief Financial Officer
Patricia Robinson, Secretary
James MacDougald, Treasurer
Ownership: Howell E Begle Jr., 50%; Jean L Scudder, 50%.
Represented (legal): Wilkinson Barker Knauer LLP.
TV Stations:
Alaska: KTVA-DT Anchorage.
Newspapers:
California: Alameda Times-Star; Azusa Herald Highlander; Chico Enterprise Record; Contra Costa Times; Covina Press-Courier Highlander; Diamond Bar Highlander; Times-Standard, Tri-City Weekly (Eureka); Ft. Bragg Advocate Ne
Connecticut: Connecticut Post (Bridgeport); The News-Times (Danbury); Darien News; Fairfield Citizen; Greenwich Citizen, Greenwich Town Crier; New Canaan News-Review; Norwalk Citizen-News; The Advocate (Stamford); Westport
Massachusetts: Public Spirit (Aver); Berkshire Advocate; Devens Commerce; Sentinel & Enterprise, Shirley Oracle (Fitchburg); Greenfield Town Crier; Groton Landmark; Harvard Hillside; The Sun, The Valley Dispatch (Lowell); Nor
Michigan: The Detroit News
Minnesota: St. Paul Pioneer Press
New Hampshire: The Broadcaster (Lowell, MA)
New Mexico: Alamogordo Daily News; Carlsbad Current-Argus; The Deming Highlight; The Daily Times, Four Corners Business Journal (Farmington); Las Cruces Sun-News; Ruidoso News; Silver City Sun News; White Sands Missile Ra
Pennsylvania: Public Opinion (Chambersburg); The Evening Sun (Hanover); Lebanon Daily News; York Daily Record, The York Dispatch
Texas: Alvarado Star; Breckenridge American; Burleson Star; Crowley Star; El Paso Times; South Tarrant Star (Everman/Kennedale); The Graham Leader, Lake Country Shopper,

The Senior Times (Graham); The Jack County Hera

Utah: The Park Record (Park City), The Salt Lake Tribune

Vermont: Bellows Falls Town Crier; Bennington Banner; Brattleboro Reformer, The Original Vermont Observer (Brattleboro); The Manchester Journal

West Virginia: Charleston Daily Mail

Radio Stations:
Alaska: KNIK-FM; KBYR (AM)
Colorado: Colorado Daily, Daily Camera (Boulder); Brush News Tribune; The Denver Post; The Fort Morgan Times; Journal-Advocate (Sterling).

MERCURY BROADCASTING CO. INC.
115 E. Travis
Suite 533
San Antonio, TX 78205
Phone: 210-222-0973
Ownership: Van H. Archer III, Pres.
TV Stations:
Kansas: KMTW-DT Hutchinson.

MEREDITH CORP.
1716 Locust St.
Des Moines, IA 50309-3023
Phone: 515-284-3000
Fax: 515-284-2514
Web site: www.meredith.com
Officers:
Stephen M. Lacy, President & Chief Executive Officer
Paul Karpowicz, President, Broadcasting Group
Douglas R. Lowe, Executive Vice President, Broadcasting Group
Joseph Ceryanec, Vice President & Chief Financial Officer
John S. Zieser, Chief Development Officer
Larry Oaks, Vice President, Technology
Joseph Snelson, Vice President, Engineering
Tom Cox, Vice President, Broadcasting Solutions
Kieran Clarke, Executive Vice President, Meredith Video Solutions
Tim Reynolds, Director, Interactive Media
Jeff Trott, Director, IT & Ad Operations
Dalton Lee, Vice President, Finance
Ownership: Katharine Meredith, 31.879% voting stock & 3.851% assets%; Edwin Meredith IV, 11.027% voting stock & 0.995% assets%; Dianne Mell Meredith Frazier, 10.462% voting stock & 0.948% assets%.
TV Stations:
Arizona: KPHO-DT Phoenix.
Connecticut: WFSB-DT Hartford.
Georgia: WGCL-DT Atlanta.
Michigan: WNEM-DT Bay City.
Missouri: KCTV-DT Kansas City; KSMO-DT Kansas City.
Nevada: KVVU-DT Henderson.
Oregon: KPTV-DT Portland.
South Carolina: WHNS-DT Greenville.
Tennessee: WSMV-DT Nashville.
Washington: KPDX-DT Vancouver.
LPTV Stations:
Arizona: K40AD Cottonwood, etc.; K50HU Flagstaff; K09KV Prescott.
Massachusetts: WSHM-LP Springfield.
Nevada: K28EU Laughlin, etc.; K53AE Pahrump.
North Carolina: W69CN Bryson City; W14AS West Asheville.
Oregon: K20DD Albany, etc.; KUBN-LP Bend; K23DB La Grande; K51FK Nehalem & Rockaway; K18EL Newburg & Tigard; K15DS Newport, etc.; K44AH Prineville, etc.; K50GG Salem; K21DE Seaside & Astoria; K51EH The Dalles; K69AH The Dalles; K35CR Tillamook, etc..
Washington: K34HK Longview; K14HN Vancouver & Camas.
Other Holdings:

Magazine: Successful Farming, Country America, Traditional Home, Country Home, Midwest Living; Ladies' Home Journal; Better Homes and Gardens

Publishing: 37 titles produced by Better Homes & Gardens Special Interest Publications. American Park Network publishes visitor guides for parks.

MID-STATE TELEVISION INC.
2900 Park Ave. W
Mansfield, OH 44906-1062
Phone: 419-529-5900
Fax: 419-529-3319
Officers:
Gunther Meisse, Chairman, President & Chief Executive Officer
Charles J. Hire, Vice President
Glenn Cheesman, Vice President, Sales
William Heichel, Secretary-Treasurer
Ownership: Gunther S. Meisse Revocable Trust, Gunther S. Meisse Trustee, 51%; Phyllis F. Hire Revocable Trust, 35%; Glenn Cheesman, 14%. Hire, Meisse & Cheesman have radio interests.
Represented (legal): Fletcher, Heald & Hildreth PLC.
TV Stations:
Ohio: WMFD-DT Mansfield.
LPTV Stations:
Ohio: WOHZ-CA Mansfield.

MIDWEST TELEVISION INC.
7677 Engineer Rd.
PO Box 85888
San Diego, CA 92186-5888
Phone: 858-495-9300
E-mail: etrimble@kfmb.com
Officers:
August C. Meyer Jr., Co-President
Jack B. Everette, Co-President, Chief Operating Officer & Treasurer
Ed Trimble, President, Western Division
Karen H. Meyer, Vice President & Secretary
Bill Lamb, Vice President
Robb Gray Jr., Vice President
Bob Bolinger, Vice President
Ownership: Elisabeth Meyer Kimmel, 51%; August C Meyer Jr., 49%.
Represented (legal): Covington & Burling.
TV Stations:
California: KFMB-DT San Diego.
Radio Stations:
California: KFMB-AM-FM San Diego

LARRY H. MILLER COMMUNICATIONS CORP.
5181 Amelia Earhart Dr.
Salt Lake City, UT 84116-2869
Phone: 801-537-1414
Fax: 801-238-6414
Officers:
Karen G. Miller, President
Denny Haslam, Chief Operating Officer
Robert Hyde, Chief Financial Officer
Larry H. Miller, Secretary-Treasurer
Ownership: Karen G Miller, 48%; Larry H Miller Irrevocable Trust, Karen G Miller, Trustee, 48%; Bryan J Miller, 1%; Gregory S Miller, 1%; Roger L Miller, 1%; Stephen F Miller, 1%.
Represented (legal): Leventhal, Senter & Lerman PLLC.
TV Stations:
Utah: KJZZ-DT Salt Lake City.
LPTV Stations:
Utah: K21DY Heber City; K18DL-D Logan; K44EL Ouray; K21EZ Price; K38GO Roosevelt; K24CY St. George; K15DI Vernal; K32EJ Woodland.

Wyoming: K50DR Evanston; K19CP Mountain View; K26DK Rock Springs.

MISSION BROADCASTING INC.
544 Red Rock Dr.
Wadsworth, OH 44281
Phone: 330-335-8808
Fax: 330-336-8454
Officers:
David S. Smith, President & Treasurer
Dennis Thatcher, Chief Operating Officer
Nancie J. Smith, Vice President & Secretary
Ownership: David S. Smith, 100% votes.
Represented (legal): Drinker Biddle.
TV Stations:
Arkansas: KTVE-DT El Dorado.
Illinois: WTVO-DT Rockford.
Indiana: WFXW-DT Terre Haute.
Missouri: KODE-DT Joplin; KOLR-DT Springfield.
Montana: KHMT-DT Hardin.
New York: WUTR-DT Utica.
Pennsylvania: WFXP-DT Erie; WYOU-DT Scranton.
Texas: KRBC-DT Abilene; KCIT-DT Amarillo; KAMC-DT Lubbock; KSAN-DT San Angelo; KJTL-DT Wichita Falls.
LPTV Stations:
New Mexico: K47DH Clovis; K30DZ San Jon.
Oklahoma: K47DK Grandfield; K53DS Lawton.
Pennsylvania: W19AR Clarks Summit; W54AV Mansfield; W66AI Pottsville, etc.; W60AH Stroudsburg; W26AT Williamsport; W55AG Williamsport.
Texas: KCPN-LP Amarillo; K35CG Bovina; KJBO-LP Wichita Falls.

THE CURATORS OF THE U. OF MISSOURI
Hwy. 63 S
Columbia, MO 65201
Phone: 573-882-8888
Fax: 573-884-8888
Represented (legal): Pillsbury Winthrop Shaw Pittman LLP.
TV Stations:
Missouri: KOMU-DT Columbia.
LPTV Stations:
Missouri: K07SD Rolla.

MMMRC LLC
3148 Mid Valley Dr
De Pere, WI 54115
Phone: 920-532-9483
Ownership: Paul B Belschner, managing member, 33.3%; Scott R Smet, member, 33.3%; Chad L Smet, member, 33.3%.
Represented (legal): Dan J. Alpert.
TV Stations:
Michigan: WZMQ-DT Marquette.

MNE BROADCASTING LLC
PO Box 370
Danville, VA 24540
Phone: 434-791-2424
Ownership: Melvin N. Eleazer.
Represented (legal): Borsari & Paxson.
TV Stations:
Virginia: WDRL-DT Danville.

MOBILE VIDEO TAPES INC.
PO Box 2906
Baton Rouge, LA 70821-2906
Phone: 225-387-2222
Officers:
Richard F. Manship, Chairman, President & Chief Executive Officer
David C. Manship, Vice Chairman & Vice President
Ray Alexander, Secretary-Treasurer
Douglas L. Manship Jr., Assistant Secretary

Ownership: Richard F. Manship, 19.34%; David C. Manship, 19.34%; Douglas L. Manship Jr., 19.34%; Dina Manship Planche, 19.34%; Grandchildren's Trust, Dina Manship Planche, Trustee, 22.63%. Manships are also principals of Louisiana Television Broadcasting LLC, see listing.
TV Stations:
Texas: KRGV-DT Weslaco.

MOKUPUNI TELEVISION CO. INC.
111-A Helikili St.
Suite 136
Kailua, HI 96734
Phone: 808-543-0925
Officers:
Susan Sims, President
Yoland Laula, Vice President
Margaret Logotaeao, Secretary-Treasurer
Ownership: Susan Sims, 33.3%; Yoland Laula, 33.3%; Margaret Logotaeao, 33.3%.
TV Stations:
Hawaii: KKAI-DT Kailua.

MORGAN MURPHY MEDIA
Box 44965
Madison, WI 53744-4965
Phone: 608-271-4321
Fax: 608-278-5553
E-mail: talkback@wisctv.com
Officers:
Elizabeth Murphy Burns, President & Chief Executive Officer
John B. Murphy, Secretary-Treasurer
George A. Nelson, Chief Financial Officer
Ownership: Evening Telegram Co.. Evening Telegram Co. also owns Spokane Television Inc., see listing.
Represented (legal): Rini Coran PC.
TV Stations:
Washington: KVEW-DT Kennewick; KXLY-DT Spokane; KAPP-DT Yakima.
Wisconsin: WKBT-DT La Crosse; WISC-DT Madison.
LPTV Stations:
Washington: K40EE Pullman; K14HT Walla Walla, etc..
Newspapers:
Minnesota: Evening Telegram Company or its shareholders own 50% of Murphy McGinnis Media Inc., which publishes daily, weekly, shopper and other publications in Kansas, Michigan, Minnesota and Wisconsin, including daily newspapers in Superior, Wisconsin; Ashland, Wis
Radio Stations:
Idaho: KVNI (AM) Coeur d'Alene, KHTQ (FM) Hayden
Iowa: KIYXA (FM) Sageville
Washington: KXLX (AM) Airway Heights; KEZE (FM), KXLY-AM-FM, KZZU-FM Spokane
Wisconsin: WGLR-AM-FM Lancaster, WPVL-AM-FM Platteville
Other Holdings:
Magazine: Madison Magazine.

MORRIS MULTIMEDIA INC.
27 Abercorn St.
Savannah, GA 31401-2715
Phones: 912-233-1281; 912-745-4141
Officers:
Charles H. Morris, Chairman
H. Dean Hinson, President
Jeffrey R. Samuels, Vice President & Chief Financial Officer
Kathy Kurazawa, Secretary
J. Wiley Ellis, Assistant Secretary
Ownership: Charles H. Morris.
Represented (legal): Fletcher, Heald & Hildreth PLC.
TV Stations:
Georgia: WMGT-DT Macon.

Kentucky: WTVQ-DT Lexington.
Mississippi: WCBI-DT Columbus; WXXV-DT Gulfport.
North Carolina: WWAY-DT Wilmington.
Tennessee: WDEF-DT Chattanooga.
Newspapers:
California: Manteca Bulletin, Newhall Signal, Sun Litho (Van Nuys), Morning Press (Vista) Newspapers published by Morris Newspaper Corp.
Florida: De Land Sun News; Florida Times Union, Jacksonville Journal (Jacksonville)
Georgia: The Webworks (Atlanta), Coastal Courier (Hinesville), Savannah Penny-Savers, Statesboro Herald
Kansas: Great Bend Tribune
South Carolina: Camden Chronicle, Florence News & Shopper
Tennessee: Franklin Review-Appeal, Southern Standard (McMinnville), Murfreesboro Daily News-Journal

MOUNTAIN BROADCASTING CORP.
500 Weldon Rd.
Box 985
Lake Hopatcong, NJ 07849-0156
Phone: 201-697-0063
Fax: 973-697-0063
Officers:
Sun Young Joo, President & Chief Executive Officer
Joon S. Joo, Vice President
Sun Hoo Joo, Vice President
Ownership: Sun Young Joo, 92.3%; Sun Hoo Joo, 7.7%.
Represented (legal): Fleischman & Harding LLP.
TV Stations:
New Jersey: WMBC-DT Newton.

MOUNTAIN LICENSES LP
2111 University Park Dr.
Suite 650
Okemos, MI 48864
Phone: 517-347-4111
Officer:
Brian W. Brady, President, General Partner
Ownership: Northwest Broadcast Inc., Gen. Partner, 1% equity, 100% votes; Mountain Broadcasting LLC, Ltd. Partner, 99%. equity; NBI ownership:; Brian W. Brady, MBLLC ownership:; Northwest Broadcasting Inc.. 100% votes; 1% equity; Northwest Broadcasting LP, 99%. equity; NBLP ownership:; Northwest Broadcasting Inc.. Gen. Partner. 100% votes; 0.07% equity; Brian W. Brady, Ltd. Partner, 99.3%. equity; NBI ownership:; Brian W. Brady. Brady is also a principal of Broadcasting Licenses LP & Stainless Broadcasting LP, see listings.
Represented (legal): Leventhal, Senter & Lerman PLLC.
TV Stations:
Oregon: KFFX-DT Pendleton.
Washington: KAYU-DT Spokane.
LPTV Stations:
Idaho: K50DM Coeur d'Alene; K19BY Grangeville; K47BW Lewiston, etc.; K52GH Sandpoint.
Washington: K44CK Chelan; K09UP Colville; K35BJ Ellisford; K19AU Omak & Okanogan; K31AH Omak, etc.; K10NQ Prosser, etc.; KBWU-LD Richland, etc.; K38IT Stemilt, etc.; KCYU-LD Yakima.

MOUNTAIN TV LLC
220 Salters Creek Rd
Hampton, VA 23661
Phone: 757-722-9736
Officer:
David A. Hanna, President
Ownership: James L. Lockwood Jr., see listing, 80%; James A. Stern, 20%.

Represented (legal): Brooks, Pierce, McLendon, Humphrey & Leonard LLP.
TV Stations:
Ohio: WQCW-DT Portsmouth.
LPTV Stations:
West Virginia: WOCW-LP Charleston; WVCW-LP Huntington.

MOUNT MANSFIELD TELEVISION INC.
P.O.Box 5408
Burlington, VT 05406-4508
Phone: 802-652-6300
Fax: 802-652-6319
E-mail: Teffner@wcax.com
Web site: www.wcax.com
Officers:
Peter Martin, President
Theodore Teffner, Vice President, Engineering
Marselis Parsons, Vice President, News
Ownership: Stuart T Martin, 49.5%; Peter R Martin, 12.46%; James S Martin, 12.46%; Marcia H Martin Boyer, 12.46%; Donald P Martin, 12.46%.
Represented (legal): Sheehey, Furlong & Behm PC.
TV Stations:
Vermont: WCAX-DT Burlington.
LPTV Stations:
Vermont: W69AR Rutland.

MULTICULTURAL TELEVISION BROADCASTING LLC
449 Broadway
New York, NY 10013
Phone: 212-431-4300
E-mail: arthurl@mrbi.net
Officers:
Arthur Liu, President & Manager
Yvonne Liu, Vice President
Young (Sean) C. Kim, Secretary-Treasurer
Ownership: Multicultural Capital Trust; MCT ownership:; Lee W Schubert LC, Trustee. As a consequence of defaulting on certain credit facilities, Multicultural Television Broadcasting has transfered ownership to Multicultural Capital Trust.
Represented (legal): Leventhal, Senter & Lerman PLLC.
TV Stations:
California: KCNS-DT San Francisco.
Connecticut: WSAH-DT Bridgeport.
Massachusetts: WMFP-DT Lawrence.
North Carolina: WRAY-DT Wilson.
Ohio: WRLM Canton.

NBC UNIVERSAL
30 Rockefeller Plaza
Room 1491E
New York, NY 10012
Phone: 212-664-4444
E-mail: nbcunisupport@nbcuni.com
Web site: www.nbcuni.com/
Officers:
Bob Wright, Chairman
Jeff Zucker, President & Chief Executive Officer
Lisa Gersh, President, Strategic Initiatives
Lynn Calpeter, Executive Vice President & Chief Financial Officer
Rick Cotton, Executive Vice President & General Counsel
Allison Gollust, Executive Vice President, Corporate Communications
Cory Shields, Executive Vice President, Global Policy Strategies & Alliances

Branch Offices:
3000 Alameda Ave
Burbank, CA 91523-0002
Phone: 818-840-4444

4001 Nebraska Ave NW
Washington, DC 20016
Phone: 202-885-4015
Ownership: General Electric Co., 80%; Vivendi Universal, 20%.
TV Stations:
Arizona: KTAZ-DT Phoenix; KHRR-DT Tucson.
California: KVEA-DT Corona; KNBC-DT Los Angeles; KWHY-DT Los Angeles; KNSO-DT Merced; KNTV-DT San Jose; KSTS-DT San Jose.
Colorado: KDEN-DT Longmont.
Connecticut: WVIT-DT New Britain.
District of Columbia: WRC-DT Washington.
Florida: WSCV-DT Fort Lauderdale; WTVJ-DT Miami.
Illinois: WMAQ-DT Chicago; WSNS-DT Chicago.
Nevada: KBLR-DT Paradise.
New Hampshire: WNEU-DT Merrimack.
New Jersey: WNJU-DT Linden.
New York: WNBC-DT New York.
Pennsylvania: WCAU-DT Philadelphia.
Puerto Rico: WKAQ-DT San Juan.
Texas: KXTX-DT Dallas; KTMD-DT Galveston; KVDA-DT San Antonio.
LPTV Stations:
Arizona: K28EY Douglas.
California: K15CU Salinas; K47GD San Luis Obispo; K46GF Santa Maria.
Colorado: KMAS-LP Denver.
Florida: W58BU Hallandale.
Nevada: K52FF Reno.
Puerto Rico: W68BU Adjuntas; W09AT Fajardo; W32AJ Utuado.
Utah: KEJT-LP Salt Lake City.
Other Holdings:
Broadcast holdings: Station Venture Operations LP, see listing, 79.62%
Cable Network: CNBC Europe; CNBC (Consumer News & Business Channel); Bravo; 50% of MSNBC; 25% of American Movie Classics; CNBC Asia; The Weather Channel; NBC Europe; 50% of National Geographic Channel Worldwide; 25% of both A & E and the History Channel
Data service: 9.9% of Telescan Internet search firm; Partner in Contentville.com; AllBusiness.com
Program source: 36% of ValueVision; NBC Studios; NBC Entertainment
Satellite programming: Rainbow Program Enterprises.

NEPSK INC.
PO Box 1149
12 Brewer Rd.
Presque Isle, ME 04769
Phone: 207-764-4461
Fax: 207-764-5329
Officers:
Gordon Wark, President
Peter P. Kozloski, Chief Executive Officer
Catherine Donovan, Vice President & Chief Financial Officer
Carole M. Kozloski, Vice President

Branch Office:
72 Main
PO Box 610
Houlton, ME 04730
Phone: 207-532-2579
Fax: 207-532-4025
Ownership: Peter P Kozloski.
Cable Systems:
MAINE: DANFORTH; HOULTON; HOWLAND; ISLAND FALLS; MEDWAY; MONTICELLO (town); OAKFIELD; PATTEN.
TV Stations:
Maine: WAGM-DT Presque Isle.
LPTV Stations:
Maine: W11AA Madawaska.

NEW AGE MEDIA
46 Public Sq
Ste 500
WIlkes-Barre, PA 18701
Phone: 570-824-7895

Ownership: Sedgwick Media LLC, 65%; Dallas Media LLC, 33.64%; Michael Yanuzzi, 1.36%; SMLLC ownership:; John Parente, 51%. votes, 18.94% assets; Charles E. & Mary M. Parente, 49%. votes, 4.06% assets; Sedgwick Co. LLC, 30.08% assets; Marlco Investment Corp., 15.4% assets; C.E. Parente Trust, U/A 9/17/1997, John J. Parente, Trustee, 7.07%. assets; Brynfan Associates, 3.85%. assets; Brian J Parente, 3.85%. assets; Charles L Parente, 3.85%. assets; Marla P Sgarlat, 3.85%. assets; DMLLC ownership:; Frank M. Henry, 85%; Frank M. Henry Jr., 5%; Scott Henry, 5%; Marjorie Henry Marquart, 5%; BA, MIC & SCLLC ownership:; Parente Family.

Represented (legal): Fletcher, Heald & Hildreth PLC.

TV Stations:
Florida: WGFL-DT High Springs.
Georgia: WTLH-DT Bainbridge.
Maine: WPXT-DT Portland.
Pennsylvania: WOLF-DT Hazleton; WQMY-DT Williamsport.
Tennessee: WDSI-DT Chattanooga.

LPTV Stations:
Florida: WYPN-CA Gainesville; WMYG-LP Lake City.
Georgia: WBFL-CA Valdosta; WBVJ-LP Valdosta.
Pennsylvania: W24DB Sayre.
Tennessee: WPDP-LP Cleveland.

NEW LIFE EVANGELISTIC CENTER INC.
PO Box 924
St. Louis, MO 63188
Phones: 314-436-2424; 314-351-7390
E-mail: knlc24jim@hereshelpnet.org
Web site: www.knlc.tv
Officers:
Lawrence W. Rice Jr., President
Raymond K. Redlich, Vice President
Charles W. Hale, Secretary-Treasurer
Ownership: Non-profit corp.--St. Louis, MO. Governed by 12 member Board of Directors.
TV Stations:
Missouri: KNLC-DT St. Louis.
LPTV Stations:
Arkansas: K54FH Green Forest.
Missouri: K61GJ Aurora; KNJD-LP Branson; K64FW Joplin; K64FQ Lebanon; K17FU Marshfield; K68EL Marshfield; K39CI Springfield; K54FX Springfield.
Radio Stations:
Arkansas: KTCN (FM) Eureka Springs, KBPB (FM) Harrison
Illinois: WINU (AM) Shelbyville
Kansas: KKLO (AM) Leavenworth
Missouri: KNLH (FM) Cedar Hill; KNLQ (FM) Cuba; KAUL (FM) Ellington; KNRF (FM), KNLM (FM) Marshfield; KNLF (FM) Potosi; KBIY (FM) Van Buren; KNLN (FM) Vienna; KKLL (FM) Webb City

NEWPORT TELEVISION LLC
50 Kennedy Plz, 18th Fl
Providence, RI 02903
Phone: 401-751-1700
Officer:
Sandy DiPasquale, President & Chief Executive Officer
Ownership: Newport Television Holdings LLC; NTHLLC ownership:; Providence Equity Partners VI (Umbrella US) LP, 55.2%; TV InvestmentCo LP, 44.8%; PEPVI (UUS)LP ownership:; Providence Equity GP VI LP, Gen. Partner. 100% votes, 0.2% equity; TVICLP ownership:; Providence VI Umbrella GP LLC, Gen. Partner. 100 % votes, 90% equity; PEGPVILP & PVIUGPLLC ownership:; Glenn M. Creamer, Managing Member, 33.3%; Jonathan M. Nelson, Managing Member, 33.3%; Paul J. Salem, Managing Member, 33.3%.
Represented (legal): Covington & Burling.

TV Stations:
Alabama: WPMI-DT Mobile.
Alaska: KTVF-DT Fairbanks.
Arkansas: KASN-DT Little Rock; KLRT-DT Little Rock.
California: KFTY-DT Santa Rosa.
Florida: WAWS-DT Jacksonville; WJTC-DT Pensacola.
Kansas: KOCW-DT Hoisington; KAAS-DT Salina; KSAS-DT Wichita.
New York: WXXA-DT Albany; WIVT-DT Binghamton; WETM-DT Elmira; WHAM-DT Rochester; WSYR-DT Syracuse; WWTI-DT Watertown.
Ohio: WKRC-DT Cincinnati.
Oklahoma: KMYT-DT Tulsa; KOKI-DT Tulsa.
Oregon: KMCB-DT Coos Bay; KMTR-DT Eugene; KTCW-DT Roseburg.
Pennsylvania: WHP-DT Harrisburg.
Tennessee: WJKT-DT Jackson; WLMT-DT Memphis; WPTY-DT Memphis.
Utah: KTVX-DT Salt Lake City.
Washington: KVOS-DT Bellingham.

LPTV Stations:
Alaska: K07NJ Delta Junction, etc.; K06LA Healy, etc..
California: KKEY-LP Bakersfield.
Kansas: KSAS-LP Dodge City; KAAS-LP Garden City.
New York: WBGH-CA Binghamton; W07BA Syracuse-DeWitt.
Oregon: K46AS Coos Bay; KMOR-LP Eugene; K03CQ Mapleton; K05DF Mapleton; K31AE Sutherlin; K22GX Tri City.
Utah: K34CX Apple Valley; K51BK-D Aurora, etc.; K18FU-D Beaver County (rural); K05BU Enterprise; K09SU Hildale, UT & Cane Beds, AZ; K11OO Pine Valley; K45FW Price, etc.; K25JS-D St. George; K69CT St. George; K31IS-D Toquerville; K13QK Virgin; K52KG-D Washington.

NEWS PRESS & GAZETTE CO.
825 Edmond St
St. Joseph, MO 64501
Phone: 816-271-8500
Fax: 816-271-8695
Web site: www.npgcable.net
Officers:
Henry H. Bradley, Chairman, Vice President & Treasurer
David R. Bradley Jr., President, Editor & Publisher
Lyle E. Leimkuhler, Vice President, Finance & Secretary
Ownership: NPG Voting Trust; NPGVT ownership:; David R. Bradley Jr., & Henry H. Bradley, Trustees, 50% each.
Represented (legal): Smithwick & Belendiuk PC.
Cable Systems:
ARIZONA: BULLHEAD CITY; FLAGSTAFF; KINGMAN; LAKE HAVASU CITY; PARKER; PAYSON; PINE; SEDONA.
CALIFORNIA: BLYTHE; JUNE LAKE; MAMMOTH LAKES.
MISSOURI: ST. JOSEPH.
TV Stations:
California: KECY-DT El Centro; KESQ-DT Palm Springs.
Colorado: KRDO-DT Colorado Springs; KJCT-DT Grand Junction.
Idaho: KIFI-DT Idaho Falls.
Oregon: KTVZ-DT Bend.
Texas: KVIA-DT El Paso.
LPTV Stations:
California: KDFX-CA Indio/Palm Springs; K27DS Yucca Valley.
Colorado: K12ME Canon City; K38FO Carbondale; KTLO-LP Colorado Springs; K42CX Cripple Creek; K42EV Glenwood Springs; KKHD-LP Grand Junction; K39CD Lake George; K28AD Montrose; KXHD-LP Montrose; K51FQ Mount Massive, etc.; K36AF

New Castle; K45AF Parachute; KTLP-LP Pueblo; K57CR Rifle; K44CI Salida, etc..
Idaho: K61AP Burley, etc.; K05CJ Challis; K13CO Fish Creek; K13RV Leadore; K61CI Leadore; K21JC-D Pocatello; K61FO Pocatello; K12MA Rexburg, etc..
New Mexico: K40BP Alamogordo; K55BT Deming; K41KY-D Las Cruces; K57BV Las Cruces & Organ.
Oregon: K27DO Bend; K45KM-D Bend; KFXO-LP Bend; K41HZ Burns; K43IH Burns; K06LI Chemult; K02JL La Pine; K05JV La Pine; K13JF La Pine; K66BC Madras & Culver; K32CC Montgomery Ranch, etc.; K38DT North La Pine; K66AZ Prineville; KQRE-LP Riley; K06JN Severance Ranch, etc.; K57CH Sun River.
Wyoming: K13LY Hoback Junction; K13FZ Jackson; K29HG-D Jackson; K36JD-D Jackson; K09LF South Park.
Newspapers:
Kansas: Atchison Daily Globe; Hiawatha World; Johnson County Sun; Louisburg Herald; Miami County Republic; Northeast Johnson County Sun; Osawatomie Graphic; Blue Valley Sun, Kansas City Jewish Chronicle, Kansas City Nu
Magazine: Wednesday Magazine (Overland Park, KS)
Missouri: Sun Tribune (Gladstone); Kearney Courier; Liberty Tribune; Platte County Sun Gazette; Raytown Tribune; Smithville Herald; Greenacres Publication, St. Joseph News-Press (St. Joseph); Daily Star Journal (Warrensb)
Radio Stations:
Colorado: KRDO-AM-FM Colorado Springs, KESQ (AM) Indio, KUNA-FM LaQuinta

NEW VISION TELEVISION LLC, DEBTOR IN POSSESSION
3500 Lenox Rd.
Suite 640
Atlanta, GA 30326
Phone: 404-995-4711
Officers:
Jason Elkin, Chairman & Chief Executive Officer
John Heinen, President & Chief Operating Officer
Eric Simontis, Chief Financial Officer
Steve Spendlove, Executive Vice President
Ownership: Jason Elkin, 2.25% votes & assets; John Heinen, 0.9% votes & assets; HBK NV LLC, 95.48% votes & assets; HBKNVLLC ownership:; HBK Management LLC; KBKMLLC ownership:; Jamiel A. Akhtar; Richard L. Booth; David C. Haley; Laurence H. Lebowitz; William E. Rose, 20% votes each.
Represented (legal): Wiley Rein LLP.
TV Stations:
Alabama: WIAT-DT Birmingham.
Georgia: WJCL-DT Savannah.
Hawaii: KHAW-DT Hilo; KHON-DT Honolulu; KAII-DT Wailuku.
Iowa: KIMT-DT Mason City.
Kansas: KSNG-DT Garden City; KSNC-DT Great Bend; KSNT-DT Topeka; KSNW-DT Wichita.
Nebraska: KSNK-DT McCook.
Ohio: WKBN-DT Youngstown.
Oregon: KOIN-DT Portland.
LPTV Stations:
Alabama: W04CB Sylacauga.
Hawaii: K55DZ Lihue.
Kansas: KETM-CA Emporia; KTLJ-CA Junction City; KMJT-CA Ogden; KSNL-LD Salina; KSNL-LP Salina; KTMJ-CA Topeka.
Ohio: WYFX-LP Youngstown.
Oregon: K34DC Astoria; KBNZ-LD Bend; K04BJ La Pine; K38CZ Lincoln City & Newport; K34AI North La Pine; K31CR-D Prineville, etc.; K52AK Prineville, etc.; K64BK The Dalles; K52ET Tillamook.

Pennsylvania: WFXI-CA Mercer.
Washington: K63AW Grays River, etc..

NEXSTAR BROADCASTING GROUP INC.
909 Lake Carolyn Pkwy.
Ste 1450
Irving, TX 75039
Phone: 972-373-8800
Officers:
Perry Sook, President & Chief Executive Officer
Duane Lammers, Executive Vice President & Chief Operating Officer
Thomas Carter, Chief Financial Officer
Timothy Busch, Senior Vice President
Brian Jones, Senior Vice President
Richard Stolpe, Vice President & Engineering Director
Susana G. Willingham, Vice President & Corporate News Director
Ownership: ABRY Broadcast Partners III LP. 55.33% votes, 16.22% assets; ABRY Broadcast Partners II LP. 37.79% votes, 11.08% assets; Perry Sook. 2.38% votes, 0.7% assets; publicly held. 4.5% votes, 12.35% assets; ABRY ownership:; Royce Yudkoff.
Represented (legal): Drinker Biddle.
TV Stations:
Alabama: WDHN-DT Dothan.
Arkansas: KFTA-DT Fort Smith; KARK-DT Little Rock; KARZ-DT Little Rock; KNWA-DT Rogers.
Illinois: WCIA-DT Champaign; WMBD-DT Peoria; WQRF-DT Rockford; WCFN-DT Springfield.
Indiana: WFFT-DT Fort Wayne; WTWO-DT Terre Haute.
Louisiana: KARD-DT West Monroe.
Maryland: WHAG-DT Hagerstown.
Missouri: KSNF-DT Joplin; KSFX-DT Springfield; KQTV-DT St. Joseph.
Montana: KSVI-DT Billings.
New York: WROC-DT Rochester; WFXV-DT Utica.
Pennsylvania: WTAJ-DT Altoona; WJET-DT Erie; WLYH-DT Lancaster; WBRE-DT Wilkes-Barre.
Texas: KTAB-DT Abilene; KAMR-DT Amarillo; KLBK-DT Lubbock; KMID-DT Midland; KBTV-DT Port Arthur; KLST-DT San Angelo; KTAL-DT Texarkana; KFDX-DT Wichita Falls.
LPTV Stations:
Montana: K25BP Billings; K27IM Billings; K58IH Colstrip, etc.; K66EQ Colstrip, etc.; K33EA Columbus; K16DZ Hardin; K16DH Miles City; K19FF Miles City.
New Mexico: K45BF Clovis; K28BA San Jon.
New York: W31BP Burlington; W53AM Utica; WPNY-LP Utica, etc.
Pennsylvania: W51BP Clarks Summit, etc.; W24BL Pottsville, etc.; W64AL Stroudsburg; W30AN Williamsport.
Texas: K12FM Fort Stockton; K44FG Snyder; K25CP Tulia.
Wyoming: K06AT Sheridan, etc..
Radio Stations:
Pennsylvania: WJET (FM)
Texas: KTAL-FM; KCMC (AM)

NORTH PACIFIC INTERNATIONAL TV INC.
2002 W. Lone Cactus Dr.
Phoenix, AZ 85027
Phone: 623-582-6550
Fax: 623-582-8229
Officers:
Kenneth Casey, President & Treasurer
Charlene F. Weh, Secretary
Ownership: Kenneth Casey, 50.1%; Allen E Hom, 40%; Charlene F Weh, 9.9%.

TV Stations:
Washington: KHCV-DT Seattle.

NORWELL TELEVISION LLC

c/o ValueVision Media Acquisitions Inc., 6740 Shady Oak Rd.
Eden Prairie, MN 55344
Phone: 952-943-6117
Officers:
Frank Elsenbast, Chairman & President
Nathan E. Farge, Secretary
Nicholas J. Vassallo, Treasurer
Ownership: ValueVision Media Inc..
Represented (legal): Wilmer Cutler Pickering Hale & Dorr LLP.
TV Stations:
Massachusetts: WWDP-DT Norwell.

OCEANIA CHRISTIAN CHURCH

PO Box 15667
Honolulu, HI 96830
Phone: 808-440-1350
Officers:
James W. Gustafson, President
Heather M. Vaikona, Vice President
Diane Sandlin, Secretary-Treasurer
Ownership: Dr. & Rev. James W. Gustafson; Diane Sandlin; Heather M Vaikona, 33.3%. votes each.
Represented (legal): Fletcher, Heald & Hildreth PLC.
TV Stations:
Hawaii: KLEI-DT Kailua Kona; KUPU-DT Waimanalo.

ORAL ROBERTS U.

7777 S. Lewis Ave.
Tulsa, OK 74171
Phone: 918-495-6161
Officer:
Walter H. Richardson, President, University Broadcasting Inc.
Ownership: Don Argue; Mary E. Banks; Frederick A. Boswell Jr.; Stanley M. Burgess; Scott A. Cordray; Harold D. Donaldson; Rick Fenimore; Mart Green; Michael A. Hammer; Robert D. Hoskins; Scott Howard; Lynette Lewis; Ron Luce; Charles W. McKinney; Glenda Payas; Oral Roberts; Russell P. Spittler; William Wilson, trustees, 5.56%. votes each.
Represented (legal): Hardy, Carey, Chautin & Balkin LLP.
TV Stations:
Oklahoma: KGEB-DT Tulsa.

LAUREN WRAY OSTENDORFF

180 Prominade Ave.
Shreveport, LA 71115
Phone: 318-861-5887
Represented (legal): Garvey Schubert Barer.
TV Stations:
Louisiana: KPXJ-DT Minden.

OTTUMWA MEDIA HOLDINGS LLC

6100 Fairview Rd.
Suite 600
Charlotte, NC 28210
Phone: 704-643-4148
Ownership: Thomas B. Henson, 90%; Macon B. Moye, managing member, 10%.
Represented (legal): Thomas B. Henson.
TV Stations:
Iowa: KYOU-DT Ottumwa.
LPTV Stations:
Missouri: K34CW Kirksville.

RAUL & CONSUELO PALAZUELOS

1138 W. Church St.
Santa Maria, CA 93458

Phone: 805-928-7700
Fax: 805-928-8606
Officer:
Raul Palazuelos, President
Represented (legal): Fletcher, Heald & Hildreth PLC.
TV Stations:
California: KVIQ-DT Eureka; KTAS-DT Santa Maria.
LPTV Stations:
California: K10HX Garberville; K11NE Hoopa; K08LD Miranda; K09UF Morro Bay; K08HJ Orleans; K10FS Rio Dell & Scotia; K07TA Santa Maria; K10KY Shelter Cove; K10EN Willow Creek.

PAPPAS TELECASTING COMPANIES

500 S. Chinowth Rd.
Visalia, CA 93277
Phone: 559-733-7800
Fax: 559-627-5363
Web site: www.pappastv.com
Officers:
Harry J. Pappas, Chairman & Chief Executive Officer
Dennis J. Davis, President, Chief Operating Officer
LeBon G. Abercrombie, Senior Executive Vice President, Planning & Development
Howard H. Shrier, Senior Executive Vice President & Chief Operating Officer, TV Stations
Peter C. Pappas, Executive Vice President, Legal & Governmental Affairs
Rich Elmendorf, Executive Vice President & Chief Financial Officer
Debbie Sweeney, Senior Vice President, Programming
Dale P. Kelly, Senior Vice President & Engineering Director, Emeritus
Dale E. Alfieris, Vice President & General Counsel
Dale Scherbring, Vice President & Engineering Director
Rosemary Danon, Vice President, Online & New Media
Gary E. Cripe, General Counsel
Rueben Cuadros, Controller
Ownership: Harry J. Pappas. On May 10, 2008, certain affiliates of Pappas Telecasting filed for Chapter 11 bankruptcy protection. Mohshin Meghji was appointed Chief Restructuring Officer for those affiliates.
Represented (legal): Fletcher, Heald & Hildreth PLC.
TV Stations:
Alabama: WLGA-DT Opelika.
Arizona: KSWT-DT Yuma.
California: KAZA-DT Avalon.
Iowa: KCWI-DT Ames; KDMI-DT Des Moines.
Nebraska: KWNB-DT Hayes Center; KHGI-DT Kearney.
Wisconsin: WWAZ-DT Fond du Lac.
LPTV Stations:
California: KBBV-CA Bakersfield; KVVB-CA Bakersfield; KBVQ-LP Eureka; KFRE-CA Tulare.
Iowa: WBVK-LP Spencer; KCWL-LP Storm Lake.
Nebraska: KBVZ-LP McCook; KWNB-LD McCook; WCWH-LP McCook; KHGI-CA North Platte; KAZK-LP O'Neill; KOAZ-LP O'Neill; KHJP-LP Valentine; WCWY-LD Valentine.
New Mexico: KIAZ-LP Gallup; KCWF-CA Las Cruces.
Texas: KXLK-CA Austin; KXCC-CA Corpus Christi; KHMV-CA Houston; KVVV-LP Houston.
Radio Stations:
California: KMPH (AM) Modesto, KTRB (AM) San Francisco

PARKER BROADCASTING INC.

5341 Tate Ave.
Plano, TX 75093
Phone: 972-403-7132
Ownership: Barry J. C. Parker, President & Secretary.
TV Stations:
Colorado: KFQX-DT Grand Junction.
Louisiana: KAQY-DT Columbia.
North Dakota: KXJB-DT Valley City.

PAXTON MEDIA GROUP INC.

201 S. 4th St.
Box 1680
Paducah, KY 42002-1680
Phone: 207-575-8630
Fax: 270-442-8188
Officers:
David Michael Paxton, President & Chief Executive Officer
Richard Edwin Paxton, Vice President, Chief Financial Officer, Treasurer & Assistant Secretary
James Fredrick Paxton Jr., Vice President & Secretary
Jay Frizzo, Vice President
David R. Mathes, Vice President & Assistant Treasurer
Frank R. Paxton, Assistant Treasurer
Ownership: David Michael Paxton, 18.4%. votes, 6.9% assets; James Frederick Paxton Jr., 17%. votes, 5.5% assets; Richard Edwin Paxton, 17%. votes, 5.5% assets; Gordon Spoor, Trustee of Trust for Louise P. Gallagher Estate, 15.1%. votes; Louise P. Gallagher Estate, 15.1%. assets; , James Frederick Paxton Estate, 11.5%. assets; George H. Sullivan, Trustee, 7.3%. votes; Patricia Paxton Brockenborough, 6.4%. votes; 6.4% assets; Mary Mitchell Canter, 4%. votes, 4% assets; Bruce Paxton Brockenborough, 3.4%. votes; 3.4% assets.
Represented (legal): Covington & Burling.
TV Stations:
Kentucky: WPSD-DT Paducah.
LPTV Stations:
Illinois: W10AH Carbondale.
Newspapers:
Arkansas: Jonesboro Sun, Paragould Daily Press, Russellville Courier, Searcy Daily Citizen
Georgia: The Bowdon Bulletin (weekly), Douglas County Sentinel, Griffin Daily News, Haralson-Gateway Beacon (weekly), The Tallapoosa Journal (weekly), The Times, Georgian, The Villa Rican (weekly)
Indiana: Connersville News-Examiner, The Times (Frankfort), Michigan City News Dispatch, New Castle Courier-Times, Peru Tribune, The Shelbyville News, Vincennes Sun Commercial, Wabash Plain Dealer
Kentucky: Messenger-Inquirer (Owensboro), The Paducah Sun, The Messenger (Madisonville)
Louisiana: Hammond Daily Star
Michigan: The Herald-Palladium (St. Joseph)
Mississippi: The Banner-Independent (weekly), The Daily Corinthian
North Carolina: Lenoir-News Topic, The Enquirer-Journal (Monroe), Henderson Daily Dispatch, The Daily Courier (Forest City), The Sanford Herald
Tennessee: The Mountain Press (Sevierville)
Other Holdings:
Publishing: Paducah, KY.

PBC TELEVISION HOLDINGS LLC, DEBTOR IN POSSESSION

11766 Wilshire Blvd
Ste 405
Los Angeles, CA 90025-6573
Phone: 310-478-3213

Ownership: Todd Parkin.
Represented (legal): Drinker Biddle.
TV Stations:
Ohio: WYTV-DT Youngstown.
South Carolina: WTGS-DT Hardeeville.

PILOT GROUP LP

745 Madison Ave., 24th Floor
New York, NY 10151
Phone: 212-486-4446
Ownership: Pilot Group GP LLC, General Partner%; PGGPLLC ownership:; Robert W. Pittman, 76.7%. votes; Mayo S. Stuntz Jr., 17.2%; Paul M. McNicol, 4.1%; Robert B. Sherman, 1.8%. votes; Katonah Pittman Ventures LLC, 72.7%. assets; KPVLLC ownership:; Robert W. Pittman. 100% votes, 51% assets.
Represented (legal): Covington & Burling.
TV Stations:
Colorado: KXRM-DT Colorado Springs.
Georgia: WFXL-DT Albany.
Illinois: WHOI-DT Peoria.
Michigan: WBSF-DT Bay City; WTOM-DT Cheboygan; WLUC-DT Marquette; WEYI-DT Saginaw; WPBN-DT Traverse City.
Missouri: KHQA-DT Hannibal; KRCG-DT Jefferson City; KTVO-DT Kirksville.
New Mexico: KVIH-DT Clovis.
New York: WSTM-DT Syracuse.
Ohio: WNWO-DT Toledo.
South Carolina: WACH-DT Columbia; WPDE-DT Florence.
Texas: KVII-DT Amarillo; KGBT-DT Harlingen.
LPTV Stations:
Colorado: KXTU-LP Colorado Springs; K28GE Woodland Park.
Michigan: W14CE Escanaba; W07DB Marquette.
Missouri: K11OJ Sedalia, etc..
New Mexico: K43BU Clovis; K24DU Dora; K26DR San Jon.
New York: WSTQ-LP Syracuse.
Texas: K57CW Friona & Bovina.

PMCM TV LLC

63 W Parish Rd
Concord, NH 03303
Phone: 732-245-4705
Officer:
Richard T Morena, Chief Financial Officer
Ownership: Alfred D Colantoni; Robert E McAllan; Richard T Morena; Jules L Plangere Jr., 25%. each.
Represented (legal): Fletcher, Heald & Hildreth PLC.
TV Stations:
Nevada: KVNV-DT Ely.
Wyoming: KJWY-DT Jackson.

POCATELLO CHANNEL 15 LLC

3654 W. Jarvis Ave.
Skokie, IL 60076
Phone: 847-674-0864
Ownership: Myoung Hwa Bae, see Hapa Media Properties LLC & KM Communications Inc..
TV Stations:
Idaho: KPIF-DT Pocatello.
Wyoming: KBEO-DT Jackson.

POST-NEWSWEEK STATIONS INC.

550 W. Lafayette
Detroit, MI 48226
Phone: 313-223-2260
E-mail: twpcoreply@washpost.com
Officers:
G. William Ryan, President & Chief Executive Officer
Robert E. Branson, Vice President, Secretary & General Counsel
Mark Effron, Vice President, News
Catherine Nierle, Vice President, Business Affairs & Treas.

Barbara Reising, Vice President, Human Resources

Ownership: The Washington Post Co.. Owns The Washington Post; The Washington Post National Weekly Edition; the Herald (Everett, WA); 26% of the Minneapolis Star & Minneapolis Tribune & the Gazette Newspapers (MD); MSO Post-Newsweek Cable; program service Pro Am Sports (PASS); Newsweek, Newsweek International & Newsweek Japan magazines. Has interests in data, manufacturing & service companies.

Represented (legal): Covington & Burling.

TV Stations:
Florida: WJXT-DT Jacksonville; WPLG-DT Miami; WKMG-DT Orlando.
Michigan: WDIV-DT Detroit.
Texas: KPRC-DT Houston; KSAT-DT San Antonio.

LPTV Stations:
Florida: W29AB Ocala.

POWER TELEVISION INTERNATIONAL LLC
5660 Southwyck Blvd
Ste 101
Toledo, OH 43614-1597
Phone: 419-861-3815
Officer:
Charles Glover, Manager
Ownership: Charles Glover, Mgr., 51%; Mitchell A Lambert, 20%; Joanne Phiels, 10%; Marlene Wisniewski, 10%; Seymour Feig, 5%.

TV Stations:
Maine: WPFO-DT Waterville.
Puerto Rico: WMEI-DT Arecibo.

LPTV Stations:
Puerto Rico: WQQZ-CA Ponce; WWKQ-LP Quebradillas.

PRIME CITIES BROADCASTING INC.
112 High Ridge Ave.
Ridgefield, CT 06877
Phone: 203-431-3366
Officer:
John B. Tupper, President & Secretary-Treasurer
Ownership: John B. Tupper, 51%; Bruce E. Fox, Dir., 46%; James R. Kelly, 3%. T.

TV Stations:
North Dakota: KNDX-DT Bismarck; KXND-DT Minot.

LPTV Stations:
North Dakota: K38HA Dickinson; K42FY Dickinson; K38HS Williston; K44HR Williston.

PRIME TIME CHRISTIAN BROADCASTING INC.
Box 61000
Midland, TX 79711
Phone: 432-563-0420
Fax: 432-563-1736
Web site: www.godslearningchannel.com
Officers:
Albert O. Cooper, Chairman
Tommie J. Cooper, Vice President & Secretary-Treasurer

Branch Offices:
2401B N Main
Clovis, NM 88101
Phone: 505-742-1800
88 East CR 112
Snyder, TX 79549
Phone: 625-573-9517
2606 S Main
Roswell, NM 88201
Phone: 505-622-5778
5604 Martin Luther
Lubbock, TX 79704
Phone: 806-747-4997
Ownership: Non-profit corp.--Midland, TX.

Represented (legal): Cohn & Marks LLP.
TV Stations:
New Mexico: KRPV-DT Roswell.
Texas: KPTF-DT Farwell; KPTB-DT Lubbock; KMLM-DT Odessa; KPCB-DT Snyder.
LPTV Stations:
New Mexico: KAPT-LP Alamogordo; KCGD-LP Carlsbad; KCVP-LP Clovis; KHLC-LP Hobbs; KLCP-LP Las Cruces; KKGD-LP Roswell; KPLP-LP Roswell; KGDR-LP Ruidoso.
Texas: KPTA-LP Abilene/Sweetwater; KKCP-LP Ballinger-Coleman; K46FO Big Spring; KPTR-LP Lamesa; K50ED McCamey & Rankin; KPDN-LP Monahans; KPGD-LP Plainview; KPKS-LP San Angelo; KSGD-LP Seminole; KWGD-LP Welch.

QUINCY NEWSPAPERS INC.
Box 909
Quincy, IL 62306
Phone: 217-223-5100
E-mail: info@qni.biz
Officers:
Dennis R. Williams, Chairman
Martin M. Lindsay, Vice Chairman
Ralph M Oakley, President, Chief Executive Officer & Assistant Secretary
Peter A Oakley, Secretary
Thomas A. Oakley, Treasurer
David A. Graff, Assistant Treasurer
Ownership: A. O. Lindsay Trust, Lela B. Lindsay & F. M. Lindsay Jr., Trustees, 26.02%; Thomas A. Oakley, Trustee of Thomas A. Oakley Revocable Trust & On Behalf of Gordon M. Smith Trust, 7.92%; Lee Lindsay Curtis, Individually & as Co-Trustee of Lindsay Trust & Beneficiary of Barbara Lee Williams Trust, 7.16%; Lucy Lindsay Smith, 5.73%; Thomas A. Oakley Grantor Irrevocable Trust, Ralph M Oakley & Mary O Winters Co-Trustees, 4.63%; Peter A Oakley Revocable Trust, Peter A Oakley Trustee, 3.00%; Martin M. Lindsay, 2.90%; Susan Oakley-Day, 2.40%; Harold B Oakley, 1.39%; Ralph M Oakley, 0.58%.
Represented (legal): Wilkinson Barker Knauer LLP.
TV Stations:
Illinois: WGEM-DT Quincy; WREX-DT Rockford.
Indiana: WSJV-DT Elkhart.
Iowa: KTIV-DT Sioux City; KWWL-DT Waterloo.
Minnesota: KTTC-DT Rochester.
West Virginia: WVVA-DT Bluefield.
Wisconsin: WYOW-DT Eagle River; WQOW-DT Eau Claire; WXOW-DT La Crosse; WKOW-DT Madison; WAOW-DT Wausau.
LPTV Stations:
Minnesota: K70DR Blue Earth; K62EV Winona.
Nebraska: K48CH Norfolk.
Wisconsin: W67CH La Crosse.
Newspapers:
Illinois: Quincy Herald-Whig
New Jersey: New Jersey Herald (Newton)
Radio Stations:
Illinois: WGEM-AM-FM Quincy
Other Holdings:
Television holdings: Holds option to purchase KXLT-TV Rochester, MN.

RADIANT LIFE MINISTRIES INC.
PO Box 1010
Marion, IL 62959-1010
Phone: 618-997-9333
Fax: 618-997-1859
E-mail: cmmay@maylawoffices.com
Officers:
Garth W. Coonce, President
Christina M. Coonce, Vice President
Michael J. Daly, Secretary
Charles Payne, Treasurer
Julie Nolan, Assistant Secretary

Ownership: Non-profit organization--Marion, IL; Garth W. Coonce; Christina M. Coonce; Charles Payne; Victoria Clark; Julie Nolan, 20%. votes each. See also listings for Faith Broadcasting Network Inc., TCT of Michigan Inc. & Tri-State Christian TV Inc.
Represented (legal): Colby M. May.
TV Stations:
North Carolina: WLXI Greensboro.
Ohio: WRLM Canton.

RADIO PERRY INC.
Box 980
Perry, GA 31069
Phone: 912-987-2980
Officers:
Lowell L. Register, President
Janice J. Register, Secretary-Treasurer
Ownership: Lowell L Register.
Represented (legal): Brown, Nietert & Kaufman Chartered.
TV Stations:
Georgia: WPGA-DT Perry.
Radio Stations:
Georgia: WPGA-AM-FM Perry

RAMAR COMMUNICATIONS INC.
PO Box 3757
9800 University Ave
Lubbock, TX 79452-3757
Phone: 806-748-9300
Fax: 806-748-1949
E-mail: dcampbell@ramarcom.com
Web site: www.ramarcom.com
Officers:
Ray Moran, Chairman
Brad Moran, President
Mary Moran, Secretary-Treasurer

Branch Office:
2400 Monroe NE
Albuquerque, NM 87190
Phone: 505-884-5353
Ownership: Ray Moran, 51%. votes, 45.3% assets; Brad Moran, 49%. votes, 49.1% assets.
Represented (legal): Leventhal, Senter & Lerman PLLC.
TV Stations:
Colorado: KTLL-DT Durango.
New Mexico: KTEL-DT Carlsbad; KUPT-DT Hobbs.
Texas: KJTV-DT Lubbock.
LPTV Stations:
New Mexico: KFAC-LP Albuquerque; KTEL-LP Albuquerque; K45IL Hobbs; K46GY Santa Fe.
Texas: K48GB Lubbock; KJTV-CA Lubbock; KMYL-LP Lubbock; KXTQ-CA Lubbock; K40FK Matador; K42ES Matador; K45FE Matador; K47GE Matador; K44GL Plainview; K17FX Seminole; K21FV Seminole; K42ET Snyder; K47IP Snyder; K49GT Snyder.
Radio Stations:
Texas: KLZK (FM) Brownfield; KJTV (AM), KXTQ-FM Lubbock; KSTQ-FM New Deal

RANCHO PALOS VERDE BROADCASTERS INC.
15304 Sunset Blvd.
No. 204
Pacific Palisades, CA 90272
Phone: 310-454-8673
Fax: 310-454-4983
Officer:
Paul A. Zevnik, President
Ownership: Paul A Zevnik, 36.4%; Terence E Crosby, 24%; Arnold Applebaum, 24%; Jim Devaney; Susan Devaney, jointly, 15.6%.
Represented (legal): Thompson Hine LLP.

TV Stations:
California: KXLA-DT Rancho Palos Verdes.

R. & F. BROADCASTING
Cermica Annex
Box 1833
Carolina, PR 00984-1833
Phone: 787-762-5500
Officers:
Rickin Sanchez Sr., Chairman, President & Chief Executive Officer
Rickin Sanchez Jr., Chief Operating Officer & Vice President, Production
Blanche Vidal, Secretary-Treasurer
Michelle Sanchez-Diaz, Chief Financial Officer
Ownership: Enrique A Sanchez, Gen. Partner, 50%; Blanca Vidal de Sanchez, 50%.
TV Stations:
Puerto Rico: WRFB-DT Carolina.

RAPID BROADCASTING CO.
2424 S. Plaza Dr.
Box 9549
Rapid City, SD 57709
Phone: 605-355-0024
Fax: 605-355-9274
Officers:
Gilbert D. Moyle, President
James F. Simpson, Chief Executive Officer
Gilbert D. Moyle III, Vice President
Clark D. Moyle, Secretary-Treasurer
Steve Mentele, Chief Financial Officer
Ownership: W. R Barbour, 25%; Charles H Lien, 25%; Gilbert D Moyle, 16.7%; Gilbert D Moyle III, 16.7%; Clark D Moyle, 16.6%.
Represented (legal): Cole, Raywid & Braverman LLP.
TV Stations:
South Dakota: KNBN-DT Rapid City.
LPTV Stations:
South Dakota: K40GS Rapid City; KKRA-LP Rapid City; KWBH-LP Rapid City.
Wyoming: K22AD Gillette.

RAYCOM MEDIA INC.
201 Monroe St.
RSA Tower, Suite 710
Montgomery, AL 36104
Phone: 334-206-1400
E-mail: info@raycommedia.com
Officers:
Paul H. McTear Jr., President & Chief Executive Officer
Wayne Daugherty, Executive Vice President & Chief Operating Officer
Mary Carole McDonnell, Executive Vice President, Programming
Marty Edelman, Vice President, Television
Leon Long, Vice President, Television
Jeff Rosser, Vice President, Television
Melissa Thurber, Vice President & Chief Financial Officer
Anne Adkins, Vice President, Marketing
J. Clyde Baucom, Vice President, Human Resources
Rebecca Bryan, Vice President & General Counsel
David Folsom, Vice President & Chief Technology Officer
Pat LaPlatney, Vice President, Digital Media
William R. McDowell, Vice President, Research
Susana Schuler, Vice President, News
Ownership: Paul H. McTear Jr., 14%. votes; qualified company employees, none with more than 5% voting interest.
Represented (legal): Covington & Burling.
TV Stations:
Alabama: WBRC-DT Birmingham; WAFF-DT Huntsville; WSFA-DT Montgomery; WDFX-DT Ozark.

Arizona: KOLD-DT Tucson.
Arkansas: KAIT-DT Jonesboro.
Florida: WPGX-DT Panama City; WFLX-DT West Palm Beach.
Georgia: WALB-DT Albany; WTVM-DT Columbus; WTOC-DT Savannah.
Hawaii: KHBC-DT Hilo; KFVE-DT Honolulu; KHNL-DT Honolulu; KOGG-DT Wailuku.
Indiana: WFIE-DT Evansville.
Kentucky: WAVE-DT Louisville; WXIX-DT Newport.
Louisiana: WAFB-DT Baton Rouge; KPLC-DT Lake Charles; KSLA-DT Shreveport.
Mississippi: WLOX-DT Biloxi; WLBT-DT Jackson; WDAM-DT Laurel.
Missouri: KFVS-DT Cape Girardeau.
North Carolina: WBTV-DT Charlotte; WECT-DT Wilmington.
Ohio: WUAB-DT Lorain; WOIO-DT Shaker Heights; WTOL-DT Toledo.
South Carolina: WCSC-DT Charleston; WIS-DT Columbia; WMBF-DT Myrtle Beach.
Tennessee: WTNZ-DT Knoxville; WMC-DT Memphis.
Texas: KCBD-DT Lubbock; KTRE-DT Lufkin; KLTV-DT Tyler.
Virginia: WTVR-DT Richmond; WWBT-DT Richmond.
LPTV Stations:
Alabama: W29AO Anniston.
Hawaii: K45CT Hilo; K63DZ Kailua-Kona; K65BV Lihue; K27DW Wailuku.
Kentucky: WQTV-LP Murray; WQWQ-LP Paducah.
Louisiana: WBXH-CA Baton Rouge.
New Mexico: K27GJ-D Farmington.
Radio Stations:
Tennessee: WMC-AM-FM.
Other Holdings:
Advertising sales company, production &.

RED LION BROADCASTING CO. INC.
PO Box 88
2900 Windsor Rd.
Red Lion, PA 17356
Phone: 717-246-1681
Fax: 717-244-9316
Web site: www.wgcbtv.com
Ownership: Estate of John H. Norris, Anna L. Plourde-Norris, Executrix, 60%; Anna L Plourde-Norris, 40%. John H. Norris died September 28, 2008.
Represented (legal): Booth Freret Imlay & Tepper PC.
TV Stations:
Pennsylvania: WGCB-DT Red Lion.
Radio Stations:
Pennsylvania: WGCB-AM-FM

RED RIVER BROADCAST CORP.
3600 S. Westport Ave.
Sioux Falls, SD 57116
Phone: 605-361-5555
Officers:
Ro Grignon, President
Myron Kunin, Chief Executive Officer
Kathy Lau, Vice President
Ownership: Curtis Squire Inc.; CSI ownership:; Curtis Squire, 90%; Ro Grignon, 10%. Grignon & Squire also own KQDS Acquisition Corp., see listing.
Represented (legal): Phillips & Potach PA; Crowell Moring LLP.
TV Stations:
Minnesota: KBRR-DT Thief River Falls.
North Dakota: KVRR-DT Fargo; KJRR-DT Jamestown.
South Dakota: KDLV-DT Mitchell; KDLT-DT Sioux Falls.
LPTV Stations:
Minnesota: K54AT Brainerd; K05IV Park Rapids.
South Dakota: K42FI Watertown.

REITEN TELEVISION
3425 S. Broadway
Minot, ND 58701
Officers:
David M. Reiten, Chairman
Kathleen Huuby, Secretary-Treasurer
Ownership: Chester Reiten & family.
Represented (legal): Pillsbury Winthrop Shaw Pittman LLP.
TV Stations:
North Dakota: KXMB-DT Bismarck; KXMA-DT Dickinson; KXMC-DT Minot; KXMD-DT Williston.
Radio Stations:
North Dakota: KMXA-FM; KCJB (AM); KYYX-FM

RKM MEDIA INC.
137 Spyglass Lane
Fayetteville, NY 13066
Phone: 315-637-5530
Ownership: The Ronald W. Philips Revocable Trust; Ronald W. Philips, Trustee.
Represented (legal): Rubin, Winston, Diercks, Harris & Cooke LLP.
TV Stations:
New York: WNYS-DT Syracuse.

MICHAEL V. ROBERTS
1408 N. Kingshighway Blvd.
Suite 300
St. Louis, MO 63113
Phones: 314-367-0090; 314-367-4600
Fax: 314-367-0174
Represented (legal): DLA Piper International.
TV Stations:
Kentucky: WAZE-DT Madisonville.
Mississippi: WRBJ-DT Magee.
South Carolina: WZRB-DT Columbia.
LPTV Stations:
Indiana: WAZE-LP Evansville; WIKY-LP Evansville, etc.; WJPS-LP Evansville, etc..
Other Holdings:
TV Stations: Roberts holds 50% of the voting equity of Roberts Brothers Broadcasting LLC, which holds 50% of the voting equity in St. Louis/Denver LLC see listing..

STEVEN C. ROBERTS
1408 N. Kingshighway Blvd.
Suite 300
St. Louis, MO 63113
Phones: 314-367-0090; 314-367-4600
Fax: 314-367-0176
Represented (legal): DLA Piper International.
TV Stations:
Kentucky: WAZE-DT Madisonville.
Mississippi: WRBJ-DT Magee.
South Carolina: WZRB-DT Columbia.
LPTV Stations:
Indiana: WAZE-LP Evansville; WIKY-LP Evansville, etc.; WJPS-LP Evansville, etc..
Other Holdings:
TV Stations: Roberts holds 50% of the voting equity of Roberts Brothers Broadcasting LLC, which holds 50% of the voting equity in St. Louis/Denver LLC see listing..

ROCKFLEET BROADCASTING LP
885 3rd Ave., 34th Floor
New York, NY 10022
Phone: 212-888-5500
Officers:
Jeffrey A. Smith, President
Bruce M. Schnelwar, Senior Vice President
David A. Pershing, Senior Vice President & Secretary
Kevin J. DeLuise, Vice President, Treasurer & Assistant Secretary

Ownership: R. Joseph Fuchs, 14.85%. equity; Rockfleet Broadcasting Inc., 1%. equity, 100% voting; SDR Rockfleet Holdings LLC, 84.15%. equity; RBI ownership:; R. Joseph Fuchs; SDRRHLLC ownership:; Randall Smith, 88%; Jeffrey Smith, 12%.
Represented (legal): Wiley Rein LLP.
TV Stations:
Maine: WVII-DT Bangor.
Wisconsin: WJFW-DT Rhinelander.
LPTV Stations:
Maine: WFVX-LP Bangor.
Wisconsin: W27AU Wausau.
Other Holdings:
Radio.

SAGA COMMUNICATIONS INC.
73 Kercheval Ave.
Suite 201
Grosse Pointe Farms, MI 48236-3559
Phone: 313-886-7070
Fax: 313-886-7150
E-mail: bwells@sagacom.com
Officers:
Edward K. Christian, Chairman, President & Chief Executive Officer
Steven J. Goldstein, Executive Vice President, Programming
Warren Lada, Senior Vice President, Operations
Samuel D. Bush, Senior Vice President, Treasurer & Chief Financial Officer
Marcia K. Lobaito, Vice President & Secretary
Ownership: Publicly held.; Edward K Christian, controlling interest.
Represented (legal): Smithwick & Belendiuk PC.
TV Stations:
Kansas: KOAM-DT Pittsburg.
Mississippi: WXVT-DT Greenville.
Texas: KAVU-DT Victoria.
LPTV Stations:
Texas: KMOL-LP Victoria; KUNU-LP Victoria; KVTX-LP Victoria; KXTS-LP Victoria.
Radio Stations:
Arkansas: KEGI (FM) Jonesboro, KDXY (FM) Lake City, KJBX (FM) Trumann
Illinois: WIXY (FM), WLRW (FM) Champaign; WXTT (FM) Danville; WYMG (FM) Jacksonville; WABZ (FM) Sherman, WDBR (FM), WQQL (FM), WTAX (AM) Springfield; WCFF (FM) Urbana
Iowa: KLTI-FM Ames; KIOA (FM), KPSZ (AM), KRNT (AM), KSTZ (FM) Des Moines; KAZR (FM) Pella; KICD (AM), KLLT (FM) Spencer
Kentucky: WCVQ (FM), WJQI (AM) Fort Campbell; WVVR (FM) Hopkinsville; WEGI (AM) Oak Grove
Maine: WVAE (AM) Biddeford; WCLZ (FM) North Yarmouth; WBAE (AM), WGAN (AM), WMGX (FM), WPOR (FM), WZAN (AM) Portland; WYNZ (FM) Westbrook
Massachusetts: WHNP (AM) East Longmeadow; WHAI (FM), WHMQ (AM), WPVQ (FM) Greenfield; WLZX (FM) Northhampton; WAQY (FM) Springfield
New Hampshire: WMLL (FM) Bedford; WFEA (AM), WZID (FM) Manchester
New York: WIII (FM) Cortland; WHCU (AM), WNYY (AM), WQNY (FM), WYXL (FM) Ithaca
North Carolina: WISE (AM) Asheville, WOXL-FM Biltmore Forest, WYSE (AM) Canton, WTMT (FM) Weaverville
Ohio: WBCO (AM), WQEL (FM) Bucyrus; WSNY (FM) Columbus; WODB (FM) Delaware; WJZK (FM) Richwood
South Dakota: KMIT (FM) Mitchell, KUQL (FM) Wessington Springs, WNAX-AM-FM Yankton
Tennessee: WKFN (AM) Clarksville
Vermont: WKVT (FM) Brattleboro, WRSY (FM) Marlboro
Virginia: WINA (AM), WQMZ (FM), WVAX (AM), WWWV (FM) Charlottesville; WCNR (FM) Keswick; WJOI (AM), WNOR (FM), WAFX (FM) Norfolk; WAFX (FM) Suffolk

Washington: KAFE (FM), KBAI (AM), KGMI (AM), KISM (FM), KPUG (AM) Bellingham
Wisconsin: WJZX (FM) Brookfield; WJMR-FM Menomonee Falls; WHQG (FM), WJYI (AM), WKLH (FM) Milwaukee

SAGAMOREHILL BROADCASTING LLC
2 Embarcadero Center, 23rd Floor
San Francisco, CA 94111
Phone: 415-788-2755
Officer:
Louis Wall, President
Ownership: Duff, Ackerman & Goodrich LP, principal..
Represented (legal): Wiley Rein LLP.
TV Stations:
Alabama: WNCF-DT Montgomery; WBMM-DT Tuskegee.
Georgia: WLTZ-DT Columbus.
Nebraska: KSTF-DT Scottsbluff.
Texas: KGNS-DT Laredo.
Wyoming: KGWN-DT Cheyenne.
LPTV Stations:
Wyoming: K19FX Laramie.

SAINTE PARTNERS II LP
Box 4159
Modesto, CA 95352-4159
Phone: 209-523-0777
Fax: 209-523-0839
Ownership: C & N Broadcast Division Inc., gen. partner, 50%. votes; 1% equity; Sainte Network Inc., gen. partner, 50%. votes; 1.34%. equity; Chester Smith, ltd. partner, 35.4%. equity; Naomi L. Smith, ltd. partner, 35.4%. equity; Albert I. & Virginia C. Chance, ltd. partners, 7.38%. equity; J. Wilmar Jensen, ltd. partner, 7.38%. equity; Sharon D. Sepulveda, ltd. partner, 2.91%. equity; Madeline J. Roddy, ltd. partner, 2.82%. equity; Center Family Trust, ltd. partner, 2.24%. equity; Dorothy Ibarra, ltd. partner, 2.24%. equity; Danny Roddy, ltd. partner, 0.94%. equity; Sean Roddy, ltd. partner, 0.94%. equity; CNBDI & SNI ownership:; Chester Smith, Pres., 50%; Naomi L. Smith, V.P., 50%; J. Wilmar Jensen, Secy.-Treas..
TV Stations:
California: KBVU-DT Eureka; KCVU-DT Paradise.
LPTV Stations:
California: K38FQ Anderson/Central Valley; KKTF-LP Chico; KUCO-LP Chico; KXVU-LP Chico; KZVU-LP Chico; K52FK Eureka; K59FW Eureka; K67GU Eureka; KEMY-LP Eureka; KEUV-LP Eureka; KUVU-LP Eureka; K14MN Fortuna; K08NH Oroville; K04QC Palermo; K46HI Redding; KRVU-LP Redding.
Oregon: K41ID Klamath Falls; KFBI-LP Medford; KMCW-LP Medford.

ST. LOUIS/DENVER LLC
Suite 300
1408 N Kingshighway Blvd
St. Louis, MO 63113
Phone: 314-367-4600
Ownership: Roberts Brothers Broadcasting LLC, 56%. assets & 50% voting rights; Telefutura, 44%. assets & 50% voting rights; RBBLLC ownership:; Michael V. Roberts, see listing, 50%. assets & voting rights; Steven C. Roberts, see listing, 50%. assets & voting rights; Telefutura ownership:; Univision Communications Inc., see listing.
TV Stations:
Colorado: KTFD-DT Boulder.
Illinois: WRBU-DT East St. Louis.

SCHURZ COMMUNICATIONS INC.
225 W. Colfax Ave.
South Bend, IN 46626
Phone: 574-287-1001

Fax: 574-287-2257

Web site: www.schurz.com

Officers:

Franklin D. Schurz Jr., Chairman

Scott C Schurz, Vice Chairman

Todd F Schurz, President & Chief Executive Officer

Marcia K. Burdick, Senior Vice President, Broadcasting

Gary N Hoipkemier, Senior Vice President, Secretary & Treasurer & Chief Financial Officer

Charles V Pittman, Senior Vice President, Publishing

James M Schurz, Senior Vice President

Sally J Brown, Vice President, Radio-Indiana

Hyler Cooper, Vice President, Digital Media

David C Ray, Vice President

Martin D Switalski, Vice President, Finance & Administration & Assistant Treasurer

Judy A Felty, Assistant Secretary

Ownership: Franklin D. Schurz Jr.; Mary Schurz; James M. Schurz; Scott C. Schurz, 75.2%. votes, Trustees; David C Ray, V.P., 15.2%. votes, 4.06% assets; Robin S Bruni, 9.6, votes, 4.37% assets%; Todd F Schurz, 7.36%. assets; Franklin D Schurz Jr, 7.14%. assets; Scott C Schurz, 3.76%. assets; Scott C Schurz Jr, 3.17%. assets.

Represented (legal): Wilmer Cutler Pickering Hale & Dorr LLP.

Cable Systems:

FLORIDA: CORAL SPRINGS; WESTON. MARYLAND: HAGERSTOWN.

TV Stations:

Alaska: KTUU-DT Anchorage.

Georgia: WAGT-DT Augusta.

Indiana: WSBT-DT South Bend.

Kansas: KBSD-DT Ensign; KBSL-DT Goodland; KBSH-DT Hays; KWCH-DT Hutchinson; KSCW-DT Wichita.

Missouri: KYTV-DT Springfield.

Virginia: WDBJ-DT Roanoke.

LPTV Stations:

Alaska: K04DS Kenai River; K10NC Kenai, etc.; K09JE Palmer.

Indiana: WBND-LD South Bend; WBND-LP South Bend.

Missouri: K17DL-D Branson; K15CZ Springfield.

Virginia: W04AG Garden City, etc..

Newspapers:

California: Adelante Valle (El Centro), Imperial Valley Press

Indiana: Times Mail (Bedford), Herald Times (Bloomington), Reporter Times (Martinsville), Mooresville-Decatur Times, Noblesville Daily Times, South Bend Tribune

Kentucky: The Advocate-Messenger (Danville), The Jessamine Journal (Nicholasville), The Interior Journal (Stanford), The Winchester Sun

Maryland: Herald-Mail (Hagerstown)

Michigan: Charlevoix Courier, Gaylord Herald Times, The Petoskey News-Review

Pennsylvania: Daily American (Somerset)

South Dakota: American News (Aberdeen)

Radio Stations:

Indiana: WASK (AM), WHKY (AM), WKDA (AM), WXXB (FM) Lafayette; WNSN (FM), WSBT (AM) South Bend

South Dakota: KFXS (FM), KKLS (AM), KKMK (FM), KOUT (FM), KRCS (FM) Rapid City; KBHB (AM) Sturgis

JOSEPH C. SCHWARTZEL

2824 Palm Beach Blvd.

Fort Myers, FL 33916

Phone: 239-337-2346

E-mail: joe.schwartzel@meridianradio.com

Represented (legal): Leibowitz & Associates PA.

TV Stations:

Florida: WXCW-DT Naples.

ERNESTO SCHWEIKERT III

3244 Georgia Ave.

Kenner, LA 70065

Phone: 504-913-1540

Represented (legal): Fletcher, Heald & Hildreth PLC.

TV Stations:

Louisiana: KGLA-DT Hammond.

E. W. SCRIPPS CO.

312 Walnut St.

28th Floor

Cincinnati, OH 45202

Phone: 513-977-3000

Fax: 513-977-3721

Web site: www.scripps.com

Officers:

Nackey Scagliotti, Chairman

Richard A. Boehne, President & Chief Executive Officer

Brian Lawlor, President, Television Division

William Appleton, Senior Vice President & General Counsel

Mark G. Contreras, Senior Vice President, Newspapers

Lisa Knutson, Senior Vice President, Human Resources

William B. Peterson, Senior Vice President, Television

Timothy E. Stautberg, Senior Vice President & Chief Financial Officer

Robert A. Carson, Vice President & Chief Information Officer

David M. Giles, Vice President, Deputy Gen. Counsel

Michael T. Hales, Vice President, Audit & Compliance

Timothy A. King, Vice President, Corporate Communications & Investor Relations

Mary Denise Kuprionis, Vice President, Secretary & Chief Compliance & Ethics Officer

Douglas F. Lyons, Vice President & Controller

Ownership: The Edward W. Scripps Trust, Edward W. Scripps, Nackey E. Scagliotti & John Burlingame, Trustees, 87.5%. votes; 35.6 assets; The John P. Scripps Trust, Paul K. Scripps, Peter R. Ladow & Barbara Scripps Evans, Trustees, 7.9%. votes; 1.4% assets; Paul K. Scripps, 0.90%. votes; remainder publicly held.. On July 1, 2008 Scripps' five cable networks (DIY Network, Fine Living Network, Food Network, Great American Country & HGTV) plus two online comparison shopping services (Shopzilla & uSwitch) split off to a publicly traded company, Scripps Networks Interactive.

Represented (legal): Baker Hostetler LLP.

TV Stations:

Arizona: KNXV-DT Phoenix.

Florida: WFTS-DT Tampa; WPTV-DT West Palm Beach.

Kansas: KMCI-DT Lawrence.

Maryland: WMAR-DT Baltimore.

Michigan: WXYZ-DT Detroit.

Missouri: KSHB-DT Kansas City.

Ohio: WCPO-DT Cincinnati; WEWS-DT Cleveland.

Oklahoma: KJRH-DT Tulsa.

LPTV Stations:

Arizona: K44CN Cottonwood; K52CM Flagstaff; K57FY Kingman; K47DJ Prescott.

Newspapers:

Alabama: Birmingham Post-Herald

California: Redding Record Searchlight, Ventura Star Newspapers

Colorado: Boulder Daily Camera, Denver Rocky Mountain News

Florida: Fort Pierce Tribune, Naples Daily News, The Stuart News, Vero Beach Press-Journal

Indiana: Evansville Courier-Press

Kentucky: The Kentucky Post

New Mexico: The Albuquerque Tribune

Ohio: The Cincinnati Post

South Carolina: Anderson Independent Mail

Tennessee: The Knoxville News Sentinel, The Commercial Appeal (Memphis)

Texas: Abilene Reporter News, Corpus Christi Caller-Times, Standard Times (San Angelo), Times Record News (Wichita Falls)

Washington: Bremerton Sun

Other Holdings:

Features syndicator: United Media, licensor & syndicator of news features & comics

Production: Scripps Productions, producer of cable programs.

SEAL ROCK BROADCASTERS LLC

351 Elliott Ave. W

Suite 300

Seattle, WA 98119-4150

Phone: 206-285-2295

Ownership: Lance W Anderson, 50%; George V Kriste, 50%.

TV Stations:

California: KCBA-DT Salinas.

SECOND GENERATION OF IOWA LTD.

3451 Bonita Bay Blvd.

Suite 101

Bonita Springs, FL 34134

Phone: 941-498-4600

Officers:

Thomas J. Embrescia, Chairman & Chief Executive Officer

Jonathan Pinch, President

Larry Blum, Chief Operating Officer

Ownership: Thomas J. Embrescia, 33.33%; Jonathan Pinch, 33.33%; Larry Blum, 33.33%.

TV Stations:

Iowa: KFXA-DT Cedar Rapids.

TIMOTHY G. SHEEHAN

17 Crooked Lane

Manchester, MA 01944

Phone: 978-526-8306

TV Stations:

Rhode Island: WNAC-DT Providence.

SHOOTINGSTAR BROADCASTING OF NEW ENGLAND LLC

3606 Camino de la Cumbre

Sherman Oaks, CA 91423

Phone: 818-788-8228

Ownership: Alta ShootingStar Corp., 95%; ShootingStar Inc., 5%; ASC ownership:; Alta Communications IX LP, 94.43%; SI ownership:; Diane Sutter; ACIXLP ownership:; Alta Communications IX Managers LLC, Gen. Partner; ACIXMLLC ownership:; Timothy L. Dibble, 20.4, Managing Member%; Brian W. McNeill, Managing Member, 20.4%.

Represented (legal): Leventhal, Senter & Lerman PLLC.

TV Stations:

New Hampshire: WZMY-DT Derry.

SILVERTON BROADCASTING CO. LLC

116 Tigertail Rd.

Los Angeles, CA 90049

Phone: 310-476-2217

Ownership: Barry Silverton, Pres..

Represented (legal): Drinker Biddle.

TV Stations:

Wyoming: KTWO-DT Casper.

LPTV Stations:

Wyoming: K69DD Bondurant; K56BT Jackson; K22CI Lander; K12IS Lusk; K55BL Sheridan, etc.; K13NZ Shoshoni; K35CV Shoshoni; K08AA Wyodak, etc..

SIMONS BROADCASTING LP, DEBTOR IN POSSESSION

510 N Valley Mills Dr

Ste 500

Waco, TX 76710

Phone: 254-741-6188

Officer:

Mike Simons, President

Ownership: Simons Asset Management LLC, Gen. Partner; SAMLLC ownership:; Mike Simons, Pres..

Represented (legal): Garvey Schubert Barer.

TV Stations:

Texas: KTAQ-DT Greenville.

JAMES F. SIMPSON

23646 Wilderness Canyon Rd

Rapid City, SD 57702

Phone: 605-355-0024

TV Stations:

South Dakota: KWSD-DT Sioux Falls.

LPTV Stations:

South Dakota: KAUN-LP Sioux Falls; KCWS-LP Sioux Falls.

SINCLAIR BROADCAST GROUP INC.

10706 Beaver Dam Rd.

Cockeysville, MD 21030

Phone: 410-568-1500

Fax: 410-568-1533

E-mail: comments@sbgi.net

Web site: www.sbgi.net

Officers:

David D. Smith, President & Chief Executive Officer

David B. Amy, Executive Vice President & Chief Financial Officer

Barry M. Faber, Executive Vice President & General Counsel

Steve Marks, Vice President & Chief Operating Officer, Television Group

J. Duncan Smith, Vice President & Secretary

Frederick G. Smith, Vice President

Nat S. Ostroff, Vice President, New Technology

Lucy Rutishauser, Vice President, Corporate Finance & Treasurer

Donald H. Thompson, Vice President, Human Resources

Tom Waters, Vice President, Purchasing

Robert Malandra, Vice President, Finance & Television, Sinclair Television Group Inc.

David R. Bochenek, Chief Accounting Officer

Ownership: David D. Smith, 24.6%. votes, 11.5% equity; J. Duncan Smith, 25.1%. votes, 11.4% equity; Frederick G. Smith, 19.2%. votes, 9.2% equity; Robert E. Smith, 17%. votes, 7.7% equity.

Represented (legal): Pillsbury Winthrop Shaw Pittman LLP.

TV Stations:

Alabama: WABM-DT Birmingham; WTTO-DT Homewood.

Florida: WFGX-DT Fort Walton Beach; WEAR-DT Pensacola; WTWC-DT Tallahassee.

Illinois: WYZZ-DT Bloomington; WICD-DT Champaign; WICS-DT Springfield.

Iowa: KGAN-DT Cedar Rapids; KDSM-DT Des Moines.

Kentucky: WDKY-DT Danville.

Maine: WGME-DT Portland.

Maryland: WBFF-DT Baltimore.

Michigan: WSMH-DT Flint.

Minnesota: WUCW-DT Minneapolis.

Missouri: KBSI-DT Cape Girardeau; KDNL-DT St. Louis.

Nevada: KVCW-DT Las Vegas; KVMY-DT Las Vegas.

New York: WNYO-DT Buffalo; WUTV-DT Buffalo; WUHF-DT Rochester; WSYT-DT Syracuse.

North Carolina: WLOS-DT Asheville; WRDC-DT Durham; WMYV-DT Greensboro; WLFL-DT Raleigh; WXLV-DT Winston-Salem.

Ohio: WSTR-DT Cincinnati; WSYX-DT Columbus; WKEF-DT Dayton.
Oklahoma: KOCB-DT Oklahoma City; KOKH-DT Oklahoma City.
Pennsylvania: WPGH-DT Pittsburgh; WPMY-DT Pittsburgh.
South Carolina: WMMP-DT Charleston.
Tennessee: WUXP-DT Nashville; WZTV-DT Nashville.
Texas: KMYS-DT Kerrville; KABB-DT San Antonio.
Virginia: WTVZ-DT Norfolk; WRLH-DT Richmond.
West Virginia: WCHS-DT Charleston.
Wisconsin: WMSN-DT Madison; WCGV-DT Milwaukee; WVTV-DT Milwaukee.

LPTV Stations:
Alabama: W62BG Birmingham.
Iowa: K13MN Washington.
Nevada: K51AC Pahrump.
New York: W16AX Ithaca.
North Carolina: W06AQ Bat Cave, etc.; W12AQ Black Mountain; W05AP Brasstown, etc.; W08AN Bryson City, etc.; W12AU Burnsville; W05AF Cherokee; W11AJ Franklin; W12CI Hot Springs; W06AP Maggie Valley, etc.; W10AP Marion, etc.; W06AL Oteen/Warren; W11AQ Robbinsville, etc.; W06AN Sapphire Valley, etc.; W06AD Spruce Pine; W05AE Sylva, etc.; W05AC Tryon, etc.; W12AR Waynesville, etc..
Ohio: W66AQ Dayton.
South Carolina: W05AO Pickens.

SMITH MEDIA LICENSE HOLDINGS LLC
One Federal St., 23rd Floor
Boston, MA 02110
Phone: 617-350-1500
Ownership: Smith Media LLC; SMLLC ownership:; Frontyard Management LLC, 55.56%. votes; Smith Television of New York Inc., 44.44%. votes; FMLLC ownership:; Barry Baker; Roy F. Coppedge III; Barbara M. Ginader, 33.3%. each; STONYI ownership:; Robert N. & Anne Smith Trust; RNAST ownership:; Leslie J. Goldman, Trustee, 25%; Anne Smith, Trustee, 25%; Jennifer Smith, Special Trustee, 25%; Michael D. Smith, Special Trustee, 25%.
Represented (legal): Dow Lohnes PLLC.
TV Stations:
Alaska: KIMO-DT Anchorage; KATN-DT Fairbanks; KJUD-DT Juneau.
California: KEYT-DT Santa Barbara.
New York: WKTV-DT Utica.
Vermont: WFFF-DT Burlington.

LPTV Stations:
Alaska: K13KU Delta Junction; K13OC Douglas, etc.; K03FW Kenai, etc.; K13MZ Usibelli, etc..
California: K57BC San Luis Obispo, etc.; KSBB-LP Santa Barbara.

SON BROADCASTING INC.
PO Box 4338
Albuquerque, NM 87196
Phone: 505-345-1991
Fax: 505-474-4998
E-mail: annette@kchf.com
Officers:
Annette Garcia, President
Richard Shakarian, Vice President
Angie Gonzales, Vice President
Marcimilliano Baca, Vice President & Treasurer
Clem M. Dixon, Secretary
Ownership: Vickie Archevque; Dinah Baca; Annette Garcia; Joanna Gonzales; Mary Kay Gonzales; Ted Gonzales; Warren Trumbly, 14.29%. votes each.
Represented (legal): Gammon & Grange PC.

TV Stations:
New Mexico: KCHF-DT Santa Fe.
LPTV Stations:
New Mexico: K51DM Antonito; K28CE Socorro; K43IA Taos.

SONSHINE FAMILY TV INC.
813 N. Fenwick St.
Allentown, PA 18101
Phones: 610-433-4400; 610-954-7501
Fax: 610-433-8251
Officers:
Patricia F. Huber, President & Chief Executive Officer
Daniel Huber, Chief Operating Officer
Ownership: Daniel P Huber; Margaret M Huber; Patricia F Huber, 33.3%.
Represented (legal): William D. Silva.
TV Stations:
Pennsylvania: WBPH-DT Bethlehem.

SOUTHERN BROADCAST CORP. OF SARASOTA
1477 10th St.
Sarasota, FL 34236
Phone: 941-923-8840
Fax: 941-924-3971
Officers:
Gary Shorts, Chairman
J. Manuel Calvo, President & General Manager
Shirley Ellis, Vice President
Sandra Hardy, Vice President & Secretary
Carolyn Smith, Vice President
Michael White, Treasurer
Ownership: Calkins Media Inc.; CMI ownership:; Shirley Ellis, V.P., 33.3%; Sandra Hardy, V.P. & Secy., 33.3%; Carolyn Smith, V.P., 33.3%. Calkins owns & operates the Intelligencer Record in Doylestown, PA; Bucks County Courier Times in Levittown, PA; Burlington County Times in Willingboro, NJ; Beaver County Times in Beaver, PA; South Dade News Leader in Homestead, FL. Hardy, Ellis & Smith have controlling interest in Union Town Newspapers Inc., publisher of the Herald Standard in Uniontown, PA.
Represented (legal): Leibowitz & Associates PA.
TV Stations:
Alabama: WAAY-DT Huntsville.
Florida: WWSB-DT Sarasota; WTXL-DT Tallahassee.

SOUTHERN BROADCASTING INC.
Box 1645
Tupelo, MS 38802
Phone: 601-842-7620
Officers:
Walter D. Spain, President
Wendell R. Robinson, Chief Operating Officer
K. M. Spain, Secretary-Treasurer
Ownership: Walter D Spain, 50%; Kyle M Spain, 50%.
Represented (legal): Garvey Schubert Barer.
TV Stations:
Mississippi: WKDH-DT Houston.

SOUTHERN TV CORP.
9661 82nd Ave. N
Seminole, FL 33777
Phone: 727-319-6100
Fax: 727-397-0785
Officers:
Dan L. Johnson, Chairman, President & Chief Executive Officer
Charles E. Robb, Chief Operating & Financial Officer
Jo Johnson, Vice President
Robert G. Keelean, Secretary-Treasurer

Ownership: Betty Johnson, 42.5%; Dan L. Johnson; Robert G. Keelean, 30%; Kim Doniel, 10%; William Doniel; Lisa Keelean, 5%; Robert G. Keelean Jr., 5%; Mabel Reed Young, 5%; Donald Chervier, 2.5%.
Represented (legal): Irwin, Campbell & Tannenwald PC.
TV Stations:
Georgia: WGSA-DT Baxley.
LPTV Stations:
Georgia: W41CR Hinesville-Richmond; WGCW-LP Savannah; WGSA-CA Savannah; W25CQ Statesboro.

SPANISH BROADCASTING SYSTEM INC.
2601 S. Bayshore Dr.
Penthouse 2
Coconut Grove, FL 33133
Phone: 305-441-6901
Officers:
Raul Alarcon Jr., Chairman, President & Chief Executive Officer
Marko Radlovic, Chief Operating Officer
Joseph A. Garcia, Executive Vice President, Secretary & Chief Financial Officer
William B. Tanner, Executive Vice President, Programming
Ownership: Raul Alarcon Jr., 78.8%. vote; 32.5% equity; Pablo Raul Alarcon Sr., 3.6%. vote; 1.5% equity.
Represented (legal): Kaye Scholer LLP.
TV Stations:
Florida: WSBS-DT Key West.
LPTV Stations:
Florida: WSBS-CA Miami.

STAINLESS BROADCASTING LP
2111 University Park Dr.
Suite 650
Okemos, MI 48864-6913
Phone: 517-347-4141
Officers:
Brian W. Brady, President & Chief Executive Officer
Fred L. Levy, Secretary
William Quarles, Chief Financial Officer & Treasurer
Ownership: Stainless Broadcasting Co., Gen. Partner, 100% votes; 1% equity; Stainless Broadcasting LLC, Ltd. Partner, 99%. equity; SBC ownership:; Brian W. Brady, SBLLC ownership:; Stainless Broadcasting Co., 100% votes; 1% equity; Northwest Broadcasting LP, 99%. equity; NBLP & SBC ownership:; Brian W. Brady. Brady is also a principal of Broadcasting Licenses LP & Mountain Licenses LP, see listings.
Represented (legal): Leventhal, Senter & Lerman PLLC.
TV Stations:
New York: WICZ-DT Binghamton.
LPTV Stations:
New York: WBPN-LP Binghamton.

STATION VENTURE OPERATIONS LP
1299 Pennsylvania Ave. NW
11th Floor
Washington, DC 20004
Phone: 202-637-4545
Ownership: NBC Telemundo License Co., Gen. Partner, 0.25%. equity, 100% votes; Station Venture Holdings LLC, Ltd. Partner, 99.75%. equity; NBCTLC ownership:; NBC Telemundo Inc.; NBCTI ownership:; NBC Telemundo Holding Co., 20%. assets, 55.6% votes; NBC Universal Inc., see listing, 80%. assets, 44.4% votes; NBCUI ownership:; NBC Holding Inc., 80%; NBCHI & NBCTHC ownership:; General Electric Co.; GEC ownership:; publicly held.; SVHLLC ownership:; NBC Telemundo License Co., 79.62%. vote; LIN Television Corp., see listing, 20.38%.

TV Stations:
California: KNSD-DT San Diego.
Texas: KXAS-DT Fort Worth.
LPTV Stations:
California: KNSD-LP La Jolla.

SUNBEAM TELEVISION CORP.
1401 79th St. Causeway
Miami, FL 33141
Phone: 305-751-6692
Officers:
Edmund Ansin, President
Robert Leider, Chief Executive & Operating Officer
Alice Jacobs, Vice President, News
Roger Metcalf, Chief Financial Officer

Branch Office:
1020 S. Andrews Ave.
Fort Lauderdale, FLPhone: 954-463-2291
Ownership: Edmund Ansin, Principal.
TV Stations:
Florida: WSVN-DT Miami.
Massachusetts: WHDH-DT Boston; WLVI-DT Cambridge.

SUNBELT COMMUNICATIONS CO.
1500 Foremaster Lane
Las Vegas, NV 89101
Phone: 702-657-3423
Fax: 702-657-3423
Officers:
James E. Rogers, Chairman & Chief Executive Officer
Beverly Rogers, Vice Chairman & Executive Officer
Ralph Toddre, President & Chief Operating Officer
Bill Fouch, Executive Vice President
Shelley Goings, Secretary
Scott Mattox, Treasurer
JoAnn Haneman, Assistant Secretary
Ownership: James E. Rogers, Trustee of the James E. Rogers Trust, 95.22%; Beverly Rogers, Trustee of the Beverly Rogers Trust, 2.66%; James E. Rogers, Trustee for the Children of Elizabeth Ruybalid, 2.12%.
Represented (legal): Luvaas Cobb PC.
TV Stations:
Arizona: KYMA-DT Yuma.
Idaho: KPVI-DT Pocatello; KXTF-DT Twin Falls.
Montana: KBBJ-DT Havre; KTVH-DT Helena; KBAO-DT Lewistown.
Nevada: KENV-DT Elko; KVBC-DT Las Vegas; KRNV-DT Reno; KWNV-DT Winnemucca.
Wyoming: KCWY-DT Casper; KCWY-DT Casper; KJWY-DT Jackson.
LPTV Stations:
California: K33CN South Lake Tahoe; K56BW Tahoe City.
Idaho: K07UL Burley; K39GV Burley, etc.; K08KV Jerome; K04NO Paul; K02NO Rupert.
Montana: KBGF-LP Great Falls.
Nevada: K06KD Austin; K52DN Carson City; K16GK Ely; K58BC Ely, etc.; K57BU Eureka; K13QV Fallon; K40CQ Laughlin; K52AC Mercury & Nevada Test Site; K50CM North Shore Lake Tahoe; K44AA Pahrump.
Wyoming: KCHY-LP Cheyenne; K14LK Laramie; KHDE-LP Laramie; KSWY-LP Sheridan.

SUNBELT TELEVISION INC.
Box 1468
Victorville, CA 92393-1468
Phone: 760-241-6464
Officer:
Peter L. White, President

Ownership: TVPlus LLC; TVPLLC ownership.; Arthur Liu, Pres. & Chief Exec. Officer, 80%; LATV Partners LLC, 20%; LATVPLLC ownership.; Lynn Welshman, 73.5%; BC Advisory LLC, 10%; Mertin Genauer, 7%; PMJ LLC, 7%; LATVPLLC ownership.; Lynn Welshman, V.P., 73.5%; Jim McPhetridge III, 2.5%; BCALLC ownership.; Hiroshi Yoshida; PMJLLC ownership.; Paul Libovitz.

Represented (legal): Wilkinson Barker Knauer LLP.

TV Stations:

California: KHIZ-DT Barstow.

SARKES TARZIAN INC.
Box 62
205 N College Ave
Bloomington, IN 47402
Phone: 812-332-7251
Officers:

Thomas Tarzian, Chairman

Thomas Tolar, Executive Vice President, TV

Geoffrey Vargo, Executive Vice President, Radio

Valerie Carney, Senior Vice President & General Counsel

Robert Davis, Senior Vice President, Financial & Accounting

Ownership: Thomas Tarzian, 63.3%; Mary Tarzian, Estate, 33.5%; U. of LaVerne & others, 3.2%.

Represented (legal): Leventhal, Senter & Lerman PLLC.

TV Stations:

Nevada: KTVN-DT Reno.
Tennessee: WRCB Chattanooga.

LPTV Stations:

California: K40JV-D Stateline, etc.; K43DB Stateline, etc..
Nevada: K06HT Ely; K29BN Silver Springs.

Radio Stations:

Indiana: WGCL (AM), WTTS (FM) Bloomington; WAJI (FM), WLDE (FM) Fort Wayne

TCM MEDIA ASSOCIATES LLC
5880 Midnight Pass Rd.
Suite 701
Siesta Key, FL 34242
Phone: 941-312-0214
Officer:

Anthony J. Malara III, Vice President & Secretary

Ownership: Estate of Anthony C. Malara, Anthony J. Malara Personal Representative, 70%; Anthony J. Malara III, 10%; Elizabeth Malara Hamilton, 10%; Margaret Malara Hamilton, 10%. Anthony J. Malara III is also principal of White Knight Holdings Inc., see listing.

Represented (legal): WolfBlock.

TV Stations:

Indiana: WPTA-DT Fort Wayne.
Minnesota: KDLH-DT Duluth.

LPTV Stations:

Minnesota: K59BQ Deer River; K63BI Grand Marais.

TCT OF MICHIGAN INC.
PO Box 1010
Marion, IL 62959-1010
Phone: 618-997-9333
Fax: 618-997-1859
E-mail: cmmay@maylawoffices.com
Officers:

Garth W. Coonce, President

Christina M. Coonce, Vice President

Michael J. Daly, Secretary

Charles Payne, Treasurer

Ownership: Non-profit organization--Marion, IL; Garth W. Coonce; Christina M. Coonce; Charles Payne; Victoria Clark, 25%. votes each. Garth & Christina Coonce, Payne & Clark are also principals of Faith Broadcasting Network Inc., Radiant Life Ministries Inc. & Tri-State Christian TV Inc., see listings.

Represented (legal): Colby M. May.

TV Stations:

Michigan: WTLJ-DT Muskegon; WAQP-DT Saginaw.

LPTV Stations:

Michigan: WDWO-CA Detroit; W26BX Kalamazoo.

TELEADORACION CHRISTIAN NETWORK INC.
Levitown Station
Box 50615
Toa Baja, PR 00950
Phone: 787-795-8113

Ownership: Jesus Velez Rivera, Pres.; Dorcas Candelaria Martinez; Wilfredo Lopez, 33.%. votes each. Formerly Iglesia Christiana Amor y Verdad Inc.

Represented (legal): Fletcher, Heald & Hildreth PLC.

TV Stations:

Puerto Rico: WDWL-DT Bayamon.

TEXAS TELEVISION INC.
5002 S Padre Island Dr
Corpus Christi, TX 78466-6669
Phone: 361-986-8300
Fax: 361-986-8411
Officers:

Michael D. McKinnon, Chairman & President

James A. Gillece, Vice President, Secretary-Treasurer

Mark McKinnon, Vice President

Michael Dean McKinnon, Vice President

Ownership: Michael D. McKinnon, Chmn. & Pres., 66.26%; C. Dan McKinnon, Dir., 17.48%; Mark Daniel McKinnon, V.P., 8.13%; Michael Dean McKinnon, V.P., 8.13%. McKinnons have interest in Channel 3 of Corpus Christi Inc., see listing.

Represented (legal): Wiley Rein LLP.

TV Stations:

California: KUSI-DT San Diego.
Texas: KBMT-DT Beaumont.

THOMAS BROADCASTING CO.
Box 3001
Oak Hill, WV 25901
Phone: 304-469-3361
Fax: 304-465-1420
Officers:

Helen Thomas, Chairman

Robert R. Thomas III, Chief Executive Officer

Ownership: Helen G Thomas, 42.7%; Robert R Thomas III, 11.4%; Helen L Thomas, 11.4%; John G Thomas, 11.4%; Barbara L. T Canterbury, 11.4%; Sarah A Thomas, 11.4%.

Represented (legal): Fletcher, Heald & Hildreth PLC.

TV Stations:

West Virginia: WOAY-DT Oak Hill.

TIME WARNER INC.
75 Rockefeller Plaza
New York, NY 10019
Phone: 212-484-8000
Officers:

Richard D. Parsons, Chairman

Jeff Bewkes, President & Chief Executive Officer

John Martin, Executive Vice President & Chief Financial Officer

Tommy Harris, Executive Vice President, AOL-TW Interactive Video

Carol Melton, Executive Vice President, Global Public Policy

Timothy A. Boggs, Senior Vice President

Pascal Desroches, Senior Vice President & Controller

James Burton, Senior Vice President, Mergers & Acquisitions

Edward Ruggiero, Senior Vice President & Treasurer

Douglas Shapiro, Senior Vice President, Investor Relations

Ownership: Publicly traded..

TV Stations:

Georgia: WPCH-DT Atlanta.

Other Holdings:

Cable: See Time Warner Cable in Cable System Ownership

Cable Channel: n-tv (49%) 24-hour German language news channel in Berlin.

Motion picture holdings: Towani Corp. (33.3%) Japanese movie production & distribution company..

TRANS AMERICA BROADCASTING CORP.
6803 West Blvd.
Inglewood, CA 90302
Phone: 213-678-3731
Fax: 213-678-9696
Officers:

Gerardo Borrego, President

Charles P. William, Vice President

Ownership: A. J. Williams T.A.B. 1997 Trust, 39.9%. votes, 39.9 assets, Clair Reis Benezra trustee; Elizabeth Williams Marital Trust, 39.9%. votes, 16.7 assets, Clair Reis Benezra trustee; Jon Marc Reeder, 20.1%. votes, 20.1 assets; Charles P. Williams, V.P., 6.2%. assets; Stephanie Messina, 5.9%. assets; Kathleen Serrano, 5.6%. assets; Gerardo Borrego, Pres., 2%. assets.

Represented (legal): Miller & Neely PC.

TV Stations:

California: KAIL-DT Fresno.

Radio Stations:

California: KTYM (AM) Inglewood

TRIBUNE BROADCASTING CO., DEBTOR-IN-POSSESSION
435 N. Michigan Ave.
No. 1800
Chicago, IL 60611
Phone: 312-222-3333
Fax: 312-222-5981
Officers:

Sam Zell, Chairman & Chief Executive Officer

Ed Wilson, President, Tribune Broadcast Group

Chandler Bigelow, Chief Financial Officer

Randy Michaels, Chief Operating Officer

Steve Gable, Executive Vice President & Chief Technology Officer

Ray Schonbak, Executive Vice President, Fox Affiliates

Gerald A. Spector, Executive Vice President & Chief Administrative Officer

Steve Charlier, Senior Vice President, News & Operations

Sean Compton, Senior Vice President, Programming & Entertainment

David Eldersveld, Senior Vice President, Deputy Counsel & Corporate Secretary

Hank Hundemer, Senior Vice President, Engineering

Dan Kazan, Senior Vice President, Development

Naomi Sachs, Senior Vice President, Strategy

Ownership: Tribune Co.; TC ownership.; Tribune Employee Stock Ownership Plan, privately held. Sam Zell, through EGI-TRB, holds a warrant to acquire up to 40% of company. Tribune Co. filed December 8, 2008 seeking relief under Chapter 11 of the Bankruptcy Code.

Represented (legal): Dow Lohnes PLLC.

TV Stations:

California: KTLA-DT Los Angeles; KTXL-DT Sacramento; KSWB-DT San Diego.
Colorado: KWGN-DT Denver.
Connecticut: WTIC-DT Hartford; WTXX-DT Waterbury.
District of Columbia: WDCW-DT Washington.
Florida: WSFL-DT Miami.
Illinois: WGN-DT Chicago.
Indiana: WTTV-DT Bloomington; WXIN-DT Indianapolis; WTTK-DT Kokomo.
Louisiana: WGNO-DT New Orleans; WNOL-DT New Orleans.
Michigan: WXMI-DT Grand Rapids.
Missouri: KPLR-DT St. Louis.
New York: WPIX-DT New York.
Oregon: KRCW-DT Salem.
Pennsylvania: WPHL-DT Philadelphia; WPMT-DT York.
Texas: KDAF-DT Dallas; KIAH-DT Houston.
Washington: KMYQ-DT Seattle; KCPQ-DT Tacoma.

LPTV Stations:

Michigan: W42CB Hesperia; W52DB Muskegon.
Oregon: K24DX Pendleton; K20ES Pendleton, etc.; KRCW-LP Portland.
Pennsylvania: W51CY Chambersburg.
Washington: K25CG Aberdeen; K25CH Centralia; K42CM Centralia, etc.; K64ES Chelan; K54DX Ellensburg-Kittitas; K29ED Everett.

Newspapers:

California: Los Angeles Times
Connecticut: The Hartford Courant
Florida: South Florida Sun-Sentinel (Fort Lauderdale), Orlando Sentinel
Illinois: Chicago Tribune, RedEye (Chicago)
Maryland: The Sun (Baltimore)
New York: amNewYork (New York City), 3% of Newsday (Long Island & New York City)
Pennsylvania: The Morning Call (Allentown, Bethlehem, Lehigh Valley)
Virginia: Daily Press (Hampton Roads)

Radio Stations:

Illinois: WGN (AM) Chicago

Other Holdings:

Features syndicator: Tribune Media Services Inc.
Magazine: Williamsburg Magazine; Chicago Magazine
Professional sports team: Chicago Cubs
Program source: ChicagoLand Television News; 29% of TV Food Network; 22.25% of WB TV Network; Tribune Entertainment.

TRINITY BROADCASTING NETWORK INC.
2442 Michelle Dr.
Tustin, CA 92780
Phone: 714-832-2950
Fax: 714-730-0661
Web site: www.tbn.org
Officers:

Paul F. Crouch Sr., President

Janice W. Crouch, Vice President

W. Ben Miller, Vice President & Engineering Director

Norman G. Juggert, Secretary-Treasurer

Branch Office:
Cable Headquarters
2900 W. Airport Freeway
Irving, TX 75062
Phone: 214-313-1333

Ownership: Janice W. Crouch; Matthew W. Crouch; Paul F. Crouch Jr.; Dr. Paul F. Crouch Sr., Directors, 25%. votes each. Non-profit organization.

Represented (legal): Colby M. May.
TV Stations:
Alabama: WTJP-DT Gadsden; WMPV-DT Mobile; WMCF-DT Montgomery.
Arizona: KPAZ-DT Phoenix.
California: KTBN-DT Santa Ana.
Colorado: KPJR-DT Greeley.
Florida: WHLV-DT Cocoa; WHFT-DT Miami.
Georgia: WELF-DT Dalton; WHSG-DT Monroe.
Hawaii: KAAH-DT Honolulu.
Illinois: WWTO-DT La Salle.
Indiana: WCLJ-DT Bloomington; WKOI-DT Richmond.
Mississippi: WBUY-DT Holly Springs.
Missouri: KTAJ-DT St. Joseph.
New Jersey: WGTW-DT Burlington.
New Mexico: KNAT-DT Albuquerque.
New York: WTBY-DT Poughkeepsie.
Ohio: WDLI-DT Canton; WSFJ-DT Newark.
Oklahoma: KDOR-DT Bartlesville; KTBO-DT Oklahoma City.
Oregon: KNMT-DT Portland.
Tennessee: WPGD-DT Hendersonville.
Texas: KDTX-DT Dallas.
Washington: KTBW-DT Tacoma.
Wisconsin: WWRS-DT Mayville.

LPTV Stations:
Alabama: W46DK Birmingham; W33CM Decatur; W41BN Dothan; W30BD Eufaula; W57BV Florence; W67CO Huntsville; W25DR Jasper; W27CV Scottsboro; W24CK Selma; W46BU Tuscaloosa.
Arizona: K51IO Bullhead City; K41ER Globe & Miami; K51HV Prescott & Cottonwood; K38CX Shonto; K07YX Tucson; K57BD Tucson, etc..
Arkansas: K15FW Batesville; K42BS Fayetteville; K16ER Fort Smith; K23GT Hot Springs; K42GX Jonesboro; K34FH Little Rock; K41HC Mountain Home; K27FC Paragould.
California: K21FP Bakersfield; K56DZ Fresno; K49EO Modesto; K40ID Palm Springs; K15CO Porterville; K50GP Redding; K22FR Sacramento; K45HC Sacramento; K45DU Ventura.
Colorado: K48FW Denver; K57BT Denver; K66FB Denver; K25FZ Grand Junction; K48CG Loveland.
Delaware: W14CM Dover; W40AZ Wilmington.
Florida: W16CJ Naples; W34DH Panama City; W17CK Port Charlotte; W48CN Sarasota; W51DY Sebring; W36CO St. Petersburg; W56EB Tampa.
Georgia: W34CZ Albany; W58CZ Augusta; W33AL Brunswick; W50DA Macon; W49DE Marietta; W57CT Savannah; W48BH Statesboro; W38CM Thomasville; W33BX Tifton; W25CP Valdosta; W14CQ Vidalia; W45CU Waycross.
Hawaii: K34HC Hilo; K38HU Kailua-Kona.
Idaho: K47BE Boise; K53FF Coeur d'Alene; K26EW Idaho Falls; K27GO Lewiston; K58GL Lewiston; K25EV Twin Falls.
Illinois: W64CQ Arlington Heights; W51CT Bloomington; W34DL Champaign; W29BG Decatur; W57DN Elgin; W51DT Galesburg; W40BY Palatine; W50DD Peoria; W25CL Rockford; W19CX Sterling-Dixon.
Indiana: W18CF Elkhart; W38BK Evansville; W51DU Lafayette; W43BV Terre Haute.
Iowa: K17ET Cedar Rapids; K61HD Davenport; K42HI Muscatine; K42AM Ottumwa; K44FK Waterloo.
Kansas: K43HN Dodge City; K52GZ Emporia; K39FW Garden City; K50GO Independence; K25DS Junction City; K31BW Manhattan; K33HZ Pittsburg; K15CN Salina; K33IC Topeka; K28JB Wichita.
Kentucky: W39CJ Elizabethtown; W22CH Hopkinsville.
Louisiana: K45IY Alexandria; K48IT Baton Rouge; K51EC Lake Charles; K45DI Mermentau; K45IM Monroe; K19FR New Iberia; K28IL New Orleans; K39JV Opelousas; K31HO Shreveport.

Maine: W36CK Bangor; W27CE Dover & Foxcroft; W21BH Machias; W34CN Medway; W32CA Portland; W51AG Presque Isle.
Maryland: W43BP Cresaptown.
Michigan: W18BT Alpena; W66BV Detroit; W20BZ Escanaba; W25CZ Grand Rapids; W27CQ Houghton; W17CS Marquette.
Minnesota: K40JT Albert Lea; K42FH Bemidji; K58CM Duluth; K25IA Minneapolis; K56HW Rochester; K19BG St. Cloud; K64FY Winona.
Mississippi: W56DY Cleveland; W25AD Columbus; W42CY Greenville; W30BY Grenada; W36AC McComb; W47CG Meridian; W27CX Natchez; W51CU Pascagoula.
Missouri: K56AU Columbia; K41OI Jefferson City; K39CP Poplar Bluff; K16FE Rolla; K41FQ Springfield; K47LH Springfield; K22HG St. Charles; K33GU St. Louis.
Montana: K31IA Great Falls; K41CX Helena; K26DD Kalispell; K42EO Missoula.
Nebraska: K29GL Lincoln; K21HS Norfolk; K26CV Ogallala.
Nevada: K19CU Carson City; K41IO Las Vegas.
New Jersey: W45CP Atlantic City.
New Mexico: K56IU Alamogordo; K36GD Carlsbad; K14MJ Farmington; K18CT Raton; K50IA Roswell.
New York: W52DF Albany; W26BS Binghamton; W59DG Elmira; W47CM Glens Falls; W20BT Ithaca; W10BH Jamestown; W30BA Massena; W30BW Olean; W26CP Potsdam; W38CY Syracuse; W51CV Utica.
North Carolina: W50CZ Asheville; W16CF Charlotte; W38CN Charlotte; W45CO Fayetteville; W63CW Goldsboro; W44CN Greenville; W35CC Lumberton; W64CN Raleigh; W45CN Rocky Mount; W21CI Statesville; W51CW-D Wilmington.
North Dakota: K46DY Bismarck; K28EP Dickinson; K35HO Fargo; K49FF Grand Forks; K21GQ Minot; K40DE Williston.
Ohio: W63CZ Cambridge; W36DG Cincinnati; W23BZ Columbus; W51BI Kirtland; W32AR Lexington; W20CL Springfield; W22CO Toledo; W52DS Youngstown; W16BT Zanesville.
Oklahoma: K44BQ Ardmore; K49GC Lawton; K25GJ Muskogee; K30IX Tahlequah.
Oregon: K33AG Bend; K33AO Coos Bay; K36HL Grants Pass; K58BG Klamath Falls; K21BC Lakeview; K49FV Roseburg.
Pennsylvania: W48CH Erie; W52BO Meadville; W65CG Pittsburgh; W26CD Scranton; W39BT Williamsport.
South Carolina: W50CL Anderson; W19CH Beaufort; W20CN Charleston; W50DX Columbia; W22CJ Jacksonville; W34CQ Myrtle Beach; W45DE Orangeburg.
South Dakota: K35FJ Aberdeen; K38CQ Huron; K43GX Madison; K33CO Rapid City; K56GF Sioux Falls; K31DP Yankton.
Tennessee: W49CQ Cookeville; W35AH Jackson; W46DC Knoxville; W61DG Morristown; W48DF Nashville.
Texas: K51CK Abilene; K25GI Amarillo; K34FM Austin; K26AP Brownwood; K47ED College Station; K57FC Corpus Christi; K46DL Kingsville; K44HH Lubbock; K17BP Palestine; K42DA Paris; K44FJ San Angelo; K20BW San Antonio; K45FJ San Antonio; K58GN Seminole; K30EA Texarkana; K15BV Uvalde; K43DV Victoria; K26DL Wichita Falls.
Utah: K41JJ Ogden; K18FJ Salt Lake City; K67HK St. George; K39AK Vernal.
Vermont: W16AL Burlington.
Virginia: W18BS Hampton; W40BM Lynchburg; W39CO Richmond; W49AP Roanoke; W24OI Virginia Beach.
Washington: K32GS Spokane; K34EM Wenatchee.
West Virginia: W31CA Charleston; W44CF Clarksburg; W36CR Huntington; W45BW Parkersburg.
Wisconsin: W49CB Green Bay; W65EE Janesville; W38CT Madison; W17CF Ripon; W36DH Waupaca.

Wyoming: K33GI Casper; K35CN Green River.

TRI-STATE CHRISTIAN TV INC.

PO Box 1010
Marion, IL 62959-1010
Phone: 618-997-9333
Fax: 618-997-1859
E-mail: cmmay@maylawoffices.com
Officers:
Garth W. Coonce, President
Christina M. Coonce, Vice President
Michael J. Daly, Secretary
Charles Payne, Treasurer
Victoria Clark, Assistant Secretary
Ownership: Non-profit organization--Marion, IL.; Garth W. Coonce, Christina M. Coonce; Victoria Clark; Charles Payne, 25%. votes each. Garth & Christina Coonce, Payne & Clark are also principals of Faith Broadcasting Network Inc., Radiant Life Ministries Inc. & TCT of Michigan Inc., see listings.
Represented (legal): Colby M. May.
TV Stations:
Illinois: WTCT-DT Marion.
Indiana: WINM-DT Angola.

LPTV Stations:
Indiana: W38EA-D Fort Wayne.
Kentucky: W54AE Paducah.
Michigan: W27CN Lansing.
Missouri: KCGI-CA Cape Girardeau.
New York: W42CO Rochester.
Tennessee: WDYR-CA Dyersburg.
Virginia: W18BG Danville.

TUCKER BROADCASTING OF TRAVERSE CITY INC.

9434 N Sunset Ridge
Fountain Hills, AZ 85268
Phone: 480-836-2181
E-mail: bentucker13@cox.net
Ownership: Tucker Media and Management Consulting LLC; TMMCLLC ownership:; Benjamin W. Tucker.
Represented (legal): Pillsbury Winthrop Shaw Pittman LLP.
TV Stations:
Michigan: WGTQ-DT Sault Ste. Marie; WGTU-DT Traverse City.

RONALD ULLOA

11322 Chalon Rd.
Los Angeles, CA 90049
Phone: 310-575-1220
TV Stations:
California: KVMD-DT Twentynine Palms.

UNITED COMMUNICATIONS CORP.

715 58th St.
Kenosha, WI 53141
Phone: 262-657-1000
E-mail: wwny@wwnytv.net
Officers:
Howard J. Brown, President & Chief Executive Officer
Eugene W. Schulte, Senior Vice President & Secretary-Treasurer
Kenneth L. Dowdell, Vice President
Ronald J. Montemurro, Vice President
Ownership: Howard J Brown, 36.05%; Elizabeth K Brown, 9.55%; Eugene W Schulte, 4.11%; other members of the Brown & Schulte families.
TV Stations:
Minnesota: KEYC-DT Mankato.
New York: WWNY-DT Carthage.
LPTV Stations:
Minnesota: K19CA St. James.
New York: WNYF-LP Massena; WNYF-CA Watertown.

Newspapers:
Massachusetts: Attleboro Sun Chronicle
Wisconsin: Kenosha News

UNIVISION COMMUNICATIONS INC.

5999 Center Dr
Ste 4083
Los Angeles, CA 90045
Phone: 310-349-3600
Officers:
Joe Uva, Chief Executive Officer
Ray Rodriguez, President & Chief Operating Officer
Joanne Lynch, President, TV Stations Group
Andrew W. Hobson, Senior Executive Vice President, Chief Strategic & Financial Officer
C. Douglas Kranwinkle, Executive Vice President & General Counsel
Peter H. Lori, Assistant Treasurer & Assistant Secretary

Branch Office:
605 3rd Ave.
12th Floor
New York, NY 10158
Phone: 212-455-5200
Ownership: Broadcast Media Partners Holdings Inc.; BMPHI ownership:; Broadcasting Media Partners Inc.. 100 % votes, 80% assets; Broadcasting Media Partners Shareholders, 20%. assets; BMPI ownership:; SCG Investments II LLC, 9.73%. votes, 7.55% assets; TPG Umbrella V LP, 9.44%. votes, 7.68% assets; Thomas H. Lee Equity Fund VI LP, 7.85%. votes, 6.38% assets; Madison Dearborn Capital Partners V-A LP, 7.84%. votes, 6.38% assets; Providence Equity Partners V (Umbrella US) LP, 7.3%. votes, 5.94% assets; TPG Umbrella International V LP, 7.09%. votes, 5.77% assets; Madison Dearborn Capital Partners IV LP, 7.05%. votes, 5.74% assets; THL Equity Fund VI Investors (Univision) LP, 6.08%. votes, 4.95% assets; TPG Umbrella IV LP, 6.03%. votes, 4.91% assets; SCGIILLC ownership:; HSAC Investments LP; HSACILP ownership:; Haim Saban, 65.52%; Cheryl Saban, 34.48; TPGUVLP, TPGUIVLP & TPGUIVLP ownership:; David Bonderman, Chmn. & Pres.; James Coulter, V.P.; THLEFVILP & THLEFVI (U)LP ownership:; Thomas H. Lee Advisors LLC; THLALLC ownership:; Todd M. Abbrecht; Charles A. Brizius; Anthony J. DiNovi; Thomas M. Hagerty; Scott L. Jaeckel; Seth W. Lawry; Soren L. Oberg; Scott A. Schoen; Scott M. Sperling; Kent R. Weldon, 10%. votes, each; MDCPV-ALP & MDCPIVLP ownership:; Madison Dearborn Partners, Gen. Partner; MDP ownership:; John A. Canning Jr., Chmn. & Chief Exec. Officer; Paul J. Finnegan, Co-Pres.; Samuel M. Mencoff, Co-Pres.; PEPV (UUS)LP ownership:; Providence Equity Partners V LLC, Gen. Partner; PEPVLLC ownership:; Glenn M. Creamer; Jonathan M. Nelsen; Paul J. Salem, Managing Members.
Represented (legal): Pillsbury Winthrop Shaw Pittman LLP.
TV Stations:
Arizona: KFTU-DT Douglas; KFPH-DT Flagstaff; KUVE-DT Green Valley; KTVW-DT Phoenix.
California: KUVI-DT Bakersfield; KFTV-DT Hanford; KMEX-DT Los Angeles; KUVS-DT Modesto; KFTR-DT Ontario; KTFF-DT Porterville; KDTV-DT San Francisco; KTFK-DT Stockton; KFSF-DT Vallejo.
Florida: WAMI-DT Hollywood; WOTF-DT Melbourne; WLTV-DT Miami; WFTT-DT Tampa.
Georgia: WUVG-DT Athens.
Illinois: WXFT-DT Aurora; WGBO-DT Joliet.
Massachusetts: WUTF-DT Marlborough.
New Jersey: WFUT-DT Newark; WXTV-DT Paterson; WUVP-DT Vineland.
New Mexico: KTFQ-DT Albuquerque.
New York: WFTY-DT Smithtown.

North Carolina: WUVC-DT Fayetteville.
Ohio: WQHS-DT Cleveland.
Puerto Rico: WLII-DT Caguas; WSTE-DT Ponce; WSUR-DT Ponce.
Texas: KFTH-DT Alvin; KNIC-DT Blanco; KUVN-DT Garland; KSTR-DT Irving; KAKW-DT Killeen; KXLN-DT Rosenberg; KWEX-DT San Antonio.
Utah: KUTH-DT Provo.
Virginia: WFDC-DT Arlington.
LPTV Stations:
Arizona: K16FB Globe; KDOS-LP Globe; KFPH-CA Phoenix; KTVW-CA Phoenix; K21GC Safford; KZOL-LP Safford; K48GX Tucson; KFTU-CA Tucson; KUVE-CA Tucson.
California: KABE-LP Bakersfield; KBTF-CA Bakersfield; KTFB-CA Bakersfield; KTFF-LP Fresno; KEXT-CA Modesto; KEZT-CA Sacramento; K35ER Santa Maria; KDTV-CA Santa Rosa.
North Carolina: WTNC-LP Durham.
Pennsylvania: WFPA-CA Philadelphia; WXTV-LP Philadelphia.
Texas: KTFO-CA Austin; K45DX Floresville; KUVN-CA Fort Worth; KFTO-CA San Antonio; KNIC-CA San Antonio.
Radio Stations:
Arizona: KKMR (FM) Arizona City, KQMR (FM) Globe, KHOT (FM) Paradise Valley, KOMR (FM) Sun City, KHOV (FM) Wickenburg
California: KOND (FM) Clovis; KSCA (FM) Glendale; KRDA (FM) Hanford; KRCD (FM) Inglewood; KLVE (FM); KTNQ (FM) Los Angeles; KLLE (FM) North Fork; KVVF (FM) Santa Clara; KSQL (FM) Santa Cruz; KLNV (FM), KLQV (FM) San Diego; KSOL (FM) S
Florida: WRTO-FM Goulds; WAMR-FM, WAQI (AM), WQBA (AM) Miami
Illinois: WRTO (AM) Chicago, WPPN (FM) Des Plaines, WOJO (FM) Evanston, WVIV-FM Highland Park, WVIX (FM) Joliet
Nevada: KRGT (FM) Indian Springs, KISF (FM) Las Vegas, KLSQ (AM) Whitney
New Jersey: WCAA (AM) Newark
New Mexico: KKRG (FM) Albuquerque; KIOT (FM) Los Lunas; KQBT (FM) Rio Rancho; KJFA (FM), KKSS (FM) Sante Fe
New York: WQBU-FM Garden City, WADO (AM) New York
Puerto Rico: WYEL (AM) Mayaguez, WUKQ-AM-FM Ponce, WKAQ-AM-FM San Juan
Texas: KDXX (FM) Benbrook, KPTI (FM) Crystal Beach, KFZO (FM) Denton; KAMA (AM), KBNA (FM), KQBU (AM) El Paso; KFLC (AM), KLNO (FM) Fort Worth; KOVE-FM Galveston; KINV (FM) Georgetown; KBTQ (FM), KGBT-AM-FM Harlingen; KLAT (AM),

VCY AMERICA INC.
3434 W. Kilbourn Ave.
Milwaukee, WI 53208
Phone: 414-935-3000
Fax: 414-935-3015
Officers:
Dr. Randall Melchert, President
Victor C. Eliason, Vice President
Walter Lecocq, Secretary-Treasurer
Ownership: Non-profit organization.
TV Stations:
Wisconsin: WVCY-DT Milwaukee.
LPTV Stations:
Wisconsin: W04CW Tigerton, etc..
Radio Stations:
Kansas: KVCY (FM) Fort Scott, KCVS (FM) Salina
Michigan: WVCM (FM) Iron Mountain
Ohio: WJIC (FM) Zanesville
South Dakota: KVCF (FM) Freeman, KVFL (FM) Pierre
Wisconsin: WVCF (FM) Eau Claire, WVFL (FM) Fond du Lac, WVCY (AM) Oshkosh, WVCX (FM) Tomah, WVRN (FM) Wittenberg

VENTURE TECHNOLOGIES GROUP LLC
5670 Wilshire Blvd
Ste 1300
Los Angeles, CA 90036
Phone: 323-965-5400
Fax: 323-965-5411
Officer:
Lawrence J. Rogow, Manager
Ownership: Lawrence H Rogow, 50%; Garry A Spire, 35%; Paul H Koplin, 15%.
Represented (legal): Fleischman & Harding LLP.
TV Stations:
California: KBBC-DT Bishop.
Illinois: WAOE-DT Peoria.
Massachusetts: WNYA-DT Pittsfield.
Michigan: WHTV-DT Jackson.
Washington: KBCB-DT Bellingham.
LPTV Stations:
Arizona: KWTA-LP Tucson.
California: KEBK-LP Bakersfield; KRMV-LP Banning; KRVD-LP Banning; KDBK-LP Caliente; KILA-LP Cherry Valley; KEFM-LP Chico; KSGO-LP Chico; KSCZ-LP Greenfield; KHTV-LP Inland Empire; KNET-CA Los Angeles; KNLA-LP Los Angeles; KSFV-CA Los Angeles; KMRZ-LP Moreno Valley; KFMD-LP Redding.
Colorado: K26HQ Estes Park; K39JT Estes Park; K42GS Estes Park.
Connecticut: WHCT-LP Hartford.
Illinois: WLFM-LP Chicago.
Indiana: W27CT Columbia.
Iowa: WBQD-LP Davenport; KSXC-LP South Sioux City.
New York: WNYA-CA Albany; W20CM Port Jervis; W26DB Port Jervis; W32DC Port Jervis; W34DI Port Jervis; W42CX Port Jervis; W46DQ Port Jervis; W52DW Port Jervis; W55DK Port Jervis; W59EA Port Jervis; WASA-LP Port Jervis.
Ohio: WXOX-LP Cleveland; WBTL-LP Toledo.
Pennsylvania: WBPA-LP Pittsburgh.
Texas: K38HP Lubbock; KFIQ-LP Lubbock; KFMP-LP Lubbock.
Washington: K38JH Bellingham.

WAITT BROADCASTING INC.
1650 Farnam St.
Omaha, NE 68102-2186
Phone: 402-346-6000
Officers:
Norman W. Waitt Jr., Chairman
Steven W. Seline, Vice Chairman
Michael J. Delich, President
Ownership: Norman W Waitt Jr..
TV Stations:
Iowa: KMEG-DT Sioux City.
LPTV Stations:
Iowa: K55FL Spencer; K40CO Storm Lake.
Nebraska: K35FM Norfolk.
Radio Stations:
Iowa: KQKQ-FM Council Bluffs
Nebraska: KYDZ (AM), KOZN (AM) Bellevue; KBLR-FM Blair; KOOO (AM) Lincoln; KKAR (AM) Omaha; KOIL (AM) Plattsmouth

FRANK WASHINGTON
5670 Wilshire Blvd.
Suite 1300
Los Angeles, CA 90036
Phone: 323-965-5400
TV Stations:
Michigan: WHTV-DT Jackson.
Washington: KBCB-DT Bellingham.

WATERMAN BROADCASTING CORP.
Box 7578
Fort Myers, FL 33911
Phone: 941-939-2020

Fax: 941-936-7771
Officers:
Bernard E. Waterman, President
Steven H. Pontius, Executive Vice President
Edith B. Waterman, Secretary-Treasurer
Ownership: Bernard E Waterman, 90%; Edith B Waterman, 10%.
Represented (legal): Cohn & Marks LLP.
TV Stations:
Florida: WBBH-DT Fort Myers.
Virginia: WVIR-DT Charlottesville.
LPTV Stations:
Virginia: W31CE Bridgewater et al.; W28BF Harrisonburg.

WBHQ COLUMBIA LLC
120-A Pontiac Business Center Dr.
Elgin, SC 29045
Phone: 803-419-6363
Fax: 803-419-6399
E-mail: srein@midlandswb4.com
Web site: www.wktctv.com
Ownership: Stefanie Rein, managing member; David Canfield, Joint Tenants, 8.18%. assets; 100% votes.
Represented (legal): Pillsbury Winthrop Shaw Pittman LLP.
TV Stations:
South Carolina: WKTC-DT Sumter.

WBKISLG LLC
2310 N Molter Rd
Ste 112
Liberty Lake, WA 99019
Phone: 502-348-1645
Officer:
Gregory W. Kunz, Manager
Ownership: National Television Investments LLC, 51.1%. voting interest; Big Hat LLC, 28.6%. voting interest; Sidney LLC, 18.7%. voting interest; Old Red Vines LLC, 1.5%. voting interest; NTI ownership:; Gregory W. Kunz Trust, 25.57%. voting interest; Enterprise Wagon Inc., 9.2%. voting interest; EWI ownership:; Gregory W. Kunz Trust; Deniis W. Brush & Anne K. Brush (Revocable Living) Trust; BHLLC ownership:; Gregory W Kunz; SLLC ownership:; William S Levine; ORVLLC ownership:; Dennis W Brush.
Represented (legal): Davis Wright Tremaine LLP.
TV Stations:
Kentucky: WBKI-DT Campbellsville.
LPTV Stations:
Kentucky: WBKI-CA Louisville.

WDBB-TV INC.
6120 W. Tropicana
A16 PMB-Suite 329
Las Vegas, NV 89103
Officer:
David Dubose, President
Ownership: H & P Communications Inc., 80%; David Dubose, 20%; H & PCI ownership:; Cecil Heftel, Co-Chmn., 50%; H. Carl Parmer, Co-Chmn. & Pres., 50%.
Represented (legal): Fletcher, Heald & Hildreth PLC.
TV Stations:
Alabama: WDBB-DT Bessemer.

WEIGEL BROADCASTING CO.
26 N Halsted St
Chicago, IL 60661
Phone: 312-705-2600
Fax: 312-705-2656
Officers:
Howard Shapiro, Chairman
Norman H. Shapiro, President & Secretary-Treasurer

Neal Sabin, Executive Vice President
William J. Lyall, Controller
Ownership: Howard Shapiro, 48%. votes; Norman H. Shapiro, 17%. votes; Fred Bishop, trustee, 29%. votes.
Represented (legal): Cohn & Marks LLP.
TV Stations:
Illinois: WCIU-DT Chicago.
Wisconsin: WDJT-DT Milwaukee; WBME-DT Racine.
LPTV Stations:
Illinois: WMEU-CA Chicago; WWME-CA Chicago; WWME-LD Chicago; WFBN-LP Rockford.
Indiana: WCWW-LD South Bend; WCWW-LP South Bend; WMYS-LD South Bend; WMYS-LP South Bend.
Wisconsin: WMLW-CA Milwaukee; WYTU-LD Milwaukee; WYTU-LP Milwaukee.

WHITE KNIGHT HOLDINGS INC.
9257 Bailey Ln
Fairfax, VA 22031-1903
Phone: 703-253-2027
Officer:
Anthony J. Malara III, President
Ownership: Malara Enterprises LLC; MELLC ownership:; Anthony J. Malara III. Malara is also principal of TCM Media Associates LLC, see listing.
Represented (legal): WolfBlock.
TV Stations:
Louisiana: WVLA-DT Baton Rouge; KSHV-DT Shreveport.
Texas: KFXK-DT Longview.
LPTV Stations:
Louisiana: KZUP-CA Baton Rouge.
Texas: KLPN-LP Longview; KFXL-LP Lufkin; KTPN-LP Tyler.

WILDERNESS COMMUNICATIONS LLC
3501 N.W. Evangeline Thruway
Carencro, LA 70520
Phone: 337-896-1600
Officers:
Paul J. Azar Jr., Co-Manager
Eddie Blanchard, Co-Manager
Charles Chatelain, Co-Manager
Ownership: Azar Family Holdings LLC, 44%. votes, 40% assets; Gulf Management LLC, 56%. votes, 60% assets; AFHLLC ownership:; Barbara Azar; Paul Azar Jr.. votes; 60% assets, jointly; Paul J. Azar III, 20%. assets; Susan Azar, 20%. assets; GMLLC ownership:; Charles Chatelain, 67.7%. votes, 34.2% assets; Eddie Blanchard, 32.7%. votes, 16.6% assets; Carolyn Chatelain, 16.4%. assets; Kerrie Chatelain, 16.4%. assets; Ann Maria Mouton, 16.4%. assets.
Represented (legal): Fletcher, Heald & Hildreth PLC.
TV Stations:
Louisiana: KBCA-DT Alexandria; KLWB-DT New Iberia.

E. ROGER WILLIAMS, TRUSTEE
114 Ferris Hill Rd
New Canaan, CT 06840
Phone: 203-972-6447
E-mail: pappastrustee@gmail.com
Represented (legal): Davis Wright Tremaine LLP.
TV Stations:
California: KTNC-DT Concord; KFRE-DT Sanger; KMPH-DT Visalia.
Iowa: KPTH-DT Sioux City.
Nebraska: KPTM-DT Omaha.
Nevada: KREN-DT Reno.
North Carolina: WCWG-DT Lexington.

Texas: KAZH-DT Baytown; KDBC-DT El Paso.
LPTV Stations:
California: KMPH-CA Merced-Mariposa; KREN-LP Susanville; KDSL-CA Ukiah.
Nebraska: KPTP-LP Norfolk; KKAZ-CA Omaha.
Nevada: KNNC-LP Battle Mountain; KRNS-CA Reno; KPMP-LP Winnemucca.
New Mexico: KKNJ-LP Alamogordo; KCWO-CA Silver City, etc..
Washington: KCWK-LP Yakima.

WINSTON BROADCASTING NETWORK INC.
Box 91660
Cleveland, OH 44101
Phone: 440-843-5555
Fax: 440-842-5597
Officers:
Lou Spangler, President
Anne Catherine Keith, Vice President
Ownership: Grace Cathedral.
Represented (legal): Dow Lohnes PLLC.
TV Stations:
Ohio: WBNX-DT Akron.

WLNY HOLDINGS INC.
270 S. Service Rd.
Suite 55
Melville, NY 11747
Phone: 631-777-8855
Fax: 631-777-8180
Officers:
Michael C. Pascucci, President
Marvin Chauvin, Chief Executive Officer
Christopher S. Pascucci, Vice President & Assistant Secretary
Ownership: Michael C. Pascucci; Jocelyn Pascucci, trustees, jointly, 44.57%; Christopher S. Pascucci, 26.81%; Michael A. Pascucci, 3.69%; Dawn Pascucci, 3.69%; Ralph P. Pascucci, 3.69%; Michael C. Pascucci, 0.72%.
Represented (legal): Cohn & Marks LLP.
TV Stations:
New York: WLNY-DT Riverhead.
LPTV Stations:
Connecticut: W27CD Stamford.
New Jersey: W54CZ Morristown.
New York: WLIG-LD Mineola.

WORD BROADCASTING NETWORK INC.
3701 Fern Valley Rd.
Louisville, KY 40219
Phone: 502-964-2121
Fax: 502-966-9692
Officers:
Robert W Rodgers, Chairman & President
Margaret E Rodgers, Vice President, Secretary & Treasurer
Ownership: Non-profit corp.-Louisville, KY.
Represented (legal): Womble, Carlyle, Sandridge & Rice.
TV Stations:
Kentucky: WBNA-DT Louisville.

WORD OF GOD FELLOWSHIP INC.
3901 Hwy 121 S
Bedford, TX 76021
Phone: 817-571-1229
Officers:
Marcus D. Lamb, President
Joni T. Lamb, Vice President
Ownership: Non-profit corp.--Colleyville, TX; Corrine Lamb, 20%; Jimmie F. Lamb, 20%; Joni T. Lamb, 20%; Marcus D. Lamb, 20%; John T. Calender, 20%.
Represented (legal): Koerner & Olender PC.

TV Stations:
Alabama: WDPM-DT Mobile.
Arkansas: KWOG-DT Springdale.
Illinois: WPXS-DT Mount Vernon.
Oklahoma: KOCM-DT Norman.
Tennessee: WMAK-DT Knoxville.
ETV Stations:
Colorado: KRMT-DT Denver.
LPTV Stations:
Alabama: WBUN-CA Birmingham.
Arizona: KPCE-LP Green Valley.
California: KPCD-LP Big Bear Lake; KSCD-LP Big Bear Lake; KDAS-LP Clarks Crossing; KACA-LP Modesto; KRJR-LP Sacramento; KDTS-LP Stockton.
Colorado: KDNF-LP Fort Collins.
District of Columbia: WDDN-LP Washington.
Florida: WSVT-CA Bradenton; WOCD-LP Dunnellon; WUJF-LP Maxville; WDTO-LP Orlando; WSLF-LP Port St. Lucie.
Georgia: WGGD-LP Cleveland; WDDA-LP Dalton; WCTD-LP Ducktown; WDTA-LP Fayetteville; WDMA-CA Macon.
Hawaii: KAUI-LP Wailuku.
Idaho: KQUP-LP Coeur d'Alene.
Kentucky: WBLU-LP Lexington.
Maine: WLLB-LP Portland.
Michigan: WUDT-CA Detroit; WUHQ-LP Grand Rapids.
Minnesota: WDMI-LP Minneapolis.
Mississippi: WJKO-LP Jackson.
Missouri: KDSI-CA Carthage; KCDN-LP Kansas City; KDTL-LP St. Louis; KUMO-LP St. Louis.
Nebraska: KOHA-LP Omaha.
Nevada: KLVD-LP Las Vegas.
New York: WDTB-LP Hamburg; WWBI-LP Plattsburgh.
North Carolina: WAEN-LP Asheville; WDMC-LP Charlotte; WACN-LP Raleigh; WWIW-LP Raleigh.
Ohio: WCDN-LP Cleveland; WCLL-CA Columbus.
Oklahoma: KDNT-LP Allen; KTZT-CA Tulsa.
Pennsylvania: WELL-LP Philadelphia.
South Carolina: WSQY-LP Spartanburg.
Tennessee: WJTD-LP Jackson; WDTT-LP Knoxville; WDNM-LP Memphis; WNTU-LP Nashville.
Texas: KDAX-LP Amarillo; KDCP-LP Corpus Christi; KADT-LP Killeen; KQVE-LP La Vernia; KDHU-LP Louise; KLOD-LP Lubbock; KPTD-LP Paris.
Utah: K45GX Salt Lake City; KUBX-LP Salt Lake City.
Virginia: W25CS Chesapeake; WDWA-LP Luray; WRID-LP Richmond.
Other Holdings:
Broadcast Holdings: Tri-State Family Broadcasting Inc., see listing.

WORLD BROADCASTING INC.
World Herald Square
Omaha, NE 68102-1138
Phone: 402-444-1000
Officers:
A. William Kernen, President
Terry Kroeger, Vice President
William E. Conley, Secretary-Treasurer
Ownership: Omaha World Herald Co.; OWHC ownership: John Gottschalk, Pres. & Chief Exec. Officer, Ames, IA, 14.9%; A. W Kernen, Sr. V.P. & Chief Financial Officer, 5.5%; Peter Kiewit Foundation, 18.9%; Others with less than 5% each.; PKF is divided between 5 Trustees. Omaha World Herald publishes newspapers in Stockton, CA; Kearney, Scottsbluff, North Platte, Lexington, Gering, Bellevue, Omaha & Papillon,.
TV Stations:
Nebraska: KFXL-TV Lincoln.

WQED MULTIMEDIA
4802 5th Ave.
Pittsburgh, PA 15213

Phone: 412-622-1300
Fax: 412-622-6413
Officers:
Herbert Bennett Conner, Chairman
George L. Miles Jr., President & Chief Executive Officer
Robert F. Petrilli, Vice President, Chief Operating Officer & Treasurer
Represented (legal): Cohen & Grigsby.
TV Stations:
Pennsylvania: WQEX-DT Pittsburgh.
ETV Stations:
Pennsylvania: WQED-DT Pittsburgh.
Radio Stations:
Pennsylvania: WQED-FM Johnstown, WQEJ-FM Pittsburgh
Other Holdings:
Magazine (Pittsburgh magazine).

WRNN-TV ASSOCIATES LP
800 Westchester Ave
Ste S640
Rye Brook, NY 10573
Phone: 914-417-2700
Officer:
Richard E. French Jr., President & Secretary of General Partner
Ownership: New Mass Media Inc., Gen. Partner, 1.5%; Hudson Valley Holdings LP, Ltd. Partner, 98.5%; NMMI ownership:; Richard E. French Jr., Pres. & Secy.; HVHLP ownership:; Sullivan & Booth Inc., Gen. Partner, 50.77%. Class A Interest; 99% Class B Interest; Richard E. French Jr., Ltd. Partner, 1%. Class B Interest; Maria Cristina French, Trustee, Richard E. French Jr. 2004 Descendants Trust, 18.78%. Class A Interest; Christian French, Ltd. Partner, 10.15%. Class A Interest; Mark French, Ltd. Partner, 10.15%. Class A Interest; Richard French III, Ltd. Partner, 10.15%. Class A Interest; SABI ownership:; Richard E. French Jr., Pres. & Secy., 39.72%. shareholder; Maria Cristina French, 39.72%. shareholder; David Ross, 11.54%. shareholder; Christian French, 3.01%. shareholder; Mark French, 3.01%. shareholder; Richard French III, 3.01%. shareholder.
TV Stations:
New York: WRNN-DT Kingston.
Pennsylvania: WTVE-DT Reading.
LPTV Stations:
New York: WRNN-LP Nyack.

YOUNG BROADCASTING INC., DEBTOR IN POSSESSION
PO Box 1800
c/o Brooks, Pierce, et al.
Raleigh, NC 27602
Phone: 919-839-0300
E-mail: invest@youngbroadcasting.com
Officers:
Vincent J. Young, Chairman & Chief Executive Officer
Deborah A McDermott, President
James A Morgan, Executive Vice President, Chief Financial Officer & Secretary
Daniel R Batchelor, Senior Vice President, Director of Sales
Chris Eisenhardt, Vice President, Assistant Secretary & Controller
Robert Petersen, Vice President, Business Development
Peter Grazioli, Vice President, Information Technology
Brian J Greif, Vice President, News
Janice E Cross, Assistant Secretary
Ownership: Publicly held; Adam Young; Vincent Young, Principals. Young Broadcasting Inc. filed for Chapter 11 bankruptcy February 13, 2009.

Represented (legal): Brooks, Pierce, McLendon, Humphrey & Leonard LLP.
TV Stations:
California: KRON-DT San Francisco.
Iowa: KWQC-DT Davenport.
Louisiana: KLFY-DT Lafayette.
Massachusetts: WCDC-DT Adams.
Michigan: WLNS-DT Lansing.
New York: WTEN-DT Albany.
South Dakota: KDLO-DT Florence; KCLO-DT Rapid City; KPLO-DT Reliance; KELO-DT Sioux Falls.
Tennessee: WATE-DT Knoxville; WKRN-DT Nashville.
Virginia: WRIC-DT Petersburg.
Wisconsin: WBAY-DT Green Bay.
LPTV Stations:
California: K25HI Santa Rosa.
New York: W04AE Herkimer.
South Dakota: K24DT Aberdeen; K57BX Lake Andes; K69DJ Philip, etc..
Other Holdings:
TV Station sales representative: Adam Young Inc..

DR. JOSEPH A. ZAVALETTA
603 E. St. Charles St.
Brownsville, TX 78520
Phone: 956-504-6699
Represented (legal): Skadden, Arps, Slate, Meagher & Flom LLP.
TV Stations:
Texas: KVAW-DT Eagle Pass.

ZGS BROADCASTING HOLDINGS INC.
2000 N. 14th St.
Suite 400
Arlington, VA 22201
Phone: 703-528-5656
E-mail: info@zgsgroup.com
Officers:
Peter Housman, President, Business & Corporate Affairs
Eduardo Zavala, President, Digital & Broadcast Operations

Branch Offices:
1650 Sand Lake Rd
Ste 215
Orlando, FL 32809
Phone: 407-888-2288
2700 W Martin Luther King
Ste 400
Tampa, FL 33607
Phone: 813-879-5757
Ownership: Eduardo Zavala, 12%. votes.
Represented (legal): Davis Wright Tremaine LLP.
TV Stations:
New Jersey: WWSI-DT Atlantic City.
New Mexico: KTDO-DT Las Cruces.
LPTV Stations:
Connecticut: WRDM-CA Hartford.
District of Columbia: WZDC-CA Washington.
Florida: WDYB-CA Daytona Beach; W50DW Gainesville; WKME-CA Kissimmee; WMVJ-CA Melbourne; WWDT-CA Naples; WTMO-CA Orlando; WWWF-LP Tallahassee; WRMD-CA Tampa.
Massachusetts: WTMU-LP Boston; WDMR-LP Springfield.
New Mexico: K48IK El Paso.
North Carolina: WZGS-CA Raleigh.
Rhode Island: WRIW-CA Providence.
Virginia: WZTD-LP Richmond.
Radio Stations:
Maryland: WILC (AM) Laurel.

Low Power Television & TV Translator Stations

As of October 1, 2009

Listing without notation indicates licensees. Solid box (■) preceding listing indicates Class A television service.

Alabama

■Alabaster—W15AZ, Ch. 15, Glen Iris Baptist Church School.

Technical Facilities: 100-w TPO, 6-kw ERP, 187-ft. above ground, 863-ft. above sea level, lat. 33° 14' 07", long. 86° 47' 07".

Transmitter: Double Oak Mountain, 2-mi. E of Alabaster.

Ownership: Glen Iris Baptist Church School.

Alexander City—WAXC-LP, Ch. 64, Venture Television LLC. Phones: 205-234-0426; 205-234-6464. Fax: 205-234-0088.

Studio: 1051 Tallapoosa St, Alexander City, AL 35010.

Technical Facilities: 12.2-kw ERP, 279-ft. above ground, 978-ft. above sea level, lat. 32° 56' 50", long. 85° 56' 31".

Transmitter: 1051 Tallapoosa St., Alexander City.

Ownership: Venture Television LLC.

Andalusia—W19BV, Ch. 19, Loflin Children's Trust-Four.

Technical Facilities: 126-w TPO, 1-kw ERP, 308-ft. above ground, 617-ft. above sea level, lat. 31° 20' 27", long. 86° 28' 02".

Transmitter: 1-mi. N of Andalusia.

Ownership: Loflin Children's Trust-One, Two & Four.

Andalusia—W36BQ, Ch. 36, Loflin Children's Trust-Four.

Technical Facilities: 126-w TPO, 1-kw ERP, 308-ft. above ground, 617-ft. above sea level, lat. 31° 20' 27", long. 86° 28' 02".

Transmitter: 1-mi. N of Andalusia.

Ownership: Loflin Children's Trust-One, Two & Four.

Andalusia—W57CC, Ch. 57, Loflin Children's Trust-Four.

Technical Facilities: 126-w TPO, 1-kw ERP, 308-ft. above ground, 617-ft. above sea level, lat. 31° 20' 27", long. 86° 28' 02".

Transmitter: 1-mi. N of Andalusia.

Ownership: Loflin Children's Trust-One, Two & Four.

Andalusia—W59CQ, Ch. 59, Loflin Children's Trust-Four.

Technical Facilities: 126-w TPO, 1-kw ERP, 308-ft. above ground, 617-ft. above sea level, lat. 31° 20' 27", long. 86° 28' 02".

Transmitter: 1-mi. N of Andalusia.

Ownership: Loflin Children's Trust-One, Two & Four.

Andalusia—W65CW, Ch. 65, David M. Loflin. Phone: 504-928-3574.

Technical Facilities: 126-w TPO, 1-kw ERP, 308-ft. above ground, 617-ft. above sea level, lat. 31° 20' 27", long. 86° 28' 02".

Transmitter: 1-mi. N of Andalusia.

Ownership: David M. Loflin.

Andalusia—WAAO-LP, Ch. 40, Three Notch Communications LLC. Phone: 301-986-4160.

Technical Facilities: 126-w TPO, 1-kw ERP, 308-ft. above ground, 617-ft. above sea level, lat. 31° 20' 27", long. 86° 28' 02".

Transmitter: 1-mi. N of Andalusia.

Began Operation: October 14, 1997.

Ownership: Three Notch Communications LLC.

Andalusia—WKNI-LP, Ch. 25, Silver Wings Broadcasting Inc. Phone: 334-427-9966.

Technical Facilities: 19.2-kw ERP, 296-ft. above ground, 627-ft. above sea level, lat. 31° 23' 04", long. 86° 28' 06".

Holds CP for change to 15-kw ERP, BDFCDTL-20070820AAU.

Ownership: Eddie Knight.

Anniston—W29AO, Ch. 29, WBRC License Subsidiary LLC. Phone: 334-206-1400.

Technical Facilities: 8.5-kw ERP, 200-ft. above ground, 2608-ft. above sea level, lat. 33° 29' 07", long. 85° 48' 33".

Ownership: Raycom Media Inc.

Ashville—W50BO, Ch. 50, Sanctuary Broadcasting Co. Inc. Phone: 256-362-6209.

Technical Facilities: 1000-w TPO, 24.6-kw ERP, 134-ft. above ground, 1253-ft. above sea level, lat. 33° 47' 51", long. 86° 12' 45".

Transmitter: Beaver Creek Mountain.

Began Operation: March 2, 1998.

Ownership: Sanctuary Broadcasting Co. Inc.

■Athens—WTZT-CA, Ch. 11, Jamie Cooper Television Inc. Phone: 256-533-1888.

Technical Facilities: 273-w TPO, 2-kw ERP, 190-ft. above ground, 879-ft. above sea level, lat. 34° 46' 58", long. 86° 55' 59".

Holds CP for change to 3-kw ERP, 480-ft. above ground, 1730-ft. above sea level, BPTVA-20030808AAD.

Transmitter: E of Interstate 65 on Hwy 72, Athens.

Ownership: Jamie Cooper Television Inc.

Personnel: Bill Shrode, Chief Engineer; Bill West, Sales Manager.

Berry—WSFG-LD, Ch. 38, Ettie Clark. Phone: 205-689-4489.

Technical Facilities: 15-kw ERP, 230-ft. above ground, 850-ft. above sea level, lat. 33° 41' 16", long. 87° 33' 55".

Ownership: Ettie Clark.

Berry—WSSF-LD, Ch. 15, Ettie Clark. Phone: 205-689-4489.

Technical Facilities: 15-kw ERP, 72-ft. above ground, 410-ft. above sea level, lat. 33° 40' 54", long. 87° 49' 24".

Ownership: Ettie Clark.

Berry—WSSF-LP, Ch. 48, Ettie Clark. Phone: 205-689-4489.

Technical Facilities: 18.9-kw ERP, 72-ft. above ground, 410-ft. above sea level, lat. 33° 40' 54", long. 87° 49' 24".

Ownership: Ettie Clark.

Birmingham—W08DC, Ch. 8, CYS Inc.

Technical Facilities: 4.4-kw ERP, 505-ft. above ground, 1510-ft. above sea level, lat. 33° 29' 04", long. 86° 48' 25".

Ownership: CYS Inc.

Personnel: Kim Dion, General Manager.

Birmingham—W34BI, Ch. 34, Ventana Television Inc. Phone: 727-872-4210.

Technical Facilities: 26.5-kw ERP, 348-ft. above ground, 1289-ft. above sea level, lat. 33° 27' 37", long. 86° 51' 07".

Holds CP for change to 30-kw ERP, 348-ft. above ground, 1288-ft. above sea level, BPTTL-20041028AIE.

Began Operation: April 12, 1993.

Ownership: Ventana Television Inc.

Birmingham—W46DK, Ch. 46, Trinity Broadcasting Network Inc. Phone: 714-832-2950. Fax: 714-730-0661.

Technical Facilities: 15.1-kw ERP, 380-ft. above ground, 1327-ft. above sea level, lat. 33° 29' 04", long. 86° 48' 25".

Holds CP for change to channel number 31, 2-kw ERP, BDISDTT-20060327ABW.

Ownership: Trinity Broadcasting Network Inc.

■Birmingham—W49AY, Ch. 49, Glen Iris Baptist Church School. Phone: 205-323-1516. Fax: 205-323-2747.

Technical Facilities: 1000-w TPO, 0.197-kw ERP, 180-ft. above ground, 1201-ft. above sea level, lat. 33° 29' 02", long. 86° 48' 35".

Holds CP for change to channel number 47, 38.6-kw ERP, 190-ft. above ground, 1201-ft. above sea level, BDISTTA-20080804AEH.

Transmitter: 1100 Railroad Ave., Birmingham.

Began Operation: April 17, 1990.

Ownership: Glen Iris Baptist Church School.

Personnel: Chris Lamb, General Manager; Ron Haas, Chief Engineer; Nathan Mills, Program Director.

Birmingham—W62BG, Ch. 62, Sinclair Broadcast Group Inc. Phone: 410-568-1500. Fax: 410-568-1533.

Technical Facilities: 1000-w TPO, 9.51-kw ERP, 131-ft. above ground, 1089-ft. above sea level, lat. 33° 28' 39", long. 86° 49' 16".

Transmitter: 600 Beacon Pkwy. W, Birmingham.

Ownership: Sinclair Broadcast Group Inc.

Personnel: Charles B. Rountree, General Manager; Rick Blevins, Operations Director; John Batson, Director, Engineering.

Birmingham—WBMA-LP, Ch. 58, TV Alabama Inc. Phone: 205-403-3340.

Technical Facilities: 916-w TPO, 8.8-kw ERP, 482-ft. above ground, 1424-ft. above sea level, lat. 33° 26' 28", long. 86° 53' 00".

Holds CP for change to channel number 11, 0.3-kw ERP, 485-ft. above ground, 1425-ft. above sea level, lat. 33° 26' 28", long. 86° 53' 02". BDISDTL-20060324ABZ.

Transmitter: WZRR(FM) tower.

Ownership: Allbritton Communications Co.

■Birmingham—WBUN-CA, Ch. 27, Word of God Fellowship Inc. Phone: 501-221-0400. Fax: 501-221-1101.

Technical Facilities: 660-w TPO, 11.8-kw ERP, 574-ft. above ground, 1525-ft. above sea level, lat. 33° 29' 04", long. 86° 48' 25".

Transmitter: Red Mountain.

Ownership: Word of God Fellowship Inc.

■Birmingham—WBXA-CA, Ch. 2, L4 Media Group LLC. Phone: 321-729-8451.

Studio: 244 Goodwin Crest Dr, Ste 111, Birmingham, AL 35209.

Technical Facilities: 1.2-kw ERP, 75-ft. above ground, 1037-ft. above sea level, lat. 33° 28' 18", long. 86° 50' 03".

Transmitter: 236 Goodwill Crest Rd., Birmingham.

Ownership: L4 Media Group LLC.

Personnel: Liz Kiley, Broadcast Vice President; Warren Reeves, Consulting Engineer; Amy Brown, Broadcast Operations Director.

Cullman—WCQT-LP, Ch. 27, First Cullman Broadcasting Inc. Phone: 256-739-6652. Fax: 256-734-5660.

Technical Facilities: 16-kw ERP, 272-ft. above ground, 1028-ft. above sea level, lat. 34° 10' 17", long. 86° 50' 39".

Holds CP for change to channel number 38, 2-kw ERP, BDISDTL-20061102ABU.

Ownership: First Cullman Broadcasting Inc.

Personnel: Andrew W. Stevens, General Manager.

Decatur—W33CM, Ch. 33, Trinity Broadcasting Network Inc. Phone: 714-832-2950. Fax: 714-730-0661.

Technical Facilities: 11.3-kw ERP, 135-ft. above ground, 955-ft. above sea level, lat. 34° 35' 22", long. 87° 06' 17".

Ownership: Trinity Broadcasting Network Inc.

■Demopolis—WJMY-CA, Ch. 25, TTI Inc. Phone: 205-553-7242. Fax: 205-349-4369.

Technical Facilities: 150-kw ERP, 433-ft. above ground, 853-ft. above sea level, lat. 32° 52' 40", long. 87° 36' 53".

Ownership: TTI Inc.

Dothan—W23DJ, Ch. 23, Equity Media Holdings Corp., Debtor in Possession. Phone: 501-219-2400.

Technical Facilities: 1-kw ERP, 16-ft. above ground, 276-ft. above sea level, lat. 31° 13' 39", long. 85° 21' 10".

Began Operation: June 22, 2007.

Ownership: Equity Media Holdings Corp., Debtor in Possession.

Dothan—W41BN, Ch. 41, Trinity Broadcasting Network. Phone: 714-832-2950. Fax: 714-730-0661.

Technical Facilities: 17.3-kw ERP, 312-ft. above ground, 571-ft. above sea level, lat. 31° 13' 39", long. 85° 21' 10".

Holds CP for change to 5-kw ERP, 312-ft. above ground, 574-ft. above sea level, lat. 31° 13' 43", long. 85° 21' 06". BDFCDTT-20060331ABX.

Ownership: Trinity Broadcasting Network Inc.

Dothan—WDTH-LP, Ch. 15, Equity Media Holdings Corp., Debtor in Possession. Phone: 501-291-2400.

Technical Facilities: 1-kw ERP, 312-ft. above ground, 571-ft. above sea level, lat. 31° 13' 39", long. 85° 21' 10".

Holds CP for change to 16-ft. above ground, 276-ft. above sea level, BMPTTL-20070511ABM.

Began Operation: June 8, 2007.

Ownership: Equity Media Holdings Corp., Debtor in Possession.

■ **Dothan**—WJJN-LP, Ch. 5, James Wilson III. Phone: 334-671-1753.

Technical Facilities: 213-w TPO, 0.5-kw ERP, 440-ft. above ground, 718-ft. above sea level, lat. 31° 12' 04", long. 86° 20' 04".

Holds CP for change to 1.18-kw ERP, 495-ft. above ground, 804-ft. above sea level, lat. 31° 14' 54", long. 85° 23' 20". BPTVA-20020730AAL.

Transmitter: Corner of Drew Rd. & U.S. Hwy. 84.

Ownership: James Wilson III.

Eufaula—W30BD, Ch. 30, Trinity Broadcasting Network Inc. Phone: 714-832-2950. Fax: 714-730-0661.

Technical Facilities: 100-w TPO, 1-kw ERP, 285-ft. above ground, 597-ft. above sea level, lat. 31° 54' 30", long. 85° 09' 51".

Transmitter: Fort Browder Rte.

Ownership: Trinity Broadcasting Network Inc.

Florence—W57BV, Ch. 57, Trinity Broadcasting Network Inc. Phone: 714-832-2950. Fax: 714-730-0661.

Technical Facilities: 5.7-kw ERP, lat. 34° 40' 24", long. 87° 42' 56".

Transmitter: 0.8-mi. WNW of junction of Jackson Hwy. & Milk Spring Rd., near Milk Spring.

Ownership: Trinity Broadcasting Network Inc.

■ **Florence**—WBCF-LP, Ch. 3, Benny Carle Broadcasting. Phone: 256-764-8170.

Studio: 525 E Tennessee St, Florence, AL 35631.

Technical Facilities: 500-w TPO, 0.018-kw ERP, 259-ft. above ground, 801-ft. above sea level, lat. 34° 48' 11", long. 87° 40' 14".

Transmitter: 525 E. Tennessee St.

Multichannel TV Sound: Stereo and separate audio program.

Ownership: BCB Inc.

Personnel: Benny Carle, General Manager; Ed Carter, Chief Engineer.

■ **Florence**—WXFL-LP, Ch. 5, Benny Carle Broadcasting. Phone: 256-764-8170.

Studio: 201 N Pine St, Florence, AL 35631.

Technical Facilities: 10-w TPO, 0.018-kw ERP, 259-ft. above ground, 801-ft. above sea level, lat. 34° 48' 11", long. 87° 40' 14".

Transmitter: 525 E. Tennessee St.

Ownership: BCB Inc.

Personnel: Benny Carle, General Manager; Ed Carter, Chief Engineer.

Gadsden—W15AP, Ch. 15, WBRC License Inc. Phone: 202-895-3088.

Technical Facilities: 17.4-kw ERP, 187-ft. above ground, 1588-ft. above sea level, lat. 33° 57' 14", long. 86° 12' 55".

Ownership: Fox Television Holdings Inc.

■ **Greensboro**—WDVZ-CA, Ch. 3, TTI Inc. Phone: 205-349-4902. Fax: 205-349-4369.

Technical Facilities: 10-w TPO, 3-kw ERP, 435-ft. above ground, 855-ft. above sea level, lat. 32° 52' 40", long. 87° 36' 53".

Transmitter: Approx. 1.5-mi. N of Greensboro.

Ownership: TTI Inc.

Gulf Shores—WGHA-LP, Ch. 66, Tiger Eye Broadcasting Corp. Phone: 954-431-3144.

Technical Facilities: 100-w TPO, 0.47-kw ERP, 187-ft. above sea level, lat. 30° 32' 48", long. 87° 34' 50".

Transmitter: Approx. 656-ft. SSE of intersection of U.S. Rte. 90 & State Rte.87, Elsanor.

Ownership: Tiger Eye Broadcasting Corp.

Hamilton—W24DC, Ch. 24, WMTY Inc. Phone: 205-921-5150.

Technical Facilities: 19.7-kw ERP, 183-ft. above ground, 904-ft. above sea level, lat. 34° 02' 22", long. 87° 57' 03".

Holds CP for change to 15-kw ERP, BDFCDTL-20080324AIP.

Ownership: WMTY Inc.

Hamilton—W46DF, Ch. 46, WMTY Inc. Phone: 205-921-5150.

Technical Facilities: 10.2-kw ERP, 191-ft. above ground, 886-ft. above sea level, lat. 34° 02' 22", long. 87° 57' 03".

Holds CP for change to 12.65-kw ERP, 191-ft. above ground, 912-ft. above sea level, BDFCDTL-20080801ASM.

Ownership: WMTY Inc.

■ **Huntsville**—W38BQ, Ch. 38, Three Angels Broadcasting Network Inc. Phone: 618-627-4651. Fax: 618-627-4155.

Technical Facilities: 1000-w TPO, 13.6-kw ERP, 883-ft. above sea level, lat. 34° 41'28", long. 86° 43' 36".

Transmitter: N of Joe Wheeler Rd., 0.62-mi. W of Sheton Rd.

Ownership: Three Angels Broadcasting Network Inc.

Personnel: Moses Primo, Chief Engineer; Linda Shelton, Program Director.

Huntsville—W67CO, Ch. 67, Trinity Broadcasting Network Inc. Phone: 714-832-2950. Fax: 714-730-0661.

Technical Facilities: 6.4-kw ERP, 420-ft. above ground, 1919-ft. above sea level, lat. 34° 40' 50", long. 86° 30' 54".

Holds CP for change to channel number 34, 10-kw ERP, 420-ft. above ground, 1931-ft. above sea level, lat. 34° 40' 50", long. 86° 39' 55". BDISTT-20060328AKO.

Transmitter: Atop Huntsville Mountain.

Ownership: Trinity Broadcasting Network Inc.

■ **Jacksonville**—WJXS-CA, Ch. 24, Alabama Heritage Communications LLC. Phone: 256-782-5133.

Technical Facilities: 11.5-kw ERP, 154-ft. above ground, 1785-ft. above sea level, lat. 33° 37' 21", long. 85° 52' 22".

Ownership: Alabama Heritage Communications LLC.

Personnel: Thomas E. Williams, Chief Executive Officer.

Jasper—W23AK, Ch. 23, WMTY Inc. Phone: 205-921-5150.

Technical Facilities: 100-w TPO, 0.879-kw ERP, 98-ft. above ground, 499-ft. above sea level, lat. 33° 48' 04", long. 87° 06' 42".

Transmitter: Off U.S. Hwy. 78, Argo.

Ownership: WMTY Inc.

Jasper—W25DR, Ch. 25, Trinity Broadcasting Network Inc. Phone: 714-832-2950. Fax: 714-730-0661.

Technical Facilities: 8.4-kw ERP, 499-ft. above ground, 889-ft. above sea level, lat. 33° 50' 42", long. 87° 18' 26".

Ownership: Trinity Broadcasting Network Inc.

Jasper—W55BJ, Ch. 55, Combs Broadcasting Inc. Phone: 205-387-8320. Fax: 205-384-0408.

Studio: 511 W 19th St, Jasper, AL 35501.

Technical Facilities: 5.7-kw ERP, 528-ft. above ground, 919-ft. above sea level, lat. 33° 50' 42", long. 87° 18' 26".

Transmitter: 7th St. NW, Bankhead tower.

Ownership: Combs Broadcasting Inc.

Personnel: Charlie Watts, General Manager; Rick Woodson, Chief Engineer.

Mobile—W30BX, Ch. 30, Ventana Television Inc. Phone: 727-872-4210.

Technical Facilities: 50-w ERP, 456-ft. above ground, 466-ft. above sea level, lat. 30° 41' 33", long. 88° 02' 30".

Began Operation: December 7, 1992.

Ownership: Ventana Television Inc.

Mobile—W50CF, Ch. 50, Franklin Media Inc. Phone: 850-433-1766.

Technical Facilities: 25.5-kw ERP, 190-ft. above ground, 203-ft. above sea level, lat. 30° 41' 23", long. 88° 03' 11".

Transmitter: On top of existing building.

Began Operation: December 29, 1992.

Ownership: Franklin Media Inc.

Mobile—WMOE-LP, Ch. 12, Tiger Eye Broadcasting Corp. Phone: 317-931-0310.

Technical Facilities: 100-w TPO, 0.54-kw ERP, 59-ft. above ground, 187-ft. above sea level, lat. 30° 32' 48", long. 87° 34' 50".

Transmitter: Approx. 656-ft. SE of intersection of U.S. Rte. 90 & SR 87, Elsanor.

Ownership: Tiger Eye Broadcasting Corp.

Mobile—WWBH-LP, Ch. 27, Tiger Eye Broadcasting Corp. Phone: 954-431-3144.

Technical Facilities: 100-w TPO, 0.49-kw ERP, 167-ft. above ground, 187-ft. above sea level, lat. 30° 32' 48", long. 87° 34' 50".

Holds CP for change to channel number 44, 1-kw ERP, 187-ft. above ground, 632-ft. above sea level, lat. 30° 37' 38.3", long. 87° 37' 31.1". BDISTTL-20060330AGA.

Transmitter: Approx. 656-ft. SE of intersection of U.S. Rte. 90 & SR 87, Elsanor.

Ownership: Tiger Eye Broadcasting Corp.

■ **Montevallo**—WOTM-LP, Ch. 19, WOTM LLC. Phone: 205-682-1019.

Technical Facilities: 1000-w TPO, 12.6-kw ERP, 98-ft. above ground, 1350-ft. above sea level, lat. 33° 09' 14", long. 86° 50' 12".

Transmitter: 0.8-mi. WNW of SR 70 & SR 119, near Montevallo.

Ownership: WOTM LLC.

Personnel: Michael A. Plaia, Manager.

■ **Montgomery**—WBXM-CA, Ch. 5, L4 Media Group LLC. Phone: 321-729-9451.

Studio: 600 Montgomery St, Ste 801, Montgomery, AL 36104.

Technical Facilities: 0.7-kw ERP, 224-ft. above ground, 403-ft. above sea level, lat. 32° 22' 34.5", long. 86° 18' 38.1".

Ownership: L4 Media Group LLC.

Personnel: Warren Reeves, Consulting Engineer; Amy Brown, Broadcast Operations Director; Liz Kiley, Broadcast Vice President.

Montgomery—WETU-LP, Ch. 39, Venture Television LLC. Phones: 205-234-0426; 205-234-6464. Fax: 205-234-0088.

Technical Facilities: 1000-w TPO, 105-kw ERP, 348-ft. above ground, 889-ft. above sea level, lat. 32° 32' 12", long. 86° 13' 01".

Transmitter: Bald Knob Hill on U.S. 231, 0.5-mi. SE of Wetumpka.

Ownership: Venture Television LLC.

Personnel: Jackson Mitchell, General Manager; Ken Jordan, Chief Engineer.

Montgomery—WFRZ-LD, Ch. 34, Frazer Memorial United Methodist Church. Phone: 334-272-8622.

Technical Facilities: 15-kw ERP, 499-ft. above ground, 679-ft. above sea level, lat. 32° 24' 12", long. 86° 11' 47".

Transmitter: WLWI-FM tower, 1.3-mi. NE of Wares Ferry Rd. as it crosses CSX RR tracks.

Began Operation: March 4, 1994.

Ownership: Frazer Memorial United Methodist Church.

Personnel: Jerry Kemp, General Manager; John Simons, Chief Engineer.

■ **Moody**—WBMG-LP, Ch. 38, Tiger Eye Broadcasting Corp.

Technical Facilities: 1000-w TPO, 30.9-kw ERP, 89-ft. above ground, 1207-ft. above sea level, lat. 33° 33' 50", long. 86° 28' 34".

Transmitter: Karr Mountain.

Ownership: Tiger Eye Broadcasting Corp.

Opelika—WQMK-LP, Ch. 18, Ben Jordan Communications Corp. Phone: 706-518-3911.

Technical Facilities: 6.1-kw ERP, 351-ft. above ground, 1010-ft. above sea level, lat. 32° 37' 19", long. 85° 30' 05".

Holds CP for change to 15-kw ERP, 351-ft. above ground, 1011-ft. above sea level, BDFCDTT-20060331ACK.

Transmitter: side of tower, 1-mi. NNE of intersection of SR 14 & SR 267, Auburn.

Ownership: Ben Jordan Communications Corp.

Phenix City, etc.—W06BH, Ch. 6, Greene Communications Inc. Phone: 205-297-1410.

Technical Facilities: 14-w TPO, 0.6-kw ERP, 125-ft. above ground, 869-ft. above sea level, lat. 32° 27' 48", long. 85° 02' 27".

Transmitter: 1.12-mi. SW of intersection of U.S. Rte. 280 & SR 8, Phenix City.

Ownership: R. M. Greene Inc.

Personnel: Lynn Heard, General Manager.

Priceville—WYAM-LP, Ch. 51, Decatur Communication Properties. Phone: 256-355-4567.

Technical Facilities: 19.6-kw ERP, 224-ft. above ground, 805-ft. above sea level, lat. 34° 34' 00", long. 86° 54' 46".

Holds CP for change to 15-kw ERP, BDFCDTL-20070912ACA.

Ownership: Decatur Communication Properties LLC.

Personnel: Terry Arnold, General Manager & Sales Manager; John Hains, Chief Engineer.

■ **Prichard**—WRBM-LP, Ch. 60, Upper Gulf Coast LLC. Phone: 361-289-0125.

Technical Facilities: 1000-w TPO, 21.28-kw ERP, 499-ft. above ground, 531-ft. above sea level, lat. 30° 44' 44", long. 88° 05' 40".

Transmitter: 2300 Smiley Lane.

Ownership: Upper Gulf Coast LLC.

Russellville—W45CW, Ch. 45, WMTY Inc. Phone: 662-728-6492.

Technical Facilities: 45-kw ERP, 183-ft. above ground, 1043-ft. above sea level, lat. 34° 30' 06", long. 87° 44' 54".

Began Operation: September 8, 1992.

Ownership: WMTY Inc.

Scottsboro—W27CV, Ch. 27, Trinity Broadcasting Network. Phone: 714-832-2950. Fax: 714-730-0661.

Technical Facilities: 11.1-kw ERP, 151-ft. above ground, 1512-ft. above sea level, lat. 34° 35' 22", long. 85° 59' 31".

Holds CP for change to 15-kw ERP, BDFCDTT-20060330AMK.

Ownership: Trinity Broadcasting Network Inc.

Selma—W24CK, Ch. 24, Trinity Broadcasting Network Inc. Phone: 714-832-2950. Fax: 714-730-0661.

Technical Facilities: 1000-w TPO, 15-kw ERP, 486-ft. above ground, 574-ft. above sea level, lat. 32° 21' 40", long. 86° 52' 28".

Transmitter: 4.7-mi. NNW of Rte. 80 & Old Town Creek.

Ownership: Trinity Broadcasting Network Inc.

■ **Somerville**—WMJN-LP, Ch. 29, Global Outreach Ministry Network Inc. Phone: 850-832-6208.

Technical Facilities: 12-kw ERP, 190-ft. above ground, 1017-ft. above sea level, lat. 34° 30' 43", long. 86° 50' 55".

Holds CP for change to 10-kw ERP, BDFCDTL-20061102ABY.

Transmitter: 2632 Chapel Hill Rd.

Ownership: Global Outreach Ministry Network Inc.

Sylacauga—W04CB, Ch. 4, NVT Birmingham Licensee LLC, Debtor in Possession. Phone: 404-995-4711.

Technical Facilities: 0.17-kw ERP, 89-ft. above ground, 919-ft. above sea level, lat. 33° 08' 23", long. 86° 15' 26".

Began Operation: March 25, 1991.

Ownership: New Vision Television LLC, Debtor in Possession.

Talladega—W63CK, Ch. 63, Joseph V. Early. Phone: 256-249-4348.

Technical Facilities: 100-w TPO, 5.5-kw ERP, 36-ft. above ground, 597-ft. above sea level, lat. 33° 26' 06", long. 86° 06' 14".

Began Operation: May 9, 1997.

Ownership: Joseph V. Early.

Personnel: Harvey Bowlin Sr., General Manager.

■ **Talladega**—WOIL-LP, Ch. 47, Joseph V. Early. Phone: 256-249-4348.

Technical Facilities: 1000-w TPO, 22.5-kw ERP, 125-ft. above ground, 1683-ft. above sea level, lat. 33° 24' 42", long. 86° 12' 27".

Transmitter: Flagpole Mountain, adjacent to Penfroe lookout tower.

Began Operation: May 31, 1995.

Ownership: Joseph V. Early.

Personnel: Jimmy Dale Abrams, General Manager.

Tuscaloosa—W46BU, Ch. 46, Trinity Broadcasting Network Inc. Phone: 714-832-2950. Fax: 714-730-0661.

Technical Facilities: 25.4-kw ERP, 551-ft. above ground, 994-ft. above sea level, lat. 33° 03' 15", long. 87° 32' 57".

Holds CP for change to 15-kw ERP, BDFCDTT-20060313AAH.

Transmitter: Side mounted on existing WTUG(FM) tower, 2.6-mi. NE of State Rd. 69 at Big Sandy Creek near Hull.

Ownership: Trinity Broadcasting Network Inc.

■ **Tuscaloosa**—WVUA-CA, Ch. 7, Board of Trustees of the U. of Alabama. Phones: 205-348-7000; 205-348-7001. Fax: 205-348-8000.

Technical Facilities: 1000-w TPO, 0.43-kw ERP, 239-ft. above ground, 843-ft. above sea level, lat. 33° 09' 36", long. 87° 30' 54".

Transmitter: Near 15th Ave & Jug Factory Rd.

Ownership: TTI Inc.

Personnel: Roy Clem, General Manager & Program Director; Dave Baughn, Chief Engineer; Lynn Brooks, News Director; Vicki Richardson, Program Director & Traffic Manager.

■ **Tuscumbia**—W46CF, Ch. 46, WMTY Inc. Phone: 205-921-5150.

Technical Facilities: 1000-w TPO, 23.4-kw ERP, 192-ft. above ground, 1152-ft. above sea level, lat. 34° 35' 07", long. 87° 48' 00".

Transmitter: Church School Yard, W of Crooked Oak Triangle, Crooked Oak.

Ownership: WMTY Inc.

Personnel: Bill Lambert, General Manager; Lealon Owens, Chief Engineer; Rick Joyner, Sales Manager.

Washington—KWTE-LP, Ch. 12, Warren Communications News. Phones: 202-872-9200; 800-771-9202. Fax: 202-296-4397.

Studio: 2115 Ward Court, NW, Washington, DC 20037.

Technical Facilities: 1000-kw ERP, 1550-ft. above ground, 1350-ft. above sea level, lat. 12° 34' 45", long. 123° 45' 50".

Transmitter: 2115 Ward Court.

Alaska

Adak—K04LY, Ch. 4, State of Alaska.

Technical Facilities: 0.43-kw ERP, 46-ft. above sea level, lat. 51° 51' 59", long. 176° 38' 31".

Ownership: State of Alaska.

Adak—K13SH, Ch. 13, State of Alaska.

Technical Facilities: 0.43-kw ERP, lat. 51° 51' 59", long. 176° 38' 31".

Ownership: State of Alaska.

Akhiok—K04LL, Ch. 4, State of Alaska.

Technical Facilities: 0.043-kw ERP, 49-ft. above sea level, lat. 56° 56' 43", long. 154° 10' 00".

Ownership: State of Alaska.

Akhiok—K09UD, Ch. 9, State of Alaska. Phone: 907-269-5744.

Technical Facilities: 0.06-kw ERP, lat. 56° 56' 43", long. 154° 10' 00".

Ownership: State of Alaska.

Akiak—K10MV, Ch. 10, State of Alaska.

Technical Facilities: 0.01-kw ERP, lat. 60° 54' 45", long. 161° 13' 00".

Ownership: State of Alaska.

Akiak—K12NS, Ch. 12, State of Alaska.

Technical Facilities: 0.009-kw ERP, 59-ft. above ground, 82-ft. above sea level, lat. 60° 54' 45", long. 161° 13' 00".

Ownership: State of Alaska.

Akutan—K04LK, Ch. 4, State of Alaska.

Technical Facilities: 0.043-kw ERP, 56-ft. above sea level, lat. 54° 08' 06", long. 165° 45' 18".

Ownership: State of Alaska.

Akutan—K09RH, Ch. 9, State of Alaska.

Technical Facilities: 10-w TPO, 0.0542-kw ERP, 20-ft. above ground, 60-ft. above sea level, lat. 54° 08' 06", long. 165° 46' 18".

Transmitter: Alascom Earth Station, Akutan.

Ownership: State of Alaska.

Alakanuk—K04ND, Ch. 4, State of Alaska.

Technical Facilities: 0.05-kw ERP, 36-ft. above sea level, lat. 62° 41' 03", long. 164° 38' 56".

Ownership: State of Alaska.

Alakanuk—K08KD, Ch. 8, State of Alaska.

Technical Facilities: 0.056-kw ERP, lat. 62° 41' 03", long. 164° 38' 56".

Ownership: State of Alaska.

Aleknagik—K08HU, Ch. 8, State of Alaska.

Technical Facilities: 0.063-kw ERP, 1273-ft. above sea level, lat. 59° 16' 37", long. 158° 32' 47".

Ownership: State of Alaska.

Aleknagik—K13RP, Ch. 13, State of Alaska.

Technical Facilities: 10-w TPO, 0.0514-kw ERP, 20-ft. above ground, 110-ft. above sea level, lat. 59° 17' 05", long. 158° 37' 50".

Transmitter: Aleknagik Community School, Aleknagik.

Ownership: State of Alaska.

Allakaket—K02KB, Ch. 2, Allakaket City Council.

Technical Facilities: 0.018-kw ERP, 371-ft. above sea level, lat. 66° 33' 53", long. 152° 38' 38".

Ownership: Allakaket City Council.

Allakaket, etc.—K09QL, Ch. 9, State of Alaska.

Technical Facilities: 10-w TPO, 0.0562-kw ERP, 20-ft. above ground, 420-ft. above sea level, lat. 66° 33' 53", long. 152° 38' 38".

Transmitter: Alascom Earth Station, Allakaket.

Ownership: State of Alaska.

Alyeska—K04GP, Ch. 4, Anchorage Broadcast Television Consortium Inc. Phone: 425-258-1440.

Technical Facilities: 0.006-kw ERP, 1020-ft. above sea level, lat. 60° 57' 20", long. 149° 06' 04".

Ownership: Anchorage Broadcast Television Consortium Inc.

Ambler—K11QI, Ch. 11, State of Alaska.

Technical Facilities: 10-w TPO, 0.056-kw ERP, 20-ft. above ground, 100-ft. above sea level, lat. 67° 05' 16", long. 157° 51' 00".

Transmitter: Alascom Earth Station, Ambler.

Ownership: State of Alaska.

Anaktuvuk Pass—K04IX, Ch. 4, State of Alaska.

Technical Facilities: 0.018-kw ERP, 2073-ft. above sea level, lat. 68° 08' 31", long. 151° 43' 51".

Ownership: State of Alaska.

Anaktuvuk Pass—K09RS, Ch. 9, State of Alaska.

Technical Facilities: 10-w TPO, 0.0562-kw ERP, 20-ft. above ground, 2085-ft. above sea level, lat. 68° 08' 31", long. 151° 43' 51".

Transmitter: Alascom Earth Station, Anaktuvuk Pass.

Ownership: State of Alaska.

Anchor Point—K51AF, Ch. 51, Anchorage Broadcast Television Consortium Inc. Phone: 425-258-1440.

Technical Facilities: 0.629-kw ERP, 98-ft. above ground, 351-ft. above sea level, lat. 59° 45' 22", long. 151° 46' 21".

Began Operation: October 8, 1986.

Ownership: Anchorage Broadcast Television Consortium Inc.

Anchorage—K22HN-D, Ch. 22, Fireweed Communications Corp. Phone: 907-339-3800.

Technical Facilities: 2.8-kw ERP, 46-ft. above ground, 1007-ft. above sea level, lat. 61° 06', long. 149° 44' 40".

Ownership: Fireweed Communications LLC.

Anchorage—K41DP, Ch. 41, Ketchikan TV LLC. Phone: 303-688-5162.

Technical Facilities: 34.5-kw ERP, 47-ft. above ground, 2,060-ft. above sea level, lat. 61° 20' 11", long. 149° 30' 48".

Ownership: Ketchikan TV LLC.

Anchorage—K45HQ, Ch. 45, Ketchikan TV LLC. Phone: 303-688-5162.

Technical Facilities: 35.5-kw ERP, 164-ft. above ground, 2060-ft. above sea level, lat. 61° 20' 11", long. 149° 30' 48".

Ownership: Ketchikan TV LLC.

Anchorage—KABA-LP, Ch. 6, Fireweed Communications Corp. Phone: 907-248-5937.
Technical Facilities: 0.92-kw ERP, 49-ft. above ground, 1473-ft. above sea level, lat. 61° 07' 34", long. 149° 42' 50".
Ownership: Fireweed Communications LLC.

Anchorage—KACN-LP, Ch. 38, Dan Etulain. Phone: 907-747-8200.
Technical Facilities: 20-kw ERP, 184-ft. above ground, 305-ft. above sea level, lat. 61° 13' 01", long. 149° 53' 34".
Ownership: Dan Etulain.

■ **Anchorage**—KCFT-LP, Ch. 20, Alaska Broadcast Television Inc. Phone: 907-337-2020. Fax: 907-333-9851.
Technical Facilities: 1000-w TPO, 20.7-kw ERP, 62-ft. above ground, 1755-ft. above sea level, lat. 61° 04' 02", long. 149° 44' 36".
Transmitter: Approx. 2-mi. NE of Seward Hwy. as it crosses Potter Creek, near Anchorage.
Ownership: Alaska Broadcast Television Inc.
Personnel: Michael D. Murray, General Manager.

■ **Anchorage**—KYEX-LP, Ch. 29, Fireweed Communications Corp. Phone: 907-339-3800. Fax: 907-243-0709.
Technical Facilities: 1000-w TPO, 103-kw ERP, 98-ft. above ground, 4339-ft. above sea level, lat. 61° 28' 05", long. 150° 44' 16".
Holds CP for change to channel number 18, 10-kw ERP, 16-ft. above ground, 4281-ft. above sea level, lat. 61° 06' 58", long. 149° 47' 59". BDFCDTT-20080716AIF.
Transmitter: Mount Susitna, 5.7-mi. NW of Alexander.
Ownership: Fireweed Communications LLC.
Personnel: Carol Schatz, General Manager; Jeremy Lansman, Chief Engineer; Carter Crawford, Sales Manager.

Angoon—K02JI, Ch. 2, State of Alaska.
Technical Facilities: 0.01-kw ERP, 20-ft. above ground, 102-ft. above sea level, lat. 57° 30' 08", long. 134° 35' 00".
Ownership: Angoon Public Schools.

Angoon—K07SS, Ch. 7, State of Alaska. Phone: 907-269-5744.
Technical Facilities: 0.053-kw ERP, 46-ft. above sea level, lat. 57° 30' 03", long. 134° 35' 00".
Ownership: State of Alaska.

Angoon—K09QF, Ch. 9, State of Alaska.
Technical Facilities: 10-w TPO, 0.0536-kw ERP, 20-ft. above ground, 45-ft. above sea level, lat. 57° 30' 03", long. 134° 35' 00".
Transmitter: Angoon Community School.
Ownership: State of Alaska.

Aniak—K02KY, Ch. 2, State of Alaska.
Technical Facilities: 10-w TPO, 0.0433-kw ERP, 20-ft. above ground, 103-ft. above sea level, lat. 61° 34' 51", long. 159° 32' 49".
Transmitter: Alascom Earth Station, Aniak.
Ownership: State of Alaska.

Aniak—K11QN, Ch. 11, State of Alaska. Phone: 907-269-5744.
Technical Facilities: 0.058-kw ERP, 75-ft. above ground, 157-ft. above sea level, lat. 61° 34' 55", long. 159° 33' 53".

Ownership: State of Alaska.

Anvik—K02JY, Ch. 2, State of Alaska.
Technical Facilities: 0.018-kw ERP, 125-ft. above sea level, lat. 62° 39' 21", long. 160° 12' 11".
Ownership: City of Anvik.

Anvik—K07RE, Ch. 7, State of Alaska.
Technical Facilities: 10-w TPO, 0.0548-kw ERP, 20-ft. above ground, 80-ft. above sea level, lat. 62° 39' 21", long. 160° 12' 11".
Transmitter: Alascom Earth Station, Anvik.
Ownership: State of Alaska.

Arctic Village—K04LI, Ch. 4, State of Alaska. Phone: 907-269-5744.
Technical Facilities: 0.042-kw ERP, 2073-ft. above sea level, lat. 68° 07' 32", long. 145° 32' 10".
Ownership: State of Alaska.

Arctic Village—K09RV, Ch. 9, State of Alaska.
Technical Facilities: 10-w TPO, 0.0536-kw ERP, 20-ft. above ground, 2080-ft. above sea level, lat. 68° 07' 32", long. 145° 32' 10".
Transmitter: Alascom Earth Station, Arctic Village.
Ownership: State of Alaska.

Atka—K04LJ, Ch. 4, State of Alaska. Phone: 907-269-5744.
Technical Facilities: 0.043-kw ERP, 75-ft. above sea level, lat. 52° 11' 59", long. 174° 11' 43".
Ownership: State of Alaska.

Atka—K09RX, Ch. 9, State of Alaska.
Technical Facilities: 10-w TPO, 0.0549-kw ERP, 20-ft. above ground, 80-ft. above sea level, lat. 52° 11' 39", long. 174° 11' 43".
Transmitter: Alascom Earth Station, Atka.
Ownership: State of Alaska.

Atkasuk—K04NH, Ch. 4, State of Alaska.
Technical Facilities: 0.04-kw ERP, lat. 70° 28' 10", long. 157° 23' 40".
Ownership: State of Alaska.

Atkasuk—K09TZ, Ch. 9, State of Alaska.
Technical Facilities: 0.55-kw ERP, lat. 70° 28' 10", long. 157° 23' 40".
Ownership: State of Alaska.

Atmautluak—K05II, Ch. 5, State of Alaska. Phone: 907-269-5744.
Technical Facilities: 0.044-kw ERP, 16-ft. above ground, 39-ft. above sea level, lat. 60° 51' 29", long. 162° 16' 37".
Ownership: State of Alaska.

Atmautluak—K12NP, Ch. 12, State of Alaska. Phone: 907-269-5744.
Technical Facilities: 20-ft. above ground, 46-ft. above sea level, lat. 60° 51' 29", long. 162° 16' 14".
Ownership: State of Alaska.

Barrow—K04KS, Ch. 4, State of Alaska.
Technical Facilities: 0.045-kw ERP, 31-ft. above ground, 56-ft. above sea level, lat. 71° 17' 32", long. 156° 47' 10".
Transmitter: 1230 Adguik St.
Ownership: State of Alaska.

Barrow—K11NN, Ch. 11, State of Alaska. Phone: 907-269-5744.
Technical Facilities: 0.06-kw ERP, lat. 71° 17' 32", long. 156° 41' 10".
Transmitter: 1230 Adguik St.
Ownership: State of Alaska.

Beaver—K04LC, Ch. 4, State of Alaska. Phone: 907-260-5744.
Technical Facilities: 0.043-kw ERP, lat. 66° 21' 33", long. 147° 23' 42".
Ownership: State of Alaska.

Beaver—K09QQ, Ch. 9, State of Alaska.
Technical Facilities: 10-w TPO, 0.0555-kw ERP, 20-ft. above ground, 380-ft. above sea level, lat. 66° 21' 33", long. 147° 23' 42".
Transmitter: Alascom Earth Station, Beaver.
Ownership: State of Alaska.

Bethel—K15AV, Ch. 15, Bethel Broadcasting Inc. Phone: 907-543-3131.
Technical Facilities: 10-w TPO, 0.662-kw ERP, 218-ft. above sea level, lat. 60° 47' 33", long. 161° 46' 22".
Transmitter: 310 Radio St., Bethel.
Ownership: Bethel Broadcasting Inc.

Bethel—K21AO, Ch. 21, Bethel Broadcasting Inc. Phone: 907-543-3131.
Technical Facilities: 0.663-kw ERP, 128-ft. above sea level, lat. 60° 47' 33", long. 161° 46' 22".
Transmitter: 310 Radio St., Bethel.
Ownership: Bethel Broadcasting Inc.

Bettles—K09TE, Ch. 9, State of Alaska.
Technical Facilities: 10-w TPO, 0.052-kw ERP, 20-ft. above ground, 610-ft. above sea level, lat. 66° 54' 25", long. 151° 40' 55".
Transmitter: Bettles High School.
Ownership: State of Alaska.

Bettles—K13TE, Ch. 13, State of Alaska. Phone: 907-269-5744.
Technical Facilities: 0.05-kw ERP, lat. 66° 54' 25", long. 151° 40' 55".
Ownership: State of Alaska.

Birch Creek—K09TD, Ch. 9, State of Alaska.
Technical Facilities: 10-w TPO, 0.55-kw ERP, 20-ft. above ground, 450-ft. above sea level, lat. 66° 15' 46", long. 149° 49' 05".
Transmitter: Birch Creek School.
Ownership: State of Alaska.

Birch Creek—K13SY, Ch. 13, State of Alaska. Phone: 907-269-5744.
Technical Facilities: 0.05-kw ERP, lat. 66° 15' 46", long. 149° 49' 05".
Ownership: State of Alaska.

Bird Creek—K67AY, Ch. 67, Alaska Public Telecommunications Inc.
Technical Facilities: 0.01-kw ERP, lat. 60° 55' 07", long. 149° 32' 09".
Ownership: Alaska Public Telecommunications Inc.

Bird Point, etc.—K09HG, Ch. 9, Anchorage Broadcast Television Consortium Inc. Phone: 425-258-1440.
Technical Facilities: 0.01-kw ERP, lat. 60° 55' 07", long. 149° 32' 13".

Ownership: Anchorage Broadcast Television Consortium Inc.

Bird Point, etc.—K57BQ, Ch. 57, Anchorage Broadcast Television Consortium Inc. Phone: 425-258-1440.
Technical Facilities: 0.21-kw ERP, 1650-ft. above sea level, lat. 60° 55' 07", long. 149° 32' 09".
Began Operation: February 15, 1983.
Ownership: Anchorage Broadcast Television Consortium Inc.

BP Alaska Camp, etc.—K08IZ, Ch. 8, Northern Television Inc. Phone: 907-257-5601.
Technical Facilities: 0.265-kw ERP, lat. 70° 17' 29", long. 148° 42' 02".
Ownership: Northern Television Inc.

Buckland—K04LU, Ch. 4, State of Alaska. Phone: 907-269-5744.
Technical Facilities: 0.041-kw ERP, lat. 65° 58' 46", long. 161° 07' 20".
Ownership: State of Alaska.

Buckland—K09RI, Ch. 9, State of Alaska.
Technical Facilities: 10-w TPO, 0.053-kw ERP, 20-ft. above ground, 50-ft. above sea level, lat. 65° 58' 46", long. 161° 07' 20".
Transmitter: Alascom Earth Station, Buckland.
Ownership: State of Alaska.

Cantwell—K02KK, Ch. 2, State of Alaska. Phone: 907-269-5744.
Technical Facilities: 0.04-kw ERP, 2251-ft. above sea level, lat. 63° 23' 14", long. 148° 52' 32".
Ownership: State of Alaska.

Cantwell—K09SI, Ch. 9, State of Alaska.
Technical Facilities: 10-w TPO, 0.052-kw ERP, 50-ft. above ground, 2300-ft. above sea level, lat. 63° 23' 14", long. 148° 52' 42".
Transmitter: State of Alaska Hwys. Garage, Cantwell.
Ownership: State of Alaska.

Cape Pole—K09NP, Ch. 9, State of Alaska.
Technical Facilities: 0.013-kw ERP, lat. 55° 57' 57", long. 133° 47' 33".
Ownership: Southeast Island School District.

Cape Pole—K13SD, Ch. 13, State of Alaska.
Technical Facilities: 10-w TPO, 0.056-kw ERP, 20-ft. above ground, 50-ft. above sea level, lat. 55° 57' 57", long. 133° 47' 33".
Transmitter: Cape Pole Commissary, Cape Pole.
Ownership: State of Alaska.

Chalkyitsik—K04JU, Ch. 4, State of Alaska. Phone: 907-269-5744.
Technical Facilities: 0.018-kw ERP, lat. 66° 39' 01", long. 143° 43' 30".
Ownership: Chalkyitsik Village Council.

Chalkyitsik—K09QG, Ch. 9, State of Alaska.
Technical Facilities: 10-w TPO, 0.0562-kw ERP, 20-ft. above ground, 595-ft. above sea level, lat. 66° 39' 01", long. 143° 43' 30".
Transmitter: Alascom Earth Station, Chalkyitsik.
Ownership: State of Alaska.

Chefornak—K02LO, Ch. 2, State of Alaska.

Technical Facilities: 10-w TPO, 0.043-kw ERP, 20-ft. above ground, 40-ft. above sea level, lat. 60° 09' 35", long. 164° 16' 40".

Transmitter: Alascom Bldg., Chefornak.

Ownership: State of Alaska.

Chefornak—K04MK, Ch. 4, State of Alaska. Phone: 907-269-5744.

Technical Facilities: 0.04-kw ERP, lat. 60° 09' 35", long. 164° 16' 40".

Ownership: State of Alaska.

Chenega—K13VV, Ch. 13, State of Alaska.

Technical Facilities: 10-w TPO, 0.054-kw ERP, 20-ft. above ground, 85-ft. above sea level, lat. 60° 03' 57", long. 148° 00' 47".

Transmitter: Chenega School.

Ownership: State of Alaska.

Chevak—K02KX, Ch. 2, State of Alaska.

Technical Facilities: 10-w TPO, 0.045-kw ERP, 31-ft. above ground, 51-ft. above sea level, lat. 61° 31' 46", long. 165° 35' 00".

Transmitter: City Office Bldg.

Ownership: State of Alaska.

Chevak—K09PO, Ch. 9, State of Alaska. Phone: 907-269-5744.

Technical Facilities: 0.018-kw ERP, lat. 61° 31' 13", long. 165° 35' 00".

Ownership: City of Chevak.

Chickaloon—K10MT, Ch. 10, State of Alaska.

Technical Facilities: 0.05-kw ERP, lat. 61° 47' 40", long. 148° 25' 19".

Ownership: State of Alaska.

Chignik—K02LK, Ch. 2, State of Alaska. Phone: 907-269-5744.

Technical Facilities: 0.043-kw ERP, lat. 56° 18' 11", long. 158° 24' 38".

Ownership: State of Alaska.

Chignik—K07RY, Ch. 7, State of Alaska.

Technical Facilities: 10-w TPO, 0.043-kw ERP, 20-ft. above ground, 45-ft. above sea level, lat. 56° 18' 11", long. 158° 24' 38".

Transmitter: Alascom site, Chignik.

Ownership: State of Alaska.

Chignik Lagoon—K04MZ, Ch. 4, State of Alaska. Phone: 907-269-5744.

Technical Facilities: 0.043-kw ERP, lat. 56° 18' 30", long. 158° 32' 11".

Ownership: State of Alaska.

Chignik Lagoon—K09SO, Ch. 9, State of Alaska.

Technical Facilities: 10-w TPO, 0.056-kw ERP, 20-ft. above ground, 50-ft. above sea level, lat. 56° 18' 30", long. 158° 32' 11".

Transmitter: Chignik Lagoon Community School.

Ownership: State of Alaska.

Chignik Lake—K02MR, Ch. 2, State of Alaska.

Technical Facilities: 10-w TPO, 0.043-kw ERP, 20-ft. above ground, 50-ft. above sea level, lat. 56° 15' 21", long. 158° 45' 49".

Transmitter: Community Hall, Chignik Lake.

Ownership: State of Alaska.

Chignik Lake—K11RQ, Ch. 11, State of Alaska. Phone: 907-269-5744.

Technical Facilities: 0.035-kw ERP, lat. 56° 15' 16", long. 158° 45' 36".

Transmitter: Chignik Lake Community Health Building.

Ownership: State of Alaska.

Chistochina—K07QZ, Ch. 7, State of Alaska.

Technical Facilities: 10-w TPO, 0.053-kw ERP, 55-ft. above ground, 1955-ft. above sea level, lat. 62° 35' 33", long. 144° 38' 47".

Transmitter: Postie's Lodge, Tok Cutoff Hwy.

Ownership: State of Alaska.

Chistochina—K09PX, Ch. 9, State of Alaska. Phone: 907-269-5744.

Technical Facilities: 0.05-kw ERP, lat. 62° 35' 33", long. 144° 38' 47".

Ownership: State of Alaska.

Chitina—K09NF, Ch. 9, State of Alaska. Phone: 907-269-5744.

Technical Facilities: 0.013-kw ERP, lat. 61° 31' 21", long. 144° 28' 07".

Ownership: Village of Chitina.

Chitina—K13SB, Ch. 13, State of Alaska.

Technical Facilities: 10-w TPO, 0.056-kw ERP, 20-ft. above ground, 970-ft. above sea level, lat. 61° 31' 05", long. 144° 26' 20".

Transmitter: Chitina Country Store.

Ownership: State of Alaska.

Chuathbaluk—K06LG, Ch. 6, State of Alaska.

Technical Facilities: 0.05-kw ERP, 105-ft. above sea level, lat. 61° 34' 51", long. 159° 14' 37".

Ownership: State of Alaska.

Chuathbaluk—K09PP, Ch. 9, State of Alaska. Phone: 907-269-5744.

Technical Facilities: 0.002-kw ERP, lat. 61° 34' 21", long. 159° 14' 37".

Ownership: Chuathbaluk City Council.

Circle—K09TT, Ch. 9, State of Alaska. Phone: 907-269-5744.

Technical Facilities: 0.055-kw ERP, lat. 65° 49' 38", long. 144° 03' 58".

Ownership: State of Alaska.

Circle—K13SI, Ch. 13, State of Alaska.

Technical Facilities: 10-w TPO, 0.055-kw ERP, 20-ft. above ground, 610-ft. above sea level, lat. 65° 49' 38", long. 144° 03' 58".

Transmitter: Circle School, Circle.

Ownership: State of Alaska.

Circle Hot Springs—K03GO, Ch. 3, State of Alaska.

Technical Facilities: 0.43-kw ERP, lat. 65° 34' 16", long. 144° 48' 58".

Ownership: State of Alaska.

Circle Hot Springs—K06LP, Ch. 6, State of Alaska.

Technical Facilities: 10-w TPO, 0.055-kw ERP, 20-ft. above ground, 760-ft. above sea level, lat. 65° 29' 08", long. 144° 37' 55".

Transmitter: Circle Hot Springs School.

Ownership: State of Alaska.

Clarks Point, etc.—K06LK, Ch. 6, State of Alaska. Phone: 907-269-5744.

Technical Facilities: 0.029-kw ERP, 26-ft. above ground, 39-ft. above sea level, lat. 58° 48' 34", long. 158° 33' 36".

Ownership: State of Alaska.

Clarks Point, etc.—K12NL, Ch. 12, State of Alaska.

Technical Facilities: 10-w TPO, 0.03-kw ERP, 20-ft. above ground, 40-ft. above sea level, lat. 58° 50' 38", long. 158° 33' 03".

Transmitter: Alascom Office, Clarks Point.

Ownership: State of Alaska.

Coffman Cave—K09TV, Ch. 9, State of Alaska.

Technical Facilities: 10-w TPO, 0.055-kw ERP, 20-ft. above ground, 40-ft. above sea level, lat. 56° 00' 57", long. 132° 02' 27".

Transmitter: Community School, Coffman Cove.

Ownership: State of Alaska.

Coffman Cove—K13SZ, Ch. 13, State of Alaska. Phone: 907-269-5744.

Technical Facilities: 0.05-kw ERP, 39-ft. above sea level, lat. 56° 00' 09", long. 132° 50' 17".

Ownership: State of Alaska.

Cold Bay—K07TM, Ch. 7, State of Alaska. Phone: 907-269-5744.

Technical Facilities: 0.524-kw ERP, lat. 55° 12' 25", long. 162° 42' 20".

Transmitter: City office bldg., Cold Bay.

Ownership: State of Alaska.

Cold Bay—K13UO, Ch. 13, State of Alaska.

Technical Facilities: 100-w TPO, 0.512-kw ERP, 28-ft. above ground, 96-ft. above sea level, lat. 55° 12' 25", long. 162° 42' 20".

Transmitter: City Office Bldg.

Ownership: State of Alaska.

Cooper Landing—K08KO, Ch. 8, State of Alaska.

Technical Facilities: 0.05-kw ERP, lat. 60° 29' 22", long. 149° 44' 09".

Ownership: State of Alaska.

Copper Center—K12MO, Ch. 12, State of Alaska.

Technical Facilities: 10-w TPO, 0.0954-kw ERP, 50-ft. above ground, 1275-ft. above sea level, lat. 62° 02' 40", long. 145° 25' 26".

Transmitter: State Hwy. Maintenance Station, Glennallen.

Ownership: State of Alaska.

Cordova—K09OR, Ch. 9, State of Alaska. Phone: 907-269-5744.

Technical Facilities: 0.013-kw ERP, lat. 60° 32' 49", long. 145° 44' 48".

Ownership: State of Alaska.

Cordova—K15AK, Ch. 15, State of Alaska.

Technical Facilities: 100-w TPO, 0.392-kw ERP, 23-ft. above ground, 2522-ft. above sea level, lat. 60° 31' 30", long. 145° 41' 36".

Transmitter: Haney Mountain, 2-mi. SE of Cordova.

Ownership: State of Alaska.

Council—K07TL, Ch. 7, State of Alaska. Phone: 907-269-5744.

Technical Facilities: 0.055-kw ERP, 112-ft. above sea level, lat. 64° 53' 42", long. 163° 40' 10".

Ownership: State of Alaska.

Council—K09UK, Ch. 9, State of Alaska.

Technical Facilities: 10-w TPO, 0.055-kw ERP, 20-ft. above ground, 90-ft. above sea level, lat. 64° 53' 42", long. 163° 40' 10".

Transmitter: Alascom Office, Council.

Ownership: State of Alaska.

Craig—K57DE, Ch. 57, State of Alaska. Phone: 907-269-5744.

Technical Facilities: 0.08-kw ERP, lat. 55° 28' 35", long. 133° 08' 30".

Ownership: State of Alaska.

Craig—K61DE, Ch. 61, State of Alaska.

Technical Facilities: 0.63-kw ERP, lat. 55° 28' 36", long. 133° 08' 14".

Ownership: State of Alaska.

Crooked Creek—K07RZ, Ch. 7, State of Alaska.

Technical Facilities: 10-w TPO, 0.056-kw ERP, 20-ft. above ground, 148-ft. above sea level, lat. 61° 52' 16", long. 158° 06' 06".

Transmitter: Crooked Creek School.

Ownership: State of Alaska.

Deering—K04LT, Ch. 4, State of Alaska. Phone: 907-269-5744.

Technical Facilities: 0.043-kw ERP, 36-ft. above sea level, lat. 66° 04' 36", long. 162° 43' 09".

Ownership: State of Alaska.

Deering—K09RN, Ch. 9, State of Alaska.

Technical Facilities: 10-w TPO, 0.0568-kw ERP, 20-ft. above ground, 40-ft. above sea level, lat. 66° 04' 36", long. 162° 43' 09".

Transmitter: Alascom Earth Station, Deering.

Ownership: State of Alaska.

Delta Junction—K05FI, Ch. 5, U. of Alaska. Phone: 907-269-5744.

Technical Facilities: 0.174-kw ERP, lat. 63° 47' 18", long. 145° 51' 35".

Ownership: U. of Alaska.

Delta Junction—K10OB, Ch. 10, R. E. Andreassen. Phone: 907-895-4352.

Technical Facilities: 10-w TPO, 0.02-kw ERP, 150-ft. above ground, 1400-ft. above sea level, lat. 64° 03' 25", long. 145° 35' 30".

Transmitter: 2.7-mi. E & 0.3-mi. N of Delta Junction, 0.2-mi. W of Mill-Tan Rd.

Ownership: R. E. Andreassen.

Delta Junction—K13KU, Ch. 13, Smith Media License Holdings LLC. Phone: 314-853-7736.

Technical Facilities: 0.27-kw ERP, lat. 63° 47' 18", long. 145° 51' 35".

Ownership: Smith Media License Holdings LLC.

Delta Junction—K17AF, Ch. 17, State of Alaska.

Technical Facilities: 20-w TPO, 0.137-kw ERP, 20-ft. above ground, 1145-ft. above sea level, lat. 64° 02' 13", long. 145° 42' 02".

Transmitter: Delta Junction Community School.

Ownership: State of Alaska.

Delta Junction, etc.—K07NJ, Ch. 7, Newport Television License LLC. Phone: 816-751-0204.

Technical Facilities: 0.284-kw ERP, 2956-ft. above sea level, lat. 63° 47' 18", long. 145° 51' 35".

Ownership: Newport Television LLC.

Dillingham—K05KF, Ch. 5, Alaska Corp. of Seventh Day Adventists.

Technical Facilities: 0.16-kw ERP, 69-ft. above ground, 151-ft. above sea level, lat. 59° 02' 38", long. 158° 29' 18".

Ownership: Alaska Corp. of Seventh Day Adventists.

Dillingham—K10LD, Ch. 10, State of Alaska.

Technical Facilities: 0.302-kw ERP, lat. 59° 03' 46", long. 158° 28' 03".

Ownership: State of Alaska.

Diomede—K13UX, Ch. 13, State of Alaska.

Technical Facilities: 0.05-kw ERP, lat. 65° 45' 30", long. 168° 58' 15".

Ownership: State of Alaska.

Dot Lake—K07RU, Ch. 7, State of Alaska. Phone: 907-269-5744.

Technical Facilities: 0.05-kw ERP, lat. 63° 39' 31", long. 144° 03' 22".

Ownership: State of Alaska.

Dot Lake—K13RM, Ch. 13, State of Alaska.

Technical Facilities: 10-w TPO, 0.0556-kw ERP, 20-ft. above ground, 1395-ft. above sea level, lat. 63° 39' 31", long. 144° 03' 22".

Transmitter: Dot Lake School, Dot Lake.

Ownership: State of Alaska.

Douglas, etc.—K13OC, Ch. 13, Smith Media License Holdings LLC. Phone: 314-853-7736.

Technical Facilities: 0.011-kw ERP, 89-ft. above sea level, lat. 58° 22' 15", long. 134° 33' 11".

Holds CP for change to 0.28-kw ERP, 98-ft. above ground, 1663-ft. above sea level, lat. 58° 22' 19", long. 134° 33' 24". BMJPTTV-20000831CKM.

Ownership: Smith Media License Holdings LLC.

Dutch Harbor—KUCB-LP, Ch. 8, Unalaska Community Television Inc. Phone: 907-581-1888.

Ownership: Unalaska Community Television Inc.

Eagle River—K16DO, Ch. 16, Anchorage Broadcast Television Consortium Inc. Phone: 425-258-1440.

Technical Facilities: 0.502-kw ERP, 59-ft. above ground, 1460-ft. above sea level, lat. 61° 18' 46", long. 149° 27' 42".

Began Operation: December 29, 1994.

Ownership: Anchorage Broadcast Television Consortium Inc.

Eagle River Road—K55DC, Ch. 55, Anchorage Broadcast Television Consortium Inc. Phone: 425-258-1440.

Technical Facilities: 0.34-kw ERP, lat. 61° 18' 46", long. 149° 27' 42".

Began Operation: September 16, 1982.

Ownership: Anchorage Broadcast Television Consortium Inc.

Eagle River Road—K58BH, Ch. 58, Anchorage Broadcast Television Consortium Inc. Phone: 425-258-1440.

Technical Facilities: 0.34-kw ERP, lat. 61° 18' 46", long. 149° 27' 42".

Began Operation: September 16, 1982.

Ownership: Anchorage Broadcast Television Consortium Inc.

Eagle River Road—K61CB, Ch. 61, Anchorage Broadcast Television Consortium Inc. Phone: 425-258-1440.

Technical Facilities: 0.34-kw ERP, 59-ft. above ground, 1440-ft. above sea level, lat. 61° 18' 46", long. 149° 27' 42".

Began Operation: September 16, 1982.

Ownership: Anchorage Broadcast Television Consortium Inc.

Eagle Village—K05IJ, Ch. 5, State of Alaska. Phone: 907-269-5744.

Technical Facilities: 0.05-kw ERP, lat. 64° 46' 48", long. 141° 06' 50".

Ownership: State of Alaska.

Eagle Village—K09RF, Ch. 9, State of Alaska.

Technical Facilities: 10-w TPO, 0.053-kw ERP, 20-ft. above ground, 895-ft. above sea level, lat. 64° 46' 48", long. 141° 06' 50".

Transmitter: Alascom Earth Station, Eagle Village.

Ownership: State of Alaska.

Eek—K09TN, Ch. 9, State of Alaska.

Technical Facilities: 10-w TPO, 0.055-kw ERP, 20-ft. above ground, 40-ft. above sea level, lat. 60° 13' 08", long. 162° 01' 11".

Transmitter: Eek High School.

Ownership: State of Alaska.

Eek—K11SD, Ch. 11, State of Alaska.

Technical Facilities: 0.055-kw ERP, lat. 60° 13' 08", long. 162° 01' 11".

Ownership: State of Alaska.

Egegik—K04KR, Ch. 4, State of Alaska.

Technical Facilities: 10-w TPO, 0.0506-kw ERP, 20-ft. above ground, 75-ft. above sea level, lat. 58° 12' 55", long. 157° 22' 27".

Transmitter: Egegik Community School.

Ownership: State of Alaska.

Egegik—K09SK, Ch. 9, State of Alaska. Phone: 907-269-5744.

Technical Facilities: 0.05-kw ERP, lat. 58° 12' 55", long. 157° 22' 27".

Ownership: State of Alaska.

Eight Fathoms Bight—K09TA, Ch. 9, State of Alaska.

Technical Facilities: 10-w TPO, 0.055-kw ERP, 20-ft. above ground, 40-ft. above sea level, lat. 58° 00' 10", long. 135° 46' 03".

Ownership: State of Alaska.

Eight Fathoms Bight—K13TG, Ch. 13, State of Alaska. Phone: 907-269-5744.

Technical Facilities: 0.05-kw ERP, lat. 57° 56' 38", long. 134° 44' 17".

Ownership: State of Alaska.

Ekwok—K04MS, Ch. 4, State of Alaska. Phone: 907-269-5744.

Technical Facilities: 0.043-kw ERP, lat. 59° 20' 59", long. 157° 28' 33".

Ekwok—K11QW, Ch. 11, State of Alaska.

Technical Facilities: 10-w TPO, 0.055-kw ERP, 20-ft. above ground, 185-ft. above sea level, lat. 59° 20' 59", long. 157° 28' 33".

Transmitter: Ekwok High School.

Ownership: State of Alaska.

Elfin Cove—K09TK, Ch. 9, State of Alaska.

Technical Facilities: 10-w TPO, 0.055-kw ERP, 20-ft. above ground, 40-ft. above sea level, lat. 58° 11' 03", long. 136° 20' 35".

Transmitter: Elfin Cove School.

Ownership: State of Alaska.

Elim—K03GA, Ch. 3, State of Alaska. Phone: 907-269-5744.

Technical Facilities: 0.043-kw ERP, 43-ft. above sea level, lat. 64° 37' 03", long. 162° 15' 20".

Ownership: State of Alaska.

Elim—K09QS, Ch. 9, State of Alaska.

Technical Facilities: 10-w TPO, 0.0555-kw ERP, 20-ft. above ground, 47-ft. above sea level, lat. 64° 37' 03", long. 162° 15' 20".

Transmitter: Alascom Earth Station, Elim.

Ownership: State of Alaska.

Emmonak—K05IH, Ch. 5, State of Alaska.

Technical Facilities: 0.05-kw ERP, lat. 62° 46' 44", long. 164° 31' 36".

Ownership: State of Alaska.

Emmonak—K07OP, Ch. 7, State of Alaska. Phone: 907-269-5744.

Technical Facilities: 0.013-kw ERP, lat. 62° 46' 33", long. 164° 31' 35".

Ownership: Village of Emmonak.

English Bay—K31AG, Ch. 31, State of Alaska. Phone: 907-269-5744.

Technical Facilities: 0.14-kw ERP, lat. 59° 21' 38", long. 151° 55' 48".

Ownership: State of Alaska.

English Bay—K43AK, Ch. 43, State of Alaska. Phone: 907-269-5744.

Technical Facilities: 0.14-kw ERP, lat. 59° 21' 38", long. 151° 55' 48".

Ownership: State of Alaska.

Ernestine—K04MY, Ch. 4, State of Alaska. Phone: 907-269-5744.

Technical Facilities: 0.04-kw ERP, lat. 61° 27' 04", long. 145° 10' 18".

Ownership: State of Alaska.

Ernestine—K11RI, Ch. 11, State of Alaska.

Technical Facilities: 10-w TPO, 0.055-kw ERP, 20-ft. above ground, 1000-ft. above sea level, lat. 61° 27' 04", long. 145° 10' 18".

Transmitter: Hwy. Maintenance Camp, Ernestine.

Ownership: State of Alaska.

■**Fairbanks**—K13XD, Ch. 13, Tanana Valley Television Co.

Technical Facilities: 3-kw ERP, 331-ft. above ground, 1713-ft. above sea level, lat. 64° 55' 20", long. 147° 42' 55".

Ownership: Tanana Valley Television Co.

Fairbanks—K14JL, Ch. 14, Tanana Valley Television Co. Phone: 907-452-3697.

Studio: 3532 International Blvd, Fairbanks, AK 99501.

Fairbanks—K16DW, Ch. 16, Tanana Valley Television Co. Phone: 907-452-3697.

Studio: 3532 International Blvd, Fairbanks, AK 99501.

Technical Facilities: 1000-w TPO, 29.5-kw ERP, 49-ft. above ground, 2415-ft. above sea level, lat. 64° 52' 44", long. 148° 03' 10".

Holds CP for change to 15-kw ERP, BMAPTTL-20000831CLY.

Transmitter: 9.3-mi. WNW of Fairbanks, on Ester Dome.

Multichannel TV Sound: Stereo only.

Ownership: Tanana Valley Television Co.

Personnel: Kate Giard, General Manager; Thomas Peak, Chief Engineer; George Quinto, Sales Manager.

Fairbanks—K22EY, Ch. 22, Tanana Valley Television Co. Phone: 907-452-3697.

Studio: 3532 International Blvd, Fairbanks, AK 99501.

Technical Facilities: 1000-w TPO, 30-kw ERP, 49-ft. above ground, 2415-ft. above sea level, lat. 64° 52' 44", long. 148° 03' 10".

Transmitter: 9.3-mi. WNW of Fairbanks, on Ester Dome.

Multichannel TV Sound: Stereo only.

Ownership: Tanana Valley Television Co.

Personnel: Kate Giard, General Manager; Thomas Peak, Chief Engineer; George Quinto, Sales Manager.

Fairbanks—K28ES, Ch. 28, Tanana Valley Television Co. Phone: 907-452-3697.

Studio: 3532 International Blvd, Fairbanks, AK 99501.

Technical Facilities: 1000-w TPO, 30-kw ERP, 49-ft. above ground, 2415-ft. above sea level, lat. 64° 52' 44", long. 148° 03' 10".

Transmitter: 9.3-mi. WNW of Fairbanks, on Ester Dome.

Multichannel TV Sound: Stereo only.

Ownership: Tanana Valley Television Co.

Personnel: Kate Giard, General Manager; Thomas Peak, Chief Engineer; George Quinto, Sales Manager.

Fairbanks—K30ET, Ch. 30, Denali Television. Phone: 907-459-2288.

Studio: 3532 International Blvd, Fairbanks, AK 99501.

Technical Facilities: 1000-w TPO, 30-kw ERP, 49-ft. above ground, 2415-ft. above sea level, lat. 64° 52' 44", long. 148° 03' 10".

Transmitter: 9.3-mi. WNW of Fairbanks, on Ester Dome.

Multichannel TV Sound: Stereo only.

Ownership: Denali Television.

Personnel: Kate Giard, General Manager; Thomas Peak, Chief Engineer; George Quinto, Sales Manager.

Fairbanks—K34EJ, Ch. 34, Denali Television. Phone: 907-459-2288.

Studio: 3532 International Blvd, Fairbanks, AK 99501.

Technical Facilities: 1000-w TPO, 30-kw ERP, 49-ft. above ground, 2415-ft. above sea level, lat. 64° 52' 44", long. 148° 03' 10".

Transmitter: 9.3-mi. WNW of Fairbanks, on Ester Dome.

Multichannel TV Sound: Stereo only.

Ownership: Denali Television.

Personnel: Kate Giard, General Manager; Thomas Peak, Chief Engineer; George Quinto, Sales Manager.

Fairbanks—K36ED, Ch. 36, Denali Television. Phone: 907-459-2288.

Studio: 3532 International Blvd, Fairbanks, AK 99501.

Technical Facilities: 1000-w TPO, 30-kw ERP, 49-ft. above ground, 2415-ft. above sea level, lat. 64° 52' 44", long. 148° 03' 10".

Transmitter: 9.3-mi. WNW of Fairbanks, on Ester Dome.

Multichannel TV Sound: Stereo only.

Ownership: Denali Television.

Personnel: Kate Giard, General Manager; Thomas Peak, Chief Engineer; George Quinto, Sales Manager.

Fairbanks—K38EL, Ch. 38, Denali Television. Phone: 907-459-2288.

Studio: 3532 International Blvd, Fairbanks, AK 99501.

Technical Facilities: 1000-w TPO, 30-kw ERP, 49-ft. above ground, 2415-ft. above sea level, lat. 64° 52' 44", long. 148° 03' 10".

Transmitter: 9.3-mi. WNW of Fairbanks, on Ester Dome.

Multichannel TV Sound: Stereo only.

Ownership: Denali Television.

Personnel: Kate Giard, General Manager; Thomas Peak, Chief Engineer; George Quinto, Sales Manager.

Fairbanks—K40EN, Ch. 40, Denali Television. Phone: 907-459-2288.

Studio: 3532 International Blvd, Fairbanks, AK 99501.

Technical Facilities: 1000-w TPO, 30-kw ERP, 49-ft. above ground, 2415-ft. above sea level, lat. 64° 52' 44", long. 148° 03' 10".

Transmitter: 9.3-mi. WNW of Fairbanks, on Ester Dome.

Multichannel TV Sound: Stereo only.

Ownership: Denali Television.

Personnel: Kate Giard, General Manager; Thomas Peak, Chief Engineer; George Quinto, Sales Manager.

Fairbanks—K42EC, Ch. 42, Denali Television. Phone: 907-459-2288.

Studio: 3532 International Blvd, Fairbanks, AK 99501.

Technical Facilities: 1000-w TPO, 30-kw ERP, 49-ft. above ground, 2415-ft. above sea level, lat. 64° 52' 44", long. 148° 03' 10".

Transmitter: 9.3-mi. WNW of Fairbanks, on Ester Dome.

Multichannel TV Sound: Stereo only.

Ownership: Denali Television.

Personnel: Kate Giard, General Manager; Thomas Peak, Chief Engineer; George Quinto, Sales Manager.

Fairbanks—K44EK, Ch. 44, Denali Television. Phone: 907-459-2288.

Studio: 3532 International Blvd, Fairbanks, AK 99501.

Technical Facilities: 1000-w TPO, 30-kw ERP, 102-ft. above ground, 2464-ft. above sea level, lat. 64° 52' 44", long. 148° 03' 10".

Transmitter: 9.3-mi. WNW of Fairbanks, on Ester Dome.

Multichannel TV Sound: Stereo only.

Ownership: Denali Television.

Personnel: Kate Giard, General Manager; Thomas Peak, Chief Engineer; George Quinto, Sales Manager.

Fairbanks—K46EH, Ch. 46, Denali Television. Phone: 907-459-2288.

Studio: 3532 International Blvd, Fairbanks, AK 99501.

Technical Facilities: 1000-w TPO, 30-kw ERP, 102-ft. above ground, 2464-ft. above sea level, lat. 64° 52' 44", long. 148° 03' 10".

Holds CP for change to 15-kw ERP, 102-ft. above ground, 2467-ft. above sea level, BMAPTTL-20000831CMA.

Transmitter: 9.3-mi. WNW of Fairbanks, on Ester Dome.

Multichannel TV Sound: Stereo only.

Ownership: Denali Television.

Personnel: Kate Giard, General Manager; Thomas Peak, Chief Engineer; George Quinto, Sales Manager.

■**Fairbanks**—K48FG, Ch. 48, Denali Television. Phone: 907-459-2288.

Studio: 3532 International Blvd, Fairbanks, AK 99501.

Technical Facilities: 1000-w TPO, 30-kw ERP, 102-ft. above ground, 2464-ft. above sea level, lat. 64° 52' 44", long. 148° 03' 10".

Transmitter: 9.3-mi. WNW of Fairbanks, on Ester Dome.

Multichannel TV Sound: Stereo only.

Ownership: Denali Television.

Personnel: Kate Giard, General Manager; Thomas Peak, Chief Engineer; George Quinto, Sales Manager.

Fairbanks—K50EH, Ch. 50, Denali Television. Phone: 907-459-2288.

Studio: 3532 International Blvd, Fairbanks, AK 99501.

Technical Facilities: 1000-w TPO, 30-kw ERP, 102-ft. above ground, 2464-ft. above sea level, lat. 64° 52' 44", long. 148° 03' 10".

Transmitter: 9.3-mi. WNW of Fairbanks, on Ester Dome.

Multichannel TV Sound: Stereo only.

Ownership: Denali Television.

Personnel: Kate Giard, General Manager; Thomas Peak, Chief Engineer; George Quinto, Sales Manager.

Fairbanks—K52EY, Ch. 52, Denali Television. Phone: 907-459-2288.

Studio: 3532 International Blvd, Fairbanks, AK 99501.

Technical Facilities: 1000-w TPO, 30-kw ERP, 102-ft. above ground, 2464-ft. above sea level, lat. 64° 52' 44", long. 148° 03' 10".

Holds CP for change to 15-kw ERP, 102-ft. above ground, 2467-ft. above sea level, BMAPTTL-20000831CNH.

Transmitter: 9.3-mi. WNW of Fairbanks, on Ester Dome.

Multichannel TV Sound: Stereo only.

Ownership: Denali Television.

Personnel: Kate Giard, Sales Manager; Thomas Peak, Chief Engineer; George Quinto, Sales Manager.

Fairbanks—K54EW, Ch. 54, Denali Television. Phone: 907-459-2288.

Studio: 3532 International Blvd, Fairbanks, AK 99501.

Technical Facilities: 1000-w TPO, 30-kw ERP, 102-ft. above ground, 2464-ft. above sea level, lat. 64° 52' 44", long. 148° 03' 10".

Transmitter: 9.3-mi. WNW of Fairbanks, on Ester Dome.

Multichannel TV Sound: Stereo only.

Ownership: Denali Television.

Personnel: Kate Giard, General Manager; Thomas Peak, Chief Engineer; George Quinto, Sales Manager.

Fairbanks—K56FX, Ch. 56, Denali Television. Phone: 907-459-2288.

Studio: 3532 International Blvd, Fairbanks, AK 99501.

Technical Facilities: 1000-w TPO, 30-kw ERP, 102-ft. above ground, 2464-ft. above sea level, lat. 64° 52' 44", long. 148° 03' 10".

Transmitter: 9.3-mi. WNW of Fairbanks, on Ester Dome.

Multichannel TV Sound: Stereo only.

Ownership: Denali Television.

Personnel: Kate Giard, General Manager; Thomas Peak, Chief Engineer; George Quinto, Sales Manager.

Fairbanks—K60FQ, Ch. 60, Denali Television. Phone: 907-459-2288.

Studio: 3532 International Blvd, Fairbanks, AK 99501.

Technical Facilities: 1000-w TPO, 30-kw ERP, 102-ft. above ground, 2464-ft. above sea level, lat. 64° 52' 44", long. 148° 03' 10".

Holds CP for change to 15-kw ERP, 102-ft. above ground, 2467-ft. above sea level, BMAPTTL-20000831CNF.

Transmitter: 9.3-mi. WNW of Fairbanks, on Ester Dome.

Multichannel TV Sound: Stereo only.

Ownership: Denali Television.

Personnel: Kate Giard, General Manager; Thomas Peak, Chief Engineer; George Quinto, Sales Manager.

Fairbanks—K62FB, Ch. 62, Denali Television. Phone: 907-459-2288.

Studio: 3532 International Blvd, Fairbanks, AK 99501.

Technical Facilities: 1000-w TPO, 30-kw ERP, 102-ft. above ground, 2464-ft. above sea level, lat. 64° 52' 44", long. 148° 03' 10".

Holds CP for change to 15-kw ERP, 102-ft. above ground, 2467-ft. above sea level, BMAPTTL-20000831CLJ.

Transmitter: 9.3-mi. WNW of Fairbanks, on Ester Dome.

Multichannel TV Sound: Stereo only.

Ownership: Denali Television.

Personnel: Kate Giard, General Manager; Thomas Peak, Chief Engineer; George Quinto, Sales Manager.

Fairbanks—K64EU, Ch. 64, Denali Television. Phone: 907-459-2288.

Studio: 3532 International Blvd, Fairbanks, AK 99501.

Technical Facilities: 1000-w TPO, 30-kw ERP, 102-ft. above ground, 2464-ft. above sea level, lat. 64° 52' 44", long. 148° 03' 10".

Transmitter: 9.3-mi. WNW of Fairbanks, on Ester Dome.

Multichannel TV Sound: Stereo only.

Ownership: Denali Television.

Personnel: Kate Giard, General Manager; Thomas Peak, Chief Engineer; George Quinto, Sales Manager.

Fairbanks—K66FG, Ch. 66, Denali Television. Phone: 907-459-2288.

Studio: 3532 International Blvd, Fairbanks, AK 99501.

Technical Facilities: 1000-w TPO, 30-kw ERP, 102-ft. above ground, 2464-ft. above sea level, lat. 64° 52' 44", long. 148° 03' 10".

Transmitter: 9.3-mi. WNW of Fairbanks, on Ester Dome.

Multichannel TV Sound: Stereo only.

Ownership: Denali Television.

Personnel: Kate Giard, General Manager; Thomas Peak, Chief Engineer; George Quinto, Sales Manager.

Fairbanks—K68EZ, Ch. 68, Denali Television. Phone: 907-459-2288.

Studio: 3532 International Blvd, Fairbanks, AK 99501.

Technical Facilities: 1000-w TPO, 30-kw ERP, 102-ft. above ground, 2464-ft. above sea level, lat. 64° 52' 44", long. 148° 03' 10".

Holds CP for change to 15-kw ERP, 102-ft. above ground, 2467-ft. above sea level, BMAPTTL-20000831CNB.

Transmitter: 9.3-mi. WNW of Fairbanks, on Ester Dome.

Multichannel TV Sound: Stereo only.

Ownership: Denali Television.

Personnel: Kate Giard, General Manager; Thomas Peak, Chief Engineer; George Quinto, Sales Manager.

Fairbanks—KDMD-LP, Ch. 22, Ketchikan TV LLC. Phone: 303-688-5162.

Studio: 6921 Brayton Dr, Ste 221, Anchorage, AK 99514.

Technical Facilities: 500-w TPO, 284-kw ERP, 102-ft. above ground, 2398-ft. above sea level, lat. 64° 52' 44", long. 148° 03' 10".

Holds CP for change to channel number 32, 11.5-kw ERP, 18-ft. above ground, 2315-ft. above sea level, BPTTL-20071009ABN.

Transmitter: End of Basher Rd.

Ownership: Ketchikan TV LLC.

Personnel: Frank Martin, General Manager.

False Pass—K04LG, Ch. 4, State of Alaska. Phone: 907-269-5744.

Technical Facilities: 0.042-kw ERP, lat. 54° 54' 23", long. 163° 24' 44".

Ownership: State of Alaska.

False Pass—K09RP, Ch. 9, State of Alaska.

Technical Facilities: 10-w TPO, 0.0542-kw ERP, 20-ft. above ground, 50-ft. above sea level, lat. 51° 54' 23", long. 163° 24' 44".

Transmitter: Alascom Earth Station, False Pass.

Ownership: State of Alaska.

Fort Yukon—K07RC, Ch. 7, State of Alaska.

Technical Facilities: 10-w TPO, 0.055-kw ERP, 20-ft. above ground, 460-ft. above sea level, lat. 66° 33' 53", long. 145° 15' 48".

Transmitter: Alascom Earth Station, Fort Yukon.

Ownership: State of Alaska.

Freshwater Bay—K09TP, Ch. 9, State of Alaska.

Technical Facilities: 10-w TPO, 0.055-kw ERP, 20-ft. above ground, 40-ft. above sea level, lat. 57° 53' 57", long. 135° 09' 21".

Transmitter: Freshwater Bay School.

Ownership: State of Alaska.

Freshwater Bay—K13TW, Ch. 13, State of Alaska. Phone: 907-269-5744.

Technical Facilities: 0.05-kw ERP, lat. 57° 53' 57", long. 135° 09' 21".

Ownership: State of Alaska.

Gakona—K11RG, Ch. 11, State of Alaska.

Technical Facilities: 10-w TPO, 0.055-kw ERP, 20-ft. above ground, 1470-ft. above sea level, lat. 62° 18' 01", long. 145° 18' 13".

Ownership: State of Alaska.

Gakona, etc.—K03FJ, Ch. 3, State of Alaska. Phone: 907-269-5744.

Technical Facilities: 0.04-kw ERP, 20-ft. above ground, 1470-ft. above sea level, lat. 62° 18' 01", long. 145° 18' 13".

Ownership: Wrangell Mountain TV Club Inc.

Galena—K04LZ, Ch. 4, State of Alaska.

Technical Facilities: 10-w TPO, 0.041-kw ERP, 30-ft. above ground, 190-ft. above sea level, lat. 64° 45' 33", long. 156° 51' 41".

Transmitter: Alexander Lake Townsite addition, Galena.

Ownership: State of Alaska.

Galena—K10LJ, Ch. 10, City of Galena. Phone: 907-656-1301.

Technical Facilities: 0.018-kw ERP, lat. 64° 45' 33", long. 156° 51' 41".

Ownership: City of Galena.

Gambell—K09QR, Ch. 9, State of Alaska.

Technical Facilities: 10-w TPO, 0.0535-kw ERP, 20-ft. above ground, 35-ft. above sea level, lat. 63° 46' 44", long. 171° 43' 54".

Transmitter: Alascom Earth Station, Gambell.

Ownership: State of Alaska.

Girdwood—K05FW, Ch. 5, Alaska Public Telecommunications Inc. Phone: 907-563-7070.

Technical Facilities: 0.061-kw ERP, lat. 60° 57' 12", long. 149° 06' 03".

Holds CP for change to 20-ft. above ground, 805-ft. above sea level, lat. 60° 57' 12", long. 149° 06' 28". BDFCDTT-20060331BEN.

Ownership: Alaska Public Telecommunications Inc.

Girdwood—K08KA, Ch. 8, Anchorage Broadcast Television Consortium Inc. Phone: 425-258-1440.

Technical Facilities: 0.055-kw ERP, lat. 60° 57' 12", long. 149° 06' 03".

Began Operation: January 6, 1983.

Ownership: Anchorage Broadcast Television Consortium Inc.

Girdwood—K10MB, Ch. 10, Anchorage Broadcast Television Consortium Inc. Phone: 425-258-1440.

Technical Facilities: 10-w TPO, 0.05-kw ERP, 60-ft. above ground, 110-ft. above sea level, lat. 60° 56' 45", long. 149° 10' 24".

Transmitter: Hwy. Maintenance Shop, Girdwood.

Began Operation: December 7, 1982.

Ownership: Anchorage Broadcast Television Consortium Inc.

Girdwood Valley—K12MM, Ch. 12, Anchorage Broadcast Television Consortium Inc. Phone: 425-258-1440.

Technical Facilities: 0.02-kw ERP, lat. 60° 57' 12", long. 149° 06' 03".

Began Operation: March 22, 1983.

Ownership: Anchorage Broadcast Television Consortium Inc.

Glenallen—K05HA, Ch. 5, State of Alaska. Phone: 907-269-5744.

Technical Facilities: 0.928-kw ERP, lat. 61° 46' 44", long. 145° 12' 25".

Ownership: State of Alaska.

Glennallen—K07QS, Ch. 7, Wrangell Mountain TV Club Inc. Phone: 907-822-3407.

Technical Facilities: 100-w TPO, 0.297-kw ERP, 90-ft. above ground, 3290-ft. above sea level, lat. 61° 46' 11", long. 145° 11' 47".

Transmitter: Willow Mountain.

Ownership: Wrangell Mountain TV Club Inc.

Glennallen & Cooper Landing—K13UB, Ch. 13, State of Alaska.

Technical Facilities: 100-w TPO, 0.47-kw ERP, 85-ft. above ground, 3284-ft. above sea level, lat. 61° 46' 44", long. 145° 12' 25".

Transmitter: Willow Mountain, Mile 88, Richardson Hwy.

Ownership: State of Alaska.

Golovin—K04LH, Ch. 4, State of Alaska. Phone: 907-269-5744.

Technical Facilities: 0.042-kw ERP, 46-ft. above sea level, lat. 64° 33' 36", long. 163° 02' 03".

Ownership: State of Alaska.

Golovin—K07QX, Ch. 7, State of Alaska.

Technical Facilities: 10-w TPO, 0.0549-kw ERP, 20-ft. above ground, 50-ft. above sea level, lat. 64° 32' 36", long. 163° 02' 03".

Transmitter: Alascom Earth Station, Golovin.

Ownership: State of Alaska.

Goodnews Bay—K04KT, Ch. 4, State of Alaska.

Technical Facilities: 10-w TPO, 0.0506-kw ERP, 20-ft. above ground, 90-ft. above sea level, lat. 59° 07' 07", long. 161° 35' 19".

Transmitter: Alascom Earth Station, Goodnews Bay.

Ownership: State of Alaska.

Goodnews Bay—K09SG, Ch. 9, State of Alaska. Phone: 907-269-5744.

Technical Facilities: 0.062-kw ERP, 30-ft. above ground, 52-ft. above sea level, lat. 59° 07' 01", long. 161° 35' 18".

Ownership: State of Alaska.

Gravina Island—K02ML, Ch. 2, State of Alaska. Phone: 907-269-5744.

Technical Facilities: 0.428-kw ERP, lat. 55° 21' 11", long. 131° 42' 04".

Transmitter: Ketchikan Borough Airport, Gravina Island.

Ownership: State of Alaska.

Gravina Island, etc.—K04NC, Ch. 4, State of Alaska.

Technical Facilities: 10-w TPO, 0.043-kw ERP, 20-ft. above ground, 40-ft. above sea level, lat. 55° 21' 22", long. 131° 42' 41".

Transmitter: Ketchikan Borough Airport Bldg., Gravina Island.

Ownership: State of Alaska.

Grayling—K09PC, Ch. 9, State of Alaska. Phone: 907-269-5744.

Technical Facilities: 0.018-kw ERP, lat. 62° 54' 11", long. 160° 03' 54".

Ownership: City of Grayling.

Grayling—K11QH, Ch. 11, State of Alaska.

Technical Facilities: 10-w TPO, 0.0534-kw ERP, 20-ft. above ground, 95-ft. above sea level, lat. 62° 54' 11", long. 160° 03' 54".

Transmitter: Alascom Earth Station, Grayling.

Ownership: State of Alaska.

Gustavus—K02LW, Ch. 2, State of Alaska.

Technical Facilities: 10-w TPO, 0.43-kw ERP, 20-ft. above ground, 50-ft. above sea level, lat. 58° 25' 04", long. 135° 42' 30".

Transmitter: Airport Maintenance Bldg., Gustavus.

Ownership: State of Alaska.

Gustavus—K04MR, Ch. 4, State of Alaska. Phone: 907-269-5744.

Technical Facilities: 0.04-kw ERP, lat. 58° 25' 04", long. 135° 42' 30".

Ownership: State of Alaska.

Haines—K03FM, Ch. 3, Lynn Canal Broadcasting. Phone: 907-269-5744.

Technical Facilities: 0.018-kw ERP, 394-ft. above sea level, lat. 59° 13' 06", long. 135° 25' 29".

Ownership: Lynn Canal Broadcasting.

Haines—K07RF, Ch. 7, State of Alaska.

Technical Facilities: 10-w TPO, 0.055-kw ERP, 20-ft. above ground, 70-ft. above sea level, lat. 59° 14' 08", long. 135° 27' 01".

Transmitter: Alascom Earth Station, Haines.

Ownership: State of Alaska.

Haines—K09PD, Ch. 9, State of Alaska. Phone: 907-269-5744.

Technical Facilities: 0.01-kw ERP, lat. 59° 14' 05", long. 135° 27' 01".

Ownership: State of Alaska.

Halibut Cove—K08JY, Ch. 8, State of Alaska. Phone: 907-269-5744.

Technical Facilities: 0.06-kw ERP, lat. 59° 35' 57", long. 151° 14' 22".

Ownership: State of Alaska.

Halibut Cove—K12NW, Ch. 12, State of Alaska.

Technical Facilities: 0.06-kw ERP, lat. 59° 35' 57", long. 151° 14' 22".

Transmitter: Halibut Cove School.

Ownership: State of Alaska.

Healy—K07ND, Ch. 7, U. of Alaska.

Technical Facilities: 0.335-kw ERP, lat. 63° 52' 30", long. 148° 51' 00".

Ownership: U. of Alaska.

Healy—K58BI, Ch. 58, State of Alaska.

Technical Facilities: 10-w TPO, 0.317-kw ERP, 20-ft. above ground, 173-ft. above sea level, lat. 63° 50' 13", long. 148° 58' 38".

Transmitter: State of Alaska Communications Site, Healy.

Ownership: State of Alaska.

Healy, etc.—K06LA, Ch. 6, Newport Television License LLC. Phone: 816-751-0204.

Technical Facilities: 0.02-kw ERP, lat. 63° 52' 30", long. 148° 51' 00".

Ownership: Newport Television LLC.

Hobart Bay—K09TB, Ch. 9, State of Alaska.

Technical Facilities: 10-w TPO, 0.055-kw ERP, 20-ft. above ground, 40-ft. above sea level, lat. 57° 24' 15", long. 133° 24' 31".

Transmitter: Hobart Bay School.

Ownership: State of Alaska.

Hobart Bay—K13TT, Ch. 13, State of Alaska. Phone: 907-269-5744.

Technical Facilities: 0.05-kw ERP, lat. 57° 24' 15", long. 133° 24' 31".

Ownership: State of Alaska.

Hollis—K08KP, Ch. 8, State of Alaska.

Technical Facilities: 0.05-kw ERP, lat. 55° 28' 58", long. 132° 38' 53".

Ownership: State of Alaska.

Hollis—K12NT, Ch. 12, State of Alaska.

Technical Facilities: 0.58-kw ERP, lat. 55° 28' 58", long. 132° 38' 53".

Ownership: State of Alaska.

Holy Cross—K07RJ, Ch. 7, State of Alaska.

Technical Facilities: 10-w TPO, 0.0556-kw ERP, 20-ft. above ground, 195-ft. above sea level, lat. 62° 11' 58", long. 159° 46' 05".

Transmitter: Alascom Earth Station, Holy Cross.

Ownership: State of Alaska.

Holy Cross—K09NJ, Ch. 9, Village of Holy Cross. Phone: 907-269-5744.

Technical Facilities: 0.013-kw ERP, lat. 62° 12' 00", long. 159° 40' 07".

Ownership: Village of Holy Cross.

Homer—K07PF, Ch. 7, Alaska Public Telecommunications Inc. Phone: 907-563-7070.

Technical Facilities: 0.18-kw ERP, lat. 59° 27' 17", long. 151° 40' 18".

Holds CP for change to 0.176-kw ERP, 105-ft. above ground, 1204-ft. above sea level, BDFCDTT-20060331BCE.

Ownership: Alaska Public Telecommunications Inc.

Homer—K09XO, Ch. 9, Fireweed Communications Corp. Phone: 907-248-5937.

Technical Facilities: 3-kw ERP, 121-ft. above ground, 1220-ft. above sea level, lat. 59° 27' 17", long. 151° 40' 18".

Ownership: Fireweed Communications LLC.

Homer & Seldovia—K02IB, Ch. 2, Anchorage Broadcast Television Consortium Inc. Phone: 425-258-1440.

Technical Facilities: 0.63-kw ERP, lat. 59° 27' 17", long. 151° 40' 18".

Began Operation: March 7, 1980.

Ownership: Anchorage Broadcast Television Consortium Inc.

Homer, etc.—K04JH, Ch. 4, Anchorage Broadcast Television Consortium Inc. Phone: 425-258-1440.

Technical Facilities: 0.75-kw ERP, lat. 59° 27' 17", long. 151° 40' 18".

Ownership: Anchorage Broadcast Television Consortium Inc.

Homer, etc.—K11RK, Ch. 11, Anchorage Broadcast Television Consortium Inc. Phone: 425-258-1440.

Technical Facilities: 100-w TPO, 0.79-kw ERP, 115-ft. above ground, 1215-ft. above sea level, lat. 59° 27' 17", long. 151° 40' 18".

Began Operation: June 14, 1983.

Ownership: Anchorage Broadcast Television Consortium Inc.

Homer, etc.—K13TR, Ch. 13, Anchorage Broadcast Television Consortium Inc. Phone: 425-258-1440.

Technical Facilities: 0.13-kw ERP, lat. 59° 27' 17", long. 151° 40' 18".

Began Operation: June 25, 1982.

Ownership: Anchorage Broadcast Television Consortium Inc.

Homer-Seldovia—K11VP, Ch. 11, Alaska Broadcasting Co. Inc. Phone: 907-273-3192.

Technical Facilities: 3-kw ERP, 112-ft. above ground, 1211-ft. above sea level, lat. 59° 27' 17", long. 151° 40' 18".

Ownership: Alaska Broadcasting Co. Inc.

Hoonah—K04MO, Ch. 4, State of Alaska. Phone: 907-269-5744.

Technical Facilities: 0.041-kw ERP, lat. 58° 06' 36", long. 135° 26' 28".

Ownership: State of Alaska.

Hoonah—K07QV, Ch. 7, State of Alaska.

Technical Facilities: 10-w TPO, 0.053-kw ERP, 70-ft. above ground, 85-ft. above sea level, lat. 58° 06' 36", long. 135° 26' 28".

Transmitter: Waste Treatment Plant, Hoonah.

Ownership: State of Alaska.

Hooper Bay—K04MC, Ch. 4, State of Alaska.

Technical Facilities: 10-w TPO, 0.043-kw ERP, 20-ft. above ground, 40-ft. above sea level, lat. 61° 31' 56", long. 166° 05' 42".

Transmitter: Alascom Earth Station, Hooper Bay.

Ownership: State of Alaska.

Hooper Bay—K07QD, Ch. 7, State of Alaska. Phone: 907-269-5744.

Technical Facilities: 0.018-kw ERP, lat. 61° 31' 56", long. 166° 05' 42".

Ownership: Hooper Bay City Council.

Hughes—K09RY, Ch. 9, State of Alaska.

Technical Facilities: 10-w TPO, 0.054-kw ERP, 20-ft. above ground, 315-ft. above sea level, lat. 66° 02' 50", long. 154° 15' 20".

Transmitter: Alascom Earth Station, Hughes.

Ownership: State of Alaska.

Huslia—K04JS, Ch. 4, State of Alaska. Phone: 907-269-5744.

Technical Facilities: 0.018-kw ERP, lat. 65° 41' 57", long. 156° 23' 50".

Ownership: Huslia Village Council.

Huslia—K09QD, Ch. 9, State of Alaska.

Technical Facilities: 10-w TPO, 0.0555-kw ERP, 20-ft. above ground, 215-ft. above sea level, lat. 65° 41' 57", long. 156° 23' 50".

Transmitter: Alascom Earth Station, Huslia.

Ownership: State of Alaska.

Hydaburg—K02JW, Ch. 2, City of Hydaburg. Phone: 907-269-5744.

Technical Facilities: 0.04-kw ERP, lat. 55° 12' 26", long. 132° 49' 14".

Ownership: City of Hydaburg.

Hydaburg—K09QI, Ch. 9, State of Alaska.

Technical Facilities: 10-w TPO, 0.055-kw ERP, 20-ft. above ground, 45-ft. above sea level, lat. 55° 12' 26", long. 132° 49' 26".

Transmitter: Hydaburg Public School.

Ownership: State of Alaska.

Hyder—K02MJ, Ch. 2, State of Alaska.

Technical Facilities: 0.04-kw ERP, lat. 55° 54' 58", long. 130° 01' 25".

Ownership: State of Alaska.

Hyder—K04MM, Ch. 4, State of Alaska. Phone: 907-269-5744.

Technical Facilities: 0.04-kw ERP, lat. 55° 54' 58", long. 130° 01' 25".

Ownership: State of Alaska.

Igiugig—K04ME, Ch. 4, State of Alaska. Phone: 907-269-5744.

Technical Facilities: 0.043-kw ERP, lat. 59° 19' 39", long. 155° 53' 33".

Ownership: State of Alaska.

Igiugig—K09SP, Ch. 9, State of Alaska.

Technical Facilities: 0.05-kw ERP, lat. 59° 19' 39", long. 155° 53' 33".

Ownership: State of Alaska.

Iliamna—K04KO, Ch. 4, State of Alaska.

Technical Facilities: 0.06-kw ERP, 33-ft. above ground, 105-ft. above sea level, lat. 59° 43' 12", long. 154° 50' 38".

Ownership: State of Alaska.

Iliamna—K07RV, Ch. 7, State of Alaska. Phone: 907-269-5744.

Technical Facilities: 0.036-kw ERP, lat. 59° 45' 12", long. 154° 50' 38".

Transmitter: Iliamna Village Council Bldg.

Ownership: State of Alaska.

Indian, etc.—K25AI, Ch. 25, Anchorage Broadcast Television Consortium Inc. Phone: 425-258-1440.

Technical Facilities: 0.6-kw ERP, lat. 61° 08' 35", long. 150° 00' 56".

Began Operation: May 10, 1983.

Ownership: Anchorage Broadcast Television Consortium Inc.

Indian, etc.—K47AM, Ch. 47, Anchorage Broadcast Television Consortium Inc. Phone: 425-258-1440.

Technical Facilities: 0.6-kw ERP, lat. 60° 55' 07", long. 149° 32' 12".

Began Operation: May 9, 1983.

Ownership: Anchorage Broadcast Television Consortium Inc.

Ivanof Bay—K04MF, Ch. 4, State of Alaska. Phone: 907-269-5744.

Technical Facilities: 0.043-kw ERP, 46-ft. above sea level, lat. 55° 154' 07", long. 159° 29' 15".

Ownership: State of Alaska.

Ivanof Bay—K09SN, Ch. 9, State of Alaska.

Technical Facilities: 10-w TPO, 0.056-kw ERP, 20-ft. above ground, 45-ft. above sea level, lat. 55° 54' 07", long. 159° 29' 15".

Transmitter: Community Hall, Ivanof Bay.

Ownership: State of Alaska.

Juneau—KCBJ-LP, Ch. 15, Juneau Alaska Communications Inc. Phone: 907-583-3680.

Technical Facilities: 0.8-kw ERP, 246-ft. above ground, 254-ft. above sea level, lat. 58° 18' 05", long. 134° 26' 25".

Began Operation: April 15, 2005.

Ownership: Juneau Alaska Communications LLC.

Juneau—KXLJ-LD, Ch. 24, GreenTV Corp. Phones: 907-586-2455; 303-688-5162. Fax: 907-586-2495.

Technical Facilities: 0.95-kw ERP, 20-ft. above ground, 28-ft. above sea level, lat. 58° 18' 05", long. 134° 26' 26".

Ownership: GreenTV Corp.

Juneau-Douglas—KATH-LP, Ch. 5, Dan Etulain. Phone: 907-586-8384. Fax: 907-586-8394.

Studio: 1107 W. 8th St, Juneau, AK 99801.

Technical Facilities: 10-w TPO, 0.054-kw ERP, 256-ft. above sea level, lat. 58° 18'13", long. 134° 24' 38".

Transmitter: 129 E. 7th St.

Ownership: Dan Etulain.

Kake—K09QP, Ch. 9, State of Alaska.

Technical Facilities: 10-w TPO, 0.0512-kw ERP, 20-ft. above ground, 95-ft. above sea level, lat. 56° 58' 39", long. 133° 56' 47".

Transmitter: Kake Public School.

Ownership: State of Alaska.

Kake—K12NR, Ch. 12, State of Alaska. Phone: 907-269-5744.

Technical Facilities: 0.05-kw ERP, 79-ft. above ground, 2218-ft. above sea level, lat. 56° 58' 53", long. 133° 48' 15".

Ownership: State of Alaska.

Kakhonak—K09TM, Ch. 9, State of Alaska.

Technical Facilities: 10-w TPO, 0.059-kw ERP, 24-ft. above ground, 75-ft. above sea level, lat. 59° 26' 30", long. 154° 45' 07".

Transmitter: Kakhonak Village office bldg.

Ownership: State of Alaska.

Kakhonak—K13TF, Ch. 13, State of Alaska. Phone: 907-269-5744.

Technical Facilities: 0.06-kw ERP, lat. 59° 26' 30", long. 154° 45' 07".

Transmitter: Kakhonak village office bldg.

Ownership: State of Alaska.

Kaktovik—K04IU, Ch. 4, State of Alaska. Phone: 907-269-5744.

Technical Facilities: 0.018-kw ERP, lat. 70° 07' 12", long. 143° 35' 52".

Ownership: State of Alaska.

Kaktovik—K09QY, Ch. 9, State of Alaska.

Technical Facilities: 10-w TPO, 0.054-kw ERP, 20-ft. above ground, 70-ft. above sea level, lat. 70° 07' 35", long. 143° 36' 55".

Transmitter: Alascom Earth Station, Kaktovik.

Ownership: State of Alaska.

Kalskag—K09TR, Ch. 9, State of Alaska.

Technical Facilities: 10-w TPO, 0.055-kw ERP, 20-ft. above ground, 82-ft. above sea level, lat. 61° 30' 48", long. 160° 21' 30".

Transmitter: Kalskag High School.

Ownership: State of Alaska.

Kalskag—K11RF, Ch. 11, State of Alaska. Phone: 907-269-5744.

Technical Facilities: 0.05-kw ERP, lat. 61° 30' 48", long. 160° 21' 30".

Ownership: State of Alaska.

Kaltag—K02KA, Ch. 2, Kaltag Village Council. Phone: 907-269-5744.

Technical Facilities: 0.018-kw ERP, lat. 64° 19' 42", long. 158° 43' 16".

Ownership: Kaltag Village Council.

Kaltag—K09TX, Ch. 9, State of Alaska.

Technical Facilities: 0.056-kw ERP, lat. 64° 19' 42", long. 158° 43' 16".

Ownership: State of Alaska.

Karluk—K04LS, Ch. 4, State of Alaska. Phone: 907-269-5744.

Technical Facilities: 0.042-kw ERP, lat. 57° 33' 53", long. 154° 25' 57".

Ownership: State of Alaska.

Karluk—K09QK, Ch. 9, State of Alaska.

Technical Facilities: 10-w TPO, 0.0549-kw ERP, 20-ft. above ground, 70-ft. above sea level, lat. 57° 33' 53", long. 154° 25' 57".

Transmitter: Alascom Earth Station, Karluk.

Ownership: State of Alaska.

Kasaan—K09SM, Ch. 9, State of Alaska.

Technical Facilities: 0.06-kw ERP, lat. 54° 32' 24", long. 132° 24' 04".

Ownership: State of Alaska.

Kasaan—K13SG, Ch. 13, State of Alaska. Phone: 907-269-5744.

Technical Facilities: 0.056-kw ERP, 49-ft. above sea level, lat. 55° 32' 44", long. 132° 24' 04".

Ownership: State of Alaska.

Kasigluk—K02LZ, Ch. 2, State of Alaska. Phone: 907-269-5744.

Technical Facilities: 0.04-kw ERP, lat. 60° 53' 44", long. 162° 31' 05".

Ownership: State of Alaska.

Kasigluk—K09UE, Ch. 9, State of Alaska.

Technical Facilities: 10-w TPO, 0.055-kw ERP, 20-ft. above ground, 50-ft. above sea level, lat. 60° 53' 44", long. 162° 31' 05".

Transmitter: Kasigluk High School.

Ownership: State of Alaska.

Kasilof—K48AC, Ch. 48, Alaska Public Telecommunications Inc. Phone: 907-550-8400.

Technical Facilities: 0.044-kw ERP, 105-ft. above ground, 564-ft. above sea level, lat. 60° 16' 31", long. 151° 18' 30".

Holds CP for change to 1.3-kw ERP, 105-ft. above ground, 152-ft. above sea level, lat. 60° 16' 32", long. 151° 18' 30". BDFCDTT-20090430ABP.

Ownership: Alaska Public Telecommunications Inc.

Kasilof—K56AQ, Ch. 56, Anchorage Broadcast Television Consortium Inc. Phone: 425-258-1440.

Technical Facilities: 0.09-kw ERP, lat. 60° 32' 32", long. 151° 18' 30".

Began Operation: February 26, 1986.

Ownership: Anchorage Broadcast Television Consortium Inc.

Kasilof—K61AN, Ch. 61, Anchorage Broadcast Television Consortium Inc. Phone: 425-258-1440.

Technical Facilities: 0.09-kw ERP, lat. 60° 16' 32", long. 151° 18' 30".

Began Operation: February 26, 1986.

Ownership: Anchorage Broadcast Television Consortium Inc.

Kasilof—K67AU, Ch. 67, Anchorage Broadcast Television Consortium Inc. Phone: 425-258-1440.

Technical Facilities: 0.09-kw ERP, lat. 60° 16' 32", long. 151° 18' 30".

Began Operation: February 26, 1986.

Ownership: Anchorage Broadcast Television Consortium Inc.

Kenai—K09QH, Ch. 9, Piedmont Television of Anchorage License LLC. Phone: 704-341-0944.

Technical Facilities: 0.121-kw ERP, 325-ft. above ground, 489-ft. above sea level, lat. 60° 31' 57", long. 151° 04' 51".

Ownership: Piedmont Television Holdings LLC.

Kenai & Soldotna—K08LW, Ch. 8, Northern Television Inc. Phone: 907-257-5601.

Technical Facilities: 0.122-kw ERP, 312-ft. above ground, 476-ft. above sea level, lat. 60° 31' 57", long. 151° 04' 51".

Ownership: Northern Television Inc.

Kenai River—K04DS, Ch. 4, Northern Lights Media Inc. Phone: 574-287-1001.

Technical Facilities: 0.039-kw ERP, lat. 60° 28' 15", long. 149° 49' 58".

Holds CP for change to 0.008-kw ERP, 13-ft. above ground, 3133-ft. above sea level, BDFCDTT-20060331BLQ.

Ownership: Schurz Communications Inc.

Kenai, etc.—K03FW, Ch. 3, Smith Media License Holdings LLC. Phone: 314-853-7736.

Technical Facilities: 0.15-kw ERP, lat. 60° 31' 57", long. 151° 04' 51".

Holds CP for change to 1.5-kw ERP, 325-ft. above ground, 487-ft. above sea level, lat. 60° 31' 58", long. 151° 04' 51". BMJPTTV-20000831CEH.

Transmitter: Mile 3.5 of Kenai Spur Hwy., Alascom Site 17, near Soldotna.

Ownership: Smith Media License Holdings LLC.

Kenai, etc.—K06MF, Ch. 6, Fireweed Communications Corp. Phone: 907-339-3800.

Technical Facilities: 1.44-kw ERP, 320-ft. above ground, 482-ft. above sea level, lat. 60° 31' 56", long. 151° 05' 00".

Transmitter: Mile 3.5 of Kenai Spur Hwy., Alascom Site 17, near Soldotna.

Ownership: Fireweed Communications LLC.

Kenai, etc.—K10NC, Ch. 10, Northern Lights Media Inc. Phone: 574-287-1001.

Technical Facilities: 0.128-kw ERP, 326-ft. above ground, 489-ft. above sea level, lat. 60° 31' 57", long. 151° 04' 51".

Transmitter: Alascom Site 17 on Spur Rd.

Ownership: Schurz Communications Inc.

Kenai, etc.—K12LA, Ch. 12, Alaska Public Telecommunications Inc. Phone: 907-563-7070.

Technical Facilities: 0.22-kw ERP, lat. 60° 31' 57", long. 151° 04' 51".

Holds CP for change to 0.118-kw ERP, 325-ft. above ground, 489-ft. above sea level, lat. 60° 31' 58", long. 151° 04' 52". BDFCDTT-20060331BBQ.

Ownership: Alaska Public Telecommunications Inc.

Kenai, etc.—K23AF, Ch. 23, Anchorage Broadcast Television Consortium Inc. Phone: 425-258-1440.

Technical Facilities: 100-w TPO, 1.4-kw ERP, 300-ft. above ground, 600-ft. above sea level, lat. 60° 32' 15", long. 150° 32' 15".

Transmitter: 0.5-mi. W of Robinson Loop Rd., Sterling.

Began Operation: November 9, 1982.

Ownership: Anchorage Broadcast Television Consortium Inc.

Ketchikan—K09OX, Ch. 9, Rainbird Community Broadcasting Corp. Phone: 907-225-9655.

Technical Facilities: 0.13-kw ERP, lat. 55° 21' 12", long. 131° 40' 51".

Ownership: Rainbird Community Broadcasting Corp.

Ketchikan—K15AR, Ch. 15, State of Alaska. Phone: 907-269-5744.

Technical Facilities: 0.69-kw ERP, lat. 55° 20' 20", long. 131° 37' 21".

Ownership: State of Alaska.

Ketchikan—K21AH, Ch. 21, State of Alaska.

Technical Facilities: 20-w TPO, 0.308-kw ERP, 20-ft. above ground, 480-ft. above sea level, lat. 55° 20' 17", long. 131° 37' 28".

Ownership: State of Alaska.

Kiana—K04IG, Ch. 4, City of Kiana. Phone: 907-269-5744.

Technical Facilities: 0.018-kw ERP, 22-ft. above ground, 223-ft. above sea level, lat. 66° 58' 35", long. 160° 25' 11".

Transmitter: Kiana Community Center.

Ownership: City of Kiana.

Kiana—K09RW, Ch. 9, State of Alaska.

Technical Facilities: 10-w TPO, 0.0559-kw ERP, 20-ft. above ground, 175-ft. above sea level, lat. 66° 58' 27", long. 160° 25' 47".

Transmitter: Alascom Earth Station, Kiana.

Ownership: State of Alaska.

King Cove—K04HR, Ch. 4, King Cove School District.

Technical Facilities: 0.033-kw ERP, lat. 55° 03' 39", long. 162° 18' 34".

Ownership: King Cove School District.

King Cove—K09QW, Ch. 9, State of Alaska.

Technical Facilities: 10-w TPO, 0.059-kw ERP, 40-ft. above ground, 70-ft. above sea level, lat. 55° 03' 37", long. 162° 18' 31".

Transmitter: City warehouse.

Ownership: State of Alaska.

King Mountain—K03GL, Ch. 3, State of Alaska. Phone: 907-269-5744.

Technical Facilities: 0.4-kw ERP, lat. 61° 47' 40", long. 148° 25' 19".

Ownership: State of Alaska.

King Salmon—K04KN, Ch. 4, State of Alaska.

Technical Facilities: 10-w TPO, 0.0491-kw ERP, 20-ft. above ground, 91-ft. above sea level, lat. 58° 40' 58", long. 156° 39' 49".

Transmitter: Alascom Earth Station, King Salmon.

Ownership: State of Alaska.

King Salmon—K08KS, Ch. 8, State of Alaska.

Technical Facilities: 0.025-kw ERP, 36-ft. above ground, 62-ft. above sea level, lat. 58° 41' 38", long. 156° 42' 00".

Ownership: State of Alaska.

Kipnuk—K04LM, Ch. 4, State of Alaska.

Technical Facilities: 10-w TPO, 0.043-kw ERP, 20-ft. above ground, 40-ft. above sea level, lat. 59° 56' 21", long. 164° 02' 28".

Transmitter: Alascom Earth Station, Kipnuk.

Ownership: State of Alaska.

Kipnuk—K07OL, Ch. 7, Village of Kipnuk. Phone: 907-269-5744.

Technical Facilities: 0.013-kw ERP, lat. 59° 56' 21", long. 164° 02' 28".

Kivalina—K04IL, Ch. 4, State of Alaska.

Technical Facilities: 0.019-kw ERP, lat. 67° 43' 34", long. 164° 31' 46".

Ownership: City of Kivalina.

Kivalina—K09QZ, Ch. 9, State of Alaska.

Technical Facilities: 10-w TPO, 0.0571-kw ERP, 20-ft. above ground, 45-ft. above sea level, lat. 67° 43' 38", long. 164° 32' 03".

Transmitter: Alascom Earth Station, Kivalina.

Ownership: State of Alaska.

Klawock—K07TI, Ch. 7, State of Alaska.

Technical Facilities: 0.05-kw ERP, lat. 55° 33' 18", long. 133° 05' 45".

Ownership: State of Alaska.

Klawock—K11RA, Ch. 11, State of Alaska. Phone: 907-269-5744.

Technical Facilities: 0.055-kw ERP, lat. 55° 33' 18", long. 133° 05' 45".

Ownership: State of Alaska.

Klukwan—K04KQ, Ch. 4, State of Alaska.

Technical Facilities: 10-w TPO, 0.0466-kw ERP, 100-ft. above ground, 300-ft. above sea level, lat. 59° 24' 08", long. 135° 53' 07".

Transmitter: Klukwan Water Storage Tank, 0.5-mi. N of Klukwan.

Ownership: State of Alaska.

Klukwan—K11RD, Ch. 11, State of Alaska. Phone: 907-269-5744.

Technical Facilities: 0.048-kw ERP, lat. 59° 24' 08", long. 135° 53' 07".

Ownership: State of Alaska.

Kobuk—K02KZ, Ch. 2, State of Alaska.

Technical Facilities: 10-w TPO, 0.0444-kw ERP, 20-ft. above ground, 150-ft. above sea level, lat. 66° 54' 29", long. 156° 52' 51".

Transmitter: Alascom Earth Station, Kobuk.

Ownership: State of Alaska.

Kobuk—K13SF, Ch. 13, State of Alaska. Phone: 907-269-5744.

Technical Facilities: 0.056-kw ERP, lat. 66° 54' 28", long. 156° 52' 51".

Ownership: State of Alaska.

Kodiak—K15AT, Ch. 15, State of Alaska. Phone: 907-269-5744.

Technical Facilities: 0.603-kw ERP, lat. 57° 47' 41", long. 152° 23' 28".

Transmitter: KMXT Generator Building, 700 Upper Mill Bay Rd.

Ownership: State of Alaska.

Kodiak—K17GQ, Ch. 17, GreenTV Corp. Phone: 303-688-5162.

Technical Facilities: 10.3-kw ERP, 80-ft. above ground, 240-ft. above sea level, lat. 57° 47' 03", long. 152° 23' 57".

Ownership: GreenTV Corp.

Kodiak—KMXT-LP, Ch. 9, Kodiak Public Broadcasting Corp.

Technical Facilities: 0.013-kw ERP, lat. 57° 47' 41", long. 152° 23' 28".

Ownership: Kodiak Public Broadcasting Corp.

Kodiak—KUBD-LP, Ch. 11, Ketchikan TV LLC. Phone: 303-688-5162.

Technical Facilities: 0.18-kw ERP, 36-ft. above ground, 107-ft. above sea level, lat. 57° 48' 04", long. 152° 22' 55".

Ownership: Ketchikan TV LLC.

Koliganek—K04JV, Ch. 4, State of Alaska. Phone: 907-269-5744.

Technical Facilities: 0.02-kw ERP, lat. 59° 43' 42", long. 157° 16' 55".

Ownership: State of Alaska.

Koliganek—K07QW, Ch. 7, State of Alaska.

Technical Facilities: 10-w TPO, 0.055-kw ERP, 20-ft. above ground, 230-ft. above sea level, lat. 59° 43' 42", long. 157° 16' 55".

Transmitter: Alascom Earth Station, Koliganek.

Ownership: State of Alaska.

Kongiganak—K04LF, Ch. 4, State of Alaska. Phone: 907-269-5744.

Technical Facilities: 0.043-kw ERP, lat. 59° 57' 36", long. 162° 53' 30".

Ownership: State of Alaska.

Kongiganak—K09RG, Ch. 9, State of Alaska.

Technical Facilities: 10-w TPO, 0.0561-kw ERP, 20-ft. above ground, 60-ft. above sea level, lat. 59° 57' 36", long. 162° 53' 30".

Transmitter: Alascom Earth Station, Kongiganak.

Ownership: State of Alaska.

Kotlik—K09SL, Ch. 9, State of Alaska.

Technical Facilities: 10-w TPO, 0.055-kw ERP, 20-ft. above ground, 40-ft. above sea level, lat. 63° 03' 00", long. 163° 33' 08".

Transmitter: Head Start Bldg., Kotlik.

Ownership: State of Alaska.

Kotzebue—K09OV, Ch. 9, State of Alaska.
Technical Facilities: 0.49-kw ERP, lat. 66° 53' 52", long. 162° 35' 46".
Ownership: Kotzebue Broadcasting Inc.

Kotzebue—K13UE, Ch. 13, State of Alaska.
Technical Facilities: 0.05-kw ERP, lat. 66° 53' 52", long. 162° 35' 46".
Ownership: State of Alaska.

Koyuk—K02MB, Ch. 2, State of Alaska.
Technical Facilities: 10-w TPO, 0.0434-kw ERP, 20-ft. above ground, 70-ft. above sea level, lat. 64° 55' 54", long. 161° 09' 23".
Transmitter: Alascom Earth Station, Koyuk.
Ownership: State of Alaska.

Koyuk—K09SA, Ch. 9, State of Alaska. Phone: 907-269-5744.
Technical Facilities: 0.036-kw ERP, 36-ft. above sea level, lat. 64° 55' 54", long. 161° 09' 23".
Ownership: Koyuk City Council.

Koyukuk—K03FZ, Ch. 3, State of Alaska.
Technical Facilities: 10-w TPO, 0.043-kw ERP, 20-ft. above ground, 150-ft. above sea level, lat. 64° 52' 58", long. 157° 42' 24".
Transmitter: Koyukuk School.
Ownership: State of Alaska.

Koyukuk—K13TQ, Ch. 13, State of Alaska. Phone: 907-269-5744.
Technical Facilities: 0.055-kw ERP, lat. 64° 52' 58", long. 157° 42' 24".
Ownership: State of Alaska.

Kwethluk—K09UJ, Ch. 9, State of Alaska.
Technical Facilities: 0.05-kw ERP, lat. 60° 48' 45", long. 161° 26' 00".
Ownership: State of Alaska.

Kwethluk—K11QY, Ch. 11, State of Alaska. Phone: 907-269-5744.
Technical Facilities: 0.055-kw ERP, lat. 60° 48' 45", long. 161° 26' 00".
Ownership: State of Alaska.

Kwigillingok—K11SC, Ch. 11, State of Alaska.
Technical Facilities: 0.05-kw ERP, lat. 59° 51' 54", long. 163° 08' 08".
Ownership: State of Alaska.

Kwigillingok—K13UK, Ch. 13, State of Alaska.
Technical Facilities: 0.055-kw ERP, lat. 59° 51' 54", long. 163° 08' 08".
Ownership: State of Alaska.

Labouchere Bay—K02MC, Ch. 2, State of Alaska. Phone: 907-269-5744.
Technical Facilities: 0.04-kw ERP, lat. 56° 18' 24", long. 133° 37' 35".
Ownership: State of Alaska.

Lake Louise, etc.—K09TU, Ch. 9, Greater Copper Valley Communications Inc. Phone: 907-822-4051.
Technical Facilities: 0.55-kw ERP, lat. 62° 06' 20", long. 146° 10' 18".
Ownership: Greater Copper Valley Communications Inc.

Lake Louise, etc.—K11RJ, Ch. 11, Greater Copper Valley Communications Inc. Phone: 907-822-4051.
Technical Facilities: 100-w TPO, 0.55-kw ERP, 20-ft. above ground, 2994-ft. above sea level, lat. 62° 06' 20", long. 146° 10' 18".
Transmitter: 28-mi. W of Glennallen.
Ownership: Greater Copper Valley Communications Inc.

Larsen Bay—K09QE, Ch. 9, State of Alaska.
Technical Facilities: 10-w TPO, 0.0534-kw ERP, 20-ft. above ground, 60-ft. above sea level, lat. 57° 32' 17", long. 153° 58' 48".
Transmitter: Alascom Earth Station, Larsen Bay.
Ownership: State of Alaska.

Lemon, etc.—K02QM-D, Ch. 2, Capital Community Broadcasting Inc. Phone: 907-586-1670.
Technical Facilities: 0.01-kw ERP, 70-ft. above ground, 77-ft. above sea level, lat. 58° 20' 41", long. 134° 31' 46".
Began Operation: March 20, 2009.
Ownership: Capital Community Broadcasting Inc.

Levelock—K02MN, Ch. 2, State of Alaska. Phone: 907-269-5744.
Technical Facilities: 0.04-kw ERP, lat. 59° 06' 54", long. 156° 51' 39".
Ownership: State of Alaska.

Levelock—K07TT, Ch. 7, State of Alaska.
Technical Facilities: 0.05-kw ERP, 29-ft. above ground, 69-ft. above sea level, lat. 59° 06' 54", long. 156° 51' 39".
Ownership: State of Alaska.

Lime Village—K07TH, Ch. 7, State of Alaska. Phone: 907-269-5744.
Technical Facilities: 0.05-kw ERP, lat. 61° 21' 22", long. 155° 26' 10".
Ownership: State of Alaska.

Lime Village—K11RW, Ch. 11, State of Alaska.
Technical Facilities: 0.05-kw ERP, lat. 61° 21' 22", long. 155° 26' 10".
Ownership: State of Alaska.

Long Island—K05IR, Ch. 5, State of Alaska. Phone: 907-269-5744.
Technical Facilities: 10-w TPO, 0.01-kw ERP, 26-ft. above ground, 46-ft. above sea level, lat. 54° 55' 43", long. 132° 44' 34".
Transmitter: Long Island School Bldg.
Ownership: State of Alaska.

Manley Hot Springs—K06JX, Ch. 6, Manley Hot Springs Park Assn.
Technical Facilities: 0.003-kw ERP, lat. 65° 01' 20", long. 150° 40' 08".
Ownership: Manley Hot Springs Park Assn.

Manley Hot Springs—K07RX, Ch. 7, State of Alaska.
Technical Facilities: 10-w TPO, 0.055-kw ERP, 20-ft. above ground, 400-ft. above sea level, lat. 64° 59' 52", long. 150° 38' 26".
Transmitter: Telco Bldg., Manley Hot Springs.
Ownership: State of Alaska.

Manley Hot Springs—K13TN, Ch. 13, State of Alaska. Phone: 907-269-5744.
Technical Facilities: 0.05-kw ERP, lat. 64° 59' 52", long. 150° 38' 26".
Ownership: State of Alaska.

Manokotak—K07LB, Ch. 7, State of Alaska. Phone: 907-269-5744.
Technical Facilities: 0.063-kw ERP, lat. 59° 04' 41", long. 159° 03' 45".
Ownership: State of Alaska.

Manokotak—K09TQ, Ch. 9, State of Alaska.
Technical Facilities: 10-w TPO, 0.055-kw ERP, 20-ft. above ground, 40-ft. above sea level, lat. 58° 58' 52", long. 159° 03' 20".
Transmitter: Manokotak School.
Ownership: State of Alaska.

Marshall—K02KV, Ch. 2, State of Alaska.
Technical Facilities: 10-w TPO, 0.0441-kw ERP, 20-ft. above ground, 70-ft. above sea level, lat. 61° 52' 53", long. 162° 05' 09".
Transmitter: Alascom Earth Station, Marshall.
Ownership: State of Alaska.

Marshall—K07TK, Ch. 7, State of Alaska. Phone: 907-269-5744.
Technical Facilities: 0.059-kw ERP, 66-ft. above sea level, lat. 61° 52' 53", long. 162° 05' 09".
Ownership: State of Alaska.

McGrath—K02JE, Ch. 2, Iditarod Area School District. Phone: 907-269-5744.
Technical Facilities: 0.019-kw ERP, lat. 62° 57' 12", long. 155° 35' 30".
Ownership: Iditarod Area School District.

McGrath—K07TJ, Ch. 7, State of Alaska. Phone: 907-269-5744.
Technical Facilities: 0.0588-kw ERP, lat. 62° 57' 02", long. 155° 35' 10".
Transmitter: Captain Snow Community Office Bldg.
Ownership: State of Alaska.

McGrath—K09QC, Ch. 9, State of Alaska.
Technical Facilities: 10-w TPO, 0.059-kw ERP, 48-ft. above ground, 135-ft. above sea level, lat. 62° 57' 02", long. 135° 35' 10".
Transmitter: Captain Snow community office bldg.
Ownership: State of Alaska.

McKinley Park—K03GK, Ch. 3, State of Alaska.
Technical Facilities: 10-w TPO, 0.497-kw ERP, 25-ft. above ground, 1700-ft. above sea level, lat. 63° 43' 40", long. 148° 54' 15".
Transmitter: 0.75-mi. off McKinley Park Hwy., McKinley Park.
Ownership: State of Alaska.

McKinley Park—K10MI, Ch. 10, State of Alaska. Phone: 907-269-5744.
Technical Facilities: 10-kw ERP, lat. 63° 43' 40", long. 148° 54' 14".
Ownership: State of Alaska.

Mekoryuk—K04MD, Ch. 4, State of Alaska.
Technical Facilities: 10-w TPO, 0.043-kw ERP, 20-ft. above ground, 40-ft. above sea level, lat. 60° 23' 12", long. 166° 11' 12".
Transmitter: Alascom Earth Station, Mekoryuk.
Ownership: State of Alaska.

Mekoryuk—K09NI, Ch. 9, State of Alaska. Phone: 907-269-5744.
Technical Facilities: 0.013-kw ERP, lat. 60° 23' 12", long. 166° 11' 12".
Ownership: City of Mekoryuk.

Mendenhall Valley, etc.—K06JZ, Ch. 6, Capital Community Broadcasting Inc.
Technical Facilities: 0.047-kw ERP, lat. 58° 21' 57", long. 134° 37' 59".
Ownership: Capital Community Broadcasting Inc.

Mentasta Lake—K07SQ, Ch. 7, State of Alaska. Phone: 907-269-5744.
Technical Facilities: 0.054-kw ERP, lat. 62° 55' 46", long. 143° 47' 40".
Ownership: State of Alaska.

Mentasta Lake—K09QJ, Ch. 9, State of Alaska.
Technical Facilities: 10-w TPO, 0.0543-kw ERP, 20-ft. above ground, 2355-ft. above sea level, lat. 62° 55' 46", long. 143° 47' 40".
Transmitter: Mentasta Lake School, Mentasta Lake.
Ownership: State of Alaska.

Metlakatla—K07SL, Ch. 7, State of Alaska.
Technical Facilities: 10-w TPO, 0.055-kw ERP, 20-ft. above ground, 40-ft. above sea level, lat. 55° 07' 42", long. 161° 34' 20".
Transmitter: Metlakatla School.
Ownership: State of Alaska.

Metlakatla—K11QZ, Ch. 11, State of Alaska. Phone: 907-269-5744.
Technical Facilities: 0.055-kw ERP, lat. 55° 07' 42", long. 131° 34' 20".
Ownership: State of Alaska.

Meyers Chuck—K09TI, Ch. 9, State of Alaska.
Technical Facilities: 10-w TPO, 0.055-kw ERP, lat. 55° 44' 28", long. 132° 15' 14".
Ownership: State of Alaska.

Meyers Chuck—K13TB, Ch. 13, State of Alaska. Phone: 907-269-5744.
Technical Facilities: 0.05-kw ERP, lat. 55° 44' 28", long. 132° 15' 14".
Ownership: State of Alaska.

Minchumina—K05IK, Ch. 5, State of Alaska. Phone: 907-269-5744.
Technical Facilities: 10-w TPO, 0.028-kw ERP, 20-ft. above ground, 670-ft. above sea level, lat. 63° 52' 59", long. 152° 18' 45".
Transmitter: Alascom Office, Minchumina.
Ownership: State of Alaska.

Minchumina—K09SZ, Ch. 9, State of Alaska.
Technical Facilities: 10-w TPO, 0.055-kw ERP, 20-ft. above ground, 670-ft. above sea level, lat. 63° 52' 59", long. 152° 18' 45".
Transmitter: Alascom Office, Minchumina.
Ownership: State of Alaska.

Minto—K05HZ, Ch. 5, State of Alaska. Phone: 907-269-5744.
Technical Facilities: 0.059-kw ERP, 489-ft. above sea level, lat. 65° 09' 10", long. 149° 20' 23".
Ownership: State of Alaska.

Minto—K07QF, Ch. 7, State of Alaska. Phone: 907-269-5744.

Technical Facilities: 0.018-kw ERP, 489-ft. above sea level, lat. 65° 09' 10", long. 149° 20' 23".

Ownership: Minto Village Council.

Minto—K13TK, Ch. 13, State of Alaska.

Technical Facilities: 10-w TPO, 0.055-kw ERP, 20-ft. above ground, 435-ft. above sea level, lat. 65° 09' 10", long. 149° 20' 23".

Transmitter: Alascom Earth Station, Minto.

Ownership: State of Alaska.

Moose Pass—K04KK, Ch. 4, Moose Pass Sportsmans Club.

Technical Facilities: 0.08-kw ERP, lat. 60° 30' 00", long. 149° 23' 30".

Ownership: Moose Pass Sportsmans Club.

Moose Pass—K07QT, Ch. 7, Moose Pass Sportsmans Club.

Technical Facilities: 0.09-kw ERP, lat. 60° 30' 00", long. 149° 23' 30".

Ownership: Moose Pass Sportsmans Club.

Moose Pass—K11QF, Ch. 11, Moose Pass Sportsmans Club.

Technical Facilities: 0.284-kw ERP, lat. 60° 20' 20", long. 149° 18' 06".

Ownership: Moose Pass Sportsmans Club.

Moose Pass—K13RL, Ch. 13, Moose Pass Sportsmans Club.

Technical Facilities: 0.284-kw ERP, lat. 60° 20' 20", long. 149° 18' 06".

Ownership: Moose Pass Sportsmans Club.

Moose Pass—K15AP, Ch. 15, State of Alaska.

Technical Facilities: 0.28-kw ERP, lat. 60° 14' 13", long. 149° 21' 28".

Ownership: State of Alaska.

Mosquito Lake—K02MW, Ch. 2, State of Alaska. Phone: 907-269-5744.

Technical Facilities: 0.05-kw ERP, 193-ft. above sea level, lat. 59° 27' 32", long. 136° 01' 24".

Ownership: State of Alaska.

Mosquito Lake—K13UM, Ch. 13, State of Alaska.

Technical Facilities: 0.06-kw ERP, lat. 59° 27' 32", long. 136° 01' 24".

Ownership: State of Alaska.

Mountain Village—K13TJ, Ch. 13, State of Alaska.

Technical Facilities: 10-w TPO, 0.055-kw ERP, 20-ft. above ground, 120-ft. above sea level, lat. 62° 05' 18", long. 163° 43' 35".

Transmitter: Alascom Earth Station, Mountain Village.

Ownership: State of Alaska.

Naknek—K13TZ, Ch. 13, State of Alaska.

Technical Facilities: 10-w TPO, 0.0436-kw ERP, 150-ft. above ground, 195-ft. above sea level, lat. 58° 44' 35", long. 156° 57' 57".

Transmitter: 1.7-mi. E of Naknek on Naknek King Solomon.

Ownership: State of Alaska.

Napakiak—K10MR, Ch. 10, State of Alaska.

Technical Facilities: 0.01-kw ERP, lat. 60° 41' 36", long. 161° 57' 50".

Ownership: State of Alaska.

Napakiak—K13UV, Ch. 13, State of Alaska. Phone: 907-269-5744.

Technical Facilities: 0.009-kw ERP, 59-ft. above ground, 79-ft. above sea level, lat. 60° 41' 36", long. 161° 57' 50".

Ownership: State of Alaska.

Napaskiak—K02MZ, Ch. 2, State of Alaska.

Technical Facilities: 0.04-kw ERP, lat. 60° 41' 48", long. 161° 57' 13".

Transmitter: Napaskiak School.

Ownership: State of Alaska.

Napaskiak—K07SJ, Ch. 7, State of Alaska.

Technical Facilities: 10-w TPO, 0.055-kw ERP, 20-ft. above ground, 40-ft. above sea level, lat. 60° 41' 48", long. 161° 57' 13".

Transmitter: Napaskiak School.

Ownership: State of Alaska.

Naukati Bay—K09TJ, Ch. 9, State of Alaska.

Technical Facilities: 10-w TPO, 0.055-kw ERP, 20-ft. above ground, 40-ft. above sea level, lat. 55° 52' 06", long. 133° 13' 03".

Transmitter: Naukati Bay School.

Ownership: State of Alaska.

Naukati Bay—K13TS, Ch. 13, State of Alaska. Phone: 907-269-5744.

Technical Facilities: 0.055-kw ERP, lat. 55° 52' 06", long. 133° 13' 03".

Ownership: State of Alaska.

Nelson Lagoon—K04LQ, Ch. 4, State of Alaska. Phone: 907-269-5744.

Technical Facilities: 0.042-kw ERP, lat. 56° 00' 07", long. 161° 12' 07".

Ownership: State of Alaska.

Nelson Lagoon—K09QM, Ch. 9, State of Alaska.

Technical Facilities: 10-w TPO, 0.0549-kw ERP, 20-ft. above ground, 50-ft. above sea level, lat. 56° 00' 07", long. 161° 12' 07".

Transmitter: Alascom Earth Station, Nelson Lagoon.

Ownership: State of Alaska.

Nenana—K05HI, Ch. 5, U. of Alaska.

Technical Facilities: 0.053-kw ERP, lat. 64° 34' 55", long. 149° 04' 36".

Ownership: U. of Alaska.

Nenana—K55DE, Ch. 55, State of Alaska.

Technical Facilities: 10-w TPO, 0.0666-kw ERP, 85-ft. above ground, 445-ft. above sea level, lat. 64° 33' 15", long. 149° 05' 06".

Transmitter: State Hwy. Maintenance Station, Nenana.

Ownership: State of Alaska.

New Stuyahok—K09QV, Ch. 9, State of Alaska.

Technical Facilities: 10-w TPO, 0.0542-kw ERP, 20-ft. above ground, 160-ft. above sea level, lat. 59° 27' 09", long. 157° 18' 31".

Transmitter: Alascom Earth Station, New Stuyahok.

Ownership: State of Alaska.

New Stuyahok—K13TO, Ch. 13, State of Alaska. Phone: 907-269-5744.

Technical Facilities: 0.054-kw ERP, lat. 59° 27' 09", long. 157° 18' 31".

Ownership: State of Alaska.

Newtok—K02LN, Ch. 2, State of Alaska.

Technical Facilities: 10-w TPO, 0.043-kw ERP, 20-ft. above ground, 40-ft. above sea level, lat. 60° 56' 29", long. 164° 37' 44".

Transmitter: Newtok School.

Ownership: State of Alaska.

Newtok—K04MT, Ch. 4, State of Alaska. Phone: 907-269-5744.

Technical Facilities: 0.043-kw ERP, 39-ft. above sea level, lat. 60° 56' 29", long. 164° 37' 41".

Ownership: State of Alaska.

Nightmute—K03GD, Ch. 3, State of Alaska. Phone: 907-269-5744.

Technical Facilities: 0.043-kw ERP, lat. 60° 29' 48", long. 164° 43' 29".

Ownership: State of Alaska.

Nightmute—K10LU, Ch. 10, State of Alaska.

Technical Facilities: 0.06-kw ERP, 30-ft. above ground, 52-ft. above sea level, lat. 60° 28' 42", long. 164° 43' 12".

Transmitter: Nightmute School Storage Bldg.

Ownership: State of Alaska.

Nikolai—K04MB, Ch. 4, State of Alaska.

Technical Facilities: 10-w TPO, 0.043-kw ERP, 30-ft. above ground, 455-ft. above sea level, lat. 63° 00' 47", long. 154° 22' 19".

Transmitter: Nikolai School Bldg.

Ownership: State of Alaska.

Nikolai—K09PR, Ch. 9, State of Alaska. Phone: 907-269-5744.

Technical Facilities: 0.05-kw ERP, lat. 63° 00' 47", long. 154° 22' 19".

Ownership: State of Alaska.

Nikolski—K04LR, Ch. 4, State of Alaska. Phone: 907-269-5744.

Technical Facilities: 0.05-kw ERP, lat. 55° 56' 17", long. 168° 52' 20".

Ownership: State of Alaska.

Nikolski—K09RK, Ch. 9, State of Alaska.

Technical Facilities: 10-w TPO, 0.056-kw ERP, 45-ft. above ground, 75-ft. above sea level, lat. 52° 56' 17", long. 168° 52' 20".

Transmitter: Chaluka Office Bldg.

Ownership: State of Alaska.

Ninilchik—K21AM, Ch. 21, Alaska Public Telecommunications Inc. Phone: 907-563-7070.

Technical Facilities: 1.4-kw ERP, lat. 60° 00' 35", long. 151° 42' 45".

Holds CP for change to 252-ft. above ground, 512-ft. above sea level, BDFCDTT-20060331AZS.

Ownership: Alaska Public Telecommunications Inc.

Ninilchik—K39AA, Ch. 39, Anchorage Broadcast Television Consortium Inc. Phone: 425-258-1440.

Technical Facilities: 200-w TPO, 1.27-kw ERP, 200-ft. above ground, 459-ft. above sea level, lat. 60° 00' 35", long. 151° 42' 45".

Transmitter: 3.2-mi. SW of Ninilchik.

Began Operation: November 28, 1978.

Ownership: Anchorage Broadcast Television Consortium Inc.

Ninilchik, etc.—K15AG, Ch. 15, Anchorage Broadcast Television Consortium Inc. Phone: 425-258-1440.

Technical Facilities: 0.872-kw ERP, 531-ft. above sea level, lat. 60° 00' 35", long. 151° 42' 45".

Began Operation: December 3, 1982.

Ownership: Anchorage Broadcast Television Consortium Inc.

Ninilchik, etc.—K27AI, Ch. 27, Anchorage Broadcast Television Consortium Inc. Phone: 425-258-1440.

Technical Facilities: 0.872-kw ERP, 509-ft. above sea level, lat. 60° 00' 35", long. 151° 42' 45".

Began Operation: December 7, 1982.

Ownership: Anchorage Broadcast Television Consortium Inc.

Ninilchik, etc.—K33AF, Ch. 33, Anchorage Broadcast Television Consortium Inc. Phone: 425-258-1440.

Technical Facilities: 0.87-kw ERP, 499-ft. above sea level, lat. 60° 00' 35", long. 151° 42' 45".

Began Operation: March 6, 2009.

Ownership: Anchorage Broadcast Television Consortium Inc.

Noatak—K07RI, Ch. 7, State of Alaska.

Technical Facilities: 10-w TPO, 0.0548-kw ERP, 20-ft. above ground, 135-ft. above sea level, lat. 67° 34' 03", long. 162° 57' 58".

Transmitter: Alascom Earth Station, Noatak.

Ownership: State of Alaska.

Noatak—K09NG, Ch. 9, State of Alaska. Phone: 907-269-5744.

Technical Facilities: 0.013-kw ERP, lat. 67° 34' 03", long. 162° 57' 58".

Ownership: City of Noatak.

Nome—K09OW, Ch. 9, State of Alaska. Phone: 907-269-5744.

Technical Facilities: 0.091-kw ERP, lat. 64° 30' 15", long. 165° 23' 52".

Transmitter: Nome Recreation Center, 6th Ave.

Ownership: State of Alaska.

Nome—K11TH, Ch. 11, Three Angels Broadcasting Network Inc. Phone: 618-627-4651. Fax: 618-627-4155.

Technical Facilities: 10-w TPO, 0.25-kw ERP, 42-ft. above ground, 170-ft. above sea level, lat. 64° 31' 11", long. 165° 22' 20".

Transmitter: Lot 6, Block 6, Icy View Subdivision.

Ownership: Three Angels Broadcasting Network Inc.

Personnel: Moses Primo, Chief Engineer.

Nome—K13UG, Ch. 13, State of Alaska.

Technical Facilities: 0.05-kw ERP, lat. 64° 29' 50", long. 165° 24' 05".

Ownership: State of Alaska.

Nondalton—K02LJ, Ch. 2, State of Alaska. Phone: 907-269-5744.

Technical Facilities: 0.042-kw ERP, 288-ft. above sea level, lat. 59° 58' 28", long. 154° 50' 49".

Ownership: State of Alaska.

Nondalton—K09RQ, Ch. 9, State of Alaska.
Technical Facilities: 10-w TPO, 0.0536-kw ERP, 20-ft. above ground, 295-ft. above sea level, lat. 59° 58' 28", long. 154° 50' 49".

Transmitter: Nondalton Community School.

Ownership: State of Alaska.

Noorvik—K04IK, Ch. 4, State of Alaska. Phone: 907-269-5744.
Technical Facilities: 0.019-kw ERP, lat. 66° 50' 18", long. 161° 01' 56".

Ownership: City of Noorvik.

Northway—K02LB, Ch. 2, State of Alaska.
Technical Facilities: 10-w TPO, 0.04985-kw ERP, 80-ft. above ground, 1796-ft. above sea level, lat. 62° 58' 04", long. 141° 53' 34".

Transmitter: Community Bldg., Northway.

Ownership: Northway Village Council.

Northway—K04KP, Ch. 4, State of Alaska.
Technical Facilities: 10-w TPO, 0.0484-kw ERP, 20-ft. above ground, 1720-ft. above sea level, lat. 62° 57' 47", long. 141° 55' 57".

Transmitter: Northway Community School.

Ownership: State of Alaska.

Nuiqsut—K04IS, Ch. 4, State of Alaska. Phone: 907-269-5744.
Technical Facilities: 0.018-kw ERP, 66-ft. above sea level, lat. 70° 30' 00", long. 151° 00' 00".

Ownership: State of Alaska.

Nuiqsut—K09RT, Ch. 9, State of Alaska.
Technical Facilities: 10-w TPO, 0.056-kw ERP, 20-ft. above ground, 70-ft. above sea level, lat. 70° 12' 39", long. 150° 59' 27".

Transmitter: Alascom Earth Station.

Ownership: State of Alaska.

Nulato—K02KW, Ch. 2, State of Alaska.
Technical Facilities: 10-w TPO, 0.043-kw ERP, 20-ft. above ground, 135-ft. above sea level, lat. 64° 43' 10", long. 158° 06' 10".

Transmitter: Alascom Earth Station.

Ownership: State of Alaska.

Nulato—K04JF, Ch. 4, Village of Nulato. Phone: 907-269-5744.
Technical Facilities: 0.014-kw ERP, lat. 64° 43' 10", long. 158° 06' 10".

Ownership: Village of Nulato.

Old Harbor—K13RN, Ch. 13, State of Alaska.
Technical Facilities: 10-w TPO, 0.06-kw ERP, 28-ft. above ground, 49-ft. above sea level, lat. 57° 12' 19", long. 153° 18' 07".

Transmitter: VPSO Office Bldg.

Ownership: State of Alaska.

Ouzinkie—K02MA, Ch. 2, State of Alaska. Phone: 907-269-5744.
Technical Facilities: 0.043-kw ERP, lat. 57° 55' 24", long. 152° 30' 00".

Ownership: State of Alaska.

Ouzinkie—K07QY, Ch. 7, State of Alaska.
Technical Facilities: 10-w TPO, 0.0555-kw ERP, 20-ft. above ground, 45-ft. above sea level, lat. 51° 55' 24", long. 152° 30' 00".

Transmitter: Ouzinkie Community School.

Palmer—K09JE, Ch. 9, Northern Lights Media Inc. Phone: 574-287-1001.
Technical Facilities: 0.058-kw ERP, lat. 61° 36' 56", long. 149° 01' 07".

Ownership: Schurz Communications Inc.

Palmer—K12OW, Ch. 12, Fireweed Communications Corp. Phone: 907-339-3800.
Technical Facilities: 0.075-kw ERP, lat. 61° 43' 17", long. 149° 25' 23".

Transmitter: Motorola Site, Beckwitt Bluff, Grubstake Ridge.

Ownership: Fireweed Communications LLC.

Palmer—K66CF, Ch. 66, Northern Television Inc.
Technical Facilities: 0.032-kw ERP, 30-ft. above ground, 899-ft. above sea level, lat. 61° 37' 18", long. 149° 01' 16".

Ownership: Northern Television Inc.

Paxson—K04MQ, Ch. 4, State of Alaska. Phone: 907-269-5744.
Technical Facilities: 0.043-kw ERP, lat. 63° 01' 54", long. 145° 29' 35".

Ownership: State of Alaska.

Paxson—K11QV, Ch. 11, State of Alaska.
Technical Facilities: 10-w TPO, 0.055-kw ERP, 20-ft. above ground, 2720-ft. above sea level, lat. 63° 01' 54", long. 145° 29' 35".

Transmitter: Paxson Hwy. 185, 0.5-mi. up Richardson Hwy.

Ownership: State of Alaska.

Pedro Bay—K09TS, Ch. 9, State of Alaska. Phone: 907-269-5744.
Technical Facilities: 0.059-kw ERP, lat. 59° 47' 07", long. 154° 46' 15".

Transmitter: Village General Maintenance Building.

Ownership: State of Alaska.

Pedro Bay—K13SV, Ch. 13, State of Alaska.
Technical Facilities: 10-w TPO, 0.054-kw ERP, 20-ft. above ground, 90-ft. above sea level, lat. 59° 47' 06", long. 154° 07' 09".

Transmitter: Alascom Office, Pedro Bay.

Ownership: State of Alaska.

Pelican—K04LB, Ch. 4, State of Alaska. Phone: 907-269-5744.
Technical Facilities: 0.042-kw ERP, lat. 57° 57' 45", long. 136° 13' 51".

Ownership: State of Alaska.

Pelican—K09RM, Ch. 9, State of Alaska.
Technical Facilities: 10-w TPO, 0.0548-kw ERP, 20-ft. above ground, 145-ft. above sea level, lat. 57° 57' 45", long. 136° 13' 51".

Transmitter: Pelican Community School.

Ownership: State of Alaska.

Perryville—K04MA, Ch. 4, State of Alaska.
Technical Facilities: 10-w TPO, 0.043-kw ERP, 20-ft. above ground, 50-ft. above sea level, lat. 55° 54' 45", long. 159° 08' 34".

Transmitter: Perryville Community Hall.

Ownership: State of Alaska.

Perryville—K09NK, Ch. 9, Village of Perryville. Phone: 907-269-5744.

Technical Facilities: 0.013-kw ERP, lat. 55° 54' 45", long. 159° 08' 34".

Ownership: Village of Perryville.

Petersburg—K09OU, Ch. 9, Narrows Broadcasting Corp.
Technical Facilities: 0.01-kw ERP, lat. 56° 48' 52", long. 132° 57' 05".

Ownership: Narrows Broadcasting Corp.

Petersburg—K11QC, Ch. 11, Narrows Broadcasting Corp.
Technical Facilities: 0.047-kw ERP, 79-ft. above sea level, lat. 56° 47' 28", long. 132° 58' 20".

Ownership: Narrows Broadcasting Corp.

Petersburg—K15AF, Ch. 15, State of Alaska. Phone: 907-269-5744.
Technical Facilities: 0.64-kw ERP, lat. 56° 48' 55", long. 132° 57' 12".

Ownership: State of Alaska.

Petersburg—K21CK, Ch. 21, State of Alaska.
Technical Facilities: 100-w TPO, 0.7-kw ERP, 105-ft. above ground, 180-ft. above sea level, lat. 56° 48' 55", long. 132° 57' 12".

Transmitter: Petersburg High School, 3rd & B Sts.

Ownership: State of Alaska.

Pilot Point—K02LI, Ch. 2, State of Alaska.
Technical Facilities: 10-w TPO, 0.042-kw ERP, 20-ft. above ground, 30-ft. above sea level, lat. 57° 33' 53", long. 157° 34' 30".

Transmitter: School Power House, Pilot Point.

Ownership: State of Alaska.

Pilot Point—K09NO, Ch. 9, Village of Pilot Point.
Technical Facilities: 0.013-kw ERP, 98-ft. above sea level, lat. 57° 33' 53", long. 157° 34' 30".

Ownership: Village of Pilot Point.

Pilot Station—K15AU, Ch. 15, State of Alaska.
Technical Facilities: 10-w TPO, 0.163-kw ERP, 20-ft. above ground, 295-ft. above sea level, lat. 61° 52' 24", long. 162° 52' 34".

Transmitter: Pump House, Pilot Station.

Ownership: State of Alaska.

Pitkas Point—K02LV, Ch. 2, State of Alaska.
Technical Facilities: 10-w TPO, 0.043-kw ERP, 20-ft. above ground, 45-ft. above sea level, lat. 62° 01' 57", long. 163° 16' 55".

Ownership: State of Alaska.

Pitkas Point—K04MW, Ch. 4, State of Alaska. Phone: 907-269-5744.
Technical Facilities: 0.04-kw ERP, lat. 62° 01' 57", long. 163° 16' 55".

Ownership: State of Alaska.

Platinum—K05HY, Ch. 5, State of Alaska. Phone: 907-269-5744.
Technical Facilities: 0.05-kw ERP, lat. 59° 00' 40", long. 161° 49' 35".

Ownership: State of Alaska.

Platinum—K13UJ, Ch. 13, State of Alaska. Phone: 907-269-5744.

Technical Facilities: 0.013-kw ERP, lat. 55° 54' 45", long. 159° 08' 34".

Ownership: Village of Perryville.

Technical Facilities: 0.057-kw ERP, 36-ft. above sea level, lat. 59° 00' 40", long. 161° 49' 35".

Ownership: State of Alaska.

Point Baker—K04MV, Ch. 4, State of Alaska. Phone: 907-269-5744.
Technical Facilities: 0.04-kw ERP, lat. 56° 21' 14", long. 133° 37' 13".

Ownership: State of Alaska.

Point Baker—K09SY, Ch. 9, State of Alaska.
Technical Facilities: 10-w TPO, 0.056-kw ERP, 20-ft. above ground, 50-ft. above sea level, lat. 56° 21' 14", long. 133° 37' 13".

Transmitter: Community Store, Point Baker.

Ownership: State of Alaska.

Point Hope—K04IQ, Ch. 4, State of Alaska. Phone: 907-269-5744.
Technical Facilities: 0.018-kw ERP, lat. 68° 21' 30", long. 160° 46' 30".

Ownership: State of Alaska.

Point Hope—K09QN, Ch. 9, State of Alaska.
Technical Facilities: 10-w TPO, 0.0536-kw ERP, 20-ft. above ground, 47-ft. above sea level, lat. 68° 20' 51", long. 166° 44' 16".

Transmitter: Alascom Earth Station, Point Hope.

Ownership: State of Alaska.

Point Lay—K04IT, Ch. 4, State of Alaska. Phone: 907-269-5744.
Technical Facilities: 0.02-kw ERP, lat. 69° 46' 00", long. 163° 04' 58".

Ownership: State of Alaska.

Point Lay—K09UC, Ch. 9, State of Alaska.
Technical Facilities: 0.05-kw ERP, lat. 69° 49' 00", long. 163° 04' 48".

Ownership: State of Alaska.

Port Alice—K09TL, Ch. 9, State of Alaska.
Technical Facilities: 10-w TPO, 0.055-kw ERP, 20-ft. above ground, 40-ft. above sea level, lat. 55° 47' 59", long. 133° 35' 13".

Transmitter: Port Alice School.

Ownership: State of Alaska.

Port Alice—K13TL, Ch. 13, State of Alaska. Fax: 907-269-5744.
Technical Facilities: 0.055-kw ERP, 39-ft. above sea level, lat. 55° 47' 59", long. 133° 35' 13".

Ownership: State of Alaska.

Port Alsworth—K07SH, Ch. 7, State of Alaska.
Technical Facilities: 10-w TPO, 0.059-kw ERP, 31-ft. above ground, 301-ft. above sea level, lat. 60° 12' 09", long. 154° 19' 08".

Transmitter: Tanalian School generator bldg.

Ownership: State of Alaska.

Port Alsworth—K13TU, Ch. 13, State of Alaska. Phone: 907-269-5744.
Technical Facilities: 0.06-kw ERP, lat. 60° 12' 09", long. 154° 19' 08".

Transmitter: Tanalian School generator bldg.

Ownership: State of Alaska.

Port Graham—K09QB, Ch. 9, State of Alaska.
Technical Facilities: 0.006-kw ERP, lat. 59° 20' 54", long. 151° 49' 29".

Transmitter: Community Center, Port Graham.

Ownership: State of Alaska.

Port Graham—K13SC, Ch. 13, State of Alaska.

Technical Facilities: 10-w TPO, 0.055-kw ERP, 57-ft. above ground, 107-ft. above sea level, lat. 59° 20' 54", long. 151° 49' 29".

Transmitter: Community Center, Port Graham.

Ownership: State of Alaska.

Port Heiden—K04JT, Ch. 4, City of Port Heiden. Phone: 907-269-5744.

Technical Facilities: 0.02-kw ERP, lat. 56° 54' 47", long. 158° 40' 54".

Ownership: City of Port Heiden.

Port Heiden—K13SA, Ch. 13, State of Alaska.

Technical Facilities: 10-w TPO, 0.0589-kw ERP, 55-ft. above ground, 124-ft. above sea level, lat. 56° 51' 04", long. 158° 35' 50".

Transmitter: Port Heiden Fire Station.

Ownership: State of Alaska.

Port Lions—K07RG, Ch. 7, State of Alaska.

Technical Facilities: 10-w TPO, 0.058-kw ERP, 47-ft. above ground, 75-ft. above sea level, lat. 57° 52' 07", long. 152° 52' 43".

Transmitter: BIA School Bldg.

Ownership: State of Alaska.

Port Lions—K09SR, Ch. 9, State of Alaska.

Technical Facilities: 10-w TPO, 0.059-kw ERP, 46-ft. above ground, 75-ft. above sea level, lat. 57° 52' 09", long. 152° 52' 43".

Transmitter: BIA School Bldg.

Ownership: State of Alaska.

Port Moller—K02LX, Ch. 2, State of Alaska. Phone: 907-269-5744.

Technical Facilities: 0.04-kw ERP, lat. 57° 59' 22", long. 160° 34' 33".

Ownership: State of Alaska.

Port Moller—K07SO, Ch. 7, State of Alaska.

Technical Facilities: 10-w TPO, 0.055-kw ERP, 20-ft. above ground, 40-ft. above sea level, lat. 57° 59' 22", long. 160° 34' 33".

Transmitter: Port Moller High School.

Ownership: State of Alaska.

Port Protection—K11QX, Ch. 11, State of Alaska.

Technical Facilities: 10-w TPO, 0.055-kw ERP, 20-ft. above ground, 40-ft. above sea level, lat. 56° 19' 23", long. 133° 36' 44".

Transmitter: Port Protection School.

Ownership: State of Alaska.

Port Protection—K13TV, Ch. 13, State of Alaska. Phone: 907-269-5744.

Technical Facilities: 0.05-kw ERP, lat. 56° 19' 23", long. 133° 36' 44".

Ownership: State of Alaska.

Portage Creek—K07TU, Ch. 7, State of Alaska.

Technical Facilities: 0.54-kw ERP, lat. 58° 54' 10", long. 157° 43' 08".

Ownership: State of Alaska.

Portage Creek—K13KY, Ch. 13, State of Alaska. Phone: 907-269-5744.

Technical Facilities: 0.106-kw ERP, lat. 58° 53' 46", long. 157° 28' 28".

Ownership: State of Alaska.

Quinhagak—K09SX, Ch. 9, State of Alaska.

Technical Facilities: 10-w TPO, 0.054-kw ERP, 20-ft. above ground, 40-ft. above sea level, lat. 59° 44' 53", long. 161° 54' 47".

Transmitter: Alascom Bldg., Quinhagak.

Ownership: State of Alaska.

Quinhagak—K13SK, Ch. 13, State of Alaska. Phone: 907-269-5744.

Technical Facilities: 0.035-kw ERP, lat. 59° 44' 53", long. 161° 54' 47".

Ownership: State of Alaska.

Rampart—K04LO, Ch. 4, State of Alaska. Phone: 907-269-5744.

Technical Facilities: 0.042-kw ERP, lat. 65° 30' 16", long. 150° 10' 09".

Ownership: State of Alaska.

Rampart—K09RD, Ch. 9, State of Alaska.

Technical Facilities: 10-w TPO, 0.0549-kw ERP, 20-ft. above ground, 335-ft. above sea level, lat. 65° 30' 16", long. 150° 10' 09".

Transmitter: Alascom Earth Station, Rampart.

Ownership: State of Alaska.

Red Devil—K02LA, Ch. 2, State of Alaska.

Technical Facilities: 10-w TPO, 0.043-kw ERP, 20-ft. above ground, 220-ft. above sea level, lat. 61° 47' 04", long. 157° 20' 00".

Transmitter: Alascom Earth Station, Red Devil.

Ownership: State of Alaska.

Rifle—K11KR, Ch. 11, State of Alaska. Phone: 907-269-5744.

Technical Facilities: 0.094-kw ERP, lat. 58° 44' 35", long. 156° 58' 58".

Ownership: State of Alaska.

Rowan Bay—K09TC, Ch. 9, State of Alaska.

Technical Facilities: 10-w TPO, 0.055-kw ERP, 20-ft. above ground, 40-ft. above sea level, lat. 56° 39' 50", long. 134° 16' 06".

Transmitter: Rowan Bay School.

Ownership: State of Alaska.

Rowan Bay—K13TM, Ch. 13, State of Alaska. Phone: 907-269-5744.

Technical Facilities: 0.055-kw ERP, lat. 56° 39' 50", long. 134° 16' 06".

Ownership: State of Alaska.

Ruby—K04KU, Ch. 4, State of Alaska.

Technical Facilities: 10-w TPO, 0.052-kw ERP, 20-ft. above ground, 260-ft. above sea level, lat. 64° 44' 23", long. 155° 29' 09".

Transmitter: Alascom Earth Station.

Ownership: State of Alaska.

Ruby—K09PK, Ch. 9, City of Ruby.

Technical Facilities: 0.018-kw ERP, lat. 64° 44' 23", long. 155° 29' 09".

Ownership: City of Ruby.

Russian Mission—K09SH, Ch. 9, State of Alaska.

Technical Facilities: 10-w TPO, 0.051-kw ERP, 20-ft. above ground, 90-ft. above sea level, lat. 61° 47' 11", long. 161° 19' 11".

Transmitter: Native Store Warehouse, Russian Mission.

Ownership: State of Alaska.

Russian Mission—K11SB, Ch. 11, State of Alaska. Phone: 907-269-5744.

Technical Facilities: 0.058-kw ERP, 20-ft. above ground, 295-ft. above sea level, lat. 61° 47' 11", long. 161° 19' 11".

Ownership: State of Alaska.

Sand Point—K04HV, Ch. 4, City of Sand Point. Phone: 907-269-5744.

Technical Facilities: 0.018-kw ERP, lat. 55° 20' 30", long. 160° 30' 00".

Ownership: City of Sand Point.

Sand Point—K09RA, Ch. 9, State of Alaska.

Technical Facilities: 10-w TPO, 0.05-kw ERP, 55-ft. above ground, 155-ft. above sea level, lat. 55° 20' 37", long. 160° 29' 15".

Transmitter: Alascom Earth Station, Sand Point.

Ownership: State of Alaska.

Savoonga—K07RD, Ch. 7, State of Alaska.

Technical Facilities: 10-w TPO, 0.056-kw ERP, 20-ft. above ground, 50-ft. above sea level, lat. 63° 41' 45", long. 170° 28' 45".

Transmitter: Alascom Earth Station, Savoonga.

Ownership: State of Alaska.

Savoonga—K09NL, Ch. 9, State of Alaska. Phone: 907-269-5744.

Technical Facilities: 0.013-kw ERP, lat. 63° 41' 45", long. 170° 28' 45".

Ownership: Village of Savoonga.

Scammon Bay—K02LS, Ch. 2, State of Alaska.

Technical Facilities: 10-w TPO, 0.045-kw ERP, 41-ft. above ground, 62-ft. above sea level, lat. 61° 50' 42", long. 165° 34' 40".

Transmitter: Village gymnasium.

Ownership: State of Alaska.

Scammon Bay—K07SR, Ch. 7, State of Alaska. Phone: 907-269-5744.

Technical Facilities: 0.05-kw ERP, lat. 61° 50' 33", long. 165° 34' 36".

Ownership: State of Alaska.

Selawik—K02JU, Ch. 2, City of Selawik. Phone: 907-269-5744.

Technical Facilities: 0.018-kw ERP, lat. 66° 35' 57", long. 160° 00' 00".

Ownership: City of Selawik.

Selawik—K09RL, Ch. 9, State of Alaska.

Technical Facilities: 10-w TPO, 0.0565-kw ERP, 20-ft. above ground, 55-ft. above sea level, lat. 66° 35' 56", long. 160° 00' 40".

Transmitter: Alascom Earth Station, Selawik.

Ownership: State of Alaska.

Seward—K03FO, Ch. 3, City of Seward.

Technical Facilities: 1.88-kw ERP, lat. 60° 06' 18", long. 149° 26' 20".

Ownership: City of Seward.

Seward—K07PG, Ch. 7, City of Seward.

Technical Facilities: 0.038-kw ERP, lat. 60° 06' 12", long. 149° 26' 12".

Ownership: City of Seward.

Seward—K55DD, Ch. 55, State of Alaska.

Technical Facilities: 10-w TPO, 0.0943-kw ERP, 71-ft. above ground, 118-ft. above sea level, lat. 60° 06' 12", long. 149° 26' 12".

Transmitter: Seward Library Bldg., 5th Ave. & Adams St.

Ownership: State of Alaska.

Shageluk—K04KY, Ch. 4, State of Alaska.

Technical Facilities: 10-w TPO, 0.053-kw ERP, 31-ft. above ground, 102-ft. above sea level, lat. 62° 39' 20", long. 159° 31' 48".

Transmitter: Community Center & City Office Bldg.

Ownership: State of Alaska.

Shageluk—K10KH, Ch. 10, State of Alaska.

Technical Facilities: 0.013-kw ERP, lat. 62° 39' 20", long. 159° 31' 48".

Transmitter: Community center & city office bldg.

Ownership: Village of Shageluk.

Shaktoolik—K02LM, Ch. 2, State of Alaska. Phone: 907-269-5744.

Technical Facilities: 0.042-kw ERP, 49-ft. above sea level, lat. 64° 12' 18", long. 161° 11' 22".

Ownership: State of Alaska.

Shaktoolik—K07QU, Ch. 7, State of Alaska.

Technical Facilities: 10-w TPO, 0.0548-kw ERP, 20-ft. above ground, 55-ft. above sea level, lat. 64° 21' 18", long. 161° 11' 22".

Transmitter: Alascom Earth Station, Shaktoolik.

Ownership: State of Alaska.

Sheep Mountain—K08KM, Ch. 8, State of Alaska.

Technical Facilities: 10-w TPO, 0.03-kw ERP, lat. 61° 47' 07", long. 147° 39' 98".

Ownership: State of Alaska.

Sheep Mountain—K12NO, Ch. 12, State of Alaska.

Technical Facilities: 0.03-kw ERP, lat. 61° 47' 07", long. 147° 39' 48".

Ownership: State of Alaska.

Sheldon Point—K03GP, Ch. 3, State of Alaska. Phone: 907-269-5744.

Technical Facilities: 26-ft. above ground, 46-ft. above sea level, lat. 62° 31' 56", long. 164° 50' 50".

Ownership: State of Alaska.

Sheldon Point—K11QR, Ch. 11, State of Alaska.

Technical Facilities: 10-w TPO, 0.055-kw ERP, 20-ft. above ground, 40-ft. above sea level, lat. 62° 31' 56", long. 164° 50' 50".

Ownership: State of Alaska.

Shishmaref—K04LD, Ch. 4, State of Alaska. Phone: 907-269-5744.

Technical Facilities: 0.042-kw ERP, 36-ft. above sea level, lat. 66° 15' 21", long. 166° 04' 10".

Ownership: State of Alaska.

Shishmaref—K09RZ, Ch. 9, State of Alaska.

Technical Facilities: 10-w TPO, 0.0536-kw ERP, 20-ft. above ground, 40-ft. above sea level, lat. 66° 15' 21", long. 166° 04' 10".

Transmitter: Alascom Earth Station, Shishmaref.

Ownership: State of Alaska.

Shungnak—K07RA, Ch. 7, State of Alaska.
Technical Facilities: 10-w TPO, 0.05-kw ERP, 55-ft. above ground, 155-ft. above sea level, lat. 55° 20' 37", long. 160° 29' 15".

Transmitter: State of Alaska Communications Building.

Ownership: State of Alaska.

Shungnak—K09NH, Ch. 9, City of Shungnak. Phone: 907-269-5744.
Technical Facilities: 0.013-kw ERP, lat. 66° 51' 51", long. 146° 40' 38".

Ownership: Village of Shungnak.

Sitka—K03GJ, Ch. 3, Sitka School District.
Technical Facilities: 10-w TPO, 0.0049-kw ERP, 80-ft. above ground, 41-ft. above sea level, lat. 57° 03' 09", long. 135° 20' 19".

Ownership: Sitka School District.

Sitka—K08KY, Ch. 8, Capital Community Broadcasting Inc.
Technical Facilities: 0.1-kw ERP, lat. 57° 03' 13", long. 135° 21' 07".

Ownership: Capital Community Broadcasting Inc.

Sitka—KSCT-LP, Ch. 5, Dan Etulain. Phones: 907-747-8200; 800-747-8488.
Technical Facilities: 10-w TPO, 0.049-kw ERP, 43-ft. above ground, 89-ft. above sea level, lat. 57° 03' 27", long. 135° 20' 20".

Transmitter: 520 Lake St.

Ownership: Dan Etulain.

Personnel: Dan Etulain, General Manager.

Skagway—K11QE, Ch. 11, State of Alaska.
Technical Facilities: 10-w TPO, 0.0489-kw ERP, 80-ft. above ground, 105-ft. above sea level, lat. 59° 27' 13", long. 135° 19' 17".

Transmitter: Waste Treatment Plant, Skagway.

Ownership: State of Alaska.

Skagway—K13QQ, Ch. 13, State of Alaska. Phone: 907-269-5744.
Technical Facilities: 0.02-kw ERP, lat. 59° 27' 13", long. 135° 19' 17".

Ownership: State of Alaska.

Slana—K04KX, Ch. 4, State of Alaska.
Technical Facilities: 10-w TPO, 0.047-kw ERP, 80-ft. above ground, 2270-ft. above sea level, lat. 62° 42' 27", long. 143° 58' 37".

Transmitter: Slana Hwy. Station, Mile 60, Tok Hwy., Slana.

Ownership: State of Alaska.

Slana—K13SM, Ch. 13, State of Alaska.
Technical Facilities: 10-w TPO, 0.049-kw ERP, 80-ft. above ground, 2270-ft. above sea level, lat. 62° 42' 27", long. 143° 58' 37".

Transmitter: Slana Hwy. Station, Mile 60, Tok Hwy., Slana.

Ownership: State of Alaska.

Sleetmute—K07SX, Ch. 7, State of Alaska.
Technical Facilities: 0.057-kw ERP, 299-ft. above sea level, lat. 61° 41' 45", long. 157° 10' 10".

Transmitter: Village Corp. Bldg.

Ownership: State of Alaska.

Sleetmute—K12MD, Ch. 12, State of Alaska. Phone: 907-269-5744.
Technical Facilities: 0.036-kw ERP, lat. 61° 42' 12", long. 157° 10' 00".

Ownership: Sleetmute Village Council.

Sparrevohn—K05IB, Ch. 5, State of Alaska. Phone: 907-269-5744.
Technical Facilities: 0.53-kw ERP, lat. 61° 06' 24", long. 155° 36' 21".

Ownership: State of Alaska.

St. George—K09RE, Ch. 9, State of Alaska.
Technical Facilities: 10-w TPO, 0.0542-kw ERP, 20-ft. above ground, 140-ft. above sea level, lat. 56° 36' 12", long. 169° 32' 57".

Transmitter: Alascom Earth Station, St. George.

Ownership: State of Alaska.

St. Mary's—K07RK, Ch. 7, City of St. Mary's. Phone: 907-269-5744.
Technical Facilities: 0.018-kw ERP, 351-ft. above sea level, lat. 62° 03' 07", long. 163° 10' 29".

Ownership: City of St. Mary's.

St. Mary's—K13SX, Ch. 13, State of Alaska.
Technical Facilities: 10-w TPO, 0.055-kw ERP, 20-ft. above ground, 135-ft. above sea level, lat. 62° 03' 07", long. 163° 10' 29".

Transmitter: Alascom Earth Station.

Ownership: State of Alaska.

St. Michaels—K02LP, Ch. 2, State of Alaska. Phone: 907-269-5744.
Technical Facilities: 0.042-kw ERP, lat. 63° 28' 43", long. 162° 02' 19".

Ownership: State of Alaska.

St. Michaels—K09QX, Ch. 9, State of Alaska.
Technical Facilities: 10-w TPO, 0.0548-kw ERP, 20-ft. above ground, 50-ft. above sea level, lat. 63° 28' 43", long. 162° 02' 19".

Transmitter: Alascom Earth Station, St. Michaels.

Ownership: State of Alaska.

St. Paul—K09RB, Ch. 9, State of Alaska.
Technical Facilities: 10-w TPO, 0.0536-kw ERP, 20-ft. above ground, 120-ft. above sea level, lat. 57° 07' 14", long. 170° 28' 45".

Transmitter: Alascom Earth Station, St. Paul.

Ownership: State of Alaska.

St. Paul Island—K04HM, Ch. 4, State of Alaska. Phone: 907-269-5744.
Technical Facilities: 0.039-kw ERP, lat. 57° 10' 08", long. 170° 16' 58".

Ownership: City of St. Paul Island.

Stebbins—K04LE, Ch. 4, State of Alaska. Phone: 907-269-5744.
Technical Facilities: 0.042-kw ERP, 30-ft. above sea level, lat. 63° 31' 10", long. 162° 17' 15".

Ownership: State of Alaska.

Stebbins—K09RR, Ch. 9, State of Alaska.
Technical Facilities: 10-w TPO, 0.0542-kw ERP, 20-ft. above ground, 35-ft. above sea level, lat. 63° 31' 10", long. 162° 17' 15".

Transmitter: Stebbins Community School.

Ownership: State of Alaska.

Stevens Village—K04NA, Ch. 4, State of Alaska. Phone: 907-269-5744.

Technical Facilities: 0.0535-kw ERP, lat. 66° 00' 26", long. 149° 05' 38".

Transmitter: Village Clinic Bldg.

Ownership: State of Alaska.

Stevens Village—K09SV, Ch. 9, State of Alaska.
Technical Facilities: 10-w TPO, 0.058-kw ERP, 17-ft. above ground, 328-ft. above sea level, lat. 66° 00' 26", long. 149° 05' 38".

Transmitter: Village Clinic Bldg.

Ownership: State of Alaska.

Stony River—K02JZ, Ch. 2, Stony River Traditional Council. Phone: 907-269-5744.
Technical Facilities: 0.018-kw ERP, lat. 61° 46' 59", long. 156° 35' 17".

Ownership: Stony River Traditional Council.

Stony River—K13SE, Ch. 13, State of Alaska.
Technical Facilities: 10-w TPO, 0.055-kw ERP, 20-ft. above ground, 250-ft. above sea level, lat. 61° 46' 59", long. 156° 35' 17".

Transmitter: Community Center, Stony River.

Ownership: State of Alaska.

Takotna—K04LN, Ch. 4, State of Alaska.
Technical Facilities: 10-w TPO, 0.043-kw ERP, 30-ft. above ground, 430-ft. above sea level, lat. 56° 59' 21", long. 156° 03' 42".

Transmitter: Takotna School Bldg.

Ownership: State of Alaska.

Takotna—K09PN, Ch. 9, State of Alaska. Phone: 907-269-5744.
Technical Facilities: 0.054-kw ERP, lat. 62° 59' 21", long. 156° 03' 42".

Ownership: State of Alaska.

Tanana—K02KM, Ch. 2, City of Tanana. Phone: 907-269-5744.
Technical Facilities: 0.018-kw ERP, 253-ft. above sea level, lat. 65° 10' 24", long. 152° 04' 31".

Ownership: City of Tanana.

Tanana—K07RB, Ch. 7, State of Alaska.
Technical Facilities: 10-w TPO, 0.054-kw ERP, 20-ft. above ground, 230-ft. above sea level, lat. 65° 10' 24", long. 152° 04' 38".

Transmitter: Alascom Earth Station, Tanana.

Ownership: State of Alaska.

Tanunak—K07SA, Ch. 7, State of Alaska. Phone: 907-269-5744.
Technical Facilities: 0.054-kw ERP, lat. 60° 35' 00", long. 165° 15' 32".

Ownership: State of Alaska.

Tanunak—K09SW, Ch. 9, State of Alaska.
Technical Facilities: 10-w TPO, 0.054-kw ERP, 20-ft. above ground, 40-ft. above sea level, lat. 60° 35' 00", long. 165° 15' 32".

Transmitter: Alascom Bldg., Tanunak.

Ownership: State of Alaska.

Tatitlek—K09NE, Ch. 9, Village of Tatitlek. Phone: 907-269-5744.
Technical Facilities: 0.013-kw ERP, lat. 60° 51' 51", long. 146° 40' 38".

Ownership: Village of Tatitlek.

Tatitlek—K13SJ, Ch. 13, State of Alaska.

Technical Facilities: 10-w TPO, 0.052-kw ERP, 20-ft. above ground, 60-ft. above sea level, lat. 60° 51' 51", long. 146° 40' 38".

Transmitter: Community School, Tatitlek.

Ownership: State of Alaska.

Telida—K11RV, Ch. 11, State of Alaska. Phone: 907-269-5744.
Technical Facilities: 0.05-kw ERP, lat. 63° 23' 03", long. 153° 16' 34".

Ownership: State of Alaska.

Telida—K13RO, Ch. 13, State of Alaska.
Technical Facilities: 10-w TPO, 0.0548-kw ERP, 20-ft. above ground, 630-ft. above sea level, lat. 63° 23' 03", long. 153° 16' 34".

Transmitter: Alascom Earth Station, Telida.

Ownership: State of Alaska.

Teller—K04LW, Ch. 4, State of Alaska. Phone: 907-269-5744.
Technical Facilities: 0.042-kw ERP, lat. 65° 15' 55", long. 166° 21' 50".

Ownership: State of Alaska.

Teller—K09RO, Ch. 9, State of Alaska.
Technical Facilities: 10-w TPO, 0.0536-kw ERP, 20-ft. above ground, 35-ft. above sea level, lat. 65° 15' 55", long. 166° 21' 50".

Transmitter: Teller Community School.

Ownership: State of Alaska.

Tenakee Springs—K07RH, Ch. 7, State of Alaska.
Technical Facilities: 10-w TPO, 0.053-kw ERP, 20-ft. above ground, 80-ft. above sea level, lat. 57° 46' 53", long. 135° 13' 08".

Transmitter: Alascom Earth Station, Tenakee Springs.

Ownership: State of Alaska.

Tenakee Springs—K10KG, Ch. 10, City of Tenakee Springs. Phone: 907-269-5744.
Technical Facilities: 0.013-kw ERP, lat. 57° 46' 51", long. 135° 13' 11".

Ownership: City of Tenakee Springs.

Tetlin—K07SP, Ch. 7, State of Alaska.
Technical Facilities: 0.05-kw ERP, lat. 63° 08' 14", long. 142° 31' 28".

Ownership: State of Alaska.

Tetlin—K11QU, Ch. 11, State of Alaska.
Technical Facilities: 10-w TPO, 0.055-kw ERP, 20-ft. above ground, 1720-ft. above sea level, lat. 63° 08' 14", long. 142° 31' 28".

Transmitter: Tetlin High School.

Ownership: State of Alaska.

Thorne Bay—K07SN, Ch. 7, State of Alaska.
Technical Facilities: 10-w TPO, 0.055-kw ERP, 20-ft. above ground, 40-ft. above sea level, lat. 55° 41' 08", long. 132° 31' 42".

Transmitter: Thorne Bay School.

Ownership: State of Alaska.

Thorne Bay—K11RC, Ch. 11, State of Alaska. Phone: 907-269-5744.
Technical Facilities: 0.055-kw ERP, lat. 55° 41' 08", long. 132° 31' 42".

Ownership: State of Alaska.

Togiak—K03FL, Ch. 3, City of Togiak. Phone: 907-269-5744.

Technical Facilities: 0.036-kw ERP, lat. 59° 03' 43", long. 160° 22' 33".

Ownership: City of Togiak.

Togiak—K09QU, Ch. 9, State of Alaska.

Technical Facilities: 10-w TPO, 0.056-kw ERP, 20-ft. above ground, 40-ft. above sea level, lat. 59° 03' 43", long. 160° 22' 33".

Transmitter: Alascom Earth Station, Togiak.

Ownership: State of Alaska.

Tok—K13RR, Ch. 13, State of Alaska.

Technical Facilities: 10-w TPO, 0.0295-kw ERP, 228-ft. above ground, 1863-ft. above sea level, lat. 63° 19' 38", long. 142° 59' 48".

Transmitter: State Hwy. maintenance station, Tok.

Ownership: State of Alaska.

Toksook Bay—K04LV, Ch. 4, State of Alaska. Phone: 907-269-5744.

Technical Facilities: 0.043-kw ERP, lat. 60° 31' 53", long. 165° 06' 19".

Ownership: State of Alaska.

Toksook Bay—K11QG, Ch. 11, State of Alaska.

Technical Facilities: 10-w TPO, 0.0561-kw ERP, 20-ft. above ground, 60-ft. above sea level, lat. 60° 31' 53", long. 165° 06' 19".

Transmitter: Alascom Earth Station, Toksook Bay.

Ownership: State of Alaska.

Trapper Creek—K16AF, Ch. 16, State of Alaska. Phone: 907-269-5744.

Technical Facilities: 1.31-kw ERP, lat. 62° 19' 05", long. 150° 19' 00".

Ownership: State of Alaska.

Trapper Creek—K24AG, Ch. 24, State of Alaska.

Technical Facilities: 1.31-kw ERP, 541-ft. above sea level, lat. 62° 19' 05", long. 150° 19' 00".

Transmitter: Trapper Creek.

Ownership: State of Alaska.

Tuluksak—K08ID, Ch. 8, State of Alaska.

Technical Facilities: 0.055-kw ERP, lat. 61° 06' 08", long. 60° 57' 30".

Ownership: State of Alaska.

Tuluksak—K11RE, Ch. 11, State of Alaska. Phone: 907-269-5744.

Technical Facilities: 0.055-kw ERP, lat. 61° 06' 08", long. 160° 57' 30".

Ownership: State of Alaska.

Tuntutuliak—K09TF, Ch. 9, State of Alaska.

Technical Facilities: 10-w TPO, 0.055-kw ERP, 20-ft. above ground, 40-ft. above sea level, lat. 60° 20' 38", long. 162° 39' 50".

Transmitter: Tuntutuliak School.

Ownership: State of Alaska.

Tuntutuliak—K13TC, Ch. 13, State of Alaska. Phone: 907-269-5744.

Technical Facilities: 0.055-kw ERP, lat. 60° 20' 38", long. 162° 39' 50".

Ownership: State of Alaska.

Unalakleet—K04JW, Ch. 4, City of Unalakleet. Phone: 907-269-5744.

Technical Facilities: 0.018-kw ERP, lat. 63° 52' 38", long. 160° 47' 15".

Ownership: City of Unalakleet.

Unalakleet—K09RC, Ch. 9, State of Alaska.

Technical Facilities: 10-w TPO, 0.0522-kw ERP, 20-ft. above ground, 60-ft. above sea level, lat. 63° 52' 38", long. 160° 47' 15".

Transmitter: Alascom Earth Station, Unalakleet.

Ownership: State of Alaska.

Unalaska—K04KV, Ch. 4, State of Alaska.

Technical Facilities: 10-w TPO, 0.049-kw ERP, 20-ft. above ground, 51-ft. above sea level, lat. 53° 52' 44", long. 166° 32' 14".

Transmitter: Alascom Earth Station, Unalaska.

Ownership: State of Alaska.

Unalaska, etc.—K02HO, Ch. 2, State of Alaska. Phone: 907-269-5744.

Technical Facilities: 2-kw ERP, 328-ft. above sea level, lat. 53° 52' 36", long. 166° 32' 20".

Ownership: State of Alaska.

Usibelli, etc.—K13MZ, Ch. 13, Smith Media License Holdings LLC.

Technical Facilities: 0.01-kw ERP, 3232-ft. above sea level, lat. 63° 52' 30", long. 148° 51' 00".

Ownership: Smith Media License Holdings LLC.

Valdez—K09OT, Ch. 9, State of Alaska. Phone: 907-269-5744.

Technical Facilities: 0.18-kw ERP, lat. 61° 08' 12", long. 146° 20' 15".

Transmitter: Dept. of Transportation Yard, Electrical/Communications Bldg.

Ownership: State of Alaska.

Valdez—K15AI, Ch. 15, State of Alaska.

Technical Facilities: 10-w TPO, 0.12-kw ERP, 95-ft. above ground, 115-ft. above sea level, lat. 61° 07' 56", long. 146° 20' 07".

Transmitter: Alascom Earth Station, Valdez.

Ownership: State of Alaska.

Venetie—K09TW, Ch. 9, State of Alaska.

Technical Facilities: 0.055-kw ERP, lat. 67° 07' 05", long. 146° 25' 14".

Ownership: State of Alaska.

Wainwright—K04IR, Ch. 4, State of Alaska. Phone: 907-269-5744.

Technical Facilities: 0.018-kw ERP, lat. 70° 37' 55", long. 160° 01' 00".

Ownership: State of Alaska.

Wales—K02LT, Ch. 2, State of Alaska.

Technical Facilities: 0.0449-kw ERP, 46-ft. above sea level, lat. 65° 36' 48", long. 168° 05' 22".

Transmitter: Cable Co. Building, 0.5-mi. N of Wales.

Ownership: State of Alaska.

Wales—K04MN, Ch. 4, State of Alaska. Phone: 907-269-5744.

Technical Facilities: 0.04-kw ERP, lat. 65° 36' 48", long. 168° 05' 22".

Ownership: State of Alaska.

Whales Pass—K07SI, Ch. 7, State of Alaska.

Technical Facilities: 10-w TPO, 0.055-kw ERP, 20-ft. above ground, 40-ft. above sea level, lat. 56° 06' 13", long. 133° 06' 40".

Transmitter: Whales Pass School.

Ownership: State of Alaska.

Whales Pass—K11RB, Ch. 11, State of Alaska. Phone: 907-269-5744.

Technical Facilities: 0.05-kw ERP, lat. 56° 06' 13", long. 133° 06' 40".

Ownership: State of Alaska.

White Mountain—K11QT, Ch. 11, State of Alaska.

Technical Facilities: 10-w TPO, 0.055-kw ERP, 20-ft. above ground, 40-ft. above sea level, lat. 64° 41' 06", long. 163° 24' 40".

Transmitter: White Mountain High School.

Ownership: State of Alaska.

White Mountain—K13TD, Ch. 13, State of Alaska. Phone: 907-269-5744.

Technical Facilities: 0.055-kw ERP, 39-ft. above sea level, lat. 64° 41' 06", long. 163° 24' 40".

Ownership: State of Alaska.

Whittier—K09UB, Ch. 9, State of Alaska.

Technical Facilities: 10-w TPO, 0.055-kw ERP, 20-ft. above ground, 15-ft. above sea level, lat. 60° 46' 33", long. 148° 41' 15".

Transmitter: Alascom Earth Station, Whittier.

Ownership: State of Alaska.

Wiseman—K13TA, Ch. 13, State of Alaska. Phone: 907-269-5744.

Technical Facilities: 0.055-kw ERP, lat. 67° 24' 40", long. 150° 06' 32".

Ownership: State of Alaska.

Womens Bay—K02ME, Ch. 2, State of Alaska.

Technical Facilities: 10-w TPO, 0.043-kw ERP, 20-ft. above ground, 100-ft. above sea level, lat. 57° 43' 23", long. 152° 31' 08".

Transmitter: Nyman Peninsula, Kodiak Coast Guard Station.

Ownership: State of Alaska.

Womens Bay—K07ST, Ch. 7, State of Alaska. Phone: 907-269-5744.

Technical Facilities: 0.05-kw ERP, lat. 57° 43' 23", long. 152° 31' 08".

Ownership: State of Alaska.

Wrangell—K09OQ, Ch. 9, Capital Community Broadcasting Inc.

Technical Facilities: 0.06-kw ERP, 112-ft. above sea level, lat. 56° 27' 14", long. 132° 22' 54".

Ownership: Capital Community Broadcasting Inc.

Wrangell—K15AJ, Ch. 15, State of Alaska. Phone: 907-269-5744.

Technical Facilities: 0.69-kw ERP, lat. 56° 27' 14", long. 132° 22' 54".

Ownership: State of Alaska.

Wrangell—K21AF, Ch. 21, State of Alaska.

Technical Facilities: 100-w TPO, 0.69-kw ERP, 135-ft. above ground, 144-ft. above sea level, lat. 56° 27' 14", long. 132° 22' 54".

Transmitter: Wrangell Cemetery.

Ownership: State of Alaska.

Yakutat—K02ID, Ch. 2, State of Alaska. Phone: 907-269-5744.

Technical Facilities: 0.03-kw ERP, lat. 59° 32' 39", long. 139° 43' 32".

Ownership: Yakutat City School District.

Yakutat—K09UA, Ch. 9, State of Alaska.

Technical Facilities: 10-w TPO, 0.0514-kw ERP, 20-ft. above ground, 65-ft. above sea level, lat. 59° 32' 00", long. 144° 10' 00".

Transmitter: Alascom Earth Station.

Ownership: State of Alaska.

Arizona

Big Sandy Valley—K27DA, Ch. 27, Mohave County Board of Supervisors.

Technical Facilities: 0.072-kw ERP, 33-ft. above ground, 7713-ft. above sea level, lat. 35° 06' 37", long. 113° 52' 55".

Ownership: Mohave County Board of Supervisors.

Bullhead City—K02HR, Ch. 2, Mohave County Board of Supervisors.

Technical Facilities: 0.115-kw ERP, lat. 35° 12' 46", long. 114° 33' 18".

Ownership: Mohave County Board of Supervisors.

Bullhead City—K04GT, Ch. 4, Mohave County Board of Supervisors.

Technical Facilities: 0.116-kw ERP, lat. 35° 12' 46", long. 114° 33' 18".

Ownership: Mohave County Board of Supervisors.

Bullhead City—K07YJ, Ch. 7, Mohave County Board of Supervisors. Phone: 928-753-0729.

Technical Facilities: 0.06-kw ERP, 20-ft. above ground, 1181-ft. above sea level, lat. 35° 12' 46", long. 114° 33' 18".

Ownership: Mohave County Board of Supervisors.

Bullhead City—K09KG, Ch. 9, Mohave County Board of Supervisors.

Technical Facilities: 0.116-kw ERP, lat. 35° 12' 46", long. 114° 33' 18".

Ownership: Mohave County Board of Supervisors.

Bullhead City—K11LX, Ch. 11, Mohave County Board of Supervisors.

Technical Facilities: 0.115-kw ERP, lat. 35° 12' 46", long. 114° 33' 18".

Ownership: Mohave County Board of Supervisors.

Bullhead City—K12OF, Ch. 12, Mohave County Board of Supervisors.

Technical Facilities: 0.115-kw ERP, lat. 35° 12' 46", long. 114° 33' 18".

Ownership: Mohave County Board of Supervisors.

Bullhead City—K16EV, Ch. 16, Mohave County Board of Supervisors.

Technical Facilities: 1.1-kw ERP, 26-ft. above ground, 4035-ft. above sea level, lat. 35° 02' 09", long. 114° 22' 14".

Ownership: Mohave County Board of Supervisors.

Bullhead City—K18CB, Ch. 18, Howard F. Roycroft. Phone: 202-637-6525.

Technical Facilities: 100-w TPO, 2.54-kw ERP, 43-ft. above ground, 485-ft. above sea level, lat. 35° 14' 50", long. 114° 44' 35".

Transmitter: 11.8-mi. NW of Bullhead City.

Ownership: Howard F. Roycroft.

Bullhead City—K24DK, Ch. 24, KAZT LLC.

Technical Facilities: 100-w TPO, 0.7-kw ERP, 39-ft. above ground, 4019-ft. above sea level, lat. 35° 02' 09", long. 114° 22' 14".

Transmitter: Oakman Electronic site, SE of Bullhead City.

Ownership: KAZT LLC.

Personnel: Richard Howe, General Manager & Sales Manager; Wally Macomber, Chief Engineer.

■**Bullhead City**—K25HD, Ch. 25, Richard D. Tatham. Phones: 928-453-8825; 928-855-9110. Fax: 928-453-2588.

Technical Facilities: 1.2-kw ERP, 27-ft. above ground, 4827-ft. above sea level, lat. 35° 14' 46", long. 114° 44' 32".

Ownership: Richard D. Tatham.

Personnel: Richard D. Tatham, General Manager; Faron Eckelbarger, Chief Engineer.

Bullhead City—K51IO, Ch. 51, Trinity Broadcasting Network Inc. Phone: 714-832-2950. Fax: 714-730-0661.

Technical Facilities: 9.99-kw ERP, 40-ft. above ground, 4699-ft. above sea level, lat. 35° 14' 58", long. 114° 44' 34".

Holds CP for change to 0.5-kw ERP, 40-ft. above ground, 4774-ft. above sea level, BDFCDTT-20070709ADE.

Transmitter: KFLG(FM) Tower, atop Christmas Tree Pass near Laughlin, NV.

Ownership: Trinity Broadcasting Network Inc.

■**Camp Verde**—K18DD, Ch. 18, Central States Communications. Phone: 928-567-3433.

Technical Facilities: 3.76-kw ERP, 92-ft. above ground, 7733-ft. above sea level, lat. 34° 41' 14", long. 112° 07' 00".

Ownership: Central States Communications.

Camp Verde—K19FD, Ch. 19, Central States Communications. Phone: 928-567-3433.

Technical Facilities: 1.22-kw ERP, 34-ft. above ground, 6560-ft. above sea level, lat. 34° 27' 51", long. 111° 52' 17".

Ownership: Central States Communications.

Camp Verde—K21GE, Ch. 21, Camp Verde TV Club. Phone: 928-567-3433.

Technical Facilities: 0.789-kw ERP, 32-ft. above ground, 6433-ft. above sea level, lat. 34° 28' 13", long. 111° 52' 21".

Ownership: Camp Verde TV Club.

Camp Verde—K23FZ, Ch. 23, Camp Verde TV Club. Phone: 928-567-3433.

Technical Facilities: 0.917-kw ERP, 32-ft. above ground, 6433-ft. above sea level, lat. 34° 28' 13", long. 111° 52' 21".

Ownership: Camp Verde TV Club.

Camp Verde—K47IK, Ch. 47, Central States Communications. Phone: 928-567-3433.

Technical Facilities: 0.077-kw ERP, 11-ft. above ground, 6411-ft. above sea level, lat. 34° 28' 13", long. 111° 52' 21".

Ownership: Camp Verde TV Club.

Camp Verde—K55IY, Ch. 55, Camp Verde TV Club. Phone: 928-567-3433.

Technical Facilities: 0.01-kw ERP, lat. 34° 28' 13", long. 111° 52' 21".

Ownership: Camp Verde TV Club.

Camp Verde, etc.—K49HP, Ch. 49, Camp Verde TV Club. Phone: 928-567-3433.

Technical Facilities: 0.079-kw ERP, 10-ft. above ground, 6411-ft. above sea level, lat. 34° 28' 13", long. 111° 52' 21".

Ownership: Camp Verde TV Club.

Casa Grande—K43CO, Ch. 43, KAZT LLC.

Technical Facilities: 53.3-kw ERP, 39-ft. above ground, 2795-ft. above sea level, lat. 33° 00' 05", long. 111° 40' 29".

Ownership: KAZT LLC.

Casa Grande—KCAB-LP, Ch. 28, Central Arizona Broadcasting LLC. Phone: 520-560-2555. Fax: 520-876-4985.

Technical Facilities: 9.99-kw ERP, 105-ft. above ground, 1509-ft. above sea level, lat. 32° 52' 19", long. 111° 44' 40".

Ownership: Central Arizona Broadcasting LLC.

Casas Adobes—K64BV, Ch. 64, KVOA Communications Inc. Phone: 520-792-2270.

Technical Facilities: 10.92-kw ERP, lat. 32° 12' 53", long. 111° 00' 20".

Ownership: KVOA Communications Inc.

Chinle—K08HQ, Ch. 8, KOB-TV LLC.

Technical Facilities: 0.01-kw ERP, lat. 36° 09' 20", long. 109° 35' 46".

Ownership: Hubbard Broadcasting Inc.

Chinle—K10IN, Ch. 10, KOAT Hearst-Argyle Television Inc. Phone: 919-839-0300.

Technical Facilities: 0.1-kw ERP, lat. 36° 09' 20", long. 109° 35' 46".

Ownership: Hearst-Argyle Television Inc.

Chinle—K13VW, Ch. 13, LIN of Colorado LLC.

Technical Facilities: 0.99-kw ERP, lat. 36° 09' 20", long. 109° 35' 46".

Ownership: LIN TV Corp.

Chinle—K51AV, Ch. 51, The Navajo Nation. Phone: 602-724-3311.

Studio: Telecommunications Dept., Tsaile, AZ 86556.

Technical Facilities: 0.58-kw ERP, lat. 36° 21' 15", long. 109° 49' 45".

Ownership: Navajo Community College.

Personnel: Curtis Sweet, General Manager.

Chloride—K30GG, Ch. 30, Mohave County Board of Supervisors.

Technical Facilities: 0.071-kw ERP, 13-ft. above ground, 4774-ft. above sea level, lat. 35° 23' 49", long. 114° 10' 16".

Ownership: Mohave County Board of Supervisors.

Chloride—K32DW, Ch. 32, Mohave County Board of Supervisors.

Technical Facilities: 0.08-kw ERP, 16-ft. above ground, 4777-ft. above sea level, lat. 35° 23' 49", long. 114° 10' 16".

Ownership: Mohave County Board of Supervisors.

Chloride—K42CQ, Ch. 42, Mohave County Board of Supervisors.

Technical Facilities: 0.032-kw ERP, lat. 35° 23' 49", long. 114° 10' 16".

Ownership: Mohave County Board of Supervisors.

Chloride—K49EU, Ch. 49, Mohave County Board of Supervisors.

Technical Facilities: 0.032-kw ERP, lat. 35° 23' 49", long. 114° 10' 16".

Ownership: Mohave County Board of Supervisors.

Colorado City—K27EJ, Ch. 27, Mohave County Board of Supervisors.

Technical Facilities: 0.8-kw ERP, lat. 36° 54' 11", long. 113° 01' 58".

Ownership: Mohave County Board of Supervisors.

Concho—KWKM-LP, Ch. 10, KM Communications Inc. Phone: 847-674-0864.

Technical Facilities: 0.795-kw ERP, 180-ft. above ground, 8563-ft. above sea level, lat. 34° 14' 58", long. 109° 35' 11".

Ownership: KM Communications Inc.

Concho—KWSJ-LP, Ch. 12, KM Communications Inc. Phone: 847-674-0864.

Technical Facilities: 0.795-kw ERP, 180-ft. above ground, 8563-ft. above sea level, lat. 34° 14' 58", long. 109° 35' 11".

Ownership: KM Communications Inc.

Cottonwood—K16BP, Ch. 16, Fox Television Stations Inc. Phone: 202-895-3088.

Technical Facilities: 5-kw ERP, 125-ft. above ground, 7775-ft. above sea level, lat. 34° 41' 14", long. 112° 07' 01".

Ownership: Fox Television Holdings Inc.

Cottonwood—K44CN, Ch. 44, Scripps Howard Broadcasting Co. Phone: 602-273-1500.

Studio: 515 N Gateway Blvd, Phoenix, AZ 85008.

Technical Facilities: 1000-w TPO, 21.385-kw ERP, 49-ft. above ground, 7703-ft. above sea level, lat. 34° 41' 12", long. 112° 07' 00".

Transmitter: Mingus Mountain.

Ownership: E. W. Scripps Co.

Personnel: Brad Nilsen, General Manager; Don Thomas, Chief Engineer; Janice Todd, General Sales Manager.

Cottonwood & Prescott—K34EE, Ch. 34, KTVK Inc.

Technical Facilities: 155-w TPO, 0.85-kw ERP, 55-ft. above ground, 7775-ft. above sea level, lat. 34° 41' 15", long. 112° 07' 02".

Transmitter: Approx. 6.8-mi. SW of Cottonwood.

Ownership: Belo Corp.

Personnel: W. Grant Hafley, President; David J. Kessell, General Manager.

Cottonwood, etc.—K38AI, Ch. 38, KTVK Inc. Phone: 602-207-3333.

Technical Facilities: 21.4-kw ERP, 59-ft. above ground, 7707-ft. above sea level, lat. 34° 41' 12", long. 112° 06' 59".

Ownership: Belo Corp.

Cottonwood, etc.—K40AD, Ch. 40, Meredith Corp. Phones: 503-239-4949; 515-284-3000. Fax: 503-239-6184.

Technical Facilities: 21.4-kw ERP, 59-ft. above ground, 7707-ft. above sea level, lat. 34° 41' 12", long. 112° 06' 59".

Holds CP for change to 2.3-kw ERP, BDFCDTT-20090501ABX.

Ownership: Meredith Corp.

Cottonwood, etc.—K42AC, Ch. 42, Arizona State Board of Regents for Arizona State U.

Technical Facilities: 7.27-kw ERP, lat. 34° 41' 12", long. 112° 06' 59".

Ownership: Arizona State Board of Regents for Arizona State U.

Dolan Springs—K35EI, Ch. 35, Mohave County Board of Supervisors.

Technical Facilities: 1.38-kw ERP, lat. 35° 35' 42", long. 114° 14' 46".

Ownership: Mohave County Board of Supervisors.

Dolan Springs—K41BZ, Ch. 41, Mohave County Board of Supervisors.

Technical Facilities: 0.35-kw ERP, lat. 35° 35' 42", long. 114° 14' 46".

Ownership: Mohave County Board of Supervisors.

Dolan Springs—K43GU, Ch. 43, Mohave County Board of Supervisors.

Technical Facilities: 1.92-kw ERP, 43-ft. above ground, 5030-ft. above sea level, lat. 35° 35' 42", long. 114° 14' 46".

Ownership: Mohave County Board of Supervisors.

Douglas—K28EY, Ch. 28, NBC Telemundo License Co. Phone: 202-637-4535.

Technical Facilities: 1.62-kw ERP, lat. 31° 28' 50", long. 109° 57' 20".

Transmitter: 5-mi. NW of Bisbee.

Ownership: NBC Universal.

Duncan—K20GG, Ch. 20, Arizona Board of Regents, U. of Arizona. Phone: 520-621-1567.

Technical Facilities: 1.33-kw ERP, lat. 32° 53' 14", long. 109° 18' 49".

Ownership: Arizona U. Board of Regents.

Duncan—K33DA, Ch. 33, Southern Greenlee County TV Assn. Inc.

Technical Facilities: 50-w TPO, 2.28-kw ERP, 39-ft. above ground, 6575-ft. above sea level, lat. 32° 53' 14", long. 109° 18' 49".

Transmitter: Guthrie Peak, 17-mi. NW of Duncan.

Ownership: Southern Greenlee County TV Assn. Inc.

Duncan—K35CP, Ch. 35, Southern Greenlee County TV Assn. Inc.

Technical Facilities: 50-w TPO, 2.28-kw ERP, 39-ft. above ground, 6575-ft. above sea level, lat. 32° 53' 14", long. 109° 18' 49".

Transmitter: Guthrie Peak, 17-mi. NW of Duncan.

Ownership: Southern Greenlee County TV Assn. Inc.

Duncan—K39CM, Ch. 39, Southern Greenlee County TV Assn. Inc.

Technical Facilities: 50-w TPO, 2.28-kw ERP, 39-ft. above ground, 6575-ft. above sea level, lat. 32° 53' 14", long. 109° 18' 49".

Transmitter: Guthrie Peak, 17-mi. NW of Duncan.

Ownership: Southern Greenlee County TV Assn. Inc.

Duncan—K41CV, Ch. 41, Southern Greenlee County TV Assn. Inc.

Technical Facilities: 100-w TPO, 2.28-kw ERP, 39-ft. above ground, 6575-ft. above sea level, lat. 32° 53' 14", long. 109° 18' 49".

Transmitter: Guthrie Peak, 17-mi. NW of Duncan.

Ownership: Southern Greenlee County TV Assn. Inc.

Duncan—K43CN, Ch. 43, Southern Greenlee County TV Assn. Inc.

Technical Facilities: 2.33-kw ERP, 16-ft. above ground, 6588-ft. above sea level, lat. 32° 53' 14", long. 109° 18' 49".

Ownership: Southern Greenlee County TV Assn. Inc.

Duncan—K47DA, Ch. 47, Southern Greenlee County TV Assn. Inc.

Technical Facilities: 930-w TPO, 2.32-kw ERP, lat. 32° 53' 14", long. 109° 18' 49".

Ownership: Southern Greenlee County TV Assn. Inc.

Duncan—K49CH, Ch. 49, Southern Greenlee County TV Assn. Inc.

Technical Facilities: 2.23-kw ERP, lat. 32° 53' 14", long. 109° 18' 49".

Ownership: Southern Greenlee County TV Assn. Inc.

Duncan—K51DG, Ch. 51, Southern Greenlee County TV Assn. Inc.

Technical Facilities: 2.32-kw ERP, 16-ft. above ground, 6588-ft. above sea level, lat. 32° 53' 14", long. 109° 18' 49".

Ownership: Southern Greenlee County TV Assn. Inc.

Duncan—K53DL, Ch. 53, Southern Greenlee County TV Assn. Inc.

Technical Facilities: 500-w TPO, 2.32-kw ERP, lat. 32° 53' 14", long. 109° 18' 49".

Ownership: Southern Greenlee County TV Assn. Inc.

Duncan, etc.—K55DM, Ch. 55, Southern Greenlee County TV Assn. Inc. Phone: 502-359-2503.

Technical Facilities: 2.32-kw ERP, 20-ft. above ground, 6591-ft. above sea level, lat. 32° 53' 14", long. 109° 18' 49".

Ownership: Southern Greenlee County TV Assn. Inc.

Duncan, etc.—K57CU, Ch. 57, Southern Greenlee County TV Assn. Inc.

Technical Facilities: 50-w TPO, 2.39-kw ERP, lat. 32° 53' 14", long. 109° 18' 49".

Ownership: Southern Greenlee County TV Assn. Inc.

Duncan, etc.—K65CM, Ch. 65, Southern Greenlee County TV Assn. Inc.

Technical Facilities: 2.67-kw ERP, lat. 32° 53' 14", long. 109° 18' 49".

Ownership: Southern Greenlee County TV Assn. Inc.

Duncan, etc.—K67CP, Ch. 67, Southern Greenlee County TV Assn. Inc.

Technical Facilities: 2.74-kw ERP, lat. 32° 53' 14", long. 109° 18' 49".

Ownership: Southern Greenlee County TV Assn. Inc.

Duncan, etc.—K69DG, Ch. 69, Southern Greenlee County TV Assn. Inc.

Technical Facilities: 2.81-kw ERP, lat. 32° 53' 14", long. 109° 18' 49".

Ownership: Southern Greenlee County TV Assn. Inc.

East Flagstaff, etc.—K39FC, Ch. 39, NW Communications of Phoenix Inc. Phone: 202-715-2350.

Technical Facilities: 0.7-kw ERP, 36-ft. above ground, 9272-ft. above sea level, lat. 35° 14' 26", long. 111° 35' 48".

Began Operation: May 10, 1983.

Ownership: Fox Television Holdings Inc.

Flagstaff—K14KK, Ch. 14, Arizona State Board of Regents for Arizona State U. Phone: 480-965-3506.

Technical Facilities: 0.6-kw ERP, 36-ft. above ground, 9294-ft. above sea level, lat. 35° 14' 26", long. 111° 35' 48".

Ownership: Arizona State Board of Regents for Arizona State U.

Flagstaff—K20HS, Ch. 20, Marcia T. Turner. Phone: 954-732-9539.

Technical Facilities: 3.5-kw ERP, 148-ft. above ground, 8612-ft. above sea level, lat. 35° 58' 07", long. 111° 30' 25".

Ownership: Marcia T. Turner.

Flagstaff—K23HB, Ch. 23, Prism Broadcasting Network Inc. Phone: 770-953-3232.

Technical Facilities: 0.005-kw ERP, 27-ft. above ground, 9147-ft. above sea level, lat. 35° 14' 28", long. 111° 36' 35".

Ownership: Prism Broadcasting Network Inc.

Flagstaff—K28CW, Ch. 28, Fox Television Stations Inc.

Technical Facilities: 1-kw ERP, lat. 35° 14' 26", long. 111° 35' 48".

Ownership: Fox Television Holdings Inc.

Flagstaff—K30DT, Ch. 30, KAZT LLC. Phone: 602-957-1650.

Technical Facilities: 1-kw ERP, 26-ft. above ground, 9281-ft. above sea level, lat. 35° 14' 26", long. 111° 35' 48".

Ownership: KAZT LLC.

Flagstaff—K35FH, Ch. 35, Jerry Marth. Phone: 405-943-9957.

Technical Facilities: 1.3-kw ERP, lat. 35° 14' 28", long. 111° 36' 35".

Holds CP for change to 15-kw ERP, 82-ft. above ground, 9281-ft. above sea level, BDFCDTT-20060329AFB.

Transmitter: Existing tower atop Mount Eldon, near Flagstaff.

Ownership: Jerry Marth.

Flagstaff—K42IQ-D, Ch. 42, EICB-TV East LLC. Phone: 972-291-3750.

Technical Facilities: 1-kw ERP, 66-ft. above ground, 9186-ft. above sea level, lat. 35° 14' 28", long. 111° 36' 35".

Began Operation: January 23, 2009.

Ownership: EICB-TV LLC.

Flagstaff—K48GI, Ch. 48, NW Communications of Phoenix Inc. Phone: 202-715-2350.

Technical Facilities: 1.44-kw ERP, 167-ft. above ground, 9285-ft. above sea level, lat. 35° 14' 34", long. 111° 36' 40".

Ownership: Fox Television Holdings Inc.

Flagstaff—K50HU, Ch. 50, Meredith Corp. Phones: 503-239-4949; 515-284-3000. Fax: 503-239-6184.

Technical Facilities: 1.04-kw ERP, 26-ft. above ground, 9324-ft. above sea level, lat. 35° 14' 26", long. 111° 35' 48".

Holds CP for change to 0.3-kw ERP, BDFCDTL-20090501ACB.

Ownership: Meredith Corp.

Flagstaff—K52CM, Ch. 52, Scripps Howard Broadcasting Co.

Technical Facilities: 0.712-kw ERP, lat. 35° 14' 26", long. 111° 35' 48".

Ownership: E. W. Scripps Co.

Flagstaff—K54GI, Ch. 54, KTVK Inc. Phone: 214-977-6606.

Technical Facilities: 1-kw ERP, 33-ft. above ground, 9370-ft. above sea level, lat. 35° 14' 26", long. 111° 35' 48".

Holds CP for change to channel number 17, BDISTT-20080117ACR.

Ownership: Belo Corp.

Fortuna—KBFY-LP, Ch. 41, Powell Meredith Communications Co. Phone: 325-829-6850.

Technical Facilities: 1000-w TPO, 1.8-kw ERP, 72-ft. above ground, 1686-ft. above sea level, lat. 32° 40' 19", long. 114° 20' 09".

Transmitter: Telegraph Peak, Telegraph Pass.

Ownership: Powell Meredith Communications Co.

Fredonia, etc.—K15DX, Ch. 15, Western Kane County Special Service District No. 1.

Technical Facilities: 0.252-kw ERP, 39-ft. above ground, 5111-ft. above sea level, lat. 36° 59' 14", long. 112° 30' 08".

Ownership: Western Kane County Special Service District No. 1.

Ganado—K09XH, Ch. 9, KOB-TV LLC.

Technical Facilities: 0.28-kw ERP, lat. 35° 40' 40", long. 109° 33' 28".

Ownership: Hubbard Broadcasting Inc.

Globe—K16FB, Ch. 16, Telefutura Partnership of Phoenix. Phone: 310-348-3600.

Technical Facilities: 9.95-kw ERP, 92-ft. above ground, 7644-ft. above sea level, lat. 33° 17' 21", long. 110° 49' 45".

Ownership: Univision Communications Inc.

Globe—KDOS-LP, Ch. 50, KTVW License Partnership GP. Phone: 310-348-3600.

Technical Facilities: 9.95-kw ERP, 92-ft. above ground, 7644-ft. above sea level, lat. 33° 17' 21", long. 110° 49' 45".

Ownership: Univision Communications Inc.

Globe—KFPB-LP, Ch. 30, Globe LPTV LLC. Phone: 805-928-8300.

Technical Facilities: 5-kw ERP, 89-ft. above ground, 2536-ft. above sea level, lat. 33° 29' 33", long. 111° 38' 26".

Holds CP for change to channel number 50, 9.9-kw ERP, 108-ft. above ground, 2758-ft. above sea level, lat. 33° 19' 57.3", long. 112° 03' 57". BDISTTL-20080801AMB.

Ownership: James L. Primm.

Globe & Miami—K41ER, Ch. 41, Trinity Broadcasting Network Inc. Phone: 714-832-2950. Fax: 714-730-0661.

Technical Facilities: 0.126-kw ERP, lat. 33° 20' 20", long. 110° 52' 16".

Ownership: Trinity Broadcasting Network Inc.

Globe & Miami—K43IB, Ch. 43, Arizona State Board of Regents for Arizona State U. Phone: 408-965-8888.

Technical Facilities: 0.16-kw ERP, 49-ft. above ground, 6581-ft. above sea level, lat. 33° 20' 20", long. 110° 52' 16".

Ownership: Arizona State Board of Regents for Arizona State U.

Globe & Miami—K57BO, Ch. 57, KTVK Inc. Phone: 214-977-6606.

Technical Facilities: 1.15-kw ERP, lat. 33° 20' 20", long. 110° 52' 16".

Holds CP for change to channel number 14, 1-kw ERP, 39-ft. above ground, 6611-ft. above sea level, lat. 33° 20' 31", long. 110° 52' 13". BDISTT-20080117ACS.

Ownership: Belo Corp.

Globe & Miami—K61FB, Ch. 61, Multimedia Holdings Corp. Phone: 703-854-6899.

Technical Facilities: 1.11-kw ERP, 33-ft. above ground, 6565-ft. above sea level, lat. 33° 20' 20", long. 110° 52' 16".

Holds CP for change to channel number 48, 2.07-kw ERP, 56-ft. above ground, 6627-ft. above sea level, lat. 33° 20' 31", long. 110° 52' 13". BDISTT-20060330AHO.

Ownership: Gannett Co. Inc.

Golden Valley—K11TA, Ch. 11, Mohave County Board of Supervisors.

Technical Facilities: 0.071-kw ERP, 20-ft. above ground, 2854-ft. above sea level, lat. 35° 13' 40", long. 114° 12' 54".

Ownership: Mohave County Board of Supervisors.

Golden Valley—K21EG, Ch. 21, Mohave County Board of Supervisors.

Technical Facilities: 0.64-kw ERP, 39-ft. above ground, 2881-ft. above sea level, lat. 35° 13' 40", long. 114° 12' 54".

Ownership: Mohave County Board of Supervisors.

Golden Valley—K46CG, Ch. 46, Mohave County Board of Supervisors.

Technical Facilities: 0.626-kw ERP, 39-ft. above ground, 2881-ft. above sea level, lat. 35° 13' 40", long. 114° 12' 54".

Ownership: Mohave County Board of Supervisors.

Green Valley—KPCE-LP, Ch. 29, Word of God Fellowship Inc. Phone: 817-571-1229.

Technical Facilities: 15-kw ERP, 164-ft. above ground, 4495-ft. above sea level, lat. 32° 14' 56", long. 111° 06' 58".

Ownership: Word of God Fellowship Inc.

Hilltop—KKAX-LP, Ch. 36, Tri-State Broadcasting LLC. Phone: 928-753-9100. Fax: 928-753-1978.

Technical Facilities: 7.5-kw ERP, 39-ft. above ground, 8359-ft. above sea level, lat. 35° 04' 53", long. 113° 54' 14".

Transmitter: Radar Hill.

Ownership: Tri-State Broadcasting LLC.

Personnel: Maurice W. Coburn, President.

Holbrook—KNLO-LP, Ch. 6, KM Communications Inc. Phone: 847-674-0864.

Technical Facilities: 0.475-kw ERP, 125-ft. above ground, 5492-ft. above sea level, lat. 34° 50' 18", long. 110° 11' 10".

Ownership: KM Communications Inc.

Kingman—K14HG, Ch. 14, Fox Television Stations Inc.

Technical Facilities: 0.8-kw ERP, lat. 35° 04' 52", long. 113° 54' 13".

Ownership: Fox Television Holdings Inc.

Kingman—K16GB, Ch. 16, Smoke and Mirrors LLC. Phone: 928-855-1051.

Technical Facilities: 0.1-kw ERP, 50-ft. above ground, 3491-ft. above sea level, lat. 35° 13' 09.2", long. 114° 00' 57.9".

Ownership: Smoke and Mirrors LLC.

Kingman—K20ID, Ch. 20, KAZT LLC. Phone: 602-224-0027.

Technical Facilities: 0.788-kw ERP, 69-ft. above ground, 8419-ft. above sea level, lat. 35° 04' 52", long. 113° 54' 13".

Ownership: KAZT LLC.

Kingman—K23FV, Ch. 23, Mohave County Board of Supervisors.

Technical Facilities: 0.227-kw ERP, 20-ft. above ground, 8409-ft. above sea level, lat. 40° 48' 21", long. 121° 57' 24".

Ownership: Mohave County Board of Supervisors.

Kingman—K25HU, Ch. 25, Gerald Benavides. Phone: 361-774-4354.

Technical Facilities: 10-kw ERP, 30-ft. above ground, 4790-ft. above sea level, lat. 35° 23' 49", long. 114° 10' 16".

Began Operation: April 17, 2006.

Ownership: Gerald G. Benavides.

Kingman—K31BI, Ch. 31, Mohave County Board of Supervisors.

Technical Facilities: 2.15-kw ERP, lat. 35° 06' 37", long. 113° 52' 55".

Ownership: Mohave County Board of Supervisors.

Kingman—K34EF, Ch. 34, Mohave County Board of Supervisors. Fax: 520-753-0729.

Technical Facilities: 0.5-kw ERP, 33-ft. above ground, 8422-ft. above sea level, lat. 35° 04' 53", long. 113° 54' 14".

Ownership: Mohave County Board of Supervisors.

Kingman—K41FT, Ch. 41, Mohave County Board of Supervisors.

Technical Facilities: 0.826-kw ERP, lat. 35° 04' 53", long. 113° 54' 14".

Ownership: Mohave County Board of Supervisors.

Kingman—K44DK, Ch. 44, Mohave County Board of Supervisors.

Technical Facilities: 0.65-kw ERP, 33-ft. above ground, 8422-ft. above sea level, lat. 35° 04' 53", long. 113° 54' 14".

Transmitter: Hayden Peak.

Ownership: Mohave County Board of Supervisors.

Kingman—K48AY, Ch. 48, Mohave County Board of Supervisors.

Technical Facilities: 1.14-kw ERP, lat. 35° 05' 30", long. 113° 54' 04".

Ownership: Mohave County Board of Supervisors.

Kingman—K49GE, Ch. 49, Mohave County Board of Supervisors.

Technical Facilities: 0.826-kw ERP, lat. 35° 04' 53", long. 113° 54' 14".

Ownership: Mohave County Board of Supervisors.

Kingman—K50CY, Ch. 50, Mohave County Board of Supervisors.

Technical Facilities: 0.64-kw ERP, lat. 35° 05' 30", long. 113° 54' 04".

Ownership: Mohave County Board of Supervisors.

Kingman—K57FY, Ch. 57, Scripps Howard Broadcasting Co.

Technical Facilities: 0.639-kw ERP, 30-ft. above ground, 8379-ft. above sea level, lat. 35° 04' 57", long. 113° 54' 13".

Ownership: E. W. Scripps Co.

Klagetoh—K43GQ, Ch. 43, KOB-TV LLC. Phone: 651-642-4212.

Technical Facilities: 0.22-kw ERP, 103-ft. above ground, 8984-ft. above sea level, lat. 35° 40' 15", long. 109° 12' 03".

Ownership: Hubbard Broadcasting Inc.

Lake Havasu City—K15CR, Ch. 15, Fox Television Stations Inc.

Technical Facilities: 1.09-kw ERP, lat. 34° 36' 09", long. 114° 22' 13".

Ownership: Fox Television Holdings Inc.

Lake Havasu City—K17DA, Ch. 17, KAZT LLC.

Technical Facilities: 2.614-kw ERP, lat. 34° 36' 09", long. 114° 22' 13".

Transmitter: Mountain Top Communication site, 1.1-mi. N of Rte. 95 & Castle Rock Bay Rd.

Ownership: KAZT LLC.

Lake Havasu City—K21EA, Ch. 21, Mohave County Board of Supervisors.

Technical Facilities: 2.44-kw ERP, 52-ft. above ground, 1339-ft. above sea level, lat. 34° 36' 09", long. 114° 22' 13".

Ownership: Mohave County Board of Supervisors.

Lake Havasu City—K23BJ, Ch. 23, Tri-State Broadcasting LLC. Phone: 928-753-9100. Fax: 928-753-1978.

Technical Facilities: 1000-w TPO, 7.4-kw ERP, 78-ft. above ground, 1286-ft. above sea level, lat. 34° 36' 11", long. 114° 22' 14".

Transmitter: Goat Hill, 9.7-mi. N of Lake Havasu City.

Ownership: Tri-State Broadcasting LLC.

Personnel: Maurice W. Coburn, President.

■ **Lake Havasu City**—K25AL, Ch. 25, Lake Havasu Christian TV. Phones: 928-453-8825; 928-855-9110. Fax: 928-453-2588.

Technical Facilities: 1.28-kw ERP, 80-ft. above ground, 500-ft. above sea level, lat. 34° 29' 28", long. 114° 19' 44".

Holds CP for change to 0.006-kw ERP, 85-ft. above ground, 807-ft. above sea level, BDFCDTA-20060330AII.

Transmitter: 510 N. Acoma Blvd., Lake Havasu City.

Ownership: Lake Havasu Christian TV.

Personnel: Richard Tatham, General Manager; Faron Eckelbarger, Chief Engineer.

■ **Lake Havasu City**—K27EC, Ch. 27, Lake Havasu Christian TV. Phones: 520-453-8825; 928-855-9110. Fax: 520-453-2588.

Technical Facilities: 100-w TPO, 1.3-kw ERP, 26-ft. above ground, 1286-ft. above sea level, lat. 34° 36' 11", long. 114° 22' 14".

Holds CP for change to 0.006-kw ERP, BDFCDTA-20060331AED.

Transmitter: BLM Electronics site near State Hwy. 95, N of Lake Havasu City.

Ownership: Lake Havasu Christian TV.

Lake Havasu City—K29FD, Ch. 29, Mohave County Board of Supervisors.

Technical Facilities: 2.21-kw ERP, 53-ft. above ground, 1338-ft. above sea level, lat. 34° 36' 09", long. 114° 22' 33".

Ownership: Mohave County Board of Supervisors.

Lake Havasu City—K31GZ, Ch. 31, Mohave County Board of Supervisors. Phone: 928-753-0729.

Technical Facilities: 2.21-kw ERP, 52-ft. above ground, 1339-ft. above sea level, lat. 34° 36' 09", long. 114° 22' 13".

Ownership: Mohave County Board of Supervisors.

■ **Lake Havasu City**—K36DU, Ch. 36, Richard D. Tatham. Phone: 928-855-9110. Fax: 928-453-2588.

Studio: 2141 Bryce Dr, Lake Havasu City, AZ 86404.

Technical Facilities: 100-w TPO, 1.53-kw ERP, 32-ft. above ground, 1293-ft. above sea level, lat. 34° 36' 11", long. 114° 22' 14".

Holds CP for change to 0.007-kw ERP, 33-ft. above ground, 1293-ft. above sea level, BDFCDTA-20060331AKF.

Transmitter: BLM electronic site, near State Hwy 95, N of Lake Havasu City.

Ownership: Richard D. Tatham.

Personnel: Richard D. Tatham, General Manager; Faron Eckelbarger, Chief Engineer.

Lake Havasu City—K38IR, Ch. 38, Mohave County Board of Supervisors. Phone: 928-753-0729.

Technical Facilities: 2.34-kw ERP, 52-ft. above ground, 1339-ft. above sea level, lat. 34° 36' 09", long. 114° 22' 16".

Ownership: Mohave County Board of Supervisors.

Lake Havasu City—K39FV, Ch. 39, Mohave County Board of Supervisors.

Technical Facilities: 2.34-kw ERP, 52-ft. above ground, 1339-ft. above sea level, lat. 34° 36' 09", long. 114° 22' 16".

Ownership: Mohave County Board of Supervisors.

Lake Havasu City—K43GJ, Ch. 43, Mohave County Board of Supervisors.

Technical Facilities: 1.16-kw ERP, 52-ft. above ground, 1339-ft. above sea level, lat. 34° 36' 09", long. 114° 22' 13".

Ownership: Mohave County Board of Supervisors.

Lake Havasu City—K46GI, Ch. 46, Mohave County Board of Supervisors.

Technical Facilities: 1.16-kw ERP, 52-ft. above ground, 1339-ft. above sea level, lat. 34° 36' 09", long. 114° 22' 13".

Ownership: Mohave County Board of Supervisors.

Lake Havasu City—KBBA-LP, Ch. 10, Smoke and Mirrors LLC. Phone: 928-855-1051.

Technical Facilities: 3-kw ERP, 52-ft. above ground, 1339-ft. above sea level, lat. 34° 36' 09", long. 114° 22' 16".

Ownership: Smoke and Mirrors LLC.

■ **Lake Havasu City**—KLHU-CA, Ch. 45, Jensen Investments FLP. Phone: 206-963-6364.

Technical Facilities: 1.4-kw ERP, 39-ft. above ground, 1281-ft. above sea level, lat. 34° 36' 09", long. 114° 22' 13".

Multichannel TV Sound: Stereo only.

Ownership: Jensen Investments FLP.

Personnel: Wayne R. Holmes, General Manager.

Le Chee, etc.—K07PH, Ch. 7, U. of Utah.

Technical Facilities: 0.106-kw ERP, 4616-ft. above sea level, lat. 36° 51' 06", long. 111° 26' 17".

Ownership: U. of Utah.

Littlefield—K30IP, Ch. 30, Hispanic Christian Community Network Inc. Phone: 214-434-6357.

Technical Facilities: 150-kw ERP, 131-ft. above ground, 1923-ft. above sea level, lat. 36° 53' 00", long. 113° 55' 29".

Ownership: Hispanic Christian Community Network Inc.

Littlefield—K31EA, Ch. 31, Mohave County Board of Supervisors.

Technical Facilities: 2.53-kw ERP, 39-ft. above ground, 7720-ft. above sea level, lat. 37° 09' 19", long. 113° 52' 57".

Ownership: Mohave County Board of Supervisors.

Madera Peak—K55BW, Ch. 55, NW Communications of Phoenix Inc. Phone: 202-715-2350.

Technical Facilities: 1.16-kw ERP, lat. 33° 20' 20", long. 110° 52' 16".

Holds CP for change to channel number 22, 1-kw ERP, 40-ft. above ground, 6677-ft. above sea level, lat. 33° 20' 24", long. 110° 52' 11.5". BDISTT-20080902ADV.

Began Operation: October 12, 1982.

Ownership: Fox Television Holdings Inc.

Many Farms—K30GL, Ch. 30, LIN of Colorado LLC. Phone: 202-462-6001.

Technical Facilities: 5.1-kw ERP, 23-ft. above ground, 9806-ft. above sea level, lat. 36° 27' 30", long. 109° 05' 37".

Ownership: LIN TV Corp.

Many Farms—K49ET, Ch. 49, KOB-TV LLC.

Technical Facilities: 3.04-kw ERP, lat. 36° 27' 30", long. 109° 05' 37".

Ownership: Hubbard Broadcasting Inc.

Many Farms—K63AE, Ch. 63, KOAT Hearst-Argyle Television Inc. Phone: 919-839-0300.

Technical Facilities: 0.1-kw ERP, lat. 36° 27' 30", long. 109° 05' 37".

Ownership: Hearst-Argyle Television Inc.

Martinez Lake—K49BX, Ch. 49, Wellton-Mohawk Irrigation & Drainage District. Phone: 520-785-3351.

Technical Facilities: 0.65-kw ERP, lat. 32° 57' 49", long. 114° 25' 37".

Ownership: Wellton-Mohawk Irrigation & Drainage District.

Meadview—K23DK, Ch. 23, Mohave County Board of Supervisors.

Technical Facilities: 1.11-kw ERP, 43-ft. above ground, 4281-ft. above sea level, lat. 35° 51' 48", long. 114° 05' 45".

Ownership: Mohave County Board of Supervisors.

Meadview—K25DH, Ch. 25, Mohave County Board of Supervisors.

Technical Facilities: 1.11-kw ERP, 43-ft. above ground, 4285-ft. above sea level, lat. 35° 51' 48", long. 114° 05' 45".

Transmitter: Meadview/Patterson Slope.

Ownership: Mohave County Board of Supervisors.

Meadview—K36FZ, Ch. 36, Mohave County Board of Supervisors.

Technical Facilities: 46-ft. above ground, 4285-ft. above sea level, lat. 35° 51' 48", long. 114° 05' 45".

Ownership: Mohave County Board of Supervisors.

Meadview—K38GR, Ch. 38, Mohave County Board of Supevisors.

Technical Facilities: 1.05-kw ERP, 46-ft. above ground, 4285-ft. above sea level, lat. 35° 51' 48", long. 114° 05' 45".

Ownership: Mohave County Board of Supervisors.

Meadview—K47HE, Ch. 47, Mohave County Board of Supervisors.

Technical Facilities: 0.998-kw ERP, lat. 35° 51' 48", long. 114° 05' 45".

Ownership: Mohave County Board of Supervisors.

Mesa—K57HX, Ch. 57, KAZT LLC.

Technical Facilities: 25.3-kw ERP, lat. 33° 29' 30", long. 111° 38' 22".

Transmitter: Usery Mountain, 6-mi. N of Main St.

Ownership: KAZT LLC.

Moccasin—K35EE, Ch. 35, Mohave County Board of Supervisors.

Technical Facilities: 2.52-kw ERP, 39-ft. above ground, 6522-ft. above sea level, lat. 36° 54' 22", long. 112° 48' 48".

Ownership: Mohave County Board of Supervisors.

Navajo Compressor Station—K66BH, Ch. 66, LIN of New Mexico LLC.

Technical Facilities: 0.239-kw ERP, lat. 35° 40' 15", long. 109° 12' 03".

Ownership: LIN TV Corp.

Oro Valley & Tucson—K16EO, Ch. 16, Journal Broadcast Corp. Phone: 702-876-1313.

Technical Facilities: 9-kw ERP, 36-ft. above ground, 3156-ft. above sea level, lat. 32° 12' 51", long. 111° 00' 19".

Ownership: Journal Communications Inc.

Parker—K02MT, Ch. 2, Arizona West Media LLC. Phone: 928-855-8358.

Studio: 912 Joshua, Parker, AZ 85344.

Technical Facilities: 5.5-w TPO, 0.06-kw ERP, 1000-ft. above ground, 1665-ft. above sea level, lat. 34° 07' 22", long. 114° 12' 40".

Transmitter: Black Peak, 4.3-mi. SE of Parker.

Multichannel TV Sound: Stereo only.

Ownership: Arizona West Media LLC.

Personnel: Gerald M. Hale, General Manager; Deborah Hale, General Sales Manager; Margaret Hale, Office Manager & Promotion Director.

Parks—K47GQ, Ch. 47, Arizona State Board of Regents for Arizona State U. Fax: 480-965-3506.

Technical Facilities: 1.22-kw ERP, 23-ft. above ground, 9265-ft. above sea level, lat. 35° 12' 01", long. 112° 12' 17".

Ownership: Arizona State Board of Regents for Arizona State U.

Payson—KPSN-LP, Ch. 22, Multimedia Holdings Corp. Phone: 520-474-4901. Fax: 520-474-4901.

Technical Facilities: 100-w TPO, 1.6-kw ERP, 40-ft. above ground, 6400-ft. above sea level, lat. 34° 17' 23", long. 111° 11' 26".

Transmitter: Diamond Point Lookout communication site.

Ownership: Gannett Co. Inc.

Peach Springs—K26GF, Ch. 26, Mohave County Board of Supervisors. Fax: 520-753-0729.

Technical Facilities: 0.07-kw ERP, 33-ft. above ground, 4954-ft. above sea level, lat. 35° 32' 10", long. 113° 25' 52".

Ownership: Mohave County Board of Supervisors.

Peach Springs—K42CP, Ch. 42, Mohave County Board of Supervisors.

Technical Facilities: 0.032-kw ERP, lat. 35° 32' 10", long. 113° 25' 52".

Ownership: Mohave County Board of Supervisors.

Phoenix—K25DM, Ch. 25, Mako Communications LLC. Phone: 361-883-1763.

Studio: 23011 N 16th Ln, Phoenix, AZ 85027-1331.

Technical Facilities: 1000-w TPO, 9.8-kw ERP, 85-ft. above ground, 2214-ft. above sea level, lat. 33° 35' 38", long. 112° 05' 10".

Holds CP for change to channel number 6, 0.95-kw ERP, 85-ft. above ground, 2300-ft. above sea level, BDISTVL-20071112ADN.

Transmitter: Shaw Butte, East Hill, Phoenix.

Ownership: Mako Communications LLC.

Personnel: Kenneth Casey, President, Chief Engineer & Sales Manager; Charlene Weh, General Manager; Chris Casey, Program Director.

Phoenix—K36AE, Ch. 36, NW Communications of Phoenix Inc. Phone: 202-715-2350.

Technical Facilities: 21.7-kw ERP, lat. 34° 41' 14", long. 112° 06' 59".

Began Operation: November 3, 1982.

Ownership: Fox Television Holdings Inc.

Phoenix—K38IZ-D, Ch. 38, Spanish Independent Broadcast Network LLC. Phone: 480-961-4353.

Technical Facilities: 9.9-kw ERP, 86-ft. above ground, 2746-ft. above sea level, lat. 33° 20' 00", long. 112° 03' 45".

Ownership: Spanish Independent Broadcast Network LLC.

Personnel: Chris Furphy, Chief Engineer.

Phoenix—K55EH, Ch. 55, KAZT LLC.

Technical Facilities: 6.66-kw ERP, lat. 33° 35' 47", long. 112° 05' 31".

Ownership: KAZT LLC.

■ **Phoenix**—KAZT-CA, Ch. 27, KAZT LLC. Phone: 602-224-0027.

Technical Facilities: 34-kw ERP, 202-ft. above ground, 2800-ft. above sea level, lat. 33° 20' 02", long. 112° 03' 41".

Ownership: KAZT LLC.

■ **Phoenix**—KCOS-LP, Ch. 28, Aracelis Ortiz Corp. Phone: 956-421-2635.

Technical Facilities: 63-kw ERP, 66-ft. above ground, 2608-ft. above sea level, lat. 33° 29' 39", long. 111° 38' 28".

Ownership: Aracelis Ortiz Corp.

Phoenix—KDPH-LP, Ch. 48, Community Television Educators Inc. Phone: 817-571-1229.

Studio: 4625 S 33rd Pl, Phoenix, AZ 85040.

Technical Facilities: 52.6-kw ERP, 171-ft. above ground, 2799-ft. above sea level, lat. 33° 20' 03", long. 112° 03' 38".

Transmitter: South Mountain, 3-mi. SE of intersection of Central Ave. & Dobbins Rd.

Ownership: Community Television Educators Inc.

Personnel: James A. Johnson, President; Victor Carranza, General Manager; Charlie Mandala, Sales Manager; Efren Padilla, Local Sales Manager; Anna Ctarza, Traffic Manager.

Phoenix—KDTP-LP, Ch. 58, Community Television Educators Inc. Phone: 817-571-1229.

Technical Facilities: 316-w TPO, 23.6-kw ERP, 70-ft. above ground, 2721-ft. above sea level, lat. 33° 20' 00", long. 112° 03' 45".

Holds CP for change to channel number 11, 0.999-kw ERP, 59-ft. above ground, 2719-ft. above sea level, lat. 33° 20' 01", long. 112° 03' 45". BDISTVL-20060706ACO.

Transmitter: South Mountain Park, Site 8, 10660 S. Central Ave.

Multichannel TV Sound: Stereo and separate audio program.

Ownership: Community Television Educators Inc.

Personnel: Brooke Temple, Vice President; Donald S. Wilson, Chief Engineer.

Phoenix—KEJR-LD, Ch. 40, HERO Licenseco LLC. Phone: 305-863-5700.

Technical Facilities: 15-kw ERP, 66-ft. above ground, 2723-ft. above sea level, lat. 33° 20' 01", long. 112° 03' 44".

Ownership: HERO Broadcasting LLC.

Phoenix—KEJR-LP, Ch. 43, HERO Licenseco LLC. Phone: 305-863-5700.

Technical Facilities: 9-kw ERP, 66-ft. above ground, 2723-ft. above sea level, lat. 33° 20' 01", long. 112° 03' 44".

Ownership: HERO Broadcasting LLC.

■ **Phoenix**—KFPH-CA, Ch. 39, Telefutura Partnership of Phoenix. Phone: 310-556-7600.

Studio: 5757 N Central Ave, Phoenix, AZ 85012.

Technical Facilities: 50-kw ERP, 79-ft. above ground, 2739-ft. above sea level, lat. 33° 20' 01", long. 112° 03' 48".

Transmitter: South Mountain, 7.5-mi. S of Phoenix.

Multichannel TV Sound: Stereo and separate audio program.

Ownership: Univision Communications Inc.

Personnel: Julian D. Roy, President; Rick Hooton, General Manager.

■ **Phoenix**—KPDF-CA, Ch. 41, Una Vez Mas Phoenix License LLC. Phone: 214-754-7008.

Technical Facilities: 2000-w TPO, 24.9-kw ERP, 49-ft. above ground, 2700-ft. above sea level, lat. 33° 20' 00", long. 112° 03' 45".

Transmitter: South Mountain Park, Site 8, 10660 S. Central Ave.

Ownership: Una Vez Mas GP LLC.

Phoenix—KPHE-LD, Ch. 16, Lotus TV of Phoenix LLC. Phone: 323-512-2225.

Technical Facilities: 15-kw ERP, 91-ft. above ground, 2751-ft. above sea level, lat. 33° 20' 01", long. 112° 03' 45".

Began Operation: March 26, 2009.

Ownership: Lotus Communications Corp.

Phoenix—KPHE-LP, Ch. 44, Lotus TV of Phoenix LLC. Phone: 323-512-2225.

Technical Facilities: 10-kw ERP, 187-ft. above ground, 2844-ft. above sea level, lat. 33° 20' 01", long. 112° 03' 44".

Ownership: Lotus Communications Corp.

Phoenix—KTVP-LP, Ch. 22, Mako Communications LLC. Phones: 361-883-1763; 361-883-3160.

Technical Facilities: 280-w TPO, 42-kw ERP, 69-ft. above ground, 2720-ft. above sea level, lat. 33° 19' 58", long. 112° 03' 59".

Transmitter: N of Main St., Mesa.

Ownership: Mako Communications LLC.

■ **Phoenix**—KTVW-CA, Ch. 6, KTVW License Partnership GP. Phone: 310-556-7600.

Studio: 5501 E Empire Ave, Flagstaff, AZ 86004.

Technical Facilities: 20-w TPO, 0.114-kw ERP, 30-ft. above ground, 9296-ft. above sea level, lat. 35° 14' 26", long. 111° 35' 48".

Transmitter: Mount Elden Electronics site, 3.1-mi. NE of Flagstaff.

Multichannel TV Sound: Separate audio program.

Ownership: Univision Communications Inc.

Personnel: J. Christian Damon, General Manager; B. MacArthur, Program Director.

Phoenix—KVPA-LP, Ch. 42, KRCA License LLC. Phone: 818-729-5300.

Technical Facilities: 11-kw ERP, 66-ft. above ground, 2694-ft. above sea level, lat. 33° 19' 57", long. 112° 03' 57".

Holds CP for change to 15-kw ERP, BDFCDTL-20081211AAW.

Ownership: Liberman Broadcasting Inc.

Prescott—K04AI, Ch. 4, NW Communications of Phoenix Inc. Phone: 202-715-2350.

Technical Facilities: 0.06-kw ERP, lat. 34° 29' 20", long. 112° 32' 15".

Ownership: Fox Television Holdings Inc.

Prescott—K06AE, Ch. 6, Multimedia Holdings Corp.

Technical Facilities: 0.03-kw ERP, lat. 34° 29' 20", long. 112° 32' 15".

Ownership: Gannett Co. Inc.

Prescott—K09KV, Ch. 9, Meredith Corp. Phone: 503-239-4949. Fax: 503-239-6184.

Technical Facilities: 0.15-kw ERP, lat. 34° 29' 20", long. 112° 32' 15".

Holds CP for change to channel number 30, 2.5-kw ERP, 23-ft. above ground, 7014-ft. above sea level, BDISDTT-20060331AUF.

Ownership: Meredith Corp.

Prescott—K11LC, Ch. 11, KTVK Inc. Phone: 602-207-3333.

Technical Facilities: 0.16-kw ERP, lat. 34° 29' 20", long. 112° 32' 15".

Ownership: Belo Corp.

Prescott—K14HC, Ch. 14, Fox Television Stations Inc. Phone: 202-895-3088.

Technical Facilities: 1.55-kw ERP, lat. 34° 32' 27", long. 112° 25' 40".

Ownership: Fox Television Holdings Inc.

Personnel: Robert Furlong, General Manager; Tom Foy, Chief Engineer; Michael Durand, Sales Manager.

Prescott—K39IT-D, Ch. 39, NW Communications of Phoenix Inc. Phone: 202-715-2350.

Technical Facilities: 1.3-kw ERP, 20-ft. above ground, 6991-ft. above sea level, lat. 34° 29' 20", long. 112° 32' 15".

Began Operation: August 3, 2007.

Ownership: Fox Television Holdings Inc.

Prescott—K47DJ, Ch. 47, Scripps Howard Broadcasting Co.

Technical Facilities: 1.35-kw ERP, 46-ft. above ground, 7146-ft. above sea level, lat. 34° 29' 25", long. 112° 32' 00".

Ownership: E. W. Scripps Co.

Prescott—K53IJ, Ch. 53, KVFW-TV LLC. Phone: 361-774-4354.

Technical Facilities: 10-kw ERP, 33-ft. above ground, 7579-ft. above sea level, lat. 34° 13' 58", long. 112° 22' 13".

Began Operation: October 30, 2006.

Ownership: Gerald G. Benavides.

Prescott—KDFQ-LP, Ch. 47, Una Vez Mas Prescott License II LLC. Phone: 214-754-7008.

Technical Facilities: 9.97-kw ERP, 98-ft. above ground, 7749-ft. above sea level, lat. 34° 41' 11", long. 112° 06' 59".

Ownership: Una Vez Mas GP LLC.

Prescott—KPVY-LD, Ch. 45, KM Communications Inc. Phone: 847-674-0864.

Technical Facilities: 0.35-kw ERP, 98-ft. above ground, 5125-ft. above sea level, lat. 34° 11' 32", long. 112° 45' 13".

Ownership: KM Communications Inc.

Prescott—KQBN-LP, Ch. 28, Una Vez Mas Prescott License I LLC. Phone: 214-754-7008.

Technical Facilities: 1000-w TPO, 56.9-kw ERP, 36-ft. above ground, 7582-ft. above sea level, lat. 34° 13' 58", long. 112° 22' 13".

Transmitter: Tower Mountain.

Ownership: Una Vez Mas GP LLC.

Prescott & Cottonwood—K51HV, Ch. 51, Trinity Broadcasting of Arizona Inc. Phones: 602-273-1477; 714-832-2950. Fax: 714-730-0661.

Technical Facilities: 2.9-kw ERP, 98-ft. above ground, 7907-ft. above sea level, lat. 34° 42' 04", long. 112° 07' 04".

Ownership: Trinity Broadcasting Network Inc.

Prescott, etc.—K55DB, Ch. 55, Arizona State Board of Regents for Arizona State U. Phone: 480-965-8888.

Technical Facilities: 1.81-kw ERP, lat. 34° 31' 59", long. 112° 29' 24".

Ownership: Arizona State Board of Regents for Arizona State U.

Quartzsite—KRPO-LP, Ch. 55, Hispanic Christian Community Network Inc. Phone: 214-434-6357.

Technical Facilities: 50-kw ERP, 98-ft. above ground, 3412-ft. above sea level, lat. 33° 34' 17", long. 114° 20' 55".

Ownership: Hispanic Christian Community Network Inc.

Safford—K21GC, Ch. 21, Telefutura Partnership of Phoenix. Phone: 310-348-3600.

Technical Facilities: 9.95-kw ERP, 102-ft. above ground, 10065-ft. above sea level, lat. 32° 39' 01", long. 109° 50' 53".

Ownership: Univision Communications Inc.

Safford—KZOL-LP, Ch. 15, KTVW License Partnership GP. Phone: 310-348-3600.

Technical Facilities: 9.95-kw ERP, 102-ft. above ground, 10065-ft. above sea level, lat. 32° 39' 01", long. 109° 50' 53".

Ownership: Univision Communications Inc.

Scottsdale—K23BY, Ch. 23, KAZT LLC. Phone: 602-957-1650.

Technical Facilities: 1.29-kw ERP, 75-ft. above ground, 1509-ft. above sea level, lat. 33° 36' 45", long. 111° 54' 46".

Ownership: KAZT LLC.

Shonto—K38CX, Ch. 38, Trinity Broadcasting Network Inc. Phone: 714-832-2950. Fax: 714-730-0661.

Technical Facilities: 100-w TPO, 1.2-kw ERP, 92-ft. above ground, 7037-ft. above sea level, lat. 36° 37' 18", long. 110° 34' 36".

Transmitter: White Post Church property, near Shonto.

Ownership: Trinity Broadcasting Network Inc.

Personnel: Paul Crouch, General Manager; Ben Miller, Chief Engineer; Rod Henke, Sales Manager.

Sierra Vista—K20FO, Ch. 20, KVOA Communications Inc.

Technical Facilities: 49.4-kw ERP, lat. 31° 29' 08", long. 109° 57' 21".

Transmitter: Mule Mountain, 2.3-mi. NNW of Bisbee.

Ownership: Evening Post Publishing Co.

Sierra Vista—K33CG, Ch. 33, Florinda Mae Balfour. Phone: 520-720-4968. Fax: 520-720-5390.

Technical Facilities: 37-w TPO, 0.001-kw ERP, 72-ft. above ground, 7231-ft. above sea level, lat. 31° 28' 58", long. 109° 57' 29".

Transmitter: Atop Mule Mountain.

Ownership: Florinda Mae Balfour.

Personnel: Richard Richards, General Manager & Sales Manager.

Snowflake, etc.—K03FB, Ch. 3, Arizona State Board of Regents for Arizona State U.

Technical Facilities: 0.027-kw ERP, lat. 34° 12' 22", long. 109° 56' 34".

Ownership: Arizona State Board of Regents for Arizona State U.

Snowflake, etc.—K07OJ, Ch. 7, NW Communications of Phoenix Inc. Phone: 202-715-2350.

Technical Facilities: 0.033-kw ERP, lat. 34° 12' 22", long. 109° 56' 34".

Began Operation: July 27, 1982.

Ownership: Fox Television Holdings Inc.

Tacna—KYPO-LP, Ch. 27, Hispanic Christian Community Network Inc. Phone: 214-434-6357.

Technical Facilities: 1-kw ERP, 49-ft. above ground, 2149-ft. above sea level, lat. 33° 45' 06.7", long. 113° 40' 29.8".

Ownership: Hispanic Christian Community Network Inc.

Topock—K21FU, Ch. 21, Mohave County Board of Supervisors.

Technical Facilities: 1.03-kw ERP, 49-ft. above ground, 4029-ft. above sea level, lat. 35° 02' 09", long. 114° 22' 14".

Ownership: Mohave County Board of Supervisors.

Topock, etc.—K42EU, Ch. 42, Mohave County Board of Supervisors.

Technical Facilities: 0.918-kw ERP, lat. 35° 02' 09", long. 114° 22' 14".

Transmitter: 0.99-mi. E of Oatman.

Ownership: Mohave County Board of Supervisors.

Tsaile—K40AP, Ch. 40, The Navajo Nation. Phone: 602-724-3311.

Technical Facilities: 0.235-kw ERP, lat. 36° 17' 13", long. 109° 11' 16".

Ownership: Navajo Nation.

Personnel: Curtis Sweet, Director.

Tucson—K07YX, Ch. 7, Trinity Broadcasting of Arizona Inc. Phones: 602-273-1477; 714-832-2950. Fax: 714-730-0661.

Technical Facilities: 0.05-kw ERP, 98-ft. above ground, 4449-ft. above sea level, lat. 32° 14' 57", long. 111° 06' 59".

Transmitter: Tucson Mountain Antenna Farm, near Tucson.

Ownership: Trinity Broadcasting Network Inc.

Tucson—K21CX, Ch. 21, Ventana Television Inc. Phone: 727-872-4210.

Technical Facilities: 800-w TPO, 10-kw ERP, 180-ft. above ground, 8658-ft. above sea level, lat. 32° 24' 54", long. 110° 42' 56".

Transmitter: Mount Bigelow electronic site, 22-mi. N of intersection of I-10 & I-19.

Began Operation: August 28, 1991.

Ownership: Ventana Television Inc.

Personnel: John Skelnik, General Manager & Chief Engineer.

Tucson—K48GX, Ch. 48, Telefutura Partnership of Tucson. Phone: 310-348-3600.

Technical Facilities: 89-ft. above ground, 4469-ft. above sea level, lat. 32° 14' 56", long. 111° 06' 58".

Ownership: Univision Communications Inc.

Tucson—K50FV, Ch. 50, KMSB-TV Inc. Phone: 520-770-1123. Fax: 520-629-7185.

Technical Facilities: 1000-w TPO, 0.6-kw ERP, 85-ft. above ground, 8615-ft. above sea level, lat. 32° 24' 55", long. 110° 42' 54".

Transmitter: Mount Bigelow electronic site.

Ownership: Belo Corp.

■ **Tucson**—KFTU-CA, Ch. 34, Telefutura Partnership of Tucson. Phone: 310-556-7600.

Technical Facilities: 200-w TPO, 9.97-kw ERP, 171-ft. above ground, 8665-ft. above sea level, lat. 32° 24' 54", long. 110° 42' 56".

Transmitter: Mount Bigelow, Pima County.

Multichannel TV Sound: Stereo only.

Ownership: Univision Communications Inc.

Personnel: Lawrence Rogow, General Manager; Donald Wilson, Chief Engineer.

Tucson—KUDF-LP, Ch. 14, Una Vez Mas Tucson License LLC. Phone: 214-754-7008.

Studio: 2919 E Broadway, Tucson, AZ 85716.

Technical Facilities: 934-w TPO, 9.99-kw ERP, 174-ft. above ground, 8665-ft. above sea level, lat. 32° 24' 54", long. 110° 42' 56".

Transmitter: Mount Bigelow, Coronado National Forest, S. G. Communication site.

Multichannel TV Sound: Separate audio progam.

Ownership: Una Vez Mas GP LLC.

Personnel: Tamara Valenzuela-Cavazos, General Manager; Steve Twisleton, Chief Engineer; Thelma Abril, Sales Manager.

■ **Tucson**—KUVE-CA, Ch. 38, Univision Tucson LLC. Phone: 520-622-0984. Fax: 520-620-0046.

Studio: 2301 N Forbes Blvd, Ste 108, Tucson, AZ 85745.

Technical Facilities: 9.9-kw ERP, 89-ft. above ground, 4468-ft. above sea level, lat. 32° 14' 56", long. 111° 06' 58".

Transmitter: Tucson communications site, approx 8.9-mi W of downtown Tucson.

Ownership: Univision Communications Inc.

Personnel: Myrna Sonora, General Manager; Gary Rogers, Chief Engineer; John Matt Gongora, Sales Manager.

Tucson—KWTA-LP, Ch. 31, Venture Technologies Group LLC. Phone: 323-904-4090.

Technical Facilities: 100-w TPO, 9.97-kw ERP, 171-ft. above ground, 8665-ft. above sea level, lat. 32° 24' 54", long. 110° 42' 56".

Holds CP for change to channel number 51, 60-kw ERP, BDISTTL-20060331ARL.

Transmitter: S.G Communications Bldg., Mount Bigelow.

Ownership: Venture Technologies Group LLC.

Personnel: Brooke Temple, Vice President.

Tucson, etc.—K57BD, Ch. 57, Trinity Broadcasting of Arizona Inc. Phones: 602-273-1477; 714-832-2950. Fax: 714-730-0661.

Technical Facilities: 100-w TPO, 1.3-kw ERP, 200-ft. above ground, 4421-ft. above sea level, lat. 32° 26' 31", long. 110° 46' 51".

Transmitter: Mount Lemmon.

Ownership: Trinity Broadcasting Network Inc.

Personnel: Paul Crouch, General Manager; Ben Miller, Chief Engineer; Rod Henke, Sales Manager.

Verde Valley, etc.—K46IL, Ch. 46, Camp Verde TV Club. Phone: 928-567-3433.

Technical Facilities: 1.186-kw ERP, 92-ft. above ground, 7733-ft. above sea level, lat. 34° 41' 14", long. 112° 07' 00".

Holds CP for change to 56-ft. above ground, 7697-ft. above sea level, BMPTTL-20080908ABG.

Began Operation: January 4, 1982.

Ownership: Camp Verde TV Club.

Verde Valley, etc.—K57DC, Ch. 57, Camp Verde TV Club. Phone: 928-567-3433.

Technical Facilities: 0.18-kw ERP, lat. 34° 28' 13", long. 111° 52' 21".

Ownership: Camp Verde TV Club.

Wellton-Mohawk—K61AX, Ch. 61, Wellton-Mohawk Irrigation & Drainage District. Phone: 520-785-3351.

Technical Facilities: 3.26-kw ERP, lat. 32° 40' 21", long. 114° 20' 07".

Ownership: Wellton-Mohawk Irrigation & Drainage District.

Wellton-Mohawk—K63AV, Ch. 63, Wellton-Mohawk Irrigation & Drainage District. Phone: 520-785-3351.

Technical Facilities: 2.48-kw ERP, lat. 32° 40' 21", long. 114° 20' 07".

Ownership: Wellton-Mohawk Irrigation & Drainage District.

Wellton-Mohawk—K65BB, Ch. 65, Wellton-Mohawk Irrigation & Drainage District. Phone: 520-785-3351.

Technical Facilities: 2.47-kw ERP, lat. 32° 40' 21", long. 114° 20' 07".

Ownership: Wellton-Mohawk Irrigation & Drainage District.

Wellton-Mohawk—K67BI, Ch. 67, Wellton-Mohawk Irrigation & Drainage District. Phone: 520-785-3351.

Technical Facilities: 2.45-kw ERP, lat. 32° 40' 21", long. 114° 20' 07".

Ownership: Wellton-Mohawk Irrigation & Drainage District.

Whiteriver—K09WY, Ch. 9, TV Board of Whiteriver, c/o George Hess.

Technical Facilities: 0.187-kw ERP, lat. 33° 45' 37", long. 109° 58' 28".

Transmitter: Electonic site, 2.2-mi. SSE of Fort Apache.

Ownership: TV Board of Whiteriver.

Whiteriver—K13XC, Ch. 13, TV Board of Whiteriver, c/o George Hess.

Technical Facilities: 0.187-kw ERP, lat. 33° 45' 37", long. 109° 58' 28".

Transmitter: Electronic Site 2.2-mi. SSE of Fort Apache.

Ownership: TV Board of Whiteriver.

Williams—K29DK, Ch. 29, KAZT LLC. Phone: 602-224-0027. Fax: 928-778-6770.

Technical Facilities: 1.16-kw ERP, 30-ft. above ground, 9272-ft. above sea level, lat. 35° 12' 01", long. 112° 12' 15".

Ownership: KAZT LLC.

Williams—K43IE, Ch. 43, NW Communications of Phoenix Inc. Phone: 202-715-2350.

Technical Facilities: 1.62-kw ERP, 46-ft. above ground, 9347-ft. above sea level, lat. 35° 12' 13", long. 112° 12' 13".

Began Operation: January 28, 1991.

Ownership: Fox Television Holdings Inc.

Williams-Ash Fork—K53GM, Ch. 53, KTVK Inc. Phone: 214-977-6606.

Technical Facilities: 1-kw ERP, 33-ft. above ground, 9275-ft. above sea level, lat. 35° 12' 01", long. 112° 12' 15".

Holds CP for change to channel number 15, BDISTT-20080117ACT.

Ownership: Belo Corp.

Williams-Ashfork—K41JE, Ch. 41, KTVK Inc. Phone: 214-976-6606.

Technical Facilities: 1-kw ERP, 33-ft. above ground, 9275-ft. above sea level, lat. 35° 12' 01", long. 112° 12' 15".

Ownership: Belo Corp.

Window Rock—K44BB, Ch. 44, Kee Long. Phone: 928-871-7350.

Technical Facilities: 4-kw ERP, 52-ft. above ground, 7388-ft. above sea level, lat. 35° 33' 36", long. 109° 06' 30".

Holds CP for change to 0.5-kw ERP, 57-ft. above ground, 6976-ft. above sea level, lat. 35° 40' 51.5", long. 109° 03' 08.1". BPTT-20080408AEW.

Ownership: Navajo Nation.

Winslow—K09JZ, Ch. 9, NW Communications of Phoenix Inc. Phone: 202-715-2350.

Technical Facilities: 0.04-kw ERP, lat. 34° 50' 26", long. 110° 54' 55".

Ownership: Fox Television Holdings Inc.

York, etc.—K02FV, Ch. 2, Southern Greenlee County TV Assn. Inc.

Technical Facilities: 0.032-kw ERP, lat. 32° 53' 14", long. 109° 18' 49".

Ownership: Southern Greenlee County TV Assn. Inc.

York, etc.—K07IR, Ch. 7, Southern Greenlee County TV Assn. Inc.

Technical Facilities: 0.139-kw ERP, lat. 32° 53' 14", long. 109° 18' 49".

Ownership: Southern Greenlee County TV Assn. Inc.

York, etc.—K11JJ, Ch. 11, Southern Greenlee County TV Assn. Inc.

Technical Facilities: 0.137-kw ERP, lat. 32° 53' 14", long. 109° 18' 49".

Ownership: Southern Greenlee County TV Assn. Inc.

Yuma—K19CX, Ch. 19, KAZT LLC. Phone: 602-840-8348.

Technical Facilities: 1.86-kw ERP, 43-ft. above ground, 1614-ft. above sea level, lat. 32° 40' 11", long. 114° 20' 05".

Ownership: KAZT LLC.

Yuma—K28FM, Ch. 28, Broadcast Group Ltd. Phone: 915-577-0045.

Technical Facilities: 500-w TPO, 0.99-kw ERP, 90-ft. above ground, 1634-ft. above sea level, lat. 32° 40' 22", long. 114° 20' 13".

Transmitter: Telegraph Pass communication site.

Ownership: Broadcast Group Ltd.

Yuma—K30HA, Ch. 30, Region 1 Translator Assn. Phone: 970-848-5301.

Technical Facilities: 392-ft. above ground, 4601-ft. above sea level, lat. 40° 08' 35", long. 102° 48' 51".

Ownership: Region 1 Translator Association.

Yuma—K52EG, Ch. 52, Three Angels Broadcasting Network Inc. Phone: 618-627-4651. Fax: 618-627-4155.

Technical Facilities: 100-w TPO, 1.24-kw ERP, 69-ft. above ground, 1348-ft. above sea level, lat. 32° 40' 23", long. 114° 20' 16".

Transmitter: Telegraph Pass, 16.2-mi. E of Yuma.

Ownership: Three Angels Broadcasting Network Inc.

Personnel: Moses Primo, Chief Engineer.

Yuma—KESE-LP, Ch. 35, Gulf-California Broadcast Co. Phone: 928-539-9990.

Studio: 1965 S 4th Ave, Yuma, AZ 85364.

Technical Facilities: 1000-w TPO, 8-kw ERP, 262-ft. above ground, 466-ft. above sea level, lat. 32° 38' 31", long. 114° 33' 34".

Transmitter: Ave. 4E at 13th St.

Ownership: Gulf-California Broadcast Co.

Personnel: Christopher Gallu, General Manager.

Yuma—KVFA-LP, Ch. 6, KM Communications Inc. Phone: 847-674-0864.

Technical Facilities: 0.05-kw ERP, 125-ft. above ground, 321-ft. above sea level, lat. 32° 41' 41", long. 114° 36' 47".

Ownership: KM Communications Inc.

Yuma—KYUM-LP, Ch. 2, Centro Cristiano Vida Abundante Inc.

Technical Facilities: 0.1-kw ERP, 98-ft. above ground, 303-ft. above sea level, lat. 32° 40' 34", long. 114° 35' 27".

Ownership: Centro Cristiano Vida Abundante Inc.

Arkansas

Batesville—K15FW, Ch. 15, Trinity Broadcasting Network Inc. Phone: 714-832-2950. Fax: 714-730-0661.

Technical Facilities: 9.2-kw ERP, 390-ft. above ground, 1250-ft. above sea level, lat. 35° 53' 27", long. 91° 44' 01".

Holds CP for change to 15-kw ERP, BDFCDTT-20060315AFC.

Ownership: Trinity Broadcasting Network Inc.

Batesville—K20EX, Ch. 20, MS Communications LLC. Phone: 414-765-9737.

Technical Facilities: 0.007-kw ERP, 105-ft. above ground, 965-ft. above sea level, lat. 35° 53' 27", long. 91° 44' 02".

Ownership: MS Communications LLC.

Batesville—K22ES, Ch. 22, MS Communications LLC. Phone: 414-765-9737.

Technical Facilities: 1000-w TPO, 0.007-kw ERP, 105-ft. above ground, 860-ft. above sea level, lat. 35° 53' 26", long. 91° 44' 00".

Transmitter: 1.5-mi. NE of Cushman.

Ownership: MS Communications LLC.

Batesville—K30EC, Ch. 30, MS Communications LLC. Phone: 414-765-9737.

Technical Facilities: 1000-w TPO, 0.007-kw ERP, 105-ft. above ground, 860-ft. above sea level, lat. 35° 53' 27", long. 91° 44' 02".

Transmitter: 1.5-mi. NE of Cushman.

Ownership: MS Communications LLC.

Batesville—K35EA, Ch. 35, MS Communications LLC. Phone: 414-765-9737.

Technical Facilities: 1000-w TPO, 0.007-kw ERP, 105-ft. above ground, 860-ft. above sea level, lat. 35° 53' 27", long. 91° 44' 02".

Transmitter: 1.5-mi. NE of Cushman.

Ownership: MS Communications LLC.

Batesville—K40DS, Ch. 40, MS Communications LLC. Phone: 414-765-9737.

Technical Facilities: 1000-w TPO, 0.007-kw ERP, 105-ft. above ground, 860-ft. above sea level, lat. 35° 53' 27", long. 91° 44' 02".

Holds CP for change to 138.5-kw ERP, 295-ft. above ground, 1155-ft. above sea level, BPTTL-20030813AFX.

Transmitter: 1.5-mi. NE of Cushman.

Ownership: MS Communications LLC.

Batesville—K46EM, Ch. 28, MS Communications LLC. Phone: 414-765-9737.

Technical Facilities: 100-w TPO, 0.007-kw ERP, 105-ft. above ground, 860-ft. above sea level, lat. 35° 53' 27", long. 91° 44' 02".

Transmitter: 1.5-mi. NE of Cushman.

Ownership: MS Communications LLC.

Batesville—K53FM, Ch. 53, MS Communications LLC. Phone: 414-765-9737.

Technical Facilities: 1000-w TPO, 0.007-kw ERP, 105-ft. above ground, 860-ft. above sea level, lat. 35° 53' 27", long. 91° 44' 02".

Transmitter: 1.5-mi. NE of Cushman.

Ownership: MS Communications LLC.

Batesville—K57FV, Ch. 57, MS Communications LLC. Phone: 414-765-9737.

Technical Facilities: 1000-w TPO, 0.007-kw ERP, 105-ft. above ground, 965-ft. above sea level, lat. 35° 53' 27", long. 91° 44' 02".

Transmitter: 1.5-mi. NE of Cushman.

Ownership: MS Communications LLC.

Batesville—K59FB, Ch. 59, MS Communications LLC. Phone: 414-765-9737.

Technical Facilities: 1000-w TPO, 0.007-kw ERP, 105-ft. above ground, 860-ft. above sea level, lat. 35° 53' 27", long. 91° 44' 02".

Transmitter: 1.5-mi. NE of Cushman.

Ownership: MS Communications LLC.

Batesville—K61FP, Ch. 61, MS Communications LLC. Phone: 414-765-9737.

Technical Facilities: 87.6-w TPO, 0.007-kw ERP, 105-ft. above ground, 860-ft. above sea level, lat. 35° 53' 27", long. 91° 44' 02".

Transmitter: 1.5-mi. NE of Cushman.

Ownership: MS Communications LLC.

Batesville—K65FN, Ch. 65, MS Communications LLC. Phone: 414-765-9737.

Technical Facilities: 1000-w TPO, 0.007-kw ERP, 32-ft. above ground, 965-ft. above sea level, lat. 35° 53' 27", long. 91° 44' 02".

Transmitter: 1.5-mi. NE of Cushman.

Ownership: MS Communications LLC.

Batesville—K67GR, Ch. 67, MS Communications LLC. Phone: 414-765-9737.

Technical Facilities: 1000-w TPO, 0.007-kw ERP, 105-ft. above ground, 860-ft. above sea level, lat. 35° 53' 27", long. 91° 44' 02".

Transmitter: 1.5-mi. NE of Cushman.

Ownership: MS Communications LLC.

Batesville—K69GT, Ch. 69, MS Communications LLC. Phone: 414-765-9737.

Technical Facilities: 1000-w TPO, 0.007-kw ERP, 105-ft. above ground, 860-ft. above sea level, lat. 35° 53' 27", long. 91° 44' 02".

Transmitter: NE of Cushman.

Ownership: MS Communications LLC.

Bentonville—K67EO, Ch. 67, Local TV Arkansas License LLC. Phone: 859-448-2707.

Technical Facilities: 1000-w TPO, 14-kw ERP, 338-ft. above ground, 1578-ft. above sea level, lat. 36° 23' 36", long. 94° 10' 53".

Holds CP for change to channel number 11, 0.8-kw ERP, 312-ft. above ground, 1578-ft. above sea level, lat. 36° 23' 37", long. 94° 10' 53". BDISTTV-20070824ADL.

Transmitter: 0.8-mi. E of J St., 0.74-mi. N of Bentonville boundary.

Ownership: Local TV Holdings LLC.

Personnel: Gene Graham, General Manager; Larry Duncan, Chief Engineer; Van Comer, Sales Manager.

■ **Bentonville**—KHMF-CA, Ch. 26, Fort Smith 46 Inc., Debtor in Possession. Phone: 501-219-2400.

Technical Facilities: 150-kw ERP, 302-ft. above ground, 1562-ft. above sea level, lat. 36° 23' 37", long. 94° 10' 57".

Began Operation: May 25, 1994.

Ownership: Equity Media Holdings Corp., Debtor in Possession.

■ **Bentonville & Rogers**—K45EI, Ch. 45, Victory Communications Inc. Phone: 479-795-4057. Fax: 501-795-4058.

Studio: 14019 Noah Rd, Gravette, AR 72736.

Technical Facilities: 35-kw ERP, 187-ft. above ground, 1558-ft. above sea level, lat. 36° 21' 56", long. 94° 20' 24".

Transmitter: 3-mi. W of Centerton & 0.4-mi. N of Hwy. 102.

Ownership: Victory Communications Inc.

Personnel: Bryan Holland, General Manager & Chief Engineer; Janice Holland, Sales Manager.

De Queen—K08KF, Ch. 8, First Assembly of God. Phone: 909-793-7800. Fax: 909-793-8821.

Technical Facilities: 0.12-kw ERP, 180-ft. above ground, 581-ft. above sea level, lat. 34° 02' 48", long. 94° 21' 40".

Ownership: First Assembly of God.

El Dorado—K18AB, Ch. 18, Hoak Media of Louisiana License LLC. Phone: 972-960-4896.

Technical Facilities: 0.828-kw ERP, lat. 33° 12' 42", long. 92° 39' 48".

Holds CP for change to 2.54-kw ERP, 89-ft. above ground, 367-ft. above sea level, BDFCDTT-20090306AFF.

Ownership: Hoak Media LLC.

El Dorado—K27FF, Ch. 27, MS Communications LLC. Phone: 414-765-9737.

Technical Facilities: 1000-w TPO, 0.007-kw ERP, 105-ft. above ground, 180-ft. above sea level, lat. 33° 16' 19", long. 92° 42' 12".

Transmitter: Hwy. 335, 5.5-mi. N of intersection with Hwy. 82.

Ownership: MS Communications LLC.

El Dorado—K29DC, Ch. 29, MS Communications LLC. Phone: 414-765-9737.

Technical Facilities: 1000-w TPO, 0.007-kw ERP, 105-ft. above ground, 285-ft. above sea level, lat. 33° 16' 19", long. 92° 42' 12".

Transmitter: Hwy. 355, 5.5-mi. N of intersection with Hwy. 82.

Ownership: MS Communications LLC.

El Dorado—K36DR, Ch. 36, MS Communications LLC. Phone: 414-765-9737.

Technical Facilities: 540-w TPO, 0.007-kw ERP, 105-ft. above ground, 285-ft. above sea level, lat. 33° 16' 19", long. 92° 42' 12".

Transmitter: Hwy. 335, 5.5-mi. N of intersection with Hwy. 82.

Ownership: MS Communications LLC.

El Dorado—K40EF, Ch. 40, MS Communications LLC. Phone: 414-765-9737.

Technical Facilities: 1000-w TPO, 0.007-kw ERP, 105-ft. above ground, 285-ft. above sea level, lat. 33° 16' 19", long. 92° 42' 12".

Transmitter: Hwy. 335, 5.5-mi. N of intersection with Hwy. 82.

Ownership: MS Communications LLC.

El Dorado—K46DT, Ch. 46, MS Communications LLC. Phone: 414-765-9737.

Technical Facilities: 1000-w TPO, 11.8-kw ERP, 562-ft. above ground, 741-ft. above sea level, lat. 33° 16' 19", long. 92° 41' 11".

Transmitter: Hwy 335, 5.5-mi. N of intersection with Hwy 82.

Ownership: MS Communications LLC.

El Dorado—K47JG, Ch. 47, Equity Media Holdings Corp., Debtor in Possession. Phone: 501-219-2400. Fax: 501-221-1101.

Technical Facilities: 1-kw ERP, 190-ft. above ground, 463-ft. above sea level, lat. 32° 59' 35", long. 92° 20' 38".

Holds CP for change to 16-ft. above ground, 289-ft. above sea level, BMPTTL-20070510ABW.

Began Operation: May 25, 2007.

Ownership: Equity Media Holdings Corp., Debtor in Possession.

El Dorado—K48EP, Ch. 48, MS Communications LLC. Phone: 414-765-9737.

Technical Facilities: 1000-w TPO, 12-kw ERP, 562-ft. above ground, 741-ft. above sea level, lat. 33° 16' 19", long. 92° 41' 11".

Transmitter: Hwy. 335, 5.5-mi. N of intersection with Hwy. 82.

Ownership: MS Communications LLC.

El Dorado—K50EK, Ch. 50, MS Communications LLC. Phone: 414-765-9737.

Technical Facilities: 1000-w TPO, 12.6-kw ERP, 562-ft. above ground, 741-ft. above sea level, lat. 33° 16' 19", long. 92° 41' 11".

Transmitter: Hwy. 335, 5.5-mi. N of intersection with Hwy. 82.

Ownership: MS Communications LLC.

El Dorado—K53FB, Ch. 53, MS Communications LLC. Phone: 414-765-9737.

Technical Facilities: 1000-w TPO, 12.8-kw ERP, 562-ft. above ground, 741-ft. above sea level, lat. 33° 16' 19", long. 92° 41' 11".

Transmitter: Hwy. 335, 5.5-mi. N of intersection with Hwy. 82.

Ownership: MS Communications LLC.

El Dorado—K57GF, Ch. 57, MS Communications LLC. Phone: 414-765-9737.

Technical Facilities: 1000-w TPO, 0.007-kw ERP, 105-ft. above ground, 285-ft. above sea level, lat. 33° 16' 19", long. 92° 42' 12".

Transmitter: Hwy. 335, 5.5-mi. N of intersection with Hwy. 82.

Ownership: MS Communications LLC.

El Dorado—K59FJ, Ch. 59, MS Communications LLC. Phone: 414-765-9737.

Technical Facilities: 1000-w TPO, 0.007-kw ERP, 105-ft. above ground, 180-ft. above sea level, lat. 33° 16' 19", long. 92° 42' 12".

Transmitter: Hwy. 335, 5.5-mi. N of intersection with Hwy. 82.

Ownership: MS Communications LLC.

El Dorado—K63FX, Ch. 63, MS Communications LLC. Phone: 414-765-9737.

Technical Facilities: 100-w TPO, 0.007-kw ERP, 105-ft. above ground, 285-ft. above sea level, lat. 33° 16' 19", long. 92° 42' 12".

Transmitter: Hwy. 335, 5.5-mi. N of intersection with Hwy. 82.

Ownership: MS Communications LLC.

El Dorado—K66EX, Ch. 66, MS Communications LLC. Phone: 414-765-9737.

Technical Facilities: 0.007-kw ERP, 105-ft. above ground, 285-ft. above sea level, lat. 33° 16' 19", long. 92° 42' 12".

Ownership: MS Communications LLC.

El Dorado—K69HO, Ch. 69, MS Communications LLC. Phone: 414-765-9737.

Technical Facilities: 0.007-kw ERP, 105-ft. above ground, 285-ft. above sea level, lat. 33° 16' 19", long. 92° 42' 12".

Ownership: MS Communications LLC.

El Dorado—KCIB-LP, Ch. 5, Immanuel Baptist Church. Phone: 501-862-4264.

Technical Facilities: 30-w TPO, 0.044-kw ERP, 144-ft. above ground, 393-ft. above sea level, lat. 33° 12' 17", long. 92° 39' 54".

Transmitter: Corner of S. West Ave. & Cross St.

Ownership: Immanuel Baptist Church.

Personnel: Jim Davidson, General Manager; Mike Miller, Chief Engineer; Tim Reames, Sales Manager.

■ **El Dorado**—KLMB-LP, Ch. 23, Louisiana Christian Broadcasting Inc. Phone: 318-322-1399.

Technical Facilities: 22.4-kw ERP, 164-ft. above ground, 453-ft. above sea level, lat. 33° 12' 22", long. 92° 39' 13".

Holds CP for change to 0.11-kw ERP, 164-ft. above ground, 449-ft. above sea level, BDFCDTA-20060331BPL.

Began Operation: March 29, 1999.

Ownership: Louisiana Christian Broadcasting Inc.

Eureka Springs—K22HS, Ch. 22, Christians Incorporated for Christ. Phone: 417-337-8747. Fax: 417-337-5503.

Technical Facilities: 10-kw ERP, 210-ft. above ground, 1850-ft. above sea level, lat. 36° 21' 38", long. 93° 44' 54".

Ownership: Christians Incorporated for Christ Inc.

Fayetteville—K42BS, Ch. 42, Trinity Broadcasting Network Inc. Phone: 714-832-2950. Fax: 714-730-0661.

Technical Facilities: 1000-w TPO, 21.6-kw ERP, 135-ft. above ground, 1653-ft. above sea level, lat. 36° 12' 16", long. 94° 06' 04".

Transmitter: Communications tower atop Dodd Mountain, near Springdale.

Ownership: Trinity Broadcasting Network Inc.

Personnel: Paul Crouch, General Manager; Ben Miller, Chief Engineer; Rod Henke, Sales Manager.

Fayetteville—K62DQ, Ch. 62, Local TV Arkansas License LLC. Phone: 859-448-2707.

Technical Facilities: 880-w TPO, 15.2-kw ERP, 387-ft. above ground, 1736-ft. above sea level, lat. 36° 08' 50", long. 94° 11' 14".

Holds CP for change to channel number 44, 23-kw ERP, 377-ft. above ground, 1736-ft. above sea level, lat. 36° 08' 50", long. 94° 11' 13". BDISTT-20070824ADM.

Transmitter: 2.6-mi. along a bearing of 137 degrees from intersection of State Rtes. 68 & 112.

Ownership: Local TV Holdings LLC.

Personnel: Gene Graham, General Manager; Larry Duncan, Chief Engineer; Van Comer, Sales Manager.

Fayetteville—KEGW-LP, Ch. 64, Fort Smith 46 Inc., Debtor in Possession. Phone: 501-219-2400. Fax: 501-221-3955.

Technical Facilities: 1000-w TPO, 24.8-kw ERP, 361-ft. above ground, 1713-ft. above sea level, lat. 36° 08' 50", long. 94° 11' 14".

Transmitter: 1-mi. E of State Rd. 112, 1-mi. NW of Johnson.

Began Operation: August 21, 2000.

Ownership: Equity Media Holdings Corp., Debtor in Possession.

■ **Fayetteville**—KFFS-CA, Ch. 36, Fort Smith 46 Inc., Debtor in Possession. Phone: 501-219-2400. Fax: 501-785-4844.

Technical Facilities: 1000-w TPO, 16.7-kw ERP, 184-ft. above ground, 1535-ft. above sea level, lat. 36° 08' 50", long. 94° 11' 14".

Transmitter: Johnson Tower Rd., 0.4-mi. NE of New Hope Church.

Began Operation: November 7, 1995.

Ownership: Equity Media Holdings Corp., Debtor in Possession.

Personnel: Karen Pharis, General Manager; Don Jones, Chief Engineer; Leo Cruz, Sales Manager.

Fort Smith—K14JJ, Ch. 14, Ellerbeck Family Partners II Ltd. Phone: 713-975-1133.

Technical Facilities: 130-w TPO, 1-kw ERP, 344-ft. above ground, 846-ft. above sea level, lat. 35° 26' 50", long. 94° 21' 54".

Transmitter: 0.9-mi. NE of Van Buren.

Ownership: Ruth E. Ellerbeck.

Fort Smith—K16ER, Ch. 16, Trinity Broadcasting Network Inc. Phone: 714-832-2950. Fax: 714-730-0661.

Technical Facilities: 2000-w TPO, 7.5-kw ERP, 190-ft. above ground, 981-ft. above sea level, lat. 35° 26' 50", long. 94° 21' 53".

Transmitter: Mount Vista, Watertank Rd., Van Buren.

Ownership: Trinity Broadcasting Network Inc.

Fort Smith—K32GH, Ch. 32, Fort Smith 46 Inc., Debtor in Possession. Phone: 501-219-2400.

Technical Facilities: 150-kw ERP, 328-ft. above ground, 2408-ft. above sea level, lat. 35° 47' 49", long. 94° 10' 04".

Began Operation: August 17, 2004.

Ownership: Equity Media Holdings Corp., Debtor in Possession.

Fort Smith—K33HE, Ch. 33, Fort Smith 46 Inc., Debtor in Possession. Phone: 501-219-2400. Fax: 501-785-4844.

Technical Facilities: 23.2-kw ERP, 164-ft. above ground, 1200-ft. above sea level, lat. 35° 18' 09", long. 93° 45' 40".

Began Operation: July 23, 1996.

Ownership: Equity Media Holdings Corp., Debtor in Possession.

Fort Smith—K36EH, Ch. 36, Ellerbeck Family Partners II Ltd. Phone: 713-975-1133.

Technical Facilities: 130-w TPO, 1-kw ERP, 240-ft. above ground, 1040-ft. above sea level, lat. 35° 26' 50", long. 94° 21' 54".

Transmitter: 1-mi. NE of Van Buren.

Ownership: Ellerbeck Family Partners II Ltd.

Fort Smith—K48FL, Ch. 48, Fort Smith 46 Inc., Debtor in Possession. Phone: 501-219-2400. Fax: 501-785-4844.

Technical Facilities: 51.8-kw ERP, 131-ft. above ground, 1771-ft. above sea level, lat. 35° 40' 09", long. 94° 48' 42".

Began Operation: July 23, 1996.

Ownership: Equity Media Holdings Corp., Debtor in Possession.

■ **Fort Smith**—KFDF-CA, Ch. 10, Fort Smith 46 Inc., Debtor in Possession. Phone: 501-219-2400.

Technical Facilities: 3-kw ERP, 165-ft. above ground, 965-ft. above sea level, lat. 35° 26' 50", long. 94° 21' 54".

Began Operation: December 8, 1989.

Ownership: Equity Media Holdings Corp., Debtor in Possession.

■ **Fort Smith**—KPBI-CA, Ch. 46, Fort Smith 46 Inc., Debtor in Possession. Phone: 501-219-2400. Fax: 501-785-4844.

Studio: 523 Garrison Ave, 2nd Fl, Fort Smith, AR 72901.

Technical Facilities: 32-kw ERP, 175-ft. above ground, 975-ft. above sea level, lat. 35° 26' 50", long. 94° 21' 54".

Began Operation: June 9, 1995.

Ownership: Equity Media Holdings Corp., Debtor in Possession.

Personnel: Karen Pharis, General Manager; Marty Houston, Station Manager; Leo Cruz, Sales; Don Patrick, Engineering; Bill Pharis, News Director.

Fort Smith—KUFS-LP, Ch. 54, Fort Smith 46 Inc., Debtor in Possession. Phone: 501-219-2400. Fax: 501-785-4844.

Technical Facilities: 23.1-kw ERP, 150-ft. above ground, 2509-ft. above sea level, lat. 35° 04' 05", long. 94° 40' 59".

Began Operation: July 23, 1996.

Ownership: Equity Media Holdings Corp., Debtor in Possession.

Fort Smith—KWFT-LP, Ch. 34, TV 34 Inc., Debtor in Possession. Phone: 501-219-2400. Fax: 501-785-4844.

Technical Facilities: 130-w TPO, 8.2-kw ERP, 154-ft. above ground, 1329-ft. above sea level, lat. 35° 31' 30", long. 94° 22' 27".

Transmitter: 1-mi. NE of Van Buren.

Began Operation: July 23, 1996.

Ownership: Equity Media Holdings Corp., Debtor in Possession.

Fort Smith—KXUN-LP, Ch. 43, Fort Smith 46 Inc., Debtor in Possession. Phone: 501-219-2400.

Technical Facilities: 5.8-kw ERP, 239-ft. above ground, 1039-ft. above sea level, lat. 35° 26' 50", long. 94° 21' 54".

Began Operation: July 23, 1996.

Ownership: Equity Media Holdings Corp., Debtor in Possession.

Fulton—K11VO, Ch. 11, Hispanic Christian Community Network Inc. Phone: 214-879-0081.

Technical Facilities: 2.5-kw ERP, 164-ft. above ground, 413-ft. above sea level, lat. 33° 36' 45", long. 93° 48' 45".

Ownership: Hispanic Christian Community Network Inc.

Fulton—KZTE-LP, Ch. 64, Hispanic Christian Community Network Inc. Phone: 214-879-0081.

Technical Facilities: 150-kw ERP, 164-ft. above ground, 413-ft. above sea level, lat. 33° 36' 45", long. 93° 48' 45".

Ownership: Hispanic Christian Community Network Inc.

Green Forest—K54FH, Ch. 54, New Life Evangelistic Center Inc. Phone: 314-436-2424.

Technical Facilities: 24.24-kw ERP, lat. 36° 17' 27", long. 93° 26' 11".

Holds CP for change to channel number 47, 7.5-kw ERP, 385-ft. above ground, 2392-ft. above sea level, lat. 36° 17' 31", long. 93° 26' 08". BDISDTL-20060331AYO.

Transmitter: Bradshaw Mountain, 1.2-mi. E of State Rd. 103.

Ownership: New Life Evangelistic Center Inc.

Harrison—K23DU, Ch. 23, Christians Incorporated for Christ Inc. Phone: 417-337-8747. Fax: 417-337-5503.

Technical Facilities: 1000-w TPO, 15.3-kw ERP, 112-ft. above ground, 2080-ft. above sea level, lat. 36° 14' 34", long. 93° 13' 15".

Holds CP for change to channel number 36, 11.9-kw ERP, BDISTTL-20061020AAO.

Transmitter: Kennedy Mountain.

Ownership: Christians Incorporated for Christ Inc.

Personnel: Keith O'Neil, Vice President.

Harrison—KTKO-LP, Ch. 8, TKO Inc. Phone: 870-741-2566.

Technical Facilities: 2-kw ERP, 148-ft. above ground, 2159-ft. above sea level, lat. 36° 10' 40", long. 93° 12' 40".

Holds CP for change to 3-kw ERP, lat. 36° 11' 28.7", long. 93° 11' 55.4". BMPTVL-20070613ADN.

Ownership: TKO Inc.

■ **Hindsville**—KRBF-CA, Ch. 41, Fort Smith 46 Inc., Debtor in Possession. Phone: 501-219-2400.

Technical Facilities: 27.4-kw ERP, 102-ft. above ground, 1812-ft. above sea level, lat. 36° 07' 37", long. 93° 51' 58".

Began Operation: May 25, 1994.

Ownership: Equity Media Holdings Corp., Debtor in Possession.

Hope—KTSS-LP, Ch. 50, Sandra May. Phone: 501-777-3548.

Technical Facilities: 1000-w TPO, 14.5-kw ERP, 395-ft. above ground, 837-ft. above sea level, lat. 33° 39' 26", long. 93° 33' 00".

Transmitter: Approx. 1.7-mi. E of Hope & 0.7-mi. N of Hwy. 4.

Ownership: Sandra A. May.

Hot Springs—K23GT, Ch. 23, Trinity Broadcasting Network. Phone: 714-832-2950. Fax: 714-730-0661.

Technical Facilities: 34.9-kw ERP, 200-ft. above ground, 1360-ft. above sea level, lat. 34° 33' 56", long. 93° 05' 03".

Ownership: Trinity Broadcasting Network Inc.

■ **Hot Springs**—KTVV-LP, Ch. 63, Arkansas 49 Inc., Debtor in Possession. Phone: 501-219-2400. Fax: 501-785-4844.

Technical Facilities: 1000-w TPO, 28.4-kw ERP, 299-ft. above ground, 1457-ft. above sea level, lat. 34° 33' 56", long. 93° 05' 03".

Holds CP for change to channel number 18, 150-kw ERP, BDISTTL-20060403AQY.

Transmitter: 2-mi. N of Hot Springs.

Ownership: Equity Media Holdings Corp., Debtor in Possession.

Jonesboro—K42GX, Ch. 42, Trinity Broadcasting Network Inc. Phone: 714-832-2950. Fax: 714-730-0661.

Technical Facilities: 14.8-kw ERP, 495-ft. above ground, 863-ft. above sea level, lat. 35° 53' 27", long. 90° 40' 26".

Transmitter: KASU(FM) tower, 1.3-mi. SSE of New Haven & Thomas Green Rds.

Ownership: Trinity Broadcasting Network Inc.

Little Rock—K27JP-D, Ch. 27, Three Angels Broadcasting Network Inc. Phone: 618-627-4651. Fax: 618-627-4155.

Technical Facilities: 1-kw ERP, 555-ft. above ground, 859-ft. above sea level, lat. 34° 44' 38", long. 92° 16' 32".

Ownership: Three Angels Broadcasting Network Inc.

Personnel: Moses Primo, Chief Engineer.

Little Rock—K34FH, Ch. 34, Trinity Christian Center of Santa Ana Inc. Phone: 714-832-2950.

Technical Facilities: 20.9-kw ERP, 499-ft. above ground, 1453-ft. above sea level, lat. 34° 47' 57", long. 92° 29' 29".

Transmitter: 0.4-mi. ESE of Two Towers & Gordon Rds., Pulaski County.

Ownership: Trinity Broadcasting Network Inc.

Little Rock—KHTE-LP, Ch. 44, Hallmark National Mortgage Corp. Phone: 501-376-0800.

Technical Facilities: 10-kw ERP, 568-ft. above ground, 873-ft. above sea level, lat. 34° 44' 38", long. 92° 16' 32".

Holds CP for change to channel number 50, 150-kw ERP, 226-ft. above ground, 816-ft. above sea level, lat. 34° 46' 20", long. 92° 21' 27". BDISTTL-20060215AAJ.

Began Operation: October 16, 1996.

Ownership: Bank of Little Rock.

Little Rock—KHUG-LP, Ch. 14, Little Rock TV-14 LLC, Debtor in Possession. Phone: 501-219-2400.

Technical Facilities: 15.5-kw ERP, 111-ft. above ground, 696-ft. above sea level, lat. 34° 49' 52", long. 92° 19' 18".

Began Operation: March 17, 1999.

Ownership: Ronald Ellerbeck; Equity Media Holdings Corp., Debtor in Possession.

■ **Little Rock**—KJLR-LP, Ch. 28, Cowsert Family LLC.

Technical Facilities: 1000-w TPO, 13.5-kw ERP, 397-ft. above ground, 880-ft. above sea level, lat. 34° 44' 38", long. 92° 16' 32".

Transmitter: TCBY Bldg., 5th St. & Broadway.

Ownership: Cowsert Family LLC.

■ **Little Rock**—KKYK-CA, Ch. 20, Arkansas 49 Inc., Debtor in Possession. Phone: 501-219-2400.

Studio: One Shackleford Dr, Ste 400, Little Rock, AR 72211.

Technical Facilities: 150-kw ERP, 607-ft. above ground, 607-ft. above sea level, lat. 34° 47' 56", long. 92° 29' 45".

Ownership: Equity Media Holdings Corp., Debtor in Possession.

Personnel: Tammy Graham, General Manager.

Little Rock—KLRA-LP, Ch. 58, Equity Media Holdings Corp., Debtor in Possession. Phone: 501-219-2400.

Technical Facilities: 50-kw ERP, 250-ft. above ground, 840-ft. above sea level, lat. 34° 46' 20", long. 92° 21' 27".

Began Operation: December 20, 1996.

Ownership: Equity Media Holdings Corp., Debtor in Possession.

Little Rock, etc.—KZJG-LP, Ch. 9, Cowsert Family LLC. Phone: 501-664-5438.

Technical Facilities: 1.5-kw ERP, 551-ft. above ground, 855-ft. above sea level, lat. 34° 37.7", long. 92° 16' 32.5".

Ownership: Cowsert Family LLC.

Personnel: Jim Cowsert, General Manager; David Cowsert, General Sales Manager; Cal Dring, National Sales Manager; Joe Elder, Chief Engineer; Ted Biggs, News Director; Joe Maggard, Business Manager.

Mountain Home—K07XL, Ch. 7, Reynolds Media Inc. Phones: 870-841-4891; 870-424-6957.

Technical Facilities: 0.7-kw ERP, 184-ft. above ground, 1299-ft. above sea level, lat. 36° 21' 00", long. 92° 24' 12".

Ownership: Dan Reynolds.

Personnel: Ian Marcus Reynolds, Operations Manager; Gil Ty Reynolds, General Manager.

Mountain Home—K26GS, Ch. 26, Reynolds Media Inc. Phones: 870-741-4891; 877-297-3435. Fax: 870-741-4891.

Technical Facilities: 150-kw ERP, 180-ft. above ground, 2398-ft. above sea level, lat. 36° 06' 41", long. 93° 01' 56".

Ownership: Reynolds Media Inc.

Personnel: Ian Reynolds, Operations Manager.

Mountain Home—K41HC, Ch. 41, Trinity Broadcasting Network Inc. Phone: 714-832-2950. Fax: 714-730-0661.

Technical Facilities: 10.2-kw ERP, 98-ft. above ground, 1197-ft. above sea level, lat. 36° 20' 55", long. 92° 24' 01".

Nashville—KJEP-CA, Ch. 23, KNVL-TV Inc. Phone: 870-845-5685.

Studio: 123 W Howard St, Nashville, AR 71852-2064.

Technical Facilities: 1000-w TPO, 20.1-kw ERP, 269-ft. above ground, 735-ft. above sea level, lat. 33° 57' 58", long. 93° 49' 36".

Holds CP for change to 0.1-kw ERP, 269-ft. above ground, 731-ft. above sea level, BDFCDTA-20070103AAQ.

Transmitter: 0.4-mi. SSE of State Rte. 27 at Howard/Hempstead county line.

Multichannel TV Sound: Stereo and separate audio program.

Ownership: KNVL-TV Inc.

Personnel: Glen Power, General Manager; Sean Harper, Chief Engineer.

Nashville—KSJA-CA, Ch. 29, KNVL-TV Inc. Phone: 870-845-5685.

Technical Facilities: 1000-w TPO, 20-kw ERP, 269-ft. above ground, 735-ft. above sea level, lat. 33° 57' 58", long. 93° 49' 36".

Holds CP for change to 269-ft. above ground, 731-ft. above sea level, BDISTTA-20080805ABF.

Transmitter: 0.4-mi. SSE of State Rte. 27 at Howard/Hempstead county line.

Multichannel TV Sound: Separate audio progam.

Ownership: KNVL-TV Inc.

Personnel: Glen Power, General Manager; Sean Harper, Chief Engineer.

Paragould—K27FC, Ch. 27, Trinity Broadcasting Network Inc. Phone: 714-832-2950. Fax: 714-730-0661.

Technical Facilities: 100-w TPO, 0.9-kw ERP, 282-ft. above ground, 613-ft. above sea level, lat. 36° 01' 52", long. 90° 30' 57".

Transmitter: 2301 Cody St.

Ownership: Trinity Broadcasting Network Inc.

Paris—KRAH-CA, Ch. 53, Fort Smith 46 Inc., Debtor in Possession. Phone: 501-219-2400.

Technical Facilities: 793-w TPO, 34.7-kw ERP, 121-ft. above ground, 2802-ft. above sea level, lat. 35° 09' 52", long. 93° 40' 52".

Transmitter: 1.4-mi. W of Signal Hill, Dripping Springs recreation area.

Began Operation: December 17, 1993.

Ownership: Equity Media Holdings Corp., Debtor in Possession.

Pine Bluff—KIPB-LP, Ch. 65, Immanuel Broadcasting Corp. Phone: 501-536-2287. Fax: 501-534-3757.

Studio: 1801 W 17th St, Pine Bluff, AR 71603.

Technical Facilities: 1000-w TPO, 16.4-kw ERP, 187-ft. above ground, 413-ft. above sea level, lat. 34° 12' 46", long. 92° 01' 14".

Transmitter: 1801 W. 17th St.

Ownership: Immanuel Broadcasting Corp.

Personnel: Charles Black, General Manager & Executive Director; James Rowe, Production Manager.

Pine Bluff—KWBK-LP, Ch. 45, Arkansas 49 Inc., Debtor in Possession. Phones: 501-219-2400; 501-221-0400. Fax: 501-785-4844.

Technical Facilities: 150-kw ERP, 479-ft. above ground, 754-ft. above sea level, lat. 34° 29' 12", long. 92° 09' 28".

Began Operation: September 15, 2000.

Ownership: Equity Media Holdings Corp., Debtor in Possession.

Searcy—KTWN-LD, Ch. 18, My Town TV Inc. Phones: 501-279-1121; 501-279-8880. Fax: 501-305-3111.

Technical Facilities: 15-kw ERP, 279-ft. above ground, 673-ft. above sea level, lat. 35° 02' 13", long. 92° 01' 02".

Multichannel TV Sound: Stereo only.

Ownership: My Town TV.

Sheridan—KEJC-LP, Ch. 5, Equity Media Holdings Corp., Debtor in Possession. Phone: 501-219-2400.

Technical Facilities: 104.6-kw ERP, 230-ft. above ground, 630-ft. above sea level, lat. 34° 30' 27", long. 92° 32' 48".

Began Operation: September 17, 1987.

Ownership: Equity Media Holdings Corp., Debtor in Possession.

Siloam Springs—KKAF-CA, Ch. 33, Fort Smith 46 Inc., Debtor in Possession. Phone: 501-219-2400.

Technical Facilities: 16.7-kw ERP, lat. 36° 09' 07", long. 94° 30' 55".

Transmitter: Intersection of Hwys. 16 & 66.

Began Operation: April 15, 1997.

Ownership: Equity Media Holdings Corp., Debtor in Possession.

Springdale—KJBW-CA, Ch. 4, Fort Smith 46 Inc., Debtor in Possession. Phone: 501-219-2400.

Technical Facilities: 3-kw ERP, 292-ft. above ground, 1650-ft. above sea level, lat. 36° 08' 50", long. 94° 11' 13".

Holds CP for change to 2.1-kw ERP, BPTVA-20040309AAA.

Transmitter: 2659 S. 56th St.

Began Operation: March 29, 1993.

Ownership: Equity Media Holdings Corp., Debtor in Possession.

Springdale—KVAQ-LP, Ch. 20, Christians Incorporated for Christ Inc. Phone: 417-337-8747. Fax: 417-337-5503.

Technical Facilities: 800-w TPO, 14.6-kw ERP, 148-ft. above ground, 1729-ft. above sea level, lat. 36° 12' 20", long. 94° 06' 06".

Transmitter: Fitzgerald Mountain.

Ownership: Christians Incorporated for Christ Inc.

Personnel: Keith O'Neill, Vice President.

Texarkana—KLFI-LP, Ch. 35, Beech Street Communications Corp. Phone: 870-774-3500. Fax: 870-774-3600.

Technical Facilities: 1000-w TPO, 10.6-kw ERP, 404-ft. above ground, 715-ft. above sea level, lat. 33° 25' 48", long. 94° 05' 08".

Transmitter: 0.1-mi. NW of W. 7th St., Texarkana.

Ownership: Beech Street Communications.

Personnel: Burns Barr, Operations Manager.

Texarkana—KTEV-LP, Ch. 13, Mulholland Media Group. Phone: 903-793-5995.

Technical Facilities: 1-kw ERP, 68-ft. above ground, 378-ft. above sea level, lat. 33° 26' 49", long. 94° 04' 25".

Ownership: Mulholland Media Group.

Winslow—KWNL-CA, Ch. 9, Fort Smith 46 Inc., Debtor in Possession. Phone: 501-219-2400. Fax: 501-785-4844.

Technical Facilities: 1000-w TPO, 3-kw ERP, 269-ft. above ground, 2349-ft. above sea level, lat. 35° 47' 49", long. 94° 10' 04".

Holds CP for change to channel number 31, 150-kw ERP, 292-ft. above ground, 1650-ft. above sea level, lat. 36° 08' 50", long. 94° 11' 13". BPTTA-20030829BDQ.

Transmitter: Signal Hill, 2-mi. W of U.S. Hwy. 71 & State Hwy. 74, Winslow.

Began Operation: December 17, 1993.

Ownership: Equity Media Holdings Corp., Debtor in Possession.

Personnel: Karen Pharis, General Manager; Don Jones, Chief Engineer; Leo Cruz, Sales Manager.

California

Altadena—KTAV-LP, Ch. 69, AlmaVision Hispanic Network Inc. Phones: 213-627-8900; 213-627-8711.

Technical Facilities: 9.98-kw ERP, 135-ft. above ground, 5843-ft. above sea level, lat. 34° 13' 35.3", long. 118° 03' 57.7".

Ownership: AlmaVision Hispanic Network Inc.

Personnel: Charles M. Harker, General Manager.

Alturas—K20DE-D, Ch. 20, Northern California Educational TV Assn. Inc. Phone: 530-243-5493.

Technical Facilities: 0.9-kw ERP, 20-ft. above ground, 7421-ft. above sea level, lat. 41° 09' 18", long. 120° 33' 46".

Ownership: Northern California Educational TV Assn. Inc.

Alturas—K60AR, Ch. 60, Freedom Broadcasting of Oregon Licensee LLC.

Technical Facilities: 0.252-kw ERP, 5419-ft. above sea level, lat. 41° 32' 18", long. 120° 21' 22".

Ownership: Freedom Communications Holdings Inc.

Alturas, etc.—K47EH, Ch. 47, Mutual Television Network. Phone: 888-482-1080.

Technical Facilities: 14.6-kw ERP, lat. 40° 43' 36", long. 123° 58' 26".

Transmitter: 1.6-mi. WNW of Keeland & Mountain Rds.

Ownership: Mutual Television Network.

Anderson/Central Valley—K38FQ, Ch. 38, Sainte Partners II LP. Phone: 209-523-0777.

Technical Facilities: 150-kw ERP, 52-ft. above ground, 3212-ft. above sea level, lat. 40° 39' 16", long. 122° 31' 13".

Holds CP for change to 15-kw ERP, 52-ft. above ground, 3213-ft. above sea level, BDFCDTL-20060329AHN.

Ownership: Sainte Partners II LP.

Atascadero—KASC-CA, Ch. 7, Una Vez Mas Atascadero License LLC. Phone: 214-754-7008.

Technical Facilities: 50-w TPO, 249-kw ERP, 75-ft. above ground, 2275-ft. above sea level, lat. 35° 26' 47", long. 120° 42' 58".

Transmitter: Falcon Rd., Frog Pond Mountain, 1.2-mi. S of Rte. 41.

Ownership: Una Vez Mas GP LLC.

Bakersfield—K08MM, Ch. 8, Three Angels Broadcasting Network Inc. Phone: 618-627-4651. Fax: 618-627-4155.

Technical Facilities: 0.46-kw ERP, 199-ft. above ground, 593-ft. above sea level, lat. 35° 21' 42", long. 119° 03' 34".

Ownership: Three Angels Broadcasting Network Inc.

Personnel: Moses Primo, Chief Engineer.

Bakersfield—K18HD-D, Ch. 18, Valley Public Television Inc. Phone: 559-266-1800.

Technical Facilities: 13-kw ERP, 59-ft. above ground, 3602-ft. above sea level, lat. 35° 26' 18", long. 118° 44' 18".

Ownership: Valley Public Television Inc.

Bakersfield—K21FP, Ch. 21, Trinity Broadcasting Network Inc. Phone: 714-832-2950. Fax: 714-730-0661.

Technical Facilities: 0.35-kw ERP, lat. 35° 26' 17", long. 118° 44' 22".

Transmitter: Mount Adelaide electronics site.

Ownership: Trinity Broadcasting Network Inc.

Bakersfield—K24GS, Ch. 24, Three Angels Broadcasting Network Inc. Phone: 618-627-4651. Fax: 618-627-4155.

Technical Facilities: 21.5-kw ERP, 260-ft. above ground, 654-ft. above sea level, lat. 35° 21' 41.8", long. 119° 03' 34.3".

Ownership: Three Angels Broadcasting Network Inc.

Personnel: Moses Primo, Chief Engineer.

Bakersfield—K46II, Ch. 46, Community TV of Southern California. Phone: 323-953-5209.

Technical Facilities: 38.4-kw ERP, 57-ft. above ground, 3581-ft. above sea level, lat. 35° 26' 16.6", long. 118° 44' 25.1".

Holds CP for change to 15-kw ERP, lat. 35° 26' 17.1", long. 118° 44' 21.7". BDFCDTT-20080221AAG.

Ownership: Community TV of Southern California.

Bakersfield—KABE-LP, Ch. 39, Univision Bakersfield LLC. Phone: 310-348-3600.

Technical Facilities: 100-kw ERP, 56-ft. above ground, 7543-ft. above sea level, lat. 35° 27' 14", long. 118° 35' 37".

Holds CP for change to 15-kw ERP, BDFCDTL-20080801BCP.

Ownership: Univision Communications Inc.

Bakersfield—KBBV-CA, Ch. 19, Hispanic Bakersfield LLC. Phone: 559-733-7800.

Technical Facilities: 7.3-kw ERP, 79-ft. above ground, 7625-ft. above sea level, lat. 35° 27' 11", long. 118° 35' 25".

Ownership: Pappas Telecasting Companies.

Bakersfield—KBFK-LP, Ch. 36, Cocola Broadcasting Companies LLC. Phone: 559-435-7000. Fax: 559-435-3201.

Technical Facilities: 150-kw ERP, 33-ft. above ground, 3432-ft. above sea level, lat. 35° 26' 16", long. 118° 44' 28".

Holds CP for change to 15-kw ERP, BDFCDTL-20081215ABE.

Began Operation: November 25, 1996.

Ownership: Cocola Broadcasting Companies LLC.

Personnel: Todd Lopes, President.

Bakersfield—KBFX-CA, Ch. 58, Fisher Broadcasting-California TV LLC. Phone: 206-404-7000.

Studio: 5035 E McKinley Ave, Fresno, CA 93727.

Technical Facilities: 4000-w TPO, 23.8-kw ERP, 69-ft. above ground, 7644-ft. above sea level, lat. 35° 27' 11", long. 118° 35' 25".

Transmitter: Breckenridge Mountain, KBAK(TV) site.

Ownership: Fisher Communications Inc.

Personnel: Teresa Burgess, Vice President & General Manager.

■ **Bakersfield**—KBTF-CA, Ch. 31, Telefutura Bakersfield LLC. Phone: 310-348-3600.

Technical Facilities: 60-kw ERP, 56-ft. above ground, 7543-ft. above sea level, lat. 35° 27' 14", long. 118° 35' 37".

Holds CP for change to 15-kw ERP, BDFCDTA-20080804AET.

Ownership: Univision Communications Inc.

Bakersfield—KCBT-LP, Ch. 34, Cocola Broadcasting Companies LLC. Phone: 559-435-7000. Fax: 559-435-3201.

Technical Facilities: 150-kw ERP, 33-ft. above ground, 3432-ft. above sea level, lat. 35° 26' 16", long. 118° 44' 28".

Began Operation: July 8, 1993.

Ownership: Cocola Broadcasting Companies LLC.

Personnel: Todd Lopes, President.

Bakersfield—KEBK-LP, Ch. 47, Venture Technologies Group LLC. Phone: 323-904-4090.

Technical Facilities: 50-kw ERP, 52-ft. above ground, 7536-ft. above sea level, lat. 35° 27' 14", long. 118° 35' 37".

Holds CP for change to 150-kw ERP, 41-ft. above ground, 7525-ft. above sea level, BPTTL-20080728AEK.

Began Operation: April 20, 2006.

Ownership: Venture Technologies Group LLC.

Bakersfield—KKEY-LP, Ch. 11, Newport Television License LLC. Phones: 209-523-0777; 816-751-0204. Fax: 209-523-0839.

Technical Facilities: 3-kw ERP, 92-ft. above ground, 3615-ft. above sea level, lat. 35° 26' 17", long. 118° 44' 22".

Ownership: Newport Television LLC.

Bakersfield—KNXT-LP, Ch. 38, Diocese of Fresno Education Corp. Phone: 559-488-7440.

Studio: 1550 N Fresno St, Fresno, CA 93703.

Technical Facilities: 65-kw ERP, 33-ft. above ground, 3432-ft. above sea level, lat. 35° 26' 16", long. 118° 44' 28".

Ownership: Diocese of Fresno Education Corp.

Personnel: Todd Lopes, President.

Bakersfield—KPMC-LP, Ch. 43, Cocola Broadcasting Companies LLC. Phone: 559-435-7000.

Technical Facilities: 150-kw ERP, 33-ft. above ground, 3432-ft. above sea level, lat. 35° 26' 16", long. 118° 44' 26".

Ownership: Cocola Broadcasting Companies LLC.

Bakersfield—KTBV-LD, Ch. 12, EICB-TV West LLC. Phone: 972-291-3750.

Technical Facilities: 0.1-kw ERP, 98-ft. above ground, 7887-ft. above sea level, lat. 34° 46' 22.37", long. 118° 58' 26.14".

Ownership: EICB-TV LLC.

■ **Bakersfield**—KTFB-CA, Ch. 4, Telefutura Bakersfield LLC. Phone: 310-348-3600.

Technical Facilities: 7.84-w TPO, 0.28-kw ERP, 36-ft. above ground, 3537-ft. above sea level, lat. 35° 26' 16", long. 118° 44' 28".

Holds CP for change to channel number 16, 15-kw ERP, 49-ft. above ground, 3570-ft. above sea level, lat. 35° 26' 20", long. 118° 44' 24". BDISDTA-20070611AKQ.

Transmitter: Mount Adelaid, ENE of Bakersfield.

Began Operation: October 26, 1998.

Ownership: Univision Communications Inc.

Personnel: Steven E. Humphries, Chief Operating Officer; James E. Foss, Chief Engineer; Del Beveridge, Sales Manager; Sylvester Rameriz, Production Director; Zilpa Barbosa, Traffic Director; Aldolfo Reyna Jr., Creative Director.

■ **Bakersfield**—KVVB-CA, Ch. 19, Hispanic Bakersfield LLC. Phone: 559-733-7800.

Technical Facilities: 7.3-kw ERP, 79-ft. above ground, 7625-ft. above sea level, lat. 35° 27' 11", long. 118° 35' 25".

Ownership: Pappas Telecasting Companies.

Personnel: Charles Pfaff, General Manager; Debbie Sweeney.

Bakersfield—KZKC-LP, Ch. 42, McGraw-Hill Broadcasting Co. Inc. Phone: 661-637-2323.

Technical Facilities: 150-kw ERP, 33-ft. above ground, 3432-ft. above sea level, lat. 35° 26' 16", long. 118° 44' 28".

Holds CP for change to channel number 23, 15-kw ERP, 46-ft. above ground, 7533-ft. above sea level, lat. 35° 27' 14", long. 118° 35' 37". BDISDTL-20090113ABQ.

Began Operation: April 15, 1999.

Ownership: McGraw-Hill Broadcasting Co. Inc.

Personnel: Steven P McEvoy, General Manager.

Banning—KRMV-LP, Ch. 45, Venture Technologies Group LLC. Phone: 323-904-4090.

Technical Facilities: 10-kw ERP, 72-ft. above ground, 7992-ft. above sea level, lat. 34° 02' 17", long. 116° 48' 47".

Ownership: Venture Technologies Group LLC.

Banning—KRVD-LP, Ch. 33, Venture Technologies Group LLC. Phone: 323-904-4090.

Technical Facilities: 1.2-kw ERP, 72-ft. above ground, 7992-ft. above sea level, lat. 34° 02' 17", long. 116° 48' 47".

Ownership: Venture Technologies Group LLC.

Barstow—K20IM, Ch. 20, EICB-TV West LLC. Phone: 972-291-3750.

Technical Facilities: 0.2-kw ERP, 26-ft. above ground, 2251-ft. above sea level, lat. 34° 53' 27", long. 117° 00' 33".

Holds CP for change to 2-kw ERP, 118-ft. above ground, 3094-ft. above sea level, lat. 34° 51' 22", long. 117° 03' 00". BPTTL-20081009ANQ.

Began Operation: August 14, 2008.

Ownership: EICB-TV LLC.

Barstow—K28IE, Ch. 28, Jeff Chang. Phone: 310-403-5039.

Technical Facilities: 2.38-kw ERP, 15-ft. above ground, 4497-ft. above sea level, lat. 34° 36' 40", long. 117° 17' 22".

Ownership: Jeff Chang.

Barstow—K36JH, Ch. 36, David Primm. Phone: 831-402-7066.

Technical Facilities: 9.5-kw ERP, 131-ft. above ground, 4498-ft. above sea level, lat. 34° 36' 43.6", long. 117° 17' 28.9".

Began Operation: January 24, 2007.

Ownership: David Primm.

Barstow—KCIO-LP, Ch. 6, Obidia Porras. Phone: 760-956-2111.

Technical Facilities: 0.99-kw ERP, 92-ft. above ground, 4652-ft. above sea level, lat. 34° 40' 10", long. 116° 55' 50.5".

Holds CP for change to 0.499-kw ERP, 23-ft. above ground, 5630-ft. above sea level, lat. 34° 15' 19", long. 117° 21' 43". BPTVL-20090415ABR.

Ownership: Obidia Porras.

Benbow, etc.—K12JJ, Ch. 12, BlueStone License Holdings Inc. Phone: 212-247-8717.

Technical Facilities: 0.014-kw ERP, 3064-ft. above sea level, lat. 40° 06' 00", long. 123° 41' 06".

Ownership: Bonten Media Group LLC.

Bieber—K06GS, Ch. 6, California-Oregon Broadcasting Inc.

Technical Facilities: 0.01-kw ERP, lat. 41° 04' 20", long. 121° 13' 00".

Ownership: California-Oregon Broadcasting Inc.

Big Bear Lake—K20IU, Ch. 20, Iglesia Jesucristo Es Mi Refugio Inc. Phone: 972-467-9791.

Technical Facilities: 4-kw ERP, 144-ft. above ground, 6913-ft. above sea level, lat. 34° 14' 34", long. 116° 54' 42".

Ownership: Iglesia Jesucristo Es Mi Refugio Inc.

Big Bear Lake—KPCD-LP, Ch. 35, Word of God Fellowship Inc. Phone: 817-571-1229. Fax: 817-571-7478.

Technical Facilities: 0.25-kw ERP, 82-ft. above ground, 9025-ft. above sea level, lat. 34° 03' 46", long. 116° 53' 34".

Holds CP for change to 33-ft. above ground, 9058-ft. above sea level, lat. 34° 03' 46", long. 116° 53' 33". BPTTL-20080122AQF.

Ownership: Word of God Fellowship Inc.

Big Bear Lake—KSCD-LP, Ch. 38, Word of God Fellowship Inc. Phone: 817-571-1229.

Technical Facilities: 3-kw ERP, 49-ft. above ground, 7897-ft. above sea level, lat. 34° 11' 49", long. 117° 02' 57".

Ownership: Word of God Fellowship Inc.

Big Bear Lake Valley—K06MU, Ch. 6, Bear Valley Broadcasting Inc. Phones: 909-878-4886; 909-522-9063. Fax: 909-866-8452.

Technical Facilities: 10-w TPO, 1-kw ERP, 50-ft. above ground, 6883-ft. above sea level, lat. 34° 14' 24", long. 116° 54' 47".

Transmitter: 351 Maple Lane.

Ownership: Bear Valley Broadcasting Inc.

Big Bend, etc.—K04EZ, Ch. 4, BlueStone License Holdings Inc. Phone: 212-247-8717.

Technical Facilities: 0.003-kw ERP, 3100-ft. above sea level, lat. 41° 00' 50", long. 121° 57' 00".

Ownership: Bonten Media Group LLC.

Blue Lake—K36BT, Ch. 36, BlueStone License Holdings Inc. Phone: 212-247-8717.

Technical Facilities: 0.11-kw ERP, lat. 40° 53' 25", long. 123° 58' 53".

Ownership: Bonten Media Group LLC.

Personnel: Bob Wise, General Manager; Jeff Knott, Chief Engineer; Dennis Siewert, Sales Manager.

Blythe—K24FA, Ch. 24, Palo Verde Valley TV Club Inc.

Technical Facilities: 0.99-kw ERP, 30-ft. above ground, 3343-ft. above sea level, lat. 33° 34' 12", long. 114° 20' 56".

Ownership: Palo Verde Valley TV Club Inc.

Blythe—K26FS, Ch. 26, Palo Verde Valley TV Club Inc.

Technical Facilities: 0.99-kw ERP, 33° 34' 12", long. 114° 20' 56".

Ownership: Palo Verde Valley TV Club Inc.

Blythe—K29EC, Ch. 29, Palo Verde Valley TV Club Inc.

Technical Facilities: 0.99-kw ERP, 29-ft. above ground, 3343-ft. above sea level, lat. 33° 34' 12", long. 114° 20' 56".

Ownership: Palo Verde Valley TV Club Inc.

Blythe—K31FE, Ch. 31, Palo Verde Valley TV Club Inc.

Technical Facilities: 0.99-kw ERP, 33° 34' 12", long. 114° 20' 56".

Ownership: Palo Verde Valley TV Club Inc.

Blythe—K33FD, Ch. 33, Palo Verde Valley TV Club Inc.

Technical Facilities: 0.99-kw ERP, 33° 34' 12", long. 114° 20' 56".

Ownership: Palo Verde Valley TV Club Inc.

Boonville, etc.—K57CT, Ch. 57, Anderson Valley TV Inc.

Technical Facilities: 0.3-kw ERP, 3022-ft. above sea level, lat. 38° 58' 20", long. 123° 16' 00".

Ownership: Anderson Valley TV Inc.

Boonville, etc.—K59CH, Ch. 59, Anderson Valley TV Inc.

Technical Facilities: 0.3-kw ERP, 3022-ft. above sea level, lat. 38° 58' 20", long. 123° 16' 00".

Ownership: Anderson Valley TV Inc.

Boonville, etc.—K61CH, Ch. 61, Anderson Valley TV Inc.

Technical Facilities: 0.3-kw ERP, 3022-ft. above sea level, lat. 38° 58' 20", long. 123° 16' 00".

Ownership: Anderson Valley TV Inc.

Boonville, etc.—K63CE, Ch. 63, Anderson Valley TV Inc.

Technical Facilities: 0.3-kw ERP, 3022-ft. above sea level, lat. 38° 58' 20", long. 123° 16' 00".

Ownership: Anderson Valley TV Inc.

Boonville, etc.—K67CC, Ch. 67, Anderson Valley TV Inc.

Technical Facilities: 0.304-kw ERP, 3022-ft. above sea level, lat. 38° 58' 20", long. 123° 16' 00".

Ownership: Anderson Valley TV Inc.

Boonville, etc.—K69CU, Ch. 69, Anderson Valley TV Inc.

Technical Facilities: 1.52-kw ERP, 3022-ft. above sea level, lat. 38° 58' 20", long. 123° 16' 00".

Ownership: Anderson Valley TV Inc.

Bridgeport, etc.—K02JX, Ch. 2, Mono County Service Area No. 5.

Technical Facilities: 0.004-kw ERP, lat. 38° 11' 10", long. 119° 19' 10".

Ownership: Mono County Service Area No. 5.

Bridgeport, etc.—K07QM, Ch. 7, Mono County Service Area No. 5.

Technical Facilities: 0.064-kw ERP, lat. 38° 23' 19", long. 119° 21' 50".

Ownership: Mono County Service Area No. 5.

Bridgeport, etc.—K11HS, Ch. 11, Mono County Service Area No. 5.

Technical Facilities: 0.033-kw ERP, lat. 38° 23' 19", long. 119° 21' 50".

Ownership: Mono County Service Area No. 5.

Bridgeport, etc.—K13EX, Ch. 13, Mono County Service Area No. 5.

Technical Facilities: 0.011-kw ERP, lat. 38° 11' 10", long. 119° 19' 10".

Ownership: Mono County Service Area No. 5.

Burney, etc.—K05DQ, Ch. 5, BlueStone License Holdings Inc. Phone: 212-247-8717.

Technical Facilities: 0.017-kw ERP, 58-ft. above ground, 4442-ft. above sea level, lat. 41° 00' 13", long. 121° 28' 52".

Transmitter: Honey Mountain, 2.5-mi. W of Fall River Mills.

Ownership: Bonten Media Group LLC.

Burnt Ranch, etc.—K12JL, Ch. 12, Pollack/Belz Broadcasting Co. LLC.

Technical Facilities: 0.026-kw ERP, 5236-ft. above sea level, lat. 40° 50' 00", long. 123° 26' 50".

Ownership: Pollack/Belz Broadcasting Co. LLC.

Calexico—K36FO, Ch. 36, Broadcast Group Ltd. Phone: 915-577-0045.

Technical Facilities: 1000-w TPO, 76-kw ERP, 312-ft. above ground, 187-ft. above sea level, lat. 32° 57' 12", long. 115° 30' 08".

Ownership: Broadcast Group Ltd.

Caliente—KDBK-LP, Ch. 41, Venture Technologies Group LLC. Phone: 323-904-4090.

Technical Facilities: 65-kw ERP, 52-ft. above ground, 7536-ft. above sea level, lat. 35° 27' 14", long. 118° 35' 37".

Began Operation: March 6, 2009.

Ownership: Venture Technologies Group LLC.

Caliente—KJOI-LP, Ch. 12, Cocola Broadcasting Companies LLC. Phone: 559-435-7000.

Technical Facilities: 1-kw ERP, 49-ft. above ground, 3448-ft. above sea level, lat. 35° 26' 16", long. 118° 44' 28".

Ownership: Cocola Broadcasting Companies LLC.

Canby—K08OR-D, Ch. 8, Northern California Educational TV Assn. Inc. Phone: 530-243-5493.

Technical Facilities: 0.019-kw ERP, 39-ft. above ground, 4879-ft. above sea level, lat. 41° 26' 26.4", long. 120° 43' 53.8".

Ownership: Northern California Educational TV Assn. Inc.

■ **Cathedral City**—KPSP-LP, Ch. 58, Desert Television LLC. Phone: 760-343-5700.

Studio: 31276 Dunham Way, Thousand Palms, CA 92276.

Technical Facilities: 750-w TPO, 10.3-kw ERP, 13-ft. above ground, 1539-ft. above sea level, lat. 33° 51' 58", long. 116° 26' 05".

Transmitter: Edom Hill, 1.7-mi. NE of I-10 & Date Palm Rd.

Ownership: Desert Television LLC.

■ **Cathedral City**—KRET-CA, Ch. 45, Charles R. Meeker.

Technical Facilities: 970-w TPO, 20-kw ERP, 43-ft. above ground, 1568-ft. above sea level, lat. 33° 51' 58", long. 116° 26' 05".

Transmitter: Edom Hill, 1.7-mi. NE of I-10 & Date Palm Rd.

Ownership: Charles R. Meeker.

Cedarville—K51KJ, Ch. 51, Surprise Valley TV Club. Phone: 530-279-2577.

Technical Facilities: 0.575-kw ERP, 23-ft. above ground, 4947-ft. above sea level, lat. 41° 37' 45", long. 120° 03' 45".

Ownership: Surprise Valley TV Club.

Chalfant Valley—K55FD, Ch. 55, Mono County Service Area No. 2.

Technical Facilities: 0.413-kw ERP, lat. 37° 36' 18", long. 118° 20' 32".

Ownership: Mono County Service Area No. 2.

Chalfant Valley—K61EJ, Ch. 61, Mono County Service Area No. 2.

Technical Facilities: 0.4-kw ERP, lat. 37° 36' 18", long. 118° 20' 32".

Ownership: Mono County Service Area No. 2.

Chalfant Valley—K64CY, Ch. 64, Mono County Service Area No. 2.

Technical Facilities: 0.394-kw ERP, lat. 37° 36' 18", long. 118° 20' 32".

Ownership: Mono County Service Area No. 2.

Cherry Village—KILA-LP, Ch. 51, Venture Technologies Group LLC. Phone: 323-904-4090.

Technical Facilities: 1.2-kw ERP, 72-ft. above ground, 7992-ft. above sea level, lat. 34° 02' 17", long. 116° 48' 47".

Holds CP for change to 0.01-kw ERP, BPTTL-20080228ACJ.

Ownership: Venture Technologies Group LLC.

Chico—K02OA, Ch. 2, Family Stations Inc. Phone: 916-641-8191.

Technical Facilities: 3-kw ERP, 142-ft. above ground, 3623-ft. above sea level, lat. 39° 57' 26.9", long. 121° 42' 47.4".

Ownership: Family Stations Inc.

Chico—K11VZ-D, Ch. 11, Family Stations Inc. Phone: 916-641-8191.

Technical Facilities: 0.3-kw ERP, 141-ft. above ground, 3635-ft. above sea level, lat. 39° 57' 29", long. 121° 42' 49".

Ownership: Family Stations Inc.

Chico—K15HV-D, Ch. 15, Three Angels Broadcasting Network Inc. Phone: 618-627-4651.

Technical Facilities: 1.04-kw ERP, 161-ft. above ground, 3655-ft. above sea level, lat. 39° 57' 29", long. 121° 42' 49".

Ownership: Three Angels Broadcasting Network Inc.

Chico—K19FY, Ch. 19, Mutual Television Network. Phone: 888-482-1080.

Studio: Media Way, Paradise, CA 95967.

Technical Facilities: 20.5-kw ERP, 269-ft. above ground, 3809-ft. above sea level, lat. 39° 57' 45", long. 121° 42' 40".

Ownership: Mutual Television Network.

Personnel: Ron Warkentin, General Manager.

Chico—K48KB, Ch. 48, Andrew Fara. Phone: 415-971-9880.

Technical Facilities: 40-kw ERP, 164-ft. above ground, 334-ft. above sea level, lat. 39° 44' 41", long. 122° 03' 22".

Began Operation: April 6, 2009.

Ownership: Andrew Fara.

Chico—KBIT-LD, Ch. 51, Paul Strieby & Matt Tuter. Phone: 510-352-3110.

Technical Facilities: 15-kw ERP, 120-ft. above ground, 3601-ft. above sea level, lat. 39° 57' 26.9", long. 121° 42' 47.4".

Holds CP for change to 35-kw ERP, lat. 39° 57' 26.5", long. 121° 42' 51.3". BPTTL-20080102ABE.

Ownership: Matt Tuter; Paul Strieby.

Chico—KEFM-LP, Ch. 6, Venture Technologies Group LLC. Phone: 323-904-4090.

Technical Facilities: 0.5-kw ERP, 125-ft. above ground, 3350-ft. above sea level, lat. 39° 48' 42", long. 121° 33' 30".

Holds CP for change to 246-ft. above ground, 1321-ft. above sea level, lat. 39° 43' 37.4", long. 121° 40' 45.1". BMPTVL-20070111ACP.

Ownership: Venture Technologies Group LLC.

■ **Chico**—KKPM-CA, Ch. 28, Family Stations Inc. Phone: 916-641-8191.

Technical Facilities: 129-kw ERP, 200-ft. above ground, 2296-ft. above sea level, lat. 39° 12' 20.4", long. 121° 49' 06.1".

Holds CP for change to 11.5-kw ERP, lat. 39° 12' 20.4", long. 121° 49' 10.1". BDFCDTA-20081031ABI.

Multichannel TV Sound: Stereo and separate audio program.

Began Operation: December 31, 1998.

Ownership: Family Stations Inc.

Personnel: Matt Tuter, General Manager; Paul Strieby, Chief Engineer.

Chico—KKTF-LP, Ch. 35, Sainte Partners II LP. Phone: 209-523-0777.

Technical Facilities: 42.2-kw ERP, 374-ft. above ground, 3953-ft. above sea level, lat. 39° 57' 49", long. 121° 42' 38".

Holds CP for change to channel number 30, 15-kw ERP, 377-ft. above ground, 3917-ft. above sea level, lat. 39° 57' 45", long. 121° 42' 40". BDISDTL-20070423AAZ.

Ownership: Sainte Partners II LP.

Chico—KMSX-LD, Ch. 29, Randall A. Weiss. Phone: 972-291-3750.

Technical Facilities: 10-kw ERP, 20-ft. above ground, 3012-ft. above sea level, lat. 39° 39' 04", long. 121° 27' 43".

Ownership: Randall A. Weiss.

Chico—KSGO-LP, Ch. 59, Venture Technologies Group LLC. Phone: 323-904-4090.

Technical Facilities: 0.5-kw ERP, 239-ft. above ground, 1314-ft. above sea level, lat. 39° 43' 37.4", long. 121° 40' 45.1".

Ownership: Venture Technologies Group LLC.

Chico—KUCO-LP, Ch. 27, Sainte Partners II LP. Phone: 530-893-1234. Fax: 530-893-1266.

Technical Facilities: 67-kw ERP, 197-ft. above ground, 3737-ft. above sea level, lat. 39° 57' 45", long. 121° 42' 40".

Holds CP for change to 15-kw ERP, BDFCDTL-20060329AEM.

Ownership: Sainte Partners II LP.

Personnel: Doug Holroyd, General Manager & General Sales Manager; Bert Westhoff, National Sales Manager; Ken Rice, Chief Engineer; Patti Bittrolff, Business Manager & Research Director; Kelly Brown, Promotion & Creative Services Director; George Robinette, Production Director; Paula Murphy, Traffic & Office Manager.

Chico—KXVU-LP, Ch. 17, Sainte Partners II LP. Phone: 209-523-0777.

Technical Facilities: 40-kw ERP, 197-ft. above ground, 3776-ft. above sea level, lat. 39° 57' 49", long. 121° 42' 38".

Holds CP for change to 10-kw ERP, BDFCDTT-20060329AEC.

Ownership: Sainte Partners II LP.

Chico—KZVU-LP, Ch. 22, Sainte Partners II LP. Phone: 209-523-0777.

Studio: 300 Main St, Chico, CA 95928.

Technical Facilities: 3000-w TPO, 60-kw ERP, 157-ft. above ground, 3697-ft. above sea level, lat. 39° 57' 45", long. 121° 42' 44".

Holds CP for change to 6-kw ERP, lat. 39° 57' 45", long. 121° 42' 40". BDFCDTL-20060329AET.

Transmitter: Cohasset Ridge, 20-mi. NE of Chico.

Ownership: Sainte Partners II LP.

Personnel: John Stall, General Manager & Sales Manager; Alan Tompkins, Chief Engineer.

China Lake, etc.—K14AT, Ch. 14, Indian Wells Valley TV Booster Inc. Phone: 760-375-0233.

Technical Facilities: 20-w TPO, 0.55-kw ERP, 20-ft. above ground, 2940-ft. above sea level, lat. 35° 39' 44", long. 117° 36' 12".

Transmitter: Lone Butte transmitter site, 1-mi. E of China Lake golf course.

Ownership: Indian Wells Valley TV Booster Inc.

Personnel: Edward R. Middlemiss, President.

Clarks Crossing—KDAS-LP, Ch. 48, Word of God Fellowship Inc. Phone: 817-571-1229.

Technical Facilities: 40-kw ERP, 49-ft. above ground, 1611-ft. above sea level, lat. 38° 32' 21", long. 122° 57' 36".

Ownership: Word of God Fellowship Inc.

Coalinga—KJKZ-LP, Ch. 27, Cocola Broadcasting Companies LLC. Phone: 559-435-7000. Fax: 559-435-3201.

Technical Facilities: 150-kw ERP, 79-ft. above ground, 3458-ft. above sea level, lat. 36° 44' 45", long. 119° 16' 57".

Ownership: Cocola Broadcasting Companies LLC.

Personnel: Todd Lopes, President.

Crescent City—K09VQ, Ch. 9, Redwood Empire Public Television Inc. Phone: 707-445-0813.

Technical Facilities: 0.039-kw ERP, lat. 41° 50' 36", long. 124° 07' 55".

Transmitter: E of Kings Valley Rd., approx. 1.6-mi. SSE of Fort Dick.

Ownership: Redwood Empire Public TV Inc.

Crescent City—K39EO, Ch. 39, Three Angels Broadcasting Network Inc. Phone: 618-627-4651. Fax: 618-627-4155.

Studio: 3391 Charley Good Rd, West Frankfort, IL 62896.

Technical Facilities: 1000-w TPO, 30.2-kw ERP, 105-ft. above ground, 840-ft. above sea level, lat. 41° 50' 36", long. 124° 07' 55".

Transmitter: 5295 Kings Valley Rd., 6.5-mi. NNE of Crescent City.

Ownership: Three Angels Broadcasting Network Inc.

Personnel: Moses Primo, Chief Engineer.

Crescent City—K44JF-D, Ch. 44, Redwood Empire Public TV Inc. Phone: 707-445-0813.

Technical Facilities: 12-kw ERP, 110-ft. above ground, 1020-ft. above sea level, lat. 41° 58' 11", long. 124° 11' 17".

Ownership: Redwood Empire Public TV Inc.

Crescent City, etc.—K34KJ, Ch. 34, California-Oregon Broadcasting Inc. Phone: 541-779-5555. Fax: 541-779-1151.

Technical Facilities: 9.15-kw ERP, 140-ft. above ground, 1093-ft. above sea level, lat. 41° 58' 10", long. 124° 11' 15".

Began Operation: December 9, 1994.

Ownership: California-Oregon Broadcasting Inc.

Personnel: Patsy Smullin, President; John Larkin, General Manager; Steve Aase, Chief Engineer.

Crowley Lake & Long Valley—K15DP, Ch. 15, Mono County Service Area No. 1. Phone: 760-934-6299.

Technical Facilities: 10-w TPO, 0.122-kw ERP, 26-ft. above ground, 8999-ft. above sea level, lat. 37° 42' 45", long. 118° 39' 27".

Transmitter: Near the intersection of the west boundary of the SE quarter of Section 3.

Ownership: Mono County Service Area No. 1.

Crowley Lake & Long Valley—K17DF, Ch. 17, Mono County Service Area No. 1. Phone: 760-934-6299.

Technical Facilities: 10-w TPO, 0.136-kw ERP, 33-ft. above ground, 8005-ft. above sea level, lat. 37° 35' 51", long. 118° 48' 34".

Transmitter: Mount Morrison, ESE of Mammoth Lakes.

Ownership: Mono County Service Area No. 1.

Crowley Lake & Long Valley—K19DI, Ch. 19, Mono County Service Area No. 1. Phone: 760-934-6299.

Technical Facilities: 10-w TPO, 0.136-kw ERP, 33-ft. above ground, 8005-ft. above sea level, lat. 37° 35' 51", long. 118° 48' 34".

Transmitter: Mount Morrison, ESE of Mammoth Lakes.

Ownership: Mono County Service Area No. 1.

Crowley Lake & Long Valley—K25EB, Ch. 25, Mono County Service Area No. 1. Phone: 760-934-6299.

Technical Facilities: 10-w TPO, 0.136-kw ERP, 43-ft. above ground, 9006-ft. above sea level, lat. 37° 42' 45", long. 118° 39' 27".

Transmitter: Rural area near Long Valley.

Ownership: Mono County Service Area No. 1.

Crowley Lake & Long Valley—K27DV, Ch. 27, Mono County Service Area No. 1. Phone: 760-934-6299.

Technical Facilities: 10-w TPO, 0.136-kw ERP, 43-ft. above ground, 9006-ft. above sea level, lat. 37° 42' 45", long. 118° 39' 27".

Transmitter: Rural area near Long Valley.

Ownership: Mono County Service Area No. 1.

Crowley Lake & Long Valley—K58BN, Ch. 58, Mono County Service Area No. 1.

Technical Facilities: 0.135-kw ERP, 30-ft. above ground, 9002-ft. above sea level, lat. 37° 42' 45", long. 118° 39' 27".

Ownership: Mono County Service Area No. 1.

Daggett—K15BZ, Ch. 15, County of San Bernardino, Area 40. Phone: 760-367-1833.

Technical Facilities: 0.91-kw ERP, lat. 34° 53' 07", long. 116° 53' 45".

Ownership: San Bernardino County.

Daggett—K19BS, Ch. 19, County of San Bernardino, Area 40. Phone: 760-367-1833.

Technical Facilities: 0.9-kw ERP, lat. 34° 53' 07", long. 116° 53' 45".

Ownership: San Bernardino County.

Daggett—K23BP, Ch. 23, County of San Bernardino, Area 40. Phone: 760-367-1833.

Technical Facilities: 1.12-kw ERP, 174-ft. above ground, 2864-ft. above sea level, lat. 34° 53' 07", long. 116° 53' 45".

Ownership: San Bernardino County.

Daggett—K35BQ, Ch. 35, County of San Bernardino, Area 40. Phone: 760-367-1833.

Technical Facilities: 1.07-kw ERP, lat. 34° 53' 07", long. 116° 53' 45".

Ownership: San Bernardino County.

Daggett—K39DW, Ch. 39, County of San Bernardino, Area 40. Phone: 760-367-1833.

Technical Facilities: 0.92-kw ERP, lat. 34° 53' 07", long. 116° 53' 45".

Transmitter: Elephant Mountain, approx. 1.7-mi. NNW of Daggett.

Ownership: San Bernardino County.

Daggett—K41CY, Ch. 41, County of San Bernardino, Area 40. Phone: 760-367-1833.

Technical Facilities: 1.15-kw ERP, 144-ft. above ground, 2835-ft. above sea level, lat. 34° 53' 07", long. 116° 53' 45".

Ownership: San Bernardino County.

Daggett—K48IP, Ch. 48, County of San Bernardino, Area 40. Phone: 760-367-1833.

Technical Facilities: 1.07-kw ERP, 192-ft. above ground, 2881-ft. above sea level, lat. 34° 53' 07", long. 116° 53' 45".

Ownership: San Bernardino County.

Daggett—K50HV, Ch. 50, County of San Bernardino, Area 40. Phone: 760-367-1833.

Technical Facilities: 0.852-kw ERP, 202-ft. above ground, 2890-ft. above sea level, lat. 34° 53' 07", long. 116° 53' 45".

Ownership: San Bernardino County.

Daggett—KTSK-LP, Ch. 17, County of San Bernardino, Area 40. Phone: 760-367-1833.

Studio: 610 E. Main St, Barstow, CA 92311.

Technical Facilities: 1000-w TPO, 9.02-kw ERP, 174-ft. above ground, 2864-ft. above sea level, lat. 34° 53' 07", long. 116° 53' 45".

Transmitter: Elephant Mountain, 1.7-mi. NNW of Daggett.

Ownership: San Bernardino County.

Daggett, etc.—K46HT, Ch. 46, County of San Bernardino, Area 40. Phone: 760-367-1833.

Technical Facilities: 0.915-kw ERP, 146-ft. above ground, 2834-ft. above sea level, lat. 34° 53' 07", long. 116° 53' 45".

Transmitter: Elephant Mountain, 7.9-mi. NNW of Daggett.

Ownership: San Bernardino County.

Dunsmuir, etc.—K02CN, Ch. 2, Freedom Broadcasting of Oregon Licensee LLC. Phone: 518-346-6666.

Technical Facilities: 0.04-kw ERP, 4839-ft. above sea level, lat. 41° 13' 30", long. 122° 18' 00".

Ownership: Freedom Communications Holdings Inc.

Dunsmuir, etc.—K05BR, Ch. 5, BlueStone License Holdings Inc. Phone: 212-247-8717.

Technical Facilities: 0.04-kw ERP, 4865-ft. above sea level, lat. 41° 13' 30", long. 122° 18' 00".

Ownership: Bonten Media Group LLC.

Eagleville—K13IU, Ch. 13, Surprise Valley Unified School District. Phone: 530-279-6141. Fax: 530-279-2210.

Technical Facilities: 0.089-kw ERP, 16-ft. above ground, 4924-ft. above sea level, lat. 41° 38' 13", long. 120° 05' 29".

Ownership: Surprise Valley Joint Unified School District.

East Weed—K33DI, Ch. 33, BlueStone License Holdings Inc. Phone: 212-247-8717.

Technical Facilities: 0.354-kw ERP, 23-ft. above ground, 3724-ft. above sea level, lat. 41° 25' 01", long. 122° 23' 34".

Ownership: Bonten Media Group LLC.

El Centro-Holtville—KHFS-LP, Ch. 56, Inspiration Television Inc.

Technical Facilities: 8.15-kw ERP, lat. 32° 47' 10", long. 115° 29' 53".

Transmitter: 2098 Hwy. 111, Holtville.

Began Operation: November 12, 1999.

Ownership: Inspiration Television Inc.

Etna—K03HX-D, Ch. 3, Northern California Educational TV Assn. Inc. Phone: 530-243-5493.

Technical Facilities: 0.0017-kw ERP, 22-ft. above ground, 5353-ft. above sea level, lat. 41° 28' 00", long. 122° 55' 40".

Ownership: Northern California Educational TV Assn. Inc.

Eureka—K27FX, Ch. 27, MS Communications LLC. Phone: 414-765-9737.

Technical Facilities: 130-w TPO, 1-kw ERP, 2497-ft. above sea level, lat. 40° 29' 52", long. 124° 17' 36".

Transmitter: 0.25-mi. S of Oil Creek.

Ownership: MS Communications LLC.

Eureka—K41FD, Ch. 41, MS Communications LLC. Phone: 414-765-9737.

Technical Facilities: 130-w TPO, 0.007-kw ERP, 33-ft. above ground, 2402-ft. above sea level, lat. 40° 29' 52", long. 124° 17' 36".

Transmitter: 0.25-mi. S of Oil Creek.

Ownership: MS Communications LLC.

Eureka—K48GP, Ch. 48, MS Communications LLC. Phone: 414-765-9737.

Technical Facilities: 130-w TPO, 0.007-kw ERP, 33-ft. above ground, 2497-ft. above sea level, lat. 40° 29' 52", long. 124° 17' 36".

Transmitter: 2.5-mi. S of Oil Creek.

Ownership: MS Communications LLC.

Eureka—K50EQ, Ch. 50, MS Communications LLC. Phone: 414-765-9737.

Technical Facilities: 130-w TPO, 0.007-kw ERP, 33-ft. above ground, 2402-ft. above sea level, lat. 40° 29' 52", long. 124° 17' 36".

Transmitter: 0.25-mi. S of Oil Creek.

Ownership: MS Communications LLC.

Eureka—K52FK, Ch. 52, Sainte Partners II LP. Phone: 209-523-0777.

Technical Facilities: 130-w TPO, 1-kw ERP, 33-ft. above ground, 2402-ft. above sea level, lat. 40° 29' 52", long. 124° 17' 36".

Transmitter: 0.25-mi. S of Oil Creek.

Ownership: Sainte Partners II LP.

Eureka—K57HB, Ch. 57, MS Communications LLC. Phone: 414-765-9737.

Technical Facilities: 130-w TPO, 0.007-kw ERP, 33-ft. above ground, 2497-ft. above sea level, lat. 40° 29' 51", long. 125° 17' 36".

Transmitter: 0.25-mi. S of Oil Creek.

Ownership: MS Communications LLC.

Eureka—K59FW, Ch. 59, Sainte Partners II LP. Phone: 209-523-0777.

Technical Facilities: 130-w TPO, 0.007-kw ERP, 33-ft. above ground, 2497-ft. above sea level, lat. 40° 29' 51", long. 124° 17' 36".

Transmitter: 0.25-mi. S of Oil Creek.

Ownership: Sainte Partners II LP.

Eureka—K63GK, Ch. 63, MS Communications LLC. Phone: 414-765-9737.

Technical Facilities: 130-w TPO, 0.007-kw ERP, 33-ft. above ground, 2497-ft. above sea level, lat. 40° 29' 51", long. 124° 17' 36".

Transmitter: 0.25-mi. S of Oil Creek.

Ownership: MS Communications LLC.

Eureka—K67GU, Ch. 67, Sainte Partners II LP. Phone: 209-523-0777.

Technical Facilities: 130-w TPO, 0.007-kw ERP, 33-ft. above ground, 2497-ft. above sea level, lat. 40° 29' 51", long. 124° 17' 36".

Holds CP for change to channel number 29, 63.2-kw ERP, 157-ft. above ground, 1913-ft. above sea level, lat. 40° 49' 32", long. 124° 00' 05". BDISTTL-20081118AEI.

Transmitter: 0.25-mi. S of Oil Creek.

Began Operation: November 30, 2000.

Ownership: Sainte Partners II LP.

Eureka—K68GT, Ch. 68, EICB-TV West LLC. Phone: 972-291-3750.

Technical Facilities: 11.22-kw ERP, 230-ft. above ground, 233-ft. above sea level, lat. 40° 48' 01", long. 124° 07' 46".

Ownership: EICB-TV LLC.

Eureka—K69IE, Ch. 69, Patrick Mbaba. Phones: 661-327-4193; 661-979-5231. Fax: 661-215-6436.

Technical Facilities: 1004-w TPO, 0.007-kw ERP, 33-ft. above ground, 2402-ft. above sea level, lat. 40° 29' 52", long. 124° 17' 36".

Holds CP for change to channel number 43, 3.79-kw ERP, 210-ft. above ground, 2860-ft. above sea level, lat. 40° 43'38.8", long. 123° 58' 16.9". BMPDTL-20081031AAM.

Transmitter: 0.25-mi. S of Oil Creek.

Ownership: Patrick Mbaba.

Personnel: D. Erickson, Consulting Engineer; A. Tapia, Customer Service; A. Mbaba, News Anchor; D. Arnson, Marketing Consultant; L. McClairen, Religious Program Director.

Eureka—KBVQ-LP, Ch. 35, TV Americas of Eureka LLC. Phone: 559-733-7800.

Technical Facilities: 50-kw ERP, 283-ft. above ground, 2955-ft. above sea level, lat. 40° 43' 36", long. 123° 58' 18".

Holds CP for change to 15-kw ERP, 283-ft. above ground, 2933-ft. above sea level, lat. 40° 43' 39", long. 123° 58' 17". BDFCDTL-20060330AFR.

Ownership: Pappas Telecasting Companies.

Eureka—KEMY-LP, Ch. 33, Sainte Partners II LP. Phone: 209-523-0777.

Technical Facilities: 21.9-kw ERP, 194-ft. above ground, 2832-ft. above sea level, lat. 40° 43' 36", long. 123° 58' 27".

Ownership: Sainte Partners II LP.

Eureka—KEUV-LP, Ch. 31, Sainte Partners II LP. Phone: 209-523-0777. Fax: 310-552-7970.

Technical Facilities: 21.9-kw ERP, 194-ft. above ground, 2831-ft. above sea level, lat. 40° 43' 36", long. 123° 58' 27".

Holds CP for change to 4-kw ERP, BDFCDTL-20060403AKS.

Ownership: Sainte Partners II LP.

Eureka—KUVU-LP, Ch. 9, Sainte Partners II LP. Phone: 209-523-0777.

Technical Facilities: 3-kw ERP, 154-ft. above ground, 2792-ft. above sea level, lat. 40° 43' 36", long. 123° 58' 27".

Holds CP for change to 0.3-kw ERP, BDFCDVL-20070220ABE.

Ownership: Sainte Partners II LP.

Fall River Mills—K28DB-D, Ch. 28, Northern California Educational TV Assn. Inc. Phone: 530-243-5493.

Technical Facilities: 0.066-kw ERP, 20-ft. above ground, 4432-ft. above sea level, lat. 41° 00' 13", long. 121° 28' 52".

Ownership: Northern California Educational TV Assn. Inc.

Fall River Mills, etc.—K11JM, Ch. 11, California Oregon Broadcasting Inc. Phone: 541-779-5555.

Technical Facilities: 0.3-kw ERP, 49-ft. above ground, 4462-ft. above sea level, lat. 41° 00' 12", long. 121° 28' 54".

Ownership: California-Oregon Broadcasting Inc.

Ford City—KSSY-LP, Ch. 20, Iglesia Jesucristo Es Mi Refugio Inc. Phone: 214-330-8700.

Technical Facilities: 100-kw ERP, 66-ft. above ground, 4616-ft. above sea level, lat. 34° 55' 12", long. 119° 24' 15".

Began Operation: December 6, 1989.

Ownership: Iglesia Jesucristo Es Mi Refugio Inc.

Personnel: Cherie Erwin, General Manager; Marty Scala, Chief Engineer.

Fort Bidwell—K04GB, Ch. 4, Surprise Valley TV Club. Phone: 530-279-2577.

Technical Facilities: 0.087-kw ERP, lat. 41° 33' 06", long. 119° 56' 03".

Ownership: Surprise Valley TV Club.

Fort Dick—K36HM, Ch. 36, Soda Mountain Broadcasting Inc. Phone: 541-485-5611.

Technical Facilities: 2.4-kw ERP, 39-ft. above ground, 1795-ft. above sea level, lat. 42° 07' 23", long. 124° 17' 56".

Ownership: Soda Mountain Broadcasting Inc.

Fort Jones, etc.—K04EQ, Ch. 4, BlueStone License Holdings Inc. Phone: 212-247-8717.

Technical Facilities: 0.02-kw ERP, lat. 41° 28' 00", long. 122° 55' 40".

Ownership: Bonten Media Group LLC.

Fort Jones, etc.—K06KA, Ch. 6, Freedom Broadcasting of Oregon Licensee LLC. Phone: 518-346-6666.

Technical Facilities: 0.02-kw ERP, lat. 41° 28' 00", long. 122° 55' 40".

Ownership: Freedom Communications Holdings Inc.

Fort Jones, etc.—K13HU, Ch. 13, California-Oregon Broadcasting Inc.

Technical Facilities: 0.022-kw ERP, lat. 41° 28' 00", long. 122° 55' 40".

Ownership: California-Oregon Broadcasting Inc.

Fortuna—K14MN, Ch. 14, Sainte Partners II LP. Phone: 209-523-0777.

Technical Facilities: 22-kw ERP, 72-ft. above ground, 3071-ft. above sea level, lat. 40° 25' 23", long. 124° 06' 21".

Ownership: Sainte Partners II LP.

Fortuna/Rio Dell—K20CN, Ch. 20, BlueStone License Holdings Inc. Phone: 212-247-8717.

Technical Facilities: 1000-w TPO, 8.07-kw ERP, 171-ft. above ground, 3251-ft. above sea level, lat. 40° 25' 12", long. 124° 05' 00".

Transmitter: Monument Ridge, 5.5-mi. S of Rio Dell.

Ownership: Bonten Media Group LLC.

Personnel: Bob Wise, General Manager; Jeff Knott, Chief Engineer; Dennis Siewert, Sales Manager.

Freshwater, etc.—K45DS, Ch. 45, BlueStone License Holdings Inc. Phone: 212-247-8717.

Technical Facilities: 0.603-kw ERP, 259-ft. above ground, 266-ft. above sea level, lat. 40° 48' 09", long. 124° 08' 20".

Ownership: Bonten Media Group LLC.

Fresno—K03HK, Ch. 3, Three Angels Broadcasting Network Inc. Phone: 618-627-4651.

Technical Facilities: 0.9-kw ERP, 72-ft. above ground, 1670-ft. above sea level, lat. 36° 55' 49", long. 119° 38' 28".

Ownership: Three Angels Broadcasting Network Inc.

■ **Fresno**—K12OZ, Ch. 12, Three Angels Broadcasting Network Inc. Phone: 618-627-2726. Fax: 618-627-4155.

Studio: 3391 Charley Good Rd, West Frankfort, IL 62896.

Technical Facilities: 10-w TPO, 0.263-kw ERP, 69-ft. above ground, 1670-ft. above sea level, lat. 36° 55' 49", long. 119° 38' 28".

Transmitter: Owens Mountain.

Ownership: Three Angels Broadcasting Network Inc.

Personnel: Moses Primo, Chief Engineer.

Fresno—K15EK, Ch. 15, Family Stations Inc.

Technical Facilities: 0.32-kw ERP, 167-ft. above ground, 4337-ft. above sea level, lat. 37° 32' 01", long. 120° 01' 50".

Ownership: Family Stations Inc.

Fresno—K15ET, Ch. 15, Family Stations Inc. Phone: 916-641-8191.

Technical Facilities: 167-ft. above ground, 4337-ft. above sea level, lat. 37° 32' 01", long. 120° 01' 50".

Holds CP for change to channel number 11, 3-kw ERP, 214-ft. above ground, 4383-ft. above sea level, BDISTVL-20060928AHX.

Ownership: Family Stations Inc.

Fresno—K56DZ, Ch. 56, Trinity Christian Center of Santa Ana Inc. Phones: 714-832-2950; 949-552-0490.

Technical Facilities: 1000-w TPO, 41-kw ERP, 98-ft. above ground, 1700-ft. above sea level, lat. 36° 55' 49", long. 119° 38' 28".

Holds CP for change to channel number 46, 2-kw ERP, 98-ft. above ground, 1699-ft. above sea level, BDISDTT-20080228ABP.

Transmitter: Owens Mountain, 2.17-mi. ESE of Auberry Rd. at Friant Kern Canal.

Ownership: Trinity Broadcasting Network Inc.

Personnel: Jane P. Duff, Manager; Mark Fountain, Chief Engineer.

Fresno—KBID-LP, Ch. 31, Cocola Broadcasting Companies LLC. Phone: 559-435-7000. Fax: 559-435-3201.

Studio: 706 W Herndon Ave, Fresno, CA 93650.

Technical Facilities: 150-kw ERP, 92-ft. above ground, 4573-ft. above sea level, lat. 37° 04' 25", long. 119° 25' 52".

Ownership: Cocola Broadcasting Companies LLC.

Personnel: Todd Lopes, President.

Fresno—KHSC-LP, Ch. 16, Cocola Broadcasting Companies LLC. Phone: 559-435-7000. Fax: 559-435-3201.

Technical Facilities: 150-kw ERP, 89-ft. above ground, 3468-ft. above sea level, lat. 36° 44' 45", long. 119° 16' 57".

Ownership: Cocola Broadcasting Companies LLC.

Fresno—KJEO-LP, Ch. 32, Cocola Broadcasting Companies LLC. Phone: 559-435-7000. Fax: 559-435-3201.

Studio: 706 W Herndon Ave, Fresno, CA 93650.

Technical Facilities: 150-kw ERP, 92-ft. above ground, 4573-ft. above sea level, lat. 37° 04' 26", long. 119° 25' 52".

Holds CP for change to 15-kw ERP, BDFCDTL-20090420ABO.

Ownership: Cocola Broadcasting Companies LLC.

Personnel: Todd Lopes, President.

Fresno—KMSG-LP, Ch. 39, Cocola Broadcasting Companies LLC. Phone: 559-435-7000. Fax: 559-435-3201.

Technical Facilities: 50-kw ERP, 37-ft. above ground, 3397-ft. above sea level, lat. 36° 44' 46", long. 119° 16' 57".

Ownership: Cocola Broadcasting Companies LLC.

Personnel: Todd Lopes, President.

Fresno—KSDI-LP, Ch. 34, Cocola Broadcasting Companies LLC. Phone: 559-435-7000. Fax: 559-435-3201.

Studio: 706 W Herndon Ave, Fresno, CA 93650.

Technical Facilities: 2000-w TPO, 21.1-kw ERP, 56-ft. above ground, 3455-ft. above sea level, lat. 36° 44' 45", long. 119° 16' 57".

Transmitter: Bear Mountain communications site.

Multichannel TV Sound: Stereo and separate audio program.

Ownership: Cocola Broadcasting Companies LLC.

Personnel: Todd Lopes, President.

■ **Fresno**—KTFF-LP, Ch. 41, Telefutura Fresno LLC. Phone: 310-348-3600.

Technical Facilities: 150-kw ERP, 141-ft. above ground, 4632-ft. above sea level, lat. 37° 04' 22", long. 119° 25' 51".

Holds CP for change to 15-kw ERP, BDFCDTL-20080801BCN.

Ownership: Univision Communications Inc.

Personnel: Todd Lopes, General Manager; Steve LeBel, Chief Engineer; Jack Cook, Sales Manager.

Fresno—KVHF-LP, Ch. 4, Cocola Broadcasting Companies LLC. Phone: 559-435-7000. Fax: 559-435-3201.

Studio: 706 W Herndon Ave, Fresno, CA 93650.

Technical Facilities: 100-w TPO, 3-kw ERP, 43-ft. above ground, 3422-ft. above sea level, lat. 36° 44' 45", long. 119° 16' 57".

Holds CP for change to channel number 42, 15-kw ERP, 120-ft. above ground, 4601-ft. above sea level, lat. 37° 04' 26", long. 119° 25' 52". BDISDTL-20090108AOE.

Transmitter: Bear Mountain communications site.

Began Operation: September 22, 1988.

Ownership: Cocola Broadcasting Companies LLC.

Personnel: Todd Lopes, President.

■ **Fresno**—KZMM-CA, Ch. 22, Caballero Acquisition Inc. Phone: 202-429-8970.

Technical Facilities: 150-kw ERP, 98-ft. above ground, 4544-ft. above sea level, lat. 37° 04' 19", long. 119° 25' 49".

Holds CP for change to 15-kw ERP, BDFCDTA-20080804ACS.

Ownership: Caballero Acquisition Inc.

Personnel: Eduardo Caballero, Chief Executive Officer.

Garberville—K10HX, Ch. 10, Raul Broadcasting Co. of Eureka Inc. Phone: 209-521-5702.

Technical Facilities: 0.01-kw ERP, lat. 40° 06' 12", long. 123° 49' 08".

Holds CP for change to 0.015-kw ERP, 10-ft. above ground, 3852-ft. above sea level, lat. 40° 07' 09", long. 123° 41' 30". BPTTV-20090108ADR.

Ownership: Raul & Consuelo Palazuelos.

Garberville, etc.—K04NX, Ch. 4, Pollack/Belz Broadcasting Co. LLC.

Technical Facilities: 0.01-kw ERP, lat. 40° 06' 06", long. 123° 48' 40".

Ownership: Pollack/Belz Broadcasting Co. LLC.

Gonzalez—KOTR-LP, Ch. 2, Mirage Media 2 LLC. Phone: 909-793-2233.

Technical Facilities: 3-kw ERP, 79-ft. above ground, 3474-ft. above sea level, lat. 36° 32' 06", long. 121° 37' 09".

Ownership: Mirage Media LLC.

Grass Valley—K16CX, Ch. 16, Sierra Joint Junior College District. Phone: 916-781-0563. Fax: 916-781-0455.

Studio: Sierra College, 5000 Rocklin Rd., Rocklin, CA 95677.

Technical Facilities: 1000-w TPO, 12-kw ERP, 171-ft. above ground, 2769-ft. above sea level, lat. 39° 08' 02", long. 121° 05' 59".

Transmitter: Wolf Mountain communications site, 5.6-mi. SSW of Grass Valley.

Ownership: Sierra Joint Community College District.

Green Point, etc.—K05EQ, Ch. 5, BlueStone License Holdings Inc. Phone: 212-247-8717.

Technical Facilities: 0.03-kw ERP, lat. 40° 52' 20", long. 123° 44' 08".

Ownership: Bonten Media Group LLC.

Greenfield—KSCZ-LP, Ch. 42, Venture Technologies Group LLC. Phone: 323-904-4090.

Technical Facilities: 1.9-kw ERP, lat. 36° 18' 19", long. 120° 24' 09".

Transmitter: Black Mountain.

Ownership: Venture Technologies Group LLC.

■ **Hanford**—KHMM-CA, Ch. 14, Caballero Television Texas LLC. Phones: 972-503-6800; 800-99-MUSIC.

Studio: 3310 Keller Springs Rd., Carrollton, TX 75006.

Technical Facilities: 2-kw ERP, 59-ft. above ground, 4541-ft. above sea level, lat. 37° 04' 10", long. 119° 24' 40".

Holds CP for change to 0.5-kw ERP, 79-ft. above ground, 4524-ft. above sea level, lat. 37° 04' 19", long. 119° 25' 49". BPTTA-20071102ATG.

Transmitter: 12592 S. Cedar Ave., Fresno.

Ownership: Caballero Television LLC.

Personnel: Rosamaria Caballero, President.

Happy Camp—K07IX, Ch. 7, Slater Butte Translator Co.

Technical Facilities: 0.056-kw ERP, lat. 41° 51' 30", long. 123° 21' 13".

Ownership: Slater Butte Translator Co.

Happy Camp, etc.—K09PI, Ch. 9, Slater Butte Translator Co.

Technical Facilities: 0.023-kw ERP, 4649-ft. above sea level, lat. 41° 51' 30", long. 123° 21' 13".

Ownership: Slater Butte Translator Co.

Happy Camp, etc.—K11GO, Ch. 11, Slater Butte Translator Co.

Technical Facilities: 0.023-kw ERP, 4682-ft. above sea level, lat. 41° 51' 30", long. 123° 21' 13".

Ownership: Slater Butte Translator Co.

Happy Camp, etc.—K13GL, Ch. 13, Slater Butte Translator Co.

Technical Facilities: 0.023-kw ERP, 4701-ft. above sea level, lat. 41° 51' 30", long. 123° 21' 13".

Ownership: Slater Butte Translator Co.

Hayfork—K05CR-D, Ch. 5, Trinity County Superintendent of Schools. Phone: 530-623-2861.

Technical Facilities: 0.007-kw ERP, 36-ft. above ground, 4324-ft. above sea level, lat. 40° 29' 34", long. 123° 11' 52".

Ownership: Trinity County Superintendent of Schools.

Hemet—KDUG-LP, Ch. 21, Louis Martinez Family Group LLC. Phone: 951-509-1751.

Technical Facilities: 9.99-kw ERP, 66-ft. above ground, 1929-ft. above sea level, lat. 33° 36' 01", long. 117° 11' 41".

Ownership: Louis Martinez Family Group LLC.

Hemet—KZSW-LP, Ch. 27, KZSW Television Inc. Phone: 951-693-0027.

Studio: 1211 W Acacia Ave, Ste H, Hemet, CA 92543.

Technical Facilities: 9.99-kw ERP, 125-ft. above ground, 1988-ft. above sea level, lat. 33° 36' 01", long. 117° 11' 41".

Ownership: KZSW Television Inc.

Personnel: Kevin Page, General Manager; Cal Willis, Chief Engineer.

Hoopa—K07GJ, Ch. 7, Pollack/Belz Broadcasting Co. LLC.

Technical Facilities: 0.009-kw ERP, lat. 41° 07' 13", long. 123° 42' 47".

Ownership: Pollack/Belz Broadcasting Co. LLC.

Hoopa—K11NE, Ch. 11, Raul Broadcasting Co. of Eureka Inc. Phone: 209-521-5702.

Technical Facilities: 0.009-kw ERP, lat. 41° 07' 13", long. 123° 42' 47".

Holds CP for change to 0.005-kw ERP, 26-ft. above ground, 1942-ft. above sea level, BDFCDVA-20060703AAW.

Ownership: Raul & Consuelo Palazuelos.

Hopland—K06FA, Ch. 6, Sanel Valley TV Association. Phone: 707-744-1722.

Technical Facilities: 0.013-kw ERP, lat. 38° 56' 06", long. 123° 06' 22".

Ownership: Sanel Valley Television Association.

Hopland—K10FZ, Ch. 10, Sanel Valley TV Association. Phone: 707-744-1722.

Technical Facilities: 0.012-kw ERP, lat. 38° 56' 06", long. 123° 06' 22".

Ownership: Sanel Valley Television Association.

Hopland—K11TD, Ch. 11, Sanel Valley TV Association. Phone: 707-744-1722.

Technical Facilities: 0.012-kw ERP, lat. 38° 55' 39", long. 123° 06' 50".

Ownership: Sanel Valley Television Association.

Hopland—K13ID, Ch. 13, Sanel Valley TV Association. Phone: 707-744-1722.

Technical Facilities: 0.012-kw ERP, lat. 38° 56' 06", long. 123° 06' 22".

Ownership: Sanel Valley Television Association.

Hopland—K35DO, Ch. 35, Rural California Broadcasting Corp.

Technical Facilities: 0.129-kw ERP, 30-ft. above ground, 1736-ft. above sea level, lat. 38° 55' 39", long. 123° 06' 50".

Ownership: Rural California Broadcasting Corp.

■ **Indio**—K06MB, Ch. 6, Business World Broadcasting Partners. Phone: 818-845-1270.

Technical Facilities: 3-kw ERP, 56-ft. above ground, 1789-ft. above sea level, lat. 33° 48' 07", long. 116° 13' 31".

Ownership: Business World Broadcasting Partners.

Personnel: Leo Kesselman, General Manager; Wayne Goff, Engineer.

■ **Indio**—KEVC-CA, Ch. 5, Entravision Holdings LLC. Phone: 310-447-3870.

Technical Facilities: 10-w TPO, 0.35-kw ERP, 56-ft. above ground, 1145-ft. above sea level, lat. 33° 48' 07", long. 116° 13' 27".

Transmitter: Indio Peak, approx. 3-mi. NW of Indio.

Ownership: Entravision Communications Corp.

Indio—KLPS-LP, Ch. 19, Palm Springs DTV LLC. Phone: 517-782-1510; 866-995-9850. Fax: 517-782-1510.

Technical Facilities: 9.932-kw ERP, 66-ft. above ground, 1667-ft. above sea level, lat. 33° 48' 07", long. 116° 13' 27".

Ownership: Local HDTV Inc.

Indio—KPDC-LP, Ch. 25, Desert Springs Inc. Phone: 760-327-2772.

Technical Facilities: 1000-w TPO, 10.4-kw ERP, 35-ft. above ground, 1575-ft. above sea level, lat. 33° 51' 56", long. 116° 25' 58".

Transmitter: Indio Hill, 5-mi. N of Indio.

Ownership: Desert Springs Inc.

Indio—KUNA-LP, Ch. 15, Gulf-California Broadcast Co. Phone: 760-773-0342.

Technical Facilities: 9.7-kw ERP, 85-ft. above ground, 1824-ft. above sea level, lat. 33° 48' 08", long. 116° 13' 30".

Ownership: Gulf-California Broadcast Co.

Personnel: Martin Serna, General Manager; Tee Thomas, Chief Engineer; Martin Serna, Sales Manager.

■ **Indio**—KVER-CA, Ch. 4, Entravision Holdings LLC. Phone: 310-447-3870.

Studio: 41601 Corporate Way, Palm Desert, CA 92260.

Technical Facilities: 10-w TPO, 0.349-kw ERP, 20-ft. above ground, 1759-ft. above sea level, lat. 33° 48' 07", long. 116° 13' 27".

Transmitter: Indio Peak, approx. 3-mi. NW of Indio.

Ownership: Entravision Communications Corp.

Personnel: Julio Lucero, General & Sales Manager; Wayne Goff, Chief Engineer.

Indio—KVPS-LP, Ch. 8, New Global Communications Inc. Phone: 201-248-9634.

Technical Facilities: 165-w TPO, 0.5-kw ERP, 43-ft. above ground, 1781-ft. above sea level, lat. 33° 48' 08", long. 116° 13' 27".

Holds CP for change to 0.5-kw ERP, 43-ft. above ground, 1568-ft. above sea level, lat. 33° 51' 58", long. 116° 26' 05". BPTVL-20080908AAL.

Transmitter: Indio Hill, 5-mi. N of Indio.

Began Operation: January 22, 2002.

Ownership: New Global Communications Inc.

■ **Indio/Palm Springs**—KDFX-CA, Ch. 33, Gulf-California Broadcast Co. Phone: 816-271-8695.

Technical Facilities: 383-w TPO, 9.6-kw ERP, 46-ft. above ground, 1601-ft. above sea level, lat. 33° 51' 58", long. 116° 26' 02".

Transmitter: 7.2-mi. NE of Mecca.

Ownership: News Press & Gazette Co.

Personnel: Bob Allen, General Manager.

Inland Empire—KHTV-LP, Ch. 38, Venture Technologies Group LLC. Phone: 323-965-5400. Fax: 323-965-5411.

Technical Facilities: 2000-w TPO, 9.8-kw ERP, 71-ft. above ground, 5512-ft. above sea level, lat. 34° 12' 45", long. 117° 41' 58".

Transmitter: Lodestar tower site, Mount Harvard, San Gabriel Mountains.

Ownership: Venture Technologies Group LLC.

Personnel: Brian Holton, General Manager; Ted Lester, Chief Engineer; Andrea Wilson, Sales Manager.

Inyokern—K19CL, Ch. 19, Victor A. Garcia. Phones: 661-324-2358; 661-324-6423. Fax: 661-324-1949.

Technical Facilities: 82-w TPO, 2.8-kw ERP, 139-ft. above ground, 4409-ft. above sea level, lat. 35° 28' 39", long. 117° 41' 58".

Transmitter: El Paso electronic site, Ridgecrest.

Ownership: Victor A. Garcia.

Personnel: Linda K. Garcia, General Manager; Ed Tippler, Chief Engineer; Victor D. Garcia, Sales Manager.

Inyokern, etc.—K06OL, Ch. 6, Robert D. Adelman. Phone: 760-371-1700.

Technical Facilities: 3-kw ERP, 33-ft. above ground, 5013-ft. above sea level, lat. 35° 26' 10", long. 117° 48' 56".

Ownership: Robert D. Adelman.

Inyokern, etc.—K47AE, Ch. 47, Indian Wells Valley TV Booster Inc. Phone: 760-375-0233.

Technical Facilities: 0.875-kw ERP, lat. 35° 28' 48", long. 117° 40' 59".

Ownership: Indian Wells Valley TV Booster Inc.

Joshua Tree—K15FC, Ch. 15, County of San Bernardino, Area 70. Phone: 760-367-1833.

Technical Facilities: 0.3-kw ERP, 25-ft. above ground, 2755-ft. above sea level, lat. 34° 08' 06.9", long. 116° 18' 27".

Ownership: San Bernardino County.

Joshua Tree—K17GJ, Ch. 17, County of San Bernardino Service Area 70. Phone: 760-367-1833.

Technical Facilities: 0.3-kw ERP, 25-ft. above ground, 2755-ft. above sea level, lat. 34° 08' 06.9", long. 116° 18' 27".

Ownership: San Bernardino County.

Joshua Tree, etc.—K21GR, Ch. 21, San Bernardino County. Phone: 760-367-1833.

Technical Facilities: 0.3-kw ERP, 25-ft. above ground, 2755-ft. above sea level, lat. 34° 08' 06.9", long. 116° 18' 27".

Ownership: San Bernardino County.

Joshua Tree, etc.—K25GK, Ch. 25, County of San Bernardino, Area 70. Phone: 760-367-1833.

Technical Facilities: 0.63-kw ERP, lat. 34° 04' 32", long. 115° 57' 18".

Transmitter: Pinto Mountain, 8-mi. SE of Twentynine Palms.

Ownership: San Bernardino County.

Klamath—K25CI, Ch. 25, BlueStone License Holdings Inc. Phone: 212-247-8717.

Technical Facilities: 0.005-kw ERP, 30-ft. above ground, 4295-ft. above sea level, lat. 41° 31' 26", long. 123° 54' 26".

Ownership: Bonten Media Group LLC.

■ **La Jolla**—K35DG, Ch. 35, The Regents of the U. of California. Phone: 510-987-0440. Fax: 510-987-0328.

Studio: U. of California, La Jolla, CA 92093.

Technical Facilities: 26.7-kw ERP, 104-ft. above ground, 823-ft. above sea level, lat. 32° 50' 25", long. 117° 14' 56".

Ownership: Regents of the U. of California.

Personnel: Rhyena Halpern, Programming & Production Director; Sherman George, Engineering Director.

La Jolla—K59AL, Ch. 59, Board of Trustees for San Diego U.

Technical Facilities: 1.9-kw ERP, lat. 32° 50' 53", long. 117° 16' 32".

Ownership: Board of Trustees for San Diego U.

La Jolla—K67AM, Ch. 67, Board of Trustees for San Diego U.

Technical Facilities: 1.25-kw ERP, lat. 32° 50' 46", long. 117° 16' 33".

Ownership: Board of Trustees for San Diego U.

La Jolla—KNSD-LP, Ch. 62, Station Venture Operations LP.

Technical Facilities: 1000-w TPO, 0.001-kw ERP, 102-ft. above ground, 823-ft. above sea level, lat. 32° 50' 24", long. 117° 14' 52".

Transmitter: KCLX-FM tower, Soledad Mountain.

Ownership: Station Venture Operations LP.

Lake City, etc.—K06FF, Ch. 6, Surprise Valley TV Club. Phone: 530-279-2577.

Technical Facilities: 0.046-kw ERP, lat. 41° 37' 45", long. 120° 03' 45".

Ownership: Surprise Valley TV Club.

Lake Shastina—K27BH, Ch. 27, BlueStone License Holdings Inc. Phone: 212-247-8717.

Technical Facilities: 20-w TPO, 0.077-kw ERP, 23-ft. above ground, 3038-ft. above sea level, lat. 41° 30' 38", long. 122° 23' 33".

Transmitter: Lake Shastina area, 5-mi. N of Weed.

Ownership: Bonten Media Group LLC.

Personnel: Bob Wise, General Manager; Dennis Siewart, Sales Manager; Jeff Knott, Operations Manager.

Lakehead—K02FF, Ch. 2, BlueStone License Holdings Inc. Phone: 212-247-8717.

Technical Facilities: 0.01-kw ERP, lat. 40° 52' 17", long. 122° 22' 31".

Ownership: Bonten Media Group LLC.

Lakehead—K14HX-D, Ch. 14, Northern California Educational TV Assn. Inc. Phone: 530-243-5493.

Technical Facilities: 0.058-kw ERP, 16-ft. above ground, 3950-ft. above sea level, lat. 40° 54' 52", long. 122° 26' 42".

Ownership: Northern California Educational TV Assn. Inc.

Lakeport—K04QR-D, Ch. 4, Mako Communications LLC. Phone: 361-883-1763.

Technical Facilities: 0.1-kw ERP, 16-ft. above ground, 1722-ft. above sea level, lat. 38° 47' 13", long. 122° 07' 20".

Holds CP for change to 0.24-kw ERP, 167-ft. above ground, 201-ft. above sea level, lat. 38° 42' 28.5", long. 121° 28' 32.5". BPDVL-20090430ABM.

Began Operation: March 17, 1980.

Ownership: Mako Communications LLC.

Lakeport—K05MI-D, Ch. 5, Mako Communications LLC. Phone: 361-883-1763.

Technical Facilities: 0.3-kw ERP, 33-ft. above ground, 3740-ft. above sea level, lat. 38° 59' 22", long. 122° 46' 04".

Ownership: Mako Communications LLC.

Lakeport—K15FJ, Ch. 15, Jesus Christ Fellowship. Phone: 707-987-0888.

Technical Facilities: 0.931-kw ERP, lat. 38° 59' 22", long. 122° 46' 04".

Transmitter: 9-mi. SE of Lakeport.

Ownership: Jesus Christ Fellowship.

Lakeport—K26GK, Ch. 26, Lake County TV Club. Phone: 707-263-9020.

Technical Facilities: 5.9-kw ERP, 98-ft. above ground, 4065-ft. above sea level, lat. 38° 59' 22", long. 122° 46' 04".

Ownership: Lake County TV Club.

■**Lakeport**—K33CH, Ch. 33, Lake County TV Club. Phone: 707-263-9020.

Technical Facilities: 0.753-kw ERP, lat. 38° 59' 23", long. 122° 45' 03".

Ownership: Lake County TV Club.

■**Lakeport**—K46DR, Ch. 46, Lake County TV Club. Phone: 707-263-9020.

Technical Facilities: 0.753-kw ERP, 95-ft. above ground, 4062-ft. above sea level, lat. 38° 59' 22", long. 122° 46' 04".

Ownership: Lake County TV Club.

Lakeport—K52AJ, Ch. 52, Lake County TV Club. Phone: 707-263-9032.

Technical Facilities: 0.38-kw ERP, lat. 38° 59' 23", long. 122° 45' 03".

Ownership: Lake County TV Club.

Lakeport—K54CY, Ch. 54, Nicholas L. Muhlhauser. Phone: 408-395-6746.

Technical Facilities: 0.753-kw ERP, 95-ft. above ground, 4062-ft. above sea level, lat. 38° 59' 22", long. 122° 46' 04".

Ownership: Nicholas L. Muhlhauser.

Lakeport—K58AW, Ch. 58, Nicholas L Muhlhauser. Phone: 408-395-6746.

Technical Facilities: 0.668-kw ERP, lat. 38° 59' 23", long. 122° 45' 03".

Ownership: Nicholas L. Muhlhauser.

Lakeport—K68AL, Ch. 68, Lake County TV Club. Phone: 707-263-9032.

Technical Facilities: 0.1-kw ERP, 4035-ft. above sea level, lat. 38° 59' 22", long. 122° 46' 04".

Ownership: Lake County TV Club.

Lakeshore, etc.—K04FL, Ch. 4, Catamount Broadcasting of Chico-Redding Inc.

Technical Facilities: 0.034-kw ERP, lat. 40° 54' 52", long. 122° 26' 43".

Ownership: Catamount Broadcast Group.

Lancaster—K26GN, Ch. 26, Obidia Porras. Phone: 760-956-2111.

Technical Facilities: 0.5-kw ERP, 20-ft. above ground, 4718-ft. above sea level, lat. 34° 32' 50", long. 118° 12' 24".

Ownership: Obidia Porras.

Lancaster—KEDD-LP, Ch. 50, Adelman Broadcasting Inc. Phone: 760-371-1700.

Technical Facilities: 26-kw ERP, 49-ft. above ground, 5249-ft. above sea level, lat. 34° 32' 50", long. 118° 12' 57".

Holds CP for change to 15-kw ERP, 322-ft. above ground, 6030-ft. above sea level, lat. 34° 13' 35", long. 118° 03' 58". BDFCDTL-20060809ALC.

Ownership: Robert D. Adelman.

Lewiston—K06EX, Ch. 6, Lewiston Translator Co.

Technical Facilities: 0.00746-kw ERP, lat. 40° 41' 17", long. 122° 49' 55".

Ownership: Lewiston Translator Co.

Lewiston—K28CY-D, Ch. 28, Northern California Educational TV Assn. Inc. Phone: 530-243-5493.

Technical Facilities: 0.014-kw ERP, 36-ft. above ground, 3251-ft. above sea level, lat. 40° 41' 27", long. 122° 49' 55".

Ownership: Northern California Educational TV Assn. Inc.

Lewiston, etc.—K03CT, Ch. 3, Lewiston Translator Co.

Technical Facilities: 0.039-kw ERP, lat. 40° 41' 27", long. 122° 49' 55".

Ownership: Lewiston Translator Co.

Likely—K05ET-D, Ch. 5, California-Oregon Broadcasting Inc. Phone: 541-779-5555.

Technical Facilities: 0.25-kw ERP, 20-ft. above ground, 7379-ft. above sea level, lat. 41° 09' 19", long. 120° 33' 45".

Ownership: California-Oregon Broadcasting Inc.

Likely—K11LD, Ch. 11, BlueStone License Holdings Inc. Phone: 212-247-8717.

Technical Facilities: 0.04-kw ERP, lat. 41° 09' 08", long. 120° 33' 14".

Ownership: Bonten Media Group LLC.

Litchfield—K34KK, Ch. 34, Honey Lake Community TV Corp. Phone: 530-257-9625.

Technical Facilities: 0.57-kw ERP, 21-ft. above ground, 7098-ft. above sea level, lat. 40° 07' 01", long. 120° 19' 06".

Began Operation: November 22, 1982.

Ownership: Honey Lake Community TV Corp.

Litchfield—K46HL, Ch. 46, Honey Lake Community TV Corp. Phone: 530-257-9625.

Technical Facilities: 1.1-kw ERP, 20-ft. above ground, 6755-ft. above sea level, lat. 40° 26' 49", long. 120° 21' 25".

Ownership: Honey Lake Community TV Corp.

Litchfield—K48DI, Ch. 48, Honey Lake Community TV Corp. Phone: 530-257-9625.

Technical Facilities: 0.82-kw ERP, 21-ft. above ground, 7098-ft. above sea level, lat. 40° 07' 01", long. 120° 19' 06".

Ownership: Honey Lake Community TV Corp.

Litchfield—K50HJ, Ch. 50, Honey Lake Community TV Corp. Phone: 530-257-9625.

Technical Facilities: 0.255-kw ERP, 26-ft. above ground, 7103-ft. above sea level, lat. 40° 07' 01", long. 120° 19' 06".

Ownership: Honey Lake Community TV Corp.

■**Lompoc**—K10OG, Ch. 10, Entravision Holdings LLC.

Technical Facilities: 5.9-w TPO, 0.162-kw ERP, 26-ft. above ground, 1266-ft. above sea level, lat. 34° 44' 25", long. 120° 26' 42".

Ownership: Entravision Communications Corp.

Lompoc—K23CL, Ch. 23, Central Coast Good News Inc.

Technical Facilities: 100-w TPO, 1.28-kw ERP, lat. 34° 44' 29", long. 120° 26' 45".

Ownership: Central Coast Good News Inc.

■**Lompoc**—KLDF-CA, Ch. 17, Una Vez Mas Lompoc License LLC. Phone: 214-754-7008.

Technical Facilities: 12.1-kw ERP, 13-ft. above ground, 1253-ft. above sea level, lat. 34° 44' 24", long. 120° 26' 42".

Ownership: Una Vez Mas GP LLC.

Long Valley—K05FR, Ch. 5, Mono County Service Area No. 1.

Technical Facilities: 0.002-kw ERP, lat. 37° 35' 51", long. 118° 48' 34".

Ownership: Mono County Service Area No. 1.

Long Valley—K49EA, Ch. 49, Mono County Service Area No. 1. Phone: 760-934-6299.

Technical Facilities: 10-w TPO, 0.12-kw ERP, 25-ft. above ground, 7997-ft. above sea level, lat. 37° 35' 51", long. 118° 48' 34".

Transmitter: Approx. 10-mi. ESE of Mammoth Lakes.

Ownership: Mono County Service Area No. 1.

Long Valley—K56BS, Ch. 56, Mono County Service Area No. 1.

Technical Facilities: 0.057-kw ERP, 9012-ft. above sea level, lat. 37° 42' 45", long. 118° 39' 27".

Ownership: Mono County Service Area No. 1.

Long Valley Region—K60BR, Ch. 60, Mono County Service Area No. 1.

Technical Facilities: 0.05-kw ERP, lat. 37° 42' 45", long. 118° 39' 27".

Ownership: Mono County Service Area No. 1.

■**Los Angeles**—KNET-CA, Ch. 25, Venture Technologies Group LLC. Phone: 323-904-4090. Fax: 323-965-5411.

Technical Facilities: 73.7-kw ERP, 167-ft. above ground, 5590-ft. above sea level, lat. 34° 12' 46.1", long. 118° 03' 41.5".

Ownership: Venture Technologies Group LLC.

Los Angeles—KNLA-LP, Ch. 68, Venture Technologies Group LLC. Phone: 323-965-5400. Fax: 323-965-5411.

Technical Facilities: 9.8-kw ERP, 71-ft. above ground, 5512-ft. above sea level, lat. 34° 12' 48", long. 118° 03' 41".

Transmitter: Lodestar tower site, Mount Harvard, San Gabriel Mountain.

Ownership: Venture Technologies Group LLC.

Personnel: Brian Holton, General Manager; Mel Maddox, Station Manager; Ted Lester, Chief Engineer.

■**Los Angeles**—KSFV-CA, Ch. 6, Venture Technologies Group LLC. Phone: 323-904-4090.

Technical Facilities: 0.499-kw ERP, 5512-ft. above sea level, lat. 34° 12' 46", long. 118° 03' 42".

Ownership: Venture Technologies Group LLC.

Los Angeles—KSMV-LP, Ch. 33, KJLA LLC. Phone: 310-943-5288. Fax: 310-943-5299.

Technical Facilities: 50-w TPO, 22.8-kw ERP, 129-ft. above ground, 5828-ft. above sea level, lat. 34° 13' 36", long. 118° 03' 57".

Transmitter: South Mountain.

Ownership: Costa de Oro Television Inc.

Los Angeles—KVTU-LP, Ch. 3, Mark C. Allen. Phone: 530-246-8782.

Technical Facilities: 0.499-kw ERP, 20-ft. above ground, 5400-ft. above sea level, lat. 34° 15' 25", long. 117° 19' 50".

Holds CP for change to 150-ft. above ground, 5852-ft. above sea level, lat. 34° 13' 35.1", long. 118° 04' 00.9". BPTVL-20080922AFN.

Ownership: Mark C. Allen.

Lucerne Valley—K15CA, Ch. 15, County of San Bernardino, Area 29. Phone: 760-367-1833.

Technical Facilities: 0.74-kw ERP, lat. 34° 27' 47", long. 116° 52' 44".

Ownership: San Bernardino County.

Lucerne Valley—K19BT, Ch. 19, County of San Bernardino, Area 29. Phone: 760-367-1833.

Technical Facilities: 0.74-kw ERP, lat. 34° 27' 47", long. 116° 52' 44".

Ownership: San Bernardino County.

Lucerne Valley—K33DK, Ch. 33, MTC Broadcasting Inc. Phone: 818-339-9575.

Technical Facilities: 1.14-kw ERP, 141-ft. above ground, 3100-ft. above sea level, lat. 34° 27' 47", long. 116° 52' 44".

Ownership: Shahram Hashemizadeh.

Lucerne Valley—K41CB, Ch. 41, County of San Bernardino, Area 29. Phone: 760-367-1833.

Technical Facilities: 0.9-kw ERP, lat. 34° 27' 47", long. 116° 52' 44".

Ownership: San Bernardino County.

Lucerne Valley—K43EE, Ch. 43, County of San Bernardino, Area 29. Phone: 760-367-1833.

Technical Facilities: 0.89-kw ERP, lat. 34° 27' 47", long. 116° 52' 44".

Transmitter: Pickaninny Butte, 5.5-mi. E of Lucerne Valley.

Ownership: San Bernardino County.

Lucerne Valley—K48AD, Ch. 48, County of San Bernardino, Area 29. Phone: 760-367-1833.

Technical Facilities: 0.91-kw ERP, lat. 34° 27' 47", long. 116° 52' 44".

Ownership: San Bernardino County.

Lucerne Valley—K54AD, Ch. 54, County of San Bernardino, Area 29. Phone: 760-367-1833.

Technical Facilities: 1.06-kw ERP, lat. 34° 27' 47", long. 116° 52' 44".

Ownership: San Bernardino County.

Lucerne Valley—KIJR-LP, Ch. 47, Birach Broadcasting Corp. Phone: 248-557-3500.

Technical Facilities: 9-kw ERP, 33-ft. above ground, 1552-ft. above sea level, lat. 33° 51' 58", long. 116° 26' 00".

Ownership: Birach Broadcasting Corp.

Mammoth Lakes—K22HB, Ch. 22, Centro Cristiano Sion. Phone: 650-367-8807.

Technical Facilities: 1.26-kw ERP, 27-ft. above ground, 7884-ft. above sea level, lat. 37° 38' 30", long. 118° 57' 42".

Ownership: Centro Cristiano Sion.

Mammoth Lakes—KSRW-LP, Ch. 33, Benett Kessler. Phone: 760-878-2381.

Technical Facilities: 1000-w TPO, 26.28-kw ERP, 75-ft. above ground, 4216-ft. above sea level, lat. 37° 22' 32", long. 118° 23' 37".

Transmitter: 1280 N. Main St.

Ownership: Benett Kessler.

Mariposa—K27GZ, Ch. 27, Mutual Television Network. Phone: 888-482-1080.

Technical Facilities: 0.25-kw ERP, lat. 37° 31' 59", long. 120° 01' 33".

Holds CP for change to channel number 45, 2-kw ERP, 151-ft. above ground, 4298-ft. above sea level, BDISDTT-20060321AFC.

Ownership: Mutual Television Network.

Martinez—K49HV, Ch. 49, Aracelis Ortiz Corp. Phone: 956-412-9101.

Technical Facilities: 5-kw ERP, 66-ft. above ground, 1798-ft. above sea level, lat. 33° 48' 07", long. 116° 13' 28".

Ownership: Aracelis Ortiz Corp.

■ **Merced-Mariposa**—KMPH-CA, Ch. 17, KMPH (TV) License LLC, Debtor-in-Possession. Phone: 559-733-7800.

Technical Facilities: 0.5-kw ERP, 79-ft. above ground, 4281-ft. above sea level, lat. 37° 33' 33", long. 120° 04' 29".

Ownership: E. Roger Williams, Trustee.

Mineral—K05JK, Ch. 5, BlueStone License Holdings Inc. Phone: 212-710-7771.

Technical Facilities: 0.029-kw ERP, 23-ft. above ground, 6916-ft. above sea level, lat. 40° 17' 57", long. 121° 36' 56".

Holds CP for change to 0.006-kw ERP, 22-ft. above ground, 6938-ft. above sea level, BDFCDTV-20090203ACS.

Began Operation: May 26, 1992.

Ownership: Bonten Media Group LLC.

Miranda—K08LD, Ch. 8, Raul Broadcasting Co. of Eureka Inc. Phone: 209-521-5702.

Technical Facilities: 0.003-kw ERP, 144-ft. above ground, 1204-ft. above sea level, lat. 40° 13' 04", long. 123° 49' 58".

Holds CP for change to 0.005-kw ERP, 36-ft. above ground, 1096-ft. above sea level, BDFCDVA-20060703AAQ.

Ownership: Raul & Consuelo Palazuelos.

Miranda—K10NU, Ch. 10, Pollack/Belz Broadcasting Co. LLC.

Technical Facilities: 0.004-kw ERP, 52-ft. above ground, 1168-ft. above sea level, lat. 40° 13' 04", long. 123° 49' 58".

Ownership: Pollack/Belz Broadcasting Co. LLC.

Modesto—K08LT, Ch. 8, CYS Inc.

Technical Facilities: 5-kw ERP, 215-ft. above ground, 320-ft. above sea level, lat. 37° 43' 45", long. 121° 11' 49".

Ownership: CYS Inc.

Personnel: Kevin Henning, General Manager.

Modesto—K49EO, Ch. 49, Trinity Broadcasting Network Inc. Phone: 714-832-2950. Fax: 714-730-0661.

Technical Facilities: 4.2-kw ERP, 328-ft. above ground, 302-ft. above sea level, lat. 37° 39' 00", long. 121° 01' 25".

Holds CP for change to channel number 44, 15-kw ERP, 458-ft. above ground, 501-ft. above sea level, lat. 37° 43' 45", long. 121° 11' 49". BDFCDTT-20060322ABD.

Ownership: Trinity Broadcasting Network Inc.

Modesto—KACA-LP, Ch. 34, Word of God Fellowship Inc. Phone: 817-571-1229.

Technical Facilities: 87-kw ERP, 459-ft. above ground, 502-ft. above sea level, lat. 37° 43' 45", long. 121° 11' 49".

Ownership: Word of God Fellowship Inc.

Modesto—KAZV-LP, Ch. 14, Frank & Linda Azevedo. Phone: 209-577-0743. Fax: 209-577-0401.

Studio: 2731 Iowa Ave, Modesto, CA 95351.

Technical Facilities: 1000-w TPO, 36.5-kw ERP, 249-ft. above ground, 2739-ft. above sea level, lat. 37° 28' 48", long. 121° 21' 02".

Holds CP for change to channel number 36, 0.5-kw ERP, 59-ft. above ground, 2739-ft. above sea level, BMPDTL-20080418AAR.

Transmitter: Mount Oso electronic site, 9-mi. SW of Westley.

Multichannel TV Sound: Separate audio program.

Ownership: Frank & Linda Azevedo.

Personnel: Frank Azevedo, General Manager; Rick Rogers, Sales Manager.

■ **Modesto**—KEXT-CA, Ch. 27, Telefutura Sacramento LLC. Phone: 310-556-7600.

Technical Facilities: 90-kw ERP, 59-ft. above ground, 2739-ft. above sea level, lat. 37° 28' 48", long. 121° 21' 02".

Holds CP for change to 15-kw ERP, BDFCDTA-20080804AER.

Ownership: Univision Communications Inc.

Monterey—KMCE-LP, Ch. 52, KMCE Inc. Phone: 831-768-8668.

Technical Facilities: 55.1-kw ERP, 136-ft. above ground, 3186-ft. above sea level, lat. 36° 45' 22", long. 121° 30' 06".

Ownership: KMCE Inc.

Monterey—KMUV-LP, Ch. 23, Cowles California Media Co. Phone: 509-459-5520.

Technical Facilities: 50-kw ERP, 197-ft. above ground, 3274-ft. above sea level, lat. 36° 45' 23", long. 121° 30' 05".

Multichannel TV Sound: Stereo and separate audio program.

Ownership: Cowles Co.

Monterey—KYMB-LD, Ch. 27, Cocola Broadcasting Companies LLC. Phone: 559-435-7000.

Technical Facilities: 5-kw ERP, 98-ft. above ground, 1290-ft. above sea level, lat. 36° 33' 09", long. 121° 47' 17".

Ownership: Cocola Broadcasting Companies LLC.

Monterey, etc.—K29AB, Ch. 29, KTVU Partnership. Phone: 408-953-3636.

Technical Facilities: 1-kw ERP, lat. 36° 32' 05", long. 121° 37' 14".

Holds CP for change to 3.1-kw ERP, 98-ft. above ground, 3166-ft. above sea level, lat. 36° 45' 22", long. 121° 30' 06". BDFCDTT-20060829BHB.

Ownership: Cox Enterprises Inc.

Moreno Valley—KMRZ-LP, Ch. 69, Venture Technologies Group LLC. Phone: 323-904-4090.

Technical Facilities: 0.4-kw ERP, 72-ft. above ground, 7992-ft. above sea level, lat. 34° 02' 17", long. 116° 48' 47".

Began Operation: December 4, 2008.

Ownership: Venture Technologies Group LLC.

Morongo Valley—K13WJ, Ch. 13, County of San Bernardino, Area 70. Phone: 760-367-1833.

Technical Facilities: 0.03-kw ERP, 180-ft. above ground, 2976-ft. above sea level, lat. 34° 03' 54", long. 116° 32' 42".

Ownership: San Bernardino County.

Morongo Valley—K14AB, Ch. 14, County of San Bernardino, Area 70. Phone: 760-367-1833.

Technical Facilities: 1.08-kw ERP, 2999-ft. above sea level, lat. 34° 03' 54", long. 116° 32' 42".

Ownership: San Bernardino County.

Morongo Valley—K16AA, Ch. 16, County of San Bernardino, Area 70. Phone: 760-367-1833.

Technical Facilities: 1.08-kw ERP, lat. 34° 03' 54", long. 116° 32' 42".

Ownership: San Bernardino County.

Morongo Valley—K21GI, Ch. 21, County of San Bernardino, Area 70. Phone: 760-367-1833.

Technical Facilities: 1.08-kw ERP, 178-ft. above ground, 2975-ft. above sea level, lat. 34° 03' 54", long. 116° 32' 42".

Ownership: San Bernardino County.

Morongo Valley—K30GU, Ch. 30, County of San Bernardino, Area 70. Phone: 760-367-1833.

Technical Facilities: 1.08-kw ERP, lat. 34° 03' 54", long. 116° 32' 42".

Ownership: San Bernardino County.

Morongo Valley—K32EM, Ch. 32, County of San Bernardino, Area 70. Phone: 760-367-1833. Fax: 760-367-4732.

Technical Facilities: 100-w TPO, 1.04-kw ERP, 190-ft. above ground, 2986-ft. above sea level, lat. 34° 03' 54", long. 116° 32' 42".

Transmitter: 3-mi. NE of Morongo Valley Post Office.

Multichannel TV Sound: Stereo only.

Ownership: San Bernardino County.

Personnel: Jim Parker, Chief Engineer.

Morongo Valley—K34EU, Ch. 34, County of San Bernardino, Area 70. Phone: 760-367-1833. Fax: 760-367-4732.

Technical Facilities: 100-w TPO, 1.04-kw ERP, 190-ft. above ground, 2986-ft. above sea level, lat. 34° 03' 54", long. 116° 32' 42".

Transmitter: 3-mi. NE of Morongo Valley Post Office.

Ownership: San Bernardino County.

Personnel: Jim Parker, Chief Engineer.

Morongo Valley—K36GO, Ch. 36, County of San Bernardino, Area 70. Phone: 760-367-1833.

Technical Facilities: 1.08-kw ERP, 178-ft. above ground, 2976-ft. above sea level, lat. 34° 03' 54", long. 116° 32' 42".

Ownership: San Bernardino County.

Morongo Valley—K40HX, Ch. 40, County of San Bernardino, Area 70. Phone: 760-367-1833.

Technical Facilities: 1.08-kw ERP, 178-ft. above ground, 2978-ft. above sea level, lat. 34° 03' 54", long. 116° 32' 42".

Ownership: San Bernardino County.

Morongo Valley—K48EM, Ch. 48, County of San Bernardino, Area 70. Phone: 760-367-1833.

Technical Facilities: 1.12-kw ERP, 154-ft. above ground, 2953-ft. above sea level, lat. 34° 03' 54", long. 116° 32' 42".

Ownership: San Bernardino County.

Morongo Valley—KJHP-LP, Ch. 18, San Bernardino Community College District. Phone: 909-384-4444.

Technical Facilities: 7.5-kw ERP, 65-ft. above ground, 1518-ft. above sea level, lat. 33° 51' 56", long. 116° 25' 58".

Ownership: San Bernardino Community College District.

■ **Morro Bay**—K09UF, Ch. 9, Raul & Consuelo Palazuelos. Phone: 805-928-7700. Fax: 805-928-8606.

Studio: 330 W Carmen Ln, Santa Maria, CA 93458.

Technical Facilities: 3-kw ERP, 85-ft. above ground, 2562-ft. above sea level, lat. 35° 21' 38", long. 120° 39' 21".

Holds CP for change to 0.002-kw ERP, BDFCDVA-20061030ADV.

Ownership: Raul & Consuelo Palazuelos.

Personnel: Sandy Keefer, General Manager & Sales Manager; Roy Keefer, Chief Engineer.

Morro Bay—K22EE, Ch. 22, Central Coast Good News Inc.

Technical Facilities: 1-kw ERP, lat. 35° 16' 51", long. 120° 48' 41".

Transmitter: 2-mi. S of Willow Dr. & Los Osos Valley Rd. intersection.

Ownership: Central Coast Good News Inc.

Mountain Gate—K03FU, Ch. 3, BlueStone License Holdings Inc. Phone: 212-247-8717.

Technical Facilities: 0.022-kw ERP, 1526-ft. above sea level, lat. 40° 45' 00", long. 122° 17' 49".

Ownership: Bonten Media Group LLC.

National City—K61GH, Ch. 61, International Communications Network Inc. Phone: 619-230-0330.

Technical Facilities: 50-kw ERP, 131-ft. above ground, 449-ft. above sea level, lat. 32° 41' 15", long. 117° 03' 56".

Ownership: International Communications Network Inc.

Needles—K17BN, Ch. 17, Mohave County Board of Supervisors.

Technical Facilities: 1.43-kw ERP, lat. 35° 02' 09", long. 114° 22' 14".

Ownership: Mohave County Board of Supervisors.

Needles—K30BQ, Ch. 30, Needles Community TV Club Inc.

Technical Facilities: 1.43-kw ERP, lat. 35° 02' 09", long. 114° 22' 14".

Ownership: Needles Community TV Club Inc.

Needles, etc.—K31HY, Ch. 31, Mohave County Baord of Supervisors. Phone: 928-753-0729.

Technical Facilities: 1.06-kw ERP, 23-ft. above ground, 4039-ft. above sea level, lat. 35° 02' 09", long. 114° 22' 14".

Ownership: Mohave County Board of Supervisors.

Newberry Springs—K03EK, Ch. 3, County of San Bernardino, Area 40. Phone: 760-367-1833.

Technical Facilities: 0.089-kw ERP, lat. 34° 50' 03", long. 116° 40' 48".

Ownership: San Bernardino County.

Newberry Springs—K06IQ, Ch. 6, County of San Bernardino, Area 40. Phone: 760-367-1833.

Technical Facilities: 0.009-kw ERP, lat. 34° 50' 03", long. 116° 40' 48".

Ownership: San Bernardino County.

Newberry Springs—K08IA, Ch. 8, County of San Bernardino, Area 40. Phone: 760-367-1833.

Technical Facilities: 0.081-kw ERP, lat. 34° 50' 03", long. 116° 40' 48".

Ownership: San Bernardino County.

Newberry Springs—K10IX, Ch. 10, County of San Bernardino, Area 40. Phone: 760-367-1833.

Technical Facilities: 0.008-kw ERP, lat. 34° 50' 03", long. 116° 40' 48".

Ownership: San Bernardino County.

Newberry Springs—K12JI, Ch. 12, County of San Bernardino, Area 40. Phone: 760-367-1833.

Technical Facilities: 0.008-kw ERP, lat. 34° 50' 03", long. 116° 40' 48".

Ownership: San Bernardino County.

Newell—K08OB-D, Ch. 8, Northern California Educational TV Assn. Inc. Phone: 530-243-5493.

Technical Facilities: 0.0043-kw ERP, 92-ft. above ground, 4147-ft. above sea level, lat. 41° 51' 16.9", long. 121° 19' 42.2".

Ownership: Northern California Educational TV Assn. Inc.

Orleans—K08HJ, Ch. 8, Raul Broadcasting Co. of Eureka Inc. Phone: 209-521-5702.

Technical Facilities: 0.01-kw ERP, lat. 41° 17' 06", long. 123° 29' 46".

Holds CP for change to 0.005-kw ERP, 10-ft. above ground, 4242-ft. above sea level, BDFCDVA-20060703AAR.

Ownership: Raul & Consuelo Palazuelos.

Orleans—K11IQ, Ch. 11, Pollack/Belz Broadcasting Co. LLC.

Technical Facilities: 0.01-kw ERP, lat. 41° 17' 06", long. 123° 29' 46".

Ownership: Pollack/Belz Broadcasting Co. LLC.

Oroville—K08NH, Ch. 8, Sainte Partners II LP. Phone: 209-523-0777.

Technical Facilities: 3-kw ERP, lat. 39° 27' 46", long. 121° 34' 49".

Holds CP for change to 0.3-kw ERP, 95-ft. above ground, 333-ft. above sea level, BDFCDTT-20060329ADT.

Ownership: Sainte Partners II LP.

Oroville—K15CX, Ch. 15, BlueStone License Holdings Inc. Phone: 212-247-8717.

Technical Facilities: 21-kw ERP, lat. 39° 27' 46", long. 121° 34' 49".

Ownership: Bonten Media Group LLC.

Oroville—K42HL, Ch. 42, Chico License LLC. Phone: 941-721-0929.

Technical Facilities: 11-kw ERP, 138-ft. above ground, 3097-ft. above sea level, lat. 39° 39' 04", long. 121° 27' 43".

Ownership: Evans Broadcasting of Chico LLC.

■ **Oxnard**—KSKP-CA, Ch. 25, Capital Broadcasting Corp. Phone: 818-884-2617.

Technical Facilities: 519-w TPO, 10-kw ERP, 57-ft. above ground, 2356-ft. above sea level, lat. 34° 19' 52", long. 119° 01' 20".

Holds CP for change to 0.07-kw ERP, 57-ft. above ground, 2052-ft. above sea level, BDFCDTA-20051017ABS.

Transmitter: South Mountain, Santa Paula.

Ownership: Capital Broadcasting Corp.

Personnel: Larry Windsor, President; Bob Ruiz, Chief Executive Officer.

Palermo—K04QC, Ch. 4, Sainte Partners II LP. Phone: 209-523-0777.

Technical Facilities: 3-kw ERP, 95-ft. above ground, 333-ft. above sea level, lat. 39° 27' 46", long. 121° 34' 49".

Holds CP for change to 0.3-kw ERP, BDFCDTT-20060329ADM.

Ownership: Sainte Partners II LP.

Palm Desert—KDUO-LP, Ch. 43, Louis Martinez Family Group LLC. Phone: 951-509-1751.

Technical Facilities: 9.5-kw ERP, 75-ft. above ground, 1640-ft. above sea level, lat. 33° 51' 58", long. 116° 25' 59".

Ownership: Louis Martinez Family Group LLC.

Palm Desert, etc.—K09XW, Ch. 9, PSTV Partners LLC. Phone: 760-325-7191. Fax: 760-325-7258.

Technical Facilities: 1.5-kw ERP, 23-ft. above ground, 7506-ft. above sea level, lat. 33° 32' 45", long. 116° 28' 06".

Holds CP for change to 60-ft. above ground, 2660-ft. above sea level, lat. 33° 52' 15", long. 116° 13' 37". BPTTV-20060331BIK.

Ownership: PSTV Partners LLC.

Palm Springs—K10OU, Ch. 10, Marcia T. Turner. Phone: 954-732-9539.

Technical Facilities: 3-kw ERP, 164-ft. above ground, 1900-ft. above sea level, lat. 33° 55' 20", long. 116° 37' 01".

Ownership: Marcia T. Turner.

Palm Springs—K20HZ, Ch. 20, Howard Mintz. Phone: 361-883-1763.

Technical Facilities: 2.5-kw ERP, 62-ft. above ground, 1630-ft. above sea level, lat. 33° 52' 02.8", long. 116° 25' 58.1".

Ownership: Howard Mintz.

Palm Springs—K40ID, Ch. 40, Trinity Broadcasting Network Inc. Phone: 714-832-2950. Fax: 714-730-0661.

Technical Facilities: 45.6-kw ERP, 26-ft. above ground, 1640-ft. above sea level, lat. 33° 52' 02", long. 116° 26' 13".

Ownership: Trinity Broadcasting Network Inc.

Palm Springs—KCWQ-LP, Ch. 2, Gulf-California Broadcast Co. Phone: 760-773-0342.

Technical Facilities: 1-kw ERP, 36-ft. above ground, 1591-ft. above sea level, lat. 33° 51' 58", long. 116° 26' 02".

Ownership: Gulf-California Broadcast Co.

Palm Springs—KODG-LP, Ch. 17, Biltmore Broadcasting Palm Springs Inc. Phone: 310-454-8673.

Technical Facilities: 1000-w TPO, 14.2-kw ERP, 59-ft. above ground, 1778-ft. above sea level, lat. 33° 48' 07", long. 116° 13' 27".

Transmitter: Indio Peak, 5.4-mi. N of Indio.

Ownership: Biltmore Broadcasting Corp.

Palm Springs—KPSE-LP, Ch. 50, Journal Broadcast Corp. Phone: 702-876-1313.

Technical Facilities: 1000-w TPO, 5.2-kw ERP, 25-ft. above ground, 1604-ft. above sea level, lat. 33° 52' 03", long. 116° 25' 59".

Transmitter: Edom Hill.

Ownership: Journal Communications Inc.

Palm Springs—KVES-LP, Ch. 28, Entravision Holdings LLC. Phone: 310-447-3870.

Technical Facilities: 1000-w TPO, 9.99-kw ERP, 50-ft. above ground, 1590-ft. above sea level, lat. 33° 51' 56", long. 116° 25' 58".

Transmitter: Edom Hill, Thousand Palms Riverside.

Ownership: Entravision Communications Corp.

Personnel: Julio Lucero, General Manager; Jose Mora, Chief Technician; Mickey Sambor, Sales Manager.

Palm Springs—KYAV-LP, Ch. 12, U-Dub Productions LLC. Phone: 760-343-5700.

Technical Facilities: 10-w TPO, 0.99-kw ERP, 30-ft. above ground, 1528-ft. above sea level, lat. 33° 51' 58", long. 116° 26' 03".

Transmitter: Edom Hill, 6-mi. NE of Palm Springs.

Ownership: U-Dub Productions LLC.

■ **Palm Springs/Indio**—K21DO, Ch. 21, Three Angels Broadcasting Network Inc. Phone: 618-627-4651. Fax: 618-627-4155.

Studio: 3391 Charley Good Rd, West Frankfort, IL 62896.

Technical Facilities: 80-w TPO, 9.2-kw ERP, 39-ft. above ground, 1634-ft. above sea level, lat. 33° 52' 12", long. 116° 25' 44".

Transmitter: Edom Hill, Palm Springs.

Ownership: Three Angels Broadcasting Network Inc.

Personnel: Moses Primo, Chief Engineer.

Palmdale—K67AO, Ch. 67, Roy William Mayhugh. Phone: 760-446-6794.

Technical Facilities: 4.57-kw ERP, lat. 35° 28' 47", long. 117° 40' 59".

Holds CP for change to channel number 12, 3-kw ERP, 33-ft. above ground, 5013-ft. above sea level, lat. 35° 26' 10", long. 117° 48' 56". BPTTV-20041129ABP.

Transmitter: Laurel Mountain electronics site.

Ownership: Roy William Mayhugh.

Palmdale—KFLA-LD, Ch. 8, Roy William Mayhugh. Phone: 760-446-6794.

Technical Facilities: 0.3-kw ERP, 164-ft. above ground, 5873-ft. above sea level, lat. 34° 13' 35.3", long. 118° 03' 57.7".

Ownership: Roy William Mayhugh.

■ **Palmdale**—KPAL-LP, Ch. 38, KPAL Television Inc. Phone: 919-844-5225.

Technical Facilities: 100-w TPO, 4.47-kw ERP, 49-ft. above ground, 5233-ft. above sea level, lat. 34° 32' 50", long. 118° 12' 53".

Transmitter: Hauser Mountain, 6.2-mi. SSW of Palmdale.

Multichannel TV Sound: Stereo and separate audio program.

Ownership: KPAL Television Inc.

Personnel: Bob Allen, General Manager; Kurt Lauchart, Chief Engineer.

Paradise—K05EM, Ch. 5, BlueStone License Holdings Inc. Phone: 212-710-7771.

Technical Facilities: 0.03-kw ERP, lat. 39° 48' 42", long. 121° 33' 30".

Holds CP for change to 0.006-kw ERP, 23-ft. above ground, 3379-ft. above sea level, BDFCDTV-20090203ABV.

Ownership: Bonten Media Group LLC.

Paradise—K49CT, Ch. 49, Catamount Broadcasting of Chico-Redding Inc.

Technical Facilities: 3.05-kw ERP, 102-ft. above ground, 3110-ft. above sea level, lat. 39° 39' 04", long. 121° 27' 43".

Ownership: Catamount Broadcast Group.

■ **Paso Robles**—K17GD, Ch. 17, Entravision Holdings LLC. Phone: 310-447-3870.

Technical Facilities: 11.6-kw ERP, 66-ft. above ground, 1867-ft. above sea level, lat. 35° 38' 45", long. 120° 44' 16".

Ownership: Entravision Communications Corp.

Paso Robles—K44DN, Ch. 44, Cowles California Media Co. Phone: 509-459-5520.

Technical Facilities: 0.603-kw ERP, 39-ft. above ground, 1841-ft. above sea level, lat. 35° 38' 45", long. 120° 44' 16".

Ownership: Cowles Co.

Paso Robles—KJCN-LP, Ch. 36, Central Coast Good News Inc. Phone: 805-239-2012.

Technical Facilities: 1000-w TPO, 25-kw ERP, 55-ft. above ground, 2525-ft. above sea level, lat. 35° 21' 38", long. 120° 39' 21".

Holds CP for change to 150-kw ERP, 82-ft. above ground, 2871-ft. above sea level, lat. 35° 57' 07", long. 121° 00' 00". BPTTL-20070918ACL.

Ownership: Central Coast Good News Inc.

Personnel: Clyde Harmon, Secretary.

Paso Robles—KMBY-LP, Ch. 22, Cocola Broadcasting Companies LLC. Phone: 559-435-7000.

Technical Facilities: 80-kw ERP, 197-ft. above ground, 5403-ft. above sea level, lat. 36° 22' 07", long. 120° 38' 33".

Ownership: Cocola Broadcasting Companies LLC.

■ **Paso Robles**—KPAO-CA, Ch. 22, Una Vez Mas Paso Robles License LLC. Phone: 214-754-7008.

Technical Facilities: 12.4-kw ERP, 85-ft. above ground, 1886-ft. above sea level, lat. 35° 38' 45", long. 120° 44' 16".

Ownership: Una Vez Mas GP LLC.

Petaluma—K14MW-D, Ch. 14, One Ministries Inc. Phone: 707-577-2225.

Technical Facilities: 4-kw ERP, 33-ft. above ground, 1634-ft. above sea level, lat. 38° 30' 31", long. 122° 39' 41".

Ownership: One Ministries Inc.

Placerville—KGTN-LP, Ch. 62, Praise the Lord Studio Chapel.

Technical Facilities: 11.7-kw ERP, 479-ft. above ground, 2506-ft. above sea level, lat. 38° 37' 49", long. 120° 51' 20".

Ownership: Praise The Lord Studio Chapel.

Porterville—K15CO, Ch. 15, Trinity Broadcasting Network Inc. Phone: 714-832-2950. Fax: 714-730-0661.

Technical Facilities: 1000-w TPO, 9.12-kw ERP, 39-ft. above ground, 5741-ft. above sea level, lat. 36° 17' 07", long. 118° 50' 19".

Holds CP for change to 15-kw ERP, 39-ft. above ground, 5619-ft. above sea level, BDFCDTT-20060329AKF.

Transmitter: Blue Ridge Lookout, 1.7-mi. E of Exeter.

Ownership: Trinity Broadcasting Network Inc.

Porterville—KVVG-LP, Ch. 54, Cocola Broadcasting Companies LLC. Phone: 559-435-7000. Fax: 559-435-3201.

Technical Facilities: 20-kw ERP, 98-ft. above ground, 5814-ft. above sea level, lat. 36° 17' 14", long. 118° 50' 17".

Ownership: Cocola Broadcasting Companies LLC.

Personnel: Todd Lopes, President.

Potter Valley—K06DK, Ch. 6, Potter Valley TV Assn. Inc.

Technical Facilities: 0.13-kw ERP, lat. 39° 14' 22", long. 122° 59' 52".

Ownership: Potter Valley Television Association Inc.

Potter Valley—K08EE, Ch. 8, Potter Valley TV Assn. Inc.

Technical Facilities: 0.135-kw ERP, lat. 39° 14' 22", long. 122° 59' 52".

Ownership: Potter Valley Television Association Inc.

Potter Valley—K10EQ, Ch. 10, Potter Valley TV Assn. Inc.

Technical Facilities: 0.135-kw ERP, lat. 39° 14' 22", long. 122° 59' 52".

Ownership: Potter Valley Television Association Inc.

Potter Valley—K12DV, Ch. 12, Potter Valley TV Assn. Inc.

Technical Facilities: 0.014-kw ERP, lat. 39° 14' 22", long. 122° 59' 52".

Ownership: Potter Valley Television Association Inc.

Potter Valley—K66DQ, Ch. 66, Potter Valley TV Assn. Inc.

Technical Facilities: 4.51-kw ERP, lat. 39° 14' 22", long. 122° 59' 52".

Ownership: Potter Valley Television Association Inc.

Potter Valley—K69DI, Ch. 69, Potter Valley TV Assn. Inc.

Technical Facilities: 0.29-kw ERP, lat. 39° 14' 22", long. 122° 59' 52".

Ownership: Potter Valley Television Association Inc.

Poway, etc.—KUAN-LP, Ch. 48, KSLS Inc.

Technical Facilities: 0.1-kw ERP, lat. 33° 00' 31", long. 116° 58' 16".

Ownership: International Media Group.

Red Bluff—KACX-LP, Ch. 3, Educational Broadcasting Network. Phone: 530-243-5622.

Technical Facilities: 1.9-kw ERP, 20-ft. above ground, 715-ft. above sea level, lat. 40° 26' 50", long. 122° 17' 50".

Holds CP for change to 0.18-kw ERP, 16-ft. above ground, 3445-ft. above sea level, lat. 40° 39' 13", long. 122° 31' 30". BMPTVL-20080909ACU.

Ownership: Educational Broadcasting Network.

Redding—K33HH, Ch. 33, Northern California Conference Assn. of SDA. Phone: 925-685-4300.

Studio: 2828 Eureka Way, Redding, CA 96001.

Technical Facilities: 1000-w TPO, 1.02-kw ERP, 104-ft. above ground, 3281-ft. above sea level, lat. 40° 39' 14", long. 122° 31' 12".

Transmitter: South Fork Mountain, 12-mi. NW of Redding.

Ownership: Northern California Conference Association of SDA.

Personnel: Robert Wilson, Chief Engineer; Sam Meek, Production Supervisor; Dick Seltzer, Program Director & Director of Station Relations.

Redding—K40HE, Ch. 40, Family Stations Inc.

Technical Facilities: 31.6-kw ERP, 89-ft. above ground, 3268-ft. above sea level, lat. 40° 39' 14", long. 122° 31' 12".

Ownership: Family Stations Inc.

Redding—K46HI, Ch. 46, Sainte Partners II LP. Phone: 209-523-0777.

Technical Facilities: 3-kw ERP, 66-ft. above ground, 3227-ft. above sea level, lat. 40° 39' 16", long. 122° 31' 13".

Holds CP for change to 1-kw ERP, BDFCDTL-20060329AIY.

Ownership: Sainte Partners II LP.

Redding—K50GP, Ch. 50, Trinity Broadcasting Network Inc. Phone: 714-832-2950. Fax: 714-730-0661.

Technical Facilities: 45.7-kw ERP, 138-ft. above ground, 741-ft. above sea level, lat. 40° 36' 37", long. 122° 22' 44".

Holds CP for change to 15-kw ERP, BDFCDTT-20060329AJR.

Ownership: Trinity Broadcasting Network Inc.

Personnel: Paul Crouch, General Manager; Ben Miller, Chief Engineer; Rod Henke, Sales Manager.

Redding—KFMD-LP, Ch. 6, Venture Technologies Group LLC. Phone: 323-904-4090.

Technical Facilities: 1.5-kw ERP, 108-ft. above ground, 3285-ft. above sea level, lat. 40° 39' 15", long. 122° 31' 13".

Holds CP for change to 0.3-kw ERP, 128-ft. above ground, 3330-ft. above sea level, lat. 40° 39' 14", long. 122° 31' 15". BMPDVL-20081219AFN.

Began Operation: September 18, 2006.

Ownership: Venture Technologies Group LLC.

Redding—KGEC-LP, Ch. 26, Cooper Communications LLC. Phones: 530 242-6158; 800 949-8826. Fax: 530 242-6186.

Technical Facilities: 1000-w TPO, 37.8-kw ERP, 89-ft. above ground, 3304-ft. above sea level, lat. 40° 39' 06", long. 122° 31' 32".

Transmitter: South Fork Mountain, 8-mi. NW of Redding.

Ownership: Cooper Communications LLC.

Personnel: Mildred D. Cooper, President, Chief Executive Officer & General Manager; Jim McKeown, Chief Engineer.

Redding—KMCA-LP, Ch. 2, Mark C. Allen. Phone: 530-246-8782.

Technical Facilities: 0.023-kw ERP, 15-ft. above ground, 770-ft. above sea level, lat. 40° 33' 51", long. 122° 26' 00".

Ownership: Mark C. Allen.

Redding—KQSX-LP, Ch. 42, EICB-TV West LLC. Phone: 972-291-3750.

Technical Facilities: 0.85-kw ERP, 16-ft. above ground, 7631-ft. above sea level, lat. 41° 21' 30", long. 122° 12' 21".

Holds CP for change to 0.3-kw ERP, 49-ft. above ground, 3609-ft. above sea level, lat. 41° 17' 34", long. 122° 18' 18". BPTTL-20090123ACS.

Began Operation: October 31, 2005.

Ownership: EICB-TV LLC.

Redding—KRDN-LP, Ch. 5, KM Communications Inc. Phone: 847-674-0864. Fax: 847-674-9188.

Technical Facilities: 0.6-kw ERP, 39-ft. above ground, 761-ft. above sea level, lat. 40° 36' 39", long. 122° 22' 48".

Holds CP for change to 0.3-kw ERP, 326-ft. above ground, 2001-ft. above sea level, lat. 40° 15' 31", long. 122° 05' 24". BDFCDVL-20080424ABP.

Ownership: KM Communications Inc.

■ **Redding**—KRDT-CA, Ch. 47, Family Stations Inc. Phone: 916-641-8191.

Technical Facilities: 47-kw ERP, 78-ft. above ground, 3162-ft. above sea level, lat. 40° 20' 41", long. 121° 56' 48".

Ownership: Family Stations Inc.

Redding—KRHT-LP, Ch. 41, Cocola Broadcasting Companies LLC. Phone: 559-435-7000.

Technical Facilities: 3-kw ERP, 49-ft. above ground, 3461-ft. above sea level, lat. 40° 39' 16", long. 122° 31' 23".

Began Operation: May 2, 2007.

Ownership: Cocola Broadcasting Companies LLC.

Redding—KRVU-LP, Ch. 21, Sainte Partners II LP. Phones: 530-893-1234; 209-523-0777. Fax: 530-893-1266.

Studio: 300 Main St, Chico, CA 95928.

Technical Facilities: 2000-w TPO, 60-kw ERP, 91-ft. above ground, 3251-ft. above sea level, lat. 40° 39' 16", long. 122° 31' 13".

Holds CP for change to 6-kw ERP, 92-ft. above ground, 3253-ft. above sea level, BDFCDTL-20060403ABG.

Transmitter: Richardson Ranch Rd., 0.6-mi. N of intersection with Placer Rd.

Ownership: Sainte Partners II LP.

Personnel: John Holroyd, General Manager & General Sales Manager; Bert Westhoff, National Sales Manager; Ken Rice, Chief Engineer; Patti Bittrolff, Business Manager & Research Director; Kelly Brown, Promotion & Creative Services Director; George Robinette, Production Director; Paula Murphy, Traffic & Office Manager.

Redding—KVFR-LP, Ch. 4, EICB-TV West LLC. Phone: 972-291-3750.

Technical Facilities: 0.6-kw ERP, 98-ft. above ground, 820-ft. above sea level, lat. 40° 36' 40", long. 122° 22' 51".

Holds CP for change to 0.3-kw ERP, 102-ft. above ground, 823-ft. above sea level, lat. 40° 36' 40", long. 122° 22' 51". BMPDVL-20090304ADR.

Began Operation: May 30, 2007.

Ownership: EICB-TV LLC.

Redlands—KLAU-LP, Ch. 66, Gerald G. Benavides. Phone: 361-241-7944.

Technical Facilities: 98-ft. above ground, 5797-ft. above sea level, lat. 34° 13' 37", long. 118° 03' 57".

Multichannel TV Sound: Separate audio program.

Ownership: Gerald G. Benavides.

Personnel: Gordon Young, General Manager; Mike Orr, Chief Engineer & Sales Manager.

Reedley—KCWB-LP, Ch. 13, Cocola Broadcasting Companies LLC. Phone: 559-435-7000. Fax: 559-435-3201.

Technical Facilities: 10-w TPO, 3-kw ERP, 52-ft. above ground, 3379-ft. above sea level, lat. 36° 44' 45", long. 119° 16' 57".

Transmitter: Bear Mountain communications site.

Ownership: Cocola Broadcasting Companies LLC.

Personnel: Todd Lopes, President.

Ridgecrest—K41GO, Ch. 41, Indian Wells Valley TV Booster Inc. Phone: 760-375-0233. Fax: 619-939-2433.

Technical Facilities: 2.38-kw ERP, 10-ft. above ground, 4468-ft. above sea level, lat. 35° 28' 47", long. 117° 40' 56".

Ownership: Indian Wells Valley TV Booster Inc.

Ridgecrest—K43AG, Ch. 43, Iglesia Jesucristo Es Mi Refugio Inc. Phone: 214-330-8700.

Technical Facilities: 3.84-kw ERP, lat. 35° 28' 29", long. 117° 41' 57".

Holds CP for change to 10-kw ERP, 164-ft. above ground, 3386-ft. above sea level, lat. 34° 55' 03", long. 117° 31' 10". BPTTL-20080114ACV.

Transmitter: El Paso Mountain Electronic site, near Inyokern.

Ownership: Iglesia Jesucristo Es Mi Refugio Inc.

Ridgecrest—K45GQ, Ch. 45, Indian Wells Valley TV Booster Inc. Phone: 760-375-0233.

Technical Facilities: 4.75-kw ERP, lat. 35° 28' 47", long. 117° 40' 56".

Transmitter: Laurel Mountain Electronics Site.

Ownership: Indian Wells Valley TV Booster Inc.

Ridgecrest, etc.—K02HY, Ch. 2, Indian Wells Valley TV Booster Inc.

Technical Facilities: 0.037-kw ERP, lat. 35° 39' 44", long. 117° 36' 12".

Ownership: Indian Wells Valley TV Booster Inc.

Ridgecrest, etc.—K04HX, Ch. 4, Indian Wells Valley TV Booster Inc.

Technical Facilities: 0.039-kw ERP, lat. 35° 39' 44", long. 117° 36' 12".

Ownership: Indian Wells Valley TV Booster Inc.

Ridgecrest, etc.—K05FO, Ch. 5, Indian Wells Valley TV Booster Inc.

Technical Facilities: 0.038-kw ERP, lat. 35° 39' 44", long. 117° 36' 12".

Ownership: Indian Wells Valley TV Booster Inc.

Ridgecrest, etc.—K07NH, Ch. 7, Indian Wells Valley TV Booster Inc.

Technical Facilities: 0.036-kw ERP, lat. 35° 39' 44", long. 117° 36' 12".

Ownership: Indian Wells Valley TV Booster Inc.

Ridgecrest, etc.—K09MG, Ch. 9, Indian Wells Valley TV Booster Inc.

Technical Facilities: 0.036-kw ERP, lat. 35° 39' 44", long. 117° 36' 12".

Ownership: Indian Wells Valley TV Booster Inc.

Ridgecrest, etc.—K11ML, Ch. 11, Indian Wells Valley TV Booster Inc.

Technical Facilities: 0.035-kw ERP, lat. 35° 39' 44", long. 117° 36' 12".

Ownership: Indian Wells Valley TV Booster Inc.

Ridgecrest, etc.—K13NF, Ch. 13, Indian Wells Valley TV Booster Inc.

Technical Facilities: 0.034-kw ERP, lat. 35° 39' 44", long. 117° 36' 12".

Ownership: Indian Wells Valley TV Booster Inc.

Ridgecrest, etc.—K33ID-D, Ch. 33, Indian Wells Valley TV Booster Inc. Phone: 760-375-0233.

Technical Facilities: 0.5-kw ERP, 10-ft. above ground, 4410-ft. above sea level, lat. 35° 28' 49", long. 117° 40' 56".

Ownership: Indian Wells Valley TV Booster Inc.

Ridgecrest, etc.—K35HO-D, Ch. 35, Indian Wells Valley TV Booster Inc. Phone: 760-375-0233.

Technical Facilities: 0.5-kw ERP, 10-ft. above ground, 4449-ft. above sea level, lat. 35° 28' 49", long. 117° 40' 56".

Ownership: Indian Wells Valley TV Booster Inc.

Ridgecrest, etc.—K39HT-D, Ch. 39, Indian Wells Valley TV Booster Inc. Phone: 760-375-0233.

Technical Facilities: 0.5-kw ERP, 10-ft. above ground, 4449-ft. above sea level, lat. 35° 28' 48", long. 117° 40' 56".

Ownership: Indian Wells Valley TV Booster Inc.

Ridgecrest, etc.—K49AA, Ch. 49, Indian Wells Valley TV Booster Inc. Phone: 760-375-0233.

Technical Facilities: 0.437-kw ERP, lat. 35° 28' 48", long. 117° 40' 59".

Ownership: Indian Wells Valley TV Booster Inc.

Ridgecrest, etc.—K51DD-D, Ch. 51, Indian Wells Valley TV Booster Inc. Phone: 760-375-0233.

Technical Facilities: 0.5-kw ERP, 10-ft. above ground, 4449-ft. above sea level, lat. 35° 28' 48", long. 117° 40' 56".

Ownership: Indian Wells Valley TV Booster Inc.

Ridgecrest, etc.—K59AO, Ch. 59, Roy William Mayhugh.

Technical Facilities: 0.275-kw ERP, lat. 35° 28' 48", long. 117° 40' 59".

Ownership: Roy William Mayhugh.

Rio Dell—K04NY, Ch. 4, Pollack/Belz Broadcasting Co. LLC.

Technical Facilities: 0.006-kw ERP, 13-ft. above ground, 3025-ft. above sea level, lat. 40° 25' 22", long. 124° 05' 51".

Ownership: Pollack/Belz Broadcasting Co. LLC.

Rio Dell & Scotia—K10FS, Ch. 10, Raul Broadcasting Co. of Eureka Inc. Phone: 209-521-5702.

Technical Facilities: 0.01-kw ERP, lat. 40° 25' 20", long. 124° 05' 40".

Holds CP for change to 0.005-kw ERP, 20-ft. above ground, 2890-ft. above sea level, BDFCDVA-20060703AAS.

Ownership: Raul & Consuelo Palazuelos.

Riverside—KBLM-LP, Ch. 25, Louis Martinez Family Group LLC. Phone: 951-509-1751.

Technical Facilities: 9.55-kw ERP, 50-ft. above ground, 3117-ft. above sea level, lat. 33° 57' 44", long. 117° 16' 48".

Began Operation: June 14, 1999.

Ownership: Louis Martinez Family Group LLC.

Sacramento—K22FR, Ch. 22, Trinity Christian Center of Santa Ana Inc. Phone: 714-832-2950.

Technical Facilities: 34.9-kw ERP, 292-ft. above ground, 397-ft. above sea level, lat. 38° 40' 21", long. 121° 19' 55".

Ownership: Trinity Broadcasting Network Inc.

■ **Sacramento**—K27EU, Ch. 27, Abundant Life Broadcasting Inc. Phones: 916-434-3880; 916-665-2187. Fax: 916-663-1483.

Technical Facilities: 2000-w TPO, 62-kw ERP, 308-ft. above ground, 442-ft. above sea level, lat. 38° 49' 58", long. 121° 19' 03".

Transmitter: KFIA(AM) tower, near Rocklin.

Ownership: Abundant Life Broadcasting Inc.

Personnel: Sam Wallington, Chief Engineer.

Sacramento—K45HC, Ch. 45, Trinity Broadcasting Network Inc. Phone: 714-832-2950. Fax: 714-730-0661.

Technical Facilities: 150-kw ERP, 597-ft. above ground, 597-ft. above sea level, lat. 38° 15' 54", long. 121° 29' 24".

Holds CP for change to 15-kw ERP, BDFCDTT-20060330AAG.

Ownership: Trinity Broadcasting Network Inc.

Personnel: Paul Crouch, General Manager; Ben Miller, Chief Engineer; Rod Henke, Sales Manager.

■ **Sacramento**—KBTV-CA, Ch. 8, Tower of Babel Sacramento Licensing LLC. Phone: 323-646-0123.

Technical Facilities: 369-w TPO, 3-kw ERP, 316-ft. above ground, 470-ft. above sea level, lat. 38° 33' 59", long. 121° 28' 47".

Holds CP for change to channel number 51, 15-kw ERP, 289-ft. above ground, 315-ft. above sea level, BDISTTA-20070104ABT.

Transmitter: 1811 22nd St.

Ownership: Tower of Babel LLC.

Personnel: Bob Suffel, General Manager.

Sacramento—KCSO-LP, Ch. 33, Sainte 51 LP. Phone: 209-523-0777. Fax: 209-523-0839.

Studio: 142 N 9th St, Ste 8, Modesto, CA 95350.

Technical Facilities: 130-kw ERP, 384-ft. above ground, 3122-ft. above sea level, lat. 38° 07' 10", long. 120° 43' 27".

Holds CP for change to channel number 5, 0.3-kw ERP, 374-ft. above ground, 3112-ft. above sea level, BMPDVL-20080619ADN.

Transmitter: Bear Mountain, approx. 5-mi. SW of San Andreas (Calaveras).

Began Operation: August 2, 1995.

Ownership: Sainte 51 LP.

Personnel: Robert T. Castro, General Manager; Paul Johnson, Chief Engineer.

■ **Sacramento**—KEZT-CA, Ch. 23, Telefutura Sacramento LLC. Phone: 310-348-3600.

Technical Facilities: 2000-w TPO, 12.2-kw ERP, 284-ft. above ground, 309-ft. above sea level, lat. 38° 33' 59", long. 121° 28' 46".

Holds CP for change to 4.5-kw ERP, 284-ft. above ground, 310-ft. above sea level, lat. 38° 33' 59", long. 121° 28' 47". BDFCDTA-20080804AEU.

Transmitter: 1811 2nd St.

Ownership: Univision Communications Inc.

Personnel: Christianne Trumbly, General Manager; Art Sanchez, Chief Engineer; Juan Meono, Sales Manager.

Sacramento—KMMK-LP, Ch. 14, Caballero Television Texas LLC. Phone: 972-503-6800. Fax: 972-503-6801.

Technical Facilities: 1.1-kw ERP, 225-ft. above ground, 2248-ft. above sea level, lat. 38° 37' 49", long. 120° 51' 20".

Holds CP for change to 2.3-kw ERP, BDFCDTL-20060331BAP.

Transmitter: Near Rancho Cordova & Mather AFB.

Ownership: Caballero Television LLC.

Personnel: Eduardo Caballero, Chief Executive Officer.

■ **Sacramento**—KMUM-CA, Ch. 15, Caballero Acquisition Inc.

Technical Facilities: 1000-w TPO, 18-kw ERP, 427-ft. above ground, 459-ft. above sea level, lat. 38° 42' 26", long. 121° 28' 33".

Transmitter: KGBY(FM) tower, Rio Linda.

Ownership: Caballero Acquisition Inc.

Personnel: Eduardo Caballero, Chief Executive Officer.

Sacramento—KRJR-LP, Ch. 44, Word of God Fellowship Inc. Phone: 817-571-1229. Fax: 817-571-7478.

Technical Facilities: 21.8-kw ERP, 351-ft. above ground, 384-ft. above sea level, lat. 38° 39' 26", long. 121° 43' 12".

Began Operation: March 2, 1992.

Ownership: Word of God Fellowship Inc.

Sacramento—KSAO-LP, Ch. 49, Cocola Broadcasting Companies LLC. Phone: 559-435-7000. Fax: 559-435-3201.

Technical Facilities: 4.5-kw ERP, 89-ft. above ground, 915-ft. above sea level, lat. 38° 38' 53", long. 121° 05' 51".

Ownership: Cocola Broadcasting Companies LLC.

Personnel: Todd Lopes, President.

Sacramento—KSTV-LP, Ch. 32, Bustos Media of California License LLC. Phone: 916-368-6300. Fax: 916-473-5324.

Technical Facilities: 150-kw ERP, 88-ft. above ground, 915-ft. above sea level, lat. 38° 38' 53", long. 121° 05' 51".

Transmitter: 14600 Clarksville Rd, Folsom.

Ownership: Bustos Media of California License LLC.

Personnel: Todd Lopes, President.

■ **Salinas**—K15CU, Ch. 15, NBC Telemundo License Co. Phone: 202-637-4535.

Technical Facilities: 7-kw ERP, 130-ft. above ground, 3207-ft. above sea level, lat. 36° 45' 23", long. 121° 30' 05".

Ownership: NBC Universal.

Salinas—K38JP, Ch. 38, Monterey County Superintendent of Schools. Phone: 805-896-7335.

Technical Facilities: 114-kw ERP, 154-ft. above ground, 3215-ft. above sea level, lat. 36° 32' 18", long. 121° 37' 31".

Ownership: Monterey County Superintendent of Schools.

Salinas—KLFB-LP, Ch. 21, Living Faith Broadcasting. Phone: 831-722-6892. Fax: 831-768-7846.

Technical Facilities: 1000-w TPO, 16.1-kw ERP, 131-ft. above ground, 3527-ft. above sea level, lat. 36° 32' 06", long. 121° 37' 09".

Transmitter: Mount Toro.

Ownership: Living Faith Broadcasting.

Personnel: Dwayne Toppenberg, Manager; William Cline, Chief Engineer.

■ **Salinas**—KMMD-CA, Ch. 3, Caballero Acquisition Inc.

Technical Facilities: 0.088-kw ERP, 16-ft. above ground, 3412-ft. above sea level, lat. 36° 32' 06", long. 121° 37' 09".

Transmitter: KKMC(AM) tower, Gonzales.

Ownership: Caballero Acquisition Inc.

Personnel: Eduardo Caballero, Chief Executive Officer.

■ **Salinas/Monterey, etc.**—KDJT-CA, Ch. 33, Entravision Holdings LLC. Phone: 408-929-2800. Fax: 408-929-0288.

Technical Facilities: 1000-w TPO, 29.1-kw ERP, 79-ft. above ground, 2493-ft. above sea level, lat. 37° 02' 25", long. 121° 45' 28".

Transmitter: Summit Rd., NW of intersection of Hwy. 152 & Summit Rd., San Martin.

Ownership: Entravision Communications Corp.

Personnel: Alex Sanchez, General Manager; Art Sanchez, Chief Engineer; Juan Meono, Sales Manager.

San Bernardino—KSGA-LP, Ch. 64, KJLA LLC. Phone: 818-757-7583. Fax: 818-757-7533.

Technical Facilities: 64.4-kw ERP, 49-ft. above ground, 2477-ft. above sea level, lat. 34° 01' 20", long. 117° 17' 46".

Ownership: KJLA LLC.

Personnel: Francis Wilkinson, General Manager; Ken Brown, Chief Engineer.

San Diego—K63EN, Ch. 63, Civic Light. Phone: 619-267-8923.

Technical Facilities: 0.8-kw ERP, 364-ft. above ground, 32-ft. above sea level, lat. 44° 05' 117", long. 09° 34' ".

Holds CP for change to channel number 7, 3-kw ERP, 49-ft. above ground, 2936-ft. above sea level, lat. 33° 00' 32", long. 116° 58' 16". BPTVL-20051019ABA.

Ownership: Civic Light Inc.

■ **San Diego**—KBNT-CA, Ch. 17, Entravision Holdings LLC. Phone: 310-447-3870.

Technical Facilities: 11.9-kw ERP, 420-ft. above ground, 430-ft. above sea level, lat. 32° 41' 40", long. 117° 07' 17".

Ownership: Entravision Communications Corp.

■ **San Diego**—KBOP-CA, Ch. 43, D.T.V. LLC. Phone: 603-520-1127.

Technical Facilities: 58.05-kw ERP, 80-ft. above ground, 2626-ft. above sea level, lat. 32° 41' 48", long. 116° 56' 10".

Ownership: D.T.V. LLC.

San Diego—KDTF-LP, Ch. 36, Entravision Holdings LLC. Phone: 310-447-3870.

Technical Facilities: 3.42-kw ERP, 82-ft. above ground, 2644-ft. above sea level, lat. 32° 41' 47", long. 116° 56' 09".

Transmitter: Union Bank Bldg.

Ownership: Entravision Communications Corp.

San Diego—KSDX-LP, Ch. 29, KRCA License LLC. Phone: 818-729-5300.

Technical Facilities: 500-w TPO, 7.4-kw ERP, 56-ft. above ground, 2551-ft. above sea level, lat. 32° 41' 53", long. 116° 56' 03".

Transmitter: Mount San Miguel.

Ownership: Liberman Broadcasting Inc.

Personnel: Winter Horton, General Manager; Ozzie Mendoza, Sales Manager; George Murray, Chief Engineer.

San Diego—KSZZ-LP, Ch. 19, Entravision Holdings LLC. Phones: 310-447-3870; 858-576-1919.

Studio: 5770 Ruppin Rd, San Diego, CA 92123.

Technical Facilities: 1000-w TPO, 31.3-kw ERP, 289-ft. above ground, 6089-ft. above sea level, lat. 33° 18' 32", long. 116° 50' 38".

Transmitter: Mount Palomar.

Multichannel TV Sound: Stereo only.

Ownership: Entravision Communications Corp.

Personnel: Philip Wilkinson, General Manager; Mike Flynn, Local Sales Manager; Hector Molina, Station Manager; Manuel Rojo, Chief Engineer.

San Diego—KTCD-LP, Ch. 46, Entravision Holdings LLC. Phone: 310-447-3870.

Technical Facilities: 2600-w TPO, 0.012-kw ERP, 59-ft. above ground, 2890-ft. above sea level, lat. 33° 00' 31", long. 116° 58' 16".

Transmitter: Mount Woodson.

Ownership: Entravision Communications Corp.

San Diego—KZSD-LP, Ch. 41, McGraw-Hill Broadcasting Co. Inc. Phone: 619-237-1010.

Technical Facilities: 15-kw ERP, 58-ft. above ground, 2953-ft. above sea level, lat. 33° 00' 33", long. 116° 58' 14".

Ownership: McGraw-Hill Broadcasting Co. Inc.

San Francisco—KMMC-LP, Ch. 40, Caballero Acquisition Inc. Phone: 202-420-8970.

Technical Facilities: 44-kw ERP, 157-ft. above ground, 1414-ft. above sea level, lat. 37° 41' 15", long. 122° 26' 01".

Holds CP for change to 3.2-kw ERP, 157-ft. above ground, 1425-ft. above sea level, lat. 37° 41' 13", long. 122° 26' 03". BDFCDTL-20080801AOG.

Ownership: Caballero Acquisition Inc.

■ **San Francisco, etc.**—KFTL-CA, Ch. 28, Polar Broadcasting Inc. Phone: 916-641-8191.

Studio: 1640 Alum Rock Ave, San Jose, CA 95116.

Technical Facilities: 90-kw ERP, 128-ft. above ground, 1385-ft. above sea level, lat. 37° 41' 15", long. 122° 26' 01".

Ownership: Family Stations Inc.

Personnel: Warren L. Trumbly, General Manager; Art Sanchez, Chief Engineer; Juan Meono, Sales Manager.

San Luis Obispo—K16FC, Ch. 16, Community TV of Southern California. Phone: 323-953-5209.

Technical Facilities: 16-kw ERP, 89-ft. above ground, 2543-ft. above sea level, lat. 35° 21' 37", long. 120° 39' 20".

Holds CP for change to 15-kw ERP, BDFCDTT-20080221AAE.

Transmitter: Cuesta Peak communications site, 5.8-mi. N of San Luis Obispo.

Ownership: Community TV of Southern California.

■ **San Luis Obispo**—K28FK, Ch. 28, Entravision Holdings, LLC.

Technical Facilities: 850-w TPO, 13.5-kw ERP, 243-ft. above ground, 2716-ft. above sea level, lat. 39° 21' 38", long. 120° 39' 21".

Transmitter: Cuesta Peak, approx. 1-mi. W of U.S. 101.

Ownership: James L. Primm.

San Luis Obispo—K47GD, Ch. 47, NBC Telemundo License Co. Phone: 202-637-4535.

Technical Facilities: 27.1-kw ERP, 93-ft. above ground, 2559-ft. above sea level, lat. 35° 21' 38", long. 120° 39' 20".

Ownership: NBC Universal.

San Luis Obispo—KCCE-LP, Ch. 20, Anet Communications. Phone: 805-545-7770.

Studio: 1026 Chorro St, San Luis Obispo, CA 93401.

Technical Facilities: 1000-w TPO, 47.9-kw ERP, 30-ft. above ground, 2539-ft. above sea level, lat. 35° 21' 40", long. 120° 39' 21".

Transmitter: Cuesta electronics site.

Ownership: Anet Communications Inc.

Personnel: Harvey Caplan, General Manager.

San Luis Obispo—KFUL-LP, Ch. 44, KJLA LLC. Phone: 818-757-7583. Fax: 818-757-7533.

Technical Facilities: 19.9-kw ERP, 43-ft. above ground, 2508-ft. above sea level, lat. 35° 21' 38", long. 120° 39' 21".

Transmitter: Questa Park Antenna Farm, 5-mi. N of San Luis Obispo.

Ownership: KJLA LLC.

Personnel: Francis Wilkinson, General Manager; Ken Brown, Chief Engineer.

■ **San Luis Obispo**—KKFX-CA, Ch. 24, Cowles California Media Co. Phone: 509-459-5520.

Technical Facilities: 1-w TPO, 2.03-kw ERP, 72-ft. above ground, 2549-ft. above sea level, lat. 35° 21' 38", long. 120° 39' 21".

Transmitter: Questa Peak antenna farm, 5-mi. N of San Luis Obispo.

Ownership: Cowles Co.

Personnel: Jeffery MacDougall, Vice President & General Manager.

■ **San Luis Obispo**—KMMA-CA, Ch. 18, Caballero Acquisition Inc. Phone: 202-429-8970.

Technical Facilities: 14.3-kw ERP, 52-ft. above ground, 2526-ft. above sea level, lat. 35° 21' 38", long. 120° 39' 21".

Holds CP for change to channel number 41, 4-kw ERP, BDFCDTA-20081110AJG.

Transmitter: 4.3-mi. N of San Luis Obispo.

Began Operation: March 20, 1998.

Ownership: Caballero Acquisition Inc.

Personnel: Eduardo Caballero, Chief Executive Officer.

San Luis Obispo—KPXA-LP, Ch. 60, Tomay Television Inc. Phone: 805-928-8300.

Technical Facilities: 21.4-kw ERP, 230-ft. above ground, 610-ft. above sea level, lat. 35° 17' 58", long. 120° 40' 20".

Holds CP for change to channel number 49, 42-kw ERP, 37-ft. above ground, 1635-ft. above sea level, lat. 34° 53' 54", long. 120° 35' 28". BDISTTL-20070320AMK.

Ownership: Tomay Television Inc.

■ **San Luis Obispo**—KSBO-CA, Ch. 42, Una Vez Mas San Luis Obispo License LLC. Phone: 214-754-7008.

Technical Facilities: 14-kw ERP, 249-ft. above ground, 2723-ft. above sea level, lat. 35° 21' 38", long. 120° 39' 21".

Ownership: Una Vez Mas GP LLC.

San Luis Obispo, etc.—K57BC, Ch. 57, Smith Media License Holdings LLC. Phone: 314-853-7736.

Technical Facilities: 0.8-kw ERP, 2513-ft. above sea level, lat. 35° 21' 38", long. 120° 39' 21".

Holds CP for change to channel number 31, 0.14-kw ERP, 46-ft. above ground, 2500-ft. above sea level, lat. 34° 53' 54", long. 120° 39' 21". BDISDTT-20080513ABH.

Ownership: Smith Media License Holdings LLC.

■ **San Marcos**—KSKT-CA, Ch. 43, Blue Skies Broadcasting Corp. Phone: 818-884-0440.

Technical Facilities: 1000-w TPO, 42.808-kw ERP, 92-ft. above ground, 1171-ft. above sea level, lat. 33° 06' 39", long. 117° 09' 13".

Transmitter: 21815 Washington, San Marcos.

Ownership: Blue Skies Broadcasting Corp.

Santa Barbara—K15DB, Ch. 15, Mutual Television Network. Phone: 888-482-1080.

Technical Facilities: 713-w TPO, 3.25-kw ERP, 13-ft. above ground, 2172-ft. above sea level, lat. 34° 27' 57", long. 119° 40' 37".

Holds CP for change to 15-kw ERP, 13-ft. above ground, 2155-ft. above sea level, BDFCDTT-20060330AAJ.

Transmitter: Gibraltar Peak, near Santa Barbara.

Ownership: Mutual Television Network.

Santa Barbara—K26FT, Ch. 26, Community TV of Southern California. Phone: 323-953-5209.

Technical Facilities: 0.397-kw ERP, lat. 34° 27' 56", long. 119° 40' 40".

Holds CP for change to 0.203-kw ERP, 13-ft. above ground, 2139-ft. above sea level, BDFCDTT-20080221AAF.

Ownership: Community TV of Southern California.

Santa Barbara—K28GY, Ch. 28, Community TV of Southern California. Phone: 323-953-5209.

Technical Facilities: 74.3-kw ERP, 56-ft. above ground, 4049-ft. above sea level, lat. 34° 31' 31", long. 119° 57' 29".

Holds CP for change to 2.6-kw ERP, BDFCDTT-20080221AAU.

Ownership: Community TV of Southern California.

Santa Barbara—K59CD, Ch. 59, KSBY Communications Inc. Phone: 843-577-7111.

Technical Facilities: 1.18-kw ERP, lat. 34° 27' 55", long. 119° 40' 38".

Holds CP for change to channel number 10, 0.1-kw ERP, 14-ft. above ground, 2146-ft. above sea level, BDISDTV-20061215AAN.

Ownership: Evening Post Publishing Co.

Santa Barbara—KBAB-LP, Ch. 51, Biltmore Broadcasting Santa Barbara Inc. Phone: 310-452-7938.

Technical Facilities: 1000-w TPO, 3.57-kw ERP, 29-ft. above ground, 2184-ft. above sea level, lat. 34° 27' 58", long. 119° 40' 37".

Transmitter: Broadcast Peak.

Ownership: Biltmore Broadcasting Corp.

■ **Santa Barbara**—KSBB-LP, Ch. 17, Smith Media License Holdings LLC. Phone: 314-853-7736.

Technical Facilities: 1.07-kw ERP, 30-ft. above ground, 230-ft. above sea level, lat. 34° 24' 27", long. 119° 42' 26".

Holds CP for change to 0.005-kw ERP, BDFCDTA-20080513ABD.

Ownership: Smith Media License Holdings LLC.

Santa Barbara—KSBT-LP, Ch. 32, Arnold N. Applebaum.

Technical Facilities: 1900-w TPO, 4.58-kw ERP, 11-ft. above ground, 2169-ft. above sea level, lat. 34° 27' 57", long. 119° 40' 38".

Transmitter: Gregory Rd., approx. 1.5-mi. N of Santa Barbara.

Ownership: Arnold N. Applebaum.

■ **Santa Barbara**—KTSB-LP, Ch. 43, Entravision Holdings LLC. Phone: 310-447-3870.

Technical Facilities: 10-kw ERP, 13-ft. above ground, 2162-ft. above sea level, lat. 34° 27' 55", long. 119° 40' 38".

Ownership: Entravision Communications Corp.

■ **Santa Barbara**—KVMM-CA, Ch. 41, Caballero Acquisition Inc. Phone: 202-429-8970.

Technical Facilities: 40-kw ERP, 12-ft. above ground, 2113-ft. above sea level, lat. 34° 27' 57", long. 119° 40' 38".

Holds CP for change to 15-kw ERP, BDFCDTA-20080804ACQ.

Ownership: Caballero Acquisition Inc.

Personnel: Eduardo Caballero, Chief Executive Officer.

Santa Barbara—KZDF-LP, Ch. 8, Una Vez Mas Santa Barbara License LLC. Phone: 214-754-7008.

Technical Facilities: 0.94-kw ERP, 40-ft. above ground, 2165-ft. above sea level, lat. 34° 27' 55", long. 119° 40' 38".

Ownership: Una Vez Mas GP LLC.

■ **Santa Clara-San Jose**—KAXT-CA, Ch. 22, Broadland Properties Inc. Phone: 916-222-5460.

Technical Facilities: 56-kw ERP, 167-ft. above ground, 1129-ft. above sea level, lat. 37° 19' 23", long. 121° 45' 15".

Began Operation: July 31, 1990.

Ownership: Broadland Properties Inc.

Personnel: Juan Meono, Sales Manager; Art Sanchez, Operations Manager.

■ **Santa Maria**—K07TA, Ch. 7, Raul & Consuelo Palazuelos. Phone: 805-928-7700. Fax: 805-928-8606.

Studio: 330 W Carmen Ln, Santa Maria, CA 93458.

Technical Facilities: 10-w TPO, 0.13-kw ERP, lat. 34° 50' 06", long. 120° 22' 56".

Holds CP for change to 0.001-kw ERP, 30-ft. above ground, 1368-ft. above sea level, BDFCDVA-20061030ADS.

Transmitter: Solomon Mountain.

Ownership: Raul & Consuelo Palazuelos.

Personnel: Sandy Keefer, General Manager & Sales Manager; Roy Keefer, Chief Engineer.

■ **Santa Maria**—K35ER, Ch. 35, Entravision Holdings LLC. Phone: 310-447-3870.

Technical Facilities: 20-kw ERP, 98-ft. above ground, 3346-ft. above sea level, lat. 34° 54' 37", long. 120° 11' 09".

Began Operation: September 2, 1998.

Ownership: Entravision Communications Corp.

Santa Maria—K46GF, Ch. 46, NBC Telemundo License Co. Phone: 202-637-4535.

Technical Facilities: 7-kw ERP, 75-ft. above ground, 3323-ft. above sea level, lat. 34° 54' 37", long. 120° 11' 08".

Transmitter: Tepusquet Peak, SE of Santa Maria.

Ownership: NBC Universal.

Santa Maria—K51GB, Ch. 51, Central Coast Good News Inc. Phone: 805-434-1848.

Technical Facilities: 5-kw ERP, lat. 34° 50' 05", long. 120° 22' 57".

Ownership: Central Coast Good News Inc.

■ **Santa Maria**—KDFS-CA, Ch. 30, Una Vez Mas Santa Maria License LLC. Phone: 214-754-7008.

Technical Facilities: 1000-w TPO, 28.4-kw ERP, 36-ft. above ground, 1637-ft. above sea level, lat. 34° 53' 54", long. 120° 35' 28".

Transmitter: 5-mi. S of Guadalupe.

Ownership: Una Vez Mas GP LLC.

Santa Maria—KKDJ-LP, Ch. 8, Cocola Broadcasting Companies LLC. Phone: 559-435-7000. Fax: 559-435-3201.

Technical Facilities: 3-kw ERP, 56-ft. above ground, 3304-ft. above sea level, lat. 34° 54' 37", long. 120° 11' 08".

Ownership: Cocola Broadcasting Companies LLC.

Personnel: Todd Lopes, President.

Santa Maria—KLFA-LP, Ch. 25, KJLA LLC. Phone: 818-757-7583. Fax: 818-757-7533.

Technical Facilities: 1000-w TPO, 16.2-kw ERP, 40-ft. above ground, 1384-ft. above sea level, lat. 34° 50' 06", long. 120° 22' 56".

Transmitter: Mount Solomon, 0.5-mi. SSE of Santa Maria.

Ownership: KJLA LLC.

Personnel: Francis Wilkinson, General Manager; Ken Brown, Chief Engineer.

■ **Santa Maria**—KQMM-CA, Ch. 14, Caballero Acquisition Inc.

Technical Facilities: 84-kw ERP, 43-ft. above ground, 3291-ft. above sea level, lat. 34° 54' 36", long. 120° 11' 10".

Ownership: Caballero Acquisition Inc.

Personnel: Eduardo Caballero, Chief Executive Officer.

Santa Maria—KQMM-LD, Ch. 29, Caballero Acquisition Inc. Phone: 202-429-8970.

Technical Facilities: 15-kw ERP, 43-ft. above ground, 3291-ft. above sea level, lat. 34° 54' 36", long. 120° 11' 10".

Ownership: Caballero Acquisition Inc.

Santa Maria—KWSM-LP, Ch. 40, Cocola Broadcasting Companies LLC. Phone: 559-435-7000. Fax: 559-435-3201.

Technical Facilities: 1000-w TPO, 150-kw ERP, 56-ft. above ground, 3304-ft. above sea level, lat. 34° 54' 37", long. 120° 11' 08".

Transmitter: 5-mi. S of Guadalupe.

Ownership: Cocola Broadcasting Companies LLC.

Personnel: Todd Lopes, President.

Santa Rosa—K25HI, Ch. 25, Young Broadcasting of San Francisco Inc., Debtor in Possessi. Phone: 919-839-0300.

Technical Facilities: 17-kw ERP, 193-ft. above ground, 1795-ft. above sea level, lat. 38° 30' 31", long. 122° 39' 41".

Began Operation: February 7, 1992.

Ownership: Young Broadcasting Inc., Debtor in Possession.

■ **Santa Rosa**—KDTV-CA, Ch. 28, KDTV License Partnership GP. Phone: 415-538-8000. Fax: 415-538-8053.

Studio: 50 Fremont St, 41st Fl, San Francisco, CA 94105.

Technical Facilities: 900-w TPO, 8.2-kw ERP, 59-ft. above ground, 3999-ft. above sea level, lat. 38° 39' 23", long. 122° 36' 54".

Transmitter: 5.6-mi. NW of Calistoga & 1-mi. N of Red Hill in Mayacamas Mountains.

Multichannel TV Sound: Stereo and separate audio program.

Ownership: Univision Communications Inc.

Personnel: Marcela Medina, Vice President & General Manager; Mike Roberts, Chief Engineer; Ernie Rizzuti, General Sales Manager; Chris Newgard, National Sales Manager; Sandi Stretch, Local Sales Manager; Sandra Thomas, News Director; Francisco Jaramillo, Creative Services Manager; Perla Rodriguez, Community & Public Affairs Manager; Melanie Wellbeloved, Research Director; Maria Rodriguez, Traffic Manager.

Santa Rosa—KQRM-LP, Ch. 40, One Ministries Inc. Phone: 707-537-9881.

Technical Facilities: 11.25-kw ERP, 36-ft. above ground, 1637-ft. above sea level, lat. 38° 30' 31", long. 122° 39' 41".

Holds CP for change to 5.5-kw ERP, 164-ft. above ground, 1765-ft. above sea level, BPTTL-20080505AAE.

Ownership: One Ministries Inc.

Santa Rosa—KTVJ-LP, Ch. 36, Fiori Media Inc. Phone: 707-446-7946.

Technical Facilities: 21.3-kw ERP, 167-ft. above ground, 1768-ft. above sea level, lat. 38° 30' 31", long. 122° 39' 41".

Holds CP for change to channel number 20, 4-kw ERP, 69-ft. above ground, 1867-ft. above sea level, lat. 38° 19' 56", long. 122° 35' 42". BDISTTL-20080428AAA.

Ownership: Fiori Media Inc.

Seiad Valley—K04NU, Ch. 4, Nolowire Inc.

Technical Facilities: 0.005-kw ERP, 20-ft. above ground, 3921-ft. above sea level, lat. 41° 50' 21", long. 123° 14' 27".

Ownership: Nolowire Inc.

Seiad Valley—K08EQ, Ch. 8, Nolowire Inc.

Technical Facilities: 0.049-kw ERP, lat. 41° 50' 21", long. 123° 14' 17".

Ownership: Nolowire Inc.

Seiad Valley—K12JD, Ch. 12, Nolowire Inc.

Technical Facilities: 0.004-kw ERP, lat. 41° 50' 21", long. 123° 14' 17".

Ownership: Nolowire Inc.

Shelter Cove—K02OD, Ch. 2, Pollack/Belz Broadcasting Co. LLC.

Technical Facilities: 0.005-kw ERP, lat. 40° 01' 56", long. 124° 02' 20".

Ownership: Pollack/Belz Broadcasting Co. LLC.

Shelter Cove—K10KY, Ch. 10, Raul Broadcasting Co. of Eureka Inc. Phone: 209-521-5702.

Technical Facilities: 0.006-kw ERP, lat. 40° 01' 56", long. 124° 02' 20".

Holds CP for change to 0.005-kw ERP, 30-ft. above ground, 2028-ft. above sea level, BDFCDVA-20060703AAV.

Ownership: Raul & Consuelo Palazuelos.

Shelter Cove—K12OV, Ch. 12, Redwood Empire Public Television Inc. Phone: 707-445-0813.

Technical Facilities: 0.003-kw ERP, 30-ft. above ground, 1991-ft. above sea level, lat. 40° 01' 56", long. 124° 02' 20".

Ownership: Redwood Empire Public TV Inc.

South Eureka & Loleta—K51EG, Ch. 51, BlueStone License Holdings Inc. Phone: 212-247-8717.

Technical Facilities: 0.301-kw ERP, lat. 40° 42' 58", long. 124° 12' 11".

Transmitter: Humboldt Hill Rd., 5-mi. SSW of Eureka.

Ownership: Bonten Media Group LLC.

South Lake Tahoe—K12PP, Ch. 12, KTVU Partnership. Phone: 775-856-1100.

Technical Facilities: 0.047-kw ERP, 36-ft. above ground, 7336-ft. above sea level, lat. 39° 04' 57", long. 120° 10' 28".

Ownership: Cox Enterprises Inc.

South Lake Tahoe—K33CN, Ch. 33, Sierra Broadcasting Co.

Technical Facilities: 0.4-kw ERP, lat. 38° 54' 37", long. 120° 02' 05".

Ownership: Sunbelt Communications Co.

South Lake Tahoe—K48LA-D, Ch. 48, KTVU Partnership. Phone: 775-856-1100.

Technical Facilities: 0.227-kw ERP, 36-ft. above ground, 7336-ft. above sea level, lat. 39° 04' 57", long. 120° 10' 28".

Began Operation: October 10, 2008.

Ownership: KTVU Partnership.

South Yreka—K47DV, Ch. 47, California Oregon Broadcasting Inc.

Technical Facilities: 1000-w TPO, 9.89-kw ERP, 3274-ft. above sea level, lat. 41° 43' 31", long. 122° 37' 32".

Transmitter: Butcher Hill communications site.

Ownership: California-Oregon Broadcasting Inc.

Stateline, etc.—K40JV-D, Ch. 40, Sarkes Tarzian Inc. Phone: 812-332-7251.

Technical Facilities: 0.122-kw ERP, 72-ft. above ground, 7323-ft. above sea level, lat. 38° 54' 37", long. 120° 02' 05".

Ownership: Sarkes Tarzian Inc.

Stateline, etc.—K43DB, Ch. 43, Sarkes Tarzian Inc. Phone: 812-332-7251.

Technical Facilities: 0.408-kw ERP, 72-ft. above ground, 7323-ft. above sea level, lat. 38° 54' 37", long. 120° 02' 05".

Ownership: Sarkes Tarzian Inc.

Stockton—KDTS-LP, Ch. 52, Word of God Fellowship Inc. Phone: 817-858-9955. Fax: 817-571-7478.

Technical Facilities: 7.68-kw ERP, 394-ft. above ground, 413-ft. above sea level, lat. 37° 59' 30", long. 121° 17' 17".

Ownership: Word of God Fellowship Inc.

Stockton—KMMW-LD, Ch. 28, Caballero Acquisition Inc. Phone: 202-429-8970.

Technical Facilities: 15-kw ERP, 248-ft. above ground, 2986-ft. above sea level, lat. 38° 07' 10", long. 120° 43' 27".

Ownership: Caballero Acquisition Inc.

Personnel: Eduardo Caballero, Chief Executive Officer.

Susanville—KREN-LP, Ch. 29, Entravision Holdings LLC. Phone: 310-447-3870.

Technical Facilities: 8-kw ERP, 164-ft. above ground, 5991-ft. above sea level, lat. 40° 27' 13", long. 120° 34' 14".

Holds CP for change to 15-kw ERP, BDFCDTTL-20060330AHK.

Began Operation: April 20, 2006.

Ownership: Entravision Communications Corp.

Susanville & Herlong—K19GA, Ch. 19, Honey Lake Community TV Corp. Phone: 530-257-9625.

Technical Facilities: 1.01-kw ERP, 25-ft. above ground, 6760-ft. above sea level, lat. 40° 26' 49", long. 120° 21' 25".

Ownership: Honey Lake Community TV Corp.

Susanville, etc.—K17HE, Ch. 17, Honey Lake Community TV Corp. Phone: 530-257-9625.

Technical Facilities: 1.01-kw ERP, 25-ft. above ground, 6760-ft. above sea level, lat. 40° 26' 49", long. 120° 21' 25".

Ownership: Honey Lake Community TV Corp.

Susanville, etc.—K31IE, Ch. 31, Honey Lake Community TV Corp. Phone: 530-257-9625.

Technical Facilities: 1-kw ERP, 25-ft. above ground, 6760-ft. above sea level, lat. 40° 26' 49", long. 120° 21' 25".

Ownership: Honey Lake Community TV Corp.

Susanville, etc.—K36HH, Ch. 36, Honey Lake Community TV Corp. Phone: 530-257-9625.

Technical Facilities: 1.17-kw ERP, 25-ft. above ground, 6760-ft. above sea level, lat. 40° 26' 49", long. 120° 21' 25".

Ownership: Honey Lake Community TV Corp.

Susanville, etc.—K38IU, Ch. 38, Honey Lake Community TV Corp. Phone: 530-257-9625.

Technical Facilities: 0.987-kw ERP, 25-ft. above ground, 6760-ft. above sea level, lat. 40° 26' 49", long. 120° 21' 25".

Ownership: Honey Lake Community TV Corp.

Susanville, etc.—K42GV, Ch. 42, Honey Lake Community TV Corp. Phone: 530-257-9625.

Technical Facilities: 1.118-kw ERP, 25-ft. above ground, 6760-ft. above sea level, lat. 40° 26' 49", long. 120° 21' 25".

Ownership: Honey Lake Community TV Corp.

Swauger Creek—K51CP, Ch. 51, Mono County Service Area No. 5.

Technical Facilities: 0.03-kw ERP, lat. 38° 23' 19", long. 119° 21' 50".

Ownership: Mono County Service Area No. 5.

Swauger Creek—K54CX, Ch. 54, Mono County Service Area No. 5.

Technical Facilities: 0.03-kw ERP, lat. 38° 23' 19", long. 119° 21' 50".

Ownership: Mono County Service Area No. 5.

Tahoe City—K23DT, Ch. 23, Ellis Communications Inc. Phone: 404-229-8080.

Technical Facilities: 5.6-kw ERP, 82-ft. above ground, 9764-ft. above sea level, lat. 39° 18' 38", long. 119° 53' 01".

Holds CP for change to 4.4-kw ERP, 53-ft. above ground, 9735-ft. above sea level, BDFCDTT-20081124ALW.

Transmitter: Atop Slide Mountain, near Incline Village.

Began Operation: September 27, 1993.

Ownership: Ellis Communications Inc.

Tahoe City—K56BW, Ch. 56, Sierra Broadcasting Co.

Technical Facilities: 10.6-kw ERP, 23-ft. above ground, 6726-ft. above sea level, lat. 39° 18' 36", long. 120° 19' 49".

Ownership: Sunbelt Communications Co.

Temecula—K12PO, Ch. 12, Channel 51 of San Diego Inc. Phone: 858-571-5151.

Technical Facilities: 1000-w TPO, 1-kw ERP, 85-ft. above ground, 1824-ft. above sea level, lat. 33° 35' 36", long. 117° 08' 53".

Transmitter: Red Mountain, 0.7-mi. NNW of Mission Rd. & Live Oak Park Rd. intersection.

Multichannel TV Sound: Stereo only.

Ownership: Channel 51 of San Diego Inc.

Personnel: Mike McKinnon, General Manager; Richard Large, Chief Engineer; Bob Sexton, Sales Manager.

Trinity Center—K39DG-D, Ch. 39, Northern California Educational TV Assn. Inc. Phone: 530-243-5493.

Technical Facilities: 0.059-kw ERP, 20-ft. above ground, 3629-ft. above sea level, lat. 40° 58' 03", long. 122° 42' 30".

Ownership: Northern California Educational TV Assn. Inc.

■**Tulare**—KFRE-CA, Ch. 40, Harry J. Pappas - Debtor-in-Possession. Phone: 775-851-8769.

Studio: 5035 E McKinley Ave, Fresno, CA 93727.

Technical Facilities: 1000-w TPO, 1.7-kw ERP, 98-ft. above ground, 5770-ft. above sea level, lat. 36° 17' 12", long. 118° 50' 20".

Transmitter: Blue Ridge, near Tulare.

Ownership: Pappas Telecasting Companies.

Twentynine Palms—K14JT, Ch. 14, Morongo Basin TV Club Inc.

Technical Facilities: 3.71-kw ERP, lat. 34° 04' 32", long. 115° 57' 18".

Transmitter: Pinto Mountain, approx. 7.9-mi. SE of Twentynine Palms.

Ownership: Morongo Basin TV Club Inc.

Twentynine Palms—K16FI, Ch. 16, County of San Bernardino Service Area 70. Phone: 760-367-1833. Fax: 760-367-4732.

Technical Facilities: 1.19-kw ERP, 23-ft. above ground, 4272-ft. above sea level, lat. 34° 04' 32", long. 115° 57' 18".

Multichannel TV Sound: Stereo only.

Ownership: County Service Area 70 TV5.

Personnel: Jim Parker, General Manager & Chief Engineer; Sharon O'Neill, Sales Manager.

Twentynine Palms—K18FH, Ch. 18, Morongo Basin TV Club Inc.

Technical Facilities: 3.71-kw ERP, lat. 34° 04' 32", long. 115° 57' 18".

Transmitter: Pinto Mountain, 7.9-mi. SE of Twentynine Palms.

Ownership: Morongo Basin TV Club Inc.

Twentynine Palms—K38EE, Ch. 38, Mutual Television Network. Phone: 888-482-1080.

Technical Facilities: 1.2-kw ERP, 16-ft. above ground, 4121-ft. above sea level, lat. 34° 04' 32", long. 115° 57' 18".

Transmitter: 5.7-mi. SW of Base Line St. & Utah Trail, near Twentynine Palms.

Ownership: Mutual Television Network.

Twentynine Palms, etc.—K29GK, Ch. 29, County of San Bernardino, Area 70. Phone: 760-367-1833.

Technical Facilities: 4-kw ERP, 30-ft. above ground, 4278-ft. above sea level, lat. 34° 04' 32", long. 115° 57' 18".

Ownership: San Bernardino County.

Twentynine Palms, etc.—K47IB, Ch. 47, County of San Bernardino, Area 70. Phone: 760-367-1833.

Technical Facilities: 3-kw ERP, 13-ft. above ground, 4262-ft. above sea level, lat. 34° 04' 32", long. 115° 57' 18".

Ownership: San Bernardino County.

Twentynine Palms, etc.—K49DC, Ch. 49, County of San Bernardino, Area 70. Phone: 760-367-1833.

Technical Facilities: 2.57-kw ERP, lat. 34° 04' 32", long. 115° 57' 18".

Ownership: San Bernardino County.

Twentynine Palms, etc.—K51DU, Ch. 51, County of San Bernardino, Area 70. Phone: 760-367-1833.

Technical Facilities: 2.57-kw ERP, lat. 34° 04' 32", long. 115° 57' 18".

Ownership: San Bernardino County.

Twin Peaks—KHIR-LP, Ch. 3, Delta Media Group Inc. Phone: 818-399-9375.

Technical Facilities: 0.5-kw ERP, 66-ft. above ground, 2987-ft. above sea level, lat. 33° 54' 30", long. 116° 59' 45".

Holds CP for change to channel number 22, 9.99-kw ERP, 23-ft. above ground, 5646-ft. above sea level, lat. 34° 15' 23.97", long. 117° 14' 22.84". BDISTTL-20071107AAD.

Ownership: Shahram Hashemizadeh.

Ukiah—K17CG, Ch. 17, Television Improvement Assn.

Technical Facilities: 2.54-kw ERP, lat. 39° 07' 03", long. 123° 05' 35".

Ownership: Television Improvement Assn.

Ukiah—K21CD, Ch. 21, Television Improvement Assn.

Technical Facilities: 2.54-kw ERP, lat. 39° 07' 03", long. 123° 05' 35".

Ownership: Television Improvement Assn.

Ukiah—K27EE, Ch. 27, Television Improvement Assn.

Technical Facilities: 2.54-kw ERP, 23-ft. above ground, 3153-ft. above sea level, lat. 39° 07' 03", long. 123° 05' 35".

Ownership: Television Improvement Assn.

Ukiah—K29DF, Ch. 29, Television Improvement Assn.

Technical Facilities: 2.54-kw ERP, 23-ft. above ground, 3153-ft. above sea level, lat. 39° 07' 03", long. 123° 05' 35".

Ownership: Television Improvement Assn.

Ukiah—K31GK, Ch. 31, Television Improvement Assn.

Technical Facilities: 2.54-kw ERP, 20-ft. above ground, 3153-ft. above sea level, lat. 39° 07' 03", long. 123° 05' 35".

Ownership: Television Improvement Assn.

Ukiah—K39AG, Ch. 39, Television Improvement Assn.

Technical Facilities: 2.53-kw ERP, lat. 39° 07' 03", long. 123° 05' 35".

Ownership: Television Improvement Assn.

Ukiah—K41AF, Ch. 41, Television Improvement Assn.

Technical Facilities: 2.53-kw ERP, lat. 39° 07' 03", long. 123° 05' 35".

Ownership: Television Improvement Assn.

Ukiah—K42HE, Ch. 42, Centro Cristiano Sion. Phone: 650-369-8707.

Technical Facilities: 70-kw ERP, 220-ft. above ground, 2559-ft. above sea level, lat. 38° 44' 00", long. 123° 17' 19".

Holds CP for change to channel number 49, 15-kw ERP, 164-ft. above ground, 2602-ft. above sea level, lat. 38° 20' 52", long. 122° 34' 35". BDISDTL-20090317ADT.

Began Operation: December 12, 2007.

Ownership: Centro Cristiano Sion.

Ukiah—K43AF, Ch. 43, Television Improvement Assn.

Technical Facilities: 2.53-kw ERP, lat. 39° 07' 03", long. 123° 05' 35".

Ownership: Television Improvement Assn.

Ukiah—K45AH, Ch. 45, Television Improvement Assn.

Technical Facilities: 2.53-kw ERP, lat. 39° 07' 03", long. 123° 05' 35".

Ownership: Television Improvement Assn.

Ukiah—K47AL, Ch. 47, Television Improvement Assn. Phone: 707-462-5733.

Technical Facilities: 100-w TPO, 2.5-kw ERP, 30-ft. above ground, 3159-ft. above sea level, lat. 39° 07' 03", long. 123° 05' 35".

Transmitter: Cow Mountain, 6.5-mi. SE of Ukiah.

Ownership: Television Improvement Assn.

Personnel: L. J. Dietz, General Manager.

Ukiah—K51AQ, Ch. 51, Television Improvement Assn.

Technical Facilities: 2.53-kw ERP, lat. 39° 07' 03", long. 123° 05' 35".

Ownership: Television Improvement Assn.

Ukiah—K55GX, Ch. 55, Television Improvement Assn.

Technical Facilities: 2.54-kw ERP, 23-ft. above ground, 3153-ft. above sea level, lat. 39° 07' 03", long. 123° 05' 35".

Ownership: Television Improvement Assn.

Ukiah—K69DF, Ch. 69, Television Improvement Assn.

Technical Facilities: 1.15-kw ERP, lat. 39° 07' 03", long. 123° 05' 35".

Ownership: Television Improvement Assn.

■**Ukiah**—KDSL-CA, Ch. 23, Concord License LLC - Debtor-in-Possession. Phone: 559-733-7800.

Technical Facilities: 12.7-kw ERP, 49-ft. above ground, 3612-ft. above sea level, lat. 39° 07' 49", long. 123° 04' 31".

Transmitter: Cow Mountain, approx. 4-mi. E of Ukiah.

Ownership: E. Roger Williams, Trustee.

Ukiah—KTJH-LP, Ch. 44, Jeff Chang. Phone: 310-403-5039.

Technical Facilities: 1.04-kw ERP, 13-ft. above ground, 2508-ft. above sea level, lat. 39° 06' 57.4", long. 123° 13' 56".

Ownership: Jeff Chang.

Van Nuys—K55KD, Ch. 55, AlmaVision Hispanic Network Inc. Phone: 213-627-8711.

Technical Facilities: 9.98-kw ERP, 141-ft. above ground, 5840-ft. above sea level, lat. 34° 13' 36", long. 118° 03' 57".

Holds CP for change to 135-ft. above ground, 5843-ft. above sea level, BPTTL-20060912AAX.

Ownership: AlmaVision Hispanic Network Inc.

■**Van Nuys**—KSKJ-CA, Ch. 38, Capital Broadcasting Corp. Phone: 818-884-2617.

Technical Facilities: 3.8-kw ERP, 200-ft. above ground, 1450-ft. above sea level, lat. 34° 17' 03", long. 118° 28' 17".

Multichannel TV Sound: Separate audio program.

Ownership: Capital Broadcasting Corp.

Personnel: Robert Ruiz, General Manager & Chief Engineer; Todd Ruiz, Sales Manager.

Van Nuys—KWJD-LP, Ch. 25, Friendly Broadcasting Co. Phone: 818-831-9333.

Technical Facilities: 1.2-kw ERP, 138-ft. above ground, 883-ft. above sea level, lat. 34° 12' 06", long. 118° 27' 19".

Ownership: Friendly Broadcasting Co.

Ventura—K45DU, Ch. 45, Trinity Christian Center of Santa Ana Inc. Phone: 714-832-2950. Fax: 714-730-0661.

Technical Facilities: 1.5-kw ERP, 26-ft. above ground, 2106-ft. above sea level, lat. 34° 20' 57", long. 119° 20' 07".

Ownership: Trinity Broadcasting Network Inc.

Personnel: Paul Crouch, General Manager; Ben Miller, Chief Engineer; Rod Henke, Sales Manager.

Ventura—KIMG-LP, Ch. 23, EBC Los Angeles Inc., Debtor in Possession. Phone: 501-219-2400.

Technical Facilities: 300-w TPO, 1.03-kw ERP, 98-ft. above ground, 2178-ft. above sea level, lat. 34° 20' 57", long. 119° 20' 07".

Transmitter: Red Top Mountain 6.2-mi. NW of Ventura.

Began Operation: June 26, 1998.

Ownership: Equity Media Holdings Corp., Debtor in Possession.

Victorville—K39GY, Ch. 39, Jeff Chang. Phone: 310-403-5039.

Technical Facilities: 1.5-kw ERP, 30-ft. above ground, 4531-ft. above sea level, lat. 34° 36' 36", long. 117° 17' 13".

Holds CP for change to 15-kw ERP, BDFCDTT-20060223AAM.

Ownership: Jeff Chang.

Personnel: Paul Crouch, General Manager; Ben Miller, Chief Engineer; Rod Henke, Sales Manager.

Victorville—K47CC, Ch. 47, Community TV of Southern California.

Technical Facilities: 0.968-kw ERP, 56-ft. above ground, 4553-ft. above sea level, lat. 34° 36' 35", long. 117° 17' 12".

Ownership: Community TV of Southern California.

Victorville—KVKV-LP, Ch. 29, Louis Martinez Family Group LLC. Phone: 951-509-1751.

Technical Facilities: 1-kw ERP, 161-ft. above ground, 4528-ft. above sea level, lat. 34° 36' 44", long. 117° 17' 29".

Holds CP for change to 7.6-kw ERP, 161-ft. above ground, 4557-ft. above sea level, BPTTL-20090227ABH.

Began Operation: July 25, 2008.

Ownership: Louis Martinez Family Group LLC.

Victorville, etc.—K21AC, Ch. 21, Victor Valley Public Translator Inc.

Technical Facilities: 1.28-kw ERP, lat. 34° 39", long. 117° 17' 12".

Ownership: Victor Valley Public Translator Inc.

Victorville, etc.—K25AD, Ch. 25, Victor Valley Public Translator Inc.

Technical Facilities: 1.28-kw ERP, 4560-ft. above sea level, lat. 34° 36' 39", long. 117° 17' 12".

Ownership: Victor Valley Public Translator Inc.

Victorville, etc.—K27AE, Ch. 27, Victor Valley Public Translator Inc.

Technical Facilities: 1.28-kw ERP, lat. 34° 36' 39", long. 117° 17' 12".

Ownership: Victor Valley Public Translator Inc.

Victorville, etc.—K31AD, Ch. 31, Victor Valley Public Translator Inc.

Technical Facilities: 1.28-kw ERP, lat. 34° 36' 39", long. 117° 17' 12".

Ownership: Victor Valley Public Translator Inc.

Victorville, etc.—K51AN, Ch. 51, Victor Valley Public Translator Inc.

Technical Facilities: 1.28-kw ERP, 4560-ft. above sea level, lat. 34° 36' 39", long. 117° 17' 12".

Ownership: Victor Valley Public Translator Inc.

■**Visalia**—KFAZ-CA, Ch. 8, Cocola Broadcasting Companies LLC. Phone: 559-435-7000. Fax: 559-435-3201.

Technical Facilities: 3-kw ERP, 98-ft. above ground, 5814-ft. above sea level, lat. 36° 17' 14", long. 118° 50' 17".

Holds CP for change to 0.139-kw ERP, BDFCDVA-20080801ANV.

Ownership: Cocola Broadcasting Companies LLC.

Visalia—KMCF-LP, Ch. 35, Cocola Broadcasting Companies LLC. Phone: 559-435-7000. Fax: 559-435-3201.

Studio: 706 W Herndon Ave, Fresno, CA 93650.

Technical Facilities: 150-kw ERP, 98-ft. above ground, 5814-ft. above sea level, lat. 36° 17' 14", long. 118° 50' 17".

Transmitter: Blue Ridge Mountain, near Milo.

Ownership: Cocola Broadcasting Companies LLC.

Personnel: Todd Lopes, President.

Vista—K26FA, Ch. 26, D'Amico Brothers Bcstg. Corp. Phone: 858-481-5686. Fax: 858-481-5686.

Studio: 155 13th St, Del Mar, CA 92014.

Technical Facilities: 7-w TPO, 0.001-kw ERP, 49-ft. above ground, 1667-ft. above sea level, lat. 36° 06' 39", long. 117° 09' 10".

Transmitter: 21851 Washingtonia, San Mareos, CA.

Ownership: D'Amico Brothers Broadcasting.

Personnel: Richard D'Amico, General Manager, Sales Manager & Chief Engineer.

Vista—KHAX-LP, Ch. 49, Entravision Holdings LLC. Phone: 310-447-3870.

Studio: 8691 Echo Dr, La Mesa, CA 92041.

Technical Facilities: 429-w TPO, 0.045-kw ERP, 69-ft. above ground, 1742-ft. above sea level, lat. 33° 12' 53", long. 117° 11' 15".

Transmitter: Blackjack Hill communications site, 3-mi. E of Vista.

Ownership: Entravision Communications Corp.

Weaverville—K04DD, Ch. 4, Weaverville Translator Corp. Phone: 530-623-5479.

Technical Facilities: 0.015-kw ERP, lat. 40° 43' 11", long. 122° 58' 46".

Holds CP for change to 35-ft. above ground, 3968-ft. above sea level, BDFCDTV-20090102ABY.

Ownership: Weaverville Translator Corp.

Weaverville, etc.—K02EE-D, Ch. 2, Trinity County Superintendent of Schools. Phone: 530-623-2861.

Technical Facilities: 0.015-kw ERP, 41-ft. above ground, 3975-ft. above sea level, lat. 40° 43' 11", long. 122° 58' 46".

Ownership: Trinity County Superintendent of Schools.

Weaverville, etc.—K05CF, Ch. 5, Weaverville Translator Co. Inc. Phone: 530-623-5479.

Technical Facilities: 0.015-kw ERP, 3934-ft. above sea level, lat. 40° 43' 11", long. 122° 58' 46".

Holds CP for change to 30-ft. above ground, 3964-ft. above sea level, BDFCDTV-20090102ABZ.

Ownership: Weaverville Translator Corp.

Weed—K06GR, Ch. 6, Northern California Educational TV Assn. Inc.

Technical Facilities: 0.001-kw ERP, 12615-ft. above sea level, lat. 41° 25' 00", long. 122° 24' 10".

Ownership: Northern California Educational TV Assn. Inc.

Westwood—K54EE, Ch. 54, Catamount Broadcasting of Chico-Redding Inc.

Technical Facilities: 2.5-kw ERP, 13-ft. above ground, 7484-ft. above sea level, lat. 40° 14' 22", long. 121° 02' 54".

Ownership: Catamount Broadcast Group.

Personnel: Raymond J. Johns, President.

Willow Creek—K08GR, Ch. 8, Pollack/Belz Broadcasting Co. LLC.

Technical Facilities: 0.01-kw ERP, lat. 40° 55' 53", long. 123° 35' 54".

Ownership: Pollack/Belz Broadcasting Co. LLC.

Willow Creek—K10EN, Ch. 10, Raul Broadcasting Co. of Eureka Inc. Phone: 209-521-5702.

Technical Facilities: 0.05-kw ERP, lat. 40° 55' 46", long. 123° 36' 06".

Holds CP for change to 0.01-kw ERP, 95-ft. above ground, 2562-ft. above sea level, BDFCDVA-20060703AAT.

Ownership: Raul & Consuelo Palazuelos.

Willow Creek—K34BW, Ch. 34, BlueStone License Holdings Inc. Phone: 212-247-8717.

Technical Facilities: 1-w TPO, 0.005-kw ERP, 26-ft. above ground, 4026-ft. above sea level, lat. 40° 58' 05", long. 123° 41' 17".

Transmitter: Brannon Mountain, 3.8-mi. NE of Willow Creek.

Ownership: Bonten Media Group LLC.

Personnel: Bob Wise, General Manager; Jeff Knott, Chief Engineer; Dennis Stewert, Sales Manager.

Yreka—K06GP, Ch. 6, Freedom Broadcasting of Oregon Licensee LLC. Phone: 518-346-6666.

Technical Facilities: 0.002-kw ERP, lat. 41° 43' 30", long. 122° 37' 45".

Ownership: Freedom Communications Holdings Inc.

Yreka—K41JB, Ch. 41, Broadcasting Licenses LP. Phone: 517-347-4141.

Technical Facilities: 10.3-kw ERP, 33-ft. above ground, 5800-ft. above sea level, lat. 41° 36' 31", long. 122° 37' 32".

Ownership: Broadcasting Licenses LP.

Yreka—K49IG, Ch. 49, Three Angels Broadcasting Network Inc. Phone: 618-627-4651.

Technical Facilities: 5.87-kw ERP, 39-ft. above ground, 4902-ft. above sea level, lat. 41° 44' 54.5", long. 122° 42' 00.5".

Ownership: Three Angels Broadcasting Network Inc.

Yreka—K53DY, Ch. 53, Freedom Broadcasting of Oregon Licensee LLC.

Technical Facilities: 10.9-kw ERP, 52-ft. above ground, 3182-ft. above sea level, lat. 41° 43' 30", long. 122° 37' 45".

Ownership: Freedom Communications Holdings Inc.

Yreka, etc.—K04HE, Ch. 4, California-Oregon Broadcasting Inc.

Technical Facilities: 0.091-kw ERP, 20-ft. above ground, 5298-ft. above sea level, lat. 41° 44' 55", long. 122° 42' 00".

Transmitter: 3-mi. W of Yreka.

Ownership: California-Oregon Broadcasting Inc.

Yreka, etc.—K13LO, Ch. 13, BlueStone License Holdings Inc. Phone: 212-247-8717.

Technical Facilities: 0.03-kw ERP, 4819-ft. above sea level, lat. 41° 44' 48", long. 122° 41' 45".

Ownership: Bonten Media Group LLC.

Yreka, etc.—K17BA, Ch. 17, Soda Mountain Broadcasting Inc. Phone: 541-485-5611.

Technical Facilities: 1.19-kw ERP, 49-ft. above ground, 5810-ft. above sea level, lat. 41° 36' 41", long. 122° 37' 26".

Ownership: Soda Mountain Broadcasting Inc.

Yreka, etc.—K19GL-D, Ch. 19, Northern California Educational TV Assn. Inc. Phone: 530-243-5493.

Technical Facilities: 0.12-kw ERP, 69-ft. above ground, 5958-ft. above sea level, lat. 41° 36' 37.3", long. 122° 37' 25.4".

Ownership: Northern California Educational TV Assn. Inc.

Yucca Valley—K27DS, Ch. 27, Gulf-California Broadcast Co.

Technical Facilities: 3.41-kw ERP, lat. 34° 02' 17", long. 116° 48' 47".

Ownership: News Press & Gazette Co.

Colorado

Aguilar—K02AC, Ch. 2, Aguilar TV Club.

Technical Facilities: 0.91-kw ERP, lat. 37° 23' 20", long. 104° 37' 40".

Ownership: Aguilar TV Club.

Aguilar—K04KB, Ch. 4, Rocky Mountain Public Broadcasting Network Inc.

Technical Facilities: 0.06-kw ERP, lat. 37° 23' 20", long. 104° 37' 40".

Ownership: Rocky Mountain Public Broadcasting Network Inc.

Aguilar—K07AG, Ch. 7, Aguilar TV Club.

Technical Facilities: 0.006-kw ERP, lat. 37° 23' 20", long. 104° 37' 40".

Ownership: Aguilar TV Club.

Aguilar—K09AH, Ch. 9, Aguilar TV Club.

Technical Facilities: 0.006-kw ERP, lat. 37° 23' 20", long. 104° 37' 40".

Ownership: Aguilar TV Club.

Akron—K08ND, Ch. 8, Region 1 Translator Assn. Phone: 970-848-5301.

Technical Facilities: 0.258-kw ERP, 275-ft. above ground, 4763-ft. above sea level, lat. 40° 16' 52", long. 103° 05' 55".

Holds CP for change to 2.5-kw ERP, BPTTV-20080912ACZ.

Began Operation: October 29, 2004.

Ownership: Region 1 Translator Association.

Akron—K11UW, Ch. 11, Region 1 Translator Assn. Phone: 970-848-5301.

Technical Facilities: 0.258-kw ERP, 275-ft. above ground, 4763-ft. above sea level, lat. 40° 16' 52", long. 103° 05' 55".

Ownership: Region 1 Translator Association.

Akron—K13XW, Ch. 13, Region 1 Translator Assn. Phone: 970-848-5301.

Technical Facilities: 0.258-kw ERP, 275-ft. above ground, 4763-ft. above sea level, lat. 40° 16' 52", long. 103° 05' 55".

Holds CP for change to 2.5-kw ERP, BPTTV-20080902AAH.

Began Operation: October 4, 2005.

Ownership: Region 1 Translator Association.

Akron—K33FI, Ch. 33, Board of Washington County Commissioners.

Technical Facilities: 0.583-kw ERP, lat. 40° 16' 52", long. 103° 05' 55".

Transmitter: Washington County Rd. 49.

Ownership: Board of Washington County Commissioners.

Akron—K35FI, Ch. 35, Board of Washington County Commissioners.

Technical Facilities: 0.583-kw ERP, lat. 40° 16' 52", long. 103° 05' 55".

Holds CP for change to 0.19-kw ERP, 310-ft. above ground, 4798-ft. above sea level, lat. 40° 16' 52", long. 103° 05' 57". BDFCDTT-20090130ANP.

Transmitter: Washington County Rd. 49.

Ownership: Board of Washington County Commissioners.

Akron—K41EV, Ch. 41, Board of Washington County Commissioners.

Technical Facilities: 0.583-kw ERP, lat. 40° 16' 52", long. 103° 05' 55".

Transmitter: Washington County Rd. 49.

Ownership: Board of Washington County Commissioners.

Akron—K43FS, Ch. 43, Board of Washington County Commissioners.

Technical Facilities: 0.583-kw ERP, 310-ft. above ground, 4800-ft. above sea level, lat. 40° 16' 52", long. 103° 05' 57".

Ownership: Board of Washington County Commissioners.

Alamosa—KENY-LP, Ch. 39, Kenneth D. Swinehart. Phone: 719-588-3132.

Technical Facilities: 5-kw ERP, 65-ft. above ground, 7614-ft. above sea level, lat. 37° 28' 06", long. 105° 51' 58".

Ownership: Kenneth D. Swinehart.

Alma—K02GX, Ch. 2, Town of Alma.

Technical Facilities: 0.014-kw ERP, lat. 39° 20' 01", long. 106° 05' 00".

Ownership: Town of Alma.

Anton—K47FT-D, Ch. 47, Board of Washington County Commissioners. Phone: 970-345-2701.

Technical Facilities: 0.435-kw ERP, 407-ft. above ground, 5381-ft. above sea level, lat. 39° 51' 17", long. 103° 20' 38".

Began Operation: November 9, 1981.

Ownership: Board of Washington County Commissioners.

Anton—K51HS-D, Ch. 51, Region 1 Translator Assn. Phone: 970-848-5301.

Technical Facilities: 0.421-kw ERP, 407-ft. above ground, 5381-ft. above sea level, lat. 39° 51' 17", long. 103° 20' 38".

Ownership: Region 1 Translator Association.

Anton—K57IL, Ch. 57, Region 1 Translator Assn. Phone: 970-848-5301.

Technical Facilities: 0.48-kw ERP, 407-ft. above ground, 5380-ft. above sea level, lat. 39° 51' 17", long. 103° 20' 38".

Holds CP for change to channel number 24, 0.436-kw ERP, 407-ft. above ground, 5381-ft. above sea level, BDISDTT-20090218ACD.

Ownership: Region 1 Translator Association.

Anton & Washington County (rural SW)—K45FD, Ch. 45, Board of Washington County Commissioners. Phone: 970-345-2701.

Technical Facilities: 0.48-kw ERP, lat. 39° 51' 17", long. 103° 20' 38".

Holds CP for change to 0.435-kw ERP, 407-ft. above sea level, lat. 39° 51' 17", long. 103° 20' 38", BDFCDTT-20081023ABM.

Ownership: Board of Washington County Commissioners.

Anton & Washington County (rural SW)—K49EX, Ch. 49, Board of Washington County Commissioners. Phone: 970-345-2701.

Technical Facilities: 0.48-kw ERP, 407-ft. above ground, 5381-ft. above sea level, lat. 39° 51' 17", long. 103° 20' 38".

Holds CP for change to 0.435-kw ERP, BDFCDTT-20081023ABT.

Ownership: Board of Washington County Commissioners.

Anton & Washington County (rural SW)—K55IB, Ch. 55, Board of Washington County Commissioners. Phone: 970-345-2701.

Technical Facilities: 0.48-kw ERP, lat. 39° 51' 17", long. 103° 20' 38".

Holds CP for change to channel number 22, 0.435-kw ERP, 407-ft. above ground, 5381-ft. above sea level, BDISDTT-20081126ALX.

Began Operation: November 9, 1981.

Ownership: Board of Washington County Commissioners.

Ashcroft—K02FW, Ch. 2, Glen C. Brand.

Technical Facilities: 0.01-kw ERP, lat. 39° 08' 48", long. 106° 52' 11".

Ownership: Glen C. Brand.

Ashcroft—K16FS, Ch. 16, Pitkin County Translator Dept. Phone: 970-920-5395.

Technical Facilities: 0.625-kw ERP, 33-ft. above ground, 9452-ft. above sea level, lat. 39° 13' 33", long. 106° 50' 00".

Ownership: Pitkin County Translator Dept.

Personnel: Terri Newland, Translator Administrator.

Ashcroft—K19FH, Ch. 19, Pitkin County Translator Dept. Phone: 970-920-5395.

Technical Facilities: 0.625-kw ERP, 33-ft. above ground, 9452-ft. above sea level, lat. 39° 13' 33", long. 106° 50' 00".

Ownership: Pitkin County Translator Dept.

Aspen—K06HU, Ch. 6, Pitkin County Translator Dept. Phone: 970-920-5395.

Technical Facilities: 0.012-kw ERP, lat. 39° 13' 33", long. 106° 50' 00".

Ownership: Pitkin County Translator Dept.

Aspen—K08HN, Ch. 8, Pitkin County Translator Dept. Phone: 970-920-5395.

Technical Facilities: 0.025-kw ERP, lat. 39° 13' 33", long. 106° 50' 00".

Ownership: Pitkin County Translator Dept.

Aspen—K50IN, Ch. 50, Pitkin County Translator Dept. Phone: 970-920-5395.

Technical Facilities: 0.06-kw ERP, 26-ft. above ground, 8691-ft. above sea level, lat. 39° 18' 37", long. 106° 56' 53".

Ownership: Pitkin County Translator Dept.

Aspen—KSZG-LP, Ch. 20, Aspen Television LLC. Phone: 212-407-4965.

Studio: 303 ABC, Ste H, Aspen, CO 61611.

Technical Facilities: 1-w TPO, 0.008-kw ERP, 26-ft. above ground, 7798-ft. above sea level, lat. 39° 13' 06", long. 106° 51' 36".

Transmitter: Red Mountain, N of Aspen.

Ownership: Aspen Television LLC.

Personnel: Carolyne Harvey, General Manager; John Dady, Chief Engineer; John Switala, Sales Manager; Alison Blair, Production Director.

Aurora—KDEO-LP, Ch. 23, Sande Family Trust. Phone: 303-368-0870.

Technical Facilities: 50.2-kw ERP, 57-ft. above ground, 7774-ft. above sea level, lat. 39° 40' 24", long. 105° 13' 03".

Holds CP for change to channel number 20, 0.005-kw ERP, BDISDTL-20060921ACM.

Ownership: Sande Family Trust.

■ **Aurora**—KQDK-CA, Ch. 39, Denver Broadcasting Inc., Debtor in Possession. Phone: 501-219-2400.

Technical Facilities: 35-kw ERP, 295-ft. above ground, 5840-ft. above sea level, lat. 39° 40' 31", long. 104° 52' 24".

Began Operation: September 26, 1994.

Ownership: Equity Media Holdings Corp., Debtor in Possession.

Banty Point—K05CM, Ch. 5, Rio Blanco County TV Assn.

Technical Facilities: 0.006-kw ERP, lat. 40° 02' 39", long. 108° 59' 32".

Ownership: Rio Blanco County TV Association.

Banty Point, etc.—K04JX, Ch. 4, Rio Blanco County TV Assn.

Technical Facilities: 0.06-kw ERP, 5604-ft. above sea level, lat. 40° 02' 39", long. 108° 59' 32".

Ownership: Rio Blanco County TV Association.

Banty Point, etc.—K07QE, Ch. 7, Rio Blanco County TV Assn.

Technical Facilities: 0.078-kw ERP, 5561-ft. above sea level, lat. 40° 02' 39", long. 108° 59' 32".

Ownership: Rio Blanco County TV Association.

Banty Point, etc.—K09VT, Ch. 9, Rio Blanco County TV Assn.

Technical Facilities: 0.078-kw ERP, 20-ft. above ground, 5561-ft. above sea level, lat. 40° 02' 39", long. 108° 59' 32".

Ownership: Rio Blanco County TV Association.

Banty Point, etc.—K11PI, Ch. 11, Rio Blanco County TV Assn.

Technical Facilities: 0.078-kw ERP, 20-ft. above ground, 5561-ft. above sea level, lat. 40° 02' 39", long. 108° 59' 32".

Ownership: Rio Blanco County TV Association.

Basalt—K05MB, Ch. 5, Pitkin County Translator Dept. Phone: 970-920-5395.

Technical Facilities: 0.028-kw ERP, 49-ft. above ground, 8307-ft. above sea level, lat. 39° 21' 10", long. 107° 05' 33".

Ownership: Pitkin County Translator Dept.

Basalt—K07KR, Ch. 7, Pitkin County Translator Dept. Phone: 970-920-5395.

Technical Facilities: 0.028-kw ERP, 33-ft. above ground, 8323-ft. above sea level, lat. 39° 21' 11", long. 107° 05' 34".

Ownership: Pitkin County Translator Dept.

Basalt—K09AG, Ch. 9, Pitkin County Translator Dept. Phone: 970-920-5395.

Technical Facilities: 0.028-kw ERP, 26-ft. above ground, 8317-ft. above sea level, lat. 39° 21' 11", long. 107° 05' 34".

Ownership: Pitkin County Translator Dept.

Basalt—K33HY, Ch. 33, Pitkin County Translator Dept. Phone: 970-920-5395.

Technical Facilities: 2.104-kw ERP, 40-ft. above ground, 8101-ft. above sea level, lat. 39° 21' 11", long. 107° 05' 34".

Holds CP for change to 0.075-kw ERP, 49-ft. above ground, 8353-ft. above sea level, lat. 39° 21' 10", long. 107° 05' 33". BDFCDTT-20090506ABH.

Ownership: Pitkin County Translator Dept.

Basalt—K36GX, Ch. 36, Pitkin County Translator Dept. Phone: 970-920-5395.

Technical Facilities: 0.08-kw ERP, 40-ft. above ground, 8101-ft. above sea level, lat. 39° 21' 11", long. 107° 05' 33".

Holds CP for change to 0.075-kw ERP, 49-ft. above ground, 8353-ft. above sea level, lat. 39° 21' 10", long. 107° 05' 33". BDFCDTT-20090506ABK.

Ownership: Pitkin County Translator Dept.

Bayfield—K46FM, Ch. 46, KOB-TV LLC. Phone: 651-642-4212.

Technical Facilities: 1.41-kw ERP, 49-ft. above ground, 8750-ft. above sea level, lat. 37° 104' 107", long. 29° 12' ".

Ownership: Hubbard Broadcasting Inc.

Bayfield—K50FS-D, Ch. 50, LIN of New Mexico LLC. Phone: 401-457-9525.

Technical Facilities: 0.24-kw ERP, 36-ft. above ground, 8881-ft. above sea level, lat. 37° 11' 03", long. 107° 29' 07".

Ownership: LIN TV Corp.

Bayfield & Ignacio—K42DI-D, Ch. 42, LIN of Colorado LLC. Phone: 401-457-9525.

Technical Facilities: 0.28-kw ERP, 56-ft. above ground, 8901-ft. above sea level, lat. 37° 11' 03", long. 107° 29' 06".

Ownership: LIN TV Corp.

Bethune & Burlington—K53AD, Ch. 53, Kit Carson County. Phone: 719-346-8139.

Technical Facilities: 0.81-kw ERP, lat. 39° 16' 20", long. 102° 23' 54".

Ownership: Kit Carson County.

Bethune & Burlington—K55AX, Ch. 55, Kit Carson County. Phone: 719-346-8139.

Technical Facilities: 0.81-kw ERP, lat. 39° 16' 20", long. 102° 23' 54".

Ownership: Kit Carson County.

Bethune & Burlington—K57AM, Ch. 57, Kit Carson County. Phone: 719-346-8139.

Technical Facilities: 0.795-kw ERP, lat. 39° 16' 20", long. 102° 23' 54".

Ownership: Kit Carson County.

Bethune & Burlington—K59AP, Ch. 59, Kit Carson County. Phone: 719-346-8139.

Technical Facilities: 0.795-kw ERP, lat. 39° 16' 20", long. 102° 23' 54".

Ownership: Kit Carson County.

Big Elk Meadows—K08JK, Ch. 8, Big Elk Meadows Assn.

Technical Facilities: 0.021-kw ERP, lat. 40° 15' 37", long. 105° 25' 32".

Ownership: Big Elk Meadows Association.

Big Elk Meadows—K11OF, Ch. 11, Big Elk Meadows Assn.

Technical Facilities: 0.002-kw ERP, lat. 40° 15' 37", long. 105° 25' 32".

Ownership: Big Elk Meadows Association.

Big Elk Meadows—K13OU, Ch. 13, Big Elk Meadows Assn.

Technical Facilities: 0.002-kw ERP, lat. 40° 15' 37", long. 105° 25' 32".

Ownership: Big Elk Meadows Association.

Blue Mountain, etc.—K10DY, Ch. 10, Rio Blanco County TV Assn.

Technical Facilities: 0.009-kw ERP, lat. 40° 09' 36", long. 108° 57' 12".

Ownership: Rio Blanco County TV Association.

Blue Mountain, etc.—K12EE, Ch. 12, Rio Blanco County TV Assn.

Technical Facilities: 0.01-kw ERP, lat. 40° 09' 36", long. 108° 57' 12".

Ownership: Rio Blanco County TV Association.

Boulder—K11QJ, Ch. 11, Colorado Public Television Inc.

Technical Facilities: 0.308-kw ERP, 5531-ft. above sea level, lat. 39° 59' 56", long. 105° 15' 06".

Ownership: Colorado Public Television Inc.

Boulder—K17CF, Ch. 17, Full Gospel Outreach Inc.

Technical Facilities: 100-w TPO, 2.69-kw ERP, lat. 40° 03' 17", long. 105° 18' 28".

Ownership: Full Gospel Outreach Inc.

Boulder—K24HQ-D, Ch. 24, Rocky Mountain Public Broadcasting Network Inc. Phone: 303-892-6666.

Technical Facilities: 0.25-kw ERP, 171-ft. above ground, 5515-ft. above sea level, lat. 39° 59' 58", long. 105° 15' 06".

Ownership: Rocky Mountain Public Broadcasting Network Inc.

Boulder—K44CT, Ch. 44, Rocky Mountain Public Broadcasting Network Inc.

Technical Facilities: 18.6-kw ERP, lat. 39° 59' 58", long. 105° 15' 06".

Ownership: Rocky Mountain Public Broadcasting Network Inc.

Boulder—K47IH, Ch. 47, Multimedia Holdings Corp. Phone: 703-854-6621.

Technical Facilities: 0.4-kw ERP, 233-ft. above ground, 5558-ft. above sea level, lat. 40° 00' 18", long. 105° 15' 21".

Ownership: Gannett Co. Inc.

Boulder—K54DK, Ch. 54, Community Television of Colorado License LLC. Phone: 859-448-2700.

Technical Facilities: 1000-w TPO, 1.18-kw ERP, 89-ft. above ground, 7969-ft. above sea level, lat. 40° 04' 19", long. 105° 21' 14".

Holds CP for change to channel number 46, 1-kw ERP, 75-ft. above ground, 5797-ft. above sea level, lat. 39° 57' 38", long. 105° 12' 44". BDISTT-20070215AAT.

Transmitter: Lee Hill, 5.3-mi. NW of Boulder.

Ownership: Local TV Holdings LLC.

Breckenridge—K10PM, Ch. 10, Summit Public Radio & TV Inc. Phone: 970-453-9293.

Technical Facilities: 0.1-kw ERP, 11-ft. above ground, 12541-ft. above sea level, lat. 39° 27' 35", long. 105° 58' 46".

Ownership: Summit Public Radio & TV Inc.

Breckenridge—K26GY, Ch. 26, Resort Television USA LLC.

Technical Facilities: 0.1-kw ERP, 46-ft. above ground, 9393-ft. above sea level, lat. 39° 36' 50", long. 106° 04' 02".

Ownership: Resort Sports Network Inc.

Breckenridge/Dillon—K28HI, Ch. 28, Resort Sports Network Inc. Phone: 207-772-5000.

Technical Facilities: 0.016-kw ERP, 33-ft. above ground, 9088-ft. above sea level, lat. 39° 33' 57", long. 106° 03' 17".

Ownership: Resort Sports Network Inc.

Broadmoor—K41JO, Ch. 41, Tuck Properties Inc. Phone: 202-293-0569.

Technical Facilities: 42.27-kw ERP, 141-ft. above ground, 6368-ft. above sea level, lat. 38° 49' 53", long. 104° 51' 33".

Holds CP for change to 1.5-kw ERP, BDFCDTL-20090515ACB.

Began Operation: July 22, 1985.

Ownership: Tuck Properties Inc.

Buford—K05GI, Ch. 5, Rio Blanco County TV Assn.

Technical Facilities: 0.078-kw ERP, lat. 39° 56' 13", long. 107° 43' 21".

Ownership: Rio Blanco County TV Association.

Buford—K07RP, Ch. 7, Rio Blanco County TV Assn.

Technical Facilities: 0.07-kw ERP, lat. 39° 56' 13", long. 107° 43' 21".

Ownership: Rio Blanco County TV Association.

Buford—K10HE, Ch. 10, Rio Blanco County TV Assn.

Technical Facilities: 0.073-kw ERP, lat. 39° 56' 13", long. 107° 43' 21".

Ownership: Rio Blanco County TV Association.

Buford, etc.—K13QU, Ch. 13, Rio Blanco County TV Assn.

Technical Facilities: 0.078-kw ERP, 7631-ft. above sea level, lat. 39° 56' 13", long. 107° 43' 21".

Ownership: Rio Blanco County TV Association.

Canon City—K10LI, Ch. 10, Gray Television Licensee LLC. Phone: 719-634-2844.

Technical Facilities: 0.109-kw ERP, lat. 38° 25' 20", long. 105° 09' 05".

Holds CP for change to channel number 13, 59-ft. above ground, 5574-ft. above sea level, BDISDTV-20081224AAQ.

Began Operation: June 19, 1980.

Ownership: Gray Television Inc.

Canon City—K12ME, Ch. 12, Pikes Peak Television inc. Phone: 719-632-1515.

Technical Facilities: 0.11-kw ERP, lat. 38° 25' 20", long. 105° 09' 05".

Ownership: News Press & Gazette Co.

Canon City—K19DY, Ch. 19, Sangre de Cristo Communications Inc.

Technical Facilities: 1.38-kw ERP, lat. 38° 25' 20", long. 105° 09' 05".

Ownership: Sangre de Cristo Communcations Inc.

Carbondale—K08GZ, Ch. 8, Garfield County.

Technical Facilities: 0.005-kw ERP, lat. 39° 23' 48", long. 107° 14' 00".

Ownership: Garfield County.

Carbondale—K10LW, Ch. 10, Garfield County.

Technical Facilities: 0.05-kw ERP, lat. 39° 23' 48", long. 107° 14' 00".

Ownership: Garfield County.

Carbondale—K29CK, Ch. 29, Pitkin County Translator Dept. Phone: 970-920-5395.

Technical Facilities: 2.3-kw ERP, 105-ft. above ground, 10669-ft. above sea level, lat. 39° 25' 23.5", long. 107° 22' 31.6".

Holds CP for change to 0.64-kw ERP, 75-ft. above ground, 10636-ft. above sea level, BDFCDTT-20090506AAW.

Ownership: Pitkin County Translator Dept.

Carbondale—K31CW, Ch. 31, Pitkin County Translator Dept. Phone: 970-920-5395.

Technical Facilities: 2.3-kw ERP, 105-ft. above ground, 10709-ft. above sea level, lat. 39° 25' 33", long. 107° 22' 25".

Holds CP for change to 0.64-kw ERP, 99-ft. above ground, 10660-ft. above sea level, lat. 39° 25' 23", long. 107° 22' 31". BDFCDTT-20090506AAX.

Ownership: Pitkin County Translator Dept.

Carbondale—K38FO, Ch. 38, Pikes Peak Television Inc. Phone: 970-245-8880.

Technical Facilities: 0.13-kw ERP, 62-ft. above ground, 10633-ft. above sea level, lat. 39° 25' 21.1", long. 107° 22' 31.4".

Ownership: News Press & Gazette Co.

Personnel: Kristy Santiago, General Manager.

Carbondale—K45HL, Ch. 45, Pitkin County Translator. Phone: 970-920-5395.

Technical Facilities: 1.4-kw ERP, 82-ft. above ground, 10646-ft. above sea level, lat. 39° 25' 24", long. 107° 22' 32".

Holds CP for change to 0.012-kw ERP, 52-ft. above ground, 8724-ft. above sea level, lat. 39° 14' 20", long. 107° 13' 02". BDFCDTT-20090506ABD.

Ownership: Pitkin County Translator Dept.

Carbondale—K48IC, Ch. 48, Pitkin County Translator Dept. Phone: 970-927-6813.

Technical Facilities: 1.4-kw ERP, 75-ft. above ground, 10640-ft. above sea level, lat. 39° 25' 23.5", long. 107° 22' 31.6".

Ownership: Pitkin County Translator Dept.

Cheyenne Wells—K60AM, Ch. 60, Cheyenne County.

Technical Facilities: 0.754-kw ERP, lat. 38° 47' 30", long. 102° 32' 57".

Ownership: Cheyenne County.

Cheyenne Wells—K62AH, Ch. 62, Cheyenne County.

Technical Facilities: 0.754-kw ERP, lat. 38° 47' 30", long. 102° 32' 57".

Ownership: Cheyenne County.

Cheyenne Wells—K64AJ, Ch. 64, Cheyenne County.

Technical Facilities: 0.754-kw ERP, 4944-ft. above sea level, lat. 38° 47' 30", long. 102° 32' 57".

Ownership: Cheyenne County.

Cheyenne Wells—K68AQ, Ch. 68, Cheyenne County.

Technical Facilities: 0.754-kw ERP, lat. 38° 47' 30", long. 102° 32' 57".

Ownership: Cheyenne County.

Cimarron—K06AM, Ch. 6, Gunnison County Metropolitan Recreation District.

Technical Facilities: 0.002-kw ERP, lat. 38° 23' 44", long. 107° 25' 44".

Ownership: Gunnison County Metropolitan Recreation District.

Cimarron Creek—K44CA, Ch. 44, Hoak Media of Colorado License LLC. Phone: 972-960-4896.

Technical Facilities: 3.42-kw ERP, lat. 38° 19' 58", long. 107° 38' 08".

Ownership: Hoak Media LLC.

Coaldale—K03FH, Ch. 3, Coaldale TV Club.

Technical Facilities: 0.004-kw ERP, lat. 38° 20' 22", long. 105° 43' 55".

Ownership: Coaldale TV Club.

Coaldale—K10AR, Ch. 10, Coaldale TV Club.

Technical Facilities: 0.006-kw ERP, lat. 38° 20' 42", long. 105° 45' 11".

Ownership: Coaldale TV Club.

Coaldale—K59CL, Ch. 59, Rocky Mountain Public Broadcasting Network Inc. Phone: 303-892-6666.

Technical Facilities: 0.01-kw ERP, lat. 38° 20' 42", long. 105° 45' 11".

Holds CP for change to channel number 33, 0.015-kw ERP, 7-ft. above ground, 7218-ft. above sea level, BDISDTT-20060331AVO.

Ownership: Rocky Mountain Public Broadcasting Network Inc.

Collbran—K02OP, Ch. 2, Mesa County.

Technical Facilities: 0.002-kw ERP, 26-ft. above ground, 6106-ft. above sea level, lat. 39° 14' 31", long. 107° 57' 52".

Ownership: Mesa County.

Collbran—K04OM, Ch. 4, Mesa County.

Technical Facilities: 0.002-kw ERP, 26-ft. above ground, 6106-ft. above sea level, lat. 39° 14' 31", long. 107° 57' 52".

Ownership: Mesa County.

Collbran—K06KJ, Ch. 6, Mesa County.

Technical Facilities: 0.004-kw ERP, lat. 39° 14' 15", long. 107° 57' 45".

Ownership: Mesa County.

Collbran—K11PS, Ch. 11, Mesa County.

Technical Facilities: 0.005-kw ERP, lat. 39° 14' 15", long. 107° 57' 45".

Ownership: Mesa County.

Collbran—K13RD, Ch. 13, Mesa County.

Technical Facilities: 0.005-kw ERP, lat. 39° 14' 15", long. 107° 57' 45".

Ownership: Mesa County.

Colorado Springs—K30AA, Ch. 30, Sangre de Cristo Communications Inc. Phone: 719-544-5781.

Technical Facilities: 126.5-kw ERP, 86-ft. above ground, 9488-ft. above sea level, lat. 38° 44' 45", long. 104° 51' 40".

Holds CP for change to 3-kw ERP, 89-ft. above ground, 9495-ft. above sea level, BDFCDTL-20061019ACU.

Ownership: Sangre de Cristo Communcations Inc.

Colorado Springs—K32EO, Ch. 32, Colorado Public Television Inc. Phone: 303-296-1212.

Technical Facilities: 109.4-kw ERP, 59-ft. above ground, 9495-ft. above sea level, lat. 38° 44' 40", long. 104° 51' 42".

Ownership: Colorado Public Television Inc.

Colorado Springs—K43CG, Ch. 43, Full Gospel Outreach Inc. Phone: 719-574-7777.

Technical Facilities: 1000-w TPO, 11.8-kw ERP, 85-ft. above ground, 9524-ft. above sea level, lat. 38° 44' 46", long. 104° 51' 42".

Transmitter: Cheyenne Mountain, approx. 6.5-mi. SSW of center of Colorado Springs.

Ownership: Full Gospel Outreach Inc.

Colorado Springs—KJCS-LP, Ch. 38, Full Gospel Outreach Inc. Phone: 719-637-1138. Fax: 719-636-2332.

Technical Facilities: 950-w TPO, 13.2-kw ERP, 98-ft. above ground, 9508-ft. above sea level, lat. 38° 44' 43", long. 104° 51' 41".

Holds CP for change to 5.3-kw ERP, BDFCDTL-20080924AKL.

Transmitter: Cheyenne Mountain, 6.4-mi. SW of Colorado Springs.

Ownership: Beta Broadcasting Inc.

Colorado Springs—KTLO-LP, Ch. 49, Pikes Peak Television Inc. Phone: 816-271-8505.

Technical Facilities: 1000-w TPO, 4.53-kw ERP, 20-ft. above ground, 9474-ft. above sea level, lat. 38° 44' 45", long. 104° 51' 40".

Holds CP for change to channel number 46, 50-kw ERP, 56-ft. above ground, 9472-ft. above sea level, BDISTTL-20080910ACG.

Transmitter: 6120 Transmitter Lane, Cheyenne Mountain.

Began Operation: June 11, 1990.

Ownership: News Press & Gazette Co.

Colorado Springs—KWHS-LP, Ch. 51, LeSea Broadcasting Corp. Phones: 303-799-8853; 574-291-8200. Fax: 303-792-5303.

Studio: 12999 E Jamison Circle, Englewood, CO 80112.

Technical Facilities: 599-w TPO, 13.6-kw ERP, 20-ft. above ground, 9403-ft. above sea level, lat. 38° 44' 45", long. 104° 51' 39".

Holds CP for change to 150-kw ERP, 100-ft. above ground, 9509-ft. above sea level, lat. 38° 44' 43", long. 104° 51' 39". BPTTL-20061129AKZ.

Transmitter: 6.5-mi. SSW of Colorado Springs.

Ownership: LeSea Broadcasting Corp.

Personnel: Mark Walker, General Manager; Ron Vincent, Chief Engineer; Graham Nash, Production Manager; Idell Stelly, Office Manager.

Colorado Springs—KXTU-LP, Ch. 57, Barrington Colorado Springs License LLC. Phone: 847-884-1877.

Technical Facilities: 135-kw ERP, 48-ft. above ground, 9457-ft. above sea level, lat. 38° 44' 44", long. 104° 51' 40".

Ownership: Pilot Group LP.

Personnel: Steve Dant, Vice President & General Manager.

Colorado Springs—KZCS-LP, Ch. 23, McGraw-Hill Broadcasting Co. Inc. Phone: 303-832-0190. Fax: 540-667-5138.

Technical Facilities: 50-kw ERP, 140-ft. above ground, 9569-ft. above sea level, lat. 38° 44' 41", long. 104° 51' 48".

Ownership: McGraw-Hill Broadcasting Co. Inc.

Personnel: Darrell Brown, General Manager.

Cortez—K06JF, Ch. 6, LIN of Colorado LLC. Phone: 202-462-6001.

Technical Facilities: 1.155-kw ERP, 33-ft. above ground, 8858-ft. above sea level, lat. 37° 19' 32", long. 108° 14' 55".

Ownership: LIN TV Corp.

Cortez—K07UY, Ch. 7, Southwest Colorado TV Translator Assn. Phone: 970-565-2129.

Technical Facilities: 1-kw ERP, 56-ft. above ground, 10357-ft. above sea level, lat. 37° 21' 00.9", long. 108° 08' 00.8".

Ownership: Southwest Colorado TV Translator Assn.

Personnel: Wayne Johnson, General Manager.

Cortez—K09DM, Ch. 9, Southwest Colorado TV Translator Assn. Phone: 970-565-2129.

Technical Facilities: 1-kw ERP, 56-ft. above ground, 10357-ft. above sea level, lat. 37° 21' 00.9", long. 108° 08' 00.8".

Ownership: Southwest Colorado TV Translator Assn.

Personnel: Wayne Johnson, General Manager.

Cortez—K14JS-D, Ch. 14, Southwest Colorado TV Translator Assn. Phone: 970-565-2129.

Technical Facilities: 2-kw ERP, 66-ft. above ground, 10361-ft. above sea level, lat. 37° 21' 54", long. 108° 08' 49".

Ownership: Southwest Colorado TV Translator Assn.

Cortez—K16CT-D, Ch. 16, Southwest Colorado TV Translator Assn. Phone: 970-565-2129.

Technical Facilities: 2-kw ERP, 66-ft. above ground, 10361-ft. above sea level, lat. 37° 21' 54", long. 108° 08' 49".

Ownership: Southwest Colorado TV Translator Assn.

Personnel: Wayne Johnson, General Manager.

Cortez—K24CH-D, Ch. 24, Southwest Colorado TV Translator Assn. Phone: 970-565-2121.

Technical Facilities: 1-kw ERP, 66-ft. above ground, 10361-ft. above sea level, lat. 37° 21' 54", long. 108° 08' 49".

Ownership: Southwest Colorado TV Translator Assn.

Personnel: Wayne Johnson, General Manager.

Cortez—K25JN-D, Ch. 25, Southwest Colorado TV Translator Assn. Phone: 970-565-2129.

Technical Facilities: 0.006-kw ERP, 33-ft. above ground, 10328-ft. above sea level, lat. 37° 21' 01", long. 108° 08' 01".

Ownership: Southwest Colorado TV Translator Assn.

Cortez—K26CI-D, Ch. 26, Southwest Colorado TV Translator Assn. Phone: 970-565-2121.

Technical Facilities: 1-kw ERP, 66-ft. above ground, 10361-ft. above sea level, lat. 37° 21' 54", long. 108° 08' 49".

Ownership: Southwest Colorado TV Translator Assn.

Personnel: Wayne Johnson, General Manager.

Cortez—K27IG-D, Ch. 27, Southwest Colorado TV Translator Assn. Phone: 970-565-2129.

Technical Facilities: 1-kw ERP, 66-ft. above ground, 10361-ft. above sea level, lat. 37° 21' 54", long. 108° 08' 49".

Ownership: Southwest Colorado TV Translator Assn.

Cortez—K29GO-D, Ch. 29, Southwest Colorado TV Translator Assn. Phone: 970-565-2129.

Technical Facilities: 2-kw ERP, 66-ft. above ground, 10361-ft. above sea level, lat. 37° 21' 54", long. 108° 08' 49".

Ownership: Southwest Colorado TV Translator Assn.

Personnel: Wayne Johnson, General Manager.

Cortez—K31CT, Ch. 31, Southwest Colorado TV Translator Assn. Phone: 970-565-2129.

Technical Facilities: 0.92-kw ERP, 52-ft. above ground, 10354-ft. above sea level, lat. 37° 21' 01", long. 108° 08' 01".

Ownership: Southwest Colorado TV Translator Assn.

Cortez—K32IJ, Ch. 32, Southwest Colorado TV Translator Assn. Phone: 970-565-2129.

Technical Facilities: 1.5-kw ERP, 34-ft. above ground, 8994-ft. above sea level, lat. 37° 13' 10", long. 108° 48' 26".

Began Operation: May 21, 2007.

Ownership: Southwest Colorado TV Translator Assn.

Cortez—K33JL-D, Ch. 33, Southwest Colorado TV Translator Assn. Phone: 970-565-2129.

Technical Facilities: 0.006-kw ERP, 33-ft. above ground, 10328-ft. above sea level, lat. 37° 21' 01", long. 108° 08' 01".

Ownership: Southwest Colorado TV Translator Assn.

Cortez—K39EY-D, Ch. 39, Southwest Colorado TV Translator Assn. Phone: 970-565-2129.

Technical Facilities: 1-kw ERP, 26-ft. above ground, 10223-ft. above sea level, lat. 37° 21' 58", long. 108° 08' 42".

Transmitter: 7.7-mi. NE of Mancos.

Ownership: Southwest Colorado TV Translator Assn.

Personnel: Wayne Johnson, General Manager.

Cortez—K49EQ-D, Ch. 49, Southwest Colorado TV Translator Assn. Phone: 970-565-2121.

Technical Facilities: 2-kw ERP, 66-ft. above ground, 10361-ft. above sea level, lat. 37° 21' 54", long. 108° 08' 49".

Ownership: Southwest Colorado TV Translator Assn.

Personnel: Wayne Johnson, General Manager.

Cortez—K50IV, Ch. 50, KOB-TV LLC. Phone: 651-642-4337.

Technical Facilities: 1.8-kw ERP, 46-ft. above ground, 8871-ft. above sea level, lat. 37° 19' 32", long. 108° 14' 55".

Ownership: Hubbard Broadcasting Inc.

Cortez—K51DB-D, Ch. 51, Southwest Colorado TV Translator Assn. Phone: 970-565-2121.

Technical Facilities: 1-kw ERP, 66-ft. above ground, 10361-ft. above sea level, lat. 37° 21' 54", long. 108° 08' 49".

Ownership: Southwest Colorado TV Translator Assn.

Personnel: Wayne Johnson, General Manager.

Cortez—K55KN-D, Ch. 55, Southwest Colorado TV Translator Assn. Phone: 970-565-2129.

Technical Facilities: 0.006-kw ERP, 33-ft. above ground, 10328-ft. above sea level, lat. 37° 21' 01", long. 108° 08' 01".

Ownership: Southwest Colorado TV Translator Assn.

Cortez & Mancos, etc.—K35CH-D, Ch. 35, Southwest Colorado TV Translator Assn. Phone: 970-565-2121.

Technical Facilities: 1.2-kw ERP, 66-ft. above ground, 10361-ft. above sea level, lat. 37° 21' 54", long. 108° 08' 49".

Ownership: Southwest Colorado TV Translator Assn.

Cortez, etc.—K11LP, Ch. 11, Southwest Colorado TV Translator Assn. Phone: 970-565-2121.

Technical Facilities: 10-w TPO, 0.306-kw ERP, lat. 37° 21' 24", long. 108° 08' 20".

Ownership: Southwest Colorado TV Translator Assn.

Personnel: Wayne Johnson, General Manager.

Cortez, etc.—K18DR-D, Ch. 18, Southwest Colorado TV Translator Assn. Phone: 970-565-2129.

Technical Facilities: 1-kw ERP, 66-ft. above ground, 10361-ft. above sea level, lat. 37° 21' 54", long. 108° 08' 49".

Ownership: Southwest Colorado TV Translator Assn.

Personnel: Wayne Johnson, General Manager.

Cortez, etc.—K22CU-D, Ch. 22, Southwest Colorado TV Translator Assn. Phone: 970-565-2121.

Technical Facilities: 1-kw ERP, 66-ft. above ground, 10361-ft. above sea level, lat. 37° 21' 54", long. 108° 08' 49".

Ownership: Southwest Colorado TV Translator Assn.

Personnel: Wayne Johnson, General Manager.

Cortez, etc.—K24HY, Ch. 24, Southwest Colorado TV Translator Assn. Phone: 970-565-2129.

Technical Facilities: 0.92-kw ERP, 52-ft. above ground, 10354-ft. above sea level, lat. 37° 21' 00.9", long. 108° 08' 00.8".

Ownership: Southwest Colorado TV Translator Assn.

Personnel: Wayne Johnson, General Manager.

Cortez, etc.—K28EB-D, Ch. 28, Southwest Colorado TV Translator Assn. Phone: 970-565-2129.

Technical Facilities: 1-kw ERP, 66-ft. above ground, 10361-ft. above sea level, lat. 37° 21' 54", long. 108° 08' 49".

Ownership: Southwest Colorado TV Translator Assn.

Cortez, etc.—K30HJ-D, Ch. 30, Southwest Colorado TV Translator Assn. Phone: 970-565-2121.

Technical Facilities: 2-kw ERP, 66-ft. above ground, 10361-ft. above sea level, lat. 37° 21' 54", long. 108° 08' 49".

Ownership: Southwest Colorado TV Translator Assn.

Personnel: Wayne Johnson, General Manager.

Cortez, etc.—K41DE, Ch. 41, San Juan Basin Technical College. Phone: 970-565-8457.

Technical Facilities: 100-w TPO, 1.17-kw ERP, 54-ft. above ground, 10300-ft. above sea level, lat. 37° 21' 58", long. 108° 08' 42".

Transmitter: 8-mi. NE of Mancos.

Ownership: San Juan Basin Technical College.

Personnel: Ken Hill, Chief Engineer.

Cortez, etc.—K52KF-D, Ch. 52, Southwest Colorado TV Translator Assn. Phone: 970-565-2129.

Technical Facilities: 0.006-kw ERP, 33-ft. above ground, 10328-ft. above sea level, lat. 37° 21' 01", long. 108° 08' 01".

Ownership: Southwest Colorado TV Translator Assn.

Cortez, etc.—K53JP-D, Ch. 53, Southwest Colorado TV Translator Assn. Phone: 970-565-2129.

Technical Facilities: 0.006-kw ERP, 33-ft. above ground, 10328-ft. above sea level, lat. 37° 21' 01", long. 108° 08' 01".

Ownership: Southwest Colorado TV Translator Assn.

Cortez, etc.—K56JI-D, Ch. 56, Southwest Colorado TV Translator Assn. Phone: 970-565-2129.

Technical Facilities: 0.006-kw ERP, 33-ft. above ground, 10328-ft. above sea level, lat. 37° 21' 01", long. 108° 08' 01".

Ownership: Southwest Colorado TV Translator Assn.

Cortez, etc.—K57KA-D, Ch. 57, Southwest Colorado TV Translator Assn. Phone: 970-565-2129.

Technical Facilities: 0.006-kw ERP, 33-ft. above ground, 10328-ft. above sea level, lat. 37° 21' 01", long. 108° 08' 01".

Ownership: Southwest Colorado TV Translator Assn.

Cortez, Mancos, etc.—K58IV-D, Ch. 58, Southwest Colorado TV Translator Assn. Phone: 970-565-2129.

Technical Facilities: 0.006-kw ERP, 33-ft. above ground, 10328-ft. above sea level, lat. 37° 21' 01", long. 108° 08' 01".

Ownership: Southwest Colorado TV Translator Assn.

Craig—K27FA, Ch. 27, Tia Shaw. Phone: 970-824-5835.

Technical Facilities: 0.522-kw ERP, lat. 40° 31' 27", long. 107° 33' 11".

Ownership: Tia Shaw.

Crested Butte—K12AK, Ch. 12, Gunnison County Metro. Recreation District.

Technical Facilities: 0.01-kw ERP, lat. 38° 52' 45", long. 106° 57' 55".

Ownership: Gunnison County Metropolitan Recreation District.

Crested Butte—K30EJ, Ch. 30, Gunnison County Metro. Recreation District.

Technical Facilities: 0.16-kw ERP, 20-ft. above ground, 9058-ft. above sea level, lat. 38° 48' 37", long. 106° 54' 30".

Ownership: Gunnison County Metropolitan Recreation District.

Crested Butte—K33EL, Ch. 33, Town of Crested Butte.

Technical Facilities: 0.125-kw ERP, lat. 38° 54' 08", long. 106° 58' 20".

Transmitter: 2.3-mi. N of Crested Butte.

Ownership: Town of Crested Butte.

Crested Butte South—K45CY, Ch. 45, Gunnison County Metro. Recreation District.

Technical Facilities: 20.3-kw ERP, lat. 38° 48' 37", long. 106° 54' 30".

Transmitter: Approx. 2-mi. SW of Crested Butte.

Ownership: Gunnison County Metropolitan Recreation District.

Crested Butte South—K49BW, Ch. 49, Gunnison County Metro. Recreation District.

Technical Facilities: 0.128-kw ERP, lat. 38° 48' 37", long. 106° 54' 30".

Transmitter: Approx. 2-mi. SW of Crested Butte.

Ownership: Gunnison County Metropolitan Recreation District.

Crested Butte, etc.—K04GS, Ch. 4, Gunnison County Metro. Recreation District.

Technical Facilities: 0.01-kw ERP, lat. 38° 54' 08", long. 106° 58' 20".

Ownership: Gunnison County Metropolitan Recreation District.

Crested Butte, etc.—K10AK, Ch. 10, Gunnison County Metro. Recreation District.

Technical Facilities: 0.01-kw ERP, lat. 38° 54' 08", long. 106° 58' 20".

Ownership: Gunnison County Metropolitan Recreation District.

Crested Butte, etc.—K41AH, Ch. 41, Gunnison County Metro. Recreation District.

Technical Facilities: 0.46-kw ERP, 9764-ft. above sea level, lat. 38° 54' 08", long. 106° 58' 20".

Ownership: Gunnison County Metropolitan Recreation District.

Crested Butte, etc.—K43AH, Ch. 43, Gunnison County Metro. Recreation District.

Technical Facilities: 0.46-kw ERP, 9774-ft. above sea level, lat. 38° 54' 08", long. 106° 58' 20".

Ownership: Gunnison County Metropolitan Recreation District.

Crested Butte, etc.—K47BL, Ch. 47, Gunnison County Metro. Recreation District.

Technical Facilities: 0.17-kw ERP, 33-ft. above ground, 9810-ft. above sea level, lat. 38° 48' 47", long. 106° 54' 30".

Transmitter: 2-mi. SW of Crested Butte South.

Ownership: Gunnison County Metropolitan Recreation District.

Cripple Creek—K42CX, Ch. 42, Pikes Peak Television Inc. Phone: 719-632-1515.

Technical Facilities: 0.12-kw ERP, 20-ft. above ground, 9810-ft. above sea level, lat. 38° 45' 00", long. 105° 11' 42".

Ownership: News Press & Gazette Co.

Cripple Creek, etc.—K05MD-D, Ch. 5, Tuck Properties Inc. Phone: 202-293-0569.

Technical Facilities: 0.3-kw ERP, 36-ft. above ground, 7290-ft. above sea level, lat. 39° 23' 06.04", long. 105° 02' 49.05".

Holds CP for change to 0.025-kw ERP, 10-ft. above ground, 7493-ft. above sea level, lat. 39° 43' 13", long. 105° 14' 37". BPDVL-20090309ACF.

Ownership: Tuck Properties Inc.

Cripple Creek, etc.—K14MH, Ch. 14, Tuck Properties Inc.

Technical Facilities: 5-kw ERP, 141-ft. above ground, 6516-ft. above sea level, lat. 38° 49' 53", long. 104° 51' 33".

Ownership: Tuck Properties Inc.

Cripple Creek, etc.—K30IK, Ch. 30, Tuck Properties Inc.

Technical Facilities: 0.5-kw ERP, 131-ft. above ground, 6824-ft. above sea level, lat. 39° 25' 39", long. 104° 51' 60".

Ownership: Tuck Properties Inc.

Crystal, etc.—K35HK, Ch. 35, Pitkin County Translator Dept. Phone: 970-920-5395.

Technical Facilities: 1.7-kw ERP, 98-ft. above ground, 10663-ft. above sea level, lat. 39° 26' 23.5", long. 107° 22' 31.6".

Ownership: Pitkin County Translator Dept.

Crystal, etc.—K40IO, Ch. 40, Pitkin County Translator Dept. Phone: 970-920-5395.

Technical Facilities: 0.5-kw ERP, 301-ft. above ground, 10656-ft. above sea level, lat. 39° 25' 23.5", long. 107° 22' 31.6".

Holds CP for change to 0.64-kw ERP, 79-ft. above ground, 10640-ft. above sea level, BDFCDTT-20090506ABA.

Ownership: Pitkin County Translator Dept.

Crystal, etc.—K56AD, Ch. 56, Pitkin County Translator Dept. Phone: 970-920-5395.

Technical Facilities: 1.7-kw ERP, 87-ft. above ground, 10651-ft. above sea level, lat. 39° 25' 24", long. 107° 22' 32".

Ownership: Pitkin County Translator Dept.

Del Norte—K02KJ, Ch. 2, Rocky Mountain Public Broadcasting Network Inc.

Technical Facilities: 0.055-kw ERP, lat. 37° 40' 30", long. 106° 14' 30".

Ownership: Rocky Mountain Public Broadcasting Network Inc.

Del Norte—K04JA, Ch. 4, Parker Hill TV Assn. Phone: 719-657-2744.

Technical Facilities: 0.126-kw ERP, lat. 37° 40' 30", long. 106° 14' 30".

Ownership: Parker Hill TV Association.

Del Norte—K06KB, Ch. 6, Parker Hill TV Assn. Phone: 719-657-2744.

Technical Facilities: 0.126-kw ERP, lat. 37° 40' 30", long. 106° 14' 30".

Ownership: Parker Hill TV Association.

Del Norte—K07KB, Ch. 7, Parker Hill TV Assn. Phone: 719-657-2744.

Technical Facilities: 0.222-kw ERP, lat. 37° 40' 30", long. 106° 14' 30".

Ownership: Parker Hill TV Association.

Del Norte—K09BU, Ch. 9, Parker Hill TV Assn. Phone: 719-657-2744.

Technical Facilities: 0.003-kw ERP, lat. 37° 40' 19", long. 106° 21' 11".

Ownership: Parker Hill TV Association.

Del Norte—K11EG, Ch. 11, Parker Hill TV Assn. Phone: 719-657-2744.

Technical Facilities: 0.215-kw ERP, lat. 37° 40' 30", long. 106° 14' 30".

Ownership: Parker Hill TV Association.

Del Norte—K13CB, Ch. 13, Parker Hill TV Assn. Phone: 719-657-2744.

Technical Facilities: 0.207-kw ERP, lat. 37° 40' 30", long. 106° 14' 30".

Ownership: Parker Hill TV Association.

Del Norte & South Fork—K41DJ, Ch. 41, South Fork TV Assn. Phone: 719-657-2744.

Technical Facilities: 0.398-kw ERP, 49-ft. above ground, 7815-ft. above sea level, lat. 37° 40' 30", long. 106° 14' 30".

Ownership: South Fork TV Association.

Delta—K52BC, Ch. 52, Rocky Mountain Public Broadcasting Network Inc.

Technical Facilities: 1.06-kw ERP, lat. 38° 44' 50", long. 108° 04' 55".

Ownership: Rocky Mountain Public Broadcasting Network Inc.

Delta—K55DR, Ch. 55, Rocky Mountain Public Broadcasting Network Inc. Phone: 303-892-6666.

Technical Facilities: 0.31-kw ERP, lat. 38° 42' 30", long. 107° 36' 15".

Holds CP for change to channel number 34, 0.22-kw ERP, 46-ft. above ground, 7408-ft. above sea level, lat. 38° 42' 40", long. 107° 36' 19". BDISDTT-20060331AVM.

Ownership: Rocky Mountain Public Broadcasting Network Inc.

Delta, etc.—K02GJ, Ch. 2, Hoak Media of Colorado License LLC. Phone: 972-960-4896.

Technical Facilities: 0.03-kw ERP, lat. 38° 44' 36", long. 108° 05' 18".

Ownership: Hoak Media LLC.

Denver—K48FW, Ch. 48, Trinity Broadcasting Network Inc. Phone: 714-832-2950. Fax: 714-730-0661.

Technical Facilities: 15.5-kw ERP, 732-ft. above ground, 5961-ft. above sea level, lat. 39° 44' 37", long. 104° 59' 18".

Holds CP for change to 15-kw ERP, 984-ft. above ground, 6053-ft. above sea level, lat. 40° 05' 57", long. 104° 53' 48". BDFCDTT-20060330AAN.

Ownership: Trinity Broadcasting Network Inc.

Denver—K57BT, Ch. 57, Trinity Broadcasting of Denver Inc. Phones: 303-650-5515; 714-832-2950. Fax: 714-730-0661.

Studio: 90th & Yates St., Westminster, CO .

Technical Facilities: 1000-w TPO, 4.9-kw ERP, 449-ft. above ground, 7333-ft. above sea level, lat. 39° 43' 59", long. 105° 14' 12".

Holds CP for change to channel number 14, 0.1-kw ERP, 59-ft. above ground, 7339-ft. above sea level, lat. 39° 43' 58", long. 105° 14' 08". BDISDTT-20081120AEE.

Transmitter: Lookout Mountain, adjacent to Cody Monument, Golden.

Began Operation: August 14, 1980.

Ownership: Trinity Broadcasting Network Inc.

Personnel: Paul Crouch, General Manager; Ben Miller, Chief Engineer; Rod Henke, Sales Manager.

Denver—K61AA, Ch. 61, Syncom Media Group Inc. Phone: 303-593-1433.

Technical Facilities: 150-kw ERP, 20-ft. above ground, 8320-ft. above sea level, lat. 39° 54' 48", long. 105° 17' 33".

Ownership: Syncom Media Group Inc.

Denver—K66FB, Ch. 66, Trinity Broadcasting Network Inc. Phones: 303-770-0400; 303-771-3926. Fax: 303-796-1322.

Studio: 8081 E Orchard Rd, Greenwood Village, CO 80111.

Technical Facilities: 47.3-kw ERP, 105-ft. above ground, 5564-ft. above sea level, lat. 39° 51' 08", long. 105° 00' 51".

Ownership: Trinity Broadcasting Network Inc.

Personnel: Joe Oestreich, Chief Engineer; Pat Rosales, Traffic Manager; Gene Steiner, Director of Media.

Denver—KDVT-LP, Ch. 36, Entravision Holdings LLC. Phone: 310-447-3870.

Studio: 777 Grant St, 5th Fl, Denver, CO 80203.

Technical Facilities: 1000-w TPO, 31.4-kw ERP, 43-ft. above ground, 7316-ft. above sea level, lat. 39° 43' 59", long. 105° 14' 12".

Transmitter: KWGN-TV transmitter site, Buffalo Bill Hwy., Lookout Mountain, Golden.

Ownership: Entravision Communications Corp.

Personnel: Yrma Rico, General Manager; Dennis Visser, Chief Engineer.

Denver—KHDT-LP, Ch. 45, Syncom Media Group Inc. Phone: 303-593-1433.

Technical Facilities: 59.5-kw ERP, 36-ft. above ground, 8337-ft. above sea level, lat. 39° 54' 48", long. 105° 17' 33".

Holds CP for change to channel number 38, 0.01-kw ERP, 33-ft. above ground, 8333-ft. above sea level, BDISTTL-20070227AEA.

Ownership: Syncom Media Group Inc.

Denver—KLPD-LP, Ch. 28, Syncom Media Group Inc. Phone: 303-593-1433. Fax: 540-667-5138.

Technical Facilities: 38.4-kw ERP, 20-ft. above ground, 8317-ft. above sea level, lat. 39° 54' 48", long. 105° 17' 33".

Ownership: Syncom Media Group Inc.

Denver—KLPT-LP, Ch. 30, Syncom Media Group. Phone: 303-593-1433.

Technical Facilities: 6-kw ERP, 20-ft. above ground, 8320-ft. above sea level, lat. 39° 54' 48", long. 105° 17' 33".

Holds CP for change to channel number 6, 0.07-kw ERP, BDISTVL-20070615ACX.

Ownership: Syncom Media Group Inc.

Denver—KMAS-LP, Ch. 33, NBC Telemundo License Co. Phone: 202-637-4535.

Technical Facilities: 13.2-kw ERP, 54-ft. above ground, 7774-ft. above sea level, lat. 39° 40' 24", long. 105° 13' 03".

Ownership: NBC Universal.

■ **Denver**—KSBS-LP, Ch. 47, Denver Digital Television LLC. Phone: 303-526-1702.

Technical Facilities: 23.2-kw ERP, 60-ft. above ground, 7280-ft. above sea level, lat. 39° 23' 06", long. 105° 02' 51".

Holds CP for change to 100-kw ERP, 46-ft. above ground, 7280-ft. above sea level, BPTTA-20080111AFX.

Transmitter: 0.99-mi. N of Woodbine Lodge.

Ownership: Denver Digital Television LLC.

Denver—KZCO-LP, Ch. 27, McGraw-Hill Broadcasting Co. Inc. Phone: 303-832-0190.

Technical Facilities: 29.5-kw ERP, 54-ft. above ground, 7774-ft. above sea level, lat. 39° 40' 24", long. 105° 13' 03".

Ownership: McGraw-Hill Broadcasting Co. Inc.

Personnel: Darrell Brown, General Manager.

Deora—K45BU, Ch. 45, Baca County.

Technical Facilities: 3.12-kw ERP, lat. 37° 37' 08", long. 102° 56' 22".

Ownership: Baca County.

Deora—K47CJ, Ch. 47, Baca County.

Technical Facilities: 3.12-kw ERP, 56-ft. above ground, 4849-ft. above sea level, lat. 37° 37' 08", long. 102° 56' 22".

Ownership: Baca County.

Deora—K49BT, Ch. 49, Baca County.

Technical Facilities: 3.12-kw ERP, 56-ft. above ground, 4849-ft. above sea level, lat. 37° 37' 08", long. 102° 56' 22".

Ownership: Baca County.

Deora, etc.—K51CL, Ch. 51, Baca County.

Technical Facilities: 0.832-kw ERP, 49-ft. above ground, 4862-ft. above sea level, lat. 37° 37' 08", long. 102° 56' 22".

Ownership: Baca County.

Divide Creek, etc.—K04GM, Ch. 4, Garfield County.

Technical Facilities: 0.047-kw ERP, 8537-ft. above sea level, lat. 39° 36' 11", long. 107° 38' 49".

Ownership: Garfield County.

Divide Creek, etc.—K06GW, Ch. 6, Rocky Mountain Public Broadcasting Network Inc. Phone: 303-892-6666.

Technical Facilities: 0.011-kw ERP, lat. 39° 36' 11", long. 107° 38' 49".

Holds CP for change to 0.005-kw ERP, 26-ft. above ground, 6365-ft. above sea level, lat. 39° 33' 56", long. 107° 31' 57". BDFCDTT-20060331AYJ.

Ownership: Rocky Mountain Public Broadcasting Network Inc.

Dolores—K02OG, Ch. 2, Southwest Colorado TV Translator Assn. Phone: 970-565-2121.

Technical Facilities: 10-w TPO, 0.04-kw ERP, 7037-ft. above sea level, lat. 37° 28' 07", long. 108° 32' 48".

Transmitter: S of Dolores.

Ownership: Southwest Colorado TV Translator Assn.

Dolores—K04NK, Ch. 4, Southwest Colorado TV Translator Assn. Phone: 970-565-2121.

Technical Facilities: 1-w TPO, 0.005-kw ERP, lat. 37° 28' 07", long. 108° 32' 48".

Transmitter: S of Dolores.

Ownership: Southwest Colorado TV Translator Assn.

Dolores—K05GA, Ch. 5, Southwest Colorado TV Translator Assn. Phone: 970-565-2121.

Technical Facilities: 0.001-kw ERP, lat. 37° 28' 07", long. 108° 32' 48".

Transmitter: S of Dolores.

Ownership: Southwest Colorado TV Translator Assn.

Dolores—K06NT, Ch. 6, Southwest Colorado TV Translator Assn. Phone: 970-565-2129.

Technical Facilities: 0.005-kw ERP, 10-ft. above ground, 7080-ft. above sea level, lat. 37° 28' 00", long. 108° 31' 26".

Ownership: Southwest Colorado TV Translator Assn.

Dolores—K08LL, Ch. 8, Southwest Colorado TV Translator Assn. Phone: 970-565-2121.

Technical Facilities: 50-w TPO, 0.05-kw ERP, lat. 37° 28' 07", long. 108° 32' 48".

Transmitter: S of Dolores.

Ownership: Southwest Colorado TV Translator Assn.

Personnel: Wayne Johnson, General Manager.

Dolores—K10MZ, Ch. 10, Southwest Colorado TV Translator Assn. Phone: 970-565-2121.

Technical Facilities: 5-w TPO, 0.005-kw ERP, lat. 37° 28' 07", long. 108° 32' 48".

Transmitter: S of Dolores.

Ownership: Southwest Colorado TV Translator Assn.

Personnel: Wayne Johnson, General Manager.

Dolores—K12QH, Ch. 12, Southwest Colorado TV Translator Assn. Phone: 970-565-2129.

Technical Facilities: 0.005-kw ERP, 10-ft. above ground, 7080-ft. above sea level, lat. 37° 28' 00", long. 108° 31' 26".

Ownership: Southwest Colorado TV Translator Assn.

Dolores—K13AT, Ch. 13, Southwest Colorado TV Translator Assn. Phone: 970-565-2121.

Technical Facilities: 1-w TPO, 0.004-kw ERP, lat. 37° 28' 07", long. 108° 32' 48".

Transmitter: S of Dolores.

Ownership: Southwest Colorado TV Translator Assn.

Personnel: Wayne Johnson, General Manager.

Dove Creek—K15GU, Ch. 15, Southwest Colorado TV Translator Assn.

Technical Facilities: 0.3-kw ERP, 89-ft. above ground, 6998-ft. above sea level, lat. 37° 45' 37", long. 108° 54' 39".

Ownership: Southwest Colorado TV Translator Assn.

Dove Creek—K17GE, Ch. 17, Southwest Colorado TV Translator Assn.

Technical Facilities: 0.3-kw ERP, 98-ft. above ground, 7004-ft. above sea level, lat. 37° 45' 55", long. 108° 54' 13".

Ownership: Southwest Colorado TV Translator Assn.

Dove Creek—K19GB, Ch. 19, Southwest Colorado TV Translator Assn. Phone: 970-565-2129.

Technical Facilities: 0.3-kw ERP, 89-ft. above ground, 6998-ft. above sea level, lat. 37° 45' 55", long. 108° 54' 10".

Ownership: Southwest Colorado TV Translator Assn.

Dove Creek—K21GT, Ch. 21, Southwest Colorado TV Translator Assn. Phone: 970-565-2129.

Technical Facilities: 0.3-kw ERP, 88-ft. above ground, 6998-ft. above sea level, lat. 37° 45' 55", long. 108° 54' 10".

Ownership: Southwest Colorado TV Translator Assn.

Dove Creek—K23GF, Ch. 23, Southwest Colorado TV Translator Assn. c/o Wayne Johnson. Phone: 970-565-2129.

Technical Facilities: 0.3-kw ERP, 89-ft. above ground, 6998-ft. above sea level, lat. 37° 45' 37", long. 108° 54' 39".

Ownership: Southwest Colorado TV Translator Assn.

Dove Creek—K30DC, Ch. 30, Southwest Colorado TV Translator Assn.

Technical Facilities: 1.17-w TPO, 118-ft. above ground, 7027-ft. above sea level, lat. 37° 45' 37", long. 108° 54' 39".

Ownership: Southwest Colorado TV Translator Assn.

Dove Creek—K32EY, Ch. 32, Southwest Colorado TV Translator Assn. Phone: 970-565-2121.

Technical Facilities: 1.17-kw ERP, 66-ft. above ground, 6863-ft. above sea level, lat. 37° 45' 37", long. 108° 54' 39".

Transmitter: 409 N. Main.

Ownership: Southwest Colorado TV Translator Assn.

Personnel: Wayne Johnson, General Manager.

Dove Creek—K34IA, Ch. 34, Southwest Colorado TV Translator Assn. Phone: 970-565-2129.

Technical Facilities: 1.17-kw ERP, 118-ft. above ground, 7027-ft. above sea level, lat. 37° 45' 37", long. 108° 54' 39".

Ownership: Southwest Colorado TV Translator Assn.

Dove Creek—K48BK, Ch. 48, Southwest Colorado TV Translator Assn. Phone: 970-565-2121.

Technical Facilities: 100-w TPO, 1.76-kw ERP, lat. 37° 48' 05", long. 109° 25' 30".

Ownership: Southwest Colorado TV Translator Assn.

Personnel: Wayne Johnson, General Manager.

Doyleville—K03EY, Ch. 3, Gunnison County Metro. Recreation District.

Technical Facilities: 0.003-kw ERP, lat. 38° 22' 25", long. 106° 40' 47".

Ownership: Gunnison County Metropolitan Recreation District.

Durango—K25GE, Ch. 25, KOB-TV LLC. Phone: 651-642-4212.

Technical Facilities: 20-kw ERP, 40-ft. above ground, 8957-ft. above sea level, lat. 37° 20' 16", long. 107° 49' 23".

Ownership: Hubbard Broadcasting Inc.

Durango—K29CZ, Ch. 29, Rocky Mountain Public Broadcasting Network Inc.

Technical Facilities: 0.6-kw ERP, lat. 37° 15' 44", long. 107° 53' 58".

Transmitter: Smelter Mountain.

Ownership: Rocky Mountain Public Broadcasting Network Inc.

Durango—K38JD, Ch. 38, EICB-TV East LLC. Phone: 972-291-3750.

Technical Facilities: 0.1-kw ERP, 26-ft. above ground, 6627-ft. above sea level, lat. 37° 17' 34", long. 107° 51' 41".

Began Operation: March 19, 2009.

Ownership: EICB-TV LLC.

Durango—K39AH-D, Ch. 39, LIN of New Mexico LLC. Phone: 401-457-9525.

Technical Facilities: 0.133-kw ERP, 46-ft. above ground, 7749-ft. above sea level, lat. 37° 15' 46", long. 107° 54' 58".

Ownership: LIN TV Corp.

Durango—K45DH, Ch. 45, KOAT Hearst-Argyle Television Inc. Phone: 919-839-0300.

Technical Facilities: 0.68-kw ERP, lat. 37° 20' 18", long. 107° 49' 21".

Ownership: Hearst-Argyle Television Inc.

Durango & Hermosa—K31FV-D, Ch. 31, LIN of Colorado LLC. Phone: 401-457-9525.

Technical Facilities: 0.399-kw ERP, 49-ft. above ground, 9062-ft. above sea level, lat. 37° 20' 18", long. 107° 49' 21".

Ownership: LIN TV Corp.

Eads—K50AA, Ch. 50, Kiowa County.

Technical Facilities: 0.888-kw ERP, lat. 38° 22' 35", long. 102° 58' 48".

Ownership: Kiowa County.

Eads—K52AA, Ch. 52, Kiowa County.

Technical Facilities: 0.89-kw ERP, lat. 38° 22' 35", long. 102° 58' 48".

Ownership: Kiowa County.

Eads—K54AB, Ch. 54, Kiowa County.

Technical Facilities: 0.89-kw ERP, lat. 38° 22' 35", long. 102° 58' 48".

Ownership: Kiowa County.

Eads—K56AG, Ch. 56, Kiowa County.

Technical Facilities: 0.888-kw ERP, lat. 38° 22' 35", long. 102° 58' 48".

Ownership: Kiowa County.

Eads, etc.—K48DW, Ch. 48, Kiowa County.

Technical Facilities: 0.75-kw ERP, lat. 38° 22' 35", long. 102° 58' 47".

Transmitter: 13-mi. SW of Eads.

Ownership: Kiowa County.

Eagle, etc.—KCXP-LP, Ch. 40, Colorado TV Marketing LLC. Phone: 970-920-9600.

Technical Facilities: 1-kw ERP, 55-ft. above ground, 10504-ft. above sea level, lat. 39° 44' 23", long. 106° 48' 04".

Holds CP for change to 70-ft. above ground, 10493-ft. above sea level, lat. 39° 13' 16", long. 106° 48' 47". BMPTTL-20071212AAW.

Ownership: Colorado TV Marketing LLC.

East Elk Creek—K08JS, Ch. 8, Garfield County.

Technical Facilities: 0.003-kw ERP, lat. 39° 36' 32", long. 107° 33' 23".

Ownership: Garfield County.

Estes Park—K26HQ, Ch. 26, Venture Technologies Group LLC. Phone: 323-904-4090.

Technical Facilities: 0.1-kw ERP, 49-ft. above ground, 8943-ft. above sea level, lat. 40° 21' 38", long. 105° 31' 12".

Ownership: Venture Technologies Group LLC.

Estes Park—K39JT, Ch. 39, Venture Technologies Group LLC. Phone: 323-904-4090.

Technical Facilities: 0.1-kw ERP, 49-ft. above ground, 8943-ft. above sea level, lat. 40° 21' 38", long. 105° 31' 12".

Ownership: Venture Technologies Group LLC.

Estes Park—K42GS, Ch. 42, Venture Technologies Group LLC. Phone: 323-904-4090.

Technical Facilities: 0.1-kw ERP, 49-ft. above ground, 8943-ft. above sea level, lat. 40° 21' 38", long. 105° 31' 12".

Ownership: Venture Technologies Group LLC.

Estes Park—K47EC, Ch. 47, Syncom Media Group Inc.

Technical Facilities: 0.12-kw ERP, lat. 40° 20' 15", long. 105° 34' 44".

Ownership: Syncom Media Group Inc.

Estes Park—K63AB, Ch. 63, Syncom Media Group Inc. Phone: 303-593-1433.

Technical Facilities: 1.24-kw ERP, lat. 40° 25' 13", long. 105° 26' 39".

Holds CP for change to channel number 26, 115-kw ERP, 20-ft. above ground, 8320-ft. above sea level, lat. 39° 54' 48", long. 105° 17' 33". BDISTTL-20070703ABO.

Ownership: Syncom Media Group Inc.

Fairplay—K11MM, Ch. 11, Twelve Mile Club.

Technical Facilities: 0.006-kw ERP, lat. 39° 07' 37", long. 106° 03' 45".

Ownership: Twelve Mile Ranch.

Flagler-Seibert—K63AJ, Ch. 63, Kit Carson County.

Technical Facilities: 0.742-kw ERP, lat. 39° 19' 05", long. 103° 06' 25".

Ownership: Kit Carson County.

Flagler-Seibert—K65AO, Ch. 65, Kit Carson County.

Technical Facilities: 0.742-kw ERP, lat. 39° 19' 05", long. 103° 06' 25".

Ownership: Kit Carson County.

Flagler-Seibert—K67AQ, Ch. 67, Kit Carson County.

Technical Facilities: 0.742-kw ERP, lat. 39° 19' 05", long. 103° 06' 25".

Ownership: Kit Carson County.

Flagler-Seibert—K69AX, Ch. 69, Kit Carson County.

Technical Facilities: 0.742-kw ERP, lat. 39° 19' 05", long. 103° 06' 25".

Ownership: Kit Carson County.

Fort Collins—K43FN, Ch. 43, Entravision Holdings LLC. Phone: 310-447-3870.

Technical Facilities: 0.1-kw ERP, 127-ft. above ground, 7289-ft. above sea level, lat. 40° 32' 46", long. 105° 11' 51".

Holds CP for change to channel number 41, 1-kw ERP, 60-ft. above ground, 7222-ft. above sea level, BDISTTL-20080312AAD.

Ownership: Entravision Communications Corp.

Fort Collins—K54IK, Ch. 54, Entravision Holdings LLC. Phone: 310-447-3870.

Technical Facilities: 76.4-kw ERP, 127-ft. above ground, 7289-ft. above sea level, lat. 40° 32' 46", long. 105° 11' 51".

Holds CP for change to channel number 49, 55-kw ERP, BPTTL-20051017ACB.

Ownership: Entravision Communications Corp.

Fort Collins—KDNF-LP, Ch. 44, Word of God Fellowship Inc. Phone: 817-571-1229.

Technical Facilities: 33.7-kw ERP, 400-ft. above ground, 7139-ft. above sea level, lat. 40° 53' 42", long. 105° 11' 38".

Ownership: Word of God Fellowship Inc.

Fort Collins—KPXH-LP, Ch. 52, ION Media LPTV Inc., Debtor in Possession. Phone: 561-682-4206. Fax: 561-659-4754.

Technical Facilities: 25-kw ERP, 69-ft. above ground, 7149-ft. above sea level, lat. 40° 32' 56", long. 105° 11' 47".

Holds CP for change to channel number 13, 0.3-kw ERP, BDISDTL-20060321ADB.

Transmitter: Horsetooth Mountain, 8-km SW of Fort Collins.

Began Operation: August 8, 1988.

Ownership: ION Media Networks Inc., Debtor in Possession.

Personnel: Catherine Goin, General Manager; Paul A. Des Chenes, Chief Engineer.

Fraser—K27CB, Ch. 27, Fraser Valley Metropolitan Recreation District.

Technical Facilities: 0.4-kw ERP, lat. 39° 51' 45", long. 105° 46' 20".

Ownership: Fraser Valley Metropolitan Recreation District.

Fraser—K33BV, Ch. 33, Fraser Valley Metropolitan Recreation District.

Technical Facilities: 0.39-kw ERP, lat. 39° 51' 45", long. 105° 46' 20".

Ownership: Fraser Valley Metropolitan Recreation District.

Fraser—K36BR, Ch. 36, Fraser Valley Metropolitan Recreation District.

Technical Facilities: 0.382-kw ERP, lat. 39° 51' 45", long. 105° 46' 20".

Ownership: Fraser Valley Metropolitan Recreation District.

Fraser—K39BT, Ch. 39, Fraser Valley Metropolitan Recreation District.

Technical Facilities: 0.371-kw ERP, lat. 39° 51' 45", long. 105° 46' 20".

Ownership: Fraser Valley Metropolitan Recreation District.

Fraser, etc.—K30CR, Ch. 30, Fraser Valley Metropolitan Recreation District.

Technical Facilities: 0.355-kw ERP, 20-ft. above ground, 11102-ft. above sea level, lat. 39° 51' 45", long. 105° 46' 20".

Ownership: Fraser Valley Metropolitan Recreation District.

Frying Pan River—K07KF, Ch. 7, Pitkin County Translator Dept. Phone: 970-920-5395.

Technical Facilities: 0.005-kw ERP, lat. 39° 21' 12", long. 106° 41' 00".

Ownership: Pitkin County Translator Dept.

Garfield, etc.—K20GE-D, Ch. 20, Garfield County. Phone: 435-676-8826.

Technical Facilities: 0.105-kw ERP, 42-ft. above ground, 11252-ft. above sea level, lat. 38° 32' 30.3", long. 112° 04' 20.2".

Ownership: Garfield County.

Gateview—K62DP, Ch. 62, Gunnison County Metropolitan Recreation District.

Technical Facilities: 0.128-kw ERP, 20-ft. above ground, 9117-ft. above sea level, lat. 38° 15' 43", long. 107° 15' 01".

Ownership: Gunnison County Metropolitan Recreation District.

Gateview, etc.—K02IK, Ch. 2, Gunnison County Metropolitan Recreation District. Phone: 970-641-8725.

Technical Facilities: 0.005-kw ERP, 9258-ft. above sea level, lat. 38° 17' 28", long. 107° 15' 06".

Ownership: Gunnison County Metropolitan Recreation District.

Gateway—K04KG, Ch. 4, Mesa County.

Technical Facilities: 0.008-kw ERP, 23-ft. above ground, 7602-ft. above sea level, lat. 38° 44' 18", long. 108° 53' 10".

Ownership: Mesa County.

Gateway—K09MR, Ch. 9, Hoak Media of Colorado License LLC. Phone: 972-960-4896.

Technical Facilities: 0.01-kw ERP, lat. 38° 38' 25", long. 108° 59' 32".

Ownership: Hoak Media LLC.

Glen Haven—K08IS, Ch. 8, Syncom Media Group Inc. Phone: 303-593-1433.

Technical Facilities: 0.005-kw ERP, lat. 40° 27' 23", long. 105° 26' 59".

Ownership: Syncom Media Group Inc.

Glen Haven—K10JY, Ch. 10, Syncom Media Group Inc. Phone: 303-593-1433.

Technical Facilities: 0.005-kw ERP, lat. 40° 27' 23", long. 105° 26' 59".

Ownership: Syncom Media Group Inc.

Glen Haven—K12KP, Ch. 12, Syncom Media Group Inc.

Technical Facilities: 0.005-kw ERP, lat. 40° 27' 23", long. 105° 26' 59".

Ownership: Syncom Media Group Inc.

Glen Haven—K13ON, Ch. 13, Syncom Media Group Inc. Phone: 303-593-1433.

Technical Facilities: 0.005-kw ERP, lat. 40° 27' 34", long. 105° 27' 48".

Ownership: Syncom Media Group Inc.

Glenwood Springs—K05HE, Ch. 5, Colorado TV Marketing LLC. Phone: 970-920-9600.

Technical Facilities: 0.02-kw ERP, lat. 39° 32' 38", long. 107° 17' 59".

Ownership: Colorado TV Marketing LLC.

Glenwood Springs—K06LX, Ch. 6, Rocky Mountain Public Broadcasting Network Inc.

Technical Facilities: 0.02-kw ERP, lat. 39° 32' 38", long. 107° 17' 59".

Ownership: Rocky Mountain Public Broadcasting Network Inc.

Glenwood Springs—K07GD-D, Ch. 7, Hoak Media of Colorado License LLC. Phone: 972-960-4896.

Technical Facilities: 0.001-kw ERP, 17-ft. above ground, 7314-ft. above sea level, lat. 39° 33' 48", long. 107° 19' 01.2".

Ownership: Hoak Media LLC.

Glenwood Springs—K09DC, Ch. 9, Garfield County.

Technical Facilities: 0.058-kw ERP, lat. 39° 32' 38", long. 107° 17' 59".

Ownership: Garfield County.

Glenwood Springs—K42EV, Ch. 42, Pikes Peak Television Inc. Phone: 970-245-8880. Fax: 970-245-8249.

Studio: 8 Foresight Cir, Grand Junction, CO 81505.

Technical Facilities: 100-w TPO, 1.23-kw ERP, 88-ft. above ground, 8123-ft. above sea level, lat. 39° 32' 36", long. 107° 17' 51".

Transmitter: 1.4-mi. E of Glenwood Springs.

Multichannel TV Sound: Stereo only.

Ownership: News Press & Gazette Co.

Personnel: Kristy Santiago, General Manager; Jay Rademacher, Chief Engineer.

Glenwood Springs—K44DF, Ch. 44, Colorado TV Marketing LLC. Phone: 970-920-9600.

Technical Facilities: 15-kw ERP, 72-ft. above ground, 8090-ft. above sea level, lat. 39° 32' 36.7", long. 107° 17' 49.3".

Holds CP for change to 60-ft. above ground, 7980-ft. above sea level, lat. 39° 32' 34", long. 107° 17' 58". BMPTTL-20071212AAS.

Ownership: Colorado TV Marketing LLC.

Glenwood Springs—KHGS-LP, Ch. 39, EICB-TV East LLC. Phone: 972-291-3750.

Technical Facilities: 2-kw ERP, 49-ft. above ground, 7510-ft. above sea level, lat. 39° 31' 57", long. 107° 20' 30".

Began Operation: March 16, 2009.

Ownership: EICB-TV LLC.

Glenwood Springs, etc.—K11DI, Ch. 11, Garfield County.

Technical Facilities: 0.014-kw ERP, lat. 39° 32' 38", long. 107° 17' 59".

Ownership: Garfield County.

Grand Junction—K02GH, Ch. 2, Gunnison County Metropolitan Recreation District.

Technical Facilities: lat. 38° 42' 47", long. 106° 48' 36".

Ownership: Gunnison County Metropolitan Recreation District.

Grand Junction—K14LS, Ch. 14, Marcia T. Turner. Phone: 954-732-9539.

Technical Facilities: 40-kw ERP, 459-ft. above ground, 5043-ft. above sea level, lat. 39° 03' 23", long. 108° 31' 48".

Ownership: Marcia T. Turner.

Grand Junction—K25FZ, Ch. 25, Trinity Broadcasting Network Inc. Phone: 714-832-2950. Fax: 714-730-0661.

Technical Facilities: 21.4-kw ERP, lat. 39° 04' 00", long. 108° 44' 41".

Holds CP for change to 15-kw ERP, 131-ft. above ground, 7198-ft. above sea level, BDFCDTT-20060330AAQ.

Transmitter: KJYE-FM tower, Black Ridge.

Ownership: Trinity Broadcasting Network Inc.

Grand Junction—K30IU, Ch. 30, EICB-TV East LLC. Phone: 972-291-3750.

Technical Facilities: 17-kw ERP, 33-ft. above ground, 7431-ft. above sea level, lat. 38° 52' 39", long. 108° 13' 36".

Began Operation: June 27, 2008.

Ownership: EICB-TV LLC.

Grand Junction—K45IT, Ch. 45, Mesa County. Phone: 970-255-7150.

Technical Facilities: 0.976-kw ERP, 46-ft. above ground, 7165-ft. above sea level, lat. 39° 03' 56", long. 108° 44' 50".

Ownership: Mesa County.

Grand Junction—K49IO, Ch. 49, Mesa County. Phone: 970-255-7150.

Technical Facilities: 0.976-kw ERP, 59-ft. above ground, 7178-ft. above sea level, lat. 39° 03' 56", long. 108° 44' 50".

Ownership: Mesa County.

■ **Grand Junction**—KGJT-LP, Ch. 27, Hoak Media of Colorado License LLC. Phone: 972-960-4896.

Technical Facilities: 150-kw ERP, lat. 39° 05' 21", long. 108° 13' 37".

Transmitter: Palisades Point, Grand Mesa.

Ownership: Hoak Media LLC.

Grand Junction—KKHD-LP, Ch. 20, Pikes Peak Television Inc. Phone: 816-271-8505.

Technical Facilities: 16-kw ERP, 135-ft. above ground, 7205-ft. above sea level, lat. 39° 04' 00", long. 108° 44' 45".

Holds CP for change to 20.4-kw ERP, 75-ft. above ground, 9997-ft. above sea level, lat. 39° 02' 55", long. 108° 15' 03". BPTTL-20070410ABQ.

Ownership: News Press & Gazette Co.

Grand Junction, etc.—K39AF, Ch. 39, Mesa County.

Technical Facilities: 1.22-kw ERP, lat. 39° 05' 20", long. 108° 13' 35".

Ownership: Mesa County.

Grand Junction, etc.—K43AB, Ch. 43, Mesa County.

Technical Facilities: 1.22-kw ERP, lat. 39° 05' 20", long. 108° 13' 25".

Ownership: Mesa County.

Grand Junction, etc.—K47JR, Ch. 47, Mesa County. Phone: 970-255-7150.

Technical Facilities: 0.976-kw ERP, 59-ft. above ground, 7178-ft. above sea level, lat. 39° 03' 56", long. 108° 44' 50".

Ownership: Mesa County.

Grand Lake—K13EL, Ch. 13, Grand Lake Metropolitan Recreation District.

Technical Facilities: 0.022-kw ERP, lat. 40° 13' 00", long. 105° 51' 51".

Ownership: Grand Lake Metropolitan Recreation District.

Grand Valley—K02HW, Ch. 2, Hoak Media of Colorado License LLC. Phone: 972-960-4896.

Technical Facilities: 0.06-kw ERP, lat. 39° 25' 48", long. 107° 57' 10".

Ownership: Hoak Media LLC.

Grand Valley—K11PR, Ch. 11, Garfield County.

Technical Facilities: 0.141-kw ERP, lat. 39° 26' 34", long. 107° 57' 57".

Ownership: Garfield County.

Grand Valley—K13QZ, Ch. 13, Colorado TV Marketing LLC. Phone: 970-920-9600.

Technical Facilities: 0.072-kw ERP, lat. 39° 26' 34", long. 107° 57' 57".

Ownership: Colorado TV Marketing LLC.

Grand Valley—K28HA, Ch. 28, Rocky Mountain Public Broadcasting Network Inc. Phone: 303-892-6666.

Technical Facilities: 0.356-kw ERP, 42-ft. above ground, 7262-ft. above sea level, lat. 39° 26' 36", long. 107° 58' 01".

Holds CP for change to 0.43-kw ERP, 43-ft. above ground, 7316-ft. above sea level, BDFCDTT-20060331AZE.

Ownership: Rocky Mountain Public Broadcasting Network Inc.

Grand Valley, etc.—K07JM, Ch. 7, Garfield County.

Technical Facilities: 0.05-kw ERP, 8130-ft. above sea level, lat. 39° 26' 34", long. 107° 57' 57".

Ownership: Garfield County.

Gunnison—K02LY, Ch. 2, Gunnison County Metro. Recreation District. Phone: 303-641-3290.

Studio: 105 N Wisconsin, Gunnison, CO 81230.

Technical Facilities: 10-w TPO, 0.024-kw ERP, 46-ft. above ground, 8666-ft. above sea level, lat. 38° 31' 45", long. 106° 54' 22".

Transmitter: Tenderfoot Mountain, 1.5-mi. SE of Gunnison.

Ownership: Gunnison County Metropolitan Recreation District.

Personnel: Carol Draper, Station Manager; Fred Jones, Chief Engineer.

Gunnison—K04DH, Ch. 4, Gunnison County Metro. Recreation District. Phone: 303-641-0196.

Technical Facilities: 0.01-kw ERP, 35-ft. above ground, 8620-ft. above sea level, lat. 38° 31' 25", long. 106° 54' 20".

Transmitter: 2-mi. SE of Gunnison.

Ownership: Gunnison County Metropolitan Recreation District.

Gunnison—K06HN, Ch. 6, Gunnison County Metropolitan Recreation District.

Technical Facilities: 0.013-kw ERP, lat. 38° 31' 25", long. 106° 54' 20".

Ownership: Gunnison County Metropolitan Recreation District.

Gunnison—K09TH, Ch. 9, Gunnison County Metropolitan Recreation District.

Technical Facilities: 0.016-kw ERP, lat. 38° 31' 25", long. 106° 54' 20".

Ownership: Gunnison County Metropolitan Recreation District.

Gunnison—K13AV, Ch. 13, Gunnison County Metropolitan Recreation District.

Technical Facilities: 0.021-kw ERP, 30-ft. above ground, 8651-ft. above sea level, lat. 38° 31' 25", long. 106° 54' 20".

Ownership: Gunnison County Metropolitan Recreation District.

Gunnison, etc.—K07BE, Ch. 7, Gunnison County Metropolitan Recreation District.

Technical Facilities: 0.01-kw ERP, lat. 38° 31' 25", long. 106° 54' 20".

Ownership: Gunnison County Metropolitan Recreation District.

Gunnison, etc.—K11AT, Ch. 11, Gunnison County Metropolitan Recreation District.

Technical Facilities: 0.024-kw ERP, lat. 38° 31' 25", long. 106° 54' 20".

Ownership: Gunnison County Metropolitan Recreation District.

Hartsel—K66AW, Ch. 66, Gunnison County Metropolitan Recreation District.

Technical Facilities: 4.6-kw ERP, lat. 39° 02' 57", long. 105° 30' 45".

Ownership: Gunnison County Metropolitan Recreation District.

Hartsel—K68AR, Ch. 68, Gunnison County Metropolitan Recreation District. Phone: 940-641-8725.

Technical Facilities: 4.62-kw ERP, lat. 39° 02' 57", long. 105° 30' 45".

Ownership: Gunnison County Metropolitan Recreation District.

Hartsel—K70FL, Ch. 70, Gunnison County Metropolitan Recreation District. Phone: 940-641-8725.

Technical Facilities: 3.4-kw ERP, 16-ft. above ground, 11309-ft. above sea level, lat. 39° 02' 57", long. 105° 30' 45".

Holds CP for change to channel number 23, BDISTT-20070926APN.

Ownership: Gunnison County Metropolitan Recreation District.

Hartsel, etc.—K64AQ, Ch. 64, Gunnison County Metropolitan Recreation District.

Technical Facilities: 4.6-kw ERP, 11306-ft. above sea level, lat. 39° 02' 57", long. 105° 30' 45".

Ownership: Gunnison County Metropolitan Recreation District.

Haxtun—K31FZ, Ch. 31, Region 1 Translator Assn. Phone: 970-848-5301.

Technical Facilities: 0.862-kw ERP, 276-ft. above ground, 4373-ft. above sea level, lat. 40° 38' 57", long. 102° 40' 58".

Ownership: Region 1 Translator Association.

Haxtun—K33GM, Ch. 33, Region 1 Translator Assn. Phone: 970-848-5301.

Technical Facilities: 0.89-kw ERP, 276-ft. above ground, 4373-ft. above sea level, lat. 40° 38' 57", long. 102° 40' 58".

Ownership: Region 1 Translator Association.

Haxtun—K35GO, Ch. 35, Region 1 Translator Assn. Phone: 970-848-5301.

Technical Facilities: 0.89-kw ERP, 276-ft. above ground, 4373-ft. above sea level, lat. 40° 38' 57", long. 102° 40' 58".

Ownership: Region 1 Translator Association.

Haxtun—K39HM, Ch. 39, Region 1 Translator Assn. Phone: 970-848-5301.

Technical Facilities: 0.89-kw ERP, 276-ft. above ground, 4373-ft. above sea level, lat. 40° 38' 57", long. 102° 40' 58".

Ownership: Region 1 Translator Association.

Haxtun—K41IT, Ch. 41, Region 1 Translator Assn. Phone: 970-848-5301.

Technical Facilities: 0.89-kw ERP, 276-ft. above ground, 4373-ft. above sea level, lat. 40° 38' 57", long. 102° 40' 58".

Ownership: Region 1 Translator Association.

Haxtun—K43JJ, Ch. 43, Region 1 Translator Assn. Phone: 970-848-5301.

Technical Facilities: 0.89-kw ERP, 276-ft. above ground, 4373-ft. above sea level, lat. 40° 38' 57", long. 102° 40' 58".

Ownership: Region 1 Translator Association.

Hayden—K06CE, Ch. 6, Yampa Valley TV Assn. Inc.

Technical Facilities: 0.072-kw ERP, lat. 40° 31' 16", long. 107° 17' 51".

Ownership: Yampa Valley TV Association Inc.

Hayden—K09NX, Ch. 9, Yampa Valley TV Assn. Inc.

Technical Facilities: 0.052-kw ERP, lat. 40° 31' 16", long. 107° 17' 51".

Ownership: Yampa Valley TV Association Inc.

Hayden—K19CF, Ch. 19, Routt County.

Technical Facilities: 0.49-kw ERP, 112-ft. above ground, 7392-ft. above sea level, lat. 40° 31' 15", long. 107° 17' 46".

Ownership: Routt County.

Hesperus—K02QI, Ch. 2, Southwest Colorado TV Translator Assn. Phone: 970-565-2129.

Technical Facilities: 0.005-kw ERP, 20-ft. above ground, 8888-ft. above sea level, lat. 37° 17' 01", long. 108° 01' 01".

Ownership: Southwest Colorado TV Translator Assn.

Hesperus—K04PJ, Ch. 4, Southwest Colorado TV Translator Assn. Phone: 970-565-2121.

Technical Facilities: 0.005-kw ERP, 20-ft. above ground, 8888-ft. above sea level, lat. 37° 17' 01", long. 108° 01' 01".

Ownership: Southwest Colorado TV Translator Assn.

Hesperus—K13XX, Ch. 13, Southwest Colorado TV Translator Assn. Phone: 970-565-2121.

Technical Facilities: 0.005-kw ERP, 20-ft. above ground, 8888-ft. above sea level, lat. 37° 17' 01", long. 108° 01' 01".

Ownership: Southwest Colorado TV Translator Assn.

Hoehne—K03DO, Ch. 3, Valley Metro Recreation District. Phone: 719-845-1315.

Technical Facilities: 0.004-kw ERP, 7375-ft. above sea level, lat. 37° 08' 35", long. 104° 26' 40".

Ownership: Valley Metro Recreation District.

Hoehne—K07HK, Ch. 7, Valley Metro Recreation District. Phone: 719-845-1315.

Technical Facilities: 0.009-kw ERP, 7365-ft. above sea level, lat. 37° 08' 35", long. 104° 26' 40".

Ownership: Valley Metro Recreation District.

Hoehne—K09HU, Ch. 9, Valley Metro Recreation District. Phone: 719-845-1315.

Technical Facilities: 0.003-kw ERP, 7365-ft. above sea level, lat. 37° 08' 35", long. 104° 26' 40".

Ownership: Valley Metro Recreation District.

Holyoke—K15FD, Ch. 15, Region 1 Translator Assn. Phone: 970-848-5301.

Technical Facilities: 3.46-kw ERP, lat. 40° 30' 37", long. 102° 21' 33".

Transmitter: 5-mi. S & 3-mi. W of Holyoke.

Ownership: Region 1 Translator Association.

Holyoke—K17EU, Ch. 17, Region 1 Translator Assn. Phone: 970-848-5301.

Technical Facilities: 0.74-kw ERP, lat. 40° 30' 37", long. 102° 21' 33".

Transmitter: 5-mi. S & 3-mi. W of Holyoke.

Ownership: Region 1 Translator Association.

Holyoke—K19EG, Ch. 19, Region 1 Translator Assn. Phone: 970-848-5301.

Technical Facilities: 3.455-kw ERP, lat. 40° 30' 37", long. 102° 21' 33".

Transmitter: 5-mi. S & 3-mi. W of Holyoke.

Ownership: Region 1 Translator Association.

Holyoke—K21FF, Ch. 21, Region 1 Translator Assn. Phone: 970-848-5301.

Technical Facilities: 3.46-kw ERP, 209-ft. above ground, 4193-ft. above sea level, lat. 40° 30' 37", long. 102° 21' 33".

Transmitter: 5-mi. S & 3-mi. W of Holyoke.

Ownership: Region 1 Translator Association.

Holyoke—K25GZ, Ch. 25, Region 1 Translator Assn. Phone: 970-848-5301.

Technical Facilities: 0.946-kw ERP, lat. 40° 30' 37", long. 102° 21' 33".

Transmitter: 5-mi. S & 3-mi. W of Holyoke.

Ownership: Region 1 Translator Association.

Holyoke—K27IH-D, Ch. 27, Region 1 Translator Association. Phone: 970-848-5301.

Technical Facilities: 0.2-kw ERP, 207-ft. above ground, 4190-ft. above sea level, lat. 40° 30' 37", long. 102° 21' 33".

Ownership: Region 1 Translator Association.

Holyoke—K29GI, Ch. 29, Region 1 Translator Assn. Phone: 970-848-5301.

Technical Facilities: 3.714-kw ERP, 209-ft. above ground, 4192-ft. above sea level, lat. 40° 30' 37", long. 102° 21' 33".

Ownership: Region 1 Translator Association.

Hotchkiss, etc.—K13ML, Ch. 13, Hoak Media of Colorado License LLC. Phone: 972-960-4896.

Technical Facilities: 0.03-kw ERP, lat. 38° 42' 48", long. 107° 36' 42".

Ownership: Hoak Media LLC.

Howard—K04IC, Ch. 4, Pleasant Valley TV Assn, c/o Fire Department. Phone: 719-942-3353.

Technical Facilities: 0.0038-kw ERP, lat. 38° 42' 48", long. 105° 48' 08".

Ownership: Pleasant Valley TV Assn.

Idalia—K14LB, Ch. 14, Region 1 Translator Assn. Phone: 970-848-5301.

Technical Facilities: 0.59-kw ERP, 409-ft. above ground, 4563-ft. above sea level, lat. 39° 43' 50", long. 102° 28' 56".

Ownership: Region 1 Translator Association.

Idalia—K18FO, Ch. 18, Region 1 Translator Assn. Phone: 970-848-5301.

Technical Facilities: 0.966-kw ERP, lat. 39° 43' 50", long. 102° 28' 56".

Transmitter: 10.5-mi. WNW of Idalia.

Ownership: Region 1 Translator Association.

Idalia—K20HM, Ch. 20, Region 1 Translator Assn. Phone: 970-848-5301.

Technical Facilities: 0.59-kw ERP, 409-ft. above ground, 4563-ft. above sea level, lat. 39° 43' 50", long. 102° 28' 56".

Ownership: Region 1 Translator Association.

Idalia—K22GQ, Ch. 22, Region 1 Translator Assn. Phone: 970-848-5301.

Technical Facilities: 0.59-kw ERP, 409-ft. above ground, 4563-ft. above sea level, lat. 39° 43' 50", long. 102° 28' 56".

Ownership: Region 1 Translator Association.

Idalia—K29HD-D, Ch. 29, Region 1 Translator Assn. Phone: 970-848-5301.

Technical Facilities: 0.154-kw ERP, 410-ft. above ground, 4567-ft. above sea level, lat. 39° 43' 50", long. 102° 28' 56".

Began Operation: March 27, 1981.

Ownership: Region 1 Translator Association.

Idalia & South Yuma County—K16EK, Ch. 16, Region 1 Translator Assn. Phone: 970-848-5301.

Technical Facilities: 0.54-kw ERP, lat. 39° 43' 50", long. 102° 28' 56".

Transmitter: 10.5-mi. WNW of Idalia.

Ownership: Region 1 Translator Association.

Idalia & South Yuma County—K24EZ, Ch. 24, Region 1 Translator Assn. Phone: 970-848-5301.

Technical Facilities: 0.966-kw ERP, lat. 39° 43' 50", long. 102° 28' 56".

Transmitter: 10.5-mi. WNW of Idalia.

Ownership: Region 1 Translator Association.

Idalia & South Yuma County—K26FP, Ch. 26, Region 1 Translator Assn. Phone: 970-848-5301.

Technical Facilities: 0.966-kw ERP, lat. 39° 43' 50", long. 102° 28' 56".

Transmitter: 10.5-mi. WNW of Idalia.

Ownership: Region 1 Translator Association.

Ignacio—K52GA, Ch. 52, Rocky Mountain Public Broadcasting Network Inc. Phone: 303-892-6666.

Technical Facilities: 0.582-kw ERP, 68-ft. above ground, 8979-ft. above sea level, lat. 37° 11' 03", long. 107° 29' 06".

Holds CP for change to channel number 36, 0.17-kw ERP, 69-ft. above ground, 8983-ft. above sea level, BDISDTT-20060331AWO.

Transmitter: Rattlesnake Ridge.

Ownership: Rocky Mountain Public Broadcasting Network Inc.

Ismay Canyon—K02OU, Ch. 2, Southwest Colorado TV Translator Assn. Phone: 970-565-2121.

Technical Facilities: 1-w TPO, 0.002-kw ERP, 10-ft. above ground, 1801-ft. above sea level, lat. 37° 15' 08", long. 108° 41' 16".

Transmitter: Approx. 8.5-mi. SW of Cortez.

Ownership: Southwest Colorado TV Translator Assn.

Ismay Canyon—K04OO, Ch. 4, Southwest Colorado TV Translator Assn. Phone: 970-565-2121. Fax: 970-565-1120.

Technical Facilities: 1-w TPO, 0.016-kw ERP, 16-ft. above ground, 5915-ft. above sea level, lat. 37° 15' 08", long. 108° 41' 16".

Transmitter: Approx. 8.5-mi. SW of Cortez.

Ownership: Southwest Colorado TV Translator Assn.

Ismay Canyon—K05JW, Ch. 5, Southwest Colorado TV Translator Assn. Phone: 970-565-2121.

Technical Facilities: 10-w TPO, 0.002-kw ERP, 23-ft. above ground, 592-ft. above sea level, lat. 37° 15' 08", long. 108° 41' 16".

Transmitter: Approx. 8.5-mi. SW of Cortez.

Ownership: Southwest Colorado TV Translator Assn.

Ismay Canyon—K10NY, Ch. 10, Southwest Colorado TV Translator Assn. Phone: 970-565-2121.

Technical Facilities: 1-w TPO, 0.2-kw ERP, 26-ft. above ground, 5925-ft. above sea level, lat. 37° 15' 08", long. 108° 41' 16".

Transmitter: Approx. 8.5-mi. SW of Cortez.

Ownership: Southwest Colorado TV Translator Assn.

Personnel: Wayne Johnson, General Manager.

Ismay Canyon—K13XG, Ch. 13, Southwest Colorado TV Translator Assn. Phone: 970-565-2121.

Technical Facilities: 1-w TPO, 0.0002-kw ERP, 30-ft. above ground, 5928-ft. above sea level, lat. 37° 15' 08", long. 108° 41' 16".

Transmitter: Approx. 8.5-mi. SW of Cortez.

Ownership: Southwest Colorado TV Translator Assn.

Personnel: Wayne Johnson, General Manager.

Jack's Cabin—K05EJ, Ch. 5, Gunnison County Metropolitan Recreation District.

Technical Facilities: 0.024-kw ERP, 30-ft. above ground, 9449-ft. above sea level, lat. 38° 42' 47", long. 106° 48' 36".

Ownership: Gunnison County Metropolitan Recreation District.

Jack's Cabin—K16DR, Ch. 16, Gunnison County Metropolitan Recreation District. Phone: 970-641-8725.

Technical Facilities: 0.074-kw ERP, 20-ft. above ground, 9439-ft. above sea level, lat. 38° 42' 47", long. 106° 48' 36".

Ownership: Gunnison County Metropolitan Recreation District.

Jack's Cabin—K67CQ, Ch. 67, Gunnison County Metropolitan Recreation District.

Technical Facilities: 0.93-kw ERP, lat. 38° 42' 47", long. 106° 48' 36".

Ownership: Gunnison County Metropolitan Recreation District.

Jack's Cabin, etc.—K08HC, Ch. 8, Gunnison County Metropolitan Recreation District.

Technical Facilities: 0.015-kw ERP, lat. 38° 42' 47", long. 106° 48' 36".

Ownership: Gunnison County Metropolitan Recreation District.

Jack's Cabin, etc.—K65CR, Ch. 65, Gunnison County Metropolitan Recreation District.

Technical Facilities: 0.93-kw ERP, lat. 38° 43' 45", long. 106° 47' 53".

Ownership: Gunnison County Metropolitan Recreation District.

Jack's Cabin, etc.—K69BU, Ch. 69, Gunnison County Metropolitan Recreation District.

Technical Facilities: 0.2-kw ERP, lat. 38° 43' 45", long. 106° 47' 53".

Ownership: Gunnison County Metropolitan Recreation District.

Julesburg—K45IS-D, Ch. 45, Region 1 Translator Association. Phone: 970-848-5301.

Technical Facilities: 0.135-kw ERP, 289-ft. above ground, 4157-ft. above sea level, lat. 40° 54' 19", long. 102° 22' 32".

Ownership: Region 1 Translator Association.

Julesburg—K47JH, Ch. 47, Region 1 Translator Assn. Phone: 970-848-5301.

Technical Facilities: 0.665-kw ERP, 289-ft. above ground, 4157-ft. above sea level, lat. 40° 54' 19", long. 102° 22' 32".

Ownership: Region 1 Translator Association.

Julesburg—K49IN, Ch. 49, Region 1 Translator Assn. Phone: 970-848-5301.

Technical Facilities: 0.665-kw ERP, 289-ft. above ground, 4157-ft. above sea level, lat. 40° 54' 19", long. 102° 22' 32".

Ownership: Region 1 Translator Association.

Julesburg—K51IL, Ch. 51, Region 1 Translator Assn. Phone: 970-848-5301.

Technical Facilities: 0.665-kw ERP, 289-ft. above ground, 4157-ft. above sea level, lat. 40° 54' 19", long. 102° 22' 32".

Ownership: Region 1 Translator Association.

Julesburg—K53IY, Ch. 53, Region 1 Translator Assn. Phone: 970-848-5301.

Technical Facilities: 0.665-kw ERP, 289-ft. above ground, 4157-ft. above sea level, lat. 40° 54' 19", long. 102° 22' 32".

Ownership: Region 1 Translator Association.

Julesburg—K55JC, Ch. 55, Region 1 Translator Assn. Phone: 970-848-5301.

Technical Facilities: 0.665-kw ERP, 289-ft. above ground, 4157-ft. above sea level, lat. 40° 54' 19", long. 102° 22' 32".

Ownership: Region 1 Translator Association.

Julesburg—K57JE, Ch. 57, Region 1 Translator Assn. Phone: 970-848-5301.

Technical Facilities: 0.665-kw ERP, 289-ft. above ground, 4157-ft. above sea level, lat. 40° 54' 19", long. 102° 22' 32".

Ownership: Region 1 Translator Association.

La Junta—K35DZ, Ch. 35, Full Gospel Outreach Inc.

Technical Facilities: 1.26-kw ERP, 138-ft. above ground, 4334-ft. above sea level, lat. 37° 56' 47", long. 103° 32' 39".

Ownership: Full Gospel Outreach Inc.

La Veta—K03FR, Ch. 3, Rocky Mountain Public Broadcasting Network Inc.

Technical Facilities: 0.006-kw ERP, lat. 37° 30' 00", long. 105° 00' 27".

Ownership: Rocky Mountain Public Broadcasting Network Inc.

Lake City—K04HG, Ch. 4, Hinsdale County Chamber of Commerce. Phone: 970-944-2527.

Technical Facilities: 0.012-kw ERP, 11220-ft. above sea level, lat. 37° 59' 35", long. 107° 19' 30".

Ownership: Hinsdale County Chamber of Commerce.

Lake City—K08GV, Ch. 8, Hinsdale County Chamber of Commerce Inc.

Technical Facilities: 0.004-kw ERP, lat. 38° 03' 16", long. 107° 14' 17".

Ownership: Hinsdale County Chamber of Commerce.

Lake City—K10EA, Ch. 10, Kinsdale County Chamber of Commerce. Phone: 970-944-2527.

Technical Facilities: 0.005-kw ERP, lat. 37° 59' 56", long. 107° 19' 35".

Ownership: Hinsdale County Chamber of Commerce.

Lake City—K12KV, Ch. 12, Hinsdale County Chamber of Commerce. Phone: 970-944-2527.

Technical Facilities: 0.01-kw ERP, 11220-ft. above sea level, lat. 37° 59' 35", long. 107° 19' 30".

Ownership: Hinsdale County Chamber of Commerce.

Lake George—K39CD, Ch. 39, Pikes Peak Televison Inc. Phone: 719-632-1515.

Technical Facilities: 2.34-kw ERP, lat. 39° 03' 01", long. 105° 30' 50".

Transmitter: Badger Mountain, 9.9-mi. NW of Lake George.

Ownership: News Press & Gazette Co.

Lake George, etc.—K58FY, Ch. 58, Rocky Mountain Public Broadcasting Network Inc. Phone: 303-892-6666.

Technical Facilities: 1.19-kw ERP, lat. 39° 03' 01", long. 105° 30' 50".

Holds CP for change to channel number 29, 0.2-kw ERP, 89-ft. above ground, 11319-ft. above sea level, BDISDTT-20060331BIM.

Ownership: Rocky Mountain Public Broadcasting Network Inc.

Lamar—K03BA, Ch. 3, City of Lamar.

Technical Facilities: 0.004-kw ERP, lat. 38° 03' 35", long. 102° 39' 04".

Ownership: City of Lamar.

Lamar—K07DH, Ch. 7, City of Lamar.

Technical Facilities: 0.01-kw ERP, lat. 38° 03' 35", long. 102° 39' 04".

Ownership: City of Lamar.

Lamar—K09DH, Ch. 9, City of Lamar.

Technical Facilities: 0.007-kw ERP, lat. 38° 03' 35", long. 102° 39' 04".

Ownership: City of Lamar.

Lamar—K42EA, Ch. 42, Full Gospel Outreach Inc.

Technical Facilities: 1.24-kw ERP, 102-ft. above ground, 3888-ft. above sea level, lat. 38° 02' 13", long. 102° 36' 02".

Ownership: Full Gospel Outreach Inc.

Lamar—K53AA, Ch. 53, Prowers County.

Technical Facilities: 0.754-kw ERP, 4196-ft. above sea level, lat. 38° 02' 05", long. 102° 26' 10".

Ownership: Prowers County.

Lamar—K55AK, Ch. 55, Prowers County.

Technical Facilities: 0.754-kw ERP, 4190-ft. above sea level, lat. 38° 02' 05", long. 102° 26' 10".

Ownership: Prowers County.

Lamar—K57AG, Ch. 57, Prowers County.

Technical Facilities: 0.754-kw ERP, 4196-ft. above sea level, lat. 38° 02' 05", long. 102° 26' 10".

Ownership: Prowers County.

Lamar—K59AH, Ch. 59, Prowers County.

Technical Facilities: 0.754-kw ERP, lat. 38° 02' 05", long. 102° 26' 10".

Ownership: Prowers County.

Las Animas—K40DP, Ch. 40, Full Gospel Outreach Inc.

Technical Facilities: 20-w TPO, 0.041-kw ERP, 144-ft. above ground, 4043-ft. above sea level, lat. 38° 04' 10", long. 103° 14' 21".

Transmitter: 29875 McBridge Ave., Las Animas.

Ownership: Full Gospel Outreach Inc.

Las Animas—K63AF, Ch. 63, Bent County.

Technical Facilities: 0.75-kw ERP, lat. 38° 01' 15", long. 102° 59' 10".

Ownership: Bent County.

Las Animas—K65AJ, Ch. 65, Bent County.

Technical Facilities: 0.754-kw ERP, lat. 38° 01' 15", long. 102° 59' 10".

Ownership: Bent County.

Las Animas—K67AH, Ch. 67, Bent County.

Technical Facilities: 0.754-kw ERP, lat. 38° 01' 15", long. 102° 59' 10".

Ownership: Bent County.

Las Animas—K69AN, Ch. 69, Bent County.

Technical Facilities: 0.754-kw ERP, lat. 38° 01' 15", long. 102° 59' 10".

Ownership: Bent County.

Leadville—K03CD, Ch. 3, Lake County TV-FM Inc.

Technical Facilities: 0.011-kw ERP, lat. 39° 15' 48", long. 106° 10' 57".

Ownership: Lake County TV-FM Inc.

Leadville—K08ER, Ch. 8, Lake County TV-FM Inc.

Technical Facilities: 0.112-kw ERP, lat. 39° 16' 15", long. 106° 11' 11".

Ownership: Lake County TV-FM Inc.

Leadville—K11GM, Ch. 11, Lake County TV-FM Inc.

Technical Facilities: 0.11-kw ERP, lat. 39° 15' 52", long. 106° 10' 54".

Ownership: Lake County TV-FM Inc.

Leadville—K13GI, Ch. 13, Lake County TV-FM Inc.

Technical Facilities: 0.11-kw ERP, lat. 39° 15' 52", long. 106° 10' 54".

Ownership: Lake County TV-FM Inc.

Loveland—K48CG, Ch. 48, Trinity Broadcasting Network Inc. Phone: 714-832-2950. Fax: 714-730-0661.

Technical Facilities: 1000-w TPO, 3-kw ERP, 367-ft. above ground, 7178-ft. above sea level, lat. 40° 32' 56", long. 105° 11' 47".

Transmitter: Horsetooth Mtn., 3.3-mi W of Drake Rd. & Overland Trail Rd, near Fort Collins.

Ownership: Trinity Broadcasting Network Inc.

Personnel: Paul Crouch, General Manager; Ben Miller, Chief Engineer; Rod Henke, Sales Manager.

Lower Frying Pan River area—K11LM, Ch. 11, Pitkin County Translator Dept. Phone: 970-920-5395.

Technical Facilities: 0.045-kw ERP, 33-ft. above ground, 12434-ft. above sea level, lat. 39° 21' 12", long. 106° 41' 00".

Ownership: Pitkin County Translator Dept.

Lower Piceance Creek—K03HG, Ch. 3, Rio Blanco County TV Assn.

Technical Facilities: 0.006-kw ERP, lat. 39° 58' 14", long. 108° 11' 29".

Transmitter: 17-mi. WSW of Meeker.

Ownership: Rio Blanco County TV Association.

Lower Piceance Creek—K13WY, Ch. 13, Rio Blanco County TV Assn.

Technical Facilities: 0.007-kw ERP, 43-ft. above ground, 5971-ft. above sea level, lat. 39° 58' 14", long. 108° 11' 29".

Ownership: Rio Blanco County TV Association.

Manitou Springs—K03AO, Ch. 3, City of Manitou Springs. Phone: 719-685-2600.

Technical Facilities: 0.001-kw ERP, lat. 38° 51' 50", long. 104° 54' 15".

Ownership: City of Manitou Springs.

Manitou Springs—K06BI, Ch. 6, City of Manitou Springs. Phone: 719-685-2600.

Technical Facilities: 0.001-kw ERP, lat. 38° 51' 50", long. 104° 54' 15".

Ownership: City of Manitou Springs.

Manitou Springs—K07PA, Ch. 7, Rocky Mountain Public Broadcasting Network Inc. Phone: 303-892-6666.

Technical Facilities: 0.037-kw ERP, lat. 38° 51' 50", long. 104° 54' 15".

Holds CP for change to 0.02-kw ERP, 23-ft. above ground, 6601-ft. above sea level, BDFCDTT-20060331AYF.

Ownership: Rocky Mountain Public Broadcasting Network Inc.

Manitou Springs—K09LH, Ch. 9, City of Manitou Springs. Phone: 719-685-2600.

Technical Facilities: 0.003-kw ERP, lat. 38° 51' 50", long. 104° 54' 15".

Ownership: City of Manitou Springs.

Manitou Springs—K47FJ, Ch. 47, Full Gospel Outreach Inc.

Technical Facilities: 0.054-kw ERP, lat. 38° 51' 50", long. 104° 54' 48".

Transmitter: Approx. 0.25-mi. NE of Manitou Springs Post Office.

Ownership: Full Gospel Outreach Inc.

Marvine Creek, etc.—K48EC, Ch. 48, Rio Blanco County TV Assn.

Technical Facilities: 0.126-kw ERP, 23-ft. above ground, 7976-ft. above sea level, lat. 40° 02' 41", long. 107° 30' 21".

Ownership: Rio Blanco County TV Association.

Maybell—K10EW, Ch. 10, Moffat County.

Technical Facilities: 0.009-kw ERP, 7959-ft. above sea level, lat. 40° 27' 15", long. 108° 01' 47".

Ownership: Moffat County.

Meeker—K30CK, Ch. 30, Rio Blanco County TV Assn.

Technical Facilities: 1.63-kw ERP, lat. 40° 05' 51", long. 108° 48' 36".

Ownership: Rio Blanco County TV Association.

Meeker—K46DO, Ch. 46, Rio Blanco County TV Assn.

Technical Facilities: 1.06-kw ERP, 20-ft. above ground, 7585-ft. above sea level, lat. 40° 02' 35", long. 107° 56' 01".

Ownership: Rio Blanco County TV Association.

Meeker—K48CL, Ch. 48, Rio Blanco County TV Assn.

Technical Facilities: 3.58-kw ERP, lat. 39° 42' 04", long. 107° 57' 05".

Ownership: Rio Blanco County TV Association.

Meeker—K64BH, Ch. 64, Rio Blanco County TV Assn.

Technical Facilities: 1.26-kw ERP, lat. 40° 02' 35", long. 107° 56' 01".

Ownership: Rio Blanco County TV Association.

Meeker, etc.—K06JJ, Ch. 6, Rio Blanco County TV Assn.

Technical Facilities: 0.011-kw ERP, lat. 40° 02' 35", long. 107° 56' 01".

Ownership: Rio Blanco County TV Association.

Meeker, etc.—K09FE, Ch. 9, Rio Blanco County TV Assn.

Technical Facilities: 0.011-kw ERP, lat. 40° 02' 35", long. 107° 56' 01".

Ownership: Rio Blanco County TV Association.

Meeker, etc.—K12LT, Ch. 12, Rio Blanco County TV Assn.

Technical Facilities: 0.011-kw ERP, 7644-ft. above sea level, lat. 40° 10' 55", long. 107° 54' 01".

Ownership: Rio Blanco County TV Association.

Meeker, Rangely, etc.—K56EZ, Ch. 56, Rio Blanco County TV Assn.

Technical Facilities: 1.36-kw ERP, lat. 40° 09' 50", long. 108° 26' 36".

Ownership: Rio Blanco County TV Association.

Mesa—K12OR, Ch. 12, Mesa County.

Technical Facilities: 0.2-kw ERP, lat. 39° 04' 55", long. 108° 12' 16".

Transmitter: SW of the town of Mesa.

Ownership: Mesa County.

Mesa—K31DW, Ch. 31, Mesa County.

Technical Facilities: 0.167-kw ERP, 20-ft. above ground, 9997-ft. above sea level, lat. 38° 04' 55", long. 108° 12' 18".

Ownership: Mesa County.

Montrose—K19CE, Ch. 19, Colorado TV Marketing LLC. Phone: 970-920-9600.

Technical Facilities: 1.3-kw ERP, 26-ft. above ground, 9938-ft. above sea level, lat. 38° 20' 21", long. 107° 38' 22".

Holds CP for change to 15-kw ERP, BPTT-20071130BCT.

Ownership: Colorado TV Marketing LLC.

Montrose—K21JK-D, Ch. 21, Pikes Peak Television Inc. Phone: 816-271-8505.

Technical Facilities: 13-kw ERP, 184-ft. above ground, 10079-ft. above sea level, lat. 38° 18' 55", long. 108° 11' 45".

Ownership: Pikes Peak Broadcasting Co.

Montrose—K28AD, Ch. 28, Pikes Peak Television Inc. Phone: 719-632-1515.

Technical Facilities: 27.6-kw ERP, lat. 38° 31' 00", long. 107° 51' 08".

Ownership: News Press & Gazette Co.

Personnel: Jay Rademacher, Chief Engineer.

Montrose—K49JX-D, Ch. 49, Gray Television Licensee LLC. Phone: 970-243-1111.

Technical Facilities: 1-kw ERP, 184-ft. above ground, 10079-ft. above sea level, lat. 38° 18' 57", long. 108° 11' 47".

Began Operation: November 25, 2008.

Ownership: Gray Television Inc.

Montrose—K50EZ, Ch. 50, Gray Television Licensee LLC. Phone: 202-719-4551.

Technical Facilities: 8.07-kw ERP, 184-ft. above ground, 10095-ft. above sea level, lat. 38° 18' 57", long. 108° 11' 47".

Ownership: Gray Television Inc.

Montrose—KXHD-LP, Ch. 36, Pikes Peak Television Inc. Phone: 816-271-8505.

Technical Facilities: 46.8-kw ERP, 92-ft. above ground, 9987-ft. above sea level, lat. 38° 18' 57", long. 108° 11' 47".

Holds CP for change to 34.3-kw ERP, 184-ft. above ground, 10079-ft. above sea level, lat. 38° 18' 55", long. 108° 11' 45". BPTTL-20081008AKN.

Ownership: News Press & Gazette Co.

Montrose, etc.—K32CW, Ch. 32, Rocky Mountain Public Broadcasting Network Inc. Phone: 303-892-6666.

Technical Facilities: 9.87-kw ERP, 217-ft. above ground, 10157-ft. above sea level, lat. 38° 18' 50", long. 108° 12' 09".

Holds CP for change to 2.5-kw ERP, BDFCDTT-20060331AXA.

Ownership: Rocky Mountain Public Broadcasting Network Inc.

Mount Carmel—K08GY, Ch. 8, Baca County.

Technical Facilities: 0.027-kw ERP, lat. 37° 04' 20", long. 102° 22' 45".

Ownership: Baca County.

Mount Carmel—K10IM, Ch. 10, Baca County.

Technical Facilities: 0.028-kw ERP, lat. 37° 04' 20", long. 102° 22' 45".

Ownership: Baca County.

Mount Carmel—K12IM, Ch. 12, Baca County.

Technical Facilities: 0.028-kw ERP, lat. 37° 04' 20", long. 102° 22' 45".

Ownership: Baca County.

Mount Carmel—K13VR, Ch. 13, Baca County.

Technical Facilities: 0.028-kw ERP, 207-ft. above ground, 4235-ft. above sea level, lat. 37° 04' 20", long. 102° 22' 45".

Ownership: Baca County.

Mount Massive, etc.—K09LT, Ch. 9, Mount Massive Lakes Inc.

Technical Facilities: 0.004-kw ERP, lat. 39° 09' 02", long. 106° 18' 05".

Ownership: Mount Massive Lakes Inc.

Mount Massive, etc.—K51FQ, Ch. 51, Pikes Peak Television Inc. Phone: 719-632-1515.

Technical Facilities: 0.043-kw ERP, 16-ft. above ground, 9590-ft. above sea level, lat. 39° 11' 46", long. 106° 19' 50".

Ownership: News Press & Gazette Co.

New Castle—K36AF, Ch. 36, Pikes Peak Television Inc. Phone: 970-245-8880. Fax: 970-245-8249.

Studio: 8 Foresight Cir, Grand Junction, CO 81505.

Technical Facilities: 20-w TPO, 0.145-kw ERP, 21-ft. above ground, 6355-ft. above sea level, lat. 39° 33' 56", long. 107° 31' 57".

Transmitter: 0.5-mi. S of New Castle.

Multichannel TV Sound: Stereo only.

Ownership: News Press & Gazette Co.

Personnel: Kristy Santiago, General Manager; Jay Rademacher, Chief Engineer.

New Castle, etc.—K05GY, Ch. 5, Colorado TV Marketing LLC. Phone: 970-920-9600.

Technical Facilities: 0.011-kw ERP, 6437-ft. above sea level, lat. 39° 33' 40", long. 107° 31' 57".

Ownership: Colorado TV Marketing LLC.

New Castle, etc.—K09JT, Ch. 9, Garfield County.

Technical Facilities: 0.049-kw ERP, 6421-ft. above sea level, lat. 39° 33' 40", long. 107° 31' 57".

Ownership: Garfield County.

New Castle, etc.—K11JZ, Ch. 11, Garfield County.

Technical Facilities: 0.047-kw ERP, 6421-ft. above sea level, lat. 39° 33' 40", long. 107° 31' 57".

Ownership: Garfield County.

Norwood—K06GQ, Ch. 6, Hoak Media of Colorado License LLC. Phone: 972-960-4896.

Technical Facilities: 0.14-kw ERP, lat. 38° 06' 00", long. 108° 13' 20".

Ownership: Hoak Media LLC.

Nucla—K13SN, Ch. 13, Rocky Mountain Public Broadcasting Network Inc. Phone: 303-892-6666.

Technical Facilities: 0.053-kw ERP, 6689-ft. above sea level, lat. 38° 15' 30", long. 108° 41' 15".

Holds CP for change to 0.02-kw ERP, 56-ft. above ground, 6903-ft. above sea level, BDFCDTT-20060331AYB.

Ownership: Rocky Mountain Public Broadcasting Network Inc.

Nucla, etc.—K02GC, Ch. 2, Hoak Media of Colorado License LLC. Phone: 972-960-4896.

Technical Facilities: 0.14-kw ERP, lat. 38° 15' 10", long. 108° 39' 30".

Ownership: Hoak Media LLC.

Nucla, etc.—K04FY, Ch. 4, Montrose County.

Technical Facilities: 0.143-kw ERP, lat. 38° 15' 30", long. 108° 41' 15".

Ownership: Montrose County.

Oak Creek—K02DY, Ch. 2, Yampa Valley TV Assn. Inc.

Technical Facilities: 0.003-kw ERP, lat. 40° 15' 20", long. 106° 56' 21".

Ownership: Yampa Valley TV Association Inc.

Oak Creek—K69DL, Ch. 69, Yampa Valley TV Assn. Inc.

Technical Facilities: 2.49-kw ERP, lat. 40° 17' 04", long. 106° 58' 07".

Ownership: Yampa Valley TV Association Inc.

Oak Creek, etc.—K06CH, Ch. 6, Yampa Valley TV Assn. Inc.

Technical Facilities: 0.002-kw ERP, 8113-ft. above sea level, lat. 40° 15' 17", long. 106° 57' 20".

Ownership: Yampa Valley TV Association Inc.

Oak Creek, etc.—K09IF, Ch. 9, Yampa Valley TV Assn. Inc.

Technical Facilities: 0.002-kw ERP, 8113-ft. above sea level, lat. 40° 15' 17", long. 106° 57' 20".

Ownership: Yampa Valley TV Association Inc.

Ouray, etc.—K09PJ, Ch. 9, Rocky Mountain Public Broadcasting Network Inc. Phone: 303-892-6666.

Technical Facilities: 0.03-kw ERP, lat. 38° 00' 57", long. 107° 39' 59".

Holds CP for change to 0.02-kw ERP, 20-ft. above ground, 8271-ft. above sea level, BDFCDTT-20060331AYD.

Ownership: Rocky Mountain Public Broadcasting Network Inc.

Ouray, etc.—K61BR, Ch. 61, Rocky Mountain Public Broadcasting Network Inc. Phone: 303-892-6666.

Technical Facilities: 0.71-kw ERP, lat. 38° 23' 12", long. 107° 40' 31".

Holds CP for change to channel number 33, 0.1-kw ERP, 46-ft. above ground, 9436-ft. above sea level, BDISDTT-20060331AUA.

Ownership: Rocky Mountain Public Broadcasting Network Inc.

Pagosa Springs—K02IL, Ch. 2, LIN of Colorado LLC.

Technical Facilities: 0.06-kw ERP, lat. 37° 15' 40", long. 107° 02' 45".

Ownership: LIN TV Corp.

Pagosa Springs—K04NS, Ch. 4, LIN of Colorado LLC.

Technical Facilities: 0.002-kw ERP, 49-ft. above ground, 7818-ft. above sea level, lat. 37° 15' 40", long. 107° 02' 45".

Ownership: LIN TV Corp.

Pagosa Springs—K31FS, Ch. 31, LIN of New Mexico LLC. Phone: 202-462-6001. Fax: 505-246-2222.

Technical Facilities: 1.3-kw ERP, 98-ft. above ground, 7618-ft. above sea level, lat. 37° 15' 40", long. 107° 02' 45".

Ownership: LIN TV Corp.

Pagosa Springs—K40GE, Ch. 40, KOB-TV LLC. Phone: 651-642-4212.

Technical Facilities: 0.62-kw ERP, 36-ft. above ground, 7959-ft. above sea level, lat. 37° 11' 36", long. 107° 05' 31".

Ownership: Hubbard Broadcasting Inc.

Pagosa Springs—K43GT, Ch. 43, LIN of Colorado LLC. Phone: 202-462-6001.

Technical Facilities: 0.444-kw ERP, 70-ft. above ground, 8751-ft. above sea level, lat. 37° 11' 32", long. 107° 05' 57".

Holds CP for change to 0.09-kw ERP, BDFCDTT-20060323AIL.

Ownership: LIN TV Corp.

Pagosa Springs—K48HA, Ch. 48, LIN of New Mexico LLC. Phone: 401-457-9525.

Technical Facilities: 1.32-kw ERP, 33-ft. above ground, 8661-ft. above sea level, lat. 37° 11' 36", long. 107° 05' 31".

Holds CP for change to 0.264-kw ERP, BDFCDTT-20081219AAF.

Ownership: LIN TV Corp.

Pagosa Springs—K58CJ, Ch. 58, Pagosa Springs TV Assn.

Technical Facilities: 0.12-kw ERP, lat. 37° 11' 36", long. 107° 05' 31".

Ownership: Pagosa Springs TV Association.

Paonia—K06HZ, Ch. 6, Hoak Media of Colorado License LLC. Phone: 972-960-4896.

Technical Facilities: 0.06-kw ERP, lat. 38° 52' 34", long. 107° 39' 29".

Ownership: Hoak Media LLC.

Paonia—K58BV, Ch. 58, Rocky Mountain Public Broadcasting Network Inc. Phone: 303-892-6666.

Technical Facilities: 2.23-kw ERP, lat. 38° 52' 20", long. 107° 39' 45".

Holds CP for change to channel number 32, 0.1-kw ERP, 43-ft. above ground, 6896-ft. above sea level, lat. 38° 52' 28", long. 107° 39' 40". BDISDTT-20060331AVT.

Ownership: Rocky Mountain Public Broadcasting Network Inc.

Paonia, etc.—K09QA, Ch. 9, Hoak Media of Colorado License LLC.

Technical Facilities: 0.04-kw ERP, 8550-ft. above sea level, lat. 38° 54' 39", long. 107° 36' 00".

Ownership: Hoak Media LLC.

Parachute—K45AF, Ch. 45, Pikes Peak Television Inc. Phone: 719-632-1515.

Technical Facilities: 0.822-kw ERP, lat. 39° 26' 34", long. 107° 57' 59".

Ownership: News Press & Gazette Co.

Parlin, etc.—K41DU, Ch. 41, Gunnison County Metropolitan Recreation District.

Technical Facilities: 0.17-kw ERP, 23-ft. above ground, 8858-ft. above sea level, lat. 38° 30' 22", long. 106° 40' 47".

Ownership: Gunnison County Metropolitan Recreation District.

Parlin, etc.—K61DC, Ch. 61, Gunnison County Metropolitan Recreation District.

Technical Facilities: 0.037-kw ERP, lat. 38° 30' 22", long. 106° 40' 47".

Transmitter: 3-mi. NE of Parlin.

Ownership: Gunnison County Metropolitan Recreation District.

Parlin, etc.—K63CX, Ch. 63, Gunnison County Metropolitan Recreation District.

Technical Facilities: 0.04-kw ERP, lat. 38° 30' 22", long. 106° 40' 47".

Ownership: Gunnison County Metropolitan Recreation District.

Parlin-Doyleville—K36GQ, Ch. 36, Gunnison County Metropolitan Recreation District. Phone: 970-641-8725.

Technical Facilities: 0.052-kw ERP, 59-ft. above ground, 8894-ft. above sea level, lat. 38° 30' 22", long. 106° 40' 47".

Ownership: Gunnison County Metropolitan Recreation District.

Parlin-Doyleville—K39DC, Ch. 39, Gunnison County Metropolitan Recreation District.

Technical Facilities: 0.052-kw ERP, 23-ft. above ground, 8858-ft. above sea level, lat. 38° 30' 22", long. 106° 40' 47".

Ownership: Gunnison County Metropolitan Recreation District.

Peetz—K14JZ-D, Ch. 14, Board of Logan County Commissioners. Phone: 970-522-0888.

Technical Facilities: 0.165-kw ERP, 209-ft. above ground, 4796-ft. above sea level, lat. 40° 53' 31", long. 103° 13' 45".

Ownership: Board of Logan County Commissioners.

Peetz—K26FM, Ch. 26, Board of Logan County Commissioners.

Technical Facilities: 0.74-kw ERP, lat. 40° 53' 31", long. 103° 13' 45".

Transmitter: 6-mi. W of Peetz.

Ownership: Board of Logan County Commissioners.

Peetz—K28FW, Ch. 28, Board of Logan County Commissioners.

Technical Facilities: 0.74-kw ERP, lat. 40° 53' 31", long. 103° 13' 45".

Transmitter: 6-mi. W of Peetz.

Ownership: Board of Logan County Commissioners.

Peetz—K30FO, Ch. 30, Board of Logan County Commissioners.

Technical Facilities: 0.74-kw ERP, lat. 40° 53' 31", long. 103° 13' 45".

Transmitter: 6-mi. W of Peetz.

Ownership: Board of Logan County Commissioners.

Peetz—K32EX, Ch. 32, Board of Logan County Commissioners. Phone: 970-522-0888.

Technical Facilities: 0.74-kw ERP, 209-ft. above ground, 4797-ft. above sea level, lat. 40° 53' 31", long. 103° 13' 45".

Ownership: Board of Logan County Commissioners.

Peetz & Logan County—K16EJ, Ch. 16, Board of Logan County Commissioners.

Technical Facilities: 0.757-kw ERP, lat. 40° 53' 31", long. 103° 13' 45".

Transmitter: 6-mi. W of Peetz.

Ownership: Board of Logan County Commissioners.

Peetz & Logan County—K18FN, Ch. 18, Board of Logan County Commissioners.

Technical Facilities: 0.757-kw ERP, lat. 40° 53' 31", long. 103° 13' 45".

Transmitter: 6-mi. W of Peetz.

Ownership: Board of Logan County Commissioners.

Peetz & Logan County—K20FS, Ch. 20, Board of Logan County Commissioners.

Technical Facilities: 0.757-kw ERP, lat. 40° 53' 31", long. 103° 13' 45".

Transmitter: 6-mi. W of Peetz.

Ownership: Board of Logan County Commissioners.

Piceance Creek—K07QB, Ch. 7, Rio Blanco County TV Assn.

Technical Facilities: 0.02-kw ERP, 7054-ft. above sea level, lat. 39° 52' 00", long. 108° 13' 55".

Ownership: Rio Blanco County TV Association.

Piceance Creek—K09WZ, Ch. 9, Rio Blanco County TV Assn.

Technical Facilities: 0.024-kw ERP, lat. 39° 52' 00", long. 108° 13' 55".

Transmitter: 19-mi. SW of Meeker.

Ownership: Rio Blanco County TV Association.

Piceance Creek—K61BD, Ch. 61, Rio Blanco County TV Assn.

Technical Facilities: 0.069-kw ERP, 7031-ft. above sea level, lat. 39° 52' 00", long. 108° 13' 55".

Ownership: Rio Blanco County TV Association.

Piceance Creek—K64AV, Ch. 64, Rio Blanco County TV Assn.

Technical Facilities: 0.068-kw ERP, lat. 39° 52' 00", long. 108° 13' 55".

Ownership: Rio Blanco County TV Association.

Piceance Creek area—K67BK, Ch. 67, Rio Blanco County TV Assn.

Technical Facilities: 0.069-kw ERP, lat. 39° 52' 00", long. 108° 13' 55".

Ownership: Rio Blanco County TV Association.

Pitkin—K05JT, Ch. 5, Gunnison County Metropolitan Recreation District.

Technical Facilities: 0.002-kw ERP, 26-ft. above ground, 10184-ft. above sea level, lat. 38° 33' 28", long. 106° 29' 32".

Ownership: Gunnison County Metropolitan Recreation District.

Pitkin—K15ED, Ch. 15, Gunnison County Metropolitan Recreation District.

Technical Facilities: 0.17-kw ERP, 23-ft. above ground, 10184-ft. above sea level, lat. 38° 33' 28", long. 106° 29' 32".

Ownership: Gunnison County Metropolitan Recreation District.

Pitkin—K17GC, Ch. 17, Gunnison County Metropolitan Recreation District. Phone: 970-641-8725.

Technical Facilities: 0.155-kw ERP, 30-ft. above ground, 9229-ft. above sea level, lat. 38° 36' 16", long. 106° 31' 40".

Ownership: Gunnison County Metropolitan Recreation District.

Pitkin—K19DS, Ch. 19, Gunnison County Metropolitan Recreation District. Phone: 940-641-8725.

Technical Facilities: 0.16-kw ERP, 20-ft. above ground, 9219-ft. above sea level, lat. 38° 36' 16", long. 106° 31' 40".

Ownership: Gunnison County Metropolitan Recreation District.

Pitkin—K21EF, Ch. 21, Gunnison County Metropolitan Recreation District. Phone: 940-641-8725.

Technical Facilities: 0.155-kw ERP, 30-ft. above ground, 9229-ft. above sea level, lat. 38° 36' 16", long. 106° 31' 40".

Ownership: Gunnison County Metropolitan Recreation District.

Pitkin—K23DX, Ch. 23, Gunnison County Metropolitan Recreation District. Phone: 940-641-8725.

Technical Facilities: 0.17-kw ERP, 13-ft. above ground, 9212-ft. above sea level, lat. 38° 36' 16", long. 106° 31' 40".

Ownership: Gunnison County Metropolitan Recreation District.

Pitkin—K43EG, Ch. 43, Gunnison County Metropolitan Recreation District. Phone: 940-641-8725.

Technical Facilities: 0.16-kw ERP, 23-ft. above ground, 9222-ft. above sea level, lat. 38° 36' 16", long. 106° 31' 40".

Ownership: Gunnison County Metropolitan Recreation District.

Pitkin & Ohio—K08JZ, Ch. 8, Gunnison County Metropolitan Recreation District.

Technical Facilities: 0.006-kw ERP, 10180-ft. above sea level, lat. 38° 33' 28", long. 106° 29' 32".

Ownership: Gunnison County Metropolitan Recreation District.

Pitkin & Ohio—K10MA, Ch. 10, Gunnison County Metropolitan Recreation District.

Technical Facilities: 0.01-kw ERP, 10180-ft. above sea level, lat. 38° 33' 28", long. 106° 29' 32".

Ownership: Gunnison County Metropolitan Recreation District.

Pitkin, etc.—K12AL, Ch. 12, Gunnison County Metropolitan Recreation District.

Technical Facilities: 0.01-kw ERP, 10180-ft. above sea level, lat. 38° 33' 28", long. 106° 29' 32".

Ownership: Gunnison County Metropolitan Recreation District.

Placerville—K03FX, Ch. 3, Hoak Media of Colorado License LLC. Phone: 972-960-4896.

Technical Facilities: 0.02-kw ERP, lat. 38° 01' 05", long. 108° 04' 02".

Ownership: Hoak Media LLC.

Pleasant Valley—K14KL, Ch. 14, Region 1 Translator Assn. Phone: 970-848-5301.

Technical Facilities: 0.214-kw ERP, 75-ft. above ground, 3805-ft. above sea level, lat. 40° 30' 35", long. 102° 06' 51".

Ownership: Region 1 Translator Association.

Pleasant Valley—K16ET, Ch. 16, Region 1 Translator Assn. Phone: 970-848-5301.

Technical Facilities: 0.214-kw ERP, 75-ft. above ground, 3802-ft. above sea level, lat. 40° 30' 35", long. 102° 06' 51".

Ownership: Region 1 Translator Association.

Pleasant Valley—K18GM, Ch. 18, Region 1 Translator Assn. Phone: 970-848-5301.

Technical Facilities: 0.214-kw ERP, 75-ft. above ground, 3802-ft. above sea level, lat. 40° 30' 35", long. 102° 06' 51".

Ownership: Region 1 Translator Association.

Pleasant Valley—K20GK, Ch. 20, Region 1 Translator Assn. Phone: 970-848-5301.

Technical Facilities: 0.214-kw ERP, 75-ft. above ground, 3805-ft. above sea level, lat. 40° 30' 35", long. 102° 06' 51".

Ownership: Region 1 Translator Association.

Pleasant Valley—K24FU-D, Ch. 24, Region 1 Translator Assn. Phone: 970-848-5301.

Technical Facilities: 0.055-kw ERP, 75-ft. above ground, 3802-ft. above sea level, lat. 40° 30' 35", long. 102° 06' 51".

Began Operation: July 13, 2005.

Ownership: Region 1 Translator Association.

Pleasant Valley—K26GX, Ch. 26, Region 1 Translator Assn. Phone: 970-848-5301.

Technical Facilities: 0.214-kw ERP, 75-ft. above ground, 3802-ft. above sea level, lat. 40° 30' 35", long. 102° 06' 51".

Ownership: Region 1 Translator Association.

Pleasant Valley—K28IX, Ch. 28, Region 1 Translator Association. Phone: 970-848-5301.

Technical Facilities: 0.214-kw ERP, 75-ft. above ground, 3806-ft. above sea level, lat. 40° 30' 35", long. 102° 06' 51".

Ownership: Region 1 Translator Association.

Pleasant Valley—K30GO, Ch. 30, Region 1 Translator Assn. Phone: 970-848-5301.

Technical Facilities: 0.214-kw ERP, 75-ft. above ground, 3803-ft. above sea level, lat. 40° 30' 35", long. 102° 06' 51".

Ownership: Region 1 Translator Association.

Powderhorn—K69AO, Ch. 69, Colorado TV Marketing LLC. Phone: 970-920-9600.

Technical Facilities: 4.47-kw ERP, lat. 39° 05' 15", long. 108° 13' 40".

Holds CP for change to channel number 34, 15-kw ERP, 33-ft. above ground, 9993-ft. above sea level, lat. 39° 05' 18", long. 108° 13' 36". BMPTT-20080107AAP.

Ownership: Colorado TV Marketing LLC.

Powderhorn Valley—K09WB, Ch. 9, Gunnison County Metropolitan Recreation District.

Technical Facilities: 0.002-kw ERP, lat. 38° 18' 30", long. 107° 09' 00".

Ownership: Gunnison County Metropolitan Recreation District.

Powderhorn Valley—K12LX, Ch. 12, Gunnison County Metropolitan Recreation District.

Technical Facilities: 0.015-kw ERP, lat. 38° 17' 53", long. 107° 07' 55".

Ownership: Gunnison County Metropolitan Recreation District.

Pueblo—K48CU, Ch. 48, Full Gospel Outreach Inc.

Technical Facilities: 100-w TPO, 1.09-kw ERP, 126-ft. above ground, 4830-ft. above sea level, lat. 38° 16' 50", long. 104° 36' 34".

Transmitter: 2109 7th Ave.

Ownership: Full Gospel Outreach Inc.

Pueblo—KTLP-LP, Ch. 34, Pikes Peak Television Inc. Phone: 816-271-8505.

Technical Facilities: 100-w TPO, 1.34-kw ERP, 72-ft. above ground, 4970-ft. above sea level, lat. 38° 18' 56", long. 104° 37' 01".

Transmitter: 3.1-mi. N of Pueblo.

Ownership: News Press & Gazette Co.

■ **Pueblo, etc.**—KGHB-CA, Ch. 27, Entravision Holdings LLC.

Technical Facilities: 7.71-kw ERP, 95-ft. above ground, 9504-ft. above sea level, lat. 38° 44' 43", long. 104° 51' 41".

Ownership: Entravision Communications Corp.

Rangely—K06IX, Ch. 6, Rio Blanco County TV Association.

Technical Facilities: 0.08-kw ERP, lat. 40° 09' 36", long. 108° 57' 12".

Ownership: Rio Blanco County TV Association.

Rangely—K22DZ, Ch. 22, Rio Blanco County TV Association.

Technical Facilities: 0.456-kw ERP, 39-ft. above ground, 5331-ft. above sea level, lat. 40° 05' 51", long. 108° 48' 36".

Ownership: Rio Blanco County TV Association.

Rangely—K24DG, Ch. 24, Rio Blanco County TV Association.

Technical Facilities: 0.456-kw ERP, 39-ft. above ground, 5331-ft. above sea level, lat. 40° 05' 51", long. 108° 48' 36".

Ownership: Rio Blanco County TV Association.

Rangely—K26DP, Ch. 26, Rio Blanco County TV Association.

Technical Facilities: 0.368-kw ERP, lat. 40° 05' 51", long. 108° 48' 36".

Ownership: Rio Blanco County TV Association.

Rangely—K28CG, Ch. 28, Rio Blanco County TV Association.

Technical Facilities: 0.456-kw ERP, 39-ft. above ground, 5331-ft. above sea level, lat. 40° 05' 51", long. 108° 48' 36".

Ownership: Rio Blanco County TV Association.

Rangely—K32AC, Ch. 32, Rio Blanco County TV Assn.

Technical Facilities: 2.05-kw ERP, lat. 40° 05' 51", long. 108° 48' 36".

Ownership: Rio Blanco County TV Association.

Rangely—K66ER, Ch. 66, Rio Blanco County TV Association.

Technical Facilities: 0.456-kw ERP, 39-ft. above ground, 5331-ft. above sea level, lat. 40° 05' 51", long. 108° 48' 36".

Ownership: Rio Blanco County TV Association.

Redstone—K04HP, Ch. 4, Pitkin County Translator Dept. Phone: 970-920-5395.

Technical Facilities: 0.045-kw ERP, 15-ft. above ground, 7921-ft. above sea level, lat. 39° 14' 20", long. 107° 13' 02".

Ownership: Pitkin County Translator Dept.

Redstone—K09XN, Ch. 9, Pitkin County Translator Dept. Phone: 970-920-5395. Fax: 970-920-5374.

Technical Facilities: 0.042-kw ERP, 39-ft. above ground, 8409-ft. above sea level, lat. 39° 14' 18", long. 107° 13' 28".

Ownership: Pitkin County Translator Dept.

Redstone—K11VC, Ch. 11, Pitkin County Translator Dept. Phone: 970-920-5395. Fax: 970-920-5374.

Technical Facilities: 0.042-kw ERP, 43-ft. above ground, 8114-ft. above sea level, lat. 39° 14' 18", long. 107° 13' 28".

Ownership: Pitkin County Translator Dept.

Redstone—K18GD, Ch. 18, Pitkin County Translator Dept. Phone: 970-920-5395.

Technical Facilities: 0.05-kw ERP, 56-ft. above ground, 8763-ft. above sea level, lat. 39° 14' 20", long. 107° 13' 02".

Holds CP for change to 0.012-kw ERP, 56-ft. above ground, 8727-ft. above sea level, BDFCDTT-20090506ABB.

Ownership: Pitkin County Translator Dept.

Redstone, etc.—K02IO, Ch. 2, Pitkin County Translator Dept. Phone: 970-920-5395.

Technical Facilities: 0.045-kw ERP, 15-ft. above ground, 7925-ft. above sea level, lat. 39° 14' 20", long. 107° 13' 02".

Ownership: Pitkin County Translator Dept.

Redstone, etc.—K06CK, Ch. 6, Pitkin County Translator Dept.

Technical Facilities: 0.113-kw ERP, lat. 39° 14' 18", long. 107° 13' 02".

Ownership: Pitkin County Translator Dept.

Redvale, etc.—K34DH, Ch. 34, Montrose County.

Technical Facilities: 0.317-kw ERP, 95-ft. above ground, 10033-ft. above sea level, lat. 38° 18' 53", long. 108° 11' 52".

Ownership: Montrose County.

Ridgway—K03AY, Ch. 3, Hoak Media of Colorado License LLC. Phone: 972-960-4896.

Technical Facilities: 0.02-kw ERP, lat. 38° 11' 11", long. 107° 46' 30".

Ownership: Hoak Media LLC.

Ridgway—K13RH, Ch. 13, City of Ouray.

Technical Facilities: 0.02-kw ERP, lat. 38° 11' 11", long. 107° 46' 30".

Ownership: City of Ouray.

Ridgway, etc.—K64BL, Ch. 64, Rocky Mountain Public Broadcasting Network Inc. Phone: 303-892-6666.

Technical Facilities: 0.63-kw ERP, lat. 38° 11' 11", long. 107° 46' 30".

Holds CP for change to channel number 31, 0.19-kw ERP, 20-ft. above ground, 8120-ft. above sea level, BDISDTT-20060331AUU.

Ownership: Rocky Mountain Public Broadcasting Network Inc.

Rifle—K57CR, Ch. 57, Pikes Peak Television Inc. Phone: 970-245-8880. Fax: 970-245-8249.

Studio: 8 Foresight Cir, Grand Junction, CO 81505.

Technical Facilities: 100-w TPO, 3.385-kw ERP, 16-ft. above ground, 8150-ft. above sea level, lat. 39° 32' 10", long. 107° 56' 56".

Holds CP for change to channel number 34, 3.88-kw ERP, 16-ft. above ground, 8153-ft. above sea level, BDISTT-20060324AFH.

Transmitter: 9-mi. W of Rifle.

Multichannel TV Sound: Stereo only.

Ownership: News Press & Gazette Co.

Personnel: Kristy Santiago, General Manager; Jay Rademacher, Chief Engineer.

Rio Blanco Valley—K36DM, Ch. 36, Rio Blanco County TV Association.

Technical Facilities: 1.57-kw ERP, 79-ft. above ground, 8432-ft. above sea level, lat. 39° 42' 04", long. 107° 57' 05".

Ownership: Rio Blanco County TV Association.

Rio Blanco Valley—K50AE, Ch. 50, Rio Blanco County TV Assn.

Technical Facilities: 0.684-kw ERP, lat. 40° 10' 55", long. 107° 54' 01".

Ownership: Rio Blanco County TV Association.

Rio Blanco Valley, etc.—K38AG, Ch. 38, Rio Blanco County TV Association.

Technical Facilities: 0.63-kw ERP, lat. 39° 42' 04", long. 107° 57' 05".

Ownership: Rio Blanco County TV Association.

Rio Blanco Valley, etc.—K44AC, Ch. 44, Rio Blanco County TV Association.

Technical Facilities: 0.63-kw ERP, lat. 39° 42' 04", long. 107° 57' 05".

Ownership: Rio Blanco County TV Association.

Rocky Ford—K39ED, Ch. 39, Full Gospel Outreach Inc.

Technical Facilities: 0.903-kw ERP, 111-ft. above ground, 4295-ft. above sea level, lat. 38° 03' 38", long. 103° 43' 53".

Ownership: Full Gospel Outreach Inc.

Romeo—K47KC, Ch. 47, Mainstreet Broadcasting Co. Inc. Phone: 719-738-3636.

Technical Facilities: 0.83-kw ERP, 72-ft. above ground, 10951-ft. above sea level, lat. 36° 51' 34", long. 106° 01' 03".

Ownership: Mainstreet Broadcasting Co. Inc.

Romeo—K63AN, Ch. 63, KOB-TV LLC. Phone: 651-642-4337.

Technical Facilities: 5.72-kw ERP, 98-ft. above ground, 11023-ft. above sea level, lat. 36° 51' 25", long. 106° 01' 12".

Ownership: Hubbard Broadcasting Inc.

Romeo, etc.—K45GD, Ch. 45, San Luis Valley TV Inc. Phone: 719-843-5883.

Technical Facilities: 1-kw ERP, lat. 36° 51' 25", long. 106° 01' 12".

Holds CP for change to 0.2-kw ERP, 98-ft. above ground, 11023-ft. above sea level, BDFCDTT-20060331ARV.

Ownership: San Luis Valley Television Inc.

Romeo, etc.—K57CB, Ch. 57, Gray TV Licensee LLC. Phone: 719-634-2844.

Technical Facilities: 7.11-kw ERP, lat. 37° 12' 25", long. 106° 01' 12".

Holds CP for change to channel number 31, 0.62-kw ERP, 112-ft. above ground, 11020-ft. above sea level, lat. 36° 51' 34", long. 106° 01' 07". BDISDTT-20060331AUH.

Ownership: Gray Television Inc.

Romeo, etc.—K61AZ, Ch. 61, San Luis Valley TV Inc.

Technical Facilities: 7.086-kw ERP, lat. 37° 12' 25", long. 106° 01' 12".

Ownership: San Luis Valley Television Inc.

Romeo, etc.—K65AS, Ch. 65, San Luis Valley TV Inc.

Technical Facilities: 6.32-kw ERP, lat. 37° 12' 25", long. 106° 01' 12".

Ownership: San Luis Valley Television Inc.

Rulison—K26FK, Ch. 26, Colorado TV Marketing LLC. Phone: 970-920-9600.

Technical Facilities: 1.69-kw ERP, 36-ft. above ground, 8986-ft. above sea level, lat. 39° 32' 05", long. 107° 57' 25".

Ownership: Colorado TV Marketing LLC.

Rulison—K40CS, Ch. 40, Hoak Media of Colorado License LLC. Phone: 972-960-4896.

Technical Facilities: 0.01-kw ERP, lat. 39° 32' 05", long. 107° 57' 25".

Ownership: Hoak Media LLC.

Rulison, etc.—K61BN, Ch. 61, Rocky Mountain Public Broadcasting Network Inc. Phone: 303-892-6666.

Technical Facilities: 1.69-iw ERP, lat. 39° 32' 05", long. 107° 57' 25".

Holds CP for change to channel number 32, 1.1-kw ERP, 36-ft. above ground, 8986-ft. above sea level, BDISDTT-20060331AVF.

Ownership: Rocky Mountain Public Broadcasting Network Inc.

Rulison, etc.—K63BM, Ch. 63, Garfield County.

Technical Facilities: 1.69-kw ERP, 8986-ft. above sea level, lat. 39° 32' 05", long. 107° 57' 25".

Ownership: Garfield County.

Rulison, etc.—K68BR, Ch. 68, Garfield County.

Technical Facilities: 1.69-kw ERP, 8986-ft. above sea level, lat. 39° 32' 05", long. 107° 57' 25".

Ownership: Garfield County.

Salida—K36HS, Ch. 36, Kenneth D. Swinehart. Phone: 719-588-3132.

Technical Facilities: 0.35-kw ERP, 33-ft. above ground, 11673-ft. above sea level, lat. 38° 26' 50", long. 106° 00' 38".

Holds CP for change to 60-ft. above ground, 11759-ft. above sea level, lat. 38° 27' 11", long. 106° 01' 02". BMPTT-20070816ABJ.

Ownership: Kenneth D. Swinehart.

Salida, etc.—K02JH, Ch. 2, Chaffee County TV Translator Assn. Phone: 719-539-2942.

Technical Facilities: 0.009-kw ERP, 10899-ft. above sea level, lat. 38° 44' 37", long. 106° 11' 50".

Ownership: Chaffee County TV Translator Assn.

Salida, etc.—K04JD, Ch. 4, Chaffee County TV Translator Assn. Phone: 719-539-2942.

Technical Facilities: 0.041-kw ERP, 10899-ft. above sea level, lat. 38° 44' 37", long. 106° 11' 50".

Ownership: Chaffee County TV Translator Assn.

Salida, etc.—K06HF, Ch. 6, Chaffee County TV Translator Assn. Phone: 719-539-2942.

Technical Facilities: 0.021-kw ERP, 10820-ft. above sea level, lat. 38° 44' 37", long. 106° 11' 50".

Ownership: Chaffee County TV Translator Assn.

Salida, etc.—K11KU, Ch. 11, Chaffee County TV Translator Assn. Phone: 719-539-2942.

Technical Facilities: 0.036-kw ERP, 10830-ft. above sea level, lat. 38° 44' 37", long. 106° 11' 50".

Ownership: Chaffee County TV Translator Assn.

Salida, etc.—K13LD, Ch. 13, Chaffee County TV Translator Assn. Phone: 719-539-2942.

Technical Facilities: 0.036-kw ERP, 10820-ft. above sea level, lat. 38° 44' 37", long. 106° 11' 50".

Ownership: Chaffee County TV Translator Assn.

Salida, etc.—K44CI, Ch. 44, Pikes Peak Television Inc. Phone: 719-632-1515.

Technical Facilities: 8.73-kw ERP, 39-ft. above ground, 11712-ft. above sea level, lat. 37° 26' 44", long. 106° 00' 35".

Ownership: News Press & Gazette Co.

Salida, etc.—K53AR, Ch. 53, Rocky Mountain Public Broadcasting Network Inc. Phone: 303-892-6666.

Technical Facilities: 2.27-kw ERP, lat. 38° 26' 48", long. 106° 00' 38".

Holds CP for change to channel number 31, 1.2-kw ERP, 36-ft. above ground, 11719-ft. above sea level, BDISDTT-20060331AWE.

Ownership: Rocky Mountain Public Broadcasting Network Inc.

San Luis—K02KI, Ch. 2, Rocky Mountain Public Broadcasting Network Inc.

Technical Facilities: 0.005-kw ERP, lat. 37° 12' 14", long. 105° 25' 37".

Ownership: Rocky Mountain Public Broadcasting Network Inc.

San Luis Valley, etc.—K55CL, Ch. 55, Rocky Mountain Public Broadcasting Network Inc. Phone: 303-892-6666.

Technical Facilities: 1.14-kw ERP, lat. 37° 12' 25", long. 106° 01' 12".

Holds CP for change to channel number 32, 1.1-kw ERP, 56-ft. above ground, 10964-ft. above sea level, BDISDTT-20061218ACA.

Ownership: Rocky Mountain Public Broadcasting Network Inc.

Sapinero—K46DB, Ch. 46, Gunnison County Metropolitan Recreation District.

Technical Facilities: 0.16-kw ERP, 20-ft. above ground, 8658-ft. above sea level, lat. 38° 26' 52", long. 107° 16' 20".

Ownership: Gunnison County Metropolitan Recreation District.

Sapinero—K48EF, Ch. 48, Gunnison County Metropolitan Recreation District.

Technical Facilities: 0.16-kw ERP, 20-ft. above ground, 8658-ft. above sea level, lat. 38° 26' 52", long. 107° 16' 20".

Ownership: Gunnison County Metropolitan Recreation District.

Sargents—K02NV, Ch. 2, Gunnison County Metropolitan Recreation District.

Technical Facilities: 0.002-kw ERP, lat. 28° 23' 26", long. 106° 24' 39".

Transmitter: 1-mi. SSE of Sargents.

Ownership: Gunnison County Metropolitan Recreation District.

Sargents—K04OF, Ch. 4, Gunnison County Metropolitan Recreation District.

Technical Facilities: 0.002-kw ERP, lat. 38° 23' 26", long. 106° 24' 39".

Transmitter: 1-mi. SSE of Sargents.

Ownership: Gunnison County Metropolitan Recreation District.

Sargents—K06NG, Ch. 6, Gunnison County Metropolitan Recreation District.

Technical Facilities: 0.003-kw ERP, 23-ft. above ground, 9262-ft. above sea level, lat. 38° 23' 26", long. 106° 24' 39".

Ownership: Gunnison County Metropolitan Recreation District.

Sargents—K07VH, Ch. 7, Gunnison County Metropolitan Recreation District.

Technical Facilities: 0.003-kw ERP, 20-ft. above ground, 9258-ft. above sea level, lat. 38° 23' 26", long. 106° 24' 39".

Ownership: Gunnison County Metropolitan Recreation District.

Sargents—K11TJ, Ch. 11, Gunnison County Metropolitan Recreation District.

Technical Facilities: 0.002-kw ERP, 20-ft. above ground, 9258-ft. above sea level, lat. 38° 23' 26", long. 106° 24' 39".

Transmitter: 1-mi. SSE of Sargents.

Ownership: Gunnison County Metropolitan Recreation District.

Sargents—K53AY, Ch. 53, Gunnison County Metropolitan Recreation District. Phone: 970-641-8725.

Technical Facilities: 0.95-kw ERP, lat. 38° 29' 56", long. 106° 19' 28".

Holds CP for change to channel number 33, 2.2-kw ERP, 16-ft. above ground, 11926-ft. above sea level, lat. 38° 29' 49.2", long. 106° 19' 11.7". BDISTT-20090210AEC.

Ownership: Gunnison County Metropolitan Recreation District.

Sargents—K57CS, Ch. 57, Gunnison County Metropolitan Recreation District. Phone: 970-641-8725.

Technical Facilities: 0.94-kw ERP, 13-ft. above ground, 11913-ft. above sea level, lat. 38° 29' 56", long. 106° 19' 28".

Holds CP for change to channel number 47, 2.2-kw ERP, 16-ft. above ground, 11926-ft. above sea level, lat. 38° 29' 49.2", long. 106° 19' 11.7". BDISTT-20090210AEF.

Ownership: Gunnison County Metropolitan Recreation District.

Sargents—K59DV, Ch. 59, Gunnison County Metropolitan Recreation District. Phone: 970-641-8725.

Technical Facilities: 0.894-kw ERP, 13-ft. above ground, 11913-ft. above sea level, lat. 38° 29' 56", long. 106° 19' 28".

Holds CP for change to channel number 49, 2.2-kw ERP, 16-ft. above ground, 11926-ft. above sea level, lat. 38° 29' 49.2", long. 106° 19' 11.7". BDISTT-20090210AEG.

Ownership: Gunnison County Metropolitan Recreation District.

Silt, etc.—K47AC, Ch. 47, Colorado TV Marketing LLC. Phone: 970-920-9600.

Technical Facilities: 0.87-kw ERP, lat. 39° 25' 45", long. 107° 23' 00".

Ownership: Colorado TV Marketing LLC.

Silt, etc.—K49AH, Ch. 49, Rocky Mountain Public Broadcasting Network Inc. Phone: 303-892-6666.

Technical Facilities: 0.869-kw ERP, lat. 39° 25' 45", long. 107° 23' 00".

Holds CP for change to 1-kw ERP, 98-ft. above ground, 10702-ft. above sea level, BDFCDTT-20060331AWR.

Ownership: Rocky Mountain Public Broadcasting Network Inc.

Snowmass at Aspen—K02HI, Ch. 2, Pitkin County Translator Dept. Phone: 970-920-5395.

Technical Facilities: 0.016-kw ERP, 28-ft. above ground, 9444-ft. above sea level, lat. 39° 13' 33", long. 106° 50' 00".

Ownership: Pitkin County Translator Dept.

Snowmass at Aspen—K04HH, Ch. 4, Pitkin County Translator Dept. Phone: 970-920-5395.

Technical Facilities: 0.016-kw ERP, 44-ft. above ground, 9463-ft. above sea level, lat. 39° 13' 33", long. 106° 50' 00".

Ownership: Pitkin County Translator Dept.

Snowmass at Aspen—K10IW, Ch. 10, Pitkin County Translator Dept. Phone: 970-920-5395.

Technical Facilities: 0.033-kw ERP, lat. 39° 13' 11", long. 106° 54' 31".

Ownership: Pitkin County Translator Dept.

Somerset—K02IJ, Ch. 2, Mesa Television Inc.

Technical Facilities: 0.009-kw ERP, lat. 38° 55' 34", long. 107° 30' 06".

Ownership: Mesa Television Inc.

Somerset—K10KK, Ch. 10, Mesa Television Inc.

Technical Facilities: 0.006-kw ERP, lat. 38° 55' 34", long. 107° 30' 06".

Ownership: Mesa Television Inc.

Somerset—K12MN, Ch. 12, Mesa Television Inc.

Technical Facilities: 0.008-kw ERP, lat. 38° 55' 34", long. 107° 30' 06".

Ownership: Mesa Television Inc.

South Fork, etc.—K02EX, Ch. 2, South Fork TV Assn.

Technical Facilities: 0.024-kw ERP, lat. 37° 41' 07", long. 106° 39' 19".

Ownership: South Fork TV Association.

South Fork, etc.—K18DE, Ch. 18, South Fork TV Assn.

Technical Facilities: 0.118-kw ERP, 26-ft. above ground, 8642-ft. above sea level, lat. 37° 41' 07", long. 106° 39' 19".

Ownership: South Fork TV Association.

South Fork, etc.—K57BW, Ch. 57, South Fork TV Assn.

Technical Facilities: 0.25-kw ERP, 30-ft. above ground, 9705-ft. above sea level, lat. 37° 41' 07", long. 106° 39' 19".

Ownership: South Fork TV Association.

Southwest Baca County—K03DZ, Ch. 3, Baca County.

Technical Facilities: 0.136-kw ERP, lat. 37° 10' 05", long. 103° 05' 55".

Ownership: Baca County.

Southwest Baca County—K06HW, Ch. 6, Baca County.

Technical Facilities: 0.136-kw ERP, lat. 37° 10' 05", long. 103° 05' 55".

Ownership: Baca County.

Southwest Baca County—K07UN, Ch. 7, Baca County.

Technical Facilities: 0.085-kw ERP, 62-ft. above ground, 5538-ft. above sea level, lat. 37° 10' 05", long. 103° 05' 55".

Ownership: Baca County.

Southwest Baca County, etc.—K09JS, Ch. 9, Baca County.

Technical Facilities: 0.136-kw ERP, lat. 37° 10' 05", long. 103° 05' 55".

Ownership: Baca County.

Spring Creek—K03HA, Ch. 3, Gunnison County Metropolitan Recreation District.

Technical Facilities: 0.003-kw ERP, lat. 38° 43' 33", long. 106° 46' 24".

Transmitter: 0.15-mi. N of Rte. 306, along Spring Creek.

Ownership: Gunnison County Metropolitan Recreation District.

Spring Creek, etc.—K11QK, Ch. 11, Gunnison County Metropolitan Recreation District.

Technical Facilities: 0.005-kw ERP, lat. 38° 43' 33", long. 106° 46' 24".

Transmitter: 800-ft. N of Rte. 306, along Spring Creek.

Ownership: Gunnison County Metropolitan Recreation District.

Spring Creek, etc.—K13RX, Ch. 13, Gunnison County Metropolitan Recreation District.

Technical Facilities: 0.005-kw ERP, lat. 38° 43' 33", long. 106° 46' 24".

Transmitter: 800-ft. N of Rte. 306, along Spring Creek.

Ownership: Gunnison County Metropolitan Recreation District.

Springfield—K62CT, Ch. 62, Baca County.

Technical Facilities: 0.932-kw ERP, lat. 37° 21' 44", long. 102° 38' 44".

Ownership: Baca County.

Springfield—K64CT, Ch. 64, Baca County.

Technical Facilities: 0.8-kw ERP, lat. 37° 21' 44", long. 102° 38' 44".

Ownership: Baca County.

Springfield—K66CW, Ch. 66, Baca County.

Technical Facilities: 0.8-kw ERP, lat. 37° 21' 44", long. 102° 38' 44".

Ownership: Baca County.

Springfield—K68CR, Ch. 68, Baca County.

Technical Facilities: 0.799-kw ERP, lat. 37° 21' 33", long. 102° 37' 20".

Ownership: Baca County.

Stadtman Mesa—K60AC, Ch. 60, Rio Blanco County TV Assn.

Technical Facilities: 1.546-kw ERP, 46-ft. above ground, 6808-ft. above sea level, lat. 40° 09' 50", long. 108° 26' 36".

Transmitter: 28.8-mi. W of Meeker.

Ownership: Rio Blanco County TV Association.

Stadtman Mesa, etc.—K58EF, Ch. 58, Rio Blanco County TV Assn.

Technical Facilities: 1.36-kw ERP, 40° 09' 50", long. 108° 26' 36".

Ownership: Rio Blanco County TV Association.

Steamboat Springs—K03CL, Ch. 3, Yampa Valley TV Assn. Inc.

Technical Facilities: 0.004-kw ERP, lat. 40° 27' 47", long. 106° 51' 10".

Ownership: Yampa Valley TV Association Inc.

Steamboat Springs—K06CF, Ch. 6, Yampa Valley TV Assn. Inc.

Technical Facilities: 0.002-kw ERP, lat. 40° 27' 36", long. 106° 51' 10".

Ownership: Yampa Valley TV Association Inc.

Steamboat Springs—K09GX, Ch. 9, Yampa Valley TV Assn. Inc.

Technical Facilities: 0.002-kw ERP, lat. 40° 27' 36", long. 106° 51' 10".

Ownership: Yampa Valley TV Association Inc.

Steamboat Springs—K11FW, Ch. 11, Moffat County.

Technical Facilities: 0.086-kw ERP, 10341-ft. above sea level, lat. 40° 27' 16", long. 106° 44' 34".

Ownership: Moffat County.

Steamboat Springs—K58AQ, Ch. 58, Moffat County.

Technical Facilities: 2.78-kw ERP, lat. 40° 27' 16", long. 106° 44' 34".

Ownership: Moffat County.

Steamboat Springs—K64AR, Ch. 64, Moffat County.

Technical Facilities: 2.78-kw ERP, lat. 40° 27' 16", long. 106° 44' 34".

Ownership: Moffat County.

Steamboat Springs—KHSB-LP, Ch. 33, EICB-TV East LLC. Phone: 972-291-3750.

Technical Facilities: 3.75-kw ERP, 44-ft. above ground, 10389-ft. above sea level, lat. 40° 27' 16", long. 106° 44' 32".

Ownership: EICB-TV LLC.

Sterling—K31IQ-D, Ch. 31, Board of Logan County Commissioners. Phone: 970-522-0888.

Technical Facilities: 0.398-kw ERP, 407-ft. above ground, 4918-ft. above sea level, lat. 40° 35' 28", long. 103° 02' 23".

Ownership: Board of Logan County Commissioners.

Sterling—K46CY, Ch. 46, Board of Logan County Commissioners. Phone: 970-522-0888.

Technical Facilities: 500-w TPO, 2.26-kw ERP, 407-ft. above ground, 4918-ft. above sea level, lat. 40° 35' 28", long. 103° 02' 23".

Transmitter: Reiradon Hill, 9.4-mi. E of Sterling.

Ownership: Board of Logan County Commissioners.

Sterling—K48DQ, Ch. 48, Board of Logan County Commissioners. Phone: 303-522-0888.

Technical Facilities: 0.45-kw ERP, 407-ft. above ground, 4918-ft. above sea level, lat. 40° 35' 28", long. 103° 02' 23".

Ownership: Board of Logan County Commissioners.

Sterling—K50EE, Ch. 50, Board of Logan County Commissioners. Phone: 970-522-0888.

Technical Facilities: 0.45-kw ERP, 407-ft. above ground, 4918-ft. above sea level, lat. 40° 35' 28", long. 103° 02' 23".

Ownership: Board of Logan County Commissioners.

Sterling—K52EW, Ch. 52, Board of Logan County Commissioners. Phone: 970-522-0888.

Technical Facilities: 0.45-kw ERP, 407-ft. above ground, 4918-ft. above sea level, lat. 40° 35' 28", long. 103° 02' 23".

Ownership: Board of Logan County Commissioners.

Sterling—K58GH, Ch. 58, Board of Logan County Commissioners.

Technical Facilities: 2.26-kw ERP, 407-ft. above ground, 4918-ft. above sea level, lat. 40° 35' 28", long. 103° 02' 23".

Ownership: Board of Logan County Commissioners.

Sterling & south Logan County—K44FL, Ch. 44, Board of Logan County Commissioners.

Technical Facilities: 0.45-kw ERP, 407-ft. above ground, 4918-ft. above sea level, lat. 40° 35' 28", long. 103° 02' 23".

Ownership: Board of Logan County Commissioners.

Sterling, etc.—K56GL, Ch. 56, Board of Logan County Commissioners.

Technical Facilities: 2.26-kw ERP, 407-ft. above ground, 4918-ft. above sea level, lat. 40° 35' 28", long. 103° 02' 23".

Ownership: Board of Logan County Commissioners.

Sunetha & Nutria—K66AV, Ch. 66, LIN of Colorado LLC.

Technical Facilities: 0.36-kw ERP, lat. 37° 11' 36", long. 107° 05' 31".

Ownership: LIN TV Corp.

Sutank, etc.—K04KC, Ch. 4, Garfield County.

Technical Facilities: 0.04-kw ERP, 6529-ft. above sea level, lat. 39° 23' 48", long. 107° 14' 00".

Ownership: Garfield County.

■ **Sweetwater Creek**—K36DB, Ch. 36, Resort Television USA LLC. Phone: 207-772-5000.

Technical Facilities: 0.001-kw ERP, 33-ft. above ground, 7461-ft. above sea level, lat. 39° 38' 07", long. 106° 32' 13".

Ownership: Resort Sports Network Inc.

Thomasville—K04PO, Ch. 4, Pitkin County Translator Dept. Phone: 970-945-4932.

Technical Facilities: 0.044-kw ERP, 50-ft. above ground, 8682-ft. above sea level, lat. 39° 21' 12", long. 106° 41' 00".

Ownership: Pitkin County Translator Dept.

Thomasville—K05JA, Ch. 5, Pitkin County Translator Dept. Phone: 970-920-5395.

Technical Facilities: 0.024-kw ERP, lat. 39° 21' 12", long. 106° 41' 00".

Ownership: Pitkin County Translator Dept.

Thomasville—K14LQ, Ch. 14, Pitkin County Translator Dept. Phone: 970-920-5395.

Technical Facilities: 0.088-kw ERP, 39-ft. above ground, 8671-ft. above sea level, lat. 39° 21' 12", long. 106° 41' 00".

Ownership: Pitkin County Translator Dept.

Thomasville—K20HR, Ch. 20, Pitkin County Translator Dept. Phone: 970-920-5395.

Technical Facilities: 0.088-kw ERP, 34-ft. above ground, 8666-ft. above sea level, lat. 39° 21' 12", long. 106° 41' 00".

Ownership: Pitkin County Translator Dept.

Toponas—K12KR, Ch. 12, Yampa Valley TV Assn.

Technical Facilities: 0.079-kw ERP, 8350-ft. above sea level, lat. 40° 03' 40", long. 106° 51' 00".

Ownership: Yampa Valley TV Association Inc.

Trinidad—K34GI, Ch. 34, Mainstreet Broadcasting Co. Inc. Phone: 719-738-3636.

Technical Facilities: 0.84-kw ERP, 86-ft. above ground, 7188-ft. above sea level, lat. 37° 14' 14", long. 104° 30' 52".

Ownership: Mainstreet Broadcasting Co. Inc.

Trinidad, Valdez, etc.—K15GL-D, Ch. 15, Rocky Mountain Public Broadcasting Network Inc. Phone: 303-892-6666.

Technical Facilities: 0.18-kw ERP, 69-ft. above ground, 7169-ft. above sea level, lat. 37° 14' 14", long. 104° 30' 52".

Ownership: Rocky Mountain Public Broadcasting Network Inc.

Upper Frying Pan River—K09LE, Ch. 9, Pitkin County Translator Dept. Phone: 970-920-5395.

Technical Facilities: 0.002-kw ERP, lat. 39° 21' 12", long. 106° 41' 00".

Ownership: Pitkin County Translator Dept.

Vail—K45IE, Ch. 45, Vail Associates Inc. dba TV 8. Phone: 970-479-4688.

Technical Facilities: 0.055-kw ERP, 33-ft. above ground, 7625-ft. above sea level, lat. 39° 38' 38", long. 106° 32' 14".

Ownership: Vail Associates Inc. dba TV 8.

Personnel: Cathleen Hancock, General Manager.

Vail—KRYD-LP, Ch. 10, Colorado TV Marketing LLC. Phone: 970-920-9600.

Technical Facilities: 0.5-kw ERP, 246-ft. above ground, 9918-ft. above sea level, lat. 39° 38' 05.5", long. 106° 26' 46.9".

Holds CP for change to 30-ft. above ground, 8931-ft. above sea level, lat. 39° 36' 58", long. 106° 26' 55". BMPTVL-20071212AAM.

Ownership: Colorado TV Marketing LLC.

Vallecito—K02ET, Ch. 2, Lake TV Assn.

Technical Facilities: 0.038-kw ERP, lat. 37° 22' 00", long. 107° 31' 30".

Ownership: Lake TV Assn.

Vallecito—K08ET, Ch. 8, Lake TV Assn.

Technical Facilities: 0.057-kw ERP, lat. 37° 22' 00", long. 107° 31' 30".

Ownership: Lake TV Assn.

Vallecito—K10AD, Ch. 10, Lake TV Assn.

Technical Facilities: 0.057-kw ERP, 9639-ft. above sea level, lat. 37° 22' 00", long. 107° 31' 30".

Ownership: Lake TV Assn.

Walsenburg—KSPK-LP, Ch. 28, Mainstreet Broadcasting Co. Inc. Phone: 719-738-3636.

Technical Facilities: 7.4-kw ERP, 131-ft. above ground, 6886-ft. above sea level, lat. 37° 37' 39", long. 104° 49' 17".

Ownership: Mainstreet Broadcasting Co. Inc.

Personnel: Paul Richards, General Manager.

Waunita Hot Springs—K51DI, Ch. 51, Gunnison County Metropolitan Recreation District. Phone: 970-641-8725.

Technical Facilities: 0.813-kw ERP, 13-ft. above ground, 11913-ft. above sea level, lat. 38° 29' 56", long. 106° 19' 28".

Holds CP for change to channel number 51, 2.2-kw ERP, 16-ft. above ground, 11926-ft. above sea level, lat. 38° 29' 49.2", long. 106° 19' 11.7". BDISTT-20090210AEH.

Ownership: Gunnison County Metropolitan Recreation District.

Waunita Hot Springs—K55BI, Ch. 55, Gunnison County Metropolitan Recreation District. Phone: 970-641-8725.

Technical Facilities: 0.004-kw ERP, lat. 38° 29' 56", long. 106° 19' 28".

Holds CP for change to channel number 45, 2.2-kw ERP, 16-ft. above ground, 11926-ft. above sea level, lat. 38° 29' 49.2", long. 106° 19' 11.7". BDISTT-20090210AEE.

Ownership: Gunnison County Metropolitan Recreation District.

Weber Canyon—K02OS, Ch. 2, Southwest Colorado TV Translator Assn. Phone: 970-565-2121.

Technical Facilities: 1-w TPO, 0.2-kw ERP, 10-ft. above ground, 7004-ft. above sea level, lat. 37° 17' 51", long. 108° 18' 02".

Transmitter: 6051 County Rte. 41, Mancos.

Ownership: Southwest Colorado TV Translator Assn.

Weber Canyon—K04ON, Ch. 4, Southwest Colorado TV Translator Assn. Phone: 970-565-2121.

Technical Facilities: 1-w TPO, 0.2-kw ERP, 7011-ft. above sea level, lat. 37° 17' 51", long. 108° 18' 02".

Transmitter: 6051 County Rte. 41, Mancos.

Ownership: Southwest Colorado TV Translator Assn.

Weber Canyon—K08MB, Ch. 8, Southwest Colorado TV Translator Assn. Phone: 970-565-2121.

Technical Facilities: 1-w TPO, 0.2-kw ERP, 7018-ft. above sea level, lat. 37° 17' 51", long. 108° 18' 02".

Transmitter: 6051 County Rte. 41, Mancos.

Ownership: Southwest Colorado TV Translator Assn.

Personnel: Wayne Johnson, General Manager.

Weber Canyon—K10OD, Ch. 10, Southwest Colorado TV Translator Assn. Phone: 970-565-2121.

Technical Facilities: 1-w TPO, 0.002-kw ERP, 26-ft. above ground, 7019-ft. above sea level, lat. 37° 17' 51", long. 108° 18' 02".

Transmitter: 6051 County Rte. 41, Mancos.

Ownership: Southwest Colorado TV Translator Assn.

Personnel: Wayne Johnson, General Manager.

Weber Canyon—K13XH, Ch. 13, Southwest Colorado TV Translator Assn. Phone: 970-565-2121.

Technical Facilities: 1-w TPO, 0.0002-kw ERP, 30-ft. above ground, 7024-ft. above sea level, lat. 37° 17' 51", long. 108° 18' 02".

Transmitter: 6051 County Rte. 41, Mancos.

Ownership: Southwest Colorado TV Translator Assn.

Personnel: Wayne Johnson, General Manager.

Westcliffe—K07BW, Ch. 7, Custer County. Phone: 719-783-2281.

Technical Facilities: 0.02-kw ERP, lat. 38° 07' 39", long. 105° 22' 08".

Ownership: Custer County Road & Bridge.

Westcliffe—K09DY, Ch. 9, Custer County Road & Bridge. Phone: 719-783-2281.

Technical Facilities: 0.02-kw ERP, lat. 38° 07' 39", long. 105° 22' 08".

Ownership: Custer County Road & Bridge.

Windsor—KZFC-LP, Ch. 36, McGraw-Hill Broadcasting Co. Inc. Phone: 303-832-0190.

Technical Facilities: 18.9-kw ERP, 341-ft. above ground, 5587-ft. above sea level, lat. 40° 38' 31", long. 104° 49' 03".

Holds CP for change to 1.75-kw ERP, BDFCDTL-20060331BJQ.

Ownership: McGraw-Hill Broadcasting Co. Inc.

Personnel: Darrell Brown, General Manager.

Wolcott—K13DE, Ch. 13, Colorado TV Marketing LLC. Phones: 970-920-9600; 866-250-6422.

Technical Facilities: 2.84-kw ERP, 55-ft. above ground, 10504-ft. above sea level, lat. 39° 44' 23", long. 106° 48' 04".

Ownership: Colorado TV Marketing LLC.

Wolcott & Eagle—K07DB, Ch. 7, Eagle Valley TV Corp.

Technical Facilities: 0.034-kw ERP, lat. 39° 44' 01", long. 106° 48' 04".

Ownership: Eagle Valley TV Corp.

Woodland Park—K28GE, Ch. 28, Barrington Colorado Springs License LLC. Phone: 847-884-1877.

Technical Facilities: 1.12-kw ERP, lat. 38° 59' 13", long. 105° 04' 08".

Transmitter: 1-mi. SW of Woodland Park Post Office.

Ownership: Pilot Group LP.

Woodland Park—K33EW, Ch. 33, Full Gospel Outreach Inc.

Technical Facilities: 0.99-kw ERP, lat. 38° 59' 12", long. 105° 04' 05".

Transmitter: 1-mi. SW of Woodland Park Post Office.

Ownership: Full Gospel Outreach Inc.

Woody Creek—K39HE, Ch. 39, Pitkin County Translator Dept.

Technical Facilities: 0.06-kw ERP, 60-ft. above ground, 8849-ft. above sea level, lat. 39° 18' 37", long. 106° 56' 53".

Ownership: Pitkin County Translator Dept.

Woody Creek—K44GQ, Ch. 44, Pitkin County Translator Dept. Phone: 970-920-5395.

Technical Facilities: 1.21-kw ERP, 34-ft. above ground, 8114-ft. above sea level, lat. 39° 18' 30", long. 106° 57' 15".

Ownership: Pitkin County Translator Dept.

Woody Creek, etc.—K07RN, Ch. 7, Pitkin County Translator Dept. Phone: 970-920-5395.

Technical Facilities: 0.001-kw ERP, 39-ft. above ground, 8140-ft. above sea level, lat. 38° 18' 30", long. 106° 57' 15".

Ownership: Pitkin County Translator Dept.

Woody Creek, etc.—K11LW, Ch. 11, Pitkin County Translator Dept. Phone: 970-920-5395.

Technical Facilities: 0.017-kw ERP, lat. 39° 18' 30", long. 106° 57' 15".

Ownership: Pitkin County Translator Dept.

Woody Creek, etc.—K13MT, Ch. 13, Pitkin County Translator Dept. Phone: 970-920-5395.

Technical Facilities: 0.003-kw ERP, lat. 39° 18' 30", long. 106° 57' 15".

Ownership: Pitkin County Translator Dept.

Wray—K31IH-D, Ch. 31, Region 1 Translator Assn. Phone: 970-848-5301.

Technical Facilities: 0.189-kw ERP, 307-ft. above ground, 4146-ft. above sea level, lat. 40° 03' 15", long. 102° 13' 32".

Ownership: Region 1 Translator Association.

Wray—K44FM, Ch. 44, Region 1 Translator Assn. Phone: 970-848-5301.

Technical Facilities: 0.616-kw ERP, lat. 40° 03' 15", long. 102° 13' 31".

Ownership: Region 1 Translator Association.

Wray—K46FF, Ch. 46, Region 1 Translator Assn. Phone: 970-848-5301.

Technical Facilities: 0.616-kw ERP, lat. 40° 03' 15", long. 102° 13' 31".

Ownership: Region 1 Translator Association.

Wray—K48GA, Ch. 48, Region 1 Translator Assn. Phone: 970-848-5301.

Technical Facilities: 0.564-kw ERP, lat. 40° 03' 15", long. 102° 13' 31".

Ownership: Region 1 Translator Association.

Wray—K50FJ, Ch. 50, Region 1 Translator Assn. Phone: 970-848-5301.

Technical Facilities: 0.564-kw ERP, lat. 40° 03' 15", long. 102° 13' 31".

Ownership: Region 1 Translator Association.

Wray—K52FZ, Ch. 52, Region 1 Translator Assn. Phone: 970-848-5301.

Technical Facilities: 0.563-kw ERP, lat. 40° 03' 15", long. 102° 13' 31".

Ownership: Region 1 Translator Association.

Wray—K56HG, Ch. 56, Region 1 Translator Assn. Phone: 970-848-5301.

Technical Facilities: 0.615-kw ERP, lat. 40° 03' 15", long. 102° 13' 32".

Ownership: Region 1 Translator Association.

Wray—K58GV, Ch. 58, Region 1 Translator Assn. Phone: 970-848-5301.

Technical Facilities: 0.615-kw ERP, 307-ft. above ground, 4146-ft. above sea level, lat. 40° 03' 15", long. 102° 13' 32".

Ownership: Region 1 Translator Association.

Yampa, etc.—K13ES, Ch. 13, Yampa Valley TV Assn. Inc.

Technical Facilities: 0.123-kw ERP, 10351-ft. above sea level, lat. 40° 27' 16", long. 106° 44' 34".

Ownership: Yampa Valley TV Association Inc.

Yuma—K28JH-D, Ch. 28, Region 1 Translator Assn. Phone: 970-848-5301.

Technical Facilities: 0.173-kw ERP, 392-ft. above ground, 4601-ft. above sea level, lat. 40° 08' 35", long. 102° 48' 51".

Ownership: Region 1 Translator Association.

Yuma—K32AB, Ch. 32, Region 1 Translator Assn. Phone: 970-848-5301.

Technical Facilities: 2.69-kw ERP, 392-ft. above ground, 4600-ft. above sea level, lat. 40° 08' 35", long. 102° 48' 51".

Ownership: Region 1 Translator Association.

Yuma—K34AC, Ch. 34, Region 1 Translator Assn. Phone: 970-848-5301.

Technical Facilities: 0.862-kw ERP, lat. 40° 08' 35", long. 102° 48' 51".

Ownership: Region 1 Translator Association.

Yuma—K36AC, Ch. 36, Region 1 Translator Assn. Phone: 970-848-5301.

Technical Facilities: 2.69-kw ERP, lat. 40° 08' 35", long. 102° 48' 51".

Ownership: Region 1 Translator Association.

Ownership: Gunnison County Metropolitan Recreation District.

Yuma—K38AD, Ch. 38, Region 1 Translator Assn. Phone: 970-848-5301.

Technical Facilities: 2.69-kw ERP, lat. 40° 08' 35", long. 102° 48' 51".

Ownership: Region 1 Translator Association.

Yuma—K40CG, Ch. 40, Region 1 Translator Assn. Phone: 970-848-5301.

Technical Facilities: 2.69-kw ERP, 392-ft. above ground, 4600-ft. above sea level, lat. 40° 08' 35", long. 102° 48' 51".

Ownership: Region 1 Translator Association.

Yuma—K42GI, Ch. 42, Region 1 Translator Assn. Phone: 970-848-5301.

Technical Facilities: 2.7-kw ERP, 392-ft. above ground, 4598-ft. above sea level, lat. 40° 08' 35", long. 102° 48' 51".

Ownership: Region 1 Translator Association.

Connecticut

■ **Allingtown**—W28AJ, Ch. 28, Paging Assoc. Inc. Phone: 203-932-3500. Fax: 203-933-2259.

Studio: 24 Rockdale Rd, West Haven, CT 06516.

Technical Facilities: 1000-w TPO, 48.8-kw ERP, 184-ft. above ground, 335-ft. above sea level, lat. 41° 17' 28", long. 72° 58' 06".

Transmitter: 24 Rockdale Rd.

Ownership: Paging Associates Inc.

Bridgeport—W65DZ, Ch. 65, Paging Assoc. Inc. Phone: 800-343-9333.

Technical Facilities: 1000-w TPO, 1.26-kw ERP, 85-ft. above ground, 102-ft. above sea level, lat. 41° 09' 58", long. 73° 13' 03".

Transmitter: 623 Pine St.

Ownership: Paging Associates Inc.

Danbury—W22BN, Ch. 22, IT Communications Inc.

Technical Facilities: 500-w TPO, 10.4-kw ERP, 88-ft. above ground, 728-ft. above sea level, lat. 41° 23' 44", long. 73° 25' 24".

Transmitter: Shelter Rock, Shelter Rock Rd.

Multichannel TV Sound: Stereo only.

Ownership: IT Communications Inc.

Personnel: David Abrantes, General Manager & Chief Engineer.

Granby—WESA-LP, Ch. 34, R and S Broadcasting LLC. Phone: 860-529-9303.

Technical Facilities: 45-kw ERP, 120-ft. above ground, 930-ft. above sea level, lat. 42° 07' 11.3", long. 72° 24' 39".

Holds CP for change to 3.5-kw ERP, BDFCDTL-20080319ACP.

Ownership: R and S Broadcasting LLC.

Hartford—WHCT-LP, Ch. 38, Venture Technologies Group LLC. Phone: 323-965-5400. Fax: 323-965-5411.

Technical Facilities: 150-kw ERP, 299-ft. above ground, 991-ft. above sea level, lat. 41° 47' 48", long. 72° 47' 52".

Ownership: Venture Technologies Group LLC.

■ **Hartford**—WRDM-CA, Ch. 50, ZGS Hartford Inc. Phone: 703-528-5656.

Studio: 886 Maple Ave, Hartford, CT 06114.

Technical Facilities: 50-kw ERP, 308-ft. above ground, 1001-ft. above sea level, lat. 41° 47' 48", long. 72° 47' 52".

Multichannel TV Sound: Stereo and separate audio program.

Ownership: ZGS Broadcasting Holdings Inc.

Personnel: Lucio C. Ruzzier Sr., President & Chief Executive Officer; Paul D'Agostino, Chief Financial Officer & Controller; William Newton, President of Sales & Program Director; Gaetano Leone, General Manager; Salvatore Minniti, Chief Engineer.

Hartford—WRNT-LP, Ch. 48, R and S Broadcasting LLC. Phone: 860-529-9303.

Studio: 18 Garden St, Hartford, CT 06105.

Technical Facilities: 60-kw ERP, 200-ft. above ground, 892-ft. above sea level, lat. 41° 47' 48", long. 72° 47' 52".

Holds CP for change to 1-kw ERP, 255-ft. above ground, 947-ft. above sea level, BDFCDTL-20080319ACK.

Ownership: R and S Broadcasting LLC.

Personnel: Louis Maisel, President, General Manager & Chief Engineer.

■ **Hartford**—WUTH-CA, Ch. 47, Entravision Holdings LLC. Phone: 310-447-3870.

Technical Facilities: 17.9-kw ERP, lat. 41° 42' 32", long. 72° 28' 30".

Ownership: Entravision Communications Corp.

Personnel: Alex Von Lichtenberg, General Manager.

New Haven—WNHX-LP, Ch. 51, Area 51 DMG Inc. Phone: 203-557-3279.

Technical Facilities: 100-kw ERP, 73-ft. above ground, 413-ft. above sea level, lat. 41° 19' 42", long. 72° 54' 25".

Ownership: Area 51 DMG Inc.

Stamford—W17CD, Ch. 17, K Licensee Inc. Phone: 718-358-4219.

Technical Facilities: 75-kw ERP, 209-ft. above ground, 329-ft. above sea level, lat. 41° 03' 54", long. 73° 32' 04".

Ownership: K Licensee Inc.

Stamford—W27CD, Ch. 27, WLNY LP. Phone: 631-777-8855. Fax: 631-777-8180.

Technical Facilities: 17.4-kw ERP, 142-ft. above ground, 218-ft. above sea level, lat. 41° 03' 41", long. 73° 32' 03".

Ownership: WLNY Holdings Inc.

Personnel: David Feinblatt, President & General Manager; Richard Mulliner, Chief Engineer; Elliott Simmons, Sales Manager.

Delaware

Dover—W14CM, Ch. 14, Trinity Broadcasting Network Inc. Phone: 714-832-2950. Fax: 714-730-0661.

Technical Facilities: 1000-w TPO, 3.5-kw ERP, 98-ft. above ground, 253-ft. above sea level, lat. 39° 11' 08", long. 75° 29' 28".

Transmitter: 2.36-mi. NW of intersection of State Rtes. 8 & 9.

Ownership: Trinity Broadcasting Network Inc.

Personnel: Paul Crouch, General Manager; Ben Miller, Chief Engineer; Rod Henke, Sales Manager.

Dover—WEVD-LP, Ch. 10, Delmarva Broadcast Service LLC. Phone: 407-423-4431.

Studio: White Oak Rd., Dover, DE 19901.

Technical Facilities: 1000-w TPO, 81.4-kw ERP, 229-ft. above ground, 255-ft. above sea level, lat. 39° 11' 10", long. 75° 29' 26".

Ownership: Delmarva Broadcast Service LLC.

Millsboro, etc.—WLWP-LP, Ch. 4, Ocean 4 Broadcasting Assn. Phone: 302-732-1400. Fax: 302-732-3933.

Technical Facilities: 200-w TPO, 0.063-kw ERP, 69-ft. above ground, 75-ft. above sea level, lat. 36° 33' 08", long. 75° 13' 23".

Transmitter: Rte. 26, Dagsboro, DE.

Ownership: Ocean Broadcasting Assn.

Personnel: Robert Neuhaus, General Manager.

Rehoboth Beach—WRDE-LD, Ch. 31, Price Hill TV LLC. Phone: 513-257-5011.

Technical Facilities: 7.1-kw ERP, 296-ft. above ground, 321-ft. above sea level, lat. 38° 42' 14", long. 75° 12' 01".

Ownership: Price Hill Television LLC.

Sussex County—WEWE-LP, Ch. 24, Ocean 60 Broadcasting Assn. Phone: 302-732-1400. Fax: 302-732-3933.

Technical Facilities: 0.97-kw ERP, 75-ft. above ground, 95-ft. above sea level, lat. 38° 33' 08", long. 75° 13' 23".

Ownership: Ocean Broadcasting Assn.

Personnel: Robert Neuhaus, General Manager.

Wilmington—W40AZ, Ch. 40, Trinity Christian Center of Santa Ana Inc. Phone: 714-832-2950.

Technical Facilities: 10.3-kw ERP, 256-ft. above ground, 646-ft. above sea level, lat. 39° 51' 03", long. 75° 29' 45".

Ownership: Trinity Broadcasting Network Inc.

District of Columbia

Washington—WDDN-LP, Ch. 23, Word of God Fellowship Inc. Phone: 817-571-1229.

Studio: 3400 Idaho Ave. NW, Washington, DC 20016.

Technical Facilities: 10-kw ERP, 656-ft. above ground, 951-ft. above sea level, lat. 39° 00' 00", long. 77° 03' 26".

Ownership: Word of God Fellowship Inc.

Washington—WIAV-LP, Ch. 58, Asiavision Inc. Phone: 301-345-2742.

Technical Facilities: 661-w TPO, 35-kw ERP, 177-ft. above ground, 325-ft. above sea level, lat. 38° 59' 29", long. 76° 52' 45".

Transmitter: 7501 Greenway Center Dr., Greenbelt, MD.

Ownership: Asiavision Inc.

■ **Washington**—WMDO-CA, Ch. 47, Entravision Holdings LLC. Phones: 202-522-8640; 310-447-3870. Fax: 202-898-1897.

Studio: 101 Constitution Ave. NW, Ste L-100, Washington, DC 20001.

Technical Facilities: 16.5-kw ERP, 308-ft. above ground, 695-ft. above sea level, lat. 38° 56' 24", long. 77° 04' 54".

Ownership: Entravision Communications Corp.

Washington—WWTD-LP, Ch. 49, DC Broadcasting Inc. Phones: 303-593-1433; 303-520-9996. Fax: 815-327-4319.

Technical Facilities: 59.2-kw ERP, 405-ft. above ground, 792-ft. above sea level, lat. 38° 56' 24", long. 77° 04' 54".

Ownership: DC Broadcasting Inc.

■ **Washington**—WZDC-CA, Ch. 25, Onda Capital Inc. Phone: 703-528-5656.

Technical Facilities: 28.3-kw ERP, 205-ft. above ground, 592-ft. above sea level, lat. 38° 56' 23.6", long. 77° 04' 54.1".

Holds CP for change to 4.6-kw ERP, BDFCDTA-20080804ACV.

Ownership: ZGS Broadcasting Holdings Inc.

Florida

Alachua, etc.—W40CQ-D, Ch. 40, Associated Christian TV System Inc. Phone: 407-263-4040.

Technical Facilities: 15-kw ERP, 440-ft. above ground, 526-ft. above sea level, lat. 29° 37' 46", long. 82° 34' 25".

Began Operation: February 27, 2009.

Ownership: Associated Christian Television System Inc.

Alachua, etc.—W69AY, Ch. 69, Associated Christian Television System Inc. Phone: 407-298-5555.

Studio: 1001 Waldo Rd, Gainesville, FL 32601.

Technical Facilities: 1000-w TPO, 38.02-kw ERP, 567-ft. above ground, 231-ft. above sea level, lat. 29° 42' 45", long. 82° 18' 08".

Transmitter: 1001 Waldo Rd., Gainesville.

Ownership: Associated Christian Television System Inc.

Personnel: Claud Bowers, Station Manager; Donna Lee, General Sales Manager; John Wasson, Chief Engineer.

Altamonte Springs—WXXU-LP, Ch. 12, Rama Communications II Ltd.

Technical Facilities: 10-w TPO, 0.42-kw ERP, 1499-ft. above ground, 1122-ft. above sea level, lat. 28° 55' 16", long. 81° 19' 09".

Transmitter: 1.3-mi. W of the intersection of Rtes. 17 & 92 & Miller Rd., Orange City.

Ownership: Rama Communications.

Big Pine—W16CA, Ch. 16, Cayo Hueso Networks LLC. Phone: 303-688-5162.

Technical Facilities: 36.7-kw ERP, 335-ft. above ground, 338-ft. above sea level, lat. 24° 39' 02", long. 81° 18' 36".

Ownership: Cayo Hueso Networks LLC.

Big Pine Key—W47AC, Ch. 47, Cayo Hueso Networks LLC. Phone: 303-688-5162.

Technical Facilities: 1.6-kw ERP, lat. 24° 40' 09", long. 81° 21' 33".

Ownership: Cayo Hueso Networks LLC.

Big Pine Key—W57AM, Ch. 57, Cayo Hueso Networks LLC. Phone: 303-688-5162.

Technical Facilities: 0.32-kw ERP, lat. 24° 40' 09", long. 81° 21' 33".

Ownership: Cayo Hueso Networks LLC.

■ **Bradenton**—WSVT-CA, Ch. 18, Word of God Fellowship Inc. Phone: 817-858-9955. Fax: 817-571-7478.

Technical Facilities: 150-kw ERP, 594-ft. above ground, 610-ft. above sea level, lat. 27° 56' 49", long. 82° 27' 34".

Ownership: Word of God Fellowship Inc.

Personnel: Nick Manassa, General Manager.

Chiefland—W33BL, Ch. 33, Suncoast Broadcasting of Lafayette County.

Technical Facilities: 22.7-kw ERP, 180-ft. above ground, 220-ft. above sea level, lat. 29° 28' 12", long. 82° 48' 20".

Ownership: Suncoast Broadcasting of Lafayette County Inc.

■ **Clearwater**—WXAX-LP, Ch. 26, Una Vez Mas Tampa License LLC. Phone: 214-754-7008.

Technical Facilities: 50-kw ERP, 1100-ft. above ground, 1175-ft. above sea level, lat. 27° 50' 52", long. 82° 15' 48".

Ownership: Una Vez Mas GP LLC.

■ **Daytona Beach**—WDYB-LP, Ch. 53, Tiger Eye Broadcasting Corp. Phone: 954-331-7866.

Technical Facilities: 1000-w TPO, 11.3-kw ERP, 327-ft. above ground, 209-ft. above sea level, lat. 29° 13' 53", long. 81° 02' 31".

Holds CP for change to channel number 28, 50-kw ERP, 250-ft. above ground, 267-ft. above sea level, lat. 29° 13' 57", long. 81° 02' 14". BDISTTA-20060922ACY.

Transmitter: 540 Corporation Dr.

Began Operation: August 9, 1999.

Ownership: Tiger Eye Broadcasting Corp.

Daytona Beach—WPXB-LD, Ch. 50, ION Media LPTV Inc., Debtor in Possession. Phone: 561-682-4206. Fax: 560-659-4754.

Technical Facilities: 15-kw ERP, 380-ft. above ground, 417-ft. above sea level, lat. 29° 10' 24", long. 81° 09' 24".

Began Operation: April 17, 1989.

Ownership: ION Media Networks Inc., Debtor in Possession.

Personnel: Frank D. Tenore, General Manager; David T. Hall, Chief Engineer.

■ **De Funiak Springs**—WWEO-CA, Ch. 24, World Evangelism Outreach. Phone: 850-892-6202. Fax: 850-892-6226.

Studio: German Club Rd, De Funiak Springs, FL 32433.

Technical Facilities: 1000-w TPO, 10.8-kw ERP, 187-ft. above ground, 404-ft. above sea level, lat. 30° 44' 18", long. 86° 06' 22".

Transmitter: 1.2-mi. NE of Courthouse, near West Sandy Creek.

Ownership: World Evangelism Outreach.

Personnel: R. W. White, President & General Manager; James Roberts, Chief Engineer & Production Manager; Elaine White, Program Director.

■ **Destin**—WDES-CA, Ch. 48, Beach TV Properties Inc. Phone: 904-234-2773.

Technical Facilities: 38.4-kw ERP, 174-ft. above ground, 190-ft. above sea level, lat. 30° 23' 49", long. 86° 30' 27".

Transmitter: 140 Palmetto.

Ownership: Beach TV Properties Inc.

Duck Key—W29CW, Ch. 29, Prism Broadcasting Network Inc. Phone: 770-953-3232.

Technical Facilities: 0.004-kw ERP, 50-ft. above ground, 54-ft. above sea level, lat. 24° 46' 02", long. 80° 56' 42".

Ownership: Prism Broadcasting Network Inc.

Dunnellon—WOCD-LP, Ch. 27, Word of God Fellowship Inc. Phone: 817-571-1229.

Technical Facilities: 30-kw ERP, 292-ft. above ground, 330-ft. above sea level, lat. 29° 05' 51", long. 82° 38' 06".

Began Operation: March 31, 2009.

Ownership: Word of God Fellowship Inc.

Fort Myers—W22CL, Ch. 22, U.S. Television LLC. Phone: 318-992-7766.

Technical Facilities: 836-w TPO, 15-kw ERP, 400-ft. above ground, 410-ft. above sea level, lat. 26° 30' 18", long. 81° 51' 14".

Transmitter: 16341 Old U.S. 41 S.

Ownership: Dean M. Mosely.

Personnel: J. R. Skinner, General Manager & Sales Manager; Loren Matthews, Chief Engineer.

■ **Fort Myers**—WEVU-CA, Ch. 4, SP Fort Myers LLC. Phone: 203-542-4200.

Technical Facilities: 3-kw ERP, 259-ft. above ground, 266-ft. above sea level, lat. 26° 38' 47", long. 81° 52' 06".

Began Operation: June 15, 1988.

Ownership: SP Television LLC.

Personnel: David Elliott, General Manager; John Garbo, General Sales Manager; Dave Taylor, News Director.

Fort Myers—WLZE-LP, Ch. 51, SP Fort Myers LLC. Phone: 203-542-4200.

Technical Facilities: 150-kw ERP, 1201-ft. above ground, 1230-ft. above sea level, lat. 26° 47' 07", long. 81° 47' 47".

Began Operation: September 9, 1997.

Ownership: SP Television LLC.

Fort Myers—WTPH-LP, Ch. 14, Tu Programmacion Hispana LLC. Phone: 239-772-1650.

Technical Facilities: 127-kw ERP, 427-ft. above ground, 444-ft. above sea level, lat. 26° 43' 36", long. 81° 47' 14".

Ownership: Tu Programmacion Hispana LLC.

Fort Pierce—W31DC-D, Ch. 31, Barry Telecommunications Inc. Phone: 561-737-8000.

Technical Facilities: 15-kw ERP, 302-ft. above ground, 335-ft. above sea level, lat. 27° 32' 46", long. 80° 22' 08".

Ownership: Barry Telecommunications Inc.

Fort Pierce—W44AY, Ch. 44, Barry Telecommunications Inc. Phone: 561-737-8000. Fax: 561-369-3067.

Studio: 3401 S Congress Ave, Boynton Beach, FL 33426.

Technical Facilities: 524.7-w TPO, 34.8-kw ERP, 341-ft. above ground, 374-ft. above sea level, lat. 27° 32' 46", long. 80° 22' 08".

Transmitter: 0.5-mi. NW of Viking.

Multichannel TV Sound: Stereo and separate audio program.

Ownership: Barry Telecommunications Inc.

Personnel: Jerry Carr, President; Bernie Henneburg, Vice President, Finance.

Fort Pierce—WFPI-LP, Ch. 8, EBC Southwest Florida Inc., Debtor in Possession. Phone: 501-219-2400.

Technical Facilities: 10-w TPO, 0.06-kw ERP, 30-ft. above ground, 49-ft. above sea level, lat. 27° 26' 05", long. 81° 21' 04".

Holds CP for change to 3-kw ERP, lat. 27° 26' 06", long. 80° 21' 03". BPTVL-20060306BBU.

Transmitter: 2609 Jersey Ave.

Began Operation: May 10, 1996.

Ownership: Equity Media Holdings Corp., Debtor in Possession.

Gainesville—W50DW, Ch. 50, ZGS Florida Inc. Phone: 703-528-5656.

Technical Facilities: 39.7-kw ERP, 240-ft. above ground, 311-ft. above sea level, lat. 29° 28' 22.6", long. 82° 35' 20.5".

Ownership: ZGS Broadcasting Holdings Inc.

■ **Gainesville**—WBXG-CA, Ch. 33, L4 Media Group LLC. Phone: 321-729-8451.

Studio: 3405-B NW 97th, Gainesville, FL 32606.

Technical Facilities: 23.6-kw ERP, 367-ft. above ground, 443-ft. above sea level, lat. 29° 38' 37", long. 82° 25' 11".

Transmitter: 7175 S.W. 8th Ave.

Ownership: L4 Media Group LLC.

Personnel: Liz Kiley, Broadcast Vice President; Warren Reeves, Consulting Engineer; Amy Brown, Broadcast Operations Director.

Gainesville—WGVT-LD, Ch. 26, Budd Broadcasting Co. Inc. Phone: 352-371-7772.

Technical Facilities: 15-kw ERP, 423-ft. above ground, 594-ft. above sea level, lat. 29° 44' 22", long. 82° 23' 09".

Began Operation: December 7, 2006.

Ownership: Budd Broadcasting Co. Inc.

Gainesville—WLUF-LP, Ch. 10, Board of Trustees, State of Florida, acting for and on behalf of the U. of Florida. Phone: 904-392-5551. Fax: 904-392-5731.

Studio: U. of Florida, Weimar Hall, Gainesville, FL 32611.

Technical Facilities: 10-w TPO, 0.057-kw ERP, 558-ft. above ground, 738-ft. above sea level, lat. 29° 43' 35", long. 82° 23' 41".

Holds CP for change to channel number 5, 0.3-kw ERP, lat. 29° 42' 34", long. 82° 23' 40". BDISDTL-20060403ANS.

Transmitter: 5.5-mi. NW of Gainesville at the Devil's Millhopper.

Ownership: U. of Florida.

Personnel: Richard A. Lehner, General Manager; Ward Lindsey, Chief Engineer; Frank Counts, Director, Production.

Gainesville—WNFT-LP, Ch. 8, Budd Broadcasting Co. Inc. Phone: 352-371-7772.

Technical Facilities: 3-kw ERP, 387-ft. above ground, 499-ft. above sea level, lat. 29° 38' 08", long. 82° 19' 35".

Holds CP for change to 2.5-kw ERP, 266-ft. above ground, 377-ft. above sea level, BPTVL-20080828AAR.

Began Operation: September 12, 2006.

Ownership: Budd Broadcasting Co. Inc.

Gainesville—WTBZ-LP, Ch. 29, Robert A. Naismith. Phone: 231-547-2696.

Technical Facilities: 15-kw ERP, 295-ft. above ground, 374-ft. above sea level, lat. 29° 25' 05", long. 82° 32' 57".

Ownership: Robert A. Naismith.

■ **Gainesville**—WYPN-CA, Ch. 45, New Age Media of Gainesville License LLC. Phone: 570-824-7895.

Technical Facilities: 1000-w TPO, 30-kw ERP, 486-ft. above ground, 95-ft. above sea level, lat. 29° 32' 09", long. 82° 19' 18".

Ownership: New Age Media.

Personnel: Jimmie Citivers, Chief Engineer; Brenda Maynard, Sales Manager.

■ **Hallandale**—W58BU, Ch. 58, NBC Telemundo License Co. Phone: 202-637-4535.

Technical Facilities: 78.3-kw ERP, lat. 25° 59' 09", long. 80° 11' 37".

Transmitter: 4991 S.W. 28th St., Pembroke Park.

Ownership: NBC Universal.

■ **Inglis/Yankeetown**—WYKE-LP, Ch. 47, Citrus County Association for Retarded Citizens Inc. Phones: 352-564-1400; 352-746-3982.

Studio: 1315 N Van Nortwick Rd, Lecanto, FL 34461.

Technical Facilities: 15-kw ERP, 277-ft. above ground, 336-ft. above sea level, lat. 28° 53' 02", long. 82° 31' 20".

Multichannel TV Sound: Stereo only.

Ownership: Citrus County Association for Retarded Citizens Inc.

Personnel: Chester V. Cole, Executive Director.

Inverness—W61AK, Ch. 61, CBS Operations Inc. Phone: 202-457-4518.

Technical Facilities: 0.015-kw ERP, 548-ft. above sea level, lat. 28° 53' 20", long. 82° 22' 59".

Holds CP for change to channel number 26, 11-kw ERP, 411-ft. above ground, 480-ft. above sea level, lat. 28° 53' 20", long. 82° 23' 00". BDISDTT-20081006ABY.

Began Operation: April 29, 1982.

Ownership: CBS Corp.

Jacksonville—W45BZ, Ch. 45, Deepak Viswanath. Phone: 908-246-3636.

Technical Facilities: 3434-w TPO, 24.7-kw ERP, 57-ft. above ground, 584-ft. above sea level, lat. 30° 16' 51", long. 81° 34' 12".

Transmitter: 8675-I Hogan Rd., Jacksonville.

Ownership: Deepak Viswanath.

Jacksonville—W50CO, Ch. 50, Three Angels Broadcasting Network Inc. Phone: 618-627-4651. Fax: 618-627-4155.

Studio: 3391 Charley Good Rd, West Frankfort, IL 62896.

Technical Facilities: 1000-w TPO, 16.5-kw ERP, 351-ft. above ground, 354-ft. above sea level, lat. 30° 19' 22", long. 81° 38' 34".

Holds CP for change to 558-ft. above ground, 564-ft. above sea level, lat. 30° 19' 32.9", long. 81° 39' 32.9". BPTTL-20071102AAD.

Transmitter: 1084 E. Adams St., Jacksonville.

Ownership: Three Angels Broadcasting Network Inc.

Personnel: Moses Primo, Chief Engineer.

Jacksonville—W54CS, Ch. 54, Ventana Television Inc. Phone: 727-872-4210.

Technical Facilities: 190-w TPO, 2.51-kw ERP, 538-ft. above ground, 545-ft. above sea level, lat. 30° 19' 33", long. 81° 39' 32".

Holds CP for change to channel number 35, 25-kw ERP, 541-ft. above ground, 548-ft. above sea level, BDISTTL-20060403APQ.

Transmitter: Independence Life Bldg., Main at Hogan.

Began Operation: February 26, 1992.

Ownership: Ventana Television Inc.

Jacksonville—W67DL, Ch. 67, Deepak Viswanath.

Technical Facilities: 1000-w TPO, 24.71-kw ERP, 350-ft. above ground, 354-ft. above sea level, lat. 30° 19' 22", long. 81° 38' 34".

Transmitter: 1084 E. Adams St., Jacksonville.

Ownership: Deepak Viswanath.

Jacksonville—WPXJ-LP, Ch. 41, ION Media License Co. LLC, Debtor in Possession. Phone: 561-682-4206. Fax: 561-659-4754.

Technical Facilities: 1000-w TPO, 12.2-kw ERP, 554-ft. above ground, 561-ft. above sea level, lat. 30° 19′ 33″, long. 81° 39′ 32″.

Holds CP for change to 15-kw ERP, 555-ft. above ground, 561-ft. above sea level, lat. 30° 19′ 33″, long. 81° 39′ 33″. BDFCDTL-20090515ABQ.

Transmitter: One Independence Dr., Jacksonville.

Began Operation: May 12, 1988.

Ownership: ION Media Networks Inc., Debtor in Possession.

Jacksonville—WUBF-LP, Ch. 69, Ummat Broadcasting Corp. Inc.

Technical Facilities: 1000-w TPO, 11.45-kw ERP, 233-ft. above ground, 253-ft. above sea level, lat. 30° 23′ 15″, long. 81° 44′ 01″.

Holds CP for change to channel number 23, 11.5-kw ERP, 184-ft. above ground, 390-ft. above sea level, lat. 30° 21′ 08″, long. 81° 43′ 04″. BDISTTL-20061024AGD.

Transmitter: 5521 Soutel Dr.

Ownership: Ummat Broadcasting Corp. Inc.

Jacksonville—WVVQ-LP, Ch. 15, Budd Broadcasting Co. Inc. Phone: 352-371-7772.

Technical Facilities: 150-kw ERP, 820-ft. above ground, 830-ft. above sea level, lat. 30° 16′ 51″, long. 81° 34′ 12″.

Began Operation: May 8, 1997.

Ownership: Budd Broadcasting Co. Inc.

Jacksonville—WWRJ-LP, Ch. 27, U.S. Television LLC. Phone: 318-992-7766.

Technical Facilities: 1000-w TPO, 11.9-kw ERP, 550-ft. above ground, 560-ft. above sea level, lat. 30° 19′ 33″, long. 81° 39′ 32″.

Holds CP for change to 130-kw ERP, 902-ft. above ground, 912-ft. above sea level, lat. 30° 16′ 51″, long. 81° 34′ 12″. BPTTL-20060403AOM.

Transmitter: Independent Square, One Independent Dr.

Ownership: Dean M. Mosely.

Personnel: Bob Joblin, General Manager; Neal Ardman, Chief Engineer.

■**Jacksonville, etc.**—WBXJ-CA, Ch. 43, L4 Media Group LLC. Phone: 321-729-8451.

Studio: 3119 Spring Glen Rd, Ste 109, Jacksonville, FL 32207.

Technical Facilities: 20-w TPO, 49-kw ERP, 217-ft. above ground, 217-ft. above sea level, lat. 30° 16′ 34″, long. 81° 33′ 53″.

Transmitter: 701 N. Ocean Blvd.

Multichannel TV Sound: Stereo only.

Ownership: L4 Media Group LLC.

Personnel: Liz Kiley, Broadcast Vice President; Warren Reeves, Consulting Engineer; Amy Brown, Broadcast Operations Director.

Jupiter—WALO-LP, Ch. 53, Spirit Productions Inc. Phone: 561-746-0170.

Technical Facilities: 40-kw ERP, 436-ft. above ground, 454-ft. above sea level, lat. 26° 35′ 20″, long. 80° 12′ 43″.

Began Operation: April 30, 1990.

Ownership: Spirit Productions Inc.

Key West—W05CJ, Ch. 5, James J. Chladek. Phone: 212-686-5386.

Technical Facilities: 0.59-kw ERP, 75-ft. above ground, 86-ft. above sea level, lat. 24° 33′ 18″, long. 81° 48′ 05″.

Ownership: James J. Chladek.

Key West—W10CQ, Ch. 10, James J. Chladek. Phone: 212-686-5386.

Technical Facilities: 0.66-kw ERP, 80-ft. above ground, 91-ft. above sea level, lat. 24° 33′ 18″, long. 81° 48′ 05″.

Ownership: James J. Chladek.

Key West—W16CL, Ch. 16, Prism Broadcasting Network Inc. Phone: 770-953-3232.

Technical Facilities: 1.8-kw ERP, 151-ft. above ground, 162-ft. above sea level, lat. 24° 33′ 18″, long. 81° 48′ 05″.

Began Operation: October 2, 2008.

Ownership: Prism Broadcasting Network Inc.

Key West—W25DQ, Ch. 25, Prism Broadcasting Network Inc. Phone: 770-953-3232.

Technical Facilities: 2.8-kw ERP, 118-ft. above ground, 120-ft. above sea level, lat. 24° 35′ 44″, long. 81° 39′ 37″.

Ownership: Prism Broadcasting Network Inc.

Key West—W39AC, Ch. 39, Mapale LLC. Phone: 202-457-7040.

Technical Facilities: 0.4-kw ERP, 90-ft. above ground, 101-ft. above sea level, lat. 24° 33′ 18″, long. 81° 48′ 05″.

Ownership: Cumbia Entertainment LLC.

Key West—W44AC, Ch. 44, Miranda Broadcasting Co. of Key West LLC. Phone: 954-709-8207.

Technical Facilities: 2.2-kw ERP, 151-ft. above ground, 162-ft. above sea level, lat. 24° 34′ 58″, long. 81° 46′ 00″.

Ownership: Miranda Broadcasting Co. of Key West LLC.

■**Key West**—WCAY-LP, Ch. 34, Beach TV Properties Inc. Phone: 850-234-2773.

Technical Facilities: 4.62-kw ERP, lat. 24° 34′ 17″, long. 81° 44′ 20″.

Holds CP for change to channel number 36, 5.44-kw ERP, 135-ft. above ground, 138-ft. above sea level, lat. 24° 34′ 05″, long. 81° 44′ 03″. BPTTA-20050610AHT.

Began Operation: December 8, 1986.

Ownership: Beach TV Properties Inc.

Key West—WEYW-LP, Ch. 19, New Colonial Broadcasting LLC. Phone: 304-222-5063.

Technical Facilities: 2-kw ERP, 46-ft. above ground, 56-ft. above sea level, lat. 24° 33′ 37″, long. 81° 47′ 51″.

Ownership: New Colonial Broadcasting LLC.

Key West—WGAY-LP, Ch. 41, Paradise TV LLC. Phone: 941-349-2165.

Studio: 1107 Keys Plz, Ste 282, Key West, FL 33040.

Technical Facilities: 10-kw ERP, 84-ft. above ground, 87-ft. above sea level, lat. 24° 34′ 19.5″, long. 81° 44′ 24.7″.

Began Operation: January 6, 2006.

Ownership: Paradise TV LLC.

Personnel: Jason Sherwood, General Manager.

Key West—WGZT-LP, Ch. 27, Global Broadcast Network Inc. Phone: 213-617-0892.

Technical Facilities: 4-kw ERP, 11-ft. above ground, 115-ft. above sea level, lat. 24° 33′ 07″, long. 81° 47′ 53″.

Holds CP for change to channel number 51, 10-kw ERP, 73-ft. above ground, 76-ft. above sea level, lat. 24° 34′ 19.5″, long. 81° 44′ 24.7″. BDISTTL-20060929AKI.

Transmitter: 0.4-mi. N of Federal Hwy. 1, W. Summerland Key, Big Pine.

Ownership: Global Broadcast Network Inc.

Key West—WKIZ-LP, Ch. 49, Cayo Hueso Networks LLC. Phone: 303-688-5162.

Technical Facilities: 2.2-kw ERP, 143-ft. above ground, 149-ft. above sea level, lat. 24° 34′ 04″, long. 81° 44′ 55″.

Ownership: Cayo Hueso Networks LLC.

Key West—WTVK-LP, Ch. 31, Mary Sparacio. Phone: 305-849-2188.

Technical Facilities: 0.5-kw ERP, 20-ft. above ground, 30-ft. above sea level, lat. 24° 34′ 24.5″, long. 81° 44′ 56.3″.

Ownership: Mary Sparacio.

■**Kissimmee**—WKME-CA, Ch. 15, ZGS Broadcasting of Orlando Inc. Phone: 703-528-5656.

Technical Facilities: 50-kw ERP, 315-ft. above ground, 417-ft. above sea level, lat. 28° 21′ 31″, long. 81° 30′ 45″.

Holds CP for change to 15-kw ERP, BDFCDTA-20080804ABP.

Began Operation: October 25, 1993.

Ownership: ZGS Broadcasting Holdings Inc.

Lake City—WMYG-LP, Ch. 11, New Age Media of Gainesville License LLC. Phone: 570-824-7895.

Technical Facilities: 3-kw ERP, 400-ft. above ground, 575-ft. above sea level, lat. 30° 12′ 50″, long. 82° 39′ 00″.

Ownership: New Age Media.

Personnel: Harvey M. Budd, General Manager.

Lakeland—WLWA-LP, Ch. 14, Tri-Media Group Inc. Phone: 407-682-7195.

Technical Facilities: 7.59-kw ERP, 276-ft. above ground, 423-ft. above sea level, lat. 28° 03′ 02″, long. 81° 47′ 58″.

Holds CP for change to channel number 31, 11.18-kw ERP, 394-ft. above ground, 535-ft. above sea level, lat. 28° 00′ 10″, long. 81° 45′ 25″. BDISTTL-20060912AAM.

Ownership: Tri Media Group Inc.

Largo, etc.—WPDS-LD, Ch. 14, Pinellas County Schools. Phone: 727-588-6402. Fax: 727-588-6347.

Studio: 301 4th St. SW, Largo, FL 33770.

Technical Facilities: 3.448-kw ERP, 49-ft. above ground, 167-ft. above sea level, lat. 27° 54′ 51″, long. 82° 47′ 37″.

Ownership: Pinellas County Schools.

Personnel: Brian Abe, General Manager; Richard Mahoney, Chief Engineer.

Lealman—W43CE, Ch. 43, Mako Communications LLC. Phone: 361-883-1763.

Technical Facilities: 45-kw ERP, 591-ft. above ground, 600-ft. above sea level, lat. 28° 02′ 21″, long. 83° 39′ 20″.

Ownership: Mako Communications LLC.

Madison—W03AO, Ch. 3, Thomas H. Greene Jr. & Ann K. Nixon. Phone: 850-973-4141.

Technical Facilities: 10-w TPO, 0.0313-kw ERP, 150-ft. above ground, 350-ft. above sea level, lat. 30° 28′ 57″, long. 83° 24′ 16″.

Transmitter: 0.24-mi. S of Madison on Hwy. 53.

Ownership: Ann K. Nixon; Thomas H. Greene Jr.

Marathon—W21CL, Ch. 21, Mapale LLC. Phone: 202-457-7040.

Technical Facilities: 85-kw ERP, 245-ft. above ground, 249-ft. above sea level, lat. 24° 46′ 02″, long. 80° 56′ 42″.

Ownership: Cumbia Entertainment LLC.

Marathon—W38AA, Ch. 38, Mapale LLC. Phone: 202-457-7040.

Technical Facilities: 1.6-kw ERP, 151-ft. above ground, 154-ft. above sea level, lat. 24° 41′ 28″, long. 81° 06′ 30″.

Ownership: Cumbia Entertainment LLC.

Marathon—W63AL, Ch. 63, Mapale LLC. Phone: 202-457-7040.

Technical Facilities: 0.17-kw ERP, 151-ft. above ground, 154-ft. above sea level, lat. 24° 41′ 28″, long. 81° 06′ 30″.

Ownership: Cumbia Entertainment LLC.

Marathon—WDFL-LP, Ch. 48, Paramount Broadcasting Communications LLC. Phone: 754-422-1719.

Technical Facilities: 12.2-kw ERP, 115-ft. above ground, 119-ft. above sea level, lat. 24° 46′ 02″, long. 80° 56′ 41″.

Holds CP for change to 118-ft. above ground, 121-ft. above sea level, BPTTL-20061025AAE.

Ownership: Francois Leconte.

Matecumbe—W40AA, Ch. 16, Luna Digital Television LLC. Phone: 303-688-5162.

Technical Facilities: 47.7-kw ERP, 394-ft. above ground, 404-ft. above sea level, lat. 25° 05′ 29″, long. 80° 26′ 37″.

Ownership: Cayo Hueso Networks LLC.

Matecumbe—W43AD, Ch. 43, Cayo Hueso Networks LLC. Phone: 303-688-5162.

Technical Facilities: 3.34-kw ERP, lat. 24° 54′ 18″, long. 80° 38′ 56″.

Ownership: Cayo Hueso Networks LLC.

Matecumbe—W43CB, Ch. 43, Ministerio Oscar Aguero Inc. Phone: 305-826-5555.

Technical Facilities: 120.5-kw ERP, 984-ft. above ground, 991-ft. above sea level, lat. 25° 32′ 24″, long. 80° 28′ 09″.

Holds CP for change to 3-kw ERP, BDFCDTL-20090203ABA.

Began Operation: November 2, 1983.

Ownership: Ministerio Oscar Aguero Inc.

Matecumbe—W57DU-D, Ch. 57, Cayo Hueso Networks LLC. Phone: 303-688-5162.

Technical Facilities: 15-kw ERP, 902-ft. above ground, 910-ft. above sea level, lat. 25° 32′ 24″, long. 80° 28′ 07″.

Began Operation: February 23, 2009.

Ownership: Cayo Hueso Networks LLC.

Maxville—WUJF-LP, Ch. 15, Word of God Fellowship Inc. Phone: 817-571-1229.

Technical Facilities: 150-kw ERP, 974-ft. above ground, 984-ft. above sea level, lat. 30° 16′ 51″, long. 81° 34′ 12″.

Began Operation: April 3, 1997.

Ownership: Word of God Fellowship Inc.

Mayo—W32DI, Ch. 32, Robert William Carr. Phone: 352-373-5752.

Technical Facilities: 150-kw ERP, 331-ft. above ground, 374-ft. above sea level, lat. 30° 00' 40", long. 83° 01' 51".

Holds CP for change to 15-kw ERP, 407-ft. above ground, 463-ft. above sea level, lat. 29° 36' 29", long. 82° 51' 01". BDFCDTL-20090408ABY.

Ownership: Robert William Carr.

Melbourne—W26BN, Ch. 26, TDI Acquisition Corp. Phone: 703-433-4000.

Technical Facilities: 4.4-kw ERP, 489-ft. above ground, 512-ft. above sea level, lat. 28° 08' 14", long. 80° 42' 11".

Ownership: Sprint Nextel Corp.

Melbourne—W32DJ-D, Ch. 32, Three Angels Broadcasting Network Inc. Phone: 618-627-4651. Fax: 618-627-4155.

Studio: 3391 Charley Good Rd, West Frankfort, IL 62896.

Technical Facilities: 1.5-kw ERP, 492-ft. above ground, 514-ft. above sea level, lat. 28° 08' 12.2", long. 80° 42' 12.6".

Ownership: Three Angels Broadcasting Network Inc.

Personnel: Moses Primo, Chief Engineer.

Melbourne—W47DA, Ch. 47, Entravision Holdings LLC. Phone: 310-447-3870.

Technical Facilities: 9.5-kw ERP, 131-ft. above ground, 4498-ft. above sea level, lat. 34° 36' 43.6", long. 117° 17' 28.9".

Began Operation: February 11, 1993.

Ownership: Entravision Communications Corp.

■ **Melbourne**—WMVJ-CA, Ch. 29, ZGS Broadcasting of Orlando Inc. Phone: 703-528-5656.

Technical Facilities: 1000-w TPO, 7.96-kw ERP, 489-ft. above ground, 512-ft. above sea level, lat. 28° 08' 14", long. 80° 42' 11".

Holds CP for change to 15-kw ERP, 417-ft. above ground, 442-ft. above sea level, lat. 28° 02' 49", long. 80° 40' 34". BDFCDTA-20080804AAZ.

Transmitter: 1865 Harlock Rd.

Ownership: ZGS Broadcasting Holdings Inc.

Melbourne—WSCF-LP, Ch. 31, James J. Chladek. Phone: 321-728-9834.

Studio: 1700 W New Haven Ave, Ste 199, Melbourne, FL 32907.

Technical Facilities: 745-w TPO, 10-kw ERP, 284-ft. above ground, 308-ft. above sea level, lat. 28° 08' 57", long. 80° 42' 15".

Transmitter: 2601 Harlock Rd.

Ownership: James J. Chladek.

Personnel: James Chladek, Chief Engineer.

Miami—W49CL, Ch. 49, Mapale LLC. Phone: 202-457-7040.

Technical Facilities: 75-kw ERP, 800-ft. above ground, 811-ft. above sea level, lat. 25° 59' 09", long. 80° 11' 37".

Ownership: Cumbia Entertainment LLC.

Miami—WEYS-LP, Ch. 56, AlmaVision Hispanic Network Inc. Phone: 213-627-8711.

Technical Facilities: 150-kw ERP, 804-ft. above ground, 809-ft. above sea level, lat. 25° 58' 15", long. 80° 12' 32".

Holds CP for change to channel number 6, 0.2-kw ERP, 217-ft. above ground, 226-ft. above sea level, lat. 25° 52' 24", long. 80° 28' 59". BDISTVL-20080501ACP.

Ownership: AlmaVision Hispanic Network Inc.

Miami—WGEN-LP, Ch. 30, Mapale LLC. Phone: 202-457-7040.

Technical Facilities: 138.2-kw ERP, 543-ft. above ground, 553-ft. above sea level, lat. 25° 46' 29", long. 80° 11' 19".

Ownership: Cumbia Entertainment LLC.

Miami—WHDT-LP, Ch. 44, Guenter Marksteiner. Phone: 561-983-6300.

Technical Facilities: 15-kw ERP, 900-ft. above ground, 905-ft. above sea level, lat. 25° 58' 15", long. 80° 12' 32".

Transmitter: 350 NW 215th St, N. Miami.

Ownership: Guenter Marksteiner.

■ **Miami**—WIMP-CA, Ch. 25, Sunshine Broadcasting Co. Inc. Phone: 603-279-4440.

Technical Facilities: 150-kw ERP, 801-ft. above ground, 811-ft. above sea level, lat. 25° 59' 09", long. 80° 11' 37".

Transmitter: 200 S. Biscayne Blvd.

Ownership: Sunshine Broadcasting Co. Inc.

■ **Miami**—WJAN-CA, Ch. 41, Sherjan Broadcasting Co. Inc. Phone: 305-592-4141. Fax: 305-592-3808.

Technical Facilities: 4000-w TPO, 101.2-kw ERP, 512-ft. above ground, 521-ft. above sea level, lat. 25° 46' 24", long. 80° 25' 22".

Transmitter: 0.87-mi. N of intersection of Tamiami Trail & S.W. 139th Ave., Sweetwater.

Multichannel TV Sound: Stereo only.

Ownership: Sherjan Broadcasting Co. Inc.

Personnel: Sherwin Grossman, President & Chief Executive Officer; Omar Romay, General Manager; Herb Esrino, General Sales Manager; Julio DeFrancesco, Chief Engineer & Director of Operations.

Miami—WLMF-LP, Ch. 53, Paging Systems Inc. Phone: 650-697-1000.

Technical Facilities: 15.8-kw ERP, 880-ft. above ground, 884-ft. above sea level, lat. 25° 58' 15", long. 80° 12' 32".

Ownership: Paging Systems Inc.

■ **Miami**—WPMF-LP, Ch. 38, James J. Chladek. Phone: 305-379-7610. Fax: 305-374-3586.

Studio: 555 NE 15th St, 7th Fl, Miami, FL 33132.

Technical Facilities: 14-kw ERP, 602-ft. above ground, 613-ft. above sea level, lat. 25° 46' 19", long. 80° 11' 31".

Transmitter: Knight Center, 100 S.E. 2nd Ave.

Ownership: James J. Chladek.

Personnel: Corrie Medor, Chief Engineer.

■ **Miami**—WSBS-CA, Ch. 50, WSBS Licensing Inc. Phones: 305-441-6901; 305-644-4800.

Studio: 9130 S Dadeland Blvd, No. 1612, Miami, FL 33156.

Technical Facilities: 126.9-kw ERP, 768-ft. above ground, 779-ft. above sea level, lat. 25° 59' 09", long. 80° 11' 37".

Began Operation: July 6, 1994.

Ownership: Spanish Broadcasting System Inc.

Personnel: Haydely Rodriguez, General Manager; Raymond Bell Jr., Chief Engineer.

Miami—WVFW-LP, Ch. 34, Claro Communications Ltd. Phone: 361-774-4354.

Technical Facilities: 120-kw ERP, 820-ft. above ground, 830-ft. above sea level, lat. 25° 59' 34", long. 80° 10' 27".

Holds CP for change to 15-kw ERP, 853-ft. above sea level, 860-ft. above sea level, BDFCDTL-20080812ABB.

Ownership: Gerald G. Benavides.

Miami, etc.—WFUN-LP, Ch. 48, CaribeVision Station Group LLC. Phone: 305-365-2030.

Technical Facilities: 150-kw ERP, 643-ft. above ground, 654-ft. above sea level, lat. 25° 59' 09", long. 80° 11' 37".

Holds CP for change to 15-kw ERP, BMPDTL-20070423ABK.

Multichannel TV Sound: Stereo and separate audio program.

Ownership: CaribeVision Holdings Inc.

Personnel: J. Rudger Skinner Jr., General Manager & Sales Manager; Loren Matthews, Chief Engineer.

Naples—W16CJ, Ch. 16, Trinity Broadcasting Network. Phone: 714-832-2950. Fax: 714-730-0661.

Technical Facilities: 26.6-kw ERP, 239-ft. above ground, sea above sea level, lat. 26° 12' 12", long. 81° 48' 54".

Transmitter: 4301 Gulf Shore Blvd N.

Ownership: Trinity Broadcasting Network Inc.

■ **Naples**—WBSP-CA, Ch. 7, EBC Southwest Florida Inc., Debtor in Possession. Phone: 501-219-2400.

Technical Facilities: 0.573-kw ERP, 381-ft. above ground, 407-ft. above sea level, lat. 26° 25' 22", long. 81° 37' 49".

Began Operation: August 2, 1990.

Ownership: Equity Media Holdings Corp., Debtor in Possession.

■ **Naples**—WUVF-CA, Ch. 2, SP Fort Myers LLC. Phone: 203-542-4200.

Technical Facilities: 3-kw ERP, 699-ft. above ground, 714-ft. above sea level, lat. 26° 19' 00", long. 81° 47' 13".

Began Operation: June 12, 1996.

Ownership: SP Television LLC.

Personnel: Warren Reeves, General Manager; Jessee Coleman, Chief Engineer.

■ **Naples**—WWDT-CA, Ch. 43, ZGS of Fort Myers-Naples Inc. Phone: 703-528-5656.

Technical Facilities: 144-kw ERP, 403-ft. above ground, 413-ft. above sea level, lat. 26° 30' 17.7", long. 81° 51' 13.7".

Holds CP for change to 15-kw ERP, BDFCDTA-20080804ABA.

Ownership: ZGS Broadcasting Holdings Inc.

Naples—WXDT-LP, Ch. 23, Guenter Marksteiner. Phones: 561-471-9200; 239-263-0450.

Technical Facilities: 1000-w TPO, 17-kw ERP, 226-ft. above ground, 233-ft. above sea level, lat. 26° 12' 07", long. 81° 48' 49".

Transmitter: 4451 Gulf Shore Blvd.

Multichannel TV Sound: Stereo and separate audio program.

Ownership: Guenter Marksteiner.

Personnel: Sonia DeBerle, General Manager; Gunter Marksteiner, Chief Engineer.

■ **Naples**—WYDT-CA, Ch. 32, Guenter Marksteiner. Phones: 561-471-9200; 239-263-0450.

Technical Facilities: 1000-w TPO, 20.5-kw ERP, 226-ft. above ground, 233-ft. above sea level, lat. 26° 12' 07", long. 81° 48' 49".

Transmitter: 4451 Gulf Shore Blvd.

Multichannel TV Sound: Stereo and separate audio program.

Ownership: Guenter Marksteiner.

Personnel: Sonia DeBeale, General Manager; Gunter Marksteiner, Chief Engineer.

Naples—WZDT-LP, Ch. 39, Guenter Marksteiner. Phone: 561-471-9200.

Technical Facilities: 20-kw ERP, 224-ft. above ground, 231-ft. above sea level, lat. 26° 12' 07", long. 81° 48' 49".

Ownership: Guenter Marksteiner.

Ocala—W07BP-D, Ch. 7, Marion County Public Schools. Phones: 352-620-7763; 352-671-7568. Fax: 352-620-7788.

Technical Facilities: 0.3-kw ERP, 295-ft. above ground, 413-ft. above sea level, lat. 29° 10' 57", long. 82° 08' 00".

Began Operation: October 9, 1984.

Ownership: Marion County Public Schools.

Personnel: Doug Joiner, General Manager; Gary Almgren, Chief Engineer.

Ocala—W29AB, Ch. 29, Post-Newsweek Stations Orlando Inc. Phone: 407-521-1200.

Technical Facilities: 15.9-kw ERP, lat. 29° 06' 05", long. 82° 07' 02".

Holds CP for change to channel number 42, 55-kw ERP, 415-ft. above ground, 489-ft. above sea level, lat. 29° 16' 11", long. 82° 11' 20". BDISTT-20070103AEI.

Transmitter: 8240 S.E. 16th Ave.

Ownership: Post-Newsweek Stations Inc.

■ **Oldsmar**—WZRA-CA, Ch. 48, Amka Broadcast Network Inc. Phones: 727-725-3500; 813-814-7575. Fax: 813-855-4100.

Technical Facilities: 150-kw ERP, 302-ft. above ground, 302-ft. above sea level, lat. 28° 15' 32", long. 82° 43' 45".

Ownership: Amka Broadcast Network Inc.

Personnel: Sotirios Agelatos, President; Sam Agelatos, General Manager.

Orient City—W15CM, Ch. 15, Mako Communications LLC. Phone: 361-883-1763.

Technical Facilities: 49-kw ERP, 397-ft. above ground, 446-ft. above sea level, lat. 27° 59' 37", long. 82° 24' 46".

Holds CP for change to 5-kw ERP, BDFCDTL-20090515ABO.

Ownership: Mako Communications LLC.

Orlando—W21AU, Ch. 21, Central Broadcast Co. Phone: 407-224-5521.

Technical Facilities: 1000-w TPO, 8.35-kw ERP, 499-ft. above ground, 594-ft. above sea level, lat. 28° 36' 23", long. 81° 27' 11".

Holds CP for change to 482-ft. above ground, 590-ft. above sea level, lat. 28° 36' 23", long. 81° 27' 24". BDFCDTL-20080826AAO.

Transmitter: Lake Sparling Rd., Orlando.

Ownership: Central Broadcast Co.

Orlando—WAWA-LP, Ch. 47, Del Caribe Orlando LLC. Phone: 828-859-6982.

Technical Facilities: 700-w TPO, 10.87-kw ERP, 400-ft. above ground, 508-ft. above sea level, lat. 28° 38' 46", long. 81° 30' 05".

Holds CP for change to 10-kw ERP, 407-ft. above ground, 495-ft. above sea level, lat. 28° 22' 01", long. 81° 23' 13". BMPDTL-20090320ABS.

Transmitter: 2121 S. Clarcona Rd., Apopka.

Began Operation: November 16, 1994.

Ownership: Del Caribe Orlando LLC.

Personnel: Otoniel Font, General Manager; Robert Sanchez, Chief Engineer.

Orlando—WDTO-LP, Ch. 50, Word of God Fellowship Inc. Phone: 817-571-1229.

Technical Facilities: 87-kw ERP, 646-ft. above ground, 771-ft. above sea level, lat. 28° 33' 34", long. 81° 35' 38".

Holds CP for change to channel number 28, 15-kw ERP, 541-ft. above ground, 607-ft. above sea level, lat. 28° 34' 51", long. 81° 04' 32". BDISDTL-20080507ACB.

Ownership: Word of God Fellowship Inc.

■ **Orlando**—WFOL-LP, Ch. 4, Native Country Broadcasting Corp. Phone: 772-562-1020.

Technical Facilities: 80-w TPO, 0.078-kw ERP, 249-ft. above ground, 335-ft. above sea level, lat. 28° 36' 22", long. 81° 17' 20".

Transmitter: Aloma Ave. & Forsyth Rd., Winter Park.

Ownership: Native Country Broadcasting Corp.

■ **Orlando**—WHDO-CA, Ch. 38, Digital TV of Orlando LLC. Phone: 517-206-0404.

Technical Facilities: 75-kw ERP, 259-ft. above ground, 348-ft. above sea level, lat. 28° 25' 30", long. 81° 27' 50".

Holds CP for change to 108-kw ERP, 443-ft. above ground, 533-ft. above sea level, lat. 28° 22' 01", long. 81° 23' 13". BPTTA-20080804AFI.

Ownership: Local HDTV Inc.

Orlando—WOKB-LP, Ch. 7, Rama Communications II Ltd.

Technical Facilities: 180-w TPO, 0.068-kw ERP, 420-ft. above ground, 528-ft. above sea level, lat. 28° 32' 22", long. 81° 22' 46".

Transmitter: Sun Bank Tower, 200 S. Orange.

Ownership: Rama Communications.

■ **Orlando**—WRCF-LP, Ch. 29, Charles S. Namey.

Technical Facilities: 307-w TPO, 5-kw ERP, 427-ft. above ground, 535-ft. above sea level, lat. 28° 32' 25", long. 81° 22' 46".

Transmitter: Sun Trust Bldg.

Ownership: OD TV Communications Inc.

■ **Orlando**—WTMO-CA, Ch. 31, ZGS Broadcasting of Orlando Inc. Phone: 703-528-5656.

Technical Facilities: 912-w TPO, 30-kw ERP, 400-ft. above ground, 511-ft. above sea level, lat. 28° 36' 23", long. 81° 27' 11".

Holds CP for change to 6.7-kw ERP, 407-ft. above ground, 512-ft. above sea level, lat. 28° 36' 21", long. 81° 27' 26". BDFCDTA-20080804ACU.

Transmitter: Lake Sparling Rd.

Ownership: ZGS Broadcasting Holdings Inc.

Personnel: Frank D. Tenore, General Manager; David T. Hall, Chief Engineer.

Orlando—WVCI-LP, Ch. 16, Entravision Holdings LLC. Phone: 310-447-3870.

Studio: 5135 Adanson St, Ste 300, Orlando, FL 32804.

Technical Facilities: 9.2-kw ERP, 351-ft. above ground, 443-ft. above sea level, lat. 28° 35' 35", long. 81° 25' 13".

Ownership: Entravision Communications Corp.

Personnel: May Nohra, General Manager; Chuck Seithel, Chief Engineer; Paul Gomache, Sales Manager.

■ **Orlando**—WZXZ-CA, Ch. 36, CaribeVision Station Group LLC. Phone: 305-565-2030.

Studio: 1800 Pembrook Dr, Ste 400, Orlando, FL 32810.

Technical Facilities: 23-kw ERP, 550-ft. above ground, 615-ft. above sea level, lat. 28° 34' 52", long. 81° 04' 31".

Multichannel TV Sound: Stereo only.

Ownership: CaribeVision Holdings Inc.

Personnel: Liz Kiley, Broadcast Vice President; Warren Reeves, Consulting Engineer; Amy Brown, Broadcast Operations Director.

■ **Palatka**—WJGV-LP, Ch. 48, Pentecostal Revival Assn. Inc. Phones: 386-325-5854; 386-325-6323. Fax: 386-325-8626.

Studio: S. State Rd. 19, Palatka, FL 32177.

Technical Facilities: 1000-w TPO, 22-kw ERP, 356-ft. above ground, 371-ft. above sea level, lat. 29° 35' 48", long. 81° 41' 59".

Holds CP for change to 1.8-kw ERP, 344-ft. above ground, 358-ft. above sea level, BDFCDTL-20080306ABS.

Transmitter: 5.47-mi. SW of Palatka.

Began Operation: November 26, 1991.

Ownership: Pentecostal Revival Assn. Inc.

Personnel: Rev. Dolly Harrell, General Manager; James L. Harrell Jr., Chief Engineer.

■ **Palm Beach**—WTCN-CA, Ch. 43, WPB TV Licensee Corp. Phone: 801-973-5402.

Technical Facilities: 150-kw ERP, 890-ft. above ground, 890-ft. above sea level, lat. 27° 01' 31", long. 80° 10' 43".

Holds CP for change to channel number 50, 1435-ft. above ground, 1464-ft. above sea level, lat. 27° 07' 19", long. 80° 23' 20". BDISTTA-20080804ADZ.

Began Operation: October 25, 1988.

Ownership: Four Points Media Group Holding LLC.

Personnel: Arika Zink, Vice President & General Manager; Larry A. Most, General Sales Manager.

Panama City—W12DE, Ch. 12, Gabriela Lopez Sanchez. Phone: 949-645-4786.

Technical Facilities: 1-kw ERP, 16-ft. above ground, 39-ft. above sea level, lat. 30° 13' 30", long. 85° 37' 20".

Ownership: Gabriela Lopez Sanchez.

Panama City—W26BV, Ch. 26, Breeze Broadcast Corp. LLC. Phone: 305-937-1010.

Technical Facilities: 120-w TPO, 1-kw ERP, 325-ft. above ground, 339-ft. above sea level, lat. 30° 24' 41", long. 86° 37' 28".

Holds CP for change to 150-kw ERP, 620-ft. above ground, 656-ft. above sea level, lat. 30° 24' 13", long. 86° 59' 34". BPTTL-20060818AAN.

Transmitter: 1-mi. N of Shalimar.

Ownership: Breeze Broadcast Corp. LLC.

Panama City—W30CF, Ch. 30, Tidalwave Holdings Inc. Phone: 888-620-6815.

Technical Facilities: 40-kw ERP, 295-ft. above ground, 331-ft. above sea level, lat. 30° 11' 42", long. 85° 37' 51".

Holds CP for change to 150-kw ERP, 328-ft. above ground, 394-ft. above sea level, lat. 30° 21' 14", long. 85° 54' 27". BPTTL-20080108ABX.

Ownership: Tidalwave Holdings Inc.

Panama City—W34DH, Ch. 34, Trinity Broadcasting Network Inc. Phone: 714-832-2950. Fax: 714-730-0661.

Technical Facilities: 5000-w TPO, 2.1-kw ERP, 175-ft. above ground, 211-ft. above sea level, lat. 30° 11' 41", long. 85° 37' 51".

Holds CP for change to 15-kw ERP, BDFCDTT-20060330AAS.

Transmitter: 3099 Ormond Ave., Hiland Park.

Ownership: Trinity Broadcasting Network Inc.

Panama City—W40BU, Ch. 40, Ralph Fytton. Phone: 954-782-6393.

Technical Facilities: 20.51-kw ERP, 308-ft. above ground, 360-ft. above sea level, lat. 30° 19' 41", long. 85° 41' 22".

Ownership: Ralph Fytton.

Panama City—W46AN, Ch. 46, Beach TV Properties Inc. Phone: 904-234-2773.

Technical Facilities: 1000-w TPO, 13.2-kw ERP, 148-ft. above ground, 158-ft. above sea level, lat. 30° 08' 50", long. 85° 45' 43".

Transmitter: 5801 Thomas Dr., Panama City.

Ownership: Beach TV Properties Inc.

Panama City—W50BP, Ch. 50, Tiger Eye Broadcasting Corp. Phone: 954-431-3144.

Technical Facilities: 1000-w TPO, 2.986-kw ERP, 162-ft. above ground, 180-ft. above sea level, lat. 30° 10' 49", long. 85° 42' 05".

Holds CP for change to channel number 44, 50-kw ERP, 290-ft. above ground, 308-ft. above sea level, lat. 30° 11' 41", long. 85° 50' 01". BDISTTL-20060306BCD.

Transmitter: 3101 W. Hwy. 98.

Ownership: Tiger Eye Broadcasting Corp.

Panama City—WCTU-LD, Ch. 46, Randall A. Weiss. Phone: 972-271-3750.

Technical Facilities: 15-kw ERP, 270-ft. above ground, 381-ft. above sea level, lat. 30° 28' 31.5", long. 87° 15' 16.2".

Holds CP for change to 5-kw ERP, 65-ft. above ground, 110-ft. above sea level, lat. 30° 24' 42", long. 86° 46' 02". BDFCDTL-20080201COZ.

Ownership: Randall A. Weiss.

Panama City—WDWY-LP, Ch. 14, Tidalwave Holdings Inc. Phone: 888-620-6815.

Technical Facilities: 98-w TPO, 1-kw ERP, 405-ft. above ground, 344-ft. above sea level, lat. 30° 10' 44", long. 85° 46' 55".

Transmitter: Laurie & Laird Rds.

Ownership: Tidalwave Holdings Inc.

Personnel: Jackson Mitchell, General Manager & Sales Manager; Bryan Baker, Chief Engineer.

Panama City—WEWA-LP, Ch. 17, Global Outreach Ministry Network Inc. Phone: 850-932-6412.

Technical Facilities: 131-w TPO, 1-kw ERP, 239-ft. above ground, 256-ft. above sea level, lat. 30° 11' 00", long. 85° 46' 33".

Holds CP for change to 150-kw ERP, 453-ft. above ground, 492-ft. above sea level, lat. 30° 08' 33", long. 85° 25' 28". BPTTL-20070305AAA.

Transmitter: Laurie & Laird Rds.

Ownership: Global Outreach Ministry Network Inc.

Panama City—WGOM-LP, Ch. 10, Global Outreach Ministry Network Inc. Phones: 850-932-6412; 800-489-9006.

Technical Facilities: 3-kw ERP, 463-ft. above ground, 515-ft. above sea level, lat. 30° 19' 41", long. 85° 41' 22".

Ownership: Global Outreach Ministry Network Inc.

Panama City—WHDY-LP, Ch. 6, Confesora Peralta. Phone: 718-801-3707.

Technical Facilities: 1-kw ERP, 16-ft. above ground, 69-ft. above sea level, lat. 30° 19' 42", long. 85° 41' 22".

Began Operation: May 2, 2007.

Ownership: Confesora Peralta.

Panama City—WPAF-LP, Ch. 2, Marcia T. Turner. Phone: 954-732-9539.

Technical Facilities: 0.127-kw ERP, 151-ft. above ground, 180-ft. above sea level, lat. 30° 08' 51", long. 85° 35' 36".

Holds CP for change to channel number 39, 75-kw ERP, BDISTTL-20060403ARH.

Ownership: Marcia T. Turner.

Panama City—WPCY-LP, Ch. 26, Tiger Eye Broadcasting Corp. Phone: 954-431-3144.

Technical Facilities: 67.6-kw ERP, 615-ft. above ground, 699-ft. above sea level, lat. 30° 21' 08", long. 85° 23' 28".

Transmitter: 3101 W. Hwy. 98.

Multichannel TV Sound: Stereo only.

Ownership: Tiger Eye Broadcasting Corp.

■ **Panama City**—WPFN-CA, Ch. 22, Beach TV Properties Inc.

Technical Facilities: 1000-w TPO, 17.1-kw ERP, 190-ft. above ground, 207-ft. above sea level, lat. 30° 10' 59", long. 85° 46' 42".

Transmitter: 5801 Thomas Dr.

Ownership: Beach TV Properties Inc.

Panama City—WXPC-LP, Ch. 23, Michael Mintz. Phone: 361-883-1763.

Technical Facilities: 20.51-kw ERP, 164-ft. above ground, 190-ft. above sea level, lat. 30° 08' 55", long. 85° 35' 45".

Ownership: Michael Mintz.

Pensacola—W19CO, Ch. 19, Ventana Television Inc. Phones: 805-969-6664; 727-872-4210.

Technical Facilities: 2000-w TPO, 23.6-kw ERP, 282-ft. above ground, 387-ft. above sea level, lat. 30° 30' 52", long. 87° 17' 46".

Transmitter: 8150 Ashland Ave., Pensacola.

Began Operation: April 28, 1993.

Ownership: Ventana Television Inc.

Pensacola—W39BP, Ch. 39, Pensacola ACTS Inc. Phone: 904-476-2203.

Technical Facilities: 1000-w TPO, 10.1-kw ERP, 250-ft. above ground, 358-ft. above sea level, lat. 30° 30' 50", long. 87° 13' 45".

Transmitter: E corner of the junction of Harold Ave. & Debby Ave.

Ownership: Pensacola ACTS Inc.

■ **Pensacola**—WBQP-CA, Ch. 12, Vernon Watson. Phone: 850-433-1210. Fax: 850-433-2537.

Studio: 3101 N R St, Pensacola, FL 32505.

Technical Facilities: 3-kw ERP, 281-ft. above ground, 392-ft. above sea level, lat. 30° 28' 31.5", long. 87° 15' 16.2".

Multichannel TV Sound: Stereo and separate audio program.

Began Operation: May 18, 1992.

Ownership: Vernon Watson.

Personnel: Vernon Watson, General Manager; David Monard, Chief Engineer; Gary Montgomery, Sales Manager.

■ **Pensacola**—WRBD-LP, Ch. 8, Upper Gulf Coast LLC. Phone: 361-289-0126.

Technical Facilities: 80-w TPO, 0.116-kw ERP, 397-ft. above ground, 482-ft. above sea level, lat. 30° 26' 43", long. 87° 14' 37".

Transmitter: 1301 N. R St.

Ownership: Upper Gulf Coast LLC.

Perry—WSFD-LP, Ch. 18, Dockins Communications Inc. Phone: 573-701-9590.

Studio: Balthrasher Rd, Perry, FL 32347.

Technical Facilities: 150-kw ERP, 269-ft. above ground, 328-ft. above sea level, lat. 30° 08' 00", long. 83° 35' 45".

Ownership: Dockins Communications Inc.

■ **Pompano Beach**—WDLP-CA, Ch. 21, Mapale LLC. Phone: 202-457-7040.

Technical Facilities: 150-kw ERP, 800-ft. above ground, 811-ft. above sea level, lat. 25° 59' 09", long. 80° 11' 37".

Ownership: Cumbia Entertainment LLC.

Port Charlotte—W17CK, Ch. 17, Trinity Broadcasting Network Inc. Phone: 714-832-2950. Fax: 714-730-0661.

Technical Facilities: 1000-w TPO, 10-kw ERP, 300-ft. above ground, 318-ft. above sea level, lat. 26° 58' 48", long. 82° 04' 03".

Holds CP for change to 15-kw ERP, 299-ft. above ground, 317-ft. above sea level, BDFCDTT-20060330ABD.

Transmitter: 1.2-mi. NNE of U.S. Rte. 41 & SR 776.

Ownership: Trinity Broadcasting Network Inc.

Port St. Lucie—WSLF-LP, Ch. 35, Word of God Fellowship Inc. Phone: 817-571-1229.

Technical Facilities: 26.8-kw ERP, 400-ft. above ground, 430-ft. above sea level, lat. 27° 07' 14", long. 80° 23' 59".

Began Operation: February 2, 2005.

Ownership: Word of God Fellowship Inc.

Reddick—WOFT-LP, Ch. 8, Budd Broadcasting Co. Inc. Phone: 352-371-7772.

Technical Facilities: 3-kw ERP, 194-ft. above ground, 387-ft. above sea level, lat. 29° 21' 25", long. 82° 17' 55".

Holds CP for change to 0.3-kw ERP, 194-ft. above ground, 276-ft. above sea level, lat. 29° 16' 05.1", long. 82° 04' 50.7". BDFCDVL-20090217ACP.

Began Operation: March 7, 2008.

Ownership: Budd Broadcasting Co. Inc.

Rock Harbor—W64AN, Ch. 64, Mapale LLC. Phone: 919-839-0300.

Technical Facilities: 15-kw ERP, 902-ft. above ground, 910-ft. above sea level, lat. 25° 35' 24", long. 80° 28' 07".

Ownership: Cumbia Entertainment LLC.

Santa Rosa Beach—WGOX-LP, Ch. 41, Harvest Ministries International. Phone: 850-682-3900.

Technical Facilities: 44-kw ERP, 492-ft. above ground, 512-ft. above sea level, lat. 30° 22' 27", long. 86° 11' 20".

Holds CP for change to channel number 43, 15-kw ERP, BDISDTL-20090324ADQ.

Began Operation: May 8, 1997.

Ownership: Harvest Ministries International.

Sarasota—W05CO, Ch. 5, Three Angels Broadcasting Network Inc. Phone: 618-627-4651.

Technical Facilities: 3-kw ERP, 338-ft. above ground, 368-ft. above sea level, lat. 27° 20' 11", long. 82° 28' 18".

Ownership: Three Angels Broadcasting Network Inc.

Sarasota—W48CN, Ch. 48, Trinity Christian Center of Santa Ana Inc. Phone: 714-832-2950.

Technical Facilities: 1000-w TPO, 26-kw ERP, 486-ft. above ground, 512-ft. above sea level, lat. 27° 20' 27", long. 82° 27' 54".

Transmitter: 5205 Fruitville Rd.

Ownership: Trinity Broadcasting Network Inc.

Personnel: Mark Fountain, Chief Engineer.

Sebring—W23CN, Ch. 23, CBS Operations Inc. Phone: 202-457-4518.

Technical Facilities: 10.1-kw ERP, lat. 27° 27' 15", long. 81° 24' 22".

Holds CP for change to 5.55-kw ERP, 410-ft. above ground, 520-ft. above sea level, lat. 27° 27' 14", long. 81° 24' 23". BDFCDTT-20081006ABW.

Transmitter: Approx. 3.5-mi. SE of Sebring.

Ownership: CBS Corp.

Sebring—W51DY, Ch. 51, Trinity Broadcasting Network Inc. Phone: 714-832-2950. Fax: 714-730-0661.

Technical Facilities: 39.6-kw ERP, 279-ft. above ground, 361-ft. above sea level, lat. 27° 24' 29", long. 81° 25' 53".

Ownership: Trinity Broadcasting Network Inc.

■ **Sebring, etc.**—WHRT-CA, Ch. 17, Trianon Broadcasting Co. Inc. Phone: 262-567-7307.

Technical Facilities: 27.5-kw ERP, 376-ft. above ground, 491-ft. above sea level, lat. 27° 29' 39", long. 81° 25' 00".

Ownership: Trianon Broadcasting Co. Inc.

■ **St. Augustine**—WQXT-CA, Ch. 22, A1A TV Inc. Phone: 904-794-6774.

Technical Facilities: 1000-w TPO, 56.1-kw ERP, 374-ft. above ground, 410-ft. above sea level, lat. 29° 54' 14", long. 81° 22' 55".

Holds CP for change to 150-kw ERP, 386-ft. above ground, 425-ft. above sea level, BDISTTA-20070625AAL.

Transmitter: Industry Center Dr.

Ownership: A1A TV Inc.

St. Petersburg—W33CC, Ch. 33, Ventana Television Inc. Phones: 805-969-6664; 727-872-4210.

Technical Facilities: 630-w TPO, 3-kw ERP, 636-ft. above ground, 545-ft. above sea level, lat. 27° 50' 53", long. 82° 45' 48".

Transmitter: 8320 Starkey Rd.

Began Operation: September 26, 1990.

Ownership: Ventana Television Inc.

Personnel: John Skelnik, General Manager.

St. Petersburg—W36CO, Ch. 36, Local HDTV Inc. Phone: 517-206-0404.

Technical Facilities: 3.8-kw ERP, 279-ft. above ground, 329-ft. above sea level, lat. 28° 03' 06", long. 82° 44' 11".

Holds CP for change to 15-kw ERP, 279-ft. above ground, 320-ft. above sea level, lat. 28° 03' 15", long. 82° 44' 17". BDFCDTL-20090427AAC.

Began Operation: October 19, 1990.

Ownership: Local HDTV Inc.

Personnel: Paul F. Crouch, General Manager; Ben Miller, Chief Engineer; Rod Henke, Sales Manager.

■ **St. Petersburg**—WSPF-CA, Ch. 35, City of St. Petersburg/ICS Communications. Phones: 727-893-7050; 727-551-3211. Fax: 727-843-7173.

Studio: 175 5th St. N, St. Petersburg, FL 33701.

Technical Facilities: 28-kw ERP, 243-ft. above ground, 266-ft. above sea level, lat. 27° 46' 23", long. 82° 38' 08".

Ownership: City of St. Petersburg.

Personnel: Cathi Brake, General Manager; David Solinske, Chief Engineer.

■ **Stuart**—WWHB-CA, Ch. 48, WPB TV Licensee Corp. Phone: 212-891-2100.

Studio: 1500 NW Federal Hwy, Stuart, FL 34994.

Technical Facilities: 60-kw ERP, 890-ft. above ground, 890-ft. above sea level, lat. 27° 01' 31", long. 80° 10' 43".

Multichannel TV Sound: Stereo only.

Ownership: Four Points Media Group Holding LLC.

Personnel: Arika Zink, Vice President & General Manager; Larry A. Most, General Sales Manager; Louis Delannoy, Chief Engineer.

Summerland Key—W28CP, Ch. 28, Hosanna Apostolic Ministries Broadcasting Corp. Phone: 520-971-9274.

Technical Facilities: 60-kw ERP, 492-ft. above ground, 496-ft. above sea level, lat. 24° 40' 35", long. 81° 30' 41".

Holds CP for change to 150-kw ERP, 131-ft. above ground, 138-ft. above sea level, lat. 24° 34' 06", long. 81° 44' 54". BPTTL-20070330BIY.

Began Operation: August 3, 2006.

Ownership: Hosanna Apostolic Ministries Broadcasting Corp.

Tallahassee—W21BK, Ch. 21, Joseph W. Shaffer. Phone: 928-717-0828.

Technical Facilities: 700-w TPO, 29.5-kw ERP, 230-ft. above ground, 430-ft. above sea level, lat. 30° 29' 35", long. 84° 17' 01".

Transmitter: 3000 N. Meridian Rd.

Ownership: Joseph W. Shaffer.

Tallahassee—W35BN, Ch. 35, Deepak Viswanath. Phone: 718-781-8555.

Technical Facilities: 1000-w TPO, 20-kw ERP, 551-ft. above ground, 791-ft. above sea level, lat. 30° 29' 32", long. 84° 17' 13".

Holds CP for change to 87-kw ERP, BPTTL-20060403AAH.

Transmitter: 123 Ridgeland Rd.

Ownership: Deepak Viswanath.

Tallahassee—WACX-LP, Ch. 9, Associated Christian Television System Inc. Phone: 407-297-0155.

Technical Facilities: 0.018-kw ERP, 190-ft. above ground, 400-ft. above sea level, lat. 30° 26' 29", long. 84° 16' 55".

Ownership: Associated Christian Television System Inc.

■ **Tallahassee**—WBXT-CA, Ch. 43, L4 Media Group LLC. Phone: 321-729-8451.

Studio: 2834 Industrial Pl, Tallahassee, FL 32301.

Technical Facilities: 49-kw ERP, 499-ft. above ground, 722-ft. above sea level, lat. 30° 29' 32", long. 84° 17' 02".

Ownership: L4 Media Group LLC.

Personnel: Liz Kiley, Broadcast Vice President; Warren Reeves, Consulting Engineer; Amy Brown, Broadcast Operations Director; Mike Plummer, Program Director.

Tallahassee—WTBC-LP, Ch. 65, Temple Baptist Church Inc. Phone: 850-386-6500. Fax: 850-385-7188.

Studio: 3000 N Meridian Rd, Tallahassee, FL 32312.

Technical Facilities: 1000-w TPO, 16.9-kw ERP, 613-ft. above ground, 712-ft. above sea level, lat. 30° 29' 15", long. 84° 16' 48".

Transmitter: Near Temple Baptist Church, Tallahassee.

Multichannel TV Sound: Stereo and separate audio program.

Ownership: Temple Baptist Church Inc.

Personnel: Daniel M. Lethers, General Manager.

■ **Tallahassee**—WVUP-CA, Ch. 45, Christian Television Corp. Inc. Phones: 850-402-1116; 727-535-5622.

Studio: 4000 County Road 12, Tallahassee, FL 32312.

Technical Facilities: 150-kw ERP, 857-ft. above ground, 1001-ft. above sea level, lat. 30° 34' 27", long. 84° 12' 09".

Holds CP for change to 15-kw ERP, BMPDTA-20080804ACB.

Began Operation: May 15, 1984.

Ownership: Christian Television Network Inc.

Personnel: Bob D'Andrea, President; Tod Cole, General Manager; Kelly Simmons, Production Supervisor; Keith Garvin, Operations Manager; Chuck Stewart, Children's Programming.

Tallahassee—WWWF-LP, Ch. 47, ZGS Florida Inc. Phone: 703-528-5656.

Technical Facilities: 1000-w TPO, 150-kw ERP, 328-ft. above ground, 554-ft. above sea level, lat. 30° 29' 32", long. 84° 17' 02".

Transmitter: High Point Center, 106 E. College Ave.

Ownership: ZGS Broadcasting Holdings Inc.

Personnel: Woody Jenkins, General Manager.

Tampa—W56EB, Ch. 56, Enlace Christian Television Inc. Phone: 469-499-0832.

Technical Facilities: 65-kw ERP, 635-ft. above ground, 695-ft. above sea level, lat. 27° 49' 10", long. 82° 15' 38".

Holds CP for change to channel number 31, 12-kw ERP, 636-ft. above ground, 712-ft. above sea level, lat. 27° 49' 10", long. 82° 15' 39". BDISDTT-20060213AAW.

Transmitter: 111 W. Fortune St.

Began Operation: October 11, 1990.

Ownership: Enlace Christian Television Inc.

Personnel: Paul F. Crouch, General Manager; Ben Miller, Chief Engineer; Rod Henke, Sales Manager.

■**Tampa**—WRMD-CA, Ch. 49, ZGS Television of Tampa Inc. Phone: 703-528-5656.

Studio: 2700 W Martin Luther King, Ste 400, Tampa, FL 33607.

Technical Facilities: 128-kw ERP, 508-ft. above ground, 524-ft. above sea level, lat. 27° 56' 50.9", long. 82° 27' 32.7".

Holds CP for change to 15-kw ERP, BDFCDTA-20080804ABO.

Multichannel TV Sound: Separate audio progam.

Ownership: ZGS Broadcasting Holdings Inc.

Personnel: Laura Santos, General Manager; Jose Torres, Sales Manager.

Tampa—WTAM-LP, Ch. 30, Lotus TV of Tampa LLC. Phone: 323-512-2225.

Technical Facilities: 68.9-kw ERP, 1251-ft. above ground, 1325-ft. above sea level, lat. 27° 49' 09.7", long. 82° 15' 38.7".

Ownership: Lotus Communications Corp.

Personnel: Bob Joblin, General Manager; Neal Ardman, Chief Engineer.

Tampa—WVEA-LP, Ch. 46, Entravision Holdings LLC. Phone: 310-447-3870.

Studio: 2942 W Columbus Dr, Ste 204, Tampa, FL 33607.

Technical Facilities: 49-kw ERP, 482-ft. above ground, 497-ft. above sea level, lat. 27° 56' 50", long. 82° 27' 35".

Ownership: Entravision Communications Corp.

Personnel: Lilly M. Gonzalez, General Manager; Edwin Castro, Sales Manager.

■**Tampa-St. Petersburg**—WARP-CA, Ch. 20, Sunshine Broadcasting Co. Inc. Phone: 603-279-4440.

Technical Facilities: 150-kw ERP, 459-ft. above ground, 464-ft. above sea level, lat. 27° 52' 00", long. 82° 37' 27".

Multichannel TV Sound: Stereo only.

Ownership: Sunshine Broadcasting Co. Inc.

Union Park—WSWF-LP, Ch. 13, Specialty Broadcasting Corp. Phone: 407-740-8422. Fax: 407-740-6589.

Technical Facilities: 30-w TPO, 0.088-kw ERP, 249-ft. above ground, 325-ft. above sea level, lat. 28° 34' 07", long. 81° 13' 56".

Holds CP for change to channel number 10, 0.3-kw ERP, 354-ft. above ground, 427-ft. above sea level, lat. 28° 34' 07", long. 81° 13' 55". BDISDVL-20080506AAE.

Transmitter: 10606 E. Colonial Dr.

Ownership: Specialty Broadcasting Corp.

Vero Beach—WMMF-LP, Ch. 19, Budd Broadcasting Co. Inc. Phone: 352-371-7772.

Technical Facilities: 14.8-kw ERP, 341-ft. above ground, 362-ft. above sea level, lat. 27° 36' 05", long. 80° 23' 34".

Ownership: Budd Broadcasting Co. Inc.

■**Vero Beach**—WWCI-CA, Ch. 10, V-1 Productions Inc. Phone: 561-978-0023. Fax: 561-978-0053.

Technical Facilities: 3-kw ERP, 430-ft. above ground, 449-ft. above sea level, lat. 27° 36' 04", long. 80° 23' 33".

Holds CP for change to 0.3-kw ERP, 430-ft. above ground, 451-ft. above sea level, lat. 27° 36' 05", long. 80° 23' 34". BDFCDVA-20080804ADJ.

Transmitter: 901 First Place.

Ownership: V-1 Productions Inc.

Personnel: Jose Guerra, General Manager; Frank Banos, Chief Engineer; Maria Guerra, Sales Manager.

West Gate—W16CC, Ch. 16, Mako Communications LLC. Phone: 361-883-1763.

Technical Facilities: 115-kw ERP, 820-ft. above ground, 830-ft. above sea level, lat. 25° 59' 35", long. 80° 10' 26".

Holds CP for change to 3-kw ERP, 410-ft. above ground, 418-ft. above sea level, lat. 25° 59' 34", long. 80° 10' 27". BDFCDTL-20090323ACC.

Began Operation: November 2, 1983.

Ownership: Mako Communications LLC.

West Palm Beach—WBWP-LP, Ch. 57, H & R Production Group LLC. Phone: 561-863-0417. Fax: 561-863-0418.

Technical Facilities: 40-kw ERP, 463-ft. above ground, 489-ft. above sea level, lat. 26° 47' 59", long. 80° 04' 33".

Ownership: H & R Production Group LLC.

Personnel: Jose Uzal, General Manager.

Williston—W56EJ, Ch. 56, Equity Media Holdings Corp., Debtor in Possession. Phone: 501-219-2400.

Technical Facilities: 8-kw ERP, 344-ft. above ground, 420-ft. above sea level, lat. 29° 24' 11", long. 82° 27' 03".

Holds CP for change to channel number 34, 75-kw ERP, 840-ft. above ground, 985-ft. above sea level, lat. 29° 21' 32", long. 82° 19' 43". BDISTTL-20071205ABE.

Began Operation: June 8, 2007.

Ownership: Equity Media Holdings Corp., Debtor in Possession.

Williston—W63DB, Ch. 63, Equity Media Holdings Corp., Debtor in Possession. Phone: 501-219-2400.

Technical Facilities: 150-kw ERP, 344-ft. above ground, 420-ft. above sea level, lat. 29° 24' 11", long. 82° 27' 03".

Holds CP for change to channel number 18, 70-kw ERP, 920-ft. above ground, 984-ft. above sea level, lat. 29° 32' 11", long. 82° 24' 00". BDISTTL-20071205ABG.

Began Operation: July 22, 2005.

Ownership: Equity Media Holdings Corp., Debtor in Possession.

Yankeetown—WGCT-LP, Ch. 17, Budd Broadcasting Co. Inc. Phone: 352-371-7772.

Technical Facilities: 87-kw ERP, 361-ft. above ground, 371-ft. above sea level, lat. 29° 01' 18", long. 82° 41' 20".

Ownership: Budd Broadcasting Co. Inc.

Zephyrhills—WGCT-LD, Ch. 45, Budd Broadcasting Co. Inc. Phone: 352-371-7772.

Technical Facilities: 15-kw ERP, 427-ft. above ground, 597-ft. above sea level, lat. 28° 30' 17", long. 82° 20' 34".

Holds CP for change to 745-ft. above ground, 820-ft. above sea level, lat. 27° 49' 10", long. 82° 15' 39". BPDTL-20090218AAB.

Began Operation: January 26, 2009.

Ownership: Budd Broadcasting Co. Inc.

Georgia

Albany—W34CZ, Ch. 34, Trinity Broadcasting Network Inc. Phone: 714-832-2950. Fax: 714-730-0661.

Technical Facilities: 6.3-kw ERP, 420-ft. above ground, 619-ft. above sea level, lat. 31° 26' 43", long. 84° 07' 53".

Holds CP for change to 15-kw ERP, lat. 31° 26' 44", long. 84° 07' 52". BDFCDTT-20060330ABG.

Ownership: Trinity Broadcasting Network Inc.

Personnel: Paul Crouch, General Manager; Ben Miller, Chief Engineer; Rod Henke, Sales Manager.

Athens—WAGC-LP, Ch. 42, C.T.S. Broadcasting. Phones: 706-543-7993; 678-576-8507. Fax: 706-543-0226.

Studio: Daniels Bridge Rd, Athens, GA 30606.

Technical Facilities: 14.2-kw ERP, 381-ft. above ground, 1119-ft. above sea level, lat. 33° 53' 38", long. 83° 25' 58".

Holds CP for change to channel number 50, 11-kw ERP, 299-ft. above ground, 997-ft. above sea level, lat. 33° 57' 47", long. 83° 27' 22". BMPTTL-20070910ABB.

Ownership: C.T.S. Broadcasting.

Personnel: Stanley R. Pulliam, Executive Chairman.

Atlanta—W23DN, Ch. 23, Ventana Television Inc. Phone: 727-872-4120.

Technical Facilities: 18.1-kw ERP, 494-ft. above ground, 1362-ft. above sea level, lat. 33° 48' 26", long. 84° 20' 22".

Began Operation: October 7, 1988.

Ownership: Ventana Television Inc.

Personnel: John Skelnik, General Manager & Chief Engineer.

■**Atlanta**—WANN-CA, Ch. 32, Prism Broadcasting Network Inc. Phone: 770-953-3232.

Technical Facilities: 12-kw ERP, 1017-ft. above ground, 2034-ft. above sea level, lat. 33° 46' 15", long. 84° 23' 10".

Ownership: Prism Broadcasting Network Inc.

■**Atlanta**—WIRE-CA, Ch. 40, D.T.V. LLC. Phone: 603-520-1127.

Technical Facilities: 55-kw ERP, 800-ft. above ground, 1769-ft. above sea level, lat. 33° 44' 41", long. 84° 21' 36".

Multichannel TV Sound: Stereo only.

Ownership: D.T.V. LLC.

■**Atlanta**—WKTB-CA, Ch. 38, Korean American TV Broadcasting Corp. Phone: 770-497-0015.

Studio: 250 Spring St, Atlanta, GA 30303.

Technical Facilities: 4.62-kw ERP, 325-ft. above ground, 1417-ft. above sea level, lat. 33° 55' 00", long. 84° 12' 07".

Began Operation: February 5, 1991.

Ownership: Korean American TV Broadcasting Corp.

Atlanta—WKTB-LD, Ch. 47, Korean American TV Broadcasting Corp. Phone: 770-497-0015.

Technical Facilities: 10-kw ERP, 325-ft. above ground, 1415-ft. above sea level, lat. 33° 55' 00", long. 84° 12' 07".

Holds CP for change to 15-kw ERP, lat. 33° 55' 01", long. 84° 12' 06". BPDTL-20090402AOZ.

Began Operation: August 28, 2008.

Ownership: Korean American TV Broadcasting Corp.

■**Atlanta**—WSKC-CA, Ch. 22, KM LPTV of Atlanta LLC. Phones: 847-674-0864; 847-674-9188. Fax: 770-645-1114.

Technical Facilities: 150-kw ERP, 112-ft. above ground, 1791-ft. above sea level, lat. 34° 04' 01", long. 84° 27' 23".

Holds CP for change to 0.8-kw ERP, BDFCDTA-20061201AJF.

Transmitter: Sweat Mountain, approx. 1.8-mi. W of Marietta.

Ownership: KM Communications Inc.

Personnel: K. C. Bae, General Manager; Stan Byers, Chief Engineer.

Atlanta—WTBS-LP, Ch. 26, Prism Broadcasting Network Inc. Phone: 770-953-3232.

Studio: 646 Mount Alto Rd, Rome, GA 30161.

Technical Facilities: 1000-w TPO, 22.2-kw ERP, 801-ft. above ground, 1870-ft. above sea level, lat. 33° 45' 34", long. 84° 23' 19".

Holds CP for change to 103.5-kw ERP, 1017-ft. above ground, 2034-ft. above sea level, lat. 33° 46' 15", long. 84° 23' 10". BPTTL-20070411ACJ.

Transmitter: 210 Peachtree St.

Ownership: Prism Broadcasting Network Inc.

Personnel: Bill Hill, General Manager; Don Patterson, Sales Manager; John Simmons, Sales Manager.

Atlanta—WTHC-LP, Ch. 42, Beach TV Properties Inc. Phones: 850-234-2773; 404-582-8887.

Technical Facilities: 7-kw ERP, 721-ft. above ground, 1790-ft. above sea level, lat. 33° 45' 34", long. 84° 23' 19".

Began Operation: July 12, 1993.

Ownership: Beach TV Properties Inc.

Personnel: J. Mitchell Johnson, General Manager.

Atlanta—WUVM-LP, Ch. 4, Una Vez Mas Atlanta License LLC. Phone: 214-754-7008.

Technical Facilities: 1000-w TPO, 2.5-kw ERP, 870-ft. above ground, 1737-ft. above sea level, lat. 33° 48' 26", long. 84° 20' 22".

Transmitter: Sweat Mountain radio site, Marietta.

Ownership: Una Vez Mas GP LLC.

■**Atlanta**—WYGA-CA, Ch. 55, Mako Communications LLC. Phone: 361-883-1763.

Technical Facilities: 1000-w TPO, 9-kw ERP, 492-ft. above ground, 1443-ft. above sea level, lat. 33° 35' 39", long. 84° 32' 06".

Transmitter: 3075 River Rd., Panthersville.

Began Operation: July 19, 1993.

Ownership: Mako Communications LLC.

Augusta—W58CZ, Ch. 58, Trinity Broadcasting Network Inc. Phone: 714-832-2950. Fax: 714-730-0661.

Technical Facilities: 1000-w TPO, 6-kw ERP, 551-ft. above ground, 1001-ft. above sea level, lat. 33° 30' 53", long. 81° 56' 23".

Holds CP for change to channel number 49, 11.9-kw ERP, BPTT-20030701AWJ.

Transmitter: Intersection of Aetna and Womrath.

Ownership: Trinity Broadcasting Network Inc.

Personnel: Paul F. Crouch, General Manager; Rod Henke, Sales Manager; Ben Miller, Chief Engineer.

Augusta—WAAU-LP, Ch. 18, Thomas J. Piper.

Technical Facilities: 50-kw ERP, 328-ft. above ground, 760-ft. above sea level, lat. 33° 26' 13", long. 82° 05' 32".

Transmitter: 7-mi. W of I-20 & I-520 intersection.

Ownership: Thomas J. Piper.

■**Augusta**—WBEK-CA, Ch. 16, AVN Inc. Phone: 706-736-6700.

Technical Facilities: 150-kw ERP, 121-ft. above ground, 593-ft. above sea level, lat. 33° 28' 25", long. 82° 02' 05".

Holds CP for change to 6.9-kw ERP, BDFCDTA-20080805AAU.

Transmitter: Water tower near Central & Highland Aves.

Ownership: AVN Inc.

Personnel: Jeremy M. Coghlan, President; Gene Diduch, Sales; James Garner, Production; Gene Wilson, Engineer.

■**Augusta**—WBPI-CA, Ch. 49, Watchmen Broadcasting Productions International Inc. Phone: 803-278-3618.

Technical Facilities: 150-kw ERP, 480-ft. above ground, 929-ft. above sea level, lat. 33° 30' 53", long. 81° 56' 23".

Holds CP for change to 15-kw ERP, 586-ft. above ground, 1035-ft. above sea level, BMPDTA-20080804ABD.

Ownership: Watchmen Broadcasting Productions International Inc.

Blairsville—WBUD-LP, Ch. 38, Robert A. Naismith. Phone: 231-547-2696.

Technical Facilities: 80-kw ERP, 131-ft. above ground, 2717-ft. above sea level, lat. 34° 30' 34", long. 83° 48' 25".

Began Operation: June 26, 2008.

Ownership: Robert A. Naismith.

Blairsville—WDWW-LP, Ch. 28, Richard C. & Lisa A. Goetz. Phone: 615-826-0792.

Technical Facilities: 87-kw ERP, 148-ft. above ground, 2733-ft. above sea level, lat. 34° 30' 32", long. 83° 48' 27".

Ownership: Richard C. & Lisa A. Goetz.

Brunswick—W33AL, Ch. 33, Trinity Broadcasting Network Inc. Phone: 714-832-2950. Fax: 714-730-0661.

Technical Facilities: 1000-w TPO, 10.4-kw ERP, 174-ft. above ground, 184-ft. above sea level, lat. 31° 10' 07", long. 81° 32' 14".

Holds CP for change to 15-kw ERP, BDFCDTT-20060331ADG.

Transmitter: State Rte. 303 & U.S. Rte. 95, near Brunswick.

Ownership: Trinity Broadcasting Network Inc.

Personnel: Paul Crouch, General Manager; Ben Miller, Chief Engineer; Rod Henke, Sales Manager.

Cairo & Thomasville—W02CI, Ch. 2, Cee Inc. Phone: 912-234-8875.

Technical Facilities: 10-w TPO, 0.018-kw ERP, 174-ft. above ground, 413-ft. above sea level, lat. 30° 52' 21", long. 84° 05' 17".

Transmitter: 7-mi. E of Cairo, on N side of Hwy. 84.

Ownership: Cee Inc.

Carrollton—W49AD, Ch. 49, Georgia Public Telecommunications Commission. Phone: 404-685-2527. Fax: 404-685-2491.

Technical Facilities: 0.008-kw ERP, lat. 33° 33' 50", long. 85° 01' 04".

Ownership: Georgia Public Telecommunications Commission.

Personnel: Mark G. Fehlig, Chief Engineer.

Clayton, etc.—W06AE, Ch. 6, WYFF Hearst-Argyle Television Inc. Phone: 919-839-0300.

Technical Facilities: 0.01-kw ERP, 3652-ft. above sea level, lat. 34° 54' 24", long. 83° 24' 56".

Began Operation: April 9, 1981.

Ownership: Hearst-Argyle Television Inc.

Cleveland—WGGD-LP, Ch. 23, Word of God Fellowship Inc. Phone: 817-571-1229.

Technical Facilities: 75-kw ERP, 699-ft. above ground, 1916-ft. above sea level, lat. 34° 07' 47", long. 83° 55' 56".

Ownership: Word of God Fellowship Inc.

Colquitt—W08DM, Ch. 8, MS Communications LLC. Phone: 414-765-9737.

Technical Facilities: 0.09-kw ERP, 30-ft. above ground, 230-ft. above sea level, lat. 31° 16' 00", long. 84° 42' 16".

Ownership: MS Communications LLC.

Colquitt—W22BV, Ch. 22, MS Communications LLC. Phone: 414-765-9737.

Technical Facilities: 0.007-kw ERP, 105-ft. above ground, 699-ft. above sea level, lat. 31° 14' 35", long. 84° 44' 55".

Ownership: MS Communications LLC.

Colquitt—W26BM, Ch. 26, MS Communications LLC. Phone: 414-765-9737.

Technical Facilities: 0.007-kw ERP, 105-ft. above ground, 699-ft. above sea level, lat. 31° 14' 35", long. 84° 44' 55".

Ownership: MS Communications LLC.

Colquitt—W30BO, Ch. 30, MS Communications LLC. Phone: 414-765-9737.

Technical Facilities: 0.007-kw ERP, 105-ft. above ground, 699-ft. above sea level, lat. 31° 14' 35", long. 84° 44' 55".

Transmitter: 1.2-mi. E of Hwy. 45 & Early-Miller County Line intersection.

Ownership: MS Communications LLC.

Colquitt—W45BL, Ch. 45, MS Communications LLC. Phone: 414-765-9737.

Technical Facilities: 0.007-kw ERP, 105-ft. above ground, 699-ft. above sea level, lat. 31° 14' 35", long. 84° 44' 55".

Ownership: MS Communications LLC.

Colquitt—W47BX, Ch. 47, MS Communications LLC. Phone: 414-765-9737.

Technical Facilities: 0.007-kw ERP, 105-ft. above ground, 699-ft. above sea level, lat. 31° 14' 35", long. 84° 44' 55".

Ownership: MS Communications LLC.

Colquitt—W51CQ, Ch. 51, MS Communications LLC. Phone: 414-765-9737.

Technical Facilities: 0.007-kw ERP, 105-ft. above ground, 699-ft. above sea level, lat. 31° 14' 35", long. 84° 44' 55".

Ownership: MS Communications LLC.

Colquitt—W69DO, Ch. 69, MS Communications LLC. Phone: 414-765-9737.

Technical Facilities: 0.007-kw ERP, 105-ft. above ground, 399-ft. above sea level, lat. 31° 14' 35", long. 84° 44' 55".

Ownership: MS Communications LLC.

Columbus—W33CN, Ch. 33, Tiger Eye Licensing LLC. Phone: 954-431-3144.

Technical Facilities: 40-kw ERP, 213-ft. above ground, 783-ft. above sea level, lat. 32° 31' 52", long. 85° 01' 37".

Ownership: Tiger Eye Broadcasting Corp.

Columbus—W61DU, Ch. 61, The Estate of John R. Powley, Caroline Kaye Smith Executrix. Phone: 850-936-6461.

Technical Facilities: 1-kw ERP, 16-ft. above ground, 558-ft. above sea level, lat. 32° 31' 52", long. 84° 57' 31".

Ownership: The Estate of John R. Powley, Caroline Kaye Smith Executrix.

Columbus—WANX-LP, Ch. 19, Prism Broadcasting Network Inc. Phone: 770-953-3232.

Technical Facilities: 0.1-kw ERP, 16-ft. above ground, 266-ft. above sea level, lat. 32° 22' 53.3", long. 84° 57' 33.7".

Ownership: Prism Broadcasting Network Inc.

Columbus—WWCG-LP, Ch. 11, MD Broadcasting LLC. Phone: 205-620-9660.

Technical Facilities: 2.5-kw ERP, 313-ft. above ground, 775-ft. above sea level, lat. 32° 30' 45", long. 85° 00' 41".

Ownership: MD Broadcasting LLC.

■**Columbus**—WYBU-CA, Ch. 16, Christian Television Network Inc. Phones: 706-323-6630; 727-535-5622. Fax: 706-323-9796.

Technical Facilities: 1000-w TPO, 8.2-kw ERP, 344-ft. above ground, 968-ft. above sea level, lat. 32° 27' 48", long. 85° 03' 23".

Holds CP for change to 15-kw ERP, 290-ft. above ground, 913-ft. above sea level, lat. 32° 27' 59", long. 85° 03' 22". BMPDTA-20080804AEN.

Transmitter: Windtree Dr., Phenix City.

Multichannel TV Sound: Stereo and separate audio program.

Began Operation: April 29, 1987.

Ownership: Christian Television Network Inc.

Personnel: Virgil Thompson, General Manager; Steven Rhodes, Chief Engineer.

Dalton—WDDA-LP, Ch. 6, Word of God Fellowship Inc. Phone: 817-571-1229.

Technical Facilities: 2.5-kw ERP, 180-ft. above ground, 883-ft. above sea level, lat. 34° 47' 21", long. 84° 57' 35".

Ownership: Word of God Fellowship Inc.

■**Dalton**—WDGA-CA, Ch. 43, North Georgia Television. Phone: 706-278-9713. Fax: 706-278-7950.

Studio: 101 S Spencer St, Dalton, GA 30721.

Technical Facilities: 1.25-kw ERP, 131-ft. above ground, 955-ft. above sea level, lat. 34° 46' 16", long. 84° 57' 51".

Ownership: North Georgia Television.

Personnel: Calvin Means, General Manager; Doug Jensen, Chief Executive Officer; Judy Elliott, Local Sales Manager.

■**Dalton**—WDNN-CA, Ch. 49, North Georgia Television. Phone: 706-278-9713. Fax: 706-278-7950.

Studio: 101 S Spencer St, Dalton, GA 30721.

Technical Facilities: 10.36-kw ERP, 69-ft. above ground, 1880-ft. above sea level, lat. 34° 44' 00", long. 85° 01' 03".

Ownership: North Georgia Television.

Personnel: Doug Jensen, Chief Executive Officer; Calvin Means, General Manager; Judy Elliott, Local Sales Manager.

Douglas—WWPD-LP, Ch. 41, KM Communications Inc. Phone: 847-674-0864.

Technical Facilities: 5.3-kw ERP, 184-ft. above ground, 433-ft. above sea level, lat. 31° 30' 41", long. 82° 51' 32".

Ownership: KM Communications Inc.

Ducktown—WCTD-LP, Ch. 22, Word of God Fellowship Inc. Phone: 817-571-1229.

Technical Facilities: 150-kw ERP, 180-ft. above ground, 2188-ft. above sea level, lat. 35° 02' 18", long. 84° 27' 13".

Ownership: Word of God Fellowship Inc.

Fayetteville—WDTA-LP, Ch. 53, Word of God Fellowship. Phone: 817-571-1229. Fax: 817-571-7478.

Technical Facilities: 1000-w TPO, 111.5-kw ERP, 1017-ft. above ground, 2034-ft. above sea level, lat. 33° 46' 15", long. 84° 23' 10".

Holds CP for change to channel number 35, 1.5-kw ERP, 853-ft. above ground, 1877-ft. above sea level, lat. 33° 45' 45", long. 84° 23' 14". BDISDTL-20081007ALW.

Transmitter: Nations Bank Bldg., Atlanta.

Began Operation: July 12, 1988.

Ownership: Word of God Fellowship Inc.

Hartwell & Royston—W22AC, Ch. 22, Georgia Public Telecommunications Commission. Phone: 404-685-2410.

Technical Facilities: 0.9-kw ERP, lat. 34° 18' 45", long. 82° 56' 15".

Holds CP for change to channel number 11, 0.15-kw ERP, 381-ft. above ground, 1199-ft. above sea level, BMPDTV-20090423AAP.

Ownership: Georgia Public Telecommunications Commission.

Hazlehurst—WVOH-LP, Ch. 56, Broadcast South LLC. Phone: 912-389-0995.

Technical Facilities: 0.76-kw ERP, 259-ft. above ground, 499-ft. above sea level, lat. 31° 51' 15", long. 82° 34' 00".

Transmitter: Hwy. 341 S.

Ownership: Broadcast South LLC.

Personnel: John Hulett, General Manager & Sales Manager; Wilbur Heath, Chief Engineer.

Hiawassee—W50AB, Ch. 50, Georgia Public Telecommunications Commission. Phone: 404-685-2457. Fax: 404-685-2491.

Technical Facilities: 1.05-kw ERP, lat. 34° 57' 15", long. 83° 43' 47".

Ownership: Georgia Public Telecommunications Commission.

Personnel: Mark G. Fehlig, Chief Engineer.

Hinesville-Richmond—W41CR, Ch. 41, Southern TV Corp. Phone: 912-692-8000.

Technical Facilities: 26.9-kw ERP, 180-ft. above ground, 270-ft. above sea level, lat. 31° 49' 52", long. 81° 47' 21".

Holds CP for change to 184-ft. above ground, 274-ft. above sea level, BMPTTL-20060705ACG.

Ownership: Southern TV Corp.

■**La Grange**—WCAG-LP, Ch. 33, Georgia-Alabama Broadcasting Inc. Phone: 706-845-8833. Fax: 706-845-8804.

Studio: No. 1 E. Lafayette Square, La Grange, GA 30240.

Technical Facilities: 1000-w TPO, 23.9-kw ERP, 223-ft. above ground, 1043-ft. above sea level, lat. 33° 03' 00", long. 85° 01' 50".

Transmitter: E of Ridley Ave., N of Mitchell Ave.

Multichannel TV Sound: Separate audio progam.

Ownership: Georgia-Alabama Broadcasting Inc.

Personnel: Peter Mallory, General Manager; Donna Martin, General Sales Manager; John Simmons, Chief Engineer.

Lafayette—WLFW-LP, Ch. 41, North Georgia Television.

Technical Facilities: 1.22-kw ERP, lat. 34° 41' 06", long. 85° 11' 46".

Transmitter: Taylor's Ridge, near Hwy. 136.

Ownership: North Georgia Television.

Macon—W50DA, Ch. 50, Radio Peach Inc. Phone: 202-783-4141.

Technical Facilities: 1000-w TPO, 13.3-kw ERP, 499-ft. above ground, 809-ft. above sea level, lat. 32° 45' 09", long. 83° 33' 35".

Transmitter: WPGA (TV) tower, Macon.

Began Operation: February 23, 1998.

Ownership: Radio Peach Inc.

■ **Macon**—WDMA-CA, Ch. 31, Word of God Fellowship Inc. Phone: 817-571-1229. Fax: 817-571-7478.

Technical Facilities: 32-kw ERP, 591-ft. above ground, 1020-ft. above sea level, lat. 32° 50' 31", long. 83° 40' 19".

Transmitter: 667 Bartlett Rd.

Ownership: Word of God Fellowship Inc.

Marietta—W49DE, Ch. 49, Trinity Broadcasting Network Inc. Phone: 714-832-2950. Fax: 714-730-0661.

Technical Facilities: 23.8-kw ERP, 126-ft. above ground, 1772-ft. above sea level, lat. 34° 03' 58", long. 84° 27' 14".

Ownership: Trinity Broadcasting Network Inc.

Moultrie—W19CP, Ch. 19, Richard C. & Lisa A. Goetz. Phone: 615-826-0792.

Technical Facilities: 300-w TPO, 2.62-kw ERP, 500-ft. above ground, 823-ft. above sea level, lat. 31° 08' 05", long. 84° 06' 16".

Transmitter: Hwy. 93, 2-mi. E. of Pelham.

Ownership: Richard C. & Lisa A. Goetz.

Personnel: James Christian Hawkins, Partner.

Pearson—WPDW-LP, Ch. 26, KM Communications Inc. Phone: 847-674-0864.

Technical Facilities: 42-kw ERP, 479-ft. above ground, 672-ft. above sea level, lat. 31° 19' 36", long. 82° 51' 54".

Ownership: KM Communications Inc.

Pearson—WPNG-LP, Ch. 3, KM Communications Inc. Phone: 847-674-0864.

Technical Facilities: 0.6-kw ERP, 427-ft. above ground, 619-ft. above sea level, lat. 31° 19' 36", long. 82° 51' 54".

Ownership: KM Communications Inc.

Savannah—W57CT, Ch. 43, Trinity Broadcasting Network Inc. Phone: 714-832-2950. Fax: 714-730-0661.

Technical Facilities: 36.5-kw ERP, 384-ft. above ground, 394-ft. above sea level, lat. 32° 02' 43", long. 81° 07' 23".

Holds CP for change to 1-kw ERP, 384-ft. above ground, 400-ft. above sea level, lat. 32° 02' 42", long. 81° 07' 21". BDFCDTT-20070402BHQ.

Ownership: Trinity Broadcasting Network Inc.

Savannah—WGCW-LP, Ch. 38, Southern TV Corp. Phone: 912-692-8000.

Technical Facilities: 7.8-kw ERP, 358-ft. above ground, 364-ft. above sea level, lat. 32° 04' 21", long. 81° 04' 45".

Ownership: Southern TV Corp.

■ **Savannah**—WGSA-CA, Ch. 50, Southern TV Corp. Phone: 912-692-8000.

Technical Facilities: 146-kw ERP, 384-ft. above ground, 390-ft. above sea level, lat. 32° 04' 21", long. 81° 04' 45".

Transmitter: 835 E. Perry Lane.

Ownership: Southern TV Corp.

Savannah—WHDS-LP, Ch. 32, Paradigm Broadcasting Group LLC. Phone: 803-419-6363.

Technical Facilities: 138-w TPO, 4.46-kw ERP, 400-ft. above ground, 322-ft. above sea level, lat. 32° 04' 07", long. 81° 05' 35".

Transmitter: 4-mi. W of Hopeton Airport.

Ownership: Paradigm Broadcasting Group LLC.

■ **Savannah**—WXSX-CA, Ch. 46, L4 Media Group LLC. Phone: 321-729-8451.

Studio: 214 Television Circle, Savannah, GA 31406.

Technical Facilities: 50-kw ERP, 430-ft. above ground, 430-ft. above sea level, lat. 32° 02' 43", long. 81° 07' 20".

Holds CP for change to 133-kw ERP, 430-ft. above ground, 446-ft. above sea level, lat. 32° 02' 42", long. 81° 07' 21". BPTTA-20060324AFD.

Ownership: L4 Media Group LLC.

Personnel: Warren Reeves, Consulting Engineer; Amy Brown, Broadcast Operations Director; Liz Kiley, Broadcast Vice President.

Statesboro—W25CQ, Ch. 25, Southern TV Corp. Phone: 912-692-8000.

Technical Facilities: 17-kw ERP, 430-ft. above ground, lat. 32° 20' 04", long. 81° 41' 15".

Transmitter: 1.1-mi. SW of intersection with State Rte. 67.

Ownership: Southern TV Corp.

Statesboro—W48BH, Ch. 48, Trinity Broadcasting Network Inc. Phone: 714-832-2950. Fax: 714-730-0661.

Technical Facilities: 100-w TPO, 13.3-kw ERP, 269-ft. above ground, 515-ft. above sea level, lat. 32° 25' 32", long. 81° 47' 43".

Transmitter: 1-mi. SSW of U.S. Hwy. 310 & State Hwy. 67 intersection.

Ownership: Trinity Broadcasting Network Inc.

Personnel: Mark Loyd, General Manager.

Summerville-Trion—WKSY-LP, Ch. 21, Audio Graphics Inc. Phone: 706-857-8504.

Technical Facilities: 1.08-kw ERP, 66-ft. above ground, 1476-ft. above sea level, lat. 34° 28' 07", long. 85° 17' 52".

Ownership: Audio Graphics Inc.

Thomasville—W38CM, Ch. 38, Trinity Christian Center of Santa Ana Inc. Phone: 714-832-2950.

Technical Facilities: 21.6-kw ERP, 30° 23' 42", long. 83° 32' 02".

Holds CP for change to channel number 29, 15-kw ERP, 282-ft. above ground, 492-ft. above sea level, lat. 30° 50' 51", long. 83° 52' 56". BDISDTT-20060329ABW.

Transmitter: NNW of State Rtes. 388 & 167 intersection, near Bennett.

Ownership: Trinity Broadcasting Network Inc.

Tifton—W12DA, Ch. 12, Richard C. & Lisa A. Goetz. Phone: 615-826-0792.

Technical Facilities: 0.1-kw ERP, 246-ft. above ground, 541-ft. above sea level, lat. 31° 34' 00", long. 82° 58' 15".

Holds CP for change to channel number 13, 0.36-kw ERP, 164-ft. above ground, 413-ft. above sea level, lat. 31° 30' 41", long. 82° 51' 32". BDISTVL-20070615ACI.

Ownership: Richard C. & Lisa A. Goetz.

Tifton—W33BX, Ch. 33, Trinity Broadcasting Network. Phone: 714-832-2950. Fax: 714-730-0661.

Technical Facilities: 21.2-kw ERP, 499-ft. above ground, 781-ft. above sea level, lat. 31° 27' 17", long. 83° 33' 37".

Holds CP for change to 15-kw ERP, 499-ft. above ground, 779-ft. above sea level, lat. 31° 27' 17", long. 83° 33' 38". BDFCDTT-20060331ADJ.

Ownership: Trinity Broadcasting Network Inc.

■ **Tifton**—W38DG, Ch. 38, Northside Baptist Church. Phones: 912-386-5151; 912-382-6855. Fax: 912-382-9542.

Technical Facilities: 1-kw ERP, 115-ft. above ground, 466-ft. above sea level, lat. 31° 28' 18", long. 83° 30' 48".

Ownership: Northside Baptist Church.

Personnel: Ricky Hobby, General Manager.

Tifton—W62DE, Ch. 62, Billy Ray Washington. Phone: 229-392-4848.

Technical Facilities: 0.16-kw ERP, 89-ft. above ground, 440-ft. above sea level, lat. 31° 26' 34", long. 83° 30' 27".

Holds CP for change to 0.19-kw ERP, 89-ft. above ground, 517-ft. above sea level, lat. 31° 25' 41.7", long. 83° 32' 01.6". BPTTL-20060724ACW.

Ownership: Billy Ray Washington.

Toccoa—W68AF, Ch. 68, Georgia Public Telecommunications Commission. Phones: 404-685-2410; 404-685-2652. Fax: 404-685-2491.

Technical Facilities: 0.867-kw ERP, lat. 34° 36' 32", long. 83° 21' 51".

Holds CP for change to channel number 8, 0.15-kw ERP, 182-ft. above ground, 1542-ft. above sea level, BMPDTV-20090226AAC.

Ownership: Georgia Public Telecommunications Commission.

Personnel: Mark G. Fehlig, Chief Engineer.

Valdosta—W25CP, Ch. 25, Trinity Broadcasting Network Inc. Phone: 714-832-2950. Fax: 714-730-0661.

Technical Facilities: 1000-w TPO, 8-kw ERP, 417-ft. above ground, 607-ft. above sea level, lat. 30° 51' 50", long. 83° 23' 40".

Transmitter: WAFT (FM) tower site, near Valdosta.

Ownership: Trinity Broadcasting Network Inc.

■ **Valdosta**—WBFL-CA, Ch. 13, New Age Media of Tallahassee License LLC. Phone: 570-824-7895.

Technical Facilities: 66.2-kw ERP, 30° 51' 50", long. 83° 23' 39".

Transmitter: S side of State Rte. 94, 4.25-mi. WNW of intersection of I-75 & State Rte. 94.

Ownership: New Age Media.

■ **Valdosta**—WBVJ-LP, Ch. 35, New Age Media of Tallahassee License LLC. Phone: 570-824-7895.

Technical Facilities: 100-w TPO, 0.439-kw ERP, 400-ft. above ground, 564-ft. above sea level, lat. 30° 50' 29", long. 83° 18' 26".

Transmitter: W. Gordon St.

Ownership: New Age Media.

Personnel: David Hinterschied, General Manager; Michael F. Brown, Chief Engineer; Don Abel, Creative Services Director.

Vidalia—W14CQ, Ch. 14, Trinity Broadcasting Network Inc. Phone: 714-832-2950. Fax: 714-730-0661.

Technical Facilities: 10-kw ERP, 308-ft. above ground, 634-ft. above sea level, lat. 32° 12' 19", long. 82° 29' 40".

Ownership: Trinity Broadcasting Network Inc.

Vidalia—W53CG, Ch. 53, ETC Communications Inc. Phone: 256-810-2497.

Technical Facilities: 2-kw ERP, 328-ft. above ground, 643-ft. above sea level, lat. 32° 12' 29", long. 82° 29' 48".

Holds CP for change to channel number 17, 143-kw ERP, BPTTL-20060123ACL.

Ownership: ETC Communications Inc.

■ **Vidalia**—WPHJ-CA, Ch. 46, Southern Media Associates Inc. Phone: 912-530-8832.

Technical Facilities: 45.7-kw ERP, 367-ft. above ground, 682-ft. above sea level, lat. 32° 12' 29", long. 82° 29' 49".

Began Operation: February 6, 1995.

Ownership: Southern Media Associates Inc.

Waycross—W45CU, Ch. 45, TCCSA Inc. dba Trinity Broadcasting Network. Phone: 714-832-2950. Fax: 714-730-0661.

Technical Facilities: 19.8-kw ERP, 253-ft. above ground, 456-ft. above sea level, lat. 31° 15' 49", long. 82° 17' 30".

Ownership: Trinity Broadcasting Network Inc.

Personnel: Paul Crouch, General Manager; Ben Miller, Chief Engineer; Rod Henke, Sales Manager.

Young Harris—W04BJ, Ch. 4, Georgia Public Telecommunications Commission. Phone: 404-685-2410.

Technical Facilities: 0.006-kw ERP, lat. 34° 55' 22", long. 83° 50' 26".

Holds CP for change to channel number 12, 0.005-kw ERP, 49-ft. above ground, 4833-ft. above sea level, lat. 34° 52' 27", long. 83° 48' 38". BMPDTV-20070417AAI.

Ownership: Georgia Public Telecommunications Commission.

Personnel: Mark G. Fehlig, Chief Engineer.

Hawaii

Anahola—K63AZ, Ch. 63, Hawaii Public Television Foundation. Phone: 808-973-1000.

Technical Facilities: 0.548-kw ERP, lat. 22° 08' 22", long. 159° 19' 14".

Holds CP for change to channel number 36, 0.11-kw ERP, 130-ft. above ground, 393-ft. above sea level, lat. 22° 08' 25", long. 159° 18' 56". BDISDTT-20060331BFW.

Ownership: Hawaii Public Television Foundation.

Hakalau—K67BA, Ch. 67, Hawaii Public Television Foundation. Phone: 808-973-1000.

Technical Facilities: 0.1-kw ERP, lat. 19° 54' 55", long. 155° 11' 07".

Holds CP for change to channel number 50, 22-ft. above ground, 1350-ft. above sea level, lat. 19° 54' 57", long. 155° 11' 06". BDISDTT-20060331BFB.

Ownership: Hawaii Public Television Foundation.

Hanalei, etc.—K68BE, Ch. 68, Hawaii Public Television Foundation.

Technical Facilities: 1.13-kw ERP, lat. 22° 12' 42", long. 159° 28' 13".

Holds CP for change to channel number 29, 0.1-kw ERP, 23-ft. above ground, 407-ft. above sea level, BDISDTT-20060331BFF.

Ownership: Hawaii Public Television Foundation.

Hanamaulu—KESU-LP, Ch. 6, Chang Broadcasting of Hawaii LLC. Phones: 808-245-9844; 866-528-2450. Fax: 808-245-9666.

Studio: 3-2600 Kaumualii Hwy. B18, Ste 532, Lihue, HI 96766.

Technical Facilities: 3-kw ERP, 98-ft. above ground, 1358-ft. above sea level, lat. 21° 56' 10", long. 159° 26' 43".

Multichannel TV Sound: Stereo only.

Ownership: Chang Broadcasting Hawaii LLC.

Personnel: Jeff Chang, President & General Manager.

Hilo—K04FE, Ch. 4, Hawaii Public Television Foundation. Phone: 808-973-1000.

Technical Facilities: 0.705-kw ERP, lat. 19° 43' 56", long. 155° 01' 00".

Ownership: Hawaii Public Television Foundation.

Hilo—K34HC, Ch. 34, Trinity Broadcasting Network Inc. Phone: 714-832-2950. Fax: 714-730-0661.

Technical Facilities: 12.5-kw ERP, 72-ft. above ground, 730-ft. above sea level, lat. 19° 50' 19", long. 155° 06' 43".

Holds CP for change to 15-kw ERP, BDFCDTT-20060331AEH.

Ownership: Trinity Broadcasting Network Inc.

Hilo—K45CT, Ch. 45, KASA License Subsidiary LLC. Phone: 334-206-1400.

Technical Facilities: 91.8-kw ERP, 46-ft. above ground, 8215-ft. above sea level, lat. 19° 35' 18", long. 155° 27' 10".

Ownership: Raycom Media Inc.

Hilo—KHHB-LP, Ch. 5, Hilo LP TV LLC. Phone: 702-477-3830.

Technical Facilities: 3-kw ERP, 75-ft. above ground, 833-ft. above sea level, lat. 19° 50' 19", long. 155° 06' 43".

Ownership: Hilo LP TV LLC.

Hilo—KHOH-LP, Ch. 38, Richard C. & Lisa A. Goetz. Phone: 615-826-0792.

Technical Facilities: 32-kw ERP, 180-ft. above ground, 1801-ft. above sea level, lat. 19° 35' 00", long. 155° 07' 26".

Ownership: Richard C. & Lisa A. Goetz.

Holualoa—K26HL, Ch. 26, Prism Broadcasting Network Inc. Phone: 770-953-3232.

Technical Facilities: 0.005-kw ERP, 26-ft. above ground, 5344-ft. above sea level, lat. 19° 43' 16", long. 155° 55' 05".

Ownership: Prism Broadcasting Network Inc.

Honolulu—K42CO, Ch. 42, Oceania Broadcasting Network Inc. Phone: 808-329-8120.

Technical Facilities: 1000-w TPO, 13.1-kw ERP, 39-ft. above ground, 164-ft. above sea level, lat. 21° 19' 49", long. 157° 45' 25".

Transmitter: SW junction of Kakaina & Waikapanaha Sts., near Waimanalo.

Ownership: Oceania Broadcasting Network Inc.

Honolulu—K56EX, Ch. 56, Victor Agmata. Phones: 808-847-1151; 808-845-0056. Fax: 808-848-2660.

Technical Facilities: 1000-w TPO, 46.9-kw ERP, 33-ft. above ground, 2234-ft. above sea level, lat. 21° 23' 45", long. 158° 05' 58".

Transmitter: Palehua Ridge.

Ownership: Victor Agmata.

Personnel: Flora Galla, General & Sales Manager; Robin Liu, Chief Engineer.

Honolulu—KHHI-LP, Ch. 48, U.S. Television LLC. Phone: 318-992-7766.

Technical Facilities: 1800-w TPO, 32.8-kw ERP, 59-ft. above ground, 2339-ft. above sea level, lat. 21° 23' 45", long. 158° 05' 58".

Transmitter: Palikea Ridge, 0.25 mi. SE of Palehua.

Ownership: Dean M. Mosely.

Personnel: Bob Joblin, General Manager; Neal Ardman, Chief Engineer.

■ **Honolulu**—KHLU-LP, Ch. 46, HTV/HTN/Hawaii Television Network. Phone: 808-878-1770.

Technical Facilities: 23.93-kw ERP, 59-ft. above ground, 2339-ft. above sea level, lat. 21° 33' 45", long. 158° 05' 58".

Holds CP for change to 0.03-kw ERP, BDFCDTA-20070530AAM.

Multichannel TV Sound: Stereo only.

Ownership: HTV/HTN/Hawaiian Television Network Ltd.

Personnel: Charlene Weh, General Manager.

Kailua-Kona—K32GJ, Ch. 32, Chang Broadcasting Hawaii LLC. Phone: 310-403-5039.

Technical Facilities: 0.16-kw ERP, 230-ft. above ground, 5548-ft. above sea level, lat. 19° 43' 04", long. 155° 55' 00".

Ownership: Chang Broadcasting Hawaii LLC.

Kailua-Kona—K38HU, Ch. 38, Trinity Broadcasting Network Inc. Phone: 714-832-2950. Fax: 714-730-0661.

Technical Facilities: 9.7-kw ERP, 131-ft. above ground, 5451-ft. above sea level, lat. 19° 43' 04", long. 155° 55' 00".

Ownership: Trinity Broadcasting Network Inc.

Kailua-Kona—K63DZ, Ch. 63, KASA License Subsidiary LLC. Phone: 334-206-1400.

Technical Facilities: 1.44-kw ERP, 49-ft. above ground, 5653-ft. above sea level, lat. 19° 42' 56", long. 155° 55' 00".

Ownership: Raycom Media Inc.

Kailua-Kona—KHIK-LP, Ch. 47, KM Communications Inc. Phone: 847-674-0864.

Technical Facilities: 150-kw ERP, 164-ft. above ground, 6161-ft. above sea level, lat. 19° 42' 56", long. 155° 55' 00".

Ownership: KM Communications Inc.

Kaumakani—K63AI, Ch. 63, Hawaii Public Television Foundation. Phone: 808-973-1000.

Technical Facilities: 0.368-kw ERP, lat. 21° 56' 27", long. 159° 32' 25".

Holds CP for change to 0.79-kw ERP, 30-ft. above ground, 841-ft. above sea level, lat. 21° 55' 10.3", long. 159° 31' 36.5". BPTT-20080401ASW.

Ownership: Hawaii Public Television Foundation.

Kilauea—K62AQ, Ch. 62, Hawaii Public Television Foundation. Phone: 808-973-1000.

Technical Facilities: 2.56-kw ERP, lat. 22° 13' 30", long. 159° 23' 44".

Holds CP for change to channel number 34, 0.12-kw ERP, 3-ft. above ground, 448-ft. above sea level, lat. 22° 13' 35.3", long. 159° 23' 51.5". BDISDTT-20060331BEX.

Ownership: Hawaii Public Television Foundation.

Kilauea Military Camp—K56BD, Ch. 56, Hawaii Public Television Foundation. Phone: 808-973-1000.

Technical Facilities: 1.32-kw ERP, lat. 19° 31' 25", long. 155° 18' 06".

Holds CP for change to channel number 41, 0.3-kw ERP, 150-ft. above ground, 5632-ft. above sea level, BDISDTT-20060331BHA.

Ownership: Hawaii Public Television Foundation.

Kula—K17GR, Ch. 17, Prism Broadcasting Network Inc. Phone: 770-953-3232.

Technical Facilities: 0.005-kw ERP, 26-ft. above ground, 4406-ft. above sea level, lat. 20° 39' 36", long. 156° 21' 50".

Ownership: Prism Broadcasting Network Inc.

Kula—K19FV, Ch. 19, Prism Broadcasting Network Inc. Phone: 770-953-3232.

Technical Facilities: 0.04-kw ERP, 66-ft. above ground, 1672-ft. above sea level, lat. 20° 50' 33", long. 156° 19' 18".

Holds CP for change to 26-ft. above ground, 4406-ft. above sea level, lat. 20° 39' 36", long. 156° 21' 50". BMPTTL-20070116ABG.

Ownership: Prism Broadcasting Network Inc.

Lihue—K51BB, Ch. 51, Hearst-Argyle Stations Inc. Phone: 919-839-0300.

Technical Facilities: 0.66-kw ERP, lat. 21° 58' 41", long. 159° 29' 55".

Ownership: Hearst-Argyle Television Inc.

Lihue—K55DZ, Ch. 55, NVT Hawaii Licensee LLC, Debtor in Possession. Phone: 404-995-4711.

Technical Facilities: 1.06-kw ERP, 49-ft. above ground, 2799-ft. above sea level, lat. 21° 58' 41", long. 159° 29' 55".

Ownership: New Vision Television LLC, Debtor in Possession.

Lihue—K65BV, Ch. 65, KASA License Subsidiary LLC. Phone: 334-206-1400.

Technical Facilities: 0.142-kw ERP, lat. 21° 58' 41", long. 159° 29' 55".

Transmitter: 8-mi. W of Lihue.

Ownership: Raycom Media Inc.

Lihue—K67AV, Ch. 67, Hawaii Public Television Foundation. Phone: 808-973-1000.

Technical Facilities: 23-kw ERP, lat. 21° 58' 41", long. 159° 29' 55".

Holds CP for change to channel number 30, 0.1-kw ERP, 10-ft. above ground, 2750-ft. above sea level, lat. 21° 58' 35.2", long. 159° 29' 54.8". BDISDTT-20060331BGC.

Ownership: Hawaii Public Television Foundation.

Lihue, etc.—K69BZ, Ch. 69, HITV License Subsidiary Inc. Phone: 703-247-7500.

Technical Facilities: 0.58-kw ERP, 17-ft. above ground, 2778-ft. above sea level, lat. 21° 58' 35.6", long. 159° 29' 54.4".

Ownership: MCG Capital Corp.

Ownership: Hawaii Public Television Foundation.

Mountain View—KOIW-LP, Ch. 22, ESI Broadcasting Corp. Phone: 561-694-1280.

Technical Facilities: 1000-w TPO, 26-kw ERP, 69-ft. above ground, 1939-ft. above sea level, lat. 19° 23' 33", long. 155° 06' 22".

Transmitter: 1.2-mi. NW of Glenwood.

Ownership: ESI Broadcasting Corp.

Naalehu, etc.—K63BB, Ch. 63, Hawaii Public Television Foundation. Phone: 808-973-1000.

Technical Facilities: 1.13-kw ERP, 682-ft. above sea level, lat. 19° 02' 40", long. 155° 35' 00".

Holds CP for change to channel number 31, 0.2-kw ERP, 16-ft. above ground, 640-ft. above sea level, lat. 19° 02' 48", long. 155° 34' 59". BDISDTT-20060331BHP.

Ownership: Hawaii Public Television Foundation.

South Point—K69CF, Ch. 69, Hawaii Public Television Foundation. Phone: 808-973-1000.

Technical Facilities: 2.31-kw ERP, lat. 19° 00' 19", long. 155° 40' 39".

Holds CP for change to channel number 35, 0.75-kw ERP, 50-ft. above ground, 1250-ft. above sea level, BDISDTT-20060331BHZ.

Ownership: Hawaii Public Television Foundation.

Wailuku—K27DW, Ch. 27, KASA License Subsidiary LLC. Phone: 334-206-1400.

Technical Facilities: 52.9-kw ERP, 36-ft. above ground, 8838-ft. above sea level, lat. 20° 33', long. 156° 15' 52".

Ownership: Raycom Media Inc.

Wailuku—KAMN-LP, Ch. 61, Juliet R. Yanklowitz.

Technical Facilities: 1000-w TPO, 10.2-kw ERP, 30-ft. above ground, 827-ft. above sea level, lat. 20° 53' 58", long. 156° 31' 15".

Ownership: Juliet R. Harvey.

Personnel: Daniel C. Yanklowitz, General Manager.

Wailuku—KAUI-LP, Ch. 51, Word of God Fellowship Inc. Phone: 817-571-1229. Fax: 817-571-7478.

Technical Facilities: 49.3-kw ERP, 121-ft. above ground, 3719-ft. above sea level, lat. 20° 39' 37", long. 156° 21' 34".

Transmitter: Puu Makua Peak, near Wailuku.

Ownership: Word of God Fellowship Inc.

Waimea—K57BI, Ch. 57, HITV License Subsidiary Inc. Phone: 703-247-7500.

Technical Facilities: 0.366-kw ERP, lat. 21° 56' 27", long. 159° 32' 25".

Holds CP for change to 0.44-kw ERP, 26-ft. above ground, 837-ft. above sea level, lat. 21° 55' 10.3", long. 159° 31' 36.5". BPTT-20080425AAN.

Ownership: MCG Capital Corp.

Waimea—K63DT, Ch. 63, Hawaii Public Television Foundation. Phone: 808-973-1000.

Technical Facilities: 2.54-kw ERP, 16-ft. above ground, 4213-ft. above sea level, lat. 19° 53' 09", long. 155° 39' 28".

Holds CP for change to channel number 28, 0.075-kw ERP, 18-ft. above ground, 4211-ft. above sea level, lat. 19° 53' 10", long. 155° 39' 29". BDISDTT-20060331BHT.

Ownership: Hawaii Public Television Foundation.

Waipake—K66AY, Ch. 66, Hawaii Public Television Foundation. Phone: 808-973-1000.

Technical Facilities: 0.28-kw ERP, lat. 22° 11' 19", long. 159° 19' 60".

Holds CP for change to channel number 21, 0.11-kw ERP, 18-ft. above ground, 347-ft. above sea level, lat. 22° 11'09.9", long. 159° 20' 09.8". BDISDTT-20060331BFM.

Ownership: Hawaii Public Television Foundation.

Idaho

Albion—K09IR, Ch. 9, Neuhoff Family LP.

Technical Facilities: 0.01-kw ERP, lat. 42° 21' 44", long. 113° 27' 13".

Ownership: Neuhoff Family LP.

Arco—K13VK, Ch. 13, Oregon Trail Broadcasting Co. Phone: 702-642-3333. Fax: 702-657-3423.

Technical Facilities: 10-w TPO, 0.17-kw ERP, 56-ft. above ground, 5358-ft. above sea level, lat. 43° 37' 17", long. 113° 17' 25".

Transmitter: Approx. 1.6-mi. NW of Country Rd. & U.S. 20/26 intersection.

Ownership: Oregon Trail Broadcasting Co.

Personnel: Bill Fouch, General Manager; Robin Estopinal, Chief Engineer.

Ashton—K13YF, Ch. 13, Oregon Trail Broadcasting Co. Phone: 702-642-3333. Fax: 702-657-3423.

Technical Facilities: 0.15-kw ERP, 59-ft. above ground, 5305-ft. above sea level, lat. 44° 03' 59", long. 111° 27' 31".

Ownership: Oregon Trail Broadcasting Co.

Personnel: Bill Fouch, General Manager; Robin Estopinal, Chief Engineer.

Blackfoot—K13VI, Ch. 13, Oregon Trail Broadcasting Co. Phone: 702-642-3333. Fax: 702-657-3423.

Technical Facilities: 10-w TPO, 0.085-kw ERP, 49-ft. above ground, 4531-ft. above sea level, lat. 43° 11' 54", long. 112° 21' 22".

Transmitter: Near corner of Jensen Grove & Parkway Dr., Blackfoot.

Ownership: Oregon Trail Broadcasting Co.

Personnel: Bill Fouch, General Manager; Robin Estopinal, Chief Engineer.

■**Boise**—K31FD, Ch. 31, Three Angels Broadcasting Network Inc. Phone: 618-627-4651. Fax: 618-627-4155.

Studio: 3391 Charley Good Rd, West Frankfort, IL 62896.

Technical Facilities: 1000-w TPO, 72-kw ERP, 200-ft. above ground, 7240-ft. above sea level, lat. 43° 45' 18", long. 116° 05' 52".

Transmitter: Deer Point antenna site, 9.5-mi. NNE of Boise.

Ownership: Three Angels Broadcasting Network Inc.

Personnel: Moses Primo, Chief Engineer.

Boise—K47BE, Ch. 47, Trinity Broadcasting Network Inc. Phone: 714-832-2950. Fax: 714-730-0611.

Technical Facilities: 900-w TPO, 59.6-kw ERP, 79-ft. above ground, 3740-ft. above sea level, lat. 43° 35' 41", long. 116° 08' 39".

Transmitter: Table Rock, approx. 1-mi. E of Boise.

Ownership: Trinity Broadcasting Network Inc.

Personnel: Paul Crouch, General Manager; Ben Miller, Chief Engineer; Rod Henke, Sales Manager.

Boise—KBTI-LP, Ch. 41, Cocola Broadcasting Companies LLC. Phone: 559-435-7000.

Technical Facilities: 150-kw ERP, 49-ft. above ground, 5905-ft. above sea level, lat. 43° 44' 23", long. 116° 08' 14".

Ownership: Cocola Broadcasting Companies LLC.

Boise—KCBB-LP, Ch. 51, Cocola Broadcasting Companies LLC. Phone: 559-435-7000.

Technical Facilities: 150-kw ERP, 98-ft. above ground, 5955-ft. above sea level, lat. 43° 44' 23", long. 116° 08' 15".

Holds CP for change to 15-kw ERP, BDFCDTL-20080923AAL.

Ownership: Cocola Broadcasting Companies LLC.

■**Boise**—KCLP-CA, Ch. 18, Alpha & Omega Communications LLC. Phone: 801-595-0056.

Studio: 309 1/2 11th Ave. S, Nampa, ID 83651.

Technical Facilities: 60-kw ERP, 135-ft. above ground, 7175-ft. above sea level, lat. 43° 45' 18", long. 116° 05' 52".

Transmitter: Deer Point antenna site, 9.5-mi. NNE of Boise.

Multichannel TV Sound: Stereo only.

Ownership: Alpha & Omega Communications LLC.

Personnel: William B. Hull, General Manager; Roy Gould, Chief Engineer.

Boise—KITL-LP, Ch. 20, Lopes Broadcasting of Boise LLC. Phone: 925-788-5930.

Technical Facilities: 150-kw ERP, 52-ft. above ground, 5905-ft. above sea level, lat. 43° 44' 23", long. 116° 08' 14".

Holds CP for change to 15-kw ERP, BDFCDTL-20060330ACS.

Ownership: Todd A. Lopes.

Boise—KIWB-LP, Ch. 43, Cocola Broadcasting Companies LLC. Phone: 559-435-7000. Fax: 559-435-3201.

Technical Facilities: 150-kw ERP, 52-ft. above ground, 5905-ft. above sea level, lat. 43° 44' 23", long. 116° 08' 14".

Transmitter: Table Rock, 1-mi. E of Boise.

Ownership: Cocola Broadcasting Companies LLC.

Personnel: Todd Lopes, President.

Boise—KKIC-LP, Ch. 16, Cocola Broadcasting Companies LLC. Phone: 559-435-7000.

Technical Facilities: 150-kw ERP, 164-ft. above ground, 6020-ft. above sea level, lat. 43° 44' 23", long. 116° 08' 15".

Holds CP for change to 15-kw ERP, BDFCDTL-20080923AAN.

Ownership: Cocola Broadcasting Companies LLC.

Boise—KYUU-LP, Ch. 35, Fisher Broadcasting Co. Phone: 206-404-7000.

Technical Facilities: 150-kw ERP, 70-ft. above ground, 7114-ft. above sea level, lat. 43° 45' 17", long. 116° 05' 53".

Ownership: Fisher Communications Inc.

Boise—KZAK-LP, Ch. 49, Cocola Broadcasting Companies LLC. Phone: 559-435-7000.

Technical Facilities: 150-kw ERP, 98-ft. above ground, 5955-ft. above sea level, lat. 43° 44' 23", long. 116° 08' 15".

Ownership: Cocola Broadcasting Companies LLC.

Boise, etc.—KBSE-LP, Ch. 33, Cocola Broadcasting Companies LLC. Phone: 559-435-7000. Fax: 559-435-3201.

Technical Facilities: 120-kw ERP, 75-ft. above ground, 5876-ft. above sea level, lat. 43° 44' 23", long. 116° 08' 14".

Transmitter: Table Rock, 1-mi. E of Boise.

Ownership: Cocola Broadcasting Companies LLC.

Personnel: Todd Lopes, President.

Bonners Ferry—K11HM, Ch. 11, Boundary County TV Translator District. Phone: 208-267-7220.

Technical Facilities: 0.014-kw ERP, lat. 48° 36' 37", long. 116° 15' 24".

Holds CP for change to 0.044-kw ERP, 85-ft. above ground, 6168-ft. above sea level, lat. 48° 36' 38", long. 116° 15' 28". BDFCDTV-20070821AAZ.

Ownership: Boundary County TV Translator District.

Bonners Ferry—K23IB, Ch. 23, Idaho State Board of Education. Phone: 208-373-7220.

Technical Facilities: 0.63-kw ERP, 20-ft. above ground, 6056-ft. above sea level, lat. 48° 36' 37", long. 116° 15' 24".

Holds CP for change to 0.1575-kw ERP, 20-ft. above ground, 6076-ft. above sea level, BDFCDTT-20081002AAY.

Began Operation: September 16, 1980.

Ownership: Idaho State Board of Education.

Bonners Ferry—K32HA, Ch. 32, Boundary County TV Translator District. Phone: 208-267-7220.

Technical Facilities: 1.1-kw ERP, 40-ft. above ground, 6123-ft. above sea level, lat. 48° 36' 37", long. 116° 15' 24".

Holds CP for change to 0.383-kw ERP, 85-ft. above ground, 6168-ft. above sea level, lat. 48° 36' 38", long. 116° 15' 28". BDFCDTT-20070821ABA.

Began Operation: September 16, 1980.

Ownership: Boundary County TV Translator District.

Bonners Ferry—K35IC, Ch. 35, Boundary County TV Translator District. Phone: 208-267-7220.

Technical Facilities: 1.1-kw ERP, 40-ft. above ground, 6123-ft. above sea level, lat. 48° 36' 37", long. 116° 15' 24".

Holds CP for change to 0.383-kw ERP, 85-ft. above ground, 6168-ft. above sea level, lat. 48° 36' 38", long. 116° 15' 28". BDFCDTT-20070821ABB.

Ownership: Boundary County TV Translator District.

Bonners Ferry—K46HZ, Ch. 46, Boundary County TV Translator District. Phone: 208-267-7220.

Technical Facilities: 1.1-kw ERP, 40-ft. above ground, 6123-ft. above sea level, lat. 48° 36' 37", long. 116° 15' 24".

Holds CP for change to 0.383-kw ERP, 85-ft. above ground, 6168-ft. above sea level, lat. 48° 36' 48", long. 116° 15' 28". BDFCDTT-20070821ABC.

Ownership: Boundary County TV Translator District.

Bonners Ferry—K50GL, Ch. 50, Boundary County TV Translator District. Phone: 208-267-7220.

Technical Facilities: 0.132-kw ERP, lat. 48° 36' 37", long. 116° 15' 24".

Holds CP for change to 0.383-kw ERP, 85-ft. above ground, 6168-ft. above sea level, lat. 48° 36' 38", long. 116° 15' 28". BDFCDTT-20070821ABD.

Ownership: Boundary County TV Translator District.

Bonners Ferry—K51IN, Ch. 51, Three Angels Broadcasting Network Inc. Phone: 618-627-4651. Fax: 618-627-4155.

Technical Facilities: 3-kw ERP, 66-ft. above ground, 6148-ft. above sea level, lat. 48° 36' 37", long. 116° 15' 24".

Ownership: Three Angels Broadcasting Network Inc.

Personnel: Moses Primo, Broadcasting Operations & Engineering Director.

Brownlee—K09OP, Ch. 9, Idaho Power Co.

Technical Facilities: 0.02-kw ERP, lat. 44° 47' 51", long. 116° 53' 06".

Ownership: Idaho Power Co.

Brownlee—K13QL, Ch. 13, Idaho Power Co.

Technical Facilities: 0.02-kw ERP, lat. 44° 47' 51", long. 116° 53' 06".

Ownership: Idaho Power Co.

Brownlee Power Plant—K11PD, Ch. 11, Idaho Power Co.

Technical Facilities: 0.02-kw ERP, lat. 44° 47' 51", long. 116° 53' 06".

Ownership: Idaho Power Co.

Burley—K07UL, Ch. 7, Falls Broadcasting Co. Phone: 702-642-3333. Fax: 702-657-3423.

Technical Facilities: 10-w TPO, 0.174-kw ERP, 56-ft. above ground, 4206-ft. above sea level, lat. 42° 32' 38", long. 113° 48' 00".

Transmitter: Near intersection of 8th St. & Yale Ave., Burley.

Ownership: Sunbelt Communications Co.

Personnel: Bill Fouch, General Manager; Robin Estopinal, Chief Engineer.

Burley, etc.—K14IC, Ch. 14, Idaho State Board of Education.

Technical Facilities: 1.28-kw ERP, 43-ft. above ground, 5239-ft. above sea level, lat. 42° 26' 08", long. 113° 37' 24".

Ownership: Idaho State Board of Education.

Burley, etc.—K39GV, Ch. 39, Falls Broadcasting Co. Phone: 702-642-3333.

Technical Facilities: 3.9-kw ERP, 26-ft. above ground, 5236-ft. above sea level, lat. 42° 26' 02", long. 113° 37' 23".

Ownership: Sunbelt Communications Co.

Burley, etc.—K59CC, Ch. 59, Neuhoff Family LP.

Technical Facilities: 1-kw ERP, 5226-ft. above sea level, lat. 42° 26' 08", long. 113° 37' 24".

Ownership: Neuhoff Family LP.

Burley, etc.—K61AP, Ch. 61, NPG of Idaho Inc. Phone: 816-271-8505.

Technical Facilities: 0.684-kw ERP, lat. 42° 26' 08", long. 113° 37' 24".

Holds CP for change to channel number 26, 4.25-kw ERP, 49-ft. above ground, 5239-ft. above sea level, BDISTT-20060324AAF.

Ownership: News Press & Gazette Co.

Burley, etc.—K65AZ, Ch. 65, Fisher Broadcasting - S.E. Idaho TV LLC.

Technical Facilities: 0.005-kw ERP, lat. 45° 04' 05", long. 113° 52' 30".

Ownership: Fisher Communications Inc.

Cambridge—K55GM, Ch. 55, Fisher Broadcasting-Idaho TV LLC. Phone: 206-404-7000.

Technical Facilities: 0.09-kw ERP, lat. 44° 31' 59", long. 116° 39' 22".

Ownership: Fisher Communications Inc.

Cambridge, etc.—K05DC, Ch. 5, KING Broadcasting Co.

Technical Facilities: 0.007-kw ERP, lat. 44° 31' 59", long. 116° 39' 22".

Ownership: Belo Corp.

Cambridge, etc.—K11PB, Ch. 11, Idaho State Board of Education.

Technical Facilities: 0.003-kw ERP, lat. 44° 31' 59", long. 116° 39' 22".

Ownership: Idaho State Board of Education.

Cascade—K09LO, Ch. 9, Idaho State Board of Education.

Technical Facilities: 0.009-kw ERP, lat. 44° 31' 25", long. 116° 02' 50".

Ownership: Idaho State Board of Education.

Cascade—K11GR, Ch. 11, Fisher Broadcasting-Idaho TV LLC. Phone: 206-404-7000.

Technical Facilities: 0.008-kw ERP, lat. 44° 31' 25", long. 116° 02' 50".

Ownership: Fisher Communications Inc.

Cascade—K13GO, Ch. 13, KING Broadcasting Co.

Technical Facilities: 0.085-kw ERP, lat. 44° 31' 25", long. 116° 02' 50".

Ownership: Belo Corp.

Challis—K04OH, Ch. 4, Oregon Trail Broadcasting Co. Phone: 702-642-3333. Fax: 702-657-3423.

Technical Facilities: 10-w TPO, 0.098-kw ERP, 8461-ft. above sea level, lat. 44° 14' 02", long. 113° 57' 23".

Transmitter: Willow Creek Summit, N of Dickey.

Ownership: Oregon Trail Broadcasting Co.

Personnel: Bill Fouch, General Manager; Robin Estopinal, Chief Engineer.

■ **Challis**—K05CJ, Ch. 5, NPG of Idaho Inc. Phone: 816-271-8404.

Technical Facilities: 0.01-kw ERP, lat. 44° 32' 46", long. 114° 04' 57".

Ownership: News Press & Gazette Co.

Challis—K07VI, Ch. 7, Oregon Trail Broadcasting Co. Phone: 702-642-3333.

Technical Facilities: 10-w TPO, 0.075-kw ERP, 20-ft. above ground, 5102-ft. above sea level, lat. 44° 30' 50", long. 114° 09' 24".

Transmitter: 3.5-mi. ENE of center of Challis, 0.9-mi. SE of Beardsley Hot Springs.

Ownership: Oregon Trail Broadcasting Co.

Challis—K10AW, Ch. 10, Fisher Broadcasting-S.E. Idaho TV LLC. Phone: 206-404-7000. Fax: 703-770-7900.

Technical Facilities: 0.01-kw ERP, 8300-ft. above sea level, lat. 44° 32' 46", long. 114° 04' 57".

Ownership: Fisher Communications Inc.

Challis & Ellis—K12LS, Ch. 12, Idaho State Board of Education.

Technical Facilities: 0.089-kw ERP, lat. 44° 32' 45", long. 114° 04' 50".

Ownership: Idaho State Board of Education.

Coeur d'Alene—K18DT, Ch. 18, KHQ Inc. Phone: 509-448-6000.

Technical Facilities: 27.03-kw ERP, lat. 47° 43' 54", long. 116° 43' 47".

Holds CP for change to 2.7-kw ERP, 102-ft. above ground, 4183-ft. above sea level, BDFCDTV-20081105ABI.

Transmitter: W. Canfield Butte, 0.9-mi. NE of Dalton.

Ownership: Cowles Co.

Coeur d'Alene—K41FJ, Ch. 41, KING Broadcasting Co. Phone: 509-448-2000.

Technical Facilities: 9.6-kw ERP, lat. 47° 43' 54", long. 116° 43' 47".

Ownership: Belo Corp.

Coeur d'Alene—K44EC, Ch. 44, Spokane School District No. 81. Phone: 509-354-7800.

Technical Facilities: 11-kw ERP, lat. 47° 43' 54", long. 116° 43' 47".

Transmitter: 0.5-mi. NNW of Coeur d'Alene at West Canfield Butte.

Ownership: Spokane School District No. 81.

Coeur d'Alene—K50DM, Ch. 50, Mountain Licenses LP. Phone: 517-347-4141.

Technical Facilities: 9.96-kw ERP, 89-ft. above ground, 4170-ft. above sea level, lat. 47° 43' 54", long. 116° 43' 47".

Ownership: Mountain Licenses LP.

Coeur d'Alene—K53FF, Ch. 53, Trinity Broadcasting Network Inc. Phone: 714-832-2950. Fax: 714-730-0661.

Technical Facilities: 100-w TPO, 1.3-kw ERP, 69-ft. above ground, 2650-ft. above sea level, lat. 47° 41' 40", long. 117° 20' 01".

Holds CP for change to channel number 51, 10-kw ERP, 34-ft. above ground, 4465-ft. above sea level, lat. 47° 39' 35", long. 116° 57' 12". BDISDTT-20060331AHA.

Transmitter: Fantcher Hill, Spokane.

Ownership: Trinity Broadcasting Network Inc.

Coeur d'Alene—KMNZ-LP, Ch. 38, Spokane Television Inc. Phone: 509-324-4000. Fax: 509-328-5274.

Technical Facilities: 11.2-kw ERP, 75-ft. above ground, 4150-ft. above sea level, lat. 47° 43' 54", long. 116° 43' 47".

Multichannel TV Sound: Stereo only.

Ownership: Spokane Television Inc.

Coeur d'Alene—KQUP-LP, Ch. 47, Word of God Fellowship Inc. Phone: 817-571-1229.

Technical Facilities: 11-kw ERP, 43-ft. above ground, 3182-ft. above sea level, lat. 47° 36' 03", long. 117° 19' 51".

Began Operation: June 10, 1999.

Ownership: Word of God Fellowship Inc.

Coeur d'Alene—KTYJ-LP, Ch. 58, Christian Broadcasting of Idaho Inc. Phone: 208-734-6633.

Technical Facilities: 1000-w TPO, 26.4-kw ERP, 66-ft. above ground, 4146-ft. above sea level, lat. 47° 43' 54", long. 116° 43' 47".

Transmitter: W. Confield Butte, 4-mi. NNE of Coeur d'Alene.

Ownership: Christian Broadcasting of Idaho Inc.

Coolin—K11UN, Ch. 11, Priest Lake Translator District. Phone: 208-443-3896.

Technical Facilities: 0.074-kw ERP, lat. 48° 35' 36", long. 116° 54' 29".

Holds CP for change to 0.016-kw ERP, 33-ft. above ground, 3455-ft. above sea level, BDFCDTV-20070529ABP.

Transmitter: 9.9-mi. NNW of Coolin.

Ownership: Priest Lake Translator District.

Coolin, etc.—K05GL, Ch. 5, Priest Lake Translator District. Phone: 208-443-3896.

Technical Facilities: 0.041-kw ERP, lat. 48° 35' 38", long. 116° 54' 30".

Holds CP for change to 0.013-kw ERP, 33-ft. above ground, 3455-ft. above sea level, lat. 48° 35' 36", long. 116° 54' 29". BDFCDTV-20070529ABN.

Ownership: Priest Lake Translator District.

Coolin, etc.—K09XY, Ch. 9, Priest Lake Translator District. Phone: 208-443-3896.

Technical Facilities: 0.237-kw ERP, 23-ft. above ground, 3445-ft. above sea level, lat. 48° 35' 35.7", long. 116° 54' 32.8".

Holds CP for change to 0.017-kw ERP, 33-ft. above ground, 3455-ft. above sea level, lat. 48° 35' 36", long. 116° 54' 29". BDFCDTV-20070529ABO.

Ownership: Priest Lake Translator District.

Coolin, etc.—K10KR, Ch. 10, Priest Lake Translator District. Phone: 208-443-3896.

Technical Facilities: 0.029-kw ERP, lat. 48° 35' 38", long. 116° 54' 30".

Holds CP for change to 0.016-kw ERP, 33-ft. above ground, 3455-ft. above sea level, lat. 48° 35' 36", long. 116° 54' 29". BDFCDTV-20070529ABM.

Ownership: Priest Lake Translator District.

Coolin, etc.—K12LF, Ch. 12, Priest Lake Translator District. Phone: 208-443-3896.

Technical Facilities: 0.028-kw ERP, lat. 48° 35' 38", long. 116° 54' 30".

Holds CP for change to 0.016-kw ERP, 33-ft. above ground, 3455-ft. above sea level, lat. 48° 35' 36", long. 116° 54' 29". BDFCDTV-20070529ABQ.

Ownership: Priest Lake Translator District.

Coolin, etc.—K31DS, Ch. 31, Priest Lake Translator District. Phone: 208-443-3896.

Technical Facilities: 0.107-kw ERP, 46-ft. above ground, 3235-ft. above sea level, lat. 48° 31' 53", long. 116° 48' 58".

Holds CP for change to 0.99-kw ERP, BDFCDTT-20070529ABR.

Ownership: Priest Lake Translator District.

Coolin, etc.—K40DJ, Ch. 40, Priest Lake Translator District. Phone: 208-443-3896.

Technical Facilities: 0.53-kw ERP, 33-ft. above ground, 3222-ft. above sea level, lat. 48° 31' 53", long. 116° 48' 58".

Holds CP for change to 0.097-kw ERP, 46-ft. above ground, 3235-ft. above sea level, BDFCDTT-20070529ABS.

Ownership: Priest Lake Translator District.

Coolin, etc.—K51EF, Ch. 51, Priest Lake Translator District. Phone: 208-443-3896.

Technical Facilities: 0.109-kw ERP, 39-ft. above ground, 3228-ft. above sea level, lat. 48° 31' 53", long. 116° 48' 58".

Holds CP for change to 0.095-kw ERP, 46-ft. above ground, 3235-ft. above sea level, BDFCDTT-20070529ABU.

Ownership: Priest Lake Translator District.

Cottonwood, etc.—K39CT, Ch. 39, Faith TV.

Technical Facilities: 1.2-kw ERP, 39-ft. above ground, 5771-ft. above sea level, lat. 46° 04' 09", long. 116° 27' 54".

Transmitter: Cottonwood Butte.

Ownership: Faith TV.

Council—K05GO, Ch. 5, Idaho State Board of Education. Phone: 208-373-7220.

Technical Facilities: 0.035-kw ERP, 3425-ft. above sea level, lat. 44° 39' 48", long. 116° 26' 24".

Ownership: Idaho State Board of Education.

Council—K09OA, Ch. 9, City of Council.

Technical Facilities: lat. 44° 39' 48", long. 116° 26' 24".

Ownership: City of Council.

Council—K11HA, Ch. 11, City of Council.

Technical Facilities: lat. 44° 39' 48", long. 116° 26' 24".

Ownership: City of Council.

Council—K13GW, Ch. 13, KING Broadcasting Co. Phone: 208-375-7277.

Technical Facilities: lat. 44° 39' 48", long. 116° 26' 24".

Ownership: Belo Corp.

Craigmont, etc.—K26CK, Ch. 26, Central Idaho TV Inc.

Technical Facilities: 1.2-kw ERP, lat. 46° 04' 09", long. 116° 27' 54".

Ownership: Central Idaho TV Inc.

Crouch, etc.—K41EO, Ch. 41, Idaho State Board of Education.

Technical Facilities: 0.007-kw ERP, 13-ft. above ground, 4915-ft. above sea level, lat. 44° 07' 49", long. 116° 00' 28".

Transmitter: 2-mi. NW of Crouch.

Ownership: Idaho State Board of Education.

Dingle, etc.—K09PL, Ch. 9, Bear Lake County TV District. Phone: 208-847-1376.

Technical Facilities: 0.012-kw ERP, 6220-ft. above sea level, lat. 42° 19' 15", long. 111° 17' 12".

Ownership: Bear Lake County T.V. District.

Dingle, etc.—K11PP, Ch. 11, Bear Lake County TV District. Phone: 208-847-1376.

Technical Facilities: 0.012-kw ERP, 6220-ft. above sea level, lat. 42° 19' 15", long. 111° 17' 12".

Ownership: Bear Lake County T.V. District.

Dingle, etc.—K13QY, Ch. 13, Bear Lake County TV District. Phone: 208-847-1376.

Technical Facilities: 0.01-kw ERP, 6220-ft. above sea level, lat. 42° 19' 15", long. 111° 17' 12".

Ownership: Bear Lake County T.V. District.

Driggs—K07QC, Ch. 7, GT Acquisitions I LLC. Phone: 307-353-2300.

Technical Facilities: 0.047-kw ERP, 9947-ft. above sea level, lat. 43° 47' 18", long. 110° 56' 02".

Ownership: GT Acquisitions I LLC.

Driggs—K51HF, Ch. 51, Oregon Trail Broadcasting Co. Phone: 702-642-3333. Fax: 702-657-3423.

Technical Facilities: 1-kw ERP, 26-ft. above ground, 9826-ft. above sea level, lat. 43° 47' 18", long. 110° 56' 02".

Transmitter: Grand Targhee Ski Resort, 8.9-mi. E of Driggs.

Ownership: Oregon Trail Broadcasting Co.

Personnel: Bill Fouch, General Manager; Robin Estopinal, Chief Engineer.

Driggs, etc.—K05GU, Ch. 5, GT Acquisitions I LLC. Phone: 307-353-2300.

Technical Facilities: 0.057-kw ERP, 9947-ft. above sea level, lat. 43° 47' 18", long. 110° 56' 02".

Ownership: GT Acquisitions I LLC.

Driggs, etc.—K13QE, Ch. 13, Idaho State Board of Education. Phone: 208-373-7220.

Technical Facilities: 0.032-kw ERP, 7323-ft. above sea level, lat. 43° 46' 08", long. 110° 59' 40".

Ownership: Idaho State Board of Education.

Elk Bend—K07SZ, Ch. 7, Elk Bend TV, Unincorporated Assn.

Technical Facilities: 0.001-kw ERP, 4524-ft. above sea level, lat. 44° 53' 57", long. 113° 57' 44".

Ownership: Elk Bend TV, Unincorporated Association.

Fairfield—K03FK, Ch. 3, Camas County TV Translator Assn.

Technical Facilities: 0.082-kw ERP, 16-ft. above ground, 5541-ft. above sea level, lat. 43° 17' 22", long. 114° 55' 24".

Ownership: Camas County TV Translator Assn.

Fairfield—K05GT, Ch. 5, Camas County TV Translator Assn.

Technical Facilities: 0.082-kw ERP, 5545-ft. above sea level, lat. 43° 17' 22", long. 114° 55' 24".

Ownership: Camas County TV Translator Assn.

Fairfield—K09OZ, Ch. 9, Camas County TV Translator Assn.

Technical Facilities: 0.082-kw ERP, 5545-ft. above sea level, lat. 43° 17' 22", long. 114° 55' 24".

Ownership: Camas County TV Translator Assn.

Fairfield—K13QP, Ch. 13, Camas County TV Translator Assn.

Technical Facilities: 0.114-kw ERP, 5545-ft. above sea level, lat. 43° 17' 22", long. 114° 55' 24".

Ownership: Camas County TV Translator Assn.

Ferdinand—K07CP, Ch. 7, Ferdinand TV Service.

Technical Facilities: 0.005-kw ERP, 4150-ft. above sea level, lat. 46° 09' 06", long. 116° 24' 15".

Ownership: Ferdinand TV Service.

Firth-Basalt—K12OE, Ch. 12, Oregon Trail Broadcasting Co. Phone: 702-642-3333. Fax: 702-657-3423.

Technical Facilities: 10-w TPO, 0.043-kw ERP, 60-ft. above ground, 4711-ft. above sea level, lat. 43° 18' 46", long. 112° 11' 08".

Transmitter: River Rd., approx. 0.46-mi. NW of intersection with Yellowstone Hwy.

Ownership: Oregon Trail Broadcasting Co.

Personnel: Bill Fouch, General Manager; Robin Estopinal, Chief Engineer.

■ **Fish Creek**—K13CO, Ch. 13, NPG of Idaho Inc. Phone: 816-271-8404.

Technical Facilities: 0.007-kw ERP, 66-ft. above ground, 6178-ft. above sea level, lat. 42° 36' 59", long. 112° 00' 08".

Ownership: News Press & Gazette Co.

Fish Creek, etc.—K11CP, Ch. 11, Fisher Broadcasting-S.E. Idaho TV LLC.

Technical Facilities: 0.004-kw ERP, 6181-ft. above sea level, lat. 42° 36' 59", long. 112° 00' 08".

Ownership: Fisher Communications Inc.

Garden Valley—K49EB, Ch. 49, Garden Valley Translator District.

Technical Facilities: 0.032-kw ERP, lat. 44° 01' 48", long. 115° 49' 35".

Transmitter: Ridge 9.2-mi. SE of Crouch.

Ownership: Garden Valley Translator District.

Garden Valley—K51FL, Ch. 51, Idaho State Board of Education.

Technical Facilities: 0.033-kw ERP, 13-ft. above ground, 5128-ft. above sea level, lat. 44° 01' 48", long. 115° 49' 35".

Ownership: Idaho State Board of Education.

Garden Valley—K55GZ, Ch. 55, Garden Valley Translator District.

Technical Facilities: 0.032-kw ERP, 13-ft. above ground, 5102-ft. above sea level, lat. 44° 01' 48", long. 115° 49' 35".

Transmitter: 9.2-mi. SE of Crouch.

Ownership: Garden Valley Translator District.

Garden Valley—K57FO, Ch. 57, Garden Valley Translator District.

Technical Facilities: 0.03-kw ERP, 44° 01' 48", long. 115° 49' 35".

Transmitter: SE of Crouch.

Ownership: Garden Valley Translator District.

Garden Valley, etc.—K53EF, Ch. 53, Garden Valley Translator District.

Technical Facilities: 0.032-kw ERP, 16-ft. above ground, 5105-ft. above sea level, lat. 44° 01' 48", long. 115° 49' 35".

Ownership: Garden Valley Translator District.

Georgetown—K15GO, Ch. 15, Idaho State Board of Education. Phone: 208-373-7220.

Technical Facilities: 0.326-kw ERP, 38-ft. above ground, 6935-ft. above sea level, lat. 42° 30' 07", long. 111° 20' 31".

Ownership: Idaho State Board of Education.

Georgetown—K16HQ-D, Ch. 16, Bear Lake Country TV District. Phone: 208-847-1376.

Technical Facilities: 0.2-kw ERP, 15-ft. above ground, 7016-ft. above sea level, lat. 42° 30' 00", long. 111° 20' 19".

Ownership: Bear Lake County T.V. District.

Georgetown—K17CO, Ch. 17, Bear Lake County TV District.

Technical Facilities: 0.088-kw ERP, 20-ft. above ground, 7001-ft. above sea level, lat. 42° 30' 00", long. 111° 20' 19".

Ownership: Bear Lake County T.V. District.

Glenns Ferry—K04EN, Ch. 4, Neuhoff Family LP. Phone: 561-625-0616.

Technical Facilities: 0.01-kw ERP, lat. 42° 55' 37", long. 115° 21' 10".

Ownership: Neuhoff Family LP.

Glenns Ferry—K05DD, Ch. 5, King Broadcasting Co.

Technical Facilities: 0.012-kw ERP, lat. 42° 55' 37", long. 115° 21' 10".

Ownership: Belo Corp.

Glenns Ferry—K09HS, Ch. 9, Fisher Broadcasting-Idaho TV LLC. Phone: 209-404-7000.

Technical Facilities: 0.009-kw ERP, lat. 42° 55' 37", long. 115° 21' 10".

Ownership: Fisher Communications Inc.

Grace, etc.—K07BK, Ch. 7, Caribou County TV Assn.

Technical Facilities: 0.03-kw ERP, lat. 42° 37' 48", long. 111° 41' 00".

Ownership: Caribou County TV Assn.

Grace, etc.—K11BC, Ch. 11, Caribou County TV Assn.

Technical Facilities: 0.27-kw ERP, lat. 42° 37' 48", long. 111° 41' 00".

Ownership: Caribou County TV Assn.

Grace, etc.—K13AY, Ch. 13, Caribou County TV Assn.

Technical Facilities: 0.26-kw ERP, lat. 42° 37' 48", long. 111° 41' 00".

Ownership: Caribou County TV Assn.

Grangeville—K19BY, Ch. 19, Mountain Licenses LP. Phone: 517-347-4111.

Technical Facilities: 0.928-kw ERP, 52-ft. above ground, 5781-ft. above sea level, lat. 46° 04' 09", long. 116° 27' 54".

Ownership: Mountain Licenses LP.

Grangeville—K46HX, Ch. 46, Idaho State Board of Education. Phone: 208-373-7220.

Technical Facilities: 1.35-kw ERP, 52-ft. above ground, 5787-ft. above sea level, lat. 46° 04' 09", long. 116° 27' 54".

Holds CP for change to 15-kw ERP, BDFCDTT-20071221ADE.

Ownership: Idaho State Board of Education.

Grangeville, etc.—K43CI, Ch. 43, Central Idaho TV Inc.

Technical Facilities: 1.26-kw ERP, lat. 46° 04' 09", long. 116° 27' 54".

Ownership: Central Idaho TV Inc.

Grangeville, etc.—K48DH, Ch. 48, Central Idaho TV Inc.

Technical Facilities: 1.19-kw ERP, lat. 46° 04' 09", long. 116° 27' 54".

Ownership: Central Idaho TV Inc.

Grangeville, etc.—K69AK, Ch. 69, Central Idaho TV Inc.

Technical Facilities: 1.237-kw ERP, lat. 46° 04' 09", long. 116° 27' 54".

Transmitter: Cottonwood Butte, 6-mi. WNW of Cottonwood.

Ownership: Central Idaho TV Inc.

Hagerman—K29GV, Ch. 29, Hagerman Translator District. Phone: 208-837-6525.

Technical Facilities: 1.43-kw ERP, 16-ft. above ground, 3415-ft. above sea level, lat. 42° 50' 56", long. 114° 54' 44".

Ownership: Hagerman Translator District.

Hagerman—K31IF, Ch. 31, Hagerman Translator District. Phone: 208-837-6525.

Technical Facilities: 1.44-kw ERP, 16-ft. above ground, 3432-ft. above sea level, lat. 42° 50' 56", long. 114° 54' 44".

Ownership: Hagerman Translator District.

Hagerman—K41JF, Ch. 41, Hagerman Translator District. Phone: 208-837-6525.

Technical Facilities: 1.43-kw ERP, 16-ft. above ground, 3432-ft. above sea level, lat. 42° 50' 56", long. 114° 54' 44".

Ownership: Hagerman Translator District.

Hagerman—K47JW, Ch. 47, Hagerman Translator District. Phone: 208-837-6525.

Technical Facilities: 1.43-kw ERP, 16-ft. above ground, 3432-ft. above sea level, lat. 42° 50' 56", long. 114° 54' 44".

Ownership: Hagerman Translator District.

Hagerman—K49IT, Ch. 49, Hagerman Translator District. Phone: 208-837-6063.

Technical Facilities: 1.43-kw ERP, 16-ft. above ground, 3432-ft. above sea level, lat. 42° 50' 56", long. 114° 54' 44".

Ownership: Hagerman Translator District.

Hagerman—K57CC, Ch. 57, Neuhoff Family LP.

Technical Facilities: 1.29-kw ERP, lat. 42° 50' 56", long. 114° 54' 44".

Ownership: Neuhoff Family LP.

■ **Hailey**—KSVX-LP, Ch. 18, Plum TV Inc. Phone: 646-292-4200.

Technical Facilities: 100-w TPO, 1.5-kw ERP, 46-ft. above ground, 8688-ft. above sea level, lat. 43° 38' 36", long. 114° 23' 49".

Transmitter: Seattle Ridge, 3.1-mi. from Ketchum.

Ownership: Plum TV Inc.

Personnel: Clint Stennett, General Manager; Maria Prekegys, Sales Manager.

Hollister—K30HK, Ch. 30, Turner Enterprises. Phone: 954-732-9539.

Technical Facilities: 0.85-kw ERP, 66-ft. above ground, 4035-ft. above sea level, lat. 42° 33' 45.3", long. 114° 43' 17.8".

Ownership: Marcia T. Turner.

Idaho Falls—K12NZ, Ch. 12, Oregon Trail Broadcasting Co. Phone: 702-642-3333. Fax: 702-657-3423.

Technical Facilities: 0.113-kw ERP, 43-ft. above ground, 4767-ft. above sea level, lat. 43° 30' 39.5", long. 112° 00' 35.3".

Ownership: Oregon Trail Broadcasting Co.

Personnel: Bill Fouch, General Manager; Robin Estopinal, Chief Engineer.

Idaho Falls—K26EW, Ch. 26, Trinity Broadcasting Network Inc. Phone: 714-832-2950. Fax: 714-730-0661.

Technical Facilities: 1000-w TPO, 23-kw ERP, 26-ft. above ground, 5561-ft. above sea level, lat. 43° 32' 37", long. 111° 53' 07".

Transmitter: Side of existing tower, 2.4-mi. NE of Iona.

Ownership: Trinity Broadcasting Network Inc.

Idaho Falls—K39HJ, Ch. 39, Marcia T. Turner. Phone: 954-732-9539.

Technical Facilities: 0.7-kw ERP, 295-ft. above ground, 5026-ft. above sea level, lat. 43° 31' 00", long. 112° 00' 40".

Ownership: Marcia T. Turner.

Inkom, etc.—K07NO, Ch. 7, Inkom TV Assn.

Technical Facilities: 0.089-kw ERP, lat. 42° 46' 38", long. 112° 10' 00".

Ownership: Inkom TV Assn.

Irwin & Swan Valley—K13QH, Ch. 13, Idaho State Board of Education. Phone: 208-373-7220.

Technical Facilities: 0.01-kw ERP, lat. 43° 24' 21", long. 111° 17' 33".

Ownership: Idaho State Board of Education.

Jerome—K08KV, Ch. 8, Falls Broadcasting Co. Phone: 702-642-3333. Fax: 702-657-3423.

Technical Facilities: 10-w TPO, 0.151-kw ERP, 56-ft. above ground, 3865-ft. above sea level, lat. 42° 43' 55", long. 114° 30' 06".

Transmitter: N side of 8th Ave., Jerome.

Ownership: Sunbelt Communications Co.

Personnel: Bill Fouch, General Manager; Robin Estopinal, Chief Engineer.

Juliaetta—K07NL, Ch. 7, Juliaetta TV Assn. Phone: 208-276-3661.

Technical Facilities: 0.007-kw ERP, lat. 46° 34' 44", long. 116° 41' 26".

Ownership: Juliaetta TV Association.

Juliaetta—K09DF, Ch. 9, Juliaetta TV Assn. Phone: 208-276-3661.

Technical Facilities: 0.007-kw ERP, lat. 46° 34' 44", long. 116° 41' 26".

Ownership: Juliaetta TV Association.

Juliaetta—K11DL, Ch. 11, Juliaetta TV Association. Phone: 208-763-3661.

Technical Facilities: 0.002-kw ERP, lat. 46° 40' 10", long. 116° 45' 10".

Ownership: Juliaetta TV Association.

Juliaetta—K41GW, Ch. 41, Juliaetta TV Assn. Phone: 208-276-3661.

Technical Facilities: 0.004-kw ERP, lat. 46° 34' 44", long. 116° 41' 26".

Ownership: Juliaetta TV Association.

Juliaetta—K43GE, Ch. 43, Idaho State Board of Education. Phone: 208-373-7220.

Technical Facilities: 0.01-kw ERP, lat. 46° 36' 31", long. 116° 41' 45".

Ownership: Idaho State Board of Education.

Juliaetta—K48HB, Ch. 48, Juliaetta TV Association. Phone: 208-276-3661.

Technical Facilities: 0.004-kw ERP, lat. 46° 34' 44", long. 116° 41' 26".

Ownership: Juliaetta TV Association.

Kamiah—K07AQ, Ch. 7, Kamiah Valley TV Inc. Phone: 208-983-1014.

Technical Facilities: 0.002-kw ERP, lat. 46° 11' 30", long. 116° 02' 00".

Ownership: Kamiah Valley TV Inc.

Kamiah—K09AL, Ch. 9, Kamiah Valley TV Inc. Phone: 208-983-1014.

Technical Facilities: 0.002-kw ERP, lat. 46° 11' 30", long. 116° 02' 00".

Ownership: Kamiah Valley TV Inc.

Kamiah—K11KO, Ch. 11, Kamiah Valley TV Inc. Phone: 208-983-1014.

Technical Facilities: 0.001-kw ERP, lat. 46° 11' 30", long. 116° 02' 00".

Ownership: Kamiah Valley TV Inc.

Kamiah—K13AP, Ch. 13, Kamiah Valley TV Inc. Phone: 208-983-1014.

Technical Facilities: 0.002-kw ERP, lat. 46° 11' 30", long. 116° 02' 00".

Ownership: Kamiah Valley TV Inc.

Kellogg—K49JD, Ch. 49, Idaho State Board of Education. Phone: 208-373-7220.

Technical Facilities: 0.065-kw ERP, 13-ft. above ground, 6227-ft. above sea level, lat. 47° 29' 32", long. 116° 08' 33".

Ownership: Idaho State Board of Education.

Ketchum—KSVT-LP, Ch. 20, Plum TV Inc. Phone: 646-292-4200.

Technical Facilities: 20-w TPO, 0.143-kw ERP, 8671-ft. above sea level, lat. 43° 38' 36", long. 114° 23' 49".

Transmitter: Seattle Ridge, 3.1-mi. from Ketchum.

Ownership: Plum TV Inc.

Personnel: Clint Stennett, General Manager; Maria Prekegys, Sales Manager.

Ketchum, etc.—K13HG, Ch. 13, Neuhoff Family LP.

Technical Facilities: 0.01-kw ERP, lat. 43° 40' 55", long. 114° 20' 51".

Ownership: Neuhoff Family LP.

Kooskia & Stites—K05GQ, Ch. 5, Idaho State Board of Education. Phone: 208-373-7220.

Technical Facilities: 0.01-kw ERP, lat. 46° 09' 23", long. 115° 58' 50".

Ownership: Idaho State Board of Education.

Lava Hot Springs—K14MC, Ch. 14, Idaho State Board of Education. Phone: 208-373-7220. Fax: 208-373-7245.

Technical Facilities: 0.007-kw ERP, 6221-ft. above ground, 12442-ft. above sea level, lat. 42° 36' 46", long. 112° 00' 05".

Ownership: Idaho State Board of Education.

■**Leadore**—K13RV, Ch. 13, NPG of Idaho Inc. Phone: 816-271-8404.

Technical Facilities: 0.007-kw ERP, lat. 44° 42' 40", long. 113° 19' 25".

Ownership: News Press & Gazette Co.

Leadore—K14IJ, Ch. 14, Idaho State Board of Education.

Technical Facilities: 0.015-kw ERP, 13-ft. above ground, 6529-ft. above sea level, lat. 44° 42' 40", long. 113° 19' 25".

Ownership: Idaho State Board of Education.

Leadore—K61CI, Ch. 61, NPG of Idaho Inc. Phone: 816-271-8505.

Technical Facilities: 0.99-kw ERP, lat. 44° 40' 02", long. 113° 34' 00".

Holds CP for change to channel number 26, 16-ft. above ground, 6037-ft. above sea level, BDISTT-20060324AAE.

Ownership: News Press & Gazette Co.

Leadore, etc.—K11BD, Ch. 11, Salmon TV Translator District. Phone: 208-756-2349.

Technical Facilities: 0.003-kw ERP, 6112-ft. above sea level, lat. 44° 42' 30", long. 113° 20' 00".

Ownership: Salmon TV Translator District.

Lemhi, etc.—K05BE, Ch. 5, Salmon TV Translator District. Phone: 208-756-2349.

Technical Facilities: 0.246-kw ERP, lat. 44° 52' 30", long. 113° 34' 40".

Ownership: Salmon TV Translator District.

Lemhi, etc.—K09SD, Ch. 9, Salmon TV Translator District. Phone: 208-756-2349.

Technical Facilities: 0.163-kw ERP, lat. 44° 55' 30", long. 113° 34' 40".

Ownership: Salmon TV Translator District.

Lewiston—K15CH, Ch. 15, Washington State U. Phone: 509-335-6536. Fax: 509-335-3772.

Technical Facilities: 0.18-kw ERP, lat. 46° 27' 04", long. 117° 02' 46".

Holds CP for change to 20-ft. above ground, 2871-ft. above sea level, BDFCDTT-20060330AIZ.

Ownership: Washington State U.

Lewiston—K21CC, Ch. 21, King Broadcasting Co. Phone: 214-977-6606.

Technical Facilities: 0.12-kw ERP, lat. 46° 27' 04", long. 117° 02' 46".

Ownership: Belo Corp.

Lewiston—K27GO, Ch. 27, Trinity Broadcasting Network Inc. Phone: 714-832-2950. Fax: 714-730-0661.

Technical Facilities: 2.2-kw ERP, lat. 46° 27' 29", long. 117° 06' 05".

Ownership: Trinity Broadcasting Network Inc.

Lewiston—K35BW, Ch. 35, KHQ Inc. Phone: 508-448-6000.

Technical Facilities: 100-w TPO, 0.617-kw ERP, 37-ft. above ground, 2877-ft. above sea level, lat. 46° 27' 04", long. 117° 02' 46".

Holds CP for change to 0.147-kw ERP, 26-ft. above ground, 2877-ft. above sea level, BDFCDTT-20081105ABJ.

Transmitter: 2.5-mi. N of Clarkston, WA.

Ownership: Cowles Co.

Lewiston—K45FZ, Ch. 45, Spokane Television Inc. Phone: 509-324-4000.

Technical Facilities: 0.634-kw ERP, 27-ft. above ground, 2875-ft. above sea level, lat. 46° 27' 04", long. 117° 02' 46".

Ownership: Spokane Television Inc.

Lewiston—K51HY, Ch. 51, Idaho State Board of Education. Phone: 208-373-7220.

Technical Facilities: 0.362-kw ERP, 38-ft. above ground, 2869-ft. above sea level, lat. 46° 27' 03", long. 117° 02' 46".

Holds CP for change to 38-ft. above ground, 2862-ft. above sea level, BDFCDTT-20081022AAG.

Ownership: Idaho State Board of Education.

Lewiston—K53GN, Ch. 53, Spokane School District No. 81. Phone: 509-354-7800.

Technical Facilities: 1.32-kw ERP, lat. 46° 27' 04", long. 117° 02' 46".

Ownership: Spokane School District No. 81.

Lewiston—K58GL, Ch. 58, Trinity Christian Center of Santa Ana Inc. Phone: 714-832-2950. Fax: 714-730-0661.

Technical Facilities: 3.5-kw ERP, lat. 46° 27' 30", long. 117° 06' 01".

Ownership: Trinity Broadcasting Network Inc.

Lewiston—KIDQ-LP, Ch. 27, KIDQ Inc. Phone: 509-758-0900.

Technical Facilities: 11.4-kw ERP, 98-ft. above ground, 2720-ft. above sea level, lat. 46° 27' 38", long. 117° 01' 00".

Ownership: KIDQ Inc.

Lewiston, etc.—K47BW, Ch. 47, Mountain Licenses LP. Phone: 517-347-4111.

Studio: 4600 S. Regal, Spokane, WA 99336.

Technical Facilities: 100-w TPO, 2.58-kw ERP, 20-ft. above ground, 2870-ft. above sea level, lat. 46° 27' 04", long. 117° 02' 47".

Transmitter: 2.5-mi. N of Clarkston.

Ownership: Mountain Licenses LP.

Lowman—K13IA, Ch. 13, Fisher Broadcasting-Idaho TV LLC.

Technical Facilities: 0.003-kw ERP, lat. 44° 05' 41", long. 115° 37' 37".

Ownership: Fisher Communications Inc.

Mackay—K15HR, Ch. 15, Idaho State Board of Education. Phone: 208-373-7220.

Technical Facilities: 0.148-kw ERP, 16-ft. above ground, 7723-ft. above sea level, lat. 43° 55' 40", long. 113° 40' 20".

Ownership: Idaho State Board of Education.

Malad—K31HS, Ch. 31, Oneida School District #351. Phone: 208-766-4405.

Technical Facilities: 1.2-kw ERP, 30-ft. above ground, 5108-ft. above sea level, lat. 42° 04' 50", long. 112° 12' 29".

Began Operation: May 3, 2004.

Ownership: Oneida School District #351.

Malad & surrounding area—K51KS-D, Ch. 51, Oneida County Translator District. Phone: 207-766-4405.

Technical Facilities: 1.6-kw ERP, 30-ft. above ground, 5138-ft. above sea level, lat. 42° 04' 50", long. 112° 12' 29".

Ownership: Oneida County Translator District.

Malad City—K19GF, Ch. 19, Oneida County Translator District. Phone: 207-766-4405.

Technical Facilities: 1.6-kw ERP, 30-ft. above ground, 5108-ft. above sea level, lat. 42° 04' 50", long. 112° 12' 29".

Holds CP for change to 1-kw ERP, BDFCDTT-20081212ACH.

Began Operation: January 25, 1993.

Ownership: Oneida County Translator District.

Malad City—K21HV, Ch. 21, Oneida County Translator District. Phone: 207-766-4405.

Technical Facilities: 1.6-kw ERP, 30-ft. above ground, 5108-ft. above sea level, lat. 42° 04' 50", long. 112° 12' 29".

Holds CP for change to 1-kw ERP, BDFCDTT-20081212ACF.

Began Operation: December 2, 1988.

Ownership: Oneida County Translator District.

Malad City—K23JA-D, Ch. 23, Oneida County Translator District. Phone: 207-766-4405.

Technical Facilities: 1-kw ERP, 30-ft. above ground, 5108-ft. above sea level, lat. 42° 04' 50", long. 112° 12' 29".

Ownership: Oneida County Translator District.

Ownership: Kamiah Valley TV Inc.

Malad City—K25IP-D, Ch. 25, Oneida County Translator District. Phone: 207-766-4405.

Technical Facilities: 1-kw ERP, 30-ft. above ground, 5108-ft. above sea level, lat. 42° 04' 50", long. 112° 12' 29".

Ownership: Oneida County Translator District.

Malad City—K27IN-D, Ch. 27, Oneida County Translator District. Phone: 208-766-4405.

Technical Facilities: 1-kw ERP, 30-ft. above ground, 5108-ft. above sea level, lat. 42° 04' 50", long. 112° 12' 29".

Ownership: Oneida County Translator District.

Malad City—K29HA, Ch. 29, Oneida County Translator District. Phone: 207-766-4405.

Technical Facilities: 1.6-kw ERP, 30-ft. above ground, 5108-ft. above sea level, lat. 42° 04' 50", long. 112° 12' 29".

Ownership: Oneida County Translator District.

Malad City—K33IM-D, Ch. 33, Oneida County Translator District. Phone: 207-766-4405.

Technical Facilities: 1-kw ERP, 30-ft. above ground, 5108-ft. above sea level, lat. 42° 04' 50", long. 112° 12' 29".

Ownership: Oneida County Translator District.

Malad City—K35GW-D, Ch. 35, Idaho State Board of Education. Phone: 208-373-7220.

Technical Facilities: 0.377-kw ERP, 23-ft. above ground, 5102-ft. above sea level, lat. 42° 04' 50", long. 112° 12' 29".

Ownership: Idaho State Board of Education.

Malad City—K49KB-D, Ch. 49, Oneida County Translator District. Phone: 207-766-4405.

Technical Facilities: 1.6-kw ERP, 30-ft. above ground, 5138-ft. above sea level, lat. 42° 04' 50", long. 112° 12' 29".

Ownership: Oneida County Translator District.

Malta, etc.—K23DO, Ch. 23, Idaho State Board of Education. Phone: 208-373-7220.

Technical Facilities: 0.087-kw ERP, 20-ft. above ground, 7129-ft. above sea level, lat. 42° 21' 42", long. 113° 27' 17".

Ownership: Idaho State Board of Education.

McCall—K20HW, Ch. 20, Plum TV Inc. Phone: 646-292-4200.

Technical Facilities: 0.19-kw ERP, 102-ft. above ground, 5161-ft. above sea level, lat. 44° 54' 40", long. 116° 05' 38".

Ownership: Plum TV Inc.

■ **McCall**—K27DX, Ch. 27, Journal Broadcast Group Inc. Phone: 414-332-9611. Fax: 414-967-5400.

Technical Facilities: 100-w TPO, 1.93-kw ERP, 26-ft. above ground, 7385-ft. above sea level, lat. 45° 00' 38", long. 116° 07' 53".

Transmitter: No Business Mountain, S of McCall.

Ownership: Journal Communications Inc.

Personnel: David Harbert, General Manager; Don Conklin, Chief Engineer; Bob Thomas, Sales Manager.

McCall—K41HS-D, Ch. 41, Idaho State Board of Education. Phone: 208-373-7220.

Technical Facilities: 0.0845-kw ERP, 63-ft. above ground, 7448-ft. above sea level, lat. 44° 45' 54", long. 116° 11' 47.6".

Ownership: Idaho State Board of Education.

McCall, etc.—K05FG, Ch. 5, Idaho State Board of Education. Phone: 208-373-7220.

Technical Facilities: 0.04-kw ERP, lat. 45° 00' 29", long. 116° 08' 00".

Ownership: Idaho State Board of Education.

McCall, etc.—K10FD, Ch. 10, Fisher Broadcasting Inc. Phone: 770-216-8277.

Technical Facilities: 0.02-kw ERP, lat. 45° 00' 07", long. 116° 08' 03".

Ownership: Fisher Communications Inc.

McCall, etc.—K13SO, Ch. 13, KING Broadcasting Co.

Technical Facilities: 0.1-kw ERP, lat. 45° 00' 07", long. 116° 08' 03".

Ownership: Belo Corp.

Mink Creek—K08EZ, Ch. 8, Franklin County Translator District #1. Phone: 208-766-4405.

Technical Facilities: 0.005-kw ERP, lat. 42° 15' 10", long. 111° 43' 45".

Holds CP for change to 0.1-kw ERP, 23-ft. above ground, 5902-ft. above sea level, BDFCDTV-20080707AHR.

Ownership: Franklin County Translator District #1.

Mink Creek—K10FF, Ch. 11, Franklin County Translator District #1. Phone: 208-766-4405.

Technical Facilities: 0.04-kw ERP, 187-ft. above ground, 6066-ft. above sea level, lat. 42° 15' 10", long. 111° 43' 45".

Holds CP for change to 0.1-kw ERP, 23-ft. above ground, 5902-ft. above sea level, BDFCDTV-20080711ADB.

Ownership: Franklin County Translator District #1.

Mink Creek—K13HA, Ch. 13, Franklin County Translator District #1. Phone: 208-766-4405.

Technical Facilities: 0.005-kw ERP, lat. 42° 15' 10", long. 111° 43' 45".

Holds CP for change to 0.1-kw ERP, 23-ft. above ground, 5902-ft. above sea level, BDFCDTV-20080707AHV.

Ownership: Franklin County Translator District #1.

Montpelier—K19DQ, Ch. 19, Bear Lake County TV District. Phone: 208-847-1376.

Technical Facilities: 0.257-kw ERP, lat. 42° 23' 22", long. 111° 23' 05".

Transmitter: 7-mi. NW of Montpelier.

Ownership: Bear Lake County T.V. District.

Montpelier—K21CE, Ch. 21, Bear Lake County TV District. Phone: 208-847-1376.

Technical Facilities: 0.257-kw ERP, lat. 42° 23' 22", long. 111° 23' 05".

Transmitter: 7-mi. NW of Montpelier.

Ownership: Bear Lake County T.V. District.

Montpelier—K23BV, Ch. 23, Bear Lake County TV District. Phone: 208-847-1376.

Technical Facilities: 0.257-kw ERP, lat. 42° 23' 22", long. 111° 23' 05".

Transmitter: 7-mi. NW of Montpelier.

Ownership: Bear Lake County T.V. District.

Montpelier—K25CK, Ch. 25, Bear Lake County TV District. Phone: 208-847-1376.

Technical Facilities: 0.44-kw ERP, lat. 42° 23' 22", long. 111° 23' 05".

Ownership: Bear Lake County T.V. District.

Montpelier—K27CS, Ch. 27, Bear Lake County TV District. Phone: 208-847-1376.

Technical Facilities: 0.257-kw ERP, lat. 42° 23' 22", long. 111° 23' 05".

Transmitter: 7-mi. NW of Montpelier.

Ownership: Bear Lake County T.V. District.

Montpelier—K29BM, Ch. 29, Bear Lake County TV District. Phone: 208-847-1376.

Technical Facilities: 0.257-kw ERP, lat. 42° 23' 22", long. 111° 23' 05".

Transmitter: 7-mi. NW of Montpelier.

Ownership: Bear Lake County T.V. District.

Montpelier—K31CI, Ch. 31, Bear Lake County TV District. Phone: 208-847-1376.

Technical Facilities: 0.257-kw ERP, lat. 42° 23' 22", long. 111° 23' 05".

Transmitter: 7-mi. NW of Montpelier.

Ownership: Bear Lake County T.V. District.

Montpelier—K33DR, Ch. 33, Bear Lake County TV District. Phone: 208-847-1376.

Technical Facilities: 0.257-kw ERP, lat. 42° 23' 22", long. 111° 23' 05".

Transmitter: 7-mi. NW of Montpelier.

Ownership: Bear Lake County T.V. District.

Montpelier—K52EC, Ch. 52, Bear Lake County TV District. Phone: 208-847-1376.

Technical Facilities: 0.2567-kw ERP, lat. 41° 23' 22", long. 111° 23' 05".

Transmitter: 7-mi. NW of Montpelier.

Ownership: Bear Lake County T.V. District.

Montpelier—K54DY, Ch. 54, Bear Lake County TV District. Phone: 208-847-1376.

Technical Facilities: 0.257-kw ERP, 16-ft. above ground, 7116-ft. above sea level, lat. 42° 23' 22", long. 111° 23' 05".

Ownership: Bear Lake County T.V. District.

Montpelier—K56FM, Ch. 56, Bear Lake County TV District. Phone: 208-847-1376.

Technical Facilities: 0.588-kw ERP, lat. 42° 30' 00", long. 111° 20' 19".

Transmitter: 1.8-mi. NE of Georgetown.

Ownership: Bear Lake County T.V. District.

Mullan—K10HC, Ch. 10, BlueStone License Holdings Inc. Phone: 212-247-8717.

Technical Facilities: 0.019-kw ERP, lat. 47° 27' 15", long. 115° 40' 23".

Ownership: Bonten Media Group LLC.

Oxbow Dam—K02JS, Ch. 2, Idaho Power Co.

Technical Facilities: 0.004-kw ERP, 2717-ft. above sea level, lat. 44° 57' 34", long. 116° 49' 57".

Ownership: Idaho Power Co.

Paul—K04NO, Ch. 4, Falls Broadcasting Co. Phone: 702-642-3333. Fax: 702-657-3423.

Technical Facilities: 10-w TPO, 0.082-kw ERP, 56-ft. above ground, 4203-ft. above sea level, lat. 42° 36' 20", long. 113° 47' 35".

Holds CP for change to 56-ft. above ground, 4275-ft. above sea level, lat. 42° 36' 22", long. 113° 47' 47". BPTTV-20060925AEA.

Transmitter: N side of Rte. 25, approx. 0.25-mi. W of 4th St.

Ownership: Sunbelt Communications Co.

Personnel: Bill Fouch, General Manager; Robin Estopinal, Chief Engineer.

■ **Payette**—K17ED, Ch. 17, Three Angels Broadcasting Network Inc. Phone: 618-627-4651. Fax: 618-627-4155.

Studio: 3391 Charley Good Rd, West Frankfort, IL 62896.

Technical Facilities: 18.18-kw ERP, 374-ft. above ground, 2854-ft. above sea level, lat. 44° 03' 44", long. 116° 54' 22".

Ownership: Three Angels Broadcasting Network Inc.

Personnel: Moses Primo, Chief Engineer.

Peck—K07BQ, Ch. 7, Peck TV Club.

Technical Facilities: 0.008-kw ERP, lat. 46° 28' 42", long. 116° 27' 30".

Ownership: Peck TV Club.

Peck—K09AX, Ch. 9, Peck TV Club.

Technical Facilities: 0.008-kw ERP, lat. 46° 28' 42", long. 116° 27' 30".

Ownership: Peck TV Club.

Pocatello—K12OA, Ch. 12, Oregon Trail Broadcasting Co. Phone: 702-642-3333. Fax: 702-657-3423.

Technical Facilities: 10-w TPO, 0.043-kw ERP, 28-ft. above ground, 4688-ft. above sea level, lat. 42° 50' 52", long. 112° 26' 24".

Transmitter: 0.5-mi. S of Main St. & Arthur Ave. intersection.

Ownership: Oregon Trail Broadcasting Co.

Personnel: Bill Fouch, General Manager; Robin Estopinal, Chief Engineer.

Pocatello—K21JC-D, Ch. 21, NPG of Idaho Inc. Phone: 816-271-8505.

Technical Facilities: 0.19-kw ERP, 23-ft. above ground, 5673-ft. above sea level, lat. 42° 51' 58", long. 112° 30' 48".

Began Operation: February 17, 2009.

Ownership: News Press & Gazette Co.

Pocatello—K41JC, Ch. 41, Mutual Television Network. Phone: 888-482-1080.

Technical Facilities: 16-kw ERP, 43-ft. above ground, 7319-ft. above sea level, lat. 42° 48' 33", long. 112° 29' 07".

Holds CP for change to 4-kw ERP, BDFCDTT-20060330ACA.

Ownership: Mutual Television Network.

Pocatello—K47JK-D, Ch. 47, Three Angels Broadcasting Network Inc. Phone: 618-627-4651.

Technical Facilities: 15-kw ERP, 217-ft. above ground, 6024-ft. above sea level, lat. 42° 51' 50", long. 112° 31' 10".

Ownership: Three Angels Broadcasting Network Inc.

Pocatello—K51HU, Ch. 51, Marcia T. Turner. Phone: 954-732-9539.

Technical Facilities: 1-kw ERP, 226-ft. above ground, 4721-ft. above sea level, lat. 43° 11' 30", long. 112° 20' 41".

Ownership: Marcia T. Turner.

Pocatello—K61FO, Ch. 61, NPG of Idaho Inc. Phone: 816-271-8505.

Technical Facilities: 0.106-kw ERP, 20-ft. above ground, 5833-ft. above sea level, lat. 42° 51' 58", long. 112° 30' 48".

Ownership: News Press & Gazette Co.

Pocatello—KXPI-LP, Ch. 24, Fisher Broadcasting Co. Phone: 206-404-7000.

Technical Facilities: 1000-w TPO, 10.2-kw ERP, 100-ft. above ground, 5917-ft. above sea level, lat. 42° 51' 58", long. 112° 30' 48".

Transmitter: Howard Mountain, approx. 3.1-mi. W of Pocatello.

Began Operation: February 2, 2001.

Ownership: Fisher Communications Inc.

Preston—K07XM, Ch. 7, Franklin County Translator District #1. Phone: 208-766-4405.

Technical Facilities: 0.08-kw ERP, 26-ft. above ground, 5846-ft. above sea level, lat. 42° 15' 10", long. 111° 43' 45".

Holds CP for change to 0.1-kw ERP, 23-ft. above ground, 5902-ft. above sea level, BDFCDTV-20080707AHY.

Began Operation: October 8, 2002.

Ownership: Franklin County Translator District #1.

Preston—K19EW-D, Ch. 19, Franklin County Translator District #1. Phone: 208-766-4405.

Technical Facilities: 1-kw ERP, 20-ft. above ground, 6221-ft. above sea level, lat. 42° 07' 30", long. 111° 46' 30".

Began Operation: October 3, 1995.

Ownership: Franklin County Translator District #1.

Preston—K21HH, Ch. 21, Franklin County Translator District #1. Phone: 208-766-4405.

Technical Facilities: 1.12-kw ERP, 89-ft. above ground, 6289-ft. above sea level, lat. 42° 07' 30", long. 111° 46' 30".

Began Operation: September 23, 1992.

Ownership: Franklin County Translator District #1.

Preston—K23GR-D, Ch. 23, Franklin County Translator District #1. Phone: 208-766-4405.

Technical Facilities: 1-kw ERP, 20-ft. above ground, 6221-ft. above sea level, lat. 42° 07' 30", long. 111° 46' 30".

Began Operation: June 14, 1982.

Ownership: Franklin County Translator District #1.

Preston—K25HG-D, Ch. 25, Franklin County Translator District #1. Phone: 208-766-4405.

Technical Facilities: 1-kw ERP, 20-ft. above ground, 6221-ft. above sea level, lat. 42° 07' 30", long. 111° 46' 30".

Began Operation: April 23, 1996.

Ownership: Franklin County Translator District #1.

Preston—K27GM-D, Ch. 27, Franklin County Translator District #1. Phone: 208-766-4405.

Technical Facilities: 1-kw ERP, 20-ft. above ground, 6221-ft. above sea level, lat. 42° 07' 30", long. 111° 46' 30".

Began Operation: June 14, 1982.

Ownership: Franklin County Translator District #1.

Preston—K29EY-D, Ch. 29, Franklin County Translator District #1. Phone: 208-766-4405.

Technical Facilities: 1-kw ERP, 20-ft. above ground, 6221-ft. above sea level, lat. 42° 07' 30", long. 111° 46' 30".

Began Operation: June 14, 1982.

Ownership: Franklin County Translator District #1.

Preston—K31FR-D, Ch. 31, Franklin County Translator District #1. Phone: 208-766-4405.

Technical Facilities: 1-kw ERP, 20-ft. above ground, 6221-ft. above sea level, lat. 42° 07' 30", long. 111° 46' 30".

Began Operation: June 14, 1982.

Ownership: Franklin County Translator District #1.

Preston—K33GF-D, Ch. 33, Franklin County Translator District #1. Phone: 208-766-4405.

Technical Facilities: 1-kw ERP, 20-ft. above ground, 6221-ft. above sea level, lat. 42° 07' 30", long. 111° 46' 30".

Ownership: Franklin County Translator District #1.

Preston—K35GJ-D, Ch. 35, Franklin County Translator District #1. Phone: 208-766-4405.

Technical Facilities: 1-kw ERP, 20-ft. above ground, 6221-ft. above sea level, lat. 42° 07' 30", long. 111° 46' 30".

Began Operation: June 14, 1982.

Ownership: Franklin County Translator District #1.

Preston—K40GZ-D, Ch. 40, Franklin County Translator District #1. Phone: 208-766-4405.

Technical Facilities: 1-kw ERP, 20-ft. above ground, 5978-ft. above sea level, lat. 41° 53' 00", long. 112° 04' 42".

Began Operation: October 8, 2002.

Ownership: Franklin County Translator District #1.

Preston—K42GN-D, Ch. 42, Franklin County Translator District #1. Phone: 208-766-4405.

Technical Facilities: 1-kw ERP, 20-ft. above ground, 5978-ft. above sea level, lat. 41° 53' 00", long. 112° 04' 42".

Began Operation: May 3, 2004.

Ownership: Franklin County Translator District #1.

Preston—K44HA-D, Ch. 44, Franklin County Translator District #1. Phone: 208-766-4405.

Technical Facilities: 1-kw ERP, 20-ft. above ground, 5978-ft. above sea level, lat. 41° 53' 00", long. 112° 04' 42".

Began Operation: November 3, 2003.

Ownership: Franklin County Translator District #1.

Preston—K46HW-D, Ch. 46, Franklin County Translator District #1. Phone: 208-766-4405.

Technical Facilities: 1-kw ERP, 20-ft. above ground, 5978-ft. above sea level, lat. 41° 53' 00", long. 112° 04' 42".

Began Operation: November 12, 2004.

Ownership: Franklin County Translator District #1.

Preston—K48IJ-D, Ch. 48, Franklin County Translator District #1. Phone: 208-766-4405.

Technical Facilities: 1-kw ERP, 20-ft. above ground, 5978-ft. above sea level, lat. 41° 53' 00", long. 112° 04' 42".

Began Operation: November 3, 2003.

Ownership: Franklin County Translator District #1.

Preston—K50IE-D, Ch. 50, Franklin County Translator District #1. Phone: 208-766-4405.

Technical Facilities: 1-kw ERP, 20-ft. above ground, 5978-ft. above sea level, lat. 41° 53' 00", long. 112° 04' 42".

Began Operation: November 12, 2004.

Ownership: Franklin County Translator District #1.

Priest Lake—K42GT, Ch. 42, Idaho State Board of Education. Phone: 208-373-7220.

Technical Facilities: 0.007-kw ERP, 20-ft. above ground, 4790-ft. above sea level, lat. 48° 35' 35.5", long. 116° 54' 32.7".

Ownership: Idaho State Board of Education.

Rexburg—K13UF-D, Ch. 13, Oregon Trail Broadcasting Co. Phones: 702-642-3333; 775-336-0604. Fax: 702-657-3423.

Technical Facilities: 0.3-kw ERP, 49-ft. above ground, 5213-ft. above sea level, lat. 43° 47' 58", long. 111° 46' 32".

Began Operation: September 13, 1984.

Ownership: Oregon Trail Broadcasting Co.

Personnel: Bill Fouch, General Manager; Robin Estopinal, Chief Engineer.

Rexburg—K43JD-D, Ch. 43, Idaho State Board of Education. Phone: 208-373-7220.

Technical Facilities: 0.0197-kw ERP, 25-ft. above ground, 5055-ft. above sea level, lat. 43° 45' 19", long. 111° 57' 59".

Ownership: Idaho State Board of Education.

■ **Rexburg, etc.**—K12MA, Ch. 12, NPG of Idaho Inc.

Technical Facilities: 0.409-kw ERP, 66-ft. above ground, 5308-ft. above sea level, lat. 43° 45' 33", long. 111° 57' 51".

Ownership: News Press & Gazette Co.

Rockland—K19CY, Ch. 19, Idaho State Board of Education. Phone: 208-373-7220.

Technical Facilities: 0.015-kw ERP, 16-ft. above ground, 4731-ft. above sea level, lat. 42° 34' 27", long. 112° 54' 00".

Holds CP for change to 0.0037-kw ERP, 16-ft. above ground, 4747-ft. above sea level, BDFCDTT-20081002ABC.

Ownership: Idaho State Board of Education.

Rupert—K02NO, Ch. 2, Falls Broadcasting Co. Phone: 702-642-3333. Fax: 702-657-3423.

Technical Facilities: 10-w TPO, 0.09-kw ERP, 60-ft. above ground, 4290-ft. above sea level, lat. 42° 37' 22", long. 113° 41' 14".

Transmitter: W of County Rte. 100, approx. 0.2-mi. N of intersection with 8th St.

Ownership: Sunbelt Communications Co.

Personnel: Bill Fouch, General Manager; Robin Estopinal, Chief Engineer.

Salmon—K07PV, Ch. 7, Salmon TV Translator District. Phone: 208-756-2349.

Technical Facilities: 0.005-kw ERP, 4780-ft. above sea level, lat. 45° 04' 05", long. 113° 32' 30".

Ownership: Salmon TV Translator District.

Salmon—K30BU, Ch. 30, Salmon TV Translator District. Phone: 208-756-2349.

Technical Facilities: 0.01-kw ERP, lat. 44° 42' 40", long. 113° 19' 25".

Ownership: Salmon TV Translator District.

Salmon—K34CB, Ch. 34, Salmon TV Translator District. Phone: 208-756-2349.

Technical Facilities: 0.15-kw ERP, lat. 44° 40' 02", long. 113° 21' 00".

Ownership: Salmon TV Translator District.

Salmon—K46EC, Ch. 46, Salmon TV Translator District. Phone: 208-756-2349.

Technical Facilities: 0.36-kw ERP, lat. 45° 08' 45", long. 114° 00' 30".

Transmitter: Baldy Mountain, 6-mi. SW of Salmon.

Ownership: Salmon TV Translator District.

Salmon—K49IC, Ch. 49, Idaho State Board of Education. Phone: 208-373-7220.

Technical Facilities: 1.79-kw ERP, 26-ft. above ground, 9176-ft. above sea level, lat. 45° 08' 44", long. 114° 00' 30".

Ownership: Idaho State Board of Education.

Salmon—K59AV, Ch. 59, Salmon TV Translator District. Phone: 208-756-2349.

Technical Facilities: 0.85-kw ERP, lat. 45° 08' 45", long. 114° 00' 30".

Ownership: Salmon TV Translator District.

Salmon—K65BG, Ch. 65, Salmon TV Translator District. Phone: 208-756-2349.

Technical Facilities: 0.85-kw ERP, lat. 45° 08' 45", long. 114° 00' 30".

Ownership: Salmon TV Translator District.

Salmon—K69CA, Ch. 69, Salmon TV Translator District.

Technical Facilities: 0.798-kw ERP, lat. 45° 08' 45", long. 114° 00' 30".

Ownership: Salmon TV Translator District.

Salmon, etc.—K11TY, Ch. 11, Salmon TV Translator District. Phone: 208-756-2349.

Technical Facilities: 0.06-kw ERP, 16-ft. above ground, 4774-ft. above sea level, lat. 45° 04' 05", long. 113° 52' 30".

Ownership: Salmon TV Translator District.

Sandpoint—K16EN, Ch. 16, Idaho State Board of Education. Phone: 208-373-7220.

Technical Facilities: 1.17-kw ERP, 68-ft. above ground, 6315-ft. above sea level, lat. 48° 19' 53", long. 116° 41' 35".

Ownership: Idaho State Board of Education.

Sandpoint—K18HQ, Ch. 18, Three Angels Broadcasting Network Inc. Phone: 618-627-4651.

Technical Facilities: 890-kw ERP, 66-ft. above ground, 6224-ft. above sea level, lat. 48° 19' 53.1", long. 116° 41' 31.9".

Ownership: Three Angels Broadcasting Network Inc.

Sandpoint—K24DW, Ch. 24, Spokane School District No. 81.

Technical Facilities: 0.561-kw ERP, 49-ft. above ground, 6243-ft. above sea level, lat. 48° 19' 53", long. 116° 41' 34".

Ownership: Spokane School District No. 81.

Sandpoint—K48DX, Ch. 48, KHQ Inc. Phone: 509-448-6000.

Technical Facilities: 0.607-kw ERP, lat. 48° 19' 54", long. 116° 41' 35".

Holds CP for change to 0.063-kw ERP, 49-ft. above ground, 6243-ft. above sea level, BDFCDTT-20081105ABK.

Transmitter: Bald Mountain.

Ownership: Cowles Co.

Sandpoint—K52GH, Ch. 52, Mountain Licenses LP. Phone: 517-347-4111.

Technical Facilities: 0.8-kw ERP, 36-ft. above ground, 6266-ft. above sea level, lat. 48° 19' 53", long. 116° 41' 34".

Transmitter: Bald Mountain.

Ownership: Mountain Licenses LP.

Shelley—K13VJ, Ch. 13, Oregon Trail Broadcasting Co. Phone: 702-642-3333. Fax: 702-657-3423.

Technical Facilities: 10-w TPO, 0.054-kw ERP, 56-ft. above ground, 1426-ft. above sea level, lat. 43° 22' 47", long. 112° 07' 59".

Transmitter: Hanson Ave. & Pine St., Shelley.

Ownership: Oregon Trail Broadcasting Co.

Personnel: Bill Fouch, General Manager; Robin Estopinal, Chief Engineer.

Soda Springs—K09ID, Ch. 9, Caribou County TV Assn. Phone: 208-648-7663. Fax: 208-641-7663.

Technical Facilities: 0.026-kw ERP, 20-ft. above ground, 7040-ft. above sea level, lat. 42° 37' 48", long. 111° 41' 00".

Ownership: Caribou County TV Assn.

Soda Springs—K39GZ, Ch. 39, Caribou County TV Assn. Phone: 208-317-0008.

Technical Facilities: 1.135-kw ERP, 85-ft. above ground, 7106-ft. above sea level, lat. 42° 37' 48", long. 111° 41' 00".

Ownership: Caribou County TV Assn.

Soda Springs—K41GK, Ch. 41, Caribou County TV Assn. Phone: 208-648-7663.

Technical Facilities: 1.19-kw ERP, 20-ft. above ground, 7041-ft. above sea level, lat. 42° 37' 48", long. 111° 41' 00".

Ownership: Caribou County TV Assn.

Soda Springs—K47HF, Ch. 47, Caribou County TV Assn. Phone: 208-648-7663.

Technical Facilities: 1.19-kw ERP, 20-ft. above ground, 7041-ft. above sea level, lat. 42° 37' 48", long. 111° 41' 00".

Ownership: Caribou County TV Assn.

Soda Springs, etc.—K12LK, Ch. 12, Caribou County TV Assn. Phone: 208-648-7663.

Technical Facilities: 0.265-kw ERP, lat. 42° 37' 48", long. 111° 41' 00".

Ownership: Caribou County TV Assn.

Soda Springs, etc.—K33HO, Ch. 33, Caribou County TV Assn. Phone: 208-317-0008.

Technical Facilities: 1.135-kw ERP, 85-ft. above ground, 7106-ft. above sea level, lat. 42° 37' 48", long. 111° 41' 00".

Ownership: Caribou County TV Assn.

Soda Springs, etc.—K35HD, Ch. 35, Caribou County TV Assn. Phone: 208-317-0008.

Technical Facilities: 1.135-kw ERP, 85-ft. above ground, 7106-ft. above sea level, lat. 42° 37' 48", long. 111° 41' 00".

Ownership: Caribou County TV Assn.

Soda Springs, etc.—K43GP, Ch. 43, Caribou County TV Assn. Phone: 208-282-2339.

Technical Facilities: 1.19-kw ERP, 20-ft. above ground, 7041-ft. above sea level, lat. 42° 37' 48", long. 111° 41' 00".

Ownership: Caribou County TV Assn.

Soda Springs, etc.—K45GG, Ch. 45, Caribou County TV Assn. Phone: 208-648-7663.

Technical Facilities: 1.19-kw ERP, 20-ft. above ground, 7041-ft. above sea level, lat. 42° 37' 48", long. 111° 41' 00".

Ownership: Caribou County TV Assn.

Soda Springs, etc.—K49HU, Ch. 49, Caribou County TV Assn. Phone: 208-317-0008.

Technical Facilities: 1.135-kw ERP, 85-ft. above ground, 7106-ft. above sea level, lat. 42° 37' 48", long. 111° 41' 00".

Ownership: Caribou County TV Assn.

Soda Springs, etc.—K51HM, Ch. 51, Caribou County TV Assn. Phone: 208-317-0008.

Technical Facilities: 1.135-kw ERP, 85-ft. above ground, 7106-ft. above sea level, lat. 42° 37' 48", long. 111° 41' 00".

Ownership: Caribou County TV Assn.

St. Anthony—K12OB, Ch. 12, Oregon Trail Broadcasting Co. Phone: 702-642-3333. Fax: 702-657-3423.

Technical Facilities: 10-w TPO, 0.03-kw ERP, 56-ft. above ground, 5016-ft. above sea level, lat. 43° 57' 30", long. 111° 41' 18".

Transmitter: S Corner of W. 8th & S. 5th Sts.

Ownership: Oregon Trail Broadcasting Co.

Personnel: Bill Fouch, General Manager; Robin Estopinal, Chief Engineer.

St. Maries—K23HT, Ch. 23, Idaho State Board of Education. Phone: 208-373-7220.

Technical Facilities: 1.13-kw ERP, 15-ft. above ground, 5842-ft. above sea level, lat. 47° 21' 49", long. 116° 24' 43".

Ownership: Idaho State Board of Education.

Tendoy & Baker—K55AI, Ch. 55, Salmon TV Translator District. Phone: 208-756-2349.

Technical Facilities: 4.2-kw ERP, lat. 44° 55' 30", long. 113° 34' 40".

Ownership: Salmon TV Translator District.

Terrace Lakes—K03ET, Ch. 3, Garden Valley Translator District.

Technical Facilities: 0.005-kw ERP, lat. 44° 07' 09", long. 116° 00' 28".

Ownership: Garden Valley Translator District.

Terrace Lakes & Crouch—K67FI, Ch. 67, Garden Valley Translator District. Phone: 208-462-3013.

Technical Facilities: 0.074-kw ERP, 16-ft. above ground, 5026-ft. above sea level, lat. 44° 07' 49", long. 116° 00' 28".

Holds CP for change to channel number 47, 0.075-kw ERP, 16-ft. above ground, 5020-ft. above sea level, BDISTT-20090302AAC.

Ownership: Garden Valley Translator District.

Terrace Lakes, etc.—K05EY, Ch. 5, Garden Valley Translator District.

Technical Facilities: 0.006-kw ERP, lat. 44° 07' 49", long. 116° 00' 28".

Ownership: Garden Valley Translator District.

Terrace Lakes, etc.—K10OA, Ch. 10, Garden Valley Translator District.

Technical Facilities: 0.006-kw ERP, lat. 44° 07' 49", long. 116° 00' 28".

Ownership: Garden Valley Translator District.

Twin Falls—K25EV, Ch. 25, Trinity Broadcasting Network Inc. Phone: 714-832-2950. Fax: 714-730-0661.

Technical Facilities: 1000-w TPO, 11.1-kw ERP, 282-ft. above ground, 4449-ft. above sea level, lat. 42° 43' 54", long. 114° 25' 04".

Holds CP for change to 15-kw ERP, 190-ft. above ground, 4488-ft. above sea level, BDFCDTT-20060331AFA.

Transmitter: Side of KZRT(FM) tower, Flat Top Butte.

Ownership: Trinity Broadcasting Network Inc.

Twin Falls—KBAX-LP, Ch. 27, Christian Broadcasting of Idaho Inc. Phone: 208-733-3133.

Technical Facilities: 975-w TPO, 16-kw ERP, 141-ft. above ground, 4413-ft. above sea level, lat. 42° 43' 44", long. 114° 24' 56".

Transmitter: 11.2-mi. N of Twin Falls on Flat Top Butte, Jerome.

Ownership: Christian Broadcasting of Idaho Inc.

Twin Falls—KCJY-LP, Ch. 55, Twin Broadcasting Inc. Phone: 208-734-5525.

Technical Facilities: 27-kw ERP, 141-ft. above ground, 4413-ft. above sea level, lat. 42° 43' 45", long. 114° 24' 55".

Ownership: Twin Broadcasting Inc.

Twin Falls—KCTF-LP, Ch. 45, Christian Broadcasting of Idaho Inc. Phone: 208-733-3133.

Technical Facilities: 942-w TPO, 16-kw ERP, 141-ft. above ground, 4413-ft. above sea level, lat. 42° 43' 44", long. 114° 24' 56".

Transmitter: Flat Top Butte, 11.2-mi. N of Twin Falls.

Ownership: Christian Broadcasting of Idaho Inc.

Twin Falls—KSAW-LP, Ch. 51, Journal Broadcast Corp. Phone: 702-876-1313.

Technical Facilities: 21.6-kw ERP, 110-ft. above ground, 4401-ft. above sea level, lat. 42° 43' 46", long. 114° 24' 53".

Holds CP for change to 15-kw ERP, BMPDTL-20080219BMB.

Ownership: Journal Communications Inc.

Personnel: Scott Eymer, General Manager; Ken Ritchie, Sales Manager; Denise Vickers, News Director; Don Conklin, Engineering Director.

Twin Falls—KTFT-LD, Ch. 20, King Broadcasting Co. Phone: 214-977-6606.

Technical Facilities: 15-kw ERP, 325-ft. above ground, 4585-ft. above sea level, lat. 42° 43' 48", long. 114° 25' 06".

Ownership: King Broadcasting Co.

Twin Falls—KTFT-LP, Ch. 38, KTVB-TV Inc.

Technical Facilities: 150-kw ERP, 325-ft. above ground, 4583-ft. above sea level, lat. 42° 43' 48", long. 114° 25' 06".

Ownership: Belo Corp.

Twin Falls—KTID-LP, Ch. 58, Neuhoff Family LP. Phone: 773-486-8914.

Technical Facilities: 946-w TPO, 50-kw ERP, 161-ft. above ground, 4459-ft. above sea level, lat. 42° 43' 47", long. 114° 24' 52".

Transmitter: Flat Top Butte, 11-mi. N of Twin Falls.

Ownership: Neuhoff Family LP.

Twin Falls—KTWT-LP, Ch. 43, Neuhoff Family LP. Phone: 773-486-8914.

Technical Facilities: 941-w TPO, 11-kw ERP, 161-ft. above ground, 4459-ft. above sea level, lat. 42° 43' 47", long. 114° 24' 52".

Transmitter: 11-mi. N of Twin Falls.

Ownership: Neuhoff Family LP.

Twin Falls—KYTL-LP, Ch. 53, Lopes Broadcasting of Twin Falls LLC. Phone: 925-788-5930.

Technical Facilities: 150-kw ERP, 125-ft. above ground, 4377-ft. above sea level, lat. 42° 43' 46", long. 114° 25' 15".

Holds CP for change to 125-ft. above ground, 4363-ft. above sea level, BMPTTL-20060703ABA.

Ownership: Todd A. Lopes.

White Bird—K09GK, Ch. 9, White Bird TV Association. Phone: 208-839-2441.

Technical Facilities: 0.001-kw ERP, lat. 45° 51' 08", long. 116° 14' 04".

Ownership: White Bird TV Association.

White Bird—K11BJ, Ch. 11, White Bird TV Association. Phone: 208-839-2441.

Technical Facilities: 0.003-kw ERP, lat. 45° 51' 08", long. 116° 14' 06".

Ownership: White Bird TV Association.

White Bird—K13JL, Ch. 13, White Bird TV Association. Phone: 208-839-2441.

Technical Facilities: 0.006-kw ERP, lat. 45° 51' 08", long. 116° 14' 06".

Ownership: White Bird TV Association.

Illinois

■ **Alton**—W50CH, Ch. 50, Liberty Communications. Phone: 618-463-5757. Fax: 618-465-4017.

Technical Facilities: 2000-w TPO, 41-kw ERP, 184-ft. above ground, 689-ft. above sea level, lat. 38° 55' 12", long. 90° 06' 18".

Transmitter: 3401 Fosterburg Rd., Alton.

Ownership: Liberty Communications (Alton, IL).

Personnel: Fred Church, General Manager & Sales Manager; Al Manning, Chief Engineer.

Arbury Hills—W25DW, Ch. 25, Marcia Cohen. Phone: 202-293-0011.

Technical Facilities: 95-kw ERP, 1214-ft. above ground, 1806-ft. above sea level, lat. 41° 53' 05.98", long. 87° 37' 17.51".

Holds CP for change to 12.5-kw ERP, BDFCDTL-20090217AAT.

Began Operation: June 6, 1995.

Ownership: Marcia Cohen.

Arlington Heights—W64CQ, Ch. 64, Trinity Broadcasting Network Inc. Phone: 714-832-2950. Fax: 714-730-0661.

Technical Facilities: 1000-w TPO, 1.4-kw ERP, 249-ft. above ground, 958-ft. above sea level, lat. 42° 08' 14", long. 87° 58' 57".

Holds CP for change to channel number 42, 150-kw ERP, 249-ft. above ground, 957-ft. above sea level, BDISTT-20070709ACL.

Transmitter: Side of existing WYLL(FM) tower.

Ownership: Trinity Broadcasting Network Inc.

■ **Arlington Heights**—WEDE-CA, Ch. 34, First United Inc. Phone: 708-633-0038.

Technical Facilities: 48-kw ERP, 1457-ft. above ground, 2051-ft. above sea level, lat. 41° 52' 44", long. 87° 38' 10".

Holds CP for change to 4.3-kw ERP, 1457-ft. above ground, 2052-ft. above sea level, BDFCDTA-20081024AAM.

Began Operation: June 11, 1999.

Ownership: First United Inc.

Ashton—WRDH-LP, Ch. 7, CHN Media LLC. Phone: 847-674-0864.

Technical Facilities: 3-kw ERP, 679-ft. above ground, 1494-ft. above sea level, lat. 41° 59' 46", long. 89° 12' 11".

Ownership: KM Communications Inc.

■ **Aurora**—WPVN-CA, Ch. 24, Polnet Communications Ltd. Phone: 773-588-6300.

Technical Facilities: 831-w TPO, 7-kw ERP, 437-ft. above ground, 1204-ft. above sea level, lat. 41° 36' 23", long. 88° 27' 09".

Transmitter: Immanuel & Legion Rds., S of Yorkville.

Began Operation: July 16, 1999.

Ownership: Polnet Communications Ltd.

Bloomington—W51CT, Ch. 51, Trinity Broadcasting Network. Phone: 714-832-2950. Fax: 714-730-0661.

Studio: 420 E Stevenson Rd, Ottawa, IL 61350.

Technical Facilities: 6.6-kw ERP, 392-ft. above ground, 1180-ft. above sea level, lat. 40° 28' 59", long. 88° 59' 43".

Transmitter: 2018 Ireland Grove Rd., Bloomington.

Ownership: Trinity Broadcasting Network Inc.

Personnel: Roger Crawford, General Manager; Charles Boyd, Chief Engineer.

Carbondale—W10AH, Ch. 10, WPSD-TV LLC. Phone: 270-575-8630.

Technical Facilities: 0.05-kw ERP, lat. 37° 42' 29", long. 89° 14' 05".

Ownership: Paxton Media Group Inc.

Carthage—WCRD-LP, Ch. 44, FXM Broadcasting LLC. Phone: 847-674-0864.

Technical Facilities: 35.5-kw ERP, 485-ft. above ground, 1300-ft. above sea level, lat. 41° 59' 46", long. 89° 12' 11".

Holds CP for change to 150-kw ERP, 509-ft. above ground, 1328-ft. above sea level, lat. 42° 17' 48", long. 89° 10' 15". BPTTL-20050627ACM.

Ownership: KM Communications Inc.

■ **Champaign**—W07DD-D, Ch. 7, Three Angels Broadcasting Network Inc. Phone: 618-627-4651. Fax: 618-627-4155.

Technical Facilities: 0.28-kw ERP, 499-ft. above ground, 1269-ft. above sea level, lat. 40° 13' 26.9", long. 88° 17' 55.8".

Ownership: Three Angels Broadcasting Network Inc.

Champaign—W32CM, Ch. 32, Ventana Television Inc.

Technical Facilities: 1000-w TPO, 12.5-kw ERP, 248-ft. above ground, 979-ft. above sea level, lat. 40° 06' 34", long. 88° 14' 06".

Transmitter: 302 E. John St.

Ownership: Ventana Television Inc.

Personnel: John Skelnik, General Manager & Chief Engineer.

Champaign—W34DL, Ch. 34, Trinity Broadcasting Network Inc. Phone: 714-832-2950. Fax: 714-730-0661.

Technical Facilities: 90-kw ERP, 400-ft. above ground, 1086-ft. above sea level, lat. 40° 09' 12", long. 88° 06' 56".

Ownership: Trinity Broadcasting Network Inc.

Champaign—W39BH, Ch. 39, Ventana Television Inc. Phone: 727-872-4210.

Technical Facilities: 12.5-kw ERP, 249-ft. above ground, 978-ft. above sea level, lat. 40° 06' 34", long. 88° 14' 06".

Began Operation: April 20, 1992.

Ownership: Ventana Television Inc.

■ **Champaign & Urbana**—WBXC-CA, Ch. 46, L4 Media Group LLC. Phone: 321-729-8451.

Studio: 4108 Fieldstone Rd, Ste C, Champaign, IL 61822.

Technical Facilities: 15-kw ERP, 274-ft. above ground, 1008-ft. above sea level, lat. 40° 06' 40", long. 88° 14' 35".

Ownership: L4 Media Group LLC.

Personnel: Liz Kiley, Broadcast Vice President; Warren Reeves, Consulting Engineer; Amy Brown, Director, Broadcast Operations.

Champaign/Urbanna—W48CU, Ch. 48, MS Communications LLC. Phone: 414-765-9737.

Technical Facilities: 0.004-kw ERP, 50-ft. above ground, 759-ft. above sea level, lat. 40° 13' 05", long. 88° 06' 55".

Ownership: MS Communications LLC.

Chana—WBKM-LP, Ch. 46, BKM Broadcasting LLC. Phone: 847-674-0864.

Technical Facilities: 35.5-kw ERP, 470-ft. above ground, 1285-ft. above sea level, lat. 41° 59' 46", long. 89° 12' 11".

Holds CP for change to channel number 21, 15-kw ERP, 328-ft. above ground, 1165-ft. above sea level, lat. 41° 53' 52", long. 89° 36' 20". BDCCDTL-20061030AMY.

Ownership: KM Communications Inc.

Chicago—WCHU-LP, Ch. 61, Venture Technologies Group LLC. Phone: 323-904-4090.

Technical Facilities: 50-kw ERP, 1257-ft. above ground, 1849-ft. above sea level, lat. 41° 53' 56", long. 87° 37' 23".

Holds CP for change to channel number 44, 15-kw ERP, 1225-ft. above ground, 1818-ft. above sea level, BMPDTL-20090514ACR.

Chicago—WLFM-LP, Ch. 55, WLFM LLC. Phone: 323-965-5400.

Technical Facilities: 50-kw ERP, 1257-ft. above ground, 1849-ft. above sea level, lat. 41° 53' 56", long. 87° 37' 23".

Holds CP for change to channel number 6, 3-kw ERP, BDISTVL-20061026AEA.

Began Operation: January 30, 2006.

Ownership: Malibu Broadcasting LLC; Venture Technologies Group LLC.

■ **Chicago**—WMEU-CA, Ch. 48, Weigel Broadcasting Co. Phone: 312-705-2600.

Studio: 19418 S 97th Ave, Mokena, IL 60448.

Technical Facilities: 20-kw ERP, 390-ft. above ground, 1099-ft. above sea level, lat. 41° 32' 11", long. 87° 51' 17".

Holds CP for change to 143-kw ERP, 1572-ft. above ground, 2165-ft. above sea level, lat. 41° 52' 44", long. 87° 38' 10". BPTTA-20080804ABH.

Ownership: Weigel Broadcasting Co.

Personnel: John Ambuul, General Manager.

■ **Chicago**—WOCH-CA, Ch. 41, KM LPTV of Chicago-28 LLC. Phone: 847-674-0864. Fax: 847-674-9188.

Technical Facilities: 25-kw ERP, 1167-ft. above ground, 1760-ft. above sea level, lat. 41° 53' 56", long. 87° 37' 23".

Holds CP for change to channel number 49, 15-kw ERP, BDISDTA-20080605ABA.

Began Operation: December 27, 1991.

Ownership: KM Communications Inc.

Personnel: K. C. Bae, General Manager; Stan Byers, Chief Engineer.

■ **Chicago**—WOCK-CA, Ch. 13, KM Communications Inc. Phone: 847-674-0864. Fax: 847-674-9188.

Technical Facilities: 10-w TPO, 3-kw ERP, 1185-ft. above ground, 1778-ft. above sea level, lat. 41° 53' 56", long. 87° 37' 23".

Transmitter: John Hancock Bldg., 875 N. Michigan Ave.

Multichannel TV Sound: Stereo only.

Ownership: KM Communications Inc.

Personnel: Stuart Mackie, General Manager; Stan Byers, Chief Engineer.

■ **Chicago**—WWME-CA, Ch. 23, Channel 23 Ltd. Partnership. Phone: 312-705-2600. Fax: 312-705-2656.

Technical Facilities: 51-kw ERP, 1503-ft. above ground, 2098-ft. above sea level, lat. 41° 52' 44", long. 87° 38' 10".

Transmitter: Sears Tower, 233 S Walker Dr.

Ownership: Weigel Broadcasting Co.

Chicago—WWME-LD, Ch. 39, Channel 23 LP. Phone: 312-705-2600.

Technical Facilities: 4.4-kw ERP, 1450-ft. above ground, 2044-ft. above sea level, lat. 41° 52' 44", long. 87° 38' 10".

Began Operation: March 18, 2008.

Ownership: Weigel Broadcasting Co.

Danville—W31BX-D, Ch. 31, WAND(TV) Partnership. Phone: 217-424-2500.

Technical Facilities: 3.08-kw ERP, 194-ft. above ground, 791-ft. above sea level, lat. 40° 07' 30", long. 87° 37' 49".

Began Operation: December 8, 1980.

Ownership: Block Communications Inc.

Decatur—W29BG, Ch. 29, Trinity Broadcasting Network Inc. Phone: 714-832-2950. Fax: 714-730-0661.

Technical Facilities: 14.9-kw ERP, 449-ft. above ground, 1125-ft. above sea level, lat. 39° 48' 35", long. 88° 59' 31".

Holds CP for change to channel number 32, 15-kw ERP, 449-ft. above ground, 1124-ft. above sea level, BDISDTT-20060329ALT.

Ownership: Trinity Broadcasting Network Inc.

Effingham—WLCF-LD, Ch. 45, Christian Television Network Inc. Phone: 727-535-5622.

Technical Facilities: 15-kw ERP, 1007-ft. above ground, 1697-ft. above sea level, lat. 39° 57' 03", long. 88° 52' 05".

Began Operation: June 7, 1993.

Ownership: Christian Television Network Inc.

Personnel: Jamie Bye, General Manager; Brian Haarmann, Chief Engineer; Gerri Bye, Sales Manager.

Elgin—W57DN, Ch. 57, Trinity Broadcasting Network Inc. Phone: 714-832-2950. Fax: 714-730-0661.

Technical Facilities: 1000-w TPO, 17.8-kw ERP, 322-ft. above ground, 1093-ft. above sea level, lat. 41° 59' 54", long. 88° 14' 33".

Holds CP for change to channel number 30, 15-kw ERP, BDISDTT-20060213ACF.

Transmitter: WJKL (FM) tower.

Ownership: Trinity Broadcasting Network Inc.

Galesburg—W51DT, Ch. 51, Trinity Broadcasting Network Inc. Phone: 714-832-2950. Fax: 714-730-0661.

Technical Facilities: 17.8-kw ERP, 322-ft. above ground, 1096-ft. above sea level, lat. 40° 56' 34", long. 90° 20' 39".

Holds CP for change to 15-kw ERP, BDFCDTT-20060331AEM.

Ownership: Trinity Broadcasting Network Inc.

■ **Johnston City**—W15BU, Ch. 15, Three Angels Broadcasting Network Inc. Phone: 618-627-4651. Fax: 618-627-4155.

Studio: 3391 Charley Good Rd, West Frankfort, IL 62896.

Technical Facilities: 1000-w TPO, 12.7-kw ERP, 466-ft. above ground, 909-ft. above sea level, lat. 37° 50' 43", long. 88° 55' 46".

Holds CP for change to 7-kw ERP, 449-ft. above ground, 892-ft. above sea level, BDFCDTA-20081209AAH.

Transmitter: 0.6-mi. E of State Rte. 37, 2-mi. N of Johnston City.

Began Operation: June 11, 1991.

Ownership: Three Angels Broadcasting Network Inc.

Personnel: Moses Primo, Chief Engineer; Linda Shelton, Program Director.

Mount Carmel—WCJT-LP, Ch. 12, Wabash Communications Inc. Phone: 618-262-4102. Fax: 618-262-4103.

Studio: 606 Market St, Mount Carmel, IL 62863.

Technical Facilities: 10-w TPO, 0.0374-kw ERP, 112-ft. above ground, 541-ft. above sea level, lat. 38° 24' 44", long. 87° 45' 46".

Transmitter: 606 Market St., Mount Carmel.

Multichannel TV Sound: Separate audio program.

Ownership: Wabash Communications Inc.

Personnel: Kyle Peach, General Manager; Kevin Madden, Sales Manager; Frank Hertel, Engineer; Robert Effland, Engineer.

Palatine—W40BY, Ch. 40, Trinity Broadcasting Network Inc. Phone: 714-832-2950. Fax: 714-730-0661.

Technical Facilities: 37.2-kw ERP, 1493-ft. above ground, 2088-ft. above sea level, lat. 41° 52' 44", long. 87° 38' 08".

Ownership: Trinity Broadcasting Network Inc.

Peoria—W50DD, Ch. 50, Trinity Broadcasting Network Inc. Phone: 714-832-2950. Fax: 714-730-0661.

Technical Facilities: 37.7-kw ERP, 302-ft. above ground, 955-ft. above sea level, lat. 40° 33' 29", long. 89° 34' 05".

Holds CP for change to channel number 33, 15-kw ERP, 302-ft. above ground, 954-ft. above sea level, BDISDTT-20060328ABW.

Ownership: Trinity Broadcasting Network Inc.

■ **Plano**—WSPY-LP, Ch. 30, WSPY-TV Inc. Phone: 630-552-1000.

Studio: One Broadcast Center, Plano, IL 60545.

Technical Facilities: 3.3-kw ERP, 475-ft. above ground, 1106-ft. above sea level, lat. 41° 39' 55", long. 88° 34' 34".

Transmitter: 2-mi. W of Plano.

Quincy—W15CT, Ch. 15, MS Communications LLC. Phone: 414-213-4629.

Technical Facilities: 0.007-kw ERP, 23-ft. above ground, 768-ft. above sea level, lat. 39° 58' 19", long. 91° 19' 40".

Ownership: MS Communications LLC.

Quincy—W17DD, Ch. 17, MS Communications LLC. Phone: 414-213-4629.

Technical Facilities: 0.007-kw ERP, 23-ft. above ground, 768-ft. above sea level, lat. 39° 58' 19", long. 91° 19' 40".

Ownership: MS Communications LLC.

Quincy—W18CJ, Ch. 18, Three Angels Broadcasting Network Inc. Phone: 618-627-4651. Fax: 618-627-4155.

Studio: 3391 Charley Good Rd, West Frankfort, IL 62896.

Technical Facilities: 1000-w TPO, 21.3-kw ERP, 1339-ft. above sea level, lat. 39° 58' 18", long. 91° 19' 42".

Transmitter: NE of Quincy.

Ownership: Three Angels Broadcasting Network Inc.

Personnel: Moses Primo, Chief Engineer; Linda Shelton, Program Director.

Quincy—W19DI, Ch. 19, MS Communications LLC. Phone: 414-213-4629.

Technical Facilities: 0.007-kw ERP, 23-ft. above ground, 768-ft. above sea level, lat. 39° 58' 19", long. 91° 19' 40".

Ownership: MS Communications LLC.

Quincy—W20CU, Ch. 20, MS Communications LLC. Phone: 414-213-4629.

Technical Facilities: 0.007-kw ERP, 23-ft. above ground, 768-ft. above sea level, lat. 39° 58' 19", long. 91° 19' 40".

Ownership: MS Communications LLC.

Quincy—W36BS, Ch. 36, MS Communications LLC. Phone: 414-213-4629.

Technical Facilities: 0.007-kw ERP, 23-ft. above ground, 768-ft. above sea level, lat. 39° 58' 19", long. 91° 19' 40".

Ownership: MS Communications LLC.

Quincy—W45BM, Ch. 45, MS Communications LLC. Phone: 414-213-4629.

Technical Facilities: 0.007-kw ERP, 23-ft. above ground, 768-ft. above sea level, lat. 39° 58' 19", long. 91° 19' 40".

Ownership: MS Communications LLC.

Quincy—W49BS, Ch. 49, MS Communications LLC. Phone: 414-213-4629.

Technical Facilities: 0.007-kw ERP, 23-ft. above ground, 768-ft. above sea level, lat. 39° 58' 19", long. 91° 19' 40".

Ownership: MS Communications LLC.

Quincy—W51EI, Ch. 51, MS Communications LLC. Phone: 414-213-4629.

Technical Facilities: 0.007-kw ERP, 23-ft. above ground, 768-ft. above sea level, lat. 39° 58' 19", long. 91° 19' 40".

Ownership: MS Communications LLC.

Robinson—W57AO, Ch. 57, Full Gospel Business Men's Fellowship.

Technical Facilities: 1000-w TPO, 9.3-kw ERP, 308-ft. above ground, 860-ft. above sea level, lat. 39° 06' 58", long. 87° 48' 29".

Transmitter: 2-mi. SSE of Annapolis.

Ownership: Full Gospel Business Men's Fellowship International.

Rochelle—WMKB-LP, Ch. 25, Diligent Broadcasting LLC. Phone: 847-674-0864.

Technical Facilities: 39.8-kw ERP, 640-ft. above ground, 1455-ft. above sea level, lat. 41° 59' 46", long. 89° 12' 11".

Ownership: KM Communications Inc.

Rockford—W25CL, Ch. 25, Trinity Broadcasting Network Inc. Phone: 714-832-2950. Fax: 714-730-0661.

Technical Facilities: 3.5-kw ERP, 184-ft. above ground, 974-ft. above sea level, lat. 42° 16' 02", long. 89° 04' 12".

Holds CP for change to channel number 38, 15-kw ERP, BDISDTT-20060330ABA.

Ownership: Trinity Broadcasting Network Inc.

■**Rockford**—WCFC-CA, Ch. 51, Christian Communications of Chicagoland Inc. Phone: 815-877-5151.

Studio: 6110 Broadcast Pkwy, Rockford, IL 61111.

Technical Facilities: 49.4-kw ERP, 367-ft. above ground, 1224-ft. above sea level, lat. 42° 19' 19.9", long. 89° 00' 40.6".

Ownership: Christian Communications of Chicagoland Inc.

Personnel: Holly Swanson, General Manager.

Rockford—WFBN-LP, Ch. 33, Weigel Broadcasting Co. Phone: 312-705-2600. Fax: 312-705-2656.

Technical Facilities: 14.4-kw ERP, 174-ft. above ground, 968-ft. above sea level, lat. 42° 16' 02", long. 89° 04' 12".

Ownership: Weigel Broadcasting Co.

■**Rockford**—WQFL-CA, Ch. 8, Family Values Organization Inc. Phone: 815-677-8000. Fax: 815-987-3975.

Studio: 721 E State St, Rockford, IL 61104.

Technical Facilities: 10-w TPO, 0.016-kw ERP, 180-ft. above ground, 991-ft. above sea level, lat. 42° 15' 51", long. 89° 01' 55".

Transmitter: 4249 E. State St.

Multichannel TV Sound: Stereo and separate audio program.

Ownership: Family Values Organization Inc.

Personnel: Joe Musser, President & General Manager; Todd Housser, Engineer.

■**Salem**—W29CI, Ch. 29, Three Angels Broadcasting Network Inc. Phone: 618-627-4651. Fax: 618-627-4155.

Studio: 3391 Charley Good Rd, West Frankfort, IL 62896.

Technical Facilities: 1000-w TPO, 12.6-kw ERP, 417-ft. above ground, 961-ft. above sea level, lat. 38° 33' 45", long. 88° 59' 57".

Transmitter: 5.3-mi. SW of city center, 0.74-mi. W of Interstate 57, Salem.

Ownership: Three Angels Broadcasting Network Inc.

Personnel: Moses Primo, Chief Engineer.

Springfield—W08DP, Ch. 8, West Central Illinois Educational Telecommunications Corp. Phone: 217-483-7887.

Technical Facilities: 0.14-kw ERP, lat. 39° 49' 44", long. 89° 35' 44".

Holds CP for change to channel number 36, 15-kw ERP, 440-ft. above ground, 1016-ft. above sea level, BDISDTA-20060630AHG.

Ownership: West Central Illinois Educational Telecommunications Corp.

Springfield—W33AY, Ch. 33, Ventana Television Inc. Phone: 727-872-4210.

Technical Facilities: 1000-w TPO, 8.52-kw ERP, 381-ft. above ground, 971-ft. above sea level, lat. 39° 46' 52", long. 89° 36' 17".

Transmitter: 1820 Dirksen Pkwy.

Began Operation: September 27, 1991.

Ownership: Ventana Television Inc.

Sterling—W48CK, Ch. 48, Black Hawk College. Phone: 309-796-2424. Fax: 309-796-2484.

Technical Facilities: 15.8-kw ERP, 351-ft. above ground, 1188-ft. above sea level, lat. 41° 53' 52", long. 89° 36' 20".

Began Operation: December 30, 1991.

Ownership: Black Hawk College.

Personnel: Rick Best, General Manager; Steve Ellis, Chief Engineer.

Sterling-Dixon—W19CX, Ch. 19, Trinity Broadcasting Network Inc. Phone: 714-832-2950. Fax: 714-730-0661.

Technical Facilities: 9.5-kw ERP, 299-ft. above ground, 1135-ft. above sea level, lat. 41° 53' 52", long. 89° 36' 20".

Ownership: Trinity Broadcasting Network Inc.

■**Sugar Grove**—W40CN, Ch. 40, Waubonsee Community College. Phone: 630-466-7900. Fax: 630-466-7799.

Studio: Rte 47 at Waubonsee Dr, Sugar Grove, IL 60554.

Technical Facilities: 23-kw ERP, 182-ft. above ground, 888-ft. above sea level, lat. 41° 47' 46", long. 88° 27' 30".

Holds CP for change to 15-kw ERP, BDFCDTL-20070301ABR.

Ownership: Waubonsee Community College.

Personnel: Michael Vester, General Manager; Steve Zahn, Chief Engineer.

Indiana

Auburn—W07CL, Ch. 7, Kovas Communications. Phone: 219-747-1511.

Studio: 5446 County Rd 29, Auburn, IN 46706.

Technical Facilities: 10-w TPO, 0.032-kw ERP, 272-ft. above ground, 1142-ft. above sea level, lat. 41° 20' 01", long. 85° 03' 08".

Transmitter: 5446 County Rd. 29, Auburn.

Ownership: Kovas Communications.

Brookston—WAJN-LP, Ch. 43, Jerald Nay. Phone: 336-665-1073.

Technical Facilities: 150-kw ERP, 164-ft. above ground, 896-ft. above sea level, lat. 40° 45' 31", long. 87° 02' 39".

Holds CP for change to 2-kw ERP, 197-ft. above ground, 866-ft. above sea level, lat. 40° 32' 48", long. 86° 50'59". BPTTL-20061103ABE.

Ownership: Jerald Nay.

Chesterton—WHCH-LD, Ch. 40, LeSea Broadcasting Corp. Phone: 574-291-8200.

Technical Facilities: 15-kw ERP, 394-ft. above ground, 1243-ft. above sea level, lat. 41° 31' 22", long. 87° 01' 28".

Ownership: LeSea Broadcasting Corp.

■**Clarksville**—WNDA-CA, Ch. 45, Dominion Media Inc. Phone: 812-949-9595.

Technical Facilities: 150-kw ERP, 302-ft. above ground, 1282-ft. above sea level, lat. 38° 22' 09", long. 85° 49' 46".

Transmitter: WAVE-TV Tower, Bald Knob Rd.

Ownership: John W. Smith Jr.

Columbia—W27CT, Ch. 27, Venture Technologies Group LLC. Phone: 323-965-5400.

Technical Facilities: 2-kw ERP, 197-ft. above ground, 1207-ft. above sea level, lat. 39° 37' 55", long. 85° 06' 10".

Ownership: Venture Technologies Group LLC.

Elkhart—W18CF, Ch. 18, Trinity Broadcasting Network Inc. Phone: 714-832-2950. Fax: 714-730-0661.

Technical Facilities: 2.9-kw ERP, lat. 41° 38' 41", long. 85° 59' 11".

Transmitter: 58555 County 7, near Elkhart.

Ownership: Trinity Broadcasting Network Inc.

■**Evansville**—W23BV, Ch. 23, Bethel Sanitarium. Phone: 812-425-6348.

Technical Facilities: 12.9-kw ERP, 472-ft. above ground, 961-ft. above sea level, lat. 38° 03' 49", long. 87° 42' 36".

Holds CP for change to 3.46-kw ERP, BDFCDTA-20080925AAV.

Ownership: Bethel Sanitarium.

Evansville—W38BK, Ch. 38, Trinity Broadcasting Network Inc. Phone: 714-832-2950. Fax: 714-730-0661.

Technical Facilities: 5-kw ERP, 476-ft. above ground, 889-ft. above sea level, lat. 37° 52' 45", long. 87° 27' 17".

Ownership: Trinity Broadcasting Network Inc.

■**Evansville**—WAZE-LP, Ch. 17, Roberts Broadcasting Co. of Evansville, IN LLC. Phone: 314-367-4600.

Studio: 1277 N St. Joe Ave, Evansville, IN 47720.

Technical Facilities: 2.74-kw ERP, 449-ft. above ground, 879-ft. above sea level, lat. 37° 59' 21", long. 87° 35' 48".

Multichannel TV Sound: Stereo only.

Began Operation: December 1, 1992.

Ownership: Steven C. Roberts; Michael V. Roberts.

Personnel: John Engelbrecht, President; Conrad L. Cagle, General Manager & Sales Manager.

Evansville—WTSN-LP, Ch. 36, Evansville Low Power Partnership. Phones: 812-464-4463; 812-471-9300. Fax: 812-465-4559.

Technical Facilities: 13.5-kw ERP, 499-ft. above ground, 912-ft. above sea level, lat. 37° 53' 17", long. 87° 32' 37".

Transmitter: WEVV Tower, 0.9-mi. E of State Rte 414 & US 41 intersection, Henderson.

Began Operation: August 21, 1997.

Ownership: Dunn Family LP; Dunn Broadcasting Co.

Personnel: Dan Robbins, General Manager; Don Hollingsworth, Chief Engineer.

Evansville—WYYW-LP, Ch. 41, Evansville Low Power Partnership. Phones: 812-471-9300; 812-471-0230.

Studio: 44 Main St, Evansville, IN 47708-1450.

Technical Facilities: 13.2-kw ERP, 499-ft. above ground, 912-ft. above sea level, lat. 37° 53' 17", long. 87° 32' 37".

Began Operation: October 15, 1993.

Ownership: Dunn Family LP; Dunn Broadcasting Co.

Personnel: Dan Robbins, General Manager; Don Hollingsworth, Chief Engineer.

Evansville, etc.—WIKY-LP, Ch. 5, Roberts Broadcasting Co. of Evansville, IN LLC. Phone: 314-367-4600.

Studio: 1162 Mt. Auburn Rd, Evansville, IN 47720.

Technical Facilities: 10-w TPO, 0.14-kw ERP, 427-ft. above ground, 856-ft. above sea level, lat. 37° 59' 21", long. 87° 35' 48".

Transmitter: Near intersection of St. Joseph Ave. & W. Maryland, Evansville.

Began Operation: May 7, 1987.

Ownership: Steven C. Roberts; Michael V. Roberts.

Personnel: Conrad Cagle, General Manager & Sales Manager; Lee Thompson, Chief Engineer.

Evansville, etc.—WJPS-LP, Ch. 4, Roberts Broadcasting Co. of Evansville, IN LLC. Phone: 314-367-4600.

Studio: 1162 Mount Auburn Rd, Evansville, IN 47720.

Technical Facilities: 10-w TPO, 0.108-kw ERP, 449-ft. above ground, 879-ft. above sea level, lat. 37° 59' 21", long. 87° 35' 48".

Transmitter: Near intersection of St. Joseph Ave. & W. Maryland.

Multichannel TV Sound: Stereo only.

Began Operation: May 7, 1987.

Ownership: Steven C. Roberts; Michael V. Roberts.

Personnel: Conrad L. Cagle, General Manager & Sales Manager; Lee Thompson, Engineering.

Fort Wayne—W38EA-D, Ch. 38, Tri-State Christian TV Inc. Phone: 618-997-9333. Fax: 618-997-1859.

Studio: 02966 CR 1, Edgerton, OH 43517.

Technical Facilities: 15-kw ERP, 584-ft. above ground, 1398-ft. above sea level, lat. 41° 06' 13", long. 85° 11' 28".

Transmitter: 3632 Butler Rd.

Ownership: Tri-State Christian TV Inc.

Personnel: Kyle Hinnerichs, Station Manager; Lee Gilbert, Chief Engineer.

■ **Fort Wayne**—WFWC-CA, Ch. 45, Tran-Star Inc.

Technical Facilities: 100-w TPO, 5.8-kw ERP, 394-ft. above ground, 1171-ft. above sea level, lat. 41° 05' 58", long. 85° 08' 43".

Transmitter: 2602 Cass St., Fort Wayne.

Ownership: Tran-Star Inc.

Gary—WHNW-LP, Ch. 18, LeSea Broadcasting Corp. Phone: 574-291-8200.

Technical Facilities: 915-w TPO, 26.3-kw ERP, 161-ft. above ground, 761-ft. above sea level, lat. 41° 36' 10", long. 87° 20' 15".

Holds CP for change to 15-kw ERP, BDFCDTL-20060331AGD.

Transmitter: 504 Broadway St., intersection of U.S. Rte. 12 & State Rd. 53, Gary.

Ownership: LeSea Broadcasting Corp.

Personnel: Peter Sumrall, General Manager; Doug Garlinger, Chief Engineer.

■ **Indianapolis**—WALV-CA, Ch. 50, VideOhio Inc. Phone: 317-636-1313. Fax: 317-636-3717.

Studio: 1000 N Meridian St, Indianapolis, IN 46204.

Technical Facilities: 1000-w TPO, 14.9-kw ERP, 833-ft. above ground, 1657-ft. above sea level, lat. 39° 55' 43", long. 86° 10' 55".

Holds CP for change to channel number 46, 46-kw ERP, 888-ft. above ground, 1712-ft. above sea level, BDISTTA-20081208AAT.

Transmitter: Ditch Rd. & 96th St.

Began Operation: April 19, 1991.

Ownership: Dispatch Broadcast Group.

Personnel: Richard Pegram, General Manager; Marc Dunlap, Station Manager; Al Grossniklaus, Engineering Director; Curt Young, Local Sales Manager.

■ **Indianapolis**—WBXI-CA, Ch. 47, Viacom International Inc. Phone: 615-833-1107. Fax: 615-833-0758.

Studio: 1800 N Meridian St, Ste 404, Indianapolis, IN 46202.

Technical Facilities: 1000-w TPO, 13.92-kw ERP, 860-ft. above ground, 1552-ft. above sea level, lat. 39° 46' 11", long. 86° 09' 26".

Transmitter: 111 Monument Circle.

Ownership: CBS Corp.

Personnel: Liz Kiley, Broadcast Vice President; Warren Reeves, Consulting Engineer; Amy Brown, Broadcast Operations Director.

■ **Indianapolis**—WDNI-LP, Ch. 65, Radio One of Indiana LLC. Phone: 301-306-1111.

Technical Facilities: 40-kw ERP, 286-ft. above ground, 730-ft. above sea level, lat. 39° 49' 29", long. 86° 09' 23".

Holds CP for change to channel number 19, 15-kw ERP, 449-ft. above ground, 1275-ft. above sea level, lat. 39° 48' 01", long. 86° 04' 39". BDFCDTA-20090206ABO.

Ownership: Radio One Licenses Inc.

Personnel: Bill Shirk, General Manager; Marty Hensley, Chief Engineer; Doug Housemeyer, Sales Manager.

■ **Indianapolis**—WIIH-CA, Ch. 17, Indiana Broadcasting LLC. Phone: 202-462-6065.

Technical Facilities: 6-w TPO, 14.5-kw ERP, 531-ft. above ground, 1348-ft. above sea level, lat. 39° 53' 25", long. 86° 12' 20".

Transmitter: 7619 Walnut Dr.

Ownership: LIN TV Corp.

Personnel: Scott Blumenthal, General Manager; Jeff White, General Sales Manager; Terry VanBibber, Chief Engineer; Rick Thedwall, Program Manager.

Indianapolis—WIPX-LP, Ch. 51, ION Media License Co. LLC, Debtor in Possession. Phone: 561-682-4206.

Technical Facilities: 588-w TPO, 6.5-kw ERP, 781-ft. above ground, 1496-ft. above sea level, lat. 39° 46' 11", long. 86° 09' 26".

Holds CP for change to channel number 34, 150-kw ERP, 949-ft. above ground, 1784-ft. above sea level, lat. 39° 53' 40", long. 86° 12' 21". BDISTTL-20071206ACU.

Transmitter: 111 Monument Circle, Bank One Center.

Began Operation: September 18, 1997.

Ownership: ION Media Networks Inc., Debtor in Possession.

Personnel: John Kawalke, Station Operations Manager; Dexter J. Wilson, Chief Engineer; Terri Durrett, Traffic Manager.

■ **Indianapolis**—WKOG-LP, Ch. 31, Kingdom of God Inc. Phone: 317-920-1000.

Technical Facilities: 55-kw ERP, 322-ft. above ground, 1040-ft. above sea level, lat. 39° 46' 01", long. 86° 09' 29".

Ownership: International Evangelical Catholic Television Network.

Personnel: Sister Sue Jenkins, President.

Jasper—WJTS-LD, Ch. 18, Paul E. Knies. Phones: 812-482-2727; 812-634-9232. Fax: 812-482-3696.

Studio: 511 Newton St, Ste 204, Jasper, IN 47546.

Technical Facilities: 15-kw ERP, 388-ft. above ground, 1008-ft. above sea level, lat. 38° 22' 53", long. 86° 52' 26".

Began Operation: February 12, 2009.

Ownership: Paul E. Knies.

Personnel: Paul Knies, General Manager; Joshua Budd, Sales Representative; Sandy Elmore, Programming Director; Jeremy Markos, Studio Production; Jesse Kluesner, Production; Kurt Gutgsell, Sports/News.

■ **Jeffersonville, etc.**—WJYL-CA, Ch. 9, Dominion Media Inc. Phone: 812-948-9843. Fax: 812-949-5056.

Technical Facilities: 3-kw ERP, 300-ft. above ground, 1273-ft. above sea level, lat. 38° 22' 08", long. 85° 49' 48".

Ownership: John W. Smith Jr.

■ **Kokomo**—WKGK-LP, Ch. 50, Kingdom of God Inc.

Technical Facilities: 10.8-kw ERP, 46-ft. above ground, 896-ft. above sea level, lat. 40° 25' 55", long. 86° 06' 37".

Ownership: International Evangelical Catholic Television Network.

Lafayette—W51DU, Ch. 51, Trinity Broadcasting Network Inc. Phone: 714-832-2950. Fax: 714-730-0661.

Technical Facilities: 35.4-kw ERP, 322-ft. above ground, 976-ft. above sea level, lat. 40° 23' 24", long. 86° 51' 53".

Ownership: Trinity Broadcasting Network Inc.

■ **Marion**—WIWU-CA, Ch. 51, Indiana Wesleyan U. Phones: 765-677-2819; 765-677-2791. Fax: 765-677-2794.

Technical Facilities: 4.3-kw ERP, 438-ft. above ground, 1302-ft. above sea level, lat. 40° 36' 56", long. 85° 38' 47".

Holds CP for change to 1.45-kw ERP, BDFCDTA-20080804AFJ.

Multichannel TV Sound: Stereo only.

Ownership: Indiana Wesleyan U.

Personnel: Terry Munday, General Manager; Marty Lewis, Technical Operations Manager; Max Nottingham, Sales Manager.

Marion—WSOT-LP, Ch. 57, Sunnycrest Media Inc. Phone: 765-668-1014.

Studio: 2172 Chapel Pike, Marion, IN 46952.

Technical Facilities: 1000-w TPO, 6.6-kw ERP, 555-ft. above ground, 1427-ft. above sea level, lat. 40° 35' 52", long. 85° 39' 21".

Holds CP for change to channel number 27, 7-kw ERP, 486-ft. above ground, 1383-ft. above sea level, lat. 40° 39' 18", long. 85° 37' 23". BDISDTL-20081230AFT.

Transmitter: Near State Rte. 9 & Harreld Rd., near Marion.

Ownership: Sunnycrest Media Inc.

Personnel: David Trimble, Vice President & General Manager; Steve Wright, Sales Manager; Gene Miller, Engineer; Nancy Newcomer, Programming Manager; Jan Walters, Production Manager.

Martinsville—WREP-LP, Ch. 15, Metropolitan School District of Martinsville. Phone: 765-342-5571. Fax: 765-349-5256.

Studio: 1360 E Gray St, Martinsville, IN 46151.

Technical Facilities: 570-w TPO, 4.6-kw ERP, 187-ft. above ground, 978-ft. above sea level, lat. 39° 26' 43", long. 86° 25' 06".

Holds CP for change to 0.2-kw ERP, 185-ft. above ground, 975-ft. above sea level, BDFCDTL-20090121ACF.

Transmitter: 1310 Lincoln Hill Rd.

Multichannel TV Sound: Stereo only.

Began Operation: August 6, 1990.

Ownership: Metropolitan School District of Martinsville.

Personnel: Eric Meyer, General Manager & Station Manager; Martin Hensley, Chief Engineer.

Muncie—WMUN-LP, Ch. 26, Full Gospel Business Men's Fellowship, Muncie, IN. Phone: 765-282-3725.

Technical Facilities: 875-w TPO, 10.4-kw ERP, 259-ft. above ground, 1211-ft. above sea level, lat. 40° 06' 43", long. 85° 28' 32".

Transmitter: State Hwy. 67 S, Muncie.

Ownership: Full Gospel Business Men's Fellowship International.

Personnel: Donald Bradley, General Manager.

Portage—WODN-LP, Ch. 13, Studio 5 Inc. Phones: 219-763-7211; 219-762-1541. Fax: 219-763-6349.

Technical Facilities: 3-kw ERP, 108-ft. above ground, 807-ft. above sea level, lat. 41° 37' 28", long. 87° 11' 28".

Transmitter: Lot 53, Hillcrest Rd., Ogden Dunes.

Multichannel TV Sound: Separate audio program.

Ownership: Studio 5 Inc.

Personnel: Thomas W. Tittle, Chief Engineer.

Princeton—W06BD, Ch. 6, North Gibson School Corp. Phones: 812-385-5292; 812-385-2591. Fax: 812-386-1531.

Studio: Old Hwy. 41 N, Princeton, IN 47676.

Technical Facilities: 10-w TPO, 0.614-kw ERP, 210-ft. above ground, 679-ft. above sea level, lat. 38° 21' 56", long. 87° 34' 54".

Transmitter: Old Hwy. 41 N, Princeton.

Multichannel TV Sound: Stereo only.

Ownership: North Gibson School Corp.

Personnel: Kyla D. Krieg, General Manager.

■ **Salem**—WHAN-LP, Ch. 17, Rebecca L. White. Phones: 812-883-5750; 812-883-3401. Fax: 812-883-2797.

Studio: 1308 Hwy. 56 E, Salem, IN 47167.

Technical Facilities: 1000-w TPO, 9-kw ERP, 256-ft. above ground, 1145-ft. above sea level, lat. 38° 35' 59", long. 86° 05' 17".

Transmitter: Existing WSLM(FM) tower.

Multichannel TV Sound: Stereo and separate audio program.

Ownership: Don Martin; Rebecca L. White.

Personnel: Don H. Martin, General Manager; J. R. Marlin, Chief Engineer.

South Bend—WBND-LD, Ch. 49, WSBT Inc. Phone: 574-233-3141.

Technical Facilities: 15-kw ERP, 997-ft. above ground, 1870-ft. above sea level, lat. 41° 36' 55", long. 86° 11' 07".

Ownership: Schurz Communications Inc.

South Bend—WBND-LP, Ch. 57, WSBT Inc. Phone: 574-233-3141.

Technical Facilities: 1000-w TPO, 58.2-kw ERP, 1020-ft. above ground, 1893-ft. above sea level, lat. 41° 36' 55", long. 86° 11' 07".

Transmitter: 16965 Johnson Rd., Mishawaka.

Ownership: Schurz Communications Inc.

Personnel: Jeff Guy, General Manager; Frank Hawkins, Sales Manager; Bernard Hoelting, Chief Engineer.

South Bend—WCWW-LD, Ch. 27, WCWW-TV LP. Phone: 312-705-2600.

Technical Facilities: 15-kw ERP, 958-ft. above ground, 1831-ft. above sea level, lat. 41° 36' 55", long. 86° 11' 07".

Ownership: Weigel Broadcasting Co.

South Bend—WCWW-LP, Ch. 25, WCWW-TV LP. Phone: 574-243-4321. Fax: 574-243-4326.

Technical Facilities: 2000-w TPO, 37.8-kw ERP, 1054-ft. above ground, 1927-ft. above sea level, lat. 41° 36' 55", long. 86° 11' 07".

Transmitter: 2814 U.S. Hwy. 31 N, Niles, MI.

Ownership: Weigel Broadcasting Co.

South Bend—WMYS-LD, Ch. 23, Weigel Broadcasting Co. Phone: 312-705-2600.

Technical Facilities: 15-kw ERP, 932-ft. above ground, 1804-ft. above sea level, lat. 41° 36' 55", long. 86° 11' 07".

Ownership: Weigel Broadcasting Co.

South Bend—WMYS-LP, Ch. 69, Weigel Broadcasting Co. Phone: 312-705-2600. Fax: 312-705-2656.

Technical Facilities: 131-kw ERP, 974-ft. above ground, 1847-ft. above sea level, lat. 41° 36' 55", long. 86° 11' 07".

Transmitter: 2.5-mi. SW of State Rte. 19 & US Hwy. 6.

Ownership: Weigel Broadcasting Co.

Sullivan—WHFE-LP, Ch. 18, KM Communications Inc. Phone: 847-674-0864. Fax: 847-674-9188.

Technical Facilities: 0.053-kw ERP, 92-ft. above ground, 623-ft. above sea level, lat. 39° 07' 12", long. 87° 24' 36".

Holds CP for change to 25-kw ERP, 591-ft. above ground, 1091-ft. above sea level, lat. 39° 20' 13", long. 89° 28' 00". BPTTL-20050714ACM.

Ownership: KM Communications Inc.

Sullivan—WIIB-LP, Ch. 7, KM Communications Inc. Phone: 847-674-0864.

Technical Facilities: 1.5-kw ERP, 100-ft. above ground, 632-ft. above sea level, lat. 39° 07' 12", long. 87° 24' 36".

Ownership: KM Communications Inc.

Sullivan—WKMF-LP, Ch. 32, KM Communications Inc. Phone: 847-674-0864.

Technical Facilities: 80-kw ERP, 602-ft. above ground, 1172-ft. above sea level, lat. 39° 13' 03", long. 87° 22' 35".

Ownership: KM Communications Inc.

Sullivan—WVGO-LP, Ch. 54, KM Communications Inc. Phone: 847-674-0864. Fax: 847-674-9188.

Technical Facilities: 0.039-kw ERP, 98-ft. above ground, 630-ft. above sea level, lat. 39° 07' 12", long. 87° 24' 36".

Holds CP for change to channel number 8, 0.3-kw ERP, BDCCDVL-20061027ABF.

Ownership: KM Communications Inc.

Terre Haute—W43BV, Ch. 43, Trinity Broadcasting Network Inc. Phone: 714-832-2950. Fax: 714-730-0661.

Technical Facilities: 11.2-kw ERP, 587-ft. above ground, 1148-ft. above sea level, lat. 39° 30' 14", long. 87° 26' 37".

Transmitter: 0.3-mi. E of Hwy. 150 on Mulberry Ave., Terre Haute.

Ownership: Trinity Broadcasting Network Inc.

Personnel: Paul F. Crouch, General Manager; Rod Henke, Sales Manager; Benn Miller, Chief Engineer.

Valparaiso—WHVI-LP, Ch. 24, LeSea Broadcasting Corp. Phone: 574-291-8200.

Technical Facilities: 1000-w TPO, 6.29-kw ERP, 348-ft. above ground, 1198-ft. above sea level, lat. 41° 31' 22", long. 87° 01' 28".

Holds CP for change to 10-kw ERP, BDFCDTL-20060331AFL.

Transmitter: NE of intersection of 600 N & 200 E, 3.9-mi. NNE of Valparaiso.

Ownership: LeSea Broadcasting Corp.

Personnel: Peter Sumrall, General Manager; Doug Garlinger, Chief Engineer.

West Lafayette—WUVI-LP, Ch. 65, Hosanna Apostolic Ministries Broadcasting Corp. Phone: 520-971-9274.

Technical Facilities: 5-kw ERP, 66-ft. above ground, 846-ft. above sea level, lat. 40° 45' 51.2", long. 87° 09' 03.3".

Began Operation: November 16, 2007.

Ownership: Hosanna Apostolic Ministries Broadcasting Corp.

Westville—WAAA-LP, Ch. 49, Aqua-Land Communications Inc. Phone: 219-762-1541. Fax: 219-763-6349.

Technical Facilities: 87-kw ERP, 312-ft. above ground, 1165-ft. above sea level, lat. 41° 31' 17", long. 87° 01' 26".

Ownership: Aqua-Land Communications Inc.

Personnel: Thomas W. Tittle, President.

Iowa

Ames—K26IY, Ch. 26, TV-45 Inc. Phone: 515-597-3138.

Technical Facilities: 8.4-kw ERP, 423-ft. above ground, 1473-ft. above sea level, lat. 41° 58' 49", long. 93° 44' 24".

Ownership: TV-45 Inc.

Ames—K48FZ, Ch. 48, TV-52 Inc.

Technical Facilities: 3-kw ERP, 423-ft. above ground, 1476-ft. above sea level, lat. 41° 58' 49", long. 93° 44' 23".

Ownership: TV-52 Inc.

Cedar Rapids—K17ET, Ch. 17, Trinity Broadcasting Network Inc. Phone: 714-832-2950. Fax: 714-730-0661.

Technical Facilities: 4-kw ERP, 299-ft. above ground, 1112-ft. above sea level, lat. 42° 02' 43", long. 91° 38' 48".

Ownership: Trinity Broadcasting Network Inc.

Cedar Rapids—KCDE-LP, Ch. 67, Tiger Eye Broadcasting Corp.

Technical Facilities: 100-w TPO, 0.51-kw ERP, 295-ft. above ground, 1135-ft. above sea level, lat. 41° 54' 33", long. 91° 39' 17".

Holds CP for change to channel number 44, 29-kw ERP, BPTTL-20060331AYS.

Transmitter: 6301 Kirkwood Blvd.

Ownership: Tiger Eye Broadcasting Corp.

Cedar Rapids—KCDR-LP, Ch. 55, Tiger Eye Broadcasting Corp. Phone: 954-431-3144.

Technical Facilities: 100-w TPO, 0.523-kw ERP, 295-ft. above ground, 1135-ft. above sea level, lat. 41° 54' 33", long. 91° 39' 17".

Transmitter: 6301 Kirkwood Blvd.

Ownership: Tiger Eye Broadcasting Corp.

Cedar Rapids—KHHH-LP, Ch. 57, Tiger Eye Broadcasting Corp. Phone: 954-431-3144.

Technical Facilities: 100-w TPO, 0.52-kw ERP, 295-ft. above ground, 1135-ft. above sea level, lat. 41° 54' 33", long. 91° 39' 17".

Transmitter: 6301 Kirkwood Blvd.

Ownership: Tiger Eye Broadcasting Corp.

Cedar Rapids—KRUB-LP, Ch. 65, Tiger Eye Broadcasting Corp. Phone: 954-431-3144.

Technical Facilities: 100-w TPO, 0.512-kw ERP, 295-ft. above ground, 1135-ft. above sea level, lat. 41° 54' 33", long. 91° 39' 17".

Holds CP for change to channel number 46, 0.1-kw ERP, BDCCDTL-20061030AOD.

Transmitter: 6301 Kirkwood Blvd.

Ownership: Tiger Eye Broadcasting Corp.

Clarinda—K56AF, Ch. 56, City of Clarinda. Phone: 712-542-2136.

Technical Facilities: 0.775-kw ERP, lat. 40° 44' 28", long. 95° 03' 37".

Ownership: City of Clarinda.

Council Bluffs—K52GP, Ch. 52, TV 45 Inc. Phone: 515-597-3531.

Technical Facilities: 2000-w TPO, 35.7-kw ERP, 108-ft. above ground, 1335-ft. above sea level, lat. 41° 15' 17", long. 95° 50' 09".

Transmitter: 5 Linn Ave.

Ownership: TV-45 Inc.

Council Bluffs—K54GL, Ch. 54, TV-45 Inc. Phone: 515-597-3531.

Technical Facilities: 4700-w TPO, 29.7-kw ERP, 108-ft. above ground, 1335-ft. above sea level, lat. 41° 15' 17", long. 95° 50' 09".

Transmitter: Omaha Communications Tower, Linn Lane.

Ownership: TV-45 Inc.

■ **Davenport**—K16EL, Ch. 16, Three Angels Broadcasting Network Inc. Phone: 618-627-4651. Fax: 618-627-4155.

Studio: 3391 Charley Good Rd, West Frankfort, IL 62896.

Technical Facilities: 1000-w TPO, 16-kw ERP, 800-ft. above ground, 1529-ft. above sea level, lat. 41° 36' 22", long. 90° 59' 35".

Transmitter: KBOB(FM) tower.

Ownership: Three Angels Broadcasting Network Inc.

Personnel: Moses Primo, Chief Engineer.

Ownership: Trinity Broadcasting Network Inc.

Cedar Rapids—KCDE-LP, Ch. 67, Tiger Eye Broadcasting Corp.

Davenport—K61HD, Ch. 61, Trinity Broadcasting Network Inc. Phone: 714-832-2950. Fax: 714-730-0661.

Technical Facilities: 2000-w TPO, 5.8-kw ERP, 541-ft. above ground, 1211-ft. above sea level, lat. 41° 32' 52", long. 90° 28' 30".

Holds CP for change to channel number 29, 15-kw ERP, lat. 41° 32' 51", long. 90° 28' 28". BDISDTT-20060328ACJ.

Transmitter: Intersection of Belmont & Middle Rds.

Ownership: Trinity Broadcasting Network Inc.

Personnel: Paul Crouch, General Manager; Ben Miller, Chief Engineer; Rod Henke, Sales Manager.

Davenport—WBQD-LP, Ch. 26, Four Seasons Peoria LLC. Phone: 323-904-4090.

Technical Facilities: 1000-w TPO, 26-kw ERP, 315-ft. above ground, 974-ft. above sea level, lat. 41° 28' 29", long. 90° 26' 45".

Holds CP for change to channel number 10, 3-kw ERP, 295-ft. above ground, 955-ft. above sea level, BMPTVL-20060403ARG.

Transmitter: 4-mi. W of Scott Community College, Bettendorf.

Ownership: Paul H. Koplin; Malibu Broadcasting LLC; Venture Technologies Group LLC.

Personnel: Julie Brinks, General Manager; Tim Harrison, Chief Engineer.

Decorah—K14AF, Ch. 14, Iowa Public Broadcasting Board. Phone: 515-242-3100.

Technical Facilities: 5.87-kw ERP, 1568-ft. above sea level, lat. 43° 18' 05", long. 91° 47' 31".

Holds CP for change to channel number 16, 126-kw ERP, 373-ft. above ground, 1532-ft. above sea level, lat. 43° 19' 30", long. 91° 46' 00". BDISTT-20060322ACJ.

Ownership: Iowa Public Broadcasting Board.

Des Moines—K29EA, Ch. 29, TV-45 Inc. Phone: 515-597-3138.

Technical Facilities: 932-w TPO, 10.9-kw ERP, 194-ft. above ground, 1155-ft. above sea level, lat. 41° 39' 54", long. 93° 35' 03".

Ownership: TV-45 Inc.

Des Moines—K41DD, Ch. 41, Ventana Television Inc. Phone: 727-872-4210.

Technical Facilities: 1000-w TPO, 33.2-kw ERP, 459-ft. above ground, 1427-ft. above sea level, lat. 41° 39' 53", long. 93° 45' 24".

Transmitter: 5750 N.W. 100th St., 1.8-mi. SE of Grimes.

Began Operation: August 17, 1992.

Ownership: Ventana Television Inc.

Personnel: John Skelnik, General Manager & Chief Engineer.

Des Moines—K46EY, Ch. 46, TV-45 Inc. Phone: 515-597-3531.

Technical Facilities: 100-w TPO, 13.03-kw ERP, 194-ft. above ground, 1135-ft. above sea level, lat. 41° 39' 54", long. 93° 35' 03".

Transmitter: 2011 N.E. 58th Ave.

Ownership: TV-45 Inc.

■ **Des Moines**—KRPG-LP, Ch. 43, Tiger Eye Broadcasting Corp. Phone: 954-431-3144.

Technical Facilities: 36.9-kw ERP, 463-ft. above ground, 1404-ft. above sea level, lat. 41° 35' 20", long. 93° 32' 18".

Ownership: Tiger Eye Broadcasting Corp.

■ **Des Moines**—WBXF-CA, Ch. 4, L4 Media Group LLC. Phone: 321-729-8451.

Studio: 319 7th St, Ste 428, Des Moines, IA 50309.

Technical Facilities: 0.015-kw ERP, 476-ft. above ground, 1289-ft. above sea level, lat. 41° 35' 13", long. 93° 37' 34".

Transmitter: Ruan Center.

Multichannel TV Sound: Stereo only.

Ownership: L4 Media Group LLC.

Personnel: Liz Kiley, Broadcast Vice President; Warren Reeves, Consulting Engineer; Amy Brown, Broadcast Operations Director.

Fort Madison, etc.—K28JD, Ch. 28, Iowa Public Broadcasting Board. Phone: 515-242-3100.

Technical Facilities: 76.6-kw ERP, 421-ft. above ground, 1081-ft. above sea level, lat. 40° 37' 55", long. 91° 26' 00".

Ownership: Iowa Public Broadcasting Board.

Iowa City—K39EX, Ch. 39, R.B. Sheldahl.

Technical Facilities: 1000-w TPO, 1.22-kw ERP, 190-ft. above ground, 942-ft. above sea level, lat. 41° 41' 12", long. 91° 33' 45".

Transmitter: 0.2-mi. NE of First Ave. & I-80, Coralville.

Ownership: Twyla P. Sheldahl Trustee, R. B. Sheldahl Estate.

Iowa Falls—K25FA, Ch. 25, Robert M. Campbell.

Technical Facilities: 1000-w TPO, 1.3-kw ERP, 480-ft. above ground, 1689-ft. above sea level, lat. 42° 20' 10", long. 93° 28' 00".

Transmitter: 1.5-mi. N & 1.5-mi. W of Radcliffe.

Ownership: Robert M. Campbell.

Iowa Falls—K47EK, Ch. 47, Robert M. Campbell. Phone: 612-937-1466.

Technical Facilities: 100-w TPO, 1.612-kw ERP, 480-ft. above ground, 1690-ft. above sea level, lat. 42° 20' 10", long. 93° 28' 00".

Transmitter: 1.5-mi. N of Radcliffe.

Ownership: Robert M. Campbell.

Iowa Falls—K53FD, Ch. 53, Robert M. Campbell. Phone: 612-937-1466.

Technical Facilities: 1.67-kw ERP, 480-ft. above ground, 1690-ft. above sea level, lat. 42° 20' 10", long. 93° 28' 00".

Transmitter: 2.25-mi. SE of Williams.

Ownership: Robert M. Campbell.

Iowa Falls, etc.—K33ED, Ch. 33, East Side Enterprises. Phone: 612-771-8865.

Technical Facilities: 1.34-kw ERP, 480-ft. above ground, 1689-ft. above sea level, lat. 42° 20' 10", long. 93° 28' 00".

Ownership: East Side Enterprises.

Iowa Falls, etc.—K55GV, Ch. 55, Robert M. Campbell. Phone: 612-937-1466.

Technical Facilities: 46-w TPO, 0.8-kw ERP, 479-ft. above ground, 1689-ft. above sea level, lat. 42° 20' 10", long. 93° 28' 00".

Transmitter: 1.5-mi. N of Radcliffe.

Ownership: Robert M. Campbell.

Iowa Falls, etc.—K61GF, Ch. 61, BSA Investment. Phone: 612-451-9197.

Technical Facilities: 46-w TPO, 0.8-kw ERP, 480-ft. above ground, 1689-ft. above sea level, lat. 42° 20' 10", long. 93° 28' 00".

Transmitter: 1.5-mi. NW of Radcliffe.

Ownership: BSA Investment.

Keokuk—K44AB, Ch. 44, Iowa Public Broadcasting Board. Phone: 515-242-3100.

Technical Facilities: 0.439-kw ERP, 167-ft. above ground, 810-ft. above sea level, lat. 40° 24' 40", long. 91° 24' 14".

Holds CP for change to 24.8-kw ERP, 167-ft. above ground, 974-ft. above sea level, BPTT-20060320AAC.

Ownership: Iowa Public Broadcasting Board.

Keokuk—K60CL, Ch. 60, Christ Vision Inc. Phone: 217-847-3348.

Studio: 228 N 4th St, Keokuk, IA 52632.

Technical Facilities: 81-w TPO, 0.65-kw ERP, 197-ft. above ground, 817-ft. above sea level, lat. 40° 22' 37", long. 91° 22' 10".

Transmitter: 4.7-mi. S of intersection of U.S. 136 & Hamilton Toll Bridge.

Ownership: Christ Vision.

Personnel: Jim Richardson, General Manager; Melvin George, Chief Engineer.

Keokuk—KXWL-LP, Ch. 46, Independent Pentecostal Christian Church Inc. Phone: 319-627-4163.

Technical Facilities: 0.3-kw ERP, 49-ft. above ground, 627-ft. above sea level, lat. 40° 24' 01.8", long. 91° 23' 07.5".

Began Operation: August 18, 2008.

Ownership: Independent Pentecostal Christian Church Inc.

Keosauqua, etc.—K54AF, Ch. 54, Iowa Public Broadcasting Board. Phone: 515-242-3100.

Technical Facilities: 0.1-kw ERP, 1142-ft. above sea level, lat. 40° 43' 04", long. 91° 56' 23".

Holds CP for change to channel number 24, 114-kw ERP, 390-ft. above ground, 1100-ft. above sea level, BDISTT-20060320AAB.

Ownership: Iowa Public Broadcasting Board.

Lansing—K41AD, Ch. 41, Iowa Public Broadcasting Board. Phone: 515-242-3100.

Technical Facilities: 16.6-kw ERP, lat. 43° 21' 10", long. 93° 13' 00".

Holds CP for change to channel number 49, 62.5-kw ERP, 256-ft. above ground, 1316-ft. above sea level, lat. 43° 20' 59", long. 91° 13' 16". BDISTT-20060221AAM.

Ownership: Iowa Public Broadcasting Board.

■ **Marshalltown**—KDAO-LP, Ch. 45, MTN Broadcasting LLC. Phone: 641-752-4122.

Studio: 1930 N Center St, Marshalltown, IA 50158.

Technical Facilities: 2.97-kw ERP, 197-ft. above ground, 1066-ft. above sea level, lat. 42° 04' 17", long. 92° 55' 19".

Transmitter: 1930 N. Center St., Marshalltown.

Ownership: MTN Broadcasting Inc.

Personnel: Mark Osmundson, General Manager.

Muscatine—K42HI, Ch. 42, Trinity Broadcasting Network Inc. Phone: 714-832-2950. Fax: 714-730-0661.

Technical Facilities: 19.6-kw ERP, 282-ft. above ground, 958-ft. above sea level, lat. 41° 26' 34", long. 91° 04' 33".

Transmitter: KWCC-FM tower.

Ownership: Trinity Broadcasting Network Inc.

Ottumwa—K18GU, Ch. 18, Iowa Public Broadcasting Board. Phone: 515-242-3100.

Technical Facilities: 100-kw ERP, 459-ft. above ground, 1230-ft. above sea level, lat. 40° 57' 40", long. 92° 22' 11".

Holds CP for change to 15-kw ERP, 446-ft. above ground, 1220-ft. above sea level, BDFCDTT-20090424AAL.

Ownership: Iowa Public Broadcasting Board.

Ottumwa—K21EM, Ch. 21, MS Communications LLC. Phone: 414-765-9737.

Technical Facilities: 100-w TPO, 0.007-kw ERP, 105-ft. above ground, 837-ft. above sea level, lat. 40° 57' 50", long. 92° 23' 51".

Transmitter: Black Hawk Rd., 2.2-mi. W of Ottumwa.

Ownership: MS Communications LLC.

Ottumwa—K23CI, Ch. 23, Ottumwa Area Translator System Inc. Phone: 641-652-7575.

Technical Facilities: 0.89-kw ERP, lat. 40° 57' 50", long. 92° 23' 50".

Ownership: Ottumwa Area Translator System Inc.

Ottumwa—K25DE, Ch. 25, Ottumwa Area Translator System Inc. Phone: 641-652-7575.

Technical Facilities: 0.89-kw ERP, 387-ft. above ground, 1129-ft. above sea level, lat. 40° 57' 50", long. 92° 23' 50".

Ownership: Ottumwa Area Translator System Inc.

Ottumwa—K27CV, Ch. 27, Ottumwa Area Translator System Inc. Phone: 641-652-7575.

Technical Facilities: 0.89-kw ERP, lat. 40° 57' 50", long. 92° 23' 50".

Ownership: Ottumwa Area Translator System Inc.

Ottumwa—K31ED, Ch. 31, MS Communications LLC. Phone: 414-765-9737.

Technical Facilities: 100-w TPO, 0.007-kw ERP, 105-ft. above ground, 837-ft. above sea level, lat. 40° 57' 50", long. 92° 23' 51".

Transmitter: Black Hawk Rd., 2.2-mi. W of Ottumwa.

Ownership: MS Communications LLC.

Ottumwa—K42AM, Ch. 42, Trinity Broadcasting Network Inc. Phone: 714-832-2950. Fax: 714-730-0661.

Technical Facilities: 1000-w TPO, 2.2-kw ERP, 302-ft. above ground, 1073-ft. above sea level, lat. 41° 01' 28", long. 92° 28' 56".

Transmitter: 0.96-mi. N of U.S. Rte. 34.

Ownership: Trinity Broadcasting Network Inc.

Personnel: Paul Crouch, General Manager; Ben Miller, Chief Engineer; Rod Henke, Sales Manager.

Ottumwa—K45EE, Ch. 45, MS Communications LLC. Phone: 414-765-9737.

Technical Facilities: 100-w TPO, 0.007-kw ERP, 105-ft. above ground, 837-ft. above sea level, lat. 40° 57' 50", long. 92° 23' 51".

Transmitter: Black Hawk Rd., 2.2-mi. W of Ottumwa.

Ownership: MS Communications LLC.

Ottumwa—K49DX, Ch. 49, MS Communications LLC. Phone: 414-765-9737.

Technical Facilities: 0.007-kw ERP, 190-ft. above ground, 961-ft. above sea level, lat. 40° 57' 50", long. 92° 23' 51".

Ownership: MS Communications LLC.

Ottumwa—K51FJ, Ch. 51, MS Communications LLC. Phone: 414-765-9737.

Technical Facilities: 100-w TPO, 0.007-kw ERP, 105-ft. above ground, 837-ft. above sea level, lat. 40° 57' 50", long. 92° 23' 51".

Transmitter: Black Hawk Rd., 2.2-mi. W of Ottumwa.

Ownership: MS Communications LLC.

Ottumwa—K53FC, Ch. 53, MS Communications LLC. Phone: 414-765-9737.

Technical Facilities: 100-w TPO, 0.007-kw ERP, 105-ft. above ground, 837-ft. above sea level, lat. 40° 57' 50", long. 92° 23' 51".

Transmitter: Black Hawk Rd., 2.2-mi. W of Ottumwa.

Ownership: MS Communications LLC.

Ottumwa—K55GS, Ch. 55, MS Communications LLC. Phone: 414-765-9737.

Technical Facilities: 100-w TPO, 0.007-kw ERP, 105-ft. above ground, 837-ft. above sea level, lat. 40° 57' 50", long. 92° 23' 51".

Transmitter: Black Hawk Rd., 2.2-mi. W of Ottumwa.

Ownership: MS Communications LLC.

Ottumwa—K58ER, Ch. 58, MS Communications LLC. Phone: 414-765-9737.

Technical Facilities: 100-w TPO, 0.007-kw ERP, 105-ft. above ground, 837-ft. above sea level, lat. 40° 57' 50", long. 92° 23' 51".

Transmitter: Black Hawk Rd., 3.5-mi. W of Ottumwa.

Ownership: MS Communications LLC.

Ottumwa—K65GA, Ch. 65, MS Communications LLC. Phone: 414-765-9737.

Technical Facilities: 100-w TPO, 0.007-kw ERP, 105-ft. above ground, 837-ft. above sea level, lat. 40° 57' 50", long. 92° 23' 51".

Transmitter: Black Hawk Rd., 2.2-mi. W of Ottumwa.

Ownership: MS Communications LLC.

Ottumwa—K67GH, Ch. 67, MS Communications LLC. Phone: 414-765-9737.

Technical Facilities: 100-w TPO, 0.007-kw ERP, 105-ft. above ground, 837-ft. above sea level, lat. 40° 57' 50", long. 92° 23' 51".

Transmitter: Black Hawk Rd., 2.2-mi. W of Ottumwa.

Ownership: MS Communications LLC.

Rock Rapids, etc.—K25AA, Ch. 25, Iowa Public Broadcasting Board. Phone: 515-242-3100.

Technical Facilities: 1-kw ERP, lat. 43° 22' 36", long. 96° 11' 46".

Holds CP for change to 126-kw ERP, 460-ft. above ground, 1885-ft. above sea level, BPTT-20060322ACU.

Ownership: Iowa Public Broadcasting Board.

Sibley, etc.—K33AB, Ch. 33, Iowa Public Broadcasting Board. Phone: 515-242-3100.

Technical Facilities: 18.6-kw ERP, lat. 43° 24' 10", long. 95° 40' 15".

Ownership: Iowa Public Broadcasting Board.

Sioux City—K54GK, Ch. 54, Cornerstone Faith Center. Phone: 712-274-7572.

Technical Facilities: 20-kw ERP, 299-ft. above ground, 1598-ft. above sea level, lat. 42° 29' 39", long. 96° 18' 21".

Ownership: Cornerstone Faith Center.

South Sioux City—KSXC-LP, Ch. 5, Venture Technologies Group LLC. Phone: 323-904-4090.

Technical Facilities: 3-kw ERP, 364-ft. above ground, 1778-ft. above sea level, lat. 42° 29' 26", long. 96° 18' 21".

Holds CP for change to 0.3-kw ERP, 388-ft. above ground, 542-ft. above sea level, lat. 42° 29' 05.5", long. 96° 18' 18.9". BDFCDVL-20090114ACF.

Began Operation: January 6, 2006.

Ownership: Venture Technologies Group LLC.

Spencer—K55FL, Ch. 55, Waitt Broadcasting Inc. Phones: 712-277-3554; 402-697-8000. Fax: 712-277-4732.

Technical Facilities: 1000-w TPO, 8.4-kw ERP, 399-ft. above ground, 1775-ft. above sea level, lat. 43° 15' 20", long. 94° 58' 36".

Transmitter: 3-mi. SSW of Terril.

Ownership: Waitt Broadcasting Inc.

Personnel: Brian McDonough, General Manager; Richard Herr, Chief Technician; Janice Jessen, Sales Manager.

Spencer—WBVK-LP, Ch. 52, Pappas Telecasting Companies. Phone: 559-733-7800.

Technical Facilities: 4.5-kw ERP, 387-ft. above ground, 1763-ft. above sea level, lat. 43° 15' 20", long. 94° 58' 35".

Ownership: Pappas Telecasting Companies.

Storm Lake—K40CO, Ch. 40, Waitt Broadcasting Inc. Phones: 712-277-3554; 402-330-2520. Fax: 712-277-4732.

Technical Facilities: 1000-w TPO, 8.3-kw ERP, 403-ft. above ground, 1695-ft. above sea level, lat. 42° 40' 07", long. 94° 59' 26".

Holds CP for change to channel number 18, 15-kw ERP, 394-ft. above ground, 1686-ft. above sea level, lat. 42° 40' 06", long. 94° 59' 35". BDISDTT-20071019AIH.

Transmitter: 5.5-mi. N of Rte. 7, 4.3-mi. NNE of Newell.

Ownership: Waitt Broadcasting Inc.

Personnel: Brian McDonough, General Manager; Richard Herr, Chief Engineer; Janice Jessen, Sales Manager.

Storm Lake—KCWL-LP, Ch. 57, Pappas Telecasting Companies. Phone: 559-733-7800.

Technical Facilities: 7.1-kw ERP, 387-ft. above ground, 1679-ft. above sea level, lat. 42° 40' 06", long. 94° 59' 35".

Ownership: Pappas Telecasting Companies.

■ **Washington**—K13MN, Ch. 13, KGAN Licensee LLC.

Technical Facilities: 0.09-kw ERP, lat. 41° 19' 00", long. 91° 41' 30".

Ownership: Sinclair Broadcast Group Inc.

Waterloo—K40GO, Ch. 40, MS Communications LLC. Phone: 414-765-9737.

Technical Facilities: 0.004-kw ERP, 50-ft. above ground, 901-ft. above sea level, lat. 42° 29' 43", long. 92° 19' 15.3".

Ownership: MS Communications LLC.

Waterloo—K44FK, Ch. 44, Trinity Broadcasting Network Inc. Phone: 714-832-2950. Fax: 714-730-0661.

Technical Facilities: 180-w TPO, 9.1-kw ERP, 322-ft. above ground, 1283-ft. above sea level, lat. 42° 26' 45", long. 92° 22' 29".

Transmitter: KKCV(FM) tower, 4719 Ansborough Ave.

Ownership: Trinity Broadcasting Network Inc.

Kansas

Chanute—K39HI, Ch. 39, Marcia T. Turner. Phone: 954-732-9539.

Technical Facilities: 6-kw ERP, 295-ft. above ground, 1253-ft. above sea level, lat. 37° 41' 15", long. 95° 24' 49".

Ownership: Marcia T. Turner.

Chanute—KJCA-LP, Ch. 40, Western Family Television Inc. Phone: 406-442-2655.

Technical Facilities: 8-kw ERP, 295-ft. above ground, 1253-ft. above sea level, lat. 37° 41' 15", long. 95° 24' 48".

Ownership: Western Family Television Inc.

Concordia—K64BS, Ch. 64, Smoky Hills Public Television Corp.

Technical Facilities: 1-kw ERP, lat. 39° 32' 20", long. 97° 41' 42".

Ownership: Smoky Hills Public Television Corp.

Dodge City—K43HN, Ch. 43, Trinity Broadcasting Network Inc. Phone: 714-832-2950. Fax: 714-730-0661.

Technical Facilities: 20-kw ERP, lat. 37° 45' 36", long. 100° 05' 53".

Ownership: Trinity Broadcasting Network Inc.

Dodge City—K50HS, Ch. 50, Marcia T. Turner. Phone: 954-732-9539.

Technical Facilities: 150-kw ERP, 427-ft. above ground, 3258-ft. above sea level, lat. 37° 52' 26", long. 100° 33' 25".

Ownership: Marcia T. Turner.

Dodge City—KSAS-LP, Ch. 29, Newport Television License LLC. Phone: 816-751-0204.

Technical Facilities: 1000-w TPO, 15-kw ERP, 354-ft. above ground, 2975-ft. above sea level, lat. 37° 46' 47", long. 100° 03' 39".

Transmitter: Rural Rte. 2, 3-mi. N of post office.

Ownership: Newport Television LLC.

Emporia—K52GZ, Ch. 52, Trinity Broadcasting Network Inc. Phone: 714-832-2950. Fax: 714-730-0661.

Technical Facilities: 10-kw ERP, 387-ft. above ground, 1283-ft. above sea level, lat. 38° 31' 47", long. 96° 05' 10".

Ownership: Trinity Broadcasting Network Inc.

■ **Emporia**—KETM-CA, Ch. 17, NVT Topeka II Licensee LLC, Debtor in Possession. Phone: 404-995-4711.

Technical Facilities: 1000-w TPO, 22.3-kw ERP, 371-ft. above ground, 1634-ft. above sea level, lat. 38° 31' 47", long. 96° 05' 09".

Transmitter: 0.6-mi. N of Hwy. 170, 0.6-mi E of Hwy. 99, Reading Twp.

Began Operation: March 8, 1991.

Ownership: New Vision Television LLC, Debtor in Possession.

Garden City—K34GG, Ch. 34, Enriqueta Garza. Phone: 956-428-7556.

Technical Facilities: 0.111-kw ERP, 52-ft. above ground, 2877-ft. above sea level, lat. 37° 57' 27", long. 100° 48' 46".

Ownership: Enriqueta Garza.

Garden City—K39FW, Ch. 39, Trinity Broadcasting Network Inc. Phone: 714-832-2950. Fax: 714-730-0661.

Technical Facilities: 10.1-kw ERP, 259-ft. above ground, 3132-ft. above sea level, lat. 37° 59' 42", long. 100° 52' 42".

Ownership: Trinity Broadcasting Network Inc.

Garden City—KAAS-LP, Ch. 31, Newport Television License LLC. Phone: 816-751-0204.

Technical Facilities: 1000-w TPO, 14.6-kw ERP, 390-ft. above ground, 3284-ft. above sea level, lat. 37° 52' 25", long. 100° 50' 44".

Transmitter: 6.5-mi. SSW of Garden City, E of Hwy. 83.

Ownership: Newport Television LLC.

Great Bend—K30GD, Ch. 30, Gray Television Licensee LLC. Phone: 316-943-4221.

Technical Facilities: 8.4-kw ERP, 342-ft. above ground, 2242-ft. above sea level, lat. 38° 24' 22", long. 98° 43' 19".

Holds CP for change to 15-kw ERP, BDFCDTT-20060331ACT.

Ownership: Gray Television Inc.

Hays—K25CV, Ch. 25, Gray Television Licensee LLC. Phone: 316-943-4221.

Technical Facilities: 8.9-kw ERP, 194-ft. above ground, 2324-ft. above sea level, lat. 38° 54' 54", long. 99° 19' 39".

Holds CP for change to 15-kw ERP, BDFCDTT-20060331ABZ.

Ownership: Gray Television Inc.

Hoxie, etc.—K69DB, Ch. 69, Sheridan County.

Technical Facilities: 0.87-kw ERP, 358-ft. above ground, 3117-ft. above sea level, lat. 39° 20' 03", long. 100° 26' 19".

Ownership: Sheridan County, KS.

Independence—K50GO, Ch. 50, Trinity Broadcasting Network. Phone: 714-832-2950. Fax: 714-730-0661.

Technical Facilities: 19-kw ERP, 279-ft. above ground, 1146-ft. above sea level, lat. 37° 09' 57", long. 95° 33' 45".

Ownership: Trinity Broadcasting Network Inc.

Personnel: Thomas Harrison, General Manager; Jim Bowles, Chief Engineer.

Iola—K30AL-D, Ch. 30, Washburn U. of Topeka. Phone: 785-670-1010.

Technical Facilities: 7.1-kw ERP, 515-ft. above ground, 1592-ft. above sea level, lat. 37° 54' 33", long. 95° 07' 23".

Ownership: Washburn U.

Junction City—K25DS, Ch. 25, Trinity Broadcasting Network Inc. Phones: 714-832-2950; 714-730-0661.

Technical Facilities: 1000-w TPO, 7.3-kw ERP, 459-ft. above ground, 1742-ft. above sea level, lat. 39° 00' 53", long. 96° 52' 15".

Transmitter: 1-mi. S of K-18 & Spring Valley Rd.

Ownership: Trinity Broadcasting Network Inc.

Personnel: Paul F. Crouch, General Manager; Rod Henke, Sales Manager; W. Ben Miller, Chief Engineer.

■ **Junction City**—KTLJ-CA, Ch. 6, NVT Topeka II Licensee LLC, Debtor in Possession. Phone: 404-995-4711.

Technical Facilities: 0.016-kw ERP, 49-ft. above ground, 1339-ft. above sea level, lat. 39° 01' 07", long. 96° 48' 14".

Began Operation: March 22, 1983.

Ownership: New Vision Television LLC, Debtor in Possession.

Lawrence—K58CX, Ch. 58, Northeast Kansas Broadcast Service Inc. Phone: 785-273-4449.

Technical Facilities: 1000-w ERP, 59-kw ERP, 282-ft. above ground, 1312-ft. above sea level, lat. 38° 53' 23", long. 95° 17' 17".

Transmitter: 2.4-mi. S of Hwy. 10 & U.S. 59, 1.2-mi. W of U.S. 59 on County Rd.

Ownership: Brechner Management Co.

Lawrence—KUJH-LP, Ch. 14, U. of Kansas. Phone: 913-864-0600. Fax: 913-864-0614.

Technical Facilities: 532-w TPO, 7.2-kw ERP, 390-ft. above ground, 1401-ft. above sea level, lat. 38° 57' 18", long. 95° 15' 57".

Transmitter: Daisy Hill, U. of Kansas, W. Campus, Lawrence.

Multichannel TV Sound: Stereo only.

Ownership: U. of Kansas.

Personnel: Gary Hawke, General Manager.

Liberal—KLKT-LP, Ch. 41, Marcia T. Turner. Phone: 702-256-8030.

Technical Facilities: 7.7-kw ERP, 492-ft. above ground, 3278-ft. above sea level, lat. 37° 03' 13", long. 100° 51' 22".

Ownership: Marcia T. Turner.

Manhattan—K31BW, Ch. 31, Trinity Broadcasting Network Inc. Phone: 714-832-2950. Fax: 714-730-0661.

Technical Facilities: 1000-w TPO, 8.7-kw ERP, 269-ft. above ground, 1549-ft. above sea level, lat. 39° 13' 34", long. 96° 37' 01".

Transmitter: 1.5-mi. SSE of intersection of Hwys. 113 & 24, near Manhattan.

Ownership: Trinity Broadcasting Network Inc.

Manhattan—K32HB, Ch. 32, EICB-TV East LLC. Phone: 972-291-3750.

Technical Facilities: 0.025-kw ERP, 33-ft. above ground, 1184-ft. above sea level, lat. 39° 12' 33", long. 96° 37' 08".

Began Operation: October 14, 2008.

Ownership: EICB-TV LLC.

Manhattan—K38GZ, Ch. 38, Marcia T. Turner. Phone: 954-732-9539.

Technical Facilities: 15-kw ERP, 246-ft. above ground, 1398-ft. above sea level, lat. 39° 12' 12", long. 96° 20' 25".

Ownership: Marcia T. Turner.

Manhattan—K40IJ-D, Ch. 40, EICB-TV East LLC. Phone: 972-291-3750.

Technical Facilities: 0.2-kw ERP, 33-ft. above ground, 1132-ft. above sea level, lat. 39° 12' 40", long. 96° 19' 56".

Holds CP for change to 5-kw ERP, 625-ft. above ground, 1704-ft. above sea level, lat. 39° 03' 50", long. 95° 45' 49". BPDTL-20080818AAG.

Ownership: EICB-TV LLC.

Manhattan—K52HZ, Ch. 52, Shahram Hashemizadeh. Phone: 818-339-6739.

Technical Facilities: 0.005-kw ERP, 33-ft. above ground, 1311-ft. above sea level, lat. 39° 13' 34", long. 96° 37' 00".

Holds CP for change to channel number 51, 75-kw ERP, BDISTTL-20071126AAP.

Ownership: Shahram Hashemizadeh.

Manhattan—KKSU-LP, Ch. 21, Kansas State U., Educational Communications. Phone: 785-532-7041. Fax: 785-532-7355.

Technical Facilities: 32-w TPO, 0.44-kw ERP, 121-ft. above ground, 1187-ft. above sea level, lat. 39° 11' 32", long. 96° 34' 45".

Transmitter: Dole Hall.

Ownership: Kansas State University.

Personnel: Mel Chastain, Director; Tracy Gibson, Chief Engineer; Susan Jagerson, Coordinator.

Natoma—K11NS, Ch. 11, City of Natoma.

Technical Facilities: 0.036-kw ERP, lat. 39° 10' 24", long. 99° 02' 04".

Ownership: City of Natoma.

Natoma—K13OM, Ch. 13, City of Natoma.

Technical Facilities: 0.003-kw ERP, lat. 39° 10' 24", long. 99° 02' 04".

Ownership: City of Natoma.

■ **Ogden**—KMJT-CA, Ch. 15, NVT Topeka II Licensee LLC, Debtor in Possession. Phone: 404-995-4711.

Technical Facilities: 1000-w TPO, 10.9-kw ERP, 220-ft. above ground, 1404-ft. above sea level, lat. 39° 09' 21", long. 96° 36' 44".

Holds CP for change to 150-kw ERP, 220-ft. above ground, 1405-ft. above sea level, BMJPTTL-20000829AUA.

Transmitter: 0.6-mi. SSW of intersection of State Rtes. 18 & 113.

Began Operation: February 3, 1994.

Ownership: New Vision Television LLC, Debtor in Possession.

Overland Park—K27FR, Ch. 27, U. of Kansas School of Journalism. Phone: 913-864-0603. Fax: 913-864-5173.

Technical Facilities: 12.2-kw ERP, 135-ft. above ground, 1175-ft. above sea level, lat. 38° 53' 58", long. 94° 43' 30".

Multichannel TV Sound: Stereo only.

Ownership: U. of Kansas.

Personnel: Gary Hawke, Provost's Representative.

Parsons—K33HW, Ch. 33, Marcia T. Turner. Phone: 954-732-9539.

Technical Facilities: 25-kw ERP, 236-ft. above ground, 1247-ft. above sea level, lat. 37° 17' 34", long. 95° 24' 43".

Ownership: Marcia T. Turner.

Phillipsburg—K66CD, Ch. 66, Smoky Hills Public Television Corp.

Technical Facilities: 2.21-kw ERP, lat. 39° 55' 10", long. 99° 19' 43".

Ownership: Smoky Hills Public Television Corp.

Pittsburg—K33HZ, Ch. 33, TCCSA Inc. dba Trinity Broadcasting Network. Phone: 714-832-2950. Fax: 714-730-0661.

Technical Facilities: 11.4-kw ERP, 148-ft. above ground, 782-ft. above sea level, lat. 37° 23' 39", long. 94° 46' 14".

Ownership: Trinity Broadcasting Network Inc.

Pittsburg—K41KX, Ch. 41, EICB-TV East LLC. Phone: 972-291-3750.

Technical Facilities: 0.025-kw ERP, 33-ft. above ground, 942-ft. above sea level, lat. 37° 25' 41", long. 94° 42' 54".

Holds CP for change to 15-kw ERP, 394-ft. above ground, 1434-ft. above sea level, lat. 37° 04' 34.4", long. 94° 32' 32.2". BDFCDTL-20080925AFC.

Began Operation: August 7, 2008.

Ownership: EICB-TV LLC.

Pittsburg—KJCJ-LP, Ch. 54, Western Family Television Inc. Phone: 406-442-2655.

Technical Facilities: 9-kw ERP, 279-ft. above ground, 1197-ft. above sea level, lat. 37° 24' 47", long. 94° 38' 14".

Holds CP for change to channel number 20, 20-kw ERP, 194-ft. above ground, 1145-ft. above sea level, lat. 37° 14' 34", long. 94° 30' 21". BDISTT-20061206ADV.

Ownership: Western Family Television Inc.

Pittsburg—KPJO-LP, Ch. 49, Dean M. Mosely. Phone: 318-992-7766.

Technical Facilities: 44.3-kw ERP, 312-ft. above ground, 1189-ft. above sea level, lat. 37° 11' 29.9", long. 94° 41' 18.2".

Ownership: Dean M. Mosely.

Pittsburg—KSPJ-LP, Ch. 59, Lamar Veasey. Phone: 916-501-7787.

Technical Facilities: 37.9-kw ERP, 131-ft. above ground, 1063-ft. above sea level, lat. 37° 23' 39", long. 94° 46' 14".

Ownership: Lamar Veasey.

Russell—K38GH, Ch. 38, Gray Television License LLC. Phone: 316-943-4221.

Technical Facilities: 7.2-kw ERP, 368-ft. above ground, 2213-ft. above sea level, lat. 38° 54' 51", long. 98° 51' 51".

Holds CP for change to 15-kw ERP, BDFCDTT-20060331AQO.

Ownership: Gray Television Inc.

Salina—K15CN, Ch. 15, Trinity Broadcasting Network Inc. Phone: 714-832-2950. Fax: 714-730-0661.

Technical Facilities: 1000-w TPO, 11.2-kw ERP, 154-ft. above ground, 1390-ft. above sea level, lat. 38° 50' 06", long. 97° 36' 24".

Holds CP for change to 15-kw ERP, 154-ft. above ground, 1391-ft. above sea level, BDFCDTT-20060329AJO.

Transmitter: 0.1-mi. NW of intersection of Santa Fe Ave. & South St.

Ownership: Trinity Broadcasting Network Inc.

Personnel: Paul Crouch, General Manager; Ben Miller, Chief Engineer; Rod Henke, Sales Manager.

Salina—K51GC, Ch. 51, Gray Television Licensee LLC. Phone: 316-943-4221.

Technical Facilities: 0.94-kw ERP, lat. 38° 50' 27", long. 97° 40' 07".

Holds CP for change to 15-kw ERP, 284-ft. above ground, 1518-ft. above sea level, BDFCDTT-20060331ART.

Ownership: Gray Television Inc.

Salina—KSKV-LP, Ch. 41, Marcia T. Turner. Phone: 305-788-5300.

Technical Facilities: 52.7-kw ERP, 313-ft. above ground, 1537-ft. above sea level, lat. 38° 53' 23", long. 97° 38' 46".

Holds CP for change to 150-kw ERP, 445-ft. above ground, 2078-ft. above sea level, lat. 38° 39' 58", long. 47° 41' 29.9". BPTTL-20060331BLM.

Ownership: Marcia T. Turner.

Salina—KSNL-LD, Ch. 47, NVT Wichita Licensee LLC, Debtor in Possession. Phones: 316-265-3333; 404-995-4711. Fax: 316-292-1197.

Technical Facilities: 15-kw ERP, 213-ft. above ground, 1447-ft. above sea level, lat. 38° 50' 29", long. 97° 40' 03".

Began Operation: June 11, 2008.

Ownership: New Vision Television LLC, Debtor in Possession.

Personnel: Al Buch, General Manager; Dan Schurtz, General Sales Manager; Marty West, Local Sales Manager.

Salina—KSNL-LP, Ch. 6, NVT Wichita Licensee LLC, Debtor in Possession. Phone: 404-995-4711.

Technical Facilities: 0.019-kw ERP, 217-ft. above ground, 1447-ft. above sea level, lat. 38° 50' 29", long. 97° 40' 03".

Ownership: New Vision Television LLC, Debtor in Possession.

Topeka—K33IC, Ch. 33, Trinity Broadcasting Network Inc. Phone: 714-832-2950. Fax: 714-730-0661.

Technical Facilities: 49.9-kw ERP, 499-ft. above ground, 1609-ft. above sea level, lat. 39° 01' 34", long. 95° 55' 01".

Ownership: Trinity Broadcasting Network Inc.

Topeka—KGKC-LP, Ch. 10, Hispanic Christian Community Network Inc. Phone: 214-434-6357.

Technical Facilities: 0.3-kw ERP, 49-ft. above ground, 1347-ft. above sea level, lat. 39° 06' 04", long. 96° 17' 28".

Began Operation: August 26, 2008.

Ownership: Hispanic Christian Community Network Inc.

■ **Topeka**—KTMJ-CA, Ch. 43, NVT Topeka II Licensee LLC, Debtor in Possession. Phone: 404-995-4711.

Technical Facilities: 1000-w TPO, 29.3-kw ERP, 425-ft. above ground, 1198-ft. above sea level, lat. 39° 03' 50", long. 95° 45' 49".

Transmitter: 4137 Lower Silver Lake Rd.

Began Operation: September 7, 1989.

Ownership: New Vision Television LLC, Debtor in Possession.

Wichita—K15DD, Ch. 15, Ventana Television Inc. Phone: 727-872-4210.

Technical Facilities: 1.3-kw ERP, 331-ft. above ground, 1630-ft. above sea level, lat. 37° 41' 53", long. 97° 19' 10".

Began Operation: October 23, 1991.

Ownership: Ventana Television Inc.

Wichita—K28JB, Ch. 28, Trinity Broadcasting Network Inc. Phone: 714-832-2950. Fax: 714-730-0661.

Technical Facilities: 8.8-kw ERP, 329-ft. above ground, 1631-ft. above sea level, lat. 37° 41' 53", long. 97° 19' 10".

Holds CP for change to channel number 38, 15-kw ERP, BDISDTT-20060328AJT.

Transmitter: 1615 Murdock Ave., Wichita.

Ownership: Trinity Broadcasting Network Inc.

Wichita—KCTU-LP, Ch. 5, River City Broadcasting Corp. Phone: 316-942-7948.

Technical Facilities: 3-kw ERP, 296-ft. above ground, 1598-ft. above sea level, lat. 37° 41' 53", long. 97° 19' 10".

Ownership: River City Broadcasting Corp.

Wichita—KFVT-LP, Ch. 40, Family Broadcasting Group Inc. Phone: 405-631-7335.

Technical Facilities: 50-kw ERP, 358-ft. above ground, 1670-ft. above sea level, lat. 37° 43' 43", long. 97° 19' 43".

Began Operation: January 19, 1996.

Ownership: Family Broadcasting Group Inc.

■ **Wichita**—KGPT-CA, Ch. 49, Great Plains Television Network LLC. Phone: 316-239-3149.

Technical Facilities: 346-w TPO, 4.8-kw ERP, 259-ft. above ground, 1561-ft. above sea level, lat. 37° 41' 13", long. 97° 20' 23".

Holds CP for change to 5.45-kw ERP, BDFCDTA-20081014AEF.

Transmitter: 300 W. Douglas, Wichita.

Ownership: Great Plains Television Network LLC.

Personnel: Mary Knecht, General Manager.

Wichita—KSMI-LP, Ch. 51, Newmark Communications LLC. Phone: 818-955-5704.

Technical Facilities: 14.1-kw ERP, 302-ft. above ground, 1604-ft. above sea level, lat. 37° 41' 53", long. 97° 19' 10".

Ownership: Newmark Communications LLC.

Kentucky

Augusta—W20CT-D, Ch. 20, Kentucky Authority for ETV. Phone: 859-258-7000.

Technical Facilities: 0.8-kw ERP, 46-ft. above ground, 771-ft. above sea level, lat. 38° 46' 04", long. 84° 00' 35".

Ownership: Kentucky Authority for ETV.

Augusta—W56AT, Ch. 56, Kentucky Authority for ETV. Phone: 859-258-7000.

Technical Facilities: 1.22-kw ERP, lat. 38° 46' 45", long. 84° 00' 33".

Ownership: Kentucky Authority for ETV.

Barbourville—W07AH, Ch. 7, Barbourville Area Television Corp.

Technical Facilities: 0.004-kw ERP, lat. 36° 51' 58", long. 83° 54' 00".

Ownership: Barbourville Area Television Corp.

■ **Campbellsville**—WLCU-CA, Ch. 4, Campbellsville U. Phone: 502-789-5210. Fax: 502-789-5095.

Studio: 217 Matthew St., Campbellsville, KY 42718.

Technical Facilities: 10-w TPO, 0.071-kw ERP, 220-ft. above ground, 1075-ft. above sea level, lat. 37° 20' 07", long. 85° 22' 33".

Ownership: Campbellsville U.

Personnel: Nallia Sabrina, Broadcast Services Director; Mike Graham, Engineering; Marc C. Whitt, Marketing & Public Relations Director.

Corbin—WVTN-LP, Ch. 48, Victory Training School Corp. Phone: 606-528-4671. Fax: 606-528-8704.

Technical Facilities: 1000-w TPO, 10.147-kw ERP, 315-ft. above ground, 1515-ft. above sea level, lat. 36° 59' 01", long. 84° 08' 01".

Transmitter: 2.9-mi. SE of Keavy, 1.3-mi. NW of Corbin.

Began Operation: March 23, 1993.

Ownership: Victory Training School Corp.

Personnel: Charles Sivley, President; Brenda Sivley, Chief Executive Officer.

East Bernstadt, etc.—WOBZ-LP, Ch. 9, Andrea Joy Kesler. Phone: 606-843-9999.

Technical Facilities: 10-w TPO, 0.174-kw ERP, 197-ft. above ground, 1398-ft. above sea level, lat. 37° 12' 32", long. 84° 09' 00".

Transmitter: Johnson Ridge, 0.3-mi. NE of Johnson Ridge School, East Bernstadt.

Ownership: Andrea J. Kesler.

Personnel: Joseph B. Kesler III, General Manager; Dewayne Morgan, Chief Engineer; Joseph B Kesler III, Sales Manager.

Elizabethtown—W39CJ, Ch. 39, Trinity Broadcasting Network Inc. Phone: 714-832-2950. Fax: 714-730-0661.

Technical Facilities: 1000-w TPO, 28-kw ERP, 450-ft. above ground, 1227-ft. above sea level, lat. 37° 40' 55", long. 85° 50' 31".

Holds CP for change to channel number 30, 5-kw ERP, 449-ft. above ground, 1226-ft. above sea level, BDISDTT-20070907AFU.

Transmitter: WKZT-TV tower, approx. 1-mi. SE of Elizabethtown.

Ownership: Trinity Broadcasting Network Inc.

Falmouth—W23DM-D, Ch. 23, Kentucky Authority for ETV. Phone: 859-258-7000.

Technical Facilities: 0.8-kw ERP, 48-ft. above ground, 818-ft. above sea level, lat. 38° 40' 09", long. 84° 19' 35".

Ownership: Kentucky Authority for ETV.

Falmouth—W56AM, Ch. 56, Kentucky Authority for ETV.

Technical Facilities: 0.485-kw ERP, lat. 38° 40' 09", long. 84° 19' 35".

Ownership: Kentucky Authority for ETV.

Glasgow—WKUG-LP, Ch. 62, Budd Broadcasting Co. Inc. Phone: 352-371-7772.

Technical Facilities: 20-kw ERP, 328-ft. above ground, 1204-ft. above sea level, lat. 36° 58' 37", long. 85° 53' 48".

Ownership: Budd Broadcasting Co. Inc.

Glasgow—WKUT-LP, Ch. 64, Budd Broadcasting Co. Inc. Phone: 352-371-7772. Fax: 352-371-9353.

Technical Facilities: 6.9-kw ERP, 328-ft. above ground, 1007-ft. above sea level, lat. 36° 57' 34", long. 86° 00' 08".

Holds CP for change to 150-kw ERP, 348-ft. above ground, 1138-ft. above sea level, lat. 36° 57' 37", long. 86° 32' 49". BPTTL-20051219ACB.

Ownership: Budd Broadcasting Co. Inc.

Hopkinsville—W22CH, Ch. 22, Trinity Broadcasting Network Inc. Phone: 714-832-2950. Fax: 714-730-0661.

Technical Facilities: 1000-w TPO, 11.9-kw ERP, 138-ft. above ground, 738-ft. above sea level, lat. 36° 53' 05", long. 87° 30' 44".

Transmitter: 0.31-mi. N of intersection US 68 & SR 91.

Ownership: Trinity Broadcasting Network Inc.

Personnel: Paul Crouch, General Manager; Ben Miller, Chief Engineer; Rod Henke, Sales Manager.

Hopkinsville—WKAG-CA, Ch. 43, Owen Broadcasting LLC. Phone: 502-885-4300. Fax: 502-886-5882.

Studio: 1616 E 9th St, Hopkinsville, KY 42240.

Technical Facilities: 1000-w TPO, 17.1-kw ERP, 300-ft. above ground, 1032-ft. above sea level, lat. 36° 55' 36", long. 87° 28' 35".

Transmitter: 4-mi. N of city center on Old Madisonville Rd.

Ownership: Owen Broadcasting LLC.

Personnel: Edward Owen, General Manager; Ron Hicks, Chief Engineer; Kim Borders, General Sales Manager; Tim Golden, News Operations.

Jamestown—W09CQ, Ch. 9, Hispanic Christian Community Network Inc. Phone: 214-879-0081.

Technical Facilities: 0.5-kw ERP, 16-ft. above ground, 1047-ft. above sea level, lat. 37° 04' 36", long. 85° 08' 12".

Ownership: Hispanic Christian Community Network Inc.

Jamestown—WESL-LP, Ch. 2, Hispanic Christian Community Network Inc. Phone: 214-879-0081.

Technical Facilities: 0.35-kw ERP, 16-ft. above ground, 1030-ft. above sea level, lat. 37° 09' 29", long. 85° 09' 50".

Began Operation: May 4, 2007.

Ownership: Hispanic Christian Community Network Inc.

Lebanon—W06AY, Ch. 6, Gary White. Phone: 502-468-7379.

Studio: 144 W Main St, Lebanon, KY 40033.

Technical Facilities: 10-w TPO, 0.07-kw ERP, 130-ft. above ground, 1010-ft. above sea level, lat. 37° 35' 12", long. 85° 12' 15".

Holds CP for change to 0.3-kw ERP, 194-ft. above ground, 1106-ft. above sea level, BDFCDVL-20070925AJU.

Transmitter: Shortline Pike.

Ownership: Gary White.

Personnel: Gary White, General Manager.

Lexington—WBLU-LP, Ch. 62, Word of God Fellowship Inc. Phone: 817-571-1229.

Studio: 155 W Tiverton Way, Ste 1A, Lexington, KY 40503.

Technical Facilities: 4-kw ERP, 410-ft. above ground, 1358-ft. above sea level, lat. 38° 02' 51", long. 84° 29' 57".

Holds CP for change to 42-kw ERP, BPTTL-20070111AAW.

Transmitter: Lex Fin Center.

Began Operation: August 20, 1998.

Ownership: Word of God Fellowship Inc.

Personnel: John R. Powley, General Manager; D. Powell, Chief Engineer; W. Smith, Sales Manager.

Louisa—W10AR, Ch. 10, Kentucky Authority for ETV.

Technical Facilities: 0.002-kw ERP, lat. 38° 06' 36", long. 82° 36' 35".

Ownership: Kentucky Authority for ETV.

Louisa—W28DD-D, Ch. 28, Kentucky Authority for ETV. Phone: 859-258-7000.

Technical Facilities: 0.11-kw ERP, 47-ft. above ground, 872-ft. above sea level, lat. 38° 06' 36", long. 82° 36' 35".

Ownership: Kentucky Authority for ETV.

Louisville—W24BW, Ch. 24, Greater Louisville Communications. Phone: 502-966-0624. Fax: 502-968-0424.

Technical Facilities: 21.8-kw ERP, 330-ft. above ground, 965-ft. above sea level, lat. 38° 21' 55", long. 85° 50' 24".

Ownership: Greater Louisville Communications.

Personnel: Bernard D. Rosenthal, General Manager; Jerome Hutchinson Jr., Sales Manager.

Louisville—W50CI, Ch. 50, South Central Communications Corp. Phone: 812-424-8284.

Technical Facilities: 1000-w TPO, 26.2-kw ERP, 367-ft. above ground, 1319-ft. above sea level, lat. 38° 21' 54", long. 85° 50' 25".

Holds CP for change to 15-kw ERP, 367-ft. above ground, 1330-ft. above sea level, lat. 38° 21' 55", long. 85° 50' 24". BDFCDTL-20090415AJP.

Transmitter: Floyds Knob.

Multichannel TV Sound: Stereo only.

Ownership: South Central Communications Corp.

Personnel: John Englebrecht, General Manager.

Louisville—WBKI-CA, Ch. 28, WBKISLG LLC. Phone: 502-809-3400.

Technical Facilities: 10-w TPO, 21.1-kw ERP, 983-ft. above ground, 1947-ft. above sea level, lat. 38° 04' 36", long. 85° 46' 10".

Transmitter: Mitchell Hill.

Began Operation: December 15, 1992.

Ownership: WBKISLG LLC.

Louisville—WBXV-CA, Ch. 13, L4 Media Group LLC. Phone: 321-729-8451.

Studio: 410 Mount Tabor Rd, New Albany, IN 47150.

Technical Facilities: 0.75-kw ERP, 249-ft. above ground, 1212-ft. above sea level, lat. 38° 21' 55", long. 85° 50' 24".

Ownership: L4 Media Group LLC.

Personnel: Warren Reeves, Consulting Engineer; Amy Brown, Broadcast Operations Director; Liz Kiley, Broadcast Vice President.

Lynch & Benham—WAPM-CA, Ch. 9, Holston Valley Broadcasting Corp.

Technical Facilities: 0.008-kw ERP, lat. 36° 54' 50", long. 82° 53' 40".

Transmitter: Black Mountain, 3.9-mi. from Lynch.

Ownership: Holston Valley Broadcasting Corp.

Martin—WVVK-LP, Ch. 45, Parker W. Tiller. Phone: 606-432-3768.

Technical Facilities: 3.3-kw ERP, 94-ft. above ground, 2814-ft. above sea level, lat. 37° 17' 05.6", long. 82° 31' 36.5".

Ownership: Parker W. Tiller.

Murray—WQTV-LP, Ch. 24, KFVS License Subsidiary LLC.

Studio: 804 Fine Arts Bldg, Murray, KY 42071.

Technical Facilities: 9.97-kw ERP, 530-ft. above ground, 1063-ft. above sea level, lat. 36° 32' 58", long. 88° 19' 52".

Ownership: Raycom Media Inc.

Personnel: Stan Marinoff, General Manager & Sales Manager; Larry Albert, Chief Engineer; Glenda Jones, Marketing & Public Relations; Shasta O'Neal, Operations; Allen Fowler, Transmitter Engineer.

Paducah—W54AE, Ch. 54, Tri-State Christian TV Inc. Phone: 618-997-9333.

Technical Facilities: 13.5-kw ERP, 456-ft. above ground, 906-ft. above sea level, lat. 37° 01' 48", long. 88° 38' 51".

Holds CP for change to channel number 38, 15-kw ERP, 279-ft. above ground, 719-ft. above sea level, lat. 37° 01' 50", long. 88° 38' 47". BDISDTT-20060331AZG.

Transmitter: Star Hill Rd., Paducah.

Ownership: Tri-State Christian TV Inc.

Paducah—WQWQ-LP, Ch. 9, KFVS License Subsidiary LLC. Phone: 207-744-8769. Fax: 207-744-0999.

Studio: 2000 McCracken Blvd, Paducah, KY 42001.

Technical Facilities: 3000-w TPO, 7.47-kw ERP, 314-ft. above ground, 336-ft. above sea level, lat. 37° 02' 55", long. 88° 35' 41".

Transmitter: W. Hovekamp Rd. End.

Multichannel TV Sound: Stereo only.

Ownership: Raycom Media Inc.

Personnel: Jean Turnbough, Station Manager; Mike Wunderlich, Operations Director; Allen Fowler, Chief Engineer; Stan Marinoff, Program Executive; Chuck Voss, Creative Services Director.

Scottsville—WPBM-LP, Ch. 31, Proclaim Broadcasting Inc. Phone: 270-618-8848. Fax: 270-618-4800.

Studio: 9406 New Glasgow Rd, Scottsville, KY 42102.

Technical Facilities: 35.6-kw ERP, 466-ft. above ground, 1166-ft. above sea level, lat. 36° 50' 00", long. 86° 05' 00".

Ownership: Proclaim Broadcasting Inc.

Personnel: Dave Benz, General Manager; Dale Howard, Chief Engineer.

Talbert—W16BI, Ch. 16, MS Communications LLC. Phone: 414-765-9737.

Technical Facilities: 1000-w TPO, 5.49-kw ERP, 550-ft. above ground, 2579-ft. above sea level, lat. 37° 11' 34", long. 83° 11' 16".

Transmitter: Buffalo Knob, 3.6-mi. S of Harvard.

Ownership: MS Communications LLC.

Talbert—W20BO, Ch. 20, MS Communications LLC. Phone: 414-765-9737.

Technical Facilities: 500-w TPO, 0.5-kw ERP, 344-ft. above ground, 1138-ft. above sea level, lat. 37° 32' 46", long. 83° 23' 42".

Transmitter: 0.4-mi. S of Jackson.

Ownership: MS Communications LLC.

Talbert—W24BT, Ch. 24, MS Communications LLC. Phone: 414-765-9737.

Technical Facilities: 1000-w TPO, 6-kw ERP, 551-ft. above ground, 2578-ft. above sea level, lat. 37° 11' 34", long. 83° 11' 16".

Transmitter: Buffalo Knob, 3.6-mi. S of Harvard.

Ownership: MS Communications LLC.

Talbert—W26BK, Ch. 26, MS Communications LLC. Phone: 414-765-9737.

Technical Facilities: 1000-w TPO, 0.007-kw ERP, 105-ft. above ground, 2005-ft. above sea level, lat. 37° 10' 18", long. 83° 07' 42".

Transmitter: Buffalo Knob, 3.6-mi. S of Harvard.

Ownership: MS Communications LLC.

Talbert—W31BU, Ch. 31, MS Communications LLC. Phone: 414-765-9737.

Technical Facilities: 1-w TPO, 0.007-kw ERP, 105-ft. above ground, 2005-ft. above sea level, lat. 37° 10' 18", long. 83° 07' 42".

Transmitter: 0.7-mi. SW of Jackson.

Ownership: MS Communications LLC.

Talbert—W51CK, Ch. 51, MS Communications LLC. Phone: 414-765-9737.

Technical Facilities: 432-w TPO, 0.007-kw ERP, 105-ft. above ground, 2005-ft. above sea level, lat. 37° 10' 18", long. 83° 07' 42".

Transmitter: Buffalo Knob, 3.6-mi. S of Harvard.

Ownership: MS Communications LLC.

Talbert—W53BQ, Ch. 53, MS Communications LLC. Phone: 414-213-4629.

Technical Facilities: 1000-w TPO, 0.007-kw ERP, 105-ft. above ground, 2005-ft. above sea level, lat. 37° 10' 18", long. 83° 07' 42".

Transmitter: Buffalo Knob, 3.5-mi. S of Harvard.

Ownership: MS Communications LLC.

Talbert—W54CI, Ch. 54, MS Communications LLC. Phone: 414-765-9737.

Technical Facilities: 63-w TPO, 0.5-kw ERP, 328-ft. above ground, 1627-ft. above sea level, lat. 37° 32' 46", long. 83° 23' 42".

Transmitter: 0.5-mi. SW of Jackson.

Ownership: MS Communications LLC.

Talbert—W64CM, Ch. 64, MS Communications LLC. Phone: 414-765-9737.

Technical Facilities: 458-w TPO, 0.007-kw ERP, 105-ft. above ground, 2005-ft. above sea level, lat. 37° 10' 18", long. 83° 07' 42".

Transmitter: Buffalo Knob, 3.6-mi. S of Harvard.

Ownership: MS Communications LLC.

Talbert—W66DA, Ch. 66, MS Communications LLC. Phone: 414-765-9737.

Technical Facilities: 466-w TPO, 0.007-kw ERP, 105-ft. above ground, 2005-ft. above sea level, lat. 37° 10' 18", long. 83° 07' 42".

Transmitter: Buffalo Knob, 3.6-mi. S of Harvard.

Ownership: MS Communications LLC.

Talbert—W69ED, Ch. 69, MS Communications LLC. Phone: 414-765-9737.

Technical Facilities: 729-w TPO, 0.007-kw ERP, 105-ft. above ground, 2005-ft. above sea level, lat. 37° 10' 18", long. 83° 07' 42".

Transmitter: Buffalo Knob, 3.6-mi. S of Harvard.

Ownership: MS Communications LLC.

Louisiana

Alexandria—K02QB, Ch. 2, Agape Broadcasters Inc. Phone: 337-783-1560.

Technical Facilities: 0.002-kw ERP, 82-ft. above ground, 157-ft. above sea level, lat. 31° 16' 04.34", long. 92° 26' 23.51".

Ownership: Agape Broadcasters Inc.

Alexandria—K16DK, Ch. 16, MS Communications LLC. Phone: 414-213-4629.

Technical Facilities: 0.007-kw ERP, 105-ft. above ground, 197-ft. above sea level, lat. 31° 18' 24", long. 92° 24' 12".

Holds CP for change to 26-ft. above ground, 118-ft. above sea level, BPTTL-20071207ACH.

Transmitter: 1736 Bayou Marie Rd, Pineville.

Ownership: MS Communications LLC.

Alexandria—K21EL, Ch. 21, MS Communications LLC. Phone: 414-213-4629.

Technical Facilities: 0.007-kw ERP, 109-ft. above ground, 197-ft. above sea level, lat. 31° 18' 24", long. 92° 26' 12".

Holds CP for change to 26-ft. above ground, 118-ft. above sea level, BPTTL-20080411AED.

Transmitter: 1736 Bayou Marie Rd., Pineville.

Ownership: MS Communications LLC.

Alexandria—K23DZ, Ch. 23, MS Communications LLC. Phone: 414-765-9737.

Technical Facilities: 1000-w TPO, 0.007-kw ERP, 105-ft. above ground, 197-ft. above sea level, lat. 31° 18' 24", long. 92° 24' 12".

Transmitter: 1736 Bayou Marie Rd., Pineville.

Ownership: MS Communications LLC.

Alexandria—K38EG, Ch. 38, MS Communications LLC. Phone: 414-765-9737.

Technical Facilities: 1000-w TPO, 0.007-kw ERP, 105-ft. above ground, 551-ft. above sea level, lat. 31° 16' 04", long. 92° 26' 24".

Ownership: MS Communications LLC.

Alexandria—K43EI, Ch. 43, MS Communications LLC. Phone: 414-765-9737.

Technical Facilities: 1000-w TPO, 0.007-kw ERP, 105-ft. above ground, 92-ft. above sea level, lat. 31° 18' 24", long. 92° 24' 12".

Ownership: MS Communications LLC.

Alexandria—K45IY, Ch. 45, Trinity Broadcasting Network. Phone: 714-832-2950. Fax: 714-730-0661.

Technical Facilities: 7.8-kw ERP, 374-ft. above ground, 449-ft. above sea level, lat. 31° 16' 04", long. 92° 26' 24".

Ownership: Trinity Broadcasting Network Inc.

Alexandria—K47DW, Ch. 47, ComCorp of Alexandria License Corp. Phone: 337-237-1142.

Technical Facilities: 13.3-kw ERP, 374-ft. above ground, 456-ft. above sea level, lat. 31° 16' 04", long. 92° 26' 24".

Ownership: Communications Corp. of America.

Alexandria—K50DW, Ch. 50, MS Communications LLC. Phone: 414-765-9737.

Technical Facilities: 1000-w TPO, 0.007-kw ERP, 105-ft. above ground, 197-ft. above sea level, lat. 31° 18' 04", long. 92° 24' 12".

Transmitter: 1736 Bayou Marie Rd., Pineville.

Ownership: MS Communications LLC.

Alexandria—K55GT, Ch. 55, MS Communications LLC. Phone: 414-213-4629.

Technical Facilities: 725-w TPO, 0.007-kw ERP, 105-ft. above ground, 551-ft. above sea level, lat. 31° 16' 04", long. 92° 26' 24".

Holds CP for change to channel number 18, 26-ft. above ground, 118-ft. above sea level, lat. 31° 18' 24", long. 92° 24' 12". BDISTTL-20071207ACB.

Ownership: MS Communications LLC.

Alexandria—K57GK, Ch. 57, MS Communications LLC. Phone: 414-213-4629.

Technical Facilities: 653-w TPO, 0.007-kw ERP, 105-ft. above ground, 92-ft. above sea level, lat. 31° 18' 24", long. 92° 24' 12".

Holds CP for change to channel number 29, 26-ft. above ground, 118-ft. above sea level, BDISTTL-20071207ACC.

Transmitter: 1736 Bayou Marie Rd., Pineville.

Ownership: MS Communications LLC.

Alexandria—K60GE, Ch. 60, MS Communications LLC. Phone: 414-213-4629.

Technical Facilities: 1000-w TPO, 0.007-kw ERP, 105-ft. above ground, 551-ft. above sea level, lat. 31° 18' 24", long. 92° 24' 12".

Holds CP for change to channel number 19, 26-ft. above ground, 118-ft. above sea level, BDISTTL-20071207ACG.

Transmitter: 1736 Bayou Marie Rd., Pineville.

Ownership: MS Communications LLC.

Alexandria—K66EY, Ch. 66, Tiger Eye Broadcasting Corp. Phone: 954-431-3144.

Technical Facilities: 0.811-kw ERP, 404-ft. above ground, 479-ft. above sea level, lat. 31° 16' 04", long. 92° 26' 24".

Ownership: Tiger Eye Broadcasting Corp.

Alexandria—KWCE-LP, Ch. 27, Pollack/Betz Communications Inc. Phone: 901-753-0768.

Technical Facilities: 12.3-kw ERP, 430-ft. above ground, 522-ft. above sea level, lat. 31° 18' 24", long. 92° 24' 12".

Ownership: Pollack/Belz Broadcasting Co. LLC.

Baton Rouge—K48IT, Ch. 48, Trinity Broadcasting Network Inc. Phone: 714-832-2950. Fax: 714-730-0661.

Technical Facilities: 12.9-kw ERP, 1007-ft. above ground, 1020-ft. above sea level, lat. 30° 19' 34", long. 91° 16' 36".

Ownership: Trinity Broadcasting Network Inc.

■ **Baton Rouge**—KBTR-CA, Ch. 41, Louisiana Television Broadcasting LLC. Phone: 225-387-2222.

Technical Facilities: 18.9-kw ERP, 190-ft. above ground, 246-ft. above sea level, lat. 30° 26' 59.3", long. 91° 07' 54.5".

Ownership: Louisiana Television Broadcasting LLC.

Baton Rouge—KPBN-LP, Ch. 11, Pelican Broadcasting Network Inc. Phone: 225-248-0049. Fax: 225-774-5004.

Technical Facilities: 195-w TPO, lat. 30° 26' 02", long. 91° 05' 09".

Ownership: Pelican Broadcasting Co.

■ **Baton Rouge**—KZUP-CA, Ch. 19, Knight Broadcasting of Baton Rouge License Corp. Phone: 703-253-2027.

Studio: 914 N Foster Dr, Baton Rouge, LA 70806.

Technical Facilities: 150-kw ERP, 700-ft. above ground, 713-ft. above sea level, lat. 30° 19' 34", long. 91° 16' 36".

Transmitter: One American Place, Baton Rouge.

Ownership: White Knight Holdings Inc.

Personnel: Tammy Traham Willeford, General Manager; Louis (Woody) Jenkins, Chairman & Sales Manager; Kris Kreutz, News Director; Edress Landry, Traffic Manager.

■ **Baton Rouge**—WBRL-CA, Ch. 21, Comcorp of Baton Rouge License Corp. Phone: 337-237-1142.

Studio: 914 N Foster Dr, Baton Rouge, LA 70806.

Technical Facilities: 150-kw ERP, 700-ft. above ground, 713-ft. above sea level, lat. 30° 19' 34", long. 91° 16' 36".

Holds CP for change to 10-kw ERP, BDFCDTA-20080826ABW.

Transmitter: 3920 LA 1 N, Port Allen.

Ownership: Communications Corp. of America.

Personnel: Woody Jenkins, General Manager; Dan Richey, News Director.

■ **Baton Rouge**—WBXH-CA, Ch. 39, WAFB License Subsidiary LLC.

Studio: 5400 Firestation Rd, Ste D, Zachary, LA 70791.

Technical Facilities: 59.5-kw ERP, 459-ft. above ground, 551-ft. above sea level, lat. 30° 36' 50", long. 91° 47' 02".

Transmitter: 6.7-mi. NW of Ryan Airport, Irene.

Ownership: Raycom Media Inc.

Personnel: Liz Kiley, Vice President, Broadcast; Warren Reeves, Consulting Engineer; Amy Brown, Director, Broadcast Operations.

Baton Rouge—WCBZ-LP, Ch. 7, Louisiana Christian Broadcasting Inc. Phone: 318-322-1399.

Technical Facilities: 3-kw ERP, 499-ft. above ground, 547-ft. above sea level, lat. 30° 30' 21.3", long. 91° 01' 24.2".

Began Operation: March 29, 1995.

Ownership: Louisiana Christian Broadcasting Inc.

Personnel: Woody Jenkins, General Manager.

■ **Baton Rouge**—WLFT-CA, Ch. 30, Bethany World Prayer Center Inc. Phone: 255-774-1700. Fax: 225-774-7780.

Technical Facilities: 150-kw ERP, 476-ft. above ground, 499-ft. above sea level, lat. 30° 22' 50", long. 91° 03' 16".

Holds CP for change to 15-kw ERP, BDFCDTA-20080804ACM.

Ownership: Bethany World Prayer Center Inc.

Personnel: Ronald L. Bennett, Vice President; Darren Ryder, General Manager; Beau Hoover, Chief Engineer.

Bunkie—K67GL, Ch. 67, ComCorp of Alexandria License Corp. Phone: 337-237-1142.

Technical Facilities: 8.87-kw ERP, 302-ft. above ground, 374-ft. above sea level, lat. 31° 00' 58", long. 92° 08' 58".

Holds CP for change to channel number 42, 0.1-kw ERP, BDISDTT-20060331ACM.

Ownership: Communications Corp. of America.

Church Point—K69HD, Ch. 69, ComCorp of Louisiana License Corp. Phone: 337-237-1142.

Technical Facilities: 4.09-kw ERP, 793-ft. above ground, 833-ft. above sea level, lat. 30° 21' 44", long. 92° 12' 53".

Holds CP for change to channel number 42, 0.1-kw ERP, BDISDTT-20060331AWF.

Ownership: Communications Corp. of America.

■ **Crowley**—KAGN-LP, Ch. 31, Agape Broadcasters Inc. Phone: 337-783-1560. Fax: 318-783-1674.

Studio: 110 W 3rd St, Crowley, LA 70526.

Technical Facilities: 17.8-kw ERP, 500-ft. above ground, 528-ft. above sea level, lat. 30° 19' 20", long. 92° 22' 40".

Transmitter: W of Hwy. 13, 0.87-mi. S of Crowley.

Ownership: Agape Broadcasters Inc.

Personnel: Barry Thompson, General Manager; Tony Evans, Chief Engineer; Bryan Rivera, Sales Manager.

■ **Hammond**—WSTY-LP, Ch. 23, Ponchatrain Investors LLC. Phone: 225-336-5995.

Technical Facilities: 1000-w TPO, 24.3-kw ERP, 529-ft. above ground, 577-ft. above sea level, lat. 30° 32' 26", long. 90° 29' 07".

Transmitter: 3795 N. Morrison Blvd.

Ownership: Ponchartrain Investors LLC.

Hicks—K61GO, Ch. 61, ComCorp of Alexandria License Corp. Phone: 337-237-1142.

Technical Facilities: 9.29-kw ERP, 282-ft. above ground, 666-ft. above sea level, lat. 31° 09' 35", long. 92° 58' 20".

Holds CP for change to channel number 42, 0.1-kw ERP, BDISDTT-20060331ACR.

Ownership: Communications Corp. of America.

■ **Houma**—KFOL-CA, Ch. 30, Folse Communications LLC. Phones: 504-928-3146; 504-876-3456. Fax: 504-923-2822.

Technical Facilities: 1000-w TPO, 40-kw ERP, 370-ft. above ground, 376-ft. above sea level, lat. 29° 38' 52", long. 90° 41' 34".

Holds CP for change to 0.55-kw ERP, 375-ft. above ground, 385-ft. above sea level, BMPDTA-20080804AEE.

Transmitter: Rte. 316 & Hwy. 90 intersection, 3-mi. N of Houma.

Ownership: Folse Communications LLC.

■ **Jennings**—KJEF-CA, Ch. 13, GAP Broadcasting Lake Charles License LLC. Phone: 214-295-3530.

Studio: 1215 S Lake Arthur Ave, Jennings, LA 70546.

Technical Facilities: 10-w TPO, 0.012-kw ERP, 220-ft. above ground, 243-ft. above sea level, lat. 30° 12' 38", long. 92° 39' 55".

Transmitter: 1215 S. Lake Arthur Ave., Jennings.

Ownership: GAP Broadcasting Lake Charles LLC.

Personnel: Gregory N. Marcantel, General Manager; Tony Evans, Chief Engineer; Charles L. Williams, Program Director; Sara Cormier, Office Manager.

■ **Lafayette**—KAJN-LP, Ch. 40, Agape Broadcasters Inc. Phone: 337-783-1560. Fax: 337-783-1674.

Studio: 704 Eraste Landry Rd, Lafayette, LA 70501.

Technical Facilities: 1000-w TPO, 150-kw ERP, 508-ft. above ground, 528-ft. above sea level, lat. 30° 02' 54", long. 91° 59' 49".

Transmitter: 0.4-mi. S of Hwys. 342 & 93.

Ownership: Agape Broadcasters Inc.

Personnel: Barry Thompson, General Manager; Tony Evans, Chief Engineer.

Lafayette—KLAF-LP, Ch. 46, ComCorp of Louisiana License Corp. Phone: 337-237-1142.

Technical Facilities: 1000-w TPO, 7.41-kw ERP, 491-ft. above ground, 522-ft. above sea level, lat. 30° 12' 49", long. 92° 04' 59".

Holds CP for change to 0.1-kw ERP, 494-ft. above ground, 522-ft. above sea level, BDFCDTL-20090505AAX.

Transmitter: 0.3-mi. NE of Rte. 93, approx. 1.2-mi. SE of Scott.

Ownership: Communications Corp. of America.

■ **Lafayette**—KXKW-CA, Ch. 21, Delta Media Corp. Phone: 337-896-1600.

Technical Facilities: 15-kw ERP, 932-ft. above ground, 955-ft. above sea level, lat. 30° 20' 32", long. 91° 58' 32".

Ownership: Delta Media Corp.

Personnel: K. Sandoval Burke, General Manager.

Lafayette—KXKW-LD, Ch. 32, Delta Media Corp. Phone: 337-896-1600.

Technical Facilities: 8.3-kw ERP, 932-ft. above ground, 955-ft. above sea level, lat. 30° 20' 32", long. 91° 57' 46".

Began Operation: March 18, 2009.

Ownership: Delta Media Corp.

Lake Charles—K22GT, Ch. 22, Foster Charitable Foundation Inc. Phone: 303-757-3199.

Technical Facilities: 9-kw ERP, 481-ft. above ground, 489-ft. above sea level, lat. 30° 05' 54", long. 93° 28' 32".

Holds CP for change to 23-kw ERP, 482-ft. above ground, 490-ft. above sea level, BPTTL-20070706ACE.

Ownership: Foster Charitable Foundation Inc.

Lake Charles—K45HY, Ch. 45, Windsong Communications Inc. Phone: 936-443-4451.

Technical Facilities: 50-kw ERP, 295-ft. above ground, 317-ft. above sea level, lat. 30° 16' 05.4", long. 93° 14' 44.8".

Ownership: Windsong Communications Inc.

Lake Charles—K51EC, Ch. 51, Trinity Christian Center of Santa Ana Inc. Phone: 714-832-2950.

Technical Facilities: 1000-w TPO, 7.6-kw ERP, 403-ft. above sea level, lat. 30° 16' 45", long. 93° 14' 45".

Transmitter: SSW junction of State Rtes. 378 & 378 Spur, near Lake Charles.

Ownership: Trinity Broadcasting Network Inc.

Personnel: Jane P. Duff, General Manager; Mark Fountain, Chief Engineer.

Lake Charles—K63HF, Ch. 63, Windsong Communications Inc. Phone: 936-443-4451.

Technical Facilities: 50-kw ERP, 295-ft. above ground, 316-ft. above sea level, lat. 30° 16' 05.4", long. 93° 14' 44.8".

Ownership: Windsong Communications Inc.

■ **Lake Charles**—KFAM-LP, Ch. 14, Agape Broadcasters Inc. Phone: 337-783-1560. Fax: 337-783-1674.

Technical Facilities: 150-kw ERP, 555-ft. above ground, 570-ft. above sea level, lat. 30° 13' 23.96", long. 93° 18' 35.94".

Ownership: Agape Broadcasters Inc.

Personnel: Barry Thompson, General Manager & Sales Manager; Tony Evans, Chief Engineer.

Lake Charles—KYHT-LP, Ch. 69, Windsong Communications Inc. Phone: 936-443-4451.

Technical Facilities: 50-kw ERP, 295-ft. above ground, 316-ft. above sea level, lat. 30° 16' 05.4", long. 93° 14' 44.8".

Ownership: Windsong Communications Inc.

■ **Leesville**—K51FO, Ch. 51, ComCorp of Alexandria License Corp. Phone: 337-237-1142.

Technical Facilities: 8.07-kw ERP, 385-ft. above ground, 755-ft. above sea level, lat. 31° 14' 08", long. 93° 12' 04".

Holds CP for change to 0.1-kw ERP, 384-ft. above ground, 751-ft. above sea level, BDISDTT-20071221ACU.

Ownership: Communications Corp. of America.

■ **Mermentau**—K45DI, Ch. 45, Trinity Broadcasting Network Inc. Phone: 714-832-2950. Fax: 714-730-0661.

Technical Facilities: 1000-w TPO, 21.9-kw ERP, 406-ft. above ground, 430-ft. above sea level, lat. 30° 11' 32", long. 92° 37' 16".

Holds CP for change to 3-kw ERP, 400-ft. above ground, 411-ft. above sea level, lat. 30° 11' 30", long. 92° 37' 17". BDFCDTT-20060331AFS.

Transmitter: 0.12-mi. S of Hwy. 90, Acadia Parish.

Ownership: Trinity Broadcasting Network Inc.

Monroe—K45IM, Ch. 45, Trinity Broadcasting Network Inc. Phones: 714-832-2950; 330-753-5542. Fax: 714-730-0661.

Technical Facilities: 28.8-kw ERP, 499-ft. above ground, 573-ft. above sea level, lat. 32° 39' 36", long. 92° 05' 15".

Holds CP for change to 15-kw ERP, BDFCDTT-20060313AAF.

Ownership: Trinity Broadcasting Network Inc.

■ **Monroe**—KMNO-LP, Ch. 22, Great Oaks Broadcasting Corp. Phone: 225-201-2121. Fax: 225-928-5097.

Technical Facilities: 18.2-kw ERP, 446-ft. above ground, 518-ft. above sea level, lat. 32° 30' 21", long. 92° 08' 54".

Ownership: Great Oaks Broadcasting Corp.

Personnel: Woody Jenkins, General Manager.

■ **Morgan City**—KJUN-CA, Ch. 7, Folse Communications LLC. Phones: 504-876-3456; 985-876-3456.

Technical Facilities: 0.013-kw ERP, 328-ft. above ground, 333-ft. above sea level, lat. 29° 45' 15", long. 91° 10' 26".

Holds CP for change to 0.3-kw ERP, BMPDVA-20080804ABK.

Ownership: Folse Communications LLC.

Morgan City—KWBJ-LD, Ch. 22, Price Media Corp. Phone: 985-384-6321.

Technical Facilities: 15-kw ERP, 190-ft. above ground, 195-ft. above sea level, lat. 29° 43' 15", long. 91° 12' 18".

Ownership: Price Media Corp.

■ **Morgan City**—KWBJ-LP, Ch. 39, Price Media Corp. Phone: 985-384-6960. Fax: 985-385-1916.

Studio: 608 Michigan St, Morgan City, LA 70380.

Technical Facilities: 1000-w TPO, 8.61-kw ERP, 200-ft. above ground, 194-ft. above sea level, lat. 29° 43' 15", long. 91° 12' 18".

Transmitter: 719-ft. NE of Shaw St. & Shaw Dr., Morgan City.

Ownership: Price Media Corp.

Personnel: David C. Price, General Manager; J. A. Price, Chief Engineer; Stacie Gravois, Sales Representative; Leda Lipari, Programming/Traffic.

Natchitoches—KAIN-LP, Ch. 55, Mary Gill Lee. Phone: 318-356-0017. Fax: 318-356-0872.

Technical Facilities: 138-w TPO, 1-kw ERP, 410-ft. above ground, 672-ft. above sea level, lat. 31° 47' 56", long. 93° 28' 54".

Transmitter: 2-mi. SE of Pleasant Hill.

Ownership: Mary Gill Lee.

Personnel: Richard Gill, General Manager; Ron Davis, Chief Engineer; David Poston, Sales Manager.

Natchitoches—KNTS-LP, Ch. 17, Richard Gill. Phone: 318-356-0017. Fax: 318-356-0872.

Technical Facilities: 138-w TPO, 1-kw ERP, 308-ft. above ground, 673-ft. above sea level, lat. 31° 47' 56", long. 93° 28' 54".

Transmitter: 2-mi. SE of Pleasant Hill.

Ownership: Richard Gill.

Personnel: Richard Gill, General Manager; Ron Davis, Chief Engineer; David Poston, Sales Manager.

Natchitoches—KNYS-LP, Ch. 27, Mary Gill Lee. Phone: 318-356-0017. Fax: 318-356-0872.

Technical Facilities: 138-w TPO, 1-kw ERP, 309-ft. above ground, 673-ft. above sea level, lat. 31° 47' 56", long. 93° 28' 54".

Transmitter: 2-mi. SE of Pleasant Hill.

Ownership: Mary Gill Lee.

New Iberia—K19FR, Ch. 19, Trinity Broadcasting Network. Phone: 714-832-2950. Fax: 714-730-0661.

Technical Facilities: 49.8-kw ERP, 325-ft. above ground, 339-ft. above sea level, lat. 30° 01' 51", long. 91° 48' 48".

Ownership: Trinity Broadcasting Network Inc.

New Iberia—K54FT, Ch. 54, ComCorp of Louisiana License Corp.

Technical Facilities: 7.58-kw ERP, 440-ft. above ground, 459-ft. above sea level, lat. 29° 57' 12", long. 91° 45' 10".

Ownership: Communications Corp. of America.

New Iberia—W08DT, Ch. 8, Native Country Broadcasting Corp. Phone: 772-465-4400.

Technical Facilities: 3-kw ERP, 492-ft. above ground, 495-ft. above sea level, lat. 29° 37' 37", long. 92° 22' 24".

Ownership: Native Country Broadcasting Corp.

New Orleans—K28IL, Ch. 28, Trinity Broadcasting Network Inc. Phone: 714-832-2950. Fax: 714-730-0661.

Technical Facilities: 1000-w TPO, 150-kw ERP, 535-ft. above ground, 535-ft. above sea level, lat. 29° 55' 11", long. 90° 01' 29".

Ownership: Trinity Broadcasting Network Inc.

Personnel: Paul Crouch, General Manager; Ben Miller, Chief Engineer; Rod Henke, Sales Manager.

New Orleans—K47JO, Ch. 47, Ventana Television Inc. Phone: 727-872-4210.

Technical Facilities: 72.8-kw ERP, 814-ft. above ground, 814-ft. above sea level, lat. 29° 55' 11", long. 90° 01' 29".

Transmitter: 1036 Old Behrman Hwy., Gretna.

Began Operation: April 13, 1992.

Ownership: Ventana Television Inc.

■ **New Orleans**—KNOV-CD, Ch. 41, Beach TV Properties Inc. Phone: 850-234-2773.

Technical Facilities: 6.3-kw ERP, 662-ft. above ground, 666-ft. above sea level, lat. 29° 57' 07", long. 90° 04' 13".

Transmitter: 201 St. Charles Ave.

Ownership: Beach TV Properties Inc.

New Orleans—W30ID, Ch. 30, MS Communications LLC. Phone: 414-765-9737.

Technical Facilities: 0.004-kw ERP, 49-ft. above ground, 49-ft. above sea level, lat. 29° 55' 11", long. 90° 01' 29".

Ownership: MS Communications LLC.

■ **New Orleans**—WBXN-CA, Ch. 18, Belo TV Inc. Phone: 214-977-6606.

Studio: 1830 St Bernard, New Orleans, LA 70116.

Technical Facilities: 500-w TPO, 5-kw ERP, 1001-ft. above ground, 1001-ft. above sea level, lat. 29° 55' 12", long. 90° 01' 29".

Holds CP for change to 2.3-kw ERP, 864-ft. above ground, 865-ft. above sea level, lat. 29° 54' 22", long. 90° 02' 22". BPTTA-20070404ABX.

Multichannel TV Sound: Stereo only.

Ownership: Belo Corp.

Personnel: Liz Kiley, Vice President, Broadcast; Warren Reeves, Consulting Engineer; Amy Brown, Director, Broadcast Operations.

New Orleans—WLPN-LP, Ch. 61, Glenn R. & Karin A. Plummer. Phone: 248-559-7778.

Technical Facilities: 1000-w TPO, 30-kw ERP, 869-ft. above ground, 869-ft. above sea level, lat. 29° 55' 11", long. 90° 01' 29".

Holds CP for change to channel number 51, 40-kw ERP, BDISTTL-20060705ACI.

Transmitter: Near Clairborne Ave. & Armon Aster Ave.

Ownership: Glenn R. & Karin A. Plummer.

Opelousas—K39JV, Ch. 39, Trinity Christian Center of Santa Ana Inc. Phone: 714-832-2950.

Technical Facilities: 15.9-kw ERP, 436-ft. above ground, 499-ft. above sea level, lat. 30° 36' 41", long. 92° 08' 24".

Holds CP for change to 15-kw ERP, BDFCDTT-20080403ABI.

Ownership: Trinity Broadcasting Network Inc.

■ **Opelousas**—KDCG-LP, Ch. 22, Acadiana Cable Advertising Inc. Phones: 337-948-7267; 888-881-5901. Fax: 318-948-9040.

Studio: 2897 South St, Opelousas, LA 70570.

Technical Facilities: 10.9-kw ERP, 269-ft. above sea level, lat. 30° 30' 02", long. 95° 05' 12".

Holds CP for change to 15-kw ERP, 207-ft. above ground, 267-ft. above sea level, BMPDTA-20080204ABF.

Transmitter: Hwy. 182 S, 1.7-mi. S of Jefferson St.

Multichannel TV Sound: Separate audio program.

Began Operation: October 13, 1994.

Ownership: Acadiana Cable Advertising Inc.

Personnel: Thom Daly, General Manager; Karl Fontenot, Chief Engineer; Roddy Dye, Sales Manager; Liz Hernandez, Program Director; Melanie Zerinque, News Director.

Opelousas—KOPP-LP, Ch. 62, ComCorp of Louisiana License Corp. Phone: 337-237-1142.

Technical Facilities: 8.93-kw ERP, 290-ft. above ground, 354-ft. above sea level, lat. 30° 31' 14", long. 92° 03' 36".

Holds CP for change to channel number 30, 0.1-kw ERP, 291-ft. above ground, 354-ft. above sea level, BDISDTL-20060331AVY.

Transmitter: 0.5-mi. SE of State Rte. 49 on Laurent St.

Ownership: Communications Corp. of America.

Personnel: Eddie Blanchard, General Manager; Tom Poehler, Sales; Keith Townsdin, Engineering.

Rayville—K26EV, Ch. 26, Don Rayburn Jr.

Technical Facilities: 126-w TPO, 1-kw ERP, 314-ft. above ground, 374-ft. above sea level, lat. 32° 27' 22", long. 91° 39' 27".

Transmitter: 1-mi. NE of Bee Bayou.

Ownership: Don Rayburn Jr.

Shreveport—K31HO, Ch. 31, Trinity Broadcasting Network Inc. Phone: 714-832-2950. Fax: 714-730-0661.

Technical Facilities: 50-kw ERP, 991-ft. above ground, 1256-ft. above sea level, lat. 32° 39' 58", long. 93° 55' 59".

Ownership: Trinity Broadcasting Network Inc.

Shreveport—K42FE, Ch. 42, Three Angels Broadcasting Network Inc. Phone: 618-627-4651. Fax: 618-627-4155.

Studio: 3391 Charley Good Rd, West Frankfort, IL 62896.

Technical Facilities: 46-kw ERP, 380-ft. above ground, 621-ft. above sea level, lat. 32° 28' 25", long. 93° 46' 13".

Ownership: Three Angels Broadcasting Network Inc.

Personnel: Moses Primo, Chief Engineer.

Shreveport—K47HO, Ch. 47, Ventana Television Inc. Phone: 727-872-4210.

Technical Facilities: 21-kw ERP, 243-ft. above ground, 463-ft. above sea level, lat. 32° 30' 32", long. 93° 45' 00".

Began Operation: June 16, 1993.

Ownership: Ventana Television Inc.

■ **Shreveport**—KADO-LP, Ch. 15, Word of Life Ministries Inc.

Technical Facilities: 1000-w TPO, 6.55-kw ERP, 275-ft. above ground, 535-ft. above sea level, lat. 32° 29' 36", long. 93° 45' 53".

Transmitter: 1903 Park Ave.

Ownership: Word of Life Ministries Inc.

■ **Shreveport**—KBXS-CA, Ch. 50, L4 Media Group LLC. Phone: 321-729-8451.

Studio: 400 Travis St., Shreveport, LA 71101.

Technical Facilities: 104-kw ERP, 274-ft. above ground, 484-ft. above sea level, lat. 32° 30' 51", long. 93° 44' 58".

Ownership: L4 Media Group LLC.

Personnel: Warren Reeves, Consulting Engineer; Amy Brown, Broadcast Operations Director; Liz Kiley, Broadcast Vice President.

Vidalia—W44CE, Ch. 44, KM Television of El Dorado LLC. Phone: 847-674-0864.

Technical Facilities: 12.7-kw ERP, 453-ft. above ground, 814-ft. above sea level, lat. 31° 27' 17", long. 91° 18' 54".

Ownership: KM Communications Inc.

West Monroe—KWMS-LP, Ch. 17, Sonrise Communications Inc. Phone: 318-323-4668.

Technical Facilities: 21-kw ERP, 246-ft. above ground, 323-ft. above sea level, lat. 32° 30' 07.2", long. 92° 07' 35.4".

Ownership: Sonrise Communications Inc.

Winnfield—KCDH-LP, Ch. 4, Cranford L. Jordan. Phone: 318-628-3892. Fax: 318-628-3818.

Studio: 171 Snowden Rd, Winnfield, LA 71483.

Technical Facilities: 10-w TPO, 0.023-kw ERP, 200-ft. above ground, 381-ft. above sea level, lat. 31° 52' 39", long. 92° 35' 11".

Transmitter: 2.5-mi. SE of Winnfield.

Multichannel TV Sound: Separate audio progam.

Ownership: Cranford L. Jordan.

Personnel: Cranford L. Jordan, General Manager; Mike Culbertson, Chief Engineer; Philip Wise, Sales Manager.

Maine

Allagash—W04BH, Ch. 4, Maine Public Broadcasting Corp. Phone: 207-783-9101.

Technical Facilities: 0.007-kw ERP, lat. 47° 04' 50", long. 69° 00' 16".

Ownership: Maine Public Broadcasting Corp.

Bangor—W31CX, Ch. 31, EICB-TV East LLC. Phone: 972-291-3750.

Technical Facilities: 0.07-kw ERP, 33-ft. above ground, 117-ft. above sea level, lat. 44° 45' 22", long. 08° 47' 28".

Began Operation: March 17, 2009.

Ownership: EICB-TV LLC.

Bangor—W36CK, Ch. 36, Trinity Broadcasting Network Inc. Phone: 714-832-2950. Fax: 714-730-0661.

Technical Facilities: 2000-w TPO, 19.8-kw ERP, 110-ft. above ground, 1047-ft. above sea level, lat. 44° 40' 39", long. 68° 45' 15".

Holds CP for change to 15-kw ERP, 351-ft. above ground, 1047-ft. above sea level, BDFCDTT-20060313AAG.

Transmitter: Side of WKIT-FM tower atop Kings Mountain.

Began Operation: April 24, 1991.

Ownership: Trinity Broadcasting Network Inc.

Bangor—W39CC, Ch. 39, MS Communications LLC. Phone: 414-765-9737.

Technical Facilities: 0.007-kw ERP, 105-ft. above ground, 981-ft. above sea level, lat. 44° 45' 36", long. 68° 33' 59".

Transmitter: Summit of Blackcap Mountain, East Eddington.

Ownership: MS Communications LLC.

Bangor—W41DD, Ch. 41, Dean M. Mosely. Phone: 318-992-7766.

Technical Facilities: 4-kw ERP, 184-ft. above ground, 486-ft. above sea level, lat. 44° 51' 09", long. 68° 47' 06".

Ownership: Dean M. Mosely.

Bangor—W42BZ, Ch. 42, MS Communications LLC. Phone: 414-765-9737.

Technical Facilities: 0.007-kw ERP, 105-ft. above ground, 699-ft. above sea level, lat. 44° 45' 36", long. 68° 33' 59".

Ownership: MS Communications LLC.

Bangor—W50BX, Ch. 50, MS Communications LLC. Phone: 414-765-9737.

Technical Facilities: 0.007-kw ERP, 105-ft. above ground, 981-ft. above sea level, lat. 44° 45' 36", long. 68° 33' 59".

Ownership: MS Communications LLC.

Bangor—W54CG, Ch. 54, MS Communications LLC. Phone: 414-765-9737.

Technical Facilities: 0.007-kw ERP, 105-ft. above ground, 1086-ft. above sea level, lat. 44° 45' 36", long. 68° 33' 59".

Transmitter: Summit of Blackcap Mountain, East Eddington.

Ownership: MS Communications LLC.

Bangor—W58CM, Ch. 58, MS Communications LLC. Phone: 414-765-9737.

Technical Facilities: 0.007-kw ERP, 105-ft. above ground, 1086-ft. above sea level, lat. 44° 45' 36", long. 68° 33' 59".

Holds CP for change to 62-ft. above ground, 1086-ft. above sea level, lat. 44° 45' 33", long. 68° 33' 58". BPTTL-20060117AEN.

Ownership: MS Communications LLC.

Bangor—W66CL, Ch. 66, MS Communications LLC. Phone: 414-765-9737.

Technical Facilities: 0.007-kw ERP, 105-ft. above ground, 981-ft. above sea level, lat. 44° 45' 36", long. 68° 33' 59".

Ownership: MS Communications LLC.

■ **Bangor**—WBGR-LP, Ch. 33, Maine Family Broadcasting Inc. Phone: 207-947-3300. Fax: 207-884-8333.

Technical Facilities: 1000-w TPO, 29.8-kw ERP, 89-ft. above ground, 883-ft. above sea level, lat. 44° 44' 16", long. 68° 42' 06".

Transmitter: Copeland Hill, East Holden.

Ownership: Maine Family Broadcasting Inc.

Bangor—WCKD-LP, Ch. 30, Western Family Television Inc. Phone: 406-442-2655.

Technical Facilities: 1000-w TPO, 33.7-kw ERP, lat. 44° 40' 39", long. 68° 45' 15".

Ownership: Western Family Television Inc.

Bangor—WFVX-LP, Ch. 22, Rockfleet Broadcasting III LLC. Phone: 212-888-5500.

Technical Facilities: 0.007-kw ERP, 105-ft. above ground, 699-ft. above sea level, lat. 44° 45' 36", long. 68° 33' 59".

Ownership: Rockfleet Broadcasting LP.

Bethel, etc.—W04BS, Ch. 4, Maine Public Broadcasting Corp. Phone: 207-783-9101.

Technical Facilities: 0.02-kw ERP, lat. 44° 25' 42", long. 70° 46' 46".

Holds CP for change to 109-ft. above ground, 1109-ft. above sea level, BDFCDTT-20060330ABS.

Ownership: Maine Public Broadcasting Corp.

Brunswick—W29CA, Ch. 29, Craig Ministries Inc. Phone: 207-989-4040.

Technical Facilities: 14.82-kw ERP, 93-ft. above ground, 354-ft. above sea level, lat. 43° 59' 35", long. 69° 58' 40".

Ownership: Craig Ministries Inc.

Calais—W57AQ, Ch. 57, Pacific & Southern Co. Inc. Phone: 703-854-6899.

Studio: 329 Mount Hope Ave, Bangor, ME 04401.

Technical Facilities: 1000-w TPO, 11-kw ERP, 118-ft. above ground, 597-ft. above sea level, lat. 45° 01' 44", long. 67° 19' 24".

Holds CP for change to channel number 8, 0.3-kw ERP, 118-ft. above ground, 608-ft. above sea level, BDISDTT-20060330AGQ.

Transmitter: Conant Hill, 0.8-mi. SE of Rtes. 191 & 214, Meddybemps.

Ownership: Gannett Co. Inc.

Calais—W61AO, Ch. 61, Community Broadcasting Service.

Technical Facilities: 3.36-kw ERP, lat. 45° 01' 44", long. 67° 19' 24".

Ownership: Maine Public Broadcasting Corp.

Dover & Foxcroft—W27CE, Ch. 27, Trinity Broadcasting Network Inc. Phone: 714-832-2950. Fax: 714-730-0661.

Technical Facilities: 100-w TPO, 1.1-kw ERP, 112-ft. above ground, 843-ft. above sea level, lat. 45° 12' 59", long. 69° 14' 37".

Transmitter: Goffs Corner.

Ownership: Trinity Broadcasting Network Inc.

Falmouth—W57AP, Ch. 57, Sherwood H. Craig. Phones: 207-866-2000; 207-989-4040. Fax: 207-898-3304.

Technical Facilities: 100-kw ERP, 194-ft. above ground, 699-ft. above sea level, lat. 43° 45' 32", long. 70° 19' 14".

Ownership: Craig Ministries Inc.

Personnel: Sherwood Craig, General Manager & Sales Manager; Howie Soule, Chief Engineer.

Farmington—WGBI-LP, Ch. 21, Global Broadcast Network Inc. Phone: 213-617-0892.

Technical Facilities: 15-kw ERP, 190-ft. above ground, 1250-ft. above sea level, lat. 44° 39' 24", long. 70° 11' 52".

Holds CP for change to 14-kw ERP, BDFCDTL-20060331BFC.

Transmitter: Voter Hill, near West Farmington.

Ownership: Global Broadcast Network Inc.

Harpswell—W14DA, Ch. 14, Harpswell Community Broadcasting Corp. Phone: 207-833-2363.

Technical Facilities: 14.5-kw ERP, 98-ft. above ground, 239-ft. above sea level, lat. 43° 48' 00", long. 69° 56' 15".

Began Operation: March 19, 2009.

Ownership: Harpswell Community Broadcasting Corp.

Harrison, etc.—W03AM, Ch. 3, Maine Public Broadcasting Corp. Phone: 207-783-9101.

Technical Facilities: 0.01-kw ERP, lat. 44° 05' 58", long. 70° 40' 22".

Holds CP for change to 0.007-kw ERP, 85-ft. above ground, 705-ft. above sea level, BDFCDTT-20060323ABI.

Ownership: Maine Public Broadcasting Corp.

Machias—W21BH, Ch. 21, Trinity Broadcasting Network Inc. Phone: 714-832-2950. Fax: 714-730-0661.

Technical Facilities: 1000-w TPO, 35.3-kw ERP, 56-ft. above ground, 725-ft. above sea level, lat. 44° 59' 14", long. 67° 28' 07".

Transmitter: Cooper Mountain.

Ownership: Trinity Broadcasting Network Inc.

Madawaska—W11AA, Ch. 11, NEPSK Inc. Phone: 207-764-4461.

Technical Facilities: 0.01-kw ERP, lat. 47° 20' 30", long. 68° 18' 51".

Ownership: NEPSK Inc.

Medway—W34CN, Ch. 34, Trinity Broadcasting Network Inc. Phone: 714-832-2950. Fax: 714-730-0661.

Technical Facilities: 100-w TPO, 0.653-kw ERP, 801-ft. above sea level, lat. 45° 34' 25", long. 68° 31' 10".

Transmitter: 0.16-mi. S of Cemetery Rd.

Ownership: Trinity Broadcasting Network Inc.

Portland—W32CA, Ch. 32, Trinity Christian Center of Santa Ana Inc. Phone: 949-552-0490.

Technical Facilities: 25-kw ERP, 400-ft. above ground, 820-ft. above sea level, lat. 43° 44' 38", long. 70° 20' 05".

Holds CP for change to 15-kw ERP, 400-ft. above ground, 815-ft. above sea level, lat. 43° 44' 38", long. 70° 20' 01". BDFCDTT-20060328ABZ.

Ownership: Trinity Broadcasting Network Inc.

Portland—WLLB-LP, Ch. 15, Word of God Fellowship Inc. Phone: 617-423-0210. Fax: 617-482-9305.

Technical Facilities: 863-w TPO, 8-kw ERP, 164-ft. above ground, 200-ft. above sea level, lat. 43° 41' 22", long. 70° 20' 06".

Transmitter: 779 Warren Ave., Portland.

Ownership: Word of God Fellowship Inc.

Personnel: Ken Carter, General Manager; Steve Callahan, Chief Engineer.

Presque Isle—W51AG, Ch. 51, Trinity Broadcasting Network Inc. Phone: 714-832-2950. Fax: 714-730-0661.

Technical Facilities: 1000-w TPO, 20-kw ERP, 72-ft. above ground, 1043-ft. above sea level, lat. 46° 44' 29", long. 67° 54' 59".

Transmitter: 6-mi. N of Presque Isle.

Ownership: Trinity Broadcasting Network Inc.

Personnel: Paul Crouch, General Manager; Ben Miller, Chief Engineer; Rod Henke, Sales Manager.

Rockland—W64BY, Ch. 64, Craig Ministries Inc. Phones: 207-989-4040; 207-866-2000. Fax: 207-866-3304.

Technical Facilities: 12.24-kw ERP, 82-ft. above ground, 394-ft. above sea level, lat. 44° 06' 30", long. 69° 09' 28".

Ownership: Craig Ministries Inc.

Personnel: Sherwood Craig, General Manager & Sales Manager; Howie Soule, Chief Engineer.

Skowhegan—WGCI-LP, Ch. 4, Pacific & Southern Co. Inc. Phones: 207-942-4821; 703-854-6899. Fax: 207-947-0992.

Studio: 329 Mount Hope Ave, Bangor, ME 04401.

Technical Facilities: 0.3-kw ERP, 151-ft. above ground, 932-ft. above sea level, lat. 44° 42' 46", long. 69° 43' 38".

Ownership: Gannett Co. Inc.

St. Francis—W04AY, Ch. 4, Maine Public Broadcasting Corp. Phone: 207-783-9101.

Technical Facilities: 0.002-kw ERP, lat. 47° 10' 08", long. 68° 51' 47".

Ownership: Maine Public Broadcasting Corp.

St. John Plantation—W11AY, Ch. 11, Town of St. John. Phone: 207-834-6444.

Technical Facilities: 0.039-kw ERP, lat. 47° 13' 30", long. 68° 42' 16".

Transmitter: Summit of Bossy Mountain.

Ownership: St. John Plantation.

Waterville—WFYW-LP, Ch. 41, Three Angels Broadcasting Network Inc. Phone: 618-627-4651. Fax: 618-627-4155.

Studio: 3391 Charley Good Rd, West Frankfort, IL 62896.

Technical Facilities: 1000-w TPO, 28.5-kw ERP, 249-ft. above ground, 673-ft. above sea level, lat. 44° 29' 04", long. 69° 39' 22".

Transmitter: NNW of Intersection of Grove Rd. & Taber Hill, Vassalboro.

Ownership: Three Angels Broadcasting Network Inc.

Personnel: Moses Primo, Chief Engineer.

Maryland

Annapolis—WRZB-LP, Ch. 31, DC Broadcasting Inc. Phones: 303-593-1433; 303-520-9996. Fax: 815-327-4319.

Technical Facilities: 67.6-kw ERP, 92-ft. above ground, 167-ft. above sea level, lat. 38° 59' 13", long. 76° 33' 12".

Ownership: DC Broadcasting Inc.

Baltimore—W28BY, Ch. 28, Information Super Station LLC. Phone: 202-457-0400.

Technical Facilities: 317-w TPO, 14-kw ERP, 413-ft. above ground, 800-ft. above sea level, lat. 38° 56' 24", long. 77° 04' 54".

Transmitter: 4001 Nebraska Ave. NW.

Multichannel TV Sound: Stereo and separate audio program.

Ownership: Information Super Station LLC.

Personnel: Dennis Dunbar, General Manager; Brian McConnaughay, Chief Engineer; Mel Hopkins, Sales Manager.

Cresaptown—W43BP, Ch. 43, Trinity Broadcasting Network Inc. Phone: 714-832-2950. Fax: 714-730-0661.

Technical Facilities: 1.3-kw ERP, 43-ft. above ground, 2936-ft. above sea level, lat. 39° 34' 56", long. 78° 53' 53".

Holds CP for change to channel number 39, 15-kw ERP, BDISDTT-20060330ALB.

Ownership: Trinity Broadcasting Network Inc.

Personnel: Paul Crouch, General Manager; Ben Miller, Chief Engineer; Rod Henke, Sales Manager.

Flintstone—W08BN, Ch. 8, Flintstone Community Television Inc.

Technical Facilities: 0.013-kw ERP, lat. 39° 41' 18", long. 78° 31' 56".

Ownership: Flintstone Community Television Inc.

Flintstone—W11AL, Ch. 11, Flintstone Community Television Inc.

Technical Facilities: 0.012-kw ERP, lat. 39° 41' 18", long. 78° 31' 56".

Ownership: Flintstone Community Television Inc.

Flintstone—W13AD, Ch. 13, Flintstone Community Television Inc.

Technical Facilities: 0.013-kw ERP, lat. 39° 41' 18", long. 78° 31' 56".

Ownership: Flintstone Community Television Inc.

Frederick—W22DA, Ch. 22, Three Angels Broadcasting Network Inc. Phone: 618-627-4651.

Technical Facilities: 37.3-kw ERP, 200-ft. above ground, 1138-ft. above sea level, lat. 39° 19' 50", long. 77° 31' 29".

Ownership: Three Angels Broadcasting Network Inc.

Hagerstown—W42CK, Ch. 42, Three Angels Broadcasting Network Inc. Phone: 618-627-4651. Fax: 618-627-4155.

Studio: 3391 Charley Good Rd, West Frankfort, IL 62896.

Technical Facilities: 1000-w TPO, 6.37-kw ERP, 699-ft. above ground, 738-ft. above sea level, lat. 39° 36' 41", long. 77° 46' 53".

Transmitter: Hwy. 81, Williamsport.

Ownership: Three Angels Broadcasting Network Inc.

Personnel: Moses Primo, Chief Engineer.

Lake Shore—WQAW-LP, Ch. 8, Una Vez Mas Lake Shore License LLC. Phone: 214-754-7008.

Technical Facilities: 3-kw ERP, 394-ft. above ground, 404-ft. above sea level, lat. 38° 58' 02", long. 76° 15' 31".

Ownership: Una Vez Mas GP LLC.

Ocean City—W35CS, Ch. 35, EICB-TV East LLC. Phone: 972-291-3750.

Technical Facilities: 0.005-kw ERP, 33-ft. above ground, 39-ft. above sea level, lat. 38° 19' 54", long. 75° 05' 10".

Holds CP for change to 6.5-kw ERP, 361-ft. above ground, 392-ft. above sea level, lat. 38° 34' 33", long. 75° 20' 18". BDFCDTL-20090324ADK.

Ownership: EICB-TV LLC.

Ocean City—W63DC, Ch. 63, Jeff Chang. Phone: 310-403-5039.

Technical Facilities: 0.2-kw ERP, 243-ft. above ground, 253-ft. above sea level, lat. 38° 24' 59", long. 75° 03' 24".

Holds CP for change to channel number 26, 0.5-kw ERP, 367-ft. above ground, 407-ft. above sea level, lat. 38° 24' 17.6", long. 75° 36' 03.3". BDFCDTL-20080305AEP.

Ownership: Jeff Chang; Chris McHale.

Ocean City—W65EF, Ch. 65, Christopher McHale. Phone: 310-709-9041.

Technical Facilities: 0.2-kw ERP, 243-ft. above ground, 253-ft. above sea level, lat. 38° 24' 59", long. 75° 03' 24".

Ownership: Chris McHale.

Ocean City—WBLP-LP, Ch. 22, Ocean 60 Broadcasting Assn. Phone: 302-732-1400.

Technical Facilities: 10-w TPO, 0.061-kw ERP, 62-ft. above sea level, lat. 38° 26' 37", long. 75° 03' 15".

Holds CP for change to 0.75-kw ERP, 125-ft. above ground, 374-ft. above sea level, BPTTL-20080505AAH.

Transmitter: Parking lot, 138th St. & Coastal Hwy.

Began Operation: November 14, 1994.

Ownership: Ocean Broadcasting Assn.

Ocean City—WRAV-LP, Ch. 8, Asiavision Inc. Phone: 301-345-2742.

Technical Facilities: 10-w TPO, 0.297-kw ERP, 279-ft. above ground, 260-ft. above sea level, lat. 38° 22' 52", long. 75° 10' 32".

Transmitter: N of Rte. 90, E of Rte. 589, Ocean Pines.

Ownership: Asiavision Inc.

Salisbury—W06CF, Ch. 6, The Estate of John R. Powley, Caroline Kaye Smith Executrix. Phone: 850-936-6461.

Technical Facilities: 1-kw ERP, 436-ft. above ground, 466-ft. above sea level, lat. 38° 23' 11.5", long. 75° 17' 26.3".

Began Operation: March 26, 2009.

Ownership: The Estate of John R. Powley, Caroline Kaye Smith Executrix.

Salisbury—W23CX, Ch. 23, Prism Broadcasting Network Inc. Phone: 770-953-3232.

Technical Facilities: 0.1-kw ERP, 23-ft. above ground, 53-ft. above sea level, lat. 38° 13' 49", long. 75° 18' 00".

Ownership: Prism Broadcasting Network Inc.

Salisbury—W23DF, Ch. 23, EICB-TV East LLC. Phone: 972-291-3750.

Technical Facilities: 3.5-kw ERP, 36-ft. above ground, 85-ft. above sea level, lat. 38° 27' 22", long. 75° 34' 22".

Holds CP for change to 15-kw ERP, 276-ft. above ground, 295-ft. above sea level, lat. 38° 32' 34", long. 75° 56' 56". BDFCDTL-20090331ASG.

Began Operation: March 16, 2009.

Ownership: EICB-TV LLC.

Salisbury—WNDC-LP, Ch. 11, Hispanic Christian Community Network Inc. Phone: 214-879-0001.

Technical Facilities: 0.1-kw ERP, 16-ft. above ground, 36-ft. above sea level, lat. 38° 20' 42", long. 75° 17' 00".

Began Operation: June 1, 2007.

Ownership: Hispanic Christian Community Network Inc.

Salisbury—WNGA-LP, Ch. 7, Hispanic Christian Community Network Inc. Phone: 214-879-0081.

Technical Facilities: 0.1-kw ERP, 16-ft. above ground, 36-ft. above sea level, lat. 38° 20' 42", long. 75° 17' 00".

Ownership: Hispanic Christian Community Network Inc.

■ **Towson**—WMJF-LP, Ch. 16, Towson U. Phone: 410-704-2447. Fax: 410-704-3744.

Studio: Media Center 102, Dept. of Electronic Media & Film, Towson U., Towson, MD 21252-0001.

Technical Facilities: 3.5-kw ERP, 154-ft. above ground, 554-ft. above sea level, lat. 39° 23' 45", long. 76° 36' 29".

Transmitter: Residence Tower, Towson U.

Ownership: Towson U.

Personnel: John MacKerron, General Manager.

Massachusetts

Adams, etc.—W38DL, Ch. 38, WNYT-TV LLC. Phone: 651-642-4334.

Technical Facilities: 6-kw ERP, 187-ft. above ground, 3625-ft. above sea level, lat. 42° 38' 14", long. 73° 10' 08".

Holds CP for change to 0.91-kw ERP, BDFCDTT-20080619AFG.

Ownership: Hubbard Broadcasting Inc.

Boston—W40BO, Ch. 40, ION Media LPTV Inc., Debtor in Possession. Phone: 561-682-4206. Fax: 561-659-4754.

Technical Facilities: 918-w TPO, 20-kw ERP, 860-ft. above ground, 958-ft. above sea level, lat. 42° 18' 27", long. 71° 13' 27".

Holds CP for change to 3.5-kw ERP, 860-ft. above ground, 954-ft. above sea level, BDFCDTT-20060322ACL.

Transmitter: 1165 Chestnut St., Newton.

Began Operation: March 22, 1991.

Ownership: ION Media Networks Inc., Debtor in Possession.

Personnel: Lon Mirolli, General Manager; David J. Raymond, Chief Engineer.

Boston—WCEA-LP, Ch. 3, Channel 19 TV Corp. Phone: 617-541-2222. Fax: 617-427-6227.

Studio: 780 Dudley St, Dorchester, MA 02125.

Technical Facilities: 5-kw ERP, 131-ft. above ground, 148-ft. above sea level, lat. 42° 19' 52", long. 71° 04' 40".

Ownership: Channel 19 TV Corp.

Personnel: Peter N. Cuenca, General Manager; Juan Hernandez, Sales Manager.

■ **Boston**—WFXZ-CA, Ch. 24, Boston Broadcasting Corp. Phone: 603-279-4440.

Technical Facilities: 90-kw ERP, 860-ft. above ground, 958-ft. above sea level, lat. 42° 18' 27", long. 71° 13' 27".

Ownership: Boston Broadcasting Corp.

Boston—WHDN-LD, Ch. 26, Guenter Marksteiner. Phones: 772-220-9886; 561-471-9200.

Technical Facilities: 15-kw ERP, 613-ft. above ground, 652-ft. above sea level, lat. 42° 21' 31", long. 71° 03' 33".

Ownership: Guenter Marksteiner.

Boston—WTMU-LP, Ch. 32, ZGS Boston Inc. Phone: 703-528-5656.

Technical Facilities: 1000-w TPO, 12.5-kw ERP, 817-ft. above ground, 800-ft. above sea level, lat. 42° 20' 50", long. 71° 04' 59".

Transmitter: Prudential Tower Bldg., 800 Boylston St.

Ownership: ZGS Broadcasting Holdings Inc.

Dennis—WMPX-LP, Ch. 33, ION Media Boston License Inc., Debtor in Possession. Phone: 561-682-4206.

Technical Facilities: 14.6-kw ERP, 259-ft. above ground, 385-ft. above sea level, lat. 41° 41' 20", long. 70° 20' 49".

Began Operation: September 23, 1983.

Ownership: ION Media Networks Inc., Debtor in Possession.

Leicester—WCRN-LP, Ch. 34, Carter Broadcasting Corp. Phone: 617-423-0810. Fax: 617-482-9305.

Technical Facilities: 909-w TPO, 7-kw ERP, 1361-ft. above sea level, lat. 42° 14' 47", long. 71° 55' 51".

Transmitter: Hwy. 9, 0.8-mi. W of Leicester.

Ownership: Carter Broadcasting Corp.

Personnel: Ken Carter, General Manager; Steve Callahan, Chief Engineer.

Pittsfield, etc.—W28DA, Ch. 28, WNYT-TV LLC. Phone: 651-642-4334.

Technical Facilities: 9.3-kw ERP, 80-ft. above ground, 1440-ft. above sea level, lat. 42° 25' 26", long. 73° 15' 57".

Holds CP for change to 2.8-kw ERP, BDFCDTT-20080611ABV.

Ownership: Hubbard Broadcasting Inc.

Plainfield—W35BK, Ch. 35, Lydia Sylvane Stockwell. Phone: 413-931-5300. Fax: 413-634-5688.

Technical Facilities: 0.28-kw ERP, 30-ft. above ground, 157-ft. above sea level, lat. 42° 31' 23", long. 72° 52' 47".

Ownership: Lydia Sylvane Stockwell.

Springfield—WDMR-LP, Ch. 51, ZGS Hartford Inc. Phone: 703-528-5656.

Studio: 886 Maple Ave, Hartford, CT 06114.

Technical Facilities: 142-kw ERP, 157-ft. above ground, 761-ft. above sea level, lat. 42° 05' 07", long. 72° 42' 12".

Holds CP for change to 15-kw ERP, BDFCDTL-20080804ACW.

Transmitter: Provin Mountain, on West St.

Multichannel TV Sound: Separate audio progam.

Ownership: ZGS Broadcasting Holdings Inc.

Personnel: Lucio C. Ruzzier Sr., President; Gaetano Leone, General Manager; Sal Minniti, Chief Engineer; William Newton, President, Sales.

■ **Springfield**—WFXQ-CA, Ch. 28, WWLP Broadcasting LLC. Phone: 401-457-9525.

Technical Facilities: 5-kw ERP, 46-ft. above ground, 1184-ft. above sea level, lat. 42° 15' 05", long. 72° 38' 43".

Holds CP for change to 125-kw ERP, 335-ft. above ground, 974-ft. above sea level, lat. 42° 05' 05", long. 72° 42' 14". BPTTA-20081017AHG.

Began Operation: February 19, 1991.

Ownership: LIN TV Corp.

Springfield—WSHM-LP, Ch. 67, Meredith Corp. Phones: 413-736-4333; 515-284-2166.

Studio: One Monarch Pl, Ste 300, Springfield, MA 01144-7012.

Technical Facilities: 1.6-kw ERP, 30-ft. above ground, 1195-ft. above sea level, lat. 42° 14' 28", long. 72° 38' 54".

Holds CP for change to channel number 41, 2-kw ERP, lat. 42° 14' 27.7", long. 72° 38' 55.7". BDCCDTL-20061018AAD.

Transmitter: side of existing WGGB-TV tower atop Mount Tom.

Ownership: Meredith Corp.

Michigan

Alpena—W18BT, Ch. 18, Trinity Broadcasting Network Inc. Phone: 714-832-2950. Fax: 714-730-0661.

Technical Facilities: 1000-w TPO, 17.4-kw ERP, 330-ft. above ground, 1079-ft. above sea level, lat. 45° 09' 22", long. 83° 37' 54".

Transmitter: 1295 E. LaComb Rd.

Ownership: Trinity Broadcasting Network Inc.

Personnel: Curt Smith, General Manager; Jim Marr, Chief Engineer; Barbara Bowen, Sales Manager.

Ann Arbor—WFHD-LP, Ch. 27, SMG Media Group. Phone: 517-782-1510.

Studio: 12880 Burt Rd, Detroit, MI 48227.

Technical Facilities: 1000-w TPO, 1.5-kw ERP, 272-ft. above ground, 1142-ft. above sea level, lat. 42° 16' 41", long. 83° 44' 32".

Holds CP for change to 3-kw ERP, BDFCDTT-20060331BBA.

Transmitter: 555 E. Williams St.

Began Operation: February 25, 1991.

Ownership: Local HDTV Inc.

Personnel: Adrian Boganey, Station Manager; Ron Booth, Chief Engineer.

■ **Battle Creek**—WOBC-CA, Ch. 14, WOOD License Co. LLC. Phone: 202-462-6065.

Technical Facilities: 9.1-kw ERP, 305-ft. above ground, 1184-ft. above sea level, lat. 42° 17' 17", long. 85° 09' 54".

Transmitter: 0.4-mi. S of Golden Ave. & Beadle Lake Rd. intersection, Kalamazoo.

Ownership: LIN TV Corp.

Berrien Springs—WYGN-LP, Ch. 12, Good News Television. Phone: 269-473-5274.

Technical Facilities: 1000-w TPO, 3-kw ERP, 450-ft. above ground, 1109-ft. above sea level, lat. 41° 57' 42", long. 86° 21' 02".

Transmitter: 1.2-mi. NW of Snow Rd. & U.S. Rte. 31/33 intersection.

Ownership: Good News Television.

Cedar—WLLZ-LP, Ch. 12, P & P Cable Holdings LLC. Phone: 231-420-1325.

Technical Facilities: 1.23-kw ERP, 100-ft. above ground, 1173-ft. above sea level, lat. 44° 45' 22", long. 85° 40' 42".

Holds CP for change to 0.893-kw ERP, 249-ft. above ground, 1322-ft. above sea level, BPTVL-20070706ACY.

Ownership: P & P Cable Holdings LLC.

Personnel: Bob Naismith, General Manager.

■ **Dearborn**—W33BY, Ch. 33, Highland Park Broadcasting LP.

Technical Facilities: 15-kw ERP, 325-ft. above ground, 948-ft. above sea level, lat. 42° 22' 40", long. 83° 14' 32".

Ownership: Highland Park Broadcasting LP.

Detroit—W48AV, Ch. 48, ION Media License Co. LLC, Debtor in Possession. Phone: 561-682-4206. Fax: 561-659-4754.

Technical Facilities: 2000-w TPO, 38.24-kw ERP, 312-ft. above ground, 892-ft. above sea level, lat. 42° 27' 43", long. 82° 52' 35".

Holds CP for change to 2-kw ERP, BDFCDTL-20060323AFZ.

Transmitter: 1500 Shore Club Dr., St. Clair Shores.

Began Operation: October 16, 1991.

Ownership: ION Media Networks Inc., Debtor in Possession.

Personnel: Michael Berman, General Manager; Robert Thompson, Chief Engineer.

Detroit—W66BV, Ch. 66, Trinity Broadcasting Network Inc. Phone: 714-832-2950. Fax: 714-730-0661.

Technical Facilities: 1-w TPO, 19.7-kw ERP, 1298-ft. above ground, 1869-ft. above sea level, lat. 42° 19' 45", long. 83° 02' 25".

Holds CP for change to channel number 47, 2.7-kw ERP, 728-ft. above ground, 1299-ft. above sea level, BDISDTT-20070105AAR.

Transmitter: Westin Hotel Bldg., Detroit.

Ownership: Trinity Broadcasting Network Inc.

■ **Detroit**—WDWO-CA, Ch. 18, TCT of Michigan Inc. Phone: 618-997-9333.

Studio: 12280 Burt Rd, Detroit, MI 48227.

Technical Facilities: 1000-w TPO, 20-kw ERP, 289-ft. above ground, 915-ft. above sea level, lat. 42° 22' 40", long. 83° 14' 37".

Transmitter: 12280 Burt Rd.

Ownership: TCT of Michigan Inc.

Personnel: Adrian Boganey, General Manager; Ronald L. Booth, Chief Engineer.

■ **Detroit**—WLPC-LP, Ch. 26, WLPC TV-26 Detroit Inc. Phone: 248-559-4200.

Technical Facilities: 2000-w TPO, 32-kw ERP, 475-ft. above ground, 1037-ft. above sea level, lat. 45° 19' 56", long. 83° 02' 42".

Transmitter: Cadillac Tower Bldg., Cadillac Square.

Ownership: Glenn R. & Karin A. Plummer.

Personnel: Glenn R. Plummer, General Manager; Timothy Hoadly, Chief Engineer.

■ **Detroit**—WUDT-CA, Ch. 23, Word of God Fellowship Inc. Phone: 817-571-1229.

Studio: 4128 W Vernor Hwy, Detroit, MI 48209-2145.

Technical Facilities: 50-kw ERP, 712-ft. above ground, 1375-ft. above sea level, lat. 42° 26' 52", long. 83° 10' 23".

Began Operation: June 25, 1990.

Ownership: Word of God Fellowship Inc.

Personnel: Liz Kiley, Vice President, Broadcast; Warren Reeves, Consulting Engineer; Amy Brown, Broadcast Operations Director.

Escanaba—W11CZ, Ch. 11, Hispanic Christian Community Network Inc. Phone: 214-879-0081.

Technical Facilities: 0.1-kw ERP, 164-ft. above ground, 787-ft. above sea level, lat. 45° 45' 48.4", long. 87° 05' 45".

Ownership: Hispanic Christian Community Network Inc.

Escanaba—W14CE, Ch. 14, Barrington Marquette License LLC. Phone: 847-884-1877.

Technical Facilities: 0.856-kw ERP, 164-ft. above ground, 758-ft. above sea level, lat. 45° 44' 43", long. 87° 03' 14".

Ownership: Pilot Group LP.

Escanaba—W20BZ, Ch. 20, Trinity Broadcasting Network Inc. Phone: 714-832-2950. Fax: 714-730-0661.

Technical Facilities: 10-kw ERP, 213-ft. above ground, 905-ft. above sea level, lat. 45° 46' 56", long. 87° 06' 04".

Ownership: Trinity Broadcasting Network Inc.

Escanaba—W40AN-D, Ch. 40, LIN of Wisconsin LLC. Phone: 401-457-9525.

Technical Facilities: 4.04-kw ERP, 233-ft. above ground, 925-ft. above sea level, lat. 45° 46' 56", long. 87° 06' 04".

Ownership: LIN TV Corp.

Flint—WHNE-LP, Ch. 32, Thomas T. Tait. Phone: 818-415-3438.

Technical Facilities: 35.4-kw ERP, 234-ft. above ground, 1015-ft. above sea level, lat. 43° 10' 23", long. 83° 40' 51".

Ownership: Thomas T. Tait.

Flint—WXON-LP, Ch. 54, P & P Cable Holdings LLC. Phone: 231-547-2696.

Technical Facilities: 2000-w TPO, 0.1-kw ERP, 30-ft. above ground, 833-ft. above sea level, lat. 43° 07' 09", long. 83° 40' 38".

Ownership: P & P Cable Holdings LLC.

Grand Rapids—W25CZ, Ch. 25, Trinity Broadcasting Network Inc. Phone: 714-832-2950. Fax: 714-730-0661.

Technical Facilities: 10-kw ERP, lat. 47° 15' 17", long. 93° 26' 03".

Ownership: Trinity Broadcasting Network Inc.

■ **Grand Rapids**—W48CL, Ch. 48, Three Angels Broadcasting Network Inc. Phone: 618-627-4651. Fax: 618-627-4155.

Technical Facilities: 1000-w TPO, 16.1-kw ERP, 308-ft. above ground, 1079-ft. above sea level, lat. 43° 01' 01", long. 85° 45' 25".

Transmitter: Near Elmridge Dr. & Three Mile Rd.

Ownership: Three Angels Broadcasting Network Inc.

Personnel: Moses Primo, General Manager; Linda Shelton, Program Director.

■ **Grand Rapids**—WOGC-CA, Ch. 25, WOOD License Co. LLC. Phone: 401-457-9525.

Technical Facilities: 30-kw ERP, 381-ft. above ground, 1030-ft. above sea level, lat. 42° 48' 59", long. 85° 57' 20".

Holds CP for change to 2.6-kw ERP, BMPDTA-20080804ADU.

Ownership: LIN TV Corp.

■ **Grand Rapids**—WOLP-CA, Ch. 27, WOOD License Co. LLC.

Technical Facilities: 1000-w TPO, 15.3-kw ERP, 138-ft. above ground, 879-ft. above sea level, lat. 42° 57' 36", long. 85° 39' 18".

Transmitter: 1.6-mi. SE of I-131 & I-196 intersection.

Ownership: LIN TV Corp.

Grand Rapids—WUHQ-LP, Ch. 29, Word of God Fellowship Inc. Phone: 817-571-1229.

Technical Facilities: 537.7-w TPO, 40-kw ERP, 392-ft. above ground, 1002-ft. above sea level, lat. 42° 57' 14", long. 85° 41' 52".

Transmitter: 0.3-mi. W of Blue Grass Rd. on U.S. Rte. 27.

Began Operation: April 4, 2003.

Ownership: Word of God Fellowship Inc.

■ **Grand Rapids**—WXSP-CA, Ch. 15, WOOD License Co. LLC. Phone: 616-456-1818. Fax: 616-643-0018.

Studio: 120 College Ave SE, Grand Rapids, MI 49503.

Technical Facilities: 9.42-kw ERP, 344-ft. above ground, 1115-ft. above sea level, lat. 43° 01' 01", long. 85° 44' 25".

Ownership: LIN TV Corp.

Hesperia—W42CB, Ch. 42, Tribune Television Holdings Inc., Debtor-In-Possession. Phone: 616-447-8722.

Technical Facilities: 7.31-kw ERP, 427-ft. above ground, 1227-ft. above sea level, lat. 43° 33' 00", long. 86° 02' 34".

Holds CP for change to 15-kw ERP, BDFCDTT-20090313AAA.

Ownership: Tribune Broadcasting Co., Debtor-In-Possession.

■ **Holland**—WOHO-CA, Ch. 33, WOOD License Co. LLC. Phone: 202-462-6065.

Technical Facilities: 1000-w TPO, 10-kw ERP, 381-ft. above ground, 1030-ft. above sea level, lat. 42° 48' 59", long. 85° 57' 20".

Transmitter: 2640 72nd Ave.

Ownership: LIN TV Corp.

Houghton—W27CQ, Ch. 27, Trinity Broadcasting Network Inc. Phone: 714-832-2950. Fax: 714-730-0661.

Technical Facilities: 10-kw ERP, 279-ft. above ground, 1340-ft. above sea level, lat. 47° 06' 06", long. 88° 34' 11".

Ownership: Trinity Broadcasting Network Inc.

Houghton Lake—W18CB, Ch. 18, MS Communications LLC. Phone: 414-765-9737.

Technical Facilities: 1000-w TPO, 0.007-kw ERP, 105-ft. above ground, 1424-ft. above sea level, lat. 44° 17' 25", long. 84° 44' 40".

Transmitter: 1-mi. S of Summit Heights.

Ownership: MS Communications LLC.

Houghton Lake—W21BS, Ch. 21, MS Communications LLC. Phone: 414-765-9737.

Technical Facilities: 132-w TPO, 0.007-kw ERP, 105-ft. above ground, 1424-ft. above sea level, lat. 44° 17' 25", long. 84° 44' 40".

Transmitter: 1-mi. S of Summit Heights.

Ownership: MS Communications LLC.

Houghton Lake—W24CG, Ch. 24, MS Communications LLC. Phone: 414-765-9737.

Technical Facilities: 132-w TPO, 0.007-kw ERP, 105-ft. above ground, 1424-ft. above sea level, lat. 44° 17' 25", long. 84° 44' 40".

Transmitter: 1-mi. S of Summit Heights.

Ownership: MS Communications LLC.

Houghton Lake—W31BN, Ch. 31, MS Communications LLC. Phone: 414-765-9737.

Technical Facilities: 132-w TPO, 0.007-kw ERP, 105-ft. above ground, 1424-ft. above sea level, lat. 44° 17' 25", long. 84° 44' 40".

Transmitter: 1-mi. S of Summit Heights.

Ownership: MS Communications LLC.

Houghton Lake—W36CE, Ch. 36, MS Communications LLC. Phone: 414-765-9737.

Technical Facilities: 132-w TPO, 0.007-kw ERP, 105-ft. above ground, 1424-ft. above sea level, lat. 44° 17' 25", long. 84° 44' 40".

Transmitter: 1-mi. S of Summit Heights.

Ownership: MS Communications LLC.

Houghton Lake—W50CD, Ch. 50, MS Communications LLC. Phone: 414-765-9737.

Technical Facilities: 132-w TPO, 0.007-kw ERP, 105-ft. above ground, 1424-ft. above sea level, lat. 44° 17' 25", long. 84° 44' 40".

Transmitter: 1-mi. S of Summit Heights.

Ownership: MS Communications LLC.

Houghton Lake—W52CO, Ch. 52, MS Communications LLC. Phone: 414-765-9737.

Technical Facilities: 132-w TPO, 0.007-kw ERP, 105-ft. above ground, 1423-ft. above sea level, lat. 44° 17' 25", long. 84° 44' 40".

Transmitter: 1-mi. S of Summit Heights.

Ownership: MS Communications LLC.

Houghton Lake—W55CH, Ch. 55, MS Communications LLC. Phone: 414-765-9737.

Technical Facilities: 132-w TPO, 0.007-kw ERP, 105-ft. above ground, 1423-ft. above sea level, lat. 44° 17' 25", long. 84° 44' 40".

Transmitter: 1-mi. S of Summit Heights.

Ownership: MS Communications LLC.

Houghton Lake—W57CQ, Ch. 57, MS Communications LLC. Phone: 414-765-9737.

Technical Facilities: 132-w TPO, 0.007-kw ERP, 105-ft. above ground, 1424-ft. above sea level, lat. 44° 17' 25", long. 84° 44' 40".

Transmitter: 1-mi. S of Summit Heights.

Ownership: MS Communications LLC.

Houghton Lake—W59DC, Ch. 59, MS Communications LLC. Phone: 414-765-9737.

Technical Facilities: 132-w TPO, 0.007-kw ERP, 105-ft. above ground, 1424-ft. above sea level, lat. 44° 17' 25", long. 84° 44' 40".

Transmitter: 1-mi. S of Summit Heights.

Ownership: MS Communications LLC.

Houghton Lake—W61CS, Ch. 61, MS Communications LLC. Phone: 414-765-9737.

Technical Facilities: 500-w TPO, 0.007-kw ERP, 105-ft. above ground, 1319-ft. above sea level, lat. 44° 17' 25", long. 84° 44' 40".

Transmitter: 1-mi. S of Summit Heights.

Ownership: MS Communications LLC.

Houghton Lake—W63CH, Ch. 63, MS Communications LLC. Phone: 414-765-9737.

Technical Facilities: 500-w TPO, 0.007-kw ERP, 105-ft. above ground, 1424-ft. above sea level, lat. 44° 17' 25", long. 84° 44' 40".

Transmitter: 1-mi. S of Summit Heights.

Ownership: MS Communications LLC.

Houghton Lake—W65DJ, Ch. 65, MS Communications LLC. Phone: 414-765-9737.

Technical Facilities: 132-w TPO, 0.007-kw ERP, 105-ft. above ground, 1424-ft. above sea level, lat. 44° 17' 25", long. 84° 44' 40".

Transmitter: 1-mi. S of Summit Heights.

Ownership: MS Communications LLC.

Houghton Lake—W67DN, Ch. 67, MS Communications LLC. Phone: 414-765-9737.

Technical Facilities: 0.007-kw ERP, 105-ft. above ground, 1424-ft. above sea level, lat. 44° 17' 25", long. 84° 44' 40".

Ownership: MS Communications LLC.

Ironwood—W32CV, Ch. 32, KQDS Acquisition Corp. Phone: 701-277-1515.

Technical Facilities: 15.9-kw ERP, 350-ft. above ground, 2010-ft. above sea level, lat. 46° 26' 28", long. 90° 11' 26".

Holds CP for change to 8.452-kw ERP, BDFCDTT-20060331BFS.

Ownership: KQDS Acquisition Corp.

Kalamazoo—W26BX, Ch. 26, TCT of Michigan Inc. Phone: 618-997-9333.

Technical Facilities: 5.3-kw ERP, 440-ft. above ground, 1355-ft. above sea level, lat. 42° 07' 43", long. 85° 20' 16".

Holds CP for change to 15-kw ERP, 440-ft. above ground, 1352-ft. above sea level, lat. 42° 07' 44", long. 85° 20' 22". BDFCDTT-20060331AYN.

Ownership: TCT of Michigan Inc.

■ **Kalamazoo**—WOKZ-CA, Ch. 50, WOOD License Co. LLC. Phone: 401-454-2880.

Technical Facilities: 14.3-kw ERP, 148-ft. above ground, 1086-ft. above sea level, lat. 42° 17' 48", long. 85° 38' 29".

Multichannel TV Sound: Separate audio progam.

Ownership: LIN TV Corp.

Personnel: Scott Blumenthal, General Manager; Mike Laemers, Director of Engineering; Diane Knowski, Sales Manager.

Lansing—W27CN, Ch. 27, Tri-State Christian TV Inc. Phone: 618-997-9333. Fax: 618-997-1859.

Studio: 2865 Trautner Dr, Saginaw, MI 48604.

Technical Facilities: 8.5-kw ERP, 340-ft. above ground, 1169-ft. above sea level, lat. 42° 43' 16", long. 84° 33' 01".

Holds CP for change to 15-kw ERP, BDFCDTT-20060331BFH.

Ownership: Tri-State Christian TV Inc.

Personnel: Mike Socier, Station Manager; Ron Booth, Chief Engineer.

Leeland, etc.—W69AV, Ch. 69, Central Michigan U. Phone: 989-774-4000.

Technical Facilities: 0.78-kw ERP, lat. 44° 58' 50", long. 85° 40' 45".

Ownership: Central Michigan U.

Ludington—W34BZ, Ch. 34, MS Communications LLC. Phone: 414-765-9737.

Michigan — Low Power TV & TV Translator Stations

Technical Facilities: 100-w TPO, 0.007-kw ERP, 105-ft. above ground, 823-ft. above sea level, lat. 44° 03' 57", long. 86° 19' 58".

Transmitter: Jebavy at Ehler.

Ownership: MS Communications LLC.

Ludington—W48BY, Ch. 48, MS Communications LLC. Phone: 414-765-9737.

Technical Facilities: 100-w TPO, 0.007-kw ERP, 105-ft. above ground, 823-ft. above sea level, lat. 44° 03' 57", long. 86° 19' 58".

Transmitter: Jebavy at Ehler.

Ownership: MS Communications LLC.

Ludington—WBWT-LP, Ch. 38, Bustos Media of Wisconsin License LLC. Phone: 916-368-6300.

Studio: 1136 S 108th St, West Allise, WI 53214.

Technical Facilities: 25-kw ERP, 650-ft. above ground, 1278-ft. above sea level, lat. 43° 05' 46", long. 87° 59' 15".

Ownership: Bustos Media of Wisconsin License LLC.

Personnel: Ana Bermudez, General Manager.

Marquette—W07DB, Ch. 7, Barrington Marquette License LLC.

Technical Facilities: 0.025-kw ERP, 115-ft. above ground, 830-ft. above sea level, lat. 46° 32' 45", long. 87° 23' 27".

Ownership: Pilot Group LP.

Marquette—W17CS, Ch. 17, Trinity Broadcasting Network Inc. Phone: 714-832-2950. Fax: 714-730-0661.

Technical Facilities: 8.9-kw ERP, 380-ft. above ground, 1625-ft. above sea level, lat. 46° 30' 52", long. 87° 28' 36".

Holds CP for change to 15-kw ERP, BDFCDTT-20060331AGV.

Began Operation: September 15, 2004.

Ownership: Trinity Broadcasting Network Inc.

Menominee—W31BK, Ch. 31, Journal Broadcast Corp. Phones: 920-494-2626; 702-876-1313. Fax: 920-494-7071.

Technical Facilities: 8.6-kw ERP, 459-ft. above ground, 1049-ft. above sea level, lat. 45° 11' 19", long. 87° 34' 08".

Multichannel TV Sound: Stereo only.

Ownership: Journal Communications Inc.

Personnel: Mike Harding, Chief Executive Officer; Mark L. Cramer, Chief Engineer; Mike Smith, Sales Manager.

Mount Pleasant—W44BQ, Ch. 44, NTN/ Saginaw Inc. Phone: 231-436-7731.

Technical Facilities: 512-w TPO, 0.242-kw ERP, 25-ft. above ground, 806-ft. above sea level, lat. 43° 41' 56", long. 84° 46' 11".

Transmitter: U.S. Rte. 27, 0.4-mi. W of Blue Grass Rd.

Ownership: NTN/Saginaw Inc.

Mount Pleasant—W60CO, Ch. 60, NTN/ Saginaw Inc. Phone: 231-436-7731.

Technical Facilities: 528.6-w TPO, 0.242-kw ERP, 257-ft. above ground, 806-ft. above sea level, lat. 43° 41' 56", long. 84° 46' 11".

Transmitter: 0.3-mi. W of Blue Grass Rd. on U.S. Rte. 27.

Ownership: Merle W. Pearce.

Mount Pleasant—W61DK, Ch. 61, NTN/ Saginaw Inc. Phone: 231-436-7731.

Technical Facilities: 1000-w TPO, 9.73-kw ERP, 1277-ft. above ground, 1164-ft. above sea level, lat. 43° 34' 33", long. 84° 46' 29".

Transmitter: BR/27, 1.5-mi. S of Mount Pleasant.

Ownership: NTN/Saginaw Inc.

Mount Pleasant—WBWM-LP, Ch. 32, P & P Cable Holdings LLC. Phone: 231-436-7731.

Technical Facilities: 515-w TPO, 0.0872-kw ERP, 50-ft. above ground, 847-ft. above sea level, lat. 43° 34' 33", long. 84° 46' 29".

Transmitter: 0.3-mi. W of Blue Grass Rd. on US Rte. 27.

Ownership: P & P Cable Holdings LLC.

Muskegon—W52DB, Ch. 52, Tribune Television Holdings Inc., Debtor-In-Possession. Phone: 206-674-1300.

Technical Facilities: 21.7-kw ERP, 420-ft. above ground, 1076-ft. above sea level, lat. 43° 18' 50", long. 86° 09' 17".

Transmitter: 5-mi. W of Big Rapids.

Ownership: Tribune Broadcasting Co., Debtor-In-Possession.

■ **Muskegon**—WMKG-LP, Ch. 38, Kelley Enterprises. Phone: 616-733-4040. Fax: 616-739-4329.

Studio: 4237 Airline Rd, North Shores, MI 49444.

Technical Facilities: 33.8-kw ERP, 187-ft. above ground, 843-ft. above sea level, lat. 43° 15' 06", long. 86° 09' 10".

Multichannel TV Sound: Stereo only.

Ownership: Kelley Enterprises.

Personnel: Fenton Kelley, General Manager & Chief Engineer.

■ **Muskegon**—WOMS-CA, Ch. 29, WOOD License Co. LLC. Phone: 401-457-9525.

Technical Facilities: 10.4-kw ERP, 440-ft. above ground, 1122-ft. above sea level, lat. 43° 15' 45", long. 86° 04' 34".

Holds CP for change to 0.7-kw ERP, BDFCDTA-20060330ALZ.

Ownership: LIN TV Corp.

Petoskey—W18BX, Ch. 18, MS Communications LLC. Phone: 414-213-4629.

Technical Facilities: 0.0124-kw ERP, 50-ft. above ground, 1321-ft. above sea level, lat. 45° 28' 40", long. 84° 57' 04".

Ownership: MS Communications LLC.

Petoskey—W20BQ, Ch. 20, MS Communications LLC. Phone: 414-213-4629.

Technical Facilities: 0.0124-kw ERP, 50-ft. above ground, 1321-ft. above sea level, lat. 45° 28' 40", long. 84° 57' 04".

Ownership: MS Communications LLC.

Petoskey—W23BM, Ch. 23, MS Communications LLC. Phone: 414-213-4629.

Technical Facilities: 0.0124-kw ERP, 50-ft. above ground, 1321-ft. above sea level, lat. 45° 28' 40", long. 84° 57' 04".

Ownership: MS Communications LLC.

Petoskey—W25CD, Ch. 25, MS Communications LLC. Phone: 414-213-4629.

Technical Facilities: 0.0124-kw ERP, 50-ft. above ground, 1321-ft. above sea level, lat. 45° 28' 40", long. 84° 57' 04".

Ownership: MS Communications LLC.

Petoskey—W31BI, Ch. 31, MS Communications LLC. Phone: 414-765-9737.

Technical Facilities: 179-w TPO, 1-kw ERP, 623-ft. above ground, 1814-ft. above sea level, lat. 45° 19' 17", long. 84° 52' 33".

Transmitter: 1-mi. N of Boyne City.

Ownership: MS Communications LLC.

Petoskey—W34CR, Ch. 34, Frank J. Catz, Trustee. Phone: 650-854-0111. Fax: 650-854-0223.

Technical Facilities: 179-w TPO, 1-kw ERP, 594-ft. above ground, 1884-ft. above sea level, lat. 45° 19' 34", long. 84° 52' 43".

Transmitter: 1-mi. N of Boyne City.

Ownership: Frank J. Catz, Trustee.

Petoskey—W36CD, Ch. 36, MS Communications LLC. Phone: 414-213-4629.

Technical Facilities: 0.0124-kw ERP, 50-ft. above ground, 1321-ft. above sea level, lat. 45° 28' 40", long. 84° 57' 04".

Ownership: MS Communications LLC.

Petoskey—W39CB, Ch. 39, MS Communications LLC. Phone: 414-213-4629.

Technical Facilities: 0.0124-kw ERP, 50-ft. above ground, 1321-ft. above sea level, lat. 45° 28' 40", long. 84° 57' 04".

Ownership: MS Communications LLC.

Petoskey—W41CK, Ch. 41, Frank J. Catz, Trustee. Phone: 650-854-0111. Fax: 650-854-0223.

Technical Facilities: 179-w TPO, 1-kw ERP, 623-ft. above ground, 1814-ft. above sea level, lat. 45° 19' 17", long. 84° 52' 33".

Transmitter: 1-mi. N of Boyne City.

Ownership: Frank J. Catz, Trustee.

Petoskey—W51CR, Ch. 51, MS Communications LLC. Phone: 414-213-4629.

Technical Facilities: 0.0124-kw ERP, 50-ft. above ground, 1321-ft. above sea level, lat. 45° 28' 40", long. 84° 57' 04".

Ownership: MS Communications LLC.

Petoskey—W53BN, Ch. 53, MS Communications LLC. Phone: 414-213-4629.

Technical Facilities: 0.0124-kw ERP, 50-ft. above ground, 1321-ft. above sea level, lat. 45° 28' 40", long. 84° 57' 04".

Ownership: MS Communications LLC.

Petoskey—W55CL, Ch. 55, MS Communications LLC. Phone: 414-213-4629.

Technical Facilities: 0.0124-kw ERP, 50-ft. above ground, 1321-ft. above sea level, lat. 45° 28' 40", long. 84° 57' 04".

Ownership: MS Communications LLC.

Petoskey—W57CP, Ch. 57, MS Communications LLC. Phone: 414-765-9737.

Technical Facilities: 179-w TPO, 4-kw ERP, 415-ft. above ground, 1686-ft. above sea level, lat. 45° 28' 40", long. 84° 57' 04".

Transmitter: 1-mi. N of Boyne City.

Ownership: MS Communications LLC.

Petoskey—W62CR, Ch. 62, MS Communications LLC. Phone: 414-213-4629.

Technical Facilities: 0.0124-kw ERP, 50-ft. above ground, 1321-ft. above sea level, lat. 45° 28' 40", long. 84° 57' 04".

Ownership: MS Communications LLC.

Petoskey—W64CK, Ch. 64, MS Communications LLC. Phone: 414-213-4629.

Technical Facilities: 0.0124-kw ERP, 50-ft. above ground, 1321-ft. above sea level, lat. 45° 28' 40", long. 84° 57' 04".

Ownership: MS Communications LLC.

Petoskey—W66CY, Ch. 66, MS Communications LLC. Phone: 414-213-4629.

Technical Facilities: 0.0124-kw ERP, 50-ft. above ground, 1321-ft. above sea level, lat. 45° 28' 40", long. 84° 57' 04".

Ownership: MS Communications LLC.

Petoskey—W68DH, Ch. 68, MS Communications LLC. Phone: 414-213-4629.

Technical Facilities: 0.0124-kw ERP, 49-ft. above ground, 1320-ft. above sea level, lat. 45° 28' 40", long. 84° 57' 04".

Ownership: MS Communications LLC.

Pickford—W43CM, Ch. 43, Cadillac Telecasting Co. Phone: 602-571-1052.

Technical Facilities: 12-kw ERP, 246-ft. above ground, 1142-ft. above sea level, lat. 46° 05' 05", long. 84° 24' 23".

Ownership: Cadillac Telecasting Co.

Pinconning—W09CK, Ch. 9, P & P Cable Holdings LLC. Phone: 231-436-7731. Fax: 231-436-7731.

Technical Facilities: 939-w TPO, 0.085-kw ERP, 26-ft. above ground, 830-ft. above sea level, lat. 43° 07' 09", long. 83° 40' 38".

Transmitter: 3685 Garfield Rd., Mount Forest Twp.

Ownership: P & P Cable Holdings LLC.

Pinconning—W15BP, Ch. 15, P & P Cable Holdings LLC. Phone: 231-436-7731. Fax: 253-540-0980.

Technical Facilities: 1000-w TPO, 0.25-kw ERP, 25-ft. above ground, 618-ft. above sea level, lat. 43° 50' 46", long. 84° 05' 32".

Transmitter: 3685 Garfield Rd., Mount Forest Twp.

Ownership: P & P Cable Holdings LLC.

Pinconning—W44BO, Ch. 44, P & P Cable Holdings LLC. Phone: 231-436-7731.

Technical Facilities: 1000-w TPO, 0.25-kw ERP, 25-ft. above ground, 618-ft. above sea level, lat. 43° 50' 46", long. 84° 05' 32".

Transmitter: 3685 Garfield Rd., Mount Forest Twp.

Ownership: P & P Cable Holdings LLC.

Pinconning—WKJF-LP, Ch. 58, P & P Cable Holdings LLC. Phone: 231-436-7731.

Technical Facilities: 931-w TPO, 0.25-kw ERP, 25-ft. above ground, 618-ft. above sea level, lat. 43° 42' 02", long. 83° 59' 17".

Transmitter: 3685 Garfield Rd., Mount Forest Twp.

Ownership: P & P Cable Holdings LLC.

Pinconning—WKNX-LP, Ch. 22, P & P Cable Holdings LLC. Phone: 231-436-7731.

Technical Facilities: 1000-w TPO, 0.25-kw ERP, 25-ft. above ground, 618-ft. above sea level, lat. 43° 42' 02", long. 83° 59' 17".

Transmitter: 3685 Garfield Rd., Mount Forest Twp.

Ownership: P & P Cable Holdings LLC.

Pinconning—WTCF-LP, Ch. 69, NTN/Saginaw Inc. Phone: 231-436-7731. Fax: 253-540-0980.

Technical Facilities: 0.25-kw ERP, 25-ft. above ground, 618-ft. above sea level, lat. 43° 50' 46", long. 84° 05' 32".

Transmitter: 3685 Garfield Rd., Mount Forest Twp.

Ownership: NTN/Saginaw Inc.

Pinconning—WUHO-LP, Ch. 36, P & P Cable Holdings LLC. Phone: 231-547-2696. Fax: 253-540-0981.

Technical Facilities: 15-kw ERP, 450-ft. above ground, 1379-ft. above sea level, lat. 42° 16' 28", long. 85° 39' 12".

Ownership: P & P Cable Holdings LLC.

Saginaw & Midland—W46CR, Ch. 46, Three Angels Broadcasting Network Inc. Phone: 618-627-4651.

Technical Facilities: 1000-w TPO, 66.4-kw ERP, 476-ft. above ground, 1164-ft. above sea level, lat. 43° 30' 56", long. 84° 32' 49".

Holds CP for change to channel number 24, 2.33-kw ERP, 252-ft. above ground, 901-ft. above sea level, lat. 43° 37' 44.5", long. 84° 10' 09.8". BDISDTL-20080918AGD.

Transmitter: 2-mi. ENE of Geneva Rd.

Began Operation: October 12, 1999.

Ownership: Three Angels Broadcasting Network Inc.

Personnel: Moses Primo, Chief Engineer.

Sault Ste. Marie—W21BN, Ch. 21, MS Communications LLC. Phone: 414-765-9737.

Technical Facilities: 132-w TPO, 0.007-kw ERP, 105-ft. above ground, 761-ft. above sea level, lat. 46° 23' 48", long. 84° 23' 52".

Transmitter: 1-mi. S of Sault Ste. Marie.

Ownership: MS Communications LLC.

Sault Ste. Marie—W32BN, Ch. 32, MS Communications LLC. Phone: 414-765-9737.

Technical Facilities: 132-w TPO, 0.007-kw ERP, 105-ft. above ground, 656-ft. above sea level, lat. 46° 23' 48", long. 84° 23' 52".

Transmitter: 1-mi. S of Sault Ste. Marie.

Ownership: MS Communications LLC.

Sault Ste. Marie—W36BV, Ch. 36, MS Communications LLC. Phone: 414-765-9737.

Technical Facilities: 132-w TPO, 0.007-kw ERP, 105-ft. above ground, 656-ft. above sea level, lat. 46° 23' 48", long. 84° 23' 52".

Transmitter: 1-mi. S of Sault Ste. Marie.

Ownership: MS Communications LLC.

Sault Ste. Marie—W39BY, Ch. 39, MS Communications LLC. Phone: 414-765-9737.

Technical Facilities: 132-w TPO, 0.007-kw ERP, 105-ft. above ground, 656-ft. above sea level, lat. 46° 23' 48", long. 84° 23' 52".

Transmitter: 1-mi. S of Sault Ste. Marie.

Ownership: MS Communications LLC.

Sault Ste. Marie—W48BZ, Ch. 48, MS Communications LLC. Phone: 414-765-9737.

Technical Facilities: 132-w TPO, 0.007-kw ERP, 105-ft. above ground, 656-ft. above sea level, lat. 46° 23' 48", long. 84° 23' 52".

Transmitter: 1-mi. S of Sault Ste. Marie.

Ownership: MS Communications LLC.

Sault Ste. Marie—W50CA, Ch. 50, MS Communications LLC. Phone: 414-765-9737.

Technical Facilities: 132-w TPO, 0.007-kw ERP, 105-ft. above ground, 656-ft. above sea level, lat. 46° 23' 48", long. 84° 23' 52".

Transmitter: 1-mi. S of Sault Ste. Marie.

Ownership: MS Communications LLC.

Sault Ste. Marie—W52CB, Ch. 52, MS Communications LLC. Phone: 414-765-9737.

Technical Facilities: 1000-w TPO, 0.007-kw ERP, 105-ft. above ground, 656-ft. above sea level, lat. 46° 23' 48", long. 84° 23' 52".

Transmitter: 1-mi. S of Sault Ste. Marie.

Ownership: MS Communications LLC.

Sault Ste. Marie—W56DI, Ch. 56, MS Communications LLC. Phone: 414-765-9737.

Technical Facilities: 132-w TPO, 0.007-kw ERP, 105-ft. above ground, 656-ft. above sea level, lat. 46° 23' 48", long. 84° 23' 52".

Transmitter: 1-mi. S of Sault Ste. Marie.

Ownership: MS Communications LLC.

Sault Ste. Marie—W58CO, Ch. 58, MS Communications LLC. Phone: 414-765-9737.

Technical Facilities: 500-w TPO, 0.007-kw ERP, 105-ft. above ground, 656-ft. above sea level, lat. 46° 23' 48", long. 84° 23' 52".

Transmitter: 1-mi. S of Sault Ste. Marie.

Ownership: MS Communications LLC.

Sault Ste. Marie—W61CR, Ch. 61, Cadillac Telecasting Co. Phone: 602-571-1052.

Technical Facilities: 10-kw ERP, lat. 46° 29' 10", long. 84° 13' 49".

Transmitter: Sugar Island Rd., 0.6-mi. W of McMahon Rd.

Ownership: Cadillac Telecasting Co.

Sault Ste. Marie—W67CS, Ch. 67, Three Angels Broadcasting Network Inc.

Technical Facilities: 10.3-kw ERP, 157-ft. above ground, 856-ft. above sea level, lat. 46° 26' 16", long. 84° 22' 42".

Ownership: Three Angels Broadcasting Network Inc.

Traverse City—W15BM, Ch. 15, MS Communications LLC. Phone: 414-765-9737.

Technical Facilities: 0.007-kw ERP, 105-ft. above ground, 1155-ft. above sea level, lat. 44° 46' 13", long. 85° 41' 43".

Ownership: MS Communications LLC.

Traverse City—W23BL, Ch. 23, MS Communications LLC. Phone: 414-765-9737.

Technical Facilities: 69-w TPO, 0.007-kw ERP, 105-ft. above ground, 1155-ft. above sea level, lat. 44° 46' 13", long. 85° 41' 43".

Transmitter: 1.5-mi. SE of Traverse City Airport.

Ownership: MS Communications LLC.

Traverse City—W25CU, Ch. 25, Edward J. & Madge E. Hess. Phone: 209-722-1976.

Technical Facilities: 0.5-kw ERP, 459-ft. above ground, 480-ft. above sea level, lat. 44° 45' 22", long. 85° 40' 42".

Ownership: Edward J. & Madge E. Hess.

Traverse City—W34CE, Ch. 34, MS Communications LLC. Phone: 414-765-9737.

Technical Facilities: 69-w TPO, 0.007-kw ERP, 105-ft. above ground, 1155-ft. above sea level, lat. 44° 46' 13", long. 85° 41' 43".

Transmitter: 1.6-mi. SE of Traverse City airport.

Ownership: MS Communications LLC.

Traverse City—W36BZ, Ch. 19, MS Communications LLC. Phone: 414-765-9737.

Technical Facilities: 0.008-kw ERP, 49-ft. above ground, 1493-ft. above sea level, lat. 44° 14' 56", long. 85° 18' 48".

Ownership: MS Communications LLC.

Traverse City—W48CC, Ch. 48, MS Communications LLC. Phone: 414-765-9737.

Technical Facilities: 69-w TPO, 0.007-kw ERP, 105-ft. above ground, 1050-ft. above sea level, lat. 44° 46' 13", long. 85° 41' 43".

Transmitter: 1.5-mi. SE of Traverse City Airport.

Ownership: MS Communications LLC.

Traverse City—W52CP, Ch. 52, MS Communications LLC. Phone: 414-765-9737.

Technical Facilities: 69-w TPO, 0.007-kw ERP, 105-ft. above ground, 1050-ft. above sea level, lat. 44° 46' 13", long. 85° 41' 43".

Transmitter: 1.5-mi. SE of Traverse City Airport.

Ownership: MS Communications LLC.

Traverse City—W54CR, Ch. 54, Cadillac Telecasting Co. Phone: 602-571-1052.

Technical Facilities: 30.45-kw ERP, 269-ft. above ground, 1318-ft. above sea level, lat. 44° 46' 13", long. 85° 41' 43".

Ownership: Cadillac Telecasting Co.

Traverse City—W56DF, Ch. 56, MS Communications LLC. Phone: 414-765-9737.

Technical Facilities: 0.007-kw ERP, 105-ft. above ground, 1155-ft. above sea level, lat. 44° 46' 13", long. 85° 41' 43".

Ownership: MS Communications LLC.

Traverse City—W58CN, Ch. 58, MS Communications LLC. Phone: 414-765-9737.

Technical Facilities: 0.007-kw ERP, 105-ft. above ground, 1050-ft. above sea level, lat. 44° 46' 13", long. 85° 41' 43".

Ownership: MS Communications LLC.

Traverse City—W62CQ, Ch. 62, MS Communications LLC. Phone: 414-765-9737.

Technical Facilities: 69-w TPO, 0.007-kw ERP, 105-ft. above ground, 1050-ft. above sea level, lat. 44° 46' 13", long. 85° 41' 43".

Transmitter: 1.5-mi. SE of Traverse City Airport.

Ownership: MS Communications LLC.

Traverse City—W66CX, Ch. 66, MS Communications LLC. Phone: 414-765-9737.

Technical Facilities: 69-w TPO, 0.007-kw ERP, 105-ft. above ground, 1050-ft. above sea level, lat. 44° 46' 13", long. 85° 41' 43".

Transmitter: 1.5-mi. SE of Traverse City Airport.

Ownership: MS Communications LLC.

Traverse City—W68DD, Ch. 68, MS Communications LLC. Phone: 414-765-9737.

Technical Facilities: 69-w TPO, 0.007-kw ERP, 105-ft. above ground, 1050-ft. above sea level, lat. 44° 46' 13", long. 85° 41' 43".

Transmitter: 1.5-mi. SE of Traverse City Airport.

Ownership: MS Communications LLC.

Traverse City, etc.—W46AD, Ch. 46, Central Michigan U. Phone: 989-774-4000.

Technical Facilities: 15.6-kw ERP, lat. 44° 46' 36", long. 85° 41' 02".

Ownership: Central Michigan U.

Minnesota

Aitkin—K39GG, Ch. 39, KQDS Acquisition Corp. Phone: 701-277-1515.

Technical Facilities: 14.3-kw ERP, 328-ft. above ground, 1545-ft. above sea level, lat. 46° 32' 05", long. 93° 50' 15".

Holds CP for change to 6.745-kw ERP, BDFCDTT-20060331BIW.

Ownership: KQDS Acquisition Corp.

Albert Lea—K40JT, Ch. 40, Trinity Broadcasting Network Inc. Phone: 714-832-2950. Fax: 714-730-0661.

Technical Facilities: 10.7-kw ERP, 197-ft. above ground, 1481-ft. above sea level, lat. 43° 37' 40", long. 93° 21' 49".

Ownership: Trinity Broadcasting Network Inc.

Alexandria—K14LZ, Ch. 14, Selective TV Inc. Phone: 320-763-5924. Fax: 320-763-9247.

Technical Facilities: 1.56-kw ERP, 354-ft. above ground, 1824-ft. above sea level, lat. 45° 55' 59", long. 95° 26' 50".

Ownership: Selective TV Inc.

Alexandria—K16CO, Ch. 16, Selective TV Inc. Phone: 320-763-5924. Fax: 320-763-9247.

Studio: 2308 S Broadway, Alexandria, MN 56308.

Technical Facilities: 100-w TPO, 1.56-kw ERP, 338-ft. above ground, 1808-ft. above sea level, lat. 45° 55' 59", long. 95° 26' 50".

Transmitter: 4-mi. NW of Alexandria.

Ownership: Selective TV Inc.

Personnel: Mike Gregor, General Manager; Dave Wilbur, Chief Engineer.

Alexandria—K18DG, Ch. 18, Selective TV Inc. Phone: 320-763-5924. Fax: 320-763-9247.

Studio: 2308 S Broadway, Alexandria, MN 56308.

Technical Facilities: 100-w TPO, 1.56-kw ERP, 338-ft. above ground, 1808-ft. above sea level, lat. 45° 55' 59", long. 95° 26' 50".

Transmitter: 4-mi. NW of Alexandria.

Ownership: Selective TV Inc.

Personnel: Mike Gregor, General Manager; Dave Wilbur, Chief Engineer.

Alexandria—K21GN, Ch. 21, Selective TV Inc. Phone: 651-642-4212.

Technical Facilities: 1.56-kw ERP, 338-ft. above ground, 1808-ft. above sea level, lat. 45° 55' 59", long. 95° 26' 50".

Ownership: Selective TV Inc.

Alexandria—K26CL, Ch. 26, Selective TV Inc. Phone: 320-763-5924. Fax: 320-763-9247.

Studio: 2308 S Broadway, Alexandria, MN 56308.

Technical Facilities: 100-w TPO, 0.745-kw ERP, 338-ft. above ground, 1808-ft. above sea level, lat. 45° 55' 59", long. 95° 26' 50".

Transmitter: 4-mi. NW of Alexandria.

Ownership: Selective TV Inc.

Personnel: Mike Gregor, General Manager; Dave Wilbur, Chief Engineer.

Alexandria—K30AF, Ch. 30, Selective TV Inc. Phone: 320-763-5924. Fax: 320-763-9247.

Studio: 2308 S Broadway, Alexandria, MN 56308.

Technical Facilities: 100-w TPO, 1.4012-kw ERP, 354-ft. above ground, 1824-ft. above sea level, lat. 45° 55' 59", long. 95° 26' 50".

Transmitter: 4-mi. NW of Alexandria.

Ownership: Selective TV Inc.

Personnel: Mike Gregor, General Manager; Dave Wilbur, Chief Engineer.

Alexandria—K32EB, Ch. 32, Selective TV Inc. Phone: 320-763-5924. Fax: 320-763-9247.

Technical Facilities: 100-w TPO, 1.63-kw ERP, 354-ft. above ground, 1807-ft. above sea level, lat. 45° 55' 59", long. 95° 26' 50".

Transmitter: 4-mi. NW of Alexandria.

Ownership: Selective TV Inc.

Personnel: Mike Gregor, General Manager; Dave Wilbur, Chief Engineer.

Alexandria—K34AF, Ch. 34, Selective TV Inc. Phone: 320-763-5924. Fax: 320-763-9247.

Studio: 2308 S Broadway, Alexandria, MN 56308.

Technical Facilities: 100-w TPO, 1.4012-kw ERP, 354-ft. above ground, 1470-ft. above sea level, lat. 45° 55' 59", long. 95° 26' 50".

Transmitter: 4-mi. NW of Alexandria.

Ownership: Selective TV Inc.

Personnel: Mike Gregor, General Manager; Dave Wilbur, Chief Engineer.

Alexandria—K38AC, Ch. 38, Selective TV Inc. Phone: 320-763-5924. Fax: 320-763-9247.

Technical Facilities: 1.4-kw ERP, 1811-ft. above sea level, lat. 45° 55' 59", long. 95° 26' 50".

Ownership: Selective TV Inc.

Alexandria—K44GH, Ch. 44, Three Angels Broadcasting Network Inc. Phone: 618-627-4651.

Technical Facilities: 1.2-kw ERP, 338-ft. above ground, 1808-ft. above sea level, lat. 45° 55' 59", long. 95° 26' 50".

Ownership: Three Angels Broadcasting Network Inc.

Alexandria—K48DV, Ch. 48, Selective TV Inc. Phone: 320-763-5924. Fax: 320-763-9247.

Studio: 2308 S Broadway, Alexandria, MN 56308.

Technical Facilities: 100-w TPO, 1.45-kw ERP, 338-ft. above ground, 1808-ft. above sea level, lat. 45° 55' 59", long. 95° 26' 50".

Transmitter: 4-mi. NW of Alexandria.

Ownership: Selective TV Inc.

Personnel: Mike Gregor, General Manager; Dave Wilbur, Chief Engineer.

Alexandria—K50DB, Ch. 50, Selective TV Inc. Phone: 320-763-5924. Fax: 320-763-9247.

Studio: 2308 S Broadway, Alexandria, MN 56308.

Technical Facilities: 100-w TPO, 1.45-kw ERP, 338-ft. above ground, 1808-ft. above sea level, lat. 45° 55' 59", long. 95° 26' 50".

Transmitter: 4-mi. NW of Alexandria.

Ownership: Selective TV Inc.

Personnel: Michael R. Gregor, President.

Alexandria—K52DZ, Ch. 52, Selective TV Inc. Phone: 320-763-5924. Fax: 320-763-9247.

Studio: 2308 S Broadway, Alexandria, MN 56308.

Technical Facilities: 100-w TPO, 1.45-kw ERP, 338-ft. above ground, 1808-ft. above sea level, lat. 45° 55' 59", long. 95° 26' 50".

Transmitter: 4-mi. NW of Alexandria.

Ownership: Selective TV Inc.

Personnel: Michael R. Gregor, General Manager; Dave Wilbur, Chief Engineer.

Alexandria—K55ID, Ch. 55, Selective TV Inc. Phone: 320-763-5924. Fax: 320-763-9247.

Technical Facilities: 1.56-kw ERP, lat. 45° 55' 59", long. 95° 26' 50".

Ownership: Selective TV Inc.

Alexandria—K58DS, Ch. 58, Selective TV Inc. Phone: 320-763-5924. Fax: 320-763-9247.

Studio: 2308 S Broadway, Alexandria, MN 56308.

Technical Facilities: 100-w TPO, 1.53-kw ERP, 338-ft. above ground, 1808-ft. above sea level, lat. 45° 55' 59", long. 95° 26' 50".

Transmitter: 4-mi. NW of Alexandria.

Ownership: Selective TV Inc.

Personnel: Michael R. Gregor, General Manager; Dave Wilbur, Chief Engineer.

Alexandria—K60EJ, Ch. 60, Selective TV Inc. Phone: 320-763-5924. Fax: 320-763-9247.

Studio: 2308 S Broadway, Alexandria, MN 56308.

Technical Facilities: 100-w TPO, 1.53-kw ERP, 338-ft. above ground, 1807-ft. above sea level, lat. 45° 55' 59", long. 95° 26' 50".

Holds CP for change to channel number 47, 1.45-kw ERP, 338-ft. above ground, 1808-ft. above sea level, BDISTTL-20060828ACD.

Transmitter: 4-mi. NW of Alexandria.

Ownership: Selective TV Inc.

Personnel: Michael R. Gregor, General Manager; Dave Wilbur, Chief Engineer.

Alexandria—K62AU, Ch. 62, Selective TV Inc. Phone: 320-763-5924. Fax: 320-763-9247.

Studio: 2308 S Broadway, Alexandria, MN 56308.

Technical Facilities: 100-w TPO, 1.4-kw ERP, lat. 45° 55' 59", long. 95° 26' 50".

Transmitter: 4-mi. NW of Alexandria.

Ownership: Selective TV Inc.

Personnel: Michael R. Gregor, General Manager; Dave Wilbur, Chief Engineer.

Alexandria—K65HD, Ch. 65, Selective TV Inc. Phone: 320-763-5924. Fax: 320-763-9247.

Studio: 2308 S Broadway, Alexandria, MN 56308.

Technical Facilities: 1.26-kw ERP, 338-ft. above ground, 1808-ft. above sea level, lat. 45° 55' 59", long. 95° 26' 50".

Holds CP for change to channel number 51, 1.45-kw ERP, BDISTTL-20060828AFF.

Ownership: Selective TV Inc.

Personnel: Michael R. Gregor, General Manager; Dave Wilbur, Chief Engineer.

Alexandria—K67HI, Ch. 67, Selective TV Inc. Phone: 320-763-5924. Fax: 320-763-9247.

Technical Facilities: 1.31-kw ERP, lat. 45° 55' 59", long. 95° 26' 50".

Ownership: Selective TV Inc.

Appleton—K15DC, Ch. 15, Prairieview TV Inc. Phone: 952-975-0548.

Technical Facilities: 1.26-kw ERP, 483-ft. above ground, 1515-ft. above sea level, lat. 45° 10' 49", long. 95° 59' 47".

Ownership: Prairieview TV Inc.

Appleton—K17CS, Ch. 17, Prairieview TV Inc. Phone: 952-975-0548.

Technical Facilities: 100-w TPO, 1.23-kw ERP, 482-ft. above ground, 1503-ft. above sea level, lat. 45° 10' 49", long. 95° 59' 47".

Transmitter: Near Hwy. 7, 1-mi. SE of Appleton.

Ownership: Prairieview TV Inc.

Personnel: Tamie Campbell, General Manager.

Appleton—K19CW, Ch. 19, Prairieview TV Inc. Phone: 952-975-0548.

Technical Facilities: 100-w TPO, 1.31-kw ERP, 482-ft. above ground, 1503-ft. above sea level, lat. 45° 10' 49", long. 95° 59' 47".

Transmitter: Near Hwy. 7, 1-mi. SE of Appleton.

Ownership: Prairieview TV Inc.

Personnel: Tamie Campbell, General Manager.

Appleton—K21AK, Ch. 21, Teleview Systems of Minnesota Inc. Phone: 952-975-0547.

Technical Facilities: 1.17-kw ERP, 489-ft. above ground, 1509-ft. above sea level, lat. 45° 10' 49", long. 95° 59' 47".

Transmitter: 0.99 mi. SE of Appleton, near Hwy. 7.

Ownership: Teleview Systems of Minnesota.

Appleton—K23DF, Ch. 23, Prairieview TV Inc. Phone: 952-975-0548.

Technical Facilities: 100-w TPO, 0.82-kw ERP, 479-ft. above ground, 1499-ft. above sea level, lat. 45° 10' 49", long. 95° 59' 47".

Transmitter: Near Hwy. 7, 1-mi. SE of Appleton.

Ownership: Prairieview TV Inc.

Personnel: Tamie Campbell, General Manager.

Appleton—K25EI, Ch. 25, Prairieview TV Inc. Phone: 952-975-0548.

Technical Facilities: 1.21-kw ERP, 483-ft. above ground, 1515-ft. above sea level, lat. 45° 10' 49", long. 95° 59' 47".

Ownership: Prairieview TV Inc.

Appleton—K29CC, Ch. 29, Prairieview TV Inc. Phone: 952-975-0548.

Technical Facilities: 0.896-kw ERP, lat. 45° 10' 49", long. 95° 59' 47".

Transmitter: Near Hwy. 7, 1-mi. SE of Appleton.

Ownership: Prairieview TV Inc.

Appleton—K33CR, Ch. 33, Prairieview TV Inc. Phone: 952-975-0548.

Technical Facilities: 100-w TPO, 0.896-kw ERP, 482-ft. above ground, 1503-ft. above sea level, lat. 45° 10' 49", long. 95° 59' 47".

Transmitter: Near Hwy. 7, 1-mi. SE of Appleton.

Ownership: Prairieview TV Inc.

Personnel: Tamie Campbell, General Manager.

Appleton—K49ED, Ch. 49, Prairieview TV Inc. Phone: 952-975-0548.

Technical Facilities: 100-w TPO, 0.98-kw ERP, 495-ft. above ground, 1516-ft. above sea level, lat. 45° 10' 49", long. 95° 59' 47".

Transmitter: Near Hwy. 7, 1-mi. SE of Appleton.

Ownership: Prairieview TV Inc.

Personnel: Tamie Campbell, General Manager.

Appleton—K52AH, Ch. 52, Prairieview TV Inc. Phone: 952-975-0548.

Technical Facilities: 1.68-kw ERP, lat. 45° 10' 49", long. 95° 59' 47".

Ownership: Prairieview TV Inc.

Appleton—K56BZ, Ch. 56, Prairieview TV Inc. Phone: 952-975-0548.

Technical Facilities: 1.17-kw ERP, 482-ft. above ground, 1503-ft. above sea level, lat. 45° 10' 49", long. 95° 59' 47".

Ownership: Prairieview TV Inc.

Appleton—K58EO, Ch. 58, Prairieview TV Inc. Phone: 952-975-0548.

Technical Facilities: 100-w TPO, 1.17-kw ERP, 483-ft. above ground, 1503-ft. above sea level, lat. 45° 10' 49", long. 95° 59' 47".

Transmitter: Near Hwy. 7, 1-mi. SE of Appleton.

Ownership: Prairieview TV Inc.

Personnel: Tamie Campbell, General Manager.

Appleton—K60AB, Ch. 60, Prairieview TV Inc. Phone: 952-975-0548.

Technical Facilities: 1.68-kw ERP, lat. 45° 10' 46", long. 95° 59' 35".

Ownership: Selective TV Inc.

Baudette—K53BL, Ch. 53, Lake of the Woods County. Phone: 218-634-2836.

Technical Facilities: 1.46-kw ERP, lat. 48° 40' 14", long. 94° 34' 24".

Ownership: Lake of the Woods County.

Baudette—K55BH, Ch. 55, Lake of the Woods County. Phone: 218-634-2836.

Technical Facilities: 1.48-kw ERP, lat. 48° 40' 14", long. 94° 34' 24".

Ownership: Lake of the Woods County.

Baudette—K57AR, Ch. 57, Lake of the Woods County. Phone: 218-634-2836.

Technical Facilities: 1.46-kw ERP, lat. 48° 40' 14", long. 94° 34' 24".

Ownership: Lake of the Woods County.

Bemidji—K28DD, Ch. 28, KSAX-TV Inc. Phone: 651-642-4334. Fax: 651-642-4103.

Technical Facilities: 16-kw ERP, 371-ft. above ground, 1850-ft. above sea level, lat. 47° 28' 07", long. 94° 49' 23".

Ownership: Hubbard Broadcasting Inc.

Bemidji—K30DK, Ch. 30, Fox Television Stations Inc.

Technical Facilities: 16-kw ERP, 371-ft. above ground, 1850-ft. above sea level, lat. 47° 28' 08", long. 94° 49' 23".

Ownership: Fox Television Holdings Inc.

Bemidji—K42FH, Ch. 42, Trinity Broadcasting Network Inc. Phone: 714-832-2950. Fax: 714-730-0611.

Technical Facilities: 8.8-kw ERP, 350-ft. above ground, 1760-ft. above sea level, lat. 47° 33' 21", long. 94° 48' 05".

Ownership: Trinity Broadcasting Network Inc.

Big Falls—W64AM, Ch. 64, County of Koochiching. Phone: 218-283-1101.

Technical Facilities: 0.812-kw ERP, lat. 48° 11' 30", long. 93° 48' 00".

Ownership: County of Koochiching.

Big Falls, etc.—K60BO, Ch. 60, County of Koochiching. Phone: 218-283-1101.

Technical Facilities: 0.81-kw ERP, lat. 48° 11' 30", long. 93° 48' 00".

Ownership: County of Koochiching.

Big Falls, etc.—K62BJ, Ch. 62, County of Koochiching. Phone: 218-283-1101.

Technical Facilities: 0.81-kw ERP, lat. 48° 11' 30", long. 93° 48' 00".

Ownership: County of Koochiching.

Bigfork, etc.—K67CA, Ch. 67, EZ-TV Inc. Phone: 218-743-3131.

Technical Facilities: 0.812-kw ERP, lat. 47° 39' 05", long. 93° 40' 24".

Ownership: EZ-TV Inc.

Bigfork, etc.—K69CR, Ch. 69, EZ-TV Inc. Phone: 218-743-3131.

Technical Facilities: 0.81-kw ERP, lat. 47° 39' 05", long. 93° 40' 24".

Ownership: EZ-TV Inc.

Birchdale, etc.—K56BO, Ch. 56, County of Koochiching. Phone: 218-283-1101.

Technical Facilities: 0.924-kw ERP, lat. 48° 29' 08", long. 94° 00' 26".

Ownership: County of Koochiching.

Birchdale, etc.—W58AI, Ch. 58, County of Koochiching. Phone: 218-283-1101.

Technical Facilities: 0.924-kw ERP, lat. 48° 29' 08", long. 94° 00' 26".

Ownership: County of Koochiching.

Blue Earth—K70DR, Ch. 70, KTTC Television Inc. Phone: 507-288-4444.

Technical Facilities: 2.68-kw ERP, lat. 43° 38' 05", long. 94° 02' 35".

Holds CP for change to channel number 16, 0.73-kw ERP, 245-ft. above ground, 1345-ft. above sea level, BDISDTT-20060331ACH.

Ownership: Quincy Newspapers Inc.

Brainerd—K16BQ, Ch. 16, KSAX-TV Inc. Phone: 651-642-4212. Fax: 651-642-4103.

Technical Facilities: 15.6-kw ERP, lat. 46° 19' 19", long. 94° 09' 55".

Ownership: Hubbard Broadcasting Inc.

Brainerd—K48IF, Ch. 48, Fox Television Stations Inc. Phone: 202-895-3088.

Technical Facilities: 1.14-kw ERP, 450-ft. above ground, 1720-ft. above sea level, lat. 46° 19' 19", long. 94° 09' 55".

Ownership: Fox Television Holdings Inc.

Brainerd—K54AT, Ch. 53, Red River Broadcast Co. LLC. Phone: 701-277-1515.

Studio: 4015 9th Ave SW, Fargo, ND 58103.

Technical Facilities: 1000-w TPO, 19.5-kw ERP, 512-ft. above ground, 1883-ft. above sea level, lat. 46° 25' 21", long. 94° 27' 41".

Holds CP for change to channel number 31, 7.36-kw ERP, 510-ft. above ground, 1881-ft. above sea level, BDISDTT-20060922ACP.

Transmitter: E of Rte. 1, 6-mi. N of intersection of Rte. 1 & Hwy. 210, Pillager.

Multichannel TV Sound: Stereo and separate audio program.

Ownership: Red River Broadcast Corp.

Breezy Point—KLKS-LP, Ch. 14, Lakes Broadcasting Group Inc. Phone: 218-562-4884. Fax: 218-562-4058.

Technical Facilities: 970-w TPO, 13.1-kw ERP, 473-ft. above ground, 1607-ft. above sea level, lat. 46° 36' 13", long. 94° 15' 04".

Transmitter: NE of Wildwood Lane & County Rd. 11, 1.68-mi. W of Breezy Point.

Ownership: Lakes Broadcasting Group Inc.

Deer River—K59BQ, Ch. 59, Malara Broadcast Group of Duluth Licensee LLC. Phone: 703-253-2020.

Technical Facilities: 11.3-kw ERP, 390-ft. above ground, 1851-ft. above sea level, lat. 47° 21' 25.1", long. 93° 45' 13.2".

Ownership: TCM Media Associates LLC.

Duluth—K50IZ, Ch. 50, Telecom Wireless LLC. Phone: 954-614-2416.

Technical Facilities: 3-kw ERP, 361-ft. above ground, 1611-ft. above sea level, lat. 46° 47' 20", long. 92° 07' 28".

Ownership: Telecom Wireless LLC.

Duluth—K58CM, Ch. 58, Trinity Broadcasting Network Inc. Phone: 714-832-2950. Fax: 714-730-0661.

Technical Facilities: 12.7-kw ERP, 492-ft. above ground, 1732-ft. above sea level, lat. 46° 47' 07", long. 92° 07' 13".

Holds CP for change to channel number 41, 3-kw ERP, 482-ft. above ground, 1722-ft. above sea level, BDISDTT-20060331ACI.

Ownership: Trinity Broadcasting Network Inc.

Duluth—KWMN-LP, Ch. 56, Duluth Datacasting Partners GP. Phone: 800-948-7101.

Technical Facilities: 288-w TPO, 1.165-kw ERP, 1538-ft. above sea level, lat. 46° 47' 19", long. 92° 06' 59".

Transmitter: 5th Ave. & W. 10th St.

Ownership: Duluth Datacasting Partners GP.

Erhard—K31CH, Ch. 31, Rural Services of Central Minnesota Inc. Phone: 218-863-4600. Fax: 218-863-1172.

Technical Facilities: 923-w TPO, 15-kw ERP, 164-ft. above ground, 1755-ft. above sea level, lat. 46° 28' 19", long. 95° 58' 13".

Transmitter: 1.3-mi. SE of intersection of Rtes. 3 & 24.

Ownership: Rural Services of Central Minnesota Inc.

Personnel: David Weakland, General Manager; Michael Ostbye, Chief Financial Officer.

Erhard—K39CJ, Ch. 39, Rural Services of Central Minnesota Inc. Phone: 218-863-4600. Fax: 218-863-1172.

Technical Facilities: 914-w TPO, 16-kw ERP, 164-ft. above ground, 1755-ft. above sea level, lat. 46° 28' 19", long. 95° 58' 13".

Transmitter: 1.3-mi. SE of intersection of Rtes. 3 & 24.

Ownership: Rural Services of Central Minnesota Inc.

Personnel: David Weakland, General Manager; Michael Ostbye, Chief Financial Officer.

Erhard—K41CS, Ch. 41, Rural Services of Central Minnesota Inc. Phone: 218-863-4600. Fax: 218-863-1172.

Technical Facilities: 908-w TPO, 16-kw ERP, 164-ft. above ground, 1755-ft. above sea level, lat. 46° 28' 19", long. 95° 58' 13".

Transmitter: 1.3-mi. SE of intersection of Rtes. 3 & 24.

Ownership: Rural Services of Central Minnesota Inc.

Personnel: David Weakland, General Manager; Michael Ostbye, Chief Financial Officer.

Erhard—K43CS, Ch. 43, Rural Services of Central Minnesota Inc. Phone: 218-863-4600. Fax: 218-863-1172.

Technical Facilities: 908-w TPO, 16.4-kw ERP, 164-ft. above ground, 1755-ft. above sea level, lat. 46° 28' 19", long. 95° 58' 13".

Transmitter: 1.3-mi. SE of intersection of County Rtes. 3 & 24.

Ownership: Rural Services of Central Minnesota Inc.

Personnel: David Weakland, General Manager; Michael Ostbye, Chief Financial Officer.

Erhard—K51DC, Ch. 51, Rural Services of Central Minnesota Inc. Phone: 218-863-4600. Fax: 218-863-1172.

Technical Facilities: 993-w TPO, 16.5-kw ERP, 167-ft. above ground, 1759-ft. above sea level, lat. 46° 28' 19", long. 95° 58' 13".

Transmitter: 1.3-mi. SE of intersection of Rtes. 3 & 24.

Ownership: Rural Services of Central Minnesota Inc.

Personnel: David Weakland, General Manager; Michael Ostbye, Chief Financial Officer.

Fergus Falls—K02MM, Ch. 2, Forum Communications Co. Phone: 701-237-6500.

Technical Facilities: 0.099-kw ERP, 1381-ft. above sea level, lat. 46° 19' 35", long. 96° 05' 25".

Ownership: Forum Communications Co.

Fergus Falls—K49FA, Ch. 49, West Central Minnesota Educational TV Co. Phone: 320-289-2622. Fax: 320-289-2627.

Technical Facilities: 1000-w TPO, 32-kw ERP, 466-ft. above ground, 2027-ft. above sea level, lat. 46° 28' 48", long. 96° 01' 45".

Transmitter: 4-mi. E of Erhard.

Ownership: West Central Minnesota ETV Corp.

Frost—K14KD, Ch. 14, South Central Electric Assn.

Technical Facilities: 1.71-kw ERP, lat. 43° 35' 09", long. 93° 55' 46".

Transmitter: 0.25-mi. W of Frost.

Ownership: South Central Electric Assn.

Frost—K18EY, Ch. 18, South Central Electric Assn. Phone: 507-375-3164.

Technical Facilities: 71-w TPO, 0.875-kw ERP, 293-ft. above ground, 1424-ft. above sea level, lat. 43° 35' 09", long. 93° 55' 46".

Transmitter: 0.25-mi. W of Frost.

Ownership: South Central Electric Assn.

Frost—K19GW, Ch. 19, South Central Electric Assn. Phone: 202-625-3500.

Technical Facilities: 0.28-kw ERP, 292-ft. above ground, 1421-ft. above sea level, lat. 43° 35' 09", long. 93° 55' 46".

Ownership: South Central Electric Assn.

Frost—K23FY, Ch. 23, Cooperative TV Assn. of Southern Minnesota. Phone: 507-387-7963.

Technical Facilities: 2-kw ERP, 245-ft. above ground, 1375-ft. above sea level, lat. 43° 35' 09", long. 93° 55' 46".

Ownership: Cooperative Television Assn. of Southern Minnesota.

Frost—K27FI, Ch. 27, South Central Electric Assn. Phone: 507-375-3164.

Technical Facilities: 71-w TPO, 0.902-kw ERP, 293-ft. above ground, 1424-ft. above sea level, lat. 43° 35' 09", long. 93° 55' 46".

Transmitter: 0.25-mi. W of Frost.

Ownership: South Central Electric Assn.

Frost—K29IF-D, Ch. 29, Blue Earth-Nicollet-Faribault Cooperative Electric Assn. Phone: 507-387-7963.

Technical Facilities: 3.1-kw ERP, 295-ft. above ground, 1424-ft. above sea level, lat. 43° 35' 09", long. 93° 55' 46".

Ownership: Blue Earth-Nicollet-Faribault Cooperative Electric Assn.

Frost—K31EF, Ch. 31, South Central Electric Assn. Phone: 507-375-3164.

Technical Facilities: 100-w TPO, 1.71-kw ERP, 305-ft. above ground, 1424-ft. above sea level, lat. 43° 35' 09", long. 93° 55' 46".

Transmitter: 0.25-mi. W of Frost.

Ownership: South Central Electric Assn.

Frost—K34JZ-D, Ch. 34, South Central Electric Assn. Phone: 202-625-3500.

Technical Facilities: 0.17-kw ERP, 292-ft. above ground, 1421-ft. above sea level, lat. 43° 35' 09", long. 93° 55' 46".

Ownership: South Central Electric Assn.

Frost—K36FI, Ch. 36, South Central Electric Assn. Phone: 507-375-3164.

Technical Facilities: 100-w TPO, 1.51-kw ERP, 293-ft. above ground, 1429-ft. above sea level, lat. 43° 35' 09", long. 93° 55' 46".

Transmitter: 0.2-mi. W of Frost.

Ownership: South Central Electric Assn.

Frost—K39JI, Ch. 39, Blue Earth-Nicollet-Faribault Cooperative Electric Assn. Phone: 507-387-7963.

Technical Facilities: 2-kw ERP, 295-ft. above ground, 1424-ft. above sea level, lat. 43° 35' 09", long. 93° 55' 46".

Ownership: Blue Earth-Nicollet-Faribault Cooperative Electric Assn.

Frost—K49JG, Ch. 49, Blue Earth-Nicollet-Faribault Cooperative Electric Assn. Phone: 507-387-7963.

Technical Facilities: 2-kw ERP, 295-ft. above ground, 1424-ft. above sea level, lat. 43° 35' 09", long. 93° 55' 46".

Ownership: Blue Earth-Nicollet-Faribault Cooperative Electric Assn.

Frost—K51KB, Ch. 51, South Central Electric Assn. Phones: 507-375-3164; 202-625-3500.

Technical Facilities: 2-kw ERP, 295-ft. above ground, 1424-ft. above sea level, lat. 43° 35' 09", long. 93° 55' 46".

Ownership: South Central Electric Assn.

Frost—K62FH, Ch. 62, Blue Earth-Nicollet-Faribault Cooperative Electric Assn. Phone: 507-387-7963.

Technical Facilities: 71-w TPO, 1.09-kw ERP, 293-ft. above ground, 1424-ft. above sea level, lat. 43° 35' 09", long. 93° 55' 46".

Holds CP for change to channel number 40, 2-kw ERP, 295-ft. above ground, 1424-ft. above sea level, BDISTTL-20060912AEO.

Transmitter: 0.25-mi. W of Frost.

Ownership: Blue Earth-Nicollet-Faribault Cooperative Electric Assn.

Geneva—K44HE, Ch. 48, Three Angels Broadcasting Network Inc. Phone: 618-627-4651.

Technical Facilities: 40-kw ERP, 295-ft. above ground, 1595-ft. above sea level, lat. 43° 49' 31", long. 93° 25' 57".

Ownership: Three Angels Broadcasting Network Inc.

Grand Marais—K63BI, Ch. 63, Malara Broadcast Group of Duluth Licensee LLC. Phone: 703-253-2020.

Technical Facilities: 0.82-kw ERP, lat. 47° 46' 13", long. 90° 21' 06".

Ownership: TCM Media Associates LLC.

Grand Marais—K67CT, Ch. 67, Duluth-Superior Area Educational TV Corp. Phone: 218-724-8567.

Technical Facilities: 2.6-kw ERP, lat. 47° 46' 04", long. 90° 20' 47".

Ownership: Duluth-Superior Area ETV Corp.

Grand Marais—W61AF, Ch. 61, WDIO-TV Inc. Phone: 651-642-4212.

Technical Facilities: 0.82-kw ERP, lat. 47° 46' 09", long. 90° 20' 49".

Ownership: Hubbard Broadcasting Inc.

Grand Portage—K55BR, Ch. 55, WDIO-TV Inc. Phone: 651-642-4212.

Technical Facilities: 0.82-kw ERP, lat. 47° 58' 30", long. 89° 45' 34".

Ownership: Hubbard Broadcasting Inc.

Grand Rapids—K29EB, Ch. 29, KQDS Acquisition Corp. Phone: 701-277-1515.

Technical Facilities: 1000-w TPO, 35.9-kw ERP, 499-ft. above ground, 1989-ft. above sea level, lat. 47° 20' 22", long. 93° 23' 48".

Holds CP for change to 14.91-kw ERP, 479-ft. above ground, 1993-ft. above sea level, BDFCDTT-20060331BGK.

Transmitter: Approx. 2-mi. NNW of Taconite.

Ownership: KQDS Acquisition Corp.

Granite Falls—K16CP, Ch. 16, Minnesota Valley TV Improvement. Phone: 320-564-4970.

Technical Facilities: 100-w TPO, 1.67-kw ERP, 312-ft. above ground, 1325-ft. above sea level, lat. 44° 48' 17", long. 95° 34' 49".

Transmitter: 1.5-mi. WSW of Granite Falls.

Ownership: Minnesota Valley TV Improvement Corp.

Granite Falls—K18DI, Ch. 18, Minnesota Valley TV Improvement Corp. Phone: 320-564-4970.

Technical Facilities: 1.67-kw ERP, 312-ft. above ground, 1325-ft. above sea level, lat. 44° 48' 17", long. 95° 34' 49".

Ownership: Minnesota Valley TV Improvement Corp.

Granite Falls—K22DO, Ch. 22, Minnesota Valley TV Improvement.

Technical Facilities: 100-w TPO, 1.65-kw ERP, 312-ft. above ground, 1325-ft. above sea level, lat. 44° 48' 17", long. 95° 34' 49".

Transmitter: 1.5-mi. WSW of Granite Falls.

Ownership: Minnesota Valley TV Improvement Corp.

Granite Falls—K24CS, Ch. 24, Minnesota Valley TV Improvement Corp. Phones: 612-564-4970; 612-564-4807. Fax: 612-564-4812.

Technical Facilities: 100-w TPO, 1.65-kw ERP, 312-ft. above ground, 1325-ft. above sea level, lat. 44° 48' 17", long. 95° 34' 49".

Transmitter: 1.5-mi. WSW of Granite Falls.

Ownership: Minnesota Valley TV Improvement Corp.

Personnel: Dan Richter, General Manager.

Granite Falls—K26DG, Ch. 26, Minnesota Valley TV Improvement Corp. Phone: 320-564-4970.

Technical Facilities: 100-w TPO, 1.65-kw ERP, 312-ft. above ground, 1325-ft. above sea level, lat. 44° 48' 17", long. 95° 34' 49".

Transmitter: 1.5-mi. WSW of Granite Falls.

Ownership: Minnesota Valley TV Improvement Corp.

Granite Falls—K32DR, Ch. 32, Minnesota Valley TV Improvement Corp. Phone: 320-564-4970.

Technical Facilities: 1.45-kw ERP, lat. 44° 48' 17", long. 95° 34' 49".

Transmitter: 1.5 mi. WSW of Granite Falls.

Ownership: Minnesota Valley TV Improvement Corp.

Granite Falls—K35DK, Ch. 35, Minnesota Valley TV Improvement Corp.

Technical Facilities: 100-w TPO, 1.45-kw ERP, 312-ft. above ground, 1325-ft. above sea level, lat. 44° 48' 17", long. 95° 34' 49".

Transmitter: 1.5-mi. WSW of Granite Falls.

Ownership: Minnesota Valley TV Improvement Corp.

Granite Falls—K45DJ, Ch. 45, Minnesota Valley TV Improvement Corp.

Technical Facilities: 100-w TPO, 1.45-kw ERP, 312-ft. above ground, 1325-ft. above sea level, lat. 44° 48' 17", long. 95° 34' 49".

Transmitter: 1.5-mi. WSW of Granite Falls.

Ownership: Minnesota Valley TV Improvement Corp.

Granite Falls—K47EA, Ch. 47, Minnesota Valley TV Improvement Corp. Phone: 320-564-4970.

Technical Facilities: 100-w TPO, 1.45-kw ERP, 1325-ft. above sea level, lat. 44° 48' 17", long. 95° 34' 49".

Transmitter: 1.5-mi. WSW of Granite Falls.

Ownership: Minnesota Valley TV Improvement Corp.

Granite Falls—K61AU, Ch. 61, Minnesota Valley TV Improvement Corp. Phone: 320-564-4970.

Technical Facilities: 1.37-kw ERP, 312-ft. above ground, 1327-ft. above sea level, lat. 44° 48' 17", long. 95° 34' 50".

Holds CP for change to channel number 14, 1.7-kw ERP, 608-ft. above ground, 1324-ft. above sea level, lat. 44° 48' 17", long. 95° 34' 49". BDISTTL-20060720ADG.

Ownership: Minnesota Valley TV Improvement Corp.

Granite Falls—K63AU, Ch. 63, Minnesota Valley TV Improvement Corp. Phone: 320-564-4970.

Technical Facilities: 1.37-kw ERP, 312-ft. above ground, 1326-ft. above sea level, lat. 44° 48' 17", long. 95° 34' 49".

Holds CP for change to channel number 23, 1.7-kw ERP, 308-ft. above ground, 1325-ft. above sea level, BDISTTL-20060720ADF.

Ownership: Minnesota Valley TV Improvement Corp.

Granite Falls—K65BA, Ch. 65, Minnesota Valley TV Improvement Corp. Phone: 320-564-4970.

Technical Facilities: 1.37-kw ERP, 312-ft. above ground, 1327-ft. above sea level, lat. 44° 48' 17", long. 95° 34' 49".

Holds CP for change to channel number 25, 1-kw ERP, 308-ft. above ground, 1324-ft. above sea level, BDISTTL-20060720ADE.

Ownership: Minnesota Valley TV Improvement Corp.

Granite Falls—K67AN, Ch. 67, Minnesota Valley TV Improvement Corp. Phone: 320-564-4970.

Technical Facilities: 0.707-kw ERP, lat. 44° 48' 01", long. 95° 34' 21".

Holds CP for change to channel number 28, 1.7-kw ERP, 308-ft. above ground, 1324-ft. above sea level, lat. 44° 48' 17", long. 95° 34' 49". BDISTTL-20060720ADC.

Ownership: Minnesota Valley TV Improvement Corp.

Granite Falls—K69DP, Ch. 69, Minnesota Valley TV Improvement Corp. Phone: 320-564-4970.

Technical Facilities: 1.37-kw ERP, 312-ft. above ground, 1325-ft. above sea level, lat. 44° 48' 17", long. 95° 34' 49".

Holds CP for change to channel number 39, 1.7-kw ERP, 308-ft. above ground, 1325-ft. above sea level, BDISTTL-20060720ADB.

Ownership: Minnesota Valley TV Improvement Corp.

Hibbing—K15GT, Ch. 15, KQDS Acquisition Corp. Phone: 701-277-1515.

Technical Facilities: 175-ft. above ground, 1819-ft. above sea level, lat. 47° 22' 52", long. 92° 57' 19".

Holds CP for change to 8.035-kw ERP, 175-ft. above ground, 1820-ft. above sea level, BDFCDTT-20060331AYZ.

Ownership: KQDS Acquisition Corp.

International Falls—K39GT, Ch. 39, Three Angels Broadcasting Network Inc. Phone: 618-627-4651. Fax: 618-627-4155.

Technical Facilities: 3.6-kw ERP, 177-ft. above ground, 1280-ft. above sea level, lat. 48° 35' 29.2", long. 93° 24' 23.4".

Ownership: Three Angels Broadcasting Network Inc.

Personnel: Moses Primo, Broadcasting Engineering & Operations Director.

International Falls—K45JD, Ch. 45, KQDS Acquisition Corp. Phone: 701-277-1515.

Technical Facilities: 8.83-kw ERP, 301-ft. above ground, 1526-ft. above sea level, lat. 48° 34' 23", long. 93° 19' 21".

Holds CP for change to 0.045-kw ERP, BDFCDTT-20060331BJW.

Ownership: KQDS Acquisition Corp.

International Falls—K49BU, Ch. 49, County of Koochiching. Phone: 218-283-1101.

Technical Facilities: 0.91-kw ERP, lat. 48° 34' 12", long. 93° 18' 30".

Ownership: County of Koochiching.

International Falls—K51CM, Ch. 51, County of Koochiching. Phone: 218-283-1101.

Technical Facilities: 0.91-kw ERP, lat. 48° 34' 23", long. 93° 19' 21".

Ownership: County of Koochiching.

International Falls—K53CQ, Ch. 53, County of Koochiching. Phone: 218-283-1101.

Technical Facilities: 0.91-kw ERP, lat. 48° 34' 12", long. 93° 18' 30".

Ownership: County of Koochiching.

International Falls—K60BT, Ch. 60, County of Koochiching. Phone: 218-283-1101.

Technical Facilities: 0.92-kw ERP, lat. 48° 29' 08", long. 94° 00' 26".

Ownership: County of Koochiching.

Jackson—K16GL, Ch. 16, Blue Earth-Nicollet-Faribault Cooperative Electric Assn. Phone: 507-387-7963.

Technical Facilities: 3-kw ERP, 338-ft. above ground, 1758-ft. above sea level, lat. 43° 36' 12", long. 94° 59' 33".

Ownership: Blue Earth-Nicollet-Faribault Cooperative Electric Assn.

Jackson—K18HP, Ch. 18, Cooperative Television Assn. of Southern Minnesota. Phone: 507-387-7963.

Technical Facilities: 3-kw ERP, 338-ft. above ground, 1758-ft. above sea level, lat. 43° 36' 12", long. 94° 59' 33".

Ownership: Cooperative Television Assn. of Southern Minnesota.

Jackson—K19FO, Ch. 19, Cooperative Television Assn. of Southern Minnesota. Phone: 507-387-7963.

Technical Facilities: 2-kw ERP, 253-ft. above ground, 1673-ft. above sea level, lat. 43° 36' 12", long. 94° 59' 33".

Ownership: Cooperative Television Assn. of Southern Minnesota.

Jackson—K23FO, Ch. 23, Federated Rural Electric Assn. Phone: 507-847-3520.

Technical Facilities: 0.8-kw ERP, 304-ft. above ground, 1722-ft. above sea level, lat. 43° 36' 12", long. 94° 59' 34".

Ownership: Federated Rural Electric Assn.

Jackson—K36IV-D, Ch. 36, Federated Rural Electric Assn. Phone: 507-847-3520.

Technical Facilities: 1.5-kw ERP, 325-ft. above ground, 1745-ft. above sea level, lat. 43° 36' 12", long. 94° 59' 33".

Ownership: Federated Rural Electric Assn.

Jackson—K40JN-D, Ch. 40, Federated Rural Electric Assn. Phone: 507-847-3520.

Technical Facilities: 1.5-kw ERP, 325-ft. above ground, 1745-ft. above sea level, lat. 43° 36' 12", long. 94° 59' 33".

Ownership: Federated Rural Electric Assn.

Jackson—K41EG, Ch. 41, Federated Rural Electric Assn. Phone: 507-847-3520.

Technical Facilities: 1.8-kw ERP, lat. 43° 36' 12", long. 94° 59' 33".

Ownership: Federated Rural Electric Assn.

Jackson—K45EH, Ch. 45, Federated Rural Electric Assn. Phone: 507-847-3520. Fax: 507-728-8366.

Technical Facilities: 90-w TPO, 1.8-kw ERP, 289-ft. above ground, 1714-ft. above sea level, lat. 43° 36' 12", long. 94° 59' 34".

Transmitter: Hwy. 71, S of Jackson.

Ownership: Federated Rural Electric Assn.

Jackson—K49JU-D, Ch. 49, Cooperative TV Assn. of Southern Minnesota. Phone: 507-387-7963.

Technical Facilities: 1.5-kw ERP, 325-ft. above ground, 1745-ft. above sea level, lat. 43° 36' 12", long. 94° 59' 33".

Ownership: Cooperative Television Assn. of Southern Minnesota.

Jackson—K51EN, Ch. 51, Federated Rural Electric Assn. Phone: 507-847-3520. Fax: 507-728-8366.

Technical Facilities: 90-w TPO, 1.8-kw ERP, 289-ft. above ground, 1714-ft. above sea level, lat. 43° 36' 12", long. 94° 59' 34".

Transmitter: Hwy. 71, S of Jackson.

Ownership: Federated Rural Electric Assn.

Jackson—K53HR, Ch. 53, Federated Rural Electric Assn. Phone: 507-847-3520. Fax: 507-728-8366.

Technical Facilities: 3-kw ERP, 302-ft. above ground, 1722-ft. above sea level, lat. 43° 36' 12", long. 94° 59' 33".

Holds CP for change to channel number 26, 338-ft. above ground, 1759-ft. above sea level, BDISTTL-20060912AEP.

Ownership: Federated Rural Electric Assn.

Jackson—K57IX, Ch. 57, Federated Rural Electric Assn. Phones: 507-847-3520; 507-728-8366.

Technical Facilities: 3-kw ERP, 302-ft. above ground, 1722-ft. above sea level, lat. 43° 36' 12", long. 94° 59' 33".

Holds CP for change to channel number 35, 338-ft. above ground, 1759-ft. above sea level, BDISTTL-20060720ACV.

Ownership: Federated Rural Electric Assn.

Jackson—K61GE, Ch. 61, Blue Earth-Nicollet-Faribault Cooperative Electric Assn. Phone: 507-387-7963.

Technical Facilities: 90-w TPO, 1.9-kw ERP, 289-ft. above ground, 1714-ft. above sea level, lat. 43° 36' 12", long. 94° 59' 34".

Holds CP for change to channel number 50, 3-kw ERP, 338-ft. above ground, 1759-ft. above sea level, lat. 43° 36' 12", long. 94° 59' 33". BDISTTL-20060720ACY.

Transmitter: Hwy. 71, S of Jackson.

Ownership: Blue Earth-Nicollet-Faribault Cooperative Electric Assn.

Kabetogama—K65EA, Ch. 65, County of Koochiching. Phone: 218-283-1101.

Technical Facilities: 0.24-kw ERP, lat. 48° 21' 40", long. 93° 00' 36".

Ownership: County of Koochiching.

Kabetogama—K67EH, Ch. 67, County of Koochiching. Phone: 218-283-1101.

Technical Facilities: 0.91-kw ERP, lat. 48° 21' 40", long. 93° 00' 36".

Ownership: County of Koochiching.

Kabetogama—K69FD, Ch. 69, County of Koochiching. Phone: 218-283-1101.

Technical Facilities: 0.91-kw ERP, lat. 48° 21' 40", long. 93° 00' 36".

Ownership: County of Koochiching.

■ **La Crescent**—KQEG-CA, Ch. 23, Magnum Radio Inc. Phone: 608-372-9600.

Studio: 505 King St., LaCrosse, WI 54601.

Technical Facilities: 3200-w TPO, 18.5-kw ERP, 449-ft. above ground, 1614-ft. above sea level, lat. 43° 44' 53", long. 91° 17' 51".

Transmitter: 5.6-mi. S of La Crescent.

Ownership: Magnum Radio Inc.

Personnel: Eleanor St. John, General Manager; Richard T. Wilson, Sales Manager.

Lake Crystal—K43JE-D, Ch. 43, Three Angels Broadcasting Network Inc. Phone: 618-627-4651.

Technical Facilities: 10.82-kw ERP, 492-ft. above ground, 1487-ft. above sea level, lat. 44° 03' 05.5", long. 94° 17' 59".

Ownership: Three Angels Broadcasting Network Inc.

Little Falls—K18GF, Ch. 18, Three Angels Broadcasting Network Inc.

Technical Facilities: 2.29-kw ERP, 131-ft. above ground, 1352-ft. above sea level, lat. 45° 56' 38.9", long. 94° 24' 01.3".

Ownership: Three Angels Broadcasting Network Inc.

Little Falls—K49KQ, Ch. 49, Fox Television Stations Inc. Phone: 202-715-2350.

Technical Facilities: 0.94-kw ERP, 282-ft. above ground, 1472-ft. above sea level, lat. 45° 52' 58", long. 94° 27' 01".

Began Operation: April 17, 1989.

Ownership: Fox Television Holdings Inc.

Mankato—KHVM-LD, Ch. 28, EICB-TV East LLC. Phone: 972-291-3750.

Technical Facilities: 15-kw ERP, 269-ft. above ground, 1319-ft. above sea level, lat. 44° 27' 40", long. 93° 35' 08".

Ownership: EICB-TV LLC.

Max, etc.—K60BL, Ch. 60, EZ-TV Inc. Phone: 218-743-3131.

Technical Facilities: 0.868-kw ERP, 1693-ft. above sea level, lat. 47° 36' 48".

Ownership: EZ-TV Inc.

Max, etc.—K62BH, Ch. 62, EZ-TV Inc. Phone: 218-743-3131.

Technical Facilities: 0.868-kw ERP, lat. 47° 39' 05", long. 93° 40' 24".

Ownership: EZ-TV Inc.

■ **Minneapolis**—K14KH, Ch. 14, Three Angels Broadcasting Network Inc. Phone: 618-627-4651. Fax: 618-627-4155.

Studio: 3391 Charley Good Rd, West Frankfort, IL 62896.

Technical Facilities: 49.8-kw ERP, 774-ft. above ground, 1624-ft. above sea level, lat. 44° 58' 34", long. 93° 16' 20".

Ownership: Three Angels Broadcasting Network Inc.

Personnel: Moses Primo, Chief Engineer; Linda Shelton, Program Director.

Minneapolis—K25IA, Ch. 25, Trinity Broadcasting Network Inc. Phone: 714-832-2950. Fax: 714-730-0661.

Technical Facilities: 100-kw ERP, 820-ft. above ground, 1674-ft. above sea level, lat. 44° 58' 34", long. 93° 16' 20".

Ownership: Trinity Broadcasting Network Inc.

Personnel: Paul Crouch, General Manager; Ben Miller, Chief Engineer; Rod Henke, Sales Manager.

Minneapolis—K43HB, Ch. 43, Ventana Television Inc. Phone: 727-872-4210.

Technical Facilities: 54.8-kw ERP, 830-ft. above ground, 1684-ft. above sea level, lat. 44° 58' 34", long. 93° 16' 21".

Began Operation: January 21, 1992.

Ownership: Ventana Television Inc.

Minneapolis—WDMI-LP, Ch. 62, Word of God Fellowship Inc. Phone: 817-571-1229. Fax: 817-571-7478.

Technical Facilities: 9.24-kw ERP, lat. 45° 03' 30", long. 93° 07' 27".

Holds CP for change to channel number 31, 150-kw ERP, 801-ft. above ground, 1655-ft. above sea level, lat. 44° 58' 34", long. 93° 16' 20". BDISTTL-20070622ADM.

Ownership: Word of God Fellowship Inc.

■ **Minneapolis**—WTMS-CA, Ch. 7, SP Minneapolis LLC. Phone: 203-542-4200.

Technical Facilities: 20-w TPO, 0.405-kw ERP, 801-ft. above ground, 1657-ft. above sea level, lat. 44° 58' 34", long. 93° 16' 20".

Transmitter: IDS Center, Nicollet Mall & 7th St., Minneapolis.

Began Operation: March 2, 1990.

Ownership: SP Television LLC.

■ **Minneapolis**—WUMN-CA, Ch. 13, SP Minneapolis LLC. Phone: 203-542-4200.

Studio: 7001 France Ave. S, Ste 200, Edina, MN 55435.

Technical Facilities: 1000-w TPO, 1.25-kw ERP, 604-ft. above ground, 1450-ft. above sea level, lat. 44° 58' 25", long. 93° 16' 13".

Began Operation: September 14, 1988.

Ownership: SP Television LLC.

Personnel: Warren Reeves, Consulting Engineer; Amy Brown, Broadcast Operations Director; Liz Kiley, Broadcast Vice President.

Northome, etc.—K55BY, Ch. 55, County of Koochiching. Phone: 218-283-1101.

Technical Facilities: 0.868-kw ERP, lat. 47° 48' 12", long. 94° 19' 51".

Ownership: County of Koochiching.

Northome, etc.—K57BK, Ch. 57, County of Koochiching. Phone: 218-283-1101.

Technical Facilities: 0.868-kw ERP, 1818-ft. above sea level, lat. 47° 49' 16", long. 94° 18' 58".

Ownership: County of Koochiching.

Olivia—K23FP, Ch. 23, Renville County TV Corp. Phone: 320-523-2448. Fax: 320-523-2799.

Technical Facilities: 1.05-kw ERP, 384-ft. above ground, 1475-ft. above sea level, lat. 44° 45' 33", long. 94° 52' 24".

Ownership: Renville County TV Corp.

Olivia—K45FR, Ch. 45, Renville County TV Corp. Phone: 320-523-2448. Fax: 320-523-2799.

Technical Facilities: 100-w TPO, 0.99-kw ERP, 384-ft. above ground, 1475-ft. above sea level, lat. 44° 45' 33", long. 94° 52' 24".

Transmitter: 1-mi. ESE of Bird Island.

Ownership: Renville County TV Corp.

Personnel: Tom Upman, Chief Engineer.

Olivia—K47JE, Ch. 47, Three Angels Broadcasting Network Inc. Phone: 618-627-4651.

Technical Facilities: 2.04-kw ERP, 394-ft. above ground, 1485-ft. above sea level, lat. 44° 45' 33", long. 94° 52' 23".

Ownership: Three Angels Broadcasting Network Inc.

Olivia—K49AJ, Ch. 49, Renville County TV Corp. Phone: 320-523-2448. Fax: 320-523-2799.

Technical Facilities: 0.96-kw ERP, lat. 44° 45' 50", long. 94° 52' 10".

Ownership: Renville County TV Corp.

Olivia—K51AL, Ch. 51, Renville County TV Corp. Phone: 320-523-2448. Fax: 320-523-2799.

Technical Facilities: 0.96-kw ERP, lat. 44° 45' 50", long. 94° 52' 10".

Ownership: Renville County TV Corp.

Olivia—K53AO, Ch. 53, Renville County TV Corp. Phone: 320-523-2448. Fax: 320-523-2799.

Technical Facilities: 0.96-kw ERP, lat. 44° 45' 50", long. 94° 52' 10".

Ownership: Renville County TV Corp.

Olivia—K55CK, Ch. 55, Renville County TV Corp. Phone: 320-523-2448. Fax: 320-523-2799.

Technical Facilities: 0.96-kw ERP, lat. 44° 45' 50", long. 94° 52' 10".

Ownership: Renville County TV Corp.

Olivia—K57AE, Ch. 57, Renville County TV Corp. Phone: 320-523-2448. Fax: 320-523-2799.

Technical Facilities: 0.955-kw ERP, 1499-ft. above sea level, lat. 44° 45' 33", long. 94° 52' 23".

Ownership: Renville County TV Corp.

Orr—K59EN, Ch. 59, Orr Area Minneonto II. Phone: 218-757-3500.

Technical Facilities: 0.994-kw ERP, 243-ft. above ground, 1732-ft. above sea level, lat. 47° 58' 41", long. 92° 49' 49".

Ownership: Orr Area Minneonto II.

Orr—K61EW, Ch. 61, Orr Area Minneonto II. Phone: 218-757-3500.

Technical Facilities: 0.99-kw ERP, lat. 47° 58' 41", long. 92° 49' 49".

Ownership: Orr Area Minneonto II.

Orr—K63DV, Ch. 63, Orr Area Minneonto II. Phone: 218-757-3500.

Technical Facilities: 0.94-kw ERP, lat. 47° 58' 41", long. 92° 49' 49".

Ownership: Orr Area Minneonto II.

Park Rapids—K05IV, Ch. 5, Red River Broadcast Co. LLC. Phone: 701-277-1515.

Technical Facilities: 10-w TPO, 0.019-kw ERP, 312-ft. above ground, 1775-ft. above sea level, lat. 46° 59' 06", long. 95° 06' 17".

Transmitter: Junction of County Rd. 32 & Minnesota State Hwy. 71, Park Rapids.

Ownership: Red River Broadcast Corp.

Park Rapids—K32FY, Ch. 32, KSAX-TV Inc. Phone: 651-642-4212. Fax: 651-642-4103.

Technical Facilities: 8.36-kw ERP, lat. 46° 55' 42", long. 95° 00' 22".

Ownership: Hubbard Broadcasting Inc.

Red Lake—K59FR, Ch. 59, Red Lake Band of Chippewa Indians. Phone: 218-679-3341.

Technical Facilities: 0.952-kw ERP, 272-ft. above ground, 1572-ft. above sea level, lat. 47° 50' 37", long. 95° 02' 18".

Ownership: Red Lake Band of Chippewa Indians.

Red Lake—K61CM, Ch. 61, Red Lake Band of Chippewa Indians. Phone: 218-679-3341.

Technical Facilities: 0.952-kw ERP, 272-ft. above ground, 1572-ft. above sea level, lat. 47° 50' 37", long. 95° 02' 18".

Ownership: Red Lake Band of Chippewa Indians.

Red Lake—K63CI, Ch. 63, Red Lake Band of Chippewa Indians. Phone: 218-679-3341.

Technical Facilities: 0.952-kw ERP, 272-ft. above ground, 1572-ft. above sea level, lat. 47° 50' 37", long. 95° 02' 18".

Ownership: Red Lake Band of Chippewa Indians.

Red Lake—K65BN, Ch. 65, Red Lake Band of Chippewa Indians. Phone: 218-679-3341.

Technical Facilities: 0.94-kw ERP, lat. 47° 50' 37", long. 95° 02' 18".

Ownership: Red Lake Band of Chippewa Indians.

Red Lake—K67BM, Ch. 67, Red Lake Band of Chippewa Indians. Phone: 218-679-3341.

Technical Facilities: 0.938-kw ERP, lat. 47° 50' 37", long. 95° 02' 18".

Ownership: Red Lake Band of Chippewa Indians.

Red Lake—K69BT, Ch. 69, Red Lake Band of Chippewa Indians. Phone: 218-679-3341.

Technical Facilities: 0.938-kw ERP, lat. 47° 50' 37", long. 95° 02' 18".

Ownership: Red Lake Band of Chippewa Indians.

Redwood Falls—K17BV, Ch. 17, Redwood TV Improvement Corp.

Technical Facilities: 100-w TPO, 0.768-kw ERP, 351-ft. above ground, 1355-ft. above sea level, lat. 44° 33' 15", long. 94° 58' 00".

Transmitter: 0.5-mi. E of Morton.

Ownership: Redwood TV Improvement Corp.

Redwood Falls—K19CV, Ch. 19, Redwood TV Improvement Corp.

Technical Facilities: 100-w TPO, 1.58-kw ERP, 302-ft. above ground, 1305-ft. above sea level, lat. 44° 33' 15", long. 94° 58' 00".

Transmitter: 0.5-mi. E of Morton.

Ownership: Redwood TV Improvement Corp.

Redwood Falls—K25II, Ch. 25, Redwood TV Improvement Corp. Phone: 507-697-6489.

Technical Facilities: 0.72-kw ERP, 328-ft. above ground, 1333-ft. above sea level, lat. 44° 33' 15", long. 94° 58' 02".

Ownership: Redwood TV Improvement Corp.

Redwood Falls—K39CH, Ch. 39, Redwood TV Improvement Corp.

Technical Facilities: 100-w TPO, 0.723-kw ERP, 328-ft. above ground, 1332-ft. above sea level, lat. 44° 33' 15", long. 94° 58' 02".

Transmitter: 0.5-mi. E of Morton.

Ownership: Redwood TV Improvement Corp.

Redwood Falls—K46FY, Ch. 46, Redwood TV Improvement Corp.

Technical Facilities: 0.839-kw ERP, 300-ft. above ground, 1305-ft. above sea level, lat. 44° 32' 59", long. 94° 58' 00".

Transmitter: 0.5-mi. E of Morton.

Ownership: Redwood TV Improvement Corp.

Redwood Falls—K48GQ, Ch. 48, Redwood TV Improvement Corp.

Technical Facilities: 1.48-kw ERP, 302-ft. above ground, 1306-ft. above sea level, lat. 44° 32' 59", long. 94° 58' 00".

Ownership: Redwood TV Improvement Corp.

Redwood Falls—K50KF, Ch. 50, Redwood TV Improvement Corp. Phone: 507-697-6489.

Technical Facilities: 0.9-kw ERP, 444-ft. above ground, 1448-ft. above sea level, lat. 44° 32' 59", long. 94° 58' 00".

Ownership: Redwood TV Improvement Corp.

Redwood Falls—K52GU, Ch. 52, Redwood TV Improvement Corp. Phone: 507-697-6489.

Technical Facilities: 0.855-kw ERP, 302-ft. above ground, 1306-ft. above sea level, lat. 44° 33' 15", long. 94° 58' 00".

Transmitter: 0.5-mi. E of Morton.

Ownership: Redwood TV Improvement Corp.

Redwood Falls—K58AS, Ch. 58, Redwood TV Improvement Corp.

Technical Facilities: 0.993-kw ERP, 1355-ft. above sea level, lat. 44° 33' 15", long. 94° 58' 00".

Ownership: Redwood TV Improvement Corp.

Redwood Falls—K62AA, Ch. 62, Redwood TV Improvement Corp.

Technical Facilities: 0.2-kw ERP, 1257-ft. above sea level, lat. 44° 33' 15", long. 94° 58' 00".

Ownership: Redwood TV Improvement Corp.

Redwood Falls—K66BB, Ch. 66, Redwood TV Improvement Corp.

Technical Facilities: 0.645-kw ERP, 1453-ft. above sea level, lat. 44° 32' 59", long. 94° 58' 00".

Ownership: Redwood TV Improvement Corp.

Redwood Falls—K68BJ, Ch. 68, Redwood TV Improvement Corp.

Technical Facilities: 0.2-kw ERP, 1257-ft. above sea level, lat. 44° 33' 15", long. 94° 58' 00".

Ownership: Redwood TV Improvement Corp.

Redwood Falls—W56EL, Ch. 56, Redwood TV Improvement Corp. Phone: 507-697-6489.

Technical Facilities: 0.9-kw ERP, 444-ft. above ground, 1448-ft. above sea level, lat. 44° 32' 59", long. 94° 58' 00".

Ownership: Redwood TV Improvement Corp.

Rochester—K52HH, Ch. 52, MS Communications LLC. Phone: 414-765-9737.

Technical Facilities: 0.004-kw ERP, 50-ft. above ground, 1216-ft. above sea level, lat. 43° 58' 16", long. 92° 24' 54".

Ownership: MS Communications LLC.

Rochester—K56HW, Ch. 56, Trinity Broadcasting Network Inc. Phone: 714-832-2950. Fax: 714-730-0661.

Technical Facilities: 75-kw ERP, 528-ft. above ground, 1784-ft. above sea level, lat. 44° 02' 32", long. 92° 20' 26".

Holds CP for change to channel number 39, 15-kw ERP, 528-ft. above ground, 1782-ft. above sea level, BDISDTT-20060330AKQ.

Ownership: Trinity Broadcasting Network Inc.

Personnel: Paul Crouch, General Manager; Ben Miller, Chief Engineer; Rod Henke, Sales Manager.

Rochester—K58GC, Ch. 58, Three Angels Broadcasting Network Inc. Phone: 618-627-4651. Fax: 618-627-4155.

Studio: 3391 Charley Good Rd, West Frankfort, IL 62896.

Technical Facilities: 29-kw ERP, 479-ft. above ground, 1735-ft. above sea level, lat. 44° 02' 32", long. 92° 20' 26".

Holds CP for change to channel number 51, 1-kw ERP, 597-ft. above ground, 1843-ft. above sea level, lat. 44° 02' 28", long. 92° 20' 25". BMPDTL-20080929AHB.

Transmitter: KWWK(FM) tower.

Ownership: Three Angels Broadcasting Network Inc.

Personnel: Moses Primo, Chief Engineer.

Roseau—K42CU, Ch. 42, Roseau County.

Technical Facilities: 2.33-kw ERP, 384-ft. above ground, 1443-ft. above sea level, lat. 48° 51' 10", long. 95° 46' 13".

Ownership: Roseau County.

Roseau—K46BV, Ch. 46, Roseau County. Phone: 218-463-1282.

Technical Facilities: 2.34-kw ERP, lat. 48° 51' 10", long. 95° 46' 13".

Ownership: Roseau County.

Roseau—K48CQ, Ch. 48, Roseau County. Phone: 218-463-1282.

Technical Facilities: 2.34-kw ERP, lat. 48° 51' 10", long. 95° 46' 13".

Ownership: Roseau County.

Roseau—K50AM, Ch. 50, Roseau County. Phone: 218-463-1282.

Technical Facilities: 2.33-kw ERP, lat. 48° 51' 10", long. 95° 46' 13".

Ownership: Roseau County.

Roseau—K52AM, Ch. 52, Roseau County. Phone: 218-463-1282.

Technical Facilities: 2.33-kw ERP, lat. 48° 51' 10", long. 95° 46' 13".

Ownership: Roseau County.

Royalton—KTCJ-LD, Ch. 30, EICB-TV East LLC. Phone: 972-291-3750.

Technical Facilities: 2-kw ERP, 157-ft. above ground, 1250-ft. above sea level, lat. 45° 20' 34", long. 93° 34' 20".

Ownership: EICB-TV LLC.

St. Cloud—K19BG, Ch. 19, Trinity Broadcasting Network Inc. Phone: 714-832-2950. Fax: 714-730-0661.

Technical Facilities: 100-w TPO, 112-kw ERP, 295-ft. above ground, 1713-ft. above sea level, lat. 45° 31' 00", long. 94° 13' 52".

Transmitter: 3-mi. SW of Wade Park on County Rd. 135.

Ownership: Trinity Broadcasting Network Inc.

Personnel: Paul Crouch, General Manager; Ben Miller, Chief Engineer; Rod Henke, Sales Manager.

St. Cloud-Sartell—WCMN-LP, Ch. 13, Starcom LLC. Phone: 320-650-1600. Fax: 320-255-5276.

Technical Facilities: 3-kw ERP, 108-ft. above ground, 1207-ft. above sea level, lat. 45° 32' 28", long. 94° 07' 48".

Ownership: Starcom Inc.

Personnel: Scott Christenson, Sales Manager.

St. James—K14KE, Ch. 14, Cooperative Television Assn. of Southern Minnesota. Phone: 507-387-7963.

Technical Facilities: 100-w TPO, 0.98-kw ERP, 600-ft. above ground, 1631-ft. above sea level, lat. 44° 06' 28", long. 94° 35' 55".

Holds CP for change to 594-ft. above ground, 1627-ft. above sea level, BPTTL-20080602AHF.

Transmitter: 2-mi. E of Godahl.

Ownership: Cooperative Television Assn. of Southern Minnesota.

St. James—K16CG, Ch. 16, Cooperative TV Assn. of Southern Minnesota. Phone: 507-387-7963.

Technical Facilities: 100-w TPO, 0.992-kw ERP, 600-ft. above ground, 1631-ft. above sea level, lat. 44° 06' 28", long. 94° 35' 55".

Holds CP for change to 594-ft. above ground, 1627-ft. above sea level, BPTTL-20080602AHH.

Ownership: Cooperative Television Assn. of Southern Minnesota.

St. James—K19CA, Ch. 19, United Communications Corp.

Technical Facilities: 39-kw ERP, lat. 44° 06' 28", long. 94° 35' 55".

Transmitter: 2-mi. E of Godahl.

Ownership: United Communications Corp.

St. James—K21DG, Ch. 21, Cooperative TV Assn. of Southern Minnesota. Phone: 507-387-7963.

Technical Facilities: 71-w TPO, 0.754-kw ERP, 600-ft. above ground, 1631-ft. above sea level, lat. 44° 06' 28", long. 94° 35' 55".

Holds CP for change to 594-ft. above ground, 1627-ft. above sea level, BPTTL-20080602AHI.

Ownership: Cooperative Television Assn. of Southern Minnesota.

St. James—K24CP, Ch. 24, Cooperative Television Assn. of Southern Minnesota. Phone: 507-387-7963.

Technical Facilities: 2-kw ERP, 598-ft. above ground, 1631-ft. above sea level, lat. 44° 06' 28", long. 94° 35' 55".

Holds CP for change to 594-ft. above ground, 1627-ft. above sea level, BPTTL-20080602AHJ.

Transmitter: 2-mi. E of Godahl.

Ownership: Cooperative Television Assn. of Southern Minnesota.

St. James—K26CS, Ch. 26, Cooperative Television Assn. of Southern Minnesota. Phone: 507-387-7963.

Technical Facilities: 2-kw ERP, 598-ft. above ground, 1631-ft. above sea level, lat. 44° 06' 28", long. 94° 35' 55".

Holds CP for change to 594-ft. above ground, 1627-ft. above sea level, BPTTL-20080602AHK.

Ownership: Cooperative Television Assn. of Southern Minnesota.

St. James—K29IE-D, Ch. 29, Cooperative Television Assn. of Southern Minnesota. Phone: 507-387-7963.

Technical Facilities: 1.5-kw ERP, 594-ft. above ground, 1627-ft. above sea level, lat. 44° 06' 28", long. 94° 35' 55".

Ownership: Cooperative Television Assn. of Southern Minnesota.

St. James—K30FN, Ch. 30, Cooperative Television Assn. of Southern Minnesota. Phone: 507-387-7963.

Technical Facilities: 12.3-kw ERP, lat. 44° 06' 27", long. 94° 35' 43".

Holds CP for change to 978-ft. above ground, 2018-ft. above sea level, lat. 44° 06' 25", long. 94° 35' 44". BPTTL-20080604AAR.

Ownership: Cooperative Television Assn. of Southern Minnesota.

St. James—K32GX-D, Ch. 32, Cooperative Television Assn. of Southern Minnesota. Phone: 507-387-7963.

Technical Facilities: 1-kw ERP, 978-ft. above ground, 2018-ft. above sea level, lat. 44° 06' 25", long. 94° 35' 44".

Ownership: Cooperative Television Assn. of Southern Minnesota.

St. James—K34JX-D, Ch. 34, Cooperative Television Assn. of Southern Minnesota. Phone: 507-387-7963.

Technical Facilities: 1.5-kw ERP, 981-ft. above ground, 2021-ft. above sea level, lat. 44° 06' 25", long. 94° 35' 44".

Ownership: Cooperative Television Assn. of Southern Minnesota.

St. James—K35DC, Ch. 35, Cooperative TV Assn. of Southern Minnesota. Phone: 507-387-7963.

Technical Facilities: 100-w TPO, 1.24-kw ERP, 600-ft. above ground, 1631-ft. above sea level, lat. 44° 06' 28", long. 94° 35' 55".

Holds CP for change to 594-ft. above ground, 1627-ft. above sea level, BPTTL-20080602AHN.

Ownership: Cooperative Television Assn. of Southern Minnesota.

St. James—K40BU, Ch. 40, Cooperative TV Assn. of Southern Minnesota. Phone: 507-387-7963.

Technical Facilities: 100-w TPO, 1.34-kw ERP, 613-ft. above ground, 1630-ft. above sea level, lat. 44° 06' 28", long. 94° 34' 55".

Holds CP for change to 594-ft. above ground, 1627-ft. above sea level, BPTTL-20080602AHQ.

Transmitter: 2-mi. E of Godahl.

Ownership: Cooperative Television Assn. of Southern Minnesota.

St. James—K41IZ, Ch. 41, Cooperative Television Assn. of Southern Minnesota. Phone: 507-387-7963.

Technical Facilities: 2-kw ERP, 981-ft. above ground, 2021-ft. above sea level, lat. 44° 06' 25", long. 94° 35' 44".

Holds CP for change to 978-ft. above ground, 2018-ft. above sea level, BPTTL-20080604AAS.

Ownership: Cooperative Television Assn. of Southern Minnesota.

St. James—K42AV, Ch. 42, Cooperative TV Assn. of Southern Minnesota. Phone: 507-387-7963.

Technical Facilities: 1.32-kw ERP, 600-ft. above ground, 1631-ft. above sea level, lat. 44° 06' 28", long. 94° 35' 55".

Holds CP for change to 594-ft. above ground, 1627-ft. above sea level, BPTTL-20080602AHS.

Ownership: Cooperative Television Assn. of Southern Minnesota.

St. James—K44AD, Ch. 44, Cooperative Television Assn. of Southern Minnesota. Phone: 507-387-7963.

Technical Facilities: 1.35-kw ERP, 600-ft. above ground, 1631-ft. above sea level, lat. 44° 06' 28", long. 94° 36' 55".

Holds CP for change to 594-ft. above ground, 1627-ft. above sea level, BPTTL-20080602AHW.

Ownership: Cooperative Television Assn. of Southern Minnesota.

St. James—K46AA, Ch. 46, Cooperative TV Assn. of Southern Minnesota. Phone: 507-387-7963.

Technical Facilities: 1.37-kw ERP, 600-ft. above ground, 1630-ft. above sea level, lat. 44° 06' 28", long. 94° 35' 55".

Holds CP for change to 594-ft. above ground, 1627-ft. above sea level, BPTTL-20080602AHX.

Ownership: Cooperative Television Assn. of Southern Minnesota.

St. James—K48AA, Ch. 48, Cooperative Television Assn. of Southern Minnesota. Phone: 507-387-7963.

Technical Facilities: 1.39-kw ERP, 600-ft. above ground, 1631-ft. above sea level, lat. 44° 06' 20", long. 94° 36' 55".

Holds CP for change to 594-ft. above ground, 1627-ft. above sea level, BPTTL-20080602AHY.

Ownership: Cooperative Television Assn. of Southern Minnesota.

St. James—K49HE, Ch. 49, Cooperative Television Assn. of Southern Minnesota. Phone: 507-387-7963.

Technical Facilities: 3-kw ERP, 981-ft. above ground, 2021-ft. above sea level, lat. 44° 06' 25", long. 94° 35' 44".

Holds CP for change to 978-ft. above ground, 2018-ft. above sea level, BPTTL-20080604AAT.

Ownership: Cooperative Television Assn. of Southern Minnesota.

St. James—K50AB, Ch. 50, Cooperative Television Assn. of Southern Minnesota. Phone: 507-387-7963.

Technical Facilities: 1.42-kw ERP, 600-ft. above ground, 1631-ft. above sea level, lat. 44° 06' 28", long. 94° 35' 55".

Holds CP for change to 594-ft. above ground, 1627-ft. above sea level, BPTTL-20080602AIA.

Ownership: Cooperative Television Assn. of Southern Minnesota.

St. James—K52AB, Ch. 52, Cooperative TV Assn. of Southern Minnesota. Phone: 507-387-7963.

Technical Facilities: 1.75-kw ERP, 598-ft. above ground, 1631-ft. above sea level, lat. 44° 06' 28", long. 94° 35' 55".

Holds CP for change to 594-ft. above ground, 1627-ft. above sea level, BPTTL-20080604AAG.

Ownership: Cooperative Television Assn. of Southern Minnesota.

St. Paul—K19ER, Ch. 19, St. Michael Broadcasting Inc. Phone: 612-240-9232.

Studio: 548 LaFond Ave, St. Paul, MN 55103.

Technical Facilities: 1000-w TPO, 4.83-kw ERP, 807-ft. above ground, 1660-ft. above sea level, lat. 44° 58' 34", long. 93° 16' 21".

Began Operation: June 6, 1989.

Ownership: St. Michael Broadcasting Inc.

Personnel: Terri Brey, General Manager.

Vesta—K51GL, Ch. 51, Three Angels Broadcasting Network Inc. Phone: 618-627-4651.

Technical Facilities: 45-kw ERP, 328-ft. above ground, 1411-ft. above sea level, lat. 44° 29' 03", long. 95° 29' 26".

Ownership: Three Angels Broadcasting Network Inc.

Virginia—K47IR, Ch. 47, KQDS Acquisition Corp. Phone: 701-277-1515.

Technical Facilities: 15.6-kw ERP, 175-ft. above ground, 1940-ft. above sea level, lat. 47° 29' 18", long. 92° 31' 12".

Holds CP for change to 0.092-kw ERP, BDFCDTT-20060331BIJ.

Ownership: KQDS Acquisition Corp.

Virginia—K66AP, Ch. 66, County of Koochiching.

Technical Facilities: 1.21-kw ERP, lat. 47° 34' 14", long. 92° 31' 20".

Ownership: County of Koochiching.

Virginia—K68AT, Ch. 68, County of Koochiching.

Technical Facilities: 1.21-kw ERP, lat. 47° 34' 14", long. 92° 31' 20".

Ownership: County of Koochiching.

Wabasha—K57CN, Ch. 57, KSTP-TV LLC. Phone: 651-642-4334.

Technical Facilities: 10.4-kw ERP, 282-ft. above ground, 1453-ft. above sea level, lat. 44° 22' 12", long. 92° 04' 47".

Holds CP for change to channel number 33, 15-kw ERP, 281-ft. above ground, 1453-ft. above sea level, lat. 44° 22' 12", long. 92° 04' 47". BDISDTT-20071128AAS.

Ownership: Hubbard Broadcasting Inc.

Wadena—K17FE, Ch. 17, KSAX-TV Inc. Phone: 651-642-4212. Fax: 651-642-4103.

Technical Facilities: 25-kw ERP, 472-ft. above ground, 1824-ft. above sea level, lat. 46° 23' 23", long. 95° 04' 03".

Ownership: Hubbard Broadcasting Inc.

Wadena—K33KC, Ch. 33, Fox Television Stations Inc. Phone: 202-715-2350.

Technical Facilities: 0.8-kw ERP, 449-ft. above ground, 1800-ft. above sea level, lat. 46° 23' 23", long. 95° 04' 03".

Began Operation: July 20, 1989.

Ownership: Fox Television Holdings Inc.

Wadena—K47JC-D, Ch. 47, Three Angels Broadcasting Network Inc. Phone: 618-627-4651.

Technical Facilities: 2.25-kw ERP, 180-ft. above ground, 1530-ft. above sea level, lat. 46° 25' 35.2", long. 95° 05' 52".

Ownership: Three Angels Broadcasting Network Inc.

Walker—K25JZ, Ch. 25, Leech Lake TV Corp. Phone: 218-224-3195.

Technical Facilities: 0.85-kw ERP, 407-ft. above ground, 1892-ft. above sea level, lat. 47° 05' 36.2", long. 94° 34' 47".

Ownership: Leech Lake TV Corp.

Walker—K49CU, Ch. 49, Fox Television Stations Inc.

Technical Facilities: 8.82-kw ERP, 499-ft. above ground, 1886-ft. above sea level, lat. 46° 56' 03", long. 94° 27' 25".

Ownership: Fox Television Holdings Inc.

Walker—K67BZ, Ch. 67, Leech Lake TV Corp. Phone: 218-224-3195.

Technical Facilities: 0.672-kw ERP, lat. 47° 05' 36", long. 94° 34' 47".

Holds CP for change to channel number 27, 0.85-kw ERP, 407-ft. above ground, 1892-ft. above sea level, BDISTT-20061012ABS.

Ownership: Leech Lake TV Corp.

Walker—K69CP, Ch. 69, Leech Lake TV Corp. Phone: 218-224-3195.

Technical Facilities: 0.672-kw ERP, lat. 47° 05' 36", long. 94° 34' 47".

Holds CP for change to channel number 51, 0.85-kw ERP, 407-ft. above ground, 1892-ft. above sea level, BDISTT-20061012ABV.

Ownership: Leech Lake TV Corp.

Williams—K61AR, Ch. 61, Lake of the Woods County.

Technical Facilities: 1.46-kw ERP, lat. 48° 51' 49", long. 94° 48' 22".

Ownership: Lake of the Woods County.

Williams—K63AS, Ch. 63, Lake of the Woods County.

Technical Facilities: 1.46-kw ERP, lat. 48° 51' 49", long. 94° 48' 22".

Ownership: Lake of the Woods County.

Williams—W59AX, Ch. 59, Lake of the Woods County.

Technical Facilities: 1.46-kw ERP, 1407-ft. above sea level, lat. 48° 51' 49", long. 94° 48' 22".

Ownership: Lake of the Woods County.

Willmar—K13YA, Ch. 13, JLBJ Productions Inc. Phone: 320-231-1013.

Technical Facilities: 1.5-kw ERP, 167-ft. above ground, 1430-ft. above sea level, lat. 45° 17' 23", long. 94° 55' 47".

Ownership: JLBJ Productions Inc.

Willmar—K14LF, Ch. 14, UHF-TV Inc. Phone: 866-214-8214.

Technical Facilities: 100-w TPO, 0.97-kw ERP, 472-ft. above ground, 1672-ft. above sea level, lat. 45° 09' 58", long. 95° 02' 37".

Ownership: UHF-TV Inc.

Willmar—K17FA, Ch. 17, UHF TV Inc. Phone: 866-214-8214.

Technical Facilities: 100-w TPO, 1-kw ERP, 472-ft. above ground, 1672-ft. above sea level, lat. 45° 09' 58", long. 95° 02' 37".

Transmitter: 3.5-mi. N of Willmar.

Ownership: UHF-TV Inc.

Personnel: Melissa Greer, General Manager.

Willmar—K20GD, Ch. 20, UHF TV Inc.

Technical Facilities: 0.8-kw ERP, lat. 45° 09' 58", long. 95° 02' 37".

Ownership: UHF-TV Inc.

Willmar—K28IF, Ch. 28, Willmar Assembly of God Church. Phone: 320-235-2529. Fax: 320-235-3837.

Technical Facilities: 1-kw ERP, 472-ft. above ground, 1673-ft. above sea level, lat. 45° 09' 58", long. 95° 02' 37".

Transmitter: 3.5-mi. N of Willmar.

Ownership: Willmar Assembly of God Church.

Personnel: Michael Jackson, General Manager; Bruce Hanson, Chief Engineer.

Willmar—K30FZ, Ch. 30, KSAX-TV Inc. Phone: 651-642-4212. Fax: 651-642-4103.

Technical Facilities: 11-kw ERP, lat. 45° 09' 58", long. 95° 02' 41".

Ownership: Hubbard Broadcasting Inc.

Willmar—K34HO, Ch. 34, UHF-TV Inc. Phone: 866-214-8214.

Technical Facilities: 100-w TPO, 1.3-kw ERP, 472-ft. above ground, 1673-ft. above sea level, lat. 45° 09' 58", long. 95° 02' 37".

Transmitter: 3.5-mi. N of Willmar.

Ownership: UHF-TV Inc.

Personnel: Melissa Greer, General Manager.

Willmar—K39FE, Ch. 39, UHF-TV Inc. Phone: 320-214-8214.

Technical Facilities: 1.3-kw ERP, 472-ft. above ground, 1673-ft. above sea level, lat. 45° 09' 58", long. 95° 02' 41".

Transmitter: 3.5-mi. N of Willmar.

Ownership: UHF-TV Inc.

Personnel: Melissa Greer, General Manager.

Willmar—K44AE, Ch. 44, UHF TV Inc.

Technical Facilities: 1.4-kw ERP, 1673-ft. above sea level, lat. 45° 09' 58", long. 95° 02' 41".

Ownership: UHF-TV Inc.

Willmar—K46AC, Ch. 46, UHF TV Inc.

Technical Facilities: 1.4-kw ERP, lat. 45° 09' 58", long. 95° 02' 41".

Ownership: UHF-TV Inc.

Willmar—K48AH, Ch. 48, UHF TV Inc.

Technical Facilities: 1.4-kw ERP, 1673-ft. above sea level, lat. 45° 09' 58", long. 95° 02' 41".

Ownership: UHF-TV Inc.

Willmar—K50HZ, Ch. 50, UHF-TV Inc. Phone: 866-214-8214.

Technical Facilities: 100-w TPO, 1.4-kw ERP, 472-ft. above ground, 1673-ft. above sea level, lat. 45° 09' 58", long. 95° 02' 37".

Transmitter: 3.5-mi. N of Willmar.

Ownership: UHF-TV Inc.

Windom—K56AH, Ch. 56, City of Windom.

Technical Facilities: 0.442-kw ERP, lat. 43° 51' 15", long. 95° 07' 30".

Ownership: City of Windom.

Windom—K58AF, Ch. 58, City of Windom.

Technical Facilities: 0.43-kw ERP, lat. 43° 51' 15", long. 95° 07' 30".

Ownership: City of Windom.

Windom—K60AD, Ch. 60, City of Windom.

Technical Facilities: 0.163-kw ERP, lat. 43° 51' 15", long. 95° 07' 30".

Ownership: City of Windom.

Windom—K62AI, Ch. 62, City of Windom.

Technical Facilities: 0.42-kw ERP, lat. 43° 51' 15", long. 95° 07' 30".

Ownership: City of Windom.

Windom—K64AK, Ch. 64, City of Windom.

Technical Facilities: 0.413-kw ERP, lat. 43° 51' 15", long. 95° 07' 30".

Ownership: City of Windom.

Winona—K62EV, Ch. 62, KTTC Television Inc. Phone: 507-288-4444.

Technical Facilities: 0.89-kw ERP, lat. 44° 01' 18", long. 91° 34' 24".

Holds CP for change to channel number 43, 3-kw ERP, 344-ft. above ground, 1545-ft. above sea level, BDISDTT-20060331ACL.

Transmitter: 1.9-mi. SE of Winona.

Ownership: Quincy Newspapers Inc.

Winona—K64FY, Ch. 64, Trinity Broadcasting Network Inc. Phone: 714-832-2950. Fax: 714-730-0661.

Technical Facilities: 1.5-kw ERP, lat. 44° 01' 52", long. 91° 38' 32".

Ownership: Trinity Broadcasting Network Inc.

Worthington—K22HJ, Ch. 22, Independent Communications Inc.

Technical Facilities: 12.3-kw ERP, 384-ft. above ground, 2085-ft. above sea level, lat. 43° 37' 02", long. 95° 41' 20".

Ownership: Independent Communications Inc.

Mississippi

■ **Booneville**—W34DV, Ch. 34, Unity Broadcasting Inc. Phone: 662-728-6492. Fax: 662-728-3530.

Studio: 504 N 3rd St, Booneville, MS 38829.

Technical Facilities: 25.5-kw ERP, 323-ft. above ground, 823-ft. above sea level, lat. 34° 39' 45", long. 88° 34' 07".

Ownership: Unity Broadcasting Inc.

Personnel: Leland Owens, President; Jewel Owens, Vice President; Bill Lambert, General Manager; Jared Owens, Chief Engineer; Dora Baker, Office Manager.

Bruce—W07BN, Ch. 7, Bruce Independent TV Inc. Phone: 662-983-2801. Fax: 662-983-2814.

Technical Facilities: 100-w TPO, 3-kw ERP, 295-ft. above ground, 669-ft. above sea level, lat. 34° 01' 17", long. 89° 21' 17".

Transmitter: 0.25-mi. N of intersection of Hwys. 9 & 9 West.

Ownership: Bruce Independent TV Inc.

Personnel: William Morgan, Station Manager; Bill Morgan, Sales.

Calhoun City—W34BJ, Ch. 34, William Earl Morgan. Phone: 662-983-2801.

Technical Facilities: 50-kw ERP, 246-ft. above ground, 620-ft. above sea level, lat. 34° 01' 17", long. 89° 21' 17".

Ownership: William Earl Morgan.

Clarksdale—WPRQ-LP, Ch. 12, David Ellington. Phone: 662-375-2654.

Technical Facilities: 3-kw ERP, 315-ft. above ground, 476-ft. above sea level, lat. 34° 10' 43", long. 90° 33' 03".

Ownership: David Ellington.

Cleveland—W56DY, Ch. 56, Trinity Broadcasting Network Inc. Phone: 714-832-2950. Fax: 714-730-0661.

Technical Facilities: 2.4-kw ERP, 259-ft. above ground, 394-ft. above sea level, lat. 33° 44' 01", long. 90° 42' 50".

Ownership: Trinity Broadcasting Network Inc.

Cleveland—WHCQ-LP, Ch. 8, David Ellington. Phone: 662-375-2654.

Studio: 1321 Hwy. 8 W, Ste 12, Cleveland, MS 38732.

Technical Facilities: 3-kw ERP, 295-ft. above ground, 433-ft. above sea level, lat. 33° 45' 28", long. 90° 42' 56".

Holds CP for change to channel number 9, 0.3-kw ERP, BDISDVL-20080627AAF.

Ownership: David Ellington.

Personnel: Chad Ellington, General Manager.

Columbia—W45AA, Ch. 45, Mississippi Authority for ETV. Phone: 601-432-6565.

Technical Facilities: 14.2-kw ERP, lat. 31° 16' 00", long. 89° 49' 56".

Ownership: Mississippi Authority for ETV.

Columbus—W25AD, Ch. 25, Trinity Broadcasting Network Inc. Phone: 714-832-2950. Fax: 714-730-0661.

Technical Facilities: 9.2-kw ERP, 358-ft. above ground, 677-ft. above sea level, lat. 33° 33' 00", long. 88° 23' 59".

Ownership: Trinity Broadcasting Network Inc.

Personnel: Paul Crouch, General Manager; Ben Miller, Chief Engineer; Rod Henke, Sales Manager.

■ **Fulton**—W39CD, Ch. 39, Unity Broadcasting Inc. Phone: 662-728-6492.

Technical Facilities: 22.9-kw ERP, 484-ft. above ground, 899-ft. above sea level, lat. 34° 03' 30", long. 88° 15' 34".

Holds CP for change to 117.8-kw ERP, BPTTA-20080916ADQ.

Began Operation: January 26, 1995.

Ownership: Unity Broadcasting Inc.

Personnel: Bill Lambert, General Manager; Lem Smith, Chief Engineer; Grady Davidson, Sales Manager.

Greenville—W42CY, Ch. 42, Trinity Broadcasting Network Inc. Phone: 714-832-2950. Fax: 714-730-0661.

Technical Facilities: 17.8-kw ERP, 341-ft. above ground, 456-ft. above sea level, lat. 33° 21' 57", long. 90° 57' 20".

Ownership: Trinity Broadcasting Network Inc.

Grenada—W12CR, Ch. 12, MS Communications LLC. Phone: 414-213-4629.

Technical Facilities: 9.5-w TPO, 0.007-kw ERP, 105-ft. above ground, 407-ft. above sea level, lat. 33° 53' 28", long. 90° 03' 09".

Holds CP for change to channel number 50, 26-ft. above ground, 328-ft. above sea level, BDISTTL-20071130BHO.

Transmitter: 7-mi. S of Charleston.

Ownership: MS Communications LLC.

Grenada—W13CS, Ch. 13, Dewey Sanford. Phones: 662-226-1354; 662-227-1494.

Technical Facilities: 10-w TPO, 0.078-kw ERP, 250-ft. above ground, 584-ft. above sea level, lat. 33° 46' 36", long. 89° 49' 23".

Transmitter: WQXB(FM) radio tower, Grenada.

Ownership: Dewey Sanford.

Personnel: Dewey Sanford, General Manager, Chief Engineer & Sales Manager.

Grenada—W28BP, Ch. 28, MS Communications LLC. Phone: 414-213-4629.

Technical Facilities: 0.007-kw ERP, 105-ft. above ground, 407-ft. above sea level, lat. 33° 53' 28", long. 90° 03' 09".

Holds CP for change to 26-ft. above ground, 328-ft. above sea level, BPTTL-20071130BGX.

Ownership: MS Communications LLC.

Grenada—W30BY, Ch. 30, Trinity Broadcasting Network Inc. Phone: 714-832-2950. Fax: 714-730-0661.

Technical Facilities: 1000-w TPO, 5.6-kw ERP, 299-ft. above ground, 1857-ft. above sea level, lat. 33° 46' 30", long. 89° 49' 12".

Transmitter: 1.4-mi. SE of junction of State Rte. 8 & U.S. Rte. 55.

Ownership: Trinity Broadcasting Network Inc.

Grenada—W36BT, Ch. 36, MS Communications LLC. Phone: 414-213-4629.

Technical Facilities: 0.007-kw ERP, 105-ft. above ground, 302-ft. above sea level, lat. 33° 53' 28", long. 90° 03' 09".

Holds CP for change to 26-ft. above ground, 328-ft. above sea level, BPTTL-20071130BHL.

Ownership: MS Communications LLC.

Grenada—W41BV, Ch. 41, MS Communications LLC. Phone: 414-765-9737.

Technical Facilities: 0.007-kw ERP, 105-ft. above ground, 302-ft. above sea level, lat. 33° 53' 28", long. 90° 03' 09".

Ownership: MS Communications LLC.

Grenada—W46CK, Ch. 46, MS Communications LLC. Phone: 414-213-4629.

Technical Facilities: 0.007-kw ERP, 105-ft. above ground, 302-ft. above sea level, lat. 33° 53' 28", long. 90° 03' 09".

Holds CP for change to 26-ft. above ground, 328-ft. above sea level, BPTTL-20071130BHC.

Ownership: MS Communications LLC.

Hattiesburg—W42CW, Ch. 42, Prism Broadcasting Network Inc. Phone: 770-953-3232.

Technical Facilities: 0.12-kw ERP, 387-ft. above ground, 763-ft. above sea level, lat. 31° 16' 21", long. 89° 21' 04".

Holds CP for change to 26-ft. above ground, 386-ft. above sea level, lat. 31° 18' 26", long. 89° 24' 47", BMPTTL-20070613ADB.

Ownership: Prism Broadcasting Network Inc.

Hattiesburg—W47BP, Ch. 47, Mississippi Authority for ETV. Phone: 601-432-6565.

Technical Facilities: 10.66-kw ERP, lat. 31° 21' 02", long. 89° 22' 12".

Holds CP for change to 55.8-kw ERP, 513-ft. above ground, 840-ft. above sea level, lat. 31° 20' 32.3", long. 89° 25' 05.5", BPTT-20081118ABV.

Began Operation: May 19, 1993.

Ownership: Mississippi Authority for ETV.

Hattiesburg—W50CX, Ch. 50, Marcia T. Turner. Phone: 954-732-9539.

Technical Facilities: 9-kw ERP, 249-ft. above ground, 420-ft. above sea level, lat. 31° 22' 16", long. 89° 19' 50".

Ownership: Marcia T. Turner.

Hattiesburg—WGVI-LP, Ch. 10, Hispanic Christian Community Network Inc. Phone: 214-434-6357.

Technical Facilities: 3-kw ERP, 164-ft. above ground, 305-ft. above sea level, lat. 31° 20' 30", long. 85° 37' 20".

Ownership: Hispanic Christian Community Network Inc.

Hattiesburg—WHGM-LP, Ch. 30, Dean M. Mosely. Phone: 713-479-3833. Fax: 713-479-3845.

Technical Facilities: 8.8-kw ERP, 370-ft. above ground, 730-ft. above sea level, lat. 31° 18' 25.6", long. 89° 24' 47.2".

Ownership: Dean M. Mosely.

Hattiesburg—WHPM-LP, Ch. 30, Hattiesburg TV LLC. Phone: 318-992-7766.

Technical Facilities: 8.8-kw ERP, 370-ft. above ground, 730-ft. above sea level, lat. 31° 18' 26", long. 89° 24' 47".

Ownership: Dean M. Mosely.

■ **Holly Springs**—WBII-CA, Ch. 20, Mid-South Broadcasting. Phone: 662-224-3220.

Technical Facilities: 1000-w TPO, 19.3-kw ERP, 292-ft. above ground, 853-ft. above sea level, lat. 34° 47' 48", long. 89° 24' 42".

Holds CP for change to 15-kw ERP, 286-ft. above ground, 919-ft. above sea level, lat. 34° 50' 07", long. 89° 10' 31". BDFCDTA-20081016AES.

Transmitter: Qwest Tower, Hwy. 4 & Finley Rd. intersection.

Ownership: Mid-South Broadcasting.

Jackson—W23BC, Ch. 23, Jackson State U.

Technical Facilities: 100-w TPO, 1-kw ERP, 522-ft. above sea level, lat. 32° 17' 47", long. 90° 12' 23".

Transmitter: 1735 Lynch St.

Ownership: Jackson State U.

Personnel: Judy Alsobrooks, General Manager; Laura Powell, Sales Manager.

■ **Jackson**—WBMS-CA, Ch. 10, Mississippi Television LLC. Phone: 601-922-1234.

Studio: 124 E. Amite St, Jackson, MS 39201.

Technical Facilities: 3-kw ERP, 650-ft. above ground, 1070-ft. above sea level, lat. 32° 12' 47", long. 90° 22' 54".

Transmitter: 210 E. Capitol St.

Began Operation: November 16, 1987.

Ownership: Mississippi Television LLC.

Personnel: Gene Blailock, General Manager; Major Norman, Chief Engineer.

Jackson—WJKO-LP, Ch. 64, Word of God Fellowship Inc. Phone: 817-571-1229.

Technical Facilities: 1000-w TPO, 5.2-kw ERP, 610-ft. above ground, 1020-ft. above sea level, lat. 32° 16' 00", long. 90° 16' 59".

Holds CP for change to channel number 43, 50-kw ERP, 1083-ft. above ground, 1549-ft. above sea level, lat. 32° 16' 53", long. 90° 17' 41". BDISTTL-20060321ADE.

Transmitter: 140 Rebel Circle.

Ownership: Word of God Fellowship Inc.

Personnel: Gary Neubert, Sales.

Jackson—WJMF-LP, Ch. 53, Kid's Television LLC. Phone: 615-975-0525.

Technical Facilities: 1000-w TPO, 20.5-kw ERP, 1000-ft. above ground, 1466-ft. above sea level, lat. 32° 16' 53", long. 90° 17' 41".

Holds CP for change to channel number 19, 120-kw ERP, 1001-ft. above ground, 1467-ft. above sea level, BDISTTL-20070220ABX.

Transmitter: 140 Alpha Rd. 1.

Began Operation: November 6, 1998.

Ownership: Kid's Television LLC.

Jackson—WJXF-LP, Ch. 49, Kid's Television LLC. Phone: 615-975-0525.

Technical Facilities: 20.5-kw ERP, 1040-ft. above ground, 1506-ft. above sea level, lat. 32° 16' 53", long. 90° 17' 41".

Transmitter: 1.4-mi. N of Forest Hill.

Began Operation: November 6, 1998.

Ownership: Equity Media Holdings Corp., Debtor in Possession.

■ **Jackson, etc.**—WBXK-CA, Ch. 8, Community Television Network LLC. Phone: 321-729-8451. Fax: 321-676-2363.

Studio: 1015 Metrocenter Mall, Jackson, MS 38209.

Technical Facilities: 10-w TPO, 0.91-kw ERP, 1007-ft. above ground, 1348-ft. above sea level, lat. 32° 16' 53", long. 90° 17' 41".

Transmitter: Off Maddox Rd., N of Hwy. 16.

Ownership: Community Television Network LLC.

Personnel: Jesse Weatherby, President; Jim Courtney, Operation Manager; Charles Flowers, Chief Engineer.

Jackson/Brandon—W46CW, Ch. 46, Mississippi Television LLC. Phone: 601-922-1234.

Technical Facilities: 1000-w TPO, 12.6-kw ERP, 137-ft. above ground, 485-ft. above sea level, lat. 32° 25' 30", long. 90° 08' 06".

Transmitter: Water Tower, Rankin & Madison.

Began Operation: August 29, 1997.

Ownership: Mississippi Television LLC.

Personnel: Gene Blailock, General Manager.

Laurel—W04DE, Ch. 4, Hispanic Christian Community Network Inc. Phone: 214-434-6357.

Technical Facilities: 0.1-kw ERP, 49-ft. above ground, 374-ft. above sea level, lat. 31° 41' 29", long. 89° 04' 25".

Ownership: Hispanic Christian Community Network Inc.

Laurel—W68DX, Ch. 68, Hispanic Christian Community Network Inc. Phone: 214-879-0081.

Technical Facilities: 1-kw ERP, 16-ft. above ground, 305-ft. above sea level, lat. 31° 41' 44", long. 89° 05' 40".

Ownership: Hispanic Christian Community Network Inc.

McComb—W36AC, Ch. 36, Trinity Broadcasting Network Inc. Phone: 714-832-2950. Fax: 714-730-0661.

Studio: Enterprise Journal Bldg, McComb, MS 39648.

Technical Facilities: 24.3-kw ERP, 515-ft. above ground, 915-ft. above sea level, lat. 31° 19' 00", long. 90° 27' 05".

Holds CP for change to 15-kw ERP, BDFCDTT-20060331AHO.

Ownership: Trinity Broadcasting Network Inc.

Meridian—W20BS, Ch. 20, MS Communications LLC. Phone: 414-213-4629.

Technical Facilities: 1.1-kw ERP, 351-ft. above ground, 1004-ft. above sea level, lat. 32° 11' 47", long. 89° 10' 32".

Holds CP for change to 0.2-kw ERP, 328-ft. above ground, 981-ft. above sea level, BPTTL-20071211ACC.

Ownership: MS Communications LLC.

Personnel: Harry Kaiser, General Manager.

Meridian—W26BR, Ch. 26, MS Communications LLC. Phone: 414-213-4629.

Technical Facilities: 1.1-kw ERP, 351-ft. above ground, 1004-ft. above sea level, lat. 32° 11' 47", long. 89° 10' 32".

Ownership: MS Communications LLC.

Meridian—W27DD, Ch. 27, MS Communications LLC. Phone: 414-213-4629.

Technical Facilities: 1.1-kw ERP, 351-ft. above ground, 1004-ft. above sea level, lat. 32° 11' 47", long. 89° 10' 32".

Holds CP for change to 0.2-kw ERP, 328-ft. above ground, 981-ft. above sea level, BPTTL-20071211ACB.

Ownership: MS Communications LLC.

Meridian—W35CQ, Ch. 35, MS Communications LLC. Phone: 414-213-4629.

Technical Facilities: 1.1-kw ERP, 351-ft. above ground, 1004-ft. above sea level, lat. 32° 11' 47", long. 89° 10' 32".

Ownership: MS Communications LLC.

Meridian—W36BY, Ch. 36, MS Communications LLC. Phone: 414-213-4629.

Technical Facilities: 1.1-kw ERP, 351-ft. above ground, 1004-ft. above sea level, lat. 32° 11' 47", long. 89° 10' 32".

Ownership: MS Communications LLC.

Meridian—W36CU, Ch. 36, MS Communications LLC. Phone: 414-765-9737.

Technical Facilities: 106.9-kw ERP, 902-ft. above ground, 1115-ft. above sea level, lat. 30° 42' 30", long. 89° 05' 06".

Ownership: MS Communications LLC.

Meridian—W42DD, Ch. 42, EICB-TV East LLC. Phone: 972-291-3750.

Technical Facilities: 0.075-kw ERP, 26-ft. above ground, 338-ft. above sea level, lat. 32° 22' 38.5", long. 88° 44' 45.8".

Holds CP for change to 2-kw ERP, 52-ft. above ground, 364-ft. above sea level, BPTTL-20090511BAT.

Began Operation: March 11, 2009.

Ownership: EICB-TV LLC.

Meridian—W46CL, Ch. 46, MS Communications LLC. Phone: 414-213-4629.

Technical Facilities: 1.1-kw ERP, 351-ft. above ground, 1004-ft. above sea level, lat. 32° 11' 47", long. 89° 10' 32".

Holds CP for change to 0.2-kw ERP, 328-ft. above ground, 981-ft. above sea level, BPTTL-20080430ADZ.

Ownership: MS Communications LLC.

Meridian—W47CG, Ch. 47, Trinity Broadcasting Network Inc. Phone: 714-832-2950. Fax: 714-730-0661.

Technical Facilities: 100-w TPO, 10.1-kw ERP, lat. 30° 24' 34", long. 87° 12' 53".

Holds CP for change to 15-kw ERP, 230-ft. above ground, 898-ft. above sea level, lat. 32° 19' 38", long. 88° 41' 28". BDFCDTT-20060317AAB.

Ownership: Trinity Broadcasting Network Inc.

Meridian—W52CS, Ch. 52, MS Communications LLC. Phone: 414-213-4629.

Technical Facilities: 1.1-kw ERP, 351-ft. above ground, 1004-ft. above sea level, lat. 32° 11' 47", long. 89° 10' 32".

Ownership: MS Communications LLC.

Meridian—W53CE, Ch. 53, MS Communications LLC. Phone: 414-213-4629.

Technical Facilities: 0.004-kw ERP, 50-ft. above ground, 342-ft. above sea level, lat. 31° 46' 05.4", long. 89° 10' 11.8".

Ownership: MS Communications LLC.

Meridian—W54CD, Ch. 54, MS Communications LLC. Phone: 414-213-4629.

Technical Facilities: 1.1-kw ERP, 351-ft. above ground, 1004-ft. above sea level, lat. 32° 11' 47", long. 89° 10' 32".

Holds CP for change to 0.2-kw ERP, 328-ft. above ground, 981-ft. above sea level, BPTTL-20071211ACD.

Ownership: MS Communications LLC.

Meridian—W59DE, Ch. 59, MS Communications LLC. Phone: 414-213-4629.

Technical Facilities: 1.1-kw ERP, 351-ft. above ground, 1004-ft. above sea level, lat. 32° 11' 47", long. 89° 10' 32".

Ownership: MS Communications LLC.

Meridian—W65DE, Ch. 65, MS Communications LLC. Phone: 414-213-4629.

Technical Facilities: 1.1-kw ERP, 351-ft. above ground, 1004-ft. above sea level, lat. 32° 11' 47", long. 89° 10' 32".

Holds CP for change to channel number 38, 0.2-kw ERP, 328-ft. above ground, 981-ft. above sea level, BDISTTL-20080430ADY.

Ownership: MS Communications LLC.

Meridian—W69DJ, Ch. 69, MS Communications LLC. Phone: 414-213-4629.

Technical Facilities: 1.1-kw ERP, 351-ft. above ground, 1004-ft. above sea level, lat. 32° 11' 47", long. 89° 10' 32".

Holds CP for change to channel number 51, 0.2-kw ERP, 328-ft. above ground, 981-ft. above sea level, BDISTTL-20071207ACV.

Ownership: MS Communications LLC.

Meridian—WMRQ-LP, Ch. 40, Norma Jean Lewis. Phone: 281-495-1886.

Technical Facilities: 0.157-kw ERP, 180-ft. above ground, 652-ft. above sea level, lat. 32° 20' 38.98", long. 88° 42' 39.94".

Holds CP for change to 0.7-w TPO, 420-ft. above ground, 1040-ft. above sea level, lat. 32° 18' 44", long. 88° 41' 33". .

Ownership: Norma Jean Lewis.

Natchez—W24CR, Ch. 24, Louisiana Christian Broadcasting Inc. Phone: 318-322-1399. Fax: 318-323-3783.

Technical Facilities: 1000-w TPO, 37.6-kw ERP, 470-ft. above ground, 810-ft. above sea level, lat. 31° 30' 19", long. 91° 19' 38".

Holds CP for change to 15-kw ERP, BDFCDTT-20060331BPW.

Transmitter: 2.9-mi. S of Natchez.

Ownership: Louisiana Christian Broadcasting Inc.

Personnel: Woody Jenkins, General Manager.

Natchez—W27CX, Ch. 27, Trinity Broadcasting Network. Phone: 714-832-2950. Fax: 714-730-0661.

Technical Facilities: 16.3-kw ERP, 449-ft. above ground, 577-ft. above sea level, lat. 31° 30' 33", long. 91° 24' 19".

Transmitter: WNTZ-TV tower.

Ownership: Trinity Broadcasting Network Inc.

Personnel: Paul Crouch, General Manager; Ben Miller, Chief Engineer; Rod Henke, Sales Manager.

Natchez—W30CC, Ch. 30, Foster Charitable Foundation Inc. Phone: 303-757-3199.

Technical Facilities: 50-kw ERP, 164-ft. above ground, 377-ft. above sea level, lat. 31° 35' 05", long. 91° 23' 18".

Holds CP for change to 25-kw ERP, 384-ft. above ground, 744-ft. above sea level, lat. 31° 27' 17.4", long. 91° 18' 53.6". BPTTL-20070706ACK.

Ownership: Foster Charitable Foundation Inc.

Natchez—WXMS-LP, Ch. 22, Jackson Television LLC. Phone: 617-262-7770.

Technical Facilities: 20.5-kw ERP, lat. 31° 30' 33", long. 91° 24' 19".

Transmitter: 625 Beltline Hwy.

Ownership: Jackson Television LLC.

Pascagoula—W51CU, Ch. 51, Trinity Broadcasting Network Inc. Phone: 714-832-2950. Fax: 714-730-0661.

Technical Facilities: 20.5-kw ERP, 266-ft. above ground, 276-ft. above sea level, lat. 30° 26' 54", long. 88° 33' 05".

Holds CP for change to 2-kw ERP, BDFCDTT-20060330ACH.

Ownership: Trinity Broadcasting Network Inc.

Personnel: Paul Crouch, General Manager; Ben Miller, Chief Engineer; Rod Henke, Sales Manager.

Pascagoula—WKFK-LD, Ch. 7, Frances S. Smith dba NCN Cable Advertising. Phones: 228-769-7767; 228-762-0464. Fax: 228-769-7771.

Technical Facilities: 0.3-kw ERP, 492-ft. above ground, 528-ft. above sea level, lat. 30° 29' 10", long. 88° 42' 53".

Ownership: Frances S. Smith.

Pontotoc—W15CG, Ch. 15, Unity Broadcasting Inc. Phone: 662-728-6492.

Technical Facilities: 36.2-kw ERP, 383-ft. above ground, 776-ft. above sea level, lat. 34° 13' 37", long. 88° 58' 53".

Ownership: Unity Broadcasting Inc.

Starkville—W05BV, Ch. 5, First United Methodist Church. Phone: 662-338-1002. Fax: 662-324-5364.

Technical Facilities: 40-w TPO, 0.066-kw ERP, 141-ft. above ground, 531-ft. above sea level, lat. 33° 27' 47", long. 88° 49' 01".

Transmitter: Wilson at Lapkin St., Starkville.

Multichannel TV Sound: Stereo only.

Ownership: First United Methodist Church.

Personnel: Chris White, General Manager, General Sales Manager & Traffic Director; Olen Booth, Chief Engineer.

Tupelo—W32BH, Ch. 32, WTVA Inc. Phone: 601-844-4083.

Technical Facilities: 310-w TPO, 3-kw ERP, 476-ft. above ground, 1338-ft. above sea level, lat. 34° 19' 24", long. 88° 42' 39".

Transmitter: 3.6-mi. N of Tupelo, on U.S. 45 at Natchez.

Ownership: WTVA Inc.

Personnel: Mark Ledbetter, General Manager; Wendell Robinson, Chief Engineer.

Tupelo—W40BZ, Ch. 40, Prism Broadcasting Network Inc. Phone: 770-953-3232.

Technical Facilities: 0.005-kw ERP, 21-ft. above ground, 264-ft. above sea level, lat. 34° 11' 55", long. 88° 39' 34".

Ownership: Prism Broadcasting Network Inc.

Tupelo—W49BK, Ch. 49, MS Communications LLC. Phone: 414-765-9737.

Technical Facilities: 0.004-kw ERP, 50-ft. above ground, 300-ft. above sea level, lat. 34° 12' 18", long. 88° 41' 49".

Ownership: MS Communications LLC.

Tylertown—W23CM, Ch. 23, Pegasus Broadcast Television Inc., Debtor-In-Possession. Phone: 610-934-7098.

Technical Facilities: 12.7-kw ERP, 295-ft. above ground, 695-ft. above sea level, lat. 31° 08' 27", long. 90° 04' 09".

Ownership: The PSC Liquidating Trust.

■ **Vicksburg**—W26BB, Ch. 26, Three Angels Broadcasting Network Inc. Phone: 618-627-4651. Fax: 618-627-4155.

Technical Facilities: 1000-w TPO, 11.89-kw ERP, 600-ft. above sea level, lat. 32° 21' 34", long. 90° 50' 08".

Transmitter: No. 1 Old Jackson Rd., 3-mi. ENE of Vicksburg.

Ownership: Three Angels Broadcasting Network Inc.

Personnel: Moses Primo, Chief Engineer; Linda Shelton, Program Director.

Webb—WEBU-LP, Ch. 11, David Ellington. Phone: 662-375-2654.

Studio: 307 John St, Webb, MS 38966.

Technical Facilities: 0.028-kw ERP, 184-ft. above ground, 335-ft. above sea level, lat. 33° 56' 38", long. 90° 20' 40".

Holds CP for change to 3-kw ERP, 381-ft. above ground, 722-ft. above sea level, lat. 33° 59' 15", long. 90° 02' 52". BPTVL-20080701AEP.

Began Operation: August 22, 1988.

Ownership: David Ellington.

Missouri

Anderson/Pineville—K53IS, Ch. 9, Deborah R. & Gary M. Kenny. Phones: 417-451-1440; 417-623-4646. Fax: 417-451-3333.

Studio: Rte. 8, PO Box 428E, Neosho, MO 64850.

Technical Facilities: 50-kw ERP, 226-ft. above ground, 1400-ft. above sea level, lat. 36° 36' 39", long. 94° 24' 28".

Transmitter: E of U.S. Hwy. 71, 0.3-mi. N of State Hwy. EE.

Ownership: Gary M. Kenny; Deborah R. Kenny.

Personnel: Deborah R. Kenny, General Manager; Gary M. Kenny, Engineer.

Asbury—KJOM-LP, Ch. 24, Marcia T. Turner. Phone: 305-788-5300.

Technical Facilities: 58-kw ERP, 370-ft. above ground, 1318-ft. above sea level, lat. 37° 26' 54.8", long. 94° 38' 11.2".

Holds CP for change to channel number 65, 150-kw ERP, 265-ft. above ground, 1115-ft. above sea level, lat. 37° 07' 57.8", long. 94° 41' 38.2". BDISTTL-20060403ARC.

Ownership: Marcia T. Turner.

Aurora—K61GJ, Ch. 61, New Life Evangelistic Center Inc. Phone: 314-436-2424.

Technical Facilities: 1000-w TPO, 32-kw ERP, 270-ft. above ground, 1844-ft. above sea level, lat. 36° 52' 50", long. 93° 42' 36".

Holds CP for change to channel number 48, 15-kw ERP, 269-ft. above ground, 1843-ft. above sea level, lat. 36° 52' 50", long. 93° 42' 37". BDISDTL-20060331AXX.

Transmitter: 0.5-mi. E of State Rd. 39, 5-mi. S of Aurora.

Ownership: New Life Evangelistic Center Inc.

Aurora—KNJE-LP, Ch. 58, EBC Harrison Inc., Debtor in Possession. Phone: 501-219-2400. Fax: 501-221-1101.

Technical Facilities: 150-kw ERP, 364-ft. above ground, 1724-ft. above sea level, lat. 36° 44' 54", long. 93° 39' 32".

Holds CP for change to channel number 40, BDISTTL-20070216ABF.

Began Operation: July 13, 1995.

Ownership: Equity Media Holdings Corp., Debtor in Possession.

Branson—K05JQ, Ch. 5, Miller Family Broadcasting LLC.

Technical Facilities: 10-w TPO, 0.015-kw ERP, 141-ft. above ground, 1227-ft. above sea level, lat. 36° 36' 40", long. 93° 14' 29".

Transmitter: 0.62-mi. S of School of the Ozarks.

Ownership: Miller Family Broadcasting LLC.

Personnel: Jerry Landers, General Manager; Dean Fagan, Chief Engineer.

Branson—K17DL-D, Ch. 17, Branson Visitors TV LLC. Phone: 417-268-3000. Fax: 417-268-3100.

Technical Facilities: 2.1-kw ERP, 476-ft. above ground, 1824-ft. above sea level, lat. 36° 44' 52", long. 93° 16' 37".

Transmitter: 0.2-mi. ESE of State Rtes. T & 76, near Branson.

Began Operation: November 13, 2001.

Ownership: Branson Visitors TV LLC.

Personnel: Michael Scott, President & General Manager; Angela Moyle, Business Manager; Bryan Cochran, General Sales Manager; Trenna Underhill, Programming Coordinator.

Branson—K25BD, Ch. 25, Christians Incorporated for Christ Inc. Phone: 417-337-8747. Fax: 417-337-5503.

Technical Facilities: 1000-w TPO, 14.2-kw ERP, 236-ft. above ground, 1206-ft. above sea level, lat. 36° 38' 24", long. 93° 14' 31".

Transmitter: Branson Heights Shopping Center, Branson.

Ownership: Christians Incorporated for Christ Inc.

Personnel: Keith O'Neil, Vice President.

■ **Branson**—KBNS-CA, Ch. 38, The Vacation Channel Inc. Phone: 417-334-1200. Fax: 417-334-5209.

Technical Facilities: 49.1-kw ERP, 423-ft. above ground, 1663-ft. above sea level, lat. 36° 46' 52", long. 93° 10' 02".

Ownership: The Vacation Channel.

Branson—KNJD-LP, Ch. 59, New Life Evangelistic Center Inc. Phone: 314-436-2424. Fax: 314-436-2434.

Technical Facilities: 740-w TPO, 10.5-kw ERP, 236-ft. above ground, 1476-ft. above sea level, lat. 36° 43' 52", long. 93° 10' 02".

Holds CP for change to channel number 42, 15-kw ERP, BDISDTL-20060331BER.

Transmitter: 1.7-mi. N of U.S. Rte. 160, 0.5-mi. NE of State Rd. 176 & U.S. 160, 2.1-mi.

Ownership: New Life Evangelistic Center Inc.

Cape Girardeau—K10KM, Ch. 10, WSIL-TV Inc. Phone: 919-839-0300.

Technical Facilities: 0.29-kw ERP, lat. 37° 22' 16", long. 89° 31' 52".

Ownership: Mel Wheeler Inc.

Cape Girardeau—K33EQ, Ch. 33, MS Communications LLC. Phone: 414-765-9737.

Technical Facilities: 0.007-kw ERP, 49-ft. above ground, 499-ft. above sea level, lat. 37° 09' 17", long. 89° 36' 39".

Transmitter: Scott County Rd. 223, Chaffee.

Ownership: MS Communications LLC.

Cape Girardeau—K47FB, Ch. 47, MS Communications LLC. Phone: 414-765-9737.

Technical Facilities: 0.007-kw ERP, 105-ft. above ground, 499-ft. above sea level, lat. 37° 09' 17", long. 89° 36' 39".

Transmitter: Scott County Rd. 223, Chaffee.

Ownership: MS Communications LLC.

Cape Girardeau—K55HL, Ch. 55, MS Communications LLC. Phone: 414-765-9737.

Technical Facilities: 100-w TPO, 1.16-kw ERP, 150-ft. above ground, 663-ft. above sea level, lat. 37° 09' 27", long. 89° 36' 20".

Transmitter: Scott County Rd. 223, Chaffee.

Ownership: MS Communications LLC.

Cape Girardeau—K58FD, Ch. 58, MS Communications LLC. Phone: 414-765-9737.

Technical Facilities: 100-w TPO, 1.16-kw ERP, 150-ft. above ground, 663-ft. above sea level, lat. 37° 09' 27", long. 89° 36' 20".

Transmitter: Scott County Rd. 223, Chaffee.

Ownership: MS Communications LLC.

Cape Girardeau—K65GP, Ch. 65, MS Communications LLC. Phone: 414-765-9737.

Technical Facilities: 100-w TPO, 1.16-kw ERP, 150-ft. above ground, 663-ft. above sea level, lat. 37° 09' 27", long. 89° 36' 20".

Transmitter: Scott County Rd. 223, Chaffee.

Ownership: MS Communications LLC.

Cape Girardeau—K67HF, Ch. 67, MS Communications LLC. Phone: 414-765-9737.

Technical Facilities: 0.007-kw ERP, 49-ft. above ground, 499-ft. above sea level, lat. 37° 09' 17", long. 89° 36' 39".

Transmitter: Scott County Rd. 223, Chaffee.

Ownership: MS Communications LLC.

Cape Girardeau—K69HT, Ch. 69, MS Communications LLC. Phone: 414-765-9737.

Technical Facilities: 100-w TPO, 1.16-kw ERP, 150-ft. above ground, 663-ft. above sea level, lat. 37° 09' 27", long. 89° 36' 20".

Transmitter: Scott County Rd. 223, Chaffee.

Ownership: MS Communications LLC.

■ **Cape Girardeau**—KCGI-CA, Ch. 45, Tri-State Christian TV Inc. Phone: 618-997-9333. Fax: 618-997-1859.

Technical Facilities: 1000-w TPO, 9.1-kw ERP, 699-ft. above ground, 1414-ft. above sea level, lat. 37° 22' 16", long. 89° 31' 52".

Transmitter: 0.68-mi. S of Bainbridge Rd., approx. 4-mi. N of Cape Girardeau.

Ownership: Tri-State Christian TV Inc.

Personnel: Fortune Brayfield, Station Manager.

■ **Carthage**—KDSI-CA, Ch. 5, Word of God Fellowship Inc. Phone: 817-858-9955. Fax: 817-571-7478.

Technical Facilities: 10-w TPO, 0.17-kw ERP, 57-ft. above ground, 1124-ft. above sea level, lat. 37° 08' 14", long. 94° 18' 49".

Transmitter: 1-mi. W of U.S. 571 & HH junction.

Ownership: Word of God Fellowship Inc.

Columbia—K02NQ, Ch. 2, JW Broadcasting LLC. Phone: 520-544-6186.

Studio: 23 S 8th St, Columbia, MO 65201.

Technical Facilities: 0.004-kw ERP, 30-ft. above ground, 780-ft. above sea level, lat. 38° 57' 53.1", long. 92° 19' 51.6".

Ownership: JW Broadcasting LLC.

Personnel: Jim Karpowicz, General Manager.

Columbia—K56AU, Ch. 56, Trinity Broadcasting Network Inc. Phone: 714-832-2950. Fax: 714-730-0661.

Technical Facilities: 1000-w TPO, 6.7-kw ERP, 440-ft. above ground, 899-ft. above sea level, lat. 38° 57' 21", long. 92° 16' 24".

Holds CP for change to channel number 46, 6.9-kw ERP, 440-ft. above ground, 1195-ft. above sea level, lat. 38° 57' 18", long. 92° 16' 20". BMPTT-20060825ACJ.

Transmitter: KARO/KFMZ tower.

Ownership: Trinity Broadcasting Network Inc.

Columbia—KQFX-LP, Ch. 32, JW Broadcasting LLC. Phone: 573-449-0917.

Technical Facilities: 33.1-kw ERP, 545-ft. above ground, 1424-ft. above sea level, lat. 38° 47' 27.9", long. 92° 17' 43.3".

Holds CP for change to channel number 22, 15-kw ERP, 1010-ft. above ground, 1818-ft. above sea level, lat. 38° 46' 29", long. 92° 33' 22". BDISDTL-20081002ABI.

Began Operation: September 6, 1990.

Ownership: JW Broadcasting LLC.

Jamestown—K63FW, Ch. 63, Roger E. Harders. Phone: 402-443-3198.

Technical Facilities: 0.5-kw ERP, 47-ft. above ground, 869-ft. above sea level, lat. 38° 46' 57", long. 92° 27' 25".

Ownership: Roger E. Harders.

Jefferson City—K05LU, Ch. 5, Hispanic Christian Community Network Inc. Phone: 214-879-0081.

Technical Facilities: 0.11-kw ERP, 164-ft. above ground, 699-ft. above sea level, lat. 38° 34' 13.8", long. 92° 03' 24.8".

Ownership: Hispanic Christian Community Network Inc.

Jefferson City—K41OI, Ch. 41, Trinity Broadcasting Network Inc. Phone: 714-832-2950. Fax: 714-730-0661.

Technical Facilities: 32.2-kw ERP, 449-ft. above ground, 1329-ft. above sea level, lat. 38° 49' 28", long. 92° 17' 43".

Ownership: Trinity Broadcasting Network Inc.

Jefferson City—KLMC-LP, Ch. 28, Prism Broadcasting Network Inc. Phone: 770-953-3232.

Technical Facilities: 0.004-kw ERP, 49-ft. above ground, 863-ft. above sea level, lat. 38° 33' 59.7", long. 92° 15' 14.2".

Ownership: Prism Broadcasting Network Inc.

Jefferson City—KZOU-LP, Ch. 38, JW Broadcasting LLC. Phone: 573-449-0917. Fax: 573-875-7078.

Studio: 501 Business Loop 70 E, Columbia, MO 65201.

Technical Facilities: 143.2-kw ERP, 514-ft. above ground, 1394-ft. above sea level, lat. 38° 47' 27", long. 92° 17' 43".

Ownership: JW Broadcasting LLC.

Joplin—K04OV, Ch. 4, MS Communications LLC. Phone: 414-765-9737.

Technical Facilities: 0.007-kw ERP, 105-ft. above ground, 1033-ft. above sea level, lat. 37° 04' 49", long. 94° 33' 25".

Transmitter: 2510 W. 20th St.

Ownership: MS Communications LLC.

Joplin—K52FC, Ch. 52, MS Communications LLC. Phone: 414-765-9737.

Technical Facilities: 143-w TPO, 0.007-kw ERP, 105-ft. above ground, 1033-ft. above sea level, lat. 37° 04' 49", long. 94° 33' 25".

Transmitter: 0.9-mi. NW of I-44.

Ownership: MS Communications LLC.

Joplin—K55HU, Ch. 55, MS Communications LLC. Phone: 414-765-9737.

Technical Facilities: 0.007-kw ERP, 105-ft. above ground, 1132-ft. above sea level, lat. 37° 04' 49", long. 94° 33' 25".

Transmitter: 2510 W. 20th St.

Ownership: MS Communications LLC.

Joplin—K64FW, Ch. 64, New Life Evangelistic Center Inc. Phone: 314-436-2424.

Technical Facilities: 1000-w TPO, 13.7-kw ERP, 450-ft. above ground, 1109-ft. above sea level, lat. 41° 57' 42", long. 86° 21' 02".

Holds CP for change to channel number 36, 1.5-kw ERP, 279-ft. above ground, 1414-ft. above sea level, lat. 36° 58' 54", long. 94° 28' 36". BDISDTL-20060331AYL.

Transmitter: 7-mi. S of Joplin, W of U.S. 71.

Ownership: New Life Evangelistic Center Inc.

Joplin—KGCS-LP, Ch. 22, Board of Governors, Missouri Southern State U. Phones: 417-625-9375; 417-625-9777. Fax: 417-625-9742.

Studio: 3950 E Newman Rd, Joplin, MO 64801-1595.

Technical Facilities: 14-kw ERP, 673-ft. above ground, 1643-ft. above sea level, lat. 37° 05' 49", long. 94° 34' 25".

Ownership: Missouri Southern State University.

Personnel: Jay R. Moorman, Executive Manager; Judy Stiles, General Manager; Don Ross, Chief Engineer.

Joplin—KJPX-LP, Ch. 47, Gary M. & Deborah R. Kenny. Phone: 417-623-4646. Fax: 417-206-4482.

Technical Facilities: 25-kw ERP, 350-ft. above ground, 1436-ft. above sea level, lat. 37° 03' 10", long. 94° 23' 20".

Holds CP for change to channel number 35, 50-kw ERP, 348-ft. above ground, 1434-ft. above sea level, lat. 37° 03' 07.8", long. 94° 23' 20.2". BDISTTL-20060329AMT.

Multichannel TV Sound: Stereo only.

Ownership: Gary M. Kenny; Deborah R. Kenny.

Personnel: Gary Kenny, Chief Engineer.

■ **Joplin-Carthage**—KCLJ-CA, Ch. 30, Gary M. & Deborah R. Kenny. Phone: 417-623-4646. Fax: 417-206-4482.

Studio: 1146 Lark, Joplin, MO 64804.

Technical Facilities: 38.1-kw ERP, 336-ft. above ground, 336-ft. above sea level, lat. 37° 03' 10", long. 94° 23' 20".

Ownership: Gary M. Kenny; Deborah R. Kenny.

Personnel: Gary Kenny, Chief Executive Officer; Deborah R. Kenny, General Manager.

Kansas City—K45IO, Ch. 45, Ventana Television Inc. Phone: 727-872-4210.

Technical Facilities: 104-kw ERP, 725-ft. above ground, 1611-ft. above sea level, lat. 39° 01' 20", long. 94° 30' 49".

Began Operation: July 17, 1991.

Ownership: Ventana Television Inc.

Personnel: John Skelnik, General Manager.

Kansas City—KCDN-LP, Ch. 35, Word of God Fellowship Inc. Phone: 817-571-1229. Fax: 817-571-7478.

Technical Facilities: 1000-w TPO, 16.8-kw ERP, 827-ft. above ground, 1709-ft. above sea level, lat. 39° 04' 24", long. 94° 29' 06".

Holds CP for change to channel number 43, 75-kw ERP, 679-ft. above ground, 1565-ft. above sea level, lat. 39° 01' 20", long. 94° 30' 49". BDISTTL-20080703ABI.

Transmitter: 2800 Wallace Ave.

Ownership: Word of God Fellowship Inc.

Kansas City—KUKC-LP, Ch. 40, SP Kansas City LLC. Phone: 203-542-4200.

Technical Facilities: 1000-w TPO, 12.7-kw ERP, 827-ft. above ground, 1709-ft. above sea level, lat. 39° 04' 24", long. 94° 29' 06".

Holds CP for change to 150-kw ERP, 699-ft. above ground, 1585-ft. above sea level, lat. 39° 01' 20", long. 94° 30' 49". BMPTTL-20070213AAE.

Transmitter: 2800 Wallace Ave.

Began Operation: August 28, 1992.

Ownership: SP Television LLC.

Kirksville—K34CW, Ch. 34, Ottumwa Media Holdings LLC. Phone: 704-643-4148.

Technical Facilities: 5.9-kw ERP, lat. 40° 13' 38", long. 92° 36' 35".

Ownership: Ottumwa Media Holdings LLC.

Lebanon—K64FQ, Ch. 64, New Life Evangelistic Center Inc. Phone: 314-436-2424.

Technical Facilities: 891-w TPO, 9.96-kw ERP, 489-ft. above ground, 1670-ft. above sea level, lat. 37° 49' 10", long. 92° 44' 51".

Holds CP for change to channel number 38, 15-kw ERP, 486-ft. above ground, 1671-ft. above sea level, BDISDTL-20060331AZM.

Transmitter: State Rds. E & D, 0.5-mi. SE of Eldridge.

Ownership: New Life Evangelistic Center Inc.

Lewistown—K09XZ, Ch. 9, Hispanic Christian Community Network Inc. Phone: 214-879-0081.

Technical Facilities: 3-kw ERP, 164-ft. above ground, 883-ft. above sea level, lat. 40° 05' 55", long. 91° 50' 36".

Ownership: Hispanic Christian Community Network Inc.

Malden—K62DA, Ch. 62, Local TV Tennessee License LLC. Phone: 859-448-2707.

Technical Facilities: 1.41-kw ERP, lat. 36° 30' 18", long. 89° 58' 15".

Ownership: Local TV Holdings LLC.

Marshfield—K17FU, Ch. 17, New Life Evangelistic Center Inc. Phone: 314-436-2424.

Technical Facilities: 36.3-kw ERP, 273-ft. above ground, 1653-ft. above sea level, lat. 37° 19' 01", long. 92° 57' 51".

Holds CP for change to 15-kw ERP, BDFCDTL-20060331BAQ.

Ownership: New Life Evangelistic Center Inc.

Marshfield—K68EL, Ch. 68, New Life Evangelistic Center Inc. Phone: 314-436-2424.

Technical Facilities: 942-w TPO, 27.6-kw ERP, 476-ft. above ground, 1916-ft. above sea level, lat. 37° 11' 10", long. 93° 01' 23".

Transmitter: 5.6-mi. NW of Fordland.

Ownership: New Life Evangelistic Center Inc.

Moberly—K05LY, Ch. 5, Hispanic Christian Community Network Inc. Phone: 214-434-6357.

Technical Facilities: 0.1-kw ERP, 49-ft. above ground, 915-ft. above sea level, lat. 39° 25' 04.5", long. 92° 26' 17".

Ownership: Hispanic Christian Community Network Inc.

Monett—K38DD, Ch. 38, Peggy L. Davis & Deborah R. Kenny. Phones: 417-451-1440; 417-623-4646. Fax: 417-451-3333.

Technical Facilities: 100-w TPO, 0.985-kw ERP, 130-ft. above ground, 1500-ft. above sea level, lat. 36° 56' 15", long. 93° 55' 30".

Transmitter: County Rd. 37 at northern city limits, Monett.

Ownership: Deborah R. Kenny; Peggy L. Davis.

Personnel: Deborah R. Kenny, General Manager; Gary M. Kenny, Chief Engineer.

■ **Neosho**—KCLG-CA, Ch. 32, Gary M. & Deborah R. Kenny. Phones: 417-623-4646; 417-451-1440. Fax: 417-206-4482.

Technical Facilities: 5-kw ERP, 151-ft. above ground, 1375-ft. above sea level, lat. 36° 52' 38", long. 94° 24' 24".

Ownership: Gary M. Kenny; Deborah R. Kenny.

Poplar Bluff—K39CP, Ch. 39, Trinity Broadcasting Network Inc. Phone: 714-832-2950. Fax: 714-730-0661.

Technical Facilities: 1000-w TPO, 20.6-kw ERP, 479-ft. above ground, 981-ft. above sea level, lat. 36° 48' 04", long. 90° 27' 06".

Transmitter: Side of existing KPOB-TV tower.

Ownership: Trinity Broadcasting Network Inc.

Personnel: Paul Crouch, General Manager; Ben Miller, Chief Engineer; Rod Henke, Sales Manager.

Rolla—K07SD, Ch. 7, The Curators of the U. of Missouri. Phone: 573-882-8888. Fax: 573-884-8888.

Studio: Hwy. 63 S, Columbia, MO 65201.

Technical Facilities: 10-w TPO, 0.15523-kw ERP, 145-ft. above ground, 1345-ft. above sea level, lat. 37° 57' 35", long. 91° 46' 19".

Transmitter: Thomas Jefferson Hall, 202 W. 18th St., Rolla.

Ownership: The Curators of the U. of Missouri.

Personnel: Martin Siddall, Manager; Lee Eggers, Chief Engineer.

Rolla—K16FE, Ch. 16, Trinity Broadcasting Network Inc. Phone: 714-832-2950. Fax: 714-730-0661.

Technical Facilities: 9.8-kw ERP, 330-ft. above ground, 1510-ft. above sea level, lat. 37° 52' 39", long. 91° 44' 45".

Holds CP for change to 15-kw ERP, BDFCDTT-20060313AEP.

Ownership: Trinity Broadcasting Network Inc.

Rolla—KROL-LP, Ch. 48, John A. McAulay. Phone: 661-944-2087.

Technical Facilities: 5.4-kw ERP, 98-ft. above ground, 1253-ft. above sea level, lat. 37° 58' 47", long. 91° 45' 42".

Ownership: John A. McAulay.

Sedalia, etc.—K11OJ, Ch. 11, Barrington Jefferson City License LLC. Phone: 847-884-1877.

Technical Facilities: 0.14-kw ERP, lat. 38° 44' 48", long. 93° 13' 56".

Ownership: Pilot Group LP.

Springfield—K08MA, Ch. 8, Metropolitan Radio Group Inc. Phone: 417-863-6371. Fax: 417-862-9079.

Studio: 1549 Greenbridge, Springfield, MO 65808.

Technical Facilities: 100-w TPO, 0.212-kw ERP, 1631-ft. above ground, lat. 37° 12' 06", long. 93° 14' 01".

Transmitter: 3000 E. Cherry St.

Ownership: Metropolitan Radio Group Inc.

Personnel: Mark Acker, General Manager; Martha Katona, Sales Manager.

Springfield—K15CZ, Ch. 15, KY3 Inc. Phone: 417-268-3000. Fax: 417-268-3100.

Studio: 999 W Sunshine, Springfield, MO 65807.

Technical Facilities: 247-w TPO, 4.56-kw ERP, 479-ft. above ground, 1863-ft. above sea level, lat. 37° 13' 25", long. 93° 14' 30".

Holds CP for change to 3.9-kw ERP, 476-ft. above ground, 1756-ft. above sea level, lat. 37° 14' 23", long. 93° 17' 07". BDFCDTL-20081014AEG.

Transmitter: 2650 E Division Rd.

Ownership: Schurz Communications Inc.

Personnel: Michael Scott, President & General Manager; Bryan Cochran, General Sales Manager; Trenna Underhill, Programming Coordinator; Angela Moyle, Business Manager.

Springfield—K39CI, Ch. 39, New Life Evangelistic Center Inc.

Technical Facilities: 8.8-kw ERP, lat. 37° 12' 47", long. 93° 17' 14".

Ownership: New Life Evangelistic Center Inc.

Springfield—K41FQ, Ch. 41, Trinity Broadcasting Network Inc. Phone: 714-832-2950. Fax: 714-730-0661.

Technical Facilities: 1000-w TPO, 76-kw ERP, 699-ft. above ground, 2276-ft. above sea level, lat. 37° 13' 08", long. 92° 56' 56".

Transmitter: side of existing KDEB-TV tower, 2.5-mi. NNE of Fordland.

Ownership: Trinity Broadcasting Network Inc.

Personnel: Paul Crouch, General Manager; Ben Miller, Chief Engineer; Rod Henke, Sales Manager.

Springfield—K47LH, Ch. 47, Trinity Broadcasting Network Inc. Phone: 714-832-2950. Fax: 714-730-0661.

Technical Facilities: 19.5-kw ERP, 266-ft. above ground, 1621-ft. above sea level, lat. 37° 12' 07", long. 93° 14' 02".

Ownership: Trinity Broadcasting Network Inc.

Springfield—K54FX, Ch. 54, New Life Evangelistic Center Inc. Phone: 314-436-2424.

Technical Facilities: 8.8-kw ERP, lat. 37° 12' 47", long. 93° 17' 14".

Holds CP for change to channel number 39, 0.5-kw ERP, 312-ft. above ground, 1590-ft. above sea level, BDISDTL-20060331AZU.

Ownership: New Life Evangelistic Center Inc.

■ **Springfield**—KBBL-CA, Ch. 56, EBC Harrison Inc., Debtor in Possession. Phone: 501-219-2400.

Studio: 1736 E Sunshine, Ste 805, Springfield, MO 65804.

Technical Facilities: 1000-w TPO, 19-kw ERP, 174-ft. above ground, 1512-ft. above sea level, lat. 37° 10' 50", long. 93° 15' 58".

Ownership: Equity Media Holdings Corp., Debtor in Possession.

Personnel: Keith Hendrix, General Manager; Neal Ardman, Chief Engineer.

St. Charles—K22HG, Ch. 22, Trinity Broadcasting Network Inc. Phone: 714-832-2950. Fax: 714-730-0661.

Technical Facilities: 20-kw ERP, 400-ft. above ground, 865-ft. above sea level, lat. 38° 45' 07", long. 90° 37' 22".

Holds CP for change to channel number 17, 15-kw ERP, BDISDTT-20060327ACC.

Ownership: Trinity Broadcasting Network Inc.

Personnel: Paul Crouch, General Manager; Ben Miller, Chief Engineer; Rod Henke, Sales Manager.

St. Louis—K33GU, Ch. 33, Trinity Broadcasting Network Inc. Phones: 330-753-5542; 714-832-2950. Fax: 714-730-0661.

Technical Facilities: 10-kw ERP, 554-ft. above ground, 1024-ft. above sea level, lat. 38° 34' 24", long. 90° 19' 30".

Ownership: Trinity Broadcasting Network Inc.

St. Louis—K38HD, Ch. 38, Ventana Television Inc. Phone: 727-872-4210.

Technical Facilities: 150-kw ERP, 259-ft. above ground, 759-ft. above sea level, lat. 38° 37' 55", long. 90° 13' 59".

Began Operation: March 7, 1991.

Ownership: Ventana Television Inc.

St. Louis—K43EU, Ch. 43, Roger E. Harders.

Technical Facilities: 0.51-kw ERP, 47-ft. above ground, 869-ft. above sea level, lat. 38° 46' 57", long. 92° 27' 25".

Ownership: Roger E. Harders.

■ **St. Louis**—K49FC, Ch. 49, Three Angels Broadcasting Network Inc. Phone: 618-627-4651. Fax: 618-627-4155.

Studio: 3391 Charley Good Rd, West Frankfort, IL 62896.

Technical Facilities: 40.9-kw ERP, 269-ft. above ground, 771-ft. above sea level, lat. 38° 37' 55", long. 90° 13' 59".

Ownership: Three Angels Broadcasting Network Inc.

Personnel: Moses Primo, Chief Engineer.

St. Louis—KDTL-LP, Ch. 16, Word of God Fellowship Inc. Phone: 817-571-1229.

Technical Facilities: 130-kw ERP, 495-ft. above ground, 965-ft. above sea level, lat. 38° 34' 24", long. 90° 19' 30".

Ownership: Word of God Fellowship Inc.

■ **St. Louis**—KEFN-CA, Ch. 62, Eternal Family Network. Phone: 636-949-2424.

Studio: 9705 Watson Rd, St. Louis, MO 63126.

Technical Facilities: 50-kw ERP, 463-ft. above ground, 1237-ft. above sea level, lat. 38° 25' 01", long. 90° 25' 59".

Ownership: Eternal Family Network.

Personnel: William Federer, General Manager.

St. Louis—KPTN-LP, Ch. 7, Mako Communications LLC. Phone: 361-883-1763.

Technical Facilities: 2.21-kw ERP, 787-ft. above ground, 1258-ft. above sea level, lat. 38° 34' 24", long. 90° 19' 30".

Transmitter: Resurrection Cemetery, 7555 MacKenzie Rd, Afton.

Ownership: Mako Communications LLC.

St. Louis—KUMO-LP, Ch. 51, WPXS Inc. Phone: 817-571-1229.

Technical Facilities: 70-kw ERP, 900-ft. above ground, 1370-ft. above sea level, lat. 38° 34' 24", long. 90° 19' 30".

Ownership: Word of God Fellowship Inc.

Warrensburg—K32FH, Ch. 32, Roger E. Harders.

Technical Facilities: 0.403-kw ERP, 49-ft. above ground, 941-ft. above sea level, lat. 38° 55' 54", long. 93° 49' 07".

Ownership: Roger E. Harders.

West Plains—K38HE, Ch. 38, Promised Land Ministries Inc./Light the World Ministries. Phone: 417-372-1129.

Technical Facilities: 30.1-kw ERP, 331-ft. above ground, 1391-ft. above sea level, lat. 36° 45' 02", long. 91° 51' 51".

Ownership: Promised Land Ministries Inc./Light the World Ministries.

Montana

Absarokee—K05EI, Ch. 5, Absarokee Community TV Club. Phone: 406-328-4654.

Technical Facilities: 0.034-kw ERP, lat. 45° 31' 45", long. 109° 25' 20".

Ownership: Absarokee Community TV Club.

Absarokee—K10MO, Ch. 10, Absarokee Community TV Club. Phone: 406-328-4654.

Technical Facilities: 10-kw ERP, lat. 45° 31' 45", long. 109° 25' 20".

Ownership: Absarokee Community TV Club.

Absarokee—K12HX, Ch. 12, Absarokee Community TV Club. Phone: 406-328-4654.

Technical Facilities: 0.034-kw ERP, lat. 45° 31' 45", long. 109° 25' 20".

Ownership: Absarokee Community TV Club.

Arlee—K48EG, Ch. 48, Salish Kootenai College. Phone: 406-275-4878.

Technical Facilities: 0.064-kw ERP, 66-ft. above ground, 6191-ft. above sea level, lat. 47° 12' 52", long. 114° 01' 43".

Holds CP for change to 0.032-kw ERP, 16-ft. above ground, 4186-ft. above sea level, lat. 47° 15' 48", long. 114° 04' 50". BDFCDTT-20081202AHG.

Began Operation: October 4, 1993.

Ownership: Salish Kootenai College.

Baker—K04IH, Ch. 4, Baker TV Tax District. Phone: 406-778-2203.

Technical Facilities: 0.01-kw ERP, lat. 46° 18' 45", long. 104° 12' 25".

Ownership: Baker TV Tax District.

Baker—K08IP, Ch. 8, Baker TV Tax District. Phone: 406-778-2203.

Technical Facilities: 0.146-kw ERP, lat. 46° 16' 30", long. 104° 13' 30".

Ownership: Baker TV Tax District.

Baker—K10JP, Ch. 10, Baker TV Tax District. Phone: 406-778-2203.

Technical Facilities: 0.144-kw ERP, lat. 46° 18' 45", long. 104° 12' 25".

Ownership: Baker TV Tax District.

Baker—K13OW, Ch. 13, Baker TV Tax District. Phone: 406-778-2203.

Technical Facilities: 0.142-kw ERP, lat. 46° 16' 30", long. 104° 13' 30".

Ownership: Baker TV Tax District.

Belgrade, etc.—K20DY, Ch. 20, Montana State U. Phones: 406-586-3280; 406-586-4135.

Technical Facilities: 6.85-kw ERP, 100-ft. above ground, 5700-ft. above sea level, lat. 45° 38' 15", long. 111° 16' 01".

Holds CP for change to 0.15-kw ERP, 102-ft. above ground, 5699-ft. above sea level, BDFCDTT-20061207ACC.

Ownership: Montana U. System Board of Regents.

Big Arm—K07VU, Ch. 7, Blacktail TV Tax District. Phone: 406-883-2975.

Technical Facilities: 0.102-kw ERP, 26-ft. above ground, 3077-ft. above sea level, lat. 47° 48' 56", long. 114° 19' 14".

Holds CP for change to 0.04-kw ERP, 26-ft. above ground, 3097-ft. above sea level, BDFCDTV-20070618ACL.

Ownership: Blacktail TV Tax District.

Big Arm—K11RX, Ch. 11, Blacktail TV Tax District. Phone: 406-883-2975.

Technical Facilities: 0.04-kw ERP, lat. 47° 49' 00", long. 114° 18' 50".

Holds CP for change to 0.035-kw ERP, 23-ft. above ground, 3094-ft. above sea level, lat. 47° 48' 56", long. 114° 19' 14". BDFCDTV-20070618ACP.

Ownership: Blacktail TV Tax District.

Big Sandy—K07IP, Ch. 7, Big Sandy TV Club. Phone: 406-378-2582.

Technical Facilities: 0.009-kw ERP, lat. 48° 09' 40", long. 110° 02' 04".

Ownership: Big Sandy TV Club.

Big Sandy—K10BK, Ch. 10, Big Sandy TV Club. Phone: 406-378-2582.

Technical Facilities: 0.001-kw ERP, lat. 48° 09' 40", long. 110° 02' 04".

Ownership: Big Sandy TV Club.

Big Sandy—K13OQ, Ch. 13, Big Sandy TV Club. Phone: 406-378-2582.

Technical Facilities: 0.001-kw ERP, lat. 48° 09' 40", long. 110° 02' 04".

Ownership: Big Sandy TV Club.

Big Timber, etc.—K69CM, Ch. 69, KTVQ Communications Inc. Phone: 406-252-5611.

Technical Facilities: 0.44-kw ERP, lat. 45° 40' 45", long. 110° 46' 21".

Holds CP for change to channel number 39, 18-ft. above ground, 7265-ft. above sea level, BDISTTL-20060331BLP.

Ownership: KTVQ Communications Inc.

Billings—K14IS, Ch. 14, Yellowstone Valley Community TV. Phone: 406-652-1288. Fax: 406-655-0696.

Technical Facilities: 1000-w TPO, 9.66-kw ERP, 168-ft. above ground, 3796-ft. above sea level, lat. 45° 46' 02", long. 108° 27' 27".

Transmitter: 2.5-mi. ESE of Billings.

Ownership: Yellowstone Valley Community TV.

Billings—K20HB, Ch. 20, Montana State U. Phone: 406-994-3437.

Technical Facilities: 51.2-kw ERP, 148-ft. above ground, 3816-ft. above sea level, lat. 45° 46' 00", long. 108° 27' 27".

Holds CP for change to 14.5-kw ERP, BDFCDTT-20061207ACB.

Ownership: Montana U. System Board of Regents.

Billings—K23HI, Ch. 23, Prism Broadcasting Network Inc. Phone: 770-953-3232.

Technical Facilities: 0.1-kw ERP, 20-ft. above ground, 3323-ft. above sea level, lat. 45° 47' 55", long. 108° 32' 30".

Ownership: Prism Broadcasting Network Inc.

Billings—K25BP, Ch. 25, Nexstar Broadcasting Inc. Phone: 972-373-8800.

Technical Facilities: 14-kw ERP, lat. 45° 46' 04", long. 108° 27' 27".

Holds CP for change to 0.09-kw ERP, 148-ft. above ground, 3780-ft. above sea level, lat. 45° 46' 05", long. 108° 27' 25". BDFCDTT-20060403AKQ.

Transmitter: 2-mi. NW of Billings.

Ownership: Nexstar Broadcasting Group Inc.

Billings—K27IM, Ch. 27, Nexstar Broadcasting Inc. Phone: 972-373-8800.

Technical Facilities: 14-kw ERP, 141-ft. above ground, 3730-ft. above sea level, lat. 45° 46' 04", long. 108° 27' 25".

Ownership: Nexstar Broadcasting Group Inc.

Billings—K30IB, Ch. 30, Marcia T. Turner. Phone: 954-732-9539.

Technical Facilities: 3-kw ERP, 262-ft. above ground, 3533-ft. above sea level, lat. 45° 39' 52", long. 108° 46' 10".

Ownership: Marcia T. Turner.

Billings—K36EZ, Ch. 36, Comanche Enterprises. Phone: 406-656-3551.

Technical Facilities: 1.05-kw ERP, 33-ft. above ground, 3658-ft. above sea level, lat. 45° 46' 06", long. 108° 27' 31".

Holds CP for change to 145.2-kw ERP, 154-ft. above ground, 3779-ft. above sea level, BMAPTTL-20000831CHP.

Ownership: Comanche Enterprises.

Billings—K45KS, Ch. 45, EICB-TV East LLC. Phone: 972-291-3750.

Technical Facilities: 1.1-kw ERP, 56-ft. above ground, 3747-ft. above sea level, lat. 45° 45' 51", long. 108° 27' 22".

Began Operation: September 2, 2008.

Ownership: EICB-TV LLC.

Billings—K48IQ, Ch. 48, Western Family Television Inc. Phone: 406-442-2655.

Technical Facilities: 9-kw ERP, 230-ft. above ground, 3921-ft. above sea level, lat. 45° 45' 37", long. 108° 27' 09".

Ownership: Western Family Television Inc.

Billings—K51KR, Ch. 51, EICB-TV East LLC. Phone: 972-291-3750.

Technical Facilities: 1.1-kw ERP, 56-ft. above ground, 3747-ft. above sea level, lat. 45° 45' 51", long. 108° 27' 22".

Began Operation: September 2, 2008.

Ownership: EICB-TV LLC.

Birney—K13RW, Ch. 13, Birney TV Club.

Technical Facilities: 0.005-kw ERP, lat. 45° 17' 27", long. 106° 31' 06".

Ownership: Birney TV Club.

Bitterroot Range, etc.—K11IL, Ch. 11, Hot Springs Community TV Inc. Phone: 406-741-2353.

Technical Facilities: 0.009-kw ERP, lat. 47° 33' 32", long. 114° 32' 42".

Ownership: Hot Springs TV District.

Blacktail, etc.—K32HH, Ch. 32, Blacktail TV Tax District. Phone: 406-883-2975.

Technical Facilities: 0.724-kw ERP, 18-ft. above ground, 6616-ft. above sea level, lat. 48° 00' 38", long. 114° 21' 46".

Holds CP for change to 0.271-kw ERP, 30-ft. above ground, 6788-ft. above sea level, lat. 48° 00' 40", long. 114° 21' 48". BDFCDTT-20070710ADA.

Ownership: Blacktail TV Tax District.

Blacktail, etc.—K44FR, Ch. 44, Blacktail TV Tax District. Phone: 406-883-2975.

Technical Facilities: 100-w TPO, 1.02-kw ERP, 43-ft. above ground, 6802-ft. above sea level, lat. 48° 01' 10", long. 114° 20' 00".

Holds CP for change to 0.271-kw ERP, 33-ft. above ground, 6792-ft. above sea level, lat. 48° 00' 40", long. 114° 21' 48". BDFCDTT-20070618ACU.

Transmitter: 6.5-mi. W of Lakeside.

Ownership: Blacktail TV Tax District.

Blacktail, etc.—K46FD, Ch. 46, Blacktail TV Tax District.

Technical Facilities: 0.28-kw ERP, 16-ft. above ground, 7054-ft. above sea level, lat. 48° 01' 10", long. 113° 52' 32".

Ownership: Blacktail TV Tax District.

Boulder—K08KT, Ch. 8, Boulder TV Assn. Phone: 406-225-3820.

Technical Facilities: 0.06-kw ERP, lat. 46° 15' 21", long. 112° 08' 53".

Ownership: Boulder TV Assn.

Boulder—K10HD, Ch. 10, Boulder TV Assn. Phone: 406-225-3820.

Technical Facilities: 0.006-kw ERP, lat. 46° 12' 42", long. 112° 06' 18".

Ownership: Boulder TV Assn.

Boulder—K13KP, Ch. 13, Boulder TV Assn. Phone: 406-225-3820.

Technical Facilities: 0.012-kw ERP, lat. 46° 16' 18", long. 112° 09' 42".

Ownership: Boulder TV Assn.

Boulder—K27CD, Ch. 27, Boulder TV Assn. Phones: 406-225-3820; 406-225-3376.

Technical Facilities: 100-w TPO, 1.24-kw ERP, 49-ft. above ground, 5968-ft. above sea level, lat. 46° 15' 34", long. 112° 09' 08".

Transmitter: 2-mi. NW of Boulder.

Ownership: Boulder TV Assn.

Boyes, etc.—K09VL, Ch. 9, Powder River County TV Board. Phone: 406-436-2361.

Technical Facilities: 0.106-kw ERP, 30-ft. above ground, 4472-ft. above sea level, lat. 45° 05' 28", long. 105° 01' 18".

Ownership: Powder River County TV Board.

Bozeman—K11UJ, Ch. 11, Murray Duffy.

Technical Facilities: 10-w TPO, 0.054-kw ERP, 5000-ft. above sea level, lat. 45° 39' 45", long. 110° 59' 55".

Transmitter: 699 Bozeman Trail Rd.

Ownership: Murray Duffy.

■**Bozeman**—K26DE, Ch. 26, KCTZ Communications Inc. Phone: 406-586-3280. Fax: 406-586-4135.

Technical Facilities: 1000-w TPO, 23.1-kw ERP, 30-ft. above ground, 5650-ft. above sea level, lat. 45° 38' 15", long. 111° 16' 01".

Transmitter: 1.9-mi. S of Rte. 84, 4.3-mi. W of Bozeman.

Ownership: Evening Post Publishing Co.

Personnel: Tim Gazy, Station & General Sales Manager; Ron Schlosser, Chief Engineer.

Bozeman—K34FI-D, Ch. 34, BlueStone License Holdings Inc. Phone: 212-247-8717.

Technical Facilities: 7.8-kw ERP, 176-ft. above ground, 6786-ft. above sea level, lat. 45° 40' 24", long. 110° 52' 02".

Ownership: Bonten Media Group LLC.

■**Bozeman**—K42BZ, Ch. 42, BlueStone License Holdings Inc. Phone: 212-710-7771.

Technical Facilities: 26.2-kw ERP, lat. 45° 40' 27", long. 110° 52' 05".

Holds CP for change to 5-kw ERP, 175-ft. above ground, 6786-ft. above sea level, lat. 45° 40' 24", long. 110° 52' 02". BDFCDTA-20080804ACA.

Ownership: Bonten Media Group LLC.

Bozeman—KHJT-LP, Ch. 54, Oasis Broadcasting Inc. Phone: 702-914-7409.

Technical Facilities: 0.165-kw ERP, 13-ft. above ground, 4934-ft. above sea level, lat. 45° 39' 33", long. 111° 03' 22".

Ownership: Oasis Broadcasting Inc.

Bozeman—KJCX-LP, Ch. 40, Western Family Television Inc. Phone: 406-442-2655.

Technical Facilities: 10-kw ERP, 104-ft. above ground, 4845-ft. above sea level, lat. 45° 41' 54", long. 111° 01' 41".

Ownership: Western Family Television Inc.

Bozeman—KWYB-LP, Ch. 28, MMM License LLC. Phone: 757-437-9800.

Technical Facilities: 297-w TPO, 10-kw ERP, 189-ft. above ground, 6752-ft. above sea level, lat. 45° 40' 24", long. 110° 52' 04".

Holds CP for change to 15-kw ERP, 180-ft. above ground, 6755-ft. above sea level, BDFCDTL-20060331BIG.

Transmitter: 1.7-mi. WNW of Brigham Canyon Rd. & E. U.S. 10 intersection, Green Mountain.

Began Operation: December 31, 1996.

Ownership: Max Media X LLC.

Personnel: Phillip Hurley, General Manager; Moe Straut, Chief Engineer; Katalin Green, Station Manager.

Bozeman, etc.—K45EB, Ch. 45, Gallatin Valley Community TV Assn. Phone: 406-587-8302. Fax: 406-585-0935.

Technical Facilities: 1000-w TPO, 10.3-kw ERP, 60-ft. above ground, 5748-ft. above sea level, lat. 45° 38' 10", long. 111° 16' 18".

Transmitter: 4.5-mi. W of Bozeman Hot Springs.

Ownership: Gallatin Valley Community TV Assn.

Bridger, etc.—K57EW, Ch. 57, Clarks Fork Valley TV District No. 1. Phone: 406-668-7633.

Technical Facilities: 1.09-kw ERP, 98-ft. above ground, 4324-ft. above sea level, lat. 45° 17' 11", long. 108° 56' 02".

Ownership: Clarks Fork Valley TV District No. 1.

Bridger, etc.—K59DT, Ch. 59, Clarks Fork Valley TV District No. 1. Phone: 406-668-7633.

Technical Facilities: 1.09-kw ERP, 98-ft. above ground, 4324-ft. above sea level, lat. 45° 17' 11", long. 108° 56' 02".

Ownership: Clarks Fork Valley TV District No. 1.

Bridger, etc.—K61EX, Ch. 61, Clarks Fork Valley TV District No. 1. Phone: 406-668-7633.

Technical Facilities: 1.09-kw ERP, 98-ft. above ground, 4324-ft. above sea level, lat. 45° 17' 11", long. 108° 56' 02".

Ownership: Clarks Fork Valley TV District No. 1.

Bridger, etc.—K63EA, Ch. 63, Clarks Fork Valley TV District No. 1. Phone: 406-668-7633.

Technical Facilities: 100-w TPO, 1.09-kw ERP, 98-ft. above ground, 4324-ft. above sea level, lat. 45° 17' 11", long. 108° 56' 02".

Transmitter: Approximately 1.24-mi. SW of Bridger.

Ownership: Clarks Fork Valley TV District No. 1.

Broadus—K03CS, Ch. 3, Powder River County TV Board. Phone: 406-436-2361.

Technical Facilities: 0.044-kw ERP, lat. 45° 24' 40", long. 105° 21' 28".

Holds CP for change to 0.012-kw ERP, 85-ft. above ground, 3517-ft. above sea level, BDFCDTV-20080923AEF.

Ownership: Powder River County TV Board.

Broadus, etc.—K06AA, Ch. 6, Powder River County TV Board. Phone: 406-436-2361.

Technical Facilities: 0.39-kw ERP, 94-ft. above ground, 3654-ft. above sea level, lat. 45° 24' 40", long. 105° 21' 28".

Ownership: Powder River County TV Board.

Broadus, etc.—K08JV, Ch. 8, Powder River County TV Board. Phone: 406-436-2361.

Technical Facilities: 0.08-kw ERP, lat. 45° 24' 40", long. 105° 21' 28".

Ownership: Powder River County TV Board.

Broadus, etc.—K10AC, Ch. 10, Powder River County TV Board. Phone: 406-436-2361.

Technical Facilities: 0.074-kw ERP, 79-ft. above ground, 4488-ft. above sea level, lat. 45° 36' 02", long. 105° 56' 15".

Ownership: Powder River County TV Board.

Broadus, etc.—K55FG, Ch. 55, Powder River County TV Board. Phone: 406-436-2361.

Technical Facilities: 1.65-kw ERP, 69-ft. above ground, 4478-ft. above sea level, lat. 45° 36' 02", long. 105° 56' 15".

Ownership: Powder River County TV Board.

Browning—K57FM, Ch. 57, Browning Public Schools. Phone: 406-338-2715. Fax: 406-338-2708.

Technical Facilities: 100-w TPO, 1.028-kw ERP, 126-ft. above ground, 4497-ft. above sea level, lat. 48° 33' 26", long. 113° 00' 51".

Transmitter: Atop Browning water tower.

Ownership: Browning Public Schools.

Brusett, etc.—K06EB, Ch. 6, Garfield TV Club. Phone: 406-557-6200.

Technical Facilities: 0.18-kw ERP, 3383-ft. above sea level, lat. 47° 24' 40", long. 107° 25' 50".

Ownership: Garfield TV Club.

Bull Lake Valley—K09KE, Ch. 9, Lake Creek TV District. Phone: 406-295-4266.

Technical Facilities: 0.077-kw ERP, 5604-ft. above sea level, lat. 48° 31' 02", long. 115° 47' 56".

Ownership: Lake Creek TV District.

Bull Lake Valley—K11KP, Ch. 11, Lake Creek TV District. Phone: 406-295-4266.

Technical Facilities: 0.077-kw ERP, lat. 48° 31' 02", long. 115° 47' 56".

Ownership: Lake Creek TV District.

Bull Lake Valley—K13KV, Ch. 13, Lake Creek TV District. Phone: 406-295-4266.

Technical Facilities: 0.077-kw ERP, lat. 48° 31' 02", long. 115° 47' 56".

Ownership: Lake Creek TV District.

Butte—K22HD, Ch. 22, Marcia T. Turner. Phone: 954-732-9539.

Technical Facilities: 113-kw ERP, 52-ft. above ground, 8783-ft. above sea level, lat. 46° 20' 17", long. 112° 17' 30".

Ownership: Marcia T. Turner.

Butte—K34II, Ch. 34, EICB-TV East LLC. Phone: 972-291-3750.

Technical Facilities: 1.8-kw ERP, 39-ft. above ground, 5502-ft. above sea level, lat. 45° 59' 23", long. 112° 32' 07".

Holds CP for change to 2-kw ERP, 118-ft. above ground, 6329-ft. above sea level, lat. 46° 01' 41", long. 112° 32' 04". BPTTL-20090203ADB.

Began Operation: August 18, 2008.

Ownership: EICB-TV LLC.

Butte—K43DU, Ch. 43, Montana State U. Phone: 406-994-3437.

Technical Facilities: 13.5-kw ERP, 50-ft. above ground, 8304-ft. above sea level, lat. 46° 00' 29", long. 112° 26' 30".

Holds CP for change to 4.55-kw ERP, BDFCDTT-20061207ACA.

Ownership: Montana U. System Board of Regents.

Castle Rock, etc.—K64EM, Ch. 64, KTVQ Communications Inc. Phone: 406-252-5611.

Technical Facilities: 22.7-kw ERP, 86-ft. above ground, 4790-ft. above sea level, lat. 45° 50' 27", long. 106° 54' 39".

Holds CP for change to channel number 29, BDISTTL-20060331BMD.

Ownership: KTVQ Communications Inc.

Checkerboard—K11CC, Ch. 11, Checkerboard TV District. Phone: 406-547-2190.

Technical Facilities: 0.014-kw ERP, lat. 46° 35' 20", long. 110° 32' 30".

Ownership: Checkerboard TV District.

Checkerboard, etc.—K07KD, Ch. 7, Checkerboard TV District. Phone: 406-547-2190.

Technical Facilities: 0.014-kw ERP, 5709-ft. above sea level, lat. 46° 35' 20", long. 110° 32' 30".

Ownership: Checkerboard TV District.

Checkerboard, etc.—K09WP, Ch. 9, Checkerboard TV District. Phone: 406-547-2190.

Technical Facilities: 0.065-kw ERP, 13-ft. above ground, 5784-ft. above sea level, lat. 46° 35' 20", long. 110° 32' 30".

Transmitter: Hwy. 12, 13.5-mi. NW of Martinsdale.

Ownership: Checkerboard TV District.

Chinook—K61BK, Ch. 61, Chinook TV Association Inc. Phone: 406-357-3212.

Technical Facilities: 1.21-kw ERP, 3005-ft. above sea level, lat. 48° 28' 13", long. 109° 16' 05".

Ownership: Chinook TV Association Inc.

Chinook—K63AR, Ch. 63, Chinook TV Association Inc. Phone: 406-357-3212.

Technical Facilities: 1.21-kw ERP, 3005-ft. above sea level, lat. 48° 28' 13", long. 109° 16' 05".

Ownership: Chinook TV Association Inc.

Chinook—K65BR, Ch. 65, Chinook TV Association Inc. Phone: 406-357-3212.

Technical Facilities: 1.21-kw ERP, 2297-ft. above sea level, lat. 48° 28' 13", long. 109° 16' 05".

Ownership: Chinook TV Association Inc.

Circle—K13BC, Ch. 13, Circle TV Booster Club Inc. Phone: 406-485-2196.

Technical Facilities: 0.12-kw ERP, lat. 47° 17' 00", long. 105° 24' 55".

Ownership: Circle TV Booster Club Inc.

Circle—K14AG, Ch. 14, Circle TV Booster Club Inc. Phone: 406-485-2196.

Technical Facilities: 0.341-kw ERP, 1069-ft. above sea level, lat. 47° 16' 60", long. 105° 24' 55".

Ownership: Circle TV Booster Club Inc.

Circle—K16GP, Ch. 16, Circle TV Booster Club Inc. Phone: 406-485-2986.

Technical Facilities: 0.84-kw ERP, 69-ft. above ground, 3533-ft. above sea level, lat. 47° 16' 04", long. 105° 23' 26".

Ownership: Circle TV Booster Club Inc.

Circle, etc.—K06KY, Ch. 6, Circle TV Booster Club Inc. Phone: 406-485-2196.

Technical Facilities: 0.98-kw ERP, 3510-ft. above sea level, lat. 47° 17' 00", long. 105° 24' 55".

Ownership: Circle TV Booster Club Inc.

Circle, etc.—K10AT, Ch. 10, Circle TV Booster Club Inc. Phone: 406-485-2196.

Technical Facilities: 0.095-kw ERP, 3510-ft. above sea level, lat. 47° 17' 00", long. 105° 24' 55".

Ownership: Circle TV Booster Club Inc.

Circle, etc.—K18CR, Ch. 18, Circle TV Booster Club Inc. Phone: 406-485-2196.

Technical Facilities: 1.12-kw ERP, 59-ft. above ground, 3527-ft. above sea level, lat. 47° 17' 00", long. 105° 24' 55".

Ownership: Circle TV Booster Club Inc.

Clancy—K36CX, Ch. 36, Boulder TV Assn. Phones: 406-225-3820; 406-225-3376.

Technical Facilities: 100-w TPO, 0.609-kw ERP, 56-ft. above ground, 5527-ft. above sea level, lat. 46° 30' 37", long. 111° 55' 55".

Transmitter: 4-mi. NE of Clancy.

Ownership: Boulder TV Assn.

Clyde Park, etc.—K44DI, Ch. 44, Shields Valley TV Tax District. Phone: 406-248-9043.

Technical Facilities: 1.73-kw ERP, 49-ft. above ground, 6548-ft. above sea level, lat. 45° 35' 52", long. 110° 32' 45".

Ownership: Shields Valley TV Tax District.

Colstrip—K07WJ, Ch. 7, Colstrip TV Tax District.

Technical Facilities: 10-w TPO, 0.106-kw ERP, 69-ft. above ground, 3369-ft. above sea level, lat. 45° 53' 42", long. 106° 37' 39".

Transmitter: Rural area, near Colstrip.

Ownership: Colstrip TV Tax District.

Colstrip—K09OY, Ch. 9, Colstrip TV Tax District. Phone: 406-346-2251.

Technical Facilities: 0.123-kw ERP, lat. 45° 53' 42", long. 106° 37' 39".

Ownership: Colstrip TV Tax District.

Colstrip—K13PV, Ch. 13, Colstrip TV Tax District. Phone: 406-346-2251.

Technical Facilities: 0.005-kw ERP, lat. 45° 53' 42", long. 106° 37' 39".

Ownership: Colstrip TV Tax District.

Colstrip, etc.—K58IH, Ch. 58, Nexstar Broadcasting Inc. Phone: 972-373-8800.

Technical Facilities: 31.9-kw ERP, 35-ft. above ground, 4819-ft. above sea level, lat. 45° 50' 20", long. 106° 54' 17".

Holds CP for change to channel number 35, 0.15-kw ERP, BDISDTT-20060403AFL.

Ownership: Nexstar Broadcasting Group Inc.

Colstrip, etc.—K61BL, Ch. 61, Colstrip TV Tax District. Phone: 406-346-2251.

Technical Facilities: 3.54-kw ERP, lat. 45° 50' 16", long. 106° 53' 47".

Ownership: Colstrip TV Tax District.

Colstrip, etc.—K66EQ, Ch. 66, Nexstar Finance Inc. Phone: 972-373-8800.

Technical Facilities: 100-w TPO, 1.722-kw ERP, 95-ft. above ground, 4879-ft. above sea level, lat. 45° 50' 20", long. 106° 54' 17".

Holds CP for change to channel number 32, 0.005-kw ERP, BDISDTT-20060403AFS.

Transmitter: 14-mi. SW of Colstrip, near Sarpy.

Ownership: Nexstar Broadcasting Group Inc.

Personnel: Dale Woods, General Manager.

Columbus—K24FL, Ch. 24, MMM License II LLC. Phone: 757-437-9800.

Technical Facilities: 0.606-kw ERP, 29-ft. above ground, 3651-ft. above sea level, lat. 45° 37' 36.2", long. 109° 15' 36.4".

Holds CP for change to 5-kw ERP, BDFCDTT-20060331BOC.

Began Operation: September 30, 2004.

Ownership: Max Media X LLC.

Columbus—K26GL, Ch. 26, KTVQ Communications Inc.

Technical Facilities: 0.635-kw ERP, 29-ft. above ground, 3651-ft. above sea level, lat. 45° 37' 36.2", long. 109° 15' 36.4".

Ownership: KTVQ Communications Inc.

Columbus—K33EA, Ch. 33, Nexstar Broadcasting Inc. Phone: 972-373-8800.

Technical Facilities: 3.8-kw ERP, 16-ft. above ground, 4111-ft. above sea level, lat. 45° 38' 37", long. 109° 17' 43".

Holds CP for change to 0.018-kw ERP, BDFCDTT-20060403AKP.

Ownership: Nexstar Broadcasting Group Inc.

Condon—K07GM, Ch. 7, Summit TV Improvement Assn.

Technical Facilities: 0.047-kw ERP, lat. 47° 23' 20", long. 113° 37' 40".

Ownership: Summit TV Improvement Association.

Conrad—K06IL, Ch. 6, Conrad TV District. Phone: 406-271-4040.

Technical Facilities: 0.013-kw ERP, lat. 48° 11' 22", long. 112° 03' 30".

Ownership: Conrad TV District.

Conrad—K08DT, Ch. 8, Conrad TV District. Phone: 406-271-4040.

Technical Facilities: 0.132-kw ERP, lat. 48° 11' 22", long. 112° 03' 30".

Ownership: Conrad TV District.

Conrad—K10DX, Ch. 10, Conrad TV District. Phone: 406-271-4040.

Technical Facilities: 0.132-kw ERP, lat. 48° 11' 22", long. 112° 03' 30".

Ownership: Conrad TV District.

Conrad—K12DJ, Ch. 12, Conrad TV District. Phone: 406-271-4040.

Technical Facilities: 0.01-kw ERP, lat. 48° 11' 22", long. 112° 03' 30".

Ownership: Conrad TV District.

Cooke City, etc.—K11GE, Ch. 11, Shoo Fly TV Translator Station Assocaition. Phone: 406-838-2166.

Technical Facilities: 0.019-kw ERP, lat. 45° 01' 30", long. 109° 54' 10".

Ownership: Shoo Fly TV Translator Station Association.

Cooke City, etc.—K13FW, Ch. 13, Shoo Fly TV Translator Station Assn. Phone: 406-838-2166.

Technical Facilities: 0.019-kw ERP, lat. 45° 01' 30", long. 109° 54' 10".

Ownership: Shoo Fly TV Translator Station Association.

Culbertson—K34GY, Ch. 34, Town of Culbertson. Phone: 406-787-5271.

Technical Facilities: 0.99-kw ERP, 89-ft. above ground, 2457-ft. above sea level, lat. 48° 12' 00", long. 104° 31' 54".

Ownership: Town of Culbertson.

Darby—K21AN, Ch. 21, Bitterroot Valley Public TV Inc. Phone: 406-961-3692.

Technical Facilities: 0.931-kw ERP, 49-ft. above ground, 4202-ft. above sea level, lat. 46° 05' 03", long. 114° 11' 14".

Ownership: Bitterroot Valley Public TV Inc.

Denton—K10HB, Ch. 10, Denton TV Association.

Technical Facilities: 0.009-kw ERP, lat. 47° 20' 18", long. 109° 55' 30".

Ownership: Denton TV Association.

Denton—K12HP, Ch. 12, Denton TV Association.

Technical Facilities: 0.009-kw ERP, lat. 47° 20' 18", long. 109° 55' 30".

Ownership: Denton TV Association.

Ownership: Nexstar Broadcasting Group Inc.

Dillon—K51DW, Ch. 51, BlueStone License Holdings Inc. Phone: 212-247-8717.

Technical Facilities: 0.101-kw ERP, 26-ft. above ground, 5882-ft. above sea level, lat. 45° 14' 21", long. 112° 40' 05".

Ownership: Bonten Media Group LLC.

Dodson—K36CW, Ch. 36, Phillips County TV Translator District. Phone: 406-383-4499.

Technical Facilities: 1.3-kw ERP, 26-ft. above ground, 2329-ft. above sea level, lat. 48° 24' 30", long. 108° 09' 15".

Ownership: Phillips County TV Translator District.

Dodson & Wagner—K08FS, Ch. 8, Phillips County TV Translator District. Phone: 406-383-4499.

Technical Facilities: 0.001-kw ERP, 2346-ft. above sea level, lat. 48° 23' 30", long. 108° 10' 00".

Ownership: Phillips County TV Translator District.

Dodson & Wagner—K10FC, Ch. 10, Phillips County TV Translator District. Phone: 406-383-4499.

Technical Facilities: 0.002-kw ERP, 2346-ft. above sea level, lat. 48° 23' 30", long. 108° 10' 00".

Ownership: Phillips County TV Translator District.

Dodson & Wagner—K12GP, Ch. 12, Phillips County TV Translator District. Phone: 406-383-4499.

Technical Facilities: 0.002-kw ERP, 2336-ft. above sea level, lat. 48° 23' 30", long. 108° 10' 00".

Ownership: Phillips County TV Translator District.

East Glacier—K08IU, Ch. 8, East Glacier TV Assn.

Technical Facilities: 0.015-kw ERP, lat. 48° 29' 30", long. 113° 12' 10".

Ownership: East Glacier TV Association.

East Glacier Park—K10MK, Ch. 10, East Glacier TV Assn.

Technical Facilities: 0.015-kw ERP, 5371-ft. above sea level, lat. 48° 29' 30", long. 113° 12' 10".

Ownership: East Glacier TV Association.

East Glacier Park—K13EJ, Ch. 13, East Glacier TV Assn.

Technical Facilities: 0.018-kw ERP, lat. 48° 29' 30", long. 113° 12' 10".

Ownership: East Glacier TV Association.

Ekalaka—K07EQ, Ch. 7, Ekalaka Community TV Club. Phone: 406-775-6618.

Technical Facilities: 0.004-kw ERP, lat. 45° 54' 03", long. 104° 32' 57".

Ownership: Ekalaka Community TV Club.

Ekalaka—K09BE, Ch. 9, Ekalaka Community TV Club. Phone: 406-775-6618.

Technical Facilities: 0.007-kw ERP, lat. 45° 54' 03", long. 104° 32' 57".

Ownership: Ekalaka Community TV Club.

Ekalaka—K13LN, Ch. 13, Ekalaka Community TV Club. Phone: 406-775-6618.

Technical Facilities: 0.01-kw ERP, lat. 45° 54' 03", long. 104° 32' 57".

Ownership: Ekalaka Community TV Club.

Ekalaka—K23DJ, Ch. 23, Plevna Public School Trustees District No. 55. Phone: 406-772-5601. Fax: 406-772-5548.

Technical Facilities: 100-w TPO, 1.294-kw ERP, 3742-ft. above sea level, lat. 45° 54' 05", long. 104° 33' 00".

Transmitter: NW of Carter County Courthouse.

Ownership: Plevna Public School Trustees District No. 55.

Elmo—K20CP, Ch. 20, Salish Kootenai College.

Technical Facilities: 1.14-kw ERP, lat. 47° 46' 25", long. 114° 16' 04".

Ownership: Salish Kootenai College.

Emigrant—K03HF, Ch. 3, Paradise Valley TV District. Phone: 406-222-3146.

Technical Facilities: 0.139-kw ERP, lat. 45° 20' 07", long. 110° 41' 21".

Ownership: Paradise Valley TV District.

Emigrant—K19CO, Ch. 19, Paradise Valley TV Association. Phone: 406-222-3146.

Technical Facilities: 10-w TPO, 0.374-kw ERP, 16-ft. above ground, 5656-ft. above sea level, lat. 45° 20' 07", long. 110° 41' 22".

Transmitter: 4-mi. SE of Emigrant.

Ownership: Paradise Valley TV District.

Emigrant—K27DL, Ch. 27, Paradise Valley TV Association. Phone: 406-222-3146.

Technical Facilities: 10-w TPO, 0.374-kw ERP, 16-ft. above ground, 5656-ft. above sea level, lat. 45° 20' 07", long. 110° 41' 22".

Transmitter: 4-mi. SE of Emigrant.

Ownership: Paradise Valley TV District.

Emigrant, etc.—K05EH, Ch. 5, Paradise Valley TV District. Phone: 406-222-3146.

Technical Facilities: 0.126-kw ERP, lat. 45° 34' 25", long. 110° 32' 40".

Ownership: Paradise Valley TV District.

Emigrant, etc.—K10AH, Ch. 10, Paradise Valley TV District. Phone: 406-222-3146.

Technical Facilities: 0.139-kw ERP, lat. 45° 20' 07", long. 110° 41' 22".

Ownership: Paradise Valley TV District.

Emigrant, etc.—K57CE, Ch. 57, Paradise Valley TV District. Phone: 406-222-3146.

Technical Facilities: 4.46-kw ERP, 30-ft. above ground, 5430-ft. above sea level, lat. 45° 20' 07", long. 110° 41' 22".

Ownership: Paradise Valley TV District.

Eureka, etc.—K02AO, Ch. 2, BlueStone License Holdings Inc. Phone: 212-247-8717.

Technical Facilities: 0.061-kw ERP, 30-ft. above ground, 4094-ft. above sea level, lat. 48° 51' 53", long. 115° 07' 27".

Ownership: Bonten Media Group LLC.

Ferndale, etc.—K12LO, Ch. 12, Swan Hill TV Inc. Phone: 406-837-2922.

Technical Facilities: 0.017-kw ERP, lat. 48° 04' 03", long. 114° 01' 10".

Holds CP for change to 0.008-kw ERP, 108-ft. above ground, 3819-ft. above sea level, lat. 48° 04' 04.5", long. 114° 02' 15.9". BDFCDTV-20080902ADU.

Ownership: Swan Hill TV Inc.

Ferndale, etc.—K24ID-D, Ch. 24, Swan Hill TV District. Phone: 406-837-2922.

Technical Facilities: 0.108-kw ERP, 106-ft. above ground, 3814-ft. above sea level, lat. 48° 04' 04.5", long. 114° 02' 15.9".

Began Operation: June 16, 1982.

Ownership: Swan Hill TV Inc.

Florence—K29CV, Ch. 29, Bitterroot Valley Public TV Inc. Phone: 406-961-3692.

Technical Facilities: 0.579-kw ERP, 82-ft. above ground, 3786-ft. above sea level, lat. 46° 37' 04", long. 114° 06' 47".

Ownership: Bitterroot Valley Public TV Inc.

Forsyth—K07LO, Ch. 7, Forsyth Community TV Relay System Inc. Phone: 406-346-2251.

Technical Facilities: 0.001-kw ERP, lat. 46° 15' 36", long. 106° 40' 15".

Ownership: Forsyth Community TV Relay System.

Forsyth—K09BW, Ch. 9, Forsyth Community TV Relay System Inc. Phone: 406-346-2251.

Technical Facilities: 0.001-kw ERP, lat. 46° 15' 36", long. 106° 40' 15".

Ownership: Forsyth Community TV Relay System.

Forsyth—K11CB, Ch. 11, Forsyth Community TV Relay System Inc. Phone: 406-346-2251.

Technical Facilities: 0.001-kw ERP, lat. 46° 15' 36", long. 106° 40' 15".

Ownership: Forsyth Community TV Relay System.

Forsyth—K12LR, Ch. 12, Forsyth T.V. Tax District. Phone: 406-346-2251.

Technical Facilities: 0.18-kw ERP, 3084-ft. above sea level, lat. 46° 19' 38", long. 106° 41' 49".

Ownership: Forsyth Community TV Relay System.

Forsyth, etc.—K04FF, Ch. 4, Forsyth Community TV Relay System Inc. Phone: 406-346-2251.

Technical Facilities: 0.048-kw ERP, lat. 46° 19' 38", long. 106° 41' 49".

Ownership: Forsyth Community TV Relay System.

Fort Peck—K51BA, Ch. 51, Valley County TV District No. 1. Phone: 406-367-9353.

Technical Facilities: 1.38-kw ERP, lat. 48° 01' 49", long. 106° 17' 48".

Ownership: Valley County TV District No. 1.

Four Buttes, etc.—K60BN, Ch. 60, Klear Vu Television District. Phone: 406-487-5485.

Technical Facilities: 0.6-kw ERP, 2126-ft. above sea level, lat. 48° 36' 02", long. 105° 17' 44".

Ownership: Klear Vu Television District.

Frenchtown—K14IU, Ch. 14, BlueStone License Holdings Inc. Phone: 212-247-8717.

Technical Facilities: 20-w TPO, 0.234-kw ERP, 276-ft. above ground, 5827-ft. above sea level, lat. 46° 51' 12", long. 113° 55' 41".

Transmitter: University Mountain, E of Missoula.

Ownership: Bonten Media Group LLC.

Personnel: Keith Sommer, General Manager; Charlie Cannaliato, Chief Engineer.

Gallatin River, etc.—K07LE, Ch. 7, Big Sky Owners Assn. Inc. Phone: 406-995-4166.

Technical Facilities: 0.045-kw ERP, lat. 45° 16' 27", long. 111° 23' 36".

Ownership: Big Sky Owners Assn. Inc.

Gallatin River, etc.—K09LP, Ch. 9, Big Sky Owners Assn. Inc. Phone: 406-995-4166.

Technical Facilities: 0.045-kw ERP, lat. 45° 16' 27", long. 111° 23' 36".

Ownership: Big Sky Owners Assn. Inc.

Glasgow—K14AR, Ch. 14, Valley County TV District No. 1. Phone: 406-367-9353.

Technical Facilities: 1.38-kw ERP, lat. 48° 12' 18", long. 106° 38' 00".

Transmitter: Northern section of Glasgow city limits.

Ownership: Valley County TV District No. 1.

Glasgow—K16AZ, Ch. 16, Valley County TV District No. 1. Phone: 406-367-9353.

Technical Facilities: 100-w TPO, 0.88-kw ERP, 148-ft. above ground, 2234-ft. above sea level, lat. 48° 12' 18", long. 106° 38' 00".

Transmitter: Northern section of Glasgow city limits.

Ownership: Valley County TV District No. 1.

Glasgow—K18BN, Ch. 18, Valley County TV District No. 1. Phone: 406-367-9353.

Technical Facilities: 100-w TPO, 0.86-kw ERP, 144-ft. above ground, 2185-ft. above sea level, lat. 48° 12' 18", long. 106° 38' 00".

Transmitter: Northern section of Glasgow city limits.

Ownership: Valley County TV District No. 1.

Glasgow—K39GF, Ch. 39, Valley County TV District No. 1. Phone: 406-367-9353.

Technical Facilities: 1.02-kw ERP, 56-ft. above ground, 2684-ft. above sea level, lat. 48° 01' 44", long. 106° 19' 06".

Ownership: Valley County TV District No. 1.

Glasgow—K45CH, Ch. 45, Valley County TV District No. 1. Phone: 406-367-9353.

Technical Facilities: 1.38-kw ERP, 39-ft. above ground, 2792-ft. above sea level, lat. 48° 01' 49", long. 106° 17' 48".

Ownership: Valley County TV District No. 1.

Glasgow, etc.—K07JG, Ch. 7, Valley County Television District No. 1. Phone: 406-367-9353.

Technical Facilities: 0.12-kw ERP, 2349-ft. above sea level, lat. 48° 12' 18", long. 106° 38' 00".

Ownership: Valley County TV District No. 1.

Glendive—K13PL, Ch. 13, Hoak Media of Dakota License LLC. Phone: 972-960-4896.

Technical Facilities: 2.36-kw ERP, lat. 47° 11' 39", long. 104° 38' 37".

Ownership: Hoak Media LLC.

Grasshopper Valley, etc.—K09MY, Ch. 9, Grasshopper TV Association.

Technical Facilities: 0.007-kw ERP, 8441-ft. above sea level, lat. 45° 26' 00", long. 113° 09' 00".

Ownership: Grasshopper TV Association.

Grasshopper, etc.—K07OC, Ch. 7, Grasshopper TV Association.

Technical Facilities: 0.007-kw ERP, 8448-ft. above sea level, lat. 45° 26' 00", long. 113° 09' 00".

Ownership: Grasshopper TV Association.

Great Falls—K31IA, Ch. 31, Trinity Broadcasting Network Inc. Phone: 714-832-2950. Fax: 714-730-0661.

Technical Facilities: 9.6-kw ERP, 279-ft. above ground, 3848-ft. above sea level, lat. 47° 31' 57", long. 111° 16' 38".

Ownership: Trinity Broadcasting Network Inc.

Personnel: Paul F. Crouch, General Manager; Rod Henke, Sales Manager; Ben Miller, Chief Engineer.

Great Falls—K33HN, Ch. 33, Marcia T. Turner. Phone: 954-732-9539.

Technical Facilities: 3-kw ERP, 328-ft. above ground, 4997-ft. above sea level, lat. 47° 22' 10", long. 112° 04' 28".

Ownership: Marcia T. Turner.

Great Falls—KBGF-LP, Ch. 50, Beartooth Communications Co. Phones: 406-771-1666; 702-642-3333.

Technical Facilities: 50-kw ERP, 320-ft. above ground, 3830-ft. above sea level, lat. 47° 32' 19", long. 111° 15' 41".

Ownership: Sunbelt Communications Co.

Hardin—K16DZ, Ch. 16, Nexstar Finance Inc. Phone: 972-373-8800.

Technical Facilities: 0.922-kw ERP, lat. 45° 44' 40", long. 107° 32' 08".

Transmitter: 0.3-mi. WNW of Hardin.

Ownership: Nexstar Broadcasting Group Inc.

Hardin—K24GD, Ch. 24, KTVQ Communications Inc. Phone: 406-252-5611.

Technical Facilities: 1.34-kw ERP, 56-ft. above ground, 3333-ft. above sea level, lat. 45° 44' 39", long. 107° 32' 08".

Ownership: KTVQ Communications Inc.

Harlowton—K10AX, Ch. 10, Harlowton TV Association.

Technical Facilities: 0.025-kw ERP, lat. 46° 19' 52", long. 109° 43' 30".

Ownership: Harlowton TV Association.

Harlowton—K13BE, Ch. 13, Harlowton TV Association.

Technical Facilities: 0.025-kw ERP, lat. 46° 19' 52", long. 109° 43' 30".

Ownership: Harlowton TV Association.

Harlowton, etc.—K57FR, Ch. 57, Marlo TV Association.

Technical Facilities: 1.28-kw ERP, 49-ft. above ground, 6476-ft. above sea level, lat. 46° 21' 05", long. 110° 08' 35".

Ownership: Marlo TV Association.

Harlowton, etc.—K59CE, Ch. 59, Marlo TV Association.

Technical Facilities: 1.28-kw ERP, 6476-ft. above sea level, lat. 46° 21' 05", long. 110° 08' 35".

Ownership: Marlo TV Association.

Harlowton, etc.—K61CE, Ch. 61, Marlo TV Association.

Technical Facilities: 1.35-kw ERP, 6476-ft. above sea level, lat. 46° 21' 05", long. 110° 08' 35".

Ownership: Marlo TV Association.

Helena—K41CX, Ch. 41, Trinity Broadcasting Network Inc. Phone: 714-832-2950. Fax: 714-730-0661.

Technical Facilities: 9.8-kw ERP, 100-ft. above ground, 4982-ft. above sea level, lat. 46° 46' 07", long. 112° 01' 21".

Ownership: Trinity Broadcasting Network Inc.

Personnel: Paul Crouch, General Manager; Ben Miller, Chief Engineer; Rod Henke, Sales Manager.

Helena—K44GE, Ch. 44, Wireless Access LLC. Phone: 914-586-3311.

Technical Facilities: 0.211-kw ERP, 43-ft. above ground, 4003-ft. above sea level, lat. 46° 35' 37", long. 111° 59' 05".

Ownership: Wireless Access LLC.

Helena—K49EH, Ch. 49, Montana State U. Phone: 406-994-3437.

Technical Facilities: 12.7-kw ERP, lat. 46° 46' 11", long. 112° 01' 25".

Holds CP for change to 3.1-kw ERP, 30-ft. above ground, 4984-ft. above sea level, BDFCDTT-20061207ABY.

Transmitter: North Ridge Electronic Site, 12-mi. N of Helena.

Ownership: Montana U. System Board of Regents.

Helena—KHBB-LD, Ch. 21, MMM License II LLC. Phone: 757-437-9800.

Technical Facilities: 5-kw ERP, 98-ft. above ground, 5020-ft. above sea level, lat. 46° 46' 12", long. 112° 01' 22".

Ownership: Max Media X LLC.

Helena—KJJC-LP, Ch. 34, Western Family Television Inc. Phone: 406-442-2655.

Technical Facilities: 10-kw ERP, 98-ft. above ground, 5102-ft. above sea level, lat. 46° 46' 11", long. 112° 01' 25".

Ownership: Western Family Television Inc.

Helena—KXLH-LP, Ch. 25, KXLF Communications Inc.

Technical Facilities: 10.4-kw ERP, 66-ft. above ground, 5020-ft. above sea level, lat. 46° 46' 12", long. 112° 01' 22".

Ownership: Evening Post Publishing Co.

Hinsdale—K05IZ, Ch. 5, Hinsdale TV Club. Phone: 406-364-2271.

Technical Facilities: 0.028-kw ERP, 36-ft. above ground, 2464-ft. above sea level, lat. 48° 21' 54", long. 106° 58' 30".

Ownership: Hinsdale TV Club.

Hinsdale—K10JK, Ch. 10, Hinsdale TV Club. Phone: 406-364-2271.

Technical Facilities: 0.224-kw ERP, 2464-ft. above sea level, lat. 48° 21' 54", long. 106° 58' 30".

Ownership: Hinsdale TV Club.

Hinsdale—K42FP, Ch. 42, Hinsdale TV District.

Technical Facilities: 0.891-kw ERP, 36-ft. above ground, 2484-ft. above sea level, lat. 48° 21' 56", long. 106° 58' 46".

Ownership: Hinsdale TV District.

Hinsdale & rural area (north)—K13JO, Ch. 13, Hinsdale TV Club. Phone: 406-364-2271.

Technical Facilities: 0.022-kw ERP, lat. 48° 21' 54", long. 106° 58' 30".

Ownership: Hinsdale TV Club.

Horse Ranch & Roy—K09CB, Ch. 9, Roy TV Tax District. Phone: 406-464-5471.

Technical Facilities: 0.007-kw ERP, 4104-ft. above sea level, lat. 47° 20' 36", long. 109° 07' 40".

Ownership: Roy TV Tax District.

Hot Springs—K05AH, Ch. 5, Hot Springs TV District. Phone: 406-741-2353.

Technical Facilities: 0.034-kw ERP, 3146-ft. above sea level, lat. 47° 37' 17", long. 114° 38' 44".

Ownership: Hot Springs TV District.

Hot Springs—K45DQ, Ch. 45, Hot Springs TV District. Phone: 406-741-2353.

Technical Facilities: 0.131-kw ERP, 23-ft. above ground, 3734-ft. above sea level, lat. 47° 37' 56", long. 114° 39' 50".

Ownership: Hot Springs TV District.

Howard—K06JU, Ch. 6, Forsyth TV Tax District. Phone: 406-346-2251.

Technical Facilities: 0.18-kw ERP, lat. 46° 19' 50", long. 106° 59' 35".

Ownership: Forsyth TV Tax District.

Howard—K10AJ, Ch. 10, Howard TV Club. Phone: 406-346-2251.

Technical Facilities: 0.008-kw ERP, 3100-ft. above sea level, lat. 46° 19' 50", long. 106° 59' 35".

Ownership: Howard TV Club.

Howard—K44DM, Ch. 44, Forsyth TV District. Phone: 406-346-2251.

Technical Facilities: 1.38-kw ERP, 26-ft. above ground, 2900-ft. above sea level, lat. 46° 14' 26", long. 106° 59' 35".

Ownership: Forsyth TV District.

Hysham—K11OS, Ch. 11, Treasure County T.V. District. Phone: 406-342-5218.

Technical Facilities: 0.12-kw ERP, lat. 46° 14' 20", long. 107° 22' 00".

Holds CP for change to channel number 8, 0.021-kw ERP, 33-ft. above ground, 3287-ft. above sea level, lat. 46° 14' 26", long. 107° 19' 34". BDISDTV-20090212ADJ.

Ownership: Treasure County T.V. District.

Hysham—K13PO, Ch. 13, Treasure County TV District. Phone: 406-342-5218.

Technical Facilities: 0.123-kw ERP, lat. 46° 14' 20", long. 107° 22' 00".

Holds CP for change to 0.021-kw ERP, 33-ft. above ground, 3287-ft. above sea level, lat. 46° 14' 26", long. 107° 19' 34". BDFCDTV-20090212ADG.

Began Operation: December 10, 1979.

Ownership: Treasure County T.V. District.

Joplin—K48AI, Ch. 48, KRTV Communications Inc.

Technical Facilities: 8.36-kw ERP, lat. 48° 51' 17", long. 111° 08' 27".

Ownership: Evening Post Publishing Co.

Joplin—K54AM-K51KO, Ch. 51, East Butte TV Club Inc. Phone: 406-434-2207.

Technical Facilities: 11.7-kw ERP, 15-ft. above ground, 6986-ft. above sea level, lat. 48° 51' 30", long. 111° 06' 28".

Ownership: East Butte TV Club Inc.

Jordan—K13YD, Ch. 13, Garfield TV Club. Phone: 406-827-3981.

Technical Facilities: 0.18-kw ERP, 33-ft. above ground, 3084-ft. above sea level, lat. 47° 19' 55", long. 107° 04' 56".

Ownership: Garfield TV Club.

Jordan, etc.—K07VA, Ch. 7, Garfield TV Club. Phone: 406-557-6200.

Technical Facilities: 0.122-kw ERP, 30-ft. above ground, 3081-ft. above sea level, lat. 47° 20' 00", long. 107° 05' 00".

Ownership: Garfield TV Club.

Jordan, etc.—K09HI, Ch. 9, Garfield TV Club. Phone: 406-557-6200.

Technical Facilities: 0.016-kw ERP, lat. 47° 20' 00", long. 107° 05' 00".

Ownership: Garfield TV Club.

Jordan, etc.—K11HE, Ch. 11, Garfield TV Club. Phone: 406-557-6200.

Technical Facilities: 0.022-kw ERP, lat. 47° 20' 00", long. 107° 05' 00".

Ownership: Garfield TV Club.

Kalispell—K15GP, Ch. 15, Blacktail TV Tax District. Phone: 406-883-2975.

Technical Facilities: 1.32-kw ERP, 30-ft. above ground, 6788-ft. above sea level, lat. 48° 00' 40", long. 114° 21' 48".

Holds CP for change to 0.275-kw ERP, BDFCDTT-20070706ADQ.

Ownership: Blacktail TV Tax District.

■ **Kalispell**—K18AJ, Ch. 18, KPAX Communications Inc. Phones: 406-542-4400; 406-756-5888. Fax: 406-543-7111.

Technical Facilities: 1000-w TPO, 45.8-kw ERP, 92-ft. above ground, 3799-ft. above sea level, lat. 48° 09' 58", long. 114° 19' 51".

Transmitter: 3-mi. SW of Kalispell, near Lone Pine State Park.

Multichannel TV Sound: Stereo only.

Ownership: Evening Post Publishing Co.

Personnel: Robert J. Hermes, General Manager; Larry Arbaugh, Chief Engineer.

Kalispell—K19GD, Ch. 19, Blacktail TV Tax District. Phone: 406-883-2975.

Technical Facilities: 0.906-kw ERP, 18-ft. above ground, 6616-ft. above sea level, lat. 48° 00' 38", long. 114° 21' 46".

Holds CP for change to 0.275-kw ERP, 30-ft. above ground, 6788-ft. above sea level, BDFCDTT-20070706ADP.

Ownership: Blacktail TV Tax District.

Kalispell—K26DD, Ch. 26, Trinity Broadcasting Network Inc. Phone: 714-832-2950. Fax: 714-730-0661.

Technical Facilities: 1000-w TPO, 11.8-kw ERP, 118-ft. above ground, 3842-ft. above sea level, lat. 48° 10' 34", long. 114° 20' 53".

Holds CP for change to 15-kw ERP, BDFCDTT-20060313AES.

Transmitter: Atop Lone Pine Mountain.

Began Operation: June 19, 1991.

Ownership: Trinity Broadcasting Network Inc.

Personnel: Paul F. Crouch, General Manager; Rod Henke, Sales Manager; Ben Miller, Chief Engineer.

Kalispell—K51HT, Ch. 51, Blacktail TV Tax District. Phone: 406-883-2975.

Technical Facilities: 1.32-kw ERP, 30-ft. above ground, 6788-ft. above sea level, lat. 48° 00' 40", long. 114° 21' 48".

Holds CP for change to 0.27-kw ERP, 33-ft. above ground, 6792-ft. above sea level, BDFCDTT-20070619AAC.

Ownership: Blacktail TV Tax District.

Kalispell—KTMF-LP, Ch. 42, MMM License LLC. Phone: 757-437-9800.

Technical Facilities: 8.4-kw ERP, 108-ft. above ground, 3832-ft. above sea level, lat. 48° 10' 34", long. 114° 20' 53".

Began Operation: June 8, 1995.

Ownership: Max Media X LLC.

Personnel: Phillip H. Hurley, General Manager; Moe Strout, Chief Engineer; Joe Elliot, Sales Manager.

King Springs, etc.—K09HY, Ch. 9, Valley County Television District No. 1. Phone: 406-367-9353.

Technical Facilities: 0.18-kw ERP, lat. 48° 12' 18", long. 106° 38' 00".

Ownership: Valley County TV District No. 1.

King Springs, etc.—K11IA, Ch. 11, Valley County Television District No. 1. Phone: 406-367-9353.

Technical Facilities: 0.015-kw ERP, lat. 48° 12' 18", long. 106° 38' 00".

Ownership: Valley County TV District No. 1.

King Springs, etc.—K13IB, Ch. 13, Valley County Television District No. 1. Phone: 406-367-9353.

Technical Facilities: 0.012-kw ERP, lat. 48° 12' 18", long. 106° 38' 00".

Ownership: Valley County TV District No. 1.

Lake McDonald, etc.—K05FC, Ch. 5, Desert Mountain TV. Phone: 406-387-5230.

Technical Facilities: 0.01-kw ERP, lat. 48° 31' 10", long. 114° 01' 15".

Ownership: Desert Mountain TV.

Lavina—K11MB, Ch. 11, Golden Valley Association No. 2 Translator District. Phone: 406-636-2025.

Technical Facilities: 0.008-kw ERP, lat. 46° 16' 50", long. 108° 53' 05".

Ownership: Golden Valley Association No. 2 Translator District.

Lavina—K13MR, Ch. 13, Golden Valley Association No. 2 Translator District. Phone: 406-636-2025.

Technical Facilities: 0.008-kw ERP, lat. 46° 16' 50", long. 108° 53' 05".

Ownership: Golden Valley Association No. 2 Translator District.

Lennep & Martinsdale—K07VK, Ch. 7, Marlo TV Association.

Technical Facilities: 0.09-kw ERP, 36-ft. above ground, 6886-ft. above sea level, lat. 46° 28' 15", long. 110° 26' 59".

Ownership: Marlo TV Association.

Lennep & Martinsdale—K11TK, Ch. 11, Marlo TV Association.

Technical Facilities: 0.09-kw ERP, 26-ft. above ground, 6877-ft. above sea level, lat. 46° 28' 15", long. 110° 26' 59".

Ownership: Marlo TV Association.

Lewistown—K43DC, Ch. 43, MMM License II LLC. Phone: 757-437-9800.

Technical Facilities: 0.1-kw ERP, lat. 47° 10' 44", long. 109° 32' 15".

Holds CP for change to 15-kw ERP, 49-ft. above ground, 5810-ft. above sea level, lat. 47° 10' 40", long. 109° 32' 06". BDFCDTT-20060331BNW.

Began Operation: April 10, 1980.

Ownership: Max Media X LLC.

■**Lewistown**—K45CS, Ch. 45, KRTV Communications Inc. Phone: 406-791-5400.

Technical Facilities: 1.05-kw ERP, 69-ft. above ground, 5856-ft. above sea level, lat. 47° 10' 39", long. 109° 32' 06".

Holds CP for change to 0.274-kw ERP, 69-ft. above ground, 5859-ft. above sea level, BDFCDTA-20090223ABA.

Began Operation: May 25, 1989.

Ownership: Evening Post Publishing Co.

Lewistown—K47DP, Ch. 47, Destiny Licenses LLC. Phone: 316-688-0069.

Technical Facilities: 0.1-kw ERP, lat. 47° 10' 44", long. 109° 32' 15".

Ownership: Destiny Communications LLC.

Libby—K60EA, Ch. 60, Libby Video Club.

Technical Facilities: 1.13-kw ERP, lat. 48° 26' 40", long. 115° 31' 20".

Ownership: Libby Video Club.

Libby—K62DL, Ch. 62, Libby Video Club.

Technical Facilities: 0.826-kw ERP, 26-ft. above ground, 2920-ft. above sea level, lat. 48° 26' 40", long. 115° 31' 20".

Ownership: Libby Video Club.

Libby—K64DL, Ch. 64, Libby Video Club.

Technical Facilities: 1.13-kw ERP, lat. 48° 26' 40", long. 115° 31' 20".

Ownership: Libby Video Club.

Libby—K66DR, Ch. 66, Libby Video Club.

Technical Facilities: 1.13-kw ERP, lat. 48° 26' 40", long. 115° 31' 20".

Ownership: Libby Video Club.

Libby—K68AS, Ch. 68, Libby Video Club.

Technical Facilities: 0.206-kw ERP, lat. 48° 26' 15", long. 115° 31' 45".

Ownership: Libby Video Club.

Livingston—K17BT, Ch. 17, Shields Valley TV Tax District.

Technical Facilities: 100-w TPO, 1.73-kw ERP, 56-ft. above ground, 6608-ft. above sea level, lat. 45° 35' 52", long. 110° 32' 45".

Transmitter: Approx. 4.5-mi. SE of Livingston on the Myers Ranch.

Ownership: Shields Valley TV Tax District.

Livingston, etc.—K55CF, Ch. 55, Paradise Valley TV District. Phone: 406-222-3146.

Technical Facilities: 2.2-kw ERP, 6601-ft. above sea level, lat. 45° 35' 52", long. 110° 32' 45".

Ownership: Paradise Valley TV District.

Livingston, etc.—K60BE, Ch. 60, Paradise Valley TV District. Phone: 406-222-3146.

Technical Facilities: 2.15-kw ERP, 6601-ft. above sea level, lat. 45° 35' 52", long. 110° 32' 45".

Ownership: Paradise Valley TV District.

Livingston, etc.—K63BV, Ch. 63, Paradise Valley TV District. Phone: 406-222-3146.

Technical Facilities: 2.13-kw ERP, 6624-ft. above sea level, lat. 45° 35' 52", long. 110° 32' 45".

Ownership: Paradise Valley TV District.

Livingston, etc.—K66BR, Ch. 66, MMM License II LLC. Phone: 757-437-9800.

Technical Facilities: 2.15-kw ERP, lat. 45° 35' 52", long. 110° 32' 45".

Transmitter: Myers Ranch, 6-mi. SE of Livingston.

Began Operation: May 5, 1981.

Ownership: Max Media X LLC.

Loma—K07AM, Ch. 7, Loma TV Club. Phone: 406-739-4224.

Technical Facilities: 0.013-kw ERP, lat. 47° 56' 25", long. 110° 29' 55".

Ownership: Loma TV Club.

Loma—K11AD, Ch. 11, Loma TV Club. Phone: 406-739-4224.

Technical Facilities: 0.013-kw ERP, lat. 47° 56' 25", long. 110° 29' 55".

Ownership: Loma TV Club.

Loring—K65AH, Ch. 65, Phillips County TV Translator District. Phone: 406-383-4499.

Technical Facilities: 3.58-kw ERP, 2864-ft. above sea level, lat. 48° 53' 45", long. 107° 58' 13".

Ownership: Phillips County TV Translator District.

Loring, etc.—K09JG, Ch. 9, Phillips County TV Translator District. Phone: 406-383-4499.

Technical Facilities: 0.002-kw ERP, 2910-ft. above sea level, lat. 48° 53' 45", long. 107° 58' 13".

Ownership: Phillips County TV Translator District.

Malta—K07IC, Ch. 7, Phillips County TV Translator District. Phone: 406-383-4499.

Technical Facilities: 0.003-kw ERP, lat. 48° 21' 02", long. 107° 51' 55".

Ownership: Phillips County TV Translator District.

Malta—K15AS, Ch. 15, Phillips County TV Translator District. Phone: 406-383-4499.

Technical Facilities: 1.38-kw ERP, lat. 48° 20' 15", long. 107° 53' 00".

Ownership: Phillips County TV Translator District.

Malta, etc.—K11IH, Ch. 11, Phillips County TV Translator District. Phone: 406-383-4499.

Technical Facilities: 0.003-kw ERP, 2395-ft. above sea level, lat. 48° 22' 02", long. 107° 51' 55".

Ownership: Phillips County TV Translator District.

Malta, etc.—K13GP, Ch. 13, Phillips County TV Translator District. Phone: 406-383-4499.

Technical Facilities: 0.007-kw ERP, 2395-ft. above sea level, lat. 48° 22' 02", long. 107° 51' 55".

Ownership: Phillips County TV Translator District.

Martinsdale-Lennep—K09LW, Ch. 9, Marlo TV Association.

Technical Facilities: 0.09-kw ERP, lat. 46° 28' 15", long. 110° 26' 59".

Transmitter: 0.7-mi. W of Martinsdale.

Ownership: Marlo TV Association.

Miles City—K06FE, Ch. 6, MMM License II LLC. Phone: 757-437-9800.

Technical Facilities: 0.79-kw ERP, lat. 46° 26' 01", long. 105° 50' 51".

Holds CP for change to 0.1-kw ERP, 39-ft. above ground, 2648-ft. above sea level, BDFCDTT-20060331BNY.

Began Operation: December 19, 1983.

Ownership: Max Media X LLC.

Miles City—K10GF, Ch. 10, KTVQ Communications Inc. Phone: 406-252-5611.

Technical Facilities: 0.69-kw ERP, lat. 46° 26' 01", long. 105° 50' 51".

Ownership: Evening Post Publishing Co.

Miles City—K16DH, Ch. 16, Nexstar Broadcasting Inc. Phone: 972-373-8800.

Technical Facilities: 15.06-kw ERP, 90-ft. above ground, 2710-ft. above sea level, lat. 46° 26' 08", long. 105° 50' 53".

Holds CP for change to 0.085-kw ERP, BDFCDTT-20060403AOK.

Ownership: Nexstar Broadcasting Group Inc.

Miles City—K19FF, Ch. 19, Nexstar Finance Inc. Phone: 972-373-8800.

Technical Facilities: 15.06-kw ERP, 90-ft. above ground, 2710-ft. above sea level, lat. 46° 26' 09", long. 105° 50' 54".

Holds CP for change to 0.083-kw ERP, lat. 46° 26' 08", long. 105° 50' 53". BDFCDTT-20060403AOL.

Ownership: Nexstar Broadcasting Group Inc.

Missoula—K32EU, Ch. 32, Spokane School District No. 81. Phone: 509-354-7800.

Technical Facilities: 5.01-kw ERP, lat. 47° 01' 04", long. 114° 00' 47".

Ownership: Spokane School District No. 81.

Missoula—K42EO, Ch. 42, Trinity Broadcasting Network Inc. Phone: 714-832-2950. Fax: 714-730-0661.

Technical Facilities: 6.7-kw ERP, 194-ft. above ground, 5873-ft. above sea level, lat. 46° 48' 30", long. 113° 58' 38".

Holds CP for change to 8-kw ERP, BDFCDTT-20060330ACL.

Ownership: Trinity Broadcasting Network Inc.

Missoula—KMTM-LP, Ch. 46, North Rocky Mountain Television Inc.

Technical Facilities: 127-w TPO, 10-kw ERP, 41-ft. above ground, 8009-ft. above sea level, lat. 47° 02' 27", long. 113° 59' 10".

Transmitter: 11-mi. NW of Missoula.

Ownership: North Rocky Mountain Television LLC.

Missoula, etc.—K50CP, Ch. 50, David A. Tucker. Phone: 406-273-6161.

Studio: 100 Glacier Dr, Ste F, Lolo, MT 59847.

Technical Facilities: 100-w TPO, 2.2-kw ERP, 98-ft. above ground, 4869-ft. above sea level, lat. 46° 47' 49", long. 114° 00' 59".

Transmitter: Mount Dean Stone communications site, 4-mi. S of Missoula.

Multichannel TV Sound: Separate audio progam.

Ownership: David A. Tucker.

Missoula, MT—KEXI-LP, Ch. 35, Montana Broadcasting Group Inc., Debtor in Possession. Phone: 501-219-2400.

Technical Facilities: 10-kw ERP, 50-ft. above ground, 6867-ft. above sea level, lat. 48° 30' 22", long. 114° 20' 49".

Began Operation: July 13, 1999.

Ownership: Equity Media Holdings Corp., Debtor in Possession.

Northfork, etc.—K10AU, Ch. 10, Garfield TV Club. Phone: 406-557-6200.

Technical Facilities: 0.019-kw ERP, 3405-ft. above sea level, lat. 47° 14' 55", long. 107° 27' 35".

Ownership: Garfield TV Club.

■ **Pablo/Ronan**—KSKC-CA, Ch. 25, Salish Kootenai College. Phone: 406-275-4878. Fax: 406-275-4801.

Studio: 52000 Hwy. 93, Box 70, Pablo, MT 59855.

Technical Facilities: 100-w TPO, 1.14-kw ERP, 112-ft. above ground, 3159-ft. above sea level, lat. 47° 31' 53", long. 114° 07' 01".

Transmitter: NE edge of Ronan.

Ownership: Salish Kootenai College.

Personnel: Frank Tyro, General Manager.

Phillips County—K20BP, Ch. 20, Phillips County TV Translator District. Phone: 406-383-4499.

Technical Facilities: 1.38-kw ERP, lat. 47° 56' 20", long. 108° 32' 40".

Ownership: Phillips County TV Translator District.

Phillips County—K46BX, Ch. 46, Phillips County TV Translator District. Phone: 406-383-4499.

Technical Facilities: 1.38-kw ERP, lat. 47° 56' 20", long. 108° 32' 40".

Ownership: Phillips County TV Translator District.

Phillips County—K53CP, Ch. 53, Phillips County TV Translator District. Phone: 406-383-4499.

Technical Facilities: 1.38-kw ERP, 30-ft. above ground, 5751-ft. above sea level, lat. 47° 56' 20", long. 108° 32' 40".

Ownership: Phillips County TV Translator District.

Pinesdale—K67EC, Ch. 67, Bitterroot Valley Public TV Inc. Phone: 406-961-3692.

Technical Facilities: 0.587-kw ERP, lat. 40° 20' 28", long. 95° 02' 36".

Holds CP for change to channel number 45, 75-ft. above ground, 4616-ft. above sea level, BDISTT-20060221AEO.

Transmitter: Hilltop location, 3.5-mi. NE of Corvallis.

Ownership: Bitterroot Valley Public TV Inc.

Pipe Creek—K13MY, Ch. 13, Libby Video Club.

Technical Facilities: 0.009-kw ERP, lat. 48° 21' 13", long. 115° 40' 42".

Ownership: Libby Video Club.

Pipe Creek, etc.—K10LL, Ch. 10, Libby Video Club Inc.

Technical Facilities: 0.017-kw ERP, 7260-ft. above sea level, lat. 48° 21' 13", long. 115° 40' 42".

Ownership: Libby Video Club.

Plains—K11JP, Ch. 11, Plains-Paradise TV District. Phone: 406-826-3417.

Technical Facilities: 0.01-kw ERP, lat. 47° 31' 15", long. 114° 57' 28".

Holds CP for change to 0.042-kw ERP, 11-ft. above ground, 4027-ft. above sea level, BDFCDTV-20081205AFS.

Ownership: Plains-Paradise TV District.

Plains & Paradise—K05GM-D, Ch. 5, Plains-Paradise TV District. Phone: 406-826-3417.

Technical Facilities: 0.017-kw ERP, 11-ft. above ground, 4020-ft. above sea level, lat. 47° 31' 30", long. 114° 57' 28".

Began Operation: June 4, 1979.

Ownership: Plains-Paradise TV District.

Plains & Paradise—K07CH-D, Ch. 7, Plains-Paradise TV District. Phone: 406-826-3417.

Technical Facilities: 0.03-kw ERP, 11-ft. above ground, 4023-ft. above sea level, lat. 47° 31' 30", long. 114° 57' 28".

Began Operation: May 22, 1979.

Ownership: Plains-Paradise TV District.

Plains, etc.—K21CA, Ch. 21, Plains-Paradise TV District. Phone: 406-826-3417.

Technical Facilities: 100-w TPO, 3.3-kw ERP, 13-ft. above ground, 3809-ft. above sea level, lat. 47° 31' 15", long. 114° 57' 28".

Transmitter: Approx. 6-mi. NW of Plains.

Ownership: Plains-Paradise TV District.

Plentywood—K46GS, Ch. 46, Sheridan County. Phone: 406-765-1660.

Technical Facilities: 1-kw ERP, 69-ft. above ground, 2661-ft. above sea level, lat. 48° 41' 35", long. 104° 35' 44".

Ownership: Sheridan County, MT.

Plevna—K03HD, Ch. 3, Plevna TV Booster Club. Phone: 406-772-5731.

Technical Facilities: 0.043-kw ERP, 36-ft. above ground, 3117-ft. above sea level, lat. 46° 20' 00", long. 104° 31' 50".

Ownership: Plevna TV Booster Club.

Plevna—K09IV, Ch. 9, Plevna TV Booster Club. Phone: 406-772-5731.

Technical Facilities: 0.012-kw ERP, lat. 46° 20' 00", long. 104° 31' 50".

Ownership: Plevna TV Booster Club.

Plevna—K13WT, Ch. 13, Plevna TV Booster Club. Phone: 406-772-5731.

Technical Facilities: 0.088-kw ERP, lat. 46° 20' 00", long. 104° 31' 50".

Transmitter: 5.5-mi. S of Plevna.

Ownership: Plevna TV Booster Club.

Plevna—K17OB, Ch. 17, Plevna Public School Trustees District No. 55. Phone: 406-772-5666.

Technical Facilities: 0.327-kw ERP, 30-ft. above ground, 3113-ft. above sea level, lat. 46° 20' 05", long. 104° 30' 45".

Ownership: Plevna Public School Trustees District No. 55.

Plevna—K24DD, Ch. 24, Plevna Public School Trustees District No. 55. Phone: 406-772-5601. Fax: 406-772-5548.

Studio: Box 158, Plevna, MT 59344.

Technical Facilities: 20-w TPO, 0.246-kw ERP, 62-ft. above ground, 2812-ft. above sea level, lat. 46° 25' 06", long. 104° 31' 03".

Transmitter: Plevna High School.

Ownership: Plevna Public School Trustees District No. 55.

Personnel: Carter Christiansen, General Manager.

Plevna—K34DP, Ch. 34, Plevna Public School Trustees District No. 55. Phone: 406-772-5666.

Technical Facilities: 0.376-kw ERP, 30-ft. above ground, 3081-ft. above sea level, lat. 46° 27' 24", long. 104° 30' 50".

Ownership: Plevna Public School Trustees District No. 55.

Polson—K03DJ, Ch. 3, Blacktail TV Tax District. Phones: 406-883-2975; 406-249-3251.

Technical Facilities: 0.15-kw ERP, 20-ft. above ground, 4091-ft. above sea level, lat. 47° 40' 39", long. 114° 08' 30".

Holds CP for change to 0.032-kw ERP, 20-ft. above ground, 3409-ft. above sea level, BDFCDTV-20070706ADF.

Ownership: Blacktail TV Tax District.

Polson—K11HO, Ch. 11, Blacktail TV Tax District. Phone: 406-883-2975.

Technical Facilities: 0.103-kw ERP, 20-ft. above ground, 3409-ft. above sea level, lat. 47° 40' 42", long. 114° 08' 36".

Holds CP for change to 0.04-kw ERP, 20-ft. above ground, 3409-ft. above sea level, BDFCDTV-20070618ACM.

Ownership: Blacktail TV Tax District.

Polson—K14LT, Ch. 14, Blacktail TV Tax District. Phone: 406-883-2975.

Technical Facilities: 0.25-kw ERP, 22-ft. above ground, 3417-ft. above sea level, lat. 47° 40' 39", long. 114° 08' 30".

Holds CP for change to 0.061-kw ERP, 33-ft. above ground, 3323-ft. above sea level, lat. 47° 40' 42", long. 114° 08' 36". BDFCDTT-20070618ACQ.

Ownership: Blacktail TV Tax District.

Polson—K16GJ, Ch. 16, Blacktail TV Tax District. Phone: 406-249-3251.

Technical Facilities: 0.25-kw ERP, 22-ft. above ground, 3421-ft. above sea level, lat. 47° 40' 39", long. 114° 08' 30".

Holds CP for change to 0.061-kw ERP, 33-ft. above ground, 3423-ft. above sea level, lat. 47° 40' 42", long. 114° 08' 36". BDFCDTT-20070619AAF.

Ownership: Blacktail TV Tax District.

Polson—K30II, Ch. 30, Blacktail TV Tax District. Phone: 406-883-2975.

Technical Facilities: 0.25-kw ERP, 22-ft. above ground, 3421-ft. above sea level, lat. 47° 40' 39", long. 114° 08' 30".

Holds CP for change to 0.06-kw ERP, 33-ft. above ground, 3423-ft. above sea level, lat. 47° 40' 42", long. 114° 08' 36". BDFCDTT-20070618ACS.

Ownership: Blacktail TV Tax District.

Polson—K41IW, Ch. 41, Blacktail TV Tax District. Phone: 406-883-2975.

Technical Facilities: 0.25-kw ERP, 22-ft. above ground, 3421-ft. above sea level, lat. 47° 40' 39", long. 114° 08' 30".

Holds CP for change to 0.061-kw ERP, 33-ft. above ground, 3423-ft. above sea level, lat. 47° 40' 42", long. 114° 08' 36". BDFCDTT-20070618ACT.

Ownership: Blacktail TV Tax District.

Polson—K50LB, Ch. 50, Blacktail TV Tax District. Phone: 406-883-2975.

Technical Facilities: 0.2-kw ERP, 19-ft. above ground, 3418-ft. above sea level, lat. 47° 40' 39", long. 114° 08' 30".

Holds CP for change to 0.1-kw ERP, BDFCDTT-20090115BJX.

Began Operation: October 1, 1981.

Ownership: Blacktail TV Tax District.

Pony—K10HZ, Ch. 10, BlueStone License Holdings Inc. Phone: 212-247-8717.

Technical Facilities: 0.005-kw ERP, lat. 45° 39' 37", long. 111° 52' 52".

Ownership: Bonten Media Group LLC.

Poplar—K05KK, Ch. 5, Poplar TV District. Phone: 406-768-3800. Fax: 406-768-3801.

Technical Facilities: 10-w TPO, 0.124-kw ERP, 36-ft. above ground, 2257-ft. above sea level, lat. 48° 07' 40", long. 105° 04' 21".

Transmitter: 5-mi. E & 1-mi. N of Poplar.

Ownership: Poplar TV District.

Poplar—K13PZ, Ch. 13, Poplar TV District. Phone: 406-768-3800.

Technical Facilities: 0.18-kw ERP, lat. 48° 08' 25", long. 105° 07' 15".

Ownership: Poplar TV District.

Poplar—K48IA, Ch. 48, Poplar TV District. Phone: 406-768-3800.

Technical Facilities: 0.818-kw ERP, 112-ft. above ground, 2749-ft. above sea level, lat. 48° 17' 28", long. 105° 15' 09".

Ownership: Poplar TV District.

Poplar—K50GU, Ch. 50, Poplar TV District. Phone: 406-768-3800.

Technical Facilities: 0.818-kw ERP, 112-ft. above ground, 2749-ft. above sea level, lat. 48° 17' 28", long. 105° 15' 09".

Ownership: Poplar TV District.

Poplar—K55BX, Ch. 55, Poplar TV District. Phone: 407-768-3800.

Technical Facilities: 0.816-kw ERP, 111-ft. above ground, 2749-ft. above sea level, lat. 48° 17' 28", long. 105° 15' 09".

Ownership: Poplar TV District.

Quartz Creek, etc.—K11MF, Ch. 11, Libby Video Club.

Technical Facilities: 0.012-kw ERP, lat. 48° 21' 13", long. 115° 40' 42".

Ownership: Libby Video Club.

Red Lodge—K39HD, Ch. 39, KTVQ Communications Inc. Phone: 406-252-5611.

Technical Facilities: 0.807-kw ERP, 23-ft. above ground, 6883-ft. above sea level, lat. 45° 07' 19", long. 109° 16' 11".

Ownership: KTVQ Communications Inc.

Rexford & Fortine—K05GC, Ch. 5, Tobacco Valley Communications. Phone: 406-889-3311. Fax: 406-889-5100.

Technical Facilities: 0.103-kw ERP, lat. 48° 54' 00", long. 115° 00' 00".

Ownership: Tobacco Valley Communications.

Richey—K13JU, Ch. 13, Richey Television District.

Technical Facilities: 0.015-kw ERP, lat. 47° 40' 00", long. 105° 03' 45".

Ownership: Richey Television District.

Rock Creek, etc.—K07DI, Ch. 7, Hinsdale TV Club. Phone: 406-364-2271.

Technical Facilities: 0.022-kw ERP, 2507-ft. above sea level, lat. 48° 21' 54", long. 106° 58' 30".

Ownership: Hinsdale TV Club.

Rosebud, etc.—K07QK, Ch. 7, Forsyth TV Tax District.

Technical Facilities: 0.18-kw ERP, 2795-ft. above sea level, lat. 46° 18' 50", long. 106° 30' 25".

Ownership: Forsyth TV Tax District.

Rosebud, etc.—K09OK, Ch. 9, Forsyth TV Tax District.

Technical Facilities: 0.18-kw ERP, 2785-ft. above sea level, lat. 46° 18' 50", long. 106° 30' 25".

Ownership: Forsyth TV Tax District.

Roundup—K07WP, Ch. 7, Roundup TV Tax District. Phone: 406-323-3554.

Technical Facilities: 0.16-kw ERP, lat. 46° 28' 02", long. 108° 33' 50".

Transmitter: 1-mi. NW of Roundup.

Ownership: Roundup TV Tax District.

Roundup—K09WS, Ch. 9, Roundup TV Tax District. Phone: 406-323-3554.

Technical Facilities: 0.16-kw ERP, lat. 46° 28' 02", long. 108° 33' 50".

Transmitter: Approx. 1-mi. NW of city limits.

Ownership: Roundup TV Tax District.

Roundup—K11FS, Ch. 11, Roundup TV Tax District. Phone: 406-323-3554.

Technical Facilities: 0.016-kw ERP, lat. 46° 28' 02", long. 108° 33' 50".

Ownership: Roundup TV Tax District.

Roundup—K13AN, Ch. 13, Roundup TV Tax District. Phone: 406-323-3554.

Technical Facilities: 0.016-kw ERP, lat. 46° 28' 02", long. 108° 33' 50".

Ownership: Roundup TV Tax District.

Roy, etc.—K11HN, Ch. 11, Roy TV Tax District. Phone: 406-464-5471.

Technical Facilities: 0.001-kw ERP, 4081-ft. above sea level, lat. 47° 20' 36", long. 109° 07' 40".

Ownership: Roy TV Tax District.

Ryegate—K06FU, Ch. 6, Golden Valley TV Association No. 1. Phone: 406-568-2251.

Technical Facilities: 0.001-kw ERP, lat. 46° 18' 06", long. 109° 15' 14".

Ownership: Golden Valley TV Association No. 1.

Ryegate—K12HB, Ch. 12, Golden Valley TV Association No. 1. Phone: 406-568-2251.

Technical Facilities: 0.022-kw ERP, lat. 46° 18' 06", long. 109° 15' 14".

Ownership: Golden Valley TV Association No. 1.

Saco, etc.—K06FI, Ch. 6, Phillips County TV Translator District. Phone: 406-383-4499.

Technical Facilities: 0.003-kw ERP, lat. 48° 27' 35", long. 107° 25' 25".

Ownership: Phillips County TV Translator District.

Saco, etc.—K09BX, Ch. 9, Phillips County TV Translator District. Phone: 406-383-4499.

Technical Facilities: 0.003-kw ERP, 2621-ft. above sea level, lat. 48° 27' 35", long. 107° 25' 25".

Ownership: Phillips County TV Translator District.

Saco, etc.—K12FB, Ch. 12, Phillips County TV Translator District. Phone: 406-383-4499.

Technical Facilities: 0.003-kw ERP, 2621-ft. above sea level, lat. 48° 27' 35", long. 107° 25' 25".

Ownership: Phillips County TV Translator District.

Sand Springs—K13HK, Ch. 13, Garfield TV Club. Phone: 406-557-6200.

Technical Facilities: 0.026-kw ERP, lat. 47° 01' 30", long. 107° 26' 00".

Ownership: Garfield TV Club.

Scobey—K03DP, Ch. 3, Klear-Vu Television District. Phone: 406-487-5485.

Technical Facilities: 0.01-kw ERP, 2956-ft. above sea level, lat. 48° 47' 51", long. 105° 21' 14".

Ownership: Klear Vu Television District.

Scobey—K13MA, Ch. 13, Klear-Vu Television District. Phone: 406-487-5485.

Technical Facilities: 0.019-kw ERP, lat. 48° 47' 51", long. 105° 21' 14".

Ownership: Klear Vu Television District.

Seeley Lake—K02OL, Ch. 2, BlueStone License Holdings Inc. Phone: 212-247-8717.

Technical Facilities: 20-ft. above ground, 4961-ft. above sea level, lat. 47° 09' 53", long. 113° 31' 49".

Ownership: Bonten Media Group LLC.

Sidney & Fairview—K13IG, Ch. 13, Glendive Broadcasting Corp.

Technical Facilities: 0.24-kw ERP, lat. 47° 47' 03", long. 104° 07' 35".

Ownership: Glendive Broadcasting Corp.

St. Ignatius—K28CF, Ch. 28, Salish Kootenai College. Phone: 406-275-4800. Fax: 406-275-4801.

Technical Facilities: 1-w TPO, 0.969-kw ERP, 154-ft. above ground, 3103-ft. above sea level, lat. 47° 19' 24", long. 114° 05' 25".

Transmitter: North edge of St. Ignatius.

Ownership: Salish Kootenai College.

Personnel: Frank Tyro, Chief Engineer; Marius McTucker, Sales Manager.

St. Regis—K05DS, Ch. 5, St. Regis TV Tax District. Phone: 406-649-2316.

Technical Facilities: 0.009-kw ERP, lat. 47° 19' 08", long. 115° 07' 04".

Holds CP for change to 0.006-kw ERP, 18-ft. above ground, 3535-ft. above sea level, BDFCDTV-20081218AFC.

Ownership: St. Regis TV Tax District.

St. Regis—K10HM, Ch. 10, St. Regis TV Tax District. Phone: 406-649-2315.

Technical Facilities: 0.024-kw ERP, lat. 47° 19' 08", long. 115° 07' 04".

Holds CP for change to 0.006-kw ERP, 18-ft. above ground, 3535-ft. above sea level, BDFCDTV-20081218AFD.

Ownership: St. Regis TV Tax District.

Stanford—K07AV, Ch. 7, Stanford TV Association. Phone: 406-566-2775.

Technical Facilities: 0.001-kw ERP, 4721-ft. above sea level, lat. 47° 10' 29", long. 110° 15' 47".

Holds CP for change to channel number 11, BDISDTV-20081010BCF.

Ownership: Stanford TV Association.

Stanford—K11AQ, Ch. 11, Stanford TV Association.

Technical Facilities: 0.001-kw ERP, lat. 47° 10' 29", long. 110° 15' 47".

Ownership: Stanford TV Association.

Sula, etc.—K03GW, Ch. 3, Sula TV District.

Technical Facilities: 0.016-kw ERP, 20-ft. above ground, 6306-ft. above sea level, lat. 45° 49' 18", long. 113° 59' 37".

Ownership: Sula TV District.

Sula, etc.—K05JE, Ch. 5, Sula TV District.

Technical Facilities: 0.018-kw ERP, 20-ft. above ground, 6306-ft. above sea level, lat. 45° 49' 18", long. 113° 59' 37".

Ownership: Sula TV District.

Sweetgrass, etc.—K61BZ, Ch. 61, East Butte TV Club. Phone: 406-434-2207.

Technical Facilities: 0.224-kw ERP, 36-ft. above ground, 3678-ft. above sea level, lat. 48° 59' 00", long. 111° 57' 30".

Ownership: East Butte TV Club Inc.

Sweetgrass, etc.—K63AQ, Ch. 63, Border TV Club. Phone: 406-434-2207.

Technical Facilities: 0.242-kw ERP, 3674-ft. above sea level, lat. 48° 59' 00", long. 111° 57' 30".

Ownership: East Butte TV Club Inc.

Sweetgrass, etc.—K65DK, Ch. 65, East Butte TV Club. Phone: 406-434-2207.

Technical Facilities: 0.22-kw ERP, 56-ft. above ground, 3674-ft. above sea level, lat. 48° 59' 00", long. 111° 57' 30".

Ownership: East Butte TV Club Inc.

Tampico—K57AJ, Ch. 57, Valley County Television District No. 1. Phone: 406-367-9353.

Technical Facilities: 3.78-kw ERP, 2595-ft. above sea level, lat. 48° 21' 42", long. 107° 08' 56".

Ownership: Valley County TV District No. 1.

Tampico, etc.—K69DN, Ch. 69, Valley County Television District No. 1. Phone: 406-367-9353.

Technical Facilities: 3.82-kw ERP, 2864-ft. above sea level, lat. 48° 21' 42", long. 107° 08' 56".

Ownership: Valley County TV District No. 1.

Thompson Falls—K07FL, Ch. 7, Thompson Falls TV District. Phone: 406-827-4100.

Technical Facilities: 0.014-kw ERP, 4734-ft. above sea level, lat. 47° 33' 00", long. 115° 21' 30".

Holds CP for change to 0.033-kw ERP, 40-ft. above ground, 5132-ft. above sea level, lat. 47° 32' 27.04", long. 115° 19' 05.71". BDFCDTV-20070806ABR.

Ownership: Thompson Falls TV District.

Thompson Falls—K09FQ, Ch. 9, Thompson Falls TV District. Phone: 406-827-4100.

Technical Facilities: 0.014-kw ERP, 4734-ft. above sea level, lat. 47° 33' 00", long. 115° 21' 30".

Holds CP for change to 0.033-kw ERP, 40-ft. above ground, 5132-ft. above sea level, lat. 47° 32' 27.04", long. 115° 19' 05.71". BDFCDTV-20070806ABS.

Ownership: Thompson Falls TV District.

Thompson Falls—K11FQ, Ch. 11, Thompson Falls TV District. Phone: 406-827-4100.

Technical Facilities: 0.013-kw ERP, 4734-ft. above sea level, lat. 47° 33' 00", long. 115° 21' 30".

Holds CP for change to 0.033-kw ERP, 40-ft. above ground, 5132-ft. above sea level, lat. 47° 32' 27.04", long. 115° 19' 05.71". BDFCDTV-20070806ABT.

Ownership: Thompson Falls TV District.

Thompson Falls—K36BW, Ch. 36, Thompson Falls TV District. Phone: 406-827-4100.

Technical Facilities: 1.19-kw ERP, 49-ft. above ground, 5039-ft. above sea level, lat. 47° 33' 00", long. 115° 21' 30".

Holds CP for change to 0.185-kw ERP, 46-ft. above ground, 5138-ft. above sea level, lat. 47° 32' 27.04", long. 115° 19' 05.71". BDFCDTL-20070806ABU.

Ownership: Thompson Falls TV District.

Three Forks—K35DJ, Ch. 35, BlueStone License Holdings Inc. Phone: 212-247-8717.

Technical Facilities: 0.326-kw ERP, 39-ft. above ground, 4321-ft. above sea level, lat. 45° 56' 21", long. 111° 29' 10".

Ownership: Bonten Media Group LLC.

Toole, etc.—K36DK, Ch. 36, East Butte TV Club Inc. Phone: 406-434-2207.

Technical Facilities: 1.26-kw ERP, 56-ft. above ground, 6972-ft. above sea level, lat. 48° 51' 30", long. 111° 06' 24".

Ownership: East Butte TV Club Inc.

Toole, etc.—K38DZ, Ch. 38, East Butte TV Club Inc. Phone: 406-434-2207.

Technical Facilities: 1.26-kw ERP, 56-ft. above ground, 6972-ft. above sea level, lat. 48° 51' 30", long. 111° 06' 24".

Ownership: East Butte TV Club Inc.

Toole, etc.—K40DG, Ch. 40, East Butte TV Club Inc. Phone: 406-434-2207.

Technical Facilities: 1.26-kw ERP, 56-ft. above ground, 6972-ft. above sea level, lat. 48° 51' 30", long. 111° 06' 24".

Ownership: East Butte TV Club Inc.

Toole, etc.—K42DD, Ch. 42, East Butte TV Club Inc. Phone: 406-434-2207.

Technical Facilities: 1.26-kw ERP, 56-ft. above ground, 6972-ft. above sea level, lat. 48° 51' 30", long. 111° 06' 24".

Ownership: East Butte TV Club Inc.

Townsend—K07EJ, Ch. 7, Townsend TV District.

Technical Facilities: 0.003-kw ERP, 4924-ft. above sea level, lat. 46° 16' 43", long. 111° 32' 55".

Ownership: Townsend TV District.

Townsend—K13KH, Ch. 13, Townsend TV District.

Technical Facilities: 0.006-kw ERP, lat. 46° 17' 00", long. 111° 33' 00".

Ownership: Townsend TV District.

Troy—K08BG, Ch. 8, Troy T.V. District. Phone: 406-295-4266.

Technical Facilities: 0.067-kw ERP, lat. 48° 31' 02", long. 115° 47' 56".

Transmitter: King Mountain, 6.25-mi. NNE of Troy.

Ownership: Troy T.V. District.

Troy—K10AF, Ch. 10, Troy T.V. District. Phone: 406-295-4266.

Technical Facilities: 0.067-kw ERP, lat. 48° 31' 02", long. 115° 47' 56".

Transmitter: King Mountain, 6.25-mi. NNE of Troy.

Ownership: Troy T.V. District.

Troy—K12AA, Ch. 12, Troy T.V. District. Phone: 406-295-4266.

Technical Facilities: 0.067-kw ERP, lat. 48° 31' 02", long. 115° 47' 56".

Transmitter: King Mountain, approx. 6.22-mi. NNE of Troy.

Ownership: Troy T.V. District.

Turner-Hogeland—K60BV, Ch. 60, Big Flat TV Association. Phone: 406-379-2293.

Technical Facilities: 0.672-kw ERP, lat. 48° 52' 24", long. 108° 57' 13".

Ownership: Big Flat TV Association.

Turner-Hogeland—K64BQ, Ch. 64, Big Flat TV Association. Phone: 406-379-2293.

Technical Facilities: 0.672-kw ERP, lat. 48° 52' 24", long. 108° 57' 13".

Ownership: Big Flat TV Association.

Turner-Hogeland—K66BZ, Ch. 66, Big Flat TV Association. Phone: 406-379-2293.

Technical Facilities: 0.672-kw ERP, lat. 48° 52' 24", long. 108° 57' 13".

Ownership: Big Flat TV Association.

Valley County—K41BT, Ch. 41, Valley County Television District No. 1. Phone: 406-367-9353.

Ownership: Valley County TV District No. 1.

Valley County—K43CQ, Ch. 43, Valley County Television District No 1. Phone: 406-367-9353.

Technical Facilities: 1.38-kw ERP, lat. 48° 01' 49", long. 106° 17' 48".

Ownership: Valley County TV District No. 1.

Valley County—K47CY, Ch. 47, Valley County Television District No. 1. Phone: 406-367-9353.

Technical Facilities: 1.38-kw ERP, 39-ft. above ground, 2792-ft. above sea level, lat. 48° 01' 49", long. 106° 17' 48".

Ownership: Valley County TV District No. 1.

Valley County—K49CF, Ch. 49, Valley County Television District No. 1. Phone: 406-367-9353.

Technical Facilities: 1.38-kw ERP, lat. 48° 01' 49", long. 106° 17' 48".

Ownership: Valley County TV District No. 1.

Virginia City—K10HL, Ch. 10, BlueStone License Holdings Inc. Phone: 212-247-8717.

Technical Facilities: 0.012-kw ERP, lat. 45° 16' 30", long. 111° 57' 15".

Ownership: Bonten Media Group LLC.

Watkins, etc.—K09KH, Ch. 9, BlueStone License Holdings Inc. Phone: 212-247-8717.

Technical Facilities: 0.012-kw ERP, 5154-ft. above sea level, lat. 45° 20' 11", long. 111° 41' 50".

Ownership: Bonten Media Group LLC.

Weeksville—K48LG, Ch. 48, Plains-Paradise TV District. Phone: 406-826-3417.

Technical Facilities: 4.1-kw ERP, 12-ft. above ground, 6846-ft. above sea level, lat. 47° 22' 20", long. 114° 51' 29".

Ownership: Plains-Paradise TV District.

Weeksville, etc.—K29ID, Ch. 29, Plains-Paradise TV District. Phone: 406-826-3417.

Technical Facilities: 0.84-kw ERP, 12-ft. above ground, 6846-ft. above sea level, lat. 47° 22' 20", long. 114° 51' 29".

Ownership: Plains-Paradise TV District.

West Glacier, etc.—K07IT, Ch. 7, Desert Mountain TV.

Technical Facilities: 0.007-kw ERP, 6214-ft. above sea level, lat. 48° 26' 30", long. 113° 58' 00".

Ownership: Desert Mountain TV.

West Glacier, etc.—K10LH, Ch. 10, Desert Mountain TV.

Technical Facilities: 0.01-kw ERP, lat. 48° 26' 30", long. 113° 58' 00".

Ownership: Desert Mountain TV.

West Glacier, etc.—K12LU, Ch. 12, Desert Mountain TV.

Technical Facilities: 0.005-kw ERP, 6214-ft. above sea level, lat. 48° 26' 30", long. 113° 58' 00".

Ownership: Desert Mountain TV.

West Yellowstone—K28AZ, Ch. 28, West Yellowstone TV Translator District. Phone: 208-238-0949.

Technical Facilities: 0.2-kw ERP, lat. 44° 45' 10", long. 111° 11' 54".

Ownership: West Yellowstone TV Translator District.

West Yellowstone—K30BC, Ch. 30, West Yellowstone TV Translator District. Phone: 208-238-0949.

Technical Facilities: 0.257-kw ERP, 62-ft. above ground, 7136-ft. above sea level, lat. 44° 45' 10", long. 111° 11' 54".

Ownership: West Yellowstone TV Translator District.

West Yellowstone—K32CG, Ch. 32, West Yellowstone TV Translator District. Phone: 208-238-0949.

Technical Facilities: 0.002-kw ERP, lat. 44° 45' 10", long. 111° 11' 54".

Ownership: West Yellowstone TV Translator District.

West Yellowstone—K34AW, Ch. 34, West Yellowstone TV Translator District. Phone: 208-238-0949.

Technical Facilities: 20-w TPO, 80-ft. above ground, 7157-ft. above sea level, lat. 44° 45' 10", long. 111° 11' 54".

Transmitter: Horse Butte, 5 miles N of West Yellowstone.

Ownership: West Yellowstone TV Translator District.

White Sulphur Springs—K06NV, Ch. 6, Meagher County Television District. Phone: 406-547-2190.

Technical Facilities: 0.065-kw ERP, 20-ft. above ground, 6066-ft. above sea level, lat. 46° 27' 44", long. 110° 51' 22".

Ownership: Meagher County Television District.

White Sulphur Springs—K07NU, Ch. 7, Meagher County Television District. Phone: 406-547-2190.

Technical Facilities: 0.018-kw ERP, lat. 46° 30' 12", long. 110° 49' 41".

Ownership: Meagher County Television District.

White Sulphur Springs—K08LI, Ch. 8, Meagher County Public TV Inc. Phone: 406-547-3803.

Technical Facilities: 0.065-kw ERP, 16-ft. above ground, 6316-ft. above sea level, lat. 46° 30' 12", long. 110° 49' 41".

Ownership: Meagher County Public TV Inc.

White Sulphur Springs—K09MH, Ch. 9, Meagher County Television District. Phone: 406-547-3612.

Technical Facilities: 0.051-kw ERP, lat. 46° 30' 12", long. 110° 49' 41".

Ownership: Meagher County Television District.

White Sulphur Springs—K11MP, Ch. 11, Meagher County Television District. Phone: 406-547-3612.

Technical Facilities: 0.007-kw ERP, lat. 46° 30' 12", long. 110° 49' 41".

Ownership: Meagher County Television District.

White Sulphur Springs—K57CX, Ch. 57, Meagher County Public TV Inc. Phone: 406-547-3803.

Technical Facilities: 1-kw ERP, 56-ft. above ground, 5138-ft. above sea level, lat. 46° 32' 40", long. 110° 54' 01".

Ownership: Meagher County Public TV Inc.

Whitefish/Columbia—K29AA, Ch. 29, Blacktail TV Tax District. Phone: 406-883-2975.

Technical Facilities: 1.79-kw ERP, lat. 48° 30' 08", long. 114° 20' 16".

Holds CP for change to 0.173-kw ERP, 120-ft. above ground, 6918-ft. above sea level, lat. 48° 30' 22", long. 114° 20' 49". BDFCDTT-20070618ACR.

Ownership: Blacktail TV Tax District.

Whitehall—K40HL, Ch. 40, Whitehall Low Power TV Inc. Phone: 406-287-2197.

Technical Facilities: 0.374-kw ERP, 40-ft. above ground, 6589-ft. above sea level, lat. 45° 55' 15", long. 112° 01' 15".

Ownership: Whitehall Low Power TV Inc.

Whitehall—K52CE, Ch. 52, Whitehall Low Power TV Inc. Phone: 406-287-3762. Fax: 406-287-3762.

Technical Facilities: 100-w TPO, 0.86-kw ERP, 118-ft. above ground, 4531-ft. above sea level, lat. 45° 52' 34", long. 112° 05' 14".

Transmitter: New water tower, adjacent to Hwy. 90 on the NE edge of Whitehall.

Ownership: Whitehall Low Power TV Inc.

Whitewater—K34DN, Ch. 34, Phillips County TV Translator District. Phone: 406-383-4499.

Technical Facilities: 1.3-kw ERP, 26-ft. above ground, 2776-ft. above sea level, lat. 48° 45' 30", long. 107° 45' 00".

Ownership: Phillips County TV Translator District.

Winifred, etc.—K07OA, Ch. 7, Winifred TV Tax District. Phone: 406-462-5383.

Technical Facilities: 0.008-kw ERP, 3570-ft. above sea level, lat. 47° 33' 40", long. 109° 21' 50".

Ownership: Winifred TV Tax District.

Winifred, etc.—K11NH, Ch. 11, Winifred TV Tax District. Phone: 406-462-5383.

Technical Facilities: 0.008-kw ERP, 3570-ft. above sea level, lat. 47° 33' 40", long. 109° 21' 50".

Ownership: Winifred TV Tax District.

Winnett—K06LF, Ch. 6, Winnett Community TV System.

Technical Facilities: 0.01-kw ERP, lat. 47° 04' 36", long. 108° 21' 43".

Ownership: Winnett Community TV System.

Winnett—K10DA, Ch. 10, Winnett Community TV System.

Technical Facilities: 0.026-kw ERP, lat. 47° 04' 36", long. 108° 21' 43".

Ownership: Winnett Community TV System.

Winnett—K12FD, Ch. 12, Winnett Community TV System.

Technical Facilities: 0.002-kw ERP, lat. 47° 04' 36", long. 108° 21' 43".

Ownership: Winnett Community TV System.

Wolf Point—K04GF, Ch. 4, Wolf Point TV District. Phone: 406-653-1427.

Technical Facilities: 0.012-kw ERP, lat. 48° 06' 44", long. 105° 41' 42".

Ownership: Wolf Point TV District.

Wolf Point—K06AV, Ch. 6, Wolf Point TV District. Phone: 406-653-1427.

Technical Facilities: 0.006-kw ERP, lat. 48° 06' 44", long. 105° 41' 42".

Ownership: Wolf Point TV District.

Wolf Point—K13FP, Ch. 13, Wolf Point TV District. Phone: 406-653-1427.

Technical Facilities: 0.005-kw ERP, lat. 48° 06' 44", long. 105° 41' 42".

Ownership: Wolf Point TV District.

Wolf Point—K25HO, Ch. 25, Wolf Point TV District.

Technical Facilities: 0.84-kw ERP, 69-ft. above ground, 2352-ft. above sea level, lat. 48° 02' 06", long. 105° 31' 12".

Ownership: Wolf Point TV District.

Wolf Point—K27JQ, Ch. 27, Wolf Point TV District. Phone: 406-653-1427.

Technical Facilities: 0.84-kw ERP, 46-ft. above ground, 2329-ft. above sea level, lat. 48° 02' 06", long. 105° 31' 12".

Ownership: Wolf Point TV District.

Wolf Point—K29FS, Ch. 29, Wolf Point TV District. Phone: 406-653-1427.

Technical Facilities: 0.84-kw ERP, 46-ft. above ground, 2349-ft. above sea level, lat. 48° 02' 06", long. 105° 31' 12".

Ownership: Wolf Point TV District.

Wolf Point—K61CP, Ch. 61, Wolf Point TV District. Phone: 406-653-1427.

Technical Facilities: 1.32-kw ERP, lat. 48° 06' 44", long. 105° 41' 42".

Ownership: Wolf Point TV District.

Woods Bay—K07EN, Ch. 7, Blacktail TV Tax District. Phone: 406-883-2975.

Technical Facilities: 0.025-kw ERP, lat. 48° 01' 15", long. 114° 03' 30".

Holds CP for change to 0.044-kw ERP, 49-ft. above ground, 3149-ft. above sea level, lat. 48° 01' 30.6", long. 114° 03' 19.2". BDFCDTV-20080711ABO.

Ownership: Blacktail TV Tax District.

Woods Bay—K11KE, Ch. 11, Blacktail TV Tax District. Phone: 406-883-2975.

Technical Facilities: 0.229-kw ERP, lat. 48° 01' 15", long. 114° 03' 30".

Holds CP for change to 0.035-kw ERP, 40-ft. above ground, 3213-ft. above sea level, BDFCDTV-20070618ACO.

Ownership: Blacktail TV Tax District.

Woods Bay—K48EO, Ch. 48, Blacktail TV Tax District. Phone: 406-883-2975.

Technical Facilities: 0.795-kw ERP, 30-ft. above ground, 3110-ft. above sea level, lat. 48° 01' 15", long. 114° 03' 30".

Holds CP for change to 0.173-kw ERP, 40-ft. above ground, 3213-ft. above sea level, BDFCDTT-20070619AAA.

Ownership: Blacktail TV Tax District.

Wynot—K13DU, Ch. 13, Phillips County TV Translator District. Phone: 406-383-4499.

Technical Facilities: 0.003-kw ERP, 2851-ft. above sea level, lat. 48° 45' 30", long. 107° 45' 00".

Ownership: Phillips County TV Translator District.

Wynot, etc.—K07IB, Ch. 7, Phillips County TV Translator District. Phone: 406-383-4499.

Technical Facilities: 0.002-kw ERP, 2821-ft. above sea level, lat. 48° 45' 30", long. 107° 45' 00".

Ownership: Phillips County TV Translator District.

Wynot, etc.—K11GX, Ch. 11, Phillips County TV Translator District. Phone: 406-383-4499.

Technical Facilities: 0.002-kw ERP, 2841-ft. above sea level, lat. 48° 45' 30", long. 107° 45' 00".

Ownership: Phillips County TV Translator District.

Nebraska

Ainsworth—K11KW, Ch. 11, City of Ainsworth. Phone: 402-387-2494.

Technical Facilities: 0.095-kw ERP, lat. 42° 33' 25", long. 99° 51' 41".

Ownership: City of Ainsworth.

Ainsworth—K13EH, Ch. 13, City of Ainsworth. Phone: 402-387-2494.

Technical Facilities: 0.071-kw ERP, lat. 42° 33' 25", long. 99° 51' 41".

Ownership: City of Ainsworth.

Bassett—K13PB, Ch. 13, City of Bassett.

Technical Facilities: 0.035-kw ERP, lat. 42° 34' 00", long. 99° 32' 00".

Ownership: City of Bassett.

Beatrice—K17CI, Ch. 17, Colins Broadcasting Co.

Technical Facilities: 0.979-kw ERP, 249-ft. above ground, 1552-ft. above sea level, lat. 40° 15' 49", long. 96° 46' 27".

Ownership: Colins Broadcasting Co.

Beatrice—K23AA-D, Ch. 23, Nebraska Educational Telecommunications Commission. Phone: 402-472-9333.

Technical Facilities: 8.8-kw ERP, 476-ft. above ground, 1919-ft. above sea level, lat. 40° 13' 07", long. 96° 54' 56".

Ownership: Nebraska Educational Telecommunications Commission.

Beaver Lake area—K20DK, Ch. 20, Hoak Media of Nebraska License LLC.

Technical Facilities: 0.84-kw ERP, lat. 42° 27' 00", long. 100° 41' 07".

Ownership: Hoak Media LLC.

Benkelman—K33FO-D, Ch. 33, Nebraska Educational Telecommunications Commission. Phone: 402-472-9333.

Technical Facilities: 15-kw ERP, 312-ft. above ground, 3412-ft. above sea level, lat. 40° 04' 27", long. 101° 23' 31".

Ownership: Nebraska Educational Telecommunications Commission.

Blair—K24GO-D, Ch. 24, Nebraska Educational Telecommunications Comm. Phone: 402-472-9333.

Technical Facilities: 0.03-kw ERP, 36-ft. above ground, 1322-ft. above sea level, lat. 41° 31' 53", long. 96° 08' 12".

Ownership: Nebraska Educational Telecommunications Commission.

Broken Bow—K04CV, Ch. 4, Broken Bow Jr. Chamber of Commerce.

Technical Facilities: 0.068-kw ERP, lat. 41° 23' 49", long. 99° 37' 03".

Ownership: Broken Bow Jr. Chamber of Commerce.

Broken Bow—K06EY, Ch. 6, Broken Bow Jr. Chamber of Commerce.

Technical Facilities: 0.053-kw ERP, lat. 41° 23' 30", long. 99° 37' 00".

Ownership: Broken Bow Jr. Chamber of Commerce.

Broken Bow—K09GW, Ch. 9, Broken Bow Jr. Chamber of Commerce.

Technical Facilities: 0.095-kw ERP, lat. 41° 23' 30", long. 99° 37' 00".

Ownership: Broken Bow Jr. Chamber of Commerce.

Broken Bow—K18DH, Ch. 18, Hoak Media of Nebraska License LLC.

Technical Facilities: 1.01-kw ERP, 295-ft. above ground, 3212-ft. above sea level, lat. 41° 25' 53", long. 99° 50' 17".

Ownership: Hoak Media LLC.

Cambridge—K30FV, Ch. 30, Gray Television Licensee LLC. Phone: 402-467-9210.

Technical Facilities: 10.7-kw ERP, lat. 40° 22' 03", long. 100° 17' 57".

Ownership: Gray Television Inc.

Chadron—K02NY, Ch. 2, City of Chadron. Phone: 308-432-0505.

Technical Facilities: 0.136-kw ERP, 154-ft. above ground, 3720-ft. above sea level, lat. 42° 48' 04", long. 103° 00' 22".

Ownership: City of Chadron.

Chadron—K06JC-D, Ch. 6, Nebraska Educational Telecommunications Commission. Phone: 402-472-9333.

Technical Facilities: 0.066-kw ERP, 220-ft. above ground, 3783-ft. above sea level, lat. 42° 48' 46.8", long. 103° 00' 22".

Ownership: Nebraska Educational Telecommunications Commission.

Columbus—K21ES, Ch. 21, David C. Broadahl. Phone: 402-443-3000.

Technical Facilities: 2.42-kw ERP, 387-ft. above ground, 2034-ft. above sea level, lat. 41° 23' 34", long. 96° 54' 37".

Ownership: David C. Broadahl.

Columbus—K31EN, Ch. 31, David C. Broadahl. Phone: 402-443-3000.

Technical Facilities: 2.32-kw ERP, 387-ft. above ground, 2034-ft. above sea level, lat. 41° 23' 34", long. 96° 54' 37".

Ownership: David C. Broadahl.

Columbus—K33EM, Ch. 33, David C. Broadahl. Phone: 402-443-3000.

Technical Facilities: 2.67-kw ERP, 387-ft. above ground, 2034-ft. above sea level, lat. 41° 23' 34", long. 96° 54' 37".

Ownership: David C. Broadahl.

Columbus—K46EE, Ch. 46, David F. Harders. Phone: 402-443-3000.

Technical Facilities: 3.04-kw ERP, 387-ft. above ground, 2034-ft. above sea level, lat. 41° 23' 34", long. 96° 54' 37".

Ownership: David F. Harders.

Columbus—K52EX, Ch. 52, Glenda R. Harders. Phone: 402-443-3000.

Technical Facilities: 49.6-kw ERP, 443-ft. above ground, 1587-ft. above sea level, lat. 40° 13' 11", long. 95° 39' 56".

Ownership: Glenda R. Harders.

Columbus—KCAZ-LP, Ch. 57, TV Americas de Omaha LLC. Phone: 402-558-4200.

Technical Facilities: 10.3-kw ERP, 180-ft. above ground, 1831-ft. above sea level, lat. 41° 18' 23", long. 97° 20' 52".

Holds CP for change to channel number 36, 15-kw ERP, BDFCDTL-20060331ADQ.

Ownership: TV Americas de Omaha LLC.

■ **Columbus & Fremont**—K41FU, Ch. 41, Roger E. Harders. Phone: 402-443-3198.

Technical Facilities: 635-w TPO, 4.13-kw ERP, 394-ft. above ground, 2040-ft. above sea level, lat. 41° 23' 34", long. 96° 54' 37".

Transmitter: 1.5-mi. SE of Linwood.

Ownership: Roger E. Harders.

■ **Columbus & Fremont**—K47FK, Ch. 47, Roger E. Harders. Phone: 402-443-3198.

Technical Facilities: 1000-w TPO, 2.05-kw ERP, 394-ft. above ground, 2040-ft. above sea level, lat. 41° 23' 34", long. 96° 54' 37".

Transmitter: 1.5-mi. SE of Linwood.

Ownership: Roger E. Harders.

■ **Columbus & Fremont**—K49FP, Ch. 49, Glenda R. Harders. Phone: 402-443-3198.

Technical Facilities: 3.03-kw ERP, 387-ft. above ground, 2034-ft. above sea level, lat. 41° 23' 34", long. 96° 54' 37".

Ownership: Glenda R. Harders.

Columbus, etc.—K48FF, Ch. 48, David F. Harders. Phone: 402-443-3000.

Technical Facilities: 1000-w TPO, 2.92-kw ERP, 410-ft. above ground, 2040-ft. above sea level, lat. 41° 23' 34", long. 96° 54' 37".

Transmitter: 1.5-mi. SE of Linwood.

Ownership: David F. Harders.

■ **Columbus, etc.**—K50EG, Ch. 50, David F. Harders.

Technical Facilities: 250-w TPO, 2.96-kw ERP, 410-ft. above ground, 2040-ft. above sea level, lat. 41° 23' 34", long. 96° 54' 37".

Transmitter: 1.5-mi. SE of Linwood.

Ownership: David F. Harders.

Columbus, etc.—K63FQ, Ch. 63, Mary E. Harders. Phone: 402-443-3000.

Technical Facilities: 3.19-kw ERP, 387-ft. above ground, 2034-ft. above sea level, lat. 41° 23' 34", long. 96° 54' 37".

Transmitter: 1.5-mi SE of Linwood.

Ownership: Mary E. Harders.

Columbus-Fremont—K28EN, Ch. 28, Glenda R. Harders. Phone: 402-443-3000.

Technical Facilities: 145-w TPO, 1.82-kw ERP, 397-ft. above ground, 2040-ft. above sea level, lat. 41° 23' 34", long. 96° 54' 37".

Transmitter: 1.5-mi. SE of Linwood.

Ownership: Glenda R. Harders.

Columbus-Fremont—K54EU, Ch. 54, Glenda R. Harders. Phone: 402-443-3000.

Technical Facilities: 116.4-kw ERP, 1472-ft. above ground, 4000-ft. above sea level, lat. 42° 20' 05", long. 99° 29' 03".

Ownership: Glenda R. Harders.

Columbus-Fremont—K55HX, Ch. 55, Roger E. Harders. Phone: 402-443-3000.

Technical Facilities: 116.4-kw ERP, 295-ft. above ground, 3208-ft. above sea level, lat. 41° 25' 53", long. 99° 50' 18".

Ownership: Roger E. Harders.

Cozad—K55AF, Ch. 55, Gray Television Licensee LLC. Phone: 402-467-4321.

Technical Facilities: 6.07-kw ERP, lat. 40° 38' 04", long. 99° 41' 51".

Holds CP for change to channel number 24, 1.1-kw ERP, 295-ft. above ground, 2881-ft. above sea level, BDISDTT-20060329ANJ.

Ownership: Gray Television Inc.

Crawford—K06KR-D, Ch. 6, Nebraska Educational Telecommunications Commission. Phone: 402-472-9333.

Technical Facilities: 0.028-kw ERP, 43-ft. above ground, 3868-ft. above sea level, lat. 42° 40' 13", long. 103° 24' 09".

Began Operation: March 14, 1984.

Ownership: Nebraska Educational Telecommunications Commission.

Decatur—K34IB-D, Ch. 34, Nebraska Educational Telecommunications Commission. Phone: 402-472-9333.

Technical Facilities: 0.03-kw ERP, 39-ft. above ground, 1273-ft. above sea level, lat. 42° 00' 21", long. 96° 15' 25".

Ownership: Nebraska Educational Telecommunications Commission.

Falls City—K46FG-D, Ch. 46, Nebraska Educational Telecommunications Commission. Phone: 402-472-9333.

Technical Facilities: 8.3-kw ERP, 479-ft. above ground, 1623-ft. above sea level, lat. 40° 13' 11", long. 95° 39' 55".

Ownership: Nebraska Educational Telecommunications Commission.

■**Fremont & Omaha**—K28FS, Ch. 28, David F. Harders.

Technical Facilities: 250-w TPO, 2.86-kw ERP, 413-ft. above ground, 2040-ft. above sea level, lat. 41° 23' 34", long. 96° 54' 37".

Transmitter: 1.5-mi. SE of Linwood.

Ownership: David F. Harders.

Gothenburg—K28GC, Ch. 28, Gray Television Licensee LLC. Phone: 715-835-1313.

Technical Facilities: 11.4-kw ERP, lat. 40° 58' 32", long. 100° 11' 23".

Ownership: Gray Television Inc.

Gothenburg—K45II, Ch. 45, Marcia T. Turner. Phone: 954-732-9539.

Technical Facilities: 150-kw ERP, 239-ft. above ground, 2858-ft. above sea level, lat. 40° 58' 30", long. 100° 16' 19".

Ownership: Marcia T. Turner.

Grand Island—K56FC, Ch. 56, Hall County. Phone: 308-385-5444. Fax: 308-355-5486.

Technical Facilities: 662-w TPO, 17.2-kw ERP, 2031-ft. above sea level, lat. 40° 55' 29", long. 98° 20' 16".

Transmitter: SW corner of Sycamore & 2nd Sts.

Ownership: Hall County.

Personnel: Dick Gorgen, A-V Technician.

Harrison—K08LN-D, Ch. 8, Nebraska Educational Telecommunications Commission. Phone: 402-472-9333.

Technical Facilities: 0.07-kw ERP, 46-ft. above ground, 5276-ft. above sea level, lat. 42° 47' 05", long. 103° 59' 46".

Began Operation: August 4, 1992.

Ownership: Nebraska Educational Telecommunications Commission.

Harrison—K09PW, Ch. 9, Harrison Community Club.

Technical Facilities: 0.03-kw ERP, lat. 42° 43' 30", long. 103° 54' 00".

Ownership: Harrison Community Club.

Holdrege—K14IY, Ch. 14, Hoak Media of Nebraska License LLC.

Technical Facilities: 9.8-kw ERP, lat. 40° 24' 25", long. 99° 19' 14".

Transmitter: 6.2-mi. E & 2.5-mi. S of Holdrege.

Ownership: Hoak Media LLC.

Kilgore—K09IW, Ch. 9, Kilgore Television Committee.

Technical Facilities: 0.008-kw ERP, lat. 42° 57' 00", long. 100° 57' 30".

Ownership: Kilgore Television Committee.

Lewellen—K07JI, Ch. 7, Village of Lewellen.

Technical Facilities: 0.005-kw ERP, lat. 41° 18' 19", long. 102° 08' 07".

Ownership: Village of Lewellen.

Lewellen—K11KC, Ch. 11, Village of Lewellen.

Technical Facilities: 0.008-kw ERP, lat. 41° 18' 19", long. 102° 08' 07".

Ownership: Village of Lewellen.

Lexington—K35AL, Ch. 35, Hoak Media of Nebraska License LLC. Phone: 972-960-4896.

Technical Facilities: 0.863-kw ERP, 2966-ft. above sea level, lat. 40° 41' 20", long. 99° 46' 31".

Ownership: Hoak Media LLC.

Lincoln—K18CD, Ch. 18, Colins Broadcasting Co.

Technical Facilities: 9.17-kw ERP, lat. 40° 51' 10", long. 96° 40' 36".

Transmitter: 4100 Industrial Ave.

Ownership: Colins Broadcasting Co.

Lincoln—K27GX, Ch. 27, Three Angels Broadcasting Network Inc. Phone: 618-627-4651. Fax: 618-627-4155.

Studio: 3391 Charley Good Rd, West Frankfort, IL 62896.

Technical Facilities: 1000-w TPO, 15.3-kw ERP, 1547-ft. above sea level, lat. 40° 51' 10", long. 96° 40' 36".

Transmitter: 4100 Industrial Ave.

Ownership: Three Angels Broadcasting Network Inc.

Personnel: Moses Primo, Chief Engineer; Linda Shelton, Program Director.

Lincoln—K29GL, Ch. 29, Trinity Broadcasting Network Inc. Phone: 714-832-2950. Fax: 714-730-0661.

Technical Facilities: 29.1-kw ERP, 331-ft. above ground, 1729-ft. above sea level, lat. 40° 43' 40", long. 96° 36' 50".

Holds CP for change to 15-kw ERP, BDFCDTT-20060330ACT.

Transmitter: 7900 Yankee Hill Rd., Lincoln.

Ownership: Trinity Broadcasting Network Inc.

Personnel: Paul Crouch, General Manager; Ben Miller, Chief Engineer; Rod Henke, Sales Manager.

Lincoln—K67CV, Ch. 67, Channel America LPTV Holdings Inc. Phone: 212-366-9880.

Technical Facilities: 70-w TPO, 1.07-kw ERP, 243-ft. above ground, 1417-ft. above sea level, lat. 40° 48' 42", long. 96° 42' 05".

Transmitter: 233 S. 13th St., Lincoln.

Ownership: Channel America LPTV License Subsidiary Inc.

Lincoln—KWAZ-LP, Ch. 35, Colins Broadcasting Co. Phone: 559-625-4234.

Technical Facilities: 7.5-kw ERP, 414-ft. above ground, 1561-ft. above sea level, lat. 40° 51' 10", long. 96° 40' 36".

Ownership: Colins Broadcasting Co.

Lynch—K02LF, Ch. 2, Lynch Community Club. Phone: 402-569-3202.

Technical Facilities: 7.3-kw ERP, lat. 42° 49' 10", long. 98° 27' 45".

Ownership: Lynch Community Club.

Lynch—K10KU, Ch. 10, Lynch Community Club. Phone: 402-569-3202.

Technical Facilities: 0.007-kw ERP, lat. 42° 49' 10", long. 98° 27' 45".

Ownership: Lynch Community Club.

Lynch—K12LH, Ch. 12, Lynch Community Club. Phone: 402-569-3202.

Technical Facilities: 0.007-kw ERP, lat. 42° 49' 10", long. 98° 27' 45".

Ownership: Lynch Community Club.

McCook—KBVZ-LP, Ch. 42, Pappas Telecasting Companies. Phone: 559-733-7800.

Technical Facilities: 8.2-kw ERP, 272-ft. above ground, 2940-ft. above sea level, lat. 40° 12' 52", long. 100° 39' 51".

Holds CP for change to 4-kw ERP, BDFCDTL-20060331AGL.

Ownership: Pappas Telecasting Companies.

Personnel: Dale Scherbring, General Manager.

McCook—KWNB-LD, Ch. 29, Pappas Telecasting Companies. Phone: 559-733-7800.

Technical Facilities: 4.7-kw ERP, 250-ft. above ground, 2918-ft. above sea level, lat. 40° 12' 52", long. 100° 39' 51".

Ownership: Pappas Telecasting Companies.

McCook—WCWH-LP, Ch. 40, Pappas Telecasting Companies. Phone: 559-733-7800.

Technical Facilities: 16.6-kw ERP, 272-ft. above ground, 2940-ft. above sea level, lat. 40° 12' 52", long. 100° 39' 51".

Holds CP for change to 15-kw ERP, BDFCDTL-20060331AGE.

Ownership: Pappas Telecasting Companies.

McCook & Culbertson—K44FN-D, Ch. 44, Nebraska Educational Telecommunications Commission. Phone: 402-472-9333.

Technical Facilities: 15-kw ERP, 256-ft. above ground, 3038-ft. above sea level, lat. 40° 15' 46", long. 100° 53' 30".

Ownership: Nebraska Educational Telecommunications Commission.

Neligh—K50IO-D, Ch. 50, Nebraska Educational Telecommunications Commission. Phone: 402-472-9333.

Technical Facilities: 0.35-kw ERP, 381-ft. above ground, 2306-ft. above sea level, lat. 42° 02' 43", long. 98° 01' 41".

Ownership: Nebraska Educational Telecommunications Commission.

Neligh—K53GC, Ch. 53, Gray Television Licensee LLC. Phone: 402-467-4321.

Technical Facilities: 10.8-kw ERP, lat. 42° 02' 43", long. 98° 01' 41".

Holds CP for change to channel number 32, 4.9-kw ERP, 423-ft. above ground, 2348-ft. above sea level, BDISDTT-20060329ANK.

Ownership: Gray Television Inc.

Newport—K25GM, Ch. 25, Gray Television Licensee LLC. Phone: 402-467-9210.

Technical Facilities: 8.7-kw ERP, lat. 42° 37' 33", long. 99° 19' 30".

Transmitter: K24AA LPTV tower, 1.7-mi. N of Newport.

Ownership: Gray Television Inc.

Niobrara—K14MI-D, Ch. 14, Nebraska Educational Telecommunications Commission. Phone: 402-472-9333.

Technical Facilities: 0.002-kw ERP, 46-ft. above ground, 1427-ft. above sea level, lat. 42° 44' 42", long. 98° 02' 00".

Ownership: Nebraska Educational Telecommunications Commission.

Norfolk—K21HS, Ch. 21, Trinity Broadcasting Network. Phone: 714-832-2950. Fax: 714-730-0661.

Technical Facilities: 1.9-kw ERP, 322-ft. above ground, 2001-ft. above sea level, lat. 42° 01' 52", long. 97° 21' 28".

Ownership: Trinity Broadcasting Network Inc.

Norfolk—K35FM, Ch. 35, Waitt Broadcasting Inc. Phone: 402-330-2520.

Technical Facilities: 3.35-kw ERP, lat. 42° 01' 43", long. 97° 21' 24".

Holds CP for change to 9.3-kw ERP, 308-ft. above ground, 2031-ft. above sea level, BMPTT-20071002AAV.

Ownership: Waitt Broadcasting Inc.

Norfolk—K48CH, Ch. 48, KTIV Television Inc. Phone: 712-223-5100.

Technical Facilities: 1.23-kw ERP, lat. 42° 02' 05", long. 97° 21' 53".

Holds CP for change to channel number 24, 15-kw ERP, 272-ft. above ground, 1922-ft. above sea level, BDISDTT-20060331AIW.

Ownership: Quincy Newspapers Inc.

Norfolk—KAZJ-LP, Ch. 46, TV Americas de Omaha LLC. Phone: 559-733-7800.

Technical Facilities: 75-kw ERP, 384-ft. above ground, 2154-ft. above sea level, lat. 42° 01' 41", long. 97° 20' 25".

Ownership: TV Americas de Omaha LLC.

Norfolk—KPTP-LP, Ch. 57, KPTH License LLC - Debtor-in-Possession. Phone: 559-773-7800. Fax: 559-627-5363.

Technical Facilities: 6.6-kw ERP, 351-ft. above ground, 2121-ft. above sea level, lat. 42° 01' 41", long. 97° 20' 25".

Ownership: E. Roger Williams, Trustee.

Personnel: Dale Scherbring, General Manager.

North Platte—K04ED, Ch. 4, City of North Platte.

Technical Facilities: 0.055-kw ERP, lat. 41° 08' 30", long. 100° 45' 30".

Ownership: City of North Platte.

■**North Platte**—K11TW, Ch. 11, Hoak Media of Nebraska License LLC. Phone: 308-532-2222. Fax: 308-532-9579.

Technical Facilities: 10-w TPO, 0.084-kw ERP, 417-ft. above ground, 3524-ft. above sea level, lat. 41° 12' 13", long. 100° 43' 58".

Transmitter: 1.1-mi. NE of State Rtes. 97 & 70 intersection.

Ownership: Hoak Media LLC.

Personnel: Lewys Carlini, General Manager; Mike McNeil, Chief Engineer.

North Platte—K45GS, Ch. 45, Mary E. Harders. Phone: 402-443-3000.

Technical Facilities: 250-w TPO, 3.12-kw ERP, 387-ft. above ground, 2034-ft. above sea level, lat. 41° 23' 34", long. 96° 54' 37".

Transmitter: 1.5-mi. SE of Linwood.

Ownership: Mary E. Harders.

North Platte—K50JI, Ch. 50, EICB-TV East LLC. Phone: 972-291-3750.

Technical Facilities: 0.08-kw ERP, 26-ft. above ground, 2848-ft. above sea level, lat. 41° 08' 01", long. 100° 47' 13".

Began Operation: March 17, 2009.

Ownership: EICB-TV LLC.

North Platte—K57CZ, Ch. 57, Gray Television Licensee LLC. Phone: 402-467-4321.

Technical Facilities: 0.13-kw ERP, lat. 41° 08' 30", long. 100° 45' 30".

Holds CP for change to channel number 25, 2.28-kw ERP, 145-ft. above ground, 2944-ft. above sea level, BDISDTT-20061208AAV.

Ownership: Gray Television Inc.

North Platte—K59FT, Ch. 59, Mary E. Harders. Phone: 402-443-3000.

Technical Facilities: 101.6-kw ERP, 590-ft. above ground, 3609-ft. above sea level, lat. 41° 12' 13", long. 100° 44' 00".

Ownership: Mary E. Harders.

■ **North Platte**—KHGI-CA, Ch. 13, Pappas Telecasting of Central Nebraska LP (A Delaware LP). Phone: 559-733-7800.

Technical Facilities: 0.018-kw ERP, 180-ft. above ground, 2982-ft. above sea level, lat. 41° 08' 30", long. 100° 45' 30".

Ownership: Pappas Telecasting Companies.

North Platte—KMBB-LP, Ch. 30, Kansas-Nebraska Association of Seventh-Day Adventists. Phone: 785-478-4726.

Technical Facilities: 0.167-kw ERP, 95-ft. above ground, 2900-ft. above sea level, lat. 41° 08' 14", long. 100° 45' 37".

Ownership: Kansas-Nebraska Association of Seventh-Day Adventists.

Ogallala—K21CY, Ch. 21, Hoak Media of Nebraska License LLC. Phone: 972-960-4896.

Technical Facilities: 11.9-kw ERP, lat. 41° 08' 30", long. 101° 43' 15".

Ownership: Hoak Media LLC.

Ogallala—K26CV, Ch. 26, Trinity Broadcasting Network Inc. Phone: 714-832-2950. Fax: 714-730-0661.

Technical Facilities: 1.1-kw ERP, 161-ft. above ground, 3481-ft. above sea level, lat. 41° 08' 02", long. 101° 41' 42".

Ownership: Trinity Broadcasting Network Inc.

Omaha—K53EY, Ch. 53, TV-45 Inc. Phone: 515-597-3531.

Technical Facilities: 1000-w TPO, 10.55-kw ERP, 174-ft. above ground, 1253-ft. above sea level, lat. 41° 12' 47", long. 96° 03' 33".

Transmitter: 9437 J St.

Ownership: TV-45 Inc.

Omaha—K61GA, Ch. 61, Three Angels Broadcasting Network Inc. Phone: 618-627-4651. Fax: 618-627-4155.

Technical Facilities: 25-w TPO, 0.179-kw ERP, 479-ft. above ground, 1509-ft. above sea level, lat. 41° 15' 20", long. 95° 56' 20".

Transmitter: 1700 Farnam St.

Ownership: Three Angels Broadcasting Network Inc.

Personnel: Moses Primo, Chief Engineer.

Omaha—KAZO-LP, Ch. 57, TV Americas de Omaha LLC. Phone: 559-735-7800.

Technical Facilities: 100-kw ERP, 351-ft. above ground, 1469-ft. above sea level, lat. 41° 15' 26", long. 95° 59' 01".

Holds CP for change to channel number 34, 50-kw ERP, BPTTL-20040727ACO.

Ownership: TV Americas de Omaha LLC.

■ **Omaha**—KKAZ-CA, Ch. 57, KPTM (TV) License LLC - Debtor-in-Possession. Phone: 559-733-7800.

Technical Facilities: 12.3-kw ERP, 351-ft. above ground, 1332-ft. above sea level, lat. 41° 15' 26", long. 95° 59' 01".

Transmitter: WOW(FM) tower, 0.5-mi. NW of Military Ave. & 72nd St. intersection.

Ownership: E. Roger Williams, Trustee.

Omaha—KOHA-LP, Ch. 48, Word of God Fellowship Inc. Phone: 817-571-1229. Fax: 817-571-7478.

Technical Facilities: 150-kw ERP, 446-ft. above ground, 1640-ft. above sea level, lat. 41° 18' 40", long. 96° 01' 37".

Holds CP for change to 447-ft. above ground, 1608-ft. above sea level, lat. 41° 18' 32", long. 96° 01' 33". BPTTL-20070917ACE.

Began Operation: November 7, 1996.

Ownership: Word of God Fellowship Inc.

Omaha—KVSS-LP, Ch. 50, VSS Catholic Communications. Phone: 402-571-0200.

Technical Facilities: 10-kw ERP, 492-ft. above ground, 1644-ft. above sea level, lat. 41° 18' 47", long. 96° 00' 36".

Ownership: VSS Catholic Communications.

O'Neill—K43FX, Ch. 43, Gray Television Licensee LLC. Phone: 402-467-9210.

Technical Facilities: 5.9-kw ERP, lat. 42° 27' 00", long. 98° 36' 52".

Ownership: Gray Television Inc.

O'Neill—KAZK-LP, Ch. 27, Pappas Telecasting Companies. Phone: 559-733-7800.

Technical Facilities: 10.3-kw ERP, 225-ft. above ground, 2195-ft. above sea level, lat. 42° 26' 57", long. 98° 36' 53".

Holds CP for change to 15-kw ERP, 225-ft. above ground, 2194-ft. above sea level, lat. 42° 26' 56", long. 98° 36' 51". BDFCDTL-20060331AHD.

Ownership: Pappas Telecasting Companies.

O'Neill—KOAZ-LP, Ch. 48, Pappas Telecasting Companies. Phone: 559-733-7800.

Technical Facilities: 9.9-kw ERP, 227-ft. above ground, 2197-ft. above sea level, lat. 42° 26' 57", long. 98° 36' 53".

Holds CP for change to 15-kw ERP, 226-ft. above ground, 2195-ft. above sea level, lat. 42° 26' 56", long. 98° 36' 51". BDFCDTL-20060331AHI.

Ownership: Pappas Telecasting Companies.

Ord—K02HJ, Ch. 2, City of Ord. Phone: 308-728-3540.

Technical Facilities: 0.032-kw ERP, lat. 41° 35' 38", long. 98° 55' 29".

Ownership: City of Ord.

Ord—K04HL, Ch. 4, City of Ord. Phone: 308-728-3540.

Technical Facilities: 0.032-kw ERP, 2178-ft. above sea level, lat. 41° 36' 00", long. 98° 36' 00".

Ownership: City of Ord.

Pawnee City—K33AC-D, Ch. 33, Nebraska Educational Telecommunications Commission. Phone: 402-472-9333.

Technical Facilities: 8.5-kw ERP, 479-ft. above ground, 1929-ft. above sea level, lat. 40° 11' 01", long. 96° 21' 04".

Ownership: Nebraska Educational Telecommunications Commission.

■ **Scottsbluff**—K02NT, Ch. 2, Duhamel Broadcasting Enterprises. Phone: 605-342-2000.

Technical Facilities: 1.38-kw ERP, 105-ft. above ground, 3966-ft. above sea level, lat. 41° 55' 44", long. 103° 39' 38".

Ownership: Duhamel Broadcasting Enterprises.

South Sioux City—KAZS-LP, Ch. 23, TV Americas de Omaha LLC. Phone: 559-733-7800.

Technical Facilities: 87.7-kw ERP, 394-ft. above ground, 1481-ft. above sea level, lat. 42° 28' 21", long. 96° 25' 20".

Ownership: TV Americas de Omaha LLC.

Stapleton—K12KW, Ch. 12, Village of Stapleton.

Technical Facilities: 0.004-kw ERP, lat. 41° 28' 40", long. 100° 30' 30".

Ownership: Village of Stapleton.

Trenton—K04EG, Ch. 4, Village of Trenton. Phone: 308-334-5488.

Technical Facilities: 0.002-kw ERP, lat. 40° 10' 44", long. 101° 00' 37".

Ownership: Village of Trenton.

Valentine—KHJP-LP, Ch. 29, Pappas Telecasting Companies. Phone: 559-733-7800.

Technical Facilities: 10.1-kw ERP, 164-ft. above ground, 2867-ft. above sea level, lat. 42° 53' 22", long. 100° 33' 15".

Holds CP for change to 15-kw ERP, BDFCDTL-20060331AEC.

Ownership: Pappas Telecasting Companies.

Valentine—WCWY-LD, Ch. 31, Pappas Telecasting Companies. Phone: 559-733-7800.

Technical Facilities: 1-kw ERP, 164-ft. above ground, 2867-ft. above sea level, lat. 42° 53' 22", long. 100° 33' 15".

Ownership: Pappas Telecasting Companies.

Verdigre—K10JW-D, Ch. 10, Nebraska Educational Telecommunications Commission. Phone: 402-472-9333.

Technical Facilities: 0.006-kw ERP, 92-ft. above ground, 1611-ft. above sea level, lat. 42° 35' 55", long. 98° 02' 30".

Began Operation: August 14, 1978.

Ownership: Nebraska Educational Telecommunications Commission.

Wallace—K33FF, Ch. 33, Gray Television Licensee LLC. Phone: 402-467-4321.

Technical Facilities: 8-kw ERP, 613-ft. above ground, 3845-ft. above sea level, lat. 41° 03' 50", long. 101° 11' 29".

Ownership: Gray Television Inc.

Wauneta—K20IJ-D, Ch. 20, Nebraska Educational Telecommunications Commission. Phone: 402-472-9333.

Technical Facilities: 0.002-kw ERP, 43-ft. above ground, 3094-ft. above sea level, lat. 40° 25' 14", long. 101° 21' 58".

Ownership: Nebraska Educational Telecommunications Commission.

Wood Lake—K13AW, Ch. 13, Village of Wood Lake.

Technical Facilities: 0.003-kw ERP, lat. 42° 38' 20", long. 100° 14' 30".

Ownership: Village of Wood Lake.

Nevada

Alamo, etc.—K10NV, Ch. 10, Clark County School District. Phone: 702-299-1010.

Technical Facilities: 0.034-kw ERP, 17-ft. above ground, 6188-ft. above sea level, lat. 37° 20' 39.9", long. 115° 15' 24.1".

Ownership: Clark County School District.

Austin—K06KD, Ch. 6, Valley Broadcasting Co. Phone: 702-642-3333.

Technical Facilities: 0.139-kw ERP, lat. 39° 27' 13", long. 117° 03' 13".

Ownership: Sunbelt Communications Co.

Austin—K10KB, Ch. 10, Austin Television Association. Phone: 775-964-2447.

Technical Facilities: 0.013-kw ERP, lat. 40° 30' 12", long. 117° 03' 48".

Ownership: Austin Television Association.

Austin—K12IX, Ch. 12, Gray Television Licensee LLC. Phone: 715-835-1313.

Technical Facilities: 0.15-kw ERP, lat. 39° 27' 13", long. 117° 03' 13".

Ownership: Gray Television Inc.

Austin—K26EH, Ch. 26, Austin Television Association. Phone: 775-964-2447.

Technical Facilities: 0.037-kw ERP, 43-ft. above ground, 6867-ft. above sea level, lat. 39° 29' 33", long. 117° 03' 45".

Ownership: Austin Television Association.

Austin—K28EI, Ch. 28, Austin Television Association. Phone: 775-964-2447.

Technical Facilities: 0.037-kw ERP, 33-ft. above ground, 6857-ft. above sea level, lat. 39° 29' 33", long. 117° 03' 45".

Ownership: Austin Television Association.

Austin—K46FB, Ch. 46, Austin Television Association. Phone: 775-964-2447.

Technical Facilities: 0.001-kw ERP, lat. 39° 20' 48", long. 117° 24' 00".

Ownership: Austin Television Association.

Austin & Reese River—K41HH, Ch. 41, Austin Television Association. Phone: 775-964-2447.

Technical Facilities: 0.043-kw ERP, 13-ft. above ground, 6903-ft. above sea level, lat. 39° 20' 48", long. 117° 24' 00".

Ownership: Austin Television Association.

Battle Mountain—K11IY, Ch. 11, Lander County General Improvement District #1. Phone: 775-635-2278.

Technical Facilities: 0.472-kw ERP, lat. 40° 35' 25", long. 116° 54' 00".

Holds CP for change to 0.102-kw ERP, 11-ft. above ground, 7334-ft. above sea level, lat. 40° 37' 04.8", long. 116° 41' 21". BPTTV-20090224ACC.

Ownership: Lander County General Improvement District No. 1.

Battle Mountain—K13JD, Ch. 13, Lander County General Improvement District No. 1. Phone: 775-635-2278.

Technical Facilities: 0.057-kw ERP, lat. 40° 35' 25", long. 116° 54' 00".

Holds CP for change to 0.102-kw ERP, 11-ft. above ground, 7334-ft. above sea level, lat. 40° 37' 04.8", long. 116° 41' 21". BPTTV-20090224ACB.

Ownership: Lander County General Improvement District No. 1.

Battle Mountain—K16FD, Ch. 16, Lander County General Improvement District 1.

Technical Facilities: 0.16-kw ERP, 20-ft. above ground, 7372-ft. above sea level, lat. 40° 37' 05", long. 116° 41' 19".

Ownership: Lander County General Improvement District No. 1.

Battle Mountain—K22GM, Ch. 22, Lander County General Improvement District 1.

Technical Facilities: 0.16-kw ERP, 23-ft. above ground, 7375-ft. above sea level, lat. 40° 37' 05", long. 116° 41' 19".

Ownership: Lander County General Improvement District No. 1.

Battle Mountain—K32CA, Ch. 32, Lander County General Improvement District No. 1.

Technical Facilities: 100-w TPO, 1.19-kw ERP, 46-ft. above ground, 4574-ft. above sea level, lat. 40° 35' 25", long. 116° 54' 00".

Transmitter: Approx. 4-mi. SE of Battle Mountain.

Ownership: Lander County General Improvement District No. 1.

Battle Mountain—K42DZ, Ch. 42, Lander County General Improvement District No. 1.

Technical Facilities: 0.732-kw ERP, lat. 40° 36' 49", long. 116° 41' 12".

Transmitter: Argentina Rim, 14-mi. at 100 degrees T from Battle Mountain.

Ownership: Lander County General Improvement District No. 1.

Battle Mountain—KNNC-LP, Ch. 3, Entravision Holdings LLC. Phone: 310-447-3870.

Technical Facilities: 3-kw ERP, 50-ft. above ground, 6999-ft. above sea level, lat. 40° 42' 39", long. 116° 49' 48".

Began Operation: May 3, 2006.

Ownership: Entravision Communications Corp.

Beowawe—K09XP, Ch. 9, Eureka County TV District. Phone: 775-237-5506.

Technical Facilities: 0.089-kw ERP, 16-ft. above ground, 7424-ft. above sea level, lat. 40° 37' 15", long. 116° 41' 17".

Ownership: Eureka County Television District.

Beowawe—K12HY, Ch. 12, Eureka County Television District.

Technical Facilities: 0.099-kw ERP, 7211-ft. above sea level, lat. 40° 38' 00", long. 116° 40' 30".

Ownership: Eureka County Television District.

Beowawe—K18GW, Ch. 18, Eureka County TV District. Phone: 775-237-5506.

Technical Facilities: 0.165-kw ERP, 16-ft. above ground, 7424-ft. above sea level, lat. 40° 37' 15", long. 116° 41' 17".

Ownership: Eureka County Television District.

Beowawe—K20HX, Ch. 20, Eureka County TV District. Phone: 775-237-5506.

Technical Facilities: 0.165-kw ERP, 16-ft. above ground, 7424-ft. above sea level, lat. 40° 37' 15", long. 116° 41' 17".

Ownership: Eureka County Television District.

Beowawe—K30HF, Ch. 30, Eureka County TV District. Phone: 775-237-5506.

Technical Facilities: 0.164-kw ERP, 16-ft. above ground, 7424-ft. above sea level, lat. 40° 37' 15", long. 116° 41' 17".

Ownership: Eureka County Television District.

Beowawe—K40CA, Ch. 40, Elko Television District. Phone: 775-738-5025.

Technical Facilities: 0.608-kw ERP, lat. 40° 36' 40", long. 116° 40' 30".

Ownership: Elko Television District.

Beowawe, etc.—K02OK, Ch. 2, Eureka County Television District No. 2.

Technical Facilities: 0.009-kw ERP, 20-ft. above ground, 7379-ft. above sea level, lat. 40° 35' 40", long. 116° 40' 30".

Ownership: Eureka County Television District.

Beowawe, etc.—K04GD, Ch. 4, Eureka County Television District.

Technical Facilities: 0.099-kw ERP, 7211-ft. above sea level, lat. 40° 38' 00", long. 116° 40' 30".

Ownership: Eureka County Television District.

Beowawe, etc.—K36DC, Ch. 36, Eureka County Television District No. 2.

Technical Facilities: 0.544-kw ERP, 20-ft. above ground, 7720-ft. above sea level, lat. 40° 43' 07", long. 116° 16' 06".

Ownership: Eureka County Television District.

Caliente—K02JO, Ch. 2, Lincoln County TV District No. 1. Phone: 775-962-5336.

Technical Facilities: 0.004-kw ERP, lat. 37° 37' 24", long. 114° 30' 25".

Ownership: Lincoln County TV District No. 1.

Caliente—K09FL, Ch. 9, Lincoln County TV District No. 1. Phone: 775-962-5336.

Technical Facilities: 0.001-kw ERP, lat. 37° 37' 24", long. 114° 30' 25".

Ownership: Lincoln County TV District No. 1.

Caliente—K11CN, Ch. 11, Lincoln County TV District No. 1. Phone: 775-962-5336.

Technical Facilities: 0.048-kw ERP, lat. 37° 37' 24", long. 114° 30' 25".

Ownership: Lincoln County TV District No. 1.

Caliente—K13LV, Ch. 13, Lincoln County TV District No. 1. Phone: 775-962-5336.

Technical Facilities: 0.008-kw ERP, lat. 37° 37' 24", long. 114° 30' 25".

Ownership: Lincoln County TV District No. 1.

Caliente—K45AL, Ch. 45, Lincoln County TV District No. 1. Phone: 775-962-5336.

Technical Facilities: 0.01-kw ERP, lat. 37° 37' 24", long. 114° 30' 25".

Ownership: Lincoln County TV District No. 1.

Carlin—K13BB, Ch. 13, Carlin Television District. Phone: 775-754-6447.

Technical Facilities: 0.138-kw ERP, lat. 40° 56' 09", long. 116° 03' 04".

Ownership: Carlin Television District.

Carlin—K27DY, Ch. 27, Carlin Television District. Phone: 775-754-6447.

Technical Facilities: 0.001-kw ERP, lat. 40° 43' 00", long. 116° 06' 40".

Transmitter: Carlin town site.

Ownership: Carlin Television District.

Carlin—K30CD, Ch. 30, Carlin Television District. Phone: 775-754-6447.

Technical Facilities: 1-w TPO, 0.003-kw ERP, 26-ft. above ground, 4980-ft. above sea level, lat. 40° 43' 00", long. 116° 06' 40".

Transmitter: NW quarter of section 27, Twp. 33 N, Range 52 E, Carlin.

Ownership: Carlin Television District.

Personnel: Howard R. Wright, General Manager.

Carlin—K33DP, Ch. 33, Carlin Television District. Phone: 775-754-6447.

Technical Facilities: 0.003-kw ERP, 20-ft. above ground, 5013-ft. above sea level, lat. 40° 43' 00", long. 116° 06' 40".

Ownership: Carlin Television District.

Carlin—K35BR, Ch. 35, Carlin Television District. Phone: 775-754-6447.

Technical Facilities: 1-w TPO, 0.003-kw ERP, 26-ft. above ground, 5013-ft. above sea level, lat. 40° 43' 00", long. 116° 06' 40".

Transmitter: NW quarter of Section 27, Twp. 33 N, Range 52 E Carlin.

Ownership: Carlin Television District.

Personnel: Howard R. Wright, General Manager.

Carlin—K44AM, Ch. 44, Carlin Television District. Phone: 775-754-6447.

Technical Facilities: 0.51-kw ERP, lat. 40° 43' 07", long. 116° 16' 06".

Ownership: Carlin Television District.

Carlin—K46KH, Ch. 46, Carlin Television District. Phone: 775-754-6447.

Technical Facilities: 0.802-kw ERP, 14-ft. above ground, 7616-ft. above sea level, lat. 40° 43' 07", long. 116° 16' 06".

Ownership: Carlin Television District.

Carlin—K48LM, Ch. 48, Carlin Television District. Phone: 775-754-6447.

Technical Facilities: 0.819-kw ERP, 14-ft. above ground, 7616-ft. above sea level, lat. 40° 43' 07", long. 116° 16' 06".

Ownership: Carlin Television District.

Carlin—K54DV, Ch. 54, Carlin Television District. Phone: 775-754-6447.

Technical Facilities: 20-w TPO, 0.87-kw ERP, 7613-ft. above sea level, lat. 40° 43' 07", long. 116° 16' 06".

Transmitter: Mary's Mountain, near Carlin.

Ownership: Carlin Television District.

Personnel: Howard R. Wright, General Manager.

Carrara—K30IG, Ch. 30, Hispanic Christian Community Network Inc. Phone: 214-879-0081.

Technical Facilities: 150-kw ERP, 131-ft. above ground, 3058-ft. above sea level, lat. 36° 48' 15", long. 116° 42' 29".

Ownership: Hispanic Christian Community Network Inc.

Carson City—K17CA-D, Ch. 17, KTVU Partnership. Phone: 775-856-1100.

Technical Facilities: 5.13-kw ERP, 89-ft. above ground, 7506-ft. above sea level, lat. 39° 15' 32", long. 119° 42' 06".

Ownership: Cox Enterprises Inc.

Carson City—K19CU, Ch. 19, Trinity Broadcasting Network Inc. Phone: 714-832-2950. Fax: 714-730-0661.

Technical Facilities: 1000-w TPO, 8.8-kw ERP, 98-ft. above ground, 7487-ft. above sea level, lat. 39° 15' 34", long. 119° 42' 21".

Transmitter: Atop McClellan Peak, near Silver City.

Ownership: Trinity Broadcasting Network Inc.

Carson City—K29ES, Ch. 29, Channel 5 Public Broadcasting Inc. Phone: 775-784-4555.

Technical Facilities: 0.757-kw ERP, 20-ft. above ground, 5951-ft. above sea level, lat. 39° 12' 50", long. 119° 46' 14".

Holds CP for change to 1.43-kw ERP, lat. 39° 12' 50", long. 119° 46' 10". BDFCDTT-20081125AFF.

Began Operation: January 14, 1985.

Ownership: Channel 5 Public Broadcasting Inc.

Carson City—K32GW-D, Ch. 32, Ellis Communications Inc. Phone: 404-229-8080.

Technical Facilities: 6.94-kw ERP, 60-ft. above ground, 7501-ft. above sea level, lat. 39° 15' 34", long. 119° 42' 16".

Ownership: Ellis Communications Inc.

Carson City—K52DN, Ch. 52, Sierra Broadcasting Co.

Technical Facilities: 0.819-kw ERP, 20-ft. above ground, 5961-ft. above sea level, lat. 39° 12' 40", long. 119° 46' 20".

Ownership: Sunbelt Communications Co.

Carson City—KNCV-LP, Ch. 48, Entravision Holdings LLC. Phone: 310-447-3870.

Technical Facilities: 1000-w TPO, 9.9-kw ERP, 89-ft. above ground, 4469-ft. above sea level, lat. 32° 14' 56", long. 111° 06' 58".

Transmitter: McClelland Peak communications site, 7.4-mi. NNE of Carson City.

Ownership: Entravision Communications Corp.

Copper Canyon, etc.—K06FQ, Ch. 6, Lander County General Improvement District No. 1. Phone: 775-635-2278.

Technical Facilities: 0.188-kw ERP, 6184-ft. above sea level, lat. 40° 35' 25", long. 116° 41' 30".

Ownership: Lander County General Improvement District No. 1.

Dayton—K06JK, Ch. 6, Lyon County Public Works. Phone: 775-463-6551.

Technical Facilities: 0.047-kw ERP, lat. 39° 11' 52", long. 119° 28' 50".

Ownership: Lyon County Public Works.

Dayton—K45GZ, Ch. 45, Lyon County Public Works. Phone: 775-463-6551.

Technical Facilities: 0.5-kw ERP, 16-ft. above ground, 8045-ft. above sea level, lat. 39° 11' 52", long. 119° 28' 50".

Ownership: Lyon County Public Works.

Duckwater, etc.—K15GS, Ch. 15, Eureka County TV District. Phone: 775-237-5506.

Technical Facilities: 0.499-kw ERP, 26-ft. above ground, 9586-ft. above sea level, lat. 39° 26' 58", long. 115° 59' 54".

Ownership: Eureka County Television District.

Duckwater, etc.—K29GM, Ch. 29, Eureka County TV District. Phone: 775-237-5506.

Technical Facilities: 0.518-kw ERP, 26-ft. above ground, 9586-ft. above sea level, lat. 39° 26' 58", long. 115° 59' 54".

Ownership: Eureka County Television District.

Elko—K05JU, Ch. 5, Elko Television District. Phone: 775-738-5025.

Technical Facilities: 0.108-kw ERP, 33-ft. above ground, 6499-ft. above sea level, lat. 40° 49' 16", long. 115° 42' 04".

Ownership: Elko Television District.

Elko—K06MK, Ch. 6, Elko Television District. Phone: 775-738-5025.

Technical Facilities: 10-w TPO, 0.054-kw ERP, 6499-ft. above sea level, lat. 40° 49' 16", long. 115° 42' 04".

Transmitter: Lamoille Summit, E of Elko.

Ownership: Elko Television District.

Elko—K08LS, Ch. 8, Elko Television District. Phone: 775-738-5025.

Technical Facilities: 0.057-kw ERP, 23-ft. above ground, 6489-ft. above sea level, lat. 40° 49' 16", long. 115° 42' 04".

Ownership: Elko Television District.

Elko—K15EE, Ch. 15, Elko Television District. Phone: 775-738-5025.

Technical Facilities: 0.341-kw ERP, lat. 40° 50' 54", long. 115° 45' 32".

Ownership: Elko Television District.

Elko—K17DT, Ch. 17, Elko Television District. Phone: 775-738-5025.

Technical Facilities: 1.13-kw ERP, 23-ft. above ground, 6489-ft. above sea level, lat. 40° 49' 16", long. 115° 42' 04".

Ownership: Elko Television District.

Elko—K19FZ, Ch. 19, Elko Television District. Phone: 775-738-5025. Fax: 775-738-4712.

Technical Facilities: 0.546-kw ERP, 30-ft. above ground, 7411-ft. above sea level, lat. 40° 42' 00", long. 115° 54' 09".

Ownership: Elko Television District.

Elko—K23FC, Ch. 23, Elko Television District. Phone: 775-738-5025.

Technical Facilities: 0.821-kw ERP, 28-ft. above ground, 7439-ft. above sea level, lat. 40° 42' 00", long. 115° 54' 09".

Ownership: Elko Television District.

Elko—K25FR, Ch. 25, Elko Television District. Phone: 775-738-5025.

Technical Facilities: 0.576-kw ERP, lat. 40° 42' 00", long. 115° 54' 09".

Ownership: Elko Television District.

Elko—K32GK, Ch. 32, Elko Television District. Phone: 775-738-5025.

Technical Facilities: 1-kw ERP, 60-ft. above ground, 6526-ft. above sea level, lat. 40° 49' 16", long. 115° 42' 04".

Ownership: Elko Television District.

Elko—K34HE, Ch. 34, Elko Television District. Phone: 775-738-5025.

Technical Facilities: 1-kw ERP, 60-ft. above ground, 6526-ft. above sea level, lat. 40° 49' 16", long. 115° 42' 04".

Ownership: Elko Television District.

Elko—K38IF, Ch. 38, Elko Television District. Phone: 775-738-5025.

Technical Facilities: 0.96-kw ERP, 40-ft. above ground, 7421-ft. above sea level, lat. 40° 42' 00", long. 115° 54' 09".

Ownership: Elko Television District.

Elko—K47HP, Ch. 47, Elko Television District. Phone: 775-738-5025.

Technical Facilities: 0.3-kw ERP, 40-ft. above ground, 6506-ft. above sea level, lat. 40° 49' 16", long. 115° 42' 04".

Ownership: Elko Television District.

Elko—K50CA, Ch. 50, Elko Television District. Phone: 775-738-5025.

Technical Facilities: 0.546-kw ERP, lat. 40° 42' 00", long. 115° 54' 09".

Ownership: Elko Television District.

Elko—K55IK, Ch. 55, Elko Television District. Phone: 775-738-5025.

Technical Facilities: 0.546-kw ERP, 30-ft. above ground, 7411-ft. above sea level, lat. 40° 42' 00", long. 115° 54' 09".

Holds CP for change to channel number 21, 1.93-kw ERP, 28-ft. above ground, 7410-ft. above sea level, BPTT-20040709ACH.

Ownership: Elko Television District.

Elko—K57GR, Ch. 57, Elko Television District. Phone: 775-738-5025.

Technical Facilities: 0.936-kw ERP, 30-ft. above ground, 7411-ft. above sea level, lat. 40° 42' 00", long. 115° 54' 09".

Ownership: Elko Television District.

Elko—K59EV, Ch. 59, Elko TV District. Phone: 775-738-5025.

Technical Facilities: 0.959-kw ERP, 30-ft. above ground, 7411-ft. above sea level, lat. 40° 42' 00", long. 115° 54' 09".

Ownership: Elko Television District.

Ely—K06HT, Ch. 6, Sarkes Tarzian Inc. Phone: 812-332-7251.

Technical Facilities: 0.025-kw ERP, lat. 39° 15' 48", long. 114° 53' 36".

Ownership: Sarkes Tarzian Inc.

Ely—K14AL, Ch. 14, White Pine Television District No. 1. Phone: 702-289-2972.

Technical Facilities: 0.324-kw ERP, 20-ft. above ground, 6302-ft. above sea level, lat. 39° 15' 00", long. 114° 53' 25".

Ownership: White Pine Television District No. 1.

Ely—K16GK, Ch. 16, Sierra Broadcasting Co. Phone: 702-642-3333.

Technical Facilities: 150-kw ERP, 131-ft. above ground, 7959-ft. above sea level, lat. 39° 14' 46", long. 114° 55' 36".

Ownership: Sunbelt Communications Co.

Ely—K24GY, Ch. 24, White Pine Television District No. 1. Phone: 775-289-4048.

Technical Facilities: 0.796-kw ERP, 10-ft. above ground, 10751-ft. above sea level, lat. 39° 09' 45", long. 114° 36' 32".

Holds CP for change to 0.199-kw ERP, 8-ft. above ground, 10759-ft. above sea level, BDFCDTT-20080225AAL.

Ownership: White Pine Television District No. 1.

Ely—K26HY, Ch. 26, White Pine Television District No. 1. Phone: 775-289-4048.

Technical Facilities: 0.796-kw ERP, 10-ft. above ground, 10751-ft. above sea level, lat. 39° 09' 45", long. 114° 36' 32".

Holds CP for change to 0.199-kw ERP, 8-ft. above ground, 10759-ft. above sea level, BDFCDTT-20080225AAS.

Ownership: White Pine Television District No. 1.

Ely—K28IZ, Ch. 28, White Pine Television District No. 1. Phone: 775-289-4048.

Technical Facilities: 0.796-kw ERP, 10-ft. above ground, 10751-ft. above sea level, lat. 39° 09' 45", long. 114° 36' 32".

Holds CP for change to 0.199-kw ERP, 8-ft. above ground, 10759-ft. above sea level, BDFCDTT-20080225AAR.

Ownership: White Pine Television District No. 1.

Ely—K30CN, Ch. 30, White Pine Television District No. 1. Phone: 775-289-4048.

Technical Facilities: 0.772-kw ERP, lat. 39° 09' 45", long. 114° 36' 32".

Holds CP for change to 0.199-kw ERP, 8-ft. above ground, 10759-ft. above sea level, BDFCDTT-20080225AAT.

Ownership: White Pine Television District No. 1.

Ely—K32CJ, Ch. 32, White Pine Television District No. 1. Phone: 775-289-4048.

Technical Facilities: 0.772-kw ERP, lat. 39° 09' 45", long. 114° 36' 32".

Holds CP for change to 0.199-kw ERP, 8-ft. above ground, 10759-ft. above sea level, BDFCDTT-20080225AAU.

Ownership: White Pine Television District No. 1.

Ely—K34CM, Ch. 34, White Pine Television District No. 1. Phone: 775-289-4048.

Technical Facilities: 0.772-kw ERP, lat. 39° 09' 45", long. 114° 36' 32".

Holds CP for change to 0.199-kw ERP, 8-ft. above ground, 10759-ft. above sea level, BDFCDTT-20080225AAV.

Ownership: White Pine Television District No. 1.

Ely, etc.—K13NR, Ch. 13, White Pine Television District No. 1. Phone: 775-289-4048.

Technical Facilities: 0.06-kw ERP, 8031-ft. above sea level, lat. 39° 15' 48", long. 114° 53' 36".

Holds CP for change to 0.015-kw ERP, 13-ft. above ground, 8045-ft. above sea level, BDFCDTV-20080303AAX.

Ownership: White Pine Television District No. 1.

Ely, etc.—K58BC, Ch. 58, Valley Broadcasting Co. Phone: 775-336-0604.

Technical Facilities: 0.28-kw ERP, 7903-ft. above sea level, lat. 39° 15' 48", long. 114° 53' 56".

Began Operation: February 9, 1981.

Ownership: Sunbelt Communications Co.

Eureka—K17FY, Ch. 17, Eureka County Television District. Phone: 775-237-5506.

Technical Facilities: 0.06-kw ERP, lat. 39° 28' 30", long. 115° 59' 33".

Ownership: Eureka County Television District.

Eureka—K40CI, Ch. 40, Eureka County Television District. Phone: 775-237-5506.

Technical Facilities: 0.25-kw ERP, lat. 39° 28' 30", long. 115° 59' 33".

Ownership: Eureka County Television District.

Eureka—K42CL, Ch. 42, Eureka County Television District. Phone: 775-237-5506.

Technical Facilities: 0.25-kw ERP, lat. 39° 28' 30", long. 115° 59' 33".

Ownership: Eureka County Television District.

Eureka—K44CP, Ch. 44, Eureka County Television District. Phone: 775-237-5506.

Technical Facilities: 20-w TPO, 0.255-kw ERP, 20-ft. above ground, 5948-ft. above sea level, lat. 39° 28' 33", long. 115° 59' 33".

Transmitter: 2.5-mi. SW of Eureka.

Ownership: Eureka County Television District.

Eureka—K47DG, Ch. 47, Eureka County Television District. Phone: 775-237-5506.

Technical Facilities: 100-w TPO, 4.17-kw ERP, 197-ft. above ground, 9590-ft. above sea level, lat. 39° 26' 59", long. 115° 59' 54".

Transmitter: Prospect Peak, 4.7-mi. S of Eureka.

Ownership: Eureka County Television District.

Eureka—K51GR, Ch. 51, Eureka County Television District. Phone: 775-237-5506.

Technical Facilities: 4.2-kw ERP, 20-ft. above ground, 8405-ft. above sea level, lat. 39° 28' 30", long. 115° 59' 33".

Ownership: Eureka County Television District.

Eureka—K57BU, Ch. 57, Valley Broadcasting Co. Phone: 702-642-3333.

Technical Facilities: 6.52-kw ERP, lat. 39° 26' 59", long. 115° 59' 54".

Ownership: Sunbelt Communications Co.

Eureka, etc.—K21GJ, Ch. 21, Eureka County Television District. Phone: 775-237-5506.

Technical Facilities: 1.36-kw ERP, 20-ft. above ground, 9590-ft. above sea level, lat. 39° 26' 58", long. 115° 59' 54".

Ownership: Eureka County Television District.

Fallon—K13QV, Ch. 13, Sierra Broadcasting Co. Phone: 702-642-3333.

Technical Facilities: 0.027-kw ERP, lat. 39° 29' 22", long. 118° 45' 09".

Ownership: Sunbelt Communications Co.

Fallon—K44BE, Ch. 44, Broadcast Development Corp. Phone: 775-856-2121.

Technical Facilities: 16.2-kw ERP, lat. 39° 29' 17", long. 118° 45' 08".

Ownership: Broadcast Development Corp.

Fallon—K51IA, Ch. 51, KTVU Partnership. Phone: 775-865-1100.

Technical Facilities: 12.72-kw ERP, 26-ft. above ground, 4209-ft. above sea level, lat. 39° 29' 17", long. 118° 45' 08".

Ownership: Cox Enterprises Inc.

Fish Lake Valley, etc.—K53EZ, Ch. 53, Fish Lake Valley Communications Foundation. Phone: 775-572-3337.

Technical Facilities: 0.9-kw ERP, 13-ft. above ground, 7333-ft. above sea level, lat. 38° 02' 00", long. 118° 12' 40".

Ownership: Fish Lake Valley Communications Foundation.

Fish Lake Valley, etc.—K55GR, Ch. 55, Fish Lake Valley Communications Foundation. Phone: 775-572-3337.

Technical Facilities: 0.882-kw ERP, 23-ft. above ground, 7342-ft. above sea level, lat. 38° 02' 00", long. 118° 12' 40".

Ownership: Fish Lake Valley Communications Foundation.

Fish Lake Valley, etc.—K57GI, Ch. 57, Fish Lake Valley Communications Foundation. Phone: 775-572-3337.

Technical Facilities: 0.862-kw ERP, 20-ft. above ground, 7336-ft. above sea level, lat. 38° 02' 00", long. 118° 12' 40".

Ownership: Fish Lake Valley Communications Foundation.

Fish Lake Valley, etc.—K59FH, Ch. 59, Fish Lake Valley Communications Foundation. Phone: 775-572-3337.

Technical Facilities: 0.862-kw ERP, 7336-ft. above sea level, lat. 38° 02' 00", long. 118° 12' 40".

Ownership: Fish Lake Valley Communications Foundation.

Fish Lake Valley, etc.—K64AE, Ch. 64, Fish Lake Valley Communications Foundation. Phone: 775-572-3337.

Technical Facilities: 0.787-kw ERP, 7342-ft. above sea level, lat. 38° 02' 00", long. 118° 12' 40".

Ownership: Fish Lake Valley Communications Foundation.

Gabbs—K06NZ, Ch. 6, City of Gabbs. Phone: 775-285-2671.

Technical Facilities: 0.057-kw ERP, 10-ft. above ground, 5649-ft. above sea level, lat. 38° 52' 02", long. 117° 53' 39".

Ownership: City of Gabbs.

Gabbs—K13YK, Ch. 13, City of Gabbs. Phone: 775-423-2543.

Technical Facilities: 0.057-kw ERP, 10-ft. above ground, 5650-ft. above sea level, lat. 38° 52' 02", long. 117° 53' 39".

Ownership: City of Gabbs.

Glendale—K23CJ, Ch. 23, Clark County School District. Phone: 702-799-1010.

Technical Facilities: 1.43-kw ERP, 16-ft. above ground, 2231-ft. above sea level, lat. 36° 41' 02", long. 114° 30' 59".

Ownership: Clark County School District.

Personnel: Darrell Brown, General Manager.

Golconda—K26GG-D, Ch. 26, Humboldt County. Phone: 775-623-6349.

Technical Facilities: 0.19-kw ERP, 36-ft. above ground, 6358-ft. above sea level, lat. 41° 09' 19", long. 117° 28' 16".

Ownership: Humboldt County.

Golconda—K28EO, Ch. 28, Humboldt County. Phone: 775-623-6349.

Technical Facilities: 0.38-kw ERP, 16-ft. above ground, 6936-ft. above sea level, lat. 41° 09' 19", long. 117° 28' 16".

Ownership: Humboldt County.

Golconda—K31FU, Ch. 31, Humboldt County. Phone: 775-623-6349.

Technical Facilities: 1.7-kw ERP, 16-ft. above ground, 6936-ft. above sea level, lat. 41° 09' 19", long. 117° 28' 16".

Ownership: Humboldt County.

Golconda—K33GB, Ch. 33, Humboldt County. Phone: 775-623-6349.

Technical Facilities: 1.7-kw ERP, 23-ft. above ground, 6942-ft. above sea level, lat. 41° 09' 19", long. 117° 28' 16".

Ownership: Humboldt County.

Golconda, etc.—K35GD, Ch. 35, Humboldt County. Phone: 775-623-6349.

Technical Facilities: 1.7-kw ERP, 20-ft. above ground, 6939-ft. above sea level, lat. 41° 09' 19", long. 117° 28' 16".

Holds CP for change to 0.19-kw ERP, 33-ft. above ground, 6355-ft. above sea level, BDFCDTT-20060330AJD.

Ownership: Humboldt County.

Hawthorne—K13WI, Ch. 13, Virginia M. Becker. Phones: 775-945-1300; 775-945-9090.

Technical Facilities: 10-w TPO, 0.017-kw ERP, 50-ft. above ground, 4327-ft. above sea level, lat. 38° 31' 56", long. 118° 37' 16".

Holds CP for change to 40-ft. above ground, 4373-ft. above sea level, lat. 38° 31' 26", long. 118° 37' 21". BPTVL-20081027ACW.

Transmitter: 996 H St.

Began Operation: April 18, 1994.

Ownership: Virginia M. Becker.

Personnel: Bob Becker, Manager; Scott Becker, Chief Engineer; Virginia Becker, Sales Manager.

Hawthorne—K20FR, Ch. 20, Mineral TV District No. 1.

Technical Facilities: 3.78-kw ERP, lat. 38° 27' 37", long. 118° 45' 39".

Ownership: Mineral Television District No. 1.

Hawthorne—K22FH, Ch. 22, KTVU Partnership.

Technical Facilities: 2.06-kw ERP, 18-ft. above ground, 10258-ft. above sea level, lat. 38° 27' 27", long. 118° 45' 49".

Ownership: KTVU Partnership.

Hawthorne—K30FS, Ch. 30, Mineral TV District No. 1. Phone: 775-423-2543.

Technical Facilities: 1.905-kw ERP, lat. 38° 27' 37", long. 118° 45' 39".

Ownership: Mineral Television District No. 1.

Hawthorne—K33GZ, Ch. 33, Mineral TV District No.1. Phone: 775-423-2543.

Technical Facilities: 0.89-kw ERP, lat. 38° 27' 37", long. 118° 45' 39".

Holds CP for change to 0.24-kw ERP, 10-ft. above ground, 10253-ft. above sea level, BDFCDTT-20090209AMA.

Began Operation: October 8, 2003.

Ownership: Mineral Television District No. 1.

Hawthorne—K48GG, Ch. 48, Mineral TV District No. 1. Phone: 775-423-2543.

Technical Facilities: 2.327-kw ERP, lat. 38° 27' 37", long. 118° 45' 39".

Ownership: Mineral Television District No. 1.

Hawthorne—K50AI, Ch. 50, Mineral TV District No. 1. Phone: 775-423-2543.

Technical Facilities: 3.78-kw ERP, 10286-ft. above sea level, lat. 38° 27' 37", long. 118° 45' 39".

Transmitter: 7000-ft. NE of Cory Peak, located W of Hawthorne.

Ownership: Mineral Television District No. 1.

Hawthorne, etc.—K35AX, Ch. 35, Ellis Communications Inc. Phone: 404-229-8080.

Technical Facilities: 0.926-kw ERP, 7-ft. above ground, 10029-ft. above sea level, lat. 38° 27' 37", long. 118° 45' 39".

Ownership: Ellis Communications Inc.

Henderson—K46GX, Ch. 46, KLAS LLC. Phone: 702-792-8888.

Technical Facilities: 0.723-kw ERP, 12-ft. above ground, 3667-ft. above sea level, lat. 35° 59' 44", long. 114° 51' 46".

Ownership: Landmark Media Enterprises LLC.

Imlay—K39CX-D, Ch. 39, Humboldt County. Phone: 775-623-6349.

Technical Facilities: 0.85-kw ERP, 33-ft. above ground, 6860-ft. above sea level, lat. 40° 07' 10", long. 118° 43' 50".

Ownership: Humboldt County.

Imlay—K41GI-D, Ch. 41, Humboldt County. Phone: 775-623-6349.

Technical Facilities: 0.19-kw ERP, 16-ft. above ground, 6007-ft. above sea level, lat. 40° 34' 50", long. 118° 13' 01".

Ownership: Humboldt County.

Incline Village—KVCJ-LP, Ch. 14, North Lake Tahoe Community Foundation. Phone: 775-741-7969.

Technical Facilities: 100-w TPO, 0.76-kw ERP, 40-ft. above ground, 7490-ft. above sea level, lat. 39° 14' 53", long. 119° 55' 17".

Transmitter: Ski Way, 1.5-mi. NE of Lake Tahoe.

Multichannel TV Sound: Stereo only.

Began Operation: December 6, 1983.

Ownership: North Lake Tahoe Community Foundation.

Personnel: Steve Baker, General Manager; Herb Primosch, Chief Engineer.

Indian Springs—K07JC, Ch. 7, Clark County School District. Phone: 702-799-1010.

Technical Facilities: 0.005-kw ERP, 3819-ft. above sea level, lat. 36° 35' 42", long. 115° 37' 58".

Holds CP for change to 12-ft. above ground, 3732-ft. above sea level, lat. 36° 35' 38.8", long. 115° 37' 52.4". BPTTV-20060329AKN.

Ownership: Clark County School District.

Jean—K23BS, Ch. 23, Clark County School District. Phone: 702-799-1010.

Technical Facilities: 0.743-kw ERP, lat. 35° 53' 36", long. 115° 29' 39".

Holds CP for change to 0.736-kw ERP, 22-ft. above ground, 6223-ft. above sea level, BPTT-20060329AKS.

Ownership: Clark County School District.

Kings River—K04GA, Ch. 4, Quinn River TV Maintenance District. Phone: 208-375-2205.

Technical Facilities: 0.032-kw ERP, lat. 41° 31' 36", long. 118° 03' 50".

Ownership: Quinn River TV Maintenance District.

Kings River, etc.—K10HJ, Ch. 10, Quinn River TV Maintenance District. Phone: 208-375-2205.

Technical Facilities: 0.035-kw ERP, 5518-ft. above sea level, lat. 41° 31' 36", long. 118° 03' 30".

Ownership: Quinn River TV Maintenance District.

Las Vegas—K41IO, Ch. 41, Enlace Christian Television Inc. Phone: 469-499-0832.

Technical Facilities: 150-kw ERP, 62-ft. above ground, 3389-ft. above sea level, lat. 36° 00' 30", long. 115° 00' 20".

Holds CP for change to 15-kw ERP, BDFCDTT-20060331AMY.

Began Operation: November 17, 1987.

Ownership: Enlace Christian Television Inc.

■**Las Vegas**—K43FO, Ch. 43, Three Angels Broadcasting Network Inc. Phone: 618-627-4651. Fax: 618-627-4155.

Studio: 3391 Charley Good Rd, West Frankfort, IL 62896.

Technical Facilities: 10.2-kw ERP, 233-ft. above ground, 3458-ft. above sea level, lat. 36° 00' 36", long. 115° 00' 20".

Holds CP for change to 14.5-kw ERP, 39-ft. above ground, 3267-ft. above sea level, BDFCDTA-20081023AAC.

Began Operation: December 29, 1998.

Ownership: Three Angels Broadcasting Network Inc.

Personnel: Moses Primo, Chief Engineer.

■**Las Vegas**—KEEN-CA, Ch. 17, Christian Communications of Chicagoland Inc. Phones: 702-636-1717; 603-801-3838. Fax: 702-636-2127.

Studio: 4511 W Cheyenne Ave, Ste 507, North Las Vegas, NV 89032.

Technical Facilities: 998-w TPO, 145-kw ERP, 141-ft. above ground, 2670-ft. above sea level, lat. 36° 17' 43", long. 115° 16' 48".

Holds CP for change to 4.1-kw ERP, 156-ft. above ground, 3384-ft. above sea level, lat. 36° 00' 36", long. 115° 00' 20". BDFCDTA-20090211AAW.

Transmitter: Off Hwy. 95, 11-mi. NW of Las Vegas.

Multichannel TV Sound: Separate audio program.

Began Operation: May 6, 1993.

Ownership: Christian Communications of Chicagoland Inc.

Personnel: Kevin Culbertson, General Manager; Mike Mulanax, Chief Engineer.

Las Vegas—KEGS-LP, Ch. 30, Mako Communications LLC. Phone: 361-883-1763.

Studio: 2675 E Flamingo Rd, Ste 6, Las Vegas, NV 89121.

Technical Facilities: 2.1-kw ERP, 82-ft. above ground, 4416-ft. above sea level, lat. 35° 56' 43", long. 115° 02' 32".

Began Operation: May 7, 1997.

Ownership: Mako Communications LLC.

Personnel: Darwin Paustian, General Manager; Neal Ardman, Chief Engineer; Elaine Dawson, Sales Manager.

Las Vegas—KELV-LP, Ch. 27, Entravision Holdings LLC.

Technical Facilities: 0.03-kw ERP, lat. 36° 00' 26", long. 115° 00' 23".

Ownership: Entravision Communications Corp.

Las Vegas—KGNG-LP, Ch. 47, King Kong Broadcasting Inc. Phone: 702-642-8847. Fax: 702-649-5588.

Technical Facilities: 13.4-kw ERP, 50-ft. above ground, 4350-ft. above sea level, lat. 35° 56' 44", long. 115° 02' 31".

Transmitter: Atop Potosi Mountain, near Las Vegas.

Ownership: King Kong Broadcasting Inc.

Personnel: Larry Hunt, General Manager & Chief Engineer; Lisa Rhodes, Sales Manager.

■**Las Vegas**—KHDF-CA, Ch. 19, Una Vez Mas Las Vegas License LLP. Phone: 214-754-7008.

Technical Facilities: 550-w TPO, 7-kw ERP, 98-ft. above ground, 3435-ft. above sea level, lat. 36° 00' 30", long. 115° 00' 20".

Transmitter: 7200 N. Rancho Rd.

Ownership: Una Vez Mas GP LLC.

Las Vegas—KLSV-LP, Ch. 50, Biltmore Broadcasting Las Vegas Inc. Phone: 310-452-7938.

Technical Facilities: 9.3-kw ERP, 94-ft. above ground, 3427-ft. above sea level, lat. 36° 00' 31", long. 115° 00' 28".

Ownership: Biltmore Broadcasting Corp.

Personnel: Larry Hunt, Chief Engineer.

Las Vegas—KLVD-LP, Ch. 23, Word of God Fellowship Inc. Phone: 817-571-1229.

Technical Facilities: 87-kw ERP, 220-ft. above ground, 3448-ft. above sea level, lat. 36° 00' 36", long. 115° 00' 20".

Ownership: Word of God Fellowship Inc.

■ **Las Vegas**—KNBX-CA, Ch. 31, Mako Communications LLC. Phone: 361-883-1776.

Technical Facilities: 149-kw ERP, 82-ft. above ground, 4416-ft. above sea level, lat. 35° 56' 43", long. 115° 02' 32".

Began Operation: January 16, 1998.

Ownership: Mako Communications LLC.

■ **Las Vegas**—KTUD-CA, Ch. 25, Las Vegas TV Partners LLC. Phone: 702-222-2225.

Technical Facilities: 2000-w TPO, 18.9-kw ERP, 35-ft. above ground, 4370-ft. above sea level, lat. 35° 56' 44", long. 115° 02' 33".

Transmitter: Black Mountain, 3.5-mi. W of Henderson.

Ownership: Las Vegas TV Partners LLC.

Personnel: Julie Neil, General Manager.

Las Vegas—KVPX-LP, Ch. 28, Mako Communications LLC. Phone: 361-883-1763.

Technical Facilities: 150-kw ERP, 121-ft. above ground, 3455-ft. above sea level, lat. 36° 00' 31", long. 115° 00' 28".

Ownership: Mako Communications LLC.

Las Vegas—KVTE-LP, Ch. 35, Mountain Ridge Communications Inc. Phone: 702-796-3535. Fax: 702-454-3043.

Technical Facilities: 150-kw ERP, 66-ft. above ground, 4400-ft. above sea level, lat. 35° 56' 44", long. 115° 02' 31".

Ownership: Mountain Ridge Holdings Inc.

Personnel: Shenandoah Merrick, Executive Vice President; Rocky Van Blaricom, Chief Engineer.

Laughlin—K22DR, Ch. 22, KLAS LLC. Phone: 702-792-8888.

Technical Facilities: 2.31-kw ERP, 30-ft. above ground, 4849-ft. above sea level, lat. 35° 14' 58", long. 114° 44' 34".

Ownership: Landmark Media Enterprises LLC.

Laughlin—K40CQ, Ch. 40, Valley Broadcasting Co. Phone: 702-642-3333.

Technical Facilities: 2.31-kw ERP, 30-ft. above ground, 4849-ft. above sea level, lat. 35° 14' 58", long. 114° 44' 34".

Ownership: Sunbelt Communications Co.

Laughlin—K53DG, Ch. 53, Clark County School District. Phone: 702-799-1010.

Technical Facilities: 0.958-kw ERP, 56-ft. above ground, 4869-ft. above sea level, lat. 35° 14' 58", long. 114° 44' 34".

Ownership: Clark County School District.

Laughlin—K57JO, Ch. 57, 9th Island Broadcasting Inc. Phone: 801-557-1322.

Technical Facilities: 0.82-kw ERP, 164-ft. above ground, 1417-ft. above sea level, lat. 35° 10' 08", long. 114° 38' 09".

Ownership: 9th Island Broadcasting Inc.

Laughlin—K59EX, Ch. 59, Journal Broadcast Corp. Phone: 702-876-1313. Fax: 702-871-1961.

Technical Facilities: 100-w TPO, 1.31-kw ERP, 4872-ft. above sea level, lat. 35° 14' 58", long. 114° 44' 34".

Transmitter: Christmas Tree Mountain, 10.5-mi. WNW of Dan's Dam.

Ownership: Journal Communications Inc.

Personnel: Kris Foate, General Manager; Roman Hlohowskyj, Chief Engineer; John Dalrymple, Sales Manager.

Laughlin—K63HJ, Ch. 63, Roger Mills. Phone: 435-884-3136.

Technical Facilities: 0.82-kw ERP, 164-ft. above sea level, lat. 35° 10' 08", long. 114° 38' 09".

Ownership: Roger Mills.

Personnel: Rubin Rodriguez Jr., President.

Laughlin—K67HO, Ch. 67, Smoke and Mirrors LLC. Phone: 928-855-1051.

Technical Facilities: 2.43-kw ERP, 23-ft. above ground, 4849-ft. above sea level, lat. 35° 14' 58", long. 114° 44' 34".

Holds CP for change to channel number 26, 147-kw ERP, 46-ft. above ground, 4885-ft. above sea level, BDISTTL-20060210ABE.

Ownership: Smoke and Mirrors LLC.

Laughlin—KNTL-LP, Ch. 47, Entravision Holdings LLC. Phone: 310-447-3870.

Technical Facilities: 1000-w TPO, 18.9-kw ERP, 23-ft. above ground, 4849-ft. above sea level, lat. 35° 14' 58", long. 114° 44' 34".

Transmitter: Electronics site, 10-mi. NW of Laughlin.

Ownership: Entravision Communications Corp.

Personnel: Gabe Quiroz, General Manager.

Laughlin, etc.—K28EU, Ch. 28, KVVU Broadcasting Corp. Phone: 515-284-3000.

Studio: 2628 Hwy. 95, Bullhead City, AZ 86442.

Technical Facilities: 1000-w TPO, 1.12-kw ERP, 53-ft. above ground, 4864-ft. above sea level, lat. 35° 14' 50", long. 114° 44' 35".

Holds CP for change to 0.35-kw ERP, 52-ft. above ground, 4865-ft. above sea level, BDFCDTT-20060310AEK.

Transmitter: Spirit Mountain electronics site.

Multichannel TV Sound: Stereo only.

Ownership: Meredith Corp.

Personnel: Earl R. Sorensen, General Manager; Brigitte Rahammer, Sales Manager.

Logan & Moapa area—K07IJ, Ch. 7, Moapa Valley TV Maintenance District. Phone: 702-397-6888.

Technical Facilities: 0.039-kw ERP, lat. 36° 40' 54", long. 114° 31' 21".

Holds CP for change to channel number 14, 1.8-kw ERP, 94-ft. above ground, 2342-ft. above sea level, lat. 36° 41' 08.8", long. 114° 31' 09.8". BDISDTL-20081121AMW.

Ownership: Moapa Valley TV Maintenance District.

Lovelock—K14KQ, Ch. 14, Pershing County School District. Phone: 775-273-7819.

Technical Facilities: 0.994-kw ERP, 71-ft. above ground, 4080-ft. above sea level, lat. 40° 11' 01", long. 118° 28' 47".

Ownership: Pershing County School District.

Lovelock—K18DP, Ch. 18, Pershing County NV TV Tax District. Fax: 775-423-2543.

Technical Facilities: 100-w TPO, 3.9-kw ERP, 44-ft. above ground, 4322-ft. above sea level, lat. 40° 07' 05", long. 118° 43' 38".

Holds CP for change to 1.2-kw ERP, 98-ft. above ground, 6959-ft. above sea level, BDFCDTT-20090223AAA.

Transmitter: Tulon Peak, 15-mi. NW of Lovelock.

Began Operation: March 25, 1987.

Ownership: Pershing County NV TV Tax District.

Lovelock—K24FF, Ch. 24, Pershing County NV TV Tax District. Phone: 775-423-2543.

Technical Facilities: 4.005-kw ERP, lat. 40° 07' 05", long. 118° 43' 38".

Holds CP for change to 1.2-kw ERP, 105-ft. above ground, 6965-ft. above sea level, BDFCDTT-20090223AAB.

Transmitter: Tulon Peak, 14.9-mi. NW of Lovelock.

Ownership: Pershing County NV TV Tax District.

Lovelock—K30DS, Ch. 30, Pershing County NV TV Tax District. Phone: 775-423-2543.

Technical Facilities: 0.62-kw ERP, lat. 40° 07' 05", long. 118° 43' 38".

Holds CP for change to 1.2-kw ERP, 112-ft. above ground, 6972-ft. above sea level, BDFCDTT-20090223AAC.

Ownership: Pershing County NV TV Tax District.

Lovelock—K34BL, Ch. 34, Ellis Communications Inc.

Technical Facilities: 3.64-kw ERP, lat. 40° 07' 05", long. 118° 43' 38".

Ownership: Ellis Communications Inc.

Lovelock—K36GL, Ch. 36, KTVU Partnership. Phone: 775-856-1100.

Technical Facilities: 3.8-kw ERP, 17-ft. above ground, 6867-ft. above sea level, lat. 40° 07' 05", long. 118° 43' 38".

Ownership: Cox Enterprises Inc.

Lund & Preston—K08CB, Ch. 8, White Pine Television District No. 1. Phone: 775-289-4048.

Technical Facilities: 0.158-kw ERP, lat. 39° 14' 59", long. 114° 59' 59".

Holds CP for change to 0.039-kw ERP, 11-ft. above ground, 8092-ft. above sea level, BDFCDTV-20080225AHD.

Ownership: White Pine Television District No. 1.

Lund & Preston—K10BU, Ch. 10, White Pine Television District No. 1. Phone: 775-289-4048.

Technical Facilities: 0.158-kw ERP, lat. 39° 14' 59", long. 114° 59' 59".

Holds CP for change to 0.039-kw ERP, 11-ft. above ground, 8089-ft. above sea level, BDFCDTV-20080225ABB.

Ownership: White Pine Television District No. 1.

Lund & Preston—K12DE, Ch. 12, White Pine Television District No. 1. Phone: 775-289-4048.

Technical Facilities: 0.158-kw ERP, lat. 39° 13' 40", long. 114° 58' 30".

Holds CP for change to 0.039-kw ERP, 11-ft. above ground, 8089-ft. above sea level, BDFCDTV-20080225ABA.

Ownership: White Pine Television District No. 1.

Lund & Preston—K45HS, Ch. 45, White Pine Television District No. 1. Phone: 775-289-4048.

Technical Facilities: 3.549-kw ERP, 15-ft. above ground, 8076-ft. above sea level, lat. 39° 13' 40", long. 114° 58' 30".

Holds CP for change to 0.887-kw ERP, 13-ft. above ground, 8094-ft. above sea level, lat. 39° 14' 59", long. 114° 59' 59". BDFCDTT-20080303ABL.

Ownership: White Pine Television District No. 1.

Lund & Preston—K47HV, Ch. 47, White Pine Television District No. 1. Phone: 775-289-4048.

Technical Facilities: 3.549-kw ERP, 15-ft. above ground, 8076-ft. above sea level, lat. 39° 13' 40", long. 114° 58' 30".

Holds CP for change to 0.887-kw ERP, 13-ft. above ground, 8087-ft. above sea level, BDFCDTT-20080303AAS.

Ownership: White Pine Television District No. 1.

Lund & Preston—K49AM, Ch. 49, White Pine Television District No. 1. Phone: 775-289-4048.

Technical Facilities: 2.56-kw ERP, lat. 39° 13' 40", long. 114° 58' 30".

Holds CP for change to 0.887-kw ERP, 11-ft. above ground, 8095-ft. above sea level, BDFCDTT-20080303AAT.

Ownership: White Pine Television District No. 1.

Manhattan—K06KQ, Ch. 6, County of Nye. Phone: 775-482-8103.

Technical Facilities: 0.02-kw ERP, lat. 38° 32' 16", long. 117° 03' 57".

Ownership: County of Nye.

Manhattan—K10LQ, Ch. 10, County of Nye. Phone: 775-482-8103.

Technical Facilities: 0.021-kw ERP, lat. 38° 32' 16", long. 117° 03' 57".

Ownership: County of Nye.

Manhattan—K12MW, Ch. 12, County of Nye. Phone: 775-482-8103.

Technical Facilities: 0.02-kw ERP, lat. 38° 32' 16", long. 117° 03' 57".

Ownership: County of Nye.

McDermitt—K48EB, Ch. 48, Quinn River TV Maintenance District. Phone: 208-375-2205.

Technical Facilities: 0.252-kw ERP, lat. 42° 10' 43", long. 117° 44' 19".

Ownership: Quinn River TV Maintenance District.

McDermitt—K50CZ, Ch. 50, Quinn River TV Maintenance District. Phone: 208-375-2205.

Technical Facilities: 0.288-kw ERP, 30-ft. above ground, 6289-ft. above sea level, lat. 42° 10' 43", long. 117° 44' 19".

Ownership: Quinn River TV Maintenance District.

McDermitt—K52DV, Ch. 52, Quinn River TV Maintenance District. Phone: 208-375-2205.

Technical Facilities: 0.05-kw ERP, lat. 42° 10' 43", long. 117° 44' 19".

Ownership: Quinn River TV Maintenance District.

McDermitt—K54DQ, Ch. 54, Quinn River TV Maintenance District. Phone: 208-375-2205.

Technical Facilities: 0.084-kw ERP, lat. 42° 10' 43", long. 117° 44' 19".

Ownership: Quinn River TV Maintenance District.

McDermitt—K58DZ, Ch. 58, Quinn River TV Maintenance District. Phone: 208-375-2205.

Technical Facilities: 0.288-kw ERP, 30-ft. above ground, 6289-ft. above sea level, lat. 42° 10' 43", long. 117° 44' 19".

Ownership: Quinn River TV Maintenance District.

McDermitt—K62EL, Ch. 62, Quinn River TV Maintenance District. Phone: 208-375-2205.

Technical Facilities: 0.288-kw ERP, 30-ft. above ground, 6289-ft. above sea level, lat. 40° 10' 42", long. 117° 44' 18".

Ownership: Quinn River TV Maintenance District.

Mercury—K02FM, Ch. 2, Clark County School District. Phone: 702-799-1010.

Technical Facilities: 0.004-kw ERP, lat. 35° 53' 36", long. 115° 29' 39".

Ownership: Clark County School District.

Mercury—K54BO, Ch. 54, Crown Castle Nevada LLC. Phone: 713-570-3000.

Technical Facilities: 3.23-kw ERP, lat. 36° 19' 07", long. 115° 34' 28".

Ownership: Crown Castle Nevada LLC.

Mercury & Nevada Test Site—K52AC, Ch. 52, Valley Broadcasting Co. Phone: 702-642-3333.

Technical Facilities: 2.43-kw ERP, 8934-ft. above sea level, lat. 36° 19' 07", long. 115° 34' 28".

Ownership: Sunbelt Communications Co.

Mercury, etc.—K45AA, Ch. 45, Crown Castle Nevada LLC. Phone: 713-570-3000.

Technical Facilities: 2.43-kw ERP, 8934-ft. above sea level, lat. 36° 19' 07", long. 115° 34' 28".

Ownership: Crown Castle Nevada LLC.

Mercury, etc.—K48AB, Ch. 48, KLAS LLC. Phone: 757-446-2660.

Technical Facilities: 2.43-kw ERP, 8934-ft. above sea level, lat. 36° 19' 07", long. 115° 34' 28".

Ownership: Landmark Media Enterprises LLC.

Mesquite—K02FN, Ch. 2, Clark County School District. Phone: 702-799-1010.

Technical Facilities: 0.282-kw ERP, 80-ft. above ground, 1964-ft. above sea level, lat. 36° 49' 55", long. 114° 03' 32".

Ownership: Clark County School District.

Mesquite, etc.—KWWB-LP, Ch. 45, Entravision Holdings LLC. Phones: 702-434-0015; 310-447-3870. Fax: 702-434-0527.

Technical Facilities: 1-kw ERP, 36-ft. above ground, 7716-ft. above sea level, lat. 37° 09' 19", long. 113° 52' 53".

Ownership: Entravision Communications Corp.
Personnel: Gabe Quiroz, General Manager.

Mina—K39EZ, Ch. 39, Mineral Television District No. 1. Phone: 775-423-2543.

Technical Facilities: 0.493-kw ERP, lat. 38° 23' 40", long. 118° 03' 00".

Ownership: Mineral Television District No. 1.

Mina & Luning—K10GT, Ch. 10, Mineral Television District No. 1. Phone: 775-423-2543.

Technical Facilities: 0.048-kw ERP, lat. 38° 23' 40", long. 118° 03' 00".

Ownership: Mineral Television District No. 1.

Mina & Luning—K40GA, Ch. 40, Mineral Television District No. 1. Phone: 775-423-2543.

Technical Facilities: 0.473-kw ERP, 10-ft. above ground, 6109-ft. above sea level, lat. 38° 23' 40", long. 118° 03' 00".

Ownership: Mineral Television District No. 1.

Mina & Luning—K43GS, Ch. 43, Mineral Television District No. 1. Phone: 775-423-2543.

Technical Facilities: 10-ft. above ground, 6109-ft. above ground, lat. 38° 23' 40", long. 118° 03' 00".

Ownership: Mineral Television District No. 1.

Mina, etc.—K05AF, Ch. 5, Mineral Television District No. 1. Phone: 775-423-2543.

Technical Facilities: 0.004-kw ERP, lat. 38° 24' 45", long. 118° 03' 55".

Ownership: Mineral Television District No. 1.

Mina-Luning—K16FU, Ch. 16, Mineral Television District No. 1. Phone: 775-423-2543.

Technical Facilities: 0.22-kw ERP, 10-ft. above ground, 6109-ft. above sea level, lat. 38° 23' 40", long. 118° 03' 00".

Ownership: Mineral Television District No. 1.

Mina-Luning—K18GG, Ch. 18, Mineral Television District No. 1. Phone: 775-423-2543.

Technical Facilities: 0.473-kw ERP, lat. 38° 23' 40", long. 118° 03' 00".

Ownership: Mineral Television District No. 1.

Moapa & Overton—K09IT, Ch. 9, Moapa Valley TV Maintenance District. Phone: 702-397-6888.

Technical Facilities: 0.039-kw ERP, 2336-ft. above sea level, lat. 36° 40' 54", long. 114° 31' 21".

Holds CP for change to channel number 18, 1.8-kw ERP, 94-ft. above ground, 2342-ft. above sea level, lat. 36° 41' 08.8", long. 114° 31' 09.8". BDISDTT-20081121ANB.

Ownership: Moapa Valley TV Maintenance District.

Murray Canyon—K11EE, Ch. 11, White Pine Television District No. 1. Phone: 775-289-4048.

Technical Facilities: 0.06-kw ERP, lat. 39° 15' 48", long. 114° 53' 36".

Holds CP for change to 0.015-kw ERP, 13-ft. above ground, 8045-ft. above sea level, lat. 39° 15' 48", long. 114° 53' 46". BDFCDTV-20080303AAU.

Ownership: White Pine Television District No. 1.

Murray Canyon, etc.—K07DU, Ch. 7, White Pine Television District No. 1. Phone: 775-289-4048.

Technical Facilities: 0.072-kw ERP, 8031-ft. above sea level, lat. 39° 15' 48", long. 114° 53' 36".

Holds CP for change to 0.015-kw ERP, 13-ft. above ground, 8045-ft. above sea level, lat. 39° 15' 48", long. 114° 53' 46". BDFCDTV-20080303AAW.

Ownership: White Pine Television District No. 1.

Murray Canyon, etc.—K09EA, Ch. 9, White Pine Television District No. 1. Phone: 775-289-4048.

Technical Facilities: 0.06-kw ERP, 8031-ft. above sea level, lat. 39° 15' 48", long. 114° 53' 36".

Holds CP for change to 0.015-kw ERP, 13-ft. above ground, 8045-ft. above sea level, lat. 39° 15' 48", long. 114° 53' 46". BDFCDTV-20080303AAV.

Ownership: White Pine Television District No. 1.

Murray Canyon, etc.—K50IY, Ch. 50, White Pine Television District No. 1. Phone: 775-289-4048.

Technical Facilities: 3.549-kw ERP, 18-ft. above ground, 8020-ft. above sea level, lat. 39° 15' 48", long. 114° 53' 36".

Holds CP for change to 0.887-kw ERP, 10-ft. above ground, 8028-ft. above sea level, lat. 39° 15' 48", long. 114° 53' 46". BDFCDTT-20080303AAY.

Ownership: White Pine Television District No. 1.

Nixon—K56IG, Ch. 56, KTVU Partnership. Phone: 775-856-1100.

Technical Facilities: 0.028-kw ERP, 69-ft. above ground, 8415-ft. above sea level, lat. 39° 45' 22", long. 119° 27' 37".

Holds CP for change to channel number 22, 6.81-kw ERP, 70-ft. above ground, 6943-ft. above sea level, lat. 39° 29' 17.3", long. 119° 17' 48.4". BDISDTT-20080804ADT.

Ownership: KTVU Partnership.

North Shore Lake Tahoe—K50CM, Ch. 50, Sierra Broadcasting Co.

Technical Facilities: 2.26-kw ERP, lat. 39° 18' 47", long. 119° 53' 00".

Ownership: Sunbelt Communications Co.

Oasis Valley—K02FJ, Ch. 2, Clark County School District.

Technical Facilities: 0.044-kw ERP, lat. 36° 41' 01", long. 114° 30' 54".

Ownership: Clark County School District.

Oasis Valley—K09OB, Ch. 9, Beatty Town Advisory Council.

Technical Facilities: 0.057-kw ERP, lat. 36° 52' 40", long. 116° 40' 30".

Ownership: Beatty Town Advisory Council.

Oasis Valley—K11OQ, Ch. 11, Beatty Town Advisory Council.

Technical Facilities: 0.055-kw ERP, lat. 36° 52' 40", long. 116° 40' 30".

Ownership: Beatty Town Advisory Council.

Oasis Valley—K13PK, Ch. 13, Beatty Town Advisory Council.

Technical Facilities: 0.055-kw ERP, lat. 36° 52' 40", long. 116° 40' 30".

Ownership: Beatty Town Advisory Council.

Orovada—K06CT, Ch. 6, Quinn River TV Maintenance District. Phone: 208-375-2205.

Technical Facilities: 0.233-kw ERP, lat. 41° 38' 59", long. 117° 43' 14".

Ownership: Quinn River TV Maintenance District.

Orovada—K08NM, Ch. 8, Quinn River TV Maintenance District. Phone: 775-375-2205.

Technical Facilities: 0.0725-kw ERP, 16-ft. above ground, 6114-ft. above sea level, lat. 41° 38' 59", long. 117° 43' 14".

Ownership: Quinn River TV Maintenance District.

Orovada—K11VB, Ch. 11, Quinn River TV Maintenance District. Phone: 208-375-2205.

Technical Facilities: 0.0725-kw ERP, 18-ft. above ground, 6117-ft. above sea level, lat. 41° 38' 59", long. 117° 43' 14".

Ownership: Quinn River TV Maintenance District.

Orovada—K13EN, Ch. 13, Quinn River TV Maintenance District. Phone: 208-375-2205.

Technical Facilities: 0.226-kw ERP, lat. 41° 38' 59", long. 117° 43' 14".

Ownership: Quinn River TV Maintenance District.

Orovada, etc.—K60AP, Ch. 60, Quinn River TV Maintenance District. Phone: 208-375-2205.

Technical Facilities: 0.77-kw ERP, 5023-ft. above sea level, lat. 41° 31' 36", long. 118° 03' 30".

Ownership: Quinn River TV Maintenance District.

Overton—K11JL, Ch. 11, Moapa Valley TV Maintenance District. Phone: 702-397-6888.

Technical Facilities: 0.038-kw ERP, lat. 36° 40' 54", long. 114° 31' 21".

Holds CP for change to channel number 20, 1.8-kw ERP, 94-ft. above ground, 2342-ft. above sea level, lat. 36° 41' 08.8", long. 114° 31' 09.8". BDISDTT-20081121ANC.

Ownership: Moapa Valley TV Maintenance District.

Overton—K44GU, Ch. 44, Moapa Valley TV Maintenance District. Phone: 702-397-6760.

Technical Facilities: 0.251-kw ERP, 20-ft. above ground, 2349-ft. above sea level, lat. 36° 40' 54", long. 114° 31' 21".

Ownership: Moapa Valley TV Maintenance District.

Overton—K48ID, Ch. 48, Moapa Valley TV Maintenance District. Phone: 702-397-6760.

Technical Facilities: 0.841-kw ERP, 20-ft. above ground, 2349-ft. above sea level, lat. 36° 40' 54", long. 114° 31' 21".

Ownership: Moapa Valley TV Maintenance District.

Overton, etc.—K46HG, Ch. 46, Moapa Valley TV Maintenance District. Phone: 702-397-6760.

Technical Facilities: 0.251-kw ERP, 20-ft. above ground, 2349-ft. above sea level, lat. 36° 40' 54", long. 114° 31' 21".

Ownership: Moapa Valley TV Maintenance District.

Overton, etc.—K50HQ, Ch. 50, Moapa Valley TV Maintenance District. Phone: 702-397-6760.

Technical Facilities: 0.251-kw ERP, 20-ft. above ground, 2349-ft. above sea level, lat. 36° 40' 54", long. 114° 31' 21".

Ownership: Moapa Valley TV Maintenance District.

Pahrump—K17CL, Ch. 17, Town of Pahrump. Phone: 775-727-5107.

Technical Facilities: 1.09-kw ERP, 187-ft. above ground, 3005-ft. above sea level, lat. 36° 12' 17", long. 115° 57' 50".

Ownership: Town of Pahrump.

Pahrump—K19BU, Ch. 19, Town of Pahrump. Phone: 775-727-5107.

Technical Facilities: 1.09-kw ERP, lat. 36° 12' 17", long. 115° 57' 50".

Ownership: Town of Pahrump.

Pahrump—K24BY, Ch. 24, Town of Pahrump. Phone: 775-727-5107.

Technical Facilities: 1.12-kw ERP, lat. 36° 12' 17", long. 115° 57' 50".

Ownership: Town of Pahrump.

Pahrump—K28CS, Ch. 28, Town of Pahrump. Phone: 775-727-5107.

Technical Facilities: 1.07-kw ERP, 187-ft. above ground, 3008-ft. above sea level, lat. 36° 12' 17", long. 115° 57' 50".

Ownership: Town of Pahrump.

Pahrump—K31HV, Ch. 31, Marcia T. Turner. Phone: 954-732-9539.

Technical Facilities: 45-kw ERP, 186-ft. above ground, 2756-ft. above sea level, lat. 36° 11' 24", long. 116° 06' 59".

Ownership: Marcia T. Turner.

Pahrump—K36BQ, Ch. 36, Town of Pahrump. Phone: 775-727-5107.

Technical Facilities: 1.11-kw ERP, lat. 36° 12' 17", long. 115° 57' 50".

Ownership: Town of Pahrump.

Pahrump—K42AA, Ch. 42, Journal Broadcast Corp. Phone: 702-876-1313.

Technical Facilities: 0.284-kw ERP, lat. 35° 58' 04", long. 115° 30' 03".

Ownership: Journal Communications Inc.

Pahrump—K44AA, Ch. 44, Valley Broadcasting Co. Phone: 702-642-3333.

Technical Facilities: 7.12-kw ERP, lat. 35° 58' 04", long. 115° 30' 03".

Ownership: Sunbelt Communications Co.

Pahrump—K49AB, Ch. 49, KLAS LLC. Phone: 757-446-2660.

Technical Facilities: 7.3-kw ERP, 13-ft. above ground, 8432-ft. above sea level, lat. 35° 57' 25", long. 115° 29' 46".

Ownership: Landmark Media Enterprises LLC.

Pahrump—K51AC, Ch. 51, Sinclair Media II Inc. Phone: 202-663-8525.

Technical Facilities: 7.12-kw ERP, lat. 35° 58' 04", long. 115° 30' 03".

Ownership: Sinclair Broadcast Group Inc.

Pahrump—K53AE, Ch. 53, KVVU Broadcasting Corp. Phone: 515-284-3000.

Technical Facilities: 7.12-kw ERP, lat. 35° 58' 04", long. 115° 30' 03".

Ownership: Meredith Corp.

Pahrump—KHMP-LP, Ch. 62, Hilltop Church Inc. Phone: 775-751-9709.

Technical Facilities: 5-kw ERP, 190-ft. above ground, 3087-ft. above sea level, lat. 36° 12' 15", long. 115° 57' 13".

Holds CP for change to channel number 18, 7.5-kw ERP, 26-ft. above ground, 8287-ft. above sea level, lat. 35° 57' 21", long. 115° 29' 42". BDFCDTL-20080821ADO.

Ownership: Hilltop Church Inc.

Pahrump—KPVM-LP, Ch. 41, Vernon Van Winkle. Phone: 775-727-9400. Fax: 775-751-5786.

Technical Facilities: 6.74-kw ERP, 187-ft. above ground, 3058-ft. above sea level, lat. 36° 12' 25", long. 115° 57' 35".

Ownership: Vernon Van Winkle.

Pahrump—KPVT-LP, Ch. 30, Hilltop Church Inc.

Technical Facilities: 45-kw ERP, 161-ft. above ground, 3058-ft. above sea level, lat. 36° 12' 15", long. 115° 57' 13".

Ownership: Hilltop Church Inc.

Panaca—K04HF, Ch. 4, Lincoln County TV District No. 1. Phone: 775-962-5336.

Technical Facilities: 0.009-kw ERP, lat. 37° 27' 20", long. 114° 28' 20".

Ownership: Lincoln County TV District No. 1.

Panaca—K06DM, Ch. 6, Lincoln County TV District No. 1. Phone: 775-962-5336.

Technical Facilities: 0.009-kw ERP, lat. 37° 27' 33", long. 114° 27' 59".

Ownership: Lincoln County TV District No. 1.

Panaca—K07CM, Ch. 7, Lincoln County TV District No. 1. Phone: 775-962-5336.

Technical Facilities: 0.008-kw ERP, lat. 37° 27' 33", long. 114° 27' 59".

Holds CP for change to channel number 41, 3.8-kw ERP, 15-ft. above ground, 7308-ft. above sea level, lat. 37° 27' 51", long. 114° 28' 12". BDISTT-20060403APB.

Ownership: Lincoln County TV District No. 1.

Panaca—K43DS, Ch. 43, Lincoln County TV District No. 1. Phone: 775-962-5336.

Technical Facilities: 6-kw ERP, 29-ft. above ground, 4871-ft. above sea level, lat. 37° 47' 33", long. 114° 25' 02".

Ownership: Lincoln County TV District No. 1.

Panaca—K55AO, Ch. 55, White Pine Television District No. 1. Phone: 775-289-4048.

Technical Facilities: 4.18-kw ERP, lat. 37° 27' 20", long. 114° 28' 20".

Ownership: White Pine Television District No. 1.

Panaca—K61AW, Ch. 61, Lincoln County TV District No. 1. Phone: 775-962-5336.

Technical Facilities: 4.32-kw ERP, lat. 37° 27' 39", long. 114° 28' 20".

Ownership: Lincoln County TV District No. 1.

Paradise Valley—K09MM, Ch. 9, Humboldt County. Phone: 775-623-6349.

Technical Facilities: 0.038-kw ERP, lat. 41° 40' 00", long. 117° 34' 00".

Ownership: Humboldt County.

Paradise Valley—K11MU, Ch. 11, Humboldt County. Phone: 775-623-6349.

Technical Facilities: 0.038-kw ERP, lat. 41° 40' 00", long. 117° 34' 00".

Ownership: Humboldt County.

Pioche—K03CM, Ch. 3, Lincoln County TV District No. 1. Phone: 775-962-5336.

Technical Facilities: 0.028-kw ERP, lat. 37° 55' 20", long. 114° 27' 03".

Ownership: Lincoln County TV District No. 1.

Pioche—K09FJ, Ch. 9, Lincoln County TV District No. 1. Phone: 775-962-5336.

Technical Facilities: 0.009-kw ERP, lat. 37° 55' 20", long. 114° 27' 03".

Ownership: Lincoln County TV District No. 1.

Pioche—K11IV, Ch. 11, Lincoln County TV District No. 1. Phone: 775-962-5336.

Technical Facilities: 0.009-kw ERP, lat. 37° 55' 20", long. 114° 27' 03".

Ownership: Lincoln County TV District No. 1.

Pioche—K13PU, Ch. 13, Lincoln County TV District No. 1. Phone: 775-962-5336.

Technical Facilities: 0.006-kw ERP, lat. 37° 55' 20", long. 114° 27' 03".

Ownership: Lincoln County TV District No. 1.

Pioche—K45AO, Ch. 45, Lincoln County TV District No. 1. Phone: 775-962-5336.

Technical Facilities: 0.01-kw ERP, lat. 37° 55' 20", long. 114° 27' 03".

Ownership: Lincoln County TV District No. 1.

Quinn River area—K40FV, Ch. 40, Humboldt County. Phone: 725-623-6349.

Technical Facilities: 0.756-kw ERP, 13-ft. above ground, 5439-ft. above sea level, lat. 41° 50' 50", long. 118° 35' 20".

Ownership: Humboldt County.

Reno—K39FF, Ch. 39, Mutual Television Network. Phone: 888-482-1080.

Technical Facilities: 1000-w TPO, 89.2-kw ERP, 121-ft. above ground, 5600-ft. above sea level, lat. 39° 35' 03", long. 119° 47' 52".

Transmitter: Existing tower atop Red Peak.

Ownership: Mutual Television Network.

Personnel: Paul Crouch, General Manager; Ben Miller, Chief Engineer; Rod Henke, Sales Manager.

Reno—K52FF, Ch. 52, NBC Telemundo License Co. Phone: 202-637-4535.

Technical Facilities: 1000-w TPO, 0.014-kw ERP, 118-ft. above ground, 5568-ft. above sea level, lat. 39° 35' 03", long. 119° 47' 52".

Holds CP for change to channel number 36, 120.6-kw ERP, 104-ft. above ground, 5567-ft. above sea level, lat. 39° 35' 03", long. 119° 47' 52". BDISTTL-20061214AAS.

Transmitter: Red Peak, 5.5-mi. N of Reno.

Ownership: NBC Universal.

Reno—KELM-LP, Ch. 43, NGen Solutions LLC. Phone: 775-333-6626.

Technical Facilities: 1000-w TPO, 28.4-kw ERP, 79-ft. above ground, 5538-ft. above sea level, lat. 39° 35' 03", long. 119° 47' 52".

Transmitter: Red Peak, 4.5-mi. N of Reno.

Began Operation: October 30, 1990.

Ownership: NGen Solutions LLC.

Reno—KNVV-LP, Ch. 41, Entravision Holdings LLC. Phone: 310-447-3870.

Technical Facilities: 23.48-kw ERP, 50-ft. above ground, 9610-ft. above sea level, lat. 39° 18' 38", long. 119° 53' 01".

Ownership: Entravision Communications Corp.

■ **Reno**—KRNS-CA, Ch. 46, Entravision Holdings LLC. Phone: 310-447-3870.

Studio: 940 Matley Ln, Ste 15, Reno, NV 89502.

Technical Facilities: 10.9-kw ERP, 75-ft. above ground, 9721-ft. above sea level, lat. 39° 18' 47", long. 119° 52' 59".

Began Operation: June 7, 1995.

Ownership: Entravision Communications Corp.

Personnel: Leo L. Ramos, General Manager; Mike Andrews, Station Manager; Domingo Miranda, Chief Engineer; Andrea Brown, Sales Manager.

Reno—KRRI-LP, Ch. 25, Eastern Sierra Broadcasting. Phone: 510-769-5904.

Technical Facilities: 1000-w TPO, 13.4-kw ERP, 115-ft. above ground, 5566-ft. above sea level, lat. 39° 35' 02", long. 119° 47' 51".

Transmitter: Red Peak, N of Reno.

Began Operation: October 28, 1998.

Ownership: Eastern Sierra Broadcasting.

Round Mountain—K42EK, Ch. 42, Smoky Valley TV District. Phone: 775-377-2044.

Technical Facilities: 20-w TPO, 0.281-kw ERP, 20-ft. above ground, 7827-ft. above sea level, lat. 38° 39' 23", long. 116° 59' 55".

Transmitter: 4.7-mi. SE of Round Mountain.

Ownership: Smoky Valley TV District.

Round Mountain—K45EY, Ch. 45, Smoky Valley TV District. Phone: 775-377-2044.

Technical Facilities: 20-w TPO, 0.389-kw ERP, 15-ft. above ground, 9826-ft. above sea level, lat. 38° 39' 23", long. 116° 59' 55".

Transmitter: 4.7-mi. SE of Round Mountain.

Ownership: Smoky Valley TV District.

Round Mountain—K55HQ, Ch. 55, Smoky Valley TV District. Phone: 775-377-2044.

Technical Facilities: 20-w TPO, 0.281-kw ERP, 1362-ft. above ground, 9823-ft. above sea level, lat. 38° 39' 23", long. 116° 59' 55".

Transmitter: Head of South Shoshone Canyon, 4.6-mi. SE of Round Mountain.

Ownership: Smoky Valley TV District.

Round Mountain—K58FM, Ch. 58, Smoky Valley TV District. Phone: 775-377-2044.

Technical Facilities: 0.389-kw ERP, lat. 38° 29' 23", long. 116° 59' 55".

Transmitter: 4.6-mi. SE of Round Mountain.

Ownership: Smoky Valley TV District.

Round Mountain—K61GL, Ch. 61, Smoky Valley TV District. Phone: 775-377-2044.

Technical Facilities: 0.389-kw ERP, 15-ft. above ground, 9831-ft. above sea level, lat. 38° 39' 23", long. 116° 59' 55".

Ownership: Smoky Valley TV District.

Round Mountain—K63FP, Ch. 63, Smoky Valley TV District. Phone: 775-377-2044.

Technical Facilities: 0.281-kw ERP, 8-ft. above ground, 9819-ft. above sea level, lat. 38° 29' 23", long. 116° 59' 55".

Transmitter: 5-mi. SE of Round Mountain.

Ownership: Smoky Valley TV District.

Ruth—K03DS, Ch. 3, White Pine Television District No. 1. Phone: 775-289-4048.

Technical Facilities: 0.005-kw ERP, lat. 39° 16' 22", long. 114° 59' 45".

Holds CP for change to 11-ft. above ground, 6960-ft. above sea level, lat. 39° 16' 27", long. 114° 59' 12". BDFCDTV-20080303ABB.

Ownership: White Pine Television District No. 1.

Ruth—K07DV, Ch. 7, White Pine Television District No. 1. Phone: 775-289-4048.

Technical Facilities: 0.008-kw ERP, lat. 39° 16' 22", long. 114° 59' 45".

Holds CP for change to 0.002-kw ERP, 11-ft. above ground, 6960-ft. above sea level, lat. 39° 16' 27", long. 114° 59' 12". BDFCDTV-20080303ABA.

Ownership: White Pine Television District No. 1.

Ruth—K09DW, Ch. 9, White Pine Television District No. 1. Phone: 775-289-4048.

Technical Facilities: 0.008-kw ERP, lat. 39° 16' 22", long. 114° 59' 45".

Holds CP for change to 0.002-kw ERP, 11-ft. above ground, 6960-ft. above sea level, lat. 39° 16' 27", long. 114° 59' 12". BDFCDTV-20080303ABC.

Ownership: White Pine Television District No. 1.

Ruth—K11ED, Ch. 11, White Pine Television District No. 1. Phone: 775-289-4048.

Technical Facilities: 0.008-kw ERP, lat. 39° 16' 22", long. 114° 59' 45".

Holds CP for change to 0.002-kw ERP, 11-ft. above ground, 6960-ft. above sea level, lat. 39° 16' 27", long. 114° 59' 12". BDFCDTV-20080303ABD.

Ownership: White Pine Television District No. 1.

Ruth—K13NQ, Ch. 13, White Pine Television District No. 1. Phone: 775-289-4048.

Technical Facilities: 0.008-kw ERP, lat. 39° 16' 22", long. 114° 59' 45".

Holds CP for change to 0.002-kw ERP, 11-ft. above ground, 6960-ft. above sea level, lat. 39° 16' 27", long. 114° 59' 12". BDFCDTV-20080303ABE.

Ownership: White Pine Television District No. 1.

Ruth—K43IL, Ch. 43, White Pine Television District No. 1. Phone: 775-289-4048.

Technical Facilities: 0.075-kw ERP, 15-ft. above ground, 7137-ft. above sea level, lat. 39° 16' 22", long. 114° 59' 45".

Holds CP for change to 0.018-kw ERP, 8-ft. above ground, 7147-ft. above sea level, BDFCDTT-20080303ABM.

Ownership: White Pine Television District No. 1.

Ryndon—K05LP, Ch. 5, Elko TV District. Phone: 775-738-5025.

Technical Facilities: 0.063-kw ERP, 12-ft. above ground, 5173-ft. above sea level, lat. 40° 57' 54", long. 115° 36' 47".

Ownership: Elko Television District.

Ryndon—K06NY, Ch. 6, Elko Television District. Phone: 775-738-5025.

Technical Facilities: 0.062-kw ERP, 25-ft. above ground, 5186-ft. above sea level, lat. 40° 57' 54", long. 115° 36' 47".

Ownership: Elko Television District.

Ryndon—K08NQ, Ch. 8, Elko Television District. Phone: 775-778-0561. Fax: 775-738-4712.

Technical Facilities: 0.073-kw ERP, 18-ft. above ground, 5179-ft. above sea level, lat. 40° 57' 54", long. 115° 36' 47".

Ownership: Elko Television District.

Ryndon—K12PT, Ch. 12, Elko TV District. Phone: 775-738-5025.

Technical Facilities: 0.07-kw ERP, 35-ft. above ground, 5196-ft. above sea level, lat. 40° 57' 54", long. 115° 36' 47".

Ownership: Elko Television District.

Ryndon—K16FV, Ch. 16, Elko TV District. Phone: 775-738-5025.

Technical Facilities: 0.154-kw ERP, 30-ft. above ground, 5190-ft. above sea level, lat. 40° 57' 54", long. 115° 36' 47".

Ownership: Elko Television District.

Ryndon—K18GT, Ch. 18, Elko Television District. Phone: 775-738-5025.

Technical Facilities: 0.156-kw ERP, 22-ft. above ground, 5184-ft. above sea level, lat. 40° 57' 54", long. 115° 36' 47".

Ownership: Elko Television District.

Ryndon, etc.—K02KS, Ch. 2, Elko Television District. Phone: 775-738-5025.

Technical Facilities: 0.013-kw ERP, 6224-ft. above sea level, lat. 41° 01' 20", long. 115° 11' 40".

Ownership: Elko Television District.

Schurz—K32CQ, Ch. 32, Walker River Paiute Tribe. Phone: 702-773-2306. Fax: 702-773-2585.

Technical Facilities: 0.158-kw ERP, 13-ft. above ground, 6174-ft. above sea level, lat. 38° 57' 58", long. 118° 53' 21".

Ownership: Walker River Paiute Tribe.

Schurz—K36FF, Ch. 36, Walker River Paiute Tribe. Phone: 702-773-2306.

Technical Facilities: 0.158-kw ERP, lat. 38° 57' 58", long. 118° 53' 21".

Ownership: Walker River Paiute Tribe.

Schurz—K39FA, Ch. 34, Walker River Paiute Tribe. Phone: 702-773-2306.

Technical Facilities: 0.15-kw ERP, 20-ft. above ground, 6178-ft. above sea level, lat. 38° 57' 58", long. 118° 53' 21".

Ownership: Walker River Paiute Tribe.

Schurz—K46CC, Ch. 46, Walker River Paiute Tribe. Phone: 702-773-2306. Fax: 702-773-2585.

Technical Facilities: 5-w TPO, lat. 38° 57' 58", long. 118° 53' 21".

Ownership: Walker River Paiute Tribe.

Schurz—K58CY, Ch. 58, Walker River Paiute Tribe. Phone: 702-773-2306.

Technical Facilities: 0.158-kw ERP, lat. 38° 57' 58", long. 118° 53' 21".

Ownership: Walker River Paiute Tribe.

Silver Springs—K29BN, Ch. 29, Sarkes Tarzian Inc. Phone: 812-332-7251.

Technical Facilities: 0.59-kw ERP, lat. 39° 29' 04", long. 119° 17' 59".

Ownership: Sarkes Tarzian Inc.

Silver Springs—K31BM, Ch. 31, Channel 5 Public Broadcasting Inc. Phone: 775-784-4555.

Technical Facilities: 0.594-kw ERP, lat. 39° 29' 04", long. 119° 17' 59".

Began Operation: August 6, 1979.

Ownership: Channel 5 Public Broadcasting Inc.

Silver Springs—K33IB, Ch. 33, KTVU Partnership.

Technical Facilities: 0.636-kw ERP, 18-ft. above ground, 6872-ft. above sea level, lat. 39° 29' 05", long. 119° 18' 07".

Ownership: KTVU Partnership.

Silver Springs—K35FL, Ch. 35, Broadcast Development Corp. Phone: 404-267-1226.

Technical Facilities: 1.21-kw ERP, 70-ft. above ground, 6750-ft. above sea level, lat. 39° 29' 05", long. 119° 18' 07".

Ownership: Broadcast Development Corp.

Smith—K10HQ, Ch. 10, Lyon County Public Works.

Technical Facilities: 0.072-kw ERP, 8241-ft. above sea level, lat. 38° 41' 08", long. 119° 11' 06".

Ownership: Lyon County Public Works.

Smith—K12IT, Ch. 12, Lyon County Public Works. Phone: 775-463-6551.

Technical Facilities: 0.044-kw ERP, 8258-ft. above sea level, lat. 38° 41' 08", long. 119° 11' 06".

Ownership: Lyon County Public Works.

Smith, etc.—K05GD, Ch. 5, Lyon County Public Works. Phone: 775-463-6551.

Technical Facilities: 0.056-kw ERP, 8248-ft. above sea level, lat. 38° 41' 08", long. 119° 11' 06".

Ownership: Lyon County Public Works.

Spring Creek Mobile Home Park—K12MS, Ch. 12, Elko TV District. Phone: 775-738-5025.

Technical Facilities: 0.004-kw ERP, lat. 40° 49' 16", long. 115° 42' 04".

Ownership: Elko Television District.

Star Valley—K33HD, Ch. 33, Elko Television District. Phone: 775-778-0561. Fax: 775-738-5025.

Technical Facilities: 0.67-kw ERP, 20-ft. above ground, 8277-ft. above sea level, lat. 41° 07' 14", long. 114° 34' 27".

Ownership: Elko Television District.

Starr Valley—K04JR, Ch. 4, Elko Television District. Phone: 775-738-5025.

Technical Facilities: 0.133-kw ERP, lat. 41° 01' 20", long. 115° 11' 40".

Ownership: Elko Television District.

Starr Valley—K39GL, Ch. 39, Elko Television District. Phone: 775-778-5025. Fax: 775-738-4712.

Technical Facilities: 0.73-kw ERP, 20-ft. above ground, 7208-ft. above sea level, lat. 41° 11' 40", long. 114° 56' 36".

Ownership: Elko Television District.

Stateline—K38FW, Ch. 38, RSN West LLC. Phone: 207-772-5000.

Technical Facilities: 12-kw ERP, 236-ft. above ground, 6519-ft. above sea level, lat. 38° 57' 35", long. 119° 56' 24".

Ownership: Resort Sports Network Inc.

Stateline—K59GM, Ch. 59, RSN West LLC. Phone: 207-772-5000.

Technical Facilities: 8-kw ERP, 36-ft. above ground, 6276-ft. above sea level, lat. 38° 56' 47", long. 119° 57' 55".

Holds CP for change to channel number 31, BDISTTL-20081125AUH.

Began Operation: August 22, 2003.

Ownership: Resort Sports Network Inc.

Stead & Lawton—K49CK, Ch. 49, Gray Television Licensee LLC. Phone: 775-858-8888.

Technical Facilities: 1.13-kw ERP, 30-ft. above ground, 8268-ft. above sea level, lat. 39° 35' 12", long. 119° 55' 52".

Holds CP for change to 0.34-kw ERP, BDFCDTT-20081020ALD.

Ownership: Gray Television Inc.

Steptoe/Ruby Valley—K08IY, Ch. 8, White Pine Television District No. 1. Phone: 775-289-4048.

Technical Facilities: 0.04-kw ERP, 11-ft. above ground, 8607-ft. above sea level, lat. 40° 19' 20", long. 114° 33' 39".

Holds CP for change to 0.01-kw ERP, 11-ft. above ground, 8620-ft. above sea level, BDFCDTV-20080303ABH.

Ownership: White Pine Television District No. 1.

Steptoe/Ruby Valley—K10KL, Ch. 10, White Pine Television District No. 1. Phone: 775-289-4048.

Technical Facilities: 0.04-kw ERP, 11-ft. above ground, 8607-ft. above sea level, lat. 40° 19' 22", long. 114° 33' 39".

Holds CP for change to 0.01-kw ERP, 11-ft. above ground, 8620-ft. above sea level, BDFCDTV-20080303ABG.

Ownership: White Pine Television District No. 1.

Steptoe/Ruby Valley—K12KO, Ch. 12, White Pine Television District No. 1. Phone: 775-289-4048.

Technical Facilities: 0.04-kw ERP, 11-ft. above ground, 8607-ft. above sea level, lat. 40° 19' 22", long. 114° 33' 39".

Holds CP for change to 0.01-kw ERP, 11-ft. above ground, 8620-ft. above sea level, BDFCDTV-20080303ABI.

Ownership: White Pine Television District No. 1.

Tonopah—K13YU, Ch. 13, Hispanic Christian Community Network Inc. Phone: 214-434-6357.

Technical Facilities: 3-kw ERP, 66-ft. above ground, 6247-ft. above sea level, lat. 38° 03' 49", long. 117° 13' 25.7".

Ownership: Hispanic Christian Community Network Inc.

Ursine—K02EG, Ch. 2, Lincoln County TV District No. 1. Phone: 775-962-5336.

Technical Facilities: 0.058-kw ERP, lat. 37° 59' 00", long. 114° 13' 20".

Ownership: Lincoln County TV District No. 1.

Ursine—K09FK, Ch. 9, Lincoln County TV District No. 1. Phone: 775-962-5336.

Technical Facilities: 0.009-kw ERP, lat. 37° 59' 00", long. 114° 13' 20".

Ownership: Lincoln County TV District No. 1.

Ursine—K11OW, Ch. 11, Lincoln County TV District No. 1. Phone: 775-962-5336.

Technical Facilities: 0.006-kw ERP, lat. 37° 59' 00", long. 114° 13' 20".

Ownership: Lincoln County TV District No. 1.

Ursine—K13LU, Ch. 13, Lincoln County TV District No. 1. Phone: 775-962-5336.

Technical Facilities: 0.009-kw ERP, lat. 37° 59' 00", long. 114° 13' 20".

Ownership: Lincoln County TV District No. 1.

Ursine—K50DA, Ch. 50, Lincoln County TV District No. 1. Phone: 775-962-5336.

Technical Facilities: 0.08-kw ERP, 10-ft. above ground, 5768-ft. above sea level, lat. 37° 59' 00", long. 114° 13' 20".

Ownership: Lincoln County TV District No. 1.

Valmy & Red House—K27GG, Ch. 27, Humboldt County. Phone: 775-623-6349.

Technical Facilities: 1.13-kw ERP, 52-ft. above ground, 5463-ft. above sea level, lat. 40° 56' 24", long. 117° 23' 36".

Ownership: Humboldt County.

Valmy & Red House—K29EV, Ch. 29, Humboldt County. Phone: 775-623-6349.

Technical Facilities: 1.13-kw ERP, 52-ft. above ground, 5463-ft. above sea level, lat. 40° 56' 24", long. 117° 23' 36".

Ownership: Humboldt County.

Valmy & Red House—K34FP, Ch. 34, Humboldt County. Phone: 725-623-6349.

Technical Facilities: 1.13-kw ERP, 13-ft. above ground, 5462-ft. above sea level, lat. 40° 56' 24", long. 117° 23' 36".

Ownership: Humboldt County.

Verdi—K10GP, Ch. 10, Washoe County TV Tax District. Phone: 775-345-0202.

Technical Facilities: 0.162-kw ERP, 7995-ft. above sea level, lat. 39° 34' 38", long. 119° 56' 19".

Ownership: Washoe County TV Tax District.

Verdi—K33ER, Ch. 33, Washoe County TV Tax District. Phone: 775-345-0202.

Technical Facilities: 1.11-kw ERP, lat. 39° 34' 38", long. 119° 56' 19".

Holds CP for change to 0.361-kw ERP, 56-ft. above ground, 8041-ft. above sea level, BDFCDTT-20080922AEY.

Transmitter: 1-mi. SSW of Pavine Peak.

Ownership: Washoe County TV Tax District.

Verdi—K42IL, Ch. 42, Channel 5 Public Broadcasting Inc. Phone: 702-784-4555. Fax: 702-784-1438.

Technical Facilities: 0.4-kw ERP, 75-ft. above ground, 7992-ft. above sea level, lat. 39° 34' 38", long. 119° 56' 19".

Ownership: Channel 5 Public Broadcasting Inc.

Verdi—K47KJ-D, Ch. 47, Channel 5 Public Broadcasting Inc. Phone: 775-784-4555.

Technical Facilities: 0.137-kw ERP, 75-ft. above ground, 7696-ft. above sea level, lat. 39° 34' 38", long. 119° 56' 19".

Began Operation: January 2, 2009.

Ownership: Channel 5 Public Broadcasting Inc.

Verdi/Mogul—K24IB-D, Ch. 24, Washoe County TV Tax District. Phone: 775-345-0202.

Technical Facilities: 0.357-kw ERP, 56-ft. above ground, 8641-ft. above sea level, lat. 39° 34' 38", long. 119° 56' 19".

Ownership: Washoe County TV Tax District.

Verdi/Mogul—K30HY-D, Ch. 30, Verdi TV Tax District. Phone: 775-345-0202.

Technical Facilities: 0.358-kw ERP, 56-ft. above ground, 8041-ft. above sea level, lat. 39° 34' 38", long. 119° 56' 19".

Ownership: Verdi TV Tax District.

Verdi/Mogul—K51DJ-D, Ch. 51, Washoe County TV Tax District. Phone: 775-345-0202.

Technical Facilities: 0.36-kw ERP, 56-ft. above ground, 8041-ft. above sea level, lat. 39° 34' 38", long. 119° 56' 19".

Ownership: Washoe County TV Tax District.

Walker Lake—K17FR, Ch. 17, Mineral Television District No. 1. Phone: 775-423-2543.

Technical Facilities: 1.774-kw ERP, lat. 36° 36' 27", long. 118° 34' 28".

Ownership: Mineral Television District No. 1.

Walker Lake—K26JC, Ch. 26, Mineral Television District No. 1. Phone: 775-423-2543.

Technical Facilities: 0.78-kw ERP, 16-ft. above ground, 4337-ft. above sea level, lat. 38° 36' 27", long. 118° 34' 28".

Ownership: Mineral Television District No. 1.

Walker Lake—K38EH, Ch. 38, Mineral Television District No. 1. Phone: 775-423-2543.

Technical Facilities: 1.77-kw ERP, lat. 38° 35' 27", long. 118° 34' 28".

Transmitter: 1.9-mi. S of Thorne.

Ownership: Mineral Television District No. 1.

Walker Lake, etc.—K14JY, Ch. 14, Mineral Television District No. 1. Phone: 775-423-2543.

Technical Facilities: 1.82-kw ERP, 26-ft. above ground, 4347-ft. above sea level, lat. 38° 36' 27", long. 118° 34' 28".

Ownership: Mineral Television District No. 1.

Walker Lake, etc.—K24EY, Ch. 24, Mineral Television District No. 1. Phone: 775-423-2543.

Technical Facilities: 1.82-kw ERP, 26-ft. above ground, 4347-ft. above sea level, lat. 38° 36' 27", long. 118° 34' 28".

Ownership: Mineral Television District No. 1.

Walker Lake, etc.—K28GX, Ch. 28, Mineral Television District No. 1. Phone: 775-423-2543.

Technical Facilities: 1.701-kw ERP, 26-ft. above ground, 4347-ft. above sea level, lat. 38° 36' 27", long. 118° 34' 28".

Ownership: Mineral Television District No. 1.

Walker Lake, etc.—K42DS, Ch. 42, Mineral Television District No. 1. Phone: 775-423-2543.

Technical Facilities: 1.82-kw ERP, 26-ft. above ground, 4347-ft. above sea level, lat. 38° 36' 27", long. 118° 34' 28".

Ownership: Mineral Television District No. 1.

Wells—K08IO, Ch. 8, Elko Television District. Phone: 775-738-5025.

Technical Facilities: 0.017-kw ERP, lat. 41° 07' 18", long. 114° 33' 57".

Ownership: Elko Television District.

Wells—K22GW, Ch. 22, Elko Television District. Phone: 775-738-5025.

Technical Facilities: 0.95-kw ERP, 87-ft. above ground, 7275-ft. above sea level, lat. 41° 11' 40", long. 114° 56' 36".

Ownership: Elko Television District.

Wells—K24GE, Ch. 24, Elko Television District. Phone: 775-738-5025.

Technical Facilities: 0.95-kw ERP, 87-ft. above ground, 7275-ft. above sea level, lat. 41° 11' 40", long. 114° 56' 36".

Ownership: Elko Television District.

Wells—K26JB, Ch. 26, Elko Television District. Phone: 775-738-5025.

Technical Facilities: 0.95-kw ERP, 87-ft. above ground, 7275-ft. above sea level, lat. 41° 11' 40", long. 114° 56' 36".

Ownership: Elko Television District.

Wells, etc.—K20JQ, Ch. 20, Elko Television District. Phone: 775-738-5025.

Technical Facilities: 0.95-kw ERP, 39-ft. above ground, 7260-ft. above sea level, lat. 41° 11' 40", long. 114° 56' 36".

Ownership: Elko Television District.

Winnemucca—K14MR-D, Ch. 14, Humboldt County. Phone: 775-623-6349.

Technical Facilities: 0.2-kw ERP, 20-ft. above ground, 6775-ft. above sea level, lat. 41° 00' 38", long. 117° 45' 40".

Ownership: Humboldt County.

Winnemucca—K15AL-D, Ch. 15, Humboldt County. Phone: 775-623-6349.

Technical Facilities: 0.2-kw ERP, 20-ft. above ground, 6755-ft. above sea level, lat. 41° 00' 38", long. 117° 45' 40".

Ownership: Humboldt County.

Personnel: Paul Burkholder, Chief Engineer.

Winnemucca—K17HB, Ch. 17, KTVU Partnership.

Technical Facilities: 0.838-kw ERP, 16-ft. above ground, 6742-ft. above sea level, lat. 41° 00' 38", long. 117° 45' 40".

Ownership: KTVU Partnership.

Winnemucca—K19EU, Ch. 19, Humboldt County. Phone: 775-623-6349.

Technical Facilities: 1.489-kw ERP, 33-ft. above ground, 6814-ft. above sea level, lat. 41° 00' 38", long. 117° 45' 40".

Ownership: Humboldt County.

Winnemucca—K21FO-D, Ch. 21, Humboldt County. Phone: 775-623-6349.

Technical Facilities: 0.2-kw ERP, 23-ft. above ground, 6758-ft. above sea level, lat. 41° 00' 38", long. 117° 45' 40".

Ownership: Humboldt County.

Winnemucca—K23FR-D, Ch. 23, Humboldt County. Phone: 775-623-6349.

Technical Facilities: 0.2-kw ERP, 33-ft. above ground, 6768-ft. above sea level, lat. 41° 00' 38", long. 117° 45' 40".

Ownership: Humboldt County.

Winnemucca—K45BJ, Ch. 45, Humboldt County. Phone: 775-623-6349.

Technical Facilities: 1.14-kw ERP, lat. 41° 00' 38", long. 117° 45' 40".

Ownership: Humboldt County.

Winnemucca—K47CH, Ch. 47, Humboldt County. Phone: 775-623-6349.

Technical Facilities: 1.14-kw ERP, lat. 41° 00' 38", long. 117° 45' 40".

Ownership: Humboldt County.

Winnemucca—K49BK-D, Ch. 49, Humboldt County. Phone: 775-623-6349.

Technical Facilities: 0.2-kw ERP, 26-ft. above ground, 6762-ft. above sea level, lat. 41° 00' 38", long. 117° 45' 40".

Ownership: Humboldt County.

Winnemucca—K51BW, Ch. 51, Humboldt County. Phone: 775-623-6349.

Technical Facilities: 1.14-kw ERP, lat. 41° 00' 38", long. 117° 45' 40".

Ownership: Humboldt County.

Winnemucca—KPMP-LP, Ch. 2, Entravision Holdings LLC. Phone: 310-447-3870.

Technical Facilities: 3-kw ERP, 170-ft. above ground, 4655-ft. above sea level, lat. 40° 57' 23.3", long. 117° 42' 47.5".

Holds CP for change to channel number 43, 15-kw ERP, 50-ft. above ground, 6785-ft. above sea level, lat. 41° 00' 40", long. 117° 46' 04". BDFCDTL-20060331ACJ.

Began Operation: April 14, 2005.

Ownership: Entravision Communications Corp.

Yerington—K06KC, Ch. 6, Lyon County Public Works. Phone: 775-463-6551.

Technical Facilities: 0.027-kw ERP, lat. 38° 59' 15", long. 119° 14' 35".

Ownership: Lyon County Public Works.

Yerington—K16GM, Ch. 16, KTVU Partnership. Phone: 775-856-1100.

Technical Facilities: 0.744-kw ERP, 18-ft. above ground, 6389-ft. above sea level, lat. 38° 59' 12", long. 119° 14' 36".

Ownership: Cox Enterprises Inc.

Yerington—K18BW, Ch. 18, Lyon County Public Works. Phone: 775-463-6551.

Technical Facilities: 0.137-kw ERP, lat. 38° 59' 15", long. 119° 14' 35".

Ownership: Lyon County Public Works.

Yerington—K40DV, Ch. 40, Lyon County Public Works. Phone: 775-463-6551.

Technical Facilities: 0.137-kw ERP, 16-ft. above ground, 6391-ft. above sea level, lat. 38° 59' 15", long. 119° 14' 35".

Ownership: Lyon County Public Works.

Yerington—K49FZ, Ch. 49, Lyon County Public Works. Phone: 775-463-6551.

Technical Facilities: 0.025-kw ERP, lat. 38° 59' 15", long. 119° 14' 35".

Ownership: Lyon County Public Works.

New Hampshire

Berlin—W27BL, Ch. 27, Hearst-Argyle Properties Inc. Phone: 919-839-0300.

Technical Facilities: 1.81-kw ERP, lat. 44° 27' 30", long. 71° 10' 02".

Began Operation: August 19, 1994.

Ownership: Hearst-Argyle Television Inc.

Charlestown, etc.—WVBQ-LP, Ch. 47, Vision 3 Broadcasting Inc. Phone: 802-258-2200.

Technical Facilities: 0.145-kw ERP, 52-ft. above ground, 643-ft. above sea level, lat. 43° 24' 12", long. 72° 25' 42".

Ownership: Vision 3 Broadcasting Inc.

Claremont—W10AC, Ch. 10, Claremont Television Inc.

Technical Facilities: 9.31-kw ERP, lat. 43° 22' 48", long. 72° 22' 04".

Ownership: Claremont Television Inc.

Claremont—W12AF, Ch. 12, Claremont Television Inc.

Technical Facilities: 0.009-kw ERP, lat. 43° 22' 48", long. 72° 22' 04".

Ownership: Claremont Television Inc.

■ **Claremont**—W17CI, Ch. 17, Convergence Entertainment & Communications LLC. Phone: 518-825-1071.

Studio: 1611 Harbor Rd, c/o WBTV, Shelburne, VT 04582.

Technical Facilities: 100-w TPO, 1.5-kw ERP, 39-ft. above ground, 2900-ft. above sea level, lat. 43° 26' 15", long. 72° 27' 08".

Transmitter: Mount Ascutney, near Windsor.

Began Operation: December 24, 1998.

Ownership: Convergence Entertainment & Communications LLC.

Personnel: Charles Kail, General Manager.

Colebrook—W26CQ, Ch. 26, University System of New Hampshire Board of Trustees. Phone: 603-868-1100.

Technical Facilities: 19.7-kw ERP, 56-ft. above ground, 2657-ft. above sea level, lat. 44° 56' 50", long. 71° 20' 28".

Began Operation: October 21, 2004.

Ownership: Hearst-Argyle Television Inc.

Concord—W39AR, Ch. 39, Center Broadcasting Corp. of New Hampshire.

Technical Facilities: 100-w TPO, 1.047-kw ERP, 74-ft. above ground, 394-ft. above sea level, lat. 43° 12' 24", long. 71° 32' 41".

Transmitter: 0.15-mi. N of the intersection of Washington St. & Center St.

Ownership: Center Broadcasting Corp. of New Hampshire.

Hanover—W50DP-D, Ch. 50, U. of New Hampshire. Phone: 603-868-1100.

Technical Facilities: 0.05-kw ERP, 404-ft. above ground, 2234-ft. above sea level, lat. 43° 42' 30", long. 72° 09' 16".

Ownership: U. of New Hampshire.

Personnel: William Bumpus, Chief Engineer.

Littleton—W38CB, Ch. 38, Hearst-Argyle Properties Inc. Phone: 919-839-0300.

Technical Facilities: 13-kw ERP, lat. 44° 09' 24", long. 71° 41' 57".

Transmitter: Cannon Mountain, 5.5-mi. SE of Franconia.

Began Operation: July 25, 1995.

Ownership: Hearst-Argyle Television Inc.

Littleton—WMUR-LP, Ch. 29, Hearst-Argyle Properties Inc. Phone: 919-839-0300.

Technical Facilities: 1000-w TPO, 9.86-kw ERP, 80-ft. above ground, 4167-ft. above sea level, lat. 44° 09' 24", long. 71° 41' 57".

Began Operation: July 25, 1995.

Ownership: Hearst-Argyle Television Inc.

Personnel: Jeff Bartlett, General Manager; Stefan Hadl, Chief Engineer; Gerry McGavick, Sales Manager.

Manchester—W28CM, Ch. 28, Center Broadcasting Corp. of New Hampshire.

Technical Facilities: 1.04-kw ERP, 110-ft. above ground, 416-ft. above sea level, lat. 42° 43' 23", long. 71° 27' 39".

Ownership: Center Broadcasting Corp. of New Hampshire.

Nashua—W33AK, Ch. 33, Center Broadcasting Corp. of New Hampshire.

Technical Facilities: 100-w TPO, 0.735-kw ERP, 134-ft. above ground, 279-ft. above sea level, lat. 42° 45' 45", long. 71° 27' 49".

Transmitter: One Indian Head Plaza, Temple St.

Ownership: Center Broadcasting Corp. of New Hampshire.

■**Nashua**—WYCN-LP, Ch. 13, Center Broadcasting Corp. of New Hampshire. Phone: 603-883-7435.

Technical Facilities: 10-w TPO, 0.04-kw ERP, 135-ft. above ground, 279-ft. above sea level, lat. 42° 45' 45", long. 71° 27' 49".

Transmitter: One Indian Head Plaza, Temple St.

Ownership: Center Broadcasting Corp. of New Hampshire.

Personnel: Gordon Jackson, General Manager; Bob Smith, Chief Engineer; Carolyn Choste, Sales Manager.

Pittsburg—W18BO, Ch. 18, U. of New Hampshire. Phone: 603-868-1100.

Technical Facilities: 4.6-kw ERP, lat. 44° 56' 50", long. 71° 20' 28".

Holds CP for change to channel number 34, 0.06-kw ERP, 69-ft. above ground, 2671-ft. above sea level, BDISDTT-20060331AZC.

Ownership: U. of New Hampshire.

Personnel: William Bumpus, Chief Engineer.

New Jersey

Atlantic City—W45CP, Ch. 45, Trinity Broadcasting Network Inc. Phone: 714-832-2950. Fax: 714-731-0661.

Technical Facilities: 22.3-kw ERP, 417-ft. above ground, 417-ft. above sea level, lat. 39° 21' 40", long. 74° 25' 05".

Ownership: Trinity Broadcasting Network Inc.

Atlantic City—WMGM-LP, Ch. 7, Access.1 New Jersey License Co. Phone: 609-927-4440. Fax: 609-927-7014.

Studio: 1601 New Rd, Linwood, NJ 08221.

Technical Facilities: 0.029-kw ERP, 210-ft. above ground, 213-ft. above sea level, lat. 39° 23' 24", long. 74° 30' 45".

Ownership: Access.1 Communications Corp.

Personnel: Jane Stark, General Manager; Ron Smith, Station Manager; Dan Merlo, Chief Engineer.

■**Atlantic City**—WQAV-LP, Ch. 34, Asiavision Inc. Phone: 301-345-2742.

Technical Facilities: 1000-w TPO, 28.6-kw ERP, 191-ft. above sea level, lat. 39° 21' 02", long. 74° 27' 26".

Holds CP for change to channel number 13, 0.5-kw ERP, 180-ft. above ground, 190-ft. above sea level, BDISTVA-20080627AAI.

Transmitter: 3815 Ventnor Ave.

Ownership: Asiavision Inc.

Belvidere—W43CG, Ch. 43, New Jersey Public Broadcasting Authority. Phone: 609-777-5000.

Technical Facilities: 1-kw ERP, 115-ft. above ground, 1342-ft. above sea level, lat. 40° 46' 14", long. 75° 03' 52".

Holds CP for change to 0.6-kw ERP, 128-ft. above ground, 1355-ft. above sea level, BDFCDTT-20061010AET.

Ownership: New Jersey Public Broadcasting Authority.

East Orange—WPXO-LD, Ch. 34, CaribeVision Station Group LLC. Phone: 305-365-2030.

Technical Facilities: 3.5-kw ERP, 1175-ft. above ground, 1226-ft. above sea level, lat. 40° 44' 54", long. 73° 59' 10".

Ownership: CaribeVision Holdings Inc.

■**Edison**—WDVB-CA, Ch. 39, Deepak Viswanath. Phone: 718-784-8180.

Technical Facilities: 35-kw ERP, 249-ft. above ground, 358-ft. above sea level, lat. 40° 31' 45", long. 74° 23' 34".

Holds CP for change to 10-kw ERP, 69-ft. above ground, 197-ft. above sea level, lat. 40° 34' 17", long. 74° 20' 47". BPTTA-20090309AAZ.

Began Operation: February 14, 1991.

Ownership: Deepak Viswanath.

Hackettstown—W23AZ, Ch. 23, Centenary College. Phone: 908-979-4355.

Studio: 100 Rte. 46, Hackettstown, NJ 07840.

Technical Facilities: 945-w TPO, 4.43-kw ERP, 85-ft. above ground, 673-ft. above sea level, lat. 40° 50' 54", long. 74° 50' 02".

Transmitter: 20 Thomas Dr., Independence Twp.

Ownership: Centenary College.

Personnel: Norman Worth, General Manager; L. J. Tighe, Chief Engineer; Pat Layton, General Sales Manager.

Hackettstown—W49BE, Ch. 49, New Jersey Public Broadcasting Authority. Phone: 609-777-5000. Fax: 609-633-2912.

Technical Facilities: 694-w TPO, 10-kw ERP, 138-ft. above ground, 1236-ft. above sea level, lat. 40° 51' 07", long. 74° 52' 36".

Transmitter: 20 Thomas Dr.

Ownership: New Jersey Public Broadcasting Authority.

Personnel: Elizabeth Christopher, General Manager; W. Schworbos, Chief Engineer.

■**Hammonton, etc.**—WPSJ-LP, Ch. 24, Engle Broadcasting. Phone: 856-767-8884. Fax: 856-768-9084.

Studio: 104 Bellevue Ave., Hammonton, NJ 08037.

Technical Facilities: 5-kw ERP, 722-ft. above ground, 834-ft. above sea level, lat. 39° 43' 41", long. 74° 50' 38".

Multichannel TV Sound: Separate audio progam.

Ownership: Engle Broadcasting.

Personnel: Barbara E. Ciric, President; Paul V. Engle, General Manager.

Morristown—W54CZ, Ch. 54, WLNY LP. Phone: 631-777-8855. Fax: 631-777-8180.

Technical Facilities: 966-w TPO, 8-kw ERP, 810-ft. above ground, 940-ft. above sea level, lat. 40° 47' 08", long. 74° 30' 41".

Holds CP for change to channel number 17, 1-kw ERP, 111-ft. above ground, 811-ft. above sea level, BMPDTL-20080123AEX.

Ownership: WLNY Holdings Inc.

Personnel: Richard Mulliner, Chief Engineer.

Pittstown—W25BB, Ch. 25, New Jersey Public Broadcasting Authority. Phone: 609-777-5000.

Technical Facilities: 1.52-kw ERP, 118-ft. above ground, 682-ft. above sea level, lat. 40° 30' 37", long. 74° 57' 29".

Ownership: New Jersey Public Broadcasting Authority.

Springville—WNAI-LP, Ch. 41, Marcia Cohen. Phone: 202-293-0011.

Technical Facilities: 140-kw ERP, 820-ft. above ground, 1112-ft. above sea level, lat. 40° 02' 30", long. 75° 14' 11".

Holds CP for change to 2.5-kw ERP, BDFCDTL-20090326ABU.

Began Operation: September 26, 2002.

Ownership: Marcia Cohen.

Sussex—W36AZ, Ch. 36, New Jersey Public Broadcasting Authority. Phone: 609-777-5000.

Technical Facilities: 14.6-kw ERP, 52-ft. above ground, 1352-ft. above sea level, lat. 41° 08' 37", long. 74° 32' 18".

Ownership: New Jersey Public Broadcasting Authority.

■**Trenton**—W25AW, Ch. 25, WZBN-TV Inc. Phone: 609-586-5088. Fax: 609-586-8221.

Technical Facilities: 10-kw ERP, 180-ft. above ground, 233-ft. above sea level, lat. 40° 14' 48", long. 74° 42' 53".

Ownership: WZBN-TV Inc.

Personnel: Louis A. Zanoni, Chairman; Gregory L. Zanoni, President & General Manager; Doreen A. Damico, Vice President & Administrator.

Trenton—W49CW-D, Ch. 49, WZBN-TV Inc. Phone: 609-586-5088.

Technical Facilities: 0.975-kw ERP, 650-ft. above ground, 710-ft. above sea level, lat. 40° 16' 58", long. 74° 41' 11".

Ownership: WZBN-TV Inc.

New Mexico

Abiquiu—K02HU, Ch. 2, Abiquiu Valley TV Association.

Technical Facilities: 0.003-kw ERP, 7470-ft. above sea level, lat. 36° 10' 52", long. 106° 20' 28".

Ownership: Abiquiu Valley TV Association.

Abiquiu—K06ME, Ch. 6, Abiquiu Valley TV Association.

Technical Facilities: 0.008-kw ERP, 20-ft. above ground, 7510-ft. above sea level, lat. 36° 10' 52", long. 106° 20' 28".

Ownership: Abiquiu Valley TV Association.

Abiquiu—K09LY, Ch. 9, Abiquiu Valley TV Association.

Technical Facilities: 0.003-kw ERP, 7500-ft. above sea level, lat. 36° 10' 52", long. 106° 20' 28".

Ownership: Abiquiu Valley TV Association.

Alamogordo—K24CT, Ch. 24, ACME Television Licenses of New Mexico LLC. Phone: 202-828-2265.

Technical Facilities: 300-w TPO, 15.2-kw ERP, 102-ft. above ground, 7851-ft. above sea level, lat. 32° 49' 45", long. 105° 52' 14".

Transmitter: Long Ridge of Mule Peak.

Ownership: ACME Communications Inc.

Alamogordo—K27HP, Ch. 27, LIN of New Mexico LLC. Phone: 401-457-9525.

Technical Facilities: 100-w TPO, 4.95-kw ERP, 50-ft. above ground, 9255-ft. above sea level, lat. 32° 49' 45", long. 105° 52' 14".

Holds CP for change to 0.374-kw ERP, 49-ft. above ground, 7812-ft. above sea level, lat. 32° 49' 48", long. 105° 53' 15". BDFCDTT-20080408AAQ.

Transmitter: Long Ridge of Mule Peak, Alamogordo.

Ownership: LIN TV Corp.

Alamogordo—K28HB, Ch. 28, ACME Television Licenses of New Mexico LLC. Phone: 202-828-2265.

Technical Facilities: 300-w TPO, 1.89-kw ERP, 69-ft. above ground, 7667-ft. above sea level, lat. 32° 49' 45", long. 105° 52' 14".

Transmitter: Long Ridge of Mule Peak.

Ownership: ACME Communications Inc.

Alamogordo—K31GJ, Ch. 31, KOB-TV LLC. Phone: 654-642-4334.

Technical Facilities: 0.675-kw ERP, lat. 32° 49' 44", long. 105° 53' 11".

Ownership: Hubbard Broadcasting Inc.

Alamogordo—K40BP, Ch. 40, NPG of Texas LP.

Technical Facilities: 2.41-kw ERP, lat. 32° 49' 47", long. 105° 53' 15".

Ownership: News Press & Gazette Co.

Alamogordo—K42EY, Ch. 42, Regents of New Mexico State U. Phone: 505-646-2222.

Technical Facilities: 0.001-kw ERP, lat. 32° 49' 47", long. 105° 53' 13".

Ownership: Regents of New Mexico State U.

Alamogordo—K49FX, Ch. 49, LIN of New Mexico LLC. Phone: 202-462-6065.

Technical Facilities: 2.106-kw ERP, 69-ft. above ground, 7857-ft. above sea level, lat. 32° 49' 47", long. 105° 53' 12".

Holds CP for change to 0.42-kw ERP, 69-ft. above ground, 7858-ft. above sea level, BDFCDTT-20060323AAJ.

Ownership: LIN TV Corp.

Alamogordo—K56IU, Ch. 56, Trinity Broadcasting Network Inc. Phone: 714-832-2950. Fax: 714-730-0661.

Technical Facilities: 9.9-kw ERP, 164-ft. above ground, 4764-ft. above sea level, lat. 32° 56' 42", long. 105° 56' 47".

Ownership: Trinity Broadcasting Network Inc.

Alamogordo—K63GU, Ch. 63, Vision Broadcasting Network Inc. Phone: 575-437-1919.

Technical Facilities: 4.1-kw ERP, 85-ft. above ground, 7867-ft. above sea level, lat. 32° 49' 45", long. 105° 52' 14".

Ownership: Vision Broadcasting Network Inc.

Personnel: William Oechsner, General Manager; John Warren, Chief Engineer; Jason Karrer, Production Manager & News Director; Ramona Chapman, Traffic; Donna Karrer, Sales.

Alamogordo—KAPT-LP, Ch. 29, Prime Time Christian Broadcasting Inc. Phone: 915-563-0420. Fax: 915-563-1736.

Technical Facilities: 100-w TPO, 1.86-kw ERP, 23-ft. above ground, 7783-ft. above sea level, lat. 32° 49' 47", long. 105° 53' 12".

Transmitter: Long Ridge electronics site, Lincoln National Forest, near Alamogordo.

Ownership: Prime Time Christian Broadcasting Inc.

Personnel: Al Cooper, General Manager; Jay Westcott, Chief Engineer; Jeff Welter, Sales Manager.

Alamogordo—KKNJ-LP, Ch. 36, KDBC License LLC - Debtor-in-Possession. Phone: 559-733-7800.

Technical Facilities: 1.6-kw ERP, 26-ft. above ground, 7775-ft. above sea level, lat. 32° 49' 45", long. 105° 53' 15".

Ownership: E. Roger Williams, Trustee.

■**Alamogordo**—KVBA-LP, Ch. 19, Vision Broadcasting Network Inc. Phone: 575-437-1919. Fax: 575-437-5353.

Studio: 1017 New York Ave, Alamogordo, NM 88310.

Technical Facilities: 9.9-kw ERP, 69-ft. above ground, 7851-ft. above sea level, lat. 32° 49' 45", long. 105° 52' 14".

Transmitter: Long Ridge Sacramento Mountains.

Ownership: Vision Broadcasting Network Inc.

Personnel: William J. Oechsner Jr., General Manager; John Warren, Chief Engineer; Jason Karrer, Production Manager & News Director; Ramona Chapman, Traffic; Donna Karrer, Sales.

Alamogordo, etc.—K34CR, Ch. 34, KOAT Hearst-Argyle Television Inc.

Technical Facilities: 1.18-kw ERP, 39-ft. above ground, 7785-ft. above sea level, lat. 32° 49' 45", long. 105° 53' 15".

Ownership: Hearst-Argyle Television Inc.

Albuquerque—K38IM, Ch. 38, Three Angels Broadcasting Network Inc. Phone: 618-627-4651. Fax: 618-627-2726.

Technical Facilities: 45.4-kw ERP, 89-ft. above ground, 1070-ft. above sea level, lat. 35° 12' 50", long. 106° 27' 01".

Ownership: Three Angels Broadcasting Network Inc.

Personnel: Danny Shelton, General Manager; Moses Primo, Broadcast Operations & Engineering Director.

Albuquerque—K43HW, Ch. 43, Joseph W. Shaffer. Phone: 928-717-0828.

Technical Facilities: 1000-w TPO, 27-kw ERP, 141-ft. above ground, 5787-ft. above sea level, lat. 35° 04' 06", long. 106° 46' 46".

Transmitter: Approx. 10-mi. W of Albuquerque.

Ownership: Joseph W. Shaffer.

Albuquerque—KFAC-LP, Ch. 39, Ramar Communications Inc. Phone: 806-748-9300. Fax: 806-748-1949.

Technical Facilities: 71.6-kw ERP, 69-ft. above ground, 10633-ft. above sea level, lat. 35° 12' 51", long. 106° 27' 02".

Holds CP for change to 8.4-kw ERP, BDFCDTL-20080303ALF.

Transmitter: Sandia Crest electronics site.

Multichannel TV Sound: Stereo only.

Ownership: Ramar Communications Inc.

Personnel: Gabriel Zavala, General Manager; Rob Ramsayer, Chief Engineer.

Albuquerque—KQDF-LP, Ch. 25, Una Vez Mas Albuquerque License LLC. Phone: 214-754-7008.

Technical Facilities: 31.1-kw ERP, 142-ft. above ground, 5949-ft. above sea level, lat. 35° 04' 06", long. 106° 46' 46".

Holds CP for change to 150-kw ERP, 180-ft. above ground, 10791-ft. above sea level, lat. 35° 12' 50", long. 106° 27' 01". BPTTL-20081230AAP.

Transmitter: 12325 Central NW.

Began Operation: April 30, 1999April 30, 1999.

Ownership: Una Vez Mas GP LLC.

■**Albuquerque**—KTEL-LP, Ch. 47, Ramar Communications Inc. Phones: 806-745-3434; 806-748-9300. Fax: 806-748-1949.

Technical Facilities: 62.8-kw ERP, 69-ft. above ground, 10633-ft. above sea level, lat. 35° 12' 51", long. 106° 27' 02".

Holds CP for change to 15-kw ERP, BDFCDTL-20080303ALE.

Multichannel TV Sound: Stereo only.

Ownership: Ramar Communications Inc.

Personnel: Rob Ramsayer, Chief Engineer.

Albuquerque—KTFA-LP, Ch. 48, Entravision Holdings LLC. Phone: 310-447-3870.

Technical Facilities: 147.1-kw ERP, 66-ft. above ground, 10705-ft. above sea level, lat. 35° 12' 41", long. 106° 26' 56".

Ownership: Entravision Communications Corp.

Albuquerque—KTVS-LP, Ch. 36, Alpha-Omega Broadcasting of Albuquerque Inc. Phone: 505-884-3855.

Technical Facilities: 30-kw ERP, 39-ft. above ground, 10659-ft. above sea level, lat. 35° 12' 51", long. 106° 27' 01".

Holds CP for change to 15-kw ERP, 110-ft. above ground, 10717-ft. above sea level, BDFCDTL-20080618ABU.

Ownership: Alpha-Omega Broadcasting of Albuquerque Inc.

■**Albuquerque**—KYNM-LP, Ch. 30, Belmax Broadcasting LLC. Phone: 505-345-1991.

Technical Facilities: 8.41-kw ERP, 92-ft. above ground, 10791-ft. above sea level, lat. 35° 12' 44", long. 106° 26' 58".

Ownership: Belmax Broadcasting LLC.

Angel Fire—K33FK, Ch. 33, Regents of the U. of New Mexico & The Board of Education of the City of Albuquerque.

Technical Facilities: 3.46-kw ERP, lat. 36° 37' 39", long. 105° 13' 41".

Ownership: Board of Education of the City of Albuquerque; Regents of New Mexico State U.

Antonito—K51DM, Ch. 51, Son Broadcasting Inc. Phone: 505-345-1991.

Technical Facilities: 2.15-kw ERP, 56-ft. above ground, 10964-ft. above sea level, lat. 36° 51' 35", long. 106° 01' 09".

Ownership: Son Broadcasting Inc.

Arrey & Derry—K34FU, Ch. 34, LIN of New Mexico LLC.

Technical Facilities: 0.647-kw ERP, 30-ft. above ground, 7559-ft. above sea level, lat. 32° 58' 16".

Ownership: LIN TV Corp.

Artesia—K29FM-D, Ch. 29, Eastern New Mexico U. Phone: 505-562-2112.

Technical Facilities: 0.9-kw ERP, 170-ft. above ground, 3618-ft. above sea level, lat. 32° 50' 23.4", long. 104° 25' 42.2".

Ownership: Eastern New Mexico U. Board of Regents.

Artesia—K46FE, Ch. 46, LIN of New Mexico LLC. Phone: 202-462-6001.

Technical Facilities: 10-kw ERP, lat. 32° 47' 39", long. 104° 12' 27".

Transmitter: Hwy. 82, 12-mi. E of Artesia.

Ownership: LIN TV Corp.

Aztec—K08FR, Ch. 8, LIN of Colorado LLC. Phone: 202-462-6001.

Technical Facilities: 0.038-kw ERP, lat. 36° 46' 20", long. 108° 01' 42".

Holds CP for change to channel number 22, 1.1-kw ERP, 20-ft. above ground, 5860-ft. above sea level, BDISTT-20060331BFE.

Ownership: LIN TV Corp.

Aztec—K38DA-D, Ch. 38, Regents of the U. of New Mexico & The Board of Education of the City of Albuquerque. Phone: 505-277-2121.

Technical Facilities: 0.395-kw ERP, 43-ft. above ground, 6834-ft. above sea level, lat. 36° 48' 53", long. 107° 53' 31".

Ownership: Board of Education of the City of Albuquerque; Regents of the U. of New Mexico.

Aztec—K44GC-D, Ch. 44, LIN of New Mexico LLC. Phone: 401-457-9525.

Technical Facilities: 0.24-kw ERP, 43-ft. above ground, 6834-ft. above sea level, lat. 36° 48' 53", long. 107° 53' 31".

Ownership: LIN TV Corp.

Aztec & Cedar Hill—K10CG-D, Ch. 10, KOAT Hearst-Argyle Television Inc. Phone: 919-839-0300.

Technical Facilities: 0.3-kw ERP, 100-ft. above ground, 6130-ft. above sea level, lat. 36° 40' 17", long. 108° 13' 53".

Began Operation: January 29, 1987.

Ownership: Hearst-Argyle Television Inc.

Bloomfield, etc.—K09JJ, Ch. 9, KOAT Hearst-Argyle Television Inc. Phone: 919-839-0300.

Technical Facilities: 0.01-kw ERP, 5794-ft. above sea level, lat. 36° 41' 03", long. 107° 51' 29".

Ownership: Hearst-Argyle Television Inc.

Bloomfield, etc.—K11JO, Ch. 11, LIN of Colorado LLC. Phone: 202-462-6001.

Technical Facilities: 0.004-kw ERP, 33-ft. above ground, 5781-ft. above sea level, lat. 36° 41' 03", long. 107° 51' 29".

Ownership: LIN TV Corp.

Buena Vista—K10LE, Ch. 10, Buena Vista TV Translator Corp.

Technical Facilities: 0.009-kw ERP, lat. 35° 53' 55", long. 105° 15' 37".

Ownership: Buena Vista TV Translator Corp.

Buena Vista—K12LQ, Ch. 12, Buena Vista TV Translator Corp.

Technical Facilities: 0.009-kw ERP, lat. 35° 53' 55", long. 105° 15' 37".

Ownership: Buena Vista TV Translator Corp.

Caballo—K20HA, Ch. 20, KOB-TV LLC.

Technical Facilities: 0.64-kw ERP, 30-ft. above ground, 7451-ft. above sea level, lat. 32° 58' 17", long. 107° 13' 25".

Ownership: Hubbard Broadcasting Inc.

Caballo—K31DR, Ch. 31, LIN of New Mexico LLC. Phone: 202-462-6001.

Technical Facilities: 9.99-kw ERP, 49-ft. above ground, 7579-ft. above sea level, lat. 32° 58' 16", long. 107° 13' 23".

Ownership: LIN TV Corp.

Caballo—K45HJ, Ch. 45, Regents of New Mexico State U. Phone: 505-646-2222.

Technical Facilities: 1.165-kw ERP, 50-ft. above ground, 7838-ft. above sea level, lat. 32° 58' 03", long. 107° 13' 35".

Ownership: Regents of New Mexico State U.

Caballo—K49CZ, Ch. 49, KOAT Hearst-Argyle Television Inc. Phone: 919-839-0300.

Technical Facilities: 0.667-kw ERP, 20-ft. above ground, 7441-ft. above sea level, lat. 32° 58' 17", long. 107° 13' 25".

Began Operation: January 23, 1991.

Ownership: Hearst-Argyle Television Inc.

Capitan & Ruidoso—K30GM, Ch. 30, KOB-TV LLC. Phone: 651-642-4334.

Technical Facilities: 4.1-kw ERP, lat. 33° 24' 14", long. 105° 46' 55".

Ownership: Hubbard Broadcasting Inc.

Capitan & Ruidoso—K33GD, Ch. 33, LIN of New Mexico LLC. Phone: 202-462-6001. Fax: 501-246-2222.

Technical Facilities: 1.4-kw ERP, 184-ft. above ground, 10955-ft. above sea level, lat. 33° 24' 14", long. 105° 46' 55".

Ownership: LIN TV Corp.

Capulin & Des Moines—K44CG, Ch. 44, Sierra Grande TV Cooperative Inc. Phone: 505-278-2101.

Technical Facilities: 0.239-kw ERP, 30-ft. above ground, 8747-ft. above sea level, lat. 36° 42' 19", long. 103° 52' 38".

Ownership: Sierra Grande TV Cooperative Inc.

Capulin & Des Moines—K48JH, Ch. 48, Sierra Grande TV Cooperative Inc. Phone: 505-278-2101.

Technical Facilities: 0.94-kw ERP, 30-ft. above ground, 8747-ft. above sea level, lat. 36° 42' 19", long. 103° 52' 38".

Ownership: Sierra Grande TV Cooperative Inc.

Capulin & Des Moines—K50DY, Ch. 50, Sierra Grande TV Cooperative Inc. Phone: 505-278-2101.

Technical Facilities: 0.94-kw ERP, 30-ft. above ground, 8747-ft. above sea level, lat. 36° 42' 19", long. 103° 52' 38".

Ownership: Sierra Grande TV Cooperative Inc.

Capulin, etc.—K33GC, Ch. 33, Regents of the U. of New Mexico & The Board of Education of the City of Albuquerque. Phone: 505-277-2121.

Technical Facilities: 0.968-kw ERP, 105-ft. above ground, 8826-ft. above sea level, lat. 36° 42' 19", long. 103° 52' 35".

Ownership: Regents of the U. of New Mexico.

Capulin, etc.—K42CH, Ch. 42, Sierra Grande TV Cooperative Inc. Phone: 505-278-2101.

Technical Facilities: 0.239-kw ERP, 30-ft. above ground, 8747-ft. above sea level, lat. 36° 42' 19", long. 103° 52' 38".

Ownership: Sierra Grande TV Cooperative Inc.

Capulin, etc.—K46BY, Ch. 46, Sierra Grande TV Cooperative Inc. Phone: 505-278-2101.

Technical Facilities: 0.239-kw ERP, 30-ft. above ground, 8747-ft. above sea level, lat. 36° 42' 19", long. 103° 52' 38".

Ownership: Sierra Grande TV Cooperative Inc.

Carlsbad—K36GD, Ch. 36, Trinity Broadcasting Network Inc. Phones: 714-832-2950; 714-730-0661.

Technical Facilities: 10-kw ERP, 295-ft. above ground, 3373-ft. above sea level, lat. 32° 24' 16", long. 104° 11' 13".

Ownership: Trinity Broadcasting Network Inc.

Carlsbad—K45GJ, Ch. 45, KOB-TV LLC. Phone: 651-642-4212.

Technical Facilities: 0.59-kw ERP, 59-ft. above ground, 3556-ft. above sea level, lat. 32° 26' 17", long. 104° 16' 42".

Ownership: Hubbard Broadcasting Inc.

Carlsbad—K47FX, Ch. 47, LIN of New Mexico LLC. Phone: 202-462-6001.

Technical Facilities: 12.1-kw ERP, 200-ft. above ground, 3481-ft. above sea level, lat. 32° 28' 28", long. 104° 11' 54".

Ownership: LIN TV Corp.

Carlsbad—K49ES, Ch. 49, Regents of Eastern New Mexico U. Phone: 505-562-2112.

Technical Facilities: 0.627-kw ERP, lat. 32° 26' 17", long. 104° 16' 42".

Ownership: Eastern New Mexico U. Board of Regents.

Carlsbad—KCGD-LP, Ch. 63, Prime Time Christian Broadcasting Inc. Phone: 915-563-0420.

Technical Facilities: 0.79-kw ERP, lat. 32° 25' 15", long. 104° 14' 24".

Transmitter: 1010 W. Mermod.

Ownership: Prime Time Christian Broadcasting Inc.

Carrizozo—K43BT, Ch. 43, KOAT Hearst-Argyle Television Inc. Phone: 919-839-0300.

Technical Facilities: 0.51-kw ERP, lat. 33° 24' 14", long. 105° 46' 55".

Ownership: Hearst-Argyle Television Inc.

Carrizozo—K51CN, Ch. 51, KOB-TV LLC. Phone: 651-642-4212.

Technical Facilities: 7-kw ERP, 36-ft. above ground, 7152-ft. above sea level, lat. 33° 25' 46", long. 105° 59' 17".

Ownership: Hubbard Broadcasting Inc.

Carrizozo, etc.—K48GY, Ch. 48, LIN of New Mexico LLC. Phone: 202-462-6065.

Technical Facilities: 27.9-kw ERP, 36-ft. above ground, 7077-ft. above sea level, lat. 33° 49' 34", long. 106° 14' 54".

Holds CP for change to 0.84-kw ERP, BDFCDTT-20060329AAE.

Ownership: LIN TV Corp.

Cebolla—K56EH, Ch. 56, KOB-TV LLC. Phone: 651-642-4212.

Technical Facilities: 0.006-kw ERP, 56-ft. above ground, 7736-ft. above sea level, lat. 36° 31' 56", long. 106° 28' 34".

Ownership: Hubbard Broadcasting Inc.

Chama—K34FD, Ch. 34, Regents of the U. of New Mexico & the Board of Education of the City of Albuquerque. Phone: 505-277-2121.

Technical Facilities: 1.251-kw ERP, lat. 36° 53' 59", long. 106° 36' 10".

Ownership: Board of Education of the City of Albuquerque; Regents of the U. of New Mexico.

Chama—K40HC, Ch. 40, LIN of New Mexico LLC. Phone: 401-457-9525.

Technical Facilities: 1.2-kw ERP, 30-ft. above ground, 8671-ft. above sea level, lat. 36° 53' 58", long. 106° 36' 05".

Holds CP for change to 0.24-kw ERP, BDFCDTT-20081219AAE.

Ownership: LIN TV Corp.

Chama—K44DD, Ch. 44, LIN of New Mexico LLC. Phone: 202-462-6065.

Technical Facilities: 3.54-kw ERP, 16-ft. above ground, 8655-ft. above sea level, lat. 36° 53' 59", long. 106° 36' 04".

Holds CP for change to 0.708-kw ERP, BDFCDTT-20060331ABK.

Ownership: LIN TV Corp.

Cimarron—K28GF, Ch. 28, Regents of U. of the New Mexico & the Board of Education of the City of Albuquerque. Phone: 505-277-2121.

Technical Facilities: 10.77-kw ERP, 67-ft. above ground, 11232-ft. above sea level, lat. 36° 33' 36", long. 105° 11' 40".

Ownership: Board of Education of the City of Albuquerque; Regents of the U. of New Mexico.

Cliff & Gila—K02KG, Ch. 2, Regents of New Mexico State U. Phone: 505-646-2222.

Technical Facilities: 0.083-kw ERP, lat. 32° 56' 46", long. 108° 42' 30".

Ownership: Regents of New Mexico State U.

Clovis—K16EX, Ch. 16, KOB-TV LLC. Phone: 651-642-4212.

Technical Facilities: 16.4-kw ERP, 351-ft. above ground, 4672-ft. above sea level, lat. 34° 26' 23", long. 103° 12' 44".

Ownership: Hubbard Broadcasting Inc.

■**Clovis**—K26CD, Ch. 26, Panhandle Telecasting LP. Phone: 806-383-1010.

Technical Facilities: 8.01-kw ERP, lat. 34° 26' 25", long. 103° 12' 37".

Ownership: Panhandle Telecasting Co.

Clovis—K29HB, Ch. 29, Panhandle Telecasting LP. Phone: 806-383-1010.

Technical Facilities: 8.5-kw ERP, 397-ft. above ground, 4708-ft. above sea level, lat. 34° 26' 25", long. 103° 12' 37".

Ownership: Panhandle Telecasting Co.

Clovis—K43BU, Ch. 43, Barrington Amarillo License LLC. Phone: 847-884-1877.

Technical Facilities: 1000-w TPO, 7.9-kw ERP, 400-ft. above ground, 4711-ft. above sea level, lat. 34° 26' 25", long. 103° 12' 37".

Transmitter: Approx. 2-mi. N of Clovis.

Ownership: Pilot Group LP.

Clovis—K45BF, Ch. 45, Nexstar Finance Inc. Phones: 806-383-3321; 972-373-8800. Fax: 806-381-2943.

Technical Facilities: 1000-w TPO, 12.9-kw ERP, lat. 34° 26' 25", long. 103° 12' 37".

Holds CP for change to 0.051-kw ERP, 404-ft. above ground, 4715-ft. above sea level, BDFCDTT-20060403AIA.

Transmitter: 7-mi. N of Clovis.

Ownership: Nexstar Broadcasting Group Inc.

Clovis—K47DH, Ch. 47, Mission Broadcasting Inc. Phone: 330-335-8808.

Technical Facilities: 7.7-kw ERP, 400-ft. above ground, 4711-ft. above sea level, lat. 34° 26' 25", long. 103° 12' 37".

Holds CP for change to 0.045-kw ERP, BDFCDTT-20060403ACN.

Ownership: Mission Broadcasting Inc.

Clovis—K49BY, Ch. 49, LIN of New Mexico LLC. Phone: 202-462-6065.

Technical Facilities: 0.801-kw ERP, lat. 34° 26' 25", long. 103° 12' 37".

Holds CP for change to 7.9-kw ERP, 299-ft. above ground, 4616-ft. above sea level, lat. 34° 26' 25", long. 103° 12' 33". BDFCDTT-20060331AUT.

Ownership: LIN TV Corp.

Clovis—K51DX, Ch. 51, Eastern New Mexico U. Phone: 505-562-2112.

Technical Facilities: 8.86-kw ERP, 348-ft. above ground, 4662-ft. above sea level, lat. 34° 26' 25", long. 103° 12' 33".

Ownership: Eastern New Mexico U. Board of Regents.

Clovis—KCVP-LP, Ch. 34, Prime Time Christian Broadcasting Inc. Phone: 915-563-0420.

Technical Facilities: 0.88-kw ERP, 309-ft. above ground, 4610-ft. above sea level, lat. 34° 26' 21", long. 103° 12' 40".

Transmitter: 2-mi. NW of Post Office, 4910 Thornton St.

Ownership: Prime Time Christian Broadcasting Inc.

Clovis—KFCL-LP, Ch. 41, Faith Christian Church Inc. Phone: 505-762-7751.

Technical Facilities: 14.4-kw ERP, 299-ft. above ground, 4606-ft. above sea level, lat. 34° 26' 21", long. 103° 12' 22".

Ownership: Faith Christian Church Inc.

Colfax—K30GJ, Ch. 30, KOB-TV LLC. Phone: 651-642-4212.

Technical Facilities: 12.7-kw ERP, 80-ft. above ground, 11244-ft. above sea level, lat. 36° 33' 36", long. 105° 11' 40".

Ownership: Hubbard Broadcasting Inc.

Colfax—K66AE, Ch. 66, KOAT Hearst-Argyle Television Inc. Phone: 919-839-0300.

Technical Facilities: 2.31-kw ERP, 62-ft. above ground, 11224-ft. above sea level, lat. 36° 33' 36", long. 105° 11' 40".

Holds CP for change to channel number 23, 47-ft. above ground, 11209-ft. above sea level, BDISDTA-20060717ABK.

Ownership: Hearst-Argyle Television Inc.

Conchas Dam—K16DN, Ch. 16, Conchas Television Association.

Technical Facilities: 0.052-kw ERP, 33-ft. above ground, 5417-ft. above sea level, lat. 35° 16' 11", long. 104° 13' 19".

Ownership: Conchas Television Association.

Conchas Dam—K18HR, Ch. 18, The Regents of the U. of New Mexico & Board of Education of the City of Albuquerque. Phone: 505-277-2121.

Technical Facilities: 0.115-kw ERP, 27-ft. above ground, 5417-ft. above sea level, lat. 35° 16' 11", long. 104° 13' 19".

Ownership: Board of Education of the City of Albuquerque; Regents of the U. of New Mexico.

Conchas Dam, etc.—K06JB, Ch. 6, Conchas Television Association.

Technical Facilities: 0.011-kw ERP, 5298-ft. above sea level, lat. 35° 15' 48", long. 104° 13' 36".

Ownership: Conchas Television Association.

Conchas Dam, etc.—K09IA, Ch. 9, Conchas Television Association.

Technical Facilities: 0.014-kw ERP, lat. 35° 15' 48", long. 104° 13' 36".

Ownership: Conchas Television Association.

Conchas Dam, etc.—K11JD, Ch. 11, Conchas Television Association.

Technical Facilities: 0.014-kw ERP, lat. 35° 15' 48", long. 104° 13' 36".

Ownership: Conchas Television Association.

Coyote Canyon—K47DI, Ch. 47, LIN of New Mexico LLC. Phone: 202-462-6065.

Technical Facilities: 1.12-kw ERP, 69-ft. above ground, 9039-ft. above sea level, lat. 35° 54' 30", long. 108° 46' 28".

Holds CP for change to 0.224-kw ERP, BDFCDTT-20060329AAI.

Ownership: LIN TV Corp.

Crownpoint—K28GT, Ch. 28, KOB-TV LLC. Phone: 651-642-4212.

Technical Facilities: 0.13-kw ERP, 21-ft. above ground, 7090-ft. above sea level, lat. 35° 40' 52", long. 108° 08' 55".

Ownership: Hubbard Broadcasting Inc.

Crownpoint—K38AU, Ch. 38, The Navajo Nation. Phone: 520-871-6655.

Technical Facilities: 100-w TPO, 0.56-kw ERP, 56-ft. above ground, 9025-ft. above sea level, lat. 35° 54' 29", long. 108° 46' 21".

Transmitter: Deza Bluff, NM.

Ownership: Navajo Community College.

Personnel: Dr. Curtis Sweet, Director.

Crownpoint—K44GD, Ch. 44, LIN of New Mexico LLC. Phone: 202-462-6065.

Technical Facilities: 0.132-kw ERP, 20-ft. above ground, 7090-ft. above sea level, lat. 35° 40' 52", long. 108° 08' 53".

Holds CP for change to 0.026-kw ERP, 20-ft. above ground, 7087-ft. above sea level, BDFCDTT-20060329AAH.

Ownership: LIN TV Corp.

Crownpoint—K65FJ, Ch. 65, KOAT Hearst-Argyle Television Inc. Phone: 919-839-0300.

Technical Facilities: 0.13-kw ERP, 20-ft. above ground, 7090-ft. above sea level, lat. 35° 40' 52", long. 108° 08' 53".

Began Operation: August 25, 1993.

Ownership: Hearst-Argyle Television Inc.

Cuba—K34HF-D, Ch. 34, Regents of the U. of New Mexico & The Board of Education of the City of Albuquerque. Phone: 505-277-2121.

Technical Facilities: 0.647-kw ERP, 67-ft. above ground, 9657-ft. above sea level, lat. 36° 00' 48", long. 106° 50' 38".

Ownership: Board of Education of the City of Albuquerque; Regents of the U. of New Mexico.

Cuba—K35GY, Ch. 35, KOB-TV LLC. Phone: 651-642-4212.

Technical Facilities: 2.2-kw ERP, 67-ft. above ground, 9657-ft. above sea level, lat. 36° 00' 48", long. 106° 50' 38".

Holds CP for change to channel number 38, 0.22-kw ERP, 66-ft. above ground, 9655-ft. above sea level, BDISDTT-20060811ABW.

Ownership: Hubbard Broadcasting Inc.

Datil/Horse Springs—K48HL, Ch. 48, KOB-TV LLC.

Technical Facilities: 1.22-kw ERP, 69-ft. above ground, 8993-ft. above sea level, lat. 33° 46' 15", long. 107° 51' 18".

Ownership: Hubbard Broadcasting Inc.

Deming—K35HB, Ch. 35, LIN of New Mexico LLC. Phone: 202-462-6065.

Technical Facilities: 2.67-kw ERP, 16-ft. above ground, 5613-ft. above sea level, lat. 32° 11' 40", long. 107° 36' 29".

Holds CP for change to 0.53-kw ERP, BDFCDTT-20060323AAT.

Ownership: LIN TV Corp.

Deming—K41FM, Ch. 41, KOB-TV LLC. Phone: 654-642-4212.

Technical Facilities: 1.72-kw ERP, 43-ft. above ground, 5643-ft. above sea level, lat. 32° 11' 40", long. 107° 36' 29".

Ownership: Hubbard Broadcasting Inc.

Deming—K43FU, Ch. 43, LIN of New Mexico LLC. Phone: 202-462-6001.

Technical Facilities: 2.5-kw ERP, 43-ft. above ground, 5643-ft. above sea level, lat. 32° 11' 40", long. 107° 36' 29".

Ownership: LIN TV Corp.

Deming—K46GU, Ch. 46, Regents of New Mexico State U. Phone: 505-646-2222.

Technical Facilities: 0.802-kw ERP, 33-ft. above ground, 5633-ft. above sea level, lat. 32° 11' 40", long. 107° 36' 29".

Ownership: Regents of New Mexico State U.

Deming—K49GV-D, Ch. 49, Regents of New Mexico State U. Phone: 505-646-2222.

Technical Facilities: 0.802-kw ERP, 33-ft. above ground, 5666-ft. above sea level, lat. 32° 11' 40", long. 107° 36' 31".

Ownership: Regents of New Mexico State U.

Deming—K51DS, Ch. 51, KOAT Hearst-Argyle Television Inc. Phone: 919-839-0300.

Technical Facilities: 100-w TPO, 2.6-kw ERP, 39-ft. above ground, 5564-ft. above sea level, lat. 32° 12' 00", long. 107° 36' 35".

Transmitter: Little Florida Mountain, 10-mi. SE of Deming.

Began Operation: March 8, 1991.

Ownership: Hearst-Argyle Television Inc.

Personnel: Wayne Godsey, General Manager; Jeffrey Sales, General Sales Manager; Charles Amy, Chief Engineer.

Deming—K55BT, Ch. 55, NPG of Texas LP. Phone: 915-496-7777.

Technical Facilities: 2.46-kw ERP, lat. 32° 11' 40", long. 107° 36' 29".

Holds CP for change to channel number 19, 0.25-kw ERP, 49-ft. above ground, 5633-ft. above sea level, BDISTT-20060324AAH.

Ownership: News Press & Gazette Co.

Dora—K24DU, Ch. 24, Barrington Amarillo License LLC. Phone: 847-884-1877.

Technical Facilities: 0.998-kw ERP, 292-ft. above ground, 4580-ft. above sea level, lat. 33° 51' 52", long. 103° 19' 59".

Ownership: Pilot Group LP.

Dora—K40GC, Ch. 40, LIN of New Mexico LLC. Phone: 202-462-6065.

Technical Facilities: 3.129-kw ERP, 65-ft. above ground, 4566-ft. above sea level, lat. 33° 54' 15", long. 103° 30' 41".

Ownership: LIN TV Corp.

Dora—K67CS, Ch. 67, Panhandle Telecasting LP. Phone: 806-383-1010.

Technical Facilities: 0.914-kw ERP, 292-ft. above ground, 4580-ft. above sea level, lat. 33° 51' 52", long. 103° 19' 59".

Ownership: Panhandle Telecasting Co.

Dulce—K22GE, Ch. 22, LIN of New Mexico LLC. Phone: 202-462-6001. Fax: 505-246-2222.

Technical Facilities: 0.98-kw ERP, 13-ft. above ground, 9006-ft. above sea level, lat. 36° 59' 00", long. 106° 58' 12".

Ownership: LIN TV Corp.

Dulce & Lumberton—K26EP, Ch. 26, LIN of Colorado LLC. Phone: 202-462-6001.

Technical Facilities: 0.202-kw ERP, lat. 36° 59' 00", long. 105° 58' 11".

Ownership: LIN TV Corp.

Dulce & Lumberton—K28ER, Ch. 28, KOAT Hearst-Argyle Television Inc. Phone: 919-839-0300.

Technical Facilities: 0.2-kw ERP, 30-ft. above ground, 9022-ft. above sea level, lat. 36° 59' 00", long. 106° 58' 11".

Began Operation: April 21, 1997.

Ownership: Hearst-Argyle Television Inc.

Dulce & Lumberton—K30EK, Ch. 30, KOB-TV LLC. Phone: 651-642-4334.

Technical Facilities: 0.269-kw ERP, 15-ft. above ground, 9009-ft. above sea level, lat. 36° 59' 00", long. 106° 58' 11".

Ownership: Hubbard Broadcasting Inc.

Eagle Nest—K09AK, Ch. 9, Eagle Nest TV Assn. Phone: 505-377-6651.

Technical Facilities: 0.009-kw ERP, 11640-ft. above sea level, lat. 36° 38' 28", long. 105° 13' 48".

Ownership: Eagle Nest TV Assn.

Eagle Nest—K20GO, Ch. 20, Eagle Nest TV Assn. Phone: 505-377-6651.

Technical Facilities: 1.44-kw ERP, lat. 36° 38' 28", long. 105° 13' 48".

Transmitter: 6-mi. N of Eagle Nest.

Ownership: Eagle Nest TV Assn.

Eagle Nest—K35BZ, Ch. 35, Eagle Nest TV Assn. Phone: 505-377-6651.

Technical Facilities: 2.88-kw ERP, lat. 36° 38' 28", long. 105° 13' 48".

Ownership: Eagle Nest TV Assn.

Eagle Nest—K48AX, Ch. 48, Eagle Nest TV Assn. Phone: 505-377-6651.

Technical Facilities: 1.32-kw ERP, lat. 36° 38' 28", long. 105° 13' 48".

Transmitter: 6-mi. N of Eagle Nest.

Ownership: Eagle Nest TV Assn.

Eagles Nest—K38EC, Ch. 38, LIN of New Mexico LLC. Phone: 202-462-6065.

Technical Facilities: 0.83-kw ERP, 59-ft. above ground, 11283-ft. above sea level, lat. 36° 33' 36", long. 105° 11' 40".

Holds CP for change to 1.66-kw ERP, BDFCDTT-20060329AAF.

Ownership: LIN TV Corp.

El Paso—K48IK, Ch. 48, ZGS EL Paso Television LP. Phone: 303-678-1844.

Studio: 10033 Carnegie, El Paso, TX 79925.

Technical Facilities: 150-kw ERP, 85-ft. above ground, 4747-ft. above sea level, lat. 31° 47' 15", long. 106° 28' 47".

Transmitter: 500 S. Main St.

Ownership: ZGS Broadcasting Holdings Inc.

Espanola—K39EJ, Ch. 39, LIN of New Mexico LLC. Phone: 401-457-9525.

Technical Facilities: 5.04-kw ERP, 66-ft. above ground, 7985-ft. above sea level, lat. 35° 53' 55", long. 105° 53' 52".

Holds CP for change to 1-kw ERP, BDFCDTT-20081024ABQ.

Ownership: LIN TV Corp.

Farmington—K14MJ, Ch. 14, Trinity Christian Center of Santa Ana Inc. Phone: 714-832-2950.

Technical Facilities: 8.5-kw ERP, 102-ft. above ground, 6125-ft. above sea level, lat. 36° 40' 16", long. 108° 13' 54".

Ownership: Trinity Broadcasting Network Inc.

Farmington—K19CM, Ch. 19, KOAT Hearst-Argyle Television Inc. Phone: 919-839-0300.

Technical Facilities: 1.21-kw ERP, 100-ft. above ground, 6130-ft. above sea level, lat. 36° 40' 17", long. 108° 13' 53".

Ownership: Hearst-Argyle Television Inc.

Farmington—K21AX, Ch. 21, LIN of Colorado LLC.

Technical Facilities: 2.11-kw ERP, lat. 36° 41' 48", long. 108° 10' 39".

Ownership: LIN TV Corp.

Farmington—K23BT, Ch. 23, Emmis Television License Corp. of Honolulu. Phone: 714-245-9499.

Technical Facilities: 7.46-kw ERP, lat. 36° 40' 16", long. 108° 13' 54".

Ownership: ACME Communications Inc.

Farmington—K27GJ-D, Ch. 27, LIN of New Mexico LLC. Phone: 401-457-9525.

Technical Facilities: 2-kw ERP, 171-ft. above ground, 6201-ft. above sea level, lat. 36° 40' 17", long. 108° 13' 53".

Ownership: Raycom Media Inc.

Farmington—K29HR-D, Ch. 29, LIN of Colorado LLC. Phone: 401-457-9525.

Technical Facilities: 4.4-kw ERP, 144-ft. above ground, 6322-ft. above sea level, lat. 36° 40' 16", long. 108° 13' 57".

Ownership: LIN TV Corp.

Farmington—K40FI-D, Ch. 40, Regents of the U. of New Mexico & The Board of Education of the City of Albuquerque. Phone: 505-277-2121.

Technical Facilities: 0.403-kw ERP, 48-ft. above ground, 7397-ft. above sea level, lat. 36° 24' 56", long. 107° 50' 40".

Ownership: Board of Education of the City of Albuquerque; Regents of the U. of New Mexico.

Farmington—K43AI, Ch. 43, Regents of the U. of New Mexico & The Board of Education of the City of Albuquerque. Phone: 505-277-2121. Fax: 505-277-9584.

Studio: 1130 University NE, Albuquerque, NM 87102.

Technical Facilities: 8.42-kw ERP, 170-ft. above ground, 6200-ft. above sea level, lat. 36° 40' 17", long. 108° 13' 53".

Ownership: Board of Education of the City of Albuquerque; Regents of the U. of New Mexico.

Personnel: Jon Cooper, General Manager.

Farmington—K47DR, Ch. 47, Christian Broadcasting Communications. Phone: 505-327-1445. Fax: 505-327-5310.

Technical Facilities: 1000-w TPO, 31.3-kw ERP, 174-ft. above ground, 5962-ft. above sea level, lat. 36° 41' 50", long. 108° 10' 42".

Transmitter: 10-mi. SE of Farmington.

Ownership: Christian Broadcasting Communications.

Personnel: Dan Harlin, Chief Engineer.

Farmington—K62CR, Ch. 62, KOAT Hearst-Argyle Television Inc. Phone: 919-839-0300.

Technical Facilities: 0.49-kw ERP, 39-ft. above ground, 7421-ft. above sea level, lat. 36° 25' 33", long. 107° 50' 39".

Ownership: Hearst-Argyle Television Inc.

Forrest—K52CR, Ch. 52, KOAT Hearst-Argyle Television Inc. Phone: 919-839-0300.

Technical Facilities: 0.97-kw ERP, 302-ft. above ground, 5266-ft. above sea level, lat. 34° 50' 32", long. 103° 42' 44".

Ownership: Hearst-Argyle Television Inc.

Forrest & McAllister—K34EZ, Ch. 34, Regents of Eastern New Mexico U. Phone: 505-562-2112.

Technical Facilities: 1.35-kw ERP, lat. 34° 49' 54", long. 103° 43' 28".

Holds CP for change to 1-kw ERP, 186-ft. above ground, 5110-ft. above sea level, BDFCDTT-20060329ANH.

Ownership: Eastern New Mexico U. Board of Regents.

Forrest, etc.—K31GC, Ch. 31, KOB-TV LLC.

Technical Facilities: 9.23-kw ERP, 274-ft. above ground, 5249-ft. above sea level, lat. 34° 50' 45", long. 103° 42' 35".

Ownership: Hubbard Broadcasting Inc.

Fort Sumner—K21IM-D, Ch. 21, Eastern New Mexico U. Phone: 575-562-2112.

Technical Facilities: 15-kw ERP, 50-ft. above ground, 4551-ft. above sea level, lat. 34° 28' 35", long. 104° 21' 24".

Began Operation: March 3, 2009.

Ownership: Eastern New Mexico U. Board of Regents.

Fort Sumner—K34GU, Ch. 34, Eastern New Mexico U. Phone: 505-562-2112.

Technical Facilities: 1.29-kw ERP, 50-ft. above ground, 4550-ft. above sea level, lat. 34° 28' 35", long. 104° 21' 24".

Ownership: Eastern New Mexico U. Board of Regents.

Gallina—K31HB, Ch. 31, Regents of the U. of New Mexico & The Board of Education of the City of Albuquerque. Phone: 505-277-2121.

Technical Facilities: 0.982-kw ERP, 105-ft. above ground, 9124-ft. above sea level, lat. 36° 13' 15", long. 106° 45' 04".

Ownership: Board of Education of the City of Albuquerque; Regents of the U. of New Mexico.

Gallina—K48GD, Ch. 48, KOB-TV LLC. Phone: 651-642-4212.

Technical Facilities: 0.425-kw ERP, 66-ft. above ground, 9111-ft. above sea level, lat. 36° 13' 14", long. 106° 45' 42".

Ownership: Hubbard Broadcasting Inc.

Gallina—K67CE, Ch. 67, LIN of New Mexico LLC.

Technical Facilities: 0.412-kw ERP, lat. 36° 13' 14", long. 106° 45' 42".

Ownership: LIN TV Corp.

Gallup—K08IJ, Ch. 8, KOAT Hearst-Argyle Television Inc. Phone: 919-839-0300.

Technical Facilities: 0.515-kw ERP, lat. 35° 54' 34", long. 108° 46' 27".

Began Operation: November 13, 1978.

Ownership: Hearst-Argyle Television Inc.

Gallup—K18HF, Ch. 18, LIN of New Mexico LLC. Phone: 401-457-9525.

Technical Facilities: 1.07-kw ERP, 71-ft. above ground, 6734-ft. above sea level, lat. 35° 32' 08", long. 108° 44' 23".

Holds CP for change to 0.214-kw ERP, BDFCDTT-20080703ABY.

Ownership: LIN TV Corp.

Gallup—K23FE, Ch. 23, Regents of the U. of New Mexico & The Board of Education of the City of Albuquerque. Phone: 505-277-2121.

Technical Facilities: 1.04-kw ERP, lat. 35° 36' 16", long. 108° 40' 49".

Ownership: Board of Education of the City of Albuquerque; Regents of the U. of New Mexico.

Gallup—K39EW, Ch. 39, KOB-TV LLC. Phone: 651-642-4212.

Technical Facilities: 0.795-kw ERP, 60-ft. above ground, 6724-ft. above sea level, lat. 35° 32' 08", long. 108° 44' 30".

Ownership: Hubbard Broadcasting Inc.

Gallup—K48GK, Ch. 48, LIN of New Mexico LLC. Phone: 202-462-6065.

Technical Facilities: 1.18-kw ERP, lat. 35° 32' 08", long. 108° 44' 28".

Holds CP for change to 0.236-kw ERP, 132-ft. above ground, 6796-ft. above sea level, BDFCDTT-20060331ADI.

Ownership: LIN TV Corp.

Gallup—K67BP, Ch. 67, KOAT Hearst-Argyle Television Inc. Phone: 919-839-0300.

Technical Facilities: 0.1-kw ERP, lat. 35° 32' 04", long. 108° 44' 26".

Holds CP for change to channel number 10, 0.3-kw ERP, 123-ft. above ground, 6786-ft. above sea level, lat. 35° 32' 08", long. 108° 44' 28". BDISDVA-20060717ABJ.

Ownership: Hearst-Argyle Television Inc.

Gallup—KIAZ-LP, Ch. 14, Pappas Telecasting Companies. Phone: 559-733-7800.

Technical Facilities: 10-kw ERP, 318-ft. above ground, 6929-ft. above sea level, lat. 35° 32' 00", long. 108° 38' 11".

Holds CP for change to 15-kw ERP, . 11, BDFCDTL-20060331ARM.

Ownership: Pappas Telecasting Companies.

Gallup & Tohatchi—K21HJ, Ch. 21, Christian Broadcasting Communications. Phone: 505-327-1445.

Technical Facilities: 1.65-kw ERP, 43-ft. above ground, 7897-ft. above sea level, lat. 35° 36' 18", long. 108° 41' 11".

Ownership: Christian Broadcasting Communications.

Grants—K46FI, Ch. 46, LIN of New Mexico LLC. Phone: 401-457-9525.

Technical Facilities: 1-kw ERP, 30-ft. above ground, 11010-ft. above sea level, lat. 35° 15' 10", long. 107° 35' 48".

Holds CP for change to 0.2-kw ERP, 30-ft. above ground, 11010-ft. above sea level, BDFCDTT-20081222AAR.

Began Operation: July 5, 1995.

Ownership: LIN TV Corp.

Grants & Milan—K33GA, Ch. 33, Regents of the U. of New Mexico & The Board of Education of the City of Albuquerque.

Technical Facilities: 0.116-kw ERP, lat. 35° 07' 00", long. 107° 54' 02".

Ownership: Board of Education of the City of Albuquerque; Regents of the U. of New Mexico.

Grants, etc.—K06CU, Ch. 6, KOB-TV LLC. Phone: 651-642-4337.

Technical Facilities: 0.005-kw ERP, 7214-ft. above sea level, lat. 35° 07' 00", long. 107° 54' 02".

Holds CP for change to channel number 36, 0.1-kw ERP, 46-ft. above ground, 7126-ft. above sea level, BDISDTT-20081215ADF.

Ownership: Hubbard Broadcasting Inc.

Grants, etc.—K09EP, Ch. 9, LIN of New Mexico LLC. Phone: 202-462-6065.

Technical Facilities: 0.009-kw ERP, lat. 35° 07' 00", long. 107° 54' 02".

Holds CP for change to 0.002-kw ERP, 30-ft. above ground, 7109-ft. above sea level, BDFCDTT-20060331ABD.

Ownership: LIN TV Corp.

Grants, etc.—K11EV, Ch. 11, KOAT Hearst-Argyle Television Inc. Phone: 919-839-0300.

Technical Facilities: 0.001-kw ERP, 6548-ft. above sea level, lat. 35° 07' 00", long. 107° 54' 02".

Ownership: Hearst-Argyle Television Inc.

Guadalupita—K09LQ, Ch. 9, KOB-TV LLC.

Technical Facilities: 0.002-kw ERP, lat. 36° 07' 21", long. 105° 13' 24".

Ownership: Hubbard Broadcasting Inc.

Guadalupita—K11NV, Ch. 11, LIN of New Mexico LLC.

Technical Facilities: 0.004-kw ERP, 52-ft. above ground, 8054-ft. above sea level, lat. 36° 07' 19", long. 105° 13' 25".

Ownership: LIN TV Corp.

Hatch—K28GJ, Ch. 28, Regents of New Mexico State U. Phone: 505-646-2222.

Technical Facilities: 1.78-kw ERP, 43-ft. above ground, 4832-ft. above sea level, lat. 32° 41' 43", long. 107° 03' 48".

Holds CP for change to 43-ft. above ground, 4876-ft. above sea level, lat. 32° 41' 43", long. 107° 03' 50". BDFCDTT-20060331BPA.

Ownership: Regents of New Mexico State U.

Hillsboro—K02IP, Ch. 2, Hillsboro TV Assn.

Technical Facilities: 0.006-kw ERP, lat. 32° 55' 45", long. 107° 32' 00".

Ownership: Hillsboro TV Association.

Hillsboro—K06DX, Ch. 6, Hillsboro TV Assn.

Technical Facilities: 0.005-kw ERP, lat. 32° 55' 45", long. 107° 32' 00".

Ownership: Hillsboro TV Association.

Hillsboro—K08LP, Ch. 8, Hillsboro TV Assn.

Technical Facilities: 16-ft. above ground, 5656-ft. above sea level, lat. 32° 55' 24", long. 107° 32' 43".

Ownership: Hillsboro TV Association.

Hillsboro—K11HB, Ch. 11, Hillsboro TV Assn.

Technical Facilities: 0.005-kw ERP, lat. 32° 55' 45", long. 107° 32' 00".

Ownership: Hillsboro TV Association.

Hillsboro—K13UL, Ch. 13, Regents of New Mexico State U. Phone: 505-646-2222.

Technical Facilities: 0.086-kw ERP, 7-ft. above ground, 5633-ft. above sea level, lat. 32° 55' 24", long. 107° 32' 43".

Ownership: Regents of New Mexico State U.

Hillsboro—K18DY, Ch. 18, LIN of New Mexico LLC. Phone: 401-457-9525.

Technical Facilities: 0.011-kw ERP, 16-ft. above ground, 5656-ft. above sea level, lat. 32° 55' 24", long. 107° 32' 43".

Holds CP for change to 0.002-kw ERP, BDFCDTT-20080418AAA.

Ownership: LIN TV Corp.

Hobbs—K12NH, Ch. 12, KOAT Hearst-Argyle Television Inc. Phone: 919-839-0300.

Technical Facilities: 0.111-kw ERP, 121-ft. above ground, 3763-ft. above sea level, lat. 32° 42' 34", long. 103° 09' 05".

Began Operation: July 29, 1986.

Ownership: Hearst-Argyle Television Inc.

Hobbs—K16EB, Ch. 16, Community Television Development. Phone: 954-614-2416.

Technical Facilities: 175-w TPO, 1-kw ERP, 614-ft. above ground, 955-ft. above sea level, lat. 32° 40' 27", long. 103° 06' 38".

Transmitter: 1.2-mi. SE of Hobbs.

Ownership: Community Television Development.

Hobbs—K27GL, Ch. 27, LIN of New Mexico LLC. Phone: 202-462-6001.

Technical Facilities: 10-kw ERP, 151-ft. above ground, 3812-ft. above sea level, lat. 32° 47' 12", long. 103° 07' 05".

Ownership: LIN TV Corp.

Hobbs—K42FX-D, Ch. 42, Eastern New Mexico U. Phone: 505-562-2112.

Technical Facilities: 15-kw ERP, 185-ft. above ground, 3860-ft. above sea level, lat. 32° 45' 40", long. 103° 11' 31".

Ownership: Eastern New Mexico U. Board of Regents.

Hobbs—K45IL, Ch. 45, Ramar Communications Inc. Phone: 806-748-9300.

Technical Facilities: 16.7-kw ERP, 492-ft. above ground, 4114-ft. above sea level, lat. 32° 43' 28", long. 103° 05' 46".

Holds CP for change to 8.35-kw ERP, 500-ft. above ground, 4119-ft. above sea level, BDFCDTT-20060825ABF.

Ownership: Ramar Communications Inc.

Hobbs—K45JA, Ch. 45, EICB-TV EAST LLC. Phone: 972-291-3750.

Technical Facilities: 0.1-kw ERP, 33-ft. above ground, 3448-ft. above sea level, lat. 32° 26' 11", long. 103° 09' 17".

Began Operation: December 4, 2008.

Ownership: EICB-TV LLC.

Hobbs—K50GM, Ch. 50, LIN of New Mexico LLC. Phone: 202-462-6001.

Technical Facilities: 93-w TPO, 10-kw ERP, 151-ft. above ground, 3812-ft. above sea level, lat. 32° 47' 12", long. 103° 07' 05".

Transmitter: Atop Mescalero Ridge, near Hobbs.

Ownership: LIN TV Corp.

Hobbs—K50IP, Ch. 50, EICB-TV East LLC. Phone: 972-291-3750.

Technical Facilities: 0.1-kw ERP, 20-ft. above ground, 3173-ft. above sea level, lat. 32° 25' 15", long. 104° 14' 41".

Ownership: EICB-TV LLC.

Hobbs—KHLC-LP, Ch. 18, Prime Time Christian Broadcasting Inc. Phone: 432-563-0420.

Technical Facilities: 7.3-kw ERP, 250-ft. above ground, 3891-ft. above sea level, lat. 32° 42' 34", long. 103° 09' 07".

Ownership: Prime Time Christian Broadcasting Inc.

Hornsby Ranch, etc.—K25HJ, Ch. 25, LIN of New Mexico LLC. Phone: 202-462-6065.

Technical Facilities: 1.028-kw ERP, 159-ft. above ground, 5735-ft. above sea level, lat. 34° 59' 07", long. 104° 08' 00".

Ownership: LIN TV Corp.

Horse Springs—K66EE, Ch. 66, KOAT Hearst-Argyle Television Inc. Phone: 919-839-0300.

Technical Facilities: 1.06-kw ERP, 52-ft. above ground, 8983-ft. above sea level, lat. 33° 46' 14", long. 107° 51' 15".

Ownership: Hearst-Argyle Television Inc.

Indian Village—K20GT, Ch. 20, KOB-TV LLC.

Technical Facilities: 1.1-kw ERP, 70-ft. above ground, 8800-ft. above sea level, lat. 35° 27' 59", long. 108° 14' 25".

Ownership: Hubbard Broadcasting Inc.

Las Cruces—K41KY-D, Ch. 41, NPG of Texas LP. Phone: 915-496-7777.

Technical Facilities: 0.25-kw ERP, 30-ft. above ground, 4426-ft. above sea level, lat. 32° 16' 41", long. 106° 54' 36".

Began Operation: April 16, 2009.

Ownership: News Press & Gazette Co.

Las Cruces—K54GR, Ch. 54, Regents of New Mexico State U.

Technical Facilities: 0.96-kw ERP, 94-ft. above ground, 4908-ft. above sea level, lat. 32° 24' 17", long. 106° 45' 38".

Ownership: Regents of New Mexico State U.

Las Cruces—KAEP-LP, Ch. 42, KOB-TV LLC. Phone: 651-642-4334.

Technical Facilities: 2.45-kw ERP, lat. 32° 16' 44", long. 106° 54' 40".

Transmitter: S of Las Cruces Airport, 9.3-mi. W of Las Cruces.

Ownership: Hubbard Broadcasting Inc.

■ **Las Cruces**—KCWF-CA, Ch. 20, KDBC License LLC - Debtor-in-Possession.

Technical Facilities: 4.56-kw ERP, lat. 32° 16' 41", long. 106° 54' 36".

Holds CP for change to 0.99-kw ERP, 85-ft. above ground, 4905-ft. above sea level, lat. 32° 24' 16", long. 106° 45' 38". BDISTTL-20071113AIB.

Ownership: Pappas Telecasting Companies.

Las Cruces—KLCP-LP, Ch. 30, Prime Time Christian Broadcasting Inc. Phone: 432-563-0420. Fax: 432-563-1736.

Technical Facilities: 1000-w TPO, 42.5-kw ERP, 98-ft. above ground, 4864-ft. above sea level, lat. 32° 24' 17", long. 106° 45' 38".

Transmitter: Twin Peaks.

Ownership: Prime Time Christian Broadcasting Inc.

Personnel: Al Cooper, General Manager; Jay Westcott, Chief Engineer; Jeff Welter, Sales Manager.

Las Cruces & Organ—K57BV, Ch. 57, NPG of Texas LP. Phone: 915-496-7777.

Technical Facilities: 44-kw ERP, lat. 32° 16' 41", long. 106° 54' 36".

Holds CP for change to channel number 16, 4.4-kw ERP, 30-ft. above ground, 4426-ft. above sea level, lat. 32° 16' 41", long. 106° 54' 36". BDISTTL-20071003AAN.

Ownership: News Press & Gazette Co.

Las Vegas—K09AI, Ch. 9, KOAT Hearst-Argyle Television Inc. Phone: 919-839-0300.

Technical Facilities: 0.02-kw ERP, lat. 35° 35' 04", long. 105° 12' 07".

Ownership: Hearst-Argyle Television Inc.

Las Vegas—K20GQ, Ch. 20, LIN of New Mexico LLC. Phone: 401-457-4525.

Technical Facilities: 1.18-kw ERP, 66-ft. above ground, 7211-ft. above sea level, lat. 35° 36' 16", long. 105° 15' 35".

Holds CP for change to 0.236-kw ERP, BDFCDTT-20090310AAC.

Began Operation: February 10, 1982.

Ownership: LIN TV Corp.

Las Vegas—K33FL, Ch. 33, Regents of U. of New Mexico & Board of Education of the City of Albuquerque. Phone: 505-277-2121.

Technical Facilities: 1.23-kw ERP, 85-ft. above ground, 6903-ft. above sea level, lat. 35° 37' 59", long. 105° 14' 10".

Ownership: Board of Education of the City of Albuquerque; Regents of the U. of New Mexico.

Las Vegas—K43FI, Ch. 43, LIN of New Mexico LLC. Phone: 202-462-6065.

Technical Facilities: 0.99-kw ERP, lat. 35° 36' 16", long. 105° 15' 35".

Transmitter: The Creston, 2.5-mi. W of Las Vegas.

Ownership: LIN TV Corp.

Las Vegas—K47GV, Ch. 47, KOB-TV LLC. Phone: 651-642-4334.

Technical Facilities: 1.2-kw ERP, lat. 35° 37' 39", long. 105° 14' 10".

Ownership: Hubbard Broadcasting Inc.

Lordsburg—K02KP, Ch. 2, Regents of New Mexico State U. Phone: 505-646-2222.

Technical Facilities: 0.04-kw ERP, lat. 32° 19' 40", long. 108° 43' 38".

Ownership: Regents of New Mexico State U.

Lordsburg—K14LO, Ch. 14, LIN of New Mexico LLC. Phone: 202-462-6065.

Technical Facilities: 0.189-kw ERP, 36-ft. above ground, 8054-ft. above sea level, lat. 32° 34' 57", long. 108° 25' 29".

Holds CP for change to 0.038-kw ERP, BDFCDTT-20060323AAL.

Ownership: LIN TV Corp.

Lordsburg—K27FN, Ch. 27, KOB-TV LLC. Phone: 651-642-4212.

Technical Facilities: 0.133-kw ERP, lat. 32° 18' 58", long. 108° 45' 20".

Transmitter: Lookout Hill, 1.9-mi. SW of Lordsburg.

Ownership: Hubbard Broadcasting Inc.

Lordsburg—K29DP, Ch. 29, LIN of New Mexico LLC. Phone: 401-457-9525.

Technical Facilities: 0.133-kw ERP, lat. 32° 18' 58", long. 108° 45' 18".

Holds CP for change to 30-ft. above ground, 4518-ft. above sea level, BPTT-20070525ACN.

Transmitter: 1.8-mi. SW of Lordsburg.

Ownership: LIN TV Corp.

Lordsburg—K31HQ, Ch. 31, LIN of New Mexico LLC. Phone: 202-462-6001.

Technical Facilities: 0.616-kw ERP, 98-ft. above ground, 8045-ft. above sea level, lat. 32° 34' 57", long. 108° 25' 26".

Ownership: LIN TV Corp.

Lordsburg—K36GA, Ch. 36, KOB-TV LLC. Phone: 651-642-4212.

Technical Facilities: 0.23-kw ERP, 15-ft. above ground, 8001-ft. above sea level, lat. 32° 34' 57", long. 108° 25' 26".

Ownership: Hubbard Broadcasting Inc.

Lordsburg—K40HJ, Ch. 40, LIN of New Mexico LLC. Phone: 202-462-6001.

Technical Facilities: 0.279-kw ERP, 30-ft. above ground, 4521-ft. above sea level, lat. 31° 19' 40", long. 108° 43' 36".

Ownership: LIN TV Corp.

Lordsburg—K61CN, Ch. 61, KOAT Hearst-Argyle Television Inc. Phone: 919-839-0300.

Technical Facilities: 0.225-kw ERP, 7999-ft. above sea level, lat. 32° 34' 57", long. 108° 25' 29".

Began Operation: April 18, 1984.

Ownership: Hearst-Argyle Television Inc.

Los Alamos/Espanola—K49KF-D, Ch. 49, Regents of the U. of New Mexico & The Board of Education of the City of Albuquerque. Phone: 505-277-2121. Fax: 505-277-2191.

Technical Facilities: 0.694-kw ERP, 174-ft. above ground, 10148-ft. above sea level, lat. 35° 53' 09.1", long. 106° 23' 13".

Began Operation: May 23, 2007.

Ownership: Board of Education of the City of Albuquerque; Regents of the U. of New Mexico.

Lovington—K46HM, Ch. 46, Eastern New Mexico U. Phone: 505-562-2112.

Technical Facilities: 1.1-kw ERP, 190-ft. above ground, 3864-ft. above sea level, lat. 32° 55' 44", long. 103° 20' 45".

Holds CP for change to channel number 39, 144-ft. above ground, 4068-ft. above sea level, lat. 32° 57' 34.4", long. 103° 21' 12.5". BDISDTT-20070816ABC.

Ownership: Eastern New Mexico U. Board of Regents.

Mescalero—K13OY, Ch. 13, LIN of New Mexico LLC. Phone: 202-462-6065.

Technical Facilities: 0.024-kw ERP, 49-ft. above ground, 7880-ft. above sea level, lat. 33° 09' 40", long. 105° 46' 30".

Holds CP for change to 0.005-kw ERP, BDFCDTT-20060323AAA.

Ownership: LIN TV Corp.

Montoya—K22EU, Ch. 22, LIN of New Mexico LLC. Phone: 401-457-9525.

Technical Facilities: 1.15-kw ERP, lat. 34° 59' 08", long. 104° 08' 00".

Holds CP for change to 0.23-kw ERP, 157-ft. above ground, 5732-ft. above sea level, BDFCDTT-20081222AAP.

Began Operation: December 5, 1995.

Ownership: LIN TV Corp.

Montoya & Newkirk—K17FK, Ch. 17, KOB-TV LLC. Phone: 651-642-4212.

Technical Facilities: 1.2-kw ERP, 160-ft. above ground, 5734-ft. above sea level, lat. 34° 59' 04", long. 104° 08' 00".

Ownership: Hubbard Broadcasting Inc.

Montoya & Newkirk—K57BR, Ch. 57, KOAT Hearst-Argyle Televison Inc. Phone: 919-839-0300.

Technical Facilities: 1.1-kw ERP, 150-ft. above ground, 5721-ft. above sea level, lat. 34° 59' 04", long. 104° 07' 59".

Holds CP for change to channel number 39, 1.15-kw ERP, 147-ft. above ground, 5715-ft. above sea level, lat. 34° 59' 04", long. 104° 08' 00". BDISDTA-20060717ABG.

Began Operation: September 14, 1981.

Ownership: Hearst-Argyle Television Inc.

Mora—K06HX, Ch. 6, LIN of New Mexico LLC. Phone: 202-462-6001.

Technical Facilities: 0.004-kw ERP, lat. 35° 57' 31", long. 105° 21' 14".

Ownership: LIN TV Corp.

Mora—K22EW, Ch. 22, LIN of New Mexico LLC. Phone: 202-462-6065.

Technical Facilities: 1.23-kw ERP, 26-ft. above ground, 8491-ft. above sea level, lat. 35° 57' 39", long. 105° 21' 13".

Holds CP for change to 0.25-kw ERP, BDFCDTT-20060327AGG.

Ownership: LIN TV Corp.

Mora—K25FI, Ch. 25, KOB-TV LLC. Phone: 651-642-4334.

Technical Facilities: 1.23-kw ERP, 26-ft. above ground, 8491-ft. above sea level, lat. 35° 57' 39", long. 105° 21' 13".

Ownership: Hubbard Broadcasting Inc.

Mora—K31EO, Ch. 31, Regents of the U. of New Mexico & the Board of Education of the City of Albuquerque. Phone: 505-277-2121.

Technical Facilities: 1.029-kw ERP, 45-ft. above ground, 8507-ft. above sea level, lat. 35° 57' 36", long. 105° 21' 12".

Transmitter: 1.6-mi. SW of Mora.

Ownership: Board of Education of the City of Albuquerque; Regents of the U. of New Mexico.

Mud Canyon—K13OX, Ch. 13, LIN of New Mexico LLC. Phone: 202-462-6065.

Technical Facilities: 0.066-kw ERP, 69-ft. above ground, 7943-ft. above sea level, lat. 33° 11' 16", long. 105° 42' 55".

Holds CP for change to 0.013-kw ERP, BDFCDTT-20060323AAB.

Ownership: LIN TV Corp.

Penasco—K06FT, Ch. 6, KOB-TV LLC.

Technical Facilities: 0.001-kw ERP, lat. 36° 13' 02", long. 105° 43' 59".

Ownership: Hubbard Broadcasting Inc.

Penasco—K44CZ, Ch. 44, Regents of the U. of New Mexico & The Board of Education of the City of Albuquerque. Phone: 505-277-2121.

Technical Facilities: 0.15-kw ERP, 13-ft. above ground, 8035-ft. above sea level, lat. 36° 13' 13", long. 105° 43' 59".

Holds CP for change to 0.21-kw ERP, 33-ft. above ground, 8786-ft. above sea level, lat. 36° 14' 06", long. 105° 43' 33". BPTT-20060331ATL.

Ownership: Regents of New Mexico State U.

Pie Town & Quemado—K31FX, Ch. 31, Regents of the U. of New Mexico & Board of Education of the city of Albuquerque. Phone: 505-277-2121.

Technical Facilities: 3.54-kw ERP, 50-ft. above ground, 9380-ft. above sea level, lat. 34° 17' 00", long. 107° 54' 44".

Ownership: Board of Education of the City of Albuquerque; Regents of the U. of New Mexico.

Portales—K14KO, Ch. 14, LIN of New Mexico LLC. Phone: 401-457-9525.

Technical Facilities: 4.4-kw ERP, 707-ft. above ground, 4775-ft. above sea level, lat. 34° 15' 08", long. 103° 14' 20".

Holds CP for change to 0.88-kw ERP, BDFCDTT-20081222AAO.

Began Operation: February 14, 1996.

Ownership: LIN TV Corp.

Portales—K46IN, Ch. 46, KOAT Hearst-Argyle Television Inc. Phone: 919-839-0300.

Technical Facilities: 5-kw ERP, 135-ft. above ground, 4577-ft. above sea level, lat. 34° 08' 06", long. 103° 36' 56".

Holds CP for change to 18-kw ERP, 707-ft. above ground, 4775-ft. above sea level, lat. 34° 15' 08", long. 103° 14' 20". BPTT-20060828ADW.

Began Operation: July 13, 1995.

Ownership: Hearst-Argyle Television Inc.

Quemado—K09JK, Ch. 9, KOB-TV LLC.

Technical Facilities: 0.009-kw ERP, lat. 34° 20' 45", long. 108° 34' 15".

Ownership: Hubbard Broadcasting Inc.

Quemado—K15FS, Ch. 15, Regents of the U. of New Mexico & the Board of Education of the City of Albuquerque. Phone: 505-277-2121.

Technical Facilities: 0.159-kw ERP, 7608-ft. above sea level, lat. 34° 19' 47", long. 108° 34' 41".

Ownership: Board of Education of the City of Albuquerque; Regents of the U. of New Mexico.

Questa—K09GR, Ch. 9, KOB-TV LLC. Phone: 651-642-4334.

Technical Facilities: 0.24-kw ERP, lat. 36° 41' 25", long. 105° 33' 43".

Transmitter: 2-mi. SE of Questa.

Ownership: Hubbard Broadcasting Inc.

Raton—K18CT, Ch. 18, Trinity Broadcasting Network Inc. Phone: 714-832-2950. Fax: 714-730-0661.

Technical Facilities: 1.2-kw ERP, 89-ft. above ground, 7375-ft. above sea level, lat. 36° 54' 12", long. 104° 27' 37".

Ownership: Trinity Broadcasting Network Inc.

Raton—K26DX, Ch. 26, KOB-TV LLC. Phone: 651-642-4334.

Technical Facilities: 1.26-kw ERP, 52-ft. above ground, 7815-ft. above sea level, lat. 36° 40' 56", long. 104° 24' 52".

Ownership: Hubbard Broadcasting Inc.

Raton—K40DI, Ch. 40, LIN of New Mexico LLC. Phone: 401-457-9525.

Technical Facilities: 1.15-kw ERP, lat. 36° 33' 36", long. 105° 11' 40".

Holds CP for change to 0.23-kw ERP, 56-ft. above ground, 11220-ft. above sea level, BDFCDTT-20090310AAE.

Transmitter: Green Mountain, 8-mi. W of Cimarron.

Began Operation: June 24, 1992.

Ownership: LIN TV Corp.

Raton, etc.—K16CH, Ch. 16, KOAT Hearst-Argyle Television Inc. Phone: 919-839-0300.

Technical Facilities: 1.28-kw ERP, 52-ft. above ground, 7815-ft. above sea level, lat. 36° 40' 56", long. 104° 24' 52".

Began Operation: November 9, 1992.

Ownership: Hearst-Argyle Television Inc.

Raton, etc.—K20CV, Ch. 20, Regents of the U. of New Mexico & the Board of Education of the City of Albuquerque. Phone: 505-277-2121.

Technical Facilities: 1.029-kw ERP, 89-ft. above ground, 7815-ft. above sea level, lat. 36° 40' 59", long. 104° 24' 51".

Ownership: Board of Education of the City of Albuquerque; Regents of the U. of New Mexico.

Raton, etc.—K43GW, Ch. 43, LIN of New Mexico LLC. Phone: 202-462-6065.

Technical Facilities: 1.274-kw ERP, 49-ft. above ground, 7811-ft. above sea level, lat. 36° 40' 56", long. 104° 24' 52".

Transmitter: Eagle Tail Mountain, 15-mi. S of Raton.

Ownership: LIN TV Corp.

Red River—K08ES, Ch. 8, LIN of New Mexico LLC. Phone: 202-462-6065.

Technical Facilities: 0.02-kw ERP, lat. 36° 41' 00", long. 105° 22' 21".

Ownership: LIN TV Corp.

Red River—K12OC, Ch. 12, KOAT Hearst-Argyle Television Inc. Phone: 919-839-0300.

Technical Facilities: 0.039-kw ERP, 46-ft. above ground, 9944-ft. above sea level, lat. 36° 41' 00", long. 105° 22' 21".

Began Operation: November 8, 1988.

Ownership: Hearst-Argyle Television Inc.

Red River—K15FV, Ch. 15, Regents of the U. of New Mexico & the Board of Education of the City of Albuquerque. Phone: 505-277-2121.

Technical Facilities: 0.042-kw ERP, 58-ft. above ground, 9980-ft. above sea level, lat. 36° 41' 00", long. 105° 22' 21".

Ownership: Board of Education of the City of Albuquerque; Regents of the U. of New Mexico.

Red River—K46GL, Ch. 46, KOB-TV LLC. Phone: 651-642-4212.

Technical Facilities: 1.4-kw ERP, 50-ft. above ground, 9991-ft. above sea level, lat. 36° 41' 00", long. 105° 22' 21".

Ownership: Hubbard Broadcasting Inc.

Roswell—K13RK, Ch. 13, KOAT Hearst-Argyle Television Inc. Phone: 919-839-0300.

Technical Facilities: 0.05-kw ERP, lat. 33° 24' 05", long. 104° 22' 45".

Began Operation: August 10, 1982.

Ownership: Hearst-Argyle Television Inc.

Roswell—K15FT, Ch. 15, LIN of New Mexico LLC. Phone: 202-462-6001.

Technical Facilities: 10-kw ERP, 85-ft. above ground, 3835-ft. above sea level, lat. 33° 24' 05", long. 104° 22' 33".

Ownership: LIN TV Corp.

Roswell—K17EM, Ch. 17, ACME Television Licenses of New Mexico LLC.

Technical Facilities: 1000-w TPO, 13.7-kw ERP, 225-ft. above ground, 1279-ft. above sea level, lat. 33° 24' 05", long. 104° 22' 45".

Transmitter: Comanche Hill, 0.9-mi. W of Pecos River Bridge.

Ownership: ACME Communications Inc.

Personnel: Dan Myers, General Manager; Tom Wimberly, Chief Engineer.

Roswell—K31GS-D, Ch. 31, Eastern New Mexico U. Phone: 505-562-2112.

Technical Facilities: 15-kw ERP, 186-ft. above ground, 3884-ft. above sea level, lat. 33° 24' 15", long. 104° 22' 48".

Ownership: Eastern New Mexico U. Board of Regents.

Roswell—K50IA, Ch. 50, Trinity Broadcasting Network Inc. Phone: 714-832-2950. Fax: 714-730-0661.

Technical Facilities: 5.4-kw ERP, 131-ft. above ground, 4101-ft. above sea level, lat. 33° 21' 47", long. 104° 38' 11".

Holds CP for change to 1-kw ERP, BDFCDTT-20060331AJT.

Ownership: Trinity Broadcasting Network Inc.

Roswell—K62AL, Ch. 62, KOAT Hearst-Argyle Television Inc. Phone: 919-839-0300.

Technical Facilities: 9.94-kw ERP, 164-ft. above ground, 3891-ft. above sea level, lat. 33° 24' 05", long. 104° 22' 45".

Ownership: Hearst-Argyle Television Inc.

Roswell—KKGD-LP, Ch. 33, Prime Time Christian Broadcasting Inc. Phone: 915-563-0420.

Technical Facilities: 1.275-kw ERP, 46-ft. above ground, 3665-ft. above sea level, lat. 33° 21' 44", long. 104° 31' 25".

Ownership: Prime Time Christian Broadcasting Inc.

Roswell—KPLP-LP, Ch. 44, Prime Time Christian Broadcasting Inc.

Technical Facilities: 0.59-kw ERP, lat. 33° 23' 34", long. 104° 31' 27".

Transmitter: N. of Maljamar on NM Rte. 172.

Ownership: Board of Education of the City of Albuquerque; Regents of the U. of New Mexico.

Roy—K06EM, Ch. 6, KOB-TV LLC. Phone: 651-642-4334.

Technical Facilities: 0.013-kw ERP, lat. 35° 57' 50", long. 104° 13' 40".

Ownership: Hubbard Broadcasting Inc.

Roy—K09AW, Ch. 9, Village of Roy.

Technical Facilities: 0.01-kw ERP, lat. 35° 55' 33", long. 104° 24' 47".

Ownership: Village of Roy.

Roy—K34FQ, Ch. 34, Regents of the U. of New Mexico & the Board of Education of the City of Albuquerque. Phone: 505-277-2121.

Technical Facilities: 1.14-kw ERP, 38° 58' 04", long. 104° 13' 51".

Transmitter: 2.6-mi. NW of Roy.

Ownership: Regents of the U. of New Mexico.

Ruidoso—K16BZ, Ch. 16, LIN of New Mexico LLC. Phone: 202-462-6065.

Technical Facilities: 6.23-kw ERP, 49-ft. above ground, 10823-ft. above sea level, lat. 33° 24' 14", long. 105° 46' 55".

Holds CP for change to 1.25-kw ERP, BDFCDTT-20060327AGI.

Ownership: LIN TV Corp.

Ruidoso—K49EW, Ch. 49, Eastern New Mexico U. Phone: 505-562-2112.

Technical Facilities: 21-kw ERP, lat. 33° 24' 14", long. 105° 46' 55".

Ownership: Eastern New Mexico U. Board of Regents.

Ruidoso—KGDR-LP, Ch. 47, Prime Time Christian Broadcasting Inc. Phone: 432-563-0420.

Technical Facilities: 1.16-kw ERP, lat. 33° 24' 14", long. 105° 46' 55".

Ownership: Prime Time Christian Broadcasting Inc.

Ruidoso, etc.—K18GQ, Ch. 18, Eastern New Mexico U. Phone: 505-562-2112.

Technical Facilities: 1.29-kw ERP, 50-ft. above ground, 10824-ft. above sea level, lat. 33° 24' 14", long. 105° 46' 55".

Holds CP for change to 10-kw ERP, 170-ft. above ground, 10938-ft. above sea level, BDFCDTT-20060301ABG.

Ownership: Eastern New Mexico U. Board of Regents.

Ruidoso, etc.—K20GU, Ch. 20, KOAT Hearst-Argyle Television Inc. Phone: 919-839-0300.

Technical Facilities: 0.712-kw ERP, 175-ft. above ground, 10939-ft. above sea level, lat. 33° 24' 14", long. 105° 46' 55".

Ownership: Hearst-Argyle Television Inc.

Ruidoso, etc.—K35GU, Ch. 35, Eastern New Mexico U. Phone: 505-562-2112.

Technical Facilities: 8.7-kw ERP, 190-ft. above ground, 10966-ft. above sea level, lat. 33° 24' 14", long. 105° 46' 55".

Ownership: Eastern New Mexico U. Board of Regents.

■ **San Jon**—K24DP, Ch. 24, Panhandle Telecasting LP. Phone: 806-383-1010.

Technical Facilities: 0.552-kw ERP, 174-ft. above ground, 4514-ft. above sea level, lat. 35° 05' 23", long. 102° 56' 24".

Ownership: Panhandle Telecasting Co.

San Jon—K26DR, Ch. 26, Barrington Amarillo License LLC. Phone: 847-884-1877.

Technical Facilities: 0.552-kw ERP, 174-ft. above ground, 4514-ft. above sea level, lat. 35° 05' 23", long. 102° 56' 24".

Ownership: Pilot Group LP.

San Jon—K28BA, Ch. 28, Nexstar Broadcasting Inc. Phone: 972-373-8800.

Technical Facilities: 0.64-kw ERP, lat. 35° 05' 23", long. 103° 56' 24".

Holds CP for change to 0.0032-kw ERP, 174-ft. above ground, 4514-ft. above sea level, BDFCDTT-20060403AIC.

Ownership: Nexstar Broadcasting Group Inc.

San Jon—K30DZ, Ch. 30, Mission Broadcasting Inc. Phone: 330-335-8808.

Technical Facilities: 0.552-kw ERP, 174-ft. above ground, 4514-ft. above sea level, lat. 35° 05' 23", long. 102° 56' 24".

Holds CP for change to 0.003-kw ERP, BDFCDTT-20060403ACP.

Ownership: Mission Broadcasting Inc.

Santa Fe—K46GY, Ch. 46, Ramar Communications Inc. Phone: 806-748-9300.

Technical Facilities: 150-kw ERP, 66-ft. above ground, 10630-ft. above sea level, lat. 35° 12' 51", long. 106° 27' 02".

Ownership: Ramar Communications Inc.

Santa Rosa—K30FP, Ch. 30, Regents of the U. of New Mexico & the Board of Education of the City of Albuquerque. Phone: 505-277-2121.

Technical Facilities: 0.899-kw ERP, 185-ft. above ground, 4982-ft. above sea level, lat. 34° 57' 20", long. 104° 40' 53".

Transmitter: 1.1-mi. N of center of Santa Rosa.

Ownership: Board of Education of the City of Albuquerque; Regents of the U. of New Mexico.

Santa Rosa—K34GL, Ch. 34, LIN of New Mexico LLC. Phone: 401-457-9525.

Technical Facilities: 0.609-kw ERP, 161-ft. above ground, 4957-ft. above sea level, lat. 34° 57' 20", long. 104° 40' 53".

Holds CP for change to 0.122-kw ERP, BDFCDTT-20070914AAD.

Ownership: LIN TV Corp.

Santa Rosa—K36DI, Ch. 36, KOB-TV LLC. Phone: 651-642-4334.

Technical Facilities: 0.554-kw ERP, lat. 34° 57' 20", long. 104° 40' 55".

Ownership: Hubbard Broadcasting Inc.

Santa Rosa—K38HR, Ch. 38, LIN of New Mexico LLC. Phone: 202-462-6065.

Technical Facilities: 0.631-kw ERP, 105-ft. above ground, 4902-ft. above sea level, lat. 34° 57' 20", long. 104° 40' 53".

Ownership: LIN TV Corp.

Santa Rosa—K64DV, Ch. 64, Santa Rosa Chamber of Commerce.

Technical Facilities: 0.55-kw ERP, lat. 34° 57' 20", long. 104° 40' 55".

Ownership: Santa Rosa Chamber of Commerce.

Santa Rosa Heights—K09KC, Ch. 9, KOB-TV LLC. Phone: 651-642-4334.

Technical Facilities: 0.009-kw ERP, lat. 34° 56' 50", long. 104° 36' 30".

Ownership: Hubbard Broadcasting Inc.

Shiprock—K45CU, Ch. 45, LIN of New Mexico LLC. Phone: 202-462-6001.

Technical Facilities: 9.95-kw ERP, lat. 36° 27' 30", long. 109° 05' 37".

Ownership: LIN TV Corp.

Shiprock—K48AW, Ch. 48, The Navajo Nation. Phone: 602-787-6132.

Technical Facilities: 100-w TPO, 0.578-kw ERP, 56-ft. above ground, 5059-ft. above sea level, lat. 36° 48' 16", long. 108° 41' 41".

Transmitter: 1.5-mi. NNW of Shiprock at Shiprock Campus of Navajo Community College.

Ownership: Navajo Nation.

Personnel: Dr. Curtis Sweet, Director.

Shiprock, NM-Chinle, AZ—K32FK, Ch. 32, Christian Broadcasting Communications. Phone: 505-327-1445.

Technical Facilities: 1.78-kw ERP, 20-ft. above ground, 9800-ft. above sea level, lat. 36° 27' 30", long. 109° 05' 37".

Ownership: Christian Broadcasting Communications.

Silver City—K25DI, Ch. 25, LIN of New Mexico LLC. Phone: 202-462-6001.

Technical Facilities: 1.14-kw ERP, 52-ft. above ground, 7602-ft. above sea level, lat. 32° 50' 40", long. 108° 14' 18".

Ownership: LIN TV Corp.

Silver City—K28GK, Ch. 28, Regents of New Mexico State U. Phone: 505-646-2222.

Technical Facilities: 9.38-kw ERP, 81-ft. above ground, 8171-ft. above sea level, lat. 32° 51' 49", long. 108° 14' 27".

Ownership: Regents of New Mexico State U.

Silver City—K45EC, Ch. 45, LIN of New Mexico LLC. Phone: 202-462-6065.

Technical Facilities: 8.29-kw ERP, 69-ft. above ground, 7618-ft. above sea level, lat. 32° 50' 40", long. 108° 14' 18".

Ownership: LIN TV Corp.

Silver City—KOOT-LP, Ch. 8, Community Access Television of Silver City. Phone: 505-534-0130.

Technical Facilities: 0.75-kw ERP, 59-ft. above ground, 6667-ft. above sea level, lat. 32° 49' 29", long. 108° 14' 54".

Ownership: Community Access Television of Silver.

Silver City—KSIL-LP, Ch. 4, James S. Bumpous. Phone: 505-574-7742.

Technical Facilities: 0.002-kw ERP, 30-ft. above ground, 7569-ft. above sea level, lat. 32° 50' 40", long. 108° 14' 19".

Holds CP for change to 0.018-kw ERP, 23-ft. above ground, 7579-ft. above sea level, BDFCDVL-20060915AOE.

Ownership: James S. Bumpous.

■ **Silver City, etc.**—KCWO-CA, Ch. 2, KDBC License LLC - Debtor-in-Possession.

Technical Facilities: 0.1-kw ERP, 7588-ft. above sea level, lat. 32° 50' 41", long. 108° 14' 18".

Ownership: E. Roger Williams, Trustee.

Socorro—K10MG, Ch. 10, KOB-TV LLC. Phone: 651-642-4334.

Technical Facilities: 0.17-kw ERP, 36-ft. above sea level, lat. 34° 04' 18", long. 106° 57' 44".

Ownership: Hubbard Broadcasting Inc.

Socorro—K28CE, Ch. 28, Son Broadcasting Inc. Phone: 505-345-1991.

Technical Facilities: 7250-w TPO, 1.9-kw ERP, 40-ft. above ground, 7270-ft. above sea level, lat. 34° 04' 18", long. 106° 57' 44".

Transmitter: Socorro Peak, 3-mi. W of Socorro.

Ownership: Son Broadcasting Inc.

Socorro—K44HJ, Ch. 44, LIN of New Mexico LLC. Phone: 202-462-6001.

Technical Facilities: 0.288-kw ERP, 30-ft. above ground, 7274-ft. above sea level, lat. 34° 04' 18", long. 106° 57' 45".

Ownership: LIN TV Corp.

Socorro—K46HY-D, Ch. 46, Regents of the U. of New Mexico & Board of Education of the City of Albuquerque. Phone: 505-277-2121. Fax: 505-277-2191.

Technical Facilities: 0.419-kw ERP, 55-ft. above ground, 7296-ft. above sea level, lat. 34° 04' 18", long. 106° 57' 44.8".

Multichannel TV Sound: Stereo and separate audio program.

Ownership: Board of Education of the City of Albuquerque; Regents of New Mexico State U.

Personnel: Ted E. Garcia, Chief Executive Officer & General Manager.

Taos—K06LE, Ch. 6, KOB-TV LLC. Phone: 651-642-4334.

Technical Facilities: 0.06-kw ERP, lat. 35° 23' 51", long. 105° 32' 34".

Ownership: Hubbard Broadcasting Inc.

Taos—K08KX, Ch. 8, KOAT Hearst-Argyle Television Inc. Phone: 919-839-0300.

Technical Facilities: 0.08-kw ERP, lat. 36° 23' 51", long. 105° 32' 34".

Began Operation: August 27, 1979.

Ownership: Hearst-Argyle Television Inc.

Taos—K12OG, Ch. 12, LIN of New Mexico LLC. Phone: 401-457-9525.

Technical Facilities: 0.14-kw ERP, 10-ft. above ground, 8409-ft. above sea level, lat. 36° 34' 58", long. 105° 35' 38".

Holds CP for change to 89-ft. above ground, 7490-ft. above sea level, lat. 36° 23' 51", long. 105° 32' 34". BPTTV-20080418AAC.

Ownership: LIN TV Corp.

Taos—K15HD-D, Ch. 15, Regents of the U. of New Mexico and the Board of Education of the City of Albuquerque. Phone: 505-277-2121.

Technical Facilities: 0.289-kw ERP, 107-ft. above ground, 7534-ft. above sea level, lat. 36° 23' 51", long. 105° 32' 34".

Ownership: Board of Education of the City of Albuquerque; Regents of the U. of New Mexico.

Taos—K21FD, Ch. 21, LIN of New Mexico LLC. Phone: 202-462-6065.

Technical Facilities: 10.3-kw ERP, lat. 36° 23' 51", long. 105° 32' 34".

Transmitter: NW slope of Devisadero Peak, 1.8-mi. E of Taos.

Ownership: LIN TV Corp.

Taos—K30HS, Ch. 30, CYS Inc. Phone: 806-745-3434.

Technical Facilities: 16.6-kw ERP, 43-ft. above ground, 7441-ft. above sea level, lat. 36° 23' 51", long. 105° 32' 34".

Ownership: CYS Inc.

Personnel: Bill Frazier, General Manager; Tom Miller, Chief Engineer.

Taos—K33BN, Ch. 33, Regents of the U. of New Mexico & the Board of Education of the City of Albuquerque. Phone: 505-277-2121.

Technical Facilities: 0.62-kw ERP, 97-ft. above ground, 7482-ft. above sea level, lat. 36° 23' 52", long. 105° 32' 35".

Ownership: Board of Education of the City of Albuquerque; Regents of the U. of New Mexico.

Taos—K43IA, Ch. 43, Son Broadcasting Inc. Phone: 505-345-1991.

Technical Facilities: 6.2-kw ERP, 66-ft. above ground, 7470-ft. above sea level, lat. 36° 23' 51", long. 105° 32' 34".

Ownership: Son Broadcasting Inc.

Tecolote—K49IL, Ch. 49, Regents of the U. of New Mexico & The Board of Education of the City of Albuquerque. Phone: 505-277-2121.

Technical Facilities: 0.825-kw ERP, 192-ft. above ground, 6944-ft. above sea level, lat. 35° 24' 15", long. 105° 11' 23".

Ownership: Board of Education of the City of Albuquerque; Regents of the U. of New Mexico.

Thoreau—K28HM, Ch. 28, LIN of New Mexico LLC. Phone: 202-462-6065.

Technical Facilities: 1.283-kw ERP, 66-ft. above ground, 8796-ft. above sea level, lat. 35° 27' 59", long. 108° 14' 25".

Holds CP for change to 0.257-kw ERP, BDFCDTT-20060331AEA.

Ownership: LIN TV Corp.

Thoreau—K31JR, Ch. 31, Regents of the U. of New Mexico & the Board of Education of the City of Albuquerque. Phone: 505-277-2121.

Technical Facilities: 1.09-kw ERP, 65-ft. above ground, 8795-ft. above sea level, lat. 35° 28' 06", long. 108° 14' 26".

Holds CP for change to 0.39-kw ERP, BDFCDTT-20090402ANE.

Transmitter: Mount Powell, approx. 4.7-mi. NNW of Thoreau.

Ownership: Board of Education of the City of Albuquerque; Regents of the U. of New Mexico.

Tierra Amarilla—K60DD, Ch. 60, KOAT Hearst-Argyle Television Inc. Phone: 919-839-0300.

Technical Facilities: 1.99-kw ERP, 13-ft. above ground, 8655-ft. above sea level, lat. 36° 53' 58", long. 106° 36' 05".

Ownership: Hearst-Argyle Television Inc.

Tierra Amarilla, etc.—K09KJ, Ch. 9, KOB-TV LLC. Phone: 651-642-4334.

Technical Facilities: 0.04-kw ERP, 8865-ft. above sea level, lat. 36° 53' 58", long. 106° 36' 05".

Ownership: Hubbard Broadcasting Inc.

Timberon—K12MP, Ch. 12, Vision Broadcasting Network Inc.

Technical Facilities: 0.076-kw ERP, 7372-ft. above sea level, lat. 32° 38' 54", long. 105° 40' 50".

Ownership: Vision Broadcasting Network Inc.

Tohatchi—K06IS, Ch. 6, KOB-TV LLC. Phone: 651-642-4337.

Technical Facilities: 0.061-kw ERP, 89-ft. above ground, 9065-ft. above sea level, lat. 35° 54' 31", long. 108° 46' 24".

Holds CP for change to channel number 42, 0.4-kw ERP, BDISTT-20070404AAH.

Ownership: Hubbard Broadcasting Inc.

Tohatchi—K41FK, Ch. 41, LIN of New Mexico LLC. Phone: 401-457-9525.

Technical Facilities: 1.15-kw ERP, 69-ft. above ground, 9039-ft. above sea level, lat. 35° 54' 30", long. 108° 46' 28".

Holds CP for change to 0.23-kw ERP, BDFCDTT-20080703ACC.

Ownership: LIN TV Corp.

Tres Piedras—K28GV, Ch. 28, Regents of the U. of New Mexico & the Board of Education of the City of Albuquerque. Phone: 505-277-2121.

Technical Facilities: 0.994-kw ERP, 107-ft. above ground, 11016-ft. above sea level, lat. 36° 51' 34", long. 106° 01' 07".

Holds CP for change to 0.37-kw ERP, BDFCDTT-20090402ALA.

Ownership: Board of Education of the City of Albuquerque; Regents of the U. of New Mexico.

Truth or Consequences—K17BH, Ch. 17, Board of Education-Truth or Consequences.

Technical Facilities: 0.63-kw ERP, lat. 33° 08' 48", long. 107° 17' 06".

Ownership: City of Truth or Consequences.

Truth or Consequences—K25HV, Ch. 25, LIN of New Mexico LLC. Phone: 202-462-6065.

Technical Facilities: 0.653-kw ERP, 30-ft. above ground, 5030-ft. above sea level, lat. 33° 08' 48", long. 107° 17' 06".

Holds CP for change to 0.13-kw ERP, 30-ft. above ground, 5029-ft. above sea level, BDFCDTT-20060327AGE.

Ownership: LIN TV Corp.

Truth or Consequences—K27BN, Ch. 27, LIN of New Mexico LLC. Phone: 202-462-6001.

Technical Facilities: 0.63-kw ERP, lat. 33° 08' 48", long. 107° 17' 06".

Ownership: LIN TV Corp.

Truth or Consequences—K40GH, Ch. 40, Regents of New Mexico State U. Phone: 505-564-2222.

Technical Facilities: 0.333-kw ERP, 40-ft. above ground, 4981-ft. above sea level, lat. 33° 08' 48", long. 107° 17' 06".

Holds CP for change to 40-ft. above ground, 5020-ft. above sea level, lat. 33° 08' 48", long. 107° 17'08". BDFCDTT-20060331BOF.

Ownership: Regents of New Mexico State U.

Truth or Consequences—K51BQ, Ch. 51, City of Truth or Consequences.

Technical Facilities: 0.74-kw ERP, lat. 33° 08' 48", long. 107° 17' 06".

Ownership: City of Truth or Consequences.

Truth or Consequences—K64CG, Ch. 64, City of Truth or Consequences.

Technical Facilities: 0.74-kw ERP, lat. 33° 08' 48", long. 107° 17' 06".

Ownership: City of Truth or Consequences.

Tucumcari—K30HD-D, Ch. 30, Eastern New Mexico U. Phone: 505-562-2112.

Technical Facilities: 12-kw ERP, 85-ft. above ground, 5032-ft. above sea level, lat. 35° 08' 03.2", long. 103° 41' 53.5".

Ownership: Eastern New Mexico U. Board of Regents.

Tucumcari—K32FE, Ch. 32, Regents of Eastern New Mexico U. Phone: 505-562-2112.

Technical Facilities: 1.29-kw ERP, lat. 35° 08' 02", long. 103° 41' 56".

Transmitter: Tucumcari Mountain, 3.8-mi. SW of Tucumcari.

Ownership: Eastern New Mexico U. Board of Regents.

Tucumcari—K35FP, Ch. 35, UHF-TV Association. Phone: 505-461-3818.

Technical Facilities: 0.66-kw ERP, 45-ft. above ground, 4787-ft. above sea level, lat. 35° 08' 20", long. 103° 41' 45".

Ownership: UHF-TV Association.

Tucumcari—K38FP, Ch. 38, UHF-TV Association. Phone: 505-461-3818.

Technical Facilities: 0.67-kw ERP, lat. 35° 08' 20", long. 103° 41' 45".

Ownership: UHF-TV Association.

Tucumcari—K40DK, Ch. 40, UHF-TV Association. Phone: 505-461-3818.

Technical Facilities: 1.22-kw ERP, 33-ft. above ground, 5020-ft. above sea level, lat. 35° 08' 20", long. 103° 41' 45".

Ownership: UHF-TV Association.

Tucumcari—K42CR, Ch. 42, UHF-TV Association. Phone: 505-461-3818.

Technical Facilities: 1.22-kw ERP, 33-ft. above ground, 5020-ft. above sea level, lat. 35° 08' 20", long. 103° 41' 45".

Ownership: UHF-TV Association.

Tucumcari—K44CJ, Ch. 44, LIN of New Mexico LLC. Phone: 202-462-6065.

Technical Facilities: 1.22-kw ERP, lat. 35° 08' 02", long. 103° 41' 56".

Ownership: LIN TV Corp.

Tucumcari—K46BU, Ch. 46, UHF-TV Association. Phone: 505-461-3818.

Technical Facilities: 0.091-kw ERP, lat. 35° 08' 20", long. 103° 41' 45".

Ownership: UHF-TV Association.

Tucumcari—K48EH, Ch. 48, LIN of New Mexico LLC. Phone: 401-457-9525.

Technical Facilities: 1.32-kw ERP, 36-ft. above ground, 4990-ft. above sea level, lat. 35° 08' 03", long. 103° 41' 55".

Holds CP for change to 0.26-kw ERP, BDFCDTT-20081030ABP.

Ownership: LIN TV Corp.

Tucumcari—K50CX, Ch. 50, UHF-TV Association. Phone: 505-461-3818.

Technical Facilities: 1.22-kw ERP, 36-ft. above ground, 5020-ft. above sea level, lat. 35° 08' 20", long. 103° 41' 45".

Ownership: UHF-TV Association.

Wagon Mound—K06BN, Ch. 6, LIN of New Mexico LLC. Phone: 202-462-6065.

Technical Facilities: 0.028-kw ERP, lat. 36° 00' 30", long. 104° 40' 55".

Ownership: LIN TV Corp.

Wagon Mound—K09CR, Ch. 9, Wagon Mound TV Club.

Technical Facilities: 0.028-kw ERP, lat. 36° 00' 30", long. 104° 40' 55".

Ownership: Wagon Mound TV Club.

Wagon Mound—K11MD, Ch. 11, Wagon Mound TV Club.

Technical Facilities: 0.003-kw ERP, lat. 36° 00' 30", long. 104° 40' 55".

Ownership: Wagon Mound TV Club.

Wagon Mound—K36FQ, Ch. 36, Regents of the U. of New Mexico & the Board of Education of the City of Albuquerque. Phone: 505-277-2121.

Technical Facilities: 0.06-kw ERP, 47-ft. above ground, 6405-ft. above sea level, lat. 36° 00' 19", long. 104° 42' 12".

Ownership: Board of Education of the City of Albuquerque; Regents of the U. of New Mexico.

White Oaks, etc.—K22FN, Ch. 22, Regents of the U. of New Mexico & The Board of Education of the City of Albuquerque. Phone: 505-277-2121.

Technical Facilities: 2.09-kw ERP, 46-ft. above ground, 7077-ft. above sea level, lat. 33° 49' 34", long. 106° 14' 54".

Ownership: Board of Education of the City of Albuquerque; Regents of New Mexico State U.

Zuni—K39FY, Ch. 39, LIN of New Mexico LLC. Phone: 202-462-6065.

Technical Facilities: 0.829-kw ERP, lat. 35° 06' 50", long. 108° 44' 06".

Ownership: LIN TV Corp.

Zuni—K43DL, Ch. 43, Zuni Public School District.

Technical Facilities: 0.76-kw ERP, 95-ft. above ground, 7195-ft. above sea level, lat. 35° 06' 50", long. 108° 44' 12".

Ownership: Zuni Public School District.

Zuni Pueblo—K09FR, Ch. 9, Zuni Communications Authority.

Technical Facilities: 0.01-kw ERP, lat. 35° 06' 50", long. 108° 44' 12".

Ownership: Zuni Communications Authority.

Zuni Pueblo—K16DL, Ch. 16, KOB-TV LLC. Phone: 651-642-4334.

Technical Facilities: 0.26-kw ERP, lat. 35° 06' 50", long. 108° 44' 12".

Transmitter: 7-mi. NE of Zuni Pueblo.

Ownership: Hubbard Broadcasting Inc.

New York

Albany—W52DF, Ch. 52, Trinity Broadcasting Network Inc. Phone: 714-832-2950. Fax: 714-730-0661.

Technical Facilities: 1.22-kw ERP, 36-ft. above ground, 5020-ft. above sea level, lat. 35° 08' 20", long. 103° 41' 45".

Ownership: UHF-TV Association.

Technical Facilities: 1-kw ERP, lat. 42° 38' 13", long. 73° 59' 43".

Holds CP for change to channel number 32, 45.6-kw ERP, 177-ft. above ground, 1696-ft. above sea level, lat. 42° 38' 13", long. 73° 59' 45". BPTT-20050405ABY.

Transmitter: WRGB(TV) Tower.

Ownership: Trinity Broadcasting Network Inc.

■ **Albany**—WNYA-CA, Ch. 15, Venture Technologies Group LLC. Phone: 323-904-4090.

Technical Facilities: 28-kw ERP, 238-ft. above ground, 1757-ft. above sea level, lat. 42° 38' 12", long. 73° 59' 45".

Holds CP for change to 15-kw ERP, BMPDTA-20081017AHE.

Began Operation: January 14, 1998.

Ownership: Venture Technologies Group LLC.

Personnel: Dan Carbonara, General Manager; Ed Dennis, Chief Engineer; Russ Clapp, Sales Manager.

Allentown, etc.—W59AH, Ch. 59, Western New York Public Broadcasting Association.

Technical Facilities: 0.12-kw ERP, 2497-ft. above sea level, lat. 42° 04' 16", long. 78° 03' 57".

Ownership: Western New York Public Broadcasting Association.

Amityville—WPXU-LP, Ch. 38, ION Media LPTV Inc., Debtor in Possession. Phones: 212-836-4045; 860-444-2626. Fax: 212-836-4048.

Technical Facilities: 1000-w TPO, 12.6-kw ERP, 253-ft. above ground, 354-ft. above sea level, lat. 40° 44' 45", long. 73° 37' 29".

Holds CP for change to channel number 12, 0.3-kw ERP, 249-ft. above ground, 354-ft. above sea level, BDISDTL-20060103ACM.

Transmitter: 260 E. 2nd St., Mineola, NY.

Began Operation: April 23, 1992.

Ownership: ION Media Networks Inc., Debtor in Possession.

Personnel: Lisa Phillips, General Manager & Sales Manager; Ron Brown, Chief Engineer.

Andover—W61AJ, Ch. 61, Western New York Public Broadcasting Association.

Technical Facilities: 0.3-kw ERP, 2306-ft. above sea level, lat. 42° 08' 25", long. 77° 49' 25".

Ownership: Western New York Public Broadcasting Association.

Angelica, etc.—W65AJ, Ch. 65, Western New York Public Broadcasting Association.

Technical Facilities: 1.82-kw ERP, 2375-ft. above sea level, lat. 42° 19' 33", long. 78° 03' 08".

Ownership: Western New York Public Broadcasting Association.

Auburn—W48AO, Ch. 48, Sonny Persad. Phone: 315-258-7377.

Technical Facilities: 100-w TPO, 1.15-kw ERP, 230-ft. above ground, 938-ft. above sea level, lat. 42° 55' 43", long. 76° 33' 39".

Transmitter: 85 Osborne St., Auburn.

Ownership: Sonny Persad.

Auburn—W54AK, Ch. 54, Sonny Persad. Phone: 315-258-7377.

Technical Facilities: 18.1-kw ERP, 180-ft. above ground, 889-ft. above sea level, lat. 42° 55' 43", long. 76° 33' 39".

Ownership: Sonny Persad.

Auburn—WNNY-LP, Ch. 52, Renard Communications Corp. Phone: 315-468-0908.

Technical Facilities: 10.2-kw ERP, 428-ft. above ground, 1998-ft. above sea level, lat. 42° 48' 05", long. 76° 26' 14".

Holds CP for change to channel number 6, 1.5-kw ERP, 194-ft. above ground, 748-ft. above sea level, lat. 42° 57' 05", long. 76° 35' 05". BDISTVL-20080222AEE.

Began Operation: July 22, 1999.

Ownership: Craig L. Fox.

Bath—W20BL, Ch. 20, WYDC Inc. Phone: 607-937-6144. Fax: 607-937-4019.

Technical Facilities: 100-w TPO, 0.7-kw ERP, 250-ft. above ground, 2090-ft. above sea level, lat. 42° 18' 28", long. 77° 13' 18".

Transmitter: O'Brien Rd. on Irish Hill.

Ownership: WYDC Inc.

Personnel: Bill Christian, General Manager; Dennis Mahon, Sales Manager.

Binghamton—W26BS, Ch. 26, Trinity Broadcasting Network Inc. Phone: 714-832-2950. Fax: 714-730-0661.

Technical Facilities: 0.74-kw ERP, lat. 42° 03' 22", long. 75° 56' 39".

Transmitter: 0.3-mi. W of Foland Rd. & Hawleyton Rd.

Ownership: Trinity Broadcasting Network Inc.

■ **Binghamton**—WBGH-CA, Ch. 20, Newport Television License LLC. Phone: 816-751-0204.

Studio: 400 Plaza Dr, Ste C, Vestal, NY 13850.

Technical Facilities: 0.161-kw ERP, 279-ft. above ground, 1949-ft. above sea level, lat. 42° 03' 39", long. 75° 56' 36".

Ownership: Newport Television LLC.

Personnel: Chris Zell, Chief Engineer; Mike Golden, General & National Sales Manager; Kathy Breno, Local Sales Manager; Scott Iddings, Program & Promotion Director; Bob Thomas, Production Manager.

Binghamton—WBPN-LP, Ch. 10, Stainless Broadcasting LP. Phone: 517-347-4141.

Technical Facilities: 1.004-kw ERP, lat. 42° 03' 22", long. 75° 56' 39".

Transmitter: 3000 Ingraham Hill Rd., 3.1-mi. SW of Binghamton.

Ownership: Stainless Broadcasting LP.

Binghamton—WXXW-LP, Ch. 6, Johnson Broadcasting Co. Inc. Phone: 410-765-3581.

Technical Facilities: 0.016-kw ERP, 164-ft. above ground, 1063-ft. above sea level, lat. 42° 06' 00", long. 75° 54' 32".

Ownership: Johnson Broadcasting Co. Inc.

Bolivar & Richburg—W68AJ, Ch. 68, Western New York Public Broadcasting Association.

Technical Facilities: 0.017-kw ERP, lat. 42° 04' 09", long. 78° 11' 04".

Ownership: Western New York Public Broadcasting Association.

Brooklyn—WBQM-LP, Ch. 3, Renard Communications Corp. Phone: 315-468-0908.

Technical Facilities: 0.75-kw ERP, 870-ft. above ground, 901-ft. above sea level, lat. 40° 45' 08", long. 73° 58' 03".

Holds CP for change to channel number 50, 2-kw ERP, 875-ft. above ground, 906-ft. above sea level, BDISDTL-20080701AEZ.

Began Operation: April 5, 2001.

Ownership: Craig L. Fox.

■ **Buffalo**—WBNF-CA, Ch. 15, Faith Broadcasting Network Inc. Phone: 618-997-9333. Fax: 618-997-1859.

Technical Facilities: 9.2-kw ERP, 551-ft. above ground, 1138-ft. above sea level, lat. 43° 01' 32", long. 78° 55' 43".

Transmitter: Existing WUTV(TV) tower, 951 Whitehaven Rd., Grand Island.

Ownership: Faith Broadcasting Network Inc.

Personnel: Colleen Brennan, Station Manager; Mike McMannus, Chief Engineer.

Buffalo—WBXZ-LP, Ch. 56, Renard Communications Corp. Phone: 315-468-0908.

Technical Facilities: 1000-w TPO, 13.7-kw ERP, 545-ft. above ground, 1148-ft. above sea level, lat. 42° 52' 47", long. 78° 52' 36".

Transmitter: Marine Midland Center, Main St., Buffalo.

Ownership: Craig L. Fox.

Buffalo—WFHW-LP, Ch. 58, Citizens Television Systems Inc. Phones: 716-884-9228; 716-884-9229.

Studio: 18 Agassiz Circle, Buffalo, NY 14214.

Technical Facilities: 1000-w TPO, 15.1-kw ERP, 576-ft. above ground, 1167-ft. above sea level, lat. 42° 52' 47", long. 78° 52' 36".

Transmitter: Marine Midland Center.

Multichannel TV Sound: Stereo and separate audio program.

Ownership: Citizens Television Systems Inc.

Personnel: Deborah Ann Heisler, General Manager; Bruce G. Alesse, Sales Manager.

Burlington—W29BJ, Ch. 29, Kevin O'Kane. Phone: 315-829-4847.

Technical Facilities: 1000-w TPO, 10.7-kw ERP, 180-ft. above ground, 2191-ft. above sea level, lat. 42° 42' 50", long. 75° 08' 45".

Transmitter: Clock Hill Rd. at Rtes. 80 & 51 intersection.

Ownership: Kevin O'Kane.

Burlington—W31BP, Ch. 31, Nexstar Broadcasting Inc. Phone: 972-373-8800.

Technical Facilities: 1000-w TPO, 37-kw ERP, 155-ft. above ground, 2174-ft. above sea level, lat. 42° 42' 53", long. 75° 08' 40".

Holds CP for change to 0.24-kw ERP, BDFCDTT-20060403AKN.

Transmitter: Klock Hill, approx. 1.1-mi. SW of Burlington.

Ownership: Nexstar Broadcasting Group Inc.

Personnel: Dan Gragg, General Manager.

Cherry Creek, etc.—W62AE, Ch. 62, Western New York Public Broadcasting Association.

Technical Facilities: 0.59-kw ERP, 2034-ft. above sea level, lat. 42° 14' 50", long. 79° 06' 48".

Ownership: Western New York Public Broadcasting Association.

Cobleskill—WUCB-LP, Ch. 41, Adullam Gospel Church. Phone: 518-234-4769.

Technical Facilities: 9.2-kw ERP, 315-ft. above ground, 1268-ft. above sea level, lat. 42° 39' 03", long. 74° 31' 25".

Ownership: Adullam Gospel Church.

Cobleskill—WYBN-LP, Ch. 57, Cable Ad Net New York Inc. Phone: 845-876-1212.

Technical Facilities: 10-kw ERP, 315-ft. above ground, 1268-ft. above sea level, lat. 42° 39' 03", long. 74° 31' 25".

Began Operation: February 15, 2007.

Ownership: Cable Ad Net New York Inc.

Corning—W41DB, Ch. 41, Vision Communications LLC. Phone: 607-937-5000.

Technical Facilities: 7-kw ERP, 405-ft. above ground, 2085-ft. above sea level, lat. 42° 08' 31", long. 77° 04' 40".

Ownership: Vision Communications LLC (New York).

Corning—WJKP-LP, Ch. 39, Vision Communications LLC. Phone: 607-937-5000.

Technical Facilities: 1.5-kw ERP, 405-ft. above ground, 2085-ft. above sea level, lat. 42° 08' 31", long. 77° 04' 40".

Ownership: Vision Communications LLC (New York).

Cuba—W60AJ, Ch. 60, Western New York Public Broadcasting Association.

Technical Facilities: 0.29-kw ERP, lat. 42° 10' 48", long. 78° 16' 17".

Ownership: Western New York Public Broadcasting Association.

■ **De Witt**—WIXT-CA, Ch. 40, Renard Communications Corp. Phone: 315-468-0908.

Technical Facilities: 10-w TPO, 0.1-kw ERP, 62-ft. above ground, 1394-ft. above sea level, lat. 42° 57' 18", long. 75° 53' 40".

Transmitter: Syracuse Rd., Rte. 92, Cazenovia.

Ownership: Craig L. Fox.

Ellenburg—W49BI, Ch. 49, Convergence Entertainment & Communications LLC. Phone: 518-825-1071.

Technical Facilities: 1000-w TPO, 0.02-kw ERP, 157-ft. above ground, 2012-ft. above sea level, lat. 44° 51' 11", long. 73° 58' 28".

Holds CP for change to 11-kw ERP, 157-ft. above ground, 2013-ft. above sea level, BPTTL-20040406ACM.

Transmitter: 3.03-mi. ENE of U.S. Hwys. 374 & 90, near Ellenburg.

Began Operation: December 20, 2000.

Ownership: Convergence Entertainment & Communications LLC.

Elmira—W21BW, Ch. 21, Three Angels Broadcasting Network Inc.

Technical Facilities: 2.4-kw ERP, lat. 42° 01' 55", long. 76° 47' 02".

Transmitter: Comfort Hill Rd. at Comfort Hill tower site, 1.9-mi. S of Elmira.

Ownership: Three Angels Broadcasting Network Inc.

Elmira—W26BF, Ch. 26, WYDC Inc. Phone: 607-937-5000.

Technical Facilities: 1.09-kw ERP, lat. 42° 07' 51", long. 76° 42' 21".

Ownership: WYDC Inc.

Elmira—W59DG, Ch. 59, Trinity Broadcasting Network Inc. Phone: 714-832-2950. Fax: 714-730-0661.

Technical Facilities: 7.7-kw ERP, 427-ft. above ground, 1266-ft. above sea level, lat. 42° 04' 29", long. 76° 46' 47".

Holds CP for change to channel number 24, 17.1-kw ERP, BPTT-20031212ADX.

Ownership: Trinity Broadcasting Network Inc.

Elmira, Watkins Glen—WMYH-LP, Ch. 6, WYDC Inc. Phone: 607-937-5000.

Technical Facilities: 0.25-kw ERP, 150-ft. above ground, 1810-ft. above sea level, lat. 42° 03' 49", long. 76° 51' 10".

Ownership: WYDC Inc.

Fillmore—W62AQ, Ch. 62, Western New York Public Broadcasting Association.

Technical Facilities: 0.01-kw ERP, lat. 42° 28' 33", long. 78° 02' 09".

Ownership: Western New York Public Broadcasting Association.

Findley Lake—W60AC, Ch. 60, Western New York Public Broadcasting Association.

Technical Facilities: 0.05-kw ERP, lat. 42° 05' 46", long. 79° 44' 15".

Ownership: Western New York Public Broadcasting Association.

Friendship & Belmont—W62AS, Ch. 62, Western New York Public Broadcasting Association.

Technical Facilities: 1.04-kw ERP, lat. 42° 12' 35", long. 78° 03' 46".

Ownership: Western New York Public Broadcasting Association.

Glasgow—WKUW-LP, Ch. 60, Budd Broadcasting Co. Inc. Phone: 352-371-7772.

Technical Facilities: 6.9-kw ERP, 328-ft. above ground, 1007-ft. above sea level, lat. 36° 57' 34", long. 86° 00' 08".

Holds CP for change to 150-kw ERP, 348-ft. above ground, 1138-ft. above sea level, lat. 36° 57' 37", long. 86° 32' 49". BPTTL-20051219ABT.

Ownership: Budd Broadcasting Co. Inc.

Glens Falls—W04BD, Ch. 4, WMHT Educational Telecommunications Inc.

Technical Facilities: 0.049-kw ERP, 1444-ft. above sea level, lat. 43° 18' 17", long. 73° 45' 07".

Ownership: WMHT Educational Telecommunications.

Glens Falls—W47CM, Ch. 47, Trinity Broadcasting Network Inc. Phone: 714-832-2950. Fax: 714-730-0661.

Technical Facilities: 1000-w TPO, 20.2-kw ERP, 203-ft. above ground, 1526-ft. above sea level, lat. 43° 18' 17", long. 73° 45' 07".

Holds CP for change to 15-kw ERP, 203-ft. above ground, 1523-ft. above sea level, lat. 43° 18' 17", long. 73° 45' 05". BDFCDTT-20060222AAR.

Transmitter: WYLR-FM Tower.

Began Operation: May 30, 1991.

Ownership: Trinity Broadcasting Network Inc.

Personnel: Paul Crouch, General Manager; Ben Miller, Chief Engineer; Rod Henke, Sales Manager.

■ **Glens Falls**—WNCE-CA, Ch. 8, Northern Broadcasting Co. Inc. Phone: 518-798-8000. Fax: 518-798-0735.

Studio: Mark Plaza, 63 Quaker Rd, Glen Falls, NY 12801.

Technical Facilities: 10-w TPO, 0.019-kw ERP, 161-ft. above ground, 489-ft. above sea level, lat. 43° 18' 29", long. 73° 38' 32".

Holds CP for change to channel number 31, 15-kw ERP, 180-ft. above ground, 1590-ft. above sea level, lat. 43° 17' 21", long. 73° 44' 38". BDISDTA-20081002AGC.

Transmitter: Jay St., Glens Falls.

Multichannel TV Sound: Stereo only.

Ownership: Northern Broadcasting Communications Inc.

Personnel: Charles F. Adams, President, General Manager & Operations Coordinator; Peter Morton, Chief Engineer.

Gloversville—W21CP, Ch. 21, WNYT-TV LLC. Phone: 651-642-4334.

Technical Facilities: 8.3-kw ERP, 132-ft. above ground, 1107-ft. above sea level, lat. 43° 02' 29", long. 74° 22' 01".

Holds CP for change to 2.5-kw ERP, BDFCDTT-20080611ABW.

Ownership: Hubbard Broadcasting Inc.

■ **Gloversville**—WFNY-CA, Ch. 49, Michael A. Sleezer. Phone: 518-725-1108.

Technical Facilities: 1000-w TPO, 7.2-kw ERP, 190-ft. above ground, 1850-ft. above sea level, lat. 43° 06' 09", long. 74° 22' 17".

Transmitter: Approx. 1.9-mi. N of Gloversville.

Ownership: Michael A. Sleezer.

■ **Greece/Rochester**—WGCE-CA, Ch. 6, Educable Corp. Phone: 585-227-7710.

Studio: 2221 Ridgeway Ave, Rochester, NY 14626.

Technical Facilities: 10-w TPO, 0.029-kw ERP, 75-ft. above ground, 581-ft. above sea level, lat. 43° 11' 14", long. 77° 42' 09".

Holds CP for change to channel number 25, 4-kw ERP, 66-ft. above ground, 571-ft. above sea level, BDISDTA-20080804AEV.

Transmitter: Long Pond/Ridgeway Ave.

Ownership: Educable Corp.

Personnel: Sal Caterino, General Manager; John Kells, Chief Engineer.

Greenwich—WVBG-LP, Ch. 41, Wireless Access LLC. Phone: 845-586-3311.

Technical Facilities: 0.1-kw ERP, 33-ft. above ground, 1302-ft. above sea level, lat. 42° 32' 42", long. 73° 58' 49".

Ownership: Wireless Access LLC.

Personnel: Dan Carbonara, General Manager; Ed Dennis, Chief Engineer; Russ Clapp, Sales Manager.

Hamburg—WDTB-LP, Ch. 39, Word of God Fellowship Inc. Phone: 817-571-1229. Fax: 817-571-7478.

Studio: 2095 Lakeview Rd, Lakeview, NY 14085.

Technical Facilities: 1000-w TPO, 16.9-kw ERP, 315-ft. above ground, 912-ft. above sea level, lat. 42° 49' 50", long. 78° 47' 54".

Holds CP for change to channel number 28, 25-kw ERP, 586-ft. above ground, 1191-ft. above sea level, lat. 42° 52' 47", long. 78° 52' 35". BDISTTL-20080903AAP.

Transmitter: Dorrance St. & Onondago Ave., West Seneca.

Ownership: Word of God Fellowship Inc.

Personnel: Tom Smardz, General Manager; Dave Grant, Chief Engineer; Elsie Delair, Sales Manager.

Hempstead—W26DC, Ch. 26, K Licensee Inc. Phone: 718-358-4219.

Technical Facilities: 12-kw ERP, 150-ft. above ground, 386-ft. above sea level, lat. 40° 47' 19", long. 73° 27' 09".

Ownership: K Licensee Inc.

Hempstead—W32DF, Ch. 32, Seventh Day Adventist Community Health Services of Greater New York. Phone: 516-627-9350.

Technical Facilities: 3-kw ERP, 95-ft. above ground, 220-ft. above sea level, lat. 40° 45' 27", long. 73° 32' 58".

Ownership: Seventh Day Adventist Community Health Services of Greater New York.

Herkimer—W04AE, Ch. 4, Young Broadcasting of Albany Inc., Debtor in Possession. Phone: 919-839-0300.

Technical Facilities: 0.01-kw ERP, lat. 43° 03' 23", long. 74° 55' 22".

Ownership: Young Broadcasting Inc., Debtor in Possession.

Hornell—W06AR, Ch. 6, Lilly Broadcasting LLC. Phone: 607-739-0345.

Technical Facilities: 0.1-kw ERP, lat. 42° 17' 32", long. 77° 40' 27".

Ownership: Lilly Broadcasting Holdings LLC.

Hornell—W16BE, Ch. 16, WYDC Inc.

Technical Facilities: 4.4-kw ERP, lat. 42° 16' 05", long. 77° 37' 51".

Transmitter: Hinckley Hill near Rush Rd.

Ownership: WYDC Inc.

Hudson et al.—WSSN-LP, Ch. 21, Hudson Valley Television Inc. Phone: 518-537-2988.

Technical Facilities: 6-kw ERP, 35-ft. above ground, 210-ft. above sea level, lat. 42° 08' 09", long. 73° 53' 11".

Ownership: Hudson Valley Television Inc.

Personnel: Sean Small, President.

Ithaca—W07BJ, Ch. 7, Lilly Broadcasting LLC. Phone: 607-739-0345.

Technical Facilities: 0.22-kw ERP, lat. 42° 25' 16", long. 76° 25' 46".

Ownership: Lilly Broadcasting Holdings LLC.

■ **Ithaca**—W16AX, Ch. 16, WSYT Licensee LP. Phone: 410-568-1500.

Studio: 1000 James St, Syracuse, NY 13203.

Technical Facilities: 1000-w TPO, 28.5-kw ERP, 89-ft. above ground, 840-ft. above sea level, lat. 42° 25' 47", long. 76° 29' 49".

Transmitter: 815 S. Aurora St.

Ownership: Sinclair Broadcast Group Inc.

Personnel: Aaron Olander, General Manager; Robert Pritchard, Chief Engineer; Don O'Connor, Sales Manager.

Ithaca—W20BT, Ch. 20, Trinity Christian Center of Santa Ana Inc. Phone: 714-832-2950.

Technical Facilities: 19.5-kw ERP, 148-ft. above ground, 1211-ft. above sea level, lat. 42° 34' 55", long. 76° 33' 22".

Ownership: Trinity Broadcasting Network Inc.

Jamestown—W10BH, Ch. 10, Trinity Broadcasting Network Inc. Phone: 714-832-2950. Fax: 714-730-0661.

Technical Facilities: 10-w TPO, 0.026-kw ERP, 85-ft. above ground, 1821-ft. above sea level, lat. 42° 07' 53", long. 79° 13' 13".

Transmitter: Near WHUG(FM) tower.

Ownership: Trinity Broadcasting Network Inc.

Kennedy—W56AD, Ch. 56, Western New York Public Broadcasting Association.

Technical Facilities: 0.03-kw ERP, lat. 42° 09' 04", long. 79° 04' 41".

Ownership: Western New York Public Broadcasting Association.

Lake Placid—W55AI, Ch. 55, Lambert Broadcasting of Burlington LLC. Phone: 310-385-4200.

Technical Facilities: 0.99-kw ERP, lat. 44° 17' 08", long. 73° 59' 13".

Ownership: Michael Lambert.

Liberty—W30AZ, Ch. 30, John Mester Income Family Trust. Phone: 718-859-0687.

Technical Facilities: 0.825-kw ERP, 243-ft. above ground, 1056-ft. above sea level, lat. 41° 45' 09", long. 74° 43' 01".

Holds CP for change to 15-kw ERP, 125-ft. above ground, 2382-ft. above sea level, lat. 41° 41' 02", long. 74° 21' 23". BMPDTL-20080801BBK.

Began Operation: October 28, 1991.

Ownership: John Mester Income Family Trust.

■ **Manhattan**—WEBR-CA, Ch. 17, K Licensee Inc. Phone: 718-358-4219.

Technical Facilities: 2000-w TPO, 2-kw ERP, 1004-ft. above ground, 1056-ft. above sea level, lat. 40° 44' 54", long. 73° 59' 10".

Transmitter: Atop Empire State Building, 350 5th Ave.

Ownership: K Licensee Inc.

■ **Manhattan**—WMBQ-CA, Ch. 46, Renard Communications Corp. Phone: 315-468-0908.

Technical Facilities: 50-kw ERP, 557-ft. above ground, 607-ft. above sea level, lat. 40° 44' 46", long. 73° 58' 52".

Holds CP for change to 21.5-kw ERP, 873-ft. above ground, 904-ft. above sea level, lat. 40° 45' 08", long. 73° 58' 03". BMPTTA-20081216BLI.

Began Operation: March 5, 1997.

Ownership: Craig L. Fox.

Massena—W14BU, Ch. 14, David Welch. Phone: 309-655-5418.

Technical Facilities: 100-w TPO, 0.84-kw ERP, 380-ft. above ground, 594-ft. above sea level, lat. 44° 54' 14", long. 74° 53' 01".

Transmitter: Rte. 420, 1-mi. S of Massena.

Ownership: David Welch.

Massena—W20BA, Ch. 20, Trinity Christian Center of Santa Ana Inc. Phone: 714-832-2950.

Technical Facilities: 9-kw ERP, 322-ft. above ground, 531-ft. above sea level, lat. 44° 54' 14", long. 74° 53' 01".

Ownership: Trinity Broadcasting Network Inc.

Massena—W36BN, Ch. 36, Nellie Gajeski. Phone: 718-278-5385.

Technical Facilities: 100-w TPO, 0.84-kw ERP, 380-ft. above ground, 594-ft. above sea level, lat. 44° 54' 14", long. 74° 53' 01".

Transmitter: Rte. 420, 1-mi. S of Massena.

Ownership: Nellie Gajeski.

Massena—WNYF-LP, Ch. 28, United Communications Corp.

Technical Facilities: 100-w TPO, 0.95-kw ERP, 358-ft. above ground, 505-ft. above sea level, lat. 44° 54' 14", long. 74° 53' 10".

Transmitter: Winthrop Rd.

Multichannel TV Sound: Stereo only.

Ownership: United Communications Corp.

Personnel: James Corbin, General Manager; Don Rohr, Chief Engineer; Charles Cusimano, Sales Manager.

Mineola—WLIG-LD, Ch. 26, WLNY LP. Phone: 631-777-8855.

Technical Facilities: 1-kw ERP, 182-ft. above ground, 242-ft. above sea level, lat. 40° 42' 59", long. 73° 34' 52".

Ownership: WLNY Holdings Inc.

Monticello—W27AL, Ch. 27, John Mester Income Family Trust. Phone: 718-859-0687.

Technical Facilities: 0.745-kw ERP, 105-ft. above ground, 1722-ft. above sea level, lat. 41° 39' 36", long. 74° 41' 05".

Holds CP for change to 0.8-kw ERP, 194-ft. above ground, 1788-ft. above sea level, lat. 41° 39' 38.7", long. 74° 41' 11". BMPDTL-20090428AAT.

Ownership: John Mester Income Family Trust.

New York—W26CE, Ch. 26, Atlantic Coast Communications Inc. Phone: 732-264-8766.

Technical Facilities: 1.5-kw ERP, 260-ft. above ground, 504-ft. above sea level, lat. 40° 51' 17.8", long. 72° 46' 10.5".

Holds CP for change to 1-kw ERP, BDFCDTL-20080111ACY.

Ownership: Atlantic Coast Communications Inc.

New York—W60AI, Ch. 60, Ventana Television Inc. Phone: 727-872-4210.

Technical Facilities: 75-kw ERP, 925-ft. above ground, 965-ft. above sea level, lat. 40° 45' 30", long. 73° 58' 15".

Holds CP for change to channel number 41, 0.09-kw ERP, 1411-ft. above ground, 1462-ft. above sea level, lat. 40° 44' 54", long. 73° 59' 10". BDISDTL-20080317AEL.

Ownership: Ventana Television Inc.

New York—WKOB-LP, Ch. 42, Nave Communications LLC. Phone: 202-293-0011.

Technical Facilities: 50-kw ERP, 732-ft. above ground, 732-ft. above sea level, lat. 40° 42' 18.6", long. 74° 00' 34.4".

Holds CP for change to channel number 2, 0.3-kw ERP, 1266-ft. above ground, 1317-ft. above sea level, lat. 40° 44' 53.6", long. 73° 59' 10.5". BDISDVL-20080819ACY.

Ownership: Nave Communications LLC.

New York—WNXY-LP, Ch. 26, Island Broadcasting Co. Phone: 516-627-5103. Fax: 516-627-4469.

Studio: 204 E 23rd St, New York, NY 10010.

Technical Facilities: 20-kw ERP, 683-ft. above ground, 699-ft. above sea level, lat. 40° 44' 50", long. 73° 56' 38".

Holds CP for change to channel number 43, 4-kw ERP, BMPDTL-20081202AEM.

Began Operation: April 4, 1989.

Ownership: Island Broadcasting Co.

Personnel: Michael Bogner, General Manager.

New York—WNYN-LP, Ch. 39, Island Braodcasting Co. Phone: 516-627-5103.

Technical Facilities: 50-kw ERP, 683-ft. above ground, 699-ft. above sea level, lat. 40° 44' 50", long. 73° 56' 38".

Ownership: Island Broadcasting Co.

Personnel: Michael Bogner, General Manager.

New York—WNYX-LP, Ch. 35, Island Broadcasting Co. Phone: 516-627-5103. Fax: 516-627-4469.

Studio: 204 E 23rd St, New York, NY 10010.

Technical Facilities: 25-kw ERP, 683-ft. above ground, 699-ft. above sea level, lat. 40° 44' 50", long. 73° 56' 38".

Holds CP for change to 120-kw ERP, BPTTL-20070705ADS.

Ownership: Island Broadcasting Co.

Personnel: Michael Bogner, General Manager.

New York—WNYZ-LP, Ch. 6, Island Broadcasting Co. Phone: 516-627-5103.

Technical Facilities: 3-kw ERP, 683-ft. above ground, 699-ft. above sea level, lat. 40° 44' 50", long. 73° 56' 38".

Holds CP for change to 0.3-kw ERP, BMPDVL-20070925AEC.

Ownership: Island Broadcasting Co.

New York—WXNY-LP, Ch. 32, Island Broadcasting Co. Phone: 516-627-5103. Fax: 516-627-4469.

Technical Facilities: 25-kw ERP, 683-ft. above ground, 699-ft. above sea level, lat. 40° 44' 50", long. 73° 56' 38".

Multichannel TV Sound: Stereo only.

Ownership: Island Broadcasting Co.

Newcomb—W12BG, Ch. 12, Town of Newcomb. Phone: 518-582-3211.

Technical Facilities: 0.008-kw ERP, 2165-ft. above sea level, lat. 43° 57' 22", long. 74° 10' 26".

Ownership: Town of Newcomb.

North Creek, etc.—W07BH, Ch. 7, Town of Johnsburg. Phone: 518-251-2421.

Technical Facilities: 0.006-kw ERP, 2251-ft. above sea level, lat. 43° 39' 14", long. 74° 00' 57".

Ownership: Town of Johnsburg.

North Creek, etc.—W09AZ, Ch. 9, Town of Johnsburg. Phone: 518-251-2421.

Technical Facilities: 0.006-kw ERP, lat. 43° 39' 14", long. 74° 00' 57".

Ownership: Town of Johnsburg.

North Creek, etc.—W11AW, Ch. 11, Town of Johnsburg. Phone: 518-251-2421.

Technical Facilities: 0.006-kw ERP, 2251-ft. above sea level, lat. 43° 39' 14", long. 74° 00' 57".

Ownership: Town of Johnsburg.

■ **Nyack**—WRNN-LP, Ch. 35, Richard D Bogner. Phone: 516-627-5103.

Technical Facilities: 1000-w TPO, 0.8-kw ERP, 92-ft. above ground, 731-ft. above sea level, lat. 41° 09' 07", long. 73° 47' 10".

Transmitter: Hardcastle Hill, near Pleasantville.

Began Operation: May 10, 1995.

Ownership: Richard D. Bogner.

Olean—W20AB, Ch. 20, Choice Olean TV Station Inc. Phone: 716-373-5838.

Technical Facilities: 12.5-kw ERP, 82-ft. above ground, 1522-ft. above sea level, lat. 42° 04' 50", long. 78° 25' 50".

Ownership: Choice Olean Television Station Inc.

Olean—W30BW, Ch. 30, Trinity Broadcasting Network Inc. Phone: 714-832-2950. Fax: 714-730-0661.

Technical Facilities: 5.9-kw ERP, 171-ft. above ground, 2321-ft. above sea level, lat. 42° 03' 04", long. 78° 25' 11".

Ownership: Trinity Broadcasting Network Inc.

Personnel: Paul Crouch, General Manager; Ben Miller, Chief Engineer; Rod Henke, Sales Manager.

Olean—WONS-LP, Ch. 25, Choice Olean Television Station Inc. Phone: 716-373-5838. Fax: 716-373-5838.

Studio: 217 N Union St, Olean, NY 14760.

Technical Facilities: 100-w TPO, 1.34-kw ERP, 180-ft. above ground, 2256-ft. above sea level, lat. 42° 03' 40", long. 78° 25' 11".

Transmitter: Savage Hollow Rd.

Ownership: Choice Olean Television Station Inc.

Personnel: Charles Bordanaro, General Manager; Richard Say, News & Public Affairs Director; Joseph Weatherall, Production & Programming Director.

■ **Oneida**—WCUL-CA, Ch. 13, Kevin O'Kane. Phone: 315-829-4848.

Technical Facilities: 10-w TPO, 0.232-kw ERP, 120-ft. above ground, 940-ft. above sea level, lat. 43° 03' 57", long. 75° 40' 04".

Transmitter: Forest Rd.

Began Operation: July 19, 1989.

Ownership: Kevin O'Kane.

Oneida—WTKO-LP, Ch. 15, Renard Communications Corp. Phone: 315-468-0908.

Technical Facilities: 11.9-kw ERP, lat. 43° 03' 57", long. 75° 40' 04".

Transmitter: Fairview Ave.

Ownership: Craig L. Fox.

Oneonta—WISF-LP, Ch. 15, Rastus Broadcast. Phone: 607-433-8815. Fax: 607-433-6786.

Studio: 3200 Chestnut St, Oneonta, NY 13820-5115.

Technical Facilities: 100-w TPO, 0.84-kw ERP, 128-ft. above ground, 2028-ft. above sea level, lat. 42° 25' 27", long. 75° 04' 04".

Transmitter: Rte. 28, S of city.

Ownership: Walter Rasmussen.

Personnel: Walter Rasmussen, General Manager.

Philadelphia—WTKJ-LP, Ch. 19, EICB-TV East LLC. Phone: 972-291-3750.

Technical Facilities: 6.3-kw ERP, 167-ft. above ground, 1178-ft. above sea level, lat. 43° 58' 04", long. 75° 48' 22".

Ownership: EICB-TV LLC.

■ **Plattsburgh**—WWBI-LP, Ch. 27, Word of God Fellowship Inc. Phone: 518-297-2727. Fax: 518-297-3377.

Technical Facilities: 1000-w TPO, 44.65-kw ERP, 98-ft. above ground, 1578-ft. above sea level, lat. 44° 46' 13", long. 73° 36' 47".

Transmitter: Rand Hill, N of Rand Rd., Jericho.

Multichannel TV Sound: Separate audio progam.

Ownership: Word of God Fellowship Inc.

Personnel: Gary Clarke, General Manager.

Port Henry—W60AO, Ch. 60, Mountain Lake Public Telecommunications Council. Phone: 518-563-9770.

Technical Facilities: 0.7-kw ERP, 39-ft. above ground, 279-ft. above sea level, lat. 44° 05' 18", long. 73° 18' 25".

Holds CP for change to channel number 46, 0.341-kw ERP, 39-ft. above ground, 280-ft. above sea level, BDISDTT-20060331AHW.

Ownership: Mountain Lake Public Telecommunications Council.

Port Jervis—W20CM, Ch. 20, Venture Technologies Group LLC. Phone: 323-904-4090.

Technical Facilities: 0.2-kw ERP, 125-ft. above ground, 561-ft. above sea level, lat. 41° 21' 49", long. 74° 40' 41".

Ownership: Venture Technologies Group LLC.

Port Jervis—W26DB, Ch. 26, Venture Technologies Group LLC. Phone: 323-904-4090.

Technical Facilities: 0.2-kw ERP, 125-ft. above ground, 561-ft. above sea level, lat. 41° 21' 49", long. 74° 40' 41".

Ownership: Venture Technologies Group LLC.

Port Jervis—W32DC, Ch. 32, Venture Technologies Group LLC. Phone: 323-904-4090.

Technical Facilities: 0.2-kw ERP, 125-ft. above ground, 561-ft. above sea level, lat. 41° 21' 49", long. 74° 40' 41".

Ownership: Venture Technologies Group LLC.

Port Jervis—W34DI, Ch. 34, Venture Technologies Group LLC. Phone: 323-904-4090.

Technical Facilities: 0.2-kw ERP, 125-ft. above ground, 561-ft. above sea level, lat. 41° 21' 49", long. 74° 40' 41".

Ownership: Venture Technologies Group LLC.

Port Jervis—W42CX, Ch. 42, Venture Technologies Group LLC. Phone: 323-904-4090.

Technical Facilities: 0.2-kw ERP, 125-ft. above ground, 561-ft. above sea level, lat. 41° 21' 49", long. 74° 40' 41".

Holds CP for change to 0.6-kw ERP, 261-ft. above ground, 1739-ft. above sea level, lat. 41° 12' 30.3", long. 74° 21' 22.6". BDFCDTL-20080215AGD.

Ownership: Venture Technologies Group LLC.

Port Jervis—W46DQ, Ch. 46, Venture Technologies Group LLC. Phone: 323-904-4090.

Technical Facilities: 0.2-kw ERP, 125-ft. above ground, 561-ft. above sea level, lat. 41° 21' 49", long. 74° 40' 41".

Ownership: Venture Technologies Group LLC.

Port Jervis—W52DW, Ch. 52, Venture Technologies Group LLC. Phone: 323-904-4090.

Technical Facilities: 0.2-kw ERP, 125-ft. above ground, 561-ft. above sea level, lat. 41° 21' 49", long. 74° 40' 41".

Ownership: Venture Technologies Group LLC.

Port Jervis—W55DK, Ch. 55, Venture Technologies Group LLC. Phone: 323-904-4090.

Technical Facilities: 0.2-kw ERP, 125-ft. above ground, 561-ft. above sea level, lat. 41° 21' 49", long. 74° 40' 41".

Ownership: Venture Technologies Group LLC.

Port Jervis—W59EA, Ch. 59, Venture Technologies Group LLC. Phone: 323-904-4090.

Technical Facilities: 0.2-kw ERP, 125-ft. above ground, 561-ft. above sea level, lat. 41° 21' 49", long. 74° 40' 41".

Ownership: Venture Technologies Group LLC.

Port Jervis—WASA-LP, Ch. 64, KRCA License LLC. Phone: 818-729-5300.

Technical Facilities: 0.02-kw ERP, 265-ft. above ground, 1598-ft. above sea level, lat. 41° 00' 35", long. 74° 35' 39".

Ownership: Venture Technologies Group LLC.

Potsdam—W26CP, Ch. 26, Trinity Broadcasting Network Inc. Phone: 714-832-2950. Fax: 714-730-0661.

Technical Facilities: 10-kw ERP, 44° 38' 54", long. 75° 01' 08".

Ownership: Trinity Broadcasting Network Inc.

Poughkeepsie—W42AE, Ch. 42, Dutchess Community College.

Technical Facilities: 19.3-kw ERP, 112-ft. above ground, 1247-ft. above sea level, lat. 41° 43' 10", long. 73° 59' 45".

Ownership: Dutchess Community College.

Rochester—W42CO, Ch. 42, Tri-State Christian TV Inc. Phone: 618-997-9333.

Technical Facilities: 11.9-kw ERP, lat. 43° 08' 07", long. 77° 35' 06".

Holds CP for change to 8-kw ERP, 115-ft. above ground, 837-ft. above sea level, lat. 43° 08' 07", long. 77° 35' 07". BDFCDTT-20060331BDS.

Ownership: Tri-State Christian TV Inc.

Rochester—WAWW-LP, Ch. 38, Squirrel Broadcasting LLC. Phone: 585-671-8576.

Studio: 184 Monroe Ave, Rochester, NY 14607.

Technical Facilities: 1000-w TPO, 27.2-kw ERP, 118-ft. above ground, 804-ft. above sea level, lat. 43° 08' 07", long. 77° 35' 07".

Transmitter: 115 Highland Ave., Rochester.

Ownership: Squirrel Broadcasting LLC.

Personnel: Steve Herbert, General Manager; Neal Ardman, Chief Engineer.

■ **Rochester**—WBGT-CA, Ch. 40, WBGT LLC. Phone: 585-235-1870. Fax: 585-235-0574.

Studio: 1320 Buffalo Rd, Ste 114, Rochester, NY 14624.

Technical Facilities: 1000-w TPO, 10-kw ERP, 449-ft. above ground, 984-ft. above sea level, lat. 43° 10' 14", long. 77° 40' 23".

Transmitter: Colfax & Ferrano Sts. intersection.

Multichannel TV Sound: Stereo only.

Ownership: WBGT LLC.

Personnel: David Grant, General Manager & Chief Engineer; Paul Mertz, Sales Manager.

■ **Rochester**—WHSH-CA, Ch. 36, Metro TV Inc. Phone: 315-468-0908.

Technical Facilities: 200-w TPO, 16-kw ERP, 151-ft. above ground, 866-ft. above sea level, lat. 43° 08' 07", long. 77° 35' 07".

Transmitter: Pinnacle Hill, Rochester.

Ownership: Craig L. Fox.

■ **Rochester**—WROH-LP, Ch. 47, Tiger Eye Broadcasting Corp. Phone: 954-431-3144.

Technical Facilities: 11-kw ERP, 118-ft. above ground, 883-ft. above sea level, lat. 43° 08' 07", long. 77° 35' 07".

Ownership: Tiger Eye Broadcasting Corp.

Personnel: Steve Herbert, General Manager; Neal Ardman, Chief Engineer.

■ **Rome**—WWDG-CA, Ch. 12, Kevin O'Kane. Phone: 315-829-4847.

Technical Facilities: 3-kw ERP, 256-ft. above ground, 676-ft. above sea level, lat. 43° 12' 18", long. 75° 28' 48".

Multichannel TV Sound: Stereo only.

Began Operation: June 14, 1993.

Ownership: Kevin O'Kane.

Saratoga Springs—W58CX, Ch. 58, Three Angels Broadcasting Network Inc. Phone: 618-627-4651. Fax: 618-627-4155.

Studio: 3391 Charley Good Rd, West Frankfort, IL 62896.

Technical Facilities: 1000-w TPO, 37.5-kw ERP, 59-ft. above ground, 1601-ft. above sea level, lat. 42° 38' 16", long. 73° 59' 55".

Holds CP for change to channel number 44, 62-ft. above ground, 1601-ft. above sea level, BDISDTL-20081216BKK.

Transmitter: Helderberg Mountain, WFLY(FM) tower, near Meadowdale.

Began Operation: November 5, 1997.

Ownership: Three Angels Broadcasting Network Inc.

Personnel: Moses Primo, Chief Engineer.

Savona—W60AD, Ch. 60, WSKG Public Telecommunications Council. Phone: 617-729-0100.

Technical Facilities: 0.65-kw ERP, 1841-ft. above sea level, lat. 42° 18' 28", long. 77° 13' 18".

Ownership: WSKG Public Telecommunications Council.

Schenectady—WNGX-LP, Ch. 42, Brian A. Larson. Phone: 518-686-0975.

Technical Facilities: 50-kw ERP, lat. 42° 38' 16", long. 73° 59' 47".

Holds CP for change to 0.14-kw ERP, 36-ft. above ground, 1306-ft. above sea level, lat. 42° 51' 00", long. 74° 03' 56". BDFCDTL-20060331AZF.

Transmitter: 0.2-mi. S of Beaver Dam & Pinnacle Rd., New Scotland.

Ownership: Brian A. Larson.

Schoharie, etc.—W04AJ, Ch. 4, WMHT Educational Telecommunications.

Technical Facilities: 0.011-kw ERP, lat. 42° 40' 38", long. 74° 19' 40".

Ownership: WMHT Educational Telecommunications.

Schroon Lake—W07BI, Ch. 7, Town of Schroon. Phone: 518-532-7737.

Technical Facilities: 0.013-kw ERP, lat. 43° 51' 56", long. 73° 43' 21".

Ownership: Town of Schroon.

Schroon Lake—W09BB, Ch. 9, Town of Schroon. Phone: 518-532-7737.

Technical Facilities: 0.013-kw ERP, lat. 43° 51' 56", long. 73° 43' 21".

Ownership: Town of Schroon.

Sherman—W64AF, Ch. 64, Western New York Public Broadcasting Association.

Technical Facilities: 1.31-kw ERP, lat. 42° 10' 15", long. 79° 35' 31".

Ownership: Western New York Public Broadcasting Association.

Sinclairville—W62AG, Ch. 62, Western New York Public Broadcasting Association.

Technical Facilities: 0.15-kw ERP, lat. 42° 13' 05", long. 79° 17' 55".

Ownership: Western New York Public Broadcasting Association.

■ **Southampton**—WVVH-CA, Ch. 50, Video Voice Inc. Phones: 212-935-4613; 631-537-0273. Fax: 212-935-4449.

Studio: 75 Industrial Rd, PO Box 769, Wainscott, NY 11975-0769.

Technical Facilities: 20-kw ERP, 52-ft. above ground, 104-ft. above sea level, lat. 40° 57' 20", long. 72° 15' 16".

Holds CP for change to 0.1-kw ERP, BDFCDTA-20051114AIV.

Multichannel TV Sound: Stereo and separate audio program.

Ownership: Video Voice Inc.

Personnel: Ernest J. Schimizzi, General Manager; Gregory F. Schimizzi, Creative Services Director; Clarence Beverage, Chief Engineer; Pamela Reid, Local Sales Manager; Gregory Patrick, Operations Manager.

Speculator, et al.—W04BK, Ch. 4, Page Hill Community Telecasters Inc.

Technical Facilities: 0.002-kw ERP, lat. 43° 30' 50", long. 74° 22' 25".

Ownership: Page Hill Community Telecasters Inc.

Syracuse—W30AJ, Ch. 30, John Mester Income Family Trust. Phone: 718-859-0687.

Studio: 109 S Warren St, Ste 1202, Syracuse, NY 13202.

Technical Facilities: 1000-w TPO, 20.1-kw ERP, 335-ft. above ground, 735-ft. above sea level, lat. 43° 03' 00", long. 76° 09' 04".

Holds CP for change to channel number 31, 44.7-kw ERP, 302-ft. above ground, 702-ft. above sea level, BPTTL-20080213ABM.

Transmitter: State Tower Bldg., 109 S. Warren St., Syracuse.

Ownership: John Mester Income Family Trust.

Syracuse—W38CY, Ch. 38, Trinity Christian Center of Santa Ana Inc. Phone: 714-832-2950.

Technical Facilities: 8.5-kw ERP, lat. 42° 56' 46", long. 76° 06' 16".

Holds CP for change to 15-kw ERP, 74-ft. above ground, 1414-ft. above sea level, lat. 42° 56' 45", long. 76° 06' 17". BDFCDTT-20060329AGG.

Transmitter: 0.62-mi. ESE of Sentinel Heights Rd. & Bull Hill Rd. intersection, near Janesville.

Began Operation: July 26, 2002.

Ownership: Trinity Broadcasting Network Inc.

■ **Syracuse**—WBLZ-LP, Ch. 13, Renard Communications Corp. Phone: 315-468-0908.

Technical Facilities: 3-kw ERP, 315-ft. above ground, 689-ft. above sea level, lat. 43° 03' 30", long. 76° 10' 00".

Ownership: Craig L. Fox.

■ **Syracuse**—WHSU-CA, Ch. 51, Renard Communications Corp. Phone: 315-468-0908.

Technical Facilities: 1000-w TPO, 21.8-kw ERP, 367-ft. above ground, 741-ft. above sea level, lat. 43° 03' 30", long. 76° 10' 00".

Transmitter: 401 W. Kirkpatrick St.

Ownership: Craig L. Fox.

Syracuse—WMBO-LP, Ch. 60, Metro TV Inc. Phone: 315-468-0908.

Technical Facilities: 74-w TPO, 1.3-kw ERP, 174-ft. above ground, 840-ft. above sea level, lat. 43° 00' 19", long. 76° 07' 46".

Holds CP for change to channel number 6, 0.3-kw ERP, 345-ft. above ground, 720-ft. above sea level, lat. 43° 03' 30", long. 76° 10' 00". BDISTVL-20060330AOD.

Transmitter: 821 E. Brighton Ave.

Ownership: Craig L. Fox.

■ **Syracuse**—WNDR-LP, Ch. 49, Metro TV Inc. Phone: 315-468-0908.

Studio: 401 W Kirkpatrick St, Syracuse, NY 13204.

Technical Facilities: 13.4-kw ERP, 174-ft. above ground, 843-ft. above sea level, lat. 43° 00' 19", long. 76° 07' 48".

Ownership: Craig L. Fox.

■ **Syracuse**—WOBX-LP, Ch. 35, Metro TV Inc. Phone: 315-468-0908.

Technical Facilities: 4.92-kw ERP, 370-ft. above ground, 745-ft. above sea level, lat. 43° 03' 30", long. 76° 10' 00".

Transmitter: 401 W. Kirkpatrick St.

Ownership: Craig L. Fox.

Syracuse—WSTQ-LP, Ch. 14, Barrington Syracuse License LLC. Phone: 847-884-1877.

Technical Facilities: 100-w TPO, 9.8-kw ERP, 293-ft. above ground, 735-ft. above sea level, lat. 43° 03' 30", long. 76° 10' 00".

Transmitter: 401 W. Kirkpatrick St.

Ownership: Pilot Group LP.

Personnel: Jim Marco.

■ **Syracuse**—WTVU-LP, Ch. 22, Renard Communications Corp. Phone: 315-468-0908.

Technical Facilities: 858-w TPO, 50-kw ERP, 360-ft. above ground, 735-ft. above sea level, lat. 43° 03' 30", long. 76° 10' 00".

Ownership: Craig L. Fox.

■ **Syracuse, etc.**—WONO-CA, Ch. 11, Renard Communications Corp. Phone: 315-468-0908.

Technical Facilities: 1.5-kw ERP, 331-ft. above ground, 705-ft. above sea level, lat. 43° 03' 30", long. 73° 10' 00".

Ownership: Craig L. Fox.

Syracuse-DeWitt—W07BA, Ch. 7, Newport Television License LLC. Phone: 816-751-0204.

Technical Facilities: 0.016-kw ERP, lat. 43° 00' 32", long. 76° 09' 46".

Ownership: Newport Television LLC.

Troy—WNGN-LP, Ch. 38, Brian A. Larson. Phone: 518-686-0975.

Technical Facilities: 8.5-kw ERP, 249-ft. above ground, 1201-ft. above sea level, lat. 42° 47' 08", long. 73° 37' 45".

Ownership: Brian A. Larson.

Personnel: Brian A. Larson, General Manager; Peter Horton, Chief Engineer; Mark Russ, Sales Manager.

Tupper Lake—W25AT, Ch. 25, Mountain Lake Public Telecommunications Council. Phone: 518-563-9770.

Technical Facilities: 0.996-kw ERP, 56-ft. above ground, 3209-ft. above sea level, lat. 44° 09' 34", long. 74° 28' 31".

Holds CP for change to 0.165-kw ERP, BDFCDTT-20060331AFB.

Began Operation: July 29, 1991.

Ownership: Mountain Lake Public Telecommunications Council.

Union Springs—W69AN, Ch. 69, Sonny Persad. Phone: 315-258-7377.

Technical Facilities: 0.33-kw ERP, 571-ft. above sea level, lat. 42° 54' 09", long. 76° 42' 46".

Ownership: Sonny Persad.

Utica—W46DY, Ch. 46, Martin Weiss. Phone: 805-896-7335.

Technical Facilities: 10-kw ERP, 98-ft. above ground, 1598-ft. above sea level, lat. 43° 08' 28", long. 75° 01' 49".

Ownership: Martin Weiss.

Utica—W51CV, Ch. 51, Trinity Broadcasting Network Inc. Phone: 714-832-2950. Fax: 714-730-0661.

Technical Facilities: 1000-w TPO, 8.3-kw ERP, 190-ft. above ground, 1398-ft. above sea level, lat. 43° 08' 39", long. 75° 10' 45".

Holds CP for change to 0.7-kw ERP, BDFCDTT-20060222ACH.

Transmitter: WIBQ-FM tower.

Began Operation: December 4, 1986.

Ownership: Trinity Broadcasting Network Inc.

Personnel: Paul Crouch, General Manager; Ben Miller, Chief Engineer; Rod Henke, Sales Manager.

Utica—W53AM, Ch. 53, Nexstar Broadcasting Inc. Phone: 972-373-8800.

Technical Facilities: 9.84-kw ERP, 218-ft. above ground, 1438-ft. above sea level, lat. 43° 08' 43", long. 75° 10' 35".

Holds CP for change to channel number 50, 0.056-kw ERP, BDISDTL-20060818ABF.

Multichannel TV Sound: Stereo and separate audio program.

Ownership: Nexstar Broadcasting Group Inc.

Personnel: Dan Gragg, General Manager; Allan Pullman, Chief Engineer; Wendy Gragg, General Sales Manager.

Utica—W59AU, Ch. 59, The Public Broadcasting Council of Central New York Inc.

Technical Facilities: 12.2-kw ERP, 427-ft. above ground, 1627-ft. above sea level, lat. 43° 08' 38", long. 75° 10' 40".

Ownership: The Public Broadcasting Council of Central New York Inc.

Utica—WVVC-LP, Ch. 40, Northeast Gospel Broadcasting Inc. Phone: 518-686-0975.

Technical Facilities: 1.5-kw ERP, 164-ft. above ground, 1585-ft. above sea level, lat. 43° 02' 15", long. 75° 11' 45".

Ownership: Northeast Gospel Broadcasting Inc.

Utica, etc.—WPNY-LP, Ch. 11, Nexstar Broadcasting Inc. Phone: 972-373-8800.

Technical Facilities: 0.094-kw ERP, 195-ft. above ground, 1415-ft. above sea level, lat. 43° 08' 43", long. 75° 10' 35".

Holds CP for change to 0.001-kw ERP, BDFCDTL-20060403AKO.

Ownership: Nexstar Broadcasting Group Inc.

Personnel: Wendy Gragg, General Sales Manager.

Victor—W26BZ, Ch. 26, WBGT LLC. Phone: 607-937-5000.

Technical Facilities: 0.036-kw ERP, lat. 42° 08' 36", long. 77° 39' 10".

Ownership: WBGT LLC.

Watertown—WBQZ-LP, Ch. 34, R. Anthony Dimarcantonio. Phone: 315-785-0869.

Technical Facilities: 100-w TPO, 0.88-kw ERP, 289-ft. above ground, 735-ft. above sea level, lat. 44° 03' 20", long. 75° 57' 15".

Transmitter: Rte. 12 & Perch Lake Rd.

Ownership: R. Anthony Dimarcantonio.

■**Watertown**—WLOT-LP, Ch. 46, NC Partners. Phone: 315-785-0869.

Technical Facilities: 19-kw ERP, 128-ft. above ground, 587-ft. above sea level, lat. 43° 58' 30", long. 75° 54' 34".

Transmitter: Rte. 12 & Perch Lake Rd.

Ownership: NC Partners.

■**Watertown**—WNYF-CA, Ch. 28, United Communications Corp.

Studio: 1222 Arsenal St, Watertown, NY 13601.

Technical Facilities: 100-w TPO, 2.61-kw ERP, 164-ft. above ground, 1165-ft. above sea level, lat. 43° 57' 23", long. 75° 50' 26".

Transmitter: State Rte. 126.

Ownership: United Communications Corp.

Personnel: Jim Corbin, General Manager; Don Rohr, Chief Engineer; Charlie Cusimano, Sales Manager.

Wellsville & Scio—W56AU, Ch. 56, Western New York Public Broadcasting Association.

Technical Facilities: 0.13-kw ERP, lat. 42° 06' 11", long. 77° 57' 23".

Ownership: Western New York Public Broadcasting Association.

White Lake—W51BN, Ch. 51, John Mester Income Family Trust. Phone: 718-859-5172. Fax: 718-469-0881.

Studio: PO Box 761, Kauneonga Lake, NY 12749.

Technical Facilities: 100-w TPO, 0.87-kw ERP, 108-ft. above ground, 1388-ft. above sea level, lat. 41° 41' 17", long. 74° 50' 04".

Holds CP for change to 15-kw ERP, 109-ft. above ground, 1429-ft. above sea level, BDFCDTL-20070607ADB.

Transmitter: County Hwy. 141, Kauneonga Lake.

Ownership: John Mester Income Family Trust.

Whitesville—W64AJ, Ch. 64, Western New York Public Broadcasting Association.

Technical Facilities: 0.01-kw ERP, lat. 42° 01' 41", long. 77° 46' 20".

Ownership: Western New York Public Broadcasting Association.

Willsboro—W67AR, Ch. 67, Mountain Lake Public Telecommunications Council. Phone: 518-563-9770.

Technical Facilities: 0.21-kw ERP, 16-ft. above ground, 1302-ft. above sea level, lat. 44° 24' 13", long. 74° 26' 03".

Holds CP for change to channel number 46, 0.182-kw ERP, 16-ft. above ground, 1301-ft. above sea level, BDISDTL-20060331AGF.

Ownership: Mountain Lake Public Telecommunications Council.

North Carolina

Andrews, etc.—W08BH, Ch. 8, WYFF Hearst-Argyle Television Inc. Phone: 919-839-0300.

Technical Facilities: 0.03-kw ERP, lat. 35° 15' 26", long. 83° 47' 43".

Ownership: Hearst-Argyle Television Inc.

Andrews, etc.—W59AD, Ch. 59, U. of North Carolina. Phone: 919-549-7000.

Technical Facilities: 36-kw ERP, 75-ft. above ground, 4787-ft. above sea level, lat. 35° 15' 26", long. 83° 47' 43".

Holds CP for change to channel number 49, 1-kw ERP, BDISDTT-20060802ASJ.

Ownership: U. of North Carolina.

Bat Cave, etc.—W05AU, Ch. 5, U. of North Carolina. Phone: 919-549-7000.

Apex—WACN-LP, Ch. 34, Word of God Fellowship Inc. Phones: 817-858-9955; 817-571-1229. Fax: 919-303-0109.

Studio: 11301 Penny Rd, Ste F, Apex, NC 27502.

Technical Facilities: 27.65-kw ERP, 984-ft. above ground, 1345-ft. above sea level, lat. 35° 40' 28", long. 78° 31' 40".

Ownership: Word of God Fellowship Inc.

Personnel: James Layton, President.

Asheville—W41BQ, Ch. 41, Three Angels Broadcasting Network Inc. Phone: 618-627-4651. Fax: 618-627-4155.

Technical Facilities: 1000-w TPO, 37.9-kw ERP, 98-ft. above ground, 3036-ft. above sea level, lat. 35° 36' 04", long. 82° 39' 06".

Transmitter: Spivey Mountain, 6.5-mi. NW of Asheville.

Ownership: Three Angels Broadcasting Network Inc.

Personnel: Moses Primo, Chief Engineer.

Asheville—W50CZ, Ch. 50, Trinity Christian Center of Santa Ana Inc. Phone: 714-832-2950.

Technical Facilities: 21-kw ERP, 46-ft. above ground, 3570-ft. above sea level, lat. 35° 35' 23", long. 82° 40' 26".

Ownership: Trinity Broadcasting Network Inc.

Asheville—WAEN-LP, Ch. 64, Word of God Fellowship Inc. Phone: 817-571-1229.

Technical Facilities: 50-kw ERP, 151-ft. above ground, 4393-ft. above sea level, lat. 35° 27' 40", long. 82° 21' 27".

Ownership: Word of God Fellowship Inc.

Asheville—WJJV-LP, Ch. 25, Carolina Christian Broadcasting Inc. Phone: 864-244-1616. Fax: 864-292-8481.

Technical Facilities: 11.9-kw ERP, 82-ft. above ground, 3481-ft. above sea level, lat. 35° 31' 39", long. 82° 29' 44".

Holds CP for change to channel number 32, 15-kw ERP, BDISDTL-20060403APL.

Transmitter: Spivey Mountain.

Ownership: Carolina Christian Broadcasting Co.

Asheville, etc.—W23BQ, Ch. 23, Carolina Christian Broadcasting Inc. Phone: 864-244-1616.

Technical Facilities: 38-kw ERP, 115-ft. above ground, 4475-ft. above sea level, lat. 35° 34' 04", long. 82° 23' 01".

Holds CP for change to 4-kw ERP, 115-ft. above ground, 4488-ft. above sea level, lat. 35° 34' 04", long. 82° 23' 02". BDFCDTL-20060403ARD.

Ownership: Carolina Christian Broadcasting Co.

Bakersville—W40CR-D, Ch. 40, U. of North Carolina. Phone: 919-549-7000.

Technical Facilities: 0.5-kw ERP, 108-ft. above ground, 4186-ft. above sea level, lat. 36° 02' 01", long. 82° 12' 08".

Ownership: U. of North Carolina.

Bakersville—W42AX, Ch. 42, U. of North Carolina. Phone: 919-549-7000.

Technical Facilities: 1.2-kw ERP, 108-ft. above ground, 4186-ft. above sea level, lat. 36° 02' 01", long. 82° 12' 08".

Ownership: U. of North Carolina.

Bat Cave, etc.—W05AU, Ch. 5, U. of North Carolina. Phone: 919-549-7000.

Technical Facilities: 0.015-kw ERP, 75-ft. above ground, 2956-ft. above sea level, lat. 35° 25' 49", long. 82° 15' 17".

Ownership: U. of North Carolina.

Bat Cave, etc.—W06AQ, Ch. 6, WLOS Licensee LLC. Phone: 202-663-8217.

Technical Facilities: 0.01-kw ERP, 2861-ft. above sea level, lat. 35° 25' 50", long. 82° 15' 18".

Ownership: Sinclair Broadcast Group Inc.

Bat Cave, etc.—W11AX, Ch. 11, WYFF Hearst-Argyle Television Inc. Phone: 919-839-0300.

Technical Facilities: 0.02-kw ERP, 2861-ft. above sea level, lat. 35° 25' 50", long. 82° 15' 18".

Began Operation: May 1, 1980.

Ownership: Hearst-Argyle Television Inc.

Bat Cave, etc.—W41DI-D, Ch. 41, U. of North Carolina. Phone: 919-549-7000.

Technical Facilities: 0.5-kw ERP, 75-ft. above ground, 2956-ft. above sea level, lat. 35° 25' 49", long. 82° 15' 17".

Ownership: U. of North Carolina.

Beaver Dam—W08BP, Ch. 8, Media General Communications Holdings LLC. Phone: 804-649-6000.

Technical Facilities: 0.1-kw ERP, 95-ft. above ground, 3494-ft. above sea level, lat. 35° 31' 39", long. 82° 29' 44".

Ownership: Media General Inc.

Biscoe—W30CR, Ch. 30, WCNC-TV Inc. Phone: 214-977-6606.

Technical Facilities: 13.8-kw ERP, 161-ft. above ground, 732-ft. above sea level, lat. 35° 16' 36", long. 79° 50' 02".

Began Operation: December 11, 1991.

Ownership: Belo Corp.

Black Mountain—W12AQ, Ch. 12, WLOS Licensee LLC. Phone: 202-663-8217.

Technical Facilities: 0.005-kw ERP, 2782-ft. above sea level, lat. 35° 37' 10", long. 82° 20' 36".

Ownership: Sinclair Broadcast Group Inc.

Black Mountain—W52BA, Ch. 52, U. of North Carolina. Phone: 919-549-7000.

Technical Facilities: 1.2-kw ERP, 167-ft. above ground, 4528-ft. above sea level, lat. 35° 34' 04", long. 82° 23' 02".

Holds CP for change to channel number 19, 0.5-kw ERP, BDISDTT-20060727AHF.

Ownership: U. of North Carolina.

Boone—W65DT, Ch. 65, U. of North Carolina. Phone: 919-549-7000.

Technical Facilities: 1.11-kw ERP, lat. 36° 11' 18", long. 81° 42' 45".

Holds CP for change to channel number 41, 0.5-kw ERP, 69-ft. above ground, 4715-ft. above sea level, lat. 36° 14' 07", long. 81° 42' 20". BDISDTT-20060727AHL.

Ownership: U. of North Carolina.

■**Boone**—WLNN-LP, Ch. 24, Carolina Rays LLC. Phone: 828-733-2409.

Technical Facilities: 6.5-kw ERP, 49-ft. above ground, 4833-ft. above sea level, lat. 36° 14' 10", long. 81° 42' 24".

Ownership: Terry Smith.

Brasstown, etc.—W05AP, Ch. 5, WLOS Licensee LLC. Phone: 202-663-8217.

Technical Facilities: 0.01-kw ERP, 2260-ft. above sea level, lat. 35° 05' 02", long. 84° 00' 58".

Ownership: Sinclair Broadcast Group Inc.

Brevard—W02AG, Ch. 2, Media General Communications Holdings LLC. Phone: 804-649-6000.

Technical Facilities: 0.06-kw ERP, 3839-ft. above sea level, lat. 35° 10' 40", long. 82° 40' 55".

Ownership: Media General Inc.

Brevard—W68DM, Ch. 68, U. of North Carolina. Phone: 919-549-7000.

Technical Facilities: 0.121-kw ERP, 148-ft. above ground, 3927-ft. above sea level, lat. 35° 10' 36", long. 82° 40' 54".

Holds CP for change to channel number 19, 0.5-kw ERP, BDISDTT-20060727AHH.

Ownership: U. of North Carolina.

Bryson City—W46AX, Ch. 46, U. of North Carolina. Phone: 919-549-7000.

Technical Facilities: 1.2-kw ERP, 108-ft. above ground, 3412-ft. above sea level, lat. 35° 24' 47", long. 83° 30' 02".

Holds CP for change to 0.5-kw ERP, BDFCDTT-20070517ADN.

Transmitter: Potato Hill, 3.5-mi. SW of Bryson City.

Ownership: U. of North Carolina.

Bryson City—W69CN, Ch. 69, Meredith Corp. Phone: 515-284-2166.

Technical Facilities: 4.3-kw ERP, 72-ft. above ground, 4567-ft. above sea level, lat. 35° 22' 53", long. 83° 24' 52".

Holds CP for change to channel number 40, 5-kw ERP, BDISDTT-20060317AED.

Ownership: Meredith Corp.

Bryson City, etc.—W05AR, Ch. 5, WYFF Hearst-Argyle Television Inc. Phone: 919-839-0300.

Technical Facilities: 0.18-kw ERP, 4564-ft. above sea level, lat. 35° 22' 53", long. 83° 24' 52".

Began Operation: April 9, 1981.

Ownership: Hearst-Argyle Television Inc.

Bryson City, etc.—W08AN, Ch. 8, WLOS Licensee LLC. Phone: 202-663-8217.

Technical Facilities: 0.01-kw ERP, 3343-ft. above sea level, lat. 35° 24' 47", long. 83° 30' 02".

Ownership: Sinclair Broadcast Group Inc.

Bryson City, etc.—W11AN, Ch. 11, Media General Communications Holdings LLC. Phone: 804-649-6000.

Technical Facilities: 0.145-kw ERP, 4616-ft. above sea level, lat. 35° 22' 53", long. 83° 24' 52".

Ownership: Media General Inc.

Burnsville—W02AT, Ch. 2, Media General Communications Holdings LLC. Phone: 804-649-6000.

Technical Facilities: 0.032-kw ERP, 4403-ft. above sea level, lat. 35° 56' 16", long. 82° 17' 48".

Ownership: Media General Inc.

Burnsville—W09AS, Ch. 9, WYFF Hearst-Argyle Television Inc. Phone: 919-839-0900.

Technical Facilities: 0.006-kw ERP, 4400-ft. above sea level, lat. 35° 56' 16", long. 82° 17' 48".

Ownership: Hearst-Argyle Television Inc.

Burnsville—W12AU, Ch. 12, WLOS Licensee LLC. Phone: 202-663-8217.

Technical Facilities: 0.005-kw ERP, 4363-ft. above sea level, lat. 35° 56' 15", long. 82° 17' 48".

Ownership: Sinclair Broadcast Group Inc.

Burnsville—W67DV, Ch. 67, U. of North Carolina. Phone: 919-549-7000.

Technical Facilities: 0.791-kw ERP, lat. 35° 56' 16", long. 82° 17' 48".

Holds CP for change to channel number 35, 0.5-kw ERP, 108-ft. above ground, 4445-ft. above sea level, BDISDTT-20060802ASG.

Ownership: U. of North Carolina.

Buxton—WHOB-LP, Ch. 50, EICB-TV East LLC. Phone: 972-291-3750.

Technical Facilities: 0.5-kw ERP, 77-ft. above ground, 80-ft. above sea level, lat. 35° 14' 55", long. 75° 36' 30".

Ownership: EICB-TV LLC.

Buxton—WPDZ-LP, Ch. 14, Ray H. Livesay. Phone: 252-985-3978.

Technical Facilities: 15-kw ERP, 266-ft. above ground, 287-ft. above sea level, lat. 35° 15' 49", long. 75° 31' 41".

Ownership: Ray H. Livesay.

Canton, etc.—W08AO, Ch. 8, Media General Communications Holdings LLC. Phone: 804-649-6000.

Technical Facilities: 0.009-kw ERP, 4534-ft. above sea level, lat. 35° 34' 34", long. 82° 54' 26".

Ownership: Media General Inc.

Canton, etc.—W11AU, Ch. 11, WYFF Hearst-Argyle Television Inc. Phone: 919-839-0300.

Technical Facilities: 0.2-kw ERP, lat. 35° 34' 06", long. 82° 54' 25".

Began Operation: April 25, 1983.

Ownership: Hearst-Argyle Television Inc.

Canton, etc.—W27AB, Ch. 27, U. of North Carolina. Phone: 919-549-7000.

Technical Facilities: 0.106-kw ERP, 4557-ft. above sea level, lat. 35° 34' 06", long. 82° 54' 25".

Ownership: U. of North Carolina.

Canton, etc.—W46EC-D, Ch. 46, U. of North Carolina. Phone: 919-549-7000.

Technical Facilities: 1-kw ERP, 66-ft. above ground, 4557-ft. above sea level, lat. 35° 34' 06", long. 82° 54' 25".

Began Operation: January 26, 2009.

Ownership: U. of North Carolina.

Cashiers—W24AU, Ch. 24, U. of North Carolina. Phone: 919-549-7000.

Technical Facilities: 1.2-kw ERP, 108-ft. above ground, 4790-ft. above sea level, lat. 35° 08' 06", long. 83° 05' 49".

Ownership: U. of North Carolina.

Cashiers—W42DF-D, Ch. 42, U. of North Carolina. Phone: 919-549-7000.

Technical Facilities: 0.6-kw ERP, 82-ft. above ground, 4764-ft. above sea level, lat. 35° 08' 06", long. 83° 05' 49".

Began Operation: February 10, 2009.

Ownership: U. of North Carolina.

Charlotte—W16CF, Ch. 16, Trinity Broadcasting Network Inc. Phone: 714-832-2950. Fax: 714-730-0661.

Technical Facilities: 44.8-kw ERP, 656-ft. above ground, 1301-ft. above sea level, lat. 35° 15' 07", long. 80° 41' 12".

Holds CP for change to channel number 45, 1-kw ERP, 656-ft. above ground, 1303-ft. above sea level, BDISDTT-20060327ACD.

Ownership: Trinity Broadcasting Network Inc.

■ **Charlotte**—W21CK-D, Ch. 21, Three Angels Broadcasting Network Inc. Phone: 618-627-4651.

Technical Facilities: 0.09-kw ERP, 476-ft. above ground, 1211-ft. above sea level, lat. 35° 11' 56.4", long. 80° 52' 35.9".

Ownership: Three Angels Broadcasting Network Inc.

Charlotte—W38CN, Ch. 38, Trinity Christian Center of Santa Ana Inc. Phone: 714-832-2950.

Technical Facilities: 1000-w TPO, 17.1-kw ERP, 499-ft. above ground, 1280-ft. above sea level, lat. 35° 20' 49", long. 81° 10' 15".

Transmitter: 0.9-mi. N of State Rte. 1804, Charlotte.

Ownership: Trinity Broadcasting Network Inc.

Personnel: Mark Fountain, Chief Engineer.

Charlotte—WDMC-LP, Ch. 25, Word of God Fellowship Inc. Phone: 817-571-1229. Fax: 817-571-7478.

Technical Facilities: 1000-w TPO, 21.912-kw ERP, 804-ft. above ground, 1440-ft. above sea level, lat. 35° 15' 06", long. 80° 41' 12".

Holds CP for change to 797-ft. above ground, 1444-ft. above sea level, BPTTL-20060323ABK.

Transmitter: Hood Rd., 10-mi. from downtown.

Ownership: Word of God Fellowship Inc.

■ **Charlotte**—WGTB-LP, Ch. 28, Victory Christian Center Inc. Phone: 704-393-1540. Fax: 704-393-1527.

Technical Facilities: 17.6-kw ERP, 1306-ft. above ground, 1952-ft. above sea level, lat. 35° 15' 07", long. 80° 41' 11".

Transmitter: 8058 Hood Rd.

Ownership: Victory Christian Center Inc.

Personnel: Terry H. Hammond, Sales Manager.

Cherokee—W05AF, Ch. 5, WLOS Licensee LLC. Phone: 202-663-8217.

Technical Facilities: 0.005-kw ERP, 2467-ft. above sea level, lat. 35° 28' 24", long. 83° 19' 28".

Ownership: Sinclair Broadcast Group Inc.

Cherokee, etc.—W08AT, Ch. 8, Media General Communications Holdings LLC. Phone: 804-649-6000.

Technical Facilities: 0.151-kw ERP, 2484-ft. above sea level, lat. 35° 28' 24", long. 83° 19' 22".

Ownership: Media General Inc.

Cherokee, etc.—W10AL, Ch. 10, WYFF Hearst-Argyle Television Inc. Phone: 919-839-0300.

Technical Facilities: 0.01-kw ERP, 3842-ft. above sea level, lat. 35° 29' 15", long. 83° 20' 02".

Ownership: Hearst-Argyle Television Inc.

Cullowhee—W23AF, Ch. 23, U. of North Carolina. Phone: 919-549-7000.

Technical Facilities: 1.12-kw ERP, 108-ft. above ground, 2657-ft. above sea level, lat. 35° 18' 12", long. 83° 10' 39".

Holds CP for change to channel number 47, 1-kw ERP, lat. 35° 18' 12", long. 83° 10' 40". BDISDTT-20070125AAV.

Ownership: U. of North Carolina.

■ **Durham**—W24CP, Ch. 24, Three Angels Broadcasting Network Inc. Phone: 618-627-4651. Fax: 618-627-4155.

Studio: 3391 Charley Good Rd, West Frankfort, IL 62896.

Technical Facilities: 1000-w TPO, 17.1-kw ERP, 344-ft. above ground, 705-ft. above sea level, lat. 36° 01' 03", long. 78° 52' 25".

Holds CP for change to 14.06-kw ERP, 407-ft. above ground, 764-ft. above sea level, lat. 36° 01' 03", long. 78° 52' 21". BDFCDTL-20081211ADV.

Transmitter: 0.4-mi. W of Intersection of SR 1709 & 1827.

Began Operation: January 10, 1994.

Ownership: Three Angels Broadcasting Network Inc.

Personnel: Moses Primo, Chief Engineer.

Durham—WTNC-LP, Ch. 26, WUVC License Partnership GP. Phone: 310-556-7600.

Technical Facilities: 150-kw ERP, 436-ft. above ground, 886-ft. above sea level, lat. 36° 03' 33", long. 78° 57' 14".

Ownership: Univision Communications Inc.

■ **Durham, etc.**—WUBX-CA, Ch. 13, L4 Media Group LLC. Phone: 321-729-8451.

Studio: 1003 Communications Dr, Durham, NC 27704.

Technical Facilities: 10-w TPO, 0.105-kw ERP, 256-ft. above ground, 650-ft. above sea level, lat. 36° 03' 58", long. 78° 53' 26".

Transmitter: 1003 Communications Dr.

Ownership: L4 Media Group LLC.

Personnel: Warren Reeves, Consulting Engineer; Liz Kiley, Broadcast Vice President; Amy Brown, Broadcast Operations Director.

Ela, etc.—W03AK, Ch. 3, WYFF Hearst-Argyle Television Inc. Phone: 919-839-0300.

Technical Facilities: 0.01-kw ERP, lat. 35° 22' 53", long. 83° 24' 52".

Ownership: Hearst-Argyle Television Inc.

Elizabeth City—W18BB, Ch. 18, Elizabeth City State U. Phone: 919-335-3690. Fax: 919-335-3770.

Technical Facilities: 880-w TPO, 19-kw ERP, 167-ft. above ground, lat. 36° 16' 55", long. 76° 12' 44".

Transmitter: Hollowell Dr., across from Williams Hill, East Carolina State U.

Ownership: Elizabeth City State U.

Personnel: Elvin Jenkins, General Manager; Ben Shaner, Chief Engineer.

Fayetteville—W45CO, Ch. 45, Trinity Broadcasting Network Inc. Phone: 714-832-2950. Fax: 714-730-0661.

Technical Facilities: 41.5-kw ERP, 233-ft. above ground, 433-ft. above sea level, lat. 35° 05' 08", long. 78° 54' 25".

Holds CP for change to channel number 34, 15-kw ERP, BDISDTT-20061010AGB.

Ownership: Trinity Broadcasting Network Inc.

Franklin—W06AJ, Ch. 6, WYFF Hearst-Argyle Television Inc. Phone: 919-839-0300.

Technical Facilities: 0.47-kw ERP, lat. 35° 10' 22", long. 83° 34' 53".

Began Operation: February 2, 1982.

Ownership: Hearst-Argyle Television Inc.

Franklin—W09AG, Ch. 9, Media General Communications Holdings LLC. Phone: 804-649-6000.

Technical Facilities: 0.467-kw ERP, 5410-ft. above sea level, lat. 35° 10' 22", long. 83° 34' 53".

Ownership: Media General Inc.

Franklin—W11AJ, Ch. 11, WLOS Licensee LLC. Phone: 202-663-8217.

Technical Facilities: 0.24-kw ERP, 5499-ft. above sea level, lat. 35° 10' 22", long. 83° 34' 53".

Ownership: Sinclair Broadcast Group Inc.

Franklin—W19DB-D, Ch. 19, U. of North Carolina. Phone: 919-549-7000.

Technical Facilities: 0.5-kw ERP, 108-ft. above ground, 5538-ft. above sea level, lat. 35° 10' 23", long. 83° 34' 52".

Ownership: U. of North Carolina.

Franklin—W28AN, Ch. 28, U. of North Carolina. Phone: 919-549-7000. Fax: 919-549-7201.

Technical Facilities: 1.05-kw ERP, 108-ft. above ground, 5538-ft. above sea level, lat. 35° 10' 23", long. 83° 34' 52".

Transmitter: Wine Spring Bald.

Ownership: U. of North Carolina.

Franklin, etc.—W60DA, Ch. 60, U. of North Carolina. Phone: 919-549-7000.

Technical Facilities: 20.6-kw ERP, 210-ft. above ground, 5151-ft. above sea level, lat. 35° 19' 40", long. 83° 20' 11".

Holds CP for change to channel number 31, 0.5-kw ERP, BDISDTT-20070910ADF.

Ownership: U. of North Carolina.

Goldsboro—W63CW, Ch. 63, Trinity Broadcasting Network Inc. Phone: 714-832-2950. Fax: 714-730-0661.

Technical Facilities: 17.2-kw ERP, 312-ft. above ground, 381-ft. above sea level, lat. 35° 21' 53", long. 78° 01' 55".

Holds CP for change to channel number 45, 15-kw ERP, 312-ft. above ground, 382-ft. above sea level, BDISDTT-20071128ANQ.

Transmitter: WHFL-LP tower.

Ownership: Trinity Broadcasting Network Inc.

■ **Goldsboro**—WHFL-LP, Ch. 43, Free Life Ministries Inc. Phone: 919-736-7729. Fax: 919-736-9042.

Technical Facilities: 100-kw ERP, 440-ft. above ground, 510-ft. above sea level, lat. 35° 21' 53", long. 78° 01' 55".

Ownership: Free Life Ministries Inc.

Personnel: Terry Johnson, General Manager.

Greenville—W44CN, Ch. 44, Trinity Broadcasting Network. Phone: 714-832-2950. Fax: 714-730-0661.

Technical Facilities: 35.2-kw ERP, 361-ft. above ground, 440-ft. above sea level, lat. 35° 36' 29", long. 77° 28' 05".

Transmitter: WRQR Tower, 0.9-mi. ENE of State Rtes. 1210 & 1200 intersection.

Ownership: Trinity Broadcasting Network Inc.

Hayesville—W29DE-D, Ch. 29, U. of North Carolina. Phone: 919-549-7000.

Technical Facilities: 0.6-kw ERP, 108-ft. above ground, 3058-ft. above sea level, lat. 34° 59' 57", long. 83° 51' 34".

Began Operation: February 10, 2009.

Ownership: U. of North Carolina.

Hayesville—W42AT, Ch. 42, U. of North Carolina. Phone: 919-549-7000.

Technical Facilities: 0.107-kw ERP, lat. 34° 59' 57", long. 83° 51' 34".

Ownership: U. of North Carolina.

Hendersonville—W31AZ, Ch. 31, Carolina Christian Broadcasting Inc. Phone: 864-244-1616.

Technical Facilities: 22.6-kw ERP, 92-ft. above ground, 3012-ft. above sea level, lat. 35° 14' 34", long. 82° 26' 08".

Holds CP for change to 4-kw ERP, BDFCDTL-20060403AQZ.

Ownership: Carolina Christian Broadcasting Co.

Highlands—W27BD, Ch. 27, U. of North Carolina. Phone: 919-549-7000.

Technical Facilities: 0.91-kw ERP, 36-ft. above ground, 4275-ft. above sea level, lat. 35° 02' 21", long. 83° 13' 04".

Ownership: U. of North Carolina.

Highlands—W35CK-D, Ch. 35, U. of North Carolina. Phone: 919-549-7000.

Technical Facilities: 0.6-kw ERP, 36-ft. above ground, 4272-ft. above sea level, lat. 35° 02' 21", long. 83° 13' 04".

Ownership: U. of North Carolina.

Hot Springs—W12CI, Ch. 12, WLOS Licensee LLC. Phone: 202-663-8217.

Technical Facilities: 0.01-kw ERP, 56-ft. above ground, 3724-ft. above sea level, lat. 35° 55' 36", long. 82° 48' 21".

Ownership: Sinclair Broadcast Group Inc.

Jefferson—W21CR-D, Ch. 21, U. of North Carolina. Phone: 919-549-7000.

Technical Facilities: 0.175-kw ERP, 108-ft. above ground, 4800-ft. above sea level, lat. 36° 27' 40", long. 81° 29' 19".

Began Operation: February 12, 2009.

Ownership: U. of North Carolina.

Jefferson—W25AY, Ch. 25, U. of North Carolina. Phone: 919-549-7000.

Technical Facilities: 1.2-kw ERP, 108-ft. above ground, 4800-ft. above sea level, lat. 36° 27' 40", long. 81° 29' 19".

Ownership: U. of North Carolina.

Lake Lure—W27AX, Ch. 27, U. of North Carolina. Phone: 919-549-7000.

Technical Facilities: 1.2-kw ERP, 108-ft. above ground, 2989-ft. above sea level, lat. 35° 25' 49", long. 82° 15' 17".

Ownership: U. of North Carolina.

Lake Lure—W51EE-D, Ch. 51, U. of North Carolina. Phone: 919-549-7000.

Technical Facilities: 0.5-kw ERP, 157-ft. above ground, 2113-ft. above sea level, lat. 35° 40' 16.9", long. 82° 00' 19.1".

Ownership: U. of North Carolina.

■ **Lenoir**—WTBL-LP, Ch. 49, Catawba Broadcasting LLC. Phone: 301-564-0490.

Technical Facilities: 38.3-kw ERP, 90-ft. above ground, 2226-ft. above sea level, lat. 35° 54' 25", long. 81° 29' 23".

Ownership: Andrew Marriott.

Lilesville & Wadesboro—W24AY, Ch. 24, WCNC-TV Inc. Phone: 214-977-6606.

Technical Facilities: 26-kw ERP, 180-ft. above ground, 705-ft. above sea level, lat. 35° 01' 09", long. 79° 56' 50".

Ownership: Belo Corp.

Lumberton—W19CA, Ch. 19, Pacific Media Corp. Phone: 843-629-1431.

Technical Facilities: 17.4-kw ERP, lat. 34° 53' 05", long. 79° 04' 31".

Transmitter: WFAY(TV) tower, 0.3-mi. SW of State Rds. 20 & 71 intersection, near Lumber Bridge.

Ownership: Pacific Media Corp.

Lumberton—W35CC, Ch. 35, Trinity Broadcasting Network Inc. Phone: 714-832-2950. Fax: 714-730-0661.

Technical Facilities: 27-kw ERP, 476-ft. above ground, 620-ft. above sea level, lat. 34° 40' 27", long. 79° 02' 21".

Holds CP for change to 8-kw ERP, BDFCDTT-20070309ADN.

Ownership: Trinity Broadcasting Network Inc.

Lumberton-Pembroke—WLPS-LD, Ch. 14, Billy Ray Locklear Evangelistic Assn. Phone: 910-521-3101.

Technical Facilities: 15-kw ERP, 360-ft. above ground, 518-ft. above sea level, lat. 34° 42' 01", long. 79° 06' 32".

Began Operation: February 17, 2009.

Ownership: Billy Ray Locklear.

■ **Lumberton-Pembroke**—WLPS-LP, Ch. 7, Billy Ray Locklear Evangelistic Assn. Phone: 910-521-3101.

Studio: State Rd. 1421, Lumberton, NC 28358.

Technical Facilities: 3-kw ERP, 98-ft. above ground, 5814-ft. above sea level, lat. 36° 17' 14", long. 118° 50' 17".

Transmitter: 1521 Oak Grove Church Rd.

Ownership: Billy Ray Locklear.

Personnel: Billy Ray Locklear, General Manager.

Maggie Valley, etc.—W06AP, Ch. 6, WLOS Licensee LLC. Phone: 202-663-8217.

Technical Facilities: 0.01-kw ERP, 4153-ft. above sea level, lat. 35° 31' 04", long. 83° 06' 56".

Ownership: Sinclair Broadcast Group Inc.

Manteo—K59ID, Ch. 59, Lawrence F. Loesch. Phone: 919-839-0300.

Technical Facilities: 10.8-kw ERP, 230-ft. above ground, 234-ft. above sea level, lat. 35° 51' 52", long. 75° 39' 01".

Ownership: Lawrence F. Loesch.

Manteo—W17CT, Ch. 17, Lawrence F. Loesch. Phone: 919-839-0300.

Technical Facilities: 10.8-kw ERP, 230-ft. above ground, 233-ft. above sea level, lat. 35° 51' 52", long. 75° 39' 01".

Ownership: Lawrence F. Loesch.

Manteo—W28CJ, Ch. 28, Lawrence F. Loesch.

Technical Facilities: 10.8-kw ERP, 253-ft. above ground, 256-ft. above sea level, lat. 35° 51' 52", long. 75° 39' 01".

Ownership: Lawrence F. Loesch.

Manteo—W45CL, Ch. 45, Lawrence F. Loesch. Phone: 919-839-0300.

Technical Facilities: 10.8-kw ERP, 230-ft. above ground, 233-ft. above sea level, lat. 35° 51' 52", long. 75° 39' 01".

Ownership: Lawrence F. Loesch.

Manteo—W51DF, Ch. 51, Lawrence F. Loesch.

Technical Facilities: 10.8-kw ERP, 230-ft. above ground, 233-ft. above sea level, lat. 35° 51' 52", long. 75° 39' 01".

Ownership: Lawrence F. Loesch.

Manteo—W56EC, Ch. 56, Lawrence F. Loesch. Phone: 919-839-0300.

Technical Facilities: 10.8-kw ERP, 230-ft. above ground, 233-ft. above sea level, lat. 35° 51' 52", long. 75° 39' 01".

Ownership: Lawrence F. Loesch.

Marion—W06AI, Ch. 6, WSOC Television Inc. Phone: 704-335-4700.

Technical Facilities: 0.003-kw ERP, 1949-ft. above sea level, lat. 35° 40' 15", long. 82° 00' 11".

Ownership: Cox Enterprises Inc.

Marion, etc.—W08BJ, Ch. 8, Media General Communications Holdings LLC. Phone: 804-649-6000.

Technical Facilities: 0.157-kw ERP, 2034-ft. above sea level, lat. 35° 40' 15", long. 82° 00' 20".

Ownership: Media General Inc.

Marion, etc.—W10AP, Ch. 10, WLOS Licensee LLC. Phone: 202-663-6217.

Technical Facilities: 0.06-kw ERP, 2024-ft. above sea level, lat. 35° 40' 10", long. 82° 00' 24".

Ownership: Sinclair Broadcast Group Inc.

Mars Hill—W02AH, Ch. 2, Media General Communications Holdings LLC. Phone: 804-649-6000.

Technical Facilities: 0.051-kw ERP, 2943-ft. above sea level, lat. 35° 51' 04", long. 82° 33' 19".

Ownership: Media General Inc.

Marshall—W08AX, Ch. 8, Media General Communications Holdings LLC. Phone: 804-649-6000.

Technical Facilities: 0.012-kw ERP, 2388-ft. above sea level, lat. 35° 48' 15", long. 82° 41' 53".

Ownership: Media General Inc.

Montreat, etc.—W10AD, Ch. 10, Media General Communications Holdings LLC. Phone: 804-649-6000.

Technical Facilities: 0.142-kw ERP, 3333-ft. above sea level, lat. 35° 37' 44", long. 82° 20' 46".

Ownership: Media General Inc.

Morehead City—W05BI, Ch. 5, Media General Communications Holdings LLC. Phone: 804-649-6000.

Technical Facilities: 0.11-kw ERP, 207-ft. above ground, 217-ft. above sea level, lat. 34° 43' 14", long. 76° 42' 53".

Ownership: Media General Inc.

Murphy—W31AN, Ch. 31, U. of North Carolina. Phones: 919-549-7000; 800-906-5050. Fax: 919-549-7201.

Studio: PO Box 14900, Research Triangle Park, NC 27709-4900.

Technical Facilities: 100-w TPO, 1.1-kw ERP, 100-ft. above ground, lat. 35° 05' 02", long. 84° 00' 58".

Holds CP for change to 0.5-kw ERP, 108-ft. above ground, 2221-ft. above sea level, BDFCDTT-20060727AFW.

Transmitter: Will Scott Mountain.

Ownership: U. of North Carolina.

Oteen/Warren—W06AL, Ch. 6, WLOS Licensee LLC. Phone: 202-663-8217.

Technical Facilities: 0.02-kw ERP, 2769-ft. above sea level, lat. 35° 35' 49", long. 82° 27' 04".

Ownership: Sinclair Broadcast Group Inc.

■ **Pinehurst**—WYBE-CA, Ch. 44, Multimedia Network of North Carolina Inc.

Technical Facilities: 100-w TPO, 0.826-kw ERP, 200-ft. above ground, 679-ft. above sea level, lat. 35° 09' 57", long. 79° 25' 12".

Transmitter: Short & Long Sts. intersection, Southern Pines, Pinehurst.

Ownership: Multimedia Network of North Carolina Inc.

Raleigh—W58CD, Ch. 58, Ventana Television Inc. Phone: 727-872-4210.

Technical Facilities: 2000-w TPO, 46.3-kw ERP, 406-ft. above ground, 751-ft. above sea level, lat. 35° 46' 43", long. 78° 38' 23".

Holds CP for change to channel number 22, 0.05-kw ERP, 407-ft. above ground, 751-ft. above sea level, BDISTTL-20060817AEP.

Transmitter: 150 Fayetteville St. Mall.

Began Operation: April 20, 1993.

Ownership: Ventana Television Inc.

Personnel: John Skelnik, General Manager & Chief Engineer.

Raleigh—W64CN, Ch. 64, Trinity Broadcasting Network Inc. Phone: 714-832-2950. Fax: 714-730-0661.

Technical Facilities: 27-kw ERP, 499-ft. above ground, 825-ft. above sea level, lat. 35° 40' 34", long. 78° 32' 08".

Holds CP for change to channel number 12, 0.3-kw ERP, 499-ft. above ground, 822-ft. above sea level, BDISDTT-20060328AKE.

Ownership: Trinity Broadcasting Network Inc.

Personnel: Paul Crouch, General Manager; Ben Miller, Chief Engineer; Rod Henke, Sales Manager.

Raleigh—W68BK, Ch. 68, St. Augustine's College. Phone: 919-516-4750. Fax: 919-516-4425.

Studio: 1315 Oakwood Ave., Raleigh, NC 27610.

Technical Facilities: 3.02-kw ERP, 279-ft. above ground, 600-ft. above sea level, lat. 35° 47' 28", long. 78° 37' 10".

Ownership: St. Augustine's College.

Personnel: Carol Jones-Hunter, General Manager; James Davis, Chief Engineer; Benny Moore, Sales Manager.

■ **Raleigh**—WBXU-CA, Ch. 13, L4 Media Group LLC. Phone: 321-729-8451.

Studio: 1003 Communications Dr, Durham, NC 27704.

Technical Facilities: 10-w TPO, 0.209-kw ERP, 374-ft. above ground, 846-ft. above sea level, lat. 35° 47' 15", long. 78° 43' 39".

Transmitter: 5721 Chapel Hill Rd., Raleigh.

Multichannel TV Sound: Stereo only.

Ownership: L4 Media Group LLC.

Personnel: Liz Kiley, Broadcast Vice President; Warren Reeves, Consulting Engineer; Amy Brown, Broadcast Operations Director.

Raleigh—WWIW-LP, Ch. 66, Word of God Fellowship Inc. Phone: 817-571-1229.

Technical Facilities: 16.7-kw ERP, 417-ft. above ground, 741-ft. above sea level, lat. 35° 46' 27", long. 78° 38' 25".

Holds CP for change to channel number 21, 15-kw ERP, BDCCDTL-20081215AAQ.

Began Operation: January 13, 1997.

Ownership: Word of God Fellowship Inc.

■ **Raleigh**—WZGS-CA, Ch. 44, ZGS Raleigh Inc. Phone: 703-622-6161.

Studio: 333 Fayetteville St, Ste 512, Raleigh, NC 27602.

Technical Facilities: 138-kw ERP, 345-ft. above ground, 815-ft. above sea level, lat. 35° 47' 13.2", long. 78° 43' 37.9".

Began Operation: January 26, 1994.

Ownership: ZGS Broadcasting Holdings Inc.

Personnel: Oscar Eatmon, General Sales Manager.

Reidsville—WGSR-LP, Ch. 39, Starnews Corp. Phones: 276-656-3900; 336-344-5539.

Studio: 115 Gilmer St, Reidsville, NC 27320.

Technical Facilities: 7-kw ERP, 134-ft. above ground, 964-ft. above sea level, lat. 36° 21' 36", long. 79° 39' 51".

Holds CP for change to channel number 47, 15-kw ERP, 479-ft. above ground, 1217-ft. above sea level, lat. 36° 14' 53.5", long. 79° 39' 20.9". BDISDTL-20071212ABC.

Began Operation: August 3, 1989.

Ownership: Star News Corp.

Personnel: Daniel Falinski, General Manager; Ed Kasovic, Chief Engineer.

■ **Roanoke Rapids**—WNVN-LP, Ch. 20, First Media Radio Inc. Phone: 252-538-0020. Fax: 252-538-0378.

Studio: 3 E 1st St, Weldon, NC 27890.

Technical Facilities: 1000-w TPO, 8.9-kw ERP, 309-ft. above ground, 595-ft. above sea level, lat. 36° 30' 12", long. 77° 44' 47".

Transmitter: Hwy. 46, 1.9-mi. E of Vultare.

Ownership: First Media Radio LLC.

Personnel: Al Haskins, General Manager; Frank White, Chief Engineer.

Robbinsville, etc.—W11AQ, Ch. 11, WLOS Licensee LLC. Phone: 202-663-8217.

Technical Facilities: 0.01-kw ERP, 4793-ft. above sea level, lat. 35° 15' 27", long. 83° 47' 48".

Ownership: Sinclair Broadcast Group Inc.

Rocky Mount—W45CN, Ch. 45, Trinity Broadcasting Network Inc. Phone: 814-832-2950. Fax: 814-730-0661.

Technical Facilities: 8.3-kw ERP, 331-ft. above ground, 431-ft. above sea level, lat. 35° 54' 44", long. 77° 50' 06".

Holds CP for change to 15-kw ERP, BDFCDTT-20060330ACW.

Ownership: Trinity Broadcasting Network Inc.

Rocky Mount—WHIG-LP, Ch. 33, Action Community Television Broadcasting Network Inc. Phone: 252-446-8857.

Technical Facilities: 9.8-kw ERP, 85-ft. above ground, 180-ft. above sea level, lat. 35° 57' 07", long. 77° 49' 12".

Holds CP for change to 5.3-kw ERP, 489-ft. above ground, 623-ft. above sea level, lat. 35° 54' 05", long. 77° 46' 50". BPTTL-20061012ABA.

Ownership: Action Community Television Broadcasting Network Inc.

Sanford—W67CD, Ch. 67, Central Carolina Broadcasting Corp. Inc. Phone: 919-776-4646. Fax: 919-776-0125.

Studio: PO Box 4646, 204 St. Clair Ct, Sanford, NC 27331.

Technical Facilities: 1000-w TPO, 10.1-kw ERP, 187-ft. above ground, 600-ft. above sea level, lat. 35° 23' 53", long. 79° 11' 36".

Transmitter: 0.12-mi. W of the intersection of State Rtes. 1156 & 1160.

Ownership: Central Carolina Broadcasting Corp. Inc.

Personnel: 1 1 1; 2 2 2; Mark D. Lilley, President & Chief Executive Officer; Pete Saunders, Marketing Director.

■ **Sanford**—WBFT-CA, Ch. 46, San-Lee Community Broadcasting Inc.

Technical Facilities: 100-w TPO, 0.93-kw ERP, 164-ft. above ground, 559-ft. above sea level, lat. 35° 28' 46", long. 79° 10' 43".

Transmitter: 204 St. Clair Court.

Ownership: San-Lee Community Broadcasting Inc.

Personnel: Burke Buchanan, General Manager; Gordon Steve, Sales Manager.

Sapphire Valley, etc.—W06AN, Ch. 6, WLOS Licensee LLC. Phone: 202-663-8217.

Technical Facilities: 0.163-kw ERP, 4806-ft. above sea level, lat. 35° 07' 54", long. 82° 59' 33".

Ownership: Sinclair Broadcast Group Inc.

Shallotte—W47CK, Ch. 47, Paradigm Broadcasting Group LLC. Phone: 803-419-6363.

Technical Facilities: 1000-w TPO, 6.8-kw ERP, 476-ft. above ground, 526-ft. above sea level, lat. 34° 02' 35", long. 78° 19' 56".

Ownership: Paradigm Broadcasting Group LLC.

■ **Smithfield/Selma**—WARZ-LP, Ch. 34, Waters & Brock Communications Inc. Phone: 919-965-5328.

Technical Facilities: 70-kw ERP, 375-ft. above ground, 529-ft. above sea level, lat. 35° 31' 46", long. 78° 18' 07".

Holds CP for change to 0.35-kw ERP, BDFCDTA-20080320ABZ.

Ownership: Waters & Brock Communications Inc.

Personnel: Gerald Waters, General Manager, Sales Manager.

Sparta—W35AD, Ch. 35, U. of North Carolina. Phone: 919-549-7000.

Technical Facilities: 1.09-kw ERP, lat. 36° 31' 13", long. 81° 07' 27".

Holds CP for change to channel number 50, 0.6-kw ERP, 102-ft. above ground, 3648-ft. above sea level, BDISDTT-20061222ABE.

Ownership: U. of North Carolina.

Spruce Pine—W06AD, Ch. 6, WLOS Licensee LLC. Phone: 202-663-8217.

Technical Facilities: 0.006-kw ERP, 3100-ft. above sea level, lat. 35° 54' 36", long. 82° 06' 03".

Ownership: Sinclair Broadcast Group Inc.

Spruce Pine—W10AK, Ch. 10, WYFF Hearst-Argyle Television Inc. Phone: 919-839-0300.

Technical Facilities: 0.01-kw ERP, lat. 35° 52' 49", long. 82° 06' 15".

Ownership: Hearst-Argyle Television Inc.

Spruce Pine—W31DI-D, Ch. 31, U. of North Carolina. Phone: 919-549-7000.

Technical Facilities: 0.5-kw ERP, 108-ft. above ground, 4278-ft. above sea level, lat. 35° 52' 47", long. 82° 06' 17".

Ownership: U. of North Carolina.

Spruce Pine, etc.—W08BF, Ch. 8, Media General Communications Holdings LLC. Phone: 804-649-6000.

Technical Facilities: 0.116-kw ERP, 4275-ft. above sea level, lat. 35° 52' 48", long. 82° 06' 15".

Ownership: Media General Inc.

Statesville—W21CI, Ch. 21, Trinity Broadcasting Network Inc. Phone: 714-832-2950. Fax: 714-730-0661.

Technical Facilities: 9-kw ERP, 266-ft. above ground, 1176-ft. above sea level, lat. 35° 48' 15", long. 80° 53' 30".

Transmitter: Existing WSIC(AM) tower, near corner of Radio Rd & Virginia Ave.

Ownership: Trinity Broadcasting Network Inc.

Sylva, etc.—W02AF, Ch. 2, WYFF Hearst-Argyle Television Inc. Phone: 919-839-0300.

Technical Facilities: 0.056-kw ERP, 2963-ft. above sea level, lat. 35° 22' 04", long. 83° 13' 17".

Ownership: Hearst-Argyle Television Inc.

Sylva, etc.—W05AE, Ch. 5, WLOS Licensee LLC. Phone: 202-663-8217.

Technical Facilities: 0.19-kw ERP, 4153-ft. above sea level, lat. 35° 24' 49", long. 83° 13' 31".

Ownership: Sinclair Broadcast Group Inc.

Sylva, etc.—W09AF, Ch. 9, Media General Communications Holdings LLC. Phone: 804-649-6000.

Technical Facilities: 0.105-kw ERP, 3005-ft. above sea level, lat. 35° 22' 03", long. 83° 13' 18".

Ownership: Media General Inc.

Tarboro—WNCR-LP, Ch. 41, On the Map Inc. Phone: 919-880-4289.

Technical Facilities: 21.6-kw ERP, 465-ft. above ground, 600-ft. above sea level, lat. 35° 54' 10", long. 77° 46' 57".

Ownership: On the Map Inc.

Tryon—W19CR, Ch. 19, U. of North Carolina. Phone: 919-549-7000. Fax: 919-549-7179.

Technical Facilities: 1.23-kw ERP, 115-ft. above ground, 3350-ft. above sea level, lat. 35° 15' 58", long. 82° 14' 40".

Holds CP for change to 0.2-kw ERP, BDFCDTT-20060727AHI.

Ownership: U. of North Carolina.

Tryon & Columbus—W11AH, Ch. 11, WYFF Hearst-Argyle Television Inc. Phone: 919-839-0300.

Technical Facilities: 0.01-kw ERP, lat. 35° 15' 44", long. 82° 14' 28".

Ownership: Hearst-Argyle Television Inc.

Tryon, etc.—W05AC, Ch. 5, WLOS Licensee LLC. Phone: 410-568-1500.

Technical Facilities: 0.07-kw ERP, 3264-ft. above sea level, lat. 35° 15' 44", long. 82° 14' 28".

Ownership: Sinclair Broadcast Group Inc.

Wanchese—WMTO-LP, Ch. 6, Ray H. Livesay. Phone: 919-303-5465.

Technical Facilities: 0.6-kw ERP, 384-ft. above ground, 390-ft. above sea level, lat. 35° 50' 48", long. 75° 37' 19".

Ownership: Ray H. Livesay.

Waynesville—W09AD, Ch. 9, Media General Communications Holdings LLC. Phone: 804-649-6000.

Technical Facilities: 0.093-kw ERP, 4134-ft. above sea level, lat. 35° 29' 05", long. 83° 02' 11".

Ownership: Media General Inc.

Waynesville, etc.—W12AR, Ch. 12, WLOS Licensee LLC. Phone: 410-568-1500.

Technical Facilities: 0.06-kw ERP, 4134-ft. above sea level, lat. 35° 29' 08", long. 83° 02' 10".

Ownership: Sinclair Broadcast Group Inc.

Weaverville—W09AR, Ch. 9, Media General Communications Holdings LLC. Phone: 804-649-6000.

Technical Facilities: 0.105-kw ERP, 3045-ft. above sea level, lat. 35° 39' 56", long. 82° 34' 24".

Ownership: Media General Inc.

West Asheville—W14AS, Ch. 14, Meredith Corp. Phone: 512-284-2166.

Technical Facilities: 17.7-kw ERP, lat. 35° 35' 00", long. 82° 32' 49".

Ownership: Meredith Corp.

Williamston—WFTB-LP, Ch. 55, Free Temple Ministries. Phones: 252-794-9453; 703-437-8400. Fax: 252-794-3466.

Technical Facilities: 1000-w TPO, 15-kw ERP, 1014-ft. above ground, lat. 35° 53' 47", long. 76° 58' 58".

Ownership: Free Temple Ministries Inc.

Personnel: Timothy L. Baylor, General Manager; Terry C. Baylor, Chief Engineer.

Wilmington—W51CW-D, Ch. 51, Trinity Broadcasting Network Inc. Phone: 714-832-2950. Fax: 714-730-0661.

Technical Facilities: 7-kw ERP, 276-ft. above ground, 285-ft. above sea level, lat. 34° 10' 15", long. 77° 56' 57".

Ownership: Trinity Broadcasting Network Inc.

Wilmington—WILM-LD, Ch. 40, WILM Inc. Phone: 919-798-0000.

Technical Facilities: 15-kw ERP, 848-ft. above ground, 877-ft. above sea level, lat. 34° 19' 16", long. 78° 13' 43".

Ownership: Capitol Broadcasting Co. Inc.

Zionville—W59AK, Ch. 59, U. of North Carolina. Phone: 919-549-7000.

Technical Facilities: 0.496-kw ERP, lat. 36° 18' 09", long. 81° 43' 20".

Holds CP for change to channel number 30, 0.6-kw ERP, 187-ft. above ground, 5364-ft. above sea level, BDISDTT-20061222ABD.

Ownership: U. of North Carolina.

North Dakota

Belcourt—K53DH, Ch. 53, Schindler Community TV Services. Phone: 701-477-5869.

Technical Facilities: 20-w TPO, 0.15-kw ERP, 246-ft. above ground, 2497-ft. above sea level, lat. 48° 51' 40", long. 99° 52' 45".

Transmitter: 1-mi. SE of Great Walker Lake School, Turtle Mountain Indian Reservation.

Multichannel TV Sound: Separate audio progam.

Ownership: Schindler Community TV Services.

Personnel: Fred Schindler, General Manager.

Belcourt—K55FH, Ch. 55, Schindler Community TV Services. Phone: 701-477-5869.

Technical Facilities: 20-w TPO, 0.16-kw ERP, 236-ft. above ground, 2487-ft. above sea level, lat. 48° 51' 40", long. 99° 52' 45".

Transmitter: 1-mi. SE of Great Walker Lake School, Turtle Mountain Indian Reservation.

Multichannel TV Sound: Separate audio progam.

Ownership: Schindler Community TV Services.

Personnel: Fred Schindler, General Manager.

Belcourt—K57EY, Ch. 57, Schindler Community TV Services. Phone: 701-477-5869.

Technical Facilities: 20-w TPO, 0.158-kw ERP, 246-ft. above ground, 2497-ft. above sea level, lat. 48° 51' 40", long. 99° 52' 45".

Transmitter: 1-mi. SE of Great Walker Lake School, Turtle Mountain Indian Reservation.

Multichannel TV Sound: Separate audio progam.

Ownership: Schindler Community TV Services.

Personnel: Fred Schindler, General Manager.

Belcourt—K59DM, Ch. 59, Schindler Community TV Services. Phone: 701-477-5869.

Technical Facilities: 20-w TPO, 0.163-kw ERP, 236-ft. above ground, 2487-ft. above sea level, lat. 48° 51' 40", long. 99° 52' 45".

Transmitter: 1-mi. SE of Great Walker Lake School, Turtle Mountain Indian Reservation.

Ownership: Schindler Community TV Services.

Personnel: Fred Schindler Jr., General Manager.

Bismarck—K43JQ, Ch. 43, EICB-TV East LLC. Phone: 972-291-3750.

Technical Facilities: 2-kw ERP, 66-ft. above ground, 1863-ft. above sea level, lat. 46° 50' 25", long. 100° 46' 31".

Ownership: EICB-TV LLC.

Bismarck—K46DY, Ch. 46, Trinity Broadcasting Network Inc. Phone: 714-832-2950. Fax: 714-730-0661.

Technical Facilities: 8.7-kw ERP, 236-ft. above ground, 2093-ft. above sea level, lat. 46° 49' 38", long. 100° 46' 28".

Holds CP for change to 15-kw ERP, BDFCDTT-20060331AIO.

Ownership: Trinity Broadcasting Network Inc.

Devils Lake—K33HB, Ch. 33, Red River Broadcast Co. LLC. Phone: 701-277-1515.

Technical Facilities: 13.2-kw ERP, 233-ft. above ground, 1690-ft. above sea level, lat. 48° 07' 22", long. 98° 50' 57".

Holds CP for change to 0.068-kw ERP, BDFCDTT-20060331BFZ.

Ownership: Red River Broadcast Co. LLC.

Dickinson—K28EP, Ch. 28, Trinity Broadcasting Network Inc. Phone: 714-832-2950. Fax: 714-730-0661.

Technical Facilities: 100-w TPO, 1.1-kw ERP, 210-ft. above ground, 2969-ft. above sea level, lat. 46° 55' 15", long. 102° 43' 42".

Transmitter: CTC Tower.

Ownership: Trinity Broadcasting Network Inc.

Dickinson—K38HA, Ch. 38, Prime Cities Broadcasting Inc. Phone: 203-431-3366.

Technical Facilities: 8.76-kw ERP, 187-ft. above ground, 2946-ft. above sea level, lat. 46° 55' 08", long. 102° 43' 47".

Holds CP for change to 3.3-kw ERP, 184-ft. above ground, 2946-ft. above sea level, BDFCDTT-20081224AAJ.

Began Operation: July 10, 2002.

Ownership: Prime Cities Broadcasting Inc.

Dickinson—K42FY, Ch. 42, Prime Cities Broadcasting Inc. Phone: 203-431-3366.

Technical Facilities: 8.71-kw ERP, 187-ft. above ground, 2946-ft. above sea level, lat. 46° 55' 08", long. 102° 43' 47".

Ownership: Prime Cities Broadcasting Inc.

Fargo—K35HO, Ch. 35, Trinity Broadcasting Network. Phone: 714-832-2950. Fax: 714-730-0661.

Technical Facilities: 19.8-kw ERP, 413-ft. above ground, 1335-ft. above sea level, lat. 46° 45' 35", long. 96° 36' 27".

Ownership: Trinity Broadcasting Network Inc.

Fargo—KVNJ-LP, Ch. 2, G.I.G. Inc. Phone: 605-335-3393.

Technical Facilities: 10-w TPO, 150-kw ERP, 175-ft. above ground, 1079-ft. above sea level, lat. 46° 51' 39", long. 96° 51' 17".

Transmitter: 603 11th St. N.

Ownership: G.I.G. Inc.

Personnel: Richard E. Blair, President & General Manager; Marty Ullman, Chief Engineer.

Grand Forks—K17HG, Ch. 17, Three Angels Broadcasting Network Inc. Phone: 618-627-4651.

Technical Facilities: 9.4-kw ERP, 320-ft. above ground, 1150-ft. above sea level, lat. 47° 57' 52", long. 97° 01' 46".

Ownership: Three Angels Broadcasting Network Inc.

Grand Forks—K49FF, Ch. 49, Trinity Broadcasting Network Inc. Phone: 714-832-2950. Fax: 714-730-0661.

Technical Facilities: 2000-w TPO, 26.3-kw ERP, 499-ft. above ground, 1191-ft. above sea level, lat. 47° 50' 43", long. 96° 50' 22".

Holds CP for change to 15-kw ERP, 348-ft. above ground, 1196-ft. above sea level, lat. 47° 50' 45", long. 96° 50' 26". BDFCDTT-20060330ADG.

Transmitter: Off State Rte. 220, near Bygland, MN.

Began Operation: January 6, 1993.

Ownership: Trinity Broadcasting Network Inc.

Hazen—K07JA, Ch. 7, City of Hazen. Phone: 701-748-2550.

Technical Facilities: 0.001-kw ERP, lat. 47° 19' 30", long. 101° 37' 49".

Ownership: City of Hazen.

Hazen—K09JR, Ch. 9, City of Hazen. Phone: 701-748-2550.

Technical Facilities: 0.001-kw ERP, lat. 47° 19' 30", long. 101° 37' 49".

Ownership: City of Hazen.

Hazen—K11QD, Ch. 11, City of Hazen. Phone: 701-748-2550.

Technical Facilities: 0.001-kw ERP, lat. 47° 19' 30", long. 101° 37' 49".

Ownership: City of Hazen.

Jamestown—K02DD, Ch. 2, Forum Communications Co. Phone: 701-237-6500.

Technical Facilities: 0.496-kw ERP, lat. 46° 53' 30", long. 98° 42' 45".

Ownership: Forum Communications Co.

Lisbon—K07NE, Ch. 7, Prairie Public Broadcasting Inc.

Technical Facilities: 0.023-kw ERP, lat. 46° 26' 59", long. 97° 40' 50".

Ownership: Prairie Public Broadcasting Inc.

Minot—K21GQ, Ch. 21, Trinity Broadcasting Network Inc. Phone: 714-832-2950. Fax: 714-730-0661.

Technical Facilities: 10-kw ERP, 289-ft. above ground, 2068-ft. above sea level, lat. 48° 09' 48", long. 101° 17' 55".

Ownership: Trinity Broadcasting Network Inc.

Minot—K47KA, Ch. 47, EICB-TV East LLC. Phone: 972-291-3750.

Technical Facilities: 1-kw ERP, 30-ft. above ground, 1742-ft. above sea level, lat. 48° 15' 39", long. 101° 17' 58".

Holds CP for change to 2-kw ERP, BPTTL-20080724ABQ.

Ownership: EICB-TV LLC.

Turtle Mountain Indian Reservation—K51EX, Ch. 51, Schindler Community TV Services. Phones: 701-477-6254; 701-477-5869.

Technical Facilities: 20-w TPO, 0.158-kw ERP, 253-ft. above ground, 2497-ft. above sea level, lat. 48° 51' 40", long. 99° 52' 45".

Transmitter: 1-mi. SE of Great Walker Lake School, Turtle Mountain Indian Res., Belcourt.

Multichannel TV Sound: Separate audio progam.

Ownership: Schindler Community TV Services.

Personnel: Fred Schindler, General Manager, Chief Engineer & Sales Manager.

Turtle Mountain Indian Reservation—K61EF, Ch. 61, Schindler Community TV Services. Phone: 701-477-5869.

Technical Facilities: 20-w TPO, 0.16-kw ERP, 246-ft. above ground, 2498-ft. above sea level, lat. 48° 51' 40", long. 99° 52' 45".

Transmitter: 1-mi. SE of Great Walker Lake School, Turtle Mtn. Indian Res., Belcourt.

Multichannel TV Sound: Separate audio progam.

Ownership: Schindler Community TV Services.

Personnel: Fred Schindler, Jr., General Manager.

Turtle Mountain Indian Reservation—K63ER, Ch. 63, Schindler Community TV Services. Phone: 701-477-5869.

Technical Facilities: 20-w TPO, 0.158-kw ERP, 2497-ft. above sea level, lat. 48° 51' 40", long. 99° 52' 45".

Transmitter: 1-mi. SE of Great Walker Lake School, Turtle Mtn. Indian Res., Belcourt.

Multichannel TV Sound: Separate audio progam.

Ownership: Schindler Community TV Services.

Personnel: Fred Schindler, General Manager, Chief Engineer & Sales Manager.

Turtle Mountain Indian Reservation—K65FE, Ch. 65, Schindler Community TV Services. Phone: 701-477-5869.

Technical Facilities: 20-w TPO, 0.158-kw ERP, 2497-ft. above sea level, lat. 48° 51' 40", long. 99° 52' 45".

Transmitter: 1-mi. SE of Great Walker Lake School, Turtle Mtn. Indian Res., Belcourt.

Multichannel TV Sound: Separate audio progam.

Ownership: Schindler Community TV Services.

Personnel: Fred Schindler, General Manager, Chief Engineer & Sales Manager.

Williston—K38HS, Ch. 38, Prime Cities Broadcasting Inc. Phone: 203-431-3366.

Technical Facilities: 20.5-kw ERP, 160-ft. above ground, 2500-ft. above sea level, lat. 48° 09' 18", long. 103° 30' 01".

Ownership: Prime Cities Broadcasting Inc.

Williston—K40DE, Ch. 40, Trinity Broadcasting Network Inc. Phone: 714-832-2950. Fax: 714-730-0661.

Technical Facilities: 100-w TPO, 0.851-kw ERP, 66-ft. above ground, 1939-ft. above sea level, lat. 48° 08' 43", long. 103° 37' 16".

Transmitter: Herrick Bldg., 122 Main St., Williston.

Ownership: Trinity Broadcasting Network Inc.

Personnel: Paul Crouch, General Manager; Ben Miller, Chief Engineer; Rod Henke, Sales Manager.

Williston—K44HR, Ch. 44, Prime Cities Broadcasting Inc. Phone: 203-431-3366.

Technical Facilities: 13.3-kw ERP, 160-ft. above ground, 2500-ft. above sea level, lat. 48° 09' 18", long. 103° 30' 01".

Ownership: Prime Cities Broadcasting Inc.

Wilton—K57JD, Ch. 57, Mark Silberman. Phone: 310-552-7970.

Technical Facilities: 0.999-kw ERP, 328-ft. above ground, 2568-ft. above sea level, lat. 47° 08' 24", long. 100° 42' 33".

Ownership: Mark Silberman.

Ohio

Akron—WAKN-LP, Ch. 11, Wellsprings Beaumont Television Inc. Phone: 409-813-1000.

Technical Facilities: 1.5-kw ERP, 801-ft. above ground, 1891-ft. above sea level, lat. 43° 03' 52.9", long. 81° 34' 58.9".

Began Operation: December 9, 1994.

Ownership: Wellsprings Beaumont TV Inc.

■ **Akron**—WAOH-LP, Ch. 29, Media-Com Television Inc. Phone: 330-673-2323. Fax: 330-673-0301.

Studio: 2449 State Rte. 59, Kent, OH 44240.

Technical Facilities: 1000-w TPO, 60.6-kw ERP, 348-ft. above ground, 1552-ft. above sea level, lat. 41° 06' 28", long. 81° 21' 19".

Transmitter: N of I-76, 2100-ft. W of intersection of I-76 & Rte. 43, Brimfield Twp.

Ownership: Media-Com Television Inc.

Personnel: Richard Klaus, President; Bill Klaus, General Manager; Bob Klaus, Sales; Bob Sassaman, Engineering.

Ashland—W33BW, Ch. 33, Christian Faith Broadcast Inc. Phone: 419-684-5311. Fax: 419-684-5378.

Studio: 2435 Mansfield Rd, Ashland, OH 44805.

Technical Facilities: 30-kw ERP, 487-ft. above ground, 1807-ft. above sea level, lat. 40° 44' 50", long. 82° 18' 54".

Multichannel TV Sound: Separate audio progam.

Ownership: Christian Faith Broadcast Inc.

Personnel: Walter R. Stampfli, Chairman; Dean Stampfli, President & General Manager; Martin Larsen, Vice President & Sales Manager; Asa Jessee, Jr., Station Operations Manager; Mark Hiner, Chief Engineer.

■ **Bridgeport**—WVTX-CA, Ch. 28, Bruno-Goodworth Network Inc. Phone: 412-922-9576.

Technical Facilities: 150-kw ERP, 100-ft. above ground, 1384-ft. above sea level, lat. 40° 03' 41", long. 80° 45' 08".

Ownership: Bruno-Goodworth Network Inc.

■ **Bucyrus**—WBKA-CA, Ch. 22, Studio 51 Multimedia Productions Ltd. Phone: 740-383-1165.

Studio: 1820 E Mansfield Rd, Bucyrus, OH 44820.

Technical Facilities: 8.2-w TPO, 23.5-kw ERP, 203-ft. above ground, 1215-ft. above sea level, lat. 40° 49' 31", long. 82° 54' 03".

Transmitter: 0.14-mi. S of intersection of Stetzer Rd. & Parcher Rd.

Ownership: Studio 51 Multimedia Productions Ltd.

Personnel: Kevin J. Pifher, Station Manager.

Cambridge—W63CZ, Ch. 63, Trinity Broadcasting Network Inc. Phone: 714-832-2950. Fax: 714-730-0661.

Technical Facilities: 8-kw ERP, lat. 40° 00' 41", long. 81° 35' 21".

Ownership: Trinity Broadcasting Network Inc.

Canton—WIVM-LP, Ch. 52, Lucinda DeVaul. Phone: 814-833-2567.

Technical Facilities: 20-w TPO, 22-kw ERP, 300-ft. above ground, 1566-ft. above sea level, lat. 40° 53' 24", long. 81° 16' 12".

Transmitter: 8200 Snowville Rd., Cleveland.

Ownership: Lucinda De Vaul.

Celina—W17AA, Ch. 17, Greater Dayton Public Television Inc. Phone: 937-220-1611.

Technical Facilities: 21.4-kw ERP, lat. 40° 33' 08", long. 84° 30' 46".

Holds CP for change to 5-kw ERP, 447-ft. above ground, 1332-ft. above sea level, lat. 40° 33' 09", long. 84° 30' 46". BDFCDTT-20060331AJJ.

Ownership: Public Media Connect.

Chillicothe—W59DL, Ch. 59, Eagle Broadcasting Group Inc. Phone: 740-286-3537.

Technical Facilities: 1000-w TPO, 37.6-kw ERP, 135-ft. above ground, 974-ft. above sea level, lat. 39° 19' 52", long. 82° 59' 49".

Transmitter: 0.49-mi. WSW of intersection of Rte. 50 & High St.

Ownership: Eagle Broadcasting Group Inc.

Personnel: Paul Crouch, General Manager; Ben Miller, Chief Engineer; Rod Henke, Sales Manager.

Cincinnati—W36DG, Ch. 36, Trinity Broadcasting Network Inc. Phone: 714-832-2950. Fax: 714-730-0661.

Technical Facilities: 22.4-kw ERP, 300-ft. above ground, 1165-ft. above sea level, lat. 39° 12' 30", long. 84° 30' 25".

Holds CP for change to 5-kw ERP, BDFCDTT-20060329AHR.

Ownership: Trinity Broadcasting Network Inc.

■ **Cincinnati**—WBQC-CA, Ch. 38, Elliott B. Block. Phone: 513-681-3800. Fax: 513-351-8898.

Studio: 2212 Losantiville Ave, Cincinnati, OH 45237.

Technical Facilities: 140-kw ERP, 679-ft. above ground, 1522-ft. above sea level, lat. 39° 07' 30", long. 84° 29' 56".

Multichannel TV Sound: Stereo only.

Ownership: Elliot B. Block.

Personnel: Matthew Gray, Station Manager; Elliott Block, Chief Executive Officer & General Manager; Grady Morgan, General Sales Manager; Wade Yuellig, Operations Manager; Karl Weidner, Director of Business Operations.

Cincinnati—WOTH-LP, Ch. 25, Elliott B. Block. Phone: 513-631-8825. Fax: 513-351-8898.

Studio: 7737 Reinhold Dr, Cincinnati, OH 45237.

Technical Facilities: 34.5-kw ERP, 679-ft. above ground, 1522-ft. above sea level, lat. 39° 07' 30", long. 84° 29' 56".

Multichannel TV Sound: Stereo only.

Ownership: Elliot B. Block.

Personnel: Elliott B. Block, General Manager.

Cincinnatti—WOTH-LD, Ch. 47, Elliott B. Block. Phone: 513-381-3838.

Technical Facilities: 15-kw ERP, 679-ft. above ground, 1522-ft. above sea level, lat. 39° 07' 30", long. 84° 29' 56".

Began Operation: May 5, 1994.

Ownership: Elliot B. Block.

■ **Cleveland**—W35AX, Ch. 35, Media-Com Television Inc. Phone: 330-673-2323. Fax: 330-673-0301.

Technical Facilities: 2000-w TPO, 11.8-kw ERP, 1001-ft. above ground, 1919-ft. above sea level, lat. 41° 23' 02", long. 81° 41' 44".

Transmitter: 2855 W. Ridgewood Dr., Parma.

Ownership: Media-Com Television Inc.

Personnel: Bill Klaus, General Manager; Bob Klaus, Sales Manager; Bob Sassaman, Chief Engineer.

Cleveland—WCDN-LP, Ch. 53, Word of God Fellowship Inc. Phone: 513-571-1229.

Technical Facilities: 767-w TPO, 11.1-kw ERP, 823-ft. above ground, 1742-ft. above sea level, lat. 41° 23' 02", long. 84° 41' 44".

Transmitter: 0.7-mi. SW of Broadway.

Ownership: Word of God Fellowship Inc.

■ **Cleveland**—WRAP-CA, Ch. 32, D.T.V. LLC. Phone: 800-536-7327.

Technical Facilities: 6.37-kw ERP, 823-ft. above ground, 1476-ft. above sea level, lat. 41° 30' 03", long. 81° 41' 39".

Transmitter: 127 Public Square.

Multichannel TV Sound: Stereo only.

Ownership: D.T.V. LLC.

Cleveland—WXOX-LP, Ch. 57, Venture Technologies Group LLC. Phone: 323-965-4090. Fax: 323-965-5411.

Technical Facilities: 1000-w TPO, 8-kw ERP, 832-ft. above ground, 1750-ft. above sea level, lat. 41° 23' 02", long. 81° 41' 44".

Holds CP for change to channel number 44, 100-kw ERP, 832-ft. above ground, 1749-ft. above sea level, lat. 41° 23' 02", long. 81° 41' 43". BDISTTL-20060207AAO.

Transmitter: 0.75-mi. SW of Broadview & Ridgewood Rds., Parma.

Ownership: Venture Technologies Group LLC.

Columbus—W23BZ, Ch. 23, National Minority TV Inc. Phone: 949-552-0490.

Technical Facilities: 17-kw ERP, lat. 39° 53' 32", long. 83° 02' 44".

Holds CP for change to 15-kw ERP, 476-ft. above ground, 1244-ft. above sea level, lat. 39° 53' 31", long. 83° 02' 44". BDFCDTT-20060329ALU.

Transmitter: Intersection of I-270 & I-71.

Ownership: Trinity Broadcasting Network Inc.

Columbus—W43BZ, Ch. 43, Ventana Television Inc. Phone: 727-872-4210.

Technical Facilities: 0.95-kw ERP, 446-ft. above ground, 1166-ft. above sea level, lat. 39° 58' 16", long. 83° 01' 40".

Began Operation: October 15, 1990.

Ownership: Ventana Television Inc.

■ **Columbus**—WCLL-CA, Ch. 19, Word of God Fellowship Inc. Phone: 917-571-1229.

Technical Facilities: 37.7-w TPO, 8-kw ERP, 518-ft. above ground, 1306-ft. above sea level, lat. 39° 57' 44", long. 83° 00' 08".

Transmitter: LeVegue Tower, 50 W. Broad St.

Ownership: Word of God Fellowship Inc.

Columbus—WCPX-LP, Ch. 48, TVO Media LLC. Phone: 941-925-2002.

Technical Facilities: 150-kw ERP, 515-ft. above ground, 1243-ft. above sea level, lat. 40° 01' 02", long. 83° 01' 11".

Holds CP for change to channel number 25, 9.5-kw ERP, BDISDTL-20080905AEC.

Ownership: TVO Media LLC.

Personnel: Luis Orozco, General Manager.

Columbus—WCSN-LP, Ch. 32, Columbus TV LLC. Phone: 972-473-2777.

Studio: 3323 Parcher Rd, Bucyrus, OH 44820.

Technical Facilities: 25-kw ERP, 574-ft. above ground, 1302-ft. above sea level, lat. 40° 01' 02", long. 83° 01' 11".

Multichannel TV Sound: Stereo and separate audio program.

Began Operation: September 25, 1986.

Ownership: Columbus TV LLC.

Personnel: Kathy Allonas, Station Manager; Bill Allonas, General Sales Manager; Bill Bowen, Chief Engineer.

■ **Columbus**—WDEM-CD, Ch. 17, Triplett & Assoc. Inc. Phones: 937-593-6591; 937-599-4672. Fax: 937-593-2867.

Studio: 1633 W Third Ave, Rm 208/210, Columbus, OH 43212.

Technical Facilities: 1.05-kw ERP, 449-ft. above ground, 1170-ft. above sea level, lat. 39° 58' 16", long. 83° 01' 40".

Transmitter: 0.4-mi. SW of intersection of Rte. 315 & Goodale St.

Began Operation: August 30, 1988.

Ownership: Triplett & Assoc. Inc.

Personnel: Marc S. Triplett, General Manager; John McKinley, Chief Engineer.

■ **Columbus**—WGCT-CA, Ch. 8, Central Ohio Assn. of Christian Broadcasters. Phone: 740-383-1794. Fax: 740-387-6647.

Technical Facilities: 0.083-kw ERP, 702-ft. above ground, 1421-ft. above sea level, lat. 39° 58' 16", long. 83° 01' 40".

Holds CP for change to 0.3-kw ERP, 318-ft. above ground, 1148-ft. above sea level, lat. 40° 00' 31", long. 83° 02' 49". BDFCDVA-20080804AAY.

Ownership: Central Ohio Assn. of Christian Broadcasters Inc.

Conneaut—W64AK, Ch. 64, Ideastream. Phone: 216-398-2800.

Technical Facilities: 0.146-kw ERP, 1227-ft. above sea level, lat. 41° 51' 39", long. 80° 40' 46".

Ownership: Media Inc.

Dayton—W66AQ, Ch. 66, WSTR Licensee Inc. Phone: 202-663-8217.

Technical Facilities: 1.6-kw ERP, 391-ft. above ground, 1345-ft. above sea level, lat. 39° 43' 15", long. 84° 15' 39".

Ownership: Sinclair Broadcast Group Inc.

Dayton—WRCX-LP, Ch. 40, Ross Communications Ltd. Phone: 937-275-7677.

Technical Facilities: 34-kw ERP, 919-ft. above ground, 1814-ft. above sea level, lat. 39° 43' 28", long. 84° 15' 18".

Holds CP for change to 0.32-kw ERP, BDFCDTL-20090507ABE.

Began Operation: July 11, 1995.

Ownership: Ross Communications Ltd.

Dayton—WWRD-LP, Ch. 32, Life Broadcasting Network. Phone: 937-272-0003.

Technical Facilities: 13-kw ERP, 312-ft. above ground, 1316-ft. above sea level, lat. 39° 04' 48", long. 84° 04' 56".

Ownership: Life Broadcasting Network.

Defiance—WDFM-LP, Ch. 26, Citicasters Licenses Inc. Phone: 918-664-4581.

Studio: 118 Clinton St, Defiance, OH 43512.

Technical Facilities: 7.5-kw ERP, 587-ft. above ground, 1296-ft. above sea level, lat. 41° 17' 29", long. 84° 32' 15".

Ownership: Clear Channel Communications Inc.

■ **Delaware**—WXCB-CA, Ch. 42, Central Ohio Assn. of Christian Broadcasters. Phone: 740-383-1794. Fax: 740-387-6647.

Studio: 501 Bowtown Rd, Delaware, OH 43015.

Technical Facilities: 1000-w TPO, 35-kw ERP, 262-ft. above ground, 1201-ft. above sea level, lat. 40° 17' 57", long. 83° 02' 45".

Holds CP for change to 0.475-kw ERP, 180-ft. above ground, 1112-ft. above sea level, lat. 40° 18' 47", long. 83° 03' 04". BDFCDTA-20080804AAX.

Transmitter: 501 Bowtown Rd.

Ownership: Central Ohio Assn. of Christian Broadcasters Inc.

Personnel: Rev. David R. Aiken, General Manager.

Eastlake, etc.—W63CT, Ch. 63, Ideastream. Phone: 216-398-2800.

Technical Facilities: 34-kw ERP, 201-ft. above ground, 1450-ft. above sea level, lat. 41° 41' 34", long. 81° 02' 50".

Transmitter: Ledgemont High School.

Ownership: Media Inc.

Findlay—W09CG, Ch. 9, National Minority TV Inc. Phone: 949-552-0490.

Technical Facilities: 0.47-kw ERP, lat. 41° 06' 40", long. 83° 38' 45".

Ownership: National Minority TV Inc.

Findlay—WFND-LP, Ch. 22, West Central Ohio Broadcasting Inc. Phone: 419-724-6212.

Studio: 418 S. Main St., Findlay, OH 45840.

Technical Facilities: 18-kw ERP, 282-ft. above ground, 1087-ft. above sea level, lat. 41° 06' 40", long. 83° 38' 54".

Transmitter: 2-mi. N of Findlay.

Multichannel TV Sound: Stereo and separate audio program.

Ownership: Block Communications Inc.

Kirtland—W51BI, Ch. 51, Trinity Broadcasting Network Inc. Phone: 714-832-2950. Fax: 714-730-0661.

Technical Facilities: 44.4-kw ERP, 476-ft. above ground, 1722-ft. above sea level, lat. 41° 27' 40", long. 81° 17' 38".

Holds CP for change to 8-kw ERP, 476-ft. above ground, 1721-ft. above sea level, BDFCDTT-20060223ABH.

Began Operation: October 13, 1994.

Ownership: Trinity Broadcasting Network Inc.

Lexington—W32AR, Ch. 32, Trinity Broadcasting Network Inc. Phone: 714-832-2950. Fax: 714-730-0661.

Technical Facilities: 1000-w TPO, 5.8-kw ERP, 361-ft. above ground, 1739-ft. above sea level, lat. 40° 45' 50", long. 82° 37' 04".

Transmitter: WVNO-FM tower, near Mansfield.

Ownership: Trinity Broadcasting Network Inc.

Lima—W23DE-D, Ch. 23, Three Angels Broadcasting Network Inc. Phone: 618-627-4651. Fax: 612-627-4155.

Studio: 3391 Charley Good Rd, West Frankfort, IL 62896.

Technical Facilities: 3-kw ERP, 623-ft. above ground, 1487-ft. above sea level, lat. 40° 38' 03", long. 84° 12' 29".

Transmitter: 19507 State Rte. 501, Cridersville.

Began Operation: November 5, 1997.

Ownership: Three Angels Broadcasting Network Inc.

Personnel: Moses Primo, Chief Engineer.

Lima—WLMO-LP, Ch. 38, West Central Ohio Broadcasting Inc. Phone: 419-724-6212.

Technical Facilities: 15-kw ERP, 623-ft. above ground, 1487-ft. above sea level, lat. 40° 38' 03", long. 84° 12' 29".

Ownership: Block Communications Inc.

Lima—WLQP-LP, Ch. 18, West Central Ohio Broadcasting Inc. Phone: 419-724-6212.

Studio: 463 S Central Ave, Lima, OH 45804.

Technical Facilities: 1000-w TPO, 18.6-kw ERP, 623-ft. above ground, 1486-ft. above sea level, lat. 40° 38' 03", long. 84° 12' 29".

Transmitter: 0.4-mi. N of intersection of Buckland-Holden Rd. & State Rte. 501.

Multichannel TV Sound: Separate audio progam.

Ownership: Block Communications Inc.

Personnel: Greg Phipps, General Manager; Ray Tanner, Chief Engineer; Mike VanMeter, General Sales Manager.

Lima—WOHL-CA, Ch. 25, West Central Ohio Broadcasting Inc. Phone: 419-724-6212.

Studio: 463 S Central Ave, Lima, OH 45805.

Technical Facilities: 866-w TPO, 16.45-kw ERP, 623-ft. above ground, 1486-ft. above sea level, lat. 40° 38' 03", long. 84° 12' 29".

Transmitter: 19507 State Rte. 501, Cridersville.

Ownership: Block Communications Inc.

Personnel: Greg Phipps, General Manager; Ray Tanner, Chief Engineer; Randall Hulsmeyer, General Sales Manager.

Loudonville—WIVX-LP, Ch. 65, Image Video Teleproductions Inc. Phone: 330-494-9303.

Technical Facilities: 0.115-kw ERP, lat. 40° 37' 59", long. 82° 11' 45".

Ownership: Image Video Teleproductions Inc.

Mansfield—W47AB, Ch. 47, The Ohio State U. Phone: 614-292-9678. Fax: 614-688-3343.

Technical Facilities: 35.7-kw ERP, 354-ft. above ground, 1719-ft. above sea level, lat. 40° 42' 32", long. 82° 29' 12".

Holds CP for change to 10-kw ERP, BDFCDTT-20061006ABG.

Ownership: Ohio State U.

Mansfield—WOHZ-CA, Ch. 41, Mid-State Television Inc. Phone: 419-529-5900. Fax: 419-529-2319.

Studio: 2900 Park Ave W, Mansfield, OH 44906.

Technical Facilities: 13.3-kw ERP, 367-ft. above ground, 1749-ft. above sea level, lat. 40° 45' 50", long. 82° 37' 04".

Ownership: Mid-State Television Inc.

Personnel: Scott Goodwin, General Sales Manager; Wayne Fick, Chief Engineer.

Maplewood, etc.—W63AH, Ch. 63, Greater Dayton Public Television Inc. Phone: 937-220-1611.

Technical Facilities: 0.14-kw ERP, lat. 40° 23' 53", long. 84° 04' 23".

Ownership: Public Media Connect.

Marietta—WVEX-LP, Ch. 22, Wood Investments LLC. Phone: 304-222-5063.

Technical Facilities: 2.02-kw ERP, 105-ft. above ground, 755-ft. above sea level, lat. 39° 24' 22.3", long. 81° 27' 05.7".

Holds CP for change to 150-kw ERP, 286-ft. above ground, 1259-ft. above sea level, lat. 39° 15' 19.8", long. 81° 23' 51". BPTTL-20080414AAS.

Ownership: Wood Investments LLC.

Marietta—WWVX-LP, Ch. 64, Wood Investments LLC. Phone: 304-222-5063.

Technical Facilities: 25-kw ERP, 50-ft. above ground, 1030-ft. above sea level, lat. 39° 20' 34.73", long. 81° 29' 52.55".

Holds CP for change to 150-kw ERP, 390-ft. above ground, 1350-ft. above sea level, lat. 39° 20' 58.7", long. 81° 33' 56.5". BPTTL-20071002ACO.

Ownership: Wood Investments LLC.

■**Marion**—WOCB-CA, Ch. 39, Central Ohio Assn. of Christian Broadcasters. Phone: 740-383-1794. Fax: 740-387-6647.

Studio: 1282 N Main St, Marion, OH 43302.

Technical Facilities: 1-kw ERP, 312-ft. above ground, 1280-ft. above sea level, lat. 40° 36' 46", long. 83° 07' 48".

Ownership: Central Ohio Assn. of Christian Broadcasters Inc.

Personnel: David Aiken, General Manager.

Millersburg—W69AO, Ch. 69, Image Video Teleproductions Inc. Phone: 330-494-9303.

Technical Facilities: 0.896-kw ERP, lat. 40° 36' 13", long. 81° 56' 13".

Ownership: Image Video Teleproductions Inc.

Newark—W31AA, Ch. 31, Ohio Educational Telecommunications Network Commission. Phone: 614-644-3085.

Technical Facilities: 0.004-kw ERP, lat. 40° 05' 28", long. 82° 24' 22".

Ownership: Ohio Educational Telecommunications Network Commission.

Newcomerstown—WIVN-LP, Ch. 29, Image Video Teleproductions Inc. Phone: 330-494-9303.

Technical Facilities: 74-kw ERP, 272-ft. above ground, 1472-ft. above sea level, lat. 40° 21' 32", long. 81° 30' 02".

Ownership: Image Video Teleproductions Inc.

Pomeroy—WJOS-LP, Ch. 58, William A. Barnhardt. Phone: 740-992-2727. Fax: 740-992-6556.

Technical Facilities: 1000-w TPO, 27-kw ERP, 95-ft. above ground, 92-ft. above sea level, lat. 39° 02' 09", long. 82° 01' 26".

Transmitter: Off Spring Ave. near St. Johns Cemetery.

Ownership: William A. Barnhardt.

Portsmouth—WTZP-LP, Ch. 50, Eagle Broadcasting Group Inc. Phones: 740-286-3537; 740-355-9663.

Technical Facilities: 12.4-kw ERP, 384-ft. above ground, 1483-ft. above sea level, lat. 38° 43' 20", long. 83° 00' 05".

Ownership: Eagle Broadcasting Group Inc.

Personnel: Paul Crouch, General Manager; Ben Miller, Chief Engineer; Rod Henke, Sales Manager.

Sandusky—W41AP, Ch. 41, Register TV News.

Technical Facilities: 1000-w TPO, 10.07-kw ERP, 138-ft. above ground, 728-ft. above sea level, lat. 41° 27' 19", long. 82° 42' 49".

Transmitter: 314 W. Market St.

Ownership: Register TV News.

Seaman—W17AY, Ch. 17, Tranquility Community Church.

Technical Facilities: 762-w TPO, 17.6-kw ERP, 226-ft. above ground, 1145-ft. above sea level, lat. 38° 52' 52", long. 83° 29' 20".

Transmitter: 0.1-mi. N of Wheat Ridge, 0.1-mi. E of Tater Ridge Rd., Wheat Ridge.

Ownership: Tranquility Community Church.

Springfield—W20CL, Ch. 20, Trinity Broadcsting Network Inc. Phone: 714-832-2950. Fax: 714-730-0661.

Technical Facilities: 8.7-kw ERP, 259-ft. above ground, 1319-ft. above sea level, lat. 39° 57' 44", long. 83° 51' 49".

Ownership: Trinity Broadcasting Network Inc.

Steubenville—WSSS-LP, Ch. 29, Abacus Television. Phone: 202-462-3680. Fax: 202-462-3781.

Technical Facilities: 26.5-kw ERP, 184-ft. above ground, 1444-ft. above sea level, lat. 40° 21' 59", long. 80° 35' 22".

Transmitter: Archer Hill, 1.5-mi. NE of Archer Heights.

Ownership: Abacus Television.

Personnel: Benjamin Perez, General Manager.

Toledo—W22CO, Ch. 22, Trinity Christian Center of Santa Ana Inc. Phone: 714-832-2950.

Technical Facilities: 6.6-kw ERP, lat. 41° 39' 12", long. 83° 32' 53".

Holds CP for change to channel number 18, 1-kw ERP, 574-ft. above ground, 1170-ft. above sea level, lat. 41° 39' 22", long. 83° 26' 41". BDISDTT-20060329ADH.

Transmitter: Owens-Corning Fiberglass Bldg., near Toledo.

Ownership: Trinity Broadcasting Network Inc.

Toledo—W38DH, Ch. 38, Ventana Television Inc. Phone: 727-872-4210.

Technical Facilities: 8.2-kw ERP, 404-ft. above ground, 1020-ft. above sea level, lat. 41° 38' 49", long. 83° 36' 18".

Began Operation: October 15, 1992.

Ownership: Ventana Television Inc.

Personnel: John Skelnik, General Manager & Chief Engineer.

Toledo—WBTL-LP, Ch. 34, Venture Technologies Group LLC.

Technical Facilities: 14.7-kw ERP, lat. 41° 39' 05", long. 83° 32' 08".

Ownership: Venture Technologies Group LLC.

■**Toledo**—WMNT-CA, Ch. 48, Matrix Broadcast Media Inc. Phone: 419-353-1062.

Studio: 716 N Westwood Ave, Toledo, OH 43607.

Technical Facilities: 11-kw ERP, 428-ft. above ground, 1017-ft. above sea level, lat. 41° 39' 13", long. 83° 31' 49".

Ownership: Matrix Broadcast Media Inc.

Personnel: Marty Miller, General Manager; William Leutz, Chief Engineer.

Youngstown—W52DS, Ch. 52, Trinity Broadcasting Network Inc. Phone: 714-832-2950. Fax: 714-730-0661.

Technical Facilities: 1000-w TPO, 3-kw ERP, 285-ft. above ground, 1337-ft. above sea level, lat. 41° 11' 04", long. 80° 41' 31".

Ownership: Trinity Broadcasting Network Inc.

■**Youngstown**—WYFX-LP, Ch. 62, NVT Youngstown Licensee LLC, Debtor in Possession. Phone: 404-995-4711.

Studio: 3930 Sunset Blvd, Youngstown, OH 44512.

Technical Facilities: 25-kw ERP, 712-ft. above ground, 1817-ft. above sea level, lat. 41° 03' 24", long. 80° 38' 44".

Began Operation: July 7, 1997.

Ownership: New Vision Television LLC, Debtor in Possession.

Youngstown, etc.—W58AM, Ch. 58, Northeastern Educational TV of Ohio Inc. Phone: 330-677-4549.

Technical Facilities: 67-kw ERP, lat. 41° 04' 46", long. 80° 38' 25".

Holds CP for change to channel number 44, 1.5-kw ERP, 640-ft. above ground, 1673-ft. above sea level, BDISDTT-20060331ARW.

Ownership: Northeastern Educational Television of Ohio.

Zanesville—W16BT, Ch. 16, Trinity Broadcasting Network Inc. Phone: 714-832-2950. Fax: 714-731-0661.

Technical Facilities: 1191-w TPO, 8.4-kw ERP, 282-ft. above ground, 1191-ft. above sea level, lat. 39° 56' 55", long. 81° 57' 48".

Transmitter: 2477 E. Pike.

Ownership: Trinity Broadcasting Network Inc.

Oklahoma

Ada—K35CU, Ch. 35, Family Broadcasting Group Inc. Phone: 405-631-7335.

Technical Facilities: 43-kw ERP, lat. 34° 41' 46", long. 96° 45' 44".

Transmitter: S of State Rte. 1, 8.1-mi. SW of Ada.

Began Operation: April 26, 1995.

Ownership: Family Broadcasting Group Inc.

Allen—KDNT-LP, Ch. 18, Word of God Fellowship Inc. Phone: 817-571-1229.

Technical Facilities: 150-kw ERP, 984-ft. above ground, 1837-ft. above sea level, lat. 34° 15' 47", long. 96° 22' 43".

Holds CP for change to 16-kw ERP, 269-ft. above ground, 1020-ft. above sea level, lat. 33° 45' 20", long. 96° 33' 47". BPTTL-20071203ADR.

Ownership: Word of God Fellowship Inc.

Altus—K19AA, Ch. 19, Oklahoma Educational Television Authority. Phone: 405-848-8501.

Technical Facilities: 4.93-kw ERP, lat. 34° 39' 12", long. 99° 20' 57".

Holds CP for change to 0.43-kw ERP, 215-ft. above ground, 1594-ft. above sea level, BDFCDTA-20060630AHU.

Ownership: Oklahoma Educational Television Authority.

Altus—K36EV, Ch. 36, Oklahoma Community Television LLC. Phone: 405-808-2509.

Technical Facilities: 0.581-kw ERP, lat. 34° 38' 20", long. 99° 21' 19".

Transmitter: 1-mi. W of Altus.

Ownership: Oklahoma Community Television LLC.

Altus—K38FJ, Ch. 38, Oklahoma Community Television LLC. Phone: 405-808-2509.

Technical Facilities: 0.581-kw ERP, lat. 34° 38' 20", long. 99° 21' 19".

Transmitter: 1-mi. W of Altus.

Ownership: Oklahoma Community Television LLC.

Altus—K40FL, Ch. 40, Oklahoma Community Television LLC. Phone: 405-808-2509.

Technical Facilities: 0.581-kw ERP, lat. 34° 38' 20", long. 99° 21' 19".

Ownership: Oklahoma Community Television LLC.

Altus—K42FL, Ch. 42, Oklahoma Community Television LLC. Phone: 405-808-2509.

Technical Facilities: 0.94-kw ERP, 308-ft. above ground, 1683-ft. above sea level, lat. 34° 38' 21", long. 99° 21' 19".

Ownership: Oklahoma Community Television LLC.

Altus—K45FH, Ch. 45, Oklahoma Community Television LLC. Phone: 405-808-2509.

Technical Facilities: 5.86-kw ERP, lat. 34° 38' 20", long. 99° 21' 19".

Ownership: Oklahoma Community Television LLC.

Altus—K49FE, Ch. 49, Oklahoma Community Television LLC. Phone: 405-808-2509.

Technical Facilities: 5.86-kw ERP, lat. 34° 38' 20", long. 99° 21' 19".

Ownership: Oklahoma Community Television LLC.

Altus—KKTM-LP, Ch. 17, KKTM License Co. LLC. Phone: 972-663-8917.

Technical Facilities: 0.212-kw ERP, 56-ft. above ground, 1509-ft. above sea level, lat. 34° 38' 34", long. 99° 20' 01".

Ownership: London Broadcasting Co. Inc.

Alva—K30AE, Ch. 30, Oklahoma Educational Television Authority. Phone: 405-848-8501.

Technical Facilities: 6.89-kw ERP, lat. 36° 47' 03", long. 98° 33' 38".

Holds CP for change to 15-kw ERP, 309-ft. above ground, 1739-ft. above sea level, lat. 36° 47' 10", long. 98° 33' 33". BDFCDTA-20060630AHT.

Ownership: Oklahoma Educational Television Authority.

Alva & Cherokee—K56FK, Ch. 56, Local TV Oklahoma License LLC. Phone: 859-448-2707.

Technical Facilities: 100-w TPO, 0.626-kw ERP, 450-ft. above ground, 1895-ft. above sea level, lat. 36° 47' 06", long. 98° 33' 33".

Transmitter: 5-mi. E of Alva.

Ownership: Local TV Holdings LLC.

Alva & Cherokee—K58EM, Ch. 58, Local TV Oklahoma License LLC. Phone: 859-448-2707.

Technical Facilities: 100-w TPO, 0.626-kw ERP, 450-ft. above ground, 1895-ft. above sea level, lat. 36° 47' 06", long. 98° 33' 33".

Transmitter: 5-mi. E of Alva.

Ownership: Local TV Holdings LLC.

Ardmore—K17FB, Ch. 17, Family Broadcasting Group Inc. Phone: 405-631-7335.

Technical Facilities: 1000-w TPO, 80-kw ERP, 290-ft. above ground, 1590-ft. above sea level, lat. 34° 26' 27", long. 97° 12' 06".

Transmitter: 9-mi. NW of Ardmore.

Began Operation: June 26, 2003.

Ownership: Family Broadcasting Group Inc.

Personnel: Jack Kroth, General Manager & Chief Engineer; Steve Easom, Sales Manager.

Ardmore—K28AC, Ch. 28, Oklahoma Educational Television Authority. Phone: 405-848-8501.

Technical Facilities: 6.89-kw ERP, lat. 34° 09' 54", long. 97° 09' 31".

Holds CP for change to 1.1-kw ERP, 410-ft. above ground, 1280-ft. above sea level, BDFCDTA-20060630AHS.

Ownership: Oklahoma Educational Television Authority.

Ardmore—K44BQ, Ch. 44, Trinity Broadcasting Network Inc. Phone: 714-832-2950. Fax: 714-730-0661.

Technical Facilities: 296-w TPO, 54.1-kw ERP, 302-ft. above ground, 1640-ft. above sea level, lat. 34° 26' 29", long. 97° 13' 36".

Transmitter: 5.5-mi. W of I-35 & State Rte. 77 overpass, near Davis.

Ownership: Trinity Broadcasting Network Inc.

Ardmore—KCYH-LP, Ch. 53, Ardmore Community Health & Education Organization Inc. Phone: 580-223-8818.

Technical Facilities: 3-kw ERP, 361-ft. above ground, 1205-ft. above sea level, lat. 34° 09' 53", long. 97° 10' 30".

Holds CP for change to channel number 41, 150-kw ERP, 367-ft. above ground, 1211-ft. above sea level, BDISTTL-20060720ACX.

Ownership: Ardmore Community Health & Education Organization Inc.

Balko—K25EG, Ch. 25, Victory Center Inc. Phone: 580-338-5616.

Technical Facilities: 8.16-kw ERP, 410-ft. above ground, 3291-ft. above sea level, lat. 36° 36' 56", long. 100° 52' 15".

Ownership: Victory Center Inc.

Beaver—K56AY, Ch. 56, Oklahoma Educational Television Authority. Phone: 405-848-8501.

Technical Facilities: 0.836-kw ERP, 2661-ft. above sea level, lat. 36° 50' 08", long. 100° 29' 38".

Holds CP for change to channel number 34, 15-kw ERP, 206-ft. above ground, 2656-ft. above sea level, lat. 36° 48' 45", long. 100° 32' 09.5". BDFCDTT-20070131ADZ.

Ownership: Oklahoma Educational Television Authority.

Boise City—K55BV, Ch. 55, Oklahoma Educational Television Authority. Phone: 405-848-8501.

Technical Facilities: 0.1-kw ERP, 4426-ft. above sea level, lat. 36° 43' 29", long. 102° 28' 48".

Holds CP for change to channel number 20, 15-kw ERP, 286-ft. above ground, 4417-ft. above sea level, BDFCDTT-20061026AEP.

Ownership: Oklahoma Educational Television Authority.

Broken Bow—K28DJ, Ch. 28, Jewel B. Callaham Revocable Trust.

Technical Facilities: 1000-w TPO, 7.63-kw ERP, 489-ft. above ground, 912-ft. above sea level, lat. 33° 56' 12", long. 94° 45' 46".

Transmitter: 1.3-mi. SSW of Broken Bow.

Ownership: Jewel B. Callaham Revocable Trust.

Buffalo—K58AX, Ch. 58, Oklahoma Educational Television Authority. Phone: 405-848-8501.

Technical Facilities: 5.13-kw ERP, 2484-ft. above sea level, lat. 36° 43' 20", long. 99° 43' 20".

Holds CP for change to channel number 48, 15-kw ERP, 206-ft. above ground, 2506-ft. above sea level, BDFCDTT-20061026AEL.

Ownership: Oklahoma Educational Television Authority.

Cherokee & Alva—K60ER, Ch. 60, Local TV Oklahoma License LLC. Phone: 859-448-2707.

Technical Facilities: 0.88-kw ERP, lat. 36° 45' 20", long. 98° 31' 40".

Ownership: Local TV Holdings LLC.

Cherokee & Alva—K62EH, Ch. 62, Local TV Oklahoma License LLC. Phone: 859-448-2707.

Technical Facilities: 0.88-kw ERP, lat. 36° 45' 20", long. 98° 31' 40".

Ownership: Local TV Holdings LLC.

Cherokee & Alva—K64EA, Ch. 64, Local TV Oklahoma License LLC. Phone: 859-448-2707.

Technical Facilities: 0.88-kw ERP, lat. 36° 45' 20", long. 98° 31' 40".

Ownership: Local TV Holdings LLC.

Duncan—K54BB, Ch. 54, Oklahoma Educational Television Authority. Phone: 405-848-8501.

Technical Facilities: 6.89-kw ERP, 1673-ft. above sea level, lat. 34° 26' 02", long. 97° 41' 06".

Holds CP for change to channel number 47, 15-kw ERP, 366-ft. above ground, 1671-ft. above sea level, lat. 34° 26' 01", long. 97° 41' 07". BDFCDTT-20061026AEQ.

Ownership: Oklahoma Educational Television Authority.

Duncan—KSWX-LP, Ch. 31, KSWO Television Co. Inc. Phone: 580-355-7000.

Technical Facilities: 0.129-kw ERP, 57-ft. above ground, 1179-ft. above sea level, lat. 34° 29' 35", long. 97° 57' 47".

Ownership: Drewry Communications.

Durant—K46AI, Ch. 46, Oklahoma Educational Television Authority. Phone: 405-848-8501.

Technical Facilities: 6.67-kw ERP, lat. 33° 59' 23", long. 96° 23' 49".

Holds CP for change to 13.4-kw ERP, 407-ft. above ground, 1060-ft. above sea level, BDFCDTA-20060630AHR.

Ownership: Oklahoma Educational Television Authority.

Durant—K64GW, Ch. 64, Iglesia Jesucristo Es Mi Refugio Inc. Phone: 214-330-8700.

Technical Facilities: 20-kw ERP, 164-ft. above ground, 849-ft. above sea level, lat. 33° 54' 56", long. 96° 26' 55".

Ownership: Iglesia Jesucristo Es Mi Refugio Inc.

Elk City—K29EI, Ch. 29, Oklahoma Community Television LLC. Phone: 405-808-2509.

Technical Facilities: 9.98-kw ERP, 292-ft. above ground, 2267-ft. above sea level, lat. 35° 21' 25", long. 99° 16' 08".

Ownership: Oklahoma Community Television LLC.

Personnel: Arnold Cruze, General Manager.

Elk City—K54CM, Ch. 54, Oklahoma Community Television LLC. Phone: 405-808-2509.

Technical Facilities: 0.633-kw ERP, 292-ft. above ground, 2267-ft. above sea level, lat. 35° 21' 25", long. 99° 16' 08".

Holds CP for change to channel number 31, 10-kw ERP, BDISTT-20070315AAL.

Ownership: Oklahoma Community Television LLC.

Elk City—K56EY, Ch. 56, Oklahoma Community Television LLC. Phone: 405-808-2509.

Technical Facilities: 0.97-kw ERP, 292-ft. above ground, 2267-ft. above sea level, lat. 35° 21' 25", long. 99° 16' 08".

Holds CP for change to channel number 33, 10-kw ERP, BDISTT-20060719ABS.

Ownership: Oklahoma Community Television LLC.

Elk City—KOKJ-LP, Ch. 2, K02MU-TV LLC.

Studio: 5th & Randall, Elk City, OK 73648.

Technical Facilities: 0.05-kw ERP, 60-ft. above ground, 2039-ft. above sea level, lat. 35° 24' 36", long. 99° 25' 01".

Ownership: K02MU-TV LLC.

Elk City, etc.—K44AP, Ch. 44, Oklahoma Community Television LLC. Phone: 405-808-2509.

Technical Facilities: 0.97-kw ERP, lat. 35° 21' 25", long. 99° 16' 08".

Ownership: Oklahoma Community Television LLC.

Elk City, etc.—K46AN, Ch. 46, Oklahoma Community Television LLC. Phone: 405-808-2509.

Technical Facilities: 0.91-kw ERP, lat. 35° 21' 25", long. 99° 16' 08".

Ownership: Oklahoma Community Television LLC.

Elk City, etc.—K48AP, Ch. 48, Oklahoma Community Television LLC. Phone: 405-808-2509.

Technical Facilities: 0.97-kw ERP, lat. 35° 21' 25", long. 99° 16' 08".

Ownership: Oklahoma Community Television LLC.

Elk City, etc.—K50AL, Ch. 50, Oklahoma Community Television LLC. Phone: 405-808-2509.

Technical Facilities: 0.97-kw ERP, 292-ft. above ground, 2267-ft. above sea level, lat. 35° 21' 25", long. 99° 16' 08".

Ownership: Oklahoma Community Television LLC.

Enid—K45EJ, Ch. 45, Family Broadcasting Group Inc. Phone: 405-631-7335.

Technical Facilities: 27.6-kw ERP, 361-ft. above ground, 1703-ft. above sea level, lat. 36° 28' 17", long. 97° 56' 23".

Began Operation: March 10, 1997.

Ownership: Family Broadcasting Group Inc.

Enid—KXOK-LD, Ch. 31, ME3 Communications Co. LLC. Phone: 405-720-1501.

Technical Facilities: 0.04-kw ERP, 261-ft. above ground, 1510-ft. above sea level, lat. 36° 23' 48", long. 97° 52' 38".

Ownership: ME3 Communications LLC.

Enid—KXOK-LP, Ch. 32, ME3 Communications LLC. Phone: 405-834-8992.

Technical Facilities: 1000-w TPO, 12.5-kw ERP, 256-ft. above ground, 1505-ft. above sea level, lat. 36° 23' 48", long. 97° 52' 38".

Transmitter: 114 E. Broadway.

Ownership: ME3 Communications LLC.

Erick—K58CS, Ch. 58, Oklahoma Community Television LLC. Phone: 405-808-2509.

Technical Facilities: 100-w TPO, 0.815-kw ERP, 414-ft. above ground, 2020-ft. above sea level, lat. 35° 09' 05", long. 99° 42' 50".

Holds CP for change to channel number 17, 1-kw ERP, 407-ft. above ground, 2427-ft. above sea level, BDISTT-20060719ABO.

Transmitter: 11-mi. SSW of Sayre.

Ownership: Oklahoma Community Television LLC.

Erick, etc.—K60CK, Ch. 60, Oklahoma Community Television LLC. Phone: 405-808-2509.

Technical Facilities: 0.81-kw ERP, 407-ft. above ground, 2428-ft. above sea level, lat. 35° 09' 05", long. 99° 42' 50".

Holds CP for change to channel number 15, 1-kw ERP, 407-ft. above ground, 2427-ft. above sea level, BDISTT-20060719ABT.

Ownership: Oklahoma Community Television LLC.

Erick, etc.—K62BQ, Ch. 62, Oklahoma Community Television LLC. Phone: 405-808-2509.

Technical Facilities: 100-w TPO, 0.815-kw ERP, 414-ft. above ground, 2434-ft. above sea level, lat. 35° 09' 05", long. 99° 42' 50".

Holds CP for change to channel number 20, 1-kw ERP, 407-ft. above ground, 2427-ft. above sea level, BDISTT-20060719ABN.

Transmitter: 11-mi. SSW of Sayre.

Ownership: Oklahoma Community Television LLC.

Erick, etc.—K64AX, Ch. 64, Oklahoma Community Television LLC. Phone: 405-808-2509.

Technical Facilities: 0.815-kw ERP, 2434-ft. above sea level, lat. 35° 09' 05", long. 99° 42' 50".

Holds CP for change to channel number 16, 1.1-kw ERP, 407-ft. above ground, 2429-ft. above sea level, lat. 35° 09' 05", long. 99° 42' 51". BPTT-20050301AAR.

Ownership: Oklahoma Community Television LLC.

Erick, etc.—K66AQ, Ch. 66, Oklahoma Community Television LLC. Phone: 405-808-2509.

Technical Facilities: 0.815-kw ERP, 2421-ft. above sea level, lat. 35° 09' 05", long. 99° 42' 50".

Holds CP for change to channel number 23, 1-kw ERP, 407-ft. above ground, 2427-ft. above sea level, BDISTT-20060719ABM.

Ownership: Oklahoma Community Television LLC.

Erick, etc.—K68AU, Ch. 68, Oklahoma Community Television LLC. Phone: 405-808-2509.

Technical Facilities: 0.815-kw ERP, lat. 35° 09' 05", long. 99° 42' 50".

Holds CP for change to channel number 21, 1.1-kw ERP, 407-ft. above ground, 2427-ft. above sea level, lat. 35° 09' 05", long. 99° 42' 51". BDISTT-20080610ACA.

Ownership: Oklahoma Community Television LLC.

Frederick—K56BQ, Ch. 56, Oklahoma Educational Television Authority. Phone: 405-848-8501.

Technical Facilities: 0.834-kw ERP, 206-ft. above ground, 1536-ft. above sea level, lat. 34° 22' 41", long. 99° 04' 17".

Holds CP for change to channel number 34, 15-kw ERP, BDFCDTT-20061026AEM.

Ownership: Oklahoma Educational Television Authority.

Gage—K16DX, Ch. 16, Local TV Oklahoma License LLC. Phone: 859-448-2707.

Technical Facilities: 0.984-kw ERP, lat. 36° 26' 03", long. 99° 46' 22".

Ownership: Local TV Holdings LLC.

Gage, etc.—K20BR, Ch. 20, Local TV Oklahoma License LLC. Phone: 859-448-2707.

Technical Facilities: 0.815-kw ERP, lat. 36° 26' 03", long. 99° 46' 22".

Ownership: Local TV Holdings LLC.

Glencoe—KOKQ-LP, Ch. 50, KOKH Television LLC.

Technical Facilities: 1000-w TPO, 11.6-kw ERP, 1260-ft. above sea level, lat. 36° 10' 24", long. 97° 58' 10".

Transmitter: Richmond Rd., W of Hwy. 108, Glencoe.

Ownership: KOKH Television LLC.

Gould—K51CV, Ch. 51, Oklahoma Community Television LLC. Phone: 405-808-2509.

Technical Facilities: 0.942-kw ERP, 292-ft. above ground, 2041-ft. above sea level, lat. 34° 44' 30", long. 99° 48' 30".

Ownership: Oklahoma Community Television LLC.

Grandfield—K47DK, Ch. 47, Mission Broadcasting Inc. Phone: 330-335-8808.

Technical Facilities: 8.58-kw ERP, 709-ft. above ground, 1821-ft. above sea level, lat. 34° 12' 06", long. 98° 43' 44".

Holds CP for change to 0.051-kw ERP, BDFCDTT-20060403ADC.

Ownership: Mission Broadcasting Inc.

Guymon—K16AB, Ch. 16, Oklahoma Educational Television Authority. Phone: 405-848-8501.

Technical Facilities: 6.37-kw ERP, lat. 36° 40' 13", long. 101° 28' 48".

Holds CP for change to 0.65-kw ERP, 522-ft. above ground, 3638-ft. above sea level, BDFCDTA-20060630AHL.

Ownership: Oklahoma Educational Television Authority.

Guymon—K28GI, Ch. 28, Guymon TV Translator Inc. Phone: 580-338-1015.

Technical Facilities: 6.47-kw ERP, lat. 36° 40' 39", long. 101° 27' 52".

Ownership: Guymon TV Translator Inc.

Guymon—K30FY, Ch. 30, Guymon TV Translator Inc. Phone: 580-338-1015.

Technical Facilities: 6.47-kw ERP, 489-ft. above ground, 3602-ft. above sea level, lat. 36° 40' 39", long. 101° 27' 52".

Ownership: Guymon TV Translator Inc.

Guymon—K53BE, Ch. 53, Victory Center Inc. Phone: 580-338-5616. Fax: 580-338-2575.

Studio: 5th & Quinn Sts, Guymon, OK 73942.

Technical Facilities: 1000-w TPO, 6.566-kw ERP, 449-ft. above ground, 3652-ft. above sea level, lat. 36° 40' 30", long. 101° 33' 58".

Holds CP for change to channel number 48, 6.6-kw ERP, 441-ft. above ground, 3652-ft. above sea level, lat. 36° 40' 35", long. 101° 33' 56". BDISTTL-20060323AGK.

Transmitter: Approx. 3.25-mi. W of Guymon Municipal Airport.

Ownership: Victory Center Inc.

Personnel: Brad Wayne Mendenhall, General Manager.

Guymon—K57HY, Ch. 57, Guymon TV Translator Inc. Phone: 580-338-1015.

Technical Facilities: 6.47-kw ERP, lat. 36° 40' 39", long. 101° 27' 52".

Ownership: Guymon TV Translator Inc.

Guymon—K59GF, Ch. 59, Guymon TV Translator Inc. Phone: 580-338-1015.

Technical Facilities: 6.47-kw ERP, 489-ft. above ground, 3602-ft. above sea level, lat. 36° 40' 39", long. 101° 27' 52".

Ownership: Guymon TV Translator Inc.

Hollis—K24GG, Ch. 24, Oklahoma Community Television LLC. Phone: 405-808-2509.

Technical Facilities: 0.98-kw ERP, 308-ft. above ground, 2051-ft. above sea level, lat. 34° 44' 30", long. 99° 48' 30".

Ownership: Oklahoma Community Television LLC.

Hollis, etc.—K53AV, Ch. 53, Oklahoma Community Television LLC. Phone: 405-808-2509.

Technical Facilities: 1.1-kw ERP, 308-ft. above ground, 2050-ft. above sea level, lat. 34° 44' 30", long. 99° 48' 30".

Holds CP for change to channel number 22, 10-kw ERP, 308-ft. above ground, 2051-ft. above sea level, BDISTT-20060719ABK.

Ownership: Oklahoma Community Television LLC.

Hollis, etc.—K55BQ, Ch. 55, Oklahoma Community Television LLC. Phone: 405-808-2509.

Technical Facilities: 0.527-kw ERP, lat. 34° 44' 30", long. 99° 48' 30".

Holds CP for change to channel number 35, 5-kw ERP, 308-ft. above ground, 1460-ft. above sea level, BDISTT-20060719ABI.

Ownership: Oklahoma Community Television LLC.

Hollis, etc.—K57BB, Ch. 57, Oklahoma Community Television LLC. Phone: 405-808-2509.

Technical Facilities: 0.52-kw ERP, lat. 34° 44' 30", long. 99° 48' 30".

Holds CP for change to channel number 30, 10-kw ERP, 308-ft. above ground, 2051-ft. above sea level, BDISTT-20060719ABH.

Ownership: Oklahoma Community Television LLC.

Hollis, etc.—K59BI, Ch. 59, Oklahoma Community Television LLC. Phone: 405-808-2509.

Technical Facilities: 0.57-kw ERP, lat. 34° 44' 30", long. 99° 48' 30".

Holds CP for change to channel number 28, 10-kw ERP, 308-ft. above ground, 2051-ft. above sea level, BDISTT-20060719ABG.

Ownership: Oklahoma Community Television LLC.

Hugo—K15AA, Ch. 15, Oklahoma Educational Television Authority. Phone: 405-848-8501.

Technical Facilities: 4.39-kw ERP, lat. 33° 59' 49", long. 95° 30' 35".

Holds CP for change to 15-kw ERP, 355-ft. above ground, 926-ft. above sea level, BDFCDTA-20060630AHM.

Ownership: Oklahoma Educational Television Authority.

Idabel—K63BA, Ch. 63, Oklahoma Educational Television Authority. Phone: 405-848-8501.

Technical Facilities: 0.305-kw ERP, 444-ft. above ground, 911-ft. above sea level, lat. 33° 53' 16", long. 94° 48' 28".

Holds CP for change to channel number 23, 11.2-kw ERP, 447-ft. above ground, 914-ft. above sea level, BDFCDTT-20061026AEJ.

Ownership: Oklahoma Educational Television Authority.

Lawton—K11VJ, Ch. 11, Marcia T. Turner. Phone: 954-732-9539.

Technical Facilities: 0.01-kw ERP, 98-ft. above ground, 1280-ft. above sea level, lat. 34° 34' 24", long. 98° 28' 40".

Ownership: Marcia T. Turner.

Lawton—K20HO, Ch. 20, Family Broadcasting Group Inc. Phone: 405-631-7335.

Technical Facilities: 20-kw ERP, 300-ft. above ground, 1530-ft. above sea level, lat. 34° 36' 27", long. 98° 16' 26".

Began Operation: December 20, 1994.

Ownership: Family Broadcasting Group Inc.

Lawton—K25IC, Ch. 25, Mosely Enterprises LLC. Phone: 318-992-7766.

Technical Facilities: 0.108-kw ERP, 49-ft. above ground, 1102-ft. above sea level, lat. 34° 33' 57", long. 98° 23' 23".

Holds CP for change to 23-kw ERP, 328-ft. above ground, 1508-ft. above sea level, lat. 34° 34' 23.7", long. 98° 28' 39.8". BPTTL-20070410ADR.

Ownership: Mosely Enterprises LLC.

Lawton—K36AB, Ch. 36, Oklahoma Educational Television Authority. Phone: 405-848-8501.

Technical Facilities: 4.89-kw ERP, lat. 34° 37' 36", long. 98° 16' 18".

Holds CP for change to 15-kw ERP, 342-ft. above ground, 1640-ft. above sea level, lat. 34° 37' 26", long. 98° 16' 15". BDFCDTA-20060630AHQ.

Ownership: Oklahoma Educational Television Authority.

■ **Lawton**—K38GL, Ch. 38, Three Angels Broadcasting Network Inc. Phone: 618-627-4651. Fax: 618-627-4155.

Studio: 3391 Charley Good Rd, West Frankfort, IL 62896.

Technical Facilities: 53-kw ERP, 505-ft. above ground, 1706-ft. above sea level, lat. 34° 32' 59", long. 98° 32' 22".

Ownership: Three Angels Broadcasting Network Inc.

Personnel: Moses Primo, Chief Engineer.

Lawton—K43LK, Ch. 43, EICB-TV East LLC. Phone: 972-291-3750.

Technical Facilities: 0.05-kw ERP, 26-ft. above ground, 1165-ft. above sea level, lat. 34° 36' 45", long. 98° 25' 32".

Ownership: EICB-TV LLC.

Lawton—K49GC, Ch. 49, Trinity Broadcasting Network Inc. Phone: 714-832-2950. Fax: 714-730-0661.

Technical Facilities: 13.2-kw ERP, 170-ft. above ground, 1280-ft. above sea level, lat. 34° 36' 12", long. 98° 23' 46".

Holds CP for change to 15-kw ERP, 171-ft. above ground, 1280-ft. above sea level, BDFCDTT-20060330ADO.

Transmitter: Hotel Lawtonian.

Ownership: Trinity Broadcasting Network Inc.

Personnel: Paul Crouch, General Manager; Ben Miller, Chief Engineer; Rod Henke, Sales Manager.

Lawton—K53DS, Ch. 53, Mission Broadcasting of Wichita Falls Inc. Phone: 330-335-8808.

Studio: 3800 Call Field Rd., Wichita Falls, TX 76308.

Technical Facilities: 1000-w TPO, 35.3-kw ERP, 449-ft. above ground, 1657-ft. above sea level, lat. 34° 33' 00", long. 98° 32' 20".

Holds CP for change to channel number 13, 0.05-kw ERP, 467-ft. above ground, 1657-ft. above sea level, BDISDTT-20060403ACZ.

Transmitter: Deyo Mission Rd., 3.5-mi. SW of Lawton.

Ownership: Mission Broadcasting Inc.

Personnel: Kyle Williams, General Manager; Ken Thomasson, Chief Engineer; Melissa Detrich, Sales Manager.

Lawton—K64GJ, Ch. 64, Equity Media Holdings Corp., Debtor in Possession. Phone: 501-219-2400.

Technical Facilities: 21.83-kw ERP, 262-ft. above ground, 1473-ft. above sea level, lat. 34° 35' 31", long. 98° 32' 56".

Holds CP for change to channel number 23, 150-kw ERP, BDISTTL-20060403APZ.

Began Operation: November 13, 2006.

Ownership: Equity Media Holdings Corp., Debtor in Possession.

May, etc.—K18BV, Ch. 18, Local TV Oklahoma License LLC. Phone: 859-448-2707.

Technical Facilities: 100-w TPO, 0.815-kw ERP, 240-ft. above ground, 2615-ft. above sea level, lat. 36° 26' 03", long. 99° 46' 22".

Transmitter: 8-mi. N of Gage.

Ownership: Local TV Holdings LLC.

May, etc.—K22BR, Ch. 22, Local TV Oklahoma License LLC. Phone: 859-448-2707.

Technical Facilities: 0.815-kw ERP, 239-ft. above ground, 2615-ft. above sea level, lat. 36° 26' 03", long. 99° 46' 22".

Ownership: Local TV Holdings LLC.

McAlester—K51EK, Ch. 51, Family Broadcasting Group Inc. Phone: 405-631-7335.

Technical Facilities: 34.3-kw ERP, 328-ft. above ground, 1234-ft. above sea level, lat. 34° 58' 37", long. 95° 43' 01".

Began Operation: December 12, 1995.

Ownership: Family Broadcasting Group Inc.

McAlester—KEGG-LP, Ch. 35, Hosanna Apostolic Ministries Broadcasting Corp. Phone: 520-971-9274.

Technical Facilities: 0.45-kw ERP, 66-ft. above ground, 807-ft. above sea level, lat. 34° 57' 22", long. 95° 46' 23".

Began Operation: October 17, 2005.

Ownership: Hosanna Apostolic Ministries Broadcasting Corp.

Medford—K46AH, Ch. 46, Oklahoma Educational Television Authority. Phone: 405-848-8501.

Technical Facilities: 5.88-kw ERP, lat. 36° 40' 48", long. 97° 53' 19".

Holds CP for change to 2.3-kw ERP, 487-ft. above ground, 1647-ft. above sea level, BDFCDTA-20060630AHP.

Ownership: Oklahoma Educational Television Authority.

Miami—KELF-LP, Ch. 48, Family Media Inc. Phone: 918-541-1934.

Studio: 310 Spring St, Grove, OK 74344.

Technical Facilities: 98.4-kw ERP, 197-ft. above ground, 1093-ft. above sea level, lat. 36° 52' 50", long. 94° 59' 26".

Multichannel TV Sound: Planned.

Ownership: Family Media Inc.

Personnel: Tony Bickel, General Manager; Thom Thompson, Chief Engineer; Nolan Williams, Sales Manager; Jean Bohannan, Program Director.

Mooreland, etc.—K61CW, Ch. 61, Local TV Oklahoma License LLC. Phone: 859-448-2707.

Technical Facilities: 0.81-kw ERP, 2421-ft. above sea level, lat. 36° 34' 06", long. 99° 16' 33".

Ownership: Local TV Holdings LLC.

Muskogee—K14LD, Ch. 14, Family Broadcasting Group Inc. Phone: 405-631-7335.

Technical Facilities: 37-kw ERP, 265-ft. above ground, 922-ft. above sea level, lat. 35° 40' 51", long. 95° 25' 19".

Began Operation: July 22, 1997.

Ownership: Family Broadcasting Group Inc.

Muskogee—K25GJ, Ch. 25, Trinity Broadcasting Network. Phone: 714-832-2950. Fax: 714-730-0661.

Technical Facilities: 11.2-kw ERP, 171-ft. above ground, 769-ft. above sea level, lat. 35° 41' 48", long. 95° 18' 26".

Holds CP for change to channel number 16, 15-kw ERP, BDISDTT-20060330ACC.

Ownership: Trinity Broadcasting Network Inc.

■ **Norman**—KUOK-CA, Ch. 11, Woodward Broadcasting Inc., Debtor in Possession. Phone: 501-219-2400.

Technical Facilities: 0.8-kw ERP, 879-ft. above ground, 1962-ft. above sea level, lat. 35° 16' 50", long. 97° 20' 14".

Ownership: Equity Media Holdings Corp., Debtor in Possession.

■ **Nowata**—KGCT-LP, Ch. 25, Murphy D. Boughner. Phones: 918-273-2212; 918-599-4535. Fax: 918-599-4252.

Studio: 137 N Washington St, Bartlesville, OK 74006.

Technical Facilities: 1000-w TPO, 11.6-kw ERP, 85-ft. above ground, 841-ft. above sea level, lat. 36° 42' 10", long. 95° 38' 24".

Transmitter: Water Tower at junction of Pecan & Shawnee Sts.

Multichannel TV Sound: Stereo only.

Ownership: Murphy D. Boughner.

Personnel: Doug Boughner, General Manager.

■ **Oklahoma City**—KCHM-LP, Ch. 59, Oklahoma Land Co. LLC. Phone: 405-429-5003.

Technical Facilities: 20-kw ERP, 401-ft. above ground, 1713-ft. above sea level, lat. 35° 22' 10", long. 97° 27' 41".

Transmitter: 89th & Bryant Sts., Moore.

Began Operation: July 9, 1997.

Ownership: Oklahoma Land Co. LLC.

■ **Oklahoma City**—KLHO-LP, Ch. 17, Aracelis Ortiz Corp. Phone: 956-412-5600.

Technical Facilities: 1000-w TPO, 37.1-kw ERP, 197-ft. above ground, 1637-ft. above sea level, lat. 35° 22' 10", long. 97° 27' 36".

Transmitter: 5-mi. S of 89th & Bryant, Moore.

Ownership: Aracelis Ortiz Corp.

■ **Oklahoma City**—KOHC-CA, Ch. 38, Sunshine State Television Networks Inc. Phones: 954-431-3144; 305-776-8240. Fax: 954-431-3591.

Technical Facilities: 10-w TPO, 50-kw ERP, 177-ft. above ground, 1444-ft. above sea level, lat. 35° 21' 46", long. 97° 26' 57".

Transmitter: 2333 E Britton Rd.

Ownership: Sunshine State Television Networks Inc.

Personnel: Charles L. Freeny Jr., Chief Engineer.

Oklahoma City—KTOU-LP, Ch. 21, Mako Communications LLC.

Technical Facilities: 1000-w TPO, 41.61-kw ERP, 427-ft. above ground, 1706-ft. above sea level, lat. 35° 23' 14", long. 97° 29' 57".

Transmitter: 3.1-mi. S of Newcastle on State Hwy. 277.

Ownership: Mako Communications LLC.

Personnel: Bryan Covey, General Manager; Ron Turner, Chief Engineer; Don Shelton, Sales Manager.

■ **Oklahoma City**—KUOT-CA, Ch. 19, EICB-TV LLC. Phone: 972-291-3750.

Technical Facilities: 23.7-kw ERP, 591-ft. above ground, 1899-ft. above sea level, lat. 35° 22' 10", long. 97° 27' 41".

Holds CP for change to 150-kw ERP, BPTTA-20060111ACN.

Ownership: EICB-TV LLC.

Oklahoma City—KWDW-LP, Ch. 48, Oklahoma Land Co. LLC. Phone: 405-429-5003.

Technical Facilities: 18.1-kw ERP, 699-ft. above ground, 1829-ft. above sea level, lat. 35° 22' 51", long. 97° 29' 30".

Began Operation: December 30, 1992.

Ownership: Oklahoma Land Co. LLC.

Personnel: Pete Sumrall, General Manager; Dave Russell, Sales Manager; Doug Gerlinger, Chief Engineer.

Oklahoma City—KXOC-LP, Ch. 41, Family Broadcasting Group Inc. Phone: 405-631-7335.

Technical Facilities: 48.8-kw ERP, 1000-ft. above ground, 2104-ft. above sea level, lat. 35° 35' 52", long. 97° 29' 22".

Began Operation: April 26, 1995.

Ownership: Family Broadcasting Group Inc.

Ponca City—K38AK, Ch. 38, Oklahoma Educational Television Authority. Phone: 405-848-8501.

Technical Facilities: 6.89-kw ERP, lat. 36° 44' 30", long. 97° 02' 36".

Holds CP for change to 15-kw ERP, 410-ft. above ground, 1475-ft. above sea level, BDFCDTA-20060630AHO.

Ownership: Oklahoma Educational Television Authority.

Ponca City—K54FZ, Ch. 54, Family Broadcasting Group Inc. Phone: 405-631-7335.

Technical Facilities: 23.8-kw ERP, 387-ft. above ground, 1453-ft. above sea level, lat. 36° 45' 35", long. 97° 09' 36".

Transmitter: N side of Hubbard Rd., 4-mi. W of Union Rd.

Began Operation: August 13, 1996.

Ownership: Family Broadcasting Group Inc.

■ **Ponca City**—KTEW-CA, Ch. 27, Oklahoma Broadcast Associates LLC. Phone: 405-833-1380.

Studio: 114 West Central, Ponca City, OK 74601.

Technical Facilities: 100-w TPO, 0.689-kw ERP, 377-ft. above ground, 1194-ft. above sea level, lat. 36° 41' 25", long. 97° 10' 20".

Transmitter: 4-mi. W of Ponca City on Hwy. 60.

Ownership: Oklahoma Broadcast Associates LLC.

Personnel: Dave Hall, General Manager; Kristina Hall, Sales Manager; Rick King, Chief Engineer.

■ **Poteau**—KSJF-CA, Ch. 59, Fort Smith 46 Inc., Debtor in Possession. Phone: 501-219-2400. Fax: 501-785-4844.

Technical Facilities: 1000-w TPO, 21.2-kw ERP, 105-ft. above ground, 2485-ft. above sea level, lat. 35° 04' 17", long. 94° 40' 47".

Transmitter: Cavanal Mountain.

Began Operation: December 27, 1994.

Ownership: Equity Media Holdings Corp., Debtor in Possession.

Personnel: Karen Pharis, General Manager; Don Jones, Chief Engineer; Leo Cruz, Sales Manager.

Sayre—K26EU, Ch. 26, Oklahoma Community Television LLC. Phone: 405-808-2509.

Technical Facilities: 0.9-kw ERP, lat. 35° 09' 05", long. 99° 42' 50".

Transmitter: 3.75-mi. W of Sayre.

Ownership: Oklahoma Community Television LLC.

Seiling—K49DO, Ch. 49, Local TV Oklahoma License LLC. Phone: 859-448-2707.

Technical Facilities: 100-w TPO, 0.77-kw ERP, 2231-ft. above sea level, lat. 36° 06' 00", long. 98° 57' 05".

Transmitter: Near Seiling.

Ownership: Local TV Holdings LLC.

Seiling—K51EB, Ch. 51, Local TV Oklahoma License LLC. Phone: 859-448-2707.

Technical Facilities: 100-w TPO, 0.77-kw ERP, 2231-ft. above sea level, lat. 36° 06' 00", long. 98° 57' 05".

Transmitter: Near Seiling.

Ownership: Local TV Holdings LLC.

Seiling—K53CI, Ch. 53, Local TV Oklahoma License LLC. Phone: 859-448-2707.

Technical Facilities: 0.815-kw ERP, 299-ft. above ground, 2257-ft. above sea level, lat. 36° 06' 00", long. 98° 57' 05".

Ownership: Local TV Holdings LLC.

Seiling—K55EZ, Ch. 55, Local TV Oklahoma License LLC. Phone: 859-448-2707.

Technical Facilities: 0.815-kw ERP, 299-ft. above ground, 2257-ft. above sea level, lat. 36° 06' 00", long. 98° 57' 05".

Ownership: Local TV Holdings LLC.

Seiling—K57EA, Ch. 57, Local TV Oklahoma License LLC. Phone: 859-448-2707.

Technical Facilities: 292-ft. above ground, 2257-ft. above sea level, lat. 36° 06' 00", long. 98° 57' 05".

Ownership: Local TV Holdings LLC.

Stillwater—K21DF, Ch. 21, Family Broadcasting Group Inc. Phone: 405-631-7335.

Technical Facilities: 36.3-kw ERP, 325-ft. above ground, 1355-ft. above sea level, lat. 36° 06' 31", long. 97° 11' 46".

Began Operation: September 21, 1994.

Ownership: Family Broadcasting Group Inc.

Stillwater—KOKG-LP, Ch. 19, KOKI Television LLC.

Technical Facilities: 100-w TPO, 1.16-kw ERP, 1037-ft. above sea level, lat. 36° 08' 13", long. 97° 01' 41".

Transmitter: 1501 N. Hightower St.

Ownership: KOKI Television LLC.

Stillwater—KOKM-LP, Ch. 7, Wellsprings TV Network Inc. Phone: 409-813-1000.

Technical Facilities: 10-w TPO, 15.9-kw ERP, 1027-ft. above sea level, lat. 36° 08' 13", long. 97° 01' 41".

Transmitter: 1505 N. Hightower St.

Ownership: Wellsprings Television Network Inc.

Personnel: Gershon Haston, Vice President & General Manager.

Stillwater—KWEM-LP, Ch. 31, Venture Media Group LLC. Phone: 405-377-8831.

Technical Facilities: 1000-w TPO, 8.9-kw ERP, 711-ft. above ground, 1742-ft. above sea level, lat. 36° 06' 31", long. 97° 11' 46".

Transmitter: 6.8-mi. W of the center of Stillwater.

Ownership: Venture Media Group LLC.

Personnel: Trace Morgan, Manager.

Strong City—K28BY, Ch. 28, Oklahoma Community Television LLC. Phone: 405-808-2509.

Technical Facilities: 0.815-kw ERP, lat. 35° 46' 58", long. 99° 35' 13".

Transmitter: 8-mi. N of Strong City.

Ownership: Oklahoma Community Television LLC.

Strong City—K30EF, Ch. 30, Oklahoma Community Television LLC. Phone: 405-808-2509.

Technical Facilities: 1.07-kw ERP, 249-ft. above ground, 2589-ft. above sea level, lat. 35° 46' 58", long. 99° 35' 13".

Ownership: Oklahoma Community Television LLC.

Strong City—K32DF, Ch. 32, Oklahoma Community Television LLC. Phone: 405-808-2509.

Technical Facilities: 1.07-kw ERP, 249-ft. above ground, 2589-ft. above sea level, lat. 35° 46' 53", long. 99° 35' 13".

Ownership: Oklahoma Community Television LLC.

Strong City—K36AJ, Ch. 36, Oklahoma Community Television LLC. Phone: 405-808-2509.

Technical Facilities: 0.847-kw ERP, 341-ft. above ground, 2680-ft. above sea level, lat. 35° 46' 50", long. 99° 35' 13".

Holds CP for change to channel number 25, 10-kw ERP, lat. 35° 46' 57.8", long. 99° 35' 12.6". BDISTT-20060719ABL.

Ownership: Oklahoma Community Television LLC.

Strong City—K38AM, Ch. 38, Oklahoma Community Television LLC. Phone: 405-808-2509.

Technical Facilities: 0.872-kw ERP, 341-ft. above ground, 2680-ft. above sea level, lat. 35° 46' 58", long. 99° 35' 13".

Ownership: Oklahoma Community Television LLC.

Strong City—K40AG, Ch. 40, Oklahoma Community Television LLC. Phone: 405-808-2509.

Technical Facilities: 0.205-kw ERP, lat. 35° 46' 58", long. 99° 35' 13".

Ownership: Oklahoma Community Television LLC.

Strong City—K42AG, Ch. 42, Oklahoma Community Television LLC. Phone: 405-808-2509.

Technical Facilities: 1.1-kw ERP, lat. 38° 30' 32", long. 113° 17' 21".

Transmitter: 18-mi. WNW of Milford.

Ownership: Oklahoma Community Television LLC.

■ **Sulphur**—KOKT-LP, Ch. 36, Oklahoma Land Co. LLC. Phone: 405-429-5003.

Studio: PO Box 944, State Hwy 7, Sulphur, OK 73086.

Technical Facilities: 1000-w TPO, 52.4-kw ERP, 299-ft. above ground, 1564-ft. above sea level, lat. 34° 22' 32", long. 97° 08' 05".

Transmitter: 0.5-mi. N of Springer.

Began Operation: December 11, 1992.

Ownership: Oklahoma Land Co. LLC.

Personnel: Beverly Orr, General Manager; Neal Ardman, Chief Engineer.

Tahlequah—K04DY, Ch. 4, Northeastern State U. Phone: 918-456-5511.

Technical Facilities: 10-w TPO, 0.07-kw ERP, lat. 35° 54' 51", long. 94° 59' 18".

Transmitter: Keetowah Hill in Tahlequah.

Ownership: Northeastern State U.

Tahlequah—K30IX, Ch. 30, Trinity Broadcasting Network. Phones: 330-753-5542; 714-832-2950. Fax: 714-730-0661.

Technical Facilities: 10-kw ERP, 269-ft. above ground, 1329-ft. above sea level, lat. 35° 59' 24", long. 94° 56' 12".

Transmitter: Approx. 1-mi. NW of McSpadden Falls.

Ownership: Trinity Broadcasting Network Inc.

Tulsa—K13XU, Ch. 13, Family Broadcasting Group Inc. Phone: 405-631-7335.

Technical Facilities: 1-kw ERP, 220-ft. above ground, 1204-ft. above sea level, lat. 36° 11' 27", long. 96° 05' 32".

Began Operation: March 10, 1997.

Ownership: Family Broadcasting Group Inc.

Tulsa—K15DA, Ch. 15, Family Broadcasting Group Inc. Phone: 405-631-7335.

Technical Facilities: 70.9-kw ERP, 154-ft. above ground, 1014-ft. above sea level, lat. 35° 58' 15", long. 96° 10' 45".

Began Operation: October 24, 1996.

Ownership: Family Broadcasting Group Inc.

Tulsa—K39CW, Ch. 39, Ventana Television Inc. Phone: 727-872-4210.

Technical Facilities: 2000-w TPO, 29.8-kw ERP, 702-ft. above ground, 1165-ft. above sea level, lat. 36° 09' 01", long. 95° 59' 25".

Transmitter: Fourth National Bank Bldg., 15 W. 6th St.

Began Operation: May 7, 1992.

Ownership: Ventana Television Inc.

Personnel: John Skelnik, General Manager & Chief Engineer.

Tulsa—K40KC-D, Ch. 40, Three Angels Broadcasting Network Inc. Phone: 618-627-4651. Fax: 618-627-4155.

Studio: 3391 Charley Good Rd, West Frankfort, IL 62896.

Technical Facilities: 1.5-kw ERP, 197-ft. above ground, 1099-ft. above sea level, lat. 36° 06' 55.7", long. 96° 01' 02".

Ownership: Three Angels Broadcasting Network Inc.

Personnel: Moses Primo, Chief Engineer.

Tulsa—K57IP, Ch. 57, MS Communications LLC. Phone: 414-765-9737.

Technical Facilities: 0.007-kw ERP, 50-ft. above ground, 924-ft. above sea level, lat. 36° 06' 38.2", long. 96° 02' 04.2".

Ownership: MS Communications LLC.

■ **Tulsa**—KTZT-CA, Ch. 29, Word of God Fellowship Inc. Phone: 817-571-1229.

Technical Facilities: 1000-w TPO, 6-kw ERP, 702-ft. above ground, 1132-ft. above sea level, lat. 16° 09' 01", long. 95° 59' 25".

Transmitter: Bank Four Bldg.

Ownership: Word of God Fellowship Inc.

■ **Tulsa**—KUTU-CA, Ch. 25, Oklahoma Land Co. LLC. Phone: 405-429-5003.

Technical Facilities: 5.06-kw ERP, 476-ft. above ground, 1198-ft. above sea level, lat. 36° 09' 01", long. 95° 59' 25".

Transmitter: Bank IV Center, 15th W. 6th St.

Began Operation: June 11, 1996.

Ownership: Oklahoma Land Co. LLC.

Tulsa—KXAP-LD, Ch. 51, Las Americas Supermercado Inc. Phone: 918-794-0720.

Technical Facilities: 15-kw ERP, 270-ft. above ground, 941-ft. above sea level, lat. 36° 05' 13", long. 95° 51' 33".

Ownership: Las Americas Supermercado Inc.

Weatherford—K17DH, Ch. 17, Oklahoma Community Television LLC. Phone: 405-808-2509.

Technical Facilities: 20-w TPO, 0.9-kw ERP, 1968-ft. above sea level, lat. 35° 29' 28", long. 98° 43' 54".

Transmitter: 2.5-mi. SSW of Weatherford.

Ownership: Oklahoma Community Television LLC.

Weatherford—K20DX, Ch. 20, Oklahoma Community Television LLC. Phone: 405-808-2509.

Technical Facilities: 20-w TPO, 0.9-kw ERP, 1968-ft. above sea level, lat. 35° 29' 28", long. 98° 43' 54".

Transmitter: 2.5-mi. SSW of Weatherford.

Ownership: Oklahoma Community Television LLC.

Weatherford—K22ED, Ch. 22, Oklahoma Community Television LLC. Phone: 405-808-2509.

Technical Facilities: 0.9-kw ERP, 1968-ft. above sea level, lat. 35° 29' 28", long. 98° 43' 54".

Transmitter: 2.5-mi. SSW of Weatherford.

Ownership: Oklahoma Community Television LLC.

Weatherford—K38HM, Ch. 38, Oklahoma Community Television LLC. Phone: 405-808-2509.

Technical Facilities: 0.7-kw ERP, 187-ft. above ground, 1968-ft. above sea level, lat. 35° 29' 28", long. 35° 29' 54".

Ownership: Oklahoma Community Television LLC.

Weatherford—K41DS, Ch. 41, Oklahoma Community Television LLC. Phone: 405-808-2509.

Technical Facilities: 0.886-kw ERP, 187-ft. above ground, 1968-ft. above sea level, lat. 35° 29' 28", long. 98° 43' 54".

Ownership: Oklahoma Community Television LLC.

Woodward—K59EE, Ch. 59, Local TV Oklahoma License LLC. Phone: 859-448-2707.

Technical Facilities: 100-w TPO, 0.815-kw ERP, 305-ft. above ground, 2428-ft. above sea level, lat. 36° 34' 06", long. 99° 16' 33".

Transmitter: 8.9-mi. NNW of Mooreland.

Ownership: Local TV Holdings LLC.

■ **Woodward**—KOMI-CD, Ch. 34, Omni Broadcasting Inc. Phone: 580-256-5400. Fax: 580-256-3825.

Technical Facilities: 15-kw ERP, 1060-ft. above ground, 3330-ft. above sea level, lat. 36° 16' 06", long. 99° 26' 56".

Ownership: 101 Television.

Personnel: Anne Coleman, General Manager; Lawrence Powell, Chief Engineer; Larry Anderson, Sales Manager.

Woodward, etc.—K63CF, Ch. 63, Local TV Oklahoma License LLC. Phone: 859-448-2707.

Technical Facilities: 0.81-kw ERP, 2421-ft. above sea level, lat. 36° 34' 06", long. 99° 16' 33".

Ownership: Local TV Holdings LLC.

Woodward, etc.—K65CO, Ch. 65, Local TV Oklahoma License LLC. Phone: 859-448-2707.

Technical Facilities: 0.81-kw ERP, 2421-ft. above sea level, lat. 36° 34' 06", long. 99° 16' 33".

Ownership: Local TV Holdings LLC.

Woodward, etc.—K67CW, Ch. 67, Local TV Oklahoma License LLC. Phone: 859-448-2707.

Technical Facilities: 0.815-kw ERP, 2425-ft. above sea level, lat. 36° 34' 06", long. 99° 16' 33".

Ownership: Local TV Holdings LLC.

Woodward, etc.—K69DH, Ch. 69, Local TV Oklahoma License LLC. Phone: 859-448-2707.

Technical Facilities: 100-w TPO, 0.815-kw ERP, 300-ft. above ground, 2420-ft. above sea level, lat. 36° 34' 06", long. 99° 16' 33".

Transmitter: Approx. 9-mi. NNW of Mooreland.

Ownership: Local TV Holdings LLC.

Oregon

Albany, etc.—K20DD, Ch. 20, Meredith Corp. Phones: 503-239-4949; 515-284-3000. Fax: 503-239-6184.

Technical Facilities: 10.7-kw ERP, 69-ft. above ground, 1489-ft. above sea level, lat. 44° 30' 18", long. 122° 57' 32".

Holds CP for change to 2-kw ERP, 69-ft. above ground, 1491-ft. above sea level, BDFCDTL-20060331BCA.

Ownership: Meredith Corp.

Altamont, etc.—K52AS, Ch. 52, Soda Mountain Broadcasting Inc. Phone: 541-773-1212. Fax: 541-779-9261.

Studio: 1090 Knutson Ave, Medford, OR 97504.

Technical Facilities: 14.3-kw ERP, lat. 42° 12' 57", long. 121° 47' 53".

Ownership: Soda Mountain Broadcasting Inc.

Personnel: Renard Maiuri, General Manager.

Applegate Valley—K02EK, Ch. 2, Freedom Broadcasting of Oregon Licensee LLC. Phone: 518-346-6666.

Technical Facilities: 0.004-kw ERP, 2720-ft. above sea level, lat. 42° 13' 12", long. 123° 01' 59".

Ownership: Freedom Communications Holdings Inc.

Applegate Valley—K04ER, Ch. 4, California-Oregon Broadcasting Inc.

Technical Facilities: 0.003-kw ERP, 2720-ft. above sea level, lat. 42° 13' 12", long. 123° 01' 59".

Ownership: California-Oregon Broadcasting Inc.

Arlington—K17GK, Ch. 17, Oregon Public Broadcasting. Phone: 503-244-9900.

Technical Facilities: 1-kw ERP, 79-ft. above ground, 1814-ft. above sea level, lat. 45° 45' 50", long. 120° 14' 40".

Holds CP for change to 0.3-kw ERP, BDFCDTT-20080325AHM.

Ownership: Oregon Public Broadcasting.

Ashland—K39EF, Ch. 39, WatchTV Inc. Phone: 503-241-2411. Fax: 503-226-3557.

Technical Facilities: 24.5-kw ERP, 79-ft. above ground, 3730-ft. above sea level, lat. 42° 17' 43", long. 122° 45' 00".

Holds CP for change to 0.83-kw ERP, 79-ft. above ground, 3881-ft. above sea level, lat. 42° 17' 53", long. 122° 45' 01". BDFCDTL-20090102ACJ.

Began Operation: February 5, 1996.

Ownership: WatchTV Inc.

Personnel: Gregory J. Herman, General Manager; Steven A. Hale, Station Manager.

Ashland, etc.—K04EO, Ch. 4, Freedom Broadcasting of Oregon Licensee LLC. Phone: 518-346-6666.

Technical Facilities: 0.08-kw ERP, 3796-ft. above sea level, lat. 42° 17' 43", long. 122° 45' 00".

Ownership: Freedom Communications Holdings Inc.

Astoria—K04PH, Ch. 4, Kenneth E. Lewetag. Phone: 503-930-7228.

Technical Facilities: 2.25-kw ERP, 69-ft. above ground, 1388-ft. above sea level, lat. 46° 17' 10", long. 123° 53' 50".

Ownership: Kenneth E. Lewetag.

Astoria—K05LE, Ch. 5, Michael L. Mattson. Phone: 503-409-2181.

Technical Facilities: 2.5-kw ERP, 69-ft. above ground, 1388-ft. above sea level, lat. 46° 17' 10", long. 123° 53' 50".

Ownership: Michael L. Mattson.

Astoria—K17HA, Ch. 17, King Broadcasting Co. Phone: 214-977-6606.

Technical Facilities: 18-kw ERP, 49-ft. above ground, 1421-ft. above sea level, lat. 46° 17' 11", long. 123° 53' 45".

Ownership: King Broadcasting Co.

Astoria—K23GK, Ch. 23, Oregon Public Broadcasting. Phone: 503-244-9900.

Technical Facilities: 15.5-kw ERP, 49-ft. above ground, 1421-ft. above sea level, lat. 46° 17' 11", long. 123° 53' 45".

Holds CP for change to 3.1-kw ERP, BDFCDTT-20080319AAQ.

Ownership: Oregon Public Broadcasting.

Astoria—K26DB, Ch. 26, Fisher Broadcasting Inc. - Portland TV LLC.

Technical Facilities: 23.8-kw ERP, 49-ft. above ground, 1375-ft. above sea level, lat. 46° 17' 10", long. 123° 53' 50".

Ownership: Fisher Communications Inc.

Astoria—K28FP, Ch. 28, WatchTV Inc. Phone: 503-241-2411. Fax: 503-226-3557.

Technical Facilities: 1000-w TPO, 13.2-kw ERP, 49-ft. above ground, 1375-ft. above sea level, lat. 46° 17' 10", long. 123° 53' 50".

Holds CP for change to 15-kw ERP, BDFCDTL-20090102ACL.

Transmitter: 2.9-mi. N of U.S. 101, 2.5-mi. ENE of Chinook.

Began Operation: July 27, 1999.

Ownership: WatchTV Inc.

Personnel: Gregory J. Herman, General Manager; Steven A. Hale, Station Manager.

Astoria—K34DC, Ch. 34, NVT Portland Licensee LLC, Debtor in Possession. Phone: 404-995-4711.

Technical Facilities: 23.6-kw ERP, 49-ft. above ground, 1375-ft. above sea level, lat. 46° 17' 10", long. 123° 53' 50".

Began Operation: May 5, 1992.

Ownership: New Vision Television LLC, Debtor in Possession.

Baker—K42AI, Ch. 42, Blue Mountain Translator District. Phone: 509-529-9149.

Technical Facilities: 1.68-kw ERP, lat. 44° 36' 32", long. 117° 46' 32".

Ownership: Blue Mountain Translator District.

Baker—K46AM, Ch. 46, Blue Mountain Translator District. Phone: 509-529-9149.

Technical Facilities: 0.1-kw ERP, lat. 44° 36' 32", long. 117° 46' 32".

Ownership: Blue Mountain Translator District.

Baker—K50FD, Ch. 50, Blue Mountain Translator District. Phone: 509-529-9149.

Technical Facilities: 0.9-kw ERP, 23-ft. above ground, 6421-ft. above sea level, lat. 44° 36' 32", long. 117° 46' 32".

Ownership: Blue Mountain Translator District.

Baker City—K55JS, Ch. 55, Blue Mountain Translator District. Phone: 509-529-9149.

Technical Facilities: 4.9-kw ERP, 36-ft. above ground, 6437-ft. above sea level, lat. 44° 35' 57", long. 117° 46' 58".

Ownership: Blue Mountain Translator District.

Baker City, etc.—K20IV-D, Ch. 20, Oregon Public Broadcasting. Phone: 503-244-9900.

Technical Facilities: 0.5-kw ERP, 30-ft. above ground, 6430-ft. above sea level, lat. 44° 35' 57", long. 117° 46' 58".

Began Operation: December 2, 2008.

Ownership: Oregon Public Broadcasting.

Baker City, etc.—K48DC, Ch. 48, Oregon Public Broadcasting. Phone: 503-244-9900.

Technical Facilities: 5-kw ERP, 30-ft. above ground, 6430-ft. above sea level, lat. 44° 35' 57", long. 117° 46' 58".

Began Operation: November 1, 1988.

Ownership: Oregon Public Broadcasting.

Baker Valley—K44AJ, Ch. 44, Blue Mountain Translator District. Phone: 509-529-9149.

Technical Facilities: 0.337-kw ERP, lat. 44° 36' 32", long. 117° 46' 32".

Ownership: Blue Mountain Translator District.

Baker Valley, etc.—K40AJ, Ch. 40, Blue Mountain Translator District. Phone: 509-529-9149.

Technical Facilities: 0.278-kw ERP, 6421-ft. above sea level, lat. 44° 36' 32", long. 117° 46' 32".

Ownership: Blue Mountain Translator District.

Bend—K27DO, Ch. 27, NPG of Oregon Inc. Phone: 816-271-8505.

Technical Facilities: 8.7-kw ERP, lat. 44° 26' 17", long. 120° 57' 13".

Holds CP for change to 5-kw ERP, 72-ft. above ground, 5705-ft. above sea level, BDFCDTA-20060703ACY.

Transmitter: Grizzly Mountain, 10-mi. NW of Prineville.

Ownership: News Press & Gazette Co.

Bend—K28JE, Ch. 28, EICB-TV East LLC. Phone: 972-291-3750.

Technical Facilities: 0.1-kw ERP, 33-ft. above ground, 3720-ft. above sea level, lat. 44° 03' 40", long. 121° 17' 23".

Holds CP for change to 2-kw ERP, 49-ft. above ground, 6519-ft. above sea level, lat. 44° 04' 43", long. 121° 33' 07". BPTTL-20090511AZL.

Began Operation: March 24, 2009.

Ownership: EICB-TV LLC.

Bend—K33AG, Ch. 33, Trinity Broadcasting Network Inc. Phone: 714-832-2950. Fax: 714-730-0661.

Technical Facilities: 2.9-kw ERP, 75-ft. above ground, 4311-ft. above sea level, lat. 44° 04' 40", long. 121° 19' 49".

Holds CP for change to 15-kw ERP, BDFCDTT-20060330ADV.

Ownership: Trinity Broadcasting Network Inc.

Bend—K45KM-D, Ch. 45, NPG of Oregon Inc. Phone: 816-271-8502.

Technical Facilities: 4.4-kw ERP, 141-ft. above ground, 4357-ft. above sea level, lat. 44° 04' 40", long. 121° 19' 49".

Ownership: News Press & Gazette Co.

Bend—K53JV, Ch. 53, Three Sisters Broadcasting LLC. Phone: 541-485-5611.

Technical Facilities: 30-kw ERP, 200-ft. above ground, 4419-ft. above sea level, lat. 44° 04' 40.6", long. 121° 19' 56.9".

Ownership: Three Sisters Broadcasting LLC.

■ **Bend**—KABH-CA, Ch. 15, WatchTV Inc. Phone: 503-241-2411. Fax: 503-226-3557.

Technical Facilities: 1000-w TPO, 84-kw ERP, 49-ft. above ground, 4327-ft. above sea level, lat. 44° 04' 30", long. 121° 19' 46".

Transmitter: Aubrey Butte, 1.4-mi. W of U.S. Rte. 20/97.

Ownership: WatchTV Inc.

Personnel: Gregory J. Hermann, General Manager; Steven A. Hale, Station Manager.

Bend—KBND-LP, Ch. 41, Combined Communications Inc. Phone: 541-382-5263.

Technical Facilities: 6.5-kw ERP, 184-ft. above ground, 4393-ft. above sea level, lat. 44° 04' 39", long. 121° 19' 57".

Holds CP for change to 2.3-kw ERP, 174-ft. above ground, 4383-ft. above sea level, BMPDTL-20090521AEQ.

Ownership: Combined Communications Inc.

Bend—KBNZ-LD, Ch. 7, NVT Portland Licensee LLC, Debtor in Possession. Phones: 503-464-0600; 404-995-4711.

Technical Facilities: 0.3-kw ERP, 289-ft. above ground, 4508-ft. above sea level, lat. 44° 04' 41", long. 121° 19' 57".

Multichannel TV Sound: Stereo and separate audio program.

Began Operation: May 6, 1988.

Ownership: New Vision Television LLC, Debtor in Possession.

■ **Bend**—KFXO-LP, Ch. 39, NPG of Oregon Inc. Phone: 816-271-8502.

Technical Facilities: 1000-w TPO, 21.6-kw ERP, 5361-ft. above sea level, lat. 44° 11' 52", long. 120° 58' 35".

Holds CP for change to 15-kw ERP, 141-ft. above ground, 4357-ft. above sea level, lat. 44° 04' 40", long. 121° 19' 49". BMPDTA-20080725ABT.

Transmitter: Powell Butte, approx. 5-mi. SSE of Powell Butte.

Began Operation: October 14, 1993.

Ownership: News Press & Gazette Co.

Bend—KUBN-LP, Ch. 50, Meredith Corp. Phones: 503-239-4949; 515-284-3000. Fax: 503-239-6184.

Technical Facilities: 11.7-kw ERP, lat. 44° 11' 51", long. 120° 58' 35".

Holds CP for change to channel number 43, 32.7-kw ERP, 68-ft. above ground, 5238-ft. above sea level, BDISTTL-20060822AIL.

Transmitter: Powell Butte, 9.4-mi. SW of Prineville.

Ownership: Meredith Corp.

Black Butte Ranch—K04HK, Ch. 4, Black Butte Ranch Association. Phone: 541-595-1501.

Technical Facilities: 0.025-kw ERP, 4071-ft. above sea level, lat. 44° 21' 07", long. 121° 41' 24".

Ownership: Black Butte Ranch Association.

Black Butte Ranch—K05GZ, Ch. 5, Black Butte Ranch Association. Phone: 541-595-1501.

Technical Facilities: 0.025-kw ERP, 4058-ft. above sea level, lat. 44° 21' 07", long. 121° 41' 24".

Transmitter: 5-Mile Butte, Deschutes County.

Ownership: Black Butte Ranch Association.

Black Butte Ranch—K64AO, Ch. 64, Black Butte Ranch Association. Phone: 541-595-1501.

Technical Facilities: 0.163-kw ERP, 4058-ft. above sea level, lat. 44° 21' 07", long. 121° 41' 24".

Ownership: Black Butte Ranch Association.

Brookings—K07JT, Ch. 7, California-Oregon Broadcasting Inc. Phone: 541-779-5555.

Technical Facilities: 0.3-kw ERP, 26-ft. above ground, 1168-ft. above sea level, lat. 42° 02' 39", long. 124° 14' 00".

Ownership: California-Oregon Broadcasting Inc.

Brookings—K10LR, Ch. 10, Freedom Broadcasting of Oregon Licensee LLC.

Technical Facilities: 0.056-kw ERP, lat. 42° 02' 39", long. 124° 13' 52".

Ownership: Freedom Communications Holdings Inc.

Brookings—K57GP, Ch. 57, Three Angels Broadcasting Network Inc. Phone: 618-627-4651. Fax: 618-627-4155.

Studio: 3391 Charley Good Rd, West Frankfort, IL 62896.

Technical Facilities: 100-w TPO, 1.869-kw ERP, 72-ft. above ground, 1890-ft. above sea level, lat. 42° 07' 23", long. 124° 17' 56".

Holds CP for change to channel number 21, 1.2-kw ERP, 72-ft. above ground, 1857-ft. above sea level, BDFCDTL-20070612ABU.

Transmitter: 5-mi. NE of Brookings.

Ownership: Three Angels Broadcasting Network Inc.

Personnel: Moses Primo, Chief Engineer.

Brookings—KBSC-LP, Ch. 49, Oregon Coast Media Inc. Phone: 707-977-0338.

Studio: 605 Railroad St, Brookings, OR 97415.

Technical Facilities: 100-w TPO, 5.6-kw ERP, 26-ft. above ground, 1368-ft. above sea level, lat. 42° 03' 08", long. 124° 14' 07".

Transmitter: 1.2-mi. E of Harbor.

Ownership: Fred McCutchan.

Personnel: Bob deGroot, Sales Manager; Dan Nelson, Chief Engineer; Dave Shaw, News Director.

Brookings, etc.—K18EP, Ch. 18, Southern Oregon Public Television Inc.

Technical Facilities: 3.21-kw ERP, 30-ft. above ground, 1781-ft. above sea level, lat. 42° 07' 23", long. 124° 17' 56".

Ownership: Southern Oregon Public Television Inc.

Brookings, etc.—K31GP, Ch. 31, Broadcasting Licenses LP. Phone: 517-347-4141.

Technical Facilities: 2.15-kw ERP, 27-ft. above ground, 182-ft. above sea level, lat. 42° 03' 09", long. 124° 16' 51".

Ownership: Broadcasting Licenses LP.

Burns—K36BA, Ch. 36, Oregon Public Broadcasting. Phone: 503-244-9900.

Technical Facilities: 0.78-kw ERP, lat. 43° 34' 26", long. 119° 07' 48".

Holds CP for change to 0.62-kw ERP, 43-ft. above ground, 5351-ft. above sea level, BDFCDTT-20090225AAC.

Ownership: Oregon Public Broadcasting.

Burns—K41HZ, Ch. 41, NPG of Oregon Inc. Phone: 816-271-8502.

Technical Facilities: 9.45-kw ERP, 92-ft. above ground, 5377-ft. above sea level, lat. 43° 34' 26", long. 119° 07' 47".

Ownership: News Press & Gazette Co.

Burns—K43IH, Ch. 43, NPG of Oregon Inc. Phone: 816-271-8502.

Technical Facilities: 9.45-kw ERP, 92-ft. above ground, 5377-ft. above sea level, lat. 43° 34' 26", long. 119° 07' 47".

Ownership: News Press & Gazette Co.

Butte Falls—K02JF, Ch. 2, Southern Oregon Public Television Inc. Phone: 541-779-0808.

Technical Facilities: 0.046-kw ERP, lat. 42° 34' 24", long. 122° 34' 15".

Ownership: Southern Oregon Public Television Inc.

Butte Falls—K04JQ, Ch. 4, Freedom Broadcasting of Oregon Licensee LLC. Phone: 518-346-6666.

Technical Facilities: 0.009-kw ERP, lat. 42° 34' 24", long. 122° 34' 15".

Ownership: Freedom Communications Holdings Inc.

■ **Camas**—KOXI-CA, Ch. 20, WatchTV Inc. Phone: 503-241-2411. Fax: 503-226-3557.

Technical Facilities: 150-kw ERP, 600-ft. above ground, 1722-ft. above sea level, lat. 45° 31' 21", long. 122° 44' 45".

Ownership: WatchTV Inc.

Personnel: Gregory J. Herman, General Manager; Steven A. Hale, Station Manager.

Camas Valley—K07PP, Ch. 7, South West Oregon TV Broadcasting Corp. Phone: 206-404-3065.

Technical Facilities: 0.046-kw ERP, lat. 42° 59' 44", long. 123° 45' 31".

Began Operation: June 10, 1980.

Ownership: California-Oregon Broadcasting Inc.; Fisher Communications Inc.

Camas Valley—K21AI, Ch. 21, Camas Valley Grange No. 521. Phone: 541-225-1110.

Technical Facilities: 0.28-kw ERP, lat. 42° 59' 44", long. 123° 45' 31".

Ownership: Camas Valley Grange No. 521.

■ **Canyonville**—K32ET, Ch. 32, Three Angels Broadcasting Network Inc. Phone: 618-627-4651. Fax: 618-627-4155.

Studio: 3391 Charley Good Rd, West Frankfort, IL 62896.

Technical Facilities: 100-w TPO, 0.6-kw ERP, 69-ft. above ground, 3538-ft. above sea level, lat. 42° 54' 06", long. 123° 17' 07".

Transmitter: 2-mi. S of Canyonville.

Ownership: Three Angels Broadcasting Network Inc.

Personnel: Moses Primo, Chief Engineer.

Canyonville—K43DI, Ch. 43, California-Oregon Broadcasting Inc. Phone: 541-779-5555.

Technical Facilities: 0.35-kw ERP, lat. 42° 54' 06", long. 123° 17' 07".

Ownership: California-Oregon Broadcasting Inc.

Canyonville, etc.—K07KT, Ch. 7, California-Oregon Broadcasting Inc. Phone: 541-779-5555.

Technical Facilities: 0.02-kw ERP, 3389-ft. above sea level, lat. 42° 54' 06", long. 123° 17' 07".

Ownership: California-Oregon Broadcasting Inc.

Carpenterville—K60BJ, Ch. 60, Freedom Broadcasting of Oregon Licensee LLC.

Technical Facilities: 0.003-kw ERP, lat. 42° 12' 32", long. 124° 13' 27".

Ownership: Freedom Communications Holdings Inc.

Cascadia—K04CX, Ch. 4, Cascadia Community TV Inc. Phone: 541-367-2927.

Technical Facilities: 0.009-kw ERP, lat. 44° 23' 19", long. 122° 28' 11".

Ownership: Cascadia Community TV Inc.

Cave Junction—K07PZ, Ch. 7, California-Oregon Broadcasting Inc. Phone: 541-779-5555.

Technical Facilities: 0.005-kw ERP, 4026-ft. above sea level, lat. 42° 15' 31", long. 123° 39' 43".

Ownership: California-Oregon Broadcasting Inc.

Cave Junction—K13PH, Ch. 13, Southern Oregon Public Television Inc. Phone: 541-779-0808.

Technical Facilities: 0.046-kw ERP, lat. 42° 15' 14", long. 123° 39' 38".

Ownership: Southern Oregon Public Television Inc.

Cave Junction—K22IQ-D, Ch. 22, Southern Oregon Public Television Inc. Phone: 541-779-0808.

Technical Facilities: 0.1-kw ERP, 23-ft. above ground, 4022-ft. above sea level, lat. 42° 15' 29", long. 123° 39' 39".

Ownership: Southern Oregon Public Television Inc.

Cave Junction—K24BV, Ch. 24, Freedom Broadcasting of Oregon Licensee LLC.

Technical Facilities: 8.9-kw ERP, lat. 42° 15' 31", long. 123° 39' 36".

Ownership: Freedom Communications Holdings Inc.

Cave Junction—K48GO, Ch. 48, Better Life Television. Phone: 541-582-8024.

Technical Facilities: 4.1-kw ERP, 89-ft. above ground, 4091-ft. above sea level, lat. 42° 15' 31", long. 123° 39' 43".

Ownership: Better Life Television Inc.

Cave Junction, etc.—K02DV, Ch. 2, Freedom Broadcasting of Oregon Licensee LLC. Phone: 518-346-6666.

Technical Facilities: 0.004-kw ERP, 2192-ft. above sea level, lat. 42° 08' 06", long. 123° 41' 42".

Ownership: Freedom Communications Holdings Inc.

Cave Junction, etc.—K51BV, Ch. 51, Soda Mountain Broadcasting Inc. Phone: 541-485-5611.

Technical Facilities: 0.616-kw ERP, 49-ft. above ground, 4049-ft. above sea level, lat. 42° 15' 31", long. 123° 39' 43".

Ownership: Soda Mountain Broadcasting Inc.

Chemult—K06LI, Ch. 6, NPG of Oregon Inc.

Technical Facilities: 0.067-kw ERP, 36-ft. above ground, 6772-ft. above sea level, lat. 43° 18' 19", long. 121° 42' 56".

Ownership: News Press & Gazette Co.

Chemult—K07PS, Ch. 7, California-Oregon Broadcasting Inc.

Technical Facilities: 0.047-kw ERP, 7100-ft. above sea level, lat. 43° 18' 19", long. 121° 42' 56".

Ownership: California-Oregon Broadcasting Inc.

Chiloquin—K06NS-D, Ch. 6, California-Oregon Broadcasting Inc. Phone: 541-779-5555.

Technical Facilities: 0.5-kw ERP, 102-ft. above ground, 4137-ft. above sea level, lat. 42° 38' 20", long. 121° 56' 03".

Holds CP for change to 0.193-kw ERP, 85-ft. above ground, 5476-ft. above sea level, lat. 42° 15' 45", long. 121° 45' 22". BDFCDTV-20080603ADE.

Ownership: California-Oregon Broadcasting Inc.

■ **Christmas Valley**—K17DU, Ch. 17, Three Angels Broadcasting Network Inc. Phone: 618-627-4651. Fax: 618-627-4155.

Studio: 3391 Charley Good Rd, West Frankfort, IL 62896.

Technical Facilities: 100-w TPO, 4.66-kw ERP, 39-ft. above ground, 5658-ft. above sea level, lat. 43° 09' 55", long. 120° 52' 45".

Transmitter: 11.5-mi. SW of Christmas Valley on Table Rock Mountain.

Ownership: Three Angels Broadcasting Network Inc.

Personnel: Moses Primo, Chief Engineer.

College Hill, etc.—K11GT, Ch. 11, KEZI Inc.

Technical Facilities: 0.35-kw ERP, 1384-ft. above sea level, lat. 44° 00' 05", long. 123° 06' 05".

Ownership: Chambers Communications Corp.

Coos Bay—K27CL, Ch. 27, KEZI Inc. Phone: 503-485-5611. Fax: 503-342-1568.

Studio: 2940 Chad Dr, Eugene, OR 97408.

Technical Facilities: 1000-w TPO, 11.1-kw ERP, 148-ft. above ground, 1007-ft. above sea level, lat. 43° 23' 26", long. 124° 07' 48".

Transmitter: Noah Butte, 3.7-mi. E of Coos Bay.

Ownership: Chambers Communications Corp.

Personnel: John Prevedello, General Manager; Dennis Hunt, Chief Engineer; Tom Anderson, Sales Manager.

Coos Bay—K30BN, Ch. 30, California-Oregon Broadcasting Inc. Phone: 541-779-5555.

Technical Facilities: 40-kw ERP, 125-ft. above ground, 925-ft. above sea level, lat. 43° 23' 30", long. 124° 07' 48".

Ownership: California-Oregon Broadcasting Inc.

Coos Bay—K33AO, Ch. 33, Trinity Broadcasting Network Inc. Phone: 714-832-2950. Fax: 714-730-0661.

Technical Facilities: 12.1-kw ERP, lat. 43° 21' 15", long. 124° 14' 32".

Transmitter: Atop Blossom Hill.

Ownership: Trinity Broadcasting Network Inc.

Coos Bay—K36BX, Ch. 36, California-Oregon Broadcasting Inc.

Technical Facilities: 12.7-kw ERP, lat. 43° 14' 40", long. 123° 18' 42".

Ownership: California-Oregon Broadcasting Inc.

Coos Bay—K44FH, Ch. 44, Better Life Television. Phone: 571-474-3089.

Technical Facilities: 5.42-kw ERP, 79-ft. above ground, 179-ft. above sea level, lat. 43° 23' 29.6", long. 124° 14' 57.1".

Began Operation: July 18, 1994.

Ownership: Better Life Television Inc.

Coos Bay—K46AS, Ch. 46, Newport Television License LLC. Phone: 816-751-0204.

Technical Facilities: 14.7-kw ERP, lat. 43° 23' 39", long. 124° 07' 56".

Ownership: Newport Television LLC.

Coos Bay—K49DM-D, Ch. 49, WatchTV Inc. Phone: 503-241-2411. Fax: 503-241-2411.

Technical Facilities: 15-kw ERP, 66-ft. above ground, 678-ft. above sea level, lat. 43° 21' 15", long. 124° 14' 32".

Began Operation: January 7, 1997.

Ownership: WatchTV Inc.

Personnel: Gregory J. Herman, General Manager; Steven A. Hale, Station Manager.

Coos Bay—K63DO, Ch. 63, California-Oregon Broadcasting Inc. Phone: 541-779-5555.

Technical Facilities: 6.23-kw ERP, lat. 43° 23' 35", long. 124° 07' 47".

Holds CP for change to channel number 14, 40-kw ERP, 46-ft. above ground, 906-ft. above sea level, BDISTTL-20060331BDF.

Transmitter: 5-mi. E of Coos Bay.

Ownership: California-Oregon Broadcasting Inc.

Coos Bay, etc.—K17AA, Ch. 17, Oregon Public Broadcasting.

Technical Facilities: 16.1-kw ERP, 810-ft. above sea level, lat. 43° 18' 42", long. 124° 14' 36".

Ownership: Oregon Public Broadcasting.

Corvallis—K14GW, Ch. 14, California-Oregon Broadcasting Inc. Phone: 503-779-5555. Fax: 503-779-1151.

Technical Facilities: 1000-w TPO, 27.3-kw ERP, 110-ft. above ground, 1623-ft. above sea level, lat. 44° 38' 25", long. 123° 16' 25".

Transmitter: Vineyard Hill, 5-mi. N of Corvallis.

Multichannel TV Sound: Stereo only.

Began Operation: April 12, 1989.

Ownership: California-Oregon Broadcasting Inc.

Personnel: Mark Metzger, Manager; Tim Hershiser, Chief Engineer.

Corvallis—K45CV, Ch. 45, Fisher Broadcasting Inc. - Portland TV LLC.

Technical Facilities: 17-kw ERP, 102-ft. above ground, 1522-ft. above sea level, lat. 44° 30' 18", long. 122° 57' 33".

Ownership: Fisher Communications Inc.

Corvallis, etc.—K26AY, Ch. 26, KGW-TV Inc.

Technical Facilities: 13.8-kw ERP, 79-ft. above ground, 1499-ft. above sea level, lat. 44° 30' 18", long. 122° 57' 33".

Ownership: King Broadcasting Co.

Cottage Grove—K14LP, Ch. 14, South Lane TV Inc. Phone: 541-942-9804.

Technical Facilities: 0.22-kw ERP, 184-ft. above ground, 1594-ft. above sea level, lat. 43° 46' 38", long. 123° 02' 33".

Holds CP for change to 186-ft. above ground, 1626-ft. above sea level, lat. 43° 46' 40.9", long. 123° 02'32.1". BDFDTL-20081003AEH.

Transmitter: 2.4-km SSE of Cottage Grove on Hansen Butte.

Began Operation: August 18, 1992.

Ownership: South Lane TV Inc.

Cottage Grove—K18EA, Ch. 18, South Lane TV Inc.

Technical Facilities: 0.22-kw ERP, lat. 43° 46' 38", long. 123° 02' 33".

Transmitter: 2.4-km SSE of Cottage Grove on Hansen Butte.

Began Operation: September 19, 1994.

Ownership: South Lane TV Inc.

Cottage Grove—K20IR-D, Ch. 20, South Lane TV Inc. Phone: 541-942-9804.

Technical Facilities: 0.2-kw ERP, 186-ft. above ground, 1626-ft. above sea level, lat. 43° 46' 40.9", long. 123° 02' 32.1".

Began Operation: May 26, 1981.

Ownership: South Lane TV Inc.

Cottage Grove—K22HO-D, Ch. 22, South Lane TV Inc. Phone: 541-942-9804.

Technical Facilities: 0.2-kw ERP, 186-ft. above ground, 1626-ft. above sea level, lat. 43° 46' 40.9", long. 123° 02' 32.1".

Began Operation: May 26, 1981.

Ownership: South Lane TV Inc.

Cottage Grove—K40IS-D, Ch. 40, South Lane TV Inc. Phone: 541-942-9804.

Technical Facilities: 0.2-kw ERP, 186-ft. above ground, 1626-ft. above sea level, lat. 43° 46' 40.9", long. 123° 02' 32.1".

Began Operation: May 26, 1981.

Ownership: South Lane TV Inc.

Cottage Grove—K42HK-D, Ch. 42, South Lane TV Inc. Phone: 541-942-9804.

Technical Facilities: 0.2-kw ERP, 186-ft. above ground, 1626-ft. above sea level, lat. 43° 46' 40.9", long. 123° 02' 32.1".

Began Operation: May 26, 1981.

Ownership: South Lane TV Inc.

Cottage Grove—K46IP-D, Ch. 46, South Lane TV Inc. Phone: 541-942-9804.

Technical Facilities: 0.2-kw ERP, 186-ft. above ground, 1626-ft. above sea level, lat. 43° 46' 40.9", long. 123° 02' 32.1".

Began Operation: May 26, 1981.

Ownership: South Lane TV Inc.

Cottage Grove—K47AV, Ch. 47, South Lane TV Inc. Phone: 541-942-9804.

Technical Facilities: 0.84-kw ERP, lat. 43° 46' 38", long. 123° 02' 33".

Holds CP for change to 0.2-kw ERP, 186-ft. above ground, 1626-ft. above sea level, lat. 43° 46' 40.9", long. 123° 02' 32.1". BDFCDTT-20081003AEI.

Ownership: South Lane TV Inc.

Cottage Grove—K48KC-D, Ch. 48, South Lane TV Inc. Phone: 541-942-9804.

Technical Facilities: 0.2-kw ERP, 186-ft. above ground, 1626-ft. above sea level, lat. 43° 46' 40.9", long. 123° 02' 32.1".

Began Operation: May 26, 1981.

Ownership: South Lane TV Inc.

Cottage Grove—K50CT, Ch. 50, South Lane TV Inc. Phone: 541-942-9804.

Technical Facilities: 0.22-kw ERP, lat. 43° 46' 38", long. 123° 02' 33".

Holds CP for change to 186-ft. above ground, 1626-ft. above sea level, lat. 43° 46' 40.9", long. 123° 02' 32.1". BDFCDTT-20081003AES.

Transmitter: 2.4-km SSE of Cottage Grove on Hansen Butte.

Began Operation: August 18, 1992.

Ownership: South Lane TV Inc.

Disston—K11KI, Ch. 11, South Lane Television Inc. Phone: 541-942-9804.

Technical Facilities: 0.017-kw ERP, lat. 43° 43' 15", long. 122° 50' 15".

Holds CP for change to 0.024-kw ERP, 154-ft. above ground, 3195-ft. above sea level, BDFCDTV-20081210AEU.

Personnel: Daniel Mooney, Chief Engineer.

Dorena—K04GR, Ch. 4, South Lane Television Inc.

Technical Facilities: 0.008-kw ERP, lat. 43° 43' 15", long. 122° 50' 15".

Began Operation: July 17, 1980.

Ownership: South Lane TV Inc.

Dorena, etc.—K02GL, Ch. 2, South Lane Television Inc.

Technical Facilities: 0.008-kw ERP, lat. 43° 43' 15", long. 122° 50' 15".

Ownership: South Lane TV Inc.

Drewsey—K09LJ, Ch. 9, Drewsey Community TV.

Technical Facilities: 0.006-kw ERP, lat. 43° 47' 34", long. 118° 22' 48".

Ownership: Drewsey Community TV.

Drewsey—K13PM, Ch. 13, Drewsey Community TV.

Technical Facilities: 0.006-kw ERP, lat. 43° 47' 34", long. 118° 22' 48".

Began Operation: July 20, 1979.

Ownership: Drewsey Community TV.

Elgin—K26FV, Ch. 26, Blue Mountain Translator District. Phone: 509-529-9149.

Technical Facilities: 1.06-kw ERP, 20-ft. above ground, 7159-ft. above sea level, lat. 45° 18' 35", long. 117° 43' 58".

Transmitter: Mount Fanny, 9.3-mi. NE of Union.

Ownership: Blue Mountain Translator District.

Elgin—K33FS, Ch. 33, Blue Mountain Translator District. Phone: 509-529-9149.

Technical Facilities: 0.25-kw ERP, 20-ft. above ground, 7159-ft. above sea level, lat. 45° 18' 35", long. 117° 43' 58".

Transmitter: Mount Fanny, 9.3-mi. NE of Union.

Began Operation: January 11, 1982.

Ownership: Blue Mountain Translator District.

Elgin—K39FD, Ch. 39, Blue Mountain Translator District. Phone: 509-529-9149.

Technical Facilities: 0.68-kw ERP, 20-ft. above ground, 7159-ft. above sea level, lat. 45° 18' 35", long. 117° 43' 58".

Transmitter: Mount Fanny, 9.3-mi. NE of Union.

Ownership: Blue Mountain Translator District.

Elkton—K11VI, Ch. 11, Oregon Public Broadcasting. Phone: 503-244-9900.

Technical Facilities: 0.037-kw ERP, 72-ft. above ground, 1319-ft. above sea level, lat. 43° 37' 16", long. 123° 32' 03".

Ownership: Oregon Public Broadcasting.

Enterprise—K28JC, Ch. 28, Oregon Public Broadcasting. Phone: 503-244-9900.

Technical Facilities: 0.55-kw ERP, 26-ft. above ground, 7027-ft. above sea level, lat. 45° 23' 58", long. 117° 23' 16".

Holds CP for change to 0.165-kw ERP, BDFCDTT-20080325AHJ.

Began Operation: July 5, 1979.

Ownership: Oregon Public Broadcasting.

Eola—KWVT-LP, Ch. 17, Michael L. Mattson. Phone: 503-930-7228.

Technical Facilities: 35-kw ERP, 66-ft. above ground, 1152-ft. above sea level, lat. 44° 58' 38", long. 123° 08' 29".

Multichannel TV Sound: Stereo only.

Ownership: Michael L. Mattson.

Personnel: Michael Mattson, Station Manager.

Eola—KXPD-LP, Ch. 52, Churchill Media II LLC. Phone: 541-343-4100.

Technical Facilities: 150-kw ERP, 850-ft. above ground, 1949-ft. above sea level, lat. 44° 59' 59", long. 122° 41' 41".

Multichannel TV Sound: Stereo only.

Began Operation: April 26, 2005.

Ownership: Churchill Media LLC.

Eugene—K04DR, Ch. 4, Fisher Broadcasting Inc. Phone: 206-404-7000.

Technical Facilities: 0.0012-kw ERP, 69-ft. above ground, 1148-ft. above sea level, lat. 44° 02' 01", long. 123° 00' 25".

Ownership: Fisher Communications Inc.

Eugene—K21FS, Ch. 21, Oregon Public Broadcasting. Phone: 503-244-9900.

Technical Facilities: 0.776-kw ERP, lat. 44° 11' 52", long. 122° 59' 06".

Holds CP for change to 1.1-kw ERP, 92-ft. above ground, 3248-ft. above sea level, lat. 44° 11' 52", long. 122° 59' 08". BDFCDTT-20090217AEV.

Began Operation: June 11, 1979.

Ownership: Oregon Public Broadcasting.

Eugene—K59DJ, Ch. 59, His Word Broadcasting Co. Phones: 541-747-5959; 541-342-7474.

Technical Facilities: 1000-w TPO, 11.7-kw ERP, lat. 44° 07' 52", long. 123° 18' 42".

Holds CP for change to channel number 38, 8-kw ERP, 112-ft. above ground, 2221-ft. above sea level, lat. 44° 06' 57", long. 122° 59' 57". BPTTL-20050601BDS.

Transmitter: Springfield.

Began Operation: April 26, 1982.

Ownership: His Word Broadcasting Co.

Personnel: Dennis Walen, General Manager.

Eugene—KAMK-LP, Ch. 53, Better Life Television Inc. Phone: 541-474-3089.

Technical Facilities: 1000-w TPO, 10.9-kw ERP, 351-ft. above ground, 1621-ft. above sea level, lat. 44° 00' 11", long. 123° 06' 48".

Holds CP for change to channel number 49, 10-kw ERP, BDISTTL-20051230AAL.

Transmitter: Blanton Rd., SW of Eugene.

Began Operation: February 1, 1993.

Ownership: Better Life Television Inc.

■ **Eugene**—KEVU-LP, Ch. 23, California-Oregon Broadcasting Inc. Phone: 541-683-3434. Fax: 541-683-8016.

Studio: 2940 Chad Dr, Eugene, OR 97408.

Technical Facilities: 19.4-kw ERP, 580-ft. above ground, 1876-ft. above sea level, lat. 44° 00' 04", long. 123° 06' 45".

Multichannel TV Sound: Stereo only.

Ownership: California-Oregon Broadcasting Inc.

Personnel: Patricia C. Smullin, President; Mark Metzger, Station Manager; Chris Breen, National Sales Coordinator; Tim Hershiser, Chief Engineer.

Eugene—KMOR-LP, Ch. 51, Newport Television License LLC. Phone: 816-751-0204.

Technical Facilities: 1000-w TPO, 10.9-kw ERP, 351-ft. above ground, 1621-ft. above sea level, lat. 44° 00' 11", long. 123° 06' 48".

Transmitter: Blanton Rd., SW of Eugene.

Multichannel TV Sound: Stereo only.

Ownership: Newport Television LLC.

Personnel: Cambra Ward, General Manager; Kurt Thelen, Chief Engineer; Dave Ulrickson, Sales Manager.

■ **Eugene**—KORY-CA, Ch. 41, WatchTV Inc. Phone: 503-241-2411. Fax: 503-226-3557.

Technical Facilities: 1000-w TPO, 10.4-kw ERP, 131-ft. above ground, 1270-ft. above sea level, lat. 44° 00' 11", long. 123° 06' 48".

Ownership: WatchTV Inc.

Personnel: Gregory J. Herman, General Manager; Steven A. Hale, Station Manager.

Eugene—KXOR-LP, Ch. 36, Churchill Media III LLC. Phone: 541-343-4100.

Technical Facilities: 16-kw ERP, 302-ft. above ground, 1572-ft. above sea level, lat. 44° 00' 11", long. 126° 06' 48".

Multichannel TV Sound: Stereo only.

Ownership: Churchill Media LLC.

■ **Eugene, etc.**—K19GH, Ch. 19, California-Oregon Broadcasting Inc. Phone: 503-779-5555. Fax: 503-779-5564.

Technical Facilities: 10-kw ERP, 59-ft. above ground, 2169-ft. above sea level, lat. 44° 06' 57", long. 122° 59' 58".

Transmitter: 2-mi. SE of Coburg.

Ownership: California-Oregon Broadcasting Inc.

Eugene, etc.—K65ER, Ch. 65, California-Oregon Broadcasting Inc.

Technical Facilities: 6.23-kw ERP, 49-ft. above ground, 751-ft. above sea level, lat. 44° 07' 28", long. 120° 00' 03".

Transmitter: 1.7-mi. SE of Coburg.

Began Operation: January 15, 1991.

Ownership: California-Oregon Broadcasting Inc.

■ **Florence**—K48GC, Ch. 48, Three Angels Broadcasting Network Inc. Phone: 618-627-4651. Fax: 618-627-4155.

Studio: 3391 Charley Good Rd, West Frankfort, IL 62896.

Technical Facilities: 100-w TPO, 2.81-kw ERP, 82-ft. above ground, 810-ft. above sea level, lat. 43° 57' 25", long. 124° 04' 25".

Transmitter: Top of Glenada Hill, 2.5-mi. SW of Florence.

Ownership: Three Angels Broadcasting Network Inc.

Personnel: Moses Primo, Chief Engineer.

Florence—K52DO, Ch. 52, West Lane Translator Inc. Phone: 541-902-2424.

Technical Facilities: 1.07-kw ERP, 115-ft. above ground, 866-ft. above sea level, lat. 43° 57' 26", long. 124° 04' 26".

Holds CP for change to channel number 51, 2.5-kw ERP, 232-ft. above ground, 940-ft. above sea level, BDFCDTT-20090202CCU.

Began Operation: January 7, 1991.

Ownership: West Lane Translator Inc.

Florence—K54DG, Ch. 54, Oregon Public Broadcasting. Phone: 503-244-9900.

Technical Facilities: 1.7-kw ERP, 115-ft. above ground, 866-ft. above sea level, lat. 43° 57' 46", long. 124° 04' 15".

Holds CP for change to channel number 32, 2.5-kw ERP, 232-ft. above ground, 940-ft. above sea level, lat. 43° 57' 26", long. 124° 04' 26". BDFCDTT-20090210AAF.

Began Operation: April 29, 1991.

Ownership: Oregon Public Broadcasting.

Florence—K56DL, Ch. 56, West Lane Translator Inc. Phone: 541-902-2424.

Technical Facilities: 0.2-kw ERP, 148-ft. above ground, 899-ft. above sea level, lat. 43° 57' 46", long. 124° 04' 15".

Holds CP for change to channel number 35, 2.5-kw ERP, 232-ft. above ground, 940-ft. above sea level, lat. 43° 57' 26", long. 124° 04' 26". BDFCDTT-20090202CCW.

Began Operation: August 5, 1988.

Ownership: West Lane Translator Inc.

Florence—K58CW, Ch. 58, West Lane Translator Inc. Phone: 541-902-2424.

Technical Facilities: 0.2-kw ERP, 148-ft. above ground, 899-ft. above sea level, lat. 43° 57' 46", long. 124° 04' 15".

Holds CP for change to channel number 40, 2.5-kw ERP, 232-ft. above ground, 940-ft. above sea level, lat. 43° 57' 26", long. 124° 04' 26". BDFCDTT-20090202CCX.

Began Operation: August 5, 1988.

Ownership: West Lane Translator Inc.

Florence—K60DQ, Ch. 60, West Lane Translator Inc. Phone: 541-902-2424.

Technical Facilities: 0.2-kw ERP, lat. 43° 57' 46", long. 124° 04' 15".

Holds CP for change to channel number 43, 2.5-kw ERP, 232-ft. above ground, 940-ft. above sea level, lat. 43° 57' 26", long. 124° 04' 26". BDFCDTT-20090202CCR.

Ownership: West Lane Translator Inc.

Glendale—K58DA, Ch. 58, South West Oregon TV Broadcasting Corp. Phone: 206-404-3065.

Technical Facilities: 1.23-kw ERP, lat. 42° 43' 45", long. 123° 23' 12".

Began Operation: July 11, 1989.

Ownership: Fisher Communications Inc.; California-Oregon Broadcasting Inc.

Glendale, etc.—K48BS, Ch. 48, Freedom Broadcasting of Oregon Licensee LLC.

Technical Facilities: 1.24-kw ERP, 49-ft. above ground, 3159-ft. above sea level, lat. 42° 43' 48", long. 123° 23' 00".

Ownership: Freedom Communications Holdings Inc.

Glide—K34IC, Ch. 34, Three Angels Broadcasting Network Inc. Phone: 618-627-4651. Fax: 618-627-4155.

Studio: 3391 Charley Good Rd, West Frankfort, IL 62896.

Technical Facilities: 4-kw ERP, 4278-ft. above ground, 8527-ft. above sea level, lat. 43° 22' 25", long. 123° 03' 50".

Transmitter: Mount Scott.

Ownership: Three Angels Broadcasting Network Inc.

Personnel: Moses Primo, Chief Engineer.

Glide, etc.—K24FH, Ch. 24, Oregon Public Broadcasting. Phone: 503-244-9900.

Technical Facilities: 0.791-kw ERP, 75-ft. above ground, 4320-ft. above sea level, lat. 43° 22' 18", long. 123° 03' 48".

Holds CP for change to 1.1-kw ERP, 75-ft. above ground, 4321-ft. above sea level, BDFCDTT-20081023AAH.

Began Operation: August 21, 1978.

Ownership: Oregon Public Broadcasting.

Glide, etc.—K26HO, Ch. 26, South West Oregon TV Broadcasting Corp. Phone: 206-404-4884.

Technical Facilities: 10.8-kw ERP, 25-ft. above ground, 4274-ft. above sea level, lat. 43° 22' 19", long. 123° 03' 48".

Ownership: California-Oregon Broadcasting Inc.; Fisher Communications Inc.

Gold Beach—K25EN, Ch. 25, California-Oregon Broadcasting Inc.

Technical Facilities: 0.47-kw ERP, lat. 42° 26' 25", long. 124° 24' 58".

Transmitter: Approx. 1.5-mi. N of Gold Beach.

Ownership: California-Oregon Broadcasting Inc.

Gold Beach—K33CP, Ch. 33, Fisher Broadcasting - Oregon TV LLC.

Technical Facilities: 0.51-kw ERP, lat. 42° 26' 05", long. 124° 25' 12".

Ownership: Fisher Communications Inc.

Gold Beach—K55CM, Ch. 55, Oregon Public Broadcasting. Phone: 503-244-9900.

Technical Facilities: 1.62-kw ERP, lat. 42° 26' 25", long. 124° 24' 58".

Holds CP for change to channel number 50, 0.68-kw ERP, 59-ft. above ground, 738-ft. above sea level, BDISTT-20060315ACC.

Transmitter: 0.75-mi. from Wedderburn Post Office.

Began Operation: August 6, 1984.

Ownership: Oregon Public Broadcasting.

Gold Beach—K68BB, Ch. 68, Soda Mountain Broadcasting Inc.

Technical Facilities: 0.48-kw ERP, lat. 42° 26' 25", long. 124° 24' 57".

Transmitter: Wedderburn Hill, 1.9-mi. N of Gold Beach.

Began Operation: January 11, 1996.

Ownership: Soda Mountain Broadcasting Inc.

Gold Hill—K02FT, Ch. 2, California-Oregon Broadcasting Inc.

Technical Facilities: 0.045-kw ERP, lat. 42° 25' 41", long. 123° 00' 04".

Ownership: California-Oregon Broadcasting Inc.

Gold Hill—K04JZ, Ch. 4, Freedom Broadcasting of Oregon Licensee LLC. Phone: 518-346-6666.

Technical Facilities: 0.012-kw ERP, lat. 42° 25' 41", long. 123° 00' 04".

Ownership: Freedom Communications Holdings Inc.

Gold Hill—K46CH, Ch. 46, Soda Mountain Broadcasting Inc.

Technical Facilities: 0.159-kw ERP, 39-ft. above ground, 2155-ft. above sea level, lat. 42° 25' 40", long. 123° 00' 03".

Began Operation: May 25, 1989.

Ownership: Soda Mountain Broadcasting Inc.

Gold Hill, etc.—K55DQ, Ch. 55, Southern Oregon Public Television Inc.

Technical Facilities: 0.034-kw ERP, 2201-ft. above sea level, lat. 42° 25' 41", long. 123° 00' 04".

Began Operation: August 8, 1983.

Ownership: Southern Oregon Public Television Inc.

Grants Pass—K12KX, Ch. 12, Southern Oregon Public Television Inc.

Technical Facilities: 0.009-kw ERP, lat. 42° 24' 39", long. 123° 16' 52".

Began Operation: June 5, 1979.

Ownership: Southern Oregon Public Television Inc.

Grants Pass—K15BP, Ch. 15, Soda Mountain Broadcasting Inc. Phone: 541-485-5611.

Technical Facilities: 0.07-kw ERP, lat. 42° 27' 06", long. 123° 17' 47".

Holds CP for change to 0.849-kw ERP, 39-ft. above ground, 2155-ft. above sea level, BDFCDTT-20090325AEI.

Ownership: Soda Mountain Broadcasting Inc.

Grants Pass—K18AN, Ch. 18, Southern Oregon Public Television Inc. Phone: 541-779-0808.

Technical Facilities: 0.63-kw ERP, lat. 42° 24' 39", long. 123° 16' 55".

Holds CP for change to 0.62-kw ERP, 30-ft. above ground, 3199-ft. above sea level, lat. 42° 29' 20", long. 123° 18' 21". BPTT-20080125ADF.

Began Operation: June 21, 1985.

Ownership: Southern Oregon Public Television Inc.

Grants Pass—K19HS-D, Ch. 19, Southern Oregon Public Television Inc. Phone: 541-779-0808.

Technical Facilities: 0.2-kw ERP, 30-ft. above ground, 3199-ft. above sea level, lat. 42° 29' 20", long. 123° 18' 21".

Ownership: Southern Oregon Public Television Inc.

Grants Pass—K20DT, Ch. 20, WatchTV Inc. Phone: 503-241-2411. Fax: 503-226-3557.

Technical Facilities: 1000-w TPO, 13.1-kw ERP, 49-ft. above ground, 2241-ft. above sea level, lat. 42° 27' 06", long. 123° 17' 47".

Transmitter: 1.7-mi. NE of Grants Pass.

Ownership: WatchTV Inc.

Personnel: Gregory J. Herman, General Manager; Steven A. Hale, Station Manager.

■ **Grants Pass**—K22FC, Ch. 22, Better Life Television. Phone: 618-627-2741.

Technical Facilities: 100-w TPO, 0.836-kw ERP, 46-ft. above ground, 2785-ft. above sea level, lat. 42° 24' 39", long. 123° 16' 52".

Transmitter: 2.5-mi. SE of Grants Pass.

Ownership: Better Life Television Inc.

Grants Pass—K36HL, Ch. 36, Trinity Broadcasting Network. Phone: 714-832-2950. Fax: 714-730-0661.

Technical Facilities: 1.1-kw ERP, 56-ft. above ground, 2792-ft. above sea level, lat. 42° 24' 43", long. 123° 16' 54".

Holds CP for change to channel number 29, 2-kw ERP, BDISDTT-20060331AJV.

Ownership: Trinity Broadcasting Network Inc.

Grants Pass—K44JB-D, Ch. 44, Broadcasting Licenses LP. Phone: 517-347-4141.

Technical Facilities: 0.75-kw ERP, 35-ft. above ground, 2155-ft. above sea level, lat. 42° 27' 05", long. 123° 17' 48".

Ownership: Broadcasting Licenses LP.

Grants Pass—K45ED, Ch. 45, Broadcasting Licenses LP. Phone: 517-347-4141.

Technical Facilities: 10.5-kw ERP, 49-ft. above ground, 2254-ft. above sea level, lat. 42° 27' 06", long. 123° 17' 47".

Ownership: Broadcasting Licenses LP.

■ **Grants Pass**—K47GI, Ch. 47, Better Life Television. Phone: 541-474-3089.

Technical Facilities: 4-kw ERP, 98-ft. above ground, 3868-ft. above sea level, lat. 42° 22' 56", long. 123° 16' 29".

Began Operation: August 13, 1990.

Ownership: Better Life Television Inc.

Grants Pass—K50FW, Ch. 50, California-Oregon Broadcasting Inc. Phone: 541-779-5555.

Technical Facilities: 2.81-kw ERP, 98-ft. above ground, 2834-ft. above sea level, lat. 42° 24' 43", long. 123° 16' 54".

Ownership: California-Oregon Broadcasting Inc.

Grants Pass—K54DM, Ch. 54, Freedom Broadcasting of Oregon Licensee LLC.

Technical Facilities: 0.577-kw ERP, 72-ft. above ground, 3858-ft. above sea level, lat. 42° 22' 56", long. 123° 16' 28".

Ownership: Freedom Communications Holdings Inc.

Grants Pass, etc.—K04EY, Ch. 4, California-Oregon Broadcasting Inc.

Technical Facilities: 0.05-kw ERP, 2739-ft. above sea level, lat. 42° 24' 39", long. 123° 16' 52".

Ownership: California-Oregon Broadcasting Inc.

Halfway—K10NF, Ch. 10, Oregon Public Bcstg.

Technical Facilities: 0.006-kw ERP, 26-ft. above ground, 2872-ft. above sea level, lat. 44° 52' 50", long. 117° 01' 45".

Ownership: Oregon Public Broadcasting.

Heppner, etc.—K28GD, Ch. 28, Oregon Public Broadcasting. Phone: 502-244-9900.

Technical Facilities: 2.1-kw ERP, 54-ft. above ground, 5984-ft. above sea level, lat. 45° 12' 47", long. 119° 17' 41".

Ownership: Oregon Public Broadcasting.

Heppner, etc.—K39ES, Ch. 39, Rural Oregon Wireless TV Inc.

Technical Facilities: 1.06-kw ERP, 52-ft. above ground, 2579-ft. above sea level, lat. 45° 46' 53", long. 120° 33' 17".

Transmitter: approx. 14-mi. SE of Goldendale, WA.

Ownership: Rural Oregon Wireless TV Inc.

Heppner, etc.—K43FH, Ch. 43, Rural Oregon Wireless TV Inc.

Technical Facilities: 1.06-kw ERP, 52-ft. above ground, 2579-ft. above sea level, lat. 45° 46' 53", long. 120° 33' 17".

Transmitter: approx. 14-mi. SE of Goldendale, WA.

Ownership: Rural Oregon Wireless TV Inc.

Heppner, etc.—K46CU, Ch. 46, Rural Oregon Wireless TV Inc.

Technical Facilities: 1.06-kw ERP, 52-ft. above ground, 2579-ft. above sea level, lat. 45° 46' 53", long. 120° 33' 17".

Transmitter: 14-mi. SE of Goldendale, WA.

Ownership: Rural Oregon Wireless TV Inc.

■ **Hermiston**—K48DZ, Ch. 48, Three Angels Broadcasting Network Inc. Phone: 618-627-4651. Fax: 618-627-4155.

Studio: 3391 Charley Good Rd, West Frankfort, IL 62896.

Technical Facilities: 1000-w TPO, 7.9-kw ERP, 46-ft. above ground, 1230-ft. above sea level, lat. 45° 58' 49", long. 119° 17' 44".

Transmitter: NE of U.S. Rte. 82 & SR 14, near Plymouth, WA.

Ownership: Three Angels Broadcasting Network Inc.

Personnel: Moses Primo, Chief Engineer; Linda Shelton, Program Director.

Hood River—K28CQ, Ch. 28, Rural Oregon Wireless TV Inc. Phone: 503-226-5004.

Technical Facilities: 0.47-kw ERP, lat. 45° 44' 45", long. 121° 34' 51".

Holds CP for change to 1.2-kw ERP, 69-ft. above ground, 2631-ft. above sea level, lat. 45° 44' 31", long. 121° 34' 43". BPTT-20070822AAQ.

Ownership: Rural Oregon Wireless TV Inc.

Hood River—K40AM, Ch. 40, Rural Oregon Wireless TV Inc. Phone: 503-226-5004.

Technical Facilities: 0.621-kw ERP, 20-ft. above ground, 2743-ft. above sea level, lat. 45° 44' 45", long. 121° 34' 51".

Holds CP for change to channel number 34, 1.2-kw ERP, 69-ft. above ground, 2631-ft. above sea level, lat. 45° 44' 31", long. 121° 34' 43". BDISTT-20070815ABG.

Ownership: Rural Oregon Wireless TV Inc.

Hood River—K50CE, Ch. 50, Rural Oregon Wireless TV Inc. Phone: 503-226-5004.

Technical Facilities: 1.2-kw ERP, lat. 45° 44' 45", long. 121° 34' 51".

Holds CP for change to 69-ft. above ground, 2631-ft. above sea level, lat. 45° 44' 31", long. 121° 34' 43". BPTT-20070822AAV.

Ownership: Rural Oregon Wireless TV Inc.

Hood River—K53EI, Ch. 53, Rural Oregon Wireless TV Inc. Phone: 503-226-5004.

Technical Facilities: 0.47-kw ERP, lat. 45° 44' 45", long. 121° 34' 51".

Holds CP for change to channel number 38, 1.2-kw ERP, 59-ft. above ground, 2621-ft. above sea level, lat. 45° 44' 31", long. 121° 34' 43". BDISTT-20070822ABB.

Ownership: Rural Oregon Wireless TV Inc.

Hood River, etc.—K36FG, Ch. 36, Oregon Public Broadcasting. Phone: 503-244-9900.

Technical Facilities: 1.2-kw ERP, 59-ft. above ground, 2621-ft. above sea level, lat. 45° 44' 31", long. 121° 34' 43".

Ownership: Oregon Public Broadcasting.

Hugo, etc.—K40BL, Ch. 40, Freedom Broadcasting of Oregon Licensee LLC.

Technical Facilities: 1.44-kw ERP, 26-ft. above ground, 3858-ft. above sea level, lat. 42° 36' 00", long. 123° 21' 51".

Ownership: Freedom Communications Holdings Inc.

Huntington—K10GQ, Ch. 10, Fisher Broadcasting Inc.

Technical Facilities: 0.015-kw ERP, lat. 44° 21' 22", long. 117° 16' 42".

Ownership: Fisher Communications Inc.

Huntington—K13SL, Ch. 13, King Broadcasting Co. Phone: 214-977-6606.

Technical Facilities: 0.015-kw ERP, lat. 44° 21' 22", long. 117° 16' 42".

Ownership: King Broadcasting Co.

Jacksonville—K02IC, Ch. 2, Freedom Broadcasting of Oregon Licensee LLC. Phone: 518-346-6666.

Technical Facilities: 0.044-kw ERP, lat. 42° 20' 15", long. 122° 58' 25".

Ownership: Freedom Communications Holdings Inc.

Jacksonville—K07RQ, Ch. 7, Southern Oregon Public Television Inc.

Technical Facilities: 0.07-kw ERP, lat. 42° 20' 21", long. 122° 55' 30".

Ownership: Southern Oregon Public Television Inc.

Jacksonville—K21BG-D, Ch. 21, Soda Mountain Broadcasting Inc. Phone: 541-485-5611.

Technical Facilities: 0.614-kw ERP, 79-ft. above ground, 3678-ft. above sea level, lat. 42° 17' 54", long. 122° 44' 57".

Ownership: Soda Mountain Broadcasting Inc.

Jacksonville, etc.—K13JR-D, Ch. 13, California-Oregon Broadcasting Inc. Phone: 541-779-5555.

Technical Facilities: 0.3-kw ERP, 72-ft. above ground, 3678-ft. above sea level, lat. 42° 17' 53.3", long. 122° 45' 01.4".

Ownership: California-Oregon Broadcasting Inc.

John Day—K02PK, Ch. 2, Three Angels Broadcasting Network Inc. Phone: 618-627-4651. Fax: 618-627-4155.

Studio: 3391 Charley Good Rd, West Frankfort, IL 62896.

Technical Facilities: 1-w TPO, 0.002-kw ERP, 100-ft. above ground, 3980-ft. above sea level, lat. 44° 26' 02", long. 118° 57' 27".

Holds CP for change to 0.02-kw ERP, 33-ft. above ground, 3195-ft. above sea level, lat. 44° 25' 28.8", long. 118° 57' 44.5". BPTVL-20070803AAC.

Transmitter: 1.2 mi. N of U.S. Rte. 395 & Rte. 26, near John Day.

Ownership: Three Angels Broadcasting Network Inc.

Personnel: Moses Primo, Chief Engineer.

John Day—K08NP, Ch. 8, Three Angels Broadcasting Network Inc. Phone: 618-627-4651.

Technical Facilities: 0.1-kw ERP, 79-ft. above ground, 3980-ft. above sea level, lat. 44° 26' 02", long. 118° 57' 27".

Holds CP for change to 33-ft. above ground, 3195-ft. above sea level, BPTVL-20070803ABO.

Ownership: Three Angels Broadcasting Network Inc.

John Day—K26FQ, Ch. 26, Oregon Public Broadcasting. Phone: 503-244-9900.

Technical Facilities: 0.638-kw ERP, 30-ft. above ground, 3914-ft. above sea level, lat. 44° 26' 03", long. 118° 57' 28".

Holds CP for change to 0.19-kw ERP, BDFCDTT-20080325AHI.

Ownership: Oregon Public Broadcasting.

Jordan Valley—K09PB, Ch. 9, Jordan Creek Viewers Inc. Phone: 541-586-2460.

Technical Facilities: 0.018-kw ERP, lat. 43° 02' 47", long. 116° 59' 30".

Ownership: Jordan Creek Viewers Inc.

Jordan Valley—K11LS, Ch. 11, Fisher Broadcasting Inc.

Technical Facilities: 0.009-kw ERP, lat. 43° 02' 47", long. 116° 59' 30".

Ownership: Fisher Communications Inc.

Jordan Valley—K13MF, Ch. 13, Jordan Creek Viewers Inc. Phone: 541-586-2460.

Technical Facilities: 0.009-kw ERP, lat. 43° 02' 47", long. 116° 59' 30".

Ownership: Jordan Creek Viewers Inc.

Klamath—K48IW, Ch. 48, Better Life Television Inc. Phone: 541-582-8024.

Technical Facilities: 12.5-kw ERP, 66-ft. above ground, 6472-ft. above sea level, lat. 42° 59' 49", long. 121° 37' 57".

Ownership: Better Life Television Inc.

Klamath Falls—K04ES, Ch. 4, California-Oregon Broadcasting Inc.

Technical Facilities: 0.01-kw ERP, lat. 42° 14' 00", long. 121° 47' 30".

Ownership: California-Oregon Broadcasting Inc.

Klamath Falls—K13UR, Ch. 13, Soda Mountain Broadcasting Inc.

Technical Facilities: 0.03-kw ERP, lat. 42° 12' 58", long. 121° 47' 55".

Ownership: Soda Mountain Broadcasting Inc.

Klamath Falls—K39DP, Ch. 39, WatchTV Inc. Phone: 503-241-2411. Fax: 503-226-3557.

Technical Facilities: 810-w TPO, 9.8-kw ERP, 112-ft. above ground, 1808-ft. above sea level, lat. 42° 13' 26", long. 121° 49' 02".

Holds CP for change to 10-kw ERP, 112-ft. above ground, 5089-ft. above sea level, BDFCDTL-20090102ACG.

Transmitter: 1.4-mi. W of County Courthouse.

Began Operation: May 31, 1996.

Ownership: WatchTV Inc.

Personnel: Gregory J. Herman, General Manager; Steven A. Hale, Station Manager.

Klamath Falls—K41ID, Ch. 41, Sainte Partners II LP. Phone: 209-523-0777.

Technical Facilities: 8.28-kw ERP, 141-ft. above ground, 6575-ft. above sea level, lat. 42° 05' 50", long. 121° 37' 59".

Holds CP for change to 2-kw ERP, BDFCDTL-20061102AAP.

Ownership: Sainte Partners II LP.

Klamath Falls—K44DZ, Ch. 44, Broadcasting Licenses LP. Phone: 517-347-4141.

Technical Facilities: 10.5-kw ERP, 49-ft. above ground, 6421-ft. above sea level, lat. 42° 05' 48", long. 121° 37' 57".

Ownership: Broadcasting Licenses LP.

Klamath Falls—K48HV, Ch. 48, Better Life Television. Phone: 541-582-8024.

Technical Facilities: 7.244-kw ERP, 65-ft. above ground, 6535-ft. above sea level, lat. 42° 05' 56", long. 121° 38' 02".

Ownership: Better Life Television Inc.

Klamath Falls—K58BG, Ch. 58, Trinity Broadcasting Network Inc. Phone: 714-832-2950. Fax: 714-730-0661.

Technical Facilities: 1.27-kw ERP, lat. 42° 08' 48", long. 121° 46' 16".

Holds CP for change to channel number 17, 15-kw ERP, 19-ft. above ground, 4616-ft. above sea level, BDISDTT-20060331BLC.

Ownership: Trinity Broadcasting Network Inc.

Klamath Falls, etc.—K07PU, Ch. 7, Freedom Broadcasting of Oregon Licensee LLC. Phone: 518-346-6666.

Technical Facilities: 0.032-kw ERP, 4544-ft. above sea level, lat. 42° 14' 17", long. 121° 45' 59".

Ownership: Freedom Communications Holdings Inc.

La Grande—K02PJ, Ch. 2, La Grande Seventh Day Adventist Church. Phones: 541-963-3345; 541-963-4018.

Studio: 2702 Adams Ave, La Grande, OR 97850.

Technical Facilities: 10-w TPO, 0.025-kw ERP, 113-ft. above ground, 2683-ft. above sea level, lat. 45° 18' 01", long. 118° 04' 01".

Transmitter: 1.5-mi. S of La Grande on Old Oregon Trail Hwy.

Ownership: La Grande Seventh Day Adventist Church.

Personnel: Boyd Hosey, General Manager; Rod Jones, Chief Engineer.

La Grande—K23DB, Ch. 23, Meredith Corp. Phones: 503-239-4949; 515-284-3000. Fax: 503-239-6184.

Technical Facilities: 100-w TPO, 1.04-kw ERP, 20-ft. above ground, 7172-ft. above sea level, lat. 45° 18' 35", long. 117° 44' 09".

Holds CP for change to 0.3-kw ERP, 20-ft. above ground, 7129-ft. above sea level, lat. 45° 18' 35", long. 117° 43' 58". BDFCDTL-20060331BCP.

Transmitter: Mount Fanny, 6.4-mi. NE of Union.

Ownership: Meredith Corp.

La Grande—K26FE, Ch. 26, Blue Mountain Translator District. Phone: 509-529-9149.

Technical Facilities: 0.88-kw ERP, 45° 26' 15", long. 118° 05' 10".

Ownership: Blue Mountain Translator District.

La Grande—K29EL, Ch. 29, Blue Mountain Translator District. Phone: 509-529-9149.

Technical Facilities: 0.3-kw ERP, lat. 45° 18' 35", long. 117° 43' 58".

Transmitter: Mount Fanny, 9.3-mi. NE of Union.

Ownership: Blue Mountain Translator District.

La Grande—K31GN, Ch. 31, Blue Mountain Translator District. Phone: 509-529-9149.

Technical Facilities: 0.5-kw ERP, 20-ft. above ground, 7159-ft. above sea level, lat. 45° 18' 35", long. 117° 43' 58".

Ownership: Blue Mountain Translator District.

La Grande—K34DI, Ch. 34, Umatilla Electric Cooperative.

Technical Facilities: 1.8-kw ERP, 59-ft. above ground, 6050-ft. above sea level, lat. 45° 12' 47", long. 119° 17' 41".

La Grande—K35GA, Ch. 35, Blue Mountain Translator District. Phone: 509-529-9149.

Technical Facilities: 0.3-kw ERP, 20-ft. above ground, 7159-ft. above sea level, lat. 45° 18' 35", long. 117° 43' 58".

Transmitter: Mount Fanny, 9.3-mi. NE of Union.

Ownership: Blue Mountain Translator District.

La Grande—K39ET, Ch. 39, Blue Mountain Translator District. Phone: 509-529-9149.

Technical Facilities: 0.79-kw ERP, 16-ft. above ground, 5016-ft. above sea level, lat. 45° 26' 23", long. 117° 53' 59".

Ownership: Blue Mountain Translator District.

La Grande—K50CI, Ch. 50, Blue Mountain Translator District. Phone: 509-529-9149.

Technical Facilities: 0.877-kw ERP, 26-ft. above ground, 5013-ft. above sea level, lat. 45° 26' 23", long. 117° 53' 59".

Ownership: Blue Mountain Translator District.

La Grande—K52DT, Ch. 52, Blue Mountain Translator District. Phone: 509-529-9149. Fax: 509-529-0661.

Technical Facilities: 0.79-kw ERP, 16-ft. above ground, 5016-ft. above sea level, lat. 45° 26' 23", long. 117° 53' 59".

Ownership: Blue Mountain Translator District.

La Grande—K56BE, Ch. 56, Blue Mountain Translator District. Phone: 509-529-9149.

Technical Facilities: 1.69-kw ERP, lat. 45° 26' 23", long. 117° 53' 59".

Ownership: Blue Mountain Translator District.

La Grande—K58AY, Ch. 58, Blue Mountain Translator District. Phone: 509-529-9149.

Technical Facilities: 0.62-kw ERP, lat. 45° 26' 23", long. 117° 53' 59".

Ownership: Blue Mountain Translator District.

La Pine—K02JL, Ch. 2, NPG of Oregon Inc. Phone: 816-271-8504.

Technical Facilities: 0.005-kw ERP, lat. 43° 39' 17", long. 121° 25' 46".

Ownership: News Press & Gazette Co.

La Pine—K04BJ, Ch. 4, NVT Portland Licensee LLC, Debtor in Possession. Phones: 503-977-7752; 404-995-4711.

Technical Facilities: 0.036-kw ERP, lat. 43° 39' 17", long. 121° 25' 46".

Ownership: New Vision Television LLC, Debtor in Possession.

La Pine—K05JV, Ch. 5, NPG of Oregon Inc. Phone: 816-271-8502.

Technical Facilities: 0.35-kw ERP, 43-ft. above ground, 4790-ft. above sea level, lat. 43° 39' 17", long. 121° 25' 46".

Ownership: News Press & Gazette Co.

La Pine—K09YE, Ch. 9, Rural Oregon Wireless Television Inc. Phone: 503-226-5004.

Technical Facilities: 0.2-kw ERP, 20-ft. above ground, 4760-ft. above sea level, lat. 43° 39' 00", long. 121° 25' 44".

Ownership: Rural Oregon Wireless TV Inc.

La Pine—K13JF, Ch. 13, NPG of Oregon Inc. Phone: 816-271-8504.

Technical Facilities: 0.036-kw ERP, lat. 43° 39' 17", long. 121° 25' 46".

Holds CP for change to 0.2-kw ERP, 20-ft. above ground, 4760-ft. above sea level, lat. 43° 39' 00", long. 121° 25' 44". BPTTV-20060323AEK.

Ownership: News Press & Gazette Co.

■**Lakeview**—K05KI, Ch. 5, Three Angels Broadcasting Network Inc. Phone: 618-627-4651. Fax: 618-627-4155.

Studio: 3391 Charley Good Rd, West Frankfort, IL 62896.

Technical Facilities: 10-w TPO, 0.017-kw ERP, 102-ft. above ground, 4892-ft. above sea level, lat. 42° 11' 47", long. 120° 21' 01".

Transmitter: 1757 S. F St., SW of Hwys. 140 & 395 Junction, Lakeview.

Ownership: Three Angels Broadcasting Network Inc.

Personnel: Moses Primo, Chief Engineer.

Lakeview—K12IH, Ch. 12, Freedom Broadcasting of Oregon Licensee LLC.

Technical Facilities: 0.071-kw ERP, lat. 42° 11' 48", long. 120° 34' 11".

Ownership: Freedom Communications Holdings Inc.

Lakeview—K15HU-D, Ch. 15, Freedom Broadcasting of Oregon Licensee LLC. Phone: 541-773-7373.

Technical Facilities: 0.075-kw ERP, 20-ft. above ground, 7697-ft. above sea level, lat. 42° 15' 10", long. 120° 38' 20".

Ownership: Freedom Communications Holdings Inc.

Lakeview—K19BK, Ch. 19, Oregon Public Broadcasting.

Technical Facilities: 3.03-kw ERP, lat. 42° 10' 42", long. 120° 21' 18".

Ownership: Oregon Public Broadcasting.

Lakeview—K21BC, Ch. 21, Trinity Broadcasting Network Inc. Phone: 714-832-2950. Fax: 714-730-0661.

Technical Facilities: 1.27-kw ERP, lat. 42° 11' 48", long. 120° 34' 11".

Ownership: Trinity Broadcasting Network Inc.

Lakeview, etc.—K07NR-D, Ch. 7, California-Oregon Broadcasting Inc. Phone: 541-779-5555.

Technical Facilities: 0.3-kw ERP, 30-ft. above ground, 6430-ft. above sea level, lat. 42° 12' 18", long. 120° 19' 37".

Ownership: California-Oregon Broadcasting Inc.

Lincoln City—K05KY, Ch. 5, Michael L. Mattson. Phone: 503-409-2181.

Technical Facilities: 2.25-kw ERP, 66-ft. above ground, 1066-ft. above sea level, lat. 44° 45' 23", long. 124° 02' 49".

Ownership: Michael L. Mattson.

Lincoln City & Newport—K38CZ, Ch. 38, NVT Portland Licensee LLC, Debtor in Possession. Phone: 404-995-4711.

Technical Facilities: 23.3-kw ERP, lat. 44° 45' 23", long. 124° 02' 49".

Began Operation: January 31, 1994.

Ownership: New Vision Television LLC, Debtor in Possession.

Lincoln City, etc.—K42CZ, Ch. 42, Fisher Broadcasting Inc.

Technical Facilities: 23.2-kw ERP, 125-ft. above ground, 1175-ft. above sea level, lat. 44° 45' 23", long. 124° 02' 49".

Ownership: Fisher Communications Inc.

London Springs—K51EY, Ch. 51, South Lane TV Inc. Phone: 541-942-9804.

Technical Facilities: 0.012-kw ERP, 148-ft. above ground, 1188-ft. above sea level, lat. 43° 38' 10", long. 123° 05' 34".

Ownership: South Lane TV Inc.

London Springs—K53FJ, Ch. 53, South Lane TV Inc. Phone: 541-942-9804.

Technical Facilities: 0.012-kw ERP, 148-ft. above ground, 1188-ft. above sea level, lat. 43° 38' 10", long. 123° 05' 34".

Holds CP for change to channel number 27, lat. 43° 38' 13", long. 123° 05' 34.3". BDISDTT-20081105ADK.

Began Operation: April 15, 1996.

Ownership: South Lane TV Inc.

London Springs—K55HE, Ch. 55, South Lane TV Inc. Phone: 541-942-9804.

Technical Facilities: 0.012-kw ERP, lat. 43° 38' 10", long. 123° 05' 34".

Holds CP for change to channel number 35, 148-ft. above ground, 1188-ft. above sea level, BDISDTT-20081105ADL.

Transmitter: 0.25-mi. NW of London Springs.

Began Operation: April 15, 1996.

Ownership: South Lane TV Inc.

London Springs—K57GW, Ch. 57, South Lane TV Inc. Phone: 541-942-9804.

Technical Facilities: 0.012-kw ERP, lat. 43° 38' 10", long. 123° 05' 34".

Holds CP for change to channel number 33, 148-ft. above ground, 1188-ft. above sea level, BDISDTT-20081105ADM.

Transmitter: 0.25-mi. NW of London Springs.

Began Operation: April 15, 1996.

Ownership: South Lane TV Inc.

London Springs—K59FS, Ch. 59, South Lane TV Inc. Phone: 541-942-9804.

Technical Facilities: 0.012-kw ERP, 148-ft. above ground, 1188-ft. above sea level, lat. 43° 38' 10", long. 123° 05' 34".

Holds CP for change to channel number 43, BDISDTT-20081105ADN.

Began Operation: April 15, 1996.

Ownership: South Lane TV Inc.

Lonerock—K10CR, Ch. 10, Lonerock TV Co.

Technical Facilities: 0.015-kw ERP, lat. 45° 05' 00", long. 119° 56' 10".

Long Creek—K04AE, Ch. 4, F.L.C.R. Community TV Inc.

Technical Facilities: 0.119-kw ERP, lat. 44° 40' 45", long. 119° 08' 55".

Long Creek—K06AB, Ch. 6, F.L.C.R. community TV Inc.

Technical Facilities: 0.119-kw ERP, lat. 44° 40' 45", long. 119° 08' 55".

Madras & Culver—K46KG-D, Ch. 46, Rural Oregon Wireless Television Inc. Phone: 503-977-7752.

Technical Facilities: 1.2-kw ERP, 62-ft. above ground, 2762-ft. above sea level, lat. 44° 34' 45", long. 121° 09' 09".

Ownership: Rural Oregon Wireless TV Inc.

Madras & Culver—K58BK, Ch. 58, Rural Oregon Wireless Television Inc.

Technical Facilities: 1.61-kw ERP, lat. 44° 34' 48", long. 121° 09' 12".

Ownership: Rural Oregon Wireless TV Inc.

Madras & Culver—K63CC, Ch. 63, Rural Oregon Wireless Television Inc.

Technical Facilities: 1.61-kw ERP, lat. 44° 34' 48", long. 121° 09' 12".

Ownership: Rural Oregon Wireless TV Inc.

Madras & Culver—K66BC, Ch. 66, NPG of Oregon Inc. Phone: 816-271-8502.

Technical Facilities: 1.42-kw ERP, 52-ft. above ground, 2801-ft. above sea level, lat. 44° 34' 48", long. 121° 09' 12".

Holds CP for change to channel number 9, 3-kw ERP, 46-ft. above ground, 5653-ft. above sea level, lat. 44° 26' 17", long. 120° 57' 14". BDISTVL-20060329AGR.

Ownership: News Press & Gazette Co.

Madras & Culver—K69BI, Ch. 69, Rural Oregon Wireless Television Inc.

Technical Facilities: 0.525-kw ERP, 48-ft. above ground, 121° 09' 12".

Ownership: Rural Oregon Wireless TV Inc.

Mapleton—K03CQ, Ch. 3, Newport Television License LLC. Phone: 816-751-0204.

Technical Facilities: 0.006-kw ERP, lat. 44° 03' 00", long. 123° 50' 45".

Ownership: Newport Television LLC.

Mapleton—K05DF, Ch. 5, Newport Television License LLC. Phone: 816-751-0204.

Technical Facilities: 0.006-kw ERP, 1519-ft. above ground, lat. 44° 03' 00", long. 123° 50' 45".

Ownership: Newport Television LLC.

Mapleton—K19EC, Ch. 19, Oregon Public Broadcasting.

Technical Facilities: 2.781-kw ERP, lat. 44° 04' 00", long. 123° 37' 42".

Transmitter: Walker Point.

Ownership: Oregon Public Broadcasting.

Maupin—K52CH, Ch. 52, Maupin Translator District.

Technical Facilities: 2.45-kw ERP, lat. 45° 10' 54", long. 121° 03' 17".

Transmitter: 1.5-mi. NE of Maupin.

Maupin—K54BK, Ch. 54, Maupin Translator District.

Technical Facilities: 2.45-kw ERP, lat. 45° 10' 54", long. 121° 03' 17".

Transmitter: 1.5-mi. NE of Maupin on Bakeoven Rd.

Maupin—K56CD, Ch. 56, Maupin Translator District.

Technical Facilities: 2.45-kw ERP, lat. 45° 10' 54", long. 121° 03' 17".

Transmitter: 1.5-mi. NE of Maupin.

Maupin—K58BU, Ch. 58, Maupin Translator District.

Technical Facilities: 1.83-kw ERP, lat. 45° 10' 54", long. 121° 03' 17".

Maupin—K60CH, Ch. 60, Maupin Translator District.

Technical Facilities: 2.45-kw ERP, lat. 45° 10' 54", long. 121° 03' 17".

Transmitter: 1.5-mi. NE of Maupin on Bakeoven Rd.

Maupin—K62EI, Ch. 62, Maupin Translator District.

Technical Facilities: 2.45-kw ERP, 49-ft. above ground, 1870-ft. above sea level, lat. 45° 10' 54", long. 121° 03' 17".

Medford—K18GB, Ch. 18, Better Life Television. Phone: 541-474-3089.

Technical Facilities: 12.6-kw ERP, 39-ft. above ground, 3425-ft. above sea level, lat. 42° 17' 43", long. 122° 45' 00".

Ownership: Better Life Television Inc.

■**Medford**—K23EX, Ch. 23, Better Life Television. Phone: 541-474-3089.

Technical Facilities: 11.4-kw ERP, 30-ft. above ground, 2835-ft. above sea level, lat. 42° 21' 23", long. 122° 58' 33".

Holds CP for change to 3.42-kw ERP, BDFCDTA-20081205AFK.

Began Operation: July 26, 1993.

Ownership: Better Life Television Inc.

Medford—K25IM, Ch. 25, Better Life Television. Phone: 541-474-3089.

Technical Facilities: 2.97-kw ERP, 39-ft. above ground, 6119-ft. above sea level, lat. 42° 03' 53", long. 122° 28' 41".

Ownership: Better Life Television Inc.

Medford—K28GG, Ch. 28, WatchTV Inc. Phone: 503-241-2411. Fax: 503-226-3557.

Technical Facilities: 24.5-kw ERP, 79-ft. above ground, 3730-ft. above sea level, lat. 42° 17' 43", long. 122° 45' 00".

Holds CP for change to 0.56-kw ERP, 79-ft. above ground, 3881-ft. above sea level, lat. 42° 17' 53", long. 122° 45' 01". BDFCDTL-20090102ACK.

Began Operation: February 5, 1996.

Ownership: WatchTV Inc.

Personnel: Gregory J. Herman, General Manager; Steven A. Hale, Station Manager.

■**Medford**—K32DY, Ch. 32, California-Oregon Broadcasting Inc. Phone: 541-779-5555.

Technical Facilities: 10.91-kw ERP, 108-ft. above ground, 3707-ft. above sea level, lat. 42° 17' 54", long. 122° 44' 57".

Holds CP for change to 15-kw ERP, BDFCDTA-20090313AAD.

Ownership: California-Oregon Broadcasting Inc.

Medford—K41IX, Ch. 41, Mutual Television Network. Phone: 888-482-1080.

Technical Facilities: 12.1-kw ERP, 89-ft. above ground, 2188-ft. above sea level, lat. 42° 25' 41", long. 123° 00' 04".

Holds CP for change to channel number 51, 10-kw ERP, BDISDTT-20060331AFP.

Ownership: Mutual Television Network.

Medford—KDOV-LP, Ch. 44, Inspiration Television Inc. Phones: 505-890-7218; 760-727-2105.

Technical Facilities: 13.8-kw ERP, 318-ft. above ground, 1883-ft. above sea level, lat. 42° 17' 44", long. 122° 48' 15".

Began Operation: August 12, 2008.

Ownership: Inspiration Television Inc.

Medford—KFBI-LP, Ch. 48, Sainte Partners II LP. Phone: 209-523-0777.

Technical Facilities: 25.8-kw ERP, 82-ft. above ground, 3881-ft. above sea level, lat. 42° 17' 54", long. 122° 44' 57".

Holds CP for change to 0.25-kw ERP, BDFCDTA-20060703AAB.

Ownership: Sainte Partners II LP.

Medford—KMCW-LP, Ch. 14, Sainte Partners II LP. Phone: 209-523-0777.

Technical Facilities: 12.4-kw ERP, 62-ft. above ground, 3862-ft. above sea level, lat. 42° 17' 54", long. 122° 44' 57".

Holds CP for change to 0.2-kw ERP, BDFCDTA-20060710AAA.

Ownership: Sainte Partners II LP.

Merlin—K29GX, Ch. 29, Better Life Television. Phone: 541-474-3089.

Technical Facilities: 5-kw ERP, 39-ft. above ground, 4806-ft. above sea level, lat. 42° 42' 59", long. 123° 11' 57".

Ownership: Better Life Television Inc.

Merlin—K33GJ, Ch. 33, Better Life Television. Phone: 541-582-3819.

Technical Facilities: 1.63-kw ERP, 49-ft. above ground, 3848-ft. above sea level, lat. 42° 35' 59", long. 123° 21' 54".

Ownership: Better Life Television Inc.

Merrill, etc.—K04KI, Ch. 4, Southern Oregon Public Television Inc.

Technical Facilities: 0.02-kw ERP, 6421-ft. above sea level, lat. 42° 05' 48", long. 121° 37' 57".

Ownership: Southern Oregon Public Television Inc.

Midland, etc.—K19HH-D, Ch. 19, Freedom Broadcasting of Oregon Licensee LLC. Phone: 541-773-7373.

Technical Facilities: 0.26-kw ERP, 59-ft. above ground, 6509-ft. above sea level, lat. 42° 05' 55", long. 121° 38' 01".

Ownership: Freedom Communications Holdings Inc.

Midland, etc.—K60BH, Ch. 60, Freedom Broadcasting of Oregon Licensee LLC.

Technical Facilities: 1.27-kw ERP, 4606-ft. above sea level, lat. 42° 08' 48", long. 121° 46' 16".

Ownership: Freedom Communications Holdings Inc.

Midland, etc.—K62BE, Ch. 62, California-Oregon Broadcasting Inc. Phone: 541-779-5555.

Technical Facilities: 1.27-kw ERP, 4610-ft. above sea level, lat. 42° 08' 48", long. 121° 46' 16".

Holds CP for change to channel number 36, 70-kw ERP, 92-ft. above ground, 6503-ft. above sea level, lat. 42° 05' 48", long. 121° 37' 57". BDISTTL-20060331BFG.

Ownership: California-Oregon Broadcasting Inc.

Milton, etc.—K29EG, Ch. 29, Citizens TV Inc. Phone: 541-938-7935.

Technical Facilities: 1.75-kw ERP, 20-ft. above ground, 3245-ft. above sea level, lat. 45° 50' 25", long. 118° 17' 10".

Milton-Freewater—K23FH, Ch. 23, Citizens TV Inc.

Technical Facilities: 1.75-kw ERP, lat. 45° 50' 25", long. 118° 17' 10".

Milton-Freewater—K35FO, Ch. 35, Citizens TV Inc.

Technical Facilities: 1.75-kw ERP, lat. 45° 50' 25", long. 118° 17' 10".

Transmitter: Approx. 10-mi. SE of Milton-Freewater.

Milton-Freewater—K40FM, Ch. 40, Citizens TV Inc.

Technical Facilities: 1-kw ERP, lat. 45° 50' 25", long. 118° 17' 10".

Milton-Freewater—K50FX, Ch. 50, Oregon Public Broadcasting.

Technical Facilities: 1.07-kw ERP, lat. 45° 49' 54", long. 118° 15' 38".

Milton-Freewater—K51DF, Ch. 51, Citizens TV Inc.

Technical Facilities: 1.97-kw ERP, 20-ft. above ground, 3241-ft. above sea level, lat. 45° 50' 25", long. 118° 17' 10".

Milton-Freewater—K53EK, Ch. 53, Citizens T.V. Inc. Phone: 541-938-7935.

Technical Facilities: 100-w TPO, 1.16-kw ERP, 3396-ft. above sea level, lat. 45° 49' 55", long. 118° 15' 37".

Transmitter: Basket Mountain electronics site, approx. 10-mi. SE of Milton-Freewater.

Began Operation: March 8, 1993.

Ownership: Citizens T.V. Inc.

Milton-Freewater—K55GC, Ch. 55, Citizens T.V. Inc. Phone: 541-938-7935.

Technical Facilities: 100-w TPO, 1.16-kw ERP, 20-ft. above ground, 3396-ft. above sea level, lat. 45° 49' 55", long. 118° 15' 37".

Transmitter: Basket Mountain electronics site, approx. 10-mi. SE of Milton-Freewater.

Began Operation: April 22, 1992.

Ownership: Citizens T.V. Inc.

Montgomery Ranch, etc.—K32CC, Ch. 32, NPG of Oregon Inc. Phone: 816-271-8504.

Technical Facilities: 0.72-kw ERP, 49-ft. above ground, 4974-ft. above sea level, lat. 43° 52' 25", long. 121° 30' 11".

Holds CP for change to 1.2-kw ERP, BPTT-20050606AIB.

Ownership: News Press & Gazette Co.

Monument—K09MZ, Ch. 9, Monument TV Inc.

Technical Facilities: 0.017-kw ERP, lat. 44° 50' 27", long. 119° 27' 50".

Monument—K11NM, Ch. 11, Monument TV Inc.

Technical Facilities: 0.017-kw ERP, lat. 44° 50' 27", long. 119° 27' 50".

Monument—K12MX, Ch. 12, Monument TV Inc.

Technical Facilities: 0.02-kw ERP, lat. 44° 50' 27", long. 119° 27' 50".

Monument—K13OH, Ch. 13, Monument TV Inc.

Technical Facilities: 0.017-kw ERP, lat. 44° 50' 27", long. 119° 27' 50".

Murphy, etc.—K34BV, Ch. 34, California-Oregon Broadcasting Inc. Phone: 541-779-5555.

Technical Facilities: lat. 42° 17' 36", long. 123° 20' 13".

Holds CP for change to channel number 49, 1.5-kw ERP, 70-ft. above ground, 2806-ft. above sea level, lat. 42° 24' 43", long. 123° 16' 54". BDISDTT-20060331BFX.

Ownership: California-Oregon Broadcasting Inc.

Myrtle Creek—K13HM, Ch. 13, South West Oregon TV Broadcasting Corp. Phone: 206-404-3065.

Technical Facilities: 0.025-kw ERP, lat. 43° 01' 05", long. 123° 18' 46".

Ownership: California-Oregon Broadcasting Inc.; Fisher Communications Inc.

Myrtle Point—K55FM, Ch. 55, Oregon Public Broadcasting. Phone: 503-244-9900.

Technical Facilities: 0.053-kw ERP, 36-ft. above ground, 236-ft. above sea level, lat. 43° 03' 50", long. 124° 07' 54".

Ownership: Oregon Public Broadcasting.

Myrtle Point, etc.—K07JP, Ch. 7, Broadbent TV Translator Inc.

Technical Facilities: 0.006-kw ERP, lat. 43° 01' 05", long. 124° 10' 36".

Myrtle Point, etc.—K13KQ, Ch. 13, Broadbent TV Translator Inc.

Technical Facilities: 0.006-kw ERP, lat. 43° 01' 05", long. 124° 10' 36".

Nehalem & Rockaway—K51FK, Ch. 51, Meredith Corp.

Technical Facilities: 200-w TPO, 0.266-kw ERP, 30-ft. above ground, 1364-ft. above sea level, lat. 45° 44' 27", long. 123° 56' 10".

Transmitter: Neahkahnie Mountain, approx. 1.2-mi. N of Nehalem.

Ownership: Meredith Corp.

Nesika Beach—K20BI, Ch. 20, Soda Mountain Broadcasting Inc.

Technical Facilities: 1.56-kw ERP, 33-ft. above ground, 2372-ft. above sea level, lat. 42° 23' 51", long. 124° 21' 51".

Ownership: Soda Mountain Broadcasting Inc.

■ **Newberg**—KOXO-CA, Ch. 51, WatchTV Inc. Phone: 503-241-2411. Fax: 503-226-3557.

Technical Facilities: 95-kw ERP, 600-ft. above ground, 1722-ft. above sea level, lat. 45° 31' 21", long. 122° 44' 45".

Holds CP for change to channel number 6, 0.012-kw ERP, BDISTVA-20081006AIS.

Began Operation: March 12, 1993.

Ownership: WatchTV Inc.

Personnel: Gregory J. Herman, General Manager; Steven A. Hale, Station Manager; Spencer French, Sales Director.

Newburg & Tigard—K18EL, Ch. 18, Meredith Corp. Phones: 503-239-4949; 515-284-3000. Fax: 503-239-6184.

Technical Facilities: 1000-w TPO, 9.17-kw ERP, 89-ft. above ground, 1571-ft. above sea level, lat. 45° 21' 17", long. 122° 59' 17".

Holds CP for change to 1.5-kw ERP, 131-ft. above ground, 1572-ft. above sea level, BDFCDTL-20060331BBL.

Transmitter: Chehalem Mountain, approx. 3.7-mi. N of Newburg.

Ownership: Meredith Corp.

Newport—K18FR, Ch. 18, Oregon Public Broadcasting. Phone: 503-244-9900.

Technical Facilities: 12-kw ERP, 89-ft. above ground, 1158-ft. above sea level, lat. 44° 45' 25", long. 124° 02' 50".

Holds CP for change to 5.4-kw ERP, 157-ft. above ground, 1194-ft. above sea level, lat. 44° 45' 23", long. 124° 02' 55". BDFCDTT-20090210AAG.

Began Operation: May 29, 1979.

Ownership: Oregon Public Broadcasting.

Newport—K29AZ, Ch. 29, King Broadcasting Co. Phone: 214-977-6606.

Technical Facilities: 19-kw ERP, 157-ft. above ground, 1194-ft. above sea level, lat. 44° 45' 23", long. 124° 02' 55".

Began Operation: August 3, 1988.

Ownership: Belo Corp.

Newport—KDLN-LP, Ch. 4, Kenneth E. Lewetag. Phone: 503-930-7228.

Technical Facilities: 2.25-kw ERP, 66-ft. above ground, 1066-ft. above sea level, lat. 44° 45' 23", long. 124° 02' 49".

Holds CP for change to channel number 24, 12-kw ERP, 66-ft. above ground, 3422-ft. above sea level, lat. 44° 16' 47.4", long. 123° 35' 01.4". BMPDTL-20080819ACW.

Multichannel TV Sound: Stereo and separate audio program.

Began Operation: March 7, 2005.

Ownership: Kenneth E. Lewetag.

Newport, etc.—K15DS, Ch. 15, Meredith Corp. Phones: 503-239-4949; 515-284-3000. Fax: 503-239-6184.

Technical Facilities: 10.4-kw ERP, lat. 44° 45' 23", long. 124° 02' 49".

Holds CP for change to 2-kw ERP, 40-ft. above ground, 1079-ft. above sea level, BDFCDTL-20060331BDX.

Ownership: Meredith Corp.

North Bend—K07JS, Ch. 7, KEZI Inc. Phone: 541-485-5611.

Holds CP for change to 3-kw ERP, 59-ft. above ground, 959-ft. above sea level, lat. 43° 23' 26", long. 124° 07' 48". BPTTV-20050803ABZ.

Ownership: Chambers Communications Corp.

North Bend & Empire—K13JQ, Ch. 13, California-Oregon Broadcasting Inc. Phone: 541-779-5555.

Technical Facilities: 2-kw ERP, 79-ft. above ground, 879-ft. above sea level, lat. 43° 23' 30", long. 142° 07' 48".

Ownership: California-Oregon Broadcasting Inc.

North La Pine—K34AI, Ch. 34, NVT Portland Licensee LLC, Debtor in Possession. Phone: 404-995-4711.

Technical Facilities: 0.72-kw ERP, lat. 43° 52' 25", long. 121° 30' 11".

Began Operation: October 13, 1988.

Ownership: New Vision Television LLC, Debtor in Possession.

North La Pine—K38DT, Ch. 38, NPG of Oregon Inc. Phone: 816-271-8504.

Technical Facilities: 0.627-kw ERP, 49-ft. above ground, 4974-ft. above sea level, lat. 43° 52' 25", long. 121° 30' 11".

Ownership: News Press & Gazette Co.

Oakland—K07IA, Ch. 7, KEZI Inc.

Technical Facilities: 0.005-kw ERP, 554-ft. above sea level, lat. 43° 25' 29", long. 123° 18' 14".

Oakland, etc.—K12IA, Ch. 12, South West Oregon TV Broadcasting Corp. Phone: 206-404-3065.

Technical Facilities: 0.021-kw ERP, lat. 43° 24' 10", long. 123° 18' 45".

Ownership: California-Oregon Broadcasting Inc.; Fisher Communications Inc.

Oakridge—K11SZ, Ch. 11, Oregon Public Broadcasting.

Technical Facilities: 0.034-kw ERP, 112-ft. above ground, 3832-ft. above sea level, lat. 43° 46' 35", long. 122° 24' 13".

Ownership: Oregon Public Broadcasting.

■ **Ontario**—KMBA-LP, Ch. 19, Treasure Valley Community College. Phone: 541-881-8822. Fax: 541-881-2717.

Technical Facilities: 76-w TPO, 0.882-kw ERP, 89-ft. above ground, 2598-ft. above sea level, lat. 44° 03' 53", long. 116° 54' 14".

Transmitter: Communications Bldg., Clay Point, Payette, ID.

Ownership: Treasure Valley Community College.

Personnel: Russell Strawn, General Manager; George Klenck, Chief Engineer.

Ontario, etc.—K15DY, Ch. 15, Oregon Public Broadcasting. Phone: 503-244-9900.

Technical Facilities: 1.157-kw ERP, 89-ft. above ground, 2598-ft. above sea level, lat. 44° 03' 53", long. 116° 54' 14".

Holds CP for change to 0.35-kw ERP, 89-ft. above ground, 2589-ft. above sea level, BDFCDTT-20081016AAC.

Oregon Canyon—K11PO, Ch. 11, Oregon Canyon TV Assn.

Technical Facilities: 0.005-kw ERP, lat. 42° 16' 05", long. 117° 49' 57".

Oregon Canyon—K13HT, Ch. 13, Oregon Canyon TV Assn.

Technical Facilities: 0.026-kw ERP, lat. 42° 19' 03", long. 117° 52' 03".

Oxbow—K06ER, Ch. 6, Idaho Power Co.

Technical Facilities: 0.012-kw ERP, 2707-ft. above sea level, lat. 44° 57' 34", long. 116° 49' 57".

Ownership: Idaho Power Co.

Oxbow Power Plant—K04ET, Ch. 4, Idaho Power Co.

Technical Facilities: 0.012-kw ERP, 2694-ft. above sea level, lat. 44° 57' 34", long. 116° 49' 57".

Ownership: Idaho Power Co.

Pacific City & Cloverdale—K19EI, Ch. 19, Oregon Public Broadcasting. Phone: 503-244-9900.

Technical Facilities: 1.14-kw ERP, lat. 45° 12' 48", long. 123° 45' 14".

Holds CP for change to 0.55-kw ERP, 59-ft. above ground, 3199-ft. above sea level, BDFCDTT-20090220ABE.

Ownership: Oregon Public Broadcasting.

Paisley—K04PK, Ch. 4, Oregon Public Broadcasting. Phone: 503-244-9900.

Technical Facilities: 0.225-kw ERP, 16-ft. above ground, 6614-ft. above sea level, lat. 42° 23' 28", long. 120° 22' 04".

Ownership: Oregon Public Broadcasting.

Paisley—K09VC, Ch. 9, Oregon Public Broadcasting.

Technical Facilities: 0.003-kw ERP, lat. 42° 41' 42", long. 120° 33' 13".

Ownership: Oregon Public Broadcasting.

Pendleton—K24DX, Ch. 24, Tribune Broadcast Holdings Inc., Debtor-In-Possession. Phone: 503-644-3232.

Technical Facilities: 100-w TPO, 2-kw ERP, 66-ft. above ground, 5998-ft. above sea level, lat. 45° 12' 47", long. 119° 17' 41".

Transmitter: Black Mountain, approx. 15.5-mi. SE of Heppner.

Ownership: Tribune Broadcasting Co., Debtor-In-Possession.

Pendleton, etc.—K20ES, Ch. 20, Tribune Broadcast Holdings Inc., Debtor-In-Possession. Phone: 503-644-3232.

Technical Facilities: 100-w TPO, 2-kw ERP, 66-ft. above ground, 5998-ft. above sea level, lat. 45° 12' 47", long. 119° 17' 41".

Transmitter: Black Mountain, approx. 15.5-mi. SE of Heppner.

Ownership: Tribune Broadcasting Co., Debtor-In-Possession.

Pendleton, etc.—K32DE, Ch. 32, Umatilla Electric Cooperative.

Technical Facilities: 2-kw ERP, 66-ft. above ground, 5997-ft. above sea level, lat. 45° 12' 47", long. 119° 17' 41".

Transmitter: Black Mountain, 15.5-mi. SE of Heppner.

Pendleton, etc.—K36DP, Ch. 36, Blue Mountain Translator District. Phone: 509-529-9149.

Technical Facilities: 2-kw ERP, 5997-ft. above sea level, lat. 45° 12' 47", long. 119° 17' 41".

Ownership: Blue Mountain Translator District.

Pendleton, etc.—K38AH, Ch. 38, Umatilla Electric Cooperative.

Technical Facilities: 0.816-kw ERP, 66-ft. above ground, 5997-ft. above sea level, lat. 45° 12' 47", long. 119° 17' 41".

Pendleton, etc.—K59BO, Ch. 59, Oregon Public Broadcasting. Phone: 503-244-9900.

Technical Facilities: 0.485-kw ERP, 3615-ft. above sea level, lat. 45° 35' 20", long. 118° 34' 54".

Holds CP for change to channel number 22, 36-ft. above ground, 3586-ft. above sea level, lat. 45° 35' 21", long. 118° 34' 44". BDISTT-20060315AET.

Ownership: Oregon Public Broadcasting.

Phoenix—K34DJ, Ch. 34, Southern Oregon Public Television Inc.

Technical Facilities: 1-kw ERP, lat. 42° 17' 55", long. 122° 44' 59".

Ownership: Southern Oregon Public Television Inc.

Phoenix & Talent—K16CU, Ch. 16, Freedom Broadcasting of Oregon Licensee LLC.

Technical Facilities: 3.62-kw ERP, 30-ft. above ground, 3789-ft. above sea level, lat. 42° 17' 43", long. 122° 45' 00".

Ownership: Freedom Communications Holdings Inc.

Phoenix & Talent—K47LD-D, Ch. 47, Freedom Broadcasting of Oregon Licensee LLC. Phone: 541-773-7373.

Technical Facilities: 0.25-kw ERP, 46-ft. above ground, 3848-ft. above sea level, lat. 42° 17' 52", long. 122° 45' 00".

Ownership: Freedom Communications Holdings Inc.

Pinehurst—K13PF, Ch. 13, Southern Oregon Public Television Inc.

Technical Facilities: 0.081-kw ERP, lat. 42° 08' 22", long. 122° 26' 25".

Ownership: Southern Oregon Public Television Inc.

Pistol River—K07PI, Ch. 7, Pistol River Translator Group.

Technical Facilities: 0.003-kw ERP, lat. 42° 25' 08", long. 124° 23' 08".

Plush—K04CB, Ch. 4, Plush TV Inc.

Technical Facilities: 0.013-kw ERP, lat. 42° 18' 30", long. 119° 52' 30".

Port Orford—K14GT, Ch. 14, Soda Mountain Bcstg. Inc.

Technical Facilities: 0.164-kw ERP, lat. 42° 44' 30", long. 124° 30' 30".

Port Orford—K61BU, Ch. 61, Oregon Public Broadcasting. Phone: 503-244-9900.

Technical Facilities: 0.79-kw ERP, lat. 42° 44' 30", long. 124° 30' 09".

Holds CP for change to channel number 47, 0.6-kw ERP, 39-ft. above ground, 328-ft. above sea level, BDISTT-20060315ACJ.

Ownership: Oregon Public Broadcasting.

Port Orford, etc.—K08AK, Ch. 8, California-Oregon Broadcasting Inc. Phone: 541-779-5555.

Technical Facilities: 0.3-kw ERP, 49-ft. above ground, 381-ft. above sea level, lat. 42° 44' 25", long. 124° 30' 17".

Ownership: California-Oregon Broadcasting Inc.

Portland—K26GJ, Ch. 26, Northwest Christian Broadcasting. Phone: 503-362-0862.

Studio: 1144 Madison NE, Salem, OR 97303.

Technical Facilities: 25.5-kw ERP, 66-ft. above ground, 1152-ft. above sea level, lat. 45° 27' 17", long. 122° 33' 01".

Ownership: Northwest Christian Broadcasting.

Personnel: Jerry Harpham, General Manager.

■ **Portland**—KKEI-CA, Ch. 38, WatchTV Inc. Phone: 503-241-2411. Fax: 503-226-3557.

Technical Facilities: 150-kw ERP, 600-ft. above ground, 1722-ft. above sea level, lat. 45° 31' 21", long. 122° 44' 45".

Ownership: WatchTV Inc.

Personnel: Gregory J. Herman, General Manager; Steven A. Hale, Station Manager; Spencer French, Sales Director.

■ **Portland**—KORK-CA, Ch. 35, WatchTV Inc. Phone: 503-241-2411. Fax: 503-226-3557.

Technical Facilities: 150-kw ERP, 600-ft. above ground, 1722-ft. above sea level, lat. 45° 31' 21", long. 122° 44' 45".

Ownership: WatchTV Inc.

Personnel: Gregory J. Herman, General Manager; Steven A. Hale, Station Manager.

Portland—KPXG-LP, Ch. 54, ION Media License Co. LLC, Debtor in Possession. Phones: 503-222-2221; 561-682-4206. Fax: 503-222-4613.

Studio: 811 SW Naito Pkwy, Ste 100, Portland, OR 97204.

Technical Facilities: 105-kw ERP, 844-ft. above ground, 1967-ft. above sea level, lat. 45° 31' 21", long. 122° 44' 45".

Holds CP for change to channel number 42, 15-kw ERP, BDISDTL-20060323AHQ.

Began Operation: August 15, 1983.

Ownership: ION Media Networks Inc., Debtor in Possession.

Personnel: Linda Messana, Station Operations Manager; Tim Mance, Chief Engineer; Mary Pierce, Traffic Manager.

Portland—KRCW-LP, Ch. 5, Tribune Broadcast Holdings Inc., Debtor-In-Possession. Phone: 503-644-3232.

Technical Facilities: 2.7-kw ERP, 600-ft. above ground, 1660-ft. above sea level, lat. 45° 30' 58", long. 122° 43' 59".

Holds CP for change to 0.3-kw ERP, 601-ft. above ground, 1660-ft. above sea level, BDFCDTT-20060328AAF.

Ownership: Tribune Broadcasting Co., Debtor-In-Possession.

Portland—KUNP-LP, Ch. 47, Fisher Radio Regional Group. Phone: 206-404-7000.

Technical Facilities: 93.6-kw ERP, 793-ft. above ground, 1744-ft. above sea level, lat. 45° 31' 14", long. 122° 44' 37".

Ownership: Fisher Communications Inc.

Personnel: John Tamerlano, General Manager.

Powers—K61EH, Ch. 61, Powers TV Translator Inc. Phone: 541-439-2313.

Technical Facilities: 0.031-kw ERP, 33-ft. above ground, 1791-ft. above sea level, lat. 42° 53' 11", long. 124° 05' 29".

Holds CP for change to channel number 34, 0.1-kw ERP, 120-ft. above ground, 1842-ft. above sea level, lat. 42° 54' 58.5", long. 124° 04' 39.7". BDISDTT-20090211ADI.

Powers—K64DA, Ch. 64, Powers TV Translator Inc. Phone: 541-439-2313.

Technical Facilities: 0.03-kw ERP, 33-ft. above ground, 1791-ft. above sea level, lat. 42° 53' 11", long. 124° 05' 29".

Holds CP for change to channel number 38, 0.1-kw ERP, 120-ft. above ground, 1842-ft. above sea level, lat. 42° 54' 58.5", long. 124° 04' 39.7". BDISDTT-20090211ADJ.

Powers—K66DG, Ch. 66, Powers TV Translator Inc. Phone: 541-439-2313.

Technical Facilities: 0.031-kw ERP, lat. 42° 53' 11", long. 124° 05' 29".

Holds CP for change to channel number 40, 0.1-kw ERP, 120-ft. above ground, 1842-ft. above sea level, lat. 42° 54' 58.5", long. 124° 04' 39.7". BDISDTT-20090211ADK.

Powers—K69AM, Ch. 69, Powers TV Translator Inc. Phone: 541-439-2313.

Technical Facilities: 0.03-kw ERP, lat. 42° 53' 11", long. 124° 05' 29".

Holds CP for change to channel number 42, 0.1-kw ERP, 120-ft. above ground, 1842-ft. above sea level, lat. 42° 54' 58.5", long. 124° 04' 39.7". BDISDTT-20090211ADL.

Prairie City—K100K, Ch. 10, Prairie City Lions Club.

Technical Facilities: 0.018-kw ERP, lat. 44° 26' 31", long. 118° 25' 15".

Transmitter: Elkhorn Mountain, 14-mi. E of Prairie City.

Prairie City—K11LT, Ch. 11, Prairie City Lions Club.

Technical Facilities: 0.017-kw ERP, lat. 44° 26' 31", long. 118° 25' 15".

Prairie City—K13MM, Ch. 13, Prairie City Lions Club.

Technical Facilities: 0.017-kw ERP, lat. 44° 26' 31", long. 118° 25' 15".

Prairie City & Unity—K05JL, Ch. 5, Oregon Public Broadcasting.

Technical Facilities: 0.025-kw ERP, 36-ft. above ground, 6755-ft. above sea level, lat. 44° 26' 25", long. 118° 25' 09".

Ownership: Oregon Public Broadcasting.

Princeton—K10IO, Ch. 10, Princeton Community TV.

Technical Facilities: 0.006-kw ERP, 4902-ft. above sea level, lat. 43° 15' 00", long. 118° 30' 00".

Princeton, etc.—K13RT, Ch. 13, Princeton Community TV.

Technical Facilities: 0.01-kw ERP, 4902-ft. above sea level, lat. 43° 15' 00", long. 118° 30' 00".

Prineville—K08KN, Ch. 8, King Broadcasting Co. Phone: 214-977-6606.

Technical Facilities: 10-w TPO, 0.12-kw ERP, 82-ft. above ground, 5299-ft. above sea level, lat. 44° 11' 51", long. 120° 58' 35".

Transmitter: Powell Butte, 10-mi. SW of Prineville.

Ownership: Belo Corp.

Prineville—K23CU, Ch. 23, Christ Loves You Broadcasting. Phone: 541-447-3794. Fax: 541-388-2252.

Technical Facilities: 100-w TPO, 0.923-kw ERP, 52-ft. above ground, 5879-ft. above sea level, lat. 44° 26' 15", long. 120° 57' 11".

Holds CP for change to 0.28-kw ERP, 52-ft. above ground, 5682-ft. above sea level, BDFCDTL-20081205AGF.

Transmitter: Grizzly Mountain, Prineville.

Began Operation: May 13, 1991.

Ownership: Christ Loves You Broadcasting.

Prineville—K54AP, Ch. 54, Fisher Broadcasting Inc.

Technical Facilities: 2.25-kw ERP, lat. 44° 26' 17", long. 120° 57' 13".

Ownership: Fisher Communications Inc.

Prineville—K66AZ, Ch. 66, NPG of Oregon Inc. Phone: 816-271-8502.

Technical Facilities: 0.375-kw ERP, 23-ft. above ground, 5656-ft. above sea level, lat. 44° 26' 05", long. 120° 57' 06".

Holds CP for change to channel number 36, 50-kw ERP, 59-ft. above ground, 5666-ft. above sea level, lat. 44° 26' 17", long. 120° 57' 14". BDISTTL-20060329AGX.

Ownership: News Press & Gazette Co.

Prineville, etc.—K16EM, Ch. 16, Oregon Public Broadcasting. Phone: 503-244-9900. Fax: 503-293-4165.

Technical Facilities: 0.66-kw ERP, 33-ft. above ground, 5574-ft. above sea level, lat. 44° 26' 07", long. 120° 57' 08".

Holds CP for change to 0.2-kw ERP, BDFCDTT-20081231AAN.

Ownership: Oregon Public Broadcasting.

Prineville, etc.—K29CI, Ch. 29, Fisher Broadcasting Inc.

Technical Facilities: 25-kw ERP, 5279-ft. above sea level, lat. 44° 11' 51", long. 120° 58' 35".

Ownership: Fisher Communications Inc.

Prineville, etc.—K31CR-D, Ch. 31, NVT Portland Licensee LLC, Debtor in Possession. Phone: 404-995-4711.

Technical Facilities: 15-kw ERP, 102-ft. above ground, 5279-ft. above sea level, lat. 44° 11' 51", long. 120° 58' 35".

Began Operation: May 5, 1992.

Ownership: New Vision Television LLC, Debtor in Possession.

Prineville, etc.—K44AH, Ch. 44, Meredith Corp. Phones: 503-239-4949; 515-284-3000. Fax: 503-239-6184.

Technical Facilities: 1.71-kw ERP, lat. 44° 26' 17", long. 120° 57' 13".

Holds CP for change to 0.115-kw ERP, 38-ft. above ground, 5671-ft. above sea level, BDFCDTT-20060331BAR.

Ownership: Meredith Corp.

Prineville, etc.—K46AK, Ch. 46, KGW-TV Inc.

Technical Facilities: 2.25-kw ERP, lat. 44° 26' 17", long. 120° 57' 06".

Prineville, etc.—K52AK, Ch. 52, NVT Portland Licensee LLC, Debtor in Possession. Phone: 404-995-4711.

Technical Facilities: 2.25-kw ERP, lat. 44° 26' 17", long. 120° 57' 13".

Holds CP for change to channel number 47, 2.43-kw ERP, 56-ft. above ground, 5689-ft. above sea level, BDISTT-20061212ABI.

Ownership: New Vision Television LLC, Debtor in Possession.

Prospect—K02JG, Ch. 2, Southern Oregon Public Television Inc. Phone: 541-779-0808.

Technical Facilities: 0.09-kw ERP, lat. 42° 43' 36", long. 122° 36' 28".

Began Operation: February 26, 1979.

Ownership: Southern Oregon Public Television Inc.

Prospect—K07GI, Ch. 7, Prospect Lions Club Inc.

Technical Facilities: 0.007-kw ERP, lat. 42° 43' 36", long. 122° 36' 28".

Prospect—K13KO, Ch. 13, California-Oregon Broadcasting Inc.

Technical Facilities: 0.02-kw ERP, lat. 43° 45' 57", long. 122° 25' 08".

Rainier—K17GV, Ch. 17, Rural Oregon Wireless TV Inc. Phone: 503-226-5004.

Technical Facilities: 2.2-kw ERP, 49-ft. above ground, 1309-ft. above sea level, lat. 46° 09' 46", long. 122° 51' 05".

Ownership: Rural Oregon Wireless TV Inc.

Rainier—K21HG, Ch. 21, Rural Oregon Wireless TV Inc. Phone: 503-226-5004.

Technical Facilities: 2.2-kw ERP, 49-ft. above ground, 1309-ft. above sea level, lat. 46° 09' 46", long. 121° 51' 05".

Ownership: Rural Oregon Wireless TV Inc.

Rainier—K28IH, Rural Oregon Wireless TV Inc. Phone: 503-226-5004.

Technical Facilities: 2.2-kw ERP, 49-ft. above ground, 1309-ft. above sea level, lat. 46° 09' 46", long. 122° 51' 05".

Ownership: Rural Oregon Wireless TV Inc.

Rainier—K31HK, Ch. 31, Rural Oregon Wireless Television Inc. Phone: 503-226-5004.

Technical Facilities: 2.2-kw ERP, 49-ft. above ground, 1309-ft. above sea level, lat. 46° 09' 46", long. 122° 51' 05".

Ownership: Rural Oregon Wireless TV Inc.

Rainier—K41IP, Ch. 41, Rural Oregon Wireless TV Inc. Phone: 503-226-5004.

Technical Facilities: 2.2-kw ERP, 49-ft. above ground, 1309-ft. above sea level, lat. 46° 09' 46", long. 122° 51' 05".

Ownership: Rural Oregon Wireless TV Inc.

Rainier—K44HM, Ch. 44, Rural Oregon Wireless TV Inc. Phone: 503-226-5004.

Technical Facilities: 2.2-kw ERP, 49-ft. above ground, 1309-ft. above sea level, lat. 46° 09' 46", long. 122° 51' 05".

Ownership: Rural Oregon Wireless TV Inc.

Redmond, etc.—K25GA, Ch. 25, WatchTV Inc. Phone: 503-241-2411. Fax: 503-226-3557.

Technical Facilities: 1000-w TPO, 11.8-kw ERP, 49-ft. above ground, 5748-ft. above sea level, lat. 44° 26' 07", long. 120° 57' 10".

Holds CP for change to 1.6-kw ERP, 49-ft. above ground, 5659-ft. above sea level, BDFCDTL-20090302AAA.

Transmitter: Grizzly Mountain, 10-mi. NW of Prineville.

Began Operation: March 1, 1995.

Ownership: WatchTV Inc.

Personnel: Gregory J. Herman, General Manager; Steve A. Hale, Station Manager.

Reedsport—K02NW, Ch. 2, Oregon Public Broadcasting.

Technical Facilities: 0.057-kw ERP, lat. 43° 43' 21", long. 124° 05' 40".

Transmitter: 123 Gardiner Hill Rd., Gardiner.

Ownership: Oregon Public Broadcasting.

Reedsport—K04OS, Ch. 4, KEZI Inc.

Technical Facilities: 0.0584-kw ERP, lat. 43° 43' 21", long. 124° 05' 40".

Transmitter: 123 Gardiner Hill Rd.

Ownership: Chambers Communications Corp.

Richland—K08KW, Ch. 8, Oregon Public Broadcasting.

Technical Facilities: 0.041-kw ERP, lat. 44° 36' 32", long. 117° 16' 40".

Riley—KQRE-LP, Ch. 19, NPG of Oregon Inc. Phone: 816-271-8502.

Technical Facilities: 125-kw ERP, 49-ft. above ground, 6391-ft. above sea level, lat. 43° 47' 29", long. 120° 56' 48".

Holds CP for change to 50-kw ERP, 59-ft. above ground, 5666-ft. above sea level, lat. 44° 26' 17", long. 120° 57' 14". BPTTL-20060403ANE.

Ownership: News Press & Gazette Co.

Rockaway—K20HT, Ch. 20, Rural Oregon Wireless Television Inc.

Technical Facilities: 2.12-kw ERP, lat. 45° 44' 27", long. 123° 56' 10".

Rockaway.—K44AV, Ch. 44, Rural Oregon Wireless Television Inc.

Technical Facilities: 2.12-kw ERP, 16-ft. above ground, 1617-ft. above sea level, lat. 45° 44' 27", long. 123° 56' 10".

Rockaway.—K47CD, Ch. 47, Rural Oregon Wireless Television Inc. Phone: 503-226-5004.

Technical Facilities: 0.533-kw ERP, 16-ft. above ground, 1617-ft. above sea level, lat. 45° 44' 38", long. 123° 56' 23".

Rockaway & vicinity—K36GU, Ch. 36, Rural Oregon Wireless Television Inc.

Technical Facilities: 0.475-kw ERP, 16-ft. above ground, 1617-ft. above sea level, lat. 45° 44' 38", long. 123° 56' 23".

Rockaway, etc.—K41GG, Ch. 41, Rural Oregon Wireless Television Inc.

Technical Facilities: 0.521-kw ERP, 16-ft. above ground, 1617-ft. above sea level, lat. 45° 44' 38", long. 123° 56' 23".

Rogue River—K03BZ, Ch. 3, Freedom Broadcasting of Oregon Licensee LLC. Phone: 518-346-6666.

Technical Facilities: 0.019-kw ERP, lat. 42° 26' 56", long. 123° 11' 22".

Ownership: Freedom Communications Holdings Inc.

Rogue River—K17EZ, Ch. 17, Better Life Television. Phone: 541-582-8024.

Technical Facilities: 1.31-kw ERP, 29-ft. above ground, 2129-ft. above sea level, lat. 42° 25' 35", long. 123° 08' 58".

Roseburg—K25FG, Ch. 25, WatchTV Inc. Phone: 503-241-2411. Fax: 503-226-3557.

Technical Facilities: 13.1-kw ERP, 89-ft. above ground, 1577-ft. above sea level, lat. 43° 14' 08", long. 123° 19' 18".

Holds CP for change to channel number 28, 15-kw ERP, BDISDTL-20090325AMA.

Began Operation: February 5, 1996.

Ownership: WatchTV Inc.

Personnel: Gregory J. Herman, General Manager; Steven A. Hale, Station Manager.

Roseburg—K33FE, Ch. 33, California-Oregon Broadcasting Inc.

Technical Facilities: 0.634-kw ERP, 109-ft. above ground, 1430-ft. above sea level, lat. 43° 12' 03", long. 123° 22' 58".

Roseburg—K47HT, Ch. 47, Better Life Television. Phone: 541-582-8024.

Technical Facilities: 100-ft. above ground, 1439-ft. above sea level, lat. 43° 12' 08", long. 123° 22' 54".

Ownership: Better Life Television Inc.

Roseburg—K49FV, Ch. 49, Trinity Broadcasting Network Inc. Phone: 714-832-2950. Fax: 714-730-0661.

Technical Facilities: 1.5-kw ERP, 78-ft. above ground, 1567-ft. above sea level, lat. 43° 14' 08", long. 123° 19' 18".

Ownership: Trinity Broadcasting Network Inc.

Roseburg—K51GJ, Ch. 51, Oregon Public Broadcasting. Phone: 503-244-9900.

Technical Facilities: 1.1-kw ERP, 108-ft. above ground, 1444-ft. above sea level, lat. 43° 12' 07", long. 123° 22' 58".

Holds CP for change to lat. 43° 12' 08", long. 123° 22' 54". BDFCDTT-20081022AAN.

Ownership: Oregon Public Broadcasting.

Roseburg—K53CU, Ch. 53, KEZI Inc. Phone: 541-485-5611.

Technical Facilities: 12.6-kw ERP, 56-ft. above ground, 1227-ft. above sea level, lat. 43° 12' 22", long. 123° 21' 56".

Holds CP for change to channel number 27, 56-ft. above ground, 1220-ft. above sea level, lat. 43° 12' 22.1", long. 123° 21' 49.6". BDISTT-20060209AEI.

Ownership: Chambers Communications Corp.

Roseburg—K62DR, Ch. 62, California-Oregon Broadcasting Inc. Phone: 541-779-5555.

Technical Facilities: 0.58-kw ERP, lat. 43° 12' 03", long. 123° 22' 58".

Holds CP for change to channel number 41, 1-kw ERP, 95-ft. above ground, 1415-ft. above sea level, BDISTTL-20060331BFR.

Transmitter: 0.6-mi. E of Bay Wagon Rd.

Ownership: California-Oregon Broadcasting Inc.

Ruch & Applegate—K13PI, Ch. 13, Southern Oregon Public Television Inc. Phone: 541-779-0808.

Technical Facilities: 0.045-kw ERP, lat. 42° 13' 17", long. 123° 01' 27".

Began Operation: January 18, 1979.

Ownership: Southern Oregon Public Television Inc.

Ruch & Applegate—K43BJ, Ch. 43, Soda Mountain Broadcasting Inc.

Technical Facilities: 0.12-kw ERP, lat. 42° 13' 09", long. 123° 01' 30".

Salem—K21GX, Ch. 21, Northwest Christian Broadcasting. Phone: 503-362-0862.

Technical Facilities: 4.46-kw ERP, 187-ft. above ground, 1211-ft. above sea level, lat. 44° 58' 40", long. 123° 08' 29".

Ownership: Northwest Christian Broadcasting.

Personnel: Jerry Harpham, Station Manager; George Britton, General Sales Manager.

Salem—K50GG, Ch. 50, Meredith Corp. Phones: 503-239-4949; 515-284-3000. Fax: 503-239-6184.

Technical Facilities: 11.1-kw ERP, lat. 44° 59' 05", long. 123° 08' 30".

Holds CP for change to 2-kw ERP, 184-ft. above ground, 1273-ft. above sea level, BDFCDTL-20060331BDH.

Ownership: Meredith Corp.

■ **Salem**—KORS-CA, Ch. 36, WatchTV Inc. Phone: 503-241-2411. Fax: 503-226-3557.

Technical Facilities: 1000-w TPO, 10.3-kw ERP, 174-ft. above ground, 1230-ft. above sea level, lat. 44° 58' 59", long. 123° 08' 39".

Holds CP for change to channel number 16, 53-kw ERP, 600-ft. above ground, 1722-ft. above sea level, lat. 45° 31' 21", long. 122° 44' 45". BPTTA-20040902AAJ.

Transmitter: Eola Hills, approx. 5.6-mi. WNW of Salem.

Began Operation: August 1, 1994.

Ownership: WatchTV Inc.

Personnel: Gregory J. Herman, General Manager; Steven A. Hale, Station Manager.

Salt Creek—KODT-LP, Ch. 14, Michael L. Mattson. Phone: 503-409-2181.

Technical Facilities: 15-kw ERP, 30-ft. above ground, 489-ft. above sea level, lat. 44° 58' 46", long. 123° 20' 57".

Began Operation: March 9, 2005.

Ownership: Michael L. Mattson.

Salt Creek—KSLM-LD, Ch. 16, Michael L. Mattson. Phone: 503-409-2181.

Technical Facilities: 2-kw ERP, 59-ft. above ground, 1145-ft. above sea level, lat. 44° 58' 38", long. 123° 08' 29".

Holds CP for change to 10-kw ERP, 62-ft. above ground, 1148-ft. above sea level, BPDTL-20090107ACQ.

Began Operation: October 9, 2008.

Ownership: Michael L. Mattson.

Scottsburg—K02DB, Ch. 2, Fisher Broadcasting Inc.

Technical Facilities: 0.073-kw ERP, lat. 43° 38' 00", long. 123° 49' 00".

Ownership: Fisher Communications Inc.

Scottsburg—K06IO, Ch. 6, KEZI Inc.

Technical Facilities: 0.056-kw ERP, lat. 43° 38' 12", long. 123° 49' 31".

Seaside & Astoria—K21DE, Ch. 21, Meredith Corp. Phones: 503-239-4949; 515-284-3000. Fax: 503-239-6184.

Technical Facilities: 12.1-kw ERP, 39-ft. above ground, 1414-ft. above sea level, lat. 46° 06' 17", long. 123° 53' 50".

Holds CP for change to 1.86-kw ERP, 39-ft. above ground, 1400-ft. above sea level, lat. 46° 17' 11", long. 123° 53' 47". BDFCDTL-20060331BEM.

Ownership: Meredith Corp.

Severance Ranch, etc.—K06JN, Ch. 6, NPG of Oregon Inc.

Technical Facilities: 0.001-kw ERP, 3468-ft. above sea level, lat. 44° 05' 44", long. 120° 25' 00".

Ownership: News Press & Gazette Co.

Shady Cove—K13PE, Ch. 13, Southern Oregon Public Television Inc. Phone: 541-779-0808.

Technical Facilities: 0.051-kw ERP, lat. 42° 42' 21", long. 122° 47' 06".

Began Operation: July 9, 1979.

Ownership: Southern Oregon Public Television Inc.

Silver Lake—K11RM, Ch. 11, Silver Lake Community TV Assn.

Technical Facilities: 0.03-kw ERP, lat. 43° 09' 55", long. 120° 52' 50".

Silver Lake, etc.—K08LG, Ch. 8, Oregon Public Broadcasting.

Technical Facilities: 0.009-kw ERP, 46-ft. above ground, 5676-ft. above sea level, lat. 43° 09' 55", long. 120° 52' 50".

Squaw Valley—K07KZ, Ch. 7, Fisher Broadcasting Inc.

Technical Facilities: 0.01-kw ERP, lat. 42° 24' 03", long. 124° 21' 29".

Squaw Valley—K13MI, Ch. 13, Community TV Assn. Inc.

Technical Facilities: 0.049-kw ERP, lat. 42° 24' 03", long. 124° 21' 29".

Squaw Valley, etc.—K02IQ, Ch. 2, Soda Mountain Broadcasting Inc.

Technical Facilities: 0.08-kw ERP, 2359-ft. above sea level, lat. 42° 24' 03", long. 124° 21' 29".

Ownership: Soda Mountain Broadcasting Inc.

Sun River—K57CH, Ch. 57, NPG of Oregon Inc. Phone: 816-271-8505.

Technical Facilities: 0.262-kw ERP, lat. 43° 52' 26", long. 121° 30' 14".

Holds CP for change to channel number 24, 4-kw ERP, 79-ft. above ground, 4964-ft. above sea level, BDISTT-20070125ADL.

Transmitter: 2.6-mi. W of Sun River.

Ownership: News Press & Gazette Co.

Sun River, etc.—K23FS, Ch. 23, Fisher Broadcasting Inc. Phone: 206-404-7000.

Technical Facilities: 1.93-kw ERP, 59-ft. above ground, 4972-ft. above sea level, lat. 43° 52' 25", long. 121° 30' 11".

Holds CP for change to 1.2-kw ERP, 49-ft. above ground, 4974-ft. above sea level, BPTT-20050621AAS.

Sutherlin—K11BX, Ch. 11, KEZI Inc.

Technical Facilities: 0.024-kw ERP, 4219-ft. above sea level, lat. 43° 21' 23", long. 123° 03' 50".

Sutherlin—K31AE, Ch. 31, Newport Television License LLC. Phone: 816-751-0204.

Technical Facilities: 0.44-kw ERP, lat. 43° 22' 19", long. 123° 03' 48".

Transmitter: SW of Roseburg.

Ownership: Newport Television LLC.

Terrebonne—K65AE, Ch. 65, Rural Oregon Wireless Television Inc. Phone: 503-977-7752.

Technical Facilities: 0.14-kw ERP, 20-ft. above ground, 3120-ft. above sea level, lat. 44° 20' 11", long. 121° 11' 15".

Holds CP for change to channel number 34, BDISTT-20061212ABJ.

Ownership: Rural Oregon Wireless TV Inc.

■ **Terrebonne-Bend**—K42BR, Ch. 42, Rodney S. Johnson. Phone: 541-923-4848.

Technical Facilities: 8.28-kw ERP, 23-ft. above ground, 5131-ft. above sea level, lat. 44° 25' 03", long. 121° 06' 01".

Ownership: Rodney S. Johnson.

Personnel: Scott C. Johnson, General Manager & Sales Manager; Mark Howard, Chief Engineer.

■ **Terrebonne-Bend**—K48BL, Ch. 48, Rodney S. Johnson. Phone: 541-923-4848.

Technical Facilities: 100-w TPO, 2.15-kw ERP, 2500-ft. above ground, 5150-ft. above sea level, lat. 44° 25' 03", long. 121° 06' 01".

Transmitter: Gray Butte, 9-mi. NE of Terrebonne.

Ownership: Rodney S. Johnson.

Personnel: Scott C. Johnson, General Manager & Sales Manager; Mark Howard, Chief Engineer.

The Dalles—K06NI, Ch. 6, Michael L. Mattson. Phone: 503-409-2181.

Technical Facilities: 0.25-kw ERP, 43-ft. above ground, 3205-ft. above sea level, lat. 45° 42' 43", long. 121° 06' 58".

Ownership: Michael L. Mattson.

The Dalles—K18HH, Ch. 18, Fisher Broadcasting - Portland TV LLC. Phone: 206-404-4884.

Technical Facilities: 1.2-kw ERP, 59-ft. above ground, 3218-ft. above sea level, lat. 45° 42' 43", long. 121° 06' 58".

Ownership: Fisher Communications Inc.

The Dalles—K51EH, Ch. 51, Meredith Corp. Phones: 503-239-4949; 515-284-3000. Fax: 503-239-6184.

Technical Facilities: 1000-w TPO, 12-kw ERP, 39-ft. above ground, 3202-ft. above sea level, lat. 45° 42' 43", long. 121° 06' 58".

Holds CP for change to 2.23-kw ERP, BMPDTL-20071012AKF.

Transmitter: Stacker Butte, off Hwy. 14, NNE of Murdock, WA.

Ownership: Meredith Corp.

The Dalles—K59EK, Ch. 59, King Broadcasting Co. Phone: 214-977-6606.

Technical Facilities: 1.19-kw ERP, 59-ft. above ground, 3218-ft. above sea level, lat. 45° 42' 43", long. 121° 06' 58".

Holds CP for change to channel number 39, 1.2-kw ERP, BDISTT-20071120AET.

Ownership: King Broadcasting Co.

The Dalles—K64BK, Ch. 64, NVT Portland Licensee LLC, Debtor in Possession. Phone: 404-995-4711.

Technical Facilities: 1.19-kw ERP, lat. 45° 42' 43", long. 121° 06' 58".

Holds CP for change to channel number 7, 0.15-kw ERP, 59-ft. above ground, 3218-ft. above sea level, BDISTTV-20061212ABK.

Began Operation: August 23, 1989.

Ownership: New Vision Television LLC, Debtor in Possession.

The Dalles—K69AH, Ch. 69, Meredith Corp. Phones: 503-239-4949; 515-284-3000. Fax: 503-239-6184.

Technical Facilities: 0.119-kw ERP, 59-ft. above ground, 3218-ft. above sea level, lat. 45° 42' 43", long. 121° 06' 58".

Holds CP for change to channel number 22, 0.361-kw ERP, 57-ft. above ground, 3218-ft. above sea level, BDISDTT-20060330AGF.

Ownership: Meredith Corp.

■ **The Dalles**—KRHP-LP, Ch. 14, Robert H. Pettitt. Phone: 541-350-0840. Fax: 541-296-6158.

Technical Facilities: 3.51-kw ERP, 13-ft. above ground, 545-ft. above sea level, lat. 45° 39' 05", long. 121° 08' 30".

Ownership: Robert H. Pettitt.

The Dalles, etc.—K31HZ, Ch. 31, Oregon Public Broadcasting. Phone: 503-244-9900.

Technical Facilities: 1.034-kw ERP, 59-ft. above ground, 3222-ft. above sea level, lat. 45° 42' 43", long. 121° 06' 58".

Ownership: Oregon Public Broadcasting.

Tillamook—K05KX, Ch. 5, Michael L. Mattson. Phone: 503-409-2181.

Technical Facilities: 0.65-kw ERP, 52-ft. above ground, 85-ft. above sea level, lat. 45° 27' 23", long. 123° 50' 34".

Ownership: Michael L. Mattson.

Tillamook—K26HS, Ch. 26, Better Life Television Inc. Phone: 541-474-3089.

Technical Facilities: 3.25-kw ERP, 30-ft. above ground, 315-ft. above sea level, lat. 45° 26' 47.7", long. 123° 47' 58.8".

Ownership: Better Life Television Inc.

Tillamook—K40EG, Ch. 40, KGW-TV Inc.

Technical Facilities: 1.13-kw ERP, lat. 45° 12' 51", long. 123° 45' 11".

Transmitter: Mount Hebo, 16.8-mi. S. of Tillamook.

Tillamook—K43EJ, Ch. 43, Fisher Broadcasting Inc.

Technical Facilities: 0.02-kw ERP, lat. 45° 12' 51", long. 123° 45' 11".

Tillamook—K52ET, Ch. 52, NVT Portland Licensee LLC, Debtor in Possession. Phone: 404-995-4711.

Technical Facilities: 0.426-kw ERP, lat. 42° 12' 51", long. 123° 45' 11".

Holds CP for change to channel number 23, 1-kw ERP, 52-ft. above ground, 3202-ft. above sea level, BDISTT-20061212ABH.

Ownership: New Vision Television LLC, Debtor in Possession.

Tillamook—KPWC-LD, Ch. 24, Kenneth E. Lewetag. Phone: 503-930-7228.

Technical Facilities: 5.5-kw ERP, 33-ft. above ground, 3268-ft. above sea level, lat. 45° 12' 51", long. 123° 45' 11".

Holds CP for change to 4-kw ERP, 52-ft. above ground, 1224-ft. above sea level, lat. 45° 20' 36.3", long. 122° 56' 31.8". BPDTL-20090203ABG.

Multichannel TV Sound: Stereo and separate audio program.

Began Operation: April 14, 2005.

Ownership: Kenneth E. Lewetag.

Tillamook, etc.—K35CR, Ch. 35, Meredith Corp. Phones: 503-239-4949; 515-284-3000. Fax: 503-239-6184.

Technical Facilities: 1.34-kw ERP, 52-ft. above ground, 3202-ft. above sea level, lat. 45° 12' 51", long. 123° 45' 11".

Holds CP for change to 0.35-kw ERP, 52-ft. above ground, 3182-ft. above sea level, BDFCDTL-20060331BEU.

Ownership: Meredith Corp.

Tolo, etc.—K03EI, Ch. 3, California-Oregon Broadcasting Inc. Phone: 541-779-5555.

Technical Facilities: 1-kw ERP, 16-ft. above ground, 1686-ft. above sea level, lat. 42° 22' 41", long. 122° 50' 43".

Ownership: California-Oregon Broadcasting Inc.

Tri City—K22GX, Ch. 22, Newport Television License LLC. Phone: 816-751-0204.

Technical Facilities: 13-kw ERP, 52-ft. above ground, 2634-ft. above sea level, lat. 43° 00' 13", long. 123° 21' 24".

Multichannel TV Sound: Stereo only.

Ownership: Newport Television LLC.

Personnel: Cambra Ward, General Manager; Kurt Thelen, Chief Engineer; Dave Ulrickson, Sales Manager.

Tri-City, etc.—K11GH, Ch. 11, South West Oregon TV Broadcasting Corp. Phone: 206-404-3065.

Technical Facilities: 0.018-kw ERP, 3409-ft. above sea level, lat. 42° 54' 06", long. 123° 17' 07".

Ownership: California-Oregon Broadcasting Inc.; Fisher Communications Inc.

Umatilla River Valley—K03AX, Ch. 3, Umatilla River TV Assn. Inc.

Technical Facilities: 0.028-kw ERP, lat. 45° 41' 33", long. 118° 21' 54".

Ownership: Umatilla River TV Association Inc.

Vale—K11MK, Ch. 11, City of Vale.

Technical Facilities: 0.005-kw ERP, lat. 43° 58' 37", long. 117° 13' 22".

Vale—K13NC, Ch. 13, City of Vale.

Technical Facilities: 0.005-kw ERP, lat. 43° 58' 37", long. 117° 13' 22".

Wallowa—K30IV, Ch. 30, Rural Oregon Wireless TV Inc. Phone: 503-226-5004.

Technical Facilities: 0.55-kw ERP, 26-ft. above ground, 7027-ft. above sea level, lat. 45° 23' 58", long. 117° 23' 16".

Ownership: Rural Oregon Wireless TV Inc.

Wallowa—K34IF, Ch. 34, Rural Oregon Wireless TV Inc. Phone: 503-226-5004.

Technical Facilities: 0.55-kw ERP, 26-ft. above ground, 7027-ft. above sea level, lat. 45° 23' 58", long. 117° 23' 16".

Ownership: Rural Oregon Wireless TV Inc.

Wallowa—K36HV, Ch. 36, Rural Oregon Wireless TV Inc. Phone: 503-226-5004.

Technical Facilities: 0.55-kw ERP, 26-ft. above ground, 7027-ft. above sea level, lat. 45° 23' 58", long. 117° 23' 16".

Ownership: Rural Oregon Wireless TV Inc.

Wallowa—K40IK, Ch. 40, Rural Oregon Wireless TV Inc. Phone: 503-226-5004.

Technical Facilities: 0.55-kw ERP, 26-ft. above ground, 7027-ft. above sea level, lat. 45° 23' 58", long. 117° 23' 16".

Ownership: Rural Oregon Wireless TV Inc.

Warrenton—KHPN-LP, Ch. 51, EICB-TV LLC. Phone: 972-291-3750.

Technical Facilities: 2-kw ERP, 49-ft. above ground, 1375-ft. above sea level, lat. 46° 17' 10", long. 123° 53' 50".

Began Operation: March 24, 2009.

Ownership: EICB-TV LLC.

Wasco—K33CJ, Ch. 33, Rural Oregon Wireless Television Inc.

Technical Facilities: 1.06-kw ERP, lat. 45° 46' 53", long. 120° 33' 17".

Transmitter: Goodnoe Hills, approx. 14.26-mi. SE of Goldendale.

Wasco—K41CL, Ch. 41, Rural Oregon Wireless Television Inc.

Technical Facilities: 1.06-kw ERP, lat. 45° 46' 53", long. 120° 33' 17".

Transmitter: Goodnoe Hills, approx. 14.26-mi. SE Goldendale.

Wasco—K67AD, Ch. 67, Rural Oregon Wireless TV Inc. Phone: 503-226-5004.

Technical Facilities: 100-w TPO, 1.45-kw ERP, 25-ft. above ground, 3169-ft. above sea level, lat. 45° 44' 26", long. 120° 43' 46".

Holds CP for change to channel number 29, 1.5-kw ERP, 59-ft. above ground, 3218-ft. above sea level, lat. 45° 42' 43", long. 121° 06' 58". BDISTT-20071121ACT.

Transmitter: 10-mi. N of Wasco.

Ownership: Rural Oregon Wireless TV Inc.

Wasco & Heppner—K15EY, Ch. 15, Oregon Public Broadcasting. Phone: 503-244-9900.

Technical Facilities: 1.06-kw ERP, 52-ft. above ground, 2579-ft. above sea level, lat. 45° 46' 53", long. 120° 33' 17".

Holds CP for change to channel number 27, 49-ft. above ground, 3212-ft. above sea level, lat. 45° 42' 43", long. 121° 06' 58". BDISDTT-20080912AAX.

Began Operation: March 29, 1979.

Ownership: Oregon Public Broadcasting.

Wasco & Heppner—K26FG, Ch. 26, Rural Oregon Wireless Television Inc.

Technical Facilities: 1.057-kw ERP, 52-ft. above ground, lat. 45° 46' 53", long. 120° 33' 17".

Transmitter: Goodnoe Hills, approx. 14.26-mi. SE of Goldendale.

Wedderburn—K04MG, Ch. 4, Oregon Public Broadcasting. Phone: 503-244-9900.

Technical Facilities: 0.05-kw ERP, lat. 42° 24' 03", long. 124° 21' 29".

Ownership: Oregon Public Broadcasting.

Williams—K02JJ, Ch. 2, Southern Oregon Public Television Inc. Phone: 541-779-0808.

Technical Facilities: 0.072-kw ERP, lat. 42° 10' 00", long. 123° 17' 53".

Began Operation: October 30, 1978.

Ownership: Southern Oregon Public Television Inc.

Williams—K04JP, Ch. 4, Freedom Broadcasting of Oregon Licensee LLC. Phone: 518-346-6666.

Technical Facilities: 0.045-kw ERP, lat. 42° 10' 00", long. 123° 17' 53".

Ownership: Freedom Communications Holdings Inc.

Williams—K07HS, Ch. 7, California-Oregon Broadcasting Inc.

Technical Facilities: 0.01-kw ERP, lat. 42° 10' 00", long. 123° 17' 53".

Winston—K07IL, Ch. 7, KEZI Inc.

Technical Facilities: 0.004-kw ERP, 1007-ft. above sea level, lat. 43° 07' 51", long. 123° 25' 06".

Yoncalla—K32FI, Ch. 32, California-Oregon Broadcasting Inc. Phone: 541-779-5555.

Technical Facilities: 0.7-kw ERP, 50-ft. above ground, 1850-ft. above sea level, lat. 43° 38' 19", long. 123° 19' 33".

Ownership: California-Oregon Broadcasting Inc.

Yoncalla—K39CL, Ch. 39, California-Oregon Broadcasting Inc.

Technical Facilities: 0.79-kw ERP, 43-ft. above ground, 1844-ft. above sea level, lat. 43° 38' 19", long. 123° 19' 33".

Pennsylvania

Allentown-Bethlehem—W07DC, Ch. 7, Local TV Pennsylvania License LLC. Phones: 570-346-7474; 859-448-2707.

Technical Facilities: 0.1-kw ERP, lat. 40° 34' 20", long. 75° 15' 51".

Holds CP for change to 0.025-kw ERP, 151-ft. above ground, 1115-ft. above sea level, BDFCDTT-20060331BFY.

Transmitter: 933 E. Rock Rd., near Allentown.

Ownership: Local TV Holdings LLC.

Allentown-Bethlehem—W46BL, Ch. 46, Maranatha Broadcasting Co. Inc.

Technical Facilities: 17-kw ERP, lat. 40° 33' 58", long. 75° 26' 06".

Transmitter: 720 E. Rock Rd.

Ownership: Maranatha Broadcasting Co.

Altoona—W41CF, Ch. 41, Pathway Community Radio Inc. Phone: 315-469-4489.

Technical Facilities: 100-w TPO, 5.9-kw ERP, 308-ft. above ground, 2837-ft. above sea level, lat. 40° 33' 58", long. 78° 26' 36".

Transmitter: 2.2 mi. N of intersection of S.R. 36 and Avalon Rd.

Ownership: Pathway Community Radio Inc.

■ **Altoona**—WTOO-CA, Ch. 32, Abacus Television. Phone: 202-462-3680.

Technical Facilities: 26.7-kw ERP, 269-ft. above ground, 2850-ft. above sea level, lat. 40° 29' 15", long. 78° 21' 09".

Transmitter: Bush Mountain, junction of Logan, Frankstowne & Tyrone Twps.

Ownership: Abacus Television.

Beaver—WNNB-LP, Ch. 66, Bruno-Goodworth Network Inc. Phone: 412-922-9576. Fax: 412-921-6937.

Technical Facilities: 1000-w TPO, 23-kw ERP, 508-ft. above ground, 1660-ft. above sea level, lat. 40° 43' 02", long. 80° 19' 07".

Transmitter: Beaver Hollow Rd., Beaver City.

Ownership: Bruno-Goodworth Network Inc.

Personnel: Ron Bruno, General Manager & Sales Manager; Ron Massung, Chief Engineer.

■ **Berwick**—W19CI, Ch. 19, Catholic Broadcasting of Scranton Inc. Phone: 570-207-2219. Fax: 570-207-2281.

Studio: 400 Wyoming Ave, Scranton, PA 18503.

Technical Facilities: 100-w TPO, 1.18-kw ERP, 135-ft. above ground, 1755-ft. above sea level, lat. 41° 00' 20", long. 76° 12' 50".

Transmitter: 4.1-mi. SSE of Berwick.

Ownership: Catholic Broadcasting of Scranton Inc.

Personnel: James Brennan, Manager; Maria Orzel, Executive Director of Communications.

■ **Berwick**—W47AO, Ch. 47, Triple J Community Broadcasting LLC. Phone: 570-459-1869. Fax: 570-459-1383.

Studio: WYLN-TV, Hazelton, PA 18201.

Technical Facilities: 1000-w TPO, 7-kw ERP, 449-ft. above ground, 1742-ft. above sea level, lat. 41° 00' 20", long. 76° 12' 50".

Transmitter: Nescopeck Mountain, approx. 3.1-mi. S of Nescopeck.

Ownership: Harron Communications LP.

Personnel: Joseph Gans, President; Terry Herron, Operations Manager; Kim Straus, Sales Manager; Barry Jais, Chief Engineer.

Brookville—W45BT, Ch. 45, Cornerstone Television Inc.

Technical Facilities: 7.2-kw ERP, 280-ft. above ground, 2058-ft. above sea level, lat. 41° 07' 11", long. 79° 06' 51".

Butler—WJMB-LP, Ch. 60, Bruno-Goodworth Network Inc. Phone: 412-922-9576.

Technical Facilities: 1000-w TPO, 10.8-kw ERP, 299-ft. above ground, 1581-ft. above sea level, lat. 40° 53' 51", long. 79° 53' 22".

Transmitter: Palmer Rd., Center Twp.

Ownership: Bruno-Goodworth Network Inc.

Chambersburg—W38AN, Ch. 38, WITF Inc. Phone: 717-704-3000.

Technical Facilities: 0.38-kw ERP, lat. 40° 03' 00", long. 77° 44' 54".

Holds CP for change to channel number 33, 5-kw ERP, 82-ft. above ground, 2362-ft. above sea level, BDISDTT-20090218ADU.

Chambersburg—W51CY, Ch. 51, WDCW Broadcasting Inc., Debtor-In-Possession. Phone: 202-965-5050.

Technical Facilities: 60-kw ERP, 108-ft. above ground, 2243-ft. above sea level, lat. 39° 41' 47", long. 77° 30' 50".

Holds CP for change to 15-kw ERP, BDFCDTT-20090505ABE.

Transmitter: 20-mi. WSW of Upper Strasburg.

Ownership: Tribune Broadcasting Co., Debtor-In-Possession.

Clarks Summit—W19AR, Ch. 19, Mission Broadcasting Inc. Phone: 330-335-8808.

Technical Facilities: 0.832-kw ERP, lat. 41° 27' 59", long. 75° 41' 09".

Holds CP for change to 0.004-kw ERP, 66-ft. above ground, 1965-ft. above sea level, BDFCDTT-20060403ADF.

Ownership: Mission Broadcasting Inc.

Clarks Summit—W48AQ, Ch. 48, Northeastern Pennsylvania ETV Association. Fax: 572-344-1244.

Technical Facilities: 1.75-kw ERP, 59-ft. above ground, 1975-ft. above sea level, lat. 41° 28' 01", long. 75° 41' 12".

Clarks Summit, etc.—W14CO, Ch. 14, Local TV Pennsylvania License LLC. Phones: 570-346-7474; 859-448-2707.

Technical Facilities: 1.84-kw ERP, 46-ft. above ground, 1946-ft. above sea level, lat. 41° 28' 01", long. 75° 41' 12".

Holds CP for change to 0.092-kw ERP, BDFCDTT-20060331BKX.

Ownership: Local TV Holdings LLC.

Clarks Summit, etc.—W51BP, Ch. 51, Nexstar Broadcasting Inc. Phone: 972-373-8800.

Technical Facilities: 1.06-kw ERP, 69-ft. above ground, 2001-ft. above sea level, lat. 41° 28' 01", long. 75° 41' 12".

Holds CP for change to 0.005-kw ERP, BDFCDTT-20060403AKM.

Ownership: Nexstar Broadcasting Group Inc.

Darby—W36DO-D, Ch. 36, Mako Communications LLC. Phone: 361-883-1763.

Technical Facilities: 3.8-kw ERP, 272-ft. above ground, 564-ft. above sea level, lat. 40° 02' 29.6", long. 75° 14' 11.5".

Began Operation: November 12, 1993.

Ownership: Mako Communications LLC.

East Stroudsburg—W24BB, Ch. 24, Triple J Community Broadcasting LLC.

Technical Facilities: 53.5-kw ERP, lat. 41° 01' 36", long. 75° 30' 17".

Transmitter: Pimple Hill, 5-mi. ESE of Lake Harmony.

Elliottsburg—W12CA, Ch. 12, Ronald E. Deitrich.

Technical Facilities: 15.6-kw ERP, lat. 40° 24' 24", long. 77° 18' 32".

Erie—W32DH-D, Ch. 32, Three Angels Broadcasting Network Inc. Phone: 618-627-4651.

Technical Facilities: 0.04-kw ERP, 492-ft. above ground, 1838-ft. above sea level, lat. 42° 02' 16", long. 80° 03' 44".

Began Operation: April 9, 2009.

Ownership: Three Angels Broadcasting Network Inc.

Erie—W48CH, Ch. 48, Trinity Broadcasting Network Inc. Phone: 714-832-2950. Fax: 714-730-0661.

Technical Facilities: 10.2-kw ERP, lat. 42° 02' 20", long. 80° 03' 45".

Holds CP for change to channel number 38, 15-kw ERP, 357-ft. above ground, 1704-ft. above sea level, lat. 42° 02' 16", long. 80° 03' 44". BDISDTT-20060330AFA.

Transmitter: WSEE-TV tower, near Erie.

Ownership: Trinity Broadcasting Network Inc.

Erie—WLEP-LP, Ch. 9, Hapa Media Properties LLC. Phone: 847-209-2705.

Technical Facilities: 0.1-kw ERP, 390-ft. above ground, 1709-ft. above sea level, lat. 42° 02' 21", long. 80° 03' 39".

Began Operation: March 27, 2008.

Ownership: Hapa Media Properties LLC.

Freedom—WWBP-LP, Ch. 31, Abacus Television.

Technical Facilities: 29-kw ERP, 116-ft. above ground, 1276-ft. above sea level, lat. 40° 41' 34", long. 80° 15' 02".

Ownership: Abacus Television.

Greensburg—WEMW-LP, Ch. 56, Bruno-Goodworth Network Inc. Phone: 412-922-9576.

Technical Facilities: 1000-w TPO, 38.1-kw ERP, 200-ft. above ground, 1558-ft. above sea level, lat. 40° 18' 14", long. 79° 35' 48".

Holds CP for change to channel number 19, 10-kw ERP, 194-ft. above ground, 1552-ft. above sea level, BDISDTL-20060823AAL.

Transmitter: 245 Brown St.

Ownership: Bruno-Goodworth Network Inc.

■ **Greensburg**—WQVC-CA, Ch. 28, Abacus Television. Phone: 202-462-3680. Fax: 202-462-3781.

Technical Facilities: 1000-w TPO, 38.96-kw ERP, 185-ft. above ground, 1562-ft. above sea level, lat. 40° 18' 14", long. 79° 35' 48".

Transmitter: W. 245 Brown St., Greensburg.

Ownership: Abacus Television.

Personnel: Benjamin Perez, General Manager.

Harrisburg—W35BT, Ch. 35, CTVN Harrisburg LLC. Phone: 412-824-3930.

Technical Facilities: 150-kw ERP, 165-ft. above ground, 1265-ft. above sea level, lat. 40° 18' 19", long. 77° 00' 28".

Holds CP for change to channel number 7, 0.25-kw ERP, BDISDVL-20080806ABM.

Began Operation: August 29, 1988.

Ownership: Cornerstone Television Inc.

Hawley, etc.—WWPS-LP, Ch. 9, John A. Franklin. Phone: 302-732-1400. Fax: 302-732-3933.

Technical Facilities: 2.25-kw ERP, 118-ft. above ground, 1562-ft. above sea level, lat. 41° 11' 32", long. 74° 45' 13".

Holds CP for change to 0.3-kw ERP, 118-ft. above ground, 1168-ft. above sea level, lat. 40° 56' 52", long. 74° 28' 19". BDFCDVL-20090507ABP.

Began Operation: January 28, 1993.

Ownership: John A. Franklin.

Personnel: Robert Neuhaus, General Manager.

■ **Hazleton**—WYLN-LP, Ch. 35, Triple J Community Broadcasting LLC. Phone: 570-459-1869. Fax: 570-459-1625.

Technical Facilities: 1000-w TPO, 8.9-kw ERP, 98-ft. above ground, 1975-ft. above sea level, lat. 40° 58' 10", long. 75° 57' 24".

Transmitter: Intersection of 10th & Thompson Sts.

Multichannel TV Sound: Separate audio progam.

Ownership: Harron Communications LP.

Personnel: Joseph Gans, President; Terry Herron, Operations Manager; Kim Straus, Sales Manager; Barry Jais, Chief Engineer.

■ **Indiana**—WLLS-LP, Ch. 49, Larry L. Schrecongost. Phone: 724-349-8849. Fax: 724-349-7330.

Studio: PO Box 1032, 1835 Oakland Ave, Indiana, PA 15701.

Technical Facilities: 1000-w TPO, 21.3-kw ERP, 259-ft. above ground, 1919-ft. above sea level, lat. 40° 37' 38", long. 79° 12' 49".

Transmitter: to 1.5-mi. W of Indiana.

Ownership: Larry L. Schrecongost.

Personnel: Larry L. Schrecongost, General Manager & Chief Engineer; Nancy W. Schrecongost, Sales Manager.

■ **Johnstown**—WBYD-CA, Ch. 35, Abacus Television. Phone: 202-462-3680. Fax: 202-462-3781.

Technical Facilities: 5.68-kw ERP, 335-ft. above ground, 1499-ft. above sea level, lat. 40° 26' 46", long. 79° 57' 51".

Ownership: Abacus Television.

Kingston—W54BO, Ch. 54, Kathy Potera.

Technical Facilities: 667-w TPO, 2-kw ERP, 85-ft. above ground, 1585-ft. above sea level, lat. 41° 18' 56", long. 75° 53' 19".

Transmitter: Atop Bunker Hill, 0.25-mi. SE of intersection of Bunker Hill & Fire Cut Rds.

Ownership: Kathy Potera.

Kittanning—W64BL, Ch. 64, Abacus Television.

Technical Facilities: 42.7-kw ERP, lat. 40° 47' 19", long. 79° 32' 05".

Transmitter: Rte. 7, Bunker Hill Rd.

■ **Kittanning**—WKHU-CA, Ch. 60, Bruno-Goodworth Network Inc. Phone: 412-922-9576.

Technical Facilities: 49-kw ERP, 194-ft. above ground, 1432-ft. above sea level, lat. 40° 47' 19", long. 79° 32' 05".

Ownership: Bruno-Goodworth Network Inc.

Mansfield—W20CP-D, Ch. 20, Northeastern Pennsylvania ETV Association. Phone: 570-602-1170.

Technical Facilities: 1.15-kw ERP, 135-ft. above ground, 2575-ft. above sea level, lat. 41° 45' 34", long. 76° 55' 31".

Began Operation: October 19, 1987.

Ownership: Northeastern Pennsylvania ETV Association.

Mansfield—W26CV, Ch. 26, Local TV Pennsylvania License LLC. Phones: 570-346-7474; 859-448-2707.

Technical Facilities: 0.64-kw ERP, 89-ft. above ground, 2526-ft. above sea level, lat. 41° 45' 34", long. 76° 55' 31".

Holds CP for change to 0.098-kw ERP, BDFCDTT-20060331BKG.

Ownership: Local TV Holdings LLC.

Mansfield—W54AV, Ch. 54, Mission Broadcasting Inc. Phone: 330-335-8808.

Technical Facilities: 2.14-kw ERP, 102-ft. above ground, 2539-ft. above sea level, lat. 41° 45' 34", long. 76° 55' 31".

Ownership: Mission Broadcasting Inc.

Meadville—W52BO, Ch. 52, Trinity Broadcasting Network Inc. Phone: 714-832-2950. Fax: 714-730-0661.

Technical Facilities: 1000-w TPO, 5.7-kw ERP, 387-ft. above ground, 1821-ft. above sea level, lat. 41° 37' 40", long. 80° 10' 15".

Holds CP for change to channel number 40, 19-kw ERP, 387-ft. above ground, 1800-ft. above sea level, lat. 41° 37' 39", long. 80° 10' 14". BDISTT-20070403ACE.

Transmitter: 0.81-mi. WSW of junction of Park Ave. & U.S. Rte. 6, near Meadville.

Ownership: Trinity Broadcasting Network Inc.

■ **Mercer**—WFXI-CA, Ch. 17, NVT Youngstown Licensee LLC, Debtor in Possession. Phone: 404-995-4711.

Technical Facilities: 9.4-kw ERP, lat. 41° 15' 10", long. 80° 21' 27".

Began Operation: March 30, 1998.

Ownership: New Vision Television LLC, Debtor in Possession.

Middleburg—W18BC, Ch. 18, Heirloom Ministries Inc.

Technical Facilities: 1000-w TPO, 1.185-kw ERP, 112-ft. above ground, 2192-ft. above sea level, lat. 40° 43' 21", long. 77° 07' 22".

Transmitter: SW of Middleburg.

Ownership: Heirloom Ministries Inc.

New Castle—WPCP-LP, Ch. 56, Bruno-Goodworth Network Inc. Phone: 412-922-9576. Fax: 412-921-6937.

Technical Facilities: 100-w TPO, 0.848-kw ERP, 453-ft. above ground, 1575-ft. above sea level, lat. 40° 59' 35", long. 80° 19' 14".

Ownership: Bruno-Goodworth Network Inc.

Newport—W67DE, Ch. 67, Triple J Community Broadcasting LLC. Phone: 570-455-6851. Fax: 570-459-1383.

Technical Facilities: 100-w TPO, 0.6-kw ERP, 118-ft. above ground, 1500-ft. above sea level, lat. 41° 09' 56", long. 76° 01' 02".

Transmitter: Penobscott Mountain SW of Nanticoke.

Ownership: Harron Communications LP.

Personnel: Joseph Gans, President; Terry Herron, Operations Manager; Kim Strous, Sales Manager; Barry Jais, Chief Engineer.

Philadelphia—WELL-LP, Ch. 45, Word of God Fellowship Inc. Phone: 817-571-1229. Fax: 817-571-7478.

Technical Facilities: 150-kw ERP, 1083-ft. above ground, 899-ft. above sea level, lat. 40° 02' 19", long. 75° 14' 14".

Began Operation: August 22, 1991.

Ownership: Word of God Fellowship Inc.

■ **Philadelphia**—WFPA-CA, Ch. 35, WXTV License Partnership GP. Phone: 215-568-2800. Fax: 215-568-2865.

Studio: 1700 Market St, Ste 1550, Philadelphia, PA 19103.

Technical Facilities: 10.9-kw ERP, lat. 40° 02' 21", long. 75° 14' 13".

Ownership: Univision Communications Inc.

Personnel: Diana Bald, General Manager & General Sales Manager; John Skelnik, Chief Engineer.

■ **Philadelphia**—WPHA-CA, Ch. 38, D.T.V. LLC. Phone: 800-536-7327.

Technical Facilities: 40-kw ERP, 699-ft. above ground, 947-ft. above sea level, lat. 40° 02' 19", long. 75° 14' 14".

Ownership: D.T.V. LLC.

■ **Philadelphia**—WTSD-CA, Ch. 14, Priority Communications Ministries Inc. Phone: 302-367-9595.

Technical Facilities: 146-kw ERP, 1138-ft. above ground, 1431-ft. above sea level, lat. 40° 02' 30", long. 75° 14' 11".

Transmitter: 0.5-mi. SW of Rte. 7 & I-95, Christiana.

Ownership: Priority Communications Ministries Inc.

Philadelphia—WWJT-LP, Ch. 7, Philadelphia Television Network Inc. Phone: 215-989-3595.

Studio: 44 Yale Ave, Morton, PA 19070.

Technical Facilities: 3-kw ERP, 499-ft. above ground, 538-ft. above sea level, lat. 39° 57' 10", long. 75° 10' 03".

Ownership: Philadelphia Television Network Inc.

Personnel: Tom Carpenter, Chief Engineer; Michael Moxley, Sales Manager; Michael J. Mitchell, Vice President & Station Manager.

■ **Philadelphia**—WXTV-LP, Ch. 28, WXTV License Partnership GP, c/o Univision. Phone: 310-556-7640.

Studio: 500 Frank W Burr Blvd, 6th Fl, Teaneck, NJ 07666.

Technical Facilities: 1000-w TPO, 10.9-kw ERP, 499-ft. above ground, 741-ft. above sea level, lat. 40° 02' 21", long. 75° 14' 14".

Transmitter: 300 Domino Lane.

Ownership: Univision Communications Inc.

Personnel: Cristina Schwarz, General Manager; Dave Barth, Chief Engineer; Michelle Liebowitz, Sales Manager.

Philadelphia—WZPA-LP, Ch. 33, Mako Communications LLC. Phone: 361-883-1763.

Technical Facilities: 150-kw ERP, 509-ft. above ground, 801-ft. above sea level, lat. 40° 02' 29.6", long. 75° 14' 11.5".

Ownership: Mako Communications LLC.

Personnel: William E. Mattis Jr., General Manager.

Pittsburgh—W29AV, Ch. 29, Abacus Television. Phone: 202-462-3680. Fax: 202-462-3781.

Technical Facilities: 715-w TPO, 20.9-kw ERP, 1703-ft. above sea level, lat. 40° 10' 50", long. 80° 16' 52".

Transmitter: Canton Twp. substation site.

Multichannel TV Sound: Stereo only.

Ownership: Abacus Television.

Pittsburgh—W61CC, Ch. 61, The Videohouse Inc. Phone: 412-921-7577. Fax: 412-921-6437.

Technical Facilities: 5.7-kw ERP, 335-ft. above ground, 1499-ft. above sea level, lat. 40° 26' 46", long. 79° 57' 51".

Multichannel TV Sound: Stereo and separate audio program.

Ownership: The VideoHouse Inc.

Personnel: Ron Bruno, General Manager.

Pittsburgh—W63AU, Ch. 63, The Bon-Tele Network. Phones: 412-531-6365; 941-383-4978. Fax: 724-942-3127.

Studio: 1461 Crane Ave., Pittsburgh, PA 15220.

Technical Facilities: 1.04-kw ERP, 1350-ft. above sea level, lat. 40° 26' 28", long. 80° 01' 32".

Holds CP for change to 15-kw ERP, 823-ft. above ground, 2020-ft. above sea level, lat. 40° 23' 34", long. 79° 46' 54". BDFCDTL-20060331AKH.

Transmitter: 1461 Crane Ave., Banksville Park.

Multichannel TV Sound: Separate audio progam.

Ownership: The Bon-Tele Network.

Personnel: Nancy B. Hahn, General & Sales Manager; Richard Williams, Chief Engineer.

Pittsburgh—W65CG, Ch. 65, Trinity Broadcasting Network Inc. Phone: 714-832-2950. Fax: 714-730-0661.

Technical Facilities: 8.7-kw ERP, 499-ft. above ground, 1637-ft. above sea level, lat. 40° 24' 42", long. 79° 55' 54".

Holds CP for change to channel number 47, 15-kw ERP, 449-ft. above ground, 1639-ft. above sea level, lat. 40° 24' 42", long. 79° 55' 53". BDFCDTT-20060331BCD.

Ownership: Trinity Broadcasting Network Inc.

Pittsburgh—WBGN-LP, Ch. 59, Bruno-Goodworth Network Inc.

Technical Facilities: 1000-w TPO, 8.16-kw ERP, 335-ft. above ground, 1500-ft. above sea level, lat. 40° 26' 46", long. 79° 57' 51".

Transmitter: WQED tower, 2850 Burthold St.

Ownership: Bruno-Goodworth Network Inc.

Personnel: Bill Saltzgiver, General Manager.

Pittsburgh—WBPA-LP, Ch. 30, Venture Technologies Group LLC. Phone: 323-904-4090.

Studio: 500-C Seco Rd., Monroeville, PA 15146.

Technical Facilities: 8.5-kw ERP, 277-ft. above ground, 1611-ft. above sea level, lat. 40° 29' 39", long. 80° 01' 13".

Holds CP for change to 25-kw ERP, BPTTL-20060215ADN.

Multichannel TV Sound: Stereo and separate audio program.

Ownership: Venture Technologies Group LLC.

Pittsburgh—WPTG-LP, Ch. 69, Abacus Television. Phone: 202-462-3680. Fax: 202-462-3781.

Technical Facilities: 8-kw ERP, 335-ft. above ground, 1499-ft. above sea level, lat. 40° 26' 46", long. 79° 57' 51".

Transmitter: WQED tower, 2850 Burthold St.

Ownership: Abacus Television.

Personnel: Benjamin Perez, General Manager.

Pottsville, etc.—W24BL, Ch. 24, Nexstar Broadcasting Inc. Phone: 972-373-8800.

Technical Facilities: 0.64-kw ERP, 115-ft. above ground, 1365-ft. above sea level, lat. 40° 40' 38", long. 76° 12' 04".

Holds CP for change to 0.003-kw ERP, BDFCDTT-20060403AKU.

Ownership: Nexstar Broadcasting Group Inc.

Pottsville, etc.—W61AG, Ch. 61, Local TV Pennsylvania License LLC. Phones: 570-346-7474; 859-448-2707.

Technical Facilities: 1.88-kw ERP, lat. 40° 40' 33", long. 76° 11' 54".

Holds CP for change to channel number 28, 0.1-kw ERP, 92-ft. above ground, 1391-ft. above sea level, BDISTTL-20080125AAK.

Ownership: Local TV Holdings LLC.

Pottsville, etc.—W66AI, Ch. 66, Mission Broadcasting Inc. Phone: 330-335-8808.

Technical Facilities: 0.1-kw ERP, 98-ft. above ground, 1391-ft. above sea level, lat. 40° 40' 33", long. 76° 11' 54".

Holds CP for change to channel number 50, 0.001-kw ERP, BDISDTT-20060403ADI.

Ownership: Mission Broadcasting Inc.

Reading—W24CS, Ch. 24, WITF Inc. Phone: 717-236-6000.

Technical Facilities: 0.365-kw ERP, 56-ft. above ground, 1155-ft. above sea level, lat. 40° 21' 14", long. 75° 53' 55".

Holds CP for change to 0.007-kw ERP, BDFCDTT-20060331AXW.

Ownership: WITF Inc.

Renovo—W40BS, Ch. 40, Local TV Pennsylvania License LLC. Phones: 570-346-7474; 859-448-2707.

Technical Facilities: 0.2-kw ERP, 69-ft. above ground, 2090-ft. above sea level, lat. 41° 18' 19", long. 77° 44' 45".

Holds CP for change to 0.031-kw ERP, BDFCDTT-20060331BJJ.

Ownership: Local TV Holdings LLC.

■ **Sayre**—W24DB, Ch. 24, New Age Media of Pennsylvania License LLC. Phone: 570-824-7895.

Technical Facilities: 17.5-kw ERP, 299-ft. above ground, 2358-ft. above sea level, lat. 41° 26' 09", long. 75° 43' 46".

Ownership: New Age Media.

Scranton—W18BN, Ch. 18, Commonwealth Telecasters. Phone: 302-732-1400. Fax: 302-732-3933.

Technical Facilities: 1000-w TPO, 6.38-kw ERP, 150-ft. above ground, 2441-ft. above sea level, lat. 41° 35' 35", long. 75° 25' 55".

Transmitter: 1-mi. N of Rte. 6, Waymart.

Multichannel TV Sound: Stereo and separate audio program.

Began Operation: November 6, 1995.

Ownership: Commonwealth Broadcasting.

Personnel: Robert Neuhaus, General Manager.

Scranton—W26CD, Ch. 26, Trinity Christian Center of Santa Ana Inc. Phone: 714-832-2950.

Technical Facilities: 2.4-kw ERP, lat. 41° 28' 00", long. 75° 41' 13".

Holds CP for change to 15-kw ERP, 82-ft. above ground, 1982-ft. above sea level, BDFCDTT-20060328ADX.

Transmitter: 0.9-mi. S of SR 9 & U.S. Rte. 11.

Ownership: Trinity Broadcasting Network Inc.

Sharon—W29CO, Ch. 29, Cornerstone Television Inc. Phone: 412-824-3930.

Technical Facilities: 8.9-kw ERP, 311-ft. above ground, 1578-ft. above sea level, lat. 41° 14' 17", long. 80° 25' 50".

Transmitter: 1-mi. E of the intersection of U.S. Rte. 62 & State Rte. 18.

Ownership: Cornerstone Television Inc.

■ **Shickshinny**—W68CE, Ch. 68, Triple J Community Broadcasting LLC. Phone: 570-459-1869. Fax: 570-459-1383.

Technical Facilities: 0.378-kw ERP, 48-ft. above ground, 1637-ft. above sea level, lat. 41° 09' 59", long. 76° 09' 08".

Ownership: Harron Communications LP.

Personnel: Joseph Gans, President; Terry Herron, Operations Manager; Kim Straus, Sales Manager; Barry Jais, Chief Engineer.

State College—W07CD, Ch. 7, WPXI Inc. Phone: 814-255-7600.

Technical Facilities: 10-w TPO, 0.281-kw ERP, 89-ft. above ground, 2169-ft. above sea level, lat. 40° 43' 03", long. 77° 53' 30".

Transmitter: Rte. 26, Tussey Mountain, Ferguson/Barree town line.

Ownership: Cox Enterprises Inc.

State College—W36BE, Ch. 36, Local TV Pennsylvania License LLC. Phones: 570-346-7474; 859-448-2707. Fax: 717-347-0359.

Studio: 16 Montage Mountain Rd., Moosic, PA 18507.

Technical Facilities: 100-w TPO, 4.1-kw ERP, 138-ft. above ground, 2218-ft. above sea level, lat. 40° 43' 03", long. 77° 53' 30".

Holds CP for change to 0.205-kw ERP, BDFCDTT-20060331BJB.

Transmitter: 1.2-mi. SSW of Pine Grove Mills, near Centre & Huntingdon County line.

Ownership: Local TV Holdings LLC.

Personnel: Lou Abitabilo, General Sales Manager; Mike Morkavage, Chief Engineer.

State College—W39BE, Ch. 39, Local TV Pennsylvania License LLC. Phones: 570-346-7474; 859-448-2707. Fax: 717-347-0359.

Studio: 16 Montage Mountain Rd., Moosic, PA 18507.

Technical Facilities: 100-w TPO, 4.1-kw ERP, 138-ft. above ground, 2218-ft. above sea level, lat. 40° 43' 03", long. 77° 53' 30".

Holds CP for change to 0.205-kw ERP, BDFCDTT-20060331BIU.

Transmitter: 1.2-mi. SSW of Pine Grove Mills, near Centre & Huntingdon County line.

Ownership: Local TV Holdings LLC.

Personnel: Rene Laspina, President & General Manager; John Gee, General Sales Manager; Ron Schacht, Chief Engineer; John Wessling, News Director.

State College—W42DG-D, Ch. 42, WPXI Inc. Phone: 814-255-7600.

Technical Facilities: 15-kw ERP, 161-ft. above ground, 2241-ft. above sea level, lat. 40° 43' 04", long. 77° 53' 28".

Ownership: Cox Enterprises Inc.

State College—W59AI, Ch. 59, Peak Media of Pennsylvania Licensee LLC. Phone: 814-266-8088.

Technical Facilities: 1.48-kw ERP, lat. 40° 53' 32", long. 77° 51' 49".

Holds CP for change to channel number 17, 15-kw ERP, 164-ft. above ground, 1934-ft. above sea level, lat. 40° 53' 34.8", long. 77° 51' 48". BDISDTT-20080527ADG.

■ **State College**—WSCP-CA, Ch. 13, Pathway Community Radio. Phone: 315-469-4489.

Technical Facilities: 0.223-kw ERP, 89-ft. above ground, 2169-ft. above sea level, lat. 40° 43' 03", long. 77° 53' 30".

Holds CP for change to 3-kw ERP, lat. 40° 43' 04", long. 77° 53' 28". BPTVA-20080804AAV.

Ownership: Pathway Community Radio Inc.

State College, etc.—WHVL-LD, Ch. 27, Channel Communications LLC. Phone: 800-692-7401.

Technical Facilities: 15-kw ERP, 121-ft. above ground, 2581-ft. above sea level, lat. 40° 55' 10", long. 77° 58' 28".

Began Operation: March 10, 2009.

Ownership: Channel Communications LLC.

State College, etc.—WHVL-LP, Ch. 29, Channel Communications LLC. Phone: 800-692-7401.

Technical Facilities: 1000-w TPO, 11.7-kw ERP, 121-ft. above ground, 2579-ft. above sea level, lat. 40° 55' 10", long. 77° 58' 28".

Transmitter: 1-mi. E of FAA Vortac, Rattlesnake Mountain.

Ownership: Channel Communications LLC.

Stroudsburg—W26DE-D, Ch. 26, Local TV Pennsylvania License LLC. Phones: 570-346-7474; 859-448-2707.

Technical Facilities: 0.105-kw ERP, 79-ft. above ground, 843-ft. above sea level, lat. 40° 58' 25", long. 75° 11' 18".

Began Operation: May 3, 1979.

Ownership: Local TV Holdings LLC.

Stroudsburg—W60AH, Ch. 60, Mission Broadcasting Inc. Phone: 330-335-8808.

Technical Facilities: 2.04-kw ERP, lat. 40° 58' 25", long. 75° 11' 18".

Holds CP for change to channel number 40, 0.008-kw ERP, 89-ft. above ground, 856-ft. above sea level, BDISDTT-20060403ADD.

Ownership: Mission Broadcasting Inc.

Stroudsburg—W64AL, Ch. 64, Nexstar Broadcasting Inc. Phone: 972-373-8800.

Technical Facilities: 2.04-kw ERP, lat. 40° 58' 25", long. 75° 11' 18".

Holds CP for change to channel number 47, 0.01-kw ERP, 89-ft. above ground, 856-ft. above sea level, BDISDTT-20060818ABH.

Ownership: Nexstar Broadcasting Group Inc.

Towanda—W10CP, Ch. 10, Local TV Pennsylvania License LLC. Phones: 570-346-7474; 859-448-2707.

Technical Facilities: 0.131-kw ERP, 39-ft. above ground, 2159-ft. above sea level, lat. 41° 40' 52", long. 76° 28' 55".

Holds CP for change to 0.066-kw ERP, BDFCDTT-20060331BHC.

Ownership: Local TV Holdings LLC.

Towanda—W15CO-D, Ch. 15, Local TV Pennsylvania License LLC. Phones: 570-346-7474; 859-448-2707.

Studio: 16 Montage Mountain Rd., Moosic, PA 18507.

Technical Facilities: 0.034-kw ERP, 66-ft. above ground, 2185-ft. above sea level, lat. 41° 40' 52", long. 76° 28' 55".

Began Operation: September 26, 1989.

Ownership: Local TV Holdings LLC.

Personnel: Rene Laspina, General Manager; Ron Schacht, Chief Engineer; John Gee, Sales Manager.

Towanda—W25AQ, Ch. 25, Northeastern Pennsylvania ETV Assn. Phone: 570-602-1170.

Technical Facilities: 2.04-kw ERP, 108-ft. above ground, 2208-ft. above sea level, lat. 41° 40' 59", long. 76° 28' 59".

Ownership: Northeastern Pennsylvania ETV Association.

■ **Uniontown**—WWAT-CA, Ch. 45, Abacus Television. Phone: 202-462-3680. Fax: 202-462-3781.

Technical Facilities: 1000-w TPO, 0.47-kw ERP, 213-ft. above ground, 2956-ft. above sea level, lat. 39° 48' 41", long. 79° 41' 30".

Transmitter: Summit Rd.

Ownership: Abacus Television.

Personnel: Benjamin Perez, General Manager.

■ **Uniontown**—WWKH-CA, Ch. 35, Bruno-Goodworth Network Inc. Phone: 412-922-9576.

Technical Facilities: 100-w TPO, 1.031-kw ERP, 141-ft. above ground, 2720-ft. above sea level, lat. 39° 51' 17", long. 79° 39' 27".

Transmitter: Tower Power Inc. tower.

Ownership: Bruno-Goodworth Network Inc.

■ **Washington**—WWLM-CA, Ch. 20, Bruno-Goodworth Network Inc. Phone: 412-922-9576.

Technical Facilities: 0.431-kw ERP, lat. 40° 11' 25", long. 80° 14' 00".

Holds CP for change to 15-kw ERP, 225-ft. above ground, 1492-ft. above sea level, BDFCDTA-20081208AAK.

Transmitter: Intersection of Rtes. 19 & 70.

Began Operation: April 13, 1999.

Ownership: Bruno-Goodworth Network Inc.

■ **Wilkes-Barre, etc.**—W07BV, Ch. 7, Catholic Broadcasting of Scranton Inc. Phone: 570-207-2219. Fax: 570-207-2281.

Studio: 400 Wyoming Ave, Scranton, PA 18503.

Technical Facilities: 10-w TPO, 0.079-kw ERP, 400-ft. above ground, 2198-ft. above sea level, lat. 41° 11' 54", long. 75° 49' 12".

Transmitter: 4.5-mi. SE of city center, N of Rte. 933.

Ownership: Catholic Broadcasting of Scranton Inc.

Personnel: James Brennan, General Manager.

■ **Williamsport**—W05BG, Ch. 5, Triple J Community Broadcasting LLC. Phone: 570-459-1869. Fax: 570-459-1383.

Studio: WYLN-TV, Hazelton, PA 18201.

Technical Facilities: 10-w TPO, 0.017-kw ERP, 174-ft. above ground, 2014-ft. above sea level, lat. 41° 13' 08", long. 76° 57' 27".

Transmitter: Bald Eagle Mountain, Skyline Dr.

Ownership: Harron Communications LP.

Personnel: Joseph Gans, President; Darlene VanBlargan, General Manager; Terry Herron, Operations Manager; Kim Straus, Sales Manager; Barry Jais, Chief Engineer; Robert Jais, Chief Engineer; Ralph Romano, Sales Manager.

Williamsport—W20AD, Ch. 20, Local TV Pennsylvania License LLC. Phones: 570-346-7474; 859-448-2707. Fax: 717-347-0359.

Technical Facilities: 100-w TPO, 0.4-kw ERP, 125-ft. above ground, 915-ft. above sea level, lat. 41° 14' 53", long. 77° 01' 58".

Holds CP for change to 0.056-kw ERP, BDFCDTT-20060331BKL.

Transmitter: Near Wildwood Cemetery, Williamsport.

Ownership: Local TV Holdings LLC.

Personnel: Rene Laspina, General Manager; Ron Schacht, Chief Engineer; John Gee, Sales Manager.

Williamsport—W26AT, Ch. 26, Mission Broadcasting Inc. Phone: 330-335-8808.

Technical Facilities: 0.88-kw ERP, 144-ft. above ground, 965-ft. above sea level, lat. 41° 14' 53", long. 77° 01' 58".

Holds CP for change to 0.0044-kw ERP, BDFCDTT-20060403ADG.

Ownership: Mission Broadcasting Inc.

Williamsport—W30AN, Ch. 30, Nexstar Broadcasting Inc. Phone: 972-373-8800.

Technical Facilities: 0.88-kw ERP, 144-ft. above ground, 965-ft. above sea level, lat. 41° 14' 53", long. 77° 01' 58".

Holds CP for change to 0.0044-kw ERP, BDFCDTT-20060403AKV.

Ownership: Nexstar Broadcasting Group Inc.

Williamsport—W39BT, Ch. 39, Trinity Broadcasting Network Inc. Phone: 714-832-2950. Fax: 714-730-0661.

Technical Facilities: 1000-w TPO, 1.6-kw ERP, 157-ft. above ground, 1778-ft. above sea level, lat. 41° 11' 57", long. 77° 07' 38".

Holds CP for change to 15-kw ERP, lat. 41° 11' 57", long. 77° 07' 39". BDFCDTT-20060331ANI.

Transmitter: Bald Eagle Mountain.

Ownership: Trinity Broadcasting Network Inc.

Personnel: Paul Crouch, General Manager; Ben Miller, Chief Engineer; Rod Henke, Sales Manager.

Williamsport—W55AG, Ch. 55, Mission Broadcasting Inc. Phone: 330-335-8808.

Technical Facilities: 1.21-kw ERP, lat. 41° 14' 53", long. 77° 01' 58".

Holds CP for change to channel number 8, 0.002-kw ERP, 144-ft. above ground, 965-ft. above sea level, BDISDTT-20060403ACY.

Ownership: Mission Broadcasting Inc.

■ **Williamsport**—W62CS, Ch. 62, Triple J Community Broadcasting LLC. Phone: 570-459-1869. Fax: 570-459-1383.

Studio: WYLN-TV, Hazelton, PA 18201.

Technical Facilities: 1000-w TPO, 8.61-kw ERP, 118-ft. above ground, 1949-ft. above sea level, lat. 41° 13' 08", long. 76° 57' 27".

Transmitter: Bald Eagle Mountain, 2.5-mi. SE of Williamsport.

Ownership: Harron Communications LP.

Personnel: Joseph Gans, President; Terry Herron, Operations Manager; Kim Straus, Sales Manager; Barry Jais, Chief Engineer.

Puerto Rico

Adjuntas—W68BU, Ch. 68, NBC Telemundo License Co. Phone: 202-637-4535.

Technical Facilities: 2.06-kw ERP, lat. 18° 10' 15", long. 66° 42' 12".

Ownership: NBC Universal.

Aguada—W63BF, Ch. 63, Asociacion Evangelistica Cristo Viene Inc.

Technical Facilities: 35.6-kw ERP, lat. 18° 19' 31", long. 67° 10' 13".

Transmitter: 2-mi. S of the mina, 1-mi. NE of Cerro Canta Gallo, Aguada, PR.

Aguadilla—WPRU-LP, Ch. 20, Dean M. Mosely. Phone: 323-930-1908.

Technical Facilities: 5-kw ERP, 184-ft. above ground, 357-ft. above sea level, lat. 18° 24' 23", long. 69° 09' 07".

Ownership: Storefront Television LLC.

Aguadilla—WSJP-LP, Ch. 30, Storefront Television. Phone: 713-479-3833.

Technical Facilities: 5-kw ERP, 184-ft. above ground, 357-ft. above sea level, lat. 18° 24' 23", long. 69° 09' 07".

Ownership: Storefront Television LLC.

Aquadilla—WSJX-LP, Ch. 24, Storefront Television LLC. Phone: 323-930-1908.

Technical Facilities: 5-kw ERP, 184-ft. above ground, 357-ft. above sea level, lat. 18° 24' 23", long. 69° 09' 07".

Ownership: Storefront Television LLC.

■ **Arecibo**—WIMN-CA, Ch. 20, Carmen Cabrera. Phone: 787-898-1668.

Technical Facilities: 796-w TPO, 10-kw ERP, 87-ft. above ground, 436-ft. above sea level, lat. 18° 27' 14", long. 66° 38' 15".

Holds CP for change to 0.035-kw ERP, 108-ft. above ground, 436-ft. above sea level, BDFCDTA-20080512AAM.

Transmitter: 109 Lorens Torres Ave.

Ownership: Carmen Cabrera.

Bayamon-San Juan—W44CK, Ch. 44, Three Angels Broadcasting Network Inc. Phone: 618-627-4651. Fax: 618-627-4155.

Studio: 3391 Charley Good Rd, West Frankfort, IL 62896.

Technical Facilities: 19.2-kw ERP, 49-ft. above ground, 1657-ft. above sea level, lat. 18° 17' 31", long. 66° 10' 30".

Transmitter: Rd. 812 intersection, Los Pomos Barrio, Guaraguas Arriba.

Ownership: Three Angels Broadcasting Network Inc.

Personnel: Moses Primo, Chief Engineer; Linda Shelton, Program Director.

Ceiba—W59CW, Ch. 59, Fajardo TV Group.

Technical Facilities: 0.3-kw ERP, lat. 18° 17' 04", long. 65° 40' 28".

Transmitter: 2.8-mi. W of State Rd. 982.

Ceiba—WIVE-LP, Ch. 42, International Broadcasting Co. Phone: 787-274-1800.

Technical Facilities: 414-w TPO, 4-kw ERP, 98-ft. above ground, 987-ft. above sea level, lat. 18° 16' 52", long. 65° 40' 09".

Transmitter: 2.8-mi. W of State Rd. 982.

Ownership: International Broadcasting Co.

Fajardo—W09AT, Ch. 9, NBC Telemundo License Co. Phone: 202-637-4535.

Technical Facilities: 0.01-kw ERP, lat. 18° 20' 31", long. 65° 39' 18".

Ownership: NBC Universal.

Guayama—W08AB, Ch. 8, La Cadena Del Milagro Inc.

Technical Facilities: 0.01-kw ERP, lat. 18° 01' 59", long. 66° 07' 09".

Guayama—WXWZ-LP, Ch. 22, PTR Television Inc. Phone: 809-752-8808.

Technical Facilities: 1000-w TPO, 11.8-kw ERP, 33-ft. above ground, 1640-ft. above sea level, lat. 18° 01' 59", long. 66° 07' 09".

Transmitter: Insular Rte. 15, 2.2-mi. N of Olimp.

Ownership: PTR Television Inc.

Isabel Segunda—WVQS-LP, Ch. 50, Juan G. Padin. Phone: 787-383-9905.

Technical Facilities: 22.3-kw ERP, 70-ft. above ground, 505-ft. above sea level, lat. 18° 07' 50", long. 65° 26' 29".

Holds CP for change to 15-kw ERP, 54-ft. above ground, 3466-ft. above sea level, lat. 18° 18' 45", long. 65° 47' 35". BDFCDTL-20080428ACH.

Transmitter: 0.3-mi. W of State Rte. 997.

Ownership: Juan G. Padin.

■ **Mayaguez**—W10BG, Ch. 10, Telecinco Inc. Phone: 787-831-5555.

Technical Facilities: 3-kw ERP, 158-ft. above ground, 171-ft. above sea level, lat. 18° 12' 28", long. 67° 08' 48".

Holds CP for change to 0.144-kw ERP, 105-ft. above ground, 1204-ft. above sea level, lat. 18° 19' 33", long. 67° 10' 13". BDFCDVA-20090105AHZ.

Ownership: Telecinco Inc.

Mayaguez—W51DJ, Ch. 51, Sean Mintz. Phone: 361-883-1763.

Technical Facilities: 7-kw ERP, 177-ft. above ground, 850-ft. above sea level, lat. 18° 13' 46.3", long. 67° 06' 36.6".

Holds CP for change to 1-kw ERP, BDFCDTL-20081208AAQ.

Began Operation: April 4, 2006.

Ownership: Sean Mintz.

Mayaguez & Anasco—WTPM-LP, Ch. 67, Corporacion Adventista del Septimo Dia del Oeste de Puerto Rico. Phone: 809-831-9200. Fax: 809-265-4044.

Technical Facilities: 1000-w TPO, 18.5-kw ERP, 253-ft. above ground, 1368-ft. above sea level, lat. 18° 18' 47", long. 67° 11' 06".

Holds CP for change to channel number 45, 1-kw ERP, BDISDTL-20060321ABJ.

Transmitter: Cerro Comtu Callo electronics site.

Multichannel TV Sound: Stereo only.

Ownership: Corporacion Adventista del Septimo Dia del Oeste de Puerto Rico.

Personnel: Julio C. Javier, General Manager; Ricardo Vega, Chief Engineer.

Mayaguez, etc.—W34CI, Ch. 34, Western Broadcasting Corp. of Puerto Rico. Phone: 787-833-1200.

Technical Facilities: 6-kw ERP, 148-ft. above ground, 1335-ft. above sea level, lat. 18° 18' 51", long. 67° 11' 30".

Holds CP for change to channel number 46, 17.1-kw ERP, BDISTT-20070828AAO.

Ponce—W36DB, Ch. 36, Howard Mintz. Phone: 361-883-1763.

Technical Facilities: 3.82-kw ERP, 187-ft. above ground, 227-ft. above sea level, lat. 18° 00' 34.1", long. 66° 36' 48.5".

Holds CP for change to 0.3-kw ERP, BDISDTL-20090203ABH.

Ownership: Howard Mintz.

■ **Ponce**—WQQZ-CA, Ch. 33, CMCG Puerto Rico License LLC. Phones: 787-895-2725; 787-895-0000. Fax: 787-895-4198.

Technical Facilities: 3-kw ERP, 74-ft. above ground, 2011-ft. above sea level, lat. 18° 04' 50", long. 66° 44' 54".

Transmitter: Barrio Santo Domingo Penuelas.

Began Operation: December 8, 1998.

Ownership: Max Media X LLC; Power Television International LLC.

Personnel: Jose J. Arzuaga, General Manager & Chief Engineer; Idalia Arrieta, Sales Manager.

■ **Quebradillas**—WQSJ-LP, Ch. 48, Wanda Rolon. Phone: 787-730-5880. Fax: 787-797-5157.

Technical Facilities: 521-w TPO, 10-kw ERP, 86-ft. above ground, 516-ft. above sea level, lat. 18° 28' 53", long. 66° 55' 36".

Holds CP for change to 4.8-kw ERP, 98-ft. above ground, 1247-ft. above sea level, lat. 18° 18' 46", long. 67° 11' 09". BDFCDTA-20080826ACX.

Transmitter: Rd. 484, San Jose.

Ownership: Wanda Rolon.

Personnel: Jacob Rivera, General Manager; Juan Padin, Chief Engineer.

Quebradillas—WWKQ-LP, Ch. 26, CMCG Puerto Rico License LLC. Phone: 787-895-2725.

Technical Facilities: 17.82-kw ERP, 107-ft. above ground, 537-ft. above sea level, lat. 18° 28' 53", long. 66° 55' 36".

Transmitter: Rd. 484, BO, San Jose, Quebradillas.

Began Operation: October 12, 1994.

Ownership: Max Media X LLC; Power Television International LLC.

San Juan—W26DK, Ch. 26, Howard Mintz. Phone: 361-883-1763.

Technical Facilities: 5-kw ERP, 213-ft. above ground, 586-ft. above sea level, lat. 18° 21' 25.2", long. 66° 11' 23.3".

Holds CP for change to 0.8-kw ERP, BDFCDTL-20081208ADX.

Began Operation: October 6, 1993.

Ownership: Howard Mintz.

■ **San Juan**—WSJN-CA, Ch. 15, Wanda Rolon. Phone: 787-730-5880. Fax: 787-797-5157.

Studio: Carretera 861, km 4.4, Barrio Pinas, Toa Alta, PR 00953.

Technical Facilities: 1000-w TPO, 38.8-kw ERP, 75-ft. above ground, 1814-ft. above sea level, lat. 18° 17' 42", long. 66° 09' 56".

Holds CP for change to channel number 20, 1.5-kw ERP, lat. 18° 17' 38", long. 66° 10' 01". BDISDTA-20090129AAF.

Transmitter: Bayamon.

Ownership: Wanda Rolon.

Personnel: Steven Hernandez, General Manager; Juan Padin, Chief Engineer; Miguel Rodriguez, Sales Manager.

San Juan—WWXY-LP, Ch. 38, Hector Marcano Martinez. Phone: 787-289-0241.

Technical Facilities: 95.1-kw ERP, 118-ft. above ground, 1759-ft. above sea level, lat. 18° 16' 49", long. 66° 06' 35".

Ownership: Hector Marcano Martinez.

Utuado—W32AJ, Ch. 32, NBC Telemundo License Co. Phone: 202-637-4535.

Technical Facilities: 1.45-kw ERP, 46-ft. above ground, 1457-ft. above sea level, lat. 18° 17' 03", long. 66° 43' 34".

Ownership: NBC Universal.

Yauco—W54AQ, Ch. 54, Asociacion Evangelistica Cristo Viene Inc.

Technical Facilities: 200-w TPO, 1.29-kw ERP, 102-ft. above ground, 2995-ft. above sea level, lat. 18° 08' 59", long. 66° 58' 59".

Transmitter: Maricao electronics site.

Ownership: Asociacion Evangelistica Cristo Viene Inc.

Rhode Island

■ **Providence**—WRIW-CA, Ch. 50, ZGS Broadcasting Holdings Inc. Phone: 703-528-5656.

Technical Facilities: 18.4-kw ERP, 392-ft. above ground, 892-ft. above sea level, lat. 41° 48' 12", long. 71° 33' 27".

Holds CP for change to 15-kw ERP, 622-ft. above ground, 820-ft. above sea level, lat. 41° 51' 53.6", long. 71° 17' 14.8". BDFCDTA-20080804ABB.

Ownership: ZGS Broadcasting Holdings Inc.

South Carolina

Anderson—W50CL, Ch. 50, Trinity Broadcasting Network Inc. Phone: 714-832-2950. Fax: 714-730-0661.

Technical Facilities: 16.8-kw ERP, lat. 34° 25' 31", long. 82° 32' 26".

Transmitter: WRIX-FM Tower.

Ownership: Trinity Broadcasting Network Inc.

Beaufort—W19CH, Ch. 19, Trinity Broadcasting Network Inc. Phone: 714-832-2950. Fax: 714-730-0661.

Technical Facilities: 1000-w TPO, 4-kw ERP, 384-ft. above ground, 394-ft. above sea level, lat. 32° 24' 05", long. 80° 44' 21".

Holds CP for change to 15-kw ERP, 354-ft. above ground, 363-ft. above sea level, lat. 32° 24' 02", long. 80° 44' 23". BDFCDTT-20060331AQP.

Transmitter: 2.2 mi. NNW Intersection of S.R. 280 & S.R. 281.

Ownership: Trinity Broadcasting Network Inc.

Beaufort, etc.—W32BJ, Ch. 32, Southern TV Corp.

Technical Facilities: 16.6-kw ERP, 371-ft. above ground, 377-ft. above sea level, lat. 32° 24' 05", long. 80° 44' 21".

Charleston—W20CN, Ch. 20, Trinity Broadcasting Network Inc. Phone: 714-832-2950. Fax: 714-730-0661.

Technical Facilities: 18.7-kw ERP, 492-ft. above ground, 506-ft. above sea level, lat. 32° 49' 04", long. 79° 50' 08".

Holds CP for change to 15-kw ERP, BDFCDTT-20060331AYW.

Ownership: Trinity Broadcasting Network Inc.

Personnel: Paul Crouch, General Manager; Ben Miller, Chief Engineer; Rod Henke, Sales Manager.

Charleston—WCHD-LP, Ch. 49, Izzo Living Trust. Phone: 562-432-3099.

Technical Facilities: 1000-w TPO, 40.3-kw ERP, 315-ft. above sea level, lat. 32° 49' 01", long. 79° 50' 06".

Transmitter: 0.76-mi. ENE of intersection of U.S. 17 & Ocean Hwy., Mount Pleasant.

Multichannel TV Sound: Stereo and separate audio program.

Ownership: Izzo Living Trust.

Personnel: Julio Izzo, General Manager; Richard Cox, Sales Manager.

Charleston—WHDC-LP, Ch. 12, Charleston DTV LLC. Phone: 517-782-1510.

Technical Facilities: 2-kw ERP, 361-ft. above ground, 377-ft. above sea level, lat. 32° 49' 16", long. 79° 57' 26".

Holds CP for change to 3-kw ERP, 575-ft. above ground, 580-ft. above sea level, lat. 32° 47' 44", long. 79° 50' 27". BPTVL-20070723ACR.

Ownership: Local HDTV Inc.

■ **Charleston**—WLCN-CA, Ch. 18, Faith Assembly of God of Summerville. Phone: 843-873-9128.

Studio: 524 Bayshore Blvd., Goose Creek, SC 29445.

Technical Facilities: 2000-w TPO, 37.8-kw ERP, 466-ft. above ground, 482-ft. above sea level, lat. 32° 49' 01", long. 79° 50' 06".

Transmitter: SE of Rte. 701.

Ownership: Faith Assembly of God of Summerville.

Columbia—W21CA, Ch. 21, Jones Broadcasting. Phone: 407-492-9928.

Technical Facilities: 1000-w TPO, 9.5-kw ERP, 476-ft. above ground, 886-ft. above sea level, lat. 34° 03' 23", long. 80° 58' 50".

Holds CP for change to 15-kw ERP, BDFCDTT-20060403AOF.

Transmitter: Corner of Gervais & Assembly Sts.

Ownership: Gregory Jones.

Columbia—W43BS, Ch. 43, Dove Broadcasting Inc.

Technical Facilities: 0.31-kw ERP, lat. 34° 00' 04", long. 81° 02' 05".

Transmitter: Corner of Gervais & Assembly Sts.

Columbia—W50DX, Ch. 50, Trinity Christian Center of Santa Ana Inc. Phone: 714-832-2950.

Technical Facilities: 16.9-kw ERP, 404-ft. above ground, 823-ft. above sea level, .

Ownership: Trinity Broadcasting Network Inc.

Columbia—W67DP, Ch. 67, Dove Broadcasting Inc. Phone: 864-244-1616.

Technical Facilities: 1000-w TPO, 21.2-kw ERP, 180-ft. above ground, 653-ft. above sea level, lat. 35° 52' 27", long. 81° 11' 05".

Transmitter: Side of existing tower, 1.4-mi. NE of inter of SR 302 & 6, near Edmond.

Ownership: Dove Broadcasting Inc.

Florence—W51DI, Ch. 51, Jones Broadcasting Inc. Phone: 407-492-9928.

Technical Facilities: 82.2-kw ERP, 312-ft. above ground, 412-ft. above sea level, lat. 34° 04' 57", long. 79° 37' 20".

Holds CP for change to 15-kw ERP, BDFCDTT-20060403APC.

Ownership: Gregory Jones.

Greenville—W10AJ, Ch. 10, Media General Communications Holdings LLC.

Technical Facilities: 0.008-kw ERP, 2001-ft. above sea level, lat. 34° 56' 30", long. 82° 25' 05".

Ownership: Media General Inc.

Hilton Head Island—W35AY, Ch. 35, Myron K. Hines.

Technical Facilities: 1000-w TPO, 43.1-kw ERP, 299-ft. above ground, 322-ft. above sea level, lat. 32° 15' 30", long. 82° 52' 48".

Transmitter: Approx. 1.6-mi. from Bluffton.

Ownership: Myron K. Hines.

■ **Hilton Head Island**—W48CX, Ch. 48, Byrne Acquisition Group LLC. Phone: 803-417-6380.

Technical Facilities: 0.015-kw ERP, 48-ft. above ground, 58-ft. above sea level, lat. 32° 09' 17", long. 80° 45' 47".

Ownership: Byrne Acquisition Group LLC.

Honea Path—W65DS, Ch. 65, Carolina Christian Broadcasting Inc. Phone: 854-244-1616.

Technical Facilities: 1000-w TPO, 2.3-kw ERP, 121-ft. above ground, 2113-ft. above sea level, lat. 34° 56' 26", long. 82° 24' 41".

Holds CP for change to channel number 28, 15-kw ERP, BDISDTL-20060331BPN.

Transmitter: WGGS-TV tower, Paris Mountain.

Ownership: Carolina Christian Broadcasting Co.

Jacksonville—W22CJ, Ch. 22, Trinity Broadcasting Network Inc. Phone: 714-832-2950. Fax: 714-730-0661.

Technical Facilities: 100-w TPO, 14.6-kw ERP, 236-ft. above ground, 246-ft. above sea level, lat. 34° 44' 56", long. 77° 24' 51".

Holds CP for change to 4.8-kw ERP, 230-ft. above ground, 245-ft. above sea level, BDFCDTT-20060329AIX.

Transmitter: Screven St., near Church St.

Ownership: Trinity Broadcasting Network Inc.

Myrtle Beach—W34CQ, Ch. 34, Trinity Broadcasting Network Inc. Phone: 714-832-2950. Fax: 714-730-0661.

Technical Facilities: 1000-w TPO, 11.8-kw ERP, 400-ft. above ground, 420-ft. above sea level, lat. 33° 35' 27", long. 79° 02' 55".

Transmitter: 1.2-mi. S of Burgess.

Ownership: Trinity Broadcasting Network Inc.

Myrtle Beach—W49AN, Ch. 49, Jones Broadcasting. Phone: 407-492-9928.

Technical Facilities: 16-kw ERP, 577-ft. above ground, 617-ft. above sea level, lat. 33° 50' 10", long. 78° 51' 08".

Ownership: Gregory Jones.

Myrtle Beach—W51AT, Ch. 51, Jones Broadcasting. Phone: 407-492-9928.

Technical Facilities: 15.5-kw ERP, lat. 33° 50' 10", long. 78° 51' 08".

Holds CP for change to 3-kw ERP, 561-ft. above ground, 602-ft. above sea level, lat. 33° 50' 12", long. 78° 51' 11". BDFCDTT-20060403APA.

Ownership: Gregory Jones.

Myrtle Beach—W68BZ, Ch. 68, Diversified Communications.

Technical Facilities: 52.5-kw ERP, lat. 33° 40' 22", long. 78° 54' 06".

Transmitter: Palace Condominium, Ocean Blvd. & 16th Ave. S, Myrtle Beach.

■ **Myrtle Beach**—WGSC-LP, Ch. 8, Beach TV of South Carolina Inc. Phone: 904-234-2733.

Technical Facilities: 10-w TPO, 0.166-kw ERP, 259-ft. above ground, 266-ft. above sea level, lat. 33° 45' 43", long. 78° 47' 11".

Transmitter: Maison-Sur-Mer Condominium, 9650 Shore Dr., Myrtle Beach.

Ownership: Beach TV of South Carolina Inc.

■ **Myrtle Beach**—WGSI-CA, Ch. 11, Beach TV of South Carolina Inc. Phone: 850-234-2773.

Technical Facilities: 3-kw ERP, 820-ft. above ground, 840-ft. above sea level, lat. 33° 35' 27", long. 79° 02' 55".

Ownership: Beach TV of South Carolina Inc.

Myrtle Beach—WWSC-LP, Ch. 28, WWSC-TV LLC. Phone: 310-394-7761.

Technical Facilities: 130-w TPO, 0.125-kw ERP, 252-ft. above ground, 264-ft. above sea level, lat. 33° 40' 23", long. 78° 54' 05".

Transmitter: 8-mi. NE of Conway.

Ownership: Timothy K. Hall.

North Charleston—WAZS-LP, Ch. 22, Thomas B. Daniels. Phone: 843-744-4297.

Technical Facilities: 150-kw ERP, 217-ft. above ground, 247-ft. above sea level, lat. 32° 55' 42", long. 80° 06' 13".

Ownership: Thomas B. Daniels.

North Charleston—WJNI-LP, Ch. 42, Thomas B. Daniels. Phones: 843-744-4297; 843-554-1063. Fax: 843-747-3922.

Technical Facilities: 150-kw ERP, 272-ft. above ground, 303-ft. above sea level, lat. 32° 55' 42", long. 80° 06' 13".

Ownership: Thomas B. Daniels.

Personnel: Cliff Fletcher, General Manager & Sales Manager.

Orangeburg—W31BS, Ch. 31, Jones Broadcasting. Phone: 407-492-9928.

Technical Facilities: 24-kw ERP, 650-ft. above ground, 974-ft. above sea level, lat. 33° 46' 52", long. 80° 55' 14".

Holds CP for change to channel number 23, 15-kw ERP, 650-ft. above ground, 975-ft. above sea level, BDISDTA-20060703ABW.

Ownership: Gregory Jones.

Orangeburg—W45DE, Ch. 45, Trinity Broadcasting Network Inc. Phone: 714-832-2950. Fax: 714-730-0661.

Technical Facilities: 14.7-kw ERP, 499-ft. above ground, 758-ft. above sea level, lat. 33° 31' 36", long. 80° 49' 44".

Ownership: Trinity Broadcasting Network Inc.

Pickens—W05AO, Ch. 5, WLOS Licensee LLC.

Technical Facilities: 0.11-kw ERP, 1736-ft. above sea level, lat. 34° 54' 02", long. 82° 39' 33".

Ownership: Sinclair Broadcast Group Inc.

Spartanburg—WSQY-LP, Ch. 51, Word of God Fellowship Inc. Phone: 817-571-1229.

Technical Facilities: 10-kw ERP, 164-ft. above ground, 2211-ft. above sea level, lat. 34° 56' 29", long. 82° 24' 41".

Ownership: Word of God Fellowship Inc.

Summerville—W26CF, Ch. 26, Jones Broadcasting. Phone: 407-492-9928.

Technical Facilities: 119-kw ERP, 348-ft. above ground, 431-ft. above sea level, lat. 33° 02' 14", long. 80° 09' 51".

Ownership: Gregory Jones.

South Dakota

Aberdeen—K07JD, Ch. 7, South Dakota Board of Directors for Educational Telecommunications.

Technical Facilities: 0.041-kw ERP, lat. 45° 27' 05", long. 98° 31' 35".

Ownership: South Dakota Board of Directors for Educational Telecommunications.

Aberdeen—K24DT, Ch. 24, Young Broadcasting of Sioux Falls Inc., Debtor in Possession. Phone: 919-839-0300.

Technical Facilities: 0.674-kw ERP, 331-ft. above ground, 1634-ft. above sea level, lat. 45° 28' 29", long. 98° 31' 17".

Began Operation: July 12, 1994.

Ownership: Young Broadcasting Inc., Debtor in Possession.

Aberdeen—K35FJ, Ch. 35, Trinity Broadcasting Network Inc. Phone: 714-832-2950. Fax: 714-730-0661.

Technical Facilities: 100-w TPO, 1.3-kw ERP, 187-ft. above ground, 1486-ft. above sea level, lat. 45° 27' 50", long. 98° 29' 17".

Transmitter: Atop the Alonzo Ward Hotel, 104 S. Main St., Aberdeen.

Ownership: Trinity Broadcasting Network Inc.

Personnel: Paul F. Crouch, General Manager; Rod Henke, Sales Manager; Ben Miller, Chief Engineer.

Aberdeen—K39CZ, Ch. 39, Independent Communications Inc.

Technical Facilities: 734-w TPO, 8.32-kw ERP, 1465-ft. above sea level, lat. 45° 28' 19", long. 98° 31' 17".

Transmitter: 1.7-mi. NW of Aberdeen.

Ownership: Independent Communications Inc.

Aberdeen—K54AH, Ch. 54, Rio Blanco County TV Assn.

Technical Facilities: 0.041-kw ERP, 1460-ft. above sea level, lat. 45° 27' 05", long. 98° 31' 35".

Ownership: Rio Blanco County TV Association.

Badger—K35GR, Ch. 35, Red River Broadcast Co. LLC. Phones: 605-361-5555; 701-277-1515. Fax: 605-361-7017.

Technical Facilities: 11.9-kw ERP, 339-ft. above ground, 2114-ft. above sea level, lat. 44° 29' 15", long. 97° 14' 20".

Holds CP for change to 6.76-kw ERP, BDFCDTT-20060331AZR.

Ownership: Red River Broadcast Co. LLC.

Personnel: Don Sturzenbecher, Chief Engineer.

Belle Fourche—K20FT, Ch. 20, South Dakota Board of Directors for Educational Telecommunications.

Technical Facilities: 0.022-kw ERP, 46-ft. above ground, 3205-ft. above sea level, lat. 44° 39' 24", long. 103° 50' 49".

Ownership: South Dakota Board of Directors for Educational Telecommunications.

Brookings—K40FZ, Ch. 40, Red River Broadcast Co. LLC. Phones: 605-361-5555; 701-277-1515. Fax: 605-361-7017.

Technical Facilities: 13.5-kw ERP, lat. 44° 20' 22", long. 96° 46' 07".

Holds CP for change to 7.014-kw ERP, 338-ft. above ground, 1957-ft. above sea level, BDFCDTT-20060331BAF.

Ownership: Red River Broadcast Co. LLC.

Brookings—K50DG, Ch. 50, Independent Communications Inc. Phone: 605-338-0017. Fax: 605-338-7173.

Technical Facilities: 50-w TPO, 0.45-kw ERP, 125-ft. above ground, 1804-ft. above sea level, lat. 44° 18' 03", long. 96° 46' 00".

Transmitter: 22nd St. & Eastbrook Dr.

Ownership: Independent Communications Inc.

Edgemont—K64AL, Ch. 64, South Dakota Board of Directors for Educational Telecommunications.

Technical Facilities: 0.36-kw ERP, 4432-ft. above sea level, lat. 43° 22' 09", long. 103° 44' 01".

Ownership: South Dakota Board of Directors for Educational Telecommunications.

Huron—K38CQ, Ch. 38, Trinity Broadcasting Network Inc. Phone: 714-832-2950. Fax: 714-730-0661.

Technical Facilities: 1000-w TPO, 9.7-kw ERP, 259-ft. above ground, 1549-ft. above sea level, lat. 44° 20' 32", long. 98° 14' 38".

Transmitter: 2.5-mi. SSW of intersection of U.S. Rte. 14 & State Rd. 37.

Ownership: Trinity Broadcasting Network Inc.

Personnel: Paul F. Crouch, General Manager; Ben Miller, Chief Engineer; Rod Henke, Sales Manager.

Ipswich—K59BL, Ch. 59, South Dakota Five County TV Translator Dist.

Technical Facilities: 1.88-kw ERP, lat. 45° 48' 07", long. 99° 12' 59".

Lake Andes—K57BX, Ch. 57, Young Broadcasting of Sioux Falls Inc., Debtor in Possession. Phone: 919-839-0300.

Technical Facilities: 1.91-kw ERP, lat. 43° 04' 59", long. 98° 28' 28".

Began Operation: January 19, 1981.

Ownership: Young Broadcasting Inc., Debtor in Possession.

Lemmon—K07FG, Ch. 7, Lemmon TV Assn. Inc.

Technical Facilities: 0.007-kw ERP, lat. 45° 56' 41", long. 102° 10' 02".

Lemmon—K09FG, Ch. 9, Lemmon TV Assn. Inc.

Technical Facilities: 0.007-kw ERP, lat. 45° 56' 41", long. 102° 10' 02".

Lowry—K56AX, Ch. 56, South Dakota Five County TV Translator District.

Technical Facilities: 32.9-kw ERP, 3035-ft. above sea level, lat. 45° 16' 34", long. 99° 59' 03".

Lowry—K62AV, Ch. 62, South Dakota Five County TV Translator Dist.

Technical Facilities: 32.2-kw ERP, lat. 45° 16' 34", long. 99° 59' 03".

Lowry—K68BM, Ch. 68, South Dakota Five County TV Translator District.

Technical Facilities: 31.5-kw ERP, lat. 45° 16' 34", long. 99° 59' 03".

Madison—K43GX, Ch. 43, Trinity Broadcasting Network Inc. Phone: 714-832-2950. Fax: 714-730-0661.

Technical Facilities: 1000-w TPO, 8.1-kw ERP, 295-ft. above ground, 2096-ft. above sea level, lat. 43° 56' 01", long. 97° 07' 54".

Transmitter: 4.5-mi. S of Madison.

Ownership: Trinity Broadcasting Network Inc.

Milbank—K47IC, Ch. 47, Red River Broadcast Co. LLC. Phone: 701-277-1515.

Technical Facilities: 7.8-kw ERP, 686-ft. above ground, 2726-ft. above sea level, lat. 45° 10' 31", long. 96° 59' 14".

Holds CP for change to 3.889-kw ERP, BDFCDTT-20060331AYC.

Ownership: Red River Broadcast Co. LLC.

Mitchell—K07QL, Ch. 7, Hoak Media of Dakota License LLC. Phone: 972-960-4896.

Technical Facilities: 0.1-kw ERP, lat. 43° 41' 54", long. 97° 55' 58".

Ownership: Hoak Media LLC.

Mitchell—K09UN, Ch. 9, South Dakota Board of Directors for Educational Telecommunications. Phone: 605-677-5861.

Technical Facilities: 0.04-kw ERP, 177-ft. above ground, 1526-ft. above sea level, lat. 43° 41' 51", long. 98° 02' 46".

Ownership: South Dakota Board of Directors for Educational Telecommunications.

Mobridge—K09KK, Ch. 9, Mobridge TV Assn.

Technical Facilities: 0.02-kw ERP, lat. 45° 32' 36", long. 100° 21' 00".

Murdo—K44GG, Ch. 44, Red River Broadcast Co. LLC. Phones: 605-361-5555; 701-277-1515. Fax: 605-361-7017.

Technical Facilities: 0.723-kw ERP, 197-ft. above ground, 2710-ft. above sea level, lat. 43° 56' 16", long. 100° 40' 42".

Holds CP for change to 0.144-kw ERP, BDFCDTT-20060331BFC.

Ownership: Red River Broadcast Co. LLC.

Personnel: Don Sturzenbecher, Chief Engineer.

Philip, etc.—K69DJ, Ch. 69, Young Broadcasting of Rapid City Inc., Debtor in Possession. Phone: 919-839-0300.

Technical Facilities: 0.742-kw ERP, 2966-ft. above sea level, lat. 43° 58' 01", long. 101° 42' 24".

Began Operation: June 1, 1982.

Ownership: Young Broadcasting Inc., Debtor in Possession.

Pierre—K14IO, Ch. 14, Independent Communications Inc. Phone: 605-338-0017.

Technical Facilities: 8-kw ERP, lat. 44° 18' 42", long. 100° 21' 10".

Pierre—K27HJ, Ch. 27, Red River Broadcast Co. LLC. Phones: 605-361-5555; 605-361-7017.

Technical Facilities: 11.6-kw ERP, 344-ft. above ground, 2085-ft. above sea level, lat. 44° 18' 42", long. 100° 21' 09".

Holds CP for change to 6.76-kw ERP, BDFCDTT-20060331AZD.

Ownership: Red River Broadcast Co. LLC.

Personnel: Don Sturzenbecher, Chief Engineer.

Pierre—K32FW, Ch. 32, Three Angels Broadcasting Network Inc. Phone: 618-627-4651. Fax: 618-627-4155.

Technical Facilities: 3.8-kw ERP, 128-ft. above ground, 2037-ft. above sea level, lat. 44° 25' 23.1", long. 100° 21' 17.5".

Ownership: Three Angels Broadcasting Network Inc.

Personnel: Moses Primo, Broadcasting Operations & Engineering Manager.

Pierre—K34GM, Ch. 34, Three Angels Broadcasting Network Inc. Phone: 618-627-4651.

Technical Facilities: 3.8-kw ERP, 128-ft. above ground, 2037-ft. above sea level, lat. 44° 25' 23.1", long. 100° 21' 17.5".

Ownership: Three Angels Broadcasting Network Inc.

Pine Ridge—K06HG, Ch. 6, South Dakota Board of Directors for Educational Telecommunications.

Technical Facilities: 0.009-kw ERP, lat. 43° 01' 06", long. 102° 33' 15".

Ownership: South Dakota Board of Directors for Educational Telecommunications.

Pringle—K55AV, Ch. 55, South Dakota Board of Directors for Educational Telecommunications.

Technical Facilities: 0.254-kw ERP, 6348-ft. above sea level, lat. 43° 44' 43", long. 103° 28' 50".

Ownership: South Dakota Board of Directors for Educational Telecommunications.

Rapid City—K33CO, Ch. 33, Trinity Broadcasting Network Inc. Phone: 714-832-2950. Fax: 714-730-0661.

Technical Facilities: 1000-w TPO, 11.4-kw ERP, 404-ft. above ground, 4232-ft. above sea level, lat. 44° 02' 48", long. 103° 14' 46".

Holds CP for change to 15-kw ERP, 361-ft. above ground, 4199-ft. above sea level, lat. 44° 02' 49", long. 103° 14' 45". BDFCDTT-20060331ATJ.

Transmitter: 3941 Skyline Dr.

Ownership: Trinity Broadcasting Network Inc.

Personnel: Paul F. Crouch, General Manager; Ben Miller, Chief Engineer; Rod Henke, Sales Manager.

Rapid City—K40GS, Ch. 40, Rapid Broadcasting Co.

Technical Facilities: 21.6-kw ERP, 472-ft. above ground, 7431-ft. above sea level, lat. 44° 19' 42", long. 103° 50' 05".

Ownership: Rapid Broadcasting Co.

Rapid City—KCPL-LP, Ch. 52, G.I.G. Inc. Phone: 605-334-0026.

Technical Facilities: 0.574-kw ERP, 192-ft. above ground, 3971-ft. above sea level, lat. 44° 01' 19", long. 103° 15' 35".

Ownership: G.I.G. Inc.

Rapid City—KKRA-LP, Ch. 24, Rapid City Broadcasting Co. Phone: 605-355-0024. Fax: 605-355-9274.

Technical Facilities: 382-w TPO, 11.8-kw ERP, 247-ft. above ground, 4006-ft. above sea level, lat. 44° 05' 33", long. 103° 14' 53".

Transmitter: 1000 Cowboy Hill.

Ownership: Rapid Broadcasting Co.

Personnel: Jim Simpson, General Manager; Mike Morgan, Development Manager; Darren Koehne, Sales Manager; John Bennett, Chief Engineer; Terry Keegan, News Director.

Rapid City—KWBH-LP, Ch. 27, Rapid City Broadcasting Co. Phone: 605-355-0024. Fax: 605-355-9274.

Studio: 2424 S. Plaza Dr., Rapid City, SD 57702.

Technical Facilities: 1000-w TPO, 57.6-kw ERP, 247-ft. above ground, 4005-ft. above sea level, lat. 44° 05' 33", long. 103° 14' 53".

Transmitter: Cowboy Hill.

Multichannel TV Sound: Stereo only.

Ownership: Rapid Broadcasting Co.

Personnel: Jim Simpson, General Manager & Station Manager; Darren Koehne, Regional Sales Manager; Rollie Baker, Chief Engineer.

Sioux Falls—K48DK, Ch. 48, Stuart E. Moen. Phone: 605-331-0029. Fax: 605-331-0029.

Studio: 101 S. Main, Suite M120, Sioux Falls, SD 57102.

Technical Facilities: 100-w TPO, 0.86-kw ERP, 98-ft. above ground, 1506-ft. above sea level, lat. 43° 32' 51", long. 96° 43' 12".

Transmitter: South Dakota Tower.

Ownership: Stuart E. Moen.

Personnel: Rey Franko, General Manager & Sales Manager.

Sioux Falls—K53EG, Ch. 53, Siouxland Christian Broadcasting. Phone: 605-332-5565.

Studio: 2520 W. 41st St., Sioux Falls, SD 57105.

Technical Facilities: 1000-w TPO, 8.58-kw ERP, 300-ft. above ground, 1798-ft. above sea level, lat. 43° 29' 20", long. 96° 45' 40".

Transmitter: 69th & Kiwanis.

Ownership: Siouxland Christian Broadcasting.

Personnel: Roy L. McGreevy, General Manager; Randy Martens, Engineering.

Sioux Falls—K56GF, Ch. 56, Trinity Broadcasting Network Inc. Phone: 714-832-2950. Fax: 714-730-0661.

Technical Facilities: 1000-w TPO, 10.1-kw ERP, 164-ft. above ground, 1473-ft. above sea level, lat. 43° 32' 39", long. 96° 33' 01".

Holds CP for change to channel number 28, 15-kw ERP, 187-ft. above ground, 1637-ft. above sea level, lat. 43° 33' 14", long. 96° 41' 05". BDISDTT-20060330AHQ.

Transmitter: Existing tower, 1.5-mi. N of Rowena.

Ownership: Trinity Broadcasting Network Inc.

Personnel: Paul Crouch, General Manager; Ben Miller, Chief Engineer; Rod Henke, Sales Manager.

Sioux Falls—KAUN-LP, Ch. 42, J. F. Broadcasting LLC. Phone: 605-355-0024.

Technical Facilities: 1000-w TPO, 0.88-kw ERP, 141-ft. above ground, 1690-ft. above sea level, lat. 43° 28' 28", long. 96° 45' 26".

Transmitter: 3-mi. S & 0.5-mi. W of I-229 & Western Ave.

Ownership: James F. Simpson.

Sioux Falls—KCPO-LP, Ch. 26, G.I.G. Inc.

Technical Facilities: 10-w TPO, 7.57-kw ERP, 120-ft. above ground, 1538-ft. above sea level, lat. 43° 32' 38", long. 96° 43' 40".

Transmitter: 314 S. Main St.

Ownership: G.I.G. Inc.

Sioux Falls—KCWS-LP, Ch. 44, J. F. Broadcasting LLC. Phone: 605-355-0024.

Technical Facilities: 100-w TPO, 0.68-kw ERP, 118-ft. above ground, 1614-ft. above sea level, lat. 43° 32' 08", long. 96° 44' 34".

Transmitter: 1100 S. Euclid.

Ownership: James F. Simpson.

Personnel: Jim Simpson, General Manager; Mike Morgan, Development Manager; Darren Koehne, Sales Manager; John Bennett, Chief Engineer.

Spearfish—K17ES, Ch. 4, South Dakota Board of Directors for Educational Telecommunications.

Technical Facilities: 0.044-kw ERP, 5003-ft. above sea level, lat. 44° 29' 20", long. 103° 50' 00".

Ownership: South Dakota Board of Directors for Educational Telecommunications.

Springfield—K33GX, Ch. 33, Red River Broadcast Co. LLC. Phones: 605-361-5555; 701-277-1515. Fax: 605-361-7017.

Technical Facilities: 13.7-kw ERP, 339-ft. above ground, 1764-ft. above sea level, lat. 42° 48' 26", long. 97° 58' 46".

Holds CP for change to 7.014-kw ERP, BDFCDTT-20060331BBJ.

Ownership: Red River Broadcast Co. LLC.

Wagner—K50FH, Ch. 50, South Dakota Board of Directors for Educational Telecommunications.

Technical Facilities: 3.35-kw ERP, lat. 43° 11' 20", long. 98° 04' 20".

Ownership: South Dakota Board of Directors for Educational Telecommunications.

Wasta—K13PN, Ch. 13, South Dakota Board of Directors for Educational Telecommunications.

Technical Facilities: 0.009-kw ERP, lat. 44° 05' 10", long. 102° 27' 35".

Ownership: South Dakota Board of Directors for Educational Telecommunications.

Watertown—K32DK, Ch. 32, Independent Communications Inc.

Technical Facilities: 1000-w TPO, 11.4-kw ERP, 298-ft. above ground, 2060-ft. above sea level, lat. 44° 52' 12", long. 97° 06' 49".

Transmitter: W of Hwy. 81 & SE of Watertown.

Ownership: Independent Communications Inc.

Watertown—K42FI, Ch. 42, Red River Broadcast Co LLC. Phones: 605-361-5555; 701-277-1515.

Technical Facilities: 10-kw ERP, 394-ft. above ground, 2119-ft. above sea level, lat. 44° 52' 16", long. 97° 06' 34".

Holds CP for change to 6.516-kw ERP, BDFCDTT-20060331BET.

Ownership: Red River Broadcast Corp.

Yankton—K21EN, Ch. 21, Independent Communications Inc.

Technical Facilities: 18.45-kw ERP, lat. 42° 56' 56", long. 97° 09' 33".

Yankton—K31DP, Ch. 31, Trinity Broadcasting Network Inc. Phone: 714-832-2950. Fax: 714-730-0661.

Technical Facilities: 1000-w TPO, 18.7-kw ERP, 276-ft. above ground, 1814-ft. above sea level, lat. 42° 43' 49", long. 97° 24' 13".

Holds CP for change to channel number 25, 15-kw ERP, 276-ft. above ground, 429-ft. above sea level, lat. 42° 43' 49", long. 97° 24' 12". BDISDTT-20060327ACG.

Transmitter: Side of KKYA(FM) tower, 0.18-mi. NE of junction of US Rte.81 & State Rte.12.

Ownership: Trinity Broadcasting Network Inc.

Personnel: Paul F. Crouch, General Manager; Rod Henke, Sales Manager; Ben Miller, Chief Engineer.

Tennessee

Acton—W14BW, Ch. 14, MS Communications LLC. Phone: 414-765-9737.

Technical Facilities: 1000-w TPO, 0.007-kw ERP, 105-ft. above ground, 466-ft. above sea level, lat. 34° 54' 36", long. 88° 31' 17".

Transmitter: Hwy. 45, Railroad Tower, 3.8-mi. N of Corinth.

Ownership: MS Communications LLC.

Acton—W20BJ, Ch. 20, MS Communications LLC. Phone: 414-765-9737.

Technical Facilities: 1000-w TPO, 0.007-kw ERP, 105-ft. above ground, 466-ft. above sea level, lat. 34° 54' 36", long. 88° 31' 17".

Transmitter: RR tower, 3.8-mi. N of Corinth, on Hwy. 45.

Ownership: MS Communications LLC.

Acton—W27CL, Ch. 27, MS Communications LLC. Phone: 414-765-9737.

Technical Facilities: 1000-w TPO, 0.007-kw ERP, 105-ft. above ground, 466-ft. above sea level, lat. 34° 54' 36", long. 88° 31' 17".

Transmitter: RR tower, 3.8-mi. N of Corinth, on Hwy. 45.

Ownership: MS Communications LLC.

Acton—W28BO, Ch. 28, Summit Media Inc. Phone: 801-577-1322.

Technical Facilities: 10-kw ERP, 231-ft. above ground, 733-ft. above sea level, lat. 34° 58' 17.8", long. 88° 30' 59".

Ownership: Summit Media Inc.

Acton—W32BG, Ch. 32, MS Communications LLC. Phone: 414-765-9737.

Technical Facilities: 1000-w TPO, 0.007-kw ERP, 105-ft. above ground, 571-ft. above sea level, lat. 34° 54' 36", long. 88° 31' 17".

Transmitter: RR tower, 3.8-mi. N of Corinth, on Hwy. 45.

Ownership: MS Communications LLC.

Acton—W34BU, Ch. 34, MS Communications LLC. Phone: 414-765-9737.

Technical Facilities: 980-w TPO, 0.007-kw ERP, 105-ft. above ground, 466-ft. above sea level, lat. 34° 54' 36", long. 88° 31' 17".

Transmitter: Hwy. 45, Railroad Tower, 3.8-mi. N of Corinth.

Ownership: MS Communications LLC.

Acton—W43BH, Ch. 43, MS Communications LLC. Phone: 414-765-9737.

Technical Facilities: 1000-w TPO, 0.007-kw ERP, 105-ft. above ground, 466-ft. above sea level, lat. 34° 54' 36", long. 88° 31' 17".

Transmitter: RR tower, 3.8-mi. N of Corinth, on Hwy. 45.

Ownership: MS Communications LLC.

Acton—W46CE, Ch. 46, MS Communications LLC. Phone: 414-765-9737.

Technical Facilities: 1000-w TPO, 0.007-kw ERP, 105-ft. above ground, 466-ft. above sea level, lat. 34° 54' 36", long. 88° 31' 17".

Transmitter: Hwy. 45, Railroad Tower, 3.8-mi. N of Corinth.

Ownership: MS Communications LLC.

Acton—W56DA, Ch. 56, MS Communications LLC. Phone: 414-765-9737.

Technical Facilities: 820-w TPO, 0.007-kw ERP, 105-ft. above ground, 571-ft. above sea level, lat. 34° 54' 36", long. 88° 31' 17".

Transmitter: Hwy. 45 railroad tower, 4-mi. N of Corinth, MS.

Ownership: MS Communications LLC.

Acton—W62CK, Ch. 62, MS Communications LLC. Phone: 414-765-9737.

Technical Facilities: 1000-w TPO, 0.007-kw ERP, 105-ft. above ground, 466-ft. above sea level, lat. 34° 54' 36", long. 88° 31' 17".

Transmitter: Hwy. 45, Railroad Tower, 3.8-mi. N of Corinth.

Ownership: MS Communications LLC.

Acton—W66CG, Ch. 66, MS Communications LLC. Phone: 414-765-9737.

Technical Facilities: 1000-w TPO, 0.007-kw ERP, 105-ft. above ground, 571-ft. above sea level, lat. 34° 54' 36", long. 88° 31' 17".

Transmitter: Hwy. 45, Railroad tower, 3.8-mi. N of Corinth, MS.

Ownership: MS Communications LLC.

Acton—W69DB, Ch. 69, MS Communications LLC. Phone: 414-765-9737.

Technical Facilities: 1000-w TPO, 0.007-kw ERP, 105-ft. above ground, 466-ft. above sea level, lat. 34° 54' 36", long. 88° 31' 17".

Transmitter: RR tower, 3.8-mi. N of Corinth, on Hwy. 45.

Ownership: MS Communications LLC.

Alexandria—WKRP-LP, Ch. 6, Richard C. & Lisa A. Goetz. Phone: 615-826-0792.

Technical Facilities: 2-kw ERP, 230-ft. above ground, 1056-ft. above sea level, lat. 36° 09' 00", long. 86° 23' 13".

Holds CP for change to channel number 19, 10-kw ERP, BDISTTL-20080616AEI.

Ownership: Richard C. & Lisa A. Goetz.

Chattanooga—W26BE, Ch. 26, Three Angels Broadcasting Network Inc.

Technical Facilities: 9.8-kw ERP, 449-ft. above ground, 2247-ft. above sea level, lat. 35° 15' 20", long. 85° 13' 34".

Ownership: Three Angels Broadcasting Network Inc.

Chattanooga—WCNT-LP, Ch. 36, Three Angels Broadcasting Network Inc.

Technical Facilities: 64.4-kw ERP, 210-ft. above ground, 1248-ft. above sea level, lat. 35° 22' 49", long. 84° 42' 45".

Ownership: Three Angels Broadcasting Network Inc.

■ **Chattanooga**—WOOT-LP, Ch. 6, Tiger Eye Broadcasting Corp. Phone: 954-431-3144.

Technical Facilities: 1.4-kw ERP, 78-ft. above ground, 2090-ft. above sea level, lat. 35° 12' 26", long. 85° 16' 52".

Ownership: Tiger Eye Broadcasting Corp.

Chattanooga—WRNG-LP, Ch. 28, North Georgia Television. Phone: 706-278-9713. Fax: 706-278-7950.

Studio: 101 S Spencer St, Dalton, GA 30721.

Technical Facilities: 3.5-kw ERP, 38-ft. above ground, 2046-ft. above sea level, lat. 34° 57' 11.7", long. 85° 22' 55.3".

Holds CP for change to 139-kw ERP, 135-ft. above ground, 2143-ft. above sea level, BPTTL-20070828ACI.

Ownership: North Georgia Television.

Personnel: Doug Jensen, President/CEO; Calvin Means, General Manager; Judy Elliott, Sales Manager.

■ **Chattanooga**—WYHB-CA, Ch. 39, Ying Hua Benns. Phone: 423-698-8839. Fax: 423-622-6039.

Studio: 4278 B Bonny Oaks Dr., Chattanooga, TN 37406.

Technical Facilities: 1000-w TPO, 10.4-kw ERP, 190-ft. above ground, 2201-ft. above sea level, lat. 35° 12' 26", long. 85° 16' 52".

Transmitter: Sawyer Cemetery Rd., Signal Mountain.

Ownership: Ying Hua Benns.

Personnel: Ying Benns, General Sales Manager; Jeff Gregorz, Chief Engineer.

Clarksville—W26CJ, Ch. 26, MS Communications LLC. Phone: 414-765-9737.

Technical Facilities: 0.004-kw ERP, 50-ft. above ground, 595-ft. above sea level, lat. 36° 33' 30", long. 87° 19' 34".

Ownership: MS Communications LLC.

Clarksville—WCKV-LP, Ch. 49, TN Media Group Inc. Phone: 931-302-2100.

Technical Facilities: 100-w TPO, 15.9-kw ERP, 449-ft. above ground, 600-ft. above sea level, lat. 36° 26' 01", long. 87° 25' 24".

Holds CP for change to 15.4-kw ERP, 60-ft. above ground, 473-ft. above sea level, lat. 36° 31' 39", long. 87° 21' 30". BPTTL-20080514ABO.

Transmitter: 3.2-mi. NE of Indian Mound.

Ownership: Mid Tennessee Media Partners GP.

■ **Cleveland**—WPDP-LP, Ch. 38, New Age Media of Tennessee License LLC. Phone: 570-824-7895.

Technical Facilities: 0.8-kw ERP, lat. 35° 08' 05", long. 84° 37' 21".

Transmitter: Oswald Dome, Oswald Dome Rd.

Ownership: New Age Media.

■ **Cleveland**—WTNB-CA, Ch. 27, PTP Holdings LLC. Phone: 423-472-8892.

Technical Facilities: 5.88-kw ERP, 151-ft. above ground, 1243-ft. above sea level, lat. 35° 12' 03", long. 84° 53' 02".

Began Operation: October 27, 1997.

Ownership: PTP Holdings LLC.

■ **Collegedale**—W21BZ, Ch. 21, Three Angels Broadcasting Network Inc. Phone: 618-627-4651. Fax: 618-627-4155.

Studio: 3391 Charley Good Rd, West Frankfort, IL 62896.

Technical Facilities: 1000-w TPO, 4.9-kw ERP, 148-ft. above ground, 1368-ft. above sea level, lat. 35° 01' 20", long. 85° 04' 32".

Holds CP for change to 46.6-kw ERP, 148-ft. above ground, 1422-ft. above sea level, lat. 35° 01' 32", long. 85° 04' 26". BPTTA-20030304AAR.

Transmitter: White Oak Mountain.

Ownership: Three Angels Broadcasting Network Inc.

Personnel: Moses Primo, Chief Engineer.

Cookeville—W49CQ, Ch. 49, Trinity Broadcasting Network. Phone: 714-832-2950. Fax: 714-730-0661.

Technical Facilities: 42.5-kw ERP, 138-ft. above ground, 1952-ft. above sea level, lat. 36° 05' 04", long. 85° 22' 40".

Holds CP for change to 10-kw ERP, BDFCDTT-20060331BGZ.

Ownership: Trinity Broadcasting Network Inc.

Personnel: Paul Crouch, General Manager; Ben Miller, Chief Engineer; Rod Henke, Sales Manager.

Del Rio—W03AL, Ch. 3, Dennis B. Freeman.

Technical Facilities: 0.01-kw ERP, lat. 35° 50' 58", long. 82° 57' 32".

■ **Dyersburg**—WDYR-CA, Ch. 33, Tri-State Christian TV Inc. Phone: 618-997-9333.

Technical Facilities: 12-kw ERP, 482-ft. above ground, 843-ft. above sea level, lat. 36° 02' 28", long. 89° 26' 19".

Ownership: Tri-State Christian TV Inc.

Farragut/Knoxville—W14CX, Ch. 14, Three Angels Broadcasting Network Inc. Phone: 618-627-4651. Fax: 618-627-4155.

Technical Facilities: 45-kw ERP, 450-ft. above ground, 1730-ft. above sea level, lat. 36° 00' 10", long. 83° 56' 40".

Holds CP for change to 4.43-kw ERP, 483-ft. above ground, 1797-ft. above sea level, lat. 35° 59' 44.1", long. 83° 57' 23.4". BDFCDTL-20081021ABF.

Ownership: Three Angels Broadcasting Network Inc.

Personnel: Moses Primo, General Manager, Sales Manager & Chief Engineer.

Gatlinburg—WDLY-LP, Ch. 36, John Colson Dash. Phone: 276-979-9200.

Technical Facilities: 15-kw ERP, 82-ft. above ground, 1450-ft. above sea level, lat. 35° 42' 29", long. 83° 31' 15".

Ownership: John Colson Dash.

Gatlinburg—WJDP-LP, Ch. 28, John Colson Dash. Phone: 276-979-9200.

Technical Facilities: 11.43-kw ERP, 66-ft. above ground, 3097-ft. above sea level, lat. 35° 48' 43", long. 83° 40' 05".

Holds CP for change to 5.16-kw ERP, 62-ft. above ground, 3117-ft. above sea level, BPTTL-20070411AAD.

Ownership: John Colson Dash.

■ **Greeneville & Blackwater, VA**—WAPG-CA, Ch. 51, Holston Valley Broadcasting Corp. Phone: 423-246-9578.

Technical Facilities: 5-kw ERP, 52-ft. above ground, 4853-ft. above sea level, lat. 36° 01' 24", long. 82° 42' 56".

Ownership: Holston Valley Broadcasting Corp.

Harrogate—W14AQ, Ch. 14, Lincoln Memorial University. Phones: 615-869-6443; 615-869-6312. Fax: 615-869-6435.

Studio: Hwy. 25 E, Harrogate, TN 37752.

Technical Facilities: 1000-w TPO, 8.5-kw ERP, 66-ft. above ground, 1864-ft. above sea level, lat. 36° 35' 10", long. 83° 39' 54".

Transmitter: Atop Little Pinnacle Mountain.

Ownership: Lincoln Memorial University.

Personnel: Denton Loving, General Manager; Bernard Leonard, Chief Engineer.

Harrogate—W18AN, Ch. 18, Lincoln Memorial U. Phone: 615-869-6443. Fax: 615-869-6435.

Technical Facilities: 8.5-kw ERP, 66-ft. above ground, 1863-ft. above sea level, lat. 36° 35' 10", long. 83° 39' 54".

Ownership: Lincoln Memorial University.

■ **Heiskell**—WFEM-LP, Ch. 12, H. Earl Marlar. Phone: 865-938-1185. Fax: 865-947-1212.

Studio: 116 W. Bull Run Valley Dr., Heiskell, TN 37754.

Technical Facilities: 10-w TPO, 0.123-kw ERP, 350-ft. above ground, 1690-ft. above sea level, lat. 36° 04' 21", long. 84° 01' 18".

Transmitter: 8815 Ventis Lane, Knoxville.

Ownership: H. Earl Marlar.

Personnel: Earl Marlar, General Manager.

Jackson—W22BR, Ch. 22, MS Communications LLC. Phone: 414-765-9737.

Technical Facilities: 0.007-kw ERP, 105-ft. above ground, 665-ft. above sea level, lat. 35° 39' 47", long. 88° 45' 24".

Ownership: MS Communications LLC.

Jackson—W25BY, Ch. 25, MS Communications LLC. Phone: 414-765-9737.

Technical Facilities: 1000-w TPO, 10.4-kw ERP, 780-ft. above ground, 1270-ft. above sea level, lat. 35° 42' 25", long. 88° 44' 34".

Transmitter: 7-mi. NE of Jackson, N of I-40 & U.S. 70 intersection.

Ownership: MS Communications LLC.

Jackson—W35AH, Ch. 35, Trinity Broadcasting Network Inc. Phone: 714-832-2950. Fax: 714-730-0661.

Technical Facilities: 7.9-kw ERP, 469-ft. above ground, 1002-ft. above sea level, lat. 35° 38' 47", long. 88° 49' 57".

Holds CP for change to 15-kw ERP, lat. 35° 38' 49", long. 88° 50' 00". BDFCDTT-20060329AGH.

Ownership: Trinity Broadcasting Network Inc.

Personnel: Paul Crouch, General Manager; Ben Miller, Chief Engineer; Rod Henke, Sales Manager.

Jackson—W38BY, Ch. 38, MS Communications LLC. Phone: 414-765-9737.

Technical Facilities: 1000-w TPO, 11.4-kw ERP, 200-ft. above ground, 1270-ft. above sea level, lat. 35° 42' 25", long. 88° 44' 34".

Transmitter: 7 mi. NE of Jackson.

Ownership: MS Communications LLC.

Jackson—W46CG, Ch. 46, MS Communications LLC. Phone: 414-765-9737.

Technical Facilities: 87-w TPO, 1-kw ERP, 200-ft. above ground, 689-ft. above sea level, lat. 35° 32' 39", long. 88° 47' 18".

Transmitter: 344 Old Pinson Rd., 3.9-mi. SE of Jackson.

Ownership: MS Communications LLC.

Jackson—W49CG, Ch. 49, Tiger Eye Licensing LLC. Phone: 954-431-3144.

Technical Facilities: 5-kw ERP, 265-ft. above ground, 745-ft. above sea level, lat. 35° 31' 55", long. 88° 46' 10".

Ownership: Tiger Eye Broadcasting Corp.

Jackson—W52CZ, Ch. 52, MS Communications LLC. Phone: 414-765-9737.

Technical Facilities: 1000-w TPO, 0.007-kw ERP, 105-ft. above ground, 561-ft. above sea level, lat. 35° 39' 47", long. 88° 45' 24".

Transmitter: 7-mi. NE of Jackson.

Ownership: MS Communications LLC.

Jackson—W54BU, Ch. 54, MS Communications LLC. Phone: 414-765-9737.

Technical Facilities: 0.007-kw ERP, 105-ft. above ground, 667-ft. above sea level, lat. 35° 39' 47", long. 88° 45' 24".

Ownership: MS Communications LLC.

Jackson—W62CJ, Ch. 62, MS Communications LLC. Phone: 414-765-9737.

Technical Facilities: 1000-w TPO, 12.6-kw ERP, 200-ft. above ground, 689-ft. above sea level, lat. 35° 42' 25", long. 88° 44' 34".

Transmitter: 7-mi. NE of Jackson.

Ownership: MS Communications LLC.

Jackson—W64BZ, Ch. 64, MS Communications LLC. Phone: 414-765-9737.

Technical Facilities: 1000-w TPO, 0.007-kw ERP, 105-ft. above ground, 665-ft. above sea level, lat. 35° 39' 47", long. 88° 45' 24".

Transmitter: 344 Old Pinson Rd., 4-mi. SE of Jackson.

Ownership: MS Communications LLC.

Jackson—WJTD-LP, Ch. 42, Word of God Fellowship Inc. Phone: 817-571-1229.

Technical Facilities: 80-kw ERP, 492-ft. above ground, 938-ft. above sea level, lat. 35° 39' 50", long. 88° 47' 23".

Ownership: Word of God Fellowship Inc.

■ **Jackson**—WJTE-LP, Ch. 19, Tiger Eye Broadcasting Corp. Phone: 954-431-3144.

Technical Facilities: 725-w TPO, 7-kw ERP, 200-ft. above ground, 942-ft. above sea level, lat. 35° 42' 17", long. 88° 44' 46".

Holds CP for change to 150-kw ERP, 463-ft. above ground, 942-ft. above sea level, BPTTA-20030108AAX.

Transmitter: 6.9-mi. NW of Jackson.

Ownership: Tiger Eye Broadcasting Corp.

■ **Kingsport**—WAPK-CA, Ch. 36, Holston Valley Broadcasting Corp. Phone: 423-246-9578. Fax: 423-246-6261.

Technical Facilities: 22.8-kw ERP, 157-ft. above ground, 4331-ft. above sea level, lat. 36° 25' 54", long. 82° 08' 15".

Multichannel TV Sound: Stereo and separate audio program.

Ownership: Holston Valley Broadcasting Corp.

Personnel: George E. DeVault Jr., President & General Manager; Ray Walker, Executive Vice President & Sales Manager; John O. Davis, Chief Engineer.

■ **Kingsport**—WKPT-LP, Ch. 25, Holston Valley Broadcasting Corp. Phone: 423-246-9578. Fax: 423-246-1863.

Technical Facilities: 0.5-kw ERP, lat. 36° 31' 36", long. 82° 35' 14".

Ownership: Holston Valley Broadcasting Corp.

■ **Kingsport**—WOPI-CA, Ch. 56, Holston Valley Broadcasting Corp. Phone: 423-246-9578. Fax: 423-246-6261.

Technical Facilities: 1000-w TPO, 13.61-kw ERP, 174-ft. above ground, 4347-ft. above sea level, lat. 36° 25' 54", long. 82° 08' 15".

Transmitter: Holston Mountain in Cherokee National Forest, near Kingsport.

Multichannel TV Sound: Separate audio program.

Ownership: Holston Valley Broadcasting Corp.

Personnel: George E. DeVault Jr., President & General Manager; Ray Walker, Executive Vice President & Sales Manager; John O. Davis, Chief Engineer.

Knoxville—W40CM, Ch. 40, Ventana Television Inc. Phone: 727-872-4210.

Technical Facilities: 50-kw ERP, 239-ft. above ground, 1554-ft. above sea level, lat. 35° 59' 44.1", long. 83° 57' 23.4".

Began Operation: June 12, 1991.

Ownership: Ventana Television Inc.

Personnel: John Skelnik, General Manager & Chief Technician.

Knoxville—W46DC, Ch. 46, Trinity Broadcasting Network Inc. Phone: 714-832-2950. Fax: 714-730-0661.

Technical Facilities: 8900-w TPO, 25-kw ERP, 899-ft. above ground, 1989-ft. above sea level, lat. 35° 59' 20", long. 83° 57' 45".

Holds CP for change to 15-kw ERP, BDFCDTT-20060331BJI.

Ownership: Trinity Broadcasting Network Inc.

Knoxville—WDTT-LP, Ch. 24, Word of God Fellowship Inc. Phone: 817-571-1229. Fax: 817-571-7478.

Studio: 106 A St. N, Lenoir City, TN 37771.

Technical Facilities: 31.5-kw ERP, 1500-ft. above ground, 2815-ft. above sea level, lat. 35° 59' 44", long. 83° 57' 23".

Holds CP for change to 10-kw ERP, 654-ft. above ground, 1968-ft. above sea level, BDCCDTL-20081215AAT.

Began Operation: September 28, 1989.

Ownership: Word of God Fellowship Inc.

Personnel: Joe Sims, Sales Manager; Jim Grimes, Chief Engineer.

■ **Knoxville**—WEEE-LP, Ch. 32, Tiger Eye Finance Inc. Phone: 954-331-7866.

Technical Facilities: 45-kw ERP, 236-ft. above ground, 1437-ft. above sea level, lat. 35° 57' 46", long. 84° 01' 23".

Transmitter: 0.6-mi. W of Texas Ave. & State Rte. 75 intersection.

Began Operation: July 17, 1998.

Ownership: Tiger Eye Broadcasting Corp.

■ **Knoxville**—WEZK-LP, Ch. 28, South Central Communications Corp. Phone: 812-424-8284.

Studio: Sharp's Ridge, Knoxville, TN 37917.

Technical Facilities: 860-w TPO, 5.2-kw ERP, 801-ft. above ground, 2057-ft. above sea level, lat. 36° 00' 36", long. 83° 55' 57".

Transmitter: 0.2-mi. NE of Sharp's Memorial Park, Knoxville.

Multichannel TV Sound: Stereo only.

Began Operation: March 15, 1990.

Ownership: South Central Communications Corp.

Personnel: John Engelbrecht, President; Bob Glen, Engineer.

■ **Lawrenceburg**—WLLP-CA, Ch. 13, ETC Communications Inc. Phone: 256-810-2497.

Technical Facilities: 3.3-kw ERP, 193-ft. above ground, 1099-ft. above sea level, lat. 35° 08' 06.4", long. 87° 22' 31.1".

Ownership: ETC Communications Inc.

Lebanon—W11BD, Ch. 11, Dr. Joe F. Bryant. Phone: 615-444-8206. Fax: 615-444-7592.

Studio: 200 E. Spring St., Lebanon, TN 37087.

Technical Facilities: 0.75-kw ERP, 82-ft. above ground, 646-ft. above sea level, lat. 36° 12' 16", long. 86° 16' 29".

Transmitter: 200 E. Spring St.

Ownership: Bryant Broadcasting Co.

Personnel: Joe F. Bryant, General Manager; Dale Howard, Engineering; Pat Bryant, Programming.

Lewisburg—W34DB, Ch. 34, Bob Smartt. Phone: 931-359-6641.

Technical Facilities: 8.9-kw ERP, 80-ft. above ground, 841-ft. above sea level, lat. 35° 26' 55", long. 86° 47' 23".

Ownership: Bob Smartt.

Livingston—WWWB-LP, Ch. 25, CommSouth Media Inc. Phone: 931-484-1057.

Technical Facilities: 25-kw ERP, 138-ft. above ground, 2037-ft. above sea level, lat. 36° 15' 42", long. 85° 16' 35".

Memphis—W15CH, Ch. 15, George S. Flinn Jr. Phone: 901-726-8970.

Technical Facilities: 116.2-kw ERP, 607-ft. above ground, 886-ft. above sea level, lat. 35° 12' 41", long. 89° 48' 54".

Holds CP for change to 103.3-kw ERP, 610-ft. above ground, 886-ft. above sea level, lat. 35° 12' 34", long. 89° 49' 01". BPTTL-20080814ABE.

Transmitter: 0.3-mi. W of Appling Rd., near Ellendale.

Began Operation: May 8, 1997.

Ownership: Flinn Broadcasting Corp.

Memphis—W26CX, Ch. 26, George S. Flinn Jr. Phone: 901-516-8970.

Technical Facilities: 105.8-kw ERP, 607-ft. above ground, 886-ft. above sea level, lat. 35° 12' 41", long. 89° 48' 54".

Holds CP for change to channel number 6, 3-kw ERP, 696-ft. above ground, 971-ft. above sea level, lat. 35° 12' 34", long. 89° 49' 01". BDISTVL-20080918ABE.

Began Operation: May 8, 1997.

Ownership: George S. Flinn Jr.

■ **Memphis**—W42BY, Ch. 42, Three Angels Broadcasting Network Inc. Phone: 618-627-4651. Fax: 618-627-4155.

Studio: 3391 Charley Good Rd, West Frankfort, IL 62896.

Technical Facilities: 2000-w TPO, 0.3-kw ERP, 436-ft. above ground, 695-ft. above sea level, lat. 35° 08' 36", long. 90° 03' 10".

Transmitter: One Commerce Square.

Ownership: Three Angels Broadcasting Network Inc.

Personnel: Moses Primo, Chief Engineer; Linda Shelton, Program Director.

■ **Memphis**—WBXP-CA, Ch. 44, L4 Media Group LLC. Phone: 321-729-8451.

Studio: 100 N. Main, Suite 2311, Memphis, TN 36103.

Technical Facilities: 13-kw ERP, 462-ft. above ground, 732-ft. above sea level, lat. 35° 09' 00", long. 90° 03' 00".

Ownership: L4 Media Group LLC.

Personnel: Warren Reeves, Consulting Engineer; Amy Brown, Broadcast Operations Director; Liz Kiley, Broadcast Vice President.

Memphis—WDNM-LP, Ch. 19, Word of God Fellowship Inc. Phone: 817-571-1229. Fax: 817-571-7478.

Technical Facilities: 6-kw ERP, 400-ft. above ground, 738-ft. above sea level, lat. 35° 06' 41", long. 90° 02' 57".

Holds CP for change to channel number 21, 15-kw ERP, 443-ft. above ground, 764-ft. above sea level, lat. 35° 06' 44", long. 89° 53' 31". BDISDTL-20081201ABC.

Transmitter: State Rte. 72, near West Brookhaven.

Began Operation: April 23, 1999.

Ownership: Word of God Fellowship Inc.

Morristown—W61DG, Ch. 61, Trinity Broadcasting Network Inc. Phone: 714-832-2950. Fax: 714-730-0661.

Technical Facilities: 1000-w TPO, 7.9-kw ERP, 66-ft. above ground, 1968-ft. above sea level, lat. 36° 13' 38", long. 83° 19' 56".

Holds CP for change to channel number 40, 1-kw ERP, 66-ft. above ground, 1969-ft. above sea level, lat. 36° 13' 38", long. 83° 19' 53". BDISDTT-20060330AJL.

Transmitter: Crockett Ridge, 1-mi. N of intersection of McBride & N. Economy Rds.

Ownership: Trinity Broadcasting Network Inc.

■ **Murfreesboro**—WETV-LP, Ch. 11, Channel Eleven Inc. Phones: 615-889-1960; 615-893-1450.

Technical Facilities: 60-w TPO, 0.614-kw ERP, 315-ft. above ground, 899-ft. above sea level, lat. 35° 50' 26", long. 86° 23' 27".

Holds CP for change to 0.001-kw ERP, BDFCDVA-20060331ABV.

Transmitter: Intersection of U.S. Hwy. 41 & U.S. Hwy. 231.

Ownership: Channel Eleven Inc.

Personnel: William O. Barry, General Manager; Bart Walker, Vice President & Sales Manager; Gary M. Brown, Chief Engineer.

Nashville—W48DF, Ch. 48, Trinity Broadcasting Network Inc. Phone: 714-832-2950. Fax: 714-730-0661.

Technical Facilities: 19.9-kw ERP, 535-ft. above ground, 1024-ft. above sea level, lat. 36° 09' 49", long. 86° 46' 45".

Transmitter: Atop building at 401 Church St.

Ownership: Trinity Broadcasting Network Inc.

Nashville—WIIW-LP, Ch. 14, U.S. Television LLC. Phone: 318-992-7766.

Technical Facilities: 1000-w TPO, 16.4-kw ERP, 371-ft. above ground, 892-ft. above sea level, lat. 36° 09' 48", long. 86° 46' 56".

Transmitter: 511 Union St.

Ownership: Dean M. Mosely.

■ **Nashville**—WJDE-LP, Ch. 24, South Central Communications Corp. Phone: 812-424-8284. Fax: 812-423-3405.

Studio: 504 Rosedale Ave., Nashville, TN 37204.

Technical Facilities: 1000-w TPO, 13.6-kw ERP, 532-ft. above ground, 1020-ft. above sea level, lat. 36° 09' 49", long. 86° 46' 45".

Transmitter: Life & Casualty Tower, 4th & Church Sts., Nashville.

Multichannel TV Sound: Stereo only.

Ownership: South Central Communications Corp.

Personnel: John Engelbrecht, President; Lee Thompson, Engineer.

Nashville—WJNK-LP, Ch. 34, Three Angels Broadcasting Network Inc. Phone: 618-627-4651. Fax: 618-627-4155.

Studio: 3391 Charley Good Rd, West Frankfort, IL 62896.

Technical Facilities: 35.8-kw ERP, 574-ft. above ground, 1332-ft. above sea level, lat. 36° 16' 05", long. 86° 47' 45".

Ownership: Three Angels Broadcasting Network Inc.

Personnel: Moses Primo, Chief Engineer.

Nashville—WNPX-LP, Ch. 20, ION Media LPTV Inc., Debtor in Possession. Phone: 561-682-4206. Fax: 561-659-4754.

Technical Facilities: 40-kw ERP, 464-ft. above ground, 1224-ft. above sea level, lat. 36° 16' 05", long. 86° 47' 45".

Holds CP for change to 10-kw ERP, BDFCDTL-20090515ABR.

Transmitter: L & C tower, 4th & Church Sts.

Began Operation: March 3, 1989.

Ownership: ION Media Networks Inc., Debtor in Possession.

Personnel: Rick Hinds, General Manager; Tim Coucke, Chief Engineer; Phillip Crichfield, Sales Manager.

Nashville—WNTU-LP, Ch. 26, Word of God Fellowship Inc. Phone: 817-571-1229.

Studio: 504 Rosedale Ave., Nashville, TN 37204.

Technical Facilities: 1000-w TPO, 11.9-kw ERP, 531-ft. above ground, 1020-ft. above sea level, lat. 36° 09' 49", long. 86° 46' 45".

Transmitter: Life & Casualty Bldg., 4th Ave. & Church St.

Multichannel TV Sound: Stereo only.

Began Operation: November 14, 1991.

Ownership: Word of God Fellowship Inc.

Personnel: John Engelbrecht, President.

Nashville—WRMX-LP, Ch. 12, South Central Communications Corp. Phone: 812-424-8284.

Technical Facilities: 80-w TPO, 0.171-kw ERP, 190-ft. above ground, 709-ft. above sea level, lat. 36° 07' 30", long. 86° 45' 26".

Transmitter: 504 Rosedale Ave.

Ownership: South Central Communications Corp.

Pigeon Forge—WDLE-LP, Ch. 46, Richard C. & Lisa A. Goetz. Phone: 615-826-0792.

Technical Facilities: 11.4-kw ERP, 66-ft. above ground, 3097-ft. above sea level, lat. 35° 48' 43", long. 83° 40' 05".

Ownership: Richard C. & Lisa A. Goetz.

Selmer—W06AW, Ch. 6, Unity Broadcasting Inc. Phone: 662-728-6492.

Studio: Adams St. extended, Selmer, .

Technical Facilities: 80-w TPO, 0.056-kw ERP, 302-ft. above ground, 801-ft. above sea level, lat. 35° 11' 27", long. 88° 35' 21".

Transmitter: Moose Lodge Rd.

Ownership: Unity Broadcasting Inc.

Personnel: Margaret E. Jordan, Vice President; Dave Jordan, Manager; Tom Howell, Sales.

■ **Sevierville**—WJZC-LP, Ch. 22, South Central Communications Corp. Phone: 812-424-8284.

Studio: 825 N. Central, Knoxville, TN 37917.

Technical Facilities: 682-w TPO, 6.3-kw ERP, 338-ft. above ground, 1519-ft. above sea level, lat. 35° 52' 48", long. 83° 33' 10".

Transmitter: 1-mi. NNE of intersection of Chapman Hwy. & Rte. 411.

Began Operation: October 17, 1990.

Ownership: South Central Communications Corp.

■ **Union City**—WUWT-CA, Ch. 9, Joseph H. Harpole Sr. Phone: 731-885-3341.

Studio: 3862 Barham Rd., Union City, TN 38261.

Technical Facilities: 915-w TPO, 24.8-kw ERP, 332-ft. above ground, 666-ft. above sea level, lat. 36° 26' 46", long. 89° 02' 12".

Transmitter: Hwy. 51 & Jordan Terrace.

Ownership: Joseph H. Harpole Sr.

Texas

■ **Abilene**—K07UF, Ch. 7, Abilene Christian U. Phone: 325-674-2441. Fax: 325-674-2417.

Studio: 1600 Campus Court, DM 110, Abilene, TX 79601.

Technical Facilities: 10-w TPO, 0.82-kw ERP, 151-ft. above ground, 1850-ft. above sea level, lat. 32° 28' 34", long. 99° 42' 22".

Transmitter: 2209 Judge Ely Rd., Abilene.

Ownership: Abilene Christian U.

Personnel: Larry L. Bradshaw, General Manager; J. R. Kessler, Operations Manager; James Thompson, Chief Engineer.

Abilene—K38JE, Ch. 38, Tiger Eye Licensing LLC. Phone: 954-431-3144.

Technical Facilities: 10-kw ERP, 325-ft. above ground, 2210-ft. above sea level, lat. 32° 25' 03.6", long. 99° 58' 15.6".

Ownership: Tiger Eye Broadcasting Corp.

Abilene—K49HT, Ch. 49, C. Dowen Johnson. Phone: 936-443-4451.

Technical Facilities: 30.99-kw ERP, 262-ft. above ground, 1581-ft. above sea level, lat. 31° 55' 13", long. 98° 32' 42".

Ownership: C. Dowen Johnson.

Abilene—K51CK, Ch. 51, Trinity Broadcasting Network Inc. Phones: 714-832-2950; 330-753-5542. Fax: 714-730-0661.

Technical Facilities: 1000-w TPO, 9-kw ERP, 249-ft. above ground, 1975-ft. above sea level, lat. 32° 28' 45", long. 99° 45' 00".

Transmitter: 0.43-mi. E of intersection of Vogel Ave. & Mockingbird Lane.

Ownership: Trinity Broadcasting Network Inc.

Abilene—K60GT, Ch. 60, Andrew Fara. Phone: 415-971-9880.

Technical Facilities: 25-kw ERP, 164-ft. above ground, 2044-ft. above sea level, lat. 32° 19' 27.9", long. 99° 45' 31.2".

Ownership: Andrew Fara.

Abilene—KAFW-LP, Ch. 48, Una Vez Mas Abilene License II LLC. Phone: 214-754-7008.

Technical Facilities: 5-kw ERP, 325-ft. above ground, 2210-ft. above sea level, lat. 32° 25' 04", long. 99° 58' 16".

Ownership: Una Vez Mas GP LLC.

■ **Abilene**—KIDZ-LP, Ch. 42, Bayou City Broadcasting LLC. Phone: 281-380-0076.

Technical Facilities: 12-kw ERP, 284-ft. above ground, 2011-ft. above sea level, lat. 32° 26' 39", long. 99° 44' 05".

Began Operation: May 26, 1992.

Ownership: Bayou City Broadcasting LLC.

Abilene—KJTN-LP, Ch. 18, Hispanic Christian Community Network Inc. Phone: 214-680-6029.

Technical Facilities: 3-kw ERP, 295-ft. above ground, 2021-ft. above sea level, lat. 32° 26' 38", long. 99° 44' 04".

Ownership: Hispanic Christian Community Network Inc.

Abilene—KKAB-LP, Ch. 22, Una Vez Mas Abilene License I LLC. Phone: 214-754-7008.

Technical Facilities: 10-kw ERP, 325-ft. above ground, 2210-ft. above sea level, lat. 32° 25' 03.6", long. 99° 58' 15.6".

Ownership: Una Vez Mas GP LLC.

Abilene—KLMH-LP, Ch. 31, Hispanic Christian Community Network Inc. Phone: 214-879-0081.

Technical Facilities: 2-kw ERP, 279-ft. above ground, 1995-ft. above sea level, lat. 32° 26' 38", long. 99° 44' 04".

Began Operation: January 24, 2008.

Ownership: Hispanic Christian Community Network Inc.

Abilene—KTES-LP, Ch. 40, Bonten Media Group Inc. Phone: 212-710-7771.

Technical Facilities: 1000-w TPO, 52.7-kw ERP, 443-ft. above ground, 2694-ft. above sea level, lat. 32° 15' 58", long. 99° 42' 27".

Transmitter: 11-mi. S of Abilene.

Ownership: Bonten Media Group LLC.

Abilene—KTXF-LP, Ch. 5, KM Communications Inc. Phone: 847-674-0864.

Technical Facilities: 0.665-kw ERP, 230-ft. above ground, 1919-ft. above sea level, lat. 32° 30' 38", long. 99° 44' 29".

Ownership: KM Communications Inc.

Abilene—KVNL-LP, Ch. 4, Cowboys Broadcasting LLC. Phone: 325-676-2121.

Technical Facilities: 2.6-kw ERP, 318-ft. above ground, 2044-ft. above sea level, lat. 32° 26' 36", long. 99° 44' 05".

Ownership: New Life Temple.

Abilene—KZAB-LP, Ch. 46, Hispanic Christian Community Network Inc. Phone: 214-434-6357.

Ownership: Trinity Broadcasting Network Inc.

Technical Facilities: 0.7-kw ERP, 279-ft. above ground, 1995-ft. above sea level, lat. 32° 26' 38", long. 99° 44' 04".

Ownership: Hispanic Christian Community Network Inc.

Abilene/Sweetwater—KPTA-LP, Ch. 56, Prime Time Christian Broadcasting Inc.

Technical Facilities: 16-kw ERP, 400-ft. above ground, 2848-ft. above sea level, lat. 32° 24' 18", long. 100° 08' 17".

Transmitter: 3.9-mi. NW of Chalk Peak, Merkle.

Ownership: Prime Time Christian Broadcasting Inc.

■ **Albany**—KIDV-LP, Ch. 34, Bayou City Broadcasting LLC. Phone: 281-380-0076.

Technical Facilities: 14.7-kw ERP, 320-ft. above ground, 2290-ft. above sea level, lat. 32° 42' 39", long. 99° 25' 18".

Began Operation: March 31, 1997.

Ownership: Bayou City Broadcasting LLC.

Alice—KAEU-LP, Ch. 34, Una Vez Mas Alice License LLC. Phone: 214-754-7008.

Technical Facilities: 10-kw ERP, 325-ft. above ground, 679-ft. above sea level, lat. 27° 43' 24.5", long. 98° 16' 13.5".

Ownership: Una Vez Mas GP LLC.

Amarillo—K17HI-D, Ch. 17, Three Angels Broadcasting Network Inc. Phone: 618-627-4651.

Technical Facilities: 1.5-kw ERP, 328-ft. above ground, 3953-ft. above sea level, lat. 35° 14' 31.2", long. 101° 48' 43".

Began Operation: April 1, 2009.

Ownership: Three Angels Broadcasting Network Inc.

Amarillo—K18HL, Ch. 18, Prism Broadcasting Network Inc. Phone: 770-953-3232.

Technical Facilities: 0.1-kw ERP, 23-ft. above ground, 3592-ft. above sea level, lat. 35° 15' 39", long. 101° 52' 54".

Ownership: Prism Broadcasting Network Inc.

Amarillo—K25GI, Ch. 25, Trinity Christian Center of Santa Ana Inc. Phone: 714-832-2950.

Technical Facilities: 11-kw ERP, lat. 35° 15' 39", long. 101° 52' 52".

Transmitter: 2.5-mi. N of State Rte. 1719 & U.S. Rte. 66 intersection.

Ownership: Trinity Broadcasting Network Inc.

Amarillo—K29GD, Ch. 29, The Estate of John R. Powley, Caroline Kaye Powley Executrix. Phone: 850-936-6461.

Technical Facilities: 1-kw ERP, 165-ft. above ground, 3665-ft. above sea level, lat. 35° 12' 25", long. 101° 50' 18".

Ownership: The Estate of John R. Powley, Caroline Kaye Smith Executrix.

Amarillo—K38IP, Ch. 38, Luken Broadcasting LLC. Phone: 423-265-5260.

Technical Facilities: 1-kw ERP, 16-ft. above ground, 3586-ft. above sea level, lat. 35° 15' 39.1", long. 101° 52' 53.6".

Ownership: Luken Broadcasting LLC.

Amarillo—K39HF, Ch. 39, Marcia T. Turner. Phone: 954-732-9539.

Technical Facilities: 2-kw ERP, 230-ft. above ground, 3757-ft. above sea level, lat. 35° 16' 27", long. 101° 34' 39".

Ownership: Marcia T. Turner.

Amarillo—K39HF, Ch. 39, Marcia T. Turner. Phone: 954-732-9539.

Technical Facilities: 2-kw ERP, 230-ft. above ground, 3757-ft. above sea level, lat. 35° 16' 27", long. 101° 34' 39".

Ownership: Marcia T. Turner.

Amarillo—K45IQ, Ch. 45, Prism Broadcasting Network Inc. Phone: 770-953-3232.

Technical Facilities: 0.1-kw ERP, 23-ft. above ground, 3550-ft. above sea level, lat. 35° 16' 27", long. 101° 34' 39".

Ownership: Prism Broadcasting Network Inc.

Amarillo—K46HQ, Ch. 46, Michael Mintz. Phone: 361-883-1763.

Technical Facilities: 0.1-kw ERP, 98-ft. above ground, 3743-ft. above sea level, lat. 35° 13' 53", long. 101° 46' 42".

Ownership: Michael Mintz.

Amarillo—K56DF, Ch. 56, Spectrum Media.

Technical Facilities: 1000-w TPO, 16.7-kw ERP, 401-ft. above ground, 3891-ft. above sea level, lat. 35° 16' 04", long. 101° 53' 06".

Transmitter: 2.5-mi. N of Amarillo at Western Blvd.

Ownership: Spectrum Media.

Amarillo—K64GK, Ch. 64, Michael Mintz. Phone: 361-884-6293.

Technical Facilities: 36-kw ERP, 427-ft. above ground, 3996-ft. above sea level, lat. 35° 15' 41", long. 101° 52' 52".

Ownership: Michael Mintz.

Amarillo—K69IH, Ch. 69, Michael Mintz. Phone: 361-884-6293.

Technical Facilities: 13.6-kw ERP, 427-ft. above ground, 3996-ft. above sea level, lat. 35° 15' 41.41", long. 101° 52' 52.12".

Ownership: Michael Mintz.

Amarillo—KAMM-LP, Ch. 30, Una Vez Mas Amarillo License I LLC. Phone: 214-754-7008.

Technical Facilities: 21.6-kw ERP, 430-ft. above ground, 4088-ft. above sea level, lat. 35° 12' 27", long. 101° 50' 19".

Ownership: Una Vez Mas GP LLC.

Amarillo—KAMT-LP, Ch. 50, Borger Broadcasting Inc., Debtor in Possession. Phone: 501-219-2400.

Technical Facilities: 150-kw ERP, 965-ft. above ground, 4397-ft. above sea level, lat. 35° 20' 33", long. 101° 49' 20".

Began Operation: February 8, 2001.

Ownership: Equity Media Holdings Corp., Debtor in Possession.

Personnel: Jim MacDonald, General Manager.

Amarillo—KCPN-LP, Ch. 33, Mission Broadcasting Inc. Phone: 330-335-8808.

Technical Facilities: 682-w TPO, 41.1-kw ERP, 545-ft. above ground, 3976-ft. above sea level, lat. 35° 20' 33", long. 101° 49' 21".

Holds CP for change to 0.248-kw ERP, BDFCDTL-20060403ACV.

Transmitter: KCIT(TV) tower, E of Hwy. 87/287.

Ownership: Mission Broadcasting Inc.

Amarillo—KDAX-LP, Ch. 13, Word of God Fellowship Inc. Phone: 817-571-1229.

Technical Facilities: 0.1-kw ERP, 180-ft. above ground, 3776-ft. above sea level, lat. 35° 06' 00", long. 101° 48' 55".

Holds CP for change to channel number 40, 35-kw ERP, 367-ft. above ground, 3937-ft. above sea level, lat. 35° 15' 41", long. 101° 52' 52". BDISTTL-20070712AAN.

Ownership: Word of God Fellowship Inc.

Amarillo—KEAM-LP, Ch. 61, Hispanic Christian Community Network Inc. Phone: 214-879-0001.

Technical Facilities: 12-kw ERP, 984-ft. above ground, 4416-ft. above sea level, lat. 35° 20' 33", long. 101° 49' 22".

Began Operation: May 5, 2009.

Ownership: Hispanic Christian Community Network Inc.

Amarillo—KEAT-LP, Ch. 22, Borger Broadcasting Inc., Debtor in Possession. Phone: 501-219-2400.

Technical Facilities: 1000-w TPO, 12.9-kw ERP, 420-ft. above ground, 4081-ft. above sea level, lat. 35° 12' 26", long. 101° 50' 20".

Transmitter: 1.4-mi. N of Hwy. 289 & Givens Ave. intersection.

Began Operation: July 27, 1999.

Ownership: Equity Media Holdings Corp., Debtor in Possession.

Amarillo—KEYU-LP, Ch. 41, Borger Broadcasting Inc., Debtor in Possession. Phone: 501-219-2400.

Technical Facilities: 123-kw ERP, 965-ft. above ground, 4397-ft. above sea level, lat. 35° 20' 33", long. 101° 49' 20".

Began Operation: September 23, 2004.

Ownership: Equity Media Holdings Corp., Debtor in Possession.

Amarillo—KTMO-LP, Ch. 36, KKTM License Co. LLC. Phone: 972-663-8917.

Technical Facilities: 1000-w TPO, 28.2-kw ERP, 577-ft. above ground, 4042-ft. above sea level, lat. 35° 18' 55", long. 101° 50' 03".

Transmitter: 1-mi. N of Amarillo.

Ownership: London Broadcasting Co. Inc.

Amarillo—KTXD-LP, Ch. 43, Una Vez Mas San Diego LLC. Phone: 214-754-7008.

Technical Facilities: 150-kw ERP, 350-ft. above ground, 3818-ft. above sea level, lat. 35° 18' 55", long. 101° 50' 03".

Ownership: Una Vez Mas GP LLC.

Amarillo—KXIT-LP, Ch. 6, George Chambers. Phone: 806-249-4747.

Technical Facilities: 3-kw ERP, 75-ft. above ground, 3724-ft. above sea level, lat. 35° 12' 25", long. 101° 50' 18".

Ownership: George Chambers.

Atlanta—KAQC-LP, Ch. 20, AQC Productions. Phones: 903-796-8820; 903-796-7430.

Technical Facilities: 150-kw ERP, 459-ft. above ground, 909-ft. above sea level, lat. 33° 11' 54", long. 94° 12' 57".

Ownership: AQC Productions.

Personnel: Randy Smith, General Manager.

Austin—K09VR, Ch. 9, U. of Texas at Austin. Phone: 512-471-3098. Fax: 512-471-1576.

Technical Facilities: 10-w TPO, 0.05-kw ERP, 331-ft. above ground, 932-ft. above sea level, lat. 30° 17' 09", long. 97° 44' 20".

Transmitter: U. of Texas at Austin, Main Bldg.

Ownership: U. of Texas-Austin.

Personnel: Kathy Lawrence, General Manager; Bob Nagy, Chief Engineer.

Austin—K34FM, Ch. 34, Enlace Christian Television Inc. Phone: 469-499-0832.

Technical Facilities: 8-kw ERP, 650-ft. above ground, 1430-ft. above sea level, lat. 30° 19' 20", long. 97° 48' 03".

Transmitter: Side of existing tower, 2-mi. SW of SR 2222 & Mt. Bonnell Rd., near Austin.

Began Operation: September 18, 1989.

Ownership: Enlace Christian Television Inc.

Austin—KADF-LP, Ch. 20, Una Vez Mas Austin License LLC. Phone: 214-754-7008.

Technical Facilities: 150-kw ERP, 564-ft. above ground, 1344-ft. above sea level, lat. 30° 19' 20.3", long. 97° 48' 03".

Ownership: Una Vez Mas GP LLC.

■ **Austin**—KBVO-CA, Ch. 51, KXAN Inc. Phones: 512-476-3636; 202-462-6065. Fax: 512-476-1520.

Technical Facilities: 13.4-kw ERP, 1000-ft. above ground, 1850-ft. above sea level, lat. 30° 19' 33", long. 97° 47' 58".

Transmitter: Trail of the Madrones Rd., 5-mi. NW of Austin.

Ownership: LIN TV Corp.

■ **Austin**—KGBS-CA, Ch. 32, Caballero Acquisition Inc. Phones: 972-503-6800; 202-429-8970.

Technical Facilities: 86-kw ERP, 650-ft. above ground, 1387-ft. above sea level, lat. 30° 19' 10", long. 97° 48' 06".

Began Operation: July 25, 1995.

Ownership: Caballero Acquisition Inc.

Personnel: Eduardo Caballero, Chief Executive Officer.

■ **Austin**—KQUX-CA, Ch. 11, Louis Martinez Family Group LLC. Phone: 951-940-1700.

Technical Facilities: 7.6-w TPO, 0.22-kw ERP, 341-ft. above ground, 1079-ft. above sea level, lat. 30° 19' 10", long. 97° 48' 06".

Transmitter: W. Lake Hills antenna farm, 1-mi.SSE of intersection of SR 360 & W. Lake Dr.

Ownership: Louis Martinez Family Group LLC.

■ **Austin**—KTFO-CA, Ch. 30, KAKW License Partnership LP. Phones: 210-227-4141; 210-227-4145. Fax: 210-220-0469.

Technical Facilities: 1000-w TPO, 17.9-kw ERP, 233-ft. above ground, 1080-ft. above sea level, lat. 30° 19' 22", long. 97° 48' 07".

Transmitter: 5.5-mi. WNW of Capitol Bldg.

Ownership: Univision Communications Inc.

Personnel: Steve Giust, General Manager; Frank Fleenor, Chief Engineer; Toni Kirk, Sales Manager.

■ **Austin**—KXLK-CA, Ch. 40, Casa of Austin LP (A Delaware LP). Phone: 559-733-7800.

Technical Facilities: 1000-w TPO, 9-kw ERP, 400-ft. above ground, 1181-ft. above sea level, lat. 30° 19' 21", long. 97° 48' 04".

Transmitter: 4-mi. W of Austin Westlake Tower.

Ownership: Pappas Telecasting Companies.

Ballinger-Coleman—KKCP-LP, Ch. 50, Prime Time Christian Broadcasting Inc. Phone: 915-563-0420. Fax: 915-563-1736.

Technical Facilities: 7.38-kw ERP, 408-ft. above ground, 2647-ft. above sea level, lat. 32° 01' 55", long. 99° 46' 29".

Transmitter: to 9.3-mi. SSW of Crews.

Ownership: Prime Time Christian Broadcasting Inc.

Personnel: Al Cooper, General Manager; Jay Westcott, Chief Engineer; Jeff Welter, Sales Manager.

■ **Bastrop**—KHPB-CA, Ch. 45, KXAN Inc. Phones: 512-476-3636; 202-462-6065. Fax: 512-476-1520.

Technical Facilities: 10.3-kw ERP, 400-ft. above ground, 869-ft. above sea level, lat. 30° 09' 00", long. 97° 13' 16".

Ownership: LIN TV Corp.

■ **Beaumont**—K36ID-D, Ch. 36, Blue Bonnet Communications Inc. Phone: 337-477-2827.

Technical Facilities: 15-kw ERP, 525-ft. above ground, 542-ft. above sea level, lat. 30° 09' 28", long. 93° 48' 06".

Began Operation: November 26, 2007.

Ownership: Blue Bonnet Communications Inc.

Beaumont—K39HG, Ch. 39, Turner Enterprises. Phone: 954-732-9539.

Technical Facilities: 100-kw ERP, 223-ft. above ground, 246-ft. above sea level, lat. 29° 59' 39", long. 94° 13' 08".

Ownership: Marcia T. Turner.

Beaumont—K47IO, Ch. 47, C. Dowen Johnson. Phone: 936-588-2832.

Technical Facilities: 0.2-kw ERP, 98-ft. above ground, 131-ft. above sea level, lat. 30° 16' 50", long. 94° 02' 28".

Ownership: C. Dowen Johnson.

Beaumont—K52IS, Ch. 52, Blue Bonnet Communications Inc. Phone: 337-477-2827.

Technical Facilities: 50-kw ERP, 525-ft. above ground, 541-ft. above sea level, lat. 30° 09' 28", long. 93° 48' 06".

Ownership: Blue Bonnet Communications Inc.

Beaumont—KAOB-LP, Ch. 69, Windsong Communications Inc. Phone: 936-443-4451.

Technical Facilities: 12-kw ERP, 335-ft. above ground, 350-ft. above sea level, lat. 30° 06' 40.2", long. 94° 03' 10.4".

Began Operation: May 25, 2007.

Ownership: Windsong Communications Inc.

Beaumont—KEBQ-LP, Ch. 9, Fountain Television Corp. Phone: 719-382-3233.

Technical Facilities: 0.059-kw ERP, 404-ft. above ground, 430-ft. above sea level, lat. 30° 00' 05", long. 94° 05' 35".

Ownership: Fountain Television Corp.

Personnel: Don Shelton, General Manager; Ron Turner, Chief Engineer.

■ **Beaumont**—KJDF-LP, Ch. 46, Carlos Ortiz Estate, Aracelis Ortiz-Executrix. Phone: 956-421-2635.

Technical Facilities: 1000-w TPO, 12.6-kw ERP, 509-ft. above ground, 529-ft. above sea level, lat. 30° 06' 50", long. 94° 01' 44".

Transmitter: Old U.S. Hwy. 90, 1-mi. SW of Vidor.

Ownership: Carlos Ortiz Estate, Aracelis Ortiz-Executrix.

■ **Beaumont**—KPPY-LP, Ch. 53, KM Communications Inc. Phone: 847-674-0864.

Technical Facilities: 2-kw ERP, 256-ft. above ground, 272-ft. above sea level, lat. 30° 04' 31", long. 94° 07' 48".

Holds CP for change to 198-ft. above ground, 214-ft. above sea level, BPTTL-20080703AHA.

Began Operation: October 13, 2006.

Ownership: KM Communications Inc.

Beaumont—KUIL-LP, Ch. 64, Blue Bonnet Communications Inc. Phone: 337-477-2827.

Technical Facilities: 150-kw ERP, 361-ft. above ground, 371-ft. above sea level, lat. 30° 00' 06", long. 94° 05' 37".

Began Operation: October 15, 2002.

Ownership: Blue Bonnet Communications Inc.

Beaumont-Orange—KUMY-LP, Ch. 22, Minority Broadcasting Co. LLC. Phone: 409-813-1000. Fax: 409-835-7250.

Technical Facilities: 138.2-kw ERP, 34-ft. above ground, 361-ft. above sea level, lat. 30° 02' 09", long. 94° 08' 31".

Ownership: Minority Broadcasting Co. II LLC.

■ **Beeville-Refugio**—K30EG, Ch. 30, KVOA Communications Inc. Phone: 361-886-6111.

Technical Facilities: 16.4-kw ERP, 344-ft. above ground, 430-ft. above sea level, lat. 28° 23' 27", long. 97° 25' 34".

Transmitter: W of intersection of State Rtes. 202 & 2441.

Beeville-Refugio—K49DV, Ch. 49, KVOA Communications Inc. Phone: 361-886-6111.

Technical Facilities: 15.2-kw ERP, 367-ft. above ground, 453-ft. above sea level, lat. 28° 23' 27", long. 97° 25' 34".

Transmitter: W of intersection of State Rtes. 202 & 2441.

Big Spring—K10HH, Ch. 10, ICA Broadcasting I Ltd. Phone: 915-334-8881.

Technical Facilities: 0.074-kw ERP, 162-ft. above ground, 2922-ft. above sea level, lat. 32° 13' 18", long. 101° 27' 30".

Ownership: ICA Broadcasting LLC.

Big Spring—K46FO, Ch. 46, Prime Time Christian Broadcasting Inc. Phone: 915-563-0420. Fax: 915-563-1736.

Technical Facilities: 100-w TPO, 0.561-kw ERP, 420-ft. above ground, 3687-ft. above sea level, lat. 32° 11' 06", long. 101° 27' 56".

Transmitter: 0.5-mi. N & 0.5-mi. E of Junction 87 & 83.

Ownership: Prime Time Christian Broadcasting Inc.

Personnel: Al Cooper, General Manager; Jay Westcott, Chief Engineer; Jeff Welter, Sales Manager.

Big Spring—K53IX, Ch. 53, Hispanic Christian Community Network Inc. Phone: 210-837-2178.

Technical Facilities: 7.9-kw ERP, 407-ft. above ground, 3167-ft. above sea level, lat. 32° 11' 00", long. 101° 27' 33".

Began Operation: August 3, 2007.

Ownership: Issac Ruiz Mora.

Big Spring—K54JQ, Ch. 54, Martin Weiss. Phone: 805-928-8300.

Technical Facilities: 15-kw ERP, 164-ft. above ground, 2913-ft. above sea level, lat. 32° 13' 13", long. 101° 26' 25".

Holds CP for change to 9.9-kw ERP, 66-ft. above sea level, BMPTTL-20080522ACE.

Ownership: Martin Weiss.

Big Spring—KABS-LP, Ch. 21, Una Vez Mas Big Spring License LLC. Phone: 214-754-7008.

Technical Facilities: 10-kw ERP, 325-ft. above ground, 3055-ft. above sea level, lat. 32° 13' 05.6", long. 101° 27' 08.6".

Ownership: Una Vez Mas GP LLC.

Booker—K47BP, Ch. 47, C L & O Translator System Inc.

Technical Facilities: 0.92-kw ERP, lat. 36° 22' 24", long. 100° 16' 00".

Ownership: C L & O Translator System Inc.

Bovina—K35CG, Ch. 35, Mission Broadcasting Inc. Phone: 330-335-8808.

Technical Facilities: 0.9-kw ERP, 308-ft. above ground, 4521-ft. above sea level, lat. 34° 35' 13", long. 102° 52' 04".

Holds CP for change to 0.005-kw ERP, BDFCDTT-20060403ACO.

Ownership: Mission Broadcasting Inc.

Bovina, etc.—K63GN, Ch. 63, Panhandle Telecasting LP. Phone: 806-383-1010.

Technical Facilities: 0.869-kw ERP, 302-ft. above ground, 4511-ft. above sea level, lat. 34° 35' 13", long. 102° 52' 06".

Holds CP for change to channel number 38, 0.39-kw ERP, BDISDTL-20081014ADP.

Began Operation: April 8, 1983.

Ownership: Panhandle Telecasting Co.

Brady, etc.—K05EF, Ch. 5, Foster Charitable Foundation Inc. Phone: 830-896-1230.

Technical Facilities: 0.068-kw ERP, 2254-ft. above sea level, lat. 31° 05' 43", long. 99° 22' 50".

Ownership: Foster Charitable Foundation Inc.

Brady/Rochelle—K02GM, Ch. 2, Foster Charitable Foundation Inc. Phone: 830-896-1230.

Technical Facilities: 0.069-kw ERP, 2297-ft. above sea level, lat. 31° 05' 43", long. 99° 22' 50".

Ownership: Foster Charitable Foundation Inc.

■ **Brady/Rochelle**—K04GI, Ch. 4, Foster Charitable Foundation Inc. Phone: 830-896-1230.

Technical Facilities: 0.069-kw ERP, lat. 31° 05' 43", long. 99° 22' 50".

Ownership: Foster Charitable Foundation Inc.

Britton—KODF-LP, Ch. 26, Mako Communications LLC. Phone: 361-883-1763. Fax: 361-883-3160.

Technical Facilities: 86-kw ERP, 591-ft. above ground, 1421-ft. above sea level, lat. 32° 35' 21", long. 96° 58' 12".

Ownership: Mako Communications LLC.

Brownsville—KBDF-LP, Ch. 64, Una Vez Mas Brownsville License LLC. Phone: 214-754-7008.

Technical Facilities: 1000-w TPO, 25.7-kw ERP, 379-ft. above ground, 409-ft. above sea level, lat. 26° 07' 25", long. 97° 29' 38".

Transmitter: 5-mi. NW of Los Fresnos.

Ownership: Una Vez Mas GP LLC.

■ **Brownsville**—KVTF-CA, Ch. 20, Entravision Holdings LLC. Phone: 310-447-3870.

Technical Facilities: 9-kw ERP, 466-ft. above ground, 489-ft. above sea level, lat. 25° 57' 49", long. 97° 31' 11".

Ownership: Entravision Communications Corp.

Brownsville—KXIV-LP, Ch. 17, Faith Pleases God Church Corp. Phone: 956-412-5600.

Technical Facilities: 20-w TPO, 0.131-kw ERP, 440-ft. above ground, 331-ft. above sea level, lat. 25° 58' 59", long. 97° 30' 40".

Transmitter: 1-mi. E of Hwy. 77 on Duncan Rd.

Ownership: Faith Pleases God Church Corp.

Personnel: Chuck Ortiz, General Manager; Carlos Macias, Chief Engineer.

Brownwood—K26AP, Ch. 26, Trinity Broadcasting Network Inc. Phone: 714-832-2950. Fax: 714-730-0661.

Technical Facilities: 1000-w TPO, 16.6-kw ERP, 259-ft. above ground, 1833-ft. above sea level, lat. 31° 39' 40", long. 99° 06' 00".

Transmitter: 6-mi. SW of Brownwood.

Ownership: Trinity Broadcasting Network Inc.

Personnel: Paul Crouch, General Manager; Ben Miller, Chief Engineer; Rod Henke, Sales Manager.

■ **Brownwood**—KIDU-LP, Ch. 17, Bayou City Broadcasting LLC. Phone: 281-380-0076.

Technical Facilities: 10-kw ERP, 312-ft. above ground, 1920-ft. above sea level, lat. 31° 52' 12", long. 99° 07' 13".

Began Operation: July 11, 1994.

Ownership: Bayou City Broadcasting LLC.

Bryan—KMAY-LP, Ch. 23, KCEN License Co. LLC. Phone: 214-812-9600.

Technical Facilities: 5-kw ERP, 561-ft. above ground, 942-ft. above sea level, lat. 30° 41' 18", long. 96° 25' 35".

Ownership: London Broadcasting Co. Inc.

■ **Bryan**—KRHD-LP, Ch. 40, Centex Television LP. Phone: 254-754-2525.

Technical Facilities: 70-kw ERP, 419-ft. above ground, 793-ft. above sea level, lat. 30° 45' 35", long. 96° 28' 00".

Ownership: Centex Television LP.

Personnel: Jerry Pursley, General Manager.

Bryan—KSCM-LP, Ch. 18, Midessa Broadcasting LP. Phones: 254-754-2525; 580-355-7000.

Technical Facilities: 54-kw ERP, 361-ft. above ground, 735-ft. above sea level, lat. 30° 45' 35", long. 96° 28' 00".

Ownership: Midessa Broadcasting LP.

Canadian—K23EC, Ch. 23, C L & O Translator System Inc.

Technical Facilities: 0.603-kw ERP, 404-ft. above ground, 3163-ft. above sea level, lat. 36° 04' 06", long. 100° 21' 01".

Canadian—K31CD, Ch. 31, C L & O Translator System Inc.

Technical Facilities: 100-w TPO, 0.728-kw ERP, 404-ft. above ground, 3205-ft. above sea level, lat. 36° 04' 06", long. 100° 21' 01".

Transmitter: 10-mi. N of Canadian.

Ownership: C L & O Translator System Inc.

Canadian, etc.—K29BR, Ch. 29, C L & O Translator System Inc.

Technical Facilities: 0.713-kw ERP, 394-ft. above ground, 3202-ft. above sea level, lat. 36° 04' 06", long. 100° 21' 01".

Canadian, etc.—K33CQ, Ch. 33, C L & O Translator System Inc.

Technical Facilities: 0.713-kw ERP, 404-ft. above ground, 3202-ft. above sea level, lat. 36° 04' 06", long. 100° 21' 01".

Canadian, etc.—K35CE, Ch. 35, C L & O Translator System Inc.

Technical Facilities: 0.71-kw ERP, 394-ft. above ground, 3202-ft. above sea level, lat. 36° 04' 06", long. 100° 21' 01".

Canyon—KZBZ-LP, Ch. 46, Panhandle Telecasting LP. Phone: 806-383-1010.

Technical Facilities: 150-kw ERP, 187-ft. above ground, 3757-ft. above sea level, lat. 34° 58' 58", long. 101° 56' 05".

Ownership: Panhandle Telecasting Co.

Carrizo Springs—KSPG-LP, Ch. 11, Aracelis Ortiz Corp. Phone: 956-421-2635.

Technical Facilities: 10-w TPO, 0.059-kw ERP, 50-ft. above ground, 672-ft. above sea level, lat. 28° 29' 17", long. 99° 53' 06".

Transmitter: 3.3-mi. SW of downtown.

Ownership: Aracelis Ortiz Corp.

Childress—K23DE, Ch. 23, Red River Valley Translator TV Assn.

Technical Facilities: 0.956-kw ERP, 285-ft. above ground, 2195-ft. above sea level, lat. 34° 25' 57", long. 100° 13' 47".

Childress—K25CQ, Ch. 25, Red River Valley Translator TV Assn.

Technical Facilities: 0.18-kw ERP, lat. 34° 25' 57", long. 100° 13' 47".

Childress—K50CQ, Ch. 50, Red River Valley Translator TV Assn.

Technical Facilities: 0.97-kw ERP, 285-ft. above ground, 2195-ft. above sea level, lat. 34° 25' 57", long. 100° 13' 47".

Childress—K52DF, Ch. 52, Red River Valley Translator TV Assn.

Technical Facilities: 0.177-kw ERP, lat. 34° 25' 57", long. 100° 13' 47".

Childress, etc.—K46CN, Ch. 46, Red River Valley Translator TV Assn.

Technical Facilities: 0.97-kw ERP, 285-ft. above ground, 2238-ft. above sea level, lat. 34° 25' 57", long. 100° 13' 47".

Childress, etc.—K48DD, Ch. 48, Red River Valley Translator TV Assn.

Technical Facilities: 0.97-kw ERP, 285-ft. above ground, 2238-ft. above sea level, lat. 34° 25' 57", long. 100° 13' 47".

Clarendon—K17DS, Ch. 17, Amarillo Junior College District.

Technical Facilities: 1.01-kw ERP, 239-ft. above ground, 3140-ft. above sea level, lat. 34° 54' 03", long. 100° 55' 50".

Clarendon—K45DM, Ch. 45, Donley County UHF TV Inc.

Technical Facilities: 1.01-kw ERP, 239-ft. above ground, 3140-ft. above sea level, lat. 34° 54' 11", long. 100° 55' 47".

Clarendon—K47BQ, Ch. 47, Donley County UHF TV Inc.

Technical Facilities: 1.01-kw ERP, lat. 34° 54' 03", long. 100° 55' 50".

Clarendon—K49AQ, Ch. 49, Donley County UHF TV Inc.

Technical Facilities: 1.01-kw ERP, lat. 34° 54' 03", long. 100° 55' 50".

Clarendon—K51CB, Ch. 51, Donley County UHF TV Inc.

Technical Facilities: 1.01-kw ERP, lat. 34° 54' 03", long. 100° 55' 50".

Clear Lake—KVDO-LP, Ch. 25, Far Eastern Telecasters. Phones: 817-430-9444; 301-299-3146.

Technical Facilities: 23.5-kw ERP, 1737-ft. above ground, 1813-ft. above sea level, lat. 29° 34' 16", long. 95° 30' 38".

Holds CP for change to 10-kw ERP, BDFCDTL-20081125AVY.

Began Operation: October 6, 1998.

Ownership: Far Eastern Telecasters.

Clear Lake City—KJIB-LP, Ch. 5, Far Eastern Telecasters. Phone: 301-299-3146.

Technical Facilities: 0.103-kw ERP, 469-ft. above ground, 479-ft. above sea level, lat. 29° 35' 33", long. 95° 03' 11".

Holds CP for change to channel number 29, 10-kw ERP, 1737-ft. above ground, 1813-ft. above sea level, lat. 29° 34' 16", long. 95° 30' 38". BDISDTL-20080514AGQ.

Ownership: Far Eastern Telecasters.

College Station—K47ED, Ch. 47, Trinity Broadcasting Network Inc. Phone: 714-832-2950. Fax: 714-730-0661.

Technical Facilities: 1000-w TPO, 11.7-kw ERP, 344-ft. above ground, 663-ft. above sea level, lat. 30° 39' 02", long. 96° 20' 57".

Holds CP for change to 15-kw ERP, lat. 30° 39' 02", long. 96° 20' 58". BDFCDTL-20060331AUB.

Transmitter: 0.5-mi. NNE of junction of State Rte. 507 & Villa Maria Rd., Bryan.

Ownership: Trinity Broadcasting Network Inc.

Corpus Christi—K29IP-D, Ch. 29, Lawrence H. Mintz. Phone: 361-883-1763.

Technical Facilities: 0.95-kw ERP, 322-ft. above ground, 364-ft. above sea level, lat. 27° 47' 26.4", long. 97° 27' 01.5".

Began Operation: February 10, 2009.

Ownership: Lawrence Howard Mintz.

■ **Corpus Christi**—K47DF, Ch. 47, KVOA Communications Inc. Phone: 361-886-6111.

Technical Facilities: 10.2-kw ERP, 164-ft. above ground, 190-ft. above sea level, lat. 27° 43' 02", long. 97° 23' 19".

Corpus Christi—K54JS, Ch. 54, Howard Mintz. Phone: 361-883-1763.

Technical Facilities: 4-kw ERP, 322-ft. above ground, 364-ft. above sea level, lat. 27° 47' 26.3", long. 97° 27' 01.5".

Holds CP for change to channel number 20, 5.5-kw ERP, BDISTTL-20080509ACA.

Ownership: Howard Mintz.

Corpus Christi—K57FC, Ch. 57, Trinity Broadcasting Network Inc. Phone: 714-832-2950. Fax: 714-730-0661.

Technical Facilities: 425-w TPO, 94.4-kw ERP, 276-ft. above ground, 312-ft. above sea level, lat. 27° 47' 48", long. 97° 23' 51".

Holds CP for change to 10-kw ERP, BPTT-20050505ACA.

Transmitter: 0.25-mi. S of Interstate 37 & U.S. Rte. 81 intersection.

Ownership: Trinity Broadcasting Network Inc.

Corpus Christi—K68DJ, Ch. 68, KVOA Communications Inc. Phone: 361-886-6111.

Technical Facilities: 1000-w TPO, 21.7-kw ERP, 175-ft. above ground, 187-ft. above sea level, lat. 27° 43' 02", long. 97° 23' 19".

Transmitter: 4518 S. Padre Island Dr.

Ownership: KVOA Communications Inc.

Corpus Christi—KADM-LP, Ch. 63, Aracelis Ortiz Corp. Phone: 956-412-9101.

Technical Facilities: 33.2-kw ERP, 246-ft. above ground, 285-ft. above sea level, lat. 27° 47' 48", long. 97° 23' 49".

Transmitter: corner of N. Carancahua & Antelope Sts.

Ownership: Aracelis Ortiz Corp.

Corpus Christi—KCBO-LP, Ch. 49, Channel 7 of Corpus Christi Inc. Phone: 361-882-1414. Fax: 361-882-1793.

Studio: 600 Leopard, Ste 1924, Corpus Christi, TX 78473.

Technical Facilities: 9.9-kw ERP, 322-ft. above ground, 361-ft. above sea level, lat. 27° 47' 46", long. 97° 23' 47".

Multichannel TV Sound: Stereo only.

Ownership: Channel 7 of Corpus Christi Inc.

Personnel: Don Gillis, General Manager; Fred Hoffmann, Chief Engineer.

Corpus Christi—KCCG-LP, Ch. 33, KM Communications Inc. Phone: 847-674-0864.

Technical Facilities: 2.6-kw ERP, 325-ft. above ground, 365-ft. above sea level, lat. 27° 47' 46", long. 97° 23' 47".

Ownership: KM Communications Inc.

Corpus Christi—KCCX-LP, Ch. 24, Mako Communications LLC. Phone: 361-883-1763.

Studio: 3930 Leopard St., Corpus Christi, TX 78408.

Technical Facilities: 9-kw ERP, 322-ft. above ground, 364-ft. above sea level, lat. 27° 47' 26.4", long. 97° 27' 01.5".

Ownership: Mako Communications LLC.

Personnel: Amanda Orrick, President; Don Shelton, General Manager & Sales Manager; Ron Turner, Chief Engineer.

Corpus Christi—KCCZ-LP, Ch. 61, Gerald G. Benavides. Phone: 361-241-7944.

Technical Facilities: 10-kw ERP, 282-ft. above ground, 315-ft. above sea level, lat. 27° 47' 48", long. 97° 24' 15".

Ownership: Gerald G. Benavides.

■ **Corpus Christi**—KCRP-CA, Ch. 41, Nicolas Communications Corp. Phone: 512-824-5812.

Technical Facilities: 12.1-kw ERP, 352-ft. above sea level, lat. 27° 47' 46", long. 96° 23' 47".

Transmitter: 102 N. Mesquite.

Ownership: Nicolas Communications Corp.

Personnel: Anita Saenz-Carvalho, General Manager.

Corpus Christi—KDCP-LP, Ch. 19, Word of God Fellowship Inc. Phone: 817-571-1229.

Technical Facilities: 150-kw ERP, 361-ft. above ground, 456-ft. above sea level, lat. 27° 56' 49", long. 97° 38' 51".

Holds CP for change to 9.999-kw ERP, 623-ft above av. terrain, 686-ft. above ground, 27-ft. above sea level, lat. 45° 32' 97", long. 36° 26' 1". BPTTL-20070507AAC.

Ownership: Word of God Fellowship Inc.

■ **Corpus Christi**—KHCC-LP, Ch. 35, Minerva R. Lopez. Phone: 361-289-8877.

Technical Facilities: 14.9-kw ERP, 292-ft. above ground, 331-ft. above sea level, lat. 27° 45' 09", long. 97° 27' 18".

Ownership: Minerva R. Lopez.

■ **Corpus Christi**—KLAO-LP, Ch. 43, Hosanna Apostolic Ministries Broadcasting Corp. Phone: 520-971-9274.

Technical Facilities: 500-w TPO, 7.28-kw ERP, 403-ft. above ground, 413-ft. above sea level, lat. 27° 47' 59", long. 97° 23' 30".

Holds CP for change to channel number 51, 10-kw ERP, BDISTTL-20070827AAN.

Began Operation: April 22, 1991.

Ownership: Hosanna Apostolic Ministries Broadcasting Corp.

Corpus Christi—KTMV-LP, Ch. 8, Minerva R. Lopez. Phone: 361-289-8877. Fax: 361-289-7722.

Technical Facilities: 10-w TPO, 0.2-kw ERP, 292-ft. above ground, 331-ft. above sea level, lat. 27° 45' 09", long. 97° 27' 18".

Holds CP for change to channel number 50, 4.2-kw ERP, 203-ft. above ground, 239-ft. above sea level, lat. 27° 45' 10", long. 97° 27' 18". BPTTL-20041220AAE.

Transmitter: 828 South Padre Island Dr.

Multichannel TV Sound: Stereo only.

Ownership: Minerva R. Lopez.

Personnel: Carlos Lopez, General Manager; Ernest Lopez, Sales Manager; Ray Lopez, Chief Engineer.

Corpus Christi—KTOV-LP, Ch. 21, GH Broadcasting Inc. Phone: 361-882-1414. Fax: 361-882-1973.

Studio: 600 Leopard St, Ste 1924, Corpus Christi, TX 78473.

Technical Facilities: 95-kw ERP, 289-ft. above ground, 328-ft. above sea level, lat. 27° 47' 46", long. 897° 23' 47".

Ownership: GH Broadcasting Inc.

Personnel: Don Gillis, General Manager; Fred Hoffman, Chief Engineer.

Corpus Christi—KVVC-LP, Ch. 69, Windsong Communications Inc. Phone: 936-443-4451.

Technical Facilities: 4-kw ERP, 322-ft. above ground, 364-ft. above sea level, lat. 22° 47' 26.3", long. 97° 27' 01.53".

Holds CP for change to channel number 42, 9.99-kw ERP, BDISTTL-20081124AED.

Ownership: Windsong Communications Inc.

■ **Corpus Christi**—KWDT-LP, Ch. 13, Clark Ortiz. Phone: 210-412-8605. Fax: 210-440-0542.

Technical Facilities: 40-w TPO, 0.202-kw ERP, 403-ft. above ground, 413-ft. above sea level, lat. 27° 47' 59", long. 97° 23' 30".

Transmitter: One Shoreline Dr.

Ownership: Clark Ortiz.

Personnel: Clark Ortiz, General Manager.

■ **Corpus Christi**—KXCC-CA, Ch. 45, Casa of Corpus Christi LP (A Delaware LP). Phones: 512-824-5812; 512-824-3435.

Technical Facilities: 1000-w TPO, 12.8-kw ERP, 371-ft. above ground, 308-ft. above sea level, lat. 27° 47' 46", long. 97° 23' 47".

Transmitter: 600 Leopard St., Corpus Christi.

Ownership: Pappas Telecasting Companies.

■ **Corpus Christi**—KXPX-CA, Ch. 14, GH Broadcasting Inc. Phone: 361-882-1414.

Studio: 5026 Old Brownsville Rd., Corpus Christi, TX 78416.

Technical Facilities: 350-w TPO, 8-kw ERP, 289-ft. above ground, 328-ft. above sea level, lat. 27° 47' 47", long. 97° 23' 48".

Transmitter: 600 Bldg., 600 Leopard St.

Ownership: Communications Transmission Network.

Corpus Christi—KYDF-LP, Ch. 34, Una Vez Mas Corpus Christi License LLC. Phone: 214-754-7008.

Technical Facilities: 14-kw ERP, 423-ft. above ground, 432-ft. above sea level, lat. 27° 47' 58.9", long. 97° 23' 30".

Ownership: Una Vez Mas GP LLC.

Corsicana—K25FW, Ch. 25, Ventana Television Inc. Phone: 727-872-4210.

Technical Facilities: 1000-w TPO, 47.2-kw ERP, 886-ft. above ground, 1669-ft. above sea level, lat. 32° 31' 52", long. 96° 56' 57".

Transmitter: 3.6-mi. N of Midlothian.

Began Operation: March 20, 2000.

Ownership: Ventana Television Inc.

Crockett—KIVY-LP, Ch. 16, Jim Gibbs. Phone: 409-544-2171. Fax: 409-544-4891.

Technical Facilities: 1000-w TPO, 8.3-kw ERP, 400-ft. above ground, 755-ft. above sea level, lat. 31° 18' 20", long. 95° 27' 06".

Transmitter: KIVY-FM transmitter site.

Ownership: Jim Gibbs.

Personnel: Jim Gibbs, General Manager.

Crockett—KTWC-LP, Ch. 12, International Broadcasting Network. Phone: 713-251-1426.

Technical Facilities: 80-w TPO, 11.143-kw ERP, 495-ft. above ground, 925-ft. above sea level, lat. 31° 17' 37", long. 95° 28' 54".

Transmitter: Near intersection of Loop 304 & FM 2110.

Ownership: International Broadcasting Network.

Dallas—KLEG-LP, Ch. 44, Deepak Viswanath. Phone: 718-479-9411.

Technical Facilities: 1190-w TPO, 20-kw ERP, 208-ft. above ground, 1358-ft. above sea level, lat. 32° 46' 48", long. 96° 48' 13".

Transmitter: Main & Lamar Sts.

Ownership: Dilip B. Viswanath.

Dallas—KSEX-LP, Ch. 57, D.T.V. LLC. Phone: 800-536-7327.

Technical Facilities: 4000-w TPO, 100-kw ERP, 801-ft. above ground, 1604-ft. above sea level, lat. 32° 35' 19", long. 96° 58' 06".

Holds CP for change to channel number 20, 35-kw ERP, 328-ft. above ground, 1038-ft. above sea level, lat. 33° 00' 48", long. 96° 46' 51". BDISTTL-20051021AGR.

Transmitter: 1310 W. Beltline Dr., Cedar Hill.

Ownership: D.T.V. LLC.

Dallas & Mesquite—KJJM-LD, Ch. 34, Mako Communications LLC. Phone: 361-883-1763.

Technical Facilities: 15-kw ERP, 853-ft. above ground, 1683-ft. above sea level, lat. 32° 35' 21", long. 96° 58' 12".

Began Operation: January 18, 2000.

Ownership: Mako Communications LLC.

Personnel: Chad Russel, General Manager.

De Soto—K31GL-D, Ch. 31, Mako Communications LLC. Phone: 361-883-1763.

Technical Facilities: 8-kw ERP, 1083-ft. above ground, 1913-ft. above sea level, lat. 32° 35' 21", long. 96° 58' 12".

Ownership: Mako Communications LLC.

De Soto—KHPK-LD, Ch. 28, Mako Communications LLC. Phone: 361-883-1763. Fax: 361-883-3160.

Technical Facilities: 0.3-kw ERP, 892-ft. above ground, 1722-ft. above sea level, lat. 32° 35' 21.5", long. 96° 58' 11.88".

Ownership: Mako Communications LLC.

Del Rio—K55HV, Ch. 55, Jose Villareal, DBA Villareal Broadcasting.

Technical Facilities: 10-w TPO, 0.053-kw ERP, 75-ft. above ground, 1000-ft. above sea level, lat. 29° 22' 25", long. 100° 50' 06".

Transmitter: 3.9-mi. E of downtown.

Ownership: Villareal Broadcasting.

DeLeon—K38IO, Ch. 38, Foster Charitable Foundation Inc. Phone: 830-896-1230.

Technical Facilities: 0.1-kw ERP, 39-ft. above ground, 1329-ft. above sea level, lat. 32° 11' 05", long. 98° 31' 38".

Ownership: Foster Charitable Foundation Inc.

Denison—KHFW-LP, Ch. 30, Hispanic Christian Community Network Inc. Phone: 214-879-0001.

Technical Facilities: 0.3-kw ERP, 49-ft. above ground, 712-ft. above sea level, lat. 33° 51' 15", long. 96° 30' 02".

Began Operation: August 13, 2008.

Ownership: Hispanic Christian Community Network Inc.

Denison—KQFW-LP, Ch. 7, Hispanic Christian Community Network Inc. Phone: 214-434-6357.

Technical Facilities: 0.5-kw ERP, 16-ft. above ground, 673-ft. above sea level, lat. 33° 52' 20", long. 96° 28' 12".

Holds CP for change to 0.3-kw ERP, 1001-ft. above ground, 1722-ft. above sea level, lat. 33° 32' 08", long. 96° 49' 54". BDVCDVL-20081006AHT.

Ownership: Hispanic Christian Community Network Inc.

DeSoto—KNAV-LP, Ch. 22, Tuck Properties Inc. Phone: 202-293-0569.

Technical Facilities: 150-kw ERP, 1142-ft. above ground, 1972-ft. above sea level, lat. 32° 35' 21", long. 96° 58' 12".

Ownership: Tuck Properties Inc.

Personnel: Brian J. Weber, Chief Engineer.

■ **Dewalt**—KUVM-CA, Ch. 34, Club Communications. Phones: 512-814-9830; 361-883-1763. Fax: 512-855-2718.

Technical Facilities: 115-kw ERP, 1148-ft. above ground, 1148-ft. above sea level, lat. 29° 34' 15", long. 95° 30' 37".

Ownership: Club Communications.

Personnel: Gerald Benavides, General Manager.

Eagle Pass—KEAP-LP, Ch. 3, CTV Broadcasting LLC. Phone: 713-358-4229.

Technical Facilities: 10-w TPO, 0.034-kw ERP, 187-ft. above ground, lat. 28° 44' 06", long. 100° 28' 55".

Transmitter: NE edge of Eagle Pass.

Ownership: CTV Broadcasting LLC.

Personnel: Chuck Ortiz, General Manager; Carlos Macias, Chief Engineer.

El Paso—K40FW, Ch. 40, BGM License LLC. Phone: 915-585-6344. Fax: 915-577-0045.

Technical Facilities: 8.75-kw ERP, 92-ft. above ground, 5843-ft. above sea level, lat. 31° 48' 57", long. 106° 29' 20".

Ownership: Broadcast Group Holdings Inc.

Evant—K57JI, Ch. 57, Mark Silberman. Phone: 310-552-7970. Fax: 310-277-3069.

Technical Facilities: 0.999-kw ERP, 216-ft. above ground, 1668-ft. above sea level, lat. 31° 27' 05", long. 98° 07' 12".

Ownership: Mark Silberman.

Falfurrias—K07TS, Ch. 7, New Covenant Church. Phone: 512-325-3434.

Technical Facilities: 10-w TPO, 0.07-kw ERP, 138-ft. above ground, 259-ft. above sea level, lat. 27° 13' 46", long. 98° 08' 52".

Ownership: New Covenant Church.

Floresville—K45DX, Ch. 45, Telefutura Partnership of Floresville. Phone: 310-556-7600.

Technical Facilities: 1000-w TPO, 5.7-kw ERP, 279-ft. above ground, 679-ft. above sea level, lat. 29° 07' 49", long. 98° 08' 54".

Transmitter: 0.5-mi. S of U.S. 181 on Hospital Blvd.

Ownership: Univision Communications Inc.

Follett—K45AU, Ch. 45, C L & O Translator System Inc.

Technical Facilities: 1.04-kw ERP, 213-ft. above ground, 2913-ft. above sea level, lat. 36° 22' 24", long. 100° 16' 00".

Follett—K49BB, Ch. 49, C L & O Translator System Inc.

Technical Facilities: 1.04-kw ERP, 213-ft. above ground, 2913-ft. above sea level, lat. 36° 22' 24", long. 100° 16' 00".

Follett—K51BC, Ch. 51, C L & O Translator System Inc.

Technical Facilities: 1.04-kw ERP, 213-ft. above ground, 2913-ft. above sea level, lat. 36° 22' 24", long. 100° 16' 00".

Follett—K53EE, Ch. 53, C L & O Translator System Inc.

Technical Facilities: 1.04-kw ERP, 213-ft. above ground, 2913-ft. above sea level, lat. 36° 22' 24", long. 100° 16' 00".

Forbes & Jasper County—K59IL, Ch. 59, Sydcom Inc. Phone: 337-477-2827.

Technical Facilities: 1.7-kw ERP, 130-ft. above ground, 187-ft. above sea level, lat. 30° 25' 49", long. 93° 58' 49".

Ownership: Sydcom Inc.

Fort Stockton—K12FM, Ch. 12, Nexstar Finance Inc. Phone: 972-373-8800.

Technical Facilities: 0.2-kw ERP, lat. 30° 52' 51", long. 102° 51' 09".

Holds CP for change to 0.0005-kw ERP, 194-ft. above ground, 3186-ft. above sea level, lat. 30° 52' 50", long. 102° 51' 07". BDFCDTT-20060403ACM.

Ownership: Nexstar Broadcasting Group Inc.

■ **Fort Worth**—KUVN-CA, Ch. 47, KUVN License Partnership LP. Phone: 214-758-2300. Fax: 214-758-2350.

Technical Facilities: 16.2-kw ERP, 574-ft. above ground, 1184-ft. above sea level, lat. 32° 45' 01", long. 97° 20' 04".

Transmitter: 801 Cherry St.

Ownership: Univision Communications Inc.

Personnel: Becky Munoz Diaz, General Manager; Page Graham, Chief Engineer; Buff Parham, Sales Manager.

Fort Worth—KVFW-LP, Ch. 38, Gerald G. Benavides. Phone: 361-774-4354.

Technical Facilities: 112.5-kw ERP, 787-ft. above ground, 1611-ft. above sea level, lat. 32° 35' 21", long. 96° 58' 12".

Holds CP for change to 15-kw ERP, 787-ft. above ground, 1617-ft. above sea level, BDFCDTL-20081205ADK.

Began Operation: February 25, 2000.

Ownership: Gerald G. Benavides.

■ **Fredericksburg**—KHPF-CA, Ch. 44, KXAN Inc. Phone: 202-462-6065. Fax: 512-476-1520.

Technical Facilities: 1000-w TPO, 9-kw ERP, 295-ft. above ground, 2054-ft. above sea level, lat. 30° 15' 35", long. 98° 53' 13".

Holds CP for change to 0.043-kw ERP, BDFCDTA-20060329AHQ.

Transmitter: On Hwy. 165, NE of Hwy. 16 & Tivydale Rd. intersection.

Ownership: LIN TV Corp.

Freeport—K10PY-D, Ch. 10, Mako Communications LLC. Phone: 361-883-1763.

Technical Facilities: 0.3-kw ERP, 961-ft. above ground, 1036-ft. above sea level, lat. 29° 33' 44.3", long. 95° 30' 34.9".

Ownership: Mako Communications LLC.

Freeport—K30DN, Ch. 30, Mako Communications LLC. Phone: 361-883-1763.

Studio: 1701 W. 2nd St., Freeport, TX 77541.

Technical Facilities: 9-kw ERP, 374-ft. above ground, 384-ft. above sea level, lat. 29° 07' 29", long. 95° 21' 24".

Ownership: Mako Communications LLC.

Personnel: Claude E. Johnson, General Manager.

Friona & Bovina—K57CW, Ch. 57, Barrington Amarillo License LLC. Phone: 847-884-1877.

Technical Facilities: 0.928-kw ERP, lat. 34° 35' 13", long. 102° 52' 04".

Ownership: Pilot Group LP.

Gainesville—KBFW-LP, Ch. 6, Gerald G. Benavides. Phone: 361-774-4354.

Technical Facilities: 3-kw ERP, 571-ft. above ground, 1184-ft. above sea level, lat. 32° 45' 01", long. 97° 20' 03".

Holds CP for change to 0.3-kw ERP, BDFCDVL-20090211AAF.

Began Operation: September 17, 2004.

Ownership: Gerald G. Benavides.

Gainesville—KPFW-LP, Ch. 61, Iglesia Jesucristo Es Mi Refugio Inc. Phone: 214-330-8700.

Technical Facilities: 100-kw ERP, 984-ft. above ground, 1667-ft. above sea level, lat. 33° 32' 08", long. 96° 49' 55".

Holds CP for change to 15-kw ERP, 932-ft. above ground, 1358-ft. above sea level, lat. 32° 46' 48", long. 96° 48' 13". BDFCDTL-20080924AJI.

Ownership: Iglesia Jesucristo Es Mi Refugio Inc.

Gainesville—KSFW-LP, Ch. 2, Hispanic Christian Community Network Inc. Phones: 214-434-6357; 214-879-0081.

Technical Facilities: 1-kw ERP, 49-ft. above ground, 948-ft. above sea level, lat. 33° 50' 19", long. 97° 07' 32".

Began Operation: August 13, 2008.

Ownership: Hispanic Christian Community Network Inc.

Garfield—KVAT-LP, Ch. 17, Mako Communications LLC. Phone: 361-883-1763. Fax: 361-883-3160.

Technical Facilities: 60-kw ERP, 643-ft. above ground, 1440-ft. above sea level, lat. 30° 19' 23.6", long. 97° 47' 58.3".

Holds CP for change to 2-kw ERP, 643-ft. above ground, 1461-ft. above sea level, BDFCDTL-20090217AAZ.

Ownership: Mako Communications LLC.

■ **Georgetown**—KHPX-CA, Ch. 28, KXAN Inc. Phone: 512-476-3636. Fax: 512-476-1520.

Technical Facilities: 7.4-kw ERP, 436-ft. above ground, 1296-ft. above sea level, lat. 30° 36' 04", long. 97° 39' 34".

Ownership: LIN TV Corp.

■ **Giddings**—KHPG-CA, Ch. 31, KXAN Inc. Phones: 512-476-3636; 202-462-6065. Fax: 512-476-1520.

Technical Facilities: 1000-w TPO, 8.65-kw ERP, 108-ft. above ground, 610-ft. above sea level, lat. 30° 10' 53", long. 96° 56' 01".

Transmitter: E of U.S. Rte. 290 & U.S. Rte. 77 intersection.

Ownership: LIN TV Corp.

Greenville—KHFD-LD, Ch. 51, EICB-TV East LLC. Phone: 972-291-3750.

Technical Facilities: 5-kw ERP, 414-ft. above ground, 991-ft. above sea level, lat. 32° 58' 07", long. 96° 20' 30".

Ownership: EICB-TV LLC.

Gruver—K38BU, Ch. 38, Hansford County TV Translator System.

Technical Facilities: 0.815-kw ERP, 410-ft. above ground, 3579-ft. above sea level, lat. 36° 15' 00", long. 101° 22' 40".

Gruver—K40DD, Ch. 40, Hansford County TV Translator System.

Technical Facilities: 0.815-kw ERP, 3579-ft. above sea level, lat. 36° 15' 00", long. 101° 22' 40".

Gruver—K42CF, Ch. 42, Hansford County TV Translator System.

Technical Facilities: 0.815-kw ERP, 410-ft. above ground, 3579-ft. above sea level, lat. 36° 15' 00", long. 101° 22' 40".

Gruver—K44CC, Ch. 44, Hansford County TV Translator System.

Technical Facilities: 0.815-kw ERP, 410-ft. above ground, 3579-ft. above sea level, lat. 36° 15' 00", long. 101° 22' 40".

Harlingen—KTIZ-LP, Ch. 52, Entravision Holdings LLC. Phone: 310-447-3870.

Technical Facilities: 1000-w TPO, 10.1-kw ERP, 295-ft. above ground, 325-ft. above sea level, lat. 26° 09' 14", long. 97° 41' 16".

Transmitter: New Hampshire Rd.

Ownership: Entravision Communications Corp.

Harper—K17GZ, Ch. 17, Foster Charitable Foundation Inc. Phone: 830-896-1230.

Technical Facilities: 0.1-kw ERP, 39-ft. above ground, 2239-ft. above sea level, lat. 30° 20' 29", long. 99° 13' 23".

Ownership: Foster Charitable Foundation Inc.

Hereford—K44GW, Ch. 44, Hosanna Apostolic Ministries Broadcasting Corp. Phone: 520-971-9274.

Technical Facilities: 3-kw ERP, 328-ft. above ground, 4154-ft. above sea level, lat. 34° 51' 02", long. 102° 23' 38".

Began Operation: August 25, 2006.

Ownership: Hosanna Apostolic Ministries Broadcasting Corp.

Houston—KBPX-LP, Ch. 33, ION Media LPTV Inc., Debtor in Possession. Phones: 713-533-5301; 561-682-4206.

Technical Facilities: 1000-w TPO, 34.3-kw ERP, 1656-ft. above ground, 1736-ft. above sea level, lat. 29° 34' 34", long. 95° 30' 36".

Began Operation: December 21, 1988.

Ownership: ION Media Networks Inc., Debtor in Possession.

Personnel: Carol Wright Holzhauer, General Manager; Bob Mardock, Chief Engineer; Mike Kay, Sales Manager.

Houston—KCVH-LP, Ch. 30, DAIJ Media LLC. Phone: 713-589-1336.

Technical Facilities: 70-kw ERP, 1040-ft. above ground, 1115-ft. above sea level, lat. 29° 33' 44", long. 95° 30' 35".

Multichannel TV Sound: Stereo only.

Began Operation: April 21, 1994.

Ownership: DAIJ Media LLC.

Personnel: Charlene Weh, General Manager; Kenneth Casey, Sales Manager & Chief Engineer.

Houston—KHLM-LP, Ch. 43, Lotus Merger Sub LLC. Phone: 323-512-2225.

Technical Facilities: 84.9-kw ERP, 1421-ft. above ground, 1495-ft. above sea level, lat. 29° 33' 44", long. 95° 30' 35".

Holds CP for change to 15-kw ERP, BDFCDTL-20090126ACD.

Began Operation: March 30, 1992.

Ownership: Lotus Communications Corp.

■ **Houston**—KHMV-CA, Ch. 28, Pappas Telecasting of the Gulf Coast LP (A Delaware LP). Phone: 559-733-7800.

Technical Facilities: 26-kw ERP, 1585-ft. above ground, 1661-ft. above sea level, lat. 29° 34' 15", long. 95° 30' 37".

Ownership: Pappas Telecasting Companies.

Houston—KVQT-LP, Ch. 21, C. Dowen Johnson. Phone: 936-436-4451.

Technical Facilities: 50-kw ERP, 449-ft. above ground, 526-ft. above sea level, lat. 29° 34' 15", long. 95° 30' 37".

Holds CP for change to 10.5-kw ERP, 1099-ft above av. terrain, 1176-ft. above ground, BDFCDTL-20081216AOI.

Ownership: C. Dowen Johnson.

Houston—KVVV-LP, Ch. 53, Pappas Telecasting of the Gulf Coast LP. Phone: 559-733-7800.

Technical Facilities: 150-kw ERP, 466-ft. above ground, 472-ft. above sea level, lat. 29° 24' 40", long. 94° 57' 04".

Holds CP for change to channel number 15, 15-kw ERP, BDISDTL-20060302AAL.

Ownership: Pappas Telecasting Companies.

Huntsville—KHTX-LP, Ch. 31, International Broadcasting Network. Phone: 513-399-7777.

Technical Facilities: 1000-w TPO, 8.83-kw ERP, 387-ft. above ground, 797-ft. above sea level, lat. 30° 42' 13", long. 95° 28' 32".

Transmitter: S of Hwy. 190, 5.5-mi. E of Walker County Courthouse.

Ownership: Laura L. Fenton; International Broadcasting Network.

Huntsville—KHXL-LP, Ch. 7, International Broadcasting Network. Phone: 281-774-9923.

Technical Facilities: 2.4-kw ERP, 427-ft. above ground, 837-ft. above sea level, lat. 30° 42' 13", long. 95° 28' 32".

Transmitter: 601 Boettcher Mill Rd.

Ownership: International Broadcasting Network.

Jasper—K54JK, Ch. 54, Grace Fellowship Church. Phone: 409-670-3656.

Technical Facilities: 15.9-kw ERP, 400-ft. above ground, 821-ft. above sea level, lat. 30° 58' 31.3", long. 93° 59' 24.3".

Began Operation: August 7, 2007.

Ownership: Grace Fellowship Church.

Jasper—KVHP-LP, Ch. 66, Blue Bonnet Communications Inc. Phone: 337-477-2827.

Technical Facilities: 20-kw ERP, 328-ft. above ground, 748-ft. above sea level, lat. 30° 58' 32", long. 93° 59' 25".

Began Operation: May 13, 2003.

Ownership: Blue Bonnet Communications Inc.

Keene—KGSW-LP, Ch. 31, Southwestern Adventist U. Phones: 817-556-4764; 817-645-3921. Fax: 817-556-4744.

Technical Facilities: 14.1-kw ERP, 154-ft. above ground, 1063-ft. above sea level, lat. 32° 24' 19", long. 97° 19' 55".

Transmitter: College Campus, 0.3-mi. W of Rte. 2280.

Ownership: Southwestern Adventist U.

Personnel: David Chapline, Chief Engineer.

Kerrville—KVHC-LP, Ch. 15, Mary R. Silver. Phone: 830-792-5942.

Technical Facilities: 7.71-kw ERP, 387-ft. above ground, 2296-ft. above sea level, lat. 30° 03' 21", long. 99° 08' 16".

Ownership: Mary R. Silver.

Kerrville—KWTC-LP, Ch. 11, International Broadcasting Network. Phone: 281-774-9922.

Technical Facilities: 100-w TPO, 2.546-kw ERP, 420-ft. above ground, 2523-ft. above sea level, lat. 30° 06' 18", long. 99° 04' 34".

Transmitter: 5-mi. NE of Kerrville, on Hwy. 16.

Ownership: International Broadcasting Network.

Killeen—KADT-LP, Ch. 16, Word of God Fellowship Inc. Phone: 817-571-1229. Fax: 817-571-7478.

Technical Facilities: 1000-w TPO, 28-kw ERP, 1230-ft. above sea level, lat. 31° 05' 52", long. 97° 45' 12".

Holds CP for change to 106.2-kw ERP, 328-ft. above ground, 1404-ft. above sea level, lat. 30° 52' 44", long. 97° 43' 27". BPTTL-20061002AUC.

Transmitter: Adjacent to Rte. 440, S of U.S. Hwy. 190.

Ownership: Word of God Fellowship Inc.

■ **Killeen**—KPLE-CA, Ch. 22, Killeen Christian Broadcasting Corp. Phone: 254-554-3683. Fax: 254-554-7385.

Technical Facilities: 1000-w TPO, 6.6-kw ERP, 276-ft. above ground, 1223-ft. above sea level, lat. 31° 04' 50", long. 97° 44' 41".

Transmitter: 0.2-mi. S of intersection of Florence & Elm Rds.

Ownership: Killeen Christian Broadcasting Corp.

Killeen—KPLE-LD, Ch. 30, Killeen Christian Broadcasting Corp. Phone: 254-554-7385.

Technical Facilities: 15-kw ERP, 276-ft. above ground, 1224-ft. above sea level, lat. 31° 04' 50", long. 97° 44' 41".

Began Operation: April 16, 2009.

Ownership: Killeen Christian Broadcasting Corp.

Kingsville—K46DL, Ch. 46, Trinity Broadcasting Network Inc. Phone: 714-832-2950. Fax: 714-730-0661.

Technical Facilities: 360-w TPO, 3.5-kw ERP, 292-ft. above ground, 351-ft. above sea level, lat. 27° 25' 47", long. 97° 51' 40".

Transmitter: K13WE tower, 1.2-mi. S of S.R. 428 & U.S. 77 intersection, near Ricardo.

Ownership: Trinity Broadcasting Network Inc.

■ **Kingsville-Alice**—K20EK, Ch. 20, KVOA Communications Inc. Phone: 361-886-6111.

Technical Facilities: 18.7-kw ERP, 246-ft. above ground, 351-ft. above sea level, lat. 27° 39' 10", long. 97° 54' 59".

Transmitter: Rte. 70, 9.6-mi. W of Bishop.

■ **Kress & Tulia**—K41CA, Ch. 41, Panhandle Telecasting LP. Phone: 806-383-1010.

Technical Facilities: 0.928-kw ERP, 308-ft. above ground, 3779-ft. above sea level, lat. 34° 32' 12", long. 101° 44' 25".

Ownership: Panhandle Telecasting Co.

■ **La Feria**—KFTN-CA, Ch. 30, Entravision Holdings LLC. Phone: 310-447-3870.

Technical Facilities: 1000-w TPO, 30.3-kw ERP, 506-ft. above ground, 571-ft. above sea level, lat. 26° 08' 28", long. 97° 50' 04".

Transmitter: 5-mi. W of La Feria.

Ownership: Entravision Communications Corp.

■ **La Grange**—KHPL-CA, Ch. 40, KXAN Inc. Phones: 512-476-3636; 202-462-6065. Fax: 512-476-1520.

Technical Facilities: 960-w TPO, 8.5-kw ERP, 85-ft. above ground, 414-ft. above sea level, lat. 29° 54' 45", long. 96° 52' 53".

Transmitter: Jefferson & Roitsh Sts.

Ownership: LIN TV Corp.

La Vernia—KQVE-LP, Ch. 46, Word of God Fellowship Inc. Phone: 817-571-1229. Fax: 817-571-7478.

Technical Facilities: 1000-w TPO, 20-kw ERP, 541-ft. above ground, 1213-ft. above sea level, lat. 29° 26' 42", long. 98° 29' 33".

Transmitter: Hwy. 87, 2.6-mi. S of La Vernia.

Ownership: Word of God Fellowship Inc.

Lamesa—KPTR-LP, Ch. 47, Prime Time Christian Broadcasting Inc.

Technical Facilities: 6.89-kw ERP, 450-ft. above ground, 3389-ft. above sea level, lat. 32° 40' 31", long. 101° 58' 56".

Ownership: Prime Time Christian Broadcasting Inc.

■ **Laredo**—KETF-CA, Ch. 25, Entravision Holdings LLC. Phone: 310-447-3870.

Technical Facilities: 1000-w TPO, 58.7-kw ERP, 433-ft. above ground, 931-ft. above sea level, lat. 27° 21' 13", long. 99° 13' 50".

Transmitter: 9.3-mi. S of State Hwy. 59.

Ownership: Entravision Communications Corp.

Laredo—KLMV-LP, Ch. 68, J. B. Salazar.

Technical Facilities: 1000-w TPO, 28.1-kw ERP, 400-ft. above ground, 797-ft. above sea level, lat. 27° 31' 27", long. 99° 31' 20".

Ownership: J. B. Salazar.

Laredo—KNEX-LP, Ch. 55, BMP 100.5 FM LP. Phones: 215-692-2000; 817-335-5999.

Technical Facilities: 1000-w TPO, 9.55-kw ERP, 439-ft. above ground, 889-ft. above sea level, lat. 27° 24' 09", long. 99° 26' 49".

Transmitter: 5.8-mi. S of Laredo on Pinta Mountain.

Began Operation: June 3, 1999.

Ownership: Border Media Partners LLC.

■ **Laredo**—KXOF-CA, Ch. 39, Entravision Holdings LLC. Phones: 310-447-3870; 956-727-0027. Fax: 956-727-2673.

Technical Facilities: 1000-w TPO, 32-kw ERP, 164-ft. above ground, 663-ft. above sea level, lat. 27° 24' 09", long. 99° 26' 49".

Transmitter: Park & Main Sts.

Ownership: Entravision Communications Corp.

Livingston—KCTL-LP, Ch. 25, International Broadcasting Network. Phone: 281-774-9923.

Technical Facilities: 1000-w TPO, 10.411-kw ERP, 623-ft. above ground, 938-ft. above sea level, lat. 30° 41' 38", long. 94° 56' 12".

Transmitter: 125 Barney Rd.

Ownership: International Broadcasting Network.

Livingston—KETX-LP, Ch. 7, Telcom Supply Inc. Phone: 936-327-4309.

Technical Facilities: 3-kw ERP, 548-ft. above ground, 751-ft. above sea level, lat. 30° 44' 18", long. 94° 55' 26".

Ownership: Telcom Supply Inc.

Personnel: Hal Haley, General Manager.

Longview—KLGV-LP, Ch. 36, International Broadcasting Network. Phone: 281-587-8900.

Technical Facilities: 10-kw ERP, 318-ft. above ground, 629-ft. above sea level, lat. 32° 26' 56", long. 94° 43' 35".

Ownership: International Broadcasting Network.

Longview—KLPN-LP, Ch. 58, Warwick Communications Inc. Phone: 703-253-2027.

Technical Facilities: 827-w TPO, 22.3-kw ERP, 740-ft. above ground, 1381-ft. above sea level, lat. 32° 36' 04", long. 94° 52' 15".

Holds CP for change to channel number 47, 0.7-kw ERP, 740-ft. above ground, 1350-ft. above sea level, BDISDTL-20070322ABF.

Transmitter: East Mountain at Intersection of Hwy 80 & FM 188, N on FM 1844.

Ownership: White Knight Holdings Inc.

Louise—KDHU-LP, Ch. 50, Word of God Fellowship Inc. Phone: 817-571-1229.

Technical Facilities: 150-kw ERP, 312-ft. above ground, 413-ft. above sea level, lat. 29° 12' 07", long. 96° 14' 57".

Holds CP for change to 10.77-kw ERP, 338-ft. above ground, 427-ft. above sea level, lat. 29° 23' 41", long. 95° 49' 16". BDFCDTL-20071226ABX.

Ownership: Word of God Fellowship Inc.

Lubbock—K24GP, Ch. 24, Mako Communications LLC. Phone: 361-883-1763.

Technical Facilities: 10-kw ERP, 394-ft. above ground, 3608-ft. above sea level, lat. 33° 30' 57", long. 101° 50' 54".

Ownership: Mako Communications LLC.

Lubbock—K38HP, Ch. 38, Venture Technologies Group LLC. Phone: 323-904-4090.

Technical Facilities: 15-kw ERP, 394-ft. above ground, 3608-ft. above sea level, lat. 33° 30' 58", long. 101° 50' 54".

Ownership: Venture Technologies Group LLC.

Lubbock—K44HH, Ch. 44, Enlace Christian Television Inc. Phone: 469-499-0832.

Technical Facilities: 5-kw ERP, 328-ft. above ground, 3525-ft. above sea level, lat. 33° 34' 48", long. 101° 50' 46".

Began Operation: August 1, 2005.

Ownership: Enlace Christian Television Inc.

Lubbock—K48GB, Ch. 48, Ramar Communications Inc. Phone: 806-748-9300. Fax: 806-748-1949.

Technical Facilities: 24.3-kw ERP, 850-ft. above ground, 4057-ft. above sea level, lat. 33° 30' 08", long. 101° 52' 20".

Ownership: Ramar Communications Inc.

Personnel: Brad Moran, General Manager; Tom Wimberly, Chief Engineer; Bret Benge, Sales Manager.

Lubbock—K67HQ, Ch. 67, Jennifer Cremeens. Phone: 407-654-2908.

Technical Facilities: 10-kw ERP, 295-ft. above ground, 3494-ft. above sea level, lat. 33° 35' 05", long. 101° 50' 54".

Ownership: Jennifer Cremeens.

Lubbock—KBZO-LP, Ch. 51, Entravision Holdings LLC. Phone: 310-447-3870.

Studio: 1220 Broadway, Suite 500, Lubbock, TX 79401.

Technical Facilities: 60-kw ERP, 656-ft. above ground, 3881-ft. above sea level, lat. 33° 31' 33", long. 101° 52' 07".

Ownership: Entravision Communications Corp.

Personnel: Mike Aradillas, General Manager & Sales Manager.

Lubbock—KDFL-LP, Ch. 69, Una Vez Mas Lubbock License LLC. Phone: 214-754-7008.

Technical Facilities: 15-kw ERP, 394-ft. above ground, 3608-ft. above sea level, lat. 33° 30' 56", long. 101° 50' 54".

Holds CP for change to channel number 17, 1.5-kw ERP, BDISDTL-20080925AGJ.

Began Operation: September 26, 2005.

Ownership: Una Vez Mas GP LLC.

Lubbock—KFIQ-LP, Ch. 4, Venture Technologies Group LLC. Phone: 323-904-4090.

Technical Facilities: 1.19-kw ERP, 656-ft. above ground, 3881-ft. above sea level, lat. 33° 31' 33", long. 101° 52' 07".

Ownership: Venture Technologies Group LLC.

Lubbock—KFMP-LP, Ch. 6, Venture Technologies Group LLC. Phone: 323-904-4090.

Technical Facilities: 3-kw ERP, 656-ft. above ground, 3881-ft. above sea level, lat. 33° 31' 33", long. 101° 52' 07".

Ownership: Venture Technologies Group LLC.

■ **Lubbock**—KGLR-LP, Ch. 30, Lubbock Television Co. Phone: 806-747-4085. Fax: 806-747-4086.

Studio: 2124 15th St., Lubbock, TX 79401.

Technical Facilities: 1000-w TPO, 14.4-kw ERP, 499-ft. above ground, 3707-ft. above sea level, lat. 33° 30' 57", long. 101° 50' 54".

Transmitter: 84th St. & Ave. L, Lubbock.

Ownership: Lubbock Television Co.

■ **Lubbock**—KJTV-CA, Ch. 32, Ramar Communications Inc. Phone: 806-745-3434. Fax: 806-748-1949.

Studio: 9800 University Ave., Lubbock, TX 79423.

Technical Facilities: 23.8-kw ERP, 850-ft. above ground, 4058-ft. above sea level, lat. 33° 30' 08", long. 101° 52' 20".

Multichannel TV Sound: Stereo only.

Ownership: Ramar Communications Inc.

Personnel: Brad Moran, General Manager; Tom Wimberly, Chief Engineer.

Lubbock—KLOD-LP, Ch. 18, Word of God Fellowship Inc. Phone: 817-571-1229.

Technical Facilities: 87-kw ERP, 328-ft. above ground, 3510-ft. above sea level, lat. 33° 25' 02", long. 101° 50' 52".

Ownership: Word of God Fellowship Inc.

Lubbock—KMYL-LP, Ch. 14, Ramar Communications Inc. Phone: 806-748-9300. Fax: 806-748-1949.

Studio: 9800 University Ave, Lubbock, TX 79452.

Technical Facilities: 28-kw ERP, 850-ft. above ground, 4057-ft. above sea level, lat. 33° 30' 08", long. 101° 52' 20".

Multichannel TV Sound: Stereo only.

Ownership: Ramar Communications Inc.

Personnel: Brad Moran, General Manager; Wynne Bodeker, Chief Engineer.

■ **Lubbock**—KXTQ-CA, Ch. 46, Ramar Communications Inc. Phone: 806-745-3434. Fax: 806-745-3434.

Studio: 9800 University Ave., Lubbock, TX 79423.

Technical Facilities: 31.6-kw ERP, 850-ft. above ground, 4057-ft. above sea level, lat. 33° 30' 08", long. 101° 52' 20".

Holds CP for change to 15-kw ERP, BDFCDTA-20080604ACE.

Multichannel TV Sound: Stereo only.

Began Operation: February 12, 1991.

Ownership: Ramar Communications Inc.

Personnel: Chuck Heinz, General Manager; Tom Wimberly, Chief Engineer; Bret Benge, Sales Manager.

Lufkin—K48IO, Ch. 48, Windsong Communications Inc. Phone: 936-443-4451.

Technical Facilities: 28.25-kw ERP, 500-ft. above ground, 886-ft. above sea level, lat. 31° 24' 29.24", long. 94° 45' 52.04".

Ownership: C. Dowen Johnson.

Lufkin—KETK-LP, Ch. 53, KM Communications Inc. Phones: 936-564-1911; 847-674-0864.

Technical Facilities: 0.9-kw ERP, 540-ft. above ground, 900-ft. above sea level, lat. 31° 21' 55", long. 94° 45' 59".

Ownership: KM Communications Inc.

Lufkin—KFXL-LP, Ch. 30, Warwick Communications Inc. Phone: 703-253-2027.

Technical Facilities: 1000-w TPO, 19.86-kw ERP, 650-ft. above ground, 1010-ft. above sea level, lat. 31° 21' 55", long. 94° 45' 59".

Transmitter: 0.5-mi. NW of Hwy. 103, W of Loop.

Multichannel TV Sound: Separate audio progam.

Ownership: White Knight Holdings Inc.

Personnel: Mark McKay, General Manager; Randy Roberts, General Sales Manager; Vicki McRae, Local Sales Manager; Randy Robinson, Sales Manager; Keith Paxton, Director, Marketing; Charles T. Small Jr., Chief Engineer.

Lufkin—KHTM-LP, Ch. 13, International Broadcasting Network. Phone: 281-587-8900.

Technical Facilities: 80-w TPO, 0.117-kw ERP, 410-ft. above ground, 751-ft. above sea level, lat. 31° 20' 18", long. 94° 41' 16".

Holds CP for change to 3-kw ERP, 636-ft. above ground, 996-ft. above sea level, lat. 31° 21' 55", long. 94° 45'59". BPTVL-20060403AND.

Transmitter: 2601 E. Lufkin Ave.

Ownership: International Broadcasting Network.

Lufkin—KIBN-LP, Ch. 14, International Broadcasting Network. Phone: 281-587-8900.

Technical Facilities: 16-kw ERP, 633-ft. above ground, 993-ft. above sea level, lat. 31° 21' 55", long. 94° 45' 59".

Holds CP for change to 15-kw ERP, BDFCDTL-20090427AAA.

Ownership: International Broadcasting Network.

Lufkin—KLNM-LP, Ch. 42, Millennium Communications & Productions. Phone: 800-501-8273.

Technical Facilities: 50-kw ERP, 592-ft. above ground, 891-ft. above sea level, lat. 31° 21' 32", long. 94° 40' 19".

Holds CP for change to 592-ft. above ground, 903-ft. above sea level, lat. 31° 20' 05", long. 94° 40' 10". BPTTL-20080624AAM.

Ownership: Millennium Communications & Productions.

Lufkin—KLUF-LP, Ch. 5, International Broadcasting Network. Phone: 281-587-8900.

Technical Facilities: 40-w TPO, 0.094-kw ERP, 440-ft. above ground, 781-ft. above sea level, lat. 31° 20' 18", long. 94° 41' 16".

Holds CP for change to 3-w TPO, 630-ft. above ground, 990-ft. above sea level, lat. 31° 21' 55", long. 94° 45'59". BPTVL-20060403ANG.

Transmitter: 2601 E. Lufkin Ave.

Ownership: International Broadcasting Network.

Mason—K34HW, Ch. 34, Foster Charitable Foundation Inc. Phone: 830-896-1230.

Technical Facilities: 0.1-kw ERP, 39-ft. above ground, 1797-ft. above sea level, lat. 30° 47' 08", long. 99° 18' 40".

Ownership: Foster Charitable Foundation Inc.

Matador—K40FK, Ch. 40, Ramar Communications Inc. Phone: 806-748-9300.

Technical Facilities: 0.55-kw ERP, 180-ft. above ground, 3030-ft. above sea level, lat. 33° 58' 54", long. 100° 54' 48".

Ownership: Ramar Communications Inc.

Matador—K42ES, Ch. 42, Ramar Communications Inc. Phone: 806-748-9300.

Technical Facilities: 0.55-kw ERP, 180-ft. above ground, 3030-ft. above sea level, lat. 33° 58' 54", long. 100° 54' 48".

Ownership: Ramar Communications Inc.

Matador—K45FE, Ch. 45, Ramar Communications Inc. Phone: 806-748-9300.

Technical Facilities: 0.55-kw ERP, 180-ft. above ground, 3031-ft. above sea level, lat. 33° 58' 54", long. 100° 54' 48".

Ownership: Ramar Communications Inc.

Matador—K47GE, Ch. 47, Ramar Communications Inc. Phone: 806-748-9300.

Technical Facilities: 0.55-kw ERP, 180-ft. above ground, 3030-ft. above sea level, lat. 33° 58' 54", long. 100° 54' 48".

Ownership: Ramar Communications Inc.

McAllen—KJST-LP, Ch. 28, CTV Broadcasting LLC. Phone: 713-358-4229.

Technical Facilities: 20-w TPO, 0.125-kw ERP, 282-ft. above ground, 380-ft. above sea level, lat. 26° 15' 23", long. 98° 13' 49".

Transmitter: 23rd St.

Ownership: CTV Broadcasting LLC.

Personnel: Chuck Ortiz, General Manager; Carlos Macias, Chief Engineer.

McAllen—KNDF-LP, Ch. 57, Una Vez Mas McAllen License LLC. Phone: 214-754-7008.

Studio: 4801 N. Cage, Pharr, TX 78577.

Technical Facilities: 940-w TPO, 7-kw ERP, 381-ft. above ground, 476-ft. above sea level, lat. 26° 15' 23", long. 98° 13' 49".

Ownership: Una Vez Mas GP LLC.

■ **McAllen**—KRZG-CA, Ch. 35, Una Vez Mas LP. Phone: 214-719-3360.

Technical Facilities: 1000-w TPO, 33.6-kw ERP, 446-ft. above ground, 429-ft. above sea level, lat. 26° 15' 23", long. 98° 13' 50".

Transmitter: 2.17-mi. N of McAllen.

Ownership: Una Vez Mas GP LLC.

McAllen—KSFE-LP, Ch. 67, Entravision Holdings LLC. Phone: 310-447-3870.

Technical Facilities: 1000-w TPO, 12.7-kw ERP, 259-ft. above ground, 381-ft. above sea level, lat. 26° 12' 04", long. 98° 13' 53".

Transmitter: McAllen Bldg., 10th St.

Ownership: Entravision Communications Corp.

McAllen—KSTI-LP, Ch. 25, Faith Pleases God Church Corp. Phones: 956-428-4848; 956-412-5600.

Technical Facilities: 20-w TPO, 0.102-kw ERP, 300-ft. above ground, 397-ft. above sea level, lat. 26° 15' 23", long. 98° 13' 49".

Transmitter: 23rd St.

Ownership: Faith Pleases God Church Corp.

Personnel: Chuck Ortiz, General Manager; Carlos Macias, Chief Engineer.

■ **McAllen**—KTFV-CA, Ch. 32, Entravision Holdings LLC. Phone: 310-447-3870.

Technical Facilities: 1000-w TPO, 12-kw ERP, 281-ft. above ground, 377-ft. above sea level, lat. 26° 15' 23", long. 98° 13' 49".

Transmitter: 3.2-mi. N of McAllen.

Ownership: Entravision Communications Corp.

McCamey & Rankin—K50ED, Ch. 50, Prime Time Christian Broadcasting Inc.

Technical Facilities: 0.76-kw ERP, 250-ft. above ground, 3367-ft. above sea level, lat. 31° 12' 42", long. 102° 16' 14".

Ownership: Prime Time Christian Broadcasting Inc.

Memphis—K30HH, Ch. 30, Northfork TV Translator System. Phones: 806-259-2879; 806-259-3500.

Technical Facilities: 358-ft. above ground, 2897-ft. above sea level, lat. 34° 48' 18", long. 100° 36' 12".

Ownership: Northfork TV Translator System.

Memphis—K32EH, Ch. 32, Caprock Translator System Inc.

Technical Facilities: 0.914-kw ERP, 344-ft. above ground, 2848-ft. above sea level, lat. 34° 48' 35", long. 100° 36' 38".

Transmitter: 5-mi. NNW of Memphis.

Memphis—K36CA, Ch. 36, Cruze Electronics.

Technical Facilities: 0.914-kw ERP, 344-ft. above ground, 2848-ft. above sea level, lat. 34° 48' 35", long. 100° 36' 38".

Memphis, etc.—K38AP, Ch. 38, Caprock Translator System Inc.

Technical Facilities: 0.81-kw ERP, 2851-ft. above sea level, lat. 34° 48' 35", long. 100° 36' 38".

Memphis, etc.—K40AL, Ch. 40, Caprock Translator System Inc.

Technical Facilities: 0.81-kw ERP, 2848-ft. above sea level, lat. 34° 48' 35", long. 100° 36' 38".

Memphis, etc.—K42AL, Ch. 42, Caprock Translator System Inc.

Technical Facilities: 0.81-kw ERP, 2848-ft. above sea level, lat. 34° 48' 35", long. 100° 36' 38".

Memphis, etc.—K44AK, Ch. 44, Cruze Electronics. Phone: 806-259-2879. Fax: 806-259-3500.

Technical Facilities: 100-w TPO, 0.843-kw ERP, 2815-ft. above sea level, lat. 34° 48' 35", long. 100° 36' 38".

Transmitter: 5-mi. NNW of Memphis.

Ownership: Cruze Electronics.

■ **Mesquite**—KATA-CA, Ch. 50, Mako Communications LLC. Phone: 361-883-1763.

Technical Facilities: 15-kw ERP, 935-ft. above ground, 1759-ft. above sea level, lat. 32° 35' 21", long. 96° 58' 12".

Holds CP for change to 853-ft. above ground, 1683-ft. above sea level, BDFCDTA-20081020AML.

Began Operation: November 15, 1993.

Ownership: Mako Communications LLC.

Midland—K21GU, Ch. 21, Prism Broadcasting Network Inc. Phone: 770-953-3232.

Technical Facilities: 0.005-kw ERP, 20-ft. above ground, 2812-ft. above sea level, lat. 32° 03' 15", long. 102° 04' 50".

Ownership: Prism Broadcasting Network Inc.

Midland—K22IZ, Ch. 22, Martin Weiss. Phone: 805-928-8300.

Technical Facilities: 9.9-kw ERP, 486-ft. above ground, 3402-ft. above sea level, lat. 32° 02' 52.1", long. 102° 17' 45.5".

Began Operation: June 6, 2008.

Ownership: Martin Weiss.

Midland—K34HH, Ch. 34, Prism Broadcasting Network Inc. Phone: 770-953-3232.

Technical Facilities: 0.001-kw ERP, 20-ft. above ground, 2812-ft. above sea level, lat. 32° 03' 15", long. 102° 04' 50".

Ownership: Prism Broadcasting Network Inc.

■ **Midland**—K40FJ, Ch. 40, Three Angels Broadcasting Network Inc. Phone: 618-627-4651.

Technical Facilities: 100-w TPO, 2.5-kw ERP, 92-ft. above ground, 5751-ft. above sea level, lat. 31° 48' 57", long. 106° 29' 20".

Ownership: Three Angels Broadcasting Network Inc.

Midland—K63GZ, Ch. 63, Windsong Communications Inc. Phone: 936-443-4451.

Technical Facilities: 9.5-kw ERP, 177-ft. above ground, 3071-ft. above sea level, lat. 31° 59' 43.6", long. 102° 15' 27.5".

Began Operation: September 22, 2008.

Ownership: Windsong Communications Inc.

Midland—K69IT, Ch. 69, Lawrence Howard Mintz. Phone: 361-883-1763.

Technical Facilities: 9.5-kw ERP, 177-ft. above ground, 3071-ft. above sea level, lat. 31° 59' 43.6", long. 102° 15' 27.5".

Ownership: Lawrence Howard Mintz.

Midland—KDFH-LP, Ch. 41, Una Vez Mas Midland License LLC. Phone: 214-754-7008.

Technical Facilities: 9.5-kw ERP, 177-ft. above ground, 3071-ft. above sea level, lat. 31° 59' 43.6", long. 102° 15' 27.5".

Holds CP for change to 100-kw ERP, BPTTL-20060216AEQ.

Ownership: Una Vez Mas GP LLC.

Mobeetie—K39AN, Ch. 39, Wheeler County Translator System Inc.

Technical Facilities: 0.95-kw ERP, lat. 35° 35' 52", long. 100° 29' 48".

Mobeetie—K41BW, Ch. 41, Wheeler County Translator System Inc.

Technical Facilities: 1-kw ERP, lat. 35° 35' 52", long. 100° 29' 48".

Monahans—KPDN-LP, Ch. 27, Prime Time Christian Broadcasting Inc. Phone: 915-563-0420. Fax: 915-563-1736.

Technical Facilities: 1000-w TPO, 7.04-kw ERP, 499-ft. above ground, 3828-ft. above sea level, lat. 31° 57' 55", long. 102° 46' 10".

Transmitter: 3.5-mi. NW of Notrees on Oil Rd., Notrees.

Multichannel TV Sound: Separate audio progam.

Ownership: Prime Time Christian Broadcasting Inc.

Personnel: Al Cooper, General Manager; Jay Westcott, Chief Engineer; Jeff Welter, Sales Manager.

Mullin—KAXW-LP, Ch. 61, Una Vez Mas Mullin License LP. Phone: 214-754-7008.

Technical Facilities: 150-kw ERP, 312-ft. above ground, 1462-ft. above sea level, lat. 31° 40' 07", long. 98° 02' 29.6".

Holds CP for change to channel number 51, 15-kw ERP, 262-ft. above ground, 972-ft. above sea level, lat. 31° 26' 40.9", long. 97° 23' 41.1". BDISDTL-20081118ALE.

Began Operation: December 13, 1985.

Ownership: Una Vez Mas GP LLC.

Nacogdoches—KNCD-LP, Ch. 2, International Broadcasting Network.

Technical Facilities: 10-w TPO, 0.62-kw ERP, 200-ft. above ground, 2575-ft. above sea level, lat. 31° 37' 45", long. 94° 40' 44".

Transmitter: 3441 Old Tyler Rd., Nacogdoches.

Ownership: International Broadcasting Network.

■ **New Braunfels**—KNTA-LP, Ch. 14, Aracelis Ortiz Corp. Phone: 956-412-9101.

Technical Facilities: 10-kw ERP, 330-ft. above ground, 1020-ft. above sea level, lat. 29° 43' 50", long. 98° 07' 12".

Ownership: Aracelis Ortiz Corp.

New Mobeetie—K43ED, Ch. 43, Wheeler County Translator Systems Inc.

Technical Facilities: 0.96-kw ERP, lat. 35° 35' 52", long. 100° 29' 48".

New Mobeetie—K45DY, Ch. 45, Wheeler County Translator Systems Inc.

Technical Facilities: 0.789-kw ERP, 289-ft. above ground, 3222-ft. above sea level, lat. 35° 35' 52", long. 100° 29' 48".

New Mobeetie—K47GM, Ch. 47, Wheeler County Translator System Inc. Phone: 806-259-2879.

Technical Facilities: 0.956-kw ERP, 289-ft. above ground, 3263-ft. above sea level, lat. 35° 35' 53", long. 100° 30' 42".

Odessa—K46HN, Ch. 46, Prism Broadcasting Network Inc. Phone: 770-953-3232.

Technical Facilities: 0.005-kw ERP, 20-ft. above ground, 2890-ft. above sea level, lat. 31° 53' 46", long. 102° 14' 50".

Holds CP for change to lat. 31° 54' 30", long. 102° 14' 29". BPTTL-20070105AET.

Ownership: Prism Broadcasting Network Inc.

Odessa—K66GG, Ch. 66, Issac Ruiz Mora. Phone: 210-837-2178.

Technical Facilities: 0.3-kw ERP, 49-ft. above ground, 2959-ft. above sea level, lat. 31° 51' 07.4", long. 102° 22' 19.5".

Began Operation: August 14, 2008.

Ownership: Issac Ruiz Mora.

Odessa—KTLD-LP, Ch. 49, KKTM License Co. LLC. Phone: 972-663-8917.

Technical Facilities: 200-w TPO, 1.72-kw ERP, 400-ft. above ground, 3169-ft. above sea level, lat. 31° 57' 30", long. 102° 03' 59".

Transmitter: E of State Rd. 349, 1-mi. S of I-20 intersection, SSE of Midland.

Ownership: London Broadcasting Co. Inc.

Odessa—KTLE-LP, Ch. 20, KKTM License Co. LLC. Phone: 972-663-8917.

Technical Facilities: 729-w TPO, 4.81-kw ERP, 289-ft. above ground, 3205-ft. above sea level, lat. 31° 51' 58", long. 102° 22' 50".

Transmitter: Odessa Junior College, University Blvd., Odessa.

Ownership: London Broadcasting Co. Inc.

Odessa—KZOD-LP, Ch. 62, Hispanic Christian Community Network Inc. Phone: 214-879-0081.

Technical Facilities: 0.3-kw ERP, 43-ft. above ground, 2953-ft. above sea level, lat. 31° 51' 07.4", long. 102° 22' 195".

Began Operation: August 14, 2008.

Ownership: Hispanic Christian Community Network Inc.

Palestine—K17BP, Ch. 17, Trinity Broadcasting Network Inc. Phone: 714-832-2950. Fax: 714-730-0661.

Technical Facilities: 1000-w TPO, 3.1-kw ERP, 279-ft. above ground, 889-ft. above sea level, lat. 31° 43' 12", long. 95° 39' 08".

Transmitter: 1.5-mi. S of intersection of Rtes. 256 & 1990.

Ownership: Trinity Broadcasting Network Inc.

Personnel: Paul Crouch, General Manager; Ben Miller, Chief Engineer; Rod Henke, Sales Manager.

Palestine—K24DS, Ch. 24, Eternal Truth Network Inc. Phone: 903-729-7274.

Technical Facilities: 1000-w TPO, 42.3-kw ERP, 420-ft. above ground, 797-ft. above sea level, lat. 31° 39' 56", long. 95° 38' 08".

Transmitter: Rte. 5.

Ownership: Eternal Truth Network Inc.

Pampa—KZFB-LP, Ch. 34, Sendas Antiguas Ministries Inc. Phone: 512-828-6862.

Technical Facilities: 120-kw ERP, 217-ft. above ground, 3655-ft. above sea level, lat. 35° 23' 00", long. 101° 18' 41".

Ownership: Sendas Antiguas Ministries Inc.

Paris—K02EQ, Ch. 2, Gray Television Licensee LLC. Phone: 715-835-1313.

Technical Facilities: 0.904-kw ERP, lat. 33° 38' 55", long. 95° 36' 16".

Ownership: Gray Television Inc.

Paris—K27GR, Ch. 27, First Baptist Church of Paris, Texas. Phone: 970-785-6431.

Technical Facilities: 30.6-kw ERP, 420-ft. above ground, 1042-ft. above sea level, lat. 33° 37' 15", long. 95° 32' 51".

Ownership: First Baptist Church of Paris, TX.

Paris—K42DA, Ch. 42, Trinity Broadcasting Network Inc. Phone: 714-832-2950. Fax: 714-730-0661.

Technical Facilities: 1000-w TPO, 13.3-kw ERP, 561-ft. above ground, 1112-ft. above sea level, lat. 33° 37' 15", long. 95° 32' 50".

Holds CP for change to 15-kw ERP, 561-ft. above ground, 1111-ft. above sea level, BDFCDTT-20060329AFX.

Transmitter: Near Loop 286 & FM 1497, Paris.

Ownership: Trinity Broadcasting Network Inc.

Personnel: Paul F. Crouch, General Manager; Rod Henke, Sales Manager; Ben Miller, Chief Engineer.

Paris—KPTD-LP, Ch. 49, Word of God Fellowship Inc. Phone: 817-571-1229.

Texas — Low Power TV & TV Translator Stations

Technical Facilities: 10-kw ERP, 492-ft. above ground, 1042-ft. above sea level, lat. 33° 37' 15", long. 95° 32' 50".

Holds CP for change to 499-ft. above ground, 1020-ft. above sea level, lat. 33° 36' 59", long. 95° 33' 16". BPTTL-20070910ADQ.

Ownership: Word of God Fellowship Inc.

Pecos—K20HD, Ch. 20, ComCorp of Texas License Corp. Phone: 337-237-1142.

Technical Facilities: 9.47-kw ERP, lat. 31° 01' 52", long. 104° 04' 38".

Ownership: Communications Corp. of America.

Perryton—K58EA, Ch. 58, C L & O Translator System Inc.

Technical Facilities: 0.77-kw ERP, 348-ft. above ground, 3337-ft. above sea level, lat. 36° 07' 04", long. 100° 48' 07".

Perryton—K62DD, Ch. 62, C L & O Translator System Inc.

Technical Facilities: 0.76-kw ERP, 348-ft. above ground, 3337-ft. above sea level, lat. 36° 07' 04", long. 100° 48' 07".

Perryton—K64AC, Ch. 64, C L & O Translator System Inc.

Technical Facilities: 0.765-kw ERP, 348-ft. above ground, 3327-ft. above sea level, lat. 36° 06' 26", long. 100° 47' 32".

Perryton—K66AB, Ch. 66, C L & O Translator System Inc.

Technical Facilities: 0.765-kw ERP, 348-ft. above ground, 3327-ft. above sea level, lat. 36° 06' 26", long. 100° 47' 32".

Perryton—K68AD, Ch. 68, C L & O Translator System Inc.

Technical Facilities: 0.765-kw ERP, 348-ft. above ground, 3327-ft. above sea level, lat. 36° 06' 26", long. 100° 47' 32".

Plainview—K18HC, Ch. 18, Iglesia Jesucristo Es Mi Refugio Inc. Phone: 972-467-9791.

Technical Facilities: 1-kw ERP, 295-ft. above ground, 3714-ft. above sea level, lat. 34° 14' 05", long. 101° 47' 25".

Ownership: Iglesia Jesucristo Es Mi Refugio Inc.

Plainview—K31IK, Ch. 31, Tiger Eye Licensing LLC. Phone: 954-431-3144.

Technical Facilities: 10-kw ERP, 322-ft. above ground, 3804-ft. above sea level, lat. 34° 12' 55.7", long. 101° 52' 59.3".

Ownership: Tiger Eye Broadcasting Corp.

Plainview—K44GL, Ch. 44, Ramar Communications Inc. Phone: 806-745-3434.

Technical Facilities: 9.6-kw ERP, 371-ft. above ground, 3747-ft. above sea level, lat. 34° 13' 14", long. 101° 42' 54".

Holds CP for change to channel number 50, 15-kw ERP, BDISDTT-20080925AGG.

Began Operation: January 9, 1991.

Ownership: Ramar Communications Inc.

Plainview—KPGD-LP, Ch. 47, Prime Time Christian Broadcasting Inc.

Technical Facilities: 0.614-kw ERP, lat. 34° 13' 05", long. 101° 42' 02".

Ownership: Prime Time Christian Broadcasting Inc.

Port Arthur—KAZP-LP, Ch. 45, Una Vez Mas Port Arthur License LLC. Phone: 214-754-7008.

Technical Facilities: 10-kw ERP, 156-ft. above ground, 158-ft. above sea level, lat. 29° 54' 12.2", long. 94° 00' 40.3".

Ownership: Una Vez Mas GP LLC.

Quanah—K27HM, Ch. 27, Northfork TV Translator System. Phone: 806-259-2879.

Technical Facilities: 0.75-kw ERP, 292-ft. above ground, 1923-ft. above sea level, lat. 34° 12' 41", long. 99° 44' 05".

Ownership: Northfork TV Translator System.

Quanah—K29FR, Ch. 29, Northfork TV Translator Systems. Phone: 806-259-2879.

Technical Facilities: 0.75-kw ERP, 292-ft. above ground, 1923-ft. above sea level, lat. 34° 12' 41", long. 99° 44' 05".

Ownership: Northfork TV Translator System.

Quanah—K31HC, Ch. 31, Northfork TV Translator System. Phone: 806-259-2879.

Technical Facilities: 0.75-kw ERP, 292-ft. above ground, 1923-ft. above sea level, lat. 34° 12' 41", long. 99° 44' 05".

Ownership: Northfork TV Translator System.

Quanah—K33HG, Ch. 33, Northfork TV Translator System. Phone: 806-259-2879.

Technical Facilities: 0.75-kw ERP, 292-ft. above ground, 1923-ft. above sea level, lat. 34° 12' 41", long. 99° 44' 05".

Ownership: Northfork TV Translator System.

Quanah—K39GH, Ch. 39, Northfolk TV Translator System. Phone: 806-259-2879.

Technical Facilities: 0.75-kw ERP, 1886-ft. above ground, 3517-ft. above sea level, lat. 34° 12' 41", long. 99° 44' 05".

Ownership: Northfork TV Translator System.

Quanah—K41HQ, Ch. 41, Northfork TV Translator System. Phone: 806-259-2879.

Technical Facilities: 0.75-kw ERP, 1886-ft. above ground, 3517-ft. above sea level, lat. 34° 12' 41", long. 99° 44' 05".

Ownership: Northfork TV Translator System.

Quanah—K43HD, Ch. 43, Northfork TV Translator System.

Technical Facilities: 0.75-kw ERP, 1886-ft. above ground, 3517-ft. above sea level, lat. 34° 12' 41", long. 99° 44' 05".

Quitaque—K35EM, Ch. 35, Amarillo Junior College.

Technical Facilities: 1.05-kw ERP, 184-ft. above ground, 3330-ft. above sea level, lat. 34° 20' 01", long. 101° 07' 11".

■ **Raymondville**—KMAO-LP, Ch. 50, Aracelis Ortiz Corp.

Technical Facilities: 100-w TPO, 0.15-kw ERP, 500-ft. above ground, 528-ft. above sea level, lat. 26° 28' 32", long. 97° 48' 30".

Transmitter: 2-mi. W of Raymondville.

Ownership: Aracelis Ortiz.

Raymondville—KRYM-LP, Ch. 46, Aracelis Ortiz Corp. Phone: 956-412-5600.

Technical Facilities: 0.1-kw ERP, 95-ft. above ground, 131-ft. above sea level, lat. 26° 29' 51", long. 97° 46' 04".

Ownership: Aracelis Ortiz Corp.

Rio Grande City—KRGT-LP, Ch. 6, CTV Broadcasting LLC. Phone: 713-358-4229.

Technical Facilities: 6.7-w TPO, 0.04-kw ERP, 70-ft. above ground, 332-ft. above sea level, lat. 26° 24' 22", long. 98° 55' 02".

Transmitter: 0.7-mi. NE of Rosita.

Ownership: CTV Broadcasting LLC.

Personnel: Chuck Ortiz, General Manager; Carlos Macias, Chief Engineer.

■ **Robstown**—KINE-LP, Ch. 44, Humberto Lopez. Phone: 361-284-8877. Fax: 361-284-7722.

Technical Facilities: 905-w TPO, 20-kw ERP, 256-ft. above ground, 306-ft. above sea level, lat. 27° 40' 39", long. 97° 38' 20".

Transmitter: 5612 Farm Rd. 665, Petronia.

Ownership: Humberto Lopez.

Personnel: Humberto L. Lopez, General Manager; Bob Reyna, Chief Engineer; Carlos Lopez, Sales Manager.

■ **Round Rock**—KHPZ-CA, Ch. 15, KXAN Inc. Phones: 512-476-3636; 202-462-6065. Fax: 512-476-1520.

Technical Facilities: 10.6-kw ERP, 436-ft. above ground, 1296-ft. above sea level, lat. 30° 36' 04", long. 97° 39' 34".

Ownership: LIN TV Corp.

Royse City—KZFW-LP, Ch. 6, Iglesia Jesucristo Es Mi Refugio Inc. Phone: 214-330-8700.

Studio: 3302 Mineola St., Greenville, TX 75401.

Technical Facilities: 3-kw ERP, 1444-ft. above ground, 2244-ft. above sea level, lat. 32° 35' 19.5", long. 96° 58' 05".

Ownership: Iglesia Jesucristo Es Mi Refugio Inc.

Personnel: Bill R. Wright, President & General Manager; Marty Choate, Sales Manager; D. W. Strahan, Chief Engineer; Jay Garrett, Marketing Director.

San Angelo—K23IA, Ch. 23, Hispanic Christian Community Network Inc. Phone: 214-879-0001.

Technical Facilities: 5-kw ERP, 66-ft. above ground, 6079-ft. above sea level, lat. 31° 28' 18.8", long. 100° 24' 46.7".

Ownership: Hispanic Christian Community Network Inc.

San Angelo—K43IQ, Ch. 43, Windsong Communications Inc. Phone: 936-443-4451.

Technical Facilities: 0.9-kw ERP, 269-ft. above ground, 2106-ft. above sea level, lat. 31° 28' 10.4", long. 100° 27' 05.7".

Ownership: Windsong Communications Inc.

San Angelo—K44FJ, Ch. 44, Trinity Broadcasting Network Inc. Phone: 714-832-2950. Fax: 714-730-0661.

Technical Facilities: 12.9-kw ERP, lat. 31° 35' 21", long. 100° 31' 00".

Holds CP for change to 3-kw ERP, 650-ft. above ground, 2683-ft. above sea level, BDFCDTT-20060329AFF.

Transmitter: State Rte. 87 & Marsh Rd. intersection.

Ownership: Trinity Broadcasting Network Inc.

San Angelo—K45HW, Ch. 45, Howard Mintz. Phone: 361-883-1793.

Technical Facilities: 0.98-kw ERP, 328-ft. above ground, 2165-ft. above sea level, lat. 31° 28' 10", long. 100° 27' 06".

Ownership: Howard Mintz.

■ **San Angelo**—KANG-CA, Ch. 41, Entravision Holdings LLC. Phone: 310-447-3870.

Technical Facilities: 1000-w TPO, 12.5-kw ERP, 490-ft. above ground, 2879-ft. above sea level, lat. 31° 29' 41", long. 100° 28' 36".

Transmitter: 3639 N. Bryant Rd.

Ownership: Entravision Communications Corp.

San Angelo—KEUS-LP, Ch. 31, Entravision Holdings LLC. Phone: 310-447-3870.

Technical Facilities: 1000-w TPO, 11.3-kw ERP, 490-ft. above ground, 2879-ft. above sea level, lat. 31° 29' 41", long. 100° 28' 36".

Transmitter: 3639 N. Bryant Rd.

Ownership: Entravision Communications Corp.

Personnel: Gerald Benavides, General Manager.

San Angelo—KPKS-LP, Ch. 51, Prime Time Christian Broadcasting Inc. Phone: 915-563-0420.

Technical Facilities: 13.78-kw ERP, 399-ft. above ground, 2433-ft. above sea level, lat. 31° 35' 21", long. 100° 31' 00".

Ownership: Prime Time Christian Broadcasting Inc.

San Angelo—KTXE-LP, Ch. 38, Bonten Media Group Inc. Phone: 212-710-7771.

Technical Facilities: 6.38-kw ERP, 390-ft. above ground, 2283-ft. above sea level, lat. 31° 29' 06", long. 100° 27' 27".

Ownership: Bonten Media Group LLC.

San Antonio—K14KI, Ch. 14, Three Angels Broadcasting Network Inc. Phone: 618-627-4651. Fax: 618-627-4155.

Studio: 3391 Charley Good Rd, West Frankfort, IL 62896.

Technical Facilities: 1000-w TPO, 21-kw ERP, 193-ft. above ground, 974-ft. above sea level, lat. 29° 22' 56", long. 98° 38' 51".

Transmitter: 4917 Ravenswood Dr.

Ownership: Three Angels Broadcasting Network Inc.

Personnel: Moses Primo, Chief Engineer.

■ **San Antonio**—K14LM, Ch. 14, Three Angels Broadcasting Network Inc. Phone: 518-627-4651.

Technical Facilities: 53.1-kw ERP, 312-ft. above ground, 991-ft. above sea level, lat. 29° 26' 29", long. 98° 30' 22".

Ownership: Three Angels Broadcasting Network Inc.

San Antonio—K20BW, Ch. 20, Trinity Broadcasting Network Inc. Phone: 714-832-2950. Fax: 714-730-0661.

Technical Facilities: 1000-w TPO, 57.9-kw ERP, 131-ft. above ground, 1161-ft. above sea level, lat. 29° 31' 10", long. 98° 34' 15".

Transmitter: Wurzbach Rd. & Fredericksburg Rd., San Antonio.

Ownership: Trinity Broadcasting Network Inc.

Personnel: Jim R. Moss, Executive Director.

San Antonio—K45FJ, Ch. 45, Trinity Broadcasting Network Inc. Phone: 714-832-2950. Fax: 714-730-0661.

Studio: 600 N. Loop 1604 E, San Antonio, TX 78232.

Technical Facilities: 1000-w TPO, 2.5-kw ERP, 266-ft. above ground, 1204-ft. above sea level, lat. 29° 37' 12", long. 98° 22' 49".

Transmitter: 5031 Judson Rd., San Antonio, 12-mi. N of Loop 1604.

TV & Cable Factbook No. 78

Ownership: Trinity Broadcasting Network Inc.

Personnel: Rick Rodriguez, Sales Representative; Dale Taylor, Chief Engineer.

■ **San Antonio**—K51JF, Ch. 51, Mintz Broadcasting. Phone: 361-883-1763.

Technical Facilities: 9.5-kw ERP, 492-ft. above ground, 1172-ft. above sea level, lat. 29° 26' 29", long. 98° 30' 22".

Ownership: Mintz Broadcasting.

Personnel: Edward Rivera, General Manager; Carlos Ortiz, Sales Manager.

San Antonio—KBNB-LP, Ch. 10, B Communications Joint Venture. Phone: 361-241-7944.

Technical Facilities: 1-kw ERP, 436-ft. above ground, 1115-ft. above sea level, lat. 29° 26' 29", long. 98° 30' 22".

Began Operation: September 22, 1987.

Ownership: B Communications Joint Venture.

■ **San Antonio**—KEVI-LP, Ch. 25, Aracelis Ortiz Corp. Phone: 956-412-5600.

Technical Facilities: 12.6-kw ERP, 299-ft. above ground, 1237-ft. above sea level, lat. 29° 37' 12", long. 98° 22' 49".

Ownership: Aracelis Ortiz Corp.

■ **San Antonio**—KFLZ-CA, Ch. 7, B Communications Joint Venture. Phone: 361-241-7944.

Technical Facilities: 10-w TPO, 0.122-kw ERP, 193-ft. above ground, 725-ft. above sea level, lat. 29° 18' 04", long. 98° 24' 59".

Holds CP for change to channel number 6, 0.5-kw ERP, 453-ft. above ground, 1132-ft. above sea level, lat. 29° 26' 29", long. 98° 30' 22". BDISTVA-20070622ACS.

Transmitter: 1-mi. SW of I-37 S on Blue Wing Rd.

Ownership: B Communications Joint Venture.

■ **San Antonio**—KFTO-CA, Ch. 67, Telefutura Partnership of San Antonio. Phone: 310-556-7600.

Technical Facilities: 10.9-kw ERP, 328-ft. above ground, 981-ft. above sea level, lat. 29° 25' 30", long. 98° 29' 03".

Ownership: Univision Communications Inc.

■ **San Antonio**—KGMM-CA, Ch. 44, Caballero Acquisition Inc.

Technical Facilities: 51-kw ERP, 899-ft. above ground, 1424-ft. above sea level, lat. 29° 17' 39", long. 98° 15' 30".

Ownership: Caballero Acquisition Inc.

Personnel: Eduardo Caballero, Chief Executive Officer.

San Antonio—KISA-LP, Ch. 40, Mako Communications LLC. Phone: 361-883-1763.

Technical Facilities: 7-kw ERP, 420-ft. above ground, 1099-ft. above sea level, lat. 29° 26' 29.06", long. 98° 30' 21.7".

Ownership: Mako Communications LLC.

Personnel: Terry Tackitt, General Manager; Victor Pfau, Chief Engineer.

San Antonio—KMHZ-LP, Ch. 11, Louis Martinez Family Group LLC. Phone: 951-940-1700.

Technical Facilities: 0.999-kw ERP, 459-ft. above ground, 1139-ft. above sea level, lat. 29° 26' 29", long. 98° 30' 22".

Ownership: Louis Martinez Family Group LLC.

San Antonio—KMXU-LP, Ch. 15, Louis Martinez Family Group LLC. Phone: 951-940-1700.

Technical Facilities: 9.99-kw ERP, 476-ft. above ground, 1155-ft. above sea level, lat. 29° 26' 29", long. 98° 30' 21.7".

Holds CP for change to 119.6-kw ERP, BMPTTL-20060321AES.

Began Operation: January 23, 2009.

Ownership: Louis Martinez Family Group LLC.

■ **San Antonio**—KNIC-CA, Ch. 17, Telefutura Parthership of San Antonio. Phone: 310-348-3600.

Technical Facilities: 1000-w TPO, 36.8-kw ERP, 548-ft. above ground, 1220-ft. above sea level, lat. 29° 25' 41", long. 98° 29' 32".

Holds CP for change to channel number 34, 9.99-kw ERP, BDISTTA-20070615ADF.

Transmitter: NBC Plaza, 112 E. Pecan, San Antonio.

Ownership: Univision Communications Inc.

Personnel: David Loving, Vice President & General Manager.

San Antonio—KOBS-LP, Ch. 19, Daniel Gomez. Phone: 214-330-8700.

Technical Facilities: 9.99-kw ERP, 397-ft. above ground, 1076-ft. above sea level, lat. 29° 26' 29", long. 98° 30' 22".

Ownership: Daniel Gomez.

■ **San Antonio**—KRYT-LP, Ch. 51, Aracelis Ortiz Corp. Phone: 956-412-5600.

Technical Facilities: 994-w TPO, 60-kw ERP, 469-ft. above ground, 1391-ft. above sea level, lat. 29° 17' 39", long. 98° 15' 30".

Holds CP for change to channel number 36, 9.999-kw ERP, 341-ft. above ground, 981-ft. above sea level, lat. 29° 25' 52", long. 98° 29' 23". BDISTTL-20070403ABU.

Transmitter: FM 1560 & Galm Rd.

Ownership: Aracelis Ortiz.

San Antonio—KSAA-LP, Ch. 28, Mako Communications LLC. Phones: 361-883-1763; 361-883-3160.

Technical Facilities: 1000-w TPO, 14.5-kw ERP, 361-ft. above ground, 1041-ft. above sea level, lat. 29° 26' 30", long. 98° 30' 23".

Transmitter: 4-mi. from Elmendorf.

Ownership: Mako Communications LLC.

San Antonio—KTDF-LP, Ch. 18, Joseph W. Shaffer. Phone: 928-717-0828.

Technical Facilities: 11.5-kw ERP, 547-ft. above ground, 1220-ft. above sea level, lat. 29° 25' 42", long. 98° 29' 33".

■ **San Antonio**—KVDF-CA, Ch. 31, Una Vez Mas San Antonio License LLC. Phone: 214-754-7008.

Technical Facilities: 1000-w TPO, 38.4-kw ERP, 469-ft. above ground, 1148-ft. above sea level, lat. 29° 26' 30", long. 98° 30' 28".

Transmitter: 1010 W. Laurel.

Ownership: Una Vez Mas GP LLC.

Personnel: Brett Huggins, Chief Engineer.

■ **San Antonio**—KXTM-LP, Ch. 21, Humberto Lopez. Phone: 361-289-8877. Fax: 361-289-7722.

Technical Facilities: 26.4-kw ERP, 801-ft. above ground, 1325-ft. above sea level, lat. 29° 17' 39", long. 98° 15' 30".

Holds CP for change to 9.9-kw ERP, 328-ft. above ground, 978-ft. above sea level, lat. 29° 25' 06", long. 98° 29' 01". BPTTA-20050728AAA.

Multichannel TV Sound: Stereo and separate audio program.

Ownership: Humberto Lopez.

■ **San Marcos**—KHPM-CA, Ch. 40, KXAN Inc. Phones: 512-476-3636; 202-462-6065. Fax: 512-476-1520.

Technical Facilities: 8-kw ERP, 39-ft. above ground, 801-ft. above sea level, lat. 29° 53' 26", long. 97° 56' 54".

Holds CP for change to 0.037-kw ERP, BDFCDTA-20060329AMA.

Ownership: LIN TV Corp.

San Marcos—KTXU-LP, Ch. 47, Gerald G. Benavides. Phone: 361-241-7944.

Technical Facilities: 3-kw ERP, 787-ft. above ground, 1609-ft. above sea level, lat. 30° 19' 23", long. 97° 47' 58".

Transmitter: Mathews & Pecan Sts.

Ownership: Gerald G. Benavides.

San Saba—K41HX, Ch. 41, Foster Charitable Foundation Inc. Phone: 830-896-1230.

Technical Facilities: 45-kw ERP, 149-ft. above ground, 1384-ft. above sea level, lat. 31° 11' 26", long. 98° 42' 55".

Ownership: Foster Charitable Foundation Inc.

Seminole—K17FX, Ch. 17, Ramar Communications Inc. Phone: 806-745-3434.

Technical Facilities: 6.8-kw ERP, 400-ft. above ground, 4012-ft. above sea level, lat. 32° 43' 30", long. 102° 38' 01".

Holds CP for change to 15-kw ERP, 200-ft. above ground, 3547-ft. above sea level, lat. 32° 57' 01", long. 102° 33' 01". BDFCDTL-20080812AAW.

Ownership: Ramar Communications Inc.

Seminole—K21FV, Ch. 21, Ramar Communications Inc. Phone: 806-745-3434. Fax: 806-745-3434.

Technical Facilities: 6.8-kw ERP, 400-ft. above ground, 3684-ft. above sea level, lat. 32° 43' 30", long. 102° 38' 01".

Holds CP for change to 15-kw ERP, 200-ft. above ground, 3547-ft. above sea level, lat. 32° 57' 01", long. 102° 33' 01". BDFCDTL-20080812ABA.

Ownership: Ramar Communications Inc.

Seminole—K58GN, Ch. 58, Trinity Broadcasting Network Inc. Phone: 714-832-2950. Fax: 714-730-0661.

Technical Facilities: 10-kw ERP, lat. 32° 43' 54", long. 102° 38' 53".

Ownership: Trinity Broadcasting Network Inc.

Seminole—KSGD-LP, Ch. 49, Prime Time Christian Broadcasting Inc.

Technical Facilities: 0.87-kw ERP, lat. 32° 44' 47", long. 102° 40' 10".

Transmitter: 2.75-mi. N & 0.75-mi. E of Seminole off of FM 214.

Ownership: Prime Time Christian Broadcasting Inc.

Sherman—KADY-LP, Ch. 34, Una Vez Mas Sherman License LLC. Phone: 214-754-7008.

Technical Facilities: 10-kw ERP, 250-ft. above ground, 970-ft. above sea level, lat. 33° 42' 09", long. 96° 34' 05".

Ownership: Una Vez Mas GP LLC.

Snyder—K42ET, Ch. 42, Ramar Communications Inc. Phone: 806-748-9300.

Technical Facilities: 9.31-kw ERP, 310-ft. above ground, 2745-ft. above sea level, lat. 32° 45' 34", long. 100° 54' 47".

Ownership: Ramar Communications Inc.

Snyder—K44FG, Ch. 44, Nexstar Finance Inc. Phone: 972-373-8800.

Technical Facilities: 0.08-kw ERP, lat. 32° 46' 52", long. 100° 53' 52".

Holds CP for change to 0.0004-kw ERP, 207-ft. above ground, 2705-ft. above sea level, BDFCDTT-20060403AIH.

Ownership: Nexstar Broadcasting Group Inc.

Snyder—K47IP, Ch. 47, Ramar Communications Inc. Phone: 806-748-9300. Fax: 806-748-1949.

Technical Facilities: 9.31-kw ERP, 310-ft. above ground, 2745-ft. above sea level, lat. 32° 45' 34", long. 100° 54' 47".

Holds CP for change to 7.89-kw ERP, 69-ft. above ground, 2755-ft. above sea level, lat. 32° 53' 07", long. 101° 06' 39". BDFCDTT-20080806ACE.

Ownership: Ramar Communications Inc.

Snyder—K49GT, Ch. 49, Ramar Communications Inc. Phone: 806-748-9300.

Technical Facilities: 9.31-kw ERP, 310-ft. above ground, 2745-ft. above sea level, lat. 32° 45' 34", long. 100° 54' 47".

Holds CP for change to 7.89-kw ERP, 69-ft. above ground, 2755-ft. above sea level, lat. 32° 53' 07", long. 101° 06' 39". BDFCDTT-20080806ACF.

Ownership: Ramar Communications Inc.

Somerville—KUTW-LP, Ch. 34, Borger Broadcasting Inc., Debtor in Possession. Phone: 501-219-2400.

Technical Facilities: 150-kw ERP, 376-ft. above ground, 689-ft. above sea level, lat. 30° 24' 51", long. 96° 25' 52".

Began Operation: August 23, 1994.

Ownership: Equity Media Holdings Corp., Debtor in Possession.

■ **Stamford**—KIDT-LP, Ch. 44, Bayou City Broadcasting LLC. Phone: 281-380-0076.

Technical Facilities: 10-kw ERP, 515-ft. above ground, 2205-ft. above sea level, lat. 32° 56' 16", long. 99° 57' 20".

Transmitter: 0.7-mi. NW of FM 1661.

Began Operation: May 1, 1996.

Ownership: Bayou City Broadcasting LLC.

Sweetwater—KASX-LP, Ch. 22, Una Vez Mas Sweetwater License I LLC. Phone: 214-754-7008.

Technical Facilities: 10-kw ERP, 636-ft. above ground, 2736-ft. above sea level, lat. 32° 29' 11", long. 100° 22' 05".

Ownership: Una Vez Mas GP LLC.

■ **Sweetwater**—KIDB-CA, Ch. 35, Bayou City Broadcasting LLC. Phone: 281-380-0076.

Technical Facilities: 7.03-kw ERP, 325-ft. above ground, 2581-ft. above sea level, lat. 32° 25' 50.3", long. 100° 16' 51".

Began Operation: June 9, 1997.

Ownership: Bayou City Broadcasting LLC.

Sweetwater—KSWR-LP, Ch. 39, Una Vez Mas Sweetwater License II LLC. Phone: 214-754-7008.

Technical Facilities: 10-kw ERP, 636-ft. above ground, 2736-ft. above sea level, lat. 32° 29' 11", long. 100° 22' 05".

Ownership: Una Vez Mas GP LLC.

Texarkana—K30EA, Ch. 30, Trinity Broadcasting Network Inc. Phone: 714-832-2950. Fax: 714-730-0661.

Technical Facilities: 13.5-kw ERP, lat. 33° 25' 48", long. 94° 05' 08".

Ownership: Trinity Broadcasting Network Inc.

■ **Texarkana**—K41EQ, Ch. 41, Three Angels Broadcasting Network Inc. Phone: 618-627-4651. Fax: 618-627-4155.

Studio: RR 3, State Rte. 34, PO Box 176A, Thompsonville, IL 62890.

Technical Facilities: 1000-w TPO, 9.08-kw ERP, 774-ft. above ground, lat. 33° 25' 48", long. 94° 05' 08".

Transmitter: SW of Rosewood St. & Westlawn Dr.

Ownership: Three Angels Broadcasting Network Inc.

Personnel: Moses Primo, Chief Engineer; Linda Shelton, Program Director.

Tulia—K25CP, Ch. 25, Nexstar Broadcasting Inc. Phone: 972-373-8800.

Technical Facilities: 7.03-kw ERP, lat. 34° 23' 27", long. 101° 38' 37".

Holds CP for change to 0.005-kw ERP, 308-ft. above ground, 3779-ft. above sea level, lat. 34° 32' 12", long. 101° 44' 25". BDFCDTT-20060403AIG.

Ownership: Nexstar Broadcasting Group Inc.

Tulia—K36CC, Ch. 36, City of Tulia.

Technical Facilities: 7.16-kw ERP, lat. 34° 23' 27", long. 101° 38' 37".

Ownership: City of Tulia.

Tulia—K55JV, Ch. 55, City of Tulia. Phone: 806-995-3547.

Technical Facilities: 0.886-kw ERP, 308-ft. above ground, 3779-ft. above sea level, lat. 34° 32' 12", long. 101° 44' 25".

Ownership: City of Tulia.

Tulia—K57JK, Ch. 57, City of Tulia. Phone: 806-995-3547.

Technical Facilities: 0.886-kw ERP, 308-ft. above ground, 3779-ft. above sea level, lat. 34° 32' 12", long. 101° 44' 25".

Ownership: City of Tulia.

Turkey, etc.—K54AW, Ch. 54, Arnold Cruze. Phone: 806-259-2879.

Technical Facilities: 0.47-kw ERP, 121-ft. above ground, 3251-ft. above sea level, lat. 34° 24' 01", long. 101° 07' 11".

Turkey, etc.—K56DM, Ch. 56, Arnold Cruze. Phone: 806-259-2879.

Technical Facilities: 0.47-kw ERP, 121-ft. above ground, 3251-ft. above sea level, lat. 34° 24' 01", long. 101° 07' 11".

Turkey, etc.—K58DF, Ch. 58, Arnold Cruze. Phone: 806-259-2879.

Technical Facilities: 0.47-kw ERP, 121-ft. above ground, 3251-ft. above sea level, lat. 34° 24' 01", long. 101° 07' 11".

Turkey, etc.—K60BW, Ch. 60, Arnold Cruze. Phone: 806-259-2879.

Technical Facilities: 2.07-kw ERP, 3251-ft. above sea level, lat. 34° 24' 01", long. 101° 07' 11".

Tuscola—K36HF, Ch. 36, Marcia T. Turner. Phone: 954-732-9539.

Technical Facilities: 50-kw ERP, 102-ft. above ground, 1909-ft. above sea level, lat. 32° 22' 21", long. 99° 47' 42".

Ownership: Marcia T. Turner.

Tyler—K20DL, Ch. 20, Progressive Cable Communications Inc.

Technical Facilities: 1000-w TPO, 8.9-kw ERP, 889-ft. above ground, lat. 32° 21' 43", long. 95° 16' 10".

Transmitter: 0.37-mi. N of Commerce St. & Loop 323.

Ownership: Progressive Communications Inc.

Tyler—KTPN-LP, Ch. 48, Warwick Communications Inc. Phone: 703-253-2027.

Technical Facilities: 988-w TPO, 17.3-kw ERP, 430-ft. above ground, 882-ft. above sea level, lat. 32° 21' 43", long. 95° 16' 10".

Transmitter: 1702 E. Commerce St., Tyler.

Ownership: White Knight Holdings Inc.

■ **Tyler-Jacksonville**—K26GA, Ch. 26, Three Angels Broadcasting Network Inc. Phone: 618-627-4651. Fax: 618-627-4155.

Studio: 3391 Charley Good Rd, West Frankfort, IL 62896.

Technical Facilities: 1000-w TPO, 36-kw ERP, 500-ft. above ground, 1083-ft. above sea level, lat. 32° 03' 40", long. 95° 18' 50".

Transmitter: 0.9-mi. W of Hwy. 69.

Ownership: Three Angels Broadcasting Network Inc.

Personnel: Moses Primo, Chief Engineer.

Uvalde—K15BV, Ch. 15, Trinity Broadcasting Network Inc. Phone: 714-832-2950. Fax: 714-730-0661.

Technical Facilities: 1000-w TPO, 0.9-kw ERP, 121-ft. above ground, 1119-ft. above sea level, lat. 29° 10' 48", long. 99° 48' 47".

Transmitter: 1.4-mi. S of US Rte. 90 & SR 481, near Uvalde.

Ownership: Trinity Broadcasting Network Inc.

Personnel: Paul F. Crouch, General Manager; Ben Miller, Chief Engineer; Rod Henke, Sales Manager.

Uvalde—K17GL, Ch. 17, J.B. Salazar. Phone: 830-278-3523. Fax: 830-591-1120.

Technical Facilities: 0.999-kw ERP, 51-ft. above ground, 1201-ft. above sea level, lat. 29° 15' 41", long. 99° 44' 54".

Holds CP for change to 312-ft. above ground, 1358-ft. above sea level, lat. 29° 21' 46", long. 99° 37' 14". BPTTL-20090406ADC.

Ownership: J. B. Salazar.

Uvalde—K42GJ, Ch. 42, J.B. Salazar. Phone: 830-278-3523.

Technical Facilities: 10-kw ERP, 351-ft. above ground, 1270-ft. above sea level, lat. 29° 31' 25", long. 98° 43' 25".

Holds CP for change to 9.99-kw ERP, 394-ft. above ground, 1621-ft. above sea level, lat. 29° 41' 06", long. 98° 26' 59". BPTTL-20090423ADD.

Began Operation: September 30, 1993.

Ownership: J. B. Salazar.

Uvalde—K45HM, Ch. 45, J.B. Salazar. Phone: 830-278-3523. Fax: 830-591-1120.

Technical Facilities: 0.999-kw ERP, 51-ft. above ground, 1201-ft. above sea level, lat. 29° 15' 41", long. 99° 44' 53".

Ownership: J. B. Salazar.

Uvalde—K47IJ, Ch. 47, J.B. Salazar. Phone: 830-278-3523. Fax: 830-591-1120.

Technical Facilities: 9.99-kw ERP, 822-ft. above ground, 2369-ft. above sea level, lat. 29° 37' 11", long. 99° 02' 56".

Began Operation: January 27, 1989.

Ownership: J. B. Salazar.

Uvalde—K49HH, Ch. 49, J.B. Salazar. Phone: 830-278-3523.

Technical Facilities: 0.999-kw ERP, 51-ft. above ground, 1201-ft. above sea level, lat. 29° 15' 40", long. 99° 44' 53".

Holds CP for change to channel number 6, 394-ft. above ground, 1440-ft. above sea level, lat. 29° 21' 46", long. 99° 37' 14". BDISTVL-20081015ABR.

Began Operation: March 30, 2006.

Ownership: J. B. Salazar.

Uvalde—KNHB-LP, Ch. 7, CTV Broadcasting LLC. Phone: 713-358-4229. Fax: 956-428-4848.

Technical Facilities: 0.108-kw ERP, 100-ft. above ground, 1007-ft. above sea level, lat. 29° 12' 25", long. 99° 47' 55".

Ownership: CTV Broadcasting LLC.

Victoria—K38IG, Ch. 38, Mosely Enterprises LLC. Phone: 318-992-7766.

Technical Facilities: 0.11-kw ERP, 50-ft. above ground, 148-ft. above sea level, lat. 28° 46' 42", long. 96° 58' 08".

Holds CP for change to channel number 18, 9.99-kw ERP, 440-ft. above ground, 538-ft. above sea level, BDISTTL-20070402KPN.

Ownership: Mosely Enterprises LLC.

Victoria—K39HB, Ch. 39, Howard Mintz. Phone: 361-883-1763.

Technical Facilities: 5-kw ERP, 443-ft. above ground, 528-ft. above sea level, lat. 28° 47' 23", long. 96° 56' 20".

Holds CP for change to 0.45-kw ERP, BDFCDTL-20090515ABP.

Ownership: Howard Mintz.

Victoria—K43DV, Ch. 43, Trinity Broadcasting Network Inc. Phone: 714-832-2950. Fax: 714-730-0661.

Technical Facilities: 8.63-kw ERP, 436-ft. above ground, 571-ft. above sea level, lat. 28° 49' 00", long. 97° 03' 57".

Ownership: Trinity Broadcasting Network Inc.

Victoria—K49IE, Ch. 49, Telecom Wireless LLC. Phone: 954-614-2416.

Technical Facilities: 1-kw ERP, 328-ft. above ground, 413-ft. above sea level, lat. 28° 46' 45", long. 96° 56' 32".

Ownership: Telecom Wireless LLC.

■ **Victoria**—KCPV-LP, Ch. 30, Club Communications. Phone: 361-883-1763.

Technical Facilities: 2-kw ERP, 443-ft. above ground, 528-ft. above sea level, lat. 28° 47' 23", long. 96° 56' 20.5".

Ownership: Club Communications.

Personnel: Gerald Benavides, General Manager.

Victoria—KMOL-LP, Ch. 17, Saga Broadcasting LLC. Phone: 313-886-7070.

Technical Facilities: 50-kw ERP, 417-ft. above ground, 559-ft. above sea level, lat. 28° 50' 42", long. 97° 07' 33".

Ownership: Saga Communications Inc.

Victoria—KSVH-LP, Ch. 23, KM Communications Inc. Phone: 847-674-0864.

Technical Facilities: 1.45-kw ERP, 299-ft. above ground, 356-ft. above sea level, lat. 28° 46' 07", long. 96° 59' 10".

Ownership: KM Communications Inc.

■ **Victoria**—KTJA-CA, Ch. 51, Una Vez Mas Victoria License LLC. Phone: 214-754-7008.

Technical Facilities: 48.8-kw ERP, 433-ft. above ground, 531-ft. above sea level, lat. 28° 46' 43", long. 96° 58' 09".

Ownership: Una Vez Mas GP LLC.

Personnel: Gerald Benavides, General Manager.

Victoria—KUNU-LP, Ch. 21, Saga Communications Inc. Phone: 313-886-7070.

Technical Facilities: 1-kw ERP, 396-ft. above ground, 486-ft. above sea level, lat. 28° 46' 37", long. 96° 57' 45".

Holds CP for change to 23.04-kw ERP, 480-ft. above ground, 569-ft. above sea level, BPTTL-20040924ACN.

Ownership: Saga Communications Inc.

Victoria—KVCV-LP, Ch. 42, Windsong Communications Inc. Phone: 936-443-4451.

Technical Facilities: 8-kw ERP, 443-ft. above ground, 528-ft. above sea level, lat. 28° 47' 23.03", long. 96° 56' 20.45".

Ownership: Windsong Communications Inc.

■ **Victoria**—KVHM-LP, Ch. 31, Humberto Lopez. Phone: 361-575-9533. Fax: 361-575-9502.

Technical Facilities: 1000-w TPO, 27-kw ERP, 324-ft. above ground, 374-ft. above sea level, lat. 28° 46' 04", long. 96° 59' 12".

Transmitter: Hand Rd., 2.8-mi. from Victoria.

Ownership: Humberto Lopez.

Personnel: Homer Lopez, General Manager; Ray Lopez, Chief Engineer; Ernest Lopez, Sales Manager.

Victoria—KVTX-LP, Ch. 45, Saga Broadcasting Corp. Phone: 313-886-7070.

Technical Facilities: 1-kw ERP, 446-ft. above ground, 535-ft. above sea level, lat. 28° 46' 37", long. 96° 57' 45".

Ownership: Saga Communications Inc.

Victoria—KXTS-LP, Ch. 41, Saga Broadcasting Corp. Phone: 313-886-7070.

Technical Facilities: 156-w TPO, 1-kw ERP, 495-ft. above ground, 574-ft. above sea level, lat. 28° 46' 41", long. 96° 57' 38".

Holds CP for change to channel number 28, 23.04-kw ERP, 480-ft. above ground, 569-ft. above sea level, lat. 28° 46' 37", long. 96° 57' 45". BPTTL-20041122AIN.

Transmitter: 5-mi. SE of Victoria.

Ownership: Saga Communications Inc.

Victoria—KXVT-LP, Ch. 47, Telecom Wireless LLC. Phone: 954-614-2416.

Technical Facilities: 50-kw ERP, 410-ft. above ground, 495-ft. above sea level, lat. 28° 46' 45", long. 96° 56' 32".

Ownership: Telecom Wireless LLC.

Victoria—KZHO-LP, Ch. 45, Hispanic Christian Community Network Inc. Phone: 214-879-0001.

Technical Facilities: 50-kw ERP, 469-ft. above ground, 518-ft. above sea level, lat. 28° 58' 11", long. 95° 59' 01".

Holds CP for change to channel number 40, 5-kw ERP, 361-ft. above ground, 397-ft. above sea level, lat. 29° 10' 50", long. 95° 40' 02". BDISDTL-20081211ABA.

Began Operation: November 15, 2007.

Ownership: Hispanic Christian Community Network Inc.

Vidor—K66GD, Ch. 66, Roger Mills. Phone: 801-250-3018.

Technical Facilities: 12-kw ERP, 335-ft. above ground, 350-ft. above sea level, lat. 30° 06' 40", long. 94° 03' 10".

Ownership: Roger Mills.

Waco—KWKO-LP, Ch. 38, Borger Broadcasting Inc., Debtor in Possession. Phone: 501-219-2400.

Technical Facilities: 41-kw ERP, lat. 31° 28' 00", long. 97° 11' 14".

Transmitter: 1.4-mi. SE of Interstate 35 as it crosses Little Elm Creek.

Began Operation: December 10, 1997.

Ownership: Equity Media Holdings Corp., Debtor in Possession.

Welch—KWGD-LP, Ch. 19, Prime Time Christian Broadcasting Inc. Phone: 432-563-0420. Fax: 432-563-1736.

Technical Facilities: 100-w TPO, 0.8-kw ERP, 210-ft. above ground, 3337-ft. above sea level, lat. 32° 57' 52", long. 102° 07' 49".

Transmitter: 2.5-mi. N of Welch, off Hwy. 137.

Ownership: Prime Time Christian Broadcasting Inc.

Personnel: Al Cooper, General Manager; Jay Wescott, Chief Engineer; Jeff Welter, Sales Manager.

Wellington, etc.—K27BZ, Ch. 27, Greenbelt TV Translator System Inc.

Technical Facilities: 20-w TPO, 0.216-kw ERP, 226-ft. above ground, 2192-ft. above sea level, lat. 34° 46' 14", long. 100° 11' 28".

Transmitter: 4-mi. S of Wellington.

Ownership: Greenbelt TV Translator System Inc.

Wellington, etc.—K29BH, Ch. 29, Greenbelt TV Translator System Inc.

Technical Facilities: 0.214-kw ERP, 220-ft. above ground, 2185-ft. above sea level, lat. 34° 46' 14", long. 100° 11' 28".

Wellington, etc.—K31BZ, Ch. 31, Greenbelt TV Translator System Inc.

Technical Facilities: 0.214-kw ERP, 220-ft. above ground, 2185-ft. above sea level, lat. 34° 46' 14", long. 100° 11' 28".

Wellington, etc.—K33CF, Ch. 33, Greenbelt TV Translator System Inc.

Technical Facilities: 0.214-kw ERP, 220-ft. above ground, 2185-ft. above sea level, lat. 34° 46' 14", long. 100° 11' 28".

■ **Wichita Falls**—K20DN, Ch. 20, Christian Family Network Television Inc. Phone: 940-322-6229.

Technical Facilities: 100-w TPO, 1.24-kw ERP, 1063-ft. above sea level, lat. 33° 54' 31", long. 98° 29' 45".

Transmitter: 1200 9th St.

Ownership: Christian Family Network Television Inc.

Personnel: Rod Payne, General Manager.

Wichita Falls—K26DL, Ch. 26, Trinity Christian Center of Santa Ana Inc. Phone: 714-832-2950.

Technical Facilities: 5.9-kw ERP, 407-ft. above ground, 1401-ft. above sea level, lat. 33° 53' 00", long. 98° 36' 10".

Ownership: Trinity Broadcasting Network Inc.

■ **Wichita Falls**—K30DJ, Ch. 30, Christian Family Network Television Inc. Phone: 940-322-6229.

Technical Facilities: 27.2-kw ERP, 440-ft. above ground, 1309-ft. above sea level, lat. 33° 53' 50", long. 98° 32' 33".

Ownership: Christian Family Network Television Inc.

Wichita Falls—K40HZ, Ch. 40, Mosely Enterprises LLC. Phone: 318-992-7766.

Technical Facilities: 0.11-kw ERP, 49-ft. above ground, 1059-ft. above sea level, lat. 33° 53' 51", long. 98° 32' 32".

Holds CP for change to 20-kw ERP, 351-ft. above ground, 1361-ft. above sea level, BPTTL-20070328AGP.

Ownership: Mosely Enterprises LLC.

Wichita Falls—K44GS, Ch. 44, North Texas Public Broadcasting Inc. Phone: 214-871-1390.

Technical Facilities: 3.34-kw ERP, 512-ft. above ground, 1529-ft. above sea level, lat. 33° 54' 04", long. 98° 32' 21".

Ownership: North Texas Public Broadcasting Inc.

Wichita Falls—K48HU, Ch. 48, Family Broadcasting Group Inc. Phone: 405-631-7335.

Technical Facilities: 8.71-kw ERP, 168-ft. above ground, 1206-ft. above sea level, lat. 33° 54' 43", long. 98° 24' 46".

Began Operation: March 31, 1998.

Ownership: Family Broadcasting Group Inc.

Wichita Falls—KAWF-LP, Ch. 51, Una Vez Mas Wichita Falls License LLC. Phone: 214-754-7008.

Technical Facilities: 7.4-kw ERP, 492-ft. above ground, 1497-ft. above sea level, lat. 33° 52' 47.7", long. 98° 35' 17.8".

Ownership: Una Vez Mas GP LLC.

Wichita Falls—KHWF-LP, Ch. 25, Hispanic Christian Community Network Inc. Phone: 214-434-6357.

Technical Facilities: 0.3-kw ERP, 49-ft. above ground, 1076-ft. above sea level, lat. 33° 58' 20", long. 98° 45' 37".

Ownership: Hispanic Christian Community Network Inc.

Wichita Falls—KJBO-LP, Ch. 35, Mission Broadcasting of Wichita Falls Inc. Phone: 330-335-8808.

Studio: 3800 Call Field Rd., Wichita Falls, TX 76308.

Technical Facilities: 1000-w TPO, 10.5-kw ERP, 400-ft. above ground, 1411-ft. above sea level, lat. 33° 53' 50", long. 98° 32' 33".

Holds CP for change to 0.062-kw ERP, BDFCDTL-20060403ADA.

Transmitter: 3700 Onaway Trail, Wichita Falls.

Ownership: Mission Broadcasting Inc.

Personnel: Pete D'Acosta, General Manager.

Wichita Falls—KTWW-LP, Ch. 68, Equity Media Holdings Corp., Debtor in Possession. Phone: 501-219-2400.

Technical Facilities: 13.7-kw ERP, 476-ft. above ground, 1481-ft. above sea level, lat. 33° 52' 48", long. 98° 35' 18".

Holds CP for change to channel number 14, 150-kw ERP, BDISTTL-20060403AQB.

Began Operation: January 30, 2006.

Ownership: Equity Media Holdings Corp., Debtor in Possession.

Wichita Falls—KUWF-LP, Ch. 36, Equity Media Holdings Corp., Debtor in Possession. Phone: 501-219-2400.

Technical Facilities: 2.5-kw ERP, 328-ft. above ground, 1333-ft. above sea level, lat. 33° 52' 48", long. 98° 35' 18".

Began Operation: January 19, 2007.

Ownership: Equity Media Holdings Corp., Debtor in Possession.

Wichita Falls—KYWF-LP, Ch. 52, Hispanic Christian Community Network Inc. Phone: 214-879-0081.

Technical Facilities: 10-kw ERP, 295-ft. above ground, 1337-ft. above sea level, lat. 33° 51' 38", long. 98° 38' 57".

Began Operation: August 1, 2007.

Ownership: Hispanic Christian Community Network Inc.

Woodville—K23HF, Ch. 23, Hosanna Apostolic Ministries Broadcasting Corp. Phone: 520-971-9274.

Technical Facilities: 1-kw ERP, 164-ft. above ground, 397-ft. above sea level, lat. 30° 46' 45", long. 94° 24' 30".

Began Operation: February 8, 2008.

Ownership: Hosanna Apostolic Ministries Broadcasting Corp.

Utah

Alton—K09NV, Ch. 9, Western Kane County Special Service District No. 1. Phone: 435-644-5089.

Technical Facilities: 0.127-kw ERP, 7920-ft. above sea level, lat. 37° 22' 26", long. 112° 32' 07".

Ownership: Western Kane County Special Service District No. 1.

Alton—K11OC, Ch. 11, Western Kane County Special Service District No. 1. Phone: 435-644-5089.

Technical Facilities: 0.122-kw ERP, 7910-ft. above sea level, lat. 37° 22' 26", long. 112° 32' 07".

Ownership: Western Kane County Special Service District No. 1.

Alton—K13OR, Ch. 13, Western Kane County Special Service District No. 1. Phone: 435-644-5089.

Technical Facilities: 0.122-kw ERP, 7910-ft. above sea level, lat. 37° 22' 26", long. 112° 32' 07".

Ownership: Western Kane County Special Service District No. 1.

Alton—K21IH-D, Ch. 21, Western Kane County Special Service District No. 1. Phone: 435-644-5089.

Technical Facilities: 0.004-kw ERP, 16-ft. above ground, 7785-ft. above sea level, lat. 37° 22' 26.2", long. 112° 32' 07.7".

Began Operation: December 15, 2008.

Ownership: Western Kane County Special Service District No. 1.

Alton—K24IH-D, Ch. 24, Western Kane County Special Service District No. 1. Phone: 435-644-5089.

Technical Facilities: 0.004-kw ERP, 16-ft. above ground, 7785-ft. above sea level, lat. 37° 22' 26.2", long. 112° 32' 07.7".

Began Operation: December 15, 2008.

Ownership: Western Kane County Special Service District No. 1.

Alton—K25KN-D, Ch. 25, Western Kane County Special Service District No. 1. Phone: 435-644-5089.

Technical Facilities: 0.004-kw ERP, 16-ft. above ground, 7785-ft. above sea level, lat. 37° 22' 26.2", long. 112° 32' 07.7".

Began Operation: December 15, 2008.

Ownership: Western Kane County Special Service District No. 1.

Alton—K34FO-D, Ch. 34, Western Kane County Special Service District No. 1. Phone: 435-644-5089.

Technical Facilities: 20-ft. above ground, 7913-ft. above sea level, lat. 37° 22' 26", long. 112° 32' 07".

Holds CP for change to 0.038-kw ERP, 42-ft. above ground, 7811-ft. above sea level, BDFCDTT-20090106AAC.

Began Operation: November 6, 1996.

Ownership: Western Kane County Special Service District No. 1.

Alton, etc.—K22HV-D, Ch. 22, U. of Utah. Phone: 801-585-3601.

Technical Facilities: 0.003-kw ERP, 16-ft. above ground, 7785-ft. above sea level, lat. 37° 22' 26.2", long. 112° 32' 07.7".

Began Operation: December 15, 2008.

Ownership: U. of Utah.

Alton, etc.—K38IN, Ch. 38, U. of Utah.

Technical Facilities: 0.068-kw ERP, 20-ft. above ground, 7933-ft. above sea level, lat. 37° 22' 26", long. 112° 32' 07".

Ownership: U. of Utah.

Antimony—K02FA, Ch. 2, Piute County. Phone: 435-577-2840.

Technical Facilities: 0.002-kw ERP, lat. 38° 10' 50", long. 112° 02' 30".

Ownership: Piute County.

Antimony—K04FG, Ch. 4, Piute County. Phone: 435-577-2840.

Technical Facilities: 0.008-kw ERP, lat. 38° 10' 50", long. 112° 02' 30".

Ownership: Piute County.

Antimony—K05DO, Ch. 5, Piute County. Phone: 435-577-2840.

Technical Facilities: 0.002-kw ERP, lat. 38° 10' 50", long. 112° 02' 30".

Ownership: Piute County.

Antimony—K36IG-D, Ch. 36, Piute County. Phone: 435-577-2840.

Technical Facilities: 0.006-kw ERP, 14-ft. above ground, 7409-ft. above sea level, lat. 38° 10' 56.8", long. 112° 02' 24.5".

Ownership: Piute County.

Antimony—K38JS-D, Ch. 38, Piute County. Phone: 435-577-2840.

Technical Facilities: 0.006-kw ERP, 14-ft. above ground, 7409-ft. above sea level, lat. 38° 10' 56.8", long. 112° 02' 24.5".

Ownership: Piute County.

Antimony—K39IZ-D, Ch. 39, U. of Utah. Phone: 801-585-3601.

Technical Facilities: 0.006-kw ERP, 14-ft. above ground, 7409-ft. above sea level, lat. 38° 10' 56.8", long. 112° 02' 24.5".

Ownership: U. of Utah.

Antimony—K40IX-D, Ch. 40, Piute County. Phone: 435-577-2840.

Technical Facilities: 0.006-kw ERP, 14-ft. above ground, 7409-ft. above sea level, lat. 38° 10' 56.8", long. 112° 02' 24.5".

Ownership: Piute County.

Antimony—K42FB, Ch. 42, Piute County. Phone: 435-577-2840.

Technical Facilities: 0.72-kw ERP, 26-ft. above ground, 7428-ft. above sea level, lat. 38° 10' 57", long. 112° 02' 25".

Ownership: Piute County.

Antimony—K44GA, Ch. 44, U. of Utah. Phone: 801-585-3601.

Technical Facilities: 0.72-kw ERP, 26-ft. above ground, 7428-ft. above sea level, lat. 38° 10' 57", long. 112° 02' 25".

Ownership: U. of Utah.

Antimony—K46IV-D, Ch. 46, Piute County. Phone: 435-577-2840.

Technical Facilities: 0.006-kw ERP, 14-ft. above ground, 7409-ft. above sea level, lat. 38° 10' 56.8", long. 112° 02' 24.5".

Ownership: Piute County.

Apple Valley—K21IL-D, Ch. 21, U. of Utah. Phone: 801-585-3601.

Technical Facilities: 0.075-kw ERP, 23-ft. above ground, 4823-ft. above sea level, lat. 37° 07' 00", long. 113° 07' 50".

Began Operation: December 2, 2008.

Ownership: U. of Utah.

Apple Valley—K30DE, Ch. 30, U. of Utah.

Technical Facilities: 0.007-kw ERP, 30-ft. above ground, 4800-ft. above sea level, lat. 37° 07' 00", long. 113° 07' 50".

Apple Valley—K34CX, Ch. 34, Newport Television License LLC. Phone: 816-751-0204.

Technical Facilities: 0.007-kw ERP, 30-ft. above ground, 4800-ft. above sea level, lat. 37° 07' 00", long. 113° 07' 50".

Ownership: Newport Television LLC.

Aurora—K53CF, Ch. 53, SLC TV Licensee Corp. Phone: 212-891-2100.

Technical Facilities: 4.18-kw ERP, 30-ft. above ground, 8514-ft. above sea level, lat. 39° 29' 31", long. 111° 49' 40".

Ownership: Four Points Media Group Holding LLC.

Aurora, etc.—K51BK-D, Ch. 51, Newport Television License LLC. Phone: 816-751-0204.

Technical Facilities: 0.25-kw ERP, 36-ft. above ground, 8396-ft. above sea level, lat. 39° 29' 31", long. 111° 49' 37".

Ownership: Newport Television LLC.

Beaver—K24FE-D, Ch. 24, Bonneville Holding Co. Phone: 801-575-7517.

Technical Facilities: 0.239-kw ERP, 49-ft. above ground, 9721-ft. above sea level, lat. 38° 31' 05", long. 113° 17' 03".

Ownership: Bonneville International Corp.

Beaver—K36FM, Ch. 36, Beaver City.

Technical Facilities: 0.75-kw ERP, 30-ft. above ground, 7871-ft. above sea level, lat. 38° 27' 04", long. 112° 39' 05".

Beaver—K40FT, Ch. 40, U. of Utah.

Technical Facilities: 0.709-kw ERP, lat. 38° 27' 04", long. 112° 39' 05".

Transmitter: Gills Hill, 12-mi. N of Beaver.

Beaver—K42EX, Ch. 42, Beaver City Corp.

Technical Facilities: 0.75-kw ERP, 30-ft. above ground, 7871-ft. above sea level, lat. 38° 27' 04", long. 112° 39' 05".

Beaver—K44HT, Ch. 44, Beaver City Corp. Phone: 435-438-2451.

Technical Facilities: 0.6-kw ERP, 26-ft. above ground, 7913-ft. above sea level, lat. 38° 27' 04", long. 112° 39' 05".

Ownership: Beaver City Corp.

Beaver—K46IB, Ch. 46, Beaver City Corp. Phone: 435-438-2451.

Technical Facilities: 0.6-kw ERP, 26-ft. above ground, 7835-ft. above sea level, lat. 38° 27' 24.2", long. 112° 29' 27.6".

Ownership: Beaver City Corp.

Beaver (rural)—K33FW, Ch. 33, Iron County. Phone: 435-477-8341.

Technical Facilities: 0.956-kw ERP, lat. 38° 31' 05", long. 113° 17' 03".

Transmitter: Frisco Peak, WNW of Milford.

Beaver (rural), etc.—K30GC-D, Ch. 30, Iron County. Phone: 435-477-8341.

Technical Facilities: 0.25-kw ERP, 49-ft. above ground, 9724-ft. above sea level, lat. 38° 31' 13.7", long. 113° 17' 12.1".

Ownership: Iron County.

Beaver City—K38GF, Ch. 38, Beaver City. Phone: 435-438-2451.

Technical Facilities: 0.75-kw ERP, 29-ft. above ground, 7871-ft. above sea level, lat. 38° 27' 04", long. 112° 39' 05".

Beaver County (rural)—K18FU-D, Ch. 18, Newport Television License LLC. Phone: 816-751-0204.

Technical Facilities: 0.135-kw ERP, 49-ft. above ground, 9724-ft. above sea level, lat. 38° 31' 14", long. 113° 17' 12".

Ownership: Newport Television LLC.

Beaver County (rural)—K19GS-D, Ch. 19, Iron County. Phone: 435-477-8341.

Technical Facilities: 0.15-kw ERP, 50-ft. above ground, 9725-ft. above sea level, lat. 38° 31' 13.7", long. 113° 17' 12.1".

Ownership: Iron County.

Beaver, etc.—K07GY, Ch. 7, Beaver City Corp. Phone: 435-438-2451.

Technical Facilities: 0.13-kw ERP, 26-ft. above ground, 7887-ft. above sea level, lat. 38° 27' 04", long. 112° 39' 05".

Ownership: Beaver City Corp.

Beaver, etc.—K09CS, Ch. 9, Beaver City Corp. Phone: 435-438-2451.

Technical Facilities: 0.13-kw ERP, 26-ft. above ground, 7887-ft. above sea level, lat. 38° 27' 04", long. 112° 39' 05".

Ownership: Beaver City Corp.

Beaver, etc.—K11CX, Ch. 11, Beaver City Corp. Phone: 435-438-2451.

Technical Facilities: 0.13-kw ERP, 26-ft. above ground, 7887-ft. above sea level, lat. 38° 27' 04", long. 112° 39' 05".

Ownership: Beaver City Corp.

Beaver, etc.—K13CV, Ch. 13, Beaver City Corp. Phone: 435-438-2451.

Technical Facilities: 0.13-kw ERP, 26-ft. above ground, 7887-ft. above sea level, lat. 38° 27' 04", long. 112° 39' 05".

Ownership: Beaver City Corp.

Beaver, etc.—K22FS-D, Ch. 22, SLC TV Licensee Corp. Phone: 212-891-2100.

Technical Facilities: 0.25-kw ERP, 49-ft. above ground, 9724-ft. above sea level, lat. 38° 31' 14", long. 113° 17' 12".

Ownership: Four Points Media Group Holding LLC.

Bicknell & Teasdale—K34GN, Ch. 34, Wayne County. Phone: 435-836-2765.

Technical Facilities: 0.009-kw ERP, 9-ft. above ground, 7218-ft. above sea level, lat. 38° 25' 58", long. 111° 37' 57".

Bicknell & Teasdale—K45JO-D, Ch. 45, Wayne County. Phone: 435-836-2765.

Technical Facilities: 0.018-kw ERP, 20-ft. above ground, 8475-ft. above sea level, lat. 38° 16' 59.8", long. 111° 30' 36.2".

Ownership: Wayne County.

Bicknell, etc.—K38CJ, Ch. 38, U. of Utah.

Technical Facilities: 0.35-kw ERP, 26-ft. above ground, 8487-ft. above sea level, lat. 38° 17' 00", long. 111° 30' 37".

Bicknell, etc.—K42AE, Ch. 42, Wayne County.

Technical Facilities: 2.15-kw ERP, 8281-ft. above sea level, lat. 38° 17' 00", long. 111° 30' 37".

Bicknell, etc.—K52JV-D, Ch. 52, U. of Utah. Phone: 801-585-3601.

Technical Facilities: 0.014-kw ERP, 20-ft. above ground, 8475-ft. above sea level, lat. 38° 16' 59.8", long. 111° 30' 36.2".

Ownership: U. of Utah.

Bicknell, etc.—K54JV-D, Ch. 54, Wayne County. Phone: 435-836-2765.

Technical Facilities: 0.018-kw ERP, 20-ft. above ground, 8475-ft. above sea level, lat. 38° 16' 59.8", long. 111° 30' 36.2".

Ownership: Wayne County.

Ownership: Iron County.

Blanding & Monticello—K36AK, Ch. 36, San Juan County.

Technical Facilities: 0.3-kw ERP, 39-ft. above ground, 11397-ft. above sea level, lat. 37° 50' 22", long. 109° 27' 42".

Ownership: San Juan County.

Blanding & Monticello—K42AD, Ch. 42, San Juan County.

Technical Facilities: 0.3-kw ERP, 39-ft. above ground, 11397-ft. above sea level, lat. 37° 50' 22", long. 109° 27' 42".

Blanding & Monticello—K45GM, Ch. 45, San Juan County.

Technical Facilities: 0.3-kw ERP, 39-ft. above ground, 11397-ft. above sea level, lat. 37° 50' 22", long. 109° 27' 42".

Blanding & Monticello—K47JI, Ch. 47, U. of Utah. Phones: 801-581-7777; 801-585-3601.

Technical Facilities: 0.35-kw ERP, 39-ft. above ground, 11397-ft. above sea level, lat. 37° 50' 22", long. 109° 27' 42".

Holds CP for change to 0.1-kw ERP, 59-ft. above ground, 11417-ft. above sea level, BDFCDTT-20081217AAV.

Began Operation: December 7, 2005.

Ownership: U. of Utah.

Blanding, etc.—K38AJ, Ch. 38, San Juan County.

Technical Facilities: 1.3-kw ERP, lat. 37° 50' 15", long. 109° 27' 55".

Ownership: San Juan County.

Blanding, etc.—K44AG, Ch. 44, San Juan County.

Technical Facilities: 1.3-kw ERP, lat. 37° 50' 15", long. 109° 27' 55".

Ownership: San Juan County.

Blanding, etc.—K46AF, Ch. 46, San Juan County.

Technical Facilities: 1.3-kw ERP, lat. 37° 50' 15", long. 109° 27' 55".

Ownership: San Juan County.

Bloomington—K20GJ-D, Ch. 20, Bonneville Holding Co. Phone: 801-575-7517.

Technical Facilities: 0.197-kw ERP, 61-ft. above ground, 3202-ft. above sea level, lat. 37° 03' 48", long. 113° 34' 26".

Ownership: Bonneville International Corp.

Bloomington—K33GE, Ch. 33, Brigham Young U. Phone: 801-422-8423.

Technical Facilities: 0.745-kw ERP, 79-ft. above ground, 3199-ft. above sea level, lat. 37° 03' 49", long. 113° 34' 20".

Bloomington—KUWB-LP, Ch. 22, High Plains Broadcasting License Co. LLC. Phone: 580-269-2215.

Technical Facilities: 0.79-kw ERP, 61-ft. above ground, 3202-ft. above sea level, lat. 37° 03' 48", long. 113° 34' 23".

Ownership: High Plains Broadcasting Inc.

Bluebell, etc.—K31DB, Ch. 31, Duchesne County.

Technical Facilities: 0.709-kw ERP, 20-ft. above ground, 6289-ft. above sea level, lat. 40° 19' 27", long. 110° 09' 19".

Bluff—K04PI, Ch. 4, San Juan County. Phone: 435-587-3223.

Technical Facilities: 0.0045-kw ERP, 15-ft. above ground, 4711-ft. above sea level, lat. 37° 16' 12", long. 109° 33' 26".

Ownership: San Juan County.

Bluff—K06MM, Ch. 6, San Juan County.

Technical Facilities: 0.002-kw ERP, 16-ft. above ground, 4715-ft. above sea level, lat. 37° 16' 12", long. 109° 33' 32".

Bluff & area—K02PU, Ch. 2, San Juan County. Phone: 435-678-3322.

Technical Facilities: 0.0045-kw ERP, 15-ft. above ground, 4713-ft. above sea level, lat. 37° 16' 12", long. 109° 33' 26".

Ownership: San Juan County.

Bluff & area—K13XS, Ch. 13, San Juan County. Phone: 435-678-3322.

Technical Facilities: 0.0045-kw ERP, 15-ft. above ground, 4713-ft. above sea level, lat. 37° 16' 12", long. 109° 33' 26".

Ownership: San Juan County.

Boulder—K08II, Ch. 8, Garfield County.

Technical Facilities: 0.001-kw ERP, lat. 37° 53' 53", long. 111° 25' 08".

Boulder—K10JG, Ch. 10, Garfield County.

Technical Facilities: 0.001-kw ERP, lat. 37° 53' 53", long. 111° 25' 08".

Boulder—K12JR, Ch. 12, Garfield County.

Technical Facilities: 0.001-kw ERP, lat. 37° 53' 53", long. 111° 25' 08".

Boulder—K18CG, Ch. 18, U. of Utah.

Technical Facilities: 0.184-kw ERP, lat. 37° 54' 37", long. 111° 23' 58".

Boulder—K31JF-D, Ch. 31, Garfield County. Phone: 435-676-8826.

Technical Facilities: 0.003-kw ERP, 16-ft. above ground, 6801-ft. above sea level, lat. 37° 53' 53.1", long. 111° 25' 07.9".

Began Operation: April 7, 2009.

Ownership: Garfield County.

Boulder—K32HQ-D, Ch. 32, Garfield County. Phone: 435-676-8826.

Technical Facilities: 0.003-kw ERP, 16-ft. above ground, 6801-ft. above sea level, lat. 37° 53' 53.1", long. 111° 25' 07.9".

Began Operation: April 7, 2009.

Ownership: Garfield County.

Boulder—K33IZ-D, Ch. 33, Garfield County. Phone: 435-676-8826.

Technical Facilities: 0.003-kw ERP, 16-ft. above ground, 6801-ft. above sea level, lat. 37° 53' 53.1", long. 111° 25' 07.9".

Began Operation: April 7, 2009.

Ownership: Garfield County.

Boulder—K34IY-D, Ch. 34, U. of Utah. Phone: 801-585-3601.

Technical Facilities: 0.003-kw ERP, 16-ft. above ground, 6801-ft. above sea level, lat. 37° 53' 53.1", long. 111° 25' 07.9".

Began Operation: April 7, 2009.

Ownership: U. of Utah.

Bullfrog—K15GN, Ch. 15, U. of Utah. Phone: 801-581-7777.

Technical Facilities: 0.6-kw ERP, 13-ft. above ground, 6893-ft. above sea level, lat. 37° 27' 15", long. 110° 43' 20".

Ownership: U. of Utah.

Caineville—K09LV, Ch. 9, Wayne County.

Technical Facilities: 0.006-kw ERP, 4747-ft. above sea level, lat. 38° 21' 40", long. 110° 53' 34".

Caineville—K11LZ, Ch. 11, Wayne County.

Technical Facilities: 0.006-kw ERP, 4751-ft. above sea level, lat. 38° 21' 40", long. 110° 53' 34".

Caineville—K13MQ, Ch. 13, Wayne County.

Technical Facilities: 0.006-kw ERP, lat. 38° 21' 40", long. 110° 53' 34".

Cane Beds, AZ & Hildale—K06OB, Ch. 6, U. of Utah. Phone: 801-585-3601.

Technical Facilities: 0.09-kw ERP, 20-ft. above ground, 5016-ft. above sea level, lat. 36° 54' 11", long. 113° 51' 08".

Ownership: U. of Utah.

Cane Beds, AZ/Hildale—K17IK-D, Ch. 17, U. of Utah. Phone: 801-585-3601.

Technical Facilities: 0.01-kw ERP, 16-ft. above ground, 5033-ft. above sea level, lat. 36° 54' 11", long. 113° 51' 08".

Began Operation: December 2, 2008.

Ownership: U. of Utah.

Cannonville—K07OB, Ch. 7, Garfield County. Phone: 435-676-8826.

Technical Facilities: 0.129-kw ERP, lat. 37° 42' 46", long. 112° 04' 37".

Ownership: Garfield County.

Cannonville—K23IK-D, Ch. 23, Garfield County. Phone: 435-676-8826.

Technical Facilities: 0.01-kw ERP, 12-ft. above ground, 8286-ft. above sea level, lat. 37° 41' 40.9", long. 112° 04' 39.4".

Ownership: Garfield County.

Capital Reef National Park (Fruita)—K08HZ, Ch. 8, Wayne County.

Technical Facilities: 0.007-kw ERP, 6220-ft. above sea level, lat. 38° 17' 47", long. 111° 17' 30".

Capital Reef National Park (Fruita)—K10IV, Ch. 10, Wayne County.

Technical Facilities: 0.007-kw ERP, 6220-ft. above sea level, lat. 38° 17' 47", long. 111° 17' 30".

Capital Reef National Park (Fruita)—K12JH, Ch. 12, Wayne County.

Technical Facilities: 0.007-kw ERP, 6224-ft. above sea level, lat. 38° 17' 47", long. 111° 17' 30".

Carbon County (rural)—K29CM, Ch. 29, U. of Utah. Phone: 801-585-3601.

Technical Facilities: 1.05-kw ERP, 59-ft. above ground, 9846-ft. above sea level, lat. 39° 45' 26", long. 110° 55' 22".

Holds CP for change to 0.49-kw ERP, 30-ft. above ground, 9862-ft. above sea level, BPTT-20020403AAX.

Castle Gate—K02FS, Ch. 2, Carbon County.

Technical Facilities: 0.006-kw ERP, lat. 39° 43' 15", long. 110° 51' 36".

Ownership: Carbon County.

Cedar Canyon—K06JA, Ch. 6, Iron County. Phone: 435-477-8341.

Technical Facilities: 0.008-kw ERP, lat. 37° 36' 02", long. 112° 51' 17".

Holds CP for change to 0.015-kw ERP, 16-ft. above ground, 10649-ft. above sea level, lat. 37° 35' 56.9", long. 112° 51' 23.2". BDFCDTV-20081217AGW.

Ownership: Iron County.

Cedar Canyon—K08MZ, Ch. 8, Iron County. Phone: 435-477-8341.

Technical Facilities: 0.009-kw ERP, 16-ft. above ground, 10679-ft. above sea level, lat. 37° 36' 02", long. 112° 51' 17".

Holds CP for change to 0.015-kw ERP, 16-ft. above ground, 10649-ft. above sea level, lat. 37° 35' 56.9", long. 112° 51' 23.2". BDFCDTV-20081217AGX.

Ownership: Iron County.

Cedar Canyon—K10MF, Ch. 10, Iron County. Phone: 435-477-8341.

Technical Facilities: 0.01-kw ERP, lat. 37° 35' 39", long. 112° 50' 52".

Holds CP for change to 0.015-kw ERP, 16-ft. above ground, 10649-ft. above sea level, lat. 37° 35' 56.9", long. 112° 51' 23.2". BDFCDTV-20081217AGZ.

Began Operation: November 2, 1984.

Ownership: Iron County.

Cedar City—K02NU, Ch. 2, Iron County. Phone: 435-477-8341.

Technical Facilities: 1.78-kw ERP, 32-ft. above ground, 8792-ft. above sea level, lat. 37° 38' 18", long. 113° 01' 52".

Ownership: Iron County.

Cedar City—K05HB, Ch. 5, Iron County.

Technical Facilities: 1.47-kw ERP, 33-ft. above ground, 8825-ft. above sea level, lat. 37° 38' 18", long. 113° 01' 52".

Ownership: Iron County.

Cedar City—K07GQ, Ch. 7, Iron County. Phone: 435-477-8341.

Technical Facilities: 0.39-kw ERP, 32-ft. above ground, 8792-ft. above sea level, lat. 37° 38' 18", long. 113° 01' 52".

Holds CP for change to 0.24-kw ERP, 39-ft. above ground, 8589-ft. above sea level, lat. 37° 38' 20.8", long. 113° 01' 52.8". BDFCDTV-20090105AAA.

Ownership: Iron County.

Cedar City—K08OE-D, Ch. 8, U. of Utah. Phone: 801-585-3601.

Technical Facilities: 0.06-kw ERP, 39-ft. above ground, 8589-ft. above sea level, lat. 37° 38' 20.8", long. 113° 01' 52.8".

Began Operation: December 2, 2008.

Ownership: U. of Utah.

Cedar City—K09CJ, Ch. 9, Iron County.

Technical Facilities: 0.39-kw ERP, 32-ft. above ground, 8792-ft. above sea level, lat. 37° 38' 18", long. 113° 01' 52".

Cedar City—K11CQ, Ch. 11, Iron County.

Technical Facilities: 0.39-kw ERP, 32-ft. above ground, 8792-ft. above sea level, lat. 37° 38' 18", long. 113° 01' 52".

Holds CP for change to 0.24-kw ERP, 39-ft. above ground, 8589-ft. above sea level, lat. 37° 38' 20.8", long. 113° 01' 52.8". BDFCDTV-20090105AAB.

Began Operation: February 27, 1981.

Ownership: Iron County.

Cedar City—K13CP, Ch. 13, Iron County.

Technical Facilities: 0.39-kw ERP, 32-ft. above ground, 8792-ft. above sea level, lat. 37° 38' 18", long. 113° 01' 52".

Cedar City—K22RK, Ch. 22, Iron County.

Technical Facilities: 0.285-kw ERP, 25-ft. above ground, 8783-ft. above sea level, lat. 37° 38' 18", long. 113° 01' 52".

Cedar City—K31EI, Ch. 31, Iron County. Phone: 435-477-8341.

Technical Facilities: 0.034-kw ERP, 16-ft. above ground, 10679-ft. above sea level, lat. 37° 36' 02", long. 112° 51' 17".

Holds CP for change to 0.2-kw ERP, 16-ft. above ground, 10649-ft. above sea level, lat. 37° 35' 56.9", long. 112° 51' 23.2". BDFCDTT-20081217AHB.

Began Operation: January 30, 1995.

Ownership: Iron County.

Cedar City—K39FQ, Ch. 39, Iron County. Phone: 435-477-8341.

Technical Facilities: 0.285-kw ERP, 25-ft. above ground, 8785-ft. above sea level, lat. 37° 38' 18", long. 113° 01' 52".

Ownership: Iron County.

Cedar City—K41GE, Ch. 41, U. of Utah. Phone: 801-585-3601.

Technical Facilities: 0.285-kw ERP, 25-ft. above ground, 8785-ft. above sea level, lat. 37° 38' 18", long. 113° 01' 52".

Holds CP for change to 1.264-kw ERP, lat. 37° 38' 20.8", long. 113° 01' 55.7". BPTT-20060719AAK.

Ownership: U. of Utah.

Cedar City—K45HD, Ch. 45, Iron County. Phone: 435-477-8341.

Technical Facilities: 1.47-kw ERP, 26-ft. above ground, 8786-ft. above sea level, lat. 37° 38' 17", long. 113° 01' 52".

Holds CP for change to 0.4-kw ERP, BDFCDTL-20080409ACR.

Ownership: Iron County.

Cedar City—K47IS, Ch. 47, Iron County. Phone: 435-477-8341.

Technical Facilities: 1.2-kw ERP, 25-ft. above ground, 8785-ft. above sea level, lat. 37° 38' 18", long. 113° 01' 52".

Holds CP for change to 0.3-kw ERP, BDFCDTT-20070130AJT.

Ownership: Iron County.

Cedar City Canyon—K12PN, Ch. 12, Iron County. Phone: 435-477-8341.

Technical Facilities: 0.009-kw ERP, 16-ft. above ground, 10679-ft. above sea level, lat. 37° 36' 02", long. 112° 51' 17".

Holds CP for change to 0.015-kw ERP, 16-ft. above ground, 10649-ft. above sea level, lat. 37° 35' 56.9", long. 112° 51' 23.2". BDFCDTV-20081217AHA.

Began Operation: August 18, 2004.

Ownership: Iron County.

Cedar City, etc.—K33EB, Ch. 33, Iron County. Phone: 435-477-8341.

Technical Facilities: 0.034-kw ERP, 16-ft. above ground, 10679-ft. above sea level, lat. 37° 36' 02", long. 112° 51' 17".

Holds CP for change to 0.2-kw ERP, 16-ft. above ground, 10649-ft. above sea level, lat. 37° 35' 56.9", long. 112° 51' 23.2". BDFCDTT-20081217AHF.

Began Operation: March 14, 1994.

Ownership: Iron County.

Cedar City, etc.—K35HG, Ch. 35, Iron County. Phone: 435-477-8341.

Technical Facilities: 1.47-kw ERP, 25-ft. above ground, 8811-ft. above sea level, lat. 37° 38' 18", long. 113° 01' 52".

Holds CP for change to 0.3-kw ERP, 46-ft. above ground, 8806-ft. above sea level, BDFCDTT-20070129ARG.

Ownership: Iron County.

Cedar City, etc.—K43JT, Ch. 43, Iron County. Phone: 435-477-8341.

Technical Facilities: 0.147-kw ERP, 26-ft. above ground, 8786-ft. above sea level, lat. 37° 38' 18", long. 113° 01' 52".

Holds CP for change to 0.38-kw ERP, 33-ft. above ground, 8583-ft. above sea level, lat. 37° 38' 20.8", long. 113° 01' 52.8". BDFCDTT-20081209AEF.

Began Operation: January 30, 2006.

Ownership: Iron County.

Circleville—K07JV, Ch. 7, U. of Utah.

Technical Facilities: 0.31-kw ERP, 6499-ft. above sea level, lat. 38° 12' 49", long. 112° 14' 23".

Circleville—K09FX, Ch. 9, Piute County.

Technical Facilities: 0.021-kw ERP, lat. 38° 12' 49", long. 112° 14' 23".

Circleville—K11FZ, Ch. 11, Piute County.

Technical Facilities: 0.021-kw ERP, lat. 38° 12' 49", long. 112° 14' 23".

Circleville—K13EK, Ch. 13, Piute County.

Technical Facilities: 0.008-kw ERP, lat. 38° 12' 49", long. 112° 14' 23".

Circleville—K17HD, Ch. 17, Piute County.

Technical Facilities: 0.08-kw ERP, 16-ft. above ground, 6512-ft. above sea level, lat. 38° 12' 49", long. 112° 14' 23".

Ownership: Piute County.

Circleville—K19GM-D, Ch. 19, Piute County. Phone: 435-577-2840.

Technical Facilities: 0.006-kw ERP, 15-ft. above ground, 6511-ft. above sea level, lat. 38° 12' 41.3", long. 112° 14' 01.8".

Ownership: Piute County.

Circleville—K21IB-D, Ch. 21, Piute County. Phone: 435-577-2840.

Technical Facilities: 0.006-kw ERP, 15-ft. above ground, 6511-ft. above sea level, lat. 38° 12' 41.3", long. 112° 14' 01.8".

Ownership: Piute County.

Circleville—K31IY-D, Ch. 31, Piute County. Phone: 435-577-2840.

Technical Facilities: 0.006-kw ERP, 15-ft. above ground, 6511-ft. above sea level, lat. 38° 12' 41.3", long. 112° 14' 01.8".

Ownership: Piute County.

Circleville—K32HN-D, Ch. 32, Piute County. Phone: 435-577-2840.

Technical Facilities: 0.006-kw ERP, 15-ft. above ground, 6511-ft. above sea level, lat. 38° 12' 41.3", long. 112° 14' 01.8".

Ownership: Piute County.

Circleville—K33JD-D, Ch. 33, U. of Utah. Phone: 801-585-3601.

Technical Facilities: 0.006-kw ERP, 15-ft. above ground, 6511-ft. above sea level, lat. 38° 12' 41.3", long. 112° 14' 01.8".

Ownership: U. of Utah.

Coalville—K07LT, Ch. 7, Summit County.

Technical Facilities: 0.141-kw ERP, 6020-ft. above sea level, lat. 40° 55' 26", long. 111° 23' 51".

Coalville—K09DP, Ch. 9, Summit County.

Technical Facilities: 0.146-kw ERP, lat. 40° 55' 26", long. 111° 23' 51".

Coalville—K11DW, Ch. 11, Summit County.

Technical Facilities: 0.146-kw ERP, 6020-ft. above sea level, lat. 40° 55' 26", long. 111° 23' 51".

Coalville—K13DP, Ch. 13, Summit County.

Technical Facilities: 0.144-kw ERP, 6020-ft. above sea level, lat. 40° 55' 26", long. 111° 23' 51".

Coalville—K35HH, Ch. 35, Summit County. Phone: 435-336-3220.

Technical Facilities: 0.14-kw ERP, 9-ft. above ground, 6009-ft. above sea level, lat. 40° 55' 26", long. 111° 23' 51".

Ownership: Summit County.

Coalville & adjacent area—K24GF, Ch. 24, Summit County. Phone: 435-336-3220.

Technical Facilities: 0.14-kw ERP, 9-ft. above ground, 6009-ft. above sea level, lat. 40° 55' 26", long. 111° 23' 51".

Ownership: Summit County.

Coalville & adjacent area—K28IP, Ch. 28, Summit County. Phone: 439-336-3220.

Technical Facilities: 0.14-kw ERP, 9-ft. above ground, 6009-ft. above sea level, lat. 40° 55' 26", long. 111° 23' 51".

Ownership: Summit County.

Coalville, etc.—K26DS, Ch. 26, Summit County.

Technical Facilities: 0.14-kw ERP, 10-ft. above ground, 6010-ft. above sea level, lat. 40° 55' 26", long. 111° 23' 51".

Columbia, etc.—K49BO, Ch. 49, U. of Utah.

Technical Facilities: 1.07-kw ERP, 36-ft. above ground, 9819-ft. above sea level, lat. 39° 45' 26", long. 110° 55' 22".

Delta—K39FR, Ch. 39, Millard County. Phone: 435-743-5227.

Technical Facilities: 2.69-kw ERP, 26-ft. above ground, 5705-ft. above sea level, lat. 39° 21' 15", long. 112° 20' 30".

Delta—K41GH, Ch. 41, U. of Utah. Phone: 801-585-3601.

Technical Facilities: 2.63-kw ERP, 25-ft. above ground, 6601-ft. above sea level, lat. 39° 21' 15", long. 112° 20' 30".

Ownership: U. of Utah.

Delta—K49HA, Ch. 49, Millard County. Phone: 435-864-1405.

Technical Facilities: 2.6-kw ERP, 23-ft. above ground, 6598-ft. above sea level, lat. 39° 21' 15", long. 112° 20' 30".

Ownership: Millard County.

Delta—K53JE-D, Ch. 53, Millard County. Phone: 435-864-1405.

Technical Facilities: 0.008-kw ERP, 25-ft. above ground, 5474-ft. above sea level, lat. 39° 21' 12.1", long. 112° 21' 05.8".

Ownership: Millard County.

Delta & Oak City—K43GN, Ch. 43, Millard County. Phone: 435-864-1405.

Technical Facilities: 2.6-kw ERP, 25-ft. above ground, 6601-ft. above sea level, lat. 39° 21' 15", long. 112° 20' 30".

Delta & Oak City—K47HM, Ch. 47, U. of Utah. Phone: 801-581-7777.

Technical Facilities: 2.5-kw ERP, 25-ft. above ground, 6601-ft. above sea level, lat. 39° 21' 15", long. 112° 20' 30".

Delta & Oak City—K54JY-D, Ch. 54, U. of Utah. Phone: 801-585-3601.

Technical Facilities: 0.01-kw ERP, 23-ft. above ground, 5482-ft. above sea level, lat. 39° 21' 12.1", long. 112° 21' 05.8".

Ownership: U. of Utah.

Delta, etc.—K31FG, Ch. 31, SLC TV Licensee Corp. Phone: 212-891-2100.

Studio: 2185 South 3600 West, Salt Lake City, UT 84119.

Technical Facilities: 2.63-kw ERP, 23-ft. above ground, 6598-ft. above sea level, lat. 39° 21' 15", long. 112° 20' 30".

Transmitter: 1.5-mi. SSW of Oak City.

Ownership: Four Points Media Group Holding LLC.

Delta, etc.—K35GC, Ch. 35, Millard County. Phone: 435-864-1405.

Technical Facilities: 2.7-kw ERP, 25-ft. above ground, 6601-ft. above sea level, lat. 39° 21' 15", long. 112° 20' 30".

Ownership: Millard County.

Delta, etc.—K38JT-D, Ch. 38, Millard County. Phone: 435-864-1405.

Technical Facilities: 0.008-kw ERP, 25-ft. above ground, 5474-ft. above sea level, lat. 39° 21' 12.1", long. 112° 21' 05.8".

Ownership: Millard County.

Delta, etc.—K40IW-D, Ch. 40, Millard County. Phone: 435-864-1405.

Technical Facilities: 0.008-kw ERP, 25-ft. above ground, 5474-ft. above sea level, lat. 39° 21' 12.1", long. 112° 21' 05.8".

Ownership: Millard County.

Delta, etc.—K44IZ-D, Ch. 44, KUTV Holdings Inc. Phone: 202-457-4505.

Technical Facilities: 0.015-kw ERP, 25-ft. above ground, 5474-ft. above sea level, lat. 39° 21' 12.1", long. 112° 21' 05.8".

Ownership: CBS Corp.

Delta, etc.—K45GE, Ch. 45, Millard County. Phone: 435-864-1405.

Technical Facilities: 2.6-kw ERP, 25-ft. above ground, 6601-ft. above sea level, lat. 39° 21' 15", long. 112° 20' 30".

Ownership: Millard County.

Delta, etc.—K46IW-D, Ch. 46, Millard County. Phone: 435-864-1405.

Technical Facilities: 0.008-kw ERP, 25-ft. above ground, 5474-ft. above sea level, lat. 39° 21' 12.1", long. 112° 21' 05.8".

Ownership: Millard County.

Delta, etc.—K48KS-D, Ch. 48, U. of Utah. Phone: 801-585-3601.

Technical Facilities: 0.01-kw ERP, 23-ft. above ground, 5472-ft. above sea level, lat. 39° 21' 12.1", long. 112° 21' 05.8".

Ownership: U. of Utah.

Delta, etc.—K48KS-D, Ch. 48, U. of Utah. Phone: 801-585-3601.

Technical Facilities: 0.01-kw ERP, 23-ft. above ground, 5472-ft. above sea level, lat. 39° 21' 12.1", long. 112° 21' 05.8".

Ownership: U. of Utah.

Delta, etc.—K51GG, Ch. 51, Millard County. Phone: 435-864-1405.

Technical Facilities: 2-kw ERP, 26-ft. above ground, 5476-ft. above sea level, lat. 39° 21' 12", long. 112° 21' 06".

Delta, Oak City, etc.—K36IK-D, Ch. 36, Millard County. Phone: 435-864-1405.

Technical Facilities: 0.008-kw ERP, 25-ft. above ground, 5474-ft. above sea level, lat. 39° 21' 12.1", long. 112° 21' 05.8".

Ownership: Millard County.

Delta, Oak City, etc.—K42HQ-D, Ch. 42, Millard County. Phone: 435-864-1405.

Technical Facilities: 0.008-kw ERP, 25-ft. above ground, 5474-ft. above sea level, lat. 39° 21' 12.1", long. 112° 21' 05.8".

Ownership: Millard County.

Duchesne—K03CN, Ch. 3, Duchesne County.

Technical Facilities: 0.004-kw ERP, lat. 40° 09' 12", long. 110° 23' 40".

Ownership: Duchesne County.

Duchesne—K08CT, Ch. 8, Duchesne County.

Technical Facilities: 0.004-kw ERP, lat. 40° 09' 12", long. 110° 23' 40".

Duchesne—K10DE, Ch. 10, Duchesne County.

Technical Facilities: 0.004-kw ERP, lat. 40° 09' 12", long. 110° 23' 40".

Duchesne—K23FT, Ch. 23, U. of Utah. Phone: 801-585-3601.

Technical Facilities: 2-kw ERP, 40-ft. above ground, 10056-ft. above sea level, lat. 40° 21' 45", long. 110° 47' 31".

Duchesne—K34FV, Ch. 34, Duchesne County.

Technical Facilities: 0.22-kw ERP, 19-ft. above ground, 5564-ft. above sea level, lat. 40° 09' 12", long. 110° 23' 40".

Duchesne—K40HS, Ch. 40, High Plains Broadcasting License Co. LLC. Phone: 580-269-2215.

Technical Facilities: 0.069-kw ERP, 33-ft. above ground, 5853-ft. above sea level, lat. 40° 09' 17.9", long. 110° 23' 29.1".

Holds CP for change to 0.035-kw ERP, BDFCDTT-20070328ACI.

Ownership: High Plains Broadcasting Inc.

Duchesne—K45AG, Ch. 45, Duchesne County.

Technical Facilities: 0.07-kw ERP, lat. 40° 09' 12", long. 110° 23' 40".

Duchesne—K47AN, Ch. 47, Duchesne County.

Technical Facilities: 0.069-kw ERP, 6919-ft. above sea level, lat. 40° 09' 12", long. 110° 23' 40".

Duchesne County (rural)—K17DM, Ch. 17, Duchesne County.

Technical Facilities: 3.12-kw ERP, 43-ft. above ground, 10059-ft. above sea level, lat. 40° 21' 45", long. 110° 47' 31".

Duchesne, etc.—K12DL, Ch. 12, Duchesne County.

Technical Facilities: 0.004-kw ERP, lat. 40° 09' 12", long. 110° 23' 40".

East Carbon County—K39CO, Ch. 39, Carbon County.

Technical Facilities: 1.42-kw ERP, 26-ft. above ground, 9829-ft. above sea level, lat. 39° 45' 22", long. 110° 59' 26".

East Price—K02OT, Ch. 2, Carbon County.

Technical Facilities: 0.002-kw ERP, lat. 39° 36' 38", long. 110° 48' 47".

Transmitter: 0.7-mi. N of Price.

Ownership: Carbon County.

East Price—K04IW, Ch. 4, Carbon County.

Technical Facilities: 0.034-kw ERP, lat. 39° 36' 38", long. 110° 48' 47".

Ownership: Carbon County.

East Price—K05GX, Ch. 5, Carbon County.

Technical Facilities: 0.03-kw ERP, lat. 39° 36' 38", long. 110° 48' 47".

Ownership: Carbon County.

East Price—K07OQ, Ch. 7, Carbon County.

Technical Facilities: 0.002-kw ERP, lat. 39° 36' 38", long. 110° 48' 47".

Ownership: Carbon County.

Echo—K35FZ, Ch. 35, Summit County.

Technical Facilities: 0.669-kw ERP, lat. 40° 58' 40", long. 111° 26' 08".

Transmitter: 0.06-mi. NE of Echo.

Emery—K17HR-D, Ch. 17, Emery County. Phone: 435-381-5678.

Technical Facilities: 0.012-kw ERP, 38-ft. above ground, 6865-ft. above sea level, lat. 38° 55' 52", long. 111° 11' 25".

Ownership: Emery County.

Emery—K19GK-D, Ch. 19, Emery County. Phone: 435-381-5678.

Technical Facilities: 0.012-kw ERP, 38-ft. above ground, 6865-ft. above sea level, lat. 38° 55' 52", long. 111° 11' 25".

Ownership: Emery County.

Emery—K21HZ-D, Ch. 21, Emery County. Phone: 435-381-5678.

Technical Facilities: 0.012-kw ERP, 38-ft. above ground, 6865-ft. above sea level, lat. 38° 55' 52", long. 111° 11' 25".

Ownership: Emery County.

Emery—K23IE-D, Ch. 23, Emery County. Phone: 435-381-5678.

Technical Facilities: 0.012-kw ERP, 38-ft. above ground, 6865-ft. above sea level, lat. 38° 55' 52", long. 111° 11' 25".

Ownership: Emery County.

Emery—K25JA-D, Ch. 25, Emery County. Phone: 435-381-5678.

Technical Facilities: 0.012-kw ERP, 38-ft. above ground, 6865-ft. above sea level, lat. 38° 55' 52", long. 111° 11' 25".

Ownership: Emery County.

Emery—K27IS-D, Ch. 27, Emery County. Phone: 435-381-5678.

Technical Facilities: 0.012-kw ERP, 38-ft. above ground, 6865-ft. above sea level, lat. 38° 55' 52", long. 111° 11' 25".

Ownership: Emery County.

Emery—K29HK-D, Ch. 29, Emery County. Phone: 435-381-5678.

Technical Facilities: 0.012-kw ERP, 38-ft. above ground, 6865-ft. above sea level, lat. 38° 55' 52", long. 111° 11' 25".

Ownership: Emery County.

Emery—K35DW, Ch. 35, Emery County. Phone: 435-381-5678.

Technical Facilities: 0.142-kw ERP, 49-ft. above ground, 6814-ft. above sea level, lat. 38° 55' 52", long. 111° 11' 25".

Ownership: Emery County.

Emery—K39DV, Ch. 39, Emery County. Phone: 435-381-5678.

Technical Facilities: 0.142-kw ERP, 46-ft. above ground, 6811-ft. above sea level, lat. 38° 55' 52", long. 111° 11' 25".

Ownership: Emery County.

Emery—K41GV, Ch. 41, Emery County. Phone: 435-381-5678.

Technical Facilities: 0.1-kw ERP, 26-ft. above ground, 6827-ft. above sea level, lat. 38° 55' 52", long. 111° 11' 25".

Ownership: Emery County.

Emery—K43EV, Ch. 43, Emery County. Phone: 435-381-5678.

Technical Facilities: 0.141-kw ERP, lat. 38° 55' 53", long. 111° 11' 25".

Transmitter: Approx. 3-mi. E of Emery City.

Ownership: Emery County.

Emery—K45GP, Ch. 45, Emery County. Phone: 435-381-5678.

Technical Facilities: 0.1-kw ERP, 26-ft. above ground, 6827-ft. above sea level, lat. 38° 55' 52", long. 111° 11' 25".

Ownership: Emery County.

Emery—K47HD, Ch. 47, Emery County. Phone: 435-381-5678.

Technical Facilities: 0.1-kw ERP, 26-ft. above ground, 6827-ft. above sea level, lat. 38° 55' 53", long. 111° 11' 25".

Emery—K49GB, Ch. 49, Emery County. Phone: 435-381-5678.

Technical Facilities: 0.1-kw ERP, 26-ft. above ground, 6827-ft. above sea level, lat. 38° 55' 52", long. 111° 11' 25".

Ownership: Emery County.

Enoch & Summit—K50HI, Ch. 50, Iron County. Phone: 435-477-8341.

Technical Facilities: 0.745-kw ERP, 37-ft. above ground, 6827-ft. above sea level, lat. 37° 50' 32", long. 112° 58' 10".

Holds CP for change to 0.25-kw ERP, 59-ft. above ground, 6778-ft. above sea level, lat. 37° 50' 30.2", long. 112° 58' 26.6". BDFCDTT-20080415ACB.

Ownership: Iron County.

Enterprise—K03BF, Ch. 3, SLC TV Licensee Corp. Phone: 212-891-2100.

Technical Facilities: 0.014-kw ERP, lat. 37° 36' 00", long. 113° 44' 00".

Ownership: Four Points Media Group Holding LLC.

Enterprise—K05BU, Ch. 5, Newport Television License LLC. Phone: 816-751-0204.

Technical Facilities: 0.014-kw ERP, lat. 37° 36' 00", long. 113° 44' 00".

Ownership: Newport Television LLC.

Enterprise—K07ED-D, Ch. 7, Bonneville Holding Co. Phone: 801-575-7517.

Technical Facilities: 0.031-kw ERP, 26-ft. above ground, 5830-ft. above sea level, lat. 37° 36' 00", long. 113° 44' 00".

Ownership: Bonneville International Corp.

Enterprise—K13HH, Ch. 13, U. of Utah.

Technical Facilities: 0.01-kw ERP, lat. 37° 36' 00", long. 113° 44' 00".

Enterprise—K42IN-D, Ch. 42, U. of Utah. Phone: 801-585-3601.

Technical Facilities: 0.01-kw ERP, 20-ft. above ground, 7132-ft. above sea level, lat. 37° 30' 22.4", long. 113° 39' 36.2".

Began Operation: December 2, 2008.

Ownership: U. of Utah.

Enterprise—KMBU-LP, Ch. 32, CCR-St. George IV LLC. Phone: 303-468-6500.

Technical Facilities: 0.079-kw ERP, 20-ft. above ground, 7218-ft. above sea level, lat. 37° 30' 46", long. 113° 39' 14".

Holds CP for change to 10-kw ERP, 39-ft. above ground, 7231-ft. above sea level, BDFCDTA-20060630AGS.

Ownership: Cherry Creek Radio LLC.

Enterprise, etc.—K34FW, Ch. 34, Brigham Young U. Phone: 801-422-8423.

Technical Facilities: 0.38-kw ERP, 33-ft. above ground, 7224-ft. above sea level, lat. 37° 30' 46", long. 113° 39' 14".

Ownership: Brigham Young U.

Escalante—K02FQ, Ch. 2, Garfield County. Phone: 435-676-8829.

Technical Facilities: 0.007-kw ERP, lat. 37° 56' 25", long. 111° 43' 40".

Ownership: Garfield County.

Escalante—K04FR, Ch. 4, Garfield County. Phone: 435-676-8826.

Technical Facilities: 0.009-kw ERP, lat. 37° 56' 25", long. 111° 43' 40".

Ownership: Garfield County.

Escalante—K05DV, Ch. 5, Garfield County. Phone: 435-676-8826.

Technical Facilities: 0.009-kw ERP, lat. 37° 56' 25", long. 111° 43' 40".

Ownership: Garfield County.

Escalante—K07JZ, Ch. 7, Garfield County. Phone: 435-676-8826.

Technical Facilities: 0.008-kw ERP, lat. 37° 56' 25", long. 111° 43' 40".

Ownership: Garfield County.

Escalante—K09WJ, Ch. 9, Garfield County. Phone: 435-676-8826.

Technical Facilities: 0.051-kw ERP, lat. 37° 47' 15", long. 111° 35' 45".

Transmitter: 1.2-mi. NNE of Escalante.

Ownership: Garfield County.

Escalante—K11SJ, Ch. 11, Garfield County. Phone: 435-676-8826.

Technical Facilities: 0.005-kw ERP, 26-ft. above ground, 6004-ft. above sea level, lat. 37° 47' 15", long. 111° 35' 45".

Ownership: Garfield County.

Escalante—K13VH, Ch. 13, Garfield County. Phone: 435-676-8826.

Technical Facilities: 0.005-w TPO, 26-ft. above ground, 6004-ft. above sea level, lat. 37° 47' 15", long. 111° 35' 45".

Ownership: Garfield County.

Escalante—K15EM, Ch. 15, U. of Utah.

Technical Facilities: 0.159-kw ERP, lat. 37° 47' 15", long. 111° 35' 45".

Transmitter: 1.24-mi. NNE of Escalante.

Eureka—K29CJ, Ch. 29, Juab County.

Technical Facilities: 0.004-kw ERP, 10-ft. above ground, 7930-ft. above sea level, lat. 39° 56' 27", long. 112° 07' 11".

Eureka—K33DL, Ch. 33, Juab County.

Technical Facilities: 0.004-kw ERP, 10-ft. above ground, 7926-ft. above sea level, lat. 39° 56' 27", long. 112° 07' 11".

Eureka—K35CZ, Ch. 35, Juab County.

Technical Facilities: 0.004-kw ERP, 10-ft. above ground, 7930-ft. above sea level, lat. 39° 56' 27", long. 112° 07' 11".

Eureka—K39CR, Ch. 39, Juab County.

Technical Facilities: 0.004-kw ERP, 10-ft. above ground, 7930-ft. above sea level, lat. 39° 56' 27", long. 112° 07' 11".

Eureka—K41DC, Ch. 41, Juab County.

Technical Facilities: 0.004-kw ERP, 10-ft. above ground, 7930-ft. above sea level, lat. 39° 56' 27", long. 112° 07' 11".

Eureka—K43DA, Ch. 43, Juab County.

Technical Facilities: 0.004-kw ERP, 10-ft. above ground, 7930-ft. above sea level, lat. 39° 56' 27", long. 112° 07' 11".

Eureka—K45DD, Ch. 45, Juab County.

Technical Facilities: 0.004-kw ERP, 10-ft. above ground, 7930-ft. above sea level, lat. 39° 56' 27", long. 112° 07' 11".

Fillmore—K23IM-D, Ch. 23, Millard County. Phone: 435-864-1405.

Technical Facilities: 0.006-kw ERP, 48-ft. above ground, 5671-ft. above sea level, lat. 39° 02' 10", long. 112° 19' 31.2".

Ownership: Millard County.

Fillmore—K32GE, Ch. 32, Millard County. Phone: 435-743-5227.

Technical Facilities: 3.2-kw ERP, 26-ft. above ground, 5731-ft. above sea level, lat. 39° 02' 10", long. 112° 19' 31".

Fillmore—K34GO, Ch. 34, Millard County. Phone: 435-743-5227.

Technical Facilities: 3.16-kw ERP, 26-ft. above ground, 5731-ft. above sea level, lat. 39° 02' 10", long. 112° 19' 31".

Fillmore—K36FY, Ch. 36, Millard County. Phone: 435-743-5227.

Technical Facilities: 3.24-kw ERP, 26-ft. above ground, 5705-ft. above sea level, lat. 39° 02' 10", long. 112° 19' 31".

Fillmore—K38GT, Ch. 38, Millard County. Phone: 435-743-5227.

Technical Facilities: 3.24-kw ERP, 26-ft. above ground, 5705-ft. above sea level, lat. 39° 02' 10", long. 112° 19' 31".

Fillmore—K40GD, Ch. 40, Millard County. Phone: 435-743-5227.

Technical Facilities: 3.24-kw ERP, 26-ft. above ground, 5705-ft. above sea level, lat. 39° 02' 10", long. 112° 19' 31".

Fillmore—K48ED, Ch. 48, Millard County School District.

Technical Facilities: 3.16-kw ERP, lat. 39° 02' 10", long. 112° 19' 31".

Fillmore—K57JU-D, Ch. 57, Millard County. Phone: 435-864-1405.

Technical Facilities: 0.006-kw ERP, 48-ft. above ground, 5671-ft. above sea level, lat. 39° 02' 10", long. 112° 19' 31.2".

Ownership: Millard County.

Fillmore, etc.—K42DR, Ch. 42, Millard County.

Technical Facilities: 3.16-kw ERP, 26-ft. above ground, 5705-ft. above sea level, lat. 39° 02' 10", long. 112° 19' 31".

Fillmore, etc.—K44EA, Ch. 44, U. of Utah.

Technical Facilities: 1.81-kw ERP, 26-ft. above ground, 5709-ft. above sea level, lat. 39° 02' 10", long. 112° 19' 31".

Fillmore, etc.—K46EI, Ch. 46, Millard County. Phone: 435-864-1405.

Technical Facilities: 3.16-kw ERP, 26-ft. above ground, 5705-ft. above sea level, lat. 39° 02' 10", long. 112° 19' 31".

Fillmore, etc.—K56JC-D, Ch. 56, Millard County. Phone: 435-864-1405.

Technical Facilities: 0.006-kw ERP, 48-ft. above ground, 5671-ft. above sea level, lat. 39° 02' 10", long. 112° 19' 31.2".

Ownership: Millard County.

Fillmore, etc.—K58IQ-D, Ch. 58, Millard County. Phone: 435-864-1405.

Technical Facilities: 0.006-kw ERP, 48-ft. above ground, 5671-ft. above sea level, lat. 39° 02' 10", long. 112° 19' 31.2".

Ownership: Millard County.

Fillmore, etc.—K59IR-D, Ch. 59, Millard County. Phone: 435-864-1405.

Technical Facilities: 0.006-kw ERP, 48-ft. above ground, 5671-ft. above sea level, lat. 39° 02' 10", long. 112° 19' 31.2".

Ownership: Millard County.

Fillmore, Meadow, etc.—K25JJ-D, Ch. 25, Millard County. Phone: 435-864-1405.

Technical Facilities: 0.006-kw ERP, 48-ft. above ground, 5671-ft. above sea level, lat. 39° 02' 10", long. 112° 19' 31.2".

Ownership: Millard County.

Fillmore, Meadow, etc.—K50DE, Ch. 50, Millard County School District.

Technical Facilities: 3.16-kw ERP, 26-ft. above ground, 5705-ft. above sea level, lat. 39° 02' 10", long. 112° 19' 31".

Fillmore, Meadow, etc.—K52JX-D, Ch. 52, Millard County. Phone: 435-864-1405.

Technical Facilities: 0.006-kw ERP, 48-ft. above ground, 5671-ft. above sea level, lat. 39° 02' 10", long. 112° 19' 31.2".

Ownership: Millard County.

Fish Lake Resort—K03DE, Ch. 3, Sevier County.

Technical Facilities: 0.01-kw ERP, lat. 38° 31' 40", long. 111° 43' 02".

Ownership: Sevier County.

Fish Lake Resort—K06FL, Ch. 6, Sevier County.

Technical Facilities: 0.018-kw ERP, lat. 38° 31' 40", long. 111° 43' 02".

Fish Lake Resort—K07IZ, Ch. 7, Sevier County.

Technical Facilities: 0.005-kw ERP, lat. 38° 31' 40", long. 111° 43' 02".

Fish Lake Resort—K09VW, Ch. 9, Sevier County.

Technical Facilities: 0.004-kw ERP, 10-ft. above ground, 9659-ft. above sea level, lat. 38° 31' 40", long. 111° 43' 02".

Fish Lake Resort—K11TG, Ch. 11, Sevier County.

Technical Facilities: 0.004-kw ERP, 10-ft. above ground, 9659-ft. above sea level, lat. 38° 31' 40", long. 111° 43' 02".

Fishlake Resort—K13YL, Ch. 13, Sevier County. Phone: 435-896-9262.

Technical Facilities: 0.004-kw ERP, 10-ft. above ground, 9531-ft. above sea level, lat. 38° 31' 13", long. 111° 43' 29".

Ownership: Sevier County.

Fremont—K12PX, Ch. 12, Wayne County. Phone: 435-836-2765.

Technical Facilities: 0.009-kw ERP, 9-ft. above ground, 7220-ft. above sea level, lat. 38° 25' 58", long. 111° 37' 57".

Ownership: Wayne County.

Fremont—K15GI-D, Ch. 15, Wayne County. Phone: 435-836-2765.

Technical Facilities: 0.01-kw ERP, 28-ft. above ground, 7252-ft. above sea level, lat. 38° 25' 58", long. 111° 37' 56.9".

Fremont—K17FQ-D, Ch. 17, Wayne County. Phone: 435-836-2765.

Technical Facilities: 0.1-kw ERP, 28-ft. above ground, 7252-ft. above sea level, lat. 38° 25' 58", long. 111° 37' 57".

Fremont—K19GO-D, Ch. 19, Wayne County. Phone: 435-836-2765.

Technical Facilities: 0.031-kw ERP, 12-ft. above ground, 7236-ft. above sea level, lat. 38° 25' 58", long. 111° 37' 56.9".

Began Operation: February 3, 2009.

Ownership: Wayne County.

Fremont—K21ID-D, Ch. 21, Wayne County. Phone: 435-836-2765.

Technical Facilities: 0.031-kw ERP, 12-ft. above ground, 7236-ft. above sea level, lat. 38° 25' 58", long. 111° 37' 56.9".

Ownership: Wayne County.

Fruitland—K08JD, Ch. 8, Duchesne County.

Technical Facilities: 0.012-kw ERP, lat. 40° 12' 14", long. 110° 53' 29".

Fruitland—K10KN, Ch. 10, Duchesne County.

Technical Facilities: 0.012-kw ERP, lat. 40° 12' 14", long. 110° 53' 29".

Fruitland—K12KZ, Ch. 12, Duchesne County.

Technical Facilities: 0.012-kw ERP, lat. 40° 12' 14", long. 110° 53' 29".

Fruitland—K50EC, Ch. 50, Duchesne County.

Technical Facilities: 16-ft. above ground, 7316-ft. above sea level, lat. 40° 12' 14", long. 110° 53' 29".

Fruitland & Currant—K41DM, Ch. 41, Duchesne County.

Technical Facilities: 0.037-kw ERP, 20-ft. above ground, 10020-ft. above sea level, lat. 40° 20' 56", long. 110° 47' 55".

Fruitland, etc.—K29EZ, Ch. 29, Duchesne County. Phone: 435-738-1100.

Technical Facilities: 0.56-kw ERP, 40-ft. above ground, 7041-ft. above sea level, lat. 40° 12' 14", long. 110° 53' 29".

Ownership: Duchesne County.

Garfield (rural)—K24FD-D, Ch. 24, U. of Utah. Phone: 801-585-3601.

Technical Facilities: 0.105-kw ERP, 35-ft. above ground, 11246-ft. above sea level, lat. 38° 32' 30.3", long. 112° 04' 20.2".

Ownership: U. of Utah.

Garfield (rural)—K55KE-D, Ch. 55, U. of Utah. Phone: 801-585-3601.

Technical Facilities: 0.004-kw ERP, 75-ft. above ground, 10561-ft. above sea level, lat. 37° 45' 21.2", long. 111° 52' 27.2".

Ownership: U. of Utah.

Garfield County—K26GD-D, Ch. 26, Garfield County. Phone: 435-676-8826.

Technical Facilities: 0.105-kw ERP, 35-ft. above ground, 11246-ft. above sea level, lat. 38° 32' 30.3", long. 112° 04' 20.2".

Ownership: Garfield County.

Garfield County—K30GA-D, Ch. 30, Garfield County. Phone: 435-676-8826.

Technical Facilities: 0.105-kw ERP, 35-ft. above ground, 11246-ft. above sea level, lat. 38° 32' 30.3", long. 112° 04' 20.2".

Ownership: Garfield County.

Garfield County (rural)—K16EQ-D, Ch. 16, Garfield County. Phone: 435-676-8826.

Technical Facilities: 0.105-kw ERP, 42-ft. above ground, 11252-ft. above sea level, lat. 38° 32' 30.3", long. 112° 04' 20.2".

Ownership: Garfield County.

Garfield County (rural)—K18FT-D, Ch. 18, Garfield County. Phone: 435-676-8826.

Technical Facilities: 0.105-kw ERP, 42-ft. above ground, 11252-ft. above sea level, lat. 38° 32' 30.3", long. 112° 04' 20.2".

Ownership: Garfield County.

Garfield County (rural)—K22FT-D, Ch. 22, U. of Utah. Phone: 801-585-3601.

Technical Facilities: 0.105-kw ERP, 42-ft. above ground, 11252-ft. above sea level, lat. 38° 32' 30.3", long. 112° 04' 20.2".

Ownership: U. of Utah.

Garfield County (rural)—K28GM-D, Ch. 28, Garfield County. Phone: 435-676-8826.

Technical Facilities: 0.105-kw ERP, 35-ft. above ground, 11246-ft. above sea level, lat. 38° 32' 30.3", long. 112° 04' 20.2".

Ownership: Garfield County.

Garfield County (rural)—K36FW, Ch. 36, U. of Utah. Phone: 801-585-3601.

Technical Facilities: 0.735-kw ERP, 75-ft. above ground, 10525-ft. above sea level, lat. 37° 45' 21", long. 111° 52' 27".

Transmitter: 15.9-mi. NE of Tropic.

Ownership: U. of Utah.

Garfield County (rural)—K41EB-D, Ch. 41, Garfield County. Phone: 435-676-8826.

Technical Facilities: 0.184-kw ERP, 118-ft. above ground, 10604-ft. above sea level, lat. 37° 45' 21.2", long. 111° 52' 27.2".

Transmitter: Barney Top Mountain.

Ownership: Garfield County.

Garfield County (rural)—K43DY, Ch. 43, U. of Utah. Phone: 801-585-3601.

Technical Facilities: 0.49-kw ERP, 74-ft. above ground, 10567-ft. above sea level, lat. 37° 45' 21", long. 111° 52' 27".

Holds CP for change to 0.15-kw ERP, 74-ft. above ground, 10559-ft. above sea level, BDFCDTT-20090105ADN.

Began Operation: August 30, 1993.

Ownership: U. of Utah.

Garfield County (rural)—K50JU-D, Ch. 50, U. of Utah. Phone: 801-585-3601.

Technical Facilities: 0.004-kw ERP, 75-ft. above ground, 10561-ft. above sea level, lat. 37° 45' 21.2", long. 111° 52' 27.2".

Ownership: U. of Utah.

Garfield County (rural)—K51AH-D, Ch. 51, Garfield County. Phone: 435-676-8826.

Technical Facilities: 0.184-kw ERP, 115-ft. above ground, 10600-ft. above sea level, lat. 37° 45' 21.2", long. 111° 52' 27.2".

Ownership: Garfield County.

Garfield, etc.—K39FT-D, Ch. 39, Garfield County. Phone: 435-676-8826.

Technical Facilities: 0.184-kw ERP, 75-ft. above ground, 10561-ft. above sea level, lat. 37° 45' 21.2", long. 111° 52' 27.2".

Ownership: Garfield County.

Garfield, etc.—K45BY-D, Ch. 45, Garfield County. Phone: 435-676-8826.

Technical Facilities: 0.184-kw ERP, 125-ft. above ground, 10610-ft. above sea level, lat. 37° 45' 21.2", long. 111° 52' 27.2".

Ownership: Garfield County.

Garfield, etc.—K47AB-D, Ch. 47, Garfield County. Phone: 435-676-8826.

Technical Facilities: 0.184-kw ERP, 125-ft. above ground, 10610-ft. above sea level, lat. 37° 45' 21.2", long. 111° 52' 27.2".

Ownership: Garfield County.

Garfield, etc.—K49AG-D, Ch. 49, Garfield County. Phone: 435-676-8826.

Technical Facilities: 0.184-kw ERP, 125-ft. above ground, 10610-ft. above sea level, lat. 37° 45' 21.2", long. 111° 52' 27.2".

Ownership: Garfield County.

Garrison—K42FU, Ch. 42, Millard County. Phone: 435-743-5227.

Technical Facilities: 0.35-kw ERP, 23-ft. above ground, 8120-ft. above sea level, lat. 38° 56' 53", long. 114° 09' 05".

Garrison—K44GP, Ch. 44, Millard County. Phone: 435-743-5227.

Technical Facilities: 0.35-kw ERP, 23-ft. above ground, 8120-ft. above sea level, lat. 38° 56' 53", long. 114° 09' 05".

Garrison, etc.—K07OH, Ch. 7, Millard County.

Technical Facilities: 0.052-kw ERP, lat. 38° 56' 53", long. 114° 09' 05".

Garrison, etc.—K09NB, Ch. 9, Millard County.

Technical Facilities: 0.052-kw ERP, lat. 38° 56' 53", long. 114° 09' 05".

Garrison, etc.—K11NP, Ch. 11, Millard County.

Technical Facilities: 0.052-kw ERP, lat. 38° 56' 53", long. 114° 09' 05".

Garrison, etc.—K13OJ, Ch. 13, Millard County.

Technical Facilities: 0.052-kw ERP, lat. 38° 56' 53", long. 114° 09' 05".

Garrison, etc.—K46GG, Ch. 46, Millard County. Phone: 435-864-1405.

Technical Facilities: 0.348-kw ERP, 23-ft. above ground, 8120-ft. above sea level, lat. 38° 56' 53", long. 114° 09' 05".

Ownership: Millard County.

Garrison, etc.—K48FH, Ch. 48, Millard County.

Technical Facilities: 0.348-kw ERP, 23-ft. above ground, 8120-ft. above sea level, lat. 38° 56' 53", long. 114° 09' 05".

Transmitter: Approx. 5-mi. SSW of Baker.

Ownership: Millard County.

Garrison, etc.—K50FC, Ch. 50, Millard County.

Technical Facilities: 0.348-kw ERP, lat. 38° 56' 53", long. 114° 09' 05".

Transmitter: approx. 5-mi. SSW of Baker.

Green River—K02BU, Ch. 2, Green River City TV.

Technical Facilities: 0.9-kw ERP, lat. 38° 58' 35", long. 110° 10' 56".

Ownership: Green River City TV.

Green River—K04BR, Ch. 4, Green River City TV.

Technical Facilities: 0.005-kw ERP, lat. 38° 58' 35", long. 110° 10' 56".

Ownership: Green River City TV.

Green River—K05BK, Ch. 5, Green River City TV.

Technical Facilities: 0.005-kw ERP, lat. 38° 58' 35", long. 110° 10' 56".

Ownership: Green River City TV.

Green River—K07OV, Ch. 7, Green River City TV.

Technical Facilities: 0.195-kw ERP, lat. 39° 10' 58", long. 110° 36' 25".

Green River—K09CX, Ch. 9, Green River City TV.

Technical Facilities: 0.195-kw ERP, 7684-ft. above sea level, lat. 39° 10' 58", long. 110° 36' 25".

Green River—K11DD, Ch. 11, Green River City TV.

Technical Facilities: 0.195-kw ERP, lat. 39° 10' 58", long. 110° 36' 25".

Green River—K13DB, Ch. 13, Green River City TV.

Technical Facilities: 0.195-kw ERP, lat. 39° 10' 58", long. 110° 36' 25".

Green River—K15HH-D, Ch. 15, Green River City TV. Phone: 435-381-5678.

Technical Facilities: 0.02-kw ERP, 15-ft. above ground, 4322-ft. above sea level, lat. 38° 58' 35", long. 110° 10' 56".

Ownership: Green River City TV.

Green River—K16HD-D, Ch. 16, Green River City TV. Phone: 435-381-5678.

Technical Facilities: 0.02-kw ERP, 15-ft. above ground, 4322-ft. above sea level, lat. 38° 58' 35", long. 110° 10' 56".

Ownership: Green River City TV.

Green River—K17HW-D, Ch. 17, Green River City TV. Phone: 435-381-5678.

Technical Facilities: 0.02-kw ERP, 15-ft. above ground, 4322-ft. above sea level, lat. 38° 58' 35", long. 110° 10' 56".

Ownership: Green River City TV.

Green River—K32FG, Ch. 32, Catamount-Idaho License LLC.

Technical Facilities: 0.195-kw ERP, lat. 39° 10' 58", long. 110° 36' 25".

Green River—K36FX, Ch. 36, Green River City TV. Phone: 435-381-5678.

Technical Facilities: 0.6-kw ERP, 16-ft. above ground, 7677-ft. above sea level, lat. 39° 10' 58", long. 110° 36' 25".

Ownership: Green River City TV.

Green River—K38GP, Ch. 38, Green River City TV. Phone: 435-381-5678.

Technical Facilities: 0.6-kw ERP, 16-ft. above ground, 7677-ft. above sea level, lat. 39° 10' 58", long. 110° 36' 25".

Ownership: Green River City TV.

Green River—K41JS-D, Ch. 41, Green River City TV. Phone: 435-381-5678.

Technical Facilities: 0.02-kw ERP, 31-ft. above ground, 7715-ft. above sea level, lat. 39° 10' 58", long. 110° 36' 25".

Ownership: Green River City TV.

Green River—K42HP-D, Ch. 42, Green River City TV. Phone: 435-381-5678.

Technical Facilities: 0.02-kw ERP, 31-ft. above ground, 7715-ft. above sea level, lat. 39° 10' 58", long. 110° 36' 25".

Ownership: Green River City TV.

Green River—K43KG-D, Ch. 43, Green River City TV. Phone: 435-381-5678.

Technical Facilities: 0.02-kw ERP, 31-ft. above ground, 7715-ft. above sea level, lat. 39° 10' 58", long. 110° 36' 25".

Ownership: Green River City TV.

Green River—K44IK-D, Ch. 44, Green River City TV. Phone: 435-381-5678.

Technical Facilities: 0.02-kw ERP, 31-ft. above ground, 7715-ft. above sea level, lat. 39° 10' 58", long. 110° 36' 25".

Ownership: Green River City TV.

Green River—K45JV-D, Ch. 45, Green River City TV. Phone: 435-381-5678.

Technical Facilities: 0.02-kw ERP, 31-ft. above ground, 7715-ft. above sea level, lat. 39° 10' 58", long. 110° 36' 25".

Ownership: Green River City TV.

Green River—K47KX-D, Ch. 47, Green River City TV. Phone: 435-381-5678.

Technical Facilities: 0.02-kw ERP, 31-ft. above ground, 7715-ft. above sea level, lat. 39° 10' 58", long. 110° 36' 25".

Ownership: Green River City TV.

Greenlake—K17FW, Ch. 17, Daggett County Television Dept.

Technical Facilities: 0.13-kw ERP, lat. 40° 57' 34", long. 109° 24' 58".

Hanksville—K07KM, Ch. 7, Wayne County.

Technical Facilities: 0.009-kw ERP, 4524-ft. above sea level, lat. 38° 22' 28", long. 110° 41' 51".

Hanksville—K09LC, Ch. 9, Wayne County.

Technical Facilities: 0.009-kw ERP, 4524-ft. above sea level, lat. 38° 22' 28", long. 110° 41' 51".

Hanksville—K11LJ, Ch. 11, Wayne County.

Technical Facilities: 0.009-kw ERP, 4524-ft. above sea level, lat. 38° 22' 28", long. 110° 41' 51".

Hanksville—K13LS, Ch. 13, Wayne County.

Technical Facilities: 0.009-kw ERP, 4524-ft. above sea level, lat. 38° 22' 28", long. 110° 41' 51".

Hanksville—K46FU, Ch. 46, Wayne County. Phone: 435-836-2765.

Technical Facilities: 0.007-kw ERP, 10-ft. above ground, 4508-ft. above sea level, lat. 38° 22' 28", long. 110° 41' 51".

Hanksville—K48GR, Ch. 48, Wayne County. Phone: 435-836-2765.

Technical Facilities: 0.007-kw ERP, 10-ft. above ground, 4508-ft. above sea level, lat. 38° 22' 28", long. 110° 41' 51".

Hanksville—K50FZ, Ch. 50, Wayne County. Phone: 435-836-2765.

Technical Facilities: 0.007-kw ERP, 10-ft. above ground, 4508-ft. above sea level, lat. 38° 22' 28", long. 110° 41' 51".

Hanna, etc.—K07NV, Ch. 7, Duchesne County.

Technical Facilities: 0.014-kw ERP, 7024-ft. above sea level, lat. 40° 23' 08", long. 110° 45' 28".

Hanna, etc.—K09MQ, Ch. 9, Duchesne County.

Technical Facilities: 0.013-kw ERP, 7024-ft. above sea level, lat. 40° 23' 08", long. 110° 45' 28".

Hanna, etc.—K11ND, Ch. 11, Duchesne County.

Technical Facilities: 0.013-kw ERP, 7024-ft. above sea level, lat. 40° 23' 08", long. 110° 45' 28".

Hatch—K09MO, Ch. 9, Garfield County. Phone: 435-676-8826.

Technical Facilities: 0.005-kw ERP, lat. 37° 40' 37", long. 112° 22' 27".

Ownership: Garfield County.

Hatch—K11NA, Ch. 11, Garfield County. Phone: 435-676-8826.

Technical Facilities: 0.005-kw ERP, lat. 37° 40' 37", long. 112° 22' 27".

Ownership: Garfield County.

Hatch—K13NT, Ch. 13, Garfield County. Phone: 435-676-8826.

Technical Facilities: 0.004-kw ERP, lat. 37° 40' 37", long. 112° 22' 27".

Ownership: Garfield County.

Hatch—K15HE-D, Ch. 15, Garfield County. Phone: 435-676-8826.

Technical Facilities: 0.028-kw ERP, 48-ft. above ground, 7226-ft. above sea level, lat. 37° 40' 36", long. 112° 22' 19.7".

Began Operation: December 23, 2008.

Ownership: Garfield County.

Hatch—K17HQ-D, Ch. 17, Garfield County. Phone: 435-676-8826.

Technical Facilities: 0.028-kw ERP, 48-ft. above ground, 7226-ft. above sea level, lat. 37° 40' 36", long. 112° 22' 19.7".

Began Operation: December 23, 2008.

Ownership: Garfield County.

Hatch—K19GJ-D, Ch. 19, Garfield County. Phone: 435-676-8826.

Technical Facilities: 0.028-kw ERP, 48-ft. above ground, 7226-ft. above sea level, lat. 37° 40' 36", long. 112° 22' 19.7".

Began Operation: December 23, 2008.

Ownership: Garfield County.

Hatch—K23IL-D, Ch. 23, U. of Utah. Phone: 801-585-3601.

Technical Facilities: 0.028-kw ERP, 48-ft. above ground, 7226-ft. above sea level, lat. 37° 40' 36", long. 112° 22' 19.7".

Began Operation: December 15, 2008.

Ownership: U. of Utah.

Hatch—K36FV, Ch. 36, U. of Utah. Phone: 801-585-3601.

Technical Facilities: 0.35-kw ERP, 36-ft. above ground, 7214-ft. above sea level, lat. 37° 40' 37", long. 112° 22' 27".

Hatch—K38GQ, Ch. 38, Garfield County. Phone: 435-676-8826.

Technical Facilities: 0.35-kw ERP, 36-ft. above ground, 7214-ft. above sea level, lat. 37° 40' 37", long. 112° 22' 27".

Holds CP for change to 0.05-kw ERP, 57-ft. above ground, 7235-ft. above sea level, lat. 37° 40' 36", long. 112° 22' 19.7". BDFCDTT-20090102ACM.

Began Operation: April 14, 1989.

Ownership: Garfield County.

Heber—K35EW, Ch. 35, Wasatch County Commissioners.

Technical Facilities: 0.039-kw ERP, lat. 40° 33' 45", long. 111° 28' 30".

Heber & Midway—K18GV, Ch. 18, Wasatch County Commissioners. Phone: 435-654-3211.

Technical Facilities: 1.43-kw ERP, 21-ft. above ground, 8422-ft. above sea level, lat. 40° 33' 45", long. 111° 28' 30".

Ownership: Wasatch County.

Heber & Midway—K27GC, Ch. 27, Wasatch County Commissioners. Phone: 435-654-3211.

Technical Facilities: 1.49-kw ERP, 20-ft. above ground, 8422-ft. above sea level, lat. 40° 33' 45", long. 111° 28' 30".

Transmitter: Wilson Peak communications site, 3-mi. N of Midway.

Heber & Midway—K31FP, Ch. 31, Wasatch County Commissioners. Phone: 435-654-3211.

Technical Facilities: 1.49-kw ERP, 20-ft. above ground, 8422-ft. above sea level, lat. 40° 33' 45", long. 111° 28' 30".

Transmitter: Wilson Peak communications site.

Heber & Midway—K33FX, Ch. 33, U. of Utah. Phone: 801-585-3601.

Technical Facilities: 1.49-kw ERP, 25-ft. above ground, 8425-ft. above sea level, lat. 40° 33' 45", long. 111° 28' 30".

Ownership: U. of Utah.

Heber City—K21DY, Ch. 21, Larry H. Miller Communications Corp. Phone: 801-537-1414.

Technical Facilities: 1.53-kw ERP, 23-ft. above ground, 8425-ft. above sea level, lat. 40° 33' 45", long. 111° 28' 30".

Began Operation: March 2, 1994.

Ownership: Larry H. Miller Communications Corp.

Heber City—K25HF, Ch. 25, Community Television of Utah License LLC. Phone: 859-448-2700.

Technical Facilities: 1.43-kw ERP, 20-ft. above ground, 8421-ft. above sea level, lat. 40° 33' 45", long. 111° 28' 30".

Ownership: Local TV Holdings LLC.

Heber/Midway—K39HS, Ch. 39, Wasatch County Commissioners. Phone: 435-654-3211.

Technical Facilities: 1.43-kw ERP, 20-ft. above ground, 8419-ft. above sea level, lat. 40° 33' 45", long. 111° 28' 30".

Ownership: Wasatch County.

Helper—K07NS, Ch. 7, Carbon County.

Technical Facilities: 0.006-kw ERP, lat. 39° 41' 06", long. 110° 50' 29".

Helper—K09BQ, Ch. 9, Carbon County.

Technical Facilities: 0.019-kw ERP, lat. 39° 41' 06", long. 110° 50' 29".

Helper—K11BV, Ch. 11, Carbon County.

Technical Facilities: 0.01-kw ERP, lat. 39° 41' 06", long. 110° 50' 29".

Helper—K13BZ, Ch. 13, Carbon County.

Technical Facilities: 0.019-kw ERP, lat. 39° 41' 06", long. 110° 50' 29".

Helper—K31HL, Ch. 31, Carbon County. Phone: 465-969-3200.

Technical Facilities: 1.73-kw ERP, 25-ft. above ground, 5825-ft. above sea level, lat. 39° 41' 06", long. 110° 50' 29".

Ownership: Carbon County.

Helper—K33HS, Ch. 33, Carbon County. Phone: 435-969-3200.

Technical Facilities: 1.73-kw ERP, 25-ft. above ground, 5825-ft. above sea level, lat. 39° 41' 06", long. 110° 50' 29".

Ownership: Carbon County.

Helper—K36HE, Ch. 36, Carbon County. Phone: 435-969-3200.

Technical Facilities: 1.73-kw ERP, 25-ft. above ground, 5825-ft. above sea level, lat. 39° 41' 06", long. 110° 50' 29".

Ownership: Carbon County.

Henefer—K06IM, Ch. 6, U. of Utah.

Technical Facilities: 0.005-kw ERP, lat. 40° 58' 40", long. 111° 26' 08".

Henefer & Echo—K29FY, Ch. 29, Summit County. Phone: 435-336-3220.

Technical Facilities: 0.26-kw ERP, 13-ft. above sea level, lat. 40° 58' 40", long. 111° 26' 08".

Ownership: Summit County.

Henefer & Echo—K31HR, Ch. 31, Summit County. Phone: 435-336-3220.

Technical Facilities: 0.26-kw ERP, 14-ft. above sea level, lat. 40° 58' 40", long. 111° 26' 08".

Ownership: Summit County.

Henefer, etc.—K08AS, Ch. 8, Summit County.

Technical Facilities: 0.008-kw ERP, 6115-ft. above sea level, lat. 40° 58' 40", long. 111° 26' 08".

Henefer, etc.—K10AY, Ch. 10, Summit County.

Technical Facilities: 0.082-kw ERP, 6115-ft. above sea level, lat. 40° 58' 40", long. 111° 26' 08".

Henefer, etc.—K12AY, Ch. 12, Summit County.

Technical Facilities: 0.008-kw ERP, 6615-ft. above sea level, lat. 40° 58' 40", long. 111° 26' 08".

Henrieville—K09XF, Ch. 9, Garfield County. Phone: 435-676-8826.

Technical Facilities: 0.007-kw ERP, lat. 37° 33' 19", long. 111° 59' 39".

Ownership: Garfield County.

Henrieville—K11UM, Ch. 11, Garfield County. Phone: 435-676-8826.

Technical Facilities: 0.007-kw ERP, lat. 37° 33' 19", long. 111° 59' 39".

Ownership: Garfield County.

Henrieville—K13XL, Ch. 13, Garfield County. Phone: 435-676-8826.

Technical Facilities: 0.007-kw ERP, lat. 37° 33' 19", long. 111° 59' 39".

Ownership: Garfield County.

Henrieville—K16FN, Ch. 16, Garfield County. Phone: 435-676-8826.

Technical Facilities: 0.008-kw ERP, 10-ft. above ground, 6089-ft. above sea level, lat. 37° 33' 13.3", long. 111° 59' 40.4".

Ownership: Garfield County.

Henrieville—K18CV, Ch. 18, U. of Utah.

Technical Facilities: 0.008-kw ERP, 13-ft. above ground, 6056-ft. above sea level, lat. 37° 33' 19", long. 111° 59' 39".

Henrieville—K20BT, Ch. 20, Garfield County. Phone: 435-676-8826.

Technical Facilities: 0.01-kw ERP, lat. 37° 33' 19", long. 111° 59' 39".

Ownership: Garfield County.

Henrieville—K22GP, Ch. 22, Garfield County. Phone: 435-676-8826.

Technical Facilities: 0.008-kw ERP, 10-ft. above ground, 6089-ft. above sea level, lat. 37° 33' 13", long. 111° 59' 40".

Ownership: Garfield County.

Henrieville—K42HS-D, Ch. 42, U. of Utah. Phone: 801-585-3601.

Technical Facilities: 0.01-kw ERP, 12-ft. above ground, 6012-ft. above sea level, lat. 37° 32' 58.9", long. 111° 59' 21.6".

Ownership: U. of Utah.

Hildale, UT & Cane Beds, AZ—K07SC, Ch. 7, SLC TV Licensee Corp. Phone: 212-891-2100.

Technical Facilities: 0.04-kw ERP, lat. 36° 54' 11", long. 113° 01' 58".

Ownership: Four Points Media Group Holding LLC.

Hildale, UT & Cane Beds, AZ—K09SU, Ch. 9, Newport Television License LLC. Phone: 816-751-0204.

Technical Facilities: 0.04-kw ERP, lat. 36° 54' 11", long. 113° 01' 58".

Ownership: Newport Television LLC.

Hildale, UT & Cane Beds, AZ—K11QQ-D, Ch. 11, Bonneville Holding Co. Phone: 801-575-7517.

Technical Facilities: 0.031-kw ERP, 20-ft. above ground, 5217-ft. above sea level, lat. 36° 54' 58", long. 113° 01' 58".

Began Operation: November 18, 1982.

Ownership: Bonneville International Corp.

Huntsville—K32HD, Ch. 32, Weber County, Ogden Valley Recreation/Transmission Special Services District. Phone: 801-745-4202.

Technical Facilities: 0.4-kw ERP, 36-ft. above ground, 6066-ft. above sea level, lat. 41° 20' 20", long. 111° 48' 56".

Ownership: Weber County, Ogden Valley Recreation/Transmission Special Services District.

Huntsville—K35GG, Ch. 35, U. of Utah.

Technical Facilities: 0.964-kw ERP, lat. 41° 20' 45", long. 111° 48' 50".

Huntsville—K45JC, Ch. 45, Weber County, Ogden Valley Recreation/Transmission Special Services District. Phone: 801-745-4202.

Technical Facilities: 0.4-kw ERP, 36-ft. above ground, 6066-ft. above sea level, lat. 41° 20' 20", long. 111° 48' 56".

Ownership: Weber County, Ogden Valley Recreation/Transmission Special Services District.

Huntsville—K47KE, Ch. 47, Weber County, Ogden Valley Recreation/Transmission Special Services District. Phone: 801-745-4202.

Technical Facilities: 0.4-kw ERP, 36-ft. above ground, 6066-ft. above sea level, lat. 41° 20' 20", long. 111° 48' 56".

Ownership: Weber County, Ogden Valley Recreation/Transmission Special Services District.

Huntsville—K51JC, Ch. 51, Weber County, Ogden Valley Recreation/Transmission Special Services District. Phone: 801-745-4202.

Technical Facilities: 0.4-kw ERP, 36-ft. above ground, 6066-ft. above sea level, lat. 41° 20' 20.2", long. 111° 48' 56.3".

Ownership: Weber County, Ogden Valley Recreation/Transmission Special Services District.

Huntsville—K58FT, Ch. 58, Alpha & Omega Communications LLC. Phone: 801-595-0056.

Technical Facilities: 0.423-kw ERP, 99-ft. above ground, 9645-ft. above sea level, lat. 41° 12' 00", long. 111° 52' 53".

Transmitter: Mount Ogden, 7.5-mi. SW of Huntsville.

Ownership: Alpha & Omega Communications LLC.

Huntsville, etc.—K10DT, Ch. 10, Ogden Valley TV Repeater Assn.

Technical Facilities: 0.07-kw ERP, lat. 41° 20' 45", long. 111° 48' 50".

Huntsville, etc.—K17IP-D, Ch. 17, Weber County, Ogden Valley Recreation/Transmission Special Services District. Phone: 801-745-4202.

Technical Facilities: 0.012-kw ERP, 36-ft. above ground, 6066-ft. above sea level, lat. 41° 20' 20.2", long. 111° 48' 56.3".

Began Operation: December 15, 2008.

Ownership: Weber County, Ogden Valley Recreation/Transmission Special Services District.

Huntsville, etc.—K23IC-D, Ch. 23, Weber County, Ogden Valley Recreation/Transmission Special Services District. Phone: 801-745-4202.

Technical Facilities: 0.012-kw ERP, 36-ft. above ground, 6066-ft. above sea level, lat. 41° 20' 20.2", long. 111° 48' 56.3".

Began Operation: December 15, 2008.

Ownership: Weber County, Ogden Valley Recreation/Transmission Special Services District.

Huntsville, etc.—K25IX-D, Ch. 25, Weber County, Ogden Valley Recreation/Transmission Special Services District. Phone: 801-745-4202.

Technical Facilities: 0.012-kw ERP, 36-ft. above ground, 6066-ft. above sea level, lat. 41° 20' 20.2", long. 111° 48' 56.3".

Began Operation: December 15, 2008.

Ownership: Weber County, Ogden Valley Recreation/Transmission Special Services District.

Huntsville, etc.—K39IS-D, Ch. 39, Weber County, Ogden Valley Recreation/Transmission Special Services District. Phone: 801-745-4202.

Technical Facilities: 0.012-kw ERP, 36-ft. above ground, 6066-ft. above sea level, lat. 41° 20' 20.2", long. 111° 48' 56.3".

Began Operation: December 15, 2008.

Ownership: Weber County, Ogden Valley Recreation/Transmission Special Services District.

Huntsville/Liberty—K28JK-D, Ch. 28, Weber County, Ogden Valley Recreation/Transmission Special Services District. Phone: 801-745-4202.

Technical Facilities: 0.012-kw ERP, 36-ft. above ground, 6066-ft. above sea level, lat. 41° 20' 20.2", long. 111° 48' 56.3".

Began Operation: December 15, 2008.

Ownership: Weber County, Ogden Valley Recreation/Transmission Special Services District.

Hurricane, Leeds, etc.—K21GW, Ch. 21, U. of Utah. Phone: 801-581-7777. Fax: 801-585-5096.

Technical Facilities: 0.34-kw ERP, 16-ft. above ground, 5134-ft. above sea level, lat. 37° 16' 21", long. 113° 16' 34".

Ownership: U. of Utah.

Iron County (rural)—K28GQ, Ch. 28, Iron County. Phone: 435-477-8341.

Technical Facilities: 0.956-kw ERP, 48-ft. above ground, 9178-ft. above sea level, lat. 38° 31' 05", long. 113° 17' 03".

Holds CP for change to 0.3-kw ERP, 49-ft. above ground, 9724-ft. above sea level, lat. 38° 31' 13.7", long. 113° 17' 12.1". BMPDTT-20080131ARK.

Ownership: Iron County.

Juab—K20DW-D, Ch. 20, U. of Utah. Phone: 801-585-3601.

Technical Facilities: 0.39-kw ERP, 48-ft. above ground, 8407-ft. above sea level, lat. 39° 29' 31", long. 111° 49' 37".

Ownership: U. of Utah.

Juab—K22EC-D, Ch. 22, Millard County. Phone: 435-864-1405.

Technical Facilities: 0.676-kw ERP, 20-ft. above ground, 8379-ft. above sea level, lat. 39° 29' 30.6", long. 111° 49' 37.4".

Ownership: Millard County.

Juab County (rural)—K47BD-D, Ch. 47, Sevier County. Phone: 435-896-9262.

Technical Facilities: 1.2-kw ERP, 39-ft. above ground, 8399-ft. above sea level, lat. 39° 29' 30.6", long. 111° 49' 37.4".

Ownership: Sevier County.

Juab County (rural)—K49AO-D, Ch. 49, U. of Utah. Phone: 801-585-3601.

Technical Facilities: 1-kw ERP, 39-ft. above ground, 8399-ft. above sea level, lat. 39° 29' 31", long. 111° 49' 37".

Ownership: U. of Utah.

Juab County (rural)—K56BB, Ch. 56, Community Television of Utah License LLC. Phone: 859-448-2700.

Technical Facilities: 1.9-kw ERP, 30-ft. above ground, 8435-ft. above sea level, lat. 39° 29' 24", long. 111° 49' 06".

Ownership: Local TV Holdings LLC.

Kanab—K02BI, Ch. 2, Western Kane County Service District No. 1.

Technical Facilities: 0.91-kw ERP, lat. 37° 03' 38", long. 112° 31' 13".

Ownership: Western Kane County Special Service District No. 1.

Kanab—K05AX, Ch. 5, Western Kane County Service District No. 1.

Technical Facilities: 0.01-kw ERP, lat. 37° 03' 38", long. 112° 31' 13".

Ownership: Western Kane County Special Service District No. 1.

Kanab—K07ES, Ch. 7, Western Kane County Service District No. 1.

Technical Facilities: 0.013-kw ERP, 5810-ft. above sea level, lat. 37° 03' 38", long. 112° 31' 13".

Kanab—K10ME, Ch. 10, Western Kane County Service District No. 1.

Technical Facilities: 0.064-kw ERP, 16-ft. above ground, 5810-ft. above sea level, lat. 37° 03' 38", long. 112° 31' 13".

Kanab—K12ND, Ch. 12, Kanab Lions Club.

Technical Facilities: 0.06-kw ERP, lat. 36° 59' 32", long. 112° 31' 39".

Ownership: Kanab Lions Club.

Kanab—K18DN, Ch. 18, Western Kane County Service District No. 1.

Technical Facilities: 0.162-kw ERP, 26-ft. above ground, 5820-ft. above sea level, lat. 37° 03' 38", long. 112° 31' 13".

Kanab—K20EC, Ch. 20, Western Kane County Service District No. 1.

Technical Facilities: 0.162-kw ERP, 26-ft. above ground, 5820-ft. above sea level, lat. 37° 03' 38", long. 112° 31' 13".

Kanab—K23DP, Ch. 23, U. of Utah.

Technical Facilities: 0.164-kw ERP, 26-ft. above ground, 5820-ft. above sea level, lat. 37° 03' 38", long. 112° 31' 13".

Kanab—K27JV-D, Ch. 27, Western Kane County Special Service District No. 1. Phone: 435-644-5089.

Technical Facilities: 0.007-kw ERP, 13-ft. above ground, 5755-ft. above sea level, lat. 37° 03' 34.6", long. 112° 31' 12.2".

Ownership: Western Kane County Special Service District No. 1.

Kanab—K28IT, Ch. 28, Western Kane County Special Service District No. 1. Phone: 435-644-5089.

Technical Facilities: 0.32-kw ERP, 18-ft. above ground, 5759-ft. above sea level, lat. 37° 03' 35", long. 112° 31' 12".

Ownership: Western Kane County Special Service District No. 1.

Kanab—K32DC, Ch. 32, Western Kane County Service District No. 1.

Technical Facilities: 0.162-kw ERP, 26-ft. above ground, 5820-ft. above sea level, lat. 37° 03' 38", long. 112° 31' 13".

Kanab—K40JM-D, Ch. 40, Western Kane County Special Service District No. 1. Phone: 435-644-5089.

Technical Facilities: 0.007-kw ERP, 13-ft. above ground, 5755-ft. above sea level, lat. 37° 03' 34.6", long. 112° 31' 12.2".

Ownership: Western Kane County Special Service District No. 1.

Kanarraville—K06KO, Ch. 6, Iron County. Phone: 435-477-8341.

Technical Facilities: 0.15-kw ERP, 31-ft. above ground, 6350-ft. above sea level, lat. 37° 29' 16", long. 113° 12' 18".

Ownership: Iron County.

Kanarraville—K08CE, Ch. 8, Iron County. Phone: 435-477-8341.

Technical Facilities: 0.15-kw ERP, 36-ft. above ground, 6355-ft. above sea level, lat. 37° 29' 16", long. 113° 12' 18".

Ownership: Iron County.

Kanarraville—K10CK, Ch. 10, Iron County. Phone: 435-477-8341.

Technical Facilities: 0.3-kw ERP, 38-ft. above ground, 6357-ft. above sea level, lat. 37° 29' 16", long. 113° 12' 18".

Ownership: Iron County.

Kanarraville—K12CD, Ch. 12, Iron County. Phone: 435-477-8341.

Technical Facilities: 0.3-kw ERP, 38-ft. above ground, 6357-ft. above sea level, lat. 37° 29' 16", long. 113° 12' 18".

Ownership: Iron County.

Kanarraville—K47HU, Ch. 47, Iron County. Phone: 435-477-8341.

Technical Facilities: 0.068-kw ERP, 16-ft. above ground, 6165-ft. above sea level, lat. 37° 29' 13", long. 113° 12' 18".

Holds CP for change to 0.04-kw ERP, 33-ft. above ground, 6181-ft. above sea level, BDFCDTT-20070129ADA.

Kanarraville, etc.—K02KN, Ch. 2, Iron County. Phone: 435-477-8341.

Technical Facilities: 0.225-kw ERP, 45-ft. above ground, 6364-ft. above sea level, lat. 37° 29' 16", long. 113° 12' 18".

Ownership: Iron County.

Koosharem—K03FF, Ch. 3, Sevier County.

Technical Facilities: 0.001-kw ERP, 8674-ft. above sea level, lat. 38° 28' 36", long. 111° 48' 54".

Ownership: Sevier County.

Koosharem—K06IG, Ch. 6, Sevier County.

Technical Facilities: 0.001-kw ERP, lat. 38° 28' 36", long. 111° 48' 54".

Koosharem—K08CL, Ch. 8, Sevier County.

Technical Facilities: 0.006-kw ERP, lat. 38° 28' 36", long. 111° 48' 54".

Koosharem—K10CU, Ch. 10, Sevier County.

Technical Facilities: 0.012-kw ERP, lat. 38° 28' 36", long. 111° 48' 54".

Koosharem—K12CT, Ch. 12, Sevier County.

Technical Facilities: 0.012-kw ERP, lat. 38° 28' 36", long. 111° 48' 54".

Koosharem—K38KA-D, Ch. 38, Sevier County. Phone: 435-896-9262.

Technical Facilities: 0.009-kw ERP, 20-ft. above ground, 8704-ft. above sea level, lat. 38° 28' 42.9", long. 111° 49' 22.4".

Ownership: Sevier County.

Koosharem—K39JD-D, Ch. 39, Sevier County. Phone: 435-896-9262.

Technical Facilities: 0.009-kw ERP, 20-ft. above ground, 8704-ft. above sea level, lat. 38° 28' 42.9", long. 111° 49' 22.4".

Ownership: Sevier County.

Koosharem—K41FZ-D, Ch. 41, Sevier County. Phone: 435-896-9262.

Technical Facilities: 0.055-kw ERP, 28-ft. above ground, 8712-ft. above sea level, lat. 38° 28' 42.9", long. 111° 49' 22.4".

Koosharem—K43KM-D, Ch. 43, Sevier County. Phone: 435-896-9262.

Technical Facilities: 0.009-kw ERP, 20-ft. above ground, 8704-ft. above sea level, lat. 38° 28' 42.9", long. 111° 49' 22.4".

Ownership: Sevier County.

Koosharem—K45FV-D, Ch. 45, Sevier County.

Technical Facilities: 0.055-kw ERP, 28-ft. above ground, 8712-ft. above sea level, lat. 38° 28' 42.9", long. 111° 49' 22.4".

Ownership: Sevier County.

Koosharem—K47KR-D, Ch. 47, Sevier County. Phone: 435-896-9262.

Technical Facilities: 0.009-kw ERP, 20-ft. above ground, 8704-ft. above sea level, lat. 38° 28' 42.9", long. 111° 49' 22.4".

Ownership: Sevier County.

Koosharem—K49JP-D, Ch. 49, Sevier County. Phone: 435-896-9262.

Technical Facilities: 0.009-kw ERP, 20-ft. above ground, 8704-ft. above sea level, lat. 38° 28' 42.9", long. 111° 49' 22.4".

Ownership: Sevier County.

Laketown—K12MI, Ch. 12, Rich County.

Technical Facilities: 0.057-kw ERP, lat. 41° 53' 05", long. 111° 16' 00".

Laketown—K38AL, Ch. 38, Rich County. Phone: 435-793-3415.

Technical Facilities: 1.2-kw ERP, 30-ft. above ground, 7592-ft. above sea level, lat. 41° 52' 57", long. 111° 16' 09".

Laketown & Garden City—K50GA, Ch. 50, Rich County. Phone: 435-793-2415.

Technical Facilities: 1.2-kw ERP, 30-ft. above ground, 7592-ft. above sea level, lat. 41° 55' 57", long. 111° 16' 09".

Transmitter: 1-mi. E of Orderville.

Laketown, etc.—K08JR, Ch. 8, Rich County.

Technical Facilities: 0.117-kw ERP, 7592-ft. above sea level, lat. 41° 53' 05", long. 111° 16' 00".

Laketown, etc.—K10LM, Ch. 10, Rich County.

Technical Facilities: 0.058-kw ERP, 7592-ft. above sea level, lat. 41° 53' 05", long. 111° 16' 00".

Laketown, etc.—K46GD, Ch. 46, U. of Utah.

Technical Facilities: 1.2-kw ERP, 30-ft. above ground, 7762-ft. above sea level, lat. 41° 52' 57", long. 111° 16' 09".

Laketown, etc.—K48GV, Ch. 48, Rich County. Phone: 435-793-2415.

Technical Facilities: 1.28-kw ERP, 30-ft. above ground, 7592-ft. above sea level, lat. 41° 52' 57", long. 111° 16' 09".

Transmitter: 5-mi. NE of Laketown.

Leamington—K08MC, Ch. 8, Millard County.

Technical Facilities: 0.044-kw ERP, lat. 39° 31' 55", long. 112° 18' 47".

Leamington—K10NW, Ch. 10, Millard County Sch.

Technical Facilities: 0.16-kw ERP, 26-ft. above ground, 4829-ft. above sea level, lat. 39° 31' 55", long. 112° 18' 47".

Leamington—K12OO, Ch. 12, Millard County Schoo.

Technical Facilities: 0.16-kw ERP, 26-ft. above ground, 4829-ft. above sea level, lat. 39° 31' 55", long. 112° 18' 47".

Leamington—K38HK, Ch. 38, Millard County. Phone: 435-743-5227.

Technical Facilities: 0.77-kw ERP, lat. 39° 31' 55", long. 112° 18' 47".

Leamington—K42FR, Ch. 42, Millard County. Phone: 435-743-5227.

Technical Facilities: 0.77-kw ERP, lat. 39° 31' 55", long. 112° 18' 47".

Leamington—K44FB, Ch. 44, Millard County.

Technical Facilities: 0.774-kw ERP, lat. 39° 31' 55", long. 112° 18' 47".

Transmitter: 1-mi. W of Leamington.

Leamington—K46DK, Ch. 46, Millard County.

Technical Facilities: 0.774-kw ERP, 26-ft. above ground, 4829-ft. above sea level, lat. 39° 31' 55", long. 112° 18' 47".

Leamington—K48FY, Ch. 48, Millard County.

Technical Facilities: 0.774-kw ERP, lat. 39° 31' 55", long. 112° 18' 47".

Leamington—K50DJ, Ch. 50, Millard County.

Technical Facilities: 0.774-kw ERP, 26-ft. above ground, 4829-ft. above sea level, lat. 39° 31' 55", long. 112° 18' 47".

Leamington—K52JW-D, Ch. 52, Millard County. Phone: 435-864-1405.

Technical Facilities: 0.01-kw ERP, 48-ft. above ground, 4857-ft. above sea level, lat. 39° 31' 55.7", long. 112° 18' 46.7".

Ownership: Millard County.

Leamington—K55KH-D, Ch. 55, Millard County. Phone: 435-864-1405.

Technical Facilities: 0.01-kw ERP, 48-ft. above ground, 4857-ft. above sea level, lat. 37° 31' 55.7", long. 112° 18' 46.7".

Ownership: Millard County.

Leamington—K56JB-D, Ch. 56, Millard County. Phone: 435-864-1405.

Technical Facilities: 0.01-kw ERP, 48-ft. above ground, 4857-ft. above sea level, lat. 39° 31' 55.7", long. 112° 18' 46.7".

Ownership: Millard County.

Leamington—K57JS-D, Ch. 57, Millard County. Phone: 435-864-1405.

Technical Facilities: 0.01-kw ERP, 48-ft. above ground, 4857-ft. above sea level, lat. 39° 31' 55.7", long. 112° 18' 46.7".

Ownership: Millard County.

Leamington—K58IP-D, Ch. 58, Millard County. Phone: 435-864-1405.

Technical Facilities: 0.01-kw ERP, 48-ft. above ground, 4857-ft. above sea level, lat. 39° 31' 55.7", long. 112° 18' 46.7".

Ownership: Millard County.

Leamington—K59IQ-D, Ch. 59, Millard County. Phone: 435-864-1405.

Technical Facilities: 0.01-kw ERP, 48-ft. above ground, 4857-ft. above sea level, lat. 39° 31' 55.7", long. 112° 18' 46.7".

Ownership: Millard County.

Levan—K18GX, Ch. 18, Town of Levan.

Technical Facilities: 0.025-kw ERP, 16-ft. above ground, 8415-ft. above sea level, lat. 39° 29' 31", long. 111° 49' 40".

Ownership: Town of Levan.

Loa, etc.—K03AU, Ch. 3, Wayne County.

Technical Facilities: 0.144-kw ERP, 8084-ft. above sea level, lat. 38° 23' 42", long. 111° 42' 39".

Ownership: Wayne County.

Loa, etc.—K06BS, Ch. 6, Wayne County.

Technical Facilities: 0.008-kw ERP, 8084-ft. above sea level, lat. 38° 23' 42", long. 111° 42' 39".

Loa, etc.—K07CT, Ch. 7, Wayne County.

Technical Facilities: 0.01-kw ERP, 8074-ft. above sea level, lat. 38° 23' 42", long. 111° 42' 39".

Loa, etc.—K23II-D, Ch. 23, Wayne County. Phone: 435-836-2765.

Technical Facilities: 0.031-kw ERP, 12-ft. above ground, 7857-ft. above sea level, lat. 38° 24' 24.5", long. 111° 41' 51.9".

Began Operation: February 3, 2009.

Ownership: Wayne County.

Loa, etc.—K25JF-D, Ch. 25, Wayne County. Phone: 435-836-2765.

Technical Facilities: 0.031-kw ERP, 12-ft. above ground, 7857-ft. above sea level, lat. 38° 24' 24.5", long. 111° 41' 51.9".

Began Operation: February 3, 2009.

Ownership: Wayne County.

Loa, etc.—K27IX-D, Ch. 27, Wayne County. Phone: 435-836-2765.

Technical Facilities: 0.031-kw ERP, 12-ft. above ground, 7857-ft. above sea level, lat. 38° 24' 24.5", long. 111° 41' 51.9".

Began Operation: February 3, 2009.

Ownership: Wayne County.

Logan—K10OX, Ch. 10, Airwaves Inc. Phone: 801-399-0012.

Technical Facilities: 0.963-kw ERP, 46-ft. above ground, 5643-ft. above sea level, lat. 41° 45' 21", long. 112° 01' 22".

Holds CP for change to 0.085-kw ERP, 45-ft. above ground, 4543-ft. above sea level, lat. 41° 47' 15", long. 111° 50' 00". BPTVL-20080325AFH.

Ownership: Airwaves Inc.

Logan—K18DL-D, Ch. 18, Larry H. Miller Communications Corp. Phone: 801-537-1414.

Technical Facilities: 0.03-kw ERP, 30-ft. above ground, 7139-ft. above sea level, lat. 41° 33' 04", long. 111° 56' 08".

Ownership: Larry H. Miller Communications Corp.

Logan—K41GQ-D, Ch. 41, Cache County. Phone: 435-716-7171.

Technical Facilities: 0.65-kw ERP, 16-ft. above ground, 7155-ft. above sea level, lat. 41° 33' 03.6", long. 111° 56' 10.4".

Ownership: Cache County.

Logan—K43GR-D, Ch. 43, Cache County. Phone: 435-716-7171.

Technical Facilities: 0.65-kw ERP, 16-ft. above ground, 7155-ft. above sea level, lat. 41° 33' 03.6", long. 111° 56' 10.4".

Ownership: Cache County.

Logan—K45GL-D, Ch. 45, Cache County. Phone: 435-716-7171.

Technical Facilities: 0.65-kw ERP, 16-ft. above ground, 7155-ft. above sea level, lat. 41° 33' 03.6", long. 111° 56' 10.4".

Ownership: Cache County.

Logan—K47GY, Ch. 47, Cache County.

Technical Facilities: 2.61-kw ERP, lat. 41° 33' 04", long. 111° 56' 08".

Logan—K47HW-D, Ch. 47, Cache County. Phone: 435-716-7171.

Technical Facilities: 0.65-kw ERP, 16-ft. above ground, 7155-ft. above sea level, lat. 41° 33' 36", long. 111° 56' 10.4".

Ownership: Cache County.

Logan—K49FS-D, Ch. 49, Cache County. Phone: 435-716-7171.

Technical Facilities: 0.65-kw ERP, 16-ft. above ground, 7155-ft. above sea level, lat. 41° 33' 03.6", long. 111° 56' 10.4".

Ownership: Cache County.

Logan—K50IB, Ch. 50, Marcia T. Turner. Phone: 954-732-9539.

Technical Facilities: 15-kw ERP, 151-ft. above ground, 5784-ft. above sea level, lat. 41° 52' 18.7", long. 111° 48' 34.9".

Ownership: Marcia T. Turner.

Logan—K51GA-D, Ch. 51, Cache County. Phone: 435-716-7171.

Technical Facilities: 0.65-kw ERP, 16-ft. above ground, 7155-ft. above sea level, lat. 41° 33' 36", long. 111° 56' 10.4".

Ownership: Cache County.

■**Logan—KCVB-CA**, Ch. 3, Cache Valley Broadcasting LLC. Phone: 435-752-7537. Fax: 435-753-5895.

Studio: 1772 N 600 W, Logan, UT 84321.

Technical Facilities: 0.291-kw ERP, 38-ft. above ground, 4505-ft. above sea level, lat. 41° 45' 54", long. 111° 50' 52".

Ownership: Cache Valley Broadcasting LLC.

Personnel: Jeff Jacobsen, General Manager; Jack Johnson, Station Manager.

Logan—KUTA-LP, Ch. 8, Airwaves Inc. Phone: 801-399-0012.

Technical Facilities: 2.41-kw ERP, 46-ft. above ground, 5643-ft. above sea level, lat. 41° 45' 21", long. 112° 01' 22".

Holds CP for change to 0.3-kw ERP, BDFCDVL-20080324AIX.

Ownership: Airwaves Inc.

Long Valley Junction—K03CX, Ch. 3, Western Kane County Special Service District No. 1. Phone: 435-644-5089.

Technical Facilities: 0.001-kw ERP, lat. 37° 30' 25", long. 112° 30' 37".

Ownership: Western Kane County Special Service District No. 1.

Long Valley Junction—K06FM, Ch. 6, Western Kane County Special Service District No. 1. Phone: 435-644-5089.

Technical Facilities: 0.033-kw ERP, lat. 37° 30' 25", long. 112° 30' 37".

Ownership: Western Kane County Special Service District No. 1.

Long Valley Junction—K46EO-D, Ch. 46, U. of Utah. Phone: 801-585-3601.

Technical Facilities: 0.015-kw ERP, 30-ft. above ground, 7910-ft. above sea level, lat. 37° 30' 25.4", long. 112° 30' 35.6".

Ownership: U. of Utah.

Long Valley Junction—K48EK-D, Ch. 48, Western Kane County Special Service District No. 1. Phone: 435-644-5089.

Technical Facilities: 0.015-kw ERP, 29-ft. above ground, 7909-ft. above sea level, lat. 37° 30' 25.4", long. 112° 30' 35.6".

Ownership: Western Kane County Special Service District No. 1.

Long Valley Junction—K50GD, Ch. 50, U. of Utah. Phone: 801-585-3601.

Technical Facilities: 0.63-kw ERP, 25-ft. above ground, 7905-ft. above sea level, lat. 37° 30' 25", long. 112° 30' 37".

Holds CP for change to channel number 50, 0.03-kw ERP, 30-ft. above ground, 7910-ft. above sea level, lat. 37° 30' 25.4", long. 112° 30' 35.6". BDFCDTT-20090108AHS.

Ownership: U. of Utah.

Manila & Dutch John—K19DV, Ch. 19, U. of Utah.

Technical Facilities: 0.38-kw ERP, 20-ft. above ground, 7218-ft. above sea level, lat. 40° 57' 34", long. 109° 24' 58".

Manila, etc.—K04HN, Ch. 4, Daggett County TV Dept.

Technical Facilities: 0.02-kw ERP, lat. 40° 57' 16", long. 109° 27' 51".

Manila, etc.—K05FJ, Ch. 5, Daggett County TV Dept.

Technical Facilities: 0.01-kw ERP, lat. 40° 57' 16", long. 109° 27' 51".

Manila, etc.—K09LZ, Ch. 9, U. of Utah.

Technical Facilities: 0.02-kw ERP, 7142-ft. above sea level, lat. 40° 57' 16", long. 109° 27' 51".

Manti & Ephraim—K25GS-D, Ch. 25, Sanpete County. Phone: 435-835-2131.

Technical Facilities: 0.14-kw ERP, 18-ft. above ground, 7249-ft. above sea level, lat. 39° 19' 23", long. 111° 46' 23".

Manti & Ephraim—K27HR, Ch. 27, U. of Utah. Phone: 801-581-7777.

Technical Facilities: 0.46-kw ERP, 69-ft. above ground, 8510-ft. above sea level, lat. 39° 19' 23", long. 111° 46' 23".

Ownership: U. of Utah.

Manti & Ephraim—K29EM, Ch. 29, Sanpete County.

Technical Facilities: 0.46-kw ERP, 50-ft. above ground, 8507-ft. above sea level, lat. 39° 19' 23", long. 111° 46' 23".

Manti & Ephraim—K30JI-D, Ch. 30, U. of Utah. Phone: 801-585-3601.

Technical Facilities: 0.006-kw ERP, 40-ft. above ground, 8498-ft. above sea level, lat. 39° 19' 23.5", long. 111° 46' 25.8".

Ownership: U. of Utah.

Manti & Ephraim—K31FN, Ch. 31, Sanpete County.

Technical Facilities: 1.85-kw ERP, lat. 39° 19' 23", long. 111° 46' 23".

Transmitter: Barton Mountain, 7.4-mi. WNW of Manti.

Manti & Ephraim—K32HS-D, Ch. 32, U. of Utah. Phone: 801-585-3601.

Technical Facilities: 0.006-kw ERP, 40-ft. above ground, 8498-ft. above sea level, lat. 39° 19' 23.5", long. 111° 46' 25.8".

Ownership: U. of Utah.

Manti & Ephraim—K33FT, Ch. 33, U. of Utah.

Technical Facilities: 0.74-kw ERP, lat. 39° 12' 06", long. 111° 43' 39".

Manti & Ephraim—K39IW-D, Ch. 39, Sanpete County. Phone: 435-835-2131.

Technical Facilities: 0.006-kw ERP, 40-ft. above ground, 8498-ft. above sea level, lat. 39° 19' 23.5", long. 111° 46' 25.8".

Ownership: Sanpete County.

Manti & Ephraim—K41JW-D, Ch. 41, Sanpete County. Phone: 435-835-2131.

Technical Facilities: 0.006-kw ERP, 40-ft. above ground, 8498-ft. above sea level, lat. 39° 19' 23.5", long. 111° 46' 25.8".

Ownership: Sanpete County.

Manti, etc.—K09FM, Ch. 9, Sanpete County. Phone: 435-835-2131.

Technical Facilities: 0.001-kw ERP, lat. 39° 14' 56", long. 111° 37' 48".

Ownership: Sanpete County.

Manti, etc.—K11FP, Ch. 11, Sanpete County. Phone: 435-835-2131.

Technical Facilities: 0.025-kw ERP, lat. 39° 14' 56", long. 111° 37' 48".

Ownership: Sanpete County.

Manti, etc.—K13FF, Ch. 13, Sanpete County. Phone: 435-835-2131.

Technical Facilities: 0.025-kw ERP, lat. 39° 14' 56", long. 111° 37' 48".

Ownership: Sanpete County.

Manti, etc.—K24HJ-D, Ch. 24, Sanpete County. Phone: 435-835-2131.

Technical Facilities: 0.009-kw ERP, 40-ft. above ground, 8498-ft. above sea level, lat. 39° 19' 23.5", long. 111° 46' 25.8".

Ownership: Sanpete County.

Manti, etc.—K26IH-D, Ch. 26, Sanpete County. Phone: 435-835-2131.

Technical Facilities: 0.009-kw ERP, 40-ft. above ground, 8498-ft. above sea level, lat. 39° 19' 23.5", long. 111° 46' 25.8".

Ownership: Sanpete County.

Manti, etc.—K28NJ-D, Ch. 28, Sanpete County. Phone: 435-835-2131.

Technical Facilities: 0.009-kw ERP, 40-ft. above ground, 8498-ft. above sea level, lat. 39° 19' 23.5", long. 111° 46' 25.8".

Ownership: Sanpete County.

Manti/Ephraim—K43JF-D, Ch. 43, High Plains Broadcasting License Co. LLC. Phone: 580-269-2215.

Technical Facilities: 0.035-kw ERP, 49-ft. above ground, 8556-ft. above sea level, lat. 39° 19' 23.5", long. 111° 46' 25.8".

Ownership: High Plains Broadcasting Inc.

Marysvale—K02BQ, Ch. 2, Piute County.

Technical Facilities: 0.92-kw ERP, lat. 38° 30' 13", long. 112° 12' 41".

Ownership: Piute County.

Marysvale—K04BO, Ch. 4, Piute County.

Technical Facilities: 0.079-kw ERP, lat. 38° 30' 13", long. 112° 12' 41".

Ownership: Piute County.

Marysvale—K05BH, Ch. 5, Piute County.

Technical Facilities: 0.007-kw ERP, lat. 38° 30' 13", long. 112° 12' 41".

Ownership: Piute County.

Marysvale—K34AL, Ch. 34, Piute County.

Technical Facilities: 0.312-kw ERP, 7621-ft. above sea level, lat. 38° 30' 27", long. 112° 11' 50".

Marysvale—K46FX, Ch. 46, U. of Utah. Phone: 801-585-3601.

Technical Facilities: 0.57-kw ERP, 18-ft. above ground, 7620-ft. above sea level, lat. 38° 30' 27", long. 112° 11' 50".

Ownership: U. of Utah.

Marysvale—K47KO-D, Ch. 47, Piute County. Phone: 435-577-2840.

Technical Facilities: 0.01-kw ERP, 15-ft. above ground, 7702-ft. above sea level, lat. 38° 30' 25.5", long. 112° 11' 48.8".

Ownership: Piute County.

Marysvale—K48GS, Ch. 48, U. of Utah. Phone: 801-585-3601.

Technical Facilities: 0.57-kw ERP, 18-ft. above ground, 7618-ft. above sea level, lat. 38° 30' 27", long. 112° 11' 50".

Ownership: U. of Utah.

Marysvale—K49JN-D, Ch. 49, U. of Utah. Phone: 801-585-3601.

Technical Facilities: 0.01-kw ERP, 15-ft. above ground, 7702-ft. above sea level, lat. 38° 30' 25.5", long. 112° 11' 48.8".

Ownership: U. of Utah.

Marysvale—K50JV-D, Ch. 50, Piute County. Phone: 435-577-2840.

Technical Facilities: 0.01-kw ERP, 15-ft. above ground, 7702-ft. above sea level, lat. 38° 30' 25.5", long. 112° 11' 48.8".

Ownership: Piute County.

Marysville—K45JM-D, Ch. 45, Piute County. Phone: 435-577-2840.

Technical Facilities: 0.01-kw ERP, 15-ft. above ground, 7702-ft. above sea level, lat. 38° 30' 25.5", long. 112° 11' 48.8".

Ownership: Piute County.

Marysville—K51JO-D, Ch. 51, U. of Utah. Phone: 801-585-3601.

Technical Facilities: 0.01-kw ERP, 15-ft. above ground, 7702-ft. above sea level, lat. 38° 30' 25.5", long. 112° 11' 48.8".

Ownership: U. of Utah.

Marysville—K52JU-D, Ch. 52, Piute County. Phone: 435-577-2840.

Technical Facilities: 0.01-kw ERP, 15-ft. above ground, 7702-ft. above sea level, lat. 38° 30' 25.5", long. 112° 11' 48.8".

Ownership: Piute County.

Mayfield—K07PE, Ch. 7, Sanpete County. Phone: 435-835-2131.

Technical Facilities: 0.014-kw ERP, lat. 39° 07' 01", long. 111° 43' 40".

Ownership: Sanpete County.

Mayfield—K09JH, Ch. 9, Sanpete County. Phone: 435-835-2131.

Technical Facilities: 0.014-kw ERP, lat. 39° 07' 01", long. 111° 43' 40".

Ownership: Sanpete County.

Mayfield—K11JK, Ch. 11, Sanpete County. Phone: 435-835-2131.

Technical Facilities: 0.014-kw ERP, lat. 39° 07' 01", long. 111° 43' 40".

Ownership: Sanpete County.

Mayfield—K13JP, Ch. 13, Sanpete County. Phone: 435-835-2131.

Technical Facilities: 0.013-kw ERP, lat. 39° 07' 01", long. 111° 43' 40".

Ownership: Sanpete County.

Mayfield—K15CD, Ch. 15, Sanpete County. Phone: 435-835-2131.

Technical Facilities: 0.033-kw ERP, lat. 39° 07' 01", long. 111° 43' 40".

Ownership: Sanpete County.

Mexican Hat—K02PT, Ch. 2, San Juan County. Phone: 435-678-3322.

Technical Facilities: 0.0045-kw ERP, 25-ft. above ground, 4224-ft. above sea level, lat. 37° 09' 00", long. 109° 51' 34".

Ownership: San Juan County.

Mexican Hat—K04PG, Ch. 4, San Juan County. Phone: 435-678-3322.

Technical Facilities: 0.0045-kw ERP, 25-ft. above ground, 4224-ft. above sea level, lat. 37° 09' 00", long. 109° 51' 34".

Ownership: San Juan County.

Mexican Hat—K06NK, Ch. 6, San Juan County. Phone: 435-678-3322.

Technical Facilities: 0.0045-kw ERP, 25-ft. above ground, 4224-ft. above sea level, lat. 37° 09' 00", long. 109° 51' 34".

Ownership: San Juan County.

Mexican Hat—K13XO, Ch. 13, San Juan County. Phone: 435-587-3223.

Technical Facilities: 0.0045-kw ERP, 25-ft. above ground, 4224-ft. above sea level, lat. 37° 09' 00", long. 109° 51' 34".

Ownership: San Juan County.

Milford, etc.—K15FQ-D, Ch. 15, Community Television of Utah License LLC. Phone: 859-448-2700.

Technical Facilities: 0.25-kw ERP, 49-ft. above ground, 9111-ft. above sea level, lat. 38° 31' 13.8", long. 113° 17' 11.5".

Ownership: Local TV Holdings LLC.

Milford, etc.—K16BO-D, Ch. 16, U. of Utah. Phone: 801-585-3601.

Technical Facilities: 0.115-kw ERP, 49-ft. above ground, 9724-ft. above sea level, lat. 38° 31' 13.7", long. 113° 17' 12.1".

Ownership: U. of Utah.

Milford, etc.—K20GH-D, Ch. 20, U. of Utah. Phone: 801-585-3601.

Technical Facilities: 0.956-kw ERP, 48-ft. above ground, 9718-ft. above sea level, lat. 38° 31' 05", long. 113° 17' 03".

Holds CP for change to 0.115-kw ERP, 49-ft. above ground, 9724-ft. above sea level, lat. 38° 31' 13.7", long. 113° 17' 12.1". BDFCDTT-20060719AAJ.

Ownership: U. of Utah.

Milford, etc.—K26EA, Ch. 26, Iron County. Phone: 435-477-8341.

Technical Facilities: 1.15-kw ERP, 46-ft. above ground, 9705-ft. above sea level, lat. 38° 31' 05", long. 113° 17' 03".

Holds CP for change to 0.3-kw ERP, 49-ft. above ground, 9724-ft. above sea level, lat. 38° 31' 13.7", long. 113° 17' 12.1". BMPDTT-20080131AQP.

Minersville—K05AT, Ch. 5, Minersville TV Committee.

Technical Facilities: 0.007-kw ERP, lat. 38° 21' 10", long. 113° 06' 40".

Ownership: Minersville Town.

Minersville—K17HX-D, Ch. 17, Minersville Town. Phone: 435-386-2242.

Technical Facilities: 0.13-kw ERP, 50-ft. above ground, 9725-ft. above sea level, lat. 38° 31' 13.7", long. 113° 17' 12.1".

Ownership: Minersville Town.

Modena—K27GB, Ch. 27, Iron County.

Technical Facilities: 0.195-kw ERP, 51-ft. above ground, 5823-ft. above sea level, lat. 37° 42' 14", long. 113° 44' 29".

Modena—K29FA, Ch. 29, Iron County. Phone: 435-477-8341.

Technical Facilities: 0.246-kw ERP, 59-ft. above ground, 5833-ft. above sea level, lat. 37° 42' 14", long. 113° 44' 29".

Modena, Beryl, etc.—K19DO, Ch. 19, Iron County.

Technical Facilities: 0.246-kw ERP, 36-ft. above ground, 5810-ft. above sea level, lat. 37° 42' 14", long. 113° 44' 29".

Modena, Beryl, etc.—K23DV, Ch. 23, Mineral Television District No. 1.

Technical Facilities: 0.246-kw ERP, 36-ft. above ground, 5810-ft. above sea level, lat. 37° 42' 14", long. 113° 44' 29".

Modena, etc.—K17FF, Ch. 17, Iron County. Phone: 435-477-8341.

Technical Facilities: 0.195-kw ERP, 51-ft. above ground, 5825-ft. above sea level, lat. 37° 42' 14", long. 113° 44' 29".

Transmitter: 4.5-mi. WSW of Beryl.

Modena, etc.—K21EI, Ch. 21, Iron County.

Technical Facilities: 0.246-kw ERP, 36-ft. above ground, 5810-ft. above sea level, lat. 37° 42' 14", long. 113° 44' 29".

Transmitter: 4.5-mi. WSW of Beryl.

Modena, etc.—K25GY, Ch. 25, Iron County.

Technical Facilities: 0.02-kw ERP, 51-ft. above ground, 5825-ft. above sea level, lat. 37° 43' 14", long. 113° 45' 29".

Montezuma Creek & Aneth—K02OI, Ch. 2, San Juan County.

Technical Facilities: 0.017-kw ERP, 20-ft. above ground, 4692-ft. above sea level, lat. 37° 16' 07", long. 109° 17' 28".

Ownership: San Juan County.

Montezuma Creek & Aneth—K05JN, Ch. 5, San Juan County.

Technical Facilities: 0.017-kw ERP, 20-ft. above ground, 4692-ft. above sea level, lat. 37° 16' 07", long. 109° 17' 28".

Ownership: San Juan County.

Montezuma Creek & Aneth—K11VR, Ch. 11, San Juan County. Phone: 435-587-3223.

Technical Facilities: 0.0455-kw ERP, 20-ft. above ground, 4689-ft. above sea level, lat. 37° 15' 36.5", long. 109° 17' 22.7".

Ownership: San Juan County.

Montezuma Creek & Aneth—K13YC, Ch. 13, San Juan County. Phone: 435-678-3322.

Technical Facilities: 0.0455-kw ERP, 20-ft. above ground, 4689-ft. above sea level, lat. 37° 15' 37", long. 109° 17' 23".

Ownership: San Juan County.

Montezuma Creek/Aneth—K10PB, Ch. 10, San Juan County. Phone: 435-678-3322.

Technical Facilities: 0.0455-kw ERP, 20-ft. above ground, 4689-ft. above sea level, lat. 37° 15' 36.5", long. 109° 17' 22.7".

Ownership: San Juan County.

Monticello, etc.—K40AF, Ch. 40, U. of Utah. Phone: 801-585-3601.

Technical Facilities: 1.28-kw ERP, lat. 37° 50' 22", long. 109° 27' 40".

Holds CP for change to 0.35-kw ERP, 59-ft. above ground, 11417-ft. above sea level, lat. 37° 50' 22.7", long. 109° 27' 42.2". BDFCDTT-20081217AAY.

Morgan—K29EP, Ch. 29, Morgan County.

Technical Facilities: 0.63-kw ERP, 15-ft. above ground, 7415-ft. above sea level, lat. 41° 04' 11", long. 111° 39' 19".

Ownership: Morgan County.

Morgan, etc.—K08GA, Ch. 8, Morgan County.

Technical Facilities: 0.06-kw ERP, lat. 41° 04' 11", long. 111° 39' 19".

Ownership: Morgan County.

Morgan, etc.—K10FW, Ch. 10, Morgan County.

Technical Facilities: 0.06-kw ERP, lat. 41° 04' 11", long. 111° 39' 19".

Ownership: Morgan County.

Morgan, etc.—K12GI, Ch. 12, Morgan County.

Technical Facilities: 0.06-kw ERP, lat. 41° 04' 11", long. 111° 39' 19".

Ownership: Morgan County.

Morgan, etc.—K27GA, Ch. 27, U. of Utah. Phone: 801-585-3601.

Technical Facilities: 0.63-kw ERP, 15-ft. above ground, 7414-ft. above sea level, lat. 41° 04' 11", long. 111° 39' 19".

Ownership: U. of Utah.

Mount Pleasant—K08CC, Ch. 8, Sanpete County. Phone: 435-835-2131.

Technical Facilities: 0.123-kw ERP, 7251-ft. above sea level, lat. 39° 32' 19", long. 111° 19' 55".

Ownership: Sanpete County.

Mount Pleasant—K10CH, Ch. 10, Sanpete County. Phone: 435-835-2131.

Technical Facilities: 0.138-kw ERP, 7251-ft. above sea level, lat. 39° 32' 19", long. 111° 19' 55".

Ownership: Sanpete County.

Mount Pleasant—K12CC, Ch. 12, Sanpete County. Phone: 435-835-2131.

Technical Facilities: 0.119-kw ERP, 7251-ft. above sea level, lat. 39° 32' 19", long. 111° 19' 55".

Ownership: Sanpete County.

Mount Pleasant—K15HG-D, Ch. 15, Sanpete County. Phone: 435-835-2131.

Technical Facilities: 0.01-kw ERP, 18-ft. above ground, 7249-ft. above sea level, lat. 39° 32' 21.7", long. 111° 23' 17.2".

Ownership: Sanpete County.

Mount Pleasant—K19GN-D, Ch. 19, Sanpete County. Phone: 435-835-2131.

Technical Facilities: 0.01-kw ERP, 18-ft. above ground, 7249-ft. above sea level, lat. 39° 32' 21.7", long. 111° 23' 17.2".

Ownership: Sanpete County.

Mount Pleasant—K21IC-D, Ch. 21, Sanpete County. Phone: 435-835-2131.

Technical Facilities: 0.01-kw ERP, 18-ft. above ground, 7249-ft. above sea level, lat. 39° 32' 21.7", long. 111° 23' 17.2".

Ownership: Sanpete County.

Mount Pleasant—K22FW, Ch. 22, Sanpete County.

Technical Facilities: 1.8-kw ERP, 27-ft. above ground, 7038-ft. above sea level, lat. 39° 32' 22", long. 111° 23' 17".

Mount Pleasant—K23JM-D, Ch. 23, Sanpete County. Phone: 435-835-2131.

Technical Facilities: 0.01-kw ERP, 18-ft. above ground, 7249-ft. above sea level, lat. 39° 32' 21.7", long. 111° 23' 17.2".

Ownership: Sanpete County.

Mount Pleasant—K46HO-D, Ch. 46, Sanpete County. Phone: 435-835-2131.

Technical Facilities: 0.055-kw ERP, 38-ft. above ground, 7269-ft. above sea level, lat. 39° 32' 21.7", long. 111° 23' 17.2".

Ownership: Sanpete County.

Mount Pleasant—K48IL-D, Ch. 48, Sanpete County. Phone: 435-835-2131.

Technical Facilities: 0.055-kw ERP, 38-ft. above ground, 7269-ft. above sea level, lat. 39° 32' 21.7", long. 111° 23' 17.2".

Ownership: Sanpete County.

Mount Pleasant—K50HL-D, Ch. 50, Sanpete County. Phone: 435-835-2131.

Technical Facilities: 0.055-kw ERP, 38-ft. above ground, 7269-ft. above sea level, lat. 39° 32' 21.7", long. 111° 23' 17.2".

Ownership: Sanpete County.

Mountain View—K25EE, Ch. 25, Daggett County TV Dept.

Technical Facilities: 0.398-kw ERP, 26-ft. above ground, 8625-ft. above sea level, lat. 41° 06' 19", long. 110° 12' 13".

Myton—K14LW, Ch. 14, High Plains Broadcasting License Co. LLC. Phone: 580-269-2215.

Technical Facilities: 0.32-kw ERP, 43-ft. above ground, 10059-ft. above sea level, lat. 40° 21' 41", long. 110° 47' 21".

Ownership: High Plains Broadcasting Inc.

Myton—K19EY, Ch. 19, Duchesne County. Phone: 435-738-1100.

Technical Facilities: 7-kw ERP, 40-ft. above ground, 10056-ft. above sea level, lat. 40° 21' 45", long. 110° 47' 31".

Ownership: Duchesne County.

Myton—K21FT, Ch. 21, Duchesne County. Phone: 435-738-1100.

Technical Facilities: 7-kw ERP, 40-ft. above ground, 10056-ft. above sea level, lat. 40° 21' 45", long. 110° 47' 31".

Ownership: Duchesne County.

Myton—K27GN, Ch. 27, Duchesne County. Phone: 435-738-1100.

Technical Facilities: 7-kw ERP, 40-ft. above ground, 10056-ft. above sea level, lat. 40° 21' 45", long. 110° 47' 31".

Ownership: Duchesne County.

Myton—K41GT, Ch. 41, Duchesne County. Phone: 435-738-1100.

Technical Facilities: 7-kw ERP, 40-ft. above ground, 10056-ft. above sea level, lat. 40° 21' 45", long. 110° 47' 31".

Ownership: Duchesne County.

Myton, etc.—K25HH, Ch. 25, Duchesne County. Phone: 435-738-1100.

Technical Facilities: 7-kw ERP, 40-ft. above ground, 10057-ft. above sea level, lat. 40° 21' 45", long. 110° 47' 31".

Ownership: Duchesne County.

Myton, etc.—K43AE, Ch. 43, SLC TV Licensee Corp. Phone: 212-891-2100.

Technical Facilities: 100-w TPO, 3.916-kw ERP, 42-ft. above ground, 10057-ft. above sea level, lat. 40° 21' 45", long. 110° 47' 31".

Transmitter: 5-mi. W of Tabiona on Tabby Mountain translator site.

Ownership: Four Points Media Group Holding LLC.

Navajo Mountain—K11TF, Ch. 11, San Juan County.

Technical Facilities: 0.028-kw ERP, 20-ft. above ground, 6099-ft. above sea level, lat. 37° 00' 52", long. 110° 46' 20".

Navajo Mountain—K13WH, Ch. 13, San Juan County.

Technical Facilities: 0.028-kw ERP, 20-ft. above ground, 6099-ft. above sea level, lat. 37° 00' 52", long. 110° 46' 20".

Navajo Mountain School—K09XX, Ch. 9, San Juan County. Phone: 435-587-3223.

Technical Facilities: 0.0455-kw ERP, 20-ft. above ground, 6099-ft. above sea level, lat. 37° 01' 16.1", long. 110° 45' 58.2".

Ownership: San Juan County.

Navajo Mountain School, etc.—K02PX, Ch. 2, San Juan County. Phone: 435-587-3223.

Technical Facilities: 0.0455-kw ERP, 20-ft. above ground, 6099-ft. above sea level, lat. 37° 01' 16", long. 110° 45' 58".

Ownership: San Juan County.

Navajo Mountain School, etc.—K04PP, Ch. 4, San Juan County. Phone: 435-678-3322.

Technical Facilities: 0.0455-kw ERP, 20-ft. above ground, 6099-ft. above sea level, lat. 37° 01' 16", long. 110° 45' 58".

Ownership: San Juan County.

Navajo Mountain School, etc.—K06NR, Ch. 6, San Juan County. Phone: 435-587-3223.

Technical Facilities: 0.045-kw ERP, 20-ft. above ground, 6099-ft. above sea level, lat. 37° 01' 16.1", long. 110° 45' 58".

Ownership: San Juan County.

Navajo Mountain School, etc.—K07XU, Ch. 7, San Juan County. Phone: 435-678-3322.

Technical Facilities: 0.0455-kw ERP, 20-ft. above ground, 6099-ft. above sea level, lat. 37° 01' 16.1", long. 110° 45' 58.2".

Ownership: San Juan County.

New Castle, etc.—K49IF, Ch. 49, Iron County. Phone: 435-477-3375.

Technical Facilities: 0.246-kw ERP, 59-ft. above ground, 5833-ft. above sea level, lat. 37° 41' 14", long. 113° 44' 29".

Ownership: Iron County.

New Castle, etc.—K51GS, Ch. 51, Iron County.

Technical Facilities: 0.246-kw ERP, 59-ft. above ground, 5833-ft. above sea level, lat. 37° 42' 14", long. 113° 44' 29".

New Harmony, etc.—K49GA, Ch. 49, Iron County School District.

Technical Facilities: 0.068-kw ERP, 16-ft. above ground, 6165-ft. above sea level, lat. 37° 29' 13", long. 113° 12' 18".

New Harmony, etc.—K51GI, Ch. 51, Iron County. Phone: 435-477-8341.

Technical Facilities: 0.068-kw ERP, 16-ft. above ground, 6165-ft. above sea level, lat. 37° 29' 13", long. 113° 12' 18".

Ogden—K41JJ, Ch. 41, Trinity Broadcasting Network Inc. Phone: 714-832-2950. Fax: 714-730-0661.

Technical Facilities: 23.3-kw ERP, 148-ft. above ground, 4688-ft. above sea level, lat. 41° 09' 49", long. 112° 01' 28".

Transmitter: 5500 South St. & 1900 West St.

Ownership: Trinity Broadcasting Network Inc.

Ogden—KQTI-LD, Ch. 68, Airwaves Inc. Phone: 801-399-0012.

Technical Facilities: 0.236-w TPO, 0.05-kw ERP, 66-ft. above ground, 6861-ft. above sea level, lat. 41° 47' 03", long. 112° 13' 55".

Began Operation: May 28, 2009.

Ownership: Airwaves Inc.

■**Ogden**—KSVN-CA, Ch. 49, Azteca Broadcasting Corp. Phone: 801-292-1799. Fax: 801-731-4445.

Technical Facilities: 15.38-kw ERP, 197-ft. above ground, 4737-ft. above sea level, lat. 41° 09' 49", long. 112° 01' 28".

Transmitter: 5508 South 1900 West.

Ownership: Azteca Broadcasting Corp.

Personnel: Alex Collantes, General Manager & Sales Manager; Dennis Silver, Chief Engineer.

■**Ogden**—KULX-CA, Ch. 51, Airwaves Inc. Phone: 801-399-0012.

Technical Facilities: 12.2-kw ERP, 77-ft. above ground, 4652-ft. above sea level, lat. 41° 09' 57", long. 112° 00' 52".

Transmitter: Reservoir area S of Ritter Dr., Riverdale.

Ogden—KULX-LD, Ch. 10, Airwaves Inc. Phone: 801-399-0012.

Technical Facilities: 0.24-kw ERP, 72-ft. above ground, 9111-ft. above sea level, lat. 40° 39' 34", long. 112° 12' 05".

Began Operation: February 26, 2009.

Ownership: Airwaves Inc.

Oljeto—K02PV, Ch. 2, San Juan County. Phone: 435-587-3223.

Technical Facilities: 0.0045-kw ERP, 15-ft. above ground, 5255-ft. above sea level, lat. 37° 02' 28", long. 110° 19' 48".

Ownership: San Juan County.

Oljeto—K04OZ, Ch. 4, San Juan County. Phone: 435-587-3223.

Technical Facilities: 0.0045-kw ERP, 15-ft. above ground, 5255-ft. above sea level, lat. 37° 02' 28", long. 110° 19' 48".

Ownership: San Juan County.

Oljeto—K05LF, Ch. 5, San Juan County. Phone: 435-587-3223.

Technical Facilities: 0.0045-kw ERP, 15-ft. above ground, 5255-ft. above sea level, lat. 37° 02' 28", long. 110° 19' 48".

Ownership: San Juan County.

Oljeto—K06NM, Ch. 6, San Juan County. Phone: 435-678-3322.

Technical Facilities: 0.0045-kw ERP, 15-ft. above ground, 5255-ft. above sea level, lat. 37° 02' 28", long. 110° 19' 48".

Ownership: San Juan County.

Oljeto—K07XO, Ch. 7, San Juan County. Phone: 435-678-3322.

Technical Facilities: 0.0045-kw ERP, 15-ft. above ground, 5255-ft. above sea level, lat. 37° 02' 28", long. 110° 19' 48".

Ownership: San Juan County.

Oljeto—K11US, Ch. 11, San Juan County. Phone: 435-587-3223.

Technical Facilities: 0.0045-kw ERP, 15-ft. above ground, 5255-ft. above sea level, lat. 37° 02' 28", long. 110° 19' 48".

Ownership: San Juan County.

Oljeto—K13XP, Ch. 13, San Juan County. Phone: 435-587-3223.

Technical Facilities: 0.0045-kw ERP, 15-ft. above ground, 5255-ft. above sea level, lat. 37° 02' 28", long. 110° 19' 48".

Ownership: San Juan County.

Orangeville—K15GQ, Ch. 15, U. of Utah.

Technical Facilities: 4-kw ERP, 33-ft. above ground, 8733-ft. above sea level, lat. 39° 12' 36", long. 111° 08' 30".

Ownership: U. of Utah.

Orangeville—K16EW, Ch. 16, Emery County. Phone: 435-381-5678.

Technical Facilities: 4-kw ERP, 36-ft. above ground, 8737-ft. above sea level, lat. 39° 12' 36", long. 111° 08' 30".

Ownership: Emery County.

Orangeville—K18FZ, Ch. 18, Emery County. Phone: 435-381-5678.

Technical Facilities: 4-kw ERP, 36-ft. above ground, 8737-ft. above sea level, lat. 39° 12' 36", long. 111° 08' 30".

Ownership: Emery County.

Orangeville—K20GP, Ch. 20, Emery County. Phone: 435-381-5678.

Technical Facilities: 3.5-kw ERP, 36-ft. above ground, 8737-ft. above sea level, lat. 39° 12' 36", long. 111° 08' 30".

Ownership: Emery County.

Orangeville—K24FI, Ch. 24, Emery County. Phone: 435-381-5678.

Technical Facilities: 4-kw ERP, 36-ft. above ground, 8737-ft. above sea level, lat. 39° 12' 36", long. 111° 08' 30".

Ownership: Emery County.

Orangeville—K26EM, Ch. 26, Emery County. Phone: 435-381-5678.

Technical Facilities: 0.342-kw ERP, lat. 39° 12' 36", long. 111° 08' 30".

Ownership: Emery County.

Orangeville—K28GZ, Ch. 28, Emery County. Phone: 435-381-5678.

Technical Facilities: 4-kw ERP, 36-ft. above ground, 8737-ft. above sea level, lat. 39° 12' 36", long. 111° 08' 30".

Ownership: Emery County.

Orangeville—K32FR, Ch. 32, Emery County. Phone: 435-381-5678.

Technical Facilities: 4-kw ERP, 36-ft. above ground, 8737-ft. above sea level, lat. 39° 12' 36", long. 111° 08' 30".

Ownership: Emery County.

Orangeville—K36IF-D, Ch. 36, Emery County. Phone: 435-381-5678.

Technical Facilities: 0.012-kw ERP, 38-ft. above ground, 8774-ft. above sea level, lat. 39° 12' 36", long. 111° 08' 30".

Ownership: Emery County.

Orangeville—K38KP-D, Ch. 38, Emery County. Phone: 435-381-5678.

Technical Facilities: 0.012-kw ERP, 38-ft. above ground, 8774-ft. above sea level, lat. 39° 12' 36", long. 111° 08' 30".

Ownership: Emery County.

Orangeville—K40KD-D, Ch. 40, Emery County. Phone: 435-381-5678.

Technical Facilities: 0.012-kw ERP, 38-ft. above ground, 8774-ft. above sea level, lat. 39° 12' 36", long. 111° 08' 30".

Ownership: Emery County.

Orangeville—K46JK-D, Ch. 46, U. of Utah. Phone: 801-585-3601.

Technical Facilities: 0.006-kw ERP, 38-ft. above ground, 8774-ft. above sea level, lat. 39° 12' 36", long. 111° 08' 30".

Ownership: U. of Utah.

Orangeville—K47KK-D, Ch. 47, Emery County. Phone: 435-381-5678.

Technical Facilities: 0.012-kw ERP, 38-ft. above ground, 8774-ft. above sea level, lat. 39° 12' 36", long. 111° 08' 30".

Ownership: Emery County.

Orangeville—K48KK-D, Ch. 48, Emery County. Phone: 435-381-5678.

Technical Facilities: 0.006-kw ERP, 28-ft. above ground, 8765-ft. above sea level, lat. 39° 12' 36", long. 111° 08' 30".

Ownership: Emery County.

Orangeville—K49JJ-D, Ch. 49, Emery County. Phone: 435-381-5678.

Technical Facilities: 0.012-kw ERP, 38-ft. above ground, 8774-ft. above sea level, lat. 39° 12' 36", long. 111° 08' 30".

Ownership: Emery County.

Orangeville—K50JS-D, Ch. 50, Emery County. Phone: 435-381-5678.

Technical Facilities: 0.012-kw ERP, 38-ft. above ground, 8774-ft. above sea level, lat. 39° 12' 36", long. 111° 08' 30".

Ownership: Emery County.

Orangeville, etc.—K22FX, Ch. 22, U. of Utah.

Technical Facilities: 4-kw ERP, 36-ft. above ground, 8737-ft. above sea level, lat. 39° 12' 36", long. 111° 08' 30".

Orangeville, etc.—K45JN-D, Ch. 45, U. of Utah. Phone: 801-585-3601.

Technical Facilities: 0.012-kw ERP, 38-ft. above ground, 8774-ft. above sea level, lat. 39° 12' 36", long. 111° 08' 30".

Ownership: U. of Utah.

Orderville—K02EN, Ch. 2, Western Kane County Special Service District No. 1. Phone: 435-644-5089.

Technical Facilities: 0.003-kw ERP, lat. 37° 16' 35", long. 112° 37' 35".

Ownership: Western Kane County Special Service District No. 1.

Orderville—K04EK, Ch. 4, Western Kane County Special Service District No. 1. Phone: 435-644-5089.

Technical Facilities: 0.003-kw ERP, lat. 37° 16' 35", long. 112° 37' 35".

Ownership: Western Kane County Special Service District No. 1.

Orderville—K05DU, Ch. 5, Western Kane County Special Service District No. 1. Phone: 435-644-5089.

Technical Facilities: 0.003-kw ERP, lat. 37° 16' 35", long. 112° 37' 35".

Ownership: Western Kane County Special Service District No. 1.

Orderville—K16BT, Ch. 16, Western Kane County Special Service District No. 1. Phone: 435-644-5089.

Technical Facilities: 0.035-kw ERP, lat. 37° 16' 35", long. 112° 37' 35".

Ownership: Western Kane County Special Service District No. 1.

Orderville—K18ET, Ch. 18, Western Kane County Service District No. 1.

Technical Facilities: 0.068-kw ERP, lat. 37° 16' 35", long. 112° 37' 35".

Transmitter: 1-mi. E of Orderville.

Orderville—K30CP, Ch. 30, Western Kane County Special Service District No. 1. Phone: 435-644-5089.

Technical Facilities: 0.036-kw ERP, 16-ft. above ground, 7910-ft. above sea level, lat. 37° 22' 26", long. 112° 35' 07".

Holds CP for change to 0.038-kw ERP, 42-ft. above ground, 7211-ft. above sea level, BDFCDTT-20090106AAB.

Began Operation: February 27, 1989.

Ownership: Western Kane County Special Service District No. 1.

Orderville—K44FU, Ch. 44, Western Kane County Special Service District No. 1. Phone: 435-644-5089.

Technical Facilities: 0.364-kw ERP, 25-ft. above ground, 7905-ft. above sea level, lat. 37° 30' 25", long. 112° 30' 37".

Holds CP for change to 0.015-kw ERP, 30-ft. above ground, 7910-ft. above sea level, lat. 37° 30' 25.4", long. 112° 30' 35.6". BDFCDTT-20090102ACH.

Began Operation: February 27, 1989.

Ownership: Western Kane County Special Service District No. 1.

Orderville, etc.—K07OY, Ch. 7, Western Kane County Special Service District No. 1. Phone: 435-644-5089.

Technical Facilities: 0.009-kw ERP, 6004-ft. above sea level, lat. 37° 16' 35", long. 112° 37' 35".

Ownership: Western Kane County Special Service District No. 1.

Ouray—K44EL, Ch. 44, Larry H. Miller Communications Corp. Phone: 801-537-1414.

Technical Facilities: 3.37-kw ERP, lat. 39° 38' 40", long. 110° 20' 51".

Transmitter: Bruin Point, 7.2-mi. NNE of Sunnyside.

Began Operation: September 5, 1995.

Ownership: Larry H. Miller Communications Corp.

Panguitch—K02BN, Ch. 2, Garfield County. Phone: 435-676-8826.

Technical Facilities: 0.85-kw ERP, lat. 37° 49' 19", long. 112° 27' 28".

Ownership: Garfield County.

Panguitch—K04AU, Ch. 4, Garfield County. Phone: 435-676-8826.

Technical Facilities: 0.002-kw ERP, lat. 37° 49' 19", long. 112° 27' 28".

Ownership: Garfield County.

Panguitch—K05BB, Ch. 5, Garfield County. Phone: 435-676-8826.

Technical Facilities: 0.002-kw ERP, lat. 37° 49' 19", long. 112° 27' 28".

Ownership: Garfield County.

Panguitch—K07JW, Ch. 7, U. of Utah.

Technical Facilities: 0.016-kw ERP, lat. 37° 49' 19", long. 112° 27' 28".

Panguitch—K12OI, Ch. 12, Garfield County. Phone: 435-676-8826.

Technical Facilities: 0.071-kw ERP, 16-ft. above ground, 6867-ft. above sea level, lat. 37° 49' 19", long. 112° 27' 28".

Ownership: Garfield County.

Panguitch—K34FN, Ch. 34, U. of Utah. Phone: 801-585-3601.

Technical Facilities: 0.065-kw ERP, 18-ft. above ground, 6867-ft. above sea level, lat. 37° 49' 19", long. 112° 27' 28".

Panguitch—K38KF-D, Ch. 38, Garfield County. Phone: 435-676-8826.

Technical Facilities: 0.006-kw ERP, 15-ft. above ground, 7030-ft. above sea level, lat. 37° 49' 15.8", long. 112° 27' 27.7".

Ownership: Garfield County.

Panguitch—K39JG-D, Ch. 39, Garfield County. Phone: 435-676-8826.

Technical Facilities: 0.006-kw ERP, 15-ft. above ground, 7029-ft. above sea level, lat. 37° 49' 15.8", long. 112° 27' 27.7".

Ownership: Garfield County.

Panguitch—K40JL-D, Ch. 40, Garfield County. Phone: 435-676-8826.

Technical Facilities: 0.006-kw ERP, 15-ft. above ground, 7029-ft. above sea level, lat. 37° 49' 15.8", long. 112° 27' 27.7".

Ownership: Garfield County.

Panguitch—K41KA-D, Ch. 41, U. of Utah. Phone: 801-585-3601.

Technical Facilities: 0.006-kw ERP, 15-ft. above ground, 7030-ft. above sea level, lat. 37° 49' 15.8", long. 112° 27' 27.7".

Ownership: U. of Utah.

Panguitch—K44IU-D, Ch. 44, Garfield County. Phone: 435-676-8826.

Technical Facilities: 0.006-kw ERP, 15-ft. above ground, 7029-ft. above sea level, lat. 37° 49' 15.8", long. 112° 27' 27.7".

Ownership: Garfield County.

Panguitch, etc.—K10LV, Ch. 10, Garfield County. Phone: 435-676-8826.

Technical Facilities: 0.001-kw ERP, 6863-ft. above sea level, lat. 37° 49' 19", long. 112° 27' 28".

Ownership: Garfield County.

Panguitch, etc.—K46JI-D, Ch. 46, Garfield County. Phone: 435-676-8826.

Technical Facilities: 0.006-kw ERP, 15-ft. above ground, 7030-ft. above sea level, lat. 37° 49' 15.8", long. 112° 27' 27.7".

Ownership: Garfield County.

Park City—K25DL, Ch. 25, U. of Utah. Phone: 801-585-3601.

Technical Facilities: 0.348-kw ERP, 46-ft. above ground, 7464-ft. above sea level, lat. 40° 40' 59", long. 111° 31' 22".

Holds CP for change to 0.077-kw ERP, 55-ft. above ground, 7519-ft. above sea level, BDFCDTT-20090323AAA.

Began Operation: April 3, 1991.

Ownership: U. of Utah.

Park City—K27GD-D, Ch. 27, Summit County. Phone: 435-336-3220.

Technical Facilities: 0.077-kw ERP, 55-ft. above ground, 7473-ft. above sea level, lat. 40° 40' 59", long. 111° 31' 22".

Began Operation: August 15, 1983.

Ownership: Summit County.

Park City—K29II-D, Ch. 29, Summit County. Phone: 435-336-3220.

Technical Facilities: 0.077-kw ERP, 55-ft. above ground, 7473-ft. above sea level, lat. 40° 40' 59", long. 11° 31' 22".

Began Operation: April 2, 2008.

Ownership: Summit County.

Park City—K31FQ-D, Ch. 31, Summit County. Phone: 435-336-3220.

Technical Facilities: 0.077-kw ERP, 55-ft. above ground, 7473-ft. above sea level, lat. 40° 40' 59", long. 111° 31' 22".

Began Operation: August 15, 1983.

Ownership: Summit County.

Park City—K33FY-D, Ch. 33, Summit County. Phone: 435-336-3220.

Technical Facilities: 0.077-kw ERP, 55-ft. above ground, 7473-ft. above sea level, lat. 40° 40' 59", long. 111° 31' 22".

Began Operation: August 15, 1983.

Ownership: Summit County.

Park City—K35OP, Ch. 35, Community Television of Utah License LLC. Phone: 859-448-2700.

Technical Facilities: 0.639-kw ERP, 39-ft. above ground, 7457-ft. above sea level, lat. 40° 40' 59", long. 111° 31' 22".

Holds CP for change to 0.08-kw ERP, BDFCDTT-20090417AAW.

Ownership: Local TV Holdings LLC.

Park City—K39HP-D, Ch. 39, Summit County. Phone: 435-336-3220.

Technical Facilities: 0.077-kw ERP, 55-ft. above ground, 7473-ft. above sea level, lat. 40° 40' 59", long. 111° 31' 22".

Began Operation: February 14, 2005.

Ownership: Summit County.

Park City—K45AX, Ch. 45, Park City Media Group LLC.

Studio: 614 Main St., Park City, UT 84060.

Technical Facilities: 0.52-kw ERP, 50-ft. above ground, 7458-ft. above sea level, lat. 40° 40' 59", long. 111° 31' 22".

Transmitter: Quarry Mountain, Park City, Summit County.

Ownership: Park City Television.

Personnel: William H. Coleman, Owner; Mary Bailey, Station Manager; Fred Helsop, Engineer; Heide Alsop, Marketing Director.

Park City—K56IQ, Ch. 56, Craig & Marilyn Caples and William Mitchell. Phone: 702-547-1010.

Technical Facilities: 0.71-kw ERP, 69-ft. above ground, 9350-ft. above sea level, lat. 40° 51' 18", long. 111° 28' 44".

Ownership: Craig & Marilyn Caples; William Mitchell.

Park City—K57JB, Ch. 57, Airwaves Inc. Phone: 801-393-0012.

Technical Facilities: 0.732-kw ERP, 56-ft. above ground, 9350-ft. above sea level, lat. 40° 51' 15", long. 111° 28' 51".

Ownership: Airwaves Inc.

Park City—KBTU-LP, Ch. 23, Bustos Media of Utah License LLC. Phone: 916-368-6300.

Technical Facilities: 95-kw ERP, 52-ft. above ground, 8891-ft. above sea level, lat. 40° 39' 09", long. 112° 12' 05".

Ownership: Bustos Media of Utah License LLC.

Park City, etc.—K15FL-D, Ch. 15, Summit County. Phone: 435-336-3220.

Technical Facilities: 0.77-kw ERP, 55-ft. above ground, 7473-ft. above sea level, lat. 40° 40' 59", long. 111° 31' 22".

Began Operation: August 15, 1983.

Ownership: Summit County.

Parowan—K32AG, Ch. 32, Iron County. Phone: 435-477-8341.

Technical Facilities: 1.3-kw ERP, lat. 37° 50' 32", long. 112° 58' 27".

Holds CP for change to 0.25-kw ERP, 59-ft. above ground, 6778-ft. above sea level, lat. 37° 50' 30.2", long. 112° 58' 26.6". BDFCDTT-20090105AAH.

Began Operation: December 13, 1982.

Ownership: Iron County.

Parowan—K34AG, Ch. 34, Iron County. Phone: 435-477-8341.

Technical Facilities: 1.3-kw ERP, lat. 37° 50' 32", long. 112° 58' 27".

Holds CP for change to 0.25-kw ERP, 59-ft. above ground, 6778-ft. above sea level, lat. 37° 50' 30.2", long. 112° 58' 26.6". BDFCDTT-20090105AAI.

Began Operation: December 13, 1982.

Ownership: Iron County.

Parowan—K36AI, Ch. 36, Iron County. Phone: 435-477-8341.

Technical Facilities: 1.3-kw ERP, lat. 37° 50' 32", long. 112° 58' 27".

Holds CP for change to 0.25-kw ERP, 59-ft. above ground, 6778-ft. above sea level, lat. 37° 58' 30.2", long. 112° 58' 26.6". BDFCDTT-20090105AAJ.

Began Operation: December 13, 1982.

Ownership: Iron County.

Parowan—K38CM, Ch. 38, Iron County. Phone: 435-477-8341.

Technical Facilities: 1-kw ERP, lat. 37° 50' 32", long. 112° 58' 10".

Holds CP for change to 0.25-kw ERP, 59-ft. above ground, 6778-ft. above sea level, lat. 37° 50' 30.2", long. 112° 58' 26.6". BDFCDTT-20090105AAK.

Began Operation: March 8, 1989.

Ownership: Iron County.

Parowan—K40CH, Ch. 40, Iron County.

Technical Facilities: 1.15-kw ERP, lat. 37° 50' 32", long. 112° 58' 27".

Parowan, Enoch, Paragonah—K49HC, Ch. 49, Iron County. Phone: 435-477-8341.

Technical Facilities: 0.97-kw ERP, 49-ft. above ground, 6765-ft. above sea level, lat. 37° 50' 32", long. 112° 58' 27".

Holds CP for change to 0.25-kw ERP, 59-ft. above ground, 6778-ft. above sea level, lat. 37° 50' 30.2", long. 112° 58' 26.6". BDFCDTT-20080410ABX.

Ownership: Iron County.

Parowan, Enoch, Paragonah—K51HQ, Ch. 51, Iron County. Phone: 435-477-8341.

Technical Facilities: 0.97-kw ERP, 49-ft. above ground, 6765-ft. above sea level, lat. 37° 50' 32", long. 112° 58' 27".

Holds CP for change to 0.25-kw ERP, 59-ft. above ground, 6778-ft. above sea level, lat. 37° 50' 30.2", long. 112° 58' 26.6". BDFCDTT-20080410ABY.

Ownership: Iron County.

Parowan, etc.—K42AF, Ch. 42, Iron County. Phone: 435-477-8341.

Technical Facilities: 1.31-kw ERP, lat. 37° 50' 32", long. 112° 58' 27".

Holds CP for change to 0.25-kw ERP, 59-ft. above ground, 6778-ft. above sea level, lat. 37° 50' 30.2", long. 112° 58' 26.6". BDFCDTT-20090105AAL.

Began Operation: July 2, 1981.

Ownership: Iron County.

Parowan, etc.—K44DR, Ch. 44, Iron County. Phone: 435-477-8341.

Technical Facilities: 1.22-kw ERP, 33-ft. above ground, 6768-ft. above sea level, lat. 37° 50' 32", long. 112° 58' 10".

Holds CP for change to 0.25-kw ERP, 59-ft. above ground, 6778-ft. above sea level, lat. 37° 50' 30.2", long. 112° 58' 26.6". BDFCDTT-20090105AAM.

Began Operation: August 9, 1993.

Ownership: Iron County.

Parowan, etc.—K46DF, Ch. 46, Iron County.

Technical Facilities: 1.22-kw ERP, 33-ft. above ground, 6768-ft. above sea level, lat. 37° 50' 32", long. 112° 58' 10".

Parowan, etc.—K48FJ, Ch. 48, Iron County. Phone: 435-477-8341.

Technical Facilities: 2.13-kw ERP, 6768-ft. above sea level, lat. 37° 50' 32", long. 112° 58' 10".

Holds CP for change to 0.25-kw ERP, 59-ft. above ground, 6778-ft. above sea level, lat. 37° 50' 30.2", long. 112° 58' 26.6". BDFCDTT-20090105AAG.

Transmitter: 6.5-mi. W of Parowan.

Began Operation: July 31, 1995.

Ownership: Iron County.

Peoa—K28GW, Ch. 28, Summit County.

Technical Facilities: 0.49-kw ERP, 226-ft. above ground, 7205-ft. above sea level, lat. 40° 43' 21", long. 111° 21' 46".

Peoa & Oakley—K08IE, Ch. 8, Summit County.

Technical Facilities: 0.04-kw ERP, 23-ft. above ground, 7205-ft. above sea level, lat. 40° 43' 21", long. 111° 21' 46".

Peoa & Oakley—K10JB, Ch. 10, Summit County.

Technical Facilities: 0.04-kw ERP, 23-ft. above ground, 7201-ft. above sea level, lat. 40° 43' 21", long. 111° 21' 46".

Peoa & Oakley—K12JM, Ch. 12, Summit County.

Technical Facilities: 0.04-kw ERP, 23-ft. above ground, 7205-ft. above sea level, lat. 40° 43' 21", long. 111° 21' 46".

Peoa & Oakley—K15FP, Ch. 15, Summit County. Phone: 435-336-3220.

Technical Facilities: 0.49-kw ERP, 23-ft. above ground, 7205-ft. above sea level, lat. 40° 43' 21", long. 111° 21' 46".

Pine Valley—K11OO, Ch. 11, Newport Television License LLC. Phone: 816-751-0204.

Technical Facilities: 0.07-kw ERP, lat. 37° 30' 46", long. 113° 39' 14".

Ownership: Newport Television LLC.

Pine Valley, etc.—K08EN-D, Ch. 8, Bonneville Holding Co. Phone: 801-575-7517.

Technical Facilities: 0.031-kw ERP, 36-ft. above ground, 7221-ft. above sea level, lat. 37° 40' 36", long. 113° 39' 14".

Ownership: Bonneville International Corp.

Price—K17GT-D, Ch. 17, High Plains Broadcasting License Co. LLC. Phone: 580-269-2215.

Technical Facilities: 0.03-kw ERP, 131-ft. above ground, 9626-ft. above sea level, lat. 39° 31' 47", long. 111° 03' 04".

Ownership: High Plains Broadcasting Inc.

Price—K18DF, Ch. 19, U. of Utah. Phone: 801-585-3601.

Technical Facilities: 0.378-kw ERP, 16-ft. above ground, 9819-ft. above sea level, lat. 39° 31' 47", long. 111° 03' 04".

Ownership: U. of Utah.

Price—K21EZ, Ch. 21, Larry H. Miller Communications Corp. Phone: 801-537-1414.

Technical Facilities: 3.31-kw ERP, lat. 39° 45' 22", long. 110° 59' 26".

Transmitter: Ford Ridge, 15-mi. NW of Price.

Began Operation: October 3, 1995.

Ownership: Larry H. Miller Communications Corp.

Price—K23GW, Ch. 23, Carbon County. Phone: 465-969-3200.

Technical Facilities: 1.73-kw ERP, 23-ft. above ground, 5912-ft. above sea level, lat. 39° 36' 38", long. 110° 48' 47".

Ownership: Carbon County.

Price—K27HU, Ch. 27, Carbon County. Phone: 435-636-3200.

Technical Facilities: 1.73-kw ERP, 23-ft. above ground, 5912-ft. above sea level, lat. 39° 36' 38", long. 110° 48' 47".

Ownership: Carbon County.

Price—K35CK, Ch. 35, Community Television of Utah License LLC. Phone: 859-448-2700.

Technical Facilities: 2.54-kw ERP, 26-ft. above ground, 9626-ft. above sea level, lat. 39° 31' 49", long. 111° 03' 03".

Ownership: Local TV Holdings LLC.

Price—K46IC, Ch. 46, Hispanic Christian Community Network Inc. Phone: 214-879-0081.

Technical Facilities: 1-kw ERP, 16-ft. above ground, 5820-ft. above sea level, lat. 39° 32' 42", long. 110° 49' 00".

Ownership: Hispanic Christian Community Network Inc.

Price—K47GP, Ch. 47, Carbon County. Phone: 435-636-3275.

Technical Facilities: 1.66-kw ERP, 59-ft. above ground, 9842-ft. above sea level, lat. 39° 45' 22", long. 110° 59' 26".

Price—K48JE, Ch. 48, Hispanic Christian Community Network Inc. Phone: 214-879-0081.

Technical Facilities: 1-kw ERP, 16-ft. above ground, 5820-ft. above sea level, lat. 39° 32' 42", long. 110° 49' 00".

Ownership: Hispanic Christian Community Network Inc.

Price, etc.—K45FW, Ch. 45, Newport Television License LLC. Phone: 816-751-0204.

Technical Facilities: 1.66-kw ERP, 59-ft. above ground, 9844-ft. above sea level, lat. 39° 45' 22", long. 110° 59' 26".

Ownership: Newport Television LLC.

Provo—K22IT, Ch. 22, Exitos Hispanic Broadcasting Inc. Phone: 801-954-8821. Fax: 801-973-7145.

Technical Facilities: 11.35-kw ERP, 30-ft. above ground, 7605-ft. above sea level, lat. 40° 16' 41", long. 111° 55' 58".

Began Operation: April 15, 1999.

Ownership: Exitos Hispanic Broadcasting Inc.

Provo—K43JV, Ch. 43, Three Angels Broadcasting Network Inc. Phone: 618-627-4651.

Technical Facilities: 4-kw ERP, 49-ft. above ground, 7592-ft. above sea level, lat. 40° 16' 24", long. 111° 55' 27".

Ownership: Three Angels Broadcasting Network Inc.

Randolph—K09BA, Ch. 9, Norris Community TV Inc.

Technical Facilities: 0.1-kw ERP, lat. 41° 39' 54", long. 111° 05' 55".

Randolph—K11BF, Ch. 11, Norris Community TV Inc.

Technical Facilities: 0.01-kw ERP, lat. 41° 39' 54", long. 111° 05' 55".

Randolph—K13QJ, Ch. 13, Rich County.

Technical Facilities: 0.07-kw ERP, 7900-ft. above sea level, lat. 41° 39' 54", long. 111° 05' 55".

Randolph & Woodruff—K24EC, Ch. 24, Rich County.

Technical Facilities: 1.94-kw ERP, lat. 41° 37' 31", long. 111° 07' 23".

Transmitter: 4-mi. ESE of Randolph.

Randolph & Woodruff—K26GH, Ch. 26, Rich County. Phone: 435-793-2415.

Technical Facilities: 1.2-kw ERP, 30-ft. above ground, 7762-ft. above sea level, lat. 41° 37' 31", long. 111° 07' 23".

Ownership: Rich County.

Randolph & Woodruff—K34FR, Ch. 34, Rich County. Phone: 435-793-2415.

Technical Facilities: 1.2-kw ERP, 30-ft. above ground, 7,762-ft. above sea level, lat. 41° 37' 31", long. 111° 07' 23".

Ownership: Rich County.

Randolph & Woodruff—K36FS, Ch. 36, Rich County. Phone: 435-793-2415.

Technical Facilities: 1.2-kw ERP, 30-ft. above ground, 7,592-ft. above sea level, lat. 41° 37' 31", long. 111° 07' 23".

Randolph & Woodruff—K38GN, Ch. 38, U. of Utah.

Technical Facilities: 0.833-kw ERP, lat. 41° 37' 31", long. 111° 07' 23".

Randolph & Woodruff—K40FY, Ch. 40, Rich County. Phone: 435-733-2415.

Technical Facilities: 1.3-kw ERP, 30-ft. above ground, 7762-ft. above sea level, lat. 41° 37' 31", long. 111° 07' 23".

Ownership: Rich County.

Richfield & Monroe—K35GQ, Ch. 35, Sevier County. Phone: 435-896-9262.

Technical Facilities: 0.6-kw ERP, 49-ft. above ground, 8773-ft. above sea level, lat. 38° 38' 06", long. 112° 03' 34".

Richfield, etc.—K03AS, Ch. 3, Sevier County.

Technical Facilities: 0.02-kw ERP, lat. 38° 38' 04", long. 112° 03' 33".

Transmitter: 3.5-mi. NE of Monroe.

Ownership: Sevier County.

Richfield, etc.—K06BQ, Ch. 6, Sevier County.

Technical Facilities: 0.052-kw ERP, lat. 38° 38' 04", long. 112° 03' 33".

Transmitter: 3.5-mi. E of Monroe.

Richfield, etc.—K07CQ, Ch. 7, Sevier County.

Technical Facilities: 0.342-kw ERP, lat. 38° 38' 04", long. 112° 03' 33".

Transmitter: 3.5-mi. E of Monroe.

Richfield, etc.—K31JI-D, Ch. 31, Sevier County. Phone: 435-896-9262.

Technical Facilities: 0.02-kw ERP, 26-ft. above ground, 8793-ft. above sea level, lat. 38° 38' 05.8", long. 112° 03' 34.1".

Ownership: Sevier County.

Richfield, etc.—K32HU-D, Ch. 32, Sevier County. Phone: 435-896-9262.

Technical Facilities: 0.02-kw ERP, 26-ft. above ground, 8793-ft. above sea level, lat. 38° 38' 05.8", long. 112° 03' 34.1".

Ownership: Sevier County.

Richfield, etc.—K33JF-D, Ch. 33, Sevier County. Phone: 435-896-9262.

Technical Facilities: 0.02-kw ERP, 26-ft. above ground, 8793-ft. above sea level, lat. 38° 38' 05.8", long. 112° 03' 34.1".

Ownership: Sevier County.

Richfield, etc.—K34JA-D, Ch. 34, Sevier County. Phone: 435-896-9262.

Technical Facilities: 0.02-kw ERP, 26-ft. above ground, 8793-ft. above sea level, lat. 38° 38' 05.8", long. 112° 03' 34.1".

Ownership: Sevier County.

Richfield, etc.—K36CB, Ch. 36, Utah State Board of Regents.

Technical Facilities: 0.3-kw ERP, lat. 38° 38' 04", long. 112° 03' 33".

Transmitter: 3.2-mi. E of Monroe.

Richfield, etc.—K38AQ, Ch. 38, Sevier County.

Technical Facilities: 0.75-kw ERP, 55-ft. above ground, 8816-ft. above sea level, lat. 38° 38' 04", long. 112° 03' 33".

Transmitter: 3.5-mi. NE of Monroe.

Richfield, etc.—K39JF-D, Ch. 39, Sevier County. Phone: 435-896-9262.

Technical Facilities: 0.02-kw ERP, 26-ft. above ground, 8793-ft. above sea level, lat. 38° 38' 05.8", long. 112° 03' 34.1".

Ownership: Sevier County.

Richfield, etc.—K40AB, Ch. 40, Sevier County.

Technical Facilities: 0.748-kw ERP, lat. 38° 38' 04", long. 112° 03' 33".

Transmitter: 3.4-mi. E of Monroe.

Richfield, etc.—K42AJ, Ch. 42, U. of Utah.

Technical Facilities: 0.748-kw ERP, 55-ft. above ground, 8816-ft. above sea level, lat. 38° 38' 04", long. 112° 03' 33".

Richfield, etc.—K44DU, Ch. 44, Sevier County.

Technical Facilities: 0.34-kw ERP, 43-ft. above ground, 8802-ft. above sea level, lat. 38° 38' 04", long. 112° 03' 33".

Richfield, etc.—K57KB-D, Ch. 57, U. of Utah. Phone: 801-585-3601.

Technical Facilities: 0.01-kw ERP, 26-ft. above ground, 8793-ft. above sea level, lat. 38° 38' 05.8", long. 112° 03' 34.1".

Ownership: U. of Utah.

Richfield, etc.—K58IR-D, Ch. 58, Sevier County. Phone: 435-896-9262.

Technical Facilities: 0.02-kw ERP, 26-ft. above ground, 8793-ft. above sea level, lat. 38° 38' 05.8", long. 112° 03' 34.1".

Ownership: Sevier County.

Richfield/Monroe—K59IS-D, Ch. 59, Sevier County. Phone: 435-896-9262.

Technical Facilities: 0.02-kw ERP, 26-ft. above ground, 8793-ft. above sea level, lat. 38° 38' 05.8", long. 112° 03' 34.1".

Ownership: Sevier County.

Rockville—K05AR-D, Ch. 5, Bonneville Holding Co. Phone: 801-575-7517.

Technical Facilities: 0.031-kw ERP, 26-ft. above ground, 4380-ft. above sea level, lat. 37° 09' 08.6", long. 113° 01' 52.2".

Began Operation: March 3, 1980.

Ownership: Bonneville International Corp.

Rockville—K07PX, Ch. 7, CCR-St. George IV LLC. Phone: 303-468-6500.

Technical Facilities: 0.131-kw ERP, lat. 37° 09' 00", long. 113° 01' 48".

Holds CP for change to 0.3-kw ERP, 33-ft. above ground, 4436-ft. above sea level, BDFCDVA-20060630AGV.

Ownership: Cherry Creek Radio LLC.

Rockville—K09CD, Ch. 9, SLC TV Licensee Corp. Phone: 212-891-2100.

Technical Facilities: 0.129-kw ERP, lat. 37° 09' 00", long. 113° 01' 48".

Ownership: Four Points Media Group Holding LLC.

Rockville—K40FU, Ch. 40, Brigham Young U. Phone: 801-422-8423.

Technical Facilities: 3.54-kw ERP, 30-ft. above ground, 4383-ft. above sea level, lat. 37° 09' 00", long. 113° 01' 48".

Ownership: Brigham Young U.

Rockville & Springdale—K38HO, Ch. 38, U. of Utah. Phone: 801-585-3601.

Technical Facilities: 0.5-kw ERP, 16-ft. above ground, 4445-ft. above sea level, lat. 37° 09' 09", long. 113° 01' 49".

Ownership: U. of Utah.

Rockville/Springdale—K33JW-D, Ch. 33, U. of Utah. Phone: 801-585-3601.

Technical Facilities: 0.13-kw ERP, 26-ft. above ground, 4380-ft. above sea level, lat. 37° 09' 08.6", long. 113° 01' 52.2".

Began Operation: December 2, 2008.

Ownership: U. of Utah.

Roosevelt—K38GO, Ch. 38, Larry H. Miller Communications Corp. Phone: 801-537-1414.

Technical Facilities: 1.12-kw ERP, 40-ft. above ground, 6041-ft. above sea level, lat. 40° 19' 27", long. 110° 09' 19".

Began Operation: March 30, 1994.

Ownership: Larry H. Miller Communications Corp.

Roosevelt—K47HA, Ch. 47, Duchesne County. Phone: 435-738-1100.

Technical Facilities: 0.03-kw ERP, 43-ft. above ground, 5134-ft. above sea level, lat. 40° 17' 56", long. 109° 58' 25".

Transmitter: 110 E. Lagoon St.

Ownership: Duchesne County.

Roosevelt—K48GZ, Ch. 48, Duchesne County.

Technical Facilities: 1.22-kw ERP, lat. 40° 19' 27", long. 110° 09' 19".

Roosevelt—K50GO, Ch. 50, Duchesne County.

Technical Facilities: 1.12-kw ERP, 40-ft. above ground, 6041-ft. above sea level, lat. 40° 19' 27", long. 110° 09' 19".

Roosevelt, etc.—K08CS, Ch. 8, Uintah County.

Technical Facilities: 0.17-kw ERP, lat. 40° 19' 27", long. 110° 09' 19".

Roosevelt, etc.—K10DD, Ch. 10, Uintah County.

Technical Facilities: 0.17-kw ERP, lat. 40° 19' 27", long. 110° 09' 19".

Roosevelt, etc.—K12FG, Ch. 12, Uintah County.

Technical Facilities: 0.17-kw ERP, lat. 40° 19' 27", long. 110° 09' 19".

Roosevelt, etc.—K45GN, Ch. 45, Uintah County.

Technical Facilities: 0.06-kw ERP, lat. 40° 19' 27", long. 110° 09' 19".

Salina—K24GK, Ch. 24, High Plains Broadcasting License Co. LLC. Phone: 580-269-2215.

Technical Facilities: 0.143-kw ERP, 46-ft. above ground, 6765-ft. above sea level, lat. 38° 52' 37", long. 111° 52' 32".

Holds CP for change to 0.035-kw ERP, BDFCDTT-20081027AAX.

Ownership: High Plains Broadcasting Inc.

Salina & Redmond—K15FF-D, Ch. 15, Sevier County. Phone: 435-896-9262.

Technical Facilities: 0.09-kw ERP, 33-ft. above ground, 6752-ft. above sea level, lat. 38° 52' 37.4", long. 111° 52' 31.5".

Ownership: Sevier County.

Salina & Redmond—K17FC-D, Ch. 17, Sevier County. Phone: 435-896-9262.

Technical Facilities: 0.09-kw ERP, 33-ft. above ground, 6752-ft. above sea level, lat. 38° 52' 37.4", long. 111° 52' 31.5".

Ownership: Sevier County.

Salina & Redmond—K18HO-D, Ch. 18, Sevier County. Phone: 435-896-9292.

Technical Facilities: 0.09-kw ERP, 33-ft. above ground, 6752-ft. above sea level, lat. 38° 52' 37.4", long. 111° 52' 31.5".

Ownership: Sevier County.

Salina & Redmond—K21FL-D, Ch. 21, Sevier County. Phone: 435-896-9262.

Technical Facilities: 0.09-kw ERP, 33-ft. above ground, 6752-ft. above sea level, lat. 38° 52' 37.4", long. 111° 52' 31.5".

Ownership: Sevier County.

Salina & Redmond—K22HY-D, Ch. 22, Sevier County. Phone: 435-896-9262.

Technical Facilities: 0.004-kw ERP, 30-ft. above ground, 6749-ft. above sea level, lat. 38° 52' 37.4", long. 111° 52' 31.5".

Ownership: Sevier County.

Salina & Redmond—K23FK-D, Ch. 23, Sevier County. Phone: 435-896-9262.

Technical Facilities: 0.09-kw ERP, 33-ft. above ground, 6752-ft. above sea level, lat. 38° 52' 37.4", long. 111° 52' 31.5".

Ownership: Sevier County.

Salt Lake City—K18FJ, Ch. 18, Trinity Christian Center of Santa Ana Inc. Phone: 714-832-2950.

Technical Facilities: 1000-w TPO, 3.55-kw ERP, 79-ft. above ground, 9117-ft. above sea level, lat. 40° 39' 35", long. 112° 12' 05".

Holds CP for change to channel number 15, 2-kw ERP, 30-ft. above ground, 33-ft. above sea level, lat. 40° 48' 27", long. 111° 53' 18". BDISDTT-20060329ACT.

Transmitter: Farnsworth Peak.

Ownership: Trinity Broadcasting Network Inc.

Personnel: Mark Fountain, Chief Engineer.

Salt Lake City—K45GX, Ch. 45, Word of God Fellowship Inc. Phone: 817-571-1229.

Technical Facilities: 1000-w TPO, 50-kw ERP, 52-ft. above ground, 8891-ft. above sea level, lat. 40° 39' 09", long. 112° 12' 05".

Transmitter: Farnsworth Peak.

Began Operation: July 18, 1990.

Ownership: Word of God Fellowship Inc.

Salt Lake City—K59GS, Ch. 59, Exitos Hispanic Broadcasting Inc. Phone: 801-954-8821. Fax: 801-973-7145.

Technical Facilities: 5.3-kw ERP, 449-ft. above ground, 4787-ft. above sea level, lat. 40° 46' 09", long. 111° 53' 17".

Began Operation: January 4, 1988.

Ownership: Exitos Hispanic Broadcasting Inc.

Salt Lake City—K66FN, Ch. 66, Azteca Broadcasting Corp. Phone: 559-686-1370.

Technical Facilities: 38-kw ERP, 134-ft. above ground, 9170-ft. above sea level, lat. 40° 39' 35", long. 112° 12' 02".

Holds CP for change to channel number 39, 15-kw ERP, BDFCDTT-20080801ANU.

Multichannel TV Sound: Stereo only.

Ownership: Azteca Broadcasting Corp.

■ **Salt Lake City**—KEJT-LP, Ch. 50, NBC Telemundo License Co. Phone: 202-637-4535.

Technical Facilities: 8.6-kw ERP, 70-ft. above ground, 9019-ft. above sea level, lat. 40° 39' 37", long. 112° 12' 05".

Ownership: NBC Universal.

Salt Lake City—KUBX-LP, Ch. 58, Word of God Fellowship Inc. Phone: 817-571-1229.

Technical Facilities: 0.42-kw ERP, 25-ft. above ground, 8863-ft. above sea level, lat. 40° 39' 09", long. 112° 12' 05".

Holds CP for change to channel number 27, 100-kw ERP, BDISTTL-20060919ACF.

Began Operation: September 25, 1995.

Ownership: Word of God Fellowship Inc.

Personnel: Bob Joblin, General Manager; Neal Ardman, Chief Engineer.

■ **Salt Lake City**—KUCL-LP, Ch. 26, Christian Life Broadcasting. Phone: 801-484-4331.

Technical Facilities: 21.4-w TPO, 1000-kw ERP, 75-ft. above ground, 4898-ft. above sea level, lat. 40° 43' 29", long. 111° 48' 46".

Transmitter: 0.1-mi. SE of intersection of South St. & Foothill Dr.

Ownership: Christian Life Broadcasting.

Personnel: John M. Peterson, General Manager & Chief Engineer.

Samak—K03HQ, Ch. 3, Summit County. Phone: 435-336-3220.

Technical Facilities: 0.072-kw ERP, 15-ft. above ground, 7193-ft. above sea level, lat. 40° 37' 56", long. 111° 15' 30".

Ownership: Summit County.

Samak—K07US, Ch. 7, Summit County.

Technical Facilities: 0.007-kw ERP, 10-ft. above ground, 7165-ft. above sea level, lat. 40° 37' 56", long. 111° 15' 30".

Samak—K09VF, Ch. 9, Summit County.

Technical Facilities: 0.006-kw ERP, 10-ft. above ground, 7165-ft. above sea level, lat. 40° 37' 56", long. 111° 15' 30".

Samak—K11SX, Ch. 11, Summit County.

Technical Facilities: 0.006-kw ERP, 10-ft. above ground, 7165-ft. above sea level, lat. 40° 37' 56", long. 111° 15' 30".

Samak—K13VT, Ch. 13, Summit County Courthouse.

Technical Facilities: 0.006-kw ERP, 10-ft. above ground, 7165-ft. above sea level, lat. 40° 37' 56", long. 111° 15' 30".

Samak—K31HH, Ch. 31, Summit County. Phone: 435-336-3220.

Technical Facilities: 0.14-kw ERP, 15-ft. above ground, 7193-ft. above sea level, lat. 40° 37' 56", long. 111° 15' 30".

Ownership: Summit County.

Samak—K33HP, Ch. 33, Summit County. Phone: 435-336-3220.

Technical Facilities: 0.14-kw ERP, 15-ft. above ground, 7193-ft. above sea level, lat. 40° 37' 56", long. 111° 15' 30".

Ownership: Summit County.

Santa Clara—K43CC, Ch. 43, Community Television of Utah License LLC. Phone: 859-448-2700.

Technical Facilities: 3.97-kw ERP, lat. 37° 09' 30", long. 113° 53' 20".

Ownership: Local TV Holdings LLC.

Santa Clara—K49AS, Ch. 49, SLC TV Licensee Corp. Phone: 212-891-2100.

Technical Facilities: 9.43-kw ERP, 7821-ft. above sea level, lat. 37° 09' 30", long. 113° 53' 20".

Holds CP for change to 0.15-kw ERP, 39-ft. above ground, 7785-ft. above sea level, lat. 37° 09' 18.8", long. 113° 52' 56.7". BDFCDTT-20061204AFP.

Ownership: Four Points Media Group Holding LLC.

Santa Clara—KVBT-LP, Ch. 41, CCR-St. George IV LLC. Phone: 303-468-6500.

Technical Facilities: 3.73-kw ERP, lat. 37° 09' 30", long. 113° 53' 20".

Ownership: Cherry Creek Radio LLC.

Santa Clara & Washington—K48JD, Ch. 48, High Plains Broadcasting License Co. LLC. Phone: 580-269-2215.

Technical Facilities: 2.24-kw ERP, 52-ft. above ground, 7746-ft. above sea level, lat. 37° 09' 15", long. 113° 51' 32".

Ownership: High Plains Broadcasting Inc.

Santa Clara, etc.—K35FS-D, Ch. 35, Bonneville Holding Co. Phone: 801-575-7517.

Technical Facilities: 0.287-kw ERP, 43-ft. above ground, 7693-ft. above sea level, lat. 37° 09' 15", long. 113° 51' 32".

Ownership: Bonneville International Corp.

Santa Clara, etc.—K36FT, Ch. 36, Brigham Young U. Phone: 801-422-8423.

Technical Facilities: 0.745-kw ERP, 49-ft. above ground, 7730-ft. above sea level, lat. 37° 09' 30", long. 113° 53' 20".

Ownership: Brigham Young U.

Scipio—K19GR-D, Ch. 19, Millard County. Phone: 435-864-1405.

Technical Facilities: 0.01-kw ERP, 23-ft. above ground, 6824-ft. above sea level, lat. 39° 12' 09.3", long. 112° 08' 34.8".

Ownership: Millard County.

Scipio—K31GT, Ch. 31, Millard County. Phone: 435-864-1405.

Technical Facilities: 0.16-kw ERP, 23-ft. above ground, 6630-ft. above sea level, lat. 39° 11' 54", long. 112° 08' 33".

Ownership: Millard County.

Scipio—K34IZ-D, Ch. 34, Millard County. Phone: 435-864-1405.

Technical Facilities: 0.01-kw ERP, 23-ft. above ground, 6824-ft. above sea level, lat. 39° 12' 09.3", long. 112° 08' 34.8".

Ownership: Millard County.

Scipio—K35IP-D, Ch. 35, Millard County. Phone: 435-864-1405.

Technical Facilities: 0.01-kw ERP, 23-ft. above ground, 6824-ft. above sea level, lat. 39° 12' 09.3", long. 112° 08' 34.8".

Ownership: Millard County.

Scipio—K36IP-D, Ch. 36, Millard County. Phone: 435-864-1405.

Technical Facilities: 0.01-kw ERP, 23-ft. above ground, 6824-ft. above sea level, lat. 39° 12' 09.3", long. 112° 08' 34.8".

Ownership: Millard County.

Scipio—K39EH, Ch. 39, Millard County.

Technical Facilities: 0.155-kw ERP, 23-ft. above ground, 6630-ft. above sea level, lat. 39° 11' 54", long. 112° 08' 33".

Scipio—K41IG, Ch. 41, Millard County. Phone: 435-864-1405.

Technical Facilities: 0.16-kw ERP, 23-ft. above ground, 6636-ft. above sea level, lat. 39° 11' 54", long. 112° 08' 33".

Ownership: Millard County.

Scipio—K43JN, Ch. 43, Millard County. Phone: 435-864-1405.

Technical Facilities: 0.16-kw ERP, 23-ft. above ground, 6630-ft. above sea level, lat. 39° 11' 54", long. 112° 08' 33".

Ownership: Millard County.

Scipio—K45EL, Ch. 45, Millard County.

Technical Facilities: 0.155-kw ERP, 23-ft. above ground, 6630-ft. above sea level, lat. 39° 11' 54", long. 112° 08' 33".

Scipio & Holden—K06DH, Ch. 6, Millard County.

Technical Facilities: 0.027-kw ERP, lat. 39° 11' 54", long. 112° 08' 33".

Scipio & Holden—K08DP, Ch. 8, Millard County.

Technical Facilities: 0.008-kw ERP, lat. 39° 11' 54", long. 112° 08' 33".

Scipio & Holden—K10EB, Ch. 10, Millard County.

Technical Facilities: 0.008-kw ERP, lat. 39° 11' 54", long. 112° 08' 33".

Scipio & Holden—K12DH, Ch. 12, Millard County.

Technical Facilities: 0.233-kw ERP, lat. 39° 11' 54", long. 112° 08' 33".

Scipio, Holden—K25JK-D, Ch. 25, Millard County. Phone: 435-864-1405.

Technical Facilities: 0.01-kw ERP, 23-ft. above ground, 6824-ft. above sea level, lat. 39° 12' 09.3", long. 112° 08' 34.8".

Ownership: Millard County.

Scipio, Holden—K29HS-D, Ch. 29, Millard County. Phone: 435-864-1405.

Technical Facilities: 0.01-kw ERP, 23-ft. above ground, 6824-ft. above sea level, lat. 39° 12' 09.3", long. 112° 08' 34.8".

Ownership: Millard County.

Scofield—K08CF, Ch. 8, Carbon County.

Technical Facilities: 0.01-kw ERP, lat. 39° 42' 40", long. 111° 09' 20".

Scofield—K10CL, Ch. 10, Carbon County.

Technical Facilities: 0.01-kw ERP, lat. 39° 42' 40", long. 111° 09' 20".

Scofield—K12CE, Ch. 12, Carbon County.

Technical Facilities: 0.014-kw ERP, lat. 39° 42' 40", long. 111° 09' 20".

Scofield—K27HV, Ch. 27, Carbon County. Phone: 435-636-3200.

Technical Facilities: 1.73-kw ERP, 23-ft. above ground, 5912-ft. above sea level, lat. 39° 42' 40", long. 111° 09' 20".

Ownership: Carbon County.

Sevier County—K35DX, Ch. 35, Sevier County.

Technical Facilities: lat. 38° 30' 38", long. 111° 47' 05".

Sevier County (rural)—K33DU, Ch. 33, Sevier County.

Technical Facilities: 0.007-kw ERP, 36-ft. above ground, 9160-ft. above sea level, lat. 38° 30' 38", long. 111° 47' 05".

Sevier County (rural)—K39GN, Ch. 39, Sevier County. Phone: 435-896-9262.

Technical Facilities: 0.007-kw ERP, 23-ft. above ground, 9107-ft. above sea level, lat. 38° 30' 44", long. 111° 47' 00".

Sevier County (rural)—K41GA, Ch. 41, Sevier County. Phone: 435-896-9262.

Technical Facilities: 0.007-kw ERP, 35-ft. above ground, 9160-ft. above sea level, lat. 38° 30' 38", long. 111° 47' 05".

Sevier County (rural)—K45FT, Ch. 45, Sevier County. Phone: 435-896-9262.

Technical Facilities: 0.07-kw ERP, 23-ft. above ground, 8674-ft. above sea level, lat. 38° 30' 36", long. 111° 48' 54".

Sigurd & Salina—K08CM, Ch. 8, Sevier County.

Technical Facilities: 0.06-kw ERP, lat. 38° 52' 37", long. 111° 52' 30".

Sigurd & Salina—K10CT, Ch. 10, Sevier County.

Technical Facilities: 0.057-kw ERP, lat. 38° 52' 37", long. 111° 52' 30".

Sigurd & Salina—K12CJ, Ch. 12, Sevier County.

Technical Facilities: 0.016-kw ERP, lat. 38° 52' 37", long. 111° 52' 30".

Sigurd & Salina—K16HE-D, Ch. 16, Sevier County. Phone: 435-896-9262.

Technical Facilities: 0.004-kw ERP, 30-ft. above ground, 6749-ft. above sea level, lat. 38° 52' 37.4", long. 111° 52' 31.5".

Ownership: Sevier County.

Sigurd & Salina—K20JA-D, Ch. 20, Sevier County. Phone: 435-896-9262.

Technical Facilities: 0.004-kw ERP, 30-ft. above ground, 6749-ft. above sea level, lat. 38° 52' 37.4", long. 111° 52' 31.5".

Ownership: Sevier County.

Sigurd & Salina—K43KN-D, Ch. 43, Sevier County. Phone: 435-896-9262.

Technical Facilities: 0.004-kw ERP, 30-ft. above ground, 6749-ft. above sea level, lat. 38° 52' 37.4", long. 111° 52' 31.5".

Ownership: Sevier County.

Spanish Fork—K49GD, Ch. 49, Exitos Hispanic Broadcasting Inc. Phone: 801-954-8821. Fax: 801-973-7145.

Technical Facilities: 7-kw ERP, 30-ft. above ground, 7605-ft. above sea level, lat. 40° 16' 41", long. 111° 55' 58".

Transmitter: Lake Mountains, 18.7-mi. WNW of Spanish Fork.

Began Operation: April 15, 1999.

Ownership: Exitos Hispanic Broadcasting Inc.

Spring Glen—K41FX, Ch. 64, SLC TV Licensee Corp. Phone: 212-891-2100.

Technical Facilities: 1.66-kw ERP, 59-ft. above ground, 9844-ft. above sea level, lat. 39° 45' 22", long. 110° 59' 26".

Ownership: Four Points Media Group Holding LLC.

Spring Glen—K51IC-D, Ch. 51, High Plains Broadcasting License Co. LLC. Phone: 580-269-2215.

Technical Facilities: 0.13-kw ERP, 59-ft. above ground, 9829-ft. above sea level, lat. 39° 45' 23", long. 110° 59' 22".

Ownership: High Plains Broadcasting Inc.

Spring Glen, etc.—K06DR, Ch. 6, Carbon County.

Technical Facilities: 0.03-kw ERP, lat. 39° 31' 49", long. 111° 03' 03".

Spring Glen, etc.—K08AU, Ch. 8, Carbon County.

Technical Facilities: 0.25-kw ERP, lat. 39° 31' 49", long. 111° 03' 03".

Spring Glen, etc.—K10AZ, Ch. 10, Carbon County.

Technical Facilities: 0.01-kw ERP, lat. 39° 31' 49", long. 111° 03' 03".

Spring Glen, etc.—K12AZ, Ch. 12, Carbon County.

Technical Facilities: 0.25-kw ERP, lat. 39° 31' 49", long. 111° 03' 03".

St. George—K16DS, Ch. 16, Southwest Media LLC. Phone: 435-467-9795.

Technical Facilities: 0.986-kw ERP, lat. 37° 03' 49", long. 113° 34' 20".

Transmitter: Web Hill.

Ownership: Southwest Media LLC.

St. George—K24CY, Ch. 24, Larry H. Miller Communications Corp. Phone: 801-537-1414.

Technical Facilities: 1.32-kw ERP, 32-ft. above ground, 3163-ft. above sea level, lat. 37° 03' 50", long. 113° 34' 19".

Began Operation: July 30, 1993.

Ownership: Larry H. Miller Communications Corp.

St. George—K25JS-D, Ch. 25, Newport Television LLC. Phone: 401-751-1700.

Technical Facilities: 0.13-kw ERP, 62-ft. above ground, 3205-ft. above sea level, lat. 37° 03' 48", long. 113° 34' 23".

Ownership: Newport Television LLC.

St. George—K67HK, Ch. 67, Trinity Christian Center of Santa Ana Inc. Phone: 760-956-2111.

Technical Facilities: 1.3-kw ERP, lat. 37° 03' 50", long. 113° 34' 23".

Holds CP for change to channel number 6, 0.35-kw ERP, 39-ft. above ground, 3146-ft. above sea level, lat. 37° 03' 49", long. 113° 34' 20". BDISTVL-20081218ABD.

Ownership: Trinity Broadcasting Network Inc.

St. George—K69CT, Ch. 69, Newport Television License LLC. Phone: 816-751-0204.

Technical Facilities: 0.734-kw ERP, 3140-ft. above sea level, lat. 37° 03' 49", long. 113° 34' 20".

Ownership: Newport Television LLC.

■ **St. George**—KDLU-LP, Ch. 26, CCR-St. George IV LLC. Phone: 303-468-6500.

Technical Facilities: 100-w TPO, 0.99-kw ERP, 36-ft. above ground, 3146-ft. above sea level, lat. 37° 03' 49", long. 113° 34' 20".

Transmitter: Webb Hill.

Ownership: Cherry Creek Radio LLC.

St. George—KKRP-LP, Ch. 46, Community Television of Utah License LLC. Phone: 859-448-2700.

Technical Facilities: 0.745-kw ERP, 85-ft. above ground, 3084-ft. above sea level, lat. 37° 04' 18", long. 113° 32' 34".

Holds CP for change to 0.3-kw ERP, lat. 37° 04' 21", long. 113° 32' 30". BDFCDTL-20090417AAX.

Ownership: Local TV Holdings LLC.

St. George—KUTG-LP, Ch. 58, Lamar Veasey. Phone: 916-501-7787.

Technical Facilities: 4.25-kw ERP, 105-ft. above ground, 3165-ft. above sea level, lat. 37° 03' 49", long. 113° 34' 29".

Ownership: Lamar Veasey.

St. George, etc.—K32FQ, Ch. 32, U. of Utah.

Technical Facilities: 0.745-kw ERP, 79-ft. above ground, 3199-ft. above sea level, lat. 37° 03' 49", long. 113° 34' 20".

St. George, etc.—K34FS, Ch. 34, Philip Alan Titus.

Technical Facilities: 0.745-kw ERP, 79-ft. above ground, 3199-ft. above sea level, lat. 37° 03' 49", long. 113° 34' 20".

St. George, etc.—K57KG-D, Ch. 57, U. of Utah. Phone: 801-585-3601.

Technical Facilities: 0.15-kw ERP, 59-ft. above ground, 3199-ft. above sea level, lat. 37° 03' 50", long. 113° 34' 20".

Began Operation: December 2, 2008.

Ownership: U. of Utah.

■ **St. George, etc.**—KDLQ-LP, Ch. 55, CCR-St. George IV LLC. Phone: 303-468-6500.

Technical Facilities: 100-w TPO, 1.193-kw ERP, 30-ft. above ground, 3169-ft. above sea level, lat. 37° 04' 50", long. 113° 34' 19".

Transmitter: Webb Hill, S of St. George.

Multichannel TV Sound: Stereo only.

Ownership: Cherry Creek Radio LLC.

Personnel: L. Brent Miner, General Manager; Dan Hobson, Chief Engineer; Daryl Farnsworth, Sales Manager.

Summit County—K41GS, Ch. 41, Summit County.

Technical Facilities: 0.8-kw ERP, lat. 40° 51' 18", long. 111° 28' 44".

Summit County—K47HB, Ch. 47, U. of Utah. Phone: 801-585-3601.

Technical Facilities: 0.765-kw ERP, 50-ft. above ground, 9361-ft. above sea level, lat. 40° 51' 18", long. 111° 28' 44".

Ownership: U. of Utah.

Summit County—K49FY, Ch. 49, Summit County.

Technical Facilities: 0.78-kw ERP, 50-ft. above ground, 9360-ft. above sea level, lat. 40° 51' 18", long. 111° 28' 44".

Ownership: Summit County.

Summit County—K51FY, Ch. 51, Summit County.

Technical Facilities: 0.784-kw ERP, 50-ft. above ground, 9361-ft. above sea level, lat. 40° 51' 18", long. 111° 28' 44".

Ownership: Summit County.

Summit County (rural)—K17DG, Ch. 17, Summit County. Phone: 435-336-3220.

Technical Facilities: 0.34-kw ERP, 46-ft. above ground, 9357-ft. above sea level, lat. 40° 51' 18", long. 111° 28' 44".

Holds CP for change to 0.0779-kw ERP, 46-ft. above ground, 9403-ft. above sea level, BDFCDTT-20090318ADJ.

Summit County (rural)—K19DU, Ch. 19, Summit County.

Technical Facilities: 0.315-kw ERP, 46-ft. above ground, 9350-ft. above sea level, lat. 40° 51' 18", long. 111° 28' 44".

Summit County (rural)—K22DM, Ch. 22, U. of Utah. Phone: 801-585-3601.

Technical Facilities: 0.988-kw ERP, 46-ft. above ground, 9350-ft. above sea level, lat. 40° 51' 18", long. 111° 28' 44".

Ownership: U. of Utah.

Summit County (rural)—K43AA, Ch. 43, Summit County.

Technical Facilities: 1.21-kw ERP, 9363-ft. above sea level, lat. 40° 51' 18", long. 111° 28' 44".

Summit County (rural)—K63GY, Ch. 63, Summit County. Phone: 435-336-3220.

Technical Facilities: 1.23-kw ERP, 50-ft. above ground, 9358-ft. above sea level, lat. 40° 51' 18", long. 111° 28' 44".

Ownership: Summit County.

Tabiona & Myton—K29EX, Ch. 29, U. of Utah. Phone: 801-585-3601.

Technical Facilities: 7-kw ERP, 40-ft. above ground, 10056-ft. above sea level, lat. 40° 21' 45", long. 110° 47' 31".

Teasdale & Torrey—K02BO, Ch. 2, Wayne County.

Technical Facilities: 0.89-kw ERP, 8261-ft. above sea level, lat. 38° 17' 00", long. 111° 30' 37".

Ownership: Wayne County.

Teasdale & Torrey—K04BN, Ch. 4, Wayne County.

Technical Facilities: 0.068-kw ERP, 8274-ft. above sea level, lat. 38° 17' 00", long. 111° 30' 37".

Ownership: Wayne County.

Teasdale & Torrey—K05BG, Ch. 5, Wayne County.

Technical Facilities: 0.034-kw ERP, 8274-ft. above sea level, lat. 38° 17' 00", long. 111° 30' 37".

Ownership: Wayne County.

Teasdale & Torrey—K39IV-D, Ch. 39, Wayne County. Phone: 435-836-2765.

Technical Facilities: 0.018-kw ERP, 20-ft. above ground, 8475-ft. above sea level, lat. 38° 16' 59.8", long. 111° 30' 36.2".

Ownership: Wayne County.

Teasdale & Torrey—K43KI-D, Ch. 43, Wayne County. Phone: 435-836-2765.

Technical Facilities: 0.018-kw ERP, 20-ft. above ground, 8475-ft. above sea level, lat. 38° 16' 59.8", long. 111° 30' 36.2".

Ownership: Wayne County.

Teasdale, etc.—K36DL, Ch. 36, Wayne County.

Technical Facilities: 1.99-kw ERP, 30-ft. above ground, 8494-ft. above sea level, lat. 38° 17' 00", long. 111° 30' 37".

Teasdale, etc.—K53JG-D, Ch. 53, Wayne County. Phone: 435-836-2765.

Technical Facilities: 0.018-kw ERP, 20-ft. above ground, 8475-ft. above sea level, lat. 38° 16' 59.8", long. 111° 30' 36.2".

Ownership: Wayne County.

Ticaboo—K02ON, Ch. 2, Garfield County.

Technical Facilities: 0.006-kw ERP, 23-ft. above ground, 7073-ft. above sea level, lat. 37° 51' 31", long. 110° 42' 06".

Ownership: Garfield County.

Ticaboo—K04OJ, Ch. 4, Garfield County.

Technical Facilities: 0.008-kw ERP, 23-ft. above ground, 7073-ft. above sea level, lat. 37° 51' 31", long. 110° 42' 06".

Ownership: Garfield County.

Ticaboo—K05JS, Ch. 5, Garfield County.

Technical Facilities: 0.008-kw ERP, 23-ft. above ground, 7073-ft. above sea level, lat. 37° 51' 31", long. 110° 42' 06".

Ownership: Garfield County.

Ticaboo—K07VE, Ch. 7, Garfield County.

Technical Facilities: 0.016-kw ERP, 23-ft. above ground, 7073-ft. above sea level, lat. 37° 51' 31", long. 110° 42' 06".

Ticaboo—K09XT, Ch. 9, U. of Utah. Phone: 801-585-3601.

Technical Facilities: 0.08-kw ERP, 26-ft. above ground, 6906-ft. above sea level, lat. 37° 51' 31", long. 110° 42' 41".

Ownership: U. of Utah.

Tooele—K22DE, Ch. 22, Community Television of Utah License LLC. Phone: 859-448-2700.

Technical Facilities: 3.02-kw ERP, 26-ft. above ground, 8996-ft. above sea level, lat. 40° 39' 33", long. 112° 12' 08".

Ownership: Local TV Holdings LLC.

Tooele—K20ER, Ch. 63, Utah State Board of Regents. Phone: 801-585-3601. Fax: 801-581-3576.

Studio: 101 Wasatch Dr., Rm 215, Salt Lake City, UT 84112.

Technical Facilities: 1.13-kw ERP, 30-ft. above ground, 8999-ft. above sea level, lat. 40° 39' 33", long. 112° 12' 08".

Ownership: U. of Utah.

Personnel: Larry Smith, General Manager; Phil Titus, Chief Engineer.

Tooele—K65HO, Ch. 65, U. of Utah. Phone: 801-585-3601. Fax: 801-581-3576.

Studio: 101 S Wasatch Dr., Room 215, Salt Lake City, UT 84112.

Technical Facilities: 1.13-kw ERP, 30-ft. above ground, 8999-ft. above sea level, lat. 40° 39' 33", long. 112° 12' 08".

Transmitter: 19-mi. NE of Tooele.

Ownership: U. of Utah.

Personnel: Fred Esplin, General Manager; Phil Titus, Chief Engineer.

Tooele & Grantsville—K52GL, Ch. 52, Brigham Young U.

Technical Facilities: 1.23-kw ERP, 40-ft. above ground, 9006-ft. above sea level, lat. 40° 39' 33", long. 112° 12' 08".

Transmitter: Farnsworth Peak.

Toquerville—K03AL, Ch. 3, SLC TV Licensee Corp. Phone: 212-891-2100.

Technical Facilities: 0.004-kw ERP, lat. 37° 16' 21", long. 113° 16' 34".

Ownership: Four Points Media Group Holding LLC.

Toquerville—K05CP, Ch. 5, U. of Utah.

Technical Facilities: 0.004-kw ERP, lat. 37° 16' 21", long. 113° 16' 34".

Ownership: U. of Utah.

Toquerville—K07CG-D, Ch. 7, Bonneville Holding Co. Phone: 801-575-7517.

Technical Facilities: 0.031-kw ERP, 36-ft. above ground, 5226-ft. above sea level, lat. 37° 16' 21", long. 113° 16' 34".

Ownership: Bonneville International Corp.

Toquerville—K09KP, Ch. 9, CCR-St. George IV LLC. Phone: 303-468-6500.

Technical Facilities: 0.109-kw ERP, lat. 37° 17' 22", long. 113° 16' 30".

Ownership: Cherry Creek Radio LLC.

Toquerville—K19HR-D, Ch. 19, U. of Utah. Phone: 801-585-3601.

Technical Facilities: 0.004-kw ERP, 26-ft. above ground, 5236-ft. above sea level, lat. 37° 17' 23.5", long. 113° 16' 31.7".

Began Operation: December 2, 2008.

Ownership: U. of Utah.

Toquerville—K31IS-D, Ch. 31, Newport Television License LLC. Phone: 816-751-0204.

Technical Facilities: 0.22-kw ERP, 62-ft. above ground, 5266-ft. above sea level, lat. 37° 17' 22", long. 113° 16' 34".

Ownership: Newport Television LLC.

Toquerville & Leeds—K23FQ, Ch. 23, Brigham Young U. Phone: 801-422-8423.

Technical Facilities: 2.57-kw ERP, 59-ft. above ground, 5262-ft. above sea level, lat. 37° 17' 22", long. 113° 16' 34".

Ownership: Brigham Young U.

Torrey—K40AH, Ch. 40, U. of Utah.

Technical Facilities: 0.79-kw ERP, lat. 38° 16' 42", long. 111° 30' 34".

Torrey—K55KG-D, Ch. 55, U. of Utah. Phone: 801-585-3601.

Technical Facilities: 0.014-kw ERP, 20-ft. above ground, 8475-ft. above sea level, lat. 38° 16' 59.8", long. 111° 30' 36.2".

Ownership: U. of Utah.

Tropic & Cannonville—K02IF, Ch. 2, Garfield County. Phone: 435-676-8826.

Technical Facilities: 0.06-kw ERP, lat. 37° 42' 46", long. 112° 04' 37".

Ownership: Garfield County.

Tropic & Cannonville—K04IN, Ch. 4, Garfield County. Phone: 435-676-8826.

Technical Facilities: 0.06-kw ERP, lat. 37° 42' 46", long. 112° 04' 37".

Ownership: Garfield County.

Tropic & Cannonville—K05FY, Ch. 5, Garfield County. Phone: 435-676-8826.

Technical Facilities: 0.06-kw ERP, lat. 37° 42' 46", long. 112° 04' 37".

Ownership: Garfield County.

Tropic & Cannonville—K24HL-D, Ch. 24, Garfield County. Phone: 435-676-8826.

Technical Facilities: 0.01-kw ERP, 12-ft. above ground, 8286-ft. above sea level, lat. 37° 42' 40.9", long. 112° 04' 39.4".

Ownership: Garfield County.

Tropic & Cannonville—K27ID, Ch. 27, Garfield County. Phone: 435-676-8826.

Technical Facilities: 0.6-kw ERP, 30-ft. above ground, 8300-ft. above sea level, lat. 37° 42' 41", long. 112° 04' 39".

Ownership: Garfield County.

Tropic & Cannonville—K29GJ, Ch. 29, Garfield County. Phone: 435-676-8826.

Technical Facilities: 0.6-kw ERP, 16-ft. above ground, 8291-ft. above sea level, lat. 37° 42' 41", long. 112° 04' 39".

Ownership: Garfield County.

Tropic & Cannonville—K33HX, Ch. 33, Garfield County. Phone: 435-676-8826.

Technical Facilities: 0.6-kw ERP, 16-ft. above ground, 8291-ft. above sea level, lat. 37° 42' 41", long. 112° 04' 39".

Ownership: Garfield County.

Tropic, etc.—K19GQ-D, Ch. 19, Garfield County. Phone: 435-676-8826.

Technical Facilities: 0.01-kw ERP, 12-ft. above ground, 8286-ft. above sea level, lat. 37° 42' 40.9", long. 112° 04' 39.4".

Ownership: Garfield County.

Tropic, etc.—K21II-D, Ch. 21, Garfield County. Phone: 435-676-8826.

Technical Facilities: 0.01-kw ERP, 12-ft. above ground, 8286-ft. above sea level, lat. 37° 42' 40.9", long. 112° 04' 39.4".

Ownership: Garfield County.

Tropic, etc.—K31EL, Ch. 31, U. of Utah.

Technical Facilities: 0.694-kw ERP, lat. 37° 42' 46", long. 112° 04' 37".

Transmitter: 6.5-mi. N of Tropic.

Tropic/Cannonville—K17HV-D, Ch. 17, Garfield County. Phone: 435-676-8826.

Technical Facilities: 0.01-kw ERP, 12-ft. above ground, 8286-ft. above sea level, lat. 37° 42' 40.9", long. 112° 04' 39.4".

Ownership: Garfield County.

Uintah County (rural)—K16DA, Ch. 16, U. of Utah.

Technical Facilities: 0.316-kw ERP, 59-ft. above ground, 9380-ft. above sea level, lat. 40° 44' 20", long. 109° 28' 58".

Utahn—K07VL, Ch. 7, Duchesne County.

Technical Facilities: 0.007-kw ERP, 30-ft. above ground, 6030-ft. above sea level, lat. 40° 16' 12", long. 110° 24' 45".

Utahn—K09VZ, Ch. 9, Duchesne County.

Technical Facilities: 0.007-kw ERP, 30-ft. above ground, 6030-ft. above sea level, lat. 40° 16' 12", long. 110° 24' 45".

Utahn—K11TL, Ch. 11, Duchesne County.

Technical Facilities: 0.006-kw ERP, 30-ft. above ground, 6030-ft. above sea level, lat. 40° 16' 12", long. 110° 24' 45".

Vernal—K15DI, Ch. 15, Larry H. Miller Communications Corp. Phone: 801-537-1414.

Technical Facilities: 1.32-kw ERP, 26-ft. above ground, 8189-ft. above sea level, lat. 40° 22' 02", long. 109° 07' 49".

Began Operation: March 28, 1994.

Ownership: Larry H. Miller Communications Corp.

Vernal—K39AK, Ch. 39, Trinity Broadcasting Network Inc. Phone: 714-832-2950. Fax: 714-731-0661.

Technical Facilities: 100-w TPO, 1.3-kw ERP, 23-ft. above ground, 8022-ft. above sea level, lat. 40° 21' 01", long. 109° 09' 49".

Transmitter: Blue Mountain Plateau, near Red-wash.

Ownership: Trinity Broadcasting Network Inc.

Personnel: Paul Crouch, General Manager; Ben Miller, Chief Engineer; Rod Henke, Sales Manager.

Vernal, etc.—K07CY, Ch. 7, Uintah County. Phone: 435-781-5361.

Technical Facilities: 0.167-kw ERP, lat. 40° 21' 01", long. 109° 09' 49".

Vernal, etc.—K09CY, Ch. 9, Uintah County. Phone: 435-781-5361.

Technical Facilities: 0.167-kw ERP, lat. 40° 21' 01", long. 109° 09' 49".

Ownership: Uintah County.

Vernal, etc.—K11DF, Ch. 11, Uintah County. Phone: 435-781-5361.

Technical Facilities: 0.167-kw ERP, lat. 40° 21' 01", long. 109° 09' 49".

Ownership: Uintah County.

Vernal, etc.—K13HF, Ch. 13, Uintah County. Phone: 435-781-5361.

Technical Facilities: 0.167-kw ERP, lat. 40° 21' 01", long. 109° 09' 49".

Ownership: Uintah County.

Vernal, etc.—K33DO, Ch. 33, U. of Utah. Phone: 801-585-3601.

Technical Facilities: 1.7-kw ERP, 26-ft. above ground, 8025-ft. above sea level, lat. 40° 21' 01", long. 109° 09' 49".

Holds CP for change to 0.49-kw ERP, 39-ft. above ground, 8071-ft. above sea level, lat. 40° 21' 03.3", long. 109° 09' 45.1". BPTT-20020403ABB.

Vernal, etc.—K49AT, Ch. 49, Uintah County.

Technical Facilities: 1.89-kw ERP, 8031-ft. above sea level, lat. 40° 21' 01", long. 109° 09' 49".

Vernal, etc.—K51AO, Ch. 51, Uintah County.

Technical Facilities: 1.89-kw ERP, 8031-ft. above sea level, lat. 40° 21' 01", long. 109° 09' 49".

Virgin—K02AW, Ch. 2, SLC TV Licensee Corp. Phone: 212-891-2100.

Technical Facilities: 0.97-kw ERP, lat. 37° 13' 24", long. 113° 12' 40".

Ownership: Four Points Media Group Holding LLC.

Virgin—K08BO-D, Ch. 8, Bonneville Holding Co. Phone: 801-575-7517.

Technical Facilities: 0.047-kw ERP, 13-ft. above ground, 5016-ft. above sea level, lat. 37° 13' 53.7", long. 113° 12' 31.3".

Ownership: Bonneville International Corp.

Virgin—K11OP, Ch. 11, CCR-St. George IV LLC.

Technical Facilities: 0.105-kw ERP, 5013-ft. above sea level, lat. 37° 13' 24", long. 113° 12' 40".

Holds CP for change to 0.3-kw ERP, 98-ft. above ground, 4295-ft. above sea level, BDFCDVA-20060630AGT.

Ownership: Cherry Creek Radio LLC.

Virgin—K13QK, Ch. 13, Newport Television License LLC. Phone: 816-751-0204. Fax: 918-664-4581.

Technical Facilities: 0.01-kw ERP, 26-ft. above sea level, lat. 37° 13' 24", long. 113° 12' 40".

Ownership: Newport Television LLC.

Virgin—K15FN, Ch. 15, Washington County Television Dept.

**Technical Facilities: 0.105-kw ERP, lat. 37° 13' 24", long. 113° 12' 40".

Virgin—K17FG, Ch. 17, Washington County Television Dept.

Technical Facilities: 0.01-kw ERP, lat. 37° 13' 24", long. 113° 12' 40".

Virgin—K22IP-D, Ch. 22, U. of Utah. Phone: 801-585-3601.

Technical Facilities: 0.125-kw ERP, 13-ft. above ground, 5016-ft. above sea level, lat. 37° 13' 53.7", long. 113° 12' 31.3".

Began Operation: December 2, 2008.

Ownership: U. of Utah.

Virgin—K25HB, Ch. 25, U. of Utah. Phone: 801-585-3601.

Technical Facilities: 0.54-kw ERP, 22-ft. above ground, 5072-ft. above sea level, lat. 37° 13' 45", long. 113° 13' 45".

Ownership: U. of Utah.

Virgin—K29GY, Ch. 29, Brigham Young U. Phone: 801-422-8450.

Technical Facilities: 0.423-kw ERP, 22-ft. above ground, 5094-ft. above sea level, lat. 37° 13' 45", long. 113° 13' 45".

Began Operation: July 11, 1980.

Ownership: Brigham Young U.

Wanship—K06JH, Ch. 6, Summit County.

Technical Facilities: 0.013-kw ERP, lat. 40° 48' 31", long. 111° 23' 41".

Wanship—K08JE, Ch. 8, Summit County.

Technical Facilities: 0.012-kw ERP, lat. 40° 48' 31", long. 111° 23' 41".

Wanship—K10KO, Ch. 10, Summit County. Phone: 435-336-3220.

Technical Facilities: 0.045-kw ERP, lat. 40° 48' 31", long. 111° 23' 41".

Wanship—K12LC, Ch. 12, Summit County.

Technical Facilities: 0.012-kw ERP, lat. 40° 48' 31", long. 111° 23' 41".

Wanship—K27GE, Ch. 27, Summit County. Phone: 435-336-3220.

Technical Facilities: 0.083-kw ERP, lat. 40° 48' 31", long. 111° 23' 41".

Transmitter: 0.75-mi. E of Wanship.

Wanship—K31HG, Ch. 31, Summit County. Phone: 435-336-3220.

Technical Facilities: 0.26-kw ERP, 10-ft. above ground, 5968-ft. above sea level, lat. 40° 48' 31", long. 111° 23' 41".

Ownership: Summit County.

Wanship—K33HQ, Ch. 33, Summit County. Phone: 435-336-3220.

Technical Facilities: 0.26-kw ERP, 10-ft. above ground, 5968-ft. above sea level, lat. 40° 48' 31", long. 111° 23' 41".

Ownership: Summit County.

Washington—K52KG-D, Ch. 52, Newport Television LLC. Phone: 401-751-1700.

Technical Facilities: 0.25-kw ERP, 39-ft. above ground, 7716-ft. above sea level, lat. 37° 09' 15", long. 113° 53' 00".

Ownership: Newport Television LLC.

Washington, etc.—K44JI-D, Ch. 44, U. of Utah. Phone: 801-585-3601.

Technical Facilities: 0.01-kw ERP, 46-ft. above ground, 7792-ft. above sea level, lat. 37° 09' 18.8", long. 113° 52' 56.7".

Began Operation: December 2, 2008.

Ownership: U. of Utah.

Washington, etc.—K47AK, Ch. 47, U. of Utah.

Technical Facilities: 1.28-kw ERP, 43-ft. above ground, 7723-ft. above sea level, lat. 37° 09' 19", long. 113° 52' 57".

Washington, etc.—K50KC-D, Ch. 50, U. of Utah. Phone: 801-585-3601.

Technical Facilities: 0.25-kw ERP, 39-ft. above ground, 7766-ft. above sea level, lat. 37° 09' 18.9", long. 113° 52' 56.4".

Began Operation: December 2, 2008.

Ownership: U. of Utah.

Washington, etc.—K51GH, Ch. 51, U. of Utah.

Technical Facilities: 2.75-kw ERP, lat. 37° 09' 15", long. 113° 53' 00".

Wayne County—K41JZ-D, Ch. 41, Wayne County. Phone: 435-836-2765.

Technical Facilities: 0.032-kw ERP, 20-ft. above ground, 8475-ft. above sea level, lat. 38° 16' 59.8", long. 111° 30' 36.2".

Ownership: Wayne County.

Wayne County (rural)—K43IJ, Ch. 43, Sevier County. Phone: 435-896-9262.

Technical Facilities: 0.007-kw ERP, 23-ft. above ground, 9107-ft. above sea level, lat. 38° 30' 44", long. 111° 47' 01".

Ownership: Sevier County.

Wendover—K08EI, Ch. 8, Wendover City.

Technical Facilities: 0.016-kw ERP, lat. 40° 44' 31", long. 114° 02' 06".

Wendover—K10ES, Ch. 10, Wendover City.

Technical Facilities: 0.016-kw ERP, lat. 40° 44' 31", long. 114° 02' 06".

Wendover—K12EB, Ch. 12, Wendover City.

Technical Facilities: 0.016-kw ERP, lat. 40° 44' 31", long. 114° 02' 06".

Wendover—K15GZ, Ch. 15, Wendover City. Phone: 435-665-2523.

Technical Facilities: 0.133-kw ERP, 10-ft. above ground, 4803-ft. above sea level, lat. 40° 44' 31", long. 114° 02' 06".

Ownership: Wendover City.

Wendover—K17HM, Ch. 17, Community Television of Utah License LLC. Phone: 859-448-2700.

Technical Facilities: 0.133-kw ERP, 10-ft. above ground, 4803-ft. above sea level, lat. 40° 44' 31", long. 114° 02' 06".

Ownership: Local TV Holdings LLC.

Woodland—K32EJ, Ch. 32, Larry H. Miller Communications Corp. Phone: 801-537-1414.

Technical Facilities: 0.45-kw ERP, 19-ft. above ground, 7578-ft. above sea level, lat. 40° 33' 59", long. 111° 14' 31".

Began Operation: September 9, 1996.

Ownership: Larry H. Miller Communications Corp.

Woodland—K44FY, Ch. 44, Larry H. Miller Communications Corp.

Technical Facilities: 0.03-kw ERP, lat. 40° 33' 27", long. 111° 14' 47".

Transmitter: 0.6-mi. SSW of Woodland.

Woodland—K46CT, Ch. 46, Summit County.

Technical Facilities: 3.48-kw ERP, 16-ft. above ground, 7598-ft. above sea level, lat. 40° 34' 00", long. 111° 14' 30".

Woodland & Kamas—K23HS, Ch. 23, Summit County. Phone: 435-336-3220.

Technical Facilities: 0.45-kw ERP, 19-ft. above ground, 7578-ft. above sea level, lat. 40° 33' 59", long. 111° 14' 31".

Ownership: Summit County.

Woodland & Kamas—K26GI, Ch. 26, Summit County. Phone: 435-336-3220.

Technical Facilities: 0.45-kw ERP, 19-ft. above ground, 7579-ft. above sea level, lat. 40° 33' 59", long. 111° 14' 31".

Woodland & Kamas—K42FA, Ch. 42, Summit County. Phone: 435-336-3220.

Technical Facilities: 0.45-kw ERP, 19-ft. above ground, 7579-ft. above sea level, lat. 40° 33' 59", long. 111° 14' 31".

Woodland & Kamas—K48AE, Ch. 48, Summit County.

Technical Facilities: 0.883-kw ERP, 7516-ft. above sea level, lat. 40° 34' 00", long. 111° 14' 30".

Woodland & Kamas—K50AC, Ch. 50, Summit County.

Technical Facilities: 0.883-kw ERP, 7516-ft. above sea level, lat. 40° 34' 00", long. 111° 14' 30".

Vermont

Barre—W54CV, Ch. 54, Convergence Entertainment & Communications LLC. Phone: 518-825-1071.

Technical Facilities: 10-w TPO, 0.06-kw ERP, 1926-ft. above sea level, lat. 44° 10' 35", long. 72° 26' 39".

Transmitter: N side of U.S. Rte. 302, 1.2-mi. NE of East Barre.

Began Operation: August 3, 1999.

Ownership: Convergence Entertainment & Communications LLC.

Personnel: Charlie Kail, General Manager; James Driscoll, Chief Engineer; Paul Hatin, Sales Manager.

Bennington, etc.—W21CQ, Ch. 21, D.T.V. LLC. Phone: 800-536-7327.

Technical Facilities: 50-kw ERP, 131-ft. above ground, 1546-ft. above sea level, lat. 43° 01' 13", long. 73° 31' 29".

Ownership: D.T.V. LLC.

Burlington—W16AL, Ch. 16, Trinity Broadcasting Network Inc. Phone: 714-832-2950. Fax: 714-730-0661.

Technical Facilities: 970-w TPO, 43.2-kw ERP, 26-ft. above ground, 2077-ft. above sea level, lat. 41° 21' 52", long. 72° 55' 53".

Holds CP for change to 12.8-kw ERP, BDFCDTT-20060313AAM.

Began Operation: July 20, 1994.

Ownership: Trinity Broadcasting Network Inc.

Burlington—W51CB, Ch. 51, Deepak Viswanath. Phone: 908-246-3636. Fax: 908-246-8380.

Technical Facilities: 1000-w TPO, 43-kw ERP, 535-ft. above sea level, lat. 44° 30' 35", long. 73° 11' 05".

Transmitter: U.S. Hwy. 7, N of Winooski.

Ownership: Deepak Viswanath.

Personnel: Deepak Viswanath, General Manager.

■ **Burlington**—WBVT-CA, Ch. 30, Convergence Entertainment & Communications LLC. Phone: 518-825-1071.

Technical Facilities: 118-w TPO, 0.065-kw ERP, 39-ft. above ground, 715-ft. above sea level, lat. 44° 27' 02", long. 72° 58' 37".

Transmitter: Approx. 10-mi. E of State Rte. 117 & 6.6-mi. S of Jericho Center.

Began Operation: August 9, 1999.

Ownership: Convergence Entertainment & Communications LLC.

Personnel: Charlie Kail, General Manager; James Driscoll, Chief Engineer; Paul Hatin, Sales Manager.

■ **Burlington**—WGMU-CA, Ch. 39, Convergence Entertainment & Communications LLC. Phone: 518-825-1071.

Technical Facilities: 60-kw ERP, 325-ft. above ground, 755-ft. above sea level, lat. 44° 18' 46", long. 73° 11' 10".

Multichannel TV Sound: Separate audio program.

Began Operation: June 20, 1994.

Ownership: Convergence Entertainment & Communications LLC.

Personnel: Charlie Kail, General Manager; James Driscoll, Chief Engineer; Paul Hatin, Sales Manager.

Killington—W18AE, Ch. 18, Killington Ltd.

Technical Facilities: 1.2-kw ERP, 39-ft. above ground, 4275-ft. above sea level, lat. 43° 36' 17", long. 72° 49' 14".

Ownership: Killington Ltd.

■ **Manchester**—WVBK-CA, Ch. 2, Vision 3 Broadcasting Inc. Phone: 802-258-2200.

Technical Facilities: 0.004-kw ERP, 20-ft. above ground, 1939-ft. above sea level, lat. 43° 12' 46", long. 72° 56' 03".

Ownership: Vision 3 Broadcasting Inc.

Manchester, etc.—W36AX, Ch. 36, Vermont ETV Inc. Phone: 802-655-4800.

Technical Facilities: 0.167-kw ERP, 90-ft. above ground, 840-ft. above sea level, lat. 43° 10' 18", long. 73° 02' 08".

Ownership: Vermont ETV Inc.

■ **Monkton**—W19BR, Ch. 19, Convergence Entertainment & Communications LLC. Phone: 518-825-1071.

Technical Facilities: 63.8-kw ERP, 325-ft. above ground, 755-ft. above sea level, lat. 44° 18' 46", long. 73° 11' 10".

Began Operation: August 11, 1999.

Ownership: Convergence Entertainment & Communications LLC.

Monkton—W25BT, Ch. 25, Mountain Lake Public Telecommunications Council. Phone: 518-563-9770.

Technical Facilities: 8.53-kw ERP, 154-ft. above ground, 1365-ft. above sea level, lat. 44° 13' 24", long. 73° 07' 27".

Holds CP for change to 0.369-kw ERP, 154-ft. above ground, 1354-ft. above sea level, BDFCDTT-20060331AFO.

Began Operation: August 27, 1993.

Ownership: Mountain Lake Public Telecommunications Council.

■ **Newport**—W14CK, Ch. 14, SMC Communications Inc. Phone: 518-297-2727. Fax: 518-297-3377.

Technical Facilities: 11.5-kw ERP, 75-ft. above ground, 3933-ft. above sea level, lat. 42° 55' 27", long. 72° 31' 34".

Transmitter: Jay Peak, Jay State Forest, Jay.

Ownership: Susan Clarke.

Newport—W36CP, Ch. 36, Convergence Entertainment & Communications LLC. Phone: 518-825-1071.

Technical Facilities: 0.048-kw ERP, 39-ft. above ground, 1122-ft. above sea level, lat. 44° 32' 02", long. 72° 01' 45".

Began Operation: May 9, 2003.

Ownership: Convergence Entertainment & Communications LLC.

Pownal, etc.—W53AS, Ch. 53, Vermont ETV Inc.

Technical Facilities: 1.8-kw ERP, 46-ft. above ground, 2346-ft. above sea level, lat. 42° 51' 47", long. 73° 13' 56".

Rutland—W61CE, Ch. 61, Convergence Entertainment & Communications LLC. Phone: 518-825-1071.

Technical Facilities: 10-kw ERP, 249-ft. above ground, 2224-ft. above sea level, lat. 43° 39' 31", long. 73° 06' 24".

Holds CP for change to channel number 35, 20-kw ERP, BDISTTL-20060105ABE.

Began Operation: July 15, 1999.

Ownership: Convergence Entertainment & Communications LLC.

Rutland—W63AD, Ch. 63, Lambert Broadcasting of Burlington LLC. Phone: 310-385-4200.

Technical Facilities: 4.46-kw ERP, lat. 43° 38' 23", long. 72° 50' 10".

Ownership: Michael Lambert.

Rutland—W69AR, Ch. 69, Mount Mansfield Television Inc. Phone: 802-652-6300.

Technical Facilities: 0.105-kw ERP, lat. 43° 34' 04", long. 73° 00' 32".

Holds CP for change to channel number 20, 0.69-kw ERP, 188-ft. above ground, 1478-ft. above sea level, BDFCDTT-20070906ADI.

Ownership: Mount Mansfield Television Inc.

St. Albans—W52CD, Ch. 52, Convergence Entertainment & Communications LLC. Phone: 518-825-1071.

Technical Facilities: 1000-w TPO, 46.1-kw ERP, 69-ft. above ground, 1318-ft. above sea level, lat. 44° 47' 00", long. 73° 03' 49".

Transmitter: Bellevue Hill, near St. Albans.

Began Operation: August 4, 1997.

Ownership: Convergence Entertainment & Communications LLC.

White River Junction—W27CP, Ch. 27, University System of New Hampshire Board of Trustees. Phone: 603-868-1100.

Technical Facilities: 24.4-kw ERP, 75-ft. above ground, 1657-ft. above sea level, lat. 43° 39' 33", long. 72° 11' 10".

Began Operation: October 21, 2004.

Ownership: University System of New Hampshire Board of Trustees.

White River Junction—W65AM, Ch. 65, Hearst-Argyle Stations Inc. Phone: 919-839-0300.

Technical Facilities: 1.1-kw ERP, lat. 43° 39' 14", long. 72° 17' 43".

Transmitter: 1-mi. ENE of West Lebanon, NH.

Began Operation: September 28, 1979.

Ownership: Hearst-Argyle Television Inc.

Windsor—W21CN, Ch. 21, Three Angels Broadcasting Network Inc. Phone: 618-627-4651. Fax: 618-627-4155.

Technical Facilities: 6.65-kw ERP, 85-ft. above ground, 3225-ft. above sea level, lat. 43° 26' 38", long. 72° 27' 17".

Ownership: Three Angels Broadcasting Network Inc.

Virginia

■ **Abingdon**—WAPW-CA, Ch. 60, Holston Valley Broadcasting Corp.

Technical Facilities: 0.1-kw ERP, lat. 36° 49' 15", long. 82° 04' 40".

Ownership: Holston Valley Broadcasting Corp.

Appomattox—W04CI, Ch. 4, Gethsemane Baptist Church. Phone: 434-845-8796.

Technical Facilities: 0.062-kw ERP, 33-ft. above ground, 1444-ft. above sea level, lat. 37° 17' 10", long. 78° 50' 30".

Began Operation: November 5, 1990.

Ownership: Gethsemane Baptist Church.

Bergton & Criders—W07BL, Ch. 7, County of Rockingham.

Technical Facilities: 0.07-kw ERP, 2890-ft. above sea level, lat. 38° 43' 32", long. 79° 00' 32".

Bergton & Criders—W11AZ, Ch. 11, County of Rockingham.

Technical Facilities: 0.07-kw ERP, 38° 43' 32", long. 79° 00' 32".

Bergton & Criders—W13BB, Ch. 13, County of Rockingham.

Technical Facilities: 0.11-kw ERP, lat. 38° 43' 32", long. 79° 00' 32".

Bridgewater et al.—W31CE, Ch. 31, Virginia Broadcasting Corp.

Technical Facilities: 27-kw ERP, 49-ft. above ground, 4370-ft. above sea level, lat. 38° 09' 56", long. 79° 18' 47".

Ownership: Waterman Broadcasting Corp.

Castlewood—W57AI, Ch. 57, Russell County Board of Supervisors.

Technical Facilities: 0.975-kw ERP, lat. 36° 56' 23", long. 82° 13' 55".

Castlewood—W58CY, Ch. 58, Russell County Board of Supervisors.

Technical Facilities: 0.971-kw ERP, lat. 36° 56' 23", long. 82° 13' 55".

Charlottesville—W14CY, Ch. 14, Core Group International Inc. Phone: 202-296-4800.

Technical Facilities: 15-kw ERP, 35-ft. above ground, 3874-ft. above sea level, lat. 38° 03' 43.9", long. 78° 24' 58".

Ownership: Core Group International Inc.

Charlottesville—W50CM, Ch. 50, Shenandoah Valley Educational TV Corp. Phone: 540-434-5391.

Technical Facilities: 36.6-kw ERP, 215-ft. above ground, 1617-ft. above sea level, lat. 37° 59' 00", long. 78° 29' 02".

Ownership: Shenandoah Valley Educational TV Corp.

■ **Charlottesville**—WAHU-CA, Ch. 27, Gray Television Licensee LLC.

Technical Facilities: 50-kw ERP, 197-ft. above ground, 1895-ft. above sea level, lat. 37° 58' 59", long. 78° 29' 02".

Ownership: Gray Television Inc.

Personnel: Paul Van Vleet, Director of Programming & Traffic Manager.

Charlottesville—WAHU-LD, Ch. 40, Gray TV Licensee Inc. Phone: 434-242-1919.

Technical Facilities: 15-kw ERP, 135-ft. above ground, 1590-ft. above sea level, lat. 37° 59' 03", long. 78° 28' 52".

Began Operation: August 17, 2007.

Ownership: Gray Television Inc.

Charlottesville—WIVC-LP, Ch. 13, Hosanna Apostolic Ministries Broadcasting Corp. Phone: 520-971-9274.

Technical Facilities: 1-kw ERP, 16-ft. above ground, 620-ft. above sea level, lat. 38° 16' 30", long. 78° 27' 37".

Began Operation: May 4, 2007.

Ownership: Hosanna Apostolic Ministries Broadcasting Corp.

Charlottesville—WVAW-LD, Ch. 16, Gray Television Licensee LLC. Phone: 434-242-1919.

Technical Facilities: 15-kw ERP, 135-ft. above ground, 1590-ft. above sea level, lat. 37° 59' 03", long. 78° 28' 52".

Began Operation: October 15, 1980.

Ownership: Gray Television Inc.

Personnel: Paul Van Vleet, Director of Programming & Traffic Manager.

■ **Chesapeake**—W25CS, Ch. 25, Word of God Fellowship Inc. Phone: 817-571-1229.

Technical Facilities: 1000-w TPO, 20-kw ERP, 338-ft. above ground, 348-ft. above sea level, lat. 36° 48' 39", long. 76° 16' 56".

Transmitter: Poindexter St. & I-464.

Ownership: Word of God Fellowship Inc.

■ **Chesapeake**—WITD-CA, Ch. 23, WAVY Broadcasting LLC. Phone: 202-462-6065.

Technical Facilities: 70-kw ERP, 636-ft. above ground, 659-ft. above sea level, lat. 36° 49' 14", long. 76° 30' 41".

Holds CP for change to 0.32-kw ERP, BDFCDTA-20060330AER.

Ownership: LIN TV Corp.

Personnel: Doug Davis, President & General Manager; Les Garrenton, Chief Engineer; John Cochran, General Sales Manager.

■ **Chesapeake**—WJGN-CA, Ch. 5, The Union Mission. Phone: 757-430-2313.

Technical Facilities: 1000-w TPO, 3-kw ERP, 351-ft. above ground, 361-ft. above sea level, lat. 36° 51' 39", long. 76° 21' 13".

Transmitter: 2221 Salem Rd., Virginia Beach.

Ownership: The Union Mission.

Concord—W33AD, Ch. 33, Gethsemane Baptist Church. Phone: 434-845-8796.

Technical Facilities: 100-w TPO, 1.134-kw ERP, 120-ft. above ground, 1000-ft. above sea level, lat. 37° 20' 30", long. 78° 59' 17".

Began Operation: November 8, 1982.

Ownership: Gethsemane Baptist Church.

Craddockville—W20CW, Ch. 20, County of Accomack. Phone: 757-787-5700.

Technical Facilities: 2.12-kw ERP, lat. 37° 36' 11", long. 75° 50' 33".

Holds CP for change to 5.5-kw ERP, 296-ft. above ground, 328-ft. above sea level, BDISTT-20071130ASA.

Ownership: County of Accomack.

Craddockville—W22DN, Ch. 22, County of Accomack. Phone: 757-787-5700.

Technical Facilities: 2.11-kw ERP, lat. 37° 36' 11", long. 75° 50' 33".

Holds CP for change to 5.5-kw ERP, 296-ft. above ground, 328-ft. above sea level, BDISTT-20071130ASG.

Ownership: County of Accomack.

Craddockville—W42DP, Ch. 42, County of Accomack. Phone: 757-787-5700.

Technical Facilities: 2.09-kw ERP, lat. 37° 36' 11", long. 75° 50' 33".

Holds CP for change to 5.2-kw ERP, 296-ft. above ground, 328-ft. above sea level, BDISTT-20071130AQW.

Ownership: County of Accomack.

Craddockville—W48DO, Ch. 68, County of Accomack. Phone: 757-787-5700.

Technical Facilities: 2.08-kw ERP, lat. 37° 36' 11", long. 75° 50' 33".

Holds CP for change to channel number 48, 5.2-kw ERP, 296-ft. above ground, 328-ft. above sea level, BDISTT-20071130AQL.

Ownership: County of Accomack.

Danville—W18BG, Ch. 18, Star News Corp. Phone: 276-656-3900.

Technical Facilities: 2-kw ERP, 200-ft. above ground, 1289-ft. above sea level, lat. 36° 44' 30", long. 79° 23' 06".

Holds CP for change to channel number 23, 9-kw ERP, 200-ft. above ground, 1290-ft. above sea level, lat. 36° 44' 30", long. 79° 23' 07". BDISDTT-20060331BHB.

Began Operation: January 22, 1993.

Ownership: Star News Corp.

Danville—W66BI, Ch. 66, Commonwealth Public Broadcasting Corp. Phone: 804-320-1301.

Technical Facilities: 0.115-kw ERP, 308-ft. above ground, 1371-ft. above sea level, lat. 36° 44' 28", long. 79° 23' 05".

Transmitter: White Oak Mountain.

Ownership: Commonwealth Public Broadcasting Corp.

Dickinsonville—W63AK, Ch. 63, Russell County Board of Supervisors.

Technical Facilities: 0.972-kw ERP, lat. 36° 50' 57", long. 82° 11' 03".

Dickinsonville—W65AR, Ch. 65, Russell County Board of Supervisors.

Technical Facilities: 0.971-kw ERP, lat. 36° 50' 57", long. 82° 11' 03".

Fairfax—WDCN-LP, Ch. 6, Signal Above LLC. Phone: 703-761-5013.

Technical Facilities: 3-kw ERP, 250-ft. above ground, 1000-ft. above sea level, lat. 38° 53' 45", long. 77° 08' 08".

Ownership: Signal Above LLC.

Farmville—WFMA-LP, Ch. 52, Tiger Eye Broadcasting Corp. Phone: 954-431-3144.

Technical Facilities: 0.298-kw ERP, 190-ft. above ground, 581-ft. above sea level, lat. 37° 19' 23", long. 78° 23' 23".

Transmitter: Rear yard of 1537 Cumberland Rd.

Ownership: Tiger Eye Broadcasting Corp.

■ **Front Royal**—WAZF-CA, Ch. 28, JLA Media and Publications LLC. Phone: 540-598-8601.

Studio: 123 E Court St, Woodstock, VA 22664.

Technical Facilities: 1000-w TPO, 72-kw ERP, 145-ft. above ground, 863-ft. above sea level, lat. 39° 11' 12", long. 78° 09' 06".

Transmitter: 550 Fairmont Ave., Winchester.

Ownership: JLA Media and Publications LLC.

Fulks Run—W45AW, Ch. 45, Shenandoah Valley Educational TV Corp. Phone: 540-434-5391. Fax: 540-434-7084.

Technical Facilities: 1.69-kw ERP, 155-ft. above ground, 2295-ft. above sea level, lat. 38° 36' 29", long. 78° 54' 11".

Ownership: Shenandoah Valley Educational TV Corp.

Garden City, etc.—W04AG, Ch. 4, WDBJ Television Inc.

Technical Facilities: 0.008-kw ERP, 1946-ft. above sea level, lat. 37° 15' 01", long. 79° 56' 00".

Ownership: Schurz Communications Inc.

Gate City, etc.—WKIN-LP, Ch. 7, Holston Valley Broadcasting Corp. Phone: 423-246-9578. Fax: 423-247-9836.

Technical Facilities: 0.05-kw ERP, 2697-ft. above sea level, lat. 36° 38' 29", long. 82° 32' 39".

Holds CP for change to 1.3-kw ERP, 125-ft. above ground, 2405-ft. above sea level, lat. 36° 31' 37", long. 82° 35'12". BPTVL-20070208ABJ.

Ownership: Holston Valley Broadcasting Corp.

Grundy—WJDG-LP, Ch. 23, John Colson Dash. Phone: 276-979-9200.

Technical Facilities: 150-kw ERP, 180-ft. above ground, 4153-ft. above sea level, lat. 37° 01' 33", long. 81° 10' 57".

Began Operation: October 30, 1995.

Ownership: John Colson Dash.

Personnel: Dave Jordan, General Manager; Gary Street, Chief Engineer; Ron Colt, Sales Manager.

Hampton—W18BS, Ch. 18, Trinity Christian Center of Santa Ana Inc. Phone: 714-832-2950.

Technical Facilities: 20.3-kw ERP, lat. 37° 05' 07", long. 76° 25' 37".

Transmitter: Existing non-broadcast communications tower, 0.5-mi. S of Bethel Rd & Bethel Reservoir intersection.

Ownership: Trinity Broadcasting Network Inc.

Hampton—W51DO, Ch. 51, The Union Mission. Phone: 757-430-2313.

Technical Facilities: 50-kw ERP, 296-ft. above ground, 325-ft. above sea level, lat. 37° 04' 41", long. 76° 26' 47".

Transmitter: 1700 Pembroke Ave.

Ownership: The Union Mission.

Hampton—WTTD-LP, Ch. 59, WAVY Television Inc.

Technical Facilities: 7-kw ERP, 226-ft. above ground, 23-ft. above sea level, lat. 37° 01' 36", long. 76° 20' 33".

Hampton, etc.—WGBS-LP, Ch. 7, Joan & Kenneth Wright. Phone: 757-639-4768.

Technical Facilities: 2.5-kw ERP, 384-ft. above ground, 394-ft. above sea level, lat. 36° 51' 39", long. 76° 21' 13".

Holds CP for change to channel number 11, 0.3-kw ERP, BDISDVL-20081007ACA.

Began Operation: April 26, 1994.

Ownership: Joan & Kenneth Wright.

Personnel: Joan T. Wright, General Manager.

Harrisonburg—W08DY, Ch. 8, Hispanic Christian Community Network Inc. Phone: 214-897-0081.

Technical Facilities: 3-kw ERP, 164-ft. above ground, 2749-ft. above sea level, lat. 38° 31' 07", long. 79° 06' 12".

Ownership: Hispanic Christian Community Network Inc.

Harrisonburg—W28BF, Ch. 28, Virginia Broadcasting Corp.

Technical Facilities: 7.79-kw ERP, lat. 38° 23' 34", long. 78° 46' 13".

Ownership: Waterman Broadcasting Corp.

■ **Harrisonburg**—WAZH-CA, Ch. 24, JLA Media and Publications LLC. Phone: 540-598-8601.

Technical Facilities: 4.89-kw ERP, 95-ft. above ground, 3136-ft. above sea level, lat. 38° 51' 33", long. 78° 48' 19".

Transmitter: Great North Mountain Upper Electronics site, George Washington National Forest.

Ownership: JLA Media and Publications LLC.

Honaker—WAPV-LP, Ch. 51, Holston Valley Broadcasting Corp.

Technical Facilities: 1.45-kw ERP, lat. 37° 03' 08", long. 82° 02' 09".

Ownership: Holston Valley Broadcasting Corp.

Honaker—WKPH-LP, Ch. 55, Holston Valley Broadcasting Corp.

Technical Facilities: 1.4-kw ERP, lat. 37° 03' 08", long. 82° 02' 09".

Ownership: Holston Valley Broadcasting Corp.

Keysville—WERI-LP, Ch. 39, Tiger Eye Broadcasting Corp. Phone: 954-431-3144.

Technical Facilities: 100-w TPO, 0.15-kw ERP, 56-ft. above ground, 705-ft. above sea level, lat. 37° 02' 24", long. 78° 29' 02".

Transmitter: 11 King St.

Ownership: Tiger Eye Broadcasting Corp.

Keysville—WSVL-LP, Ch. 48, Tiger Eye Broadcasting Corp. Phone: 954-431-3144.

Technical Facilities: 10-w TPO, 0.15-kw ERP, 56-ft. above ground, 630-ft. above sea level, lat. 37° 00' 20", long. 78° 27' 54".

Transmitter: 5249-ft. E of State Rte. 360 on County Rd. 629.

Ownership: Tiger Eye Broadcasting Corp.

Lovingston—W70AP, Ch. 70, Commonwealth Public Broadcasting Corp. Phone: 804-320-1301.

Technical Facilities: 2.26-kw ERP, lat. 37° 47' 52", long. 78° 54' 02".

Ownership: Commonwealth Public Broadcasting Corp.

Luray—W38AV, Ch. 38, Shenandoah Valley Educational TV Corp.

Technical Facilities: 2.47-kw ERP, lat. 38° 36' 05", long. 78° 37' 57".

Luray—WAZC-LP, Ch. 16, JLA Media and Publications LLC. Phone: 540-598-8601.

Technical Facilities: 2.1-kw ERP, lat. 38° 38' 27", long. 78° 36' 51".

Holds CP for change to channel number 35, 15-kw ERP, 39-ft. above ground, 2021-ft. above sea level, BDISDTL-20060331BBM.

Ownership: JLA Media and Publications LLC.

Luray—WDWA-LP, Ch. 23, Word of God Fellowship Inc. Phone: 817-571-1229.

Technical Facilities: 132-kw ERP, 98-ft. above ground, 1066-ft. above sea level, lat. 38° 44' 27", long. 77° 50' 09".

Ownership: Word of God Fellowship Inc.

Lynchburg—W40BM, Ch. 40, Trinity Broadcasting Network Inc. Phone: 714-832-2950. Fax: 714-730-0661.

Technical Facilities: 2-kw ERP, lat. 37° 28' 15", long. 79° 22' 34".

Holds CP for change to channel number 47, 3-kw ERP, 121-ft. above ground, 2871-ft. above sea level, BDISDTT-20060330ALW.

Ownership: Trinity Broadcasting Network Inc.

Lynchburg—WDRG-LP, Ch. 2, Paul H. Passink. Phone: 804-993-3300.

Technical Facilities: 10-w TPO, 75-kw ERP, 80-ft. above ground, lat. 37° 17' 10", long. 79° 05' 30".

Transmitter: Long Mountain, Rustburg.

Ownership: Paul H. Passink.

■**Lynchburg**—WTLU-CA, Ch. 50, Liberty U. Inc. Phones: 434-582-2718; 800-332-1883. Fax: 434-582-2741.

Studio: 1971 University Blvd., Lynchburg, VA 24502-2269.

Technical Facilities: 40.6-kw ERP, 479-ft. above ground, 1810-ft. above sea level, lat. 37° 11' 51", long. 79° 21' 07".

Ownership: Liberty University Inc.

Personnel: Sandra Wagner, General Manager; Milt Ridgeway, Engineering Manager.

■**Mappsville**—WPMC-CA, Ch. 36, WAVY Broadcasting LLC. Phone: 202-462-6065.

Technical Facilities: 1000-w TPO, 15.2-kw ERP, 348-ft. above ground, 394-ft. above sea level, lat. 37° 50' 27", long. 75° 34' 21".

Transmitter: Off U.S. Rte. 13, 0.4-mi. S of Mappsville.

Ownership: LIN TV Corp.

Personnel: Doug Davis, President & General Manager; Les Garrenton, Chief Engineer; David Rogers, General Sales Manager.

Marion—W43BO, Ch. 43, Aurora License Holdings Inc. Phone: 630-789-0090.

Technical Facilities: 10.8-kw ERP, lat. 36° 54' 08", long. 81° 32' 33".

Transmitter: Walker Mountain.

Ownership: Esteem Broadcasting LLC.

Martinsville—WYAT-LP, Ch. 40, Martinsville Media Inc. Phone: 276-632-9811.

Technical Facilities: 70-kw ERP, 328-ft. above ground, 1467-ft. above sea level, lat. 36° 42' 00", long. 79° 51' 07".

Holds CP for change to 14-kw ERP, 131-ft. above ground, 1270-ft. above sea level, BPTTL-20070416AAE.

Ownership: Martinsville Media Inc.

Monterey, etc.—W08CW, Ch. 8, Shenandoah Valley Educational TV Corp.

Technical Facilities: 0.064-kw ERP, 151-ft. above ground, 4400-ft. above sea level, lat. 38° 20' 39", long. 79° 35' 47".

Norfolk—W30BV, Ch. 30, Deepak Viswanath. Phone: 718-479-9411.

Technical Facilities: 25.7-kw ERP, 394-ft. above ground, 410-ft. above sea level, lat. 36° 46' 32", long. 76° 23' 11".

Transmitter: 4001 S. Military Hwy., Norfolk.

Ownership: B. N. Viswanath.

■**Norfolk**—WNLO-CA, Ch. 45, WAVY Broadcasting LLC. Phone: 401-454-2880. Fax: 401-454-2817.

Technical Facilities: 15-kw ERP, 728-ft. above ground, 751-ft. above sea level, lat. 36° 49' 14", long. 76° 30' 41".

Ownership: LIN TV Corp.

Onancock—W25AA, Ch. 25, County of Accomack. Phone: 757-787-5700.

Technical Facilities: 19.7-kw ERP, 452-ft. above ground, 498-ft. above sea level, lat. 37° 50' 32", long. 75° 34' 17".

Ownership: County of Accomack.

Onancock—W30CI, Ch. 30, County of Accomack. Phone: 757-787-5700.

Technical Facilities: 19.4-kw ERP, 454-ft. above ground, 500-ft. above sea level, lat. 37° 50' 32", long. 75° 34' 17".

Ownership: County of Accomack.

Onancock—W34DN, Ch. 34, County of Accomack. Phone: 757-787-5700.

Technical Facilities: 19.2-kw ERP, 454-ft. above ground, 500-ft. above sea level, lat. 37° 50' 32", long. 75° 34' 17".

Ownership: County of Accomack.

Onancock—W39CS, Ch. 39, County of Accomack. Phone: 757-787-5700.

Technical Facilities: 19-kw ERP, 454-ft. above ground, 500-ft. above sea level, lat. 37° 50' 32", long. 75° 34' 17".

Ownership: County of Accomack.

■**Pennington Gap**—WMEV-LP, Ch. 4, Holston Valley Broadcasting Corp.

Technical Facilities: 0.004-kw ERP, lat. 36° 45' 00", long. 83° 01' 37".

Ownership: Holston Valley Broadcasting Corp.

Portsmouth—W14DC, Ch. 14, Ventana Television Inc. Phone: 727-872-4210.

Technical Facilities: 65.5-kw ERP, 279-ft. above ground, 288-ft. above sea level, lat. 36° 50' 40", long. 76° 18' 57".

Began Operation: December 1, 1992.

Ownership: Ventana Television Inc.

■**Portsmouth**—WKTD-CA, Ch. 17, WAVY Broadcasting LLC. Phone: 202-462-6065.

Technical Facilities: 14.35-kw ERP, 728-ft. above ground, 751-ft. above sea level, lat. 36° 49' 14", long. 76° 30' 41".

Ownership: LIN TV Corp.

Personnel: Doug Davis, President & General Manager; Les Garrenton, Director of Engineering; John Cochran, General Sales Manager.

Richmond—W39CO, Ch. 39, Trinity Christian Center of Santa Ana Inc. Phone: 714-832-2950.

Technical Facilities: 31-kw ERP, 463-ft. above ground, 692-ft. above sea level, lat. 37° 30' 52", long. 77° 30' 28".

Transmitter: German School Rd. & Wainwright Dr., approx. 0.5-mi. S of Jahnke Rd.

Ownership: Trinity Broadcasting Network Inc.

Richmond—WRID-LP, Ch. 48, Word of God Fellowship Inc. Phone: 817-858-9955. Fax: 817-571-7478.

Technical Facilities: 785-w TPO, 30-kw ERP, 453-ft. above ground, 466-ft. above sea level, lat. 37° 26' 21", long. 77° 25' 57".

Transmitter: 2001 Station Rd.

Ownership: Word of God Fellowship Inc.

■**Richmond**—WXOB-LP, Ch. 17, KM Broadcasting. Phone: 202-293-3831.

Technical Facilities: 1000-w TPO, 22.8-kw ERP, 663-ft. above ground, 682-ft. above sea level, lat. 37° 36' 52", long. 77° 30' 56".

Transmitter: 3245 Basie Rd.

Ownership: KM Broadcasting Inc.

Richmond—WZTD-LP, Ch. 45, Onda Capital Inc. Phone: 703-528-5656.

Technical Facilities: 72.6-kw ERP, 495-ft. above ground, 853-ft. above sea level, lat. 37° 30' 45", long. 77° 36' 04.9".

Holds CP for change to 15-kw ERP, lat. 37° 30' 45", long. 77° 36' 05.7". BDFCDTL-20080826ACD.

Ownership: ZGS Broadcasting Holdings Inc.

Roanoke—W05AA, Ch. 5, WSET Inc. Phone: 435-528-1313.

Technical Facilities: 0.261-kw ERP, lat. 37° 13' 56", long. 80° 02' 51".

Holds CP for change to 0.3-kw ERP, 49-ft. above ground, 1989-ft. above sea level, BDFCDTV-20090323ACK.

Ownership: Allbritton Communications Co.

Roanoke—W44CL, Ch. 44, Ventana Television Inc. Phone: 727-872-4210.

Technical Facilities: 84-kw ERP, 59-ft. above ground, 2287-ft. above sea level, lat. 37° 22' 23", long. 79° 55' 40".

Transmitter: Tinker Mountain.

Began Operation: August 7, 1992.

Ownership: Ventana Television Inc.

Roanoke—W49AP, Ch. 49, Trinity Broadcasting Network Inc. Phone: 714-832-2950. Fax: 714-730-0661.

Technical Facilities: 1000-w TPO, 36.2-kw ERP, 121-ft. above ground, 2083-ft. above sea level, lat. 37° 13' 56", long. 80° 02' 51".

Transmitter: Approx. 3-mi. W of Roanoke.

Ownership: Trinity Broadcasting Network Inc.

Personnel: Paul Crouch, General Manager; Ben Miller, Chief Engineer; Rod Henke, Sales Manager.

Roanoke—WEDD-LP, Ch. 54, Brunson/Ross Communications LLC. Phone: 410-563-1709.

Technical Facilities: 80-kw ERP, 131-ft. above ground, 3891-ft. above sea level, lat. 37° 11' 37", long. 80° 09' 25".

Holds CP for change to channel number 25, 150-kw ERP, 82-ft. above ground, 3842-ft. above sea level, lat. 37° 11' 35", long. 80° 09' 23". BDISTTL-20070123ABM.

Ownership: Brunson/Ross Communications LLC.

■**Roanoke**—WRKV-LP, Ch. 43, Tiger Eye Broadcasting Corp. Phone: 954-431-3144.

Technical Facilities: 45.8-kw ERP, 52-ft. above ground, 1073-ft. above sea level, lat. 37° 10' 43", long. 80° 09' 45".

Ownership: Tiger Eye Broadcasting Corp.

Rockfish Valley—W39AK, Ch. 39, Commonwealth Public Broadcasting Corp. Phone: 804-320-1301.

Technical Facilities: 0.315-kw ERP, 66-ft. above ground, 3222-ft. above sea level, lat. 37° 54' 20", long. 78° 55' 54".

Ownership: Commonwealth Public Broadcasting Corp.

Rockingham County (central)—W21AC, Ch. 21, County of Rockingham.

Technical Facilities: 2.14-kw ERP, lat. 38° 36' 31", long. 78° 54' 07".

Rockingham County (central)—W33AC, Ch. 33, County of Rockingham.

Technical Facilities: 2.2-kw ERP, 2241-ft. above sea level, lat. 38° 36' 31", long. 78° 54' 07".

Rockingham County (central)—W39AD, Ch. 39, County of Rockingham.

Technical Facilities: 2.14-kw ERP, lat. 38° 36' 31", long. 78° 54' 07".

Rockingham County (southern)—W18AA, Ch. 18, County of Rockingham.

Technical Facilities: 0.75-kw ERP, lat. 38° 23' 34", long. 78° 46' 13".

Rockingham County (southern)—W46AE, Ch. 46, County of Rockingham.

Technical Facilities: 0.73-kw ERP, lat. 38° 23' 34", long. 78° 46' 13".

Ruckersville, etc.—W58DK, Ch. 58, Shenandoah Valley Educational TV Corp. Phone: 540-434-5391.

Technical Facilities: 10.6-kw ERP, 79-ft. above ground, 3907-ft. above sea level, lat. 38° 28' 43", long. 78° 24' 58".

Rustburg—W60BM, Ch. 60, Commonwealth Public Broadcasting Corp. Phone: 804-320-1301.

Technical Facilities: 15.3-kw ERP, 89-ft. above ground, 1378-ft. above sea level, lat. 37° 17' 07", long. 79° 05' 25".

Ownership: Commonwealth Public Broadcasting Corp.

South Boston, etc.—W73AJ, Ch. 73, Commonwealth Public Broadcasting Corp. Phone: 804-320-1301.

Technical Facilities: 0.132-kw ERP, lat. 36° 45' 25", long. 78° 58' 29".

Ownership: Commonwealth Public Broadcasting Corp.

■**Staunton & Waynesboro**—WAZM-CA, Ch. 25, JLA Media and Publications LLC. Phone: 540-598-8601.

Technical Facilities: 44-kw ERP, 69-ft. above ground, 2969-ft. above sea level, lat. 38° 23' 35", long. 78° 46' 14".

Ownership: JLA Media and Publications LLC.

■**Suffolk**—WBTD-LP, Ch. 52, WAVY Broadcasting LLC. Phone: 757-393-1010.

Technical Facilities: 12.8-kw ERP, 472-ft. above ground, 495-ft. above sea level, lat. 36° 49' 15", long. 76° 30' 40".

Ownership: LIN TV Corp.

Personnel: Edward L. Munson, Jr., President & General Manager; Les Garrenton, Director of Engineering; David Rogers, General Sales Manager.

Tazewell—WJDW-LP, Ch. 21, John Colson Dash. Phone: 276-979-9200.

Technical Facilities: 27.5-kw ERP, 141-ft. above ground, 3261-ft. above sea level, lat. 37° 11' 27", long. 81° 31' 49".

Holds CP for change to 150-kw ERP, BPTTL-20060327AIW.

Ownership: John Colson Dash.

Virginia Beach—W24OI, Ch. 24, Trinity Broadcasting Network Inc. Phone: 714-832-2950. Fax: 714-730-0661.

Technical Facilities: 1000-w TPO, 25.1-kw ERP, 194-ft. above ground, 210-ft. above sea level, lat. 36° 51' 45", long. 75° 58' 54".

Holds CP for change to 15-kw ERP, 194-ft. above ground, 209-ft. above sea level, BDFCDTT-20060329AKQ.

Transmitter: 205 34th St.

Ownership: Trinity Broadcasting Network Inc.

Personnel: Paul Crouch, General Manager; Ben Miller, Chief Engineer; Rod Henke, Sales Manager.

■**Virginia Beach**—WCTX-CA, Ch. 35, WAVY Broadcasting LLC. Phone: 202-462-6065.

Technical Facilities: 1000-w TPO, 23-kw ERP, 148-ft. above ground, 161-ft. above sea level, lat. 36° 50' 33", long. 76° 07' 06".

Transmitter: One Columbus Beach Blvd.

Ownership: LIN TV Corp.

Personnel: Edward L. Munson Jr., President & General Manager; Les Garrenton, Director of Engineering; David Rogers, General Sales Manager.

Virginia Beach—WVBN-LP, Ch. 18, Izzo Living Trust. Phone: 562-432-3099.

Technical Facilities: 70-kw ERP, 249-ft. above ground, 266-ft. above sea level, lat. 36° 45' 39", long. 76° 07' 21".

Transmitter: 2233 Salem Rd.

Ownership: Izzo Living Trust.

■**Winchester**—WAZW-CA, Ch. 48, JLA Media and Publications LLC. Phone: 540-598-8601.

Technical Facilities: 36.8-kw ERP, 144-ft. above ground, 1014-ft. above sea level, lat. 39° 11' 46", long. 78° 10' 45".

Transmitter: 550 Fairmont Ave.

Ownership: JLA Media and Publications LLC.

■**Woodstock**—WAZT-CA, Ch. 10, JLA Media and Publications LLC. Phone: 540-598-8601.

Studio: 123 E Court St, Woodstock, VA 22664.

Technical Facilities: 115-ft. above ground, 1125-ft. above sea level, lat. 38° 57' 50", long. 78° 25' 46".

Multichannel TV Sound: Stereo only.

Ownership: JLA Media and Publications LLC.

Personnel: Arthur D. Stamler, General Manager; Larry Ritchie Sr., Chief Engineer; Phil Luttrell, News Director; Ron Croom, Program Director; Mitzi W. Jones, Controller.

■**Wytheville, etc.**—WKPZ-LP, Ch. 41, Holston Valley Broadcasting Corp. Phone: 423-246-9578. Fax: 423-246-6261.

Technical Facilities: 0.28-kw ERP, lat. 36° 54' 30", long. 81° 04' 15".

Ownership: Holston Valley Broadcasting Corp.

■**Yorktown**—WYSJ-CA, Ch. 19, JBS Inc. Phone: 757-249-9545.

Technical Facilities: 150-kw ERP, 288-ft. above ground, 318-ft. above sea level, lat. 37° 04' 41", long. 76° 26' 47".

Ownership: JBS Inc.

Washington

Aberdeen—K25CG, Ch. 25, Tribune Television Northwest Inc., Debtor-In-Possession. Phone: 206-674-1300.

Technical Facilities: 4.07-kw ERP, lat. 46° 55' 53", long. 123° 44' 02".

Holds CP for change to 15-kw ERP, 60-ft. above ground, 577-ft. above sea level, lat. 46° 55' 41", long. 123° 44' 11". BDFCDTT-20060301ABQ.

Ownership: Tribune Broadcasting Co., Debtor-In-Possession.

Aberdeen—KRUM-LD, Ch. 23, Fiori Media Inc. Phone: 707-324-9167.

Technical Facilities: 1.2-kw ERP, 98-ft. above ground, 623-ft. above sea level, lat. 46° 55' 55", long. 123° 44' 05".

Holds CP for change to 0.3-kw ERP, 69-ft. above ground, 2717-ft. above sea level, lat. 46° 58' 31", long. 123° 08' 16". BDFCDTL-20090130ABN.

Ownership: Fiori Media Inc.

Personnel: Paul F. Crouch, General Manager; Ben Miller, Chief Engineer; Rod Henke, Sales Manager.

Ardenvoir—K08AX, Ch. 8, TV Reception Improvement District. Phone: 509-663-0254.

Technical Facilities: 0.003-kw ERP, 1624-ft. above sea level, lat. 47° 44' 26", long. 120° 22' 05".

Ardenvoir—K10BB, Ch. 10, TV Reception Improvement District. Phone: 509-663-0254.

Technical Facilities: 0.003-kw ERP, 1624-ft. above sea level, lat. 47° 44' 26", long. 120° 22' 05".

Ardenvoir—K12BF, Ch. 12, TV Reception Improvement District. Phone: 509-663-0254.

Technical Facilities: 0.003-kw ERP, 1624-ft. above sea level, lat. 47° 44' 26", long. 120° 22' 05".

Baker Flats area—K57BA, Ch. 57, Apple Valley TV Association Inc. Phone: 509-293-4403.

Technical Facilities: 0.681-kw ERP, 2365-ft. above sea level, lat. 47° 29' 37", long. 120° 19' 14".

Holds CP for change to channel number 43, 13-ft. above ground, 2379-ft. above sea level, BPTT-20060928AIG.

Ownership: Apple Valley TV Association Inc.

Baker Flats area—K59BF, Ch. 59, Apple Valley TV Association Inc. Phone: 509-293-4403.

Technical Facilities: 0.681-kw ERP, 2365-ft. above sea level, lat. 47° 29' 37", long. 120° 19' 14".

Holds CP for change to channel number 6, 0.01-kw ERP, 20-ft. above ground, 2385-ft. above sea level, BDISTTV-20080225AAD.

Ownership: Apple Valley TV Association Inc.

Baker Flats area—K61AY, Ch. 61, Spokane School District No. 81. Phone: 509-354-7800.

Technical Facilities: 0.681-kw ERP, 2365-ft. above sea level, lat. 47° 19' 12", long. 120° 14' 18".

Ownership: Spokane School District No. 81.

Bellingham—K38JH, Ch. 38, Venture Technologies Group LLC. Phone: 323-904-4090.

Technical Facilities: 0.1-kw ERP, 66-ft. above ground, 230-ft. above sea level, lat. 48° 47' 34.3", long. 122° 29' 02.6".

Began Operation: November 3, 2008.

Ownership: Venture Technologies Group LLC.

Bremerton—K26IC-D, Ch. 26, KIRO-TV Inc. Phone: 206-728-7777.

Technical Facilities: 0.9-kw ERP, 79-ft. above ground, 620-ft. above sea level, lat. 47° 38' 27", long. 122° 43' 28".

Transmitter: 1-mi. SW of Silverdale, off of Dickey Rd. NW.

Ownership: Cox Enterprises Inc.

Brewster & Pateros—K56BK, Ch. 56, TV Reception District No. 3, Okanogan County.

Technical Facilities: 0.3-kw ERP, lat. 48° 01' 00", long. 119° 51' 51".

Brewster, etc.—K53CX, Ch. 53, TV Reception District No. 3, Okanogan County.

Technical Facilities: 0.43-kw ERP, 16-ft. above ground, 5249-ft. above sea level, lat. 48° 01' 10", long. 119° 58' 35".

Bridgeport—K07BC, Ch. 7, Chief Joseph Community Services Inc.

Technical Facilities: 0.001-kw ERP, lat. 48° 02' 54", long. 119° 42' 39".

Bridgeport—K11AS, Ch. 11, Chief Joseph Community Services Inc.

Technical Facilities: 0.004-kw ERP, lat. 48° 02' 54", long. 119° 42' 39".

Bridgeport—K13DL, Ch. 13, Chief Joseph Community Services Inc.

Technical Facilities: 0.004-kw ERP, lat. 48° 02' 54", long. 119° 42' 39".

Cashmere—K09ES, Ch. 9, Apple Valley TV Association Inc. Phone: 509-293-4403.

Technical Facilities: 0.001-kw ERP, lat. 47° 31' 53", long. 120° 29' 10".

Ownership: Apple Valley TV Association Inc.

Cashmere—K11EZ, Ch. 11, Apple Valley TV Association Inc. Phone: 509-293-4403.

Technical Facilities: 0.004-kw ERP, lat. 47° 31' 53", long. 120° 29' 10".

Ownership: Apple Valley TV Association Inc.

Cashmere—K13ER, Ch. 13, Apple Valley TV Association Inc. Phone: 509-293-4403.

Technical Facilities: 0.002-kw ERP, lat. 47° 31' 53", long. 120° 29' 10".

Ownership: Apple Valley TV Association Inc.

Cashmere—K40AE, Ch. 40, Apple Valley TV Association Inc. Phone: 509-293-4403.

Technical Facilities: lat. 47° 31' 31", long. 120° 31' 31".

Ownership: Apple Valley TV Association Inc.

Centralia—K25CH, Ch. 25, Tribune Television Holdings Inc., Debtor-In-Possession. Phone: 206-674-1300.

Technical Facilities: 6.1-kw ERP, 128-ft. above ground, 1575-ft. above sea level, lat. 46° 33' 16", long. 123° 03' 26".

Holds CP for change to 15-kw ERP, BDFCDTT-20060222ABH.

Ownership: Tribune Broadcasting Co., Debtor-In-Possession.

Centralia, etc.—K42CM, Ch. 42, Tribune Television Northwest Inc., Debtor-In-Possession. Phone: 206-674-1300.

Technical Facilities: 10.2-kw ERP, 151-ft. above ground, 1598-ft. above sea level, lat. 46° 33' 16", long. 123° 03' 26".

Holds CP for change to 12-kw ERP, BDFCDTT-20060227ADV.

Ownership: Tribune Broadcasting Co., Debtor-In-Possession.

Centralia, etc.—K53AZ, Ch. 53, KIRO-TV Inc. Phone: 206-728-7777.

Technical Facilities: 5.16-kw ERP, lat. 46° 33' 39", long. 123° 03' 29".

Holds CP for change to channel number 29, 1.1-kw ERP, 46-ft. above ground, 1248-ft. above sea level, lat. 46° 33' 38", long. 123° 03' 29". BDISDTT-20061107ADK.

Ownership: Cox Enterprises Inc.

Chelan—K44CK, Ch. 44, Mountain Licenses LP. Phone: 517-347-4111.

Studio: 4600 S. Regal, Spokane, WA 99223.

Technical Facilities: 100-w TPO, 0.78-kw ERP, 39-ft. above ground, 3871-ft. above sea level, lat. 47° 48' 26", long. 120° 01' 59".

Transmitter: Atop Slide Ridge, Chelan.

Ownership: Mountain Licenses LP.

Chelan—K64ES, Ch. 64, Tribune Television Northwest Inc., Debtor-In-Possession. Phone: 206-674-1313. Fax: 206-674-1777.

Technical Facilities: 100-w TPO, 1.38-kw ERP, 17-ft. above ground, 3854-ft. above sea level, lat. 47° 48' 27", long. 120° 02' 00".

Transmitter: Chelan Butte, approx. 2.5-mi. SSW of Chelan.

Ownership: Tribune Broadcasting Co., Debtor-In-Possession.

Personnel: Larry Brandt, Chief Engineer.

Chelan Butte—K03DI, Ch. 3, Apple Valley TV Association Inc. Phone: 509-293-4403.

Technical Facilities: 0.003-kw ERP, 1168-ft. above sea level, lat. 47° 47' 00", long. 120° 07' 18".

Ownership: Apple Valley TV Association Inc.

Chelan Butte—K07JO, Ch. 7, Apple Valley TV Association Inc. Phone: 509-293-4403.

Technical Facilities: 0.002-kw ERP, 1168-ft. above sea level, lat. 47° 47' 00", long. 120° 07' 18".

Ownership: Apple Valley TV Association Inc.

Chelan Butte—KCEM-LP, Ch. 5, Apple Valley TV Association Inc. Phone: 509-293-4403.

Technical Facilities: 0.014-kw ERP, 1168-ft. above sea level, lat. 47° 46' 42", long. 120° 08' 18".

Ownership: Apple Valley TV Association Inc.

Clarkston—K49EV, Ch. 49, Upper Columbia Media Assn. Phone: 509-758-5451.

Technical Facilities: 100-w TPO, 1.05-kw ERP, 20-ft. above ground, 2848-ft. above sea level, lat. 46° 27' 04", long. 117° 02' 48".

Transmitter: 2.4-mi. N of Clarkston.

Ownership: Upper Columbia Media Assn.

■**Clarkston**—KVBI-LP, Ch. 42, Life of Victory TV Inc. Phone: 208-743-4072.

Technical Facilities: 2.61-kw ERP, 20-ft. above ground, 2871-ft. above sea level, lat. 46° 27' 04", long. 117° 02' 47".

Ownership: Life of Victory TV Inc.

College Place—K36EW-D, Ch. 36, Blue Mountain Broadcasting Assn. Inc. Phone: 509-529-9149. Fax: 509-529-0661.

Studio: Corner 12th & Larch, College Place, .

Technical Facilities: 0.226-kw ERP, 88-ft. above ground, 938-ft. above sea level, lat. 46° 02' 30", long. 118° 22' 00".

Ownership: Blue Mountain Broadcasting Assn. Inc.

Personnel: Lynelle Ellis, Station Manager; Jim Roe, Chief Engineer.

Colville—K09UP, Ch. 9, Mountain Licenses LP. Phone: 517-347-4141.

Studio: 4600 S. Regal St., Spokane, WA 99223.

Technical Facilities: 1.25-kw ERP, 70-ft. above ground, 2881-ft. above sea level, lat. 48° 34' 30", long. 117° 55' 00".

Ownership: Mountain Licenses LP.

Coulee City—K12CS, Ch. 12, Town of Coulee City.

Technical Facilities: 0.005-kw ERP, lat. 47° 39' 06", long. 119° 22' 45".

Curlew & Malo—K09MP, Ch. 9, Franson Peak TV Assn. Inc.

Technical Facilities: 0.013-kw ERP, lat. 48° 51' 21", long. 118° 37' 51".

Curlew & Malo—K11NB, Ch. 11, Franson Peak TV Assn. Inc.

Technical Facilities: 0.013-kw ERP, lat. 48° 51' 21", long. 118° 37' 51".

Curlew & Malo—K13NV, Ch. 13, Franson Peak TV Assn. Inc.

Technical Facilities: 0.027-kw ERP, lat. 48° 51' 21", long. 118° 37' 51".

Douglas—K09EO, Ch. 9, Douglas TV Assn. Inc.

Technical Facilities: 0.008-kw ERP, 3678-ft. above sea level, lat. 47° 28' 55", long. 120° 01' 05".

Douglas—K11FC, Ch. 11, Douglas TV Assn. Inc.

Technical Facilities: 0.008-kw ERP, 3678-ft. above sea level, lat. 47° 28' 55", long. 120° 01' 05".

Douglas—K13CH, Ch. 13, Douglas TV Assn. Inc.

Technical Facilities: 0.008-kw ERP, 3678-ft. above sea level, lat. 47° 28' 55", long. 120° 01' 05".

Dryden—K08JP, Ch. 8, Apple Valley TV Association Inc. Phone: 509-293-4403.

Technical Facilities: 0.016-kw ERP, lat. 47° 36' 00", long. 120° 30' 29".

Ownership: Apple Valley TV Association Inc.

Dryden—K10LG, Ch. 10, Apple Valley TV Association Inc. Phone: 509-293-4403.

Technical Facilities: 0.018-kw ERP, lat. 47° 36' 00", long. 120° 30' 29".

Ownership: Apple Valley TV Association Inc.

Dryden—K12LV, Ch. 12, Apple Valley TV Association Inc. Phone: 509-293-4403.

Technical Facilities: 0.018-kw ERP, lat. 47° 36' 00", long. 120° 30' 29".

Ownership: Apple Valley TV Association Inc.

Dryden—K52ER, Ch. 52, Apple Valley TV Association Inc. Phone: 509-293-4403.

Technical Facilities: 0.268-kw ERP, 16-ft. above ground, 4705-ft. above sea level, lat. 47° 36' 07", long. 120° 30' 32".

Transmitter: 4.9-km NE of Dryden.

Ownership: Apple Valley TV Association Inc.

Dryden—K57AY, Ch. 57, Apple Valley TV Association Inc. Phone: 509-293-4403.

Technical Facilities: 0.78-kw ERP, lat. 47° 36' 00", long. 120° 30' 29".

Holds CP for change to channel number 43, 16-ft. above ground, 4734-ft. above sea level, BPTT-20060928AJG.

Ownership: Apple Valley TV Association Inc.

East Wenatchee—K53DN, Ch. 53, Apple Valley TV Association Inc. Phone: 509-293-4403.

Technical Facilities: 1.18-kw ERP, 16-ft. above ground, 3783-ft. above sea level, lat. 47° 19' 21", long. 120° 14' 23".

Holds CP for change to channel number 42, 16-ft. above ground, 3799-ft. above sea level, BPTT-20060928AKJ.

Ownership: Apple Valley TV Association Inc.

East Wenatchee—K55FO, Ch. 55, Apple Valley TV Association Inc. Phone: 509-293-4403.

Technical Facilities: 5.27-kw ERP, lat. 47° 19' 21", long. 120° 14' 23".

Holds CP for change to channel number 16, 3.28-kw ERP, 16-ft. above ground, 3799-ft. above sea level, BPTT-20060928AKP.

Ownership: Apple Valley TV Association Inc.

East Wenatchee, etc.—K18AD, Ch. 18, KCTS Television. Phone: 206-728-6463.

Technical Facilities: 0.65-kw ERP, lat. 47° 16' 27", long. 120° 24' 18".

Holds CP for change to 20-ft. above ground, 6778-ft. above sea level, BDFCDTT-20060329AKH.

Ownership: KCTS Television.

■**Ellensburg**—K25FP, Ch. 25, Three Angels Broadcasting Network Inc. Phone: 618-627-4651. Fax: 618-627-4155.

Studio: 3391 Charley Good Rd, West Frankfort, IL 62896.

Technical Facilities: 100-w TPO, 0.65-kw ERP, 49-ft. above ground, 3219-ft. above sea level, lat. 46° 53' 13", long. 120° 26' 26".

Transmitter: Manastash Ridge, near Wymer.

Ownership: Three Angels Broadcasting Network Inc.

Personnel: Moses Primo, Chief Engineer.

Ellensburg—K39DM, Ch. 39, Christian Broadcasting of Yakima. Phones: 509-972-0926; 509-248-0194. Fax: 509-577-0301.

Technical Facilities: 100-w TPO, 0.67-kw ERP, 20-ft. above ground, 3140-ft. above sea level, lat. 46° 53' 24", long. 120° 26' 38".

Holds CP for change to 10-kw ERP, 20-ft. above ground, 3159-ft. above sea level, BPTTL-20060127ARI.

Transmitter: Atop Manastash Ridge, near Ellensburg.

Ownership: Christian Broadcasting of Yakima.

Personnel: Ric McClary, General Manager; Moe Broom, Chief Engineer.

Ellensburg—K41CK, Ch. 41, Kittitas County TV Reception Improvement.

Technical Facilities: 0.68-kw ERP, lat. 46° 53' 24", long. 120° 26' 38".

Ellensburg—K50KK-D, Ch. 50, Kittitas County TV Improvement District #1. Phone: 202-296-2007.

Technical Facilities: 0.05-kw ERP, 39-ft. above ground, 3258-ft. above sea level, lat. 46° 53' 15", long. 120° 26' 29".

Ownership: Kittitas County TV Improvement District #1.

Ellensburg, etc.—K17IL-D, Ch. 17, Kittitas County TV Improvement District #1. Phone: 202-296-2007.

Technical Facilities: 0.105-kw ERP, 39-ft. above ground, 3258-ft. above sea level, lat. 46° 53' 15", long. 120° 26' 29".

Ownership: Kittitas County TV Improvement District #1.

Ellensburg, etc.—K20JL-D, Ch. 20, Kittitas County TV Improvement District #1. Phone: 202-296-2007.

Technical Facilities: 0.105-kw ERP, 39-ft. above ground, 3258-ft. above sea level, lat. 46° 53' 15", long. 120° 26' 29".

Ownership: Kittitas County TV Improvement District #1.

Ellensburg, etc.—K31AK, Ch. 31, Kittitas County TV Reception Improvement District.

Technical Facilities: 0.3-kw ERP, lat. 46° 53' 24", long. 120° 26' 38".

Ellensburg, etc.—K32IG-D, Ch. 32, Kittitas County TV Improvement District #1. Phone: 202-296-2007.

Technical Facilities: 0.03-kw ERP, 39-ft. above ground, 3258-ft. above sea level, lat. 46° 53' 15", long. 120° 26' 29".

Ownership: Kittitas County TV Improvement District #1.

Ellensburg, etc.—K51BD, Ch. 51, Kittitas County TV Improvement District #1.

Technical Facilities: 1.28-kw ERP, lat. 46° 53' 24", long. 120° 26' 38".

Ownership: Kittitas County TV Improvement District #1.

Ellensburg, etc.—K63BZ, Ch. 63, Kittitas County TV Improvement District #1. Phone: 202-296-2007.

Technical Facilities: 1.33-kw ERP, lat. 46° 53' 24", long. 120° 26' 38".

Holds CP for change to channel number 19, 1.1-kw ERP, 39-ft. above ground, 3258-ft. above sea level, lat. 46° 53' 15", long. 120° 26' 29". BDISTT-20061002AEP.

Ownership: Kittitas County TV Improvement District #1.

■**Ellensburg, etc.**—KWWA-CA, Ch. 49, Fisher Radio Regional Group Inc. Phone: 206-404-4884.

Technical Facilities: 8-kw ERP, 45-ft. above ground, 6785-ft. above sea level, lat. 47° 16' 30", long. 120° 24' 15".

Ownership: Fisher Communications Inc.

Personnel: Gregory J. Herman, General Manager; Steven A. Hale, Station Manager.

Ellensburg-Kittitas—K54DX, Ch. 54, Tribune Television Northwest Inc., Debtor-In-Possession. Phones: 206-674-1313; 206-674-1300. Fax: 206-674-1777.

Technical Facilities: 100-w TPO, 0.61-kw ERP, 20-ft. above ground, 3235-ft. above sea level, lat. 46° 53' 15", long. 120° 26' 30".

Transmitter: On Manastash Ridge, approx. 0.6-mi. W of I-82, Ellensburg.

Multichannel TV Sound: Stereo only.

Ownership: Tribune Broadcasting Co., Debtor-In-Possession.

Personnel: Larry Brandt, Chief Engineer.

Ellisford—K35BJ, Ch. 35, Mountain Licenses LP. Phone: 517-347-4111.

Studio: 4600 S. Regal St., Spokane, WA 99223.

Technical Facilities: 10-w TPO, 0.19-kw ERP, 20-ft. above ground, 2600-ft. above sea level, lat. 48° 46' 53", long. 119° 23' 10".

Transmitter: Pickens Mountain.

Ownership: Mountain Licenses LP.

Entiat—K09BJ, Ch. 9, TV Reception Improvement District. Phone: 509-663-0254.

Technical Facilities: 0.014-kw ERP, 3524-ft. above sea level, lat. 47° 38' 10", long. 120° 16' 00".

Entiat—K11BI, Ch. 11, TV Reception Improvement District. Phone: 509-663-0254.

Technical Facilities: 0.014-kw ERP, 3524-ft. above sea level, lat. 47° 38' 10", long. 120° 16' 00".

Entiat—K13BI, Ch. 13, TV Reception Improvement District. Phone: 509-663-0254.

Technical Facilities: 0.014-kw ERP, 3524-ft. above sea level, lat. 47° 38' 10", long. 120° 16' 00".

Everett—K29ED, Ch. 29, Tribune Television Holdings Inc., Debtor-In-Possession. Phone: 206-674-1300.

Technical Facilities: 8.7-kw ERP, 59-ft. above ground, 367-ft. above sea level, lat. 47° 58' 27", long. 122° 07' 24".

Holds CP for change to 15-kw ERP, 15-ft. above ground, 284-ft. above sea level, BDFCDTT-20060309AAN.

Ownership: Tribune Broadcasting Co., Debtor-In-Possession.

Everett—K58BW, Ch. 58, KIRO-TV Inc. Phone: 678-645-0000.

Technical Facilities: 1.38-kw ERP, lat. 48° 01' 58", long. 122° 08' 08".

Ownership: Cox Enterprises Inc.

Grand Coulee—K12BZ, Ch. 12, Grand Coulee TV Inc.

Technical Facilities: 0.007-kw ERP, lat. 47° 56' 50", long. 118° 57' 18".

Grand Coulee, etc.—K08BY, Ch. 8, Grand Coulee TV Inc.

Technical Facilities: 0.009-kw ERP, 2064-ft. above sea level, lat. 47° 56' 50", long. 118° 57' 18".

Grand Coulee, etc.—K10FV, Ch. 10, Grand Coulee TV Inc.

Technical Facilities: 0.009-kw ERP, 2073-ft. above sea level, lat. 47° 57' 18", long. 118° 57' 18".

Grays River, etc.—K35HU, Ch. 35, KING Broadcasting Co. Phone: 214-977-6606.

Technical Facilities: 1.73-kw ERP, 49-ft. above ground, 2890-ft. above sea level, lat. 46° 27' 40", long. 123° 32' 58".

Ownership: Belo Corp.

Grays River, etc.—K59BX, Ch. 59, Oregon Public Broadcasting. Phone: 503-244-9900.

Technical Facilities: 0.696-kw ERP, 3025-ft. above sea level, lat. 46° 27' 44", long. 123° 32' 56".

Holds CP for change to channel number 31, 0.8-kw ERP, 49-ft. above ground, 2890-ft. above sea level, lat. 46° 27' 40", long. 123° 32' 58". BDFCDTT-20090213AAK.

Ownership: Oregon Public Broadcasting.

Grays River, etc.—K63AW, Ch. 63, NVT Portland Licensee LLC, Debtor in Possession. Phone: 404-995-4711.

Technical Facilities: 1.39-kw ERP, 36-ft. above ground, 2871-ft. above sea level, lat. 46° 27' 40", long. 123° 32' 58".

Holds CP for change to channel number 29, BDISTT-20061212ABF.

Ownership: New Vision Television LLC, Debtor in Possession.

Grays River, etc.—K65BU, Ch. 65, Bates Technical College. Phone: 253-680-7702.

Technical Facilities: 0.89-kw ERP, lat. 46° 27' 44", long. 123° 32' 56".

Holds CP for change to channel number 41, 0.5-kw ERP, 49-ft. above ground, 2890-ft. above sea level, lat. 46° 27' 40", long. 123° 32' 58". BDFCDTT-20090513ACB.

Ownership: Bates Technical College.

Grays River/Lebam—K38GS, Ch. 38, Fisher Broadcasting - Portland TV LLC. Phone: 206-404-7000.

Technical Facilities: 1.33-kw ERP, 36-ft. above ground, 2871-ft. above sea level, lat. 46° 27' 40", long. 123° 32' 58".

Hoquiam—KCST-LP, Ch. 47, Duane J. Polich & Elaine F. Clemenson-Polich. Phone: 206-852-3096.

Technical Facilities: 0.125-kw ERP, 16-ft. above ground, 39-ft. above sea level, lat. 47° 00' 46", long. 124° 09' 39".

Began Operation: March 30, 2009.

Ownership: Duane J. Polich & Elaine F. Clemenson-Polich.

Personnel: Duane J Polich, General Manager.

Issaquah, etc.—K03FA, Ch. 3, King County TV Reception District #2. Phone: 425-392-5760.

Technical Facilities: 0.032-kw ERP, 1450-ft. above sea level, lat. 47° 27' 56", long. 121° 59' 14".

Began Operation: March 20, 1981.

Ownership: King County TV Reception District #2.

Issaquah, etc.—K10LA, Ch. 10, TV Reception District 2.

Technical Facilities: 0.034-kw ERP, lat. 47° 27' 49", long. 121° 58' 24".

Kennewick—K29FF, Ch. 29, Ron Bevins.

Technical Facilities: 12.3-kw ERP, 23-ft. above ground, 2215-ft. above sea level, lat. 46° 06' 14", long. 119° 07' 49".

Ownership: Ronald A. Bevins.

Kennewick & Pasco—K23FU, Ch. 23, Ron Bevins.

Technical Facilities: 7.75-kw ERP, 23-ft. above ground, 2215-ft. above sea level, lat. 46° 06' 14", long. 119° 07' 49".

Ownership: Ronald A. Bevins.

■ **Kennewick, etc.**—KVVK-CA, Ch. 15, Fisher Radio Regional Group Inc. Phone: 206-404-4884.

Technical Facilities: 1000-w TPO, 23.7-kw ERP, 98-ft. above ground, 1676-ft. above sea level, lat. 46° 14' 10", long. 119° 19' 55".

Holds CP for change to 15-kw ERP, 290-ft. above ground, 2325-ft. above sea level, lat. 46° 05' 51", long. 119° 11' 29". BDFCDTA-20081203AFC.

Transmitter: Badger Mountain.

Began Operation: February 5, 1996.

Ownership: Fisher Communications Inc.

Personnel: Gregory J. Herman, General Manager; Steven A. Hale, Station Manager.

Lake Wenatchee—K13SQ, Ch. 13, Lake Wenatchee TV Inc.

Technical Facilities: 0.011-kw ERP, lat. 47° 46' 45", long. 120° 41' 30".

Lake Wenatchee, etc.—K10KE, Ch. 10, Lake Wenatchee TV Inc.

Technical Facilities: 0.011-kw ERP, lat. 47° 46' 45", long. 120° 41' 38".

Laurier—K08GG, Ch. 8, Laurier TV Club.

Technical Facilities: 0.006-kw ERP, lat. 48° 58' 40", long. 118° 14' 10".

Laurier—K10GH, Ch. 10, Laurier TV Club.

Technical Facilities: 0.006-kw ERP, lat. 48° 58' 40", long. 118° 14' 10".

Laurier—K12GM, Ch. 12, Laurier TV Club.

Technical Facilities: 0.006-kw ERP, lat. 48° 58' 40", long. 118° 14' 10".

Long Lake & Suncrest—K11NT, Ch. 11, Spokane TV Inc.

Technical Facilities: 0.004-kw ERP, lat. 47° 47' 30", long. 117° 31' 49".

Longview—K34HK, Ch. 34, Meredith Corp. Phones: 503-239-4949; 515-284-3000. Fax: 503-239-6184.

Technical Facilities: 10.45-kw ERP, 124-ft. above ground, 1039-ft. above sea level, lat. 46° 10' 55.3", long. 122° 56' 57.6".

Ownership: Meredith Corp.

Longview—KEVE-LP, Ch. 36, Fiori Media Inc. Phone: 707-324-9167.

Technical Facilities: 1000-w TPO, 11.4-kw ERP, 131-ft. above ground, 1430-ft. above sea level, lat. 46° 09' 20", long. 122° 51' 09".

Holds CP for change to 7-kw ERP, 367-ft. above ground, 1490-ft. above sea level, lat. 45° 31' 21", long. 122° 44' 45". BDFCDTL-20090130ACF.

Transmitter: 0.9-mi. NE of junction of Harris & Allen Rds., near Kelso.

Began Operation: December 2, 1993.

Ownership: Fiori Media Inc.

Personnel: Mark Fountain, Chief Engineer.

Malaga, etc.—K12CF, Ch. 12, Apple Valley TV Association Inc. Phone: 509-293-4403.

Technical Facilities: 0.196-kw ERP, lat. 47° 27' 50", long. 120° 12' 50".

Ownership: Apple Valley TV Association Inc.

Malaga, etc.—KNEE-LP, Ch. 10, Apple Valley TV Association Inc. Phone: 509-293-4403.

Technical Facilities: 0.197-kw ERP, lat. 47° 27' 50", long. 120° 12' 50".

Ownership: Apple Valley TV Association Inc.

Malaga, etc.—KWVC-LP, Ch. 8, Apple Valley TV Association Inc. Phone: 509-293-4403.

Technical Facilities: 0.199-kw ERP, lat. 47° 27' 50", long. 120° 12' 50".

Ownership: Apple Valley TV Association Inc.

Malott & Wakefield, etc.—K08CW, Ch. 8, TV Reception Improvement District 1.

Technical Facilities: 0.03-kw ERP, lat. 48° 19' 36", long. 119° 42' 06".

Malott & Wakefield, etc.—K10DK, Ch. 10, TV Reception Improvement District 1.

Technical Facilities: 0.002-kw ERP, 2963-ft. above sea level, lat. 48° 19' 36", long. 119° 42' 06".

Malott & Wakefield, etc.—K12CW, Ch. 12, TV Reception Improvement District 1.

Technical Facilities: 0.002-kw ERP, 2966-ft. above sea level, lat. 48° 19' 36", long. 119° 42' 06".

Marcus-Evans, etc.—K08HY, Ch. 8, Bisbee Mountain Translator Assn.

Technical Facilities: 0.03-kw ERP, lat. 48° 37' 55", long. 118° 09' 13".

Marcus-Evans, etc.—K10GJ, Ch. 10, Bisbee Mountain Translator Assn.

Technical Facilities: 0.02-kw ERP, lat. 48° 37' 55", long. 118° 09' 13".

Marcus-Evans, etc.—K13IQ, Ch. 13, Bisbee Mountain Translator Assn.

Technical Facilities: 0.02-kw ERP, 4206-ft. above sea level, lat. 48° 37' 55", long. 118° 09' 13".

Mazama—K02FZ, Ch. 2, TV District #2 of Okanogan County. Phone: 509-997-2033.

Technical Facilities: 0.005-kw ERP, lat. 48° 34' 00", long. 120° 18' 00".

Ownership: TV District #2 of Okanogan County.

Mazama—K04FT, Ch. 4, TV District No. 2 of Okanogan County. Phone: 509-997-2033.

Technical Facilities: 0.005-kw ERP, lat. 48° 34' 00", long. 120° 18' 00".

Mazama—K05EK, Ch. 5, TV District No. 2 of Okanogan County. Phone: 509-997-2033.

Technical Facilities: 0.005-kw ERP, lat. 48° 34' 00", long. 120° 18' 00".

Methow—K09BI, Ch. 9, Upper Methow Valley TV Assn. Inc.

Technical Facilities: 0.002-kw ERP, lat. 48° 01' 20", long. 119° 58' 30".

Methow—K11BM, Ch. 11, Upper Methow Valley TV Assn. Inc.

Technical Facilities: 0.002-kw ERP, lat. 48° 01' 20", long. 119° 58' 30".

Methow—K44EN, Ch. 44, TV Reception District 2 of Okanogan County.

Technical Facilities: 0.86-kw ERP, lat. 48° 02' 13", long. 119° 59' 70".

Transmitter: Goat Mountain, 4.5-mi. SW of Pateros.

Molson—K09BM, Ch. 9, Oroville TV Assn. Inc.

Technical Facilities: 0.003-kw ERP, lat. 48° 56' 25", long. 119° 11' 30".

Molson—K11BT, Ch. 11, Oroville TV Assn. Inc.

Technical Facilities: 0.003-kw ERP, lat. 48° 56' 25", long. 119° 11' 30".

Molson—K13RU, Ch. 13, Oroville TV Assn. Inc.

Technical Facilities: 0.003-kw ERP, 4997-ft. above sea level, lat. 48° 56' 25", long. 119° 11' 30".

Monitor, etc.—K51AE, Ch. 51, Apple Valley TV Association Inc. Phone: 509-293-4403.

Technical Facilities: 0.234-kw ERP, lat. 47° 30' 55", long. 120° 26' 22".

Ownership: Apple Valley TV Association Inc.

Monitor, etc.—K53AH, Ch. 53, Apple Valley TV Association Inc. Phone: 509-293-4403.

Technical Facilities: 0.234-kw ERP, lat. 47° 30' 55", long. 120° 26' 22".

Ownership: Apple Valley TV Association Inc.

Monitor, etc.—K55BN, Ch. 55, Apple Valley TV Association Inc. Phone: 509-293-4403.

Technical Facilities: 0.234-kw ERP, lat. 47° 30' 55", long. 120° 26' 22".

Ownership: Apple Valley TV Association Inc.

Moses Lake—K39DL, Ch. 39, Three Angels Broadcasting Network Inc. Phone: 618-627-4651. Fax: 618-627-4155.

Studio: 3391 Charley Good Rd, West Frankfort, IL 62896.

Technical Facilities: 1000-w TPO, 2.7-kw ERP, 56-ft. above ground, 2717-ft. above sea level, lat. 46° 48' 24", long. 119° 33' 30".

Transmitter: Wahatis Peak, near Royal City.

Ownership: Three Angels Broadcasting Network Inc.

Personnel: Moses Primo, Chief Engineer; Linda Shelton, Program Director.

Moses Lake—KUMN-LP, Ch. 43, Spokane Television Inc. Phone: 509-324-4000.

Technical Facilities: 2.5-kw ERP, 26-ft. above ground, 2746-ft. above sea level, lat. 46° 48' 23", long. 119° 33' 25".

Ownership: Spokane Television Inc.

Moses Lake, etc.—K59IA, Ch. 59, Peoples TV Assn. Phone: 509-633-2888.

Technical Facilities: 100-w TPO, 2.3-kw ERP, 43-ft. above ground, 2740-ft. above sea level, lat. 46° 48' 23", long. 119° 33' 25".

Transmitter: 25-mi. SSW of Moses Lake.

Ownership: Peoples TV Assn.

Odessa—K09AR, Ch. 9, Odessa TV Club.

Technical Facilities: 0.006-kw ERP, lat. 47° 20' 45", long. 118° 41' 38".

Odessa—K11AR, Ch. 11, Odessa TV Club.

Technical Facilities: 0.006-kw ERP, lat. 47° 20' 45", long. 118° 41' 38".

Odessa—K13IJ, Ch. 13, Odessa TV Club.

Technical Facilities: 0.003-kw ERP, lat. 47° 20' 45", long. 118° 41' 38".

Odessa—K64AB, Ch. 64, Odessa TV Club.

Technical Facilities: 0.36-kw ERP, lat. 47° 20' 45", long. 118° 41' 38".

Omak—K17EV, Ch. 17, TV Reception Improvement District 1.

Technical Facilities: 0.02-kw ERP, 5239-ft. above sea level, lat. 48° 27' 15", long. 119° 18' 30".

Omak—K26GV, Ch. 26, Three Angels Broadcasting Network Inc. Phone: 618-627-4651. Fax: 618-627-4155.

Technical Facilities: 15-kw ERP, 49-ft. above ground, 622-ft. above sea level, lat. 48° 26' 57.4", long. 119° 18' 27.8".

Ownership: Three Angels Broadcasting Network Inc.

Omak & Okanogan—K19AU, Ch. 19, Mountain Licenses LP. Phone: 517-347-4111.

Technical Facilities: 2.45-kw ERP, lat. 48° 27' 40", long. 119° 17' 30".

Ownership: Mountain Licenses LP.

Omak, etc.—K07DG, Ch. 7, TV Reception Improvement District 1.

Technical Facilities: 0.026-kw ERP, 14-ft. above ground, 5761-ft. above sea level, lat. 48° 27' 15", long. 119° 18' 30".

Transmitter: Omak Mountain, 11-mi. ENE of Omak.

Omak, etc.—K09DG, Ch. 9, TV Reception Improvement District 1.

Technical Facilities: 0.051-kw ERP, 14-ft. above ground, 5761-ft. above sea level, lat. 48° 27' 15", long. 119° 18' 30".

Transmitter: Omak Mountain, 11-mi. ENE of Omak.

Omak, etc.—K11DM, Ch. 11, TV Reception Improvement District 1.

Technical Facilities: 0.017-kw ERP, 5787-ft. above sea level, lat. 48° 27' 15", long. 119° 18' 30".

Omak, etc.—K31AH, Ch. 31, Mountain Licenses LP.

Technical Facilities: 1.5-kw ERP, 5777-ft. above sea level, lat. 48° 26' 59", long. 119° 18' 28".

Ownership: Mountain Licenses LP.

Orondo & Entiat—K12BE, Ch. 12, TV Reception Improvement District. Phone: 509-663-0254.

Technical Facilities: 0.003-kw ERP, 1476-ft. above sea level, lat. 47° 40' 00", long. 120° 10' 12".

Orondo, etc.—K08BA, Ch. 8, TV Reception Improvement District. Phone: 509-663-0254.

Technical Facilities: 0.003-kw ERP, 1476-ft. above sea level, lat. 47° 40' 00", long. 120° 10' 12".

Orondo, etc.—K10BA, Ch. 10, TV Reception Improvement District. Phone: 509-663-0254.

Technical Facilities: 0.003-kw ERP, 1476-ft. above sea level, lat. 47° 40' 00", long. 120° 10' 12".

Oroville—K02MO, Ch. 2, Oroville TV Association Inc.

Technical Facilities: 0.01-kw ERP, lat. 48° 57' 30", long. 119° 24' 12".

Ownership: Oroville TV Association Inc.

Oroville—K04KZ, Ch. 4, Oroville TV Assn. Inc.

Technical Facilities: 0.002-kw ERP, 2106-ft. above sea level, lat. 48° 57' 30", long. 119° 24' 12".

Ownership: Oroville TV Association Inc.

Oroville—K06JR, Ch. 6, Oroville TV Assn. Inc.

Technical Facilities: 0.003-kw ERP, lat. 48° 57' 30", long. 119° 24' 12".

Oroville—K07SB, Ch. 7, Oroville TV Assn. Inc.

Technical Facilities: 0.002-kw ERP, 2106-ft. above sea level, lat. 48° 57' 30", long. 119° 24' 12".

Pasco & Kennewick—K04OI, Ch. 4, Ron Bevins.

Technical Facilities: 10-w TPO, 0.085-kw ERP, 1594-ft. above sea level, lat. 46° 14' 10", long. 119° 19' 15".

Transmitter: Badger Mountain tower site, SSW of Richland.

Ownership: Ronald A. Bevins.

Pateros—K10AP, Ch. 10, TV Reception District No. 3, Okanogan County.

Technical Facilities: 0.004-kw ERP, lat. 48° 01' 00", long. 119° 58' 51".

Pateros—K21HL, Ch. 21, Three Angels Broadcasting Network Inc. Phone: 618-627-4651.

Technical Facilities: 12.5-kw ERP, 46-ft. above ground, 5351-ft. above sea level, lat. 48° 00' 53", long. 119° 59' 02.7".

Ownership: Three Angels Broadcasting Network Inc.

Pateros & Mansfield—K08AP, Ch. 8, TV Reception District No. 3, Okanogan County.

Technical Facilities: 0.003-kw ERP, lat. 48° 01' 00", long. 119° 58' 51".

Pateros, etc.—K12AV, Ch. 12, TV Reception District No. 3, Okanogan County.

Technical Facilities: 0.032-kw ERP, lat. 48° 01' 00", long. 119° 58' 51".

Plain—K07WQ, Ch. 7, Lake Wenatchee TV Inc.

Technical Facilities: 0.033-kw ERP, lat. 47° 46' 51", long. 120° 41' 32".

Transmitter: 2-mi. NW of Plain.

Plain, etc.—K08FC, Ch. 8, Lake Wenatchee TV Inc.

Technical Facilities: 0.01-kw ERP, 3297-ft. above sea level, lat. 47° 46' 45", long. 120° 41' 30".

Point Pulley, etc.—K67GJ, Ch. 67, KIRO-TV Inc. Phone: 206-728-7777.

Technical Facilities: 1.5-kw ERP, lat. 47° 25' 43", long. 122° 26' 16".

Holds CP for change to channel number 47, 1.1-kw ERP, 75-ft. above ground, 302-ft. above sea level, BDISDTT-20061006AAY.

Transmitter: 0.2-mi. SW of Klahanie.

Ownership: Cox Enterprises Inc.

Port Angeles—K30FL, Ch. 30, KIRO-TV Inc. Phone: 206-728-7777.

Technical Facilities: 1.34-kw ERP, lat. 48° 07' 11", long. 123° 27' 44".

Holds CP for change to 39-ft. above ground, 358-ft. above sea level, BDFCDTT-20060919AAE.

Transmitter: 11th & E Sts.

Ownership: Cox Enterprises Inc.

Port Townsend—K62FS, Ch. 62, UPN Television Stations Inc.

Technical Facilities: 28.4-kw ERP, 43-ft. above ground, 2165-ft. above sea level, lat. 48° 00' 59", long. 122° 55' 31".

Prosser, etc.—K10NQ, Ch. 10, Mountain Licenses LP. Phone: 517-347-4141.

Technical Facilities: 1.1-kw ERP, 26-ft. above ground, 1886-ft. above sea level, lat. 46° 11' 12", long. 119° 45' 13".

Ownership: Mountain Licenses LP.

Pullman—K40EE, Ch. 40, Spokane Television Inc.

Technical Facilities: 12.2-kw ERP, 108-ft. above ground, 3707-ft. above sea level, lat. 46° 51' 43", long. 117° 10' 26".

Ownership: Morgan Murphy Media.

Pullman—KPMT-LP, Ch. 46, Duane J. Polich & Elaine F. Clemenson-Polich. Phone: 206-852-3096.

Technical Facilities: 0.125-kw ERP, 30-ft. above ground, 2470-ft. above sea level, lat. 46° 42' 51", long. 117° 10' 15".

Holds CP for change to channel number 14, 2.8-kw ERP, 49-ft. above ground, 4560-ft. above sea level, lat. 46° 48' 41", long. 116° 55' 03". BDISTTL-20080104ACG.

Ownership: Duane J. Polich & Elaine F. Clemenson-Polich.

Puyallup—K54GS, Ch. 54, KIRO-TV Inc. Phone: 206-728-7777.

Technical Facilities: 1.5-kw ERP, lat. 47° 10' 25", long. 122° 15' 51".

Holds CP for change to channel number 49, 2.2-kw ERP, 79-ft. above ground, 459-ft. above sea level, BDFCDTT-20060919ADD.

Ownership: Cox Enterprises Inc.

Quincy—K21AJ, Ch. 21, Quincy Valley TV Inc.

Technical Facilities: 2.43-kw ERP, lat. 47° 19' 14", long. 119° 48' 00".

Transmitter: 6.3-mi. NE of Quincy.

Quincy—K24AI, Ch. 24, Quincy Valley TV Inc.

Technical Facilities: 2.43-kw ERP, lat. 47° 19' 14", long. 119° 48' 00".

Quincy—K33EH, Ch. 33, Quincy Valley TV Inc.

Technical Facilities: 2.45-kw ERP, 20-ft. above ground, 2907-ft. above sea level, lat. 47° 19' 14", long. 119° 48' 00".

Quincy—K48BY, Ch. 48, Quincy Valley TV Inc.

Technical Facilities: 2.43-kw ERP, 13-ft. above ground, 2904-ft. above sea level, lat. 47° 19' 14", long. 119° 48' 00".

Quincy—K50BO, Ch. 50, Quincy Valley TV Inc.

Technical Facilities: 2.43-kw ERP, 16-ft. above ground, 2904-ft. above sea level, lat. 47° 19' 14", long. 119° 48' 00".

Richland—K54DU, Ch. 54, Three Angels Broadcasting Network Inc. Phone: 618-627-4651. Fax: 618-627-4155.

Studio: 3391 Charley Good Rd, West Frankfort, IL 62896.

Technical Facilities: 1000-w TPO, 0.7-kw ERP, 89-ft. above ground, 1640-ft. above sea level, lat. 46° 14' 10", long. 119° 19' 15".

Transmitter: On Badger Mountain, SW of Richland.

Ownership: Three Angels Broadcasting Network Inc.

Personnel: Moses Primo, Chief Engineer.

Richland—KRLB-LP, Ch. 49, Radiant Light Broadcasting. Phone: 509-943-9919. Fax: 509-946-8507.

Studio: 704 A Symons St., Richland, WA 99352.

Technical Facilities: 19.7-kw ERP, lat. 46° 14' 10", long. 119° 19' 15".

Holds CP for change to 4.9-kw ERP, 118-ft. above ground, 1670-ft. above sea level, BDFCDTL-20080922ADM.

Transmitter: On Badger Mountain, SW of Richland.

Ownership: Radiant Light Broadcasting.

Personnel: Richard O. Tedeschi, General Manager; William Carey, Chief Engineer; Maria Norman, Sales Manager.

Richland, etc.—KBWU-LD, Ch. 36, Mountain Licenses LP. Phone: 517-347-4141.

Technical Facilities: 13.3-kw ERP, 39-ft. above ground, 2219-ft. above sea level, lat. 46° 06' 15", long. 119° 07' 48".

Holds CP for change to 5.6-kw ERP, 25-ft. above ground, 1207-ft. above sea level, lat. 46° 09' 44", long. 119° 09' 13". BPDTL-20090324AAG.

Began Operation: July 26, 1985.

Ownership: Mountain Licenses LP.

Riverside—K08CY, Ch. 8, TV Reception Improvement District 1.

Technical Facilities: 0.0002-kw ERP, lat. 48° 29' 50", long. 119° 30' 45".

Transmitter: Mount Olive, 1-mi. S of Riverside.

Riverside—K10DM, Ch. 10, TV Reception Improvement District 1.

Technical Facilities: 0.002-kw ERP, 1503-ft. above sea level, lat. 48° 29' 50", long. 119° 30' 45".

Riverside—K12CV, Ch. 12, TV Reception Improvement District 1.

Technical Facilities: 0.001-kw ERP, lat. 48° 29' 50", long. 119° 30' 45".

Rock Island, etc.—K09CL, Ch. 9, Apple Valley TV Association Inc. Phone: 509-293-4403.

Technical Facilities: 0.01-kw ERP, 2159-ft. above sea level, lat. 47° 22' 00", long. 120° 16' 35".

Ownership: Apple Valley TV Association Inc.

Rock Island, etc.—K11CS, Ch. 11, Apple Valley TV Association Inc. Phone: 509-293-4403.

Technical Facilities: 0.01-kw ERP, 2159-ft. above sea level, lat. 47° 22' 00", long. 120° 16' 35".

Ownership: Apple Valley TV Association Inc.

Rock Island, etc.—K13CQ, Ch. 13, Apple Valley TV Association Inc. Phone: 509-293-4403.

Technical Facilities: 0.01-kw ERP, 2159-ft. above sea level, lat. 47° 22' 00", long. 120° 16' 35".

Ownership: Apple Valley TV Association Inc.

Seattle—K08OU-D, Ch. 8, Three Angels Broadcasting Network Inc. Phone: 618-627-4651. Fax: 618-627-4155.

Studio: 3391 Charley Good Rd, West Frankfort, IL 62896.

Technical Facilities: 0.25-kw ERP, 400-ft. above ground, 810-ft. above sea level, lat. 47° 36' 57", long. 122° 18' 26".

Ownership: Three Angels Broadcasting Network Inc.

Personnel: Moses Primo, Chief Engineer.

Seattle—KUSE-LP, Ch. 58, Mako Communications LLC. Phone: 361-883-1763.

Technical Facilities: 204-w TPO, 4.07-kw ERP, 948-ft. above ground, 1054-ft. above sea level, lat. 47° 36' 17", long. 122° 19' 46".

Transmitter: 701 5th Ave., Seattle.

Began Operation: November 12, 1997.

Ownership: Mako Communications LLC.

Spokane—K32GS, Ch. 32, Trinity Broadcasting Network. Phone: 714-832-2950. Fax: 714-730-0661.

Technical Facilities: 9.6-kw ERP, 62-ft. above ground, 2618-ft. above sea level, lat. 47° 41' 40", long. 117° 20' 01".

Ownership: Trinity Broadcasting Network Inc.

Spokane—K43GZ, Ch. 43, Ventana Television Inc. Phone: 727-872-4210.

Technical Facilities: 2.2-kw ERP, 171-ft. above ground, 3809-ft. above sea level, lat. 47° 34' 45", long. 117° 17' 51".

Began Operation: July 27, 1993.

Ownership: Ventana Television Inc.

Spokane—KHBA-LP, Ch. 39, He's Alive Broadcasting Assn. Phones: 509-838-2761; 509-622-4780. Fax: 509-838-4882.

Technical Facilities: 11.5-kw ERP, 213-ft. above ground, 3894-ft. above sea level, lat. 47° 34' 46", long. 117° 17' 51".

Holds CP for change to 3.1-kw ERP, BPDTL-20081210AAA.

Transmitter: Atop Browne Mountain, near Spokane.

Began Operation: December 2, 1993.

Ownership: He's Alive Broadcasting Assn.

Personnel: Marlo E. Fralick, General Manager; Ray Lenz, Chief Engineer.

Spokane, etc.—KXMN-LD, Ch. 9, Spokane Television Inc. Phone: 509-324-4000.

Technical Facilities: 0.2-kw ERP, 476-ft. above ground, 4104-ft. above sea level, lat. 47° 34' 34", long. 117° 17' 58".

Ownership: Spokane Television Inc.

Spokane, etc.—KXMN-LP, Ch. 11, Spokane Television Inc. Phone: 509-324-4000. Fax: 509-328-5274.

Technical Facilities: 1-kw ERP, 476-ft. above ground, 4104-ft. above sea level, lat. 47° 34' 34", long. 117° 17' 58".

Multichannel TV Sound: Stereo only.

Ownership: Spokane Television Inc.

Squilchuck State Park—K09FF, Ch. 9, Apple Valley TV Association Inc. Phone: 509-293-4403.

Technical Facilities: 0.001-kw ERP, lat. 47° 21' 05", long. 120° 19' 05".

Ownership: Apple Valley TV Association Inc.

Squilchuck State Park—K11FJ, Ch. 11, Apple Valley TV Association Inc. Phone: 509-293-4403.

Technical Facilities: 0.001-kw ERP, lat. 47° 21' 05", long. 120° 19' 05".

Ownership: Apple Valley TV Association Inc.

Squilchuck State Park—K13EZ, Ch. 13, Apple Valley TV Association Inc. Phone: 509-293-4403.

Technical Facilities: 0.001-kw ERP, lat. 47° 21' 05", long. 120° 19' 05".

Ownership: Apple Valley TV Association Inc.

Stemilt, etc.—K38IT, Ch. 38, Mountain Licenses LP. Phone: 517-347-4111.

Technical Facilities: 14.3-kw ERP, 20-ft. above ground, 6775-ft. above sea level, lat. 47° 16' 27", long. 120° 24' 18".

Ownership: Mountain Licenses LP.

Stemilt, etc.—K65AU, Ch. 65, Apple Valley TV Association Inc. Phone: 509-293-4403.

Technical Facilities: 1.08-kw ERP, 6778-ft. above sea level, lat. 47° 16' 27", long. 120° 24' 18".

Ownership: Apple Valley TV Association Inc.

Stemilt, etc.—K67CD, Ch. 67, Apple Valley TV Association Inc. Phone: 509-293-4403.

Technical Facilities: 1.2-kw ERP, lat. 47° 16' 27", long. 120° 24' 18".

Ownership: Apple Valley TV Association Inc.

Sunnyside—K13WP, Ch. 13, Ronald A. Bevins. Phone: 509-248-5971. Fax: 509-248-7499.

Technical Facilities: 10-w TPO, 0.68-kw ERP, 43-ft. above ground, 1903-ft. above sea level, lat. 46° 11' 11", long. 119° 45' 14".

Transmitter: Prosser tower site, 2-mi. SSE of Prosser.

Ownership: Ronald A. Bevins.

Sunnyside & Prosser—K05JO, Ch. 5, Three Angels Broadcasting Network Inc. Phone: 618-627-4651. Fax: 618-627-4155.

Studio: 3391 Charley Good Rd, West Frankfort, IL 62896.

Technical Facilities: 10-w TPO, 0.097-kw ERP, 26-ft. above ground, 1926-ft. above sea level, lat. 46° 11' 12", long. 119° 45' 14".

Transmitter: Prosser Butte.

Ownership: Three Angels Broadcasting Network Inc.

Personnel: Moses Primo, Chief Engineer; Linda Shelton, Program Director.

Sunnyside-Grandview—K08LU, Ch. 8, Ronald A. Bevins.

Technical Facilities: 10-w TPO, 0.169-kw ERP, 43-ft. above ground, 1903-ft. above sea level, lat. 46° 11' 11", long. 119° 45' 14".

Transmitter: Prosser tower site, approx. 2-mi. SSW of Prosser.

Ownership: Ronald A. Bevins.

Tonasket—K10DL, Ch. 10, TV Reception Improvement District 1.

Technical Facilities: 0.015-kw ERP, lat. 48° 46' 53", long. 119° 23' 10".

Transmitter: 7-mi. NNE of Tonasket.

Tonasket—K12CX, Ch. 12, TV Reception Improvement District 1.

Technical Facilities: 0.015-kw ERP, lat. 48° 46' 53", long. 119° 23' 10".

Transmitter: 7-mi. NNE of Tonasket.

Tonasket, etc.—K08CX, Ch. 8, TV Reception Improvement District 1.

Technical Facilities: 0.015-kw ERP, lat. 48° 46' 53", long. 119° 23' 10".

Transmitter: 7-mi. NNE of Tonasket.

Trout Lake—K04GC, Ch. 4, Trout Lake TV Assn.

Technical Facilities: 0.006-kw ERP, lat. 45° 59' 56", long. 121° 29' 13".

Trout Lake—K05AP, Ch. 5, Trout Lake TV Assn.

Technical Facilities: 0.005-kw ERP, lat. 45° 59' 45", long. 121° 28' 46".

Trout Lake—K09KW, Ch. 9, Trout Lake TV Assn.

Technical Facilities: 0.003-kw ERP, lat. 46° 00' 20", long. 121° 29' 37".

Vancouver & Camas—K14HN, Ch. 14, Meredith Corp. Phones: 503-239-4949; 515-284-3000. Fax: 503-239-6184.

Technical Facilities: 1000-w TPO, 10.7-kw ERP, 1079-ft. above ground, 1929-ft. above sea level, lat. 45° 41' 30", long. 122° 21' 40".

Holds CP for change to 2.5-kw ERP, 89-ft. above ground, 1929-ft. above sea level, BDFCDTL-20060331BBD.

Transmitter: Spud Mountain, approx. 3.7-mi. N of Fern Prairie.

Ownership: Meredith Corp.

Walla Walla—K21EK, Ch. 21, Blue Mountain Broadcasting Assn. Inc. Phone: 509-529-9149. Fax: 509-529-0661.

Technical Facilities: 3.58-kw ERP, 36-ft. above ground, 3711-ft. above sea level, lat. 45° 59' 20", long. 118° 10' 29".

Transmitter: Weston Mountain, approx. 1.8-mi. SE of Weston.

Ownership: Blue Mountain Broadcasting Assn. Inc.

■**Walla Walla**—K22BI, Ch. 22, Blue Mountain Broadcasting Assn. Inc. Phone: 509-529-9149. Fax: 509-529-0661.

Studio: 12th & Larch St, College Place, .

Technical Facilities: 100-w TPO, 1.11-kw ERP, 36-ft. above ground, 3711-ft. above sea level, lat. 45° 59' 20", long. 118° 10' 29".

Holds CP for change to channel number 21, 1.36-kw ERP, BDISDTA-20080711AED.

Transmitter: Pikes Peak, 11-mi. ENE of Milton-Freewater & 11-mi. SE of College Place.

Began Operation: August 13, 1990.

Ownership: Blue Mountain Broadcasting Assn. Inc.

Personnel: Lynelle Ellis, General Manager; Jim Roe, Chief Engineer.

■**Walla Walla**—K28FT, Ch. 28, Blue Mountain Broadcasting Assn. Inc. Phone: 509-529-9149. Fax: 509-529-0661.

Technical Facilities: 2.9-kw ERP, 968-ft. above sea level, lat. 46° 03' 44", long. 118° 23' 02".

Ownership: Blue Mountain Broadcasting Assn. Inc.

Personnel: Lynelle Ellis, General Manager; Jim Roe, Chief Engineer.

■**Walla Walla**—K33EJ, Ch. 33, Three Angels Broadcasting Network Inc. Phone: 618-627-4651. Fax: 618-627-4155.

Studio: 3391 Charley Good Rd, West Frankfort, IL 62896.

Technical Facilities: 1000-w TPO, 1.7-kw ERP, 79-ft. above ground, 3937-ft. above sea level, lat. 45° 59' 04", long. 118° 10' 08".

Transmitter: KNLT(FM) tower, Pikes Peak, near Walla Walla.

Ownership: Three Angels Broadcasting Network Inc.

Personnel: Moses Primo, Chief Engineer.

Walla Walla—K46FL, Ch. 46, Citizens TV Inc.

Technical Facilities: 1.74-kw ERP, lat. 45° 49' 55", long. 118° 15' 37".

Transmitter: Near Milton-Freewater.

■**Walla Walla**—KORX-CA, Ch. 16, Fisher Radio Regional Group Inc. Phone: 206-404-4884.

Technical Facilities: 84.8-kw ERP, 49-ft. above ground, 3907-ft. above sea level, lat. 45° 59' 04", long. 118° 10' 08".

Ownership: Fisher Communications Inc.

Personnel: Gregory J. Herman, General Manager; Steven A. Hale, Station Manager.

Walla Walla—KWWO-LP, Ch. 47, Radiant Light Broadcasting. Phone: 509-943-9919. Fax: 509-946-8507.

Technical Facilities: 1000-w TPO, 15.2-kw ERP, 26-ft. above ground, 3015-ft. above sea level, lat. 45° 47' 52", long. 118° 22' 07".

Holds CP for change to 1.9-kw ERP, 16-ft. above ground, 3015-ft. above sea level, BDFCDTL-20080922ADN.

Transmitter: Weston Mountain, 2.5-mi. SE of Weston.

Ownership: Radiant Light Broadcasting.

Personnel: Richard O. Tedeschi, General Manager; William Carey, Chief Engineer; Marguerite Yoshino, Sales Manager.

Walla Walla, etc.—K14HT, Ch. 14, Apple Valley Broadcasting Inc. Phone: 509-453-0351.

Technical Facilities: 2-kw ERP, 20-ft. above ground, 3238-ft. above sea level, lat. 45° 50' 25", long. 118° 17' 10".

Ownership: Morgan Murphy Media.

Wenatchee—K14BF, Ch. 14, Jumpoff Ridge LLC. Phone: 425-788-2600.

Technical Facilities: 0.78-kw ERP, lat. 47° 27' 51", long. 120° 12' 26".

Holds CP for change to 15-kw ERP, 14-ft. above ground, 3439-ft. above sea level, lat. 47° 27' 54", long. 120° 12' 32". BDFCDTT-20060323AAQ.

Ownership: Jumpoff Ridge LLC.

Wenatchee—K24EX, Ch. 24, Spokane Television Inc.

Technical Facilities: 0.679-kw ERP, 15-ft. above ground, 2034-ft. above sea level, lat. 47° 22' 52", long. 120° 17' 16".

Transmitter: Wenatchee Heights, 1.5-mi. from Wenatchee.

Wenatchee—K32FN, Ch. 32, Spokane Television Inc. Phone: 509-324-4000.

Technical Facilities: 0.89-kw ERP, 16-ft. above ground, 6778-ft. above sea level, lat. 47° 16' 27", long. 120° 24' 18".

Ownership: Spokane Television Inc.

Wenatchee—K34EM, Ch. 34, Trinity Broadcasting Network Inc. Phone: 714-832-2950. Fax: 714-730-0661.

Technical Facilities: 1000-w TPO, 12.2-kw ERP, 89-ft. above ground, 3293-ft. above sea level, lat. 47° 26' 22", long. 120° 10' 55".

Holds CP for change to 15-kw ERP, 62-ft. above ground, 3202-ft. above sea level, lat. 47° 26' 16", long. 120° 10' 42". BDFCDTT-20060329AES.

Transmitter: Clark-Badger Mountain tower site.

Began Operation: October 30, 1997.

Ownership: Trinity Broadcasting Network Inc.

Wenatchee—K45AC, Ch. 45, KREM-TV Inc.

Technical Facilities: 0.791-kw ERP, lat. 47° 16' 27", long. 120° 24' 18".

Wenatchee—K51DR, Ch. 51, Apple Valley TV Association Inc. Phone: 509-293-4403.

Technical Facilities: 5.51-kw ERP, lat. 47° 19' 11", long. 120° 14' 23".

Ownership: Apple Valley TV Association Inc.

Wenatchee—KWCC-LP, Ch. 47, Apple Valley TV Association Inc. Phone: 509-293-4403.

Technical Facilities: 6-w TPO, 0.194-kw ERP, 80-ft. above ground, 889-ft. above sea level, lat. 47° 22' 10", long. 120° 13' 30".

Transmitter: 205 1st St., First/Chelan Bldg.

Ownership: Apple Valley TV Association Inc.

Winthrop & Twisp—K08AY, Ch. 8, TV Reception District 2 of Okanogan County.

Technical Facilities: 0.098-kw ERP, lat. 48° 18' 56", long. 120° 06' 54".

Winthrop & Twisp—K10BD, Ch. 10, TV Reception District 2 of Okanogan County.

Technical Facilities: 0.098-kw ERP, lat. 48° 18' 56", long. 120° 06' 54".

Winthrop & Twisp—K12BA, Ch. 12, TV Reception District 2 of Okanogan County.

Technical Facilities: 0.098-kw ERP, lat. 48° 18' 56", long. 120° 06' 54".

Winton & Merritt—K09XB, Ch. 9, W-M TV Assn.

Technical Facilities: 0.004-kw ERP, 18-ft. above ground, 4199-ft. above sea level, lat. 47° 47' 08", long. 120° 48' 31".

Transmitter: 1/3-mi. W of Merritt.

Winton, etc.—K03EC, Ch. 3, W-M TV Assn.

Technical Facilities: 0.01-kw ERP, 4163-ft. above sea level, lat. 47° 47' 00", long. 120° 48' 00".

Ownership: W-M TV Association.

Winton, etc.—K05FN, Ch. 5, W-M TV Assn.

Technical Facilities: 0.01-kw ERP, 4163-ft. above sea level, lat. 47° 47' 00", long. 120° 48' 00".

Yakima—K39FU, Ch. 39, Ron Bevins. Phone: 509-452-8817.

Technical Facilities: 24.5-kw ERP, 43-ft. above ground, 1863-ft. above sea level, lat. 46° 31' 57", long. 120° 29' 45".

Holds CP for change to 15-kw ERP, lat. 46° 31' 58", long. 120° 29' 41". BDFCDTL-20080709AKQ.

Ownership: Ronald A. Bevins.

Yakima—K43GY, Ch. 43, Ronald A. Bevins. Phone: 509-452-8817. Fax: 509-248-7499.

Studio: 713 W. Yakima Ave., Yakima, WA 98902.

Technical Facilities: 18.6-kw ERP, 43-ft. above ground, 1863-ft. above sea level, lat. 46° 31' 57", long. 120° 29' 45".

Ownership: Ronald A. Bevins.

Personnel: Ronald Bevins, General Manager; Don Mitchell, Operations Manager; Ricardo Barrientes, Production Manager.

Yakima—KCWK-LP, Ch. 27, KCWK License LLC - Debtor-in-Possession. Phone: 509-575-0999.

Technical Facilities: 44-kw ERP, 39-ft. above ground, 2014-ft. above sea level, lat. 46° 31' 57", long. 120° 30' 37".

Ownership: E. Roger Williams, Trustee.

Yakima—KCYU-LD, Ch. 41, Mountain Licenses LP. Phone: 517-347-4141.

Technical Facilities: 12.9-kw ERP, 39-ft. above ground, 2015-ft. above sea level, lat. 46° 31' 57", long. 120° 30' 37".

Began Operation: May 17, 1993.

Ownership: Mountain Licenses LP.

■**Yakima**—KDHW-LP, Ch. 45, Christian Broadcasting of Yakima Inc. Phone: 509-972-0926. Fax: 509-577-0301.

Technical Facilities: 100-w TPO, 12.5-kw ERP, lat. 46° 31' 49", long. 120° 27' 15".

Holds CP for change to 36-kw ERP, 33-ft. above ground, 1801-ft. above sea level, lat. 46° 31' 58.8", long. 120° 29' 30.6". BPTTA-20040525ADF.

Ownership: Christian Broadcasting Network.

Personnel: Ric McClary, General Manager; Moe Broom, Chief Engineer.

■**Yakima**—KUNW-CA, Ch. 2, Fisher Radio Regional Group Inc. Phone: 206-404-4884.

Technical Facilities: 1000-w TPO, 0.8-kw ERP, 19-ft. above ground, 2188-ft. above sea level, lat. 46° 31' 40", long. 120° 33' 06".

Holds CP for change to 1-kw ERP, 34-ft. above ground, 2034-ft. above sea level, lat. 46° 31' 58", long. 120° 30' 33". BMPTVA-20070625ADO.

Transmitter: Approx 3.6-mi. S of Yakima on Ahtanum Ridge.

Ownership: Fisher Communications Inc.

Personnel: Gregory J. Herman, General Manager; Steven A. Hale, Station Manager.

Yakima, etc.—K49GF, Ch. 49, Ronald A. Bevins. Phone: 509-452-8817. Fax: 509-248-7499.

Technical Facilities: 2.48-kw ERP, 43-ft. above ground, 1863-ft. above sea level, lat. 46° 31' 57", long. 120° 29' 45".

Ownership: Ronald A. Bevins.

Yakima-Toppenish—K58DL, Ch. 58, Three Angels Broadcasting Network Inc. Phone: 618-627-4651.

Studio: 3391 Charley Good Rd, West Frankfort, IL 62896.

Technical Facilities: 1000-w TPO, 19-kw ERP, 98-ft. above ground, 2129-ft. above sea level, lat. 46° 31' 42", long. 120° 31' 16".

Holds CP for change to channel number 51, 49.75-kw ERP, 190-ft. above ground, 1909-ft. above sea level, lat. 46° 31' 51", long. 120° 27' 24". BMPTTL-20080411AEG.

Transmitter: Ahtanum Ridge, near Yakima.

Began Operation: June 25, 1990.

Ownership: Three Angels Broadcasting Network Inc.

Personnel: Moses Primo, Chief Engineer; Linda Shelton, Program Director.

West Virginia

Beckley—WCIR-LP, Ch. 2, Family Television Inc. Phone: 304-222-5063.

Technical Facilities: 3-kw ERP, 146-ft. above ground, 2634-ft. above sea level, lat. 37° 47' 06", long. 81° 06' 48".

Holds CP for change to 164-ft. above ground, 3383-ft. above sea level, lat. 37° 56' 50.6", long. 81° 18' 28.61". BPTVL-20070719ABU.

Ownership: Family Television Inc.

Charleston—W16CE, Ch. 16, Gray Television Licensee LLC. Phone: 818-973-2722.

Technical Facilities: 22.9-kw ERP, 164-ft. above ground, 1174-ft. above sea level, lat. 38° 22' 31", long. 81° 39' 22".

Transmitter: End of Garfield St.

Multichannel TV Sound: Stereo and separate audio program.

Ownership: Gray Television Inc.

Personnel: Don Ray, General Manager; Bill Galloway, Chief Engineer; Chris Aidrich, Sales Manager.

Charleston—W31CA, Ch. 31, Trinity Christian Center of Santa Ana Inc. Phone: 714-832-2950.

Technical Facilities: 11.2-kw ERP, lat. 38° 22' 36", long. 81° 42' 09".

Holds CP for change to channel number 27, 15-kw ERP, 154-ft. above ground, 1095-ft. above sea level, BDISDTT-20060329ABP.

Began Operation: April 25, 1994.

Ownership: Trinity Broadcasting Network Inc.

Charleston—WOCW-LP, Ch. 21, Mountain TV LLC. Phone: 757-722-9736.

Technical Facilities: 25-kw ERP, 249-ft. above ground, 1211-ft. above sea level, lat. 38° 22' 34", long. 81° 39' 24".

Ownership: Mountain TV LLC.

Clarksburg—W21CJ, Ch. 21, Cornerstone Television Inc. Phone: 412-824-3930.

Technical Facilities: 10-kw ERP, 266-ft. above ground, 1831-ft. above sea level, lat. 39° 16' 32", long. 80° 17' 43".

Ownership: Cornerstone Television Inc.

Clarksburg—W22CY, Ch. 22, Withers Broadcasting Co. of West Virginia. Phone: 304-848-5000. Fax: 304-842-7501.

Studio: 5 Television Dr., PO Box 480, Bridgeport, WV 26330.

Technical Facilities: 13-kw ERP, 266-ft. above ground, 1831-ft. above sea level, lat. 39° 16' 32", long. 80° 17' 43".

Ownership: W. Russell Withers Jr.

Clarksburg—W30CH, Ch. 30, W. Russell Withers Jr. Phone: 618-242-3500.

Technical Facilities: 1-kw ERP, 328-ft. above ground, 1688-ft. above sea level, lat. 39° 18' 02", long. 80° 20' 37".

Ownership: W. Russell Withers Jr.

Clarksburg—W44CF, Ch. 44, Trinity Broadcasting Network Inc. Phone: 714-832-2950. Fax: 714/730-0661.

Technical Facilities: 11.2-kw ERP, 157-ft. above ground, 1722-ft. above sea level, lat. 39° 16' 32", long. 80° 17' 43".

Ownership: Trinity Broadcasting Network Inc.

Clarksburg—W62DF, Ch. 62, Greenbrier Valley TV LLC. Phone: 304-645-5210.

Technical Facilities: 6-kw ERP, 164-ft. above ground, 1729-ft. above sea level, lat. 39° 16' 31.7", long. 80° 17' 43.7".

Ownership: Greenbrier Valley TV LLC.

Clarksburg—W64CZ, Ch. 64, TKMI Broadcasting. Phone: 304-986-2896. Fax: 304-986-2895.

Technical Facilities: 2-kw ERP, 249-ft. above ground, 1808-ft. above sea level, lat. 39° 17' 53", long. 80° 17' 59".

Ownership: TKMI Broadcasting.

Clarksburg—WVUX-LP, Ch. 56, Wood Investments LLC. Phone: 304-222-5063.

Technical Facilities: 149-kw ERP, 161-ft. above ground, 1726-ft. above sea level, lat. 39° 16' 31.67", long. 80° 17' 43.68".

Ownership: Wood Investments LLC.

Elkins—W31CQ, Ch. 31, Withers Broadcasting Co. of West Virginia. Phones: 936-854-2044; 888-322-5291.

Technical Facilities: 2.7-kw ERP, 180-ft. above ground, 3461-ft. above sea level, lat. 38° 51' 41", long. 79° 56' 01".

Ownership: W. Russell Withers Jr.

Hampshire, etc.—W34DW-D, Ch. 34, West Virginia Educational Broadcasting Authority. Phone: 304-556-4900.

Technical Facilities: 12-kw ERP, 175-ft. above ground, 2760-ft. above sea level, lat. 39° 26' 39", long. 78° 20' 52".

Began Operation: April 16, 2009.

Ownership: West Virginia Educational Broadcasting Authority.

Hampshire, etc.—W41AO, Ch. 41, West Virginia Educational Bcstg. Authority.

Technical Facilities: 2.73-kw ERP, 164-ft. above ground, 2684-ft. above sea level, lat. 39° 27' 03", long. 78° 20' 53".

Huntington—W14CU, Ch. 14, Ventana Television Inc. Phone: 727-872-4210.

Technical Facilities: 50-kw ERP, 423-ft. above ground, 1266-ft. above sea level, lat. 38° 25' 11", long. 82° 24' 06".

Began Operation: November 14, 1991.

Ownership: Ventana Television Inc.

Personnel: John Skelnik, General Manager & Chief Engineer.

Huntington—W36CR, Ch. 36, Trinity Christian Center of Santa Ana Inc. Phone: 714-832-2950.

Technical Facilities: 1000-w TPO, 9.8-kw ERP, 282-ft. above ground, 1142-ft. above sea level, lat. 38° 25' 17", long. 82° 23' 47".

Holds CP for change to 15-kw ERP, 282-ft. above ground, 1138-ft. above sea level, BDFCDTT-20060328AJY.

Transmitter: Rotary Park Antenna Farm.

Ownership: Trinity Broadcasting Network Inc.

Personnel: Mark Fountain, Chief Engineer.

Huntington—WVCW-LP, Ch. 69, Mountain TV LLC. Phone: 757-722-9736.

Technical Facilities: 1000-w TPO, 20.8-kw ERP, 445-ft. above ground, 1385-ft. above sea level, lat. 38° 29' 41", long. 82° 12' 03".

Transmitter: 1373 Grandview Dr., Kenova.

Ownership: Mountain TV LLC.

Keyser—W41DK-D, Ch. 41, West Virginia Educational Broadcasting Authority. Phone: 304-556-4900.

Technical Facilities: 7-kw ERP, 39-ft. above ground, 3100-ft. above sea level, lat. 39° 22' 55", long. 79° 04' 46".

Ownership: West Virginia Educational Broadcasting Authority.

Keyser—W48AA, Ch. 48, West Virginia Educational Bcstg. Authority.

Technical Facilities: 26.3-kw ERP, lat. 39° 22' 55", long. 79° 04' 46".

Ownership: West Virginia Educational Broadcasting Authority.

Martinsburg—W08EE-D, Ch. 8, West Virginia Educational Broadcasting Authority. Phone: 304-556-4900.

Technical Facilities: 0.3-kw ERP, 155-ft. above ground, 1615-ft. above sea level, lat. 39° 27' 36", long. 78° 03' 45".

Ownership: West Virginia Educational Broadcasting Authority.

Martinsburg—W44AA, Ch. 44, West Virginia Educational Bcstg. Authority.

Technical Facilities: 26.8-kw ERP, lat. 39° 27' 35", long. 78° 03' 49".

Mathias—W17AL, Ch. 17, West Virginia Educational Bcstg. Authority.

Technical Facilities: 1.62-kw ERP, lat. 38° 49' 15", long. 78° 53' 56".

Mathias, etc.—W09CT-D, Ch. 9, West Virginia Educational Broadcasting Authority. Phone: 304-556-4900.

Technical Facilities: 0.24-kw ERP, 110-ft. above ground, 2590-ft. above sea level, lat. 38° 49' 15", long. 78° 53' 56".

Began Operation: January 21, 2009.

Ownership: West Virginia Educational Broadcasting Authority.

Moorefield—W22CV, Ch. 22, Valley TV Cooperative Inc. Phone: 304-538-6033.

Technical Facilities: 0.035-kw ERP, 20-ft. above ground, 3284-ft. above sea level, lat. 38° 58' 57", long. 78° 54' 31".

Moorefield—W40AS, Ch. 40, Valley TV Cooperative Inc.

Technical Facilities: 0.6-kw ERP, 20-ft. above ground, 3284-ft. above sea level, lat. 38° 58' 57", long. 78° 54' 31".

Transmitter: Branch Mountain.

Moorefield—W46BR, Ch. 46, Valley TV Cooperative Inc.

Technical Facilities: 0.334-kw ERP, 20-ft. above ground, 3284-ft. above sea level, lat. 38° 58' 57", long. 78° 54' 31".

Moorefield—W50BD, Ch. 50, Valley TV Cooperative Inc.

Technical Facilities: 0.6-kw ERP, 20-ft. above ground, 3284-ft. above sea level, lat. 38° 58' 57", long. 78° 54' 31".

Moorefield—W54BG, Ch. 54, Valley TV Cooperative Inc.

Technical Facilities: 0.6-kw ERP, 20-ft. above ground, 3284-ft. above sea level, lat. 38° 58' 57", long. 78° 54' 31".

Parkersburg—W45BW, Ch. 45, Trinity Broadcasting Network Inc. Phone: 714-832-2950. Fax: 714-730-0661.

Technical Facilities: 1000-w TPO, 12.9-kw ERP, 427-ft. above ground, 1217-ft. above sea level, lat. 39° 19' 27", long. 81° 37' 33".

Holds CP for change to 15-kw ERP, BDFCDTT-20060329AEP.

Transmitter: 0.2-mi. WNW of Ward Rd. & Farson St. intersection, Dunlap Twp.

Ownership: Trinity Broadcasting Network Inc.

Parkersburg—W57AG, Ch. 57, West Virginia Educational Bcstg. Authority. Phone: 304-556-4900.

Technical Facilities: 0.861-kw ERP, lat. 39° 12' 43", long. 81° 35' 31".

Ownership: West Virginia Educational Broadcasting Authority.

Romney—W69AC, Ch. 69, West Virginia Educational Broadcasting Authority. Phone: 304-556-4900.

Technical Facilities: 1-kw ERP, 83-ft. above ground, 1963-ft. above sea level, lat. 39° 18' 56", long. 78° 43' 04".

Ownership: West Virginia Educational Broadcasting Authority.

Wardensville—W15AD, Ch. 15, West Virginia Educational Bcstg. Authority.

Technical Facilities: 2.4-kw ERP, lat. 39° 06' 59", long. 78° 28' 25".

Wardensville, etc.—W07DN-D, Ch. 7, West Virginia Educational Broadcasting Authority. Phone: 304-556-4900.

Technical Facilities: 0.3-kw ERP, 69-ft. above ground, 2884-ft. above sea level, lat. 39° 08' 38", long. 78° 26' 09".

Ownership: West Virginia Educational Broadcasting Authority.

■ **Weirtown**—WJPW-CA, Ch. 18, Bruno-Goodworth Network Inc. Phone: 412-922-9576.

Technical Facilities: 150-kw ERP, 100-ft. above ground, 1362-ft. above sea level, lat. 40° 21' 59", long. 80° 35' 22".

Transmitter: Archer Hill, 1.5-mi. NE of Archer Heights.

Ownership: Bruno-Goodworth Network Inc.

Wheeling—W41AA, Ch. 41, West Virginia Educational Bcstg. Authority.

Technical Facilities: 77.8-kw ERP, lat. 40° 03' 41", long. 80° 45' 08".

Wheeling—WWVW-LP, Ch. 56, Abacus Television. Phone: 202-462-3680.

Technical Facilities: 12.1-kw ERP, 215-ft. above ground, 1499-ft. above sea level, lat. 40° 03' 41", long. 80° 45' 08".

Ownership: Abacus Television.

Wisconsin

Ashland—W45CI, Ch. 45, KQDS Acquisition Corp. Phone: 701-277-1515.

Technical Facilities: 15.9-kw ERP, 235-ft. above ground, 931-ft. above sea level, lat. 46° 35' 24", long. 90° 50' 06".

Holds CP for change to 9.332-kw ERP, 235-ft. above ground, 935-ft. above sea level, BDFCDTT-20060331BJF.

Ownership: KQDS Acquisition Corp.

Ashland—WAST-LP, Ch. 25, True North TV 25 LLC. Phone: 715-682-8811.

Technical Facilities: 52-kw ERP, 125-ft. above ground, 1126-ft. above sea level, lat. 46° 41' 17", long. 90° 54' 23".

Ownership: True North TV 25 LLC.

Bloomington—W22CI, Ch. 22, State of Wisconsin-Educational Communications Board. Phone: 715-632-2827.

Technical Facilities: 1.346-kw ERP, 492-ft. above ground, 1492-ft. above sea level, lat. 42° 54' 12", long. 90° 57' 01".

Ownership: Wisconsin Educational Communications Board.

Coloma—W48DB-D, Ch. 48, State of Wisconsin Educational Communications Board. Phone: 715-632-2827.

Technical Facilities: 4.89-kw ERP, 458-ft. above ground, 1588-ft. above sea level, lat. 44° 01' 13", long. 89° 33' 29".

Ownership: Wisconsin Educational Communications Board.

Darlington—W56AB, Ch. 56, City of Darlington.

Technical Facilities: 0.654-kw ERP, lat. 42° 40' 47", long. 90° 07' 37".

Elk Mound—W45CF, Ch. 45, Magnum Radio Inc. Phone: 608-372-9600.

Technical Facilities: 1-kw ERP, 459-ft. above ground, 1378-ft. above sea level, lat. 44° 53' 05", long. 91° 23' 27".

Ownership: Magnum Radio Inc.

Fence—W45CD-D, Ch. 45, State of Wisconsin-Educational Communications Board. Phone: 715-632-2827.

Technical Facilities: 1.18-kw ERP, 492-ft. above ground, 2042-ft. above sea level, lat. 45° 44' 08", long. 88° 25' 40".

Began Operation: October 3, 1988.

Ownership: Wisconsin Educational Communications Board.

Grantsburg—W24CL-D, Ch. 24, State of Wisconsin-Educational Communications Board. Phone: 715-632-2827.

Technical Facilities: 1.56-kw ERP, 404-ft. above ground, 1470-ft. above sea level, lat. 45° 50' 29", long. 92° 28' 15".

Began Operation: January 3, 1989.

Ownership: Wisconsin Educational Communications Board.

Green Bay—W30BU, Ch. 30, Three Angels Broadcasting Network Inc. Phone: 618-627-4651. Fax: 618-627-4155.

Studio: 3391 Charley Good Rd, West Frankfort, IL 62896.

Technical Facilities: 0.33-w TPO, 14.7-kw ERP, 459-ft. above ground, 1420-ft. above sea level, lat. 44° 21' 32", long. 87° 59' 07".

Transmitter: 3237 Shirley Rd.

Ownership: Three Angels Broadcasting Network Inc.

Personnel: Moses Primo, Chief Engineer; Linda Shelton, Program Director.

Green Bay—W49CB, Ch. 49, Trinity Broadcasting Network Inc. Phone: 714-832-2950. Fax: 714-730-0661.

Technical Facilities: 1000-w TPO, 22.3-kw ERP, 587-ft. above ground, 1476-ft. above sea level, lat. 44° 24' 32", long. 87° 59' 31".

Transmitter: Glenmore Rd., 4.4-mi. SE of Depere Twp.

Ownership: Trinity Broadcasting Network Inc.

Personnel: Paul Crouch, General Manager; Ben Miller, Chief Engineer; Rod Henke, Sales Manager.

Hayward—K31GH, Ch. 31, KQDS Acquisition Corp. Phone: 701-277-1515.

Technical Facilities: 16.4-kw ERP, 252-ft. above ground, 1722-ft. above sea level, lat. 45° 59' 52", long. 91° 24' 14".

Holds CP for change to 9.484-kw ERP, BDFCDTT-20060331BGD.

Ownership: KQDS Acquisition Corp.

Janesville—W65EE, Ch. 65, Trinity Broadcasting Network. Phone: 714-832-2950. Fax: 714-730-0661.

Technical Facilities: 20.3-kw ERP, 180-ft. above ground, 1150-ft. above sea level, lat. 42° 41' 09", long. 89° 09' 05".

Ownership: Trinity Broadcasting Network Inc.

La Crosse—W44BF, Ch. 44, Douglas L. Sheldahl. Phone: 515-597-3531.

Technical Facilities: 1000-w TPO, 7.31-kw ERP, 405-ft. above ground, 1620-ft. above sea level, lat. 43° 48' 16", long. 91° 22' 18".

Transmitter: WLAX(TV) tower, 1000 Tschaxper Ridge Rd., La Crescent, MN.

Ownership: Douglas L. Sheldahl.

La Crosse—W58DQ, Ch. 58, Western Family Television Inc. Phone: 406-442-2655.

Technical Facilities: 0.002-kw ERP, 20-ft. above ground, 689-ft. above sea level, lat. 43° 49' 59", long. 91° 14' 56".

Ownership: Western Family Television Inc.

La Crosse—W67CH, Ch. 67, KTTC Television Inc. Phone: 217-223-5100.

Technical Facilities: 2.76-kw ERP, lat. 43° 45' 25", long. 91° 17' 40".

Holds CP for change to channel number 50, 15-kw ERP, 740-ft. above ground, 1966-ft. above sea level, lat. 43° 48' 23", long. 91° 22' 02". BMPDTT-20080721AAL.

Ownership: Quincy Newspapers Inc.

■ **Madison**—W23BW, Ch. 23, Three Angels Broadcasting Network Inc. Phone: 618-627-4651. Fax: 618-627-4155.

Studio: 3391 Charley Good Rd, West Frankfort, IL 62896.

Technical Facilities: 38.5-kw ERP, 300-ft. above ground, 1367-ft. above sea level, lat. 43° 03' 09", long. 89° 28' 42".

Transmitter: TCBY Bldg., Downtown Little Rock.

Ownership: Three Angels Broadcasting Network Inc.

Personnel: Moses Primo, Chief Engineer; Linda Shelton, Program Director.

Madison—W38CT, Ch. 38, Trinity Broadcasting Network Inc. Phone: 714-832-2950. Fax: 714-730-0661.

Technical Facilities: 14.1-kw ERP, 282-ft. above ground, 1438-ft. above sea level, lat. 43° 03' 09", long. 89° 28' 42".

Ownership: Trinity Broadcasting Network Inc.

Madison-Middleton—W08CK, Ch. 8, Science of Identity Foundation. Phone: 808-261-8815.

Technical Facilities: 10-w TPO, 0.036-kw ERP, 180-ft. above ground, 1132-ft. above sea level, lat. 43° 04' 30", long. 89° 22' 52".

Transmitter: 3 Pinckney St., Madison.

Ownership: Science of Identity Foundation.

■ **Milwaukee**—WMKE-CA, Ch. 7, KM LPTV of Milwaukee LLC. Phone: 847-674-0864. Fax: 847-674-9188.

Technical Facilities: 500-w TPO, 3-kw ERP, 591-ft. above ground, 1201-ft. above sea level, lat. 43° 02' 20", long. 87° 55' 04".

Transmitter: Marc Plaza, 509 W. Wisconsin Ave.

Multichannel TV Sound: Stereo only.

Ownership: KM Communications Inc.

Personnel: K. C. Bae, General Manager; Stan Byers, Chief Engineer.

■ **Milwaukee**—WMLW-CA, Ch. 41, Channel 43 & 63 LP. Phones: 312-705-2600; 414-777-5800. Fax: 414-777-5802.

Studio: 809 S. 60th St., Milwaukee, WI 53214.

Technical Facilities: 37-kw ERP, 1086-ft. above ground, 1709-ft. above sea level, lat. 43° 06' 42", long. 87° 55' 50".

Ownership: Weigel Broadcasting Co.

Personnel: Norman H. Shapiro, General Manager; Peter Zomaya, Sales Manager; Jim Hall, Chief Engineer.

Milwaukee—WMLW-LD, Ch. 13, Channel 41 & 63 Ltd. Partnership. Phone: 312-705-2600.

Technical Facilities: 0.3-kw ERP, 909-ft. above ground, 1532-ft. above sea level, lat. 43° 06' 42", long. 87° 55' 50".

Milwaukee—WYTU-LD, Ch. 17, Channel 41 & 63 LP. Phone: 312-705-2600.

Technical Facilities: 2.1-kw ERP, 938-ft. above ground, 1562-ft. above sea level, lat. 43° 06' 42", long. 87° 55' 50".

Ownership: Weigel Broadcasting Co.

Milwaukee—WYTU-LP, Ch. 63, Channel 41 & 63 LP. Phone: 312-705-2600.

Technical Facilities: 137-kw ERP, 1073-ft. above ground, 1696-ft. above sea level, lat. 43° 06' 42", long. 87° 55' 50".

Holds CP for change to channel number 49, BDISTTL-20080801AXK.

Began Operation: May 13, 1983February 2, 1983.

Ownership: Weigel Broadcasting Co.

Minocqua—W02CF, Ch. 2, Three Angels Broadcasting Network Inc. Phone: 618-627-4651. Fax: 618-627-4155.

Technical Facilities: 10-w TPO, 0.294-kw ERP, 1739-ft. above sea level, lat. 45° 53' 05", long. 89° 46' 50".

Transmitter: 8674 Pine Hurst Dr.

Ownership: Three Angels Broadcasting Network Inc.

Personnel: Moses Primo, Chief Engineer.

Minocqua—W31BA, Ch. 31, Three Angels Broadcasting Network Inc. Phone: 618-627-4651. Fax: 618-627-4155.

Studio: 3391 Charley Good Rd, West Frankfort, IL 62896.

Technical Facilities: 1000-w TPO, 15.6-kw ERP, 479-ft. above ground, 2080-ft. above sea level, lat. 45° 53' 21", long. 89° 47' 58".

Transmitter: 0.2-mi. NE of SR 70 & Mercer Lake Rd.

Ownership: Three Angels Broadcasting Network Inc.

Personnel: Moses Primo, Chief Engineer.

Ripon—W17CF, Ch. 17, Trinity Broadcasting Network Inc. Phone: 714-832-2950. Fax: 714-730-0661.

Technical Facilities: 1000-w TPO, 49.9-kw ERP, 299-ft. above ground, 1053-ft. above sea level, lat. 44° 03' 51", long. 88° 31' 43".

Transmitter: 3480 N. Shore Dr.

Ownership: Trinity Broadcasting Network Inc.

River Falls—W47CO-D, Ch. 47, State of Wisconsin-Educational Communications Board. Phone: 715-632-2827.

Technical Facilities: 1.6-kw ERP, 351-ft. above ground, 1391-ft. above sea level, lat. 44° 54' 10", long. 92° 41' 28".

Ownership: Wisconsin Educational Communications Board.

Sayner & Vilas County—W57AR, Ch. 57, Gray Television Licensee LLC. Phone: 715-835-1313.

Technical Facilities: 1.72-kw ERP, lat. 46° 01' 55", long. 89° 31' 48".

Ownership: Gray Television Inc.

Sheboygan—W29DJ, Ch. 29, Polnet Communications Ltd. Phone: 773-588-6300.

Technical Facilities: 43-kw ERP, 198-ft. above ground, 1050-ft. above sea level, lat. 43° 31' 14", long. 87° 56' 11".

Holds CP for change to 8.7-kw ERP, 771-ft. above ground, 1399-ft. above sea level, lat. 43° 05' 46", long. 87° 54' 15". BDFCDTL-20080240ABL.

Began Operation: August 23, 1990.

Ownership: Polnet Communications Ltd.

Personnel: Paul Crouch, General Manager; Ben Miller, Chief Engineer; Rod Henke, Sales Manager.

Sister Bay—W18CU-D, Ch. 18, State of Wisconsin-Educational Communications Board. Phone: 715-632-2827.

Technical Facilities: 1.95-kw ERP, 490-ft. above ground, 1270-ft. above sea level, lat. 45° 14' 19", long. 87° 05' 27".

Ownership: Wisconsin Educational Communications Board.

■ **Sturgeon Bay**—W22BW, Ch. 22, Journal Broadcast Corp.

Technical Facilities: 8.8-kw ERP, lat. 44° 54' 14", long. 872° 21' 03".

Transmitter: Door County Hwy., 4.5-mi N of Sturgeon Bay.

Ownership: Journal Communications Inc.

Tigerton, etc.—W04CW, Ch. 4, VCY America Inc. Phone: 414-935-3000.

Technical Facilities: 0.251-kw ERP, 185-ft. above ground, 1302-ft. above sea level, lat. 44° 42' 03.9", long. 88° 53' 24.4".

Began Operation: January 18, 1994.

Ownership: VCY America Inc.

Personnel: Jack Badalk Sr., General Manager.

Tomah—WIBU-LP, Ch. 51, Magnum Radio Inc. Phone: 608-372-9600. Fax: 608-372-7566.

Technical Facilities: 150-kw ERP, 470-ft. above ground, 1910-ft. above sea level, lat. 43° 53' 50", long. 90° 34' 57".

Transmitter: 1.3-mi. at a bearing of 315 degrees T from Ridgeville.

Ownership: David R. Magnum.

Waukesha—WTAS-LP, Ch. 47, Waukesha Tower Assoc. Phone: 262-783-8800.

Technical Facilities: 39.7-kw ERP, 449-ft. above ground, 1493-ft. above sea level, lat. 42° 58' 05", long. 88° 11' 24".

Ownership: Waukesha Tower Assoc.

Personnel: Robert von Bereghy, General Manager; Nancy Taft, Station Manager; Bob Truscott, Chief Engineer.

Waupaca—W36DH, Ch. 36, Trinity Broadcasting Network. Phone: 714-832-2950. Fax: 714-730-0661.

Technical Facilities: 16.3-kw ERP, 433-ft. above ground, 1313-ft. above sea level, lat. 44° 25' 03", long. 88° 55' 03".

Ownership: Trinity Broadcasting Network Inc.

Personnel: Paul Crouch, General Manager; Ben Miller, Chief Engineer; Rod Henke, Sales Manager.

Wausau—W27AU, Ch. 27, Northland Television LLC. Phone: 212-888-5500.

Technical Facilities: 10.4-kw ERP, lat. 44° 53' 17", long. 89° 39' 07".

Holds CP for change to 1.1-kw ERP, 194-ft. above ground, 1765-ft. above sea level, BDFCDTL-20080403ADE.

Ownership: Rockfleet Broadcasting LP.

Whiting—W06BU, Ch. 6, MS Communications LLC. Phone: 414-765-9737.

Technical Facilities: 10-w TPO, 0.007-kw ERP, 105-ft. above ground, 1191-ft. above sea level, lat. 44° 32' 36", long. 89° 40' 07".

Transmitter: 0.25-mi N of Dear Lane & County Trunk E junction.

Ownership: MS Communications LLC.

Whiting—W16AY, Ch. 16, MS Communications LLC. Phone: 414-765-9737.

Technical Facilities: 0.007-kw ERP, 105-ft. above ground, 1191-ft. above sea level, lat. 44° 32' 36", long. 89° 40' 07".

Transmitter: 6.4-mi. WNW of downtown Whiting.

Ownership: MS Communications LLC.

Whiting—W18CS, Ch. 43, MS Communications LLC. Phone: 414-765-9737.

Technical Facilities: 0.007-kw ERP, 105-ft. above ground, 1191-ft. above sea level, lat. 44° 32' 36", long. 89° 40' 07".

Transmitter: 6.4-mi. WNW of Whiting.

Ownership: MS Communications LLC.

Whiting—W24BV, Ch. 24, MS Communications LLC. Phone: 414-765-9737.

Technical Facilities: 1000-w TPO, 0.007-kw ERP, 105-ft. above ground, 1086-ft. above sea level, lat. 44° 32' 36", long. 89° 40' 07".

Transmitter: 6.4-mi. WNW of Whiting.

Ownership: MS Communications LLC.

Whiting—W31CI, Ch. 31, MS Communications LLC. Phone: 414-765-9737.

Technical Facilities: 1000-w TPO, 0.007-kw ERP, 105-ft. above ground, 1086-ft. above sea level, lat. 44° 32' 36", long. 89° 40' 07".

Transmitter: Deer Lane, 0.25-mi. N of County Trunk E junction.

Ownership: MS Communications LLC.

Whiting—W40BC, Ch. 40, MS Communications LLC. Phone: 414-765-9737.

Technical Facilities: 1000-w TPO, 0.007-kw ERP, 105-ft. above ground, 1191-ft. above sea level, lat. 44° 32' 36", long. 89° 40' 07".

Transmitter: 6.4-mi. WNW of Whiting.

Ownership: MS Communications LLC.

Whiting—W60CI, Ch. 60, MS Communications LLC. Phone: 414-765-9737.

Technical Facilities: 87-w TPO, 0.007-kw ERP, 105-ft. above ground, 1191-ft. above sea level, lat. 44° 32' 36", long. 89° 40' 07".

Transmitter: Deer Lane, 0.25-mi. N of County Trunk E Junction.

Ownership: MS Communications LLC.

Whiting—W62DA, Ch. 62, MS Communications LLC. Phone: 414-765-9737.

Technical Facilities: 0.007-kw ERP, 105-ft. above ground, 1086-ft. above sea level, lat. 44° 32' 36", long. 89° 40' 07".

Transmitter: 6.4-mi. WNW of downtown Whiting.

Ownership: MS Communications LLC.

Wyoming

Big Laramie, etc.—K03CR, Ch. 3, Laramie Plains Antenna TV Assn Inc.

Technical Facilities: 10-w TPO, 0.06-kw ERP, lat. 41° 14' 16", long. 105° 27' 48".

Ownership: Laramie Plains Antenna TV Assn. Inc.

Big Laramie, etc.—K12FY, Ch. 12, Laramie Plains Antenna TV Assn. Inc.

Technical Facilities: 10-w TPO, 0.1-kw ERP, lat. 41° 14' 16", long. 105° 27' 48".

Ownership: Laramie Plains Antenna TV Assn. Inc.

Big Piney, etc.—K07HM, Ch. 7, Upper Green River TV System.

Technical Facilities: 0.01-kw ERP, 7506-ft. above sea level, lat. 42° 34' 11", long. 109° 54' 39".

Big Piney, etc.—K10HO, Ch. 10, Upper Green River TV System.

Technical Facilities: 0.049-kw ERP, lat. 42° 34' 11", long. 109° 54' 39".

Big Piney, etc.—K12AH, Ch. 12, Upper Green River TV System.

Technical Facilities: 0.01-kw ERP, lat. 42° 34' 11", long. 109° 54' 39".

Big Piney, etc.—K24DA, Ch. 24, Sublette County. Phone: 307-276-3486.

Technical Facilities: 0.067-kw ERP, 59-ft. above ground, 7539-ft. above sea level, lat. 42° 34' 11", long. 109° 54' 39".

Ownership: Sublette County.

Big Piney, etc.—K33JQ-D, Ch. 33, Sublette County. Phone: 307-276-3486.

Technical Facilities: 0.02-kw ERP, 66-ft. above ground, 7546-ft. above sea level, lat. 42° 34' 11", long. 109° 54' 39".

Ownership: Sublette County.

Bigelow Bench area—K36DD, Ch. 36, Daggett County TV Dept.

Technical Facilities: 0.45-kw ERP, 10-ft. above ground, 8291-ft. above sea level, lat. 41° 21' 01", long. 110° 54' 24".

Bigelow Bench area—K38BZ, Ch. 38, Daggett County TV Dept.

Technical Facilities: 0.32-kw ERP, 10-ft. above ground, 8281-ft. above sea level, lat. 41° 21' 01", long. 110° 54' 24".

Bigelow Bench area—K40BX, Ch. 40, Daggett County TV Dept.

Technical Facilities: 0.33-kw ERP, 10-ft. above ground, 8281-ft. above sea level, lat. 41° 21' 01", long. 110° 54' 24".

Bondurant—K69DD, Ch. 69, Silverton Broadcasting Co. LLC. Phone: 310-476-2217.

Technical Facilities: 2.37-kw ERP, lat. 43° 06' 22", long. 110° 13' 46".

Ownership: Silverton Broadcasting Co. LLC.

Buffalo—K11UT, Ch. 11, Central Wyoming College.

Technical Facilities: 0.075-kw ERP, 20-ft. above ground, 4820-ft. above sea level, lat. 44° 19' 44", long. 106° 41' 30".

Ownership: Central Wyoming College.

Carter—K08HB, Ch. 8, Upper Bear River TV Service.

Technical Facilities: 0.06-kw ERP, lat. 41° 21' 14", long. 110° 54' 38".

Casper—K06KH, Ch. 6, Casper Community College District. Phone: 307-268-2547. Fax: 307-235-1461.

Technical Facilities: 100-w TPO, 0.162-kw ERP, 102-ft. above ground, 8118-ft. above sea level, lat. 42° 44' 26", long. 106° 21' 34".

Transmitter: 7.5-mi. S of Casper, on Casper Mountain.

Ownership: Casper Community College District.

Casper—K07YF, Ch. 7, Hispanic Christian Community Network Inc. Phone: 214-434-6357.

Technical Facilities: 1-kw ERP, 72-ft. above ground, 8094-ft. above sea level, lat. 42° 44' 26", long. 106° 21' 34".

Ownership: Hispanic Christian Community Network Inc.

Casper—K23HQ, Ch. 23, Telecom Wireless LLC. Phone: 951-614-2416.

Technical Facilities: 10-kw ERP, 214-ft. above ground, 5379-ft. above sea level, lat. 42° 50' 32.1", long. 106° 13' 04.92".

Ownership: Telecom Wireless LLC.

Casper—K26ES, Ch. 26, Wyomedia Corp. Phone: 307-577-5923. Fax: 307-577-5928.

Technical Facilities: 117-w TPO, 0.904-kw ERP, 281-ft. above ground, 8298-ft. above sea level, lat. 42° 44' 37", long. 106° 18' 26".

Transmitter: 1-mi. SW of State Rte. 251.

Ownership: Wyomedia Corp.

Personnel: Mark Nelbone, General Manager; Roger Latrance, Chief Engineer; Tina Nelbone, Sales Manager.

Casper—K31HT, Ch. 31, EICB-TV East LLC. Phone: 214-770-7770.

Technical Facilities: 0.015-kw ERP, 120-ft. above ground, 8204-ft. above sea level, lat. 42° 44' 26", long. 106° 21' 43".

Holds CP for change to 16-ft. above ground, 7953-ft. above sea level, BMPTTL-20070517AFC.

Ownership: EICB-TV LLC.

Casper—K33GI, Ch. 33, Trinity Broadcasting Network Inc. Phone: 714-832-2950. Fax: 714-730-0661.

Technical Facilities: 20-kw ERP, 164-ft. above ground, 8182-ft. above sea level, lat. 42° 44' 26", long. 106° 21' 36".

Holds CP for change to 15-kw ERP, lat. 42° 44' 26", long. 106° 21' 34". BDFCDTT-20060331AVD.

Ownership: Trinity Broadcasting Network Inc.

Casper—K36GT, Ch. 36, Turner Enterprises. Phone: 954-732-9539.

Technical Facilities: 20-kw ERP, 164-ft. above ground, 8202-ft. above sea level, lat. 42° 44' 30", long. 106° 18' 29".

Ownership: Marcia T. Turner.

Casper—K47HQ, Ch. 47, Manna Media Corp. Phone: 307-237-3391.

Studio: 2251 Mariposa Blvd., Casper, WY 82604.

Technical Facilities: 0.03-kw ERP, 195-ft. above ground, 5169-ft. above sea level, lat. 42° 52' 55", long. 106° 17' 11".

Transmitter: 2370 N. Station Rd., Casper.

Ownership: Manna Media Corp.

Personnel: Fred Hildebrand, Chief Engineer; John S. Runge, Business Manager.

Cheyenne—K14LV, Ch. 14, Hosanna Apostolic Ministries Broadcasting Corp. Phone: 520-971-9274.

Technical Facilities: 11.2-kw ERP, 30-ft. above ground, 6201-ft. above sea level, lat. 41° 10' 01", long. 104° 45' 21".

Began Operation: May 2, 2007.

Ownership: Hosanna Apostolic Ministries Broadcasting Corp.

Cheyenne—K49AY, Ch. 49, Echonet Corp. Phone: 720-266-1040.

Studio: 912 Central Ave., Cheyenne, WY 82001.

Technical Facilities: 1000-w TPO, 9.7-kw ERP, 116-ft. above ground, 6174-ft. above sea level, lat. 41° 08' 04", long. 104° 49' 02".

Transmitter: 18th & Carey, Cheyenne.

Ownership: Echonet Corp.

Personnel: Clara Rivas, General & Sales Manager; Gunter Auerbach, Chief Engineer.

Cheyenne—KCHY-LP, Ch. 13, Bozeman Trail Communications Co. Phone: 702-642-3333.

Technical Facilities: 3-kw ERP, 137-ft. above ground, 6249-ft. above sea level, lat. 41° 09' 34", long. 104° 43' 21".

Ownership: Sunbelt Communications Co.

Cheyenne—KDEV-LP, Ch. 40, Denver Broadcasting Inc., Debtor in Possession. Phone: 501-219-2400.

Technical Facilities: 10-kw ERP, 197-ft. above ground, 6657-ft. above sea level, lat. 41° 08' 55", long. 104° 57' 24".

Holds CP for change to 150-kw ERP, lat. 41° 08' 55", long. 104° 57' 22". BMPTTL-20080408AES.

Began Operation: March 15, 2007.

Ownership: Equity Media Holdings Corp., Debtor in Possession.

Cheyenne—KGSC-LP, Ch. 47, The Spirit of the Lord Ministries. Phone: 307-632-5882.

Technical Facilities: 20-kw ERP, 108-ft. above ground, 6223-ft. above sea level, lat. 41° 09' 34", long. 104° 43' 19".

Holds CP for change to 4.58-kw ERP, BDFCDTL-20090414ACG.

Ownership: The Spirit of the Lord Ministries.

Cheyenne—KKRR-LP, Ch. 45, Robert R. Rule.

Technical Facilities: 10.3-kw ERP, 62-ft. above ground, 6233-ft. above sea level, lat. 41° 10' 01", long. 104° 45' 21".

■**Cheyenne**—KMAH-LP, Ch. 39, Robert R. Rule.

Technical Facilities: 1000-w TPO, 10.25-kw ERP, 6204-ft. above sea level, lat. 41° 10' 01", long. 104° 45' 21".

Transmitter: 5318 Braehill Rd.

Ownership: Rule Communications.

Chugwater—K12QG, Ch. 12, Town of Chugwater. Phone: 307-422-3493.

Technical Facilities: 3-kw ERP, 138-ft. above ground, 5699-ft. above sea level, lat. 41° 46' 02", long. 104° 48' 57".

Ownership: Town of Chugwater.

Clareton—K68DC, Ch. 68, Mark III Media Inc. Phone: 307-235-3962.

Technical Facilities: 6.96-kw ERP, 49-ft. above ground, 5446-ft. above sea level, lat. 43° 42' 09", long. 105° 06' 05".

Ownership: Mark III Media Inc.

Clark, etc.—K07QA, Ch. 7, Central Wyoming College. Phone: 307-856-6944.

Technical Facilities: 0.127-kw ERP, lat. 44° 56' 20", long. 109° 07' 00".

Ownership: Central Wyoming College.

Clark, etc.—K09OH, Ch. 9, Park County.

Technical Facilities: 0.127-kw ERP, 4423-ft. above sea level, lat. 44° 56' 20", long. 109° 07' 00".

Clark, etc.—K11PK, Ch. 11, Park County.

Technical Facilities: 0.127-kw ERP, 4423-ft. above sea level, lat. 44° 56' 20", long. 109° 07' 00".

Clark, etc.—K13QA, Ch. 13, Park County.

Technical Facilities: 0.123-kw ERP, lat. 44° 56' 20", long. 109° 07' 00".

Clarks Fork, etc.—K02LH, Ch. 2, Central Wyoming College. Phone: 307-856-6944.

Technical Facilities: 0.05-kw ERP, lat. 44° 53' 37", long. 109° 38' 22".

Ownership: Central Wyoming College.

Clarks Fork, etc.—K06KT, Ch. 6, Park County.

Technical Facilities: 0.05-kw ERP, lat. 44° 53' 37", long. 109° 38' 22".

Clarks Fork, etc.—K07GG, Ch. 7, Park County.

Technical Facilities: 0.01-kw ERP, lat. 44° 53' 42", long. 109° 38' 12".

Clarks Fork, etc.—K09GI, Ch. 9, Park County.

Technical Facilities: 0.012-kw ERP, lat. 44° 53' 42", long. 109° 38' 12".

Cody—K15AD, Ch. 15, Rob-Art Inc.

Technical Facilities: 1.46-kw ERP, 7651-ft. above sea level, lat. 44° 29' 48", long. 109° 09' 07".

Cody—K34HZ, Ch. 34, EICB-TV East LLC. Phone: 214-770-7770.

Technical Facilities: 0.05-kw ERP, 20-ft. above ground, 7625-ft. above sea level, lat. 44° 29' 48", long. 109° 09' 07".

Holds CP for change to 5-kw ERP, BDFCDTL-20080403ACV.

Ownership: EICB-TV LLC.

Cody—K45BW, Ch. 45, Park County.

Technical Facilities: 1.28-kw ERP, 20-ft. above ground, 6568-ft. above sea level, lat. 44° 36' 25", long. 108° 51' 30".

Cody—K53AL, Ch. 53, Park County.

Technical Facilities: 1.18-kw ERP, 6575-ft. above sea level, lat. 44° 36' 25", long. 108° 51' 30".

Cody & Powell—K40JU-D, Ch. 40, Central Wyoming College. Phone: 307-856-6944.

Technical Facilities: 0.25-kw ERP, 36-ft. above ground, 6581-ft. above sea level, lat. 44° 35' 14", long. 108° 51' 08".

Ownership: Central Wyoming College.

Cody & Powell—K49AI, Ch. 49, Central Wyoming College. Phone: 307-856-6944.

Technical Facilities: 1-kw ERP, 6581-ft. above sea level, lat. 44° 35' 14", long. 108° 51' 08".

Ownership: Central Wyoming College.

Cody, etc.—K47AD, Ch. 47, Park County.

Technical Facilities: 0.1-kw ERP, 6558-ft. above sea level, lat. 44° 36' 25", long. 108° 51' 30".

Cody, etc.—K51AK, Ch. 51, Park County.

Technical Facilities: 1.18-kw ERP, 6575-ft. above sea level, lat. 44° 36' 25", long. 108° 51' 30".

Cody, etc.—K55CA, Ch. 55, Park County.

Technical Facilities: 1.18-kw ERP, 6575-ft. above sea level, lat. 44° 36' 25", long. 108° 51' 30".

Cora, etc.—K05DK, Ch. 5, Cora Peak TV Assn. Phone: 307-276-3486.

Technical Facilities: 0.04-kw ERP, lat. 42° 55' 09", long. 110° 00' 52".

Holds CP for change to channel number 22, 0.27-kw ERP, 71-ft. above ground, 7971-ft. above sea level, BDISTT-20080317AIG.

Diamond Basin—K04DA, Ch. 4, Park County.

Technical Facilities: 0.021-kw ERP, lat. 44° 29' 29", long. 109° 10' 08".

Diamond Basin, etc.—K05CB, Ch. 5, Park County.

Technical Facilities: 0.158-kw ERP, 7930-ft. above sea level, lat. 44° 29' 29", long. 109° 10' 08".

Douglas—K09XL, Ch. 9, Wyomedia Corp. Phone: 307-577-5923.

Technical Facilities: 0.05-kw ERP, 20-ft. above ground, 5046-ft. above sea level, lat. 42° 45' 47", long. 105° 25' 12".

Ownership: Wyomedia Corp.

Douglas—K11RN, Ch. 11, Wyomedia Corp. Phone: 307-577-5923.

Technical Facilities: 0.01-kw ERP, lat. 42° 45' 52", long. 105° 25' 03".

Holds CP for change to 0.16-kw ERP, 52-ft. above ground, 5079-ft. above sea level, lat. 42° 45' 47", long. 105° 25' 13". BDFCDTV-20081114AAR.

Ownership: Wyomedia Corp.

Dubois, etc.—K25AU, Ch. 25, Central Wyoming College.

Technical Facilities: 0.31-kw ERP, 69-ft. above ground, 9967-ft. above sea level, lat. 43° 29' 58", long. 109° 41' 16".

Dubois, etc.—K47LK-D, Ch. 47, Central Wyoming College. Phone: 307-856-6944.

Technical Facilities: 0.1-kw ERP, 69-ft. above ground, 9967-ft. above sea level, lat. 43° 29' 58", long. 109° 41' 16".

Ownership: Central Wyoming College.

Encampment—K06BR, Ch. 6, Elk Mountain TV Co.

Technical Facilities: 0.095-kw ERP, lat. 41° 17' 10", long. 106° 44' 00".

Encampment—K08CP, Ch. 8, Elk Mountain TV Co.

Technical Facilities: 0.095-kw ERP, lat. 41° 17' 10", long. 106° 44' 00".

Evanston—K23DS-D, Ch. 23, Central Wyoming College. Phone: 307-856-6944.

Technical Facilities: 0.23-kw ERP, 75-ft. above ground, 8455-ft. above sea level, lat. 41° 21' 01", long. 110° 54' 16".

Multichannel TV Sound: Stereo only.

Ownership: Central Wyoming College.

Personnel: Bob Spain, Chief Engineer; Ruby Calvert, General Manager.

Evanston—K28DV, Ch. 28, High Plains Broadcasting License Co. LLC. Phone: 580-269-2215.

Technical Facilities: 2.15-kw ERP, 20-ft. above ground, 8510-ft. above sea level, lat. 41° 21' 06", long. 110° 54' 20".

Ownership: High Plains Broadcasting Inc.

Evanston—K32DS, Ch. 32, Central Wyoming College. Phone: 307-856-6944.

Technical Facilities: 2.15-kw ERP, 20-ft. above ground, 8510-ft. above sea level, lat. 41° 21' 06", long. 110° 54' 20".

Ownership: Central Wyoming College.

Evanston—K50DR, Ch. 50, Larry H. Miller Communications Corp. Phone: 801-537-1414.

Technical Facilities: 100-w TPO, 2.12-kw ERP, 20-ft. above ground, 8507-ft. above sea level, lat. 41° 21' 06", long. 110° 54' 20".

Transmitter: Medicine Butte.

Ownership: Larry H. Miller Communications Corp.

Evanston—K54EH, Ch. 54, Central Wyoming College. Phone: 307-856-6944. Fax: 307-856-3893.

Technical Facilities: 100-w TPO, 2.12-kw ERP, 20-ft. above ground, 8510-ft. above sea level, lat. 41° 21' 06", long. 110° 54' 20".

Transmitter: Medicine Butte.

Ownership: Central Wyoming College.

Personnel: Greg Ray, General Manager; Roger A. Hicks, Chief Engineer.

Evanston, etc.—K15FR, Ch. 15, U. of Utah. Phone: 801-585-3601.

Technical Facilities: 1.02-kw ERP, 30-ft. above ground, 8567-ft. above sea level, lat. 41° 21' 04", long. 11° 53' 50".

Transmitter: Approx. 6.2-mi. NE of Evanston.

Freedom—K31DC, Ch. 31, Lower Star Valley Non-Profit TV Assn.

Technical Facilities: 0.2-kw ERP, 13-ft. above ground, 8924-ft. above sea level, lat. 43° 07' 08", long. 111° 07' 46".

Freedom, etc.—K66DU, Ch. 66, Lower Star Valley Non-Profit TV Assn.

Technical Facilities: 0.045-kw ERP, 39-ft. above ground, 8943-ft. above sea level, lat. 43° 06' 40", long. 111° 07' 25".

Freedom-Etna—K33DS, Ch. 33, Lower Star Valley Non-Profit TV Assn.

Technical Facilities: 0.72-kw ERP, 16-ft. above ground, 6430-ft. above sea level, lat. 43° 01' 23", long. 111° 04' 21".

■**Gillette**—K06JM, Ch. 6, Duhamel Broadcasting Enterprises. Phone: 605-342-2000.

Technical Facilities: 3-kw ERP, 128-ft. above ground, 5003-ft. above sea level, lat. 44° 15' 24", long. 105° 41' 40".

Ownership: Duhamel Broadcasting Enterprises.

Gillette—K10PC, Ch. 10, Telecom Wireless LLC. Phone: 954-614-2416.

Technical Facilities: 2-kw ERP, 417-ft. above ground, 5027-ft. above sea level, lat. 44° 18' 10", long. 105° 27' 00".

Ownership: Telecom Wireless LLC.

Gillette—K16AE, Ch. 16, Mark III Media Inc. Phone: 307-235-3962.

Technical Facilities: 1.26-kw ERP, 5151-ft. above sea level, lat. 44° 12' 33", long. 105° 28' 05".

Ownership: Mark III Media Inc.

Gillette—K22AD, Ch. 22, Rapid Broadcasting Co.

Technical Facilities: 27.5-kw ERP, 98-ft. above ground, 4806-ft. above sea level, lat. 44° 14' 53", long. 105° 29' 42".

Ownership: Rapid Broadcasting Co.

Gillette—K28CH, Ch. 28, Central Wyoming College.

Technical Facilities: 12.2-kw ERP, lat. 44° 18' 17", long. 105° 33' 53".

Gillette—K43KW-D, Ch. 43, Central Wyoming College. Phone: 307-856-6944.

Technical Facilities: 3.2-kw ERP, 59-ft. above ground, 4954-ft. above sea level, lat. 44° 18' 17", long. 105° 33' 53".

Began Operation: April 1, 2009.

Ownership: Central Wyoming College.

Glendo—K21HQ, Ch. 21, Central Wyoming College. Phone: 307-856-6944.

Technical Facilities: 0.999-kw ERP, 197-ft. above ground, 5426-ft. above sea level, lat. 42° 20' 44", long. 105° 01' 54".

Ownership: Central Wyoming College.

Green River—K35CN, Ch. 35, Trinity Broadcasting Network Inc. Phone: 714-832-2950. Fax: 714-730-0661.

Technical Facilities: 1000-w TPO, 10.5-kw ERP, 92-ft. above ground, 7736-ft. above sea level, lat. 41° 29' 50", long. 109° 20' 36".

Transmitter: Wilkens Peak, 6.8-mi. SE of Green River.

Ownership: Trinity Broadcasting Network Inc.

Personnel: Paul F. Crouch, General Manager; Ben Miller, Chief Engineer; Rod Henke, Sales Manager.

Greybull—K41KM-D, Ch. 41, Central Wyoming College. Phone: 307-856-6944.

Technical Facilities: 0.25-kw ERP, 66-ft. above ground, 4639-ft. above sea level, lat. 44° 24' 47", long. 107° 59' 49".

Ownership: Central Wyoming College.

Greybull—K50JC, Ch. 50, Central Wyoming College. Phone: 307-856-6944.

Technical Facilities: 0.999-kw ERP, 69-ft. above ground, 4642-ft. above sea level, lat. 44° 24' 47", long. 107° 59' 49".

Ownership: Central Wyoming College.

■**Hoback Junction**—K13LY, Ch. 13, NPG of Idaho Inc.

Technical Facilities: 0.1-kw ERP, lat. 43° 22' 00", long. 110° 44' 00".

Ownership: News Press & Gazette Co.

■**Jackson**—K13FZ, Ch. 13, NPG of Idaho Inc. Phone: 816-271-8505.

Technical Facilities: 0.101-kw ERP, 23-ft. above ground, 7992-ft. above sea level, lat. 43° 27' 43", long. 110° 45' 12".

Ownership: News Press & Gazette Co.

Jackson—K29HG-D, Ch. 29, NPG of Idaho Inc. Phone: 816-271-8505.

Technical Facilities: 0.128-kw ERP, 20-ft. above ground, 10469-ft. above sea level, lat. 43° 35' 50", long. 110° 52' 12".

Began Operation: September 17, 1991.

Ownership: News Press & Gazette Co.

Jackson—K36JD-D, Ch. 36, NPG of Idaho Inc. Phone: 816-271-8505.

Technical Facilities: 12.5-kw ERP, 46-ft. above ground, 8015-ft. above sea level, lat. 43° 27' 43", long. 110° 45' 12".

Began Operation: February 17, 2009.

Ownership: News Press & Gazette Co.

Jackson—K50BL, Ch. 50, Central Wyoming College.

Technical Facilities: 0.35-kw ERP, lat. 43° 27' 45", long. 110° 45' 03".

Jackson—K56BT, Ch. 56, Silverton Broadcasting Co. LLC. Phone: 310-476-2217.

Technical Facilities: 0.36-kw ERP, lat. 43° 35' 50", long. 110° 52' 13".

Ownership: Silverton Broadcasting Co. LLC.

Jeffrey City—K07NI, Ch. 7, Riverton Fremont TV Club Inc.

Technical Facilities: 0.123-kw ERP, lat. 42° 23' 57", long. 107° 57' 20".

Transmitter: 10-mi. SW of Jeffrey City.

Jeffrey City—K09MI, Ch. 9, Riverton Fremont TV Club Inc.

Technical Facilities: 0.123-kw ERP, lat. 42° 24' 39", long. 107° 57' 20".

Jeffrey City—K11MN, Ch. 11, Riverton Fremont TV Club Inc.

Technical Facilities: 0.123-kw ERP, lat. 42° 23' 57", long. 107° 57' 20".

Jeffrey City—K13NW, Ch. 13, Riverton Fremont TV Club Inc.

Technical Facilities: 0.123-kw ERP, 840-ft. above sea level, lat. 42° 23' 57", long. 107° 57' 20".

Kemmerer—K24GT-D, Ch. 24, Central Wyoming College. Phone: 307-856-6944.

Technical Facilities: 0.37-kw ERP, 25-ft. above ground, 8035-ft. above sea level, lat. 41° 50' 17", long. 110° 30' 11".

Ownership: Central Wyoming College.

La Barge—K02GE, Ch. 2, Central Wyoming College. Phone: 307-856-6944.

Technical Facilities: 0.013-kw ERP, lat. 42° 18' 45", long. 110° 19' 35".

Ownership: Central Wyoming College.

La Barge—K09IJ, Ch. 9, Central Wyoming College. Phone: 307-856-6944.

Technical Facilities: 0.02-kw ERP, lat. 42° 19' 26", long. 110° 19' 08".

Ownership: Central Wyoming College.

La Barge—K62CS, Ch. 62, Central Wyoming College. Phone: 307-856-6944.

Technical Facilities: 0.333-kw ERP, lat. 42° 19' 28", long. 110° 18' 27".

Ownership: Central Wyoming College.

La Barge & Big Piney—K06FD, Ch. 6, Central Wyoming College. Phone: 307-856-6944.

Technical Facilities: 0.07-kw ERP, 9032-ft. above sea level, lat. 42° 19' 27", long. 110° 19' 35".

Ownership: Central Wyoming College.

La Barge, etc.—K29HV-D, Ch. 29, Central Wyoming College. Phone: 307-856-6944.

Technical Facilities: 0.25-kw ERP, 23-ft. above ground, 9055-ft. above sea level, lat. 42° 09' 27", long. 110° 19' 39".

Ownership: Central Wyoming College.

La Barge, etc.—K42GZ, Ch. 42, Central Wyoming College. Phone: 307-856-6944.

Technical Facilities: 1-kw ERP, 23-ft. above ground, 9055-ft. above sea level, lat. 42° 09' 27", long. 110° 19' 39".

Ownership: Central Wyoming College.

Lander—K12HM, Ch. 12, Lander Valley TV Assn.

Technical Facilities: 0.005-kw ERP, 5643-ft. above sea level, lat. 42° 52' 32", long. 108° 41' 42".

Lander—K22CI, Ch. 22, Silverton Broadcasting Co. LLC. Phone: 310-476-2217.

Technical Facilities: 0.875-kw ERP, 108-ft. above ground, 5905-ft. above sea level, lat. 42° 54' 19", long. 108° 42' 34".

Ownership: Silverton Broadcasting Co. LLC.

Laramie—K14LK, Ch. 14, Bozeman Trail Communications Co. Phone: 702-642-3333.

Technical Facilities: 11-kw ERP, 101-ft. above ground, 8920-ft. above sea level, lat. 41° 17' 17", long. 105° 26' 42".

Ownership: Sunbelt Communications Co.

Laramie—K19FX, Ch. 19, SagamoreHill Broadcasting of Wyoming/Northern Colorado LLC. Phone: 706-855-8506.

Technical Facilities: 2.31-kw ERP, 56-ft. above ground, 8855-ft. above sea level, lat. 41° 17' 06", long. 105° 26' 41".

Holds CP for change to 0.68-kw ERP, BDFCDTT-20081031ABC.

Ownership: SagamoreHill Broadcasting LLC.

Laramie—K57AF, Ch. 57, Laramie Plains Antenna TV Assn. Inc.

Technical Facilities: 100-w TPO, 5.04-kw ERP, lat. 41° 14' 16", long. 105° 27' 48".

Ownership: Laramie Plains Antenna TV Assn. Inc.

Laramie—K59AM, Ch. 59, Laramie Plains Antenna TV Assn. Inc.

Technical Facilities: 4.73-kw ERP, lat. 41° 14' 16", long. 105° 27' 48".

Laramie—K61DX, Ch. 61, Denver Broadcasting Inc., Debtor in Possession. Phone: 501-219-2400.

Technical Facilities: 4.27-kw ERP, lat. 41° 16' 04", long. 105° 26' 00".

Ownership: Equity Media Holdings Corp., Debtor in Possession.

Laramie—KHDE-LP, Ch. 25, Hispanic Christian Community Network Inc. Phone: 214-434-6357.

Technical Facilities: 10-kw ERP, 164-ft. above ground, 8048-ft. above sea level, lat. 41° 04' 53.2", long. 105° 29' 03.9".

Ownership: Sunbelt Communications Co.

Laramie—KPAH-LP, Ch. 24, Robert R. Rule. Phone: 307-637-7777.

Technical Facilities: 4.2-kw ERP, 46-ft. above ground, 8845-ft. above sea level, lat. 41° 17' 06", long. 105° 26' 41".

Transmitter: Hill 8821, Sherman Mountains, E of Laramie.

Ownership: Rule Communications.

Laramie & Bosler—K10FQ, Ch. 10, Laramie Plains Antenna TV Assn. Inc.

Technical Facilities: 10-w TPO, 0.1-kw ERP, lat. 41° 14' 16", long. 105° 27' 48".

Ownership: Laramie Plains Antenna TV Assn. Inc.

Little America, etc.—K45GO, Ch. 45, Bridger Valley Services Board.

Technical Facilities: 1.02-kw ERP, 30-ft. above ground, 8628-ft. above sea level, lat. 41° 06' 19", long. 110° 12' 13".

Lusk—K12IS, Ch. 12, Silverton Broadcasting Co. LLC. Phone: 310-476-2217.

Technical Facilities: 0.007-kw ERP, lat. 42° 47' 37", long. 104° 25' 20".

Ownership: Silverton Broadcasting Co. LLC.

Manderson—K06KW, Ch. 6, Town of Manderson.

Technical Facilities: 0.005-kw ERP, 4075-ft. above sea level, lat. 44° 15' 44", long. 107° 56' 36".

Manderson, etc.—K03GF, Ch. 3, Town of Manderson. Phone: 307-568-2680.

Technical Facilities: 0.005-kw ERP, 4075-ft. above sea level, lat. 44° 15' 44", long. 107° 56' 36".

Began Operation: April 19, 1983.
Ownership: Town of Manderson.

Manderson, etc.—K07SU, Ch. 7, Town of Manderson.

Technical Facilities: 0.01-kw ERP, lat. 44° 15' 44", long. 107° 56' 36".

Manderson, etc.—K13TX, Ch. 13, Town of Manderson.

Technical Facilities: 0.01-kw ERP, lat. 44° 15' 44", long. 107° 56' 36".

McKinnon, etc.—K27DZ, Ch. 27, Daggett County TV Dept.

Technical Facilities: 3.78-kw ERP, 26-ft. above ground, 8625-ft. above sea level, lat. 41° 06' 19", long. 110° 12' 13".

McKinnon, etc.—K29CR, Ch. 29, Daggett County TV Dept.

Technical Facilities: 3.78-kw ERP, 26-ft. above ground, 8625-ft. above sea level, lat. 41° 06' 19", long. 110° 12' 13".

Medicine Bow—K07LI, Ch. 7, Town of Medicine Bow.

Technical Facilities: 0.032-kw ERP, lat. 41° 52' 50", long. 106° 04' 28".

Medicine Bow—K09LS, Ch. 9, Town of Medicine Bow.

Technical Facilities: 0.028-kw ERP, lat. 41° 52' 50", long. 106° 04' 28".

Medicine Bow—K13MP, Ch. 13, Town of Medicine Bow.

Technical Facilities: 0.026-kw ERP, lat. 41° 52' 50", long. 106° 04' 28".

Meeteetse, etc.—K29IH-D, Ch. 29, Central Wyoming College. Phone: 307-856-6944.

Technical Facilities: 1-kw ERP, 49-ft. above ground, 6466-ft. above sea level, lat. 44° 08' 45", long. 108° 54' 15".

Began Operation: December 12, 2008.
Ownership: Central Wyoming College.

Meeteetse, etc.—K63BO, Ch. 63, Central Wyoming College. Phone: 307-856-6944.

Technical Facilities: 2.9-kw ERP, lat. 44° 08' 45", long. 108° 54' 15".

Ownership: Central Wyoming College.

Meeteetse, etc.—K65BW, Ch. 65, Park County.

Technical Facilities: 2.9-kw ERP, lat. 44° 08' 45", long. 108° 54' 15".

Meeteetse, etc.—K67CB, Ch. 67, Park County.

Technical Facilities: 2.9-kw ERP, lat. 44° 08' 45", long. 108° 54' 15".

Meeteetse, etc.—K69CS, Ch. 69, Park County.

Technical Facilities: 2.9-kw ERP, lat. 44° 08' 45", long. 108° 54' 15".

Mountain View—K03GX, Ch. 3, Central Wyoming College. Phone: 307-856-6944.

Technical Facilities: 0.05-kw ERP, 10-ft. above ground, 8569-ft. above sea level, lat. 41° 06' 43", long. 110° 13' 00".

Ownership: Central Wyoming College.

Mountain View—K19CP, Ch. 19, Larry H. Miller Communications Corp. Phone: 801-537-1414.

Technical Facilities: 1.02-kw ERP, 30-ft. above ground, 8629-ft. above sea level, lat. 41° 06' 19", long. 110° 12' 13".

Began Operation: February 19, 1991.
Ownership: Larry H. Miller Communications Corp.

Mountain View—K31FW, Ch. 31, High Plains Broadcasting License Co. LLC. Phone: 580-269-2215.

Technical Facilities: 1.377-kw ERP, 30-ft. above ground, 8629-ft. above sea level, lat. 41° 06' 19", long. 110° 12' 13".

Ownership: High Plains Broadcasting Inc.

Mountain View, etc.—K09DI, Ch. 9, Central Wyoming College. Phone: 307-856-6944.

Technical Facilities: 0.354-kw ERP, 8622-ft. above sea level, lat. 41° 06' 50", long. 110° 14' 00".

Ownership: Central Wyoming College.

Mountain View, etc.—K11DN, Ch. 11, Central Wyoming College. Phone: 307-856-6944.

Technical Facilities: 0.354-kw ERP, 8622-ft. above sea level, lat. 41° 06' 50", long. 110° 14' 00".

Ownership: Central Wyoming College.

North Fork—K07RS, Ch. 7, Central Wyoming College. Phone: 307-856-6944.

Technical Facilities: 0.09-kw ERP, lat. 44° 29' 08", long. 109° 10' 29".

Ownership: Central Wyoming College.

North Fork—K09SF, Ch. 9, Park County.

Technical Facilities: 0.09-kw ERP, lat. 44° 29' 08", long. 109° 10' 29".

North Fork, etc.—K32IF-D, Ch. 32, Central Wyoming College. Phone: 307-856-6944.

Technical Facilities: 0.2-kw ERP, 85-ft. above ground, 7903-ft. above sea level, lat. 44° 29' 37", long. 109° 10' 07".

Began Operation: December 12, 2008.

Ownership: Central Wyoming College.

Parkersburg—W51EG-D, Ch. 51, West Virginia Educational Broadcasting Authority. Phone: 304-556-4900.

Technical Facilities: 15-kw ERP, 187-ft. above ground, 1106-ft. above sea level, lat. 39° 12' 43", long. 81° 35' 31".

Ownership: West Virginia Educational Broadcasting Authority.

Pinedale—KKBT-LP, Ch. 39, Rule Communications. Phone: 307-637-7777.

Technical Facilities: 0.25-kw ERP, 39-ft. above ground, 7739-ft. above sea level, lat. 42° 50' 40", long. 109° 55' 24".

Ownership: Rule Communications.

Pinedale, etc.—K14IL, Ch. 14, Sublette County. Phone: 307-276-3486.

Technical Facilities: 0.262-kw ERP, 66-ft. above ground, 7969-ft. above sea level, lat. 42° 55' 09", long. 110° 00' 52".

Ownership: Sublette County.

Pinedale, etc.—K16CS, Ch. 16, Sublette County. Phone: 307-276-3486.

Technical Facilities: 0.262-kw ERP, 66-ft. above ground, 7969-ft. above sea level, lat. 42° 55' 09", long. 110° 00' 52".

Ownership: Sublette County.

Pinedale, etc.—K19HJ-D, Ch. 19, Sublette County. Phone: 307-276-3486.

Technical Facilities: 0.1-kw ERP, 66-ft. above ground, 7969-ft. above sea level, lat. 42° 55' 09", long. 110° 00' 52".

Ownership: Sublette County.

Rawlins—K21CV, Ch. 21, Denver Broadcasting Inc., Debtor in Possession. Phone: 501-219-2400.

Technical Facilities: 1.12-kw ERP, 30-ft. above ground, 7228-ft. above sea level, lat. 41° 46' 15", long. 107° 14' 17".

Began Operation: February 25, 1991.
Ownership: Equity Media Holdings Corp., Debtor in Possession.

Rawlins—K26HV, Ch. 26, Central Wyoming College. Phone: 307-856-6944.

Technical Facilities: 0.037-kw ERP, 26-ft. above ground, 7224-ft. above sea level, lat. 41° 46' 15.7", long. 107° 14' 16.9".

Ownership: Central Wyoming College.

Rawlins, etc.—K51IZ, Ch. 51, Central Wyoming College. Phone: 307-856-6944.

Technical Facilities: 0.23-kw ERP, 30-ft. above ground, 8205-ft. above sea level, lat. 41° 40' 48", long. 107° 14' 12".

Holds CP for change to 20-ft. above ground, 8195-ft. above sea level, BDFCDTT-20060920AEN.

Ownership: Central Wyoming College.

Rawlins, etc.—K58AM, Ch. 58, Central Wyoming College. Phone: 307-856-6944.

Technical Facilities: 1.39-kw ERP, 8176-ft. above sea level, lat. 41° 40' 48", long. 107° 14' 12".

Ownership: Central Wyoming College.

Riverton—K28HL, Ch. 28, Riverton Fremont TV Club Inc.

Technical Facilities: 1.188-kw ERP, 19-ft. above ground, 7237-ft. above sea level, lat. 43° 27' 00", long. 108° 14' 00".

Ownership: Riverton Fremont TV Club Inc.

Riverton, etc.—K03ER, Ch. 3, Riverton Fremont TV Club Inc.

Technical Facilities: 0.116-kw ERP, 7237-ft. above sea level, lat. 42° 43' 05", long. 108° 09' 10".

Ownership: Riverton Fremont TV Club Inc.

Riverton, etc.—K07UZ, Ch. 7, Riverton Fremont TV Club Inc.

Technical Facilities: 0.442-kw ERP, 46-ft. above ground, 5256-ft. above sea level, lat. 43° 02' 22", long. 108° 26' 15".

Ownership: Riverton Fremont TV Club Inc.

Riverton, etc.—K12MJ, Ch. 12, Riverton Fremont TV Club Inc.

Technical Facilities: 0.22-kw ERP, lat. 43° 02' 22", long. 108° 26' 15".

Rock River—K04KW, Ch. 4, Town of Rock River.

Technical Facilities: 0.08-kw ERP, lat. 41° 42' 24", long. 105° 54' 53".

Rock River—K06LU, Ch. 6, Town of Rock River.

Technical Facilities: 0.005-kw ERP, 36-ft. above ground, 7395-ft. above sea level, lat. 41° 42' 24", long. 105° 54' 53".

Rock River—K07JE, Ch. 7, Town of Rock River.

Technical Facilities: 0.021-kw ERP, lat. 41° 42' 24", long. 105° 54' 55".

Rock River—K13KE, Ch. 13, Town of Rock River.

Technical Facilities: 0.02-kw ERP, lat. 41° 42' 24", long. 105° 54' 55".

Rock Springs—K18ER, Ch. 18, Loflin Children's Trust-Two. Phone: 504-928-3574.

Technical Facilities: 1000-w TPO, 0.09-kw ERP, 41-ft. above ground, 7352-ft. above sea level, lat. 41° 29' 50", long. 109° 20' 36".

Transmitter: Wilkens Peak Rd., approx. 11.3-mi. ESE of Green River.

Ownership: Loflin Children's Trust-One, Two & Four.

Rock Springs—K20FA, Ch. 20, Loflin Children's Trust-Two. Phone: 504-928-3574.

Technical Facilities: 1000-w TPO, 0.09-kw ERP, 41-ft. above ground, 7352-ft. above sea level, lat. 41° 29' 50", long. 109° 20' 36".

Transmitter: Wilkens Peak Rd., approx. 11.3-mi. ESE of Green River.

Ownership: Loflin Children's Trust-One, Two & Four.

Rock Springs—K24GZ, Ch. 24, EICB-TV East LLC. Phone: 972-291-3750.

Technical Facilities: 0.05-kw ERP, 26-ft. above ground, 6388-ft. above sea level, lat. 41° 37' 25", long. 109° 13' 41".

Holds CP for change to 2.2-kw ERP, 30-ft. above ground, 7671-ft. above sea level, lat. 41° 29' 50", long. 109° 20' 36". BPTTL-20081023ABQ.

Began Operation: July 21, 2008.

Ownership: EICB-TV LLC.

Rock Springs—K26DK, Ch. 26, Larry H. Miller Communications Corp. Phone: 801-537-1414.

Technical Facilities: 1.32-kw ERP, 23-ft. above ground, 8678-ft. above sea level, lat. 41° 26' 05", long. 109° 07' 00".

Began Operation: October 6, 1993.

Ownership: Larry H. Miller Communications Corp.

Rock Springs—K30EQ, Ch. 30, Loflin Children's Trust-Two. Phone: 504-928-3574.

Technical Facilities: 1000-w TPO, 0.09-kw ERP, 41-ft. above ground, 7349-ft. above sea level, lat. 41° 29' 50", long. 109° 20' 36".

Transmitter: Wilkens Peak Rd., approx. 11.3-mi. ESE of Green River.

Ownership: Loflin Children's Trust-One, Two & Four.

Rock Springs—K45IA, Ch. 45, High Plains Broadcasting License Co. LLC. Phone: 580-269-2215.

Technical Facilities: 1-kw ERP, 26-ft. above ground, 8720-ft. above sea level, lat. 41° 26' 05", long. 109° 07' 00".

Ownership: High Plains Broadcasting Inc.

Rock Springs—K48FE, Ch. 48, Loflin Children's Trust-One. Phone: 504-928-3574.

Technical Facilities: 1000-w TPO, 0.09-kw ERP, 41-ft. above ground, 7352-ft. above sea level, lat. 41° 29' 50", long. 109° 20' 36".

Transmitter: Wilkens Peak Rd., approx. 11.3-mi. ESE of Green River.

Ownership: Loflin Children's Trust-One, Two & Four.

Rock Springs—K56FV, Ch. 56, Loflin Children's Trust-One. Phone: 504-928-3574.

Technical Facilities: 1000-w TPO, 0.09-kw ERP, 42-ft. above ground, 7352-ft. above sea level, lat. 41° 29' 50", long. 109° 20' 36".

Transmitter: Wilkens Peak Rd., approx. 11.3-mi. ESE of Green River.

Ownership: Loflin Children's Trust-One, Two & Four.

Rock Springs—K58EW, Ch. 58, Loflin Children's Trust-One. Phone: 504-928-3574.

Technical Facilities: 1000-w TPO, 0.09-kw ERP, 41-ft. above ground, 7352-ft. above sea level, lat. 41° 29' 50", long. 109° 20' 36".

Transmitter: Wilkens Peak Rd., approx. 11.3-mi. ESE of Green River.

Ownership: Loflin Children's Trust-One, Two & Four.

Rock Springs—K64EP, Ch. 64, Loflin Children's Trust-One. Phone: 504-928-3574.

Technical Facilities: 1000-w TPO, 0.09-kw ERP, 42-ft. above ground, 7352-ft. above sea level, lat. 41° 29' 50", long. 109° 20' 36".

Transmitter: Wilkens Peak Rd., approx. 11.3-mi. ESE of Green River.

Ownership: Loflin Children's Trust-One, Two & Four.

Rock Springs, etc.—K22BK, Ch. 22, Central Wyoming College. Phone: 307-856-6944.

Technical Facilities: 0.83-kw ERP, 59-ft. above ground, 7703-ft. above sea level, lat. 41° 29' 50", long. 109° 20' 36".

Holds CP for change to 0.96-kw ERP, 328-ft. above ground, 7946-ft. above sea level, lat. 41° 34' 43", long. 109° 19' 12". BPTTL-20080717ANV.

Transmitter: Wilkins Peak, approx. 7-mi. ESE of Green River.

Began Operation: February 21, 1990.

Ownership: Central Wyoming College.

Rock Springs, etc.—K28JU-D, Ch. 28, Central Wyoming College. Phone: 307-856-6944.

Technical Facilities: 0.5-kw ERP, 325-ft. above ground, 7943-ft. above sea level, lat. 41° 34' 43", long. 109° 19' 12".

Ownership: Central Wyoming College.

Saratoga—K11ER, Ch. 11, Elk Mountain TV Co.

Technical Facilities: 0.021-kw ERP, 7549-ft. above sea level, lat. 41° 25' 50", long. 106° 41' 40".

Saratoga—K13EI, Ch. 13, Elk Mountain TV Co.

Technical Facilities: 0.095-kw ERP, 7529-ft. above sea level, lat. 41° 25' 50", long. 106° 41' 40".

Saratoga, etc.—K07NT, Ch. 7, Central Wyoming College. Phone: 307-856-6944.

Studio: 2660 Peck Ave., Riverton, WY 82501.

Technical Facilities: 0.06-kw ERP, lat. 41° 19' 03", long. 106° 21' 18".

Multichannel TV Sound: Stereo only.

Ownership: Central Wyoming College.

Personnel: Ruby Calvert, General Manager.

Saratoga, etc.—K09OC, Ch. 9, Central Wyoming College. Phone: 307-856-6944.

Technical Facilities: 0.061-kw ERP, lat. 41° 19' 03", long. 106° 21' 18".

Ownership: Central Wyoming College.

Sheridan—K09XK, Ch. 7, KTVQ Communications Inc.

Technical Facilities: 2.06-kw ERP, lat. 44° 37' 37", long. 107° 06' 51".

Sheridan—K26BE, Ch. 26, Central Wyoming College.

Technical Facilities: 12.1-kw ERP, lat. 44° 36' 07", long. 106° 55' 54".

Transmitter: 2.5-mi. NW of Storey.

Sheridan—KSWY-LP, Ch. 29, Bozeman Trail Communications Co. Phone: 775-360-0604.

Technical Facilities: 8-kw ERP, 66-ft. above ground, 7749-ft. above sea level, lat. 44° 37' 20", long. 107° 06' 57".

Began Operation: September 12, 2005.

Ownership: Sunbelt Communications Co.

Sheridan, etc.—K06AT, Ch. 6, Nexstar Broadcasting Inc. Phone: 972-373-8800.

Technical Facilities: 0.23-kw ERP, lat. 44° 37' 24", long. 107° 06' 59".

Ownership: Nexstar Broadcasting Group Inc.

Sheridan, etc.—K55BL, Ch. 55, Silverton Broadcasting Co. LLC. Phone: 310-476-2217.

Technical Facilities: 4.35-kw ERP, lat. 44° 36' 07", long. 106° 55' 54".

Ownership: Silverton Broadcasting Co. LLC.

Shoshoni—K13NZ, Ch. 13, Silverton Broadcasting Co. LLC. Phone: 310-476-2217.

Technical Facilities: 0.012-kw ERP, lat. 43° 26' 15", long. 108° 00' 02".

Ownership: Silverton Broadcasting Co. LLC.

Shoshoni—K30GV, Ch. 30, Riverton-Fremont TV Club Inc.

Technical Facilities: 1.188-kw ERP, 19-ft. above ground, 7237-ft. above sea level, lat. 43° 27' 00", long. 108° 14' 00".

Shoshoni—K32EL, Ch. 32, Riverton-Fremont TV Club Inc.

Technical Facilities: 100-w TPO, 1.18-kw ERP, 28-ft. above ground, 7236-ft. above sea level, lat. 43° 27' 00", long. 108° 14' 00".

Ownership: Riverton Fremont TV Club Inc.

Shoshoni—K35CV, Ch. 35, Silverton Broadcasting Co. LLC. Phone: 310-476-2217.

Technical Facilities: 1.09-kw ERP, 39-ft. above ground, 8271-ft. above sea level, lat. 43° 26' 15", long. 107° 59' 51".

Ownership: Silverton Broadcasting Co. LLC.

Shoshoni—K42ER, Ch. 42, Riverton Fremont TV Club Inc.

Technical Facilities: 1.19-kw ERP, lat. 43° 27' 00", long. 108° 14' 00".

Transmitter: Boysen Peak, approx. 6.94-mi. NW of Shoshoni.

Shoshoni, etc.—K38EK, Ch. 38, Riverton Fremont TV Club Inc. Phone: 307-856-3322.

Technical Facilities: 100-w TPO, 1.2-kw ERP, 18-ft. above ground, 7237-ft. above sea level, lat. 43° 27' 00", long. 108° 14' 00".

Transmitter: 7-mi. NW of Shoshoni, on Boysen Peak.

Ownership: Riverton Fremont TV Club Inc.

Shoshoni, etc.—K40AQ, Ch. 40, Riverton Fremont TV Club Inc.

Technical Facilities: 1.188-kw ERP, lat. 43° 27' 00", long. 108° 14' 00".

Transmitter: Boysen Peak, approx. 7-mi. NW of Shoshoni.

South Fork—K02LG, Ch. 2, Central Wyoming College. Phone: 307-856-6944.

Technical Facilities: 0.05-kw ERP, lat. 44° 14' 30", long. 109° 31' 30".

Ownership: Central Wyoming College.

South Fork—K06KS, Ch. 6, Park County.

Technical Facilities: 0.04-kw ERP, lat. 44° 14' 03", long. 109° 31' 30".

South Fork—K11GG, Ch. 11, Park County.

Technical Facilities: 0.036-kw ERP, lat. 44° 14' 30", long. 109° 31' 30".

South Fork, etc.—K13FX, Ch. 13, Park County.

Technical Facilities: 0.036-kw ERP, 6335-ft. above sea level, lat. 44° 14' 30", long. 109° 31' 30".

■ **South Park**—K09LF, Ch. 9, NPG of Idaho Inc.

Technical Facilities: 0.01-kw ERP, lat. 43° 23' 20", long. 110° 44' 15".

Ownership: News Press & Gazette Co.

Sundance, etc.—K09AC, Ch. 9, Sundance Community TV Assn.

Technical Facilities: 0.002-kw ERP, 5840-ft. above sea level, lat. 44° 23' 18", long. 104° 20' 33".

Sunlight Basin, etc.—K04DB, Ch. 4, Park County.

Technical Facilities: 0.079-kw ERP, lat. 44° 45' 25", long. 109° 22' 21".

Sunlight Basin, etc.—K05CC, Ch. 5, Park County.

Technical Facilities: 0.079-kw ERP, lat. 44° 45' 25", long. 109° 22' 21".

Sunlight Basin, etc.—K11QL, Ch. 11, Central Wyoming College. Phone: 307-856-6944.

Technical Facilities: 0.12-kw ERP, lat. 44° 45' 25", long. 109° 22' 21".

Ownership: Central Wyoming College.

Sunlight Basin, etc.—K13SP, Ch. 13, Park County.

Technical Facilities: 0.009-kw ERP, 8674-ft. above sea level, lat. 44° 45' 25", long. 109° 22' 21".

Teton Village—K19FG, Ch. 19, Central Wyoming College. Phone: 308-856-6944.

Technical Facilities: 0.137-kw ERP, 20-ft. above ground, 6758-ft. above sea level, lat. 43° 32' 06", long. 110° 44' 28".

Teton Village—K25ID, Ch. 25, Central Wyoming College.

Technical Facilities: 0.298-kw ERP, 27-ft. above ground, 10437-ft. above sea level, lat. 43° 35' 50", long. 110° 52' 13".

Ownership: Central Wyoming College.

Thayne, etc.—K05GJ, Ch. 5, Lower Star Valley Non-Profit TV Assn.

Technical Facilities: 0.216-kw ERP, 6430-ft. above sea level, lat. 43° 01' 23", long. 111° 04' 21".

Thayne, etc.—K07PB, Ch. 7, Lower Star Valley Non-Profit TV Assn.

Technical Facilities: 0.261-kw ERP, 6430-ft. above sea level, lat. 43° 01' 23", long. 111° 04' 21".

Thayne, etc.—K12LI, Ch. 12, Lower Star Valley Non-Profit TV Assn.

Technical Facilities: 0.261-kw ERP, 6430-ft. above sea level, lat. 43° 01' 23", long. 111° 04' 21".

Upper Bear Valley, etc.—K09JL, Ch. 9, Upper Bear River TV Service.

Technical Facilities: 0.115-kw ERP, lat. 41° 21' 14", long. 110° 54' 38".

Upper Bear Valley, etc.—K11JQ, Ch. 11, Upper Bear River TV Service.

Technical Facilities: 0.023-kw ERP, lat. 41° 21' 14", long. 110° 54' 38".

Wood River—K07RT, Ch. 7, Central Wyoming College. Phone: 307-856-6944.

Technical Facilities: 0.09-kw ERP, lat. 44° 04' 30", long. 108° 56' 10".

Ownership: Central Wyoming College.

Wood River, etc.—K04LA, Ch. 4, Park County.

Technical Facilities: 0.09-kw ERP, lat. 44° 04' 30", long. 108° 56' 10".

Wood River, etc.—K06DJ, Ch. 6, Park County.

Technical Facilities: 0.048-kw ERP, lat. 44° 04' 30", long. 108° 56' 10".

Wood River, etc.—K13FO, Ch. 13, Park County.

Technical Facilities: 0.05-kw ERP, lat. 44° 04' 30", long. 108° 56' 10".

Wood River, etc.—K31JO-D, Ch. 31, Central Wyoming College. Phone: 307-856-6944.

Technical Facilities: 0.25-kw ERP, 62-ft. above ground, 7178-ft. above sea level, lat. 44° 04' 30", long. 108° 56' 10".

Began Operation: December 12, 2008.

Ownership: Central Wyoming College.

Worland—K04DZ, Ch. 4, Farmers TV Assn.

Technical Facilities: 0.009-kw ERP, lat. 43° 56' 14", long. 107° 54' 45".

Worland—K12BK, Ch. 12, Farmers TV Assn.

Technical Facilities: 0.009-kw ERP, lat. 43° 56' 14", long. 107° 54' 45".

Wyodak, etc.—K08AA, Ch. 8, Silverton Broadcasting Co. LLC. Phone: 310-476-2217.

Technical Facilities: 0.01-kw ERP, lat. 44° 12' 35", long. 105° 28' 00".

Ownership: Silverton Broadcasting Co. LLC.

Guam

Agana—K28HS, Ch. 28, E. C. Development Ventures. Phone: 671-637-5826.

Technical Facilities: 0.15-kw ERP, 49-ft. above ground, 131-ft. above sea level, lat. 13° 29' 13.8", long. 144° 46' 50".

Began Operation: October 14, 2005.

Ownership: E. C. Development Ventures.

Agana—K30HB, Ch. 30, E. C. Development Ventures. Phone: 671-637-5826.

Technical Facilities: 0.15-kw ERP, 49-ft. above ground, 131-ft. above sea level, lat. 13° 29' 13.8", long. 144° 46' 50".

Began Operation: October 14, 2005.

Ownership: E. C. Development Ventures.

Agana—K32GB, Ch. 32, E. C. Development Ventures. Phone: 671-637-5826.

Technical Facilities: 0.15-kw ERP, 49-ft. above ground, 131-ft. above sea level, lat. 13° 29' 13.8", long. 144° 46' 50".

Began Operation: October 14, 2005.

Ownership: E. C. Development Ventures.

Agana—K36GJ, Ch. 36, E. C. Development Ventures. Phone: 671-637-5826.

Technical Facilities: 0.15-kw ERP, 49-ft. above ground, 131-ft. above sea level, lat. 13° 29' 13.8", long. 144° 46' 50".

Began Operation: October 14, 2005.

Ownership: E. C. Development Ventures.

Dededo—KEQI-LP, Ch. 22, Sorensen Television Systems Inc. Phone: 671-477-5700.

Technical Facilities: 0.97-kw ERP, 85-ft. above ground, 725-ft. above sea level, lat. 13° 29' 17", long. 144° 49' 30".

Holds CP for change to 1.95-kw ERP, 66-ft. above ground, 705-ft. above sea level, BDFCDTL-20081229AAN.

Began Operation: February 14, 2005.

Ownership: Sorensen Television Systems Inc.

Tamuning—KTKB-LP, Ch. 26, KM Broadcasting of Guam LLC. Phone: 847-674-0864.

Technical Facilities: 54-kw ERP, 138-ft. above ground, 797-ft. above sea level, lat. 13° 29' 16", long. 144° 49' 36".

Ownership: KM Communications Inc.

Tamuning—KUAM-LP, Ch. 20, Pacific Telestations Inc. Phone: 671-637-5826. Fax: 671-637-9865.

Studio: 600 Harmon Loop Rd, Ste 102, Dededo, GU 96912.

Technical Facilities: 1000-w TPO, 13.1-kw ERP, 174-ft. above ground, 371-ft. above sea level, lat. 13° 30' 34", long. 144° 48' 36".

Transmitter: 193 Tumon Lane.

Ownership: Micronesia Broadcasting Corp.

Personnel: Jason Salas, Web Development Manager; Joseph G. Calvo, General Manager; Richard Garman, Chief Engineer; Marie Calvo Monge; Sabrina Salas Matanane, News Director.

Mariana Islands

Garapan & Saipan—KPPI-LP, Ch. 7, Sorensen Television Systems Inc.

Technical Facilities: 0.78-kw ERP, 79-ft. above ground, 212-ft. above sea level, lat. 15° 11' 25", long. 145° 42' 59".

Ownership: Sorensen Television Systems Inc.

Virgin Islands

Charlotte Amalie—WBIV-LP, Ch. 38, Virgin Islands Telecommunications Ventures.

Technical Facilities: 1000-w TPO, 20-kw ERP, 1667-ft. above sea level, lat. 18° 21' 33", long. 64° 58' 18".

Transmitter: Crown Mountain.

Ownership: Virgin Islands Telecommunications Ventures LLC.

Charlotte Amalie—WMNS-LP, Ch. 22, V. I. Christian Ministries Inc. Phone: 340-714-4399.

Technical Facilities: 10-kw ERP, 29-ft. above ground, 1509-ft. above sea level, lat. 18° 21' 17", long. 64° 56' 51".

Holds CP for change to 5-kw ERP, 98-ft. above ground, 1562-ft. above sea level, lat. 18° 21' 28", long. 64° 56' 53". BDFCDTL-20060327AIN.

Ownership: V.I. Christian Ministries Inc.

Charlotte Amalie—WVGN-LP, Ch. 14, LKK Group Corp. Phone: 800-275-6437.

Technical Facilities: 0.7-kw ERP, 197-ft. above ground, 1687-ft. above sea level, lat. 18° 21' 26", long. 64° 58' 17".

Ownership: LKK Group Corp.

Christainsted—W05AW, Ch. 5, Virgin Islands Public Television System.

Technical Facilities: 0.06-kw ERP, lat. 17° 45' 25", long. 64° 47' 59".

Christiansted—W21AA, Ch. 21, Virgin Islands Public Television System.

Technical Facilities: lat. 17° 44' 07", long. 64° 40' 46".

Christiansted—WEYA-LP, Ch. 52, Frontline Missions International Inc. Phone: 340-715-7729.

Technical Facilities: 2.5-kw ERP, 131-ft. above ground, 891-ft. above sea level, lat. 17° 43' 46", long. 64° 41' 16".

Holds CP for change to channel number 10, 3-kw ERP, 94-ft. above ground, 1094-ft. above sea level, lat. 17° 45' 22", long. 64° 47' 57". BPTVL-20050926AEH.

Ownership: Frontline Missions International Inc.

Christiansted—WJWM-LP, Ch. 34, Seventh Trumpet Broadcasting Corp. Phone: 340-778-4621.

Technical Facilities: 7.5-kw ERP, 46-ft. above ground, 1142-ft. above sea level, lat. 17° 45' 24", long. 64° 48' 00".

Ownership: Seventh Trumpet Broadcasting Corp.

Frederiksted—WEON-LP, Ch. 60, LKK Group Corp. Phone: 323-934-8283.

Technical Facilities: 10-kw ERP, 197-ft. above ground, 257-ft. above sea level, lat. 17° 41' 43", long. 64° 52' 57".

Holds CP for change to channel number 42, 15-kw ERP, 197-ft. above ground, 255-ft. above sea level, lat. 17° 41' 50", long. 64° 52' 58". BDISDTL-20070103ADR.

Ownership: LKK Group Corp.

St. Thomas—W29CB, Ch. 29, Three Angels Broadcasting Network Inc. Phones: 618-627-4651; 800-752-3226. Fax: 618-627-4155.

Studio: 3391 Charley Good Rd, West Frankfort, IL 62896.

Technical Facilities: 1000-w TPO, 35.02-kw ERP, 200-ft. above ground, 1592-ft. above sea level, lat. 18° 21' 25", long. 64° 58' 00".

Transmitter: Estate Dorothea 22A.

Ownership: Three Angels Broadcasting Network Inc.

Personnel: Moses Primo, Chief Engineer.

Ownership of Low Power Television/Translator Stations

Includes licensees and permittees. Lottery grantees not included.

101 TELEVISION
101 Centre, Suite G
Williams & Downs Ave.
Woodward, OK 73801
Phone: 580-256-3694
Fax: 580-256-3825
Officers:
J. Douglas William, Chairman, President &
Chief Executive Officer
Mike Mitchel, Secretary-Treasurer
Julia Hart, Chief Financial Officer
Ownership: Omni Broadcasting.
Represented (legal): Pillsbury Winthrop Shaw
Pittman LLP.
LPTV Stations:
Oklahoma: KOMI-CD Woodward.

NORTH LAKE TAHOE COMMUNITY FOUNDATION
5165 Driftstone Ave
Reno, NV 89523
Phone: 775-741-7969
E-mail: jrdahle@yahoo.com
Ownership: Jeff Dahle, Board Member.
LPTV Stations:
Nevada: KVCJ-LP Incline Village.

DEL CARIBE ORLANDO LLC
426 S River Rd
Tryon, NC 28782-7879
Phone: 828-859-6982
Ownership: Mark Jorgenson, Managing Member.
LPTV Stations:
Florida: WAWA-LP Orlando.

OROVILLE TV ASSOCIATION INC.

LPTV Stations:
Washington: K02MO Oroville; K04KZ Oroville.

A1A TV INC.
126 Hercules Rd.
St. Augustine, FL 32086-6718
Phone: 904-794-6774
Ownership: Fred Campbell.
LPTV Stations:
Florida: WQXT-CA St. Augustine.

ABACUS TELEVISION
1801 Columbia Rd NW
Ste 101
Washington, DC 20009-2031
Phones: 202-462-3680; 800-499-4120
Fax: 202-462-3781

Branch Office:
514 Chautauqua St.
Pittsburgh, PA 15214
Phone: 412-322-5526
Ownership: Benjamin Perez, Pres..
LPTV Stations:
Ohio: WSSS-LP Steubenville.
Pennsylvania: WTOO-CA Altoona; WWBP-LP
Freedom; WQVC-CA Greensburg; WBYD-CA
Johnstown; W29AV Pittsburgh; WPTG-LP
Pittsburgh; WWAT-CA Uniontown.

West Virginia: WWVW-LP Wheeling.

ABILENE CHRISTIAN U.
1600 Campus Court
ACU Box 27820
Abilene, TX 79699
Phone: 325-674-2441
Fax: 325-674-2417
E-mail: kesslerj@acu.edu
Web site: www.acu.edu
Officers:
J.R. Kessler, Operations Director
Larry Bradshaw, Chief Operating Officer
LPTV Stations:
Texas: K07UF Abilene.

ABIQUIU VALLEY TV ASSOCIATION
PO Box 63
Abiquiu, NM 87501
LPTV Stations:
New Mexico: K02HU Abiquiu; K06ME Abiquiu;
K09LY Abiquiu.

ABSAROKEE COMMUNITY TV CLUB
PO Box 546
Absarokee, MT 59001-0546
Phone: 406-328-4654
E-mail: ganddshell@yahoo.com
Officer:
Gary L. Shelley, President
LPTV Stations:
Montana: K05EI Absarokee; K10MO Absarokee;
K12HX Absarokee.

ABUNDANT LIFE BROADCASTING INC.
914 Cirby Way
Roseville, CA 95661
Phone: 916-786-8350
LPTV Stations:
California: K27EU Sacramento.

ACADIANA CABLE ADVERTISING INC.
Drawer 7186
Opelousas, LA 70571
Phone: 319-948-7267
Officers:
Frank T. Daly Jr., President
J. E. Brignac, Secretary-Treasurer
LPTV Stations:
Louisiana: KDCG-LP Opelousas.

ACCESS.1 COMMUNICATIONS CORP.
11 Penn Plaza, 16th Floor
New York, NY 10001
Phone: 212-714-1000
Officers:
Sydney L. Small, Chairman & Chief Executive
Officer
Chesley Maddox-Dorsey, President & Chief
Operating Officer
Adriane Gaines, Secretary

Ownership: Sydney L. Small, 50.16%; Chesley
Maddox-Dorsey, 5.28%; Adriane Gaines,
3.44%.
Represented (legal): Rubin, Winston, Diercks,
Harris & Cooke LLP.
LPTV Stations:
New Jersey: WMGM-LP Atlantic City.
Commercial TV Stations:
New Jersey: WMGM-DT Wildwood.
Other Holdings:
Radio: SupeRadio, producer & distributer if
radio programming.

COUNTY OF ACCOMACK
Box 388
Accomack, VA 23301-0388
LPTV Stations:
Virginia: W20CW Craddockville; W22DN Crad-
dockville; W42DP Craddockville; W48DO
Craddockville; W25AA Onancock; W30CI
Onancock; W34DN Onancock; W39CS Onan-
cock.

ACME COMMUNICATIONS INC.
2101 E. 4th St.
Suite 202A
Santa Ana, CA 92705
Phone: 715-245-9499
E-mail: contactus@newmexicoswbcw.tv
Officers:
Jamie Kellner, Chairman & Chief Executive
Officer
Douglas Gealy, President & Chief Operating
Officer
Tom Allen, Executive Vice President, Secretary
& Chief Financial Officer
Ownership: Gabelli Capital LLC, 10.11%; CEA
Capital Partners USA LP, 9.57%; James
Collis, 9.57%; Brian McNeill, 9.57%; Cannell
Capital LLC, 8.62%; Dimensional Fund
Advisors Inc., 7.2%; Alta Communications
VI LP, 6.72%; Wynnefield Capital, 5.68%;
Jamie Kellner, 4.72%; Douglas Gealy,
3.39%; Thomas D. Allen, 3.38%; Thomas
Embrescia, 0.90%.
Represented (legal): O'Melveny & Myers LLP;
Dickstein Shapiro LLP.
LPTV Stations:
New Mexico: K24CT Alamogordo; K28HB
Alamogordo; K23BT Farmington; K17EM
Roswell.
Commercial TV Stations:
New Mexico: KASY-DT Albuquerque; KRWB-DT
Roswell; KWBQ-DT Santa Fe.
Ohio: WBDT-DT Springfield.
Tennessee: WBXX-DT Crossville.
Wisconsin: WBUW-DT Janesville; WIWB-DT
Suring.

ACTION COMMUNITY TELEVISION BROADCASTING NETWORK INC.
1701 Sunset Blvd.
Suite 205
Rocky Mount, NC 27804
Phone: 252-446-8857
Officer:
Herbert Greenberg, President
Represented (legal): Reddy, Begley & Mc-
Cormick LLP.

LPTV Stations:
North Carolina: WHIG-LP Rocky Mount.

ROBERT D. ADELMAN
731 N. Balsam
Ridgecrest, CA 93555
Phone: 760-371-1700
Represented (legal): Putbrese, Hunsaker &
Trent PC.
LPTV Stations:
California: K06OL Inyokern, etc.; KEDD-LP
Lancaster.

ADULLAM GOSPEL CHURCH
RR1
Box 26
Richmondville, NY 12149
Phone: 518-234-4769
LPTV Stations:
New York: WUCB-LP Cobleskill; WYBN-LP
Cobleskill.

AGAPE BROADCASTERS INC.
PO Box 1469
Crowley, LA 70527-1469
Phone: 337-783-1560
Fax: 337-783-1674
Officers:
Barry D. Thompson Sr., Chairman, President,
Chief Executive & Operating Officer
R. S. King Jr., Secretary
Annette G. Thompson, Treasurer & Chief
Financial Officer
Ownership: Barry D Thompson Sr., 70%.
Represented (legal): Pillsbury Winthrop Shaw
Pittman LLP.
LPTV Stations:
Louisiana: K02QB Alexandria; KAGN-LP Crow-
ley; KAJN-LP Lafayette; KFAM-LP Lake
Charles.
Radio Stations:
Louisiana: KAJN-FM Crowley

VICTOR AGMATA
1170 N. King St.
Honolulu, HI 96817
Phone: 808-847-1151
LPTV Stations:
Hawaii: K56EX Honolulu.

AGUILAR TV CLUB
Box 199
Aguilar, CO 81020-0199
Phone: 719-547-0639
Officer:
Bruce E. Merritt, Information Contact
LPTV Stations:
Colorado: K02AC Aguilar; K07AG Aguilar;
K09AH Aguilar.

CITY OF AINSWORTH
PO Box 165
Ainsworth, NE 69210-0165
Phone: 402-387-2494

LPTV Stations:
Nebraska: K11KW Ainsworth; K13EH Ainsworth.

AIRWAVES INC.
c/o John C. Terrill
453 Simoron Dr.
Ogden, UT 84404
Phone: 801-393-0012
Web site: www.telemundo-utah.com
Officer:
John C. Terrill, President
LPTV Stations:
Utah: K10OX Logan; KUTA-LP Logan; KQTI-LD Ogden; KULX-LD Ogden; K57JB Park City.

ALABAMA HERITAGE COMMUNICATIONS LLC
Box 10
Jacksonville, AL 36265
Phone: 256-782-5133
Ownership: Forney McMichael, 66.81%; Mickey Shadrix, 15.13%; Rebecca Wilson, 10%; Steven Lynch, 8.06%.
Represented (legal): Fletcher, Heald & Hildreth PLC.
LPTV Stations:
Alabama: WJXS-CA Jacksonville.

ALASKA BROADCASTING CO. INC.
1007 W. 32nd Ave.
Anchorage, AK 99503
Phone: 907-273-3192
Officer:
Jerry M. Bever, Vice President
Represented (legal): Wilkinson Barker Knauer LLP.
LPTV Stations:
Alaska: K11VP Homer-Seldovia.

ALASKA BROADCAST TELEVISION INC.
Box 210830
Anchorage, AK 99521
Phone: 907-337-2020
Fax: 907-333-9851
Officers:
Dr. Jerry L. Prevo, President
Floyd Damron, Vice President
Mark Runkle, Secretary
Ron Hoffman, Treasurer
Ownership: Curt Beytebien; Floyd Damron; Steve Gilbert; Ron Hoffman; Larry Linegar; Mike Paulsen; Dr. Jerry L. Prevo; Mark Runkle, 12.5%. votes each.
Represented (legal): Joseph E. Dunne III.
LPTV Stations:
Alaska: KCFT-LP Anchorage.

ALASKA CORP. OF SEVENTH DAY ADVENTISTS
6100 O'Malley Rd.
Anchorage, AK 99516
Phone: 907-346-1004
LPTV Stations:
Alaska: K05KF Dillingham.

ALASKA PUBLIC TELECOMMUNICATIONS INC.
3877 University Dr.
Anchorage, AK 99508
Phone: 907-563-7070
Fax: 907-273-9192
Officers:
Tom Williams, Chairman
Susan Satin, President
Paul Stankavich, General Manager
Ronnie Dent, Development Manager & Public Information Officer

Patsy Parker, Finance Manager
Ownership: Non-profit organization.
LPTV Stations:
Alaska: K67AY Bird Creek; K05FW Girdwood; K07PF Homer; K48AC Kasilof; K12LA Kenai, etc.; K21AM Ninilchik.
ETV Stations:
Alaska: KAKM-DT Anchorage.

STATE OF ALASKA
5900 E. Tudor Rd.
Division of Information Services
Anchorage, AK 99507
Phone: 907-269-5744
Officer:
John Morrone, Deputy Director
Ownership: State government.
LPTV Stations:
Alaska: K04LY Adak; K13SH Adak; K04LL Akhiok; K09UD Akhiok; K10MV Akiak; K12NS Akiak; K04LK Akutan; K09RH Akutan; K04ND Alakanuk; K08KD Alakanuk; K08HU Aleknagik; K13RP Aleknagik; K09QL Allakaket, etc.; K04GP Alyeska; K11QI Ambler; K04IX Anaktuvuk Pass; K09RS Anaktuvuk Pass; K51AF Anchor Point; K07SS Angoon; K09QF Angoon; K02KY Aniak; K11QN Aniak; K07RE Anvik; K04LI Arctic Village; K09RV Arctic Village; K04LJ Atka; K09RX Atka; K04NH Atkasuk; K09TZ Atkasuk; K05II Atmautluak; K12NP Atmautluak; K04KS Barrow; K11NN Barrow; K04LC Beaver; K09QQ Beaver; K09TE Bettles; K13TE Bettles; K09TD Birch Creek; K13SY Birch Creek; K09HG Bird Point, etc.; K57BQ Bird Point, etc.; K04LU Buckland; K09RI Buckland; K02KK Cantwell; K09SI Cantwell; K13SD Cape Pole; K09QG Chalkyitsik; K02LO Chefornak; K04MK Chefornak; K13VV Chenega; K02KX Chevak; K10MT Chickaloon; K02LK Chignik; K07RY Chignik; K04MZ Chignik Lagoon; K09SO Chignik Lagoon; K02MR Chignik Lake; K11RQ Chignik Lake; K07QZ Chistochina; K09PX Chistochina; K13SB Chitina; K06LG Chuathbaluk; K09TT Circle; K13SI Circle; K03GO Circle Hot Springs; K06LP Circle Hot Springs; K06LK Clarks Point, etc.; K12NL Clarks Point, etc.; K09TV Coffman Cove; K13SZ Coffman Cove; K07TM Cold Bay; K13UO Cold Bay; K08KO Cooper Landing; K12MO Copper Center; K09OR Cordova; K15AK Cordova; K07TL Council; K09UK Council; K57DE Craig; K61DE Craig; K07RZ Crooked Creek; K04LT Deering; K09RN Deering; K17AF Delta Junction; K10LD Dillingham; K13UX Diomede; K07RU Dot Lake; K13RM Dot Lake; K16DO Eagle River; K55DC Eagle River Road; K58BH Eagle River Road; K61CB Eagle River Road; K05IJ Eagle Village; K09RF Eagle Village; K09TN Eek; K11SD Eek; K04KR Egegik; K09SK Egegik; K09TA Eight Fathoms Bight; K13TG Eight Fathoms Bight; K04MS Ekwok; K11QW Ekwok; K09TK Elfin Cove; K03GA Elim; K09QS Elim; K05IH Emmonak; K31AG English Bay; K43AK English Bay; K04MY Ernestine; K11RI Ernestine; K04LG False Pass; K09RP False Pass; K07RC Fort Yukon; K09TP Freshwater Bay; K13TW Freshwater Bay; K11RG Gakona; K04LZ Galena; K09QR Gambell; K08KA Girdwood; K10MB Girdwood; K12MM Girdwood Valley; K05HA Glenallen; K13UB Glennallen & Cooper Landing; K04LH Golovin; K07QX Golovin; K04KT Goodnews Bay; K09SG Goodnews Bay; K02ML Gravina Island; K04NC Gravina Island, etc.; K11QH Grayling; K02LW Gustavus; K04MR Gustavus; K07RF Haines; K09PD Haines; K08JY Halibut Cove; K12NW Halibut Cove; K58BI Healy; K09TB Hobart Bay; K13TT Hobart Bay; K08KP Hollis; K12NT Hollis; K07RJ Holy Cross; K02IB Homer & Seldovia; K04JH Homer, etc.; K11RK Homer, etc.; K13TR Homer, etc.; K04MO Hoonah; K07QV Hoonah; K04MC

Hooper Bay; K09RY Hughes; K09QD Huslia; K09QI Hydaburg; K02MJ Hyder; K04MM Hyder; K04ME Igiugig; K09SP Igiugig; K04KO Iliamna; K07RV Iliamna; K25AI Indian, etc.; K47AM Indian, etc.; K04MF Ivanof Bay; K09SN Ivanof Bay; K09QP Kake; K12NR Kake; K09TM Kahkonak; K13TF Kahonak; K04IU Kaktovik; K09QY Kaktovik; K09TR Kalskag; K11RF Kalskag; K09TX Kaltag; K04LS Karluk; K09QK Karluk; K09SM Kasaan; K13SG Kasaan; K02LZ Kasigluk; K09UE Kasigluk; K56AQ Kasilof; K61AN Kasilof; K67AU Kasilof; K23AF Kenai, etc.; K25AH Ketchikan; K21AH Ketchikan; K09RW Kiana; K09QW King Cove; K03GL King Mountain; K04KN King Salmon; K08KS King Salmon; K04LM Kipnuk; K09QZ Kivalina; K07TI Klawock; K11RA Klawock; K04KQ Klukwan; K11RD Klukwan; K02KZ Kobuk; K13SF Kobuk; K15AT Kodiak; K04JV Koliganek; K07QW Koliganek; K04LF Kongiganak; K09RG Kongiganak; K09SL Kotlik; K13UE Kotzebue; K02MB Koyuk; K03FZ Koyukuk; K13TQ Koyukuk; K09UJ Kwethluk; K11QY Kwethluk; K11SC Kwigillingok; K13UK Kwigillingok; K02MC Labouchere Bay; K09QE Larsen Bay; K02MN Levelock; K07TT Levelock; K07TH Lime Village; K11RW Lime Village; K05IR Long Island; K07RX Manley Hot Springs; K13TN Manley Hot Springs; K07LB Manokotak; K09TQ Manokotak; K02KV Marshall; K07TK Marshall; K07TJ McGrath; K09QC McGrath; K03GK McKinley Park; K10MI McKinley Park; K04MD Mekoryuk; K07SQ Mentasta Lake; K09QJ Mentasta Lake; K07SL Metlakatla; K11QZ Metlakatla; K09TI Meyers Chuck; K13TB Meyers Chuck; K05IK Minchumina; K09SZ Minchumina; K05HZ Minto; K13TK Minto; K09AP Moose Pass; K02MW Mosquito Lake; K13UM Mosquito Lake; K13TJ Mountain Village; K13TZ Naknek; K10MR Napakiak; K13UV Napakiak; K02MZ Napaskiak; K07SJ Napaskiak; K09TJ Naukati Bay; K13TS Naukati Bay; K04LQ Nelson Lagoon; K09QM Nelson Lagoon; K55DE Nenana; K09QV New Stuyahok; K13TO New Stuyahok; K02LN Newtok; K04MT Newtok; K03GD Nightmute; K10LU Nightmute; K04MB Nikolai; K09PR Nikolai; K04LR Nikolski; K09RK Nikolski; K39AA Ninilchik, etc.; K15AG Ninilchik, etc.; K27AI Ninilchik, etc.; K33AF Ninilchik, etc.; K07RI Noatak; K09OW Nome; K13UG Nome; K02LJ Nondalton; K09RQ Nondalton; K04KP Northway; K04IS Nuiqsut; K09RT Nuiqsut; K02KW Nulato; K13RN Old Harbor; K02MA Ouzinkie; K07QY Ouzinkie; K04MQ Paxson; K11QV Paxson; K09TS Pedro Bay; K13SV Pedro Bay; K04LB Pelican; K09RM Pelican; K04MA Perryville; K15AF Petersburg; K21CK Petersburg; K02LI Pilot Point; K15AU Pilot Station; K07LV Pitkas Point; K04MW Pitkas Point; K05HY Platinum; K13UJ Platinum; K04MV Point Baker; K09SY Point Baker; K04IQ Point Hope; K09QN Point Hope; K04IT Point Lay; K09UC Point Lay; K09TL Port Alice; K13TL Port Alice; K07SH Port Alsworth; K13TU Port Alsworth; K09QB Port Graham; K13SC Port Graham; K13SA Port Heiden; K07RG Port Lions; K09SP Port Lions; K02LX Port Moller; K07SO Port Moller; K11QX Port Protection; K13TV Port Protection; K07TU Portage Creek; K13KY Portage Creek; K09SX Quinhagak; K13SK Quinhagak; K04LO Rampart; K09RD Rampart; K02LA Red Devil; K11KR Rifle; K09TC Rowan Bay; K13TM Rowan Bay; K04KU Ruby; K09SH Russian Mission; K11SB Russian Mission; K09RA Sand Point; K07RD Savoonga; K02LS Scammon Bay; K07SR Scammon Bay; K09RL Selawik; K55DD Seward; K04KY Shageluk; K02LM Shaktoolik; K07QU Shaktoolik; K08KM Sheep Mountain; K12NO Sheep Mountain; K03GP Sheldon Point; K11QR Sheldon Point; K04LD Shishmaref; K09RZ Shishmaref; K07RA Shungnak; K11QE Skagway; K13QQ Skagway; K04KX Slana;

K13SM Slana; K07SX Sleetmute; K05IB Sparrevohn; K09RE St. George; K13SX St. Mary's; K09QX St. Michael; K02LP St. Michaels; K09RB St. Paul; K04LE Stebbins; K09RR Stebbins; K04NA Stevens Village; K09SV Stevens Village; K13SE Stony River; K04LN Takotna; K09PN Takotna; K07RB Tanana; K07SA Tanunak; K09SW Tanunak; K13SJ Tatitlek; K11RV Telida; K13RO Telida; K04LW Teller; K09RO Teller; K07RH Tenakee Springs; K07SP Tetlin; K11QU Tetlin; K07SN Thorne Bay; K11RC Thorne Bay; K09QU Togiak; K13RR Tok; K04LV Toksook Bay; K11QG Toksook Bay; K16AF Trapper Creek; K24AG Trapper Creek; K08ID Tuluksak; K11RE Tuluksak; K09TF Tuntutuliak; K13TC Tuntutuliak; K09RC Unalakleet; K04KV Unalaska; K02HO Unalaska, etc.; K09OT Valdez; K15AI Valdez; K09TW Venetie; K04IR Wainwright; K02LT Wales; K04MN Wales; K07SI Whales Pass; K11RB Whales Pass; K11QT White Mountain; K13TD White Mountain; K09UB Whittier; K13TA Wiseman; K02ME Womens Bay; K07ST Womens Bay; K15AJ Wrangell; K21AF Wrangell; K09UA Yakutat.

BOARD OF EDUCATION OF THE CITY OF ALBUQUERQUE
1130 University Blvd. NE
Albuquerque, NM 87102-1798
Phone: 505-277-2121
Fax: 505-277-2191
Represented (legal): Dow Lohnes PLLC.
LPTV Stations:
New Mexico: K33FK Angel Fire; K38DA-D Aztec; K34FD Chama; K28GF Cimarron; K18HR Conchas Dam; K34HF-D Cuba; K40FI-D Farmington; K43AI Farmington; K31HB Gallina; K24FT-D Gallup; K33GA Grants & Milan; K33FL Las Vegas; K49KF-D Los Alamos/Espanola; K31EO Mora; K31FX Pie Town & Quemado; K15FS Quemado; K20CV Raton, etc.; K15FV Red River; K30FP Santa Rosa; K46HY-D Socorro; K15HD-D Taos; K33BN Taos; K49IL Tecolote; K31JR Thoreau; K28GV Tres Piedras; K36FQ Wagon Mound; K22FN White Oaks, etc..
ETV Stations:
New Mexico: KNME-DT Albuquerque; KNMD-DT Santa Fe.

ALLAKAKET CITY COUNCIL
5900 E. Tudor Rd.
Anchorage, AK 99507
LPTV Stations:
Alaska: K02KB Allakaket.

ALLBRITTON COMMUNICATIONS CO.
1000 Wilson Blvd.
Suite 2700
Arlington, VA 22209
Phone: 703-647-8700
Fax: 703-647-8707
E-mail: jfritz@allbrittontv.com
Officers:
Joe L. Allbritton, Chairman of Executive Committee
Robert L. Allbritton, Chairman & Chief Executive Officer
Lawrence I. Hebert, Vice Chairman
Frederick J. Ryan Jr., Vice Chairman, President & Chief Executive Officer
Jerald N. Fritz, Senior Vice President, Legal & Strategic Affairs
Stephen P. Gibson, Senior Vice President & Chief Financial Officer
Ownership: Joe L Allbritton, 49%; Robert Lewis Allbritton 1996 Trust, 49%; Barbara B. Allbritton 2008 Marital Trust, 2%.
LPTV Stations:
Alabama: WBMA-LP Birmingham.

Virginia: W05AA Roanoke.
Commercial TV Stations:
Alabama: WJSU-DT Anniston; WCFT-DT Tuscaloosa.
Arkansas: KATV-DT Little Rock.
District of Columbia: WJLA-DT Washington.
Oklahoma: KTUL-DT Tulsa.
Pennsylvania: WHTM-DT Harrisburg.
South Carolina: WCIV-DT Charleston.
Virginia: WSET-DT Lynchburg.
Newspapers:
Connecticut: Enfield Press
Massachusetts: Longmeadow News, Wallace Pennysaver, The Westfield Evening News (published by Allbritton affiliate Westfield News Advertiser Inc.)

MARK C. ALLEN
4531 Shannon Place
Redding, CA 96001
Phone: 530-246-8782
Fax: 530-547-4925
LPTV Stations:
California: KVTU-LP Los Angeles; KMCA-LP Redding.

TOWN OF ALMA
Box 1050
Alma, CO 80420
LPTV Stations:
Colorado: K02GX Alma.

ALMAVISION HISPANIC NETWORK INC.
Box 341440
Los Angeles, CA 90034
Phone: 213-622-4445
Fax: 213-622-4443
Officer:
Juan Bruno Caamano, President
Represented (legal): Katten, Munchin & Rosenman LLP.
LPTV Stations:
California: KTAV-LP Altadena; K55KD Van Nuys.
Florida: WEYS-LP Miami.

ALPHA & OMEGA COMMUNICATIONS LLC
PO Box 352
Salt Lake City, UT 84110
Phone: 801-973-8820
Ownership: Isaac Max Jaramillo; Patricia Jaramillo; Connie Whitney, 33.3%. each.
Represented (legal): Wood, Maines & Nolan Chartered.
LPTV Stations:
Idaho: KCLP-CA Boise.
Utah: K58FT Huntsville; K22IT Provo; K59GS Salt Lake City; K49GD Spanish Fork.
Commercial TV Stations:
Utah: KTMW-DT Salt Lake City.

ALPHA-OMEGA BROADCASTING OF ALBUQUERQUE INC.
4501 Montgomery NE
Albuquerque, NM 87109
Phones: 505-883-1300; 505-884-8355
Officers:
Raymond L. Franks Jr., Chairman
Brenton D. Franks, Vice President
Dan Segura, Vice President
Ownership: Eugene Agnes; Tomey Anaya; Bethal J. Franks; Brenton Franks; Raymond L. Franks; Ruth Franks; Clifford Qualls; Dan Segura; Dale Shamblin; Eugene Shiplet, 10%. each.
Represented (legal): Midlen Law Center.

LPTV Stations:
New Mexico: KTVS-LP Albuquerque.
ETV Stations:
New Mexico: KAZQ-DT Albuquerque.

AMKA BROADCAST NETWORK INC.
109 Bayview Blvd.
Suite A
Oldsmar, FL 34677
Phone: 727-725-3500
Fax: 813-814-7575
Officer:
Sotirios Agelatos, President & Chief Executive Officer
LPTV Stations:
Florida: WZRA-CA Oldsmar.

ANCHORAGE BROADCAST TELEVISION CONSORTIUM INC.
701 E Tudor Rd
Ste 220
Anchorage, AK 99503
Phone: 425-258-1440
Officer:
Alvin O Bramstedt, President
Represented (legal): Pillsbury Winthrop Shaw Pittman LLP.
LPTV Stations:
Alaska: K04GP Alyeska; K51AF Anchor Point; K09HG Bird Point, etc.; K57BQ Bird Point, etc.; K16DO Eagle River; K55DC Eagle River Road; K58BH Eagle River Road; K61CB Eagle River Road; K08KA Girdwood; K10MB Girdwood; K12MM Girdwood Valley; K02IB Homer & Seldovia; K04JH Homer, etc.; K11RK Homer, etc.; K13TR Homer, etc.; K25AI Indian, etc.; K47AM Indian, etc.; K56AQ Kasilof; K61AN Kasilof; K67AU Kasilof; K23AF Kenai, etc.; K39AA Ninilchik; K15AG Ninilchik, etc.; K27AI Ninilchik, etc.; K33AF Ninilchik, etc..

ANDERSON VALLEY TV INC.
Box 391
Boonville, CA 95415
LPTV Stations:
California: K57CT Boonville, etc.; K59CH Boonville, etc.; K61CH Boonville, etc.; K63CE Boonville, etc.; K67CC Boonville, etc.; K69CU Boonville, etc..

R. E. ANDREASSEN
HC 60
Box 4860
Delta Junction, AK 99737
Phone: 907-895-5100
LPTV Stations:
Alaska: K100B Delta Junction.

ANET COMMUNICATIONS INC.
1026 Chorro St.
No. 2
San Luis Obispo, CA 93401
LPTV Stations:
California: KCCE-LP San Luis Obispo.

ANGOON PUBLIC SCHOOLS
5900 E. Tuor Rd.
Anchorage, AK 99507
LPTV Stations:
Alaska: K02JI Angoon.

CITY OF ANVIK
5900 E. Tudor Rd.
Anchorage, AK 99507
LPTV Stations:
Alaska: K02JV Anvik.

ARNOLD N. APPLEBAUM
14830 Valley View Ave.
La Mirada, CA 90638

LPTV Stations:
California: KSBT-LP Santa Barbara.

APPLE VALLEY TV ASSOCIATION INC.
Box 582
Wenatchee, WA 98807-0582
Phone: 509-293-4403
E-mail: lonnie@kwcctv.com
Officer:
Lonnie K. England, President & Chief Executive Officer
LPTV Stations:
Washington: K57BA Baker Flats area; K59BF Baker Flats area; K09ES Cashmere; K11EZ Cashmere; K13ER Cashmere; K40AE Cashmere; K03DI Chelan Butte; K07JO Chelan Butte; KCEM-LP Chelan Butte; K08JP Dryden; K10LG Dryden; K12LV Dryden; K52ER Dryden; K57AY Dryden; K53DN East Wenatchee; K55FO East Wenatchee; K12CF Malaga, etc.; KNEE-LP Malaga, etc.; KWVC-LP Malaga, etc.; K51AE Monitor, etc.; K53AH Monitor, etc.; K55BN Monitor, etc.; K09CL Rock Island, etc.; K11CS Rock Island, etc.; K13CQ Rock Island, etc.; K09FF Squilchuck State Park; K11FJ Squilchuck State Park; K13EZ Squilchuck State Park; K65AU Stemilt, etc.; K67CD Stemilt, etc.; K51DR Wenatchee; KWCC-LP Wenatchee.

AQC PRODUCTIONS
Box 753
Atlanta, TX 75551
Phone: 903-796-8820
Fax: 903-796-1786
Web site: www.aqctv.com
LPTV Stations:
Texas: KAQC-LP Atlanta.

AQUA-LAND COMMUNICATIONS INC.
60 Stage Coach Rd.
Portage, IN 46368
Phone: 219-767-1541
Officer:
Thomas W. Tittle, President & Chief Operating Officer
LPTV Stations:
Indiana: WAAA-LP Westville.

ARACELIS ORTIZ CORP.
PO Box 532979
Harlingen, TX 78552
Phone: 956-412-5600
E-mail: jackie@lafamiliatv.com
Officers:
Aracelis Ortiz, President
Julie Mejia, Vice President
Veronica Ortiz, Treasurer
Ownership: Aracelis Ortiz, see listing, 46%; Julie Mejia, 27%; Veronica Ortiz, 27%.
LPTV Stations:
Arizona: KCOS-LP Phoenix.
California: K49HV Martinez.
Oklahoma: KLHO-LP Oklahoma City.
Texas: KSPG-LP Carrizo Springs; KADM-LP Corpus Christi; KNTA-LP New Braunfels; KRYM-LP Raymondville; KEVI-LP San Antonio.

ARDMORE COMMUNITY HEALTH & EDUCATION ORGANIZATION INC.
Box 7
Ardmore, OK 73401
Phone: 580-223-8077

LPTV Stations:
Oklahoma: KCYH-LP Ardmore.

AREA 51 DMG INC.
1025 Thomas Jefferson St NW, Ste 700
c/o Katten Muchin Rosenman LLP
Washington, DC 20007-5201
Phone: 203-557-3279
Ownership: Allen Christopher, Pres., 20%. shares; remainder held by ten private investors. Christopher is also principal of IT Communications Inc., see listing.
Represented (legal): Katten, Munchin & Rosenman LLP.
LPTV Stations:
Connecticut: WNHX-LP New Haven.

ARIZONA STATE BOARD OF REGENTS FOR ARIZONA STATE U.
c/o Elizabeth Craft
Tempe, AZ 85287-2904
Phones: 480-965-3506; 480-965-6738
Fax: 480-965-1371
E-mail: eight@asu.edu
Officers:
Charles R. Allen, General Manager
Ray Murdock, Finance & Administration Manager
Represented (legal): Covington & Burling.
LPTV Stations:
Arizona: K42AC Cottonwood, etc.; K14KK Flagstaff; K43IB Globe & Miami; K47GQ Parks; K55DB Prescott, etc.; K03FB Snowflake, etc..
ETV Stations:
Arizona: KAET-DT Phoenix.

ARIZONA U. BOARD OF REGENTS
Modern Languages Bldg.
No. 225
Tucson, AZ 85721
Phone: 602-621-7365
Officers:
Rudy Campbell, President
Kurt Davis, Secretary
George Amos, Treasurer
John Platt, Assistant Treasurer
LPTV Stations:
Arizona: K20GG Duncan.

ARIZONA WEST MEDIA LLC
1930 Mesquite, No. 3A
Lake Havasu City, AZ 86403
Phone: 928-855-8358
E-mail: alpacajer@frontiernet.net
Officer:
Maurice W. Coburn, President
LPTV Stations:
Arizona: K02MT Parker.

ASIAVISION INC.
7501 Greenway Center Dr
Ste 740
Greenbelt, MD 20770
Phone: 301-345-2742
Officer:
Salvador Serrano, Vice President
Ownership: Julia S. Cuevo; Benita S. Querubin, majority owners.
Represented (legal): Dan J. Alpert.
LPTV Stations:
District of Columbia: WIAV-LP Washington.
Maryland: WRAV-LP Ocean City.
New Jersey: WQAV-LP Atlantic City.

ASOCIACION EVANGELISTICA CRISTO VIENE INC.
Box 949
Camuy, PR 00627

Phone: 787-898-5120
Fax: 787-898-0529
Officers:
Jose J. Avila, President
Esther Robles, Secretary
Ownership: Tito Apiles, 25%; Jose J Avila, 25%; Edwin Tavarez, 25%; Vincente Vales, 25%.
LPTV Stations:
Puerto Rico: W54AQ Yauco.
Commercial TV Stations:
Puerto Rico: WCCV-DT Arecibo.

ASPEN TELEVISION LLC
c/o Plum TV, 75 Industrial Rd.
Box 610
Wainscott, NY 11975
Phone: 212-407-4965
Officer:
Chris Clowacki, President
Represented (legal): Katten, Munchin & Rosenman LLP.
LPTV Stations:
Colorado: KSZG-LP Aspen.

ASSOCIATED CHRISTIAN TELEVISION SYSTEM INC.
4520 Parkbreeze Court
Orlando, FL 32808
Phone: 407-298-5555
Officers:
Claud Bowers, Chairman, President & Chief Executive Officer
Angela Courte, Vice President, Operations
P. B. Howell Jr., Vice President
Freeda Bowers, Secretary-Treasurer & Chief Financial Officer
Ownership: Non-profit organization.
Represented (legal): Koerner & Olender PC.
LPTV Stations:
Florida: W40CQ-D Alachua, etc.; W69AY Alachua, etc.; WACX-LP Tallahassee.
Commercial TV Stations:
Florida: WACX-DT Leesburg.

ATLANTIC COAST COMMUNICATIONS INC.
Box 340
Holmdel, NJ 07733
Phone: 732-264-8766
LPTV Stations:
New York: W26CE New York.

AUDIO GRAPHICS INC.
PO Box 735
Summerville, GA 30747
Phone: 706-857-8504
E-mail: terryadams@windstream.net
Officer:
Terry Adams, President
LPTV Stations:
Georgia: WKSY-LP Summerville-Trion.

AUSTIN TELEVISION ASSOCIATION
PO Box 10
Austin, NV 89310
LPTV Stations:
Nevada: K10KB Austin; K26EH Austin; K28EI Austin; K46FB Austin; K41HH Austin & Reese River.

AVN INC.
2567 Central Ave.
Augusta, GA 30904
Phone: 706-736-6700
Officers:
Jeremy M. Coghlan, President & Programming Director

M. J. Groothand, Executive Vice President, Marketing
Ownership: Jeremy M Coghlan.
LPTV Stations:
Georgia: WBEK-CA Augusta.

FRANK & LINDA AZEVEDO
2731 Iowa Ave.
Modesto, CA 95351
Phone: 204-577-0743
Officers:
Frank Azevedo, Chairman, Chief Executive & Operating Officer
Linda Azevedo, President, Secretary-Treasurer & Chief Financial Officer
LPTV Stations:
California: KAZV-LP Modesto.

AZTECA BROADCASTING CORP.
323 E. San Joaquin St.
Tulare, CA 93274
Phone: 559-686-1370
Ownership: Rolando Collantes, Pres..
LPTV Stations:
Utah: KSVN-CA Ogden; K66FN Salt Lake City.

BACA COUNTY
741 Main St.
Springfield, CO 81073
Phone: 719-523-6532
Fax: 719-523-6584
LPTV Stations:
Colorado: K45BU Deora; K47CJ Deora; K49BT Deora; K51CL Deora, etc.; K08GY Mount Carmel; K10IM Mount Carmel; K12IM Mount Carmel; K13VR Mount Carmel; K03DZ Southwest Baca County; K06HW Southwest Baca County; K07UN Southwest Baca County; K09JS Southwest Baca County, etc.; K62CT Springfield; K64CT Springfield; K66CW Springfield; K68CR Springfield.

BAKER TV TAX DISTRICT
PO Box 1135
8 Prairie View Dr
Baker, MT 59313-1135
Phone: 406-778-2203
E-mail: dvgustaf@midrivers.com
Officer:
David H. Gustafson, President
LPTV Stations:
Montana: K04IH Baker; K08IP Baker; K10JP Baker; K13OW Baker.

FLORINDA MAE BALFOUR
3517 Pinetree Ter
Falls Church, VA 22041-1417
Phone: 202-461-5825
E-mail: flossunrise@netzero.net
Represented (legal): Fletcher, Heald & Hildreth PLC.
LPTV Stations:
Arizona: K33CG Sierra Vista.

BANK OF LITTLE ROCK
200 N Main St
Little Rock, AR 72201
Phone: 501-376-0800
Officer:
Eugene L Maris, Chairman & Chief Executive Officer
LPTV Stations:
Arkansas: KHTE-LP Little Rock.

BARBOURVILLE AREA TELEVISION CORP.
PO Box 1600
Barbourville, KY 40906

LPTV Stations:
Kentucky: W07AH Barbourville.

WILLIAM A. BARNHARDT
212 Rock St.
Pomeroy, OH 45769
Phone: 740-992-6558
Fax: 740-992-6556
LPTV Stations:
Ohio: WJOS-LP Pomeroy.

BARRY TELECOMMUNICATIONS INC.
Box 6607
West Palm Beach, FL 33405
Phone: 561-737-8000
Fax: 561-369-3067
Officers:
Jeanne O'Laughlin, Chairman
Jerry Carr, President & Chief Executive Officer
Phil DiComo, Vice President, Development
Bernard Henneberg, Vice President, Finance
Represented (legal): Schwartz, Woods & Miller.
LPTV Stations:
Florida: W31DC-D Fort Pierce; W44AY Fort Pierce.
ETV Stations:
Florida: WXEL-DT West Palm Beach.
Radio Stations:
Florida: WXEL (FM) West Palm Beach

CITY OF BASSETT
PO Box 383
Bassett, NE 68714
LPTV Stations:
Nebraska: K13PB Bassett.

BATES TECHNICAL COLLEGE
1101 S. Yakima Ave.
Tacoma, WA 98405
Phone: 253-596-1528
Fax: 253-596-1623
Ownership: Board of Trustees:; Mike Grunwald, Chmn.; Karen Seinfeld, Vice Chmn.; Calvin Pearson Jr., Board Member; Theresa Pan-Hosley, Board Member; Stanley Rumbaugh, Board Member.
Represented (legal): Akin, Gump, Strauss, Hauer & Feld LLP.
LPTV Stations:
Washington: K65BU Grays River, etc..
ETV Stations:
Washington: KCKA-DT Centralia; KBTC-DT Tacoma.

BAYOU CITY BROADCASTING LLC
1300 Post Oak Blvd
Ste 830
Houston, TX 77056
Phone: 281-380-0076
Ownership: Dr. Oliver Hunter, 50%; DuJuan McCoy, 50%.
Represented (legal): Fletcher, Heald & Hildreth PLC.
LPTV Stations:
Texas: KIDZ-LP Abilene; KIDV-LP Albany; KIDU-LP Brownwood; KIDT-LP Stamford; KIDB-CA Sweetwater.
Commercial TV Stations:
Texas: KXVA-DT Abilene; KIDY-DT San Angelo.

BCB INC.
525 E. Tennessee St.
Florence, AL 35630
Phone: 256-764-8170
Fax: 256-764-8340
Officers:
Benny Carle, Chairman & Chief Executive Officer

Benjy Carle, Chief Operating Officer
Jay Carle, Chief Financial Officer
Ownership: Benny Carle.
LPTV Stations:
Alabama: WBCF-LP Florence; WXFL-LP Florence.
Radio Stations:
Alabama: WBCF (AM) Florence

B COMMUNICATIONS JOINT VENTURE
11737 Nelon St.
Corpus Christi, TX 78410
Phone: 361-289-0125
Ownership: Gerald Benavides, 50%; Albert Benavides, 25%; Rick Benavides, 25%.
LPTV Stations:
Texas: KBNB-LP San Antonio; KFLZ-CA San Antonio.

BEACH TV OF SOUTH CAROLINA INC.
Box 9556
Panama City Beach, FL 32407
Phone: 904-234-2773
LPTV Stations:
South Carolina: WGSC-LP Myrtle Beach; WGSI-CA Myrtle Beach.

BEACH TV PROPERTIES INC.
8317 Front Beach Rd.
Suite 23
Panama City, FL 32407
Phone: 850-234-2773
Officers:
Byron J. Colley Jr., President
Tonita Davis, Secretary-Treasurer
Ownership: Jud Colley, 50%; Tonita Davis, 50%.
LPTV Stations:
Florida: WDES-CA Destin; WCAY-LP Key West; W46AN Panama City; WPFN-CA Panama City.
Georgia: WTHC-LP Atlanta.
Louisiana: KNOV-CD New Orleans.
Commercial TV Stations:
Florida: WAWD-DT Fort Walton Beach; WPCT-DT Panama City Beach.

BEAR LAKE COUNTY T.V. DISTRICT
PO Box 184
Montpelier, ID 83254
Phone: 208-847-1376
LPTV Stations:
Idaho: K09PL Dingle, etc.; K11PP Dingle, etc.; K13QY Dingle, etc.; K16HQ-D Georgetown; K17CO Georgetown; K19DQ Montpelier; K21CE Montpelier; K23BV Montpelier; K25CK Montpelier; K27CS Montpelier; K29BM Montpelier; K31CI Montpelier; K33DR Montpelier; K52EC Montpelier; K54DY Montpelier; K56FM Montpelier.

BEAR VALLEY BROADCASTING INC.
41506 Big Bear Blvd.
Box 1634
Big Bear Lake, CA 92315
Phones: 909-878-4886; 909-522-9063
Fax: 909-866-8452
LPTV Stations:
California: K06MU Big Bear Lake Valley.

BEATTY TOWN ADVISORY COUNCIL
PO Box 837
Beatty, NV 89003

LPTV Stations:
Nevada: K09OB Oasis Valley; K11OQ Oasis Valley; K13PK Oasis Valley.

BEAVER CITY CORP.
60 W. Center St.
Beaver, UT 84713
Phone: 435-438-2451
LPTV Stations:
Utah: K44HT Beaver; K46IB Beaver; K07GY Beaver, etc.; K09CS Beaver, etc.; K11CX Beaver, etc.; K13CV Beaver, etc..

VIRGINIA M. BECKER
Box 1300
Hawthorne, NV 89415
Phone: 702-945-1300
LPTV Stations:
Nevada: K13WI Hawthorne.

BEECH STREET COMMUNICATIONS
601 Beech St.
Box 1469
Texarkana, AR 75504
Phone: 870-774-3500
Fax: 870-774-3600
Officers:
Bill Steeger, President
Burns Barr, Chief Executive Officer
Larry Crank, Chief Financial Officer
Ownership: Dan Brown, 11%. votes; Robert Brown, 11%. votes; Maxine Crow, 11%. votes; Tim Day, 11%. votes; Carolyn Eppinette, 11%. votes; Jane Qualls, 11%. votes; Larry West, 11%. votes; Norman Wolf, 11%. votes; Dick Young, 11%. votes.
Represented (legal): Joseph E. Dunne III.
LPTV Stations:
Arkansas: KLFI-LP Texarkana.

BELO CORP.
Box 655237
Dallas, TX 75265
Phone: 214-977-6606
Fax: 214-977-6603
E-mail: nhulcy@belo.com
Web site: www.belo.com
Officers:
Robert W. Decherd, Chairman
Dunia A. Shive, President & Chief Executive Officer
Dennis A. Williamson, Executive Vice President & Chief Financial Officer
Peter Diaz, Executive Vice President, Television Operations
Guy H. Kerr, Executive Vice President, Law & Government and Secretary
Kathy Clements, Senior Vice President, Television Operations
Russell F Coleman, Senior Vice President & General Counsel
Marian Spitzberg, Senior Vice President, Human Resources
Paul Fry, Vice President, Investor Relations & Corporate Communications
Ownership: Publicly held. On February 8, 2008, all newspaper holdings and related assets were spun-off to a new publicly traded company, A. H. Belo Corp.
LPTV Stations:
Arizona: K34EE Cottonwood & Prescott; K38AI Cottonwood, etc.; K54GI Flagstaff; K57BO Globe & Miami; K11LC Prescott; K50FV Tucson; K53GM Williams-Ash Fork; K41JE Williams-Ashfork.
Idaho: K05DC Cambridge, etc.; K13GO Cascade; K41FJ Coeur d'Alene; K13GW Council; K05DD Glenns Ferry; K21CC Lewiston; K13SO McCall, etc.; KTFT-LP Twin Falls.
Louisiana: WBXN-CA New Orleans.

North Carolina: W30CR Biscoe; W24AY Lilesville & Wadesboro.
Oregon: K29AZ Newport; K08KN Prineville.
Washington: K35HU Grays River, etc..
Commercial TV Stations:
Arizona: KASW-DT Phoenix; KTVK-DT Phoenix; KMSB Tucson; KTTU-DT Tucson.
Idaho: KTVB-DT Boise.
Kentucky: WHAS-DT Louisville.
Louisiana: WWL-DT New Orleans; WUPL-DT Slidell.
Missouri: KMOV-DT St. Louis.
North Carolina: WCNC-DT Charlotte.
Oregon: KGW-DT Portland.
Texas: KVUE-DT Austin; WFAA Dallas; KHOU Houston; KENS San Antonio.
Virginia: WVEC Hampton.
Washington: KONG Everett; KING-DT Seattle; KREM Spokane; KSKN-DT Spokane.
Newspapers:
California: La Prensa, The Business Press, The Press-Enterprise, This Week in the Desert (Riverside)
Rhode Island: Rhode Island Monthly, The Providence Journal (Providence)
Texas: al dia, Denton Record Chronicle, Quick, Texas Almanac, The Dallas Morning News (Dallas/Ft. Worth)
Other Holdings:
Cable Network: 24/7 NewsChannel (Boise, ID); Texas Cable News; Local News on Cable (Norfolk-Hampton, VA); NewsWatch on Channel 15 (New Orleans, LA); Northwest Cable News Network
Data service: Belo Interactive Inc..

GERALD G. BENAVIDES
11737 Nelon Dr.
Corpus Christi, TX 78410
Phone: 361-241-7794
Fax: 361-241-7945
E-mail: jb12@sbcglobal.net
Represented (legal): Booth Freret Imlay & Tepper PC.
LPTV Stations:
Arizona: K25HU Kingman; K53IJ Prescott.
California: KLAU-LP Redlands.
Florida: WVFW-LP Miami.
Texas: KCCZ-LP Corpus Christi; KVFW-LP Fort Worth; KBFW-LP Gainesville; KTXU-LP San Marcos.

YING HUA BENNS
1225 Connecticut Ave. NW
Washington, DC 20036
LPTV Stations:
Tennessee: WYHB-CA Chattanooga.

BENT COUNTY
County Courthouse
PO Box 350
Las Animas, CO 81054
LPTV Stations:
Colorado: K63AF Las Animas; K65AJ Las Animas; K67AH Las Animas; K69AN Las Animas.

BETA BROADCASTING INC.
5050 Edison Ave.
No. 219
Colorado Springs, CO 80915
Phone: 719-578-0517
Fax: 719-574-7776
Officers:
Jack Connelly, Chairman & President
Jack Manning, Secretary-Treasurer
Ownership: Jack Connelly; Zoe Connelly; Jack Manning; Norma Dee Manning.

LPTV Stations:
Colorado: KJCS-LP Colorado Springs.

BETHANY WORLD PRAYER CENTER INC.
13855 Plank Rd.
Baker, LA 70714
Phone: 225-774-1700
Fax: 225-774-7785
LPTV Stations:
Louisiana: WLFT-CA Baton Rouge.

BETHEL BROADCASTING INC.
Box 468
Bethel, AK 99559
Phone: 907-543-3131
Fax: 907-543-3130
Officers:
Andrew Guy, President
John A. McDonald, Chief Operating Officer
Jan Debnam, Chief Financial Officer
Represented (legal): Wilkinson Barker Knauer LLP.
LPTV Stations:
Alaska: K15AV Bethel; K21AO Bethel.
Radio Stations:
Alaska: KYUK (AM) Bethel

BETHEL SANITARIUM
5825 Kuiken
Evansville, IN 47710
Phone: 812-428-6348
LPTV Stations:
Indiana: W23BV Evansville.

BETTER LIFE TELEVISION INC.
PO Box 776
Grants Pass, OR 97528
Phone: 541-474-3089
Fax: 541-474-9409
E-mail: rondavis@betterlifetv.tv
Web site: www.betterlifetv.tv
Officers:
Robert Heisler, President
Delmer Wagner, Vice President
Ron Davis, Secretary
Don Eisner, Treasurer
Ownership: Keith Babcock; Duane Corwin; Ron Davis; Don Eisner; Glenn Gingery, 5.5%. votes each.; Paul Gordon; Robert L Heisler; Patty Hyland; Walter MacPhee; Bob McReynolds; Olen Nations; Perry Parks; Judy Randahl; Willard Register; Holly Rueb; Richard Surroz; Delmer Wagner; George White.
Represented (legal): Donald E. Martin.
LPTV Stations:
Oregon: K48GO Cave Junction; K44FH Coos Bay; KAMK-LP Eugene; K22FC Grants Pass; K47GI Grants Pass; K48IW Kalmath; K48HV Klamath Falls; K16GB Medford; K23EX Medford; K25IM Medford; K29GX Merlin; K33GJ Merlin; K47HT Roseburg; K26HS Tillamook.
Commercial TV Stations:
Oregon: KBLN-DT Grants Pass; KTVC-DT Roseburg.

RONALD A. BEVINS
713 W. Yakima Ave.
Yakima, WA 98902
Phone: 509-452-8817
Fax: 509-248-7499
LPTV Stations:
Washington: K29FF Kennewick; K23FU Kennewick & Pasco; K04OI Pasco & Kennewick;

K13WP Sunnyside; K08LU Sunnyside-Grandview; K39FU Yakima; K43GY Yakima; K49GF Yakima, etc..

BIG ELK MEADOWS ASSOCIATION
Box 440
Lyons, CO 80540
LPTV Stations:
Colorado: K08JK Big Elk Meadows; K11OF Big Elk Meadows; K13OU Big Elk Meadows.

BIG FLAT TV ASSOCIATION
PO Box 136
Turner, MT 59542
Phone: 406-379-2293
E-mail: tfairbank@co.blaine.mt.us
Officer:
Tom Fairbank, TV Board Chairman
LPTV Stations:
Montana: K60BV Turner-Hogeland; K64BQ Turner-Hogeland; K66BZ Turner-Hogeland.

BIG SANDY TV CLUB
PO Box 494
Big Sandy, MT 59520-0494
Phone: 406-378-2582
Officer:
Cynthia J. Desrosier, Secretary-Treasurer
LPTV Stations:
Montana: K07IP Big Sandy; K10BK Big Sandy; K13OQ Big Sandy.

BIG SKY OWNERS ASSN. INC.
PO Box 160057
Big Sky, MT 59716
Phone: 406-995-4166
E-mail: bsoamj@3rivers.net
Officer:
Mary Jane McGarity, Executive Director
LPTV Stations:
Montana: K07LE Gallatin River, etc.; K09LP Gallatin River, etc..

BILTMORE BROADCASTING CORP.
15304 Sunset Blvd.
Suite 204
Pacific Palisades, CA 90272
Phone: 310-454-8673
Fax: 310-454-4983
Officers:
Paul A. Zevnik, President & Secretary
Walter F. Ulloa, Vice President
Ownership: Walter F Ulloa, 50%. assets; Paul A Zevnik, 50%. assets, 100% voting. See also Costa de Oro Television Inc. & Entravision Communications Co. LLC.
Represented (legal): Thompson Hine LLP.
LPTV Stations:
California: KODG-LP Palm Springs; KBAB-LP Santa Barbara.
Nevada: KLSV-LP Las Vegas.

BIRACH BROADCASTING CORP.
21700 Northwestern Hwy., Tower 14
Suite 1190
Southfield, MI 48075
Phone: 248-557-3500
LPTV Stations:
California: KIJR-LP Lucerne Valley.

BIRNEY TV CLUB
PO Box 551
Birney, MT 59012

LPTV Stations:
Montana: K13RW Birney.

BITTERROOT VALLEY PUBLIC TV INC.
PO Box 838
Hamilton, MT 59840
Phone: 406-961-3692
Officer:
Mike Looney, Board Member
LPTV Stations:
Montana: K21AN Darby; K29CV Florence; K67EC Pinesdale.

BLACK BUTTE RANCH ASSOCIATION
PO Box 8000
Black Butte Ranch, OR 97759
Phone: 541-595-1501
LPTV Stations:
Oregon: K04HK Black Butte Ranch; K05GZ Black Butte Ranch; K64AO Black Butte Ranch.

BLACK HAWK COLLEGE
6600 34th St.
Moline, IL 61265-5899
Phone: 309-796-2424
Fax: 309-796-2484
Officers:
Steve Spivey, Chairman
Glenn Doyle, Vice Chairman
Keith Miller, President
LPTV Stations:
Illinois: W48CK Sterling.
ETV Stations:
Illinois: WQPT-DT Moline.

BLACKTAIL TV TAX DISTRICT
Box 609
Lakeside, MT 59922
Phone: 406-857-2131
LPTV Stations:
Montana: K07VU Big Arm; K11RX Big Arm; K32HH Blacktail, etc.; K44FR Blacktail, etc.; K46FD Blacktail, etc.; K15GP Kalispell; K19GD Kalispell; K51HT Kalispell; K03DJ Polson; K11HO Polson; K14LT Polson; K16GJ Polson; K30II Polson; K41IW Polson; K50LB Polson; K29AA Whitefish/Columbia; K07EN Woods Bay; K11KE Woods Bay; K48EO Woods Bay.

BELMAX BROADCASTING LLC
5010 4th St NW
Albuquerque, NM 87107
Phone: 505-345-1991
Ownership: Belarmino Gonzalez Estate, 50%; Isaac Max Jaramillo, 16.6%; Pat Jaramillo, 16.6%; Connie Whitney, 16.6%.
Represented (legal): Gammon & Grange PC.
LPTV Stations:
New Mexico: KYNM-LP Albuquerque.

BLOCK COMMUNICATIONS INC.
6450 Monroe St.
Sylvania, OH 43560
Phones: 419-724-9802; 419-724-6035
Fax: 419-724-6167
Web site: www.blockcommunications.com
Officers:
Allan J Block, Chairman
John R Block, Vice Chairman
Gary J Blair, President
David M. Beihoff, Vice President, Newspaper Operations
Jodi L. Miehls, Assistant Secretary
Ownership: Allan J Block, 25%; John R Block, 25%; William Block Jr., 25%; Karen D. Johnese, 25%. votes.

Represented (legal): Dow Lohnes PLLC.
LPTV Stations:
Illinois: W31BX-D Danville.
Ohio: WFND-LP Findlay; WLMO-LP Lima; WLQP-LP Lima; WOHL-CA Sylvania.
Commercial TV Stations:
Idaho: KTRV-DT Nampa.
Illinois: WAND-DT Decatur.
Indiana: WMYO-DT Salem.
Kentucky: WDRB-DT Louisville.
Ohio: WLIO-DT Lima.
Cable Systems:
OHIO: SANDUSKY; TOLEDO.
Newspapers:
Ohio: Toledo Blade
Pennsylvania: Pittsburgh Post-Gazette
Other Holdings:
Outdoor advertising: Community Communications Services, advertising distribution company..

ELLIOT B. BLOCK
2212 Losantiville Ave.
Cincinnati, OH 45237
Phone: 513-531-8835
Fax: 513-351-8898
LPTV Stations:
Ohio: WBQC-CA Cincinnati; WOTH-LP Cincinnati; WOTH-LD Cincinnatti.

BLUE BONNET COMMUNICATIONS INC.
205 W. College St.
Lake Charles, LA 70605
Phone: 337-477-2827
Officers:
Syd Dyer Jr., President
Lester Langley Jr., Chief Financial Officer
Ownership: Syd Dyer Jr., 60%; Lester Langley Jr., 40%.
Represented (legal): Koerner & Olender PC.
LPTV Stations:
Texas: K36ID-D Beaumont; K52IS Beaumont; KUIL-LP Beaumont; KVHP-LP Jasper.
Other Holdings:
Sydcom Inc., owner of 3 non-operating LPTV stations.

BLUE EARTH-NICOLLET-FARIBAULT COOPERATIVE ELECTRIC ASSN.
Frost-Benco-Wells Electric
PO Box 8
Mankato, MN 56002
Phone: 507-387-7963
Officer:
Bradley Leiding, President
LPTV Stations:
Minnesota: K29IF-D Frost; K39JI Frost; K49JG Frost; K62FH Frost; K16GL Jackson; K61GE Jackson.

BLUE MOUNTAIN BROADCASTING ASSN. INC.
715 S.E. 12th St.
Box 205
College Place, WA 99324
Phone: 509-529-9149
Fax: 509-529-0661
Web site: www.bluemttv.com
Officers:
John Cress, President
Jim Forsyth, Secretary
Ben Wiedemann, Treasurer
Ownership: Walla Walla Valley Seventh-Day Adventist Churches.

LPTV Stations:
Washington: K36EW-D College Place; K21EK Walla Walla; K22BI Walla Walla; K28FT Walla Walla.

BLUE MOUNTAIN TRANSLATOR DISTRICT
Box 901
La Grande, OR 97850
Phone: 541-963-0196
LPTV Stations:
Oregon: K42AI Baker; K46AM Baker; K50FD Baker; K55JS Baker City; K44AJ Baker Valley; K40AJ Baker Valley, etc.; K26FV Elgin; K33FS Elgin; K39FD Elgin; K26FE La Grande; K29EL La Grande; K31GN La Grande; K35GA La Grande; K39ET La Grande; K50CI La Grande; K52DT La Grande; K56BE La Grande; K58AY La Grande; K36DP Pendleton, etc..

BLUE SKIES BROADCASTING CORP.
5220 Campo Rd.
Woodland Hills, CA 91364
Phone: 818-884-0440
Ownership: Robert Ruiz.
LPTV Stations:
California: KSKT-CA San Marcos.

RICHARD D. BOGNER
4 Hunters Ln
Roslyn, NY 11576
Phone: 516-627-5103
Represented (legal): Dickstein Shapiro LLP.
LPTV Stations:
New York: WRNN-LP Nyack.

BONNEVILLE INTERNATIONAL CORP.
55 North 300 West, Box 1160
Broadcast House
Salt Lake City, UT 84110-1160
Phone: 801-575-7500
Fax: 801-575-7548
Officers:
James B. Jacobson, Chairman
Bruce T. Reese, President & Chief Executive Officer
Robert A. Johnson, Executive Vice President & Chief Operating Officer
Glenn N. Larkin, Senior Vice President & Chief Financial Officer
David K. Redd, Vice President, Secretary & General Counsel
Ownership: Deseret Management Corp.; DMC ownership:; The First Presidency of the Jesus Christ of the Latter-Day Saints..
Represented (legal): Wilkinson Barker Knauer LLP.
LPTV Stations:
Utah: K24FE-D Beaver, etc.; K20GJ-D Bloomington; K07ED-D Enterprise; K11QQ-D Hildale, UT & Cane Beds, AZ; K08EN-D Pine Valley, etc.; K05AR-D Rockville; K35FS-D Santa Clara, etc.; K07CG-D Toquerville; K08BO-D Virgin.
Commercial TV Stations:
Utah: KSL-DT Salt Lake City.
Newspapers:
Utah: The Deseret News, Salt Lake City (operated by Deseret News Publishing)
Radio Stations:
Arizona: KMVP (AM), KPKX (FM), KTAR-AM-FM Phoenix
District of Columbia: WTOP (AM), WWWT-AM-FM
Illinois: WDRV (FM), WILV (FM) Chicago; WMVN (FM) East St. Louis; WARH (FM) Granite City; WTMX (FM) Skokie
Kentucky: WYGY (FM) Fort Thomas
Maryland: WFED (AM) Silver Spring

Missouri: WIL-AM-FM St. Louis
Ohio: WKRQ (FM), WUVE-FM CIncinnati; WSWD (FM) Fairfield
Utah: KSF (FM), KSL-AM-FM, KRSP-FM Salt Lake City; KUTR (AM) Taylorsville
Other Holdings:
Production: Video West (Salt Lake City)
Service company: Media/Paymaster Plus Corp. (Salt Lake City) provide payroll and signatory services; Bonneville Entertainment Co. (Los Angeles); Bonneville Communications (Salt Lake City) provides advertising agency services.

THE BON-TELE NETWORK
168 Canterbury Lane
McMurray, PA 15317
Phone: 412-531-6678
Fax: 412-531-5727
Ownership: Nancy B Hahn.
LPTV Stations:
Pennsylvania: W63AU Pittsburgh.

BONTEN MEDIA GROUP LLC
280 Park Ave
25th Floor, E Tower
New York, NY 10017
Phone: 212-247-8717
E-mail: info@dchold.com
Officers:
Randall D. Bongarten, President
David M. Wittels, Vice President
Scott Schneider, Vice President
Stephen M. Bassford, Vice President
Kyle N. Cruz, Vice President
Ownership: Diamond Castle Partners IV LP. votes, 69.6% assets; Bonten/DiamondCastle LLC, 29.8% assets; DCPIVLP & BDCLLC ownership:; DCP IV GP LP, Gen. Partner; DCPIVGPLP ownership:; DCP IV GP-GP LLC, Gen. Partner; DCPIVGPGPLLC ownership:; Michael W. Ranger, Managing Member, 50%. votes; Lawrence M.v.D. Schloss, Managing Member, 50%. votes.
Represented (legal): Covington & Burling.
LPTV Stations:
California: K12JJ Benbow, etc.; K04EZ Big Bend, etc.; K36BT Blue Lake; K05DQ Burney, etc.; K05BR Dunsmuir, etc.; K33DI East Weed; K04EQ Fort Jones, etc.; K20CN Fortuna/Rio Dell; K45DS Freshwater, etc.; K05EQ Green Point, etc.; K25CI Klamath; K27BH Lake Shastina; K02FF Lakehead; K11LD Likely; K05JK Mineral; K03FU Mountain Gate; K15CX Oroville; K05EM Paradise; K51EG South Eureka & Loleta; K34BW Willow Creek; K13LO Yreka, etc..
Idaho: K10HC Mullan.
Montana: K34FI-D Bozeman; K42BZ Bozeman; K51DW Dillon; K02AO Eureka, etc.; K14IU Frenchtown; K10HZ Pony; K02OL Seeley Lake; K35DJ Three Forks; K10HL Virginia City; K09KH Watkins, etc..
Texas: KTES-LP Abilene; KTXE-LP Abilene.
Commercial TV Stations:
California: KAEF-DT Arcata; KRCR-DT Redding.
Montana: KTVM-DT Butte; KCFW-DT Kalispell; KECI-DT Missoula.
North Carolina: WCTI-DT New Bern.
Texas: KTXS-DT Sweetwater.
Virginia: WCYB-DT Bristol.

BORDER MEDIA PARTNERS LLC
8750 N Central Expy
Ste 650
Dallas, TX 75231
Phone: 214-692-2000
Ownership: The Goldman Sachs Group Inc., 30%. votes; Vestar Capital Partners IV LP., 30%. votes; Thomas Castro, 10%. votes; DBVA BMP Holdings LLC, 10%. votes; BuenaVentura Communications Inc., 10%. votes; RGG Radio LLC, 10%. votes.
Represented (legal): Fletcher, Heald & Hildreth PLC.

LPTV Stations:
Texas: KNEX-LP Laredo.

BOSTON BROADCASTING CORP.
1903 S. Greeley Hwy.
Suite 127
Cheyenne, WY 82007
Phone: 603-279-4440
Officer:
Randolph Weigner, President
LPTV Stations:
Massachusetts: WFXZ-CA Boston.
Other Holdings:
LPTV stations: See also D.T.V. LLC & Sunshine Broadcasting Co. Inc..

MURPHY D. BOUGHNER
305 N. Pine St.
Box 186
Nowata, OK 74048
Phone: 918-273-2212
Fax: 918-599-4252
LPTV Stations:
Oklahoma: KGCT-LP Nowata.

BOULDER TV ASSN.
Box 146
215 N Madison
Boulder, MT 59632-0146
Phones: 406-225-3376; 406-225-3820
Officers:
Ralph R. Simons, President & Secretary-Treasurer
William Shoquist, Chief Operating Officer
LPTV Stations:
Montana: K08KT Boulder; K10HD Boulder; K13KP Boulder; K27CD Boulder; K36CX Clancy.

BOUNDARY COUNTY TV TRANSLATOR DISTRICT
PO Box 894
Bonners Ferry, ID 83805
Phone: 208-267-7220
E-mail: general@elautomationinc.com
LPTV Stations:
Idaho: K11HM Bonners Ferry; K32HA Bonners Ferry; K35IC Bonners Ferry; K46HZ Bonners Ferry; K50GL Bonners Ferry.

GLEN C. BRAND
530 E. Main St.
Aspen, CO 81611
LPTV Stations:
Colorado: K02FW Ashcroft.

BRANSON VISITORS TV LLC
PO Box 3500
Springfield, MO 65808-3500
Phone: 417-268-3010
Officers:
Steven L. Presley, President
Michael A. Scott, Vice President
Ownership: Mary Chalender; Angela Moyle; John Presley; Nick Presley; Steven L. Presley; Michael A. Scott, Board of Managers.
Represented (legal): Wilmer Cutler Pickering Hale & Dorr LLP.
LPTV Stations:
Missouri: K17DL-D Branson.

BRECHNER MANAGEMENT CO.
Box 531103
Orlando, FL 32853
Phone: 407-423-4431
Fax: 407-843-0704
Officers:
Marion B. Brechner, President

Berl Brechner, Vice President & Treasurer
Ownership: Marion Brechner; Berl Brechner. Brechners also have interest in Delmarva Broadcast Service GP, see listing.
Represented (legal): Cohn & Marks LLP.
LPTV Stations:
Kansas: K58CX Lawrence.
Other Holdings:
Outdoor Advertising (Great Outdoor Advertising Inc., Wilmington, OH).

BRIGHAM YOUNG U.
C-302 HFAC
Provo, UT 84602
Phone: 801-378-3551
Officers:
Newell Dayley, Dean
Duane Roberts, TV Group Manager
Ownership:.
Represented (legal): Wilkinson Barker Knauer LLP.
LPTV Stations:
Utah: K34FW Enterprise, etc.; K40FU Rockville; K36FT Santa Clara, etc.; K23FQ Toquerville & Leeds; K29GY Virgin.
ETV Stations:
Utah: KBYU-DT Provo.
Radio Stations:
Utah: KBYU-FM.

DAVID C. BROADAHL
PO Box 93
Wahoo, NE 68066
Phone: 402-443-3000
LPTV Stations:
Nebraska: K21ES Columbus; K31EN Columbus; K33EM Columbus.

BROADCAST DEVELOPMENT CORP.
4920 Brookside Ct
Reno, NV 89502
Phone: 775-856-2121
Officer:
Raymond L. Stofer, Chief Operator
Represented (legal): Goldberg, Godles, Wiener & Wright.
LPTV Stations:
Nevada: K44BE Fallon; K35FL Silver Springs.

BROADCAST GROUP HOLDINGS INC.
5925 Cromo Dr
El Paso, TX 79912
Phone: 915-585-6344
Ownership: Cabada Holdings LLC, 75%; CHLLC ownership:; Alfonso Cabada; Sergio Cabada, 50%. each.
Represented (legal): Fletcher, Heald & Hildreth PLC.
LPTV Stations:
Texas: K40FW El Paso.

BROADCAST GROUP LTD.
5925 Cromo Dr.
El Paso, TX 79912
Phone: 915-585-6344
Officer:
Sergio Cabada, President
Ownership: Broadcast Group Management LLC, Gen. Partner. 100% votes; 1% equity; Alfonso Cabada, Ltd. Partner, 54%. equity; Sergio Cabada A, Ltd. Partner, 25%. equity; Cabafam Inc., Ltd. Partner, 20%. equity.
Represented (legal): Fletcher, Heald & Hildreth PLC.
LPTV Stations:
Arizona: K28FM Yuma.

California: K36FO Calexico.

BROADCASTING LICENSES LP
2111 University Park Dr.
Suite 650
Okemos, MI 48864-6913
Phone: 517-347-4111
Ownership: Northwest Broadcasting Inc., Gern. Partner. 100% votes; 1% equity; Broadcasting Communications LLC, Ltd. Partner, 99%. equity; NBI ownership:; Brian W. Brady; BCLLC ownership:; Northwest Broadcasting Inc.. 100% votes; 1% equity; Northwest Broadcasting LP, 99%. equity; NBLP ownership:; Northwest Broadcasting Inc., Gen. Partner. 100% votes; 0.07% equity; Brian W. Brady, Ltd. Partner, 99.3%. equity; NBI ownership:; Brian W. Brady. Brady is also a principal of Mountain Licenses LP & Stainless Licenses LP, see listings.
LPTV Stations:
California: K41JB Yreka.
Oregon: K31GP Brookings, etc.; K44JB-D Grants Pass; K45ED Grants Pass; K44DZ Klamath Falls.
Commercial TV Stations:
Oregon: KMVU-DT Medford.

BROADCAST SOUTH LLC
1931 Georgia Hwy 32 E
Douglas, GA 31533
Phone: 912-389-0995
E-mail: johnovidhiggs@hotmail.com
Officer:
John Ovid Higgs, President
Ownership: John O. Higgs, 25%; Kerry Van Moore, 25%; B. Gene Waldron, 25%; Nearly Famous Properties LLC, 25%; NFPLLC ownersahip:; Brian Vaughn, 51%; Cindy J. Vaughn, 49%.
Represented (legal): Fletcher, Heald & Hildreth PLC.
LPTV Stations:
Georgia: WVOH-LP Hazlehurst.

BROADLAND PROPERTIES INC.
Box 11757
Zephyr Cove, NV 89448-4757
Phone: 775-586-1515
Officers:
Linda K. Trumbly, President
Warren L. Trumbly, Vice President & Secretary-Treasurer
Ownership: Linda K. Trumbly.
Represented (legal): Irwin, Campbell & Tannenwald PC.
LPTV Stations:
California: KAXT-CA Santa Clara-San Jose.

BROKEN BOW JR. CHAMBER OF COMMERCE
PO Box 101
Broken Bow, OK 68822
LPTV Stations:
Nebraska: K04CV Broken Bow; K06EY Broken Bow; K09GW Broken Bow.

BROWNING PUBLIC SCHOOLS
129 First Ave. SE
Browning, MT 59417
Phone: 406-338-2475
E-mail: julieh@bps.k12.mt.us
Officer:
Don Barcus, Information Contact
LPTV Stations:
Montana: K57FM Browning.

BREEZE BROADCAST CORP. LLC
6583 Berry Hill Rd.
Milton, FL 32570

E-mail: lordfulwood@hotmail.com
Officer:
Baroness Maxine Ann Agasim-Pereira, President
LPTV Stations:
Florida: W26BV Panama City.

BRUCE INDEPENDENT TV INC.
403 W. Calhoun
Bruce, MS 38915-0580
Phone: 662-983-2801
Fax: 662-983-2814
Officers:
William E. Morgan, President & Chief Executive Officer
Bill Morgan, Chief Operating Officer
Ann Morgan, Chief Financial Officer
Ownership: William E Morgan.
LPTV Stations:
Mississippi: W07BN Bruce.

BRUNO-GOODWORTH NETWORK INC.
975 Greentree Rd.
Pittsburgh, PA 15220
Phone: 412-922-9576
E-mail: debbie@wbgn.com
Ownership: Ron Bruno; Debra A. Goodworth, jointly.
LPTV Stations:
Ohio: WVTX-CA Bridgeport.
Pennsylvania: WNNB-LP Beaver; WJMB-LP Butler; WEMW-LP Greensburg; WKHU-CA Kittanning; WPCP-LP New Castle; WBGN-LP Pittsburgh; WWKH-CA Uniontown; WWLM-CA Washington.
West Virginia: WJPW-CA Weirton.

BRUNSON/ROSS COMMUNICATIONS LLC
1265 E. Fayette St.
Baltimore, MD 21202
Phone: 410-563-1709
Ownership: Edward Brunson.
Represented (legal): Wood, Maines & Nolan Chartered.
LPTV Stations:
Virginia: WEDD-LP Roanoke.

BRYANT BROADCASTING CO.
200 E. Spring St.
Lebanon, TN 37087
Phones: 615-444-7211; 615-444-8206
Fax: 615-444-7215
Ownership: Dr. Joe F Bryant, Chairman, President & Chief Executive Officer.
LPTV Stations:
Tennessee: W11BD Lebanon.
Commercial TV Stations:
Tennessee: WJFB-DT Lebanon.

BSA INVESTMENT
11 Alice Court
South St. Paul, MN 55075
Phone: 612-451-9197
LPTV Stations:
Iowa: K61GF Iowa Falls, etc..

BUDD BROADCASTING CO. INC.
4150 N.W. 93rd Ave.
Gainesville, FL 32653
Phone: 352-371-7772
Fax: 352-371-9353
E-mail: buddman@gru.net
Officers:
Harvey M. Budd, President
Ilene S. Budd, Vice President & Secretary-Treasurer
Ownership: Harvey M Budd, 50%; Ilene Budd, 50%.

Represented (legal): Shainis & Peltzman Chartered.
LPTV Stations:
Florida: WGVT-LD Gainesville; WNFT-LP Gainesville; WVVQ-LP Jacksonville; WOFT-LP Reddick; WMMF-LP Vero Beach; WGCT-LP Yankeetown; WGCT-LD Zephyrhills.
Kentucky: WKUG-LP Glasgow; WKUT-LP Glasgow.
New York: WKUW-LP Glasgow.
Commercial TV Stations:
Florida: WFXU-DT Live Oak.

BUENA VISTA TV TRANSLATOR CORP.
General Delivery
Buena Vista, NM 87712
LPTV Stations:
New Mexico: K10LE Buena Vista; K12LQ Buena Vista.

JAMES S. BUMPOUS
707 W. College Ave.
Silver City, NM 88061
Phone: 505-574-7742
Represented (legal): Shainis & Peltzman Chartered.
LPTV Stations:
New Mexico: KSIL-LP Silver City.
Other Holdings:
Broadcasting: Jackalope Broadcasters Bumpous has 50% interest in company..

BUSINESS WORLD BROADCASTING PARTNERS
2706 W. Burbank Blvd.
Burbank, CA 91505
Phone: 818-845-1270
Ownership: Miguel Torresblanco, Gen. Partner.
Represented (legal): Michael Couzens.
LPTV Stations:
California: K06MB Indio.

BUSTOS MEDIA OF CALIFORNIA LICENSE LLC
500 Media Pl
Sacramento, CA 95815
Phone: 916-368-6300
E-mail: abustos@bustosmedia.com
Officer:
Amador Bustos, Chairman, President & Chief Executive Officer
Represented (legal): Fletcher, Heald & Hildreth PLC.
LPTV Stations:
California: KSTV-LP Sacramento.

BUSTOS MEDIA OF UTAH LICENSE LLC
500 Media Pl
Sacramento, CA 95815
Phone: 916-368-6300
Ownership: Amador Bustos, Pres. of ultimate parent co..
Represented (legal): Fletcher, Heald & Hildreth PLC.
LPTV Stations:
Utah: KBTU-LP Park City.

BUSTOS MEDIA OF WISCONSIN LICENSE LLC
3100 Fite Circle
Suite 101
Sacramento, CA 95827
Phone: 916-368-6300
E-mail: abustos@bustosmedia.com
Officer:
Amador Bustos, President
Ownership: Providence Equity Partners Inc., principal.

Represented (legal): Fletcher, Heald & Hildreth PLC.
LPTV Stations:
Michigan: WBWT-LP Ludington.
Radio Stations:
Michigan: WDDW (FM)

BYRNE ACQUISITION GROUP LLC
454 S. Anderson Rd.
Suite 130
Rock Hill, SC 29730
Phone: 803-417-6380
E-mail: jbyrne@anglerschannel.com
Officer:
John Byrne, President
LPTV Stations:
South Carolina: W48CX Hilton Head Island.

CABALLERO ACQUISITION INC.
2000 K St. NW
Suite 725
Washington, DC 20006
Phone: 202-457-4518
Officers:
Sumner M. Redstone, Executive Chairman & Founder
Tom Freston, President & Chief Executive Officer
Robert M. Bakish, Executive Vice President, Operations & Viacom Enterprises
Michael J. Dolan, Executive Vice President & Chief Financial Officer
Carl D. Folta, Executive Vice President, Office of the Chairman
Michael D. Fricklas, Executive Vice President, General Counsel & Secretary
JoAnne Adams Griffith, Executive Vice President, Human Resources
DeDe Lea, Executive Vice President, Government Affairs
Carole Robinson, Executive Vice President, Corporate Relations
James Bombassei, Senior Vice President, Investor Relations
Wade Davis, Senior Vice President, Mergers & Acquisitions
Jacques Tortoroli, Senior Vice President, Corporate Controller & Chief Accounting Officer
Ownership: NAIRI Inc., 69.5%. voting stock; remainder publicly held.; NI ownership:; National Amusements Inc.'; NAI ownership:; The Sumner M. Redstone Trust, 66.66%; Brent D. Redstone, 16.66%; Shari Redstone, 16.66. Viacom has extensive programming services in cable including BET, CMT; Country Music Television, Comedy Central, Logo, MTV, MTV2, MTVU, Nickelodeon, Nick at Nite, Noggin, The N, Spike TV, TV Land & VH1. See Pay TV & Satellite Services for additional information.
Represented (legal): Leventhal, Senter & Lerman PLLC.
LPTV Stations:
California: KZMM-CA Fresno; KMUM-CA Sacramento; KMMD-CA Salinas; KMMC-LP San Francisco; KMMA-CA San Luis Obispo; KVMM-CA Santa Barbara; KQMM-CA Santa Maria; KQMM-LD Santa Maria; KMMW-LD Stockton.
Texas: KGBS-CA Austin; KGMM-CA San Antonio.
Other Holdings:
See also listing for CBS Corp.

CABALLERO TELEVISION LLC
299 Alhambra Circle
No. 510
Coral Gables, FL 33134
Phone: 305-648-0065
Fax: 305-648-0068
E-mail: eduardo@caballero.com
Web site: www.masmusica.tv

Officers:
Eduardo Caballero, Chief Executive Officer
Rosamaria Caballero, President
Peter J. Stafford, Chief Financial Officer

Branch Office:
3310 Keller Springs Rd.
No. 105
Carrollton, TX 75006
Phone: 972-503-6800
Ownership: Eduardo Caballero; Rosamaria Caballero.
LPTV Stations:
California: KHMM-CA Hanford; KMMK-LP Sacramento.
Other Holdings:
Caballero TV & Cable Sales Inc. Rep firm for independent Spanish -language TV stations.; Mas Musica TeVe Network Youth-oriented Spanish language music programming.

CABLE AD NET NEW YORK INC.
5 Cambridge Dr
Red Hook, NY 12571-1604
Phone: 845-876-1212
Officer:
Daniel F Viles Jr, President
Represented (legal): Fletcher, Heald & Hildreth PLC.
LPTV Stations:
New York: WYBN-LP Cobleskill.

CARMEN CABRERA
PO Box 1350
Hatillo, PR 00659
Phone: 787-898-1668
E-mail: riquelmek@xsn.net
LPTV Stations:
Puerto Rico: WIMN-CA Arecibo.

CACHE COUNTY
199 N. Main St.
Logan, UT 84321
Phone: 435-716-7171
E-mail: lynn.lemons@cachecounty.org
Officer:
M. Lynn Lemon, County Executive
LPTV Stations:
Utah: K41GQ-D Logan; K43GR-D Logan; K45GL-D Logan; K47HW-D Logan; K49FS-D Logan; K51GA-D Logan.

CACHE VALLEY BROADCASTING LLC
1772 N 600 W
Logan, UT 84321
Phone: 435-752-7537
E-mail: earl@thevalleychannel.com
Ownership: Earl S. Rouse, Managing Member.
Represented (legal): Irwin, Campbell & Tannenwald PC.
LPTV Stations:
Utah: KCVB-CA Logan.

CADILLAC TELECASTING CO.
22713 N Galacia Dr
Sun City West, AZ 85375-2361
Phone: 602-571-1052
E-mail: jrnbolea@aol.com
Ownership: Alexander Bolea, President & Secretary-Treasurer.
Represented (legal): Womble, Carlyle, Sandridge & Rice.
LPTV Stations:
Michigan: W43CM Pickford; W61CR Sault Ste. Marie; W54CR Traverse City.
Commercial TV Stations:
Michigan: WFQX-DT Cadillac; WFUP-DT Vanderbilt.

CALIFORNIA-OREGON BROADCASTING INC.
PO Box 1489
125 S. Fir St.
Medford, OR 97501
Phones: 541-779-5555; 1-800-821-8108
Fax: 541-779-1151
Web site: www.kobi5.com
Ownership: Patricia C Smullin, Pres..
Represented (legal): Wiley Rein LLP.
LPTV Stations:
California: K06GS Bieber; K34KJ Crescent City, etc.; K11JM Fall River Mills, etc.; K13HU Fort Jones, etc.; K05ET-D Likely; K47DV South Yreka; K04HE Yreka, etc..
Oregon: K04ER Applegate Valley; K07JT Brookings; K07PP Camas Valley; K43DI Canyonville; K07KT Canyonville, etc.; K07PZ Cave Junction; K07PS Chemult; K06NS-D Chiloquin; K30BN Coos Bay; K36BX Coos Bay; K63DO Coos Bay; K14GW Corvallis; KEVU-LP Eugene; K19GH Eugene, etc.; K65ER Eugene, etc.; K58DA Glendale; K26HO Glide,etc.; K25EN Gold Beach; K02FT Gold Hill; K50FW Grants Pass; K04EY Grants Pass, etc.; K13JR-D Jacksonville, etc.; K04ES Klamath Falls; K07NR-D Lakeview, etc.; K32DY Medford; K62BE Midland, etc.; K34BV Murphy, etc.; K13HM Myrtle Creek; K13JQ North Bend & Empire; K12IA Oakland, etc.; K08AK Port Orford, etc.; K62DR Roseburg; K03EI Tolo, etc.; K11GH Tri-City, etc.; K32FI Yoncalla.
Commercial TV Stations:
Oregon: KLSR-DT Eugene; KOTI-DT Klamath Falls; KOBI-DT Medford; KPIC-DT Roseburg.
Cable Systems:
OREGON: ENTERPRISE; LA PINE; MADRAS; PRINEVILLE.

REGENTS OF THE U. OF CALIFORNIA
300 Lakeside Dr., 8th Floor
Office of the President
Oakland, CA 94612-3550
Phone: 510-987-0373
LPTV Stations:
California: K35DG La Jolla.

JEWEL B. CALLAHAM REVOCABLE TRUST
PO Box 548
Broken Bow, OK 74728
Phone: 580-584-3340
E-mail: jane@pinetelephone.com
Ownership: Esta Callaham; John B Callaham; Angela G Wisenhunt.
LPTV Stations:
Oklahoma: K28DJ Broken Bow.
Cable Systems:
OKLAHOMA: BROKEN BOW.
Other Holdings:
Telephone: Pine Telephone Co. Inc.

CAMAS COUNTY TV TRANSLATOR ASSN.
PO Box 152
Fairfield, ID 83327
LPTV Stations:
Idaho: K03FK Fairfield; K05GT Fairfield; K09OZ Fairfield; K13QP Fairfield.

CAMAS VALLEY GRANGE NO. 521
PO Box 37
Camas Valley, OR 97416
Phone: 541-225-1110
E-mail: dhunt@cmc.net
Officer:
Dennis Hunt, Information Contact

LPTV Stations:
Oregon: K21AI Camas Valley.

ROBERT M. CAMPBELL
15560 Edgewood Court
Eden Prairie, MN 55346
Phone: 612-937-1466
LPTV Stations:
Iowa: K25FA Iowa Falls; K47EK Iowa Falls; K53FD Iowa Falls; K55GV Iowa Falls, etc..

CAMPBELLSVILLE U.
One University Dr.
Campbellsville, KY 42718
Phone: 502-465-8158
LPTV Stations:
Kentucky: WLCU-CA Campbellsville.
Other Holdings:
Radio.

CAMP VERDE TV CLUB
1575 S. Roadrunner Lane
Cam Verde, AZ 86322
Phone: 928-567-3433
LPTV Stations:
Arizona: K21GE Camp Verde; K23FZ Camp Verde; K47IK Camp Verde; K55IY Camp Verde; K49HP Camp Verde, etc.; K46IL Verde Valley, etc.; K57DC Verde Valley, etc..

CAPITAL BROADCASTING CORP.
5220 Campo Rd.
Woodland Hills, CA 91364
Phone: 818-884-2617
E-mail: ruizbob@pacbell.net
Ownership: Robert Ruiz, President, majority owner.
Represented (legal): Irwin, Campbell & Tannenwald PC.
LPTV Stations:
California: KSKP-CA Oxnard; KSKJ-CA Van Nuys.
Radio Stations:
North Carolina: WRAL (FM) Raleigh

CAPITAL COMMUNITY BROADCASTING INC.
360 Egan Dr.
Juneau, AK 99801-1198
Phone: 907-586-1670
Fax: 907-586-3612
Officers:
Jay Lyon, Chairman
Bill Legere, President & General Manager
Maxine Richert, Treasurer
Don Jones, Vice President, Engineering
Represented (legal): Schwartz, Woods & Miller.
LPTV Stations:
Alaska: K02QM-D Lemon, etc.; K06JZ Mendenhall Valley, etc.; K08KY Sitka; K09OQ Wrangell.
ETV Stations:
Alaska: KTOO-DT Juneau.
Radio Stations:
Alaska: KRNN (FM), KTOO (FM), KXLL (FM) Juneau

CAPITOL BROADCASTING CO. INC.
2619 Western Blvd
Raleigh, NC 27606
Phone: 919-890-6000
Fax: 919-890-6095
E-mail: webmaster@cbc-raleigh.com
Web site: www.cbc-raleigh.com
Officers:
Jim Goodmon, President & Chief Executive Officer

Jimmy Goodmon, Vice President, CBC New Media Group
George W. Habel, Vice President, Radio Networks/Sports
Michael D. Hill, Vice President, General Counsel
Ardie Gregory, Vice President, General Manager, WRAL-FM & WCMC-FM
Jim Hefner, Vice President & General Manager, WRAL-TV
Dan McGrath, Vice President, Finance & Treasurer
Vicki Murray, Corporate Secretary
Jan Sharp, Vice President, Human Resources
Tom McLaughlin, Corporate Controller & Assistant Secretary-Assistant Treasurer
Ownership: Capitol Holding Co. Inc., 96.4%; A.J. Fletcher Foundation, 3.6%; CHCI ownership:; James F. Goodmon, 96%.
Represented (legal): Fletcher, Heald & Hildreth PLC.
LPTV Stations:
North Carolina: WILM-LD Wilmington.
Commercial TV Stations:
North Carolina: WJZY-DT Belmont; WRAL-DT Raleigh; WRAZ-DT Raleigh.
South Carolina: WMYT-DT Rock Hill.
Radio Stations:
North Carolina: WRAL (FM) Raleigh
Other Holdings:
Telecommunications company (Microspace Communications Corp.).

CRAIG & MARILYN CAPLES
3325 W Wigwam Ave
c/o Caples Production
Las Vegas, NV 89139-7882
Phone: 702-547-1010
LPTV Stations:
Utah: K56IQ Park City.

CARBON COUNTY
120 E. Main
Price, UT 84501
Phone: 435-636-3200
LPTV Stations:
Utah: K02FS Castle Gate; K02OT East Price; K04IW East Price; K05GX East Price; K31HL Helper; K33HS Helper; K36HE Helper; K23GW Price; K27HU Price; K27HV Scofield.

CARIBEVISION HOLDINGS INC.
1401 Brickell Ave
Ste 500
Miami, FL 33131
Phone: 305-365-2030
Officers:
Alejandro Burillo, Chairman
Carlos Barba, President & Chief Executive Officer
Enrique de la Campa, Vice President & Secretary-Treasurer
Ownership: Barba TV Group LLC, 80.73%; BTVGLLC ownership:; Barba Television Co., 91.65%; Pedro Gonzales, 5.44%; Maria Barba-Farshchian, 2.91%; BTC ownership:; Carlos Barba, 50%; Teresa Barba, 50%.
Represented (legal): Fletcher, Heald & Hildreth PLC.
LPTV Stations:
Florida: WFUN-LP Miami, etc.; WZXZ-CA Orlando.
New Jersey: WPXO-LD East Orange.
Commercial TV Stations:
Puerto Rico: WKPV-DT Ponce; WJPX-DT San Juan; WJWN-DT San Sebastian; WIRS-DT Yauco.

CARIBOU COUNTY TV ASSN.
c/o Doris Hayden
2041 Lund Rd.
Bancroft, ID 83217

Phone: 208-648-7663
E-mail: greedavi@isu.edu
Officer:
Doris Hayden, President
LPTV Stations:
Idaho: K07BK Grace, etc.; K11BC Grace, etc.; K13AY Grace, etc.; K09ID Soda Springs; K39GZ Soda Springs; K41GK Soda Springs; K47HF Soda Springs; K49HU Soda Springs; K12LK Soda Springs, etc.; K33HO Soda Springs, etc.; K35HD Soda Springs, etc.; K43GP Soda Springs, etc.; K45GG Soda Springs, etc.; K51HM Soda Springs, etc..

CARLIN TELEVISION DISTRICT
Box 787
Carlin, NV 89822
Phone: 702-754-6897
Officers:
Howard R. Wright, Chairman
LaDawn Lawson, Secretary
Ownership: Community owned--Carlin, NV.
LPTV Stations:
Nevada: K13BB Carlin; K27DY Carlin; K30CD Carlin; K33DP Carlin; K35BR Carlin; K44AM Carlin; K46KH Carlin; K48LM Carlin; K54DV Carlin.

CAROLINA CHRISTIAN BROADCASTING CO.
Box 1616
Greenville, SC 29602
Phone: 864-244-1616
Fax: 864-292-8481
Officers:
James H. Thompson, President & General Manager
Norvin C. Duncan, Assistant to the President
Ownership: James H Thompson, 92%; remainder unissued.
Represented (legal): Bechtel & Cole Chartered.
LPTV Stations:
North Carolina: WJJV-LP Asheville; W23BQ Asheville, etc.; W31AZ Hendersonville.
South Carolina: W65DS Honea Path.
Commercial TV Stations:
South Carolina: WGGS-DT Greenville.

ROBERT WILLIAM CARR
4818 NW 17th Pl
Gainesville, FL 32605
Phone: 352-373-5752
E-mail: rcarr@wuft.org
Represented (legal): Fletcher, Heald & Hildreth PLC.
LPTV Stations:
Florida: W32DI Mayo.

CARTER BROADCASTING CORP.
20 Park Plaza
Suite 720
Boston, MA 02116
Phone: 617-423-0210
Officers:
Kenneth R. Carberry, President
Lorayne Carberry, Vice President
Joyce Scott, Secretary
Dale O'Hayer, Treasurer
Ownership: Kenneth R Carberry.
Represented (legal): Garvey Schubert Barer.
LPTV Stations:
Massachusetts: WCRN-LP Leicester.
Radio Stations:
Massachusetts: WACE (AM) Chicopee, WCRN (AM) Worcester

CASCADIA COMMUNITY TV INC.
PO Box 704
26995 Dobbin Creek Rd
Cascadia, OR 97329-0704

Phone: 541-367-2927
E-mail: mgross@dswebnet.com
Officer:
Michael A. Gross, Translator Engineer
LPTV Stations:
Oregon: K04CX Cascadia.

CASPER COMMUNITY COLLEGE DISTRICT
125 College Dr.
Casper, WY 82601
LPTV Stations:
Wyoming: K06KH Casper.

CATAMOUNT BROADCAST GROUP
71 East Ave.
Norwalk, CT 06851
Phone: 203-852-7164
Fax: 203-852-7163
Officers:
Ralph E. Becker, President & Chief Executive Officer
Daniel J. Duman, Chief Financial Officer
Ownership: BCI Partners Inc., Principal.
Represented (legal): Fletcher, Heald & Hildreth PLC.
LPTV Stations:
California: K04FL Lakeshore, etc.; K49CT Paradise; K54EE Westwood.
Commercial TV Stations:
California: KHSL-DT Chico.

CATHOLIC BROADCASTING OF SCRANTON INC.
400 Wyoming Ave.
Scranton, PA 18503
Phone: 570-207-2219
Fax: 570-346-8958
Officers:
Rev. James C. Timlin, President
Maria Orzel, Executive Director, Communications
James Brennan, CTV Manager
Ownership: Bishop James C Timlin, Trustee.
Represented (legal): Womble, Carlyle, Sandridge & Rice.
LPTV Stations:
Pennsylvania: W19CI Berwick; W07BV Wilkes-Barre, etc..

CATHOLIC VIEWS BROADCASTS INC.
50 S. Franklin Turnpike
Ramsey, NJ 07446
Phone: 201-236-9336
LPTV Stations:
Minnesota: K19ER St. Paul.

FRANK J. CATZ, TRUSTEE
1276 Sharon Park Dr.
Menlo Park, CA 94025-7030
Phone: 650-854-0111
Fax: 650-854-0223
LPTV Stations:
Michigan: W34CR Petoskey; W41CK Petoskey.

CAYO HUESO NETWORKS LLC
PO Box 348
2539 N Hwy 67
Sedalia, CO 80135
Phone: 303-688-5162
E-mail: dmdsat@aol.com
Ownership: Penny M. Drucker, 87.5%; David M. Drucker, 12.5%. Druckers also have interest in Denver Digital Television LLC, Echonet Corp., GreenTV Corp., Ketchikan TV LLC & Polar Communications.
Represented (legal): Rini Coran PC.

LPTV Stations:
Florida: W16CA Big Pine; W47AC Big Pine Key; W57AM Big Pine Key; WKIZ-LP Key West; W40AA Matecumbe; W43AD Matecumbe; W57DU-D Matecumbe.

CBS CORP.
51 W. 52nd St.
New York, NY 10019-6188
Phone: 212-975-4321
Fax: 212-975-4516
Web site: www.cbscorporation.com
Officers:
Sumner M. Redstone, Chairman
Leslie Moonves, President & Chief Executive Officer
Anthony G. Ambrosio, Executive Vice President, Human Resources & Administration
Louis J. Briskman, Executive Vice President & General Counsel
Martin D. Franks, Executive Vice President, Planning, Policy & Government Relations
Gil Schwartz, Executive Vice President, Corporate Communications
Martin M. Shea, Executive Vice President, Investor Relations
Susan C. Gordon, Senior Vice President, Corporate Controller & Chief Accounting Officer
Angeline C. Straka, Senior Vice President, Deputy General Counsel & Secretary
Joseph R. Ianniello, Senior Vice President, Finance & Treasurer

Branch Office:
Paramount Stations Group Inc.
5555 Melrose Ave.
Los Angeles, CA 90038
Phone: 323-956-8100
Fax: 323-862-0121
Ownership: NAIRI Inc., 69.5% voting stock; remainder publicly held.%; NI ownership:; National Amusements Inc.; NAI ownership:; The Sumner M. Redstone Trust, 80%; Shari Redstone, 20%.
LPTV Stations:
Florida: W61AK Inverness; W23CN Sebring.
Indiana: WBXI-CA Indianapolis.
Utah: K44IZ-D Delta, etc..
Commercial TV Stations:
California: KCAL-DT Los Angeles; KCBS-DT Los Angeles; KMAX-DT Sacramento; KBCW-DT San Francisco; KPIX-DT San Francisco; KOVR-DT Stockton.
Colorado: KCNC-DT Denver.
Florida: WBFS-DT Miami; WFOR-DT Miami; WTOG-DT St. Petersburg.
Georgia: WUPA-DT Atlanta.
Illinois: WBBM-DT Chicago.
Maryland: WJZ-DT Baltimore.
Massachusetts: WBZ-DT Boston; WSBK-DT Boston.
Michigan: WKBD-DT Detroit; WWJ-DT Detroit.
Minnesota: KCCO-DT Alexandria; WCCO-DT Minneapolis; KCCW-DT Walker.
New York: WCBS-DT New York.
Pennsylvania: WPCW-DT Jeannette; KYW-DT Philadelphia; WPSG-DT Philadelphia; KDKA-DT Pittsburgh.
Texas: KTVT-DT Fort Worth; KTXA-DT Fort Worth.
Virginia: WGNT-DT Portsmouth.
Washington: KSTW-DT Tacoma.
Radio Stations:
Arizona: KMLE (FM) Chandler; KOOL-FM, KZON (FM) Phoenix
California: KCBS-AM-FM, KFWB (AM), KLSX (FM), KNX (AM), KRTH (FM), KTWV (FM) Los Angeles; KROQ-FM Pasadena; KQJK (FM) Roseville; KHTK-AM, KNCI (FM), KYMX (FM), KZZO (FM) Sacramento; KFRG (FM) San Bernardino; KSCF (FM), KYXY (FM) San D
Colorado: KIMN-FM, KWLI, KXKL-FM Denver

Connecticut: WTIC-AM-FM, WZMX (FM) Hartford; WRCH (FM) New Britain
District of Columbia: WPGC-AM-FM
Florida: WJHM (FM) Daytona Beach; WOCL (FM) DeLand; WLLD (FM) Holmes Beach; WPBZ (FM) Indiantown; WMBX (FM) Jensen Beach; WNEW (FM) Jupiter; WSJT (FM) Lakeland; WOMX-FM Orlando; WYUU (FM) Safety Harbor; WQYK-AM-FM Seffner; WRBQ (FM) Tampa
Georgia: WAOK (AM), WVEE (FM), WZGC (FM) Atlanta
Illinois: WBBM-AM-FM, WJMK (FM), WSCR (AM), WUSN (FM), WXRT-FM Chicago; WCFS-FM Elmwood Park
Kansas: KXNT (AM) Topeka
Maryland: WLZL (FM) Annapolis; WJFK-AM-FM, WLIF (FM), WQSR (FM), WWMX (FM) Baltimore; WTGB-FM Bethesda; WHFS (FM) Catonsville; WPGC (AM) Morningside
Massachusetts: WBCN (FM), WBMX (FM), WBZ (AM), WODS (FM), WZLX-FM Boston
Michigan: WOMC (FM), WVMV (FM), WWJ (AM), WXYT-AM-FM, WYCD (FM) Detroit
Minnesota: WCCO (AM), WLTE (FM) Minneapolis; KZJK (FM) St. Louis Park
Missouri: KEZK-FM, KMOX (AM), KYKY (FM) St. Louis
Nevada: KKJ (FM), KMXB (FM) Henderson; KLUC-FM Las Vegas; KSFN (AM) North Las Vegas; KXTE (FM) Pahrump
New York: WCBS-AM-FM, WFAN (AM), WINS (AM), WWFS (FM), WXRK (FM) New York
North Carolina: WFNA (FM), WFNZ (AM), WKQC (FM), WNKS (FM), WSOC-FM Charlotte; WPEG (FM) Concord; WBAV-FM Gastonia; WKRK (FM) Murphy
Ohio: WDOK (FM), WNCX (FM), WQAL (FM) Cleveland
Oregon: KVMX (FM) Banks; KLTH (FM) Lake Oswego; KCMD (AM), KINK-FM, KUFO-FM, KUPL-FM Portland
Pennsylvania: WZPT (FM) New Kensington; KYW (AM), WIP (AM), WPHT (AM), WYSP (FM) Philadelphia; KDKA (AM), WBZW-FM, WDSY-FM Pittsburgh
Texas: KJKK (FM), KLLI (FM), KLUV (FM), KRLD (AM), KVIL (FM) Dallas; KMVK (FM) Fort Worth; KHJZ (FM), KILT-AM-FM Houston; KIKK (AM) Pasadena
Washington: KJAQ (FM), KMPS-FM, KPTK (AM), KZOK-FM Seattle; KBKS-FM Tacoma
Other Holdings:
Advertising on out-of-door media: CBS Outdoor.
Broadcast holdings: Caballero Acquisition Inc., see listing.
Consumer Products: CBS Consumer Products.
Digital Media: CBS Digital Media & CSTV Networks.
Publishing holdings: Simon & Schuster.
Television Production & Syndication: CBS Paramount Television & King World.
Theme Parks: Paramount Parks..

CEE INC.
Box 28
Cairo, GA 31728
Ownership: Anna P Searcy; Floyd H Searcy.
LPTV Stations:
Georgia: W02CI Cairo & Thomasville.

CENTENARY COLLEGE
400 Jefferson St.
Hackettstown, PA 07840
Phone: 908-852-1400
LPTV Stations:
New Jersey: W23AZ Hackettstown.

CENTER BROADCASTING CORP. OF NEW HAMPSHIRE
81 N. State Rd.
Concord, NH 03301

LPTV Stations:
New Hampshire: W39AR Concord; W28CM Manchester; W33AK Nashua; WYCN-LP Nashua.

CENTEX TELEVISION LP
PO Box 2522
Waco, TX 76702
Phone: 254-754-2525
Officer:
Robert H. Drewry, President
Represented (legal): Davis Wright Tremaine LLP.
LPTV Stations:
Texas: KRHD-LP Bryan.

CENTRAL ARIZONA BROADCASTING LLC
719 E. Cottonwood Lane
Suite B
Casa Grande, AZ 85222
Phone: 520-876-4080
Fax: 520-876-4985
Officers:
Brett F. Eisele, President
John W. McEvoy, Chief Executive Officer
Nancy A. McEvoy, Secretary
Eddie F. Higginbotham, Chief Financial Officer
Ownership: Beatrice Lueck, 16.67%%; Brett F. Eisele, 16.67%%; Eddie F. Higginbotham, 16.67%%; John W. McEvoy, 16.67%%; Nancy A. McEvoy, 16.67%%; Jack A. Salvatore, 16.67%.
LPTV Stations:
Arizona: KCAB-LP Casa Grande.

CENTRAL BROADCAST CO.
2333 Ponce de Leon Blvd.
PH-1120
Coral Gables, FL 33134
Phone: 305-448-4747
LPTV Stations:
Florida: W21AU Orlando.

CENTRAL CAROLINA BROADCASTING CORP. INC.
151 S. Horner Blvd.
Box 2563
Sanford, NC 27330
Phone: 919-708-6775
Fax: 919-775-5612
Officer:
Joseph F. Tucker Jr., President & General Manager
LPTV Stations:
North Carolina: W67CD Sanford.

CENTRAL COAST GOOD NEWS INC.
Box 17
Santa Maria, CA 93456
Phone: 805-925-1140
Officer:
Clyde Harmon, Secretary
Ownership: Non-profit corp--Santa Monica, CA..
LPTV Stations:
California: K23CL Lompoc; K22EE Morro Bay; KJCN-LP Paso Robles; K51GB Santa Maria.

CENTRAL IDAHO TV INC.
Rte. 2
PO Box 726
Grangeville, ID 83530

LPTV Stations:
Idaho: K26CK Craigmont, etc.; K43CI Grangeville, etc.; K48DH Grangeville, etc.; K69AK Grangeville, etc..

CENTRAL MICHIGAN U.
3965 E. Broomfield Rd.
Mount Pleasant, MI 48859
Phone: 989-774-3105
Fax: 989-774-4427
Officers:
Thomas J. Endres, Director, Fundraising
Rick Schudiske, Director, TV
Represented (legal): Dow Lohnes PLLC.
LPTV Stations:
Michigan: W69AV Leeland, etc.; W46AD Traverse City, etc..
ETV Stations:
Michigan: WCML-DT Alpena; WCMV-DT Cadillac; WCMW-DT Manistee; WCMU-DT Mount Pleasant.
Radio Stations:
Michigan: WCMU-FM; WCML-FM

CENTRAL OHIO ASSN. OF CHRISTIAN BROADCASTERS INC.
1282 N. Main St.
Marion, OH 43302
Phone: 740-383-1794
Fax: 740-387-6647
Officer:
David R. Aiken, President & General Manager
Ownership: Non-profit corp.--Marion, OH.
LPTV Stations:
Ohio: WGCT-CA Columbus; WXCB-CA Delaware; WOCB-CA Marion.

CENTRAL STATES COMMUNICATIONS
1575 S. Roadrunner Lane
Box 750
Camp Verde, AZ 86322
Phone: 928-567-3433
LPTV Stations:
Arizona: K18DD Camp Verde; K19FD Camp Verde.

CENTRAL WYOMING COLLEGE
2660 Peck Ave.
Riverton, WY 82501
Phone: 307-856-6944
Officers:
Daniel Schiedel, General Manager
Roger A Hicks, Chief Operator
LPTV Stations:
Wyoming: K11UT Buffalo; K07QA Clark, etc.; K02LH Clarks Fork, etc.; K40JU-D Cody & Powell; K49AI Cody & Powell; K49AI Cody & Powell; K47LK-D Dubois, etc.; K23DS-D Evanston; K32DS Evanston; K54EH Evanston; K43KW-D Gillette; K21HQ Glendo; K41KM-D Greybull; K50JC Greybull; K24GT-D Kemmerer; K02GE La Barge; K09IJ La Barge; K62CS La Barge; K06FD La Barge & Big Piney; K29HV-D La Barge, etc.; K42GZ La Barge, etc.; K63BO Meeteetse, etc.; K29IH-D Meeteetse, etc.; K03GX Mountain View; K09DI Mountain View, etc.; K11DN Mountain View, etc.; K07RS North Fork; K32IF-D North Fork, etc.; K26HV Rawlins; K51IZ Rawlins, etc.; K58AM Rawlins, etc.; K22BK Rock Springs, etc.; K28JU-D Rock Springs, etc.; K07NT Saratoga, etc.; K09OC Saratoga, etc.; K02LG South Fork; K11QL Sunlight Basin, etc.; K25ID Teton Village; K07RT Wood River; K31JO-D Wood River, etc..
ETV Stations:
Wyoming: KCWC-DT Lander; KWYP-DT Laramie.

CENTRO CRISTIANO SION
1662 Broadway Ave
Redwood City, CA 94063
Phone: 650-367-8807
Officer:
David de la Quintana, Pastor
LPTV Stations:
California: K22HB Mammoth Lakes; K42HE Ukiah.

CENTRO CRISTIANO VIDA ABUNDANTE INC.
121 W. Alvin Ave.
Santa Maria, CA 93458
Officer:
Manuel Sanchez, President
LPTV Stations:
Arizona: KYUM-LP Yuma.

CITY OF CHADRON
234 Main St.
Chadron, NE 69337
Phone: 308-432-0505
Officer:
Alfred Vicanti, City Manager
LPTV Stations:
Nebraska: K02NY Chadron.

CHAFFEE COUNTY TV TRANSLATOR ASSN.
5375 Hwy. 50 E
Salida, CO 81201
Phone: 719-539-2942
LPTV Stations:
Colorado: K02JH Salida, etc.; K04JD Salida, etc.; K06HF Salida, etc.; K11KU Salida, etc.; K13LD Salida, etc..

CHALKYITSIK VILLAGE COUNCIL
5900 E. Tudor Rd.
Anchorage, AK 99507
Phone: 907-269-5744
LPTV Stations:
Alaska: K04JU Chalkyitsik.

CHAMBERS COMMUNICATIONS CORP.
PO Box 7009
2295 Coburg Rd., Suite 200
Eugene, OR 97401
Phone: 541-485-5611
Fax: 541-342-2695
E-mail: mpuckett@adpronetworks.com
Web site: www.chamberscable.com; www.cmc.net/~chambers/
Ownership: Carolyn S Chambers, Chmn. & Chief Exec. Officer, see also Soda Mountain Broadcasting Inc..
Represented (legal): Arnold, Gallagher, Saydack, Percell, Roberts & Potter PC.
LPTV Stations:
Oregon: K11GT College Hill, etc.; K27CL Coos Bay; K07JS North Bend; K04OS Reedsport; K53CU Roseburg.
Commercial TV Stations:
Oregon: KOHD-DT Bend; KEZI-DT Eugene; KDKF-DT Klamath Falls; KDRV-DT Medford.
Cable Systems:
OREGON: SUNRIVER.
Other Holdings:
Multimedia: Chambers Production Group, Chambers Multimedia Connection Inc..

GEORGE CHAMBERS
1806 Monte Vista
Dalhart, TX 79022
Phone: 806-249-4747
E-mail: kxit@xit.net

LPTV Stations:
Texas: KXIT-LP Amarillo.

CHANG BROADCASTING HAWAII LLC
269 S. Beverly Dr.
PMB 704
Beverly Hills, CA 90212
Phone: 310-403-5039
Fax: 310-388-1353
Represented (legal): Irwin, Campbell & Tannenwald PC.
LPTV Stations:
Hawaii: KESU-LP Hanamaulu; K32GJ Kailua-Kona.

JEFF CHANG
269 S. Beverly Dr.
PMB 704
Beverly Hills, CA 90212
Phone: 310-403-5039
Represented (legal): Irwin, Campbell & Tannenwald PC.
LPTV Stations:
California: K28IE Barstow; KTJH-LP Ukiah; K39GY Victorville.
Maryland: W63DC Ocean City.

CHANNEL 5 PUBLIC BROADCASTING INC.
1670 N. Virginia St.
Reno, NV 89503
Phone: 702-784-4555
Officers:
Richard W. Schneider, President & Chief Executive Officer
Fred Ihlow, Vice President, Technology
Lee Nicholson, Chief Financial Officer
Ownership: Non-profit organization--Reno, NV..
Represented (legal): Schwartz, Woods & Miller.
LPTV Stations:
Nevada: K29ES Carson City; K31BM Silver Springs; K42IL Verdi; K47KJ-D Verdi.
ETV Stations:
Nevada: KNPB-DT Reno.

CHANNEL 7 OF CORPUS CHRISTI INC.
600 Leopard St.
Suite 1924
Corpus Christi, TX 78473
Phone: 361-882-1414
LPTV Stations:
Texas: KCBO-LP Corpus Christi.

CHANNEL ELEVEN INC.
1617 Lebanon Rd
Nashville, TN 37210
Phone: 615-889-1960

Branch Office:
MURFREESBORO, TN
306 S. Church St.
Murfreesboro, TN 37130
Phone: 615-893-1450
Ownership: S. Bart Walker, President & Secretary.
Represented (legal): Fletcher, Heald & Hildreth PLC.
LPTV Stations:
Tennessee: WETV-LP Murfreesboro.

CHANNEL 19 TV CORP.
911 Massachusetts Ave.
Boston, MA 02118
Phone: 617-541-2222
Fax: 617-427-6227
Officers:
Peter N. Cuenca, President & General Manager

Juan Hernandez, Vice President, Marketing
Ownership: Peter N Cuenca.
Represented (legal): Luvaas Cobb PC.
LPTV Stations:
Massachusetts: WCEA-LP Boston.
Newspapers:
Massachusetts: La Semana (Spanish weekly, Dorchester)

CHANNEL 51 OF SAN DIEGO INC.
4575 Viewridge Ave.
San Diego, CA 92123
Phone: 858-571-5151
LPTV Stations:
California: K12PO Temecula.

CHANNEL AMERICA LPTV LICENSE SUBSIDIARY INC.
19 W. 21st St.
Suite 204
New York, NY 10010
Officers:
David Post, Chairman
Robert Mauro, President
Represented (legal): Rosenman & Colin LLP.
LPTV Stations:
Nebraska: K67CV Lincoln.
Other Holdings:
Program source: Channel America.

CHANNEL COMMUNICATIONS LLC
Box 1317
Lewistown, PA 17044-3317
Phone: 800-692-7401
LPTV Stations:
Pennsylvania: WHVL-LD State College, etc.; WHVL-LP State College, etc..

CHECKERBOARD TV DISTRICT
425 Camas Creek Rd
White Sulphur Springs, MT 59645
Phone: 406-547-2190
E-mail: camascr@mtintouch.net
Officer:
Jock H. Doggett, Information Contact
LPTV Stations:
Montana: K11CC Checkerboard; K07KD Checkerboard, etc.; K09WP Checkerboard, etc..

CHERRY CREEK RADIO LLC
501 S Cherry St
Ste 480
Denver, CO 80246
Phone: 303-468-6500
E-mail: lbarnhill@cherrycreekradio.com
Web site: www.cherrycreekradio.com
Officer:
Joseph Schwartz, President & Chief Executive Officer
Ownership: Arlington Capital Partners LP, 80.29%. assets, 97.2% votes; ACPLP ownership:; Arlington Capital Group LLC; ACGLLC ownership:; Raymond W. Smith, 35.56%. assets, 25% votes; Paul G. Stern, 35.56%. assets, 25% votes; Robert I. Knibb, 17.77%. assets, 25% votes; Jeffrey H. Freed, 11.11%. assets, 25% votes; Perry W. Steiner, Managing Dir..
Represented (legal): Drinker Biddle.
LPTV Stations:
Utah: KMBU-LP Enterprise; K07PX Rockville; KVBT-LP Santa Clara; KDLU-LP St. George; KDLQ-LP St. George, etc.; K09KP Toquerville; K11OP Virgin.
Radio Stations:
Montana: KHLN (FM) Montana City

CITY OF CHEVAK
5900 E. Tudor Rd.
Anchorage, AK 99507

Phone: 907-269-5744
LPTV Stations:
Alaska: K09PO Chevak.

CHEYENNE COUNTY
County Courthouse
PO Box 67
Cheyenne Wells, CO 80810
LPTV Stations:
Colorado: K60AM Cheyenne Wells; K62AH Cheyenne Wells; K64AJ Cheyenne Wells; K68AQ Cheyenne Wells.

CHINOOK TV ASSOCIATION INC.
PO Box 492
Chinook, MT 59523
Phone: 406-357-3212
Officer:
Myrla McCoy, Treasurer
LPTV Stations:
Montana: K61BK Chinook; K63AR Chinook; K65BR Chinook.

VILLAGE OF CHITINA
5900 E. Tudor Rd.
Anchorage, AK 99507
Phone: 907-269-5744
LPTV Stations:
Alaska: K09NF Chitina.

JAMES J. CHLADEK
204 E. 23rd St., 2nd Floor
New York, NY 10010
Phone: 212-686-5386
Fax: 212-576-1839
Represented (legal): Rosenman & Colin LLP.
LPTV Stations:
Florida: W05CJ Key West; W10CQ Key West; WSCF-LP Melbourne; WPMF-LP Miami.
Radio Stations:
New Jersey: WXMC (AM) Parsippany-Troy Hill

CHOICE OLEAN TELEVISION STATION INC.
217 N. Union St.
Olean, NY 14760
Phone: 716-373-5838
Fax: 716-373-5838
Officer:
Charles X. Bordonaro, President
Ownership: Choice Olean Television Inc..
LPTV Stations:
New York: W20AB Olean; WONS-LP Olean.

CHRISTIAN BROADCASTING COMMUNICATIONS
PO Box 3704
3881 Southside River Rd
Farmington, NM 87499
Phone: 505-327-1445
Officer:
John M. Holland, President
LPTV Stations:
Colorado: K32IJ Cortez.
New Mexico: K47DR Farmington; K21HJ Gallup & Tohatchi; K32FK Shiprock-Chinle, AZ.

CHRISTIAN BROADCASTING NETWORK
5135 Lyons Loop
Yakima, WA 98903
Phones: 509-248-1700; 509-248-1701
Fax: 509-248-0887
Officers:
Jere Irwin, President
Eleanor Fasano, Secretary-Treasurer
Represented (legal): Joseph E. Dunne III.

LPTV Stations:
Washington: KDHW-LP Yakima.
Other Holdings:
Program source: 8.7% interest in International Family Entertainment Inc..

CHRISTIAN BROADCASTING OF IDAHO INC.
4002 North 3300 East
Twin Falls, ID 83301-0354
Phone: 208-733-3133
Officers:
Michael Kestler, President
Danny R. Basham, Vice President
Nora Kestler, Secretary-Treasurer
LPTV Stations:
Idaho: KTYJ-LP Coeur d'Alene; KBAX-LP Twin Falls; KCTF-LP Twin Falls.

CHRISTIAN BROADCASTING OF YAKIMA
Box 10745
Yakima, WA 98909-1745
Phone: 509-248-0194
E-mail: rafael@irwinresearch.com
Officer:
Rafael Fernandez, Chief Engineer
LPTV Stations:
Washington: K39DM Ellensburg.

CHRISTIAN COMMUNICATIONS OF CHICAGOLAND INC.
38 S. Peoria
Chicago, IL 60607
Phone: 312-433-3838
Fax: 312-433-3839
Officers:
Jerry K. Rose, Chairman & Chief Executive Officer
Jim Nichols, Chief Financial Officer
Peter Edgers, Director, Network Operations
Holly Swanson, Cable, Affiliate Director

Branch Office:
San Francisco Office:
400 Tamal Plaza
Corte Madera, CA 94925
Phone: 415-924-7500
Represented (legal): Pillsbury Winthrop Shaw Pittman LLP.
LPTV Stations:
Illinois: WCFC-CA Rockford.
Nevada: KEEN-CA Las Vegas.
Commercial TV Stations:
California: KTLN-DT Novato.

CHRISTIAN FAITH BROADCAST INC.
PO Box 247
3809 Maple Ave
Castalia, OH 44824
Phone: 419-684-5311
Fax: 419-684-5378
Officers:
Shelby Gilliam, President
Debra Yost, Secretary
LPTV Stations:
Ohio: W33BW Ashland.
Commercial TV Stations:
Michigan: WLLA-DT Kalamazoo.
Ohio: WGGN-DT Sandusky.
Radio Stations:
Ohio: WJKW (FM) Athens, WGGN (FM) Castalia, WLRD (FM) Willard

CHRISTIAN FAMILY NETWORK TELEVISION INC.
1200 9th St.
Wichita Falls, TX 76301
Phone: 940-322-6229

E-mail: cfntk30@yahoo.com
Web site: www.cfnt.org
Officers:
Rod Payne, President & Chief Operating Officer
Steve Cookingham, Chief Executive Officer
Susan Anderson, Public & Children's Liaison
Bobby Redwine, Chief Financial Officer
Represented (legal): Joseph E. Dunne III.
LPTV Stations:
Texas: K20DN Wichita Falls; K30DJ Wichita Falls.

CHRISTIAN LIFE BROADCASTING
2125 West 900 South
West Jordan, UT 84088
Phone: 801-484-4331
Officers:
John M. Peterson, President
Tom Schwartz, Vice President
Debbie Bess, Secretary
Robert Scharffenberg, Chief Financial Officer
LPTV Stations:
Utah: KUCL-LP Salt Lake City.

CHRISTIANS INCORPORATED FOR CHRIST INC.
Box 7940
Branson, MO 65615-7940
Phones: 417-336-3945; 417-337-5503
Officers:
Anna Lee Fuller, President
Keith O'Neil, Vice President & Chief Operating Officer
Jimmie Sue Smith, Secretary-Treasurer
Ownership: Keith O'Neil.
LPTV Stations:
Arkansas: K22HS Eureka Springs; K23DU Harrison; KVAQ-LP Springdale.
Missouri: K25BD Branson.

CHRISTIAN TELEVISION NETWORK INC.
6922 142nd Ave. N
Largo, FL 33771
Phone: 727-535-5622
Fax: 727-531-2497
E-mail: comments@ctnonline.com
Officers:
Robert D'Andrea, President
Virginia Oliver, Secretary
Jimmy Smith, Treasurer
Ownership: Robert D'Andrea; Virginia Oliver; Jimmy Smith; Wayne Wetzel; Robert S. Young, 20%. votes each.
Represented (legal): Hardy, Carey, Chautin & Balkin LLP.
LPTV Stations:
Florida: WVUP-CA Tallahassee.
Georgia: WYBU-CA Columbus.
Illinois: WLCF-LD Effingham.
Commercial TV Stations:
Florida: WCLF-DT Clearwater; WFGC-DT Palm Beach; WHBR-DT Pensacola; WRXY-DT Tice.
Georgia: WGNM-DT Macon.
Illinois: WTJR-DT Quincy.
Iowa: KFXB-DT Dubuque.
Missouri: KNLJ-DT Jefferson City.
Tennessee: WHTN-DT Murfreesboro; WVLR-DT Tazewell.

CHRIST LOVES YOU BROADCASTING
Box 490
Redmond, OR 97756
LPTV Stations:
Oregon: K23CU Prineville.

CHRIST VISION
Box 787
Keokuk, IA 52632

Phone: 217-847-3348
Officers:
Melvin George, President
Donette Douglas, Vice President
Judy Sheffler, Secretary
Donna Benson, Treasurer
Ownership: Community owned--Keokuk, IA.
LPTV Stations:
Iowa: K60CL Keokuk.

CHUATHBALUK CITY COUNCIL
5900 E. Tudor Rd.
Anchorage, AK 99507
Phone: 907-269-5744
LPTV Stations:
Alaska: K09PP Chuathbaluk.

TOWN OF CHUGWATER
PO Box 243
Chugwater, WY 82210-0243
Phone: 307-422-3493
LPTV Stations:
Wyoming: K12QG Chugwater.

CHURCHILL MEDIA LLC
871 Country Club Rd
Eugene, OR 97401
Phone: 541-343-4100
Officers:
Suzanne K. Arlie, Managing Member
Scott M. Diehl, Vice President
Ownership: Suzanne K. Arlie, Sole Board Member.
Represented (legal): J. Dominic Monahan.
LPTV Stations:
Oregon: KXPD-LP Eola; KXOR-LP Eugene.
Washington: K58DL Yakima-Toppenish.

CIRCLE TV BOOSTER CLUB INC.
PO Box 153
Circle, MT 59215-0153
Phone: 406-485-2196
E-mail: skywaytv@midrivers.com
Officers:
Douglas Shennum, Chairman
Dale Bond, President
Edwin Moos, Vice President
Robert T. Hoover, Secretary
Eugene Schull, Treasurer
LPTV Stations:
Montana: K13BC Circle; K14AG Circle; K16GP Circle; K06KY Circle, etc.; K10AT Circle, etc.; K18CR Circle, etc..

CITIZENS TELEVISION SYSTEMS INC.
919 18th St. NW, 10th Floor
Washington, DC 20006
LPTV Stations:
New York: WFHW-LP Buffalo.

CITIZENS T.V. INC.
PO Box 2
Milton-Freewater, OR 97862
Phone: 541-938-7935
Officers:
John Kelly, President
Alvin Adams, Vice President
Larry Anderson, Secretary-Treasurer
Ownership: Alvin Adams; Jennifer Anderson; Larry Anderson; Alan Benz; Mike Greer; Dave Houchin; John Kelly; Craig Lane; Merle Sherman, Board Members.

LPTV Stations:
Oregon: K53EK Milton-Freewater; K55GC Milton-Freewater.

CITRUS COUNTY ASSOCIATION FOR RETARDED CITIZENS INC.
130 Heights Ave.
Inverness, FL 34452
Phones: 352-746-3982; 352-795-4919
Fax: 352-746-3984
Officer:
Thomas Franklin, General Manager
LPTV Stations:
Florida: WYKE-LP Inglis/Yankeetown.

CITY OF WINDOM
PO Box 38
444 9th St.
Windom, MN 56101
LPTV Stations:
Minnesota: K56AH Windom; K58AF Windom; K60AD Windom; K62AI Windom; K64AK Windom.

CIVIC LIGHT INC.
2999 Morningside St.
San Diego, CA 92139
Phone: 619-299-6363
Fax: 619-298-5371
Officers:
John M. Willkie, President & Chief Executive Officer
Karl Fackler, Chief Financial Officer
Ownership: John M Willkie, 39.28%; Karl F Fackler, 38.27%; Eric Kravitz, 4.29%.
LPTV Stations:
California: K63EN San Diego.

C L & O TRANSLATOR SYSTEM INC.
Box 87
Lipscomb, TX 79056
LPTV Stations:
Texas: K47BP Booker; K31CD Canadian.

CLAREMONT TELEVISION INC.
141 Hanover St
Claremont, NH 03743
LPTV Stations:
New Hampshire: W10AC Claremont; W12AF Claremont.

CITY OF CLARINDA
200 S. 15th St.
Clarinda, IA 51632
Phone: 712-542-2136
E-mail: clarindamanager@iowatelecom.net
Officer:
Gary R. Walter, City Manager
LPTV Stations:
Iowa: K56AF Clarinda.

CLARK COUNTY SCHOOL DISTRICT
4210 E. Channel 10 Dr.
Las Vegas, NV 89119
Officers:
Thomas Axtel, General Manager
Lee Solonche, Director, Instructional Television
Represented (legal): Wiley Rein LLP.
LPTV Stations:
Nevada: K10NV Alamo, etc.; K23CJ Glendale; K07JC Indian Springs; K23BS Jean; K53DG Laughlin; K02FM Mercury; K02FN Mesquite; K02FJ Oasis Valley.
ETV Stations:
Nevada: KLVX-DT Las Vegas.

SUSAN CLARKE
87 Lake St.
Plattsburgh, NY 12901
Phone: 518-297-2727
Fax: 518-297-3377
E-mail: wwbitv27@hotmail.com
LPTV Stations:
Vermont: W14CK Newport.

ETTIE CLARK
660 County Rd. 123
Berry, AL 35546
Phone: 205-689-5218
Fax: 205-932-2299
LPTV Stations:
Alabama: WSFG-LD Berry; WSSF-LD Berry;
WSSF-LP Berry.

**CLARKS FORK VALLEY TV
DISTRICT NO. 1**
PO Box 30
Bridger, MT 59014
Phone: 406-668-7633
E-mail: chambersmules@yahoo.com
Officer:
Laura J. Chambers, Secretary
LPTV Stations:
Montana: K57EW Bridger, etc.; K59DT Bridger,
etc.; K61EX Bridger, etc.; K63EA Bridger,
etc..

**CLEAR CHANNEL
COMMUNICATIONS INC.**
200 Basse Rd.
San Antonio, TX 78209
Phone: 210-822-2828
E-mail: lisacdollinger@clearchannel.com
Officers:
L. Lowry Mays, Chairman
Mark Mays, Chief Executive Officer
Randall Mays, President
Craig Millar, Interim President, Clear Channel
Television
Lisa Dollinger, Chief Communications Officer
Rip Riordan, Executive Vice President
Herbert W. Hill Jr., Senior Vice President &
Chief Accounting Officer
Kenneth E. Wyker, Senior Vice President &
Secretary
Hal Capron, Vice President
David D'Antuono, Vice President
John Feeser, Vice President
Donald C. McGraw, Vice President
Sharon Moloney, Vice President
Jack Peck, Vice President
R. Randolph Pratt, Vice President
Debbie Sinay, Vice President
Steve Spendlove, Vice President
Jerry Whitener, Vice President
Ownership:L. Lowry Mays, controlling stock-
holder.
Represented (legal): Wiley Rein LLP.
LPTV Stations:
Ohio: WDFM-LP Defiance.
Other Holdings:
Radio..

CLUB COMMUNICATIONS
1129 Comal Dr.
Corpus Christi, TX 78407
Phones: 512-575-5555; 512-814-9830
Fax: 512-855-2718
Ownership: Dr. Michael Mintz, see listing,
49.9%; Ben Benavides, 25.1%; Jerald
Benavides, 25%.

LPTV Stations:
Texas: KUVM-CA Dewalt; KCPV-LP Victoria.

COALDALE TV CLUB
PO Box 2
Coaldale, CO 81222
LPTV Stations:
Colorado: K03FH Coaldale; K10AR Coaldale.

**COCOLA BROADCASTING
COMPANIES LLC**
706 W. Herndon Ave.
Fresno, CA 93650-1033
Phone: 559-435-7000
Fax: 559-435-3201
Web site: www.cocolatv.com
Officers:
Gary M. Cocola, Chairman & Chief Executive
Officer
Todd Lopes, President
Colleen Crouch, Administrative Assistant
Ownership: Gary M. Cocola, sole member &
manager.
Represented (legal): Dow Lohnes PLLC.
LPTV Stations:
California: KBFK-LP Bakersfield; KCBT-LP
Bakersfield; KPMC-LP Bakersfield; KJOI-LP
Caliente; KJKZ-LP Coalinga; KBID-LP Fresno;
KHSC-LP Fresno; KJEO-LP Fresno; KMSG-LP
Fresno; KSDI-LP Fresno; KVHF-LP Fresno;
KYMB-LD Monterey; KMBY-LP Paso Robles;
KVVG-LP Porterville; KRHT-LP Redding;
KCWB-LP Reedley; KSAO-LP Sacramento;
KKDJ-LP Santa Maria; KWSM-LP Santa
Maria; KFAZ-CA Visalia; KMCF-LP Visalia.
Idaho: KBTI-LP Boise; KCBB-LP Boise; KIWB-
LP Boise; KKIC-LP Boise; KZAK-LP Boise;
KBSE-LP Boise, etc..
Commercial TV Stations:
California: KBBC-DT Bishop; KGMC-DT Clovis.
Other Holdings:
Boise Telecasters LP, see listing.

MARCIA COHEN
71 Walnut Rd.
Weston, MA 02493
Phones: 781-431-7002; 202-293-0011
LPTV Stations:
Illinois: W25DW Arbury Hills.
New Jersey: WNAI-LP Springville.

COLINS BROADCASTING CO.
205 S. West St.
Suite A
Visalia, CA 93291
Phone: 209-625-4234
Officers:
Thomas F. Mitts, President
Russell T. Mitts, Vice President
Linda K. Mitts, Secretary
Mary A. Maddox, Assistant Secretary
Ownership: Thomas F. Mitts.
LPTV Stations:
Nebraska: K17CI Beatrice; K18CD Lincoln;
KWAZ-LP Lincoln.
Commercial TV Stations:
Nebraska: KSNB-DT Superior.

**COLORADO PUBLIC TELEVISION
INC.**
2900 Welton St., First Floor
Denver, CO 80205
Phone: 303-296-1212
Fax: 303-296-6680
Officers:
Scott Shirai, Chairman
Gary Burandt, Vice Chairman
Willard D. Rowland, Jr., President & General
Manager

Kim Johnson, Vice President, Braodcast
Nancy Bell, Secretary-Treasurer
Paula DeGroat, Chief Financial Officer
Represented (legal): Mintz Levin Cohn Ferris
Glovsky & Popeo.
LPTV Stations:
Colorado: K11QJ Boulder; K32EO Colorado
Springs.

COLORADO TV MARKETING LLC
PO Box 1223
Aspen, CO 81612
Phone: 866-250-6422
Represented (legal): Cohn & Marks LLP.
LPTV Stations:
Colorado: KCXP-LP Eagle, etc.; K05HE
Glenwood Springs; K44DF Glenwood Springs;
K13QZ Grand Valley; K19CE Montrose; K05GY
New Castle, etc.; K69AO Powderhorn; K26FK
Rulison; K47AC Silt, etc.; KRYD-LP Vail;
K13DE Wolcott.

COLSTRIP TV TAX DISTRICT
PO Box 47
Rosebud County Courthouse
Colstrip, MT 59323-0047
Phone: 406-346-2251
E-mail: rcc@rangeweb.net
Officer:
Daniel D. Watson, Secretary-Treasurer
LPTV Stations:
Montana: K07WJ Colstrip; K09OY Colstrip;
K13PV Colstrip; K61BL Colstrip, etc..

COLUMBUS TV LLC
5805 Farr Oak Dr
Plano, TX 75093
Phone: 972-473-2777
Officer:
James J Joynt, Manager
LPTV Stations:
Ohio: WCSN-LP Columbus.

COMANCHE ENTERPRISES
Box 30552
Billings, MT 59107
Phone: 406-656-3551
LPTV Stations:
Montana: K36EZ Billings.

COMBINED COMMUNICATIONS INC.
PO Box 5037
Bend, OR 97708
Phone: 541-382-5263
Ownership: Charles V. Chackel Trust, Charles
V. & Kathryn F. Chackel Trustees, 49%;
Kathryn F. Chackel Trust, Charles V. &
Kathryn F. Chackel Trustees, 49%; Geoffrey
Chackel, 1%; Ryan Chackel, 1%.
LPTV Stations:
Oregon: KBND-LP Bend.
Radio Stations:
Oregon: KBND (AM), KMTK (FM), KTWS (FM)
Bend; KLRR (FM) Redmond

COMBS BROADCASTING INC.
1812 5th Ave S
Jasper, AL 35501
Phone: 205-387-8320
Fax: 205-384-0408
Officers:
Tommy Combs, President
Linda C. Combs, Secretary-Treasurer
Ownership: Tommy Combs.
Represented (legal): Hardy, Carey, Chautin &
Balkin LLP.

LPTV Stations:
Alabama: W55BJ Jasper.

COMMONWEALTH BROADCASTING
277 Garrison Ave.
Staten Island, NY 10314
Officers:
Robert Neuhaus, Chairman & Chief Operating
Officer
John Davenport, President
Richard Franklin, Chief Executive Officer
Barbara Neuhaus, Vice President, Pennsylvania
& Secretary
Gregory Argila, Treasurer
Joseph Scaramuzzo, Chief Financial Officer

Branch Offices:
Box 824
Keysville, VA 23947
Phone: 800-442-3085
Box 796
Milford, PA 18337
Phone: 717-296-4338
Represented (legal): National Association of
Regulatory Utility Commissioners (NARUC)
LPTV Stations:
Pennsylvania: W18BN Honesdale.

**COMMONWEALTH PUBLIC
BROADCASTING CORP.**
23 Sesame St.
Richmond, VA 23235
Phone: 804-320-1301
Fax: 804-320-8729
Officers:
Charles W. Sydnor Jr., President & Chief
Executive Officer
Frederick W. Thomas, Executive Vice President

Branch Offices:
8101 Lee Hwy.
Falls Church, VA 22042
Phone: 703-698-9682
Box 2021
Charlottesville, VA 22902
Phone: 434-295-7671
Ownership: Non-profit, non-stock corp..
Represented (legal): Wiley Rein LLP.
LPTV Stations:
Virginia: W66BI Danville; W70AP Lovingston;
W39AK Rockfish Valley; W60BM Rustburg;
W73AJ South Boston, etc..
ETV Stations:
Virginia: WHTJ-DT Charlottesville; WNVT-DT
Goldvein; WCVE-DT Richmond; WCVW-DT
Richmond.

**COMMUNICATIONS CORP. OF
AMERICA**
Box 53708
Lafayette, LA 70505
Phone: 337-237-1142
Fax: 337-237-1373
Officer:
Steve Pruett, Chief Executive Officer
Ownership: SP ComCorp LLC, 75%; SPCCLLC
ownership:; SP ComCorp Investments LLC,
Member & Mgr.. 100% votes; SP ComCorp
Holdco 1 LLC, Member, 99%. assets;
SP ComCorp Holdco 2 LLC, 1%. assets;
SPCCILLC ownership:; Edward Mule', 50%.
votes; Robert O'Shea, 50%. votes; SPCCH
1 & 2 LLC ownership:; Edward Mule',
40%. votes; Robert O'Shea, 40%. votes;
Michael Gatto, 20%. votes.
Represented (legal): Dow Lohnes PLLC.
LPTV Stations:
Louisiana: K47DW Alexandria; WBRL-CA Baton
Rouge; K67GL Bunkie; K69HD Church Point;
K61GO Hicks; KLAF-LP Lafayette; K51FO
Leesville; K54FT New Iberia; KOPP-LP
Opelousas.

Texas: K20HD Pecos.
Commercial TV Stations:
Indiana: WEVV-DT Evansville.
Louisiana: WGMB-DT Baton Rouge; KADN-DT Lafayette; KMSS-DT Shreveport.
Mississippi: WNTZ-DT Natchez.
Texas: KVEO-DT Brownsville; KYLE-DT Bryan; KTSM-DT El Paso; KETK-DT Jacksonville; KPEJ-DT Odessa; KWKT-DT Waco.

COMMUNICATIONS TRANSMISSION NETWORK
1905 N. Rancho Rd.
Las Vegas, NV 89106
Phone: 702-896-5457
LPTV Stations:
Texas: KXPX-CA Corpus Christi.

COMMUNITY ACCESS TELEVISION OF SILVER
213 N. Bullard St.
Silver City, NM 88061
Phone: 505-534-0130
E-mail: cats-communityac@qwest.net
Officer:
Herbert W. Marsden, President, Board of Directors
LPTV Stations:
New Mexico: KOOT-LP Silver City.

COMMUNITY TELEVISION DEVELOPMENT
5722 Flamingo Rd.
Suite 229
Fort Lauderdale, FL 33330
LPTV Stations:
New Mexico: K16EB Hobbs.

COMMUNITY TELEVISION EDUCATORS INC.
Box 612066
Dallas, TX 75261
Phone: 214-432-0029
Fax: 817-571-7458
Officers:
Marcus D. Lamb, President
Jonnie F. Lamb, Vice President
Joni Trammel, Secretary
John T. Calender, Director
Ownership: Marcus D Lamb, 25%; John T Calender, 25%; Jonnie F Lamb, 25%; Joni Trammel, 25%.
Represented (legal): Koerner & Olender PC.
LPTV Stations:
Arizona: KDPH-LP Phoenix; KDTP-LP Phoenix.

COMMUNITY TELEVISION NETWORK LLC
219 Salt Grass Place
Melbourne Beach, FL 32951
Phone: 321-729-8451
Officer:
Mark C. Mayo, Chief Executive Officer
Represented (legal): Irwin, Campbell & Tannenwald PC.
LPTV Stations:
Mississippi: WBXK-CA Jackson, etc..

COMMUNITY TV OF SOUTHERN CALIFORNIA
4401 Sunset Blvd.
Los Angeles, CA 90027
Phone: 323-666-6500
Officers:
Bruce M. Ramer, Chairman
Al Jerome, President & Chief Executive Officer
Debbi Hinton, Executive Vice President & Chief Financial Officer

Mary Mazur, Senior Vice President, Programming
Barbara Goen, Senior Vice President, Public Information
Represented (legal): Arent Fox LLP.
LPTV Stations:
California: K46II Bakersfield; K16FC San Luis Obispo; K26FT Santa Barbara; K28GY Santa Barbara; K47CC Victorville.
ETV Stations:
California: KCET-DT Los Angeles.

COMUNIDAD MISIONERA DE ADORACION INC.
17090 N.W. 22nd
Pembroke, FL 33028
Phone: 954-442-0195
Officer:
Pastor Pedro Rivera, President
LPTV Stations:
Florida: W28CP Summerland Key.
Texas: K44GW Hereford.
Wyoming: K14LV Cheyenne.

CONCHAS TELEVISION ASSOCIATION
PO Box 961
Conchas Dam, NM 88416
LPTV Stations:
New Mexico: K16DN Conchas Dam; K06JB Conchas Dam, etc.; K09IA Conchas Dam, etc.; K11JD Conchas Dam, etc..

CONRAD TV DISTRICT
20 SW 4th Ave
Conrad, MT 59425
Phone: 406-271-4040
E-mail: pondes@3rivers.net
Ownership: Cindy Mullaney, Board Member.
LPTV Stations:
Montana: K06IL Conrad; K08DT Conrad; K10DX Conrad; K12DJ Conrad.

CONVERGENCE ENTERTAINMENT & COMMUNICATIONS LLC
PO Box 2423
Plattsburgh, NY 12901
Phone: 518-825-1071
Officer:
Jeff Loper, Manager
Ownership: Jeff Loper, 85%; Harrison Uhl, 15%.
Represented (legal): Scott C. Cinnamon PLLC.
LPTV Stations:
New Hampshire: W17CI Claremont.
New York: W49BI Ellenburg.
Vermont: W54CV Barre; WBVT-CA Burlington; WGMU-CA Burlington; W19BR Monkton; W36CP Newport; W61CE Rutland; W52CD St. Albans.

COOPERATIVE TELEVISION ASSN. OF SOUTHERN MINNESOTA
Benco Electric
PO Box 8
Mankato, MN 56002-0008
Phone: 507-387-7963
Fax: 507-387-1269
Officer:
Dave Sunderman, Manager
LPTV Stations:
Minnesota: K23FY Frost; K18HP Jackson; K19FO Jackson; K49JU-D Jackson; K14KE St. James; K16CG St. James; K21DG St. James; K24CP St. James; K26CS St. James; K29IE-D St. James; K30FN St. James; K32GX-D St. James; K34JX-D St. James; K35DC St. James; K40BU St. James; K41IZ St. James; K42AV St. James; K44AD St. James; K46AA St. James; K48AA

St. James; K49HE St. James; K50AB St. James; K52AB St. James.

COOPER COMMUNICATIONS LLC
215 Lake Blvd.
Suite 26
Redding, CA 96003
Phone: 800-949-8826
Fax: 559-277-9188
E-mail: mcooper@kgec.tv
Officer:
Mildred D. Cooper, Managing Member
Ownership: Mildred D. Cooper, 90%; James Phillips; Tracey Phillips, 10%. jointly.
Represented (legal): Irwin, Campbell & Tannenwald PC.
LPTV Stations:
California: KGEC-LP Redding.

CORE GROUP INTERNATIONAL INC.
2101 L St NW
Ste 402
Washington, DC 20036
Phone: 202-296-4800
E-mail: grb@baplaw.com
Officers:
George R. Borsari, President
Anne Thomas Paxson, Vice President
Ownership: George R. Borsari.
Represented (legal): Borsari & Paxson.
LPTV Stations:
Virginia: W14CY Charlottesville.

CORNERSTONE FAITH CENTER
6000 E. Gordon Dr.
Sioux City, IA 51106
Officer:
Douglas R. Daniels, Chief Financial Officer
LPTV Stations:
Iowa: K54GK Sioux City.

CORNERSTONE TELEVISION INC.
One Signal Hill Dr.
Wall, PA 15148-1499
Phone: 412-824-3930
Fax: 412-824-5442
Web site: www.ctvn.org
Officers:
Oleen Eagle, Chief Executive Officer
David Skeba, Vice President & Director, Programming
Blake Richert, Vice President & Director, Engineering
Dee Richert, Secretary
Ron Hembree, Chief Ministerial Officer
Ownership: Non-profit organization.; Michele Agatston; Oleen Eagle; Dr. William Kofmehl; Dr. Mitchel Nickols; Richard Simmons; Gary Tustin, jointly.
Represented (legal): Pillsbury Winthrop Shaw Pittman LLP.
LPTV Stations:
Pennsylvania: W35BT Harrisburg; W29CO Sharon.
West Virginia: W21CJ Clarksburg.
Commercial TV Stations:
Pennsylvania: WKBS-DT Altoona; WPCB-DT Greensburg.

CORPORACION ADVENTISTA DEL SEPTIMO DIA DEL OESTE DE PUERTO RICO
Box 1629
Mayaguez, PR 00681
Represented (legal): Fletcher, Heald & Hildreth PLC.

LPTV Stations:
Puerto Rico: WTPM-LP Mayaguez & Anasco.

COSTA DE ORO TELEVISION INC.
2323 Corinth Ave.
West Los Angeles, CA 90064
Phone: 310-943-5288
Fax: 310-943-5299
Ownership: Walter F Ulloa, Pres. & Chief Exec. Officer. Ulloa also has interest in Biltmore Broadcasting & Entravision Communications Corp., see listings.
Represented (legal): Thompson Hine LLP.
LPTV Stations:
California: KSMV-LP Los Angeles.
Commercial TV Stations:
California: KJLA-DT Ventura.

CITY OF COUNCIL
PO Box 527
Council, ID 83612
LPTV Stations:
Idaho: K09OA Council; K11HA Council.

COUNTY SERVICE AREA 70 TV5
Box 864
73658 Old Dale Rd.
Twentynine Palms, CA 92277-3280
Phone: 760-367-1833
Officers:
Craig Duckworth, Supervisor, Admin. Services
Jim Parker, Chief Engineer
LPTV Stations:
California: K16FI Twentynine Palms.

COWLES CO.
W 999 Riverside Ave
Spokane, WA 99201-1006
Phone: 509-459-5520
E-mail: q6news@khq.com
Officers:
Elizabeth Allison Cowles, Chairman
William Stacey Cowles, President
Steven R. Rector, Secretary-Treasurer
Ownership: James P Cowles; William Stacey Cowles, Co-Trustees of Various Cowles Family Trusts.
Represented (legal): Skadden, Arps, Slate, Meagher & Flom LLP.
LPTV Stations:
California: KMUV-LP Monterey; K44DN Paso Robles; KKFX-CA San Luis Obispo.
Idaho: K18DT Coeur d'Alene; K35BW Lewiston; K48DX Sandpoint.
Commercial TV Stations:
California: KION-DT Monterey; KCOY-DT Santa Maria.
Washington: KNDU-DT Richland; KHQ-DT Spokane; KNDO-DT Yakima.
Newspapers:
Washington: Spokesman Review; Spokane Journal of Business

COWSERT FAMILY LLC
2400 N. Taylor
Little Rock, AR 72207
LPTV Stations:
Arkansas: KJLR-LP Little Rock; KZJG-LP Little Rock, etc..

COX ENTERPRISES INC.
1400 Lake Hearn Dr. NE
Atlanta, GA 30319
Phone: 404-843-5000
Fax: 404-843-5142
Officers:
James C. Kennedy, Chairman
David E. Easterly, Vice Chairman
Jimmy W Hayes, Chief Executive Officer

G. Dennis Berry, President & Chief Operating Officer

Bruce Baker, President, Cox TV

John M. Dyer, Executive Vice President & Chief Financial Officer

John G. Boyette, Senior Vice President, Investments & Administration

Dale Hughes, Senior Vice President, Strategic Investments & Real Estate Planning.

Timothy W. Hughes, Senior Vice President, Administration

Alexander V. Netchvolodoff, Senior Vice President, Public Policy

Branch Offices:
Public Policy
1225 19th St. NW
Suite 450
Washington, DC 20036
Phone: 202-296-4933
Newspaper
2000 Pennsylvania Ave. NW
Suite 10000
Washington, DC 20006
Phone: 202-331-0900

Broadcasting
400 N. Capitol St.
Suite 189
Washington, DC 20001
Phone: 202-737-0277
Ownership: Dayton Cox Trust-A, 41.06%; Barbara Cox Anthony Atlanta Trust, 28.94%; Anne Cox Chambers Atlanta Trust, 28.94%.
Represented (legal): Dow Lohnes PLLC.
LPTV Stations:
California: K29AB Monterey, etc.; K12PP South Lake Tahoe.
Nevada: K17CA-D Carson City; K51IA Fallon; K36GL Lovelock; K16GM Yerington.
North Carolina: W06AI Marion.
Pennsylvania: W07CD State College; W42DG-D State College.
Washington: K26IC-D Bremerton; K53AZ Centralia, etc.; K58BW Everett; K67GJ Point Pulley, etc.; K30FL Port Angeles; K54GS Puyallup.
Commercial TV Stations:
Florida: WFTV-DT Orlando; WRDQ-DT Orlando.
Georgia: WSB-DT Atlanta.
North Carolina: WSOC-DT Charlotte; WAXN-DT Kannapolis.
Ohio: WHIO-DT Dayton; WTOV-DT Steubenville.
Pennsylvania: WJAC-DT Johnstown; WPXI-DT Pittsburgh.
Washington: KIRO-DT Seattle.
Newspapers:
Colorado: The Daily Sentinel, The Nickel (Grand Junction)
Florida: Palm Beach Daily News; The Palm Beach Post, Florida Pennysaver, LaPalma (West Palm Beach)
Georgia: The Atlanta Journal Constitution, Mundo Hispãnico (Atlanta)
Ohio: Dayton Daily News, JournalNews (Hamilton), Western Star (Lebanon), Fairfield Echo (Liberty Township), Pulse-Journal (Mason), The Middletown Journal, Oxford Press, Springfield News-Sun
Texas: Austin American-Statesman, íahora sf!, Lake Travis View (Austin); Bastrop Advertiser; Longview News-Journal; The Lufkin Daily News; The Marshall News Messenger; The Daily Sentinel (Nacogdoches); North Lake Trav
Radio Stations:
Alabama: WAGG (AM), WZZK-FM Birmingham; WNCB (FM) Gardendale; WBPT (FM) Homewood; WBHJ (FM) Midfield; WBHK (FM) Warrior
Connecticut: WEZN-FM Bridgeport; WPLR (FM) New Haven; WFOX (FM), WNLK (AM) Norwalk; WSTC (AM) Stamford
Florida: WFYV-FM Atlantic Beach; WHQT (FM) Coral Gables; WCFB (FM) Daytona Beach; WSUN-FM Holiday; WAPE-FM, WJGL (FM), WMXQ (FM), WOKV-AM-FM Jacksonville;

WPYD (FM) Maitland; WEDR (FM), WFLC (FM), WHDR (FM) Miami; WDUV (FM) New
Georgia: WSB-AM-FM Atlanta, WBTS (FM) Dora, WSRV (FM) Gainesville, WALR-FM Greenville
Hawaii: KCCN-FM, KINE-FM, KRTR-AM-FM Honolulu; KPHW (FM) Kaneohe; KKNE (AM) Waipahu
Indiana: WSFR (FM) Corydon
Kentucky: WPTI (FM) Louisville; WRKA (FM), WVEZ (FM) St. Matthews
New York: WBAB (FM) Babylon, WBLI (FM) Patchogue, WCTZ (FM) Port Chester
Ohio: WHIO (AM), WHKO (FM) Dayton; WZLR (FM) Xenia
Oklahoma: KKCM (FM) Sand Springs; KJSR (FM), KRAV-FM, KRMG (AM), KWEN (FM) Tulsa
South Carolina: WJMZ-FM Anderson, WHZT (FM) Seneca
Texas: KTHT (FM) Cleveland; KHPT (FM) Conroe; KHTC (FM) Lake Jackson; KKBQ-FM Pasadena; KCYY (FM), KISS-FM, KKYX (AM), KONO (AM) San Antonio; KSMG (FM) Seguin; KPWT (FM) Terrell Hills
Virginia: WDYL (FM) Chester, WKHK (FM) Colonial Heights, WKLR (FM) Fort Lee, WMXB (FM) Richmond
Other Holdings:
Auction company: Manheim Auctions
Cable advertising representative: CableRep Inc.
Production: Rysher Entertainment
Program source: 10.4% E! Entertainment TV Network
Publishing: Auto Trader, Auto Mart & Truck Trader.
Telecommunications company: Interactive Studios: Cox Interactive Media Inc.
TV Station sales representative: TeleRep Inc.; MMT Sales; Harrington, Righter & Parsons.

CRAIG MINISTRIES INC.
345 Main Rd.
Orono, ME 04473
Phone: 207-866-2000
Fax: 207-866-0860
Officers:
Sherwood Craig, Chairman & Chief Executive Officer
Vern Craig, Vice President
LPTV Stations:
Maine: W29CA Brunswick; W57AP Falmouth; W64BY Rockland.

JENNIFER CREMEENS
1017 Autumn Leaf Dr.
Winter Gardens, FL 34787
Phone: 407-654-2908
Represented (legal): Booth Freret Imlay & Tepper PC.
LPTV Stations:
Texas: K67HQ Lubbock.

TOWN OF CRESTED BUTTE
Crested Butte Town Hall, 308 3rd St.
Crested Butte, CO 81224
LPTV Stations:
Colorado: K33EL Crested Butte.

CROWN CASTLE NEVADA LLC
510 Bering Dr.
Houston, TX 77057
Phone: 713-570-3000
E-mail: blake.hawk@crowncastle.com
Officers:
John P. Kelly, Chief Executive Officer
Don Reid, Secretary

LPTV Stations:
Nevada: K54BO Mercury; K45AA Mercury, etc..

CRUZE ELECTRONICS
1905 Palo Dr.
Box 397
Memphis, TX 79245
Phone: 806-259-2879
Ownership: Arnold Cruze.
LPTV Stations:
Texas: K44AK Memphis, etc..

C.T.S. BROADCASTING
5202 Charlemagne
Lilburn, GA 30047
Phone: 678-576-8507
E-mail: masontwoinc@aol.com
Officer:
Jack Mason Taylor, President
LPTV Stations:
Georgia: WAGC-LP Athens.

CTV BROADCASTING LLC
7001 N. 10th
Suite A1
McAllen, TX 78504
Phone: 713-358-4229
Officer:
John A. Orfanos, President
LPTV Stations:
Texas: KEAP-LP Eagle Pass; KJST-LP McAllen; KRGT-LP Rio Grande City; KNHB-LP Uvalde.

TOWN OF CULBERTSON
PO Box 351
Culbertson, MT 59218
Phone: 406-787-5271
LPTV Stations:
Montana: K34GY Culbertson.

CUMBIA ENTERTAINMENT LLC
c/o Charles R. Naftalin, Holland & Knight LLP
2099 Pennsylvania Ave. NW, Suite 100
Washington, DC 20006-6801
Phone: 202-457-7040
E-mail: charles.naftalin@hklaw.com
Officer:
Alejandro Santo Domingo, President & Manager
Ownership: Wepahe Entertainment LLC, 75%; Caracol TV America Corp., 25%; WELLC ownership: Alejandro Santo Domingo; CTAC ownership:; Caracol Television SA (Columbia).
Represented (legal): Holland & Knight LLP.
LPTV Stations:
Florida: W39AC Key West; W21CL Marathon; W38AA Marathon; W63AL Marathon; W49CL Miami; WGEN-LP Miami; WDLP-CA Pompano Beach; W64AN Rock Harbor.
Commercial TV Stations:
Florida: WGEN-DT Key West.

CUSTER COUNTY ROAD & BRIDGE
Box 1669
Westcliffe, CO 81252
Phone: 719-783-2281
E-mail: rboffice@centurytel.net
Officer:
Roger Squire, Information Contact
LPTV Stations:
Colorado: K07BW Westcliffe; K09DY Westcliffe.

CYS INC.
2358 Gatetree Lane SE
Grand Rapids, MI 49546-7590
LPTV Stations:
Alabama: W08DC Birmingham.
California: K08LT Modesto.

New Mexico: K30HS Taos.
Cable Systems:
WISCONSIN: RICHLAND CENTER.

DAIJ MEDIA LLC
912 Curtis St
Pasadena, TX 77502
Phone: 713-589-1336
Ownership: Ruben Villarreal, member.
Represented (legal): Dan J. Alpert.
LPTV Stations:
Texas: KCVH-LP Houston.

D'AMICO BROTHERS BROADCASTING
155 13th St.
Del Mar, CA 92014
Officer:
Richard D'Amico, President
LPTV Stations:
California: K26FA Vista.

THOMAS B. DANIELS
5081 Rivers Ave.
North Charleston, SC 29418
Phone: 843-744-7497
LPTV Stations:
South Carolina: WAZS-LP North Charleston; WJNI-LP North Charleston.

JOHN COLSON DASH
PO Box 100
Bishop, VA 24604
Phone: 276-979-9200
E-mail: johndash@wjdw.net
LPTV Stations:
Tennessee: WDLY-LP Gatlinburg; WJDP-LP Gatlinburg.
Virginia: WJDG-LP Grundy; WJDW-LP Tazewell.

PEGGY L. DAVIS
Box 932
Neosho, MO 64850
Phone: 417-451-1440
LPTV Stations:
Missouri: K38DD Monett.

DC BROADCASTING INC.
4056 W. 107th Court
Westminster, CO 80031
Phones: 303-593-1433; 303-520-9996
Fax: 815-327-4319
Officer:
J. Christopher Blair, President
Represented (legal): Irwin, Campbell & Tannenwald PC.
LPTV Stations:
District of Columbia: WWTD-LP Washington.
Maryland: WRZB-LP Annapolis.

DECATUR COMMUNICATION PROPERTIES LLC
1301 Central Pkwy.
Decatur, AL 35601
Phone: 256-355-4567
LPTV Stations:
Alabama: WYAM-LP Priceville.

DELMARVA BROADCAST SERVICE LLC
222 Pasadena Place
Orlando, FL 32803
Phone: 407-423-4431
Ownership: Marion Brechner, 51%; Berl Brechner, 49%. Brechners also have interest in Brechner Management Co., see listing.
Represented (legal): Fletcher, Heald & Hildreth PLC.

LPTV Stations:
Delaware: WEVD-LP Dover.
Commercial TV Stations:
Maryland: WMDT-DT Salisbury.

DELTA MEDIA CORP.
3501 NW Evangeline Thruway
Carencro, LA 70520
Phone: 337-896-1600
Officer:
Eddie Blanchard, Vice President
Represented (legal): Fletcher, Heald & Hildreth PLC.
LPTV Stations:
Louisiana: KXKW-CA Lafayette; KXKW-LD Lafayette.

DENALI TELEVISION
3002 #2 Industrial Ave.
Fairbanks, AK 99701
Phone: 907-459-2288
E-mail: denalitv@alaska.net
LPTV Stations:
Alaska: K30ET Fairbanks; K34EJ Fairbanks; K36ED Fairbanks; K38EL Fairbanks; K40EN Fairbanks; K42EC Fairbanks; K44EK Fairbanks; K46EH Fairbanks; K48FG Fairbanks; K50EH Fairbanks; K52EY Fairbanks; K54EW Fairbanks; K56FX Fairbanks; K60FQ Fairbanks; K62FB Fairbanks; K64EU Fairbanks; K66FG Fairbanks; K68EZ Fairbanks.

DENTON TV ASSOCIATION
PO Box 887
Denton, MT 59430
LPTV Stations:
Montana: K10HB Denton; K12HP Denton.

DENVER DIGITAL TELEVISION LLC
PO Box 1471
Evergreen, CO 80437
Phone: 303-526-1702
E-mail: ddrucker@wildblue.net
Officer:
David M. Drucker, Manager
Ownership: David M. Drucker, 70%; Penny Drucker, 10%; Ena Lukes Family Trust, 20%.
LPTV Stations:
Colorado: KSBS-LP Denver.
Other Holdings:
Druckers also have interest in Cayo Hueso Networks LLC, Echonet Corp. GreenTV Corp., Ketchikan TV LLC & Polar Communications, see listings..

DESERT MOUNTAIN TV
PO Box 260242
Martin City, MT 59926
Phone: 406-387-5230
E-mail: wa7ywl@msn.com
Officer:
John Barnett, Information Contact
LPTV Stations:
Montana: K05FC Lake McDonald, etc.; K07IT West Glacier, etc.; K10LH West Glacier, etc.; K12LU West Glacier, etc..

DESERT SPRINGS INC.
630 S. Sunrise Way
Palm Springs, CA 92264
Phone: 760-327-2772
LPTV Stations:
California: KPDC-LP Indio.

DESERT TELEVISION LLC
1000 E. Tahquitz Canyon Way
Suite C
Palm Springs, CA 92262
Phone: 760-322-2519
LPTV Stations:
California: KPSP-LP Cathedral City.

DESTINY COMMUNICATIONS LLC
2824 S. Osage
Suite 302
Wichita, KS 67217
Phone: 316-524-5620
Ownership: Darnell Washington.
Represented (legal): Garvey Schubert Barer.
LPTV Stations:
Montana: K47DP Lewistown.
Commercial TV Stations:
Montana: KTGF-DT Great Falls.

LUCINDA DE VAUL
5257 Sandy Circle NW
Canton, OH 44718
Phone: 330-494-9303
Represented (legal): Irwin, Campbell & Tannenwald PC.
LPTV Stations:
Ohio: WIVM-LP Canton.

R. ANTHONY DIMARCANTONIO
95 Public Square
Ste 505
Watertown, NY 13601
Phone: 315-785-0869
Represented (legal): Wiley Rein LLP.
LPTV Stations:
New York: WBQZ-LP Watertown.

DISPATCH BROADCAST GROUP
Box 1010
Columbus, OH 43216
Phone: 614-460-3700
Fax: 614-460-2812
Officers:
Michael J. Fiorile, President & Chief Executive Officer
Thomas S. Stewart, Vice President & General Manager
Marvin Born, Vice President Engineering
Gerald E. Cary, Chief Financial Officer
Ownership: Dispatch Printing Co..
Represented (legal): Sidley Austin LLP.
LPTV Stations:
Indiana: WALV-CA Indianapolis.
Commercial TV Stations:
Indiana: WTHR-DT Indianapolis.
Ohio: WBNS-DT Columbus.
Newspapers:
Ohio: Columbus Dispatch
Radio Stations:
Ohio: WBNS-AM-FM-Columbus

DOCKINS COMMUNICATIONS INC.
540 Maple Valley Dr.
Farmington, MO 64640
Phone: 573-701-9590
Officer:
Fred Dockins, President
LPTV Stations:
Florida: WSFD-LP Perry.

DOVE BROADCASTING INC.
Box 1616
Greenville, SC 29602
Phone: 864-244-1616
Officers:
James H. Thompson, President
Joanne U. Thompson, Vice President
Fred Crain, Secretary
Ownership: James H Thompson, 20%; Joanne U Thompson, 20%; Fred Crain, 20%; Frances Crain, 20%; Cliff Claeson, 20%.

LPTV Stations:
South Carolina: W67DP Columbia.

DREWRY COMMUNICATIONS
811 S.W. D Ave.
Lawton, OK 73501
Phone: 580-355-2250
Fax: 580-355-7531
Web site: www.lcisp.com
Officers:
Robert H. Drewry, Vice President
Larry Patton, Vice President
Ownership: Drewry Family, controlling interest. Drewrys also have interest in Adelante Television Limited Partnership & Panhandle Television, see listings.
LPTV Stations:
Oklahoma: KSWX-LP Duncan.
Commercial TV Stations:
Oklahoma: KSWO-DT Lawton.
Texas: KFDA-DT Amarillo; KWAB-DT Big Spring; KWES-DT Odessa; KXXV-DT Waco.
Other Holdings:
Radio.

DREWSEY COMMUNITY TV
341 N Broadway Ave
Burns, OR 97720
LPTV Stations:
Oregon: K09LJ Drewsey; K13PM Drewsey.

D.T.V. LLC
1903 S. Greeley Hwy.
Suite 127
Cheyenne, WY 82007
Phones: 603-520-1127; 800-536-7327
E-mail: dtv@usa.com
Ownership: Randolph Weigner, Pres..
Represented (legal): Irwin, Campbell & Tannenwald PC.
LPTV Stations:
California: KBOP-CA San Diego.
Georgia: WIRE-CA Atlanta.
Ohio: WRAP-CA Cleveland.
Pennsylvania: WPHA-CA Philadelphia.
Texas: KSEX-LP Dallas.
Vermont: W21CQ Bennington, etc..
Other Holdings:
LPTV Stations: See also Boston Broadcasting Corp. & Sunshine Broadcasting Co. Inc..

DUCHESNE COUNTY
Box 270
Duchesne, UT 84021
Officers:
Larry A. Ross, Chairman & Commissioner
Guy Thayne, Commissioner
Diane Freston, Duchesne County Clerk
LPTV Stations:
Utah: K03CN Duchesne; K29EZ Fruitland, etc.; K19EY Myton; K27GN Myton; K41GT Myton; K25HH Myton, etc.; K47HA Roosevelt.

MURRAY DUFFY
699 Bozeman
Box 777
Bozeman, MT 59715
LPTV Stations:
Montana: K11UJ Bozeman.

DUHAMEL BROADCASTING ENTERPRISES
Box 1760
Rapid City, SD 57709-1760
Phone: 605-342-2000
Fax: 605-342-7305
Officers:
William F. Duhamel Sr., President & Chief Executive Officer
Dr. Peter A. Duhamel, Vice President

Monte Loos, Chief Operating Officer
Susan Hastings, Chief Financial Officer
Ownership: William F Duhamel Sr., 63%; Dr. Peter A Duhamel, 37%.
Represented (legal): Pillsbury Winthrop Shaw Pittman LLP.
LPTV Stations:
Nebraska: K02NT Scottsbluff.
Wyoming: K06JM Gillette.
Commercial TV Stations:
Nebraska: KDUH-DT Scottsbluff.
South Dakota: KHSD-DT Lead; KOTA-DT Rapid City.
Wyoming: KSGW-DT Sheridan.
Radio Stations:
South Dakota: KOTA (AM), KQRQ (FM) Rapid City; KDDX (FM) Spearfish

DULUTH DATACASTING PARTNERS GP
860 U.S. Hwy. 1
Suite 108
North Palm Beach, FL 33408
Phone: 800-948-7101
LPTV Stations:
Minnesota: KWMN-LP Duluth.

DULUTH-SUPERIOR AREA ETV CORP.
1202 E. University Circle
Duluth, MN 55811
Phone: 218-724-8567
Officers:
Gilbert E. Sidney, President
Dale W. App, Vice President
Edward K. Blanck Jr., Secretary-Treasurer
Ownership: Non-profit corp..
Represented (legal): Arent Fox LLP.
LPTV Stations:
Minnesota: K67CT Grand Marais.
ETV Stations:
Minnesota: WDSE-DT Duluth.

DUNN BROADCASTING CO
300 SE Riverside Dr
Ste 100
Evansville, IN 47713-1036
Phone: 812-471-9300
Fax: 812-471-0230
E-mail: jmdunn@dunnhospitality.com
Ownership: John M Dunn, Pres.. See also Dunn Family LP.
Represented (legal): Irwin, Campbell & Tannenwald PC.
LPTV Stations:
Indiana: WTSN-LP Evansville; WYYW-LP Evansville.

DUNN FAMILY LP
300 SE Riverside Dr
Ste 100
Evansville, IN 47713-1026
Phone: 812-471-9300
Fax: 812-471-0230
Ownership: Kathy Dunn Jagielski, 30%; Heather Dunn Niemeier, 30%; Holly Dunn Pendleton, 30%; John M Dunn, 10%. John M Dunn is also principal of Dunn Broadcasting Co., see listing.
Represented (legal): Fletcher, Heald & Hildreth PLC.
LPTV Stations:
Indiana: WTSN-LP Evansville; WYYW-LP Evansville.

DUTCHESS COMMUNITY COLLEGE
53 Pendell Rd.
Poughkeepsie, NY 12601-1595
Phone: 845-431-8947
Fax: 845-431-8985

Web site: www.tv42.org
Officers:
D. David Conklin, President & Chief Executive Officer
W. John Dunn, Chief Financial Officer
Ownership: SUNY-State University of New York, (Dutchess County, NY).
Represented (legal): Schwartz, Woods & Miller.
LPTV Stations:
New York: W42AE Poughkeepsie.

EAGLE BROADCASTING GROUP INC.
PO Box 573
227 E Main St
Jackson, OH 45640
Phone: 740-286-3537
Officer:
Joseph D Kirby, Secretary
LPTV Stations:
Ohio: W59DL Chillicothe; WTZP-LP Portsmouth.

EAGLE NEST TV ASSN.
Box 372
Angel Fire, NM 87710
Phone: 505-377-6651
E-mail: ncountry@angelfirenm.us
Officer:
Stanley R. Samuels, President
Represented (legal): Fletcher, Heald & Hildreth PLC.
LPTV Stations:
New Mexico: K09AK Eagle Nest; K20GO Eagle Nest; K35BZ Eagle Nest; K48AX Eagle Nest.

EAGLE VALLEY TV CORP.
PO Box 101
Eagle, CO 18130
Phone: 970-328-6244
Officer:
Sally Metcalf, Director
LPTV Stations:
Colorado: K07DB Wolcott & Eagle.

JOSEPH V. EARLY
One S Main
Sylacauga, AL 35150
Phone: 256-249-4348
Represented (legal): Hall Estill.
LPTV Stations:
Alabama: W63CK Talladega; WOIL-LP Talladega.

EAST BUTTE TV CLUB INC.
303 Galletin St
Shelby, MT 59474-1681
Phone: 406-434-2207
E-mail: mcranch@hughes.net
Ownership: Larry McCormick, Trustee.
LPTV Stations:
Montana: K54AMK51KO Joplin; K61BZ Sweetgrass, etc.; K63AQ Sweetgrass, etc.; K65DK Sweetgrass, etc.; K36DK Toole, etc.; K38DZ Toole, etc.; K40DG Toole, etc.; K42DD Toole, etc..

EASTERN NEW MEXICO U. BOARD OF REGENTS
52 Broadcast Center
Portales, NM 88130-9989
Phone: 505-562-2112
Fax: 505-562-2590
Officers:
Jay Gurley, Chairman, Board of Regents
Blaine Hess, President, Board of Regents
Dr. Steven G. Gamble, President
Tanya Miller, Secretary-Treasurer
LPTV Stations:
New Mexico: K29FM-D Artesia; K49ES Carlsbad; K51DX Clovis; K34EZ Forrest & McAllister;

K21IM-D Fort Sumner; K34GU Fort Sumner; K42FX-D Hobbs; K46HM Lovington; K31GS-D Roswell; K49EW Ruidoso; K18GQ Ruidoso, etc.; K35GU Ruidoso, etc.; K30HD-D Tucumcari; K32FE Tucumcari.
ETV Stations:
New Mexico: KENW-DT Portales.
Other Holdings:
Radio.

EASTERN SIERRA BROADCASTING
PO Box 1254
Alameda, CA 94501
Phone: 510-769-5904
Officer:
Chris Kidd, President
LPTV Stations:
Nevada: KRRI-LP Reno.

EAST GLACIER TV ASSOCIATION
PO Box 175
East Glacier, MT 59434
LPTV Stations:
Montana: K08IU East Glacier; K10MK East Glacier Park; K13EJ East Glacier Park.

EAST SIDE ENTERPRISES
857 Daisy Circle
Hudson, WI 54016
LPTV Stations:
Iowa: K33ED Iowa Falls, etc..

E. C. DEVELOPMENT VENTURES
600 Harmon Loop Rd
Dededo, MP 96929
Phone: 671-637-5826
Officer:
Jay Lather, Chief Executive Officer
Ownership: Carmen T. Calvo, 20%; Eduardo A. Calvo, 20%; John T. Calvo, 20%; Joseph G. Calvo, 20%; Leonard P. Calvo, 20%.
LPTV Stations:
Guam: K28HS Agana; K30HB Agana; K32GB Agana; K36GJ Agana.

ECHONET CORP.
400 Inverness Pkwy
Ste 250
Englewood, CO 80112
Phone: 720-266-1040
Officers:
David M. Drucker, President
Candy M. Ergen, Secretary-Treasurer
Ownership: Candy M. Ergen, 40%; Charles Ergen, 40%; David M. Drucker, 20%. Drucker also has interest in Cayo Hueso Networks LLC, Denver Digital Television LLC, GreenTV Corp., Ketchikan TV LLC & Polar Communications, see listings.
LPTV Stations:
Wyoming: K49AY Cheyenne.

EDUCABLE CORP.
240 Woodcrest Rd.
Rochester, NY 14616
Phone: 585-227-7710
Officers:
Brian J. Caterino, President
Angelina L. Caterino, Vice President
John Kells, Secretary-Treasurer
Represented (legal): Irwin, Campbell & Tannenwald PC.
LPTV Stations:
New York: WGCE-CA Greece/Rochester.

EDUCATIONAL BROADCASTING NETWORK
38 New Dawn Circle
Chico, CA 95928

Phone: 530-243-5622
Officers:
Mark C. Allen, Co-Chairman
Russ Thane, Co-Chairman
LPTV Stations:
California: KACX-LP Red Bluff.

EICB-TV LLC
406 Copeland Dr.
Cedar Hill, TX 75104
Phone: 972-291-3750
E-mail: randy@crosstalk.org
Officer:
Dr. Randall A. Weiss, Manager
LPTV Stations:
Arizona: K42IQ-D Flagstaff.
California: KTBV-LD Bakersfield; K20IM Barstow; K68GT Eureka; KQSX-LP Redding; KVFR-LP Redding.
Colorado: K38JD Durango; KHGS-LP Glenwood Springs; K30IU Grand Junction; KHSB-LP Steamboat Springs.
Kansas: K32HB Manhattan; K40IJ-D Manhattan; K41KX Pittsburg.
Maine: W31CX Bangor.
Maryland: W35CS Ocean City; W23DF Salisbury.
Minnesota: KHVM-LD Mankato; KTCJ-LD Royalton.
Mississippi: W42DD Meridian.
Montana: K45KS Billings; K51KR Billings; K34II Butte.
Nebraska: K50JI North Platte.
New Mexico: K45JA Hobbs; K50IP Hobbs.
New York: WTKJ-LP Philadelphia.
North Carolina: WHOB-LP Buxton.
North Dakota: K43JQ Bismarck; K47KA Minot.
Oklahoma: K43LK Lawton; KUOT-CA Oklahoma City.
Oregon: K28JE Bend; KHPN-LP Warrenton.
Texas: KHFD-LD Greenville.
Wyoming: K31HT Casper; K34HZ Cody; K24GZ Rock Springs.

EKALAKA COMMUNITY TV CLUB
PO Box 14
Ekalaka, MT 59324-0014
Phone: 406-775-6618
E-mail: delmarj@midrivers.com
Officer:
Louise Dague, Secretary-Treasurer
LPTV Stations:
Montana: K07EQ Ekalaka; K09BE Ekalaka; K13LN Ekalaka.

ELIZABETH CITY STATE U.
1704 Weeksville Rd.
Elizabeth City, NC 27909
Phone: 252-335-3690
Fax: 252-335-3770
LPTV Stations:
North Carolina: W18BB Elizabeth City.

ELK BEND TV, UNINCORPORATED ASSOCIATION
H.C. 61
PO Box 72
Slamon, ID 83467
LPTV Stations:
Idaho: K07SZ Elk Bend.

ELKO TELEVISION DISTRICT
881 5th St
Elko, NV 89801-3503
Phone: 775-738-5025
Fax: 775-738-4712
Officers:
Charles E. d'Asto, President
Stanley A. Zunino, Secretary-Treasurer
LPTV Stations:
Nevada: K40CA Beowawe; K05JU Elko; K06MK Elko; K08LS Elko; K15EE Elko; K17DT Elko;

K19FZ Elko; K23FC Elko; K25FR Elko; K32GK Elko; K34HE Elko; K38IF Elko; K47HP Elko; K50CA Elko; K55IK Elko; K57GR Elko; K59EV Elko; K05LP Ryndon; K06NY Ryndon; K08NQ Ryndon; K12PT Ryndon; K16FV Ryndon; K18GT Ryndon; K02KS Ryndon, etc.; K12MS Spring Creek Mobile Home Park; K33HD Star Valley; K04JR Star Valley; K39GL Star Valley; K08IO Wells; K22GW Wells; K24GE Wells; K26JB Wells; K20JQ Wells, etc..

ELLERBECK FAMILY PARTNERS II LTD.
720 N Post Oak Rd
Ste 230
Houston, TX 77024
Phone: 713-975-1133
LPTV Stations:
Arkansas: K36EH Fort Smith.

RUTH E. ELLERBECK
710 N Post Oak Rd
Ste 350
Houston, TX 77024
Phone: 713-975-1133
LPTV Stations:
Arkansas: K14JJ Fort Smith.

DAVID ELLINGTON
Box 617
Webb, MS 38966
Phone: 601-375-9212
LPTV Stations:
Mississippi: WPRQ-LP Clarksdale; WHCQ-LP Cleveland; WEBU-LP Webb.

ELLIS COMMUNICATIONS INC.
1180 Northmoor Ct
Atlanta, GA 30327
Phone: 404-229-8080
Officers:
U. Bertram Ellis Jr., President
James Altenbach, Secretary
Ownership: U. Bertram Ellis Jr..
Represented (legal): Goldberg, Godles, Wiener & Wright.
LPTV Stations:
California: K23DT Tahoe City.
Nevada: K32GW-D Carson City; K35AX Hawthorne, etc.; K34BL Lovelock.
Commercial TV Stations:
Nevada: KAME-DT Reno.

EMERY COUNTY
PO Box 817
Castle Dale, UT 84513-0817
Phone: 435-381-5678
E-mail: bmills1@ecso.com
Officer:
R. Bret Mills, Communications Specialist
LPTV Stations:
Utah: K17HR-D Emery; K19GK-D Emery; K21HZ-D Emery; K23IE-D Emery; K25JA-D Emery; K27IS-D Emery; K29HK-D Emery; K35DW Emery; K39DV Emery; K41GV Emery; K43EV Emery; K45GP Emery; K47HD Emery; K49GB Emery; K16EW Orangeville; K18FZ Orangeville; K20GP Orangeville; K24FI Orangeville; K26EM Orangeville; K28GZ Orangeville; K32FR Orangeville; K36IF-D Orangeville; K38KP-D Orangeville; K40KD-D Orangeville; K47KK-D Orangeville; K48KK-D Orangeville; K49JJ-D Orangeville; K50JS-D Orangeville.

VILLAGE OF EMMONAK
5900 E. Tudor Rd.
Anchorage, AK 99507
Phone: 907-269-5744

LPTV Stations:
Alaska: K07OP Emmonak.

ENGLE BROADCASTING
PO Box 288
Cedar Brook, NJ 08018
Phone: 856-767-8884
Fax: 856-768-9084
Ownership: Barbara E. Ciric;   Paul Engle,
Partners.
LPTV Stations:
New Jersey: WPSJ-LP Hammonton, etc..

ENLACE CHRISTIAN TELEVISION INC
2021 S Harvard St
Irving, TX 75061
Phone: 469-499-0832
Officer:
Jonas Gonzalez, President
LPTV Stations:
Florida: W56EB Tampa.
Nevada: K41IO Las Vegas.
Texas: K34FM Austin; K44HH Lubbock.

ENTRAVISION COMMUNICATIONS CORP.
2425 Olympic Blvd.
Suite 6000 W
Santa Monica, CA 90404
Phone: 310-447-3870
Officers:
Walter F. Ulloa, Chairman & Chief Executive
Officer
Philip C. Wilkinson, President & Chief Operating
Officer
Christopher T. Young, Executive Vice President,
Treasurer & Chief Financial Officer
Larry E. Safir, Executive Vice President
Jeffrey A. Liberman, President, Radio Division
Paul A. Zevnik, Secretary
Mark A. Boelke, General Counsel, Vice
President, Legal Affairs & Secretary
Ownership: Walter F Ulloa, 12.36%;   Philip
C Wilkinson, 7.2%;   Paul A Zevnik,
4.52%;   Univision Communications Inc.,
16%;   remainder publicly held. See also
listings for Biltmore Broadcasting & Costa
de Oro Television Inc.
Represented (legal): Thompson Hine LLP.
LPTV Stations:
California: KEVC-CA Indio; KVER-CA Indio;
K100G Lompoc; KVES-LP Palm Springs;
K17GO Paso Robles; KDJT-CA Salinas/
Monterey, etc.; KBNT-CA San Diego; KDTF-
LP San Diego; KSZZ-LP San Diego; KTCD-LP
San Diego; KTSB-LP Santa Barbara; K35ER
Santa Maria; KREN-LP Susanville; KHAX-LP
Vista.
Colorado: KDVT-LP Denver; K43FN Fort Collins;
K54IK Fort Collins; KGHB-CA Pueblo, etc..
Connecticut: WUTH-CA Hartford.
District of Columbia: WMDO-CA Washington.
Florida: W47DA Melbourne; WVCI-LP Orlando;
WVEA-LP Tampa.
Nevada: KNNC-LP Battle Mountain; KELV-LP
Las Vegas; KNTL-LP Laughlin; KWWB-LP
Mesquite, etc.; KNCV-LP Reno; KNVV-
LP Reno; KRNS-CA Reno; KPMP-LP
Winnemucca.
New Mexico: KTFA-LP Albuquerque.
Texas: KVTF-CA Brownsville; KTIZ-LP Harlingen;
KFTN-CA La Feria; KETF-CA Laredo; KXOF-
CA Laredo; KBZO-LP Lubbock; KSFE-LP
McAllen; KTFV-CA McAllen; KANG-CA San
Angelo; KEUS-LP San Angelo.
Commercial TV Stations:
California: KVYE-DT El Centro; KSMS-DT
Monterey; KPMR-DT Santa Barbara.
Colorado: KCEC-DT Denver; KVSN-DT Pueblo.
Connecticut: WUVN-DT Hartford.

Florida: WVEN-DT Daytona Beach; WVEA-DT
Venice.
Kansas: KDCU-DT Derby.
Maryland: WJAL-DT Hagerstown.
Massachusetts: WUNI-DT Worcester.
Nevada: KINC-DT Las Vegas; KREN-DT Reno.
New Mexico: KLUZ-DT Albuquerque.
Texas: KORO-DT Corpus Christi; KINT-DT El
Paso; KTFN-DT El Paso; KLDO-DT Laredo;
KNVO-DT McAllen; KUPB-DT Midland.
Radio Stations:
Arizona: KVVA-FM Apache Junction, KMIA
(AM) Black Canyon City, KDVA (FM)
Buckeye
California: KSSE (FM) Arcadia, KSEH (FM)
Brawley, KXSE (FM) Davis, KWST (AM)
El Centro, KSSD (FM) Fallbrook, KMXX
(FM) Imperial, KCVR (AM) Lodi, KRCX-FM
Marysville, KDLE (FM) Newport Beach,
KTSE-FM Patterson, KLYY (FM) Riverside,
K
Colorado: KPVW (FM) Aspen, KMXA (AM)
Aurora, KJMN (FM) Castle Rock, KXPK
(FM) Evergreen
Nevada: KRRN (FM) Dolan Springs, KQRT
(FM) Las Vegas, KRNV-FM Reno
New Mexico: KRZY-AM-FM Albuquerque
Texas: KKPS (FM) Brownsville; KVLY (FM)
Edinburg; KHRO (AM), KINT-FM, KOFX (FM),
KSVE (AM), KYSE (FM) El Paso; KFRQ
(FM) Harlingen; KGOL (AM) Humble; KBZO
(AM) Lubbock; KNVO-FM Port Isabel; KAIQ
(FM) Wolfforth
Other Holdings:
Television holdings: Limited voting interest
in licensees of XHAS-TV, San Diego,
CA-Tijuana, Mexico & XUPN-TV, Tecate,
Baja California, Mexico..

EQUITY MEDIA HOLDINGS CORP., DEBTOR IN POSSESSION
One Shackleford Dr.
Suite 400
Little Rock, AR 72211
Phones: 501-219-2400; 501-221-0400
Fax: 501-221-1101
Officers:
John E. Oxendine, Chief Executive Officer
Larry E Morton, President & Chief Executive
Officer, Retro Programming Services Inc.
Gregory W. Fess, Senior Vice President &
Chief Operating Officer
Mario B. Ferrari, Chief Strategic Officer
Thomas M Arnost, President & Chief Executive
Officer, Equity Broadcasting Corp.
Mark Dvornik, Executive Vice President, Retro
Television Network
James H. Hearnsberger, Vice President,
Administration & Finance
Patrick Doran, Chief Financial Officer
Glenn Charlesworth, Vice President & Chief
Accounting Officer
Lori Withrow, Corporate Secretary
Ownership: Harry G. Luken III, 16.08%;
Greg Fess, 5.91%;   RPCP Investments
LLC, 5.89%. Luken has interest in Luken
Broadcasting LLC & Luken Communications
LLC, see listings. Equity filed for Chapter 11
bankruptcy protection December 8, 2008.
Chief Restructuring Officer is Kim Kelly.
Represented (legal): Irwin, Campbell &
Tannenwald PC.
LPTV Stations:
Alabama: W23DJ Dothan; WDTH-LP Dothan.
Arkansas: KHMF-CA Bentonville; K47JG El
Dorado; KEGW-LP Fayetteville; KFFS-CA
Fayetteville; K32GH Fort Smith; K33HE
Fort Smith; K48FL Fort Smith; KFDF-CA
Fort Smith; KPBI-CA Fort Smith; KUFS-LP
Fort Smith; KWFT-LP Fort Smith; KXUN-LP
Fort Smith; KRBF-CA Hindsville; KTVV-
LP Hot Springs; KHUG-LP Little Rock;
KKYK-CA Little Rock; KLRA-LP Little Rock;

KRAH-CA Paris; KWBK-LP Pine Bluff; KEJC-
LP Sheridan; KKAF-CA Siloam Springs;
KJBW-CA Springdale; KWNL-CA Winslow.
California: KIMG-LP Ventura.
Colorado: KQDK-CA Aurora.
Florida: WFPI-LP Fort Pierce; WBSP-CA Naples;
W56EJ Williston; W63DB Williston.
Mississippi: WJXF-LP Jackson.
Missouri: KNJE-LP Aurora; KBBL-CA Springfield.
Montana: KEXI-LP Kalispell.
Oklahoma: K64GJ Lawton; KUOK-CA Norman;
KSJF-CA Poteau.
Texas: KAMT-LP Amarillo; KEAT-LP Amarillo;
KEYU-LP Amarillo; KUTW-LP Somerville;
KWKO-LP Waco; KTWW-LP Wichita Falls;
KUWF-LP Wichita Falls.
Wyoming: KDEV-LP Cheyenne; K61DX Laramie;
K21CV Rawlins.
Commercial TV Stations:
Nebraska: KTUW-DT Scottsbluff.
Nevada: KBNY-DT Ely.
Texas: KEYU-DT Borger.
Wyoming: KQCK-DT Cheyenne.

ESI BROADCASTING CORP.
860 U.S. Hwy. 1
Suite 108
North Palm Beach, FL 33408
Phone: 561-694-1280
Officers:
Mike Stocklin, President
Kevin Hessee, Vice President
Claudia Hessee, Chief Financial Officer
Ownership: Mike Stocklin, 50%; Kevin Hessee,
50%.
Represented (legal): Rini Coran PC.
LPTV Stations:
Hawaii: KOIW-LP Mountain View.

ESTEEM BROADCASTING LLC
13865 E Elliott Dr
Marshall, IL 62441
Phone: 217-826-6095
Ownership: David L. Bailey, Pres..
Represented (legal): Drinker Biddle.
LPTV Stations:
Virginia: W43BO Marion.
Commercial TV Stations:
North Carolina: WFXI-DT Morehead City.
Tennessee: WEMT-DT Greeneville.

ETC COMMUNICATIONS INC.
PO Box 850
Sheffield, AL 35660-0850
Phone: 256-810-2497
Fax: 888-817-9950
Officer:
Karen Snead-White, Chief Executive Officer
Ownership: Karen Snead-White, Executrix,
Lester W. White Estate. Lester W. White
died December 14, 2005.
Represented (legal): Irwin, Campbell &
Tannenwald PC.
LPTV Stations:
Georgia: W53CG Vidalia.
Tennessee: WLLP-CA Lawrenceburg.

ETERNAL FAMILY NETWORK
201 S. 5th St.
St. Louis, MO 63301
LPTV Stations:
Missouri: KEFN-CA St. Louis.

ETERNAL TRUTH NETWORK INC.
Rte. 1
Box 230-B
Grapeland, TX 75844
Phone: 409-687-4310

LPTV Stations:
Texas: K24DS Palestine.

DAN ETULAIN
520 Lake St.
Sitka, AK 99835
Phone: 907-747-8200
Represented (legal): Garvey Schubert Barer.
LPTV Stations:
Alaska: KACN-LP Anchorage; KATH-LP Juneau-
Douglas; KSCT-LP Sitka.

EUREKA COUNTY TELEVISION DISTRICT
PO Box 633
110 S Main St
Eureka, NV 89316
LPTV Stations:
Nevada: K09XP Beowawe; K12HY Beowawe;
K18GW Beowawe; K20HX Beowawe; K30HF
Beowawe; K02OK Beowawe, etc.; K04GD
Beowawe, etc.; K36DC Beowawe, etc.;
K15GS Duckwater, etc.; K29GM Duckwater,
etc.; K17FY Eureka; K40CI Eureka; K42CL
Eureka; K44CP Eureka; K47DG Eureka;
K51GR Eureka; K21GJ Eureka, etc..

EVANS BROADCASTING OF CHICO LLC
308 8th Ave E
Palmetto, FL 34221
Phone: 941-721-0929
Officers:
William Guy Evans, President
Janice Atkinson Evans, Secretary
Ownership: William Guy Evans, 51%; Janice
Atkinson Evans, 49%.
Represented (legal): Fletcher, Heald & Hildreth
PLC.
LPTV Stations:
California: K42HL Oroville.
Commercial TV Stations:
California: KNVN-DT Chico.

EVENING POST PUBLISHING CO.
134 Columbus St.
Charleston, SC 29403-4800
Phone: 843-577-7111
E-mail: publiceditor@postandcourier.com
Officers:
Peter Manigault, Chairman
Ivan V. Anderson Jr., President & Chief
Executive Officer
Terrance F. Hurley, TV Group President
Travis O. Rockey, Executive Vice President &
Chief Operating Officer
Arthur M. Wilcox, Secretary
James W. Martin, Treasurer & Chief Financial
Officer
Mary M. Gilbreth, Assistant Secretary

Branch Office:
Cordillera Communications Inc.
11 E. Superior St.
Suite 518
Duluth, MN 55802
Phone: 218-625-2260
Fax: 218-625-2261
Ownership: Peter Manigault, Principal.
Represented (legal): Dow Lohnes PLLC.
LPTV Stations:
Arizona: K20FO Sierra Vista.
California: K59CD Santa Barbara.
Montana: K26DE Bozeman; KXLH-LP Helena;
K48AI Joplin; K18AJ Kalispell; K45CS
Lewistown; K10GF Miles City.
Commercial TV Stations:
Arizona: KVOA-DT Tucson.
California: KSBY-DT San Luis Obispo.
Colorado: KOAA-DT Pueblo.
Kentucky: WLEX-DT Lexington.

Louisiana: KATC-DT Lafayette.
Montana: KTVQ-DT Billings; KBZK-DT Bozeman; KXLF-DT Butte; KRTV-DT Great Falls; KPAX-DT Missoula.
Texas: KRIS-DT Corpus Christi.
Newspapers:
North Carolina: The Clemmons Courier, Davie County Enterprise, The Salisbury Post
South Carolina: Aiken Standard; The Charleston Mercury, The Post and Courier (Charleston); The Georgetown Times; Goose Creek Gazette; The Journal (James Island-Folly Beach); The (Kingtree) News; The Berkeley Independent (Monck
Texas: The Eagle (Bryan-College Station)
Other Holdings:
Features syndicator: Editor's Press Service Inc. (International)
Service company: White Oak Forestry Corp. (timberland management).

EXITOS HISPANIC BROADCASTING INC.
314 S Redwood Rd
Salt Lake City, UT 84104
Phone: 801-954-8821
Fax: 801-973-7145
Officer:
Victor Galindo, President
LPTV Stations:
Utah: K22IT Provo; K59GS Salt Lake City; K49GD Spanish Fork.

EZ-TV INC.
PO Box 227
Bigfork, MN 56628
Phone: 218-743-3131
Officer:
Jeffrey J. Ortman, Chief Executive Officer
LPTV Stations:
Minnesota: K67CA Bigfork, etc.; K69CR Bigfork, etc.; K60BL Max, etc.; K62BH Max, etc..

FAITH ASSEMBLY OF GOD OF SUMMERVILLE
337 Farmington Rd
Summerville, SC 29483
Phone: 843-873-9128
Officer:
Larry Burgbacher, Chairman
Represented (legal): Shelbourne Law.
LPTV Stations:
South Carolina: WLCN-CA Charleston.

FAITH BROADCASTING NETWORK INC.
Box 1010
Marion, IL 62959-1010
Phone: 618-997-9333
Fax: 618-997-1859
E-mail: cmmay@maylawoffices.com
Officers:
Garth W. Coonce, President
Christina M. Coonce, Vice President
Michael J. Daly, Secretary
Charles Payne, Treasurer
Julie Nolan, Assistant Secretary
Ownership: Non-profit organization--Marion, IL; Garth W. Coonce; Christina M. Coonce; Charles Payne; Victoria Clark; Julie Nolan, 20%. votes, each.
Represented (legal): Colby M. May.
LPTV Stations:
New York: WBNF-CA Buffalo.
Commercial TV Stations:
New York: WNYB-DT Jamestown.

FAITH CHRISTIAN CHURCH INC.
3401 N. Norris
Clovis, NM 88101
Phone: 505-762-7751
Officer:
Virginia McCreery, Secretary
Represented (legal): Fletcher, Heald & Hildreth PLC.
LPTV Stations:
New Mexico: KFCL-LP Clovis.

FAITH PLEASES GOD CHURCH CORP.
Box 530777
Harlingen, TX 78553-0777
Phone: 956-428-4848
Officers:
John Jacobson, Vice President
Aracelis Ortiz, Vice President-Secretary
Minerva Jacobson, Treasurer
Ownership: Aracelis Ortiz, see listing; John Jacobson; Minerva Jacobson.
LPTV Stations:
Texas: KXIV-LP Brownsville; KSTI-LP McAllen.

FAITH TV
PO Box 1227
Lewiston, ID 83501
Officer:
Rev. Ray Tucker, Information Contact
LPTV Stations:
Idaho: K39CT Cottonwood, etc..

FAMILY BROADCASTING GROUP INC.
Box 95188
Oklahoma City, OK 73143
Phone: 405-631-7335
E-mail: info@ksbitv.com
Officers:
Brady M. Brus, President
Brenda Deimund, Vice President
Angela Brus, Secretary-Treasurer
Ownership: Brady M. Brus, 21.18%; Angela Brus, 20.54%; Seekfirst Media Partners LLC, 14.4%; Janet S Bowie Trust, 12.84%; Aubrey K McClendon, 12.4%; Ward Family Enterprises LP, c/o Tom L. Ward, 12.4%; McClendon Venture Co, c/o Aubrey K McClendon, 3.1%; TLW Venture Co LLC, c/o Tom L. Ward, 3.1%.
Represented (legal): Booth Freret Imlay & Tepper PC.
LPTV Stations:
Kansas: KFVT-LP Wichita.
Oklahoma: K35CU Ada; K17FB Ardmore; K45EJ Enid; K20HO Lawton; K51EK McAlester; K14LD Muskogee; KXOC-LP Oklahoma City; K54FZ Ponca City; K21DF Stillwater; K13XU Tulsa; K15DA Tulsa.
Texas: K48HU Wichita Falls.
Commercial TV Stations:
Oklahoma: KSBI-DT Oklahoma City.

FAMILY MEDIA INC.
PO Box 108
Miami, OK 74355
Phones: 918-541-1934; 800-383-8491
Fax: 918-541-1939
E-mail: jerryturner@familymediainc.com
Web site: www.greencountrytv.com
Officer:
Jerry R. Turner, President
LPTV Stations:
Oklahoma: KELF-LP Miami.

FAMILY STATIONS INC.
4135 Northgate Blvd.
Suite One
Sacramento, CA 95834

Phone: 916-641-8191
Fax: 916-641-8238
E-mail: info@familyradio.org
Officers:
Harold Camping, President
Richard Van Dyk, Secretary-Treasurer
Ownership: Harold Camping; Richard Van Dyke; David Morrell; William Thornton.
Represented (legal): Irwin, Campbell & Tannenwald PC.
LPTV Stations:
California: K02OA Chico; K11VZ-D Chico; KKPM-CA Chico; K15EK Fresno; K15ET Fresno; K40HE Redding; KRDT-CA Redding; KFTL-CA San Francisco, etc..
ETV Stations:
New Jersey: WFME-DT West Milford.
Radio Stations:
Alabama: WBFR (FM) Birmingham
Arizona: KPHF (FM) Phoenix
California: KFRB (FM) Bakersfield, KHAP (FM) Chico, KFRP (FM) Coalinga, KECR (AM) El Cajon, KFNO (FM) Fresno, KEFR (FM) Le Grand, KFRN (AM) Long Beach, KEBR (AM) Rocklin, KEAR-AM-FM San Francisco, KHFR (FM) Santa Maria, KFRS (FM) So
Colorado: KFRY (FM) Pueblo
Connecticut: WCTF (AM) Vernon
Florida: WMFL (FM) Florida City, WJFR (FM) Jacksonville, WFTI-FM St. Petersburg, WWFR (FM) Stuart
Georgia: WFRP (FM) Americus
Illinois: WJCH (FM) Joliet
Iowa: KDFR (FM) Des Moines, KEGR (FM) Fort Dodge, KYFR (AM) Shenandoah
Kansas: KPOR (FM) Emporia
Maryland: WFSI (FM) Annapolis; WBMD (AM), WBGR (AM) Baltimore
Michigan: WOFR (FM) Schoolcraft
Montana: KFRD (FM) Butte, KFRW (FM) Great Falls
New Jersey: WKDN (FM) Camden, WFME (FM) Newark
New York: WFBF (FM) Buffalo, WFRH (FM) Kingston, WFRS (FM) Smithtown, WFRW (FM) Webster
North Dakota: KBFR (FM) Bismarck
Ohio: WCUE (AM) Cuyahoga Falls, WOTL (FM) Toledo, WYTN (FM) Youngstown
Oregon: KYOR (FM) Newport, KPFR (FM) Pine Grove, KQFE (FM) Springfield
Pennsylvania: WEFR (FM) Erie, WFRJ (FM) Johnstown
South Carolina: WFCH (FM) Charleston
South Dakota: KKAA (AM) Aberdeen, KQFR (FM) Rapid City, KQKD (AM) Redfield
Texas: KEDR (FM) Bay City, KTXB (FM) Beaumont
Utah: KUFR (FM) Salt Lake City
Washington: KARR (AM) Kirkland, KJVH (FM) Longview
Wisconsin: WMWK (FM) Milwaukee

FAMILY TELEVISION INC.
54 Osprey Rd.
Beckley, WV 25801
Phone: 304-222-5063
Officer:
Tom Syner, President
Represented (legal): Shainis & Peltzman Chartered.
LPTV Stations:
West Virginia: WCIR-LP Beckley.

FAMILY VALUES ORGANIZATION INC.
5375 Pebble Creek Rd.
Rockford, IL 61111
Phone: 815-677-8000
Fax: 815-987-3971

LPTV Stations:
Illinois: WQFL-CA Rockford.

ANDREW FARA
1360 Leavenworth
San Francisco, CA 94109
Phone: 415-921-1390
LPTV Stations:
California: K48KB Chico.
Texas: K60GT Abilene.

FAR EASTERN TELECASTERS
1110 NASA Rd. 1
Suite 501
Houston, TX 77058
LPTV Stations:
Texas: KVDO-LP Clear Lake; KJIB-LP Clear Lake City.

FEDERATED RURAL ELECTRIC ASSN.
Hwy. 71
Box 69
Jackson, MN 56143
Phone: 507-847-3520
Officers:
Martin Rose, Chairman & President
Richard Burud, Chief Executive Officer
David Post, Secretary-Treasurer
Ownership: Cooperative.
Represented (legal): Rosenman & Colin LLP.
LPTV Stations:
Minnesota: K23FO Jackson; K36IV-D Jackson; K40JN-D Jackson; K41EG Jackson; K45EH Jackson; K51EN Jackson; K53HR Jackson; K57IX Jackson.

LAURA L. FENTON
Box 691111
Houston, TX 77269
LPTV Stations:
Texas: KHTX-LP Huntsville.

FERDINAND TV SERVICE
PO Box 115
Ferdinand, ID 83526
LPTV Stations:
Idaho: K07CP Ferdinand.

FIORI MEDIA INC.
Box 911
Vacaville, CA 95696
Phone: 707-324-9167
Officer:
John Fiori, President
LPTV Stations:
California: KTVJ-LP Santa Rosa.
Washington: KRUM-LD Aberdeen; KEVE-LP Longview.

FIREWEED COMMUNICATIONS LLC
3700 Woodland Dr.
Suite 800
Anchorage, AK 99517
Phone: 907-248-5937
Fax: 907-339-3889
Web site: www.kyes.com
Officers:
Jeremy Lansman, President
Carol Schatz, Chief Executive Officer
Ownership: Jeremy Lansman, 55.14%; Carol Schatz, 44.86%.
LPTV Stations:
Alaska: K22HN-D Anchorage; KABA-LP Anchorage; KYEX-LP Anchorage; K09XO Homer; K06MF Kenai, etc.; K12OW Palmer.
Commercial TV Stations:
Alaska: KYES-DT Anchorage.

FIRST ASSEMBLY OF GOD
1445 Ford St.
Redlands, CA 92373
Phone: 909-793-7800

Fax: 909-793-8821

LPTV Stations:

Arkansas: K08KF De Queen.

FIRST BAPTIST CHURCH OF PARIS, TX
Box 489
Paris, TX 75461
Phone: 903-785-6431

Officer:

Gary Pirtle, President

LPTV Stations:

Texas: K27GR Paris.

FIRST CULLMAN BROADCASTING INC.
501 2nd Ave.
Cullman, AL 35055
Phone: 205-734-5632

LPTV Stations:

Alabama: WCQT-LP Cullman.

FIRST MEDIA RADIO LLC
306 Port St.
Easton, MD 21601
Phone: 410-822-3301

LPTV Stations:

North Carolina: WNVN-LP Roanoke Rapids.

FIRST UNITED INC.
18600 S. Oak Park Ave.
Tinley Park, IL 60477
Phone: 708-633-0001

LPTV Stations:

Illinois: WEDE-CA Arlington Heights.

FIRST UNITED METHODIST CHURCH
Box 728
Starkville, MS 39759
Phone: 662-338-1002

Fax: 662-324-5364

LPTV Stations:

Mississippi: W05BV Starkville.

FISHER COMMUNICATIONS INC.
100 4th Ave. N
Suite 510
Seattle, WA 98109
Phone: 206-404-7000

Fax: 206-404-6037

E-mail: info@fsci.com

Web site: www.fsci.com

Officers:

Phelps K. Fisher, Chairman

Colleen B. Brown, President & Chief Executive Officer

Christopher Bellavia, Senior Vice President, General Counsel & Corporate Secretary

Joseph Lovejoy, Acting Chief Financial Officer

Branch Office:
444 N. Capitol St. NW
Suite 601-A
Washington, DC 20001
Phone: 202-783-0322

Ownership: GAMCO Investors Inc., 16.28%; Donald G. Graham Jr., 9.3263%; Reed, Conner & Birdwell LLC, 6.7%; George D. Fisher, 6.1%; Edward A. Gowey, 6%; Robin J. Campbell Knepper, 5.3468%; William H. Gates III, 5.24%; Donald G. Graham III, 5.1884%; O.D. Fisher Investment Co., 5.0228%; TowerView LLC, 5%; Phelps K. Fisher, 3%; GAMCO ownership:; Mario Gabelli, controlling interest; RC&BLLC ownership:; Donn B. Conner; Jeffrey Bronchick, principals; ODFIC ownership:; Donald G. Graham Jr., Pres.; TVLLC ownership:; Daniel R. Tisch, principal.

Represented (legal): Irwin, Campbell & Tannenwald PC.

LPTV Stations:

California: KBFX-CA Bakersfield.
Idaho: KYUU-LP Boise; K65AZ Burley, etc.; K55GM Cambridge; K11GR Cascade; K10AW Challis; K11CP Fish Creek, etc.; K09HS Glenns Ferry; K13IA Lowman; K10FD McCall, etc.; KXPI-LP Pocatello.
Oregon: K26DB Astoria; K07PP Camas Valley; K45CV Corvallis; K04DR Eugene; K58DA Glendale; K26HO Glide,etc.; K33CP Gold Beach; K10GQ Huntington; K11LS Jordan Valley; K42CZ Lincoln City, etc.; K13HM Myrtle Creek; K12IA Oakland, etc.; KUNP-LP Portland; K54AP Prineville; K29CI Prineville, etc.; K02DB Scottsburg; K18HH The Dalles; K11GH Tri-City, etc..
Washington: KWWA-CA Ellensburg, etc.; KVVK-CA Kennewick, etc.; KORX-CA Walla Walla; KUNW-CA Yakima.

Commercial TV Stations:

California: KBAK-DT Bakersfield.
Idaho: KBCI-DT Boise; KIDK-DT Idaho Falls; KLEW-DT Lewiston.
Oregon: KCBY-DT Coos Bay; KVAL-DT Eugene; KUNP-DT La Grande; KATU-DT Portland; KPIC-DT Roseburg.
Washington: KUNS-DT Bellevue; KEPR-DT Pasco; KOMO-DT Seattle; KIMA-DT Yakima.

Radio Stations:

Montana: KIKF (FM), KINX (FM) Cascade; KQDI-AM-FM, KXGF (AM) Great Falls
Washington: KOMO (AM), KPLZ-FM, KVI (AM) Seattle

FISH LAKE VALLEY COMMUNICATIONS FOUNDATION
PO Box 333
Dyer, NV 89010-0333
Phone: 775-572-3337

E-mail: alfalfaqueen@gbis.com

Officer:

E. Mark Hartman, President

LPTV Stations:

Nevada: K53EZ Fish Lake Valley, etc.; K55GR Fish Lake Valley, etc.; K57GI Fish Lake Valley, etc.; K59FH Fish Lake Valley, etc.; K64AE Fish Lake Valley, etc..

FLINN BROADCASTING CORP.
188 S. Bellevue
No. 222
Memphis, TN 38104
Phone: 901-375-9324

Officers:

George S. Flinn Jr., President & Treasurer

Mark Hopper, Chief Operating Officer

Branch Offices:
4124 Baldwin Sq
Memphis, TN 38117
Phone: 901-324-0861

483 S Highland
Memphis, TN 38111
Phone: 901-458-8255

Ownership: George S Flinn Jr., see listing. Flinn also has interest in Broadcasting for the Challenged Inc., TV applicant.

LPTV Stations:

Tennessee: W15CH Memphis.

Commercial TV Stations:

Alabama: WBIH-DT Selma.

Radio Stations:

Arkansas: KFLI (FM) Des Arc, KVHU (FM) Judsonia, KXHT (FM) Marion, KWLR (FM) Maumelle, KWBF-FM North Little Rock
California: KWCA (FM) Weaverville
Georgia: WWWD (FM) Bolingbroke
Iowa: KRQN (FM) Vinton
Louisiana: KEDG (FM) Alexandria
Mississippi: WMUT (FM) Grenada, KBUD (FM) Sardis, WAVN (AM) Southaven, WQJB State College, WIVG (FM) Tunica, WJXN-FM Utica
Missouri: KPPL (FM) Poplar Bluff
Montana: KLSK (FM) Great Falls
Nevada: KBDB (AM) Sparks, KWNZ (FM) Sun Valley
Oklahoma: KPAK (FM) Alva
Tennessee: WMPS (AM) Barlett; WOWW (AM) Germantown; WGSF (AM), WHBQ-AM-FM Memphis; WYDL (FM) Middleton

GEORGE S. FLINN JR.
188 S. Bellevue
Suite 222
Memphis, TN 38104
Phone: 901-726-8970

LPTV Stations:

Tennessee: W26CX Memphis.

Commercial TV Stations:

Florida: WFBD-DT Destin.
Mississippi: WWJX-DT Jackson.

Other Holdings:

Flinn Broadcasting Corp., see listing..

FLINTSTONE COMMUNITY TELEVISION INC.
General Delivery
Flintstone, MD 21530

LPTV Stations:

Maryland: W08BN Flintstone; W11AL Flintstone; W13AD Flintstone.

FOLSE COMMUNICATIONS LLC
1202 St. Charles Ave.
Houma, LA 70360
Phones: 504-928-3146; 504-923-2822

LPTV Stations:

Louisiana: KFOL-CA Houma; KJUN-CA Morgan City.

FORSYTH COMMUNITY TV RELAY SYSTEM
PO Box 47
Rosebud County Courthouse
Forsyth, MT 59327-0047
Phone: 406-346-2251

E-mail: rcc@rangeweb.net

Officer:

Daniel D. Watson, Secretary-Treasurer

LPTV Stations:

Montana: K07LO Forsyth; K09BW Forsyth; K11CB Forsyth; K12LR Forsyth; K04FF Forsyth, etc..

FORSYTH TV TAX DISTRICT
PO Box 47
Rosebud County Courthouse
Forsyth, MT 59327-0047
Phone: 406-346-2251

E-mail: rcc@rangeweb.net

Officer:

Daniel D. Watson, Secretary-Treasurer

LPTV Stations:

Montana: K06JU Howard; K44DM Howard; K07QK Rosebud, etc.; K09OK Rosebud, etc..

FORUM COMMUNICATIONS CO.
Box 2020
Fargo, ND 58103
Phone: 701-235-7311

E-mail: kbmykmcy@btinet.net

Officers:

William C. Marcil, President & Chief Executive Officer

Lloyd Case, Vice President & Chief Operating Officer

Charles Bohnet, Vice President

Jane B. Marcil, Secretary-Treasurer

Ownership: Jane B Marcil; William C Marcil.
Represented (legal): Wiley Rein LLP.

LPTV Stations:

Minnesota: K02MM Fergus Falls.
North Dakota: K02DD Jamestown.

Commercial TV Stations:

North Dakota: KBMY-DT Bismarck; WDAZ-DT Devils Lake; WDAY-DT Fargo; KMCY-DT Minot.

Newspapers:

Minnesota: Alexandria Echo Press; The Pioneer (Bemidji); The Pine Journal (Cloquet); Duluth News Tribune; Duluth Budgeteer News; Detroit Lakes Tribune, Becker County Record, Lake Area Press (Detroit Lakes); The Farmington
North Dakota: The Dickinson Press, The Forum (Fargo), Grand Forks Herald, The Jamestown Sun, The West Fargo Pioneer
South Dakota: The Daily Republic (Mitchell)
Wisconsin: Hudson Star-Observer, New Richmond News, Pierce County Herald, River Falls Journal, The Daily Telegram (Superior)

Radio Stations:

North Dakota: WDAY (AM) Fargo

FOSTER CHARITABLE FOUNDATION INC.
2125 Sidney Baker N
Kerrville, TX 78028
Phone: 830-896-1230

Officers:

David Larry Greenwald, President

Sherry Wheeler, Secretary

Ownership: David Carmen; David Larry Greenwald; Harry Herzog; Jana Smith, Dirs..
Represented (legal): Shainis & Peltzman Chartered.

LPTV Stations:

Louisiana: K22GT Lake Charles.
Mississippi: W30CC Natchez.
Texas: K05EF Brady, etc.; K02GM Brady/Rochelle; K04GI Brady/Rochelle; K38IO DeLeon; K17GZ Harper; K34HW Mason; K41HX San Saba.

FOUNTAIN TELEVISION CORP.
8850 Link Rd.
Fountain, CO 80817
Phone: 719-382-3233

Officer:

Jerry Powell, President

LPTV Stations:

Texas: KEBQ-LP Beaumont.

FOUR POINTS MEDIA GROUP HOLDING LLC
299 Park Ave
c/o Cerberus Capital Management LP
New York, NY 10171
Phone: 212-891-2100

Officers:

Christopher A Holt, Vice President

Mark Ploof, Vice President

Richard Reingold, Vice President

Ownership: Four Points Media Group LLC; FPMGLLC ownership:; TV Stations Investors LLC, managing member. 100% votes, not less than 90% assets; TVSILLC ownership:; TV Manager LLC. 100% votes; TVMLLC ownership:; Insulated Members. 100% assets; Stephen Feinberg; IM ownership:; Affiliates of Cerberus Capital Management LP; AOCCMLP ownership:; Stephen Feinberg, managing member%.

Represented (legal): Wiley Rein LLP.

LPTV Stations:

Florida: WTCN-CA Palm Beach; WWHB-CA Stuart.

Utah: K53CF Aurora; K22FS-D Beaver, etc.; K31FG Delta, etc.; K03BF Enterprise; K07SC Hildale, UT & Cane Beds, AZ; K43AE Myton, etc.; K09CD Rockville; K49AS Santa Clara; K41FX Spring Glen; K03AL Toquerville; K02AW Virgin.

Commercial TV Stations:

Florida: WTVX-DT Fort Pierce.

Massachusetts: WLWC-DT New Bedford.

Texas: KEYE-DT Austin.

Utah: KUTV-DT Salt Lake City; KUSG-DT St. George.

CRAIG L. FOX
4853 Manor Hill Dr.
Syracuse, NY 13215-1336
Phone: 315-468-0908
Represented (legal): James L. Oyster.

LPTV Stations:

New York: WNNY-LP Auburn; WBQM-LP Brooklyn; WBXZ-LP Buffalo; WIXT-CA De Witt; WMBQ-CA Manhattan; WTKO-LP Oneida; WHSH-CA Rochester; WBLZ-LP Syracuse; WHSU-CA Syracuse; WMBO-LP Syracuse; WNDR-LP Syracuse; WOBX-LP Syracuse; WTVU-LP Syracuse; WONO-CA Syracuse, etc.

Radio Stations:

New York: WVOA (FM) Mexico

FOX TELEVISION HOLDINGS INC.
444 N Capitol St NW, Ste 740
c/o Dianne Smith (News Corp.)
Washington, DC 20001
Phone: 202-715-2350
E-mail: mollyp@foxtv.com

Officers:

K. Rupert Murdoch, Chairman & Chief Operating Officer

Lawrence A. Jacobs, Executive Vice President & Secretary

Raymond L. Parrish, Vice President & Assistant Treasurer

Joseph DiScipio, Vice President, Legal & FCC Compliance

Paula M. Wardynski, Vice President

David E. Miller, Treasurer

Bonnie I. Bogin, Assistant Secretary

Elizabeth Casey, Assistant Secretary

Jon Del Barrio, Assistant Secretary

Randall F. Kender, Assistant Secretary

Gary D. Roberts, Assistant Secretary

Branch Offices:
5151 Wisconsin Ave NW
Washington, DC 20016
Phone: 202-244-5151
1211 Avenue of the Americas
21st Fl
New York, NY 10036
Phone: 212-301-3545

Ownership: Fox Entertainment Group Inc., 85.2%. votes, 99.9% equity; K. Rupert Murdoch, 14.8%. votes, 0.1% equity; FEGI ownership:; News Corp.; NC ownership:; K. Rupert Murdoch, Chmn. & Chief Exec. Officer, 5.7%. asserts, 38.6% votes; Murdoch Family Trust, Cruden Financial Services LLC, Trustee, 5.4%. assets; 37.2 % votes; HRH Prince Alwaleed Bin Talal Bin Abdulaziz Alsaud, 1%. assets, 7% votes.

Represented (legal): Skadden, Arps, Slate, Meagher & Flom LLP.

LPTV Stations:

Alabama: W15AP Gadsden.

Arizona: K16BP Cottonwood; K39FC East Flagstaff, etc.; K28CW Flagstaff; K48GI Flagstaff; K14HG Kingman; K15CR Lake Havasu City; K55BW Madera Peak; K36AE Phoenix; K04AI Prescott; K14HC Prescott; K39IT-D Prescott; K07OJ Snowflake, etc.; K43IE Williams; K09JZ Winslow.

Minnesota: K30DK Bemidji; K48IF Brainerd; K49KQ Little Falls; K33KC Wadena; K49CU Walker.

Commercial TV Stations:

Arizona: KSAZ-DT Phoenix; KUTP-DT Phoenix.

California: KCOP-DT Los Angeles; KTTV-DT Los Angeles.

District of Columbia: WDCA-DT Washington; WTTG-DT Washington.

Florida: WOGX-DT Ocala; WOFL-DT Orlando; WRBW-DT Orlando; WTVT-DT Tampa.

Georgia: WAGA-DT Atlanta.

Illinois: WFLD-DT Chicago.

Indiana: WPWR-DT Gary.

Maryland: WUTB-DT Baltimore.

Massachusetts: WFXT-DT Boston.

Michigan: WJBK-DT Detroit.

Minnesota: KFTC-DT Bemidji; KMSP-DT Minneapolis; WFTC-DT Minneapolis.

New Jersey: WWOR-DT Secaucus.

New York: WNYW-DT New York.

Pennsylvania: WTXF-DT Philadelphia.

Tennessee: WHBQ-DT Memphis.

Texas: KTBC-DT Austin; KDFI-DT Dallas; KDFW-DT Dallas; KRIV-DT Houston; KTXH-DT Houston.

Radio Stations:

Illinois: WSBC (AM) Chicago, WCFJ (AM) Chicago Heights

Other Holdings:

Television holdings: Equity interest in Davis Television Inc., see listing.

FRANKLIN COUNTY TRANSLATOR DISTRICT 1
Box 168
Preston, ID 83263-0168
Phone: 208-766-4405
E-mail: greedavl@lsu.edu
Officer:
Norm Jaussi, Engineer

LPTV Stations:

Idaho: K08EZ Mink Creek; K10FF Mink Creek; K13HA Mink Creek; K07XM Preston; K19EW-D Preston; K21HH Preston; K23GR-D Preston; K25HG-D Preston; K27GM-D Preston; K29EY-D Preston; K31FR-D Preston; K33GF-D Preston; K35GJ-D Preston; K40GZ-D Preston; K42GN-D Preston; K44HA-D Preston; K46HW-D Preston; K48IJ-D Preston; K50IE-D Preston.

JOHN A. FRANKLIN
30329 Vines Creek Rd
Dagsboro, DE 19939-9809
Phone: 302-732-1400

Branch Office:
706 Crest Dr.
Hawley, PA 18428
Phone: 717-226-4108

LPTV Stations:

Pennsylvania: WWPS-LP Hawley, etc..

FRANKLIN MEDIA INC.
Box 18126
Pensacola, FL 32523
Phone: 850-433-1766

Officers:

John L. Franklin, President

Delores A. Franklin, Secretary

LPTV Stations:

Alabama: W50CF Mobile.

Commercial TV Stations:

Florida: WPAN-DT Fort Walton Beach.

FRASER VALLEY METROPOLITAN RECREATION DISTRICT
PO Box 3348
Winter Park, CO 80482-3348
Phone: 970-726-8968
E-mail: scott@fraservalleyrec.org

Officer:

Scott Ledin, Director, Parks & Recreation

LPTV Stations:

Colorado: K27CB Fraser; K33BV Fraser; K36BR Fraser; K39BT Fraser; K30CR Fraser, etc..

FRAZER MEMORIAL UNITED METHODIST CHURCH
6000 Atlanta Hwy.
Montgomery, AL 36124-1347
Phone: 334-272-8622

Officer:

Jerry T. Kemp, President

LPTV Stations:

Alabama: WFRZ-LD Montgomery.

FREEDOM COMMUNICATIONS HOLDINGS INC.
17666 Fitch
Irvine, CA 92614
Phone: 949-253-2313
Fax: 949-253-2349
E-mail: staff@wpecnews12.com

Officers:

Scott N. Flanders, President & Chief Executive Officer

N. Christian Anderson III, Senior Vice President & President, Metro Information Div.

Michael J. Mathieu, Senior Vice President & President, Interactive Division

Jonathan Segal, Senior Vice President & President, Community Newspapers Division

Doreen D. Wade, Senior Vice President & President, Broadcast Division

Marcy E. Bruskin, Vice President, Human Resources & Organizational Development

Richard A. Wallace, Vice President & Secretary

Michael Brown, Vice President & Chief Information Officer

Joanne Norton, Vice President, Shareholder Relations & Assistant Secretary

Rachel L. Sagan, Vice President & General Counsel

Nancy S. Trillo, Vice President, Treasurer & Controller

Katherine Bartzoff, Assistant Secretary

Ownership: Blackstone FC Communications Partners LP, 16.81%. votes; Providence Equity Partners IV LP, 15.93%. votes; Mary Elizabeth Hoiles Bassett, 9.33%. votes; Threshie Ltd., 8.44%. votes; Robin J. Hardie, 6.93%. votes; Janet Baker Nardie, 6.8%. votes; Douglas R. Hardie, 6.39%. votes; Blackstone FC Capital Partners IV LP, 5.6%. votes; Thomas W. Bassett, 5.59%. votes; Richard A. Wallace, 3.75%. votes; David A. Threshie, 0.79%. votes; Raymond C. H. Bryan, 0.36%. votes; BFCCPLP & BFCCPIVLP ownership:; Peter G. Peterson, Founding Member; Stephen A. Schwarzman, Founding Member; PEPIVLP ownership:; Glenn M. Creamer; Jonathan M. Nelson; Paul J. Salem, principals; TL ownership:; Threshie Family Trusts.

Represented (legal): Latham & Watkins.

LPTV Stations:

California: K60AR Alturas; K02CN Dunsmuir, etc.; K06KA Fort Jones, etc.; K06GP Yreka; K53DY Yreka.

Oregon: K02EK Applegate Valley; K04EO Ashland, etc.; K10LR Brookings; K04JQ Butte Falls; K60BJ Carpenterville; K24BV Cave Junction; K02DV Cave Junction, etc.; K48BS Glendale, etc.; K04JZ Gold Hill; K54DM Grants Pass; K40BL Hugo, etc.; K02IC Jacksonville; K07PU Klamath Falls, etc.; K12IH Lakeview; K15HU-D Lakeview; K19HH-D Midland, etc.; K60BH Midland, etc.; K16CU Phoenix & Talent; K47LD-D Phoenix & Talent; K03BZ Rogue River; K04JP Williams.

Commercial TV Stations:

Florida: WPEC-DT West Palm Beach.

Michigan: WWMT-DT Kalamazoo; WLAJ-DT Lansing.

New York: WCWN-DT Schenectady; WRGB-DT Schenectady.

Oregon: KTVL-DT Medford.

Tennessee: WTVC-DT Chattanooga.

Texas: KFDM-DT Beaumont.

Newspapers:

Arizona: East Valley Tribune (Mesa); Daily News-Sun (Sun City); The Sun, Bajo El Sol (Yuma)

California: Desert Dispatch (Barstow); Colusa Sun Herald; Corning Observer; Hesperia Star; Appeal-Democrat (Marysville); The Orange County Register; Orland Press Register; The Porterville Recorder, Noticieros Semanal (Port

Colorado: The Gazette (Colorado Springs)

Florida: Holmes County Times-Advertiser (Bonifay), The Crestview News Bulletin, The Destin Log, Northwest Florida Daily News (Fort Walton Beach), Santa Rosa Press Gazette/Santa Rosa Free Press (Milton), The News Herald

Illinois: The Telegraph (Alton), Journal-Courier (Jacksonville)

Indiana: The Tribune (Seymour)

Missouri: The Sedalia Democrat

New Mexico: Clovis News Journal, Portales News-Tribune, Quay County Sun

North Carolina: Times-News (Burlington), The Gaston Gazette, Havelock News, The Daily News (Jacksonville), Free Press (Kinston), Sun Journal (New Bern), The Shelby Star, The Topsail Advertiser (Surf City), Jones Post (Trenton)

Ohio: The Lima News

Texas: The Brownsville Herald, El Nuevo Heraldo (Brownsville); Valley Morning Star, La Estrella (Harlingen); The Monitor, La Frontera (McAllen); Odessa American, El Semanario (Odessa); Mid Valley Town Crier (Weslaco)

Other Holdings:

Magazine: Clinical Geriatrics; CRM Magazine; Field Force Automation; Home HealthCare Consultant; The Journal of Gender Specific Medicine; Latin Trade; MODE Magazine; Revista Latin Trade; Small Business Computing; The Annals of Long-Term Care.

FREE LIFE MINISTRIES INC.
708 N. William
Box 282
Goldsboro, NC 27533-0282
Phone: 919-736-7729
Fax: 919-736-9042
Officers:
Dennis Jacobs, Chairman
Delbert Taylor, Vice Chairman
Terry Johnson, Secretary
Thelma Jean Smith, Treasurer
Ownership: Non-profit corp.--Goldsboro, NC.
Represented (legal): Rini Coran PC.
LPTV Stations:
North Carolina: WHFL-LP Goldsboro.

FREE TEMPLE MINISTRIES INC.
211 Morning Rd.
Box 208
Windsor, NC 27983
Phone: 252-794-9453
Fax: 252-794-3466
Officers:
Timothy Lloyd Baylor Sr., President
Timothy Baylor, Chief Executive Officer
Carolyn Spivey, Chief Operating Officer
Linda Raynor, Secretary-Treasurer
T. L. Baylor Sr., Chief Financial Officer
LPTV Stations:
North Carolina: WFTB-LP Williamston.

DIOCESE OF FRESNO EDUCATION CORP.
1550 N. Fresno St.
Fresno, CA 93703
Phone: 209-486-4949
Officers:
John T. Steinbock, President & Treasurer
Marvin Harrison, General Manager
Myron Cotta, Secretary-Treasurer
Marv Harrison, Programming Director
Steve LeBel, Engineering Consultant
Ownership: Sergio Negro, Secy.; Rt. Rev.
  John Steinbock, Pres..
Represented (legal): Kelley Drye & Warren LLP.
LPTV Stations:
California: KNXT-LP Bakersfield.
ETV Stations:
California: KNXT-DT Visalia.

FRIENDLY BROADCASTING CO.
1304 Courthouse Court
Mansfield, TX 76063
LPTV Stations:
California: KWJD-LP Van Nuys.

FRONTLINE MISSIONS INTERNATIONAL INC.
Box 892
Christiansted, VI 00821-0892
Phone: 340-719-1400
Officer:
Antony W. Whitehead, Executive Director
LPTV Stations:
Virgin Islands: WEYA-LP Christiansted.

FULL GOSPEL BUSINESS MEN'S FELLOWSHIP INTERNATIONAL
Box 2357
Muncie, IN 47307
Phones: 503-362-0682; 503-364-5227
LPTV Stations:
Illinois: W57AO Robinson.

Indiana: WMUN-LP Muncie.

FULL GOSPEL OUTREACH INC.
5050 Edison Ave.
Suite 219
Colorado Springs, CO 80915
Phone: 719-574-7777
LPTV Stations:
Colorado: K17CF Boulder; K43CG Colorado
  Springs; K35DZ La Junta; K42EA Lamar;
  K40DP Las Animas; K47FJ Manitou Springs;
  K48CU Pueblo; K39ED Rocky Ford; K33EW
  Woodland Park.

RALPH FYTTON
2805 E. Oakland Park Blvd.
Suite 363
Fort Lauderdale, FL 33306
Phone: 954-782-6393
E-mail: lptv@internetinformation.com
LPTV Stations:
Florida: W40BU Panama City.

CITY OF GABBS
Box 86
Gabbs, NV 89409-0086
Phone: 775-285-2671
LPTV Stations:
Nevada: K06NZ Gabbs; K13YK Gabbs.

NELLIE GAJESKI
20-37 Hazen St.
Jackson Heights, NY 11370
Phone: 718-278-5385
LPTV Stations:
New York: W36BN Massena.
Other Holdings:
Cellular telephone: Touchtone Cellular.

CITY OF GALENA
Box 149
Galena, AK 99741
Phone: 907-656-1301
Ownership: Community owned--Galena, AK.
LPTV Stations:
Alaska: K10LJ Galena.

GALLATIN VALLEY COMMUNITY TV ASSN.
101 Arrowhead
Bozeman, MT 59715
Phone: 406-585-9689
LPTV Stations:
Montana: K45EB Bozeman, etc..

GANNETT CO. INC.
7950 Jones Bridge Dr.
McLean, VA 22107
Phone: 703-854-6899
E-mail: gcishare@gannett.com
Officers:
Craig A. Dubow, Chairman, President & Chief
  Executive Officer
Dave Lougee, President, Broadcast Division
Garcia C. Martore, Executive Vice President
  & Chief Financial Officer
Todd A. Mayman, Senior Vice President,
  Secretary & General Counsel
Christopher W. Baldwin, Vice President, Taxes
Jose A. Berrios, Vice President, Leadership
  Development & Diversity
Tara J. Connell, Vice President, Corporate
  Communications
Daniel S. Ehrman Jr., Vice President, Planning
  & Development
George R. Gavagan, Vice President & Controller
Michael A. Hart, Vice President & Treasurer
Roxanne V. Horning, Vice President, Human
  Resources

Darryll Green, Vice President, Program
  Development
Wendell J. Van Lare, Vice President, Senior
  Labor Counsel
Barbara W. Wall, Vice President, Senior
  Associate General Counsel
Ownership: Publicly held.
Represented (legal): Wiley Rein LLP.
LPTV Stations:
Arizona: K61FB Globe & Miami; KPSN-LP
  Payson; K06AE Prescott.
Colorado: K47IH Boulder.
Maine: W57AQ Calais; WGCI-LP Skowhegan.
Commercial TV Stations:
Arizona: KNAZ-DT Flagstaff; KPNX-DT Mesa.
Arkansas: KTHV-DT Little Rock.
California: KXTV-DT Sacramento.
Colorado: KTVD-DT Denver; KUSA-DT Denver.
District of Columbia: WUSA-DT Washington.
Florida: WTLV-DT Jacksonville; WJXX-DT
  Orange Park; WTSP-DT St. Petersburg.
Georgia: WATL-DT Atlanta; WXIA-DT Atlanta;
  WMAZ-DT Macon.
Maine: WLBZ-DT Bangor; WCSH-DT Portland.
Michigan: WZZM Grand Rapids.
Minnesota: KARE-DT Minneapolis.
Missouri: KSDK-DT St. Louis.
New York: WGRZ Buffalo.
North Carolina: WFMY-DT Greensboro.
Ohio: WKYC Cleveland.
South Carolina: WLTX-DT Columbia.
Tennessee: WBIR-DT Knoxville.
Newspapers:
Alabama: The Montgomery Advertiser
Arizona: The Arizona Republic (Phoenix),
  Tucson Citizen
Arkansas: Baxter Bulletin (Mountain Home)
California: The Desert Sun (Palm Springs), The
  Salinas Californian, Tulare Advance-Register,
  Visalia Times-Delta
Colorado: Fort Collins Coloradoan
Delaware: The News Journal (Wilmington)
Florida: Florida Today (Brevard County), The
  News-Press (Fort Myers), Pensacola News
  Journal, Tallahasee Democrat
Guam: Pacific Daily News (Hagatna)
Hawaii: The Honolulu Advertiser
Indiana: The Indianapolis Star, Journal and
  Courier (Lafayette), The Star Press (Muncie),
  Palladium-Item (Richmond)
Iowa: The Des Moines Register, Iowa City
  Press-Citizen
Kentucky: The Courier-Journal (Louisville)
Louisiana: The Town Talk (Alexandria), The
  Daily Advertiser (Lafayette), The News-Star
  (Monroe), Daily World (Opelousas), The
  Times (Shreveport)
Maryland: The Daily Times (Salisbury)
Michigan: Battle Creek Enquirer, Detroit Free
  Press, Lansing State Journal, Daily Press
  & Argus (Livingston County), Observer
  & Eccentric Newspapers (Livonia), Times
  Herald (Port Huron)
Minnesota: St. Cloud Times
Mississippi: Hattiesburg American, The Clarion-
  Ledger (Jackson)
Missouri: Springfield News-Leader
Montana: Great Falls Tribune
Nevada: Reno Gazette-Journal
New Jersey: Asbury Park Press, Courier-News
  (Bridgewater), Courier-Post (Cherry Hill),
  Home News Tribune (East Brunswick), Daily
  Record (Morristown), The Daily Journal
  (Vineland)
New York: Press and Sun-Bulletin (Bing-
  hamton), Star-Gazette (Elmira), The Ithaca
  Journal, Poughkeepsie Journal, Rochester
  Democrat and Chronicle, The Journal News
  (Westchester County)
North Carolina: Asheville Citizen-Times
Ohio: Telegraph-Forum (Bucyrus), Chillicothe
  Gazette, The Cincinnati Enquirer, Newspaper
  Network of Central Ohio (Columbus),
  Coshocton Tribune, The News-Messenger
  (Fremont), Lancaster Eagle-Gazette, News
  Journal (Man

Oregon: Statesman Journal (Salem)
South Carolina: The Greenville News
South Dakota: Argus Leader (Sioux Falls)
Tennessee: The Leaf-Chronicle (Clarksville),
  The Jackson Sun, The Daily News Journal
  (Murfreesboro), The Tennessean (Nashville)
Utah: The Spectrum (St. George)
Vermont: The Burlington Free Press
Virginia: Staunton Daily News-Leader
Wisconsin: The Port-Crescent (Appleton);
  Action Advertising Inc., The Reporter (Fond
  du Lac); Green Bay Press-Gazette; Herald
  Times Reporter (Manitowoc); Marshfield
  News-Herald; Oshkosh Northwestern; The
  Sheboygan Press;
Other Holdings:
Magazine: Military Times; Army Times; Armed
  Forces Journal; Navy Times; Marine Corps
  Times; Air Force Times; Federal Times;
  Defense News
National Newspaper: USA Today Over 300
  non-daily publications.

GAP BROADCASTING LAKE CHARLES LLC
12900 Preston Rd
Ste 525
Dallas, TX 75230
Phone: 214-295-3530
Officer:
George Laughlin, President & Secretary
Ownership: B. James Ford; George Laughlin;
  David Quick; Andrew Salter; Neal Schore,
  Board of Managers.
Represented (legal): Drinker Biddle.
LPTV Stations:
Louisiana: KJEF-CA Jennings.
Other Holdings:
Radio.

VICTOR A. GARCIA
1315 La Puente Dr.
Bakersfield, CA 93308
Phone: 805-324-2358

Branch Office:
Victor Broadcasting Co.
700 Chester Ave
Bakersfield, CA 93301-5422
Phone: 805-324-6423
Represented (legal): J. J. Gianquinto Law
  Offices.
LPTV Stations:
California: K19CL Inyokern.

GARDEN VALLEY TRANSLATOR DISTRICT
PO Box 711
Garden Valley, ID 83622
LPTV Stations:
Idaho: K49EB Garden Valley; K55GZ Garden
  Valley; K57FO Garden Valley; K53EF Garden
  Valley, etc.; K03ET Terrace Lakes; K67FI
  Terrace Lakes & Crouch; K05EY Terrace
  Lakes, etc.; K100A Terrace Lakes, etc..

GARFIELD COUNTY
55 S. Main
Box 77
Panguitch, UT 84759
Phone: 435-676-8826
Fax: 435-676-8239
E-mail: resources@uen.org
LPTV Stations:
Colorado: K08GZ Carbondale; K10LW Car-
  bondale; K04GM Divide Creek, etc.; K08JS
  East Elk Creek; K20GE-D Garfield, etc.;
  K09DC Glenwood Springs; K11DI Glenwood
  Springs, etc.; K11PR Grand Valley; K07JM
  Grand Valley, etc.; K09JT New Castle;
  K11JZ New Castle, etc.; K63BM Rulison,

etc.; K68BR Rulison, etc.; K04KC Sutank, etc..

Utah: K31JF-D Boulder; K32HQ-D Boulder; K33IZ-D Boulder; K07OB Cannonville; K23IK-D Cannonville; K02FQ Escalante; K04FR Escalante; K05DV Escalante; K07JZ Escalante; K09WJ Escalante; K11SJ Escalante; K13VH Escalante; K26GD-D Garfield County; K30GA-D Garfield County; K16EQ-D Garfield County (rural); K18FT-D Garfield County (rural); K28GM-D Garfield County (rural); K41EB-D Garfield County (rural); K51AH-D Garfield County (rural); K39FT-D Garfield, etc.; K45BY-D Garfield, etc.; K47AB-D Garfield, etc.; K49AG-D Garfield, etc.; K09MO Hatch; K11NA Hatch; K13NT Hatch; K15HE-D Hatch; K17HQ-D Hatch; K19GJ-D Hatch; K38GQ Hatch; K09XF Henrieville; K11UM Henrieville; K13XL Henrieville; K16FN Henrieville; K20BT Henrieville; K22GP Henrieville; K02BN Panguitch; K04AU Panguitch; K05BB Panguitch; K12OI Panguitch; K38KF-D Panguitch; K39JG-D Panguitch; K40JL-D Panguitch; K44IU-D Panguitch; K10LV Panguitch, etc.; K46JI-D Panguitch, etc.; K02ON Ticaboo; K04OJ Ticaboo; K05JS Ticaboo; K02IF Tropic & Cannonville; K04IN Tropic & Cannonville; K05FY Tropic & Cannonville; K24HL-D Tropic & Cannonville; K27ID Tropic & Cannonville; K29GJ Tropic & Cannonville; K33HX Tropic & Cannonville; K19GQ-D Tropic, etc.; K21II-D Tropic, etc.; K17HV-D Tropic/Cannonville.

GARFIELD TV CLUB
PO Box 436
Jordan, MT 59337
Phone: 406-557-6200
Officer:
George Fitzgerald, Chairman
LPTV Stations:
Montana: K06EB Brusett, etc.; K13YD Jordan; K07VA Jordan, etc.; K09HI Jordan, etc.; K11HE Jordan, etc.; K10AU Northfork, etc.; K13HK Sand Springs.

ENRIQUETA GARZA
168 Meadowbrook Lane
Apt. B
San Benito, TX 78586
Phone: 956-428-7556
LPTV Stations:
Kansas: K34GG Garden City.

GEORGIA-ALABAMA BROADCASTING INC.
Box 2830
La Grange, GA 30240
Phone: 404-845-8833
Officer:
Sarah Beth Mallory, President
Ownership: Sarah Beth Mallory; Mallory Communications.
Represented (legal): Cole, Raywid & Braverman LLP.
LPTV Stations:
Georgia: WCAG-LP La Grange.

GEORGIA PUBLIC TELECOMMUNICATIONS COMMISSION
260 14th St. NW
Atlanta, GA 30318
Phone: 404-685-2410
Fax: 404-685-2417
E-mail: ask@gpb.org
Officer:
Richard W. Harrell, Chairman
Ownership: Richard W. Harrell; Ann C. Dorsey; Jeanne R. Ferst; Arthur J. Morris; Cheryl Smith Moultrie; Janice F. Paul; Lowell L. Register/Board Members.

LPTV Stations:
Georgia: W49AD Carrollton; W22AC Hartwell & Royston; W50AB Hiawassee; W68AF Toccoa; W04BJ Young Harris.
Other Holdings:
Radio.

GETHSEMANE BAPTIST CHURCH
411 Blue Ridge St
Lynchburg, VA 24501
Phone: 434-845-8796
E-mail: seeaduck@aol.com
Ownership: Carlton A Duck, Pastor & Trustee.
Represented (legal): Putbrese, Hunsaker & Trent PC.
LPTV Stations:
Virginia: W04CI Appomattox; W33AD Concord.

GH BROADCASTING INC.
2866 Lawnview
Corpus Christi, TX 78404
Phone: 361-882-1414
LPTV Stations:
Texas: KTOV-LP Corpus Christi.

JIM GIBBS
Box 1109
Crockett, TX 75835
Phone: 936-544-2171
Fax: 936-544-4891
LPTV Stations:
Texas: KIVY-LP Crockett.

G.I.G. INC.
PO Box 88336
Sioux Falls, SD 57109
Phone: 605-335-3393
Officer:
Charles D. Poppen, President
LPTV Stations:
North Dakota: KVNJ-LP Fargo.
South Dakota: KCPL-LP Rapid City; KCPO-LP Sioux Falls.

RICHARD GILL
Box 270
Pleasant Hill, LA 71065
Phone: 318-352-7628
LPTV Stations:
Louisiana: KNTS-LP Natchitoches.

GLENDIVE BROADCASTING CORP.
210 S. Douglas St.
Glendive, MT 59330
Phone: 406-365-3377
Fax: 406-365-3378
Officers:
Stephen A. Marks, President
Dan Frenzel, Vice President
Jerry Cook, Secretary
Ownership: Stephen A Marks. Marks is 88.5% owner of Thunder Bay Broadcasting Corp., see listing.
Represented (legal): Fleischman & Harding LLP.
LPTV Stations:
Montana: K13IG Sidney & Fairview.
Commercial TV Stations:
Montana: KXGN-DT Glendive; KYUS-DT Miles City.
Radio Stations:
North Dakota: KDZN-FM, KXGN (AM) Glendive.

GLEN IRIS BAPTIST CHURCH SCHOOL
1137 10th Place S
Birmingham, AL 35205
Phone: 205-323-1516

Fax: 205-323-2747
LPTV Stations:
Alabama: W15AZ Alabaster; W49AY Birmingham.

GLOBAL BROADCAST NETWORK INC.
880 W First St
Ste 306
Los Angeles, CA 90012
Phone: 213-617-0892
E-mail: nameofmysong@aol.com
Officer:
Kenta Rooks, President
Represented (legal): Dan J. Alpert.
LPTV Stations:
Florida: WGZT-LP Key West.
Maine: WGBI-LP Farmington.

GLOBAL OUTREACH MINISTRY NETWORK INC.
390 Tyndall Pkwy.
Suite 135
Panama City, FL 32405
Phones: 850-832-6208; 800-489-9006
E-mail: mljubilee@aol.com
Web site: www.gbn.cc
Officers:
Michael A. Lee, President
Kimberly D. Lee, Vice President

Branch Office:
GBN Stream
247 Brockton Dr.
Madison, AL 35758
Phone: 256-325-9956
Ownership: Michael A. Lee, 33.3%. votes; Kimberly D. Lee, 33.3%. votes; Victoria Anderson, 33.3%. votes.
LPTV Stations:
Alabama: WMJN-LP Somerville.
Florida: WEWA-LP Panama City; WGOM-LP Panama City.

RICHARD C. & LISA A. GOETZ
116 Beaumont Dr.
Hendersonville, TN 37075
Phone: 615-826-0792
Fax: 615-824-3282
Web site: www.rlmediasystems.com
LPTV Stations:
Georgia: WDWW-LP Blairsville; W19CP Moultrie; W12DA Tifton.
Hawaii: KHOH-LP Hilo.
Tennessee: WKRP-LP Alexandria; WDLE-LP Pigeon Forge.

GOLDEN VALLEY ASSOCIATION NO. 2 TRANSLATOR DISTRICT
PO Box 181
Lavina, MT 59046
Phone: 406-636-2025
E-mail: lavina@midrivers.com
Officer:
Wanda Kalgren, Director
LPTV Stations:
Montana: K11MB Lavina; K13MR Lavina.

GOLDEN VALLEY TV ASSOCIATION NO. 1
PO Box 163
Ryegate, MT 59074
Phone: 406-568-2251
E-mail: rpsad@midrivers.com
LPTV Stations:
Montana: K06FU Ryegate; K12HB Ryegate.

DANIEL GOMEZ
1629 Old Hickory Trl
Desoto, TX 75115

Phone: 214-330-8700
Represented (legal): Dan J. Alpert.
LPTV Stations:
Texas: KOBS-LP San Antonio.

GOOD NEWS TELEVISION
8940 Grove Ave
Berrien Springs, MI 49103-8940
Phone: 269-473-5274
Officer:
Ernest F. Herford, President
LPTV Stations:
Michigan: WYGN-LP Berrien Springs.

GRACE FELLOWSHIP CHURCH
PO Box 1561
Orange, TX 77631
Phone: 409-670-3656
E-mail: ricktallent1973@yahoo.com
Ownership: Rev. Jerry Brittain; Audrey L. Tallent; Carol Tallent; Rev. Richard S. Tallent, Dirs..
LPTV Stations:
Texas: K54JK Jasper.

GRAND LAKE METROPOLITAN RECREATION DISTRICT
PO Box 590
1415 County Rd 48
Grand Lake, CO 80447
LPTV Stations:
Colorado: K13EL Grand Lake.

GRASSHOPPER TV ASSOCIATION
D L Ranch
Polaris, MT 59746
LPTV Stations:
Montana: K09MY Grasshopper Valley, etc.; K07OC Grasshopper, etc..

CITY OF GRAYLING
5900 E. Tudor Rd.
Anchorage, AK 99507
Phone: 907-269-5744
Ownership: Community owned--Grayling, AK.
LPTV Stations:
Alaska: K09PC Grayling.

GRAY TELEVISION INC.
126 N. Washington St.
Albany, GA 31702-0048
Phones: 229-888-9390; 404-504-9828
Fax: 229-888-9374
Web site: www.graycommunications.com
Officers:
Hilton Howell, Chief Executive Officer
Robert S. Prather Jr., President & Chief Operating Officer
James C. Ryan, Senior Vice President & Chief Financial Officer
Robert A. Beizer, Vice President, Law & Development
Jackson S. Cowart IV, Chief Accounting Officer & Assistant Secretary
Martha E. Gilbert, Assistant Vice President, Benefis
Vance F. Luke, Controller & Assistant Secretary
Ownership: Datasouth Computer Corp., 15.25%; Bull Run Corp., 10.86%; Robert S. Prather Jr., 2.86%; DCC ownership: Bull Run Corp.; BRC ownership: J. Mack Robinson, 16.67%; Samuel R. Shapiro, 10.9%; Robinson-Prather Partnership, 7.16%; James W. Busby, 5.72%; W. James Host, 3.16%.
Represented (legal): Venable LLP.
LPTV Stations:
Colorado: K10LI Canon City; K49JX-D Montrose; K50EZ Montrose; K57CB Romeo, etc..
Kansas: K30GD Great Bend; K25CV Hays; K38GH Russell; K51GC Salina.

Nebraska: K30FV Cambridge; K55AF Cozad; K28GC Gothenburg; K53GC Neligh; K25GM Newport; K57CZ North Platte; K43FX O'Neill; K33FF Wallace.

Nevada: K12IX Austin; K49CK Stead & Lawton.

Texas: K02EQ Paris.

Virginia: WAHU-CA Charlottesville; WAHU-LD Charlottesville; WVAW-LD Charlottesville.

West Virginia: W16CE Charleston.

Wisconsin: W57AR Sayner & Vilas County.

Commercial TV Stations:
Alabama: WTVY-DT Dothan.

Colorado: KKTV-DT Colorado Springs; KKCO-DT Grand Junction.

Florida: WJHG-DT Panama City.

Georgia: WRDW-DT Augusta; WCTV-DT Thomasville; WSWG-DT Valdosta.

Illinois: WIFR-DT Freeport.

Indiana: WNDU-DT South Bend.

Kansas: KLBY-DT Colby; KUPK-DT Garden City; WIBW-DT Topeka; KAKE-DT Wichita.

Kentucky: WBKO-DT Bowling Green; WYMT-DT Hazard; WKYT-DT Lexington.

Michigan: WILX-DT Onondaga.

Mississippi: WTOK-DT Meridian.

Nebraska: KGIN-DT Grand Island; KOLN-DT Lincoln; WOWT-DT Omaha.

Nevada: KOLO-DT Reno.

North Carolina: WITN-DT Washington.

Tennessee: WVLT-DT Knoxville.

Texas: KBTX-DT Bryan; KXII-DT Sherman; KWTX-DT Waco.

Virginia: WCAV-DT Charlottesville; WHSV-DT Harrisonburg.

West Virginia: WSAZ-DT Huntington; WTAP-DT Parkersburg.

Wisconsin: WEAU-DT Eau Claire; WMTV-DT Madison; WSAW-DT Wausau.

Radio Stations:
Colorado: KRYD-FM

GREATER COPPER VALLEY COMMUNICATIONS INC.
HC01 Box 1942
Glennallen, AK 99588
Phone: 907-822-4051
Officer:
Randall Struck, President
LPTV Stations:
Alaska: K09TU Lake Louise, etc.; K11RJ Lake Louise, etc..

GREATER LOUISVILLE COMMUNICATIONS
4300 Outer Loop
Suite 10
Louisville, KY 40219
Phone: 502-966-0624
Officers:
Greg Kunz, Chairman
Richard H. Williams, Chief Executive Officer
Ken Karaszkiewicz, Chief Financial Officer

Branch Office:
Cascade Broadcasting
100 Dickinson
Suite 270
Chaddsford, PA 19317
Phone: 610-558-2500
LPTV Stations:
Kentucky: W24BW Louisville.

GREAT OAKS BROADCASTING CORP.
914 N. Foster Dr.
Baton Rouge, LA 70806
Phone: 225-928-3146
Fax: 225-928-5097
Officers:
Louis (Woody) Jenkins, Chairman & Chief Executive Officer
Diane Jenkins, President

Ownership: Louis Jenkins, 51%; Tammy Trahan-Willeford, 1%; remainder undisclosed.
LPTV Stations:
Louisiana: KMNO-LP Monroe.

GREAT PLAINS TELEVISION NETWORK LLC
110 S. Main
Suite 800
Wichita, KS 67202
Phone: 316-267-8660
Officers:
Kyle C. Bauer, President
Kent L. Moore, Vice President
Thomas Bowles, Secretary-Treasurer
Ownership: Thomas Bowles, 25%; S. Bismarck Brackett, 25%; Kent L. Moore, 25%; Taylor Communications Inc., 25%; TCI ownership:; Kyle C. Bauer, Secy.-Treas., 40%; Walter Lent Lips, Pres., 40%; Scott Patterson, V.P., 20%.
LPTV Stations:
Kansas: KGPT-CA Wichita.

GREENBELT TV TRANSLATOR SYSTEM INC.
Marshall Peters
Box 272
Wellington, TX 79095
LPTV Stations:
Texas: K27BZ Wellington, etc..

GREENBRIER VALLEY TV LLC
1107 Pocahontas Ave.
Ronceverte, WV 24970
Phone: 304-645-5210
Officer:
Joe Sharp, Manager
Ownership: Joe Sharp, 80%; Thomas C. Syner, 20%.
Represented (legal): Shainis & Peltzman Chartered.
LPTV Stations:
West Virginia: W62DF Clarksburg.

R. M. GREENE INC.
PO Box 130
2400 Sportsman Dr.
Phenix City, AL 36867
Phone: 334-298-7000
Fax: 334-298-0833
Web site: www.phenixcable.net
Officers:
Roy M. Greene, Chairman
Lynne G. Frakes, President
Vicki Abbot, Chief Operating Officer
LPTV Stations:
Alabama: W06BH Phenix City, etc..
Cable Systems:
ALABAMA: PHENIX CITY.

THOMAS H. GREENE JR.
State Rd. 53 S
Madison, FL 32340
LPTV Stations:
Florida: W03AO Madison.

GREEN RIVER CITY TV
Box 620
Green River, UT 84525
LPTV Stations:
Utah: K02BU Green River; K04BR Green River; K05BK Green River; K15HH-D Green River; K16HD-D Green River; K17HW-D Green River; K36FX Green River; K38GP Green River; K41JS-D Green River; K42HP-D Green River; K43KG-D Green River; K44IK-D Green

River; K45JV-D Green River; K47KX-D Green River.

GREENTV CORP.
PO Box 348
2539 N. Hwy. 67
Sedalia, CO 80135
Phone: 303-688-5162
Officers:
David M. Drucker, Chairman, President & Chief Executive Officer
Penny Drucker, Secretary-Treasurer
Ownership: David M Drucker. Drucker also has interest in Cayo Hueso Networks LLC, Denver Digital Television LLC, Echonet Corp. & Ketchikan TV LLC, see listings.
Represented (legal): Rini Coran PC.
LPTV Stations:
Alaska: KXLJ-LD Juneau; K17GQ Kodiak.

GT ACQUISITIONS I LLC
Box Ski
Alta, WY 83515
Phone: 307-353-2300
Officer:
Larry H. Williamson, President
Represented (legal): Womble, Carlyle, Sandridge & Rice.
LPTV Stations:
Idaho: K07QC Driggs; K05GU Driggs, etc..

GULF-CALIFORNIA BROADCAST CO.
42-650 Melanie Place
Palm Desert, CA 92211
Phone: 760-773-0342
Officers:
David Bradley Jr., Chairman
John Kuenekse, President, Broadcasting
Bob Allen, Chief Executive Officer & Executive Vice President
Lyle Leimkuhler, Secretary-Treasurer & Chief Financial Officer
Ownership: David Bradley; Hank Bradley.
LPTV Stations:
Arizona: KESE-LP Yuma.
California: KUNA-LP Indio; KCWQ-LP Palm Springs.

GUNNISON COUNTY METROPOLITAN RECREATION DISTRICT
PO Box 1382
Gunnison, CO 81230
Phone: 940-641-8725
Officers:
Paul Wayne Foreman, Chairman
Jerry Vosburg, President
Peter Kennel, Secretary-Treasurer
Ownership: State-owned.
LPTV Stations:
Colorado: K06AM Cimarron; K12AK Crested Butte; K30EJ Crested Butte; K45CY Crested Butte South; K49BW Crested Butte South; K04GS Crested Butte, etc.; K10AK Crested Butte, etc.; K41AH Crested Butte, etc.; K43AH Crested Butte, etc.; K47BL Crested Butte, etc.; K03EY Doyleville; K62DP Gateview; K02IK Gateview, etc.; K02GH Grand Junction; K02LY Gunnison; K04DH Gunnison; K06HN Gunnison; K09TH Gunnison; K13AV Gunnison; K07BE Gunnison, etc.; K11AT Gunnison, etc.; K66AW Hartsel; K68AR Hartsel; K70FL Hartsel; K64AQ Hartsel, etc.; K05EJ Jack's Cabin; K16DR Jack's Cabin; K67CQ Jack's Cabin; K08HC Jack's Cabin, etc.; K65CR Jack's Cabin, etc.; K69BU Jack's Cabin, etc.; K41DU Parlin, etc.; K61DC Parlin, etc.; K63CX Parlin, etc.; K36GQ Parlin-Doyleville; K39DC Parlin-Doyleville; K05JT Pitkin; K15ED Pitkin; K17GC Pitkin; K19DS Pitkin; K21EF Pitkin;

K23DX Pitkin; K43EG Pitkin; K08JZ Pitkin & Ohio; K10MA Pitkin & Ohio; K12AL Pitkin, etc.; K09WB Powderhorn Valley; K12LX Powderhorn Valley; K46DB Sapinero; K48EF Sapinero; K02NV Sargents; K04OF Sargents; K06NG Sargents; K07VH Sargents; K11TJ Sargents; K53AY Sargents; K57CS Sargents; K59DV Sargents; K03HA Spring Creek; K11QK Spring Creek, etc.; K13RX Spring Creek, etc.; K51DI Waunita Hot Springs; K55BI Waunita Hot Springs.

GUYMON TV TRANSLATOR INC.
PO Box 613
Guymon, OK 73942
Phone: 580-338-1015
E-mail: acruze@valornet.com
Officer:
Steve Smith, President
LPTV Stations:
Oklahoma: K28GI Guymon; K30FY Guymon; K57HY Guymon; K59GF Guymon.

HAGERMAN TRANSLATOR DISTRICT
Box 151
Hagerman, ID 83332
LPTV Stations:
Idaho: K29GV Hagerman; K31IF Hagerman; K41JF Hagerman; K47JW Hagerman; K49IT Hagerman.

HALL COUNTY
Box 1968
Grand Island, NE 68802
Phone: 308-385-5444
Fax: 308-385-5486
LPTV Stations:
Nebraska: K56FC Grand Island.

TIMOTHY K. HALL
Box 7519
Santa Monica, CA 90406
Phone: 310-394-7761
LPTV Stations:
South Carolina: WWSC-LP Myrtle Beach.

H & R PRODUCTION GROUP LLC
Rte. 106
Box 574
Belmont, NH 03220
Phone: 603-267-7778
LPTV Stations:
Florida: WBWP-LP West Palm Beach.

HAPA MEDIA PROPERTIES LLC
Box 513
Glenview, IL 60025
Phone: 847-209-2705
Officer:
Kevin J. Bae, President & Manager
Represented (legal): Jeffrey L. Timmons.
LPTV Stations:
Pennsylvania: WLEP-LP Erie.
Other Holdings:
See KM Communications & Pocatello Channel 15 LLC.

DAVID F. HARDERS
530 N. Broadway
Box 93
Wahoo, NE 68066
Phones: 402-443-3000; 402-443-3198
LPTV Stations:
Nebraska: K46EE Columbus; K48FF Columbus, etc.; K50EG Columbus, etc.; K28FS Fremont & Omaha.

GLENDA R. HARDERS
530 N. Broadway
Box 93
Wahoo, NE 68066

Phones: 402-443-3000; 402-443-3198
LPTV Stations:
Nebraska: K52EX Columbus; K49FP Columbus & Fremont; K28EN Columbus-Fremont; K54EU Columbus-Fremont.

MARY E. HARDERS
926 N. Beach
Wahoo, NE 68066
Phone: 402-443-3000
LPTV Stations:
Nebraska: K63FQ Columbus, etc.; K45GS North Platte; K59FT North Platte.

ROGER E. HARDERS
530 N. Broadway
Box 93
Wahoo, NE 68066
Phones: 402-443-3000; 402-443-3198
LPTV Stations:
Missouri: K63FW Jamestown; K43EU St. Louis; K32FH Warrensburg.
Nebraska: K41FU Columbus & Fremont; K47FK Columbus & Fremont; K55HX Columbus/Fremont.

HARLOWTON TV ASSOCIATION
PO Box 567
Harlowton, MT 59036
LPTV Stations:
Montana: K10AX Harlowton; K13BE Harlowton.

JOSEPH H. HARPOLE SR.
1200 Bishop St.
Box 709
Union City, TN 38261
Phone: 901-885-3341
LPTV Stations:
Tennessee: WUWT-CA Union City.
Other Holdings:
Microwave holdings.

HARPSWELL COMMUNITY BROADCASTING CORP.
PO Box 99
10 Community Dr
Harswell, ME 04079
Phone: 207-833-2363
LPTV Stations:
Maine: W14DA Harpswell.

HARRISON COMMUNITY CLUB
PO Box 156
Harrison, NE 69346
LPTV Stations:
Nebraska: K09PW Harrison.

HARRON COMMUNICATIONS LP
70 E. Lancaster Ave.
Frazer, PA 19355
Phone: 610-644-7500
Fax: 610-993-1100
E-mail: lstuchell@harron.com
Web site: www.harron.com
Officers:
James J Bruder Jr., Chairman & Chief Executive Officer
Thomas M Marturano, President & Chief Operating Officer
Ryan F Pearson, Executive Vice President & General Counsel
Shawn P Flannery, Chief Financial Officer & Treasurer
Steve A Murdough, Vice President, Operations
William Lee Jr, Vice President, Engineering
Joshua S Barstow, Vice President, Advanced Services
Linda C Stuchell, Vice President, Programming & Marketing

Constance S Prince, Chief Administrative Officer
LPTV Stations:
Pennsylvania: W47AO Berwick; WYLN-LP Hazleton; W67DE Newport; W68CE Shickshinny; W05BG Williamsport; W62CS Williamsport.
Cable Systems:
ALABAMA: RED BAY.
CONNECTICUT: NEW LONDON.
MAINE: SANFORD.
MARYLAND: ST. MARY'S COUNTY.
MISSISSIPPI: ABERDEEN; AMORY; ASHLAND; BALDWYN; BOONEVILLE; BRUCE; CALHOUN CITY; CARTHAGE; COFFEEVILLE; FOREST; HICKORY FLAT; HOLLY SPRINGS; IUKA; KOSCIUSKO; MABEN; NETTLETON; NEW ALBANY; OXFORD; PHILADELPHIA; PONTOTOC; POTTS CAMP; RALEIGH; STARKVILLE.
NEW HAMPSHIRE: BELMONT; ROCHESTER.
PENNSYLVANIA: BERWICK; POCONO; SCHUYLKILL TWP.; SPRUCE CREEK TWP.; SUGAR GROVE; THREE SPRINGS.
SOUTH CAROLINA: BENNETTSVILLE.
VIRGINIA: BOWLING GREEN; COLONIAL BEACH; KING GEORGE; LANCASTER COUNTY; MIDDLESEX COUNTY; NORTHUMBERLAND COUNTY; TAPPAHANNOCK; WARSAW.
Other Holdings:
Boston Ventures communications equity firm.

HARVEST MINISTRIES INTERNATIONAL
PO Box 688
Crestview, FL 32536
Phone: 850-682-3900
Officer:
Rev. William B. Franklin, President
LPTV Stations:
Florida: WGOX-LP Santa Rosa Beach.

JULIET R. HARVEY
Box 6386
Kahului, HI 96733
Phone: 808-877-4990
LPTV Stations:
Hawaii: KAMN-LP Wailuku.

SHAHRAM HASHEMIZADEH
4570 Van Nuys Blvd.
#234
Sherman Oaks, CA 91403
Phone: 818-339-9575
Web site: www.mellitv.com
LPTV Stations:
California: K33DK Lucerne Valley; KHIR-LP Twin Peaks.
Kansas: K52HZ Manhattan.

HAWAII PUBLIC TELEVISION FOUNDATION
Box 11673
Honolulu, HI 96828
Phone: 808-973-1000
Fax: 808-973-1090
Officers:
Neil J. Hannahs, Chairman
Mike McCartney, President & Chief Executive Officer
Ed McNulty, Vice President, Programming
Rick Tsujimura, Secretary
Robert A. Alm, Treasurer
Karen Yamamoto, Chief Financial Officer
LPTV Stations:
Hawaii: K63AZ Anahola; K67BA Hakalau; K68BE Hanalei, etc.; K04FE Hilo; K63AI Kaumakani; K62AQ Kilauea; K56BD Kilauea Military Camp; K67AV Lihue; K63BB Naalehu, etc.; K69CF South Point; K63DT Waimea; K66AY Waipake.
ETV Stations:
Hawaii: KHET-DT Honolulu.

CITY OF HAZEN
PO Box 717
Hazen, ND 58545
Phone: 701-748-2550
E-mail: hazndste@westriv.com
Officer:
Steve Provarp, City Planner
LPTV Stations:
North Dakota: K07JA Hazen; K09JR Hazen; K11QD Hazen.

HEARST-ARGYLE TELEVISION INC.
888 7th Ave.
New York, NY 10106
Phone: 212-887-6800
Fax: 212-887-6875
Officers:
Frank A Bennack Jr, Chairman
David J. Barrett, President & Chief Executive Officer
Harry T. Hawks, Executive Vice President, Chief Financial Officer & Asstistant Secretary
Steven IA. Hobbs, Executive Vice President & Chief Legal & Development Officer
Roger Keating, Senior Vice President, Digital Media
Philip M. Stolz, Senior Vice President
Brian Bracco, Senior Vice President, News
Jonathan C. Mintzer, Vice President, General Counsel & Corporate Secretary
Ownership: Hearst Broadcasting Inc.; HBI ownership:; Hearst Holdings Inc.; HHI ownership:; The Hearst Corp.; THC ownership:; Stock is vested in trust with 13 trustees..
Represented (legal): Clifford Chance; Brooks, Pierce, McLendon, Humphrey & Leonard LLP.
LPTV Stations:
Arizona: K10IN Chinle; K63AE Many Farms.
Colorado: K45DH Durango.
Georgia: W06AE Clayton, etc..
Hawaii: K51BB Lihue.
New Hampshire: W27BL Berlin; W26CQ Colebrook; W38CB Littleton; WMUR-LP Littleton.
New Mexico: K34CR Alamogordo, etc.; K10CG-D Aztec & Cedar Hill; K09JJ Bloomfield, etc.; K49CZ Caballo; K43BT Carrizozo; K66AE Colfax; K65FJ Crownpoint; K51DS Deming; K28ER Dulce & Lumberton; K19CM Farmington; K62CR Farmington; K52CR Forrest, etc.; K08IJ Gallup; K67BP Gallup; K11EV Grants, etc.; K12NH Hobbs; K66EE Horse Springs; K09AI Las Vegas; K61CN Lordsburg; K57BR Montoya & Newkirk; K46IN Portales; K16CH Raton, etc.; K12OC Red River; K13RK Roswell; K62AL Roswell; K20GU Ruidoso, etc.; K08KX Taos; K60DD Tierra Amarilla.
North Carolina: W08BH Andrews, etc.; W11AX Bat Cave, etc.; W05AR Bryson City, etc.; W09AS Burnsville; W11AU Canton, etc.; W10AL Cherokee, etc.; W03AK Ela, etc.; W06AJ Franklin; W06AI Marion; W10AK Spruce Pine; W02AF Sylva, etc.; W11AH Tryon & Columbus.
Vermont: W27CP White River Junction; W65AM White River Junction.
Commercial TV Stations:
Arkansas: KHOG-DT Fayetteville; KHBS-DT Fort Smith.
California: KCRA-DT Sacramento; KSBW-DT Salinas; KQCA-DT Stockton.
Florida: WKCF-DT Clermont; WESH-DT Daytona Beach.
Hawaii: KHVO-DT Hilo; KITV-DT Honolulu; KMAU-DT Wailuku.
Iowa: KCCI-DT Des Moines.
Kentucky: WLKY-DT Louisville.
Louisiana: WDSU-DT New Orleans.
Maine: WMTW-DT Poland Spring.
Maryland: WBAL-DT Baltimore.
Massachusetts: WCVB-DT Boston.

Mississippi: WAPT-DT Jackson.
Missouri: KMBC-DT Kansas City.
Nebraska: KETV-DT Omaha.
New Hampshire: WMUR-DT Manchester.
New Mexico: KOAT-DT Albuquerque; KOCT-DT Carlsbad; KOVT-DT Silver City.
New York: WPTZ-DT North Pole.
North Carolina: WXII-DT Winston-Salem.
Ohio: WLWT-DT Cincinnati.
Oklahoma: KOCO-DT Oklahoma City.
Pennsylvania: WGAL-DT Lancaster; WTAE-DT Pittsburgh.
South Carolina: WYFF-DT Greenville.
Vermont: WNNE-DT Hartford.
Wisconsin: WISN-DT Milwaukee.
Radio Stations:
Maryland: WBAL (AM), WIYY (FM) Baltimore

HEIRLOOM MINISTRIES INC.
Rte. 1
Box 155K
Elliottsburg, PA 17024
LPTV Stations:
Pennsylvania: W18BC Middleburg.

HERO BROADCASTING LLC
14450 Commerce Way
Miami Lakes, FL 33016
Phone: 305-863-5700
E-mail: bbehar@belallc.com
Officers:
Robert Behar, President & Chief Executive Officer
Marisol Messir, Secretary-Treasurer & Chief Financial Officer
Ownership: Robert Behar. votes, 70.6% assets.
Represented (legal): Dow Lohnes PLLC.
LPTV Stations:
Arizona: KEJR-LD Phoenix; KEJR-LP Phoenix.
Commercial TV Stations:
Arizona: KMOH-DT Kingman.
California: KBEH-DT Oxnard.

HE'S ALIVE BROADCASTING ASSN.
Box 19039
Spokane, WA 99219-9039
Phones: 509-622-4780; 509-838-2761
Fax: 509-838-4882
Officers:
Marlo E. Fralick, Vice President
Tom Katsma, Secretary
Dwayne House, Treasurer
Ownership: Non-profit corp.--Spokane, WA.
LPTV Stations:
Washington: KHBA-LP Spokane.

EDWARD J. & MADGE E. HESS
6985 Cane Lane
Valley Springs, CA 95252
Phone: 209-722-1976
LPTV Stations:
Michigan: W25CU Traverse City.

HIGHLAND PARK BROADCASTING LP
15851 Woodland
Highland Park, MI 48203
LPTV Stations:
Michigan: W33BY Dearborn.

HIGH PLAINS BROADCASTING INC.
Po Box 288
120 Oak Dr
Kaw City, OK 74641
Phone: 580-269-2215
Ownership: James H. Martin, Pres.
Represented (legal): Pillsbury Winthrop Shaw Pittman LLP.

LPTV Stations:

Utah: KUWB-LP Bloomington; K40HS Duchesne; K43JF-D Manti/Ephraim; K14LW Myton; K17GT-D Price; K24GK Salina; K48JD Santa Clara & Washington; K51IC-D Spring Glen. Wyoming: K28DV Evanston; K31FW Mountain View; K45IA Rock Springs.

Commercial TV Stations:

California: KGET-DT Bakersfield; KGPE-DT Fresno; KFTY-DT Santa Rosa.

Florida: WTEV-DT Jacksonville.

Texas: WOAI-DT San Antonio.

Utah: KUCW-DT Ogden.

HILLSBORO TV ASSOCIATION

Box 485
Hillsboro, NM 88042

LPTV Stations:

New Mexico: K02IP Hillsboro; K06DX Hillsboro; K08LP Hillsboro; K11HB Hillsboro.

HILLTOP CHURCH INC.

250 W. Nopah Vista Ave.
Pahrump, NV 89060
Phone: 775-751-9709

LPTV Stations:

Nevada: KHMP-LP Pahrump; KPVT-LP Pahrump.

HILO LP TV LLC

1111 W Bonanza Rd
Las Vegas, NV 89106
Phone: 702-477-3830

Officer:

Michael R. Ferguson, President

Represented (legal): Garvey Schubert Barer.

LPTV Stations:

Hawaii: KHHB-LP Hilo.

MYRON K. HINES

8317 W. Alternate 98
Suite 23
Panama City, FL 32407

LPTV Stations:

South Carolina: W35AY Hilton Head Island.

HINSDALE COUNTY CHAMBER OF COMMERCE

PO Box 430
Lake City, CO 81235
Phone: 970-944-2527

Officer:

Alena Haskell, Information Contact

LPTV Stations:

Colorado: K04HG Lake City; K08GV Lake City; K10EA Lake City; K12KV Lake City.

HINSDALE TV CLUB

PO Box 296
Hinsdale, MT 59241
Phone: 406-364-2271
E-mail: 2jtoll@nemontel.net

Officer:

Jim Tollefson, Secretary

LPTV Stations:

Montana: K05IZ Hinsdale; K10JK Hinsdale; K13JO Hinsdale & rural area (north); K07DI Rock Creek, etc..

HINSDALE TV DISTRICT

Box 278
Hinsdale, MT 59241
Phone: 406-364-2241

Officer:

Tom Fisher, Chairman

LPTV Stations:

Montana: K42FP Hinsdale.

HISPANIC CHRISTIAN COMMUNITY NETWORK INC.

8500 N Stemmons Fwy
Suite 2024
Dallas, TX 75247-3830
Phone: 214-879-0081

Officer:

Antonio Cesar Guel, President

LPTV Stations:

Arizona: K30IP Littlefield; KRPO-LP Quartzsite; KYPO-LP Tacna.

Arkansas: K11VO Fulton; KZTE-LP Fulton.

Florida: WHDY-LP Panama City.

Indiana: WUVI-LP West Lafayette.

Iowa: KXWL-LP Keokuk.

Kansas: KGKC-LP Topeka.

Kentucky: W09CQ Jamestown; WESL-LP Jamestown.

Maryland: WNDC-LP Salisbury; WNGA-LP Salisbury.

Michigan: W11CZ Escanaba.

Mississippi: WGVI-LP Hattiesburg; W04DE Laurel; W68DX Laurel.

Missouri: K05LU Jefferson City; K09XZ Lewistown; K05LY Moberly.

Nevada: K30IG Carrara; K13YU Tonopah.

Oklahoma: KEGG-LP McAlester.

Texas: KJTN-LP Abilene; KLMH-LP Abilene; KZAB-LP Abilene; KEAM-LP Amarillo; K53IX Big Spring; KHFW-LP Denison; KQFW-LP Denison; KSFW-LP Gainesville; K66GG Odessa; KZOD-LP Odessa; K23IA San Angelo; KZHO-LP Victoria; KHWF-LP Wichita Falls; KYWF-LP Wichita Falls; K23HF Woodville.

Utah: K46IC Price; K48JE Price.

Virginia: WIVC-LP Charlottesville; W08DY Harrisonburg.

Wyoming: K07YF Casper.

HIS WORD BROADCASTING CO.

640 Elwood Court
Eugene, OR 97401
Phone: 541-342-7474
E-mail: jhhorn@hotmail.com

Officers:

John H. Horn, President

Dennis B. Walen, Secretary-Treasurer

Ownership: Floyd Dixon; Dan Holt; John H. Horn; Charles Marshall; Dennis B. Walen, 20% each.

LPTV Stations:

Oregon: K59DJ Eugene.

HOAK MEDIA LLC

500 Crescent Ct
Ste 220
Dallas, TX 75201
Phone: 972-960-4896

Officers:

James M. Hoak, Chairman

Eric Van den Branden, President & Manager

Kelly Slayton, Secretary

Ownership: James M. Hoak, 30.3%. votes; 9.3%. assets; Centennial Hoak Media Inc., 36.4%. votes, 11.4%. assets; Columbia Hoak Partners III Inc., 26.2%. votes, 8.2%. assets; Columbia Hoak Partners III LLC, 5.1%. votes, 1.6%. assets; Lanny Martin, 1.3%. votes, 0.4% assets; Charles A. Anderson, 0.3%. votes, 0.1%. assets; Richard A. Anderson, 0.3%. votes, 0.1%. assets; Hoak & Co., 0.1%. votes; CHMI ownership:; Duncan T. Butler Jr., 25%. votes, 15% assets; Steven C. Halstedt, 25%. votes, 17% assets; David C. Hull Jr., 25%. votes, 15% assets; Jeffrey H. Schutz, 25%. votes, 15.25% assets; CHPIII & CHPIIIL ownership:; James B. Fleming Jr., 33.3%. votes, 11.21%. assets; R. Philip Herget III, 33.3%. votes, 15.7% assets; Harry F. Hopper III, 33.3%. votes, 27.67% assets; HAC ownership:; James M. Hoak, Chmn., 10%; Nancy J. Hoak, 90%.

Represented (legal): Akin, Gump, Strauss, Hauer & Feld LLP.

LPTV Stations:

Arkansas: K18AB El Dorado.

Colorado: K44CA Cimarron Creek; K02GJ Delta, etc.; K09MR Gateway; K07GD-D Glenwood Springs; KGJT-LP Grand Junction; K02HW Grand Valley; K13ML Hotchkiss, etc.; K06GG Norwood; K02GC Nucla, etc.; K06HZ Paonia; K09QA Paonia, etc.; K03FX Placerville; K03AY Ridgway; K40CS Rulison.

Montana: K13PL Glendive.

Nebraska: K20DK Beaver Lake area; K18DH Broken Bow; K14IY Holdrege; K35AL Lexington; K11TW North Platte; K21CY Ogallala.

South Dakota: K07QL Mitchell.

Commercial TV Stations:

Colorado: KREG-DT Glenwood Springs; KREX-DT Grand Junction; KREY-DT Montrose.

Florida: WMBB-DT Panama City.

Louisiana: KALB-DT Alexandria; KNOE-DT Monroe.

Nebraska: KHAS-DT Hastings; KNOP-DT North Platte.

North Dakota: KFYR-DT Bismarck; KQCD-DT Dickinson; KVLY-DT Fargo; KMOT-DT Minot; KUMV-DT Williston.

South Dakota: KABY-DT Aberdeen; KPRY-DT Pierre; KSFY-DT Sioux Falls.

Texas: KAUZ-DT Wichita Falls.

Radio Stations:

Louisiana: KNOE-AM-FM Monroe

HOLSTON VALLEY BROADCASTING CORP.

222 Commerce St
Kingsport, TN 37660
Phone: 423-246-9578
Fax: 423-246-6261

Officers:

William M. Boyd, Chairman

George E. DeVault Jr., President

Joseph D. Fontana, Senior Vice President

Janet L. Bragg, Secretary

Bette Lawson, Treasurer

Ownership: William M Boyd, 31.25%; George E. Devault Jr., 0.84%; N. David Widener, Dir., 0.84%; Joseph D. Foantana, 0.42%; Walter P. Nelson, Dir., 0.33%; Hugh N. Boyd (Deceased) Trust, William M. Boyd & Thomas J. McGrath, Trustees, 37.09%; Ruth O'Day Ridder (Deceased) Trust, William M. Boyd, Trustee, 10.32%.

Represented (legal): Wiley Rein LLP; Cordon & Kelly.

LPTV Stations:

Kentucky: WAPM-CA Lynch & Benham.

Tennessee: WAPG-CA Greeneville & Blackwater, VA; WAPK-CA Kingsport; WKPT-LP Kingsport; WOPI-CA Kingsport.

Virginia: WAPW-CA Abingdon; WKIN-LP Gate City, etc.; WAPV-LP Honaker; WKPH-LP Honaker; WMEV-LP Pennington Gap; WKPZ-LP Wytheville, etc..

Commercial TV Stations:

Tennessee: WKPT-DT Kingsport.

Radio Stations:

Tennessee: WOPI (AM) Bristol; WKPT (AM), WTFM (FM) Kingsport

Virginia: WMEV-AM-FM Marion

VILLAGE OF HOLY CROSS

5900 E. Tudor Rd.
Anchorage, AK 99507
Phone: 907-269-5744

LPTV Stations:

Alaska: K09NJ Holy Cross.

HONEY LAKE COMMUNITY TV CORP.

2301 Main St.
Susanville, CA 96130
Phone: 530-257-9625
E-mail: marshall@psln.com

Officer:

Tom Brown, President

LPTV Stations:

California: K34KK Litchfield; K46HL Litchfield; K48DI Litchfield; K50HJ Litchfield; K19GA Susanville & Herlong; K17HE Susanville, etc.; K31IE Susanville, etc.; K36HH Susanville, etc.; K38IU Susanville, etc.; K42GV Susanville, etc..

HOOPER BAY CITY COUNCIL

5900 E. Tudor Rd.
Anchorage, AK 99507
Phone: 907-269-5744

LPTV Stations:

Alaska: K07QD Hooper Bay.

HOSANNA APOSTOLIC MINISTRIES BROADCASTING CORP.

2605 Hyacinth Dr
Mesquite, TX 75181
Phone: 520-971-9274

Officer:

Gaspar Cota, President

Represented (legal): Dan J. Alpert.

LPTV Stations:

Florida: W28CP Summerland Key.

Indiana: WUVI-LP West Lafayette.

Oklahoma: KEGG-LP McAlester.

Texas: KLAO-LP Corpus Christi; K44GW Hereford; K23HF Woodville.

Virginia: WIVC-LP Charlottesville.

Wyoming: K14LV Cheyenne.

HOT SPRINGS TV DISTRICT

PO Box 154
Hot Springs, MT 59845
Phone: 406-741-2353
E-mail: clerk@hotsprgs.net

Officer:

Bev Bangen, Secretary-Treasurer

LPTV Stations:

Montana: K11IL Bitterroot Range, etc.; K05AH Hot Springs; K45DQ Hot Springs.

HOWARD TV CLUB

PO Box 47
Rosebud County Courthouse
Forsyth, MT 59327-0047
Phone: 406-346-2251

Officer:

Daniel D. Watson, Information Contact

LPTV Stations:
Montana: K10AJ Howard.

HTV/HTN/HAWAIIAN TELEVISION NETWORK LTD.
Box 1239
Kula, HI 96790
Phone: 808-878-1770
Officers:
C. T. Ryder, Chairman
John Roth, Secretary
Ownership: C. T Ryder, 91.4%; Lisa Hawley, 1.1%; Stanley S Gima, 0.4%; Alfred S Gima, 0.4%; ETV/Hawaii/Elephant Television Inc., 3.9%; , others with less than 1.1% each.
Represented (legal): Irwin, Campbell & Tannenwald PC.
LPTV Stations:
Hawaii: KHLU-LP Honolulu.

HUBBARD BROADCASTING INC.
3415 University Ave.
St. Paul, MN 55114
Phone: 651-642-4212
Fax: 651-642-4103
E-mail: promotion@kstp.com
Officers:
Stanley S. Hubbard, Chairman, President & Chief Executive Officer
Virginia Hubbard Morris, President, Radio Group
Gerald D. Deeney, Vice President
Robert W. Hubbard, Vice President & President, Television Group
Stanley E. Hubbard II, Vice President & President, Hubbard Media Group
John Soucheray, Vice President & General Manager, Hubbard Radio Network
Ronald L. Lindwall, Vice President & Chief Financial Officer
John Mayasich, Vice President, Public Affairs
Harold Crump, Vice President, Corporate Affairs
Kathryn Hubbard Rominski, Secretary
James A. Barnum, Deputy General Counsel
Ownership: Stanley E. Hubbard Grandchildren's Trust, Stanley S. Hubbard, Trustee, 27.61%; Stanley S. Hubbard Trust, Stanley S. Hubbard, Trustee, 17.83%; Stanley E. Hubbard Residuary Trust, Stanley S. Hubbard, Trustee, 16.57%; Stanley S. Hubbard, 15.25%; Stanley E. Hubbard, 6.2%; Kathryn H. Rominski, 6.2%; Julia D. Coyte, 3.44%; Robert W. Hubbard, 3.44%; Virginia H. Morris, 3.44%.
Represented (legal): Holland & Knight LLP.
LPTV Stations:
Arizona: K08HQ Chinle; K09XH Ganado; K43GQ Klagetoh; K49ET Many Farms.
Colorado: K46FM Bayfield; K50IV Cortez; K25GE Durango; K40GE Pagosa Springs; K63AN Romeo.
Massachusetts: W38DL Adams, etc..; W28DA Pittsfield, etc..
Minnesota: K28DD Bemidji; K16BQ Brainerd; W61AF Grand Marais; K55BR Grand Portage; K32FY Park Rapids; K57CN Wabasha; K17FE Wadena; K30FZ Willmar.
New Mexico: K31GJ Alamogordo; K20HA Caballo; K30GM Capitan & Ruidoso; K45GJ Carlsbad; K51CN Carrizozo; K56EH Cebolla; K16EX Clovis; K30GJ Colfax; K28GT Crownpoint; K35GY Cuba; K48HL Datil/Horse Springs; K41FM Deming; K30EK Dulce & Lumberton; K31GC Forrest, etc.; K48GD Gallina; K39EW Gallup; K06CU Grants, etc.; K09LQ Guadalupita; K20GT Indian Village; KAEP-LP Las Cruces; K47GV Las Vegas; K27FN Lordsburg; K36GA Lordsburg; K17FK Montoya & Newkirk; K25FI Mora; K06FT Penasco; K09JK Quemado; K09GR Questa; K26DX Raton; K46GL Red River; K06EM

Roy; K36DI Santa Rosa; K09KC Santa Rosa Heights; K10MG Socorro; K06LE Taos; K09KJ Tierra Amarilla, etc.; K06IS Tohatchi; K16DL Zuni Pueblo.
New York: W21CP Gloversville.
Commercial TV Stations:
Minnesota: KSAX-DT Alexandria; KAAL-DT Austin; WDIO-DT Duluth; WIRT-DT Hibbing; KSTC-DT Minneapolis; KRWF-DT Redwood Falls; KSTP-DT St. Paul.
New Mexico: KOB-DT Albuquerque; KOBF-DT Farmington; KOBR-DT Roswell; KOBG-DT Silver City.
New York: WNYT-DT Albany; WHEC-DT Rochester.
Radio Stations:
Minnesota: WFMP (FM) Coon Rapids, KSTP-AM-FM St. Paul.
Other Holdings:
Data service (Conus Communications).

HUDSON VALLEY TELEVISION INC
75 Palatine Park Rd.
Suite 6
Germantown, NY 12526-5310
Phone: 518-537-2988
E-mail: contact@thehudsonchannel.com
Officer:
Sean Small, President
Represented (legal): Irwin, Campbell & Tannenwald PC.
LPTV Stations:
New York: WSSN-LP Hudson et al..

HUMBOLDT COUNTY
25 W. 4th St.
Winnemucca, NV 89445
Phone: 775-623-6349
Ownership: Garley Amos; Dan Cassinelli; Charles Giordano; Tom Fransway; John Milton, 20 voting, each%.
LPTV Stations:
Nevada: K26GG-D Golconda; K28EO Golconda; K31FU Golconda; K33GB Golconda; K35GD Golconda, etc.; K39CX-D Imlay; K41GI-D Imlay; K09MM Paradise Valley; K11MU Paradise Valley; K40FV Quinn River area; K27GG Valmy & Red House; K34FP Valmy & Red House; K29EV Valmy/Red House; K14MR-D Winnemucca; K15AL-D Winnemucca; K19EU Winnemucca; K21FO-D Winnemucca; K23FR-D Winnemucca; K45BJ Winnemucca; K47CH Winnemucca; K49BK-D Winnemucca; K51BW Winnemucca.

HUSLIA VILLAGE COUNCIL
5900 E. Tudor Rd.
Anchorage, AK 99507
Phone: 907-269-5744
LPTV Stations:
Alaska: K04JS Huslia.

CITY OF HYDABURG
Box 49
Hydaburg, AK 99922
Ownership: Municipally owned--Hydaburg, AK.
LPTV Stations:
Alaska: K02JW Hydaburg.

ICA BROADCASTING LLC
700 N. Grant St.
Odessa, TX 79761
Phone: 915-334-8881
Officers:
John Bushman, Chairman
Terry A. Lee, President
Ed Lasater, Executive Vice President
John C. Nichols, Vice President
Sherry Wingate, Secretary

Ownership: John Bushman, 70%; Jeff Bushman, 10%; Brad Bushman, 10%; Jason Bushman, 10%.
LPTV Stations:
Texas: K10HH Big Spring.
Commercial TV Stations:
Texas: KOSA-DT Odessa.

IDAHO POWER CO.
PO Box 70
Boise, ID 83707
LPTV Stations:
Idaho: K09OP Brownlee; K13QL Brownlee; K11PD Brownlee Power Plant; K02JS Oxbow Dam.
Oregon: K06ER Oxbow; K04ET Oxbow Power Plant.

IDAHO STATE BOARD OF EDUCATION
Box 83720
Boise, ID 83720-0037
Phone: 208-334-2270
Fax: 208-334-2632
Officer:
Nancy Zaofran, Executive Director
LPTV Stations:
Idaho: K23IB Bonners Ferry; K14IC Burley, etc.; K11PB Cambridge, etc.; K09LO Cascade; K12LS Challis & Ellis; K05GO Council; K41EO Crouch, etc.; K13QE Driggs, etc.; K51FL Garden Valley; K15GO Georgetown; K46HX Grangeville; K13QH Irwin & Swan Valley; K43GE Juliaetta; K49JD Kellogg; K05GQ Kooskia & Stites; K14MC Lava Hot Springs; K14IJ Leadore; K51HY Lewiston; K15HR Mackay; K35GW-D Malad City; K23DO Malta, etc.; K41HS-D McCall; K05FG McCall, etc.; K42GT Priest Lake; K43JD-D Rexburg; K19CY Rockland; K49IC Salmon; K16EN Sandpoint; K23HT St. Maries.
ETV Stations:
Idaho: KAID-DT Boise; KCDT-DT Coeur d'Alene; KISU-DT Pocatello; KIPT-DT Twin Falls.

IDITAROD AREA SCHOOL DISTRICT
5900 E. Tudor Rd.
Anchorage, AK 99507
Phone: 907-269-5744
LPTV Stations:
Alaska: K02JE McGrath.

IGLESIA JESUCRISTO ES MI REFUGIO INC.
2929 S. Westmoreland Rd.
PO Box 223985
Dallas, TX 75222-3985
Phone: 972-467-9791
Ownership: Roberto Gomez, Pres., 20%; Julio Cesar Calles, 20%; Daniel Gomez, 20%; Elva Rosa Gomez, 20%; Gilberto Lopez, 20%.
LPTV Stations:
California: K20IU Big Bear Lake; KSSY-LP Ford City; K43AG Ridgecrest.
Oklahoma: K64GW Durant.
Texas: KPFW-LP Gainesville; K18HC Plainview; KZFW-LP Royse City.

IGLESIA MANMIN TODA LA CREACION USA INC.
900-B W Flagler St
Miami, FL 33130
Phone: 305-921-0039
Officer:
Esteban Jose Handal, President
Represented (legal): Robert E. Levine.
LPTV Stations:
Maryland: WNDC-LP Salisbury.

Texas: KHFW-LP Denison; KZHO-LP Victoria.

IMAGE VIDEO TELEPRODUCTIONS INC.
6755 Freedom Ave NW
North Canton, OH 44720
Phone: 330-494-9303
E-mail: mctonges@aol.com
Officer:
Michael A. Tonges, President
Represented (legal): Fletcher, Heald & Hildreth PLC.
LPTV Stations:
Ohio: WIVX-LP Loudonville; W69AO Millersburg; WIVN-LP Newcomerstown.

IMMANUEL BAPTIST CHURCH
701 S. West Ave.
El Dorado, AR 71730
Phone: 501-862-4624
LPTV Stations:
Arkansas: KCIB-LP El Dorado.

IMMANUEL BROADCASTING CORP.
1801 W. 17th St.
Pine Bluff, AR 71603
Phone: 870-536-2287
Fax: 870-534-3757
Officers:
W. E. Bobo, President
Joe Clement, Chief Financial Officer
LPTV Stations:
Arkansas: KIPB-LP Pine Bluff.

INDEPENDENT COMMUNICATIONS INC.
2817 W 11th St
Sioux Falls, SD 57104
Phones: 605-338-0017; 800-568-4340
Fax: 605-338-7173
Web site: www.kttw.com
Officers:
Charles D. Poppen, President
Richard T. DeVaney, Vice President
Thomas J. Whalen, Secretary-Treasurer
Ownership: ElJim Co., 43.4%; RiBob Co., 43.4%; Charles D Poppen, 8.7%; Richard T DeVaney, 1.5%; Jerry Noonan, 1%; E. C Stangland, 1%. Stangland owns KIWA-AM-FM, Sheldon, IA; Thomas J Whalen, 1%; EC ownership:; James W Elmen; Robert C Elmen; RC ownership: James W Elmen; Robert C Elmen.
LPTV Stations:
Minnesota: K22HJ Worthington.
South Dakota: K39CZ Aberdeen; K50DG Brookings; K32DK Watertown.
Commercial TV Stations:
South Dakota: KTTM-DT Huron; KTTW-DT Sioux Falls.

INDEPENDENT PENTECOSTAL CHRISTIAN CHURCH INC.
711 E 4th St
West Liberty, IA 52776
Phone: 319-627-4163
Officer:
Concepcion Rivera, President
LPTV Stations:
Iowa: KXWL-LP Keokuk.

INDIANA WESLEYAN U.
4201 S. Washington St.
Marion, IN 46953-4974
Phones: 765-677-2819; 765-677-2791
Fax: 765-677-2794
Officers:
Leonard Mills, Chairman
James Barnes, President

Jeffrey W. Gnagey, Chief Operating Officer
Jerry Munday, Vice President, Advancement

Ownership: Indiana Wesleyan U..

Represented (legal): Irwin, Campbell & Tannenwald PC.

LPTV Stations:
Indiana: WIWU-CA Marion.

INDIAN WELLS VALLEY TV BOOSTER INC.

PO Box 562
Ridgecrest, CA 93556-0562
Phone: 703-375-0233
E-mail: contact@iwvtvbooster.org
Web site: www.iwvtvbooster.org

LPTV Stations:
California: K14AT China Lake, etc.; K47AE Inyokern, etc.; K41GO Ridgecrest; K45GQ Ridgecrest; K02HY Ridgecrest, etc.; K04HX Ridgecrest, etc.; K05FO Ridgecrest, etc.; K07NH Ridgecrest, etc.; K09MG Ridgecrest, etc.; K11ML Ridgecrest, etc.; K13NF Ridgecrest, etc.; K33ID-D Ridgecrest, etc.; K35HO-D Ridgecrest, etc.; K39HT-D Ridgecrest, etc.; K49AA Ridgecrest, etc.; K51DD-D Ridgecrest, etc..

INFORMATION SUPER STATION LLC

1025 Connecticut Ave. NW
Suite 1201
Washington, DC 20036-5414
Phone: 202-457-0400

LPTV Stations:
Maryland: W28BY Baltimore.

INKOM TV ASSN.

PO Box 13
Inkom, ID 83245

LPTV Stations:
Idaho: K07NO Inkom, etc..

INSPIRATION TELEVISION INC.

1111 Cottontail Rd.
Vista, CA 92081-8620
Phones: 760-727-2105; 505-228-8785
Fax: 760-727-0712

Officer:
George D. Sebastian, Chairman

LPTV Stations:
California: KHFS-LP El Centro-Holtville.
Oregon: KDOV-LP Medford.

INTERNATIONAL BROADCASTING CO.

1554 Bori St.
San Juan, PR 00936-6113
Phone: 787-274-1800

LPTV Stations:
Puerto Rico: WIVE-LP Ceiba.

INTERNATIONAL BROADCASTING NETWORK

Box 691111
Houston, TX 77269
Phone: 281-774-9923

Officers:
Dr. Paul J. Broyles, President
Pershing Paul Stringer, Vice President

Ownership: Non-profit corp.--Houston, TX.

LPTV Stations:
Texas: KTWC-LP Crockett; KHTX-LP Huntsville; KHXL-LP Huntsville; KWTC-LP Kerrville; KCTL-LP Livingston; KLGV-LP Longview;

KHTM-LP Lufkin; KIBN-LP Lufkin; KLUF-LP Lufkin; KNCD-LP Nacogdoches.

INTERNATIONAL COMMUNICATIONS NETWORK INC.

160 Thorn St.
Suite 200
San Diego, CA 92103
Phone: 619-230-0330

Officer:
Maxwell C. Agha, Chief Executive Officer

Ownership: Maxwell C. Agha, 54.01%; Regina Mendoza, 10.87%; Teresita Bascani, 9.17%; Ofelia Mationg-Merlau, 7.38%; Sarah Lowery, 6.05%.

Represented (legal): Katten, Munchin & Rosenman LLP.

LPTV Stations:
California: K61GH National City.

INTERNATIONAL EVANGELICAL CATHOLIC TELEVISION NETWORK

PO Box 44007
Indianapolis, IN 46244-0007
Phone: 317-920-1000
Fax: 317-920-1000
Web site: www.catholic-television.tv

Officer:
Sister Sue Jenkins, President

LPTV Stations:
Indiana: WKOG-LP Indianapolis; WKGK-LP Kokomo.

INTERNATIONAL MEDIA GROUP

1990 S. Bundy Dr.
Suite 850
Los Angeles, CA 90025
Phone: 310-478-1818
Fax: 310-479-8118

Officers:
Ray Beindorf, Chairman Emeritus
Jon Yasuda, President & Chief Operating Officer
Richard Millet, Vice President, Station Manager
Tony Cortese, Vice President & Chief Financial Officer
Bill Welty, Vice President, Engineering

Branch Office:
New York Sales Office
1180 Avenue of the Americas
New York, NY 10036
Phone: 212-999-5448

Ownership: AMG Intermediate LLC, 69.42%; Ray L. Beindorf, 25.5%; AMGI ownership; Asian Media Investors I LP, 64.28%; Korea Times Los Angeles Inc., 19.99%; AMI ownership; GEI Capital III LLC; KTLAI ownership:; Jae Min Chang, Pres., 50%; Jae Ku Change, 50%; GEIC ownership; Leonard Green, 30.7%; Johnathan Sokoloff, 20.8%; John Danhakl, 18.7%; Peter Nolan, 18.7%; Greg Annick, 8.6%; Jonathan Seiffer, 2.5%.

Represented (legal): Skadden, Arps, Slate, Meagher & Flom LLP.

LPTV Stations:
California: KUAN-LP Poway, etc..

Commercial TV Stations:
California: KSCI-DT Long Beach.
Hawaii: KIKU-DT Honolulu.

ION MEDIA NETWORKS INC., DEBTOR IN POSSESSION

601 Clearwater Park Rd.
West Palm Beach, FL 33401-6233
Phone: 561-659-4122
Fax: 561-659-4754
E-mail: pressroom@ionmedia.tv
Web site: www.ionmedia.com

Officers:

R Brandon Burgess, Chairman & Chief Executive Officer
Richard Garcia, Senior Vice President & Chief Financial Officer
Kristine Hunsinger, Senior Vice President, Planning, Scheduling & Acquisitions
Blaine Rominger, Senior Vice President, National, Local, Cable Long-Form Sales
Adam K. Weinstein, Senior Vice President, Secretary & Chief Legal Officer
Stephen P. Appel, President, Sales & Marketing
Douglas C. Barker, President., Bcst. Distribution & Southern Region
Steven J. Friedman, President, Cable
David A. Glenn, President, Engineering
Joseph Koker, President, TV Stations Group
Tammy G. Hedge, Vice President, Chief Accounting Officer & Controller
Brett Jenkins, Vice President, Technology
Robert Marino, Vice President, National Sales
Jeffrey J Quinn, Vice President & Treasurer

Branch Office:
Sales Offices:
1330 Avenue of the Americas
32nd Floor
New York, NY 10019
Phone: 212-603-8451
Fax: 212-956-0920

Ownership: CIG Media LLC; CIGMLLC ownership:; Citadel Wellington LLC, 79%. equity; Citadel Kensington Global Strategies Fund Ltd., 21%. equity; CWLLC & CKGSFL ownership:; Citadel LP; CLP ownership:; Citadel Investment Group LLC, Gen. Partner; CIGLLC ownership:; Kenneth Griffin. Paxson Communications Corp. became ION Media Networks Inc. effective June 26, 2006. ION Media Networks Inc. filed for Chapter 11 bankruptcy protection May 20, 2009.

Represented (legal): Dow Lohnes PLLC.

LPTV Stations:
Colorado: KPXH-LP Fort Collins.
Florida: WPXB-LD Daytona Beach; WPXJ-LP Jacksonville.
Indiana: WIPX-LP Indianapolis.
Massachusetts: W40BO Boston; WMPX-LP Dennis.
Michigan: W48AV Detroit.
New York: WPXU-LP Amityville.
Oregon: KPXG-LP Portland.
Tennessee: WNPX-LP Nashville.
Texas: KBPX-LP Houston.

Commercial TV Stations:
Alabama: WPXH-TV Gadsden.
Arizona: KPPX-DT Tolleson.
California: KSPX-TV Sacramento; KPXN-TV San Bernardino; KKPX-TV San Jose.
Colorado: KPXC-DT Denver.
Connecticut: WHPX-DT New London.
Delaware: WPPX-TV Wilmington.
Florida: WXPX-TV Bradenton; WPXP-TV Lake Worth; WOPX-TV Melbourne; WPXM-DT Miami.
Georgia: WPXC-DT Brunswick; WPXA-TV Rome.
Hawaii: KPXO-DT Kaneohe.
Illinois: WCPX-TV Chicago.
Indiana: WIPX-TV Bloomington.
Iowa: KPXR-TV Cedar Rapids; KFPX-TV Newton.
Kentucky: WUPX-DT Morehead.
Louisiana: WPXL-TV New Orleans.
Massachusetts: WBPX-TV Boston; WDPX-TV Vineyard Haven.
Michigan: WPXD-DT Ann Arbor; WZPX-TV Battle Creek.
Minnesota: KPXM-TV St. Cloud.
Missouri: KPXE-TV Kansas City.
New Hampshire: WPXG-TV Concord.
New York: WYPX-DT Amsterdam; WPXJ-DT Batavia; WPXN-DT New York; WSPX-DT Syracuse.
North Carolina: WGPX-TV Burlington; WFPX-TV Fayetteville; WEPX-TV Greenville; WPXU-DT Jacksonville; WRPX-TV Rocky Mount.
Ohio: WVPX-TV Akron.

Oklahoma: KOPX-TV Oklahoma City; KTPX-TV Okmulgee.
Oregon: KPXG-DT Salem.
Pennsylvania: WQPX-TV Scranton.
Rhode Island: WPXQ-TV Block Island.
Tennessee: WNPX-TV Cookeville; WPXK-TV Jellico; WPXX-DT Memphis.
Texas: KPXD-TV Arlington; KPXB-TV Conroe; KPXL-TV Uvalde.
Utah: KUPX-TV Provo.
Virginia: WPXW-TV Manassas; WPXV-TV Norfolk; WPXR-TV Roanoke.
Washington: KWPX-DT Bellevue; KGPX-TV Spokane.
West Virginia: WLPX-DT Charleston; WWPX-TV Martinsburg.
Wisconsin: WTPX-DT Antigo; WPXE-TV Kenosha.

IOWA PUBLIC BROADCASTING BOARD

6450 Corporate Dr.
Johnston, IA 50131
Phone: 515-242-3100

Officers:
Betty Jean Furgerson, President
John Blong, Vice President

Represented (legal): Dow Lohnes PLLC.

LPTV Stations:
Iowa: K14AF Decorah; K28JD Fort Madison, etc.; K44AB Keokuk; K54AF Keosauqua, etc.; K41AD Lansing; K18GU Ottumwa; K25AA Rock Rapids, etc.; K33AB Sibley, etc..

IRON COUNTY

68 South 100 East
Parowan, UT 84761
Phone: 435-477-3375

LPTV Stations:
Utah: K30GC-D Beaver (rural), etc.; K19GS-D Beaver County (rural); K06JA Cedar Canyon; K08MZ Cedar Canyon; K10MF Cedar Canyon; K02NU Cedar City; K05HB Cedar City; K07GQ Cedar City; K11CQ Cedar City; K31EI Cedar City; K39FQ Cedar City; K45HD Cedar City; K47IS Cedar City; K12PN Cedar City Canyon; K33EB Cedar City, etc.; K35HG Cedar City, etc.; K43JT Cedar City, etc.; K50HI Enoch & Summit; K28GQ Iron County (rural); K06KO Kanarraville; K08CE Kanarraville; K10CK Kanarraville; K12CD Kanarraville; K02KN Kanarraville, etc.; K49IF New Castle, etc.; K32AG Parowan; K34AG Parowan; K36AI Parowan; K38CM Parowan; K49HC Parowan, Enoch, Paragonah; K51HQ Parowan, Enoch, Paragonah; K42AF Parowan, etc.; K44DR Parowan, etc.; K48FJ Parowan, etc..

ISLAND BROADCASTING CO.

4 Hunters Lane
Roslyn, NY 11576-1306
Phone: 516-627-5103
Fax: 516-627-4469

Ownership: Richard D Bogner; Leonard H King.

Represented (legal): Rosenman & Colin LLP.

LPTV Stations:
New York: WNXY-LP New York; WNYN-LP New York; WNYX-LP New York; WNYZ-LP New York; WXNY-LP New York.

IT COMMUNICATIONS INC.

1025 Jefferson St. NW, Ste 700
c/o Katten Muchin Rosenman LLP
Washington, DC 20007-5201
Phone: 202-625-3719

Officer:
Allen Christopher, President

Ownership: Allen Christopher; George Horowitz; Douglas McAward; Sean Stanton, 90%. collectively. Christopher is also principal of Area 51 DMG Inc., see listing.
Represented (legal): Katten, Munchin & Rosenman LLP.
LPTV Stations:
Connecticut: W22BN Danbury.

IZZO LIVING TRUST
616 W. 4th St.
Long Beach, CA 90802
Phone: 562-432-3099
Ownership: Xenia Renatta Izzo.
LPTV Stations:
South Carolina: WCHD-LP Charleston.
Virginia: WVBN-LP Virginia Beach.

JACKSON STATE U.
1400 J.R. Lynch St.
Jackson, MS 39217
Officers:
Dr. James E. Lyons Sr., President
Dr. Elualee Banks, Executive Vice President
Dr. Mildred J. Allen, Executive Vice President
Dr. Dora Washington, Vice President, Academic Affairs
Kevin Appleton, Vice President, Finance
Lillian Taylor, Treasurer & Assistant Vice President, Fiscal Affairs
LPTV Stations:
Mississippi: W23BC Jackson.

JACKSON TELEVISION LLC
200 Clarendon St.
51st Floor
Boston, MA 02116
Phone: 617-262-7770
Ownership: Atla Communications VIII LP, 93.2%; ACVIIILP ownership:; Alta Communications VIII Managers LLC, Gen Partner. votes, 1% assets; ACVIIIMLLC ownership:; Timothy L. Dibble, Managing Member, 50%. votes, 20% assets; Brian W. McNeill, Managing Member, 50%. votes, 20% assets; William P. Egan, 7.5%. votes; Robert Emmert, 6.25%. votes; B. Lane MacDonald, 6.25%. votes; Philip L. Thompson, 6.25%. votes; Eileen McCarthy, 5% votes; Patrick D. Brubaker, 1.25%. votes.
Represented (legal): Pillsbury Winthrop Shaw Pittman LLP.
LPTV Stations:
Mississippi: WXMS-LP Natchez.
Commercial TV Stations:
Mississippi: WDBD-DT Jackson.

JAMIE COOPER TELEVISION INC.
Box 206
Huntsville, AL 35804
Phone: 256-533-1888
LPTV Stations:
Alabama: WTZT-CA Athens.

JBS INC.
708-A Thimble Shoals Blvd.
Newport News, VA 23606
Phone: 757-249-9545
Ownership: Sam Jacobs, Principal.
LPTV Stations:
Virginia: WYSJ-CA Yorktown.

JENSEN INVESTMENTS FLP
1507 Queen Anne Ave. N
#202
Seattle, WA 98109
Phone: 206-963-6364
E-mail: locationx3@msn.com
Ownership: Mark Jensen, Managing Partner.

LPTV Stations:
Arizona: KLHU-CA Lake Havasu City.

JESUS CHRIST FELLOWSHIP
PO Box 246
21091 Powder Horn Rd
Middletown, CA 95461
Phone: 707-987-0888
E-mail: info@jesuschristfellowship.com
Officer:
Jeff Daly, President
LPTV Stations:
California: K15FJ Lakeport.

JLA MEDIA AND PUBLICATIONS LLC
PO Box 4
High View, WV 26808
Phone: 540-598-8601
Ownership: James L. Ahlemann, Managing Member.
Represented (legal): Borsari & Paxson.
LPTV Stations:
Virginia: WAZF-CA Front Royal; WAZH-CA Harrisonburg; WAZC-LP Luray; WAZM-CA Staunton & Waynesboro; WAZW-CA Winchester; WAZT-CA Woodstock.

JLBJ PRODUCTIONS INC.
1424 S.W. 18th St.
Willmar, MN 56201
Phone: 320-231-1013
LPTV Stations:
Minnesota: K13YA Willmar.

TOWN OF JOHNSBURG
PO Box 7
North Creek, NY 12853
Phone: 518-251-2421
Officer:
William H. Thomas, Supervisor
LPTV Stations:
New York: W07BH North Creek, etc.; W09AZ North Creek, etc.; W11AW North Creek, etc..

JOHNSON BROADCASTING CO. INC.
Box 56
Endicott, NY 13760
Phone: 410-765-3581
E-mail: johnso1303@aol.com
LPTV Stations:
New York: WXXW-LP Binghamton.

C. DOWEN JOHNSON
103 Stones Edge
Montgomery, TX 77356
Phone: 936-588-2832
LPTV Stations:
Texas: K49HT Abilene; K47IO Beaumont; KVQT-LP Houston; K48IO Lufkin.

RODNEY S. JOHNSON
Box 1
9263 S. Copley Rd.
Powell Butte, OR 97753
Phone: 541-923-4848
LPTV Stations:
Oregon: K42BR Terrebonne-Bend; K48BL Terrebonne-Bend.

GREGORY JONES
1416 Langford Rd
Gwynn Oak, MD 21207
Phone: 407-492-9928
LPTV Stations:
South Carolina: W21CA Columbia; W51DI Florence; W51AT Mrytle Beach; W49AN

Myrtle Beach; W31BS Orangeburg; W26CF Summerville.

BEN JORDAN COMMUNICATIONS CORP.
828 20th St SW
Lanett, AL 36863
Phone: 706-518-3911
E-mail: benrayjordan@yahoo.com
Officer:
Benjamin Ray Jordan, President
Represented (legal): Dan J. Alpert.
LPTV Stations:
Alabama: WQMK-LP Opelika.

CRANFORD L. JORDAN
Box 30
Winnfield, LA 71483
Phone: 318-628-3892
Fax: 318-628-3818
LPTV Stations:
Louisiana: KCDH-LP Winnfield.

JORDAN CREEK VIEWERS INC.
PO Box 189
Jordan Creek, OR 97910
Phone: 541-586-2460
LPTV Stations:
Oregon: K09PB Jordan Valley; K13MF Jordan Valley.

JOURNAL COMMUNICATIONS INC.
333 W State St
Milwaukee, WI 53203
Phone: 414-332-9611
Fax: 414-967-5400
Officers:
Steven J. Smith, Chairman & Chief Executive Officer
Douglas G. Kiel, President
Paul M. Bonaiuto, Executive Vice President & Chief Financial Officer
Elizabeth F. Brenner, Executive Vice President
Mary Hill Leahy, Senior Vice President, General Counsel, Chief Compliance Officer & Secretary
Anne M. Bauer, Vice President
Carl D. Gardner, Vice President
Mark J. Keefe, Vice President
Kenneth L. Kozminski, Vice President
James P. Prather, Vice President
Steven H. Wexler, Vice President
Karen O. Trickle, Vice President & Treasurer
Ownership: Publicly held..
Represented (legal): Leventhal, Senter & Lerman PLLC.
LPTV Stations:
Arizona: K16EO Oro Valley & Tucson.
California: KPSE-LP Palm Springs.
Idaho: K27DX McCall; KSAW-LP Twin Falls.
Michigan: W31BK Menominee.
Nevada: K59EX Laughlin; K42AA Pahrump.
Wisconsin: W22BW Sturgeon Bay.
Commercial TV Stations:
Arizona: KWBA-TV Sierra Vista; KGUN-DT Tucson.
California: KMIR-DT Palm Springs.
Florida: WFTX-TV Cape Coral.
Idaho: KNIN-DT Caldwell; KIVI-TV Nampa.
Michigan: WSYM-DT Lansing.
Nebraska: KMTV-TV Omaha.
Nevada: KTNV-TV Las Vegas.
Wisconsin: WGBA-TV Green Bay; WTMJ-DT Milwaukee.
Newspapers:
Florida: St. John's Recorder (Fruit Cove), Clay Today (Orange Park), Ponte Vedra Recorder (Ponte Vedra Beach), Pelican Press (Sarasota)

Wisconsin: Brookfield News; Cudahy-St. Francis Reminder-Enterprise; Elm Grove Elm Leaves; Franklin Hub; Germantown Banner-Press; Greendale Village Life; Greenfield Observer; Hales Corners Village Hub; Kettle Moraine Index
Radio Stations:
Arizona: KGMG (FM) Oracle; KFFN (AM), KMXZ-FM, KQTH (FM) Tucson
Idaho: KGEM (AM), KJOT (FM) Boise; KCID (AM), KTHI (FM) Caldwell; KRVB (FM) Nampa; KQXR (FM) Payette
Kansas: KYQQ (FM) Arkansas City; KFXJ (FM) Augusta; KFDI-FM, KFTI (AM), KICT-FM Wichita
Missouri: KZRQ (FM) Mount Vernon; KSPW (FM) Sparta; KSGF (AM), KTTS-FM Springfield
Nebraska: KEZO-FM, KKCD (FM), KQCH (FM), KSRZ (FM), KXSP (AM) Omaha
Oklahoma: KXBL (FM) Henryetta; KFAQ (AM), KVOO-FM Tulsa
Tennessee: WMYU (FM) Karns, WKHT (FM) Knoxville, WQBB (AM) Powell, WWST (FM) Sevierville
Wisconsin: WKTI-FM, WTMJ (AM) Milwaukee

JULIAETTA TV ASSOCIATION
PO Box 441
Juliaetta, ID 83535
Phone: 208-276-3661
E-mail: rjgroseclose@tds.net
Officer:
Janice Groseclose, Information Contact
LPTV Stations:
Idaho: K07NL Juliaetta; K09DF Juliaetta; K11DL Juliaetta; K41GW Juliaetta; K48HB Juliaetta.

JUMPOFF RIDGE LLC
PO Box 1229
Monroe, WA 98272
Phone: 425-788-2600
Ownership: John D. Wallace, Managing Member.
Represented (legal): Pillsbury Winthrop Shaw Pittman LLP.
LPTV Stations:
Washington: K14BF Wenatchee.

JUNEAU ALASKA COMMUNICATIONS LLC
3161 Channel Dr
Juneau, AK 99801
Phone: 907-583-3680
Officer:
Richard Burns, Group Chief Executive Officer
Represented (legal): Davis Wright Tremaine LLP.
LPTV Stations:
Alaska: KCBJ-LP Juneau.

JW BROADCASTING LLC
11109 N Pusch Ridge Vistas Dr
Tucson, AZ 85737-7311
Phone: 520-544-6186
Ownership: Alta/JW Broadcasting Investor Corp., 52.38%; DJ Broadcasting LLC, 47.62%; AJWBIC ownership:; Timothy L. Dibble, 20.9385%; Brian W. McNeill, 20.9385%; Robert Emmert, 10.7415%; B. Lane McDonald, 10.7415%; William P. Egan, 7.5735%; Philip L. Thompson, 7.5735%; Patrick D. Brubaker, 6.3855%; Andrew T. Mulderry, 5.94%; Eileen McCarthy, 4.9995%; DJBLLC ownership:; James W. Wood, 50%. votes, 48% assets; David Joseph, 50%. votes, 7% assets. Joseph & Woods have interest in MississippiTelevision LLC, which holds controlling interest in Mississippi Television LLC, see listing.
Represented (legal): Wiley Rein LLP.

LPTV Stations:
Missouri: K02NQ Columbia; KQFX-LP Columbia; KZOU-LP Jefferson City.
Commercial TV Stations:
Missouri: KMIZ-DT Columbia.

K02MU-TV LLC
226 Sussex Ave.
Morristown, NJ 07960
LPTV Stations:
Oklahoma: KOKJ-LP Elk City.

KALTAG VILLAGE COUNCIL
5900 E. Tudor Rd.
Anchorage, AK 99507
Phone: 907-269-5744
LPTV Stations:
Alaska: K02KA Kaltag.

KAMIAH VALLEY TV INC.
PO Box 144
Kamiah, ID 83536
Phone: 208-983-1014
E-mail: benniegw@cybrquest.com
Officer:
Benita G. Weddle, Secretary-Treasurer
LPTV Stations:
Idaho: K07AQ Kamiah; K09AL Kamiah; K11KO Kamiah; K13AP Kamiah.

KANAB LIONS CLUB
359 North 100 West
Kanab, UT 84741
LPTV Stations:
Utah: K12ND Kanab.

KANSAS-NEBRASKA ASSOCIATION OF SEVENTH-DAY ADVENTISTS
3440 S.W. Urish Rd.
Topeka, KS 66614
Phone: 785-478-4726
E-mail: rcarlson@ks-ne.org
Officer:
Ron Carlson, President
Represented (legal): Donald E. Martin.
LPTV Stations:
Nebraska: KMBB-LP North Platte.

KANSAS STATE UNIVERSITY
Bob Dole Hall
Educational Communications Center
Manhattan, KS 66506
Phone: 785-532-7041
Fax: 785-532-7355
Web site: www.ksu.edu/ecc
Officer:
Doug VonFeldt, Interim Director, Educational Communications Center
LPTV Stations:
Kansas: KKSU-LP Manhattan.

KAZT LLC
4343 E. Camelback Rd.
Suite 400
Phoenix, AZ 85018
Phone: 602-957-1650
Fax: 602-224-2284
Ownership: Londen Insurance Group Inc., 99%; Ron Bergamo, 1%; LIG ownership:; Jack Londen, 96.52%; Thomas Londen, 3.48%.
Represented (legal): Pillsbury Winthrop Shaw Pittman LLP.
LPTV Stations:
Arizona: K24DK Bullhead City; K43CO Casa Grande; K30DT Flagstaff; K20ID Kingman; K17DA Lake Havasu City; K57HX Mesa;

K55EH Phoenix; KAZT-CA Phoenix; K23BY Scottsdale; K29DK Williams; K19CX Yuma.
Commercial TV Stations:
Arizona: KAZT-DT Phoenix.

KCTS TELEVISION
401 Mercer St.
Seattle, WA 98109
Phone: 206-728-6463
Officers:
Doug Beighle, Chairman
Nancy Evans, Vice Chairman
Burnill F. Clark, President & Chief Executive Officer
Walter Parsons, Senior Vice President & Chief Operating Officer
Jean Gardner, Secretary
James M. Costello, Treasurer
Jacqueline Boettcher, Chief Financial Officer
Monica Reisner, Assistant Secretary

Branch Office:
555 W. Hastings
Suite 2220
Vancouver, B.C. V6B 5K3Phone: 604-291-5101
Ownership: Non-profit corp..
Represented (legal): Dow Lohnes PLLC.
LPTV Stations:
Washington: K18AD East Wenatchee, etc..
ETV Stations:
Washington: KCTS-DT Seattle; KYVE-DT Yakima.

KELLEY ENTERPRISES
4237 Airline Rd.
Muskegon, MI 49444
Phones: 231-733-4040; 616-733-4944
Fax: 231-739-4329
Officers:
Fenton Kelley, Chairman, President & Chief Executive Officer
Channa W. Kelley, Chief Operating Officer
Michelle K. Kelley, Vice President
Ownership: Kelley Enterprises of Muskegon Inc.; Fenton L Kelley; Michelle K Kelley.
LPTV Stations:
Michigan: WMKG-LP Muskegon.

DEBORAH R. KENNY
1146 Lark Rd.
Joplin, MO 64804
Phone: 417-623-4646
Fax: 417-206-4482
LPTV Stations:
Missouri: K53IS Anderson/Pineville; KJPX-LP Joplin; KCLJ-CA Joplin-Carthage; K38DD Monett; KCLG-CA Neosho.

GARY M. KENNY
1146 Lark Rd.
Joplin, MO 64804
Phones: 417-451-1440; 417-623-4646
Fax: 417-206-4482
E-mail: Garykenny@cableone.net
LPTV Stations:
Missouri: K53IS Anderson/Pineville; KJPX-LP Joplin; KCLJ-CA Joplin-Carthage; KCLG-CA Neosho.

KENTUCKY AUTHORITY FOR ETV
600 Cooper Dr.
Lexington, KY 40502
Phone: 606-233-3000
Officers:
Steven Newberry, Chairman
Virginia Gaines Fox, Executive Director & Chief Executive Officer
Donna Moore, Deputy Executive Director, Production & Planning

Sally Hamilton, Deputy Executive Director, Administration & Support
Bill Wilson, Deputy Executive Director, Education & Outreach
Ownership: Governing Board of Kentucky Authority for ETV.
Represented (legal): Dinsmore & Shohl LLP.
LPTV Stations:
Kentucky: W20CT-D Augusta; W56AT Augusta; W23DM-D Falmouth; W56AM Falmouth; W10AR Louisa; W28DD-D Louisa.
ETV Stations:
Kentucky: WKAS-DT Ashland; WCVN-DT Covington; WKZT-DT Elizabethtown; WKLE-DT Lexington; WKMJ-DT Louisville; WKPC-DT Louisville; WKMA-DT Madisonville; WKMR-DT Morehead; WKMU-DT Murray; WKOH-DT Owensboro; WKON-DT Owenton; WKPD-DT Paducah; WKPI-DT Pikeville; WKSO-DT Somerset.

ANDREA J. KESLER
Rte. 1
Box 313
East Bernstadt, KY 40729
LPTV Stations:
Kentucky: WOBZ-LP East Bernstadt, etc..

BENETT KESSLER
Box 275
Independence, CA 93526
Phone: 760-878-2381
Ownership: Sierra Broadcasters LLC.
LPTV Stations:
California: KSRW-LP Bishop.

KETCHIKAN TV LLC
PO Box 348
2539 N Hwy 67
Sedalia, CO 80135
Phone: 303-688-5162
Officer:
David M. Drucker, President
Ownership: David M. Drucker, 75%; ENA Lukes Family Trust, 25%. Drucker also has interest in Cayo Hueso Networks LLC, Denver Digital Television LLC, Echonet Corp., GreenTV Corp. & Polar Communications, see listings.
Represented (legal): Rini Coran PC.
LPTV Stations:
Alaska: K41DP Anchorage; K45HQ Anchorage; KDMD-LP Fairbanks; KUBD-LP Kodiak.
Commercial TV Stations:
Alaska: KDMD-DT Anchorage; KUBD-DT Ketchikan; KTNL-DT Sitka.

CITY OF KIANA
5900 E. Tudor Rd.
Anchorage, AK 99507
Phone: 907-269-5744
LPTV Stations:
Alaska: K04IG Kiana.

KIDQ INC.
906 6th St
Clarkston, WA 99403
Phone: 509-758-0900
E-mail: jarel@jpiworldwide.com
Ownership: Jarel Pittman, Pres..
Represented (legal): Irwin, Campbell & Tannenwald PC.
LPTV Stations:
Idaho: KIDQ-LP Lewiston.

KID'S TELEVISION LLC
PO Box 3160
Meridian, MS 39303
Phone: 615-975-0525
Officer:

Kenneth R Rainey Sr, President
Represented (legal): Wiley Rein LLP.
LPTV Stations:
Mississippi: WJMF-LP Jackson.

KILGORE TELEVISION COMMITTEE
PO Box 135
Kilgore, NE 69216
LPTV Stations:
Nebraska: K09IW Kilgore.

KILLEEN CHRISTIAN BROADCASTING CORP.
Box 11031
Killeen, TX 76547-1031
Phone: 254-554-3683
Fax: 254-554-7385
Officers:
Catherine Mason, President
Susan Mooney, Secretary-Treasurer
Represented (legal): Brooks, Pierce, McLendon, Humphrey & Leonard LLP.
LPTV Stations:
Texas: KPLE-CA Killeen; KPLE-LD Killeen.

KILLINGTON LTD.
RR 1
Box 2450
Killington, VT 05751
Phones: 802-422-3333; 802-422-4488
Fax: 802-422-6765
Ownership: LBO Resort Enterprises.
LPTV Stations:
Vermont: W18AE Killington.

KING BROADCASTING CO.
400 S. Record St.
Dallas, TX 75202
LPTV Stations:
Idaho: KTFT-LD Twin Falls.
Oregon: K17HA Astoria; K26AY Corvallis, etc.; K13SL Huntington; K59EK The Dalles.

KING COUNTY TV RECEPTION DISTRICT 2
25230 SE Mirrormont Dr
Issaquah, WA 98027
Phone: 425-392-5760
Officer:
Barrie Austin, Director
LPTV Stations:
Washington: K03FA Issaquah, etc..

KING COVE SCHOOL DISTRICT
5900 E. Tudor Rd.
Anchorage, AK 99507
Phone: 907-269-5744
LPTV Stations:
Alaska: K04HR King Cove.

KING KONG BROADCASTING INC.
4609 Crimson Rock Way
Las Vegas, NV 89031
Phone: 702-642-8847
Officers:
Larry Hunt, Chairman, President & Chief Operating Officer
Lisa Rhodes, Vice President, Chief Executive & Financial Officer
Jeff Gotts, Vice President, Engineering
Ownership: Larry Hunt; Lisa Hunt, jointly.
LPTV Stations:
Nevada: KGNG-LP Las Vegas.

KIOWA COUNTY
Kiowa County Courthouse
PO Box 591
Eads, CO 81036

LPTV Stations:
Colorado: K50AA Eads; K52AA Eads; K54AB Eads; K56AG Eads; K48DW Eads, etc..

KIT CARSON COUNTY
Box 160
Burlington, CO 80807-0160
Phone: 719-346-8139
E-mail: kccadmin@kitcarsoncounty.org
Officer:
Lyn Brownfield, County Administrator
LPTV Stations:
Colorado: K53AD Bethune & Burlington; K55AX Bethune & Burlington; K57AM Bethune & Burlington; K59AP Bethune & Burlington; K63AJ Flagler-Seibert; K65AO Flagler-Seibert; K67AQ Flagler-Seibert; K69AX Flagler-Seibert.

KITTITAS COUNTY TV IMPROVEMENT DISTRICT 1
Box 337
Ellensburg, WA 98926
LPTV Stations:
Washington: K50KK-D Ellensburg; K17IL-D Ellensburg, etc.; K20JL-D Ellensburg, etc.; K32IG-D Ellensburg, etc.; K51BD Ellensburg, etc.; K63BZ Ellensburg, etc..

CITY OF KIVALINA
5900 E. Tudor Rd.
Anchorage, AK 99507
Phone: 907-269-5744
LPTV Stations:
Alaska: K04IL Kivalina.

KJLA LLC
2323 Corinth Ave.
West Los Angeles, CA 90064
Phone: 818-757-7583
LPTV Stations:
California: KSGA-LP San Bernardino; KFUL-LP San Luis Obispo; KLFA-LP Santa Maria.

KLEAR VU TELEVISION DISTRICT
PO Box 376
Scobey, MT 59263
Phone: 406-487-5485
LPTV Stations:
Montana: K60BN Four Buttes, etc.; K03DP Scobey; K13MA Scobey.

K LICENSEE INC.
136-56 39th Ave., 4th Floor
Flushing, NY 11354
Phone: 718-358-4219
E-mail: dokny@aol.com
Officer:
Young D. Kwon, President
Represented (legal): Garvey Schubert Barer.
LPTV Stations:
Connecticut: W17CD Stamford.
New York: W26DC Hempstead; WEBR-CA Manhattan.

KM BROADCASTING INC.
Box 119
Annandale, VA 22003-0019
Phone: 703-447-3117
Ownership: Robert E Kelly, 50%; Peter B Martine, 50%.
LPTV Stations:
Virginia: WXOB-LP Richmond.

KMCE INC.
540 Hauer Apple Way
Aptos, CA 95003-9315
Phone: 831-768-8668
Officer:

Martin Jackson, President
LPTV Stations:
California: KMCE-LP Monterey.

KM COMMUNICATIONS INC.
3654 W. Jarvis Ave.
Skokie, IL 60076
Phone: 847-674-0864
Fax: 847-674-9188
Officers:
Myoung Hwa Bae, President & Treasurer
Kevin Joel Bae, Secretary
Ownership: Myoung Hwa Bae, see Hapa Media Properties LLC & Pocatello Channel 15 LLC..
Represented (legal): Irwin, Campbell & Tannenwald PC.
LPTV Stations:
Arizona: KWKM-LP Concho; KWSJ-LP Concho; KNLO-LP Holbrook; KPVY-LD Prescott; KVFA-LP Yuma.
California: KRDN-LP Redding.
Georgia: WSKC-CA Atlanta; WWPD-LP Douglas; WPDW-LP Pearson; WPNG-LP Pearson.
Guam: KTKB-LP Tamuning.
Hawaii: KHIK-LP Kailua-Kona.
Illinois: WRDH-LP Ashton; WCRD-LP Carthage; WBKM-LP Chana; WOCH-CA Chicago; WOCK-CA Chicago; WMKB-LP Rochelle.
Indiana: WHFE-LP Sullivan; WIIB-LP Sullivan; WKMF-LP Sullivan; WVGO-LP Sullivan.
Louisiana: W44CE Vidalia.
Pennsylvania: WLEP-LP Erie.
Texas: KTXF-LP Abilene; KPPY-LP Beaumont; KCCG-LP Corpus Christi; KETK-LP Lufkin; KSVH-LP Victoria.
Wisconsin: WMKE-CA Milwaukee.
Commercial TV Stations:
Arizona: KCFG-DT Flagstaff.
Arkansas: KEJB-DT El Dorado.
Iowa: KWKB-DT Iowa City.

PAUL E. KNIES
PO Box 1009
Jasper, IN 47547-1009
Phone: 812-634-9232
E-mail: pknies@psci.net
Represented (legal): Miller & Neely PC.
LPTV Stations:
Indiana: WJTS-LD Jasper.

EDDIE KNIGHT
1033 E. 3 Notch St.
Andalusia, AL 36420
Phone: 334-427-9966
E-mail: wkni@wkni.net
Represented (legal): Dan J. Alpert.
LPTV Stations:
Alabama: WKNI-LP Andalusia.

KNVL-TV INC.
Box 1020
Nashville, AR 71852-1020
Phone: 870-845-5685
Officers:
Jerry Jacobs, President
Glen Power, Chief Executive Officer
Anna Blase, Secretary
Ronny Woods, Chief Financial Officer
Represented (legal): Joseph E. Dunne III.
LPTV Stations:
Arkansas: KJEP-CA Nashville; KSJA-CA Nashville.

KODIAK PUBLIC BROADCASTING CORP.
620 Egan Way
Kodiak, AK 99615

LPTV Stations:
Alaska: KMXT-LP Kodiak.

KOKH TELEVISION LLC
226 Sussex Ave.
Morristown, NJ 07960
LPTV Stations:
Oklahoma: KOKQ-LP Glencoe.

KOKI TELEVISION LLC
226 Sussex Ave.
Morristown, NJ 07960
LPTV Stations:
Oklahoma: KOKG-LP Stillwater.

COUNTY OF KOOCHICHING
715 4th St.
International Falls, MN 56649
Phone: 218-283-1101
Officer:
Robert Peterson, Treasurer
LPTV Stations:
Minnesota: W64AM Big Falls; K60BO Big Falls, etc.; K62BJ Big Falls, etc.; K56BO Birchdale, etc.; W58AI Birchdale, etc.; K49BU International Falls; K51CM International Falls; K53CQ International Falls; K60BT International Falls; K65EA Kabetogama; K67EH Kabetogama; K69FD Kabetogama; K55BY Northome, etc.; K57BK Northome, etc.; K66AP Virginia; K68AT Virginia.

PAUL H. KOPLIN
1207 Oak St.
Santa Monica, CA 90405
Phone: 323-965-5400
LPTV Stations:
Iowa: WBQD-LP Davenport.
Commercial TV Stations:
Illinois: WAOE-DT Peoria.

KOREAN AMERICAN TV BROADCASTING CORP.
4675 River Green Pkwy
Duluth, GA 30096
Phone: 770-497-0015
Ownership: Susan Sim Oh, Pres. & Secy., 51%; Coline K. Sim, V.P. & Treas., 49%; Brenda S Sim, Director.
Represented (legal): Fletcher, Heald & Hildreth PLC.
LPTV Stations:
Georgia: WKTB-CA Atlanta; WKTB-LD Atlanta.

KOTZEBUE BROADCASTING INC.
Box 78
Kotzebue, AK 99752
LPTV Stations:
Alaska: K09OV Kotzebue.

KOVAS COMMUNICATIONS
2000 Lower Huntington Rd
Fort Wayne, IN 46819
Phone: 219-747-1511
LPTV Stations:
Indiana: W07CL Auburn.
Radio Stations:
Illinois: WONX (AM) Evanston, WMCW (AM) Harvard, WKKD (AM) Silvis
Michigan: WCGO (AM) Jenison

KOYUK CITY COUNCIL
5900 E. Tudor Rd.
Anchorage, AK 99507
Phone: 907-269-5744

LPTV Stations:
Alaska: K09SA Koyuk.

KPAL TELEVISION INC.
308 Dunwoody Dr.
Raleigh, NC 27615
Phone: 919-844-5225
Officers:
Gloria L. Horn, President
Timothy C. Wicker, Secretary-Treasurer
Charles R. Wicker, Director
Ownership: Gloria L. Horn, 25%; Timothy C. Wicker, 25%; Charles R. Wicker, 25%.
Represented (legal): Borsari & Paxson.
LPTV Stations:
California: KPAL-LP Palmdale.

KQDS ACQUISITION CORP.
PO Box 9115
Fargo, ND 58106
Phone: 701-277-1515
Fax: 701-277-1830
Officer:
Ro D. Grignon, President
Ownership: Ro D Grignon, 15%; Curtis Squire, 85%. Grignon & Squire also own Red River Broadcast Corp., see listing.
Represented (legal): Pillsbury Winthrop Shaw Pittman LLP.
LPTV Stations:
Michigan: W32CV Ironwood.
Minnesota: K39GG Aitkin; K29EB Grand Rapids; K15GT Hibbing; K45JD International Falls; K47IR Virginia.
Wisconsin: W45CI Ashland; K31GH Hayward.
Commercial TV Stations:
Minnesota: KQDS-DT Duluth.

KTVQ COMMUNICATIONS INC.
3203 3rd Ave. N
Billings, MT 59101-1953
Phone: 406-252-5611
LPTV Stations:
Montana: K69CM Big Timber, etc.; K64EM Castle Rock, etc.; K26GL Columbus; K24GD Hardin; K39HD Red Lodge.

KTVU PARTNERSHIP
6205 Peachtree Dunwoody Rd.
Atlanta, GA 30328
Phone: 678-645-0000
Officer:
Andrew A. Merdek, Secretary
Ownership: KTVU Inc., 55%; Anthony Family Partnership, 22.5%; ACC Family Partnership LP, 22.5%; KTVUI ownership:; Cox Broadcasting Inc.; AFC ownership:; Kennedy Children's Trust, James C. Kennedy & R. Dale Hughes, Trustees, 39.19%; Parry-Okeden Children's Trust, Blair K. Parry-Okeden & R. Dale Hughes, Trustees, 26.13%; Blair D. Parry-Okeden Trust, James C. Kennedy & R. Dale Hughes, Trustees, 14.84%; KTVU-JCK Inc., 14.84%; KTVU-BCA Inc., 5%; ACCFPLP ownership:; KTVU-ACC Inc., Gen. Partner, 5%; CBI ownership:; Dayton Cox Trust-A, Barbara Cox Anthony, Anne Cox Chambers & Richard L. Braunstein, Trustees, 41.1%; Anne Cox Chambers Atlanta Trust, Barbara Cox Anthony, Trustee, 28.95%; Barbara Cox Anthony Atlanta Trust, Anne Cox Chambers, Trustee, 28.95%; KTVUACCI ownership:; Anne Cox Chambers; KTVUBCAI ownership:; Barbara Cox Anthony; KTVUJCKI ownership:; James C. Kennedy.
Represented (legal): Dow Lohnes PLLC.
LPTV Stations:
California: K48LA-D South Lake Tahoe.

Nevada: K22FH Hawthorne; K56IG Nixon; K33IB Silver Springs; K17HB Winnemucca.
Commercial TV Stations:
California: KTVU-DT Oakland; KICU-DT San Jose.
Nevada: KRXI-DT Reno.
Texas: KFOX-DT El Paso.

KVOA COMMUNICATIONS INC.
209 W. Elm St.
Tucson, AZ 85705
Phone: 520-624-7957
LPTV Stations:
Arizona: K64BV Casas Adobes.
Texas: K68DJ Corpus Christi.

KZSW TELEVISION INC.
43225 Business Park Dr.
Temecula, CA 92590
Phone: 951-693-0027
E-mail: kpage@kzswtv.com
Officer:
Kevin Page, Chief Executive Officer
LPTV Stations:
California: KZSW-LP Hemet.

L4 MEDIA GROUP LLC
219 Salt Grass Place
Melbourne Beach, FL 32951
Phone: 321-729-8451
Officer:
Rick Ehrman, Chairman
Represented (legal): Irwin, Campbell & Tannenwald PC.
LPTV Stations:
Alabama: WBXA-CA Birmingham; WBXM-CA Montgomery.
Florida: WBXG-CA Gainesville; WBXJ-CA Jacksonville, etc.; WBXT-CA Tallahassee.
Georgia: WXSX-CA Savannah.
Illinois: WBXC-CA Champaign & Urbana.
Iowa: WBXF-CA Des Moines.
Kentucky: WBXV-CA Louisville.
Louisiana: KBXS-CA Shreveport.
North Carolina: WUBX-CA Durham, etc.; WBXU-CA Raleigh.
Tennessee: WBXP-CA Memphis.

LA GRANDE SEVENTH DAY ADVENTIST CHURCH
2702 Adams Ave.
Box 1025
La Grande, OR 97850
Phone: 541-963-4018
Officers:
Buck Schaffer, Chairman
David Kramer, Chief Operating Officer
Sherri Shelman, Secretary
David Riley, Chief Financial Officer
LPTV Stations:
Oregon: K02PJ La Grande.

LAKE COUNTY TV CLUB
95 Oak Knoll
PO Box 906
Lakeport, CA 95453
Phone: 707-263-9020
Officer:
Mike Salter, President
Represented (legal): Borsari & Paxson.
LPTV Stations:
California: K26GK Lakeport; K33CH Lakeport; K46DR Lakeport; K52AJ Lakeport; K68AL Lakeport.

LAKE COUNTY TV-FM INC.
PO Box 44
Leadville, CO 80461

LPTV Stations:
Colorado: K03CD Leadville; K08ER Leadville; K11GM Leadville; K13GI Leadville.

LAKE CREEK TV DISTRICT
PO Box 906
Troy, MT 59935
Phone: 406-295-4266
E-mail: jay@libby.org
LPTV Stations:
Montana: K09KE Bull Lake Valley; K11KP Bull Lake Valley; K13KV Bull Lake Valley.

LAKE HAVASU CHRISTIAN TV
510 N. Acoma Blvd.
Box 747
Lake Havasu City, AZ 86403
Phone: 928-453-8825
Fax: 928-453-2588
Officers:
Richard D. Tatham, Chief Executive Officer & General Manager
Grace M. Tatham, Treasurer
Ownership: Advance Ministries Inc.; AMI ownership:; Richard D Tatham; Grace M Tatham.
Represented (legal): Arent Fox LLP.
LPTV Stations:
Arizona: K25AL Lake Havasu City; K27EC Lake Havasu City.
Radio Stations:
Arizona: KNLB (FM) Lake Havasu City

LAKE OF THE WOODS COUNTY
PO BOX 808
Baudette, MN 56623
Phone: 218-634-2836
Officer:
John W. Horscheid, County Auditor
LPTV Stations:
Minnesota: K53BL Baudette; K55BH Baudette; K57AR Baudette; K61AR Williams; K63AS Williams; W59AX Williams.

LAKES BROADCASTING GROUP INC.
Box 300
Breezy Point, MN 56472
Ownership: Shareholder owned--Breezy Point, MN.
LPTV Stations:
Minnesota: KLKS-LP Breezy Point.

LAKE TV ASSN.
898 Vallecito Creek Rd.
Bayfield, CO 81122
LPTV Stations:
Colorado: K02ET Vallecito; K08ET Vallecito; K10AD Vallecito.

CITY OF LAMAR
102 E. Perimeter
Lamar, CO 81052
LPTV Stations:
Colorado: K03BA Lamar; K07DH Lamar; K09DH Lamar.

MICHAEL LAMBERT
100 N. Crescent Dr.
Suite 200
Beverly Hills, CA 90210
Phone: 310-385-4200
Represented (legal): Covington & Burling.
LPTV Stations:
New York: W55AI Lake Placid.
Vermont: W63AD Rutland.
Commercial TV Stations:
Vermont: WVNY-DT Burlington.
Other Holdings:
TV Stations: Lambert Broadcasting of Tennessee, see listing..

LANDER COUNTY GENERAL IMPROVEMENT DISTRICT NO. 1
Box 565
Battle Mountain, NV 89820
Phone: 775-635-2885
Fax: 775-635-0604
Officers:
Mark D. Lake, Chairman
Walt Brown, Vice Chairman
Elizabeth Baker, Secretary-Treasurer
LPTV Stations:
Nevada: K11IY Battle Mountain; K13JD Battle Mountain; K16FD Battle Mountain; K22GM Battle Mountain; K32CA Battle Mountain; K42DZ Battle Mountain; K06FQ Copper Canyon, etc..

LANDMARK MEDIA ENTERPRISES LLC
150 W Brambleton Ave
Norfolk, VA 23510-2075
Phones: 757-446-2010; 800-446-2004
Fax: 757-446-2489
Web site: www.landmarkcom.com
Officers:
Frank Batten Sr., Chairman of Executive Committee
Frank Batten Jr., Chairman & Chief Executive Officer
Richard F. Barry III, Vice Chairman
Decker Anstrom, President & Chief Operating Officer
Debora Wilson, President, The Weather Channel
R. Bruce Bradley, Executive Vice President, Landmark Publishing Group
Guy Friddell III, Executive Vice President, Corporate Secretary & Counsel
Charlie W. Hill, Executive Vice President, Human Resources
Lemuel E. Lewis, Executive Vice President & Chief Financial Officer
Colleen R. Pittman, Vice President, Finance
Michael Alston, Vice President, Corporate Development & New Ventures
Ownership: Frank Batten Jr. Trust, Frank Batten Jr, Trustee, 36.27%. votes; Fay M. Slover Trust, Bank of America N.A. & Frank Batten, Trustees, 35.10%. votes, 24.37 % assets; Frank Batten 1986 Family Trust, Frank Batten Jr., Trustee, 18.25%. votes; William S. Glennan Trust, J. Allen Tyler, Trustee, 8.42%. votes; 6.52 assets; Frank Batten Trust, Frank Batten, Trustee, 18.47%. assets; Dorothy Batten Rolph Revocable Trust, 5.59%. assets. Formerly Landmark Communications Inc.
Represented (legal): Wiley Rein LLP.
LPTV Stations:
Nevada: K46GX Henderson; K22DR Laughlin; K48AB Mercury, etc.; K49AB Pahrump.
Commercial TV Stations:
Nevada: KLAS-DT Las Vegas.
Tennessee: WTVF-DT Nashville.
Newspapers:
Colorado: Metrowest (Brighton), The Canyon Courier (Evergreen), Clear Creek Courant (Idaho Springs), Columbine Community Courier (Littleton), The Hustler (Pine)
Florida: The Visitor (Beverly Hills), Cedar Key Beacon, Chiefland Citizen, The Wakulla News (Crawfordville), Riverland News (Dunnellon), South Marion Citizen (Ocala), Sumter County Times, The Osceola (Tallahasee), Willi
Illinois: Vandalia Leader-Union
Indiana: Mt. Vernon Democrat, Perry County News, Spencer County Journal-Democrat (Rockport)
Iowa: Opinion-Tribune (Glenwood), Red Oak Express
Kentucky: The Kentucky Standard, PLG-TV (Bardstown); Trimble Banner (Bedford); Central Kentucky News-Journal (Campbellsville); Carrollton News-Democrat; Casey

County News; Cynthiana Democrat; The News-Enterprise (Elizabe
Maryland: The Capital (Annapolis); Carroll County Times, Community Times (Westminster)
Mississippi: New Albany Gazette
New Mexico: Las Vegas Optic, Los Alamos Monitor
North Carolina: News & Record (Greensboro), Brunswick Beacon (Shallotte)
South Carolina: Chester News and Reporter, The Lancaster News, Pageland Progressive-Journal
Tennessee: LaFollette Press, Morgan County News, Roane County News
Virginia: The Bedford Bulletin, The Gazette (Galax), Declaration (Independence), Loudon Easterner, The Virginian-Pilot (Norfolk), The Roanoke Times
Other Holdings:
Career Schools: Landmark Education Serivces Inc.
Data Network Service: Continental Broadband Inc.
Databases: Alliant Cooperative Data Solutions LLC
Franchise Broker Service: FranchiseBuyer
Franchise Coordinator: Franchise Solutions
Franchise Referrals: FranchiseOpportunities.com
Magazine: The Cats' Pause (Lexington, KY); Voice of the Hawkeyes (North Liberty, IA); Florida Special Publications (Beverly Hills, FL); Gator Bait (Williston, FL); Real Estate News Citrus (Beverly Hills, FL); Citrus County Chronicle (Crystal River); Inside Indiana (Shelbyville, KY); Tri-State Homes (Cynthiana, KY); Greater Baltimore Homes (Westminster, MD); West Virginia Real Estate Guide (Martinsburg, WV); Eastern Panhandle Real Estate Guide (WV) (Westminster, MD); Eastern Panhandle Homes (WV) (Westminster, MD); Dulles Homes (Westminster, MD); Roane Real Estate Review (Kingston, TN); Carolina Gateway (Lancaster, SC); Homes of York/Adams Counties (PA) (Westminster, MD); Carolina Blue (Durham, NC); Homes & Property (Los Alamos, NM); Huskers Illustrated (Lincoln, NE); Mississippi Homes (New Albany); Real Estate News Hernando/Pasco (Beverly Hills, FL); Guide to Homes (Westminster, MD); Central Kentucky Homes (Elizabethtown, KY); Baltimore/Harford/Cecil Homes (Westminster, MD); Kentucky Homes Bullitt/Nelson/Spencer (Cynthiana, KY); Kentucky Homes Central (Cynthiana, KY); Kentucky Homes Garrard/Lincoln/Rockcastle (Cynthiana, KY); Kentucky Homes Madison/Estill (Cynthiana, KY); Kentucky Homes Northern (Cynthiana, KY); Kentucky Homes Pulaski/Wayne (Cynthiana, KY); Shelby County Home Finder's Guide (Shelbyville, KY); Frederick/Washington Co. Homes (Westminster, MD); Central Maryland Homes (Westminster, MD); 1st Choice Properties (Westminster, MD); Marion/Washington Homes (Lebanon, KY)
On-Demand Video: TotalVid Inc.
On-Line Auction Service: Naxcom.com
On-Line Marketing Services: Q Interactive
Publishing: Trader Publishing Co.; Washingtonian Magazine.

LARAMIE PLAINS ANTENNA TV ASSN. INC.
Box 188
Laramie, WY 82070
LPTV Stations:
Wyoming: K03CR Big Laramie, etc.; K12FY Big Laramie, etc.; K57AF Laramie; K10FQ Laramie & Bosler.

BRIAN A. LARSON
The Kings Rd.
Box 36
Buskirk, NY 12028
Phone: 518-686-0975

Fax: 518-686-0975

Branch Office:
2063 NY 67
Valley Falls, NY 12185
Phone: 518-753-0975
LPTV Stations:
New York: WNGX-LP Schenectady; WNGN-LP Troy.

LAS AMERICAS SUPERMERCADO INC.
2415 E Admiral Pl
Tulsa, OK 74110
Phone: 918-520-4447
Officer:
Antonio Perez, President
LPTV Stations:
Oklahoma: KXAP-LD Tulsa.

LAS VEGAS TV PARTNERS LLC
901 N. Green Valley Pkwy.
Suite 210
Henderson, NV 89074
Phone: 702-259-4023
Officer:
Phillip C. Peckman, Co-Manager
Ownership: Las Vegas TV Partners Holdings LLC; LVTVPHLLC ownership:; Greenspun Broadcasting LLC, 50%; Catalyst Investors LP; Catalyst Investors Advisors Fund LP; Catalyst Investors (QP) LP, 50%; GBLLC ownership:; Jonathan Fine Legacy Trust; James Greenspun Legacy Trust; Moira Greenspun Legacy Trust; Jesse Gale Legacy Trust; Ariel Gale Legacy Trust; Harrison Gale Legacy Trust; Jeffrey Fine Legacy Trust; Alyson Fine Legacy Trust; Amy Greenspun Legacy Trust; Kathryn Fine Legacy Trust.
Represented (legal): Drinker Biddle.
LPTV Stations:
Nevada: KTUD-CA Las Vegas.

FRANCOIS LECONTE
16280 N.W. 17th St.
Pembroke Pines, FL 33028
Phone: 754-422-1719
E-mail: fleconte@mdeinc.org
LPTV Stations:
Florida: WDFL-LP Marathon.

LEECH LAKE TV CORP.
PO Box 493
Walker, MN 56484
Phone: 218-224-3195
Officer:
Tom Knight, President
LPTV Stations:
Minnesota: K25JZ Walker; K67BZ Walker; K69CP Walker.

MARY GILL LEE
Box 270
Pleasant Hill, LA 71065
Phone: 318-352-7628
LPTV Stations:
Louisiana: KAIN-LP Natchitoches; KNYS-LP Natchitoches.

LESEA BROADCASTING CORP.
61300 S. Ironwood Rd.
South Bend, IN 46614
Phone: 574-291-8200
Fax: 574-291-9043
Officers:
Peter Sumrall, President
Stephen Sumrall, Secretary
David Sumrall, Treasurer

Ownership: David Sumrall; Peter Sumrall; Stephen Sumrall, each, 33.33%.
Represented (legal): Hardy, Carey, Chautin & Balkin LLP.
LPTV Stations:
Colorado: KWHS-LP Colorado Springs.
Indiana: WHCH-LP Chesterton; WHNW-LP Gary; WHVI-LP Valparaiso.
Commercial TV Stations:
Colorado: KWHD-DT Castle Rock.
Hawaii: KWHH-DT Hilo; KWHE-DT Honolulu; KWHM-DT Wailuku.
Indiana: WHMB-DT Indianapolis; WHME-DT South Bend.
Louisiana: WHNO-DT New Orleans.
Oklahoma: KWHB-DT Tulsa.
Radio Stations:
Indiana: WHME (FM) South Bend
Other Holdings:
Broadcast Holdings: Shortwave operations.

TOWN OF LEVAN
296 East 5th South
Box 163
Monroe, UT 84754
Phone: 435-527-3566
Officer:
Mauri K. Parsons, Technical Advisor
LPTV Stations:
Utah: K18GX Levan.

VILLAGE OF LEWELLEN
PO Box 275
Lewellen, NE 69147
LPTV Stations:
Nebraska: K07JI Lewellen; K11KC Lewellen.

KENNETH E. LEWETAG
17980 Brown Rd.
Dallas, OR 97338
Phone: 503-930-7228
Web site: www.kwvtsalem.com
LPTV Stations:
Oregon: K04PH Astoria; KDLN-LP Newport; KPWC-LD Tillamook.

NORMA JEAN LEWIS
9400 Coventry Square Dr
Ste 1516
Houston, TX 77099
Phone: 281-495-1886
LPTV Stations:
Mississippi: WMRQ-LP Meridian.

LEWISTON TRANSLATOR CO.
Box 517
Lewiston, CA 96052
LPTV Stations:
California: K06EX Lewiston; K03CT Lewiston, etc..

LIBBY VIDEO CLUB
PO Box 856
613 Dakota Ave.
Libby, MT 59923
LPTV Stations:
Montana: K60EA Libby; K62DL Libby; K64DL Libby; K66DR Libby; K68AS Libby; K13MY Pipe Creek; K10LL Pipe Creek, etc.; K11MF Quartz Creek, etc..

LIBERMAN BROADCASTING INC.
1845 Empire Ave.
Burbank, CA 91504
Phone: 818-729-5300
E-mail: LBIinfo@lbimedia.com
Officers:
Jose Liberman, President
Lenard Liberman, Executive Vice President, Secretary & Chief Financial Officer

Andrew Wallace, Vice President, Midwest National Sales
Ownership: Lenard D. Liberman, 63.13%. votes, 41.03% equity; The Liberman Trust, Jose Liberman Trustee, approximately 30%. votes, approximately 20% equity.
Represented (legal): Latham & Watkins.
LPTV Stations:
Arizona: KVPA-LP Phoenix.
California: KSDX-LP San Diego.
Commercial TV Stations:
California: KRCA-DT Riverside.
Texas: KMPX-DT Decatur; KZJL-DT Houston.
Utah: KPNZ-DT Ogden.
Other Holdings:
Radio.

LIBERTY COMMUNICATIONS (ALTON, IL)
3401 Fosterburg Rd.
Alton, IL 62002
Phone: 618-465-4000
Fax: 618-465-4717
E-mail: liberty7@ezl.com
LPTV Stations:
Illinois: W50CH Alton.

LIBERTY UNIVERSITY INC.
1971 University Blvd.
Lynchburg, VA 24502-2269
Phone: 434-582-2722
Fax: 434-582-2918
Officers:
John M. Borek, President
George Rogers, Chief Financial Officer
LPTV Stations:
Virginia: WTLU-CA Lynchburg.
Radio Stations:
Virginia: WRLV (FM), WWMC (FM) Lynchburg

LIFE BROADCASTING NETWORK
85 E. Yellow Springs
Fairborn, OH 45324
Phone: 513-754-0085
LPTV Stations:
Ohio: WWRD-LP Dayton.

LIFE OF VICTORY TV INC.
Box 1227
Lewiston, ID 83501
Phone: 208-743-4072
E-mail: victorytv@syringa.net
LPTV Stations:
Washington: KVBI-LP Clarkston.

LILLY BROADCASTING HOLDINGS LLC
2 Eastleigh Lane
Natick, MA 01760
Phone: 508-545-1995
Officer:
Kevin T Lilly, President
Ownership: Kevin T Lilly, 50%. votes, 13.14 assets; Brian M Lilly, 50%. votes, 11.99 assets; Mercury Capital Partners LP, 53.32%. assets.
LPTV Stations:
New York: W06AR Hornell; W07BJ Ithaca.
Commercial TV Stations:
New York: WENY-DT Elmira.
Radio Stations:
New York: WENY-AM-FM

LINCOLN COUNTY TV DISTRICT NO. 1
Box 216
Pioche, NV 89043-0216
Phone: 775-962-5336
Officer:

Terry Jones, President
Represented (legal): Bennet & Bennet PLLC.
LPTV Stations:
Nevada: K02JO Caliente; K09FL Caliente; K11CN Caliente; K13LV Caliente; K45AL Caliente; K04HF Panaca; K06DM Panaca; K07CM Panaca; K43DS Panaca; K61AW Panaca; K03CM Pioche; K09FJ Pioche; K11IV Pioche; K13PU Pioche; K45AO Pioche; K02EG Ursine; K09FK Ursine; K11OW Ursine; K13LU Ursine; K50DA Ursine.

LINCOLN MEMORIAL UNIVERSITY
Hwy. 25 E
Harrogate, TN 37752
Phones: 423-869-2653; 423-869-6312
Fax: 423-869-4825
Officers:
Harold M. Finley, Chairman
Sam A. Mars Jr., Vice Chairman
Scott D. Miller, President
D. D. Thompson, Vice President, Finance & Treasurer
E. Oscar Robertson, Secretary
LPTV Stations:
Tennessee: W14AQ Harrogate; W18AN Harrogate.

LIN TV CORP.
4 Richmond Sq
Ste 200
Providence, RI 02906
Phone: 401-454-2880
Fax: 401-454-2817
E-mail: edward.munson@lintv.com
Web site: www.lintv.com
Officers:
Vincent L. Sadusky, President & Chief Executive Officer
Scott Blumenthal, Executive Vice President, TV
Richard Schmaeling, Senior Vice President & Chief Financial Officer
Robert Richter, Senior Vice President, New Media
Nicholas Mohamed, Vice President & Controller
Peter E. Maloney, Vice President, Benefits & Special Projects
Edward Munson, Vice President, Station Sales
Denise M. Parent, Vice President & General Counsel

Branch Office:
11 Dupont Circle
Suite 365
Washington, DC 20036
Phone: 202-462-6065
Fax: 202-462-8285
Ownership: Hicks, Muse, Tate & Furst, 70%. voting rights; Publicly held, 30%. voting rights.
Represented (legal): Covington & Burling.
LPTV Stations:
Arizona: K13VW Chinle; K30GL Many Farms; K66BH Navajo Compressor Station.
Colorado: K50FS-D Bayfield; K42DI-D Bayfield & Ignacio; K06JF Cortez; K39AH-D Durango; K31FV-D Durango & Hermosa; K02IL Pagosa Springs; K04NS Pagosa Springs; K31FS Pagosa Springs; K43GT Pagosa Springs; K48HA Pagosa Springs; K66AV Sunetha & Nutria.
Indiana: WIIH-CA Indianapolis.
Massachusetts: WFXQ-CA Springfield.
Michigan: WOBC-CA Battle Creek; W40AN-D Escanaba; WOGC-CA Grand Rapids; WOLP-CA Grand Rapids; WXSP-CA Grand Rapids; WOHO-CA Holland; WOKZ-CA Kalamazoo; WOMS-CA Muskegon.
New Mexico: K27HP Alamogordo; K49FX Alamogordo; K34FU Arrey & Derry; K46FE Artesia; K08FR Aztec; K44GC-D Aztec;

K11JO Bloomfield, etc.; K31DR Caballo; K33GD Capitan & Ruidoso; K47FX Carlsbad; K48GY Carrizozo, etc.; K40HC Chama; K44DD Chama; K49BY Clovis; K47DI Coyote Canyon; K44GD Crownpoint; K35HB Deming; K43FU Deming; K40GC Dora; K22GE Dulce; K26EP Dulce & Lumberton; K38EC Eagles Nest; K39EJ Espanola; K21AX Farmington; K29HR-D Farmington; K67CE Gallina; K18HF Gallup; K48GK Gallup; K46FI Grants; K09EP Grants, etc.; K11NV Guadalupita; K18DY Hillsboro; K27GL Hobbs; K50GM Hobbs; K25HJ Hornsby Ranch, etc.; K20GQ Las Vegas; K43FI Las Vegas; K14LO Lordsburg; K29DP Lordsburg; K31HQ Lordsburg; K40HJ Lordsburg; K13OY Mescalero; K22EU Montoya; K06HX Mora; K22EW Mora; K13OX Mud Canyon; K14KO Portales; K40DI Raton; K43GW Raton, etc.; K08ES Red River; K15FT Roswell; K16BZ Ruidoso; K34GL Santa Rosa; K38HR Santa Rosa; K45CU Shiprock; K25DI Silver City; K45EC Silver City; K44HJ Socorro; K12OG Taos; K21FD Taos; K28HM Thoreau; K41FK Tohatchi; K25HV Truth or Consequences; K27BN Truth or Consequences; K44CJ Tucumcari; K48EH Tucumcari; K06BN Wagon Mound; K39FY Zuni.

Texas: KBVO-CA Austin; KHPB-CA Bastrop; KHPF-CA Fredericksburg; KHPX-CA Georgetown; KHPG-CA Giddings; KHPL-CA La Grange; KHPZ-CA Round Rock; KHPM-CA San Marcos.

Virginia: WITD-CA Chesapeake; WPMC-CA Mappsville; WKTD-CA Portsmouth; WBTD-LP Suffolk; WCTX-CA Virginia Beach; WNLO-CA Virginia Beach.

Commercial TV Stations:
Alabama: WBPG-DT Gulf Shores; WALA-DT Mobile.
Colorado: KREZ-DT Durango.
Connecticut: WCTX-DT New Haven; WTNH-DT New Haven.
Indiana: WANE-DT Fort Wayne; WISH-DT Indianapolis; WLFI-DT Lafayette; WNDY-DT Marion; WTHI-DT Terre Haute.
Massachusetts: WWLP-DT Springfield.
Michigan: WOTV-DT Battle Creek; WOOD-DT Grand Rapids.
New Mexico: KRQE-DT Albuquerque; KBIM-DT Roswell; KASA-DT Santa Fe.
New York: WIVB-DT Buffalo; WNLO-DT Buffalo.
Ohio: WWHO-DT Chillicothe; WDTN-DT Dayton; WUPW-DT Toledo.
Rhode Island: WPRI-DT Providence.
Texas: KXAN-DT Austin; KBVO Llano.
Virginia: WAVY-DT Portsmouth; WVBT-DT Virginia Beach.
Wisconsin: WLUK-DT Green Bay.
Radio Stations:
Indiana: WTHI-FM; WWVR-FM
Other Holdings:
Broadcast holdings: 54 Broadcasting Inc., see listing, 4.49% interest.; Station Venture Holdings LLC, 20.38% equity interest, limited partner of Station Venture Operations LP, see listing..

RAY H. LIVESAY
1141 Tarboro St.
Rocky Mount, NC 27801
Phone: 252-985-3978
LPTV Stations:
North Carolina: WPDZ-LP Buxton; WMTO-LP Wanchese.

LIVING FAITH BROADCASTING
407 Rico st.
Salinas, CA 93907
Phone: 831-394-8456
Fax: 831-899-7136

LPTV Stations:
California: KLFB-LP Salinas.

LKK GROUP CORP.
5657 Wilshire Blvd.
Suite 280
Los Angeles, CA 90036
Phone: 323-934-8283
LPTV Stations:
Virgin Islands: WVGN-LP Charlotte Amalie; WEON-LP Frederiksted.

LOCAL HDTV INC.
180 W Michigan Ave
Ste 702
Jackson, MI 49201
Phone: 517-206-0404
E-mail: johnwjkn@comcast.net
Ownership: John Salov, Pres..
LPTV Stations:
California: KLPS-LP Indio.
Florida: WHDO-CA Orlando; W36CO St. Petersburg.
Michigan: WFHD-LP Ann Arbor.
South Carolina: WHDC-LP Charleston.

LOCAL TV HOLDINGS LLC
1717 Dixie Hwy
Ste 650
Fort Wright, KY 41011
Phone: 859-448-2707
E-mail: klatek@dowlohnes.com
Officers:
Robert L Lawrence, President & Chief Executive Officer
Pamela Taylor, Chief Operating Officer
Theodore Kuhlman, Chief Financial Officer
Benjamin Diesbach, Vice President
Jonathan Friesel, Vice President
Kevin G. Levy, Vice President
Ownership: Oak Hill Capital Partners III LTV A LLC, 39.57%; Oak Hill Capital Partners II LP, 28.27%; Oak Hill Capital Partners LTV C Inc., 15.05%; Local TV B-Corp A Inc., 9.71%; OHCPIIILTVA & OHCPIIILTVC ownership:; J. Taylor Crandall; John Fant; Steven B. Gruber; Kevin G. Levy; Dennis J. Nayden; Ray L. Pinson; Mark A. Wolfson, Mgrs., 14.29%. each; OHCPILP & LTVBCAI ownership:; J. Taylor Crandall; John Fant; Steven B. Gruber; Greg Kent; Kevin G. Levy; Dennis J. Nayden; Ray L. Pinson; Mark A. Wolfson, shareholders, 12.5%. each.
Represented (legal): Dow Lohnes PLLC.
LPTV Stations:
Alabama: W29AO Anniston.
Arkansas: K67EO Bentonville; K62DQ Fayetteville.
Colorado: K54DK Boulder.
Missouri: K62DA Malden.
Oklahoma: K56FK Alva & Cherokee; K58EM Alva & Cherokee; K60ER Cherokee & Alva; K62EH Cherokee & Alva; K64EA Cherokee & Alva; K16DX Gage; K20BR Gage, etc.; K18BV May, etc.; K22BR May, etc.; K61CW Mooreland, etc.; K49DO Seiling; K51EB Seiling; K53CI Seiling; K55EZ Seiling; K57EA Seiling; K59EE Woodward; K63CF Woodward, etc.; K65CO Woodward, etc.; K67CW Woodward, etc.; K69DH Woodward, etc.
Pennsylvania: W07DC Allentown-Bethlehem; W14CO Clarks Summit, etc.; W26CV Mansfield; W61AG Pottsville, etc.; W40BS Renova; W36BE State College; W39BE State College; W26DE-D Stroudsburg; W10CP Towanda; W15CO-D Towanda; W20AD Williamsport.
Utah: K25HF Heber City; K56BB Juab County (rural); K15FQ-D Milford, etc.; K35OP Park City; K35CK Price; K43CC Santa Clara;

KKRP-LP St. George; K22DE Tooele; K17HM Wendover.
Commercial TV Stations:
Alabama: WBRC-DT Birmingham; WHNT-DT Huntsville.
Arkansas: KFSM-DT Fort Smith.
Colorado: KDVR-DT Denver; KFCT-DT Fort Collins.
Illinois: WQAD-DT Moline.
Iowa: WHO-DT Des Moines.
Missouri: WDAF-DT Kansas City; KTVI-DT St. Louis.
North Carolina: WGHP-DT High Point.
Ohio: WJW-DT Cleveland.
Oklahoma: KAUT-DT Oklahoma City; KFOR-DT Oklahoma City.
Pennsylvania: WNEP-DT Scranton.
Tennessee: WREG-DT Memphis.
Utah: KSTU-DT Salt Lake City.
Virginia: WTKR-DT Norfolk; WTVR-DT Richmond.
Wisconsin: WITI-DT Milwaukee.

BILLY RAY LOCKLEAR
3463 Oak Grove Church Rd.
Lumberton, NC 28358
Phone: 910-521-3101
LPTV Stations:
North Carolina: WLPS-LP Lumberton; WLPS-LD Lumberton-Pembroke.

LAWRENCE F. LOESCH
c/o Brooks, Pierce, McLendon, Humphrey & Leonard LLP
PO Box 1800
Raleigh, NC 27602
Phone: 919-839-0300
Represented (legal): Brooks, Pierce, McLendon, Humphrey & Leonard LLP.
LPTV Stations:
North Carolina: K59ID Manteo; W17CT Manteo; W28CJ Manteo; W45CL Manteo; W51DF Manteo; W56EC Manteo.

LOFLIN CHILDREN'S TRUST-ONE, TWO & FOUR
Box 40483
Baton Rouge, LA 70835
LPTV Stations:
Alabama: W19BV Andalusia; W36BQ Andalusia; W57CC Andalusia; W59CQ Andalusia.
Wyoming: K18ER Rock Springs; K20FA Rock Springs; K30EQ Rock Springs; K48FE Rock Springs; K56FV Rock Springs; K58EW Rock Springs; K64EP Rock Springs.

DAVID M. LOFLIN
Box 40483
Baton Rouge, LA 70835
LPTV Stations:
Alabama: W65CW Andalusia.

BOARD OF LOGAN COUNTY COMMISSIONERS
315 Main St.
Sterling, CO 80751
Phone: 970-522-0888
E-mail: commissioners@loganco.gov
Officer:
Lyle Schumacher, Chairman
LPTV Stations:
Colorado: K14JZ-D Peetz; K26FM Peetz; K28FW Peetz; K30FO Peetz; K32EX Peetz; K16EJ Peetz & Logan County; K18FN Peetz & Logan County; K20FS Peetz & Logan County; K31IQ-D Sterling; K46CY Sterling; K48DQ Sterling; K50EE Sterling; K52EW

Sterling; K58GH Sterling; K44FL Sterling & south Logan County; K56GL Sterling, etc..

LOMA TV CLUB
PO Box 207
Loma, MT 59460-0207
Phone: 406-739-4224
E-mail: 7outhome@ttc-cmc.net
Officer:
Garvey C Wood, Information Contact
LPTV Stations:
Montana: K07AM Loma; K11AD Loma.

LONDON BROADCASTING CO. INC.
2 Lincoln Centre
5420 LBJ Fwy, Ste 1000
Dallas, TX 75240
Phone: 972-663-8917
Officers:
Ned N. Fleming III, Chairman
Terry E. London, President & Chief Executive Officer
Phillip Hurley, Chief Operating Officer
Carl Kornmeyer, Chief Financial Officer
Barrett N. Bruce, Secretary
Benjamin D. Eakes, Treasurer
Ownership: SunTx LBC Holdings LP, 67.21%; SunTx Fulcrum Fund II--SBIC LP, 30.37%; STLBCHLP ownership:; SunTx Capital Partners II GP, LP, Gen. Partner; STFFII-SBICLP ownership:; SunTx Capital SBIC LP; STCPIIGPLP & STCSBICLP ownership:; Ned N. Fleming III, Pres. & Chief Exec. Officer.
Represented (legal): Wiley Rein LLP.
LPTV Stations:
Oklahoma: KKTM-LP Altus.
Texas: KTMO-LP Amarillo; KMAY-LP Bryan; KTLD-LP Odessa; KTLE-LP Odessa.
Commercial TV Stations:
Texas: KBMT-DT Beaumont; KYTX-DT Nacogdoches; KCEN-DT Temple.

TODD A. LOPES
1144 E. Province Dr.
Fresno, CA 93720
Represented (legal): Dow Lohnes PLLC.
LPTV Stations:
Idaho: KITL-LP Boise; KYTL-LP Twin Falls.

HUMBERTO LOPEZ
115 West Ave.
Robstown, TX 78380
Phone: 512-387-4861
Fax: 512-387-5396
LPTV Stations:
Texas: KINE-LP Robstown; KXTM-LP San Antonio; KVHM-LP Victoria.

MINERVA R. LOPEZ
115 West Ave
Robstown, TX 78380
Phone: 512-387-4861
Fax: 361-289-7122
LPTV Stations:
Texas: KHCC-LP Corpus Christi; KTMV-LP Corpus Christi.

LOTUS COMMUNICATIONS CORP.
3301 Barham Blvd.
Suite 200
Los Angeles, CA 90068
Phone: 323-512-2225
Officers:
Howard A. Kalmenson, President
Jerry Roy, Senior Vice President & Secretary
William H. Shriftman, Senior Vice President & Treasurer
Lynden L. Williams, Senior Vice President

James Kalmenson, Vice President
Lilli Kalmenson Rosenbloom, Vice President
Jay Levine, Assistant Secretary

Ownership: Howard A. Kalmenson. votes;
The Howard A. Kalmenson Trust, 42.66%.
equity; The Lilli Kalmenson Rosenbloom
Trust, 42.66%. equity; Diane K. Levine,
13.82%. equity; , Burton Levine Estate,
Diane K. Levine, Executrix., 0.86%. equity.

Represented (legal): Bryan Cave LLP.

LPTV Stations:
Arizona: KPHE-LD Phoenix; KPHE-LP Phoenix.
Florida: WTAM-LP Tampa.
Texas: KHLM-LP Houston.

LOUISIANA CHRISTIAN BROADCASTING INC.
701 Parkwood Dr.
West Monroe, LA 71201
Phone: 318-322-1399
Fax: 318-323-3783

Ownership: Lamb Broadcasting Inc.; LBI
ownership; Joel Dyke; Billy Haisty; Gerald
Lewis; Mike Reed, Dirs.

Represented (legal): Hardy, Carey, Chautin &
Balkin LLP.

LPTV Stations:
Arkansas: KLMB-LP El Dorado.
Louisiana: WCBZ-LP Baton Rouge.
Mississippi: W24CR Natchez.

Commercial TV Stations:
Louisiana: KMCT-DT West Monroe.

LOUISIANA TELEVISION BROADCASTING LLC
PO Box 2906
Baton Rouge, LA 70821-2906
Phone: 225-387-2222
Fax: 225-336-2246

Officers:
Richard F. Manship, President & Chief Executive Officer
David C. Manship, Vice Chairman & Vice President
Douglas L. Manship Jr., Secretary

Ownership: Dina Manship Planche, 28.04%;
Richard F. Manship, 25.89%; David C.
Manship, 23.71%; Douglas L. Manship
Jr., 22.36. Manships are also principals of
Mobile Video Tapes Inc., see listing.

Represented (legal): Cohn & Marks LLP.

LPTV Stations:
Louisiana: KBTR-CA Baton Rouge.

Commercial TV Stations:
Louisiana: WBRZ-DT Baton Rouge.

Newspapers:
Louisiana: The Advocate (Baton Rouge)

LOUIS MARTINEZ FAMILY GROUP LLC
17511 Santa Rosa Rd.
Perris, CA 92570-7760
Phone: 951-940-1700
E-mail: dmartinez2000@sbcglobal.net

Ownership: Donna J. Martinez, Co-Executor,
50%. votes, 10% assets; Susan Martinez,
Co-Executor, 50%. votes, 10% assets;
Betsy H. Martinez, 20%. assets; Susan B.
Martinez, 16.5%. assets; Donna J. Martinez,
14.5%. assets; Karen A. Martinez Brorson,
14.5%. assets; Steven L. Martinez, 14.5%.
assets.

Represented (legal): Irwin, Campbell &
Tannenwald PC.

LPTV Stations:
California: KDUG-LP Hemet; KDUO-LP Palm
Desert; KBLM-LP Riverside; KVKV-LP Vic-
torville.

Texas: KQUX-CA Austin; KMHZ-LP San Antonio;
KMXU-LP San Antonio.

LUBBOCK TELEVISION CO.
2124 15th St.
Lubbock, TX 79401
Phone: 806-747-4085
Fax: 806-747-4086
E-mail: glarryrice@aol.com

Officers:
Larry Rice, President & Chief Financial Officer
Brian Henegar, Chief Operating Officer

LPTV Stations:
Texas: KGLR-LP Lubbock.

LUKEN BROADCASTING LLC
One Central Plz, 6th Fl
835 Georgia Ave
Chattanooga, TN 37402
Phone: 423-265-2560

Ownership: Henry G. Luken III. Luken has
interest in Equity Media Holdings Corp. &
Luken Communications LLC, see listings.

LPTV Stations:
Florida: WEVU-CA Fort Myers; WLZE-LP Fort
Myers; WBSP-CA Naples; WUVF-CA Naples.
Minnesota: WUMN-CA Minneapolis.
Oklahoma: KWDW-LP Oklahoma City.
Texas: K38IP Amarillo.

LYNCH COMMUNITY CLUB
PO Box 165
Lynch, NE 68746-0165
Phone: 402-569-3202

LPTV Stations:
Nebraska: K02LF Lynch; K10KU Lynch; K12LH
Lynch.

LYNN CANAL BROADCASTING
Box 245
Haines, AK 99827

LPTV Stations:
Alaska: K03FM Haines.

LYON COUNTY PUBLIC WORKS
18 Hwy 95A N
Yerington, NV 89447
Phone: 775-463-6551

LPTV Stations:
Nevada: K06JK Dayton; K45GZ Dayton; K10HQ
Smith; K12IT Smith; K05GD Smith, etc.;
K06KC Yerington; K18BW Yerington; K40DV
Yerington; K49FZ Yerington.

DAVID R. MAGNUM
1021 N. Superior Ave.
#5
Tomah, WI 54660
Phone: 608-372-9600
Fax: 608-372-7566

Ownership:Magnum is majority owner of
Magnum Radio Inc., see listing.

Represented (legal): Denise B. Moline.

LPTV Stations:
Wisconsin: WIBU-LP Tomah.

Radio Stations:
Wisconsin: WBOG (AM), WTMB (FM), WXYM
(FM) Tomah.

MAGNUM RADIO INC.
1021 N Superior Ave
#5
Tomah, WI 54660
Phone: 608-372-9600

Ownership: Dennis R Magnum, Pres., 87.91%;
Reid Magnum Family Trust, 4.03%; Ty
Magnum Family Trust, Del M Reynolds
Trustee, 4.03%; Ty Magnum Family Trust,
Del M Reynolds Trustee, 4.03%; Weiss-
Magnum Family Trust, Del M Reynolds
Trustee, 4.03%. David R. Magnum, see
listing.

Represented (legal): Denise B. Moline.

LPTV Stations:
Minnesota: KQEG-CA La Crescent.
Wisconsin: W45CF Elk Mound.

MAINE FAMILY BROADCASTING INC.
2881 Ohio St.
Suite 6
Bangor, ME 04401
Phone: 207-873-6100

Officers:
James W. McLeod, President & Chief Financial
Officer
Bethshan McLeod, Secretary-Treasurer

Ownership: James McLeod.

LPTV Stations:
Maine: WBGR-LP Bangor.

MAINE PUBLIC BROADCASTING CORP.
1450 Lisbon St.
Lewiston, ME 04240
Phone: 207-783-9101

Officers:
Robert Edwards, Chairman
Neil Rolde, Vice Chairman
Robert H. Gardiner, President

Branch Offices:
309 Marginal Way
Portland, ME 04104
Phone: 207-874-6570

65 Texas Ave.
Bangor, ME 04401
Phone: 207-941-1010

LPTV Stations:
Maine: W04BH Allagash; W04BS Bethel, etc.;
W61AO Calais; W03AM Harrison, etc.;
W04AY St. Francis.

ETV Stations:
Maine: WCBB-DT Augusta; WMEA-DT Biddeford;
WMED-DT Calais; WMEB-DT Orono; WMEM-
DT Presque Isle.

Other Holdings:
Radio.

MAINSTREET BROADCASTING CO. INC.
516 Main St.
Walsenburg, CO 81089
Phone: 719-738-3636

LPTV Stations:
Colorado: K47KC Romeo; K34GI Trinidad;
KSPK-LP Walsenburg.

MAKO COMMUNICATIONS LLC
Box 1513
Corpus Christi, TX 78403
Phones: 361-883-1763; 361-883-3160

Ownership: Amanda Mintz, 50%; Laurie Mintz,
26.25%; Sean Mintz, 7.25%; Julie Mintz,
4.75%; Libby Mintz, 4.75%; Josh Mintz,
4.75%; Howard Mintz, 2.25%.

Represented (legal): Shainis & Peltzman
Chartered.

LPTV Stations:
Arizona: K25DM Phoenix; KTVP-LP Phoenix.
California: K04QR-D Lakeport; K05MI-D Lake-
port.
Florida: W43CE Lealman; W15CM Orient City;
W16CC West Gate.
Georgia: WYGA-CA Atlanta.
Missouri: KPTN-LP St. Louis.
Nevada: KEGS-LP Las Vegas; KNBX-CA Las
Vegas; KVPX-LP Las Vegas.
Oklahoma: KTOU-LP Oklahoma City.
Pennsylvania: WZPA-LP Camden; W36DO-D
Darby.
Texas: KCCX-LP Corpus Christi; KJJM-LD
Dallas & Mesquite; K31GL-D De Soto;

KHPK-LD De Soto; K10PY-D Freeport;
K30DN Freeport; KVAT-LP Garfield; K24GP
Lubbock; KATA-CA Mesquite; KODF-LP
Mullin; KISA-LP San Antonio; KSAA-LP San
Antonio.
Washington: KUSE-LP Seattle.

MALIBU BROADCASTING LLC
Second Generation Pl
3029 Prospect Ave
Cleveland, OH 44115
Phone: 323-965-5400

Ownership: Thomas J Wilson.

Represented (legal): Wiley Rein LLP.

LPTV Stations:
Illinois: WLFM-LP Chicago.
Iowa: WBQD-LP Davenport.

Commercial TV Stations:
Illinois: WAOE-DT Peoria.

TOWN OF MANDERSON
PO Box 96
Manderson, WY 82432
Phone: 307-568-2680

LPTV Stations:
Wyoming: K03GF Manderson, etc..

CITY OF MANITOU SPRINGS
606 Manitou Ave.
Manitou Springs, CO 80829
Phone: 719-685-2600
E-mail: msjkf@ci.manitou-springs.co.us

Officer:
John K. Forsett, Information Services Administrator

LPTV Stations:
Colorado: K03AO Manitou Springs; K06BI
Manitou Springs; K09LH Manitou Springs.

MANLEY HOT SPRINGS PARK ASSN.
Box 107
Manley Hot Springs, AK 99756

Ownership: Carol Groves, Pres.; Dian Gurtler;
Bob Lee; Damaris Mortvedt; Charles
Parker, V.P.; Pam Redington, Secy.-Treas.;
Caty Zeitler, Board Members.

LPTV Stations:
Alaska: K06JX Manley Hot Springs.

MANNA MEDIA CORP.
PO Box 2595
2251 Mariposa Blvd
Casper, WY 82602
Phone: 307-265-4453

Officers:
Carl A. Wolosin, President
Margaret Wyatt, Vice President
John S. Runge, Secretary-Treasurer

Ownership: Non-profit corp.--Casper, WY.

LPTV Stations:
Wyoming: K47HQ Casper.

MARANATHA BROADCASTING CO.
E. Rock Rd.
Allentown, PA 18103
Phone: 610-797-4530

Officers:
Richard C. Dean, President
Barry Fisher, Vice President, TV
David Hinson, Vice President, Radio
Mike Kulp, Chief Financial Officer

Ownership: Richard C Dean, 54%; Jennifer
Dean, 8%; Rick Allen Dean, 8%; Wendy
Shubert, 8%; Rebecca Watrous, 8%; Barry
Fisher, 5%; David G Hinson, 5%; Mike
Kulp, 4%.

LPTV Stations:
Pennsylvania: W46BL Allentown-Bethlehem.
Commercial TV Stations:
Pennsylvania: WFMZ-DT Allentown.
Radio Stations:
Pennsylvania: WEST (AM)

MARION COUNTY PUBLIC SCHOOLS
420 S.E. Alvarez Ave.
Suite B
Ocala, FL 34471-2287
LPTV Stations:
Florida: W07BP-D Ocala.

GUENTER MARKSTEINER
1601 Forum Place, 12th Floor
West Palm Beach, FL 33401
Phone: 561-471-9200
LPTV Stations:
Florida: WHDT-LP Miami; WXDT-LP Naples;
WYDT-CA Naples; WZDT-LP Naples.
Massachusetts: WHDN-LD Boston.
Commercial TV Stations:
Florida: WHDT-DT Stuart.

MARK III MEDIA INC.
2312 Sagewood
Casper, WY 82601
Phone: 307-235-3962
Officers:
Julie Jaffe, President
Mark R. Nalbone, Secretary-Treasurer
Ownership: Julie Jaffe, 35%; Jennifer Lechter,
35%; Mark R. Nalbone, 30%.
Represented (legal): Borsari & Associates
PLLC.
LPTV Stations:
Wyoming: K68DC Clareton; K16AE Gillette.
Commercial TV Stations:
Wyoming: KGWC-DT Casper; KGWL-DT Lander;
KGWR-DT Rock Springs.

H. EARL MARLAR
Box 121
Heiskell, TN 37754
Represented (legal): Larry D. Perry.
LPTV Stations:
Tennessee: WFEM-LP Heiskell.

MARLO TV ASSOCIATION
PO Box 567
Harlowton, MT 59036
LPTV Stations:
Montana: K57FR Harlowton, etc.; K59CE
Harlowton, etc.; K61CE Harlowton, etc.;
K07VK Lennep & Martinsdale; K11TK Lennep
& Martinsdale; K09LW Martinsdale-Lennep.

ANDREW MARRIOTT
10312 Strathmore Hall St
Ste 401
North Bethesda, MD 20852
Phone: 301-564-0490
Represented (legal): Shainis & Peltzman
Chartered.
LPTV Stations:
North Carolina: WTBL-LP Lenoir.

JERRY MARTH
3512 Windsor Terrace
Oklahoma City, OK 73122
Phone: 405-943-9957
Represented (legal): Irwin, Campbell &
Tannenwald PC.
LPTV Stations:
Arizona: K35FH Flagstaff.

DON MARTIN
Box 385
Salem, IN 47167

Phones: 812-883-3401; 812-883-5750
Fax: 812-883-2797
Represented (legal): Allen, Allen & Allen.
LPTV Stations:
Indiana: WHAN-LP Salem.

HECTOR MARCANO MARTINEZ
c/o MTVE Inc., 1311 Ponce de Leon Ave.
Marcom Tower Bldg., Suite 600
San Juan, PR 00907
LPTV Stations:
Puerto Rico: WWXY-LP San Juan.

MARTINSVILLE MEDIA INC.
512 Mulberry Rd
Martinsville, VA 24112
Phone: 276-632-9811
E-mail: bill@martinsvillemedia.com
Ownership: WIlliam D. Wyatt Jr., President.
Represented (legal): Dan J. Alpert.
LPTV Stations:
Virginia: WYAT-LP Martinsville.
Radio Stations:
Virginia: WHEE (AM), WMVA (AM) Martinsville

MATRIX BROADCAST MEDIA INC.
519 W Wooster St
c/o Victor Ten Brink
Bowling Green, OH 43402
Phone: 419-353-1062
E-mail: vtb@tthslaw.com
Officers:
Jerry Jones, President
John H. Livingston, Secretary
Ownership: John H. Livingston, 50%. votes.
LPTV Stations:
Ohio: WMNT-CA Toledo.

MICHAEL L. MATTSON
15740 May Rd.
Dallas, OR 97338
Phone: 503-409-2181
LPTV Stations:
Oregon: K05LE Astoria; KWVT-LP Dallas;
K05KY Lincoln City; KODT-LP Salt Creek;
KSLM-LD Salt Creek; K06NI The Dalles;
K05KX Tillamook.

MAX MEDIA X LLC
900 Laskin Rd.
Virginia Beach, VA 23451
Phone: 757-437-9800
Fax: 757-437-0034
Officer:
A. Eugene Loving Jr., President & Chief
Executive Officer

Ownership: Max Media LLC, Member/Mgr.,
90%; Max Management X LLC, Member,
10%; MMLLC ownership:; MBG-GG
LLC, 42.0345%; MBG Quad-C Investors
I Inc., 41.41133%; Aardvarks Also LLC,
6.1967%; Colonnade Max Investors Inc.,
4.8671%; Quad-C Max Investors Inc.,
4.6799%; MGLLC ownership:; Kenneth
Diekroeger, 49.99%. equity; 50% voting;
Jesse Rogers, 49.99%. equity, 50% voting;
Alan Nichols, 0.0002%. equity; MQIII
ownership:; Terrence D. Daniels, Mgr.,
29.51%. equity, 50% voting; Gary A. Binning,
20%. equity, 16.67% voting; Stephen M.
Burns, 20%. equity, 16.67 voting; Anthony
R. Ignaczak, 20%. equity, 16.67 voting;
AALLC ownership:; LaMaSa Airwaves LLC,
21.407%; Bay Shore Enterprises LLC,
19.648%; A. Eugene Loving Jr., Secy.,
19.648%; Steamboat SPGS LLC, 19.648%;
John A. Trinder, Pres., 16.701%; James
C. Trinder, 2.947%; CMII ownership:;
Commonwealth Investors II LP, 96.37%;
Allen B. Rider III, Chmn., Pres. & Chief
Exec. Officer, 1.04%; James C. Wheat III,
V.P., 1.04%; QCMII ownership:; Terrence
C. Daniels, Mgr., 40%. equity, 57.14 voting;
Stephen M. Burns, 15%. equity, 10.71%
voting; Edward T. Harvey, 15%. equity,
10.71% voting; Anthony R. Ignaczak, 15%.
equity, 10.71% voting; Gary A. Binning,
12%. equity, 8.57% voting; MMXLLC
ownership:; A Eugene Loving Jr, Chief
Exec. Officer, Secy. & Mgr., 20%; Allen B
Rider III, Mgr., 20%; Timothy B Robertson,
20%; John A Trinder, Chief Operating
Officer, Pres. & Mgr., 20%; David J
Wilhelm, V.P., Chief Financial Officer &
Asst. Secy., 20%.
Represented (legal): Williams Mullen.
LPTV Stations:
Montana: KWYB-LP Bozeman; K24FL Columbus;
KHBB-LD Helena; KTMF-LP Kalispell; K43DC
Lewistown; K66BR Livingston, etc.; K06FE
Miles City.
Puerto Rico: WQQZ-CA Ponce; WWKQ-LP
Quebradillas.
Commercial TV Stations:
Kentucky: WNKY-DT Bowling Green.
Maine: WPFO-DT Waterville.
Montana: KULR-DT Billings; KWYB-DT Butte;
KFBB-DT Great Falls; KTMF-DT Missoula.
Puerto Rico: WMEI-DT Arecibo.

ROY WILLIAM MAYHUGH
701 Perdew Ave.
Ridgecrest, CA 93555-2422
Phone: 760-446-6794
Represented (legal): Smithwick & Belendiuk
PC.
LPTV Stations:
California: K67AO Palmdale; KFLA-LD Palmdale;
K59AO Ridgecrest, etc..

SANDRA A. MAY
401 S Walnut
Hope, AR 71801
Phone: 870-619-4344
E-mail: jonkevinmck@yahoo.com
LPTV Stations:
Arkansas: KTSS-LP Hope.

PATRICK MBABA
1400 Easton Dr.
Suite 105
Bakersfield, CA 93309
Phone: 661-979-5231
LPTV Stations:
California: K69IE Eureka.

JOHN A. MCAULAY
31180 96th St. E
Littlerock, CA 93543-3624
Phone: 661-944-2087
E-mail: john@mcaulay.net

Represented (legal): Irwin, Campbell &
Tannenwald PC.
LPTV Stations:
Missouri: KROL-LP Rolla.

FRED MCCUTCHAN
17701 Foothill Court
Hidden Valley Lake, CA 95467
Phone: 707-987-0338
LPTV Stations:
Oregon: KBSC-LP Brookings.

MCG CAPITAL CORP.
1100 Wilson Blvd
Ste 3000
Arlington, VA 22209
Phone: 703-247-7500
Officers:
Kenneth J. O'Keefe, Chairman
Steven F. Tunney, President & Chief Executive
Officer
Robert J. Merrick, Executive Vice President &
Chief Investment Officer
Michael R. McDonnell, Executive Vice President,
Chief Operating & Financial Officer & Treasurer
B. Hagen Seville, Executive Vice President,
Business Development
Derek R. Thomas, Executive Vice President,
Risk Management & Underwriting
Samuel G. Rubenstein, Exec. V.P., Gen.
Counsel & Chief Legal Officer, Chief
Compliance Officer & Corp. Secy.
Robert S. Grazioli, Senior Vice President &
Chief Information Officer
John C. Wellons, Senior Vice President, Chief
Accounting Officer & Assistant Treasurer
Ownership: Publicly held..
Represented (legal): Dow Lohnes PLLC.
LPTV Stations:
Hawaii: K69BZ Lihue, etc.; K57BI Waimea.
Commercial TV Stations:
Hawaii: KGMD-DT Hilo; KGMB-DT Honolulu;
KGMV-DT Wailuku.

MCGRAW-HILL BROADCASTING CO.
INC.
4600 Air Way
San Diego, CA 92102
Phone: 619-237-6212
Fax: 619-262-8842
Officers:
Darrell K. Brown, President
Bruce Stein, Vice President, Sales
Mark Limbach, Group Controller
Ownership: The McGraw-Hill Companies. The
McGraw-Hill Companies also have interest
in financial services; information and
media services; educational & professional
publishing.
Represented (legal): Holland & Knight LLP.
LPTV Stations:
California: KZKC-LP Bakersfield; KZSD-LP San
Diego.
Colorado: KZCS-LP Colorado Springs; KZCO-LP
Denver; KZFC-LP Windsor.
Commercial TV Stations:
California: KERO-DT Bakersfield; KGTV-DT San
Diego.
Colorado: KMGH-DT Denver.
Indiana: WRTV-DT Indianapolis.

CHRIS MCHALE
269 S. Beverly Dr.
No. 1042
Beverly Hills, CA 90212
Phone: 310-709-9041
E-mail: mchalemedia@erthlink.net
Represented (legal): Irwin, Campbell &
Tannenwald PC.

LPTV Stations:
Maryland: W63DC Ocean City; W65EF Ocean City.

MD BROADCASTING LLC
125 Hampton Lake Dr.
Pelham, AL 35124
Phone: 205-620-9660
E-mail: mark.snow@psi-rep.
Ownership: Diane B. Snow; Mark M. Snow, Gen. Partners.
LPTV Stations:
Georgia: WWCG-LP Columbus.

ME3 COMMUNICATIONS LLC
13121 Box Canyon Rd
Oklahoma City, OK 73142-6203
Phone: 405-720-1501
Ownership: Jack Mills, Managing Member.
LPTV Stations:
Oklahoma: KXOK-LD Enid; KXOK-LP Enid.

MEAGHER COUNTY PUBLIC TV INC.
PO Box 503
501 2nd Ave SE
White Sulphur Springs, MT 59645
Phone: 406-547-3803
E-mail: bjhawkins@msn.com
Ownership: B J Hawkins, Board Member.
LPTV Stations:
Montana: K08LI White Sulphur Springs; K57CX White Sulphur Springs.

MEAGHER COUNTY TELEVISION DISTRICT
PO Box 309
White Sulphur Springs, MT 59645-0309
Phone: 406-547-2190
LPTV Stations:
Montana: K06NV White Sulphur Springs; K07NU White Sulphur Springs; K09MH White Sulphur Springs; K11MP White Sulphur Springs.

MEDIA-COM TELEVISION INC.
Box 2170
Akron, OH 44309-2170
Phone: 330-673-2323
Fax: 330-673-0301
Officers:
Richard Klaus, President
William R. Klaus, Chief Operating Officer
Robert A. Klaus, Vice President, Sales
LPTV Stations:
Ohio: WAOH-LP Akron; W35AX Cleveland.

MEDIA GENERAL INC.
Box 85333
Richmond, VA 23293-0001
Phones: 804-649-6000; 804-649-6103
Officers:
J. Stewart Bryan III, Chairman
Marshall N. Morton, President & Chief Executive Officer
Reid Ashe, Executive Vice President & Chief Operating Officer
Neal F. Fondren, Vice President & President, Interactive Media Division
H. Graham Woodlief Jr., Vice President & President, Publishing Division
James A. Zimmerman, Vice President & President, Broadcast Div.
Lou Anne Nabhan, Vice President, Corporate Communications
George L. Mahoney, Vice President, Secretary & General Counsel
John A. Schauss, Vice President, Finance, Treasurer & Chief Financial Officer
Ownership: Publicly held.

LPTV Stations:
North Carolina: W08BP Beaver Dam; W02AG Brevard; W11AN Bryson City, etc.; W02AT Burnsville; W08AO Canton, etc.; W08AT Cherokee, etc.; W09AG Franklin; W08BJ Marion, etc.; W02AH Mars Hill; W08AX Marshall; W10AD Montreat, etc.; W05BI Morehead City; W08BF Spruce Pine, etc.; W09AF Sylva, etc.; W09AD Waynesville; W09AR Weaverville.
South Carolina: W10AJ Greenville.
Commercial TV Stations:
Alabama: WVTM-DT Birmingham; WKRG-DT Mobile.
Florida: WCWJ-DT Jacksonville; WFLA-DT Tampa.
Georgia: WJBF-DT Augusta; WRBL-DT Columbus; WSAV-DT Savannah.
Mississippi: WHLT-DT Hattiesburg; WJTV-DT Jackson.
North Carolina: WYCW-DT Asheville; WNCN-DT Goldsboro; WNCT-DT Greenville.
Ohio: WCMH-DT Columbus.
Rhode Island: WJAR-DT Providence.
South Carolina: WCBD-DT Charleston; WBTW-DT Florence; WSPA-DT Spartanburg.
Tennessee: WJHL-DT Johnson City.
Virginia: WSLS-DT Roanoke.
Newspapers:
Alabama: Dothan Eagle, The Enterprise Ledger, Opelika-Auburn News
Florida: Hernando Today (Brooksville), Jackson County Floridian, Highlands Today (Sebring), The Tampa Tribune
North Carolina: (Concord & Kannapolis) Independent Tribune, The (Eden) Daily News, Hickory Daily Record, The (Marion) McDowell News, The (Morganton) News Herald, The Reidsville Review, Statesville Record & Landmark, Winston-Sa
South Carolina: (Florence) Morning News
Virginia: Bristol Herald Courier, The (Charlottesville) Daily Progress, Culpeper Star-Exponent, Danville Register & Bee, The (Lynchburg) News & Advance, Manassas Journal Messenger, Potomac (Woodbridge) News, Richmond Tim
Radio Stations:
Georgia: WNEG (AM)
Other Holdings:
Data service: TBO.com, timesdispatch.com, JournalNow.com, FlorenceMyrtleBeach.com, Tri-Cities-News.com
Finance service: Media General Financial Services-Richmond
Magazine: Virginia Business Magazine
Printing company: SP Newsprint Co. (33%), Duslin, GA and Newberg, OR.

MEDIA INC.
4300 Brookpark Rd.
Cleveland, OH 44134
Phone: 216-398-2800
Ownership: Governing Board; William E MacDonald III, Chmn.; Adrian T Dillon, Vice Chmn.; Jerrold F Wareham, Chief Exec. Officer; Kathryn P Jensen, Chief Operating Officer; William R Stewart, Secy.; Edward P Campbell, Treas..
LPTV Stations:
Ohio: W64AK Conneaut; W63CT Eastlake, etc..

CHARLES R. MEEKER
41-625 Eclectic St.
Suite J-1
Palm Desert, CA 92260
Phone: 760-674-8550
LPTV Stations:
California: KRET-CA Cathedral City.

CITY OF MEKORYUK
5900 E Tudor Rd
Anchorage, AK 99507

Phone: 907-269-5744
LPTV Stations:
Alaska: K09NI Mekoryuk.

MEREDITH CORP.
1716 Locust St.
Des Moines, IA 50309-3023
Phone: 515-284-3000
Fax: 515-284-2514
Web site: www.meredith.com
Officers:
Stephen M. Lacy, President & Chief Executive Officer
Paul Karpowicz, President, Broadcasting Group
Douglas R. Lowe, Executive Vice President, Broadcasting Group
Joseph Ceryanec, Vice President & Chief Financial Officer
John S. Zieser, Chief Development Officer
Larry Oaks, Vice President, Technology
Joseph Snelson, Vice President, Engineering
Tom Cox, Vice President, Broadcasting Solutions
Kieran Clarke, Executive Vice President, Meredith Video Solutions
Tim Reynolds, Director, Interactive Media
Jeff Trott, Director, IT & Ad Operations
Dalton Lee, Vice President, Finance
Ownership: Katharine Meredith, 31.879% voting stock & 3.851% assets%; Edwin Meredith IV, 11.027% voting stock & 0.995% assets%; Dianne Mell Meredith Frazier, 10.462% voting stock & 0.948% assets%.
LPTV Stations:
Arizona: K40AD Cottonwood, etc.; K50HU Flagstaff; K09KV Prescott.
Massachusetts: WSHM-LP Springfield.
Nevada: K28EU Laughlin, etc.; K53AE Pahrump.
North Carolina: W69CN Bryson City; W14AS West Asheville.
Oregon: K20DD Albany, etc.; KUBN-LP Bend; K23DB La Grande; K51FK Nehalem & Rockaway; K18EL Newburg & Tigard; K15DS Newport, etc.; K44AH Prineville, etc.; K50GG Salem; K21DE Seaside & Astoria; K51EH The Dalles; K69AH The Dalles; K35CR Tillamook, etc..
Washington: K34HK Longview; K14HN Vancouver & Camas.
Commercial TV Stations:
Arizona: KPHO-DT Phoenix.
Connecticut: WFSB-DT Hartford.
Georgia: WGCL-DT Atlanta.
Michigan: WNEM-DT Bay City.
Missouri: KCTV-DT Kansas City; KSMO-DT Kansas City.
Nevada: KVVU-DT Henderson.
Oregon: KPTV-DT Portland.
South Carolina: WHNS-DT Greenville.
Tennessee: WSMV-DT Nashville.
Washington: KPDX-DT Vancouver.
Other Holdings:
Magazine: Successful Farming, Country America, Traditional Home, Country Home, Midwest Living; Ladies' Home Journal, Better Homes and Gardens
Publishing: 37 titles produced by Better Homes & Gardens Special Interest Publications. American Park Network publishes visitor guides for parks.

MESA COUNTY
Box 20000
Grand Junction, CO 81501
Phone: 970-255-7150
LPTV Stations:
Colorado: K02OP Collbran; K04OM Collbran; K06KJ Collbran; K11PS Collbran; K13RD Collbran; K04KG Gateway; K45IT Grand Junction; K49IO Grand Junction; K39AF Grand Junction, etc.; K43AB Grand Junction,

etc.; K47JR Grand Junction, etc.; K12OR Mesa; K31DW Mesa.

MESA TELEVISION INC.
PO Box 789
Grand Junction, CO 81502
LPTV Stations:
Colorado: K02IJ Somerset; K10KK Somerset; K12MN Somerset.

JOHN MESTER INCOME FAMILY TRUST
682 Argyle Rd.
Brooklyn, NY 11230-0406
Phone: 718-859-5172
LPTV Stations:
New York: W30AZ Liberty; W27AL Monticello; W30AJ Syracuse; W51BN White Lake.

METROPOLITAN RADIO GROUP INC.
3801 Skillern Blvd.
Flower Mound, TX 77028
Phone: 817-430-3548

Branch Office:
1549 Greenbridge
Ozark, MO 65721
Phone: 417-581-5595
Fax: 417-581-5596
Ownership: Mark Acker, Secy.-Treas.. Personal representative for the Gary Acker Estate.
LPTV Stations:
Missouri: K08MA Springfield.
Radio Stations:
Arkansas: KGHT (AM) Sheridan
Colorado: KNKN (FM), KRMX (FM) Pueblo
Louisiana: KJVC (FM), KORI (FM) Mansfield; KIOU (AM) Shreveport; KBSF (AM), KTSF (AM) Springhill
Texas: KIJN-AM-FM Farwell

METROPOLITAN SCHOOL DISTRICT OF MARTINSVILLE
460 S. Main
Martinsville, IN 46151
Phone: 765-342-5571
Fax: 765-349-5256
LPTV Stations:
Indiana: WREP-LP Martinsville.

MICRONESIA BROADCASTING CORP.
138 Martyr St.
Suite 200
Agana, GU 96910
Phone: 671-637-5826
Fax: 671-637-9865
Officers:
Joseph G. Calvo, President
John T. Calvo, Vice President
Edward A. Calvo, Secretary
Leonard P. Calvo, Treasurer
Ownership: Calvo Enterprises Inc., 49.6%; Frances M. Calvo, 16.7%; Paul M Calvo, 16.7, 33%; Thomas J. M. Calvo, 16.7%; CEI ownership:; Eduardo M. Calvo & Frances B. Calvo Lifetime Trust, Eduardo A. Calvo Trustee, 33.3%; Paul M. Calvo & Rosa B. Calvo Lifetime Trust, Paul M. Calvo Trustee, 33.3%; Thomas J. M. & Rosario C. Calvo Lifetime Trust, Thomas J. M. Calvo Trustee., 33.3%.
LPTV Stations:
Guam: KUAM-LP Tamuning.
Commercial TV Stations:
Guam: KUAM-DT Agana.
Radio Stations:
Guam: KUAM-AM-FM Agana

MIDESSA BROADCASTING LP
PO Box 708
Lawton, OK 73502
Phone: 580-355-7000
Officer:
Robert H. Drewry, President
Represented (legal): Davis Wright Tremaine LLP.
LPTV Stations:
Texas: KSCM-LP Bryan.

MID-SOUTH BROADCASTING
Box 8
Ashland, MS 38603
Phone: 601-224-6420
LPTV Stations:
Mississippi: WBII-CA Holly Springs.

MID-STATE TELEVISION INC.
2900 Park Ave. W
Mansfield, OH 44906-1062
Phone: 419-529-5900
Fax: 419-529-3319
Officers:
Gunther Meisse, Chairman, President & Chief Executive Officer
Charles J. Hire, Vice President
Glenn Cheesman, Vice President, Sales
William Heichel, Secretary-Treasurer
Ownership: Gunther S. Meisse Revocable Trust, Gunther S. Meisse Trustee, 51%; Phyllis E. Hire Revocable Trust, 35%; Glenn Cheesman, 14%. Hire, Meisse & Cheesman have radio interests.
Represented (legal): Fletcher, Heald & Hildreth PLC.
LPTV Stations:
Ohio: WOHZ-CA Mansfield.
Commercial TV Stations:
Ohio: WMFD-DT Mansfield.

MID TENNESSEE MEDIA PARTNERS GP
122 Abbottsford
Nashville, TN 37215
LPTV Stations:
Tennessee: WCKV-LP Clarksville.

MILLARD COUNTY
50 S. Main
Fillmore, UT 84631
Phone: 435-864-1405
LPTV Stations:
Utah: K49HA Delta; K53JE-D Delta; K35GC Delta, etc.; K38JT-D Delta, etc.; K40IW-D Delta, etc.; K45GE Delta, etc.; K46IW-D Delta, etc.; K36IK-D Delta, Oak City, etc.; K42HQ-D Delta, Oak City, etc.; K23IM-D Fillmore; K57JU-D Fillmore; K56JC-D Fillmore, etc.; K58IQ-D Fillmore, etc.; K59IR-D Fillmore, etc.; K52JX-D Fillmore, Meadow, etc.; K25JJ-D Filmore, Meadow, etc.; K46GG Garrison, etc.; K48FH Garrison, etc.; K22EC-D Juab; K52JW-D Leamington; K55KH-D Leamington; K56JB-D Leamington; K57JS-D Leamington; K58IP-D Leamington; K59IQ-D Leamington; K19GR-D Scipio; K31GT Scipio; K34IZ-D Scipio; K35IP-D Scipio; K36IP-D Scipio; K41IG Scipio; K43JN Scipio; K25JK-D Scipio, Holden; K29HS-D Scipio, Holden.

MILLENNIUM COMMUNICATIONS & PRODUCTIONS
PO Box 532
Etoile, TX 75944
Phone: 936-854-2044
Fax: 936-854-2077
E-mail: klnm@lcc.net
Officers:

Janella Martin, Chairman, Secretary-Treasurer & Chief Financial Officer
Marshall Martin, President & Chief Operating Officer
Ownership: Marshall Martin.
Represented (legal): Shainis & Peltzman Chartered.
LPTV Stations:
Texas: KLNM-LP Lufkin.

MILLER FAMILY BROADCASTING LLC
118 State Dr.
Hollister, MO 65672
LPTV Stations:
Missouri: K05JQ Branson.

LARRY H. MILLER COMMUNICATIONS CORP.
5181 Amelia Earhart Dr.
Salt Lake City, UT 84116-2869
Phone: 801-537-1414
Fax: 801-238-6414
Officers:
Karen G. Miller, President
Denny Haslam, Chief Operating Officer
Robert Hyde, Chief Financial Officer
Larry H. Miller, Secretary-Treasurer
Ownership: Karen G Miller, 48%; Larry H Miller Irrevocable Trust, Karen G Miller, Trustee, 48%; Bryan J Miller, 1%; Gregory S Miller, 1%; Roger L Miller, 1%; Stephen F Miller, 1%.
Represented (legal): Leventhal, Senter & Lerman PLLC.
LPTV Stations:
Utah: K21DY Heber City; K18DL-D Logan; K44EL Ouray; K21EZ Price; K38GO Roosevelt; K24CY St. George; K15DI Vernal; K32EJ Woodland.
Wyoming: K50DR Evanston; K19CP Mountain View; K26DK Rock Springs.
Commercial TV Stations:
Utah: KJZZ-DT Salt Lake City.

ROGER MILLS
103 S. Hale St.
Grantsville, UT 84029
Phone: 435-884-3136
Represented (legal): Dan J. Alpert.
LPTV Stations:
Nevada: K63HJ Laughlin.
Texas: K66GD Vidor.

MINERAL TELEVISION DISTRICT NO. 1
Box 1991
Hawthorne, NV 89415-1991
Phone: 775-423-2543
Ownership: Karen Boyles; Jim Fitzgerald; Cal Lattin, 33.3%. votes each.
LPTV Stations:
Nevada: K20FR Hawthorne; K30FS Hawthorne; K33GZ Hawthorne; K48GG Hawthorne; K50AI Hawthorne; K39EZ Mina; K10GT Mina & Luning; K40GA Mina & Luning; K43GS Mina & Luning; K05AF Mina, etc.; K16FU Mina-Luning; K18GG Mina-Luning; K31BM Silver Springs; K17FR Walker Lake; K26JC Walker Lake; K38EH Walker Lake; K14JY Walker Lake, etc.; K24EY Walker Lake, etc.; K28GX Walker Lake, etc.; K42DS Walker Lake, etc..

MINERSVILLE TOWN
60 W Main
Mineersville, UT 84752
Phone: 435-386-2242
E-mail: djohnson@netutah.com

LPTV Stations:
Utah: K05AT Minersville; K17HX-D Minersville.

MINISTERIO OSCAR AGUERO INC.
6050 W. 20th Ave.
Hialeah, FL 33016
Phone: 305-826-5555
Officer:
Oscar Aguero, President
Represented (legal): Fletcher, Heald & Hildreth PLC.
LPTV Stations:
Florida: W43CB Matecumbe.

MINNESOTA VALLEY TV IMPROVEMENT CORP.
PO Box A
Granite Falls, MN 56241
Phone: 320-564-4970
Web site: www.mvtvwireless.com
Officer:
Daniel L. Richter, President
Represented (legal): Katten, Munchin & Rosenman LLP.
LPTV Stations:
Minnesota: K16CP Granite Falls; K18DI Granite Falls; K22DO Granite Falls; K24CS Granite Falls; K26DG Granite Falls; K32DR Granite Falls; K35DK Granite Falls; K45DJ Granite Falls; K47EA Granite Falls; K61AU Granite Falls; K63AU Granite Falls; K65BA Granite Falls; K67AN Granite Falls; K69DP Granite Falls.

MINORITY BROADCASTING CO. II LLC
1280 Bowie St.
Beaumont, TX 77701
Phone: 409-813-1000
E-mail: gershon7@juno.com
Officer:
Gershon Haston, Vice President, Business Manager
Represented (legal): Irwin, Campbell & Tannenwald PC.
LPTV Stations:
Texas: KUMY-LP Beaumont-Orange.

MINTO VILLAGE COUNCIL
5900 E. Tudor Rd.
Anchorage, AK 99507
Phone: 907-269-5744
LPTV Stations:
Alaska: K07QF Minto.

MINTZ BROADCASTING
518 Peoples St.
Corpus Christi, TX 78401
Phone: 361-883-1763
Ownership: Laurie Mintz, Partner.
Represented (legal): Shainis & Peltzman Chartered.
LPTV Stations:
Texas: K51JF San Antonio.

HOWARD MINTZ
4895 Ocean Dr.
Corpus Christi, TX 78412
Phone: 361-906-1001
LPTV Stations:
California: K20HZ Palm Springs.
Puerto Rico: W36DB Ponce; W26DK San Juan.
Texas: K54JS Corpus Christi; K45HW San Angelo; K39HB Victoria.

LAWRENCE HOWARD MINTZ
4895 Ocean Dr.
Corpus Christi, TX 78412

Phone: 361-906-1001
LPTV Stations:
Texas: K29IP-D Corpus Christi; K69IT Midland.

MICHAEL MINTZ
141 Kush Lane
Corpus Christi, TX 78404
Phone: 361-884-6293
LPTV Stations:
Florida: WXPC-LP Panama City.
Texas: K46HQ Amarillo; K64GK Amarillo; K69IH Amarillo.
Other Holdings:
See Club Communications..

SEAN MINTZ
141 Kush Lane
Corpus Christi, TX 78404
Phone: 361-884-6293
LPTV Stations:
Puerto Rico: W51DJ Mayaguez.

MIRAGE MEDIA LLC
1615 Orange Tree Ln
Ste 102
Redlands, CA 92374
Phone: 909-793-2233
Ownership: The Jaeger Trust, William J. Jaeger Trustee. votes, 40% equity; The Donald Jaeger Revocable Trust, Donald Jaeger Trustee, 30%. equity; Bart Pearce, 30%. equity.
Represented (legal): Wiley Rein LLP.
LPTV Stations:
California: KOTR-LP Gonzalez.

MIRANDA BROADCASTING CO. OF KEY WEST LLC
1001 NE 125th St
Suite 101
Miami, FL 33161
Phone: 954-709-8207
E-mail: tony@miratv.tv
Officer:
Tony Miranda, President
LPTV Stations:
Florida: W44AC Key West.

MISSION BROADCASTING INC.
544 Red Rock Dr.
Wadsworth, OH 44281
Phone: 330-335-8808
Fax: 330-336-8454
Officers:
David S. Smith, President & Treasurer
Dennis Thatcher, Chief Operating Officer
Nancie J. Smith, Vice President & Secretary
Ownership: David S. Smith. 100% votes.
Represented (legal): Drinker Biddle.
LPTV Stations:
New Mexico: K47DH Clovis; K30DZ San Jon.
Oklahoma: K47DK Grandfield; K53DS Lawton.
Pennsylvania: W19AR Clarks Summit; W54AV Mansfield; W66AI Pottsville, etc.; W60AH Stroudsburg; W26AT Williamsport; W55AG Williamsport.
Texas: KCPN-LP Amarillo; K35CG Bovina; KJBO-LP Wichita Falls.
Commercial TV Stations:
Arkansas: KTVE-DT El Dorado.
Illinois: WTVO-DT Rockford.
Indiana: WFXW-DT Terre Haute.
Missouri: KODE-DT Joplin; KOLR-DT Springfield.
Montana: KHMT-DT Hardin.
New York: WUTR-DT Utica.
Pennsylvania: WFXP-DT Erie; WYOU-DT Scranton.
Texas: KRBC-DT Abilene; KCIT-DT Amarillo; KAMC-DT Lubbock; KSAN-DT San Angelo; KJTL-DT Wichita Falls.

MISSISSIPPI AUTHORITY FOR ETV
3825 Ridgewood Rd.
Jackson, MS 39211
Phone: 601-432-6565
E-mail: marie.antoon@mpbonline.org
Officers:
Marie Antoon, Interim Executive Director
Rickie Felder, Chief Financial Officer
Represented (legal): Schwartz, Woods & Miller.
LPTV Stations:
Mississippi: W45AA Columbia; W47BP Hattiesburg.
ETV Stations:
Mississippi: WMAH-DT Biloxi; WMAU-DT Bude; WMAB-DT Mississippi State.

MISSISSIPPI TELEVISION LLC
700 St John St
Ste 301
Lafayette, LA 70501
Phone: 337-237-9965
Ownership: JW Mississippi LLC; JWMLLC ownership:; David Joseph, 50%. votes, 57.5% assets; James W. Wood, 50%. votes, 42.5% assets. Joseph and Woods are indirect principals of JW Broadcasting LLC, see listing.
Represented (legal): Pillsbury Winthrop Shaw Pittman LLP.
LPTV Stations:
Mississippi: WBMS-CA Jackson; W46CW Jackson/Brandon.
Commercial TV Stations:
Mississippi: WUFX-DT Vicksburg.
Other Holdings:
Galloway owns White Knight Holdings Inc., see listing..

MISSOURI SOUTHERN STATE UNIVERSITY
3950 E. Newman Rd.
Joplin, MO 64801
Phone: 417-625-9375
Fax: 417-625-9742
Ownership: Board of Regents.
LPTV Stations:
Missouri: KGCS-LP Joplin.
Other Holdings:
Radio.

THE CURATORS OF THE U. OF MISSOURI
Hwy. 63 S
Columbia, MO 65201
Phone: 573-882-8888
Fax: 573-884-8888
Represented (legal): Pillsbury Winthrop Shaw Pittman LLP.
LPTV Stations:
Missouri: K07SD Rolla.
Commercial TV Stations:
Missouri: KOMU-DT Columbia.

WILLIAM MITCHELL
7659 Hampton Peak Ave
Las Vegas, NV 89113
Phone: 702-278-2711
LPTV Stations:
Utah: K56IQ Park City.

MOAPA VALLEY TV MAINTENANCE DISTRICT
Box 553
Overton, NV 89040
Phone: 702-397-6760
LPTV Stations:
Nevada: K07IJ Logan & Moapa area; K09IT Moapa & Overton; K11JL Overton; K44GU

Overton; K48ID Overton; K46HG Overton, etc.; K50HQ Overton, etc..

STUART E. MOEN
415 Barren Springs Dr.
Houston, TX 77090
LPTV Stations:
South Dakota: K48DK Sioux Falls.

MOFFAT COUNTY
221 W. Victory Way
Craig, CO 81625
LPTV Stations:
Colorado: K10EW Maybell; K11FW Steamboat Springs; K58AQ Steamboat Springs; K64AR Steamboat Springs.

MOHAVE COUNTY BOARD OF SUPERVISORS
Box 7000
Kingman, AZ 86402-7000
Phone: 928-753-0729
LPTV Stations:
Arizona: K27DA Big Sandy Valley; K02HR Bullhead City; K04GT Bullhead City; K07YJ Bullhead City; K09KG Bullhead City; K11LX Bullhead City; K12OF Bullhead City; K16EV Bullhead City; K30GG Chloride; K32DW Chloride; K42CQ Chloride; K49EU Chloride; K27EJ Colorado City; K35EI Dolan Springs; K41BZ Dolan Springs; K43GU Dolan Springs; K11TA Golden Valley; K21EG Golden Valley; K46CG Golden Valley; K23FV Kingman; K31BI Kingman; K34EF Kingman; K41FT Kingman; K44DK Kingman; K48AY Kingman; K49GE Kingman; K50CY Kingman; K21EA Lake Havasu City; K29FD Lake Havasu City; K31GZ Lake Havasu City; K38IR Lake Havasu City; K39FV Lake Havasu City; K43GJ Lake Havasu City; K46GI Lake Havasu City; K31EA Littlefield; K23DK Meadview; K25DH Meadview; K36FZ Meadview; K38GR Meadview; K47HE Meadview; K35EE Moccasin; K26GF Peach Springs; K42CP Peach Springs; K21FU Topock; K42EU Topock, etc..
California: K17BN Needles; K31HY Needles, etc..

MONO COUNTY SERVICE AREA NO. 1
Box 3861
Mammoth Lakes, CA 93546
Phone: 760-934-6299
E-mail: commdev@mono.ca.gov
Officers:
Guntram Jordan, President
Patricia Fisher, Chief Executive Officer
Gary Williams, Chief Operating Officer
Marianne O'Connor, Secretary-Treasurer
Represented (legal): Fleischman & Harding LLP.
LPTV Stations:
California: K15DP Crowley Lake & Long Valley; K17DF Crowley Lake & Long Valley; K19DI Crowley Lake & Long Valley; K25EB Crowley Lake & Long Valley; K27DV Crowley Lake & Long Valley; K58BN Crowley Lake & Long Valley; K05FR Long Valley; K49EA Long Valley; K56BS Long Valley; K60BR Long Valley Region.

MONO COUNTY SERVICE AREA NO. 2
123 Valley Rd.
Chalfant, CA 93514

LPTV Stations:
California: K55FD Chalfant Valley; K61EJ Chalfant Valley; K64CY Chalfant Valley.

MONO COUNTY SERVICE AREA NO. 5
Box 675
Bridgeport, CA 93517
LPTV Stations:
California: K02JX Bridgeport, etc.; K07QM Bridgeport, etc.; K11HS Bridgeport, etc.; K13EX Bridgeport, etc.; K51CP Swauger Creek; K54CX Swauger Creek.

MONTANA U. SYSTEM BOARD OF REGENTS
Visual Communications Bldg.
Room 183
Bozeman, MT 59717-3340
Phone: 406-994-3437
Officers:
Lynn Morrison-Hamilton, Chairman, Board of Regents
Stephen M. Barrett, Vice Chairman, Board of Regents
Geoff Gamble, President, Montana State U.
David M. Dooley, Provost, Montana State U.
Craig Roloff, Vice President, Admin. & Finance
Ownership: Board of Regents.
Represented (legal): Dow Lohnes PLLC.
LPTV Stations:
Montana: K20DY Belgrade, etc.; K20HB Billings; K43DU Butte; K49EH Helena.
ETV Stations:
Montana: KUSM-DT Bozeman; KUFM-DT Missoula.

MONTEREY COUNTY SUPERINTENDENT OF SCHOOLS
901 Blanco Circle
Box 80851
Salinas, CA 93912
Phones: 831-755-0383; 831-755-0389
Fax: 831-753-7888
Officers:
William Barr, Superintendent
Mike Mellon, Chief Operating Officer
LPTV Stations:
California: K38JP Salinas.

MONTROSE COUNTY
PO Box 1289
Montrose, CO 81401
LPTV Stations:
Colorado: K04FY Nucla, etc.; K34DH Redvale, etc..

MOOSE PASS SPORTSMANS CLUB
Box 72
Moose Pass, AK 99631
LPTV Stations:
Alaska: K04KK Moose Pass; K07QT Moose Pass; K11QF Moose Pass; K13RL Moose Pass.

ISSAC RUIZ MORA
606 S Birdsong
San Antonio, TX 78258
Phone: 210-837-2178
LPTV Stations:
Texas: K53IX Big Spring; K66GG Odessa.

WILLIAM EARL MORGAN
403 W Calhoun St
Bruce, MS 38915-0580
Phone: 662-983-2801

LPTV Stations:
Mississippi: W34BJ Calhoun City.

MORGAN COUNTY
886 Morgan County Courthouse
Morgan, UT 84050
Phone: 801-829-3338
LPTV Stations:
Utah: K29EP Morgan; K08GA Morgan, etc.; K10FW Morgan, etc.; K12GI Morgan, etc..

MORGAN MURPHY MEDIA
Box 44965
Madison, WI 53744-4965
Phone: 608-271-4321
Fax: 608-278-5553
E-mail: talkback@wisctv.com
Officers:
Elizabeth Murphy Burns, President & Chief Executive Officer
John B. Murphy, Secretary-Treasurer
George A. Nelson, Chief Financial Officer
Ownership: Evening Telegram Co.. Evening Telegram Co. also owns Spokane Television Inc., see listing.
Represented (legal): Rini Coran PC.
LPTV Stations:
Washington: K40EE Pullman; K14HT Walla Walla, etc..
Commercial TV Stations:
Washington: KVEW-DT Kennewick; KXLY-DT Spokane; KAPP-DT Yakima.
Wisconsin: WKBT-DT La Crosse; WISC-DT Madison.
Newspapers:
Minnesota: Evening Telegram Company or its shareholders own 50% of Murphy McGinnis Media Inc., which publishes daily, weekly, shopper and other publications in Kansas, Michigan, Minnesota and Wisconsin, including daily newspapers in Superior, Wisconsin; Ashland, Wis
Radio Stations:
Idaho: KVNI (AM) Coeur d'Alene, KHTQ (FM) Hayden
Iowa: KIYXA (FM) Sageville
Washington: KXLX (AM) Airway Heights; KEZE (FM), KXLY-AM-FM, KZZU-FM Spokane
Wisconsin: WGLR-AM-FM Lancaster, WPVL-AM-FM Platteville
Other Holdings:
Magazine: Madison Magazine.

MORONGO BASIN TV CLUB INC.
73658 Old Dale Rd.
Twentynine Palms, CA 92277-3280
LPTV Stations:
California: K14JT Twentynine Palms; K18FH Twentynine Palms.

DEAN M. MOSELY
PO Box 3041
Jena, LA 71342
Phone: 318-992-7766
Web site: www.panamericatv.com
Represented (legal): Wiley Rein LLP.
LPTV Stations:
Florida: W22CL Fort Myers; WWRJ-LP Jacksonville.
Hawaii: KHHI-LP Honolulu.
Kansas: KPJO-LP Pittsburg.
Maine: W41DD Bangor.
Mississippi: WHGM-LP Hattiesburg; WHPM-LP Hattiesburg.
Tennessee: WIIW-LP Nashville.
Other Holdings:
Broadcasting: Mosely Enterprises LLC, see listing..

MOSELY ENTERPRISES LLC
4316 Claycut Rd.
Baton Rouge, LA 70806

Phone: 318-992-7766

E-mail: deanmosely@centurytel.net

Ownership: Dean M. Mosely, see listing,, Managing Member. 100% voting & 50% equity; Russell Long Mosely, Member, 50%. equity.

Represented (legal): Wiley Rein LLP.

LPTV Stations:

Oklahoma: K25IC Lawton.

Texas: K38IG Victoria; K40HZ Wichita Falls.

MOUNTAIN LAKE PUBLIC TELECOMMUNICATIONS COUNCIL

One Sesame St.

Plattsburgh, NY 12901

Phone: 518-563-9770

Fax: 518-561-1928

E-mail: charlie_zarbo@mountainlake.pbs.org

Officers:

Ted Kowalczyk, Chairman

Howard Lowe, President & General Manager

Samuel E. Ravit, Secretary-Treasurer

John Flanzer, Vice President & Programming Director

Alice Recore, Director, Finance Administration

Represented (legal): Dow Lohnes PLLC.

LPTV Stations:

New York: W60AO Port Henry; W25AT Tupper Lake; W67AR Willsboro.

Vermont: W25BT Monkton.

ETV Stations:

New York: WCFE-DT Plattsburgh.

MOUNTAIN LICENSES LP

2111 University Park Dr.

Suite 650

Okemos, MI 48864

Phone: 517-347-4111

Officer:

Brian W. Brady, President, General Partner

Ownership: Northwest Broadcast Inc., Gen. Partner, 1%. equity, 100% votes; Mountain Broadcasting LLC, Ltd. Partner, 99%. equity, NBI ownership:; Brian W. Brady; MBLLC ownership:; Northwest Broadcasting Inc. 100% votes; 1% equity; Northwest Broadcasting LP, 99%. equity; NBLP ownership:; Northwest Broadcasting Inc., Gen. Partner. 100% votes; 0.07% equity; Brian W. Brady, Ltd. Partner, 99.3%. equity; NBI ownership:; Brian W. Brady. Brady is also a principal of Broadcasting Licenses LP & Stainless Broadcasting LP, see listings.

Represented (legal): Leventhal, Senter & Lerman PLLC.

LPTV Stations:

Idaho: K50DM Coeur d'Alene; K19BY Grangeville; K47BW Lewiston, etc.; K52GH Sandpoint.

Washington: K44CK Chelan; K09UP Colville; K35BJ Ellisford; K19AU Omak & Okanogan; K31AH Omak, etc.; K10NQ Prosser, etc.; KBWU-LD Richland, etc.; K38IT Stemilt, etc.; KCYU-LD Yakima.

Commercial TV Stations:

Oregon: KFFX-DT Pendleton.

Washington: KAYU-DT Spokane.

MOUNTAIN RIDGE HOLDINGS INC.

6363 South Pecos Rd

Ste 109

Las Vegas, NV 89120

Phone: 702-796-3535

Web site: www.vegas35tv.com

LPTV Stations:

Nevada: KVTE-LP Las Vegas.

MOUNTAIN TV LLC

220 Salters Creek Rd

Hampton, VA 23661

Phone: 757-722-9736

Officer:

David A. Hanna, President

Ownership: James L. Lockwood Jr., see listing, 80%; James A. Stern, 20%.

Represented (legal): Brooks, Pierce, McLendon, Humphrey & Leonard LLP.

LPTV Stations:

West Virginia: WOCW-LP Charleston; WVCW-LP Huntington.

Commercial TV Stations:

Ohio: WQCW-DT Portsmouth.

MOUNT MANSFIELD TELEVISION INC.

P.O.Box 5408

Burlington, VT 05406-4508

Phone: 802-652-6300

Fax: 802-652-6319

E-mail: Teffner@wcax.com

Web site: www.wcax.com

Officers:

Peter Martin, President

Theodore Teffner, Vice President, Engineering

Marselis Parsons, Vice President, News

Ownership: Stuart T Martin, 49.5%; Peter R Martin, 12.46%; James S Martin, 12.46%; Marcia H Martin Boyer, 12.46%; Donald P Martin, 12.46%.

Represented (legal): Sheehey, Furlong & Behm PC.

LPTV Stations:

Vermont: W69AR Rutland.

Commercial TV Stations:

Vermont: WCAX-DT Burlington.

MOUNT MASSIVE LAKES INC.

PO Box 27

Leadville, CO 80461

Phone: 970-486-1075

LPTV Stations:

Colorado: K09LT Mount Massive, etc..

MS COMMUNICATIONS LLC

1121 N. Waverly Place

Milwaukee, WI 53202

Phone: 414-765-9737

E-mail: brettmaz@tds.net

Officer:

Brett Mazzone, Managing Partner

Represented (legal): Womble, Carlyle, Sandridge & Rice.

LPTV Stations:

Arkansas: K20EX Batesville; K22ES Batesville; K30EC Batesville; K35EA Batesville; K40DS Batesville; K46EM Batesville; K53FM Batesville; K57FV Batesville; K59FB Batesville; K61FP Batesville; K65FN Batesville; K67GR Batesville; K69GT Batesville; K27FF El Dorado; K29DC El Dorado; K36DR El Dorado; K40EF El Dorado; K46DT El Dorado; K48EP El Dorado; K50EK El Dorado; K53FB El Dorado; K57GF El Dorado; K59FJ El Dorado; K63FX El Dorado; K66EX El Dorado; K69HO El Dorado.

California: K27FX Eureka; K41FD Eureka; K48GP Eureka; K50EQ Eureka; K57HB Eureka; K63GK Eureka.

Georgia: W08DM Colquitt; W22BV Colquitt; W26BM Colquitt; W30BO Colquitt; W45BL Colquitt; W47BX Colquitt; W51CQ Colquitt; W69DO Colquitt.

Illinois: W48CU Champaign/Urbana; W15CT Quincy; W17DD Quincy; W19DI Quincy; W20CU Quincy; W36BS Quincy; W45BM Quincy; W49BS Quincy; W51EI Quincy.

Iowa: K21EM Ottumwa; K31ED Ottumwa; K45EE Ottumwa; K49DX Ottumwa; K51FJ Ottumwa; K53FC Ottumwa; K55GS Ottumwa; K58ER Ottumwa; K65GA Ottumwa; K67GH Ottumwa; K40GO Waterloo.

Kentucky: W16BI Talbert; W20BO Talbert; W24BT Talbert; W26BK Talbert; W31BU Talbert; W51CK Talbert; W53BQ Talbert;

W54CI Talbert; W64CM Talbert; W66DA Talbert; W69ED Talbert.

Louisiana: K16DK Alexandria; K21EL Alexandria; K23DZ Alexandria; K38EG Alexandria; K43EI Alexandria; K50DW Alexandria; K55GT Alexandria; K57GK Alexandria; K60GE Alexandria; W30ID New Orleans.

Maine: W39CC Bangor; W42BZ Bangor; W50BX Bangor; W54CG Bangor; W58CM Bangor; W66CL Bangor.

Michigan: W18CB Houghton Lake; W21BS Houghton Lake; W24CG Houghton Lake; W31BN Houghton Lake; W36CE Houghton Lake; W50CD Houghton Lake; W52CO Houghton Lake; W55CH Houghton Lake; W57CQ Houghton Lake; W59DC Houghton Lake; W61CS Houghton Lake; W63CH Houghton Lake; W65DJ Houghton Lake; W67DN Houghton Lake; W34BZ Ludington; W48BY Ludington; W18BX Petoskey; W20BQ Petoskey; W23BM Petoskey; W25CD Petoskey; W31BI Petoskey; W36CD Petoskey; W39CB Petoskey; W51CR Petoskey; W53BN Petoskey; W55CL Petoskey; W57CP Petoskey; W62CR Petoskey; W64CK Petoskey; W66CY Petoskey; W68DH Petoskey; W21BN Sault Ste. Marie; W32BN Sault Ste. Marie; W36BV Sault Ste. Marie; W39BY Sault Ste. Marie; W48BZ Sault Ste. Marie; W50CA Sault Ste. Marie; W52CB Sault Ste. Marie; W56DI Sault Ste. Marie; W58CO Sault Ste. Marie; W15BM Traverse City; W23BL Traverse City; W34CE Traverse City; W36BZ Traverse City; W48CC Traverse City; W52CP Traverse City; W56DF Traverse City; W58CN Traverse City; W62CQ Traverse City; W66CX Traverse City; W68DD Traverse City.

Minnesota: K52HH Rochester.

Mississippi: W12CR Grenada; W28BP Grenada; W36BT Grenada; W41BV Grenada; W46CK Grenada; W20BS Meridian; W26BR Meridian; W27DD Meridian; W35CQ Meridian; W36BY Meridian; W36CU Meridian; W46CL Meridian; W52CS Meridian; W53CE Meridian; W54CD Meridian; W59DE Meridian; W65DE Meridian; W69DJ Meridian; W49BK Tupelo.

Missouri: K33EQ Cape Girardeau; K47FB Cape Girardeau; K55HL Cape Girardeau; K58FD Cape Girardeau; K65GP Cape Girardeau; K67HF Cape Girardeau; K69HT Cape Girardeau; K04OV Joplin; K52FC Joplin; K55HU Joplin.

Oklahoma: K57IP Tulsa.

Tennessee: W14BW Acton; W20BJ Acton; W27CL Acton; W32BG Acton; W34BU Acton; W43BH Acton; W46CE Acton; W56DA Acton; W62CK Acton; W66CG Acton; W69DB Acton; W22BR Jackson; W25BY Jackson; W26CJ Jackson; W38BY Jackson; W46CG Jackson; W52CZ Jackson; W54BU Jackson; W62CJ Jackson; W64BZ Jackson.

Wisconsin: W06BU Whiting; W16AY Whiting; W18CS Whiting; W24BV Whiting; W31CI Whiting; W40BC Whiting; W60CI Whiting; W62DA Whiting.

MTN BROADCASTING INC.

Box 538

Marshalltown, IA 50158

Phone: 641-752-4122

Fax: 641-752-5121

Officer:

Mark K. Osmundson, President

LPTV Stations:

Iowa: KDAO-LP Marshalltown.

NICHOLAS L. MUHLHAUSER

315 Nicholson Ave

Los Gatos, CA 95030

Phone: 408-395-6746

LPTV Stations:

California: K54CY Lakeport; K58AW Lakeport.

MULHOLLAND MEDIA GROUP

2409 College Ave

Texarkana, TX 75501

Phone: 903-793-5995

Officer:

Rodney B. Davis, General Manager & Chief Executive Officer

LPTV Stations:

Arkansas: KTEV-LP Texarkana.

MULTIMEDIA NETWORK OF NORTH CAROLINA INC.

110 Torrey Pines Lane

Pinehurst, NC 28374

LPTV Stations:

North Carolina: WYBE-CA Pinehurst.

MUTUAL TELEVISION NETWORK

Box 601261

Sacramento, CA 95860

Phone: 888-482-1080

Officer:

Ronald E Hodges, President

LPTV Stations:

California: K47EH Alturas, etc.; K19FY Chico; K27GZ Mariposa; K15DB Santa Barbara; K38EE Twentynine Palms.

Idaho: K41JC Pocatello.

Nevada: K39FF Reno.

Oregon: K41IX Medford.

MY TOWN TV

1903 W. Beebe Capps

Searcy, AR 72143

Phone: 501-279-1121

E-mail: kyle@mytowntv.net

Officer:

T. Kyle Reeves, President

LPTV Stations:

Arkansas: KTWN-LD Searcy.

ROBERT A. NAISMITH

PO Box 97

1102 Bridge St.

Charlevoix, MI 49720

Phone: 231-547-2696

Web site: www.wuhw.com

LPTV Stations:

Florida: WTBZ-LP Gainesville.

Georgia: WBUD-LP Blairsville.

NARROWS BROADCASTING CORP.

Box 149

Petersburg, AK 99833

LPTV Stations:

Alaska: K09OU Petersburg; K11QC Petersburg.

NATIONAL MINORITY TV INC.

PO Box 53575

Irvine, CA 92619-3575

Phone: 949-552-0490

Web site: www.nmtv.org

Officers:

Dr. Paul F. Crouch, President

Janice W. Crouch, Vice President

Ruth Brown, Secretary-Treasurer

John B. Casoria, Assistant Secretary

Paul F. Crouch, Jr., Assistant Secretary

Ownership: Janice W. Crouch, 33.3%; Dr. Paul F. Crouch Sr., 33.3%; Paul F. Crouch Jr., 33.3%.

Represented (legal): Colby M. May.

LPTV Stations:

Ohio: W09CG Findlay.

NATIVE COUNTRY BROADCASTING CORP.

2025 Surfside Terrace

Vero Beach, FL 32963

Phone: 775-562-1020

LPTV Stations:
Florida: WFOL-LP Orlando.
Louisiana: W08DT New Iberia.

CITY OF NATOMA
514 N. 2nd
Natoma, KS 67651
LPTV Stations:
Kansas: K11NS Natoma; K13OM Natoma.

NAVAJO COMMUNITY COLLEGE
Hatathli Cultural Center
Tsaile, AZ 86556
Phone: 602-724-3311
LPTV Stations:
Arizona: K51AV Chinle.
New Mexico: K38AU Crownpoint.

NAVAJO NATION
Box 2310
Window Rock, AZ 86515
LPTV Stations:
Arizona: K40AP Tsaile; K44BB Window Rock.
New Mexico: K48AW Shiprock.

NAVE COMMUNICATIONS LLC
518 Peoples St.
Corpus Christi, TX 78401
Phone: 202-293-0569
Officer:
Avinash Ahuja, Member
LPTV Stations:
New York: WKOB-LP New York.

JERALD NAY
3202 South 1050 West
Westville, IN 46391-9532
Phone: 219-785-4091
LPTV Stations:
Indiana: WAJN-LP Brookston.

NBC UNIVERSAL
30 Rockefeller Plaza
Room 1491E
New York, NY 10012
Phone: 212-664-4444
E-mail: nbcunisupport@nbcuni.com
Web site: www.nbcuni.com/
Officers:
Bob Wright, Chairman
Jeff Zucker, President & Chief Executive Officer
Lisa Gersh, President, Strategic Initiatives
Lynn Calpeter, Executive Vice President & Chief Financial Officer
Rick Cotton, Executive Vice President & General Counsel
Allison Gollust, Executive Vice President, Corporate Communications
Cory Shields, Executive Vice President, Global Policy Strategies & Alliances

Branch Offices:
3000 Alameda Ave
Burbank, CA 91523-0002
Phone: 818-840-4444
4001 Nebraska Ave NW
Washington, DC 20016
Phone: 202-885-4015
Ownership: General Electric Co., 80%; Vivendi Universal, 20%.
LPTV Stations:
Arizona: K28EY Douglas.
California: K15CU Salinas; K47GD San Luis Obispo; K46GF Santa Maria.
Colorado: KMAS-LP Denver.
Florida: W58BU Hallandale.
Nevada: K52FF Reno.
Puerto Rico: W68BU Adjuntas; W09AT Fajardo; W32AJ Utuado.

Utah: KEJT-LP Salt Lake City.
Commercial TV Stations:
Arizona: KTAZ-DT Phoenix; KHRR-DT Tucson.
California: KVEA-DT Corona; KNBC-DT Los Angeles; KWHY-DT Los Angeles; KNSO-DT Merced; KNTV-DT San Jose; KSTS-DT San Jose.
Colorado: KDEN-DT Longmont.
Connecticut: WVIT-DT New Britain.
District of Columbia: WRC-DT Washington.
Florida: WSCV-DT Fort Lauderdale; WTVJ-DT Miami.
Illinois: WMAQ-DT Chicago; WSNS-DT Chicago.
Nevada: KBLR-DT Paradise.
New Hampshire: WNEU-DT Merrimack.
New Jersey: WNJU-DT Linden.
New York: WNBC-DT New York.
Pennsylvania: WCAU-DT Philadelphia.
Puerto Rico: WKAQ-DT San Juan.
Texas: KXTX-DT Dallas; KTMD-DT Galveston; KVDA-DT San Antonio.
Other Holdings:
Broadcast holdings: Station Venture Operations LP, see listing, 79.62%.
Cable Network: CNBC Europe; CNBC (Consumer News & Business Channel); Bravo; 50% of MSNBC; 25% of American Movie Classics; CNBC Asia; The Weather Channel; NBC Europe; 50% of National Geographic Channel Worldwide; 25% of both A & E and the History Channel
Data service: 9.9% of Telescan Internet search firm; Partner in Contentville.com; AllBusiness.com
Program source: 36% of ValueVision; NBC Studios; NBC Entertainment
Satellite programming: Rainbow Program Enterprises.

NC PARTNERS
95 Public Square
Suite 505
Watertown, NY 13601-2607
Phone: 315-785-0869
Ownership: R. Anthony Dimarcantonio, 60%; Bart S. Bonner Estate, 40%.
Represented (legal): Irwin, Campbell & Tannenwald PC.
LPTV Stations:
New York: WLOT-LP Watertown.

NEBRASKA EDUCATIONAL TELECOMMUNICATIONS COMMISSION
1800 N. 33rd St.
Lincoln, NE 68583
Phone: 402-472-3611
Fax: 402-472-1785
E-mail: tv@netnebraska.org
Officer:
John Heil, Chairman
Ownership: State of Nebraska.
Represented (legal): Dow Lohnes PLLC.
LPTV Stations:
Nebraska: K23AA-D Beatrice; K33FO-D Benkelman; K24GO-D Blair; K06JC-D Chadron; K06KR-D Crawford; K34IB-D Decatur; K46FG-D Falls City; K08LN-D Harrison; K44FN-D McCook & Culbertson; K50IO-D Neligh; K14MI-D Niobrara; K33AC-D Pawnee City; K10JW-D Verdigre; K20IJ-D Wauneta.
ETV Stations:
Nebraska: KTNE-DT Alliance; KMNE-DT Bassett; KHNE-DT Hastings; KLNE-DT Lexington; KRNE-DT Merriman; KXNE-DT Norfolk; KPNE-DT North Platte; KYNE-DT Omaha.
Radio Stations:
Nebraska: KXNE-FM; KTNE-FM; KRNE-FM; KPNE-FM; KLNE-FM; KHNE-FM

NEEDLES COMMUNITY TV CLUB INC.
Box 617
Needles, CA 92363
LPTV Stations:
California: K30BQ Needles.

NEPSK INC.
PO Box 1149
12 Brewer Rd.
Presque Isle, ME 04769
Phone: 207-764-4461
Fax: 207-764-5329
Officers:
Gordon Wark, President
Peter P. Kozloski, Chief Executive Officer
Catherine Donovan, Vice President & Chief Financial Officer
Carole M. Kozloski, Vice President

Branch Office:
72 Main
PO Box 610
Houlton, ME 04730
Phone: 207-532-2579
Fax: 207-532-4025
Ownership: Peter P Kozloski.
LPTV Stations:
Maine: W11AA Madawaska.
Commercial TV Stations:
Maine: WAGM-DT Presque Isle.
Cable Systems:
MAINE: DANFORTH; HOULTON; HOWLAND; ISLAND FALLS; MEDWAY; MONTICELLO (town); OAKFIELD; PATTEN.

NEUHOFF FAMILY LP
11793 Lake House Court
North Palm Beach, FL 33408
Phone: 561-625-0616
Ownership: Neuhoff Corp., Gen. Partner, 1%. equity, 100% voting; Marian T. Hickman; Alexander A. Neuhoff; Eric A. Neuhoff; Geoffrey H. Neuhoff, Ltd. Partners, 24.75%. equity each; NC ownership:; Roger A. Neuhoff; Louise Neuhoff, 50%. voting each.
Represented (legal): Schwartz, Woods & Miller.
LPTV Stations:
Idaho: K09IR Albion; K59CC Burley, etc.; K04EN Glenns Ferry; K57CC Hagerman; K13HG Ketchum, etc.; KTID-LP Twin Falls; KTWT-LP Twin Falls.
Commercial TV Stations:
Idaho: KMVT-DT Twin Falls.

NEW AGE MEDIA
46 Public Sq
Ste 500
WIlkes-Barre, PA 18701
Phone: 570-824-7895
Ownership: Sedgwick Media LLC, 65%; Dallas Media LLC, 33.64%; Michael Yanuzzi, 1.36%; SMLLC ownership:; John Parente, 51%. votes, 18.94% assets; Charles E. & Mary M. Parente, 49%. votes, 4.06% assets; Sedgwick Co. LLC, 30.08%. assets; Marlco Investment Corp., 15.4%. assets; C.E. Parente Trust, U/A 9/17/1997, John J. Parente, Trustee, 7.07%. assets; Brynfan Associates, 3.85%. assets; Brian J Parente, 3.85%. assets; Charles L Parente, 3.85%. assets; Marla P Sgarlat, 3.85%. assets; DMLLC ownership:; Frank M. Henry, 85%; Frank M. Henry Jr., 5%; Scott Henry, 5%; Marjorie Henry Marquart, 5%; BA, MIC & SCLLC ownership:; Parente Family.
Represented (legal): Fletcher, Heald & Hildreth PLC.
LPTV Stations:
Florida: WYPN-CA Gainesville; WMYG-LP Lake City.
Georgia: WBFL-CA Valdosta; WBVJ-LP Valdosta.
Pennsylvania: W24DB Sayre.

Tennessee: WPDP-LP Cleveland.
Commercial TV Stations:
Florida: WGFL-DT High Springs.
Georgia: WTLH-DT Bainbridge.
Maine: WPXT-DT Portland.
Pennsylvania: WOLF-DT Hazleton; WQMY-DT Williamsport.
Tennessee: WDSI-DT Chattanooga.

NEW COLONIAL BROADCASTING LLC
901 Edgewood Dr
Charleston, WV 25302
Phone: 304-549-2047
Ownership: Mark A. Hunt, Managing Member.
Represented (legal): Shainis & Peltzman Chartered.
LPTV Stations:
Florida: WEYW-LP Key West.

TOWN OF NEWCOMB
Town Hall
Newcomb, NY 12852
Phone: 518-582-3211
LPTV Stations:
New York: W12BG Newcomb.

NEW COVENANT CHURCH
110 Magnolia Heights
Falfurrias, TX 78355-3204
Phone: 512-325-5641
LPTV Stations:
Texas: K07TS Falfurrias.

NEW GLOBAL COMMUNICATIONS INC.
20 Main St
Sparta, NJ 07871
Phone: 201-248-9634
E-mail: josephpratti@yahoo.com
Officer:
Joseph P. Ratti, Secretary
Represented (legal): James L. Primm.
LPTV Stations:
California: KVPS-LP Indio.

UNIVERSITY SYSTEM OF NEW HAMPSHIRE BOARD OF TRUSTEES
268 Mast Rd
Durham, NH 03824-4601
Phone: 603-868-1100
Officer:
Peter A Frid, President & Chief Executive Officer
Represented (legal): Schwartz, Woods & Miller.
LPTV Stations:
Vermont: W27CP White River Junction.

NEW JERSEY PUBLIC BROADCASTING AUTHORITY
25 S. Stockton St.
CN777
Trenton, NJ 08625-0777
Phone: 609-777-5001
Fax: 609-633-2912
Officers:
M. Joseph Montuoro, Chairman
Elizabeth G. Christopherson, Executive Director
Eric Luskin, Director, TV Broadcasting

Branch Offices:
Jimmy Leeds Rd.
Pomona, NJ 08540
Phone: 609-652-8385
50 Park Place
Newark, NJ 07102
Phone: 201-648-3630
Represented (legal): Schwartz, Woods & Miller.

LPTV Stations:
New Jersey: W43CG Belvidere; W49BE Hackettstown; W25BB Pittstown; W36AZ Sussex.
ETV Stations:
New Jersey: WNJS-DT Camden; WNJN-DT Montclair; WNJT-DT Trenton.
Other Holdings:
Radio.

NEW LIFE EVANGELISTIC CENTER INC.
PO Box 924
St. Louis, MO 63188
Phones: 314-436-2424; 314-351-7390
E-mail: knlc24jim@hereshelpnet.org
Web site: www.knlc.tv
Officers:
Lawrence W. Rice Jr., President
Raymond K. Redlich, Vice President
Charles W. Hale, Secretary-Treasurer
Ownership: Non-profit corp.--St. Louis, MO. Governed by 12 member Board of Directors.
LPTV Stations:
Arkansas: K54FH Green Forest.
Missouri: K61GJ Aurora; KNJD-LP Branson; K64FW Joplin; K64FQ Lebanon; K17FU Marshfield; K68EL Marshfield; K39CI Springfield; K54FX Springfield.
Commercial TV Stations:
Missouri: KNLC-DT St. Louis.
Radio Stations:
Arkansas: KTCN (FM) Eureka Springs, KBPB (FM) Harrison
Illinois: WINU (AM) Shelbyville
Kansas: KKLO (AM) Leavenworth
Missouri: KNLH (FM) Cedar Hill; KNLQ (FM) Cuba; KAUL (FM) Ellington; KNRF (FM), KNLM (FM) Marshfield; KNLF (FM) Potosi; KBIY (FM) Van Buren; KNLN (FM) Vienna; KKLL (FM) Webb City

NEW LIFE TEMPLE
2465 Old Anson Rd.
Abilene, TX 79603
Phone: 325-676-2121
Fax: 325-670-9127
E-mail: cfuentes7168@hotmail.com
Officer:
Carlos S. Fuentes, General Manager
LPTV Stations:
Texas: KVNL-LP Abilene.

NEWMARK COMMUNICATIONS LLC
400 S. Victory Blvd.
Suite 300
Burbank, CA 91502
Phone: 818-955-5704
Represented (legal): Wiley Rein LLP.
LPTV Stations:
Kansas: KSMI-LP Wichita.

REGENTS OF NEW MEXICO STATE U.
MSC: TV22 NMSU
Box 30001
Las Cruces, NM 88003-0001
Phone: 505-646-2222
Fax: 505-646-1924
Represented (legal): Dow Lohnes PLLC.
LPTV Stations:
New Mexico: K42EY Alamogordo; K33FK Angel Fire; K45HJ Caballo; K02KG Cliff & Gila; K46GU Deming; K49GV-D Deming; K28GJ Hatch; K13UL Hillsboro; K54GR Las Cruces; K02KP Lordsburg; K44CZ Penasco; K28GK Silver City; K46HY-D Socorro; K40GH Truth or Consequences; K22FN White Oaks, etc..
ETV Stations:
New Mexico: KRWG-DT Las Cruces.

Radio Stations:
New Mexico: KRWG-FM

NEWPORT TELEVISION LLC
50 Kennedy Plz, 18th Fl
Providence, RI 02903
Phone: 401-751-1700
Officer:
Sandy DiPasquale, President & Chief Executive Officer
Ownership: Newport Television Holdings LLC; NTHLLC ownership:; Providence Equity Partners VI (Umbrella US) LP, 55.2%; TV InvestmentCo LP, 44.8%; PEPVI (UUS)LP ownership:; Providence Equity GP VI LP, Gen. Partner. 100% votes, 0.2% equity; TVICLP ownership:; Providence VI Umbrella GP LLC, Gen. Partner. 100 % votes, 90% equity; PEGPVILP & PVIUGPLLC ownership:; Glenn M. Creamer, Managing Member, 33.3%; Jonathan M. Nelson, Managing Member, 33.3%; Paul J. Salem, Managing Member, 33.3%.
Represented (legal): Covington & Burling.
LPTV Stations:
Alaska: K07NJ Delta Junction, etc.; K06LA Healy, etc.
California: KKEY-LP Bakersfield.
Kansas: KSAS-LP Dodge City; KAAS-LP Garden City.
New York: WBGH-CA Binghamton; W07BA Syracuse-DeWitt.
Oregon: K46AS Coos Bay; KMOR-LP Eugene; K03CQ Mapleton; K05DF Mapleton; K31AE Sutherlin; K22GX Tri City.
Utah: K34CX Apple Valley; K51BK-D Aurora, etc.; K18FU-D Beaver County (rural); K05BU Enterprise; K09SU Hildale, UT & Cane Beds, AZ; K11OO Pine Valley; K45FW Price, etc.; K25JS-D St. George; K69CT St. George; K31IS-D Toquerville; K13QK Virgin; K52KG-D Washington.
Commercial TV Stations:
Alabama: WPMI-DT Mobile.
Alaska: KTVF-DT Fairbanks.
Arkansas: KASN-DT Little Rock; KLRT-DT Little Rock.
California: KFTY-DT Santa Rosa.
Florida: WAWS-DT Jacksonville; WJTC-DT Pensacola.
Kansas: KOCW-DT Hoisington; KAAS-DT Salina; KSAS-DT Wichita.
New York: WXXA-DT Albany; WIVT-DT Binghamton; WETM-DT Elmira; WHAM-DT Rochester; WSYR-DT Syracuse; WWTI-DT Watertown.
Ohio: WKRC-DT Cincinnati.
Oklahoma: KMYT-DT Tulsa; KOKI-DT Tulsa.
Oregon: KMCB-DT Coos Bay; KMTR-DT Eugene; KTCW-DT Roseburg.
Pennsylvania: WHP-DT Harrisburg.
Tennessee: WJKT-DT Jackson; WLMT-DT Memphis; WPTY-DT Memphis.
Utah: KTVX-DT Salt Lake City.
Washington: KVOS-DT Bellingham.

NEWS PRESS & GAZETTE CO.
825 Edmond St
St. Joseph, MO 64501
Phone: 816-271-8500
Fax: 816-271-8695
Web site: www.npgcable.net
Officers:
Henry H. Bradley, Chairman, Vice President & Treasurer
David R. Bradley Jr., President, Editor & Publisher
Lyle E. Leimkuhler, Vice President, Finance & Secretary
Ownership: NPG Voting Trust; NPGVT ownership:; David R. Bradley Jr.; Henry H. Bradley, Trustees, 50%. each.
Represented (legal): Smithwick & Belendiuk PC.

LPTV Stations:
California: KDFX-CA Indio/Palm Springs; K27DS Yucca Valley.
Colorado: K12ME Canon City; K38FO Carbondale; KTLO-LP Colorado Springs; K42CX Cripple Creek; K42EV Glenwood Springs; KKHD-LP Grand Junction; K39CD Lake George; K28AD Montrose; KXHD-LP Montrose; K51FQ Mount Massive, etc.; K36AF New Castle; K45AF Parachute; KTLP-LP Pueblo; K57CR Rifle; K44CI Salida, etc. & Organ.
Idaho: K61AP Burley, etc.; K05CJ Challis; K13CO Fish Creek; K13RV Leadore; K61CI Leadore; K21JC-D Pocatello; K61FO Pocatello; K12MA Rexburg, etc..
New Mexico: K40BP Alamogordo; K55BT Deming; K41KY-D Las Cruces; K57BV Las Cruces & Organ.
Oregon: K27DO Bend; K45KM-D Bend; KFXO-LP Bend; K41HZ Burns; K43IH Burns; K06LI Chemult; K02JL La Pine; K05JV La Pine; K13JF La Pine; K66BC Madras & Culver; K32CC Montgomery Ranch, etc.; K38DT North La Pine; K66AZ Prineville; KQRE-LP Riley; K06JN Severance Ranch, etc.; K57CH Sun River.
Wyoming: K13LY Hoback Junction; K13FZ Jackson; K29HG-D Jackson; K36JD-D Jackson; K09LF South Park.
Commercial TV Stations:
California: KECY-DT El Centro; KESQ-DT Palm Springs.
Colorado: KRDO-DT Colorado Springs; KJCT-DT Grand Junction.
Idaho: KIFI-DT Idaho Falls.
Oregon: KTVZ-DT Bend.
Texas: KVIA-DT El Paso.
Cable Systems:
ARIZONA: BULLHEAD CITY; FLAGSTAFF; KINGMAN; LAKE HAVASU CITY; PARKER; PAYSON; PINE; SEDONA.
CALIFORNIA: BLYTHE; JUNE LAKE; MAMMOTH LAKES.
MISSOURI: ST. JOSEPH.
Newspapers:
Kansas: Atchison Daily Globe; Hiawatha World; Johnson County Sun; Louisburg Herald; Miami County Republic; Northeast Johnson County Sun; Osawatomie Graphic; Blue Valley Sun, Kansas City Jewish Chronicle, Kansas City Nu
Magazine: Wednesday Magazine (Overland Park, KS)
Missouri: Sun Tribune (Gladstone); Kearney Courier; Liberty Tribune; Platte County Sun Gazette; Raytown Tribune; Smithville Herald; Greenacres Publication, St. Joseph News-Press (St. Joseph); Daily Star Journal (Warrensb
Radio Stations:
Colorado: KRDO-AM-FM Colorado Springs, KESQ (AM) Indio, KUNA-FM LaQuinta

NEW VISION TELEVISION LLC, DEBTOR IN POSSESSION
3500 Lenox Rd.
Suite 640
Atlanta, GA 30326
Phone: 404-995-4711
Officers:
Jason Elkin, Chairman & Chief Executive Officer
John Heinen, President & Chief Operating Officer
Eric Simontis, Chief Financial Officer
Steve Spendlove, Executive Vice President
Ownership: Jason Elkin, 2.25%. votes & assets; John Heinen, 0.9%. votes & assets; HBK NV LLC, 95.48%. votes & assets; HBKNVLLC ownership:; HBK Management LLC; KBKMLLC ownership:; Jamiel A. Akhtar; Richard L. Booth; David C. Haley; Laurence H. Lebowitz; William E. Rose, 20%. votes each.
Represented (legal): Wiley Rein LLP.

LPTV Stations:
Alabama: W04CB Sylacauga.
Hawaii: K55DZ Lihue.
Kansas: KETM-CA Emporia; KTLJ-CA Junction City; KMJT-CA Ogden; KSNL-LD Salina; KSNL-LP Salina; KTMJ-CA Topeka.
Ohio: WYFX-LP Youngstown.
Oregon: K34DC Astoria; KBNZ-LD Bend; K04BJ La Pine; K38CZ Lincoln City & Newport; K34AI North La Pine; K31CR-D Prineville, etc.; K52AK Prineville, etc.; K64BK The Dalles; K52ET Tillamook.
Pennsylvania: WFXI-CA Mercer.
Washington: K63AW Grays River, etc..
Commercial TV Stations:
Alabama: WIAT-DT Birmingham.
Georgia: WJCL-DT Savannah.
Hawaii: KHAW-DT Hilo; KHON-DT Honolulu; KAII-DT Wailuku.
Iowa: KIMT-DT Mason City.
Kansas: KSNG-DT Garden City; KSNC-DT Great Bend; KSNT-DT Topeka; KSNW-DT Wichita.
Nebraska: KSNK-DT McCook.
Ohio: WKBN-DT Youngstown.
Oregon: KOIN-DT Portland.

NEXSTAR BROADCASTING GROUP INC.
909 Lake Carolyn Pkwy.
Ste 1450
Irving, TX 75039
Phone: 972-373-8800
Officers:
Perry Sook, President & Chief Executive Officer
Duane Lammers, Executive Vice President & Chief Operating Officer
Thomas Carter, Chief Financial Officer
Timothy Busch, Senior Vice President
Brian Jones, Senior Vice President
Richard Stolpe, Vice President & Engineering Director
Susana G. Willingham, Vice President & Corporate News Director
Ownership: ABRY Broadcast Partners III LP. 55.33% votes, 16.22% assets; ABRY Broadcast Partners II LP. 37.79% votes, 11.08% assets; Perry Sook. 2.38% votes, 0.7% assets; publicly held. 4.5% votes, 12.35% assets; ABRY ownership:; Royce Yudkoff.
Represented (legal): Drinker Biddle.
LPTV Stations:
Montana: K25BP Billings; K27IM Billings; K58IH Colstrip, etc.; K66EQ Colstrip, etc.; K33EA Columbus; K16DZ Hardin; K16DH Miles City; K19FF Miles City.
New Mexico: K45BF Clovis; K28BA San Jon.
New York: W31BP Burlington; W53AM Utica; WPNY-LP Utica, etc..
Pennsylvania: W51BP Clarks Summit, etc.; W24BL Pottsville, etc.; W64AL Stroudsburg; W30AN Williamsport.
Texas: K12FM Fort Stockton; K44FG Snyder; K25CP Tulia.
Wyoming: K06AT Sheridan, etc..
Commercial TV Stations:
Alabama: WDHN-DT Dothan.
Arkansas: KFTA-DT Fort Smith; KARK-DT Little Rock; KARZ-DT Little Rock; KNWA-DT Rogers.
Illinois: WCIA-DT Champaign; WMBD-DT Peoria; WQRF-DT Rockford; WCFN-DT Springfield.
Indiana: WFFT-DT Fort Wayne; WTWO-DT Terre Haute.
Louisiana: KARD-DT West Monroe.
Maryland: WHAG-DT Hagerstown.
Missouri: KSNF-DT Joplin; KSFX-DT Springfield; KQTV-DT St. Joseph.
Montana: KSVI-DT Billings.
New York: WROC-DT Rochester; WFXV-DT Utica.
Pennsylvania: WTAJ-DT Altoona; WJET-DT Erie; WLYH-DT Lancaster; WBRE-DT Wilkes-Barre.

Texas: KTAB-DT Abilene; KAMR-DT Amarillo; KLBK-DT Lubbock; KMID-DT Midland; KBTV-DT Port Arthur; KLST-DT San Angelo; KTAL-DT Texarkana; KFDX-DT Wichita Falls.
Radio Stations:
Pennsylvania: WJET (FM)
Texas: KTAL-FM; KCMC (AM)

NICOLAS COMMUNICATIONS CORP.
111 Paseo Encinal
San Antonio, TX 78212
Phone: 210-824-5812
Officer:
Emilio Nicolas, President
Ownership: Emilio R Nicolas; Guillermo Nicolas; Emilio Nicolas Jr..
LPTV Stations:
Texas: KCRP-CA Corpus Christi.

9TH ISLAND BROADCASTING INC.
1491 Walker Ln
Farmington, UT 84025
Phone: 801-557-1322
E-mail: tvinmotion@msn.com
Officer:
Rubin Rodriguez, President
Represented (legal): Dan J. Alpert.
LPTV Stations:
Nevada: K57JO Laughlin.

ANN K. NIXON
Box 772
Madison, FL 32341
LPTV Stations:
Florida: W03AO Madison.

CITY OF NOATAK
5900 E. Tudor Rd.
Anchorage, AK 99507
Phone: 907-269-5744
LPTV Stations:
Alaska: K09NG Noatak.

NOLOWIRE INC.
Box 501
Seiad Valley, CA 96086
LPTV Stations:
California: K04NU Seiad Valley; K08EQ Seiad Valley; K12JD Seiad Valley.

CITY OF NOORVIK
5900 E Tudor Rd
Anchorage, AK 99507
Phone: 907-269-5744
LPTV Stations:
Alaska: K04IK Noorvik.

NORTHEASTERN EDUCATIONAL TELEVISION OF OHIO
1750 Campus Center Dr.
Box 5191
Kent, OH 44240-5191
Phone: 216-677-4549
Officers:
William E. Glaeser, President & General Manager
Pat Vitone, Chief Operating Officer
Ownership: Non-profit corporation.
Represented (legal): Dow Lohnes PLLC.
LPTV Stations:
Ohio: W58AM Youngstown, etc..
ETV Stations:
Ohio: WEAO-DT Akron; WNEO-DT Alliance.

NORTHEASTERN PENNSYLVANIA ETV ASSOCIATION
100 WVIA Way
Pittston, PA 18640-6197

Phone: 570-344-1244
Fax: 570-655-1180
Officers:
Bart E. Ecker, Chairman
Bill Kelly, President & Chief Executive Officer
Mollie Worrell, Vice President, Development
Joseph Glynn, Vice President Engineering
Mark Thomas, Vice President, Programming
Chris Norton, Vice President, Radio
Mike Burnside, Vice President, Corporate Communications
Ramona Alley, Secretary
Donald Broderick, Treasurer
Ownership: Non-profit association.
Represented (legal): Dow Lohnes PLLC.
LPTV Stations:
Pennsylvania: W20CP-D Mansfield; W25AQ Towanda.
ETV Stations:
Pennsylvania: WVIA-DT Scranton.
Radio Stations:
Pennsylvania: WVIA-FM

NORTHEASTERN STATE U
610 N Grand Ave
NET Bldg/Video Tech
Tahlequah, OK 74464
Phone: 918-456-5511
E-mail: jett@nsuok.edu
Officer:
Michael Jett, Director, Video Technology
LPTV Stations:
Oklahoma: K04DY Tahlequah.

NORTHEAST GOSPEL BROADCASTING INC.
Box 36
Kings Rd.
Buskirk, NY 12028
Phone: 518-686-0975
Officers:
Brian A. Larson, President
William Dagle, Vice President
Kevin Call, Treasurer
Ownership: Brian A. Larson, 33.3%; William Dagle, 33.3%; Kevin Call, 33.3%.
LPTV Stations:
New York: WVVC-LP Utica.

NORTHERN BROADCASTING COMMUNICATIONS INC.
126 Glen St
Glens Falls, NY 12801
Phone: 518-798-8000
Fax: 518-798-0735
Ownership: Michael Collins, President.
LPTV Stations:
New York: WNCE-CA Glens Falls.

NORTHERN CALIFORNIA CONFERENCE ASSOCIATION OF SDA
Box 23165
401 Taylor Ave.
Pleasant Hill, CA 94523-0165
Phone: 925-685-4300
Officers:
Robert Spurgeon, Chairman
Richard Seltzer, Secretary
LPTV Stations:
California: K33HH Redding.

NORTHERN CALIFORNIA EDUCATIONAL TV ASSN. INC.
603 N. Market St.
Redding, CA 96003
Phone: 916-243-5493
Officers:

Robert Meyer, President
Alvin Cibula, Secretary-Treasurer
Nancy Tucker, Chief Financial Officer

Branch Office:
Library-Chico State University
Chico, CA 95928
Phone: 916-891-5493
Represented (legal): Schwartz, Woods & Miller; Carr, Kennedy, Peterson & Frost.
LPTV Stations:
California: K20DE-D Alturas; K08OR-D Canby; K03HX-D Etna; K28DB-D Fall River Mills; K14HX-D Lakehead; K28CY-D Lewiston; K08OB-D Newell; K39DG-D Trinity Center; K06GR Weed; K19GL-D Yreka, etc..

NORTHERN TELEVISION INC.
630 W. 4th Ave.
Suite 300
Anchorage, AK 99501
Phone: 907-257-5601
LPTV Stations:
Alaska: K08IZ BP Alaska Camp, etc.; K08LW Kenai & Soldotna; K66CF Palmer.

NORTHFORK TV TRANSLATOR SYSTEM
PO Box 397
1905 Palo Duro St.
Memphis, TX 79245
Phone: 806-259-2879
Fax: 806-259-3500
Ownership: Arnold Cruze.
LPTV Stations:
Texas: K30HH Memphis; K27HM Quanah; K29FR Quanah; K31HC Quanah; K33HG Quanah; K39GH Quanah; K41HQ Quanah.

NORTH GEORGIA TELEVISION
101 S. Spencer St.
Dalton, GA 30721
Phone: 706-278-9713
Fax: 706-278-7950
Officers:
Doug Jensen, Chief Executive Officer
Doug Smith, Chief Operating Officer
Sherry Wein, Vice President, News
Doug Hoskins, Chief Financial Officer
Ownership: Life Ministries Inc..
LPTV Stations:
Georgia: WDGA-CA Dalton; WDNN-CA Dalton; WLFW-LP Lafayette.
Tennessee: WRNG-LP Chattanooga.

NORTH GIBSON SCHOOL CORP.
PO Box 49
RR 4
Princeton, IN 47670
Phone: 812-385-4851
Fax: 812-386-1531
Officers:
David Oldham, President
Sandra Nixon, Chief Executive Officer
Mary Key, Vice President, School Board
Jerry Whitehead, Secretary-Treasurer
Marlene Fisher, Chief Financial Officer
Represented (legal): Arent Fox LLP.
LPTV Stations:
Indiana: W06BD Princeton.

CITY OF NORTH PLATTE
211 W 3rd St
North Platte, NE 69101

LPTV Stations:
Nebraska: K04ED North Platte.

NORTH ROCKY MOUNTAIN TELEVISION LLC
860 U.S. Hwy. 1
Suite 108
North Palm Beach, FL 33408
Phones: 561-694-1280; 800-948-7101
LPTV Stations:
Montana: KMTM-LP Missoula.

NORTHSIDE BAPTIST CHURCH
302 W. 20th St.
Tifton, GA 31794
Phones: 912-386-5151; 912-382-6855
Fax: 912-382-9542
LPTV Stations:
Georgia: W38DG Tifton.

NORTH TEXAS PUBLIC BROADCASTING INC.
3000 Harry Hines Blvd.
Dallas, TX 75201
Phone: 214-871-1390
Fax: 214-754-0635
Officers:
Richard Rogers, Chairman
Gary Ferrell, President & Chief Executive Officer
Samuel Cheng, Vice President, Finance & Administration
Kevin Martin, Executive Vice President
Jeff Luchsinger, Vice President & Radio Station Manager
Rick Owen, Vice President, Engineering
Yvette Harris, Vice President, Marketing
Patricia Lyons, Vice President, Development
Sylvia Komatsu, Vice President, Production
Sharon Philippart, Vice President, Corporate Communications & Design, Web Management
Ownership: North Texas Public Broadcasting Inc..
Represented (legal): Schwartz, Woods & Miller.
LPTV Stations:
Texas: K44GS Wichita Falls.
ETV Stations:
Texas: KERA-DT Dallas.
Radio Stations:
Texas: KERA-FM

NORTHWAY VILLAGE COUNCIL
Box 516
Northway, AK 99764
Phone: 907-778-2311
Officers:
Lee Titus, Chairman
Lorraine Felix, President
Jimmy Demit, Vice President
LPTV Stations:
Alaska: K02LB Northway.

NORTHWEST CHRISTIAN BROADCASTING
Box 7749
Salem, OR 97303-0146
Phone: 503-362-0862
Officer:
Dr. Richard Synowski, President
LPTV Stations:
Oregon: K26GJ Portland; K21GX Salem.

NTN/SAGINAW INC.
812 Cadillac St
Box 939
Mackinaw City, MI 49701
Phone: 231-436-7731
Fax: 253-540-0980

E-mail: bobtv@nmo.net
Officer:
Robert A. Naismith, President
LPTV Stations:
Michigan: W44BQ Mount Pleasant; W61DK
Mount Pleasant; WTCF-LP Pinconning.

VILLAGE OF NULATO
Pouch AC
Office of Governor-Telecom
Juneau, AK 99811
LPTV Stations:
Alaska: K04JF Nulato.

COUNTY OF NYE
PO Box 153
Tonopah, NV 89049
Phone: 775-482-8103
LPTV Stations:
Nevada: K06KQ Manhattan; K10LQ Manhattan;
K12MW Manhattan.

OASIS BROADCASTING INC.
2880 Bicentennial Pkwy
Ste 100, #244
Henderson, NV 89044
Phone: 702-914-7409
Officer:
Linda C. Macon, President
LPTV Stations:
Montana: KHJT-LP Bozeman.

OCEAN BROADCASTING ASSN.
RR3
Box 33
Dagsboro, DE 19939
Phone: 302-732-3933
Officers:
Elizabeth Neuhaus, President
Robert Neuhaus, Chief Executive Officer
John Franklin, Vice President, Sales
Joseph Scaramuzzo, Secretary-Treasurer
Ownership: Elizabeth Neuhaus; John Franklin;
Joseph Scaramuzzo, Principals.
Represented (legal): National Association of
Regulatory Utility Commissioners (NARUC).
LPTV Stations:
Delaware: WLWP-LP Millsboro, etc.; WEWE-LP
Sussex County.
Maryland: WBLP-LP Ocean City.

OCEANIA BROADCASTING
NETWORK INC.
875 Waimanu St.
Suite 110
Honolulu, HI 96813
Phone: 808-329-8120
Officers:
Christopher J. Racine, President
Wayne Kraiss, Vice President
Judith L. Racine, Secretary
Kenneth Wayman, Treasurer
LPTV Stations:
Hawaii: K42CO Honolulu.

OD TV COMMUNICATIONS INC.
200 E. Robinson St.
Suite 500
Orlando, FL 32801
Phone: 407-843-5880
LPTV Stations:
Florida: WRCF-LP Orlando.

OHIO EDUCATIONAL
TELECOMMUNICATIONS NETWORK
COMMISSION
2470 N Star Rd
Columbus, OH 43221-3405

Phone: 614-644-3085
Officer:
Denos Christofi, Executive Director
Represented (legal): Cohn & Marks LLP.
LPTV Stations:
Ohio: W31AA Newark.

OHIO STATE U.
2400 Olentangy River Rd
Columbus, OH 43210
Phone: 614-292-9678
Fax: 614-688-3343
Officer:
William J. Shkurti, Senior Vice President,
Business & Finance
Represented (legal): Dow Lohnes PLLC.
LPTV Stations:
Ohio: W47AB Mansfield.
ETV Stations:
Ohio: WOSU-DT Columbus; WPBO-DT Portsmouth.
Radio Stations:
Ohio: WOSP (FM); WOSU-AM-FM

KEVIN O'KANE
4811 Jenkins Rd.
Vernon, NY 13476
Phone: 315-829-4847
LPTV Stations:
New York: W29BJ Burlington; WCUL-CA
Oneida; WWDG-CA Rome.

OKLAHOMA BROADCAST
ASSOCIATES LLC
PO Box 10094
Enid, OK 73706
Phone: 405-833-1380
Ownership: B. Curly V. Corwin, Co-Trustee of
the Corwin Family LLC, 90%; Steve Ebey,
10%.
Represented (legal): Booth Freret Imlay &
Tepper PC.
LPTV Stations:
Oklahoma: KTEW-CA Ponca City.

OKLAHOMA COMMUNITY
TELEVISION LLC
Box 398
Sayre, OK 73662-0398
Phone: 405-808-2509
Officers:
Marvin Shirley, Chairman, Board of Managers
Steve P. Foerster, President
Ted W. Strickland, Vice President, Secretary-
Treasurer
Ownership: Griffin Communications LLC,
99.49%. see listing; Marvin Shirley, 0.51%.
Represented (legal): Holland & Knight LLP.
LPTV Stations:
Oklahoma: K36EV Altus; K38FJ Altus; K40FL
Altus; K42FL Altus; K45FH Altus; K49FE
Altus; K29EI Elk City; K54CM Elk City;
K56EY Elk City; K44AP Elk City, etc.;
K46AN Elk City, etc.; K48AP Elk City, etc.;
K50AL Elk City, etc.; K58CS Erick; K60CK
Erick, etc.; K62BQ Erick, etc.; K64AX Erick,
etc.; K66AQ Erick, etc.; K68AU Erick, etc.;
K51CV Gould; K24GG Hollis; K53AV Hollis,
etc.; K55BQ Hollis, etc.; K57BB Hollis, etc.;
K59BI Hollis, etc.; K26EU Sayre; K28BY
Strong City; K30EF Strong City; K32DF
Strong City; K36AJ Strong City; K38AM
Strong City; K40AG Strong City; K42AG
Strong City; K17DH Weatherford; K20DX
Weatherford; K22ED Weatherford; K38HM
Weatherford; K41DS Weatherford.

OKLAHOMA EDUCATIONAL
TELEVISION AUTHORITY
Box 14190
Oklahoma City, OK 73113

Phone: 405-848-8501
Fax: 405-841-9216
E-mail: info@oeta.tv
Officer:
Bill Thrash, Deputy Director, Programming &
Production
Ownership: Statutory corporation, established
by Oklahoma State Legislature.
Represented (legal): Cohn & Marks LLP.
LPTV Stations:
Oklahoma: K19AA Altus; K30AE Alva; K28AC
Ardmore; K56AY Beaver; K55BV Boise
City; K58AX Buffalo; K54BB Duncan; K46AI
Durant; K56BQ Frederick; K16AB Guymon;
K15AA Hugo; K63BA Idabel; K36AB Lawton;
K46AH Medford; K38AK Ponca City.
ETV Stations:
Oklahoma: KWET-DT Cheyenne; KOED-DT
Tulsa.

OKLAHOMA LAND CO. LLC
5101 Shields Blvd
Oklahoma City, OK 73129
Phone: 405-429-5003
E-mail: tony.t@tylermedia.com
Officer:
Tony Tyler, President
Ownership: Tony J. Tyler, 50%; Ty A. Tyler,
50%.
Represented (legal): Sidley Austin LLP.
LPTV Stations:
Oklahoma: KCHM-LP Oklahoma City; KWDW-LP
Oklahoma City; KOKT-LP Sulphur; KUTU-CA
Tulsa.
Commercial TV Stations:
Oklahoma: KTUZ-DT Shawnee.

ONEIDA COUNTY TRANSLATOR
DISTRICT
10 Court St.
Malad City, ID 83252
Phone: 208-766-4405
LPTV Stations:
Idaho: K51KS-D Malad & surrounding area;
K19GF Malad City; K21HV Malad City;
K23JA-D Malad City; K25IP-D Malad City;
K27IN-D Malad City; K29HA Malad City;
K33IM-D Malad City; K49KB-D Malad City.

ONE MINISTRIES INC.
Box 1118
Santa Rosa, CA 95402
Phone: 707-537-9881
Officer:
Keith J. Leitch, President
Represented (legal): James L. Oyster.
LPTV Stations:
California: K14MW-D Petaluma; KQRM-LP
Santa Rosa.

ON THE MAP INC.
102 Bainbridge Court
Apex, NC 27502
Phone: 919-303-5465
LPTV Stations:
North Carolina: WNCR-LP Tarboro.

CITY OF ORD
PO Box 96
Ord, NE 68862
Phone: 308-728-3540
E-mail: skruml@nctc.net
Officer:
Sandy Kruml, City Clerk & Treasurer
LPTV Stations:
Nebraska: K02HJ Ord; K04HL Ord.

OREGON PUBLIC BROADCASTING
7140 S.W. Macadam Ave.
Portland, OR 97219-3099

Phone: 503-244-9900
Fax: 503-293-4165
Officers:
Maynard Orme, President & Chief Executive
Officer
Jack Galiniche, Chief Operating Officer
Tom Doggett, Vice President, TV Programming
Jan Heskiss, Chief Financial Officer
Ownership: Oregon Public Broadcasting.
Represented (legal): Schwartz, Woods & Miller.
LPTV Stations:
Oregon: K17GK Arlington; K23GK Astoria;
K20IV-D Baker City, etc.; K48DC Baker
City, etc.; K36BA Burns; K17AA Coos
Bay, etc.; K11VI Elkton; K28JC Enterprise;
K21FS Eugene; K54DG Florence; K24FH
Glide, etc.; K55CM Gold Beach; K10NF
Halfway; K28GD Heppner, etc.; K36FG
Hood River, etc.; K26FQ John Day; K19BK
Lakeview; K19EC Mapleton; K55FM Myrtle
Point; K18FR Newport; K11SZ Oakridge;
K19EI Pacific City & Cloverdale; K04PK
Paisley; K09VC Paisley; K59BO Pendleton,
etc.; K61BU Port Orford; K05JL Prairie City
& Unity; K16EM Prineville, etc.; K02NW
Reedsport; K51GJ Roseburg; K31HZ The
Dalles, etc.; K15EY Wasco & Heppner;
K04MG Wedderburn.
Washington: K59BX Grays River, etc..
ETV Stations:
Oregon: KOAB-DT Bend; KOAC-DT Corvallis;
KEPB-DT Eugene; KTVR-DT La Grande;
KOPB-DT Portland.
Radio Stations:
Oregon: KOAB (FM) Bend, KOAC (FM)
Corvallis, KOPB-FM Eugene

OREGON TRAIL BROADCASTING CO.
1500 Foremaster Lane
Las Vegas, NV 89116
LPTV Stations:
Idaho: K13VK Arco; K13YF Ashton; K13VI
Blackfoot; K04OH Challis; K07VI Challis;
K51HF Driggs; K12OE Firth-Basalt; K12NZ
Idaho Falls; K12OA Pocatello; K13UF-
D Rexburg; K13VJ Shelley; K12OB St.
Anthony.

ORR AREA MINNEONTO II
PO Box 1
Orr, MN 55771
Phone: 218-757-3500
E-mail: ncglass@gmail.com
Officer:
N. Curtis Glass, Secretary-Treasurer
LPTV Stations:
Minnesota: K59EN Orr; K61EW Orr; K63DV
Orr.

ARACELIS ORTIZ
PO Box 530391
Harlingen, TX 78553
Phone: 956-421-2635
Fax: 956-440-0471
LPTV Stations:
Texas: KMAO-LP Raymondville; KRYT-LP San
Antonio.
Other Holdings:
Broadcast holdings: See listings for Aracelis
Ortiz Corp. & Faith Pleases God Church.

CARLOS ORTIZ ESTATE, ARACELIS
ORTIZ-EXECUTRIX
PO Box 1975
San Benito, TX 78586
Phone: 956-421-2635
Fax: 956-440-0471
LPTV Stations:
Texas: KJDF-LP Beaumont.
Other Holdings:
Broadcast holdings: See listing for Aracelis
Ortiz.

CLARK ORTIZ
PO Box 530391
Harlingen, TX 78553
Phone: 956-421-2635
Fax: 956-440-0542
LPTV Stations:
Texas: KWDT-LP Corpus Christi.

OTTUMWA AREA TRANSLATOR SYSTEM INC.
Box 423
Ottumwa, IA 52501
Phone: 641-652-7575
E-mail: ghughes@netins.net
Officers:
Glenn Hughes, President
Jerry Harshman, Vice President
Max Willhoit, Secretary
Joyce A. Amos, Treasurer
Ownership: Controlled by 11 member Board of Directors.
LPTV Stations:
Iowa: K23CI Ottumwa; K25DE Ottumwa; K27CV Ottumwa.

OTTUMWA MEDIA HOLDINGS LLC
6100 Fairview Rd.
Suite 600
Charlotte, NC 28210
Phone: 704-643-4148
Ownership: Thomas B. Henson, 90%; Macon B. Moye, managing member, 10%.
Represented (legal): Thomas B. Henson.
LPTV Stations:
Missouri: K34CW Kirksville.
Commercial TV Stations:
Iowa: KYOU-DT Ottumwa.

CITY OF OURAY
PO Box 468
Ouray, CO 81427
LPTV Stations:
Colorado: K13RH Ridgway.

OWEN BROADCASTING LLC
Box 4300
Hopkinsville, KY 42241-4300
Phone: 270-885-4300
Represented (legal): Irwin, Campbell & Tannenwald PC.
LPTV Stations:
Kentucky: WKAG-CA Hopkinsville.

PACIFIC CHANNEL SAMOA
Box 340
Pago Pago, AS 96799
Phone: 684-633-2623
LPTV Stations:
American Samoa: K11UU Pago Pago.

PACIFIC MEDIA CORP.
2425 Walker Swinton Rd
Timmonsville, SC 29161
Phone: 843-629-1431
E-mail: psieler@aol.com
Officer:
Peter G. Sieler, Vice President
Represented (legal): Koerner & Olender PC.
LPTV Stations:
North Carolina: W19CA Lumberton.

JUAN G. PADIN
PO Box 142755
Arecibo, PR 00614
Phone: 787-383-9905
E-mail: jgpadin@prtc.net

LPTV Stations:
Puerto Rico: WVQS-LP Isabel Segunda.

PAGE HILL COMMUNITY TELECASTERS INC.
PO Box 11
Rte 8
Lake Pleasant, NY 12108
LPTV Stations:
New York: W04BK Speculator, et al..

PAGING ASSOCIATES INC.
24 Rockdale Rd.
West Haven, CT 06516
Phone: 203-932-3500
Fax: 203-933-2259
LPTV Stations:
Connecticut: W28AJ Allingtown; W65DZ Bridgeport.

PAGING SYSTEMS INC.
PO Box 4249
Burlingame, CA 94011-4249
Phone: 650-697-1000
Fax: 650-347-7243
LPTV Stations:
Florida: WLMF-LP Miami.

PAGOSA SPRINGS TV ASSOCIATION
PO Box 15
Pagosa Springs, CO 81147
LPTV Stations:
Colorado: K58CJ Pagosa Springs.

TOWN OF PAHRUMP
400 N Hwy 160
Pahrump, NV 89060
Phone: 775-727-5107
Officer:
David Richards, Town Manager
LPTV Stations:
Nevada: K17CL Pahrump; K19BU Pahrump; K24BY Pahrump; K28CS Pahrump; K36BQ Pahrump.

RAUL & CONSUELO PALAZUELOS
1138 W. Church St.
Santa Maria, CA 93458
Phone: 805-928-7700
Fax: 805-928-8606
Officer:
Raul Palazuelos, President
Represented (legal): Fletcher, Heald & Hildreth PLC.
LPTV Stations:
California: K10HX Garberville; K11NE Hoopa; K08LD Miranda; K09UF Morro Bay; K08HJ Orleans; K10FS Rio Dell & Scotia; K07TA Santa Maria; K10KY Shelter Cove; K10EN Willow Creek.
Commercial TV Stations:
California: KVIQ-DT Eureka; KTAS-DT Santa Maria.

PALO VERDE VALLEY TV CLUB INC.
Box 874
Blythe, CA 92225
Phone: 760-922-4150
Officer:
Bart Fisher, President
Represented (legal): Fletcher, Heald & Hildreth PLC.
LPTV Stations:
California: K24FA Blythe; K26FS Blythe; K29EC Blythe; K31FE Blythe; K33FD Blythe.

P & P CABLE HOLDINGS LLC
PO Box 97
Charlevoix, MI 49720

Phone: 231-547-2696
E-mail: tvbobn@charter.net
Officers:
Dan Pearce, President
Robert A. Naismith, Vice President & Chief Operating Officer
Ownership: Daniel Pearce, Managing Member.
Represented (legal): Kenneth E. Hardman.
LPTV Stations:
Michigan: WLLZ-LP Cedar; WXON-LP Flint; WBWM-LP Mount Pleasant; W09CK Pinconning; W15BP Pinconning; W44BO Pinconning; WKJF-LP Pinconning; WKNX-LP Pinconning; WUHO-LP Pinconning.

PANHANDLE TELECASTING CO.
PO Box 10
Amarillo, TX 79105-0010
Phone: 806-383-1010
Ownership: Robert H. Drewry; William T. Drewry; Susan Drewry Battaglia. Drewry family has interest in Adelante Television Limited Partnership & Drewry Communications, see listing.
Represented (legal): Davis Wright Tremaine LLP.
LPTV Stations:
New Mexico: K26CD Clovis; K29HB Clovis; K67CS Dora; K24DP San Jon.
Texas: K63GN Bovina, etc.; KZBZ-LP Canyon; K41CA Kress & Tulia.

PAPPAS TELECASTING COMPANIES
500 S. Chinowth Rd.
Visalia, CA 93277
Phone: 559-733-7800
Fax: 559-627-5363
Web site: www.pappastv.com
Officers:
Harry J. Pappas, Chairman & Chief Executive Officer
Dennis J. Davis, President, Chief Operating Officer
LeBon G. Abercrombie, Senior Executive Vice President, Planning & Development
Howard H. Shrier, Senior Executive Vice President & Chief Operating Officer, TV Stations
Peter C. Pappas, Executive Vice President, Legal & Governmental Affairs
Rich Elmendorf, Executive Vice President & Chief Financial Officer
Debbie Sweeney, Senior Vice President, Programming
Dale P. Kelly, Senior Vice President & Engineering Director, Emeritus
Dale E. Alfieris, Vice President & General Counsel
Dale Scherbring, Vice President & Engineering Director
Rosemary Danon, Vice President, Online & New Media
Gary E. Cripe, General Counsel
Rueben Cuadros, Controller
Ownership: Harry J. Pappas. On May 10, 2008, certain affiliates of Pappas Telecasting filed for Chapter 11 bankruptcy protection. Mohshin Meghji was appointed Chief Restructuring Officer for those affiliates.
Represented (legal): Fletcher, Heald & Hildreth PLC.
LPTV Stations:
California: KBBV-CA Bakersfield; KVVB-CA Bakersfield; KBVQ-LP Eureka; KFRE-CA Tulare.
Iowa: WBVK-LP Spencer; KCWL-LP Storm Lake.
Nebraska: KBVZ-LP McCook; KWNB-LD McCook; WCWH-LP McCook; KHGI-CA North Platte; KAZK-LP O'Neill; KOAZ-LP O'Neill; KHJP-LP Valentine; WCWY-LD Valentine.
New Mexico: KIAZ-LP Gallup; KCWF-CA Las Cruces.

Texas: KXLK-CA Austin; KXCC-CA Corpus Christi; KHMV-CA Houston; KVVV-LP Houston.
Commercial TV Stations:
Alabama: WLGA-DT Opelika.
Arizona: KSWT-DT Yuma.
California: KAZA-DT Avalon.
Iowa: KCWI-DT Ames.
Nebraska: KWNB-DT Hayes Center; KHGI-DT Kearney.
Radio Stations:
California: KMPH (AM) Modesto, KTRB (AM) San Francisco

PARADIGM BROADCASTING GROUP LLC
120-A Pontiac Business Center Dr.
Elgin, SC 29045
Phone: 803-419-6363
E-mail: srein@midlandswb4.com
Officers:
Stefanie Rein, President
David Canfield, Vice President
Ownership: Stefanie Rein, 51%; David Canfield, 49%.
Represented (legal): Pillsbury Winthrop Shaw Pittman LLP.
LPTV Stations:
Georgia: WHDS-LP Savannah.
North Carolina: W47CK Shallotte.

PARADISE TV LLC
1107 Keys Plaza
Suite 282
Key West, FL 33040
Phone: 305-296-6069
Fax: 305-296-3027
E-mail: bohica1@comcast.net
Web site: www.wgay.tv
Officer:
Burton J. Sherwood, Managing Member
Ownership: Tuxedo Property LLC, 53.75%; Sherwood Family Trust, 33.75%; Keys TV LLC, 7.5%; Stanley Lipp; Evelyn Lipp, 5%. jointly.
Represented (legal): Miller & Neely PC.
LPTV Stations:
Florida: WGAY-LP Key West.

PARADISE VALLEY TV DISTRICT
414 E Callender St
Livingston, MT 59047-2746
Phone: 406-222-3146
LPTV Stations:
Montana: K03HF Emigrant; K19CO Emigrant; K27DL Emigrant; K05EH Emigrant, etc.; K10AH Emigrant, etc.; K57CE Emigrant, etc.; K55CF Livingston, etc.; K60BE Livingston, etc.; K63BV Livingston, etc..

PARK CITY TELEVISION
111 E. Broadway
Suite 1080
Salt Lake City, UT 84111
Phones: 801-649-0045; 801-649-4501
Fax: 801-649-5696
Ownership: Park City Media Group LLC; Steve Marriott; Ron Shapiro, Principals.
LPTV Stations:
Utah: K45AX Park City.

PARKER HILL TV ASSOCIATION
925 6th St.
Room 207
Del Norte, CO 81132-3243
Phone: 719-657-2744
E-mail: rgcommissioner@riograndecounty.org

LPTV Stations:
Colorado: K04JA Del Norte; K06KB Del Norte; K07KB Del Norte; K09BU Del Norte; K11EG Del Norte; K13CB Del Norte.

PARKER W. TILLER
533 Ratliff's Creek Rd.
Pikeville, KY 41501
Phones: 606-432-3768; 606-424-3132
Fax: 606-285-5142
Web site: www.WVVK.Com
LPTV Stations:
Kentucky: WVVK-LP Martin.

PAUL H. PASSINK
Box 350
Concord, VA 24538
LPTV Stations:
Virginia: WDRG-LP Lynchburg.

PATHWAY COMMUNITY RADIO INC.
6936 Henderson Rd.
Jamesville, NY 13078
Phone: 315-673-1269
Represented (legal): James L. Oyster.
LPTV Stations:
Pennsylvania: W41CF Altoona; WSCP-CA State College.

PAXTON MEDIA GROUP INC.
201 S. 4th St.
Box 1680
Paducah, KY 42002-1680
Phone: 207-575-8630
Fax: 270-442-8188
Officers:
David Michael Paxton, President & Chief Executive Officer
Richard Edwin Paxton, Vice President, Chief Financial Officer, Treasurer & Assistant Secretary
James Fredrick Paxton Jr., Vice President & Secretary
Jay Frizzo, Vice President
David R. Mathes, Vice President & Assistant Treasurer
Frank R. Paxton, Assistant Treasurer
Ownership: David Michael Paxton, 18.4%. votes, 6.9%. assets; James Frederick Paxton Jr., 17%. votes, 5.5% assets; Richard Edwin Paxton, 17%. votes, 5.5% assets; Gordon Spoor, Trustee of Trust for Louise P. Gallagher Estate, 15.1%. votes; Louise P. Gallagher Estate, 15.1%. assets; , James Frederick Paxton Estate, 11.5%. assets; George H. Sullivan, Trustee, 7.3%. votes; Patricia Paxton Brockenborough, 6.4%. votes; 6.4% assets; Mary Mitchell Canter, 4%. votes, 4% assets; Bruce Paxton Brockenborough, 3.4%. votes; 3.4% assets.
Represented (legal): Covington & Burling.
LPTV Stations:
Illinois: W10AH Carbondale.
Commercial TV Stations:
Kentucky: WPSD-DT Paducah.
Newspapers:
Arkansas: Jonesboro Sun, Paragould Daily Press, Russellville Courier, Searcy Daily Citizen
Georgia: The Bowdon Bulletin (weekly), Douglas County Sentinel, Griffin Daily News, Haralson-Gateway Beacon (weekly), The Tallapoosa Journal, The Times, Georgian, The Villa Rican (weekly)
Indiana: Connersville News-Examiner, The Times (Frankfort), Michigan City News Dispatch, New Castle Courier-Times, Peru Tribune, The Shelbyville News, Vincennes Sun Commercial, Wabash Plain Dealer
Kentucky: Messenger-Inquirer (Owensboro), The Paducah Sun, The Messenger (Madisonville)

Louisiana: Hammond Daily Star
Michigan: The Herald-Palladium (St. Joseph)
Mississippi: The Banner-Independent (weekly), The Daily Corinthian
North Carolina: Lenoir-News Topic, The Enquirer-Journal (Monroe), Henderson Daily Dispatch, The Daily Courier (Forest City), The Sanford Herald
Tennessee: The Mountain Press (Sevierville)
Other Holdings:
Publishing: Paducah, KY.

MERLE W. PEARCE
185 S. Brooks Rd.
Muskegon, MI 49442
LPTV Stations:
Michigan: W60CO Mount Pleasant.

PECK TV CLUB
PO Box 4
Peck, ID 83545
LPTV Stations:
Idaho: K07BQ Peck; K09AX Peck.

PELICAN BROADCASTING CO.
1660 W. 2nd St.
800 Skylight Office Tower
Cleveland, OH 44113-1495
Phone: 216-781-5096
Officers:
David B. Maltz, President
Stuart Shorenstein, Secretary-Treasurer
Ownership: David B Maltz.
Represented (legal): Kaye Scholer LLP.
LPTV Stations:
Louisiana: KPBN-LP Baton Rouge.

PENSACOLA ACTS INC.
1836 Olive Rd.
Pensacola, FL 32514
Phone: 904-476-2203
LPTV Stations:
Florida: W39BP Pensacola.

PENTECOSTAL REVIVAL ASSN. INC.
Rte. 4
Box 1506
Palatka, FL 32177
Phones: 904-325-5854; 904-325-6323
Officers:
Rev. Dolly Harrell, President
James L. Harrell Sr., Vice President
James L. Harrell Jr., Vice President
Ella Shiflett, Secretary-Treasurer
Ownership: Rev. Dolly Harrell, 25%; James L Harrell Sr., 25%; James L Harrell Jr., 25%; Ella Shiflett, 25%.
LPTV Stations:
Florida: WJGV-LP Palatka.

PEOPLES TV ASSN.
Box AG
Moses Lake, WA 98837
Phone: 509-765-8658
Officers:
Jess Morris, President
Eve Runnels, Chief Executive Officer
Vern Corkins, Chief Operating Officer
Ownership: Non-profit corp.--Moses Lake, WA.
LPTV Stations:
Washington: K59IA Moses Lake, etc..

CONFESORA PERALTA
1549 Townsend Ave
Apt 6G
Bronx, NY 10452
Phone: 718-801-3707

LPTV Stations:
Florida: WHDY-LP Panama City.

VILLAGE OF PERRYVILLE
Pouch AC
Office of Governor-Telecom
Juneau, AK 99811
LPTV Stations:
Alaska: K09NK Perryville.

SONNY PERSAD
7339 Owasco Rd.
Auburn, NY 13021
Phone: 315-258-7377
LPTV Stations:
New York: W48AO Auburn; W54AK Auburn; W69AN Union Springs.

PERSHING COUNTY NV TV TAX DISTRICT
PO Box 1428
Lovelock, NV 89419-1428
Phone: 775-273-2613
LPTV Stations:
Nevada: K18DP Lovelock; K24FF Lovelock; K30DS Lovelock.

PERSHING COUNTY SCHOOL DISTRICT
PO Box 389
1150 Elmhurst Ave
Lovelock, NV 89419
Phone: 775-273-7819
E-mail: pseager@pershing.k12.nv.us
Officers:
Daniel W. Fox, Superintendent
Phillip Seager, Information Contact
LPTV Stations:
Nevada: K14KQ Lovelock.

ROBERT H. PETTITT
1052 Fisher Hill Rd.
Appleton, WA 98602
Phones: 541-296-2711; 509-365-2313
Fax: 541-296-6158
LPTV Stations:
Oregon: KRHP-LP The Dalles.

PHILADELPHIA TELEVISION NETWORK INC.
1515 Market St.
Philadelphia, PA 19102
LPTV Stations:
Pennsylvania: WWJT-LP Philadelphia.

PHILLIPS COUNTY TV TRANSLATOR DISTRICT
PO Box 387
Malta, MT 59538
Phone: 406-383-4499
Officer:
Robert B. Williamson, Chairman
LPTV Stations:
Montana: K36CW Dodson; K08FS Dodson & Wagner; K10FC Dodson & Wagner; K12GP Dodson & Wagner; K65AH Loring; K09JG Loring, etc.; K07IC Malta; K15AS Malta; K11IH Malta, etc.; K13GP Malta, etc.; K20BP Phillips County; K46BX Phillips County; K53CP Phillips County; K06FI Saco, etc.; K09BX Saco, etc.; K12FB Saco, etc.; K34DN Whitewater; K13DU Wynot; K07IB Wynot, etc.; K11GX Wynot, etc..

PIEDMONT TELEVISION HOLDINGS LLC
7621 Little Ave.
Suite 506
Charlotte, NC 28226

Phone: 704-341-0944
Officers:
Paul Brissette, President, Chief Executive Officer & Treasurer
Stephen J. Eley, Secretary
William A. Fielder III, Chief Financial Officer
Barbara Cash, Assistant Secretary
Ownership: Wachovia Capital Partners Inc., 36.81%; BCI Growth V LP, 29.83%; BCI Growth IV LP, 25.6%; Wendell S. Reilly, 5.12%; GOCOM Broadcasting Corp., 2.16%; BCI Investors LLC, 0.49%; WCPI ownership; Wachovia National Bank; BCIG-VLP ownership; Glenpointe Associates LLC-I, Gen. Partner; BCIG-IVLP ownership; Glenpointe Associates LLC-II, Gen. Partner; GBC ownership; Richard L. Gorman, Pres. & Treas., 51%; Katherine L. Gorman, Secy., 49%; BCIILLC ownership:; Donald P. Remey, Managing Member, 16.79%; Stephen J. Eley, Managing Member, 16.79%; Theodore T. Horton Jr., Managing Member, 14.63%; J. Barton Goodwin, Managing Member, 13.20%; Hoyt J. Goodrich, Managing Member, 12.93%; Peter Wilde, 10.33%; Mark Hastings, 10.33%; Thomas J. Cusick, 5.00%.
Represented (legal): Fletcher, Heald & Hildreth PLC.
LPTV Stations:
Alaska: K09QH Kenai.

PILOT GROUP LP
745 Madison Ave., 24th Floor
New York, NY 10151
Phone: 212-486-4446
Ownership: Pilot Group GP LLC, General Partner%; PGGPLLC ownership:; Robert W. Pittman, 76.7%. votes; Mayo S. Stuntz Jr., 17.2%; Paul M. McNicol, 4.1%; Robert B. Sherman, 1.8%. votes; Katonah Pittman Ventures LLC, 72.7%. assets; KPVLLC ownership:; Robert W. Pittman. 100% votes, 51% assets.
Represented (legal): Covington & Burling.
LPTV Stations:
Colorado: KXTU-LP Colorado Springs; K28GE Woodland Park.
Michigan: W14CE Escanaba; W07DB Marquette.
Missouri: K11OJ Sedalia, etc..
New Mexico: K43BU Clovis; K24DU Dora; K26DR San Jon.
New York: WSTQ-LP Syracuse.
Texas: K57CW Friona & Bovina.
Commercial TV Stations:
Colorado: KXRM-DT Colorado Springs.
Georgia: WFXL-DT Albany.
Illinois: WHOI-DT Peoria.
Michigan: WBSF-DT Bay City; WTOM-DT Cheboygan; WLUC-DT Marquette; WEYI-DT Saginaw; WPBN-DT Traverse City.
Missouri: KHQA-DT Hannibal; KRCG-DT Jefferson City; KTVO-DT Kirksville.
New Mexico: KVIH-DT Clovis.
New York: WSTM-DT Syracuse.
Ohio: WNWO-DT Toledo.
South Carolina: WACH-DT Columbia; WPDE-DT Florence.
Texas: KVII-DT Amarillo; KGBT-DT Harlingen.

VILLAGE OF PILOT POINT
Pouch AC
Office of Governor-Telecom
Juneau, AK 99811
LPTV Stations:
Alaska: K09NO Pilot Point.

PINELLAS COUNTY SCHOOLS
301 4th St. SW
Largo, FL 34649-2942
Phone: 727-588-6357
Fax: 727-588-6202
Officer:
Brian Abe, ITV Programs & Production Supervisor

LPTV Stations:
Florida: WPDS-LD Largo, etc..

THOMAS J. PIPER
1547 N. 121st St.
Wauwatosa, WI 53226
Phone: 414-547-6624
LPTV Stations:
Georgia: WAAU-LP Augusta.

PITKIN COUNTY TRANSLATOR DEPT.
76 Service Center Rd.
Aspen, CO 81611
Phone: 970-920-5395
Fax: 970-920-5374
E-mail: reneeh@co.pitkin.co.us
Web site: www.aspenpitkin.com/depts/32
Officer:
Renee Nofziger, Translator Administrator
LPTV Stations:
Colorado: K16FS Ashcroft; K19FH Ashcroft; K06HU Aspen; K08HN Aspen; K50IN Aspen; K05MB Basalt; K07KR Basalt; K09AG Basalt; K33HY Basalt; K36GX Basalt; K29CK Carbondale; K31CW Carbondale; K45HL Carbondale; K48IC Carbondale; K35HK Crystal, etc.; K40IO Crystal, etc.; K56AD Crystal, etc.; K07KF Frying Pan River; K11LM Lower Frying Pan River; K04HP Redstone; K09XN Redstone; K11VC Redstone; K18GD Redstone; K02IO Redstone, etc.; K06CK Redstone, etc.; K02HI Snowmass at Aspen; K04HH Snowmass at Aspen; K10IW Snowmass at Aspen; K04PO Thomasville; K05JA Thomasville; K14LQ Thomasville; K20HR Thomasville; K09LE Upper Frying Pan River; K39HE Woody Creek; K44GQ Woody Creek; K07RN Woody Creek, etc.; K11LW Woody Creek, etc.; K13MT Woody Creek, etc..

PIUTE COUNTY
Courthouse Bldg.
Junction, UT 84740
Phone: 435-577-2840
LPTV Stations:
Utah: K02FA Antimony; K04FG Antimony; K05DO Antimony; K36IG-D Antimony; K38JS-D Antimony; K40IX-D Antimony; K42FB Antimony; K46IV-D Antimony; K17HD Circleville; K19GM-D Circleville; K21IB-D Circleville; K31IY-D Circleville; K32HN-D Circleville; K02BQ Marysvale; K04BO Marysvale; K05BH Marysvale; K47KO-D Marysvale; K50JV-D Marysvale; K52JU-D Marysvale; K45JM-D Marysville.

PLAINS-PARADISE TV DISTRICT
PO Box 1
Plains, MT 59859
Phone: 406-826-3417
E-mail: melva@blackfoot.net
Ownership: Richard Welty, Board Member.
LPTV Stations:
Montana: K11JP Plains; K05GM-D Plains & Paradise; K07CH-D Plains & Paradise; K21CA Plains, etc.; K48LG Weeksville; K29ID Weeksville, etc..

PLEASANT VALLEY TV ASSN.
c/o Fire Department
PO Box 154
Howard, CO 81233
LPTV Stations:
Colorado: K04IC Howard.

PLEVNA PUBLIC SCHOOL TRUSTEES DISTRICT NO. 55
Box 158
Plevna, MT 59344

Phone: 406-772-5666
Fax: 406-772-5548
Officer:
Douglas Rowe, Chairman
LPTV Stations:
Montana: K23DJ Ekalaka; K17OB Plevna; K24DD Plevna; K34DP Plevna.

PLEVNA TV BOOSTER CLUB
PO Box 116
Plevna, MT 59344
Phone: 406-772-5731
E-mail: skywaytv@midrivers.com
Officer:
Gordon Heimbach, Chairman
LPTV Stations:
Montana: K03HD Plevna; K09IV Plevna; K13WT Plevna.

GLENN R. & KARIN A. PLUMMER
15565 Northland Dr.
No. 900 W
Southfield, MI 48075
Phone: 810-559-4200
LPTV Stations:
Louisiana: WLPN-LP New Orleans.
Michigan: WLPC-LP Detroit.

PLUM TV INC.
419 Lafayette
New York, NY 10003
Phone: 646-292-4200
Officer:
Chris Glowacki, President
Represented (legal): Rubin, Winston, Diercks, Harris & Cooke LLP.
LPTV Stations:
Idaho: KSVX-LP Hailey; KSVT-LP Ketchum; K20HW McCall.

DUANE J. POLICH & ELAINE F. CLEMENSON-POLICH
PO Box 37
Bellevue, WA 98009-0037
Phone: 206-852-3096
E-mail: duane@combonate.com
Ownership: Duane J. Polich; Elaine F. Clemenson-Polich, Partners.
LPTV Stations:
Washington: KCST-LP Hoquiam; KPMT-LP Pullman.

POLLACK/BELZ BROADCASTING CO. LLC
Suite 200
6655 Poplar Ave
Germantown, TN 38138
Phone: 318-473-0031
Fax: 318-442-4646
E-mail: kiem-tv@humboldt1.com
Officers:
William H. Pollack, President & Chief Executive Officer
Martin S. Belz, Vice President
David L. Pollack, Treasurer
Ownership: William H Pollack, 33.33%; Martin S Belz, 33.33%; David L Pollack, 33.33%.
LPTV Stations:
California: K12JL Burnt Ranch, etc.; K04NX Garberville, etc.; K07GJ Hoopa; K10NU Miranda; K11IQ Orleans; K04NY Rio Dell; K02OD Shelter Cove; K08GR Willow Creek.
Louisiana: KWCE-LP Alexandria.
Commercial TV Stations:
California: KIEM-DT Eureka.
Louisiana: KLAX-DT Alexandria.

POLNET COMMUNICATIONS LTD
3656 W Belmont Ave
Chicago, IL 60618

Phone: 773-588-6300
Officers:
Walter K Kotaba, President & Treasurer
Joanna Bochenek, Vice President & Secretary
Lauane C Addis, Assistant Secretary
Ownership: Walter K Kotaba.
Represented (legal): Wiley Rein LLP.
LPTV Stations:
Illinois: WPVN-CA Aurora.
Wisconsin: W29DJ Sheboygan.

PONCHARTRAIN INVESTORS LLC
910 N. Foster
Baton Rouge, LA 70806
Phone: 225-336-5885
E-mail: greatoaks001@hotmail.com
Ownership: Margaret Savoye, 70%; Jerry Plough, 30%.
LPTV Stations:
Louisiana: WSTY-LP Hammond.

POPLAR TV DISTRICT
Box 128
Poplar, MT 59255
Phone: 406-768-3800
LPTV Stations:
Montana: K05KK Poplar; K13PZ Poplar; K48IA Poplar; K50GU Poplar; K55BX Poplar.

OBIDIA PORRAS
126201 El Dorado Pl
Victorville, CA 92392-8066
Phone: 760-956-2111
Represented (legal): Katten, Munchin & Rosenman LLP.
LPTV Stations:
California: KCIO-LP Barstow; K26GN Lancaster.

CITY OF PORT HEIDEN
5900 E. Tudor Rd.
Anchorage, AK 99507
Phone: 907-269-5744
LPTV Stations:
Alaska: K04JT Port Heiden.

POST-NEWSWEEK STATIONS INC.
550 W. Lafayette
Detroit, MI 48226
Phone: 313-223-2260
E-mail: twpcoreply@washpost.com
Officers:
G. William Ryan, President & Chief Executive Officer
Robert E. Branson, Vice President, Secretary & General Counsel
Mark Effron, Vice President, News
Catherine Nierle, Vice President, Business Affairs & Treas.
Barbara Reising, Vice President, Human Resources
Ownership: The Washington Post Co.. Owns The Washington Post; The Washington Post National Weekly Edition; the Herald (Everett, WA); 26% of the Minneapolis Star & Minneapolis Tribune & the Gazette Newspapers (MD); MSO Post-Newsweek Cable; program service Pro Am Sports (PASS); Newsweek, Newsweek International & Newsweek Japan magazines. Has interests in data, manufacturing & service companies.
Represented (legal): Covington & Burling.
LPTV Stations:
Florida: W29AB Ocala.
Commercial TV Stations:
Florida: WJXT-DT Jacksonville; WPLG-DT Miami; WKMG-DT Orlando.
Michigan: WDIV-DT Detroit.
Texas: KPRC-DT Houston; KSAT-DT San Antonio.

KATHY POTERA
157 Bunker Hill Rd.
Wyoming, PA 18644
LPTV Stations:
Pennsylvania: W54BO Kingston.

POTTER VALLEY TELEVISION ASSOCIATION INC.
Box 157
Potter Valley, CA 95469
LPTV Stations:
California: K06DK Potter Valley; K08EE Potter Valley; K10EQ Potter Valley; K12DV Potter Valley; K66DQ Potter Valley; K69DI Potter Valley.

POWDER RIVER COUNTY TV BOARD
PO Box 270
c/o Powder River County Clerk & Recorder
Broadus, MT 59317
Phone: 406-436-2361
E-mail: kamende@prco.mt.gov
Officer:
Karen D. Amende, Powder River County Clerk & Recorder
LPTV Stations:
Montana: K09VL Boyes, etc.; K03CS Broadus; K06AA Broadus, etc.; K08JV Broadus, etc.; K10AC Broadus, etc.; K55FG Broadus, etc..

POWELL MEREDITH COMMUNICATIONS CO.
3301 S. 14th St.
Suite A-10
Abilene, TX 79605
Phone: 915-695-9898
Officers:
Amy Meredith, President
Scott Powell, Vice President
Represented (legal): Shainis & Peltzman Chartered.
LPTV Stations:
Arizona: KBFY-LP Fortuna.

POWER TELEVISION INTERNATIONAL LLC
5660 Southwyck Blvd
Ste 101
Toledo, OH 43614-1597
Phone: 419-861-3815
Officer:
Charles Glover, Manager
Ownership: Charles Glover, Mgr., 51%; Mitchell A Lambert, 20%; Joanne Phiels, 10%; Marlene Wisniewski, 10%; Seymour Feig, 5%.
LPTV Stations:
Puerto Rico: WQQZ-CA Ponce; WWKQ-LP Quebradillas.
Commercial TV Stations:
Maine: WPFO-DT Waterville.
Puerto Rico: WMEI-DT Arecibo.

THE ESTATE OF JOHN R. POWLEY, CAROLINE KAYE SMITH EXECUTRIX
7588 Manatee St
Navarre, FL 32566
Phone: 850-936-6461
E-mail: 850-936-6461
Ownership: Caroline Kaye Smith, Executrix. John R. Powley died April 6, 2008.
Represented (legal): Dan J. Alpert.
LPTV Stations:
Georgia: W61DU Columbus.
Maryland: W06CF Salisbury.

Texas: K29GD Amarillo.

PRAIRIE PUBLIC BROADCASTING INC.
207 N. 5th St.
Box 3240
Fargo, ND 58108-3240
Phone: 701-241-6900
Fax: 701-239-7650
Officers:
Paul E. Nyren, Chairman
Kathleen A. Pavelko, President & Chief Executive Officer
Richard J. Veit, Vice President
Ryn Pitts, Secretary

Branch Office:
Prairie Public Radio
1814 N. 15th St.
Bismarck, ND 58501
Phone: 701-224-1700
Ownership:, Prairie Public Broadcasting Inc..
Represented (legal): Dow Lohnes PLLC.
LPTV Stations:
North Dakota: K07NE Lisbon.
ETV Stations:
Minnesota: KCGE-DT Crookston.
North Dakota: KBME-DT Bismarck; KMDE-DT Devils Lake; KDSE-DT Dickinson; KJRE-DT Ellendale; KFME-DT Fargo; KSRE-DT Minot; KWSE-DT Williston.
Other Holdings:
Radio.

PRAIRIEVIEW TV INC.
6545 Cecilia Circle
Minneapolis, MN 55435
Phone: 612-975-0548
Officer:
Tamara K. Campbell, Chief Executive Officer
Ownership: Tamara K Campbell; James Rittenour.
LPTV Stations:
Minnesota: K17CS Appleton; K19CW Appleton; K23DF Appleton; K25EI Appleton; K29CC Appleton; K33CR Appleton; K49ED Appleton; K52AH Appleton; K56BZ Appleton; K58EO Appleton; K15DC Eden Prairie.

PRAISE THE LORD STUDIO CHAPEL
Box 1606
Placerville, CA 95667
Phone: 916-626-5322
Officers:
John R. Hartman, President
Jack W. Hartman, Vice President
Mary Hartman, Secretary-Treasurer
LPTV Stations:
California: KGTN-LP Placerville.

PRICE HILL TELEVISION LLC
5856 Glenway Ave
Cincinnati, OH 45238
Phone: 513-257-5011
Officer:
Robert Backman, Member
LPTV Stations:
Delaware: WRDE-LD Rehobeth Beach.

PRICE MEDIA CORP.
Box 2642
Morgan City, LA 70381
Phone: 504-384-6960
Fax: 504-385-1916
Ownership: Ginger A Price.

LPTV Stations:
Louisiana: KWBJ-LD Morgan City; KWBJ-LP Morgan City.

PRIEST LAKE TRANSLATOR DISTRICT
PO Box 53
Coolin, ID 83821
Phone: 208-443-3896
LPTV Stations:
Idaho: K11UN Coolin; K05GL Coolin, etc.; K09XY Coolin, etc.; K10KR Coolin, etc.; K12LF Coolin, etc.; K31DS Coolin, etc.; K40DJ Coolin, etc.; K51EF Coolin, etc..

PRIME CITIES BROADCASTING INC.
112 High Ridge Ave.
Ridgefield, CT 06877
Phone: 203-431-3366
Officer:
John B. Tupper, President & Secretary-Treasurer
Ownership: John B. Tupper, 51%; Bruce E. Fox, Dir., 46%; James R. Kelly, 3%. T.
LPTV Stations:
North Dakota: K38HA Dickinson; K42FY Dickinson; K38HS Williston; K44HR Williston.
Commercial TV Stations:
North Dakota: KNDX-DT Bismarck; KXND-DT Minot.

PRIME TIME CHRISTIAN BROADCASTING INC.
Box 61000
Midland, TX 79711
Phone: 432-563-0420
Fax: 432-563-1736
Web site: www.godslearningchannel.com
Officers:
Albert O. Cooper, Chairman
Tommie J. Cooper, Vice President & Secretary-Treasurer

Branch Offices:
2401B N Main
Clovis, NM 88101
Phone: 505-742-1800
88 East CR 112
Snyder, TX 79549
Phone: 625-573-9517
2606 S Main
Roswell, NM 88201
Phone: 505-622-5778
5604 Martin Luther
Lubbock, TX 79704
Phone: 806-747-4997
Ownership: Non-profit corp.--Midland, TX.
Represented (legal): Cohn & Marks LLP.
LPTV Stations:
New Mexico: KAPT-LP Alamogordo; KCGD-LP Carlsbad; KCVP-LP Clovis; KHLC-LP Hobbs; KLCP-LP Las Cruces; KKGD-LP Roswell; KPLP-LP Roswell; KGDR-LP Ruidoso.
Texas: KPTA-LP Abilene/Sweetwater; KKCP-LP Ballinger-Coleman; K46FO Big Spring; KPTR-LP Lamesa; K50ED McCamey & Rankin; KPDN-LP Monahans; KPGD-LP Plainview; KPKS-LP San Angelo; KSGD-LP Seminole; KWGD-LP Welch.
Commercial TV Stations:
New Mexico: KRPV-DT Roswell.
Texas: KPTF-DT Farwell; KPTB-DT Lubbock; KMLM-DT Odessa; KPCB-DT Snyder.

DAVID PRIMM
41-625 Eclectic St
Ste J1
Palm Desert, CA 92260
Phone: 760-674-8550

LPTV Stations:
California: K36JH Barstow.

JAMES L. PRIMM
41-645 Eclectic St.
Suite J-1
Palm Desert, CA 92260
LPTV Stations:
Arizona: KFPB-LP Globe.
California: K28FK San Luis Obispo.

PRIORITY COMMUNICATIONS MINISTRIES INC.
2207 Concord Pike
Suite 1710
Wilmington, DE 19803-2908
Phone: 302-367-9595
Officer:
Kingsley D. King, Secretary-Treasurer
Ownership: Jennifer Hare, 33.3%; Rev. Steve Hare, 33.3%; Kingsley D. King, 33.3%.
Represented (legal): Booth Freret Imlay & Tepper PC.
LPTV Stations:
Pennsylvania: WTSD-CA Philadelphia.

PRISM BROADCASTING NETWORK INC.
7742 Spalding Dr.
Suite 475
Norcross, GA 30092
Phone: 770-953-3232
Fax: 770-953-3211
E-mail: vcastelli@earthlink.net
Officers:
Vincent Castelli, President
Mary Castelli, Chief Executive Officer
Abelardo Alvarez, Vice President
Ownership: Mary Castelli.
LPTV Stations:
Arizona: K23HB Flagstaff.
Florida: W29CW Duck Key; W16CL Key West; W25DQ Key West.
Georgia: WANN-CA Atlanta; WTBS-LP Atlanta; WANX-LP Columbus.
Hawaii: K26HL Holualoa; K17GR Kula; K19FV Kula.
Maryland: W23CX Salisbury.
Mississippi: W42CW Hattiesburg; W40BZ Tupelo.
Missouri: KLMC-LP Jefferson City.
Montana: K23HI Billings.
Texas: K18HL Amarillo; K45IQ Amarillo; K21GU Midland; K34HH Midland; K46HN Odessa.

PROCLAIM BROADCASTING INC.
9406 New Glasgow Rd.
Scottsville, KY 42102
Phone: 270-618-8848
Fax: 270-618-4800
Officer:
Marvey Wood, President
LPTV Stations:
Kentucky: WPBM-LP Scottsville.

PROGRESSIVE COMMUNICATIONS INC.
7617 Reading Rd.
Suite 214
Cincinnati, OH 45237
Officers:
Henry R. Riggins, President
Darlene Riggins, Secretary-Treasurer
Represented (legal): Brown, Nietert & Kaufman Chartered.

LPTV Stations:
Texas: K20DL Tyler.

PROMISED LAND MINISTRIES INC./ LIGHT THE WORLD MINISTRIES
PO Box 498
West Plains, MO 65775
Phone: 417-372-1129
E-mail: revdanduncan@hotmail.com
Officer:
Rev. Earl Duncan, President
LPTV Stations:
Missouri: K38HE West Plains.

PROWERS COUNTY
County Courthouse
PO Box 1046
Lamar, CO 81052
LPTV Stations:
Colorado: K53AA Lamar; K55AK Lamar; K57AG Lamar; K59AH Lamar.

THE PSC LIQUIDATING TRUST
c/o Ocean Ridge Capital Advisors LLC, 56 Harrison St.
Suite 203A
New Rochelle, NY 10801
Phone: 914-235-1075
E-mail: ocean.ridge@earthlink.net
Ownership: The PSC Liquidating Trust; TPSCLT ownership;; Ocean Ridge Capital Advisors LLC; ORCALLC ownership; Bradley E. Scher, managing member & majority interest.
LPTV Stations:
Mississippi: W23CM Tylertown.

PSTV PARTNERS LLC
1053 S. Palm Canyon Dr.
Palm Springs, CA 92264
Phone: 760-325-7191
Officer:
Mitchell Sussman, Manager & Member
Represented (legal): Fletcher, Heald & Hildreth PLC.
LPTV Stations:
California: K09XW Palm Desert, etc..

PTP HOLDINGS LLC
PO Box 0083
Cleveland, TN 37364
Phone: 423-472-8892
Officer:
Joe Palo, Manager
Ownership: Joe Palo; Robert S Thompson.
LPTV Stations:
Tennessee: WTNB-CA Cleveland.

PTR TELEVISION INC.
Box 601
Cidra, PR 00739
LPTV Stations:
Puerto Rico: WXWZ-LP Guayama.

THE PUBLIC BROADCASTING COUNCIL OF CENTRAL NEW YORK INC.
506 Old Liverpool Rd.
Box 2400
Syracuse, NY 13220-2400
Phone: 315-453-2424
Fax: 315-451-8824
Officers:
John Lucksinger Jr., Chairman
Michael W. Fields, President & Chief Executive Officer
Ownership: Non-profit corporation.
Represented (legal): Dow Lohnes PLLC.

LPTV Stations:
New York: W59AU Utica.
ETV Stations:
New York: WCNY-DT Syracuse.
Radio Stations:
New York: WUNY-FM; WJNY-FM.

PUBLIC MEDIA CONNECT
1223 Central Pkwy.
Cincinnati, OH 45214-2890
Phone: 937-220-1611
Officers:
Bryan Dunn, Chairman
John Danis, Vice Chairman
Jerry Kathman, Vice Chairman
David Fogarty, President
David Hoguet, Secretary
Albert W Leland, Secretary
Ownership: Board of directors comprised of 31 members.
Represented (legal): Dow Lohnes PLLC.
LPTV Stations:
Ohio: W17AA Celina; W63AH Maplewood, etc..
ETV Stations:
Ohio: WCET-DT Cincinnati; WPTD-DT Dayton; WPTO-DT Oxford.

QUINCY NEWSPAPERS INC.
Box 909
Quincy, IL 62306
Phone: 217-223-5100
E-mail: info@qni.biz
Officers:
Dennis R. Williams, Chairman
Martin M. Lindsay, Vice Chairman
Ralph M Oakley, President, Chief Executive Officer & Assistant Secretary
Peter A Oakley, Secretary
Thomas A. Oakley, Treasurer
David A. Graff, Assistant Treasurer
Ownership: A. O. Lindsay Trust, Lela B. Lindsay & F. M. Lindsay Jr., Trustees, 26.02%; Thomas A. Oakley, Trustee of Thomas A. Oakley Revocable Trust & On Behalf of Gordon M. Smith Trust, 7.92%; Lee Lindsay Curtis, Individually & as Co-Trustee of Lindsay Trust & Beneficiary of Barbara Lee Williams Trust, 7.16%; Lucy Lindsay Smith, 5.73%; Thomas A. Oakley Grantor Irrevocable Trust, Ralph M Oakley & Mary O Winters Co-Trustees, 4.63%; Peter A Oakley Revocable Trust, Peter A Oakley Trustee, 3.00%; Martin M. Lindsay, 2.90%; Susan Oakley-Day, 2.40%; Harold B Oakley, 1.39%; Ralph M Oakley, 0.58%.
Represented (legal): Wilkinson Barker Knauer LLP.
LPTV Stations:
Minnesota: K70DR Blue Earth; K62EV Winona.
Nebraska: K48CH Norfolk.
Wisconsin: W67CH La Crosse.
Commercial TV Stations:
Illinois: WGEM-DT Quincy; WREX-DT Rockford.
Indiana: WSJV-DT Elkhart.
Iowa: KTIV-DT Sioux City; KWWL-DT Waterloo.
Minnesota: KTTC-DT Rochester.
West Virginia: WVVA-DT Bluefield.
Wisconsin: WYOW-DT Eagle River; WQOW-DT Eau Claire; WXOW-DT La Crosse; WKOW-DT Madison; WAOW-DT Wausau.
Newspapers:
Illinois: Quincy Herald-Whig
New Jersey: New Jersey Herald (Newton)
Radio Stations:
Illinois: WGEM-AM-FM Quincy
Other Holdings:
Television holdings: Holds option to purchase KXLT-TV Rochester, MN.

QUINN RIVER TV MAINTENANCE DISTRICT
PO Box 127
Orovada, NV 89425-0158
Phone: 208-375-2205
E-mail: l-e.smith@worldnet.att.net
Officer:
Larry E. Smith, Technical Director
LPTV Stations:
Nevada: K04GA Kings River; K10HJ Kings River, etc.; K48EB McDermitt; K50CZ McDermitt; K52DV McDermitt; K54DQ McDermitt; K58DZ McDermitt; K62EL McDermitt; K06CT Orovada; K08NM Orovada; K11VB Orovada; K13EN Orovada; K60AP Orovada, etc..

RADIANT LIGHT BROADCASTING
Box 301
Richland, WA 99352-0301
Phone: 509-943-9919
Officers:
Richard O. Tedeschi, Chairman
Allan Rither, Vice President
Douglas Campbell, Chief Financial Officer
LPTV Stations:
Washington: KRLB-LP Richland; KWWO-LP Walla Walla.

RADIO ONE LICENSES INC.
5900 Princess Garden Pkwy., 8th Floor
Lanham, MD 20706
Officers:
Catherine L. Hughes, Chairman & Secretary
Alfred C. Liggins III, President, Chief Executive Officer & Treasurer
Scott R. Royster, Executive Vice President & Chief Financial Officer
Linda J. Eckard Vilardo, Vice President & Assistant Secretary
John W. Jones, Assistant Secretary
Ownership: Catherine L. Hughes; Alfred C. Liggins III, 56.6%. voting stock, jointly.
LPTV Stations:
Indiana: WDNI-LP Indianapolis.

RADIO PEACH INC
2300 N St NW, Ste 700
c/o David O'Connor
Washington, DC 20037
Phone: 202-783-4141
Officer:
Lowell L Register, President
Represented (legal): Wilkinson Barker Knauer LLP.
LPTV Stations:
Georgia: W50DA Macon.

RAINBIRD COMMUNITY BROADCASTING CORP.
123 Stedman St.
Ketchikan, AK 99901-6523
Phone: 907-225-9655
LPTV Stations:
Alaska: K09OX Ketchikan.

RAMA COMMUNICATIONS
4938 W. Colonial Dr.
Orlando, FL 32808
LPTV Stations:
Florida: WXXU-LP Altamonte Springs; WOKB-LP Orlando.

RAMAR COMMUNICATIONS INC.
PO Box 3757
9800 University Ave
Lubbock, TX 79452-3757
Phone: 806-748-9300
Fax: 806-748-1949
E-mail: dcampbell@ramarcom.com

Web site: www.ramarcom.com
Officers:
Ray Moran, Chairman
Brad Moran, President
Mary Moran, Secretary-Treasurer
Branch Office:
2400 Monroe NE
Albuquerque, NM 87190
Phone: 505-884-5353
Ownership: Ray Moran, 51%. votes, 45.3% assets; Brad Moran, 49%. votes, 49.1% assets.
Represented (legal): Leventhal, Senter & Lerman PLLC.
LPTV Stations:
New Mexico: KFAC-LP Albuquerque; KTEL-LP Albuquerque; K45IL Hobbs; K46GY Santa Fe.
Texas: K48GB Lubbock; KJTV-CA Lubbock; KMYL-LP Lubbock; KXTQ-CA Lubbock; K40FK Matador; K42ES Matador; K45FE Matador; K47GE Matador; K44GL Plainview; K17FX Seminole; K21FV Seminole; K42ET Snyder; K47IP Snyder; K49GT Snyder.
Commercial TV Stations:
Colorado: KTTL-DT Durango.
New Mexico: KTEL-DT Carlsbad; KUPT-DT Hobbs.
Texas: KJTV-DT Lubbock.
Radio Stations:
Texas: KLZK (FM) Brownfield; KJTV (AM), KXTQ-FM Lubbock; KSTQ-FM New Deal.

R AND S BROADCASTING LLC
144 Crest St.
Wethersfield, CT 06109-2217
Phone: 860-529-9303
Ownership: Rita Minniti; Salvatore Minniti, Equity Members.
Represented (legal): Cohn & Marks LLP.
LPTV Stations:
Connecticut: WESA-LP Granby; WRNT-LP Hartford.

RAPID BROADCASTING CO.
2424 S. Plaza Dr.
Box 9549
Rapid City, SD 57709
Phone: 605-355-0024
Fax: 605-355-9274
Officers:
Gilbert D. Moyle, President
James F. Simpson, Chief Executive Officer
Gilbert D. Moyle III, Vice President
Clark D. Moyle, Secretary-Treasurer
Steve Mentele, Chief Financial Officer
Ownership: W. R Barbour, 25%; Charles H Lien, 25%; Gilbert D Moyle, 16.7%; Gilbert D Moyle III, 16.7%; Clark D Moyle, 16.6%.
Represented (legal): Cole, Raywid & Braverman LLP.
LPTV Stations:
South Dakota: K40GS Rapid City; KKRA-LP Rapid City; KWBH-LP Rapid City.
Wyoming: K22AD Gillette.
Commercial TV Stations:
South Dakota: KNBN-DT Rapid City.

WALTER RASMUSSEN
3200 Chestnut St.
Box 1115
Oneonta, NY 13820-5115
Phones: 607-433-8815; 607-286-3346
Fax: 607-286-7146
Represented (legal): David Tillotson.
LPTV Stations:
New York: WISF-LP Oneonta.

DON RAYBURN JR.
Box 73272
Baton Rouge, LA 70874

LPTV Stations:
Louisiana: K26EV Rayville.

RAYCOM MEDIA INC.
201 Monroe St.
RSA Tower, Suite 710
Montgomery, AL 36104
Phone: 334-206-1400
E-mail: info@raycommedia.com
Officers:
Paul H. McTear Jr., President & Chief Executive Officer
Wayne Daugherty, Executive Vice President & Chief Operating Officer
Mary Carole McDonnell, Executive Vice President, Programming
Marty Edelman, Vice President, Television
Leon Long, Vice President, Television
Jeff Rosser, Vice President, Television
Melissa Thurber, Vice President & Chief Financial Officer
Anne Adkins, Vice President, Marketing
J. Clyde Baucom, Vice President, Human Resources
Rebecca Bryan, Vice President & General Counsel
David Folsom, Vice President & Chief Technology Officer
Pat LaPlatney, Vice President, Digital Media
William R. McDowell, Vice President, Research
Susana Schuler, Vice President, News
Ownership: Paul H. McTear Jr., 14%. votes; qualified company employees, none with more than 5% voting interest.
Represented (legal): Covington & Burling.
LPTV Stations:
Alabama: W29AO Anniston.
Hawaii: K45CT Hilo; K63DZ Kailua-Kona; K65BV Lihue; K27DW Wailuku.
Kentucky: WQTV-LP Murray; WQWQ-LP Paducah.
Louisiana: WBXH-CA Baton Rouge.
New Mexico: K27GJ-D Farmington.
Commercial TV Stations:
Alabama: WBRC-DT Birmingham; WAFF-DT Huntsville; WSFA-DT Montgomery; WDFX-DT Ozark.
Arizona: KOLD-DT Tucson.
Arkansas: KAIT-DT Jonesboro.
Florida: WPGX-DT Panama City; WFLX-DT West Palm Beach.
Georgia: WALB-DT Albany; WTVM-DT Columbus; WTOC-DT Savannah.
Hawaii: KHBC-DT Hilo; KFVE-DT Honolulu; KHNL-DT Honolulu; KOGG-DT Wailuku.
Indiana: WFIE-DT Evansville.
Kentucky: WAVE-DT Louisville; WXIX-DT Newport.
Louisiana: WAFB-DT Baton Rouge; KPLC-DT Lake Charles; KSLA-DT Shreveport.
Mississippi: WLOX-DT Biloxi; WLBT-DT Jackson; WDAM-DT Laurel.
Missouri: KFVS-DT Cape Girardeau.
North Carolina: WBTV-DT Charlotte; WECT-DT Wilmington.
Ohio: WUAB-DT Lorain; WOIO-DT Shaker Heights; WTOL-DT Toledo.
South Carolina: WCSC-DT Charleston; WIS-DT Columbia; WMBF-DT Myrtle Beach.
Tennessee: WTNZ-DT Knoxville; WMC-DT Memphis.
Texas: KCBD-DT Lubbock; KTRE-DT Lufkin; KLTV-DT Tyler.
Virginia: WTVR-DT Richmond; WWBT-DT Richmond.
Radio Stations:
Tennessee: WMC-AM-FM.
Other Holdings:
Advertising sales company, production &.

RED LAKE BAND OF CHIPPEWA INDIANS
PO Box 550
Red Lake, MN 56671
Phone: 218-679-3341

Officer:
Judy Roy, Tribal Secretary
LPTV Stations:
Minnesota: K59FR Red Lake; K61CM Red Lake; K63CI Red Lake; K65BN Red Lake; K67BM Red Lake; K69BT Red Lake.

RED RIVER BROADCAST CO. LLC
Box 9115
Fargo, ND 58106
Phone: 701-277-1515
LPTV Stations:
North Dakota: K33HB Devils Lake.
South Dakota: K35GR Badger; K40FZ Brookings; K47IC Milbank; K44GG Murdo; K27HJ Pierre; K33GX Springfield.

RED RIVER BROADCAST CORP.
3600 S. Westport Ave.
Sioux Falls, SD 57116
Phone: 605-361-5555
Officers:
Ro Grignon, President
Myron Kunin, Chief Executive Officer
Kathy Lau, Vice President
Ownership: Curtis Squire Inc.; CSI ownership:; Curtis Squire, 90%; Ro Grignon, 10%. Grignon & Squire also own KQDS Acquisition Corp., see listing.
Represented (legal): Phillips & Potach PA; Crowell Moring LLP.
LPTV Stations:
Minnesota: K54AT Brainerd; K05IV Park Rapids.
South Dakota: K42FI Watertown.
Commercial TV Stations:
Minnesota: KBRR-DT Thief River Falls.
North Dakota: KVRR-DT Fargo; KJRR-DT Jamestown.
South Dakota: KDLV-DT Mitchell; KDLT-DT Sioux Falls.

REDWOOD EMPIRE PUBLIC TV INC.
Box 13
Eureka, CA 95502-0013
Phone: 707-445-0813
Ownership: J. Michael Brown; John Campbell; Roy Corsetti; Dee Daneri; Ron Harris; Carol Johnson; Nancy Kay; Pamela Kessler; Leslie G. Lawson; W. Timothy Needham; Joseph R. Orazco; Cheryl A. Seidner; James N. Stanfield; Patrick Swartz, Board members.
LPTV Stations:
California: K09VQ Crescent City; K44JF-D Crescent City; K12OV Shelter Cove.
ETV Stations:
California: KEET-DT Eureka.

REDWOOD TV IMPROVEMENT CORP.
PO Box 120
Morton, MN 56270
Phone: 507-697-6489
Officer:
Ed Downs, President
LPTV Stations:
Minnesota: K17BV Redwood Falls; K19CV Redwood Falls; K25II Redwood Falls; K39CH Redwood Falls; K46FY Redwood Falls; K48GQ Redwood Falls; K50KF Redwood Falls; K52GU Redwood Falls; K58AS Redwood Falls; K62AA Redwood Falls; K66BB Redwood Falls; K68BJ Redwood Falls; W56EL Redwood Falls.

REGION 1 TRANSLATOR ASSOCIATION
320 E. 10th Ave.
Yuma, CO 80759 - 3002
Phone: 970-848-5301
Officers:

Richard Starkebaum, President
Chuck Powell, Vice President
Stanley E. Shafer, Secretary-Treasurer
Ownership: Richard Starkebaum, 33.3%. of votes; Chuck Powell, 33.3%. of votes; Stanley E. Shafer, 33.3%. of votes.
LPTV Stations:
Arizona: K30HA Yuma.
Colorado: K08ND Akron; K11UW Akron; K13XW Akron; K51HS-D Anton; K57IL Anton; K31FZ Haxtun; K33GM Haxtun; K35GO Haxtun; K39HM Haxtun; K41IT Haxtun; K43JJ Haxtun; K15FD Holyoke; K17EU Holyoke; K19EG Holyoke; K21FF Holyoke; K25GZ Holyoke; K27IH-D Holyoke; K29GI Holyoke; K14LB Idalia; K18FO Idalia; K20HM Idalia; K22GQ Idalia; K29HD-D Idalia; K16EK Idalia & South Yuma County; K24EZ Idalia & South Yuma County; K26FP Idalia & South Yuma County; K45IS-D Julesburg; K47JH Julesburg; K49IN Julesburg; K51IL Julesburg; K53IY Julesburg; K55JC Julesburg; K57JE Julesburg; K14LC Pleasant Valley; K16ET Pleasant Valley; K18GM Pleasant Valley; K20GK Pleasant Valley; K24FU-D Pleasant Valley; K26GX Pleasant Valley; K28IX Pleasant Valley; K30GO Pleasant Valley; K31IH-D Wray; K44FM Wray; K46FF Wray; K48GA Wray; K50FJ Wray; K52FZ Wray; K56HG Wray; K58GV Wray; K28JH-D Yuma; K32AB Yuma; K34AC Yuma; K36AC Yuma; K38AD Yuma; K40CG Yuma; K42GI Yuma.

REGISTER TV NEWS
314 W. Market St.
Sandusky, OH 44870
Phone: 419-625-5500
Officers:
Robert E. Pifer, President & Chief Executive Officer
David E. Hahn Jr., Chief Operating Officer
Ownership: Sandusky Newspapers Inc..
LPTV Stations:
Ohio: W41AP Sandusky.
Newspapers:
Michigan: Grand Haven Tribune
Ohio: Norwalk Reflector, Sandusky Register
Tennessee: Kingsport Times News

RENVILLE COUNTY TV CORP.
800 E. Depue Ave.
Olivia, MN 56277
Phone: 320-523-2448
LPTV Stations:
Minnesota: K23FP Olivia; K45FR Olivia; K49AJ Olivia; K51AL Olivia; K53AO Olivia; K55CK Olivia; K57AE Olivia.

RESORT SPORTS NETWORK INC.
PO Box 7528
Portland, ME 04112
Phone: 207-772-5000
Fax: 207-775-3658
Officers:
Jeffrey L. Dumais, President
Walter W. Crites, Controller
Ownership: Mogul Network LLC, 65.4%; Mark A. Burchill, 16.68%; Leonard T. Conway, 9.68%; John Cooney, 4.13%; J.P. Sachs Associates, 4.13%; MNLLC ownership:; Cumming Investment Co. LC, 25%; David Cumming, 25%; John Cumming, 25%; Joe Steinberg, 25%; JPSA ownership:; Kathryn S. Conway, 32.34%; Christopher H. Sachs, 32.34%; Susan F. Sachs, 32.34%; John P. Sachs, 1.49%; Mary K. Sachs, 1.49%; CICLC ownership:; Annette P. Cumming, 50%; Ian Cumming, 50%.
Represented (legal): Davis Wright Tremaine LLP.
LPTV Stations:
Colorado: K26GY Breckenridge; K28HI Breckenridge/Dillon; K36DB Sweetwater Creek.

Nevada: K38FW Stateline; K59GM Stateline.

DAN REYNOLDS
7828 Newton Line Rd.
Harrison, AR 72601
Phones: 870-741-4891; 870-424-6957
Fax: 870-365-7354
Web site: www.XL7tv.com
LPTV Stations:
Arkansas: K07XL Mountain Home.

REYNOLDS MEDIA INC.
7828 Newton Line Rd.
Harrison, AR 72601
Phone: 870-741-4891
E-mail: danr@alltel.net
Officer:
Dan Reynolds, President
LPTV Stations:
Arkansas: K26GS Mountain Home.

RICH COUNTY
County Courthouse
Randolph, UT 84064
Phone: 435-793-2415
LPTV Stations:
Utah: K26GH Randolph & Woodruff; K34FR Randolph & Woodruff; K40FY Randolph & Woodruff.

RICHEY TELEVISION DISTRICT
PO Box 114
Richey, MT 59259
LPTV Stations:
Montana: K13JU Richey.

RIO BLANCO COUNTY TV ASSOCIATION
17497 Hwy. 64
Rangely, CO 81648
E-mail: infosystems@co.rio-blanco.co.us
LPTV Stations:
Colorado: K05CM Banty Point; K04JX Banty Point, etc.; K07QE Banty Point, etc.; K09VT Banty Point, etc.; K11PI Banty Point, etc.; K10DY Blue Mountain, etc.; K12EE Blue Mountain, etc.; K05GI Buford; K07RP Buford; K10HE Buford; K13QU Buford, etc.; K03HG Lower Piceance Creek; K13WY Lower Piceance Creek; K48EC Marvine Creek, etc.; K30CK Meeker; K46DO Meeker; K48CL Meeker; K64BH Meeker; K06JJ Meeker, etc.; K09FE Meeker, etc.; K12LT Meeker, etc.; K56EZ Meeker, Rangely, etc.; K07QB Piceance Creek; K09WZ Piceance Creek; K61BD Piceance Creek; K64AV Piceance Creek; K67BK Piceance Creek area; K06IX Rangely; K22DZ Rangely; K24DG Rangely; K26DP Rangely; K28CG Rangely; K32AC Rangely; K66ER Rangely; K36DM Rio Blanco Valley; K50AE Rio Blanco Valley; K38AG Rio Blanco Valley, etc.; K44AC Rio Blanco Valley, etc.; K60AC Stadtman Mesa; K58EF Stadtman Mesa, etc..
South Dakota: K54AH Aberdeen.

RIVER CITY BROADCASTING CORP.
111 W. Douglas Ave.
Suite 102
Wichita, KS 67202
Phone: 316-942-7948
LPTV Stations:
Kansas: KCTU-LP Wichita.
Radio Stations:
Iowa: KCJJ (AM) Iowa City

RIVERTON FREMONT TV CLUB INC.
113 S. 2nd E
Box 628
Riverton, WY 82501

Phone: 307-856-3322
Officer:
Bill Willman, President
LPTV Stations:
Wyoming: K28HL Riverton; K03ER Riverton, etc.; K32EL Shoshoni; K38EK Shoshoni, etc..

MICHAEL V. ROBERTS
1408 N. Kingshighway Blvd.
Suite 300
St. Louis, MO 63113
Phones: 314-367-0090; 314-367-4600
Fax: 314-367-0174
Represented (legal): DLA Piper International.
LPTV Stations:
Indiana: WAZE-LP Evansville; WIKY-LP Evansville, etc.; WJPS-LP Evansville, etc..
Commercial TV Stations:
Kentucky: WAZE-DT Madisonville.
Mississippi: WRBJ-DT Magee.
South Carolina: WZRB-DT Columbia.
Other Holdings:
TV Stations: Roberts holds 50% of the voting equity of Roberts Brothers Broadcasting LLC, which holds 50% of the voting equity in St. Louis/Denver LLC see listing..

STEVEN C. ROBERTS
1408 N. Kingshighway Blvd.
Suite 300
St. Louis, MO 63113
Phones: 314-367-0090; 314-367-4600
Fax: 314-367-0176
Represented (legal): DLA Piper International.
LPTV Stations:
Indiana: WAZE-LP Evansville; WIKY-LP Evansville, etc.; WJPS-LP Evansville, etc..
Commercial TV Stations:
Kentucky: WAZE-DT Madisonville.
Mississippi: WRBJ-DT Magee.
South Carolina: WZRB-DT Columbia.
Other Holdings:
TV Stations: Roberts holds 50% of the voting equity of Roberts Brothers Broadcasting LLC, which holds 50% of the voting equity in St. Louis/Denver LLC see listing..

ROCKFLEET BROADCASTING LP
885 3rd Ave., 34th Floor
New York, NY 10022
Phone: 212-888-5500
Officers:
Jeffrey A. Smith, President
Bruce M. Schnelwar, Senior Vice President
David A. Pershing, Senior Vice President & Secretary
Kevin J. DeLuise, Vice President, Treasurer & Assistant Secretary
Ownership: R. Joseph Fuchs, 14.85%. equity; Rockfleet Broadcasting Inc., 1%. equity, 100% voting; SDR Rockfleet Holdings LLC, 84.15%. equity; RBI ownership:; R. Joseph Fuchs; SDRRHLLC ownership:; Randall Smith, 88%; Jeffrey Smith, 12%.
Represented (legal): Wiley Rein LLP.
LPTV Stations:
Maine: WFVX-LP Bangor.
Wisconsin: W27AU Wausau.
Commercial TV Stations:
Maine: WVII-DT Bangor.
Wisconsin: WJFW-DT Rhinelander.
Other Holdings:
Radio.

ROCKY MOUNTAIN PUBLIC BROADCASTING NETWORK INC.
1089 Bannock St.
Denver, CO 80204-9972
Phone: 303-620-5625
Fax: 303-620-5600

Officers:
James Morgese, General Manager
Donna Sanford, Programming Director
Bud Rath, Director, Network Engineering
Dan Flenniken, Director, Education
Betsy Boudreau, Director, Development
Tiffany Q. Tyson, Director, Communications
LPTV Stations:
Colorado: K04KB Aguilar; K24HQ-D Boulder; K44CT Boulder; K59CL Coaldale; K02KJ Del Norte; K52BC Delta; K55DR Delta; K06GW Divide Creek, etc.; K29CZ Durango; K06LX Glenwood Springs; K28HA Grand Valley; K52GA Ignacio; K03FR La Veta; K58FY Lake George, etc.; K07PA Manitou Springs; K32CW Montrose, etc.; K13SN Nucla; K09PJ Ouray, etc.; K61BR Ouray, etc.; K58BV Paonia; K64BL Ridgway, etc.; K61BN Rulison, etc.; K53AR Salida, etc.; K02KI San Luis; K55CL San Luis Valley, etc.; K49AH Silt, etc.; K15GL-D Trinidad, Valdez, etc..

ETV Stations:
Colorado: KRMA-DT Denver; KRMJ-DT Grand Junction; KTSC-DT Pueblo; KRMZ-DT Steamboat Springs.

WANDA ROLON
Box 24
Toa Alta, PR 00954
Phone: 787-730-5880
Fax: 787-797-5157
LPTV Stations:
Puerto Rico: WQSJ-LP Quebradillas; WSJN-CA San Juan.

ROSEAU COUNTY
606 5th Ave. SW
Room 16
Roseau, MN 56751
LPTV Stations:
Minnesota: K42CU Roseau; K46BV Roseau; K48CQ Roseau; K50AM Roseau; K52AM Roseau.

ROSS COMMUNICATIONS LTD.
708 W. Hillcrest Ave.
Dayton, OH 45406
Phone: 937-275-7677
LPTV Stations:
Ohio: WRCX-LP Dayton.

ROUNDUP TV TAX DISTRICT
506 Main St
Courthouse
Roundup, MT 59072
Phone: 406-323-3554
E-mail: rsolberg@midrivers.com
Ownership: Ronald Jay Solberg, Board Member.
LPTV Stations:
Montana: K07WP Roundup; K09WS Roundup; K11FS Roundup; K13AN Roundup.

ROUTT COUNTY
PO Box 773598
Steamboat Springs, CO 80477
LPTV Stations:
Colorado: K19CF Hayden.

HOWARD F. ROYCROFT
555 13th St. NW
Washington, DC 20004
Phone: 202-637-6525
Represented (legal): Hogan & Hartson LLP.
LPTV Stations:
Arizona: K18CB Bullhead City.

ROY TV TAX DISTRICT
117 W Main
Roy, MT 59471

Phone: 406-464-5471
Officer:
Kenneth Siroky, Information Contact
LPTV Stations:
Montana: K09CB Horse Ranch & Roy; K11HN Roy, etc..

VILLAGE OF ROY
PO Box 8
Roy, NM 87743
LPTV Stations:
New Mexico: K09AW Roy.

CITY OF RUBY
Box 90
Ruby, AK 99768
LPTV Stations:
Alaska: K09PK Ruby.

RULE COMMUNICATIONS
2232 Dell Range Blvd.
Suite 306
Cheyenne, WY 82009-4994
Phone: 307-637-7777
Fax: 307-635-1771
E-mail: kpin@wyoming.com
Represented (legal): Womble, Carlyle, Sandridge & Rice.
LPTV Stations:
Wyoming: KMAH-LP Cheyenne; KPAH-LP Laramie; KKBT-LP Pinedale.
Radio Stations:
Wyoming: KPIN (FM) Pinedale

RURAL CALIFORNIA BROADCASTING CORP.
5850 Labath Ave.
Rohnert Park, CA 94928
Phone: 707-585-8522
Fax: 707-585-1363
Officers:
Howard Nurse, Chairman
Susan Nix, Vice Chair
Nancy Dobbs, President & Chief Executive Officer
Terry Sterling, Secretary
Alice Gunn, Treasurer
LPTV Stations:
California: K35DO Hopland.
ETV Stations:
California: KRCB-DT Cotati.
Other Holdings:
Radio.

RURAL OREGON WIRELESS TV INC.
Box 442
Lake Oswego, OR 97034
Phone: 503-226-5004
E-mail: edausman@kgw.com
Officer:
P. Eric Dausman, President
Represented (legal): Wiley Rein LLP.
LPTV Stations:
Oregon: K39ES Heppner, etc.; K43FH Heppner, etc.; K46CU Heppner, etc.; K28CQ Hood River; K40AM Hood River; K50CE Hood River; K53EI Hood River; K04BJ La Pine; K09YE La Pine; K46KG-D Madras & Culver; K58BK Madras & Culver; K63CC Madras & Culver; K69BI Madras & Culver; K34AI North La Pine; K17GV Rainier; K21HG Rainier; K28IH Rainier; K31HK Rainier; K41IP Rainier; K44HM Rainier; K65AE Terrebonne; K30IV Wallowa; K34IF Wallowa; K36HV Wallowa; K40IK Wallowa; K67AD Wasco.

RURAL SERVICES OF CENTRAL MINNESOTA INC.
1401 S. Broadway
Pelican Rapids, MN 56572

Phone: 218-863-4600
Fax: 218-863-1172
Officers:
Dave Weaklend, President
Michael Ostbye, Chief Financial Officer
Ownership: Lake Region Electric Cooperative.
LPTV Stations:
Minnesota: K31CH Erhard; K39CJ Erhard; K41CS Erhard; K43CS Erhard; K51DC Erhard.

SAGA COMMUNICATIONS INC.
73 Kercheval Ave.
Suite 201
Grosse Pointe Farms, MI 48236-3559
Phone: 313-886-7070
Fax: 313-886-7150
E-mail: bwells@sagacom.com
Officers:
Edward K. Christian, Chairman, President & Chief Executive Officer
Steven J. Goldstein, Executive Vice President, Programming
Warren Lada, Senior Vice President, Operations
Samuel D. Bush, Vice President, Treasurer & Chief Financial Officer
Marcia K. Lobaito, Vice President & Secretary
Ownership: Publicly held.; Edward K Christian, controlling interest.
Represented (legal): Smithwick & Belendiuk PC.
LPTV Stations:
Texas: KMOL-LP Victoria; KUNU-LP Victoria; KVTX-LP Victoria; KXTS-LP Victoria.
Commercial TV Stations:
Kansas: KOAM-DT Pittsburg.
Mississippi: WXVT-DT Greenville.
Texas: KAVU-DT Victoria.
Radio Stations:
Arkansas: KEGI (FM) Jonesboro, KDXY (FM) Lake City, KJBX (FM) Trumann
Illinois: WIXY (FM), WLRW (FM) Champaign; WXTT (FM) Danville; WYMG (FM) Jacksonville; WABZ (FM) Sherman; WDBR (FM), WQQL (FM), WTAX (AM) Springfield; WCFF (FM) Urbana
Iowa: KLTI-FM Ames; KIOA (FM), KPSZ (AM), KRNT (AM), KSTZ (FM) Des Moines; KAZR (FM) Pella; KICD (AM), KLLT (FM) Spencer
Kentucky: WCVQ (FM), WJQI (AM) Fort Campbell; WVVR (FM) Hopkinsville; WEGI (AM) Oak Grove
Maine: WVAE (AM) Biddeford; WCLZ (FM) North Yarmouth; WBAE (AM), WGAN (AM), WMGX (FM), WPOR (FM), WZAN (AM) Portland; WYNZ (FM) Westbrook
Massachusetts: WHNP (AM) East Longmeadow; WHAI (FM), WHMQ (AM), WPVQ (FM) Greenfield; WLZX (FM) Northhampton; WAQY (FM) Springfield
New Hampshire: WMLL (FM) Bedford; WFEA (AM), WZID (FM) Manchester
New York: WIII (FM) Cortland; WHCU (AM), WNYY (AM), WQNY (FM), WYXL (FM) Ithaca
North Carolina: WISE (AM) Asheville, WOXL-FM Biltmore Forest, WYSE (AM) Canton, WTMT (FM) Weaverville
Ohio: WBCO (AM), WQEL (FM) Bucyrus; WSNY (FM) Columbus; WODB (FM) Delaware; WJZK (FM) Richwood
South Dakota: KMIT (FM) Mitchell, KUQL (FM) Wessington Springs, WNAX-AM-FM Yankton
Tennessee: WKFN (AM) Clarksville
Vermont: WKVT (AM) Brattleboro, WRSY (FM) Marlboro
Virginia: WINA (AM), WQMZ (FM), WVAX (AM), WWWV (FM) Charlottesville; WCNR (FM) Keswick; WJOI (AM), WNOR (FM) Norfolk; WAFX (FM) Suffolk
Washington: KAFE (FM), KBAI (AM), KGMI (AM), KISM (AM), KPUG (AM) Bellingham
Wisconsin: WJZX (FM); WJMR-FM Brookfield; WJMR-FM Menomonee Falls; WHQG (FM), WJYI (AM), WKLH (FM) Milwaukee

SAGAMOREHILL BROADCASTING LLC
2 Embarcadero Center, 23rd Floor
San Francisco, CA 94111
Phone: 415-788-2755
Officer:
Louis Wall, President
Ownership: Duff, Ackerman & Goodrich LP, principal..
Represented (legal): Wiley Rein LLP.
LPTV Stations:
Wyoming: K19FX Laramie.
Commercial TV Stations:
Alabama: WNCF-DT Montgomery; WBMM-DT Tuskegee.
Georgia: WLTZ-DT Columbus.
Nebraska: KSTF-DT Scottsbluff.
Texas: KGNS-DT Laredo.
Wyoming: KGWN-DT Cheyenne.

SAINTE 51 LP
Box 4159
Modesto, CA 95352-4159
Phone: 209-523-0777
Officer:
Chester Smith, President
Ownership: C & N Broadcast Division Inc., gen. partner; Sainte Network Inc., gen. partner; CNBDI & SNI ownership:; Chester Smith, Pres., 50%; Naomi L. Smith, V.P., 50%; J. Wilmer Jensen, Secy.-Treas..
Represented (legal): Womble, Carlyle, Sandridge & Rice.
LPTV Stations:
California: KCSO-LP Sacramento.

SAINTE PARTNERS II LP
Box 4159
Modesto, CA 95352-4159
Phone: 209-523-0777
Fax: 209-523-0839
Ownership: C & N Broadcast Division Inc., gen. partner, 50%. votes; 1% equity; Sainte Network Inc., gen. partner, 50%. votes; 1.34%. equity; Chester Smith, ltd. partner, 35.4%. equity; Naomi L. Smith, ltd. partner, 35.4%. equity; Albert I. & Virginia C. Chance, ltd. partners, 7.38%. equity; J. Wilmar Jensen, ltd. partner, 7.38%. equity; Sharon D. Sepulveda, ltd. partner, 2.91%. equity; Madeline J. Roddy, ltd. partner, 2.82%. equity; Center Family Trust, ltd. partner, 2.24%. equity; Dorothy Ibarra, ltd. partner, 2.24%. equity; Danny Roddy, ltd. partner, 0.94%. equity; Sean Roddy, ltd. partner, 0.94%. equity; CNBDI & SNI ownership:; Chester Smith, Pres., 50%; Naomi L. Smith, V.P., 50%; J. Wilmar Jensen, Secy.-Treas..
LPTV Stations:
California: K38FQ Anderson/Central Valley; KKTF-LP Chico; KUCO-LP Chico; KXVU-LP Chico; KZVU-LP Chico; K52FK Eureka; K59FW Eureka; K67GU Eureka; KEMY-LP Eureka; KEUV-LP Eureka; KUVU-LP Eureka; K14MN Fortuna; K08NH Oroville; K04QC Palermo; K46HI Redding; KRVU-LP Redding.
Oregon: K41ID Klamath Falls; KFBI-LP Medford; KMCW-LP Medford.
Commercial TV Stations:
California: KBVU-DT Eureka; KCVU-DT Paradise.

CITY OF ST. PAUL ISLAND
5900 E Tudor Rd
Anchorage, AK 99507
Phone: 907-269-5744

LPTV Stations:
Alaska: K04HM St. Paul Island.

CITY OF ST. PETERSBURG
175 5th St. N
St. Petersburg, FL 33701
Phone: 813-893-7050
LPTV Stations:
Florida: WSPF-CA St. Petersburg.

ST. REGIS TV TAX DISTRICT
PO Box 156
St. Regis, MT 59866
Phone: 406-649-2316
E-mail: commissioner@blackfoot.net
Officer:
Judy A. Stang, Information Contact
LPTV Stations:
Montana: K05DS St. Regis; K10HM St. Regis.

ST. AUGUSTINE'S COLLEGE
1315 Oakwood Ave.
Raleigh, NC 27611
Phone: 919-516-4750
Fax: 919-516-4425
Officers:
James N. Wade, Chairman
Dr. Bernard W. Franklin, President & Chief Executive Officer
Eugene Nicholas, Chief Financial Officer
LPTV Stations:
North Carolina: W68BK Raleigh.
Other Holdings:
Radio.

ST. JOHN PLANTATION
1774 St John Rd
St. John Plantation, ME 04743
Phone: 207-834-6444
E-mail: stjohn@sjv.net
Officer:
Patrick J. Nadeau, Information Contact
LPTV Stations:
Maine: W11AY St. John Plantation.

J. B. SALAZAR
139 W. Nopal St.
Uvalde, TX 78801
Phone: 830-591-1120
LPTV Stations:
Texas: KLMV-LP Laredo; K17GL Uvalde; K42GJ Uvalde; K45HM Uvalde; K47IJ Uvalde; K49HH Uvalde.

SALISH KOOTENAI COLLEGE
Hwy. 93
Box 117
Pablo, MT 59855
Phone: 406-675-4800
Fax: 406-675-4801
Officers:
Joe McDonald, Chief Executive Officer
Audrey Reed, Chief Financial Officer
Represented (legal): Schwartz, Woods & Miller.
LPTV Stations:
Montana: K48EG Arlee; K20CP Elmo; KSKC-CA Pablo/Ronan; K28CF St. Ignatius.

SALMON TV TRANSLATOR DISTRICT
PO Box 2308
Salmon, ID 83467
Phone: 208-756-2349
Officer:
Jackie Winterowd, Executive Secretary
LPTV Stations:
Idaho: K11BD Leadore, etc.; K05BE Lemhi, etc.; K09SD Lemhi, etc.; K07PV Salmon;

K30BU Salmon; K34CB Salmon; K46EC Salmon; K59AV Salmon; K65BG Salmon; K69CA Salmon; K11TY Salmon, etc.; K55AI Tendoy & Baker.

SAN BERNARDINO COMMUNITY COLLEGE DISTRICT
701 S. Mount Vernon Ave.
San Bernardino, CA 92410
Phone: 909-888-6511
Officers:
Stephanie Cereceres, Chairman
Stuart M. Bundy, Chancellor
LPTV Stations:
California: KJHP-LP Morongo Valley.
ETV Stations:
California: KVCR-DT San Bernardino.
Radio Stations:
California: KVCR (FM)

SAN BERNARDINO COUNTY
73658 Old Dale Rd.
Twentynine Palms, CA 92277-3280
Phone: 760-367-1833
E-mail: tv5@verizon.net
Officer:
James Parker, Senior Area Manager
LPTV Stations:
California: K15BZ Daggett; K19BS Daggett; K23BP Daggett; K35BQ Daggett; K39DW Daggett; K41CY Daggett; K48IP Daggett; K50HV Daggett; KTSK-LP Daggett; K46HT Daggett, etc.; K15FC Joshua Tree; K17GJ Joshua Tree; K21GR Joshua Tree, etc.; K25GK Joshua Tree, etc.; K15CA Lucerne Valley; K19BT Lucerne Valley; K41CB Lucerne Valley; K43EE Lucerne Valley; K48AD Lucerne Valley; K54AD Lucerne Valley; K13WJ Morongo Valley; K14AB Morongo Valley; K16AA Morongo Valley; K21GI Morongo Valley; K30GU Morongo Valley; K32EM Morongo Valley; K34EU Morongo Valley; K36GO Morongo Valley; K40HX Morongo Valley; K48EM Morongo Valley; K03EK Newberry Springs; K06IQ Newberry Springs; K08IA Newberry Springs; K10IX Newberry Springs; K12JI Newberry Springs; K29GK Twentynine Palms, etc.; K47IB Twentynine Palms, etc.; K49DC Twentynine Palms, etc.; K51DU Twentynine Palms, etc..

GABRIELA LOPEZ SANCHEZ
1084 Glen Circle
Costa Mesa, CA 92627
Phone: 949-645-4786
LPTV Stations:
Florida: W12DE Panama City.

SANCTUARY BROADCASTING CO. INC.
PO Box 853
Sylacauga, AL 35150-0853
Phone: 256-207-2464
Officer:
Freddie L. Edwards, President
Ownership: Sanctuary Church of God; , SCOG ownership:; Thomas E. Cox; Bobby Ray Davis; Freddie L. Edwards; Cindy Ogle, Dirs..
Represented (legal): Hall Estill.
LPTV Stations:
Alabama: W50BO Ashville; W63CK Talladega; WOIL-LP Talladega.

SANDE FAMILY TRUST
16922 E. Harvard Ave.
Aurora, CO 80013
Phone: 303-368-0870

Ownership: Harriet S. Van De Sande, Trustee; Jean B. Van De Sande, Trustee.
LPTV Stations:
Colorado: KDEO-LP Aurora.

BOARD OF TRUSTEES FOR SAN DIEGO U.
5200 Campanile Dr.
MC 5400
San Diego, CA 92182
Represented (legal): Dow Lohnes PLLC.
LPTV Stations:
California: K59AL La Jolla; K67AM La Jolla.

CITY OF SAND POINT
Box 16
Sand Point, AK 99661
LPTV Stations:
Alaska: K04HV Sand Point.

SANEL VALLEY TELEVISION ASSOCIATION
13750 Mount House Rd.
Hopland, CA 95449
Phone: 707-744-1722
LPTV Stations:
California: K06FA Hopland; K10FZ Hopland; K11TD Hopland; K13ID Hopland.

DEWEY SANFORD
1354 Sunset Dr.
Box 550
Grenada, MS 38901-0550
Phones: 662-226-1354; 662-227-1494
LPTV Stations:
Mississippi: W13CS Grenada.

SANGRE DE CRISTO COMMUNCATIONS INC.
2200 7th St.
Pueblo, CO 81003
Phone: 719-544-5781
Officers:
David Whitaker, President & General Manager
Quentin Henry, Chief Engineer
Represented (legal): Dow Lohnes PLLC.
LPTV Stations:
Colorado: K19DY Canon City; K30AA Colorado Springs.

SAN JUAN BASIN TECHNICAL COLLEGE
33057 Hwy 160
Mancos, CO 81328
Phone: 970-769-0808
Officer:
Sherri Wright, President
Ownership: State of Colorado/Montezuma County School Districts.
LPTV Stations:
Colorado: K41DE Cortez, etc..

SAN JUAN COUNTY
117 S. Main
Monticello, UT 84535
Phone: 435-587-3223
LPTV Stations:
Utah: K36AK Blanding & Monticello; K38AJ Blanding, etc.; K44AG Blanding, etc.; K46AF Blanding, etc.; K04PI Bluff; K02PU Bluff & area; K13XS Bluff & area; K02PT Mexican Hat; K04PG Mexican Hat; K06NK Mexican Hat; K13XO Mexican Hat; K02OI Montezuma Creek & Aneth; K05JN Montezuma Creek & Aneth; K11VR Montezuma Creek & Aneth; K13YC Montezuma Creek & Aneth; K10PB Montezuma Creek/Aneth; K09XX Navajo Mountain School; K02PX Navajo Mountain School, etc.; K04PP Navajo Mountain School,

etc.; K06NR Navajo Mountain School, etc.; K07XU Navajo Mountain School, etc.; K02PV Oljeto; K04OZ Oljeto; K05LF Oljeto; K06NM Oljeto; K07XO Oljeto; K11US Oljeto; K13XP Oljeto.

SAN-LEE COMMUNITY BROADCASTING INC.
Box 4646
Sanford, NC 27331
Phone: 919-776-4646
Fax: 919-776-0125
Officers:
Rudy Holland, Chairman
Dennis Maddox, President
Donald Perrell, Chief Executive Officer
David Yarborough, Secretary
Charlie Welborn, Chief Financial Officer
LPTV Stations:
North Carolina: WBFT-CA Sanford.

SAN LUIS VALLEY TELEVISION INC.
PO Box 241
La Jara, CO 81140
Phone: 719-843-5883
Officer:
Jim Horton, President
LPTV Stations:
Colorado: K45GD Romeo, etc.; K61AZ Romeo, etc.; K65AS Romeo, etc..

SANPETE COUNTY
160 N. Main
Manti, UT 84642
Phone: 435-835-2131
LPTV Stations:
Utah: K39IW-D Manti & Ephraim; K41JW-D Manti & Ephraim; K09FM Manti, etc.; K11FP Manti, etc.; K13FF Manti, etc.; K24HJ-D Manti, etc.; K26IH-D Manti, etc.; K28NJ-D Manti, etc.; K07PE Mayfield; K09JH Mayfield; K11JK Mayfield; K13JP Mayfield; K15CD Mayfield; K08CC Mount Pleasant; K10CH Mount Pleasant; K12CC Mount Pleasant; K15HG-D Mount Pleasant; K19GN-D Mount Pleasant; K21IC-D Mount Pleasant; K23JM-D Mount Pleasant; K46HO-D Mount Pleasant; K48IL-D Mount Pleasant.

SANTA ROSA CHAMBER OF COMMERCE
PO Box 429
486 Parker Ave
Santa Rosa, NM 88435
LPTV Stations:
New Mexico: K64DV Santa Rosa.

VILLAGE OF SAVOONGA
5900 E. Tudor Rd.
Anchorage, AK 99507
Phone: 907-269-5744
LPTV Stations:
Alaska: K09NL Savoonga.

SCHINDLER COMMUNITY TV SERVICES
Box 297
Belcourt, ND 58316
Officers:
Fred Schindler Jr., Chairman
Sharon Trottier, Secretary-Treasurer
LPTV Stations:
North Dakota: K53DH Belcourt; K55FH Belcourt; K57EY Belcourt; K59DM Belcourt; K51EX Turtle Mountain Indian Reservation; K61EF Turtle Mountain Indian Reservation; K63ER

Turtle Mountain Indian Reservation; K65FE Turtle Mountain Indian Reservation.

LARRY L. SCHRECONGOST

Box 1032
Indiana, PA 15701-1032
Phone: 724-349-8849
LPTV Stations:
Pennsylvania: WLLS-LP Indiana.
Other Holdings:
Radio.

TOWN OF SCHROON

PO Box 578
Schroon Lake, NY 12870
Phone: 518-532-7737
LPTV Stations:
New York: W07BI Schroon Lake; W09BB Schroon Lake.

SCHURZ COMMUNICATIONS INC.

225 W. Colfax Ave.
South Bend, IN 46626
Phone: 574-287-1001
Fax: 574-287-2257
Web site: www.schurz.com
Officers:
Franklin D. Schurz Jr., Chairman
Scott C Schurz, Vice Chairman
Todd F Schurz, President & Chief Executive Officer
Marcia K. Burdick, Senior Vice President, Broadcasting
Gary N Hoipkemier, Senior Vice President, Secretary & Treasurer & Chief Financial Officer
Charles V Pittman, Senior Vice President, Publishing
James M Schurz, Senior Vice President
Sally J Brown, Vice President, Radio-Indiana
Hyler Cooper, Vice President, Digital Media
David C Ray, Vice President
Martin D Switalski, Vice President, Finance & Administration & Assistant Treasurer
Judy A Felty, Assistant Secretary
Ownership: Franklin D. Schurz Jr.; Mary Schurz; James M. Schurz; Scott C. Schurz, 75.2%. votes, Trustees; David C Ray, V.P., 15.2%. votes, 4.06% assets; Robin S Bruni, 9.6, votes, 4.37% assets%; Todd F Schurz, 7.36%. assets; Franklin D Schurz Jr, 7.14%. assets; Scott C Schurz, 3.76%. assets; Scott C Schurz Jr, 3.17%. assets.
Represented (legal): Wilmer Cutler Pickering Hale & Dorr LLP.
LPTV Stations:
Alaska: K04DS Kenai River; K10NC Kenai, etc.; K09JE Palmer.
Indiana: WBND-LD South Bend; WBND-LP South Bend.
Missouri: K17DL-D Branson; K15CZ Springfield.
Virginia: W04AG Garden City, etc..
Commercial TV Stations:
Alaska: KTUU-DT Anchorage.
Georgia: WAGT-DT Augusta.
Indiana: WSBT-DT South Bend.
Kansas: KBSD-DT Ensign; KBSL-DT Goodland; KBSH-DT Hays; KWCH-DT Hutchinson; KSCW-DT Wichita.
Missouri: KYTV-DT Springfield.
Virginia: WDBJ-DT Roanoke.
Cable Systems:
FLORIDA: CORAL SPRINGS; WESTON.
MARYLAND: HAGERSTOWN.
Newspapers:
California: Adelante Valle (El Centro), Imperial Valley Press
Indiana: Times Mail (Bedford), Herald Times (Bloomington), Reporter Times (Martinsville), Mooresville-Decatur Times, Noblesville Daily Times, South Bend Tribune

Kentucky: The Advocate-Messenger (Danville), The Jessamine Journal (Nicholasville), The Interior Journal (Stanford), The Winchester Sun
Maryland: Herald-Mail (Hagerstown)
Michigan: Charlevoix Courier, Gaylord Herald Times, The Petoskey News-Review
Pennsylvania: Daily American (Somerset)
South Dakota: American News (Aberdeen)
Radio Stations:
Indiana: WASK (AM), WHKY (AM), WKDA (AM), WXXB (FM) Lafayette; WNSN (FM), WSBT (AM) South Bend
South Dakota: KFXS (FM), KKLS (AM), KKMK (FM), KOUT (FM), KRCS (FM) Rapid City; KBHB (AM) Sturgis

SCIENCE OF IDENTITY FOUNDATION

PO Box 270450
Honolulu, HI 96827
Phone: 808-261-8815
Officer:
Jeannie Bishop, President
LPTV Stations:
Wisconsin: W08CK Madison-Middleton.

E. W. SCRIPPS CO.

312 Walnut St.
28th Floor
Cincinnati, OH 45202
Phone: 513-977-3000
Fax: 513-977-3721
Web site: www.scripps.com
Officers:
Nackey Scagliotti, Chairman
Richard A. Boehne, President & Chief Executive Officer
Brian Lawlor, President, Television Division
William Appleton, Senior Vice President & General Counsel
Mark G. Contreras, Senior Vice President, Newspapers
Lisa Knutson, Senior Vice President, Human Resources
William B. Peterson, Senior Vice President, Television
Timothy E. Stautberg, Senior Vice President & Chief Financial Officer
Robert A. Carson, Vice President & Chief Information Officer
David M. Giles, Vice President, Deputy Gen. Counsel
Michael T. Hales, Vice President, Audit & Compliance
Timothy A. King, Vice President, Corporate Communications & Investor Relations
Mary Denise Kuprionis, Vice President, Secretary & Chief Compliance & Ethics Officer
Douglas F. Lyons, Vice President & Controller
Ownership: The Edward W. Scripps Trust; Edward W. Scripps, Nackey E. Scagliotti & John Burlingame, Trustees, 87.5%. votes; 35.6 assets; The John P. Scripps Trust, Paul K. Scripps, Peter R. Ladow & Barbara Scripps Evans, Trustees, 7.9%. votes; 1.4% assets; Paul K. Scripps, 0.90% votes; remainder publicly held.. On July 1, 2008 Scripps' five cable networks (DIY Network, Fine Living Network, Food Network, Great American Country & HGTV) plus two online comparison shopping services (Shopzilla & uSwitch) split off to a publicly traded company, Scripps Networks Interactive.
Represented (legal): Baker Hostetler LLP.
LPTV Stations:
Arizona: K44CN Cottonwood; K52CM Flagstaff; K57FY Kingman; K47DJ Prescott.
Commercial TV Stations:
Arizona: KNXV-DT Phoenix.
Florida: WFTS-DT Tampa; WPTV-DT West Palm Beach.
Kansas: KMCI-DT Lawrence.
Maryland: WMAR-DT Baltimore.

Michigan: WXYZ-DT Detroit.
Missouri: KSHB-DT Kansas City.
Ohio: WCPO-DT Cincinnati; WEWS-DT Cleveland.
Oklahoma: KJRH-DT Tulsa.
Newspapers:
Alabama: Birmingham Post-Herald
California: Redding Record Searchlight, Ventura Star Newspapers
Colorado: Boulder Daily Camera, Denver Rocky Mountain News
Florida: Fort Pierce Tribune, Naples Daily News, The Stuart News, Vero Beach Press-Journal
Indiana: Evansville Courier-Press
Kentucky: The Kentucky Post
New Mexico: The Albuquerque Tribune
Ohio: The Cincinnati Post
South Carolina: Anderson Independent Mail
Tennessee: The Knoxville News Sentinel, The Commercial Appeal (Memphis)
Texas: Abilene Reporter News, Corpus Christi Caller-Times, Standard Times (San Angelo), Times Record News (Wichita Falls)
Washington: Bremerton Sun
Other Holdings:
Features syndicator: United Media, licensor & syndicator of news features & comics
Production: Scripps Productions, producer of cable programs.

CITY OF SELAWIK

Box 49
Selawik, AK 99770
Phone: 907-269-5744
LPTV Stations:
Alaska: K02JU Selawik.

SELECTIVE TV INC.

2308 S. Broadway
Box 665
Alexandria, MN 56308
Phone: 320-763-5924
Officers:
Merv Mock, President
Ann Malmgren, Secretary-Treasurer
Ownership: Non-profit organization--Alexandria, MN.
Represented (legal): Rosenman & Colin LLP.
LPTV Stations:
Minnesota: K14LZ Alexandria; K16CO Alexandria; K18DG Alexandria; K21GN Alexandria; K26CL Alexandria; K30AF Alexandria; K32EB Alexandria; K34AF Alexandria; K38AC Alexandria; K48DV Alexandria; K50DB Alexandria; K52DZ Alexandria; K55ID Alexandria; K58DS Alexandria; K60EJ Alexandria; K62AU Alexandria; K65HD Alexandria; K67HI Alexandria; K60AB Appleton.

SENDAS ANTIGUAS MINISTRIES INC.

1850 Mathias Ln
Kyle, TX 78640
Phone: 512-828-6862
Officer:
Gillermo Alvarez, President
LPTV Stations:
Texas: KZFB-LP Pampa.

SEVENTH DAY ADVENTIST COMMUNITY HEALTH SERVICES OF GREATER NEW YORK

351 Jackson St.
No. 9
Hempstead, NY 11550
Phone: 516-627-2210
Officers:
Richard Marker, President
Earl G. Knight, Executive Secretary
Rubin Merino, Director, Communications Services

Benjamin Santana, Treasurer
Ownership: Non-profit organization. Greater New York Corp. of Seventh Day Adventists.
Represented (legal): Donald E. Martin.
LPTV Stations:
New York: W32DF Hempstead.

SEVENTH TRUMPET BROADCASTING CORP.

Box 809
Kingshill, VI 00851
Phone: 340-778-4621
LPTV Stations:
Virgin Islands: WJWM-LP Christiansted.

SEVIER COUNTY

Courthouse Bldg.
Richfield, UT 84701
Phone: 435-896-9262
Officer:
Johnny C. Parsons, Technical Advisor
LPTV Stations:
Utah: K03DE Fish Lake Resort; K13YL Fishlake Resort; K47BD-D Juab County (rural); K03FF Koosharem; K38KA-D Koosharem; K39JD-D Koosharem; K43KM-D Koosharem; K47KR-D Koosharem; K49JP-D Koosharem; K03AS Richfield, etc.; K31JI-D Richfield, etc.; K32HU-D Richfield, etc.; K33JF-D Richfield, etc.; K34JA-D Richfield, etc.; K39JF-D Richfield, etc.; K58IR-D Richfield, etc.; K59IS-D Richfield/Monroe; K15FF-D Salina & Redmond; K17FC-D Salina & Redmond; K18HO-D Salina & Redmond; K22HY-D Salina & Redmond; K23FK-D Salina & Redmond; K16HE-D Sigurd & Salina; K20JA-D Sigurd & Salina; K43KN-D Sigurd & Salina; K43IJ Wayne County (rural).

CITY OF SEWARD

Box 167
Seward, AK 99664
LPTV Stations:
Alaska: K03FO Seward; K07PG Seward.

JOSEPH W. SHAFFER

Box 10310
Prescott, AZ 86304-0310
Phone: 928-717-0828
LPTV Stations:
Florida: W21BK Tallahassee.
New Mexico: K43HW Albuquerque.

VILLAGE OF SHAGELUK

5900 E. Tudor Rd.
Anchorage, AK 99507
Phone: 907-269-5744
LPTV Stations:
Alaska: K10KH Shageluk.

TIA SHAW

788 Riford Rd.
Craig, CO 81625
Phone: 970-826-2662
LPTV Stations:
Colorado: K27FA Craig.

DOUGLAS L. SHELDAHL

Box 201
Huxley, IA 50124
Phone: 515-597-3138
LPTV Stations:
Wisconsin: W44BF La Crosse.
Other Holdings:
TV-45 Inc., see listing.

TWYLA P. SHELDAHL TRUSTEE, R. B. SHELDAHL ESTATE
6825 N.W. 100th St.
Johnston, IA 50131
Phone: 515-986-3355
LPTV Stations:
Iowa: K39EX Iowa City.

SHENANDOAH VALLEY EDUCATIONAL TV CORP.
298 Port Republic Rd.
Harrisonburg, VA 22801
Phone: 703-434-5391
Officer:
Maurice J. Bresnahan, Chief Executive Officer
Ownership: Community owned.
Represented (legal): Covington & Burling.
LPTV Stations:
Virginia: W50CM Charlottesville; W45AW Fulks Run.
ETV Stations:
Virginia: WVPY-DT Front Royal; WVPT-DT Staunton.

SHERIDAN COUNTY, KS
PO Box 899
Hoxie, KS 67740
LPTV Stations:
Kansas: K69DB Hoxie, etc..

SHERIDAN COUNTY, MT
100 W. Laurel Ave.
Plentywood, MT 59254
Phone: 406-765-1660
LPTV Stations:
Montana: K46GS Plentywood.

SHERJAN BROADCASTING CO. INC.
1520 N.W. 79th Ave.
Miami, FL 33126
Phone: 305-381-8417
Officers:
Omar Romay, Chairman & Chief Executive Officer
Sherwin Grossman, President
Julio Defrancesco, Chief Operating Officer
Marcelo Soldano, Chief Financial Officer
Represented (legal): Freeman, Haber, Rojas & Stanham LLP.
LPTV Stations:
Florida: WJAN-CA Miami.

SHIELDS VALLEY TV TAX DISTRICT
439 Flathead Creek Rd.
Wilsall, MT 59086
Phone: 406-578-2066
Officers:
Bob Queen, Chairman
Tom Sarrazin, President
Kelly Woosley, Secretary-Treasurer
LPTV Stations:
Montana: K44DI Clyde Park, etc.; K17BT Livingston.

SHOO FLY TV TRANSLATOR STATION ASSOCIATION
PO Box 1011
Cooke City, MT 59020-1011
Phone: 406-838-2166
E-mail: sliebl@juno.com
LPTV Stations:
Montana: K11GE Cooke City, etc.; K13FW Cooke City, etc..

VILLAGE OF SHUNGNAK
Shungnak, AK 99773

LPTV Stations:
Alaska: K09NH Shungnak.

SIERRA GRANDE TV COOPERATIVE INC.
Box 187
Des Moines, NM 88418
LPTV Stations:
New Mexico: K44CG Capulin & Des Moines; K48JH Capulin & Des Moines; K50DY Capulin & Des Moines; K42CH Capulin, etc.; K46BY Capulin, etc..

SIERRA JOINT COMMUNITY COLLEGE DISTRICT
5000 Rocklin Rd.
Rocklin, CA 95677
Phone: 916-781-0406
Fax: 916-781-0455
Officers:
Kevin M. Ramirez, President & District Superintendent
Brian Haley, Dean, Learning Resources Center
Deborah Blue, Vice President, Instruction
John DeLury, Chief Financial Officer
LPTV Stations:
California: K16CX Grass Valley.

SIGNAL ABOVE LLC
8280 Greensboro Dr, 7th Fl
McLean, VA 22102-3807
Phone: 703-761-5013
Ownership: A. Wray Fitch III, 33.3%. votes, 16.67 assets; James A. Gammon, 33.3%. votes, 16.67 assets; George R. Grange II, 33.3%. votes, 16.67 assets; Elizabeth B. Fitch, 16.67%. assets; Joanne M. Gammon, 16.67%. assets; Kathy M. Grange, 16.67%. assets.
Represented (legal): Gammon & Grange PC.
LPTV Stations:
Virginia: WDCN-LP Fairfax.

MARK SILBERMAN
c/o MS Communications LLC, 1121 N. Waverly Place
Milwaukee, WI 53202
Phone: 414-765-9737
Represented (legal): Womble, Carlyle, Sandridge & Rice.
LPTV Stations:
North Dakota: K57JD Wilton.
Texas: K57JI Evant.
Other Holdings:
MS Communications LLC, see listing..

MARY R. SILVER
425 McFarland
Kerrville, TX 78029
Phones: 830-792-5842; 830-792-5100
Web site: www.kvhc.com
LPTV Stations:
Texas: KVHC-LP Kerrville.

SILVERTON BROADCASTING CO. LLC
116 Tigertail Rd.
Los Angeles, CA 90049
Phone: 310-476-2217
Ownership: Barry Silverton, Pres..
Represented (legal): Drinker Biddle.
LPTV Stations:
Wyoming: K69DD Bondurant; K56BT Jackson; K22CI Lander; K12IS Lusk; K55BL Sheridan, etc.; K13NZ Shoshoni; K35CV Shoshoni; K08AA Wyodak, etc..
Commercial TV Stations:
Wyoming: KTWO-DT Casper.

JAMES F. SIMPSON
23646 Wilderness Canyon Rd
Rapid City, SD 57702
Phone: 605-355-0024
LPTV Stations:
South Dakota: KAUN-LP Sioux Falls; KCWS-LP Sioux Falls.
Commercial TV Stations:
South Dakota: KWSD-DT Sioux Falls.

SINCLAIR BROADCAST GROUP INC.
10706 Beaver Dam Rd.
Cockeysville, MD 21030
Phone: 410-568-1500
Fax: 410-568-1533
E-mail: comments@sbgi.net
Web site: www.sbgi.net
Officers:
David D. Smith, President & Chief Executive Officer
David B. Amy, Executive Vice President & Chief Financial Officer
Barry M. Faber, Executive Vice President & General Counsel
Steve Marks, Vice President & Chief Operating Officer, Television Group
J. Duncan Smith, Vice President & Secretary
Frederick G. Smith, Vice President
Nat S. Ostroff, Vice President, New Technology
Lucy Rutishauser, Vice President, Corporate Finance & Treasurer
Donald H. Thompson, Vice President, Human Resources
Tom Waters, Vice President, Purchasing
Robert Malandra, Vice President, Finance & Television, Sinclair Television Group Inc.
David R. Bochenek, Chief Accounting Officer
Ownership: David D. Smith, 24.6% votes, 11.5% equity; J. Duncan Smith, 25.1%. votes, 11.4% equity; Frederick G. Smith, 19.2%. votes, 9.2% equity; Robert E. Smith, 17%. votes, 7.7% equity.
Represented (legal): Pillsbury Winthrop Shaw Pittman LLP.
LPTV Stations:
Alabama: W62BG Birmingham.
Iowa: K13MN Washington.
Nevada: K51AC Pahrump.
New York: W16AX Ithaca.
North Carolina: W06AQ Bat Cave, etc.; W12AQ Black Mountain; W05AP Brasstown, etc.; W08AN Bryson City, etc.; W12AU Burnsville; W05AF Cherokee; W11AJ Franklin; W12CI Hot Springs; W06AP Maggie Valley, etc.; W10AP Marion, etc.; W06AL Oteen/Warren; W11AQ Robbinsville, etc.; W06AN Sapphire Valley, etc.; W06AD Spruce Pine; W05AE Sylva, etc.; W05AC Tryon, etc.; W12AR Waynesville, etc..
Ohio: W66AQ Dayton.
South Carolina: W05AO Pickens.
Commercial TV Stations:
Alabama: WABM-DT Birmingham; WTTO-DT Homewood.
Florida: WFGX-DT Fort Walton Beach; WEAR-DT Pensacola; WTWC-DT Tallahassee.
Illinois: WYZZ-DT Bloomington; WICD-DT Champaign; WICS-DT Springfield.
Iowa: KGAN-DT Cedar Rapids; KDSM-DT Des Moines.
Kentucky: WDKY-DT Danville.
Maine: WGME-DT Portland.
Maryland: WBFF-DT Baltimore.
Michigan: WSMH-DT Flint.
Minnesota: WUCW-DT Minneapolis.
Missouri: KBSI-DT Cape Girardeau; KDNL-DT St. Louis.
Nevada: KVCW-DT Las Vegas; KVMY-DT Las Vegas.
New York: WNYO-DT Buffalo; WUTV-DT Buffalo; WUHF-DT Rochester; WSYT-DT Syracuse.
North Carolina: WLOS-DT Asheville; WRDC-DT Durham; WMYV-DT Greensboro; WLFL-DT Raleigh; WXLV-DT Winston-Salem.
Ohio: WSTR-DT Cincinnati; WSYX-DT Columbus; WKEF-DT Dayton.
Oklahoma: KOCB-DT Oklahoma City; KOKH-DT Oklahoma City.
Pennsylvania: WPGH-DT Pittsburgh; WPMY-DT Pittsburgh.
South Carolina: WMMP-DT Charleston.
Tennessee: WUXP-DT Nashville; WZTV-DT Nashville.
Texas: KMYS-DT Kerrville; KABB-DT San Antonio.
Virginia: WTVZ-DT Norfolk; WRLH-DT Richmond.
West Virginia: WCHS-DT Charleston.
Wisconsin: WMSN-DT Madison; WCGV-DT Milwaukee; WVTV-DT Milwaukee.

SIOUXLAND CHRISTIAN BROADCASTING
1000 E. 41st St.
Sioux Falls, SD 57105
Phone: 605-332-5565
Officers:
Mike Nichols, Chairman
Roy L. McGreevy, Chief Executive Officer
Roger Swanson, Secretary-Treasurer
Ownership: Non-profit corp--Sioux Falls, SD.
Represented (legal): Woods, Fuller, Shultz & Smith PC.
LPTV Stations:
South Dakota: K53EG Sioux Falls.

SITKA SCHOOL DISTRICT
300 Kostromenioff St.
Sitka, AK 99835
Phone: 907-747-8622
Fax: 907-966-1260
Officer:
John Holst, Superintendent
LPTV Stations:
Alaska: K03GJ Sitka.

SLATER BUTTE TRANSLATOR CO.
Box 185
Happy Camp, CA 96039-0185
LPTV Stations:
California: K07IX Happy Camp; K09PI Happy Camp, etc.; K11GO Happy Camp, etc.; K13GL Happy Camp, etc..

SLEETMUTE VILLAGE COUNCIL
5900 E. Tudor Rd.
Anchorage, AK 99507
Phone: 907-269-5744
LPTV Stations:
Alaska: K12MD Sleetmute.

MICHAEL A. SLEEZER
101 Park St.
Gloversville, NY 12078
LPTV Stations:
New York: WFNY-CA Gloversville.

BOB SMARTT
217 W. Commerce St.
Lewisburg, TN 37091
Phone: 931-359-6641
LPTV Stations:
Tennessee: W34DB Lewisburg.

FRANCES S. SMITH
c/o NCN Cable Advertising
2911 Shortcut Rd.
Pascagoula, MS 39567
Phone: 228-762-0464
Fax: 228-769-7771
Web site: www.WKFK.com

LPTV Stations:
Mississippi: WKFK-LD Pascagoula.

JOHN W. SMITH JR.
515 Potters Lane
Clarksville, IN 47129
Phone: 812-284-9595
Represented (legal): Hardy, Carey, Chautin & Balkin LLP.
LPTV Stations:
Indiana: WNDA-CA Clarksville; WJYL-CA Jeffersonville, etc..

SMITH MEDIA LICENSE HOLDINGS LLC
One Federal St., 23rd Floor
Boston, MA 02110
Phone: 617-350-1500
Ownership: Smith Media LLC; SMLLC ownership:; Frontyard Management LLC, 55.56%. votes; Smith Television of New York Inc., 44.44%. votes; FMLLC ownership:; Barry Baker; Roy F. Coppedge III; Barbara M. Ginader, 33.3%. each; STONYI ownership:; Robert N. & Anne Smith Trust; RNAST ownership:; Leslie J. Goldman, Trustee, 25%; Anne Smith, Trustee, 25%; Jennifer Smith, Special Trustee, 25%; Michael D. Smith, Special Trustee, 25%.
Represented (legal): Dow Lohnes PLLC.
LPTV Stations:
Alaska: K13KU Delta Junction; K13OC Douglas, etc.; K03FW Kenai, etc.; K13MZ Usibelli, etc..
California: K57BC San Luis Obispo, etc.; KSBB-LP Santa Barbara.
Commercial TV Stations:
Alaska: KIMO-DT Anchorage; KATN-DT Fairbanks; KJUD-DT Juneau.
California: KEYT-DT Santa Barbara.
New York: WKTV-DT Utica.
Vermont: WFFF-DT Burlington.

TERRY SMITH
PO Box 67
Linville, NC 28646
Phone: 828-733-2409
LPTV Stations:
North Carolina: WLNN-LP Boone.

SMOKE AND MIRRORS LLC
No. 10 Media Center Dr.
Lake Havasu City, AZ 86403
Phone: 928-855-1051
Ownership: Rick L. Murphy, Managing Member.
Represented (legal): Koerner & Olender PC.
LPTV Stations:
Arizona: K16GB Kingman; KBBA-LP Lake Havasu City.
Nevada: K67HO Laughlin.

SMOKY HILLS PUBLIC TELEVISION CORP.
604 Elm St.
Box 9
Bunker Hill, KS 67626
Phone: 785-483-6990
Fax: 785-483-4605
Officers:
Belita Donahue, Chairman
Lawrence Holden, Chief Executive Officer
Nicholas V. Slechta, Executive Director & General Manager
Russell Townsley, Secretary
Weller Randall, Secretary
Mary Anderson, Treasurer
Mitchell O'Leary, Treasurer
Represented (legal): Dow Lohnes PLLC.

LPTV Stations:
Kansas: K64BS Concordia; K66CD Phillipsburg.
ETV Stations:
Kansas: KWKS-DT Colby; KDCK-DT Dodge City; KOOD-DT Hays; KSWK-DT Lakin.

SMOKY VALLEY TV DISTRICT
Box 1517
Round Mountain, NV 89045-1517
Phone: 702-377-2044
Officers:
Charles H. Coleman, Chairman & Technical Director
Dan Zampirro, Vice Chairman
Ben Canfield, Secretary-Treasurer
Ownership: Non-profit, community-supported organization.
LPTV Stations:
Nevada: K42EK Round Mountain; K45EY Round Mountain; K55HQ Round Mountain; K58FM Round Mountain; K61GL Round Mountain; K63FP Round Mountain.

SODA MOUNTAIN BROADCASTING INC.
2295 Coburg Rd.
Suite 200
Eugene, OR 97401
Phone: 541-485-5611
Officers:
Carolyn S. Chambers, Chairman & Chief Executive Officer
Scott Chambers, President & Chief Operating Officer
John C. Ohm, Secretary-Treasurer
James Plummer, Chief Financial Officer
Ownership: Carolyn S. Chambers, see Chambers Communications Corp.
LPTV Stations:
California: K36HM Fort Dick; K17BA Yreka, etc..
Oregon: K52AS Altamont, etc.; K51BV Cave Junction, etc.; K68BB Gold Beach; K46CH Gold Hill; K15BP Grants Pass; K21BG-D Jacksonville; K13UR Klamath Falls; K20BI Nesika Beach; K02IQ Squaw Valley, etc..

SON BROADCASTING INC.
PO Box 4338
Albuquerque, NM 87196
Phone: 505-345-1991
Fax: 505-474-4998
E-mail: annette@kchf.com
Officers:
Annette Garcia, President
Richard Shakarian, Vice President
Angie Gonzales, Vice President
Marcimilliano Baca, Vice President & Treasurer
Clem M. Dixon, Secretary
Ownership: Vickie Archeveque; Dinah Baca; Annette Garcia; Joanna Gonzales; Mary Kay Gonzales; Ted Gonzales; Warren Trumbly, 14.29%. votes each.
Represented (legal): Gammon & Grange PC.
LPTV Stations:
New Mexico: K51DM Antonito; K28CE Socorro; K43IA Taos.
Commercial TV Stations:
New Mexico: KCHF-DT Santa Fe.

SONRISE COMMUNICATIONS INC.
308 Pine St.
West Monroe, LA 71291
Phone: 318-323-4668

LPTV Stations:
Louisiana: KWMS-LP West Monroe.

SORENSEN TELEVISION SYSTEMS INC.
111 Chalen Santo Papa
Suite 800
Hagatna, GU 96910
Phone: 671-477-5700
Officers:
Rex W. Sorensen, Chairman & President
John Anderson, President, News Division
Curtis Dancoe, Vice President
Margaret Agulto, Secretary
Ownership: Rex W. Sorensen, 97.58%; John Anderson, 2.4%; Curtis Dancoe, .02%.
Represented (legal): Kaye Scholer LLP.
LPTV Stations:
Guam: KEQI-LP Dededo.
Mariana Islands: KPPI-LP Garapan & Saipan.
Commercial TV Stations:
Guam: KTGM-DT Tamuning.

SOUTH CENTRAL COMMUNICATIONS CORP.
PO Box 3848
Evansville, IN 47736-3848
Phone: 812-424-8284
Officers:
John D. Engelbrecht, President, Chief Executive & Operating Officer
Robert Shirel, Chief Financial Officer

Branch Offices:
1100 Sharps Ridge
Box 27100
Knoxville, TN 37927
Phone: 865-525-6000
504 Rosedale Ave
Box 40506
Nashville, TN 37204
Phone: 615-259-9393
Ownership: John D Engelbrecht, 80%; John P Engelbrecht, 19%; Bettie A Engelbrecht, 1%.
Represented (legal): Fletcher, Heald & Hildreth PLC.
LPTV Stations:
Kentucky: W50CI Louisville.
Tennessee: WEZK-LP Knoxville; WJDE-LP Nashville; WRMX-LP Nashville; WJZC-LP Sevierville.
Radio Stations:
Indiana: WABX (FM), WEOA (AM), WIKY-FM, WLFW (FM) Evansville.
Kentucky: WSTO (FM) Owensboro.
Tennessee: WIMZ-FM, WJXB-FM Knoxville; WQJK (FM) Marysville; WCJK (FM) Murfreesboro; WJXA (FM) Nashville; WRJK (FM) Norris

SOUTH CENTRAL ELECTRIC ASSN.
County Rd. W
Box 150
St. James, MN 56081
Phone: 507-375-3164
LPTV Stations:
Minnesota: K14KD Frost; K18EY Frost; K19GW Frost; K27FI Frost; K31EF Frost; K34JZ-D Frost; K36FI Frost; K51KB Frost.

SOUTH DAKOTA BOARD OF DIRECTORS FOR EDUCATIONAL TELECOMMUNICATIONS
Cherry & Dakota Sts.
Box 5000
Vermillion, SD 57069-5000
Phone: 605-677-5861
Fax: 605-677-5010
Web site: www.sdpb.org
Officers:

Julie Anderson, Executive Director
Bob Bosse, Television Director
Terry Spencer, Development Director
Fritz Miller, Marketing Director
Carol Robertson, Marketing Director
Brian Blevins, Promotion Producer
Amber Anders, Continuity Manager
Ownership: Julie Andersen; Otto Doll; Joseph Dondelinger; Kay Jorgensen; Rick Knobe; David Law; Robert Perry; Mark Shlanta; Sue White; Glenda Woodburn, Directors.
Represented (legal): Cohn & Marks LLP.
LPTV Stations:
South Dakota: K07JD Aberdeen; K20FT Belle Fourche; K64AL Edgemont; K09UN Mitchell; K06HG Pine Ridge; K55AV Pringle; K17ES Spearfish; K50FH Wagner; K13PN Wasta.
ETV Stations:
South Dakota: KDSD-DT Aberdeen; KESD-DT Brookings; KPSD-DT Eagle Butte; KQSD-DT Lowry; KZSD-DT Martin; KTSD-DT Pierre; KBHE-DT Rapid City; KCSD-DT Sioux Falls; KUSD-DT Vermillion.
Radio Stations:
South Dakota: KZSD-FM; KUSD-FM; KTSD-FM; KQSD-FM; KPSD-FM; KHBE (FM); KESD (FM); KDSD (FM)

SOUTHEAST ISLAND SCHOOL DISTRICT
5900 E. Tudor Rd.
Anchorage, AK 99507
Phone: 907-269-5744
LPTV Stations:
Alaska: K09NP Cape Pole.

SOUTHERN GREENLEE COUNTY TV ASSN. INC.
Box 440
222 N. Hwy. 75
Duncan, AZ 85534
Phone: 520-359-2503
LPTV Stations:
Arizona: K33DA Duncan; K35CP Duncan; K39CM Duncan; K41CV Duncan; K43CN Duncan; K47DA Duncan; K49CH Duncan; K51DG Duncan; K53DL Duncan; K55DM Duncan, etc.; K57CU Duncan, etc.; K65CM Duncan, etc.; K67CP Duncan, etc.; K69DG Duncan, etc.; K02FV York, etc.; K07IR York, etc.; K11JJ York, etc..

SOUTHERN MEDIA ASSOCIATES INC.
192 W Pine St
Jessup, GA 31545
Phone: 912-294-2130
Officer:
Bill G. Garlen, President
LPTV Stations:
Georgia: WPHJ-CA Vidalia.

SOUTHERN OREGON PUBLIC TELEVISION INC.
34 S. Fir St.
Box 4688
Medford, OR 97501
Phone: 541-779-0808
Fax: 541-779-2178
Officers:
William R. Campbell, President & Chief Executive Officer
Patrick Drysdale, Chief Financial Officer
Don McKay, Chief Operating Officer & Engineering Director
Peter Sage, Secretary
Rick Holcom, Treasurer
LPTV Stations:
Oregon: K18EP Brookings, etc.; K02JF Butte Falls; K13PH Cave Junction; K22IQ-D

Cave Junction; K55DQ Gold Hill, etc.; K12KX Grants Pass; K18AN Grants Pass; K19HS-D Grants Pass; K07RQ Jacksonville; K04KI Merrill, etc.; K34DJ Phoenix; K13PF Pinehurst; K02JG Prospect; K13PI Ruch & Applegate; K13PE Shady Cove; K02JJ Williams.

ETV Stations:
Oregon: KFTS-DT Klamath Falls.

SOUTHERN TV CORP.
9661 82nd Ave. N
Seminole, FL 33777
Phone: 727-319-6100
Fax: 727-397-0785
Officers:
Dan L. Johnson, Chairman, President & Chief Executive Officer
Charles E. Robb, Chief Operating & Financial Officer
Jo Johnson, Vice President
Robert G. Keelean, Secretary-Treasurer
Ownership: Betty Johnson, 42.5%; Dan L. Johnson; Robert G. Keelean, 30%; Kim Doniel, 10%; William Doniel; Lisa Keelean, 5%; Robert G. Keelean Jr., 5%; Mabel Reed Young, 5%; Donald Chervier, 2.5%.
Represented (legal): Irwin, Campbell & Tannenwald PC.
LPTV Stations:
Georgia: W41CR Hinesville-Richmond; WGCW-LP Savannah; WGSA-CA Savannah; W25CQ Statesboro.
Commercial TV Stations:
Georgia: WGSA-DT Baxley.

SOUTH FORK TV ASSOCIATION
925 6th St.
Room 207
Del Norte, CO 81132-3243
Phone: 719-657-2744
E-mail: rgcommissioner@riograndecounty.org
LPTV Stations:
Colorado: K41DJ Del Norte & South Fork; K02EX South Fork, etc.; K18DE South Fork, etc.; K57BW South Fork, etc..

SOUTH LANE TV INC.
PO Box 301
Cottage Grove, OR 97424
Phone: 541-942-9804
E-mail: mark_buckbee@blm.gov
LPTV Stations:
Oregon: K14LP Cottage Grove; K18EA Cottage Grove; K20IR-D Cottage Grove; K22HO-D Cottage Grove; K40IS-D Cottage Grove; K42HK-D Cottage Grove; K46IP-D Cottage Grove; K47AV Cottage Grove; K48KC-D Cottage Grove; K50CT Cottage Grove; K11KI Disston; K04GR Dorena; K02GL Dorena, etc.; K51EY London Springs; K53FJ London Springs; K55HE London Springs; K57GW London Springs; K59FS London Springs.

SOUTH SEAS BROADCASTING INC.
9408 Grand Gate St.
Las Vegas, NV 89143-1397
Phone: 702-898-4669
Fax: 208-567-6865
Web site: www.southseasbroadcasting.com
Officer:
Larry G. Fuss, President
LPTV Stations:
American Samoa: KKHJ-LP Pago Pago.
Radio Stations:
American Samoa: KKHJ (FM); WVUV (AM)

SOUTHWEST COLORADO TV TRANSLATOR ASSN.
c/o Wayne Johnson
Box 1570
Cortez, CO 81321-1570
Phone: 970-565-2129
Web site: www.swcotv.org
Ownership: State government entity.
Represented (legal): Garvey Schubert Barer.
LPTV Stations:
Colorado: K07UY Cortez; K09DM Cortez; K14JS-D Cortez; K16CT-D Cortez; K24CH-D Cortez; K25JN-D Cortez; K26CI-D Cortez; K27IG-D Cortez; K29GO-D Cortez; K31CT Cortez; K32IJ Cortez; K33JL-D Cortez; K39EY-D Cortez; K49EQ-D Cortez; K51DB-D Cortez; K55KN-D Cortez; K35CH-D Cortez & Mancos, etc.; K11LP Cortez; K18DR-D Cortez, etc.; K22CU-D Cortez, etc.; K24HY Cortez, etc.; K28EB-D Cortez, etc.; K30HJ-D Cortez, etc.; K52KF-D Cortez, etc.; K53JP-D Cortez, etc.; K56JI-D Cortez, etc.; K57KA-D Cortez, etc.; K58IV-D Cortez, Mancos, etc.; K02OG Dolores; K04NK Dolores; K05GA Dolores; K06NT Dolores; K08LL Dolores; K10MZ Dolores; K12QH Dolores; K13AT Dolores; K15GU Dove Creek; K17GE Dove Creek; K19GB Dove Creek; K21GT Dove Creek; K23GF Dove Creek; K30DC Dove Creek; K32EY Dove Creek; K34IA Dove Creek; K48BK Dove Creek; K02QI Hesperus; K04PJ Hesperus; K13XX Hesperus; K02OU Ismay Canyon; K04OO Ismay Canyon; K05JW Ismay Canyon; K10NY Ismay Canyon; K13XG Ismay Canyon; K02OS Weber Canyon; K04ON Weber Canyon; K08MB Weber Canyon; K10OD Weber Canyon; K13XH Weber Canyon.

SOUTHWESTERN ADVENTIST U.
Keene, TX 76059
Phone: 817-556-4764
Fax: 817-556-4744
LPTV Stations:
Texas: KGSW-LP Keene.

SOUTHWEST MEDIA LLC
845 E Red Hills Pkwy
St. George, UT 84770
Phone: 435-634-7500
Ownership: Stephen W Wade, Mgr.. votes; 6.98% assets.
Represented (legal): Garvey Schubert Barer.
LPTV Stations:
Utah: K16DS St. George.
Commercial TV Stations:
Utah: KCSG-DT Cedar City.

SPANISH BROADCASTING SYSTEM INC.
2601 S. Bayshore Dr.
Penthouse 2
Coconut Grove, FL 33133
Phone: 305-441-6901
Officers:
Raul Alarcon Jr., Chairman, President & Chief Executive Officer
Marko Radlovic, Chief Operating Officer
Joseph A. Garcia, Executive Vice President, Secretary & Chief Financial Officer
William B. Tanner, Executive Vice President, Programming
Ownership: Raul Alarcon Jr., 78.8%. vote; 32.5% equity; Pablo Raul Alarcon Sr., 3.6%. vote; 1.5% equity.
Represented (legal): Kaye Scholer LLP.
LPTV Stations:
Florida: WSBS-CA Miami.
Commercial TV Stations:
Florida: WSBS-DT Key West.

SPANISH INDEPENDENT BROADCAST NETWORK LLC
5030 E. Warner Rd.
Suite 3
Phoenix, AZ 85044-3372
Phone: 480-961-4353
LPTV Stations:
Arizona: K38IZ-D Phoenix.

MARY SPARACIO
813 Eaton Ln
Rear House Down the Lane
Key West, FL 33040
Phone: 305-849-2188
LPTV Stations:
Florida: WTVK-LP Key West.

SPECIALTY BROADCASTING CORP.
Box 418
Winter Park, FL 32790
Phone: 407-740-8422
LPTV Stations:
Florida: WSWF-LP Union Park.

SPECTRUM MEDIA
605 Green Meadow
Colleyville, TX 76034
Ownership: Mary H Atkins.
LPTV Stations:
Texas: K56DF Amarillo.

THE SPIRIT OF THE LORD MINISTRIES
PO Box 21058
Cheyenne, WY 82003
Phone: 307-632-5882
E-mail: tsotlordm@aol.com
Officer:
Andrew Baktamarian, President
LPTV Stations:
Wyoming: KGSC-LP Cheyenne.

SPIRIT PRODUCTIONS INC.
Box 3161
Tequesta, FL 33469
Phone: 561-746-0170
Fax: 561-575-5360
LPTV Stations:
Florida: WALO-LP Jupiter.

SPOKANE SCHOOL DISTRICT NO. 81
N. 200 Bernard St.
Spokane, WA 99201
Phone: 509-353-5777
Ownership: Public school district governed by 5 elected dirs..
LPTV Stations:
Idaho: K44EC Coeur d'Alene; K53GN Lewiston; K24DW Sandpoint.
Montana: K32EU Missoula.
Washington: K61AY Baker Flats area.
ETV Stations:
Washington: KSPS-DT Spokane.

SPOKANE TELEVISION INC.
500 W. Boone Ave.
Spokane, WA 99201
Phone: 509-324-4000
Fax: 509-328-5274
Ownership: Evening Telegram Co.. ETC is also principal of Morgan Murphy Stations, see listing.
Represented (legal): Rini Coran PC.
LPTV Stations:
Idaho: KMNZ-LP Coeur d'Alene; K45FZ Lewiston.

Washington: KUMN-LP Moses Lake; KXMN-LD Spokane, etc.; KXMN-LP Spokane, etc.; K32FN Wenatchee.

SPRINT NEXTEL CORP.
2001 Edmund Halley Dr
Attn: Robin Cohen
Reston, VA 20191
Phone: 703-433-4000
E-mail: robin.cohen@sprint.com
Officer:
Lawrence R. Krevor, Vice President
Ownership: Sprint Nextel Corp..
LPTV Stations:
Florida: W26BN Melbourne.

SP TELEVISION LLC
2 Greenwich Plaza
Greenwich, CT 06830
Phone: 203-542-4200
Ownership: Edward Mule'; Robert O'Shea, Members & mgrs.. Both Mule' and O'Shea are principals of Granite Broadcasting Corp., see listing.
Represented (legal): Dow Lohnes PLLC.
LPTV Stations:
Florida: WEVU-CA Fort Myers; WLZE-LP Fort Myers; WUVF-CA Naples.
Minnesota: WTMS-CA Minneapolis; WUMN-CA Minneapolis.
Missouri: KUKC-LP Kansas City.

SQUIRREL BROADCASTING LLC
16 San Filippo Circle
Rochester, NY 14625
Phone: 585-671-8576
E-mail: djsmiz@rochester.rr.com
Ownership: Craig L. Fox, 50%; James J. Smisloff, 50%.
Represented (legal): James L. Oyster.
LPTV Stations:
New York: WAWW-LP Rochester.

CITY OF ST. MARY'S
5900 E. Tudor Rd.
Anchorage, AK 99507
Phone: 907-269-5744
LPTV Stations:
Alaska: K07RK St. Mary's.

STAINLESS BROADCASTING LP
2111 University Park Dr.
Suite 650
Okemos, MI 48864-6913
Phone: 517-347-4141
Officers:
Brian W. Brady, President & Chief Executive Officer
Fred L. Levy, Secretary
William Quarles, Chief Financial Officer & Treasurer
Ownership: Stainless Broadcasting Co., Gen. Partner. 100% votes; 1% equity; Stainless Broadcasting LLC, Ltd. Partner, 99%. equity; SBC ownership:; Brian W. Brady, SBLLC ownership:; Stainless Broadcasting Co.. 100% votes; 1% equity; Northwest Broadcasting LP, 99%. equity; NBLP & SBC ownership:; Brian W. Brady. Brady is also a principal of Broadcasting Licenses LP & Mountain Licenses LP, see listings.
Represented (legal): Leventhal, Senter & Lerman PLLC.
LPTV Stations:
New York: WBPN-LP Binghamton.
Commercial TV Stations:
New York: WICZ-DT Binghamton.

STANFORD TV ASSOCIATION
PO Box 507
Stanford, MT 59479

LPTV Stations:
Montana: K07AV Stanford; K11AQ Stanford.

VILLAGE OF STAPLETON
PO Box 86
Stapleton, NE 69163
LPTV Stations:
Nebraska: K12KW Stapleton.

STARCOM INC.
1986 Julep Rd.
St. Cloud, MN 56301
Phone: 320-650-1600
Fax: 320-255-5276
Officers:
Dennis Carpenter, President & Chief Executive Officer
Bart Ward, Secretary-Treasurer
LPTV Stations:
Minnesota: WCMN-LP St. Cloud-Sartell.

STAR NEWS CORP.
PO Box 5146
6 Hollywood Blvd
Martinsville, VA 24115
Phone: 276-656-3900
Officers:
Azile Roark, President
Charles Roark, Vice President
Represented (legal): Wood, Maines & Nolan Chartered.
LPTV Stations:
North Carolina: WGSR-LP Reidsville.
Virginia: W18BG Danville.

STATION VENTURE OPERATIONS LP
1299 Pennsylvania Ave. NW
11th Floor
Washington, DC 20004
Phone: 202-637-4545
Ownership: NBC Telemundo License Co., Gen. Partner, 0.25% equity, 100% votes; Station Venture Holdings LLC, Ltd. Partner, 99.75% equity; NBCTLC ownership:; NBC Telemundo Inc.; NBCTI ownership:; NBC Telemundo Holding Co., 20% assets, 55.6% votes; NBC Universal Inc., see listing, 80% assets, 44.4% votes; NBCUI ownership:; NBC Holding Inc., 80%; NBCHI & NBCTHC ownership:; General Electric Co.; GEC ownership:; publicly held.; SVHLLC ownership:; NBC Telemundo License Co., 79.62%; LIN Television Corp., see listing, 20.38%.
LPTV Stations:
California: KNSD-LP La Jolla.
Commercial TV Stations:
California: KNSD-DT San Diego.
Texas: KXAS-DT Fort Worth.

LYDIA SYLVANE STOCKWELL
107 Grant St.
Plainfield, MA 01070
Phone: 413-634-5688
Fax: 413-634-5638
LPTV Stations:
Massachusetts: W35BK Plainfield.

STONY RIVER TRADITIONAL COUNCIL
5900 E. Tudor Rd.
Anchorage, AK 99507
Phone: 907-269-5744
LPTV Stations:
Alaska: K02JZ Stony River.

STOREFRONT TELEVISION LLC
1040 N. Las Palmas
Hollywood, CA 90038
Phone: 323-930-1908

Fax: 323-933-1191
E-mail: bass@lkkgroup.com
Web site: www.lkkgroup.com
Ownership: LKK Group Corp., 50%%; Bluewater LLC, 50%%; LKKGC ownership:; Keith Bass, 50%; Paulette Bass, 50%; BLLC ownership:; Scott Adelson; Michael Kramer; John Mavredakis, 33.3% each.
Represented (legal): Womble, Carlyle, Sandridge & Rice.
LPTV Stations:
Puerto Rico: WSJP-LP Aguadilla; WPRU-LP Aquadilla; WSJX-LP Aquadilla.
Commercial TV Stations:
Virgin Islands: WVXF-DT Charlotte Amalie.

PAUL STRIEBY
502 Sterling Dr.
San Leandro, CA 94578
Phone: 510-352-3110
LPTV Stations:
California: KBIT-LD Chico.

STUDIO 51 MULTIMEDIA PRODUCTIONS LTD.
390 E Center St
Marion, OH 43302
Phone: 740-383-1165
E-mail: office@marionohio.tv
Officers:
Ron Scheiderer, President
Andy Russell, Vice President, Managing Member
Dennis Potts, Vice President
Herbert Reed, Vice President
Richard Rees, Vice President
Anita C. Ritchie, Vice President
Lynn A. Thomas, Vice President
Ownership: Ron Scheiderer, 81.63%; Herbert Reed, 5.44%; Dennis Potts, 3.8%; Richard Rees, 3.8%; Andy Russell, 2.17%; Anita C. Ritchie, 2.07%; Lynn A. Thomas, 1.09%.
LPTV Stations:
Ohio: WBKA-CA Bucyrus.

STUDIO 5 INC.
72 Hillcrest Rd.
Portage, IN 46368
Phone: 219-763-7211
Fax: 219-763-6349
E-mail: ttittle@magnetsigns.com
Officer:
Thomas W. Tittle, Secretary-Treasurer
LPTV Stations:
Indiana: WODN-LP Portage.

SUBLETTE COUNTY
PO Box 98
Big Piney, WY 83113
Phone: 307-276-3486
Officer:
Jane Wardell, Chairman
LPTV Stations:
Wyoming: K24DA Big Piney, etc.; K33JQ-D Big Piney, etc.; K14IL Pinedale, etc.; K16CS Pinedale, etc.; K19HJ-D Pinedale, etc..

SULA TV DISTRICT
PO Box 15
Sula, MT 59871
LPTV Stations:
Montana: K03GW Sula, etc.; K05JE Sula, etc..

SUMMIT COUNTY
County Courthouse
Coalville, UT 84017
Phone: 435-336-3220

LPTV Stations:
Utah: K35HH Coalville; K24GF Coalville & adjacent area; K28IP Coalville & adjacent area; K29FY Henefer & Echo; K31HR Henefer & Echo; K31FQ-D Park City; K33FY-D Park City; K39HP-D Park City; K15FL-D Park City, etc.; K27GD-D Park City, etc.; K29II-D Park City, etc.; K03HQ Samak; K31HH Samak; K33HP Samak; K49FY Summit County; K51FY Summit County; K63GY Summit County (rural); K31HG Wanship; K33HQ Wanship; K23HS Woodland & Kamas.

SUMMIT MEDIA INC.
4766 S Holiday Blvd
Holiday, UT 84117
Phone: 801-577-1322
Ownership: Rubin Rodriguez Jr., Pres..
LPTV Stations:
Tennessee: W28BO Acton.

SUMMIT PUBLIC RADIO & TV INC.
PO Box 6392
Breckenridge, CO 80424-6392
Phone: 970-453-1236
LPTV Stations:
Colorado: K10PM Breckenridge.

SUMMIT TV IMPROVEMENT ASSOCIATION
324 Matthew Loop
Condon, MT 59826
LPTV Stations:
Montana: K07GM Condon.

SUNBELT COMMUNICATIONS CO.
1500 Foremaster Lane
Las Vegas, NV 89101
Phone: 702-657-3423
Fax: 702-657-3423
Officers:
James E. Rogers, Chairman & Chief Executive Officer
Beverly Rogers, Vice Chairman & Executive Officer
Ralph Toddre, President & Chief Operating Officer
Bill Fouch, Executive Vice President
Shelley Goings, Secretary
Scott Mattox, Treasurer
JoAnn Haneman, Assistant Secretary
Ownership: James E. Rogers, Trustee of the James E. Rogers Trust, 95.22%; Beverly Rogers, Trustee of the Beverly Rogers Trust, 2.66%; James E. Rogers, Trustee for the Children of Elizabeth Ruybalid, 2.12%.
Represented (legal): Luvaas Cobb PC.
LPTV Stations:
California: K33CN South Lake Tahoe; K56BW Tahoe City.
Idaho: K07UL Burley; K39GV Burley, etc.; K08KV Jerome; K04NO Paul; K02NO Rupert.
Montana: KBGF-LP Great Falls.
Nevada: K06KD Austin; K52DN Carson City; K16GK Ely; K58BC Ely, etc.; K57BU Eureka; K13QV Fallon; K40CQ Laughlin; K52AC Mercury & Nevada Test Site; K50CM North Shore Lake Tahoe; K44AA Pahrump.
Wyoming: KCHY-LP Cheyenne; K14LK Laramie; KHDE-LP Laramie; KSWY-LP Sheridan.
Commercial TV Stations:
Arizona: KYMA-DT Yuma.
Idaho: KPVI-DT Pocatello; KXTF-DT Twin Falls.
Montana: KBBJ-DT Havre; KTVH-DT Helena; KBAO-DT Lewistown.
Nevada: KENV-DT Elko; KVBC-DT Las Vegas; KRNV-DT Reno; KWNV-DT Winnemucca.
Wyoming: KCWY-DT Casper; KCWY-DT Casper; KJWY-DT Jackson.

SUNCOAST BROADCASTING OF LAFAYETTE COUNTY INC.
Box 644
Mayo, FL 32066
Phone: 904-294-2525
LPTV Stations:
Florida: W33BL Chiefland.

SUNNYCREST MEDIA INC.
2172 Chapel Pike
Marion, IN 46952
Phone: 765-668-1014
Officers:
Ron B. Smith, President
David Trimble, Vice President
Ray Bradford, Secretary-Treasurer
Ownership: Sunnycrest Baptist Church.
LPTV Stations:
Indiana: WSOT-LP Marion.

SUNSHINE BROADCASTING CO. INC.
1903 S. Greeley Hwy.
Suite 127
Cheyenne, WY 82007
Phone: 603-279-4440
Officer:
Randolph Weigner, President
LPTV Stations:
Florida: WIMP-CA Miami; WARP-CA Tampa-St. Petersburg.
Other Holdings:
LPTV Stations.: See also Boston Broadcasting Corp. & D.T.V. LLC..

SUNSHINE STATE TELEVISION NETWORKS INC.
999 Brickell Bay Dr.
Suite 1908
Miami, FL 33134
Phone: 305-776-8240
Officer:
Jorge Rossi, President
LPTV Stations:
Oklahoma: KOHC-CA Oklahoma City.

SURPRISE VALLEY JOINT UNIFIED SCHOOL DISTRICT
Box 100
Cedarville, CA 96104
Phone: 530-279-6141
Fax: 530-279-2210
Officer:
Lynn Uchida, Business Manager
LPTV Stations:
California: K13IU Eagleville.

SURPRISE VALLEY TV CLUB
Box 53
Cedarville, CA 96104
Phone: 530-279-2577
LPTV Stations:
California: K51KJ Cedarville; K04GB Fort Bidwell; K06FF Lake City, etc..

SWAN HILL TV INC.
PO Box 530
Bigfork, MT 59911
Phone: 406-837-2922
E-mail: rerpswanr@cyberport.net
Ownership: Russell Pickett, Trustee.
LPTV Stations:
Montana: K12LO Ferndale, etc.; K24ID-D Ferndale, etc..

KENNETH D. SWINEHART
625 Main St.
Alamosa, CO 81101

Phone: 719-588-3132
Represented (legal): Putbrese, Hunsaker & Trent PC.
LPTV Stations:
Colorado: KENY-LP Alamosa; K36HS Salida.

SYDCOM INC.
205 W. College St.
Lake Charles, LA 70605
Phone: 337-477-2827
Ownership: Syd Dyer Jr., Owner.
Represented (legal): Koerner & Olender PC.
LPTV Stations:
Texas: K59IL Forbes & Jasper County.
Other Holdings:
LPTV station.: Blue Bonnet Communications Inc..

SYNCOM MEDIA GROUP INC.
4056 W. 107th Ct.
Westminster, CO 80031
Phones: 303-520-9996; 303-593-1433
Fax: 815-327-4319
Officer:
J. Christopher Blair, President
LPTV Stations:
Colorado: K61AA Denver; KHDT-LP Denver; KLPD-LP Denver; KLPT-LP Denver; K47EC Estes Park; K63AB Estes Park; K08IS Glen Haven; K10JY Glen Haven; K12KP Glen Haven; K13ON Glen Haven.

THOMAS T. TAIT
12205 Brookmont Ave.
Sylmar, CA 91342
Phone: 217-202-7554
LPTV Stations:
Michigan: WHNE-LP Flint.

CITY OF TANANA
5900 E Tudor Rd
Anchorage, AK 99507
Phone: 907-269-5744
LPTV Stations:
Alaska: K02KM Tanana.

TANANA VALLEY TELEVISION CO.
3650 Bradock St.
Suite 2
Fairbanks, AK 99701
Phone: 907-452-3697
Fax: 907-456-3428
Officers:
William St. Pierre, President
David Wike, Vice President
Mike Young, Secretary-Treasurer
Ownership: William St. Pierre, 68%; Bill Damel, 5.2%; Gene Gardener, 4.22%; Vilma Grassi, 4.09%; Loreen Parker, 3.9%; Mike Young, 3.25%; David Wike, 2.6%; John Minder, 2.6%; Greg Wagner, 1.62%; Gary R Wilken, 1.3%; Preston Smith, 1.3%; Tom Clark, 0.98%; Frank Eagle, 0.81%; Steven Smith, 0.13%.
Represented (legal): Pillsbury Winthrop Shaw Pittman LLP.
LPTV Stations:
Alaska: K13XD Fairbanks; K14JL Fairbanks; K16DW Fairbanks; K22EY Fairbanks; K28ES Fairbanks.
Commercial TV Stations:
Alaska: KFXF-DT Fairbanks.

SARKES TARZIAN INC.
Box 62
205 N College Ave
Bloomington, IN 47402
Phone: 812-332-7251
Officers:
Thomas Tarzian, Chairman

Thomas Tolar, Executive Vice President, TV
Geoffrey Vargo, Executive Vice President, Radio
Valerie Carney, Senior Vice President & General Counsel
Robert Davis, Senior Vice President, Financial & Accounting
Ownership: Thomas Tarzian, 63.3%; Mary Tarzian, Estate, 33.5%; U. of LaVerne & others, 3.2%.
Represented (legal): Leventhal, Senter & Lerman PLLC.
LPTV Stations:
California: K40JV-D Stateline, etc.; K43DB Stateline, etc.
Nevada: K06HT Ely; K29BN Silver Springs.
Commercial TV Stations:
Nevada: KTVN-DT Reno.
Tennessee: WRCB Chattanooga.
Radio Stations:
Indiana: WGCL (AM), WTTS (FM) Bloomington; WAJI (FM), WLDE (FM) Fort Wayne

RICHARD D. TATHAM
2141 Bryce Dr.
Box 747-86405
Lake Havasu City, AZ 86406
Phones: 928-453-8825; 928-855-3246
Fax: 928-453-2588
LPTV Stations:
Arizona: K25HD Bullhead City; K36DU Lake Havasu City.

VILLAGE OF TATITLEK
5900 E Tudor Rd
Anchorage, AK 99507
Phone: 907-269-5744
LPTV Stations:
Alaska: K09NE Tatitlek.

TCM MEDIA ASSOCIATES LLC
5880 Midnight Pass Rd.
Suite 701
Siesta Key, FL 34242
Phone: 941-312-0214
Officer:
Anthony J. Malara III, Vice President & Secretary
Ownership: Estate of Anthony C. Malara, Anthony J. Malara Personal Representative, 70%; Anthony J. Malara III, 10%; Elizabeth Malara Hamilton, 10%; Margaret Malara Hamilton, 10%. Anthony J. Malara III is also principal of White Knight Holdings Inc., see listing.
Represented (legal): WolfBlock.
LPTV Stations:
Minnesota: K59BQ Deer River; K63BI Grand Marais.
Commercial TV Stations:
Indiana: WPTA-DT Fort Wayne.
Minnesota: KDLH-DT Duluth.

TCT OF MICHIGAN INC.
PO Box 1010
Marion, IL 62959-1010
Phone: 618-997-9333
Fax: 618-997-1859
E-mail: cmmay@maylawoffices.com
Officers:
Garth W. Coonce, President
Christina M. Coonce, Vice President
Michael J. Daly, Secretary
Charles Payne, Treasurer
Ownership: Non-profit organization--Marion, IL.; Garth W. Coonce; Christina M. Coonce; Charles Payne; Victoria Clark, 25%. votes each. Garth & Christina Coonce, Payne & Clark are also principals of Faith Broadcasting Network Inc., Radiant Life Ministries Inc. & Tri-State Christian TV Inc., see listings.

Represented (legal): Colby M. May.
LPTV Stations:
Michigan: WDWO-CA Detroit; W26BX Kalamazoo.
Commercial TV Stations:
Michigan: WTLJ-DT Muskegon; WAQP-DT Saginaw.

TELCOM SUPPLY INC.
701 W Church St
Livingston, TX 77351
Phone: 936-327-4309
E-mail: peggysmarsh@comcast.net
Officer:
Curtis G. Walzel, President
Represented (legal): Katten Muchin Rosenman LLP.
LPTV Stations:
Texas: KETX-LP Livingston.

TELECINCO INC.
Box 43
Mayaguez, PR 00681-0043
Phone: 787-831-5555
Officer:
Jose A. Vizcarrondo, Vice President

Branch Office:
First Federal Bldg.
Santurce, PR 00908
Phone: 787-721-4054
Ownership: Gloria R. de Arellano, Trustee, 61.75%; Alfred R. de Arellano III, 12.75%; Gloria R. de Arellano, 12.75%; Josefina R. de Arellano, 12.75%.
Represented (legal): Fletcher, Heald & Hildreth PLC.
LPTV Stations:
Puerto Rico: W10BG Mayaguez.
Commercial TV Stations:
Puerto Rico: WORA-DT Mayaguez.

TELECOM WIRELESS LLC
170-B Old Naples Rd.
Hendersonville, NC 28792
Phone: 954-478-7333
Officer:
Andrew Cambron, President
Ownership: Erick L. Mathe, Managing Member.
LPTV Stations:
Minnesota: K50IZ Duluth.
Texas: K49IE Victoria; KXVT-LP Victoria.
Wyoming: K23HQ Casper; K10PC Gillette.

TELEVIEW SYSTEMS OF MINNESOTA
15560 Edgewood Court
Eden Prairie, MN 55346
Phone: 612-975-0548
Ownership: Todd Communications Inc..
LPTV Stations:
Minnesota: K21AK Appleton.

TELEVISION IMPROVEMENT ASSN.
Box 342
Ukiah, CA 95482
Ownership: Community owned--Ukiah, CA.
LPTV Stations:
California: K17CG Ukiah; K21CD Ukiah; K27EE Ukiah; K29DF Ukiah; K31GK Ukiah; K39AG Ukiah; K41AF Ukiah; K43AF Ukiah; K45AH Ukiah; K47AL Ukiah; K51AQ Ukiah; K55GX Ukiah; K69DF Ukiah.

TEMPLE BAPTIST CHURCH INC.
3000 N. Meridian Rd.
Tallahassee, FL 32312
Phone: 850-385-7181
Fax: 850-385-7188

Officer:
Dr. Randy Ray, President
LPTV Stations:
Florida: WTBC-LP Tallahassee.

CITY OF TENAKEE SPRINGS
5900 E Tudor Rd
Anchorage, AK 99507
Phone: 907-269-5744
LPTV Stations:
Alaska: K10KG Tenakee Springs.

THOMPSON FALLS TV DISTRICT
Box 746
Thompson Falls, MT 59873
LPTV Stations:
Montana: K07FL Thompson Falls; K09FQ Thompson Falls; K11FQ Thompson Falls; K36BW Thompson Falls.

THREE ANGELS BROADCASTING NETWORK INC.
3391 Charley Good Rd.
Box 220
West Frankfort, IL 62896
Phones: 618-627-4651; 800-752-3226
Fax: 618-627-4155
Web site: www.3abn.org
Officers:
Dr. Walter Thompson, Chairman
Danny L. Shelton, President & Chief Executive Officer
Linda Shelton, Executive Vice President
Larry Ewing, Chief Financial Officer
Represented (legal): Cole, Raywid & Braverman LLP.
LPTV Stations:
Alabama: W38BQ Huntsville.
Alaska: K11TH Nome.
Arizona: K52EG Yuma.
Arkansas: K27JP-D Little Rock.
California: K08MM Bakersfield; K24GS Bakersfield; K15HV-D Chico; K39EO Crescent City; K03HK Fresno; K12OZ Fresno; K21DO Palm Springs/Indio; K49IG Yreka.
Florida: W50CO Jacksonville; W32DJ-D Melbourne; W05CO Sarasota.
Idaho: K31FD Boise; K51IN Bonners Ferry; K17ED Payette; K47JK-D Pocatello; K18HQ Sandpoint.
Illinois: W07DD-D Champaign; W15BU Johnson City; W18CJ Quincy; W29CI Salem.
Iowa: K16EL Davenport.
Louisiana: K42FE Shreveport.
Maine: WFYW-LP Waterville.
Maryland: W22DA Frederick; W42CK Hagerstown.
Michigan: W48CL Grand Rapids; W46CR Saginaw & Midland; W67CS Sault Ste. Marie.
Minnesota: K44GH Alexandria; K44HE Geneva; K39GT International Falls; K43JE-D Lake Crystal; K18GF Little Falls; K14KH Minneapolis; K47JE Olivia; K58GC Rochester; K51GL Vesta; K47JC-D Wadena.
Mississippi: W26BB Vicksburg.
Missouri: K49FC St. Louis.
Nebraska: K27GX Lincoln; K61GA Omaha.
Nevada: K43FO Las Vegas.
New Mexico: K38IM Albuquerque.
New York: W21BW Elmira; W58CX Saratoga Springs.
North Carolina: W41BQ Asheville; W21CK-D Charlotte; W24CP Durham.
North Dakota: K17HG Grand Forks.
Ohio: W23DE-D Lima.
Oklahoma: K38GL Lawton; K40KC-D Tulsa.
Oregon: K57GP Brookings; K32ET Canyonville; K17DU Christmas Valley; K48GC Florence; K34IC Glide; K48DZ Hermiston; K02PK John Day; K08NP John Day; K05KI Lakeview.
Pennsylvania: W32DH-D Erie.
Puerto Rico: W44CK Bayamon-San Juan.
South Dakota: K32FW Pierre; K34GM Pierre.

Tennessee: W26BE Chattanooga; WCNT-LP Chattanooga; W21BZ Collegedale; W14CX Farragut/Knoxville; W42BY Memphis; WJNK-LP Nashville.
Texas: K17HI-D Amarillo; K40FJ Midland; K14KI San Antonio; K14LM San Antonio; K41EQ Texarkana; K26GA Tyler-Jacksonville.
Utah: K43JV Provo.
Vermont: W21CN Windsor.
Virgin Islands: W29CB St. Thomas.
Washington: K25FP Ellensburg; K39DL Moses Lake; K26GV Omak; K21HL Pateros; K54DU Richland; K08OU-D Seattle; K05JO Sunnyside & Prosser; K33EJ Walla Walla; K58DL Yakima-Toppenish.
Wisconsin: W30BU Green Bay; W23BW Madison; W02CF Minocqua; W31BA Minocqua.

THREE NOTCH COMMUNICATIONS LLC
PO Box 987
Andalusia, AL 36420
Ownership: Blaine Wilson, Managing Member.
Represented (legal): Miller & Neely PC.
LPTV Stations:
Alabama: WAAO-LP Andalusia.

THREE SISTERS BROADCASTING LLC
PO Box 7009
Eugene, OR 97401
Phone: 541-485-5611
Officer:
Scott Chambers, President & Managing Member
Represented (legal): Katten, Munchin & Rosenman LLP.
LPTV Stations:
Oregon: K53JV Bend.

TIDALWAVE HOLDINGS INC.
3711 W County Hwy 30-A
Santa Rosa Beach, FL 32459
Phone: 888-620-6815
E-mail: jhbeebe@msn.com
Officer:
John H. Beebe, President
LPTV Stations:
Florida: W30CF Panama City; WDWY-LP Panama City.

TIGER EYE BROADCASTING CORP.
3400 Lakeside Dr.
Suite 500
Miramar, FL 33027
Phone: 954-431-3144
Fax: 954-431-3591
E-mail: jgallagher@unitedtelemedia.com
Officers:
John M. Kyle, Chairman & President
Diane Mercer, Secretary-Treasurer
Ownership: John N Kyle, 47.72%; John Roehrs, 8.32%; Erick L. Mathe, 7.88%; Leroy Hagenbuch, 3.9%; Keith McClendon, 2.79%; Dennis Hayes, 2.67%; Norman Cloutier, 2.14%; Brad Simon, 1.47%; Jeffrey King, 1.28%; John Linke, 1.28%.
LPTV Stations:
Alabama: WGHA-LP Gulf Shores; WMOE-LP Mobile; WWBH-LP Mobile; WBMG-LP Moody.
Florida: WDYB-LP Daytona Beach; W50BP Panama City; WPCY-LP Panama City.
Georgia: W33CN Columbus.
Iowa: KCDE-LP Cedar Rapids; KCDR-LP Cedar Rapids; KHHH-LP Cedar Rapids; KRUB-LP Cedar Rapids; KRPG-LP Des Moines.
Louisiana: K66EY Alexandria.
New York: WROH-LP Rochester.
Tennessee: WOOT-LP Chattanooga; W49CG Jackson; WJTE-LP Jackson; WEEE-LP Knoxville.

Texas: K38JE Abilene; K31IK Plainview.
Virginia: WFMA-LP Farmville; WERI-LP Keysville; WSVL-LP Keysville; WRKV-LP Roanoke.

TKMI BROADCASTING
101-115 Buffalo St.
Mannington, WV 26582
Phone: 304-986-2896
E-mail: tvtkm@westco.net
Officer:
Rev. Nicholas T. Lalli, President
LPTV Stations:
West Virginia: W64CZ Clarksburg.

TKO INC.
500 N. Main St.
Suite B
Harrison, AR 72601
Phone: 870-741-2566
Fax: 870-741-4727
E-mail: tko8@alltel.net
Web site: www.tko8.com
Ownership: Dennis King, Pres..
Represented (legal): Irwin, Campbell & Tannenwald PC.
LPTV Stations:
Arkansas: KTKO-LP Harrison.

TOBACCO VALLEY COMMUNICATIONS
PO Box 648
Dewey Ave
Eureka, MT 59917-0648
Phone: 406-889-3311
E-mail: rlittle@interbel.com
Officer:
Robert Little, OPS Manager
LPTV Stations:
Montana: K05GC Rexford & Fortine.

CITY OF TOGIAK
5900 E Tudor Rd
Anchorage, AK 99507
Phone: 907-269-5744
LPTV Stations:
Alaska: K03FL Togiak.

TOMAY TELEVISION INC.
PO Box 3174
Pismo Beach, CA 93420
Phone: 805-928-8300
Officer:
Peggy E. Tomay, President
LPTV Stations:
California: KPXA-LP San Luis Obispo.

TOWER OF BABEL LLC
601 University Ave.
Suite 211
Sacramento, CA 95825
Phone: 916-921-2290
Officer:
Frank Washington, Chief Executive Officer
LPTV Stations:
California: KBTV-CA Sacramento.

TOWNSEND TV DISTRICT
PO Box 489
515 Broadway
Townsend, MT 59644
LPTV Stations:
Montana: K07EJ Townsend; K13KH Townsend.

TOWSON U.
Dept. of Electronic Media & Film
Towson, MD 21252-0001
Phone: 410-704-2447

Fax: 410-830-3744
E-mail: jmackerron@towson.edu
Officer:
Dr. John MacKerron, Chairman & Chief Executive Officer
Ownership: Board of Regents, U. of Maryland.
LPTV Stations:
Maryland: WMJF-LP Towson.

TRANQUILITY COMMUNITY CHURCH
Box 48
Seaman, OH 45679
LPTV Stations:
Ohio: W17AY Seaman.

TRAN-STAR INC.
716 N. Westwood Ave.
Toledo, OH 43607
LPTV Stations:
Indiana: WFWC-CA Fort Wayne.

TREASURE COUNTY T.V. DISTRICT
PO Box 111
Hysham, MT 59038-0111
Phone: 406-342-5218
E-mail: rosco@rangeweb.net
Officer:
Ronald W. Thomas, Information Contact
LPTV Stations:
Montana: K11OS Hysham; K13PO Hysham.

TREASURE VALLEY COMMUNITY COLLEGE
650 College Blvd., Weese Bldg.
Ontario, OR 97914-3423
Phone: 541-881-8822
Fax: 541-881-2717
LPTV Stations:
Oregon: KMBA-LP Ontario.

VILLAGE OF TRENTON
PO Box 68
402 Main St.
Trenton, NE 69044-0068
Phone: 308-334-5488
E-mail: vtrenton@gpcom.net
LPTV Stations:
Nebraska: K04EG Trenton.

TRIANON BROADCASTING CO. INC.
Box 129
Sebring, FL 33871
Phone: 262-567-7307
Officer:
Warren Thurow, President
Represented (legal): Fletcher, Heald & Hildreth PLC.
LPTV Stations:
Florida: WHRT-CA Sebring, etc..

TRIBUNE BROADCASTING CO., DEBTOR-IN-POSSESSION
435 N. Michigan Ave.
No. 1800
Chicago, IL 60611
Phone: 312-222-3333
Fax: 312-222-5981
Officers:
Sam Zell, Chairman & Chief Executive Officer
Ed Wilson, President, Tribune Broadcast Group
Chandler Bigelow, Chief Financial Officer
Randy Michaels, Chief Operating Officer
Steve Gable, Executive Vice President & Chief Technology Officer
Ray Schonbak, Executive Vice President, Fox Affiliates
Gerald A. Spector, Executive Vice President & Chief Administrative Officer

Steve Charlier, Senior Vice President, News & Operations
Sean Compton, Senior Vice President, Programming & Entertainment
David Eldersveld, Senior Vice President, Deputy Counsel & Corporate Secretary
Hank Hundemer, Senior Vice President, Engineering
Dan Kazan, Senior Vice President, Development
Naomi Sachs, Senior Vice President, Strategy
Ownership: Tribune Co.; TC ownership:; Tribune Employee Stock Ownership Plan, privately held. Sam Zell, through EGI-TRB, holds a warrant to acquire up to 40% of company. Tribune Co. filed December 8, 2008 seeking relief under Chapter 11 of the Bankruptcy Code.
Represented (legal): Dow Lohnes PLLC.
LPTV Stations:
Michigan: W42CB Hesperia; W52DB Muskegon.
Oregon: K24DX Pendleton; K20ES Pendleton, etc.; KRCW-LP Portland.
Pennsylvania: W51CY Chambersburg.
Washington: K25CG Aberdeen; K25CH Centralia; K42CM Centralia, etc.; K64ES Chelan; K54DX Ellensburg-Kittitas; K29ED Everett.
Commercial TV Stations:
California: KTLA-DT Los Angeles; KTXL-DT Sacramento; KSWB-DT San Diego.
Colorado: KWGN-DT Denver.
Connecticut: WTIC-DT Hartford; WTXX-DT Waterbury.
District of Columbia: WDCW-DT Washington.
Florida: WSFL-DT Miami.
Illinois: WGN-DT Chicago.
Indiana: WTTV-DT Bloomington; WXIN-DT Indianapolis; WTTK-DT Kokomo.
Louisiana: WGNO-DT New Orleans; WNOL-DT New Orleans.
Michigan: WXMI-DT Grand Rapids.
Missouri: KPLR-DT St. Louis.
New York: WPIX-DT New York.
Oregon: KRCW-DT Salem.
Pennsylvania: WPHL-DT Philadelphia; WPMT-DT York.
Texas: KDAF-DT Dallas; KIAH-DT Houston.
Washington: KMYQ-DT Seattle; KCPQ-DT Tacoma.
Newspapers:
California: Los Angeles Times
Connecticut: The Hartford Courant
Florida: South Florida Sun-Sentinel (Fort Lauderdale), Orlando Sentinel
Illinois: Chicago Tribune, RedEye (Chicago)
Maryland: The Sun (Baltimore)
New York: amNewYork (New York City), 3% of Newsday (Long Island & New York City)
Pennsylvania: The Morning Call (Allentown, Bethlehem, Lehigh Valley)
Virginia: Daily Press (Hampton Roads)
Radio Stations:
Illinois: WGN (AM) Chicago
Other Holdings:
Features syndicator: Tribune Media Services Inc.
Magazine: Williamsburg Magazine; Chicago Magazine
Professional sports team: Chicago Cubs
Program source: ChicagoLand Television News; 29% of TV Food Network; 22.25% of WB TV Network; Tribune Entertainment.

TRI MEDIA GROUP INC.
PO Box 161447
Altamonte Springs, FL 32716
Phone: 407-682-7195
E-mail: sp8301@aol.com
Officer:
Marie O. Price, President
LPTV Stations:
Florida: WLWA-LP Lakeland.

TRINITY BROADCASTING NETWORK INC.
2442 Michelle Dr.
Tustin, CA 92780

Phone: 714-832-2950
Fax: 714-730-0661
Web site: www.tbn.org
Officers:
Paul F. Crouch Sr., President
Janice W. Crouch, Vice President
W. Ben Miller, Vice President & Engineering Director
Norman G. Juggert, Secretary-Treasurer

Branch Office:
Cable Headquarters
2900 W. Airport Freeway
Irving, TX 75062
Phone: 214-313-1333
Ownership: Janice W. Crouch; Matthew W. Crouch; Paul F. Crouch Jr.; Dr. Paul F. Crouch Sr., Directors, 25%. votes each. Non-profit organization.
Represented (legal): Colby M. May.
LPTV Stations:
Alabama: W46DK Birmingham; W33CM Decatur; W41BN Dothan; W30BD Eufaula; W57BV Florence; W67CO Huntsville; W25DR Jasper; W27CV Scottsboro; W24CK Selma; W46BU Tuscaloosa.
Arizona: K51IO Bullhead City; K41ER Globe & Miami; K51HV Prescott & Cottonwood; K38CX Shonto; K07YX Tucson; K57BD Tucson, etc..
Arkansas: K15FW Batesville; K42BS Fayetteville; K16ER Fort Smith; K23GT Hot Springs; K42GX Jonesboro; K34FH Little Rock; K41HC Mountain Home; K27FC Paragould.
California: K21FP Bakersfield; K56DZ Fresno; K49EO Modesto; K40ID Palm Springs; K15CO Porterville; K50GP Redding; K22FR Sacramento; K45HC Sacramento; K45DU Ventura.
Colorado: K48FW Denver; K57BT Denver; K66FB Denver; K25FZ Grand Junction; K48CG Loveland.
Delaware: W14CM Dover; W40AZ Wilmington.
Florida: W16CJ Naples; W34DH Panama City; W17CK Port Charlotte; W48CN Sarasota; W51DY Sebring; W36CO St. Petersburg; W56EB Tampa.
Georgia: W34CZ Albany; W58CZ Augusta; W33AL Brunswick; W50DA Macon; W49DE Marietta; W57CT Savannah; W48BH Statesboro; W38CM Thomasville; W33BX Tifton; W25CP Valdosta; W14CQ Vidalia; W45CU Waycross.
Hawaii: K34HC Hilo; K38HU Kailua-Kona.
Idaho: K47BE Boise; K53FF Coeur d'Alene; K26EW Idaho Falls; K27GO Lewiston; K58GL Lewiston; K25EV Twin Falls.
Illinois: W64CQ Arlington Heights; W51CT Bloomington; W34DL Champaign; W29BG Decatur; W57DN Elgin; W51DT Galesburg; W40BY Palatine; W50DD Peoria; W25CL Rockford; W19CX Sterling-Dixon.
Indiana: W18CF Elkhart; W38BK Evansville; W51DU Lafayette; W43BV Terre Haute.
Iowa: K17ET Cedar Rapids; K61HD Davenport; K42HI Muscatine; K42AM Ottumwa; K44FK Waterloo.
Kansas: K43HN Dodge City; K52GZ Emporia; K39FW Garden City; K50GO Independence; K25DS Junction City; K31BW Manhattan; K33HZ Pittsburg; K15CN Salina; K33IC Topeka; K28JB Wichita.
Kentucky: W39CJ Elizabethtown; W22CH Hopkinsville.
Louisiana: K45IY Alexandria; K48IT Baton Rouge; K51EC Lake Charles; K45DI Mermentau; K45IM Monroe; K19CR New Iberia; K28IL New Orleans; K39JV Opelousas; K31HO Shreveport.
Maine: W36CK Bangor; W27CE Dover & Foxcroft; W21BH Machias; W34CN Medway; W32CA Portland; W51AG Presque Isle.
Maryland: W43BP Cresaptown.
Michigan: W18BT Alpena; W66BV Detroit; W20BZ Escanaba; W25CZ Grand Rapids; W27CQ Houghton; W17CS Marquette.

Minnesota: K40JT Albert Lea; K42FH Bemidji; K58CM Duluth; K25IA Minneapolis; K56HW Rochester; K19BG St. Cloud; K64FY Winona.
Mississippi: W56DY Cleveland; W25AD Columbus; W42CY Greenville; W30BY Grenada; W36AC McComb; W47CG Meridian; W27CX Natchez; W51CU Pascagoula.
Missouri: K56AU Columbia; K41OI Jefferson City; K39CP Poplar Bluff; K16FE Rolla; K41FQ Springfield; K47LH Springfield; K22HG St. Charles; K33GU St. Louis.
Montana: K31IA Great Falls; K41CX Helena; K26DD Kalispell; K42EO Missoula.
Nebraska: K29GL Lincoln; K21HS Norfolk; K26CV Ogallala.
Nevada: K19CU Carson City; K41IO Las Vegas.
New Jersey: W45CP Atlantic City.
New Mexico: K56IU Alamogordo; K36GD Carlsbad; K14MJ Farmington; K18CT Raton; K50IA Roswell.
New York: W52DF Albany; W26BS Binghamton; W59DG Elmira; W47CM Glens Falls; W20BT Ithaca; W10BH Jamestown; W20BA Massena; W30BW Olean; W26CP Potsdam; W38CY Syracuse; W51CV Utica.
North Carolina: W50CZ Asheville; W16CF Charlotte; W38CN Charlotte; W45CO Fayetteville; W63CW Goldsboro; W44CN Greenville; W35CC Lumberton; W45CN Raleigh; W45CN Rocky Mount; W21CI Statesville; W51CW-D Wilmington.
North Dakota: K46DY Bismarck; K28EP Dickinson; K35HO Fargo; K49FF Grand Forks; K21GQ Minot; K40DE Williston.
Ohio: W63CZ Cambridge; W36DG Cincinnati; W23BZ Columbus; W51BI Kirtland; W32AR Lexington; W20CL Springfield; W22CO Toledo; W52DS Youngstown; W16BT Zanesville.
Oklahoma: K44BQ Ardmore; K49GC Lawton; K25GJ Muskogee; K30IX Tahlequah.
Oregon: K33AG Bend; K33AO Coos Bay; K36HL Grants Pass; K58BG Klamath Falls; K21BC Lakeview; K49FV Roseburg.
Pennsylvania: W48CH Erie; W52BO Meadville; W65CG Pittsburgh; W26CD Scranton; W39BT Williamsport.
South Carolina: W50CL Anderson; W19CH Beaufort; W20CN Charleston; W50DX Columbia; W22CJ Jacksonville; W34CQ Myrtle Beach; W45DE Orangeburg.
South Dakota: K35FJ Aberdeen; K38CQ Huron; K43GX Madison; K33CO Rapid City; K56GF Sioux Falls; K31DP Yankton.
Tennessee: W49CQ Cookeville; W35AH Jackson; W46DC Knoxville; W61DG Morristown; W48DF Nashville.
Texas: K51CK Abilene; K25GI Amarillo; K34FM Austin; K26AP Brownwood; K47ED College Station; K57FC Corpus Christi; K46DL Kingsville; K44HH Lubbock; K17BP Palestine; K42AD Paris; K44FJ San Angelo; K20BW San Antonio; K45FJ San Antonio; K58GN Seminole; K30EA Texarkana; K15BV Uvalde; K43DV Victoria; K26DL Wichita Falls.
Utah: K41JJ Ogden; K18FJ Salt Lake City; K67HK St. George; K39AK Vernal.
Vermont: W16AL Burlington.
Virginia: W18BS Hampton; W40BM Lynchburg; W39CO Richmond; W49AP Roanoke; W24OI Virginia Beach.
Washington: K32GS Spokane; K34EM Wenatchee.
West Virginia: W31CA Charleston; W44CF Clarksburg; W36CR Huntington; W45BW Parkersburg.
Wisconsin: W49CB Green Bay; W65EE Janesville; W38CT Madison; W17CF Ripon; W36DH Waupaca.
Wyoming: K33GI Casper; K35CN Green River.
Commercial TV Stations:
Alabama: WTJP-DT Gadsden; WMPV-DT Mobile; WMCF-DT Montgomery.
Arizona: KPAZ-DT Phoenix.
California: KTBN-DT Santa Ana.
Colorado: KPJR-DT Greeley.

Florida: WHLV-DT Cocoa; WHFT-DT Miami.
Georgia: WELF-DT Dalton; WHSG-DT Monroe.
Hawaii: KAAH-DT Honolulu.
Illinois: WWTO-DT La Salle.
Indiana: WCLJ-DT Bloomington; WKOI-DT Richmond.
Mississippi: WBUY-DT Holly Springs.
Missouri: KTAJ-DT St. Joseph.
New Jersey: WGTW-DT Burlington.
New Mexico: KNAT-DT Albuquerque.
New York: WTBY-DT Poughkeepsie.
Ohio: WDLI-DT Canton; WSFJ-DT Newark.
Oklahoma: KDOR-DT Bartlesville; KTBO-DT Oklahoma City.
Oregon: KNMT-DT Portland.
Tennessee: WPGD-DT Hendersonville.
Texas: KDTX-DT Dallas.
Washington: KTBW-DT Tacoma.
Wisconsin: WWRS-DT Mayville.

TRINITY COUNTY SUPERINTENDENT OF SCHOOLS
Box 1256
Weaverville, CA 96093
LPTV Stations:
California: K05CR-D Hayfork; K02EE-D Weaverville, etc..

TRIPLETT & ASSOC. INC.
Box 356
Bellefontaine, OH 43311
Phone: 937-593-6591
Officers:
Marc S. Triplett, President
Donna J. Triplett, Secretary-Treasurer
LPTV Stations:
Ohio: WDEM-CD Columbus.

TRI-STATE BROADCASTING LLC
812 E. Beale St.
Kingman, AZ 86401
Phone: 928-753-9100
Fax: 928-753-1978
LPTV Stations:
Arizona: KKAX-LP Hilltop; K23BJ Lake Havasu City.

TRI-STATE CHRISTIAN TV INC.
PO Box 1010
Marion, IL 62959-1010
Phone: 618-997-9333
Fax: 618-997-1859
E-mail: cmmay@maylawoffices.com
Officers:
Garth W. Coonce, President
Christina M. Coonce, Vice President
Michael J. Daly, Secretary
Charles Payne, Treasurer
Victoria Clark, Assistant Secretary
Ownership: Non-profit organization--Marion, IL.; Garth W. Coonce; Christina M. Coonce; Victoria Clark; Charles Payne, 25%. votes each. Garth & Christina Coonce, Payne & Clark are also principals of Faith Broadcasting Network Inc., Radiant Life Ministries Inc. & TCT of Michigan Inc., see listings.
Represented (legal): Colby M. May.
LPTV Stations:
Indiana: W38EA-D Fort Wayne.
Kentucky: W54AE Paducah.
Michigan: W27CN Lansing.
Missouri: KCGI-CA Cape Girardeau.
New York: W42CO Rochester.
Tennessee: WDYR-CA Dyersburg.
Virginia: W18BG Danville.
Commercial TV Stations:
Illinois: WTCT-DT Marion.
Indiana: WINM-DT Angola.

TROY T.V. DISTRICT
PO Box 906
225 Estate Dr
Troy, MT 59935
Phone: 406-295-4266
E-mail: jay@libby.org
Officer:
Jay Olsen, Information Contact
LPTV Stations:
Montana: K08BG Troy; K10AF Troy; K12AA Troy.

TRUE NORTH TV 25 LLC
101 W. Main St.
Box 841
Ashland, WI 54806
Phone: 715-682-8811
Ownership: Henry C. Martinsen.
LPTV Stations:
Wisconsin: WAST-LP Ashland.

CITY OF TRUTH OR CONSEQUENCES
PO Box 865
Williamsburg, NM 87942
LPTV Stations:
New Mexico: K17BH Truth or Consequences; K51BQ Truth or Consequences; K64CG Truth or Consequences.

TTI INC.
5455 Jug Factory Rd.
Box 70937
Tuscaloosa, AL 35407
Phone: 205-342-9948
Fax: 205-366-9480
E-mail: dave@pb.ua.edu
Officers:
James E. Shaw, President
David Baughn, Secretary-Treasurer
Represented (legal): Gardner Carton & Douglas.
LPTV Stations:
Alabama: WJMY-CA Demopolis; WDVZ-CA Greensboro; WVUA-CA Tuscaloosa.

DAVID A. TUCKER
Box 421
Lewiston, ID 85301
Phone: 208-746-0310

Branch Office:
101 Brooks St.
Missoula, MT 59801
Phone: 406-728-0007
LPTV Stations:
Montana: K50CP Missoula, etc..

TUCK PROPERTIES INC.
1850 M. St. NW
Suite 240
Washington, DC 20036
Phone: 202-293-0569
Officer:
Norwood Orrick, Secretary
Represented (legal): Shainis & Peltzman Chartered.
LPTV Stations:
Colorado: K41JO Broadmoor; K14MH Cripple Creek; K05MD-D Cripple Creek, etc.; K30IK Cripple Creek, etc..
Texas: KNAV-LP DeSoto.

CITY OF TULIA
201 N. Maxwell
Tulia, TX 79088
Phone: 806-995-3547
Officer:
Paula Wilson, City Manager

LPTV Stations:
Texas: K36CC Tulia; K55JV Tulia; K57JK Tulia.

TU PROGRAMMACION HISPANA LLC
114 Del Prado Blvd. S
Cape Coral, FL 33990
Phone: 239-772-1650
Officer:
Gaston Cantens, President
LPTV Stations:
Florida: WTPH-LP Fort Myers.

MARCIA T. TURNER
PO Box 435
Long Key, FL 33001-0435
Phone: 954-732-9539
Represented (legal): Shainis & Peltzman Chartered.
LPTV Stations:
Arizona: K20HS Flagstaff.
California: K100U Palm Springs.
Colorado: K14LS Grand Junction.
Florida: WPAF-LP Panama City.
Idaho: K30HK Hollister; K39HJ Idaho Falls; K51HU Pocatello.
Kansas: K39HI Chanute; K50HS Dodge City; KLKT-LP Liberal; K38GZ Manhattan; K33HW Parsons; KSKV-LP Salina.
Mississippi: W50CX Hattiesburg.
Missouri: KJOM-LP Asbury.
Montana: K30IB Billings; K22HD Butte; K33HN Great Falls.
Nebraska: K45II Gothenburg.
Nevada: K31HV Pahrump.
Oklahoma: K11VJ Lawton.
Texas: Amarillo; K39HF Amarillo; K39HG Beaumont; K36HF Tuscola.
Utah: K50IB Logan.
Wyoming: K36GT Casper.

MATT TUTER
502 Sterling Dr.
San Leandro, CA 94578
Phone: 510-352-3110
LPTV Stations:
California: KBIT-LD Chico.

TV-45 INC.
Box 201
Huxley, IA 50124
Phone: 515-597-3531
Ownership: Douglas Sheldahl, see listing..
LPTV Stations:
Iowa: K26IY Ames; K52GP Council Bluffs; K54GL Council Bluffs; K29EA Des Moines; K46EY Des Moines.
Nebraska: K53EY Omaha.

TV-52 INC.
PO Box 201
Huxley, IA 50124-0201
Phone: 515-597-3138
Officer:
Douglas Sheldahl, President
LPTV Stations:
Iowa: K48FZ Ames.

TV AMERICAS DE OMAHA LLC
500 S. Chinowth Rd.
Visalia, CA 93277
Phone: 559-733-7800
E-mail: fccmail@pappastv.com
Web site: www.pappastv.com
Ownership: Pappas Telecasting of Nebraska Inc., Managing Member, 2%; Harry J. Pappas, 94%; LeBon Abercrombie, 2%; Dennis J. Davis, 2%; PTONI ownership:; Harry J. Pappas. Pappas is principal of Pappas Telecasting Companies, see listing.

Represented (legal): Paul Hastings.
LPTV Stations:
Nebraska: KCAZ-LP Columbus; KAZJ-LP Norfolk; KAZO-LP Omaha; KAZS-LP South Sioux City.

TV BOARD OF WHITERIVER
c/o George Hess
Box 700
Whiteriver, AZ 85941
LPTV Stations:
Arizona: K09WY Whiteriver; K13XC Whiteriver.

TV DISTRICT 2 OF OKANOGAN COUNTY
PO Box 441
Twisp, WA 98856
Phone: 509-997-2033
LPTV Stations:
Washington: K02FZ Mazama.

TVO MEDIA LLC
3718 Boca Pointe Dr
Sarasota, FL 34238
Phone: 941-925-2002
Officer:
Steve Marriott, Manager
Represented (legal): Shainis & Peltzman Chartered.
LPTV Stations:
Ohio: WCPX-LP Columbus.

TWELVE MILE RANCH
3075 Wild Horse Rd.
Colorado Springs, CO 80926
LPTV Stations:
Colorado: K11MM Fairplay.

TWIN BROADCASTING INC.
4002 North 3300 East
Twin Falls, ID 83301
Phone: 208-734-5525
LPTV Stations:
Idaho: KCJY-LP Twin Falls.

U-DUB PRODUCTIONS LLC
31276 Dunham Way
Thousand Palms, CA 92276
Phone: 760-343-5700
Officer:
David Rennie, Chief Financial Officer
Represented (legal): Arnold & Porter.
LPTV Stations:
California: KYAV-LP Palm Springs.

UHF-TV ASSOCIATION
PO Box 187
Tucumcari, NM 88401-0187
Phone: 505-461-3818
E-mail: mwflint@plateautel.net
Officer:
Doyle Frasier, President
Represented (legal): Fletcher, Heald & Hildreth PLC.
LPTV Stations:
New Mexico: K35FP Tucumcari; K38FP Tucumcari; K40DK Tucumcari; K42CR Tucumcari; K46BU Tucumcari; K50CX Tucumcari.

UHF-TV INC.
Box 728
Spicer, MN 56288
Phone: 866-214-8214
Officers:
William C. Marcil, President & Treasurer
Charles T. Bohnet, Vice President & Secretary

LPTV Stations:
Minnesota: K14LF Willmar; K17FA Willmar; K20GD Willmar; K34HO Willmar; K39FE Willmar; K44AE Willmar; K46AC Willmar; K48AH Willmar; K50HZ Willmar.

UINTAH COUNTY
152 East 100 North
Vernal, UT 84078
Phone: 435-781-5361
Officer:
Dave Haslem, Chairman
LPTV Stations:
Utah: K09CY Vernal, etc.; K11DF Vernal, etc.; K13HF Vernal, etc..

UMATILLA RIVER TV ASSOCIATION INC.
53017 Cayuse Rd
Adams, OR 97810
LPTV Stations:
Oregon: K03AX Umatilla River Valley.

UMMAT BROADCASTING CORP. INC.
5521 Soutel Dr.
Box 40181
Jacksonville, FL 32203
Phone: 904-354-8573
LPTV Stations:
Florida: WUBF-LP Jacksonville.

CITY OF UNALAKLEET
5900 E Tudor Rd
Anachorage, AK 99507
Phone: 907-269-5744
LPTV Stations:
Alaska: K04JW Unalakleet.

UNALASKA COMMUNITY TELEVISION INC.
Box 181
Unalaska, AK 99685
Phone: 907-581-1888
E-mail: arcstech@pobox.alaska.net
Officer:
Christopher Bobbitt, Chairman
Represented (legal): Schwartz, Woods & Miller.
LPTV Stations:
Alaska: KUCB-LP Dutch Harbor.

UNA VEZ MAS GP LLC
703 McKinney Ave.
Suite 240
Dallas, TX 75202
Phone: 214-754-7008
Officers:
Terry Crosby, Chairman & Chief Executive Officer
Randy Nonberg, President
David L. Haymore, Chief Operating Officer
Ownership: Terry Crosby; Jay Hoker; Brian McNeill; Andrew Mulderry; Randy Nonberg, board members.
Represented (legal): Wiley Rein LLP.
LPTV Stations:
Arizona: KPDF-CA Phoenix; KDFQ-LP Prescott; KQBN-LP Prescott; KUDF-LP Tucson.
California: KASC-CA Atascadero; KLDF-CA Lompoc; KPAO-CA Paso Robles; KSBO-CA San Luis Obispo; KZDF-LP Santa Barbara; KDFS-CA Santa Maria.
Florida: WXAX-LP Clearwater.
Georgia: WUVM-LP Atlanta.
Maryland: WQAW-LP Lake Shore.
Nevada: KHDF-CA Las Vegas.
New Mexico: KQDF-LP Albuquerque.
Texas: KAFW-LP Abilene; KKAB-LP Abilene; KAEU-LP Alice; KAMM-LP Amarillo; KTXD-LP Amarillo; KADF-LP Austin; KABS-LP

Big Spring; KBDF-LP Brownsville; KYDF-LP Corpus Christi; KDFL-LP Lubbock; KNDF-LP McAllen; KRZG-CA McAllen; KDFH-LP Midland; KAXW-LP Mullin; KAZP-LP Port Arthur; KVDF-CA San Antonio; KADY-LP Sherman; KASX-LP Sweetwater; KSWR-LP Sweetwater; KTJA-CA Victoria; KAWF-LP Wichita Falls.

THE UNION MISSION
130 Brooke Ave.
Norfolk, VA 23510-3203
Phone: 757-430-2313
Officers:
Howard R. McPherson, Chairman & President
James R. Herndon, First Vice President
Murray G. Wade Jr., Second Vice President
S. Paul Hobbs, Secretary
Harry J. Brown, Treasurer
Ownership: Howard R McPherson; James R Herndon; Murray G Wade Jr.; S. Paul Hobbs; Theodore A Bashford; Harry J Brown.
LPTV Stations:
Virginia: WJGN-CA Chesapeake; W51DO Hampton.

UNITED COMMUNICATIONS CORP.
715 58th St.
Kenosha, WI 53141
Phone: 262-657-1000
E-mail: wwny@wwnytv.net
Officers:
Howard J. Brown, President & Chief Executive Officer
Eugene W. Schulte, Senior Vice President & Secretary-Treasurer
Kenneth L. Dowdell, Vice President
Ronald J. Montemurro, Vice President
Ownership: Howard J Brown, 36.05%; Elizabeth K Brown, 9.55%; Eugene W Schulte, 4.11%; other members of the Brown & Schulte families.
LPTV Stations:
Minnesota: K19CA St. James.
New York: WNYF-LP Massena; WNYF-CA Watertown.
Commercial TV Stations:
Minnesota: KEYC-DT Mankato.
New York: WWNY-DT Carthage.
Newspapers:
Massachusetts: Attleboro Sun Chronicle
Wisconsin: Kenosha News

UNITY BROADCASTING INC.
504 N. 3rd St.
Box 790
Booneville, MS 38829-0790
Phones: 662-728-5359; 662-728-6492
Fax: 662-728-3530
Web site: www.ubntv.org
Officers:
Bill Lambert, Chairman & Chief Executive Officer
Dora Baker, Secretary-Treasurer & Chief Financial Officer
LPTV Stations:
Alabama: W45CW Russellville; W46CF Tuscumbia.
Mississippi: W34DV Booneville; W39CD Fulton; W15CG Pontotoc.
Tennessee: W06AW Selmer.

U. OF ALASKA
Box 755620
KUAC-TV
Fairbanks, AK 99775-5620
Phone: 907-474-7491
Ownership: Public educational institution.

LPTV Stations:
Alaska: K05FI Delta Junction; K07ND Healy; K05HI Nenana.
ETV Stations:
Alaska: KUAC-DT Fairbanks.
Radio Stations:
Alaska: KUAC-FM

U. OF FLORIDA
2000 Weimer Hall
WUFT-TV
Gainesville, FL 32611
Phone: 352-392-5551
Officers:
Richard A. Lehner, Chief Executive Officer
Liz McArthur, Chief Financial Officer
Represented (legal): Schwartz, Woods & Miller.
LPTV Stations:
Florida: WLUF-LP Gainesville.
Radio Stations:
Florida: WUFT-FM

U. OF KANSAS
2051 Dole Center
School of Journalism
Lawrence, KS 66045
Phone: 785-864-0600
Fax: 785-864-0614
E-mail: tv14@ku.edu
Officers:
James K. Gentry, Dean
Gary Hawke, Chief Operating Officer
LPTV Stations:
Kansas: KUJH-LP Lawrence; K27FR Overland Park.

U. OF NEW HAMPSHIRE
268 Mast Rd.
Durham, NH 03824-3546
Phone: 603-868-1100
Fax: 603-868-7552
E-mail: themailbox@nhptv.org
Officers:
Joan Leitzel, President
Peter A. Frid, Chief Executive Officer
Steve Baker, Chief Financial Officer
William Bumpus, Chief Engineer
Represented (legal): Schwartz, Woods & Miller.
LPTV Stations:
New Hampshire: W50DP-D Hanover; W18BO Pittsburg.
ETV Stations:
New Hampshire: WENH-DT Durham; WEKW-DT Keene; WLED-DT Littleton.

REGENTS OF THE U. OF NEW MEXICO
1130 University Blvd. NE
Albuquerque, NM 87102
Phone: 505-277-2121
Fax: 505-277-2191
Officers:
Penny T. Rembe, President
Barbara G. Brazil, Vice President
Eric Thomas, Secretary-Treasurer
Represented (legal): Dow Lohnes PLLC.
LPTV Stations:
New Mexico: K38DA-D Aztec; K33GC Capulin, etc.; K34FD Chama; K28GF Cimarron; K18HR Conchas Dam; K34HF-D Cuba; K40FI-D Farmington; K43AI Farmington; K31HB Gallina; K23FE Gallup; K33GA Grants & Milan; K33FL Las Vegas; K49KF-D Los Alamos/Espanola; K31EO Mora; K31FX Pie Town & Quemado; K15FS Quemado; K20CV Raton, etc.; K15FV Red River; K34FQ Roy; K30FP Santa Rosa; K15HD-D Taos; K33BN

Taos; K49IL Tecolote; K31JR Thoreau; K28GV Tres Piedras; K36FQ Wagon Mound.
ETV Stations:
New Mexico: KNME-DT Albuquerque; KNMD-DT Santa Fe.

U. OF NORTH CAROLINA
910 Raleigh Rd.
Chapel Hill, NC 27514
Phone: 919-962-1000
Fax: 919-549-7201
E-mail: viewer@unctv.org
Officer:
C. D. Spangler Jr., President
Represented (legal): Schwartz, Woods & Miller.
LPTV Stations:
North Carolina: W59AD Andrews, etc.; W40CR-D Bakersville; W42AX Bakersville; W05AU Bat Cave, etc.; W41DI-D Bat Cave, etc.; W52BA Black Mountain; W65DT Boone; W68DM Brevard; W46AX Bryson City; W67DV Burnsville; W27AB Canton, etc.; W46EC-D Canton, etc.; W24AU Cashiers; W42DF-D Cashiers; W23AF Cullowhee; W19DB-D Franklin; W28AN Franklin; W60DA Franklin, etc.; W29DE-D Hayesville; W42AT Hayesville; W27BD Highlands; W35CK-D Highlands; W21CR-D Jefferson; W25AY Jefferson; W27AX Lake Lure; W51EE-D Lake Lure; W31AN Murphy; W35AD Sparta; W31DI-D Spruce Pine; W19CR Tryon; W59AK Zionville.
ETV Stations:
North Carolina: WUNF-DT Asheville; WUNC-DT Chapel Hill; WUNG-DT Concord; WUND-DT Edenton; WUNK-DT Greenville; WUNM-DT Jacksonville; WUNE-DT Linville; WUNU-DT Lumberton; WUNP-DT Roanoke Rapids; WUNJ-DT Wilmington; WUNL-DT Winston-Salem.

U. OF TEXAS-AUSTIN
Box D
Austin, TX 78713
LPTV Stations:
Texas: K09VR Austin.

U. OF UTAH
101 Wasatch Dr.
Salt Lake City, UT 84112
Phone: 801-581-7777
Fax: 801-585-5096
Ownership: Public educational institution.
Represented (legal): Jones, Waldo, Holbrook & McDonough PC.
LPTV Stations:
Arizona: K07PH Le Chee, etc..
Utah: K22HV-D Alton, etc.; K38IN Alton, etc.; K39IZ-D Antimony; K44GA Antimony; K21IL-D Apple Valley; K52JV-D Bicknell, etc.; K47JI Blanding & Monticello; K34IY-D Boulder; K15GN Bullfrog; K06OB Cane Beds, AZ & Hildale; K17IK-D Cane Beds, AZ/Hildale; K08OE-D Cedar City; K41GE Cedar City; K33JD-D Circleville; K41GH Delta; K54JY-D Delta & Oak City; K48KS-D Delta, etc.; K48KS-D Delta, etc.; K42IN-D Enterprise; K24FD-D Garfield (rural); K55KE-D Garfield (rural); K22FT-D Garfield County (rural); K36FW Garfield County (rural); K43DY Garfield County (rural); K50JU-D Garfield County (rural); K23IL-D Hatch; K33FX Heber & Midway; K42HS-D Henrieville; K21GW Hurricane, Leeds, etc.; K20DW-D Juab; K49AO-D Juab County (rural); K46EO-D Long Valley Junction; K50GD Long Valley Junction; K27HR Manti & Ephraim; K30JI-D Manti & Ephraim; K32HS-D Manti & Ephraim; K46FX Marysvale; K48GS Marysvale; K49JN-D Marysvale; K51JO-D Marysvale; K16BO-D Milford, etc.; K20GH-D Milford, etc.; K27GA Morgan, etc.; K15GQ Orangeville; K46JK-D Orangeville; K45JN-D Orangeville,

etc.; K41KA-D Panguitch; K25DL Park City; K18DF Price; K57KB-D Richfield, etc.; K38HO Rockville & Springdale; K33JW-D Rockville/Springdale; K57KG-D St. George, etc.; K47HB Summit County; K22DM Summit County (rural areas); K09XT Ticaboo; K20ER Tooele; K65HO Tooele; K05CP Toquerville; K19HR-D Toquerville; K55KG-D Torrey; K22IP-D Virgin; K25HB Virgin; K44JI-D Washington, etc.; K50KC-D Washington, etc..
ETV Stations:
Utah: KUEN-DT Ogden; KUES-DT Richfield; KUED-DT Salt Lake City; KUEW-DT St. George.
Radio Stations:
Utah: KUER (FM)
Other Holdings:
Television holdings: Construction permit for Ch. 15 Price & application for Ch. 17 Vernal, UT..

UNIVISION COMMUNICATIONS INC.
5999 Center Dr
Ste 4083
Los Angeles, CA 90045
Phone: 310-349-3600
Officers:
Joe Uva, Chief Executive Officer
Ray Rodriguez, President & Chief Operating Officer
Joanne Lynch, President, TV Stations Group
Andrew W. Hobson, Senior Executive Vice President, Chief Strategic & Financial Officer
C. Douglas Kranwinkle, Executive Vice President & General Counsel
Peter H. Lori, Assistant Treasurer & Assistant Secretary
Branch Office:
605 3rd Ave.
12th Floor
New York, NY 10158
Phone: 212-455-5200
Ownership: Broadcast Media Partners Holdings Inc.; BMPHI ownership:; Broadcasting Media Partners Inc.. 100 % votes, 80% assets; Broadcasting Media Partners Shareholders, 20%. assets; BMPI ownership:; SCG Investments II LLC, 9.73%. votes, 7.55% assets; TPG Umbrella V LP, 9.44%. votes, 7.68% assets; Thomas H. Lee Equity Fund VI LP, 7.85%. votes, 6.38% assets; Madison Dearborn Capital Partners V-A LP, 7.84%. votes, 6.38% assets; Providence Equity Partners V (Umbrella US) LP, 7.3%. votes, 5.94% assets; TPG Umbrella International V LP, 7.09%. votes, 5.77% assets; Madison Dearborn Capital Partners IV LP, 7.05%. votes, 5.74% assets; THL Equity Fund VI Investors (Univision) LP, 6.08%. votes, 4.95% assets; TPG Umbrella IV LP, 6.03%. votes, 4.91% assets; SCGIILLC ownership:; HSAC Investments LP; HSACILP ownership:; Haim Saban, 65.52%; Cheryl Saban, 34.48; TPGUVLP, TPGUIVLP & TPGIVLP ownership:; David Bonderman, Chmn. & Pres.; James Coulter, V.P.; THLEFVILP & THLEFVI (U)LP ownership:; Thomas H. Lee Advisors LLC; THLALLC ownership:; Todd M. Abbrecht; Charles A. Brizius; Anthony J. DiNovi; Thomas M. Hagerty; Scott L. Jaeckel; Seth W. Lawry; Soren L. Oberg; Scott A. Schoen; Scott M. Sperling; Kent R. Weldon, 10%. votes, each; MDCPV-ALP & MDCPIVLP ownership:; Madison Dearborn Partners, Gen. Partner; MDP ownership:; John A. Canning Jr., Chmn. & Chief Exec. Officer; Paul J. Finnegan, Co-Pres.; Samuel M. Mencoff, Co-Pres.; PEPV (UUS)LP ownership:; Providence Equity Partners V LLC, Gen. Partner; PEPVLLC ownership:; Glenn M. Creamer; Jonathan M. Nelsen; Paul J. Salem, Managing Members.
Represented (legal): Pillsbury Winthrop Shaw Pittman LLP.

LPTV Stations:
Arizona: K16FB Globe; KDOS-LP Globe; KFPH-CA Phoenix; KTVW-CA Phoenix; K21GC Safford; KZOL-LP Safford; K48GX Tucson; KFTU-CA Tucson; KUVE-CA Tucson.
California: KABE-LP Bakersfield; KBTF-CA Bakersfield; KTFB-CA Bakersfield; KTFF-LP Fresno; KEXT-CA Modesto; KEZT-CA Sacramento; K35ER Santa Maria; KDTV-CA Santa Rosa.
North Carolina: WTNC-LP Durham.
Pennsylvania: WFPA-CA Philadelphia; WXTV-LP Philadelphia.
Texas: KTFO-CA Austin; K45DX Floresville; KUVN-CA Fort Worth; KFTO-CA San Antonio; KNIC-CA San Antonio.
Commercial TV Stations:
Arizona: KFTU-DT Douglas; KFPH-DT Flagstaff; KUVE-DT Green Valley; KTVW-DT Phoenix.
California: KUVI-DT Bakersfield; KFTV-DT Hanford; KMEX-DT Los Angeles; KUVS-DT Modesto; KFTR-DT Ontario; KTFF-DT Porterville; KDTV-DT San Francisco; KTFK-DT Stockton; KFSF-DT Vallejo.
Florida: WAMI-DT Hollywood; WOTF-DT Melbourne; WLTV-DT Miami; WFTT-DT Tampa.
Georgia: WUVG-DT Athens.
Illinois: WXFT-DT Aurora; WGBO-DT Joliet.
Massachusetts: WUTF-DT Marlborough.
New Jersey: WFUT-DT Newark; WXTV-DT Paterson; WUVP-DT Vineland.
New Mexico: KTFQ-DT Albuquerque.
New York: WFTY-DT Smithtown.
North Carolina: WUVC-DT Fayetteville.
Ohio: WQHS-DT Cleveland.
Puerto Rico: WLII-DT Caguas; WSTE-DT Ponce; WSUR-DT Ponce.
Texas: KFTH-DT Alvin; KNIC-DT Blanco; KUVN-DT Garland; KSTR-DT Irving; KAKW-DT Killeen; KXLN-DT Rosenberg; KWEX-DT San Antonio.
Utah: KUTH-DT Provo.
Virginia: WFDC-DT Arlington.
Radio Stations:
Arizona: KKMR (FM) Arizona City, KQMR (FM) Globe, KHOT (FM) Paradise Valley, KOMR (FM) Sun City, KHOV (FM) Wickenburg
California: KOND (FM) Clovis, KSCA (FM) Glendale, KRDA (FM) Hanford, KRCD (FM) Inglewood, KLVE (FM), KTNQ (FM) Los Angeles, KLLE (FM) North Fork, KVVF (FM) Santa Clara, KSQL (FM) Santa Cruz, KLNV (FM), KLQV (FM) San Diego, KSOL (FM) S
Florida: WRTO-FM Goulds, WAMR-FM, WAQI (AM), WQBA (AM) Miami
Illinois: WRTO (AM) Chicago, WPPN (FM) Des Plaines, WOJO (FM) Evanston, WVIV-FM Highland Park, WVIX (FM) Joliet
Nevada: KRGT (FM) Indian Springs, KISF (FM) Las Vegas, KLSQ (AM) Whitney
New Jersey: WCAA (FM) Newark
New Mexico: KKRG (FM) Albuquerque; KIOT (FM) Los Lunas, KQBT (FM) Rio Rancho; KJFA (FM), KKSS (FM) Sante Fe
New York: WQBU-FM Garden City, WADO (AM) New York
Puerto Rico: WYEL (AM) Mayaguez, WUKQ-AM-FM Ponce, WKAQ-AM-FM San Juan
Texas: KDXX (FM) Benbrook, KPTI (FM) Crystal Beach; KFZO (FM) Denton; KAMA (AM), KBNA (FM), KQBU (AM) El Paso; KFLC (AM), KLNO (FM) Fort Worth; KOVE-FM Galveston; KINV (FM) Georgetown; KBTQ (FM), KGBT-AM-FM Harlingen; KLAT (AM),

UPPER COLUMBIA MEDIA ASSN.
Box 19039
Spokane, WA 99219
Phone: 509-747-1999
Officer:
Max Torkelsen II, President
LPTV Stations:
Washington: K49EV Clarkston.

UPPER GULF COAST LLC
1106 Concho Dr.
Corpus Christi, TX 78407
Phone: 361-289-0125

LPTV Stations:
Alabama: WRBM-LP Prichard.
Florida: WRBD-LP Pensacola.

V-1 PRODUCTIONS INC.
1082 12th St
Vero Beach, FL 32960
Phone: 772-978-0023
Fax: 772-978-0053
Officers:
Jose Guerra, President & General Manager
Maria Guerra, Vice President & Station Manager
Patricia Davis, Assistant General Manager
LPTV Stations:
Florida: WWCI-CA Vero Beach.

THE VACATION CHANNEL
282 Wintergreen Rd.
Branson, MO 65616
Phone: 417-334-1200
LPTV Stations:
Missouri: KBNS-CA Branson.

VAIL ASSOCIATES INC. DBA TV 8
Box 7
Vail, CO 81658
Phone: 970-479-4688
Officer:
William A. Jensen, Senior Vice President
LPTV Stations:
Colorado: K45IE Vail.

VALLEY COUNTY TV DISTRICT NO. 1
PO Box 2
501 Court Sq
Glasgow, MT 59230
Phone: 406-367-9353
Officers:
George Kolstad, Chairman
Terry Lightizer, Director
LPTV Stations:
Montana: K51BA Fort Peck; K14AR Glasgow; K16AZ Glasgow; K18BN Glasgow; K39GF Glasgow; K45CH Glasgow; K07JG Glasgow, etc.; K09HY King Springs, etc.; K11IA King Springs, etc.; K13IB King Springs, etc.; K57AJ Tampico; K69DN Tampico, etc.; K41BT Valley County; K43CQ Valley County; K47CY Valley County; K49CF Valley County.

VALLEY METRO RECREATION DISTRICT
18400 Hwy 350
Trinidad, CO 81082
Phone: 719-845-1315
Represented (legal): Garvey Schubert Barer.
LPTV Stations:
Colorado: K03DO Hoehne; K07HK Hoehne; K09HU Hoehne.

VALLEY PUBLIC TELEVISION INC.
1544 Van Ness Ave.
Fresno, CA 93721
Phone: 559-266-1800
Fax: 559-443-5433
Officers:
Armen D. Bacon, Chairman
Michael A. Carpenter, Vice Chairman & Chief Financial Officer
Colin Dougherty, Chief Executive Officer
Jo Ann Ross, Secretary
Represented (legal): Fletcher, Heald & Hildreth PLC.
LPTV Stations:
California: K18HD-D Bakersfield.
ETV Stations:
California: KVPT-DT Fresno.

VCY AMERICA INC.
3434 W. Kilbourn Ave.
Milwaukee, WI 53208
Phone: 414-935-3000
Fax: 414-935-3015
Officers:
Dr. Randall Melchert, President
Victor C. Eliason, Vice President
Walter Lecocq, Secretary-Treasurer
Ownership: Non-profit organization.
LPTV Stations:
Wisconsin: W04CW Tigerton, etc..
Commercial TV Stations:
Wisconsin: WVCY-DT Milwaukee.
Radio Stations:
Kansas: KVCY (FM) Fort Scott, KCVS (FM) Salina
Michigan: WVCM (FM) Iron Mountain
Ohio: WJIC (FM) Zanesville
South Dakota: KVCF (FM) Freeman, KVFL (FM) Pierre
Wisconsin: WVCF (FM) Eau Claire, WVFL (FM) Fond du Lac, WVCY (AM) Oshkosh, WVCX (FM) Tomah, WVRN (FM) Wittenberg

LAMAR VEASEY
7314 Butterball Way
Sacramento, CA 95842-4342
Phone: 916-501-7787
E-mail: lveasey@kspj.tv
LPTV Stations:
Kansas: KSPJ-LP Pittsburg.
Utah: KUTG-LP St. George.

VENTANA TELEVISION INC.
1031 E. Mountain Dr.
Santa Barbara, CA 93108
Phone: 805-969-6664
LPTV Stations:
Alabama: W34BI Birmingham; W30BX Mobile.
Arizona: K21CX Tucson.
Florida: W54CS Jacksonville; W19CO Pensacola; W33CC St. Petersburg.
Georgia: W23DN Atlanta.
Illinois: W32CM Champaign; W39BH Champaign; W33AY Springfield.
Iowa: K41DD Des Moines.
Kansas: K15DD Wichita.
Louisiana: K47JO New Orleans; K47HO Shreveport.
Minnesota: K43HB Minneapolis.
Missouri: K45IO Kansas City; K38HD St. Louis.
New York: W60AI New York.
North Carolina: W58CD Raleigh.
Ohio: W43BZ Columbus; W38DH Toledo.
Oklahoma: K39CW Tulsa.
Tennessee: W40CM Knoxville.
Texas: K25FW Corsicana.
Virginia: W14DC Portsmouth; W44CL Roanoke.
Washington: K43GZ Spokane.
West Virginia: W14CU Huntington.

VENTURE MEDIA GROUP LLC
Box 1507
Stillwater, OK 74076
Ownership: Trace Morgan, Chmn.
LPTV Stations:
Oklahoma: KWEM-LP Stillwater.

VENTURE TECHNOLOGIES GROUP LLC
5670 Wilshire Blvd
Ste 1300
Los Angeles, CA 90036
Phone: 323-965-5400
Fax: 323-965-5411
Officer:
Lawrence J. Rogow, Manager
Ownership: Lawrence H Rogow, 50%; Garry A Spire, 35%; Paul H Koplin, 15%.

Represented (legal): Fleischman & Harding LLP.
LPTV Stations:
Arizona: KWTA-LP Tucson.
California: KEBK-LP Bakersfield; KRMV-LP Banning; KRVD-LP Banning; KDBK-LP Caliente; KILA-LP Cherry Valley; KEFM-LP Chico; KSGO-LP Chico; KSCZ-LP Greenfield; KHTV-LP Inland Empire; KNET-CA Los Angeles; KNLA-LP Los Angeles; KSFV-CA Los Angeles; KMRZ-LP Moreno Valley; KFMD-LP Redding.
Colorado: K26HQ Estes Park; K39JT Estes Park; K42GS Estes Park.
Connecticut: WHCT-LP Hartford.
Illinois: WLFM-LP Chicago.
Indiana: W27CT Columbia.
Iowa: WBQD-LP Davenport; KSXC-LP South Sioux City.
New York: WNYA-CA Albany; W20CM Port Jervis; W26DB Port Jervis; W32DC Port Jervis; W34DI Port Jervis; W42CX Port Jervis; W46DQ Port Jervis; W52DW Port Jervis; W55DK Port Jervis; W59EA Port Jervis; WASA-LP Port Jervis.
Ohio: WXOX-LP Cleveland; WBTL-LP Toledo.
Pennsylvania: WBPA-LP Pittsburgh.
Texas: K38HP Lubbock; KFIQ-LP Lubbock; KFMP-LP Lubbock.
Washington: K38JH Bellingham.
Commercial TV Stations:
California: KBBC-DT Bishop.
Illinois: WAOE-DT Peoria.
Massachusetts: WNYA-DT Pittsfield.
Michigan: WHTV-DT Jackson.
Washington: KBCB-DT Bellingham.

VENTURE TELEVISION LLC
2310 Marin Dr.
Birmingham, AL 35243
Phone: 205-682-1019
Officer:
Michael D. Plaia, Manager
Represented (legal): Hall Estill.
LPTV Stations:
Alabama: WAXC-LP Alexander City; WETU-LP Wetumpka.

VERDI TV TAX DISTRICT
Box 221
Verdi, NV 89439
Phone: 775-345-0202
LPTV Stations:
Nevada: K30HY-D Verdi/Mogul.

VERMONT ETV INC.
88 Ethan Allen Ave.
Colchester, VT 05446-3129
Phone: 802-655-4800
Officers:
Helen Riehle, Chairman
John E. King, President & Chief Executive Officer
Lee Ann Lee, Vice President, Marketing & Development
Kelly Luoma, Vice President, Programming
Wayne Rosberg, Vice President, Engineering
Don Harvey, Vice President, Production
Andrea Bergeron, Vice President, Finance & Administration
Ownership: Non-profit corporation.
Represented (legal): Covington & Burling.
LPTV Stations:
Vermont: W36AX Manchester, etc..
ETV Stations:
Vermont: WETK-DT Burlington; WVER-DT Rutland; WVTB-DT St. Johnsbury.

VERNON VAN WINKLE
890 S. Higley Dr.
Pahrump, NV 89048

Phone: 775-727-9400
Fax: 775-727-8750
LPTV Stations:
Nevada: KPVM-LP Pahrump.

V.I. CHRISTIAN MINISTRIES INC.
105 Bolongo Bay
St. Thomas, VI 00802
Phone: 304-774-4904
Web site: www.vichristianministries.org
Officer:
Adelle Brown, President
Ownership: Adelle Brown; Audain Brown.
LPTV Stations:
Virgin Islands: WMNS-LP Charlotte Amalie.

VICTOR VALLEY PUBLIC TRANSLATOR INC.
PO Box 401055
Hesperia, CA 92340
Phone: 760-244-1007
E-mail: d_webb@hisperiaparks.com
Web site: www.hesperiaparks.com
LPTV Stations:
California: K21AC Victorville, etc.; K25AD Victorville, etc.; K27AE Victorville, etc.; K31AD Victorville, etc.; K51AN Victorville, etc..

VICTORY CENTER INC.
5th & Quinn
Box 14
Guymon, OK 73952
Phone: 405-338-5616
Fax: 405-338-2575
Officer:
Charles Mendenhall, President
Ownership: Non-profit corp.--Guymon, OK.
LPTV Stations:
Oklahoma: K25EG Balko; K53BE Guymon.

VICTORY CHRISTIAN CENTER INC.
Box 16408
Charlotte, NC 28224
Phone: 704-393-1540
Fax: 704-393-1527
Officers:
Robyn Gool, President
Wayne Hammond, Chief Executive Officer
LPTV Stations:
North Carolina: WGTB-LP Charlotte.
Radio Stations:
North Carolina: WOGR (AM) Charlotte, WGAS (AM) South Gastonia

VICTORY COMMUNICATIONS INC.
Box 177
Centerton, AR 72719
Phone: 479-795-4057
Officers:
Edward E. Hollowell, Chairman
Bryan Holland, President
Nancy H. Duke, Secretary
Bruce W. Johnson, Treasurer
Ownership: Non-profit corp.--Centerton, AR.
LPTV Stations:
Arkansas: K45EI Bentonville & Rogers.

VICTORY TRAINING SCHOOL CORP.
968 W City Dam Rd
Keavy, KY 40737
Phone: 606-528-4671
Fax: 606-528-8704
Ownership: Brenda Kay Sivley, 50%. votes; Charles Sivley Jr., 50%. votes.
Represented (legal): Fletcher, Heald & Hildreth PLC.

LPTV Stations:
Kentucky: WVTN-LP Corbin.

THE VIDEOHOUSE INC.
975 Greentree Rd.
Pittsburgh, PA 15220
Phone: 412-921-7577
Fax: 412-921-6937
Ownership: Ronald J Bruno, Pres..
LPTV Stations:
Pennsylvania: W61CC Pittsburgh.

VIDEO VOICE INC.
123 E. 54th St.
Suite 5G
New York, NY 10022-4506
Phone: 212-935-4613
Officers:
Gregory F. Schimizzi, Chairman & Chief Operating Officer
Ernest J. Schimizzi, President, Chief Executive & Financial Officer
Represented (legal): Cohn & Marks LLP.
LPTV Stations:
New York: WVVH-CA Southampton.

VILLAREAL BROADCASTING
Box 1975
San Benito, TX 78586
LPTV Stations:
Texas: K55HV Del Rio.

VIRGIN ISLANDS TELECOMMUNICATIONS VENTURES LLC
2099 Pennsylvania Ave. NW
Suite 1000
Washington, DC 20006
LPTV Stations:
Virgin Islands: WBIV-LP Charlotte Amalie.

VISION BROADCASTING NETWORK INC.
1017 New York Ave.
Alamogordo, NM 88310
Phone: 505-437-1919
Fax: 505-437-5353
E-mail: bill@kvbatv.com
Officers:
Bill Oechsner, President
Jim Forney, Vice President
Jack Brock, Chief Financial Officer
LPTV Stations:
New Mexico: K63GU Alamogordo; KVBA-LP Alamogordo; K12MP Timberon.

VISION COMMUNICATIONS LLC (NEW YORK)
33 E Market St
Corning, NY 14830
Phone: 607-937-5000
Ownership: William Christian, Pres., 20%. equity; 100% votes.
Represented (legal): Drinker Biddle.
LPTV Stations:
New York: W41DB Corning; WJKP-LP Corning.

VISION 3 BROADCASTING INC.
Suite 200
1300 Putney Rd.
Brattleboro, VT 05301-9063
Phone: 802-258-2200
LPTV Stations:
New Hampshire: WVBQ-LP Charlestown, etc..

Vermont: WVBK-CA Manchester.

B. N. VISWANATH
8696 Palermo St.
Holliswood, NY 11423
Phone: 718-479-9411
LPTV Stations:
Virginia: W30BV Norfolk.

DEEPAK VISWANATH
Box 286
East Elmhurst, NY 11369
Phone: 718-774-6869
LPTV Stations:
Florida: W45BZ Jacksonville; W67DL Jacksonville; W35BN Tallahassee.
New Jersey: WDVB-CA Edison.
Vermont: W51CB Burlington.
Other Holdings:
Program source: The Indian Channel.

DILIP B. VISWANATH
8694 Palermo St.
Holliswood, NY 11423
Phone: 718-479-9411
LPTV Stations:
Texas: KLEG-LP Dallas.

VSS CATHOLIC COMMUNICATIONS
5829 N. 60th St.
Omaha, NE 68014
Phone: 402-571-0200
LPTV Stations:
Nebraska: KVSS-LP Omaha.

WABASH COMMUNICATIONS INC.
606 Market St.
Mount Carmel, IL 62863
Phone: 618-262-4102
Fax: 618-262-4103
Officers:
Kevin C. Williams, President
Michael S. Bever, Chief Executive Officer
Scott R. McCallen, Chief Operating Officer
LPTV Stations:
Illinois: WCJT-LP Mount Carmel.
Radio Stations:
Illinois: WVMC (AM) Mount Carmel

WAGON MOUND TV CLUB
PO Box 68
Wagon Mound, NM 87752
LPTV Stations:
New Mexico: K09CR Wagon Mound; K11MD Wagon Mound.

WAITT BROADCASTING INC.
1650 Farnam St.
Omaha, NE 68102-2186
Phone: 402-346-6000
Officers:
Norman W. Waitt Jr., Chairman
Steven W. Seline, Vice Chairman
Michael J. Delich, President
Ownership: Norman W Waitt Jr..
LPTV Stations:
Iowa: K55FL Spencer; K40CO Storm Lake.
Nebraska: K35FM Norfolk.
Commercial TV Stations:
Iowa: KMEG-DT Sioux City.
Radio Stations:
Iowa: KQKQ-FM Council Bluffs
Nebraska: KYDZ (AM), KOZN (AM) Bellevue; KBLR-FM Blair; KOOO (AM) Lincoln; KKAR (AM) Omaha; KOIL (AM) Plattsmouth

WALKER RIVER PAIUTE TRIBE
Walker River Reservation
Schurz, NV 89427

Phone: 702-773-2306
Fax: 702-773-2585
Officers:
Harold Miller, Chairman
Anita M. Collins, Chief Executive Officer
LeRoy Hicks, Vice President
Patricia Hicks, Secretary
Lou Lockwood, Treasurer
Janet Thom, Chief Financial Officer
LPTV Stations:
Nevada: K32CQ Schurz; K36FF Schurz; K39FA Schurz; K46CC Schurz; K58CY Schurz.

WASATCH COUNTY
25 N. Main
Heber City, UT 84032
Phone: 435-654-3211
LPTV Stations:
Utah: K18GV Heber & Midway; K39HS Heber/Midway.

WASHBURN U.
1700 SW College Ave
Topeka, KS 66621
Phone: 785-670-1111
Fax: 785-231-1112
Officers:
Nancy Paul, Chairman, Board of Regents
Maggie Warren, Vice Chairman, Board of Regents
Ownership: Municipal university, directed by board of 9 regents.
LPTV Stations:
Kansas: K30AL-D Iola.
ETV Stations:
Kansas: KTWU-DT Topeka.

BILLY RAY WASHINGTON
1214 W. Golden Rd.
Box 366
Tiftin, GA 31794
Phone: 229-386-8642
LPTV Stations:
Georgia: W62DE Tifton.

BOARD OF WASHINGTON COUNTY COMMISSIONERS
Washington County Courthouse
Akron, CO 80720-1510
Phone: 970-345-2701
LPTV Stations:
Colorado: K33FI Akron; K35FI Akron; K41EV Akron; K43FS Akron; K47FT-D Anton; K45FD Anton & Washington County (rural SW); K49EX Anton & Washington County (rural SW); K55IB Anton & Washington County (rural SW).

WASHINGTON STATE U.
Murrow Communications Center
Pullman, WA 99164-2530
Phone: 509-335-6588
Fax: 509-335-3772
Officer:
Kenneth Alhadeff, President, Board of Regents

Branch Office:
2710 University Dr.
Richland, WA 99352-1671
Phone: 509-372-7000
Ownership: Public educational institution.
Represented (legal): Dow Lohnes PLLC.
LPTV Stations:
Idaho: K15CH Lewiston.
ETV Stations:
Washington: KWSU-DT Pullman; KTNW-DT Richland.
Radio Stations:
Idaho: KWSU (AM) Moscow

Washington: KRFA-FM Pullman, KFAE-FM Richland
Other Holdings:
Washington Higher Education Telecommunication System, statewide interactive instructional video system.

WASHOE COUNTY TV TAX DISTRICT
PO Box 221
Verdi, NV 89439
Phone: 775-345-0202
LPTV Stations:
Nevada: K10GP Verdi; K33ER Verdi; K24IB-D Verdi/Mogul; K51DJ-D Verdi/Mogul.

WATCHMEN BROADCASTING PRODUCTIONS INTERNATIONAL INC.
Box 3618
Augusta, GA 30914
Phone: 803-278-3618
Web site: www.watchmenbroadcasting.com
Officer:
Dorothy Spaulding, President
Represented (legal): Hardy, Carey, Chautin & Balkin LLP.
LPTV Stations:
Georgia: WBPI-CA Augusta.

WATCHTV INC.
1628 N.W. Everett St.
Portland, OR 97209
Phone: 503-241-2411
Fax: 503-226-3557
Web site: www.watchtvinc.com/ WatchTV,%20Inc/Welcome.html
Ownership: Gregory J Herman, President.
LPTV Stations:
Oregon: K39EF Ashland; K28FP Astoria; KABH-CA Bend; KOXI-CA Camas; K49DM-D Coos Bay; KORY-CA Eugene; K20DT Grants Pass; K39DP Klamath Falls; K28GG Medford; KOXO-CA Newberg; KKEI-CA Portland; KORK-CA Portland; K25GA Redmond, etc.; K25FG Roseburg; KORS-CA Salem.

WATERMAN BROADCASTING CORP.
Box 7578
Fort Myers, FL 33911
Phone: 941-939-2020
Fax: 941-936-7771
Officers:
Bernard E. Waterman, President
Steven H. Pontius, Executive Vice President
Edith B. Waterman, Secretary-Treasurer
Ownership: Bernard E Waterman, 90%; Edith B Waterman, 10%.
Represented (legal): Cohn & Marks LLP.
LPTV Stations:
Virginia: W31CE Bridgewater et al.; W28BF Harrisonburg.
Commercial TV Stations:
Florida: WBBH-DT Fort Myers.
Virginia: WVIR-DT Charlottesville.

WATERS & BROCK COMMUNICATIONS INC.
PO Box 1826
Smithfield, NC 27577
Phone: 919-965-5328
E-mail: tv34@mindspring.com
Officer:
Sarah Waters, Secretary
Ownership: Gerald Waters.

LPTV Stations:
North Carolina: WARZ-LP Smithfield/Selma.

VERNON WATSON
3101 North R St.
6582 Oakcliff Rd
Pensacola, FL 32505-5101
Phone: 850-433-1210
Fax: 850-433-2537
Represented (legal): Louis F. Ray Jr..
LPTV Stations:
Florida: WBQP-CA Pensacola.

WAUBONSEE COMMUNITY COLLEGE
6213 Middleton Springs Dr.
Communications Technology Inc.
Middleton, WI 53562
LPTV Stations:
Illinois: W40CN Sugar Grove.

WAUKESHA TOWER ASSOC.
11950 W. Lake Park Dr.
Milwaukee, WI 53224
Phone: 414-359-1800
Fax: 414-359-9075
Ownership: Robert J Von Bereghy; Martin T Franke; Maurice S Meyers.
LPTV Stations:
Wisconsin: WTAS-LP Waukesha.

WAYNE COUNTY
18 S. Main
Loa, UT 84747
Phone: 435-836-2765
LPTV Stations:
Utah: K45JO-D Bicknell & Teasdale; K54JV-D Bicknell, etc.; K12PX Fremont; K19GO-D Fremont; K21ID-D Fremont; K03AU Loa, etc.; K23II-D Loa, etc.; K25JF-D Loa, etc.; K27IX-D Loa, etc.; K02BO Teasdale & Torrey; K04BN Teasdale & Torrey; K05BG Teasdale & Torrey; K39IV-D Teasdale & Torrey; K43KI-D Teasdale & Torrey; K53JG-D Teasdale, etc.; K41JZ-D Wayne County.

WBGT LLC
33 E. Market St.
Corning, NY 14830
Phone: 607-937-5000
Ownership: Vision Communications LLC (New York); VCLLC ownership:; William Christian, Pres., 20%. equity; 100% votes.
Represented (legal): Drinker Biddle.
LPTV Stations:
New York: WBGT-CA Rochester; W26BZ Victor.

WBKISLG LLC
2310 N Molter Rd
Ste 112
Liberty Lake, WA 99019
Phone: 502-348-1645
Officer:
Gregory W. Kunz, Manager
Ownership: National Television Investments LLC, 51.1%. voting interest; Big Hat LLC, 28.6%. voting interest; Sidney LLC, 18.7%. voting interest; Old Red Vines LLC, 1.5%. voting interest; NTI ownership:; Gregory W. Kunz Trust, 25.57%. voting interest; Enterprise Wagon Inc., 9.2%. voting interest; EWI ownership:; Gregory W. Kunz Trust; Deniis W. Brush & Anne K. Brush (Revocable Living) Trust; BHLLC ownership:; Gregory W Kunz; SLLC ownership:; William S Levine; ORVLLC ownership:; Dennis W Brush.
Represented (legal): Davis Wright Tremaine LLP.
LPTV Stations:
Kentucky: WBKI-CA Louisville.
Commercial TV Stations:
Kentucky: WBKI-DT Campbellsville.

WEAVERVILLE TRANSLATOR CORP.
Box 1269
Weaverville, CA 96093-1269
Phone: 530-623-4607
E-mail: r.laudahl@snowcrest.net
Officer:
Richard Laudahl, Chairman
LPTV Stations:
California: K04DD Weaverville; K05CF Weaverville, etc..

WEBER COUNTY, OGDEN VALLEY RECREATION/TRANSMISSION SPECIAL SERVICES DISTRICT
Box 336
Eden, UT 84310
Phone: 801-745-3484
Officers:
John W. Howell, Chairman
Kay Richins, Secretary
LPTV Stations:
Utah: K32HD Huntsville; K45JC Huntsville; K47KE Huntsville; K51JC Huntsville; K17IP-D Huntsville, etc.; K23IC-D Huntsville, etc.; K25IX-D Huntsville, etc.; K39IS-D Huntsville, etc.; K28JK-D Huntsville/Liberty.

WEIGEL BROADCASTING CO.
26 N Halsted St
Chicago, IL 60661
Phone: 312-705-2600
Fax: 312-705-2656
Officers:
Howard Shapiro, Chairman
Norman H. Shapiro, President & Secretary-Treasurer
Neal Sabin, Executive Vice President
William J. Lyall, Controller
Ownership: Howard Shapiro, 48%. votes; Norman H. Shapiro, 17%. votes; Fred Bishop, trustee, 29%. votes.
Represented (legal): Cohn & Marks LLP.
LPTV Stations:
Illinois: WMEU-CA Chicago; WWME-CA Chicago; WWME-LD Chicago; WFBN-LP Rockford.
Indiana: WCWW-LD South Bend; WCWW-LP South Bend; WMYS-LD South Bend; WMYS-LP South Bend.
Wisconsin: WMLW-CA Milwaukee; WYTU-LD Milwaukee; WYTU-LP Milwaukee.
Commercial TV Stations:
Illinois: WCIU-DT Chicago.
Wisconsin: WDJT-DT Milwaukee; WBME-DT Racine.

MARTIN WEISS
3460 Torrance Blvd.
Suite 100
Torrance, CA 90503
Phone: 310-373-9647
LPTV Stations:
New York: W46DY Utica.
Texas: K54JQ Big Spring; K22IZ Midland.

RANDALL A. WEISS
406 Copeland Dr.
Cedar Hill, TX 75104
Phone: 972-291-3750
E-mail: randy@axcesstech.net
LPTV Stations:
California: KMSX-LD Chico.
Florida: WCTU-LD Panama City.

DAVID WELCH
5917 N. Isabell
Peoria, IL 61614
Phone: 309-655-5418

LPTV Stations:
New York: W14BU Massena.

WELLSPRINGS BEAUMONT TV INC.
PO Box 7519
Santa Monica, CA 90406
Phone: 409-813-1000
Officer:
Gershon Haston, Manager
LPTV Stations:
Ohio: WAKN-LP Akron.

WELLSPRINGS TELEVISION NETWORK INC.
1280 Bowie St.
Beaumont, TX 77701
Phone: 409-813-1000
LPTV Stations:
Oklahoma: KOKM-LP Stillwater.

WELLTON-MOHAWK IRRIGATION & DRAINAGE DISTRICT
30570 Wellton-Mohawk Dr.
Wellton, AZ 85356
LPTV Stations:
Arizona: K49BX Martinez Lake; K61AX Wellton-Mohawk; K63AV Wellton-Mohawk; K65BB Wellton-Mohawk; K67BI Wellton-Mohawk.

WENDOVER CITY
100 S. 9th St.
Wendover, UT 84083
Phone: 435-665-2523
Officer:
Glen Wadsworth, City Administrator
LPTV Stations:
Utah: K15GZ Wendover.

WEST CENTRAL ILLINOIS EDUCATIONAL TELECOMMUNICATIONS CORP.
Box 6248
WMEC/WQEC/WSEC
Springfield, IL 62708
Phone: 217-483-7887
Fax: 217-483-1112
Officers:
Robert Weirather, Chairman
Keith Bradbury, Vice Chairman
Lea Hudson, 2nd Vice Chairman
Robert Fluent, 3rd Vice Chairman
Jerold Gruebel, President & Chief Executive Officer
Richard Liebig, Secretary
Elwin Basquin, Treasurer
Carol Posegate, Assistant Secretary
Ownership: Non-profit organization.
Represented (legal): Dow Lohnes PLLC.
LPTV Stations:
Illinois: W08DP Springfield.
ETV Stations:
Illinois: WSEC-DT Jacksonville; WMEC-DT Macomb; WQEC-DT Quincy.

WEST CENTRAL MINNESOTA ETV CORP.
120 W. Schlieman
Appleton, MN 56208
Phone: 320-289-2622
Fax: 320-289-2634
Officers:
Craig Wilkening, Chairman
Ray Millett, 1st Vice Chairman
Loy J. Woelber, 2nd Vice Chairman
Glen Cerny, President
Rebecca Webb, Secretary-Treasurer
Ownership: Non-profit corp.--Appleton, MN.

LPTV Stations:
Minnesota: K49FA Fergus Falls.
ETV Stations:
Minnesota: KWCM-DT Appleton; KSMN-DT Worthington.

WESTERN NEW YORK PUBLIC BROADCASTING ASSOCIATION
Horizons Plaza
Box 1263
Buffalo, NY 14240
Phone: 716-845-7000
Officers:
Mary Ann Lauricella, Chairman
Donald Boswell, President & Chief Executive Officer
LPTV Stations:
New York: W59AH Allentown, etc.; W61AJ Andover; W65AJ Angelica, etc.; W68AJ Bolivar & Richburg; W62AE Cherry Creek, etc.; W60AJ Cuba; W62AQ Fillmore; W60AC Findley Lake; W62AS Friendship & Belmont; W56AD Kennedy; W64AF Sherman; W62AS Sinclairville; W56AU Wellsville & Scio; W64AJ Whitesville.
ETV Stations:
New York: WNED-DT Buffalo.
Radio Stations:
New York: WNED-AM-FM

WESTERN FAMILY TELEVISION INC.
PO Box 4218
Helena, MT 59604-4218
Phone: 406-442-2655
E-mail: tvinvestor@gmail.com
Officer:
Roger Lonnquist, President
Ownership: Roger Lonnquist, 34%. votes; Janice Lonnquist, 33%; Verdell Lonnquist, 33%.
LPTV Stations:
American Samoa: KJCP-LP Pago Pago.
Kansas: KJCA-LP Chanute; KJCJ-LP Pittsburg.
Maine: WCKD-LP Bangor.
Montana: K48IQ Billings; KJCX-LP Bozeman; KJJC-LP Helena.
Wisconsin: W58DQ La Crosse.
Wyoming: KSWY-LP Sheridan.

WESTERN KANE COUNTY SPECIAL SERVICE DISTRICT NO. 1
28 N. Main
Kanab, UT 84741
Phone: 435-527-3566
LPTV Stations:
Arizona: K15DX Fredonia, etc..
Utah: K09NV Alton; K110C Alton; K130R Alton; K21IH-D Alton; K24IH-D Alton; K25KN-D Alton; K34FO-D Alton; K02BI Kanab; K05AX Kanab; K27JV-D Kanab; K28IT Kanab; K40JM-D Kanab; K03CX Long Valley Junction; K06FM Long Valley Junction; K48EK-D Long Valley Junction; K02EN Orderville; K04EK Orderville; K05DU Orderville; K16BT Orderville; K30CP Orderville; K44FU Orderville; K07OY Orderville, etc..

WEST LANE TRANSLATOR INC.
PO Box 91
Florence, OR 97439
Phone: 541-902-0339
Officer:
Larry Bloomfield, President
LPTV Stations:
Oregon: K52DO Florence; K56DL Florence; K58CW Florence; K60DQ Florence.

WEST VIRGINIA EDUCATIONAL BROADCASTING AUTHORITY
600 Capitol St.
Charleston, WV 25301

Phone: 304-295-6511
Fax: 304-293-2642
Ownership: State of West Virginia.
Represented (legal): William D. Silva.
LPTV Stations:
West Virginia: W34DW-D Hampshire, etc.;
W41DK-D Keyser; W08EE-D Martinsburg;
W09CT-D Mathias, etc.; W57AG Parkersburg;
W69AC Romney; W07DN-D Wardensville,
etc..
Wyoming: W51EG-D Parkersburg.
ETV Stations:
West Virginia: WPBY-DT Huntington; WNPB-DT
Morgantown.
Other Holdings:
Radio.

WEST YELLOWSTONE TV TRANSLATOR DISTRICT
PO Box 536
11 Bonnie View Circle
West Yellowstone, MT 59758-0536
Phone: 208-238-0949
LPTV Stations:
Montana: K28AZ West Yellowstone; K30BC
West Yellowstone; K32CG West Yellowstone;
K34AW West Yellowstone.

MEL WHEELER INC.
c/o Brooks, Pierce, McLendon, Humphrey &
Leonard LLP
PO Box 1800
Raleigh, NC 27602
Phone: 919-839-0300
Officer:
Stephen Wheeler, President
Ownership: Leonard E. Wheeler, 34.7%. assets;
Stephen J. Wheeler, 33.3%. assets; Clark
V. Wheeler, 31.6%. assets; Daniel Wheeler,
0.2%. assets; Joseph Wheeler, 0.2%.
Represented (legal): Brooks, Pierce, McLendon,
Humphrey & Leonard LLP.
LPTV Stations:
Missouri: K10KM Cape Girardeau.
Commercial TV Stations:
Illinois: WSIL-DT Harrisburg.
Missouri: KPOB-DT Poplar Bluff.
Radio Stations:
Virginia: WFIR (AM), WSLC-FM, WSLQ (FM),
WVBE-AM-FM, WXLK (FM) Roanoke.

WHITE BIRD TV ASSOCIATION
PO Box 151
White Bird, ID 83554
Phone: 208-839-2441
Officer:
William Shuck, Information Contact
LPTV Stations:
Idaho: K09GK White Bird; K11BJ White Bird;
K13JL White Bird.

GARY WHITE
Box 515
Lebanon, KY 40033
Phone: 270-692-0237
Fax: 270-692-6915
LPTV Stations:
Kentucky: W06AY Lebanon.

WHITEHALL LOW POWER TV INC.
Box 487
Whitehall, MT 59759
LPTV Stations:
Montana: K40HL Whitehall; K52CE Whitehall.

WHITE KNIGHT HOLDINGS INC.
9257 Bailey Ln
Fairfax, VA 22031-1903
Phone: 703-253-2027

Officer:
Anthony J. Malara III, President
Ownership: Malara Enterprises LLC; MELLC
ownership:; Anthony J. Malara III. Malara
is also principal of TCM Media Associates
LLC, see listing.
Represented (legal): WolfBlock.
LPTV Stations:
Louisiana: KZUP-CA Baton Rouge.
Texas: KLPN-LP Longview; KFXL-LP Lufkin;
KTPN-LP Tyler.
Commercial TV Stations:
Louisiana: WVLA-DT Baton Rouge; KSHV-DT
Shreveport.
Texas: KFXK-DT Longview.

WHITE PINE TELEVISION DISTRICT NO. 1
PO Box 151704
Ely, NV 89315
Phone: 775-289-4048
Officer:
R. E. Swain, Chairman
LPTV Stations:
Nevada: K14AL Ely; K24GY Ely; K26HY Ely;
K28IZ Ely; K30CN Ely; K32CJ Ely; K34CM
Ely; K13NR Ely, etc.; K08CB Lund &
Preston; K10BU Lund & Preston; K12DE
Lund & Preston; K45HS Lund & Preston;
K47HV Lund & Preston; K49AM Lund &
Preston; K11EE Murray Canyon; K07DU
Murray Canyon, etc.; K09EA Murray Canyon,
etc.; K50IY Murray Canyon, etc.; K55AO
Panaca; K03DS Ruth; K07DV Ruth; K09DW
Ruth; K11ED Ruth; K13NQ Ruth; K43IL
Ruth; K08IY Steptoe/Ruby Valley; K10KL
Steptoe/Ruby Valley; K12KO Steptoe/Ruby
Valley.

REBECCA L. WHITE
3191 Marlin Rd.
Box 385
Salem, IN 47167
Phones: 812-883-3401; 812-883-5750
Fax: 812-883-2797
Represented (legal): Koerner & Olender PC.
LPTV Stations:
Indiana: WHAN-LP Salem.
Radio Stations:
Indiana: WSLM-AM-FM Salem

E. ROGER WILLIAMS, TRUSTEE
114 Ferris Hill Rd
New Canaan, CT 06840
Phone: 203-972-6447
E-mail: pappastrustee@gmail.com
Represented (legal): Davis Wright Tremaine
LLP.
LPTV Stations:
California: KMPH-CA Merced-Mariposa; KREN-
LP Susanville; KDSL-CA Ukiah.
Nebraska: KPTP-LP Norfolk; KKAZ-CA Omaha.
Nevada: KNNC-LP Battle Mountain; KRNS-CA
Reno; KPMP-LP Winnemucca.
New Mexico: KKNJ-LP Alamogordo; KCWO-CA
Silver City, etc..
Washington: KCWK-LP Yakima.
Commercial TV Stations:
California: KTNC-DT Concord; KFRE-DT Sanger;
KMPH-DT Visalia.
Iowa: KPTH-DT Sioux City.
Nebraska: KPTM-DT Omaha.
Nevada: KREN-DT Reno.
North Carolina: WCWG-DT Lexington.
Texas: KAZH-DT Baytown; KDBC-DT El Paso.

WILLMAR ASSEMBLY OF GOD CHURCH
3023 15th St. SW
Willmar, MN 56201
Phone: 612-235-2200

Fax: 612-235-3837
Officer:
Dale Lindquist, Chief Operating Officer
LPTV Stations:
Minnesota: K28IF Willmar.

JAMES WILSON III
805 N. Oates St.
Suite 13
Dothan, AL 36303
Phone: 205-671-1753
LPTV Stations:
Alabama: WJJN-LP Dothan.

WINDSONG COMMUNICATIONS INC.
104 Woodmont
Montgomery, TX 77356
Phone: 936-443-4451
E-mail: cdowenj1@cs.com
Officer:
C. Dowen Johnson, Member
Represented (legal): James L. Oyster.
LPTV Stations:
Louisiana: K45HY Lake Charles; K63HF Lake
Charles; KYHT-LP Lake Charles.
Texas: KAOB-LP Beaumont; KVVC-LP Corpus
Christi; K63GZ Midland; K43IQ San Angelo;
KVCV-LP Victoria.

WINIFRED TV TAX DISTRICT
PO Box 142
Winifred, MT 59489-0142
Phone: 406-462-5383
E-mail: tlunde@ttc-cmc.net
Officer:
Twila Lunde, Information Contact
LPTV Stations:
Montana: K07OA Winifred, etc.; K11NH
Winifred, etc..

WINNETT COMMUNITY TV SYSTEM
PO Box 147
203 W. Rowley
Winnett, MT 59087
LPTV Stations:
Montana: K06LF Winnett; K10DA Winnett;
K12FD Winnett.

WIRELESS ACCESS LLC
55 Swart St.
Margaretville, NY 12455
Phone: 914-586-3311
LPTV Stations:
Montana: K44GE Helena.
New York: WVBG-LP Greenwich.

WISCONSIN EDUCATIONAL COMMUNICATIONS BOARD
3319 W. Beltline Hwy.
Madison, WI 53713-4296
Phone: 608-264-9600
Fax: 608-264-9622
Officers:
Thomas L. Fletemeyer, Chief Executive &
Operating Officer
Ted Tobie, Chief Financial Officer
Ownership: State of Wisconsin.
LPTV Stations:
Wisconsin: W22CI Bloomington; W48DB-
D Coloma; W45CD-D Fence; W24CL-D
Grantsburg; W47CO-D River Falls; W18CU-
D Sister Bay.
ETV Stations:
Wisconsin: WPNE-TV Green Bay; WHLA-DT La
Crosse; WHWC-DT Menomonie; WLEF-DT
Park Falls; WHRM-DT Wausau.

WITF INC.
1982 Locust Lane
Harrisburg, PA 17109

Phone: 717-236-6000
Fax: 717-236-4628
Officers:
Bruce Bartels, Chairman
Gregory C. Poland, Chief Financial Officer
Represented (legal): Dow Lohnes PLLC.
LPTV Stations:
Pennsylvania: W24CS Reading.
ETV Stations:
Pennsylvania: WITF-DT Harrisburg.
Radio Stations:
Pennsylvania: WITF-FM Harrisburg
Other Holdings:
Magazine: Central PAmagazine.

W. RUSSELL WITHERS JR.
Box 1508
Mount Vernon, IL 62864-1508
Phone: 618-242-3500
Represented (legal): Dennis J. Kelly.
LPTV Stations:
West Virginia: W22CY Clarksburg; W30CH
Clarksburg; W31CQ Elkins.
Commercial TV Stations:
Michigan: WDHS-DT Iron Mountain.
West Virginia: WVFX-DT Clarksburg; WDTV-DT
Weston.
Radio Stations:
Alaska: KOKX (AM) Keokuk
Illinois: WKIB (FM) Anna; WROY (AM), WRUL
(FM) Carmi; WILY (AM), WRXX (FM)
Centralia; WISH-FM Galatia; WYNG (FM)
Mount Carmel
Kentucky: WGKY (FM) Wickliffe
Missouri: KJXX (AM) Jackson

WLNY HOLDINGS INC.
270 S. Service Rd.
Suite 55
Melville, NY 11747
Phone: 631-777-8855
Fax: 631-777-8180
Officers:
Michael C. Pascucci, President
Marvin Chauvin, Chief Executive Officer
Christopher S. Pascucci, Vice President &
Assistant Secretary
Ownership: Michael C. Pascucci; Jocelyn
Pascucci, trustees, jointly, 44.57%; Christo-
pher S. Pascucci, 26.81%; Michael A.
Pascucci, 3.69%; Dawn Pascucci, 3.69%;
Ralph P. Pascucci, 3.69%; Michael C.
Pascucci, 0.72%.
Represented (legal): Cohn & Marks LLP.
LPTV Stations:
Connecticut: W27CD Stamford.
New Jersey: W54CZ Morristown.
New York: WLIG-LD Mineola.
Commercial TV Stations:
New York: WLNY-DT Riverhead.

WMHT EDUCATIONAL TELECOMMUNICATIONS
17 Fern Ave.
Box 17
Schenectady, NY 12301-0017
Phone: 518-356-1700
Fax: 518-357-1709
Officer:
Bill Fibiger, Chairman
Represented (legal): Schwartz, Woods & Miller.
LPTV Stations:
New York: W04BD Glens Falls; W04AJ
Schoharie, etc..
ETV Stations:
New York: WMHT-DT Schenectady.
Radio Stations:
New York: WEXT (FM) Amsterdam, WRHV
(FM) Poughkeepsie, WMHT-FM Schenectady

W-M TV ASSOCIATION
18595 Karl Rd
Leavenworth, WA 98826
LPTV Stations:
Washington: K03EC Winton, etc..

WMTY INC.
156 2nd Ave NE
Hamilton, AL 35570
Phone: 205-921-5150
Officer:
William E Nichols, President
LPTV Stations:
Alabama: W24DC Hamilton; W46DF Hamilton; W23AK Jasper; W45CW Russellville; W46CF Tuscumbia.

WOLF POINT TV DISTRICT
139 E. Johnson St.
Wolf Point, MT 59201
Phone: 406-653-1427
LPTV Stations:
Montana: K04GF Wolf Point; K06AV Wolf Point; K13FP Wolf Point; K25HO Wolf Point; K27JQ Wolf Point; K29FS Wolf Point; K61CP Wolf Point.

WOOD INVESTMENTS LLC
122 Capitol St.
Suite 200
Charleston, WV 25301
Phone: 304-552-2064
Officer:
Tom Susman, Manager
LPTV Stations:
Ohio: WVEX-LP Marietta; WWVX-LP Marietta.
West Virginia: WVUX-LP Clarksburg.

VILLAGE OF WOOD LAKE
PO Box 788
Wood Lake, NE 69221
LPTV Stations:
Nebraska: K13AW Wood Lake.

WORD OF GOD FELLOWSHIP INC.
3901 Hwy 121 S
Bedford, TX 76021
Phone: 817-571-1229
Officers:
Marcus D. Lamb, President
Joni T. Lamb, Vice President
Ownership: Non-profit corp.--Colleyville, TX; Corrine Lamb, 20%; Jimmie F. Lamb, 20%; Joni T. Lamb, 20%; Marcus D. Lamb, 20%; John T. Calender, 20%.
Represented (legal): Koerner & Olender PC.
LPTV Stations:
Alabama: WBUN-CA Birmingham.
Arizona: KPCE-LP Green Valley.
California: KPCD-LP Big Bear Lake; KSCD-LP Big Bear Lake; KDAS-LP Clarks Crossing; KACA-LP Modesto; KRJR-LP Sacramento; KDTS-LP Stockton.
Colorado: KDNF-LP Fort Collins.
District of Columbia: WDDN-LP Washington.
Florida: WSVT-CA Bradenton; WOCD-LP Dunnellon; WUJF-LP Maxville; WDTO-LP Orlando; WSLF-LP Port St. Lucie.
Georgia: WGGD-LP Cleveland; WDDA-LP Dalton; WCTD-LP Ducktown; WDTA-LP Fayetteville; WDMA-CA Macon.
Hawaii: KAUI-LP Wailuku.
Idaho: KQUP-LP Coeur d'Alene.
Kentucky: WBLU-LP Lexington.
Maine: WLLB-LP Portland.
Michigan: WUDT-CA Detroit; WUHQ-LP Grand Rapids.
Minnesota: WDMI-LP Minneapolis.
Mississippi: WJKO-LP Jackson.
Missouri: KDSI-CA Carthage; KCDN-LP Kansas City; KDTL-LP St. Louis; KUMO-LP St. Louis.

Nebraska: KOHA-LP Omaha.
Nevada: KLVD-LP Las Vegas.
New York: WDTB-LP Hamburg; WWBI-LP Plattsburgh.
North Carolina: WAEN-LP Asheville; WDMC-LP Charlotte; WACN-LP Raleigh; WWIW-LP Raleigh.
Ohio: WCDN-LP Cleveland; WCLL-CA Columbus.
Oklahoma: KDNT-LP Allen; KTZT-CA Tulsa.
Pennsylvania: WELL-LP Philadelphia.
South Carolina: WSQY-LP Spartanburg.
Tennessee: WJTD-LP Jackson; WDTT-LP Knoxville; WDNM-LP Memphis; WNTU-LP Nashville.
Texas: KDAX-LP Amarillo; KDCP-LP Corpus Christi; KADT-LP Killeen; KQVE-LP La Vernia; KDHU-LP Louise; KLOD-LP Lubbock; KPTD-LP Paris.
Utah: K45GX Salt Lake City; KUBX-LP Salt Lake City.
Virginia: W25CS Chesapeake; WDWA-LP Luray; WRID-LP Richmond.
Commercial TV Stations:
Alabama: WDPM-DT Mobile.
Arkansas: KWOG-DT Springdale.
Illinois: WPXS-DT Mount Vernon.
Oklahoma: KOCM-DT Norman.
Tennessee: WMAK-DT Knoxville.
ETV Stations:
Colorado: KRMT-DT Denver.
Other Holdings:
Broadcast Holdings: Tri-State Family Broadcasting Inc., see listing.

WORD OF LIFE MINISTRIES INC.
Box 18862
Shreveport, LA 71138
LPTV Stations:
Louisiana: KADO-LP Shreveport.

WORLD EVANGELISM OUTREACH
85 N. Davis Lane
De Funiak Springs, FL 32433
Phone: 850-892-6202
Fax: 850-892-6226
Officers:
R. Wayne White, Manager
James Roberts, Vice President
Elaine White, Secretary
Roger White, Chief Financial Officer
Ownership: World Evangelism Outreach Church.
LPTV Stations:
Florida: WWEO-CA De Funiak Springs.

WOTM LLC
1012 Lake Heather Rd.
Birmingham, AL 35242
Phone: 205-682-1019
Officer:
Michael A. Plaia, Manager
Ownership: James Donald Earley, 25%.
LPTV Stations:
Alabama: WOTM-LP Montevallo.

WRANGELL MOUNTAIN TV CLUB INC.
Box 647
Glennallen, AK 99588
Phone: 907-822-3407
LPTV Stations:
Alaska: K03FJ Gakona, etc.; K07QS Glennallen.

JOAN & KENNETH WRIGHT
Box 8222
Hampton, VA 23666
Phone: 757-639-4768

LPTV Stations:
Virginia: WGBS-LP Hampton, etc..

WRNN-TV ASSOCIATES LP
800 Westchester Ave
Ste S640
Rye Brook, NY 10573
Phone: 914-417-2700
Officer:
Richard E. French Jr., President & Secretary of General Partner
Ownership: New Mass Media Inc., Gen. Partner, 1.5%; Hudson Valley Holdings LP, Ltd. Partner, 98.5%; NMMI ownership:; Richard E. French Jr., Pres. & Secy.; HVHLP ownership:; Sullivan & Booth Inc., Gen. Partner, 50.77%. Class A Interest; 99% Class B Interest; Richard E. French Jr., Ltd. Partner, 1%. Class B Interest; Maria Cristina French, Trustee, Richard E. French Jr. 2004 Descendants Trust, 18.78%. Class A Interest; Christian French, Ltd. Partner, 10.15%. Class A Interest; Mark French, Ltd. Partner, 10.15%. Class A Interest; Richard French III, Ltd. Partner, 10.15%. Class A Interest; SABI ownership:; Richard E. French Jr., Pres. & Secy., 39.72%. shareholder; Maria Cristina French, 39.72%. shareholder; David Ross, 11.54%. shareholder; Christian French, 3.01%. shareholder; Mark French, 3.01%. shareholder; Richard French III, 3.01%. shareholder.
LPTV Stations:
New York: WRNN-LP Nyack.
Commercial TV Stations:
New York: WRNN-DT Kingston.
Pennsylvania: WTVE-DT Reading.

WSKG PUBLIC TELECOMMUNICATIONS COUNCIL
Box 3000
Binghamton, NY 13902-3000
Phone: 607-729-0100
Fax: 607-729-7328
Officers:
Clover Drinkwater, Chairman, Board of Trustees
Suzanne Miller-Cormier, Director, Development
Gary Reinbolt, Chief Executive Officer
Naomi Rupright, Business Office Manager
Represented (legal): Dow Lohnes PLLC.
LPTV Stations:
New York: W60AD Savona.
ETV Stations:
New York: WSKG-DT Binghamton; WSKA-DT Corning.
Radio Stations:
New York: WSKG-FM, WSQX-FM Binghamton; WSQE (FM) Corning; WSQA (FM) Hornell; WSQG-FMIthaca; WSQC-FM Oneonta

WTVA INC.
Box 350
Tupelo, MS 38802
Phone: 662-842-7620
Fax: 662-844-7061
Ownership: Mary Jane Spain, 51%; Margaret H. Spain, 40%; Estate of Frank K. Spain, see listing, 9%.
Represented (legal): Garvey Schubert Barer.
LPTV Stations:
Mississippi: W32BH Tupelo.
Commercial TV Stations:
Mississippi: WTVA-DT Tupelo.

WYDC INC.
33 E. Market St.
Corning, NY 14830
Phone: 607-937-6144
Fax: 607-937-4269
Ownership: Bill Christian, President.

Represented (legal): Putney, Twombly, Hall & Hirson LLP.
LPTV Stations:
New York: W20BL Bath; W26BF Elmira; WMYH-LP Elmira, Watkins Glen; W16BE Hornell.
Commercial TV Stations:
New York: WYDC-DT Corning.

WYOMEDIA CORP.
1856 Skyview Dr.
Casper, WY 82601
Phone: 307-577-5923
Officers:
Marvin Gussman, Chairman & President
Toni Lattea, Secretary-Treasurer
Ownership: Marvin Gussman.
Represented (legal): Borsari & Associates PLC.
LPTV Stations:
Wyoming: K26ES Casper; K09XL Douglas; K11RN Douglas.
Commercial TV Stations:
Wyoming: KFNB-DT Casper; KLWY-DT Cheyenne; KFNR-DT Rawlins; KFNE-DT Riverton.

WZBN-TV INC.
77 Shady Lane
Trenton, NJ 08619
Phone: 609-586-5088
Fax: 609-586-8221
Officers:
Louis A. Zanoni, Chairman
Gregory L. Zanoni, President
Doreen Damico, Chief Financial Officer
Ownership: Gregory L Zanoni, 55%; Doreen Damico, 15%; Diana Zanoni, 14%; Louis A Zanoni, 15%.
Represented (legal): Irwin, Campbell & Tannenwald PC.
LPTV Stations:
New Jersey: W25AW Trenton; W49CW-D Trenton.

CHANNEL 6 INC.
[Out of business.], AL
LPTV Stations:
Texas: KMAY-LP Bryan.
Commercial TV Stations:
Texas: KCEN-DT Temple.

PIKES PEAK BROADCASTING CO.
[Out of business.],
LPTV Stations:
Colorado: K21JK-D Montrose.
Other Holdings:
TV Stations..

SAGE BROADCASTING CORP.
[Out of business.],
LPTV Stations:
Texas: KIDZ-LP Abilene; KIDV-LP Albany; KIDU-LP Brownwood; KIDT-LP Stamford; KIDB-CA Sweetwater.
Commercial TV Stations:
Texas: KXVA-DT Abilene; KIDY-DT San Angelo.

YAKUTAT CITY SCHOOL DISTRICT
5900 E. Tudor Rd.
Anchorage, AK 99507
Phone: 907-269-5744
LPTV Stations:
Alaska: K02ID Yakutat.

YAMPA VALLEY TV ASSOCIATION INC.
PO Box 773598
Steamboat Springs, CO 80477

LPTV Stations:
Colorado: K06CE Hayden; K09NX Hayden; K02DY Oak Creek; K69DL Oak Creek; K06CH Oak Creek, etc.; K09IF Oak Creek, etc.; K03CL Steamboat Springs; K06CF Steamboat Springs; K09GX Steamboat Springs; K12KR Toponas; K13ES Yampa, etc..

YELLOWSTONE VALLEY COMMUNITY TV

Box 21157
Billings, MT 59104
Phone: 406-652-1288
Fax: 406-655-9401
Officers:
Gail Edward Craig, President
Hilton McClendon, Vice President
Jay Simpson, Secretary-Treasurer
LPTV Stations:
Montana: K14IS Billings.

YOUNG BROADCASTING INC., DEBTOR IN POSSESSION

PO Box 1800
c/o Brooks, Pierce, et al.
Raleigh, NC 27602
Phone: 919-839-0300
E-mail: invest@youngbroadcasting.com
Officers:
Vincent J. Young, Chairman & Chief Executive Officer
Deborah A McDermott, President
James A Morgan, Executive Vice President, Chief Financial Officer & Secretary
Daniel R Batchelor, Senior Vice President, Director of Sales
Chris Eisenhardt, Vice President, Assistant Secretary & Controller
Robert Petersen, Vice President, Business Development
Peter Grazioli, Vice President, Information Technology
Brian J Greif, Vice President, News
Janice E Cross, Assistant Secretary
Ownership: Publicly held; Adam Young; Vincent Young, Principals. Young Broadcasting Inc. filed for Chapter 11 bankruptcy February 13, 2009.
Represented (legal): Brooks, Pierce, McLendon, Humphrey & Leonard LLP.
LPTV Stations:
California: K25HI Santa Rosa.
New York: W04AE Herkimer.
South Dakota: K24DT Aberdeen; K57BX Lake Andes; K69DJ Philip, etc..
Commercial TV Stations:
California: KRON-DT San Francisco.
Iowa: KWQC-DT Davenport.
Louisiana: KLFY-DT Lafayette.
Massachusetts: WCDC-DT Adams.
Michigan: WLNS-DT Lansing.
New York: WTEN-DT Albany.
South Dakota: KDLO-DT Florence; KCLO-DT Rapid City; KPLO-DT Reliance; KELO-DT Sioux Falls.
Tennessee: WATE-DT Knoxville; WKRN-DT Nashville.
Virginia: WRIC-DT Petersburg.
Wisconsin: WBAY-DT Green Bay.
Other Holdings:
TV Station sales representative: Adam Young Inc..

ZGS BROADCASTING HOLDINGS INC.

2000 N. 14th St.
Suite 400
Arlington, VA 22201
Phone: 703-528-5656
E-mail: info@zgsgroup.com
Officers:
Peter Housman, President, Business & Corporate Affairs
Eduardo Zavala, President, Digital & Broadcast Operations

Branch Offices:
1650 Sand Lake Rd
Ste 215
Orlando, FL 32809
Phone: 407-888-2288
2700 W Martin Luther King
Ste 400
Tampa, FL 33607
Phone: 813-879-5757
Ownership: Eduardo Zavala, 12%. votes.
Represented (legal): Davis Wright Tremaine LLP.

LPTV Stations:
Connecticut: WRDM-CA Hartford.
District of Columbia: WZDC-CA Washington.
Florida: WDYB-LP Daytona Beach; W50DW Gainesville; WKME-CA Kissimmee; WMVJ-CA Melbourne; WWDT-CA Naples; WTMO-CA Orlando; WWWF-LP Tallahassee; WRMD-CA Tampa.
Massachusetts: WTMU-LP Boston; WDMR-LP Springfield.
New Mexico: K48IK El Paso.
North Carolina: WZGS-CA Raleigh.
Rhode Island: WRIW-CA Providence.
Virginia: WZTD-LP Richmond.
Commercial TV Stations:
New Jersey: WWSI-DT Atlantic City.
New Mexico: KTDO-DT Las Cruces.
Radio Stations:
Maryland: WILC (AM) Laurel

ZUNI COMMUNICATIONS AUTHORITY

PO Box 339
Zuni, NM 87327
LPTV Stations:
New Mexico: K09FR Zuni Pueblo.

ZUNI PUBLIC SCHOOL DISTRICT

PO Box A
Zuni, NM 87327
LPTV Stations:
New Mexico: K43DL Zuni.

TELEVISION STATIONS ON AIR

1946-2009

Year	VHF Commercial	VHF ETV	Total VHF	UHF Commercial	UHF ETV	Total UHF	Total Commercial	Total ETV	Grand Total
1946			*6			—			*6
1947			12			—			12
1948			16			—			16
1949			51			—			51
1950			98			—			98
1951			107			—			107
1952			108			—			108
1953			120			6			126
1954	233	1	234	121	1	122	354	2	356
1955	297	8	305	114	3	117	411	11	422
1956	344	13	357	97	5	102	441	18	459
1957	381	17	398	90	6	96	471	23	494
1958	411	22	433	84	6	90	495	28	523
1959	433	28	461	77	7	84	510	35	545
1960	440	34	474	75	10	85	515	44	559
1961	451	37	488	76	15	91	527	52	579
1962	458	43	501	83	19	102	541	62	603
1963	466	46	512	91	22	113	557	68	625
1964	476	53	529	88	32	120	564	85	649
1965	481	58	539	88	41	129	569	99	668
1966	486	65	551	99	49	148	585	114	699
1967	492	71	563	118	56	174	610	127	737
1968	499	75	574	136	75	211	635	150	785
1969	499	78	577	163	97	260	662	175	837
1970	501	80	581	176	105	281	677	185	862
1971	503	86	589	179	113	292	682	199	881
1972	508	90	598	185	123	308	693	213	906
1973	510	93	603	187	137	324	697	230	927
1974	513	92	605	184	149	333	697	241	938
1975	514	95	609	192	152	344	706	247	953
1976	511	97	608	190	162	352	701	259	960
1977	515	101	616	196	160	356	711	261	972
1978	515	102	617	201	164	365	716	266	982
1979	515	107	622	209	167	376	724	274	998
1980	516	109	625	218	168	386	734	277	1011
1981	519	111	630	237	171	408	756	282	1038
1982	517	112	629	260	176	436	777	288	1065
1983	519	114	633	294	179	473	813	293	1106
1984	523	117	640	318	180	498	841	297	1138
1985	520	121	641	363	193	556	883	314	1197
1986	522	121	643	397	195	592	919	316	1235
1987	524	121	645	444	201	645	968	322	1290
1988	539	122	661	489	212	701	1028	334	1362
1989	545	124	669	516	218	734	1061	342	1403
1990	547	125	672	545	225	770	1092	350	1442
1991	547	126	673	551	235	786	1098	361	1459
1992	551	126	677	567	237	804	1118	363	1481
1993	552	127	679	586	241	827	1138	368	1506
1994	561	126	687	584	241	825	1145	367	1512
1995	562	126	688	599	245	844	1161	371	1532
1996	554	122	676	620	237	857	1174	359	1533
1997	560	127	687	645	242	887	1205	369	1574
1998	562	124	686	642	244	886	1204	368	1572
1999	562	124	686	654	245	899	1216	369	1585
2000	564	124	688	684	247	931	1248	371	1619
2001	571	116	687	731	258	989	1302	374	1676

Year	VHF Commercial	VHF ETV	Total VHF	UHF Commercial	UHF ETV	Total UHF	Total Commercial	Total ETV	Grand Total
2002	571	116	687	732	258	990	1303	374	1677
2003	586	127	713	755	254	1009	1341	381	1722
2004	591	127	718	770	252	1022	1361	379	1740
2005	594	128	722	781	250	1031	1375	378	1753
2006	585	128	713	787	249	1036	1372	377	1749
2007	584	128	712	780	246	1026	1364	374	1738
2008	578	127	705	775	248	1023	1353	375	1728
2009	364	102	466	1,015	290	1,305	1,379	392	1,771

*Does not include 1 CP operating intermittently.

Parent/Satellite Commercial Full Power Stations

Alabama

WTTO, Homewood, parent
WDBB, Bessemer, satellite

Alaska

KIMO, Anchorage, parent
KATN, Fairbanks, satellite

Arizona

KPNX, Mesa, parent
KNAZ-TV, Flagstaff, satellite

Arkansas

KHBS, Fort Smith, parent
KHOG-TV, Fayetteville, satellite

KFTA-TV, Fort Smith, parent
KNWA-TV, Rogers, satellite

California

KUNO-TV, Fort Bragg, parent
KTNC-TV, Concord, satellite

Colorado

KDVR, Denver, parent
KFCT, Fort Collins, satellite

KREX-TV, Grand Junction, parent
KREG-TV, Glenwood Springs, satellite
KREY-TV, Montrose, satellite

Florida

WFXU, Live Oak, parent
WTLF-DT, Tallahassee, satellite

Hawaii

KGMB, Honolulu, parent
KGMD-TV, Hilo, satellite
KGMV, Wailuku, satellite

KHNL, Honolulu, parent
KHBC-TV, Hilo, satellite
KOGG, Wailuku, satellite

KHON-TV, Honolulu, parent
KHAW-TV, Hilo, satellite
KAII-TV, Wailuku, satellite

KITV, Honolulu, parent
KHVO, Hilo, satellite
KMAU, Wailuku, satellite

KWHE, Honolulu, parent
KWHH, Hilo, satellite
KWHM, Wailuku, satellite

KPXO-DT, Kaneohe, parent
KLEI, Kailua-Kona, satellite

Idaho

KPIF, Pocatello, parent
KBEO, Jackson, WY, satellite

KPVI, Pocatello, parent
KJWY, Jackson, WY, satellite

Illinois

WCIA, Champaign, parent
WCFN, Springfield, satellite

WSIL-TV, Harrisburg, parent
KPOB-TV, Poplar Bluff, MO, satellite

WICS, Springfield, parent
WICD, Champaign, satellite

WRSP-TV, Springfield, parent
WCCU, Urbana, satellite

Indiana

WTTV, Bloomington, parent
WTTK, Kokomo, satellite

Kansas

KAKE-TV, Wichita, parent
KLBY-DT, Colby, satellite
KUPK-TV, Garden City, satellite

KSAS-TV, Wichita, parent
KOCW, Hoisington, satellite
KAAS-TV, Salina, satellite

KSNW, Wichita, parent
KSNC-DT, Great Bend, satellite
KSNG, Garden City, satellite
KSNK, McCook, NE, satellite

KWCH-TV, Hutchinson, parent
KBSD-TV, Ensign, satellite
KBSL-TV, Goodland, satellite
KBSH-TV, Hays, satellite

Louisiana

KADN, Lafayette, parent
WNTZ, Natchez, MS, satellite

Massachusetts

WBPX, Boston, parent
WPXG, Concord, NH, satellite
WDPX, Vineyard Haven, satellite

Michigan

WFQX-TV, Cadillac, parent
WFUP, Vanderbilt, satellite

WWTV, Cadillac, parent
WWUP-TV, Sault Ste. Marie, satellite

WGTU, Traverse City, parent
WGTQ, Sault Ste. Marie, satellite

WPBN-TV, Traverse City, parent
WTOM-TV, Cheboygan, satellite

Minnesota

WDIO-TV, Duluth, parent
WIRT, Hibbing, satellite

WCCO-TV, Minneapolis, parent
KCCO-TV, Alexandria, satellite
KCCW-TV, Walker, satellite

WFTC, Minneapolis, parent
KFTC, Bemidji, satellite

KSTP-TV, St. Paul, parent
KSAX, Alexandria, satellite
KRWF, Redwood Falls, satellite

Mississippi

WJTV, Jackson, parent
WHLT, Hattiesburg, satellite

Montana

KECI-TV, Missoula, parent
KTVM, Butte, satellite
KCFW-TV, Kalispell, satellite

KULR-TV, Billings, parent
KYUS-TV, Miles City, satellite

Nebraska

KHGI-TV, Kearney, parent
KWNB-TV, Hayes Center, satellite

KTVG, Grand Island, parent
KSNB-TV, Superior, satellite

KOLN, Lincoln, parent
KGIN, Grand Island, satellite

Nevada

KVBC, Las Vegas, parent
KVNV. Ely, satellite

New Jersey

WFUT-TV, Newark, parent
WFTY-TV, Smithtown, NY, satellite

New Mexico

KOAT-TV, Albuquerque, parent
KOCT, Carlsbad, satellite
KOVT, Silver City, satellite

KOB-TV, Albuquerque, parent
KOBF, Farmington, satellite
KOBR, Roswell, satellite
KOBG-TV, Silver City, satellite

KRQE, Albuquerque, parent
KREZ-TV, Durango, CO, satellite
KBIM-TV, Roswell, satellite

KFAC-LP, Albuquerque, parent
KTEL-TV, Carlsbad, satellite
KTLL-TV, Durango, CO, satellite

KWBQ, Santa Fe, parent
KRWB-TV, Roswell, satellite

New York

WTEN, Albany, parent
WCDC, Adams, MA, satellite

WPTZ, Plattsburgh, parent
WNNE, Hartford, VT, satellite

North Carolina

WEPX, Greenville, parent
WPXU-TV, Jacksonville, satellite

WFXI, Morehead City, parent
WYDO, Greenville, satellite

WRPX, Rocky Mount, parent
WFPX, Fayetteville, satellite

North Dakota

KBMY, Bismarck, parent
KMCY, Minot, satellite

KFYR-TV, Bismarck, parent
KQCD-TV, Dickinson, satellite
KMOT, Minot, satellite
KUMV-TV, Williston, satellite

KNDX, Bismarck, parent
KXND, Minot, satellite

KVRR, Fargo, parent
KJRR, Jamestown, satellite
KNRR, Pembina, satellite
KBRR, Thief River Falls, MN, satellite

WDAY-TV, Fargo, parent
WDAZ-TV, Devils Lake, satellite

KXMC-TV, Minot, parent
KXMB-TV, Bismarck, satellite
KXMA-TV, Dickinson, satellite
KXMD-TV, Williston, satellite

Oregon

KMTR, Eugene, parent
KMCB, Coos Bay, satellite
KTCW, Roseburg, satellite

KVAL-TV, Eugene, parent
KCBY-TV, Coos Bay, satellite
KPIC, Roseburg, satellite

KDRV, Medford, parent
KDKF, Klamath Falls, satellite

KOBI, Medford, parent
KOTI, Klamath Falls, satellite

Pennsylvania

WPCB-TV, Greensburg, parent
WKBS-TV, Altoona, satellite

South Dakota

KEVN-TV, Rapid City, parent
KIVV-TV, Lead, satellite

KOTA-TV, Rapid City, parent
KHSD-TV, Lead, satellite
KDUH-TV, Scottsbluff, NE, satellite
KSGW-TV, Sheridan, WY, satellite

KDLT-TV, Sioux Falls, parent
KDLV-TV, Mitchell, satellite

KELO-TV, Sioux Falls, parent
KDLO-TV, Florence, satellite
KCLO-TV, Rapid City, satellite
KPLO-TV, Reliance, satellite

KSFY-TV, Sioux Falls, parent
KABY-TV, Aberdeen, satellite
KPRY-TV, Pierre, satellite

KTTW, Sioux Falls, parent
KTTM, Huron, satellite

Tennessee

WLMT, Memphis, parent
WJKT, Jackson, satellite

Texas

KRBC-TV, Abilene, parent
KSAN-TV, San Angelo, satellite

KVII-TV, Amarillo, parent
KVIH-TV, Clovis, NM, satellite

KXAN-TV, Austin, parent
KXAM-TV, Llano, satellite

KZTV, Corpus Christi, parent
KVTV, Laredo, satellite

KWES-TV, Odessa, parent
KWAB-TV, Big Spring, satellite

KLTV, Tyler, parent
KTRE, Lufkin-Nacogdoches, satellite

KWKT Waco, parent
KYLE, Bryan, satellite

KWTX-TV, Waco, parent
KBTX-TV, Bryan, satellite

Virginia

WFXR-TV, Roanoke, parent
WWCW, Lynchburg, satellite

Washington

KAPP, Yakima, parent
KVEW, Kennewick, satellite

KIMA-TV, Yakima, parent
KEPR-TV, Pasco, satellite
KLEW-TV, Lewiston, ID, satellite

KNDO, Yakima, parent
KNDU, Richland, satellite

Wisconsin

WFRV-TV, Green Bay, parent
WJMN-TV, Escanaba, MI, satellite

WLAX, La Crosse, parent
WEUX, Chippewa Falls, satellite

WXOW-TV, La Crosse, parent
WQOW-TV, Eau Claire, satellite

KBJR-TV, Superior, parent
KRII, Chisholm, MN, satellite

WAOW-TV, Wausau, parent
WYOW, Eagle River, satellite

Wyoming

KCWY, Casper, parent
KCHY-LP, Cheyenne, satellite
KSWY, Sheridan, satellite

KFNB, Casper, parent
KFNR, Rawlins, satellite
KFNE, Riverton, satellite

KGWC-TV, Casper, parent
KGWL-TV, Lander, satellite
KGWR-TV, Rock Springs, satellite

KTWO-TV, Casper, parent
KDEV-LP, Cheyenne, satellite

KGWN-TV, Cheyenne, parent
KSTF, Scottsbluff, NE, satellite

Puerto Rico

WLII, Caguas, satellite
WORA-TV, Mayaguez, satellite
WSUR-TV, Ponce, satellite

WAPA-TV, San Juan, parent
WNJX-TV, Mayaguez, satellite
WTIN, Ponce, satellite

WJPX, San Juan, parent
WKPV, Ponce, satellite
WJWN-TV, San Sebastian, satellite
WIRS, Yauco, satellite

WTCV, San Juan, parent
WVEO, Aguadilla, satellite
WVOZ-TV, Ponce, satellite

Affiliations by Market for TV Stations

as of October 1, 2009

Market	Rank	Network (ABC, CBS, FOX, NBC)	Independent/ Other Networks	Public/Educational	Total
New York, NY	1	4	12	7	23
Los Angeles, CA	2	4	18	4	26
Chicago, IL	3	4	10	3	17
Philadelphia, PA	4	5	10	5	20
Dallas-Fort Worth, TX	5	4	13	2	19
San Francisco-Oakland-San Jose, CA	6	4	13	5	22
Boston, MA-Manchester, NH	7	5	11	5	21
Atlanta, GA	8	4	6	3	13
Washington, DC (Hagerstown, MD)	9	6	6	7	19
Houston, TX	10	4	11	2	17
Detroit, MI	11	4	4	1	9
Phoenix (Prescott), AZ	12	5	11	2	18
Seattle-Tacoma, WA	13	4	10	4	18
Tampa-St. Petersburg (Sarasota), FL	14	5	7	2	14
Minneapolis-St. Paul, MN	15	8	5	6	19
Denver, CO	16	7	8	7	22
Miami-Fort Lauderdale, FL	17	4	9	3	16
Cleveland-Akron (Canton), OH	18	4	8	3	15
Orlando-Daytona Beach-Melbourne, FL	19	5	8	4	17
Sacramento-Stockton-Modesto, CA	20	4	5	2	11
Total First 20		**94**	**185**	**77**	**356**
St. Louis, MO	21	4	3	1	8
Portland, OR	22	4	5	2	11
Pittsburgh, PA	23	4	5	3	12
Charlotte, NC	24	4	4	4	12
Indianapolis, IN	25	4	7	3	14
Raleigh-Durham (Fayetteville), NC	26	4	6	2	12
Baltimore, MD	27	4	3	2	9
San Diego, CA	28	4	1	1	6
Nashville, TN	29	4	7	2	13
Hartford & New Haven, CT	30	4	4	2	10
Salt Lake City, UT	31	7	8	5	20
Kansas City, MO	32	4	4	2	10
Cincinnati, OH	33	4	2	4	10
Columbus, OH	34	4	3	2	9
Milwaukee, WI	35	4	6	2	12
Greenville-Spartanburg-Anderson, SC-Asheville, NC	36	5	3	4	12
San Antonio, TX	37	4	7	1	12
West Palm Beach-Fort Pierce, FL	38	4	4	2	10
Harrisburg-Lancaster-Lebanon-York, PA	39	4	3	1	8
Birmingham (Anniston & Tuscaloosa), AL	40	5	6	2	13
Grand Rapids-Kalamazoo-Battle Creek, MI	41	5	4	2	11
Las Vegas, NV	42	4	5	1	10
Norfolk-Portsmouth-Newport News, VA	43	4	5	1	10
Albuquerque-Santa Fe, NM	44	10	9	4	23
Oklahoma City, OK	45	4	7	2	13
Greensboro-High Point-Winston Salem, NC	46	4	4	1	9
Jacksonville, FL	47	4	4	3	11
Austin, TX	48	5	4	1	10
Louisville, KY	49	4	3	3	10
Memphis, TN	50	4	4	3	11
Total First 50		**227**	**325**	**145**	**697**
New Orleans, LA	51	4	5	2	11
Buffalo, NY	52	4	4	1	9
Providence, RI-New Bedford, MA	53	4	2	2	8
Wilkes Barre-Scranton, PA	54	4	5	1	10
Fresno-Visalia, CA	55	4	6	2	12

Affiliations by Market

Market	Rank	Network (ABC, CBS, FOX, NBC)	Independent/ Other Networks	Public/Educational	Total
Little Rock-Pine Bluff, AR	56	4	4	5	13
Albany-Schenectady-Troy, NY	57	5	3	1	9
Richmond-Petersburg, VA	58	4	2	2	8
Knoxville, TN	59	4	6	2	12
Mobile, AL-Pensacola (Fort Walton Beach), FL	60	4	8	2	14
Tulsa, OK	61	4	6	3	13
Lexington, KY	62	5	4	4	13
Charleston-Huntington, WV	63	4	4	4	12
Fort Myers-Naples, FL	64	4	2	1	7
Dayton, OH	65	4	3	1	8
Tucson (Sierra Vista), AZ	66	4	5	2	11
Roanoke-Lynchburg, VA	67	5	5	1	11
Flint-Saginaw-Bay City, MI	68	4	4	3	11
Wichita-Hutchinson Plus, KS	69	13	3	5	21
Green Bay-Appleton, WI	70	4	2	1	7
Honolulu, HI	71	12	13	4	29
Des Moines-Ames, IA	72	4	2	3	9
Toledo, OH	73	4	1	2	7
Springfield, MO	74	4	2	1	7
Spokane, WA	75	5	3	4	12
Omaha, NE	76	4	3	3	10
Portland-Auburn, ME	77	4	2	2	8
Paducah, KY-Cape Girardeau-Harrisburg, MO-Mount Vernon, IL	78	5	4	3	12
Columbia, SC	79	4	2	2	8
Rochester, NY	80	4	1	1	6
Huntsville-Decatur (Florence), AL	81	4	2	2	8
Shreveport, LA	82	4	2	1	7
Syracuse, NY	83	4	1	1	6
Champaign & Springfield-Decatur, IL	84	6	2	3	11
Madison, WI	85	4	2	1	7
Chattanooga, TN	86	4	3	2	9
Harlingen-Weslaco-Brownsville-McAllen, TX	87	3	3	1	7
Cedar Rapids-Waterloo-Iowa City-Dubuque, IA	88	4	4	2	10
Waco-Temple-Bryan, TX	89	5	5	3	13
Jackson, MS	90	5	4	2	11
South Bend-Elkhart, IN	91	3	2	1	6
Colorado Springs-Pueblo, CO	92	4	2	1	7
Tri-Cities (Bristol, VA-Kingsport-Johnson City, TN)	93	4	2	2	8
Burlington, VT-Plattsburgh, NY	94	5	0	6	11
Baton Rouge, LA	95	4	0	1	5
Savannah, GA	96	4	2	2	8
Charleston, SC	97	4	2	1	7
El Paso, TX-Las Cruces, NM	98	4	6	4	14
Davenport, IA-Rock Island-Moline, IL	99	4	2	2	8
Fort Smith-Fayetteville-Springdale-Rogers, AR	100	5	1	1	7
Total First 100		**453**	**488**	**254**	**1,195**
Johnstown-Altoona-State College, PA	101	4	1	1	6
Evansville, IN	102	4	2	3	9
Greenville-New Bern-Washington, NC	103	4	6	3	13
Myrtle Beach-Florence, SC	104	4	1	3	8
Lincoln & Hastings-Kearney, NE	105	10	2	4	16
Tallahassee, FL-Thomasville, GA	106	6	5	1	12
Fort Wayne, IN	107	4	3	1	8
Reno, NV	108	5	2	1	8
Tyler-Longview (Lufkin & Nacogdoches), TX	109	5	2	0	7
Youngstown, OH	110	3	2	0	5
Springfield-Holyoke, MA	111	2	0	1	3
Boise, ID	112	4	2	1	7
Sioux Falls (Mitchell), SD	113	10	4	8	22
Augusta, GA-Aiken, SC	114	4	2	2	8
Lansing, MI	115	4	2	1	7
Peoria-Bloomington, IL	116	4	2	1	7

Market	Rank	Network (ABC, CBS, FOX, NBC)	Independent/ Other Networks	Public/Educational	Total
Traverse City-Cadillac, MI	117	8	1	2	11
Montgomery-Selma, AL	118	4	3	3	10
Eugene, OR	119	8	2	2	12
Santa Barbara-Santa Maria-San Luis Obispo, CA	120	3	4	0	7
Fargo-Valley City, ND	121	7	2	5	14
Macon, GA	122	4	2	1	7
Lafayette, LA	123	3	1	1	5
Monterey-Salinas, CA	124	3	2	1	6
Bakersfield, CA	125	3	2	0	5
Yakima-Pasco-Richland-Kennewick, WA	126	7	2	2	11
La Crosse-Eau Claire, WI	127	6	3	1	10
Columbus, GA-Opelika, AL	128	4	2	2	8
Corpus Christi, TX	129	4	2	1	7
Chico-Redding, CA	130	4	1	1	6
Amarillo, TX	131	5	3	2	10
Wilmington, NC	132	3	0	1	4
Columbus-Tupelo-West Point-Houston, MS	133	4	2	2	8
Rockford, IL	134	4	2	0	6
Wausau-Rhinelander, WI	135	5	4	2	11
Topeka, KS	136	3	2	1	6
Columbia-Jefferson City, MO	137	3	2	0	5
Monroe, LA-El Dorado, AR	138	4	3	1	8
Duluth, MN-Superior, WI	139	6	2	2	10
Medford-Klamath Falls, OR	140	6	2	2	10
Beaumont-Port Arthur, TX	141	3	2	0	5
Palm Springs, CA	142	2	1	0	3
Lubbock, TX	143	4	2	1	7
Salisbury, MD	144	2	1	2	5
Albany, GA	145	2	1	2	5
Erie, PA	146	4	1	1	6
Joplin, MO-Pittsburg, KS	147	4	0	1	5
Sioux City, IA	148	4	2	2	8
Wichita Falls, TX & Lawton, OK	149	4	1	0	5
Anchorage, AK	150	4	3	2	9
Panama City, FL	151	3	3	1	7
Terre Haute, IN	152	3	0	2	5
Rochester, MN-Mason City, IA-Austin, MN	153	4	2	2	8
Bangor, ME	154	3	1	2	6
Odessa-Midland, TX	155	5	5	1	11
Bluefield-Beckley-Oak Hill, WV	156	3	2	1	6
Binghamton, NY	157	3	1	1	5
Minot-Bismarck-Dickinson, ND	158	12	0	4	16
Wheeling, WV-Steubenville, OH	159	2	0	1	3
Gainesville, FL	160	3	2	1	6
Sherman, TX-Ada, OK	161	3	2	0	5
Idaho Falls-Pocatello, ID	162	5	0	0	5
Biloxi-Gulfport, MS	163	2	0	1	3
Yuma, AZ-El Centro, CA	164	4	5	0	9
Abilene-Sweetwater, TX	165	4	3	0	7
Missoula, MT	166	5	1	1	7
Hattiesburg-Laurel, MS	167	2	0	0	2
Clarksburg-Weston, WV	168	3	1	0	4
Billings, MT	169	5	1	1	7
Utica, NY	170	3	1	0	4
Quincy, IL-Hannibal, MO-Keokuk, IA	171	3	2	2	7
Dothan, AL	172	3	2	0	5
Jackson, TN	173	2	0	1	3
Rapid City, SD	174	7	0	2	9
Lake Charles, LA	175	2	0	1	3
Elmira (Corning), NY	176	3	3	1	7
Watertown, NY	177	2	1	2	5
Harrisonburg, VA	178	1	1	1	3
Alexandria, LA	179	3	1	1	5
Marquette, MI	180	5	2	1	8

Affiliations by Market

Market	Rank	Network (ABC, CBS, FOX, NBC)	Independent/ Other Networks	Public/Educational	Total
Jonesboro, AR	181	1	1	1	3
Bowling Green, KY	182	3	1	2	6
Charlottesville, VA	183	2	1	1	4
Grand Junction-Montrose, CO	184	5	3	1	9
Meridian, MS	185	4	2	1	7
Lima, OH	186	1	2	0	3
Greenwood-Greenville, MS	187	2	0	1	3
Laredo, TX	188	3	2	0	5
Bend, OR	189	2	1	1	4
Butte-Bozeman, MT	190	5	1	1	7
Lafayette, IN	191	1	0	0	1
Great Falls, MT	192	5	2	0	7
Twin Falls, ID	193	2	0	1	3
Parkersburg, WV	194	2	1	0	3
Eureka, CA	195	4	1	1	6
Casper-Riverton, WY	196	7	0	1	8
Cheyenne, WY-Scottsbluff, NE	197	4	4	0	8
San Angelo, TX	198	3	0	0	3
Mankato, MN	199	2	0	0	2
Ottumwa, IA-Kirksville, MO	200	2	0	0	2
St. Joseph, MO	201	1	1	0	2
Fairbanks, AK	202	3	2	1	6
Zanesville, OH	203	1	0	0	1
Victoria, TX	204	2	0	0	2
Presque Isle, ME	205	1	0	1	2
Helena, MT	206	1	1	0	2
Juneau, AK	207	3	3	1	7
Alpena, MI	208	1	0	1	2
North Platte, NE	209	1	0	1	2
Glendive, MT	210	2	0	0	2
Grand Total		**858**	**662**	**379**	**1,899**

NIELSEN GEOGRAPHIC REGIONS SUMMARY
TV OWNERSHIP BY REGIONS AND STATES
2009 vs. 1960

Region	SEPTEMBER 2009 Total HOUSEHOLDS	SEPTEMBER 2009 TV HOUSEHOLDS	SEPTEMBER 2009 % TV Penetration	SPRING 1960 Total HOUSEHOLDS	SPRING 1960 TV HOUSEHOLDS	SPRING 1960 % TV Penetration
NORTHEAST	20,959,100	20,734,110	99	12,859,800	10,548,160	82.0
New England	5,599,100	5,547,720	99	2,949,800	2,374,400	80.5
Connecticut	1,347,600	1,336,070	99	688,800	565,490	82.1
Maine	554,900	549,680	99	263,200	188,510	71.6
Massachusetts	2,518,400	2,496,570	99	1,474,200	1,212,460	82.2
New Hampshire	515,300	509,660	99	164,200	124,510	75.8
Rhode Island	410,000	407,690	99	249,800	213,390	85.4
Vermont	252,900	248,050	98	109,600	70,040	63.9
Middle Atlantic	15,360,000	15,186,390	99	9,910,000	8,173,760	82.5
New Jersey	3,177,800	3,156,660	99	1,672,100	1,404,970	84.0
New York	7,264,900	7,154,400	98	5,011,400	4,139,470	82.6
Pennsylvania	4,917,300	4,875,330	99	3,226,500	2,629,320	81.5
NORTH CENTRAL	26,004,800	25,818,890	99	14,816,100	11,630,760	78.5
East North Central	17,984,700	17,859,740	99	10,232,500	8,463,740	82.7
Illinois	4,798,300	4,759,710	99	2,983,300	2,445,000	82.0
Indiana	2,504,400	2,484,650	99	1,348,000	1,073,630	79.6
Michigan	3,852,200	3,828,100	99	2,148,000	1,805,000	84.0
Ohio	4,573,600	4,544,040	99	2,670,500	2,328,000	87.2
Wisconsin	2,256,200	2,243,240	99	1,082,700	812,110	75.0
West North Central	8,020,100	7,959,150	99	4,583,600	3,167,020	69.1
Iowa	1,205,400	1,197,840	99	830,600	635,180	76.5
Kansas	1,098,600	1,089,730	99	688,900	435,330	63.2
Minnesota	2,059,300	2,043,360	99	929,200	661,450	71.2
Missouri	2,366,800	2,346,920	99	1,332,500	973,720	73.1
Nebraska	705,500	701,290	99	433,100	290,390	67.0
North Dakota	266,600	264,740	99	169,900	84,400	49.7
South Dakota	317,900	315,270	99	199,400	86,550	43.4
SOUTH	43,529,400	43,115,600	99	13,723,000	8,440,010	61.5
South Atlantic	23,172,700	22,957,310	99	6,179,800	4,030,450	65.2
Delaware	343,600	340,960	99	1,089,900	687,440	63.1
District of Columbia	262,600	257,560	98	108,300	92,960	85.8
Florida	7,458,500	7,384,390	99	253,000	209,990	83.0
Georgia	3,638,900	3,604,300	99	948,900	584,880	61.6
Maryland	2,130,800	2,113,570	99	748,700	607,820	81.2
North Carolina	3,726,300	3,695,370	99	1,041,200	620,290	59.6
South Carolina	1,806,500	1,792,510	99	559,500	308,190	55.1
Virginia	3,042,700	3,014,420	99	927,900	614,850	66.3
West Virginia	762,800	754,230	99	502,400	304,030	60.5
East South Central	7,267,900	7,201,650	99	3,072,700	1,655,700	53.9
Alabama	1,883,800	1,868,690	99	803,200	444,070	55.3
Kentucky	1,746,000	1,730,240	99	811,900	463,810	57.1
Mississippi	1,115,100	1,101,920	99	558,600	211,820	37.9
Tennessee	2,523,000	2,500,800	99	899,000	536,000	59.6
West South Central	13,088,800	12,956,640	99	4,470,500	2,753,860	61.6
Arkansas	1,139,400	1,126,980	99	509,600	234,610	46.0
Louisiana	1,705,300	1,690,040	99	804,400	488,110	60.7
Oklahoma	1,444,200	1,431,680	99	668,500	444,930	66.6
Texas	8,799,900	8,707,940	99	2,488,000	1,586,210	63.8
WEST	25,649,700	25,197,780	98	7,385,700	4,876,400	66.0
Mountain	8,251,400	8,121,590	98	1,715,100	882,560	51.5
Arizona	2,461,400	2,423,720	98	292,200	168,460	57.7
Colorado	1,941,900	1,912,670	98	465,900	271,050	58.2
Idaho	575,900	566,490	98	173,800	87,570	50.4
Montana	394,500	385,750	98	200,400	63,260	31.6
Nevada	996,300	983,910	99	71,200	33,010	46.4
New Mexico	767,600	750,170	98	210,100	89,830	42.8
Utah	894,200	883,230	99	209,400	145,630	69.5
Wyoming	219,600	215,650	98	92,100	23,750	25.8
Pacific	16,732,100	16,429,890	98	5,670,600	3,993,840	70.4
California	12,639,600	12,426,720	98	4,312,300	3,177,350	73.7
Oregon	1,513,400	1,482,020	98	537,700	285,550	53.1
Washington	2,579,100	2,521,150	98	820,600	530,940	64.7
Alaska	221,400	213,060	96	—	—	—
Hawaii	444,800	433,240	97	—	—	—
TOTAL CONTINENTAL U.S.	115,476,800	114,220,080	99	48,784,600	35,495,330	72.8
TOTAL U.S.	116,143,000	114,866,380	99	—	—	—

Notes: Figures for Continental U.S. exclude Alaska & Hawaii. Figures for Alaska include Anchorage, Fairbanks & Juneau DMAs only.

Nielsen TV Household Estimates Ranked by DMA

(Data as of September 2009)

New York, NY	1	7,493,530
Los Angeles, CA	2	5,659,170
Chicago, IL	3	3,501,010
Philadelphia, PA	4	2,955,190
Dallas-Fort Worth, TX	5	2,544,410
San Francisco-Oakland-San Jose, CA	6	2,503,400
Boston, MA-Manchester, NH	7	2,410,180
Atlanta, GA	8	2,387,520
Washington, DC (Hagerstown, MD)	9	2,335,040
Houston, TX	10	2,123,460
Detroit, MI	11	1,890,220
Phoenix (Prescott), AZ	12	1,873,930
Seattle-Tacoma, WA	13	1,833,990
Tampa-St. Petersburg (Sarasota), FL	14	1,805,810
Minneapolis-St. Paul, MN	15	1,732,050
Denver, CO	16	1,539,380
Miami-Fort Lauderdale, FL	17	1,538,090
Cleveland-Akron (Canton), OH	18	1,520,750
Orlando-Daytona Beach-Melbourne, FL	19	1,455,620
Sacramento-Stockton-Modesto, CA	20	1,404,580
St. Louis, MO	21	1,249,450
Portland, OR	22	1,188,770
Pittsburgh, PA	23	1,154,950
Charlotte, NC	24	1,147,910
Indianapolis, IN	25	1,119,760
Raleigh-Durham (Fayetteville), NC	26	1,107,820
Baltimore, MD	27	1,093,170
San Diego, CA	28	1,073,390
Nashville, TN	29	1,019,010
Hartford & New Haven, CT	30	1,010,630
Salt Lake City, UT	31	944,060
Kansas City, MO	32	941,360
Cincinnati, OH	33	918,670
Columbus, OH	34	904,030
Milwaukee, WI	35	901,790
Greenville-Spartanburg-Anderson, SC-Asheville, NC	36	865,810
San Antonio, TX	37	830,000
West Palm Beach-Fort Pierce, FL	38	776,080
Harrisburg-Lancaster-Lebanon-York, PA	39	743,420
Birmingham (Anniston & Tuscaloosa), AL	40	742,140
Grand Rapids-Kalamazoo-Battle Creek, MI	41	740,430
Las Vegas, NV	42	721,780
Norfolk-Portsmouth-Newport News, VA	43	709,880
Albuquerque-Santa Fe, NM	44	694,040
Oklahoma City, OK	45	694,030
Greensboro-High Point-Winston Salem, NC	46	691,380
Jacksonville, FL	47	679,120
Austin, TX	48	678,730
Louisville, KY	49	668,310
Memphis, TN	50	667,660
New Orleans, LA	51	633,930
Buffalo, NY	52	633,220
Providence, RI-New Bedford, MA	53	619,610
Wilkes Barre-Scranton, PA	54	593,480
Fresno-Visalia, CA	55	579,180
Little Rock-Pine Bluff, AR	56	564,490
Albany-Schenectady-Troy, NY	57	554,070
Richmond-Petersburg, VA	58	553,950
Knoxville, TN	59	552,380
Mobile, AL-Pensacola (Fort Walton Beach), FL	60	534,730
Tulsa, OK	61	528,070
Lexington, KY	62	506,340
Charleston-Huntington, WV	63	501,530
Fort Myers-Naples, FL	64	500,110
Dayton, OH	65	482,590
Tucson (Sierra Vista), AZ	66	465,100
Roanoke-Lynchburg, VA	67	461,220
Flint-Saginaw-Bay City, MI	68	458,020
Wichita-Hutchinson, KS	69	452,710
Green Bay-Appleton, WI	70	443,420
Honolulu, HI	71	433,240
Des Moines-Ames, IA	72	432,310
Toledo, OH	73	423,100
Springfield, MO	74	422,740
Spokane, WA	75	419,350
Omaha, NE	76	410,350
Portland-Auburn, ME	77	408,120
Paducah, KY-Cape Girardeau, MO-Harrisburg, IL	78	399,690
Columbia, SC	79	398,620
Rochester, NY	80	392,190
Huntsville-Decatur (Florence), AL	81	390,900
Shreveport, LA	82	386,180
Syracuse, NY	83	385,440
Champaign & Springfield-Decatur, IL	84	384,620
Madison, WI	85	377,260
Chattanooga, TN	86	365,400
Harlingen-Weslaco-Brownsville-McAllen, TX	87	354,150
Cedar Rapids-Waterloo-Iowa City-Dubuque, IA	88	346,030
Waco-Temple-Bryan, TX	89	339,570
Jackson, MS	90	336,520
South Bend-Elkhart, IN	91	336,130
Colorado Springs-Pueblo, CO	92	334,710
Tri-Cities (Bristol, VA-Kingsport-Johnson City, TN)	93	334,620
Burlington, VT-Plattsburgh, NY	94	330,650
Baton Rouge, LA	95	326,890
Savannah, GA	96	322,030
Charleston, SC	97	311,190
El Paso, TX-Las Cruces, NM	98	310,760
Davenport, IA-Rock Island-Moline, IL	99	308,910
Fort Smith-Fayetteville-Springdale-Rogers, AR	100	298,330
Johnstown-Altoona-State College, PA	101	294,350
Evansville, IN	102	291,830
Greenville-New Bern-Washington, NC	103	290,280
Myrtle Beach-Florence, SC	104	287,400
Lincoln & Hastings-Kearney, NE	105	281,590
Tallahassee, FL-Thomasville, GA	106	280,710
Fort Wayne, IN	107	273,860
Reno, NV	108	270,500
Tyler-Longview (Lufkin & Nacogdoches), TX	109	267,890
Youngstown, OH	110	266,560
Springfield-Holyoke, MA	111	262,960
Boise, ID	112	262,800
Sioux Falls (Mitchell), SD	113	261,100
Augusta, GA-Aiken, SC	114	255,950
Lansing, MI	115	253,690
Peoria-Bloomington, IL	116	247,830
Traverse City-Cadillac, MI	117	245,000
Montgomery-Selma, AL	118	244,750
Eugene, OR	119	241,730
Santa Barbara-Santa Maria-San Luis Obispo, CA	120	241,370
Fargo-Valley City, ND	121	240,330
Macon, GA	122	239,330
Lafayette, LA	123	230,180
Monterey-Salinas, CA	124	227,390
Bakersfield, CA	125	222,910
Yakima-Pasco-Richland-Kennewick, WA	126	219,510
La Crosse-Eau Claire, WI	127	214,820
Columbus, GA-Opelika, AL	128	213,880
Corpus Christi, TX	129	199,560
Chico-Redding, CA	130	197,970
Amarillo, TX	131	192,490
Wilmington, NC	132	189,950
Columbus-Tupelo-West Point-Houston, MS	133	189,460
Rockford, IL	134	189,160
Wausau-Rhinelander, WI	135	184,720
Topeka, KS	136	180,090
Columbia-Jefferson City, MO	137	178,810
Monroe, LA-El Dorado, AR	138	177,200

Duluth, MN-Superior, WI	139	174,360	Lake Charles, LA	175	95,900
Medford-Klamath Falls, OR.	140	172,900	Elmira (Corning), NY	176	95,790
Beaumont-Port Arthur, TX	141	167,330	Watertown, NY.	177	93,970
Palm Springs, CA.	142	161,110	Harrisonburg, VA	178	93,400
Lubbock, TX.	143	158,360	Alexandria, LA	179	90,740
Salisbury, MD	144	158,340	Marquette, MI.	180	88,490
Albany, GA.	145	156,890	Jonesboro, AR	181	82,300
Erie, PA	146	156,520	Bowling Green, KY	182	81,650
Joplin, MO-Pittsburg, KS	147	155,670	Charlottesville, VA	183	75,920
Sioux City, IA	148	154,810	Grand Junction-Montrose, CO	184	75,030
Wichita Falls, TX & Lawton, OK	149	154,450	Meridian, MS	185	72,180
Anchorage, AK.	150	151,470	Lima, OH	186	71,380
Panama City, FL.	151	147,440	Greenwood-Greenville, MS.	187	70,350
Terre Haute, IN.	152	145,550	Laredo, TX	188	69,790
Rochester, MN-Mason City, IA-Austin, MN.	153	144,300	Bend, OR.	189	66,980
Bangor, ME	154	144,230	Butte-Bozeman, MT	190	66,260
Odessa-Midland, TX.	155	143,710	Lafayette, IN.	191	66,180
Bluefield-Beckley-Oak Hill, WV	156	142,570	Great Falls, MT.	192	65,000
Binghamton, NY.	157	137,240	Twin Falls, ID	193	64,740
Minot-Bismarck-Dickinson, ND	158	136,540	Parkersburg, WV	194	64,060
Wheeling, WV-Steubenville, OH	159	133,110	Eureka, CA.	195	61,090
Gainesville, FL	160	128,400	Casper-Riverton, WY	196	55,620
Sherman, TX-Ada, OK	161	127,990	Cheyenne, WY-Scottsbluff, NE	197	54,710
Idaho Falls-Pocatello, ID-Jackson, WY	162	126,880	San Angelo, TX	198	54,580
Biloxi-Gulfport, MS	163	122,740	Mankato, MN	199	52,230
Yuma, AZ-El Centro, CA	164	118,300	Ottumwa, IA-Kirksville, MO.	200	51,370
Abilene-Sweetwater, TX	165	116,190	St. Joseph, MO	201	48,440
Missoula, MT	166	111,940	Fairbanks, AK.	202	36,250
Hattiesburg-Laurel, MS.	167	111,610	Zanesville, OH	203	32,350
Clarksburg-Weston, WV	168	110,050	Victoria, TX	204	31,560
Billings, MT	169	107,420	Presque Isle, ME	205	31,070
Utica, NY	170	104,890	Helena, MT	206	27,630
Quincy, IL-Hannibal, MO-Keokuk, IA.	171	102,710	Juneau, AK	207	25,340
Dothan, AL.	172	101,840	Alpena, MI	208	17,420
Jackson, TN.	173	98,250	North Platte, NE	209	15,350
Rapid City, SD	174	98,240	Glendive, MT	210	3,940

Television Households by States and Counties

A.C. Nielsen Data as of September 2009
Household estimates compiled by Market Statistics Inc.
Figures Updated from 2000 U.S. Census.

Reprinted with permission of copyright holder, The Nielsen Company.

State and County	Total Households	Total TV Households	%
ALABAMA			
AUTAUGA	19,600	19,480	99
BALDWIN	73,000	72,380	99
BARBOUR	10,700	10,600	99
BIBB	8,100	7,980	99
BLOUNT	22,400	22,210	99
BULLOCK	3,700	3,610	98
BUTLER	8,200	8,100	99
CALHOUN	47,700	47,420	99
CHAMBERS	14,100	14,020	99
CHEROKEE	10,400	10,330	99
CHILTON	16,900	16,740	99
CHOCTAW	5,900	5,790	98
CLARKE	10,400	10,300	99
CLAY	5,800	5,720	99
CLEBURNE	6,100	6,040	99
COFFEE	20,300	20,130	99
COLBERT	23,100	22,900	99
CONECUH	5,600	5,520	99
COOSA	4,400	4,350	99
COVINGTON	15,800	15,640	99
CRENSHAW	5,800	5,750	99
CULLMAN	32,900	32,740	100
DALE	19,300	19,140	99
DALLAS	17,100	16,910	99
DE KALB	26,700	26,460	99
ELMORE	27,500	27,320	99
ESCAMBIA	14,300	14,140	99
ETOWAH	43,000	42,720	99
FAYETTE	7,400	7,340	99
FRANKLIN	12,200	12,100	99
GENEVA	10,900	10,800	99
GREENE	3,800	3,670	97
HALE	6,700	6,530	97
HENRY	6,900	6,850	99
HOUSTON	40,600	40,360	99
JACKSON	22,200	22,000	99
JEFFERSON	267,700	265,760	99
LAMAR	5,900	5,830	99
LAUDERDALE	37,500	37,220	99
LAWRENCE	13,900	13,770	99
LEE	56,800	56,250	99
LIMESTONE	29,400	29,260	100
LOWNDES	4,900	4,800	98
MACON	8,600	8,500	99
MADISON	132,800	132,060	99
MARENGO	8,600	8,460	98
MARION	12,300	12,210	99
MARSHALL	35,300	35,070	99
MOBILE	157,100	155,860	99
MONROE	9,100	8,970	99
MONTGOMERY	88,900	88,260	99
MORGAN	46,800	46,490	99
PERRY	4,000	3,900	98
PICKENS	7,700	7,620	99
PIKE	12,600	12,460	99
RANDOLPH	8,900	8,850	99
RUSSELL	21,000	20,800	99
SAINT CLAIR	30,800	30,610	99
SHELBY	76,400	75,950	99
SUMTER	5,300	5,230	99
TALLADEGA	31,900	31,620	99
TALLAPOOSA	16,900	16,680	99
TUSCALOOSA	73,900	73,260	99
WALKER	27,600	27,430	99
WASHINGTON	6,700	6,600	99
WILCOX	5,000	4,880	98
WINSTON	10,000	9,930	99
ALASKA			
ANCHORAGE	104,200	102,110	98
FAIRBNKS-PLUS	37,900	36,250	96
JUNEAU-PLUS	27,200	25,340	93
KENAI-PENSLA	20,800	19,650	94
MATANKA-SUSTN	31,300	29,710	95
ARIZONA			
APACHE-N	16,100	14,450	90
APACHE-S	5,600	5,030	90
COCHISE	51,700	50,690	98
COCONINO	47,600	45,220	95
GILA	21,900	21,240	97
GRAHAM	12,000	11,470	96
GREENLEE	3,200	3,140	98
LA PAZ	9,400	9,010	96
MARICOPA	1,453,600	1,439,330	99
MOHAVE	81,300	79,970	98
NAVAJO	37,000	34,710	94
PIMA	406,400	400,220	98
PINAL	135,200	133,480	99
SANTA CRUZ	14,500	14,190	98
YAVAPAI	94,400	91,330	97
YUMA	71,500	70,240	98
ARKANSAS			
ARKANSAS	8,000	7,820	98
ASHLEY	8,800	8,750	99
BAXTER	19,400	19,060	98
BENTON	81,900	80,860	99
BOONE	15,700	15,440	98
BRADLEY	4,600	4,550	99
CALHOUN	2,300	2,260	98
CARROLL	11,200	11,010	98
CHICOT	4,400	4,310	98
CLARK	9,200	9,120	99
CLAY	6,600	6,550	99
CLEBURNE	11,100	10,910	98
CLEVELAND	3,400	3,340	98
COLUMBIA	9,500	9,390	99
CONWAY	8,400	8,330	99
CRAIGHEAD	38,100	37,800	99
CRAWFORD	22,900	22,650	99
CRITTENDEN	20,000	19,790	99
CROSS	7,400	7,250	98
DALLAS	3,100	3,090	100
DESHA	5,400	5,310	98
DREW	7,600	7,500	99
FAULKNER	41,200	40,950	99
FRANKLIN	7,200	7,120	99
FULTON	4,900	4,780	98
GARLAND	41,700	41,180	99
GRANT	7,000	6,910	99
GREENE	16,500	16,400	99
HEMPSTEAD	8,600	8,500	99
HOT SPRING	12,500	12,370	99
HOWARD	5,600	5,470	98
INDEPENDENCE	14,000	13,850	99
IZARD	5,400	5,330	99
JACKSON	6,200	6,130	99
JEFFERSON	28,300	28,070	99
JOHNSON	9,600	9,490	99
LAFAYETTE	3,200	3,160	99
LAWRENCE	6,800	6,680	98

State and County	Total Households	Total TV Households	%
LEE	3,600	3,530	98
LINCOLN	3,900	3,840	98
LITTLE RIVER	5,400	5,290	98
LOGAN	8,900	8,830	99
LONOKE	25,200	24,960	99
MADISON	6,200	6,050	98
MARION	7,200	7,100	99
MILLER	17,400	17,070	98
MISSISSIPPI	17,800	17,630	99
MONROE	3,400	3,320	98
MONTGOMERY	3,700	3,600	97
NEVADA	3,600	3,550	99
NEWTON	3,600	3,500	97
OUACHITA	10,500	10,400	99
PERRY	4,100	4,070	99
PHILLIPS	7,800	7,670	99
PIKE	4,300	4,260	99
POINSETT	9,800	9,700	99
POLK	8,100	8,000	98
POPE	23,100	22,830	99
PRAIRIE	3,600	3,570	99
PULASKI	157,700	156,530	99
RANDOLPH	7,400	7,320	99
ST FRANCIS	9,000	8,890	99
SALINE	39,200	39,050	100
SCOTT	4,500	4,450	99
SEARCY	3,600	3,480	97
SEBASTIAN	48,500	48,170	99
SEVIER	5,900	5,830	99
SHARP	7,700	7,550	98
STONE	5,200	5,010	96
UNION	17,300	17,180	99
VAN BUREN	7,200	7,120	99
WASHINGTON	77,300	76,580	99
WHITE	28,800	28,590	99
WOODRUFF	3,000	2,950	98
YELL	8,200	8,130	99

CALIFORNIA

State and County	Total Households	Total TV Households	%
ALAMEDA	539,000	525,780	98
ALPINE	400	370	93
AMADOR	14,300	13,840	97
BUTTE	86,700	84,790	98
CALAVERAS	19,500	18,990	97
COLUSA	6,900	6,820	99
CONTRA COSTA	376,300	371,750	99
DEL NORTE	10,000	9,590	96
EL DORADO-E	14,500	13,880	96
EL DORADO-W	54,200	53,030	98
FRESNO	290,300	286,900	99
GLENN	9,900	9,710	98
HUMBOLDT	53,900	51,500	96
IMPERIAL	48,800	48,060	98
INYO	7,500	7,120	95
KERN-E	28,800	28,260	98
KERN-W	226,000	222,910	99
KINGS	39,900	39,590	99
LAKE	26,700	25,820	97
LASSEN	9,800	9,470	97
LOS ANGELES	3,290,100	3,242,580	99
MADERA	44,600	44,150	99
MARIN	102,700	99,220	97
MARIPOSA	7,100	6,690	94
MENDOCINO	34,200	31,610	92
MERCED	75,800	74,630	98
MODOC	3,900	3,680	94
MONO	5,400	4,950	92
MONTEREY	124,800	122,090	98
NAPA	49,600	48,720	98
NEVADA	40,100	38,900	97
ORANGE	996,500	987,440	99
PLACER	133,900	131,980	99
PLUMAS	9,100	8,580	94
RIVERSIDE-E	6,200	6,060	98
RIVERSIDE-W	521,900	514,930	99
SACRAMENTO	524,100	517,380	99
SAN BENITO	16,400	16,160	99
SAN BERNARDNO	617,800	612,040	99
SAN DIEGO	1,091,800	1,073,390	98

State and County	Total Households	Total TV Households	%
SAN FRANCISCO	347,300	330,550	95
SAN JOAQUIN	220,300	217,920	99
SAN LUIS OBPO	104,800	102,030	97
SAN MATEO	257,400	252,580	98
SANTA BRBRA-N	68,100	67,000	98
SANTA BRBRA-S	75,200	72,340	96
SANTA CLARA	603,500	593,360	98
SANTA CRUZ	93,100	89,140	96
SHASTA	71,600	70,590	99
SIERRA	1,400	1,380	99
SISKIYOU	19,600	18,720	96
SOLANO-E	86,700	85,330	98
SOLANO-W	50,900	50,320	99
SONOMA	179,100	173,690	97
STANISLAUS	165,500	163,120	99
SUTTER	32,200	31,730	99
TEHAMA	23,500	23,200	99
TRINITY	6,500	6,000	92
TULARE	128,700	127,220	99
TUOLUMNE	22,100	21,840	99
VENTURA	263,500	260,450	99
YOLO	70,100	69,000	98
YUBA	25,300	24,740	98
RIVERSIDE-C	163,800	161,110	98

COLORADO

State and County	Total Households	Total TV Households	%
ADAMS	150,700	149,800	99
ALAMOSA	6,000	5,790	97
ARAPAHOE	221,700	220,530	99
ARCHULETA	5,600	5,170	92
BACA	1,700	1,640	96
BENT	1,700	1,680	99
BOULDER	112,800	108,850	96
BROOMFIELD	21,000	20,640	98
CHAFFEE	7,200	7,050	98
CHEYENNE	700	670	96
CLEAR CREEK	4,000	3,950	99
CONEJOS	3,000	2,860	95
COSTILLA	1,500	1,450	97
CROWLEY	1,400	1,390	99
CUSTER	1,800	1,730	96
DELTA	12,700	12,430	98
DENVER	256,800	252,640	98
DOLORES	900	820	91
DOUGLAS	104,600	103,470	99
EAGLE	19,600	18,730	96
ELBERT	7,900	7,790	99
EL PASO	226,700	224,670	99
FREMONT	16,000	15,810	99
GARFIELD	21,500	21,100	98
GILPIN	2,300	2,220	97
GRAND	6,100	5,860	96
GUNNISON	6,500	6,140	94
HINSDALE	400	400	100
HUERFANO	3,100	3,060	99
JACKSON	600	580	97
JEFFERSON	216,500	214,640	99
KIOWA	600	590	98
KIT CARSON	2,800	2,750	98
LAKE	3,100	2,910	94
LA PLATA	21,200	20,130	95
LARIMER	118,000	115,730	98
LAS ANIMAS	6,700	6,510	97
LINCOLN	1,800	1,780	99
LOGAN	7,800	7,680	98
MESA	59,300	58,590	99
MINERAL	500	490	98
MOFFAT	5,500	5,320	97
MONTEZUMA	10,500	10,190	97
MONTROSE	16,700	16,440	99
MORGAN	9,600	9,550	99
OTERO	7,500	7,440	99
OURAY	2,000	1,830	92
PARK	7,300	6,980	96
PHILLIPS	1,800	1,790	99
PITKIN	7,600	6,730	89
PROWERS	4,700	4,650	99
PUEBLO	61,900	61,380	99
RIO BLANCO	2,600	2,550	98

State and County	Total Households	Total TV Households	%
RIO GRANDE	4,700	4,640	99
ROUTT	9,900	9,540	96
SAGUACHE	3,000	2,810	94
SAN JUAN	300	290	97
SAN MIGUEL	3,800	3,450	91
SEDGWICK	1,000	990	99
SUMMIT	11,100	10,680	96
TELLER	9,000	8,810	98
WASHINGTON	1,800	1,780	99
WELD	91,000	90,360	99
YUMA	3,800	3,750	99

CONNECTICUT

State and County	Total Households	Total TV Households	%
FAIRFIELD	328,000	325,440	99
HARTFORD	345,500	342,990	99
LITCHFIELD	74,600	73,790	99
MIDDLESEX	66,500	65,810	99
NEW HAVEN	329,300	326,330	99
NEW LONDON	104,300	103,250	99
TOLLAND	54,500	54,060	99
WINDHAM	44,900	44,400	99

DELAWARE

State and County	Total Households	Total TV Households	%
KENT	61,600	61,170	99
NEW CASTLE	202,800	201,560	99
SUSSEX	79,200	78,230	99

DISTRICT OF COLUMBIA

State and County	Total Households	Total TV Households	%
DISTRICT OF COLUMBIA	262,600	257,560	98

FLORIDA

State and County	Total Households	Total TV Households	%
ALACHUA	101,900	99,710	98
BAKER	8,700	8,650	99
BAY	71,300	70,760	99
BRADFORD	9,700	9,610	99
BREVARD	231,200	229,300	99
BROWARD	681,600	676,610	99
CALHOUN	5,000	4,910	98
CHARLOTTE	73,100	72,680	99
CITRUS	64,100	63,450	99
CLAY	69,500	68,990	99
COLLIER	133,000	131,260	99
COLUMBIA	25,800	25,610	99
MIAMI-DADE	843,700	830,350	98
DE SOTO	11,300	11,110	98
DIXIE	6,000	5,900	98
DUVAL	353,800	350,480	99
ESCAMBIA	118,700	117,470	99
FLAGLER	43,600	43,110	99
FRANKLIN	4,600	4,500	98
GADSDEN	17,900	17,720	99
GILCHRIST	6,300	6,200	98
GLADES	4,000	3,910	98
GULF	5,500	5,420	99
HAMILTON	4,600	4,490	98
HARDEE	8,300	8,230	99
HENDRY	12,100	12,000	99
HERNANDO	72,400	71,810	99
HIGHLANDS	43,200	42,890	99
HILLSBOROUGH	477,000	472,430	99
HOLMES	7,500	7,450	99
INDIAN RIVER	61,900	61,290	99
JACKSON	18,700	18,470	99
JEFFERSON	5,300	5,240	99
LAFAYETTE	2,400	2,340	98
LAKE	128,000	127,210	99
LEE	270,900	269,150	99
LEON	113,500	111,930	99
LEVY	16,900	16,590	98
LIBERTY	2,700	2,640	98
MADISON	7,200	7,100	98
MANATEE	135,200	134,350	99
MARION	140,000	138,790	99

State and County	Total Households	Total TV Households	%
MARTIN	62,400	61,750	99
MONROE	32,300	31,130	96
NASSAU	28,900	28,610	99
OKALOOSA	76,800	76,290	99
OKEECHOBEE	14,400	14,220	99
ORANGE	414,900	410,900	99
OSCEOLA	100,400	99,830	99
PALM BEACH-N	325,100	321,530	99
PALM BEACH-S	206,600	204,590	99
PASCO	195,900	194,670	99
PINELLAS	411,500	408,260	99
POLK	234,000	231,930	99
PUTNAM	29,800	29,360	99
ST JOHNS	75,700	74,850	99
ST LUCIE	113,800	112,700	99
SANTA ROSA	55,600	54,920	99
SARASOTA	179,500	177,790	99
SEMINOLE	162,400	161,430	99
SUMTER	36,200	35,880	99
SUWANNEE	16,200	15,630	96
TAYLOR	8,100	7,940	98
UNION	3,800	3,750	99
VOLUSIA	210,400	209,170	99
WAKULLA	12,000	11,860	99
WALTON	24,400	24,070	99
WASHINGTON	9,300	9,220	99

GEORGIA

State and County	Total Households	Total TV Households	%
APPLING	7,000	6,880	98
ATKINSON	3,000	2,950	98
BACON	4,000	3,950	99
BAKER	1,400	1,380	99
BALDWIN	15,900	15,770	99
BANKS	6,400	6,330	99
BARROW	26,500	26,410	100
BARTOW	35,600	35,300	99
BEN HILL	6,900	6,740	98
BERRIEN	6,900	6,800	99
BIBB	60,500	60,030	99
BLECKLEY	4,600	4,580	100
BRANTLEY	6,100	6,050	99
BROOKS	6,400	6,360	99
BRYAN	11,600	11,480	99
BULLOCH	27,000	26,700	99
BURKE	8,300	8,180	99
BUTTS	8,700	8,470	97
CALHOUN	1,900	1,870	98
CAMDEN	17,100	16,940	99
CANDLER	3,700	3,650	99
CARROLL	43,100	42,690	99
CATOOSA	25,100	24,940	99
CHARLTON	3,500	3,470	99
CHATHAM	99,500	98,490	99
CHATTAHOOCHEE	2,700	2,690	100
CHATTOOGA	10,500	10,420	99
CHEROKEE	78,700	77,910	99
CLARKE	45,900	44,950	98
CLAY	1,400	1,380	99
CLAYTON	93,900	93,570	100
CLINCH	2,700	2,680	99
COBB	263,200	261,460	99
COFFEE	14,500	14,270	98
COLQUITT	17,200	17,060	99
COLUMBIA	40,600	40,390	99
COOK	6,400	6,360	99
COWETA	45,000	44,630	99
CRAWFORD	4,600	4,540	99
CRISP	8,600	8,530	99
DADE	6,200	6,100	98
DAWSON	9,000	8,940	99
DECATUR	10,800	10,700	99
DE KALB	277,000	274,970	99
DODGE	7,600	7,520	99
DOOLY	3,900	3,850	99
DOUGHERTY	36,700	36,420	99
DOUGLAS	47,800	47,380	99
EARLY	4,600	4,560	99
ECHOLS	1,300	1,280	99
EFFINGHAM	19,400	19,210	99

State and County	Total Households	Total TV Households	%
ELBERT	8,200	8,160	100
EMANUEL	8,700	8,600	99
EVANS	4,300	4,270	99
FANNIN	10,100	9,800	97
FAYETTE	38,000	37,670	99
FLOYD	35,700	35,270	99
FORSYTH	62,600	61,900	99
FRANKLIN	8,700	8,590	99
FULTON	401,600	397,830	99
GILMER	11,400	11,180	98
GLASCOCK	1,200	1,190	99
GLYNN	32,100	31,730	99
GORDON	20,000	19,840	99
GRADY	9,600	9,530	99
GREENE	6,400	6,350	99
GWINNETT	274,300	272,090	99
HABERSHAM	16,500	16,300	99
HALL	63,000	62,330	99
HANCOCK	3,100	3,050	98
HARALSON	11,400	11,300	99
HARRIS	11,500	11,340	99
HART	9,900	9,860	100
HEARD	4,300	4,200	98
HENRY	70,800	70,070	99
HOUSTON	50,900	50,650	100
IRWIN	3,700	3,670	99
JACKSON	24,000	23,580	98
JASPER	5,300	5,250	99
JEFF DAVIS	5,400	5,280	98
JEFFERSON	6,200	6,020	97
JENKINS	3,300	3,250	98
JOHNSON	3,200	3,150	98
JONES	10,600	10,520	99
LAMAR	6,400	6,330	99
LANIER	3,200	3,170	99
LAURENS	18,900	18,640	99
LEE	11,900	11,780	99
LIBERTY	18,800	18,600	99
LINCOLN	3,300	3,250	98
LONG	4,000	3,940	99
LOWNDES	39,200	38,750	99
LUMPKIN	10,300	9,980	97
MC DUFFIE	8,400	8,320	99
MC INTOSH	4,700	4,610	98
MACON	4,800	4,640	97
MADISON	11,100	10,970	99
MARION	2,700	2,660	99
MERIWETHER	8,700	8,630	99
MILLER	2,500	2,470	99
MITCHELL	8,400	8,320	99
MONROE	9,300	9,220	99
MONTGOMERY	3,200	3,110	97
MORGAN	7,100	6,950	98
MURRAY	14,900	14,810	99
MUSCOGEE	72,200	71,780	99
NEWTON	37,000	36,410	98
OCONEE	11,500	11,390	99
OGLETHORPE	5,700	5,600	98
PAULDING	50,500	49,950	99
PEACH	9,900	9,830	99
PICKENS	13,000	12,760	98
PIERCE	7,300	7,180	98
PIKE	6,400	6,310	99
POLK	15,800	15,750	100
PULASKI	3,500	3,480	99
PUTNAM	8,500	8,380	99
QUITMAN	1,100	1,090	99
RABUN	7,100	6,850	96
RANDOLPH	2,700	2,670	99
RICHMOND	76,100	75,550	99
ROCKDALE	29,000	28,790	99
SCHLEY	1,700	1,680	99
SCREVEN	5,700	5,600	98
SEMINOLE	3,600	3,570	99
SPALDING	24,400	24,180	99
STEPHENS	10,200	10,150	100
STEWART	1,900	1,870	98
SUMTER	11,800	11,690	99
TALBOT	2,600	2,570	99
TALIAFERRO	800	790	99

State and County	Total Households	Total TV Households	%
TATTNALL	7,800	7,700	99
TAYLOR	3,400	3,350	99
TELFAIR	4,100	4,030	98
TERRELL	3,700	3,660	99
THOMAS	18,100	17,950	99
TIFT	15,800	15,680	99
TOOMBS	11,100	10,940	99
TOWNS	5,000	4,980	100
TREUTLEN	2,700	2,660	99
TROUP	24,300	24,030	99
TURNER	3,400	3,380	99
TWIGGS	3,800	3,760	99
UNION	9,500	9,290	98
UPSON	10,900	10,800	99
WALKER	25,900	25,690	99
WALTON	31,300	31,010	99
WARE	14,000	13,840	99
WARREN	2,400	2,370	99
WASHINGTON	7,500	7,440	99
WAYNE	10,800	10,670	99
WEBSTER	800	790	99
WHEELER	2,100	2,080	99
WHITE	10,200	10,000	98
WHITFIELD	32,600	32,390	99
WILCOX	2,700	2,690	100
WILKES	4,300	4,230	98
WILKINSON	3,900	3,850	99
WORTH	8,100	8,020	99

HAWAII

State and County	Total Households	Total TV Households	%
HAWAII	66,400	63,320	95
HONOLULU	303,900	298,700	98
KAUAI	23,500	22,390	95
MAUI	51,000	48,830	96

IDAHO

State and County	Total Households	Total TV Households	%
ADA	149,400	147,990	99
ADAMS	1,500	1,430	95
BANNOCK	30,200	29,950	99
BEAR LAKE	2,100	1,990	95
BENEWAH	3,800	3,680	97
BINGHAM	14,500	14,370	99
BLAINE	9,100	8,840	97
BOISE	3,000	2,850	95
BONNER	17,100	16,370	96
BONNEVILLE	36,900	36,540	99
BOUNDARY	4,400	4,030	92
BUTTE	1,100	1,080	98
CAMAS	500	490	98
CANYON	66,500	65,680	99
CARIBOU	2,500	2,460	98
CASSIA	7,200	7,100	99
CLARK	300	290	97
CLEARWATER	3,200	3,080	96
CUSTER	1,900	1,810	95
ELMORE	9,300	9,200	99
FRANKLIN	3,900	3,880	99
FREMONT	4,300	4,210	98
GEM	6,000	5,930	99
GOODING	5,000	4,950	99
IDAHO	6,200	5,940	96
JEFFERSON	8,000	7,900	99
JEROME	7,100	7,020	99
KOOTENAI	54,900	54,090	99
LATAH	13,700	12,910	94
LEMHI	3,400	3,280	96
LEWIS	1,500	1,460	97
LINCOLN	1,600	1,580	99
MADISON	10,500	10,310	98
MINIDOKA	6,600	6,510	99
NEZ PERCE	16,200	16,010	99
ONEIDA	1,500	1,470	98
OWYHEE	3,800	3,710	98
PAYETTE	8,300	8,120	98
POWER	2,700	2,660	99
SHOSHONE	5,700	5,570	98
TETON	3,400	3,350	99

State and County	Total Households	Total TV Households	%
TWIN FALLS	29,200	28,740	98
VALLEY	4,000	3,850	96
WASHINGTON	3,900	3,810	98

ILLINOIS

State and County	Total Households	Total TV Households	%
ADAMS	26,900	26,790	100
ALEXANDER	3,300	3,280	99
BOND	6,400	6,350	99
BOONE	19,400	19,270	99
BROWN	1,900	1,880	99
BUREAU	14,200	14,120	99
CALHOUN	2,100	2,090	100
CARROLL	6,500	6,450	99
CASS	5,300	5,270	99
CHAMPAIGN	77,300	76,090	98
CHRISTIAN	13,700	13,630	99
CLARK	7,000	6,970	100
CLAY	5,600	5,540	99
CLINTON	13,800	13,750	100
COLES	20,800	20,700	100
COOK	1,937,600	1,918,110	99
CRAWFORD	7,500	7,470	100
CUMBERLAND	4,300	4,260	99
DE KALB	38,200	37,860	99
DE WITT	6,700	6,670	100
DOUGLAS	7,500	7,420	99
DU PAGE	338,600	336,840	99
EDGAR	7,500	7,450	99
EDWARDS	2,700	2,690	100
EFFINGHAM	13,400	13,320	99
FAYETTE	8,100	8,020	99
FORD	5,600	5,580	100
FRANKLIN	16,900	16,750	99
FULTON	14,300	14,240	100
GALLATIN	2,600	2,580	99
GREENE	5,400	5,350	99
GRUNDY	19,300	19,100	99
HAMILTON	3,300	3,270	99
HANCOCK	7,500	7,450	99
HARDIN	1,800	1,780	99
HENDERSON	3,100	3,100	100
HENRY	19,800	19,750	100
IROQUOIS	11,900	11,800	99
JACKSON	24,800	24,460	99
JASPER	3,800	3,770	99
JEFFERSON	15,600	15,500	99
JERSEY	8,800	8,760	100
JO DAVIESS	9,600	9,510	99
JOHNSON	4,400	4,350	99
KANE	171,200	169,860	99
KANKAKEE	42,100	41,820	99
KENDALL	38,900	38,850	100
KNOX	20,500	20,350	99
LAKE	240,300	239,010	99
LA SALLE	45,000	44,720	99
LAWRENCE	6,000	5,930	99
LEE	13,400	13,290	99
LIVINGSTON	14,000	13,600	97
LOGAN	10,600	10,560	100
MCDONOUGH	11,800	11,730	99
MCHENRY	111,600	110,900	99
MCLEAN	64,100	63,620	99
MACON	44,800	44,590	100
MACOUPIN	19,100	19,050	100
MADISON	109,000	108,070	99
MARION	15,800	15,690	99
MARSHALL	5,100	5,050	99
MASON	6,000	5,970	100
MASSAC	6,300	6,260	99
MENARD	5,000	4,980	100
MERCER	6,500	6,480	100
MONROE	12,600	12,530	99
MONTGOMERY	11,300	11,160	99
MORGAN	13,600	13,520	99
MOULTRIE	5,500	5,470	99
OGLE	21,200	21,120	100
PEORIA	73,900	73,470	99
PERRY	8,400	8,350	99
PIATT	6,700	6,680	100

State and County	Total Households	Total TV Households	%
PIKE	6,600	6,570	100
POPE	1,700	1,690	99
PULASKI	2,500	2,470	99
PUTNAM	2,400	2,390	100
RANDOLPH	11,900	11,860	100
RICHLAND	6,400	6,320	99
ROCK ISLAND	60,000	59,730	100
ST CLAIR	102,300	101,590	99
SALINE	10,700	10,620	99
SANGAMON	83,400	82,880	99
SCHUYLER	2,900	2,880	99
SCOTT	2,100	2,090	100
SHELBY	8,700	8,660	99
STARK	2,500	2,480	99
STEPHENSON	18,800	18,750	100
TAZEWELL	53,300	52,940	99
UNION	7,300	7,260	99
VERMILION	32,000	31,830	99
WABASH	4,900	4,870	99
WARREN	6,500	6,480	100
WASHINGTON	5,700	5,600	98
WAYNE	7,000	6,900	99
WHITE	6,300	6,260	99
WHITESIDE	23,600	23,540	100
WILL	234,300	232,770	99
WILLIAMSON	27,600	27,410	99
WINNEBAGO	117,400	116,730	99
WOODFORD	14,400	14,070	98

INDIANA

State and County	Total Households	Total TV Households	%
ADAMS	12,200	12,070	99
ALLEN	138,700	138,130	100
BARTHOLOMEW	30,000	29,680	99
BENTON	3,300	3,280	99
BLACKFORD	5,400	5,360	99
BOONE	21,200	21,090	99
BROWN	5,800	5,710	98
CARROLL	7,600	7,430	98
CASS	15,000	14,900	99
CLARK	45,200	44,890	99
CLAY	10,300	10,230	99
CLINTON	12,700	12,610	99
CRAWFORD	4,200	4,130	98
DAVIESS	11,100	10,590	95
DEARBORN	18,900	18,770	99
DECATUR	10,000	9,850	99
DE KALB	16,200	16,100	99
DELAWARE	46,700	46,280	99
DUBOIS	16,100	16,030	100
ELKHART	72,700	71,610	99
FAYETTE	9,900	9,800	99
FLOYD	29,600	29,400	99
FOUNTAIN	6,700	6,650	99
FRANKLIN	8,600	8,470	98
FULTON	8,100	8,080	100
GIBSON	13,100	13,030	99
GRANT	26,600	26,360	99
GREENE	13,300	13,170	99
HAMILTON	102,200	101,820	100
HANCOCK	26,600	26,390	99
HARRISON	14,600	14,530	100
HENDRICKS	52,700	52,450	100
HENRY	18,900	18,790	99
HOWARD	35,500	35,290	99
HUNTINGTON	14,200	14,150	100
JACKSON	16,900	16,720	99
JASPER	12,000	11,920	99
JAY	8,300	8,240	99
JEFFERSON	13,000	12,890	99
JENNINGS	10,500	10,460	100
JOHNSON	54,600	54,260	99
KNOX	15,400	15,280	99
KOSCIUSKO	29,300	29,060	99
LAGRANGE	12,200	11,740	96
LAKE	189,900	188,420	99
LA PORTE	42,400	42,200	100
LAWRENCE	19,200	18,940	99
MADISON	52,200	52,110	99
MARION	363,700	361,260	99

State and County	Total Households	Total TV Households	%
MARSHALL	17,400	17,270	99
MARTIN	4,200	4,040	96
MIAMI	13,300	13,180	99
MONROE	52,000	50,690	97
MONTGOMERY	14,800	14,730	100
MORGAN	26,500	26,230	99
NEWTON	5,200	5,150	99
NOBLE	17,400	17,310	99
OHIO	2,300	2,290	100
ORANGE	8,000	7,910	99
OWEN	8,700	8,590	99
PARKE	6,200	6,130	99
PERRY	7,500	7,470	100
PIKE	5,000	4,950	99
PORTER	63,800	63,480	99
POSEY	9,900	9,850	99
PULASKI	5,200	5,160	99
PUTNAM	12,800	12,730	99
RANDOLPH	10,400	10,330	99
RIPLEY	10,400	10,320	99
RUSH	6,600	6,520	99
ST JOSEPH	101,700	101,270	100
SCOTT	9,400	9,320	99
SHELBY	17,400	17,300	99
SPENCER	7,600	7,540	99
STARKE	9,000	8,940	99
STEUBEN	13,000	12,870	99
SULLIVAN	7,700	7,670	100
SWITZERLAND	3,800	3,790	100
TIPPECANOE	63,900	62,900	98
TIPTON	6,300	6,280	100
UNION	2,800	2,770	99
VANDERBURGH	72,800	72,530	100
VERMILLION	6,600	6,560	99
VIGO	41,700	41,420	99
WABASH	12,500	12,400	99
WARREN	3,300	3,260	99
WARRICK	22,500	22,390	100
WASHINGTON	10,800	10,730	99
WAYNE	27,400	27,120	99
WELLS	10,800	10,650	99
WHITE	9,100	9,030	99
WHITLEY	13,000	12,960	100

IOWA

State and County	Total Households	Total TV Households	%
ADAIR	3,100	3,090	100
ADAMS	1,700	1,690	99
ALLAMAKEE	5,800	5,720	99
APPANOOSE	5,400	5,330	99
AUDUBON	2,400	2,380	99
BENTON	10,300	10,260	100
BLACK HAWK	51,200	51,020	100
BOONE	10,500	10,480	100
BREMER	9,200	9,170	100
BUCHANAN	8,100	8,060	100
BUENA VISTA	7,200	7,170	100
BUTLER	6,100	6,070	100
CALHOUN	3,900	3,900	100
CARROLL	8,600	8,560	100
CASS	5,800	5,780	100
CEDAR	7,200	7,180	100
CERRO GORDO	18,400	18,330	100
CHEROKEE	4,800	4,790	100
CHICKASAW	4,900	4,860	99
CLARKE	3,500	3,470	99
CLAY	7,100	7,080	100
CLAYTON	7,100	7,030	99
CLINTON	20,000	19,940	100
CRAWFORD	6,200	6,180	100
DALLAS	24,600	24,430	99
DAVIS	3,200	3,130	98
DECATUR	3,200	3,160	99
DELAWARE	6,500	6,480	100
DES MOINES	16,900	16,750	99
DICKINSON	7,400	7,380	100
DUBUQUE	36,600	36,420	100
EMMET	4,300	4,280	100
FAYETTE	8,100	8,070	100
FLOYD	6,600	6,580	100
FRANKLIN	4,300	4,290	100
FREMONT	3,000	2,980	99
GREENE	3,600	3,590	100
GRUNDY	5,000	4,970	99
GUTHRIE	4,500	4,480	100
HAMILTON	6,200	6,180	100
HANCOCK	4,500	4,460	99
HARDIN	7,000	6,960	99
HARRISON	5,900	5,880	100
HENRY	7,600	7,530	99
HOWARD	3,800	3,770	99
HUMBOLDT	3,900	3,860	99
IDA	2,900	2,890	100
IOWA	6,300	6,270	100
JACKSON	8,200	8,160	100
JASPER	14,600	14,550	100
JEFFERSON	6,400	6,250	98
JOHNSON	53,300	52,350	98
JONES	7,800	7,740	99
KEOKUK	4,300	4,260	99
KOSSUTH	6,400	6,350	99
LEE	14,100	14,030	100
LINN	87,700	87,230	99
LOUISA	4,300	4,270	99
LUCAS	3,700	3,680	99
LYON	4,300	4,080	95
MADISON	6,100	6,060	99
MAHASKA	9,000	8,910	99
MARION	12,400	12,330	99
MARSHALL	15,500	15,430	100
MILLS	5,700	5,680	100
MITCHELL	4,200	4,170	99
MONONA	3,800	3,790	100
MONROE	3,100	3,060	99
MONTGOMERY	4,500	4,480	100
MUSCATINE	16,500	16,430	100
OBRIEN	5,500	5,480	100
OSCEOLA	2,600	2,580	99
PAGE	6,000	5,940	99
PALO ALTO	3,800	3,780	99
PLYMOUTH	9,300	9,280	100
POCAHONTAS	3,200	3,190	100
POLK	174,300	173,500	100
POTTAWATTAMIE	35,700	35,490	99
POWESHIEK	7,400	7,330	99
RINGGOLD	2,100	2,080	99
SAC	4,300	4,290	100
SCOTT	66,700	66,320	99
SHELBY	4,800	4,780	100
SIOUX	11,100	10,910	98
STORY	32,600	32,360	99
TAMA	6,800	6,770	100
TAYLOR	2,500	2,470	99
UNION	5,400	5,360	99
VAN BUREN	3,200	3,180	99
WAPELLO	14,700	14,600	99
WARREN	17,000	16,970	100
WASHINGTON	8,500	8,350	98
WAYNE	2,600	2,550	98
WEBSTER	15,100	15,030	100
WINNEBAGO	4,500	4,490	100
WINNESHIEK	7,800	7,750	99
WOODBURY	39,100	38,960	100
WORTH	3,200	3,180	99
WRIGHT	5,300	5,250	99

KANSAS

State and County	Total Households	Total TV Households	%
ALLEN	5,400	5,350	99
ANDERSON	3,200	3,130	98
ATCHISON	6,200	6,170	100
BARBER	2,000	1,980	99
BARTON	11,300	11,260	100
BOURBON	6,000	5,930	99
BROWN	4,100	4,040	99
BUTLER	23,400	23,210	99
CHASE	1,100	1,060	96
CHAUTAUQUA	1,500	1,470	98
CHEROKEE	8,200	8,150	99
CHEYENNE	1,200	1,190	99

State and County	Total Households	Total TV Households	%
CLARK	800	790	99
CLAY	3,700	3,680	99
CLOUD	3,800	3,710	98
COFFEY	3,300	3,250	98
COMANCHE	900	890	99
COWLEY	13,200	13,060	99
CRAWFORD	15,800	15,700	99
DECATUR	1,200	1,190	99
DICKINSON	8,100	8,050	99
DONIPHAN	3,000	2,990	100
DOUGLAS	46,200	45,510	99
EDWARDS	1,300	1,290	99
ELK	1,300	1,240	95
ELLIS	11,800	11,740	99
ELLSWORTH	2,400	2,390	100
FINNEY	13,000	12,820	99
FORD	10,800	10,690	99
FRANKLIN	10,300	10,180	99
GEARY	12,500	12,280	98
GOVE	1,000	960	96
GRAHAM	1,100	1,090	99
GRANT	2,600	2,550	98
GRAY	1,900	1,840	97
GREELEY	500	490	98
GREENWOOD	2,800	2,760	99
HAMILTON	1,000	990	99
HARPER	2,500	2,460	98
HARVEY	13,100	12,880	98
HASKELL	1,300	1,280	98
HODGEMAN	700	690	99
JACKSON	5,000	4,970	99
JEFFERSON	6,800	6,750	99
JEWELL	1,400	1,390	99
JOHNSON	212,300	211,650	100
KEARNY	1,400	1,390	99
KINGMAN	2,900	2,880	99
KIOWA	1,000	950	95
LABETTE	8,900	8,800	99
LANE	700	690	99
LEAVENWORTH	26,000	25,840	99
LINCOLN	1,400	1,390	99
LINN	3,800	3,770	99
LOGAN	1,000	980	98
LYON	13,500	13,340	99
MCPHERSON	11,000	10,640	97
MARION	4,500	4,410	98
MARSHALL	4,100	4,070	99
MEADE	1,600	1,590	99
MIAMI	11,500	11,420	99
MITCHELL	2,600	2,560	98
MONTGOMERY	14,300	14,130	99
MORRIS	2,600	2,560	98
MORTON	1,100	1,080	98
NEMAHA	3,700	3,620	98
NEOSHO	6,400	6,370	100
NESS	1,300	1,290	99
NORTON	2,000	2,000	100
OSAGE	6,300	6,270	100
OSBORNE	1,600	1,580	99
OTTAWA	2,400	2,380	99
PAWNEE	2,300	2,290	100
PHILLIPS	2,200	2,180	99
POTTAWATOMIE	7,500	7,420	99
PRATT	3,900	3,860	99
RAWLINS	1,100	1,090	99
RENO	25,200	24,930	99
REPUBLIC	2,100	2,080	99
RICE	3,700	3,690	100
RILEY	26,800	26,520	99
ROOKS	2,100	2,090	100
RUSH	1,400	1,390	99
RUSSELL	2,900	2,890	100
SALINE	22,000	21,810	99
SCOTT	1,900	1,870	98
SEDGWICK	192,000	190,710	99
SEWARD	7,400	7,340	99
SHAWNEE	72,900	72,560	100
SHERIDAN	1,000	990	99
SHERMAN	2,500	2,480	99
SMITH	1,600	1,590	99
STAFFORD	1,800	1,790	99
STANTON	800	790	99
STEVENS	1,800	1,780	99
SUMNER	8,900	8,820	99
THOMAS	2,900	2,890	100
TREGO	1,300	1,280	98
WABAUNSEE	2,700	2,680	99
WALLACE	500	490	98
WASHINGTON	2,400	2,370	99
WICHITA	800	790	99
WILSON	3,900	3,790	97
WOODSON	1,400	1,360	97
WYANDOTTE	58,300	57,980	99

KENTUCKY

State and County	Total Households	Total TV Households	%
ADAIR	7,200	7,060	98
ALLEN	7,600	7,550	99
ANDERSON	8,500	8,470	100
BALLARD	3,500	3,480	99
BARREN	17,500	17,350	99
BATH	4,900	4,860	99
BELL	12,300	12,070	98
BOONE	44,000	43,770	99
BOURBON	8,200	8,150	99
BOYD	20,000	19,920	100
BOYLE	11,500	11,410	99
BRACKEN	3,400	3,390	100
BREATHITT	6,400	6,060	95
BRECKINRIDGE	7,800	7,700	99
BULLITT	29,400	29,180	99
BUTLER	5,300	5,260	99
CALDWELL	5,500	5,430	99
CALLOWAY	15,300	15,170	99
CAMPBELL	35,700	35,560	100
CARLISLE	2,200	2,190	100
CARROLL	4,300	4,260	99
CARTER	11,100	11,010	99
CASEY	6,900	6,720	97
CHRISTIAN	27,300	27,090	99
CLARK	14,700	14,630	100
CLAY	8,900	8,620	97
CLINTON	4,300	4,200	98
CRITTENDEN	3,900	3,880	99
CUMBERLAND	2,900	2,710	93
DAVIESS	39,200	39,050	100
EDMONSON	5,100	5,010	98
ELLIOTT	3,100	3,030	98
ESTILL	6,300	6,150	98
FAYETTE	122,200	121,530	99
FLEMING	5,900	5,780	98
FLOYD	18,000	17,790	99
FRANKLIN	21,300	21,170	99
FULTON	2,900	2,880	99
GALLATIN	3,000	2,970	99
GARRARD	6,800	6,760	99
GRANT	9,700	9,630	99
GRAVES	15,200	15,050	99
GRAYSON	10,600	10,460	99
GREEN	4,900	4,850	99
GREENUP	15,500	15,410	99
HANCOCK	3,500	3,460	99
HARDIN	37,500	37,280	99
HARLAN	13,000	12,810	99
HARRISON	7,500	7,450	99
HART	7,400	7,240	98
HENDERSON	19,000	18,920	100
HENRY	6,200	6,140	99
HICKMAN	2,100	2,090	100
HOPKINS	19,400	19,240	99
JACKSON	5,600	5,430	97
JEFFERSON	302,700	301,040	99
JESSAMINE	17,600	17,470	99
JOHNSON	9,800	9,730	99
KENTON	64,300	63,960	99
KNOTT	7,100	6,930	98
KNOX	13,600	13,450	99
LARUE	5,500	5,440	99
LAUREL	23,600	23,310	99
LAWRENCE	6,600	6,510	99

State and County	Total Households	Total TV Households	%
LEE	2,900	2,800	97
LESLIE	4,900	4,780	98
LETCHER	10,100	9,960	99
LEWIS	5,500	5,430	99
LINCOLN	10,300	10,140	98
LIVINGSTON	4,000	3,960	99
LOGAN	11,000	10,860	99
LYON	3,000	2,980	99
MCCRACKEN	28,400	28,240	99
MCCREARY	7,000	6,800	97
MCLEAN	4,000	3,960	99
MADISON	32,500	32,150	99
MAGOFFIN	5,300	5,200	98
MARION	7,300	7,230	99
MARSHALL	13,200	13,150	100
MARTIN	4,700	4,650	99
MASON	7,400	7,340	99
MEADE	10,100	10,060	100
MENIFEE	2,700	2,660	99
MERCER	9,200	9,120	99
METCALFE	4,300	4,260	99
MONROE	4,700	4,660	99
MONTGOMERY	10,700	10,610	99
MORGAN	5,000	4,880	98
MUHLENBERG	12,500	12,270	98
NELSON	17,100	16,940	99
NICHOLAS	2,700	2,670	99
OHIO	9,600	9,520	99
OLDHAM	19,500	19,420	100
OWEN	4,500	4,430	98
OWSLEY	1,900	1,830	96
PENDLETON	5,400	5,380	100
PERRY	12,300	12,060	98
PIKE	28,100	27,790	99
POWELL	5,700	5,550	97
PULASKI	25,900	25,540	99
ROBERTSON	800	790	99
ROCKCASTLE	7,000	6,780	97
ROWAN	8,500	8,400	99
RUSSELL	7,700	7,570	98
SCOTT	17,700	17,590	99
SHELBY	15,600	15,510	99
SIMPSON	6,800	6,760	99
SPENCER	6,700	6,660	99
TAYLOR	10,100	9,960	99
TODD	4,700	4,610	98
TRIGG	5,800	5,750	99
TRIMBLE	3,600	3,580	99
UNION	5,600	5,580	100
WARREN	42,800	42,530	99
WASHINGTON	4,600	4,560	99
WAYNE	8,600	8,380	97
WEBSTER	5,400	5,320	99
WHITLEY	15,600	15,360	98
WOLFE	2,900	2,850	98
WOODFORD	9,900	9,850	99

LOUISIANA

State and County	Total Households	Total TV Households	%
ACADIA	22,200	22,040	99
ALLEN	8,500	8,370	98
ASCENSION	38,100	37,880	99
ASSUMPTION	8,400	8,360	100
AVOYELLES	15,700	15,560	99
BEAUREGARD	13,500	13,180	98
BIENVILLE	5,800	5,750	99
BOSSIER	43,200	42,950	99
CADDO	100,500	99,680	99
CALCASIEU	72,400	71,680	99
CALDWELL	4,000	3,930	98
CAMERON	2,700	2,670	99
CATAHOULA	4,100	4,040	99
CLAIBORNE	5,900	5,850	99
CONCORDIA	7,300	7,210	99
DE SOTO	10,400	10,250	99
E BATON ROUGE	167,500	166,270	99
EAST CARROLL	2,600	2,500	96
E FELICIANA	6,900	6,820	99
EVANGELINE	13,200	13,100	99
FRANKLIN	7,500	7,350	98

State and County	Total Households	Total TV Households	%
GRANT	7,900	7,820	99
IBERIA	26,700	26,470	99
IBERVILLE	10,700	10,630	99
JACKSON	6,200	6,130	99
JEFFERSON	170,200	169,210	99
JEFF DAVIS	11,800	11,730	99
LAFAYETTE	82,600	82,000	99
LAFOURCHE	33,800	33,640	100
LA SALLE	5,300	5,220	98
LINCOLN	16,000	15,810	99
LIVINGSTON	44,700	44,320	99
MADISON	4,000	3,960	99
MOREHOUSE	10,800	10,700	99
NATCHITOCHES	15,200	14,950	98
ORLEANS	145,100	143,120	99
OUACHITA	56,600	56,080	99
PLAQUEMINES	7,600	7,530	99
POINTE COUPEE	8,700	8,600	99
RAPIDES	52,500	52,010	99
RED RIVER	3,200	3,160	99
RICHLAND	7,600	7,520	99
SABINE	9,700	9,560	99
ST BERNARD	15,500	15,440	100
ST CHARLES	17,800	17,710	99
ST HELENA	4,100	4,060	99
ST JAMES	7,300	7,250	99
ST JOHN BAPT	16,100	16,030	100
ST LANDRY	34,700	34,350	99
ST MARTIN	19,400	19,220	99
ST MARY	19,200	19,080	99
ST TAMMANY	86,300	85,750	99
TANGIPAHOA	44,100	43,490	99
TENSAS	2,100	2,070	99
TERREBONNE	39,000	38,760	99
UNION	9,200	9,160	100
VERMILION	21,400	21,270	99
VERNON	15,600	15,350	98
WASHINGTON	17,900	17,450	97
WEBSTER	16,500	16,390	99
W BATON ROUGE	8,400	8,360	100
WEST CARROLL	4,200	4,160	99
W FELICIANA	3,700	3,650	99
WINN	5,500	5,430	99

MAINE

State and County	Total Households	Total TV Households	%
ANDROSCOGGIN	45,500	45,250	99
AROOSTOOK	31,400	31,070	99
CUMBERLAND	114,700	113,520	99
FRANKLIN	12,400	12,210	98
HANCOCK	23,500	23,170	99
KENNEBEC	50,900	50,490	99
KNOX	17,600	17,300	98
LINCOLN	15,200	15,070	99
OXFORD	24,200	23,850	99
PENOBSCOT	62,400	61,960	99
PISCATAQUIS	7,500	7,420	99
SAGADAHOC	15,100	14,970	99
SOMERSET	21,800	21,550	99
WALDO	16,300	16,110	99
WASHINGTON	14,200	14,020	99
YORK	82,200	81,720	99

MARYLAND

State and County	Total Households	Total TV Households	%
ALLEGANY	28,300	27,940	99
ANNE ARUNDEL	192,700	191,700	99
BALTIMORE	315,000	312,750	99
CALVERT	30,800	30,450	99
CAROLINE	12,700	12,600	99
CARROLL	60,400	59,900	99
CECIL	37,400	37,040	99
CHARLES	50,700	50,270	99
DORCHESTER	13,700	13,570	99
FREDERICK	83,400	82,840	99
GARRETT	11,900	11,400	96
HARFORD	91,000	90,610	99
HOWARD	101,300	100,980	100
KENT	8,500	8,370	98

State and County	Total Households	Total TV Households	%
MONTGOMERY	356,100	353,670	99
PRINCE GEORGE	293,100	291,040	99
QUEEN ANNES	18,500	18,320	99
ST MARYS	38,100	37,500	98
SOMERSET	8,900	8,820	99
TALBOT	15,700	15,530	99
WASHINGTON	56,000	55,180	99
WICOMICO	36,800	36,520	99
WORCESTER	21,500	21,200	99
BALTIMRE CITY	248,300	245,370	99

MASSACHUSETTS

State and County	Total Households	Total TV Households	%
BARNSTABLE	95,000	94,070	99
BERKSHIRE	55,100	54,310	99
BRISTOL	212,700	211,920	100
DUKES	6,700	6,630	99
ESSEX	280,500	278,580	99
FRANKLIN	29,900	29,200	98
HAMPDEN	177,500	176,340	99
HAMPSHIRE	58,500	57,420	98
MIDDLESEX	573,500	568,640	99
NANTUCKET	4,400	4,360	99
NORFOLK	256,500	255,070	99
PLYMOUTH	177,800	177,070	100
SUFFOLK	292,100	286,110	98
WORCESTER	298,200	296,850	100

MICHIGAN

State and County	Total Households	Total TV Households	%
ALCONA	5,200	5,140	99
ALGER	3,700	3,670	99
ALLEGAN	41,700	41,450	99
ALPENA	12,400	12,280	99
ANTRIM	9,800	9,640	98
ARENAC	6,400	6,350	99
BARAGA	3,200	3,160	99
BARRY	22,300	22,160	99
BAY	44,200	44,040	100
BENZIE	7,300	7,120	98
BERRIEN	63,800	63,310	99
BRANCH	16,000	15,850	99
CALHOUN	53,300	53,080	100
CASS	19,800	19,690	99
CHARLEVOIX	10,500	10,420	99
CHEBOYGAN	11,100	11,010	99
CHIPPEWA	13,900	13,750	99
CLARE	12,500	12,420	99
CLINTON	26,500	26,310	99
CRAWFORD	5,800	5,760	99
DELTA	15,800	15,710	99
DICKINSON	11,400	11,350	100
EATON	42,700	42,450	99
EMMET	14,000	13,770	98
GENESEE	168,300	167,600	100
GLADWIN	10,800	10,710	99
GOGEBIC	6,600	6,460	98
GR TRAVERSE	35,100	34,880	99
GRATIOT	14,500	14,350	99
HILLSDALE	17,500	17,310	99
HOUGHTON	13,700	13,040	95
HURON	13,500	13,380	99
INGHAM	109,400	108,570	99
IONIA	21,600	21,490	99
IOSCO	11,700	11,620	99
IRON	5,200	5,130	99
ISABELLA	24,800	24,550	99
JACKSON	59,300	59,050	100
KALAMAZOO	99,700	99,100	99
KALKASKA	6,900	6,810	99
KENT	228,400	226,490	99
KEWEENAW	1,000	990	99
LAKE	4,700	4,660	99
LAPEER	32,300	32,160	100
LEELANAU	9,000	8,930	99
LENAWEE	37,400	37,210	99
LIVINGSTON	67,500	67,190	100
LUCE	2,300	2,260	98
MACKINAC	4,600	4,530	98

State and County	Total Households	Total TV Households	%
MACOMB	336,800	336,090	100
MANISTEE	9,900	9,820	99
MARQUETTE	27,100	26,830	99
MASON	11,900	11,750	99
MECOSTA	16,000	15,880	99
MENOMINEE	10,400	10,350	100
MIDLAND	32,500	32,380	100
MISSAUKEE	5,800	5,780	100
MONROE	58,100	57,930	100
MONTCALM	23,100	22,870	99
MONTMORENCY	4,600	4,530	98
MUSKEGON	65,700	65,310	99
NEWAYGO	18,200	18,020	99
OAKLAND	483,600	481,790	100
OCEANA	10,200	10,070	99
OGEMAW	8,800	8,770	100
ONTONAGON	3,100	3,060	99
OSCEOLA	8,900	8,810	99
OSCODA	3,700	3,570	96
OTSEGO	9,400	9,320	99
OTTAWA	92,600	92,000	99
PRESQUE ISLE	6,100	5,990	98
ROSCOMMON	11,100	11,040	99
SAGINAW	76,100	75,860	100
ST CLAIR	65,000	64,730	100
ST JOSEPH	23,600	23,250	99
SANILAC	16,500	16,300	99
SCHOOLCRAFT	3,400	3,360	99
SHIAWASSEE	27,400	27,320	100
TUSCOLA	21,200	21,090	99
VAN BUREN	29,500	29,290	99
WASHTENAW	136,400	134,910	99
WAYNE	703,800	699,120	99
WEXFORD	12,600	12,550	100

MINNESOTA

State and County	Total Households	Total TV Households	%
AITKIN	7,100	6,990	98
ANOKA	122,900	122,380	100
BECKER	13,100	12,920	99
BELTRAMI	16,500	16,320	99
BENTON	16,000	15,930	100
BIG STONE	2,200	2,190	100
BL ERTH-NCL-S	29,300	29,050	99
BROWN	10,500	10,440	99
CARLTON	13,400	13,330	99
CARVER	32,300	32,220	100
CASS	11,900	11,750	99
CHIPPEWA	5,100	5,080	100
CHISAGO	18,100	18,030	100
CLAY	21,400	21,340	100
CLEARWATER	3,400	3,300	97
COOK	2,600	2,490	96
COTTONWOOD	4,500	4,460	99
CROW WING	26,000	25,620	99
DAKOTA	150,600	150,170	100
DODGE	7,400	7,360	99
DOUGLAS	15,300	15,140	99
FARIBAULT	6,000	5,980	100
FILLMORE	8,200	8,160	100
FREEBORN	12,800	12,760	100
GOODHUE	18,000	17,850	99
GRANT	2,400	2,390	100
HENNEPIN	470,500	465,800	99
HOUSTON	7,600	7,550	99
HUBBARD	7,800	7,650	99
ISANTI	14,900	14,700	99
ITASCA	18,700	18,500	99
JACKSON	4,400	4,380	100
KANABEC	6,400	6,330	99
KANDIYOHI	16,200	16,080	99
KITTSON	1,800	1,790	99
KOOCHICHING	5,800	5,710	98
LAC QUI PARLE	3,000	2,990	100
LAKE	4,600	4,570	99
LAKE OF WOODS	1,700	1,660	98
LE SUEUR	11,000	10,890	99
LINCOLN	2,400	2,390	100
LYON	9,600	9,550	99
MCLEOD	14,800	14,690	99

State and County	Total Households	Total TV Households	%
MAHNOMEN	2,000	1,990	100
MARSHALL	3,900	3,880	99
MARTIN	8,600	8,560	100
MEEKER	9,000	8,860	98
MILLE LACS	10,700	10,580	99
MORRISON	12,700	12,540	99
MOWER	15,300	15,260	100
MURRAY	3,400	3,380	99
NICOLLET-N	6,300	6,250	99
NOBLES	7,700	7,650	99
NORMAN	2,700	2,680	99
OLMSTED	56,400	55,780	99
OTTER TAIL	23,000	22,780	99
PENNINGTON	5,700	5,660	99
PINE	10,800	10,670	99
PIPESTONE	3,900	3,860	99
POLK	12,100	12,020	99
POPE	4,500	4,480	100
RAMSEY	200,000	198,630	99
RED LAKE	1,700	1,680	99
REDWOOD	6,200	6,150	99
RENVILLE	6,300	6,260	99
RICE	21,400	21,270	99
ROCK	3,800	3,760	99
ROSEAU	6,200	6,120	99
ST LOUIS	82,400	81,680	99
SCOTT	45,800	45,560	99
SHERBURNE	30,900	30,740	99
SIBLEY	5,700	5,670	99
STEARNS	56,200	55,670	99
STEELE	14,400	14,320	99
STEVENS	3,700	3,660	99
SWIFT	3,800	3,750	99
TODD	9,400	9,270	99
TRAVERSE	1,500	1,490	99
WABASHA	8,600	8,530	99
WADENA	5,400	5,280	98
WASECA	7,100	7,050	99
WASHINGTON	87,000	86,740	100
WATONWAN	4,200	4,180	100
WILKIN	2,400	2,390	100
WINONA	18,900	18,770	99
WRIGHT	45,400	45,020	99
YELLOW MED	4,000	3,960	99

MISSISSIPPI

State and County	Total Households	Total TV Households	%
ADAMS	12,700	12,520	99
ALCORN	15,200	15,010	99
AMITE	5,300	5,230	99
ATTALA	7,800	7,720	99
BENTON	3,200	3,180	99
BOLIVAR	13,000	12,760	98
CALHOUN	5,900	5,840	99
CARROLL	4,000	3,950	99
CHICKASAW	7,100	7,000	99
CHOCTAW	3,600	3,530	98
CLAIBORNE	3,600	3,510	98
CLARKE	7,000	6,940	99
CLAY	8,000	7,920	99
COAHOMA	9,400	9,220	98
COPIAH	10,600	10,440	98
COVINGTON	7,900	7,740	98
DE SOTO	60,400	59,890	99
FORREST	30,400	30,160	99
FRANKLIN	3,200	3,140	98
GEORGE	8,100	7,920	98
GREENE	4,400	4,350	99
GRENADA	9,100	8,990	99
HANCOCK	16,500	16,320	99
HARRISON	69,000	68,350	99
HINDS	90,200	89,270	99
HOLMES	7,000	6,850	98
HUMPHREYS	3,400	3,360	99
ISSAQUENA	500	490	98
ITAWAMBA	9,100	9,020	99
JACKSON	49,100	48,680	99
JASPER	7,000	6,940	99
JEFFERSON	3,100	3,060	99
JEFF DAVIS	4,900	4,860	99
JONES	26,100	25,910	99
KEMPER	3,700	3,610	98
LAFAYETTE	17,300	17,190	99
LAMAR	19,300	19,020	99
LAUDERDALE	30,500	30,240	99
LAWRENCE	5,200	5,130	99
LEAKE	8,000	7,850	98
LEE	31,900	31,740	99
LEFLORE	12,100	11,940	99
LINCOLN	13,600	13,390	98
LOWNDES	22,400	22,180	99
MADISON	35,100	34,710	99
MARION	9,700	9,480	98
MARSHALL	13,600	13,370	98
MONROE	14,700	14,540	99
MONTGOMERY	4,400	4,270	97
NESHOBA	11,900	11,750	99
NEWTON	8,700	8,620	99
NOXUBEE	4,400	4,000	91
OKTIBBEHA	17,300	17,150	99
PANOLA	13,300	13,140	99
PEARL RIVER	22,500	22,230	99
PERRY	4,600	4,550	99
PIKE	15,700	15,480	99
PONTOTOC	11,100	10,950	99
PRENTISS	10,200	10,120	99
QUITMAN	3,000	2,950	98
RANKIN	54,600	54,090	99
SCOTT	10,500	10,320	98
SHARKEY	1,900	1,870	98
SIMPSON	10,500	10,340	99
SMITH	6,000	5,960	99
STONE	5,800	5,710	98
SUNFLOWER	8,500	8,400	99
TALLAHATCHIE	4,600	4,500	98
TATE	10,000	9,910	99
TIPPAH	8,600	8,480	99
TISHOMINGO	8,000	7,870	98
TUNICA	4,000	3,890	97
UNION	10,800	10,700	99
WALTHALL	5,900	5,780	98
WARREN	18,400	18,210	99
WASHINGTON	19,600	19,320	99
WAYNE	7,900	7,810	99
WEBSTER	3,800	3,760	99
WILKINSON	3,700	3,630	98
WINSTON	7,500	7,450	99
YALOBUSHA	5,700	5,590	98
YAZOO	8,800	8,660	98

MISSOURI

State and County	Total Households	Total TV Households	%
ADAIR	9,900	9,720	98
ANDREW	6,600	6,580	100
ATCHISON	2,600	2,570	99
AUDRAIN	9,800	9,720	99
BARRY	14,400	14,250	99
BARTON	4,800	4,730	99
BATES	6,700	6,610	99
BENTON	8,100	8,020	99
BOLLINGER	4,600	4,560	99
BOONE	64,100	63,540	99
BUCHANAN	35,600	35,390	99
BUTLER	17,300	17,140	99
CALDWELL	3,700	3,660	99
CALLAWAY	16,000	15,870	99
CAMDEN	18,000	17,780	99
CPE GIRARDEAU	29,900	29,720	99
CARROLL	3,900	3,850	99
CARTER	2,400	2,300	96
CASS	37,600	37,410	99
CEDAR	5,600	5,510	98
CHARITON	3,200	3,160	99
CHRISTIAN	30,400	30,160	99
CLARK	3,000	2,980	99
CLAY	86,900	86,560	100
CLINTON	8,100	8,060	100
COLE	29,600	29,460	100
COOPER	6,400	6,320	99
CRAWFORD	9,500	9,380	99

State and County	Total Households	Total TV Households	%	State and County	Total Households	Total TV Households	%
DADE	3,000	2,980	99	WARREN	12,400	12,330	99
DALLAS	6,500	6,380	98	WASHINGTON	9,300	9,230	99
DAVIESS	3,200	3,150	98	WAYNE	5,400	5,330	99
DE KALB	3,500	3,480	99	WEBSTER	13,500	13,300	99
DENT	6,300	6,160	98	WORTH	800	790	99
DOUGLAS	5,500	5,430	99	WRIGHT	7,400	7,320	99
DUNKLIN	12,800	12,640	99	ST LOUIS-IND	148,600	146,710	99
FRANKLIN	38,600	38,360	99				
GASCONADE	6,200	6,160	99	**MONTANA**			
GENTRY	2,400	2,380	99				
GREENE	114,500	113,650	99	BEAVERHEAD	3,700	3,440	93
GRUNDY	4,300	4,260	99	BIG HORN	4,100	4,010	98
HARRISON	3,600	3,560	99	BLAINE	2,300	2,230	97
HENRY	9,300	9,180	99	BROADWATER	2,000	1,940	97
HICKORY	4,000	3,940	99	CARBON	4,200	4,120	98
HOLT	2,100	2,080	99	CARTER	500	490	98
HOWARD	3,700	3,680	99	CASCADE	33,400	33,090	99
HOWELL	15,800	15,370	97	CHOUTEAU	1,900	1,880	99
IRON	3,900	3,840	98	CUSTER	4,600	4,530	98
JACKSON	276,000	273,660	99	DANIELS	700	690	99
JASPER	46,100	45,790	99	DAWSON	3,500	3,450	99
JEFFERSON	81,700	81,200	99	DEER LODGE	3,700	3,650	99
JOHNSON	19,100	18,880	99	FALLON	1,200	1,160	97
KNOX	1,600	1,550	97	FERGUS	4,700	4,540	97
LACLEDE	14,300	14,160	99	FLATHEAD	35,900	34,760	97
LAFAYETTE	12,700	12,630	99	GALLATIN	36,900	35,530	96
LAWRENCE	14,600	14,440	99	GARFIELD	500	490	98
LEWIS	3,700	3,670	99	GLACIER	4,300	4,230	98
LINCOLN	19,700	19,540	99	GOLDEN VALLEY	400	390	98
LINN	5,100	5,040	99	GRANITE	1,200	1,180	98
LIVINGSTON	5,700	5,640	99	HILL	6,500	6,310	97
MCDONALD	8,500	8,380	99	JEFFERSON	4,400	4,310	98
MACON	6,600	6,500	98	JUDITH BASIN	800	780	98
MADISON	5,000	4,950	99	LAKE	11,400	11,210	98
MARIES	3,700	3,660	99	LEWIS & CLARK	26,100	25,690	98
MARION	11,200	11,140	99	LIBERTY	600	590	98
MERCER	1,500	1,480	99	LINCOLN	8,300	7,940	96
MILLER	10,100	10,030	99	MCCONE	700	690	99
MISSISSIPPI	5,300	5,280	100	MADISON	3,400	3,320	98
MONITEAU	5,400	5,330	99	MEAGHER	800	780	98
MONROE	3,600	3,580	99	MINERAL	1,600	1,560	98
MONTGOMERY	4,700	4,660	99	MISSOULA	43,500	42,210	97
MORGAN	8,600	8,260	96	MUSSELSHELL	1,900	1,840	97
NEW MADRID	7,100	6,990	98	PARK	7,500	7,170	96
NEWTON	21,800	21,640	99	PETROLEUM	200	190	95
NODAWAY	8,500	8,410	99	PHILLIPS	1,600	1,570	98
OREGON	4,300	4,200	98	PONDERA	2,200	2,170	99
OSAGE	5,300	5,290	100	POWDER RIVER	700	690	99
OZARK	3,800	3,750	99	POWELL	2,300	2,240	97
PEMISCOT	7,300	7,210	99	PRAIRIE	500	490	98
PERRY	7,300	7,260	99	RAVALLI	16,600	16,210	98
PETTIS	16,400	16,240	99	RICHLAND	3,900	3,870	99
PHELPS	17,000	16,530	97	ROOSEVELT	3,400	3,350	99
PIKE	6,600	6,550	99	ROSEBUD	3,400	3,330	98
PLATTE	35,100	34,880	99	SANDERS	4,900	4,810	98
POLK	11,400	11,240	99	SHERIDAN	1,400	1,380	99
PULASKI	14,300	14,250	100	SILVER BOW	13,900	13,770	99
PUTNAM	2,000	1,980	99	STILLWATER	3,500	3,450	99
RALLS	3,900	3,890	100	SWEET GRASS	1,600	1,500	94
RANDOLPH	9,900	9,830	99	TETON	2,400	2,320	97
RAY	8,900	8,850	99	TOOLE	1,800	1,750	97
REYNOLDS	2,700	2,650	98	TREASURE	300	290	97
RIPLEY	5,500	5,350	97	VALLEY	2,900	2,850	98
ST CHARLES	132,000	131,580	100	WHEATLAND	800	780	98
ST CLAIR	3,900	3,860	99	WIBAUX	300	290	97
ST FRANCOIS	23,700	23,500	99	YELLOWSTONE	58,700	58,250	99
ST LOUIS	402,200	399,820	99				
STE GENEVIEVE	6,700	6,660	99	**NEBRASKA**			
SALINE	8,500	8,450	99				
SCHUYLER	1,700	1,690	99	ADAMS	13,100	13,070	100
SCOTLAND	1,800	1,760	98	ANTELOPE	2,700	2,680	99
SCOTT	16,000	15,900	99	ARTHUR	100	100	100
SHANNON	3,500	3,430	98	BANNER	300	300	100
SHELBY	2,500	2,480	99	BLAINE	200	190	95
STODDARD	12,200	12,120	99	BOONE	2,100	2,090	100
STONE	13,200	13,080	99	BOX BUTTE	4,500	4,490	100
SULLIVAN	2,600	2,560	98	BOYD	900	880	98
TANEY	19,900	19,700	99	BROWN	1,400	1,380	99
TEXAS	9,700	9,490	98	BUFFALO	17,700	17,650	100
VERNON	7,800	7,700	99				

State and County	Total Households	Total TV Households	%
BURT	2,800	2,790	100
BUTLER	3,300	3,280	99
CASS	9,900	9,880	100
CEDAR	3,200	3,180	99
CHASE	1,500	1,490	99
CHERRY	2,300	2,280	99
CHEYENNE	4,200	4,180	100
CLAY	2,400	2,390	100
COLFAX	3,400	3,370	99
CUMING	3,600	3,590	100
CUSTER	4,400	4,370	99
DAKOTA	6,900	6,890	100
DAWES	3,500	3,440	98
DAWSON	8,600	8,530	99
DEUEL	800	800	100
DIXON	2,400	2,390	100
DODGE	14,500	14,440	100
DOUGLAS	199,700	198,380	99
DUNDY	800	790	99
FILLMORE	2,400	2,380	99
FRANKLIN	1,200	1,190	99
FRONTIER	1,000	990	99
FURNAS	1,900	1,890	99
GAGE	9,400	9,360	100
GARDEN	800	790	99
GARFIELD	700	700	100
GOSPER	800	790	99
GRANT	200	190	95
GREELEY	900	890	99
HALL	21,800	21,660	99
HAMILTON	3,500	3,480	99
HARLAN	1,400	1,390	99
HAYES	400	400	100
HITCHCOCK	1,200	1,190	99
HOLT	4,200	4,160	99
HOOKER	300	290	97
HOWARD	2,600	2,580	99
JEFFERSON	3,100	3,080	99
JOHNSON	1,700	1,690	99
KEARNEY	2,500	2,490	100
KEITH	3,300	3,280	99
KEYA PAHA	300	290	97
KIMBALL	1,500	1,490	99
KNOX	3,400	3,350	99
LANCASTER	113,000	112,330	99
LINCOLN	15,000	14,850	99
LOGAN	300	300	100
LOUP	200	200	100
MCPHERSON	200	200	100
MADISON	12,900	12,820	99
MERRICK	3,000	2,990	100
MORRILL	2,000	1,980	99
NANCE	1,400	1,390	99
NEMAHA	2,900	2,880	99
NUCKOLLS	2,000	1,980	99
OTOE	6,100	6,080	99
PAWNEE	1,100	1,090	99
PERKINS	1,200	1,190	99
PHELPS	3,600	3,580	99
PIERCE	2,700	2,680	99
PLATTE	12,600	12,540	100
POLK	2,000	1,990	100
RED WILLOW	4,400	4,360	99
RICHARDSON	3,400	3,360	99
ROCK	700	700	100
SALINE	5,100	5,080	100
SARPY	58,500	58,320	100
SAUNDERS	7,600	7,580	100
SCOTTS BLUFF	15,100	14,960	99
SEWARD	6,300	6,250	99
SHERIDAN	2,200	2,180	99
SHERMAN	1,300	1,290	99
SIOUX	500	490	98
STANTON	2,300	2,280	99
THAYER	2,100	2,090	100
THOMAS	300	290	97
THURSTON	2,200	2,190	100
VALLEY	1,700	1,680	99
WASHINGTON	7,400	7,380	100
WAYNE	3,200	3,190	100
WEBSTER	1,400	1,390	99
WHEELER	300	300	100
YORK	5,600	5,580	100

NEVADA

State and County	Total Households	Total TV Households	%
CHURCHILL	9,400	9,260	99
CLARK	707,900	700,990	99
DOUGLAS	18,500	18,330	99
ELKO	16,400	15,890	97
ESMERALDA	300	290	97
EUREKA	700	670	96
HUMBOLDT	6,500	6,350	98
LANDER	1,900	1,800	95
LINCOLN	2,000	1,950	98
LYON	21,000	20,650	98
MINERAL	2,100	2,040	97
NYE	19,300	18,840	98
PERSHING	1,800	1,780	99
STOREY	2,000	1,930	97
WASHOE	162,000	159,030	98
WHITE PINE	3,500	3,450	99
CARSON CITY	21,000	20,660	98

NEW HAMPSHIRE

State and County	Total Households	Total TV Households	%
BELKNAP	25,300	25,000	99
CARROLL	20,600	20,000	97
CHESHIRE	30,000	29,460	98
COOS	13,900	13,740	99
GRAFTON	34,000	33,080	97
HILLSBOROUGH	154,700	153,730	99
MERRIMACK	57,000	56,250	99
ROCKINGHAM	114,500	113,740	99
STRAFFORD	47,200	46,890	99
SULLIVAN	18,100	17,770	98

NEW JERSEY

State and County	Total Households	Total TV Households	%
ATLANTIC	103,800	102,680	99
BERGEN	334,800	333,240	100
BURLINGTON	166,900	166,310	100
CAMDEN	193,600	192,650	100
CAPE MAY	39,600	39,320	99
CUMBERLAND	52,600	52,290	99
ESSEX	273,500	270,900	99
GLOUCESTER	105,800	105,540	100
HUDSON	225,700	222,570	99
HUNTERDON	47,800	47,510	99
MERCER	129,700	128,540	99
MIDDLESEX	279,300	277,760	99
MONMOUTH	235,600	234,550	100
MORRIS	177,700	177,340	100
OCEAN	227,300	225,080	99
PASSAIC	160,500	158,960	99
SALEM	25,700	25,590	100
SOMERSET	117,700	117,050	99
SUSSEX	54,400	54,010	99
UNION	183,100	182,330	100
WARREN	42,700	42,440	99

NEW MEXICO

State and County	Total Households	Total TV Households	%
BERNALILLO	262,400	258,490	99
CATRON	1,700	1,430	84
CHAVES	23,500	23,230	99
CIBOLA	9,000	8,650	96
COLFAX	5,500	5,330	97
CURRY	16,500	16,380	99
DE BACA	800	750	94
DONA ANA	71,900	70,550	98
EDDY	19,900	19,730	99
GRANT	12,500	12,110	97
GUADALUPE	1,500	1,460	97
HARDING	300	270	90
HIDALGO	1,800	1,750	97
LEA-N	20,000	19,810	99

State and County	Total Households	Total TV Households	%
LEA-S	2,100	2,090	100
LINCOLN	9,200	8,890	97
LOS ALAMOS	7,500	7,420	99
LUNA	10,400	10,240	98
MCKINLEY	20,900	19,860	95
MORA	2,100	1,980	94
OTERO	23,400	23,070	99
QUAY	3,800	3,750	99
RIO ARRIBA	15,700	15,160	97
ROOSEVELT	6,700	6,580	98
SANDOVAL	47,000	46,170	98
SAN JUAN	41,400	40,450	98
SAN MIGUEL	11,100	10,400	94
SANTA FE	58,600	56,420	96
SIERRA	5,800	5,560	96
SOCORRO	6,900	6,620	96
TAOS	14,500	12,990	90
TORRANCE	5,800	5,590	96
UNION	1,600	1,550	97
VALENCIA	25,800	25,440	99

NEW YORK

State and County	Total Households	Total TV Households	%
ALBANY	123,100	122,300	99
ALLEGANY	18,200	17,900	98
BRONX	481,800	473,790	98
BROOME	79,500	78,960	99
CATTARAUGUS	31,200	30,920	99
CAYUGA	31,200	30,980	99
CHAUTAUQUA	53,600	53,150	99
CHEMUNG	34,700	34,520	99
CHENANGO	20,300	20,110	99
CLINTON	31,400	31,180	99
COLUMBIA	25,100	24,840	99
CORTLAND	18,500	18,340	99
DELAWARE	19,000	18,630	98
DUTCHESS	104,100	102,750	99
ERIE	369,900	368,520	100
ESSEX	15,100	14,930	99
FRANKLIN	18,400	18,050	98
FULTON	22,600	22,440	99
GENESEE	22,200	22,090	100
GREENE	19,100	18,860	99
HAMILTON	2,300	2,290	100
HERKIMER	25,500	25,340	99
JEFFERSON	43,500	43,320	100
KINGS	911,300	877,680	96
LEWIS	10,100	10,010	99
LIVINGSTON	21,900	21,760	99
MADISON	26,400	26,190	99
MONROE-REM	196,500	195,790	100
ROCHESTR CITY	89,900	89,310	99
MONTGOMERY	20,100	19,950	99
NASSAU	450,500	448,980	100
NEW YORK	773,500	745,850	96
NIAGARA	88,300	88,000	100
ONONDAGA	181,100	180,250	100
ONTARIO	41,200	40,930	99
ORANGE	129,700	128,210	99
ORLEANS	15,000	14,870	99
OSWEGO	46,000	45,780	100
OTSEGO	23,700	23,410	99
PUTNAM	34,500	34,340	100
QUEENS	786,900	776,340	99
RENSSELAER	62,300	61,930	99
RICHMOND	175,800	174,940	100
ROCKLAND	97,400	95,530	98
ST LAWRENCE	41,100	40,640	99
SARATOGA	88,000	87,470	99
SCHENECTADY	61,000	60,750	100
SCHOHARIE	12,600	12,440	99
SCHUYLER	7,400	7,300	99
SENECA	12,600	12,510	99
STEUBEN	38,800	38,240	99
SUFFOLK	506,500	504,360	100
SULLIVAN	29,600	28,780	97
TIOGA	19,700	19,540	99
TOMPKINS	38,900	36,950	95
ULSTER	69,900	68,070	97
WARREN	27,900	27,600	99

State and County	Total Households	Total TV Households	%
WASHINGTON	24,400	24,210	99
WAYNE	35,600	35,490	100
WESTCHESTER	343,600	341,670	99
WYOMING	14,700	14,630	100
YATES	9,000	8,910	99
ONEIDA-E	56,500	56,140	99
ONEIDA-W	34,700	34,440	99

NORTH CAROLINA

State and County	Total Households	Total TV Households	%
ALAMANCE	60,600	60,260	99
ALEXANDER	14,400	14,320	99
ALLEGHANY	4,900	4,880	100
ANSON	8,900	8,860	100
ASHE	11,600	11,320	98
AVERY	6,800	6,580	97
BEAUFORT	19,700	19,540	99
BERTIE	7,600	7,460	98
BLADEN	13,400	13,250	99
BRUNSWICK	48,200	47,690	99
BUNCOMBE	98,500	96,550	98
BURKE	34,700	34,420	99
CABARRUS	66,900	66,600	100
CALDWELL	32,200	31,830	99
CAMDEN	4,000	3,980	100
CARTERET	27,800	27,520	99
CASWELL	8,700	8,640	99
CATAWBA	62,400	62,000	99
CHATHAM	26,500	26,320	99
CHEROKEE	12,000	11,720	98
CHOWAN	5,900	5,800	98
CLAY	5,000	4,900	98
CLEVELAND	38,200	38,040	100
COLUMBUS	21,900	21,690	99
CRAVEN	39,400	39,130	99
CUMBERLAND	116,000	115,360	99
CURRITUCK	9,700	9,630	99
DARE	14,500	14,290	99
DAVIDSON	64,500	63,980	99
DAVIE	16,800	16,620	99
DUPLIN	20,200	20,030	99
DURHAM	108,800	107,280	99
EDGECOMBE	19,400	19,230	99
FORSYTH	141,900	140,990	99
FRANKLIN	23,300	23,110	99
GASTON	83,100	82,580	99
GATES	4,500	4,460	99
GRAHAM	3,500	3,380	97
GRANVILLE	20,200	20,070	99
GREENE	7,100	7,060	99
GUILFORD	195,900	194,860	99
HALIFAX	21,800	21,590	99
HARNETT	43,200	42,950	99
HAYWOOD	25,000	24,730	99
HENDERSON	44,900	44,480	99
HERTFORD	8,800	8,680	99
HOKE	15,700	15,540	99
HYDE	1,900	1,850	97
IREDELL	62,600	62,130	99
JACKSON	15,500	15,180	98
JOHNSTON	63,900	63,560	99
JONES	4,100	4,060	99
LEE	22,900	22,680	99
LENOIR	23,300	23,150	99
LINCOLN	29,600	29,510	100
MCDOWELL	17,900	17,660	99
MACON	14,700	14,410	98
MADISON	8,700	8,370	96
MARTIN	9,300	9,240	99
MECKLENBURG	371,000	368,710	99
MITCHELL	6,800	6,740	99
MONTGOMERY	10,300	10,220	99
MOORE	36,700	36,390	99
NASH	37,400	37,100	99
NEW HANOVER	86,700	86,090	99
NORTHAMPTON	8,400	8,280	99
ONSLOW	54,300	53,850	99
ORANGE	49,600	48,710	98
PAMLICO	5,100	5,060	99
PASQUOTANK	15,900	15,800	99

State and County	Total Households	Total TV Households	%
PENDER	21,500	21,230	99
PERQUIMANS	5,700	5,620	99
PERSON	15,300	15,140	99
PITT	66,100	65,600	99
POLK	8,400	8,310	99
RANDOLPH	55,600	55,210	99
RICHMOND	17,900	17,790	99
ROBESON	45,800	45,380	99
ROCKINGHAM	37,900	37,660	99
ROWAN	54,500	54,080	99
RUTHERFORD	26,100	25,910	99
SAMPSON	24,100	23,970	99
SCOTLAND	13,700	13,590	99
STANLY	23,100	23,000	100
STOKES	18,700	18,600	99
SURRY	29,100	28,940	99
SWAIN	5,600	5,520	99
TRANSYLVANIA	13,300	13,220	99
TYRRELL	1,500	1,480	99
UNION	72,200	71,590	99
VANCE	16,500	16,400	99
WAKE	350,200	348,170	99
WARREN	7,700	7,630	99
WASHINGTON	5,300	5,250	99
WATAUGA	18,400	17,900	97
WAYNE	44,400	44,150	99
WILKES	27,500	27,140	99
WILSON	31,200	31,020	99
YADKIN	15,300	15,190	99
YANCEY	8,100	7,730	95

NORTH DAKOTA

State and County	Total Households	Total TV Households	%
ADAMS	1,000	990	99
BARNES	4,500	4,480	100
BENSON	2,300	2,280	99
BILLINGS	400	400	100
BOTTINEAU	2,700	2,690	100
BOWMAN	1,300	1,290	99
BURKE	800	790	99
BURLEIGH	33,400	33,240	100
CASS	62,600	62,060	99
CAVALIER	1,600	1,590	99
DICKEY	2,000	1,990	100
DIVIDE	900	890	99
DUNN	1,300	1,280	98
EDDY	1,000	990	99
EMMONS	1,400	1,390	99
FOSTER	1,400	1,390	99
GOLDEN VALLEY	600	600	100
GRAND FORKS	25,900	25,750	99
GRANT	1,000	990	99
GRIGGS	1,000	1,000	100
HETTINGER	1,000	990	99
KIDDER	1,000	1,000	100
LA MOURE	1,700	1,690	99
LOGAN	800	790	99
MCHENRY	2,200	2,190	100
MCINTOSH	1,100	1,090	99
MCKENZIE	2,200	2,180	99
MCLEAN	3,600	3,580	99
MERCER	3,100	3,060	99
MORTON	10,800	10,730	99
MOUNTRAIL	2,600	2,580	99
NELSON	1,400	1,390	99
OLIVER	700	690	99
PEMBINA	3,100	3,030	98
PIERCE	1,700	1,690	99
RAMSEY	4,700	4,680	100
RANSOM	2,300	2,280	99
RENVILLE	1,000	1,000	100
RICHLAND	6,400	6,360	99
ROLETTE	4,600	4,550	99
SARGENT	1,700	1,680	99
SHERIDAN	500	490	98
SIOUX	1,200	1,180	98
SLOPE	300	290	97
STARK	9,300	9,260	100
STEELE	700	690	99
STUTSMAN	8,400	8,340	99

State and County	Total Households	Total TV Households	%
TOWNER	900	890	99
TRAILL	3,100	3,080	99
WALSH	4,500	4,480	100
WARD	22,500	22,390	100
WELLS	1,800	1,780	99
WILLIAMS	8,600	8,560	100

OHIO

State and County	Total Households	Total TV Households	%
ADAMS	11,300	11,070	98
ALLEN	41,200	40,910	99
ASHLAND	21,000	20,820	99
ASHTABULA	38,600	38,360	99
ATHENS	23,500	22,950	98
AUGLAIZE	17,900	17,830	100
BELMONT	27,700	27,600	100
BROWN	16,600	16,450	99
BUTLER	137,400	136,540	99
CARROLL	11,200	11,120	99
CHAMPAIGN	15,700	15,580	99
CLARK	55,100	54,860	100
CLERMONT	75,400	74,860	99
CLINTON	16,900	16,820	100
COLUMBIANA	41,200	40,750	99
COSHOCTON	14,200	13,960	98
CRAWFORD	17,900	17,790	99
CUYAHOGA	525,500	522,360	99
DARKE	20,500	20,250	99
DEFIANCE	15,400	15,320	99
DELAWARE	63,600	63,330	100
ERIE	31,800	31,670	100
FAIRFIELD	54,700	54,460	100
FAYETTE	11,300	11,230	99
FRANKLIN	472,700	470,420	100
FULTON	16,100	16,010	99
GALLIA	12,400	12,320	99
GEAUGA	33,800	33,290	98
GREENE	62,800	62,530	100
GUERNSEY	16,000	15,790	99
HAMILTON	348,800	346,820	99
HANCOCK	30,600	30,390	99
HARDIN	12,000	11,920	99
HARRISON	6,400	6,360	99
HENRY	11,100	11,060	100
HIGHLAND	16,400	16,210	99
HOCKING	11,500	11,340	99
HOLMES	12,300	9,920	81
HURON	22,900	22,810	100
JACKSON	13,200	13,070	99
JEFFERSON	28,800	28,690	99
KNOX	22,100	21,990	100
LAKE	95,600	95,290	100
LAWRENCE	25,900	25,800	100
LICKING	61,300	60,900	99
LOGAN	18,400	18,270	99
LORAIN	115,700	115,420	100
LUCAS	178,500	177,820	100
MADISON	14,700	14,550	99
MAHONING	95,900	95,560	100
MARION	24,800	24,650	99
MEDINA	64,500	64,260	100
MEIGS	9,400	9,300	99
MERCER	15,300	15,240	100
MIAMI	40,300	40,040	99
MONROE	5,800	5,690	98
MONTGOMERY	222,000	221,150	100
MORGAN	6,000	5,960	99
MORROW	13,000	12,890	99
MUSKINGUM	32,600	32,350	99
NOBLE	4,600	4,550	99
OTTAWA	16,900	16,830	100
PAULDING	7,600	7,510	99
PERRY	13,200	13,090	99
PICKAWAY	19,500	19,400	99
PIKE	10,800	10,670	99
PORTAGE	60,500	60,170	99
PREBLE	16,200	16,040	99
PUTNAM	12,700	12,640	100
RICHLAND	48,400	47,870	99
ROSS	28,100	27,880	99

State and County	Total Households	Total TV Households	%
SANDUSKY	24,000	23,930	100
SCIOTO	30,500	30,210	99
SENECA	22,000	21,890	100
SHELBY	18,700	18,630	100
STARK	151,500	150,480	99
SUMMIT	220,700	219,700	100
TRUMBULL	85,300	84,900	100
TUSCARAWAS	36,300	35,730	98
UNION	17,400	17,260	99
VAN WERT	11,500	11,470	100
VINTON	5,200	5,120	98
WARREN	76,700	76,270	99
WASHINGTON	24,900	24,710	99
WAYNE	42,200	41,480	98
WILLIAMS	15,100	14,990	99
WOOD	49,000	48,790	100
WYANDOT	8,900	8,860	100

OKLAHOMA

State and County	Total Households	Total TV Households	%
ADAIR	7,900	7,750	98
ALFALFA	2,000	1,960	98
ATOKA	5,500	5,450	99
BEAVER	2,000	1,970	99
BECKHAM	8,300	8,220	99
BLAINE	4,000	3,960	99
BRYAN	16,300	16,110	99
CADDO	10,500	10,420	99
CANADIAN	40,400	40,130	99
CARTER	19,400	19,230	99
CHEROKEE	18,000	17,810	99
CHOCTAW	6,100	5,950	98
CIMARRON	1,000	970	97
CLEVELAND	95,600	95,090	99
COAL	2,200	2,170	99
COMANCHE	39,500	39,190	99
COTTON	2,400	2,390	100
CRAIG	5,700	5,640	99
CREEK	26,800	26,410	99
CUSTER	10,700	10,610	99
DELAWARE	16,600	16,390	99
DEWEY	1,900	1,880	99
ELLIS	1,800	1,760	98
GARFIELD	23,700	23,530	99
GARVIN	11,000	10,880	99
GRADY	20,200	20,030	99
GRANT	1,800	1,780	99
GREER	2,100	2,090	100
HARMON	1,100	1,080	98
HARPER	1,400	1,370	98
HASKELL	4,800	4,730	99
HUGHES	5,100	5,090	100
JACKSON	9,300	9,220	99
JEFFERSON	2,400	2,380	99
JOHNSTON	4,000	3,970	99
KAY	18,100	17,920	99
KINGFISHER	5,500	5,450	99
KIOWA	3,900	3,870	99
LATIMER	4,000	3,950	99
LE FLORE	18,800	18,530	99
LINCOLN	12,400	12,260	99
LOGAN	14,700	14,540	99
LOVE	3,600	3,560	99
MCCLAIN	12,600	12,420	99
MCCURTAIN	13,300	12,950	97
MCINTOSH	8,300	8,200	99
MAJOR	2,900	2,860	99
MARSHALL	6,200	6,140	99
MAYES	15,800	15,570	99
MURRAY	5,200	5,170	99
MUSKOGEE	27,500	27,240	99
NOBLE	4,500	4,450	99
NOWATA	4,200	4,160	99
OKFUSKEE	4,000	3,860	97
OKLAHOMA	290,100	288,490	99
OKMULGEE	15,100	14,970	99
OSAGE	17,300	17,180	99
OTTAWA	12,100	11,980	99
PAWNEE	6,200	6,160	99
PAYNE	30,500	30,220	99

State and County	Total Households	Total TV Households	%
PITTSBURG	17,900	17,710	99
PONTOTOC	15,100	14,940	99
POTTAWATOMIE	26,300	26,120	99
PUSHMATAHA	4,900	4,730	97
ROGER MILLS	1,500	1,470	98
ROGERS	31,100	30,830	99
SEMINOLE	9,400	9,330	99
SEQUOYAH	16,000	15,600	98
STEPHENS	18,000	17,850	99
TEXAS	7,000	6,920	99
TILLMAN	3,000	2,980	99
TULSA	241,800	240,120	99
WAGONER	26,600	26,360	99
WASHINGTON	21,400	21,290	99
WASHITA	4,700	4,620	98
WOODS	3,400	3,370	99
WOODWARD	7,800	7,730	99

OREGON

State and County	Total Households	Total TV Households	%
BAKER	6,800	6,680	98
BENTON	33,800	32,680	97
CLACKAMAS	146,600	144,640	99
CLATSOP	16,000	15,230	95
COLUMBIA	18,900	18,660	99
COOS	27,300	26,610	97
CROOK	9,900	9,700	98
CURRY	10,000	9,610	96
DESCHUTES	68,600	66,980	98
DOUGLAS	42,800	41,890	98
GILLIAM	800	770	96
GRANT	3,000	2,810	94
HARNEY	2,900	2,670	92
HOOD RIVER	7,600	7,270	96
JACKSON	82,900	81,410	98
JEFFERSON	7,800	7,640	98
JOSEPHINE	35,000	33,960	97
KLAMATH	26,600	26,140	98
LAKE	3,200	3,060	96
LANE	143,800	140,550	98
LINCOLN	20,200	19,550	97
LINN	44,900	43,820	98
MALHEUR	9,900	9,740	98
MARION	113,400	111,680	98
MORROW	3,900	3,800	97
MULTNOMAH	302,200	294,630	97
POLK	27,100	26,790	99
SHERMAN	700	670	96
TILLAMOOK	11,000	10,610	96
UMATILLA	26,000	25,470	98
UNION	10,300	9,890	96
WALLOWA	3,000	2,910	97
WASCO	9,600	9,340	97
WASHINGTON	202,700	200,560	99
WHEELER	600	580	97
YAMHILL	33,600	33,020	98

PENNSYLVANIA

State and County	Total Households	Total TV Households	%
ADAMS	38,700	38,430	99
ALLEGHENY	514,600	511,990	99
ARMSTRONG	28,600	28,490	100
BEAVER	69,500	69,190	100
BEDFORD	20,300	19,960	98
BERKS	153,100	151,390	99
BLAIR	50,900	50,580	99
BRADFORD	24,600	24,360	99
BUCKS	233,500	232,390	100
BUTLER	71,300	71,060	100
CAMBRIA	57,500	57,280	100
CAMERON	2,200	2,190	100
CARBON	26,700	26,550	99
CENTRE	53,800	52,930	98
CHESTER	183,900	182,890	99
CLARION	16,100	15,910	99
CLEARFIELD	33,200	32,930	99
CLINTON	14,900	14,660	99
COLUMBIA	25,800	25,620	99
CRAWFORD	34,200	33,690	99

State and County	Total Households	Total TV Households	%
CUMBERLAND	92,600	91,960	99
DAUPHIN	106,900	106,140	99
DELAWARE	207,900	207,240	100
ELK	13,300	13,230	99
ERIE	106,800	106,330	100
FAYETTE	58,200	57,820	99
FOREST	1,900	1,860	98
FRANKLIN	59,000	57,500	97
FULTON	6,200	6,120	99
GREENE	14,900	14,820	99
HUNTINGDON	17,200	16,850	98
INDIANA	34,900	34,600	99
JEFFERSON	18,500	18,370	99
JUNIATA	8,800	8,680	99
LACKAWANNA	87,100	86,760	100
LANCASTER	190,700	185,140	97
LAWRENCE	35,700	35,490	99
LEBANON	51,500	50,460	98
LEHIGH	134,400	133,610	99
LUZERNE	129,500	129,080	100
LYCOMING	46,800	46,240	99
MCKEAN	17,100	16,890	99
MERCER	45,700	45,350	99
MIFFLIN	18,600	18,120	97
MONROE	60,300	59,690	99
MONTGOMERY	300,500	299,340	100
MONTOUR	7,000	6,870	98
NORTHAMPTON	115,500	114,610	99
NORTHUMBERLND	38,000	37,560	99
PERRY	18,000	17,690	98
PHILADELPHIA	564,200	558,070	99
PIKE	23,200	23,060	99
POTTER	6,500	6,250	96
SCHUYLKILL	59,700	59,190	99
SNYDER	14,300	13,960	98
SOMERSET	30,300	30,030	99
SULLIVAN	2,500	2,420	97
SUSQUEHANNA	16,400	16,130	98
TIOGA	16,100	15,730	98
UNION	14,000	13,630	97
VENANGO	21,900	21,630	99
WARREN	16,700	16,500	99
WASHINGTON	83,700	83,370	100
WAYNE	20,300	19,900	98
WESTMORELAND	149,100	148,390	100
WYOMING	11,000	10,860	99
YORK	170,500	169,300	99

RHODE ISLAND

State and County	Total Households	Total TV Households	%
BRISTOL	19,200	19,120	100
KENT	68,900	68,690	100
NEWPORT	33,500	33,320	99
PROVIDENCE	239,500	238,010	99
WASHINGTON	48,900	48,550	99

SOUTH CAROLINA

State and County	Total Households	Total TV Households	%
ABBEVILLE	10,000	9,810	98
AIKEN	63,000	62,520	99
ALLENDALE	3,700	3,660	99
ANDERSON	75,000	74,540	99
BAMBERG	5,900	5,810	98
BARNWELL	9,300	9,180	99
BEAUFORT	62,000	61,470	99
BERKELEY	64,600	64,010	99
CALHOUN	6,000	5,960	99
CHARLESTON	146,400	145,080	99
CHEROKEE	22,100	21,970	99
CHESTER	12,800	12,700	99
CHESTERFIELD	17,300	17,170	99
CLARENDON	12,900	12,720	99
COLLETON	15,500	15,310	99
DARLINGTON	25,900	25,690	99
DILLON	11,700	11,600	99
DORCHESTER	48,900	48,590	99
EDGEFIELD	8,800	8,760	100
FAIRFIELD	9,400	9,310	99
FLORENCE	51,800	51,530	99

State and County	Total Households	Total TV Households	%
GEORGETOWN	25,500	25,280	99
GREENVILLE	180,300	178,990	99
GREENWOOD	26,400	26,280	100
HAMPTON	7,700	7,600	99
HORRY	117,500	116,390	99
JASPER	8,000	7,880	99
KERSHAW	23,900	23,710	99
LANCASTER	30,700	30,560	100
LAURENS	26,900	26,780	100
LEE	7,100	6,990	98
LEXINGTON	101,600	100,930	99
MCCORMICK	3,900	3,880	99
MARION	13,300	13,200	99
MARLBORO	10,100	10,020	99
NEWBERRY	15,300	15,180	99
OCONEE	30,500	30,230	99
ORANGEBURG	35,100	34,720	99
PICKENS	46,000	45,680	99
RICHLAND	143,900	142,790	99
SALUDA	7,100	7,050	99
SPARTANBURG	111,800	111,050	99
SUMTER	39,600	39,260	99
UNION	11,600	11,530	99
WILLIAMSBURG	13,000	12,920	99
YORK	86,700	86,220	99

SOUTH DAKOTA

State and County	Total Households	Total TV Households	%
AURORA	1,100	1,080	98
BEADLE	7,000	6,930	99
BENNETT	1,000	980	98
BON HOMME	2,400	2,390	100
BROOKINGS	11,500	11,370	99
BROWN	15,100	15,050	100
BRULE	2,000	1,990	100
BUFFALO	600	580	97
BUTTE	3,800	3,730	98
CAMPBELL	500	490	98
CHARLES MIX	3,200	3,180	99
CLARK	1,300	1,280	98
CLAY	5,000	4,970	99
CODINGTON	10,800	10,740	99
CORSON	1,200	1,180	98
CUSTER	3,400	3,330	98
DAVISON	7,700	7,640	99
DAY	2,300	2,280	99
DEUEL	1,800	1,780	99
DEWEY	1,900	1,840	97
DOUGLAS	1,100	1,070	97
EDMUNDS	1,500	1,490	99
FALL RIVER	3,100	3,020	97
FAULK	800	790	99
GRANT	2,900	2,860	99
GREGORY	1,800	1,790	99
HAAKON	800	790	99
HAMLIN	2,100	2,050	98
HAND	1,400	1,390	99
HANSON	1,300	1,290	99
HARDING	500	480	96
HUGHES	6,700	6,660	99
HUTCHINSON	2,800	2,770	99
HYDE	600	590	98
JACKSON	900	890	99
JERAULD	900	890	99
JONES	400	390	98
KINGSBURY	2,300	2,280	99
LAKE	4,800	4,780	100
LAWRENCE	10,100	9,960	99
LINCOLN	15,700	15,620	99
LYMAN	1,400	1,390	99
MCCOOK	2,100	2,090	100
MCPHERSON	1,000	990	99
MARSHALL	1,800	1,780	99
MEADE	9,200	9,130	99
MELLETTE	700	690	99
MINER	1,000	990	99
MINNEHAHA	72,400	72,120	100
MOODY	2,500	2,500	100
PENNINGTON	40,200	39,920	99
PERKINS	1,200	1,190	99

TV Households

State and County	Total Households	Total TV Households	%
POTTER	900	890	99
ROBERTS	3,600	3,560	99
SANBORN	1,000	980	98
SHANNON	3,100	3,010	97
SPINK	2,500	2,480	99
STANLEY	1,100	1,090	99
SULLY	500	490	98
TODD	2,900	2,800	97
TRIPP	2,300	2,290	100
TURNER	3,300	3,280	99
UNION	5,800	5,760	99
WALWORTH	2,200	2,170	99
YANKTON	8,300	8,240	99
ZIEBACH	800	780	98

TENNESSEE

State and County	Total Households	Total TV Households	%
ANDERSON	32,000	31,800	99
BEDFORD	16,800	16,740	100
BENTON	6,900	6,790	98
BLEDSOE	4,900	4,800	98
BLOUNT	50,600	50,220	99
BRADLEY	39,100	38,680	99
CAMPBELL	17,500	17,260	99
CANNON	5,600	5,530	99
CARROLL	11,500	11,370	99
CARTER	24,900	24,750	99
CHEATHAM	14,600	14,490	99
CHESTER	6,200	6,130	99
CLAIBORNE	13,100	12,950	99
CLAY	3,400	3,330	98
COCKE	15,400	15,190	99
COFFEE	21,100	20,930	99
CROCKETT	5,500	5,470	99
CUMBERLAND	23,900	23,560	99
DAVIDSON	264,900	262,560	99
DECATUR	4,800	4,630	96
DE KALB	7,700	7,650	99
DICKSON	18,900	18,680	99
DYER	15,000	14,850	99
FAYETTE	15,400	15,150	98
FENTRESS	7,600	7,310	96
FRANKLIN	16,300	16,150	99
GIBSON	20,600	20,450	99
GILES	11,900	11,720	98
GRAINGER	9,600	9,480	99
GREENE	27,800	27,610	99
GRUNDY	5,800	5,680	98
HAMBLEN	25,800	25,610	99
HAMILTON	138,600	137,750	99
HANCOCK	2,900	2,860	99
HARDEMAN	9,600	9,520	99
HARDIN	11,200	11,050	99
HAWKINS	24,800	24,530	99
HAYWOOD	7,500	7,420	99
HENDERSON	11,300	11,150	99
HENRY	13,600	13,420	99
HICKMAN	8,800	8,730	99
HOUSTON	3,300	3,260	99
HUMPHREYS	7,600	7,550	99
JACKSON	4,500	4,430	98
JEFFERSON	20,800	20,610	99
JOHNSON	7,300	7,190	98
KNOX	185,700	184,260	99
LAKE	2,100	2,080	99
LAUDERDALE	9,600	9,510	99
LAWRENCE	16,200	16,020	99
LEWIS	4,500	4,460	99
LINCOLN	13,700	13,570	99
LOUDON	20,200	20,090	99
MCMINN	21,900	21,800	100
MCNAIRY	10,800	10,650	99
MACON	8,600	8,530	99
MADISON	38,400	38,100	99
MARION	11,800	11,640	99
MARSHALL	11,800	11,690	99
MAURY	33,100	32,860	99
MEIGS	4,700	4,660	99
MONROE	19,100	18,930	99
MONTGOMERY	58,900	58,510	99

State and County	Total Households	Total TV Households	%
MOORE	2,500	2,470	99
MORGAN	7,600	7,400	97
OBION	13,000	12,920	99
OVERTON	8,800	8,680	99
PERRY	3,200	3,180	99
PICKETT	2,100	2,070	99
POLK	6,600	6,530	99
PUTNAM	28,900	28,470	99
RHEA	12,700	12,570	99
ROANE	22,600	22,450	99
ROBERTSON	24,900	24,740	99
RUTHERFORD	98,100	97,280	99
SCOTT	9,100	8,970	99
SEQUATCHIE	5,700	5,640	99
SEVIER	34,600	34,310	99
SHELBY	345,900	342,880	99
SMITH	7,700	7,640	99
STEWART	5,400	5,350	99
SULLIVAN	66,500	66,200	100
SUMNER	62,100	61,660	99
TIPTON	21,700	21,520	99
TROUSDALE	3,100	3,080	99
UNICOI	7,900	7,830	99
UNION	7,500	7,440	99
VAN BUREN	2,300	2,280	99
WARREN	16,300	16,040	98
WASHINGTON	50,600	50,220	99
WAYNE	6,000	5,880	98
WEAKLEY	13,500	13,410	99
WHITE	10,500	10,330	98
WILLIAMSON	64,000	63,750	100
WILSON	43,600	43,260	99

TEXAS

State and County	Total Households	Total TV Households	%
ANDERSON	16,600	16,290	98
ANDREWS	5,100	5,090	100
ANGELINA	30,500	30,110	99
ARANSAS	10,800	10,640	99
ARCHER	3,500	3,480	99
ARMSTRONG	800	790	99
ATASCOSA	15,000	14,830	99
AUSTIN	10,200	10,050	99
BAILEY	2,200	2,150	98
BANDERA	8,300	8,120	98
BASTROP	26,100	25,720	99
BAYLOR	1,700	1,680	99
BEE	9,300	9,110	98
BELL	104,300	103,590	99
BEXAR	582,400	575,370	99
BLANCO	3,700	3,640	98
BORDEN	300	290	97
BOSQUE	7,200	7,150	99
BOWIE	34,600	34,270	99
BRAZORIA	107,100	106,440	99
BRAZOS	64,800	63,990	99
BREWSTER	4,000	3,510	88
BRISCOE	600	590	98
BROOKS	2,700	2,650	98
BROWN	15,000	14,780	99
BURLESON	6,800	6,700	99
BURNET	17,400	17,270	99
CALDWELL	12,600	12,470	99
CALHOUN	7,600	7,430	98
CALLAHAN	5,500	5,450	99
CAMERON	120,500	118,540	98
CAMP	4,900	4,850	99
CARSON	2,500	2,490	100
CASS	12,500	12,380	99
CASTRO	2,500	2,490	100
CHAMBERS	11,600	11,500	99
CHEROKEE	17,500	17,310	99
CHILDRESS	2,400	2,360	98
CLAY	4,400	4,380	100
COCHRAN	1,100	1,080	98
COKE	1,500	1,480	99
COLEMAN	3,600	3,560	99
COLLIN	296,700	294,400	99
COLLINGSWORTH	1,200	1,180	98
COLORADO	8,100	7,960	98

State and County	Total Households	Total TV Households	%	State and County	Total Households	Total TV Households	%
COMAL	43,400	43,060	99	JOHNSON	54,600	54,150	99
COMANCHE	5,500	5,370	98	JONES	5,600	5,560	99
CONCHO	900	890	99	KARNES	4,600	4,550	99
COOKE	15,000	14,870	99	KAUFMAN	36,100	35,880	99
CORYELL	19,700	19,560	99	KENDALL	12,600	12,330	98
COTTLE	700	690	99	KENEDY	100	100	100
CRANE	1,400	1,390	99	KENT	300	290	97
CROCKETT	1,600	1,580	99	KERR	20,200	19,840	98
CROSBY	2,200	2,190	100	KIMBLE	2,000	1,950	98
CULBERSON	900	890	99	KING	100	90	90
DALLAM	2,300	2,210	96	KINNEY	1,300	1,260	97
DALLAS	863,600	856,220	99	KLEBERG	10,700	10,490	98
DAWSON	4,400	4,330	98	KNOX	1,400	1,380	99
DEAF SMITH	6,400	6,310	99	LAMAR	20,000	19,400	97
DELTA	2,200	2,160	98	LAMB	5,100	5,060	99
DENTON	244,800	242,550	99	LAMPASAS	8,100	8,000	99
DE WITT	7,200	7,070	98	LA SALLE	1,900	1,790	94
DICKENS	900	870	97	LAVACA	7,800	7,580	97
DIMMIT	3,400	3,260	96	LEE	6,200	6,120	99
DONLEY	1,600	1,580	99	LEON	6,900	6,750	98
DUVAL	4,100	4,010	98	LIBERTY	25,900	25,670	99
EASTLAND	7,300	7,180	98	LIMESTONE	7,900	7,850	99
ECTOR	48,300	47,990	99	LIPSCOMB	1,200	1,180	98
EDWARDS	700	680	97	LIVE OAK	4,100	4,050	99
ELLIS	50,500	50,150	99	LLANO	9,000	8,900	99
EL PASO	239,800	238,260	99	LOVING	100	100	100
ERATH	13,600	13,340	98	LUBBOCK	104,800	104,040	99
FALLS	6,000	5,900	98	LYNN	2,100	2,090	100
FANNIN	12,300	12,200	99	MCCULLOCH	3,300	3,230	98
FAYETTE	9,600	9,430	98	MCLENNAN	85,200	84,560	99
FISHER	1,700	1,690	99	MCMULLEN	400	390	98
FLOYD	2,400	2,360	98	MADISON	4,300	4,230	98
FOARD	600	600	100	MARION	4,500	4,480	100
FORT BEND	177,600	176,180	99	MARTIN	1,700	1,690	99
FRANKLIN	4,500	4,430	98	MASON	1,700	1,640	96
FREESTONE	7,400	7,310	99	MATAGORDA	13,900	13,750	99
FRIO	5,000	4,880	98	MAVERICK	15,100	14,580	97
GAINES	5,100	4,900	96	MEDINA	15,000	14,850	99
GALVESTON	113,400	112,410	99	MENARD	900	880	98
GARZA	1,700	1,690	99	MIDLAND	48,900	48,560	99
GILLESPIE	10,400	10,200	98	MILAM	9,700	9,550	98
GLASSCOCK	400	400	100	MILLS	2,000	1,960	98
GOLIAD	2,900	2,850	98	MITCHELL	2,700	2,670	99
GONZALES	7,100	7,040	99	MONTAGUE	8,200	8,110	99
GRAY	8,900	8,840	99	MONTGOMERY	156,900	155,340	99
GRAYSON	46,200	45,740	99	MOORE	6,800	6,780	100
GREGG	46,100	45,710	99	MORRIS	5,400	5,300	99
GRIMES	8,700	8,590	99	MOTLEY	600	590	98
GUADALUPE	42,800	42,340	99	NACOGDOCHES	23,900	23,610	99
HALE	11,600	11,530	99	NAVARRO	18,100	17,950	99
HALL	1,400	1,390	99	NEWTON	5,300	5,220	98
HAMILTON	3,400	3,360	99	NOLAN	5,900	5,860	99
HANSFORD	2,000	1,980	99	NUECES	117,200	116,040	99
HARDEMAN	1,700	1,690	99	OCHILTREE	3,500	3,460	99
HARDIN	20,100	19,780	98	OLDHAM	700	690	99
HARRIS	1,415,000	1,399,720	99	ORANGE	32,300	32,000	99
HARRISON	24,500	24,290	99	PALO PINTO	11,100	11,000	99
HARTLEY	1,600	1,590	99	PANOLA	9,300	9,190	99
HASKELL	2,300	2,280	99	PARKER	40,100	39,580	99
HAYS	52,300	51,440	98	PARMER	3,100	3,080	99
HEMPHILL	1,500	1,480	99	PECOS	5,300	5,190	98
HENDERSON	31,200	30,700	98	POLK	17,700	17,420	98
HIDALGO	215,200	212,390	99	POTTER	42,600	42,320	99
HILL	13,600	13,450	99	PRESIDIO	2,800	2,720	97
HOCKLEY	8,200	8,150	99	RAINS	4,500	4,440	99
HOOD	21,100	20,990	99	RANDALL	46,400	46,190	100
HOPKINS	13,400	13,160	98	REAGAN	1,200	1,190	99
HOUSTON	8,400	8,220	98	REAL	1,300	1,190	92
HOWARD	11,200	11,130	99	RED RIVER	5,400	5,340	99
HUDSPETH	1,100	1,060	96	REEVES	3,500	3,460	99
HUNT	31,000	30,740	99	REFUGIO	2,900	2,880	99
HUTCHINSON	8,700	8,660	100	ROBERTS	400	400	100
IRION	700	680	97	ROBERTSON	6,300	6,210	99
JACK	3,100	3,060	99	ROCKWALL	27,400	27,290	100
JACKSON	5,400	5,210	96	RUNNELS	4,000	3,990	100
JASPER	13,600	13,360	98	RUSK	18,300	18,170	99
JEFF DAVIS	1,100	1,000	91	SABINE	4,500	4,400	98
JEFFERSON	90,000	89,200	99	SAN AUGUSTINE	3,600	3,560	99
JIM HOGG	1,800	1,760	98	SAN JACINTO	10,300	9,870	96
JIM WELLS	14,100	13,890	99	SAN PATRICIO	24,200	23,940	99

State and County	Total Households	Total TV Households	%
SAN SABA	2,200	2,130	97
SCHLEICHER	1,200	1,180	98
SCURRY	5,900	5,850	99
SHACKELFORD	1,300	1,290	99
SHELBY	10,000	9,870	99
SHERMAN	1,000	980	98
SMITH	76,200	75,430	99
SOMERVELL	3,000	2,960	99
STARR	17,900	17,310	97
STEPHENS	3,700	3,660	99
STERLING	500	490	98
STONEWALL	600	590	98
SUTTON	1,700	1,660	98
SWISHER	2,700	2,680	99
TARRANT	652,000	647,900	99
TAYLOR	50,000	49,710	99
TERRELL	400	380	95
TERRY	4,200	4,180	100
THROCKMORTON	700	690	99
TITUS	10,300	10,200	99
TOM GREEN	40,900	40,560	99
TRAVIS	397,100	391,550	99
TRINITY	6,100	5,970	98
TYLER	7,900	7,770	98
UPSHUR	14,800	14,640	99
UPTON	1,300	1,280	98
UVALDE	8,800	8,580	98
VAL VERDE	15,700	15,330	98
VAN ZANDT	20,200	19,870	98
VICTORIA	32,000	31,560	99
WALKER	19,200	18,910	98
WALLER	12,600	12,420	99
WARD	4,000	3,960	99
WASHINGTON	12,500	12,270	98
WEBB	65,900	65,120	99
WHARTON	15,100	14,940	99
WHEELER	2,000	1,980	99
WICHITA	48,000	47,730	99
WILBARGER	5,500	5,460	99
WILLACY	6,000	5,910	99
WILLIAMSON	141,800	140,350	99
WILSON	14,900	14,740	99
WINKLER	2,600	2,580	99
WISE	21,300	21,180	99
WOOD	17,600	17,450	99
YOAKUM	2,600	2,570	99
YOUNG	7,300	7,220	99
ZAPATA	4,800	4,670	97
ZAVALA	3,700	3,490	94

UTAH

State and County	Total Households	Total TV Households	%
BEAVER	2,100	2,030	97
BOX ELDER	15,700	15,610	99
CACHE	34,900	34,060	98
CARBON	7,500	7,430	99
DAGGETT	400	370	93
DAVIS	94,700	94,240	100
DUCHESNE	5,900	5,820	99
EMERY	3,600	3,570	99
GARFIELD	1,700	1,630	96
GRAND	4,100	3,610	88
IRON	15,100	14,910	99
JUAB	3,000	2,980	99
KANE	2,700	2,470	91
MILLARD	4,100	4,080	100
MORGAN	2,800	2,750	98
PIUTE	500	490	98
RICH	800	780	98
SALT LAKE	345,200	341,960	99
SAN JUAN	4,600	4,230	92
SANPETE	7,700	7,570	98
SEVIER	6,800	6,740	99
SUMMIT	13,700	13,520	99
TOOELE	18,700	18,590	99
UINTAH	10,700	10,660	100
UTAH	150,800	148,560	99
WASATCH	7,300	7,170	98
WASHINGTON	50,800	49,550	98

State and County	Total Households	Total TV Households	%
WAYNE	1,000	990	99
WEBER	77,300	76,860	99

VERMONT

State and County	Total Households	Total TV Households	%
ADDISON	13,700	13,460	98
BENNINGTON	15,000	14,680	98
CALEDONIA	12,400	12,140	98
CHITTENDEN	60,600	59,760	99
ESSEX	2,700	2,650	98
FRANKLIN	18,100	17,960	99
GRAND ISLE	3,200	3,180	99
LAMOILLE	10,200	10,020	98
ORANGE	11,600	11,400	98
ORLEANS	11,400	11,280	99
RUTLAND	26,300	25,770	98
WASHINGTON	24,800	24,290	98
WINDHAM	18,500	17,730	96
WINDSOR	24,400	23,730	97

VIRGINIA

State and County	Total Households	Total TV Households	%
ACCOMACK	15,400	15,180	99
ALBEMARLE	55,400	53,940	97
ALLEGHANY	9,600	9,430	98
AMELIA	5,100	5,060	99
AMHERST	12,800	12,610	99
APPOMATTOX	5,900	5,870	99
ARLINGTON	162,600	160,330	99
AUGUSTA	48,400	47,770	99
BATH	1,900	1,880	99
BEDFORD	30,000	29,810	99
BLAND	2,800	2,770	99
BOTETOURT	12,900	12,820	99
BRUNSWICK	6,300	6,250	99
BUCHANAN	9,700	9,560	99
BUCKINGHAM	5,800	5,730	99
CAMPBELL	49,600	49,160	99
CAROLINE	10,800	10,690	99
CARROLL	15,900	15,720	99
CHARLOTTE	5,100	5,050	99
CHARLES CITY	2,900	2,860	99
CHESTERFIELD	122,600	122,210	100
CLARKE	6,200	6,110	99
CRAIG	2,200	2,140	97
CULPEPER	17,900	17,710	99
CUMBERLAND	4,100	3,990	97
DICKENSON	7,200	7,130	99
DINWIDDIE	23,700	23,450	99
ESSEX	4,600	4,550	99
FAIRFAX	386,800	384,600	99
FAUQUIER	25,000	24,640	99
FLOYD	6,500	6,400	98
FLUVANNA	10,200	10,090	99
FRANKLIN	21,900	21,480	99
FREDERICK	39,900	39,660	99
GILES	7,400	7,270	98
GLOUCESTER	14,600	14,460	99
GOOCHLAND	8,300	8,180	99
GRAYSON	7,200	7,040	98
GREENE	6,700	6,560	98
GREENSVILLE	6,000	5,930	99
HALIFAX	15,000	14,810	99
HANOVER	36,500	36,220	99
HENRICO	122,700	121,850	99
HENRY	29,600	29,460	100
HIGHLAND	1,100	1,080	98
ISLE OF WIGHT	14,100	13,950	99
JAMES CITY	30,600	30,350	99
KING & QUEEN	2,900	2,860	99
KING GEORGE	9,000	8,960	100
KING WILLIAM	6,200	6,130	99
LANCASTER	5,200	5,140	99
LEE	10,700	10,510	98
LOUDOUN	108,000	107,380	99
LOUISA	13,500	13,320	99
LUNENBURG	5,200	5,150	99
MADISON	5,600	5,330	95
MATHEWS	4,000	3,940	99

State and County	Total Households	Total TV Households	%
MECKLENBURG	13,300	13,170	99
MIDDLESEX	4,600	4,560	99
MONTGOMERY	40,900	40,090	98
NELSON	6,700	6,440	96
NEW KENT	6,800	6,740	99
NORTHAMPTON	5,600	5,550	99
NORTHUMBERLND	6,100	5,960	98
NOTTOWAY	5,800	5,750	99
ORANGE	14,000	13,770	98
PAGE	10,200	10,050	99
PATRICK	8,300	8,190	99
PITTSYLVANIA	45,200	44,750	99
POWHATAN	9,700	9,620	99
PRINCE EDWARD	7,400	7,340	99
PRINCE GEORGE	20,900	20,820	100
PRINCE WM.	147,700	147,250	100
PULASKI	15,100	14,980	99
RAPPAHANNOCK	2,900	2,760	95
RICHMOND	3,300	3,260	99
ROANOKE	91,100	90,470	99
ROCKBRIDGE	14,000	13,840	99
ROCKINGHAM	43,900	42,590	97
RUSSELL	12,300	12,070	98
SCOTT	10,200	10,070	99
SHENANDOAH	17,500	17,320	99
SMYTH	13,500	13,400	99
SOUTHAMPTON	10,600	10,460	99
SPOTSYLVANIA	54,500	53,970	99
STAFFORD	41,400	41,010	99
SUFFOLK CITY	31,400	31,030	99
SURRY	2,800	2,780	99
SUSSEX	4,100	4,080	100
TAZEWELL	19,100	18,860	99
VIRGINIA BCH	161,900	161,060	99
WARREN	14,300	14,040	98
WASHINGTON	31,100	30,620	98
WESTMORELAND	7,400	7,220	98
WISE	18,400	18,190	99
WYTHE	12,500	12,420	99
YORK	27,500	27,310	99
CHSPEAKE CITY	78,900	78,390	99
NORFOLK CITY	85,300	84,720	99
PRTSMUTH CITY	37,700	37,440	99
HAMPTON CITY	53,000	52,700	99
NWPRT NWS CTY	72,700	72,300	99
RICHMOND-IND	83,300	82,480	99

WASHINGTON

State and County	Total Households	Total TV Households	%
ADAMS	5,500	5,360	97
ASOTIN	8,900	8,780	99
BENTON	61,200	60,510	99
CHELAN	26,800	25,910	97
CLALLAM	30,900	29,790	96
CLARK	159,200	156,050	98
COLUMBIA	1,700	1,630	96
COWLITZ	39,200	38,390	98
DOUGLAS	13,300	13,080	98
FERRY	3,100	2,950	95
FRANKLIN	21,900	21,390	98
GARFIELD	900	880	98
GRANT	28,600	27,960	98
GRAYS HARBOR	27,600	26,780	97
ISLAND	32,300	31,540	98
JEFFERSON	13,500	12,920	96
KING	782,100	762,520	97
KITSAP	91,500	89,900	98
KITTITAS	16,000	14,890	93
KLICKITAT	8,200	7,660	93
LEWIS	29,300	28,200	96
LINCOLN	4,300	4,250	99
MASON	22,600	22,070	98
OKANOGAN	15,300	14,710	96
PACIFIC	9,600	9,370	98
PEND OREILLE	5,300	5,180	98
PIERCE	302,900	298,260	98
SAN JUAN	7,500	7,170	96
SKAGIT	45,100	43,700	97
SKAMANIA	4,200	4,060	97
SNOHOMISH	264,600	259,710	98

State and County	Total Households	Total TV Households	%
SPOKANE	184,400	181,930	99
STEVENS	16,600	15,960	96
THURSTON	100,700	98,510	98
WAHKIAKUM	1,700	1,600	94
WALLA WALLA	21,000	20,400	97
WHATCOM	77,400	74,560	96
WHITMAN	16,600	15,770	95
YAKIMA	77,600	76,850	99

WEST VIRGINIA

State and County	Total Households	Total TV Households	%
BARBOUR	6,400	6,330	99
BERKELEY	41,700	41,320	99
BOONE	10,500	10,390	99
BRAXTON	6,000	5,830	97
BROOKE	9,900	9,850	99
CABELL	40,200	39,890	99
CALHOUN	3,000	2,890	96
CLAY	4,100	4,030	98
DODDRIDGE	2,800	2,730	98
FAYETTE	19,000	18,840	99
GILMER	2,800	2,730	98
GRANT	5,200	5,030	97
GREENBRIER	15,200	15,020	99
HAMPSHIRE	9,300	9,000	97
HANCOCK	12,900	12,840	100
HARDY	5,800	5,680	98
HARRISON	28,800	28,640	99
JACKSON	11,500	11,440	99
JEFFERSON	21,100	20,780	98
KANAWHA	83,300	82,630	99
LEWIS	7,400	7,330	99
LINCOLN	9,300	9,140	98
LOGAN	14,900	14,790	99
MCDOWELL	9,700	9,600	99
MARION	24,300	24,090	99
MARSHALL	13,300	13,250	100
MASON	10,900	10,820	99
MERCER	27,200	26,990	99
MINERAL	11,100	10,870	98
MINGO	11,200	11,000	98
MONONGALIA	37,000	36,510	99
MONROE	6,000	5,910	99
MORGAN	7,000	6,780	97
NICHOLAS	11,100	10,900	98
OHIO	18,600	18,520	100
PENDLETON	3,200	3,040	95
PLEASANTS	2,800	2,790	100
POCAHONTAS	3,600	3,430	95
PRESTON	12,600	12,420	99
PUTNAM	22,600	22,410	99
RALEIGH	32,600	32,250	99
RANDOLPH	11,400	11,190	98
RITCHIE	4,300	4,210	98
ROANE	6,200	6,110	99
SUMMERS	5,100	4,990	98
TAYLOR	6,500	6,450	99
TUCKER	3,000	2,960	99
TYLER	3,600	3,580	99
UPSHUR	9,500	9,370	99
WAYNE	17,100	16,950	99
WEBSTER	4,100	4,020	98
WETZEL	6,800	6,730	99
WIRT	2,300	2,270	99
WOOD	36,800	36,560	99
WYOMING	10,200	10,110	99

WISCONSIN

State and County	Total Households	Total TV Households	%
ADAMS	8,600	8,530	99
ASHLAND	6,700	6,570	98
BARRON	19,100	18,840	99
BAYFIELD	6,600	6,450	98
BROWN	97,400	97,150	100
BUFFALO	5,700	5,650	99
BURNETT	7,200	7,090	98
CALUMET	17,600	17,550	100
CHIPPEWA	24,100	24,020	100
CLARK	12,300	12,110	98

State and County	Total Households	Total TV Households	%
COLUMBIA	22,400	22,190	99
CRAWFORD	6,800	6,720	99
DANE	196,500	194,610	99
DODGE	33,800	33,690	100
DOOR	12,900	12,840	100
DOUGLAS	18,500	18,410	100
DUNN	16,000	15,830	99
EAU CLAIRE	39,100	38,860	99
FLORENCE	2,200	2,190	100
FOND DU LAC	39,500	39,380	100
FOREST	4,300	4,290	100
GRANT	19,200	19,030	99
GREEN	14,700	14,620	99
GREEN LAKE	7,800	7,750	99
IOWA	9,500	9,430	99
IRON	3,000	2,990	100
JACKSON	7,600	7,530	99
JEFFERSON	31,400	31,220	99
JUNEAU	10,600	10,480	99
KENOSHA	63,200	62,860	99
KEWAUNEE	8,100	8,080	100
LA CROSSE	45,100	44,890	100
LAFAYETTE	6,400	6,370	100
LANGLADE	8,700	8,620	99
LINCOLN	12,200	12,140	100
MANITOWOC	33,800	33,690	100
MARATHON	52,900	52,720	100
MARINETTE	18,400	18,340	100
MARQUETTE	6,500	6,440	99
MENOMINEE	1,400	1,400	100
MILWAUKEE	379,600	377,700	99
MONROE	17,100	16,960	99
OCONTO	15,600	15,510	99
ONEIDA	16,000	15,830	99
OUTAGAMIE	68,600	68,470	100
OZAUKEE	34,100	33,990	100
PEPIN	2,900	2,880	99
PIERCE	14,800	14,640	99
POLK	18,400	18,240	99
PORTAGE	27,100	26,940	99
PRICE	6,500	6,430	99
RACINE	76,100	75,880	100
RICHLAND	7,400	7,250	98
ROCK	63,000	62,690	100
RUSK	6,200	6,130	99
ST CROIX	32,500	32,360	100
SAUK	24,400	24,150	99
SAWYER	7,400	7,200	97
SHAWANO	16,800	16,700	99
SHEBOYGAN	46,600	46,410	100
TAYLOR	7,900	7,840	99
TREMPEALEAU	11,500	11,430	99
VERNON	11,500	11,320	98
VILAS	10,000	9,890	99
WALWORTH	38,800	38,600	99
WASHBURN	7,300	7,090	97
WASHINGTON	51,900	51,600	99
WAUKESHA	150,200	149,840	100
WAUPACA	20,800	20,700	100
WAUSHARA	10,000	9,880	99
WINNEBAGO	65,800	65,630	100
WOOD	31,600	31,490	100

WYOMING

State and County	Total Households	Total TV Households	%
ALBANY	14,100	13,540	96
BIG HORN	4,300	4,190	97
CAMPBELL	16,300	16,230	100
CARBON	6,700	6,520	97
CONVERSE	5,600	5,480	98
CROOK	2,800	2,750	98
FREMONT	15,300	14,950	98
GOSHEN	5,100	5,050	99
HOT SPRINGS	2,100	2,030	97
JOHNSON	3,800	3,700	97
LARAMIE	35,000	34,700	99
LINCOLN	6,600	6,420	97
NATRONA	30,300	30,030	99
NIOBRARA	1,000	980	98
PARK	11,600	11,420	98
PLATTE	3,500	3,480	99
SHERIDAN	12,700	12,410	98
SUBLETTE	3,800	3,680	97
SWEETWATER	16,100	15,830	98
TETON	9,000	8,670	96
UINTA	7,700	7,550	98
WASHAKIE	3,200	3,130	98
WESTON	3,000	2,910	97

Description of Station Directory Section

THE STATION MAPS

The only official and uniform rough guide to a station's physical coverage is found in the files of the Federal Communications Commission. Each TV station grantee is required to submit to the Commission its coverage contours predicted on the basis of engineering formulas designated by the Commission. The FCC specifies the grade of service as a general indication of the probable quality of reception.

The FCC does not intend or expect the predicted coverage contour, submitted by each station, to reflect whether a signal is received or not received at any specific location. Rather, the Commission regards the contours as a general guide to probable reception. The basic use made by the Commission of the contours is as a tool to determine where to allocate channels to minimize interference among stations.

Though all stations and applicants are required to submit predicted contours to the FCC, stations may also file contours based on actual measurements of transmitted signals. Under FCC rules, such filings are not mandatory, and only a relatively few stations have offered such measurements voluntarily. The Commission has no official or uniform rules for measuring service contours; such submissions are associated with stations' files but are not given official status by the Commission.

The maps are intended to serve as guides. It should be emphasized that the use of maps for legal proceedings, such as those before the FCC, may require precision greater than that reasonably obtainable in maps of the size employed in the *Factbook*.

The standards for predicted contours as required by the FCC are as follows:

Digital Service: Satisfactory service expected at least 90% of the time for at least 50% of the receiving locations.

Principal City Service: Satisfactory service expected at least 90% of the time for at least 90% of the receiving locations.

We obtained the predicted contour maps from the FCC files or from the stations.

Due to the delayed conversion to digital format, most stations in this edition of the Factbook appear with a "-DT" suffix. A complete list of post-conversion call letters were not available at press time. Please refer to the Online Factbook (http://www.tvcablefactbook.com) for the most current information.

(The television station coverage maps and all other contents of this book are copyrighted by Warren Communications News, publishers of **Television & Cable Factbook.** *Reproduction in whole or part is prohibited without written permission.)*

NIELSEN TV STATION CIRCULATION

The *Average Weekly Circulation* estimates are based on NSI (Nielsen Station Index) diary households from the most recent February, May, July and November survey periods. These Sunday-Saturday 7 a.m.-1 a.m. average quarter-hour tuning shares are based on commercial television stations only.

All viewing numbers include only those estimates which surpass 5%. The *Station DMA Total* estimates are for viewing within the station's Designated Market Area, as defined by Nielsen. The *Other DMA Total* estimates are for viewing in a Designated Market Area other than the station's. The *Grand Total* estimates are a sum of the Station and Other DMA totals. Some stations have no viewing over 5% outside the station DMA, and therefore do not show all three categories.

DEFINITIONS OF NIELSEN TERMS

Designated Market Area—An area comprised of all counties wherein the combined share of audience for the home market commercial station(s) is larger than the combined share of audience for any station(s) assigned to another home market. In a few instances, a county has a marked division in household viewing patterns, so that the county is split by Nielsen, and each portion assigned to a DMA.

Television Households—A television household is an occupied dwelling unit having one or more television sets. Updated estimates of TV households in each county, rounded and expressed in tens, are prepared annually by the Nielsen Research Department. Those estimates are derived by applying percent television set ownership estimates, county by county, to the estimates of total households made by Market Statistics.

Cable Television Households—A cable television household is an occupied dwelling unit which subscribes to some level of delivery service for television signals, rounded and expressed in tens.

Non-Cable Television Households—A television household which receives broadcast television signals, rounded and expressed in tens.

TV Penetration—The percent of total homes having one or more television sets at the time of the surveys. TV penetration uses current regional penetration estimates derived by the Advertising Research Foundation from U.S. Bureau of the Census surveys conducted in accordance with ARF specifications.

Average Weekly Circulation—The estimated average number of different television households viewing a particular station at least once per week, Monday-Sunday, Sign-on to Sign-off.

Average Daily Circulation—The estimated average number of different television households reached by a particular station on each day of the week, Sign-on to Sign-off.

NIELSEN SURVEY METHODS

Nielsen measures viewing in over 200 television markets across the United States 4 times each year. Nielsen's national TV sample, composed of a cross-section of representative homes throughout the United States, is measured by a combination of set meters and People Meters as well as diaries.

Electronic metering is the heart of the Nielsen rating process and Nielsen uses two types. Set meters capture what channel is being tuned and People Meters go a step further to gather information about who is watching in addition to the channel tuned. Raw data from the electronic meters is transmitted from the home to Nielsen where it is analyzed and validated. In some mid-size markets, dairies provide viewer information for up to three additional "sweeps" months (October, January and March).

Diaries are used to collect viewing information from sample homes in many television markets and smaller markets are measured by paper diaries only. Each year, Nielsen processes approximately 2 million paper diaries for the months of November, February, May and July. Seven-day diaries (or eight-day diaries in homes with DVRs) are mailed to homes to keep a tally of what is watched on each television set and by whom. Over the course of a sweeps period, diaries are mailed to a new panel of homes each week. At the end of the month, all of the viewing data from the individual weeks is aggregated.

EXPLANATION OF FCC SYMBOLS

FCC Filing Symbols:

1. DOC: Docket (designation applied by FCC to hearing cases).

2. BPCDT: Broadcast Permit Commercial Digital Television.

3. BMPCDT: Broadcast Modification of Permit Commercial Digital Television.

4. GRANTED: Date of authorization by FCC.

Note: "BPCDT" and "BMPCDT" designations, accompanied by numbers, are affixed by the FCC to applications for new or changed station facilities to identify each when it is accepted for filing. They therefore constitute file numbers. Each map in the Factbook is accompanied with its file number to help reference the Commission's official files. In each case, the file number used is the one affixed to the application for facilities which were subsequently authorized by the FCC and in use at the time this Factbook was published. "Docket" numbers are used in those few cases where the application was in a hearing status and a file number had not been assigned. The "granted" date indicates when the FCC approved construction of facilities involved.

After a station is completed according to the terms of its construction permit, it receives a license; this is identified by a number with a "BLCDT" (Broadcast License Commercial Digital Television) prefix. When a license is renewed, a number with a "BRCDT" (Broadcast Renewal Commercial Digital Television) prefix is employed. Applications for licenses or license renewals do not include requests for changes in facilities, thus do not affect predicted contours. Therefore, they are not employed as references in the Factbook.

The service contours on the maps are predicted by station engineers according to the formulas designated by the FCC, as previously explained. They are based on facilities authorized or in use by stations at the time of Factbook publication.